-Date – Free 30-Day Test-Drive!

Get Instant Updates, Free Research Requests,
Postage Refunds, Insider Information & More
For 60 Days Free Using the Activation Link Below:

http://contactanycelebrity.com/free

You'll get **INSTANT ACCESS** to the Best Mailing Address,
Agent, Manager, Publicist, Production Company and Charitable Cause
For Over 60,000 Celebrities & Public Figures Worldwide!

You'll Get Instant Access To All This:

Easy-To-Use, Fully-Searchable Online Database
60,000+ Celebrities & Public Figures Worldwide
Agent, Manager & Publicist Information
Celebrity Causes Database
Daily Real-Time Updates
Free Research Requests
Postage Refund Guarantee
Professional Tips & Advice
Toll-Free 24/7 Customer Service
Celebrity Gift Bag Opportunities
Plus Much More!

Activate Your 30-Day Test-Drive:

http://contactanycelebrity.com/free

Look What People Are Saying:

"The best resource and a great deal."
- Peter Shankman, HARO (Help A Reporter Out)

"This online directory will help you find any celebrity in the world."
- Timothy Ferriss (The 4-Hour Workweek)

The Celebrity Black Book 2012: Over 60,000+ Accurate Celebrity Addresses for Autographs, Charity Donations, Signed Memorabilia, Celebrity Endorsements, Media Interviews and More!

Mega Niche Media LLC
8721 Santa Monica Boulevard, #431
Los Angeles, CA 90069-4507
310-388-6084 (Phone/Fax)
info@meganiche.com
www.meganiche.com

All addresses verified by the U.S. Postal Service NCOA (National Change of Address) System.

Printed and bound in the United States of America.

Please visit http://contactanycelebrity.com for updates and new additions.

ISBN: 978-1-60487-009-1

Edited by Jordan McAuley – http://contactanycelebrity.com
Interior by Data Management, Inc. – http://dbman.com

Buzz For *The Celebrity Black Book*

"The range is amazing – this thing is huge!"
- *CNN*

"I can do so much with this!"
- Perez Hilton

"Many small businesses, publicists, and marketers want to get their products into celebrities' hands. This book is the solution."
- Entrepreneur Magazine

"Of all the resources for celebrity addresses, this book is far and away the most useful. It is essential for any serious autograph collector. Indispensable!"
- Autograph Magazine

"Similar titles do not boast as many entries. If your library needs a current celebrity address book, this would be good. Recommended for all libraries."
- Library Journal

"A superb, quick and easy-to-use reference for entertainment professionals and fans alike."
- Midwest Book Review

"This guide offers priceless information that would otherwise take hours to research. Owning this book is like cutting six degrees of separation down to one simple degree."
- Curled Up With A Good Book

"The time saved by already having the celebrity's contact information rather than Googling and cold-calling will certainly pay for this book in the long run."
- Absolute Write

"Some of the best money you'll ever spend. This book is an excellent value and provides you (and me) with great publicity opportunities."
- Paul Hartunian, Free Publicity Information Center

"The most helpful book I have ever owned. Worth every penny."
- Jill Jackson, Syndicated Columnist, Jill Jackson's Hollywood

"If you opt to pursue a celebrity or celebrities on your own or to use in your advertising, or to get a 'blurb' from for your book, this is the place to get contact information."
- Dan Kennedy, No B.S. Guide to Marketing to the Affluent

*** Visit http://contactanycelebrity.com/testimonials for more testimonials and success stories!**

About The Editor

Known as the "King of Celebrity Contacts," Jordan McAuley's Contact Any Celebrity (http://contactanycelebrity.com) service is one of the most respected celebrity contact resources in the world, with a blue-chip roster marketers, publicists, nonprofits and media clients who rely on it daily.

McAuley has been featured by *USA Today*, *The Associated Press*, *Investor's Business Daily*, *Entertainment Weekly*, *Star Magazine*, *Village Voice*, *Entrepreneur Magazine*, *Out Magazine*, *Instinct Magazine*, and *Publishers Weekly* plus other local and national media.

He has also appeared on CNN, E! Online, National Public Radio (NPR), Q Television, Better TV, and Sirius/XM Satellite Radio.

McAuley got his start as an intern in the publicity departments of CNN and Turner Entertainment in Atlanta. He also worked at a prominent modeling agency in South Beach, Miami; a film production company in Hollywood, California; and a top talent agency in Beverly Hills.

McAuley is featured in several best-selling books including Timothy Ferris' *The 4-Hour Workweek*, Dan Kennedy's *Marketing to the Affluent*, Dan Poynter's *Publishing Encyclopedia*, John Kremer's *1001 Ways to Market Your Books*, Robin Blakely's *Get PR Therapy*, and Tsufit's *Step Into the Spotlight: A Guide to Getting Noticed.*

McAuley is the author of the best-selling annual directory, *The Celebrity Black Book*, plus *Secrets to Contacting Celebrities: 101 Ways to Reach the Rich & Famous* and *Celebrity Leverage: Insider Secrets to Getting Celebrity Endorsements, Instant Credibility, and Star-Powered Publicity.*

He is a member of the Public Relations Society of America (PRSA), the Independent Book Publishers Association (IBPA), the GLAAD Media Circle, the Information Marketing Association (IMA) and the Association of Fundraising Professionals (AFP).

Jordan McAuley was born and raised in Atlanta, Georgia. He graduated with a Bachelor of Science in Communication (Motion Picture Business and English Literature) from the University of Miami in 2000.

Introduction

Welcome to the *Celebrity Black Book 2012*!

Whether you're a fan, journalist, nonprofit, entrepreneur, author, marketer, publicist, or event planner, you're bound to find this book useful. Inside you'll discover the best, mailing addresses for over 60,000+ celebrities and public figures worldwide, all verified by the U.S. Postal Service NCOA (National Change of Address) System.

Everyone who is anyone is included: actors, athletes, musicians, politicians, world leaders, authors, artists, television hosts… even reality TV stars! The list goes on and on as you'll see once you begin browsing the following pages.

The Celebrity Black Book 2012 is a staple for fans who wish to request autographs, nonprofits who want to hold an autograph auction to raise money for their cause, businesses who want to get their products and services into the hands of celebrities, authors who want to get celebrity endorsements for their books, and members of the media who want to get an interview.

There are so many uses, the possibilities are endless!

Of course, with over 60,000 celebrities who move and change addresses on a daily basis, this book cannot possibly be 100% accurate. That's why we let you join Contact Any Celebrity's online database for just $1, so you can get real-time, immediate updates!

Our online database contains the best mailing address, agent, manager, publicist, production company and charitable cause for each celebrity, plus contact information for over 8,000 personal representatives and 5,000 entertainment companies with phone, fax and email contacts.

Activate your free 30-day test-drive here: http://contactanycelebrity.com/free

You may be wondering how to write a fan letter, request an autograph, or get your product and service in the hands of celebrities. To find out, I recommend my other books available on Amazon and Kindle:

Secrets to Contacting Celebrities: 101 Ways to Reach the Rich & Famous
http://tinyurl.com/77euph4

Celebrity Leverage: Insider Secrets to Getting Celebrity Endorsements
http://tinyurl.com/7ac6jf3

Enjoy your *Celebrity Black Book 2012*, and let me know your success stories!

Reach for the stars,

Jordan McAuley, Founder
Contact Any Celebrity
http://contactanycelebrity.com | jordan@contactanycelebrity.com

112 (Musician)
c/o Staff Member *Richard De La Font Agency*
3808 W South Park Blvd
Broken Arrow, OK 74011-1261, USA

3 (Three) Doors Down (Music Group)
c/o Kim Estlund *Baker Winokur Ryder Public Relations (BWR-LA)*
9100 Wilshire Blvd Ste 500 PMB WEST
Beverly Hills, CA 90212-3426, USA

311 (Music Group)
c/o Peter Raspler *Raspler Management*
2049 Century Park E Ste 2550
Los Angeles, CA 90067-3139, USA

50 Cent (Actor, Musician)
c/o Chris Lighty *Violator Management*
36 W 25th St Fl 11
New York, NY 10010-2752, USA

A

A Night At The Opera (Music Group, Musician)
c/o Staff Member *Agency for the Performing Arts (APA-LA)*
405 S Beverly Dr Ste 500
Beverly Hills, CA 90212-4425, USA

A3 (Music Group)
c/o Staff Member *Paradigm (Monterey)*
404 W Franklin St
Monterey, CA 93940-2303, USA

Aaker, Lee (Actor)
31806 Cienega Springs Rd
Parker, AZ 85344-8401, USA

Aalto, Antti (Athlete, Hockey Player)
300 Ocean Ave
Seal Beach, CA 90740-6031, USA

Aames, Willie (Actor)
c/o Staff Member *Jeff Ballard PR*
4814 Lemona Ave
Sherman Oaks, CA 91403-2010, USA

Aardsma, David (Athlete, Baseball Player)
22 Grogans Point Rd
Spring, TX 77380-2697, USA

Aaron, Caroline (Actor)
9057-C Nemo St
W Hollywood, CA 90069, USA

Aaron, Chester (Writer)
PO Box 388
Occidental, CA 95465-0388, USA

Aaron, Hank (Athlete, Baseball Player)
c/o Staff Member *HarperCollins Publishers*
10 E 53rd St C/O Author Mail Floor 7
New York, NY 10022, USA

Aaron, Paul (Director)
c/o Staff Member *Elsboy Entertainment*
1581 N Crescent Heights Blvd
West Hollywood, CA 90046-2405, USA

Aaron, Quinton
853 7th Ave Apt 8D
New York, NY 10019-5222, USA

Aaron, Tommy (Athlete, Golfer)
440 E Lake Dr
Gainesville, GA 30506-1740, USA

Aase, Donald W (Don) (Athlete, Baseball Player)
5055 Via Ricardo
Yorba Linda, CA 92886-4526, USA

Abad, Andy (Athlete, Baseball Player)
118 Bonaire Ln
Jupiter, FL 33458-8223, USA

Abagnale Jr, Frank W
PO Box 701290
Tulsa, OK 74170-1290, USA

Abair, Mindi (Musician)
c/o Bud Harner *Chapman Management*
14011 Ventura Blvd
Sherman Oaks, CA 91423-3533, USA

Abatantuono, Diego (Actor)
c/o Staff Member *Moviement*
Via P Cavallini 24
Rome 193, ITALY

ABBA (Music Group, Musician)
c/o Staff Member *Mono Music AB*
Södra Brobänken 41A
Stockholm 111 49, Sweden

Abbado, Claudio (Conductor, Musician)
c/o Staff Member *Askonas Holt Ltd*
Lincoln House 300 High Holborn
London WC1V 7JH, UK

Abbatiello, Carmine (Athlete)
176 Stone Hill Rd
Colts Neck, NJ 07722-1730, USA

Abbe, Elfriede M (Artist)
Applewood
Manchester Center, VT 5255

Abbett, Robert (Artist)
PO Box 126
Bridgewater, CT 06752-0126, USA

Abbey, Joe (Athlete, Football Player)
1814 S Bonnie Brae St
Denton, TX 76207-2051, USA

Abbington, Amanda (Actor)
c/o Staff Member *Lip Service Casting Ltd*
60-66 Wardour St
London W1F 0TA, UK

Abbot, Jim (Athlete, Baseball Player)
3449 Quiet Cv
Corona Del Mar, CA 92625-1637, USA

Abbott, Bruce (Actor)
c/o Staff Member *Metropolitan (MTA)*
4526 Wilshire Blvd
Los Angeles, CA 90010-3801, USA

Abbott, Christie
c/o Marie Mathews *Marie Mathews Management*
8730 W Sunset Blvd Ste 200
Los Angeles, CA 90069-2275, USA

Abbott, D Thomas (Business Person)
333 Ludlow St
Stamford, CT 06902-6987, USA

Abbott, Diahnne (Actor)
460 W Avenue 46
Los Angeles, CA 90065-5006

Abbott, Glenn (Athlete, Baseball Player)
4413 Dawson Dr
North Little Rock, AR 72116-7037, USA

Abbott, Gregory (Musician)
PO Box 68
Bergenfield, NJ 07621-0068, USA

Abbott, Jeff (Athlete, Baseball Player)
1095 Stonegate Ct
Roswell, GA 30075-2265, USA

Abbott, Josh (Musician)
c/o Joey Lee *WmE2 (WMA-TN)*
1600 Division St Ste 300
Nashville, TN 37203-2755, USA

Abbott, Kurt (Athlete, Baseball Player)
1609 SE Pomeroy St Unit 6-4
Stuart, FL 34997-3901, USA

Abbott, Kyle (Athlete, Baseball Player)
332 Springfield Bnd
Argyle, TX 76226-6848, USA

Abbott, Paul (Athlete, Baseball Player)
1809 Yermo Pl
Fullerton, CA 92833-1866, USA

Abbott, Preston S (Doctor)
1305 Namassin Rd
Alexandria, VA 22308-1043

Abbott, Reg (Athlete, Hockey Player)
5239 Hanover Pl
Victoria, BC V8Y 2C7, CANADA

Abbott, Vince (Athlete, Football Player)
121 Via Waziers
Newport Beach, CA 92663-5517, USA

Abboud, A Robert (Business Person)
212 Stone Hill Ctr
Lake Zurich, IL 60047, USA

Abboud, Joseph M (Designer, Fashion Designer)
650 5th Ave # 2700
New York, NY 10019-6108, USA

Abdnor, James (Ex-Senator, Politician)
PO Box 217
Kennebec, SD 57544-0217, USA

Abdoo, Rose (Actor)
c/o Judy Orbach *Judy O Productions*
6136 Glen Holly St
Hollywood, CA 90068-2338, USA

Abdrashitov, Vadim Y (Director)
3D Frunzenskaya 8 #211
Moscow 119270, RUSSIA

Abdul, Paula (Actor, Musician, Reality TV Star)
c/o Michael Gagliardo *PMK/BNC Public Relations (PMK-NY)*
622 3rd Ave Fl 8
New York, NY 10017-6707, USA

Abdul-Aziz, Zaid (Athlete, Basketball Player)
PO Box 75184
Seattle, WA 98175-0184, USA

Abdul-Jabbar, Kareem (Athlete, Basketball Player, Coach)
1436 Summitridge Dr
Beverly Hills, CA 90210-2246, USA

Abdul-Jabbar, Karim (Athlete, Football Player)
c/o Staff Member *Kareem Productions*
20434 S Santa Fe Ave Ste 194
Long Beach, CA 90810-1121, USA

Abdullah, Khalid (Athlete, Football Player)
7634 Wexford Club Dr E
Jacksonville, FL 32256-2330, USA

Abdullah, Rabih (Athlete, Football Player)
12810 Wallingford Dr
Tampa, FL 33624-6354, USA

Abdullah, Rahim (Athlete, Football Player)
7634 Wexford Club Dr E
Jacksonville, FL 32256-2330, USA

Abdulov, Aleksandr G (Actor)
Peschanaya Str 4 #3
Moscow 125252, RUSSIA

Abdul-Saboor, Mikal (Athlete, Football Player)
5465 Derby Chase Ct
Alpharetta, GA 30005-7882, USA

Abdur-Rahim, Shareef (Athlete, Basketball Player)
c/o Staff Member *Atlanta Hawks*
190 Marietta St NW Ste 405
Atlanta, GA 30303-2717, USA

Abeal, Marcelo ""Bonny"" (Actor)
Arenales 2756 1° Apt B
Buenos Aires 1425, Argentina

Abed, Rodrigo (Actor)
c/o Gabriel Blanco *Gabriel Blanco Iglesias (Mexico)*
Rio Balsas 35-32 Colonia Cuauhtemoc
DF 6500, Mexico

Abeernethy, Tom (Athlete, Basketball Player)
5905 William Conner Way
Carmel, IN 46033-8826, USA

Abel (DJ)
c/o Len Evans *Project Publicity*
312 W 53rd St Ste 202
New York, NY 10019-5743, USA

Abel, Gerald (Athlete, Hockey Player)
23570 Samoset Trl
Southfield, MI 48033-2820, USA

Abel, Jake (Actor)
c/o Cynthia Campos-Greenberg *Anthem Entertainment*
9595 Wilshire Blvd Ste 900
Beverly Hills, CA 90212-2509, USA

Abel, Jessica (Artist)
c/o Staff Member *Fantagraphics Books*
7563 Lake City Way NE
Seattle, WA 98115-4218, USA

Abel, Joy (Bowler)
PO Box 296
Lansing, IL 60438, USA

Abell, Bud (Athlete, Football Player)
919 E 25th Plz
Panama City, FL 32405-5255, USA

Abell, Tim (Actor)
c/o Staff Member *Gold Levin*
8424 Santa Monica Blvd Ste 706 # A
Los Angeles, CA 90069-6233, USA

Abelson, John (Biologist, Scientist)
112 Laidley St
San Francisco, CA 94131-2735, USA

Abelson, Robert P (Doctor)
1155 Whitney Ave
Hamden, CT 06517-3434

Abercrombie, Ian (Actor)
c/o Anne Geddes *Geddes Agency, The*
8430 Santa Monica Blvd Ste 200
Los Angeles, CA 90069-4253, USA

Abercrombie, John L (Musician)
300 Mercer St Apt 3J
New York, NY 10003-6732, USA

Abercrombie, Neil (Governor)
Governor, State of Hawaii Executive Chambers, State Capitol
Honolulu, HI 96813, USA

Abercrombie, Neil (Government Official)
1050 Ala Moana Blvd Ste D28
Honolulu, HI 96814-4905, HAWAII

Abercrombie, Neil (Congressman, Politician)
300 Ala Moana Blvd Rm 4104
Honolulu, HI 96850-4104, USA

Abercrombie, Reggie (Athlete, Baseball Player)
5920 Buxton Dr
Columbus, GA 31907-3635, USA

Abercrombie, Walter (Athlete, Coach, Football Coach, Football Player)
217 Westlane Cir
Woodway, TX 76712-3186, USA

Abernathy, Brent (Athlete, Baseball Player)
1787 Bridgeport Colony Ln
Fort Walton Beach, FL 32547-5711, USA

Abernathy, Frederick H (Engineer)
43 Islington Rd
Newton, MA 2166, USA

Abernathy, Robert (Athlete, Baseball Player)
2491 Walker Ln
Nashville, TN 37207-4213, USA

Abernethy, Tom (Athlete)
5268 Woodfield Dr N
Carmel, IN 46033-8794, USA

Abert, Donald B (Publisher)
333 W State St
Milwaukee, WI 53203-1305

Abgrall, Dennis (Athlete, Hockey Player)
16607 S 12th Pl
Phoenix, AZ 85048-4703, USA

Abigail (Musician)
c/o Staff Member *Diva Central Inc*
7510 W Sunset Blvd Ste 1445
Los Angeles, CA 90046-3408, USA

Abiodun, Oyewole (Musician)
c/o Staff Member *Agency Group Ltd, The (UK)*
361-373 City Rd
London EC1V 1PQ, UK

Abir, Lili (Stylist)
48 Greene St Fl 4
New York, NY 10013-2663, USA

Abizaid, John P (General)
Commander US Central Command
MacDill Air Force Base, FL 33621, USA

Able, Forest (Athlete, Basketball Player)
11102 Mitchell Hill Rd
Fairdale, KY 40118-9425, USA

Able, Whitney (Actor)
c/o Lena Roklin *Luber Roklin Management*
8530 Wilshire Blvd Ste 550
Beverly Hills, CA 90211-3133, USA

Ableson, Andrew (Actor)
c/o Stephanie Blume *Imperium 7 Talent Agency*
5455 Wilshire Blvd Ste 1706
Los Angeles, CA 90036-4217, USA

Ablon, Ralph E (Business Person)
PO Box 2615
Fairfield, NJ 7004, USA

Ablow, Keith (Doctor)
c/o Greg Lipstone *WmE2 (WMA-LA)*
1 William Morris Pl
Beverly Hills, CA 90212-4261, USA

Abner, Shawn (Athlete, Baseball Player)
1443 Olde Oak Ct
Mechanicsburg, PA 17050-9198, USA

Abney Culberson, John (Congressman, Politician)
2352 Rayburn Hob
Washington, DC 20515-2201, USA

Aboitiz, Gemina (Stylist)
c/o Staff Member *Cloutier Agency*
2632 La Cienega Ave
Los Angeles, CA 90034-2641, USA

Aboulhosn, Hassan (Athlete, Football Player)
2703 Oaklawn Blvd
Hopewell, VA 23860-4934, USA

Abourezk, James G (Ex-Senator, Politician)
21 Dupont Cir NW # 400
Washington, DC 20036-1109, USA

Abragam, Anatole (Scientist)
33 Rue Croulebarbe
Paris 75013, FRANCE

Abraham, Clifton (Athlete, Football Player)
1413 Dutchman Creek Dr
Desoto, TX 75115-3659, USA

Abraham, Donnie (Athlete, Football Player)
3038 Wentworth Way
Tarpon Springs, FL 34688-8445, USA

Abraham, F Murray (Actor)
c/o Staff Member *Paradigm (LA)*
360 N Crescent Dr
Beverly Hills, CA 90210-4874, USA

Abraham, Jay
c/o Staff Member *NASCAR Media Group*
4205 Stuart Andrew Blvd Ste B
Charlotte, NC 28217-1572, USA

Abraham, John (Athlete, Football Player)
c/o Anthony J. Agnone *Eastern Athletic Services*
11350 McCormick Road - Executive Plz
Suite 800
Hunt Valley, MD 21031, USA

Abraham, John (Actor)
A1 418 Lower Parel
Mumbai 400013, India

Abraham, Nate (Athlete, Football Player)
3038 Wentworth Way
Tarpon Springs, FL 34688-8445, USA

Abraham, Robert (Athlete, Football Player)
831 Canal St
Myrtle Beach, SC 29577-3455, USA

Abraham, Spencer E (Ex-Senator, Politician)
1000 Independence Ave SW
Washington, DC 20585-0001, USA

Abrahamian, Emil (Cartoonist)
147 Woodleaf Dr
Winter Springs, FL 32708-6159, USA

Abrahams, Jim S (Director)
c/o Staff Member *International Creative Management (ICM-LA)*
10250 Constellation Blvd Fl 7
Los Angeles, CA 90067-6207, USA

Abrahams, Jon (Actor)
c/o Christian Donatelli *Schiff Company, The*
8440 Warner Dr Ste B1
Culver City, CA 90232-2461, USA

Abrahamse, Taylor (Musician)
146 Shuter St Studio B
Toronto, ON M5A 1V9, Canada

Abrahamson, James A (Business Person, General)
3557 Havercamp Rd
Hibbing, MN 55746-8142, USA

Abram, Norm (Television Host)
PO Box 2284
South Burlington, VT 05407-2284

Abramovich, Roman (Business Person)
Stamford Bridge Fulham Road
London SW6 1HS, UK

Abramowicz, Daniel (Danny) (Athlete, Football Player)
479 N Harlem Ave Apt 801
Oak Park, IL 60301-6409, USA

Abramowicz, Sidney (Athlete, Football Player)
200 Sycamore Ln Apt 306
Woodstock, GA 30188-7311, USA

Abrams, Bobby (Athlete, Football Player)
1470 Pampas Dr
Montgomery, AL 36117-2310, USA

Abrams, Casey (Musician)
c/o Simon Fuller *XIX Entertainment*
33/32 Ransomes Dock 35-37 Parkgate Rd
London SW11 4NP, UK

Abrams, Elliott (Government Official)
10607 Dogwood Farm Ln
Great Falls, VA 22066-2937, USA

Abrams, Elliott (Government Official)
10607 Dogwood Farm Ln
Great Falls, VA 22066-2937, USA

Abrams, Jeffrey (JJ) (Actor, Producer, Writer)
c/o David Lonner *Oasis Media Group*
8730 W Sunset Blvd Ste 700
Los Angeles, CA 90069-2249, USA

Abrams, Kevin (Athlete, Football Player)
1314 E Wilder Ave
Tampa, FL 33603-2433, USA

Abramson, Leslie (Actor)
4929 Wilshire Blvd
Los Angeles, CA 90010-3808, USA

Abramson, Neil (Director, Writer)
c/o Staff Member *United Talent Agency (UTA)*
9560 Wilshire Blvd Fl 5
Beverly Hills, CA 90212-2400, USA

Abrego, Johnny (Athlete, Baseball Player)
PO Box 681144
San Antonio, TX 78268-1144, USA

Abreu, Aldo (Musician)
850 7th Ave # 1205
New York, NY 10019-5230, USA

Abreu, Bobby (Athlete, Baseball Player)
310 E 53rd St Apt 108
New York, NY 10022-5216, USA

Abreu, Irina (Actor)
c/o Staff Member *Televisa*
Blvd Adolfo Lopez Mateos 232 Colonia
San Angel INN
DF CP 01060, MEXICO

Abrikosov, Alexei A (Nobel Prize Laureate)
804 Houston St
Lemont, IL 60439-4338, USA

Abril, Victoria (Actor)
1 Rue du Louvre
Paris 75001, FRANCE

Abroms, Edward M (Director)
1866 Marlowe St
Thousand Oaks, CA 91360-3331, USA

Abronzino, Umberto (Soccer Player)
1336 Settle Ave
San Jose, CA 95125-2363, USA

Abrue, Bobby (Athlete, Baseball Player)
c/o Staff Member *Los Angeles Dodgers (LA Dodgers)*
1000 Elysian Park Ave
Los Angeles, CA 90090-1112, USA

Abrunhosa, Pedro (Musician)
Worldwide Plaza 825 8th Ave
New York, NY 10019, USA

Abruzzese, Ray (Athlete, Football Player)
3031 N Ocean Blvd Apt 1906
Fort Lauderdale, FL 33308-7331, USA

Abruzzo, Ray (Actor)
c/o Staff Member *Peter Strain & Associates Inc (LA)*
5455 Wilshire Blvd Ste 1812
Los Angeles, CA 90036-4268, USA

Absher, Dick (Athlete, Football Player)
353 Tavistock Dr
Saint Augustine, FL 32095-8401, USA

Abshire, David M (Diplomat)
1800 K St NW
Washington, DC 20006-2202, USA

abtahi, omid (Actor)

Abul-Ragheb, Ali (Prime Minister)
PO Box 80
Amman 35215, JORDAN

Accardo, Jeremy (Athlete, Baseball Player)
1543 S Gibson St
Gilbert, AZ 85296-4290, USA

Accola, Candice (Actor)
c/o Katie Rhodes *Untitled Entertainment (LA)*
350 S Beverly Dr Ste 200
Beverly Hills, CA 90212-4819, USA

Accola, Paul (Skier)
Bolgenstr 17
Davos Platz 7270, SWITZERLAND

Acconci, Vito (Artist)
20 Jay St Ste 215
Brooklyn, NY 11201-8319, USA

AC/DC (Music Group, Musician)
c/o Christopher Dalston *Creative Artists Agency (CAA-LA)*
2000 Avenue of the Stars Ste 100
Los Angeles, CA 90067-4705, USA

Ace, Buddy (Musician)
1048 Tattnall St
Macon, GA 31201-1537

Ace Hood (Musician)
c/o Staff Member *Island Def Jam Music Group*
825 8th Ave Fl 28
New York, NY 10019-7416

Ace of Base (Music Group, Musician)
c/o John Orlando *Urbania Group (Sweden)*
Box 3184
Stockholm 103 63, Stockholm

Acevedo, Hernan F (Scientist)
320 E North Ave
Pittsburgh, PA 15212-4756

Acevedo, Juan (Athlete, Baseball Player)
143 Madera Cir
Carpentersville, IL 60110-1110, USA

Acevedo, Kirk (Actor)
c/o Chris Schmidt *Paradigm (LA)*
360 N Crescent Dr
Beverly Hills, CA 90210-4874, USA

Ache, Steve (Athlete, Football Player)
22 Lashley Estates Dr
Swansea, IL 62226-2502, USA

Achebe, Chinua (Writer)
PO Box 41
Annandale, NY 12504-0041, USA

Achica, George (Athlete, Football Player)
3165 Lone Bluff Way
San Jose, CA 95111-1264, USA

Achtymichuk, Gene (Athlete, Hockey Player)
305-9985 93 Ave
Fort Saskatchewan, AB T8L 1N5, Canada

Acid Test (Music Group)
83 Riverside Dr
New York, NY 10024-5713, USA

Ackeman, Leslie (Actor)
950 2nd St Apt 201
Santa Monica, CA 90403-2439, USA

Acker, Amy (Actor)
c/o Matthew Lesher *Insight*
1134 S Cloverdale Ave
Los Angeles, CA 90019-6737, USA

Acker, Bill (Athlete, Football Player)
1809 Walker Dr
Alice, TX 78332-4126, USA

Acker, Jack (Athlete, Baseball Player)
8120 E Del Joya Dr
Scottsdale, AZ 85258-2203, USA

Acker, Jim (Athlete, Baseball Player)
PO Box 214
Freer, TX 78357-0214, USA

Acker, Joseph E (Doctor)
1307 Old Weisgarber Rd
Knoxville, TN 37909

Acker, Tom (Athlete, Baseball Player)
118 Gloucester Rd
Stuarts Draft, VA 24477-3328, USA

Ackeren, Robert V (Director)
Kurfurstendamm 132A
Berlin 10711, GERMANY

Acker-Macosko, Anna (Athlete, Golfer)
304 Earl Dr
Kerrville, TX 78028-7019, USA

Ackerman, Buddy (Athlete, Basketball Player)
27 Nassau Rd
Oceanside, NY 11572-3016, USA

Ackerman, Gary (Congressman, Politician)
2111 Rayburn Hob
Washington, DC 20515-0201, USA

Ackerman, Joshua (Actor)
c/o Joanna (Joanie) Burstein *Burstein Company, The*
15304 W Sunset Blvd Ste 208
Pacific Palisades, CA 90272-3656, USA

Ackerman, Malin (Actor)
c/o Staff Member *Sanders Armstrong Caserta*
2120 Colorado Ave Ste 120
Santa Monica, CA 90404-3561, USA

Ackerman, Michael W (General)
Hqusa Inspector General
Washington, DC 20310-0001, USA

Ackerman, Rick (Athlete, Football Player)
125 Zog Ln
Laramie, WY 82072-9546, USA

Ackerman, Roger G (Business Person)
Houghton Park
Corning, NY 14831-0001, USA

Ackerman, Thomas E (Cinematographer)
1644 San Leandro Ln
Montecito, CA 93108-2638, USA

Ackerman, Tom (Athlete, Football Player)
17511 N Greenbluff Rd
Colbert, WA 99005-9505, USA

Ackerman, William (Composer)
177 Woodland Ave
Westwood, NJ 07675-3218, USA

Ackermann, Rosemarie (Athlete, Track Athlete)
Str der Jugend 72
Cottbus 3050, GERMANY

Ackland, Joss (Actor)
c/o Staff Member *Jonathan Altaras Assoc Ltd*
11 Garrick Street Covent Garden
London WC2E 9AT, UNITED KINGDOM (UK)

Ackles, Jensen (Actor)
c/o Lainie Sorkin Becky *Management 360*
9111 Wilshire Blvd
Beverly Hills, CA 90210-5508, USA

Ackroyd, David (Actor)
PO Box 9041
Kalispell, MT 59904-2041, USA

Ackroyd, Peter (Writer)
43 Doughty St
London WC1N 2LF, UNITED KINGDOM (UK)

Acks, Ron (Athlete, Football Player)
563 Licklog Rdg
Hayesville, NC 28904-4879, USA

Acomb, Doug (Athlete, Hockey Player)
18 Millstone Ct
Markham, ON L3R 7M4, Canada

Acorah, Derek (Actor)
PO Box 32 Ormskirk
Lancashire L40 9SN, UNITED KINGDOM

Acord, Lance (Cinematographer)
c/o Staff Member *Dattner Dispoto and Associates*
10635 Santa Monica Blvd Ste 165
Los Angeles, CA 90025-8306, USA

Acosta, Eduardo (Ed) (Athlete, Baseball Player)
22822 Boltana
Mission Viejo, CA 92691-1717, USA

Acovone, Jay (Actor)
c/o Richard Lewis *Geddes Agency, The*
8430 Santa Monica Blvd Ste 200
Los Angeles, CA 90069-4253, USA

Acre, Mark (Athlete, Baseball Player)
840 E Riviera Pl
Chandler, AZ 85249-6970, USA

Acres, Mark (Athlete, Basketball Player)
233 6th St
Manhattan Beach, CA 90266-5735, USA

Acrivos, Andreas (Scientist)
145 W 67th St
New York, NY 10023-5923, USA

Acta, Manny (Athlete, Baseball Player, Coach)
6427 Shoreline Dr
Saint Cloud, FL 34771-8786, USA

Acton, Bud (Athlete, Basketball Player)
PO Box 87
Empire, MI 49630-0087, USA

Acton, Keith (Athlete, Coach, Hockey Player)
400-40 Bay St Attn Coaching Staff
Toronto, ON M5J 2X2, Canada

Acton, Loren W (Astronaut)
PO Box 1857
Bozeman, MT 59771-1857, USA

Acuff, Amy
4102 Bobwhite
Robstown, TX 78380-6060, USA

Acuna, Alicia (Correspondent)
c/o Staff Member *Fox News Channel (NY)*
1211 Ave Of The Americas Level C1
New York, NY 10036-8701, USA

Acuna, Jason (Wee Man) (Actor)
c/o Alan Somers *Pure Arts Entertainment*
1925 Century Park E Ste 2320
Los Angeles, CA 90067-2724, USA

Aczel, Janos D (Mathematician)
97 McCarron Crescent
Waterloo ON N2L 5M9, CANADA

Adade, Manohar (Actor, Bollywood)
199 Vellala Street Purasawakkam
Chennai, TN 600 084, INDIA

Adair, Deborah (Actor)
c/o Staff Member *Cast Images*
2530 J St Ste 330
Sacramento, CA 95816-4849, USA

Adair, Tatum (Actor)
10929 Vanowen St Ste 138
North Hollywood, CA 91605-6435, USA

Adam, Robert (Architect)
9 Upper High St Winchester
Hants S023 8UT, UNITED KINGDOM (UK)

Adam, Russ (Athlete, Hockey Player)
69 Old Petty Harbour Rd
St. John's, NL A1G 1H6, Canada

Adam, Theo (Opera Singer)
Schillerstr 14
Dresden 1326, GERMANY

Adamchik, Ed (Athlete, Football Player)
234 Princeton Ave
Pittsburgh, PA 15229-1516, USA

Adamkus, Valdas (Politician, President)
Gediminas 53
Vilnius 232026, LITHUANIA

Adams, Alvan (Athlete, Basketball Player)
5617 N Palo Cristi Rd
Paradise Valley, AZ 85253-7544, USA

Adams, Amy (Actor)
c/o Stacy O'Neil *Brillstein Entertainment Partners*
9150 Wilshire Blvd Ste 350
Beverly Hills, CA 90212-3453, USA

Adams, Bob (Athlete, Baseball Player)
31713 157th St E
Llano, CA 93544-1222, USA

Adams, Brent (Athlete, Football Player)
3615 Parkmont Ct
Norcross, GA 30092-4521, USA

Adams, Brooke (Actor)
248 S Van Ness Ave
Los Angeles, CA 90004-3921

Adams, Bryan (Musician)
c/o Bruce Allen *Bruce Allen Talent*
425 Carrall St Suite 500
Vancouver, BC V6B 6E3, Canada

Adams, Bryan (Athlete, Hockey Player)
c/o Staff Member *Sports Personnel Services*
125 Lake St W Ste 200
Wayzata, MN 55391-1573, USA

Adams, Charles (Athlete, Baseball Player)
6058 Puerto Dr
Rancho Murieta, CA 95683-9314, USA

Adams, Charles J (Religious Leader)
601 50th St NE
Washington, DC 20019-5450

Adams, Craig (Athlete, Hockey Player)
8030 Sherwood Dr
Presto, PA 15142-1078, USA

Adams, Curtis (Athlete, Football Player)
258 W Towering Oaks Cir
Muskegon, MI 49442-8442, USA

Adams, David (Dave) (Athlete, Football Player)
2780 N La Cienega Dr
Tucson, AZ 85715-3504, USA

Adams, Dick (Athlete, Baseball Player)
4650 Dulin Rd Spc 136
Fallbrook, CA 92028-9362, USA

Adams, Doug (Athlete, Baseball Player)
1129 Harmony Cir NE
Janesville, WI 53545-2072, USA

Adams, Earnest (Athlete, Football Player)
1061 NW 25th Way
Fort Lauderdale, FL 33311-5710, USA

Adams, Evan (Actor)
c/o Staff Member *Characters Talent Agency, The (Vancouver)*
1505 W 2nd Ave #200
Vancouver, BC V6H 3Y4, Canada

Adams, Flozell (Athlete, Football Player)
5201 Reflection Ct
Flower Mound, TX 75022-8144, USA

Adams, Gaines (Athlete, Football Player)
PO Box 49397
Greenwood, SC 29649-0007, USA

Adams, George (Athlete, Football Player)
2410 Damsel Katie Dr
Lewisville, TX 75056-5801, USA

Adams, George (Athlete, Basketball Player)
508 Watergate Cir
Gastonia, NC 28052-7718, USA

Adams, George R (Musician)
300 Mercer St Apt 3J
New York, NY 10003-6732

Adams, Gerard (Gerry) (Politician)
51/55 Falls Rd
Belfast, Northern Ireland BT 12, United Kingdom

Adams, Glenn (Athlete, Baseball Player)
12333 E Tecumseh Rd
Norman, OK 73026-8640, USA

Adams, Greg (Athlete, Hockey Player)
c/o Staff Member *Cowichan Valley Capitals*
2687 James St
Duncan, BC V9L 2X5, Canada

Adams, Greg (Athlete, Hockey Player)
19864 N 83rd Pl
Scottsdale, AZ 85255-3915, USA

Adams, Hank (Athlete, Football Player)
53 4th St
California, PA 15419-1109, USA

Adams, Henry
53 4th St
California, PA 15419-1109, USA

Adams, Herb (Athlete, Baseball Player)
4021 E 84th St
Tulsa, OK 74137-1724, USA

Adams, Jane (Actor)
c/o Staff Member *Framework Entertainment (LA)*
9057 Nemo St Ste C
West Hollywood, CA 90069-5511, USA

Adams, Jeb Stuart (Actor)
1163 Calle Vista Dr
Beverly Hills, CA 90210-2507, USA

Adams, Joey Lauren (Actor)
c/o Staff Member *Caliber Media Company*
9229 W Sunset Blvd Ste 705
West Hollywood, CA 90069-3407, USA

Adams, John (Athlete, Hockey Player)
109 Nottingham Crst
Thunder Bay, ON P7G 1B4, Canada

Adams, John (Athlete, Golfer)
4610 County Road 42200
Paris, TX 75462-1391, USA

Adams, John C (Musician)
c/o Staff Member *Elektra Records*
75 Rockefeller Plz Fl 17
New York, NY 10019-6927, USA

Adams, John H (Religious Leader)
1134 11th St NW
Washington, DC 20001-4316

Adams, Julie (Actor)
145 S Fairfax Ave Ste 310
Los Angeles, CA 90036-2176

Adams, Julius (Athlete, Football Player)
2135 Jefferson Davis St
Macon, GA 31201, USA

Adams, Keith (Athlete, Football Player)
9 N 9th St Unit 712
Philadelphia, PA 19107-3156, USA

Adams, Kenneth S (Bud) (Athlete, Football Player)
c/o Team Member *Tennessee Titans*
1 Titans Way
Nashville, TN 37213-1234

Adams, Kevyn (Athlete, Hockey Player)
9172 Curry Ln
Clarence Center, NY 14032-9504, USA

Adams, Linda
c/o Staff Member *Crews*
828 Clemont Dr NE
Atlanta, GA 30306-3694, USA

Adams, Lorraine (Journalist)
1150 15th St
Washington, DC 20071-0001

Adams, Lynn (Athlete, Golfer)
2445 Brant St Unit 207
San Diego, CA 92101-1364, USA

Adams, Mark (Artist)
209 10th Ave
San Francisco, CA 94118-2212, USA

Adams, Mary Kay (Actor)
PO Box 2023
Fairfield, IA 52556-0034, USA

Adams, Maud (Actor)
c/o Staff Member *Bondstars.com*
Pinewood Studios Iver Heath
Bucks SL0 0NH, UNITED KINGDOM

Adams, Michael F (Educator)
President S Ofc
Athens, GA 30602-0001, USA

Adams, Michele (Stylist)
c/o Staff Member *Marnie Rose Agency*
37 Lower Shad Rd
Pound Ridge, NY 10576-2216, USA

Adams, Mike (Athlete, Baseball Player)
13205 Jo Ln NE
Albuquerque, NM 87111-7112, USA

Adams, Mike (Athlete, Baseball Player)
800 Booty St
Sinton, TX 78387-3210, USA

Adams, Mike (Athlete, Football Player)
228 Flinn St
Hutto, TX 78634-3298, USA

Adams, Mike (Athlete, Football Player)
70 Graham Ave
Paterson, NJ 07524-2423, USA

Adams, Neal (Producer)
15 W 39th St Fl 9
New York, NY 10018-0631, USA

Adams, Neile McQueen (Actor)
10128 Empyrean Way Apt 203
Los Angeles, CA 90067-3801, USA

Adams, Noah (Correspondent)
635 Massachusetts Ave NW
Washington, DC 20001-3740, USA

Adams, Oleta (Music Group)
209 10th Ave South Dr # 429B
Nashville, TN 37203, USA

Adams, Pat (Artist)
370 Elm St
Bennington, VT 05201-2214, USA

Adams, Patch (Doctor)
6855 Washington Blvd
Arlington, VA 22213-1120, USA

Adams, Patrick (Actor)
c/o Andy Corren *Andy Corren Management*
Prefers to be contacted via email or telephone
CA, USA

Adams, Pete (Athlete, Football Player)
1443 Hygeia Ave
Encinitas, CA 92024-1624, USA

Adams, Ranald T Jr (General)
1002 Emerald Dr
Alexandria, VA 22308-2626, USA

Adams, Red (Athlete, Baseball Player)
6058 Puerto Dr
Rancho Murieta, CA 95683-9314, USA

Adams, Richard G (Writer)
26 Church St Whitechurch
Hants RG28 7AR, UNITED KINGDOM (UK)

Adams, Richard N (Doctor, Misc)
PO Box Zz
Basalt, CO 81621-0800, USA

Adams, Ricky (Athlete, Baseball Player)
6437 Garnet St
Rancho Cucamonga, CA 91701-4009, USA

Adams, Russ (Athlete, Baseball Player)
2342 Lake Heather Heights Ct
Dunedin, FL 34698-5647, USA

Adams, Ryan (Music Group, Songwriter, Writer)
751 Bridgeway # 300
Sausalito, CA 94965-2102, USA

Adams, Sam (Athlete, Football Player)
218 Main St Apt 514
Kirkland, WA 98033-6108, USA

Adams, Sam E (Athlete, Football Player)
12010 Holly Stone Dr
Houston, TX 77070-5420, USA

Adams, Sandy (Congressman, Politician)
216 Cannon Hob
Washington, DC 20515-4325, USA

Adams, Scott (Cartoonist)
10 E 53rd St
New York, NY 10022-5244, USA

Adams, Scott (Athlete, Football Player)
1171 Middlebrooks Rd
Watkinsville, GA 30677-3820, USA

Adams, Stan (Athlete, Football Player)
502 S Highland Dr
Cedar Hill, TX 75104-2873, USA

Adams, Stefon (Athlete)
1734 Trotters Ln
Stone Mountain, GA 30087-2337, USA

Adams, Tag (Adult Film Star)
c/o Staff Member *Diva Central Inc*
7510 W Sunset Blvd Ste 1445
Los Angeles, CA 90046-3408, USA

Adams, Terry (Athlete, Baseball Player)
11315 Howells Ferry Rd
Semmes, AL 36575-6655, USA

Adams, Theo (Athlete, Football Player)
9555 Highland Park Dr
Roseville, CA 95678-2911, USA

Adams, Tom (Athlete, Football Player)
20606 Crystal Springs Loop
Grand Rapids, MN 55744-5183, USA

Adams, Tony (Athlete, Football Player)
14012 Juniper St
Overland Park, KS 66224-3578, USA

Adams, Trace (Music Group)
1222 16th Ave S Ste 23
Nashville, TN 37212-2926, USA

Adams, Vashone (Athlete, Football Player)
2940 S Parker Ct
Aurora, CO 80014-3018, USA

Adams, William J (Athlete, Football Player)
12 Willowby Way
Lynnfield, MA 01940-1022, USA

Adams, Willie (Athlete, Baseball Player)
11903 Kibbee Ave
La Mirada, CA 90638-1518, USA

Adams, Willie J (Athlete, Football Player)
2513 Forest Creek Dr
Fort Worth, TX 76123-1145, USA

Adams, Willis (Athlete, Football Player)
7831 Quail Meadow Dr
Houston, TX 77071-2337, USA

Adams, Yolanda (Music Group, Musician)
c/o Lynn Jeter *Lynn Jeter & Associates*
3699 Wilshire Blvd Ste 850
Los Angeles, CA 90010-2737, USA

Adams, Yolonda (Musician)
75 Rockefeller Plz
New York, NY 10019-6908

Adams Jr, Robert McCornick (Misc)
PO Box Zz
Basalt, CO 81621-0800, USA

Adamson, Andrew (Director)
c/o Jeremy Zimmer *United Talent Agency (UTA)*
9560 Wilshire Blvd Fl 5
Beverly Hills, CA 90212-2400, USA

Adamson, Joel (Athlete, Baseball Player)
14832 S 46th Pl
Phoenix, AZ 85044-6872, USA

Adamson, Ken (Athlete, Football Player)
5061 Jardin Ln
Carmichael, CA 95608-6070, USA

Adamson, Mike (Athlete, Baseball Player)
17610 Canterbury Dr
Monument, CO 80132-8310, USA

Adamson IV, Robert (Actor)
c/o Theo Asweissen *Koopman Management*
851 Oreo Pl
Pacific Palisades, CA 90272-2457, USA

Adamson Jr, Robert E (Admiral)
1709 Bohnhoff Ct
Virginia Beach, VA 23454-2520, USA

Adar, Nir (Stylist)
c/o Celebrity Stylist *Zenobia Agency Inc*
PO Box 909
Groveland, CA 95321-0909, USA

Addai, Joseph (Athlete, Football Player)
11826 Elkington Ct
Houston, TX 77071-3287, USA

Addams, Abe (Athlete, Football Player)
477 Colesburg Rd
Elizabethtown, KY 42701-6144, USA

Addams, Calpernia (Actor, Reality TV Star)
c/o Staff Member *Deep Stealth Productions*
5419 Hollywood Blvd # C-142
Los Angeles, CA 90027-3480, USA

Addeney, Herb (Athlete, Football Player)
1058 Tristram Cir
Mantua, NJ 08051-2204, USA

Adderly, Herbert A (Herb) (Athlete, Football Player)
1058 Tristram Cir
Mantua, NJ 08051-2204, USA

Addis, Bob (Athlete, Baseball Player)
7466 Hollycroft Ln
Mentor, OH 44060-5611, USA

Addison, Rafael (Athlete, Basketball Player)
6 Bernadette Ct
East Hanover, NJ 07936-3425, USA

Addison, Tom (Athlete, Football Player)
47 Devant Dr E
Okatie, SC 29909-4537, USA

Adduci, Jim (Athlete, Baseball Player)
16314 Crescent Lake Dr
Crest Hill, IL 60403-1643, USA

Adduono, Rick (Athlete, Hockey Player)
153 Donald St W
Thunder Bay, ON P7E 5X8, Canada

Addy, Mark (Actor)
c/o Staff Member *ID PR (LA)*
7060 Hollywood Blvd Fl 8
Los Angeles, CA 90028-6014, USA

Ade, King Sunny (Music Group)
200 W Superior St Ste 202
Chicago, IL 60654-3554, USA

Adebayor, Emmanuel (Athlete, Soccer Player)
c/o Staff Member *Manchester City FC*
City of Manchester Stadium SportCity
Manchester M11 3FF, UK

Adedapo, Naima (Musician)
c/o Simon Fuller *XIX Entertainment*
33/32 Ransomes Dock 35-37 Parkgate Rd
London SW11 4NP, UK

Adele (Musician)
c/o Lucy Dickins *International Talent Booking*
1st Floor, Ariel House 74A Charlotte St
London W1T 4QJ, UNITED KINGDOM

Adelman, Kenneth L (Government Official)
4018 27th St N
Arlington, VA 22207-5207, USA

Adelman, Rick (Athlete, Basketball Player, Coach)
11919 SW Breyman Ave
Portland, OR 97219-8412, USA

Adelson, Sheldon (Business Person)
3355 Las Vegas Blvd S
Las Vegas, NV 89109-8941, USA

Adelstein, Paul (Actor)
c/o Marsha McManus *Principal Entertainment (LA)*
1964 Westwood Blvd Ste 400
Los Angeles, CA 90025-4695, USA

Adem (Music Group)
c/o Staff Member *Paradigm (Monterey)*
404 W Franklin St
Monterey, CA 93940-2303, USA

Aderholt, Robert (Congressman, Politician)
205 4th Ave NE Ste 104
Cullman, AL 35055-1965, USA

Adey, Christopher
137 Anson Road
Willesden Green NW2 4AH, UNITED KINGDOM (UK)

Adeyamju, Victor (Athlete, Football Player)
5375 S Maplewood Ave
Chicago, IL 60632-1537, USA

Adickes, John M (Athlete, Football Player)
205 W Fair Oaks Pl
San Antonio, TX 78209-3710, USA

Adickes, Mark (Athlete, Football Player)
6146 Bordley Dr
Houston, TX 77057-1124, USA

Adie, Kate (Journalist)
c/o Staff Member *Peller Artistes Limited*
39 Princes Ave
London N3 2DA, UK

Adiga, Aravind (Writer)
c/o Staff Member *Penguin Group (Australia)*
P.O. Box 701
Hawthorn VIC 3122, Australia

Adjani, Isabelle (Actor)
c/o Staff Member *ArtMedia*
20 avenue Rapp
Paris 75008, France

Adjodhia, Jules (Prime Minister)
Kleine Combeweg 1
Paramaribo, SURINAME

Adkins, Adele Laurie Blue (Adele) (Musician)
c/o Staff Member *September Management*
80/82 Chiswick High Rd
London W4 1SY, UK

Adkins, James (Athlete, Baseball Player)
185 Cedar Ridge Ct
Coppell, TX 75019-2981, USA

Adkins, Jon (Athlete, Baseball Player)
5322 Fisher Bowen Branch Rd
Wayne, WV 25570-5946, USA

Adkins, Kevin (Athlete, Football Player)
185 Cedar Ridge Ct
Coppell, TX 75019-2981, USA

Adkins, Margene (Athlete, Football Player)
2312 Donnyville Ct
Fort Worth, TX 76119-3111, USA

Adkins, Sam (Athlete, Football Player)
15912 NE 160th St
Woodinville, WA 98072-8910, USA

Adkins, Seth (Actor)
c/o Alisa Adler *Paradigm (LA)*
360 N Crescent Dr
Beverly Hills, CA 90210-4874, USA

Adkins, Trace (Musician)
PO Box 121889
Nashville, TN 37212-1889, USA

Adkisson, Perry L (Educator, Misc)
9211 Lake Forest Ct N
College Station, TX 77845-8757, USA

Adleman, Leonard (Scientist)
Computer Math Dept
Los Angeles, CA 90089-0001, USA

Adler, Andy (Sportscaster)
c/o Staff Member *WmE2 (WMA-LA)*
1 William Morris Pl
Beverly Hills, CA 90212-4261, USA

Adler, Brian (Composer)
2316 Delaware Ave Ste 266
Buffalo, NY 14216-2606, USA

Adler, Charles (Actor)
c/o Luanne Salandy-Regis *Innovative Artists (LA)*
1505 10th St
Santa Monica, CA 90401-2805, USA

Adler, Jerry (Actor)
c/o Alisa Adler *Paradigm (LA)*
360 N Crescent Dr
Beverly Hills, CA 90210-4874, USA

Adler, Lee (Artist)
Lime Kiln Farm
Climax, NY 12042, USA

Adler, Lou (Actor, Director, Producer)
3969 Villa Costera
Malibu, CA 90265-5151, USA

Adler, Matt
PO Box 1866
Studio City, CA 91614-0866, USA

Adler, Richard (Composer, Musician)
PO Box 1151
Southampton, NY 11969-1151, USA

Adler, Stephen L (Physicist)
Einstein Lane
Princeton, NJ 8540, USA

Adler, Steven (Music Group)
PO Box 8074
Huntington Beach, CA 92615-8074, USA

Adlesh, Dave (Athlete, Baseball Player)
9770 Avenida Monterey
Cypress, CA 90630-3446, USA

Adlon, Pamela (Actor, Voice Over Artist)
c/o Staff Member *Meghan Schumacher Management*
13351D Riverside Dr # 387
Sherman Oaks, CA 91423-2508, USA

Adni, Daniel (Musician)
64A Menelik Road
London NW2 3RH, UNITED KINGDOM (UK)

Adoboli, Koffi Eugene (Prime Minister)
BP 5618
Lome, TOGO

Adoor, Gopalkrishnan (Director)
Darsanam
Trivandrum, Kerala 695017, INDIA

Adorf, Mario (Actor)
Perlacher Str 28
Grunwald D-82031, GERMANY

Adoti, Rasaaq (Actor)
c/o Staff Member *Coast to Coast Talent Group*
3350 Barham Blvd
Los Angeles, CA 90068-1404, USA

Adoti, Razaaq (Actor, Producer)
c/o Staff Member *Coast II Coast Entertainment*
8671 Wilshire Blvd Ste 500
Beverly Hills, CA 90211-2943, USA

Adotta, Kip (Actor, Comedian)
PO Box 5734
Santa Rosa, CA 95402-5734, USA

Adria, Ferran (Chef)
En Cala Montjoi Roses
Girona 17480, SPAIN

Adu, Helen Folasade (Sade) (Actor, Musician)
c/o Staff Member *RCA Records (UK)*
9 Derry St
London W8 5HY, UNITED KINGDOM (UK)

Adu, Sade (Musician)
c/o Steven Manzano *RDWM America*
1158 26th St Ste 564
Santa Monica, CA 90403-4698, USA

Adubato, Richie (Athlete, Basketball Player, Coach)
290 Chiswell Pl
Lake Mary, FL 32746-4123, USA

Adulyadey, King (King, Politician)
BhumibolVilla Chitralada
Bangkok, THAILAND

Adway, Dwayne (Actor)
c/o Mark Schumacher *Schumacher Management*
1122 San Vicente Blvd
Santa Monica, CA 90402-2008, USA

Adyrkhayeva, Svetlana D (Ballerina)
1 Smolensky Pereulor 9 #74
Moscow 121099, RUSSIA

Aebischer, David (Athlete, Hockey Player)
365 Jackson St
Denver, CO 80206-4538, USA

Aedo, Daniela (Actor)
c/o Staff Member *Televisa*
Blvd Adolfo Lopez Mateos 232 Colonia San Angel INN
DF CP 01060, MEXICO

Aerle, Taree (Artist, Music Group)
1325 Avenue of the Americas
New York, NY 10019-6026, USA

Aerosmith (Music Group)
c/o Irving Azoff *Azoff Music Management/ Front Line*
1100 Glendon Ave
Los Angeles, CA 90024-3503, USA

Afanasenkov, Dimitry (Athlete, Hockey Player)
5235 Brighton Shore Dr
Apollo Beach, FL 33572-3318, USA

Afanasiyev, Viktor M (Cosmonaut)
Moskovskoi Oblasti
Syvisdny Goroduk 141160, RUSSIA

Afenir, Troy (Athlete, Baseball Player)
459 Old Via Rancho Dr
Escondido, CA 92029-7959, USA

Affeldt, Jeremy (Athlete, Baseball Player)
10111 S Green Gate Ln
Medical Lake, WA 99022-8531, USA

Affholter, Erik (Athlete, Football Player)
40514 N Hawk Ridge Trl
Phoenix, AZ 85086-2921, USA

Affleck, Ben (Actor)
c/o Shawn Sachs *Sunshine, Sachs & Associates*
149 5th Ave Fl 7
New York, NY 10010-6824, USA

Affleck, Bruce (Athlete, Hockey Player)
1847 Oxborough Ct
Chesterfield, MO 63017-8037, USA

Affleck, Casey (Actor, Producer, Writer)
c/o Cynthia Pett-Dante *Brillstein Entertainment Partners*
9150 Wilshire Blvd Ste 350
Beverly Hills, CA 90212-3453, USA

Affleck, James G (Business Person)
5 Giralda Farms
Madison, NJ 07940-1027, USA

Afghan Raiders (Music Group)
c/o David Benveniste *Velvet Hammer*
9014 Melrose Ave
West Hollywood, CA 90069-5610, USA

AFI (Music Group)
c/o Staff Member *Leave Home Booking*
1400 Foothill Dr Ste 34
Salt Lake City, UT 84108-2392, USA

Afinogenov, Maxim (Athlete, Hockey Player)
3700 S Ocean Blvd Apt 1502
Highland Beach, FL 33487-3376, USA

Afrika, Bambaataa (Artist, Musician)
70A Greenwich Ave # 441
New York, NY 10011-8300, USA

Afrojack (Musician)
c/o Joel Zimmerman *WmE2 (WMA-NY)*
1325 Avenue of the Americas
New York, NY 10019-6026, USA

Afroman (Artist, Music Group)
20 Music Sq W
Nashville, TN 37203-3200, USA

Aftermath (Music Group)
c/o Tom Workman *Starcrest Entertainment Corp*
4585 N River Rd
Zanesville, OH 43701-7768, USA

Aga Khan IV, Prince Karim (Religious Leader)
Aiglemont
Gouvieux 60270, FRANCE

Agajanian, Benjamin (Ben) (Athlete, Football Player)
27950 Avenida Terrazo
Cathedral Cty, CA 92234-9401, USA

Agam, Yaacov (Artist)
26 Rue Boulard
Paris 75014, FRANCE

Agarwal, Anu (Actor, Bollywood)
503 Godavari Khan Pochkhawala Road Worli
Mumbai, MS 400025, INDIA

Agassi, Andre (Tennis Player)
8921 Andre Dr
Las Vegas, NV 89148-1405, USA

Agbayani, Benny (Athlete, Baseball Player)
66-948 Kolu Pl
Waialua, HI 96791-9743, USA

Age, Louis (Athlete, Football Player)
4012 Llano Dr
Bourg, LA 70343-3628, USA

Agee, Mel (Athlete, Football Player)
3843 Dragon Fly Ln
Loganville, GA 30052-9085, USA

Agee, Tommie (Athlete, Football Player)
1505 Blackhawk Dr
Opelika, AL 36801-3513, USA

Agena, Keiko (Actor)
c/o Staff Member *Fenton Kritzer Entertainment*
8840 Wilshire Blvd Fl 3
Beverly Hills, CA 90211-2606, USA

Ager, Nikita (Actor)
c/o Kim Byrd *Innovative Artists (LA)*
1505 10th St
Santa Monica, CA 90401-2805, USA

Aghdashloo, Shohreh (Actor)
c/o Tamara Houston *Round Table Entertainment*
15301 Ventura Blvd Ste 400BLDG PMB D
Sherman Oaks, CA 91403-3102, USA

Agna, Tom (Actor, Producer, Writer)
c/o Lisa Harrison *WmE2 (Endeavor-LA)*
9601 Wilshire Blvd Fl 3
Beverly Hills, CA 90210-5219, USA

Agnello Jr, Carmine (Actor)
c/o Staff Member *Britto Agency PR*
234 W 56th St PH
New York, NY 10019-4302, USA

Agnelo, Geraldo Majella Cardinal (Religious Leader)
Rue Martin Alfanso de Souza 270
Salvador, BA 40100-050, BRAZIL

Agnew, Harold M (Physicist)
322 Punta Baja Dr
Solana Beach, CA 92075-1720, USA

Agnew, Jim (Athlete, Hockey Player)
10080 Equestrian Way
Missoula, MT 59808-8578, USA

Agnew Jr, Ray (Athlete, Football Player)
2215 Cline St
Winston Salem, NC 27107-2411, USA

Agnihotri, Atul (Actor, Bollywood)
Ashwini Pali Mala Road Bandra
Mumbai, MS 400050, INDIA

Agnus, Michael (Business Person)
Whitbread PLC Chiswell St
London EC1Y 4SD, UNITED KINGDOM (UK)

Agoos, Jeff (Athlete, Soccer Player)
235 Pascack Rd
Park Ridge, NJ 07656-1125, USA

Agostini, Didier (Actor)
36 Rue de Ponthieu
Paris 75008, FRANCE

Agosto, Ben (Figure Skater)
c/o Staff Member *Champions on Ice*
3500 W 80th St Ste 200
Minneapolis, MN 55431-1090, USA

Agosto, Juan (Athlete, Baseball Player)
4748 Sweetmeadow Cir
Sarasota, FL 34238-3396, USA

Agranoff, Bernard W (Biologist, Doctor)
1942 Boulder Dr
Ann Arbor, MI 48104-4164, USA

Agre, Bernard Cardinal (Religious Leader)
Archeveche Ave Jean-Paul II
Abidjan 01 BP 1287, IVORY COAST

Agre, Peter (Nobel Prize Laureate)
7033 Kenleigh Rd
Baltimore, MD 21212-1904, USA

Agron, Dianna (Actor)
c/o Jessica Kolstad *WKT Public Relations (WKT-LA)*
9350 Wilshire Blvd Ste 450
Beverly Hills, CA 90212-3230, USA

Agt, Andries A M Van (Prime Minister)
Europa House 9-15 Sambancho
Chiyodaku
Tokyo 102, JAPAN

Aguayo, Luis (Athlete, Baseball Player)
PO Box 1427
Vega Baja, PR 00694-1427, USA

Aguiar, Louie (Athlete, Football Player)
1411 Palmer Creek Dr
Columbia, IL 62236-2747, USA

Aguila, Chris (Athlete, Baseball Player)
3955 Falling Water Dr
Reno, NV 89519-2143, USA

Aguilar, Pepe (Musician)
c/o Staff Member *Agency Group Ltd, The (NY)*
142 W 57th St Fl 6
New York, NY 10019-3300, USA

Aguilera, Christina (Musician)
c/o Allison Statter *Azoff Music Management/Front Line*
1100 Glendon Ave
Los Angeles, CA 90024-3503, USA

Aguilera, Hellweg Max (Artist, Photographer)
PO Box 289
White Plains, NY 10605-0289, USA

Aguilera, Richard W (Rick) (Athlete, Baseball Player)
PO Box 174
Rancho Santa Fe, CA 92067-0174, USA

Aguirre, Beatriz (Actor)
c/o Staff Member *Televisa*
Blvd Adolfo Lopez Mateos 232 Colonia San Angel INN
DF CP 01060, MEXICO

Aguirre, Mark A (Athlete, Basketball Player)
10281 Highland Ct
Frisco, TX 75033-2415, USA

Agustoni, Gilberto Cardinal (Religious Leader)
Piazzi della Citla Leorina 9
Rome 193, ITALY

Agutter, Jenny (Actor)
c/o Staff Member *Marmont Management*
Langham House 308 Regent St
London W1B 3AT, UNITED KINGDOM (UK)

Agyeman, Freema (Actor)
c/o Sarah Camlett *Independent Talent Group (ITG-UK)*
Oxford House 76 Oxford St
London W1D 1BS, UK

Ahanotu, Chidi (Athlete, Football Player)
301 W Platt St
Tampa, FL 33606-2292, USA

Ahdout, Jonathan (Actor)
c/o Leonard Torgan *Collective*
8383 Wilshire Blvd Ste 1050
Beverly Hills, CA 90211-2415, USA

Aheam, Kevin (Athlete, Hockey Player)
174 Marlborough St
Boston, MA 02116-1822, USA

Ahearne, Pat (Athlete, Baseball Player)
246 Milam Ln
Bastrop, TX 78602-3108, USA

Ahem, Jim (Golfer)
314 E Wagon Wheel Dr
Phoenix, AZ 85020-4066, USA

Ahern, Bertie (Prime Minister)
Upper Merrion St
Dublin, IRELAND

Ahern, Cecelia (Writer)
c/o Staff Member *Bazar Forlag*
Hammarby Fabriksvag 25
Stockholm 12033, Sweden

Ahern, Fred (Athlete, Hockey Player)
807 E 5th St
Boston, MA 02127-3217, USA

Ahern, Jim (Athlete, Golfer)
130 E Glendale Ave
Phoenix, AZ 85020-4824, USA

Ahern, Neal (Producer)
c/o Staff Member *WmE2 (WMA-LA)*
1 William Morris Pl
Beverly Hills, CA 90212-4261, USA

Ahith, Kumar (Actor)
8/10 Norton Apartment Floor I PMB MANDAVELLI
Chennai, TN 600 028, INDIA

Ahmed, Kazi Zafar (Prime Minister)
Jatiya Sangsad
Dhaka, BANGLADESH

Ahmed, Riz
c/o Kate Bryden *Gordon and French*
12-13 Poland St
London W1F 8QB, UNITED KINGDOM (UK)

Aho, Esko (Prime Minister)
Pursimiehenkatu 15
Helsinki 150, FINLAND

Ahrens, David (Dave) (Athlete, Football Player)
5864 Manchester Ct
Pittsboro, IN 46167-9064, USA

Ahrens, Lynn (Musician)
c/o Staff Member *Gersh (LA)*
9465 Wilshire Blvd Ste 600
Beverly Hills, CA 90212-2612, USA

Ahrens, Thomas J (Geophysicist, Physicist)
Seismology Laboratory
Pasadena, CA 91125-0001, USA

Ahronovitch, Yuri
Hotorget 8
Stockholm, SWEDEN

Ahtisaari, Martti (Nobel Prize Laureate)
Erottajankatu 11 A
Helsinki 130, Finland

Ahuja, Shiney (Actor)
c/o Bunty Behl *Artist International Management*
304-305 Oberoi Chambers II B Wing Off New Link Road
Anderhi West, Mumbai 400053, India

Aida, Takefumi (Architect)
1-3-2 Okubo Shinjukuku
Tokyo 169, JAPAN

Aiello, Anthony (Athlete, Football Player)
11 Henry St
Norwalk, OH 44857-2406, USA

Aiello, Danny (Actor, Director, Producer)
c/o Johnnie Planco *Parseghian Planco LLC*
322 8th Ave Ste 601
New York, NY 10001-6715, USA

Aiken, Clay (Musician)
c/o Simon Renshaw *Strategics Artist Management*
1100 Glendon Ave Ste 1000
Los Angeles, CA 90024-3514, USA

Aiken, John (Athlete, Hockey Player)
18 Pinetree Rd
Billerica, MA 01821-3446, USA

Alken, Liam (Actor)
c/o Ellen Gilbert *Abrams Artists Agency (NY)*
275 7th Ave Fl 26
New York, NY 10001-6708, USA

Aiken, Linda H (Activist)
2209 Lombard St
Philadelphia, PA 19146-1107, USA

Aiken, Sam (Athlete, Football Player)
103 New Bingham Ct
Cary, NC 27513-4093, USA

Aikens, Carl (Athlete, Football Player)
931 W Arquilla Dr Apt 114
Glenwood, IL 60425-1143, USA

Aikens, Curtis (Chef)
68 Baca Vis
Novato, CA 94947-2102, USA

Aikens, Willie (Athlete, Baseball Player)
PO Box 150160
Atlanta, GA 30315-0160, USA

Aikman, Laura Holly (Actor)
551 Green Lanes Palmers Green
London N13 3DR, UNITED KINGDOM (UK)

Aikman, Troy (Athlete, Football Player)
4425 Highland Dr
Dallas, TX 75205-3817, USA

Aikman-Smith, Valerie (Stylist)
2110 E Live Oak Dr
Los Angeles, CA 90068-3639, USA

Ailes, Roger E (Business Person)
c/o Staff Member *Fox News Channel (NY)*
1211 Ave Of The Americas Level C1
New York, NY 10036-8701, USA

Aimee, Anouk (Actor)
c/o Staff Member *ArtMedia*
20 avenue Rapp
Paris 75008, France

Aimi, Milton (Athlete, Soccer Player)
19927 Stonelodge St
Katy, TX 77450-5201, USA

Ainge, Daniel R (Danny) (Athlete, Basketball Player)
140 Wellesley Ave
Wellesley Hills, MA 02481-7209, USA

Ainge, Danny (Athlete, Baseball Player)
140 Wellesley Ave
Wellesley Hills, MA 02481-7209, USA

Ainge, Erik (Athlete, Football Player)
634 NE Kathleen Ct
Hillsboro, OR 97124-4029, USA

Ainsleigh, H Gordon (Athlete, Track Athlete)
17119 Placer Hills Rd
Meadow Vista, CA 95722-9508, USA

Ainsworth, Kurt (Athlete, Baseball Player)
15220 Memorial Tower Dr
Baton Rouge, LA 70810-0301, USA

Air, Donna (Model, Television Host)
c/o Staff Member *The Richard Stone Partnership*
2 Henrietta St
London WC2E 8PS, UK

Air Supply (Music Group, Musician)
c/o Staff Member *Agency for the Performing Arts (APA-LA)*
405 S Beverly Dr Ste 500
Beverly Hills, CA 90212-4425, USA

Airborne Toxic Event, The (Music Group)
c/o Staff Member *Paradigm (Monterey)*
404 W Franklin St
Monterey, CA 93940-2303, USA

Airpushers (Music Group)
c/o Staff Member *Paradigm (Monterey)*
404 W Franklin St
Monterey, CA 93940-2303, USA

Aitay, Victor (Musician)
800 Deerfield Rd Apt 203
Highland Park, IL 60035-3548, USA

Aitch, Matt (Athlete, Basketball Player)
1525 Bentbrook Cir
Lansing, MI 48917-1402, USA

Aitken, Brad (Athlete, Hockey Player)
825 Royal Orchard Dr
Oshawa, ON L1K 1Z8, Canada

Aitken, Ellie Mae (Stylist)
c/o Staff Member *Fred Segal Beauty*
PO Box 5304
Beverly Hills, CA 90209-5304, USA

Aitken, John (Artist)
Slade Art School
London WC1E 6BT, UNITED KINGDOM (UK)

Aivazoff, Micah (Athlete, Hockey Player)
6916 Hammond St
Powell River, BC V8A 1R4, Canada

Aizenberg Selove, Fay (Physicist)
118 Cherry Ln
Wynnewood, PA 19096-1209, USA

Aizley, Carrie (Actor)
c/o Staff Member *Much and House Public Relations*
8075 W 3rd St Ste 500
Los Angeles, CA 90048-4325, USA

Ajayrathnam (Actor)
78 Gajapathy Street Shenoy Nagar
Chennai, TN 600 030, INDIA

Akaka, Daniel K. (Senator)
141 Hart Senate Ofc Building
Washington, DC 20510-0001, USA

Akayev, Askar (President)
Government House
Bishkek 720003, KYRGYZSTAN

Akbar, Hakim (Athlete, Football Player)
29869 Vanderbilt St Apt 4
Hayward, CA 94544-6873, USA

Akbar, Taufik (Astronaut)
Jalan Simp Pahlawan III/24
Bandung 40124, INDONESIA

Akebono (Wrestler)
4-6-4 Higashi Komagala Ryogoku
Tokyo, JAPAN

Akens, Jewel (Musician)
5228 Marburn Ave
Los Angeles, CA 90043-2103, USA

Aker, Jack (Athlete, Baseball Player)
5911 E Bloomfield Rd
Scottsdale, AZ 85254-4338, USA

Akerfelds, Darrel (Athlete, Baseball Player)
10858 W Buccaneer Dr
Sun City, AZ 85351-2641, USA

Akerlof, George A (Nobel Prize Laureate)
Economics Dept Evans Hall
Berkeley, CA 94720-0001, USA

Akerlund, Jonas (Director)
c/o Staff Member *International Creative Management (ICM-LA)*
10250 Constellation Blvd Fl 7
Los Angeles, CA 90067-6207, USA

Akerman, Malin (Actor)
c/o Steve Caserta *Sanders Armstrong Caserta*
2120 Colorado Ave Ste 120
Santa Monica, CA 90404-3561, USA

Akers, David (Athlete, Football Player)
16 Penhale Psge
Medford, NJ 08055-3357, USA

Akers, Fred (Coach, Football Coach)
Athletic Dept
West Lafayette, IN 47907, USA

Akers, John F (Business Person)
PO Box 194
Pebble Beach, CA 93953-0194, USA

Akers, Michelle (Soccer Player)
c/o Staff Member *US Soccer Federation*
1801 S Prairie Ave
Chicago, IL 60616-1356, USA

Akhtar, Farhan (Producer)
205 Devroop Bldg, 36 Turner Rd
Opposite Tava Restaurant, Bandra West
Mumbai 400 050, India

Akhtar, Javed (Songwriter, Writer)
702 Sagar Samrat Green Field Road Near Juhu P O Juhu
Bombay, MS 400 049, INDIA

Akihito (King)
1-1 Chiyoda Chiyodaku
Tokyo 100, JAPAN

Akihoto, EmperorThe Palace
1-1 ChiyodaChiyoda-Ku
Tokyo, JAPAN

Akil, Mara Brock (Producer, Writer)
c/o Andrea Nelson-Meigs *International Creative Management (ICM-LA)*
10250 Constellation Blvd Fl 7
Los Angeles, CA 90067-6207, USA

Akil, Salim (Director)
c/o Staff Member *International Creative Management (ICM-LA)*
10250 Constellation Blvd Fl 7
Los Angeles, CA 90067-6207, USA

Akili, Samaji (Athlete, Football Player)
10605 Caminito Cascara
San Diego, CA 92108-2601, USA

Akin, Harold (Athlete, Football Player)
12608 Cobblestone Pkwy
Oklahoma City, OK 73142-2217, USA

Akin, Henry (Athlete, Basketball Player)
18924 40th Pi NE
Lake Forest Park, WA 98155, USA

Akin, W. Todd (Congressman, Politician)
117 Cannon Hob
Washington, DC 20515-2502, USA

Akinnuoye-Agbaje, Adewale (Actor)
c/o Pamela Kohl *3 Arts Entertainment Inc*
9460 Wilshire Blvd Fl 7
Beverly Hills, CA 90212-2713, USA

Akins, Chris (Athlete, Football Player)
60 Gold Mine Springs Rd
Conway, AR 72032-8204, USA

Akins, Rhett (Musician)
209 10th Ave S Ste 229
Nashville, TN 37203-0721, USA

Akiu, Mike (Athlete, Football Player)
PO Box 1845
Kailua, HI 96734-8845, USA

Akiyama, Kazuyoshi (Conductor)
165 W 57th St
New York, NY 10019-2201, USA

Akiyama, Toyohiro (Astronaut, Journalist)
3-6-5 Akasaka Minaloku
Tokyo 107, JAPAN

Akiyoshi, Toshiko (Composer, Musician)
2608 9th St
Berkeley, CA 94710-2550, USA

Akon (Musician)
PO Box 190022
Atlanta, GA 31119-0022, USA

Akoshino (Royalty)
Tokyo, JAPAN

Akroyd, Dan (Actor, Musician, Producer, Writer)
c/o Fred Specktor *Creative Artists Agency (CAA-LA)*
2000 Avenue of the Stars Ste 100
Los Angeles, CA 90067-4705, USA

Aksyonov, Vassily P (Writer)
1745 Broadway # B1
New York, NY 10019-4368, USA

Aksyonov, Vladimir V (Cosmonaut)
Astrakhansky Per 5 Kv 100
Moscow 129010, RUSSIA

Al and the Transamericans (Music Group)
c/o Staff Member *Paradigm (Monterey)*
404 W Franklin St
Monterey, CA 93940-2303, USA

Al Fayed, Mohammed
The Ritz Hotel Place Vendome
Paris, FRANCE

Al Hussein, HH King Abdullah (Royalty)
The Royal Hashemite Court
Amman, Jordan

Al Maktum, Muhammad bin Raschid
Royal Palace P.O.Box 899
Abu Dhabi, United Arabian Emirates

Al Maktum, Sheikh Muhammad bin Raschid (Government Official)
Royal Palace P.O. Box 899
Abu Dhabi, United Arabian Emirates

Al Nahyan, Mansour bin Zayed (Business Person)
P.O. Box 6316
Abu Dhabi, United Arab Emirates

Al Nahyan, Sheikh Khalifa Bin Zayed (Royalty)
President°s Office Manhal Palace
Abu Dhabi, United Arab Emirates

Al Saud, HRH Crown Prince Emir Bandar Ibn Sultan (Royalty)
Council of Minister
Murabba, Riyadh 11121, Saudi Arabia

Al Saud, King Abdullah bin Abdul Aziz (Royalty)
Council of Minister
Murabba, Riyadh 11121, Saudi Arabia

Alabama (Music Group)
c/o Dale Morris *Morris Management Group, Inc*
818 19th Ave S
Nashville, TN 37203-3202, USA

Alagna, Roberto (Opera Singer)
2 Rue du Prieure
Nyon 1260, SWITZERLAND

Alaia, Azzeddine (Designer, Fashion Designer)
18 Rue de la Verrerie
Paris 75008, FRANCE

Alaigal, Selvakumar (Actor)
9A Pari St Avvai Nagar Choolaimedu
Chennai, TN 600 094, INDIA

Alaimo, Doris (Stylist)
2560 Greencastle Ct
Oxnard, CA 93035-2901, USA

Alaina, Lauren (Musician)
c/o Simon Fuller *XIX Entertainment*
33/32 Ransomes Dock 35-37 Parkgate Rd
London SW11 4NP, UK

Alan, Buddy (Musician)
600 E Gilbert Dr
Tempe, AZ 85281-2021, USA

Alan, Lori (Voice Over Artist)
9200 W Sunset Blvd Ste 1130
Los Angeles, CA 90069-3606, USA

Alarcon, Arthur L (Judge)
312 N Spring St
Los Angeles, CA 90012-4701, USA

Alarie, Mark (Athlete, Basketball Player)
8514 Country Club Dr
Bethesda, MD 20817-4581, USA

Al-Assad, Bashar (Politician, President)
c/o Staff Member *Presidential Office (Syria)*
Muharreem Abu Rumanch Al-Rashid Street
Damascas, Syria

Alatorre, Javier (Actor)
c/o Staff Member *TV Azteca*
Periferico Sur 4121 Colonia Fuentes del Pedregal
DF CP 14141, Mexico

al-Aziz, Abdullah Ibn Abdul (Prince)
Murabba
Riyadh 11121, SAUDI ARABIA

Alazraqui, Carlos (Actor)
c/o Heidi Rotbart *Heidi Rotbart Management*
1810 Malcolm Ave Apt 207
Los Angeles, CA 90025-7610, USA

Alba, Gibson (Athlete, Baseball Player)
87 E 17th St
Paterson, NJ 07524-1516, USA

Alba, Jessica (Actor)
c/o Brad Cafarelli *PMK/BNC - LA*
8687 Melrose Ave Ste 8
West Hollywood, CA 90069-5746, USA

Alban, Richard (Dick) (Athlete, Football Player)
306 Belpaire Ct
Newtown Square, PA 19073-2128, USA

Albanese, Licia (Opera Singer)
Nathan Hale Dr Wilson Point
South Norwalk, CT 6854, USA

Albarn, Damon (Musician, Songwriter, Writer)
Ransomes Dock 35 Parkgale Road #32
London SW11 4NP, UNITED KINGDOM (UK)

Albea, Troy (Athlete, Football Player)
1070 L and N Rd
Lincolnton, GA 30817-4724, USA

Albeck, Stan (Athlete, Basketball Player, Coach)
130 Tall Oak Dr
San Antonio, TX 78232-1316, USA

Albee, Edward (Writer)
14 Harrison St
New York, NY 10013-2842, USA

Albee, Edward F (Writer)
14 Harrison St
New York, NY 10013-2842, USA

Albelin, Tommy (Athlete, Coach, Hockey Player)
c/o Staff Member *New Jersey Devils*
165 Mulberry St
Newark, NJ 07102-3607, USA

Alberghetti, Anna Maria (Actor, Musician)
2800 28th St Ste 101
Santa Monica, CA 90405-6212, USA

Alberghini, Tom (Athlete, Football Player)
8514 Hempstead Ave
Bethesda, MD 20817-6710, USA

Alberoni, Sherry (Actor)
PO Box 161936
Altamonte Springs, FL 32716-1936, USA

Albers, Hans (Business Person)
Carl-Bosch-Str 38
Ludwigshafen 78351, GERMANY

Albers, Kristi (Athlete, Golfer)
5872 Via Cuesta Dr
El Paso, TX 79912-6608, USA

Albers, Matthew James (Athlete, Baseball Player)
15 S Swanwick Pl
Tomball, TX 77375-4478, USA

Alberstein, Chara (Musician)
PO Box 2728
Bala Cynwyd, PA 19004-6728, USA

Albert, Calvin (Artist)
6525 Brandywine Dr S
Margate, FL 33063-5538, USA

Albert, John G (General)
Albert Farms RR2
Monroe, VA 24574, USA

Albert, Marv (Sportscaster)
1050 Techwood Dr NW
Atlanta, GA 30318-5604, USA

Albert II (King)
Rue de Brederode
Brussels 1000, BELGIUM

Albert (Prince) (Royalty)
Palais de Monaco Boite Postale 518
Monacode Cedex 98015, MONACO

Alberti, Micah (Actor)
c/o David Dean Portelli *Precision Entertainment*
6338 Wilshire Blvd
Los Angeles, CA 90048-5002, USA

Alberto, Padre (Actor)
c/o Staff Member *Telemundo*
2470 W 8th Ave
Hialeah, FL 33010-2000, USA

Alberts, Andrew (Athlete, Hockey Player)
601 Laurel Oak Rd
Voorhees, NJ 08043-4423, USA

Alberts, Francis (Butch) (Athlete, Baseball Player)
3063 Amberlea Ln
Baldwinsville, NY 13027-1613, USA

Alberts, Trev (Athlete, Football Player)
10430 E Hickory Ridge Dr
Rochelle, IL 61068-9790, USA

Albinski, Gillian V (Stylist)
5927 Pepperhill Rd
Charlotte, NC 28212-4638, USA

Albita (Musician)
6205 Bird Rd
Miami, FL 33155-4823, USA

Albom, Mitch (Writer)
25600 Franklin Park Dr
Franklin, MI 48025-1211, USA

Albrecht, A Chim (Wrestler)
9668 Moss Glen Ave
Fountain Valley, CA 92708-1053, USA

Albrecht, Alex (Actor)
c/o Mieke Gotha *Agentur Gotha*
Elisabethstrasse 19
München 80796, Germany

Albrecht, Gerd
535 El Camino Del Mar
San Francisco, CA 94121-1041, USA

Albrecht, Karl (Business Person)
1200 N Kirk Rd
Batavia, IL 60510-1443, USA

Albrecht, Kate (Actor)
c/o Brad Petrigala *Brillstein Entertainment Partners*
9150 Wilshire Blvd Ste 350
Beverly Hills, CA 90212-3453, USA

Albrecht, Ted (Athlete, Football Player)
1205 Cherry St
Winnetka, IL 60093-2116, USA

Albrecht, Theo (Business Person)
1200 N Kirk Rd
Batavia, IL 60510-1443, USA

Albright, Ethan (Athlete, Football Player)
PO Box 38337
Greensboro, NC 27438-8337, USA

Albright, Gerald (Musician)
c/o Ron Moss *Chapman Management*
14011 Ventura Blvd
Sherman Oaks, CA 91423-3533, USA

Albright, Ira (Athlete, Football Player)
4019 Wind River Dr
Dallas, TX 75216-6064, USA

Albright, Irene (Stylist)
62 Cooper Sq # 200
New York, NY 10003-7101, USA

Albright, Lola (Actor)
213 N Valley St # 136
Burbank, CA 91505, USA

Albright, Madeleine (Politician, Secretary)
1101 New York Ave NW
Washington, DC 20005-4269, USA

Albright, Tenley E (Doctor)
186 Windswept Way
Osterville, MA 2655, USA

Albright, William (Bill) (Athlete, Football Player)
315 Bolands Private Dr
Shell Lake, WI 54871-8723, USA

Albuquerque, Lita (Artist)
305 Boyd St
Los Angeles, CA 90013-1509, USA

Albury, Victor (Vic) (Athlete, Baseball Player)
9411 N Nebraska Ave
Tampa, FL 33612-8024, USA

Albus, Jim (Athlete, Golfer)
3972 Somerset Dr Unit 1
Sarasota, FL 34242-1110, USA

Alcala, Santo (Athlete, Baseball Player)
Ramon Mota #18
San Pedro de Macoris, Dominican Republic

Alcantara, Izzy (Athlete, Baseball Player)
4059 240th Pl SE
Issaquah, WA 98029-6304, USA

Alcaraz, Lalo (Cartoonist, Editor)
PO Box 63052
Los Angeles, CA 90063-0052, USA

Alcaraz, Luis (Athlete, Baseball Player)
678 Calle Chihuahua
San Juan, PR 00926-4615, USA

Alcorn, Gary (Athlete, Basketball Player)
2552 Trenton Ave
Clovis, CA 93619-4249, USA

Alcorn, Randy (Motivational Speaker, Writer)
39085 Pioneer Blvd Ste 206
Sandy, OR 97055-8062, USA

Alcott, Amy S (Athlete, Golfer)
323 Amalfi Dr
Santa Monica, CA 90402-1127, USA

Alda, Alan (Actor)
c/o Toni Howard *International Creative Management (ICM-LA)*
10250 Constellation Blvd Fl 7
Los Angeles, CA 90067-6207, USA

Alda, Rutanya (Actor)
c/o Hazel Shallon *Shallon Star Management*
14320 Ventura Blvd # 624
Sherman Oaks, CA 91423-2717, USA

Aldcorn, Gary (Athlete, Hockey Player)
P.O. Box 5072 RPO Claremont
Claremont, ON L1Y 1Z8, Canada

Aldean, Jason (Musician)
c/o Chris Parr *Spalding Entertainment*
1025 16th A S Suite 393
Nashville, TN 37212, USA

Alden, Bruce (Producer)
c/o Staff Member *Vision Art Management*
9465 Wilshire Blvd Ste 870
Beverly Hills, CA 90212-2610, USA

Alden, Ginger (Actor, Model, Musician)
79 Shelley Renee Ln
Cordova, TN 38018-7377, USA

Alden, Norman (Actor)
c/o John Frazier *Amsel, Eisenstadt & Frazier Talent Agency (AEF)*
5055 Wilshire Blvd Ste 860
Los Angeles, CA 90036-6108, USA

Alden Robinson, Phil (Director, Producer, Writer)
4000 Warner Blvd Bldg 1
Burbank, CA 91522-0001, USA

Alderete, Loretta (Athlete, Golfer)
80194 Delphi Ct
Indio, CA 92201-8430, USA

Alderfer-Benner, Gertrude (Athlete, Baseball Player)
2191 County Line Rd
East Greenville, PA 18041-2700, USA

Alderman, Darrell (Race Car Driver)
8145 Flemingsburg Rd
Morehead, KY 40351, USA

Alderman, Grady (Athlete, Football Player)
62 Elk Valley Way
Evergreen, CO 80439-4951, USA

Alderson, Kristen (Actor)
c/o Staff Member *One Life to Live*
56 E 66th St
New York, NY 10065-6538, USA

Alderton, John (Athlete, Football Player)
12314 Williams Rd SE
Cumberland, MD 21502-7961, USA

Aldisert, Ruggero J (Judge)
120 Cremona Dr # 0
Goleta, CA 93117-5511, USA

Aldiss, Brian W (Writer)
39 Saint Andrews Road Old Headington
Oxford OX3 9DL, UNITED KINGDOM (UK)

Aldred, Scott (Athlete, Baseball Player)
13435 Lakebrook Dr
Fenton, MI 48430-8420, USA

Aldred, Sophie (Actor)
1 Duchess St #1
London S1N 3EE, UNITED KINGDOM (UK)

Aldredge, Theoni V (Designer)
425 Lafayette St
New York, NY 10003-7021, USA

Aldrete, Mike (Athlete, Baseball Player)
22160 Toro Hills Dr
Salinas, CA 93908-1131, USA

Aldrich, Cole (Athlete, Basketball Player)
c/o Jeff Schwartz *Excel Sports Management*
9665 Wilshire Blvd Ste 500
Beverly Hills, CA 90212-2312, USA

Aldrich, Jay (Athlete, Baseball Player)
9209 S 51st St
Franklin, WI 53132-9275, USA

Aldrich, John H (Politician, Scientist)
Political Science
Durham, NC 27708-0001, USA

Aldridge, Cory (Athlete, Baseball Player)
417 Penrose Dr
Abilene, TX 79601-6228, USA

Aldridge, Donald O (General)
1004 Lincoln Rd # 168
Bellevue, NE 68005-2341, USA

Aldridge, Edward C (pete) Jr (Government Official)
2350 E El Segundo Blvd
El Segundo, CA 90245-4609, USA

Aldridge, Jerry (Athlete, Football Player)
297 Ellis
Jacksonville, TX 75766, USA

Aldridge, Keith (Athlete, Hockey Player)
80 Joslyn Rd
Lake Orion, MI 48362-2215, USA

Aldridge, Kevin (Athlete, Football Player)
734 Rosecrans St
San Diego, CA 92106-3013, USA

Aldridge, Melvin (Athlete, Football Player)
14618 Braden Dr E
Houston, TX 77047-6752, USA

Aldridge, Sabrina (Actor)
c/o Allee Newhoff *Elite Model Management*
119 Washington Ave Ste 501
Miami Beach, FL 33139-7228, USA

Aldridge Jr, Allen (Athlete, Football Player)
2111 Hammerwood Dr
Missouri City, TX 77489-4137, USA

Aldridge Sr, Allen (Athlete, Football Player)
2111 Hammerwood Dr
Missouri City, TX 77489-4137, USA

Aldrin, Edwin (Buzz) (Astronaut)
c/o Staff Member *Cunningham Escott Slevin & Doherty (CESD-LA)*
10635 Santa Monica Blvd Ste 130
Los Angeles, CA 90025-8306, USA

Ale, Arnold (Athlete, Football Player)
308 E Desford St
Carson, CA 90745-2111, USA

Aleaga, Ink (Athlete, Football Player)
14612 22nd Ave SW
Burien, WA 98166-1610, USA

Aleandro, Norma (Actor)
Blanco Encalada 1150
Buenos Aires 1428, ARGENTINA

Alechinsky, Pierre (Artist)
2 Bis Rue Henri Barbusse
Bougival 78380, FRANCE

Alejandro, Kevin (Actor)
c/o Stewart Strunk *Main Title Entertainment*
2225 Wilshire Blvd Suite 500
Los Angeles, CA 90036, USA

Alekperov, Vagit (Business Person)
11, Sretensky Blvd
Moscow 101000, Russia

Aleksander, Grant (Actor)
c/o Robert Attermann *Abrams Artists Agency (LA)*
9200 W Sunset Blvd PH 11
Los Angeles, CA 90069-3601, USA

Aleksinas, Charles (Chuck) (Athlete, Basketball Player)
16 Litchfield Rd
Morris, CT 06763-1522, USA

Aleksiy II (Religious Leader)
Chisty Per 5
Moscow 119034, RUSSIA

Aleno, Charles (Athlete, Baseball Player)
601 Marion Ct
Deland, FL 32720-3217, USA

Alerlol, George (Nobel Prize Laureate)
Economics
Berkeley, CA 94720-0001, USA

Alesi, Jean (Race Car Driver)
Benzstr 8
Affalterbach 71563, GERMANY

Alessandri, Mary Beth (Stylist)
c/o Staff Member *Zenobia Agency Inc*
PO Box 909
Groveland, CA 95321-0909, USA

Alessi, Raquel (Actor)
c/o Rhonda Price *Gersh (NY)*
41 Madison Ave
New York, NY 10010-2202, USA

Alex (Actor)
2 Rajaji Street Pushpa Nagar
Nungambakkam N
Chennai, TN 600 034, USA

Alex, Keith (Athlete, Football Player)
6985 Reno Cir
Beaumont, TX 77708-3594, USA

Alexakis, Art (Musician)
30 Glenn St
White Plains, NY 10603-3254, USA

Alexakos, Steve (Athlete, Football Player)
306 W Linden St
Boise, ID 83706-4830, USA

Alexander, A Lamar (Ex-Governor, Senator)
455 Dirksen Senate Ofc Building
Washington, DC 20510-0001, USA

Alexander, Brent (Athlete, Football Player)
349 Remington Ave
Gallatin, TN 37066-7536, USA

Alexander, Brooke (Actor)
c/o Staff Member *Abrams Artists Agency (LA)*
9200 W Sunset Blvd PH 11
Los Angeles, CA 90069-3601, USA

Alexander, Bruce (Athlete, Football Player)
508 Englewood Dr
Lufkin, TX 75901-5844, USA

Alexander, Charles (Athlete, Football Player)
3711 Heritage Colony Dr
Missouri City, TX 77459-4055, USA

Alexander, Christopher W J (Architect)
2701 Shasta Rd
Berkeley, CA 94708-1923, USA

Alexander, Claire (Athlete, Hockey Player)
11 Tammy Cir
St.Catherines, ON L1Y 1R2, Canada

Alexander, Clifford L Jr (Government Official)
412 A St SE
Washington, DC 20003-3807, USA

Alexander, Corey (Athlete, Basketball Player)
440 Alpha St
Waynesboro, VA 22980-3904, USA

Alexander, Dan (Athlete, Football Player)
58520 Saint Clement Ave
Plaquemine, LA 70764-3532, USA

Alexander, Dan (Athlete, Football Player)
407 Knob Ct
Franklin, TN 37064-2390, USA

Alexander, David (Athlete, Football Player)
11420 S Granite Pl
Tulsa, OK 74137-8113, USA

Alexander, Denise (Actor)
270 N Canon Dr # 1919
Beverly Hills, CA 90210-5323, USA

Alexander, Derrick S (Athlete, Football Player)
25381 W 149th Ct
Olathe, KS 66061-8531, USA

Alexander, Doyle
5416 Hunter Park Ct
Arlington, TX 76017-3557, USA

Alexander, Doyle (Athlete, Baseball Player)
5416 Hunter Park Ct
Arlington, TX 76017-3557, USA

Alexander, Elijah (Athlete, Football Player)
4800 Longvue Dr
Frisco, TX 75034-7550, USA

Alexander, Eric (Musician)
300 Mercer St Apt 3J
New York, NY 10003-6732, USA

Alexander, Erika (Actor)
c/o Staff Member *Untitled Entertainment (LA)*
350 S Beverly Dr Ste 200
Beverly Hills, CA 90212-4819, USA

Alexander, Flex (Actor)
c/o Joel Zadak *Principato/Young Management*
9465 Wilshire Blvd Ste 430
Beverly Hills, CA 90212-2613, USA

Alexander, Gary (Athlete, Baseball Player)
5420 Senford Ave
Los Angeles, CA 90056 1029, USA

Alexander, Gerald (Athlete, Baseball Player)
307 Woodland Dr
Donaldsonville, LA 70346-9752, USA

Alexander, Harold (Athlete, Football Player)
590 J D Dr
Pickens, SC 29671-9035, USA

Alexander, J (Reality TV Star, Television Host)
c/o Staff Member *Bankable Productions*
226 W 26th St Fl 4
New York, NY 10001-6700, USA

Alexander, Jaimie (Actor)
c/o Randy James *James/Levy/Jacobson Management Inc*
3500 W Olive Ave Ste 1470
Burbank, CA 91505-5514, USA

Alexander, Jamie (Actor)
c/o Alicia Gelernt *Alicia Gelernt*
275 Madison Ave Fl 28
New York, NY 10016-1101, USA

Alexander, Jane (Actor, Government Official)
1325 Ave Of Americans
New York, NY 10019, USA

Alexander, Jason (Actor, Comedian, Producer)
c/o Lisa Strelchuk *Paradigm (LA)*
360 N Crescent Dr
Beverly Hills, CA 90210-4874, USA

Alexander, Jeff (Athlete, Football Player)
5283 Elkhart St
Denver, CO 80239-6042, USA

Alexander, John (Athlete, Football Player)
312 Lee Pl
Plainfield, NJ 07063-1337, USA

Alexander, Jules (Musician)
1924 Spring St
Paso Robles, CA 93446-1620, USA

Alexander, Keith (Actor)
c/o Staff Member *Cunningham Escott Slevin & Doherty (CESD-LA)*
10635 Santa Monica Blvd Ste 130
Los Angeles, CA 90025-8306, USA

Alexander, Kermit (Athlete, Football Player)
16651 Stallion Pl
Riverside, CA 92504-5872, USA

Alexander, Khandi (Actor)
c/o Lee Wallman *Wallman Public Relations*
10323 Santa Monica Blvd Ste 109
Los Angeles, CA 90025-5056, USA

Alexander, Lloyd (Writer)
c/o Staff Member *Random House Publicity*
1745 Broadway
New York, NY 10019-4368, USA

Alexander, Manny (Athlete, Baseball Player)
3660 N Lake Dr Apt 2664
Chicago, IL 60613, USA

Alexander, Matt (Athlete, Baseball Player)
2419 Stonewall St
Shreveport, LA 71103-3451, USA

alexander, maximillian (Actor)
c/o Staff Member *Schumacher Management*
1122 San Vicente Blvd
Santa Monica, CA 90402-2008, USA

Alexander, Monty (Musician)
1282 RR 376
Wappingers Falls, NY 12590, USA

Alexander, Nicole (Hoopz) (Actor)
9611 Victoria Ln
Taylor, MI 48180-7520, USA

Alexander, Patrise (Athlete, Football Player)
15035 Westpark Dr Apt 514
Houston, TX 77082-3942, USA

Alexander, R Minter (General)
824 Eden Ct
Alexandria, VA 22308-2034, USA

Alexander, Ray (Athlete, Football Player)
1631 Royal Palm Dr
Edgewater, FL 32132-3213, USA

Alexander, Robert (Athlete, Football Player)
10147 Tramore Ave Apt B
Englewood, FL 34224-9303, USA

Alexander, Robert M (Misc)
14 Moor Park Mount
Leeds LS6 4BU, UNITED KINGDOM (UK)

Alexander, Roc (Athlete, Football Player)
22020 E Belleview Pl
Aurora, CO 80015-6597, USA

Alexander, Rodney (Congressman, Politician)
316 Cannon Hob
Washington, DC 20515-1805, USA

Alexander, Rogers (Athlete, Football Player)
8182 Rainwater Cir
Manassas, VA 20111-5231, USA

Alexander, Sarah (Actor)
c/o Jane Brand *Independent Talent Group (ITG-UK)*
Oxford House 76 Oxford St
London W1D 1BS, UK

Alexander, Sasha (Actor, Producer)
c/o Frank Frattaroli *Dontanville/Frattaroli (D/F)*
270 Lafayette St Ste 402
New York, NY 10012-3327, USA

Alexander, Shasha (Actor, Producer)
c/o Steve Dontanville *Dontanville/ Frattaroli (D/F)*
8609 Washington Blvd # 8607
Culver City, CA 90232-7441, USA

Alexander, Shaun (Athlete, Football Player)
c/o Ben Dogra *CAA - St. Louis*
222 S Central Ave Ste 1008
Saint Louis, MO 63105-3509, USA

Alexander, Stephen (Athlete, Football Player)
3492 Westbrook Ln
Highlands Ranch, CO 80129-1527, USA

Alexander, Susana (Actor)
c/o Staff Member *TV Azteca*
Periferico Sur 4121 Colonia Fuentes del Pedregal
DF CP 14141, Mexico

Alexander, Victor (Athlete, Basketball Player)
3450 Holly Trail Ln
Alpharetta, GA 30022-5943, USA

Alexander, Vincent (Athlete, Football Player)
622 W 30th Ave
Covington, LA 70433-2012, USA

Alexander, Willie (Musician)
894 Mayville Rd
Bethel, ME 04217-4605, USA

Alexander, Willie (Athlete, Football Player)
7219 Holder Forest Cir
Houston, TX 77088-7431, USA

Alexander of Weedon, Robert S (Financier)
41 Lothbury
London EC2P 2BP, UNITED KINGDOM (UK)

Alexander (Prince Yogoslavia) (Prince)
36 Park Lane
London W1Y 3LE, UNITED KINGDOM (UK)

Alexandre, Boniface (Judge, President)
Palacio Nacional
Port-au-Prince, HAITI

Alexandrov, Alexander P (Cosmonaut)
Hovanskaya Ul 3 #27
Moscow 129515, RUSSIA

Alexeev, Nikita (Athlete, Hockey Player)
PO Box 3342
Riverview, FL 33568-3342, USA

Alexie, Sherman (Writer)
PO Box 376
Wellpinit, WA 99040-0376, USA

Alexis, Alton (Athlete, Football Player)
PO Box 16153
Fort Worth, TX 76162-0153, USA

Alexis, Kim (Actor)
PO Box 1490
Wayne, NJ 07474-1490, USA

Alfaro, Jason (Athlete)
7409 Pensacola Ave
Fort Worth, TX 76116-7834, USA

Alferov, Zhores (Nobel Prize Laureate)
26 Polyteknicheskaya
Saint Petersburg 194021, RUSSIA

Alfieri, Janet (Cartoonist)
15 Bumpus Rd
Plymouth, MA 02360-3511, USA

Alflen, Ted (Athlete, Football Player)
960 NE 27th Ave
Pompano Beach, FL 33062-4214, USA

Alfonseca, Antonio (Athlete, Baseball Player)
3020 SW 189th Ter
Miramar, FL 33029-5861, USA

Alfonsi, Sharyn (Correspondent)
c/o Staff Member *ABC News*
77 W 66th St Fl 3
New York, NY 10023-6201, USA

Alfonso, Kristian (Actor)
c/o Jack Gilardi *International Creative Management (ICM-LA)*
10250 Constellation Blvd Fl 7
Los Angeles, CA 90067-6207, USA

Alfonzo, Edgardo (Athlete, Baseball Player)
3745 Marietta Way
Saint Cloud, FL 34772-8714, USA

Alford, Brian (Athlete, Football Player)
21011 Kenosha St
Oak Park, MI 48237-3813, USA

Alford, Bruce (Athlete, Football Player)
3201 River Park Dr Apt 756
Fort Worth, TX 76116-9516, USA

Alford, Bruce (Athlete, Football Player)
105 County Road 2965
Kopperl, TX 76652-4610, USA

Alford, Darnell (Athlete, Football Player)
5806 Danielle Dr
Fredericksburg, VA 22407-6485, USA

Alford, Lynwood (Athlete, Football Player)
355 Moon Clinton Rd Apt 2
Coraopolis, PA 15108-2486, USA

Alford, Mike (Athlete, Football Player)
801 Valparaiso Blvd
Niceville, FL 32578-3406, USA

Alford, Steve (Athlete, Basketball Player)
11600 Zinfandel Ave NE
Albuquerque, NM 87122-7104, USA

Alfredsson, Daniel (Athlete, Hockey Player)
c/o Staff Member *C A A Hockey*
822 11th Ave SW Suite 204
Calgary, AB T2R 0E5, Canada

Alfredsson, Helen (Athlete, Golfer)
9034 Crichton Wood Dr
Orlando, FL 32819-4836, USA

Algabid, Hamid (President)
Vice President's Office
Niamey, NIGER

Al-Hoss, Selim (Prime Minister)
Serail Place de l'Eloile
Beirut, LEBANON

Ali, Laila (Athlete, Boxer)
c/o Gary Uberstine *Premier Sports Management*
1401 Ocean Ave Ste 302
Santa Monica, CA 90401-2161, USA

Ali, May May (Actor)
c/o Kristene Wallis *Wallis Agency*
210 N Pass Ave Ste 205
Burbank, CA 91505-3936, USA

Ali, Muhammad (Athlete, Boxer)
PO Box 187
Berrien Springs, MI 49103-0187, USA

Ali, Somy (Actor, Bollywood)
208 Vindhyachal 22 Mount Mary Road Bandra
Bombay, MS 400 050, INDIA

Ali, Tariq (Writer)
c/o Anthony Arnove *Roam Agency*
45 Main St Ste 727
Brooklyn, NY 11201-1076

Ali, Tatyana (Actor)
c/o James Weir *Anderson Group Public Relations*
8060 Melrose Ave Fl 4
Los Angeles, CA 90046-7038, USA

Ali Khan, Saif (Actor, Bollywood)
c/o Jai Khanna *Brillstein Entertainment Partners*
9150 Wilshire Blvd Ste 350
Beverly Hills, CA 90212-3453, USA

Alia, Alyssa (Stylist)
3 Edgewood Ct
North Caldwell, NJ 07006-4313, USA

Alice In Chains (Music Group)
c/o David Benveniste *Velvet Hammer*
9014 Melrose Ave
West Hollywood, CA 90069-5610, USA

Alicea, Luis (Athlete, Baseball Player)
2140 C Rd
Loxahatchee, FL 33470-3837, USA

Alicea, Wilmer (Baby Rasta) (Musician)
c/o Staff Member *Universal Music Publishing Group*
2440 S Sepulveda Blvd Ste 100
Los Angeles, CA 90064-1744, USA

Alien Ant Farm (Music Group)
c/o David Gibson *New Ocean Media*
270 Doug Baker Blvd Ste 700
Birmingham, AL 35242-8300, USA

Aliens, The (Music Group)
c/o Staff Member *Paradigm (Monterey)*
404 W Franklin St
Monterey, CA 93940-2303, USA

Alikhan, Anwar (Actor)
Parkavi Apartments Phase IV No 15-F 18
Mariamman Koil Street West K K Nagar
Chennai, TN 600 078, INDIA

Alington, William H (Architect)
60 Homewood Crescent
Wellington, NEW ZEALAND

Alipate, Tuineau (Athlete, Football Player)
801 E 101st St
Minneapolis, MN 55420-5121, USA

Alisha (Musician)
250 W 57th St
New York, NY 10107-0001, USA

Alison, Jane (Writer)
19 Union Sq W
New York, NY 10003-3304, USA

Alito, Samuel A Jr (Judge)
50 Walnut St
Newark, NJ 07102-3551, USA

Aliyev, Ilham (President)
Baku 370066, AZERBAIJAN

Alkan, Erol (Musician)
c/o Joel Zimmerman *WmE2 (WMA-NY)*
1325 Avenue of the Americas
New York, NY 10019-6026, USA

Al-Kharafi, Nasser (Business Person)
Shuwaikh Industrial Area P.O. Box 886
Kuwait Safat 13009, Kuwait

All For One / All-4-One (Music Group)
c/o Staff Member *Performers Of the World/ Management Interests Associates (POW/MIA)*
8901 Melrose Ave Fl 2
West Hollywood, CA 90069-5605, USA

All Saints (Music Group)
72 Chancellors Rd
London W6 9SG, UNITED KINGDOM (UK)

All Time Low (Music Group)
PO Box 7495
Van Nuys, CA 91409-7495, USA

Allaben, Maureen (Stylist)
6536 Jamestown Pl
Tucker, GA 30084-1517, USA

Allais, Emile (Skier)
Imeuble Cassiopee
Cluses 7430, FRANCE

Allais, Maurice (Nobel Prize Laureate)
60 Blvd Saint-Michel
Paris 75006, FRANCE

Allam, Roger (Actor)
2 Henrietta St
London WC2E 8PS, UNITED KINGDOM

Allan, Gabrielle (Producer)
c/o Staff Member *United Talent Agency (UTA)*
9560 Wilshire Blvd Fl 5
Beverly Hills, CA 90212-2400, USA

Allan, Gary (Musician)
c/o Staff Member *WmE2 (Endeavor-LA)*
9601 Wilshire Blvd Fl 3
Beverly Hills, CA 90210-5219, USA

Allan, Jed (Actor)
c/o Monique Moss *Warren Cowan & Associates PR*
8899 Beverly Blvd Ste 918
Los Angeles, CA 90048-2427, USA

Allan, Nancy Mayer (Stylist)
c/o Staff Member *The Milton Agency (LA)*
6715 Hollywood Blvd Ste 204
Los Angeles, CA 90028-4656, USA

Allan, Stephen D (Steve) (Golfer)
c/o Staff Member *Pro-Sport Management*
8355 E Hartford Dr Ste 105
Scottsdale, AZ 85255-2533, USA

Allanson, Andy (Athlete, Baseball Player)
1337 Cheetah Way
Palmdale, CA 93551-4351, USA

Allard, Beatrice (Athlete, Baseball Player)
1040 Ridgewood Dr
Lillian, AL 36549-5334, USA

Allard, Brian (Athlete, Baseball Player)
22102 N Perry Rd
Colbert, WA 99005-9488, USA

Allawi, Iyad (Prime Minister)
Karradat Mariam
Baghdad, IRAQ

Allbaugh, Joseph (Government Official)
500 C St SW
Washington, DC 20472-0007, USA

Allegre, Claude J (Misc)
110 Rue Grenelle
Paris 75700, FRANCE

Allegre, Raul (Athlete, Football Player)
6500 Rain Creek Pkwy
Austin, TX 78759-6147, USA

Allem, Fulton (Athlete, Golfer)
6876 Hidden Glade Pl
Sanford, FL 32771-6429, USA

Allen, Agnes (Athlete, Baseball Player)
48226 232nd St
Flandreau, SD 57028-6651, USA

Allen, Aleisha (Actor)
c/o Jan Jarrett *Jordan Gill & Dornbaum*
150 5th Ave Ste 308
New York, NY 10011-4311, USA

Allen, Anthony (Athlete, Football Player)
956 20th Ave
Seattle, WA 98122-4736, USA

Allen, Bernie (Athlete, Baseball Player)
3725 Coventry Way
Carmel, IN 46033-3026, USA

Allen, Beth (Athlete, Golfer)
1602 Peacock Ave
Sunnyvale, CA 94087-4917, USA

Allen, Betty (Opera Singer)
645 Saint Nicholas Ave
New York, NY 10030-1001, USA

Allen, Bob (Athlete, Baseball Player)
PO Box 677
Tatum, TX 75691-0677, USA

Allen, Bob (Athlete, Basketball Player)
485 Marblerock Way
Lexington, KY 40503-6319, USA

Allen, Bruce (Race Car Driver)
1120 Enterprise Pl
Arlington, TX 76001-7138, USA

Allen, Bryan (Athlete, Hockey Player)
7085 Spyglass Ave
Parkland, FL 33076-3965, USA

Allen, Buddy (Athlete, Football Player)
3689 Westmoreland Dr
Mays Landing, NJ 08330-3240, USA

Allen, Byron (Comedian)
c/o Eric Schwartzman *Schwartzman & Associates PR*
1925 Century Park E Ste 2300
Los Angeles, CA 90067-2724, USA

Allen, C Keith (Athlete, Hockey Player)
10000 Highland Ave
Long Beach Township, NJ 08008-3166, USA

Allen, Carl (Athlete, Football Player)
1614 Hornsby Ave
Saint Louis, MO 63147-1410, USA

Allen, Chad (Actor)
c/o Lori Swift *Kazarian, Spencer & Associates (KSA-NY)*
311 W 43rd St Ste 1107
New York, NY 10036-6007, USA

Allen, Chad (Athlete, Baseball Player)
7152 Blackwood Dr
Dallas, TX 75231-5604, USA

Allen, Christa B. (Actor)
c/o Holly Williams *Williams Unlimited*
5010 Buffalo Ave
Sherman Oaks, CA 91423-1414

Allen, Clarence R (Scientist)
1763 Royal Oaks Dr Apt F306
Duarte, CA 91010-1987, USA

Allen, Danielle Sherie (Actor)
c/o Staff Member *Privilege Talent Agency*
PO Box 260860
Encino, CA 91426-0860, USA

Allen, Deborah (Debbie) (Actor, Choreographer)
c/o Staff Member *Red Bird Productions*
3623 Hayden Ave
Culver City, CA 90232-2458, USA

Allen, Derek (Athlete, Football Player)
6206 Woodward Ln
Milton, FL 32570-4577, USA

Allen, Dick (Athlete, Baseball Player)
PO Box 254
Wampum, PA 16157-0254, USA

Allen, Don (Athlete, Football Player)
17303 Kermier Rd
Hockley, TX 77447-9100, USA

Allen, Doug (Artist)
c/o Staff Member *Fantagraphics Books*
7563 Lake City Way NE
Seattle, WA 98115-4218, USA

Allen, Doug (Athlete, Football Player)
10245 Collins Ave Apt 8A
Bal Harbour, FL 33154-1406, USA

Allen, Duane D (Musician)
88 New Shackle Island Rd
Hendersonville, TN 37075-2393, USA

Allen, Dusty (Athlete, Baseball Player)
913 Estrella Vista St
Las Vegas, NV 89138-7578, USA

Allen, Earl (Athlete, Football Player)
8015 Duffield Ln
Houston, TX 77071-2016, USA

Allen, Egypt (Athlete, Football Player)
2115 Rubens Dr
Dallas, TX 75224-4146, USA

Allen, Eric (Athlete, Football Player)
484 San Elijo St
San Diego, CA 92106-3463, USA

Allen, Frances E (Scientist)
Finney Farm
Croton on Hudson, NY 10520, USA

Allen, George F (Ex-Governor, Ex-Senator)
F.M. Kirby Freedom Center 110 Eden St
Herndon, VA 20170, USA

Allen, Geri (Composer, Musician)
307 Lake St
San Francisco, CA 94118-1320, USA

Allen, Grady (Athlete, Football Player)
317 Circleview Dr N
Hurst, TX 76054-3518, USA

Allen, Greg (Athlete, Football Player)
5006 Persimmon Hollow Rd
Milton, FL 32583-2739, USA

Allen, Hank (Athlete, Baseball Player)
PO Box 4612
Upper Marlboro, MD 20775-0612, USA

Allen, Henry (Critic)
1150 15th St NW
Washington, DC 20071-0001, USA

Allen, Herb (Business Person)
711 5th Ave Fl 9
New York, NY 10022-3168, USA

Allen, Ian (Athlete, Football Player)
11 Havenhill Rd
Hamburg, NJ 07419-1271, USA

Allen, J Presson (Producer, Writer)
1501 Broadway Ste 1614
New York, NY 10036-5600, USA

Allen, Jackie (Athlete, Football Player)
7152 Blackwood Dr
Dallas, TX 75231-5604, USA

Allen, Jamie (Athlete, Baseball Player)
1920 E Belmont Dr
Tempe, AZ 85284-1719, USA

Allen, Jared (Athlete, Football Player)
c/o Denise White *EAG Sports Management*
12910 Agustin Pl
Playa Vista, CA 90094-2301, USA

Allen, Jared (Athlete, Football Player)
c/o Ken Harris *Optimum Sports Management*
3225 S Macdill Ave Ste 330
Tampa, FL 33629-8171, USA

Allen, Jason (Athlete, Football Player)
2002 Edwards Ave
Muscle Shoals, AL 35661-1918, USA

Allen, Jeff (Athlete, Football Player)
7808 State Route 177
Camden, OH 45311-9680, USA

Allen, Jimmy (Athlete, Football Player)
830 Maine Ave
Long Beach, CA 90813-4025, USA

Allen, Joan (Actor)
c/o Simon Halls *Slate Public Relations*
9000 W Sunset Blvd Ste 915
West Hollywood, CA 90069-5809, USA

Allen, Johnny (Athlete, Football Player)
21 Fishermans Cv
Lake Placid, FL 33852-6258, USA

Allen, Jonelle (Actor)
c/o Staff Member *Silver Massetti & Szatmary (SMS) Talent Inc*
8730 W Sunset Blvd Ste 440
Los Angeles, CA 90069-2277, USA

Allen, Joseph P (Astronaut)
c/o Astronaut Office 2101 NASA Rd 1
Houston, TX 77058, USA

Allen, Karen (Actor)
8 Railroad St
Great Barrington, MA 01230-1521, USA

Allen, Keith (Athlete, Hockey Player)
10000 Highland Ave
Long Beach Township, NJ 08008-3166, USA

Allen, Kenderick (Athlete, Football Player)
1931 Southpointe Dr
Baton Rouge, LA 70808-4156, USA

Allen, Kevin (Director)
52/53 Poland Place
London W1F 7LX, UNITED KINGDOM (UK)

Allen, Kevin (Athlete, Football Player)
2422 Hazelcrest Ln
Cincinnati, OH 45231-1132, USA

Allen, Kim (Athlete, Baseball Player)
2705 La Praix St
Highland, CA 92346-1928, USA

Allen, Kris (Musician)
c/o Staff Member *19 Entertainment*
33/32 Ransomes Dock 35-37 Parkgate Rd
London SW11 4NP, UK

Allen, Krista (Actor)
c/o Todd Eisner *Agency for the Performing Arts (APA-LA)*
405 S Beverly Dr Ste 500
Beverly Hills, CA 90212-4425, USA

Allen, Larry C (Athlete, Football Player)
401 Kingswood Ln
Danville, CA 94506-6066, USA

Allen, Leo (Writer)
c/o Staff Member *Saturday Night Live*
30 Rockefeller Plz Fl 2
New York, NY 10112-0044, USA

Allen, Lew Jr (General)
555 Technology Sq
Cambridge, MA 02139-3539, USA

Allen, Lily (Musician)
c/o Staff Member *Paradigm (Monterey)*
404 W Franklin St
Monterey, CA 93940-2303, USA

Allen, Linwood (Stylist)
c/o Staff Member *Axis Models & Talent*
PO Box 367
Ringwood, NJ 07456-0367, USA

Allen, Lloyd (Athlete, Baseball Player)
2340 Castlewood Dr
Toledo, OH 43613-3923, USA

Allen, Lou (Athlete, Football Player)
1309 Hobbs Rd
Greensboro, NC 27410-4823, USA

Allen, Loy Jr (Race Car Driver)
1508 Kildaire Farm Rd
Cary, NC 27511-6552, USA

Allen, Lucius (Athlete, Basketball Player)
1915 Buckingham Rd
Los Angeles, CA 90016-1701, USA

Allen, Luke (Athlete, Baseball Player)
255 Mitchell Rd
Covington, GA 30014-6171, USA

Allen, Marcus (Athlete, Football Player)
c/o Jamie Fritz *Fritz Martin Management*
1801 Avenue of the Stars Ste 250
Los Angeles, CA 90067-5914, USA

Allen, Marty (Actor, Comedian)
c/o Staff Member *Lomar Productions*
5750 Wilshire Blvd Ste 580
Los Angeles, CA 90036-3695, USA

Allen, Marvin (Athlete, Football Player)
1806 Las Cruces Ln
Wichita Falls, TX 76306-5205, USA

Allen, Maryon P (Ex-Senator, Politician)
1551 Creekstone Cir
Birmingham, AL 35243-2827, USA

Allen, Michael (Athlete, Golfer)
5827 E Anderson Dr
Scottsdale, AZ 85254-5941, USA

Allen, Michael (Athlete, Football Player)
8839 NE 147th St
Kenmore, WA 98028-4727, USA

Allen, Nancy (Activist, Actor)
13520 Ventura Blvd
Sherman Oaks, CA 91423-3802, USA

Allen, Natalie (Correspondent)
1050 Techwood Dr NW
Atlanta, GA 30318-5604, USA

Allen, Neil (Athlete, Baseball Player)
3619 Torrey Pines Blvd
Sarasota, FL 34238-2828, USA

Allen, Pam (Athlete, Golfer)
809 Delphinium Dr
Billings, MT 59102-3409, USA

Allen, Patrick (Athlete, Football Player)
427 20th Ave E
Seattle, WA 98112-5313, USA

Allen, Paul (Business Person)
505 5th Ave S Ste 900
Seattle, WA 98104-3821, USA

Allen, Rae (Actor)
c/o Staff Member *Kyle Fritz Management*
6325 Heather Dr
Los Angeles, CA 90068-1633, USA

Allen, Randy (Athlete, Basketball Player)
10185 Nichols Lake Rd
Milton, FL 32583-9267, USA

Allen, Rax Jr (Music Group)
209 10th Ave # 527
Nashville, TN 37203, USA

Allen, Ray (Actor, Athlete, Basketball Player)
c/o Staff Member *3 Arts Entertainment Inc*
9460 Wilshire Blvd Fl 7
Beverly Hills, CA 90212-2713, USA

Allen, Richard (Actor)
89 Saltergate
Chesterfield S40 IUS, UNITED KINGDOM (UK)

Allen, Richard A (Richie) (Athlete, Baseball Player)
RR2 Possum Hollow Rd
Wampum, PA 16157, USA

Allen, Richard J (Rick) (Music Group, Musician)
9595 Wilshire Blvd Ste 900
Beverly Hills, CA 90212-2509, USA

Allen, Richard V (Government Official)
905 16th St NW
Washington, DC 20006-1703, USA

Allen, Robert (Business Person, Writer)
5072 N 300 W
Provo, UT 84604-5652, USA

Allen, Rod (Athlete, Baseball Player)
6115 Orchard Lake Rd Apt 202
West Bloomfield, MI 48322-2310, USA

Allen, Ron (Athlete, Baseball Player)
917 Winona Dr
Youngstown, OH 44511-1404, USA

Allen, Rosalind (Actor)
c/o John Carrabino *John Carrabino Management*
5900 Wilshire Blvd Ste 406
Los Angeles, CA 90036-5015, USA

Allen, Sam (Athlete, Baseball Player)
2734 Gate House Rd Apt 108
Norfolk, VA 23504-4057, USA

Allen, Scott (Figure Skater)
511 Knickerbocker Rd
Tenafly, NJ 07670-1452, USA

Allen, Sian Barbara (Actor, Writer)
1411 NE 16th Ave Apt 219
Portland, OR 97232-4410, USA

Allen, Taje (Athlete, Football Player)
1209 Valorie Ct
Cedar Park, TX 78613-4023, USA

Allen, Ted (Chef, Television Host)
c/o Staff Member *WmE2 (WMA-LA)*
1 William Morris Pl
Beverly Hills, CA 90212-4261, USA

Allen, Terry (Athlete, Football Player)
3176 Sable Ridge Dr
Buford, GA 30519-7681, USA

Allen, Tessa (Actor)
c/o Staff Member *Bobby Ball Talent Agency*
4116 W Magnolia Blvd Ste 205
Burbank, CA 91505-2700, USA

Allen, Thomas B (Opera Singer)
40 W 57th St
New York, NY 10019-4001, USA

Allen, Tim (Actor, Comedian, Producer)
c/o Rick Messina *Messina Baker/ Entertainment*
955 Carrillo Dr Ste 100
Los Angeles, CA 90048-5400, USA

Allen, Todd (Actor, Producer)
c/o David (Dave) Fleming *Mosaic Media Group*
9200 W Sunset Blvd Ste 10
Los Angeles, CA 90069-3608, USA

Allen, Tremayne (Athlete, Football Player)
529 S Parsons Ave
Brandon, FL 33511-6069, USA

Allen, Will (Athlete, Football Player)
15 Fox Hill Dr
Wayne, NJ 07470-2539, USA

Allen, Will (Athlete, Football Player)
2325 SW 105th Ter
Davie, FL 33324-7608, USA

Allen, Will (Athlete, Football Player)
12721 Tar Flower Dr
Tampa, FL 33626-2341, USA

Allen, Willard M (Doctor)
211 Key Haighway
Baltimore, MD 21230, USA

Allen, William L (Editor)
& 17th M NW
Washington, DC 20036, USA

Allen, Woody (Actor, Comedian, Director, Writer)
c/o Stephen Tenenbaum *Morra Brezner Steinberg & Tenenbaum (MBST) Entertainment*
345 N Maple Dr Ste 200
Beverly Hills, CA 90210-5174, USA

Allen Jr, Rex (Musician)
PO Box 13436
Wichita, KS 67213-0436, USA

Allenby, Robert (Athlete, Golfer)
105 Quayside Dr
Jupiter, FL 33477-4020, USA

Allende, Fernando (Actor)
c/o Staff Member *El Dorado Pictures*
725 Arizona Ave Ste 100
Santa Monica, CA 90401-1734, USA

Allende, Isabel (Writer)
116 Caledonia St
Sausalito, CA 94965-1925, USA

Allen-Mullins, Doreen (Athlete, Baseball Player)
1104 Somonauk St
Sycamore, IL 60178-2521, USA

Allenson, Gary (Athlete, Baseball Player)
711 SE 34th St
Cape Coral, FL 33904-4900, USA

Allensworth, Jermaine (Athlete, Baseball Player)
1824 Euclid Dr
Anderson, IN 46011-3937, USA

Allerman, Kurt (Athlete, Football Player)
2511 Blue Heron Dr
Hudson, OH 44236-1866, USA

Allert, Ty (Athlete, Football Player)
1504 County Road 308
Lexington, TX 78947-4113, USA

Allevi, Giovanni (Composer)
Via Arrigo Boito 9
Ascoli Piceno 63100, Italy

Alley, Alphonse (President)
Carre 181-182 BP 48
Cotonou, BENIN

Alley, Donald (Athlete, Football Player)
3258 W Parade Cir
Colorado Springs, CO 80917-2931, USA

Alley, Gene (Athlete, Baseball Player)
10236 Steuben Dr
Glen Allen, VA 23060-3072, USA

Alley, Kirstie (Actor, Producer)
c/o Jason Weinberg *Untitled Entertainment (LA)*
350 S Beverly Dr Ste 200
Beverly Hills, CA 90212-4819, USA

Alley, Steve (Athlete, Hockey Player)
545 College Rd
Lake Forest, IL 60045-2319, USA

Alley Cats, The (Music Group, Musician)
c/o Staff Member *Harmony Artists*
6399 Wilshire Blvd Ste 914
Los Angeles, CA 90048-5712, USA

Allfrey, Vincent G (Misc)
24 Winthrop Ct
Tenafly, NJ 07670-1616, USA

Allgaier, Justin (Race Car Driver)
c/o Staff Member *Penske Racing South*
200 Penske Way
Mooresville, NC 28115-8022, USA

Allgood, Lonnie (Athlete, Football Player)
12 Drake Rd
Somerset, NJ 08873-2369, USA

Allie, Gair (Athlete, Baseball Player)
11818 Button Willow Cv
San Antonio, TX 78213-1220, USA

Allietta, Bob (Athlete, Baseball Player)
25 Robinson Rd
Falmouth, MA 02540-3840, USA

Allimadi, E Otema (Prime Minister)
PO Box Gulu
Gulu District, UGANDA

Allinson, Michael (Actor)
112 Knollwood Dr
Larchmont, NY 10538, USA

Allione, Tsultrim (Religious Leader)
PO Box 3040
Pagosa Springs, CO 81147-3040, USA

Allison, Bobby (Race Car Driver)
PO Box 3696
Mooresville, NC 28117-3696, USA

Allison, Dana (Athlete, Baseball Player)
322 Thomas Dr
Middletown, VA 22645-3992, USA

Allison, Dave (Athlete, Coach, Hockey Player)
c/o Staff Member *Iowa Stars*
833 5th Ave
Des Moines, IA 50309-1399, USA

Allison, Donnie (Race Car Driver)
355 Quail Dr
Salisbury, NC 28147-8860, USA

Allison, Glenn (Bowler)
1844 S Haster St Spc 138
Anaheim, CA 92802-3750, USA

Allison, Henry (Hank) (Athlete, Football Player)
458 W Ellis Ave
Inglewood, CA 90302-1109, USA

Allison, Herbert M (Business Person)
730 3rd Ave
New York, NY 10017-3206, USA

Allison, Jason (Athlete, Hockey Player)
Cooks Rd RR 2
Parry Sound, ON P2A 2O0, Canada

Allison, Jerry (Musician, Songwriter, Writer)
8455 New Bethel Rd
Lyles, TN 37098-1909, USA

Allison, Jim (Athlete, Football Player)
1359 Akiahala St
Kailua, HI 96734-4231, USA

Allison, John A IV (Financier)
200 W 2nd St
Winston Salem, NC 27101-4019, USA

Allison, Kate (Athlete, Golfer)
349 Canterbury Ln
Wyckoff, NJ 07481-2305, USA

Allison, Mike (Athlete, Hockey Player)
PO Box 1416
International Falls, MN 56649-1416, USA

Allison, Mose J Jr (Composer, Musician)
82 Ballad Ct
Eastport, NY 11941-1602, USA

Allison, Odis (Athlete, Basketball Player)
3162 Majestic Shadows Ave
Henderson, NV 89052-3041, USA

Allison, Ray (Athlete, Hockey Player)
106 N Valleybrook Rd
Cherry Hill, NJ 08034-3809, USA

Allison, Richard C (Judge)
24 Circle Dr
Manhasset, NY 11030-1121, USA

Allison, Robert J Jr
1201 Lake Robbins Dr
Spring, TX 77380-1181, USA

Allison, Stacy (Mountaineer)
6633 SE 29th Ave
Portland, OR 97202-8721, USA

Allison Jr, Graham T (Educator)
69 Pinehurst Rd
Belmont, MA 02478-1502, USA

Alliss, Peter (Sportscaster)
1 Erieview Plaza 1360 East 9th St # 1300
Cleveland, OH 44114, USA

Alliston, Vaughn (Buddy) (Athlete, Football Player)
7493 Apple Yard Ln
Cordova, TN 38016-8770, USA

Allman, Greg (Musician)
706 Buckland Hall Rd
Richmond Hill, GA 31324-5352, USA

Allman, Jamie Anne (Actor)
c/o Jordyn Borczon *Persona PR*
8840 Wilshire Blvd Ste 109
Beverly Hills, CA 90211-2606, USA

Allman, Marshall (Actor)
c/o Nate Steadman *Gersh (LA)*
9465 Wilshire Blvd Ste 600
Beverly Hills, CA 90212-2612, USA

Allor, Kristin
11940 Willow Ridge Dr
Willow Springs, IL 60480-1187, USA

Allouache, Merzak (Director)
Cite des Asphodeles Bt D15 183 Ben Aknoun
Algiers, ALGERIA

Allport, Chris M (Actor)
1324 Pine St
Santa Monica, CA 90405-2612, USA

Allport, Christopher (Actor)
c/o Staff Member *Pakula/King & Associates*
9229 W Sunset Blvd Ste 315
Los Angeles, CA 90069-3403, USA

Allred, Beau (Athlete, Baseball Player)
2094 S Shannon Rd
Safford, AZ 85546-9344, USA

Allred, Brian (Athlete, Football Player)
16470 Ed Warfield Rd
Woodbine, MD 21797-7806, USA

Allred, Gloria R (Attorney, Lawyer)
c/o Gloria Allred *Allred, Maroko & Goldberg*
6300 Wilshire Blvd Ste 1500
Los Angeles, CA 90048-5217, USA

Allred, Jason (Athlete, Golfer)
10239 E Salt Bush Dr
Scottsdale, AZ 85255-8637, USA

Allred, John (Athlete, Football Player)
PO Box 748
Del Mar, CA 92014-0748, USA

Allsopp, Kirstie (Actor)
c/o Staff Member *Arlington Enterprises Ltd*
1-3 Charlotte St
London W1P 1HD, UNITED KINGDOM (UK)

Allstar Weekend (Music Group, Musician)
c/o Staff Member *Hollywood Records*
500 S Buena Vista St
Burbank, CA 91521-0002, USA

Allsup, Mike (Music Group, Musician)
5171 Caliente St Unit 134
Las Vegas, NV 89119-2198, USA

Allsup, Tommy (Music Group)
PO Box 1547
Arlington, TX 76004-1547, USA

Allums, Darrell (Athlete, Basketball Player)
3584 Brenton Ave Apt B
Lynwood, CA 90262-2054, USA

Almanza, Armando (Athlete, Baseball Player)
1717 Villa Santos Cir
El Paso, TX 79935-3506, USA

Almanzar, Carlos (Athlete, Baseball Player)
c/o Staff Member *San Diego Padres*
100 Park Blvd
San Diego, CA 92101-7405, USA

Almee, Anouk (Actor)
37 Rue de Acacias
Paris 75017, FRANCE

Almen, Lowell G (Religious Leader)
8765 W Higgins Rd
Chicago, IL 60631-4101, USA

Almirola, Aric (Race Car Driver)
1675 Coddle Creek Hwy
Mooresville, NC 28115-8245, USA

Almodovar, Pedro (Director)
El Deseo SA Ruiz Perello 25
Madrid 28028, SPAIN

Almon, Bill (Athlete, Baseball Player)
42 Channel Vw Unit 4
Warwick, RI 02889-6544, USA

Almond, David (Writer)
c/o Staff Member *Doubleday/ RandomHouse*
1745 Broadway
New York, NY 10019-4368, USA

Almond, Marc (Musician)
105 Shad Row Ste B
Piermont, NY 10968-3001, USA

Almonte, Edwin (Athlete, Baseball Player)
21910 SW 100th Pl
Cutler Bay, FL 33190-1100, USA

Almonte, Hector (Athlete, Baseball Player)
16742 SW 12th St
Pembroke Pines, FL 33027-1408, USA

Almunia, Amann Joaquin (Government Official)
Piaza de las Cortes #9 4A Planta
Madrid 28014, SPAIN

Almy, Brook (Actor)
c/o Nyle Brenner *Brenner Management*
9171 Wilshire Blvd Ste 441
Beverly Hills, CA 90210-5516, USA

Alois (Prince)
Vaduz 9490, LIECHTENSTEIN

Alomar, Roberto (Athlete, Baseball Player)
PO Box 367
Salinas, PR 00751-0367, USA

Alomar Jr, Sandy (Athlete, Baseball Player)
PO Box 367
Salinas, PR 00751-0367, USA

Alomar Sr, Sandy (Athlete, Baseball Player)
PO Box 367
Salinas, PR 00751-0367, USA

Alonsa, Alicia (Ballerina)
Calzada 510 Entre D & E
El Vedada, Havana CP 10400, CUBA

Alonso, Adrian (Actor)
c/o Staff Member *Featured Artists Agency*
6210 Wilshire Blvd Ste 311
Los Angeles, CA 90048-5122, USA

Alonso, Alicia (Ballerina)
510 Entre D & El Vedada E
Havana, CP 10400, CUBA

Alonso, Anabel (Actor)
Calles Fuencarral 17
Madrid 28004, SPAIN

Alonso, Daniella (Actor)
c/o Staff Member *Gersh (LA)*
9465 Wilshire Blvd Ste 600
Beverly Hills, CA 90212-2612, USA

Alonso, Fernando (Race Car Driver)
67 Villamiana
Miami, FL 33199-0001, SPAIN

Alonso, Laz (Actor)
c/o Ron West *Thruline Entertainment*
9250 Wilshire Blvd Ground Fl
Beverly Hills, CA 90212, USA

Alonso, Maria Conchita (Actor, Musician)
c/o Rona Menashe *Guttman Associates*
118 S Beverly Dr Ste 201
Beverly Hills, CA 90212-3016, USA

Alosio, Ryan (Actor)
c/o Steve Rodriquez *McGowan Management*
8733 W Sunset Blvd Ste 103
West Hollywood, CA 90069-2241, USA

Alou, Felipe (Athlete, Baseball Player)
6891 Cobia Cir
Boynton Beach, FL 33437-3639, USA

Alou, Jesus (Athlete, Baseball Player)
Apartado Postal 539/2 Lafaria
Santo Domingo, Dominican Republic

Alou, Mateo (Athlete, Baseball Player)
P.O. Box 30063 MDJ Troncuso #16 Paraiso
Santo Domingo, DOMINICAN REPUBLIC

Alou, Matty (Athlete, Baseball Player)
Manuel De Jesus Troncuso #16 P.O. Box 30063
Santo Domingo, Dominican Republic

Alou, Moises (Athlete, Baseball Player)
13095 NW 13th St
Pembroke Pines, FL 33028-2711, USA

Alpay, David (Actor)
c/o Brian Wilkins *Kritzer Levine Wilkins Entertainment*
11872 La Grange Ave Fl 1
Los Angeles, CA 90025-5283, USA

Alpert, Herb (Musician)
31930 Pacific Coast Hwy
Malibu, CA 90265-2524, USA

Alpert, Joseph S (Doctor)
3440 E Cathedral Rock Cir
Tucson, AZ 85718-1379, USA

Alphand, Luc (Skier)
Chalet Le Balme Chantemarie
Sierra Chavalier 5330, FRANCE

Alpher, Ralph A (Physicist)
253 Ascot Ln
Schenectady, NY 12309-4964, USA

Alsgaard, Thomas (Skier)
Cathinka Guldbergsveg 16
Holter 2034, NORWAY

Alsop, Marin (Musician)
c/o Staff Member *International Creative Management (ICM-LA)*
10250 Constellation Blvd Fl 7
Los Angeles, CA 90067-6207, USA

Alsop, Will (Architect)
Bishop's Wharf 39-49 Parkgate Road
London SW11 4NP, UNITED KINGDOM (UK)

Alston, Alyce Carolyn (Publisher)
Pleasantville, NY 10570, USA

Alston, Barbara (Music Group)
PO Box 371371
Las Vegas, NV 89137-1371, USA

Alston, Dell (Athlete, Baseball Player)
1107 Harwall Rd
Gwynn Oak, MD 21207-4904, USA

Alston, Garvin (Athlete, Baseball Player)
4705 E Thunderhill Pl
Phoenix, AZ 85044-4905, USA

Alston, Lyneal (Athlete, Football Player)
9303 Connecticut Ct Apt B
Clovis, NM 88101-8690, USA

Alston, Mack (Athlete, Football Player)
5421 Echols Ave
Alexandria, VA 22311-1344, USA

Alston, Rafer (Athlete, Basketball Player)
c/o Staff Member *Toronto Raptors*
400-40 Bay St
Toronto, Ontario M5J 2X2, Canada

Alston, Reeves Shirley (Music Group)
6014 N Pointe Pl
Woodland Hills, CA 91367-5500, USA

Alstott, Mike (Athlete, Football Player)
7800 9th Ave S
Saint Petersburg, FL 33707-2731, USA

Alt, Carol (Actor)
c/o Scott Hart *Scott Hart Entertainment*
14622 Ventura Blvd # 746
Sherman Oaks, CA 91403-3600, USA

Alt, John M (Athlete, Football Player)
21 Crescent Ln
Saint Paul, MN 55127-6358, USA

Altamirano, Porfi (Athlete, Baseball Player)
2010 Woodvine Dr
Houston, TX 77055-1712, USA

Altberg, Jonas Erik (Basshunter) (Musician)
c/o Staff Member *Hackford Jones PR*
19 Nassau St
London W1W 7AF, UK

Altenberg, Wolfgang (General)
Birkenhof 44
Brenen-Saint-Magnus 28759, GERMANY

Alther, Lisa (Writer)
1086 Silver St
Hinesburg, VT 05461-9450, USA

Althoff, James (Jim) (Athlete, Football Player)
508 N Green St
McHenry, IL 60050-5684, USA

Altman, Chelsea (Actor)
c/o Matthew Sullivan *Sullivan Talent Group*
305 W 105th St Apt 3B
New York, NY 10025-9116, USA

Altman, George (Athlete, Baseball Player)
915 Midpoint Dr
O Fallon, MO 63366-5906, USA

Altman, Jeff (Actor)
c/o Staff Member *Richard De La Font Agency*
3808 W South Park Blvd
Broken Arrow, OK 74011-1261, USA

Altman, Scott D (Astronaut)
1247 33rd St NW
Washington, DC 20007-3228, USA

Altman, Sidney (Nobel Prize Laureate)
71 Blake Rd
Hamden, CT 06517-3404, USA

Altman, Stuart H (Educator)
11 Bakers Hill Rd
Weston, MA 02493-1708, USA

Altmeyer, Jeannine T (Opera Singer)
Im Muhlader
Herrliberg 8709, SWITZERLAND

Altmire, Jason (Congressman, Politician)
332 Cannon Hob
Washington, DC 20515-3226, USA

Altobelli, Joe (Athlete, Baseball Player, Coach)
10 Stowell Dr Apt 3
Rochester, NY 14616-1889, USA

Altuna, Charlie (Stylist)
c/o Celebrity Stylist *Celestine - CA*
1666 20th St Ste 200B
Santa Monica, CA 90404-3828, USA

Alusik, George (Athlete, Baseball Player)
PO Box 454
Woodbridge, NJ 07095-0454, USA

Alva, Luigi (Opera Singer)
via Moscova 46/3
Mailand, Italy 20121

Alvarado, Allen (Actor)
c/o Scott Appel *Scott Appel Public Relations*
13547 Ventura Blvd # 203
Sherman Oaks, CA 91423-3825, USA

Alvarado, Natividad (Naty) (Misc)
2700 N Main St
Santa Ana, CA 92705-6634, USA

Alvarez, Barry (Coach, Football Coach)
Athletic Dept
Medison, WI 53711, USA

Alvarez, Gabe (Athlete, Baseball Player)
4401 La Madera Ave
El Monte, CA 91732-2009, USA

Alvarez, Isabel (Athlete, Baseball Player)
2402 Monmouth Ave
Fort Wayne, IN 46809-1732, USA

Alvarez, Jose (Athlete, Baseball Player)
210 Murphy Ln
Greenville, SC 29607-4934, USA

Alvarez, Juan (Athlete, Baseball Player)
10995 SW 107th Ave
Miami, FL 33176-3444, USA

Alvarez, Mario Roberto (Architect)
Solis 370
Buenos Aires, ARGENTINA

Alvarez, Orlando (Athlete, Baseball Player)
Cummunidad Dolores 37
Rio Grande, PR 745, USA

Alvarez, Rogelio (Athlete, Baseball Player)
5010 NW 183rd St
Miami Gardens, FL 33055-2929, USA

Alvarez, Victor (Athlete, Baseball Player)
c/o Staff Member *Los Angeles Dodgers (LA Dodgers)*
1000 Elysian Park Ave
Los Angeles, CA 90090-1112, USA

Alvarez, Wilson (Athlete, Baseball Player)
108 Business Services Coaching Staff Bldg ATTN
University Park, PA 16802, USA

Alvarez Martinez, Francisco Cardinal (Religious Leader)
Arco de Palacio 3
Toledo 45002, SPAIN

Alvarez-Buylla, Arturo (Biologist)
Medical Center 1230 York Ave
New York, NY 10021, USA

Alvers, Steve (Athlete, Football Player)
9751 SW 115th Ave
Miami, FL 33176-2553, USA

Alves, Camila (Model)
Webgasse 1/12
Vienna 1060, AUSTRIA

Alves, Joe (Director)
4176 Rosario Rd
Woodland Hills, CA 91364-6025, USA

Alvim, Anna (Actor)
c/o Jean Fox *Fox-Albert Management*
390 W End Ave
New York, NY 10024-6107, USA

Alvin, Dave (Musician, Songwriter, Writer)
5000 Oak Bluff Ct
Atlanta, GA 30350-1069, USA

Alvina, Anicee (Actor)
41 Rue de l'Echese
Le Visinet 75008, FRANCE

Alvis, Max (Athlete, Baseball Player)
806 Hunterwood Dr
Jasper, TX 75951-2820, USA

Alvord, Steve (Athlete, Football Player)
2907 Cherrywood Ave
Bellingham, WA 98225-1210, USA

Alward, Tom (Athlete, Football Player)
5051 Bensett Trl
Davison, MI 48423-8781, USA

Alworth, Lance (Athlete, Football Player)
990 Highland Dr Ste 300
Solana Beach, CA 92075-2438, USA

Al-Yawer, Sheik Ghazi Mashal Ajll (President)
Al-Sijound Majalis Karradat Mariam
Baghdad, IRAQ

Alyea, Brant (Athlete, Baseball Player)
119 Lockhardt Rd
Tryon, NC 28782, USA

Alyson, Jocelyn E (Musician)
c/o Staff Member *Diva Central Inc*
7510 W Sunset Blvd Ste 1445
Los Angeles, CA 90046-3408, USA

al-Zubi, Mahmoud (Prime Minister)
Damascas
SYRIA

Ama, Shola (Musician)
Executive Suite 20 Damien St
London E1 2HX, UNITED KINGDOM (UK)

Amaechi, John (Athlete, Basketball Player)
5747 E Aire Libre Ave
Scottsdale, AZ 85254-1206, USA

Amaker, Tommy (Athlete, Basketball Player, Coach)
Athletic Dept
Ann Arbor, MI 48109, USA

Amalfitano, J Joseph (Joey) (Athlete, Baseball Player, Coach)
60 Sheath Dr
Sedona, AZ 86336-6510, USA

Amalou, J K (Director)
52/53 Poland Place
London W1F 7LX, UNITED KINGDOM (UK)

Aman, Zeenat (Actor, Bollywood)
Neelam Apartments 3rd Floor Mount Mary Road Bandra
Bombay, MS 400 050, INDIA

Amanar, Simona (Gymnast)
Str Vasile Conta 16
Budapest 70139, ROMANIA

Amandes, Tom (Actor)
c/o Staff Member *Magnolia Entertainment (LA)*
9595 Wilshire Blvd Ste 601
Beverly Hills, CA 90212-2506, USA

Amano, Eugene (Athlete, Football Player)
8354 Lochinver Park Ln
Brentwood, TN 37027-9121, USA

Amanpour, Christiane (Correspondent, Journalist)
c/o Staff Member *CNN (Atlanta)*
1 Cnn Ctr NW
Atlanta, GA 30303-2762, USA

Amara, Lucine (Opera Singer)
260 W End Ave Apt 7A
New York, NY 10023-3659, USA

Amaral, Bob (Actor)
c/o Staff Member *Professional Artists Agency*
321 W 44th St Ste 605
New York, NY 10036-5432, USA

Amaral, Richard L (Rich) (Athlete, Baseball Player)
3122 Country Club Dr
Costa Mesa, CA 92626-2344, USA

Amarjargal, Rinchinnyamiyn (Prime Minister)
Ulan Bator, Great Hural 12, MONGOLIA

Amaro Jr, Ruben (Athlete, Baseball Player)
1063 Country Hills Rd
Yardley, PA 19067-6024, USA

Amaro Sr, Ruben (Athlete, Baseball Player)
4098 Cinnamon Way
Weston, FL 33331-3810, USA

Amash, Justin (Congressman, Politician)
114 Cannon Hob
Washington, DC 20515-3601, USA

Amato, Giuliano (Prime Minister)
Piazza di Montecitorio
Rome 186, ITALY

Amato, Joe (Race Car Driver)
1 Amato Dr
Moosic, PA 18507-1788, USA

Amato, Ken (Athlete, Football Player)
9290 Wardley Park Ln
Brentwood, TN 37027-4465, USA

Amaya, Armando (Artist)
Lopex 137 Depto 1
Mexico City 06070 CP, MEXICO

Amazing Jonathan, The (Actor)
c/o Staff Member *International Creative Management (ICM-LA)*
10250 Constellation Blvd Fl 7
Los Angeles, CA 90067-6207, USA

Amazing Rhythm Aces (Music Group)
c/o Staff Member *Fat City Artists*
1906 Chet Atkins Pl Apt 502
Nashville, TN 37212-2122, USA

Ambani, Anil (Business Person)
'H' Block 1st Floor
Dhirubhai Ambani Knowledge City, Navi Mumbai 400 710, INDIA

Ambani, Mukesh (Business Person)
Makers Chambers - IV Nariman Point
Mumbai 400 021, India

Ambasz, Emilio (Architect)
295 Central Park W Apt 14D
New York, NY 10024-3023, USA

Amber (Musician)
PO Box 35
Pawling, NY 12564-0035, USA

Ambres, Chip (Athlete, Baseball Player)
4460 Beale St
Beaumont, TX 77705-4705, USA

Ambro, Thomas L (Judge)
844 N King St
Wilmington, DE 19801-3519, USA

Ambrose, Ashley (Athlete, Football Player)
2726 Eudora Trl
Duluth, GA 30097-6284, USA

Ambrose, Lauren (Actor)
c/o Billy Lazarus *United Talent Agency (UTA)*
9560 Wilshire Blvd Fl 5
Beverly Hills, CA 90212-2400, USA

Ambrose, Richard (Dick) (Athlete, Football Player)
24049 Stonehedge Dr
Cleveland, OH 44145-4864, USA

Ambrosio, Alessandra (Model)
c/o Staff Member *Elite Model Management (NY)*
404 Park Ave S Fl 9
New York, NY 10016-8412, USA

Ambrosius, Marsha (Musician)
c/o Staff Member *WmE2 (WMA-LA)*
1 William Morris Pl
Beverly Hills, CA 90212-4261, USA

Ambroziak, Peter (Athlete, Hockey Player)
PO Box 830
Ogdensburg, NY 13669-0830, USA

Ambrozic, Aloysius Matthew Cardinal (Religious Leader)
1155 Yonge St
Toronto, ON M4T 1W2, CANADA

Ambuehl, Clindy (Actor)
9300 Wilshire Blvd Ste 555
Beverly Hills, CA 90212-3211, USA

Ambulance Ltd (Music Group)
c/o Staff Member *Paradigm (Monterey)*
404 W Franklin St
Monterey, CA 93940-2303, USA

Amedori, John Patrick (Actor)
c/o Anne Woodward *ROAR (LA)*
9701 Wilshire Blvd Fl 8
Beverly Hills, CA 90212-2008, USA

Ameling, Elly (Music Group, Musician)
65 W 90th St Apt 13F
New York, NY 10024-1510, USA

Amelio, Gilbert F (Business Person)
13416 Middle Fork Ln
Los Altos Hills, CA 94022-2420, USA

Amelung, Ed (Athlete, Baseball Player)
16681 Cedar Cir
Fountain Valley, CA 92708-2310, USA

Amen, Irving (Artist)
PO Box 812365
Boca Raton, FL 33481-2365, USA

Amenabar, Alejandro (Director, Musician, Writer)
c/o Sunmin Park *Maxmedia*
1620 Broadway
Santa Monica, CA 90404-2776, USA

Amend, Bill (Artist, Cartoonist)
1130 Walnut St
Kansas City, MO 64106-2109, USA

Amendola, Tony (Actor)
c/o Staff Member *Beacon Talent Agency*
170 Apple Ridge Rd
Woodcliff Lake, NJ 07677-8149, USA

Ament, Jeff (Musician)
207 1/2 1st Ave S # 300
Seattle, WA 98104, USA

Amer, Nicolas (Actor)
14 Great Russell St Flat 1
London WC1B 3NH, UK

America (Musician)
c/o Staff Member *WmE2 (WMA-LA)*
1 William Morris Pl
Beverly Hills, CA 90212-4261, USA

American Gladiators (Reality TV Star)
10250 Constellation Blvd
Los Angeles, CA 90067-6200, USA

Amerie (Musician)
c/o Richard Murphy *International Creative Management (ICM-NY)*
40 W 57th St
New York, NY 10019-4001, USA

Amerson, Glenn (Athlete, Football Player)
4857 Mustang Rd
Brenham, TX 77833-8746, USA

Ames, Aldrich (Government Official)
PO Box 3000
White Deer, PA 17887-3000, USA

Ames, Bruce N (Misc)
1324 Spruce St
Berkeley, CA 94709-1435, USA

Ames, David (Athlete, Football Player)
7909 Alvarado Rd
Richmond, VA 23229-4208, USA

Ames, Denise (Actor)
1328 12th St
Santa Monica, CA 90401-2051, USA

Ames, Ed (Actor, Musician)
c/o Staff Member *Paradise Artists*
PO Box 1821
Ojai, CA 93024-1821, USA

Ames, Frank Anthony (Musician)
1235 Potomac St NW
Washington, DC 20007-3230, USA

Ames, Rachel (Actor)
8040 Ventura Canyon Ave
Panorama City, CA 91402-6313, USA

Amey, VInce (Athlete, Football Player)
4433 Callecita Ct
Union City, CA 94587-3829, USA

Amick, Madchen (Actor)
c/o Kesha Williams *Affirmative Entertainment*
425 N Robertson Blvd
West Hollywood, CA 90048-1735, USA

Amiel, Jon (Director)
c/o Dave Brown *Artist International Management (LA)*
9595 Wilshire Blvd Fl 9
Beverly Hills, CA 90212-2512, USA

Amiez, Sebastien (Skier)
Ave Chasse-Foret
Pralognan, FRANCE

Amigo Vallejo, Carlos Cardinal (Religious Leader)
Piaza Virgin de los Reyes S/N
Seville 41004, SPAIN

Amiina (Musician)
c/o Staff Member *Paradigm (Monterey)*
404 W Franklin St
Monterey, CA 93940-2303, USA

Amini (Actor, Bollywood)
6 Parthasarathipuram T Nagar
Chennai, TN 600017, INDIA

Amis, Martin (Journalist, Writer)
Drury House 34-43 Russell St
London WC2B 5HA, UNITED KINGDOM (UK)

Amis, Suzy (Actor, Model)
c/o Davien Littlefield *Davien Littlefield Management*
33 W 67th St PH
New York, NY 10023-6224, USA

Amlong, Joe (Athlete)
HC 36 Box 73
Sand Coulee, MT 59472, USA

Amlong, Thomas (Athlete)
166 Four Mile River Rd
Old Lyme, CT 06371-1325, USA

Ammaccapane, Danielle (Athlete, Golfer)
13214 N 13th St
Phoenix, AZ 85022-4936, USA

Ammaccapane, Dina (Athlete, Golfer)
4407 E Blanche Dr
Phoenix, AZ 85032-4881, USA

Ammachi (Religious Leader)
Ettimadai
Coimbatore, Tamil Nadu 641105, INDIA

Amman, Richard (Athlete, Football Player)
2907 Lake Joanna Dr
Eustis, FL 32726-7824, USA

Ammann, Simon (Speed Skater)
Worbstr 52
Muri 3074, SWITZERLAND

Amodeo, Mike (Athlete, Hockey Player)
1481 Skyview St
Oshawa, ON L1K 2S2, Canada

Among the Oak & Asj (Music Group, Musician)
c/o Staff Member *MCT Management*
520 8th Ave Rm 2205
New York, NY 10018-4160, USA

Amons, Mary Schmidt (Reality TV Star)
c/o Staff Member *Bravo (NY)*
30 Rockefeller Plz
New York, NY 10112-0015, USA

Amonte, Tony (Athlete, Hockey Player)
PO Box 771
Humarock, MA 02047-0771, USA

Amor, Vincente (Athlete, Baseball Player)
13871 SW 52nd St
Miramar, FL 33027-5945, USA

Amorosi, Vanessa (Musician)
PO Box 51
Caulfield South, VIC, AUSTRALIA

Amos, John (Actor)
c/o Belinda Foster *AWJ Platinum PR*
8350 Wilshire Blvd Ste 200
Beverly Hills, CA 90211-2348, USA

Amos, Paul S (Business Person)
1932 Wynnton Rd
Columbus, GA 31999-0001, USA

Amos, Tori (Musician)
c/o Chelsea Laird *The Bridge Entertainment Group*
Prefers to be contacted via telephone
Santa Monica, CA, USA

Amos, Wally (Famous) (Business Person)
PO Box 897
Kailua, HI 96734-0897, USA

Amoyal, Pierre A W (Musician)
252 Rue de Faubourg Saint-Honore
Paris 75008, FRANCE

Amplas, John (Actor)
443 Meridian Dr
Pittsburgh, PA 15228-2613, USA

Amram, David W III (Composer, Musician)
Peekskill Hollow Farm Peekskill Hollow Road
Putnam Valley, NY 10579, USA

Amrapurkar, Sadashiv (Actor, Bollywood, Comedian)
A/201 Panchdhara Off Yari Road Versova Andheri
Bombay, MS 400 058, INDIA

Amritraj, Vijay (Tennis Player)
7277 Hayvenhurst Ave
Van Nuys, CA 91406-2860, USA

Amsler, Marty (Athlete, Football Player)
4009 Fairfax Rd
Evansville, IN 47710-3718, USA

Amsterdam, Anthony G (Attorney, Attorney General, Educator, General)
68 Middle Line Hwy
Southampton, NY 11968-1645, USA

Amstrong, Otis (Athlete, Football Player)
7183 S Newport Way
Centennial, CO 80112-1613, USA

Amstutz, Joe (Athlete, Football Player)
24840 Arrow Ct Apt 29
Tehachapi, CA 93561-7124, USA

Amte, Baba (Religious Leader)
Maharogi Sewa Samiti Waora Anandwan Dist Chandrapur, Maharashtra 442914, INDIA

Amukamura, Prince (Football Player)
c/o Todd France *France AllPro Athlete Management*
3500 Lenox Rd NE
Atlanta, GA 30326-4228, USA

Amundsen, Norman (Athlete, Football Player)
3901 Hemlock Dr
Valparaiso, IN 46383-1813, USA

Amurri, Eva (Actor)
c/o JJ Harris *One Talent Management*
9220 W Sunset Blvd Ste 306
Los Angeles, CA 90069-3503, USA

Amzallag, Manuela (Stylist)
c/o Staff Member *Ennis*
119 Braintree St
Boston, MA 02134-1628, USA

Ana-Alicia (Actor)
1801 Avenue of the Stars Ste 902
Los Angeles, CA 90067-5981, USA

Anagarano, Michael (Actor)
c/o Staff Member *Coast to Coast Talent Group*
3350 Barham Blvd
Los Angeles, CA 90068-1404, USA

Anagnostopoulos, Constantine E (Doctor)
3959 Mount Vernon Dr
Bloomfield Hills, MI 48301-3227, USA

Anahi (Actor)
c/o Staff Member *Televisa*
Blvd Adolfo Lopez Mateos 232 Colonia San Angel INN
DF CP 01060, MEXICO

Anakin, Douglas (Athlete)
PO Box 27
Windermere, BC V0B 2L, CANADA

Anand, Babu N (Actor)
1 A Officers Defence Colony St Thomas Mt
Chennai, TN 600 097, INDIA

Anand, J N (Actor)
No 8 B N Reddy Road T Nagar
Chennai, TN 600 017, INDIA

Anand, Sabita (Actor, Bollywood)
61 Sivan Koil Ist Cross Street Kodambakkam
Chennai, TN 600024, INDIA

Anand, Tinnu (Actor, Bollywood, Director, Filmmaker)
101 Lakshadeep Glmohar Cross Road No 4 Jvpd Scheme
Bombay, MS 400 049, INDIA

Anand, Tinu (Actor, Bollywood, Director)
101 Lakshyadeep 4th X Road Juhu Scheme
Mumbai, MS 400049, INDIA

Anand, Vijay (Actor, Bollywood, Director, Filmmaker, Producer)
Ketnav 17 Union Park Pali Hill Khar
Bombay, MS 400 052, INDIA

Ananiashvill, Nina G (Ballerina)
1 Ploschad Sverdlove
Moscow 103009, RUSSIA

Anantha, Raaj (Actor)
25 2nd Cross Street Lake Area
Chennai, TN 600 034, INDIA

Anapau, Kristina (Actor)
c/o Staff Member *One Talent Management*
9220 W Sunset Blvd Ste 306
Los Angeles, CA 90069-3503, USA

Anastasio, Trey (Musician)
c/o Patrick Jordan *Red Light Management (NY)*
44 Wall St Fl 22
New York, NY 10005-2401, USA

Anaya, Rudolfo (Writer)
5324 Canada Vista Pl NW
Albuquerque, NM 87120-2412, USA

Anaya, Toney (Ex-Governor)
200 W De Vargas St
Santa Fe, NM 87501-2643, USA

Anbusrinivas (Actor)
12 Ramanajum Street Nungambakkam
Chennai, TN 600 034, INDIA

Ancheta, Bernie (Director, Writer)
c/o Staff Member *Lenhoff & Lenhoff*
830 Palm Ave
West Hollywood, CA 90069-4009

Anchia, Juan-Ruiz (Cinematographer)
1015 Gayley Ave
Los Angeles, CA 90024-3413, USA

Ancker-Johnson, Betsy (Physicist)
222 Harbour Dr Apt 311
Naples, FL 34103-4087, USA

Andabaker, Rudy (Athlete, Football Player)
450 8th St
Donora, PA 15033-2108, USA

Andere, Jacqueline (Actor)
c/o Staff Member *Televisa*
Blvd Adolfo Lopez Mateos 232 Colonia San Angel INN
DF CP 01060, MEXICO

Anderegg, Bob (Athlete, Basketball Player)
11708 E Onyx Ave
Scottsdale, AZ 85259-5017, USA

Anders, Andrea (Actor)
c/o Wendi Green *Paradigm (LA)*
9200 W Sunset Blvd PH 11
Los Angeles, CA 90069-3601, USA

Anders, David (Actor)
c/o Kay Liberman *Liberman/Zerman Management*
252 N Larchmont Blvd Ste 200
Los Angeles, CA 90004-3754, USA

Anders, Ernie (Athlete, Basketball Player)
5714 Garden Lakes Dr
Bradenton, FL 34203-7226, USA

Anders, Kimble (Athlete, Football Player)
801 Landing Blvd
League City, TX 77573-3315, USA

Anders, Sean (Director, Producer, Writer)
c/o John Elliott *Mosaic Media Group*
9200 W Sunset Blvd Ste 10
Los Angeles, CA 90069-3608, USA

Anders, William A (Astronaut, General)
c/o Staff Member *NASA*
2101 Nasa Pkwy Spc Center
Houston, TX 77058-3696, USA

Andersen, Anthony (Actor)
1619 Broadway # 900
New York, NY 10019-7412, USA

Andersen, Barbara (Actor)
PO Box 10118
Santa Fe, NM 87504, USA

Andersen, Eric (Musician, Songwriter, Writer)
177 Woodland Ave
Westwood, NJ 07675-3218, USA

Andersen, Greta (Swimmer)
16222 Monterey Ln Spc 264
Huntington Beach, CA 92649-2248, USA

Andersen, Hjalmar (Hjallis) (Speed Skater)
Trondheimsvn 2
Oslo 5 560, NORWAY

Andersen, Jason (Athlete, Football Player)
4530 County Road 16 Apt 410
Canandaigua, NY 14424-8316, USA

Andersen, Larry (Athlete, Baseball Player)
2043 Sunray Cir
West Linn, OR 97068-4802, USA

Andersen, Linda (Yachtsman)
Aroysund
Torod 3135, NORWAY

Andersen, Mogens (Athlete, Football Player)
Strandagervej 28
Hellerup, Copenhagen 2900, Denmark

Andersen, Morten (Athlete, Football Player)
6501 Old Shadburn Ferry Rd
Buford, GA 30518-1137, USA

Andersen, Reidar (Skier)
PO Box 191
Ishpeming, MI 49849-0191, USA

Andersen, Watts Teresa (Swimmer)
2582 Marsha Way
San Jose, CA 95125-4029, USA

Andersion, Robert P (Athlete, Football Player)
244 Carmel Dr
Melbourne, FL 32940-7782, USA

Anderson, Alfred (Athlete, Football Player)
6704 Manchaca Rd Unit 8
Austin, TX 78745-4978, USA

Anderson, Allan (Athlete, Baseball Player)
1491 Lancaster Kirkersville Rd NW
Lancaster, OH 43130-8969, USA

Anderson, Anthony (Athlete, Football Player)
33 Dryden Rd
New Castle, DE 19720-2314, USA

Anderson, Anthony (Actor, Producer)
c/o E Brian Dobbins *Principato/Young Management*
9465 Wilshire Blvd Ste 430
Beverly Hills, CA 90212-2613, USA

Anderson, Antonio (Athlete, Football Player)
514 Southridge Way
Irving, TX 75063-4200, USA

Anderson, Aric (Athlete, Football Player)
16306 Rolling View Trl
Cypress, TX 77433-5856, USA

Anderson, Audrey (Stylist)
c/o Staff Member *Koko Represents*
166 Geary St Ste 1007
San Francisco, CA 94108-5623, USA

Anderson, Audrey Marie (Actor)
c/o Staff Member *Untitled Entertainment (NY)*
322 8th Ave Ste 601
New York, NY 10001-6715, USA

Anderson, Bennie (Athlete, Football Player)
6450 Virginia Ave
Saint Louis, MO 63111-2705, USA

Anderson, Bill (Musician, Songwriter)
PO Box 81036
Phoenix, AZ 85069-1036, USA

Anderson, Bill (Athlete, Football Player)
6924 Lark Ln
Knoxville, TN 37919-5928, USA

Anderson, Bob (Athlete, Baseball Player)
3140 E 89th St
Tulsa, OK 74137-3361, USA

Anderson, Bob (Athlete, Football Player)
244 Carmel Dr
Melbourne, FL 32940-7782, USA

Anderson, Bobby (Athlete, Football Player)
79125 Big Horn Trl
La Quinta, CA 92253-4523, USA

Anderson, Bonnie (Stylist)
c/o Staff Member *Team*
423 W Broadway Ste 406
Boston, MA 02127-2265, USA

Anderson, Brad (Race Car Driver)
1240 S Cucamonga Ave
Ontario, CA 91761-4505, USA

Anderson, Brad (Director)
422 Santa Monica Ct
Escondido, CA 92029, USA

Anderson, Brad (Athlete, Football Player)
6121 N 34th Pl
Paradise Valley, AZ 85253-3751, USA

Anderson, Bradford (Actor)
c/o Staff Member *General Hospital*
4151 Prospect Ave
Los Angeles, CA 90027-4524, USA

Anderson, Bradley J (Brad) (Cartoonist)
13022 Wood Harbour Dr
Montgomery, TX 77356-8046, USA

Anderson, Brady (Athlete, Baseball Player)
17736 Saint Andrews Dr
Poway, CA 92064-1026, USA

Anderson, Brett (Musician)
c/o Molly Neuman *Lookout! Records*
PO Box 11374
Berkeley, CA 94712-2374, USA

Anderson, Brian (Athlete, Baseball Player)
3571 N Myers Rd
Geneva, OH 44041-9165, USA

Anderson, Brian (Athlete, Baseball Player)
9553 N Corte Roca De Plata
Tucson, AZ 85704-8609, USA

Anderson, Bruce A (Athlete, Football Player)
910 NE Parkview Ct
Roseburg, OR 97470-2136, USA

Anderson, Bud (Athlete, Baseball Player)
240 Twin Ln E
Wantagh, NY 11793-1963, USA

Anderson, Camille (Actor)
c/o Steven Neibert *Imperium 7 Talent Agency*
5455 Wilshire Blvd Ste 1706
Los Angeles, CA 90036-4217, USA

Anderson, Chantelle (Athlete, Basketball Player)
1 Center Ct
Cleveland, OH 44115-4001, USA

Anderson, Charlie (Athlete, Football Player)
2323 Melrose Ave
Bossier City, LA 71111-5952, USA

Anderson, Chet (Athlete, Football Player)
4066 Johnny Cake Ridge Rd
Saint Paul, MN 55122-4207, USA

Anderson, Chris (Business Person, Writer)
1165 Miller Ave
Berkeley, CA 94708-1754, USA

Anderson, Chris (Athlete, Golfer)
5801 Caymus Loop
Windermere, FL 34786-5313, USA

Anderson, Christine (Psychic, Radio Personality)
PO Box 8464
Minneapolis, MN 55408-0464, USA

Anderson, Clayton C (Astronaut)
1909 Summer Reef Dr
League City, TX 77573-6659, USA

Anderson, Clifford (Athlete, Basketball Player)
2096A S John Russell Cir
Elkins Park, PA 19027-1017, USA

Anderson, Courtney (Athlete, Football Player)
609 Windsor
Hercules, CA 94547-3832, USA

Anderson, Craig (Athlete, Baseball Player)
19217 SW 96th Loop
Dunnellon, FL 34432-4201, USA

Anderson, Curtis (Athlete, Football Player)
967 Kemper Meadow Dr
Cincinnati, OH 45240-1463, USA

Anderson, Dale (Athlete, Hockey Player)
2217 Haultain Ave
Saskatoon, SK S7J 1P7, Canada

Anderson, Damien (Athlete, Football Player)
1374 E Locust Dr
Chandler, AZ 85286-2578, USA

Anderson, Dan (Athlete, Basketball Player)
19000 NW Squirrel Tail Loop
Bend, OR 97701-6784, USA

Anderson, Dan (Athlete, Basketball Player)
423 River St
Minneapolis, MN 55401-2515, USA

Anderson, Darren (Athlete, Football Player)
7328 Overland Park Ct
West Chester, OH 45069-5560, USA

Anderson, Daryl (Actor)
24136 Friar St
Woodland Hills, CA 91367-1240, USA

Anderson, Dave (Athlete, Baseball Player)
7300 Rough Riders Trl Attn Managers
Frisco, TX 75034-9088, USA

Anderson, David (Athlete, Baseball Player)
207 Athletic Office Bldg
Memphis, TN 38152-3730, USA

Anderson, David P (Dave) (Writer)
8 Inness Rd
Tenafly, NJ 07670-2715, USA

Anderson, Dennis (Race Car Driver)
495 N Commons Dr Ste 200
Aurora, IL 60504-8295, USA

Anderson, Dick (Athlete, Football Player)
4603 Santa Maria St
Miami, FL 33146-1132, USA

Anderson, Dion (Actor)
1801 Avenue of the Stars Ste 902
Los Angeles, CA 90067-5981, USA

Anderson, Don (Athlete, Football Player)
10090 Beechdale St
Detroit, MI 48204-2567, USA

Anderson, Don L (Misc)
PO Box 1417
Cambria, CA 93428-1417, USA

Anderson, Donny (Athlete, Football Player)
111 S Saint Joseph St
South Bend, IN 46601-1901, USA

Anderson, Drew (Athlete, Baseball Player)
1033 11th Ave
Saint Paul, NE 68873-6840, USA

Anderson, Duwayne M (Scientist)
6119 139th Pl SE
Bellevue, WA 98006-4384, USA

Anderson, Dwain (Athlete, Baseball Player)
1807 Fallbrook Dr
Alamo, CA 94507-2810, USA

Anderson, Earl (Athlete, Hockey Player)
602 3rd Ave NE
Roseau, MN 56751-1809, USA

Anderson, Eddie Lee (Athlete, Football Player)
PO Box 6363
Warner Robins, GA 31095-6363, USA

Anderson, Edward G (Ed) III (General)
Senior Representative United Nations Military Committee
Washington, DC 20318-0001, USA

Anderson, Eric (Athlete, Basketball Player)
18017 Kinder Oak Dr
Noblesville, IN 46062-7529, USA

Anderson, Erich (Actor)
10100 Santa Monica Blvd Ste 2500
Los Angeles, CA 90067-4116, USA

Anderson, Erick (Athlete, Football Player)
2919 Attleboro Rd
Cleveland, OH 44120-1815, USA

Anderson, Erriestine I (Musician)
11761 E Speedway Blvd
Tucson, AZ 85748-2017, USA

Anderson, Flipper (Athlete, Football Player)
190 Abbey Hill Rd
Suwanee, GA 30024-1976, USA

Anderson, Fred (Athlete, Football Player)
11810 NE 48th Pl
Kirkland, WA 98033-8750, USA

Anderson, Garret J (Athlete, Baseball Player)
36 Boulder Vw
Irvine, CA 92603-0410, USA

Anderson, Gary (Athlete, Fisherman, Football Player)
265 Miskow Close
Canmore, Alberta T1W 3G7, Canada

Anderson, Gary W (Athlete, Football Player)
1 Ridgefield Ct
Little Rock, AR 72223-4608, USA

Anderson, Gayle (Correspondent)
5800 W Sunset Blvd
Los Angeles, CA 90028-6607, USA

Anderson, Gerry (Director, Entertainer)
332 Lytham Road
Blackpool FY4 1DW, UNITED KINGDOM (UK)

Anderson, Gillian (Actor)
c/o Constance Freiberg *Envision Entertainment*
8840 Wilshire Blvd Fl 3
Beverly Hills, CA 90211-2606, USA

Anderson, Glenn (Athlete, Hockey Player)
42 W 69th St Apt 2A
New York, NY 10023-5265, USA

Anderson, H George (Religious Leader)
8765 W Higgins Rd
Chicago, IL 60631-4101, USA

Anderson, Hans Christian (Scientist)
Chemistry Dept
Stanford, CA 94305, USA

Anderson, Harry (Actor, Magician)

Anderson, Ho Che (Artist)
c/o Staff Member *Fantagraphics Books*
7563 Lake City Way NE
Seattle, WA 98115-4218, USA

Anderson, Howard A (Actor)
PO Box 2230
Los Angeles, CA 90028, USA

Anderson, Howard A Jr (Cinematographer)
c/o Staff Member *Howard Anderson Company*
5161 Lankershim Blvd
Valley Vlg, CA 91601-4962, USA

Anderson, Ian (Musician, Songwriter, Writer)
43 Brook Green
London W6 7ER, UNITED KINGDOM (UK)

Anderson, J C (Athlete, Golfer)
232 Fairway Green Dr
O Fallon, MO 63368-4268, USA

Anderson, Jamal (Athlete, Football Player)
10540 Montclair Way
Duluth, GA 30097-1840, USA

Anderson, James (Cricketer)
c/o Staff Member *International Sports Management Ltd (ISM UK)*
Cherry Tree Farm Cherry Tree Lane
Rostherne, Cheshire WA14 3RZ, UNITED KINGDOM

Anderson, James (Athlete, Football Player)
1544 Taylor Point Dr
Chesapeake, VA 23321-0181, USA

Anderson, James F (Religious Leader)
12 Surf Ave
Ocean Grove, NJ 07756-1629, USA

Anderson, James G (Misc)
Eatrh-Planetary Physics Center
Cambridge, MA 2138, USA

Anderson, James W (Doctor)
Medical Center Endocrinology Dept
Lexington, KY 40506-0001, USA

Anderson, Jamie (Actor)
c/o Craig Wyckoff *Epstein-Wyckoff-Corsa-Ross & Associates (LA)*
11350 Ventura Blvd Ste 100
Studio City, CA 91604-3140, USA

Anderson, Janet (Athlete, Golfer)
4311 W Ardmore Rd
Laveen, AZ 85339-2112, USA

Anderson, Jason (Athlete, Baseball Player)
3512 Wyoga Lake Rd Apt 104
Stow, OH 44224-6816, USA

Anderson, Jeff (Actor, Director)
c/o Staff Member *Imperium 7 Talent Agency*
5455 Wilshire Blvd Ste 1706
Los Angeles, CA 90036-4217, USA

Anderson, Jim (Athlete, Baseball Player)
2111 Bennington Ct
Thousand Oaks, CA 91360-1977, USA

Anderson, Jimmy (Athlete, Hockey Player)
4H Castle Hill Rd
Agawam, MA 01001-2460, USA

Anderson, Jimmy (Athlete, Baseball Player)
214 Pennington Blvd
Portsmouth, VA 23701-1226, USA

Anderson, Jo (Actor)
c/o Staff Member *Innovative Artists (LA)*
1505 10th St
Santa Monica, CA 90401-2805, USA

Anderson, Joe (Actor)
c/o Lindy King *United Agents*
12-26 Lexington St
London W1F OLE, UK

Anderson, John (Musician, Songwriter, Writer)
PO Box 1547
Goodlettsville, TN 37070-1547, USA

Anderson, John (Athlete, Football Player)
14730 Crestwood Ct
Elm Grove, WI 53122-1603, USA

Anderson, John (Athlete, Hockey Player)
260 Sunset Ave
Glen Ellyn, IL 60137-5358, USA

Anderson, John B (Misc)
4120 48th St NW
Washington, DC 20016-2336, USA

Anderson, John E (Attorney, Attorney General, General)
555 S Flower St # 2601
Los Angeles, CA 90071-2300, USA

Anderson, John Jr (Ex-Governor)
16609 W 133rd St
Olathe, KS 66062-1575, USA

Anderson, Jon (Musician)
9 Hillgate St
London W8 7SP, UNITED KINGDOM (UK)

Anderson, June (Opera Singer)
119 W 57th St Ste 1505
New York, NY 10019-2403, USA

Anderson, Kalen (Athlete, Golfer)
c/o Jim Lehrman *SFX Golf*
36855 W Main St Ste 200
Purcellville, VA 20132-3561, USA

Anderson, Keith (Musician)
c/o Staff Member *Fitzgerald-Hartley*
34 N Palm St Ste 100
Ventura, CA 93001-2610, USA

Anderson, Kenny (Athlete, Basketball Player)
270 N Canon Dr # 1289
Beverly Hills, CA 90210-5323, USA

Anderson, Kent (Athlete, Baseball Player)
925 E Twin Church Rd
Timmonsville, SC 29161-8528, USA

Anderson, Kevin (Actor)
c/o Staff Member *International Creative Management (ICM-LA)*
10250 Constellation Blvd Fl 7
Los Angeles, CA 90067-6207, USA

Anderson, Kevin J (Writer)
175 5th Ave
New York, NY 10010-7703, USA

Anderson, Kim (Athlete, Basketball Player)
602 Somerset Dr
Warrensburg, MO 64093-1674, USA

Anderson, Kim S (Athlete, Football Player)
6709 La Tijera Blvd
Los Angeles, CA 90045-2017, USA

Anderson, Larry (Athlete, Baseball Player)
815 Opal Cir
Arroyo Grande, CA 93420-4408, USA

Anderson, Laurie (Musician)
195 Chrystie St # 501F
New York, NY 10002-1214, USA

Anderson, Lawrence A (Larry) (Athlete, Football Player)
5610 Buncombe Rd Apt 1011
Shreveport, LA 71129-3619, USA

Anderson, Loni (Actor)
c/o Stephen (Steve) LaManna *Innovative Artists (LA)*
1505 10th St
Santa Monica, CA 90401-2805, USA

Anderson, Louie (Actor, Comedian, Producer, Writer)
c/o Jackie Miller-Knobbe *Agency for the Performing Arts (APA-LA)*
405 S Beverly Dr Ste 500
Beverly Hills, CA 90212-4425, USA

Anderson, Loule (Actor, Comedian)
8033 W Sunset Blvd # 605
West Hollywood, CA 90046-2401, USA

Anderson, Lynn (Musician)
c/o Staff Member *Wolfman Jack Entertainment*
105 River Shore Dr
Hertford, NC 27944-8015, USA

Anderson, Marina (Actor)
c/o Nancy Harding *Powerhouse Talent*
PO Box 261939
Encino, CA 91426-1939, USA

Anderson, Mark (Athlete, Football Player)
PO Box 27551
Tulsa, OK 74149-0551, USA

Anderson, Marlon (Athlete, Baseball Player)
1603 Turning Leaf Ct
Sugar Land, TX 77479-6489, USA

Anderson, Marques (Athlete, Football Player)
213 W Gardner St
Long Beach, CA 90805-2034, USA

Anderson, Mary (Actor)
1127 N Norman Pl
Los Angeles, CA 90049-1538, USA

Anderson, Matt (Athlete, Baseball Player)
14626 Anderson Woods Trce
Louisville, KY 40245-8428, USA

Anderson, Matt (Athlete, Golfer)
c/o Jim Lehrman *SFX Golf*
36855 W Main St Ste 200
Purcellville, VA 20132-3561, USA

Anderson, May (Model)
c/o Lewis, Joffe & Company 10880
Wilshire Boulevard Suite 520
Los Angeles, CA 90024, USA

Anderson, Melissa Sue (Actor, Producer)
c/o Staff Member *Bret Adams Agency*
448 W 44th St
New York, NY 10036-5220, USA

Anderson, Melody (Actor)
PO Box 24483
Los Angeles, CA 90024-0483, USA

Anderson, Michael (Musician, Songwriter, Writer)
7106 Moores Ln # 200
Brentwood, TN 37027-2903, USA

Anderson, Michael H (Physicist)
Physics
Boulder, CO 80309-0001, USA

Anderson, Michael J (Director)
52 Yorkminster Rd
North York, ON M2P 1M3, CANADA

Anderson, Mike (Athlete, Baseball Player)
407 Prairie Grass Ct
Hartland, WI 53029-8562, USA

Anderson, Mike (Athlete, Baseball Player)
4112 Westbrook Dr
Florence, SC 29501-8724, USA

Anderson, Mike (Athlete, Coach, Football Player)
PO Box 12753
Chandler, AZ 85248-0030, USA

Anderson, Mitchell (Actor)
931 Monroe Dr NE Ste A106
Atlanta, GA 30308-1795, USA

Anderson, Murray (Athlete, Hockey Player)
38 Head Ave P O Stn Main Box 38
The Pas, MB R9A 1K3, Canada

Anderson, Neal (Athlete, Football Player)
10626 SW 41st Pl
Gainesville, FL 32608-7126, USA

Anderson, Neil T. (Writer)
9051 Executive Park Dr Ste 503
Knoxville, TN 37923-4632, USA

Anderson, Neilson (Athlete, Basketball Player)
163 Harbor Isle Cir N
Memphis, TN 38103-0841, USA

Anderson, Nick (Athlete, Basketball Player)
6672 Cherry Grove Cir
Orlando, FL 32809-6658, USA

Anderson, Nick (Cartoonist, Editor)
525 W Broadway
Louisville, KY 40202-2206, USA

Anderson, Nicole (Actor)
c/o Todd Justice *Marshak/Zachary Company, The*
8840 Wilshire Blvd Fl 1
Beverly Hills, CA 90211-2606, USA

Anderson, Nikki (Stylist)
c/o Staff Member *Crews*
828 Clemont Dr NE
Atlanta, GA 30306-3694, USA

Anderson, Ottis (Athlete, Football Player)
9636 Guehring Dr
Saint Louis, MO 63123-7122, USA

Anderson, Ottis J (O J) (Athlete, Football Player)
PO Box 399
Orange, NJ 07051-0399, USA

Anderson, Paige (Stylist)
c/o Staff Member *Independent Artists*
448 E Riverdale Ave
Orange, CA 92865-1302, USA

Anderson, Pamela (Actor)
c/o Chris Smith *International Creative Management (ICM-LA)*
10250 Constellation Blvd Fl 7
Los Angeles, CA 90067-6207, USA

Anderson, Paul Thomas (Director, Writer)
c/o Bryan Lourd *Creative Artists Agency (CAA-LA)*
2000 Avenue of the Stars Ste 100
Los Angeles, CA 90067-4705, USA

Anderson, Paul W S (Director)
c/o Ken Kamins *Key Creatives*
1800 N Highland Ave Fl 5
Los Angeles, CA 90028-4523, USA

Anderson, Perry (Athlete, Hockey Player)
3311 E Oregon Ave
Phoenix, AZ 85018-1437, USA

Anderson, Philip W (Nobel Prize Laureate)
Physics
Princeton, NJ 08544-0001, USA

Anderson, R Lanier III (Judge)
56 Forsyth St NW
Atlanta, GA 30303-2218, USA

Anderson, Ralph (Athlete, Football Player)
908 Hilltop Dr Apt C
Irving, TX 75060-3925, USA

Anderson, Randy (Race Car Driver)
1240 S Cucamonga Ave
Ontario, CA 91761-4505, USA

Anderson, Rashard (Athlete, Football Player)
676 N First Ave
Forest, MS 39074-3637, USA

Anderson, Ray (Musician)
318 Wynn Ln
Port Jefferson, NY 11777-1670, USA

Anderson, Reid B (Dancer, Director)
Ober Schlossgarten 6
Stuttgart 70173, GERMANY

Anderson, Renee (Actor)
2818 Laurel Canyon Blvd
Los Angeles, CA 90046, USA

Anderson, Richard (Actor)
10120 Cielo Dr
Beverly Hills, CA 90210-2037, USA

Anderson, Richard Dean (Actor)
c/o Leigh Brillstein *International Creative Management (ICM-LA)*
10250 Constellation Blvd Fl 7
Los Angeles, CA 90067-6207, USA

Anderson, Richard (Dick) J (Athlete, Football Player)
206 Baker St
Lodi, OH 44254-1407, USA

Anderson, Richard P (Dick) (Athlete, Football Player)
4603 Santa Maria St
Coral Gables, FL 33146-1132, USA

Anderson, Richie (Athlete, Football Player)
6311 Meandering Woods Ct
Frederick, MD 21701-4955, USA

Anderson, Rick (Athlete, Baseball Player)
3929 Benjamin Dr
Saint Paul, MN 55125-3396, USA

Anderson, Robert G W (Misc)
Great Russell St
London WC1B 3DG, UNITED KINGDOM (UK)

Anderson, Robert W (Writer)
14 Sutton Pl S
New York, NY 10022-3071, USA

Anderson, Ron (Athlete, Hockey Player)
72 Woodside Close
Airdrie, AB T4B 2C7, Canada

Anderson, Ron (Athlete, Hockey Player)
11 Wallace Rd
Lynn, MA 01902-2011, USA

Anderson, Ross (Journalist)
1120 John St
Seattle, WA 98109-5321, USA

Anderson, Russ (Athlete, Hockey Player)
76 Fern Dr
Plantsville, CT 06479-1810, USA

Anderson, Sam (Actor)
c/o Staff Member *TalentWorks (LA)*
3500 W Olive Ave Ste 1400
Burbank, CA 91505-5512, USA

Anderson, Scot (Writer)
c/o Staff Member *Premiere Speakers Bureau*
109 International Dr Ste 300
Franklin, TN 37067-1764, USA

Anderson, Scott (Athlete, Baseball Player)
13061 Amber Pl
Lake Oswego, OR 97034-1524, USA

Anderson, Scott (Athlete, Football Player)
2524 Marsh Ave
Hannibal, MO 63401-2412, USA

Anderson, Scotty (Athlete, Football Player)
1405 Leon Dr
Jonesboro, LA 71251-2213, USA

Anderson, Shandon (Athlete, Basketball Player)
63 Mangum St SW Unit 6
Atlanta, GA 30313-1355, USA

Anderson, Shawn (Athlete, Hockey Player)
19 51st Ave
Notre-Dame-De-L'ile-Perrot, QC J7V 7L8, Canada

Anderson, Shelly (Race Car Driver)
1240 S Cucamonga Ave
Ontario, CA 91761-4505, USA

Anderson, Stephen H (Judge)
125 S State St
Salt Lake City, UT 84138-1102, USA

Anderson, Sterling (Writer)
c/o Abram Nalibotsky *Gersh (LA)*
9465 Wilshire Blvd Ste 600
Beverly Hills, CA 90212-2612, USA

Anderson, Stevie (Athlete, Football Player)
1405 Leon Dr
Jonesboro, LA 71251-2213, USA

Anderson, Stuart (Athlete, Football Player)
100 Careys Ln
Cardinal, VA 23025-2006, USA

Anderson, Susan (Psychic, Radio Personality)
PO Box 8464
Minneapolis, MN 55408-0464, USA

Anderson, Taz (Athlete, Football Player)
2931 Paces Ferry Rd SE Ste 150
Atlanta, GA 30339-3735, USA

Anderson, Terence (Terry) (Journalist)
17 Sunlight Hl
Yonkers, NY 10704-2903, USA

Anderson, Terry (Producer)
Iverheath Iver
Bucks SL0 0NH, UNITED KINGDOM (UK)

Anderson, Theodore W (Economist, Mathematician)
746 Santa Ynez St
Stanford, CA 94305-8441, USA

Anderson, Tom (Actor, Producer, Writer)
c/o Staff Member *Gersh (LA)*
9465 Wilshire Blvd Ste 600
Beverly Hills, CA 90212-2612, USA

Anderson, Tom (Business Person)
6060 Center Dr Ste 300
Los Angeles, CA 90045-8842, USA

Anderson, Tracy (Fitness Expert)
408 Greenwich St Fl 3
New York, NY 10013-2077, USA

Anderson, Vickey Ray (Athlete, Football Player)
9308 S Harvey Ave
Oklahoma City, OK 73139-8636, USA

Anderson, W French (Misc)
144 E Lake View Ter
Los Angeles, CA 90039, USA

Anderson, W William (Athlete, Football Player)
6924 Lark Ln
Knoxville, TN 37919-5928, USA

Anderson, Warren M (Business Person)
270 Park Ave
New York, NY 10017-2014, USA

Anderson, Webster (War Hero)
3044 US Highway 321 N
Winnsboro, SC 29180-8346, USA

Anderson, Wendell (Athlete, Hockey Player)
108 Chevy Chase Dr
Wayzata, MN 55391-1054, USA

Anderson, Wes (Director, Writer)
c/o Leslee Dart *42West (NY)*
220 W 42nd St Fl 12
New York, NY 10036-7200, USA

Anderson, Wessell (Musician)
1906 Chet Atkins Pl Apt 502
Nashville, TN 37212-2122, USA

Anderson, Weston (Physicist)
611 Hansen Way
Palo Alto, CA 94304-1015, USA

Anderson, Wilford C (War Hero)
3585 Round Barn Blvd
Santa Rosa, CA 95403-0134, USA

Anderson, William R (Misc)
10505 Miller Rd
Oakton, VA 22124-1709, USA

Anderson, Willie (Athlete, Basketball Player)
Air Canada Center 40 Bay St
Toronto, ON M5J 2N8, Canada

Anderson, Willie (Athlete, Football Player)
1490 Meadowcreek Ct
Atlanta, GA 30338-3803, USA

Anderson III, N Christian (Editor, Publisher)
30 S Prospect St
Colorado Springs, CO 80903-3638, USA

Anderson-Perkin, Janet (Athlete, Baseball Player)
244 Ottawa St N
Regina, SK S4R 2V3, CANADA

Anderson-Sheriffs, Vivian (Athlete, Baseball Player)
2654 N 117th St
Wauwatosa, WI 53226-1124, USA

Andersson, Benny (Composer, Musician)
Sodra Brobaeken 41-A
Stockholm 111 49, SWEDEN

Andersson, Bibi (Actor)
201 Faubourg Saint Honore
Paris 75008, FRANCE

Andersson, Erik (Athlete, Hockey Player)
Persilijav 9
Karlstad S-65351, Sweden

Andersson, Harriet (Actor)
Roslagsgatan 14/6
Stockholm 113 55, Sweden

Andersson, Henrik (Musician)
6404 Wilshire Blvd Ste 505
Los Angeles, CA 90048-5507, USA

Andersson, Kent-Erik (Athlete, Hockey Player)
Persiljav-9
Karlstad S-65351, Sweden

Andersson, Mikael (Athlete, Hockey Player)
c/o Staff Member *Tampa Bay Lightning*
401 Channelside Dr
Tampa, FL 33602-5400, USA

Anderszewski, Piotr (Conductor, Musician)
90 University Pl
New York, NY 10003-4665

Anderzunas, Wally (Athlete, Basketball Player)
3609 F St
Omaha, NE 68107-1345, USA

Andes, Karen (Misc)
375 Hudson St
New York, NY 10014-3658, USA

Andino, Robert (Athlete, Baseball Player)
2250 NW 2nd St
Miami, FL 33125-5206, USA

Ando, Hiromi (Stylist)
c/o Staff Member *Mercury Artists*
8460 Higuera St Fl 2
Culver City, CA 90232-2520, USA

Ando, Tadao (Architect)
5-23-2 Toyosaki
Kitaku, Osaka 531, JAPAN

Andov, Stojan (President)
Sobranje 11 Oktombri Blvd
Skopje 91000, MACEDONIA

Andrade, Sergio (Musician)
9268 W 3rd St
Beverly Hills, CA 90210-3713, USA

Andrade, William T (Billy) (Athlete, Golfer)
4439 E Brookhaven Dr NE
Atlanta, GA 30319-1007, USA

Andrascik, Steve (Athlete, Hockey Player)
32 Early Ln
Annville, PA 17003-8623, USA

Andre, Carl (Artist)
689 Crown St
Brooklyn, NY 11213-5303, USA

Andre, Maurice (Musician)
Presles-en-Brie
Tournan-en-Brie 77220, FRANCE

Andre, Peter (Musician, Television Host)
55 Drury Ln
London 4217, UNITED KINGDOM

Andrea, Paul (Athlete, Hockey Player)
136 Regent St
North Sydney, NS B2A 2G5, Canada

Andreas, Dwayne O (Business Person)
181 Southmoreland Pl
Decatur, IL 62521-3738, USA

Andreas, G Allen (Business Person)
4666 E Faries Pkwy
Decatur, IL 62526-5630, USA

Andreasen, Nancy C (Doctor)
200 Hawkins Dr
Iowa City, IA 52242-1009, USA

Andreason, Larry (Yachtsman)
10874 Kyle St
Los Alamitos, CA 90720, USA

Andre-Deshays, Claudie (Misc)
Rhumatologie Dept
Paris 75000, FRANCE

Andreeff, Starr (Actor)
1875 Century Park E Ste 2250
Los Angeles, CA 90067-2563, USA

Andreessen, Marc (Designer)
599 N Mathilda Ave
Sunnyvale, CA 94085-3505, USA

Andrei, Alessandro (Athlete, Track Athlete)
Via V Bellini 1
Scandicci, Firenze 50018, ITALY

Andreotti, Giulio (Government Official)
Piazza Montecitorio 13,1
Rome I-00186, Italy

Andress, Tuck (Musician)
PO Box 5501
Beverly Hills, CA 90209-5501, USA

Andress, Ursula (Actor)
Via Francesco Siacci 38
Rome 186, ITALY

Andretti, John (Race Car Driver)
107 Keats Rd
Mooresville, NC 28117-8769, USA

Andretti, Marco (Race Car Driver)
c/o John Caponigro *Sports Management Network, Inc.*
1668 S Telegraph Rd Ste 200
Bloomfield Hills, MI 48302-0016, USA

Andretti, Mario (Race Car Driver)
457 Rose Inn Ave
Nazareth, PA 18064-9234, USA

Andretti, Michael M (Athlete, Race Car Driver)
7615 Zionsville Rd
Indianapolis, IN 46268-2174, USA

Andrew, C Robert (Rob) (Athlete, Misc)
Newcastle-upon-Tyne NE3 2DT, UNITED KINGDOM (UK)

Andrew, HRH (Prince)
Sunninghill Park
Windsor, England

Andrew, Kim (Athlete, Baseball Player)
17018 Germain St
Granada Hills, CA 91344-6212, USA

Andrew, Phillip (Actor)
c/o Bonnie Liedtke *Principato/Young Management*
9465 Wilshire Blvd Ste 430
Beverly Hills, CA 90212-2613, USA

Andrew, Prince (Prince, Royalty)
Buckingham Palace
London SW1A 1AA, UNITED KINGDOM (UK)

Andrews, Al (Athlete, Boxer)
1119 River St
Rhinelander, WI 54501-2404, USA

Andrews, Al (Athlete, Football Player)
PO Box 82256
Atlanta, GA 30354-0256, USA

Andrews, Amy (Stylist)
2815 W Fargo Ave
Chicago, IL 60645-1221, USA

Andrews, Amy Leigh (Model)
PO Box 3184
Manhattan Beach, CA 90266-1184, USA

Andrews, Andy (Actor, Comedian)
PO Box 17321
Nashville, TN 37217-0321, USA

Andrews, Anthony (Actor)
13 Manor Place
Oxford, Oxon, UNITED KINGDOM (UK)

Andrews, Billy (Athlete, Football Player)
PO Box 703
Clinton, LA 70722-0703, USA

Andrews, Clayton (Athlete, Baseball Player)
1952 Elaine Dr
Clearwater, Fl 33760-1742, USA

Andrews, Donna (Athlete, Golfer)
2301 Hawthorne Rd
Lynchburg, VA 24503-2903, USA

Andrews, Erin (Sportscaster)
c/o Alejandra Cristina *Ace PR*
4122 Sunnyslope Ave
Sherman Oaks, CA 91423-4308, USA

Andrews, Fred (Athlete, Baseball Player)
PO Box 898
Wedowee, AL 36278-0898, USA

Andrews, Giuseppe (Actor)
PO Box 24561
Ventura, CA 93002-4561, USA

Andrews, Hub (Athlete, Baseball Player)
2305 N 2nd Ave
Dodge City, KS 67801-2534, USA

Andrews, Inez (Musician)
330 W 56th St Apt 18M
New York, NY 10019-4222, USA

Andrews, James (Doctor)
1313 13th St S
Birmingham, AL 35205-5327, USA

Andrews, James E (Misc)
100 Witherspoon St
Louisville, KY 40202-1396, USA

Andrews, Jessica (Musician)
c/o Rodney Essig *Creative Artists Agency (CAA-TN)*
3310 W End Ave Fl 5
Nashville, TN 37203-1028, USA

Andrews, John (Athlete, Baseball Player)
9292 Gordon Ave
La Habra, CA 90631-2452, USA

Andrews, John H (Architect)
PO Box 7087
McMahon's Point, NSW 2060, AUSTRALIA

Andrews, John M (Athlete, Football Player)
7306 Summer Trail Dr
Sugar Land, TX 77479-6233, USA

Andrews, John V (Athlete, Football Player)
7306 Summer Trail Dr
Sugar Land, TX 77479-6233, USA

Andrews, Julie (Actor, Musician)
c/o Steve Sauer *Media Four*
8840 Wilshire Blvd Fl 2
Beverly Hills, CA 90211-2606, USA

Andrews, Ken (Musician)
c/o Staff Member *Paradigm (Monterey)*
404 W Franklin St
Monterey, CA 93940-2303, USA

Andrews, Lee (Musician)
27 L Ambiance Ct
Bardonia, NY 10954-1421, USA

Andrews, Mark (Ex-Senator, Politician)
3354 165th Ave SE
Mapleton, ND 58059-9746, USA

Andrews, Mike (Athlete, Baseball Player)
375 Longwood Ave
Boston, MA 02215-5395, USA

Andrews, Mitch (Athlete, Football Player)
PO Box 672
Washington, LA 70589-0672, USA

Andrews, Naveen (Actor)
c/o Renee Jennett *Renee Jennett Management*
10028 Farragut Dr
Culver City, CA 90232-3228, USA

Andrews, Patricia (Patt) (Musician)
9823 Aldea Ave
Northridge, CA 91325-1915, USA

Andrews, Patricia (Patti) (Musician)
9823 Aldea Ave
Northridge, CA 91325-1915, USA

Andrews, Patty (Musician)
9823 Aldea Ave
Northridge, CA 91325-1915, USA

Andrews, Rob (Athlete, Baseball Player)
1280 Mountbatten Ct
Concord, CA 94518-3927, USA

Andrews, Robert (Writer)
375 Hudson St
New York, NY 10014-3658, USA

Andrews, Robert E (Congressman, Politician)
2265 Rayburn Hob
Washington, DC 20515-0552, USA

Andrews, Robert F (Misc)
5879 Beulah Land
Lakeland, FL 33810, USA

Andrews, Russell (Actor)

Andrews, Shane (Athlete, Baseball Player)
1816 N Guadalupe St
Carlsbad, NM 88220-8813, USA

Andrews, Shawn (Actor)
c/o Laura Berwick *Hofflund/Polone*
9465 Wilshire Blvd Ste 420
Beverly Hills, CA 90212-2603, USA

Andrews, Shawn (Athlete, Football Player)
6 Jacob Pl
Little Rock, AR 72211-2156, USA

Andrews, Stacy (Athlete, Football Player)
6 Jacob Pl
Little Rock, AR 72211-2156, USA

Andrews, Theresa (Swimmer)
2004 Homewood Rd
Annapolis, MD 21402, USA

Andrews, Thomas (Tom) (Athlete, Football Player)
1918 Wickham Way
Louisville, KY 40223-1059, USA

Andrews, Tina (Actor)
c/o Staff Member *Sharp & Associates Public Relations*
1516 N Fairfax Ave
Los Angeles, CA 90046-2608, USA

Andrews, William D (Athlete, Football Player)
PO Box 703
Clinton, LA 70722-0703, USA

Andrews, William L (Athlete, Football Player)
3916 Toccoa Falls Dr
Duluth, GA 30097-8104, USA

Andrews II, George E (Athlete, Football Player)
10195 Overhill Dr
Santa Ana, CA 92705-1515, USA

Andreychuk, Dave (Athlete, Hockey Player)
18130 Longwater Run Dr
Tampa, FL 33647-2211, USA

Andrianarivo, Tantely (Prime Minister)
Mahazoarivo, Antananarivo, MADAGASCAR

Andrie, George J (Athlete, Football Player)
26356 E Zeerip Dr
Drummond Island, MI 49726-9597, USA

Andriessen, Louis (Composer)
75 Rockefeller Plz
New York, NY 10019-6908, USA

Andrieu, Sebastien (Actor, Model)
c/o Staff Member *Creature Entertainment*
11766 Wilshire Blvd Ste 1610
Los Angeles, CA 90025-6565, USA

Andros, Plato (Athlete, Football Player)
1707 Crown Point Ave
Norman, OK 73072-5865, USA

Androsky, Carol (Actor)
8285 W Sunset Blvd Ste 1
West Hollywood, CA 90046-2420, USA

Andruff, Ron (Athlete, Hockey Player)
72 1/2 Irving Pl Apt 1F
New York, NY 10003-2223, USA

Andrulis, Greg (Coach, Football Coach)
2121 Velma Ave
Columbus, OH 43211-2085, USA

Andrus, Cecil (Ex-Governor, Ex-Senator)
1280 Candleridge Dr
Boise, ID 83712-6504, USA

Andrus, Lou
739 W 550 S
Orem, UT 84058-6070, USA

Andrus, Lou (Athlete, Football Player)
739 W 550 S
Orem, UT 84058-6070, USA

Andrus, Sheldon (Athlete, Football Player)
210 Belle Meade Blvd
Thibodaux, LA 70301-4908, USA

Andrusak, Greg (Athlete, Hockey Player)
5240 Hwy 3A
Nelson, BC V1L 6N6, Canada

Andrusyshsyn, Zenon (Athlete, Football Player)
2823 Lake Saxon Dr
Land O Lakes, FL 34639-6620, USA

Andruzzi, Joe (Athlete, Football Player)
682 Bellmore Ave
East Meadow, NY 11554-4746, USA

Andujar, Joaquin (Athlete, Baseball Player)
Ave L, Amiama Tio #47
San Pedro de Macoris, Dominican Republic

Ane, Charles T (Charlie) III (Athlete, Football Player)
749 16th Ave
Honolulu, HI 96816-4121, USA

Anemone (Actor)
82 rue Bonaparte
Paris 75006, France

Ang, Stephen (Stylist)
37 W 20th St Ste 603
New York, NY 10011-3718, USA

Angarano, Michael (Actor)
c/o Tracey Jacobs *United Talent Agency (UTA)*
9560 Wilshire Blvd Fl 5
Beverly Hills, CA 90212-2400, USA

Angel, Ashley Parker (Musician)
c/o Chuck James *International Creative Management (ICM-LA)*
10250 Constellation Blvd Fl 7
Los Angeles, CA 90067-6207, USA

Angel, Criss (Magician, Musician)
c/o David (Dave) Baram *Yorn Management Group*
2000 Avenue Of The Stars 3rd Tower Floor NORTH
Los Angeles, CA 90067, USA

Angel, Heather H (Photographer)
Highways 6 Vicarage Hill
Farnham, Surrey GU9 8HJ, UNITED KINGDOM (UK)

Angel, James R P (Astronomer)
Steward Observatory
Tucson, AZ 85721-0001, USA

Angel, Joe (Athlete, Baseball Player, Sportscaster)
4900 Moreau Ct
El Dorado Hills, CA 95762-7625, USA

Angel, Ryland (Musician)
c/o Staff Member *Paradigm (Monterey)*
404 W Franklin St
Monterey, CA 93940-2303, USA

Angel, Vanessa (Actor)
c/o Staff Member *Tappan Entertainment*
8324 Fountain Ave Apt C
Los Angeles, CA 90069-2916, USA

Angeli, Donna Lee (Stylist)
234 E 52nd St Apt 2D
New York, NY 10022-6215, USA

Angelil, Rene (Actor, Writer)
c/o Staff Member *United Talent Agency (UTA)*
9560 Wilshire Blvd Fl 5
Beverly Hills, CA 90212-2400, USA

Angelini, Florenzo Cardinal (Religious Leader)
Via Anneo Lucano 47
Rome 136, ITALY

Angelini, Norm (Athlete, Baseball Player)
15063 E Chenango Pl
Aurora, CO 80015-2136, USA

Angell, Wayne D (Financier, Government Official)
383 Madison Ave
New York, NY 10017-3217, USA

Angelopoulos, Theodoros (Theo) (Actor, Director, Producer, Writer)
Solmou 18 106 82
Athens, GREECE

Angelos, Peter (Athlete, Baseball Player)
100 N Charles St
Baltimore, MD 21201-3804, USA

Angelou, Maya (Writer)
3240 Valley Rd
Winston Salem, NC 27106-2504, USA

Angels, Anaheim
Edison Field 2000 Gene Autry Way
Anaheim, CA 92806, USA

Angels & Airwaves (Music Group)
c/o Staff Member *Geffen Records*
9126 Sunset Blvd
West Hollywood, CA 90069, USA

Angelycal Musical (Music Group)
c/o Staff Member *Sony Music Miami*
605 Lincoln Rd Ste 700
Miami Beach, FL 33139-2901, USA

Angelyne (Actor, Artist, Model)
c/o Staff Member *Angelyne Management*
5670 Wilshire Blvd Fl 22
Los Angeles, CA 90036-5679, USA

Angerer, Paul (Composer)
Esteplatz 3/26
Vienna 1030, AUSTRIA

Angerer, Peter (Athlete)
Wagenau 2
Hammer 17326, GERMANY

Angle, Kurt (Athlete, Wrestler)
PO Box 97007
Pittsburgh, PA 15229-0007, USA

Anglim, Philip (Actor)
2404 Grand Canal
Venice, CA 90291-4508, USA

Anglin, Jennifer (Actor)
651 N Kilkea Dr
Los Angeles, CA 90048-2213, USA

Angotti, Lou (Athlete, Hockey Player)
2850 NE 14th Street Cswy Apt 401B
Pompano Beach, FL 33062-3640, USA

Anguiano, Raul (Artist)
Anaxagoras 1326 Colonia Narvate
Mexico City 13 DF, MEXICO

Angullo, Richard (Athlete, Football Player)
4801 W Libby St
Glendale, AZ 85308-1436, USA

Angus & Julia Stone (Music Group, Musician)
c/o Dan Efram *The Muse Box - NY*
650 Broadway Fl 4
New York, NY 10012-2315, USA

Anholt, Christien (Actor)
4237 Morro Dr
Woodland Hills, CA 91364-5521, USA

Anholt, Darrell (Athlete, Hockey Player)
4935 49th St
Hughenden, AB T0B 2E0, Canada

Anikulap-Kuti, Femi (Musician, Songwriter, Writer)
70 Universal City Plz
Universal City, CA 91608-1011, USA

Animals, The (Music Group)
PO Box 1821
Ojai, CA 93024-1821, USA

Anissina, Marina (Figure Skater)
c/o Staff Member *Champions on Ice*
3500 W 80th St Ste 200
Minneapolis, MN 55431-1090, USA

Aniston, Jennifer (Actor)
c/o Aleen Keshishian *Brillstein Entertainment Partners*
9150 Wilshire Blvd Ste 350
Beverly Hills, CA 90212-3453, USA

Aniston, John (Actor)
PO Box 514 5520 Platt Ave
West Hills, CA 91307, USA

Anjali (Actor, Bollywood)
14 Ganapathi Colony 1 Street Gopalpuram
Chennai, TN 600006, INDIA

Anjali, Devi (Actor, Bollywood)
6 Bags Road Raja Annamalai Puram
Chennai, TN 600028, INDIA

Anju (Actor, Bollywood)
37 Nagarathanammal Nagar Janaki Nagar
Chennai, TN 600017, INDIA

Anka, Paul (Actor, Musician, Writer)
2674 Stafford Rd
Thousand Oaks, CA 91361-5039, USA

Ankiel, Rick (Athlete, Baseball Player)
8695 SE Compass Island Way
Jupiter, FL 33458-1102, USA

Ankrom, Scott (Athlete, Football Player)
1206 Harvest Cyn
San Antonio, TX 78258-3836, USA

Anlyan, William G (Doctor)
100 Seeley Mudd Bldg 109
Durham, NC 27710-0001, USA

Annable, David (Dave) (Actor)
c/o Sue Leibman *Barking Dog Entertainment*
9 Desbrosses St Fl 2
New York, NY 10013-1701, USA

Annan, Kofi A (Secretary)
Rue de Varembé 9-11
Geneva 1202, Switzerland

Annan, Kofi A (Politician, Secretary)
1 United Nations Plz
New York, NY 10017-3515, USA

Annaud, Jean-Jacques (Director)
16 Rue Saint-Vincent
Paris 75018, FRANCE

Anne (Royalty)
Gatecombe Park
Gloucestershire, UNITED KINGDOM (UK)

Anne of Bourbon-Palma (Royalty)
77 Chemin Louis-Degallier
Versoix-Geneva 1290, SWITZERLAND

Annenberg, Wallis (Publisher)
10273 Century Woods Dr
Los Angeles, CA 90067-6312, USA

Annett, Chloe (Actor)
c/o Staff Member *Innovative Artists (LA)*
1505 10th St
Santa Monica, CA 90401-2805, USA

Annis, Francesca (Actor)
c/o Staff Member *Independent Talent Group (ITG-UK)*
Oxford House 76 Oxford St
London W1D 1BS, UK

Anno, Sam (Athlete, Football Player)
12934 Ferndale Ave
Los Angeles, CA 90066-3520, USA

Annu, Kapoor (Actor, Bollywood)
F-19 Flat No. 504 Green Crest Yamuna Nagar Opp Parasrampuria Tower Andheri(W)
Mumbai, MS 400053, INDIA

Annunziata, Robert (Business Person)
Wessex House 45 Reid St
Hamilton, HM 12, BERMUDA

Ansara, Edward (Actor)
5118 Vineland Ave # 102
North Hollywood, CA 91601-3814, USA

Ansara, Michael (Actor)
4624 Park Mirasol
Calabasas, CA 91302-1731, USA

Ansari, Anousheh (Astronaut)
6101 W Plano Pkwy # 210
Plano, TX 75093-8201, USA

Ansari, Aziz (Comedian)
c/o David (Dave) Becky *3 Arts Entertainment Inc*
9460 Wilshire Blvd Fl 7
Beverly Hills, CA 90212-2713, USA

Anschutz, Jody (Athlete, Golfer)
27307 N Palo Fierro Rd
Rio Verde, AZ 85263-5087, USA

Anschutz, Philip F (Business Person)
c/o Staff Member *Anschutz Film Group*
1888 Century Park E Ste 1400
Century City, CA 90067-1718, USA

Anschutz, Philip F. (Business Person)
555 17th St Ste 2400
Denver, CO 80202-3941, USA

Anselmo, Philip (Musician)
361 W Broadway # 200
New York, NY 10013-2209, USA

Anspach, Susan (Actor)
PO Box 5605
Santa Monica, CA 90409-5605, USA

Anspaugh, David (Director, Producer)
c/o John Burnham *International Creative Management (ICM-LA)*
10250 Constellation Blvd Fl 7
Los Angeles, CA 90067-6207, USA

Ant, Adam (Musician)
c/o Staff Member *The Rights House (UK)*
Drury House 34-43 Russell St
London WC2B 5HA, UK

Antal, Nimrod (Director)
c/o Scott Greenberg *Creative Artists Agency (CAA-LA)*
2000 Avenue of the Stars Ste 100
Los Angeles, CA 90067-4705, USA

Antes, Horst (Artist)
Hohenbergstr 11
Karlsruhe (Wolfartsweier 76228, GERMANY

Anthony, Allyson (Stylist)
1980 15th St
San Francisco, CA 94114-1728, USA

Anthony, Carl (Misc)
Kennedy Government School
Cambridge, MA 2138, USA

Anthony, Carmelo (Athlete, Basketball Player)
c/o Leon Rose *CAA - NJ*
308 Harper Dr Ste 210
Moorestown, NJ 08057-3245, USA

Anthony, Charles (Athlete, Football Player)
38709 Farwell Dr
Fremont, CA 94536-7218, USA

Anthony, Edward (Athlete, Football Player)
3433 Mill Run Ln
Pfafftown, NC 27040 9478, USA

Anthony, Eric (Athlete, Baseball Player)
42 Fosters Ct
Sugar Land, TX 77479, USA

Anthony, Greg (Athlete, Basketball Player)
520 S 4th St
Las Vegas, NV 89101-6520, USA

Anthony, Jasmine Jessica (Actor)
c/o Adam Griffin *Kritzer Levine Wilkins Entertainment*
11872 La Grange Ave Fl 1
Los Angeles, CA 90025-5283, USA

Anthony, Jason (Model)
c/o Staff Member *Boss Models*
80 8th Ave
New York, NY 10011-5126, USA

Anthony, Jeff (Stylist)
918 10th St
Wilmette, IL 60091-1766, USA

Anthony, Lysette (Actor)
46 Old Compton St
London WV 5PB, UNITED KINGDOM (UK)

Anthony, Marc (Actor, Musician, Songwriter, Writer)
489 5th Ave Ste 24A
New York, NY 10017-6109, USA

Anthony, Mark (Stylist)
c/o Staff Member *ESP (London)*
63 Charlotte St. 1st Floor
London W11 4PG, UK

Anthony, Michael (Musician)
10100 Santa Monica Blvd Ste 1300
Los Angeles, CA 90067-4114, USA

Anthony, Piers (Writer)
PO Box 2289
Inverness, FL 34451-2289

Anthony, Plers (Writer)
PO Box 2289
Inverness, FL 34451-2289, USA

Anthony, Ray (Musician)
9288 Kinglet Dr
Los Angeles, CA 90069-1114, USA

Anthony, Reidel (Athlete, Football Player)
PO Box 23
South Bay, FL 33493-0023, USA

Anthony, Terry (Athlete, Football Player)
625 Dartford Ct
Debary, FL 32713-2144, USA

Anthrax (Music Group)
c/o Dave Kirby *Agency Group Ltd, The (LA)*
1880 Century Park E Ste 711
Los Angeles, CA 90067-1618, USA

Antin, Jonathan (Reality TV Star, Stylist)
901 Westbourne Dr
West Hollywood, CA 90069-4113, USA

Antin, Robin (Actor, Choreographer)
c/o Cheryl McLean *Creative Public Relations*
3385 Oak Glen Dr
Los Angeles, CA 90068-1311, USA

Antin, Steve (Actor, Writer)
c/o Doug MacLaren *International Creative Management (ICM-LA)*
10250 Constellation Blvd Fl 7
Los Angeles, CA 90067-6207, USA

Antistia, Azlea (Adult Film Star)
29 Harley St Suite B
London W1G 9QR, UK

Antoine, Daphne (Stylist)
2416 NE 10th St
Hallandale Beach, FL 33009-2873, USA

Antoine, Lionel (Athlete, Football Player)
1455 Glencliff Dr
Dallas, TX 75217-2686, USA

Antoine, Tamlin (Athlete, Football Player)
5452 New Grange Garth
Columbia, MD 21045-2422, USA

Anton, Alan (Musician)
c/o Staff Member *Macklam Feldman Mgmt*
1505 W 2nd Ave Suite 200
Vancouver BC V6H 3Y4, Canada

Anton, Craig (Actor)
c/o Staff Member *United Talent Agency (UTA)*
9560 Wilshire Blvd Fl 5
Beverly Hills, CA 90212-2400, USA

Anton, Susan (Actor, Producer)
10300 W Charleston Blvd Ste 13
Las Vegas, NV 89135-5008, USA

Antonakakis, Dimitris (Architect)
Emm Benaki 118
Athens 114-73, GREECE

Antonakakis, Suzana M (Architect)
Emm Benaki 118
Athens 114-73, GREECE

Antonelli, Dominic A (Astronaut)
4106 Oak Blossom Ct
Houston, TX 77059-3264, USA

Antonelli, Ennio Cardinal (Religious Leader)
Piazza S Giovanni 3
Florence 50129, ITALY

Antonelli, Johnny (Athlete, Baseball Player)
18 Tobey Ct
Pittsford, NY 14534-1854, USA

Antonelli, Laura (Actor)
Via B Buozzi 51
Rome 197, ITALY

Antonetti, Lorenzo Cardinal (Religious Leader)
Palazzo Apostolico
Vatican City 120

Antonio (Dancer)
Caslada 7
Madrid, SPAIN

Antonio, Lou (Actor)
530 S Gaylord Dr
Burbank, CA 91505-4714, USA

Antonio dos Santos R, Eanes (General, President)
Travessa do Falo 9
Lisbon 1200, Portugal

Antonovich, Mike (Athlete, Hockey Player)
415 Congdon Ave
Coleraine, MN 55722, USA

Antony and the Johnsons (Music Group, Musician)
c/o Staff Member *Alias Production*
22, Rue Douai
Paris F-75009, France

Antoski, Shawn (Athlete, Hockey Player)
285 Tannery Rd RR 2
Madoc, ON K0K 2K0, Canada

Antoun (Khouri), Bishop (Religious Leader)
358 Mountain Rd
Englewood, NJ 07631-3727, USA

Antuofermo, Vito (Boxer)
16019 81st St
Howard Beach, NY 11414-2924, USA

Antwine, Houston (Athlete, Football Player)
6627 Laurel Valley Dr
Memphis, TN 38135-1576, USA

Anu, Christine (Musician)
432 Tyagarah Rd
Myocum, NSW 2481, AUSTRALIA

Anuja (Actor, Bollywood)
4-B Periyar Street Happee Home Apts
Gandhi Nagar Saligram
Chennai, TN 600093, INDIA

Anusha (Actor, Bollywood)
Flat Non 202 II Floor 167 Eldams Road
Chennai, TN 600018, INDIA

Anuszkiewicz, Richard J (Artist)
76 Chestnut St
Englewood, NJ 07631-3045, USA

Anwar, Gabrielle (Actor)
c/o Bradley Kramer *Kramer Management*
5699 Kanan Rd # 275
Agoura Hills, CA 91301-3358, USA

Anzulot, Cynthia (Athlete, Golfer)
21 Spring Creek Mnr
Hershey, PA 17033-1327, USA

Aoki, Chieko N (Business Person)
777 Westchester Ave
White Plains, NY 10604-3520, USA

Aoki, Devon (Actor)
c/o Mimi DiTrani *Schiff Company, The*
8440 Warner Dr Ste B1
Culver City, CA 90232-2461, USA

Aoki, Isao (Athlete, Golfer)
1360 E 9th St Ste 100
Cleveland, OH 44114-1730, USA

Aoki, Rocky (Athlete, Business Person)
8685 NW 53rd Ter Ste 201
Miami, FL 33166-4568, USA

Aoloo Sunshine (Music Group)
c/o Staff Member *Paradigm (Monterey)*
404 W Franklin St
Monterey, CA 93940-2303, USA

Aouita, Said (Athlete, Track Athlete)
9 Rue Soivissi Loubira
Rabat, MOROCCO

Apap, Gilles (Musician)
165 W 57th St
New York, NY 10019-2201, USA

Aparicio, Luis E (Athlete, Baseball Player)
333 W Camden St Attn Alumniassociation
Baltimore, MD 21201-2496, USA

Apatow, Judd (Director, Producer, Writer)
c/o Jimmy Miller *Mosaic Media Group*
9200 W Sunset Blvd Ste 10
Los Angeles, CA 90069-3608, USA

Apel, Katrin (Athlete)
Suedlung 9
Grafenroda 99330, GERMANY

Apke, Steve (Athlete, Football Player)
427 Kenmont Ave
Pittsburgh, PA 15228-1405, USA

Apodaca, Bob (Athlete, Baseball Player)
2999 SW Van Buren Ter
Port Saint Lucie, FL 34953-4262, USA

Apodaca, Raymond S (Jerry) (Ex-Governor)
1477 Miracerros Loop N
Santa Fe, NM 87505-4021, USA

Aponte Martinez, Luis Cardinal (Misc)
201 Calle San Jorge Apatado S-1967
Santurce, PR 00912-3405, USA

Appel, Deena (Designer)
c/o Jon Furie *Montana Artists Agency*
9150 Wilshire Blvd Ste 100
Beverly Hills, CA 90212-3459, USA

Appetite for Destruction (Music Group, Musician)

Appice, Carmine (Musician)
568 SE Woodbright # 234
Boynton Beach, FL 33435, USA

Appier, Kevin (Athlete, Baseball Player)
30743 Victory Rd
Paola, KS 66071-9477, USA

Apple, Fiona (Musician)
c/o Staff Member *Paradigm (LA)*
360 N Crescent Dr
Beverly Hills, CA 90210-4874, USA

Appleby, Shiri (Actor)
c/o John Carrabino *John Carrabino Management*
5900 Wilshire Blvd Ste 406
Los Angeles, CA 90036-5015, USA

Appleby, Stuart (Athlete, Golfer)
9724 Chestnut Ridge Dr
Windermere, FL 34786-8943, USA

Applegate, Christina (Actor)
c/o Eric Kranzler *Management 360*
9111 Wilshire Blvd
Beverly Hills, CA 90210-5508, USA

Applegate, Eddie (Actor)
1328 12th St
Santa Monica, CA 90401-2051, USA

Applegate, Gideon (Athlete, Baseball Player)
7 Jenness Dr
South Newfane, VT 05351-9753, USA

Applegate, Jodi (Correspondent)
205 E 67th St
New York, NY 10065-6050, USA

Applegren, Amy (Athlete, Baseball Player)
1245 Sunset Dr
East Peoria, IL 61611-1169, USA

Applen, Henry E (Misc)
25510 Kelly Rd
Roseville, MI 48066-4932, USA

Appleton, James R (Educator)
President's Office
Redlands, CA 92373, USA

Appleton, Myra (Editor)
224 W 57th St
New York, NY 10019-3212, USA

Appleton, Steven R (Business Person)
2805 E Columbia Rd
Boise, ID 83716-9624, USA

Applewhite, Major (Athlete, Football Player)
3911 Willow Bay Dr
Baton Rouge, LA 70809-2670, USA

Appolonia (Kotero) (Actor)
c/o Staff Member *TalentWorks (LA)*
3500 W Olive Ave Ste 1400
Burbank, CA 91505-5512, USA

Apps Jr, Syl (Athlete, Hockey Player)
36 Pennock Crst
Markham, ON L3R 3M4, Canada

Aprea, John (Actor)
401 S Detroit St Apt 113
Los Angeles, CA 90036-3618, USA

April, Johnny (Musician)
c/o Staff Member *Mitch Schneider Organization, The*
14724 Ventura Blvd Ste 410
Sherman Oaks, CA 91403-3537, USA

Apt, Jerome (Jay) (Astronaut)
4 Shadycourt Dr
Pittsburgh, PA 15232-2914, USA

Apted, Michael D (Director)
c/o Brian Siberell *Creative Artists Agency (CAA-LA)*
2000 Avenue of the Stars Ste 100
Los Angeles, CA 90067-4705, USA

Apuna, Ben (Athlete, Football Player)
950 Lehua Ave Apt 804
Pearl City, HI 96782-3339, USA

Aqualung (Music Group)
c/o Staff Member *Paradigm (Monterey)*
404 W Franklin St
Monterey, CA 93940-2303, USA

Aquarium Rescue Unit (Music Group, Musician)
c/o Staff Member *Skyline Music*
28 Union St
Whitefield, NH 03598-3503, USA

Aquilino, Thomas J Jr (Judge)
1 Federal Plz
New York, NY 10278-0001, USA

Aquino, Amy (Actor)
c/o August Kammer *TalentWorks (LA)*
3500 W Olive Ave Ste 1400
Burbank, CA 91505-5512, USA

Aquino, Amy (Actor)
c/o Staff Member *Gersh (LA)*
9465 Wilshire Blvd Ste 600
Beverly Hills, CA 90212-2612, USA

Aquino, Corazon C (Nobel Prize Laureate, President)
119 de la Rosa Comer Castro St
Makati City, Manila, PHILIPPINES

Aquino, Luis (Athlete, Baseball Player)
17201 Collins Ave Apt 606
Sunny Isles Beach, FL 33160-3476, USA

Arad, Avi (Producer, Writer)
c/o Staff Member *Marvel Studios Inc*
1600 Rosecrans Ave Bldg 7STE PMB 110
Manhattan Beach, CA 90266-3708, USA

Aragaki-Van Horn, Kathy (Stylist)
7523 Kenton Ave
Skokie, IL 60076-3839, USA

Aragall Garriga, Glacomo (Opera Singer)
6 Barham Close Weybridge
Surrey KT1 9PR, UNITED KINGDOM (UK)

Aragon, Art (Boxer)
19050 Wells Dr
Tarzana, CA 91356-3937, USA

Aragon, Frank (Director)
c/o Reyna Trevino *Trevino Enterprises*
10 Universal City Plz Fl 20
Universal City, CA 91608-1074, USA

Aragones, Sergio (Cartoonist)
PO Box 696
Ojai, CA 93024-0696, USA

Araguz, Leo (Athlete, Football Player)
3201 Leo Araguz St
Harlingen, TX 78552-7835, USA

Araiza, Francisco (Opera Singer)
165 W 57th St
New York, NY 10019-2201, USA

Arakawa, Toyozo (Artist)
4-101 O-Hatacho
Tokyo, JAPAN

Araki, Gregg (Director)
c/o Brian Young *Untitled Entertainment (LA)*
350 S Beverly Dr Ste 200
Beverly Hills, CA 90212-4819, USA

Arambulo, Angela (Stylist)
c/o Staff Member *Stockland Martel*
343 E 18th St
New York, NY 10003-2802, USA

Aramburu, Juan Carlos Cardinal (Religious Leader)
Arzobispado Suipacha 1034
Buenos Aires 1008, ARGENTINA

Arana, Facundo (Actor)
c/o Staff Member *Telefe - Argentina*
Pavon 2444 (C1248AAT)
Buenos Aires, ARGENTINA

Arana, Tomas (Actor)
c/o Melanie Greene *Affirmative Entertainment*
425 N Robertson Blvd
West Hollywood, CA 90048-1735, USA

Arango, Juan Carlos (Actor)
c/o Gabriel Blanco *Gabriel Blanco Iglesias (Mexico)*
Rio Balsas 35-32 Colonia Cuauhtemoc
DF 6500, Mexico

Arapostathis, Evan (Athlete, Football Player)
4338 Macronald Dr
La Mesa, CA 91941-5608, USA

Ararktsyan, Babken G (Government Official)
Marshal Bagzamyan Prosp # 26
Memphis, TN 37501-0001, ARMENIA

Arashi, Qadi Abdul Karim al
Sana'a, Yemen

Arau, Alfonso (Director)
Privada Rafael Oliva 8
Coyoacan 4120, MEXICO

Arau, Fernando (Actor)
c/o Staff Member *Sanctuary Artist Management (UK)*
Sanctuary House 45-53 Sinclair Road
London W14 0NS, UNITED KINGDOM

Araujo, Serafim Fernandes de Cardinal (Religious Leader)
Av Brasil 2079
Belo Horizonte, MG 30240-002, Brazil

Aravind, Ramesh (Actor, Bollywood)
F1 4th Block Bajaj Apartments Nandanam Extn
Chennai, TN 600035, INDIA

Araya, Zeudy (Actor)
Via Giuseppe Pisanelli
Rome 196, ITALY

Arbaaz, Ali Khan (Actor, Bollywood)
602 Sea King Apts Band Stand Bandra W
Mumbai, MS 400050, INDIA

Arbanas, Frederick V (Fred) (Athlete, Football Player)
3350 SW Hook Rd
Lees Summit, MO 64082-1524, USA

Arbeid, Murray (Designer, Fashion Designer)
202 Ebury St
London SW1W 8UN, UNITED KINGDOM (UK)

Arber, Werner (Nobel Prize Laureate)
70 Klingelbergstr
Basel 4056, SWITZERLAND

Arbour, Al (Athlete, Hockey Player)
2071 Harbour Links Dr
Longboat Key, FL 34228-4281, USA

Arbour, John (Athlete, Hockey Player)
125 Waterloo St
Fort Erie, ON L2A 3K1, Canada

Arbour, Louise (Government Official)
1 United Nations Plz
New York, NY 10017-3515, USA

Arbour-Parrott, Beatrice (Athlete, Baseball Player)
691 Elm St
Somerset, MA 02726-4034, USA

Arbubakrr, Hasson (Athlete, Football Player)
76 Custer Ave
Newark, NJ 07112-2510, USA

Arbuckle, Charles (Athlete, Football Player)
805 Oak Park Dr
Round Rock, TX 78681-4077, USA

Arbulu Galliani, Guillermo (Prime Minister)
Urb Corpac Calle 1 Oesta S/N
Lima 27, PERU

Arbus, Alan (Actor)
2208 N Beverly Glen Blvd
Los Angeles, CA 90077-2502, USA

Arbus, Loreen (Producer)
8383 Wilshire Blvd Ste 240
Beverly Hills, CA 90211-2445, USA

Arcade Fire (Music Group, Musician)
c/o Scott Rodger *Quest Management*
36 Warple Way Unit 1D
London W3 0RG, UK

Arch, Lisa (Actor)
c/o Staff Member *The Paradise Group*
PO Box 69451
West Hollywood, CA 90069-0451, USA

Archambault, Lee J (Astronaut)
4318 Sweet Cicely Ct
Houston, TX 77059-3126, USA

Archambeau, Lester (Athlete, Football Player)
10520 Montclair Way
Duluth, GA 30097-1840, USA

Archana (Actor, Bollywood)
8 N Cresent Road T Nagar
Chennai, TN 600017, INDIA

Archer, Anne (Actor)
PO Box 57593
Sherman Oaks, CA 91413-2593, USA

Archer, Beverly (Actor)
606 N Larchmont Blvd Ste 309
Los Angeles, CA 90004-1309, USA

Archer, Dan (Athlete, Football Player)
65 Sunnyside Ave
Mill Valley, CA 94941-1924, USA

Archer, David (Athlete, Football Player)
3831 Upland Dr
Marietta, GA 30066-3064, USA

Archer, Glenn L Jr (Judge)
717 Madison Pl NW
Washington, DC 20439-0001, USA

Archer, Jeffrey (Actor, Writer)
c/o Staff Member *Curtis Brown Ltd*
Hay Market House 28-29 Hay Market
London SW1Y 4SP, UK

Archer, Jim (Athlete, Baseball Player)
1414 Oleander Dr
Tarpon Springs, FL 34689-2308, USA

Archer, John (Writer)
10901 176th Cir NE # 3601
Redmond, WA 98052-7218, USA

Archer, Tasmin (Musician)
c/o Staff Member *Mushroom Music Publishing*
9 Dundas Ln P.O. Box 158
Albert Park VIC 3206, Australia

Archer of Weston-Super-Mare, Jeffrey H (Government Official, Writer)
93 Albert Embankment
London SE1 7TY, UNITED KINGDOM (UK)

Archibaid, Nathaniel (Nate) (Athlete, Basketball Player)
2920 Holland Ave
Bronx, NY 10467-8304, USA

Archibald, Dave (Athlete, Hockey Player)
P.O. Box 2108 STN Sardis Main
Chillwack, BC V2R 1A6, Canada

Archibald, Nolan D (Business Person)
701 E Joppa Rd
Towson, MD 21286-5559, USA

Archie, Mike (Athlete, Football Player)
1178 Old Hickory Blvd
Brentwood, TN 37027-4221, USA

Archipoeski, Ken (Musician)
PO Box 656507
Fresh Meadows, NY 11365-6507, USA

Architecture in Helsinki (Music Group)
c/o Staff Member *Paradigm (Monterey)*
404 W Franklin St
Monterey, CA 93940-2303, USA

Archuleta, Adam (Athlete, Football Player)
1237 W Galveston St
Chandler, AZ 85224-4335, USA

Archuleta, David (Musician)
c/o Irving Azoff *Azoff Music Management/ Front Line*
1100 Glendon Ave
Los Angeles, CA 90024-3503, USA

Arcia, Jose (Athlete, Baseball Player)
7325 NW 3rd St
Miami, FL 33126-4211, USA

Arcieri, Leila (Actor)
c/o Staff Member *Paradigm (LA)*
360 N Crescent Dr
Beverly Hills, CA 90210-4874, USA

Arcineiga, Tomas A (Educator)
President's Office
Bakersfield, CA 9331, USA

Arctic Monkeys (Music Group)
c/o Staff Member *Paradigm (Monterey)*
404 W Franklin St
Monterey, CA 93940-2303, USA

Arcuri, Mike (Congressman, Politician)
10 Broad St Rm 330
Utica, NY 13501-1233, USA

Ard, Johnny (Athlete, Baseball Player)
3815 Edinburg Cir
Valdosta, GA 31605-7858, USA

Ard, William D (Bill) (Athlete, Football Player)
41 Vail Ln
Watchung, NJ 07069-6149, USA

Ardalan, Nader (Architect)
PO Box 3679
Safat 13037, KUWAIT

Ardant, Fanny (Actor)
c/o Staff Member *ArtMedia*
20 avenue Rapp
Paris 75008, France

Ardell, Dan (Athlete, Baseball Player)
554 Hazel Dr
Corona Del Mar, CA 92625-2535, USA

Ardell, Donald B (Doctor)
288 Beach Dr NE Apt 11C
St Petersburg, FL 33701-3481, USA

Arden, Alicia (Actor)
c/o Vance Payton *Advance LA*
7904 Santa Monica Blvd Ste 200
West Hollywood, CA 90046-5170

Arden, Jann (Musician, Songwriter, Writer)
1505 W 2nd Ave # 200
Vancouver, BC V6H 3Y4, CANADA

Arden, John (Writer)
60/66 Wardour St
London W1V 4ND, UNITED KINGDOM (UK)

Arden, Michael (Actor)
c/o Biff Liff *WmE2 (WMA-NY)*
1325 Avenue of the Americas
New York, NY 10019-6026, USA

Arden, Toni (Musician)
1 N Golfview Rd Apt 300
Lake Worth, FL 33460-3948, USA

Arditi, Pierre (Actor)
c/o Staff Member *VMA*
20 Avenue Rapp
Paris 75007, France

Ardito Barletta, Nicolas (President)
PO Box 7737
Panama City 9, PANAMA

Arditti, Irvine (Musician)
109 Boul Saint-Joseph Quest
Montreal, PA H2T 2P7, CANADA

Ardizoia, Rinaldo (Athlete, Baseball Player)
130 Santa Rosa Ave
San Francisco, CA 94112-1930, USA

Ardizzone, Anthony (Tony) (Athlete, Football Player)
27 S Farview Ave
Paramus, NJ 07652-2629, USA

Ardoin, Danny (Athlete, Baseball Player)
1524 Lee St
Ville Platte, LA 70586-6364, USA

Ardolino, Todd (Director)
c/o Staff Member *Creative Artists Agency (CAA-LA)*
2000 Avenue of the Stars Ste 100
Los Angeles, CA 90067-4705, USA

Ardolino, Tom (Musician)
200 W Sunset Blvd # 202
Chicago, IL 60610, USA

Aregood, Richards L (Journalist)
400 N Broad St
Philadelphia, PA 19130-4015, USA

Arellano, Stephanie (Actor)
c/o Ken Jacobson *Ken Jacobson Management*
3500 W Olive Ave Ste 1470
Burbank, CA 91505-5514, USA

Arena, Tina (Musician)
5 Darley St
Neutral Bay, NSW 2089, AUSTRALIA

Arenas, Gilbert (Athlete, Basketball Player)
c/o Staff Member *Washington Wizards*
601 F St NW
Washington, DC 20004-1605, USA

Arenas, Joe (Athlete, Football Player)
780 W Bay Area Blvd Apt 1215
Webster, TX 77598-4057, USA

Arenberg, Lee (Actor)
c/o Staff Member *Gage Group, The (LA)*
14724 Ventura Blvd Ste 505
Sherman Oaks, CA 91403-3505, USA

Arend, Geoffrey (Actor)
c/o Jason Newman *Untitled Entertainment (LA)*
350 S Beverly Dr Ste 200
Beverly Hills, CA 90212-4819, USA

Arens, Moshe (Government Official)
Rehov Kapian
Hakirya, Tel-Aviv 67695, ISRAEL

Aresco, Joey (Actor)
C/O Lisa King 2888 Birch St Unit #1
Vancouver V6H 2T6, CANADA

Areshenkoff, Ron (Athlete, Hockey Player)
329 12th Ave
Estevan, SK S4A 1E3, Canada

Aretsky, Ken (Business Person)
21 W 52nd St
New York, NY 10019-6101, USA

Arfons, Arthur E (Art) (Race Car Driver)
PO Box 1409
Saint Charles, MO 63302-1409, USA

Argento, Asia (Actor)
Via P Cavallini 24
Rome 193, ITALY

Argento, Dario (Director)
Via Balemonti 2
Rome, ITALY

Argento, Dominick (Composer)
Music Dept Ferguson Hall
Minneapolis, MN 55455, USA

Argenziano, Carmen (Actor)
c/o Staff Member *TalentWorks (LA)*
3500 W Olive Ave Ste 1400
Burbank, CA 91505-5512, USA

Argerich, Martha (Musician)
252 Rue Faubourg Saint Honore
Paris 75008, FRANCE

Argota, Ashley (Actor)
c/o Monique Moss *Moss Public Relations*
8060 Melrose Ave Fl 4
Los Angeles, CA 90046-7038, USA

Argott, Don (Director, Producer)
c/o David Gersh *Gersh (LA)*
9465 Wilshire Blvd Ste 600
Beverly Hills, CA 90212-2612, USA

Argov, Sherry (Writer)
PO Box 10865
Marina Del Rey, CA 90295-6865, USA

Arian, David (Misc)
1188 Franklin St
San Francisco, CA 94109-6800, USA

Arias, Alex (Athlete, Baseball Player)
37 Edmund Rd
West Park, FL 33023-5231, USA

Arias, George (Athlete, Baseball Player)
4343 W Tellurite Dr
Tucson, AZ 85745-4193, USA

Arias, Mariana (Actor)
c/o Staff Member *Telefe - Argentina*
Pavon 2444 (C1248AAT)
Buenos Aires, ARGENTINA

Arias, Moises (Actor)
c/o Matt Fletcher *Greene & Associates*
1901 Avenue Of The Stars Ste 130
Los Angeles, CA 90067-6030, USA

Arias, Ricardo M (President)
Apdo 4549
Panama City, PANAMA

Arias, Rudy (Athlete, Baseball Player)
3911 NW 11th St
Miami, FL 33126-3614, USA

Arias, Silvana (Actor)
838 N Fairfax Ave
Los Angeles, CA 90046-7208, USA

Arias, Yancey (Actor)
c/o Chris Henze *Thruline Entertainment*
9250 Wilshire Blvd Ground Fl
Beverly Hills, CA 90212, USA

Arias-Sanchez, Oscar (Nobel Prize Laureate, Politician, President)
Apdo 8-6410-1000
San Jose, COSTA RICA

Arie, India (Musician, Songwriter)
c/o Staff Member *Paradigm (Monterey)*
404 W Franklin St
Monterey, CA 93940-2303, USA

Aries, Jacqueline Pinol (Actor)
c/o Tracy Quinn *Quinn Management*
17328 Ventura Blvd Ste 416
Encino, CA 91316-3904, USA

Ariey, Mike (Athlete, Football Player)
PO Box 708
Bakersfield, CA 93302-0708, USA

Arigoni, Dulio (Misc)
Im Glockenacker 42
Zurich 8053, SWITZERLAND

Arima, Akito (Physicist)
Hirosawa 2-1
Wakoshi, Saltarna 351-01, JAPAN

Arinze, Cardinal Francis (Religious Leader)
Vatican City 193

Arison, M Micky (Business Person)
3655 NW 87th Ave
Doral, FL 33178-2418, USA

Aristide, Jean-Bertrand (President)
Palace du Gouvernement
Port-Au-Prince, HAITI

Ariyoshi, George R (Ex-Governor)
144 Ragsdale Pl
Honolulu, HI 96817-1008, USA

Ariza, Trevor (Athlete, Basketball Player)
c/o David Lee *Players Rep Sports Management*
34208 Aurora Rd # 250
Cleveland, OH 44139-3803, USA

Arjun (Actor)
B3-C Block 109 G N Chetty Road T Nagar
Chennai, TN 600 017, INDIA

Ark, The (Music Group)
c/o Staff Member *Paradigm (Monterey)*
404 W Franklin St
Monterey, CA 93940-2303, USA

Arkadius (Designer, Fashion Designer)
c/o Staff Member *Arkadius*
41 Brondesbury Road
London, England NW6 6BP, United Kingdom

Arkangel R-15 (Music Group)
c/o Staff Member *Sony Music Miami*
605 Lincoln Rd Ste 700
Miami Beach, FL 33139-2901, USA

Arkhipov, Denis (Athlete, Hockey Player)
716 Sweet Cherry Ct
Nashville, TN 37215-6174, USA

Arkhipova, Irina K (Opera Singer)
Bryusov Per 2/14 #27
Moscow 103009, RUSSIA

Arkin, Adam (Actor)
3531 Coldwater Canyon Ave
Studio City, CA 91604-4060, USA

Arkin, Alan (Actor)
c/o Estelle Lasher *Principal Entertainment (LA)*
1964 Westwood Blvd Ste 400
Los Angeles, CA 90025-4695, USA

Arlauckas, Joe (Athlete, Basketball Player)
917 Night Heron Dr
Mt Pleasant, SC 29464-4105, USA

Arlich, Don (Athlete, Baseball Player)
7877 73rd St S
Cottage Grove, MN 55016-1919, USA

Arlin, Steve (Athlete, Baseball Player)
6819 Claremore Ave
San Diego, CA 92120-3125, USA

Arlovski, Andrei (Athlete, Boxer)
c/o Staff Member *John Lewis Entertainment Group*
3071 S Valley View Blvd
Las Vegas, NV 89102-7889, USA

Arlt, Lynn (Stylist)
c/o Staff Member *Anyway Productions*
870 Avenue of the Americas
New York, NY 10001-4111, USA

Arm, Mark (Musician)
7 Trinity Row
Florence, MA 01062-1931, USA

Armacost, Michael H (Diplomat)
2201 C St NW
Washington, DC 20520-0099, USA

Arman (Artist)
430 Washington St
New York, NY 10013-1721, USA

Armani, Giorgio (Designer, Fashion Designer)
Via Borgonuovo 11
Milan 20121, Italy

Armaou, Lindsay (Musician)
55 Drury Lane Covent Garden
London WC2B 5SQ, UNITED KINGDOM (UK)

Armas, Antonio R (Tony) (Athlete, Baseball Player)
Los Mercedes #37 P Piruto-Edo
Anzoatequi, VENEZUELA

Armas, Chris (Soccer Player)
980 N Michigan Ave Ste 1998
Chicago, IL 60611-7504, USA

Armas, Marcos (Athlete, Baseball Player)
Calle Las Mercedes #37
Puerto Piritu, VENEZUELA

Armas, Tony (Athlete, Baseball Player)
c/o Staff Member *Washington Nationals*
1500 S Capitol St SE
Washington, DC 20003-3599, USA

Armato, Ange (Athlete, Baseball Player)
5082 Valley Pines Dr
Rockford, IL 61109-3774, USA

Armatrading, Joan (Musician, Songwriter, Writer)
21 Ramilles St
London W1V 1DF, UNITED KINGDOM (UK)

Armbrister, Ed (Athlete, Baseball Player)
McQuay St Box 2003
Nassau, Bahamas, WEST INDIES

Armdt-Proefrock, Ellen (Athlete, Baseball Player)
905 Alpine St
Brodhead, WI 53520-1052, USA

Armenante, Jilian (Actor)
121A N San Vicente Blvd
Beverly Hills, CA 90211-2303, USA

Armenante, Jillian (Actor)
c/o Staff Member *Metropolitan (MTA)*
4526 Wilshire Blvd
Los Angeles, CA 90010-3801, USA

Armisen, Fred (Actor, Comedian)
c/o Tim Sarkes *Brillstein Entertainment Partners*
9150 Wilshire Blvd Ste 350
Beverly Hills, CA 90212-3453, USA

Armitage, Alison (Actor, Model)
c/o Staff Member *Schiowitz Connor Ankrum Wolf*
1680 Vine St Ste 1016
Los Angeles, CA 90028-8800, USA

Armitage, Karole (Choreographer, Dancer)
350 W 21st St
New York, NY 10011-3318, USA

Armitage, Richard (Actor)
c/o Duncan Millership *Management 360*
9111 Wilshire Blvd
Beverly Hills, CA 90210-5508, USA

Armour, Jojuan (Athlete, Football Player)
1625 Avondale Ave
Toledo, OH 43607-3909, USA

Armour, Justin (Athlete, Football Player)
8 Crystal Park Pl Unit B
Manitou Springs, CO 80829-2654, USA

Armour, Thomas D (Tommy) III (Athlete, Golfer)
3006 Woodside St Apt 8017
Dallas, TX 75204-8538, USA

Arms, Russell (Actor, Musician)
312 Hillcrest Dr
Hamilton, IL 62341-1106, USA

Armstead, Jessie (Athlete, Football Player)
1316 Mill Stream Dr
Dallas, TX 75232-4604, USA

Armstrong, A James (Misc)
1100 W 42nd St
Indianapolis, IN 46208-3346, USA

Armstrong, Adger (Athlete, Football Player)
6403 Paddington St
Houston, TX 77085-3000, USA

Armstrong, Alan (Actor)
Julian House 4 Windmill St
London W1P 1HF, UNITED KINGDOM (UK)

Armstrong, Antonio (Athlete, Football Player)
5314 Palmetto St
Houston, TX 77081-4614, USA

Armstrong, Bess (Actor)
c/o Tim Angle *Don Buchwald & Associates Inc (LA)*
6500 Wilshire Blvd Ste 2200
Los Angeles, CA 90048-4942, USA

Armstrong, Billie Joe (Musician, Songwriter)
c/o John Dehais *Pat's Management Company*
543 Encinitas Blvd Ste 101
Encinitas, CA 92024-3744, USA

Armstrong, BJ (Athlete, Basketball Player)
1550 Hawthorne Ln
Highland Park, IL 60035-3404, USA

Armstrong, Brad (Adult Film Star)
c/o Staff Member *Vivid Entertainment*
3599 Cahuenga Blvd W # 400
Los Angeles, CA 90068-1397, USA

Armstrong, Bruce (Athlete, Football Player)
12543 Brookwood Ct
Davie, FL 33330-1207, USA

Armstrong, Charlotte (Athlete, Baseball Player)
7937 E Luke Ln
Scottsdale, AZ 85250-6526, USA

Armstrong, Clay M (Scientist)
3400 Spruce St
Philadelphia, PA 19104-4206, USA

Armstrong, Curtis (Actor)
3867 Shannon Rd
Los Angeles, CA 90027-1441, USA

Armstrong, Darrell (Athlete, Basketball Player)
337 Broadmoor Way
McDonough, GA 30253-4290, USA

Armstrong, Deborah (Debbie) (Athlete, Skier)
PO Box 770925
Steamboat Springs, CO 80477-0925, USA

Armstrong, Derek (Athlete, Hockey Player)
869 Sunset Dr
Hermosa Beach, CA 90254-4249, USA

Armstrong, Dwight (Actor)
c/o Paul Greenstone *Paul Greenstone Entertainment*
3008 Sorrelwood Dr
San Ramon, CA 94582-5008, USA

Armstrong, George (Athlete, Hockey Player)
22 St Cuthbert's Rd
East York, ON M4G 1V1, Canada

Armstrong, Gillian (Director)
500 Oxford St
Bondi Junction, NSW 2022, AUSTRALIA

Armstrong, Harvey (Athlete, Football Player)
2840 Olde Town Park Dr
Norcross, GA 30071-1837, USA

Armstrong, Hilton (Athlete, Basketball Player)
c/o Jeff Schwartz *Excel Sports Management*
9665 Wilshire Blvd Ste 500
Beverly Hills, CA 90212-2312, USA

Armstrong, Jack (Athlete, Baseball Player)
272 E River Park Dr
Jupiter, FL 33477-9381, USA

Armstrong, Jonas (Actor)
c/o Staff Member *Artists Rights Group (ARG)*
4 Great Portland St
London W1W 8PA, UNITED KINGDOM (UK)

Armstrong, Karen (Writer)
c/o Staff Member *Random House*
1540 Broadway
New York, NY 10036-4039, USA

Armstrong, Kelley (Writer)
RR 4
Aylmer, ON N5H 2R3, CANADA

Armstrong, Kerry (Actor)
261 Miller St
North Sydney, NSW 2060, AUSTRALIA

Armstrong, Lance (Athlete)
2201 E 6th St
Austin, TX 78702-3456, USA

Armstrong, Matthew John (Actor)
c/o David Ginsberg *Insight*
1134 S Cloverdale Ave
Los Angeles, CA 90019-6737, USA

Armstrong, Mike (Athlete, Baseball Player)
525 Ashbrook Ct
Athens, GA 30605-3985, USA

Armstrong, Murray A (Athlete, Coach, Hockey Player)
607 Mulligan Way
Saint Augustine, FL 32080-5812, USA

Armstrong, Neil (Referee)
1169 Sherwood Trl
Sarnia, ON N7V 2H3, CANADA

Armstrong, Neil (Athlete, Hockey Player)
1169 Sherwood Trl
Sarnia, ON N7V 2H3, Canada

Armstrong, Neil (Astronaut)
PO Box 436
Lebanon, OH 45036-0436, USA

Armstrong, Neill (Athlete, Football Player)
312 Lakewood Dr
Roanoke, TX 76262-5292, USA

Armstrong, Otis (Athlete, Football Player)
9951 E Idaho Cir Apt 202
Denver, CO 80247-6293, USA

Armstrong, Quincy (Athlete, Football Player)
5801 E FM 4
Grandview, TX 76050-3005, USA

Armstrong, RG (Actor)
3856 Reklaw Dr
Studio City, CA 91604-3831, USA

Armstrong, Robb (Cartoonist)
200 Madison Ave
New York, NY 10016-3903, USA

Armstrong, Robert (Bob) (Athlete, Basketball Player)
6802 Packer Dr NE
Belmont, MI 49306-9240, USA

Armstrong, Russell P (War Hero)
425 Bench Rd
Fallon, NV 89406-6334, USA

Armstrong, Samaire (Actor)
c/o Susan Calogerakis *Thruline Entertainment*
9250 Wilshire Blvd Ground Fl
Beverly Hills, CA 90212, USA

Armstrong, Sheila A (Musician, Opera Singer)
Harvesters Tilford Road Hindhead
Surrey GU26 6SQ, UNITED KINGDOM (UK)

Armstrong, Spence M (General)
9714 Bluedale St
Alexandria, VA 22308, USA

Armstrong, Tate (Athlete, Basketball Player)
14704 Westbury Rd
Rockville, MD 20853-1610, USA

Armstrong, Taylor (Reality TV Star)
c/o Staff Member *Bravo (LA)*
3000 W Alameda Ave
Burbank, CA 91523-0001, USA

Armstrong, Thomas (Race Car Driver)
150 Gasoline Alley Rd
Indianapolis, IN 46222, USA

Armstrong, Thomas H W (Misc)
1 East St Olney
Bucks MK46 4AP, UNITED KINGDOM (UK)

Armstrong, Trace (Athlete, Football Player)
8691 SW 28th Ln
Gainesville, FL 32608-9315, USA

Armstrong, Ty (Athlete, Golfer)
11529 Kensington Dr
Eden Prairie, MN 55347-4943, USA

Armstrong, Valorie (Actor)
610 Santa Monica Blvd Ste 202
Santa Monica, CA 90401-1645, USA

Armstrong, Vaughn (Actor)
c/o Staff Member *Gage Group, The (LA)*
14724 Ventura Blvd Ste 505
Sherman Oaks, CA 91403-3505, USA

Armstrong, Wally (Athlete, Golfer)
4150 Olson Memorial Hwy Ste 110
Minneapolis, MN 55422-4804, USA

Armstrong, William (Writer)
6 Roland St
Newton, MA 02461-1920, USA

Armstrong, William L (Ex-Senator, Politician)
23 Sedgwick Dr
Englewood, CO 80113-4109, USA

Arnason, Chuck (Athlete, Hockey Player)
39 Grimston Rd
Winnipeg, MB R3T 3T2, Canada

Arnason, Tyler (Athlete, Hockey Player)
881 N La Salle Dr
Chicago, IL 60610-3259, USA

Arnatt, John (Actor)
3 Warren Cottage Woodland Way
Surrey KT2 6NN, UK

Arnaud, Jean-Loup (Government Official)
55 Rue de Seine
Paris 75006, FRANCE

Arnault, Bernard (Business Person)
30 Ave Hoche
Paris 75008, FRANCE

Arnaz, Lucie (Actor)
c/o Scott Stander *Scott Stander & Associates*
4533 Van Nuys Blvd Ste 401
Sherman Oaks, CA 91403-2950, USA

Arnaz Jr, Desi (Actor)
PO Box 60684
Boulder City, NV 89006-0684, USA

Arndt, Denis (Actor)
c/o Suzanne DeWalt *Dewalt & Musik Management*
623 N Parish Pl
Burbank, CA 91506-1701, USA

Arndt, Larry (Athlete, Baseball Player)
5970 E West Miramar Dr
Tucson, AZ 85715-3024, USA

Arndt, Michael (Writer)
c/o Tom Strickler *WmE2 (Endeavor-LA)*
9601 Wilshire Blvd Fl 3
Beverly Hills, CA 90210-5219, USA

Arndt, Richard (Athlete, Football Player)
2130 Parkdale Dr
Kingwood, TX 77339-2351, USA

Arneil, Richard A S (Composer)
Benhall Lodge Benhall
Suffolk IP17 1DJ, UNITED KINGDOM (UK)

Arnelle, Jesse (Athlete, Basketball Player)
400 Urbano Dr
San Francisco, CA 94127-2827, USA

Arnesen, Lasse (Athlete, Skier)
Fagerborggata 34
Oslo N-0360, Norway

Arnesen, Liv (Skier)
119 N 4th St Ste 406
Minneapolis, MN 55401-1790, USA

Arneson, Jim (Athlete, Football Player)
12649 S 71st St
Tempe, AZ 85284-3105, USA

Arneson, Mark (Athlete, Football Player)
15902 Wetherburn Rd
Chesterfield, MO 63017-7341, USA

Arnett, Angie (Stylist)
11403 NE 8th Ave
Biscayne Park, FL 33161-6319, USA

Arnett, Jon D (Athlete, Football Player)
16869 65th Ave Unit 330
Lake Oswego, OR 97035-7865, USA

Arnett, Will (Actor)
c/o Peter Principato *Principato/Young Management*
9465 Wilshire Blvd Ste 430
Beverly Hills, CA 90212-2613, USA

Arnette, Jay (Athlete, Basketball Player)
2 Hillside Ct
Austin, TX 78746-6436, USA

Arnette, Jeanetta (Actor)
466 N Harper Ave
Los Angeles, CA 90048-2221, USA

Arnez J (Comedian)
c/o Staff Member *International Creative Management (ICM-LA)*
10250 Constellation Blvd Fl 7
Los Angeles, CA 90067-6207, USA

Arngrim, Alison (Actor)
PO Box 98
Tujunga, CA 91043-0098, USA

Arniel, Scott (Athlete, Hockey Player)
11 Shoreline Dr
Winnipeg, MB R3P 2B4, Canada

Arning, Lisa (Actor)
c/o Julie Wolff *Morgan Agency, The*
1200 N Doheny Dr
Los Angeles, CA 90069-1723, USA

Arno, Ed
11220 72nd Dr
Flushing, NY 11375-5631, USA

Arnold, Anna Bing (Philanthropist)
9700 W Pico Blvd
Los Angeles, CA 90035-4711, USA

Arnold, Ben (Musician)
227 Pine St
Philadelphia, PA 19106-4326, USA

Arnold, Brian A (General)
Commander Space & Missile Systems Center
Los Angeles Air Force Base, CA 90245, USA

Arnold, Charles (Athlete, Baseball Player)
19537 Beaverland St
Detroit, MI 48219-5507, USA

Arnold, Charlotte (Actor)
c/o Norbert Abrams *Noble Caplan Abrams*
1260 Yonge St 2nd Floor
Toronto ON M4T 1W6, Canada

Arnold, Chris (Athlete, Baseball Player)
2219 El Capitan Ave
Arcadia, CA 91006-5110, USA

Arnold, David (Athlete, Football Player)
1615 Stanley St
New Britain, CT 06053-2439, USA

Arnold, Debbie (Actor)
12 Cambridge Park Ease Twickenham
Middx TW1 2PF, UNITED KINGDOM (UK)

Arnold, Dr Jennifer (Doctor, Reality TV Star)
6621 Fannin St
Houston, TX 77030-2303, USA

Arnold, Eve (Photographer)
5 Old St
London EC1V 9HL, UNITED KINGDOM (UK)

Arnold, Francis (Athlete, Football Player)
3312 W 80th St
Inglewood, CA 90305-1354, USA

Arnold, Gary H (Critic)
5133 1st St N
Arlington, VA 22203-1207, USA

Arnold, Jackson D (Admiral, War Hero)
Los Pinos Box 185
Rancho Santa Fe, CA 92067, USA

Arnold, Jahine (Athlete, Football Player)
4534 W Beachway Dr
Tampa, FL 33609-4234, USA

Arnold, James E (Athlete, Football Player)
223 Boxwood Dr
Franklin, TN 37069-6979, USA

Arnold, James R (Misc)
Chemistry Dept Code # 524
La Jolla, CA 92093-0001, USA

Arnold, Jamie (Athlete, Baseball Player)
11716 Meredith Dr
Temple, AZ 76502, USA

Arnold, Kristine (Music Group)
5101 Overton Rd
Nashville, TN 37220-1920, USA

Arnold, Lenna (Athlete, Baseball Player)
4312 Dodge Ave
Fort Wayne, IN 46815-6925, USA

Arnold, Louise (Athlete, Baseball Player)
52806 Brandel Ave
South Bend, IN 46635-1250, USA

Arnold, Monica (Actor, Musician)
c/o Cara Lewis *WmE2 (WMA-NY)*
1325 Avenue of the Americas
New York, NY 10019-6026, USA

Arnold, Murray (Athlete, Basketball Player, Coach)
Athletic Dept
Bowling Green, KY 42101, USA

Arnold, Pam (Stylist)
9767 S Gribble Rd
Canby, OR 97013-9363, USA

Arnold, Scott (Athlete, Baseball Player)
2936 Runnymede Way
Lexington, KY 40503-2813, USA

Arnold, Stuart (Publisher)
Rockefeller Center
New York, NY 10020, USA

Arnold, Tichina (Actor)
c/o Geoff Cheddy *Brillstein Entertainment Partners*
9150 Wilshire Blvd Ste 350
Beverly Hills, CA 90212-3453, USA

Arnold, Tom (Actor, Comedian)
c/o Erik Kritzer *Kritzer Levine Wilkins Entertainment*
11872 La Grange Ave Fl 1
Los Angeles, CA 90025-5283, USA

Arnold, Tony (Athlete, Baseball Player)
5708 Vineyard Ln
Mc Kinney, TX 75070-9569, USA

Arnold, Walt (Athlete, Football Player)
8503 La Sala Grande NE
Albuquerque, NM 87111-4564, USA

Arnold Jr, Harry L (Doctor, Writer)
250 Laurel St Apt 301
San Francisco, CA 94118-2045, USA

Arnoldi, Charles A (Artist)
721 Hampton Dr
Venice, CA 90291-3018, USA

Arnott, Jason (Athlete, Hockey Player)
47 Governors Way
Brentwood, TN 37027-8926, USA

Arnoul, Francoise (Actor)
53 Rue Censier
Paris 75005, FRANCE

Arns, Paulo E Cardinal (Religious Leader)
Alvenida Higienopolos 890 CP 6778
Sao Paulo, SP 1064, BRAZIL

Arnsberg, Brad (Athlete, Baseball Player)
706 Chaffee Ct
Arlington, TX 76006-2001, USA

Arnsparger, Bill (Athlete, Football Coach, Football Player)
1574 Pine Needles Ln
Lexington, KY 40513-1503, USA

Arnstein, Rolly (Music Group)
1540 Broadway Ste 3000
New York, NY 10036-4039, USA

Arntz, Jason (Athlete)
891 Crimson Ct
Morganville, NJ 07751-1753, USA

Arnzen, Robert (Athlete, Basketball Player)
8 Grand Lake Dr
Fort Thomas, KY 41075-4100, USA

Arocha, Rene (Athlete, Baseball Player)
14273 SW 24th St
Miami, FL 33175-8001, USA

Aronofsky, Darren (Director)
c/o Karen Samfilippo *Image Management PR*
1810 14th St Ste 205
Santa Monica, CA 90404-4662, USA

Arons, Arnold B (Physicist)
10313 Lake Shore Blvd NE
Seattle, WA 98125-8160, USA

Aronson, Judie (Actor)
c/o Staff Member *ATA Management*
12 Desbrosses St
New York, NY 10013-1704, USA

Arora, Amrita (Actor, Bollywood)
c/o Bunty Bahl *Carving Dreams Entertainment*
304-305, Oberoi Chambers II B Wing, Off New Link Road, Andheri West
Mumbai 400053, INDIA

Arp, Halton C (Astronomer)
Garching Munich 84518, GERMANY

Arpel, Adrien (Beauty Pageant Winner)
400 Hackensack Ave
Hackensack, NJ 07601-6310, USA

Arpey, Gerard (Business Person)
433 Amon Carter Blvd
Forth Worth, TX 76155, USA

Arpino, Gerald P (Choreographer)
70 E Lake St Ste 1300
Chicago, IL 60601-7458, USA

Arquette, Alexis (Actor)
c/o Staff Member *Innovative Artists (LA)*
1505 10th St
Santa Monica, CA 90401-2805, USA

Arquette, David (Actor, Director, Producer)
c/o Eric Kranzler *Management 360*
9111 Wilshire Blvd
Beverly Hills, CA 90210-5508, USA

Arquette, Patricia (Actor)
c/o Molly Madden *3 Arts Entertainment Inc*
9460 Wilshire Blvd Fl 7
Beverly Hills, CA 90212-2713, USA

Arquette, Rosanna (Actor)
c/o Laina Cohn *Laina Cohn Management*
15066 Sutton St
Sherman Oaks, CA 91403-4020, USA

Arrants, Rod (Actor)
115 Maitland Dr
Alameda, CA 94502-6725, USA

Arras, Maria Celeste (Actor)
c/o Staff Member *Telemundo*
2470 W 8th Ave
Hialeah, FL 33010-2000, USA

Arredondo, Rosa (Actor)
c/o Suzanne (Sue) Wohl *TalentWorks (LA)*
3500 W Olive Ave Ste 1400
Burbank, CA 91505-5512, USA

Arrigo, Gerry (Athlete, Baseball Player)
3740 Redthorne Dr
Amelia, OH 45102, USA

Arrindell, Clement A (Ex-Governor)
Lark
Bird Rock, Saint Christopher And Nevis, West Indies

Arrington, Buddy (Race Car Driver)
2620 Kings Mountain Rd
Martinsville, VA 24112, USA

Arrington, J J (Athlete, Football Player)
1599 E Beretta Pl
Chandler, AZ 85286-1152, USA

Arrington, Jill (Sportscaster)
51 W 52nd St
New York, NY 10019-6119, USA

Arrington, LaVar (Athlete, Football Player)
1514 Cedar Lane Farm Rd
Annapolis, MD 21409-5625, USA

Arrington, Michael (Internet Star)
3800 the Strand Apt 6
Manhattan Beach, CA 90266-3136, USA

Arrington, Richard (Athlete, Football Player)
2585 King Cir SE
Conyers, GA 30013-1981, USA

Arriola, Dante (Director)
c/o Staff Member *MJZ*
2201 S Carmelina Ave
Los Angeles, CA 90064-1001, USA

Arriola, Gus (Cartoonist)
PO Box 3275
Carmel, CA 93921-3275

Arriota, Gus (Cartoonist)
PO Box 3275
Carmel, CA 93921-3275, USA

Arrobio, Charles (Chuck) (Athlete, Football Player)
35 Essex St Apt 5A
New York, NY 10002-4716, USA

Arrojo, Luis (Athlete, Baseball Player)
5684 36th Ave N
Saint Petersburg, FL 33710-1914, USA

Arrow, Kenneth J (Nobel Prize Laureate)
620 Sand Hill Rd Apt 406C
Palo Alto, CA 94304-2093, USA

Arroyo, Bronson (Athlete, Baseball Player)
47 Olive St
Brooksville, FL 34601-2125, USA

Arroyo, Carlos (Athlete, Basketball Player)
6447 Lake Burden View Dr
Windermere, FL 34786-5649, USA

Arroyo, Fernando (Athlete, Baseball Player)
702 Hampton Woods Ln SW
Vero Beach, FL 32962-7052, USA

Arroyo, Jose (Writer)
c/o Staff Member *Kaplan Stahler Agency*
8383 Wilshire Blvd Ste 923
Beverly Hills, CA 90211-2443, USA

Arroyo, Luis E (Athlete, Baseball Player)
PO Box 354
Penuelas, PR 00624-0354, USA

Arroyo, Martina (Opera Singer)
20 Alfred Dr
Pittsfield, MA 01201-8430, USA

Arroyo, Rudolph (Athlete, Baseball Player)
28799 Sequoia Ct
Coarsegold, CA 93614-9161, USA

Arsenault, Kelly (Stylist)
c/o Staff Member *Judy Inc*
1 Yorkville Ave
Toronto ON M4W 1L1, Canada

Arsmstrong, Colby (Athlete, Hockey Player)
8030 Sherwood Dr
Presto, PA 15142-1078, USA

Art of Noise, The (Music Group)
PO Box 199
London W11 4AN, UNITED KINGDOM (UK)

Arteage, Rosalia (President)
Gobiemo Palacio
Garcia Morena, Quito, ECUADOR

Artemas, Cole (Cartoonist)
15 Regency Mnr Apt 15-8
Rutland, VT 05701-5310, USA

Arterburn, Elmer (Athlete, Football Player)
3819 29th St
Lubbock, TX 79410-2508, USA

Arterburn, Stephen (Writer)
PO Box 1018
Laguna Beach, CA 92652-1018, USA

Arterton, Gemma (Actor)
c/o Pippa Beng *Premier PR (UK)*
91 Berwick St
London W1F 0NE, UK

Artest, Ron (Athlete, Basketball Player)
5617 Ridge Park Dr
Loomis, CA 95650-9487, USA

Arteta, Miguel (Director)
c/o David Lubliner *WmE2 (WMA-LA)*
1 William Morris Pl
Beverly Hills, CA 90212-4261, USA

Arthur, Fred (Athlete, Hockey Player)
203-1408 Ernest Ave
London, ON N6E 3B2, Canada

Arthur, Joseph (Musician)
c/o Staff Member *Primary Talent International (UK)*
The Primary Building 10-11 Jockeys Fields
London WC1R 4BN, UK

Arthur, Maureen (Actor)
9171 Wilshire Blvd # 530
Beverly Hills, CA 90210-5530, USA

Arthur, Michelle (Actor)
c/o Steven Neibert *Imperium 7 Talent Agency*
5455 Wilshire Blvd Ste 1706
Los Angeles, CA 90036-4217, USA

Arthur, Mike (Athlete, Football Player)
10445 Sharondale Rd
Cincinnati, OH 45241-3077, USA

Arthur, Owen (Prime Minister)
Bay St Saint Michael
Bridgetown, BARBADOS

Arthur, Perry (Athlete, Golfer)
7513 Zurich Dr
Plano, TX 75025-3118, USA

Arthur, Rebeca (Actor)
280 S Beverly Dr Ste 400
Beverly Hills, CA 90212-3904, USA

Arthurs, John (Athlete, Basketball Player)
1429 Henry Clay Ave
New Orleans, LA 70118-6059, USA

Arthurs, Paul (Bonehead) (Musician)
54 Linhope St
London NW1 6HL, UNITED KINGDOM (UK)

Artoe, Mike (Athlete, Football Player)
17 Canterbury Ct
Wilmette, IL 60091-2822, USA

Artschwager, Richard E (Artist)
PO Box 12
Hudson, NY 12534-0012, USA

Artsebarsky, Anatoli P (Cosmonaut)
Moskovskoi Oblasti
Syvisdny Goroduk 141160, RUSSIA

Arturo, Lisa (Actor)
c/o Mitch Clem *Shadow Entertainment*
10 Universal City Plz Fl 20
Universal City, CA 91608-1074, USA

Artzt, Alice J (Musician)
51 Hawthorne Ave
Princeton, NJ 08540-3803, USA

Artzt, Edwin L (Business Person)
3849 Hedgewood Dr
Lawrenceburg, IN 47025-8047, USA

Arulmani (Actor)
15 Pookara Street Saidapet
Chennai, TN 600 015, INDIA

Arulpragasam, Maya (M.I.A) (Musician)
c/o Todd Jacobs *WmE2 (Endeavor-LA)*
9601 Wilshire Blvd Fl 3
Beverly Hills, CA 90210-5219, USA

Arum, Robert (Bob) (Boxer)
36 Gulf Stream Ct
Las Vegas, NV 89113-1354, USA

Arun, Ila (Actor, Bollywood)
401 Paradise Apartments 7th Road
Santacruz E
Bombay, MS 400055, INDIA

Arvesen, Nina (Actor)
412 Culver Blvd Apt 9
Playa Del Rey, CA 90293-7765, USA

Arvie, Herman (Athlete, Football Player)
33844 Canterbury Rd
Solon, OH 44139-5617, USA

Arvind, V (Actor)
1 65th Street 12th Avenue Ashok Nagar
Chennai, TN 600 083, INDIA

Arvindasamy (Actor)
29A Muthiah Street Cathedral Rd
Chennai, TN 600 086, INDIA

Arya (Actor)
c/o Staff Member *The Harbour Agency*
135 Forbes St
Woolloomooloo NSW 2011, Australia

Arzu Irigoyen, Alvaro E (President)
Palacio Nacional
Guatemala City, GUATAMALA

As I Lay Dying (Music Group, Musician)
c/o Staff Member *Strong Management*
17625 Union Tpke # 405
Fresh Meadows, NY 11366-1515, USA

As Tall as Lions (Music Group)
c/o Staff Member *Paradigm (Monterey)*
404 W Franklin St
Monterey, CA 93940-2303, USA

Asadoor, Randy (Athlete, Baseball Player)
4857 E Richmond Ave
Clovis, CA 93619-8673, USA

Asay, Chuck (Cartoonist)
303 S Prospect St
Colorado Springs, CO 80903-3748, USA

Asbury, Kelly (Actor)
c/o Staff Member *Creative Artists Agency (CAA-LA)*
2000 Avenue of the Stars Ste 100
Los Angeles, CA 90067-4705, USA

Asbury, Martin (Cartoonist)
Stoneworld Pitch Green
Princes Risborough, Bucks HP27 9QG, UNITED KINGDOM (UK)

Asbury, Willie (Athlete, Football Player)
119 Wildernest Ln
Port Matilda, PA 16870-7107, USA

Ascencio, Nelson (Actor)
c/o Heidi Rotbart *Heidi Rotbart Management*
1810 Malcolm Ave Apt 207
Los Angeles, CA 90025-7610, USA

Aschbacher, Darrel (Athlete, Football Player)
915 NE Wyoming Dr
Prineville, OR 97754-7905, USA

Aschenbrenner, Frank (Athlete, Football Player)
16372 E Jacklin Dr
Fountain Hills, AZ 85268-5608, USA

Aschwege, David (Athlete, Baseball Player)
7500 Tiffany Rd
Lincoln, NE 68506-3056, USA

Ash, Brian (Producer, Writer)
c/o Simon Millar *Rumble Media*
1620 Broadway Ste C
Santa Monica, CA 90404-2777, USA

Ash, Leslie (Actor)
c/o Michelle Milburn *International Artistes*
Holborn Hall - 4th Floor
London WC1V 7BD, UK

Ash, Nadine (Athlete, Golfer)
5625 E Wethersfield Rd
Scottsdale, AZ 85254-4317, USA

Ash, Roy L (Business Person, Government Official)
655 Funchal Rd
Los Angeles, CA 90077-3211, USA

Asham, Arron (Athlete, Hockey Player)
c/o Staff Member *Pro-Rep Entertainment Consulting*
113-276 Midpark Way SE
Calgary, AB T2X 1J6, Canada

Ashanti (Musician)
c/o Alan Nierob *Rogers & Cowan PR (LA)*
Pacific Design Center 8687 Melrose Ave, 7th Floor
West Hollywood, CA 90069, USA

Ashbery, John L (Writer)
326 Belmont Ave
Buffalo, NY 14223-1550, USA

Ashbrook, Dana (Actor)
1180 S Beverly Dr Ste 601
Los Angeles, CA 90035-1158, USA

Ashbrook, Daphne (Actor)
1505 10th St
Santa Monica, CA 90401-2805, USA

Ashbrook, Stephen (Musician)
2280 NW Thurman St
Portland, OR 97210-2519, USA

Ashby, Alan (Athlete, Baseball Player)
12011 Cypress Creek Lakes Dr
Cypress, TX 77433-1872, USA

Ashby, Andy (Athlete, Baseball Player)
5701 NW Parkdale Cir
Kansas City, MO 64151-3281, USA

Ashby, Jeffrey S (Astronaut)
2101 Nasa Pkwy Spc Center
Houston, TX 77058-3607, USA

Ashby, Linden (Actor)
639 N Larchmont Blvd Ste 207
Los Angeles, CA 90004-1323, USA

Ashcroft, John D (Ex-Governor, Ex-Senator)
1399 New York Ave NW Ste 950
Washington, DC 20005-4762, USA

Ashcroft, Richard (Musician, Songwriter)
c/o Staff Member *Paradigm (NY)*
360 Park Ave S Fl 16
New York, NY 10010-1708, USA

Ashdown, J J D (Paddy) (Government Official)
Vane Cottage Norton Sub Hamdon
Somerset TA14 6SG, UNITED KINGDOM (UK)

Ashe, Chrstopher (Actor)
c/o Paul Greenstone *Paul Greenstone Entertainment*
3008 Sorrelwood Dr
San Ramon, CA 94582-5008, USA

Ashenfelter III, Horace (Athlete, Track Athlete)
100 Hawthome Ave
Glen Ridge, NJ 7028, USA

Asher, Barry (Bowler)
719 2nd Ave Ste 701
Seattle, WA 98104-1747, USA

Asher, Jane (Actor)
24 Cale St
London SW3 3QU, UNITED KINGDOM (UK)

Asher, Phyllis (Stylist)
c/o Staff Member *Sydney Represents*
280 Mott St
New York, NY 10012-3439, USA

Asher, Robert (Bob) (Athlete, Football Player)
4800 S Chicago Beach Dr Apt 612S
Chicago, IL 60615-3569, USA

Asherson, Renee (Actor)
28 Elsworthy Road
London NW3, UNITED KINGDOM (UK)

Ashford, Mandy (Music Group)
1776 Broadway # 1500
New York, NY 10019-2002, USA

Ashford, Michelle (Producer, Writer)
c/o Staff Member *WmE2 (WMA-LA)*
1 William Morris Pl
Beverly Hills, CA 90212-4261, USA

Ashford, Rob (Actor)
c/o Staff Member *Creative Artists Agency (CAA-LA)*
2000 Avenue of the Stars Ste 100
Los Angeles, CA 90067-4705, USA

Ashford, Roslyn (Music Group)
11761 E Speedway Blvd
Tucson, AZ 85748-2017, USA

Ashford, Tucker (Athlete, Baseball Player)
502 S Maple St
Covington, TN 38019-2830, USA

Ashford, Washington Evelyn (Athlete, Track Athlete)
38997 Cherry Point Ln
Murrieta, CA 92563-8814, USA

Ashida, Jun (Designer, Fashion Designer)
1-3-3 Aobadai Meguroku
Tokyo 153, JAPAN

Ashihara, Yoshinobu (Architect)
31-15 Sakuragaokacho Shibuyaku
Tokyo 150, JAPAN

Ashkenasi, Shmuel (Musician)
3800 N Lake Shore Dr
Chicago, IL 60613-3301, USA

Ashkenazy, Vladimir D (Musician)
Savinka Kappelistr 15
Meggen 6045, SWITZERLAND

Ashley, Billy (Athlete, Baseball Player)
4331 W Mariposa Grande
Glendale, AZ 85310-3947, USA

Ashley, Elizabeth (Actor)
1223 N Ogden Dr
West Hollywood, CA 90046-4706, USA

Ashley, Jennifer (Actor)
129 W Wilson St Ste 202
Costa Mesa, CA 92627-1586, USA

Ashley, John (Athlete, Hockey Player, Referee)
1662 Erbs Rd
St Agatha, ON N0B 2L0, Canada

Ashley, Leon (Musician)
PO Box 567
Hendersonville, TN 37077-0567, USA

Ashley, Walker (Athlete, Football Player)
4A Dwight St
Jersey City, NJ 07305-4139, USA

Ashlund, Hilary (Stylist)
219 17th St
Wilmette, IL 60091-3221, USA

Ashman, Duane (Athlete, Football Player)
2625 Antler Ct
Silver Spring, MD 20904-7157, USA

Ashmore, Aaron (Actor)
55 1/2 Sumach St
Toronto, ON M5A 3J6, Canada

Ashmore, Darryl (Athlete, Football Player)
8695 Thornbrook Terrace Pt
Boynton Beach, FL 33473-4882, USA

Ashmore, Edward B (Admiral)
Victor Bldg HM Naval Base
Portsmouth, Hants, UNITED KINGDOM (UK)

Ashmore, Frank (Actor)
c/o Staff Member *Howard Talent West*
10657 Riverside Dr
Toluca Lake, CA 91602-2341, USA

Ashmore, Shawn (Actor)
c/o Staff Member *KG Talent*
55 1/2 Sumach St
Toronto, Ontario M5A 3J6, Canada

Ashrawl, Hanan (Politician)
PO Box 17360
Jerusalem, West Bank, ISRAEL

Ashton, Brent (Athlete, Hockey Player)
311 Brabant Crst
Saskatoon, SK S7J 3Y9, Canada

Ashton, Dean (Actor)
c/o Staff Member *Laine Management*
Laine House 131 victoria road
Salford M6 8LF, UNITED KINGDOM

Ashton, John (Actor)
PO Box 272489
Fort Collins, CO 80527-2489, USA

Ashton, Peter S (Scientist)
233 Heald Rd
Carlisle, MA 01741-1440, USA

Ashton, Susan (Music Group)
713 18th Ave S
Nashville, TN 37203-3214, USA

Ashworth, Frank (Athlete, Hockey Player)
5110 Hot Spg
Fairmont Hot Springs, BC V0B 1L0, Canada

Ashworth, Gerald (Gerry) (Athlete, Track Athlete)
PO Box 2
Ogunquit, ME 03907-0002, USA

Ashworth, Jeanne C (Speed Skater)
Whiteface Highway
Wilmington, NY 12997, USA

Ashworth, Thomas (Athlete, Football Player)
7329 S Xanthia Way
Centennial, CO 80112-1962, USA

Asia (Music Group)
7715 W Sunset Blvd Fl 3
Los Angeles, CA 90046-3912, USA

Asian Dub Foundation (Music Group)
c/o Staff Member *Paradigm (Monterey)*
404 W Franklin St
Monterey, CA 93940-2303, USA

Askea, Mike (Athlete, Football Player)
8402 Front Gate Cir
Ooltewah, TN 37363-9511, USA

Askew, B J (Athlete, Football Player)
4216 Lantana Dr
Lebanon, OH 45036-4022, USA

Askew, Desmond (Actor)
c/o Staff Member *Envision Management*
8840 Wilshire Blvd Fl 3
Beverly Hills, CA 90211-2606, USA

Askew, Luke (Actor)
3059 Green Canyon Rd
Fallbrook, CA 92028-8244, USA

Askew, Matthias (Athlete, Football Player)
220 Greenup St
Covington, KY 41011-1787, USA

Askew, Reubin O (Ex-Governor)
255 S Orange Ave
Orlando, FL 32801-3445, USA

Askey, Tom (Athlete, Hockey Player)
1076 South Ave
Rochester, NY 14620, USA

Askson, Bert (Athlete, Football Player)
7713 Charlesmont St
Houston, TX 77016-3927, USA

Asleep At The Wheel
PO Box 463
Austin, TX 78767-0463, USA

Aslyn (Musician)
c/o Staff Member *Paradigm (Monterey)*
404 W Franklin St
Monterey, CA 93940-2303, USA

Asmonga, Don (Athlete, Basketball Player)
124 Naylor Dr
Belle Vernon, PA 15012-4729, USA

Asner, Edward (Ed) (Actor)
11802 Otsego St
North Hollywood, CA 91607-3223, USA

Asner, Jules (Producer, Television Host)
c/o John Ferriter *Octagon Entertainment*
8687 Melrose Ave Ste 7
West Hollywood, CA 90069-5721, USA

Asomugha, Nnamdi (Athlete, Football Player)
1050 Armitage St
Alameda, CA 94502-7931, USA

Aspen, Jennifer (Actor)
c/o Joel Stevens *Joel Stevens Entertainment*
5627 Allott Ave
Van Nuys, CA 91401-4502, USA

Aspromonte, Bob
1000 Uptown Park Blvd Apt 241
Houston, TX 77056-3243, USA

Aspromonte, Kenneth J (Ken) (Athlete, Baseball Player, Coach)
2 Derham Parc St
Houston, TX 77024-5200, USA

Asrani (Actor, Bollywood)
B3 Beach House Apartments Gandhigram Rd Juhu
Mumbai, MS 400049, INDIA

Assante, Armand (Actor)
c/o Michael Kaliski *Omniquest Entertainment (LA)*
1416 N La Brea Ave
Hollywood, CA 90028-7506, USA

Asselstine, Brian (Athlete, Baseball Player)
1488 Country Ct
Santa Ynez, CA 93460-9754, USA

Assenmacher, Ivan (Doctor)
419 Ave d'Occitanie
Montpellier 34090, FRANCE

Assenmacher, Paul (Athlete, Baseball Player)
500 Covington Cv
Alpharetta, GA 30022-5574, USA

Assouline, Pierre (Writer)
78 Bd Flandrin
Paris 75116, France

Assuras, Thalia (Television Host)
c/o Staff Member *CBS News Productions*
524 W 57th St Fl 8
New York, NY 10019-2930, USA

Astacio, Pedro (Athlete, Baseball Player)
666 Dundee Rd Ste 704
Northbrook, IL 60062-2734, USA

Astanova, Lola (Musician)
c/o Gail Parenteau *Parenteau Guidance*
132 E 35th St # 3J
New York, NY 10016-3892, USA

Astin, John (Actor, Director)
c/o Staff Member *Elinor Berger & Associates*
1010 Hammond St Apt 306
W Hollywood, CA 90069-3851, USA

Astin, Mackenzie (Actor)
c/o Staff Member *WmE2 (WMA-LA)*
1 William Morris Pl
Beverly Hills, CA 90212-4261, USA

Astin, Sean (Actor, Director, Producer)
c/o Brian Medavoy *Jackson-Medavoy Entertainment*
10203 Santa Monica Blvd Fl 4
Los Angeles, CA 90067-6439, USA

Astley, Rick (Musician)
Unit 4 Plato St 72-74 Saint Dionis Road
London SW6 4UT, UNITED KINGDOM (UK)

Aston, Lottie (Athlete, Model)
PO Box 9272
Truckee, CA 96162-7272, USA

Astor, Brooke (Misc)
405 Park Ave
New York, NY 10022-4405, USA

Astrom, Hardy (Athlete, Hockey Player)
Bonasvagen 19B
Ornskoldsvik S-89072, Sweden

Astrom-Defina, Marianna (Stylist)
123 Union St
San Rafael, CA 94901-3439, USA

Astroth, Joe C (Athlete, Baseball Player)
6035 Verde Trl S Apt J310
Boca Raton, FL 33433-4435, USA

Asturaga, Nova (Government Official)
820 2nd Ave Rm 801
New York, NY 10017-4526, USA

Asuma, Linda (Actor)
c/o JR Dibbs *Malaky International*
205 S Beverly Dr Ste 211
Beverly Hills, CA 90212-3893, USA

Aswanikumar, G (Actor)
Plot 780 29th Street T N H B Korattur
Chennai, TN 600 080, INDIA

Atack, Emily (Actor)
c/o Malcolm Browning *International Artistes*
Holborn Hall - 4th Floor
London WC1V 7BD, UK

Atchison, Scott (Race Car Driver)
3112 Olympic Dr
Bakersfield, CA 93308-1533, USA

Atchley, Justin (Athlete, Baseball Player)
17958 Cove Ln
Mount Vernon, WA 98274-8126, USA

Aterciopelados (Musician)
c/o Staff Member *BMG*
1540 Broadway
New York, NY 10036-4039, USA

Atessis, Bill (Athlete, Football Player)
PO Box 616
Phoenix, AZ 85001-0616, USA

Atha, Richard (Athlete, Basketball Player)
PO Box 256
Oxford, IN 47971-0256, USA

Athas, Pete (Athlete, Football Player)
11390 NE 8th Ave
Biscayne Park, FL 33161-6318, USA

Atherton, Keith (Athlete, Baseball Player)
1014 Cobbs Creek Ln
Cobbs Creek, VA 23035-2137, USA

Atherton, William (Actor)
5102 San Feliciano Dr
Woodland Hills, CA 91364-1624, USA

Athfield, Ian C (Architect)
105 Amritser St Khandallah
Wellington, NEW ZEALAND

Athlete (Music Group)
c/o Staff Member *Paradigm (Monterey)*
404 W Franklin St
Monterey, CA 93940-2303, USA

Athow, Kirk L (Misc)
2104 Crestview Ct
Lafayette, IN 47905-2152, USA

Atias, Moran (Actor)
c/o Evan Hainey *Untitled Entertainment (LA)*
350 S Beverly Dr Ste 200
Beverly Hills, CA 90212-4819, USA

Atiyeh, Victor (Ex-Governor)
509 SW Park Ave # 205
Portland, OR 97205, USA

Atkeson, Dale
4308 Crest Dr
Manhattan Beach, CA 90266-3082, USA

Atkin, Harvey (Actor)
527 S Curson Ave
Los Angeles, CA 90036-3252, USA

Atkins, Bob (Athlete, Football Player)
15871 Misty Loch Ln
Houston, TX 77084-6795, USA

Atkins, Christopher
c/o Melanie Sharp *Sharp Talent*
117 N Orlando Ave
Los Angeles, CA 90048-3403, USA

Atkins, Dave (Athlete, Football Player)
737 W Wildwood Dr
Phoenix, AZ 85045-0632, USA

Atkins, Doug (Athlete, Football Player)
5312 Sunset Rd
Knoxville, TN 37914-4304, USA

Atkins, Eileen (Actor, Writer)
c/o Staff Member *International Creative Management (ICM-LA)*
10250 Constellation Blvd Fl 7
Los Angeles, CA 90067-6207, USA

Atkins, Essence (Actor)
c/o Marni Goldman *Abrams Artists Agency (LA)*
9200 W Sunset Blvd PH 11
Los Angeles, CA 90069-3601, USA

Atkins, Garrett (Athlete, Baseball Player)
31 Cezanne
Irvine, CA 92603-0207, USA

Atkins, Gene (Athlete, Football Player)
3515 Sunnyside Dr
Tallahassee, FL 32305-6964, USA

Atkins, George (Athlete, Football Player)
3445 Polo Downs
Birmingham, AL 35226-3371, USA

Atkins, Jeffrey (Ja Rule) (Actor, Musician)
c/o Staff Member *Handprint Entertainment*
1100 Glendon Ave Ste 100
Los Angeles, CA 90024-3593, USA

Atkins, Jim (Athlete, Baseball Player)
PO Box 1437
Cullman, AL 35056-1437, USA

Atkins, Kelvin (Athlete, Football Player)
4978 Timber Ridge Trl
Ocoee, FL 34761-8460, USA

Atkins, Larry (Athlete, Football Player)
911 Broadway St
Venice, CA 90291-3409, USA

Atkins, Pervis (Athlete, Football Player)
639 S Commonwealth Ave
Los Angeles, CA 90005-4008, USA

Atkins, Rodney (Musician)
c/o Staff Member *Red Light Management (Nashville)*
39 Music Sq E
Nashville, TN 37203-4322, USA

Atkins, Sharif (Actor)
c/o Christopher (Chris) Wright *Christopher Wright Management*
3207 Winnie Dr
Los Angeles, CA 90068-1439, USA

Atkins, Tom (Actor)
10100 Santa Monica Blvd Ste 2500
Los Angeles, CA 90067-4116, USA

Atkins, Veronica (Business Person)
100 Park Ave Rm 1600
New York, NY 10017-5538, USA

Atkinson, Al (Athlete, Football Player)
218 Wells Ln
Springfield, PA 19064-3038, USA

Atkinson, Bill (Athlete, Baseball Player)
15 Argyle Cres
Chatham, ON N7L 4T7, CANADA

Atkinson, Frank (Athlete, Football Player)
7 Franciscan Rdg
Portola Valley, CA 94028-8043, USA

Atkinson, George (Athlete, Football Player)
3570 Caldeira Dr
Livermore, CA 94550-6563, USA

Atkinson, Jayne (Actor)
1505 10th St
Santa Monica, CA 90401-2805, USA

Atkinson, Jess (Athlete, Football Player)
2913 S Haven Dr
Annapolis, MD 21401-7125, USA

Atkinson, Ray N (Business Person)
1001 Bayhill Dr
San Bruno, CA 94066-3062, USA

Atkinson, Rick (Journalist, Writer)
1729 Grand Blvd
Kansas City, MO 64108-1413, USA

Atkinson, Ron (Soccer Player)
Pavillion Road Bridgeford
Nottingham N62 5JF, UNITED KINGDOM (UK)

Atkinson, Rowan (Actor)
Drury Ln Theatre Royal
Catherine St WC2B 5JF, UK

Atkisson, Sharyl (Correspondent)
News Dept 1051 Techwood Dr NW
Atlanta, GA 30318, USA

Atkov, Oleg Y (Cosmonaut)
Moskovskoi Oblasti
Syvisdny Goroduk 141160, RUSSIA

Atogwe, Oshiomogho (Athlete, Football Player)
43263 Parkers Ridge Dr
Leesburg, VA 20176-5108, USA

Atomic Kitten (Music Group)
c/o Staff Member *Concorde Intl Artists Ltd*
101 Shepherds Bush Rd
London W6 7LP, UNITED KINGDOM (UK)

Attal, Yvan (Actor, Director)
20 Ave Rapp
Paris 75007, FRANCE

Attanasio, Paul (Producer, Writer)
c/o David O'Connor *Creative Artists Agency (CAA-LA)*
2000 Avenue of the Stars Ste 100
Los Angeles, CA 90067-4705, USA

Attardi, Michael (Athlete, Football Player)
1330 Whitney Isles Dr
Windermere, FL 34786-6064, USA

Attell, Dave (Comedian)
c/o Staff Member *Gersh (NY)*
41 Madison Ave
New York, NY 10010-2202, USA

Attenborough, David F (Business Person, Writer)
5 Park Rd
Richmond, Surrey TW10 6NS, UK

Attenborough, Richard S (Actor, Director)
Old Farms Beaver Lodge
Richmond Green, Surrey TW9 1NQ, UNITED KINGDOM (UK)

Atterton, Edward (Actor)
Drury House 34-43 Russell St
London WC2B 5HA, UNITED KINGDOM (UK)

Attlee, Frank III (Business Person)
800 N Lindbergh Blvd
Saint Louis, MO 63167-0001, USA

Attles, Al (Athlete, Basketball Player, Coach)
195 Villanova Dr
Oakland, CA 94611-1108, USA

Attwell, Bob (Athlete, Hockey Player)
270 Whitehead Crst
Bolton, ON L7E 3Y2, Canada

Attwell, Ron (Athlete, Hockey Player)
P.O. Box 292
Sundridge, ON P0A 1Z0, Canada

Atun, Hakki (Prime Minister)
North Cyprus Republic Via Mersin 10
Lefkosa, TURKEY

Atwater, Stephen D (Steve) (Athlete, Football Player)
2510 Sugarloaf Club Dr
Duluth, GA 30097-7407, USA

Atwater Rhodes, Amelia (Writer)
c/o Staff Member *Random House Publicity*
1745 Broadway
New York, NY 10019-4368, USA

Atwell, Alfred (Astronaut)
3253 Ennis Ct
Las Vegas, NV 89121-5761, USA

Atwood, Casey (Race Car Driver)
PO Box 37
Central City, KY 42330-0037, USA

Atwood, Jensen (Actor)
c/o Staff Member *Noah's Arc*
75 Charles Rowen House Merlin Street
London WC1X OEJ, UNITED KINGDOM

Atwood, Margaret E (Writer)
481 University Ave # 900
Toronto, ON M5G 2E9, CANADA

Atwood, Susie (Sue) (Swimmer)
5624 E 2nd St
Long Beach, CA 90803-3904, USA

Atzmon, Moshe
Marignanostr 12
Basel 4059, SWITZERLAND

Auber, Brigitte
56 rue Guy-Moquet
Paris F-75017, France

Auberjonois, Rene (Actor)
c/o Staff Member *Peter Strain & Associates Inc (LA)*
5455 Wilshire Blvd Ste 1812
Los Angeles, CA 90036-4268, USA

Aubert, KD (Actor)
c/o Scott Karp *Crystal Sky Pictures*
10203 Santa Monica Blvd Ste 500
Los Angeles, CA 90067-6416, USA

Aubin, Normand (Athlete, Hockey Player)
1287 Rue Des Berges
Sorel-Tracy, QC J3P 7X5, Canada

Aubin, Serge (Athlete, Hockey Player)
PO Box 105366
Atlanta, GA 30348-5366, USA

Auboin, Jean A (Misc)
27 Ave des Baumettes
Nice 6000, FRANCE

Aubrey, Emlyn (Athlete, Golfer)
2013 Surrey Ln
Bossier City, LA 71111-5534, USA

Aubrey, James (Actor)
18-21 Jermyn St #300
London SW1Y 6HP, UNITED KINGDOM (UK)

Aubry, Cristina (Actor)
Via Giuseppe Pisanelli
Rome 196, ITALY

Aubry, Eugene E (Architect)
8021 Marina Isles Ln
Holmes Beach, FL 34217-1063, USA

Aubry, Gabriel (Model)
c/o Staff Member *LW1*
7257 Beverly Blvd Ste 200
Los Angeles, CA 90036-2567, USA

Aubry, Pierre (Athlete, Hockey Player)
110 Rue Buisson
Trois-Rivieres, QC G8V 1K4, Canada

Aubuchon, Remi (Producer)
c/o Staff Member *United Talent Agency (UTA)*
9560 Wilshire Blvd Fl 5
Beverly Hills, CA 90212-2400, USA

Auburn, David (Writer)
97 W Elmwood Ave
Clawson, MI 48017-1228, USA

Aucoin, Adrian (Athlete, Hockey Player)
421 N Grant St
Hinsdale, IL 60521-3339, USA

AuCoin, Les (Misc)
601 13th St NW # 370
Washington, DC 20005-3807, USA

Aude, Rich (Athlete, Baseball Player)
4817 Natoma Ave
Woodland Hills, CA 91364-3416, USA

Audette, Donald (Athlete, Hockey Player)
15 Rue De Chinon
Blainville, QC J7B 1Y2, Canada

Audick, Daniel (Athlete, Football Player)
13253 Sparren Ave
San Diego, CA 92129-2324, USA

Audran, Stephane (Actor)
2F De Marthod
11 Rue Chanez 70016E, FRANCE

Auel, Jean M (Writer)
PO Box 8278
Portland, OR 97207-8278, USA

Auer, Barbara (Actor)
Neurieder Str 1C
Planegg 82152, GERMANY

Auer, Joe (Athlete, Football Player)
1138 Washington Ave
Winter Park, FL 32789-5657, USA

Auer, Scott (Athlete, Football Player)
2921 Burge Dr
Crown Point, IN 46307-8172, USA

Auerbach, Frank (Artist)
6 Albermarle St
London W1X 4BY, UNITED KINGDOM (UK)

Auerbach, Rick (Athlete, Baseball Player)
2139 Stunt Rd
Calabasas, CA 91302-2358, USA

Auerbach, Stanley I (Misc)
3314 W End Ave Apt 202
Nashville, TN 37203-0916, USA

Auermann, Nadia (Model)
4 Rue de la Paiz
Paris 75002, FRANCE

Auermann, Nadja (Model)
c/o Staff Member *Models 1*
12 Macklin St Covent Gardens
London WC2B 5SZ, UK

AufDerMaur, Melissa (Music Group, Musician)
9560 Wilshire Blvd # 400
Beverly Hills, CA 90212-2427, USA

Auge, Andrea (Stylist)
1825 NE 58th St
Seattle, WA 98105-2440, USA

Auger, Brian (Music Group, Musician)
8306 Wilshire Blvd # 981
Beverly Hills, CA 90211-2382, USA

Auger, Claudine (Actor)
20 Ave Rapp
Paris 75007, FRANCE

Auger, Pierre V (Physicist)
12 Rue Emile Faguet
Paris 75014, FRANCE

Aughtman, Dowe (Athlete, Football Player)
2 Buckhead Ln
Opelika, AL 36804-7645, USA

Augmon, Stacey (Athlete, Basketball Player)
687 Neldome St
Altadena, CA 91001-5257, USA

August, Bille (Director)
2800 Lyngby
DENMARK

August, Don (Athlete, Baseball Player)
28372 Lorente
Mission Viejo, CA 92692-2240, USA

August, John (Director, Musician, Producer)
c/o David Kramer *United Talent Agency (UTA)*
9560 Wilshire Blvd Fl 5
Beverly Hills, CA 90212-2400, USA

August, Pernilla (Actor)
Box 5037
Stockholm 102 41, SWEDEN

August, Steve (Athlete, Football Player)
7704 E 86th St
Tulsa, OK 74133-6651, USA

Augusta, Kim (Athlete, Golfer)
16 Rachella Ct
East Providence, RI 02914-3063, USA

Augusta, Patrik (Athlete, Hockey Player)
c/o Staff Member *Phoenix Coyotes*
6751 N Sunset Blvd Ste 200
Glendale, AZ 85305-3124, USA

Augustain, Ira (Actor)
c/o Staff Member *Diamond Artists*
9200 W Sunset Blvd Ste 701
W Hollywood, CA 90069-3602, USA

Augustana (Musician)
c/o Staff Member *Paradigm (Monterey)*
404 W Franklin St
Monterey, CA 93940-2303, USA

Augustine, Dave (Athlete, Baseball Player)
PO Box 1114
Saint Albans, WV 25177-1114, USA

Augustine, Jerry (Athlete, Baseball Player)
S74W13490 Courtland Ln
Muskego, WI 53150-3937, USA

Augustine, Norman R (Business Person)
300 E St SW
Washington, DC 20024-3210, USA

Augustnyiak, Jerry (Music Group, Musician)
9200 W Sunset Blvd Ste 900
Los Angeles, CA 90069-3604, USA

Augustus, Seimone (Athlete, Basketball Player)
3638 American River Dr
Sacramento, CA 95864-5901, USA

Augustus, Sherman (Actor)
c/o Steven Jensen *Independent Group, The*
6363 Wilshire Blvd Ste 115
Los Angeles, CA 90048-5734, USA

Augustyniak, Jerry (Musician)
c/o Staff Member *Agency for the Performing Arts (APA-LA)*
405 S Beverly Dr Ste 500
Beverly Hills, CA 90212-4425, USA

Augustyniak, Mike (Athlete, Football Player)
13846 Atlantic Blvd Apt 953
Jacksonville, FL 32225-3288, USA

Auktyon (Music Group, Musician)
c/o Staff Member *Skyline Music*
28 Union St
Whitefield, NH 03598-3503, USA

Aulby, Michael (Mike) (Bowler)
1591 Springmill Ponds Cir
Carmel, IN 46032-8552, USA

Aulby, Mike (Bowler)
1591 Springmill Ponds Cir
Carmel, IN 46032-8552, USA

Auld, Alex (Athlete, Hockey Player)
2205 Swallow Cres
Thunder Bay, ON P7C 4T9, Canada

Aulenti, Gae (Architect)
4 Piazza San Marco
Milan 20121, ITALY

Ault, Chris (Coach, Football Coach)
Athletic
Reno, NV 89557-0001, USA

Ault, James M (Religious Leader)
1 Amoskegan Dr
Brunswick, ME 04011-9524, USA

Aumont, Michel (Actor)
c/o Staff Member *ArtMedia*
20 avenue Rapp
Paris 75008, France

Auriemma, Geno (Athlete, Basketball Player, Coach)
180 Garth Rd
Manchester, CT 06040-5644, USA

Aurilla, Rich (Athlete, Baseball Player)
5448 E Mariposa St
Phoenix, AZ 85018-3124, USA

Ausanio, Joe (Athlete, Baseball Player)
646 Delaware Ave
Kingston, NY 12401-5141, USA

Ausbie, Hubert (Athlete, Basketball Player)
902 Arthur Dr
Little Rock, AR 72204-1524, USA

Ausmus, Brad (Athlete, Baseball Player)
1644 Stratford Way
Del Mar, CA 92014-2444, USA

Ausoin, Derek (Athlete, Baseball Player)
233 W 77th St Apt 5E
New York, NY 10024-6809, USA

Aust, Dennis (Athlete, Baseball Player)
16252 Estuary Ct
Bokeelia, FL 33922-1535, USA

Auster, Paul (Director, Writer)
c/o Ron Bernstein *International Creative Management (ICM-LA)*
10250 Constellation Blvd Fl 7
Los Angeles, CA 90067-6207, USA

Austin, A Woody (Athlete, Golfer)
10906 W Havenhurst St
Maize, KS 67101-3712, USA

Austin, Alana (Actor)
c/o Lena Roklin *Luber Roklin Management*
8530 Wilshire Blvd Ste 550
Beverly Hills, CA 90211-3133, USA

Austin, Andrea (Stylist)
c/o Staff Member *Sally Bjornsen Represents*
2008 3rd Ave N
Seattle, WA 98109-2510, USA

Austin, Bill (Athlete, Football Player)
9412 Shellfish Ct
Las Vegas, NV 89117-0267, USA

Austin, Billy (Athlete, Football Player)
3435 Westheimer Rd Apt 711
Houston, TX 77027-5359, USA

Austin, Charles (Athlete, Track Athlete)
514 Duncan Dr
San Marcos, TX 78666-4900, USA

Austin, Cliff (Athlete, Football Player)
1652 Valencia Rd
Decatur, GA 30032-5263, USA

Austin, Dallas (Musician, Producer, Songwriter)
c/o Charles King *WmE2 (Endeavor-LA)*
9601 Wilshire Blvd Fl 3
Beverly Hills, CA 90210-5219, USA

Austin, Darlene (Musician, Songwriter)
PO Box 171143
Nashville, TN 37217-8143, USA

Austin, Darrell (Athlete, Football Player)
268 Austin Rd
Union, SC 29379-7658, USA

Austin, Debbie (Athlete, Golfer)
6733 Bittersweet Ln
Orlando, FL 32819-4635, USA

Austin, Denise (Fitness Expert)
610 Thimble Shoals Blvd
Newport News, VA 23606-2573, USA

Austin, Hise (Athlete, Football Player)
53 N Deerfoot Cir
Spring, TX 77380-1523, USA

Austin, Ike (Athlete, Basketball Player)
1221 S 800 E
Salt Lake City, UT 84105-1207, USA

Austin, Jake (Actor)
c/o Ryan Bartlett *Paradigm (LA)*
360 N Crescent Dr
Beverly Hills, CA 90210-4874, USA

Austin, Jeff (Athlete, Baseball Player)
190 Rutherford Ave
Redwood City, CA 94061-3511, USA

Austin, Jeff (Musician)
c/o Staff Member *Paradigm (Monterey)*
404 W Franklin St
Monterey, CA 93940-2303, USA

Austin, Jim (Athlete, Baseball Player)
20974 Rootstown Ter
Ashburn, VA 20147-4839, USA

Austin, John (Athlete, Basketball Player)
1330 Riggs St NW
Washington, DC 20009-4325, USA

Austin, Johnny (Athlete, Basketball Player)
1330 Riggs St NW
Washington, DC 20009-4325, USA

Austin, Kent (Athlete, Football Player)
704 Legends Crest Dr
Franklin, TN 37069-4659, USA

Austin, Miles (Athlete, Football Player)
c/o David Dunn *Athletes First, LLC*
3300 Irvine Ave Ste 300
Newport Beach, CA 92660-3108, USA

Austin, Ocie (Athlete, Football Player)
750 MacArthur Blvd Apt 301
Oakland, CA 94610-3702, USA

Austin, Oona (Stylist)
7681 Willow Glen Rd
Los Angeles, CA 90046-1656, USA

Austin, Patti (Music Group)
3 Loudon Dr Unit 8
Fishkill, NY 12524-1870, USA

Austin, Reggie (Athlete, Football Player)
3339 Deerwood Ln
Rex, GA 30273-2475, USA

Austin, Rick (Athlete, Baseball Player)
6509 Claret Ct
Kansas City, MO 64152-6084, USA

Austin, Sherrie (Musician)
1520 16th Ave S Unit 2
Nashville, TN 37212-2938, USA

Austin, Steve (Stone Cold) (Athlete, Wrestler)
c/o Dallas Sonnier *Caliber Media Company*
9229 W Sunset Blvd Ste 705
West Hollywood, CA 90069-3407, USA

Austin, Teri (Actor)
4245 Laurelgrove Ave
Studio City, CA 91604-1624, USA

Austin, Thomas (Athlete, Football Player)
500 Almer Rd Apt 306
Burlingame, CA 94010-3966, USA

Austin, Tracy (Tennis Player)
1751 Pinnacle Dr Ste 1500
McLean, VA 22102-3833, USA

Austin Jr, M P (Business Person)
2101 Citywest Blvd
Houston, TX 77042-2829, USA

Auston, Jim (Musician)
c/o Staff Member *Curb Records (Nashville)*
48 Music Sq E
Nashville, TN 37203-4639, USA

Austregesilo de Athayde, Belarmino M (Journalist)
Rua Cosme Velho 599
Rio de Janeiro RJ, BRAZIL

Austria, Steve (Congressman, Politician)
439 Cannon Hob
Washington, DC 20515-2801, USA

Austrian, Robert (Physicist)
Med Center 36 Hamilton Circle
Philadelphia, PA 19130, USA

Auteuil, Daniel (Actor)
20 Ave Rapp
Paris 75007, FRANCE

Auth, Tony (Cartoonist, Editor)
c/o Staff Member *Universal Press Syndicate*
1130 Walnut St
Kansas City, MO 64106-2109, USA

Autrey, Billy (Athlete, Football Player)
9810 Knoboak Dr
Houston, TX 77080-6432, USA

Autry, Alan (Actor)
c/o Staff Member *David Shapira & Associates*
193 N Robertson Blvd
Beverly Hills, CA 90211-2103, USA

Autry, Albert (Al) (Athlete, Baseball Player)
3108 Lennox Dr
El Dorado Hills, CA 95762-5662, USA

Autry, Jim (Golfer, Misc)
PO Box 109601
Palm Beach Gardens, FL 33410-9601, USA

Auyeung, Jin (Musician)
c/o Staff Member *Virgin Records (NY)*
150 5th Ave Fl 7
New York, NY 10011-4372, USA

Auzenne, Troy (Athlete, Football Player)
1501 Bluff Ct
Diamond Bar, CA 91765-4301, USA

Avalon (Music Group)
PO Box 150867
Nashville, TN 37215-0867, USA

Avalon, Frankie (Actor, Musician)
4303 Spring Forest Ln
Westlake Village, CA 91362-5605, USA

Avant, Jason (Athlete, Football Player)
12136 S State St
Chicago, IL 60628-6629, USA

Avants, Nick (Athlete, Baseball Player)
3914 Mount Carmel Rd
Bryant, AR 72022-6209, USA

Avari, Erick (Actor)
c/o Michael Greene *Greene & Associates*
1901 Avenue Of The Stars Ste 130
Los Angeles, CA 90067-6030, USA

Avary, Roger (Director)
c/o Brian Siberell *Creative Artists Agency (CAA-LA)*
2000 Avenue of the Stars Ste 100
Los Angeles, CA 90067-4705, USA

Avdelsayed, Gabriel (Religious Leader)
427 W Side Ave
Jersey City, NJ 07304-1403, USA

Avdeyev, Sergei V (Cosmonaut)
Moskovskoi Oblasti
Syvisdny Goroduk 141160, RUSSIA

Avedon, Doe (Actor)
4333 Hayvenhurst Ave
Encino, CA 91436-3537, USA

Avedon, Gregg (Model)
PO Box 266401
Weston, FL 33326-6401, USA

Avellan, Elizabeth (Producer)
c/o Staff Member *International Creative Management (ICM-LA)*
10250 Constellation Blvd Fl 7
Los Angeles, CA 90067-6207, USA

Avellini, Bob (Athlete, Football Player)
1085 Flamingo Dr
Roselle, IL 60172-4731, USA

Aven, Bruce (Athlete, Baseball Player)
4223 SW 141st Ave
Davie, FL 33330-5724, USA

Avenged Sevenfold (Music Group)
c/o Staff Member *Warner Music Germany GmbH (WMI-Germany)*
Alter Wandrahm 14
Hamburg D - 20457, Germany

Averell, Tom (Athlete, Football Player)
100 Highland Pines Ct Apt 32
Pittsburgh, PA 15237-2038, USA

Averill Jr., Earl (Athlete, Baseball Player)
1806 19th Sr NE
Auburn, WA 98002, USA

Averno, Sisto (Athlete, Football Player)
4759 Bonnie Brae Rd
Baltimore, MD 21208-2017, USA

Averre, Berton (Music Group, Musician)
17510 Posetano Rd
Pacific Palisades, CA 90272-4175, USA

Avery, Eric (Actor, Musician)
c/o Jeff Frasco *Creative Artists Agency (CAA-LA)*
2000 Avenue of the Stars Ste 100
Los Angeles, CA 90067-4705, USA

Avery, James (Actor)
c/o Joel King *Pakula/King & Associates*
9229 W Sunset Blvd Ste 315
Los Angeles, CA 90069-3403, USA

Avery, John (Athlete, Football Player)
1301 Kensington Pl Apt B
Asheville, NC 28803-2393, USA

Avery, Ken (Athlete, Football Player)
625 Indian Ridge Dr
Nashville, TN 37221-4035, USA

Avery, Margaret (Actor)
c/o Staff Member *LAX & Company*
PO Box 241207
Los Angeles, CA 90024-1207, USA

Avery, Mary Ellen (Doctor, Physicist)
52 Liberty St
Plymouth, MA 02360-4176, USA

Avery, Phyllis (Actor)
37 Glenflow Ct
Glendale, CA 91206-1731, USA

Avery, Sean (Athlete, Hockey Player)
c/o Staff Member *Los Angeles Kings*
1111 S Figueroa St Ste 3100
Los Angeles, CA 90015-1333, USA

Avery, Shondrella (Actor)
c/o Vincent Cirrincione *Vincent Cirrincione Associates*
1516 N Fairfax Ave
Los Angeles, CA 90046-2608, USA

Avery, Steve (Athlete, Football Player)
339 Central Dr
Cranberry Twp, PA 16066-4415, USA

Avery, Steven T (Steve) (Athlete, Baseball Player)
2 Gleneagles Ct
Dearborn, MI 48120-1165, USA

Avery, Susan (Stylist)
6636 Mission Club Blvd Apt 305
Orlando, FL 32821-6922, USA

Avery, Tom (Athlete, Mountaineer)
c/o Staff Member *WmE2 (WMA-LA)*
1 William Morris Pl
Beverly Hills, CA 90212-4261, USA

Avery, Val (Actor)
84 Grove St Apt 19
New York, NY 10014-3567, USA

Avery, William J (Business Person)
1 Crown Way
Philadelphia, PA 19154-4501, USA

Avezzano, Joe (Athlete, Football Player)
1208 Lakeridge Ln
Irving, TX 75063-5080, USA

Aviance, Kevin (Musician)
115 E 57th St Fl 11
New York, NY 10022-2120, USA

Avila, Alejandro (Actor)
c/o Staff Member *Televisa*
Blvd Adolfo Lopez Mateos 232 Colonia San Angel INN
DF CP 01060, MEXICO

Avila, Mariana (Actor)
c/o Staff Member *Televisa*
Blvd Adolfo Lopez Mateos 232 Colonia San Angel INN
DF CP 01060, MEXICO

Avildsen, John G (Director)
2423 Briarcrest Rd
Beverly Hills, CA 90210-1819, USA

Aviles, Ramon (Athlete, Baseball Player)
C19 Calle Juan Morell Campos
Manati, PR 00674-6618, USA

Avinger, Clarence (Athlete, Football Player)
1228 Parliament Ln
Vestavia, AL 35216-2718, USA

Avital, Mili (Actor)
c/o Craig Shapiro *International Creative Management (ICM-LA)*
10250 Constellation Blvd Fl 7
Los Angeles, CA 90067-6207, USA

Aviva (Actor)
c/o Meredith Fine *Coast to Coast Talent Group*
3350 Barham Blvd
Los Angeles, CA 90068-1404, USA

Avnet, Jon (Director, Producer)
3815 Hughes Ave
Culver City, CA 90232-2715, USA

Avni, Aki
c/o Staff Member *Marshak/Zachary Company, The*
8840 Wilshire Blvd Fl 1
Beverly Hills, CA 90211-2606, USA

Avory, Mike (Musician)
29 Rushton Mews
London W11 1RB, UNITED KINGDOM (UK)

Awalt, Rob (Athlete, Football Player)
5011 Highgrove Ct
Granite Bay, CA 95746-7101, USA

Awasom, Adrian (Athlete, Football Player)
12330 Grove Meadow Dr
Stafford, TX 77477-2204, USA

Awesome 3 (Music Group, Musician)
c/o Staff Member *Mission Control Artists Agency*
Unit 3 City Business Centre St Olav's Court, Lower Road
London SE16 2XB, UNITED KINGDOM (UK)

Awrey, Donald W (Don) (Athlete, Hockey Player)
1015 Alaska Ave
Lehigh Acres, FL 33971-6447, USA

Awtrey, Dennis (Athlete, Basketball Player)
38245 James Rd
Nehalem, OR 97131-9602, USA

Ax, Emmanuel (Music Group, Musician)
c/o Staff Member *Askonas Holt Ltd*
Lincoln House 300 High Holborn
London WC1V 7JH, UK

Axel, Richard (Nobel Prize Laureate)
Columbia University, Hammer Health Sciences Center 701 W 168th St., Room 1014
New York, NY 10032, USA

Axelrod, Jack (Actor)
c/o Jennifer Lee Garland *Circle Talent Associates*
433 N Camden Dr Ste 400
Beverly Hills, CA 90210-4408, USA

Axelrod, Jonathan H (Biologist)
10100 Ntorrey Pines Rd
La Jolla, CA 92037, USA

Axelsson, PJ (Athlete, Hockey Player)
121 Mount Vernon St
Boston, MA 02108-1104, USA

Axley, Eric (Athlete, Golfer)
3745 Shipwatch Ln
Knoxville, TN 37920-7137, USA

Axtell, George C (War Hero)
615 Laurel Lake Dr Apt A103
Columbus, NC 28722-7425, USA

Ayala, Alexis (Actor)
c/o Staff Member *Televisa*
Blvd Adolfo Lopez Mateos 232 Colonia San Angel INN
DF CP 01060, MEXICO

Ayala, Bobby (Athlete, Baseball Player)
11011 W Cottonwood Ln
Avondale, AZ 85392-4324, USA

Ayala, Fransisco J (Biologist, Misc)
2 Locke Ct
Irvine, CA 92617-4034, USA

Ayala, Paul (Boxer)
7524 Creek Meadow Dr
Fort Worth, TX 76123-1980, USA

Ayanbadejo, Brendon (Athlete, Football Player)
2800 NE 30th St Apt 2
Fort Lauderdale, FL 33306-1998, USA

Ayanbadejo, Obafemi (Athlete, Football Player)
301 W G St Unit 134
San Diego, CA 92101-6055, USA

Ayanna, Charlotte (Actor)
955 Carrillo Dr Ste 300
Los Angeles, CA 90048-5400, USA

Aybar, Manny (Athlete)
401 E Jefferson St
Phoenix, AZ 85004-2438

Aybar, Manuel (Athlete, Baseball Player)
3020 SW 189th Ter
Miramar, FL 33029-5861, USA

Ayckbourn, Alan (Director, Writer)
14A Goodwins Ct Saint Martin's Lane
London WC2N 4LL, UNITED KINGDOM (UK)

Aycock, Alice (Artist)
62 Greene St
New York, NY 10012-4346, USA

Aycock, H David (Business Person)
2100 Rexford Rd
Charlotte, NC 28211-3589, USA

Aycock, Thomas (Misc)
2124 Glendale Ave
Texarkana, AR 71854-3564, USA

Aycox, Nicki (Actor)
c/o Jeb Brandon *Kritzer Levine Wilkins Entertainment*
11872 La Grange Ave Fl 1
Los Angeles, CA 90025-5283, USA

Aydelette, William (Athlete, Football Player)
7988 Wynwood Rd
Trussville, AL 35173-2270, USA

Ayer, David (Producer, Writer)
3312 W Sunset Blvd
Los Angeles, CA 90026-2118, USA

Ayers, Chuck (Cartoonist)
4520 Main St
Kansas City, MO 64111-1876, USA

Ayers, Dick (Cartoonist)
64 Beech St W
White Plains, NY 10604-2230, USA

Ayers, Randy (Athlete, Basketball Player, Coach)
1st Union Center 3601 South Broad St
Philadelphia, PA 19148, USA

Ayers, Roy E Jr (Music Group, Musician)
209 W 97th St Apt 4D
New York, NY 10025-5602, USA

Ayers, Sam (Actor)
c/o Staff Member *Bobby Ball Talent Agency*
4116 W Magnolia Blvd Ste 205
Burbank, CA 91505-2700, USA

Aykroyd, Dan (Actor, Comedian)
c/o Susan Patricola *Patricola Lust PR*
9171 Wilshire Blvd Ste 390
Beverly Hills, CA 90210-5515, USA

Aylesworth, Reiko (Actor)
c/o Staff Member *Innovative Artists (LA)*
1505 10th St
Santa Monica, CA 90401-2805, USA

Aylward, John (Actor)
c/o Staff Member *Mitchell K Stubbs & Assoc (MKS)*
8675 Washington Blvd Ste 203
Culver City, CA 90232-7486, USA

Aylwin Azocar, Patricio (President)
Teresa Salas 786
Providencia, Santiago, CHILE

Ayodele, Akin (Athlete, Football Player)
7105 David Ln
Colleyville, TX 76034-6664, USA

Ayotte, Kelly (Senator)
188 Russell Senate Ofc Building
Washington, DC 20510-0001, USA

Ayrault, Bob (Athlete, Baseball Player)
3353 Skyline Blvd
Reno, NV 89509-5671, USA

Ayrault, Joe (Athlete, Baseball Player)
2338 Vintage St
Sarasota, FL 34240-8317, USA

Ayre, Calvin (Business Person)
Oficentro Ejecutivo Sabana Sur Edificio 7, 5 Piso
San Jose 0, Costa Rica

Ayres, Robert Temple (Artist)
9186 Avenida Miravilla
Cherry Valley, CA 92223-3833, USA

Ayres, Rosalind (Actor)
c/o Staff Member *Lou Coulson Agency*
37 Berwick St 1st Floor
London W1F 8RS, UK

Ayres Kalish, Leah (Actor)
15718 Milbank St
Encino, CA 91436-1637, USA

Aytes, Rochelle (Actor)
c/o Ryan Daly *Zero Gravity Management*
11578 Canton Dr
Studio City, CA 91604-4160, USA

Azad, Afshan (Actor)
c/o Staff Member *Gordon and French*
12-13 Poland St
London W1F 8QB, UNITED KINGDOM (UK)

Azar, Steve (Music Group)
2 Music Cir S Ste 212
Nashville, TN 37203-5708, USA

Azaria, Hank (Actor)
c/o Nancy Sanders *Sanders Armstrong Caserta*
2120 Colorado Ave Ste 120
Santa Monica, CA 90404-3561, USA

Azcue, Jose (Joe) (Athlete, Baseball Player)
7609 W 115th St
Overland Park, KS 66210-2614, USA

Azelby, Joe (Athlete, Football Player)
14 Pierce Ave
Cresskill, NJ 07626-1126, USA

Azimov, Yakhyo (Prime Minister)
Rudaki Prosp 42
Dushaube 743051, TAJIKISTAN

Azinger, Paul (Athlete, Golfer)
7847 Chick Evans Pl
Sarasota, FL 34240-8752, USA

Aziz, Tariq (Prime Minister)
Karadat Mariam
Baghdad, IRAQ

Azizi, Anthony (Actor)
c/o Karen Embry *Sky Unlimited Arts*
7510 W Sunset Blvd # 554
Los Angeles, CA 90046-3408, USA

Azlan, Muhibuddin Shah (King)
Istana Bukit Serene
Kuala Lumpur, MALAYSIA

Azlynn, Valerie (Actor)
c/o Devon Jackson *Trademark Talent*
4758 Allott Ave
Sherman Oaks, CA 91423-2403, USA

Azmi, Shabana (Actor, Bollywood)
702 Sagar Samrat Greenfields Juhu
Mumbai, MS 400049, INDIA

Aznar, Jose Maria (Prime Minister)
Complejo de las Moncloa
Madrid 28071, SPAIN

Aznavour, Charles (Actor, Musician, Songwriter, Writer)
210 rue du Faubourg st
Honore, PARIS, FRANCE

Azria, Max (Designer, Fashion Designer)
2761 Fruitland Ave
Vernon, CA 90058-3607, USA

Azul Azul (Music Group)
c/o Staff Member *Sony Music Miami*
605 Lincoln Rd Ste 700
Miami Beach, FL 33139-2901, USA

Azuma, Norio (Artist)
276 Riverside Dr
New York, NY 10025-5204, USA

Azuma, Takamitsu (Architect)
3-6-1 Minami-Aoyama Minatoku
Tokyo 107, JAPAN

Azumah, Jerry (Athlete, Football Player)
462 W Superior St
Chicago, IL 60654-3497, USA

Azzara, Candice (Actor)

Azzaro, Chrissy (Designer, Fashion Designer)
c/o Staff Member *Perception Public Relations LLC*
3940 Laurel Canyon Blvd Ste 169
Studio City, CA 91604-3709, USA

Azzi, Jennifer (Athlete, Basketball Player)
407 10th Ave
Salt Lake City, UT 84103-2825, USA

B

B, Jon (Musician, Songwriter, Writer)
6399 Wilshire Blvd Ste 426
Los Angeles, CA 90048-5714, USA

B. Anderholf, Robert (Congressman, Politician)
2264 Rayburn Hob
Washington, DC 20515-3217, USA

B. Jones, Walter (Congressman, Politician)
2333 Rayburn Hob
Washington, DC 20515-3223, USA

B. Larson, John (Congressman, Politician)
1501 Longworth Hob
Washington, DC 20515-4708, USA

B. Maloney, Carolyn (Congressman, Politician)
2332 Rayburn Hob
Washington, DC 20515-3513, USA

B. McKinley, David (Congressman, Politician)
313 Cannon Hob
Washington, DC 20515-0925, USA

B. Nugent, Richard (Congressman, Politician)
1517 Longworth Hob
Washington, DC 20515-1004, USA

B2K (Music Group)
c/o Staff Member *Pyramid Entertainment Group*
377 Rector Pl Apt 21A
New York, NY 10280-1439, USA

B-52's (Music Group)
c/o Staff Member *Astralwerks Records*
150 5th Ave Fl 7
New York, NY 10011-4372, USA

Baab, Mike (Athlete, Football Player)
411 Westover Dr
Euless, TX 76039-2039, USA

Baack, Steve (Athlete, Football Player)
12322 SW Autumn View St
Portland, OR 97224-2581, USA

Baas, David (Athlete, Football Player)
7004 Lacantera Cir
Lakewood Ranch, FL 34202-5116, USA

Baba, Enclik Abdul Ghafar Bin (Prime Minister)
Jalan Raja Laut
Kuala Lumpur 50606, MALAYSIA

Babando, Pete (Athlete, Hockey Player)
50 Sterling Ave W
Timmins, ON P4N 3K3, Canada

Babashoff, Jack (Swimmer)
4859 Monroe Ave
San Diego, CA 92115-3246, USA

Babashoff, Shirley (Swimmer)
17254 Santa Clara St
Fountain Valley, CA 92708-3337, USA

Babatunde, Obba (Actor)
6500 Wilshire Blvd # 550
Los Angeles, CA 90048-4920, USA

Babb, Charlie (Athlete, Football Player)
371 Heron Ave
Naples, FL 34108-2115, USA

Babb, Eugene (Gene) (Athlete, Football Player)
5110 W 9th Ave
Stillwater, OK 74074-1465, USA

Babbar, Raj (Actor, Bollywood)
Nepathaya Plot 20 Gulmohar Road JVPD Scheme
Mumbai, MS 400049, INDIA

Babbit, Jamie (Director, Producer, Writer)
c/o Staff Member *Innovative Artists (LA)*
1505 10th St
Santa Monica, CA 90401-2805, USA

Babbitt, Bruce E (Ex-Governor)
5169 Watson St NW
Washington, DC 20016-5330, USA

Babbitt, Milton B (Composer, Musician)
3 Gordon Way
Princeton, NJ 08540-3925, USA

Babbs, Durrell (Tank) (Musician)
c/o Amy Malone *GIC Public Relations*
Prefers to be contacted via email or telephone
Los Angeles, CA 90069, USA

Babb-Sprague, Kristen (Swimmer)
4677 Pine Valley Cir
Stockton, CA 95219-1881, USA

Babcock, Barbara (Actor)
PO Box 222271
Carmel, CA 93922-2271, USA

Babcock, Bob (Athlete, Baseball Player)
7123 Fairway Dr
Butler, PA 16001-8597, USA

Babcock, Mike (Athlete, Coach, Hockey Player)
c/o Staff Member *Detroit Red Wings*
600 Civic Center Dr
Detroit, MI 48226-4419, USA

Babcock, Tim M (Ex-Governor)
1625 Highland St
Helena, MT 59601-5248, USA

Babcock, Todd (Actor)
c/o Staff Member *Gage Group, The (LA)*
14724 Ventura Blvd Ste 505
Sherman Oaks, CA 91403-3505, USA

Babe, Warren (Athlete, Hockey Player)
15 Rocky Mountain Blvd W
Lethbridge, AB T1K 6V7, Canada

Babenco, Hector E (Director)
c/o Johnnie Planco *Parseghian Planco LLC*
322 8th Ave Ste 601
New York, NY 10001-6715, USA

Baber, Billy (Athlete, Football Player)
5614 Hill Top St
Crozet, VA 22932, USA

Babers, Roderick (Athlete, Football Player)
11838 Murr Way
Houston, TX 77048-2528, USA

Babic, Milos (Athlete, Basketball Player)
1500 Doris Dr
Cookeville, TN 38501-2026, USA

Babich, Bob (Athlete, Football Player)
4994 Mount Ashmun Dr
San Diego, CA 92111-3930, USA

Babilonia, Tai (Figure Skater)
13889 Valley Vista Blvd
Sherman Oaks, CA 91423-4662, USA

Babin, Jason (Athlete, Football Player)
5680 Highway 6 # 320
Missouri City, TX 77459-4188, USA

Babin, Mitch (Athlete, Hockey Player)
519 Pleasant St
Leominster, MA 01453-6219, USA

Babin, Rex (Cartoonist, Editor)
Editorial Dept 21st & Q Sts
Sacramento, CA 95852, USA

Babineaux, Jonathan (Athlete, Football Player)
5659 Legends Club Cir
Braselton, GA 30517-6029, USA

Babineaux, Jordan (Athlete, Football Player)
801 Dewalt Ave
Port Arthur, TX 77640-4814, USA

Babinecz, John (Athlete, Football Player)
810 Trout Run Dr
Malvern, PA 19355-3148, USA

Babitt, Shooty (Athlete, Baseball Player)
4912 Plaza Way
Richmond, CA 94804-4346, USA

Babu, Ganesh (Actor)
No 1 Janaki Avenue Abhiramapuram
Chennai, TN 600 028, INDIA

Baby, John (Athlete, Hockey Player)
252 Brebeut Ave
Sudbury, ON P3C 5H1, Canada

Baby, Peggy (Actor)
2219 Canyon Brook Ln
Newman, CA 95360-2407, USA

Babych, Dave (Athlete, Hockey Player)
1315 Wellington Crst
Winnipeg, MB R3N 0A9, Canada

Babych, Wayne (Athlete, Hockey Player)
1315 Wellington Crst
Winnipeg, MB R3N 0A9, Canada

Baca, Jimmy Santiago (Writer)
c/o Staff Member *Blue Flower Arts*
PO Box 1361
Millbrook, NY 12545-1361, USA

Baca, Joe (Congressman, Politician)
2366 Rayburn Hob
Washington, DC 20515-3509, USA

Baca, John P (War Hero)
PO Box 154
Julian, CA 92036-0154, USA

Bacall, Lauren (Actor)
1 W 72nd St Apt 43
New York, NY 10023-3418, USA

Bacashihua, Jason (Athlete, Hockey Player)
23411 Annapolis St
Dearborn Heights, MI 48125-2200, USA

Baccaglio, Marty (Athlete, Football Player)
15030 Montebello Rd
Cupertino, CA 95014-5470, USA

Baccarin, Morena (Actor)
c/o Sarah Jackson *Seven Summits Pictures & Management*
8906 W Olympic Blvd Ground Floor
Beverly Hills, CA 90211, USA

Bach, Barbara (Actor)
2 Glynde Mews
London SW3 1SB, UNITED KINGDOM (UK)

Bach, Catherine (Actor)
c/o Steve Rohr *Lexicon Public Relations*
1901 Avenue of the Stars Fl 2
Los Angeles, CA 90067-6001, USA

Bach, David (Writer)
c/o Jan Miller *Dupree Miller & Associates*
100 Highland Park Vlg Ste 350
Dallas, TX 75205-2784, USA

Bach, Emmanuelle (Actor)
20 Ave Rapp
Paris 75007, FRANCE

Bach, Jillian (Actor)
c/o Staff Member *Metropolitan (MTA)*
4526 Wilshire Blvd
Los Angeles, CA 90010-3801, USA

Bach, John (Athlete, Basketball Player)
2300 Clarendon Blvd Ste 306
Arlington, VA 22201-3367, USA

Bach, Pamela (Actor)
c/o Nelson Parks *ESI Network*
6399 Wilshire Blvd Ste 300
Los Angeles, CA 90048-5706, United States

Bach, Richard (Writer)
1540 Broadway
New York, NY 10036-4039, USA

Bach, Sebastian (Actor, Music Group)
c/o Rick Sales *Rick Sales Entertainment Group*
5355 Cartwright Ave
North Hollywood, CA 91601-3481, USA

Bachan, Abhishek (Bollywood)
Pratiksha, 10th Rd JVPD Scheme
Mumbai 400049, INDIA

Bacharach, Burt (Composer, Musician)
681 Amalfi Dr
Pacific Palisades, CA 90272-4507, USA

Bachardy, Don (Writer)
145 Adelaide Dr
Santa Monica, CA 90402-1223, USA

Bachchan, Abhishek (Actor, Bollywood)
c/o Simone Sheffield *Canyon Entertainment*
PO Box 256
Palm Springs, CA 92263-0256, USA

Bachchan, Amitabh (Actor, Bollywood)
Pratiksha 10th Road Juhu Scheme
Mumbai, MS 400049, India

Bachchan, Jaya (Actor, Bollywood)
Pratiksha 10rh Road JVPD Scheme
Mumbai, MS 400049, INDIA

Bacher, Avron (Ali) (Cricketer, Misc)
PO Box 55009
Boston, MA 02205-5009, SOUTH AFRICA

Bachleda-Curus, Alicja (Actor)
c/o Judy Hofflund *Hofflund/Polone*
9465 Wilshire Blvd Ste 420
Beverly Hills, CA 90212-2603, USA

Bachman, Jay (Athlete, Football Player)
4602 Delphene Cir
Louisville, KY 40241-6109, USA

Bachman, Michelle (Congressman, Politician)
103 Cannon Hob
Washington, DC 20515-2303, USA

Bachman, Randy (Music Group, Songwriter, Writer)
6400 Pleasant Park Dr
Chanhassen, MN 55317-8804, USA

Bachman, Tal (Music Group, Musician, Songwriter, Writer)
729 7th Ave Ste 1600
New York, NY 10019-6880, USA

Bachman, Ted (Athlete, Football Player)
2890 Huntington Blvd Apt 110
Fresno, CA 93721-2346, USA

Bachmann, Maria (Music Group, Musician)
c/o Staff Member *Above the Line*
Goethestr 17
Munich D-80336, GERMANY

Bachmann, Michele (Congressman, Politician)
412 Cannon Hob
Washington, DC 20515-2509, USA

Bachrach, Louis F Jr (Photographer)
647 Boylston St # 2
Boston, MA 02116-2804, USA

Bachus, Spencer (Congressman, Politician)
2246 Rayburn Hob
Washington, DC 20515-3224, USA

Bacic, Steve (Actor, Producer)
c/o Staff Member *Pipeline Productions*
25715 Haskell St
Taylor, MI 48180-2076, USA

Baciocco, Albert Juozas Cardinal (Admiral)
747 Pitt St
Mount Pleasant, SC 29464-5022, USA

Backe, Brandon (Athlete, Baseball Player)
2550 Quaker Dr
Texas City, TX 77590-3740, USA

Backe, John D (Business Person)
83 General Warren Blvd Ste 100
Malvern, PA 19355-1252, USA

Backis, Audrys Juozas Cardinal (Religious Leader)
Sventaragio 4
Vilnius, LITHUANIA

Backley, Stephen (Steve) (Athlete, Track Athlete)
56A-60 Glenhurst Ave
Bexley, Kent DA5 3QN, UNITED KINGDOM (UK)

Backlund, Bob (Athlete, Wrestler)
PO Box 973
Glastonbury, CT 06033-0973

Backman, Christian (Athlete, Hockey Player)
784 Bellerive Manor Dr
Saint Louis, MO 63141-6065, USA

Backman, Jules (Economist, Writer)
59 Crane Rd
Scarsdale, NY 10583-4347, USA

Backman, Mike (Athlete, Hockey Player)
50 Pond Pl
Cos Cob, CT 06807-2220, USA

Backman, Walter W (Wally) (Athlete, Baseball Player)
241 SE Mercury Ln
Prineville, OR 97754-2803, USA

Backstreet Boys (Music Group)
c/o John Marx *WmE2 (Endeavor-LA)*
9601 Wilshire Blvd Fl 3
Beverly Hills, CA 90210-5219, USA

Backstrom, Ralph (Athlete, Hockey Player)
1625 Pelican Lakes Pt
Windsor, CO 80550-6236, USA

Backus, Billy (Boxer)
308 N Main St
Canastota, NY 13032-1070, USA

Backus, George E (Geophysicist, Physicist)
9362 La Jolla Farms Rd
La Jolla, CA 92037-1125, USA

Backus, Gus (Musician)
PO Box 770850
Orlando, FL 32877-0850, USA

Backus, Jeff (Athlete, Football Player)
48075 Bellagio Ct
Northville, MI 48167-9808, USA

Backus, John (Mathematician)
970 Garden Way
Ashland, OR 97520-3416, USA

Backus, Sharon (Coach)
Athletic Dept
Los Angeles, CA 90024, USA

Bacon, Coy (Athlete, Football Player)
1017 S 8th St
Ironton, OH 45638-1944, USA

Bacon, Edmund N (Architect)
1025 N 4th St Apt D
Philadelphia, PA 19123-1533, USA

Bacon, Henry (Athlete, Basketball Player)
10103 Grand Ave Apt 218
Louisville, KY 40299-3145, USA

Bacon, Kelvin (Actor)
PO Box 668
Sharon, CT 06069-0668, USA

Bacon, Kevin (Actor)
c/o David Schiff *Schiff Company, The*
8440 Warner Dr Ste B1
Culver City, CA 90232-2461, USA

Bacon, Michael (Actor)
c/o Jennifer Lee Garland *Circle Talent Associates*
433 N Camden Dr Ste 400
Beverly Hills, CA 90210-4408, USA

Bacon, Nicky D (War Hero)
40 Patriots Point Rd
Mount Pleasant, SC 29464-4377, USA

Bacon, Roger F (Admiral)
24285 Johnson Rd NW
Poulsbo, WA 98370-9606, USA

Bacon, Waine (Athlete, Football Player)
2900 McFarland Blvd E Apt 516
Tuscaloosa, AL 35405, USA

Bacon Brothers, The (Music Group)
c/o Staff Member *Paradigm (Monterey)*
404 W Franklin St
Monterey, CA 93940-2303, USA

Bacot, J Carter (Financier)
48 Porter Pl
Montclair, NJ 07042-2036, USA

Bacs, Ludovic (Composer)
31 D Golescu Sc III E7 V Ap 87
Bucharest 1, ROMANIA

Bacsik, Mike (Athlete, Baseball Player)
4014 Falcon Lake Dr
Arlington, TX 76016-4126, USA

Bacsik, Mike (Athlete, Baseball Player)
1126 N Clinton Ave
Dallas, TX 75208-3613, USA

Bacuicchi, Antonello (Misc)
Government Palace
San Marino 47031, SAN MARINO

Bada, Jeffrey (Misc)
Chemistry
La Jolla, CA 92093-0001, USA

Badalamenti, Angelo (Composer, Musician)
11 Fidelian Way
Lincoln Park, NJ 07035-1534, USA

Badalucco, Michael (Actor)
1600 Rosecrans Ave # 1A
Manhattan Beach, CA 90266-3708, USA

Badar, Rich (Athlete, Football Player)
5877 Riceland Dr
Newburgh, IN 47630-1892, USA

Badawi, Abdullah Ahamad (Prime Minister)
Jalan Dato Onn
Kuala Lumpur 50502, MALAYSIA

Baddeley, Aaron (Athlete, Golfer)
8606 E Via Del Sol Dr
Scottsdale, AZ 85255-5253, USA

Baddiel, David (Actor, Writer)
c/o Staff Member *Lip Service Casting Ltd*
60-66 Wardour St
London W1F 0TA, UK

Baddoo, Agnes (Stylist)
c/o Staff Member *Rex Agency, The*
6311 Romaine St
Los Angeles, CA 90038-2617, USA

Baddour, Raymond F (Engineer)
8 Bayberry Ln
Belmont, MA 02478-1051, USA

Badel, Sarah (Actor)
c/o Staff Member *The Rights House (UK)*
Drury House 34-43 Russell St
London WC2B 5HA, UK

Badelt, Klaus (Musician)
c/o John Tempereau *Soundtrack Music Assoc*
1460 4th St Ste 308
Santa Monica, CA 90401-3483, USA

Bader, Beth (Athlete, Golfer)
713 S 7th St
Eldridge, IA 52748-1537, USA

Bader, Diedrich (Actor)
c/o Joel Rudnick *Paradigm (LA)*
360 N Crescent Dr
Beverly Hills, CA 90210-4874, USA

Bader, Larry (Athlete, Hockey Player)
1413 Westwood Dr SW
Faribault, MN 55021-6741, USA

Baderinwa, Sade (Correspondent)
7 Lincoln Sq
New York NY, 1003

Badger, Brad (Athlete, Football Player)
2552 Milleford Ct
Pleasanton, CA 94588, USA

Badgley, Mark (Fashion Designer)
c/o Staff Member *Badgley Mischka*
1412 Broadway Rm 1200
New York, NY 10018-9295, USA

Badgley, Penn (Actor)
c/o Doug Wald *Anonymous Content (AC-LA)*
545 Veteran Ave
Los Angeles, CA 90024-1915, USA

Badham, John M (Director)
344 Clerendon Rd
Beverly Hills, CA 90210, USA

Badham, Mary (Actor)
3720 Whitehall Rd
Sandy Hook, VA 23153-2204, USA

Badie, Mina (Actor)
c/o Staff Member *Rugolo Entertainment*
195 S Beverly Dr Ste 400
Beverly Hills, CA 90212-3044, USA

Badly Drawn Boy (Music Group)
c/o Staff Member *Paradigm (Monterey)*
404 W Franklin St
Monterey, CA 93940-2303, USA

Badnarik, Michael (Politician)
6633 E Highway 290
Austin, TX 78723-1134, USA

Badu, Erykah (Musician, Songwriter, Writer)
P.O. 25092
Arlington, VT 22202, USA

Badura-Skoda, Paul (Composer, Musician)
Zuckerkandlgass 14
Vienna 1190, AUSTRIA

Baechtold, James (Jim) (Athlete, Basketball Player)
225 W Irvine St
Richmond, KY 40475-2702, USA

Baeling, Becky (Musician)
c/o Staff Member *Diva Central Inc*
7510 W Sunset Blvd Ste 1445
Los Angeles, CA 90046-3408, USA

Baena, Marisa (Athlete, Golfer)
4036 Lantana Ln
Plano, TX 75093-7097, USA

Baer, Gordy (Bowler)
8577 Tullamore Dr
Tinley Park, IL 60487-4774, USA

Baer, Laurie (Stylist)
580 N Raymond Ave Apt 2
Pasadena, CA 91103-4318, USA

Baer, Neal (Actor, Producer, Writer)
100 Universal City Plz Bldg 2252
Universal City, CA 91608-1002, USA

Baer, Robert J (Jacob) (General)
111 Jerdone Pl
Yorktown, VA 23692-4255, USA

Baerga, Carlos (Athlete, Baseball Player)
PO Box 1667
Bayamon, PR 00960-1667, USA

Baerwald, David (Musician)

Baez, Danys (Athlete, Baseball Player)
6190 SW 114th St
Miami, FL 33156-4953, USA

Baez, Eddie (DJ)
c/o Staff Member *Diva Central Inc*
7510 W Sunset Blvd Ste 1445
Los Angeles, CA 90046-3408, USA

Baez, Joan (Musician, Songwriter)
c/o Mark Spector *The Mark Spector Company*
826 Broadway Fl 4
New York, NY 10003-4826, 212-277-7175

Baez, Jose (Athlete, Baseball Player)
1028 E Jersey St Apt 2
Elizabeth, NJ 07201-2532, USA

Baez, Kevin (Athlete, Baseball Player)
72 Hollywood Dr
Oakdale, NY 11769-1941, USA

Baeza, Braulio (Jockey)
214 S George St
Ranson, WV 25438-1415, USA

Baeza, Paloma (Actor)
Drury House 34-43 Russell St
London WC2B 5HA, USA

Bafaro, Michael (Director, Writer)
c/o Staff Member *Lenhoff & Lenhoff*
830 Palm Ave
West Hollywood, CA 90069-4009

Baffert, Bob (Misc)
1050 S Prairie Ave
Inglewood, CA 90301-4120, USA

Bagabandi, Ntsaagiyn (President)
Great Hural
Ulan Bator, MONGOLIA

Bagach, Irene (Actor, Model)
12 Macklin St Covent Garden
London WC2B 5SZ, UNITED KINGDOM

Bagdasarian Jr, Ross (Actor, Producer)
c/o Staff Member *Bagdasarian Productions*
1192 E Mountain Dr
Montecito, CA 93108-1119

Bagge, Peter (Artist)
c/o Staff Member *Fantagraphics Books*
7563 Lake City Way NE
Seattle, WA 98115-4218, USA

Baggetta, Vincent (Actor)
4812 Ranchito Ave
Sherman Oaks, CA 91423-1913, USA

Baggio, Roberto (Soccer Player)
Via Casteldebole 10
Bologna 40132, ITALY

Bagian, James P (Astronaut)
21537 Holmbury Rd
Northville, MI 48167-1021, USA

Bagley, John (Athlete, Basketball Player)
826 Patricia Ave
Elgin, IL 60120-3176, USA

Baglietto, Tara (Actor)
c/o Staff Member *Innovative Artists (NY)*
235 Park Ave S Fl 7
New York, NY 10003-1404, USA

Bagnal, Charles W (General)
221 W Springs Rd
Columbia, SC 29223-6948, USA

Bagwell, Jeffrey R (Jeff) (Athlete, Baseball Player)
405 Timberwilde Ln
Houston, TX 77024-6927, USA

Baham, Curtis (Athlete, Football Player)
5936 Oxford Pl
New Orleans, LA 70131-3908, USA

Bahns, Maxine (Actor)
c/o Steven Jensen *Independent Group, The*
6363 Wilshire Blvd Ste 115
Los Angeles, CA 90048-5734, USA

Bahnsen, Ken (Athlete, Football Player)
671 N Masch Branch Rd
Denton, TX 76207-3633, USA

Bahnsen, Stan (Athlete, Baseball Player)
3500 Blue Lake Dr Apt 402
Pompano Beach, FL 33064-2026, USA

Bahouth, Peter (Misc)
702 H St NW
Washington, DC 20001-3874, USA

Bahr, Chris (Athlete, Football Player)
122 Kaywood Dr
Boalsburg, PA 16827-1686, USA

Bahr, Egon (Government Official)
Ollenhauerster 1
Bonn 53113, GERMANY

Bahr, Matthew D (Matt) (Athlete, Football Player)
53 Parkridge Ln
Pittsburgh, PA 15228-1105, USA

Bahr, Morton (Misc)
501 3rd St NW
Washington, DC 20001-2760, USA

Bahr, Sherry (Stylist)
c/o Staff Member *Arlene Wilson Management*
807 N Jefferson St # 200
Milwaukee, WI 53202-8150, USA

Bahr, Walter (Soccer Player)
250 Elks Rd
Boalsburg, PA 16827, USA

Bai, Pandari (Actor, Bollywood)
54 Pillayar Koil Street Vadapalani
Chennai, TN 600026, INDIA

Bai, Yang (Actor)
Shanghai 200050, CHINA

Bailar, Benjamin F (Educator, Government Official)
410 Walnut Rd
Lake Forest, IL 60045-2254, USA

Bailes, Scott (Athlete, Baseball Player)
5895 S Teters Ct
Springfield, MO 65804-7720, USA

Bailey, Ben (Actor, Television Host)
PO Box 113
Brookside, NJ 07926-0113, USA

Bailey, Bob (Athlete, Baseball Player)
312 Granada Ave
Long Beach, CA 90814-3119, USA

Bailey, Claron (Athlete, Football Player)
9624 E Navarro Ave
Mesa, AZ 85209-2491, USA

Bailey, Cory (Athlete, Baseball Player)
1310 NW 82nd St
Kansas City, MO 64118-6433, USA

Bailey, Damon (Athlete, Basketball Player)
723 Diamond Rd
Heltonville, IN 47436-8559, USA

Bailey, David (Athlete, Football Player)
1916 NE 29th St
Oklahoma City, OK 73111-3346, USA

Bailey, Don (Athlete, Football Player)
14831 NW 7th Ave
Miami, FL 33168-3105, USA

Bailey, Edwin (Athlete, Football Player)
3677 Cypress Point Dr
Augusta, GA 30907-9021, USA

Bailey, Eion (Actor)
c/o Staff Member *Susan Smith Company, The*
1344 N Wetherly Dr
Los Angeles, CA 90069-1817, USA

Bailey, Elmer (Athlete, Football Player)
13390 NE 7th Ave Apt 406
North Miami, FL 33161-7562, USA

Bailey, F Lee (Attorney, Attorney General, General)
823 N Olive Ave
West Palm Beach, FL 33401-3709, USA

Bailey, G W (Actor)
c/o Staff Member *Leavitt Talent Group*
8255 W Sunset Blvd
West Hollywood, CA 90046-2417, USA

Bailey, Harold (Athlete, Football Player)
22502 Prince George St
Katy, TX 77449-2723, USA

Bailey, Howard (Athlete, Baseball Player)
11674 156th Ave
West Olive, MI 49460-9388, USA

Bailey, Jennifer (Stylist)
22606 Ironwood Rd
Lakeville, MN 55044-8176, USA

Bailey, Jim (Athlete, Football Player)
5219 Stone Creek Ct
Lawrence, KS 66049-4792, USA

Bailey, Jim (Athlete, Baseball Player)
250 Cade Rd
Ten Mile, TN 37880-2149, USA

Bailey, John (Cinematographer)
9560 Wilshire Blvd Ste 500
Beverly Hills, CA 90212-2401, USA

Bailey, Johnny L (Athlete, Football Player)
9400 Bellaire Blvd Unit 109
Houston, TX 77036-4552, USA

Bailey, Karsten (Athlete, Football Player)
16 Salbide Ave
Newnan, GA 30263-2501, USA

Bailey, Keith E (Business Person)
1 One Williams Ctr
Tulsa, OK 74172-0140, USA

Bailey, Leonard L (Doctor)
Medical School
Loma Linda, CA 92350-0001, USA

Bailey, Mark (Athlete, Baseball Player)
32703 Waltham Xing
Fulshear, TX 77441-4203, USA

Bailey, Mark (Athlete, Football Player)
3229 Corniche Ln
Roseville, CA 95661-3970, USA

Bailey, Maxwell C (General)
4704 W Pearl Ave
Tampa, FL 33611-5628, USA

Bailey, Michael (Doctor)
Psychology
Evanston, IL 60208-0001, USA

Bailey, Norman S (Opera Singer)
84 Warham Rd
South Croydon, Surrey CR2 6LB, UNITED KINGDOM (UK)

Bailey, Otha (Athlete, Baseball Player)
937 6th Pl SW
Birmingham, AL 35211-1743, USA

Bailey, Paul (Writer)
79 Davisville Road
London W12 9SH, UNITED KINGDOM (UK)

Bailey, Philip (Musician)
c/o Staff Member *Richard De La Font Agency*
3808 W South Park Blvd
Broken Arrow, OK 74011-1261, USA

Bailey, Preston (Actor)
c/o Staff Member *Elements Entertainment*
312 W 5th St Apt 815
Los Angeles, CA 90013-1750, USA

Bailey, Razzy (Musician, Songwriter, Writer)
PO Box 62
Geneva, NE 68361-0062, USA

Bailey, Robert M (Athlete, Football Player)
15325 SW 99th Ave
Miami, FL 33157-1708, USA

Bailey, Roger (Athlete, Baseball Player)
1445 Forest Trails Dr
Castle Pines, CO 80108-8298, USA

Bailey, Roland (Champ) (Athlete, Football Player)
80 Cherry Hills Farm Dr
Englewood, CO 80113-7114, USA

Bailey, Scott (Actor)
c/o Staff Member *Stone Manners Salners Agency (LA)*
9911 W Pico Blvd Ste 1400
Los Angeles, CA 90035-2715, USA

Bailey, Sean (Producer)
c/o Patrick Whitesell *WmE2 (Endeavor-LA)*
9601 Wilshire Blvd Fl 3
Beverly Hills, CA 90210-5219, USA

Bailey, Stacey (Athlete, Football Player)
3400 Lakewind Way
Alpharetta, GA 30005-6943, USA

Bailey, Steve (Athlete, Baseball Player)
4600 Queen Anne Ave
Lorain, OH 44052-5648, USA

Bailey, Steven W (Reality TV Star)
c/o Scott Fedro *Lone Star Entertainment*
139 S Beverly Dr Ste 314
Beverly Hills, CA 90212-3040, USA

Bailey, T Wayne (Activist, Politician)
Political Science Dept
Stetson, FL 32720, USA

Bailey, Teddy (Athlete, Football Player)
7825 Elbrook Ave
Cincinnati, OH 45237-2207, USA

Bailey, Thomas H (Financier)
720 S Colorado Blvd Ste 290A
Denver, CO 80246-1929, USA

Bailey, Thurl (Athlete, Basketball Player)
10265 N 6960 W
Highland, UT 84003-9337, USA

Bailey, Victor (Athlete, Football Player)
1405 Ogelthorpe Ave
Urbana, IL 61802-4749, USA

Bailey II, Irving W (Business Person)
400 W Market St
Louisville, KY 40202-3346, USA

Bailey Rae, Corinne (Musician)
14 Victoria Rd
Douglas, Isle of Man IM2 4ER, BRITISH ISLES

Baillargeon, Joel (Athlete, Hockey Player)
165B Rue Du Coutelier
Saint-Augustin-De-Desmaures, QC G3A 2J7, Canada

Bailon, Adrienne (Actor, Musician)
c/o Joann Mignano *Krupp Kommunications*
45 E 20th St Fl 5B
New York, NY 10003-1308, USA

Bailor, Bob (Athlete, Baseball Player)
1950 Swan Ln
Palm Harbor, FL 34683-6275, USA

Baily, Kirk (Actor)
c/o Staff Member *Independent Artists Agency*
9601 Wilshire Blvd Ste 750
Beverly Hills, CA 90210-5228, USA

Bailyn, Bernard (Historian)
170 Clifton St
Belmont, MA 02478-2604, USA

Bain, Barbara (Actor)
c/o Barry Krost *Barry Krost Management*
9220 W Sunset Blvd Ste 106
West Hollywood, CA 90069-3500, USA

Bain, Conrad (Actor)
900 E Stanley Blvd Unit 183
Livermore, CA 94550-4235, USA

Bain, William E (Bill) (Athlete, Football Player)
27661 Paseo Barona
San Juan Capistrano, CA 92675-2851, USA

Bainbridge, Beryl (Actor, Writer)
42 Albert St
London NW1 7NU, UNITED KINGDOM (UK)

Bainbridge, Merril (Musician, Songwriter, Writer)
PO Box 1760
Collingswood, VIC 3068, AUSTRALIA

Baines, Harold D (Athlete, Baseball Player)
PO Box 10
Saint Michaels, MD 21663-0010, USA

Baio, Scott (Actor)
c/o Harry Gold *TalentWorks (LA)*
3500 W Olive Ave Ste 1400
Burbank, CA 91505-5512, USA

Baiocchi, Hugh (Athlete, Golfer)
142 Royal Saint Georges Way
Rancho Mirage, CA 92270-5642, USA

Bair, Doug (Athlete, Baseball Player)
11545 Kemper Woods Dr
Cincinnati, OH 45249-1753, USA

Baird, Bill (Athlete, Football Player)
6050 E Heaton Ave
Fresno, CA 93727-5606, USA

Baird, Briny (Athlete, Golfer)
3340 SW Rivers End Way
Palm City, FL 34990-7603, USA

Baird, Butch (Athlete, Golfer)
PO Box 2663
Carefree, AZ 85377-2663, USA

Baird, Diora (Actor)
c/o Lena Roklin *Luber Roklin Management*
8530 Wilshire Blvd Ste 550
Beverly Hills, CA 90211-3133, USA

Baird, James M (Religious Leader)
PO Box 1428
Decatur, GA 30031-1428, USA

baird, jenni (Actor)
c/o Michael P Levine *Levine Management*
9028 W Sunset Blvd PH 1
Los Angeles, CA 90069-1830, USA

Baird, Ken (Athlete, Hockey Player)
Lot 4 Berry Bay
Snow Lake, MB R0B 1M0, Canada

Baird, Stuart (Director)
c/o Staff Member *Mirisch Agency*
8840 Wilshire Blvd Ste 100
Beverly Hills, CA 90211-2606, USA

Bairstow, Scott H (Actor)
c/o Andrea Pett-Joseph *Brillstein Entertainment Partners*
9150 Wilshire Blvd Ste 350
Beverly Hills, CA 90212-3453, USA

Baisden, Michael (Producer, Radio Personality, Writer)
13901 Midway Rd # 102-274
Dallas, TX 75244-4359, USa

Baitz, Jon Robin (Producer)
c/o Simon Halls *Slate Public Relations*
9000 W Sunset Blvd Ste 915
West Hollywood, CA 90069-5809, USA

Baiul, Oksana (Figure Skater)
c/o Phil Viardo *The Viardo Agency*
8484 Wilshire Blvd Ste 220
Beverly Hills, CA 90211-3223, USA

Bajanowsky, Louis J (Architect)
1050 Massachusetts Ave
Cambridge, MA 02138-5359, USA

Bajardi, Lane (Television Host)
c/o Staff Member *Bloomberg Television*
731 Lexington Ave
New York, NY 10022-1331, USA

Bajcsy, Ruzena (Engineer)
Electrical Engineering
Berkeley, CA 94720-0001, USA

Bajema, Billy (Athlete, Football Player)
2605 SW 120th St
Oklahoma City, OK 73170-4735, USA

Bajenaru, Jeff (Athlete, Baseball Player)
3717 E Megan St
Gilbert, AZ 85295-4818, USA

Bajpai, Manoj (Actor, Bollywood)
304 Victoria Shastrinagar Lokhandwala Complex Andheri W
Mumbai, MS 4000593, INDIA

Bakalyan, Richard (Actor)
1070 S Bedford St
Los Angeles, CA 90035-2102, USA

Bakatin, Vadim V (Government Official)
Kotelnicheskaya Nab 17
Moscow 103240, RUSSIA

Bakay, Nick (Actor)
c/o Staff Member *United Talent Agency (UTA)*
9560 Wilshire Blvd Fl 5
Beverly Hills, CA 90212-2400, USA

Bakenhaster, Dave (Athlete, Baseball Player)
3710 Rome Corners Rd
Galena, OH 43021-9490, USA

Baker, Al (Athlete, Football Player)
2784 Trinity Ct
Avon, OH 44011-1951, USA

Baker, Anita (Actor, Musician, Songwriter)
c/o Staff Member *WmE2 (WMA-LA)*
1 William Morris Pl
Beverly Hills, CA 90212-4261, USA

Baker, Art (Athlete, Football Player)
24 Quail Hollow Rd # B
Mashpee, MA 02649-2824, USA

Baker, Blanche (Actor)
4695 Independence Ave
Bronx, NY 10471-3538, USA

Baker, Brenda (Actor)
9200 W Sunset Blvd Ste 900
Los Angeles, CA 90069-3604, USA

Baker, Buddy (Race Car Driver)
4860 Moonlite Bay Dr
Sherrills Ford, NC 28673-9242, USA

Baker, Carroll (Actor)
9200 W Sunset Blvd Ste 1125
Los Angeles, CA 90069-3610, USA

Baker, Charles (Actor)
c/o Linda McAlister *Linda McAlister Talent*
100 Oak Ln
Waxahachie, TX 75167-8412, USA

Baker, Charles (Charlie) (Athlete, Football Player)
PO Box 112593
Carrollton, TX 75011-2593, USA

Baker, Christine (Stylist)
c/o Celebrity Stylist *Artists by Timothy Priano (NY)*
15 Watts St Fl 6
New York, NY 10013-1677, USA

Baker, Chuck (Athlete, Baseball Player)
3035 Mescalero Dr
Lake Havasu City, AZ 86404-9605, USA

Baker, Colin (Actor)
100 Fawe Park Road
London SW15 2EA, UNITED KINGDOM (UK)

Baker, Danny (Radio Personality)
c/o Staff Member *Noel Gay Artists*
19 Denmark St
London WC2H 8NA, United Kingdom

Baker, Dave (Athlete, Baseball Player)
22234 S23 Hwy
Lacona, IA 50139-6669, USA

Baker, Diane (Actor)
2733 Outpost Dr
Los Angeles, CA 90068-2061, USA

Baker, Donald K (Cinematographer)
144 Sierra Sunrise Way
Auburn, CA 95603-3272, USA

Baker, Doug (Athlete, Baseball Player)
116 Woodthrush Ln
Fallbrook, CA 92028-4149, USA

Baker, Dylan (Actor)
c/o Lisa Loosemore *Viking Entertainment*
445 W 23rd St Ste 1A
New York, NY 10011-1445, USA

Baker, Earl P Jr (War Hero)
10100 Cypress Cove Dr
Fort Myers, FL 33908-7638, USA

Baker, Edward (Athlete, Football Player)
45 Smull Ave
Caldwell, NJ 07006-5099, USA

Baker, Ellen Shulman (Astronaut)
2207 Garden Stream Ct
Houston, TX 77062-3650, USA

Baker, Frank (Athlete, Baseball Player)
PO Box 3066
Meridian, MS 39303-3066, USA

Baker, Ginger (Musician)
4230 Del Rey Ave # 621
Marina Del Rey, CA 90292-5603, USA

Baker, Graham (Director)
10 Buckingham St
London WC2, UNITED KINGDOM (UK)

Baker, Jack (Athlete, Baseball Player)
5513 Hunters Hill Rd
Irondale, AL 35210-3011, USA

Baker, James A (Bubba) (Athlete, Football Player)
2784 Trinity Ct
Avon, OH 44011-1951, USA

Baker, Jamie (Athlete, Hockey Player)
116 Mozart Ave
Los Gatos, CA 95032-1948, USA

Baker, Janet A (Musician, Opera Singer)
8 Bristol Gardens
London W9 2JG, UNITED KINGDOM (UK)

Baker, Jason (Athlete, Football Player)
435 S Tryon St Unit 906
Charlotte, NC 28202-1922, USA

Baker, Jerry (Athlete, Football Player)
7780 W 38th Ave Apt 305
Wheat Ridge, CO 80033-6103, USA

Baker, Joe Don (Actor)
c/o Michael Livingston *Leavitt Talent Group*
8255 W Sunset Blvd
West Hollywood, CA 90046-2417, USA

Baker, John (Athlete, Football Player)
1616 Battery Dr
Raleigh, NC 27610-3365, USA

Baker, John F Jr (War Hero)
104 Founders Ridge Rd
Columbia, SC 29229-7617, USA

Baker, John R (General)
Vice Commander Air Mobility Command
Scott Air Force Base, IL 62225, USA

Baker, John W (Athlete, Football Player)
72 Oak Village Blvd S
Homosassa, FL 34446-5945, USA

Baker, Johnnie B (Dusty) (Athlete, Baseball Player, Coach)
40 Livingston Terrace Dr
San Bruno, CA 94066-2800, USA

Baker, Kathy (Actor)
c/o Rebecca (Becca) Kovacik *Hofflund/Polone*
9465 Wilshire Blvd Ste 420
Beverly Hills, CA 90212-2603, USA

Baker, Keith (Athlete, Football Player)
3203 S Marsalis Ave
Dallas, TX 75216-5203, USA

Baker, Kendall L (Educator)
525 S Main St Lehr Memorial 201A
Ada, OH 45810-6000, USA

Baker, Kenny (Actor)
51 Mulgrave Rd Avenue Ashton
Preston, Lancashire PR2 1HJ, UK

Baker, Kitana (Actor)
c/o Jason Newman *Untitled Entertainment (LA)*
350 S Beverly Dr Ste 200
Beverly Hills, CA 90212-4819, USA

Baker, Laurie (Athlete, Hockey Player)
67 Prairie St
Concord, MA 01742-2924, USA

Baker, Lewis (Musician)
PO Box 1017
Turnersville, NJ 08012-0837, USA

Baker, Loris (Athlete, Football Player)
1009 Brentwood Pl
Fircrest, WA 98466-5922, USA

Baker, Michael A (Mike) (Astronaut)
2101 Nasa Pkwy Spc Center
Houston, TX 77058-3607, USA

Baker, Myron (Athlete, Football Player)
297 Peart Rd
Alexandria, LA 71302-9344, USA

Baker, Paul T (Misc)
1000 Escalon Ave Apt A3005
Sunnyvale, CA 94085-1638, USA

Baker, Peter (Athlete, Golfer)
1360 E 9th St Ste 100
Cleveland, OH 44114-1730, USA

Baker, Rae (Actor)
c/o Staff Member *Marmont Management*
Langham House 308 Regent St
London W1B 3AT, UNITED KINGDOM (UK)

Baker, Ralph (Athlete, Football Player)
36 Sunshine Cir
Lewistown, PA 17044-9264, USA

Baker, Raymond (Actor)
253A 26th St # 312
Santa Monica, CA 90402, USA

Baker, Rick (Stylist)
c/o Staff Member *Cinovation Studios*
6527 San Fernando Rd
Glendale, CA 91201-2108, USA

Baker, Robby (Musician)
219 Dufferin St # 309B
Toronto, ON M5K 3J1, CANADA

Baker, Robert (Actor)
c/o Amanda Glazer *Kohner Agency, The*
9300 Wilshire Blvd Ste 555
Beverly Hills, CA 90212-3211, USA

Baker, Robert (Attorney, Attorney General, General)
2850 Ocean Park Blvd
Santa Monica, CA 90405-2955, USA

Baker, Ron (Athlete, Football Player)
1119 S Main St
Stillwater, OK 74074-4639, USA

Baker, Roy Ward (Director)
c/o Staff Member *Directors Guild Of Great Britain*
4 Windmill St
London W1T 2HZ, UK

Baker, Scott (Athlete, Baseball Player)
327 Lingering Ln
Henderson, NV 89012-3262, USA

Baker, Scott (Athlete, Baseball Player)
9785 Bayou Bend Dr
Shreveport, LA 71115-8518, USA

Baker, Scott Thompson (Actor)
17651 Sidwell St
Granada Hills, CA 91344-1054, USA

Baker, Shaun (Actor)
c/o Staff Member *Brady, Brannon & Rich Talent*
5670 Wilshire Blvd Ste 820
Los Angeles, CA 90036-5613, USA

Baker, Simon (Actor)
c/o Beth Holden-Garland *Untitled Entertainment (LA)*
350 S Beverly Dr Ste 200
Beverly Hills, CA 90212-4819, USA

Baker, Stephen (Athlete, Football Player)
280 Water St
Perth Amboy, NJ 08861-4427, USA

Baker, Steve (Athlete, Baseball Player)
27527 Easy Acres Dr
Eugene, OR 97405-4500, USA

Baker, Steve (Athlete, Hockey Player)
2431 E Cheryl Dr
Phoenix, AZ 85028-4316, USA

Baker, Terry (Athlete, Football Player)
3208 SW Fairmount Blvd
Portland, OR 97239-1443, USA

Baker, Terry (Athlete, Football Player)
3208 SW Fairmount Blvd
Portland, OR 97239-1443, USA

Baker, Tom (Actor, Writer)
c/o Edward Hill *Edward Hill Management*
Dolphin House 2-5 Manchester Street
London BN2 1TF, United Kingdom

Baker, Vernon J (War Hero)
650 Vemon Ln
Saint Maries, ID 83861, USA

Baker, Vin (Athlete, Basketball Player)
PO Box 179
Old Saybrook, CT 06475-0179, USA

Baker, W Thane (Athlete, Track Athlete)
6704 Saint John Ct
Granbury, TX 76049-4520, USA

Baker, Wayne (Athlete, Football Player)
209 Needmore Rd
Waco, KY 40385-9030, USA

Baker, William (Bill) (Athlete, Hockey Player)
5638 Ojibwa Rd
Brainerd, MN 56401-7017, USA

Baker, William O (Misc)
600 Mountain Ave
New Providence, NJ 07974-2008, USA

Baker III, James A (Politician)
One Shell Plz # 910
Houston, TX 77002-4916, USA

Baker Jr, Howard H (Diplomat, Ex-Senator, Politician)
10-1-1 Akasaka Minatoku
Tokyo 7-Jan, JAPAN

Baker Jr, Leslie M (Business Person, Financier)
1166 Avenue of the Americas
New York, NY 10036-2708, USA

Baker-Finch, Ian (Athlete, Golfer)
849 Harbour Isle Pl
West Palm Beach, FL 33410-4408, USA

Bakhtair, Rudi (Correspondent)
1050 Techwood Dr NW
Atlanta, GA 30318-5604, USA

Bakke, Brenda (Actor)
c/o Staff Member *House of Representatives, The*
1434 6th St Ste 1
Santa Monica, CA 90401-2527, USA

Bakkedahl, Dan (Actor)
c/o Christie Smith *Mosaic Media Group*
9200 W Sunset Blvd Ste 10
Los Angeles, CA 90069-3608, USA

Bakken, Earl (Doctor, Inventor)
68-1399 Mauna Lani Dr
Kamuela, HI 96743-9785, USA

Bakken, James L (Jim) (Athlete, Football Player)
4801 Holiday Dr
Madison, WI 53711-1329, USA

Bakker, James O (Jim) (Religious Leader)
180 Grace Chapel Rd Unit 201
Blue Eye, MO 65611-4207, USA

Bako, Brigitte (Actor)
c/o Staff Member *Characters Talent Agency, The (Vancouver)*
1505 W 2nd Ave #200
Vancouver, BC V6H 3Y4, Canada

Bako, Paul (Athlete, Baseball Player)
500 Princeton Woods Loop
Lafayette, LA 70508-6672, USA

Bakovic, Pete (Athlete, Hockey Player)
7991 S 47th St
Franklin, WI 53132-8468, USA

Bakula, Scott (Actor)
c/o Jay Schwartz *Jay D Schwartz & Associates*
3151 Cahuenga Blvd W Ste 220
Los Angeles, CA 90068-1749, USA

Bala, Chris (Athlete, Hockey Player)
271 Beacon Dr
Phoenixville, PA 19460-2046, USA

Balaban, Bob (Director, Producer)
c/o Staff Member *Chicago Films*
101 5th Ave Fl 8
New York, NY 10003-1008, USA

Balaban, Liane (Actor)
c/o Ralph Zimmerman *Great North Artists Management Inc (Canada)*
350 Duponte
Tononto, Ontario M5R 1V9, Canada

Baladmenti, Angelo (Composer)
4146 Lankershim Blvd Ste 401
North Hollywood, CA 91602-2832, USA

Balambika (Actor, Bollywood)
3 Indira Gandhi St
Chennai, TN 600093, INDIA

Balandin, Aleksandr N (Cosmonaut)
Moskovskoi Oblasti
Syvisdny Goroduk 141160, RUSSIA

Balas, Mike
8807 Bluehaw Mdw Ln
Katy, TX 77494-0479, USA

Balassa, Sandor (Composer)
18 Sumegvar Str
Budapest 1118, HUNGARY

Balasubramaniyam, S P (Actor, Musician)
16 Kamdar Nagar Nungambakkam
Chennai, TN 600 034, INDIA

Balaz, John (Athlete, Baseball Player)
2916 Worden St
San Diego, CA 92110-5708, USA

Balazs, Andre (Business Person)
295 Lafayette St
New York, NY 10012-2701, USA

Balboa, Marcelo (Soccer Player)
13139 Hedda Dr
Cerritos, CA 90703-6146, USA

Balboni, Steve (Athlete, Baseball Player)
117 Burlington Rd
New Providence, NJ 07974-2709, USA

Balcazar, Javier Hernández (Athlete, Soccer Player)
c/o Staff Member *Manchester United PLC*
Sir Matt Busby Way Old Trafford
Manchester M160RA, UNITED KINGDOM

Balcer, Rene (Producer, Writer)
c/o Adam Berkowitz *Creative Artists Agency (CAA-LA)*
2000 Avenue of the Stars Ste 100
Los Angeles, CA 90067-4705, USA

Baldacci, David (Writer)
c/o Aaron Priest *Aaron M. Priest Literary Agency*
708 3rd Ave Rm 2301
New York, NY 10017-4212, USA

Baldacci, Lou (Athlete, Football Player)
983 Coral Dr
Pebble Beach, CA 93953-2538, USA

Baldassin, Mike (Athlete, Football Player)
7914 Interlaaken Dr SW
Lakewood, WA 98498-5707, USA

Baldavin, Barbara (Actor)
228 17th St
Manhattan Beach, CA 90266-4634, USA

Baldelli, Rocco (Athlete, Baseball Player)
8455 13th St N Apt D
Saint Petersburg, FL 33702-7950, USA

Balderis, Helmut (Athlete, Hockey Player)
Raunas lela 23
Riga LV-1039, Latvia

Balderstone, James S (Business Person)
115 Mont Albert Rd
Canterbuy, VIC 3126, AUSTRALIA

Baldeschwieler, John D (Misc)
PO Box 50065
Pasadena, CA 91115-0065, USA

Baldessari, John (Artist)
626 Vernon Ave
Venice, CA 90291-2737, USA

Balding, Rebecca (Actor)
2001 Winnetka Pl
Woodland Hills, CA 91364, USA

Baldinger, Brian (Athlete, Football Player, Sportscaster)
21 S Elmwood Rd
Marlton, NJ 08053-2562, USA

Baldinger, Gary (Athlete, Football Player)
114 Adam Rd
Massapequa, NY 11758-8102, USA

Baldinger, Rich (Athlete, Football Player)
5401 Phelps Rd
Kansas City, MO 64136-1224, USA

Baldischwiler, Karl (Athlete, Football Player)
3033 N Willow Dr
Newcastle, OK 73065-6456, USA

Baldissin, Mike (Athlete, Football Player)
13834 Bandix Rd SE
Olalla, WA 98359-9467, USA

Baldock, Bobby R (Judge)
PO Box 2388
Roswell, NM 88202-2388, USA

Baldoni, Justin (Actor)
c/o Adam Griffin *Kritzer Levine Wilkins Entertainment*
11872 La Grange Ave Fl 1
Los Angeles, CA 90025-5283, USA

Baldridge, Letitia (Business Person, Writer)
2339 Massachusetts Ave NW
Washington, DC 20008-2803, USA

Baldrige, Leticia (Writer)
2339 Massachusetts Ave NW
Washington, DC 20008-2803, USA

Baldry, Long John (Musician)
1505 W 2nd Ave # 200
Vancouver, BC V6H 3Y4, CANADA

Baldschun, Jack E (Athlete, Baseball Player)
311 Erie Rd
Green Bay, WI 54311-7706, USA

Baldwin, Adam (Actor)
c/o Abe Hoch *A Management Company*
9107 Wilshire Blvd Ste 650
Beverly Hills, CA 90210-5544, USA

Baldwin, Alec (Actor)
c/o Matthew Hiltzik *Hiltzik Strategies*
381 Park Ave S Rm 1201
New York, NY 10016-8820, USA

Baldwin, Billy (Athlete, Baseball Player)
878 Packard Dr
Akron, OH 44320-2816, USA

Baldwin, Burr (Athlete, Football Player)
219 S Plateau Dr
West Covina, CA 91791-2230, USA

Baldwin, Daniel (Actor)
c/o John McGalliard *Chaotik*
1568 N Serrano Ave
Los Angeles, CA 90027-4873, USA

Baldwin, Dave (Athlete, Baseball Player)
PO Box 190
Yachats, OR 97498-0190, USA

Baldwin, Don (Athlete, Football Player)
3624 Wind Chime Ln
Saint Charles, MO 63301-7405, USA

Baldwin, Doug (Athlete, Hockey Player)
180 Cook Ave
Gimli, MB R0C 1B0, Canada

Baldwin, Howard (Producer)
c/o Staff Member *Baldwin Entertainment*
9200 W Sunset Blvd Ste 550
West Hollywood, CA 90069-3611, USA

Baldwin, Jack (Race Car Driver)
4748 Balmoral Way NE
Marietta, GA 30068-1604, USA

Baldwin, Jack E (Misc)
Dyson Perrins Lab S Park Rd
Oxford OX1 3QY, UNITED KINGDOM (UK)

Baldwin, James (Athlete, Baseball Player)
18 Monteith Pl
Pinehurst, NC 28374-8542, USA

Baldwin, Jeff (Athlete, Baseball Player)
70 Goodwill Rd
Huntington, WV 25704-8820, USA

Baldwin, Jerry (Business Person)
1400 Park Ave
Emeryville, CA 94608-3520, USA

Baldwin, John A (Jack) Jr (Admiral)
1371 Millersville Rd
Millersville, MD 21108-2120, USA

Baldwin, John W (Historian)
History Dept
Baltimore, MD 21218, USA

Baldwin, Jonathan (Football Player)
c/o Ken Zuckerman *Priority Sports & Entertainment - (LA)*
15233 Ventura Blvd Ste 718
Sherman Oaks, CA 91403-2237, USA

Baldwin, Judy (Actor)
c/o Larry Metzger *Grant Savic Kopaloff & Associates*
6399 Wilshire Blvd Ste 414
Los Angeles, CA 90048-5716, USA

Baldwin, Keith M (Athlete, Football Player)
124 Leonardville Rd
Belford, NJ 07718-1131, USA

Baldwin, Margaret (Writer)
PO Box 1106
Williams Bay, WI 53191-1106, USA

Baldwin, Matisha (Actor)
c/o Marianne Golan *Marianne Golan Management*
6528 W 6th St
Los Angeles, CA 90048-4716, USA

Baldwin, Randy (Athlete, Football Player)
862 S 9th St
Griffin, GA 30224-4823, USA

Baldwin, Reggie (Athlete, Baseball Player)
PO Box 970816
Ypsilanti, MI 48197-0116, USA

Baldwin, Rick (Athlete, Baseball Player)
2601 Stoneridge Dr
Modesto, CA 95355-3454, USA

Baldwin, Robert E (Economist)
125 Nautilus Dr
Madison, WI 53705-4329, USA

Baldwin, Stephen (Actor)
c/o Alex D'Andrea *Edmonds Management*
1635 N Cahuenga Blvd Fl 5
Los Angeles, CA 90028-6201, USA

Baldwin, Tammy (Congressman, Politician)
2446 Rayburn Hob
Washington, DC 20515-3703, USA

Baldwin, William (Editor)
60 5th Ave
New York, NY 10011-8868, USA

Baldwin, William (Billy) (Actor)
c/o Daniel (Danny) Sussman *Brillstein Entertainment Partners*
9150 Wilshire Blvd Ste 350
Beverly Hills, CA 90212-3453, USA

Bale, Christian (Actor)
c/o Jennifer Allen *Viewpoint Inc*
8820 Wilshire Blvd Ste 220
Beverly Hills, CA 90211-2622, USA

Bale, John (Athlete, Baseball Player)
PO Box 806
Crestview, FL 32536-0806, USA

Bales, Lee (Athlete, Baseball Player)
7422 Greatwood Lake Dr
Sugar Land, TX 77479-6302, USA

Bales, Michael (Athlete, Hockey Player)
470 Brunswick Ave
Toronto, ON M5R 2Z5, Canada

Balfour, Earl (Athlete, Hockey Player)
71 Beasley Cres
Cambridge, ON N1T 1P5, Canada

Balfour, Eric (Actor)
c/o David Gardner *Principato/Young Management*
9465 Wilshire Blvd Ste 430
Beverly Hills, CA 90212-2613, USA

Balfour, Grant (Athlete, Baseball Player)
2276 Lauren Ln
Clearwater, FL 33759-1437, USA

Balgimbayev, Nurlan (Prime Minister)
Pl im Vl Lenina
Astana 148008, KAZAKHSTAN

Baliani, Marco (Actor)
Via Giuseppe Pisanelli
Rome 196, ITALY

Baliles, Gerald L (Ex-Governor)
Riverfront Plaza East Tower 951 E Byrd St
Richmond, VA 23219, USA

Balitran, Celine (Model)
c/o Staff Member *Ford Models (NY)*
238 E 4th St
New York, NY 10009-7425

Balk, Fairuza (Actor)
1180 S Beverly Dr Ste 601
Los Angeles, CA 90035-1158, USA

Balkenende, Jan-Peter (Prime Minister)
Binnenhof 20 Postbus 20001
EA Hague, NETHERLANDS

Balkenhol, Klaus (Athlete)
Narzissenweg 11A
Hilden 40723, GERMANY

Ball, Alan (Producer)
c/o Andrew Cannava *United Talent Agency (UTA)*
9560 Wilshire Blvd Fl 5
Beverly Hills, CA 90212-2400, USA

Ball, Dave (Athlete, Football Player)
9234 Carrisbrook Ln
Brentwood, TN 37027-4883, USA

Ball, David (Musician)
38 Music Sq E Ste 300
Nashville, TN 37203-4304, USA

Ball, Edward (Writer)
19 Union Sq W
New York, NY 10003-3304, USA

Ball, Eric C (Athlete, Football Player)
10614 Margate Ter
Cincinnati, OH 45241-3000, USA

Ball, Ian (Musician)
c/o Staff Member *Paradigm (Monterey)*
404 W Franklin St
Monterey, CA 93940-2303, USA

Ball, Jason (Athlete, Football Player)
325 S Jessie Doe
Durham, NH 3824, USA

Ball, Jeff (Athlete, Baseball Player)
740 18th Pl
Vero Beach, FL 32960-5408, USA

Ball, Jerry L (Athlete, Football Player)
3311 Meadowside Dr
Sugar Land, TX 77478-4051, USA

Ball, Larry (Athlete, Football Player)
8830 SW 57th St
Cooper City, FL 33328-5100, USA

Ball, Marcia (Musician)
PO Box 2629
Austin, TX 78768-2629, USA

Ball, Michael A (Actor, Musician)
PO Box 2073
Colchester, Essex CO4 3WS, UNITED KINGDOM (UK)

Ball, Robert (Athlete, Football Player)
6412 E Claire Dr
Scottsdale, AZ 85254-2623, USA

Ball, Sam (Actor)
232 N Canon Dr
Beverly Hills, CA 90210-5302, USA

Ball, Sam (Athlete, Football Player)
1220 Glenshiel Dr
Henderson, KY 42420-2530, USA

Ball, Taylor (Actor)
c/o Shannon Barr *Shannon Barr Public Relations*
3313 N Sepulveda Blvd
Manhattan Beach, CA 90266-3626, USA

Ball, Terry (Athlete, Hockey Player)
4502 Torrington Ave
Parma, OH 44134-2163, USA

Balladur, Edouard (Prime Minister)
5 Rue Jean Formige
Paris 75015, FRANCE

Ballantine, Sara (Actor)
5670 Wilshire Blvd Ste 820
Los Angeles, CA 90036-5613, USA

Ballantyne (Designer, Fashion Designer)
c/o Staff Member *Ballantyne*
4-6 Savile Road
London, England W1S 3PD, United Kingdom

Ballard, Carroll (Director)
PO Box 556
Saint Helena, CA 94574-5056, USA

Ballard, Del Jr (Bowler)
PO Box 746
Hopkinsville, KY 42241-0746, USA

Ballard, Donald E (War Hero)
PO Box 34593
North Kansas City, MO 64116-0993, USA

Ballard, Florence (Musician)
c/o Staff Member *Diva Central Inc*
7510 W Sunset Blvd Ste 1445
Los Angeles, CA 90046-3408, USA

Ballard, Greg (Athlete, Basketball Player)
100 Arborcrest Ct
Tyrone, GA 30290-1555, USA

Ballard, Howard (Athlete, Football Player)
PO Box 584
Ashland, AL 36251-0584, USA

Ballard, Jeff (Athlete, Baseball Player)
4828 Rimrock Rd
Billings, MT 59106-1317, USA

Ballard, Kaye (Actor)
PO Box 922
Rancho Mirage, CA 92270-0922, USA

Ballard, Keith (Athlete, Hockey Player)
2336 River Pointe Cir
Minneapolis, MN 55411-4414, USA

Ballard, Quinton (Athlete, Football Player)
4005 Saint Patrick Dr
Greensboro, NC 27406-6420, USA

Ballard, Robert D (Oceanographer)
55 Coogan Blvd
Mystic, CT 06355-1927, USA

Ballas, Mark (Dancer, Reality TV Star)
c/o Jessica Cohen *JCPR*
9903 Santa Monica Blvd Ste 983
Beverly Hills, CA 90212-1671, USA

Ballatore, Antonio (Stylist)
c/o Celebrity Stylist *Creative Exchange Agency*
53 Gansevoort St Ste 3
New York, NY 10014-1414, USA

Baller, Jay (Athlete, Baseball Player)
303 Spring Valley Rd
Reading, PA 19605-2747, USA

Ballerini, Edoardo (Actor)
c/o Gina Rugolo-Judd *Rugolo Entertainment*
195 S Beverly Dr Ste 400
Beverly Hills, CA 90212-3044, USA

Ballesteros, Roberto (Actor)
c/o Staff Member *Televisa*
Blvd Adolfo Lopez Mateos 232 Colonia San Angel INN
DF CP 01060, MEXICO

Ballesteros, Seveiano (Seve) (Athlete, Golfer)
C/Padaje del Pena no 2 Curata Planta
Santander E-39008, Spain

Ballestros, Anderson (Actor)
c/o J R Heermans *LatinActors*
920 Leavenworth St Apt 302
San Francisco, CA 94109-4907

Balley, Otha (Athlete, Baseball Player)
937 6th Pl SW
Birmingham, AL 35211-1743, USA

Ballhaus, Florian M (Cinematographer)
115 Berkeley Pl
Brooklyn, NY 11217-3603, USA

Ballhaus, Michael (Cinematographer)
11 Elm Pl
Rye, NY 10580-2918, USA

Ballingall, Chris (Athlete, Baseball Player)
52879 25th St
Mattawan, MI 49071-8803, USA

Ballinger, Mark (Athlete, Baseball Player)
1212 SW 5th Ave
Okeechobee, FL 34974-5014, USA

Ballmer, Steven A (Business Person)
1 Microsoft Way
Redmond, WA 98052-8300, USA

Ballon, Adrienne (Actor)
c/o Staff Member *International Creative Management (ICM-LA)*
10250 Constellation Blvd Fl 7
Los Angeles, CA 90067-6207, USA

Ballou, Mark (Actor)
c/o Staff Member *Imperium 7 Talent Agency*
5455 Wilshire Blvd Ste 1706
Los Angeles, CA 90036-4217, USA

Ballou, Tyson (Model)
c/o Staff Member *IMG*
304 Park Ave S Fl 12
New York, NY 10010-4314, USA

Balmaseda, Liz (Journalist)
1 Herald Plz
Miami, FL 33132-1609, USA

Balmer, Jean-Francois (Actor, Director)
c/o Staff Member *ArtMedia*
20 avenue Rapp
Paris 75008, France

Balog, Bob (Athlete, Football Player)
331 Monongahela Ave
Glassport, PA 15045-1439, USA

Balraaj, Anand (Actor, Bollywood)
7 2/1 Av Villa Kakori Camp Aram Nagar
Seven Bungalows Versova Andheri
Mumbai, MS 400058, INDIA

Balsam, Talia (Actor)
c/o Sue Leibman *Barking Dog Entertainment*
9 Desbrosses St Fl 2
New York, NY 10013-1701, USA

Balsamo, Tony (Athlete, Baseball Player)
15 Doral Ln
Bay Shore, NY 11706-8840, USA

Balsley, Philip E (Musician)
191 Abbington Rd
Swoope, VA 24479-2217, USA

Baltes, Jameson (Actor)
PO Box 64249
Los Angeles, CA 90064-0249, USA

Baltica, Kremerata (Musician)
c/o Staff Member *International Creative Management (ICM-LA)*
10250 Constellation Blvd Fl 7
Los Angeles, CA 90067-6207, USA

Baltimore, Bryon (Athlete, Hockey Player)
2401-10088 102 Ave NW
Edmonton, AB T5J 2Z1, Canada

Baltimore, David (Educator, Nobel Prize Laureate)
31460 Beach Park Rd
Malibu, CA 90265, USA

Baltray, Charies (Astronomer)
Astronomy Dept
New Haven, CT 6520, USA

Baltron, Donna (Actor)
1925 Century Park E Ste 750
Los Angeles, CA 90067-2708, USA

Baltsa, Agnes (Opera Singer)
Wasagasse 12/1/3
Vienna 1090, AUSTRIA

Baltz, Lewis (Photographer)
11693 San Vicente Blvd # 527
Los Angeles, CA 90049-5105, USA

Baluik, Stan (Athlete, Hockey Player)
46 Kent St
Cumberland, RI 02864-7032, USA

Balukas, Jean (Billiards Player)
9818 4th Ave
Brooklyn, NY 11209-8102, USA

Balul, Oksana (Figure Skater)
PO Box 988
Niantic, CT 06357-0988, USA

Bama, James (Artist)
27 Dunn Creek Rd
Cody, WY 82414-7878, USA

Bama, Jim (Artist)
27 Dunn Creek Rd
Cody, WY 82414-7878, USA

Bamber, Jamie
c/o Alan Siegel *Alan Siegel Entertainment*
345 N Maple Dr Ste 375
Beverly Hills, CA 90210-5174, USA

Bamberger, Hal (Athlete, Baseball Player)
480 Mountz Rd
Birdsboro, PA 19508-8011, USA

Bamford, Maria (Actor)
c/o Bob Read *ReBar Management*
10061 Riverside Dr # 722
Toluca Lake, CA 91602-2560

Bana, Eric (Actor, Comedian)
c/o Lauren Bergman *Lauren Bergman Management*
37 Browns Road, Main Ridge
Victoria 3227, Australia

Banach, Edward (Ed) (Wrestler)
2128 Country Club Blvd
Ames, IA 50014-7061, USA

Banach, Louis (Lou) (Wrestler)
3276 E Fairfax Rd
Cleveland Heights, OH 44118-4206, USA

Banachowski, Andy (Athlete, Coach, Volleyball Player)
Athletic Dept - J.D. Morgan Center P.O. Box 24044
Los Angeles, CA 90024, USA

Banaszak, John A (Athlete, Football Player)
420 Robinhood Ln
Canonsburg, PA 15317-2717, USA

Banaszak, Pete (Athlete, Football Player)
1021 Inverness Dr
Saint Augustine, FL 32092-2787, USA

Banaszek, Cas (Athlete, Football Player)
1018 Cohen Ct
Petaluma, CA 94952-5263, USA

Banaszek, Nancy Koutek (Stylist)
5448 N Lakewood Ave
Chicago, IL 60640-1303, USA

Banaszynski, Jacqui (Journalist)
345 Cedar St
Saint Paul, MN 55101-1004, USA

Banbury, F H Frith (Director)
18 Park Saint James Prince Albert Road
London NW8 7LE, UNITED KINGDOM (UK)

Bancroft, Cameron (Actor)
c/o Staff Member *Gersh (LA)*
9465 Wilshire Blvd Ste 600
Beverly Hills, CA 90212-2612, USA

Band, Richard H (Composer)
24053 Bessemer St
Woodland Hills, CA 91367-2919, USA

Band of Bees, A (Music Group)
c/o Staff Member *Paradigm (Monterey)*
404 W Franklin St
Monterey, CA 93940-2303, USA

Banda El Limon, Arrolladora (Music Group)
c/o Staff Member *Sony Music Miami*
605 Lincoln Rd Ste 700
Miami Beach, FL 33139-2901, USA

Banda Imperio (Music Group, Musician)
c/o Staff Member *Morena Music*
5021 Columbus Ave
Sherman Oaks, CA 91403-1251, USA

Banda Pachuco (Music Group)
c/o Staff Member *Sony Music Miami*
605 Lincoln Rd Ste 700
Miami Beach, FL 33139-2901, USA

Banderas, Antonio (Actor, Director, Musician, Producer)
c/o Robin Baum *Slate Public Relations*
9000 W Sunset Blvd Ste 915
West Hollywood, CA 90069-5809, USA

Bandholz, Antonio (Misc)
Sohnholm 92
Westerholz 24977, GERMANY

Bandiera, Bob (Bobby) (Musician)
104 Ocean Blvd
Atlantic Highlands, NJ 07716-1523, USA

Bando, Chris (Athlete, Baseball Player)
638 Walsall Rd
El Cajon, CA 92019-2667, USA

Bando, Salvatore L (Sal) (Athlete, Baseball Player)
W308N6225 Shore Acres Rd
Hartland, WI 53029-8723, USA

Bandura, Jeff (Athlete, Hockey Player)
1306 Cambria Dr
Joliet, IL 60431-7542, USA

Bandy, Don (Athlete, Football Player)
215 E Calvin St
Taft, CA 93268-2915, USA

Bandy, Moe (Musician, Songwriter, Writer)
PO Box 5331
Sevierville, TN 37864-5331, USA

Bane (Music Group, Musician)
c/o Mike Pike *Kenmore Agency, The*
59 Park St Ste 2
Beverly, MA 01915-4255, USA

Bane, Eddie (Athlete, Baseball Player)
1132 Los Campaneros
San Marcos, CA 92078-5225, USA

Banes, Lisa (Actor)
c/o Tim Angle *Don Buchwald & Associates Inc (LA)*
6500 Wilshire Blvd Ste 2200
Los Angeles, CA 90048-4942, USA

Baney, Dick (Athlete, Baseball Player)
2231 Northup Dr
Tustin, CA 92782-1028, USA

Banfield, Ashleigh (Correspondent)
c/o Staff Member *NBC Universal (NY)*
30 Rockefeller Plz Fl 270E
New York, NY 10112-0299, USA

Bang, Molly (Writer)
43 Drumlin Rd
Falmouth, MA 02540-2505, USA

Bang Lime (Music Group)
c/o Staff Member *Paradigm (Monterey)*
404 W Franklin St
Monterey, CA 93940-2303, USA

Bangemann, Martin (Government Official)
200 Rue de la Loi
Brussels 1049, BELGIUM

Bangles, The (Music Group)
c/o Staff Member *Agency Group Ltd, The (UK)*
361-373 City Rd
London EC1V 1PQ, UK

Banham, Frank (Athlete, Hockey Player)
139 W Grayling Ln
Suffield, CT 06078-1960, USA

Banhart, Bobby (Reality TV Star)
c/o Elizabeth Much *Much and House Public Relations*
8075 W 3rd St Ste 500
Los Angeles, CA 90048-4325, USA

Bani, John (President)
Port Vila, VANUATU

Banister, Jeff (Athlete, Baseball Player)
5228 Hidden Brook Ln
League City, TX 77573-5783, USA

Bank, Frank (Actor)
PO Box 902
N Palm Springs, CA 92258, USA

Bank, Melissa (Producer, Writer)
c/o Sylvie Rabineau *Rabineau Wachter and Sanford Literary Agency*
1107 1/2 Glendon Ave
Los Angeles, CA 90024-3501, USA

Banke, Paul (Boxer)
1926 Bobolink Way
Pomona, CA 91767-2828, USA

Banker, Ted (Athlete, Football Player)
1862 Park Ave
East Meadow, NY 11554-4007, USA

Bankhead, Scott (Athlete, Baseball Player)
1236 Idlewood Dr
Asheboro, NC 27205-4119, USA

Banks, Brian (Athlete, Baseball Player)
2232 E 900 S
Salt Lake City, UT 84108-1404, USA

Banks, Brian (Stylist)
c/o Staff Member *Rex Agency, The*
6311 Romaine St
Los Angeles, CA 90038-2617, USA

Banks, Brianna (Adult Film Star)
c/o Staff Member *Atlas Multimedia Inc*
9005 Eton Ave Ste C
Canoga Park, CA 91304-6533, USA

Banks, Carl (Athlete, Football Player)
7 Glenview Dr
Warren, NJ 07059-5476, USA

Banks, Chip (Athlete, Football Player)
55 Fair Haven Way SE
Smyrna, GA 30080-8087, USA

Banks, Chuck (Athlete, Football Player)
3705 Valley Hill Dr
Randallstown, MD 21133-4822, USA

Banks, Darren (Athlete, Hockey Player)
11 Millington Rd
Pleasant Ridge, MI 48069-1108, USA

Banks, David (Actor)
2-5 Stedham Pl Bloomsbury
London WC1A 1BU, ENGLAND

Banks, Dennis (Misc)
Oglala, SD 57764, USA

Banks, Elizabeth (Actor)
c/o Alissa Vradenburg *Untitled Entertainment (LA)*
350 S Beverly Dr Ste 200
Beverly Hills, CA 90212-4819, USA

Banks, Ernie (Athlete, Baseball Player)
27 N Wacker Dr # 466
Chicago, IL 60606-2800, USA

Banks, Fred (Athlete, Football Player)
5665 Orly Ter
Atlanta, GA 30349-3807, USA

Banks, Gene (Athlete, Basketball Player)
219 Rock St
Bluefield, WV 24701-2100, USA

Banks, Gene (Athlete, Basketball Player)
1210 Sloan St
Greensboro, NC 27401-3442, USA

Banks, Gordon (Athlete, Football Player)
2644 E Trinity Mills Rd
Carrollton, TX 75006-2136, USA

Banks, John (Athlete, Baseball Player)
902 Somerdale Rd
Voorhees, NJ 08043-1318, USA

Banks, Jonathan (Actor)
909 Euclid St Apt 8
Santa Monica, CA 90403-3097, USA

Banks, Lloyd (Musician)
c/o Staff Member *Interscope Records (LA) - Main*
2220 Colorado Ave
Santa Monica, CA 90404-3506, USA

Banks, Morwenna (Actor, Writer)
c/o Staff Member *International Creative Management (ICM-LA)*
10250 Constellation Blvd Fl 7
Los Angeles, CA 90067-6207, USA

Banks, Robert (Athlete, Football Player)
2412 Laguard Dr
Hampton, VA 23661-2418, USA

Banks, Russell (Writer)
English Debt
Princeton, NJ 08544-0001, USA

Banks, Skeeter (Athlete, Baseball Player)
3810 Castlewood Rd
Richmond, VA 23234-2612, USA

Banks, Steven (Actor, Comedian)
232 N Canon Dr
Beverly Hills, CA 90210-5302, USA

Banks, Steven Gary (Producer, Writer)
c/o Staff Member *Evolution Entertainment (LA)*
901 N Highland Ave
Los Angeles, CA 90038-2412, USA

Banks, Ted (Coach)
Athletic Dept
Riverside, CA 92506, USA

Banks, Tom (Athlete, Football Player)
358 Wisteria St
Fairhope, AL 36532-1729, USA

Banks, Tony (Athlete, Football Player)
735 Laguna
Irving, TX 75039-3218, USA

Banks, Tyra (Actor, Model, Producer)
c/o Charlie Dougiello *The Door*
246 Withers St Apt 1B
Brooklyn, NY 11211-1570, USA

Banks, Walker (Athlete, Basketball Player)
3207 Brentwood Dr
Champaign, IL 61821-3482, USA

Banks, Willie (Athlete, Baseball Player)
13 Michael St
Jamesburg, NJ 08831-1659, USA

Bankston, Michael (Athlete, Football Player)
938 Kingwood Dr Apt 220
Humble, TX 77339-4446, USA

Bankston, Warren (Athlete, Football Player)
4201 Bordeaux Dr
Kenner, LA 70065-1739, USA

Bannatyne, Duncan
Powerhouse, Haughton Rd Attn: Kim Crowther
Darlington DL1 1ST, UK

Banner, David (Actor, Musician, Producer)
c/o Peter Schwartz *Agency Group Ltd, The (NY)*
142 W 57th St Fl 6
New York, NY 10019-3300, USA

Bannerman, Bill (Director, Producer)
c/o Lawrence Mirisch 1875 Century Park E Ste 2025
Los Angeles, CA 90067, USA

Bannerman, Isabella (Cartoonist)
41 South Dr
Hastings On Hudson, NY 10706-1813, USA

Bannerman, Murray (Athlete, Hockey Player)
7222 Kiowa Rd
Larkspur, CO 80118-9110, USA

Bannister, Alan (Athlete, Baseball Player)
405 48th St NW
Bradenton, FL 34209-1921, USA

Bannister, Alan (Athlete, Baseball Player)
6349 N 78th St Unit 129
Scottsdale, AZ 85250-4771, USA

Bannister, Brian (Athlete, Baseball Player)
6701 E Caballo Dr
Paradise Valley, AZ 85253-2706, USA

Bannister, Floyd F (Athlete, Baseball Player)
6701 E Caballo Dr
Paradise Valley, AZ 85253-2706, USA

Bannister, Ken (Athlete, Basketball Player)
2322 Broadgreen Dr
Missouri City, TX 77489-5002, USA

Bannister, Reggie (Actor, Musician)
4450 California Pl # 315
Long Beach, CA 90807-2209, USA

Bannister, Roger G (Athlete, Scientist, Track Athlete)
21 Bardwell Road
Oxford OX2 6SV, UNITED KINGDOM (UK)

Bannister, Trevor (Actor)
68 Old Brompton Road
London SW7 3LQ, UNITED KINGDOM (UK)

Bannon, Bruce (Athlete, Football Player)
5765 Valley Stream Dr
Doylestown, PA 18902-9417, USA

Bannon, Jack (Actor)
6470 E Sunnyside Rd
Coeur D Alene, ID 83814-9503, USA

Bannon, Shaun (Musician)
9560 Wilshire Blvd # 400
Beverly Hills, CA 90212-2427, USA

Banois, Vincent J (Athlete, Football Player)
24256J Tamarack Trl
Southfield, MI 48075, USA

Banowsky, William S (Business Person, Educator)
PO Box 25125
Oklahoma City, OK 73125-0125, USA

Bansavage, Al (Athlete, Football Player)
PO Box 1172
Jensen Beach, FL 34958-1172, USA

Banta, Brad (Athlete, Football Player)
1100 Smith Ave
Birmingham, MI 48009-2031, USA

Bantock, Nick (Writer)
85 2nd St
San Francisco, CA 94105-3453, USA

Bantom, Mike (Athlete, Basketball Player)
418 Egret Ln
Secaucus, NJ 07094-2219, USA

Bantu, Inanna M (Stylist)
10945 Burbank Blvd # 173
North Hollywood, CA 91601-2524, USA

Banuchandar (Actor)
26 N B Reddy Rd
Chennai, TN 600 017, INDIA

Banx, Brooke (Model)
8491 W Sunset Blvd # 285
W Hollywood, CA 90069-1911, USA

Bao, Joseph Y (Doctor)
17436 Terry Lyn Ln
Cerritos, CA 90703-8522, USA

Bapitha (Actor, Bollywood)
7 Ayyappan Nagar 2nd Street Cinmaya Nagar
Chennai, TN 600111, INDIA

Baptist, Travis (Athlete, Baseball Player)
12269 Deersong Dr
Jacksonville, FL 32218-9038, USA

Baptista, Juan Alfonso (Actor)
c/o Gabriel Blanco *Gabriel Blanco Iglesias (Mexico)*
Rio Balsas 35-32 Colonia Cuauhtemoc
DF 6500, Mexico

Baptiste, Baron (Athlete)
c/o Staff Member *St Martins Press*
175 5th Ave
New York, NY 10010-7703, USA

Baquero, Ivana (Actor)
c/o Tom Drumm *The Safran Company*
8748 Holloway Dr
West Hollywood, CA 90069-2327, USA

Bar, Olaf (Opera Singer)
16 Ave FD Roosevelt
Paris 75008, FRANCE

Barahona, Ralph (Athlete, Hockey Player)
317 1/2 E Plymouth St
Long Beach, CA 90805-5915, USA

Barajas, Rod (Athlete, Baseball Player)
723 Avocado Pl
Del Mar, CA 92014-3943, USA

Barak, Ehud (General, Prime Minister)
16 Hayarkon St
Tel-Aviv 63571, ISRAEL

Baranova, Anastasia (Actor)
c/o Staff Member *Gersh (LA)*
9465 Wilshire Blvd Ste 600
Beverly Hills, CA 90212-2612, USA

Baranski, Christine (Actor)
c/o Lisa Loosemore *Viking Entertainment*
445 W 23rd St Ste 1A
New York, NY 10011-1445, USA

Barany, Istvan (Swimmer)
I Attila Utca 87
Budapest 1012, HUNGARY

Barash, Brandon (Actor)
c/o Martin Berneman *Precision Entertainment*
6338 Wilshire Blvd
Los Angeles, CA 90048-5002, USA

Baratta, Adam (Actor)
c/o Gary Raskin *Raskin Peter Rubin & Simon*
9100 Wilshire Blvd Ste 880W
Beverly Hills, CA 90212-3434, USA

Barbacid, Mariano (Misc)
Melchor Fernandez Almagro 3
Madrid 28029, SPAIN

Barbara, Kingsolver E (Writer)
c/o Staff Member *HarperCollins Publishers*
10 E 53rd St C/O Author Mail Floor 7
New York, NY 10022, USA

Barbarin, Phillipe X I Cardinal (Religious Leader)
1 Place de Fouriere
Lyon Cedex 05 69321, FRANCE

Barbaro, Gary W (Athlete, Football Player)
1000 Giuffrias Ave
Metairie, LA 70001-3649, USA

Barbat, Roxanne (Director, Producer, Writer)
c/o Staff Member *Fantastic Films*
3854 Clayton Ave
Los Angeles, CA 90027-4720, USA

Barbay, Roland (Athlete, Football Player)
1025 Breckenridge Dr
Slidell, LA 70461-5313, USA

Barbeau, Adrienne (Actor, Musician)
8808 S Ridgeley Dr
Los Angeles, CA 90036, USA

Barber, Aaron (Athlete, Basketball Player)
2830 Fillmore St NE
Minneapolis, MN 55418-2936, USA

Barber, Andrea (Actor)
6212 Banner Ave
Los Angeles, CA 90038-2802, USA

Barber, Bill (Athlete, Hockey Player)
1112 Peppertree Ct Unit 223
Sarasota, FL 34242-2236, USA

Barber, Brian (Athlete, Baseball Player)
347 Blue Stone Cir
Winter Garden, FL 34787-5231, USA

Barber, Chris (Musician)
45 High St Huntington
Cambridgeshire PE29 3TE, UNITED KINGDOM (UK)

Barber, Christopher E (Athlete, Football Player)
2621 Monaco Cove Cir
Orlando, FL 32825-8442, USA

Barber, Don (Athlete, Hockey Player)
1275 Park Ave
Washington, PA 15301-5949, USA

Barber, Glynis (Actor)
11-12 Dover St Mayfair
London W1S 4LJ, UK

Barber, John (Athlete, Basketball Player)
1554 Mahan St
Orangeburg, SC 29118-3546, USA

Barber, Kurt (Athlete, Football Player)
400 E Main St
Frankfort, KY 40601-2334, USA

Barber, Marion (Athlete, Football Player)
PO Box 46106
Minneapolis, MN 55446-0106, USA

Barber, Michael (Athlete, Football Player)
3020 Prosperity Church Rd Ste 1
Charlotte, NC 28269-7197, USA

Barber, Mike (Athlete, Football Player)
1526 W Pleasant Run Rd
Desoto, TX 75115-2702, USA

Barber, Miller (Athlete, Golfer)
8215 N 54th St
Paradise Valley, AZ 85253-2522, USA

Barber, Paul (Actor, Producer, Writer)
c/o Staff Member *Paradigm (LA)*
360 N Crescent Dr
Beverly Hills, CA 90210-4874, USA

Barber, Ronde (Athlete, Football Player)
17119 Journeys End Dr
Odessa, FL 33556-2442, USA

Barber, Rudy (Athlete, Football Player)
1411 NW 175th St
Miami, FL 33169-4660, USA

Barber, Shawn (Athlete, Football Player)
20035 Canterbury Dr
Stilwell, KS 66085-9394, USA

Barber, Steve (Athlete, Baseball Player)
902 San Eduardo Ave
Henderson, NV 89002-8900, USA

Barber, Stewart C (Stew) (Athlete, Football Player)
2138 Country Manor Dr
Mount Pleasant, SC 29466-7448, USA

Barber, Tiki (Athlete, Football Player, Sportscaster)
c/o Mark Lepselter *Maxx Sports & Entertainment*
546 5th Ave Fl 6
New York, NY 10036-5000, USA

Barber, William (Cinematographer)
2509 Whitechapel Pl
Thousand Oaks, CA 91362-5356, USA

Barbera, Catrina (Stylist)
4431 133rd Ave SE
Bellevue, WA 98006-2135, USA

Barberie, Bret (Athlete, Baseball Player)
11607 Bos St
Cerritos, CA 90703-6744, USA

Barberie, Jillian (Actor, Television Host)

Barberio, Nicholas (Stylist)
c/o Staff Member *AFG Management*
62 Chelsea Piers Ste 203
New York, NY 10011-1015, USA

Barberos, Alessandro (Business Person)
Corso G Marconi 10/20
New York, NY 10125-0001, ITALY

Barbi, Shane (Model)
c/o Jeffery LeBeau *Peacock & LeBeau*
3741 E 4th St
Long Beach, CA 90814-1628, CA

Barbi, Sia (Model)
c/o Jeffery LeBeau *Peacock & LeBeau*
3741 E 4th St
Long Beach, CA 90814-1628, CA

Barbieri, Anastasia (Stylist)
c/o Staff Member *Art Partner*
145 Hudson St Frnt 2
New York, NY 10013-2122, USA

Barbieri, Gato (Musician)
123 Hardvard Ave
Staten Island, NY 10301, USA

Barbieri, Jim (Athlete, Baseball Player)
13619 E 5th Ave
Spokane Valley, WA 99216-0600, USA

Barbon, Roberto (Athlete, Baseball Player)
Gabukun Dencho-2-Chome 6-Ban 460
Nishinomiya City
Hyogok, JAPAN

Barbosa, Derek Keith (Chino XL) (Musician)
c/o Staff Member *Universal Music Publishing Group (Latin)*
420 Lincoln Rd Ste 200
Miami Beach, FL 33139-3014, USA

Barbosa, Leandro (Athlete, Basketball Player)
2209 Plaza Dr Ste 100
Rocklin, CA 95765-4419, USA

Barbot, Ivan (Lawyer)
4 Rue Marguerite
Paris 75017, FRANCE

Barbour, Haley R (Governor)
PO Box 139
Jackson, MS 39205-0139, USA

Barbour, Ian (Physicist, Scientist)
Theology Dept
Northfield, MN 55057, USA

Barbour, John (Actor, Comedian, Writer)
10309 Denman St
Las Vegas, NV 89178-8031, USA

Barbour, Ross (Musician)
PO Box 93534
Las Vegas, NV 89193-3534, USA

Barbutti, Pete (Musician)
11761 E Speedway Blvd
Tucson, AZ 85748-2017, USA

Barcelo, Lorenzo (Athlete, Baseball Player)
1402 E Manlove St Apt 35
Tucson, AZ 85719-6143, USA

Barcelo, Rich (Athlete, Basketball Player)
5195 N Spring View Dr
Tucson, AZ 85749-7107, USA

Barcelona, Custo (Designer, Fashion Designer)
c/o Staff Member *Custo Barcelona*
2 Michael Road 1927 Bldg, North Entrance
London, England SW6 2AD, United Kingdom

Barclay, Dave (Actor)
c/o Staff Member *Coolwaters Productions*
10061 Riverside Dr # 531
Toluca Lake, CA 91602-2560, USA

Barclay, Paris (Actor)
c/o Steve Lovett *Lovett Management*
1327 Brinkley Ave
Los Angeles, CA 90049-3619, USA

Bard, Allen J (Misc)
6202 Mountainclimb Dr
Austin, TX 78731-3906, USA

Bard, Josh (Athlete, Baseball Player)
2139 Beechnut Pl
Castle Rock, CO 80108-7827, USA

Bardem, Javier E (Actor, Producer)
c/o Kelly Bush *ID PR (LA)*
7060 Hollywood Blvd Fl 8
Los Angeles, CA 90028-6014, USA

Bardo, Cori (Stylist)
c/o Staff Member *Rex Agency, The*
6311 Romaine St
Los Angeles, CA 90038-2617, USA

Bardole, Kirk (Stylist)
c/o Staff Member *Blink Management*
421 Washington Ave Ste 202
Miami Beach, FL 33139-6612, USA

Bardot, Brigitte (Actor)
La Madrague
St. Tropez F-83990, France

Bare, Bobby (Musician)
PO Box 1547
Goodlettsville, TN 37070-1547, USA

Bare, Robert J (Bobby) (Musician, Songwriter, Writer)
2401 Music Valley Dr
Nashville, TN 37214-1002, USA

Barefoot, Ken (Athlete, Football Player)
1204 Lawrence Grey Dr
Virginia Beach, VA 23455-5605, USA

Bareikis, Arija (Actor)
c/o Rhonda Price *Gersh (NY)*
41 Madison Ave
New York, NY 10010-2202, USA

Bareikis, Arlia (Actor)
360 W 23rd St
New York, NY 10011-2258, USA

Bareilles, Sara (Musician)
c/o Ian Sales *International Talent Booking*
1st Floor, Ariel House 74A Charlotte St
London W1T 4QJ, UNITED KINGDOM

Barenaked Ladies (Music Group)
c/o Jordan Feldstein *Career Artist Management*
1100 Glendon Ave Ste 1100
Los Angeles, CA 90024-3515, USA

Barenboim, Daniel (Conductor, Musician)
29 Rue de la Coulouvreeniere
Geneva 1206, SWITZERLAND

Baretto, Ray (Musician)
181 Christle St # 300
New York, NY 10002, USA

Barfield, Amanda (Actor)
6409 Primrose Ave Ste 7
Los Angeles, CA 90068-2865, USA

Barfield, Jesse L (Athlete, Baseball Player)
5814 Spanish Moss Ct
Spring, TX 77379-6482, USA

Barfield, John (Athlete, Baseball Player)
2107 Hobson Ave
Hot Springs National Park, AR 71913-3037, USA

Barfield, Josh (Athlete, Baseball Player)
5814 Spanish Moss Ct
Spring, TX 77379-6482, USA

Barfield, Ron (Race Car Driver)
PO Box 6495
Florence, SC 29502-6495, USA

Barfod, Hakon (Yachtsman)
Jon Ostensensy 15
Nesbru 1360, NORWAY

Barfoot, Van T (War Hero)
11815 Coat Bridge Ln
Henrico, VA 23238-3438, USA

Bargar, Greg (Athlete, Baseball Player)
902 Felbar Ave
Torrance, CA 90503-5128, USA

Barger, Ralph (Sonny) (Actor)
c/o Staff Member *HarperCollins Publishers*
10 E 53rd St C/O Author Mail Floor 7
New York, NY 10022, USA

Bargnani, Andrea (Athlete, Basketball Player)
c/o Leon Rose *CAA - NJ*
2000 Avenue of the Stars
Los Angeles, CA 90067-4700, USA

Barhorst, Barney (Athlete, Basketball Player)
8004 River Bay Dr E
Indianapolis, IN 46240-2994, USA

Barinholtz, Ike (Comedian)
c/o Jai Khanna *Brillstein Entertainment Partners*
9150 Wilshire Blvd Ste 350
Beverly Hills, CA 90212-3453, USA

Barisich, Carl J (Athlete, Football Player)
1744 N 134th Ln
Goodyear, AZ 85395-2282, USA

Barjatya, Sooraj (Bollywood, Director, Producer)
Bhana 1st Floor 422 Veer Sawarkar Road
Prabhadevi Dadar
Mumbai, MS 400025, INDIA

Bar-Josef, Ofer (Archaeologist)
Archaeology Dept
Cambridge, MA 2138, USA

Bark, Brian (Athlete, Baseball Player)
12308 Silver Cup Ct
Reisterstown, MD 21136-6481, USA

Barkauskas, Antanas S (President)
Akmenu 71
Vilnus, LITHUANIA

Barker, Bob
200 N Larchmont Blvd Ste 3
Los Angeles, CA 90004-3707, USA

Barker, Bryan (Athlete, Football Player)
620 Beach Ave
Atlantic Beach, FL 32233-5326, USA

Barker, Clive (Director, Writer)
c/o Ben Smith *International Creative Management (ICM-LA)*
10250 Constellation Blvd Fl 7
Los Angeles, CA 90067-6207, USA

Barker, Clyde F (Doctor)
3 Coopertown Rd
Haverford, PA 19041-1012, USA

Barker, David J P (Biologist)
Manor Farm East Dean near Salisbury
Wilts SP5 1HB, UNITED KINGDOM (UK)

Barker, Ed (Athlete, Football Player)
12002 Clover Creek Dr SW
Lakewood, WA 98499-5210, USA

Barker, Glen (Athlete, Baseball Player)
18222 Thicket Grove Rd
Houston, TX 77084-7598, USA

Barker, Jordan (Actor)
c/o Staff Member *Select Artists Ltd (CA-Westside Office)*
1138 12th St Apt 1
Santa Monica, CA 90403-5459, USA

Barker, Kevin (Athlete, Baseball Player)
PO Box 96
Mendota, VA 24270-0096, USA

Barker, Len (Athlete, Baseball Player)
10690 Locust Grove Dr
Chardon, OH 44024-8870, USA

Barker, Leo (Athlete, Football Player)
25 Via Lucena
San Clemente, CA 92673-7045, USA

Barker, Lois (Athlete, Baseball Player)
195 W Main St Apt 6
Chester, NJ 07930-2451, USA

Barker, Nigel (Photographer)
c/o Staff Member *WmE2 (WMA-LA)*
1 William Morris Pl
Beverly Hills, CA 90212-4261, USA

Barker, Pat (Writer)
29 Fernshaw Road
London SW10 0TG, UNITED KINGDOM (UK)

Barker, Ray (Athlete, Baseball Player)
303 Greenbriar Rd
Martinsburg, WV 25401-2827, USA

Barker, Rich (Athlete, Baseball Player)
17 Landers Rd
Stoneham, MA 02180-1409, USA

Barker, Richard A (Religious Leader)
PO Box P
Willow Grove, PA 19090, USA

Barker, Roy (Athlete, Football Player)
23 Saint Marks Cir
Islandia, NY 11749-1728, USA

Barker, Sue (Athlete, Tennis Player)
c/o Staff Member *BBC Artist Mail*
PO Box 1116
Belfast BT2 7AJ, United Kingdom

Barker, Tom (Actor)
2-4 Noel St
London W1V 3RB, UNITED KINGDOM (UK)

Barker, Travis (Musician)
c/o Jenni Weinman *Patricola Lust PR*
9171 Wilshire Blvd Ste 390
Beverly Hills, CA 90210-5515, USA

Barker-Lequia, Joan (Athlete, Baseball Player)
3236 34th St SW
Grandville, MI 49418-1905, USA

Barkett, Andy (Athlete, Baseball Player)
1016 Willa Lake Cir
Oviedo, FL 32765-6445, USA

Barkin, Ellen (Actor)
c/o Stephen Huvane *Slate Public Relations*
9000 W Sunset Blvd Ste 915
West Hollywood, CA 90069-5809, USA

Barkley, Brian (Athlete, Baseball Player)
9208 Spring Ridge Cir
Woodway, TX 76712-8764, USA

Barkley, Charles W (Athlete, Basketball Player, Television Host)
c/o Marc Perman *Perman Management*
Prefers to be contacted via telephone
CA, USA

Barkley, Dean M (Politician)
1732 Jonquil Ln N
Minneapolis, MN 55441-4021, USA

Barkley, Doug (Athlete, Hockey Player)
523-3131 63 Ave SE
Calgary, AB T3E 6N4, Canada

Barkley, Iran (Boxer)
2645 3rd Ave
Bronx, NY 10451-6329, USA

Barkley, Jeff (Athlete, Baseball Player)
264 3rd Ave NE
Hickory, NC 28601-5016, USA

Barkman, Tyler Jane (Janie) (Swimmer)
Athletic
Princeton, NJ 08544-0001, USA

Barksdale, James (Jim) (Business Person)
2730 Sand Hill Rd
Menlo Park, CA 94025-7071, USA

Barksdale, Lance (Athlete, Baseball Player)
4507 Pine Lake Dr
Terry, MS 39170-8741, USA

Barksdale, LaQuanda (Athlete, Basketball Player)
1 at and T Center Pkwy
San Antonio, TX 78219-3604, USA

Barksdale, Rhesa H (Judge)
245 E Capitol St
Jackson, MS 39201-2409, USA

Barkum, Jerome P (Athlete, Football Player)
2720 Palmer Dr Apt J5
Gulfport, MS 39507-2854, USA

Barletta, Joseph (Publisher)
100 Matsonford Rd
Radnor, PA 19087-4559, USA

Barletta, Lou (Congressman, Politician)
510 Cannon Hob
Washington, DC 20515-1402, USA

Barlow, Bob (Athlete, Hockey Player)
4912 Wesley Rd
Victoria, BC V8Y 1Y5, Canada

Barlow, Corey (Athlete, Football Player)
1009 Narrows Point Dr
Birmingham, AL 35242-8675, USA

Barlow, Craig (Athlete, Golfer)
644 Desert Passage St
Henderson, NV 89002-6592, USA

Barlow, Elizabeth J (Betty) (Stylist)
2304 Barker Cir
West Chester, PA 19380-6183, USA

Barlow, Gary (Musician, Songwriter, Writer)
Beaumont House, Avonmore Road, Kensington Village
London W14 8TS, UK

Barlow, Kevan (Athlete, Football Player)
82 Waterfront Dr
Pittsburgh, PA 15222-4735, USA

Barlow, Mike (Athlete, Baseball Player)
4524 Francis Rd
Cazenovia, NY 13035-8470, USA

Barlow, Perry (Cartoonist)
4 Times Sq
New York, NY 10036-6515, USA

Barlow, Reggie (Athlete, Football Player)
8311 Timber Trace Ln
Pike Road, AL 36064-3444, USA

BarlowGirl (Music Group, Musician)
c/o Greg Oliver *Greg Oliver Agency*
1710 General George Patton Dr Ste 104
Brentwood, TN 37027-2904, USA

Barmes, Bruce (Athlete, Baseball Player)
509 McDonald Ave
Charlotte, NC 28203-5321, USA

Barmore, Leon (Athlete, Basketball Player)
1100 Brookhaven Ave
Ruston, LA 71270-8505, USA

Barnaby, Matthew (Athlete, Hockey Player)
134 King Anthony Way
Getzville, NY 14068-1414, USA

Barndt, Tom (Athlete, Football Player)
11041 Romola St
Las Vegas, NV 89141-3410, USA

Barnes, Al (Athlete, Football Player)
5635 Criollo Dr
Las Vegas, NV 89122-3454, USA

Barnes, Ben (Actor)
c/o Lena Roklin *Luber Roklin Management*
8530 Wilshire Blvd Ste 550
Beverly Hills, CA 90211-3133, USA

Barnes, Benny J (Athlete, Football Player)
5003 Fleming Ave
Richmond, CA 94804-4718, USA

Barnes, Billy Ray (Athlete, Football Player)
501 W Ryder Ave
Landis, NC 28088-1238, USA

Barnes, Blair (Athlete, Hockey Player)
McIntosh Pt
Christopher Lake, SK S0J 0N0, Canada

Barnes, Brandon (Athlete, Football Player)
912 Westview Dr
Sikeston, MO 63801-4661, USA

Barnes, Brian (Athlete, Baseball Player)
860 River Cove Dr
Dacula, GA 30019-2090, USA

Barnes, Bruce (Athlete, Football Player)
7129 Alexandria Pl
Stockton, CA 95207-1503, USA

Barnes, Christopher Daniel (Actor)
3824 Fairway Ave
Studio City, CA 91604-2303, USA

Barnes, Darian (Athlete, Football Player)
554 Clifton Ave
Toms River, NJ 08753-6791, USA

Barnes, Erich (Athlete, Football Player)
712 Warburton Ave
Yonkers, NY 10701-1501, USA

Barnes, Ernest E (Athlete, Football Player)
4435 Camellia Ave
North Hollywood, CA 91602-1905, USA

Barnes, Frank (Athlete, Baseball Player)
1508 Brazil St
Greenville, MS 38701-2622, USA

Barnes, Frank S (Engineer)
Engineering
Boulder, CO 80309-0001, USA

Barnes, Gary (Athlete, Football Player)
849 Tiger Blvd Unit 406
Clemson, SC 29631-1580, USA

Barnes, Jeff (Athlete, Football Player)
10738 Versailles Blvd
Clermont, FL 34711-7342, USA

Barnes, Jhane (Designer, Fashion Designer)
140 W 57th St Ste 5B
New York, NY 10019-3326, USA

Barnes, Jimmy (Musician)
135 Forbes St
Wooloomooloo, NSW 2011, AUSTRALIA

Barnes, Joanna (Actor)
PO Box 1103
Gualala, CA 95445-1103, USA

Barnes, Joe (Athlete, Football Player)
PO Box 1154
Frisco, TX 75034-0020, USA

Barnes, John (Athlete, Baseball Player)
1455 Godell St
Templeton, CA 93465-9424, USA

Barnes, Johnnie (Athlete, Football Player)
212 Charlemagne Dr
Suffolk, VA 23435-1453, USA

Barnes, Julian P (Writer)
34-43 Russell St
London WC2B 5HA, UNITED KINGDOM (UK)

Barnes, Khalif (Athlete, Football Player)
7967 Monterey Bay Dr
Jacksonville, FL 32256-2927, USA

Barnes, Kim (Writer)
c/o Staff Member *Knopf Publishing Group*
1745 Broadway
New York, NY 10019-4368, USA

Barnes, Larry (Athlete, Football Player)
410 Navajo Ave
Simla, CO 80835, USA

Barnes, Larry (Athlete, Football Player)
4734 Belle Chase Cir
Tampa, FL 33634-4256, USA

Barnes, Larry (Athlete, Baseball Player)
11906 Crockett Ct
Bakersfield, CA 93312-5710, USA

Barnes, Linda (Writer)
56 Seaver St
Brookline, MA 02445-5749, USA

Barnes, Lute (Athlete, Baseball Player)
35911 Donny Cir
Palm Desert, CA 92211-2657, USA

Barnes, Marlon (Athlete, Football Player)
6018 Madre Ct NE
Albuquerque, NM 87111-1135, USA

Barnes, Marvin (Athlete, Basketball Player)
4707 High St W
Portsmouth, VA 23703-4221, USA

Barnes, Matt (Athlete, Basketball Player)
c/o Aaron Goodwin *Goodwin Sports Management*
Prefers to be contacted via email or telephone
Seattle, WA, USA

Barnes, Mike H (Athlete, Football Player)
205 Cindy St S
Keller, TX 76248-2341, USA

Barnes, Mike J (Athlete, Football Player)
27474 Plank Rd
Guys Mills, PA 16327-5434, USA

Barnes, Norm (Athlete, Hockey Player)
17 Meadow Xing
Simsbury, CT 06070-1006, USA

Barnes, Pat (Athlete, Football Player)
5 Willowglade
Trabuco Canyon, CA 92679-3813, USA

Barnes, Pricilla (Actor)
c/o Staff Member *GVA Talent Agency Inc*
8981 W Sunset Blvd Ste 101
Los Angeles, CA 90069-1850, USA

Barnes, Rashidi (Athlete, Football Player)
8748 Kentshire Way
Sacramento, CA 95828-6173, USA

Barnes, Reggie (Athlete, Football Player)
3110 Merrimac Ct
Southlake, TX 76092-8109, USA

Barnes, Rich (Athlete, Baseball Player)
2845 Wilderness Rd
West Palm Beach, FL 33409-2030, USA

Barnes, Rick (Athlete, Basketball Player)
Athletic Dept
Austin, TX 78713, USA

Barnes, Robert H (Psychic)
PO Box 4349
Lubbock, TX 79409-0004, USA

Barnes, Rod (Athlete, Basketball Player)
Athletic Dept
Mississippi State, MS 39762, USA

Barnes, Rodrigo (Athlete, Football Player)
PO Box 302
Waco, TX 76703-0302, USA

Barnes, Ron (Athlete, Baseball Player)
5304 MacDonald Ave
El Cerrito, CA 94530-1636, USA

Barnes, Skeeter (Athlete, Baseball Player)
11544 Winding Wood Dr
Indianapolis, IN 46235-9731, USA

Barnes, Stu (Athlete, Hockey Player)
5069 Royal Creek Ln
Plano, TX 75093-4069, USA

Barnes, Tomur (Athlete, Football Player)
2518 Broad St
Baytown, TX 77521-1265, USA

Barnes, Wallace (Business Person)
123 Main St
Bristol, CT 06010-6307, USA

Barnes, Walt (Athlete, Football Player)
P.O. Box 1383
Steamboat Springs, CO 80487, USA

Barnes, William (Athlete, Baseball Player)
19792 Ardmore St
Detroit, MI 48235-1503, USA

Barnes Jr, Harry G (Diplomat)
Hapenny Road
Peacham, VT 5862, USA

Barnes Jr, Roosevelt (Athlete, Football Player)
3128 Covington Manor Rd
Fort Wayne, IN 46814-9126, USA

Barnes-McCoy, Joyce (Athlete, Baseball Player)
1313 E 19th Ave
Hutchinson, KS 67502-5061, USA

Barnet, Lisa (Stylist)
Prefers to be contact via telephone or email
Los Angeles, CA 90069, USA

Barnet, Will (Artist, Educator)
15 Gramercy Park S
New York, NY 10003-1705, USA

Barnett, Dean (Athlete, Football Player)
8 Cozy Glen Cir
Henderson, NV 89074-1563, USA

Barnett, Dick (Athlete, Basketball Player)
1227 Pine Rdg
Bushkill, PA 18324-9794, USA

Barnett, Douglas (Athlete, Football Player)
651 Park Ln
Billings, MT 59102-1930, USA

Barnett, Doyle (Writer)
c/o Staff Member *New World Library*
14 Pamaron Way Ste 1
Novato, CA 94949-6215, USA

Barnett, Fred (Athlete, Football Player)
PO Box 604
Bala Cynwyd, PA 19004-0604, USA

Barnett, Gary (Coach, Football Coach)
Athletic
Boulder, CO 80309-0001, USA

Barnett, Jim (Athlete, Basketball Player)
7 Kittiwake Rd
Orinda, CA 94563-1716, USA

Barnett, Jonathan (Architect)
4501 Connecticut Ave NW
Washington, DC 20008-3738, USA

Barnett, Larry (Athlete, Baseball Player)
6298 Hughes Rd
Prospect, OH 43342-9602, USA

Barnett, Nate (Athlete, Basketball Player)
PO Box 144
Douglas, GA 31534-0144, USA

Barnett, Nick (Athlete, Football Player)
3496 Country Winds Ct
Green Bay, WI 54311-6906, USA

Barnett, Oliver (Athlete, Football Player)
1133 Autumn Ridge Dr
Lexington, KY 40509-2055, USA

Barnett, Pam (Athlete, Golfer)
4908 E Rancho Tierra Dr
Cave Creek, AZ 85331-5912, USA

Barnett, Sloan (Correspondent, Writer)
c/o Staff Member *Simon & Schuster*
1230 Avenue of the Americas Fl CONC1
New York, NY 10020-1586, USA

Barnett, Steven (Steve) (Athlete, Football Player)
308 Romae Ct
Danville, CA 94526-1863, USA

Barnett, Walter (Stylist)
c/o Celebrity Stylist *Smashbox Beauty*
8549 Higuera St Bldg B
Culver City, CA 90232-2521, USA

Barnette, Curtis H (Business Person)
1170 8th Ave
Bethlehem, PA 18018-2255, USA

Barney, Edith (Athlete, Baseball Player)
329 Blackburn Blvd
Venice, FL 34287-1507, USA

Barney, Matthew (Artist, Entertainer)
W 24th St Barbara Gladstone Gallery 515
New York, NY 10011-1792

Barney, Tamra (Reality TV Star)
c/o Pamela Hicks *Hicks and Associates*
Prefers to be contacted via email or telephone
Los Angeles, CA 90069, USA

Barney Jr, Lemuel J (Lem) (Athlete, Football Player)
775 Kentbrook Dr
Commerce Township, MI 48382-5013, USA

Barnhardt, Tom (Athlete, Football Player)
503 Park St
China Grove, NC 28023-2154, USA

Barnhart, Vic (Athlete, Baseball Player)
13102 Unger Rd
Hagerstown, MD 21742-1428, USA

Barnhill, Herbert (Athlete, Baseball Player)
3712 Owen Ave
Jacksonville, FL 32208-2910, USA

Barnhill, Norton (Athlete, Basketball Player)
3631 Emma Ave
Winston Salem, NC 27127-6023, USA

Barnhill, Scott (Model)
c/o Staff Member *IMG*
304 Park Ave S Fl 12
New York, NY 10010-4314, USA

Barnowski, Ed (Athlete, Baseball Player)
2380 Lake Lucy Rd
Chanhassen, MN 55317-7561, USA

Barnum, HC Barney (War Hero)
12008 Walnut Branch Rd
Herndon, VA 20194-5617, USA

Barnwell, Chris (Athlete, Baseball Player)
PO Box 600070
Jacksonville, FL 32260-0070, USA

Barnwell, Malcolm (Athlete, Football Player)
4045 Gullah Ave Apt 103
North Charleston, SC 29405-6379, USA

Barnwell, Ysaye (Musician)
PO Box 600099
Newtonville, MA 02460-0001, USA

Barocco, Rocco (Designer, Fashion Designer)
Via Occhio Marion
Capri/Napoli 80773, ITALY

Baron, Caroline (Producer)
c/o Paul Hook *International Creative Management (ICM-LA)*
10250 Constellation Blvd Fl 7
Los Angeles, CA 90067-6207, USA

Baron, Crespo Enrique (Government Official)
97/113 Rue Velliard
Brussels 1040, BELGIUM

Baron, Jimmy (Athlete, Baseball Player)
7402 Conner Ln
Edwardsville, IL 62025-4668, USA

Baron, Martin D (Editor)
Editorial Dept 135 WT Morrissey Blvd
Dorchester, MA 2125, USA

Baron, Murray (Athlete, Hockey Player)
7026 E Blue Sky Dr
Scottsdale, AZ 85266-7518, USA

Baron, Natalia (Actor)
c/o Tiffany Kuzon *Evolution Entertainment (LA)*
901 N Highland Ave
Los Angeles, CA 90038-2412, USA

Barone, Dick (Athlete, Baseball Player)
968 Forest St
Shasta Lake, CA 96019-9576, USA

Baron-Reid, Colette Baron-Reid (Writer)
c/o Staff Member *Hay House, Inc*
PO Box 5100
Carlsbad, CA 92018-5100, USA

Barr, Bob (Business Person, Politician)
4401 Northside Pkwy NW # 100
Atlanta, GA 30327-3065, USA

Barr, Brenda (Stylist)
c/o Staff Member *Illusions Management*
129 W 27th St Fl 12
New York, NY 10001-6206, USA

Barr, Dave (Golfer)
10620 Southdale Rd
Richmond, BC V7A 2W7, CANADA

Barr, Dave (Athlete, Hockey Player)
c/o Staff Member *Guelph Storm Hockey Club*
55 Wyndham St N
Guelph, ON N1H 7T8, Canada

Barr, Doris (Athlete, Baseball Player)
312-1712 Portage Ave
Winnipeg, MB R3J 0E3, CANADA

Barr, Doug (Actor)
PO Box 63
Rutherford, CA 94573-0063, USA

Barr, Jim (Athlete, Baseball Player)
6335 Oak Hill Dr
Granite Bay, CA 95746-8908, USA

Barr, Julia (Actor)
c/o Robert Attermann *Abrams Artists Agency (LA)*
9200 W Sunset Blvd PH 11
Los Angeles, CA 90069-3601, USA

Barr, Matt (Actor)
c/o Matt Luber *Luber Roklin Management*
8530 Wilshire Blvd Ste 550
Beverly Hills, CA 90211-3133, USA

Barr, Mike (Athlete, Basketball Player)
350 38th St NW
Canton, OH 44709-1523, USA

Barr, Nevada (Writer)
375 Hudson St
New York, NY 10014-3658, USA

Barr, Office of Bob (Ex-Congressman, Politician)
900 Circle 75 Pkwy SE Ste 1280
Atlanta, GA 30339-6016, USA

Barr, Roseanne (Actor, Comedian, Producer)
c/o James Kellem *JKA Talent*
12725 Ventura Blvd Ste H
Studio City, CA 91604-2437, USA

Barr, Steve (Athlete, Baseball Player)
470 Village Cir SW
Winter Haven, FL 33880-1668, USA

Barragan, Cuno (Athlete, Baseball Player)
1824 Saint Ann Ct
Carmichael, CA 95608-5643, USA

Barranca, German (Athlete, Baseball Player)
199 Kreidler Ave
York, PA 17402-4976, USA

Barrasso, John (Senator)
307 Dirksen Senate Ofc Building
Washington, DC 20510-0001, USA

Barrasso, Thomas (Tom) (Athlete, Hockey Player)
12820 Rosalie St
Raleigh, NC 27614-7970, USA

Barratt, Michael R (Astronaut)
2102 Pleasant Palm Cir
League City, TX 77573-6670, USA

Barrault, Doug (Athlete, Hockey Player)
527 10th St S
Golden, BC V0A 1H0, CANADA

Barrault, Marie-Christine (Actor)
36 Rue de Ponthlieu
Paris 75008, FRANCE

Barraza, Adriana (Actor)
c/o Craig Shapiro *International Creative Management (ICM-LA)*
10250 Constellation Blvd Fl 7
Los Angeles, CA 90067-6207, USA

Barraza, Maria (Actor)
c/o Staff Member *TV Caracol*
Calle 76 #11 - 35 Piso 10AA
Bogota DC 26484, COLOMBIA

Barre, Raymond (Prime Minister)
4-6 Ave Emile-Acollas
Paris 75007, FRANCE

Barrese, Sasha (Actor)
c/o Erik Kritzer *Kritzer Levine Wilkins Entertainment*
11872 La Grange Ave Fl 1
Los Angeles, CA 90025-5283, USA

Barreto, Alexandra (Actor)
c/o Robert Marsala *Global Creative*
1051 Cole Ave # B
Los Angeles, CA 90038-2601, USA

Barreto, Bruno (Director)
c/o Martin Spencer *Creative Artists Agency (CAA-LA)*
2000 Avenue of the Stars Ste 100
Los Angeles, CA 90067-4705, USA

Barrett, Alice (Actor)
9171 Wilshire Blvd Ste 441
Beverly Hills, CA 90210-5516, USA

Barrett, Bo (Actor)
c/o Staff Member *Badass Haircut Productions*
2718 Lakewood Ave
Los Angeles, CA 90039-2619, USA

Barrett, Brendan Ryan (Actor)
c/o Carol Elsner *Gage Group, The (LA)*
14724 Ventura Blvd Ste 505
Sherman Oaks, CA 91403-3505, USA

Barrett, Brendon Ryan (Actor)
9255 W Sunset Blvd Ste 1010
West Hollywood, CA 90069-3307, USA

Barrett, Colleen (Business Person)
PO Box 36611
Dallas, TX 75235-1611, USA

Barrett, Craig R (Business Person)
2200 Mission College Blvd
Santa Clara, CA 95054-1537, USA

Barrett, David (Athlete, Football Player)
1423 E Rose St
Blytheville, AR 72315-3714, USA

Barrett, Ernie (Athlete, Basketball Player)
2105 Grand Ridge Ct
Manhattan, KS 66503-8695, USA

Barrett, Fred (Athlete, Hockey Player)
3016 Leitrim Rd
Gloucester, ON K1T 3V9, Canada

Barrett, Jacinda (Actor)
c/o Joan Green *Joan Green Management*
1836 Courtney Ter
Los Angeles, CA 90046-2106, USA

Barrett, James E (Judge)
2120 Capitol Ave
Cheyenne, WY 82001-3633, USA

Barrett, Jean (Athlete, Football Player)
7494 S Sleepy Hollow Dr
Tulsa, OK 74136-5919, USA

Barrett, Malcolm (Actor)
c/o Craig Dorfman *Frontline Management*
5670 Wilshire Blvd Ste 1370
Los Angeles, CA 90036-5679, USA

Barrett, Mario (Actor, Musician)
c/o Tammy Brook *FYI Public Relations*
174 5th Ave Ste 400
New York, NY 10010-5935, USA

Barrett, Martin G (Marty) (Athlete, Baseball Player)
3552 Ridge Meadow St
Las Vegas, NV 89135-7811, USA

Barrett, Michael (Athlete, Baseball Player)
126 Circle Dr
Port Saint Joe, FL 32456, USA

Barrett, Michael (Mike) (Athlete, Basketball Player)
5721 Templegate Dr
Nashville, TN 37221-4108, USA

Barrett, Stephen (Activist, Doctor)
PO Box 1747
Allentown, PA 18105-1747, USA

Barrett, Ted (Athlete, Baseball Player)
4380 E Sundance Ct
Gilbert, AZ 85297-9640, USA

Barrett, Thomas J (Admiral)
Vice Commandant US Court Guard 2100 2nd St SW
Washington, DC 20593-0001, USA

Barrett, Tim (Athlete, Baseball Player)
5588 Jandel Dr
Aurora, IN 47001-3010, USA

Barrett, Tom (Athlete, Baseball Player)
5306 W Jupiter Way
Chandler, AZ 85226-8622, USA

Barrett, Wade (Soccer Player)
Mads Stangs gate 20
Fredrikstad N-1610, NORWAY

Barrett, William (Misc)
34 Harwood Ave
Sleepy Hollow, NY 10591-1309, USA

Barrichello, Rubens (Race Car Driver)
c/o Staff Member *Jaguar Racing Ltd*
Bradbourne Drive Tilbrook
Milton Keynes MK7 8BJ, United Kingdom

Barrie, Barbara (Actor)
c/o Staff Member *Innovative Artists (LA)*
1505 10th St
Santa Monica, CA 90401-2805, USA

Barrie, Chris (Actor, Comedian)
76 Oxford St
London W1N 0AX, UNITED KINGDOM (UK)

Barrie, Doug (Athlete, Hockey Player)
12130 46 St NW
Edmonton, AB T5W 2W4, Canada

Barrie, Len (Athlete, Hockey Player)
208-2800 Bryn Maur Rd
Victoria, BC V9B 3T4, Canada

Barrie, Sebastian (Athlete, Football Player)
52 Seneca Ln
San Ramon, CA 94583-4305, USA

Barrile, Anthony (Actor)
9171 Wilshire Blvd Ste 441
Beverly Hills, CA 90210-5516, USA

Barrileaux, James (Misc)
PO Box 273
Edwards, CA 93523 0273, USA

Barrino, Fantasia (Musician)
c/o Brian Dickens *BD Management*
16605 Pleasant Colony Dr
Upper Marlboro, MD 20774-8802, USA

Barrios, Jose (Athlete, Baseball Player)
6484 SW 25th St
Miami, FL 33155-2958, USA

Barris, Chuck (Television Host)
c/o Staff Member *Hyperion Books*
77 W 66th St Fl 11
New York, NY 10023-6201, USA

Barris, George (Designer, Misc)
10811 Riverside Dr
North Hollywood, CA 91602-2308, USA

Barritt, Randi (Stylist)
315 W 23rd St Apt 6D
New York, NY 10011-2253, USA

Barriw, Barbara (Actor)
15 W 72nd St Apt 2A
New York, NY 10023-3419, USA

Barron, Alex (Athlete, Football Player)
630 Emerson Rd Apt 206
Saint Louis, MO 63141-6751, USA

Barron, Alex (Race Car Driver)
2334 S Broadway
Santa Ana, CA 92707-3250, USA

Barron, Chris (Music Group, Musician)
c/o Staff Member *Skyline Music*
28 Union St
Whitefield, NH 03598-3503, USA

Barron, Dana (Actor)
c/o Kevin Turner *Coast to Coast Talent Group*
3350 Barham Blvd
Los Angeles, CA 90068-1404, USA

Barron, Doug (Athlete, Golfer)
5080 Peg Ln
Memphis, TN 38117-2147, USA

Barron, Kenneth (Kenny) (Composer, Musician)
300 Mercer St Apt 3J
New York, NY 10003-6732, USA

Barron, Lynn (Stylist)
c/o Staff Member *Rex Agency, The*
6311 Romaine St
Los Angeles, CA 90038-2617, USA

Barron, Mark (Athlete, Baseball Player)
110 N Randolph Ave
Clarksville, IN 47129-2761, USA

Barron, Tony (Athlete, Baseball Player)
16014 123rd Avenue Ct E
Puyallup, WA 98374-9649, USA

Barros, Dana (Athlete, Basketball Player)
67 Fairfield Cir
Norwood, MA 02062-5564, USA

Barrow, Barbara (Athlete, Golfer)
11427 Mayapple Way
San Diego, CA 92131-2928, USA

Barrow, Dean (Prime Minister)
Office Of The Prime Minister Sir Edney Cain Building
Belmopan, Belize

Barrow, Geoff (Musician)
Saga Center 326 Kensal Road
London W10 5BZ, UNITED KINGDOM (UK)

Barrow, Michael C (Athlete, Football Player)
1115 S Alhambra Cir
Coral Gables, FL 33146-3711, USA

Barrowman, John (Actor)
c/o Staff Member *Gavin Barker Assoc*
2D Wimpole St
London W1G 0EB, UK

Barrowman, Mike (Swimmer)
706 N Wamer St
Bay City, MI 48706, USA

Barrows, Scott (Athlete, Football Player)
3600 Kern Rd
Lake Orion, MI 48360-2351, USA

Barrows, Sydney Biddle (Business Person, Writer)
210 W 70th St Apt 209
New York, NY 10023-4363, USA

Barrueco, Manuel (Musician)
165 W 57th St
New York, NY 10019-2201, USA

Barry, A L (Religious Leader)
1333 S Kirkwood Rd
Saint Louis, MO 63122-7226, USA

Barry, Allan (Athlete, Football Player)
301 N Lake Ave Ste 410
Pasadena, CA 91101-5121, USA

Barry, Brent (Athlete, Basketball Player)
712 the Strand
Hermosa Beach, CA 90254-4457, USA

Barry, Daniel T (Dan) (Astronaut)
46 Ashton Ln
South Hadley, MA 01075-2143, USA

Barry, Dave (Journalist, Writer)
1 Herald Plz
Miami, FL 33132-1609, USA

Barry, Ed (Athlete, Hockey Player)
61 Pleasant St
Needham, MA 02492-2950, USA

Barry, Jeff (Composer)
8730 W Sunset Blvd # 300W
Los Angeles, CA 90069-2210, USA

Barry, Jeff (Athlete, Baseball Player)
322 N Barneburg Rd
Medford, OR 97504-6683, USA

Barry, Jon (Athlete, Basketball Player)
4555 Club Dr NE
Atlanta, GA 30319-1123, USA

Barry, Kevin (Athlete, Baseball Player)
71 Penn Lyle Rd
Princeton Junction, NJ 08550-1627, USA

Barry, Len (Musician)
1161 NW 76th Ave
Plantation, FL 33322-5120, USA

Barry, Lynda (Cartoonist)
PO Box 447
Footville, WI 53537-0447, USA

Barry, Marion S (Politician)
161 Raleigh St SE
Washington, DC 20032-1528, USA

Barry, Max (Writer)
c/o Staff Member *Scribe Publications Pty Ltd*
595 Drummond St
Carlton North Vic 3054, Australia

Barry, Odell (Athlete, Football Player)
2561 Ranch Reserve Rdg
Denver, CO 80234-2695, USA

Barry, Patricia (Actor)
12742 Highwood St
Los Angeles, CA 90049-2624, USA

Barry, Paul (Athlete, Football Player)
409 Kingswood Dr
El Paso, TX 79932-2217, USA

Barry, Pauline (Stylist)
Prefers to be contacted via telephone or email
San Francisco, CA, USA

Barry, Randy (Reality TV Star)
c/o Michael Martin *MM Agency*
3937 Nobel Dr
San Diego, CA 92122-6156, USA

Barry, Raymond J (Actor)
c/o Bob McGowan *McGowan Management*
8733 W Sunset Blvd Ste 103
West Hollywood, CA 90069-2241, USA

Barry, Rich (Athlete, Baseball Player)
12020 Hoffman St Apt K
Studio City, CA 91604-4760, USA

Barry, Rick (Athlete, Basketball Player)
5240 Broadmoor Bluffs Dr
Colorado Springs, CO 80906-7912, USA

Barry, Rod (Adult Film Star)
c/o Staff Member *Diva Central Inc*
7510 W Sunset Blvd Ste 1445
Los Angeles, CA 90046-3408, USA

Barry, Scott (Athlete, Baseball Player)
148 Lukesport Dr
Quincy, MI 49082-9595, USA

Barry, Seymour (Sy) (Artist, Cartoonist)
225 Fairfield Dr E
Holbrook, NY 11741-2866, USA

Barry, Todd (Comedian)
c/o David (Dave) Becky *3 Arts Entertainment Inc*
9460 Wilshire Blvd Fl 7
Beverly Hills, CA 90212-2713, USA

Barry III, Richard F D (Rick) (Athlete, Basketball Player)
55 Hawthorne St Ste 1100
San Francisco, CA 94105-3914, USA

Barrymore, Drew (Actor, Producer)
c/o Chris Miller *Flower Films Inc*
7360 Santa Monica Blvd
West Hollywood, CA 90046-6619, USA

Barrymore, Rhonda (Stylist)
c/o Staff Member *Help Me Rhonda*
541 10th St NW # 294
Atlanta, GA 30318-5713, USA

Barsh, Gregory S (Doctor)
Medical Center Pediatrics Dept
Stanford, CA 94305, USA

Barsotti, Charles (Cartoonist)
419 E 55th St
Kansas City, MO 64110-2453, USA

Bart, Peter (Writer)
c/o Daniel A (Dan) Strone *Trident Media Group LLC*
41 Madison Ave Fl 36
New York, NY 10010-2257, USA

Bart, Roger (Actor)
c/o Michael Baum *Impression Entertainment*
9229 W Sunset Blvd Ste 700
West Hollywood, CA 90069-3407, USA

Bartecko, Lubos (Athlete, Hockey Player)
121 Windy Acres Estates Dr
Ballwin, MO 63021-4232, USA

Bartee, Kimera (Athlete, Baseball Player)
10808 N 57th Dr
Glendale, AZ 85304-3864, USA

Bartee, William (Athlete, Football Player)
17 Talaquah Blvd
Ormond Beach, FL 32174-3705, USA

Bartek, Steve (Musician)
c/o Staff Member *Kraft-Engel Management*
15233 Ventura Blvd Ste 200
Sherman Oaks, CA 91403-2244, USA

Bartel, Jean (Beauty Pageant Winner)
229 Bronwood Ave
Los Angeles, CA 90049-3103, USA

Bartel, Robin (Athlete, Hockey Player)
210 Forsyth Crt
Saskatoon, SK S7N 4H2, Canada

Bartels, Wolfgang (Skier)
Womdihof Hintersee
Ransau 83486, GERMANY

Barth, Robert (Religious Leader)
PO Box 30
Circleville, OH 43113-0030, USA

Bartha, Justin (Actor, Producer)
c/o Megan Silverman *WmE2 (Endeavor-LA)*
9601 Wilshire Blvd Fl 3
Beverly Hills, CA 90210-5219, USA

Bartholomay, William C (Athlete, Baseball Player)
180 E Pearson St Apt 3307
Chicago, IL 60611-6730, USA

Bartholomew, Brent (Athlete, Football Player)
809 N Lake Pleasant Rd
Apopka, FL 32712-3219, USA

Bartholomew, Jean (Athlete, Golfer)
411 Capistrano Dr
Palm Beach Gardens, FL 33410-4301, USA

Bartholomew, Logan (Actor)
c/o Beverly Strong *Strong Management*
9350 Wilshire Blvd Ste 224
Beverly Hills, CA 90212-3204, USA

Bartholomew, Reginald (Diplomat)
2201 C St NW
Washington, DC 20520-0099, USA

Bartilson, Lynsey (Actor)
c/o Staff Member *Talent Company, The*
135 E Olive Ave # 4227
Burbank, CA 91502-1820, USA

Bartirome, Tony (Athlete, Baseball Player)
1104 Palma Sola Blvd
Bradenton, FL 34209-3342, USA

Bartiromo, Maria (Correspondent)
c/o Staff Member *CNBC (DC)*
400 N Capitol St NW Ste 850
Washington, DC 20001-1555, USA

Bartkowski, Steven J (Steve) (Athlete, Football Player)
10745 Bell Rd
Duluth, GA 30097-1801, USA

Bartle, Cheryl (Actor)
8281 Melrose Ave Ste 200
Los Angeles, CA 90046-6890, USA

Bartles, Edward (Athlete, Basketball Player)
105 Hemlock Dr
Killingworth, CT 06419-2225, USA

Bartlett, Bonnie (Actor, Musician)
12805 Hortense St
Studio City, CA 91604-1124, USA

Bartlett, Doug (Athlete, Football Player)
9133 26th St
Brookfield, IL 60513-1006, USA

Bartlett, Erinn (Actor)
c/o Randy James *James/Levy/Jacobson Management Inc*
3500 W Olive Ave Ste 1470
Burbank, CA 91505-5514, USA

Bartlett, Jason (Athlete, Baseball Player)
248 River Oaks Dr
Lodi, CA 95240-0562, USA

Bartlett, Jennifer L (Artist)
534 W 21st St
New York, NY 10011-2812, USA

Bartlett, Jim (Athlete, Hockey Player)
8718 Chadwick Dr
Tampa, FL 33635-6212, USA

Bartlett, Murray (Actor)
c/o Rosanne Quezada *Paradigm (LA)*
360 N Crescent Dr
Beverly Hills, CA 90210-4874, USA

Bartlett, Neil (Misc)
6 Oak Dr
Orinda, CA 94563-3912, USA

Bartlett, Robin (Actor)
c/o Staff Member *Gersh (LA)*
9465 Wilshire Blvd Ste 600
Beverly Hills, CA 90212-2612, USA

Bartlett, Thomas A (Educator)
1209 SW 6th Ave Unit 904
Portland, OR 97204-1031, USA

Bartlett O'Reilly, Alison (Actor)
c/o Carolyn Anthony *Anthony & Associates*
PO Box 910
New York, NY 10108-1201

Bartletti, Don (Journalist)
202 W 1st St
Los Angeles, CA 90012-4105, USA

Bartley, Boyd (Athlete, Baseball Player)
7500 Noreast Dr
North Richland Hills, TX 76180-6736, USA

Bartley, Ephesians (Athlete, Football Player)
3552 Kittery Dr
Snellville, GA 30039-6033, USA

Bartmann, Bill (Business Person)
8556 E 101st St Ste C
Tulsa, OK 74133-7036, USA

Bartoe, John-David F (Astronaut)
2724 Lighthouse Dr
Houston, TX 77058-4318, USA

Bartoletti, Bruno (Conductor)
20 N Wacker Dr
Chicago, IL 60606-2806, USA

Bartoletti, Louis (Athlete, Golfer)
1450 Longlea Ter
Wellington, FL 33414-9017, USA

Bartoli, Cecilia (Musician)
8 St James's Square
London SW1Y 4JU, UNITED KINGDOM

Bartolome, Victor (Athlete, Basketball Player)
1025A Rinconada Rd
Santa Barbara, CA 93101-1424, USA

Barton, Austin (Artist)
100 N Lake St
Joseph, OR 97846-8500, USA

Barton, Bob (Athlete, Baseball Player)
37193 Stardust Way
Murrieta, CA 92563-5076, USA

Barton, Daric (Athlete, Baseball Player)
958 Naples Dr
Corona, CA 92882-6350, USA

Barton, Dorie (Actor)
c/o Dan Spilo *Industry Entertainment Partners*
955 Carrillo Dr Ste 300
Los Angeles, CA 90048-5400, USA

Barton, Eric (Athlete, Football Player)
23 Hayes Hill Dr
Northport, NY 11768-1331, USA

Barton, Glenys (Artist)
199-205 Richmond Road
London E8 3NJ, UNITED KINGDOM (UK)

Barton, Gregory (Greg) (Athlete, Football Player)
190 College St S
Monmouth, OR 97361-2003, USA

Barton, Harris S (Athlete, Football Player)
334 Lincoln Ave
Palo Alto, CA 94301-2730, USA

Barton, James (Jim) (Athlete, Football Player)
9375 Gulf Shore Dr Apt 204
Naples, FL 34108-2156, USA

Barton, Joe (Congressman, Politician)
2109 Rayburn Hob
Washington, DC 20515-4306, USA

Barton, Katie (Stylist)
c/o Kristy Charroin *Straub Collaborative Inc*
2503 N Albina Ave
Portland, OR 97227-1761, USA

Barton, Lou Ann (Musician)
2010 Kinney Ave
Austin, TX 78704-4008, USA

Barton, Mischa (Actor)
c/o Nuala Barton *Mania*
2001 Wilshire Blvd Ste 250
Santa Monica, CA 90403-5681, USA

Barton, Rachel (Musician)
40 W 57th St
New York, NY 10019-4001, USA

Barton, Shawn (Athlete, Baseball Player)
1009 Helm Ln
Reading, PA 19605-3313, USA

Bartosh, Cliff (Athlete, Baseball Player)
939 Fairlawn Dr
Duncanville, TX 75116-3003, USA

Bartosik, Alison (Swimmer)
c/o Staff Member *Premier Management Group (PMG Sports)*
115 Crescent Commons Dr Ste 250
Cary, NC 27518-8134, USA

Bartovic, Milan (Athlete, Hockey Player)
141 Bennington Hills Ct
West Henrietta, NY 14586-9768, USA

Bartrum, Mike (Athlete, Football Player)
43375 Carlton Pl
Pomeroy, OH 45769-9462, USA

Bartucelli, Jean-Louis (Actor)
9 rue Benard
Paris F-75014, France

Bartz, Carol A (Business Person)
111 McInnis Pkwy
San Rafael, CA 94903-2773, USA

Bartz, Gary L (Composer, Musician)
300 Mercer St Apt 3J
New York, NY 10003-6732, USA

Baruch, Lisa (Stylist)
c/o Staff Member *Ford Models (Chicago)*
311 W Superior St
Chicago, IL 60654-3548, USA

Baruchel, Jay (Actor)
c/o Willie Mercer *Thruline Entertainment*
9250 Wilshire Blvd Ground Fl
Beverly Hills, CA 90212, USA

Baryshnikov, Mikhail (Actor, Dancer)
450 W 37th St Ste 501
New York, NY 10018-4016, USA

Barzilauskas, Carl (Athlete, Football Player)
4444 Lower Schooner Rd
Nashville, IN 47448-9476, USA

Basa??ez, Sergio (Actor)
c/o Staff Member *TV Azteca*
Periferico Sur 4121 Colonia Fuentes del Pedregal
DF CP 14141, Mexico

Basana, Fred (Athlete, Baseball Player)
222 Diamond Oaks Rd
Roseville, CA 95678-1007, USA

Basaraba, Gary (Actor)
26 Rue Albus
Toulouse 31300, FRANCE

Basch, Harry (Actor)
920 1/2 S Serrano Ave
Los Angeles, CA 90006-1108, USA

Basche, David (Actor)
c/o Mark Rousso *New Wave Entertainment (LA)*
2660 W Olive Ave
Burbank, CA 91505-4525, USA

Basche, David Alan (Actor)
c/o Brad Mendelsohn *New Wave Entertainment (LA)*
2660 W Olive Ave
Burbank, CA 91505-4525, USA

Baschnagel, Brian D (Athlete, Football Player)
1824 Ridgewood Ln W
Glenview, IL 60025-2206, USA

Basco, Dante (Actor)
6500 Wilshire Blvd Ste 2200
Los Angeles, CA 90048-4942, USA

Basco, Derek (Actor)
c/o Staff Member *GVA Talent Agency Inc*
8981 W Sunset Blvd Ste 101
Los Angeles, CA 90069-1850, USA

Basco, Dion (Actor)
1680 Vine St Ste 1016
Los Angeles, CA 90028-8800, USA

Basgall, Monty (Athlete, Baseball Player)
1321 Buckhorn Cir
Sierra Vista, AZ 85635-0902, USA

Bashir, Idrees (Athlete, Football Player)
5579 Mountain View Pass
Stone Mountain, GA 30087-6020, USA

Bashir, Martin (Correspondent, Journalist, Television Host)
c/o Staff Member *Nightline*
1717 Desales St NW
Washington, DC 20036-4401, USA

Bashkirov, Dmitri A (Musician)
25 Martirez Oblatos Pozuelo
Madrid, SPAIN

Basia (Music Group)
c/o Staff Member *Creative Artists Agency (CAA-LA)*
2000 Avenue of the Stars Ste 100
Los Angeles, CA 90067-4705, USA

Basilio, Carmen (Boxer)
67 Boxwood Dr
Rochester, NY 14617-4002, USA

Basinger, Kim (Actor)
4833 Don Juan Pl
Woodland Hills, CA 91364-4705, USA

Basinski, Ed (Athlete, Baseball Player)
8530 SW Curry Dr Unit B
Wilsonville, OR 97070-8448, USA

Baska, Richard (Rick) (Athlete, Football Player)
14132 Hereford St
Westminster, CA 92683-3529, USA

Basralian, Stephanie (Stylist)
Prefers to be contacted via telephone or email

Bass, Anthony (Athlete, Football Player)
120 Ridgewood Frst
Saint Albans, WV 25177-9502, USA

Bass, Bob (Athlete, Basketball Player, Coach)
2266 Deerfield Dr
Fort Mill, SC 29715-6941, USA

Bass, Doug (Actor)
c/o Jana Marimpietri *Mosaic Media Group*
9200 W Sunset Blvd Ste 10
Los Angeles, CA 90069-3608, USA

Bass, Fontella (Music Group, Musician)
c/o Staff Member *Nonesuch Records*
75 Rockefeller Plz Fl 8
New York, NY 10019-6908, USA

Bass, George F (Archaeologist)
1600 Dominik Dr
College Station, TX 77840-3623, USA

Bass, Glenn (Athlete, Football Player)
4185 Diplomacy Cir
Tallahassee, FL 32308-8720, USA

Bass, Jules (Director, Musician, Producer, Writer)
c/o Staff Member *Rankin/Bass Productions*
24 W 55th St
New York, NY 10019-5456, USA

Bass, Karen (Congressman, Politician)
405 Cannon Hob
Washington, DC 20515-4309, USA

Bass, Kevin (Athlete, Baseball Player)
3630 Maranatha Dr
Sugar Land, TX 77479-9665, USA

Bass, Lance (Musician)
c/o Jessica Berger *Sunshine, Sachs & Associates*
149 5th Ave Fl 7
New York, NY 10010-6824, USA

Bass, Michael T (Athlete, Football Player)
4703 NW 36th St
Gainesville, FL 32605-1017, USA

Bass, Norm (Athlete, Baseball Player)
8814 S 3rd Ave
Inglewood, CA 90305-2802, USA

Bass, Norm (Athlete, Football Player)
8814 S 3rd Ave
Inglewood, CA 90305-2802, USA

Bass, Randy (Athlete, Baseball Player)
2709 SW Coombs Rd
Lawton, OK 73505-0809, USA

Bass, Ronald (Writer)
c/o Staff Member *Creative Artists Agency (CAA-LA)*
2000 Avenue of the Stars Ste 100
Los Angeles, CA 90067-4705, USA

Bass, Ronald (Ron) (Actor, Producer, Writer)
c/o Staff Member *Writers Co-Op*
4000 Warner Blvd Bldg 1
Burbank, CA 91522-0001, USA

Bassen, Bob (Athlete, Coach, Hockey Player)
12 Chapman Chase
Windsor Locks, CT 06096-1343, USA

Bassett, Angela (Actor)
69 Fremont Pl
Los Angeles, CA 90005-3857, USA

Bassett, Brian (Cartoonist, Editor)
1120 John St
Seattle, WA 98109-5321, USA

Bassett, Leslie R (Composer, Musician)
5433 Ashmoore Ln
Flowery Branch, GA 30542-2777, USA

Bassett, Tim (Athlete, Basketball Player)
1143 Dorsey Pl
Plainfield, NJ 07062-2207, USA

Bassey, Dame Shirley (Musician)
24 Avenue Princess Grace
Monte Carlo 1200, Monaco

Bassey, Jennifer (Actor)
12 E 86th St Apt 1728
New York, NY 10028-0517, USA

Bassingthwaighte, Natalie (Actor)
c/o Staff Member *Mark Byrne Management*
1/2 Cooper St Double Bay
Sydney, NSW 2028, Australia

Basslitz, Georg (Artist)
Schloss Demeberg
Holle 31188, GERMANY

Bassman, Herman (Red) (Athlete, Football Player)
7860 Rolling Woods Ct Apt 305
Springfield, VA 22152-3629, USA

Basso, Gabriel (Actor)
c/o David Eisenberg *Protege Entertainment*
710 E Angeleno Ave
Burbank, CA 91501-2213, USA

Bast, William (Producer)
6691 Whitley Ter
Los Angeles, CA 90068-3220, USA

Bastedo, Alexandra (Actor)
68 Old Brompton Rd #280
London SW7 3LQ, UNITED KINGDOM (UK)

Bastel, Emily (Athlete, Golfer)
5377 County Highway 330
Upper Sandusky, OH 43351-9772, USA

Bastista, Rafael (Athlete, Baseball Player)
Box 211
San Pedro de Macoris, Dominican Republic

Basu, Bipasha (Actor)
c/o Simone Sheffield *Canyon Entertainment*
PO Box 256
Palm Springs, CA 92263-0256, USA

Bat for Lashes (Music Group)
c/o Staff Member *Red Light Management (LA)*
8439 W Sunset Blvd Ste 2
Los Angeles, CA 90069-1925, USA

Batali, Dean (Writer)
c/o Michael Van Dyck *Genesis*
360 N Crescent Dr
Beverly Hills, CA 90210-4874, USA

Batali, Mario (Chef, Television Host)
1 5th Ave
New York, NY 10003-4312, USA

Batalla, Rick (Actor)
c/o Staff Member *Halpern Management*
PO Box 5042
Santa Monica, CA 90409-5042, USA

Batch, Charlie (Athlete, Football Player)
1844 Willow Oak Dr
Wexford, PA 15090-2506, USA

Batchelor, Rich (Athlete, Baseball Player)
1004 Pineneedle Rd
Hartsville, SC 29550-8452, USA

Bateman, Brian (Athlete, Golfer)
100 Brunswick Ave
Saint Simons Island, GA 31522-2605, USA

Bateman, Jason (Actor)
c/o Michael Rotenberg *3 Arts Entertainment Inc*
9460 Wilshire Blvd Fl 7
Beverly Hills, CA 90212-2713, USA

Bateman, Justine (Actor)
c/o Stephen (Steve) LaManna *Innovative Artists (LA)*
1505 10th St
Santa Monica, CA 90401-2805, USA

Bateman, Marv (Athlete, Football Player)
1022 W Smithsonian Way
Apple Valley, UT 84737-4830, USA

Bates, Alfred (Athlete, Track Athlete)
4506 Mulberry St
Philadelphia, PA 19124-3724, USA

Bates, Bill (Athlete, Football Player)
5454 County Rd # 126
Celina, TX 75009, USA

Bates, Billy (Athlete, Basketball Player)
23727 Farm Hill Rd
Spring, TX 77373-5818, USA

Bates, Billy Ray (Athlete, Basketball Player)
8051 Gibbon St
Daniel Island, SC 29492-8351, USA

Bates, Charles C (Oceanographer)
750 S La Posada Cir Apt 77
Green Valley, AZ 85614-6432, USA

Bates, Del (Athlete, Baseball Player)
8213 NE 115th Way
Kirkland, WA 98034-3506, USA

Bates, Dick (Athlete, Baseball Player)
5859 W Cielo Grande
Glendale, AZ 85310-3631, USA

Bates, Dwayne (Athlete, Football Player)
76 Houston Loop
Jackson, SC 29831-3119, USA

Bates, Emma (Actor)
c/o Marianne Golan *Marianne Golan Management*
6528 W 6th St
Los Angeles, CA 90048-4716, USA

Bates, Jason (Athlete, Baseball Player)
9856 W Freiburg Dr Unit F
Littleton, CO 80127-5949, USA

Bates, Kathy (Actor)
c/o Susan Smith *Susan Smith Company, The*
1344 N Wetherly Dr
Los Angeles, CA 90069-1817, USA

Bates, Mario (Athlete, Football Player)
PO Box 5832
Scottsdale, AZ 85261-5832, USA

Bates, Michael (Athlete, Football Player)
16432 S 18th Ave
Phoenix, AZ 85045-1720, USA

Bates, Pat (Athlete, Golfer)
215 Ward Cir Ste 200
Brentwood, TN 37027-2306, USA

Bates, Patrick J (Athlete, Football Player)
2745 N Collins St Apt 11123
Arlington, TX 76006-7108, USA

Bates, Robert T (Misc)
601 W Golf Rd
Mount Prospect, IL 60056-4276, USA

Bates, Shawn (Athlete, Hockey Player)
35 Bradshaw St
Medford, MA 02155-4819, USA

Bates, Ted (Athlete, Football Player)
4036 Paige St
Los Angeles, CA 90031-1437, USA

Bathe, Bill (Athlete, Baseball Player)
5378 N Ridge Spring Pl
Tucson, AZ 85749-7106, USA

Bathe, Frank (Athlete, Hockey Player)
2 Meadowood Dr
Scarborough, ME 04074-9421, USA

Bathe, Ryan Michelle (Actor)
c/o Nick Campbell *Commonwealth Talent Group*
PO Box 36514
Los Angeles, CA 90036-0514, USA

Bathgate, Andy (Athlete, Hockey Player)
43 Brentwood Dr
Brampton, ON L6T 1R1, Canada

Bathgate, Frank (Athlete, Hockey Player)
602-330 Mill St S
Brampton, ON L6Y 3V3, Canada

Batikis, Annastasia (Athlete, Baseball Player)
1023 Crab Tree Ln
Racine, WI 53406-4109, USA

Batinkoff, Randall (Actor)
1330 4th St
Santa Monica, CA 90401-1302, USA

Batista, Cardinal Giovanni (Religious Leader)
Piazza Pio XII #10
Roma I-00193, ITALY

Batista, Dave (Wrestler)
2020 Pennsylvania Ave NW # 179
Washington, DC 20006-1811, USA

Batista, Eike (Business Person)
Praia Do Flamengo, 66, 10º Andar
Flamengo
Rio De Janerio, RJ 22210-903, Brazil

Batista, Tony (Athlete)
333 W Camden St
Baltimore, MD 21201-2496

Batiste, Kevin (Athlete, Baseball Player)
3624 Avenue M
Galveston, TX 77550-4145, USA

Batiste, Kim (Athlete, Baseball Player)
16163 Aikens Rd
Prairieville, LA 70769-4903, USA

Batiste, Michael (Athlete, Football Player)
2720 Edmonds St
Beaumont, TX 77705-1437, USA

Batiuk, Thomas M (Tom) (Cartoonist)
4520 Main St
Kansas City, MO 64111-1876, USA

Batra, Pooja (Actor, Bollywood)
403H Gokul Vihar II Thakur Complex
Kandivli E
Mumbai, MS 400068, INDIA

Batt, Bryan (Actor)
c/o Marc Chancer *Origin Talent Agency*
4705 Laurel Canyon Blvd Ste 306
Studio City, CA 91607-5940, USA

Battaglia, Bates (Athlete, Hockey Player)
832 Graham St
Raleigh, NC 27605-1125, USA

Battaglia, Marco (Athlete, Football Player)
15832 79th St
Howard Beach, NY 11414-2907, USA

Battaglia, Matt (Actor)
c/o Stewart Strunk *Main Title Entertainment*
2225 Wilshire Blvd Suite 500
Los Angeles, CA 90036, USA

Battaglia, Rik (Actor)
Viale Montegrappa 10 Colle Verde
Guidonia
Rome 12, ITALY

Batten, Patrick (Athlete, Football Player)
9403 E 64th Ter
Raytown, MO 64133-4916, USA

Batterman, Barbara Jo (Misc)
9171 Placer Bullion Ave
Las Vegas, NV 89178-6200, USA

Battie, Demetrius (Tony) (Athlete, Basketball Player)
11264 Bridge House Rd
Windermere, FL 34786-5405, USA

Battier, Shane (Athlete, Basketball Player)
490 Bruin Lake Rd
Gregory, MI 48137-9648, USA

Battifarano, AJ (Stylist)
235 W 75th St Apt 10G
New York, NY 10023-1763, USA

Battista, Bobbie
c/o Staff Member *Atamira*
3400 Peachtree Rd NE Ste 300
Atlanta, GA 30326-1107, USA

Battle, Allen (Athlete, Baseball Player)
106 Donette Loop
Daphne, AL 36526-7764, USA

Battle, Arnaz (Athlete, Football Player)
1091 Broadmoore Ln
Prosper, TX 75078-8940, USA

Battle, Howard (Athlete, Baseball Player)
238 Romana Ave SE
Albuquerque, NM 87102-5039, USA

Battle, James (Athlete, Football Player)
5 Oasis Ct
St Albert, AB T8N 6X2, Canada

Battle, John (Athlete, Basketball Player)
125 Glen Beigh Run
Tyrone, GA 30290-1874, USA

Battle, Julian (Athlete, Football Player)
196 Monterey Way
West Palm Beach, FL 33411-7817, USA

Battle, Kenny (Athlete, Basketball Player)
835 W Warner Rd Ste 101-445
Gilbert, AZ 85233-7296, USA

Battle, Lois (Writer)
375 Hudson St
New York, NY 10014-3658, USA

Battle, Mike (Athlete, Football Player)
712 Rodes Valley Dr
Nellysford, VA 22958-8049, USA

Battle, Ralph (Athlete, Football Player)
184 Timber Oak Rd
Huntsville, AL 35806-4110, USA

Battle, Terry (Athlete, Football Player)
37678 Rushing Wind Ct
Murrieta, CA 92563-2734, USA

Battles, Ainsley (Athlete, Football Player)
2859 Yellow Pine Dr
Jacksonville, FL 32277-3462, USA

Battles, Zoe (Stylist)
c/o Staff Member *LA Rep*
8312 Utica Dr
Los Angeles, CA 90046-7716, USA

Batton, Chris (Athlete, Baseball Player)
29806 Yorkton Rd
Murrieta, CA 92563-4748, USA

Batton, Dave (Athlete, Basketball Player)
6506 Bayonne Dr
Spring, TX 77389-3607, USA

Batts, Lloyd (Athlete, Basketball Player)
500 S Denton Ave
Glenwood, IL 60425, USA

Batts, Matt (Athlete, Baseball Player)
17927 Silver Creek Ct
Baton Rouge, LA 70810-8918, USA

Batts, Warren L (Business Person)
3600 W Lake Ave
Glenview, IL 60026-1215, USA

Baty, Greg (Athlete, Football Player)
4 King St
Redwood City, CA 94062-1938, USA

Bauchau, Patrick (Actor)
c/o Richard Schwartz *Richard Schwartz Management*
2934 1/2 N Beverly Glen Cir # 107
Los Angeles, CA 90077-1724, USA

Baucus, Max (Senator)
511 Hart Senate Ofc Bldg
Washington, DC 20510-0001, USA

Baudry, Patrick
305 Ave Mairie
Eaunas 31600, FRANCE

Bauer, Alice (Athlete, Golfer)
77165 Avenida Arteaga
La Quinta, CA 92253-2552, USA

Bauer, Belinda (Actor)
c/o Staff Member *The Rights House (UK)*
Drury House 34-43 Russell St
London WC2B 5HA, UK

Bauer, Chris (Actor)
c/o Peg Donegan *Framework Entertainment (LA)*
9057 Nemo St Ste C
West Hollywood, CA 90069-5511, USA

Bauer, Donna (Business Person)
11006 Reading Rd Ste 201
Cincinnati, OH 45241-1980, USA

Bauer, Erwin A (Photographer)
8880 SE 19th Avenue Rd
Ocala, FL 34480-5711, USA

Bauer, Hank (Athlete, Football Player)
11150 Alejo Pl
San Diego, CA 92124-1521, USA

Bauer, Jaime Lyn (Actor)
5116 Lankershim Blvd
North Hollywood, CA 91601-3717, USA

Bauer, John (Athlete, Football Player)
9764 Cambridge Cir
Mokena, IL 60448-7726, USA

Bauer, Kristen (Actor)
c/o Arthur Toretsky *Paradigm (LA)*
360 N Crescent Dr
Beverly Hills, CA 90210-4874, USA

Bauer, Kristin (Actor)
c/o Sheree Cohen *Kohner Agency, The*
9300 Wilshire Blvd Ste 555
Beverly Hills, CA 90212-3211, USA

Bauer, Linda Susan (Actor)
2476 Glendale Cir SE
Smyrna, GA 30080-1830, USA

Bauer, Peggy (Photographer)
8880 SE 19th Avenue Rd
Ocala, FL 34480-5711, USA

Bauer, Peter (Publisher)
Time-Life Building Rockefeller Center
New York, NY 10020, USA

Bauer, Rick (Athlete, Baseball Player)
6643 W Limelight Dr
Boise, ID 83714-6109, USA

Bauer, Steven (Actor)
c/o Staff Member *Innovative Artists (LA)*
1505 10th St
Santa Monica, CA 90401-2805, USA

Bauer, William J (Judge)
111 N Canal St
Chicago, IL 60606-7218, USA

Bauer van Straten, Kristin (Actor)
c/o Ben Levine *Kritzer Levine Wilkins Entertainment*
11872 La Grange Ave Fl 1
Los Angeles, CA 90025-5283, USA

Baugh, Gavin (Athlete, Baseball Player)
3605 Pasadena Dr
San Mateo, CA 94403-2947, USA

Baugh, Laura (Athlete, Golfer)
5225 Timberview Ter
Orlando, FL 32819-3924, USA

Baugh, Sammy (Athlete, Football Coach, Football Player)
General Delivery
Rotan, TX 79546-9999, USA

Baugh, Tom (Athlete, Football Player)
14716 S Bynum Rd
Lone Jack, MO 64070-9286, USA

Baughan, Maxie C (Athlete, Coach, Football Player)
3355 Lawndale Rd
Reisterstown, MD 21136-4026, USA

Baughman, J Ross (Journalist, Misc, Photographer)
31101 Harbour Vista Cir
Saint Augustine, FL 32080-5138, USA

Baughman, Justin (Athlete, Baseball Player)
4052 NE 21st Ave
Portland, OR 97212-1433, USA

Baum, Herbert M (Business Person)
700 Milam St
Houston, TX 77002-2806, USA

Baum, John (Athlete, Basketball Player)
8216 Fenton Rd
Glenside, PA 19038-7144, USA

Baum, Justine (Stylist)
11 Cushing Dr
Mill Valley, CA 94941-1060, USA

Baum, Rich (Stylist)
8562 Gunner Way
Fair Oaks, CA 95628-5346, USA

Bauman, Jon (Bowzer) (Musician)
3168 Oakshire Dr
Los Angeles, CA 90068-1743, USA

Bauman, Jon (Bowzer) (Music Group)
1161 NW 76th Street Ave
Plantation, FL 33322, USA

Bauman, Rashad (Athlete, Football Player)
14724 SE Loren Ln
Portland, OR 97267-1700, USA

Baumann, Frank M (Athlete, Baseball Player)
7712 Sunray Ln
Saint Louis, MO 63123-1938, USA

Baumann, Herbert K W (Composer)
Franziskaserster 16 #1419
Munich 81669, GERMANY

Baumann, Kenny (Actor)
c/o Michael Valeo *Valeo Entertainment*
8265 W Sunset Blvd Ste 103
West Hollywood, CA 90046-2433, USA

Baumbach, Noah (Actor)
c/o Brad Gross *Brad Gross Agency, The*
161 S Arden Blvd
Los Angeles, CA 90004-3716, USA

Baumgardner, Larry (Athlete, Football Player)
1125 Loma Ave
Coronado, CA 92118-2835, USA

Baumgarten, Ross (Athlete, Baseball Player)
1020 Bluff Rd
Glencoe, IL 60022-1152, USA

Baumgartner, Bruce (Motivational Speaker, Wrestler)
12765 Forrest Dr
Edinboro, PA 16412-1281, USA

Baumgartner, John (Athlete, Baseball Player)
1215 Oxford Ct
Birmingham, AL 35242-4676, USA

Baumgartner, Ken (Athlete, Hockey Player)
39 Court St Apt 1
Newton, MA 02458-1372, USA

Baumgartner, Mary (Athlete, Baseball Player)
60 Lane 440 Jimmerson Lk
Fremont, IN 46737-9634, USA

Baumgartner, Mike (Athlete, Hockey Player)
39998 290th St
Roseau, MN 56751-8321, USA

Baumgartner, Steve (Athlete, Football Player)
144 Brookside Dr
Mandeville, LA 70471-3202, USA

Baumgartner, William (Doctor)
600 N Wolfe St
Baltimore, MD 21287-0005, USA

Baumhower, Robert G (Bob) (Athlete, Football Player)
21201 Ayrshire Ln
Fairhope, AL 36532-4479, USA

Baumler, Hans-Jurgen (Actor)
18 chemin du Castellar
Le Rouret F-06650, France

Baun, Bob (Athlete, Hockey Player)
35 Pittman Crst
Ajax, ON L1S 3G4, CANADA

Bauta, Ed (Athlete, Baseball Player)
1400 S Nova Rd Apt 104
Daytona Beach, FL 32114-5845, USA

Baute, Joseph A (Business Person)
11 Trafalgar Sq Ste 200
Nashua, NH 03063-1991, USA

Bautista, Danny (Athlete, Baseball Player)
901 E Van Buren St Apt 1063
Phoenix, AZ 85006-4014, USA

Bautista, David (Athlete, Wrestler)
c/o Staff Member *World Wrestling Entertainment (WWE)*
1241 E Main St
Stamford, CT 06902-3520, USA

Bautista, Francisco Javier Jr (Frankie J) (Musician)
c/o Staff Member *BMG*
1540 Broadway
New York, NY 10036-4039, USA

Bautista, Jose (Athlete, Baseball Player)
15766 NW 11th St
Pembroke Pines, FL 33028-1600, USA

Bautista, Jose (Athlete, Baseball Player)
100 Shockoe Slip Fl 4
Richmond, VA 23219-4100, USA

Bavaro, David (Athlete, Football Player)
55 Ash St Unit 14
Danvers, MA 01923-2710, USA

Bavaro, Mark (Athlete, Football Player)
17 Long Hl
Boxford, MA 01921-2453, USA

Bawel, Edward (Athlete, Football Player)
1169 2nd Ave
Jasper, IN 47546-3411, USA

Bax, Kylie (Actor, Model)
c/o Staff Member *Storm Model Management*
5 Jubilee Pl 1st Floor
London SW3 3TD, UNITED KINGDOM

Baxendale, Helen (Actor)
c/o Staff Member *Yakety Yak*
8-A Bloomsbury Sq
London WC1A 2NE, UNITED KINGDOM (UK)

Baxes, Mike (Athlete, Baseball Player)
303 Wickham Dr
Mill Valley, CA 94941-3443, USA

Baxley, Rob (Athlete, Football Player)
39 Oak Creek Dr
Yorkville, IL 60560-9779, USA

Baxter, Fred (Athlete, Football Player)
PO Box 14
Brundidge, AL 36010-0014, USA

Baxter, James (Animator)
100 University City Plz
University City, CA 91608, USA

Baxter, Jeff (Skunk) (Music Group, Musician)
509 Hartnell St
Monterey, CA 93940-2825, USA

Baxter, Lea-Anne (Stylist)
c/o Staff Member *Judy Inc*
1 Yorkville Ave
Toronto ON M4W 1L1, Canada

Baxter, Lloyd (Athlete, Football Player)
718 Minturn Ln
Austin, TX 78748-6568, USA

Baxter, Meredith (Actor)
c/o Alan Iezman *Shelter Entertainment*
9454 Wilshire Blvd Ste 715
Beverly Hills, CA 90212-2925, USA

Baxter, Paul (Athlete, Hockey Player)
1610 Saint John St
Wichita Falls, TX 76302-3315, USA

Baxter, Stephen (Writer)
175 5th Ave
New York, NY 10010-7703, USA

Baxter-Johnson, Patricia (Athlete, Golfer)
111 Bryn Mawr Dr
Lake Worth, FL 33460-6311, USA

Bay, Jason (Athlete, Baseball Player)
c/o Joe Urbon *Creative Artists Agency (CAA-NY)*
162 5th Ave Fl 6
New York, NY 10010-6047, USA

Bay, Michael (Actor, Director, Producer)
c/o Rob Carlson *WmE2 (Endeavor-LA)*
1 William Morris Pl
Beverly Hills, CA 90212-4261, USA

Bay, Susan (Actor)
801 Stone Canyon Rd
Los Angeles, CA 90077-2911, USA

Bay, Willow
1050 Techwood Dr NW
Atlanta, GA 30318-5604

Bay City Rollers (Music Group)
297 Kinderkamack Rd Ste 101
Oradell, NJ 07649-1535, USA

Baye, Nathalie (Actor)
Théâtre De L'Atelier 1 Place Charles Dullin
Paris F-75 018, France

Bayer, Samuel (Director)
c/o Doreen Wilcox Little *Anonymous Content (AC-LA)*
3531 Hayden Ave
Culver City, CA 90232, USA

Bayle, Silvia (Actor)
c/o Staff Member *Telefe - Argentina*
Pavon 2444 (C1248AAT)
Buenos Aires, ARGENTINA

Bayless, Jerryd (Athlete, Basketball Player)
c/o Jeff Schwartz *Excel Sports Management*
9665 Wilshire Blvd Ste 500
Beverly Hills, CA 90212-2312, USA

Bayless, Martin (Athlete, Football Player)
757 Ernroe Dr
Dayton, OH 45417-3507, USA

Bayless, Rick (Athlete, Football Player)
2068 Tesuque Ct
Reno, NV 89511-3600, USA

Bayliss, Jonah (Athlete, Baseball Player)
182 Petitt Dr
Pownal, VT 05261-4433, USA

Bayliss, Rachel (Musician)
Somerset Park Farm
Congelton Chelshire, UK

Baylon, Noah (Writer)
c/o James (Jamie) Feldman *Lichter Grossman Nichols Adler & Goodman*
9200 W Sunset Blvd Ste 1200
Los Angeles, CA 90069-3607, USA

Baylor, Don (Athlete, Baseball Player, Coach)
56325 Riviera
La Quinta, CA 92253-5008, USA

Baylor, Elgin (Athlete, Basketball Player)
2480 Briarcrest Rd
Beverly Hills, CA 90210-1820, USA

Baylor, John (Athlete, Football Player)
211 Oak St
Hattiesburg, MS 39401-2372, USA

Baylor, Raymond (Athlete, Football Player)
5302 Heathercrest St
Houston, TX 77045-5230, USA

Baylor, Tim (Athlete, Football Player)
1302 Douglas Ave
Minneapolis, MN 55403-2904, USA

Bayne, Howard (Athlete, Basketball Player)
11840 Yarnell Rd
Knoxville, TN 37932-2354, USA

Baynham, Craig (Athlete, Football Player)
1 7th St Apt 1102
Augusta, GA 30901-1397, USA

Bayo, Maria (Opera Singer)
Maxifilianstr 22
Munich 80539, GERMANY

Bayona, Alvaro (Actor)
c/o Gabriel Blanco *Gabriel Blanco Iglesias (Mexico)*
Rio Balsas 35-32 Colonia Cuauhtemoc
DF 6500, Mexico

Bayona, Juan Antonio (Director, Producer, Writer)
c/o Robert Newman *WmE2 (Endeavor-LA)*
9601 Wilshire Blvd Fl 3
Beverly Hills, CA 90210-5219, USA

Bays, Brandon (Motivational Speaker)
P.O. Box 2
Cowbridge CF71 7WN, United Kingdom

Baz, Farouk El- (Geophysicist, Physicist)
Remot Sensing Center
Boston, MA 2215, USA

Baze, Winiford (Athlete, Football Player)
5317 New Copeland Rd Apt 119
Tyler, TX 75703-3964, USA

Bazell, Robert J (Correspondent)
4001 Nebraska Ave NW
Washington, DC 20016-2733, USA

Bazer, Fuller W (Scientist)
8600 Creekview Ct
College Station, TX 77845-5560, USA

BB Mak (Music Group)
c/o Staff Member *Hollywood Records*
500 S Buena Vista St
Burbank, CA 91521-0002, USA

BBMAK (Musician)
P.O. Box 22580
London W86YR, UK

Beach, Adam (Actor)
c/o Dan Spilo *Industry Entertainment Partners*
955 Carrillo Dr Ste 300
Los Angeles, CA 90048-5400, USA

Beach, Bill (Bowler)
3715 Lee Run Rd
Hermitage, PA 16148-6185, USA

Beach, Ed (Athlete, Football Player)
938 Sedgewick Ave
Westfield, NJ 7090, USA

Beach, Gary (Actor)
122 Andalusia Way
Palm Beach Gardens, FL 33418-1723, USA

Beach, Michael (Actor)
1823 Virginia Rd
Los Angeles, CA 90019-5938, USA

Beach, Pat (Athlete, Football Player)
2523 W Beach Rd
Oak Harbor, WA 98277-8865, USA

Beach, Roger C (Business Person)
2141 Rosecrans Ave
El Segundo, CA 90245-4747, USA

Beach, Sanjay (Athlete, Football Player)
2989 Riviera Ln
Westlake, OH 44145-6844, USA

Beacham, Stephanie (Actor)
c/o Staff Member *The Rights House (UK)*
Drury House 34-43 Russell St
London WC2B 5HA, UK

Beacher, Jeff (Producer, Television Host)
5275 Arville St Ste 348
Las Vegas, NV 89118-4948, USA

Beachy, Roger N (Scientist)
526 W Polo Dr
Saint Louis, MO 63105, USA

Beadle, Carol (Stylist)
c/o Staff Member *Rex Agency, The*
6311 Romaine St
Los Angeles, CA 90038-2617, USA

Beagle, Ronald G (Ron) (Athlete, Football Player)
3830 San Ysidro Way
Sacramento, CA 95864-5260, USA

Beahan, Kate (Actor)
c/o Suzan Bymel *Management 360*
9111 Wilshire Blvd
Beverly Hills, CA 90210-5508, USA

Beal, Jack (Artist)
80 Epps Rd
Oneonta, NY 13820-6440, USA

Beal, Jeff (Composer)
c/o Staff Member *Gorfaine/Schwartz Agency Inc*
4111 W Alameda Ave Ste 509
Burbank, CA 91505-4171, USA

Beal, Norm (Athlete, Football Player)
21246 Jade Dr
Rocky Mount, MO 65072-2953, USA

Beale, Betty (Writer)
2926 Garfield St NW
Washington, DC 20008-3536, USA

Beale, Simon Russell (Actor)
c/o Tony Lipp *Anonymous Content (AC-LA)*
2000 Avenue of the Stars
Los Angeles, CA 90067-4700, USA

Beall, Bob (Athlete, Baseball Player)
513 NE Birchwood Rd
Hillsboro, OR 97124-3374, USA

Beals, Jennifer (Actor)
c/o David Lust *Patricola Lust PR*
9171 Wilshire Blvd Ste 390
Beverly Hills, CA 90210-5515, USA

Beals, Shawn (Athlete, Football Player)
250 Edward Ave
Pittsburg, CA 94565-4107, USA

Beals, Vaughn L Jr (Business Person)
3700 W Juneau Ave
Milwaukee, WI 53208-2818, USA

Beam, C Arien (Judge)
100 Centennial Mall N
Lincoln, NE 68508-3859, USA

Beam, T J (Athlete, Baseball Player)
8505 E Pepper Tree Ln
Scottsdale, AZ 85250-4912, USA

Beaman, Lee Anne (Actor)
178 S Victory Blvd Ste 205
Burbank, CA 91502-2881, USA

Beamer, Frank (Coach, Football Coach)
Athletic
Blacksburg, VA 24061-0001, USA

Beamer, Lisa (Writer)
9 Cubberly Ct
Cranbury, NJ 08512-2821

Beamon, Autry Jr (Athlete, Football Player)
12200 River Ridge Blvd
Burnsville, MN 55337-1608, USA

Beamon, Trey (Athlete, Baseball Player)
914 Ridgegate Dr
Dallas, TX 75232-3524, USA

Beamon Jr, Charlie (Athlete, Baseball Player)
5522 Fox Sparrow Ct
Stockton, CA 95207-5403, USA

Beamon Sr, Charlie (Athlete, Baseball Player)
355 W Grant Line Rd Apt 212
Tracy, CA 95376-2579, USA

Bean, Alan L (Astronaut)
9173 Briar Forest Dr
Houston, TX 77024-7222, USA

Bean, Andy (Athlete, Golfer)
2912 Grasslands Dr
Lakeland, FL 33803-5418, USA

Bean, Bill (Athlete, Baseball Player)
3253 Courtney Dr
Lompoc, CA 93436-2358, USA

Bean, Bubba (Athlete, Football Player)
1117 Todd Trl
College Station, TX 77845-5145, USA

Bean, Colter (Athlete, Baseball Player)
2116 Shades Crest Rd
Vestavia, AL 35216-1534, USA

Bean, Dawn Pawson (Swimmer)
11902 Red Hill Ave
Santa Ana, CA 92705-3106, USA

Bean, Ed (Athlete, Baseball Player)
'827 3rd Ct SE
Winter Haven, FL 33880, USA

Bean, Henry (Director)
c/o Staff Member *Fuller Films*
625 Santa Clara Ave
Venice, CA 90291-3445, USA

Bean, Noah (Actor)
c/o Nick Campbell *Commonwealth Talent Group*
PO Box 36514
Los Angeles, CA 90036-0514, USA

Bean, Orson (Actor, Comedian)
444 Carroll Canal
Venice, CA 90291-4682, USA

Bean, Robert (Athlete, Football Player)
4197 Summit Crossing Dr
Decatur, GA 30034-3544, USA

Bean, Sean (Actor)
c/o Julie Nathanson *Rogers & Cowan PR (LA)*
Pacific Design Center 8687 Melrose Ave, 7th Floor
West Hollywood, CA 90069, USA

Bean, Shoshana (Actor, Musician)
c/o Tim Marshal *Bauman Redanty & Shaul Agency*
5757 Wilshire Blvd Suite 473
Beverly Hills, CA 90212, USA

Beane, Billy (Athlete, Baseball Player)
33 Brightwood Ln E
Danville, CA 94506-1926, USA

Bear, Greg
c/o Vince Gerardis *Created By*
1041 N Formosa Ave Formosa Bldg Room 10
West Hollywood, CA 90046, USA

Beard, Al (Athlete, Basketball Player)
1201 Orange St Apt 201
Fort Valley, GA 31030-3427, USA

Beard, Alana (Athlete, Basketball Player)
MCI Center 601 F St NW
Washington, DC 20004, USA

Beard, Alfred (Butch) (Athlete, Basketball Player, Coach)
3834 Berleigh Hill Ct
Burtonsville, MD 20866-1392, USA

Beard, Amanda (Swimmer)
c/o Staff Member *Premier Management Group (PMG Sports)*
115 Crescent Commons Dr Ste 250
Cary, NC 27518-8134, USA

Beard, Beverly (Stylist)
c/o Staff Member *Crews*
828 Clemont Dr NE
Atlanta, GA 30306-3694, USA

Beard, Dave (Athlete, Baseball Player)
5325 Derby Chase Ct
Alpharetta, GA 30005-7883, USA

Beard, Ed (Athlete, Football Player)
4110 2nd St
Chesapeake, VA 23324-1547, USA

Beard, Frank (Athlete, Golfer)
73895 Shadow Mountain Dr Apt 4
Palm Desert, CA 92260-4824, USA

Beard, Frank (Musician)
PO Box 163690
Austin, TX 78716-3690, USA

Beard, Mike (Athlete, Baseball Player)
400 Walnut St
Little Rock, AR 72205-4042, USA

Beard, Ted (Athlete, Baseball Player)
10517 Stelor Ln
Fishers, IN 46037-9673, USA

Beard, Tom (Athlete, Football Player)
164 Gale Rd
Mason, MI 48854-9735, USA

Beardsley, Marni (Stylist)
852 NW Albemarle Ter
Portland, OR 97210-3117, USA

Beare, Gary (Athlete, Baseball Player)
17666 Tatia Ct
San Diego, CA 92128-2082, USA

Bearse, Amanda (Actor)
1750 Carroll Dr NW
Atlanta, GA 30318-3673, USA

Bearse, Kevin (Athlete, Baseball Player)
656 Saint Andrews Pl
Manalapan, NJ 07726-9551, USA

Beart, Emmanuelle (Actor)
c/o Staff Member *Agence Artistique Adequat*
80 Rue D'Amsterdam
Paris 75009, France

Beart, Guy (Musician, Songwriter, Writer)
2 Rue du Marquis de Mores
Garches 92380, FRANCE

Beasley, Aaron (Athlete, Football Player)
1635 Braid Hills Dr
Pasadena, MD 21122-3533, USA

Beasley, Allyce (Actor)
145 S Fairfax Ave Ste 310
Los Angeles, CA 90036-2176, USA

Beasley, Alyce (Actor)
c/o Staff Member *TalentWorks (LA)*
3500 W Olive Ave Ste 1400
Burbank, CA 91505-5512, USA

Beasley, Bruce M (Artist)
322 Lewis St
Oakland, CA 94607-1236, USA

Beasley, Charles (Athlete, Basketball Player)
6308 Winton St
Dallas, TX 75214-2645, USA

Beasley, Chris (Athlete, Baseball Player)
1013 W Cooley Dr
Gilbert, AZ 85233-2540, USA

Beasley, Derrick (Athlete, Football Player)
141 North St
Andover, MA 01810-1131, USA

Beasley, Fred (Athlete, Football Player)
PO Box 210931
Montgomery, AL 36121-0931, USA

Beasley, John (Actor)
c/o Staff Member *Bauman Redanty & Shaul Agency*
5757 Wilshire Blvd Suite 473
Beverly Hills, CA 90212, USA

Beasley, John (Athlete, Basketball Player)
113 Oak Acres Dr W
Malakoff, TX 75148-3163, USA

Beasley, Lew (Athlete, Baseball Player)
24653 Newtown Rd
Bowling Green, VA 22427-2725, USA

Beasley, Michael (Athlete, Basketball Player)
c/o Jeff Schwartz *Excel Sports Management*
9665 Wilshire Blvd Ste 500
Beverly Hills, CA 90212-2312, USA

Beasley, Terry P (Athlete, Football Player)
4052 Wellington Way
Moody, AL 35004-3507, USA

Beasley, Tom (Athlete, Football Player)
301 Riding Ridge Rd
Annapolis, MD 21403-1653, USA

Beastie Boys (Music Group)
c/o Staff Member *Nasty Little Man*
110 Greene St Ste 605
New York, NY 10012-3838, USA

Beathard, Pete (Athlete, Football Player)
3770 Drake St
Houston, TX 77005-1118, USA

Beaton, Frank (Athlete, Hockey Player)
3327 Chapel Hills Pkwy
Fultondale, AL 35068-1596, USA

Beatrix, HM Queen (Royalty)
Kabinet Van De Koningin Korte Vijverberg 3
The Hague 2513 AB, The Netherlands

Beattie, Jim (Athlete, Baseball Player)
PO Box 231
Quechee, VT 05059-0231, USA

Beattie, Joseph (Actor)
36 - 40 Glasshouse St
London W1B 5DL, UNITED KINGDOM

Beattle, Ann (Writer)
445 Park Ave # 1300
New York, NY 10022-2606, USA

Beattle, Bob (Skier)
210 Aabc Ste N
Aspen, CO 81611-3537, USA

Beattle, Bruce (Cartoonist)
901 6th St
Daytona Beach, FL 32117-3352, USA

Beatty, Blaine (Athlete, Baseball Player)
867 Kolodzey Rd
Victoria, TX 77905-2520, USA

Beatty, Charles (Athlete, Football Player)
PO Box 2634
Waxahachie, TX 75168-8634, USA

Beatty, Jim (Athlete, Track Athlete)
1516 Larochelle Ln
Charlotte, NC 28226-6868, USA

Beatty, Ned (Actor)
2706 N Beachwood Dr
Los Angeles, CA 90068-1922, USA

Beatty, Warren (Actor, Director, Producer)
c/o Richard Lovett *Creative Artists Agency (CAA-LA)*
2000 Avenue of the Stars Ste 100
Los Angeles, CA 90067-4705, USA

Beaty, Zelmo (Athlete, Basketball Player)
2808 120th Ave NE
Bellevue, WA 98005-1515, USA

Beatz, Swizz (Musician, Producer)
c/o Keith Estabrook *Estabrook Group LLC*
55 Broad St
New York, NY 10004-2501, US

Beau Brummels, The (Music Group, Musician)
PO Box 53664
Indianapolis, IN 46253-0664, USA

Beauchamp, Jim (Athlete, Baseball Player)
105 Paula Dr
Tyrone, GA 30290-2612, USA

Beauchamp, Joe (Athlete, Football Player)
4805 N 24th Pl
Milwaukee, WI 53209-5630, USA

Beauchamp, Rolando (Stylist)
c/o Staff Member *Independent NY*
15 E 30th St Apt 401
New York, NY 10016-7031, USA

Beaudin, Norm (Athlete, Hockey Player)
8625 Stone Harbour Loop
Bradenton, FL 34212-6322, USA

Beaudoin, Doug (Athlete, Football Player)
15143 Springview St
Tampa, FL 33624-2374, USA

Beaudoin, Jocelyne (Stylist)
c/o Celebrity Stylist *Jean Gabriel Kauss/ JGK*
161 Avenue of the Americas Fl 13
New York, NY 10013-1205, USA

Beaufait, Mark (Athlete, Hockey Player)
5454 Longwood Ct SE
Ada, MI 49301-7755, USA

Beauford, Carter (Musician)
3302 Lobban Pl
Charlottesville, VA 22903-7069, USA

Beaufoy, Simon (Director, Producer, Writer)
c/o Staff Member *The Rod Hall agency*
6th Floor Fairgate House 78 New Oxford Street
London WC1A 1HB, United Kingdom

Beaumon, Sterling (Actor)
c/o Staff Member *Stevenson Talent Management*
22838 Epsilon St
Woodland Hills, CA 91364-2813, USA

Beaumont, Jimmy (Musician)
2002 Duquesne Ave
McKeesport, PA 15132-5103, USA

Beaumont, Thomas (Actor)
c/o Staff Member *Scott Stander & Associates*
4533 Van Nuys Blvd Ste 401
Sherman Oaks, CA 91403-2950, USA

Beaupre, Don (Athlete, Hockey Player)
5020 Scriver Rd
Minneapolis, MN 55436-1158, USA

Beauregard, Stephane (Athlete, Hockey Player)
175 Rue Des Plaines
Cowansville, QC J2K 3T8, Canada

Beauvais-Nilon, Garcelle (Actor)
c/o Staff Member *Luber Roklin Management*
8530 Wilshire Blvd Ste 550
Beverly Hills, CA 90211-3133, USA

Beaver, Jim (Actor)
1180 S Beverly Dr Ste 301
Los Angeles, CA 90035-1154, USA

Beaver, Joe (Rodeo Rider)
PO Box 1595
Huntsville, TX 77342-1595, USA

Beaver, Terry (Actor)
10100 Santa Monica Blvd Ste 2500
Los Angeles, CA 90067-4116, USA

Beavers, Scott (Athlete, Football Player)
4030 Pittman Rd
College Park, GA 30349-1439, USA

Beban, Gary J (Athlete, Football Player)
20 Timber Ln
Northbrook, IL 60062-3716, USA

Bebout, Nick (Athlete, Football Player)
1606 Major Ave
Riverton, WY 82501-8900, USA

Becerra, Xavier (Congressman, Politician)
1226 Longworth Hob
Washington, DC 20515-4208, USA

Bech, Debra (Actor)
480 Cedar St
Saint Paul, MN 55101-2217, USA

Becherer, Hans W (Business Person)
1 John Deere Pl
Moline, IL 61265-8010, USA

Becht, Anthony (Athlete, Football Player)
911 Morgan Ave
Drexel Hill, PA 19026-3316, USA

Bechtel, Riley P (Business Person)
50 Beale St
San Francisco, CA 94105-1813, USA

Bechtel, Stephen D Jr (Business Person)
50 Beale St
San Francisco, CA 94105-1813, USA

Beck, Aaron T (Doctor)
3600 Market St Ste 700
Philadelphia, PA 19104-2650, USA

Beck, Barry (Athlete, Hockey Player)
c/o Staff Member *Osoyoos Storm*
2 Kildeer Pl
Osoyoos, BC V0H 1V5, Canada

Beck, Braden (Athlete, Football Player)
691 Milverton Rd
Los Altos, CA 94022-3928, USA

Beck, Byron (Athlete, Basketball Player)
1909 S Williams St
Kennewick, WA 99338-1820, USA

Beck, Chip (Athlete, Golfer)
11 Pembroke Dr
Lake Forest, IL 60045-2147, USA

Beck, Ernie (Athlete, Basketball Player)
1523 Brierwood Rd
Havertown, PA 19083-2910, USA

Beck, Glenn (Radio Personality, Television Host)
c/o George Hiltzik *N.S. Bienstock*
1740 Broadway Fl 24
New York, NY 10019-4315, USA

Beck, Jeff (Musician)
c/o Staff Member *Creative Artists Agency (CAA-LA)*
2000 Avenue of the Stars Ste 100
Los Angeles, CA 90067-4705, USA

Beck, John E (Athlete, Football Player)
PO Box 530930
San Diego, CA 92153-0930, USA

Beck, Laurie Jean (Stylist)
81 Mallard Dr
Avon, CT 06001-4544, USA

Beck, Maria (Actor)
c/o Staff Member *Shamon Freitas Talent Agency*
3916 Oregon St
San Diego, CA 92104-2806, USA

Beck, Martha (Writer)
18011 N 14th Pl
Phoenix, AZ 85022-7201, USA

Beck, Martin (Actor)
c/o Dale Garrick *Dale Garrick International Agency*
928 N San Vicente Blvd Apt 201
West Hollywood, CA 90069-3850, USA

Beck, Mat (Cinematographer)
621 Via De La Paz
Pacific Palisades, CA 90272-4365, USA

Beck, Michael (Actor)
c/o Staff Member *Paradigm (LA)*
360 N Crescent Dr
Beverly Hills, CA 90210-4874, USA

Beck, Rich (Athlete, Baseball Player)
8218 N Sumter Ct
Spokane, WA 99208-5749, USA

Beck, Robin (Musician)
156 W 56th St # 1803
New York, NY 10019-3800, USA

Beck, Rod (Athlete, Baseball Player)
8623 E Mescal St
Scottsdale, AZ 85260-6632, USA

Beckel, Heather (Writer)
4203 Guadalupe St
Austin, TX 78751-4224, USA

Beckel, Robert D (General)
Superintendent's Office
Roswell, NM 88201, USA

Beckenbauer, Franz (Soccer Player)
Postfach 90 04 51
München 81504, Germany

Becker, Arthur (Athlete, Basketball Player)
1879 E Brentrup Dr
Tempe, AZ 85283-4275, USA

Becker, Beth (Stylist)
c/o Staff Member *Blink Management*
421 Washington Ave Ste 202
Miami Beach, FL 33139-6612, USA

Becker, Boris (Athlete, Tennis Player)
c/o Staff Member *IMG (Cleveland)*
1360 E 9th St Ste 100
Cleveland, OH 44114-1730, USA

Becker, Donna (Athlete, Baseball Player)
5316 40th Ave
Kenosha, WI 53144-2707, USA

Becker, Doug (Athlete, Football Player)
6716 Lincoln Ave
Evansville, IN 47715-6920, USA

Becker, Edward R (Judge)
601 Market St
Philadelphia, PA 19106-1737, USA

Becker, Gary S (Nobel Prize Laureate)
1308 E 58th St
Chicago, IL 60637-1717, USA

Becker, George (Misc)
5 Gateway Ctr
Pittsburgh, PA 15222, USA

Becker, Gerry (Actor)
c/o Oliver Mossi *Paradigm (LA)*
360 N Crescent Dr
Beverly Hills, CA 90210-4874, USA

Becker, Gretchen (Actor)
4727 Wilshire Blvd Ste 333
Los Angeles, CA 90010-3874, USA

Becker, Harold (Director, Producer)
c/o Jack Gilardi *International Creative Management (ICM-LA)*
10250 Constellation Blvd Fl 7
Los Angeles, CA 90067-6207, USA

Becker, Isaura (Actor)
c/o Staff Member *Televisa*
Blvd Adolfo Lopez Mateos 232 Colonia San Angel INN
DF CP 01060, MEXICO

Becker, Kuno (Actor)
c/o Ivan De Paz *DePaz Management*
2011 N Vermont Ave
Los Angeles, CA 90027-1931, USA

Becker, Kurt (Athlete, Football Player)
49W412 Scott Rd
Big Rock, IL 60511-9489, USA

Becker, Margaret (Musician)
101 Winners Cir N
Brentwood, TN 37027-5352, USA

Becker, Quinn H (Doctor, General)
2111 Peninsula Dr
San Antonio, TX 78239-3077, USA

Becker, Rich (Athlete, Baseball Player)
210 Mary Senica Ct
La Salle, IL 61301-9676, USA

Becker, Rob (Actor, Comedian)
c/o Staff Member *WmE2 (WMA-LA)*
1 William Morris Pl
Beverly Hills, CA 90212-4261, USA

Becker, Robert J (Misc)
2200 S Ocean Ln Apt 1905
Fort Lauderdale, FL 33316-3832, USA

Becker, Thomas (Athlete)
Hagedomweg 6A
Solingen 42697, GERMANY

Becker, Tony (Actor)
c/o Bonnie Howard 10657 Riverside Dr
Toluca Lake, CA 91602, USA

Becker, Walt (Director)
c/o Matt Luber *Luber Roklin Management*
8530 Wilshire Blvd Ste 550
Beverly Hills, CA 90211-3133, USA

Beckert, Glenn (Athlete, Baseball Player)
1953 Arkansas Ave
Englewood, FL 34224-5505, USA

Becket, MacDonald G (Architect)
2501 Colorado Ave
Santa Monica, CA 90404-3500, USA

Beckett, Bob (Athlete, Hockey Player)
38 Fonthill Blvd
Markham, ON L3R 1V7, Canada

Beckett, Josh (Athlete, Baseball Player)
1 Avery St Apt 20B
Boston, MA 02111-1025, USA

Beckett, Robbie (Athlete, Baseball Player)
15625 Harry Lind Rd
Elgin, TX 78621-3824, USA

Beckett, Rogers (Athlete, Football Player)
635 Gaelic Ct
Apopka, FL 32712-4724, USA

Beckett, Wendy (Sister)
Center Wood Ln
London, ENGLAND W12 7R3

Beckett, William (Musician)
c/o Staff Member *Fueled By Ramen*
PO Box 1803
Tampa, FL 33601-1803, USA

Beckford, Roxanne (Actor)
9255 W Sunset Blvd Ste 401
Los Angeles, CA 90069-3302, USA

Beckford, Tyson (Actor, Model)
388 2nd Ave # 223
New York, NY 10010-5616, USA

Beckham, Brice (Actor)
6561 E Espanita St
Long Beach, CA 90815-4635

Beckham, David (Athlete, Soccer Player)
c/o Simon Fuller *XIX Entertainment*
35-37 Parkgate Rd 32/33 Ransomes Dock
London SW11 4NP, UK

Beckham, Victoria (Actor, Musician)
c/o Simon Fuller *XIX Entertainment*
35-37 Parkgate Rd 32/33 Ransomes Dock
London SW11 4NP, UK

Beckinsale, Kate (Actor)
c/o Cynthia Pett-Dante *Brillstein Entertainment Partners*
9150 Wilshire Blvd Ste 350
Beverly Hills, CA 90212-3453, USA

Beckless, Ian (Athlete, Football Player)
4915 Andros Dr
Tampa, FL 33629-4801, USA

Beckley, Gerry (Music Group, Musician)
9200 W Sunset Blvd Ste 900
Los Angeles, CA 90069-3604, USA

Beckman, Cameron (Athlete, Golfer)
23303 Wilderness Cv
San Antonio, TX 78261-3030, USA

Beckman, Ed (Athlete, Football Player)
4295 18th St NE
Naples, FL 34120-6409, USA

Beckman, Stefan (Stylist)
c/o Staff Member *Exposure NY*
177 Prince St Fl 5
New York, NY 10012-2946, USA

Beckman, Thomas (Athlete, Football Player)
3672 Cedar Shake Dr
Rochester Hills, MI 48309-1013, USA

Beckum, Travis (Athlete, Football Player)
c/o Roosevelt Barnes *Maximum Sports Management*
6435 W Jefferson Blvd # 197
Fort Wayne, IN 46804-6203, USA

Beckwith, Alan (Actor)
3928 Carpenter Ave
Studio City, CA 91604-3764, USA

Beckwith, Darry (Athlete, Football Player)
c/o Jimmy Sexton *SportsTrust Advisors - TN*
1100 Ridgeway Loop Rd Fl 5
Memphis, TN 38120-4053, USA

Beckwith, Joe (Athlete, Baseball Player)
2057 Country Squire Rd
Auburn, AL 36830, USA

Becquer, Julio (Athlete, Baseball Player)
829 Vincent Ave N
Minneapolis, MN 55411-3545, USA

Becton, C W (Religious Leader)
8855 Dunn Rd
Hazelwood, MO 63042-2212, USA

Becton, Julius W Jr (Educator, General)
President's Office
Prairie View, TX 77446, USA

Bedard, Irene (Actor)
6500 Wilshire Blvd Ste 2200
Los Angeles, CA 90048-4942, USA

Bedard, James A (Athlete, Hockey Player)
c/o Staff Member *Detroit Red Wings*
600 Civic Center Dr
Detroit, MI 48226-4419, USA

Bedard, James L (Athlete, Hockey Player)
317 Crawford Ave E
Melfort, SK S0E 1A0, Canada

Bedard, Myriam (Athlete)
3329 Pinecourt
Neufchatel, QC G2B 2E4, CANADA

Bedelia, Bonnie (Actor)
c/o Nevin Dolcefino *Innovative Artists (LA)*
1505 10th St
Santa Monica, CA 90401-2805, USA

Bedell, Bob (Athlete, Basketball Player)
3107 Kipling Way
Louisville, KY 40205-3005, USA

Bedell, Brad (Athlete, Football Player)
545 N Altura Rd
Arcadia, CA 91007-6059, USA

Bedell, Howie (Athlete, Baseball Player)
1187 Crestwood Dr
Pottstown, PA 19464-2931, USA

Bedford, Brian (Actor)
1133 Broadway Ste 1025
New York, NY 10010-7985, USA

Bedford, Steuart J R
12 Penzance Place
London W11 4PA, UNITED KINGDOM (UK)

Bedford, Vance (Athlete, Football Player)
13264 SW 7th Ave
Newberry, FL 32669-3345, USA

Bedi, Kabir (Actor, Bollywood)
B4 Beach House Apt Gandhigram Road
Mumbai, MS 400054, INDIA

Bedingfield, Daniel (Musician)
825 8th Ave
New York, NY 10019-7416

Bedingfield, Natasha (Musician)
c/o Marcel Pariseau *True Public Relations*
6725 W Sunset Blvd Ste 470
Los Angeles, CA 90028-7180, USA

Bednarik, Charles P (Chuck) (Athlete, Football Player)
6379 Winding Rd
Coopersburg, PA 18036-9410, USA

Bednarski, John (Athlete, Hockey Player)
1005 Windfaire Pl
Roswell, GA 30076-3310, USA

Bedore, Thomas (Athlete, Football Player)
211 73rd St
Niagara Falls, NY 14304-4028, USA

Bedrosian, Stephen W (Steve) (Athlete, Baseball Player)
3915 Gordon Rd
Senoia, GA 30276-3041, USA

Bedsole, Harold (Hal) (Athlete, Football Player)
78661 Rainswept Way
Palm Desert, CA 92211-3035, USA

Bee, Samantha (Actor, Producer, Writer)
c/o Brian Stern *Stern Entertainment Group (Brillstein Entertainment Partners)*
14 E 38th St Fl 7
New York, NY 10016-0005, USA

Bee Gees, The (Music Group)
c/o Staff Member *United Talent Agency (UTA)*
9560 Wilshire Blvd Fl 5
Beverly Hills, CA 90212-2400, USA

Beeba, Mike (Governor)
State Capitol Room 250
Little Rock, AR 72201, USA

Beebe, Dion (Cinematographer)
8942 Wilshire Blvd # 219
Beverly Hills, CA 90211-1908, USA

Beebe, Don (Athlete, Football Player)
301 Snow St
Sugar Grove, IL 60554-5209, USA

Beeby, Thomas H (Architect)
440 N Wells St
Chicago, IL 60654-4545, USA

Beech, Matt (Athlete, Baseball Player)
516 Sheffield Dr
Richardson, TX 75081-5610, USA

Beechen, Adam (Writer)
c/o Staff Member *Natural Talent Inc*
3331 Ocean Park Blvd Ste 203
Santa Monica, CA 90405-3225, USA

Beede, Frank (Athlete, Football Player)
1645 Somerset Pl
Antioch, CA 94509-2183, USA

Beekley, Bruce (Athlete, Football Player)
1351 Eaton Ave
San Carlos, CA 94070-4940, USA

Beem, Rich (Athlete, Golfer)
104 Bella Cima Dr
Austin, TX 78734-2670, USA

Beeman, Greg (Actor, Director, Producer, Writer)
c/o Jay Sures *United Talent Agency (UTA)*
9560 Wilshire Blvd Fl 5
Beverly Hills, CA 90212-2400, USA

Beene, Andy (Athlete, Baseball Player)
113 Forest Brook St
Red Oak, TX 75154-6028, USA

Beene, Fred (Athlete, Baseball Player)
PO Box 143
Oakhurst, TX 77359-0143, USA

Beer, A M (Editor)
Editorial Dept 44 Frid St
Hamilton, ON L8N 3G3, CANADA

Beer, Samantha (Stylist)
c/o Staff Member *Jam Arts, Inc*
154 W 57th St
New York, NY 10019-3321, USA

Beer, Tom (Athlete, Football Player)
292 Changebridge Rd Apt 3
Pine Brook, NJ 07058-9543, USA

Beering, Steven C (Educator)
President's Office
West Lafayette, IN 47907, USA

Beers, Bob (Athlete, Hockey Player)
97 Blake Rd
Lexington, MA 02420-3212, USA

Beers, Gary (Musician)
8 Hayes St #1
Neutral Bay, NSW 20891, USA

Beesley, Max (Actor)
c/o Beth Holden-Garland *Untitled Entertainment (LA)*
350 S Beverly Dr Ste 200
Beverly Hills, CA 90212-4819, USA

Beeson, Jack H (Composer, Musician)
PO Box 256
Greenport, NY 11944-0256, USA

Beeson, Paul B (Doctor, Physicist)
7 Riverwoods Dr Apt F125
Exeter, NH 03833-4385, USA

Beeson, Terry (Athlete, Football Player)
1302 Hibbard St
Coffeyville, KS 67337-1412, USA

Beezer, Robert R (Judge)
5th Ave US Courthouse 1010
Seattle, WA 98104-3191, USA

Bega, Leslie (Actor)
31 1/2 Buccaneer St
Marina Del Rey, CA 90292-5103, USA

Bega, Lou (Musician)
c/o Staff Member *Unicade Music*
Truderingerstrasse 259
Munchen 81821, Germany

Begala, Paul (Television Host)
c/o Staff Member *Crossfire*
820 1st St NE Fl 10
Washington, DC 20002-4243, USA

Begay, Notah (Athlete, Golfer)
3620 Vista Del Sur St NW
Albuquerque, NM 87120-1583, USA

Begert, William J (General)
Commander Pacific Air Force
Hickam Air Force Base, HI 96853, USA

Begg, Varyl (Admiral)
Copyhold Cottage Chilbotton Stockbridge
Hants, UNITED KINGDOM (UK)

Beggs, James M (Government Official, Misc)
1177 N Great Southwest Pkwy
Grand Prairie, TX 75050-2629, USA

Beghe, Renato (Judge)
400 2 NT St NW
Washington, DC 20217-0001, USA

Begich, Mark
111 Russell Senate Ofc Building
Washington, DC 20510-0001, USA

Begler, Michael (Producer)
c/o Staff Member *WmE2 (WMA-LA)*
1 William Morris Pl
Beverly Hills, CA 90212-4261, USA

Begley Jr, Ed (Actor, Director)
c/o Stephen Roseberry *Sterling/Winters Company, The*
10877 Wilshire Blvd Fl 15
Los Angeles, CA 90024-4341, USA

Begovich, Mike (Actor)
c/o Beverly Strong *Strong Management*
3532 Hayden Ave
Culver City, CA 90232-2413, USA

Behagen, Ron (Athlete, Basketball Player)
1101 Juniper St NE Apt 401
Atlanta, GA 30309-7655, USA

Behar, Joy (Actor)
c/o Bill Stankey *Westport Entertainment Associates*
1700 Post Rd Ste C15
Fairfield, CT 06824-5726, USA

Beharie, Nicole (Actor)
c/o Andrew Rogers *International Creative Management (ICM-LA)*
10250 Constellation Blvd Fl 7
Los Angeles, CA 90067-6207, USA

Behe, Michael (Writer)
Biochemistry Dept
Bethlehem, PA 18015, USA

Behenna, Rick (Athlete, Baseball Player)
164 Bradford Station Dr
Sharpsburg, GA 30277-2035, USA

Behl, Mohnish (Actor, Bollywood)
Sagar Sangeet 30th Floor Opp Colaba Post Office
Bombay, MS 400 005, INDIA

Behle, Jochen (Skier)
Sonnenhof 1
Willingen 34508, GERMANY

Behm, Forrest E (Athlete, Football Player)
3 Briarcliff Dr
Corning, NY 14830-3328, USA

Behney, Mel (Athlete, Baseball Player)
2800 Woodshire Dr
Arlington, TX 76016-1553, USA

Behnke, Elmer (Athlete, Basketball Player)
3412 Ivy Chase Cir
Birmingham, AL 35226-2276, USA

Behnken, Robert L (Astronaut)
43708 Dejay St
Lancaster, CA 93536-5781, USA

Behr, Aaron (Actor)
c/o Staff Member *Acme Talent & Literary (LA)*
1400 Atlantic Ave Ste 274
Long Beach, CA 90813-2013, USA

Behr, Daniel (Politician)
C/O Deutscher Bundestag Platz Der Republik, 1
Berlin D-11011, Germany

Behr, Jason (Actor)
c/o Robert Stein *Robert Stein Management*
PO Box 3797
Beverly Hills, CA 90212-0797, USA

Behrend, Marc (Athlete, Hockey Player)
1808 Savannah Way
Waunakee, WI 53597-2307, USA

Behrendt, Greg (Comedian, Radio Personality)
9336 Washington Blvd
Culver City, CA 90232-2628, USA

Behrendt, Greg (Actor, Writer)
c/o Staff Member *Simon & Schuster*
1230 Avenue of the Americas Fl CONC1
New York, NY 10020-1586, USA

Behrens, Sam (Actor)
530 Bryant Dr
Canoga Park, CA 91304-1019, USA

Behrman, Dave (Athlete, Football Player)
10187 25 1/2 Mile Rd
Albion, MI 49224-9751, USA

Behrs, Beth (Actor)
c/o Chuck Binder *Binder & Associates*
1465 Lindacrest Dr
Beverly Hills, CA 90210-2519, USA

Beier, Thomas (Athlete, Football Player)
5055 Hammock Lake Dr
Coral Gables, FL 33156-2221, USA

Beilina, Nina (Musician)
400 W 43rd St Apt 7D
New York, NY 10036-6304, USA

Beimel, Joe (Athlete, Baseball Player)
291 Fairview Rd
Kersey, PA 15846-8915, USA

Beirne, Jim (Athlete, Football Player)
11173 Cox Rd
Conroe, TX 77385-7319, USA

Beirne, Kevin (Athlete, Baseball Player)
2 Cedar Chase Pl
Spring, TX 77381-3030, USA

Beisel, Monty (Athlete, Football Player)
608 Herkimer St
Oskaloosa, KS 66066-5014, USA

Beisler, Randy (Athlete, Football Player)
899 Northgate Dr Ste 500
San Rafael, CA 94903-3667, USA

Bejo, Berenice (Actor)
c/o Chris Harris *Actual Management Company*
7 Great Russell Street
London WC1B 3NH, United Kingdom

Bel Biv Devoe (Music Group, Musician)
8942 Wilshire Blvd
Beverly Hills, CA 90211-1908, USA

Belafonte, Harry (Actor, Musician)
c/o Julie Colbert *WmE2 (Endeavor-LA)*
9601 Wilshire Blvd Fl 3
Beverly Hills, CA 90210-5219, USA

Belafonte, Shari (Actor, Musician)
c/o Rick Hersh *Celebrity Consultants LLC*
3340 Ocean Park Blvd Ste 1030
Santa Monica, CA 90405-3259, USA

Belaga, Julie (Activist, Financier)
553 Farmington Ave Ste 201
Hartford, CT 06105-3048, USA

Belak, Wade (Athlete, Hockey Player)
P.O. Box 1167
Battleford, SK S0M 0E0, Canada

Belanger, Ken (Athlete, Hockey Player)
143-A Great Northern Rd Suite 133
Sault Ste Marie, ON P6B 4Y9, Canada

Belanova (Music Group, Musician)
c/o Staff Member *APA Talent and Literary Agency*
9200 W Sunset Blvd Ste 900
Los Angeles, CA 90069-3604, USA

Belanova (Music Group, Musician)

Belbin, Tanith (Figure Skater)
c/o Staff Member *Champions on Ice*
3500 W 80th St Ste 200
Minneapolis, MN 55431-1090, USA

Belcher, Kevin (Athlete, Baseball Player)
2208 Highway 121
Bedford, TX 76021-5981, USA

Belcher, Tim (Athlete, Baseball Player)
PO Box 153
Sparta, OH 43350-0153, USA

Belchlavek, Jiri (Conductor)
Alsovo Nabr 12
Prague 11001, CZECH REPUBLIC

Belden, Bob (Athlete, Football Player)
6701 Militia Hill St NW
Canton, OH 44718-1391, USA

Belew, Adrian (Musician)
2612 Erie Ave
Cincinnati, OH 45208-2002, USA

Belfi, Jordan (Actor)
c/o Mark Schumacher *Schumacher Management*
1122 San Vicente Blvd
Santa Monica, CA 90402-2008, USA

Belford, Christina (Actor)
10635 Santa Monica Blvd Ste 130
Los Angeles, CA 90025-8306, USA

Belfour, Edward (Ed) (Athlete, Hockey Player)
7260 Wisteria Ave
Parkland, FL 33076-3968, USA

Belhumeur, Michel (Athlete, Hockey Player)
58 Little Falls Ln
Rockville, VA 23146-2123, USA

Belichick, Bill (Athlete, Football Coach, Football Player)
5028 Calais Dr
Columbus, OH 43221-5685, USA

Belichik, William S (Bill) (Coach, Football Coach)
60 Washington St Gillette Stadium RR1
Foxboro, MA 02035-1388, USA

Belin, Gaspard D (Attorney, Attorney General, General)
4 Willard St
Cambridge, MA 02138-4837, USA

Belinda, Stan (Athlete, Baseball Player)
454 Sylvan Dr
State College, PA 16803-1514, USA

Belisle, Danny (Athlete, Hockey Player)
3967 Glen Oaks Manor Dr
Sarasota, FL 34232-1045, USA

Belisle, Matt (Athlete, Baseball Player)
4009 Sierra Dr
Austin, TX 78731-3913, USA

Belitz, Todd (Athlete, Baseball Player)
17901 N Colton Ct
Colbert, WA 99005-9174, USA

Beliveau, Jean (Athlete, Hockey Player)
c/o Staff Member *Montreal Canadiens*
1275 Rue Saint-Antoine O
Montreal, QB H3C 5L2, Canada

Belk, Anthony (Athlete, Football Player)
1207 Park Rd NW Apt 201
Washington, DC 20010-2027, USA

Belk, Bill (Athlete, Football Player)
12 Ricemill Fry
Columbia, SC 29229-9034, USA

Belk, Tim (Athlete, Baseball Player)
14714 Carolcrest Dr
Houston, TX 77079-6408, USA

Belka, Marek (Prime Minister)
Ul Wiejska 4/8
Warsaw 00-583, POLAND

Belknap, Anna (Actor)
c/o Steve Stone *Cornerstone Talent Agency*
37 W 20th St
New York, NY 10011-3706, USA

Bell, Albert (Athlete, Football Player)
16222 Hunsaker Ave
Paramount, CA 90723-4762, USA

Bell, Anthony D (Athlete, Football Player)
1564 Fitzgerald Dr
Pinole, CA 94564-2229, USA

Bell, Art (Business Person)
c/o Staff Member *Court TV*
600 3rd Ave Fl 2
New York, NY 10016-1919, USA

Bell, Bill (Athlete, Baseball Player)
3401 Urbandale Ave
Des Moines, IA 50310-4006, USA

Bell, Billy Ray (Athlete, Football Player)
4006 Mossy Grove Ct
Humble, TX 77346-2498, USA

Bell, Bob (Athlete, Football Player)
7415 N 12th St
Elkins Park, PA 19027-3052, USA

Bell, Bobby (Athlete, Football Player)
208 NW Shagbark St
Lees Summit, MO 64064-1445, USA

Bell, Brad (Athlete, Golfer)
6255 Oakridge Way
Sacramento, CA 95831-1829, USA

Bell, Byron (Athlete, Basketball Player)
2210 30th St
Rock Island, IL 61201-5003, USA

Bell, C Gordon (Scientist)
1 Microsoft Way
Redmond, WA 98052-8300, USA

Bell, Carlos (Athlete, Football Player)
14411 Hartshill Dr
Houston, TX 77044-4925, USA

Bell, Catherine (Actor)
c/o Daniel (Danny) Sussman *Brillstein Entertainment Partners*
9150 Wilshire Blvd Ste 350
Beverly Hills, CA 90212-3453, USA

Bell, Charles (Business Person)
1 McDonald's Plaza 1 Kroc Dr
Oak Brook, IL 60523, USA

Bell, Coby (Actor)
c/o Staff Member *Jenny Delaney Management*
3238 Fond Dr
Encino, CA 91436-4206, USA

Bell, Coleman (Athlete, Football Player)
4426 Hidden Shadow Dr
Tampa, FL 33614-1470, USA

Bell, David G (Buddy) (Athlete, Baseball Player, Coach)
244 W Goldfinch Way
Chandler, AZ 85286-4547, USA

Bell, Dennis (Athlete, Basketball Player)
111 Springfield Pike
Cincinnati, OH 45215-4263, USA

Bell, Derek N (Athlete, Baseball Player)
8316 N Fremont Ave
Tampa, FL 33604-2708, USA

Bell, Drake (Actor)
c/o Noelle Keshishian *PMK/BNC Public Relations (PMK-LA)*
8687 Melrose Ave Ste 8
West Hollywood, CA 90069-5746, USA

Bell, Drew Tyler (Actor, Director, Producer, Writer)
c/o Beverly Strong *Strong Management*
3532 Hayden Ave
Culver City, CA 90232-2413, USA

Bell, Eddie A (Actor)
4529 Tacoma Ter
Fort Worth, TX 76123-4005, USA

Bell, Eddie B (Athlete, Football Player)
515 W Chelten Ave Apt 1308
Philadelphia, PA 19144-4427, USA

Bell, Emma (Actor)
c/o Scott Wexler *Brillstein Entertainment Partners*
9150 Wilshire Blvd Ste 350
Beverly Hills, CA 90212-3453, USA

Bell, Eric (Athlete, Baseball Player)
1140 S 124th St
Chandler, AZ 85286-1121, USA

Bell, Fifi (Stylist)
c/o Celebrity Stylist *Oliver Piro Inc*
725 Riverside Dr Apt 3A
New York, NY 10031-2460, USA

Bell, Gary (Athlete, Baseball Player)
2107 Oak Rnch
San Antonio, TX 78259-1819, USA

Bell, Gerard (Athlete, Football Player)
1347 Deerbourne Dr
Zephyrhills, FL 33543-6754, USA

Bell, Glen (Business Person)
PO Box 642
Rancho Santa Fe, CA 92067-0642, USA

Bell, Grantis (Athlete, Football Player)
3049 La Mirage Dr
Lauderhill, FL 33319-4246, USA

Bell, Greg (Athlete, Football Player)
5849 Azalea Way
Goleta, CA 93117-2158, USA

Bell, Greg (Athlete, Track Athlete)
831 W Miami Ave
Logansport, IN 46947-2543, USA

Bell, Harry (Athlete, Hockey Player)
199 Alport Cres
Regina, SK S4R 7Y7, Canada

Bell, Heath (Athlete, Baseball Player)
11427 SW Kingslake Cir
Port St Lucie, FL 34987-2766, USA

Bell, Hilari (Writer)
PO Box 877
Chestertown, MD 21620-0877, USA

Bell, Jaime (Actor)
c/o Staff Member *WmE2 (Endeavor-LA)*
9601 Wilshire Blvd Fl 3
Beverly Hills, CA 90210-5219, USA

Bell, James D (Diplomat)
4512 San Marino Dr
Davis, CA 95618-5015, USA

Bell, Jamie (Actor)
c/o Brian Swardstrom *WmE2 (Endeavor-LA)*
9601 Wilshire Blvd Fl 3
Beverly Hills, CA 90210-5219, USA

Bell, Janice (Stylist)
915 W Gunnison St
Chicago, IL 60640-3735, USA

Bell, Jason (Athlete, Football Player)
2903 Sierra Dr
Carrollton, TX 75007-5626, USA

Bell, Jay S (Athlete, Baseball Player)
PO Box 50249
Phoenix, AZ 85076-0249, USA

Bell, Jerry (Athlete, Baseball Player)
631 Audrey Rd
Mount Juliet, TN 37122-3844, USA

Bell, Jerry (Athlete, Football Player)
1347 Deerbourne Dr
Zephyrhills, FL 33543-6754, USA

Bell, Joe (Athlete, Hockey Player)
11501 15th Ave NE Apt 127
Seattle, WA 98125-6330, USA

Bell, John (Musician)
400 Foundry St
Athens, GA 30601-2623, USA

Bell, John Anthony (Actor, Director)
88 George St Level 1
Rocks, NSW 200, AUSTRALIA

Bell, Jorge A M (George) (Athlete, Baseball Player)
Lamiama #14 Bell 2nd Planto
San Pedro de Macoris, Dominican Republic

Bell, Joshua (Musician)
c/o Staff Member *IMG Artists Worldwide (UK)*
The Light Box 111 Power Road
London W4 5PY, United Kingdom

Bell, Kendrell (Athlete, Football Player)
400 W Peachtree St NW Unit 1211
Atlanta, GA 30308-3547, USA

Bell, Kerwin (Athlete, Football Player)
525 3rd St N Apt 508
Jacksonville Beach, FL 32250-7039, USA

Bell, Kevin (Athlete, Baseball Player)
621 Sue St
Little Chute, WI 54140-2424, USA

Bell, Kevin (Athlete, Football Player)
5780 Phyllis Ln
Beaumont, TX 77713-9539, USA

Bell, Kristen (Actor)
c/o Emily Gerson Saines *Brookside Artists Management (NY)*
250 W 57th St Ste 2303
New York, NY 10107-2399, USA

Bell, Lake (Actor)
c/o Joanna (Joanie) Burstein *Burstein Company, The*
15304 W Sunset Blvd Ste 208
Pacific Palisades, CA 90272-3656, USA

Bell, Larry S (Artist)
PO Box 4101
Taos, NM 87571, USA

Bell, Lauralee (Actor)
c/o Brenda Feldman *Feldman PR*
13636 Ventura Blvd # 440
Sherman Oaks, CA 91423-3700, USA

Bell, Lynette (Swimmer)
149 Henry St
Merwether NSW 22, Australia

Bell, Madison Smartt (Writer)
1745 Broadway # B1
New York, NY 10019-4368, USA

Bell, Marcus (Athlete, Football Player)
678 S School Bus Rd
Eagar, AZ 85925-9678, USA

Bell, Mark E (Athlete, Football Player)
2701 N Wild Rose St
Wichita, KS 67205-1607, USA

Bell, Marshall (Actor)
8730 W Sunset Blvd Ste 490
Los Angeles, CA 90069-2248, USA

Bell, Michael (Actor)
6442 Coldwater Canyon Ave Ste 206
Valley Glen, CA 91606-1174, USA

Bell, Michelle (Athlete, Golfer)
18895 Pond Cypress Ct
Jupiter, FL 33458-3735, USA

Bell, Mike (Race Car Driver)
13515 Yarmouth Dr
Pickerington, OH 43147-8214, USA

Bell, Mike (Athlete, Baseball Player)
1331 Noah Ave
Spring Hill, FL 34608-5767, USA

Bell, Mike J (Athlete, Football Player)
7405 W Lakewood Cir
Wichita, KS 67205-1608, USA

Bell, Mikw (Athlete)
244 W Goldfinch Way
Chandler, AZ 85286-4547, USA

Bell, Myron (Athlete, Football Player)
1012 Kinder Rd
Toledo, OH 43615-6814, USA

Bell, Nick (Athlete, Football Player)
1641 Minorca Dr
Costa Mesa, CA 92626-4854, USA

Bell, Peggy (Athlete, Golfer)
400 Grove Rd
Southern Pines, NC 28387-2839, USA

Bell, Raja (Athlete, Basketball Player)
601 NE 36th St Apt 1812
Miami, FL 33137-3968, USA

Bell, Richard T (Athlete, Football Player)
12106 City View Ln SE
Chatfield, MN 55923-1719, USA

Bell, Ricky (Athlete, Football Player)
4805 Barrington Dr
Columbia, SC 29203-3413, USA

Bell, Ricky (Musician)
c/o Staff Member *Sosincere Entertainment*
2054 Nostrand Ave Apt 4F
Brooklyn, NY 11210-2526, USA

Bell, Rini (Actor)
c/o Sherry Marsh *Marsh Entertainment*
12444 Ventura Blvd Ste 203
Studio City, CA 91604-2409, USA

Bell, Rob (Athlete, Baseball Player)
28 Blossom Hill Dr
Marlboro, NY 12542-6000, USA

Bell, Robert (Musician)
c/o Staff Member *J Bird Entertainment Agency*
4905 S Atlantic Ave
Ponce Inlet, FL 32127-7311, USA

Bell, Robert F (Athlete, Football Player)
7415 N 12th St
Melrose Park, PA 19027-3052, USA

Bell, Roxanne (Stylist)
c/o Staff Member *Maximum Talent*
1873 S Bellaire St Ste 915
Denver, CO 80222-4356, USA

Bell, Sam (Coach)
2310 E Woodstock Pl
Bloomington, IN 47401-6179, USA

Bell, Sean (Actor)
c/o Daniel Sladek *Daniel Sladek Entertainment Corporation*
8306 Wilshire Blvd # 510
Beverly Hills, CA 90211-2382, USA

Bell, Terry (Athlete, Baseball Player)
8352 Normandy Creek Dr
Dayton, OH 45458-3284, USA

Bell, Tobin (Actor)
c/o Alan Saffron *Saffron Management*
9171 Wilshire Blvd Ste 441
Beverly Hills, CA 90210-5516, USA

Bell, Tom (Actor)
13 Randor Walk
London SW3 4BP, UNITED KINGDOM (uk)

Bell, Tom (Stylist)
c/o Staff Member *Jed Root Inc*
61-A Walker St
New York, NY 10013, USA

Bell, Tommy (Astronaut)
205 S Redondo Ave
Manhattan Beach, CA 90266-7039, USA

Bell, Wally (Athlete, Baseball Player)
725 Purdue Ave
Youngstown, OH 44515-4220, USA

Bell, Zoe (Actor)
c/o Todd Diener *Collective*
8383 Wilshire Blvd Ste 1050
Beverly Hills, CA 90211-2415, USA

Bell Biv Devoe (Music Group, Musician)
c/o Staff Member *International Creative Management (ICM-LA)*
10250 Constellation Blvd Fl 7
Los Angeles, CA 90067-6207, USA

Bell Calloway, Vanessa (Actor)
c/o Staff Member *Nine Yards Entertainment*
8530 Wilshire Blvd Ste 550
Beverly Hills, CA 90211-3133, USA

Bell Jr, Bobby Lee (Athlete, Football Player)
208 NW Shagbark St
Lees Summit, MO 64064-1445, USA

Bell X1 (Music Group)
c/o Staff Member *Paradigm (Monterey)*
404 W Franklin St
Monterey, CA 93940-2303, USA

Bella, Ivan (Cosmonaut)
Moskovskoi Oblasti
Syvisdny Goroduk 141160, RUSSIA

Bella, John (Athlete, Baseball Player)
409 N Cypress Dr Apt 7
Jupiter, FL 33469-2656, USA

Bella, Rachael (Actor)
c/o Leonard Torgan *Collective*
8383 Wilshire Blvd Ste 1050
Beverly Hills, CA 90211-2415, USA

Bellamy, Bill (Actor, Comedian)
c/o Staff Member *Evolution Entertainment (LA)*
901 N Highland Ave
Los Angeles, CA 90038-2412, USA

Bellamy, Carol (Misc)
3 United Nations Plz
New York, NY 10017-4414, USA

Bellamy, David J (Writer)
Mill House Bedbum Bishop Auckland
County Durham DL13 3NN, UNITED KINGDOM (UK)

Bellamy, Ned (Actor)
c/o Laina Cohn *Laina Cohn Management*
15066 Sutton St
Sherman Oaks, CA 91403-4020, USA

Bellamy, Walt (Athlete, Basketball Player)
PO Box 42751
Atlanta, GA 30311-0751, USA

Belland, Neil (Athlete, Hockey Player)
868 Renaissance Dr
Oshawa, ON L1J 8K9, Canada

Belle, Albert J (Athlete, Baseball Player)
9299 E Mariposa Grande Dr
Scottsdale, AZ 85255-3789, USA

Belle, Camilla (Actor)
c/o Brad Cafarelli *PMK/BNC - LA*
8687 Melrose Ave Ste 8
West Hollywood, CA 90069-5746, USA

Belle, Regina (Musician)
PO Box 3172
Beverly Hills, CA 90212-0172, USA

Belleci, Tory (Special Effects Designer)
1268 Missouri St
San Francisco, CA 94107-3310, USA

Bellecourt, Vernon (Activist)
1209 4th St SE
Minneapolis, MN 55414-2026, USA

Bellefeuille, Blake (Athlete, Hockey Player)
1 Angelica Ln
Southborough, MA 01772-1339, USA

Beller, Kathleen (Actor)
PO Box 806
Half Moon Bay, CA 94019-0806, USA

Bellflower, Nellie (Actor, Producer)
c/o Staff Member *Keylight Entertainment Group*
200 E 61st St Apt 10E
New York, NY 10065-8585, USA

Bellhorn, Mark (Athlete, Basketball Player)
1447 Palomino Way
Oviedo, FL 32765-9304, USA

Bellhorn, Mark (Athlete, Baseball Player)
19550 N Grayhawk Dr Unit 1083
Scottsdale, AZ 85255-3993, USA

Belliard, Rafael (Athlete, Baseball Player)
10846 King Bay Dr
Boca Raton, FL 33498-4548, USA

Belliard, Ronnie (Athlete, Baseball Player)
2999 NW 96th St
Miami, FL 33147-2337, USA

Bellinger, Clay (Athlete, Baseball Player)
1390 E Horseshoe Dr
Chandler, AZ 85249-4761, USA

Bellinger, Rodney (Athlete, Football Player)
7913 SW 104th St Apt G107
Miami, FL 33156-3656, USA

Bellingham, Lynda (Actor)
c/o Staff Member *Yakety Yak*
8-A Bloomsbury Sq
London WC1A 2NE, UNITED KINGDOM (UK)

Bellingham, Norman (Misc)
208 Morgan St NW
Washington, DC 20001-1292, USA

Bellini, Mario (Architect)
66 Portland Place
London W1, UNITED KINGDOM (UK)

Bellino, Alexis (Reality TV Star)
c/o Michael Schweiger *CEG Talent*
251 W 39th St Fl 7
New York, NY 10018-3171, USA

Bellino, Joe (Athlete, Football Player)
45 Hayden Ln
Bedford, MA 01730-1140, USA

Bellisario, Donald P (Actor, Director, Producer, Writer)
c/o Bob Broder *International Creative Management (ICM-LA)*
10250 Constellation Blvd
Los Angeles, CA 90067-6200, USA

Bellisario, Troian (Actor)
c/o Matthew Lesher *Insight*
1134 S Cloverdale Ave
Los Angeles, CA 90019-6737, USA

Bell-Lundy, Sandra (Cartoonist)
255 Northwood Dr
Welland ON L3C 6V1, Canada

Bellman, Gina (Actor)
c/o Matthew Lesher *Insight*
1134 S Cloverdale Ave
Los Angeles, CA 90019-6737, USA

Bellman-Balchunas, Lois (Athlete, Baseball Player)
5200 Westview Ln
Lisle, IL 60532-2420, USA

Bello, Maria (Actor)
c/o Kim Hodgert *Creative Artists Agency (CAA-LA)*
2000 Avenue of the Stars Ste 100
Los Angeles, CA 90067-4705, USA

Belloir, Rob (Athlete, Baseball Player)
PO Box 2933
Savannah, GA 31402-2933, USA

Bellotti, Mike (Coach, Football Coach)
Athletic Dept
Eugen, OR 97403, USA

Bellovin, Steven M (Scientist)
PO Box 971
Florham Park, NJ 07932-0971, USA

Bellows, Brian (Athlete, Hockey Player)
5205 Mirror Lakes Dr
Minneapolis, MN 55436-2050, USA

Bellows, Gil (Actor)
c/o Emily Gerson Saines *Brookside Artists Management (NY)*
250 W 57th St Ste 2303
New York, NY 10107-2399, USA

Bellucci, Monica (Actor, Model)
c/o Laurent Gregoire *Agence Artistique Adequat*
80 Rue D'Amsterdam
Paris 75009, France

Bellugi, Piero
50027 Strada In Chianti
Florence ITALY

Bellwood, Pamela (Actor)
c/o Richard Murphy *Personal Management Company*
425 N Robertson Blvd
West Hollywood, CA 90048-1735, USA

Belm, Michaela (Model)
Ohmstr 5
Munich 80802, GERMANY

Belmares, Roland (DJ)
c/o Staff Member *Diva Central Inc*
7510 W Sunset Blvd Ste 1445
Los Angeles, CA 90046-3408, USA

Belmondo, Jean-Paul (Actor)
9 Rue des Saint Peres
Paris 75007, FRANCE

Belo, Carlos Filipe Ximenes (Nobel Prize Laureate, Religious Leader)
EAST TIMOR

Belote Hamlin, Melissa (Swimmer)
7311 Exmore St
Springfield, VA 22150-4025, USA

Belotti, George (Athlete, Football Player)
330 E Algrove St
Covina, CA 91723-2608, USA

Belousova, Ludmila (Figure Skater)
Chalet Hubel
Grindelwald 3818, SWITZERLAND

Belov, Sergei (Athlete, Basketball Player)
Naismith Memorial Basketball Hall of Fame 100 W Columbus Ave
Springfield, MA 1105, USA

Belser, Ceaser (Athlete, Football Player)
317 Cooper Dr
Hurst, TX 76053-6130, USA

Belser, Jason (Athlete, Football Player)
20474 Middlebury St
Ashburn, VA 20147-3674, USA

Beltrami, Marco (Composer)
c/o Staff Member *Greenspan Artist Management*
8760 W Sunset Blvd
West Hollywood, CA 90069-2206, USA

Beltran, Carlos (Athlete, Baseball Player)
18 Paseo Alcala
Manati, PR 00674-5766, USA

Beltran, Rigoberto (Athlete, Baseball Player)
3950 Laurelwood Ln
Delray Beach, FL 33445-3503, USA

Beltran, Robert (Actor)
2210 Talmadge St
Los Angeles, CA 90027-2918, USA

Beltre, Adrian (Athlete, Baseball Player)
1204 Suncast Ln Ste 2
El Dorado Hills, CA 95762-9665, USA

Belushi, James (Jim) (Actor)
c/o Marc Gurvitz *Brillstein Entertainment Partners*
9150 Wilshire Blvd Ste 350
Beverly Hills, CA 90212-3453, USA

Belvin, Art (Athlete, Football Player)
6506 Centre Place Cir
Spring, TX 77379-2937, USA

Belzer, Richard (Actor, Comedian)
c/o Eric Gardner *Panacea Entertainment*
13587 Andalusia Dr
Santa Rosa Valley, CA 93012-9226, USA

Beman, Deane R (Athlete, Golfer)
255 Deer Haven Dr
Ponte Vedra Beach, FL 32082-2108, USA

Bemhard (Prince)
Baarn, NETHERLANDS

Bemiller, Al
5002 Armor Duells Rd
Orchard Park, NY 14127-4401, USA

Bemis, Cliff (Actor)
11271 Ventura Blvd PMB 366
Studio City, CA 91604-3136, USA

Bemvenuti, Luciana (Athlete, Golfer)
3673 Wickford Ln
Duluth, GA 30096-2409, USA

Ben Ali, Zine al-Abidine (General)
Palais Presidentiel
Tunis, TUNISIA

Benacerraf, Baruj (Nobel Prize Laureate)
111 Perkins St
Boston, MA 02130-4313, USA

Benackova, Gabriela (Opera Singer)
Maximilianstr 22
Munich 80539, GERMANY

Benade Leo, Edward (General)
417 Pine Ridge Rd # A
Carthage, NC 28327, USA

Benami, Didi (Musician)
c/o Simon Fuller *XIX Entertainment*
33/32 Ransomes Dock 35-37 Parkgate Rd
London SW11 4NP, UK

Benanti, Laura (Actor)
c/o Staff Member *Creative Artists Agency (CAA-LA)*
2000 Avenue of the Stars Ste 100
Los Angeles, CA 90067-4705, USA

Benard, Marvin (Athlete, Baseball Player)
2806 S 38th Ave
West Richland, WA 99353-7317, USA

Benard, Maurice (Actor)
c/o Staff Member *Stone Manners Salners Agency (LA)*
9911 W Pico Blvd Ste 1400
Los Angeles, CA 90035-2715, USA

Benassi, Benny (Musician)
c/o Staff Member *Mission Control Artists Agency*
Unit 3 City Business Centre St Olav's Court, Lower Road
London SE16 2XB, UNITED KINGDOM (UK)

Benatar, Pat (Musician, Songwriter)
250 W 57th St # 1830
New York, NY 10107-0001, USA

Benavides, Fortunato P (Pete) (Judge)
903 San Jacinto Blvd
Austin, TX 78701-2449, USA

Benavides, Freddie (Athlete, Baseball Player)
3007 Wincrest Cir
Laredo, TX 78045-8149, USA

Benavides, Osvaldo (Actor)
c/o Staff Member *Televisa*
Blvd Adolfo Lopez Mateos 232 Colonia San Angel INN
DF CP 01060, MEXICO

Benben, Brian (Actor)
c/o Staff Member *Gersh (LA)*
9465 Wilshire Blvd Ste 600
Beverly Hills, CA 90212-2612, USA

Bench, Johnny (Athlete, Baseball Player)
528 4 Mile Rd
Cincinnati, OH 45230-5209, USA

Benchoff, Dennis L (Den) (General)
380 Arbor Rd
Lancaster, PA 17601-3204, USA

Bender, Carey (Athlete, Football Player)
840 S 15th St
Marion, IA 52302-5001, USA

Bender, Gary N (Sportscaster)
1050 Techwood Dr NW
Atlanta, GA 30318-5604, USA

Bender, Thomas (Historian)
54 Washington Mews
New York, NY 10003-6608, USA

Bender, Wes (Athlete, Football Player)
150 S Glenoaks Blvd Apt 9127
Burbank, CA 91502-1314, USA

Bendix, Simone (Actor)
2/19 Plaza 535 Kings Road
London SW10 0SZ, UNITED KINGDOM (UK)

Bendlin, Kurt (Athlete, Track Athlete)
Asfelder Str 27
Leverkusen 64289, GERMANY

Bendre, Sonali (Actor, Bollywood)
A/203 43 Paradise Apts Swami Samarth Nagar 1st Cross Lane Andheri(W)
Mumbai, MS 400053, INDIA

Bendross, Jesse (Athlete, Football Player)
5226 SW 22nd St
West Park, FL 33023-3118, USA

Bene, Bill (Athlete, Baseball Player)
1063 Bella Vista Ave
San Gabriel, CA 91775-2548, USA

Benedek, George B (Physicist)
Physics Dept
Cambridge, MA 2139, USA

Benedek, Joana (Actor)
c/o Staff Member *Televisa*
Blvd Adolfo Lopez Mateos 232 Colonia
San Angel INN
DF CP 01060, MEXICO

Benedeti, Paulo (Actor)
4201 N Ocean Blvd Apt C505
Boca Raton, FL 33431-5362, USA

Benedict, Bruce (Athlete, Baseball Player)
335 Quiet Water Ln
Atlanta, GA 30350-3724, USA

Benedict, Dirk (Actor, Director, Writer)
c/o Staff Member *Acme Talent & Literary (LA)*
1400 Atlantic Ave Ste 274
Long Beach, CA 90813-2013, USA

Benedict, Manson (Engineer)
410 E Las Olas Blvd
Fort Lauderdale, FL 33301-2210, USA

Benedict, Robert Patrick (Actor)
c/o Charles Silver *Silver Massetti & Szatmary (SMS) Talent Inc*
8730 W Sunset Blvd Ste 440
Los Angeles, CA 90069-2277, USA

Benedict XVI, Pope (Religious Leader)
Apostolic Palace
Vatican City 120, ITALY

Benedicto, Lourdes (Actor)
c/o Bob McGowan *McGowan Management*
8733 W Sunset Blvd Ste 103
West Hollywood, CA 90069-2241, USA

Benefield, Daved (Athlete, Football Player)
420 N Rodeo Dr Apt 15281
Beverly Hills, CA 90210-4502, USA

Benepe, Jim (Athlete, Golfer)
602 Mountain Shadows Blvd
Sheridan, WY 82801-9355, USA

Benes, Alan (Athlete, Baseball Player)
754 Kraffel Ln
Chesterfield, MO 63017-8057, USA

Benes, Andrew C (Andy) (Athlete, Baseball Player)
1127 Highland Pointe Dr
Saint Louis, MO 63131-1420, USA

Benet, Eric (Actor, Musician)
c/o Shelley Wiseman *Avnet Management*
20455 Chase St
Winnetka, CA 91306-1311, USA

Benet, Kiki (Stylist)
c/o Staff Member *Rex Agency, The*
6311 Romaine St
Los Angeles, CA 90038-2617, USA

Benetton, Giuliana (Business Person)
Via Minelli
Ponzano Treviso 31050, ITALY

Benetton, Lucianno (Business Person)
Villa Minelli Ponzano
Treviso 31050, Italy

Benetton, Luciano (Business Person)
Via Minelli
Ponzano Treviso 31050, ITALY

Benfatti, Lou (Athlete, Football Player)
19 Pleasant Ln
Newfoundland, NJ 07435-1105, USA

Benflis, Ali (Prime Minister)
Palais du Gouvernement
Algiers, ALGERIA

Benford, Gregory (Writer)
c/o Vince Gerardis *Created By*
1041 N Formosa Ave Formosa Bldg Room 10
West Hollywood, CA 90046, USA

Bengis, Fred (Athlete, Baseball Player)
546 Quail Ct
Longs, SC 29568-8638, USA

Benglis, Lynda (Artist)
222 Bowery
New York, NY 10012-4203, USA

Bengston, Billy Al (Artist)
805 Hampton Dr
Venice, CA 90291-3020, USA

Bengston, Michelle (Olympic Athlete)
2362 W Betty Elyse Ln
Phoenix, AZ 85023-4218, USA

Bengtson, Michelle (Stylist)
2220 W Mission Ln Apt 2259
Phoenix, AZ 85021-5801, USA

Benhima, Mohamed (Prime Minister)
Route des Zaers
Rabat, MOROCCO

Benigni, Roberto (Actor, Director)
Via Ludovisi, 35
Rome IT-00187, Italy

Benignl, Roberto (Actor, Director)
Via Traversa 44 Vergaglio
Provinz di Prato, ITALY

Bening, Annette (Actor)
c/o Simon Halls *Slate Public Relations*
9000 W Sunset Blvd Ste 915
West Hollywood, CA 90069-5809, USA

Benioff, David (Producer, Writer)
c/o Guymon Casady *Management 360*
9111 Wilshire Blvd
Beverly Hills, CA 90210-5508, USA

Beniquez, Juan (Athlete, Baseball Player)
Villa Carolina 87-12 Calle 99A
Carolina, PR 985, USA

Benirschke, Rolf J (Athlete, Football Player)
PO Box 9922
Rancho Santa Fe, CA 92067-4922, USA

Benish, Dan (Athlete, Football Player)
2885 Cross Creek Dr
Cumming, GA 30040-6344, USA

Benishek, Dan (Congressman, Politician)
514 Cannon Hob
Washington, DC 20515-0103, USA

Benitez, Armando G (Athlete, Baseball Player)
1201 Estates Ln
Bayside, NY 11360-1141, USA

Benitez, Elsa (Model)
c/o Staff Member *M Fashion Model Management*
80 Monte Rosa Via
Ashburn, VA 20149-0001, Italy

Benitez, Jellybean (Musician)
235 Park Ave S
New York, NY 10003-1405, USA

Benitez, Wilfred (Athlete, Boxer)
PO Box 2338
Temecula, CA 92593-2338, USA

Benitez, Yamil (Athlete, Baseball Player)
Calle 13 Bo 918 Caperra Terrace
San Juan, PR 921, USA

Benitz, Max (Actor)
c/o Michael Baum *Impression Entertainment*
9229 W Sunset Blvd Ste 700
West Hollywood, CA 90069-3407, USA

Benjamin, Andre (Andre 3000) (Artist, Musician)
c/o Charles King *WmE2 (Endeavor-LA)*
9601 Wilshire Blvd Fl 3
Beverly Hills, CA 90210-5219, USA

Benjamin, Benoit (Athlete, Basketball Player)
28 Morning Grn
San Antonio, TX 78257-2602, USA

Benjamin, Guy (Athlete, Football Player)
1337 Lower Campus Rd
Honolulu, HI 96822-2352, USA

Benjamin, Jill (Actor)
c/o Staff Member *Principato/Young Management*
9465 Wilshire Blvd Ste 430
Beverly Hills, CA 90212-2613, USA

Benjamin, Mike (Athlete, Baseball Player)
25608 S 182nd Pl
Queen Creek, AZ 85142-8188, USA

Benjamin, Richard (Actor, Director)
c/o Staff Member *Gersh (LA)*
9465 Wilshire Blvd Ste 600
Beverly Hills, CA 90212-2612, USA

Benjamin, Ryan (Athlete, Football Player)
PO Box 289
Pixley, CA 93256-0289, USA

Benjamin, Stan (Athlete, Baseball Player)
15 Speak Way
Harwich, MA 02645-2324, USA

Benjamin, Stephen (Athlete, Yachtsman)
PO Box 399
Norwalk, CT 06856-0399, USA

Benkovic, Stephen J (Misc)
771 Teaberry Ln
State College, PA 16803-3183, USA

Benmosche, Robert H (Business Person)
1 Madison Ave
New York, NY 10010-3603, USA

Benn, Anthony N W (Tony) (Government Official)
Westminster
London SW1A 0AA, UNITED KINGDOM (UK)

Benn, Nigel (Boxer)
10 Western Road
Romford Essex RM1 3JT, UNITED KINGDOM

Benner, Dyne (Stylist)
311 E 60th St
New York, NY 10022-1572, USA

Benners, Fred (Athlete, Football Player)
5211 Shadywood Ln
Dallas, TX 75209-2207, USA

Bennet, Michael F. (Senator)
458 Russell Senate Ofc Building
Washington, DC 20510-0001, USA

Bennett, A L (Athlete, Basketball Player)
523 N Willow Pl
Jenks, OK 74037-3489, USA

Bennett, Adam (Athlete, Hockey Player)
7 Stockman Cres
Georgetown, ON L7G 1J5, Canada

Bennett, Barry (Athlete, Football Player)
22047 Ginseng Rd
Long Prairie, MN 56347-4754, USA

Bennett, Bill (DJ)
c/o Staff Member *Diva Central Inc*
7510 W Sunset Blvd Ste 1445
Los Angeles, CA 90046-3408, USA

Bennett, Bill (Athlete, Hockey Player)
75 Tucker Ave
Cranston, RI 02905-3314, USA

Bennett, Bob (Musician, Songwriter, Writer)
c/o Vicki Jennette *The Benjamin Artist Agency*
PO Box 92348
Nashville, TN 37209-8348, USA

Bennett, Brooke (Swimmer)
2585 Rowe Rd
Milford, MI 48380-2337, USA

Bennett, Carl (Athlete, Basketball Player)
2834 Little River Run
Fort Wayne, IN 46804-2573, USA

Bennett, Charles A (Athlete, Football Player)
19804 Bobolink Dr
Hialeah, FL 33015-2112, USA

Bennett, Clay (Cartoonist)
Editorial Dept 1 Norway St
Boston, MA 2115, USA

Bennett, Curt (Athlete, Hockey Player)
44 Polale St
Kihei, HI 96753-8283, USA

Bennett, Darren (Athlete, Football Player)
5299 Soledad Mountain Rd
San Diego, CA 92109, USA

Bennett, Dave (Athlete, Baseball Player)
408 N Fairchild St
Yreka, CA 96097-2219, USA

Bennett, Dennis (Athlete, Baseball Player)
630 N 5th St
Klamath Falls, OR 97601-3028, USA

Bennett, Donnell (Athlete, Football Player)
8055 W Leitner Dr
Coral Springs, FL 33067-2013, USA

Bennett, Edgar (Athlete, Football Player)
1880 Horseshoe Ln
De Pere, WI 54115-7947, USA

Bennett, Elmer (Athlete, Basketball Player)
2820 Avenue of the Woods
Louisville, KY 40241-6232, USA

Bennett, Erik (Athlete, Baseball Player)
PO Box 884
Yreka, CA 96097-0884, USA

Bennett, Fran (Actor)
749 N La Fayette Park Pl
Los Angeles, CA 90026-2917, USA

Bennett, Gary (Athlete, Baseball Player)
1403 W Beach Rd
Waukegan, IL 60087-1512, USA

Bennett, Haley (Actor)
c/o Mimi DiTrani *Schiff Company, The*
8440 Warner Dr Ste B1
Culver City, CA 90232-2461, USA

Bennett, Hywel (Actor)
45 S Molton St
London W1Y 3RD, UNITED KINGDOM (UK)

Bennett, Jeff (Athlete, Baseball Player)
18 Blue Bird Dr
Brush Creek, TN 38547-5005, USA

Bennett, Jimmy (Actor)
c/o Jason Newman *Untitled Entertainment (LA)*
350 S Beverly Dr Ste 200
Beverly Hills, CA 90212-4819, USA

Bennett, Joe C (Educator)
4101 Altamont Rd
Birmingham, AL 35213-2813, USA

Bennett, Joel (Athlete, Baseball Player)
401 Riley Rd
Windsor, NY 13865-1043, USA

Bennett, Jonathan (Actor)
c/o Staff Member *Amplitude Entertainment*
8033 W Sunset Blvd # 823
Los Angeles, CA 90046-2401

Bennett, Leeman (Athlete, Football Coach, Football Player)
6795 Kinnity Ct
Cumming, GA 30040-5793, USA

Bennett, Michael (Athlete, Football Player)
9520 Viking Dr
Eden Prairie, MN 55344-3825, USA

Bennett, Monte (Athlete, Football Player)
2075 Avenue U
Sterling, KS 67579-8917, USA

Bennett, Nelson (Skier)
807 S 20th Ave
Yakima, WA 98902-4228, USA

Bennett, Nigel (Actor)
c/o Larry Goldhar *Characters Talent Agency, The (Toronto)*
1505 W 2nd Ave #200
Vancouver, BC V6H 3Y4, Canada

Bennett, Paris (Musician)

Bennett, Richard Rodney (Composer)
8-9 Firth St
London W1V 5TZ, UNITED KINGDOM (UK)

Bennett, Rick (Athlete, Hockey Player)
55 Evergreen Ave
Clifton Park, NY 12065-4032, USA

Bennett, Robert (Bob) (Swimmer)
70 Rivo Alto Canal
Long Beach, CA 90803-4047, USA

Bennett, Robert R (Business Person)
2501 118th Ave N
Saint Petersburg, FL 33716-1920, USA

Bennett, Robert S (Attorney, Attorney General, General)
1840 24th St NW
Washington, DC 20008-4024, USA

Bennett, Roy (Athlete, Football Player)
455 Wynbrooke Pkwy
Stone Mountain, GA 30087-4765, USA

Bennett, Sean (Athlete, Football Player)
12163 E State Road 62
Saint Meinrad, IN 47577 9673, USA

Bennett, Shayne (Athlete, Baseball Player)
6718 Meade Pl
Downers Grove, IL 60516-3179, USA

Bennett, Tony (Musician)
48 W 10th St
New York, NY 10011-8702, USA

Bennett, Tony (Athlete, Basketball Player)
3408 Cesford Grange
Keswick, VA 22947-9126, USA

Bennett, Tracie (Actor)
9 Newburgh St
London W1V 1LA, UNITED KINGDOM (UK)

Bennett, William J. (Politician, Radio Personality, Secretary)
1901 N Moore St Ste 201B
Arlington, VA 22209-1706, USA

Bennett, Winston (Athlete, Basketball Player)
54 Barrington Cir
Paducah, KY 42003-8895, USA

Bennett Jr, Harvey (Athlete, Hockey Player)
1096 Warwick Neck Ave
Warwick, RI 02889-6815, USA

Bennie, Dan (Musician)
22121 Cleveland St
Dearborn, MI 48124-3462, USA

Benning, Brian (Athlete, Hockey Player)
Interstate Batteries 11216 156 St NW
Edmonton, AB T5M 1Y3, Canada

Benning, Jim (Athlete, Hockey Player)
PO Box 1264
Sherwood, OR 97140-1264, USA

Bennington, Chester (Musician)
c/o Staff Member *Warner Bros Records (LA)*
PO Box 6868
Burbank, CA 91510-6868, USA

Benny, Joan
1131 Coldwater Canyon Dr
Beverly Hills, CA 90210-2402

Benoit, David (Musician)
34 N Palm St Ste 100
Ventura, CA 93001-2610, USA

Benoit, Morgan (Actor)
c/o Staff Member *Bluestone Entertainment*
5639 Vista Del Monte Ave
Van Nuys, CA 91411-3356, USA

Benoit-Samuelson, Joan (Athlete, Track Athlete)
95 Lower Flying Point Rd
Freeport, ME 04032-6305, USA

Benrubi, Abraham (Actor)
c/o Erik Kritzer *Kritzer Levine Wilkins Entertainment*
11872 La Grange Ave Fl 1
Los Angeles, CA 90025-5283, USA

Bensimon, Kelly Killoren (Model, Reality TV Star, Writer)
c/o Staff Member *Bravo (NY)*
30 Rockefeller Plz
New York, NY 10112-0015, USA

Benson, Amber (Actor)
c/o Staff Member *United Talent Agency (UTA)*
9560 Wilshire Blvd Fl 5
Beverly Hills, CA 90212-2400, USA

Benson, Andrew A (Misc)
6044 Folsom Dr
La Jolla, CA 92037-6711, USA

Benson, Anna (Model)
6025 Sandy Springs Cir NE # 313
Atlanta, GA 30328-3863, USA

Benson, Ashley (Actor)
c/o JoAnne Colonna *Brillstein Entertainment Partners*
9150 Wilshire Blvd Ste 350
Beverly Hills, CA 90212-3453, USA

Benson, Brad (Athlete, Football Player)
3905 Route 1 S
Monmouth Junction, NJ 8852, USA

Benson, Cedric (Athlete, Football Player)
18 Hook Mountain Rd
Pine Brook, NJ 07058-9798, USA

Benson, Charles (Athlete, Football Player)
9440 Gross St
Beaumont, TX 77707-1147, USA

Benson, Cliff (Athlete, Football Player)
6520 Tennessee Ave
Willowbrook, IL 60527-1861, USA

Benson, Darren (Athlete, Football Player)
PO Box 742614
Dallas, TX 75374-2614, USA

Benson, Doug (Comedian)
c/o Staff Member *OmniPop Talent Group*
10700 Ventura Blvd Fl 2
Studio City, CA 91604-3561, USA

Benson, George (Actor, Musician)
c/o Dennis Turner *Turner Management Group*
9200 W Sunset Blvd Ste 600
West Hollywood, CA 90069-3196, USA

Benson, Harry (Photographer)
181 E 73rd St Apt 18A
New York, NY 10021-3566, USA

Benson, Herbert (Doctor)
Beth Israel Hospital
Brookline, MA 2146, USA

Benson, Jodi (Voice Over Artist)
c/o Staff Member *Innovative Artists (LA)*
1505 10th St
Santa Monica, CA 90401-2805, USA

Benson, Joyce (Athlete, Golfer)
5310 Papaya Cir
Harlingen, TX 78552-8956, USA

Benson, Kent (Athlete, Basketball Player)
3921 W Maybury Mall Apt 12
Bloomington, IN 47403-3738, USA

Benson, Kris (Athlete, Baseball Player)
c/o Jon Orlando *WNWN Media*
348 Hauser Blvd # PH414
Los Angeles, CA 90036-3276, USA

Benson, Robby (Actor)
c/o Staff Member *Creative Artists Agency (CAA-LA)*
2000 Avenue of the Stars Ste 100
Los Angeles, CA 90067-4705, USA

Benson, Stephen R (Steve) (Cartoonist)
200 E Van Buren St
Phoenix, AZ 85004-2238, USA

Benson, Sydney W (Misc)
1110 N Bundy Dr
Los Angeles, CA 90049-1513, USA

Benson, Thomas (Athlete, Football Player)
PO Box 701341
Dallas, TX 75370-1341, USA

Benson, Troy (Athlete, Football Player)
1038 Victoria Pl
Gibsonia, PA 15044-9200, USA

Benson, Vern (Athlete, Baseball Player, Coach)
PO Box 127
Granite Quarry, NC 28072-0127, USA

Benson Jr, Johnny (Race Car Driver)
3128 Bird Ave NE
Grand Rapids, MI 49525-3108, USA

Benson-Landes, Wendy (Actor)
c/o Staff Member *Northern Exposure Talent Management*
2888 Birch Street Unit #1
Vancouver BC V6H 2T6, Canada

Bent, Lyriq (Actor)
c/o Staff Member *Stone Manners Salners Agency (LA)*
9911 W Pico Blvd Ste 1400
Los Angeles, CA 90035-2715, USA

Bentley, Albert (Athlete, Football Player)
1835 E 5th St
Anderson, IN 46012-3522, USA

Bentley, Dierks (Musician)
c/o Staff Member *Lustig Talent Enterprises Inc*
PO Box 770850
Orlando, FL 32877-0850, USA

Bentley, Eric (Writer)
194 Riverside Dr
New York, NY 10025-7259, USA

Bentley, Lecharles (Athlete, Football Player)
1177 Windsor Ave
Columbus, OH 43211-2837, USA

Bentley, Ray (Athlete, Football Player, Sportscaster)
4050 Redbush Dr SW
Grandville, MI 49418-3041, USA

Bentley, Robert (Governor)
11 S Union St
Montgomery, AL 36130-2102, USA

Bentley, Stacey (Misc)
PO Box 26
Santa Monica, CA 90406-0026, USA

Bentley, Wes (Actor)
c/o Scott Lambert *WmE2 (WMA-LA)*
1 William Morris Pl
Beverly Hills, CA 90212-4261, USA

Benton, Andrew K (Educator)
President's Office
Malibu, CA 90263, USA

Benton, Barbi (Actor, Model)
840 N Starwood Dr
Aspen, CO 81611-9717, USA

Benton, Brad (Adult Film Star)
c/o Staff Member *Diva Central Inc*
7510 W Sunset Blvd Ste 1445
Los Angeles, CA 90046-3408, USA

Benton, Butch (Athlete, Baseball Player)
12314 SE 60th Ave
Belleview, FL 34420-5200, USA

Benton, Fletcher (Artist)
250 Dore St
San Francisco, CA 94103-4308, USA

Benton, Robert (Writer)
930 3rd Ave Fl 26
New York, NY 10022-3601, USA

Bentz, Chad (Athlete, Baseball Player)
150 Holly St
Rutland, VT 05701-2206, USA

Benvenuti, Giovanni (Nino) (Boxer)
FPI Viaie Tiziano 70
Rome 196, ITALY

Benvenuti, Leo (Director, Producer, Writer)
c/o John Elliott *Mosaic Media Group*
9200 W Sunset Blvd Ste 10
Los Angeles, CA 90069-3608, USA

Ben-Victor, Paul (Actor)
c/o Michael Garnett *Leverage Management*
3030 Pennsylvania Ave
Santa Monica, CA 90404-4112, USA

Benymon, Chico (Actor)
c/o Staff Member *Gersh (LA)*
9465 Wilshire Blvd Ste 600
Beverly Hills, CA 90212-2612, USA

Benz, Amy (Athlete, Golfer)
85133 Shinnecock Hills Dr
Fernandina Beach, FL 32034-8177, USA

Benz, Julia (Actor)
1505 10th St
Santa Monica, CA 90401-2805, USA

Benz, Julie (Actor)
c/o Vincent Cirrincione *Vincent Cirrincione Associates*
1516 N Fairfax Ave
Los Angeles, CA 90046-2608, USA

Benz, Larry (Athlete, Football Player)
1526 Brummel St
Evanston, IL 60202-3708, USA

Benz, Sepp (Athlete)
Kiefernweg 37
Zurich 8057, SWITZERLAND

Benza, AJ (Actor)
5670 Wilshire Blvd # 400W
Los Angeles, CA 90036-5679, USA

Benzali, Daniel (Actor)
c/o Staff Member *WmE2 (Endeavor-LA)*
9601 Wilshire Blvd Fl 3
Beverly Hills, CA 90210-5219, USA

Benzi, Roberto
12 Villa Sainte Foy
Neuilly-sur-Seine 92200, FRANCE

Benzinger, Todd (Athlete, Baseball Player)
1047 Shore Point Ct
Loveland, OH 45140-6970, USA

Beotti, Valentina (Actor)
Via Giuseppe Pisanelli
Rome 196, ITALY

Beracasa, Fabiola
415 Madison Ave Fl 19
New York, NY 10017-7948, USA

Beranek, Josef (Athlete, Hockey Player)
66 Mario Lemieux Pl
Pittsburgh, PA 15219-3504, USA

Berard, Bryan (Athlete, Hockey Player)
9 Holly Ln
Cumberland, RI 02864-3328, USA

Berblinger, Jeff (Athlete, Baseball Player)
102 Swanee Dr
Goddard, KS 67052-9420, USA

Bercaw, John E (Misc)
Chemistry
Pasadena, CA 91125-0001, USA

Berce, Gene (Athlete, Basketball Player)
1119 Hawthorne Pl Apt G
Pewaukee, WI 53072-6576, USA

Bercich, Bob (Athlete, Football Player)
19017 Edward Pkwy
Mokena, IL 60448-8565, USA

Bercich, Pete (Athlete, Football Player)
RR 1 Box 369
New Lenox, IL 60451, USA

Bercu, Michaela (Actor, Model)
c/o Staff Member *Elite Model Management (NY)*
404 Park Ave S Fl 9
New York, NY 10016-8412, USA

Berdahl, Robert M (Educator)
Chancellor S Ofc
Berkeley, CA 94720-0001, USA

Berdy, Sean (Actor)
c/o Liz Hanley *Bicoastal Talent & Literary Agency*
210 N Pass Ave Ste 204
Burbank, CA 91505-3936, USA

Berdych, Thomas (Athlete, Tennis Player)
c/o Staff Member *ATP Tour*
201 Atp Tour Blvd
Ponte Vedra Beach, FL 32082-3211, USA

Bere, Jason (Athlete, Baseball Player)
40 Berrington Pl
North Andover, MA 01845-2152, USA

Berehowsky, Drake (Athlete, Hockey Player)
20455 N 95th St
Scottsdale, AZ 85255-6629, USA

Berenblum, Isaac (Doctor)
Pathology Dept
Rehovot, ISRAEL

Berendt, John (Writer)
c/o Suzanne Gluck *WmE2 (WMA-NY)*
1325 Avenue of the Americas
New York, NY 10019-6026, USA

Berendzen, Richard E (Educator)
1300 Crystal Dr
Arlington, VA 22202-3234, USA

Berenger, Tom (Actor)
c/o Colton Gramm *Brillstein Entertainment Partners*
9150 Wilshire Blvd Ste 350
Beverly Hills, CA 90212-3453, USA

Berenguer, Juan (Athlete, Baseball Player)
8616 Alisa Ct
Chanhassen, MN 55317-9373, USA

Berens, Ricky (Athlete, Swimmer)
1 Olympic Plz
Colorado Springs, CO 80909-5780, USA

Berenson, Ken (Red) (Athlete, Coach, Hockey Player)
3555 Daleview Dr
Ann Arbor, MI 48105-9686, USA

Berenyl, Bruce (Athlete, Baseball Player)
PO Box 133
Sherwood, OH 43556-0133, USA

Berenzweig, Andrew (Athlete, Hockey Player)
4603 Brookside Rd
Ottawa Hills, OH 43615-2207, USA

Beresford, Bruce (Director)
c/o Steve Kenis *Steve Kenis & Company*
Royalty House 72-74 Dean St
London W1D 3SG, UK

Beresford, Meg (Activist)
Wiston Lodge Wiston
Biggar ML12 6HT, SCOTLAND

Bereson, Karin (Stylist)
c/o Celebrity Stylists *Utopia*
12 W End Ave Fl 2
New York, NY 10023, USA

Berezan, Perry (Athlete, Hockey Player)
Wellington West Capital 1100-255 5 Ave SW
Calgary, AB T2P 3G6, Canada

Berezhnaya, Yelena (Figure Skater)
111 Midtown Bridge Approac
Hackensack, NJ 07601-7505, USA

Berezin, Sergei (Athlete, Hockey Player)
1645 SW 4th Ave
Boca Raton, FL 33432-7232, USA

Berezney, Peter (Athlete, Football Player)
PO Box 10
Saint Bonaventure, NY 14778-0010, USA

Berezovsky, Boris V (Musician)
3 Burlington Lane Chiswick
London W4 2TH, UNITED KINGDOM (UK)

Berezovy, Anatoli N (Cosmonaut)
Moskovskoi Oblasti
Syvisdny Goroduk 141160, RUSSIA

Berfield, Justin (Actor, Director, Producer)

Berg, Aki (Athlete, Hockey Player)
7400 Metro Blvd Ste 280
Minneapolis, MN 55439-2363, USA

Berg, Aki-Petteri (Athlete, Hockey Player)
1751 Pinnacle Dr Ste 1500
McLean, VA 22102-3833, USA

Berg, Bill (Athlete, Hockey Player)
c/o Staff Member *The NHL Network*
9 Channel Nine Ct
Toronto, ON M1S 4B5, Canada

Berg, Dave (Athlete, Baseball Player)
1917 Stonecastle Dr
Keller, TX 76262-4912, USA

Berg, Eric (Stylist)
c/o Staff Member *Rex Agency, The*
6311 Romaine St
Los Angeles, CA 90038-2617, USA

Berg, Kevin (Business Person)
c/o Staff Member *CBS Paramount Network Television*
4024 Radford Ave
Studio City, CA 91604-2190, USA

Berg, Matraca (Musician)
4405 Belmont Park Ter
Nashville, TN 37215-3609, USA

Berg, Paul (Nobel Prize Laureate)
Medical School Beckman Center
Stanford, CA 94305, USA

Berg, Peter (Actor)
c/o Staff Member *Film 44*
1526 Cloverfield Blvd # D
Santa Monica, CA 90404-3502, USA

Berg, Rick (Congressman, Politician)
323 Cannon Hob
Washington, DC 20515-0924, USA

Berg, Steve (Actor)
c/o Ilan Breil *Mosaic Media Group*
9200 W Sunset Blvd Ste 10
Los Angeles, CA 90069-3608, USA

Berg, Yehuda (Religious Leader)
1066 S La Cienega Blvd
Los Angeles, CA 90035-2508, USA

Berganio, David Jr (Athlete, Golfer)
17811 Lahey St
Granada Hills, CA 91344-4030, USA

Berganza, Teresa (Opera Singer)
La Rossinlana Archanda 5 28200 San Lorenzo del Escorial
Madrid, SPAIN

Berge, Francine (Actor)
36 Rue de Ponthiew
Paris 75008, FRANCE

Berge, Ole M (Misc)
12050 Woodward Ave
Detroit, MI 48203-3578, USA

Berge, Pierre V G (Business Person)
5 Ave Marceau
Paris 75116, FRANCE

Bergen, Candice (Actor)
c/o Heidi Schaeffer *PMK/BNC Public Relations (PMK-LA)*
8687 Melrose Ave Ste 8
West Hollywood, CA 90069-5746, USA

Bergen, Danny (Actor)
c/o Staff Member *Paul Lane Entertainment*
468 N Camden Dr
Beverly Hills, CA 90210-4507, USA

Bergen, Gary (Athlete, Basketball Player)
1386 Graham Cir
Erie, CO 80516-3617, USA

Bergen, Polly (Actor, Musician, Producer, Writer)
1746 S Britain Rd
Southbury, CT 06488-3200, USA

Berger, Brandon (Athlete, Baseball Player)
2276 Dixie Hwy
Ft Mitchell, KY 41017-2949, USA

Berger, Gerhard (Race Car Driver)
Postfach 1121
Vaduz 9490, AUSTRIA

Berger, Helmut (Actor)
Viale Parioli 50
Rome 197, ITALY

Berger, John (Writer)
Quincy Mieussy
Taninges 74440, FRANCE

Berger, Lee (Actor)
57 Fellows Rd
Brentwood, NH 03833-6130, USA

Berger, Ronald (Athlete, Football Player)
6000 Lagorce Dr
Miami Beach, FL 33140-2117, USA

Berger, Senta (Actor)
Gebsattelstr 30
Munich 81541, GERMANY

Berger, Thomas L (Writer)
PO Box 11
Palisades, NY 10964-0011, USA

Berger-Brown, Barbara (Baseball Player)
1633 Farmer Ave
Murray, KY 42071-2234, USA

Berger-Knebl, Joan (Baseball Player)
16 Home Pl
Lodi, NJ 07644-1512, USA

Bergeron, J C (Athlete, Hockey Player)
c/o Staff Member *Reebok / CCM*
3400 Raymond-Lasnier St
Montreal, QC H4R 3L3, Canada

Bergeron, Michel (Coach)
CHL T630 25 Rue Bryant
Sherbrooke QC J1J 3Z5, CANADA

Bergeron, Patrice (Athlete, Hockey Player)
c/o Staff Member *Boston Bruins*
TD Banknorth Garden 100 Legends Way, Suite 250
Boston, MA 2114, USA

Bergeron, Peter (Athlete, Baseball Player)
3495 Manatee Dr SE
Saint Petersburg, FL 33705-4144, USA

Bergeron, Tom (Actor, Producer)
c/o Staff Member *IMG Artists Worldwide (NY)*
825 7th Ave
New York, NY 10019-6014, USA

Bergeron, Yves (Athlete, Hockey Player)
1035 Clearwater Ave
Bathurst, NB E2A 4H5, Canada

Berger-Taylor, Norma (Baseball Player)
529 N Bierman Ave
Villa Park, IL 60181-1437, USA

Bergeson, Eric (Athlete, Football Player)
2579 Sherwood Dr
Salt Lake City, UT 84108-2457, USA

Bergevin, Marc (Athlete, Hockey Player)
404 Canterbury Ct
Hinsdale, IL 60521-2826, USA

Bergey, Bruce (Athlete, Football Player)
7700 SW River Rd
Hillsboro, OR 97123-9108, USA

Bergey, John (Inventor)
1807 Mayflower Cir
Lancaster, PA 17603-6039, USA

Bergey, William E (Bill) (Athlete, Football Player)
2 Hickory Ln
Chadds Ford, PA 19317-9715, USA

Berggren, Jenny (Musician)
Norrtullsgatan 51
Stockholm 113 45, SWEDEN

Berggren, Jonas (Musician)
Norrtullsgatan 51
Stockholm 11345, SWEDEN

Berggren, Malin (Musician)
Norrtullsgatan 51
Stockholm 11345, SWEDEN

Berggren, Thommy (Actor)
PO Box 27126
Stockholm 102 52, SWEDEN

Bergh, Kate (Stylist)
Prefers to be contacted via telephone

Bergh, Larry (Athlete, Basketball Player)
7020 Peoto Ln
Crossville, TN 38572-4501, USA

Bergi, Emily (Actor)
1505 10th St
Santa Monica, CA 90401-2805, USA

Bergin, Michael (Actor, Model)
c/o Tom Chasin *Chasin Agency, The*
8899 Beverly Blvd Ste 714
Los Angeles, CA 90048-2449, USA

Bergin, Patrick (Actor)
25 Sea Colony Dr
Santa Monica, CA 90405-5495, USA

Bergkamp, Dennis (Soccer Player)
Arsenal Stadium Avenell Road
London N5 1BU, UNITED KINGDOM (UK)

Bergl, Emily (Actor)
c/o Craig Shapiro *International Creative Management (ICM-LA)*
10250 Constellation Blvd Fl 7
Los Angeles, CA 90067-6207, USA

Bergland, Robert S (Bob) (Secretary)
1104 7th Ave SE
Roseau, MN 56751-2313, USA

Bergland, Tim (Athlete, Hockey Player)
721 Labree Ave N
Thief River Falls, MN 56701-1632, USA

Berglind (Icey) (Television Host)
c/o Staff Member *E! Entertainment Television (LA)*
5750 Wilshire Blvd
Los Angeles, CA 90036-3697, USA

Bergloff, Bob (Athlete, Hockey Player)
10200 Harriet Ave S
Minneapolis, MN 55420-5233, USA

Berglund, Bo (Athlete, Hockey Player)
c/o Staff Member *Buffalo Sabres*
1 Seymour H Knox III Plz Ste 1
Buffalo, NY 14203-3096, USA

Berglund, Paavo A E (Conductor)
Munkkiniemenranta 41
Helsinki 33 330, FINLAND

Bergman, Alan (Musician)
714 N Maple Dr
Beverly Hills, CA 90210-3411, USA

Bergman, Andrew C (Director, Writer)
c/o Robert (Bob) Bookman *Creative Artists Agency (CAA-LA)*
2000 Avenue of the Stars Ste 100
Los Angeles, CA 90067-4705, USA

Bergman, Arnfinn (Skier)
Nils Collett Vogtsv 58
Oslo 7 765, NORWAY

Bergman, Bridget (Stylist)
Prefers to be contacted via telephone or email

Bergman, Dave (Athlete, Baseball Player)
728 Canterbury Ct
Grosse Pointe Woods, MI 48236-1294, USA

Bergman, Dusty (Athlete, Baseball Player)
1549 Koontz Ln
Carson City, NV 89701-6504, USA

Bergman, Jaime
c/o Holly Shelton *Precision Entertainment*
6338 Wilshire Blvd
Los Angeles, CA 90048-5002, USA

Bergman, Jamie (Actor, Model)
c/o Staff Member *Special Artists Agency*
9465 Wilshire Blvd Ste 820
Beverly Hills, CA 90212-2607, USA

Bergman, Marilyn K (Musician)
714 N Maple Dr
Beverly Hills, CA 90210-3411, USA

Bergman, Martin (Producer)
641 Lexington Ave
New York, NY 10022-4503, USA

Bergman, Peter (Actor)
4799 White Oak Ave
Encino, CA 91316-3719, USA

Bergman, Robert G (Misc)
501 Coventry Rd
Kensington, CA 94707-1316, USA

Bergman, Rushka (Stylist)
c/o Staff Member *Katy Barker Agency Inc*
6606 10th Ave Apt 3R
Brooklyn, NY 11219-5804, USA

Bergman, Sean (Athlete, Baseball Player)
14421 Scott Rd
Bryan, OH 43506-9624, USA

Bergman, Thommie (Athlete, Hockey Player)
c/o Staff Member *Toronto Maple Leafs*
Air Canada Centre 400-40 Bay St
Toronto, ON M5J 2X2, Canada

Bergmann, Erma (Baseball Player)
6613 Morganford Rd
Saint Louis, MO 63116-2835, USA

Bergmann, Jay (Athlete, Baseball Player)
12202 Bainbridge Way
Freehold, NJ 07728-4859, USA

Bergoglio, Jose Mario Cardinal (Religious Leader)
Rivadavia 415
Buenos Aires 1002, ARGENTINA

Bergomi, Giuseppe (Athlete, Football Player)
via Trento 1
Settala (MI) I-20090, Italy

Bergonzi, Caroline (Stylist)
c/o Staff Member *Jean Jacques Visual Representation*
7118 River Rd
Prospect, KY 40059-9618, USA

Bergoust, Eric (Skier)
228 W Main St
Missoula, MT 59802-4345, USA

Bergquist, Curt (Doctor)
Valinge 2090
Angelhoim 262 92, SWEDEN

Bergstein, Eleanor (Director, Producer, Writer)
c/o Staff Member *Creative Artists Agency (CAA-LA)*
2000 Avenue of the Stars Ste 100
Los Angeles, CA 90067-4705, USA

Bergsten, C Fred (Economist)
4106 Sleepy Hollow Rd
Annandale, VA 22003-2042, USA

Berhendt, Greg (Actor, Comedian)
c/o Staff Member *Avalon Management*
4A Exmoor St
London W10 6BD, UK

Beristain, Gabriel L (Cinematographer)
9560 Wilshire Blvd Ste 500
Beverly Hills, CA 90212-2401, USA

Berkeley, Michael F (Composer)
20 Powis Mews
London W11 1JN, UNITED KINGDOM (UK)

Berkeley, Xander (Actor, Producer)
c/o David (Dave) Fleming *Mosaic Media Group*
9200 W Sunset Blvd Ste 10
Los Angeles, CA 90069-3608, USA

Berkley, Elizabeth (Actor, Producer)
c/o Adam Griffin *Kritzer Levine Wilkins Entertainment*
11872 La Grange Ave Fl 1
Los Angeles, CA 90025-5283, USA

Berkley, Shelley (Congressman, Politician)
405 Cannon Hob
Washington, DC 20515-4309, USA

Berkman, Lance (Athlete, Baseball Player)
5 Farnham Park Dr
Houston, TX 77024-7501, USA

Berkner, Laurie (Musician)
PO Box 250774
New York, NY 10025-1529, USA

Berkoff, David (Swimmer)
Athletic Dept
Cambridge, MA 2138, USA

Berkowitz, Bob (Entertainer)
2200 Fletcher Ave
Fort Lee, NJ 07024-5005, USA

Berkus, Nate (Designer, Television Host)
406 N Wood St
Chicago, IL 60622-6260, USA

Berlanti, Greg (Producer)

Berlin, Clay (Publisher)
2935 Franciscan Way
Carmel, CA 93923-9216, USA

Berlin, Eddie (Athlete, Football Player)
604 44th St
Des Moines, IA 50312-2302, USA

Berlin, Mike (Bowler)
12 Coventry Ln
Muscatine, IA 52761-5659, USA

Berlin, Steve (Musician)
c/o Staff Member *Paradigm (Monterey)*
404 W Franklin St
Monterey, CA 93940-2303, USA

Berliner, Alain (Director)
9560 Wilshire Blvd Ste 500
Beverly Hills, CA 90212-2401, USA

Berlinger, Warren (Actor)
10642 Arnel Pl
Chatsworth, CA 91311-2501, USA

Berlinsky, Dmitri (Musician)
35 W 64th St Apt 7F
New York, NY 10023-6757, USA

Berlioux, Daniel (Actor)
36 Rue de Ponthieu
Paris 75008, FRANCE

Berlusconi, Silvio (Politician, Prime Minister)
Via Del Plebiscito 102
Rome I-00186, Italy

Berman, Andy (Actor)
c/o Staff Member *Gersh (LA)*
9465 Wilshire Blvd Ste 600
Beverly Hills, CA 90212-2612, USA

Berman, Benica (Stylist)
399 E 72nd St Apt 11F
New York, NY 10021-4652, USA

Berman, Boris (Musician)
165 W 57th St
New York, NY 10019-2201, USA

Berman, Chris (Sportscaster)
c/o Staff Member *ESPN (Main)*
ESPN Plaza 935 Middle St
Bristol, CT 06010-1001, USA

Berman, Jennifer (Doctor)
Women's Sexual Health Center
Los Angeles, CA 90024, USA

Berman, Josh (Producer)
c/o Staff Member *Creative Artists Agency (CAA-LA)*
2000 Avenue of the Stars Ste 100
Los Angeles, CA 90067-4705, USA

Berman, Julie (Actor)
c/o Nicole Nassar *Nicole Nassar PR*
1111 10th St Unit 104
Santa Monica, CA 90403-5363, USA

Berman, Laura (Doctor)
Women's Sexual Health Center
Los Angeles, CA 90024, USA

Berman, Lazar N (Musician)
12 Nicola Ln
Nesconset, NY 11767-1550, USA

Berman, Shari Springer (Director)
c/o Staff Member *Creative Artists Agency (CAA-LA)*
2000 Avenue of the Stars Ste 100
Los Angeles, CA 90067-4705, USA

Berman, Shelley (Actor, Comedian)
268 Bell Canyon Rd
Bell Canyon, CA 91307-1112, USA

Bermudez, Carolina (Musician)
c/o Staff Member *Don Buchwald & Associates Inc (LA)*
6500 Wilshire Blvd Ste 2200
Los Angeles, CA 90048-4942, USA

Bermudez, Gustavo (Actor)
c/o Staff Member *Telefe - Argentina*
Pavon 2444 (C1248AAT)
Buenos Aires, ARGENTINA

Bermudez, Joe (DJ)
c/o Staff Member *Diva Central Inc*
7510 W Sunset Blvd Ste 1445
Los Angeles, CA 90046-3408, USA

Bern, Howard A (Biologist)
1010 Shattuck Ave
Berkeley, CA 94707-2626, USA

Bernadotte, Princess Marianne (Royalty)
Villagatan 10
Stockholm S-11432, Sweden

Bernal, Gael Garcia (Actor)
c/o Staff Member *Canana Films*
Jose Maria Tornel #14 Colonia San Miguel Chapultepec
Mexico City 11850, MEXICO

Bernard, Betsy (Business Person)
32 Avenue of the Americas
New York, NY 10013-2473, USA

Bernard, Carlos (Actor)
c/o Lewis Kay *PMK/BNC - LA*
8687 Melrose Ave Ste 8
West Hollywood, CA 90069-5746, USA

Bernard, Claire M A (Musician)
53 Rue Rabelais
Lyon 69003, FRANCE

Bernard, Crystal (Actor, Musician, Songwriter, Writer)
c/o Staff Member *IFA Talent Agency*
8730 W Sunset Blvd Ste 490
Los Angeles, CA 90069-2248, USA

Bernard, Dwight (Athlete, Baseball Player)
5120 N Norwich Ln
Belle Rive, IL 62810-2703, USA

Bernard, Ed (Actor)
PO Box 7965
Northridge, CA 91327-7965, USA

Bernard, Henry (Architect)
44 Av D'llena
Paris 75116, FRANCE

Bernard, Robyn (Actor)
PO Box 202
Montrose, CA 91021-0202, USA

Bernardi, Barry (Producer)
c/o Staff Member *Gersh (LA)*
9465 Wilshire Blvd Ste 600
Beverly Hills, CA 90212-2612, USA

Bernardi, Frank (Athlete, Football Player)
PO Box 1015
Broomfield, CO 80038-1015, USA

Bernazard, Tony (Athlete, Baseball Player)
D-25 Santa Av Urb Santa Elvira
Caguas, PR 725, USA

Berner, Robert A (Misc)
15 Hickory Hill Rd
North Haven, CT 06473-2916, USA

Bernero, Adam (Athlete, Baseball Player)
19391 Titleist Way
Redding, CA 96003-8627, USA

Bernero, Edward Allen (Writer)
c/o Staff Member *WmE2 (Endeavor-LA)*
9601 Wilshire Blvd Fl 3
Beverly Hills, CA 90210-5219, USA

Berners-Lee, Timothy J (Scientist)
Computer Sci Lab
Cambridge, MA 2139, USA

Bernet, Ed (Athlete, Football Player)
7967 Caruth Ct
Dallas, TX 75225-8135, USA

Bernet, Lee (Athlete, Football Player)
4689 Stoddart Ln
Saint Paul, MN 55127-2334, USA

Berney, Bob (President)
c/o Staff Member *Newmarket Films*
597 5th Ave Fl 7
New York, NY 10017-8264, USA

Bernhard, Ruth (Photographer)
1826 Loyola Dr
Burlingame, CA 94010-5749, USA

Bernhard, Sandra (Actor, Comedian, Musician)
c/o Tim Curtis *WmE2 (Endeavor-LA)*
9601 Wilshire Blvd Fl 3
Beverly Hills, CA 90210-5219, USA

Bernhardt, Daniel (Actor)
6500 Wilshire Blvd Ste 2200
Los Angeles, CA 90048-4942

Bernhardt, Juan (Athlete, Baseball Player)
Eduardo Brito 13
San Pedro de Macoris, Dominican Republic

Bernhardt, Kevin (Writer)
c/o Luke Rivett *Anonymous Content (AC-LA)*
3531 Hayden Ave
Culver City, CA 90232, USA

Bernhardt, Roger (Athlete, Football Player)
PO Box 4631
Lawrence, KS 66046-1631, USA

Bernhardt, Tim (Athlete, Hockey Player)
RR 1
Schomberg, ON L0G 1T0, Canada

Bernheimer, Martin (Musician)
17350 W Sunset Blvd Apt 702C
Pacific Palisades, CA 90272-4109, USA

Bernice Johnson, Eddie (Congressman, Politician)
2468 Rayburn Hob
Washington, DC 20515-3306, USA

Bernich, Ken (Athlete, Football Player)
504 Woodland Park Cir
Mary Esther, FL 32569-1577, USA

Bernier, Serge (Athlete, Hockey Player)
534 Rue Elisabeth
Rimouski, QC G5L 3M9, Canada

Bernier, Sylvie (Race Car Driver)
Cite du Harve
Montreal QC H3C 3R4, CANADA

Berning, Susie (Athlete, Golfer)
80413 Portobello Dr
Indio, CA 92201-1877, USA

Berns, Rick (Athlete, Football Player)
632 Canyon Springs Dr
Canyon Lake, TX 78133-4301, USA

Bernsen, Corbin (Actor)
c/o Randy James *James/Levy/Jacobson Management Inc*
3500 W Olive Ave Ste 1470
Burbank, CA 91505-5514, USA

Bernstein, Assaf (Director)
c/o Brad Kaplan *Evolution Entertainment (LA)*
901 N Highland Ave
Los Angeles, CA 90038-2412, USA

Bernstein, Besil (Misc)
90 Farquhar Road
Dulwich SE19 1LT, UNITED KINGDOM (UK)

Bernstein, Bonnie (Television Host)
c/o Staff Member *CBS Television*
51 W 52nd St
New York, NY 10019-6119, USA

Bernstein, Carl (Journalist, Writer)
c/o Suzanne Gluck *WmE2 (WMA-NY)*
1325 Avenue of the Americas
New York, NY 10019-6026, USA

Bernstein, Charles (Composer, Musician)
c/o John Tempereau *Soundtrack Music Assoc*
1460 4th St Ste 308
Santa Monica, CA 90401-3483, USA

Bernstein, Fred (Stylist)
c/o Staff Member *Artists by Timothy Priano (CA)*
8447 Wilshire Blvd Ste 301
Beverly Hills, CA 90211-3206, USA

Bernstein, Josh (Television Host)
c/o Jim Ornstein *WmE2 (WMA-NY)*
1325 Avenue of the Americas
New York, NY 10019-6026, USA

Bernstein, Kenny (Race Car Driver)
26231 Dimension Dr
Lake Forest, CA 92630-7805, USA

Bernstine, Rod (Athlete, Football Player)
552 Washington Ave
Carnegie, PA 15106-2848, USA

Bernthal, Jon (Actor)
c/o Joanna (Joanie) Burstein *Burstein Company, The*
15304 W Sunset Blvd Ste 208
Pacific Palisades, CA 90272-3656, USA

Berov, Lyuben (Prime Minister)
Tzarigradsko Shosse 47/1
Sofia 1408, BULGARIA

Berra, Dale (Athlete, Baseball Player)
164 Eagle Rock Way
Montclair, NJ 07042-1623, USA

Berra, Lawrence P (Yogi) (Athlete, Baseball Player, Coach)
8 Quarry Rd
Little Falls, NJ 07424-2161, USA

Berra, Tim (Athlete, Football Player)
23 Wilson Ter
West Caldwell, NJ 07006-7953, USA

Berresford, Josh (Actor)
PO Box 601
Homewood, IL 60430-8601

Berresford, Susan V (Misc)
320 E 43rd St
New York, NY 10017-4801, USA

Berri, Claude (Director, Producer)
7 Rue de Lille
Paris 75007, FRANCE

Berridge, Elizabeth (Actor)
606 N Larchmont Blvd Ste 309
Los Angeles, CA 90004-1309, USA

Berridge, Michael J (Biologist)
13 Home Close Histon
Cambridge CB4 4JL, UNITED KINGDOM (UK)

Berrigan, Daniel (Activist)
147 Thompson St
New York, NY 10012-3110, USA

Berroa, Geronimo (Athlete, Baseball Player)
3681 Broadway Apt 23
New York, NY 10031-1539, USA

Berruti, Livio (Activist)
45 Avigliana Via
New York, NY 10138-0001, ITALY

Berry, Adam (Composer, Musician)
c/o Staff Member *Greenspan Artist Management*
8760 W Sunset Blvd
West Hollywood, CA 90069-2206, USA

Berry, Bert (Athlete, Football Player)
1402 E Coral Cove Dr
Gilbert, AZ 85234-2600, USA

Berry, Bill (Musician)
170 College Ave
Athens, GA 30601-2805, USA

Berry, Bill (Baseball Player)
2231 Dickinson St
Philadelphia, PA 19146-4204, USA

Berry, Bob (Athlete, Football Player)
1351 Wilson Cir
Gardnerville, NV 89410-6022, USA

Berry, Brad (Athlete, Hockey Player)
PO Box 5182
Grand Forks, ND 58206-5182, USA

Berry, Chuck (Musician, Songwriter, Writer)
Berry Park 691 Buckner Rd
Wentzville, MO 63385, USA

Berry, David (Actor)
5903 Winton St
Dallas, TX 75206-5536, USA

Berry, Ed (Athlete, Football Player)
4215 Skymont Dr
Belmont, CA 94002-1245, USA

Berry, Eric (Athlete, Football Player)
c/o Chad Speck *Allegiant Athletic Agency*
35 Market Sq Ste 201
Knoxville, TN 37902-1420, USA

Berry, Glen (Actor)
c/o Staff Member *The Rights House (UK)*
Drury House 34-43 Russell St
London WC2B 5HA, UK

Berry, Halle (Actor, Model)
c/o Vincent Cirrincione *Vincent Cirrincione Associates*
1516 N Fairfax Ave
Los Angeles, CA 90046-2608, USA

Berry, Jadagrace (Actor)
c/o Monique Moss *Moss Public Relations*
8060 Melrose Ave Fl 4
Los Angeles, CA 90046-7038, USA

Berry, Jennifer (Beauty Pageant Winner)
c/o Staff Member *The Miss America Organization*
2 Convention Blvd Ste 1000
Atlantic City, NJ 08401-4137, USA

Berry, Jim (Cartoonist)
200 Madison Ave
New York, NY 10016-3903, USA

Berry, John (Musician)
14724 Ventura Blvd PH
Sherman Oaks, CA 91403-3513, USA

Berry, Joy (Writer)
c/o Staff Member *Trident Media Group LLC*
41 Madison Ave Fl 36
New York, NY 10010-2257, USA

Berry, Ken (Athlete, Baseball Player)
1131 SW Camden Ln
Topeka, KS 66604-1980, USA

Berry, Kevin (Swimmer)
28 George St
Manly, NSW 2295, AUSTRALIA

Berry, Latin (Athlete, Football Player)
925 Prater Rd
Sulphur, LA 70663-4243, USA

Berry, Michael J (Misc)
7801 Comfort Cv
Austin, TX 78731-1471, USA

Berry, Neil (Athlete, Baseball Player)
407 Inkster Ave
Kalamazoo, MI 49001-4220, USA

Berry, R Stephen (Misc)
5317 S University Ave
Chicago, IL 60615-5105, USA

Berry, Raymond E (Athlete, Football Coach, Football Player)
1110 SE Broad St
Murfreesboro, TN 37130-5027, USA

Berry, Reggie (Athlete, Football Player)
1803 E Ocean Blvd Unit 402
Long Beach, CA 90802-6045, USA

Berry, Robert V (Bob) (Athlete, Coach, Hockey Player)
110 The Village Unit 505
Redondo Beach, CA 90277-2553, USA

Berry, Royce (Athlete, Football Player)
PO Box 909
Comfort, TX 78013-0909, USA

Berry, Sean (Athlete, Baseball Player)
307 Susannah Ln
Paso Robles, CA 93446-7114, USA

Berry, Vincent (Actor)
4942 Vineland Ave Ste 103
North Hollywood, CA 91601-5639, USA

Berry, Walter (Athlete, Basketball Player)
5206 Village Ct
Union City, GA 30291-5146, USA

Berry, Wendell E (Writer)
River Road
Port Royal, KY 40058, USA

Berryhill, Damon (Athlete, Baseball Player)
11 Springbrook Rd
Laguna Niguel, CA 92677-5719, USA

Berryman, Michael (Actor)
PO Box 697
Clearlake, CA 95422-0697, USA

Berschet, Marv (Athlete, Football Player)
8396 Clifton Rd
South Charleston, OH 45368-8653, USA

Bersia, John (Journalist)
633 N Orange Ave
Orlando, FL 32801-1300, USA

Bertaina, Frank (Athlete, Baseball Player)
1129 Burghley Ln
Brentwood, CA 94513-6969, USA

Bertelmann, Fred (Actor, Musician)
Am Hohenberg 9
Berg/Starnberger D-82335, Germany

Bertelsen, Jim (Athlete, Football Player)
1001 Golds Rd
Wimberley, TX 78676-6053, USA

Berteotti, Missy (Athlete, Golfer)
3065 Annandale Dr
Presto, PA 15142, USA

Berthiaume, Daniel (Athlete, Hockey Player)
PO Box 673
Hardy, VA 24101-0673, USA

Berthiaume-Wicken, Elizabeth (Baseball Player)
52 E 20th Ave
Vancouver, BC V5V 1L6, CANADA

Berthold, Helmut (Misc)
Meyerstr 21
Hamburg 21075, GERMANY

Berti, Joel (Actor)
c/o Melissa Hirschenson *Innovative Artists (LA)*
1505 10th St
Santa Monica, CA 90401-2805, USA

Bertie, Diego (Musician)
c/o Gabriel Blanco *Gabriel Blanco Iglesias (Mexico)*
Rio Balsas 35-32 Colonia Cuauhtemoc
DF 6500, Mexico

Bertil (Prince)
Hert Av Halland Kungl Slottel
Stockholm 1130, SWEDEN

Bertinelli, Valerie (Actor)
c/o Heidi Schaeffer *PMK/BNC Public Relations (PMK-LA)*
8687 Melrose Ave Ste 8
West Hollywood, CA 90069-5746, USA

Bertini, Catherine (Misc)
1 United Nations Plz
New York, NY 10017-3515, USA

Bertoia, Reno (Athlete, Baseball Player)
705-5125 Riverside Dr E
Windsor, ON N8S 4L8, Canada

Bertolucci, Bernardo (Actor)
Via Della Lungara 3
Rome 165, ITALY

Bertolucci, Irene (Stylist)
2514 Prairie Ave Apt 2B
Evanston, IL 60201-5844, USA

Bertone, Cardinal Tarcisio (Religious Leader)
Rome 193, ITALY

Bertotti, Mike (Athlete, Baseball Player)
14 Jupiter Rd
Highland Mls, NY 10930-2916, USA

Bertram, Laura (Actor)
c/o Staff Member *Lucas Talent Inc*
100 W. Pender St Sun Tower, 7th Floor
Vancouver, BC V6B 1R8, Canada

Bertsch, Jackie (Athlete, Golfer)
8215 E Bronco Trl
Scottsdale, AZ 85255-2171, USA

Bertuca, Tony (Athlete, Football Player)
2014 N Newcastle Ave
Chicago, IL 60707-3332, USA

Bertuzzi, Todd (Athlete, Hockey Player)
900 Deer Ridge Ct
Kitchener, ON N2P 2L3, Canada

Berube, Craig (Athlete, Hockey Player)
1341 Durham Rd
New Hope, PA 18938-9479, USA

Berumen, Andres (Athlete, Baseball Player)
PO Box 1436
Banning, CA 92220-0010, USA

Berzon, Marsha S (Judge)
Court Building 95 7th St
San Francisco, CA 94103, USA

Besana, Fred (Baseball Player)
222 Diamond Oaks Rd
Roseville, CA 95678-1007, USA

Beschorner-Baskovich, Mary (Baseball Player)
211 Sandy Ln
Plano, IL 60545-2054, USA

Besedin, Vladimir (Figure Skater)
c/o Staff Member *Champions on Ice*
3500 W 80th St Ste 200
Minneapolis, MN 55431-1090, USA

Beshear, Steve (Governor)
700 Capitol Ave Ste 100
Frankfort, KY 40601-3410, USA

Beshore, Del (Athlete, Basketball Player)
287 N Ezie Ave
Fresno, CA 93727-3555, USA

Bess, Daniel (Actor)
c/o Raelle Koota *Anonymous Content (AC-LA)*
3531 Hayden Ave
Culver City, CA 90232, USA

Bess, Rufus (Athlete, Football Player)
8685 Magnolia Trl Apt 214
Eden Prairie, MN 55344-7664, USA

Bessey, Joe
PO Box 525
Scarborough, ME 04070-0525, USA

Bessillieu, Donald A (Don) (Athlete, Football Player)
4787 Gardiner Dr
Columbus, GA 31907-3441, USA

Bessmertnova, Natalia (Ballerina)
Sretenskii Blvd 6/1 #9
Moscow 101000, RUSSIA

Bessmertnykh, Aleksandr (Government Official)
Yelizarova Str 10
Moscow 103064, RUSSIA

Besson, Luc (Director, Producer, Writer)
c/o Staff Member *Europa Corp*
137 Rue du Faubourg Saint-Honor
Paris 75008, FRANCE

Bessone, Amo (Athlete, Hockey Player)
263 Staab St
Santa Fe, NM 87501-1842, USA

Best, Art (Athlete, Football Player)
420 Lockville Rd
Pickerington, OH 43147-1360, USA

Best, Grady (Stylist)
309 E 108th St Apt 2H
New York, NY 10029-4208, USA

Best, Greg (Athlete, Football Player)
2859 Darlington Rd
Beaver Falls, PA 15010-1054, USA

Best, Jahvid (Athlete, Football Player)
c/o Tony Fleming *Impact Sports - LA*
11331 Ventura Blvd Ste 1A
Studio City, CA 91604-3147, USA

Best, John O (Soccer Player)
1065 Lomita Blvd
Harbor City, CA 90710-1901, USA

Best, Karl (Athlete, Baseball Player)
PO Box 1790
Snohomish, WA 98291-1790, USA

Best, Kevin (Artist)
27 Dartford Rd
Thornleigh 2120, Australia

Best, Pete (Musician)
8 Hymans Green W Derby
Liverpool 12, UNITED KINGDOM (UK)

Best, Travis (Athlete, Basketball Player)
703 Bradley Rd
Springfield, MA 01109-1424, USA

Bestar, Maria (Musician)
c/o Staff Member *Sony Music Miami*
605 Lincoln Rd Ste 700
Miami Beach, FL 33139-2901, USA

Bester, Allan (Athlete, Hockey Player)
12527 Crayford Ave
Orlando, FL 32837-8536, USA

Bestwicke, Martine (Actor)
1156 S Carmelina Ave # B
Los Angeles, CA 90049-5812, USA

Beswick, Jim (Athlete, Baseball Player)
6911 Buckhorn Dr
Columbus, GA 31904-3212, USA

Beswicke, Martine (Actor)
1156 S Carmelina Ave # 8
Los Angeles, CA 90049-5812, USA

Betancourt, Jeff (Director)
c/o Staff Member *Broder Webb Chervin Silbermann Agency, The (BWCS)*
10250 Constellation Blvd
Los Angeles, CA 90067-6200, USA

Betancourt, Yuniesky (Athlete, Baseball Player)
1001 Brickell Bay Dr Ste 1710
Miami, FL 33131-4939, USA

Betancurt, Natalia (Actor)
c/o Staff Member *TV Caracol*
Calle 76 #11 - 35 Piso 10AA
Bogota DC 26484, COLOMBIA

Bethea, Bill (Athlete, Baseball Player)
106 Penny Ln
Georgetown, TX 78633, USA

Bethea, Ellen (Actor)
505 8th Ave Ste 2208
New York, NY 10018-6505, USA

Bethea, Elvin L (Athlete, Football Player)
16211 Leslie Ln
Missouri City, TX 77489-1012, USA

Bethell, Tabrett (Actor)
c/o El Erdmane *RGM Artist Group*
64-76 Kippax St Level 2, Suite 202 & 206
Surry Hills, NSW 2010, Australia

Bethke, Jim (Athlete, Baseball Player)
4305 N Jarboe Ct
Kansas City, MO 64116-4655, USA

Bethune, Bobby (Athlete, Football Player)
PO Box 692
Leeds, AL 35094-0011, USA

Bethune, George (Athlete, Football Player)
2817 Gaslight Ln W
Mobile, AL 36695-3130, USA

Bethune, Patricia (Actor)
c/o Peter Himberger *Impact Artists Group LLC*
42 Hamilton Ter
New York, NY 10031-6403, USA

Bethune, Zina (Actor)
3096 Lake Hollywood Dr
Los Angeles, CA 90068-1565, USA

Bets, Maxim (Athlete, Hockey Player)
5566 Candlelight Dr
La Jolla, CA 92037-7711, USA

Betsill, Roscoe (Stylist)
270 Park Ave S Apt 11D
New York, NY 10010-6106, USA

Bettany, Paul (Actor)
c/o Melanie Greene *Affirmative Entertainment*
425 N Robertson Blvd
West Hollywood, CA 90048-1735, USA

Bettencourt, Liliane (Business Person)
18 Rue Delabordere
Neuilly-sur-Seine F-92 200, France

Bettendorf, Jeff (Athlete, Baseball Player)
2381 Highway Ee
Mansfield, MO 65704-8447, USA

Bettenhausen, Gary (Race Car Driver)
2741 Chesterfield Dr
Bettendorf, IA 52722-6251, USA

Betters, Doug L (Athlete, Football Player)
77 Better Way
Whitefish, MT 59937-3471, USA

Betterson, Doug (Athlete, Football Player)
2442 46th St
Pennsauken, NJ 08110-2018, USA

Betterson, James (Athlete, Football Player)
234 Allens Ln
Mullica Hill, NJ 08062-2005, USA

Bettiga, Mike (Athlete, Football Player)
1165 Vista Dr
Fortuna, CA 95540-1514, USA

Bettio, Silvio (Athlete, Hockey Player)
1405 Wedgewood Dr
Sudbury, ON P3A 3E3, Canada

Bettis, Angela (Actor)
c/o Ryan Revel *Benderspink*
5870 W Jefferson Blvd Ste E
Los Angeles, CA 90016-3159, USA

Bettis, Jerome (Actor, Athlete)
c/o Lou Oppenheim *Headline Media Management*
888 7th Ave Ste 503
New York, NY 10106-0501, USA

Bettis, Tom (Athlete, Football Coach, Football Player)
24001 Cinco Village Center Blvd Apt 3116
Katy, TX 77494-8423, USA

Bettman, Gary B (Misc)
1251 Avenue of the Americas
New York, NY 10020-1104, USA

Bettridge, Ed (Athlete, Football Player)
200 Seaward Way
Avon Lake, OH 44012-2414, USA

Betts, Austin W (General)
8003 North Holw Unit 204
San Antonio, TX 78240-2360, USA

Betts, Dickey (Musician)
c/o Staff Member *Intrepid Artists*
Midtown Plz 1300 Baxter St #405
Charlotte, NC 28204, USA

Betts, Dickie (Musician)
PO Box 604
Chagrin Falls, OH 44022-0604, USA

Betts, Jack (Actor)
c/o Jon Simmons *Simmons & Scott Entertainment*
7942 Mulholland Dr
Los Angeles, CA 90046-1225, USA

Betts, Katherine (Editor)
Editorial Dept 1770 Broadway
New York, NY 10019, USA

Beuchel, Ted (Musician)
1924 Spring St
Paso Robles, CA 93446-1620, USA

Beuerlein, Stephen T (Steve) (Athlete, Football Player)
15624 McCullers Ct
Charlotte, NC 28277-1478, USA

Beukeboom, Jeff (Athlete, Hockey Player)
c/o Staff Member *Lindsay Muskies*
Lindsay Recreation Complex
Lindsay, ON K9V 4S3, Canada

Beutler, Ernest (Doctor)
2707 Costebelle Dr
La Jolla, CA 92037-3518, USA

Beutler, Tom (Athlete, Football Player)
654 Stacey Ln
Maumee, OH 43537-2429, USA

Bevacqua, Kurt (Athlete, Baseball Player)
7679 Sitio Manana
Carlsbad, CA 92009-8960, USA

Bevan, Tim (Actor, Producer)
c/o Staff Member *Working Title Films*
9720 Wilshire Blvd Fl 4
Beverly Hills, CA 90212-2000, USA

Bevan, Timothy H (Financier)
54 Lombard St
London EC3P 3AH, UNITED KINGDOM (UK)

Beverley, Frankie (Musician)
115 Cherokee Rose Ln
Fayetteville, GA 30214-2659, USA

Beverley, Nick (Athlete, Coach, Hockey Player)
c/o Staff Member *Nashville Predators*
501 Broadway
Nashville, TN 37203-3980, USA

Beverley Sisters (Actor, Music Group)
80 Highcroft Ave Bispham
Blackpool, Lancashire FY20BW, UNITED KINGDOM

Beverlin, Jason (Athlete, Baseball Player)
6921 Vintage Ln
Port Orange, FL 32128-4095, USA

Beverly, David (Athlete, Football Player)
1919 Ford St
Llano, TX 78643-2907, USA

Beverly, Eric (Athlete, Football Player)
PO Box 492433
Lawrenceville, GA 30049-0041, USA

Beverly, Randy (Athlete, Football Player)
PO Box 193
Monroe Township, NJ 08831-0193, USA

Beverly Jr, Ed (Athlete, Football Player)
13051 Golansville Rd
Ruther Glen, VA 22546-4029, USA

Bevil, Brian (Athlete, Baseball Player)
12655 Kuykendahl Rd Apt 7108
Houston, TX 77090-6940, USA

Bevill, Lisa (Musician)
206 Bluebird Dr
Goodlettsville, TN 37072-2302, USA

Bevington, Terry P (Athlete, Baseball Player, Coach)
2600 Halle Pkwy
Collierville, TN 38017-8888, USA

Bevis, Muriel (Baseball Player)
538 Idlewood Dr
Mount Juliet, TN 37122-2118, USA

Bey, Andy (Musician)
PO Box 779
New Hope, PA 18938-0779, USA

Bey, Richard (Entertainer)
445 Park Ave # 1000
New York, NY 10022-2606, USA

Bey, Turhan (Actor)
Paradisgasse Ave 47
Vienna, XIX 1190, AUSTRIA

Beyer, Brad (Actor)
c/o Jeff Hunter *WmE2 (WMA-NY)*
1325 Avenue of the Americas
New York, NY 10019-6026, USA

Beyer, Troy (Actor)
c/o David Saunders *Agency for the Performing Arts (APA-LA)*
405 S Beverly Dr Ste 500
Beverly Hills, CA 90212-4425, USA

Beymer, Richard (Actor)
147 N Ridgewood Pl
Los Angeles, CA 90004-4002, USA

Bezic, Sandra (Figure Skater, Sportscaster)
c/o Staff Member *NBC Sports (NY)*
30 Rockefeller Plz Fl 270E
New York, NY 10112-0299, USA

Bezos, Jeffrey (Business Person)
100 Enterprise Way Ste A200
Scotts Valley, CA 95066-3266, USA

Bezucha, Tom (Director)
c/o Simon Halls *Slate Public Relations*
9000 W Sunset Blvd Ste 915
West Hollywood, CA 90069-5809, USA

Bhagwan (Actor, Bollywood)
25 Lallubhai Mansion Shankarrao Palav Marg
Mumbai, MS 400014, INDIA

Bhagwati, Jagdish N (Economist)
Economics Dept
New York, NY 10027, USA

Bhagyashree (Actor, Bollywood)
96/B Hirak Society Sv Rd Vile Parle
Mumbai, MS 400056, INDIA

Bhakta, Raj (Business Person)
238 E 50th St
New York, NY 10022-7704, USA

Bhan Bhagta Gurung (War Hero)
Old Admiralty Building
London SW1A 2BL, UNITED KINGDOM (UK)

Bhanu, Prakash (Bharathan) (Actor)
1 2/2 Circular Road United India Colony Kodambakkam
Chennai, TN 600 024, INDIA

Bhanupriya (Actor, Bollywood)
4 1st Cross Street Vijayaraghava Rd
Chennai, TN 600017, INDIA

Bhaskar, Sanjeev (Actor)
c/o Staff Member *BBC Artist Mail*
PO Box 1116
Belfast BT2 7AJ, United Kingdom

Bhatnagar, Deepti (Actor, Bollywood)
42 Ashok Apts Gandhigram Road Juhu
Mumbai, MS 400049, INDIA

Bhatnagar, Dipti (Actor, Bollywood)
42 Ashoka Apts Gandhigram Rd Juhu
Mumbai, MS 400049, INDIA

Bhatt, Brinda (Actor)
c/o Staff Member *Innovative Artists (LA)*
1505 10th St
Santa Monica, CA 90401-2805, USA

Bhatt, Mahesh (Bollywood, Director, Filmmaker)
205 Silver Beach Apartments Near Sun-N-Sand Hotel Juhu
Bombay, MS 400049, INDIA

Bhatt, Mukesh (Bollywood, Director, Filmmaker, Producer)
10 Shubh Jeevan Co-Op Society Jvpd Scheme
Bombay, MS 400 049, INDIA

Bhattacharya, Basu (Actor, Bollywood, Director)
36 Carter Road Bandra
Mumbai, MS 400050, INDIA

Bhave, Ashwini (Actor, Bollywood)
A-9 Green View Suburban Soc Shiv Shrushti
Mumbai, MS 400024, INDIA

Bhavsar, Raj (Athlete, Gymnast)
Pan American Plaza, Suite 300 201 South Capitol Avenue
Indianapolis, IN 46225

Bhumibol, Adulyadej (King)
Chirtalad a Villa
Bangkok, THAILAND

Biafra, Jello (Musician)
c/o Staff Member *Simon & Schuster*
1230 Avenue of the Americas Fl CONC1
New York, NY 10020-1586, USA

Biagiotti, Laura (Designer, Fashion Designer)
Via Borgopesco 19
Milan 20121, ITALY

Biakabutuka, Tshimanga (Tim) (Athlete, Football Player)
110 Sonnys Way
Fort Mill, SC 29708-6415, USA

Bialik, Mayim (Actor)
c/o Tiffany Kuzon *Evolution Entertainment (LA)*
901 N Highland Ave
Los Angeles, CA 90038-2412, USA

Bialosuknia, Wesley (Athlete, Basketball Player)
29 Bayberry Dr
Bristol, CT 06010-7604, USA

Bialowas, Dwight (Athlete, Hockey Player)
15616 Park Terrace Dr
Eden Prairie, MN 55346-2429, USA

Bialowas, Frank (Athlete, Hockey Player)
1640 New Brooklyn Rd
Williamstown, NJ 08094-3717, USA

Biancalana, Buddy (Athlete, Baseball Player)
1204 Lakeview Dr
Fairfield, IA 52556-9670, USA

Bianchi, Rosa Maria (Actor)
c/o Staff Member *Televisa*
Blvd Adolfo Lopez Mateos 232 Colonia San Angel INN
DF CP 01060, MEXICO

Bianchin, Wayne (Athlete, Hockey Player)
2091 Wellington Rd E
Nanaimo, BC V9S 5V2, Canada

Bianchl, Alfred (Al) (Athlete, Basketball Player, Coach)
601 Biscayne Blvd
Miami, FL 33132-1801, USA

Bianco, Tom (Athlete, Baseball Player)
12 Knolltop Dr
Nesconset, NY 11767-2222, USA

Biasucci, Dean (Athlete, Football Player)
3484 Sandy Beach Dr
Canandaigua, NY 14424-2348, USA

Bibb, John (Writer)
1100 Broadway
Nashville, TN 37203-3116, USA

Bibb, Laslie (Actor)
9615 Brighton Way Ste 300
Beverly Hills, CA 90210-5118, USA

Bibb, Leslie (Actor)
c/o John Carrabino *John Carrabino Management*
5900 Wilshire Blvd Ste 406
Los Angeles, CA 90036-5015, USA

Bibby, Henry (Athlete, Basketball Player)
University of Southern California Athletic
Los Angeles, CA 90089-0001, USA

Bibby, Jim (Athlete, Baseball Player)
1826 S Coolwell Rd
Madison Heights, VA 24572-4567, USA

Bibby, Mike (Athlete, Basketball Player)
c/o David Falk *F.A.M.E*
Prefers to be contacted via telephone
Washington, DC, USA

Bice, Bo (Musician)
c/o Staff Member *Webster & Associates PR*
3573 Couchville Pike
Hermitage, TN 37076-4012, USA

Bichette, Dante (Athlete, Baseball Player)
1830 Gipson Green Ln
Winter Park, FL 32789-1480, USA

Bichir, Demian (Actor)
c/o Sekka Scher *Sekka Scher Management*
Prefers to be contacted via telephone
New York, NY 10012, USA

Bickerstaff, Bernard T (Bernie) (Coach)
129 W Trade St Ste 700
Charlotte, NC 28202-5301, USA

Bickett, Duane (Athlete, Football Player)
508 Van Dyke Ave
Del Mar, CA 92014-2545, USA

Bickford, Valerie (Actor)
c/o Staff Member *The Learning Channel (TLC)*
10100 Santa Monica Blvd Ste 1500
Los Angeles, CA 90067-4117, USA

Bickle, Mike (Religious Leader)
3535 E Red Bridge Rd
Kansas City, MO 64137-2135, USA

Bickle, Rich (Race Car Driver)
3700 Teaberry Ct
Charlotte, NC 28227-8656, USA

Bicknell, Charlie (Athlete, Baseball Player)
109 Creekside Ln
Chapel Hill, TN 37034-7049, USA

Bidart, Frank (Writer)
106 Central St
Wellesley, MA 02481-8203, USA

Biddle, Dennis (Bose) (Athlete, Baseball Player)
9418 N Green Bay Rd Apt 241
Milwaukee, WI 53209-1070, USA

Biddle, Martin (Archaeologist)
19 Hamilton Road
Oxford OX2 7OY, UNITED KINGDOM (UK)

Biddle, Melvin E (War Hero)
5013 Gurneyville Rd
Wilmington, OH 45177-9423, USA

Biddle, Rocky (Athlete, Baseball Player)
2031 E Rancho Culebra Dr
Covina, CA 91724-3331, USA

Biden, Jill (Misc)
1600 Pennsylvania Ave NW
Washington, DC 20500-0005, USA

Biden, Joseph (Joe) (Ex-Senator, Politician, Vice President)
1600 Pennsylvania Ave NW
Washington, DC 20500-0005, USA

Bidner, Todd (Athlete, Hockey Player)
434 Oozloffsky
Petrolia, ON N0N 1R0, Canada

Bidwell, Charles E (Misc)
5835 S Kimbark Ave
Chicago, IL 60637-1635, USA

Bidwell, Josh (Athlete, Football Player)
1380 W 40th Ave
Eugene, OR 97405-2001, USA

Bieber, Justin (Musician)
c/o Melissa Victor *Island Def Jam Music Group*
825 8th Ave Fl 28
New York, NY 10019-7416

Bieber, Nita (Actor)
PO Box 1889
Avalon, CA 90704-1889, USA

Bieber, Owen F (Misc)
8000 E Jefferson Ave
Detroit, MI 48214-3963, USA

Biebl-Prelevic, Heidi (Skier)
Haus Olympia
Oberstaufen 87534, GERMANY

Biedenbach, Edward (Athlete, Basketball Player)
92 Kimberly Ave
Asheville, NC 28804-3607, USA

Biederman, Charles J (Artist)
5840 Collischan Rd
Red Wing, MN 55066-1113, USA

Biedermann, Jeanette (Actor)
Postfach 121004
Berlin 10599, Germany

Biedermann, Leo (Athlete, Football Player)
11527 Noors Ave
Las Vegas, NV 89138-1547, USA

Biegler, David W (Business Person)
Energy Plaza 1601 Bryan St
Dallas, TX 75201, USA

Biehn, Michael (Actor)
c/o Judy Hofflund *Hofflund/Polone*
9465 Wilshire Blvd Ste 420
Beverly Hills, CA 90212-2603, USA

Bieka, Silverstre Siale (Prime Minister)
Malabo, EQUATORIAL GUINEA

Biekert, Gregory (Athlete, Football Player)
2360 Fish Creek Pl
Danville, CA 94506-2063, USA

Biel, Jessica (Actor)
c/o Nicole King *Management 360*
9111 Wilshire Blvd
Beverly Hills, CA 90210-5508, USA

Bielecki, J Krzysztof (Prime Minister)
Al Ujazdowskie 9
Warsaw 00-918, POLAND

Bielecki, Mike (Athlete, Baseball Player)
1505 Habersham Pl
Crownsville, MD 21032-2230, USA

Bielke, Don (Athlete, Basketball Player)
3769 Corte Cancion
Thousand Oaks, CA 91360, USA

Biellmann, Denise (Figure Skater)
Im Brachli 25
Zurich 8053, SWITZERLAND

Bielski, Dick (Athlete, Football Player)
27 Malibu Ct
Towson, MD 21204-2047, USA

Bienen, Andy (Writer)
c/o Staff Member *United Talent Agency (UTA)*
9560 Wilshire Blvd Fl 5
Beverly Hills, CA 90212-2400, USA

Bieniemy, Eric (Athlete, Football Player)
5313 Westridge Dr
Boulder, CO 80301-6502, USA

Bierbrodt, Nick (Athlete, Baseball Player)
1200 White Hawk Ranch Dr
Boulder, CO 80303-1668, USA

Biercevicz, Greg (Baseball Player)
21 Mead Farm Rd
Seymour, CT 06483-2453, USA

Bierko, Craig (Actor, Musician)
c/o Jill Littman *Impression Entertainment*
9229 W Sunset Blvd Ste 700
West Hollywood, CA 90069-3407, USA

Bies, Don (Athlete, Golfer)
1262 NW Blakely Ct
Seattle, WA 98177-4340, USA

Bies Susan, Schmidt (Government Official)
20th St & Constitution Ave
Washington, DC 20551-0001, USA

Bieser, Steve (Athlete, Baseball Player)
11770 Royal Oak Ct
Sainte Genevieve, MO 63670-8690, USA

Bieshu, Mariya L (Opera Singer)
24 Pushkin Str
Chisinau 2012, MOLDOVA

Bietila, Walter (Skier)
Iron Mountain, MI 49801, USA

Biffen, John (Government Official)
Tanat House Llanyblodwel Oswestry
Shropshire SY10 8NQ, UNITED KINGDOM (UK)

Biffi, Giacomo Cardinal (Religious Leader)
Archdiocese of Bologna Via Altabella 6
Bologna 40126, ITALY

Biffle, Greg (Race Car Driver)
319 Doolie Rd
Mooresville, NC 28117-5801, USA

Biffle, Jerome (Athlete, Track Athlete)
3205 Monaco Pkwy
Denver, CO 80207-2203, USA

Big & Rich (Music Group)
c/o Keith Miller *WmE2 (WMA-TN)*
1600 Division St Ste 300
Nashville, TN 37203-2755, USA

Big Bad Voodoo Daddy (Music Group, Musician)
c/o Staff Member *Vanguard Records*
11400 W Olympic Blvd Ste 1450
Los Angeles, CA 90064-1649, USA

Big Dismal (Music Group)
c/o Staff Member *Wind-up Records*
72 Madison Ave Fl 8
New York, NY 10016-8731, USA

Big Preach (Musician)
c/o Staff Member *UGF Entertainment Inc*
3105 S Martin Luther King Jr Blvd # 313
Lansing, MI 48910-2939, USA

Big Tigger (Television Host)
c/o Staff Member *Britto Agency PR*
234 W 56th St PH
New York, NY 10019-4302, USA

Big Time Rush (Music Group)
c/o Pearl Servat *PMK/BNC Public Relations (PMK-LA)*
8687 Melrose Ave Ste 8
West Hollywood, CA 90069-5746, USA

Big Tymers (Music Group)
c/o Staff Member *International Creative Management (ICM-LA)*
10250 Constellation Blvd Fl 7
Los Angeles, CA 90067-6207, USA

Bigbie, Larry (Athlete, Baseball Player)
101 Margaret Dr
Stevensville, MD 21666-3653, USA

Bigelow, Kathryn (Director, Producer, Writer)
c/o Susan Ciccone *42West (LA)*
11400 W Olympic Blvd Ste 1100
Los Angeles, CA 90064-1579, USA

Biggerstaff, Sean (Actor)
c/o Jeff Morrone *Jeff Morrone Entertainment*
9350 Wilshire Blvd Ste 224
Beverly Hills, CA 90212-3204, USA

Biggert, Judy (Congressman, Politician)
2113 Rayburn Hob
Washington, DC 20515-0706, USA

Biggins, Al-Mela (Reality TV Star)
c/o Staff Member *Trading Spouses*
3151 Cahuenga Blvd W Ste 300
Los Angeles, CA 90068-1768, USA

Biggio, Craig (Athlete, Baseball Player)
c/o St. Thomas High School 4500 Memorial Dr
Houston, TX 77007, USA

Bigglo, Craig A (Baseball Player)
6520 Belmont St
Houston, TX 77005-3804, USA

Biggs, Don (Athlete, Hockey Player)
10050 Somerset Dr
Loveland, OH 45140-1863, USA

Biggs, Jason (Actor)
c/o Peter Kiernan *Management 360*
9111 Wilshire Blvd
Beverly Hills, CA 90210-5508, USA

Biggs, John H (Business Person)
240 E 47th St # 47D
New York, NY 10017-2131, USA

Biggs, Peter M
Willows London Road
Saint Ives, Huntingdon Cam PE17 4ES, UNITED KINGDOM (UK)

Biggs-Dawson, Roxann (Actor)
1505 10th St
Santa Monica, CA 90401-2805, USA

Biggs-Dawson, Rozann
c/o Staff Member *Innovative Artists (LA)*
1505 10th St
Santa Monica, CA 90401-2805, USA

Bigley, Thomas J (Admiral)
1329 Carpers Ferry Way
Vienna, VA 22182, USA

Bignotti, George (Race Car Driver)
9413 Steeplehill Dr
Las Vegas, NV 89117-7271, USA

Biittner, Larry (Athlete, Baseball Player)
915 3rd Ave NW
Pocahontas, IA 50574-1413, USA

Bijan (Designer, Fashion Designer)
420 N Rodeo Dr
Beverly Hills, CA 90210-4502, USA

Bikel, Theodore (Actor)
11661 San Vicente Blvd Ste 1000
Los Angeles, CA 90049-5118, USA

Bila, Lucie (Actor, Musician)
Karlova Ul 8
Prague 1 110 00, CZECH REPUBLIC

Bilardello, Dann (Athlete, Baseball Player)
2 Dolphin Dr
Vero Beach, FL 32960-5209, USA

Bilderback, Nicole (Actor)
c/o Jeff Morrone *Jeff Morrone Entertainment*
9350 Wilshire Blvd Ste 224
Beverly Hills, CA 90212-3204, USA

Bildt, Carl (Prime Minister)
Svenges Riksdag
Stockholm 10012, SWEDEN

Biletnikoff, Frederick (Fred) (Athlete, Football Player)
1736 Avondale Dr
Roseville, CA 95747-8389, USA

Bilheimer, Robert S (Religious Leader)
15256 Knightwood Rd
Cold Spring, MN 56320-9649, USA

Bill, Tony (Actor, Director, Producer)
73 Market St
Venice, CA 90291-3603, USA

Bill Wyman's Rhythm Kings (Music Group, Musician)
c/o Staff Member *Concerted Efforts*
PO Box 440326
Somerville, MA 02144-0004, USA

Billard, Lani (Actor)
c/o Staff Member *Insight Production Company LTD*
489 King St W Suite 401
Toronto, Ontario M5V 1K4, Canada

Billick, Brian (Athlete, Football Coach, Football Player)
836 Stagwell Rd
Queenstown, MD 21658-2402, USA

Billie (Musician)
Concorde House 101 Sherpherds Bush Road
London W6 7LP, UNITED KINGDOM (UK)

Billingham, John E (Jack) (Athlete, Baseball Player)
625 Faulkner St
New Smyrna Beach, FL 32168-6421, USA

Billings, Dick (Athlete, Baseball Player)
1917 Creek Wood Dr
Arlington, TX 76006-6611, USA

Billings, Earl (Actor)
c/o Staff Member *Stone Manners Salners Agency (LA)*
9911 W Pico Blvd Ste 1400
Los Angeles, CA 90035-2715, USA

Billings, Marland P (Misc)
Westside Road RFD
North Conway, NH 3860, USA

Billingslea, Beau (Actor)
6025 Sepulveda Blvd Ste 201
Van Nuys, CA 91411-2513, USA

Billingslea, Shavonda (Reality TV Star)
c/o Michael Martin *MM Agency*
3937 Nobel Dr
San Diego, CA 92122-6156, USA

Billingsley, Brent (Athlete, Baseball Player)
16112 Medlar Ln
Chino Hills, CA 91709-3625, USA

Billingsley, Chad (Athlete, Baseball Player)
25686 N Sandstone Way
Surprise, AZ 85387-6841, USA

Billingsley, John (Actor)
c/o Camilla Fluxman-Pines *Muse Management*
1541 Ocean Ave Ste 200
Santa Monica, CA 90401-2104, USA

Billingsley, John (Athlete, Baseball Player)
3614 N 24th Pl
Milwaukee, WI 53206-1325, USA

Billingsley, Peter (Director)
c/o Mitch Smelkinson *Stone, Meyer, Genow, Smelkinson and Binder*
9665 Wilshire Blvd Ste 500
Beverly Hills, CA 90212-2312, USA

Billingsley, Ray (Cartoonist)
c/o Staff Member *King Features Syndication*
300 W 57th St Fl 15
New York, NY 10019-5238, USA

Billingsley, Ron (Athlete, Football Player)
PO Box 2455
Gadsden, AL 35903-0455, USA

Billingsley, Sam (Baseball Player)
1426 W State St
Milwaukee, WI 53233-1249, USA

Billington, Craig (Athlete, Hockey Player)
c/o Staff Member *Colorado Avalanche*
Pepsi Center 1000 Chopper Cir
Denver, CO 80204, USA

Billington, David P (Engineer)
45 Hodge Rd
Princeton, NJ 08540-3011, USA

Billington, Kevin (Director)
33 Courtnell St
London W2 5BU, UNITED KINGDOM (UK)

Billman, John (Athlete, Football Player)
16205 36th Ave N Apt 334
Minneapolis, MN 55446-3388, USA

Billups, Chauncey (Athlete, Basketball Player)
c/o Andy Miller *ASM Sports*
920 Undercliff Ave
Edgewater, NJ 07020-1558, USA

Billups, Terry (Athlete, Football Player)
1801 E 12th St Apt 1721
Cleveland, OH 44114-3528, USA

Billy Talent (Music Group)
1650 West 2nd Ave
Vancouver V6J 4R3, CANADA

Billy Vera and the Beaters (Music Group)
c/o Troy Blakely *Agency for the Performing Arts (APA-LA)*
405 S Beverly Dr Ste 500
Beverly Hills, CA 90212-4425, USA

Bilodeau, Jean-Luc (Actor)
c/o Allan Grifka *Alchemy Entertainment*
7024 Melrose Ave Ste 420
Los Angeles, CA 90038-3394, USA

Bilson, Bruce (Director)
12505 Sarah St
Studio City, CA 91604-1113, USA

Bilson, Malcolm (Musician)
132 N Sunset Dr
Ithaca, NY 14850-1460, USA

Bilson, Rachel (Actor)
c/o Jason Weinberg *Untitled Entertainment (LA)*
350 S Beverly Dr Ste 200
Beverly Hills, CA 90212-4819, USA

bin Abdul Aziz Al-Saud, Alwaleed Bin Talal (Royalty)
P.O. Box 1
Riyadh 11321, Kingdom of Saudi Arabia

bin Abdul-Aziz, Sheikh Sulaiman Al-Rajhi (Business Person)
P.O. Box 22330
Riyadh 11495, Saudi Arabia

Binchy, Maeve (Writer)
11-15 D'Olier St
Dublin 2, Ireland

Binder, John (Religious Leader)
1S210 Summit Ave
Oakbrook Terrace, IL 60181-3933, USA

Binder, Mike (Actor, Director, Writer)
9460 Wilshire Blvd Ste 700
Beverly Hills, CA 90212-2713, USA

Binder, Steve (Director)
c/o Staff Member *Freeman, Heinecke and Sutton*
8961 W Sunset Blvd
Los Angeles, CA 90069-1807, USA

Binder, Theodor (Physicist)
Taos Canyon
Taos, NM 87571, USA

Bindler, Robb (Director, Writer)
c/o Susan Weaving *WmE2 (WMA-NY)*
1325 Avenue of the Americas
New York, NY 10019-6026, USA

Bindu (Actor, Bollywood)
C1-2 Eden Hall Opp Lotus Cinema Worli
Mumbai, MS 400018, INDIA

Bindugosh (Actor, Bollywood)
76A 1st Cross Street Ventatesa Nagar
Chennai, TN 600093, INDIA

Bing, Dave (Athlete, Basketball Player)
29555 Woodhaven Ln
Southfield, MI 48076-5281, USA

Bing, Jonathan
c/o Daniel A (Dan) Strone *Trident Media Group LLC*
41 Madison Ave Fl 36
New York, NY 10010-2257, USA

Bingaman, Jeff (Senator)
703 Hart Senate Ofc Bldg
Washington, DC 20510-0001, USA

Bingham, Craig (Athlete, Football Player)
179 Black Oak Dr
Pittsburgh, PA 15220-2007, USA

Bingham, Gregory R (Greg) (Athlete, Football Player)
3710 W Valley Dr
Missouri City, TX 77459-4320, USA

Bingham, Guy (Athlete, Football Player)
9214 Keegan Trl
Missoula, MT 59808-9382, USA

Bingham, Ryan (Musician)
c/o Jenna Adler *Creative Artists Agency (CAA-LA)*
2000 Avenue of the Stars Ste 100
Los Angeles, CA 90067-4705, USA

Bingham, Traci (Actor, Model)
c/o Staff Member *Abrams Artists Agency (LA)*
9200 W Sunset Blvd PH 11
Los Angeles, CA 90069-3601, USA

Bingle, Lara (Model)
c/o Staff Member *TCN Nine Publicity*
TCN Nine Publicity
Willoughby, NSW 2068, Australia

Binkley, Gregg (Actor)
c/o Staff Member *Schachter Entertainment*
1157 S Beverly Dr Fl 2
Los Angeles, CA 90035-1119, USA

Binkley, Leslie J (Les) (Athlete, Hockey Player)
RR 3 Main Station
Hanover, ON N4N 3B9, Canada

Binks, George (Athlete, Baseball Player)
4803 Belmont Rd
Downers Grove, IL 60515-3219, USA

Binmore, Kenneth G (Economist)
Newsmills Whitebrooks
Monmouth, Gwent NP5 4TY, UNITED KINGDOM (UK)

Binn, Dave (Athlete, Football Player)
2005 Loring St
San Diego, CA 92109-1407, USA

Binnig, Gerd K (Nobel Prize Laureate)
Saumerstr 4
Ruschlikon 8803, SWITZERLAND

Binns, Malcolm (Musician)
233 Court Rd
Orpington, Kent BR6 9BY, UNITED KINGDOM (UK)

Binoche, Juliette (Actor)
c/o Jason Weinberg *Untitled Entertainment (LA)*
350 S Beverly Dr Ste 200
Beverly Hills, CA 90212-4819, USA

Binotto, John (Athlete, Football Player)
277 E McMurray Rd
Canonsburg, PA 15317-2929, USA

Bintley, David (Choreographer)
Covent Garden Bow St
London WC2E 9DD, UNITED KINGDOM (UK)

Biodrowski, Denny (Athlete, Football Player)
2305 Grizzly Run Ln
Euless, TX 76039-6073, USA

Biondi, Frank J Jr (Business Person)
1430 Peel St
Monstreal, QC H3A 1S9, CANADA

Biondi, Matthew N (Matt) (Swimmer)
1404 Rimer Dr
Moraga, CA 94556-2555, USA

Birch, L Charles (Misc)
5A/73 Yarranabbe Rd
Darling Point, NSW 2027, AUSTRALIA

Birch, Stanley F Jr (Judge)
56 Forsyth St NW
Atlanta, GA 30303-2218, USA

Birch, Thora (Actor)
c/o Jack Birch *Keep the Peace Productions*
PO Box 691576
West Hollywood, CA 90069-9576, USA

Birchard, Bruce (Religious Leader)
1216 Arch St
Philadelphia, PA 19107-2835, USA

Birck, Michael J (Business Person)
1415 W Diehl Rd
Naperville, IL 60563-2349, USA

Bird, Antonia (Director)
76 Oxford St
London W1N 0AX, UNITED KINGDOM (UK)

Bird, Brad (Director, Writer)
c/o Staff Member *Pixar Animation Studios*
1200 Park Ave
Emeryville, CA 94608-3677, USA

Bird, Cory (Athlete, Football Player)
4618 Harding Hwy
Mays Landing, NJ 08330-2736, USA

Bird, Doug (Athlete, Baseball Player)
11821 Lady Anne Cir
Cape Coral, FL 33991-7548, USA

Bird, Forrest M (Inventor)
212 NW Cerritos Dr
Palm Springs, CA 92262-6538, USA

Bird, Jerry Lee (Athlete, Basketball Player)
114 Scenic View Dr
Corbin, KY 40701, USA

Bird, Larry J (Athlete, Basketball Player, Coach)
4715 Ellery Ln
Indianapolis, IN 46250-5677, USA

Bird, Lester B (Prime Minister)
Factory Road
Saint John's, ANTIGUA

Bird, R Byron (Engineer)
Chemical Engineering Dept
Madison, WI 53706, USA

Bird, Rodger (Athlete, Football Player)
215 S Elm St
Henderson, KY 42420-3510, USA

Bird, Sue (Athlete, Basketball Player)
c/o Dan Levy *Wasserman Media Group*
10960 Wilshire Blvd Fl 22
Los Angeles, CA 90024-3808, USA

Bird, Thora (Actor)
Old Loft 21 Leinster Mews Lancaster Gate
London W2, UNITED KINGDOM (UK)

Bird-Phillips, Nalda (Baseball Player)
2033 Honeydew Ln NW
Kennesaw, GA 30152-5852, USA

Birdsell, Lilli (Actor)
c/o John Crosby *Crosby/Spilo Management*
1310 N Spaulding Ave
Los Angeles, CA 90046-4010, USA

Birdsong, Carl (Athlete, Football Player)
1807 Clubview Dr
Amarillo, TX 79124-1731, USA

Birdsong, Cindy (Musician)
c/o Staff Member *Diva Central Inc*
7510 W Sunset Blvd Ste 1445
Los Angeles, CA 90046-3408, USA

Birdsong, Mary (Actor, Writer)
c/o Stacy Abrams *Abrams Entertainment*
5225 Wilshire Blvd # Suite 515 PMB 515
Los Angeles, CA 90036, USA

Birdsong, Otis (Athlete, Basketball Player)
PO Box 316
Little Rock, AR 72203-0316, USA

Bires, Kelly (Race Car Driver)
7201 Caldwell Rd
Harrisburg, NC 28075-7480, USA

Birk, Matt (Athlete, Football Player)
620 Hidden Creek Trl
Saint Paul, MN 55118-3753, USA

Birk, Roger E (Business Person)
3900 Wisconsin Ave NW
Washington, DC 20016-2806, USA

Birkavs, Valdis (Prime Minister)
Brivbas Blvd 36
Riga 1395, LATVIA

Birkbeck, Mike (Athlete, Baseball Player)
1705 W Hill Dr
Orrville, OH 44667-1331, USA

Birkell, Lauren (Actor)
c/o Tiffany Kuzon *Evolution Entertainment (LA)*
901 N Highland Ave
Los Angeles, CA 90038-2412, USA

Birkerts, Gunnar (Architect)
28105 Greenfield Rd
Southfield, MI 48076-3046, USA

Birkett, Zoe (Musician)
Palace Theatre Shaftesbury Ave
London W1V 8AY, UK

Birkhead, Larry
PO Box 99800
Emeryville, CA 94662-9809, USA

Birkin, David (Actor)
c/o Scott Zimmerman *Evolution Entertainment (LA)*
901 N Highland Ave
Los Angeles, CA 90038-2412, USA

Birkin, Jane (Actor)
36 Rue de Ponthieu
Paris 75008, FRANCE

Birkins, Kurt (Athlete, Baseball Player)
24106 Vanowen St
West Hills, CA 91307-2932, USA

Birman, Len (Actor)
617 S Olive St Ste 311
Los Angeles, CA 90014-1624, USA

Birmingham, Stephen (Writer)
1501 Broadway
New York, NY 10036-5601, USA

Birnes, William J. (Writer)
c/o Staff Member *Simon & Schuster*
1230 Avenue of the Americas Fl CONC1
New York, NY 10020-1586, USA

Birney, David (Actor)
20 Ocean Park Blvd # 118
Santa Monica, CA 90405-3589, USA

Birney, Earle (Writer)
1204-130 Carlton St
Toronto, ON M5A 4K3, CANADA

Birney, Frank (Actor)
c/o Staff Member *Bauman Redanty & Shaul Agency*
5757 Wilshire Blvd Suite 473
Beverly Hills, CA 90212, USA

Biron, Martin (Athlete, Hockey Player)
93 Whippoorwill Rd
Armonk, NY 10504-1108, USA

Biron, Mathieu (Athlete, Hockey Player)
5723 NW 199th Dr
Coral Springs, FL 33076, USA

Birren, James E (Misc)
Borun Gerontology Center
Los Angeles, CA 90024, USA

Birrer, Babe (Athlete, Baseball Player)
9705 the Maples
Clarence, NY 14031-1594, USA

Birthistle, Eva (Actor)
c/o Staff Member *WmE2 (Endeavor-LA)*
9601 Wilshire Blvd Fl 3
Beverly Hills, CA 90210-5219, USA

Birtsas, Tim (Athlete, Baseball Player)
PO Box 96
Clarkston, MI 48347-0096, USA

Birturk, Ricia (Stylist)
12 Queen Ave S
Minneapolis, MN 55405-1923, USA

Birtwistle, Harrison (Composer)
42 Montpelier Square
London SW7 1JZ, UNITED KINGDOM (UK)

Biscaha, Joe (Athlete, Football Player)
700 N Delaware Ave Apt 3
Beach Haven, NJ 8008, USA

Bishe, Kerry (Actor)
c/o Staff Member *Brookside Artists Management (NY)*
250 W 57th St Ste 2303
New York, NY 10107-2399, USA

Bisher, J Furman (Writer)
431 Lester Rd
Fayetteville, GA 30215-4930, USA

Bishil, Summer (Actor)
c/o Brian Swardstrom *WmE2 (Endeavor-LA)*
9601 Wilshire Blvd Fl 3
Beverly Hills, CA 90210-5219, USA

Bishop, Elvin (Musician)
4031 Panama Ct
Piedmont, CA 94611-4930, USA

Bishop, Greg (Athlete, Football Player)
PO Box 2263
Lodi, CA 95241-2263, USA

Bishop, Harold (Athlete, Football Player)
2709 20th Street Ensley
Birmingham, AL 35208-2203, USA

Bishop, J Michael (Nobel Prize Laureate)
Hooper Foundation
San Francisco, CA 94143-0001, USA

Bishop, Keith (Athlete, Football Player)
PO Box 133111
Spring, TX 77393-3111, USA

Bishop, Kelly (Actor)
c/o Robert Attermann *Abrams Artists Agency (LA)*
9200 W Sunset Blvd PH 11
Los Angeles, CA 90069-3601, USA

Bishop, Kevin (Actor)
c/o Staff Member *Gavin Barker Assoc*
2D Wimpole St
London W1G 0EB, UK

Bishop, Michael (Athlete, Football Player)
113 Philpot St
Willis, TX 77378, USA

Bishop, Rob (Congressman, Politician)
123 Cannon Hob
Washington, DC 20515-3805, USA

Bishop, Sonny (Athlete, Football Player)
22843 Hale Rd
Land O Lakes, FL 34639-4030, USA

Bisplinghoff, Raymond L (Engineer)
273 Corporate Dr # 100
Portsmouth, NH 03801-6807, USA

Bissell, Charles O (Cartoonist, Editor)
1006 Tower Pl
Nashville, TN 37204-4135, USA

Bissell, Charles P (Phil) (Cartoonist)
4 Cross Hill Cir
Forestdale, MA 02644-1630, USA

Bissell, Jean G (Judge)
717 Madison Pl NW
Washington, DC 20439-0001, USA

Bissell, Mina J (Physicist)
1 Cyclotron Rd
Berkeley, CA 94720-8099, USA

Bisset, Jacqueline (Actor)
1815 Benedict Canyon Dr
Beverly Hills, CA 90210-2006, USA

Bissett, Josie (Actor)
c/o Darris Hatch *Daris Hatch Management*
10027 Rossbury Pl
Los Angeles, CA 90064-4825, USA

Bissinger, Buzz (Writer)
222 Berkeley St Fl 8
Boston, MA 02116-3748, USA

Bisson, Yannick (Actor)
c/o Jamie Levitt *Lauren Levitt & Associates Inc*
1525 W 8th St 3rd Fl
Vancouver V6J 1T5, British Columbia

Bista, Kirti Nidhi (Prime Minister)
Gyaneshawor
Kathmandu, NEPAL

Bisutti, Kylie (Model)
c/o Anne Watkins *Lizzie Grubman Public Relations*
270 Lafayette St Ste 504
New York, NY 10012-0048, USA

Bitker, Joe (Athlete, Baseball Player)
39 Blackstone Ct
Chico, CA 95928-9428, USA

Bitterlich, Don (Athlete, Football Player)
101 Medinah Dr
Blue Bell, PA 19422-3213, USA

Bitterman, Shem (Writer)
6616 Colgate Ave
Los Angeles, CA 90048-4205, USA

Bittiger, Jeff (Athlete, Baseball Player)
2163 Valley View Dr S
Saylorsburg, PA 18353-8359, USA

Bittinger, Ned (Designer)
1323 Escalante St
Santa Fe, NM 87505-4121, USA

Bittle, Ryan (Actor)
3518 Cahuenga Blvd W # 103
Los Angeles, CA 90068-1304, USA

Bittner, Armin (Skier)
Rauchbergstr 30
Izell 83334, GERMANY

Bittner, Jayne (Baseball Player)
15536 Northville Forest Dr Apt U250
Plymouth, MI 48170-4901, USA

Bittner, Lauren (Actor)
c/o Jill McGrath *Abrams Artists Agency (NY)*
275 7th Ave Fl 26
New York, NY 10001-6708, USA

Bivens, Heidi (Stylist)
61 Carmine St Apt 2C
New York, NY 10014-4322, USA

Biya, Paul (President)
Rue de L'Exploration
Yaounde, CAMEROON REPUBLIC

Bizkit, Limp (Music Group)
c/o Rod MacSween *International Talent Booking*
1st Floor, Ariel House 74A Charlotte St
London W1T 4QJ, UNITED KINGDOM

Bizzy, Bone (Actor, Artist, Composer, Musician)
c/o Mary Bowlin *7th Sign Records*
145 Baker St
Marion, OH 43302-4111, USA

Bjarni V, Tryggvason (Astronaut)
6767 Route De Aeroport
Saint Hubert, QC J3Y 8Y9, CANADA

Bjedov-Gabrilo, Djurdjica (Swimmer)
Brace Santini 33 5800 Split
Serbia & Montenegro, SERBIA & MONTENEGRO

Bjorge, Jamie (Actor)
10061 Riverside Dr # 113
Toluca Lake, CA 91602-2560

Bjork (Musician)
c/o Staff Member *Nonesuch Records*
75 Rockefeller Plz Fl 8
New York, NY 10019-6908, USA

Bjork, Anita (Actor)
AB Baggensgatan 9
Stockholm 111 31, SWEDEN

Bjorklund, Anders (Doctor)
Neurology Dept
Lund, SWEDEN

Bjorkman, George (Athlete, Baseball Player)
3525 Teakwood Ln
Plano, TX 75075-1783, USA

Bjorkman, Jonas (Tennis Player)
1751 Pinnacle Dr Ste 1500
McLean, VA 22102-3833, USA

Bjorkman, Olle E (Biologist)
3040 Greer Rd
Palo Alto, CA 94303-4007, USA

Bjorlin, Nadia (Actor)
c/o Howie Simon *MLC PR*
7080 Hollywood Blvd Ste 903
Los Angeles, CA 90028-6936, USA

Bjornson, Eric (Athlete, Football Player)
40 Orchard Rd
Orinda, CA 94563-3421, USA

Bjugstad, Scott (Athlete, Hockey Player)
2874 Lisbon Ave N
Lake Elmo, MN 55042-8554, USA

Blab, Uwe (Athlete, Basketball Player)
5993 Mount Gainor
Wimberley, TX 78676-4278, USA

Blachnik, Gabriele (Designer, Fashion Designer)
Marstallstr 8
Munich 80539, GERMANY

Black, Alex (Actor)
c/o Staff Member *Innovative Artists (LA)*
1505 10th St
Santa Monica, CA 90401-2805, USA

Black, Barbara A (Attorney, Attorney General, Educator, General)
435 W 116th St
New York, NY 10027-7237, USA

Black, Bibi (Musician)
165 W 57th St
New York, NY 10019-2201, USA

Black, BiBi (Musician)
c/o Staff Member *EMI Recorded Music (EMI Group - NY)*
150 5th Ave Fl 7
New York, NY 10011-4372, USA

Black, Bill (Baseball Player)
264 Braeshire Dr
Ballwin, MO 63021-5659, USA

Black, Brantley (Actor)
c/o Taylor Jacobs *Cinema Talent Agency*
468 N Camden Dr # 200
Beverly Hills, CA 90210-4507, USA

Black, Bud (Athlete, Baseball Player, Coach)
PO Box 2133
Rancho Santa Fe, CA 92067-2133, USA

Black, Carole (Business Person)
c/o Staff Member *Lifetime Entertainment Services*
111 8th Ave Lbby 2
New York, NY 10011-5201, USA

Black, Cathie (Business Person, Writer)
c/o Staff Member *Hearst Magazines*
959 8th Ave Sutie 100
New York, NY 10019-3737, USA

Black, Cilla (Actor, Musician)
c/o Nick Fiveash *The Works PR*
11 Marshalsea Rd
London SE1 1EN, UK

Black, Claudia (Actor)
c/o Staff Member *Artists Independent Management (LA)*
825 Nowita Pl
Venice, CA 90291-3836, USA

Black, Clint (Actor, Musician)
c/o Jim Morey *Morey Management Group*
1100 Glendon Ave Ste 1100
Los Angeles, CA 90024-3515, USA

Black, Conrad M (Publisher)
1 Canada Square Canary Wharf
London E14 5DT, UNITED KINGDOM (UK)

Black, David (Producer, Writer)
c/o Johnnie Planco *Parseghian Planco LLC*
322 8th Ave Ste 601
New York, NY 10001-6715, USA

Black, Debbie (Stylist)
c/o Staff Member *Directions USA*
3717 W Market St Ste C
Greensboro, NC 27403-1155, USA

Black, Diane (Congressman, Politician)
1531 Longworth Hob
Washington, DC 20515-1310, USA

Black, Dustin Lance (Producer, Writer)
c/o Craig Gering *Creative Artists Agency (CAA-LA)*
2000 Avenue of the Stars Ste 100
Los Angeles, CA 90067-4705, USA

Black, Frank (Musician)
c/o Staff Member *Paradigm (Monterey)*
404 W Franklin St
Monterey, CA 93940-2303, USA

Black, Holly (Writer)
10 Pleasant Ct
Amherst, MA 01002-1513, USA

Black, Jack (Actor, Comedian, Musician)
c/o Matthew (Matt) Labov *Forefront Media*
8500 Melrose Ave Ste 205
West Hollywood, CA 90069-5169, USA

Black, James (Athlete, Hockey Player)
235 Callingwood Pl NW
Edmonton, AB T5T 2C6, Canada

Black, James W (Nobel Prize Laureate)
3 Ferrings Dulwich
London SE21 7LU, UNITED KINGDOM (UK)

Black, Jay (Musician)
c/o Staff Member *Charles Rapp Enterprises Inc*
88 Pine St
New York, NY 10005-1801, USA

Black, Karen (Actor, Director, Producer, Writer)
c/o Brian McCabe *Venture IAB*
3211 Cahuenga Blvd W Ste 104
Los Angeles, CA 90068-1372, USA

Black, Leonard (Athlete, Football Player)
2705 Preston Woods Ln Apt 12
Fayetteville, NC 28304-3629, USA

Black, Lewis (Actor, Comedian)
c/o Staff Member *Agency for the Performing Arts (APA-LA)*
405 S Beverly Dr Ste 500
Beverly Hills, CA 90212-4425, USA

Black, Lisa Hartman (Actor)
c/o Marnie Sparer *Innovative Artists (LA)*
1505 10th St
Santa Monica, CA 90401-2805, USA

Black, Lucas (Actor)
c/o Staff Member *Agency for the Performing Arts (APA-LA)*
405 S Beverly Dr Ste 500
Beverly Hills, CA 90212-4425, USA

Black, Marina (Actor)
c/o Matt Schwartz *Christopher Wright Management*
3207 Winnie Dr
Los Angeles, CA 90068-1439, USA

Black, Mary (Musician)
278 S Main St # 400
Gloucester, MA 1930, USA

Black, Michael Ian (Actor, Architect)
9560 Wilshire Blvd Ste 500
Beverly Hills, CA 90212-2401, USA

Black, Mike (Athlete, Football Player)
608 Andalusia St
Los Angeles, CA 90065-2547, USA

Black, Mike D (Athlete, Football Player)
609 Grider Dr
Roseville, CA 95678-1244, USA

Black, Pippa (Actor)
c/o Kimberlin Dalehite *Magnolia Entertainment (LA)*
9595 Wilshire Blvd Ste 601
Beverly Hills, CA 90212-2506, USA

Black, Rebecca (Musician)
c/o Debra Baum *DB Entertainment Group*
8033 W Sunset Blvd # 1062
Los Angeles, CA 90046-2401, USA

Black, Ronnie (Athlete, Golfer)
5565 N Campbell Ave
Tucson, AZ 85718-4911, USA

Black, Shane (Writer)
c/o Staff Member *WmE2 (Endeavor-LA)*
9601 Wilshire Blvd Fl 3
Beverly Hills, CA 90210-5219, USA

Black, Stan (Athlete, Football Player)
470 Johnstone Dr
Madison, MS 39110-7586, USA

Black, Steve (Athlete, Hockey Player)
417 Amethyst Cres
Thunder Bay, ON P7C 1T2, Canada

Black, Thought (Musician)
1325 Avenue of the Americas
New York, NY 10019-6026, USA

Black, Tim (Athlete, Football Player)
10520 Kilo Rd
Clarendon, TX 79226-5100, USA

Black, Todd (Producer)
c/o Staff Member *International Creative Management (ICM-LA)*
10250 Constellation Blvd Fl 7
Los Angeles, CA 90067-6207, USA

Black 47 (Music Group, Musician)
c/o Staff Member *Skyline Music*
28 Union St
Whitefield, NH 03598-3503, USA

Black Box Recorder (Music Group)
c/o Staff Member *Paradigm (Monterey)*
404 W Franklin St
Monterey, CA 93940-2303, USA

Black Crowes (Music Group)
c/o Staff Member *Paradigm (Monterey)*
404 W Franklin St
Monterey, CA 93940-2303, USA

Black Eyed Peas, The (Music Group, Musician)
c/o David Sonenberg *DAS Communications*
83 Riverside Dr
New York, NY 10024-5713, USA

Black Sabbath (Music Group)
c/o Rob Light *Creative Artists Agency (CAA-LA)*
2000 Avenue of the Stars Ste 100
Los Angeles, CA 90067-4705, USA

Black Veil Brides (Music Group)
c/o Ash Avildsen *The Pantheon Agency*
14930 Ventura Blvd Ste 340
Sherman Oaks, CA 91403-3489, USA

Blackaby, Ethan (Athlete, Baseball Player)
2308 E Orangewood Ave
Phoenix, AZ 85020-4730, USA

Blackburn, Bob (Athlete, Hockey Player)
141 Robert St P O Box 1761
New Liskeard, ON P0J 1P0, Canada

Blackburn, Dan (Athlete, Hockey Player)
12 Carey Dr
Bedford, NY 10506-2025, USA

Blackburn, Don (Athlete, Hockey Player)
637 S Owl Dr
Sarasota, FL 34236-1907, USA

Blackburn, Elizabeth (Nobel Prize Laureate)
600 16th St # 2200
San Francisco, CA 94158-2517, USA

Blackburn, Greta (Actor)
6442 Coldwater Canyon Ave Ste 206
Valley Glen, CA 91606-1174, USA

Blackburn, Marsha (Congressman, Politician)
217 Cannon Hob
Washington, DC 20515-2507, USA

Blackburn, Woody (Athlete, Golfer)
PO Box 215
Orange Park, FL 32067-0215, USA

Blackiston, Caroline (Actor)
125 Gloucester Road
London SW7 4IE, UNITED KINGDOM (UK)

Blackledge, Todd A (Athlete, Football Player, Sportscaster)
2711 Glenmont Rd NW
Canton, OH 44708-1345, USA

Blackman, Don (Athlete, Football Player)
48 Shire Dr S
East Amherst, NY 14051-1814, USA

Blackman, Honor (Actor)
c/o Staff Member *Natasha Stevenson Mgmt*
Studio 7C Clapham North Arts Centre
Voltaire Rd
London SW4 6DH, UK

Blackman, Robert (Athlete, Football Player)
70 Glenwood N
Van Vleck, TX 77482-6292, USA

Blackman, Robert R Jr (General)
Commanding General III Expeditionary Force Okinawa
FPO, AP 96602, USA

Blackman, Rolando (Athlete, Basketball Player, Sportscaster)
18008 Creek Vista Ct
Dallas, TX 75252-5622, USA

Blackmar, Phil (Athlete, Golfer)
4420 Janssen Dr
Corpus Christi, TX 78411-2817, USA

Blackmon, Will (Athlete, Football Player)
c/o Eugene Parker *Maximum Sports Management*
6435 W Jefferson Blvd # 197
Fort Wayne, IN 46804-6203, USA

Blackmore, Billie (Stylist)
220 E 18th St
New York, NY 10003-3650, USA

Blackmore, Ritchie (Musician)
PO Box 735
Nesconset, NY 11767-0735, USA

Blacknall, Hubert (Athlete, Baseball Player)
46 Avenue A
Freehold, NJ 07728-1738, USA

Blackshear, Jeff (Athlete, Football Player)
9229 Christo Ct
Owings Mills, MD 21117-3596, USA

Blackthorne, Paul (Actor)
c/o Sarah Jackson *Seven Summits Pictures & Management*
8906 W Olympic Blvd Ground Floor
Beverly Hills, CA 90211, USA

Blackwelder, Myra (Athlete, Golfer)
2009 Hill Gail Way
Versailles, KY 40383-9132, USA

Blackwell, Alois (Athlete, Football Player)
1617 Fannin St Apt 2310
Houston, TX 77002-7654, USA

Blackwell, Chris (Business Person, Musician)
6 Hadley Gardens C F Blackwell
London W4 4NX, UNITED KINGDOM

Blackwell, Harolyn (Opera Singer)
165 W 57th St
New York, NY 10019-2201, USA

Blackwell, Nathaniel (Athlete, Basketball Player)
1716 Manor Pl
Clementon, NJ 08021-5811, USA

Blackwell, Tim (Athlete, Baseball Player)
8854 Whiteport Ln
San Diego, CA 92119-2135, USA

Blackwell, Will (Athlete, Football Player)
6450 Dougherty Rd Apt 336
Dublin, CA 94568-7614, USA

Blackwood, Glenn (Athlete, Football Player)
3480 Ambassador Dr
Wellington, FL 33414-6815, USA

Blackwood, Lyle (Athlete, Football Player)
18020 Windtop Ln
Dallas, TX 75287-6658, USA

Blackwood, Nina (Entertainer)
c/o Danny Sheridan *Marquee Management*
The Gatehouse 188 Oxford St Studio B
Paddington NSW 2021, Australia

Blackwood, Sarah (Musician)
2-12 Petonville Road
London N1 9PL, UNITED KINGDOM (UK)

Blackwood, Vas (Actor)
c/o David Ginsberg *Insight*
1134 S Cloverdale Ave
Los Angeles, CA 90019-6737, USA

Blacque, Taurean (Actor)
5049 Rock Springs Rd
Lithonia, GA 30038-2239, USA

Bladd, Stephen Jo (Musician)
652 N Doheny Dr
Los Angeles, CA 90069-5526, USA

Blade, Brian (Musician)
173 Brighton Ave
Boston, MA 02134-2003, USA

Blade, Willie (Athlete, Football Player)
331 Cobblestone Rd
Auburn, GA 30011-3022, USA

Blades, Brian K (Athlete, Football Player)
1900 SW 70th Ter
Plantation, FL 33317-5010, USA

Blades, H Benedict (Bennie) (Athlete, Football Player)
1900 SW 70th Ter
Plantation, FL 33317-5010, USA

Blades, Ruben (Actor, Composer)
Apartado 4421 Centro De Convenciones Atlapa
Vía Israel, San Francisco, Republic Of Panam

Bladt, Rick (Athlete, Baseball Player)
525 Maple St
Mount Angel, OR 97362-9616, USA

Blagojevich, Rod (Politician)
c/o Staff Member *NBC Universal (LA)*
100 Universal City Plz
Universal City, CA 91608-1002, USA

Blaha, John E (Astronaut)
18219 Indian Row
San Antonio, TX 78259, USA

Blahak, Joseph (Athlete, Football Player)
4040 N 21st St
Lincoln, NE 68521-1203, USA

Blahnik, Manolo (Designer, Fashion Designer)
49-51 Old Church St
London SW3 5BS, UNITED KINGDOM (UK)

Blahoski, Alana (Athlete, Hockey Player)
550 Grand St Apt 1
Brooklyn, NY 11211-3574, USA

Blaine, David (Magician)
c/o Jill Fritzo *PMK/BNC Public Relations (PMK-NY)*
622 3rd Ave Fl 8
New York, NY 10017-6707, USA

Blaine, Ed (Athlete, Football Player)
4 E Clarkson Rd
Columbia, MO 65203-3520, USA

Blair, Anthony C L (Tony) (Politician, Prime Minister)
P.O. Box 60519
London W2 7JU, UK

Blair, Barry (Cartoonist)
PO Box 612
New York, NY 10156-0612, USA

Blair, Bonnie (Speed Skater)
1223 Aspen Ct
Delafield, WI 53018-1300, USA

Blair, Charles (Athlete, Hockey Player)
869 Niagara Pky
Fort Erie, ON L2A 5M4, Canada

Blair, Dennis (Athlete, Baseball Player)
1706 Aurora Dr
Richardson, TX 75081-2115, USA

Blair, George (Athlete, Hockey Player)
61 Kingsmill St
Fort Erie, ON L2A 4E5, Canada

Blair, George L (Athlete, Football Player)
1233 Karen Dr
Laurel, MS 39440-2186, USA

Blair, Isla (Actor)
Grafton House 2/3 Golden House
London W1R 3AD, UNITED KINGDOM (UK)

Blair, Ken (Athlete, Football Player)
1837 NE 51st St
Oklahoma City, OK 73111-7005, USA

Blair, Kimberly (Actor)
c/o John Elliott *Mosaic Media Group*
9200 W Sunset Blvd Ste 10
Los Angeles, CA 90069-3608, USA

Blair, Linda (Actor)
c/o Anthony Anzaldo *Good Guy Entertainment*
3733 Oakfield Dr
Sherman Oaks, CA 91423-4430, USA

Blair, Lionel (Dancer)
68 Old Brompton Rd # 200
London, England SW7 3LQ, United Kingdom

Blair, Maybelle (Athlete, Baseball Player)
39220 Palm Greens Pkwy
Palm Desert, CA 92260-1362, USA

Blair, Natalie (Actor)
c/o Staff Member *RGM Artist Group*
64-76 Kippax St Level 2, Suite 202 & 206
Surry Hills, NSW 2010, Australia

Blair, Paul (Athlete, Baseball Player)
10808 Enfield Dr
Woodstock, MD 21163-1471, USA

Blair, Paul (Athlete, Football Player)
345 Abilene Ave
Edmond, OK 73003-6313, USA

Blair, Selma (Actor)
c/o Peter Levine *Creative Artists Agency (CAA-LA)*
2000 Avenue of the Stars Ste 100
Los Angeles, CA 90067-4705, USA

Blair, Stanley (Athlete, Football Player)
901 Deer Run N
Pine Bluff, AR 71603-8158, USA

Blair, William (Director)
c/o Staff Member *New Star Entertainment*
PO Box 84172
San Diego, CA 92138-4172, USA

Blair, William (Athlete, Baseball Player)
1411 E Red Bird Ln
Dallas, TX 75241-2111, USA

Blair, William Draper Jr (Attorney, Attorney General, Diplomat, General)
435 E 52nd St # 6B
New York, NY 10022-6445, USA

Blair, Willie (Athlete, Baseball Player)
62 Elder Ln
Pikeville, KY 41501-3119, USA

Blais, Madeleine H (Journalist)
1 Herald Plz
Miami, FL 33132-1609, USA

Blaisdell, Mike (Athlete, Hockey Player)
458 Nicholl Ave
Regina Beach, SK S0G 4C0, Canada

Blaise, Kerlin (Athlete, Football Player)
37026 Aspen Dr
Farmington Hills, MI 48335-5482, USA

Blake, Andre (Actor)
c/o Staff Member *Kerin-Goldberg Associates*
155 E 55th St Ste 5D
New York, NY 10022-4038, USA

Blake, Asha (Correspondent)
30 Rockefeller Plz
New York, NY 10112-0015, USA

Blake, Bob (Athlete, Hockey Player)
75 Dwyer St
Buffalo, NY 14224-1113, USA

Blake, Casey (Athlete, Baseball Player)
1857 Wyndgale Ct
Westlake, OH 44145, USA

Blake, David (DJ Quik) (Musician)
c/o Linda Jones *The Mass Appeal*
3940 Laurel Canyon Blvd Unit 447
Studio City, CA 91604-3709, USA

Blake, Ed (Athlete, Baseball Player)
100 Rosewood Village Dr
Swansea, IL 62226-2301, USA

Blake, Geoffrey (Writer)
c/o Staff Member *Creative Artists Agency (CAA-LA)*
2000 Avenue of the Stars Ste 100
Los Angeles, CA 90067-4705, USA

Blake, George R (Editor)
617 Vine St
Cincinnati, OH 45202-2416, USA

Blake, Hamish (Radio Personality, Talk Show Host)
Level 15 50 Goulburn St
Sydney, NSW 2000, Australia

Blake, James (Tennis Player)
c/o Staff Member *ATP Tour*
201 Atp Tour Blvd
Ponte Vedra Beach, FL 32082-3211, USA

Blake, Jay Don (Athlete, Golfer)
2859 Calle Del Sol
Saint George, UT 84790-7968, USA

Blake, Jeff (Athlete, Football Player)
1 Novacare Way
Philadelphia, PA 19145-5900, USA

Blake, John C (Artist)
Oz Voorburgwal 131
Amsterdam 1012 ER, NETHERLANDS

Blake, Josh (Actor)
c/o Staff Member *Pakula/King & Associates*
9229 W Sunset Blvd Ste 315
Los Angeles, CA 90069-3403, USA

Blake, Julian W (Bud) (Cartoonist)
13 Highland Ct
Gloucester, MA 01930-3808, USA

Blake, Kayla (Actor)
c/o Todd Diener *Collective*
8383 Wilshire Blvd Ste 1050
Beverly Hills, CA 90211-2415, USA

Blake, Marcia (Writer)
c/o Staff Member *Creative Artists Agency (CAA-LA)*
2000 Avenue of the Stars Ste 100
Los Angeles, CA 90067-4705, USA

Blake, Norman (Musician)
433 E Cucharras St
Colorado Springs, CO 80903-3609, USA

Blake, Peter (Architect)
404 8th Ave Apt 3B
Brooklyn, NY 11215-8008, USA

Blake, Peter T (Artist)
11 Cork St
London W1X 1PD, UNITED KINGDOM (UK)

Blake, Quentin (Artist, Philanthropist)
92 High Street Great Missenden
Buckinghamshire HP16 0AN, United Kingdom

Blake, Ricky (Athlete, Football Player)
13 Harper Dr
Fayetteville, TN 37334-6679, USA

Blake, Rob (Athlete, Hockey Player)
3020 the Strand
Manhattan Beach, CA 90266-3952, USA

Blake, Rockwell (Opera Singer)
1 Onondaga Ln
Plattsburgh, NY 12901-1130, USA

Blake, Stephanie (Actor)
1631 N Bristol St # 820
Santa Ana, CA 92706-3342, USA

Blake, Susan (Correspondent)
1001 Van Ness Ave
San Francisco, CA 94109-6913, USA

Blake, Tchad (Musician)
200 W Superior St Ste 202
Chicago, IL 60654-3554, USA

Blake, Teresa (Actor)
6500 Wilshire Blvd # 550
Los Angeles, CA 90048-4920, USA

Blake, Theo (Adult Film Star)
c/o Staff Member *Diva Central Inc*
7510 W Sunset Blvd Ste 1445
Los Angeles, CA 90046-3408, USA

Blake, Tom (Athlete, Football Player)
2017 Tullis Dr
Middletown, OH 45042-2962, USA

Blake, Victoria (Actor)
23801 Calabasas Rd Ste 2023
Calabasas, CA 91302-1558, USA

Blakeley, Ronee (Actor, Musician)
8033 W Sunset Blvd # 693
West Hollywood, CA 90046-2401, USA

Blakely, Rachel (Actor)
c/o Staff Member *Morrissey Management*
77 Glebe Point Road
Sydney NSW 2037, AUSTRALIA

Blakely, Sara (Business Person)
3391 Peachtree Rd NE Ste 105
Atlanta, GA 30326-1014, USA

Blakely, Susan (Actor, Model)
c/o Kim Dorr *Defining Artists Agency*
10 Universal City Plz Ste 2000
Universal City, CA 91608-1074, USA

Blakemore, Colin B (Doctor)
Parks Road
Oxford OX1 3PT, UNITED KINGDOM (UK)

Blakemore, Michael (Actor, Director, Writer)
18 Upper Park Rd
London NW3 2UP, UNITED KINGDOM (UK)

Blakemore, Sean (Actor)
c/o Steven Jang *SDB Partners Inc*
1801 Avenue of the Stars Ste 902
Los Angeles, CA 90067-5981, USA

Blaker, Clay (Musician, Songwriter, Writer)
2317 Pecan St
Dickinson, TX 77539-4949, USA

Blakey, Marion (Government Official)
800 Independence Ave SW
Washington, DC 20591-0001, USA

Blalack, Robert (Cinematographer)
12251 Huston St
North Hollywood, CA 91607-3616, USA

Blalock, Hank (Athlete, Baseball Player)
8797 Adobe Bluffs Dr
San Diego, CA 92129-4448, USA

Blalock, Jane (Athlete, Golfer)
197 8th St Ste 300
Charlestown, MA 02129-4236, USA

Blalock, Jolene (Actor)
c/o Gina Hoffman *Baker Winokur Ryder Public Relations (BWR-LA)*
9100 Wilshire Blvd Ste 500 PMB WEST
Beverly Hills, CA 90212-3426, USA

Blamire, Larry (Actor, Director, Writer)
10878 Bloomfield St
Toluca Lake, CA 91602-2213, USA

Blanc, Georges (Chef)
Le Mere Blanc
Vonnas, Ain 1540, FRANCE

Blanc, Jennifer (Actor)
c/o Melanie Sharp *Sharp Talent*
117 N Orlando Ave
Los Angeles, CA 90048-3403, USA

Blanc, Michel (Actor)
c/o Dominique Besnehard *ArtMedia*
20 avenue Rapp
Paris 75008, France

Blanc, Raymond R A (Chef)
Church Road
Great Milton, Oxford OX44 7PD, UNITED KINGDOM (UK)

Blancas, Homero (Athlete, Golfer)
6826 Queensclub Dr
Houston, TX 77069-1216, USA

Blanchard, Cary (Athlete, Football Player)
7208 NW 131st St
Oklahoma City, OK 73142-2540, USA

Blanchard, Felix A (Doc) (Athlete, Football Player, General)
30395 Olympus
Bulverde, TX 78163-2726, USA

Blanchard, George S (General)
9160 Belvoir Woods Pkwy
Fort Belvoir, VA 22060-2703, USA

Blanchard, James H (Financier)
PO Box 120
Columbus, GA 31902-0120, USA

Blanchard, James J (Diplomat, Ex-Governor)
888 17th St NW Ste 306
Washington, DC 20006-3307, USA

Blanchard, John A (Business Person)
3680 Victoria St N
Shoreview, MN 55126-2906, USA

Blanchard, Ken (Business Person, Writer)
125 State Pl
Escondido, CA 92029-1323, USA

Blanchard, Nina (Misc)
5098 Cathedral Oaks Rd
Santa Barbara, CA 93111-1202, USA

Blanchard, Rachel (Actor)
c/o Christian Donatelli *Schiff Company, The*
8440 Warner Dr Ste B1
Culver City, CA 90232-2461, USA

Blanchard, Tammy (Actor)
c/o Carol Bodie *International Creative Management (ICM-LA)*
10250 Constellation Blvd Fl 7
Los Angeles, CA 90067-6207, USA

Blanchard, Terence (Composer, Musician)
8730 W Sunset Blvd # 300W
Los Angeles, CA 90069-2210, USA

Blanchard, Tim (Religious Leader)
1501 W Mineral Ave # B
Littleton, CO 80120-5612, USA

Blanchard, Tom (Athlete, Football Player)
1410 NE Heritage Dr
Grants Pass, OR 97526-3534, USA

Blanchett, Cate (Actor)
c/o Lisa Kasteler *WKT Public Relations (WKT-LA)*
9350 Wilshire Blvd Ste 450
Beverly Hills, CA 90212-3230, USA

Blanco, Gil (Athlete, Baseball Player)
18403 N 16th Pl
Phoenix, AZ 85022-1355, USA

Blanco, Henry (Athlete, Baseball Player)
5510 N 132nd Dr
Litchfield Park, AZ 85340-8328, USA

Blanco-Cervantes, Raul (President)
Apdo 918
San Jose, COSTA RICA

Bland, Anthony (Tony) (Athlete, Football Player)
20429 Walnut Grove Ln
Tampa, FL 33647-3352, USA

Bland, Bobby Blue (Musician)
c/o Staff Member *Wenig-LaMonica Associates*
580 White Plains Rd Ste 130
Tarrytown, NY 10591-5106, USA

Bland, Carl (Athlete, Football Player)
1985 Crossbridge Ct
Saint Charles, MO 63303-4810, USA

Bland, John (Athlete, Golfer)
PO Box 451436
Westlake, OH 44145-0638, USA

Bland, Nate (Athlete, Baseball Player)
2752 Southwood Ln
Bessemer, AL 35022-5692, USA

Blandford, Roger D (Astronomer)
Astrophysics
Pasadena, CA 91125-0001, USA

Blandi, Oscar (Business Person)
746 Madison Ave
New York, NY 10065-7052, USA

Blandon, Roberto (Actor)
c/o Staff Member *TV Azteca*
Periferico Sur 4121 Colonia Fuentes del Pedregal
DF CP 14141, Mexico

Blaney, Dave (Race Car Driver)
1751 W Lexington Ave
High Point, NC 27262-7115, USA

Blaney, George (Athlete, Basketball Player)
1633 Main St
Glastonbury, CT 06033-3133, USA

Blank, Barbie (Actor, Wrestler)
c/o Staff Member *World Wrestling Entertainment (WWE)*
1241 E Main St
Stamford, CT 06902-3520, USA

Blank, Matt (Athlete, Baseball Player)
5226 Overridge Dr
Arlington, TX 76017-1211, USA

Blankenship, Greg (Athlete, Football Player)
2067 La Con Ct Apt 1
Campbell, CA 95008-4315, USA

Blankenship, Kevin (Athlete, Baseball Player)
5014 Regency Dr
Rocklin, CA 95677-4420, USA

Blankenship, Lance (Athlete, Baseball Player)
340 Kimberwicke Ct
Alamo, CA 94507-2703, USA

Blankers-Koen, Fanny (Athlete, Track Athlete)
Surinamestraat 33
La Harve 2585, NETHERLANDS

Blankley, Anthony (Tony) (Correspondent)
International Square 1875 Eye St, NW Suite 900
Washington, DC 20006, USA

Blanks, Billy (Actor, Athlete)
c/o Staff Member *WmE2 (WMA-LA)*
1 William Morris Pl
Beverly Hills, CA 90212-4261, USA

Blanks, Jamie (Composer, Director, Editor)
c/o Simon Millar *Rumble Media*
1620 Broadway Ste C
Santa Monica, CA 90404-2777, USA

Blanks, Larvell (Athlete, Baseball Player)
PO Box 562
Del Rio, TX 78841-0562, USA

Blanks, Sid (Athlete, Football Player)
PO Box 130551
Spring, TX 77393-0551, USA

Blanton, Jerry (Athlete, Football Player)
1942 Calumet Ave
Toledo, OH 43607-1605, USA

Blarikfield, Mark (Actor)
10 100 Santa Monica Blvd # 2490
Los Angeles, CA 90067, USA

Blasberg, Erica (Athlete, Golfer)
2280 Treemont Pl Apt 206
Corona, CA 92879-7868, USA

Blasco, Chuck (Musician)
423 6th Ave
Huntington, WV 25701-1935, USA

Blasdel, Wendy (Stylist)
c/o Staff Member *Edible Style*
4476 Dyer St
La Crescenta, CA 91214-3410, USA

Blashford-Snell, John N (Misc)
Motcome Shaftesbury
Dorset SP7 9PB, UNITED KINGDOM (UK)

Blasi, Rosa (Actor)
c/o Evan Hainey *Untitled Entertainment (LA)*
350 S Beverly Dr Ste 200
Beverly Hills, CA 90212-4819, USA

Blasingame, Wade (Athlete, Baseball Player)
5207 Riverhill Rd NE
Marietta, GA 30068-4865, USA

Blass, Stephen R (Steve) (Athlete, Baseball Player)
1756 Quigg Dr
Pittsburgh, PA 15241-2023, USA

Blasucci, Dick (Producer)
c/o Staff Member *Kaplan Stahler Agency*
8383 Wilshire Blvd Ste 923
Beverly Hills, CA 90211-2443, USA

Blateric, Steve (Athlete, Baseball Player)
2855 S Monaco Pkwy Apt 2-304
Denver, CO 80222-7191, USA

Blatnick, Jeffrey C (Jeff) (Athlete, Wrestler)
848 Whitney Dr
Schenectady, NY 12309-3020, USA

Blatny, Zdenek (Athlete, Hockey Player)
c/o Staff Member *International Sports Advisors*
878 Ridge View Way
Franklin Lakes, NJ 07417-1524, USA

Blatt, Melanie (Musician)
c/o Staff Member *Concorde Intl Artists Ltd*
101 Shepherds Bush Rd
London W6 7LP, UNITED KINGDOM (UK)

Blatter, Joseph (Sepp) (Football Executive)
PO Box 85
Gloucester City, NJ 08030-0085, SWITZERLAND

Blattner, Buddy (Athlete, Baseball Player)
2335 Manor Grove Dr Apt 2
Chesterfield, MO 63017-7861, USA

Blatty, William Peter (Writer)
7018 Longwood Dr
Bethesda, MD 20817-2118, USA

Blatz, Kelly (Actor)
c/o Lena Roklin *Luber Roklin Management*
8530 Wilshire Blvd Ste 550
Beverly Hills, CA 90211-3133, USA

Blau, Daniel (Artist)
Belgradstr 26
Munich 80796, GERMANY

Blauser, Jeff (Athlete, Baseball Player)
6080 Carlisle Ln
Alpharetta, GA 30022-6279, USA

Blaylock, Anthony (Athlete, Football Player)
88 Brighton Dr
Garner, NC 27529-6872, USA

Blaylock, Bob (Athlete, Baseball Player)
36460 N 4030 Rd
Talala, OK 74080-3509, USA

Blaylock, Caroline (Athlete, Golfer)
232 Hennon Dr NW
Rome, GA 30165-9725, USA

Blaylock, Daron (Mookie) (Athlete, Basketball Player)
7601 Belmount Rd
Rowlett, TX 75089-7479, USA

Blaylock, Gary (Athlete, Baseball Player)
PO Box 241
Malden, MO 63863-0241, USA

Blazejowski, Carol (Athlete, Basketball Player)
126 Walnut St
Nutley, NJ 07110-2851, USA

Blazelowski, Carol A (Athlete, Basketball Player)
Madison Square Garden 2 Penn Plaza
New York, NY 10121, USA

Blazier, Ron (Athlete, Baseball Player)
610 N 9th St
Bellwood, PA 16617-1524, USA

Blazitz, Micael (Athlete, Football Player)
27100 Bunert Rd
Warren, MI 48088-6013, USA

Bleak, David B (War Hero)
355 Louise Dr
Arco, ID 83213-8743, USA

Bleaney, Brebis (Physicist)
Garford House Garford Road
Oxford OX1 3PU, UNITED KINGDOM (UK)

Bledel, Alexis (Actor, Model)
c/o Paul M. Brown *New Wave Entertainment (LA)*
2660 W Olive Ave
Burbank, CA 91505-4525, USA

Bledsoe, Curtis (Athlete, Football Player)
1012 Red Oak Pl
Chula Vista, CA 91910-6750, USA

Bledsoe, Drew (Athlete, Football Player)
845 Delrey Rd
Whitefish, MT 59937-8020, USA

Bledsoe, Tempestt (Actor)
c/o Staff Member *GVA Talent Agency Inc*
8981 W Sunset Blvd Ste 101
Los Angeles, CA 90069-1850, USA

Bleek (Cox), Memphis (Malik) (Artist, Musician)
PO Box 3172
Beverly Hills, CA 90212-0172, USA

Blegen, Judith (Opera Singer)
91 Central Park W Apt 1B
New York, NY 10023-4609, USA

Bleick, Tom (Athlete, Football Player)
PO Box 187
Talladega, AL 35161-0187, USA

Bleier, Robert P (Rocky) (Athlete, Football Player)
929 Osage Rd
Pittsburgh, PA 15243-1011, USA

Bleiler, Gretchen (Snowboarder)
1 Olympic Plz
Colorado Springs, CO 80909-5780, USA

Blessed, Brian (Actor)
5 Denmark St
London WC2H 8LP, UNITED KINGDOM (UK)

Blessen, Karen A (Journalist)
6327 Vickery Blvd
Dallas, TX 75214-3348, USA

Blessing, Jack (Actor)
c/o Marianne Golan *Marianne Golan Management*
6528 W 6th St
Los Angeles, CA 90048-4716, USA

Blessitt, Ike (Athlete, Baseball Player)
19712 Anglin St
Detroit, MI 48234-1469, USA

Blethen, Frank A (Publisher)
1120 John St
Seattle, WA 98109-5321, USA

Blethyn, Brenda A (Actor)
61-63 Portobello Road
London W1N OAX, UNITED KINGDOM (UK)

Bleu, Corbin (Actor)
c/o Randy James *James/Levy/Jacobson Management Inc*
3500 W Olive Ave Ste 1470
Burbank, CA 91505-5514, USA

Blevins, Jerry (Athlete, Baseball Player)
117 Jarrett Buck Loop
Johnson City, TN 37601-7137, USA

Blevins, Michael (Actor)
13 W 100th St Apt 2C
New York, NY 10025-4815, USA

Bley, Carla B (Composer, Musician)
PO Box 67
Willow, NY 12495-0218, USA

Bley, Paul (Composer, Musician)
550 Madison Ave # 1700
New York, NY 10022-3211, USA

Blick, Richard (Dick) (Athlete, Swimmer)
1602 N Nye Ave
Fremont, NE 68025-3328, USA

Blier, Bertrand (Director)
11 Rue Margueritte
Paris 75017, FRANCE

Blige, Mary J (Musician)
c/o Carrie Gordon *42West (NY)*
220 W 42nd St Fl 12
New York, NY 10036-7200, USA

Bligen, Dennis (Athlete, Football Player)
PO Box 101
West Hempstead, NY 11552-0101, USA

Blim, Richard D (Doctor)
304 W 172nd St
Belton, MO 64012, USA

Blind Boys of Alabama, The (Music Group, Musician)
c/o Eric (Ricky) McKinnie 192 Warren St. SE
Atlanta, GA 30317, USA

Blinder, Alan S (Financier, Government Official)
Economics
Princeton, NJ 08544-0001, USA

Blink 182 (Music Group)
c/o Karen Wiessen *Universal Music Group*
1755 Broadway Fl 6
New York, NY 10019-3768, USA

Blinka, Stan (Athlete, Football Player)
3304 Carriage Cir
Export, PA 15632-9213, USA

Bliss, Boti Anne (Actor)
3400 San Marino St # A
Los Angeles, CA 90006-1106

Bliss, Caroline (Actor)
c/o Staff Member *The Rights House (UK)*
Drury House 34-43 Russell St
London WC2B 5HA, UK

Blitt, Ricky (Writer)
c/o Nick Reed *International Creative Management (ICM-LA)*
10250 Constellation Blvd Fl 7
Los Angeles, CA 90067-6207, USA

Blittner, Larry (Baseball Player)
915 3rd Ave NW
Pocahontas, IA 50574-1413, USA

Blitz, Andy (Writer)
c/o Staff Member *3 Arts Entertainment Inc*
9460 Wilshire Blvd Fl 7
Beverly Hills, CA 90212-2713, USA

Blitzer, Wolf (Correspondent, Television Host)
820 1st St NE
Washington, DC 20002-4243, USA

Blobel, Gunter K J (Nobel Prize Laureate)
1230 York Ave
New York, NY 10065-6307, USA

Bloch, Erich (Engineer, Scientist)
1800 C St NE
Washington, DC 20002-6604, USA

Bloch, Henry W (Business Person)
4410 Main St
Kansas City, MO 64111-1812, USA

Bloch, Phillip (Stylist, Television Host)
c/o Chantal Cloutier *Cloutier Agency*
2632 La Cienega Ave
Los Angeles, CA 90034-2641, USA

Blochwitz, Hans-Peter (Opera Singer)
18 Allison Ave
Staten Island, NY 10306-2806, USA

Block, Francesca Lia (Writer)
c/o Angela Cheng Caplan *Cheng Caplan Co*
3136 S Bentley Ave
Los Angeles, CA 90034-3008, USA

Block, Hunt (Actor)
PO Box 462
Greens Farms, CT 06838-0462, USA

Block, John (Athlete, Basketball Player)
3900 Lomaland Dr Attn Athletic
San Diego, CA 92106-2810, USA

Block, John R (Secretary)
201 Park Washington Ct
Falls Church, VA 22046-4527, USA

Block, Ken (Athlete, Hockey Player)
4901 Windrift Way
Carmel, IN 46033-9510, USA

Block, Lawrence (Writer)
299 W 12th St Apt 12D
New York, NY 10014-1829, USA

Block, Ned J (Misc)
29 Washington Sq W
New York, NY 10011-9180, USA

Blocker, Dirk (Actor)
5063 La Ramada Dr
Santa Barbara, CA 93111-1846, USA

Blocker, Terry (Athlete, Baseball Player)
745 Guide Post Ln
Stone Mountain, GA 30088-1943, USA

Bloemberg, Jeff (Athlete, Hockey Player)
170 Diagonal Rd
Wingham, ON N0G 1W0, Canada

Bloemstedt, Herbert T
Plankengasse 7
Vienna 1010, AUSTRIA

Blomberg, Ron (Athlete, Baseball Player)
11660 Mountain Laurel Dr
Roswell, GA 30075-1329, USA

Blombergen, Nicolaas (Nobel Prize Laureate)
13835 E Langtry Ln
Tucson, AZ 85747-9637, USA

Blomdahl, Ben (Athlete, Baseball Player)
9 Emmy Ln
Ladera Ranch, CA 92694-1521, USA

Blomgren, Michael (Actor)
c/o Staff Member *Select Artists Ltd (CA-Westside Office)*
1138 12th St Apt 1
Santa Monica, CA 90403-5459, USA

Blomquist, Rich (Actor)
c/o Staff Member *Creative Artists Agency (CAA-LA)*
2000 Avenue of the Stars Ste 100
Los Angeles, CA 90067-4705, USA

Blomqvist, Timo (Athlete, Hockey Player)
HIFK Helsinki Ligaforeningen HIFK rd
Mantytie 23
Helsinki SF-00270, Finland

Blomsten, Arto (Athlete, Hockey Player)
c/o Staff Member *Canal + Television*
Teleluddsvagen 7
Stockholm S-11584, Sweden

Blonde streak (Music Group)
c/o John Elias *Three Twins Entertainment, Inc*
PO Box 100210
Staten Island, NY 10310-0210, USA

Blondie (Musician)
c/o Staff Member *10th Street Entertainment (NY)*
38 W 21st St Rm 300
New York, NY 10010-6979, USA

Blong, Jenni (Actor)
c/o Susan Smith *Susan Smith Company, The*
1344 N Wetherly Dr
Los Angeles, CA 90069-1817, USA

Blonsky, Nikki (Actor)
c/o Teal Cannaday *Rogers & Cowan PR (LA)*
Pacific Design Center 8687 Melrose Ave, 7th Floor
West Hollywood, CA 90069, USA

Blood, Edward J (Skier)
2 Beech Hill Rd
Durham, NH 03824-1803, USA

Bloodgood, Moon (Actor)
c/o Staff Member *Caliber Media Company*
9229 W Sunset Blvd Ste 705
West Hollywood, CA 90069-3407, USA

Bloodworth-Thomason, Linda (Producer, Writer)
c/o Staff Member *Mozark Productions*
4024 Radford Ave Bldg 5 PMB 104
Studio City, CA 91604, USA

Bloom, Alfred H (Educator)
President's Office
Swarthmore, PA 19081, USA

Bloom, Anne (Actor)
9200 W Sunset Blvd Ste 1125
Los Angeles, CA 90069-3610, USA

Bloom, Brian (Actor)
c/o Konrad Leh *Creative Talent Group*
1900 Avenue of the Stars Ste 2475
Los Angeles, CA 90067-4512, USA

Bloom, Claire (Actor)
c/o Staff Member *Conway van Gelder*
8-12 Broadwick St
London W1F 8HW, UK

Bloom, Floyd E (Physicist)
628 Pacific View Dr
San Diego, CA 92109-1768, USA

Bloom, Jeremy (Athlete, Olympic Athlete, Sportscaster)
c/o Staff Member *Maxx Sports & Entertainment*
546 5th Ave Fl 6
New York, NY 10036-5000, USA

Bloom, Lisa (Television Host)
c/o Staff Member *Court TV*
600 3rd Ave Fl 2
New York, NY 10016-1919, USA

Bloom, Luka (Music Group)
Derryneel Ballinalee
Longford, IRELAND

Bloom, Mike (Athlete, Hockey Player)
139 Peppertree Pl
Marina, CA 93933-2139, USA

Bloom, Orlando (Actor)
c/o Aleen Keshishian *Brillstein Entertainment Partners*
9150 Wilshire Blvd Ste 350
Beverly Hills, CA 90212-3453, USA

Bloom, Samantha (Actor)
c/o Paul Lyon-Maris *Independent Talent Group (ITG-UK)*
Oxford House 76 Oxford St
London W1D 1BS, UK

Bloom, Ursula (Writer)
Newton House Walls Dr Ravenglass
Cumbria, UNITED KINGDOM (UK)

Bloom, Verna (Actor)
327 E 82nd St
New York, NY 10028-4659, USA

Bloomberg, Michael R (Politician)
City Hall
New York, NY 10007, USA

Bloomfield, Clyde (Bud) (Athlete, Baseball Player)
300 Madison 8744
Huntsville, AR 72740-9503, USA

Bloomfield, Michael J (Mike) (Astronaut)
14302 Autumn Canyon Trce
Houston, TX 77062-2193, USA

Bloomfield, Sara (Director, Misc)
100 Wallenberg Pl SW
Washington, DC 20024, USA

Bloomfield, Willie (Athlete, Baseball Player)
3145 NE Magnolia St
Issaquah, WA 98029-3603, USA

Bloor, James E (Stylist)
117 W 15th St Apt 1FE
New York, NY 10011-9544, USA

Blosser, Greg (Athlete, Baseball Player)
5525 47th Ct E
Bradenton, FL 34203-5655, USA

Blount, Alvin (Athlete, Football Player)
11102 Belton St
Upper Marlboro, MD 20774-1404, USA

Blount, Corie (Athlete, Basketball Player)
5427 Kyles Ln
Liberty Township, OH 45044-9462, USA

Blount, Eric (Athlete, Football Player)
202 King St
Ayden, NC 28513, USA

Blount, John E (Athlete, Football Player)
1212 Daffodil Ln
Longview, TX 75604-2834, USA

Blount, Melvin C (Mel) (Athlete, Football Executive, Football Player)
6 Mel Blount Dr
Claysville, PA 15323-1329, USA

Blount, Winton M III (Business Person)
4909 SE International Way
Portland, OR 97222-4601, USA

Blout, Elkan R (Misc)
1010 Memorial Dr Apt 12A
Cambridge, MA 02138-4856, USA

Blow, Kurtis (Music Group)
2409 21st Ave S Ste 100
Nashville, TN 37212-5317, USA

Blowers, Mike (Athlete, Baseball Player)
22211 42nd Ave E
Spanaway, WA 98387-6889, USA

Blu, D K (Musician)
c/o Mike Rosen *Working Artists Agency*
13525 Ventura Blvd
Sherman Oaks, CA 91423-3801

Blucas, Marc (Actor)
c/o Sandra Chang *Industry Entertainment Partners*
955 Carrillo Dr Ste 300
Los Angeles, CA 90048-5400, USA

Blue (Musician)
c/o Staff Member *Concorde Intl Artists Ltd*
101 Shepherds Bush Rd
London W6 7LP, UNITED KINGDOM (UK)

Blue, Callum (Actor)
c/o Staff Member *Untitled Entertainment (LA)*
350 S Beverly Dr Ste 200
Beverly Hills, CA 90212-4819, USA

Blue, Forrest (Athlete, Football Player)
5225 Windham Way
Rocklin, CA 95765-5311, USA

Blue, Janice (Stylist)
1708 Rosewood St
Houston, TX 77004-4935, USA

Blue, John (Athlete, Hockey Player)
2301 Half Moon Ln
Costa Mesa, CA 92627-6738, USA

Blue, Luther (Athlete, Football Player)
6952 Ravines Cir
West Bloomfield, MI 48322-2757, USA

Blue, Vida (Athlete, Baseball Player)
PO Box 1449
Pleasanton, CA 94566-0349, USA

Blues Traveler (Music Group)
c/o Keith Sarkisian *WmE2 (Endeavor-LA)*
9601 Wilshire Blvd Fl 3
Beverly Hills, CA 90210-5219, USA

Bluford, Guion (Astronaut)
PO Box 549
North Olmsted, OH 44070-0549, USA

Bluhm, Kay (Athlete)
Bahnorstr 104
Potsdam 14480, GERMANY

Blum, Arlene (Mountaineer)
Biochemistry
Berkeley, CA 94720-0001, USA

Blum, Geoff (Athlete, Baseball Player)
1302 Waugh Dr
Houston, TX 77019-3908, USA

Blum, H Steven (General)
Hqusa Pentagon
Washington, DC 20310-0001, USA

Blum, John (Athlete, Coach, Hockey Player)
416 Marlborough St
Boston, MA 02115-1544, USA

Blum, Stephanie (Comedian)
c/o Staff Member *Don Buchwald & Associates Inc (LA)*
6500 Wilshire Blvd Ste 2200
Los Angeles, CA 90048-4942, USA

Blum, Steve (Actor)
c/o Staff Member *Arlene Thornton & Associates*
12711 Ventura Blvd Ste 490
Studio City, CA 91604-2477, USA

Bluma, Jaime (Athlete, Baseball Player)
15219 Reeds St
Overland Park, KS 66223-3241, USA

Blumas, Trevor (Actor)
c/o Staff Member *Premier Artists Management Ltd*
1502 Stoneybrook Cresc
London ON N5X 1C5, CANADA

Blume, Bernard (Athlete, Basketball Player)
29248 SE Powell Valley Rd
Gresham, OR 97080-9040, USA

Blume, Judy (Writer)
C/o Tashmoo Productions 244 Fifth Ave 11th Fl
New York, NY 10001, USA

Blume, Martin (Physicist)
2 Center St
Upton, NY 11973-9700, USA

Blumenauer, Earl (Congressman, Politician)
1502 Longworth Hob
Washington, DC 20515-1101, USA

Blumenthal, Richard (Senator)
702 Hart Senate Ofc Bldg
Washington, DC 20510-0001, USA

Blumenthal, W Michael (Financier, Misc, Secretary)
227 Ridgeview Rd
Princeton, NJ 08540-7666, USA

Blundell, Mark (Race Car Driver)
4001 Methanol Ln
Indianapolis, IN 46268-4855, USA

Blundell, Pamela (Designer, Fashion Designer)
14 Cheshire St
London E2 6EH, UNITED KINGDOM (UK)

Blundin, Matt (Athlete, Football Player)
731 Milmont Ave
Swarthmore, PA 19081-2519, USA

Blunstone, Colin (Music Group)
21A Cliftown Southend-on-Sea
Sussex SS1 1AB, UNITED KINGDOM (UK)

Blunt, Emily (Actor)
c/o Rupert Fowler *ID Public Relations*
Pall Mall Deposit 124-128 Barlby Rd Unit 27A
London W10 6BL, UK

Blunt, James (Musician)
c/o Todd Interland *Twenty-First Artists Ltd (UK)*
1 Blythe Rd
London W14 OHG, UK

Blunt, Matt (Ex-Governor)
1399 New York Ave NW Ste 950
Washington, DC 20005-4762, USA

Blunt, Roy (Senator)
260 Russell Senate Ofc Building
Washington, DC 20510-0001, USA

Blur (Music Group)
c/o Staff Member *United Talent Agency (UTA)*
9560 Wilshire Blvd Fl 5
Beverly Hills, CA 90212-2400, USA

Blurth, Ray (Bowler)
569 Beauford Dr
Saint Louis, MO 63122-1413, USA

BLVD (Music Group, Musician)
c/o Staff Member *Skyline Music*
28 Union St
Whitefield, NH 03598-3503, USA

Bly, Dre' (Athlete, Football Player)
4312 Topsail Lndg
Chesapeake, VA 23321-6601, USA

Bly, Robert (Bob) (Business Person, Writer)
1904 Girard Ave S
Minneapolis, MN 55403-2945, USA

Blyleven, Bert (Athlete, Baseball Player)
1855 Katrinka Rd
Hamel, MN 55340-9005, USA

Blyth, Ann (Actor, Music Group)
PO Box 9754
Rancho Santa Fe, CA 92067-4754, USA

Blyth, Chay (Misc, Yachtsman)
Inmans House 12 London Road Sheet Petersfield
Hamps GU31 4BE, UNITED KINGDOM (UK)

Blythe, Jamie (Reality TV Star)
c/o Michael (Mike) Esterman *Esterman.Com, LLC*
Prefers to be contacted via email
MD, USA

Boal, Mark (Writer)
c/o Staff Member *Creative Artists Agency (CAA-LA)*
2000 Avenue of the Stars Ste 100
Los Angeles, CA 90067-4705, USA

Board, Dwaine (Athlete, Football Player)
651 Arlington Rd
Redwood City, CA 94062-1842, USA

Boath, Freddie (Actor)
c/o Staff Member *Sasha Leslie Management*
34 Pember Rd
London NW10 5LS, UNITED KINGDOM

Boatman, Michael (Actor)
c/o Nancy Sanders *Sanders Armstrong Caserta*
2120 Colorado Ave Ste 120
Santa Monica, CA 90404-3561, USA

Boatwright, Ron (Athlete, Football Player)
1801 E Main St
Henderson, TX 75652-3324, USA

Bob, Tim (Music Group, Musician)
c/o Staff Member *ArtistDirect*
9046 Lindblade St
Culver City, CA 90232-2513, USA

Bobby Chacon, Bobby Chacon (Boxer)
752 S Main St
Los Angeles, CA 90014-2013, USA

Bobek, Nicole (Figure Skater)
19220 Seaview Rd # 100
Jupiter, FL 33469-2402, USA

Bobko, Karol J (Astronaut)
91 Turnberry Rd
Half Moon Bay, CA 94019-2604, USA

Bobo, DJ (Music Group)
Postfach
Wauwil 6242, SWITZERLAND

Bobo, Jonah (Actor)
c/o Ellen Gilbert *Abrams Artists Agency (LA)*
9200 W Sunset Blvd PH 11
Los Angeles, CA 90069-3601, USA

Bocachica, Hiram (Athlete, Baseball Player)
2340 CARR 2 URB REXVILLE Apt 2
Bayamon, PR 961, USA

Bocanegra, Carlos (Athlete, Soccer Player)
c/o Lyle York *Proactive Sports Management USA*
3233 M St NW
Washington, DC 20007-3556, USA

Boccabella, John (Athlete, Baseball Player)
1035 Lea Dr
San Rafael, CA 94903-3747, USA

Bocek, Milt (Athlete, Baseball Player)
1317 Elmwood Ave
Berwyn, IL 60402-1138, USA

Bocelli, Andrea (Music Group, Musician)
Vittoria Apuana
Forte dei Marmi 55042, ITALY

Bochco, Steven (Producer, Writer)
c/o Staff Member *Steven Bochco Productions*
3000 Olympic Blvd # 1310
Santa Monica, CA 90404-5073

Bochenski, Brandon (Athlete, Hockey Player)
10590 Kumquat St NW Apt 3
Minneapolis, MN 55448-1516, USA

Bochner, Hart (Actor)
232 N Canon Dr
Beverly Hills, CA 90210-5302, USA

Bochte, Bruce (Athlete, Baseball Player)
80 Century Ln
Petaluma, CA 94952-1218, USA

Bochtler, Doug (Athlete, Baseball Player)
154 Narrow Gate Rd
Maryville, TN 37801-1077, USA

Bochy, Bruce (Athlete, Baseball Player, Coach)
16144 Brittany Park Ln
Poway, CA 92064-2069, USA

Bock, Charles (Writer)
c/o Staff Member *The Rights House (UK)*
Drury House 34-43 Russell St
London WC2B 5HA, UK

Bock, Charles Jr (Misc)
PO Box 4197
Incline Village, NV 89450-4197, USA

Bock, Edward J (Athlete, Business Person, Football Player)
2232 Clifton Forge Dr
Saint Louis, MO 63131-3107, USA

Bock, Jerrold L (Jerry) (Composer)
145 Wellington Ave
New Rochelle, NY 10804-3705, USA

Bock, John (Athlete, Football Player)
627 Cambridge Ter
Weston, FL 33326-3568, USA

Bock, Joseph (Athlete, Football Player)
12 Heron Way N
Fairport, NY 14450-3318, USA

Bockhorn, Arlen (Athlete, Basketball Player)
3540 Big Tree Rd
Bellbrook, OH 45305-1971, USA

Bockman, Eddie (Athlete, Baseball Player)
1400 Millbrae Ave Apt 2
Millbrae, CA 94030-2831, USA

Bockus, Randy (Athlete, Baseball Player)
560 Helena Dr
Tallmadge, OH 44278-2667, USA

Bocuse, Paul (Business Person, Misc)
40 Rue de la Plage
Collonges-au-Mont d'Or 69660, FRANCE

Bodden, Alonzo (Actor, Comedian)
c/o Staff Member *Rozon/Mercer Management*
9250 Wilshire Blvd Ste 100
Beverly Hills, CA 90212-3343, USA

Boddicker, Michael J (Mike) (Athlete, Basketball Player)
11324 W 121st Ter
Overland Park, KS 66213-1978, USA

Boddicker, Mike (Athlete, Baseball Player)
11324 W 121st Ter
Overland Park, KS 66213-1978, USA

Boddy, Gregg (Athlete, Hockey Player)
2271 Sorrento Dr
Coquitlam, BC V3K 6P4, Canada

Bode, John R (War Hero)
1100 Warm Sands Dr SE
Albuquerque, NM 87123-4329, USA

Bode, Ken (Correspondent, Educator)
Journalism School
Evanston, IL 60206, USA

Boden, Lynn (Athlete, Football Player)
7103 N 146th St
Bennington, NE 68007-1527, USA

Boden, Margaret A (Misc)
Cognitive Science School
Brighton BN1 9QH, UNITED KINGDOM (UK)

Bodenheimer, George W. (Business Person)
c/o Staff Member *ESPN (Main)*
ESPN Plaza 935 Middle St
Bristol, CT 06010-1001, USA

Bodett, Tom (Entertainer, Writer)
PO Box 268
Putney, VT 05346-0268, USA

Bodger, Doug (Athlete, Hockey Player)
Eddy's Hockey Shop 2827 James St
Duncan, BC V9L 2X9, Canada

Bodine, Geoff (Athlete, Race Car Driver)
2029 E Lawyers Rd
Monroe, NC 28110-7458, USA

Bodine, Todd (Athlete, Race Car Driver)
PO Box 419
Mooresville, NC 28115-0419, USA

Bodison, Wolfgang (Actor)
c/o Amy Macnow *Envoy Entertainment*
2637 Centinela Ave Apt 8
Santa Monica, CA 90405-3162, USA

Bodmer, Walter F (Misc, Scientist)
Hertford College
Oxford OX1 3BW, UNITED KINGDOM (UK)

Bodrov, Sergei (Director)
c/o Steve Rabineau *United Talent Agency (UTA)*
9560 Wilshire Blvd Fl 5
Beverly Hills, CA 90212-2400, USA

Boede, Marvin J (Misc)
901 Massachusetts Ave NW
Washington, DC 20001-4307, USA

Boedeker, Bill (Athlete, Football Player)
1632 Thistle Ln
Fort Wayne, IN 46825-2960, USA

Boehm, Gottfried K (Architect, Historian)
Sevogelplatz 1
Basel 4052, SWITZERLAND

Boehm, Ron (Athlete, Hockey Player)
235 Simons Rd NW
Calgary, AB T2K 2X4, Canada

Boehmer, Len (Athlete, Baseball Player)
206 Townview Ct
Wentzville, MO 63385-2925, USA

Boehne, Edward G (Financier)
Independance Mall 100 N 6th St
Philadelphia, PA 19106, USA

Boehner, John (Congressman, Politician)
1011 Longworth Hob
Washington, DC 20515-3508, USA

Boehringer, Brian (Athlete, Baseball Player)
10 Sunset Dr
Fenton, MO 63026-4959, USA

Boehrs, Jessica (Actor)
Am Kliepesch 13a 50859
Cologne, Germany

Boeke, Jim (Athlete, Football Player)
18914 San Blas St
Fountain Valley, CA 92708-7430, USA

Boen, Earl (Actor)
3015 Kalakaua Ave
Honolulu, HI 96815-4703, USA

Boerner, Jacqueline (Speed Skater)
Bemhard-Bastlein-Str 55
Berlin 10367, USA

Boerwinkle, Tom (Athlete, Basketball Player)
8524 Walredon Ave
Burr Ridge, IL 60527-8344, USA

Boeschenstein, William W (Business Person)
10617 Cardiff Rd
Perrysburg, OH 43551-3404, USA

Boesel, Raul (Athlete, Race Car Driver)
150 SE 25th Rd Apt 4E
Miami, FL 33129-2403, USA

Boesen, Dannis L (Astronaut)
6613 Sandra Ave NE
Albuquerque, NM 87109-3639, USA

Boever, Joe (Athlete, Baseball Player)
416 Savannah Way
Franklin, TN 37067-2630, USA

Boff, Leonardo G D (Misc)
Prairie M Leao 12/204 Alto Vale Encantado
Washington, DC 20531-0001, BRAZIL

Boffill, Angela (Music Group)
1385 York Ave Apt 6B
New York, NY 10021-3906, USA

Bofill, Ricardo (Architect)
14 Ave de la Indurstria
Barcelona 8960, SPAIN

Bofinger, Heinz (Architect)
Beibricher Allee 49
Wiesbaden 65187, GERMANY

Bogar, Tim (Athlete, Baseball Player)
194 Gray St
North Andover, MA 01845-6302, USA

Bogart, Andrea (Actor)
c/o Staff Member *Kazarian Spencer Ruskin & Assoc.*
11969 Ventura Blvd Ste 300
Studio City, CA 91604-2619, USA

Bogart, Paul (Director, Television Host)
1801 Century Park E Ste 2160
Los Angeles, CA 90067-2343, USA

Bogdanovich, Peter (Director)
c/o Staff Member *Media Talent Group*
9200 W Sunset Blvd Ste 550
Los Angeles, CA 90069-3611, USA

Bogeberg, J B (Misc)
11 Elvaston Place #300
London SW7 5QC, UNITED KINGDOM (UK)

Bogener, Terry (Athlete, Baseball Player)
411 E McCabe Ave
Palmyra, MO 63461-2012, USA

Boggs, Haskell (Cinematographer)
3710 Goodland Ave
Studio City, CA 91604-2312, USA

Boggs, Tommy (Athlete, Baseball Player)
1450 Long Mdw
Salado, TX 76571-5367, USA

Boggs, Wade A (Athlete, Baseball Player)
6006 Windham Pl
Tampa, FL 33647-1149, USA

Bogguss, Suzy (Music Group, Songwriter, Writer)
c/o John Huie *Creative Artists Agency (CAA-TN)*
3310 W End Ave Fl 5
Nashville, TN 37203-1028, USA

Bogle, John C (Financier)
612 Shipton Ln
Bryn Mawr, PA 19010-3647, USA

Bogle, Warren (Athlete, Baseball Player)
3400 Gulf Shore Blvd N Apt M8
Naples, FL 34103-3609, USA

Bogner, Willy (Designer, Fashion Designer)
Saint-Veit-Str 4
Munich 81673, GERMANY

Bogosian, Eric (Actor, Artist, Writer)
c/o Emily Gerson Saines *Brookside Artists Management (NY)*
250 W 57th St Ste 2303
New York, NY 10107-2399, USA

Bogues, Muggsy (Athlete, Basketball Player)
527 E 83rd St Apt 2W
New York, NY 10028-7281, USA

Boguniecki, Eric (Athlete, Hockey Player)
58 Hine St
West Haven, CT 06516-4707, USA

Bogush, Elizabeth (Actor)
c/o Craig Shapiro *International Creative Management (ICM-LA)*
10250 Constellation Blvd Fl 7
Los Angeles, CA 90067-6207, USA

Bohan, Marc (Designer, Fashion Designer)
35 Rue du Bourg a Mont
Chatillon Sur Seine 21400, FRANCE

Bohannon, Fred (Athlete, Football Player)
5312 Goldmar Dr
Irondale, AL 35210-2812, USA

Bohanon, Brian (Athlete, Baseball Player)
243 W Thorn Way
Houston, TX 77015-2069, USA

Bohay, Heidi (Actor)
48 Main St
South Bound Brook, NJ 08880-1448, USA

Bohbot, Daniel (Designer)
2140 E 25th St
Vernon, CA 90058-1126, USA

Bohem, Les (Producer, Writer)
c/o Staff Member *United Talent Agency (UTA)*
9560 Wilshire Blvd Fl 5
Beverly Hills, CA 90212-2400, USA

Bohigas, Guardiola Oriol (Architect)
Calle Calvert 71
Barcelona 21, SPAIN

Bohling, Dewey (Athlete, Football Player)
5705 Cambria Rd NW
Albuquerque, NM 87120-2317, USA

Bohlinger, Rob (Athlete, Football Player)
12650 69th Ave N
Maple Grove, MN 55369-5438, USA

Bohlke, Sanders (Musician)
c/o Staff Member *Paradigm (Monterey)*
404 W Franklin St
Monterey, CA 93940-2303, USA

Bohlmann, Ralph A (Religious Leader)
1333 S Kirkwood Rd
Saint Louis, MO 63122-7226, USA

Bohn, Jason (Athlete, Golfer)
757 Carl Sanders Dr
Acworth, GA 30101-9580, USA

Bohn, Parker III (Bowler)
25 Pitney Ln
Jackson, NJ 08527-2933, USA

Bohn, Stephanie (Stylist)
c/o Staff Member *Clutts Agency, The*
1400 Turtle Creek Blvd # 171
Dallas, TX 75207-3337, USA

Bohn, T J (Athlete, Baseball Player)
11E Pfautz Rd
Duncannon, PA 17020-9204, USA

Bohne, Petra (Stylist)
c/o Staff Member *Stephanie Louise Inc*
17 Little West 12th St Ste 205C
New York, NY 10014-1312, USA

Bohnet, John (Athlete, Baseball Player)
224 Panorama Dr
Benicia, CA 94510-1523, USA

Bohovich, Reed (Athlete, Football Player)
11574 SE Plandome Dr
Hobe Sound, FL 33455-7901, USA

Bohr, Aage N (Nobel Prize Laureate)
Strangade 34 1-Sal
Copenhagen 1401, DENMARK

Bohrer, Thomas (Athlete)
77 Crest St
Concord, MA 01742-3006, USA

Bohringer, Romane (Actor)
c/o Staff Member *Agence Artistique Adequat*
80 Rue D'Amsterdam
Paris 75009, France

Boi, Big (Artist, Music Group, Musician)
c/o Charles King *WmE2 (Endeavor-LA)*
9601 Wilshire Blvd Fl 3
Beverly Hills, CA 90210-5219, USA

Boikov, Alexandre (Athlete, Hockey Player)
2138 Charleys Creek Rd
Culloden, WV 25510, USA

Boileau, Linda (Cartoonist, Editor)
321 W Main St
Frankfort, KY 40601-1890, USA

Boimistruck, Fred (Athlete, Hockey Player)
20 Cedar Ave P O Box 92
Hornepayne, ON P0M 1Z0, Canada

Boireau, Michael (Athlete, Football Player)
1729 SW 101st Way
Miramar, FL 33025-6537, USA

Boisclair, Bruce (Athlete, Baseball Player)
5423 Spanish Oak Ln Unit D
Oak Park, CA 91377-3728, USA

Boisson, Christine (Actor)
21 Ave Rapp
Paris 75007, FRANCE

Boisvert, Gilles (Athlete, Hockey Player)
10213 Greenside Dr
Cockeysville, MD 21030-3332, USA

Boitano, Brian (Athlete, Figure Skater)
10545 W Loyola Dr
Los Altos, CA 94024-6512, USA

Boitano, Danny (Athlete, Baseball Player)
15400 Winchester Blvd Apt 43
Los Gatos, CA 95030-2346, USA

Boiteux, Jean (Swimmer)
51 Ave De Merignac
Bordeaux, Cauderan 33200, FRANCE

Boivin, Leo (Athlete, Hockey Player)
P.O. Box 406
Prescott, ON K0E 1T0, Canada

Boivin, Leo J (Athlete, Hockey Player)
P.O. Box 406
Prescott, ON K0E 1T0, Canada

Bojovic, Novo (Athlete, Football Player)
22097 Worcester Dr
Novi, MI 48374-3956, USA

Bok, Arthur (Athlete, Football Player)
3280 Early Rd
Dayton, OH 45415-2705, USA

Bok, Bart J (Astronomer, Educator)
200 N Sierra Vista Dr
Tucson, AZ 85719-3841, USA

Bok, Chip (Cartoonist, Editor)
709 Castle Blvd
Akron, OH 44313-5709, USA

Bok, Derek C (Educator)
Kennedy Government School
Cambridge, MA 2138, USA

Bok, Sissela (Misc)
75 Cambridge Pkwy # 610
Cambridge, MA 02142-1229, USA

Bokadia, K C (Bollywood, Director, Filmmaker, Producer)
A12 Neha Apartments Juhu Tara Road Juhu
Bombay, MS 400 049, INDIA

Bokamper, Kim (Athlete, Football Player)
301 NW 127th Ave
Plantation, FL 33325-2318, USA

Bokelmann, Dick (Athlete, Baseball Player)
629 N Belmont Ave
Arlington Heights, IL 60004-5601, USA

Bola??os, Enrique (President)
Casa de Gobierno #2398
Managua, Nicaragua

Bolcom, William E (Composer)
3080 Whitmore Lake Rd
Ann Arbor, MI 48105-9649, USA

Bolden, Charles F Jr (Astronaut, General)
1505 Crystal Dr Apt 1105
Arlington, VA 22202-4172, USA

Bolden, Rickey (Athlete, Football Player)
301 High Pointe Dr
Lagrange, GA 30240-9718, USA

Boldirev, Ivan (Athlete, Hockey Player)
2003 Woodmere Dr
Valparaiso, IN 46383-6680, USA

Boldon, Ato (Athlete, Track Athlete)
PO Box 3703
Santa Cruz, Trinidad, TRINIDAD & TOBAGO

Bolduc, Dan (Athlete, Hockey Player)
27 Daisy Ln
Sidney, ME 04330-1809, USA

Boles, Carl (Athlete, Baseball Player)
5618 Pine Bay Dr
Tampa, FL 33625-4025, USA

Boles, John E (Athlete, Baseball Player, Coach)
7901 Timberlake Dr
West Melbourne, FL 32904-2151, USA

Boleyn, Brook (Stylist)
c/o Staff Member *Campbell Agency, The*
3838 Oak Lawn Ave Ste 900
Dallas, TX 75219-4510, USA

Bolger, Bill (Athlete, Basketball Player)
525 Ahlstrand Rd
Glen Ellyn, IL 60137-6926, USA

Bolger, Emma (Actor)
c/o Abby Bluestone *Innovative Artists (LA)*
1505 10th St
Santa Monica, CA 90401-2805, USA

Bolger, James B (Jim) (Prime Minister)
37 Observatory Cir NW
Washington, DC 20008-3627, USA

Bolger, Jim (Athlete, Baseball Player)
5524 Sidney Rd
Cincinnati, OH 45238-3215, USA

Bolger, Sarah (Actor)
c/o Hylda Queally *Creative Artists Agency (CAA-LA)*
2000 Avenue of the Stars Ste 100
Los Angeles, CA 90067-4705, USA

Bolick, Frank (Athlete, Baseball Player)
381 Virginia Ln
Kulpmont, PA 17834-2024, USA

Bolin, Bobby D (Athlete, Baseball Player)
100 Medinah Dr
Easley, SC 29642-3126, USA

Bolkiah, Hassanal (Royalty)
Istana Nurul Iman
Bandar Seri, Begawan BA1000, Brunei

Bolkiah, Mu'izuddin Waddaulah (Misc)
Istana Darul Hana, Brunei Darussalam

Bolkovac, Nick (Athlete, Football Player)
1418 Humbolt Ave
Youngstown, OH 44502-2755, USA

Boll, Don (Athlete, Football Player)
PO Box 131
Scribner, NE 68057-0131, USA

Bolleau, Linda (Cartoonist, Editor)
321 W Main St
Frankfort, KY 40601-1890, USA

Bollen, Roger (Cartoonist)
435 N Michigan Ave Ste 1500
Chicago, IL 60611-4012, USA

Bolles, Richard N (Writer)
10 Stirling Dr
Danville, CA 94526-2921, USA

Bollettieri, Nick (Coach, Tennis Player)
5500 34th St W
Bradenton, FL 34210-3506, USA

Bolli, Justin (Athlete, Golfer)
136 Ramsford Ln
Simpsonville, SC 29681-3650, USA

Bolliger, Beat (Stylist)
c/o Staff Member *Art Partner*
145 Hudson St Frnt 2
New York, NY 10013-2122, USA

Bolling, Claude (Composer, Music Group)
20 Ave de Lorrainne
Garches, FRANCE

Bolling, Frank (Athlete, Baseball Player)
171 Fenwick Rd
Mobile, AL 36608-1743, USA

Bolling, Milt (Athlete, Baseball Player)
4363 Old Shell Rd Apt 302
Mobile, AL 36608-2038, USA

Bolling, Tiffany (Actor)
12483 Braddock Dr
Los Angeles, CA 90066-6813, USA

Bollinger, Brian (Athlete, Football Player)
763 Malibu Ln
Indialantic, FL 32903-3617, USA

Bollinger, Brooks (Athlete, Football Player)
3549 Birchpond Rd
Saint Paul, MN 55122-4900, USA

Bollinger, Danielle (Musician)
c/o Len Evans *Project Publicity*
312 W 53rd St Ste 202
New York, NY 10019-5743, USA

Bollinger, Lee C (Educator)
President's Office
New York, NY 10027, USA

Bollman, Ryan (Actor)
c/o Staff Member *Lichtman/Salners Company*
12216 Moorpark St
Studio City, CA 91604-5228, USA

Bollo, Greg (Athlete, Baseball Player)
31032 Birchlawn St
Garden City, MI 48135-1957, USA

Bologna, Joseph (Actor, Director, Writer)
21800 Oxnard St Ste 460
Woodland Hills, CA 91367-7533, USA

Bolonchuk, Larry (Athlete, Hockey Player)
385 Woodlawn St
Winnipeg, MB R3J 2J2, Canada

Bolstorff, Douglas (Athlete, Basketball Player)
1553 Skyline Ct
Saint Paul, MN 55121-1148, USA

Bolt, Jackson (Actor)
c/o Jack Scagnetti *Jack Scagnetti Agency*
5118 Vineland Ave
North Hollywood, CA 91601-3814, USA

Bolt, Jeremy (Producer)
c/o Ken Kamins *Key Creatives*
1800 N Highland Ave Fl 5
Los Angeles, CA 90028-4523, USA

Bolt, Mae (Athlete, Bowler)
1516 Robinhood Ln
La Grange Park, IL 60526-1129, USA

Bolt, Tommy (Athlete, Golfer)
8 Whispering Winds Tc
Cherokee Village, AR 72529, USA

Bolt, Usain (Athlete)
c/o Grainne O'Dea *Pace Sports Management*
6 The Causeway
Teddington, Middlesex TW11 oHE, UK

Bolten, Joshua (Government Official)
Executive Ofc Building
Washington, DC 20503-0001, USA

Bolton, Michael (Musician, Songwriter)
c/o Staff Member *International Artists Holland*
PO Box 32
West Wardsboro, VT 05360-0032, The Netherlands

Bolton, Rodney (Athlete, Baseball Player)
2195 Ooltewah Ringgold Rd
Ooltewah, TN 37363-9392, USA

Bolton, Ron (Athlete, Football Player)
408 Maiden Ln
Chesapeake, VA 23325-4607, USA

Bolton, Scott (Athlete, Football Player)
1635 Ashmoor Dr E
Mobile, AL 36695-4345, USA

Bolton, Tom (Athlete, Baseball Player)
2288 Rolling Hills Dr
Nolensville, TN 37135-9483, USA

Bolton-Holifield, Ruthie (Athlete, Basketball Player)
1 Sports Pkwy
Sacramento, CA 95834-2300, USA

Boltz, Ray (Musician)
c/o Staff Member *Ray Boltz Music*
1767 NE 16th St
Fort Lauderdale, FL 33304-1357, USA

Bolyard, Bob (Athlete, Basketball Player)
10607 Wild Flower Pl
Fort Wayne, IN 46845-1687, USA

Bolzan, Scott (Athlete, Football Player)
1417 Ashford Ln
Aurora, IL 60502-1363, USA

Bomback, Mark (Athlete, Baseball Player)
2482 Riverside Ave
Somerset, MA 02726-5149, USA

Bombardir, Brad (Athlete, Hockey Player)
8959 Baywatch Trl NW
Walker, MN 56484-2063, USA

Bomer, Matthew (Actor)
c/o Mandi Warren *Viewpoint Inc. - NY*
Prefers to be contacted via telephone
New York, NY 10012, USA

Bon Jovi, Jon (Actor, Composer, Musician, Songwriter)
c/o Tiffany Shipp *Sunshine, Sachs & Associates*
149 5th Ave Fl 7
New York, NY 10010-6824, USA

Bonaduce, Danny (Actor, Music Group, Producer)
c/o Staff Member *Rebel Entertainment Partners*
5700 Wilshire Blvd Ste 456
Los Angeles, CA 90036-3648, USA

Bonaly, Surya (Figure Skater)
c/o Staff Member *Champions on Ice*
3500 W 80th St Ste 200
Minneapolis, MN 55431-1090, USA

Bonamy, James (Musician)
15 Music Sq W
Nashville, TN 37203-6200, USA

Bonanno, Louis (Louie) (Actor)
PO Box 583
Laguna Beach, CA 92652-0583, USA

Bonazzi, Noemi (Stylist)
c/o Staff Member *Marek & Associates Inc*
508 W 26th St Rm 12C
New York, NY 10001-5541, USA

Bond, Alan (Business Person, Yachtsman)
89 Watkins Rd
Dalkeith, WA 6069, AUSTRALIA

Bond, Christopher S (Kit) (Ex-Governor, Ex-Senator)
14 Jefferson Rd
Mexico, MO 65265-3732, USA

Bond, Edward (Writer)
Orchard Way
Great Wilbraham, Cambridge CB1 5KA, UNITED KINGDOM (UK)

Bond, H Julian (Activist)
54435 41st Pl NW
Washington, DC 20015, USA

Bond, J Max Jr (Architect)
100 E 42nd St
New York, NY 10017-5529, USA

Bond, Larry (Writer)
c/o Robert Gottlieb *Trident Media Group LLC*
41 Madison Ave Fl 36
New York, NY 10010-2257, USA

Bond, Phillip (Phil) (Athlete, Basketball Player)
208 Northwestern Pkwy
Louisville, KY 40212-2732, USA

Bond, Samantha (Actor)
18-21 Jermyn St
London SW1Y 6NB, UNITED KINGDOM (UK)

Bond, Samatha (Actor)
c/o Staff Member *Innovative Artists (LA)*
1505 10th St
Santa Monica, CA 90401-2805, USA

Bond, Victoria A (Composer)
541 Luck Ave SW Ste 200
Roanoke, VA 24016-5055, USA

Bond, Walter (Athlete, Basketball Player)
PO Box 87
Hamel, MN 55340-0087, USA

Bondar, Roberta L (Astronaut)
P O Box 7014 Station V
Vanier, ON K1L8E2, CANADA

Bonderman, Jeremy (Athlete, Baseball Player)
2100 Woodward Ave Attn Autographsforacause
Detroit, MI 48201-3470, USA

Bondevik, Kjell Magne (Prime Minister)
Postboks 8001 Dep
Oslo 30, Norway

Bondi, Hermann (Mathematician)
61 Mill Ln
Impington, Cambridgeshire CB4 4XN, UNITED KINGDOM (UK)

Bondra, Peter (Athlete, Hockey Player)
372 Carriage Park Way
Annapolis, MD 21401-7709, USA

Bonds, Barry (Athlete, Baseball Player)
44 Beverly Park Cir
Beverly Hills, CA 90210-1565, USA

Bonds, Gary U S (Music Group)
875 Avenue of the Americas # 1908
New York, NY 10001-3507, USA

Bondy, A.A. (Musician)
c/o Ken Weinstein *Big Hassle*
44 Wall St Ste 2201
New York, NY 10005-2427, USA

Bone Thugs-N-Harmony (Music Group)
c/o Staff Member *Sony Music Entertainment*
555 Madison Ave
New York, NY 10022-3301, USA

Boneham, Rupert (Reality TV Star)
c/o Staff Member *Abrams Artists Agency (NY)*
275 7th Ave Fl 26
New York, NY 10001-6708, USA

Bonehman, Rupert (Actor)
c/o Staff Member *Ruth Webb Enterprises*
10580 Des Moines Ave
Northridge, CA 91326-2926, USA

Bonell, Carlos A (Composer, Music Group)
Sutton Business Centre
Wallington, Surrey SM6 7AH, UNITED KINGDOM (UK)

Bonelli, Ernest (Athlete, Football Player)
1200 E Peppertree Ln Apt 602
Sarasota, FL 34242-8712, USA

Bonerz, Peter (Actor, Comedian, Director)
3637 Lowry Rd
Los Angeles, CA 90027-1435, USA

Bones, Ricky (Athlete, Baseball Player)
2 Villa Rosa St Apt A19
Guayama, PR 654, USA

Bonet, Lisa (Actor)
c/o Jillian Neal *Untitled Entertainment (LA)*
350 S Beverly Dr Ste 200
Beverly Hills, CA 90212-4819, USA

Bonet, Pep (Architect)
C/Pujades 62
Barcelona 8005, SPAIN

Boneta, Diego (Actor)
c/o Lena Roklin *Luber Roklin Management*
8530 Wilshire Blvd Ste 550
Beverly Hills, CA 90211-3133, USA

Bong, Jung (Baseball Player)
2917 Asteria Pointe
Duluth, GA 30097-5221, USA

Bongiovi, Tony (Producer)
649 SW Whitmore Dr
Port St Lucie, FL 34984-3567, USA

Bongo, Albert-Bernard Omar (President)
Blvd de Independence
Libreville BP 546, GABON

Bonham, Bill (Athlete, Baseball Player)
2135 Holly Ln
Solvang, CA 93463-2207, USA

Bonham, Jason (Musician)
c/o Steve Martin *Agency Group Ltd, The (NY)*
142 W 57th St Fl 6
New York, NY 10019-3300, USA

Bonham, Ron (Athlete, Basketball Player)
8020 S County Road 700 E
Selma, IN 47383-9621, USA

Bonham, Shane (Athlete, Football Player)
321 Clover Hill Rd
Maryville, TN 37801-9587, USA

Bonham, Tracy (Music Group, Songwriter)
c/o Staff Member *Paradigm (Monterey)*
404 W Franklin St
Monterey, CA 93940-2303, USA

Bonham Carter, Helena (Actor)
c/o Shelley Browning *Magnolia Entertainment (LA)*
9595 Wilshire Blvd Ste 601
Beverly Hills, CA 90212-2506, USA

Bonifant, J Evan (Actor)
c/o Staff Member *Pacific Artists Management*
1285 W Broadway Suite 685
Vancouver, BC V6H 3X8, Canada

Bonikowski, Joe (Athlete, Baseball Player)
6701 Old Reid Rd
Charlotte, NC 28210-4622, USA

Bonilla, Hector (Actor)
c/o Staff Member *TV Azteca*
Periferico Sur 4121 Colonia Fuentes del Pedregal
DF CP 14141, Mexico

Bonilla, Juan (Athlete, Baseball Player)
2902 Orchidcrest Dr
Crestview, FL 32539-8528, USA

Bonilla, Roberto M A (Bobby) (Athlete, Baseball Player)
1403 Kenilworth St
Sarasota, FL 34231-3521, USA

Bonin, Brian (Athlete, Hockey Player)
4660 Highway 61 N
Saint Paul, MN 55110-3421, USA

Bonin, Gordie (Race Car Driver)
12471 Sanford St
Los Angeles, CA 90066-6940, USA

Bonin, Greg (Athlete, Baseball Player)
509 Boulder Creek Pkwy
Lafayette, LA 70508-1717, USA

Bonin, Marcel (Athlete, Hockey Player)
408 Rue Precieux-Sang
Joliette, QC J6E 2M5, Canada

Bonington, Christian J S (Mountaineer)
Badger Hill Nether Row Hesket Newmarket
Cumbria, UNITED KINGDON (UK)

Bonjour, Daniel (Actor)
c/o Staff Member *Tinoco Management*
8033 W Sunset Blvd Ste 573
West Hollywood, CA 90046-2401, USA

Bonk, Radek (Athlete, Hockey Player)
16390 Braeburn Ridge Trl
Delray Beach, FL 33446-9508, USA

Bonnaire, Sandrine (Actor)
36 Rue De Ponthieu
Paris, FRANCE F-75008

Bonnell, Barry (Athlete, Baseball Player)
2102 179th Ct NE
Redmond, WA 98052-6064, USA

Bonner, Anthony (Athlete, Basketball Player)
5854 Elmbank Ave
Saint Louis, MO 63120-1116, USA

Bonner, Bobby (Athlete, Baseball Player)
990 Manitou Rd
Hilton, NY 14468-9390, USA

Bonner, Frank (Actor)
6500 Wilshire Blvd # 550
Los Angeles, CA 90048-4920, USA

Bonner, Jo (Congressman, Politician)
2236 Rayburn Hob
Washington, DC 20515-3312, USA

Bonner, John T (Biologist)
52 Patton Ave # A
Princeton, NJ 08540-5252, USA

Bonner, Melvin (Athlete, Football Player)
PO Box 474
Bay City, TX 77404-0474, USA

Bonness, Rik (Athlete, Football Player)
1650 Farnam St
Omaha, NE 68102-2104, USA

Bonneville, Hugh (Actor)
c/o Staff Member *Paradigm (LA)*
360 N Crescent Dr
Beverly Hills, CA 90210-4874, USA

Bonney, Barbara (Opera Singer)
Gunnarsbyn
Edane 671 94, SWEDEN

Bono (Music Group, Songwriter, Writer)
4 Windmill Lane
Dublin 2, Ireland

Bono, Chaz (Actor, Musician, Writer)
c/o Howard Bragman *Fifteen Minutes (LA)*
8436 W 3rd St Ste 650
Los Angeles, CA 90048-4131, USA

Bono, Mary (Politician)
PO Box 3370
Palm Springs, CA 92263-3370, USA

Bono, Steven C (Steve) (Athlete, Football Player)
1100 Hamilton Ave
Palo Alto, CA 94301-2216, USA

Bono Mack, Mary (Congressman, Politician)
104 Cannon Hob
Washington, DC 20515-0916, USA

Bonoff, Karla (Music Group, Songwriter, Writer)
2122 E Valley Rd
Santa Barbara, CA 93108-1513, USA

Bonsall, Joseph S (Joe) Jr (Music Group)
PO Box 726
Green Forest, AR 72638-0726, USA

Bonsalle, George (Athlete, Basketball Player)
11804 Del Rey Ave NE
Albuquerque, NM 87122-2417, USA

Bonser, Boof (Athlete, Baseball Player)
9251 126th Ave
Largo, FL 33773-1247, USA

Bonsignore, Jason (Athlete, Hockey Player)
2152 Edgemere Dr
Rochester, NY 14612-1102, USA

Bontemps, Ronald (Ron) (Athlete, Basketball Player, Olympic Athlete)
133 S Illinois Ave
Morton, IL 61550-2683, USA

Bonvicini, Joan (Athlete, Basketball Player, Coach)
McKale Memorial Center Atheletic Dept
Tucson, AZ 85721-0001, USA

Bonynge, Richard A
Chale Monet Rte de Sonloup
Les Avants, 1833 SWITZERLAN

Boo, Jim (Athlete, Hockey Player)
416 4th St S
Stillwater, MN 55082-4912, USA

Boo, Katherine (Journalist)
1150 15th St NW
Washington, DC 20071-0001, USA

Boochever, Robert (Judge)
125 S Grand Ave
Pasadena, CA 91105-1643, USA

Book, Asher (Actor)
c/o Bryan Leder *Management 101*
9107 1/2 Cahuenga Blvd
N Hollywood, CA 91601-2920, USA

Booka Shade (Music Group)
c/o Joel Zimmerman *WmE2 (WMA-NY)*
1325 Avenue of the Americas
New York, NY 10019-6026, USA

Booker, Buddy (Athlete, Baseball Player)
PO Box 59
Brookneal, VA 24528-0059, USA

Booker, Butch (Athlete, Basketball Player)
305 Barker Ave
Lansdowne, PA 19050-1215, USA

Booker, Chris (Correspondent)
c/o Staff Member *Entertainment Tonight (ET)*
4024 Radford Ave
Studio City, CA 91604-2101, USA

Booker, Chris (Athlete, Baseball Player)
2052 Perryville Rd
Monroeville, AL 36460-6852, USA

Booker, Greg (Athlete, Baseball Player)
1535 Charleigh Ct
Elon, NC 27244-9770, USA

Booker, Rod (Athlete, Baseball Player)
526 W Altadena Dr
Altadena, CA 91001-4204, USA

Booker, Vaughn (Athlete, Football Player)
1620 Powers St
Cincinnati, OH 45223-2658, USA

Booko, Daniel (Actor)
c/o Glenn Hughes III *Gem Entertainment Group*
10701 Wilshire Blvd Apt 1202
Los Angeles, CA 90024-4437, USA

Bookwalter, JR (Director)
PO Box 6573
Akron, OH 44312-0573, USA

Boom, Benn (Actor)
c/o Staff Member *WmE2 (WMA-LA)*
1 William Morris Pl
Beverly Hills, CA 90212-4261, USA

Boomer, Linwood (Producer, Writer)
c/o Philip Raskind *WmE2 (Endeavor-LA)*
9601 Wilshire Blvd Fl 3
Beverly Hills, CA 90210-5219, USA

Boon, David C (Cricketer)
Chester-le-Street
County Durham DH3 3QR, UNITED KINGDON (UK)

Boone, Aaron (Athlete, Baseball Player)
19860 N 97th St
Scottsdale, AZ 85255-6682, USA

Boone, Bob (Athlete, Baseball Player, Coach)
1432 Misty Sea Way
San Marcos, CA 92078-1010, USA

Boone, Bret (Athlete, Baseball Player)
6383 Calle Ponte Bella
Rancho Santa Fe, CA 92091-0288, USA

Boone, Danny (Athlete, Baseball Player)
320 Minnesota Ave
El Cajon, CA 92020-6118, USA

Boone, Debby (Actor, Musician)
4334 Kester Ave
Sherman Oaks, CA 91403-4135, USA

Boone, J R (Athlete, Football Player)
3731 Allan St
Selma, CA 93662-2203, USA

Boone, James (Athlete, Football Player)
2529 Butler Bay Dr N
Windermere, FL 34786-6111, USA

Boone, Pat (Actor, Musician)
c/o Staff Member *Solters & Digney*
1680 Vine St Ste 1105
Hollywood, CA 90028-8844, USA

Boone, Randy (Actor)
4150 Arch Dr Apt 223
Studio City, CA 91604-3236, USA

Boone, Ron (Athlete, Basketball Player)
48 W Broadway Apt 2404
Salt Lake City, UT 84101-2023, USA

Boone, Steve (Music Group, Musician)
620 16th Ave S
Hopkins, MN 55343-7833, USA

Boorem, Mikaela Juliette (Mike) (Actor)
c/o Mimi DiTrani *Schiff Company, The*
8440 Warner Dr Ste B1
Culver City, CA 90232-2461, USA

Boorman, Charley (Actor, Producer, Writer)
c/o Lindy King *United Agents*
12-26 Lexington St
London W1F OLE, UK

Boorman, John (Director)
16 Upper Pembroke St
Dublin 2, IRELAND

Booros, James (Athlete, Golfer)
2615 W Pennsylvania St
Allentown, PA 18104-2921, USA

Boortz, Neal (Radio Personality)
1601 W Peachtree St NE
Atlanta, GA 30309-2641, USA

Boose, Dorian (Athlete, Football Player)
4448 Oakdale Crescent Ct Apt 221
Fairfax, VA 22030-6739, USA

Boosler, Elayne (Actor, Comedian)
c/o Bill Siddons *Core/Lapides Lear Entertainment*
14724 Ventura Blvd PH
Sherman Oaks, CA 91403-3513, USA

Bootcheck, Chris (Athlete, Baseball Player)
1204 Suncast Ln Ste 2
El Dorado Hills, CA 95762-9665, USA

Booth, Adrian (Actor)
3922 Glenridge Dr
Sherman Oaks, CA 91423-4645, USA

Booth, Brad (Athlete, Football Player)
3101 Plaza Del Amo Unit 3
Torrance, CA 90503-7142, USA

Booth, Clarence (Athlete, Football Player)
33 Cor Dale Ct
Lafayette, IN 47904-1043, USA

Booth, Connie (Actor)
Primrose Hill Studios Fitzroy Rd
London NW1 8TR, UNITED KINGDOM (UK)

Booth, George (Cartoonist)
PO Box 1539
Stony Brook, NY 11790-0830, USA

Booth, Kellee (Athlete, Golfer)
4804 Goldeneyes Ln
McKinney, TX 75070-9037, USA

Booth, Kristin (Actor)
c/o Vicki McCarty *Covington International*
4237 Morro Dr
Woodland Hills, CA 91364-5521, USA

Booth, Lindy (Actor)
c/o Ronda Cooper *Characters Talent Agency, The (Vancouver)*
1505 W 2nd Ave #200
Vancouver, BC V6H 3Y4, Canada

Boothe, Powers (Actor)
PO Box 9236
Calabasas, CA 91372-9236, USA

Boothroyd, Betty (Government Official)
Westminster
London SW1A 0AA, UNITED KINGDON (UK)

Booty, John (Athlete, Football Player)
16401 Governor Bridge Rd Apt 407
Bowie, MD 20716-3717, USA

Booty, Josh (Athlete, Football Player)
9335 S Highway A1A
Melbourne Beach, FL 32951-4104, USA

Booty, Josh (Athlete, Baseball Player)
6248 N Windermere Dr
Shreveport, LA 71129-3423, USA

Boozer, Carlos (Athlete, Basketball Player)
c/o Rob Pelinka *Landmark Sports Agency*
10990 Wilshire Blvd Ste 1000
Los Angeles, CA 90024-3924, USA

Boozer, Emerson (Athlete, Football Player)
25 Windham Dr
Huntington Station, NY 11746-4541, USA

Boozer, Robert (Bob) (Athlete, Basketball Player)
PO Box 94754
Lincoln, NE 68509-4754, USA

Boozman, John
320 Hart Senate Ofc Building
Washington, DC 20510-0001, USA

Borbon, Pedro (Athlete, Baseball Player)
60 Enoch Crosby Rd
Brewster, NY 10509-2107, USA

Borchard, Joe (Athlete, Baseball Player)
3028 Luke Crossing Dr
Charlotte, NC 28226-3374, USA

Borchardt, Jon (Athlete, Football Player)
18815 201st Ave NE
Woodinville, WA 98077-5953, USA

Borcherds, Richard E (Mathematician)
Mathematics
Berkeley, CA 94720-0001, USA

Borcky, Dennis (Athlete, Football Player)
18 Weathervane Rd
Aston, PA 19014-2616, USA

Bordaberry, Arocena Juan M (President)
Juaquin Suarez 2868
Montevideo, URUGUAY

Bordano, Chris (Athlete, Football Player)
2788 Morning Moon
New Braunfels, TX 78132-4785, USA

Bordeleau, Christian (Athlete, Hockey Player)
NHL Scouting Service 50 Bay St, 11th Floor
Toronto, ON M5J 2X8, Canada

Bordeleau, J P (Athlete, Hockey Player)
91 Regal Dr
Dartmouth, NS B2W 4E9, Canada

Bordeleau, Paulin (Athlete, Hockey Player)
281A Rue Principale
La Sarre, QC J9Z 1Z1, Canada

Bordelon, Kenneth (Athlete, Football Player)
1224 Octavia St
New Orleans, LA 70115-4223, USA

Borden, Amanda (Gymnast)
3536 Woodridge Blvd
Fairfield, OH 45014, USA

Borden, Lynn (Actor)
6399 Wilshire Blvd Ste 211
Los Angeles, CA 90048-5705, USA

Borden, Robert (Producer)
c/o Staff Member *United Talent Agency (UTA)*
9560 Wilshire Blvd Fl 5
Beverly Hills, CA 90212-2400, USA

Borden, Scott (Actor)
c/o Staff Member *Progressive Artists Agency*
1041 N Formosa Ave
West Hollywood, CA 90046-6703, USA

Borden, Steve (Sting) (Wrestler)
16654 Soledad Canyon Rd # 315
Canyon Country, CA 91387-3217, USA

Border, Allan R (Cricketer)
90 Jolimont St
Jolimont VIC 3002, AUSTRATIA

Borders, Pat (Athlete, Baseball Player)
1135 S Lakeshore Blvd
Lake Wales, FL 33853-4244, USA

Bordi, Rich (Athlete, Baseball Player)
1133 Hailey Ct
Rohnert Park, CA 94928-1875, USA

Bordick, Mike (Athlete, Baseball Player)
1302 Locust Ave
Towson, MD 21204-6619, USA

Bordley, Bill (Athlete, Baseball Player)
39 Moccasin Ln
Rolling Hills Estates, CA 90274-2506, USA

Boreanaz, David (Actor)
c/o Tom Parziali *Visionary Entertainment*
1558 N Stanley Ave
Los Angeles, CA 90046-2711, USA

Borel, Calvin (Jockey)
16502 Briston Avon Ln
Louisville, KY 40245-4280, USA

Boren, Dan (Congressman, Politician)
2447 Rayburn Hob
Washington, DC 20515-4203, USA

Boren, David L (Ex-Governor, Ex-Senator)
Ofc 101
Norman, OK 73019-0001, USA

Boren, Matt (Actor)
c/o Steven Jensen *Independent Group, The*
6363 Wilshire Blvd Ste 115
Los Angeles, CA 90048-5734, USA

Borg, Bjorn R (Tennis Player)
Pier House Chiswick
London W4M 3NN, UNITED KINGDON (UK)

Borg, Kim (Opera Singer)
Osterbrogade 158
Copenhagen 2100, DENMARK

Borg-Aplin, Lorraine (Baseball Player)
5827 Laverne Cir Apt 2
Baxter, MN 56425-8231, USA

Borghi, Frank (Soccer Player)
4123 Poepping St
Saint Louis, MO 63123-7726, USA

Borgman, James A (Jim) (Cartoonist, Editor)
c/o Staff Member *King Features Syndication*
300 W 57th St Fl 15
New York, NY 10019-5238, USA

Borgmann, Glenn (Athlete, Baseball Player)
16 Lundy Ter
Butler, NJ 07405-1926, USA

Borgnine, Ernest (Actor)
3055 Lake Glen Dr
Beverly Hills, CA 90210-1313, USA

Borgognone, Dirk (Athlete, Football Player)
7148 Voyage Dr
Sparks, NV 89436-5427, USA

Boris, Angel (Actor)
c/o Staff Member *Acme Talent & Literary (LA)*
1400 Atlantic Ave Ste 274
Long Beach, CA 90813-2013, USA

Boris, Paul (Athlete, Baseball Player)
28 Sunnyside Ln
Hillsborough, NJ 08844-4738, USA

Boris, Ruthanna (Ballerina, Choreographer)
6510 Gladys Ave
El Cerrito, CA 94530-2210, USA

Bork, Erik (Producer, Writer)
c/o Staff Member *Creative Artists Agency (CAA-LA)*
2000 Avenue of the Stars Ste 100
Los Angeles, CA 90067-4705, USA

Bork, Frank (Athlete, Baseball Player)
8488 Dunsinane Dr
Dublin, OH 43017-9420, USA

Bork, George (Athlete, Football Player)
7316 Coventry Dr S
Spring Grove, IL 60081-9379, USA

Bork, Robert H (Judge)
c/o Staff Member *Simon & Schuster*
1230 Avenue of the Americas Fl CONC1
New York, NY 10020-1586, USA

Borkh, Inge (Opera Singer)
Haus Weitblick
Wienacht 9405, SWITZERLAND

Borkowski, Bob (Athlete, Baseball Player)
1031 Gerhard St
Dayton, OH 45404-2052, USA

Borkowski, David (Dave) (Athlete, Baseball Player)
35308 Monza Ct
Sterling Heights, MI 48312-4060, USA

Borland, Toby (Athlete, Baseball Player)
8642 Quitman Hwy
Quitman, LA 71268-1282, USA

Borland, Tom (Athlete, Baseball Player)
624 W Cherokee Ave
Stillwater, OK 74075-1405, USA

Borlaug, Norman E (Nobel Prize Laureate)
P O Box 6-641
Mexico City DF SP 06600, MEXICO

Borlenghi, Matthew (Actor)
c/o Marv Dauer *Marv Dauer Management*
11661 San Vicente Blvd Ste 104
Los Angeles, CA 90049-5150, USA

Borman, Frank (Astronaut, Business Person)
PO Box 64
Bighorn, MT 59010-0064, USA

Born, Ruth (Athlete, Baseball Player)
4205 Meridian Woods Dr
Valparaiso, IN 46385-7014, USA

Bornheimer, Kyle (Actor, Comedian)
c/o Brady McKay *Flutie Entertainment (LA)*
9320 Wilshire Blvd Ste 202
Beverly Hills, CA 90212-3217, USA

Bornstein, Jonathan (Athlete, Soccer Player)
c/o Lyle York *Proactive Sports Management USA*
3233 M St NW
Washington, DC 20007-3556, USA

Borntrager, Mary Christner (Writer)
c/o Staff Member *Herald Press*
1251 Virginia Ave
Harrisonburg, VA 22802-2434, USA

Borodina, Olga V (Opera Singer)
6 Henrietta St
London WC2E 8LA, UNITED KINGDON (UK)

Borom, Red (Athlete, Baseball Player)
827 Highland Oaks Dr
Dallas, TX 75232-1211, USA

Boron, Kathrin (Athlete)
An Der Pirschheide
Potsdam 14471, GERMANY

Boros, Guy (Athlete, Golfer)
2900 NE 40th St
Fort Lauderdale, FL 33308-5743, USA

Boros, Steve (Athlete, Baseball Player, Coach)
401 Heron Point Way
Deland, FL 32724-7303, USA

Boross, Peter (Prime Minister)
Kossouth Lajos Ter 1-3
Budapest 1055, HUNGARY

Borotsik, Jack (Athlete, Hockey Player)
Lot 17 1st Street N
Wasagaming, MB R0J 2H0, Canada

Borowski, Joe (Athlete, Baseball Player)
13782 E Gail Rd
Scottsdale, AZ 85259-4642, USA

Borrego, Jesse (Actor)
c/o Kay Liberman *Liberman/Zerman Management*
252 N Larchmont Blvd Ste 200
Los Angeles, CA 90004-3754, USA

Borrero, Alejandra (Actor)
c/o Gabriel Blanco *Gabriel Blanco Iglesias (Mexico)*
Rio Balsas 35-32 Colonia Cuauhtemoc
DF 6500, Mexico

Borresen, Richard (Athlete, Football Player)
2291 Jefferson St
East Meadow, NY 11554-1907, USA

Borris, Angel (Actor)
c/o Lara Rosenstock *Lara Rosenstock Management*
8371 Blackburn Ave Apt 1
Los Angeles, CA 90048-4245, USA

Borsato, Luciano (Athlete, Hockey Player)
200-4 Tortoise Crt
Brampton, ON L6P 0A1, Canada

Borsavage, Ike (Athlete, Basketball Player)
219 Doris Ave
Southampton, PA 18966-2771, USA

Borschevsky, Nikolai (Athlete, Hockey Player)
3 Geranium Crt
Richmond Hill, ON L4C 7M7, Canada

Borschman, Laurie (Athlete, Hockey Player)
27 Delamere Dr
Stittsville, ON K2S 1G7, Canada

Borst, Plet (Misc)
Meentweg 87
Bussum 1406 KE, NETHERLANDS

Borstein, Alex (Actor)
c/o Brandon Liebman *WmE2 (Endeavor-LA)*
9601 Wilshire Blvd Fl 3
Beverly Hills, CA 90210-5219, USA

Borth, Michelle (Actor)
c/o Mark Rousso *New Wave Entertainment (LA)*
2660 W Olive Ave
Burbank, CA 91505-4525, USA

Bortnick, Ethan (Actor, Musician)
c/o Michael Katcher *Creative Artists Agency (CAA-LA)*
2000 Avenue of the Stars Ste 100
Los Angeles, CA 90067-4705, USA

Borton, Della (D B) (Writer)
Dept of English
Delaware, OH 43015, USA

Bortz, Mark (Athlete, Football Player)
PO Box 3504
Quincy, IL 62305-3504, USA

Boryla, Mike (Athlete, Football Player)
7781 Oakview Pl
Castle Pines, CO 80108-8868, USA

Boryla, Vince (Athlete, Basketball Player)
5577 S Emporia Cir
Greenwood Village, CO 80111-3543, USA

Borysenko, Joan (Doctor, Writer)
393 Dixon Rd
Boulder, CO 80302-9769, USA

Borzov, Valeri F (Athlete, Track Athlete)
Esplanadna St 42
Kiev 23 252023, UKRAINE

Bosa, John (Athlete, Football Player)
2400 Magnolia Dr
North Miami, FL 33181-2221, USA

Bosarge, Wade (Athlete, Football Player)
7463 Tara Dr N
Mobile, AL 36619-1113, USA

Bosch, Don (Athlete, Baseball Player)
14446 N State Highway 3
Fort Jones, CA 96032-9773, USA

Bosch, Francisco (Actor)
c/o Suzanne Gielgud Victoria House 125 Queens Rd
Brighton BN1 3WB, UNOTED KINGDOM

Boschman, Ed (Religious Leader)
PO Box 347
Newton, KS 67114-0347, USA

Bosco, Philip (Actor)
606 N Larchmont Blvd Ste 309
Los Angeles, CA 90004-1309, USA

Bose, Amar G (Inventor)
Framingham, MA 1701, USA

Bose, Bimal K (Engineer)
215 Ski Mountain Rd
Gatlinburg, TN 37738-3142, USA

Bose, Eleanora (Model)
304 Park Ave S # 1200
New York, NY 10010-4301, USA

Bose, Miguel (Actor, Music Group, Songwriter, Writer)
Puerto Santa Maria 65
Madrid 28043, SPAIN

Bose, Rahul (Actor, Writer)

Boselll, Tony (Athlete, Football Player)
6 Glendenning Ln
Houston, TX 77024-6827, USA

Boselli, Tony (Athlete, Football Player)
12400 W Highway 71
Bee Cave, TX 78738-6517, USA

Bosetti, Rick (Athlete, Baseball Player)
1471 Arroyo Manor Dr
Redding, CA 96003-9215, USA

Bosh, Chris (Athlete, Basketball Player)
c/o Tammy Brook *FYI Public Relations*
174 5th Ave Ste 400
New York, NY 10010-5935, USA

Boshard, Lisa (Stylist)
4574 Wellington St
Holladay, UT 84117-4331, USA

Bosio, Chris (Athlete, Baseball Player)
PO Box 599
Appleton, WI 54912-0599, USA

Boskie, Shawn (Athlete, Baseball Player)
10220 N 55th St
Paradise Valley, AZ 85253-1168, USA

Boskin, Michael J (Government Official)
Hoover Instution
Stanford, CA 94305, USA

Bosley, Thad (Athlete, Baseball Player)
19440 Amhurst Ct
Cerritos, CA 90703-6787, USA

Bosman, Dick (Athlete, Baseball Player)
3511 Landmark Trl
Palm Harbor, FL 34684-5015, USA

Boso, Casper (Athlete, Football Player)
8811 Calumet Dr
Indianapolis, IN 46236-9031, USA

Bossard, Andre (Judge, Lawyer, Misc)
228 Rue de la Convention
Paris 75015, FRANCE

Bosseler, Don J (Athlete, Football Player)
7782 SW 54th Ave
Miami, FL 33143-5851, USA

Bosson, Barbara (Actor)
694 Amalfi Dr
Pacific Palisades, CA 90272-4506, USA

Bossy, Michael (Mike) (Athlete, Hockey Player)
136 Place Ducharne
Rosemere, QC J7A 4H8, Canada

Bostelle, Tom (Artist)
PO Box 8
Pocopson, PA 19366-0008, USA

Bostic, Jeff (Athlete, Football Player)
8250 Royal Saint Georges Ln
Duluth, GA 30097-1649, USA

Bostic, Jim (Athlete, Basketball Player)
111 Valentine Ln Apt 2D
Yonkers, NY 10705-3426, USA

Bostic, Joe (Athlete, Football Player)
3507 Bromley Wood Ln
Greensboro, NC 27410-2182, USA

Bostic, John (Athlete, Football Player)
611 Canaveral Ave
Titusville, FL 32796-7615, USA

Bostic, Keith (Athlete, Football Player)
2419 Duchess Way
Stafford, TX 77477-6227, USA

Boston (Music Group, Musician)
c/o Staff Member *Agency for the Performing Arts (APA-LA)*
405 S Beverly Dr Ste 500
Beverly Hills, CA 90212-4425, USA

Boston, Daryl (Athlete, Baseball Player)
1016 Valley Ln
Cincinnati, OH 45229-1932, USA

Boston, David (Athlete, Football Player)
3738 Mykonos Ln Unit 127
San Diego, CA 92130-5543, USA

Boston, Lawrence (Athlete, Basketball Player)
6362 Holiday Hills Ct
Bedford, OH 44146-3159, USA

Boston, McKinley (Athlete, Football Player)
1986 Coyote Ridge Dr
Las Cruces, NM 88011-4042, USA

Boston, Rachel (Actor)
c/o Vera Mihailovich *Forward Entertainment*
9255 W Sunset Blvd Ste 805
Los Angeles, CA 90069-3305, USA

Bostridge, Ian (Musician)
c/o Staff Member *International Creative Management (ICM-LA)*
10250 Constellation Blvd Fl 7
Los Angeles, CA 90067-6207, USA

Bostrom, Zachary (Actor)
11365 Ventura Blvd Ste 100 PMB 7403
Studio City, CA 91604-3148

Bostwick, Barry (Actor, Musician)
c/o Staff Member *Vanguard Management Group*
8060 Melrose Ave Fl 4
Los Angeles, CA 90046-7038, USA

Bostwick, Dunbar (Race Car Driver)
1623 Dewey Ave
Pompano Beach, FL 33060, USA

Bostwick, Jackson
PO Box 1452
Mount Juliet, TN 37121-1452, USA

Boswell, David W (Dave) (Athlete, Baseball Player)
309 Roxbury Ct
Joppa, MD 21085-4744, USA

Boswell, Ken (Athlete, Baseball Player)
3104 Golf Course Dr
Horseshoe Bay, TX 78657-5943, USA

Boswell, Thomas M (Writer)
1150 15th St NW
Washington, DC 20071-0001, USA

Boswell, Tom (Athlete, Basketball Player)
341 N Anton Dr
Montgomery, AL 36105-2112, USA

Bosworth, Brian (Actor, Athlete, Football Player)
4400 Arlen Ct
Plano, TX 75093-6701, USA

Bosworth, Kate (Actor)
c/o JJ Harris *One Talent Management*
9220 W Sunset Blvd Ste 306
Los Angeles, CA 90069-3503, USA

Bosworth, Lauren (Lo) (Reality TV Star)
c/o Nicole Perez *PMK/BNC Public Relations (PMK-LA)*
Pacific Design Center 8687 Melrose Ave, 7th Floor
West Hollywood, CA 90069, USA

Botchan, Ron (Athlete, Football Player)
55 Toscana Way E
Rancho Mirage, CA 92270-1977, USA

Boteach, Rabbi Shmuley (Activist, Writer)
c/o Robert Gottlieb *Trident Media Group LLC*
41 Madison Ave Fl 36
New York, NY 10010-2257, USA

Botehho, Joao (Director)
Rua de Palmeira 7 R/C
Lisbon 1200, PORTUGAL

Botelho, Derek (Athlete, Baseball Player)
1819 Orchard St
Burlington, IA 52601-6136, USA

Botero, Fernando (Artist)
2 Rue Honore Labarde
Principaute De Monaco 98 000, Monaco

Botes, Liz (Stylist)
c/o Staff Member *Legend Inc*
8855 Hollywood Blvd
Los Angeles, CA 90069-1306, USA

Botha, Francois (Frans) (Boxer)
PO Box 3982
Clearwater, FL 33767-8982, USA

Botha, Pieter W (President)
Die Anker
Wildemess, 6560 SOUTH AFRI

Botha, Roelof F (Government Official)
P O Box 16176
Pretoria North 116, SOUTH AFRICA

Botham, Ian T (Cricketer)
33 Tooley St
London SE1 2QF, UNITED KINGDOM (UK)

Bothwell, Tim (Athlete, Coach, Hockey Player)
14 Billings Ct
Burlington, VT 05408-1104, USA

Botkin, Kirk (Athlete, Football Player)
9018 Augusta St
Beach City, TX 77523-9767, USA

Botsford, Beth (Athlete, Swimmer)
2210 River Bend Ct
White Hall, MD 21161-9214, USA

Botsford, Sara (Actor)
8490 W Sunset Blvd # 403
West Hollywood, CA 90069-1912, USA

Bott, Raoul (Mathematician)
1 Richdale Ave Unit 9
Cambridge, MA 02140-2610, USA

Botta, Mario (Architect)
Via Ciani 16
Lugano 6904, SWITZERLAND

Bottalico, Ricky (Athlete, Baseball Player)
10 Rocamora Rd
Rocky Hill, CT 06067-2069, USA

Bottcher, Martin (Composer)
Postfach 96
Brusino Arsizio CH-6827, Switzerland

Bottenfield, Kent (Athlete, Baseball Player)
12168 142nd Ct N
West Palm Beach, FL 33418-7901, USA

Botterill, Jason (Athlete, Hockey Player)
236 Sunnyside Dr
Toledo, OH 43612-3625, USA

Botti, Chris (Musician)
c/o Bobby Colomby *The Colomby Group*
2110 Main St Ste 302
Santa Monica, CA 90405-2276, USA

Botting, Ralph (Athlete, Baseball Player)
7 Somerset
Trabuco Canyon, CA 92679-3701, USA

Bottom, Joe (Swimmer)
PO Box 3840
Chico, CA 95927-3840, USA

Bottomley, Virginia (Government Official)
Westminster
London SW1A 0AA, UNITED KINGDOM (UK)

Bottoms, Joseph (Actor)
c/o Belle Zwerdling *Progressive Artists Agency*
1041 N Formosa Ave
West Hollywood, CA 90046-6703, USA

Bottoms, Timothy (Actor)
c/o Darryl Marshak *Marshak/Zachary Company, The*
8840 Wilshire Blvd Fl 1
Beverly Hills, CA 90211-2606, USA

Bottrell, David Dean (Actor, Writer)
c/o Alan Gasmer *Alan Gasmer Management Company*
10877 Wilshire Blvd Ste 603
Los Angeles, CA 90024-4348, USA

Botts, Jason (Athlete, Baseball Player)
405 Peachtree Ln
Paso Robles, CA 93446-2869, USA

Botz, Bob (Athlete, Baseball Player)
14229 Desert Fire Ct
Horizon City, TX 79928-6422, USA

Boublil, Alain A (Songwriter, Writer)
1 Bedford Square
London WCIB 3RA, UNITED KINGDOM (UK)

Boucha, Henry (Athlete, Hockey Player)
PO Box 757
Warroad, MN 56763-0757, USA

Bouchard, Dan (Athlete, Hockey Player)
3111 Hillsdale Ct SE
Marietta, GA 30067-5431, USA

Bouchard, Emile J (Butch) (Athlete, Hockey Player)
1216-1705 Av Victoria
Saint-Lambert, QC J4R 2T7, Canada

Bouchard, Marc (Producer)
c/o Staff Member *Cirque du Soleil Inc*
8400 2e Avenue
Montreal QB H1Z 4M6, CANADA

Bouchard, Pierre (Athlete, Hockey Player)
208 Marie-Victorian
Vercheres, QC J0L 2R0, Canada

Bouchee, Ed
1621 E Tremaine Ave
Gilbert, AZ 85234-8140, USA

Bouchee, Ed (Athlete, Baseball Player)
1621 E Tremaine Ave
Gilbert, AZ 85234-8140, USA

Boucher, Brian (Athlete, Hockey Player)
3009 Allansford Ln
Raleigh, NC 27613-5468, USA

Boucher, Denis (Athlete, Baseball Player)
201-644 36E Av
Lachine, Quebec H8T 3M1, Canada

Boucher, Gaetan (Speed Skater)
3850 Edger
Saint Hubert, QC J4T 368, CANADA

Boucher, Philippe (Athlete, Hockey Player)
5057 Castle Creek Ln
Plano, TX 75093-4067, USA

Boucher, Pierre (Photographer)
L'Ermitage 7th Ave Massoul
Faremountiers
Coulomiers 77120, FRANCE

Boucher, Savannah (Actor)
3500 W Olive Ave Ste 1400
Burbank, CA 91505-5512, USA

Bouchez, Elodie (Actor)
c/o Scott Zimmerman *Evolution Entertainment (LA)*
901 N Highland Ave
Los Angeles, CA 90038-2412, USA

Bouck, Brittany Paige (Actor)
c/o Henry Penner *Penner PR*
8225 Santa Monica Blvd
West Hollywood, CA 90046-5912

Boudart, Michel (Engineer, Misc)
512 Gerona Rd
Stanford, CA 94305-8449, USA

Boudia, David (Athlete, Olympic Athlete)
Pan American Plaza #430 201 South Capitol Ave
Indianapolis, IN 46225, USA

Boudin, Michael (Judge)
McCormack Federal Building
Boston, MA 2109, USA

Boudreau, Bruce (Athlete, Hockey Player)
PO Box 59727
Potomac, MD 20859-9727, USA

Boudrias, Andre (Athlete, Hockey Player)
1008-4300 Place Des Cageux
Laval, QC H7W 423, Canada

Bouffard, Danielle (Actor)
c/o Staff Member *King Talent*
303-228 E 4th Ave
Vancouver V5T-1G5, CANADA

Bouffard, Danielle (Actor)

Bouggess, Lee (Athlete, Football Player)
171 Villa Knoll Ct
Sicklerville, NJ 08081-2923, USA

Boughner, Barry (Athlete, Hockey Player)
52 Locke Ave
St Thomas, ON N5P 3X7, Canada

Boughner, Bob (Athlete, Hockey Player)
c/o Staff Member *Windsor Spitfires*
334 Wyandotte St E
Windsor, ON N9A 3H6, Canada

Boujenah, Michel (Actor)
c/o Staff Member *ArtMedia*
20 avenue Rapp
Paris 75008, France

Boukadakis, Joey (Director, Producer, Writer)
c/o Michael Lasker *Mosaic Media Group*
9200 W Sunset Blvd Ste 10
Los Angeles, CA 90069-3608, USA

Bouklas, Penelope (Stylist)
4414 Newtown Rd Apt 2B
Astoria, NY 11103-2254, USA

Boulanger, Pierre (Actor)
c/o Paul Nelson *Mosaic Media Group*
9200 W Sunset Blvd Ste 10
Los Angeles, CA 90069-3608, USA

Bouldin, Carl (Athlete, Baseball Player)
42 Fairway Dr
Southgate, KY 41071-3024, USA

Boulerice, Jesse (Athlete, Hockey Player)
502 Oak Island Dr
Cary, NC 27513-2236, USA

Boulez, Pierre (Composer, Conductor)
1 Place Igor Stravinsky
Paris 75004, FRANCE

Boullion, Jean-Christophe (Race Car Driver)
40 bis rue fabert
Paris F-75007, France

Boulos, Frenchy (Soccer Player)
20 Elvin St
Staten Island, NY 10314-4049, USA

Boulter, Roy (Actor, Producer, Writer)
c/o Peter MacFarlane *MacFarlane Chard Associates*
33 ercy St
London W1T 2DF, UK

Boulud, David (Chef)
60 E 65th St
New York, NY 10065-7056, USA

Boulware, Michael (Athlete, Football Player)
c/o Eugene Parker *Maximum Sports Management*
6435 W Jefferson Blvd # 197
Fort Wayne, IN 46804-6203, USA

Boulware, Peter (Athlete, Football Player)
305 Leaning Tree Rd
Columbia, SC 29223-3010, USA

Bouman, Todd (Athlete, Football Player)
3070 Dartmouth Dr
Excelsior, MN 55331-7849, USA

Bouquet, Carole (Actor, Model)
201 Faubourg Saint Honore
Paris 75008, FRANCE

Bourbonnais, Rick (Athlete, Hockey Player)
643 E Parkway Ct
Boise, ID 83706-6526, USA

Bourcier, Jean-Louis (Athlete, Hockey Player)
623 Rg St Laurent
St-Etienne-Beauharnois, QC J0S 1S0, Canada

Bourdain, Anthony (Chef, Television Host)
c/o Kimberly Witherspoon *Inkwell Management*
521 5th Ave
New York, NY 10175-0003, USA

Bourdeaux, Brandy (Actor)
c/o Staff Member *Coralie Jr Theatrical Agency*
907 S Victory Blvd
Burbank, CA 91502-2430, USA

Bourdeaux, Michael (Religious Leader)
Heathfield Road Keston
Kent BR2 6BA, UNITED KINGDOM (UK)

Bourdian, Anthony (Chef)
1180 Avenue of the Americas # 1200
New York, NY 10036-8401, USA

Boures, Emil (Athlete, Football Player)
426 W Swissvale Ave
Pittsburgh, PA 15218-1637, USA

Bourgeois, Charles (Athlete, Hockey Player)
P.O. Box 1481 Stn Main
Moncton, NB E1C 8T6, Canada

Bourgeois, Steve (Athlete, Baseball Player)
PO Box 143
Paulina, LA 70763-0143, USA

Bourgignon, Serge (Director)
18 Rue de General-Malterre
Paris 75016, FRANCE

Bourgoin, Louise (Actor)
c/o Jessica Kovacevic *WmE2 (Endeavor-LA)*
9601 Wilshire Blvd Fl 3
Beverly Hills, CA 90210-5219, USA

Bourjaily, Vance (Writer)
Redbird Farm RR 3
Iowa City, IA 52240, USA

Bourjos, Chris (Athlete, Baseball Player)
10345 E Dreyfus Ave
Scottsdale, AZ 85260-9006, USA

Bourn, Michael (Athlete, Baseball Player)
20718 Beigewood Dr
Humble, TX 77338-2736, USA

Bourne, Bob (Athlete, Hockey Player)
1-1890 Cooper Rd
Kelowna, BC V1Y 8B7, Canada

Bourne, JR (Actor)
c/o John Elliott *Mosaic Media Group*
9200 W Sunset Blvd Ste 10
Los Angeles, CA 90069-3608, USA

Bourne, Martin (Stylist)
c/o Staff Member *Judy Casey Inc*
114 E 13th St
New York, NY 10003-5329, USA

Bourne, Shae-Lynn (Figure Skater)
300 Alumni Rd
Newington, CT 06111-1868, USA

Bournigal, Rafael (Athlete, Baseball Player)
230 Canterwood Ln
Mulberry, FL 33860-7637, USA

Bournissen, Chantal (Skier)
1983 Evolene
SWITZERLAND

Bourque, Pat (Athlete, Baseball Player)
2001 N Chipmunk Ct
Flagstaff, AZ 86004-7587, USA

Bourque, Phil (Athlete, Hockey Player)
5117 Yale Dr
Aliquippa, PA 15001-4949, USA

Bourque, Pierre (Misc)
275 Rue Notre Dame Est
Montreal, QC H2Y 1C6, CANADA

Bourque, Raymond J (Athlete, Hockey Player)
47C Dana Rd
Boxford, MA 01921-2661, USA

Bourret, Caprice (Actor)
c/o Nadja Koglin *Richard Schwartz Management*
2934 1/2 N Beverly Glen Cir # 107
Los Angeles, CA 90077-1724, USA

Boushka, Richard (Dick) (Athlete, Basketball Player, Olympic Athlete)
5414 W 145th St
Overland Park, KS 66224-3756, USA

Bouteflika, Abdul Aziz (President)
Al-Mouradia
Algiers, Algeria

Boutette, Pat (Athlete, Hockey Player)
The Doctor's House Restaurant 21 Nashville Rd
Kleinburg, ON L0J 1C0, Canada

Boutilier, Paul (Athlete, Hockey Player)
35 Elgin Ln
Bedford, NS B4A 2K2, Canada

Bouton, Jim (Athlete, Baseball Player)
P.O. Box 188
North Egremont, MA 1252, USA

Boutros-Ghali, Boutros (Secretary)
28 Rue de Bourgogne
Paris 75007, FRANCE

Boutte, Denise (Actor)
c/o Charles Newman *Newman-Thomas Management*
8306 Wilshire Blvd # 996
Beverly Hills, CA 90211-2382, USA

Boutwell, Thomas (Athlete, Football Player)
32353 Oaken Wood St
Denham Springs, LA 70726-1666, USA

Bouvet, Didier (Skier)
Abondance 74360, FRANCE

Bouvia, Gloria (Bowler)
658 NE 23rd Pl
Gresham, OR 97030, USA

Bouwmeester, Jay (Athlete, Hockey Player)
7824 NW 123rd Ave
Parkland, FL 33076-4546, USA

Bouyer, Willie (Athlete, Football Player)
6560 Chesterbrook Dr
Elk Grove, CA 95758-6326, USA

Bouza, Matt (Athlete, Football Player)
1042 Via Nueva
Lafayette, CA 94549-2726, USA

Bouzeos, Phil (Athlete, Football Player)
10 Pembroke Ln
Oak Brook, IL 60523-1727, USA

Bova, Raoul (Actor)
c/o Alan Siegel *Alan Siegel Entertainment*
345 N Maple Dr Ste 375
Beverly Hills, CA 90210-5174, USA

Bovee, Mike (Athlete, Baseball Player)
11405 Affinity Ct Unit 236
San Diego, CA 92131-2718, USA

Boven, Don (Athlete, Basketball Player)
4434 Garth Rd
Charlottesville, VA 22901-5103, USA

Bowa, Lawrence R (Larry) (Athlete, Baseball Player, Coach)
129 Upper Gulph Rd
Radnor, PA 19087-4625, USA

Bowab, John (Actor)
2598 Greenvalley Rd
Los Angeles, CA 90046-1438, USA

Bowdell III, Gordon (Athlete, Football Player)
10929 Stoney Point Dr
South Lyon, MI 48178-9296, USA

Bowden, Craig (Athlete, Golfer)
4651 S Amber Dr
Bloomington, IN 47401-8359, USA

Bowden, Katrina (Actor)
c/o William Choi *Management 360*
9111 Wilshire Blvd
Beverly Hills, CA 90210-5508, USA

Bowden, Mark (Director, Writer)
c/o Ron Bernstein *International Creative Management (ICM-LA)*
10250 Constellation Blvd Fl 7
Los Angeles, CA 90067-6207, USA

Bowden, Robert (Bobby) (Athlete, Coach, Football Coach, Football Player)
2813 Shamrock St N
Tallahassee, FL 32309-2231, USA

Bowden, Terry (Coach, Football Coach, Sportscaster)
77 W 66th St
New York, NY 10023-6201, USA

Bowden, Tommy (Coach, Football Coach)
Athletic Dept
Clemson, SC 29364, USA

Bowdler, William G (Diplomat)
2201 C St NW
Washington, DC 20520-0099, USA

Bowe, David (Actor)
329 N Wetherly Dr Ste 101
Beverly Hills, CA 90211-1674, USA

Bowe, Riddick L (Boxer)
714 Amer Dr
Fort Washington, MD 20744-5943, USA

Bowe, Rosemarie (Actor)
321 St Pierre Rd
Los Angeles, CA 90077-3432, USA

Bowen, Andrea (Actor)
c/o Mary Ellen Mulcahy *Framework Entertainment (LA)*
9057 Nemo St Ste C
West Hollywood, CA 90069-5511, USA

Bowen, Bruce (Athlete, Basketball Player)
18847 Calle Cierra
San Antonio, TX 78258-4032, USA

Bowen, Heather (Stylist)
5120 SW Richardson Dr
Portland, OR 97239-2054, USA

Bowen, Jason (Athlete, Hockey Player)
4900 W 14th Ave
Kennewick, WA 99338-1723, USA

Bowen, Jimmy (Music Group, Musician)
PO Box 454
Lebanon, TN 37088-0454, USA

Bowen, Julie (Actor)
c/o Kay Liberman *Liberman/Zerman Management*
252 N Larchmont Blvd Ste 200
Los Angeles, CA 90004-3754, USA

Bowen, Michael (Actor)
1875 Century Park E Ste 2250
Los Angeles, CA 90067-2563, USA

Bowen, Nanci (Athlete, Golfer)
201 Carolina Point Pkwy Apt 1119
Greenville, SC 29607-6580, USA

Bowen, Otis R (Secretary)
2791 2B Rd
Bremen, IN 46506-9047, USA

Bowen, Pamela (Actor)
c/o Staff Member *Henderson Hogan Agency (LA)*
850 7th Ave Ste 1003
New York, NY 10019-5230, USA

Bowen, Rob (Athlete, Baseball Player)
2055 S Park Pl SE
Atlanta, GA 30339-2014, USA

Bowen, Ryan (Athlete, Baseball Player)
3702 Frankford Rd Apt 18203
Dallas, TX 75287-7811, USA

Bowen, Sam (Athlete, Baseball Player)
8219 Victory Trl
Brentwood, TN 37027-7374, USA

Bowen, Wade (Musician)
c/o Joey Lee *WmE2 (WMA-TN)*
1600 Division St Ste 300
Nashville, TN 37203-2755, USA

Bowen, William G (Educator, Misc)
140 E 62nd St
New York, NY 10065-8124, USA

Bowens, Tim (Athlete, Football Player)
PO Box 93
Okolona, MS 38860-0093, USA

Bowens, Tom (Athlete, Basketball Player)
19788 Wildwood Dr
West Linn, OR 97068-2252, USA

Bower, Antoinette (Actor)
1529 N Beverly Glen Blvd
Los Angeles, CA 90077-3129, USA

Bower, Jaime Campbell (Actor)
c/o Simon Beresford *Dalzell & Beresford Ltd*
26 Astwood Mews
London SW7 4DE, UNITED KINGDOM (UK)

Bower, Johnny (Athlete, Hockey Player)
3937 Parkgate Dr
Mississauga, ON L5N 7B4, Canada

Bower, Michael (Actor)
c/o Dora Whitaker *Whitaker Agency, The*
4924 Vineland Ave
N Hollywood, CA 91601-3847, USA

Bower, Robert W (Inventor)
Microelectronics Dept
Davis, CA 95616, USA

Bowers, Brent (Athlete, Baseball Player)
19257 Manchester Dr
Mokena, IL 60448-7747, USA

Bowers, Chris (Actor)
c/o Staff Member *Gersh (LA)*
9465 Wilshire Blvd Ste 600
Beverly Hills, CA 90212-2612, USA

Bowers, Dane (Actor, Musician)
Penshurst Place 90-92 SouthBridge Rd
Croydon, Surrey CRO 1AF, UNITED KINGDOM

Bowers, John (Misc)
17 Battery Pl
New York, NY 10004-1207, USA

Bowers, John W (Religious Leader)
1100 Glendale Blvd
Los Angeles, CA 90026-3203, USA

Bowers, Shane (Athlete, Baseball Player)
791 S Rancho Simi Dr
Covina, CA 91724-3361, USA

Bowers, William (Athlete, Football Player)
43295 Lacovia Dr
Indio, CA 92203-8016, USA

Bowersox, Crystal (Musician)
c/o Simon Fuller *XIX Entertainment*
33/32 Ransomes Dock 35-37 Parkgate Rd
London SW11 4NP, UK

Bowersox, Kenneth D (Astronaut)
16907 Soaring Forest Dr
Houston, TX 77059-4003, USA

Bowick, Vantonio (Athlete, Football Player)
PO Box 234
Slocomb, AL 36375-0234, USA

Bowie, David (Actor, Musician)
c/o Mitch Schneider *Mitch Schneider Organization, The*
14724 Ventura Blvd Ste 410
Sherman Oaks, CA 91403-3537, USA

Bowie, Heather (Athlete, Golfer)
3017 Elm River Dr
Ft Worth, TX 76116-0697, USA

Bowie, Jim (Athlete, Baseball Player)
620 Suisun St
Suisun City, CA 94585-2438, USA

Bowie, Larry D (Athlete, Football Player)
1609 Parkwin Ave
Anniston, AL 36201-3460, USA

Bowie, Larry G (Athlete, Football Player)
739 Echo Shores Ct
Saint Paul, MN 55115-1473, USA

Bowie, Micah (Athlete, Baseball Player)
2039 Small Town Dr
New Braunfels, TX 78130-9063, USA

Bowie, Sam (Athlete, Basketball Player)
901 Curtilage
Lexington, KY 40502, USA

Bowker, Albert H (Educator)
1523 New Hampshire Ave NW
Washington, DC 20036-1203, USA

Bowker, Gordon (Business Person, Writer)
c/o Staff Member *Little, Brown Book Group*
100 Victoria Embankment
London EC4Y 0DY, UK

Bowker, Judi (Actor)
66 Berkeley House 5 Hay Hill
London W1X 7LH, UNITED KINGDOM (UK)

Bowlby, April (Actor)
c/o Brian Wilkins *Kritzer Levine Wilkins Entertainment*
11872 La Grange Ave Fl 1
Los Angeles, CA 90025-5283, USA

Bowles, Brian (Athlete, Baseball Player)
2001 Flournoy Rd
Manhattan Beach, CA 90266-2534, USA

Bowles, Charlie (Athlete, Golfer)
42009 Cherry Hill Rd
Novi, MI 48375-2518, USA

Bowles, Crandall C (Business Person)
205 N White St
Fort Mill, SC 29715-1654, USA

Bowles, Erskine B (Government Official)
6725 Old Providence Rd
Charlotte, NC 28226-7735, USA

Bowles, Lauren (Actor)
c/o Staff Member *Main Title Entertainment*
2225 Wilshire Blvd Suite 500
Los Angeles, CA 90036, USA

Bowles, Peter (Actor)
c/o Staff Member *Conway van Gelder*
8-12 Broadwick St
London W1F 8HW, UK

Bowlin, Weldon (Hoss) (Athlete, Baseball Player)
PO Box 1026
Livingston, AL 35470-1026, USA

Bowling, Andy (Athlete, Football Player)
7421 Straightstone Rd
Long Island, VA 24569-2945, USA

Bowling, Orbie (Athlete, Basketball Player)
10179 Frank Rd
Collierville, TN 38017-3623, USA

Bowling, Steve (Athlete, Baseball Player)
524 E 117th St S
Jenks, OK 74037-3618, USA

Bowling for Soup (Music Group)
c/o Staff Member *Agency Group Ltd, The (UK)*
361-373 City Rd
London EC1V 1PQ, UK

Bowman, Bob (Athlete, Baseball Player)
8340 Riesling Way
San Jose, CA 95135-1435, USA

Bowman, Elizabeth (Athlete, Golfer)
82 Davidson St
Chula Vista, CA 91910-3002, USA

Bowman, Ernie (Athlete, Baseball Player)
123 Carter Dr Apt 8
Johnson City, TN 37601-2973, USA

Bowman, Harry W (Business Person)
PO Box 410
Waukegan, IL 60079-0410, USA

Bowman, Jim (Athlete, Football Player)
12 Stony Field Rd
Norton, MA 02766-1143, USA

Bowman, Joshua (Actor)
c/o Duncan Millership *Management 360*
9111 Wilshire Blvd
Beverly Hills, CA 90210-5508, USA

Bowman, Ken (Athlete, Football Player)
2278 E Celosia Way
Oro Valley, AZ 85755-7166, USA

Bowman, Kirk (Athlete, Hockey Player)
740 Point Pelee Dr RR 1
Leamington, ON N8H 3V4, Canada

Bowman, Pasco M II (Judge)
811 Grand Blvd
Kansas City, MO 64106-1938, USA

Bowman, W Scott (Scotty) (Athlete, Coach, Hockey Player, Misc)
56 Halston Pkwy
East Amherst, NY 14051-1842, USA

Bownass, Jack (Athlete, Hockey Player)
PO Box 117 GD
Belair, MB R0E 0E0, Canada

Bownes, Fabien (Athlete, Football Player)
8127 149th Pl NE Unit B112
Redmond, WA 98052-6582, USA

Bowness, Rick (Athlete, Hockey Player)
10 Shadowstone Ln
Lawrence Township, NJ 08648-1027, USA

Bowsfield, Ted (Athlete, Baseball Player)
980 Briar Rose Ln
Nipomo, CA 93444-8989, USA

Bowyer, William (Artist)
12 Cleveland Ave Chiswick
London W4 1SN, UNITED KINGDOM (UK)

Bowyer Jr, Walter (Athlete, Football Player)
203 Main St N
Bethlehem, CT 06751-1400, USA

Boxberger, Loa (Bowler)
PO Box 708
Russell, KS 67665-0708, USA

Boxer, Barbara (Senator)
112 Hart Senate Ofc Building
Washington, DC 20510-0001, USA

Boxerbaum, David (Actor)
c/o Staff Member *Agency for the Performing Arts (APA-Nashville)*
3017 Poston Ave
Nashville, TN 37203-1313

Boxleitner, Bruce (Actor)
PO Box 5513
Sherman Oaks, CA 91413-5513, USA

Boy, Soulja (Musician)
c/o Chris Lighty *Violator Management*
36 W 25th St Fl 11
New York, NY 10010-2752, USA

Boy Hits Car (Music Group)
c/o Staff Member *Wind-up Records*
72 Madison Ave Fl 8
New York, NY 10016-8731, USA

Boyar, Lombardo (Actor)
526 N Larchmont Blvd # 201
Los Angeles, CA 90004-1300

Boyarsky, Jerry (Athlete, Football Player)
229 Boyarsky Rd
Scott Township, PA 18447-7710, USA

Boyce, Kim (Music Group)
200 Nathan Dr
Hollister, MO 65672-6123, USA

Boycott, Geoffrey (Cricketer)
Headingley Cricket Ground Leeds
Yorks LS6 3BY, UNITED KINGDOM (UK)

Boyd, Alan S (Misc, Secretary)
116 Fairview Ave N Unit 735
Seattle, WA 98109-5374, USA

Boyd, Billy (Actor)
c/o Sarah Jackson *Seven Summits Pictures & Management*
8906 W Olympic Blvd Ground Floor
Beverly Hills, CA 90211, USA

Boyd, Bob (Athlete, Football Player)
2105 Lansdowne Dr
Garland, TX 75040-3343, USA

Boyd, Brandon (Musician)
c/o Marlene Tsuchii *Creative Artists Agency (CAA-LA)*
2000 Avenue of the Stars Ste 100
Los Angeles, CA 90067-4705, USA

Boyd, Brent (Athlete, Football Player)
948 N Coast Highway 101 Apt 185
Encinitas, CA 92024-2078, USA

Boyd, Carrie Griffin (Stylist)
c/o Staff Member *Fifty8 Artists*
58 W Huron St
Chicago, IL 60654-3806, USA

Boyd, Cayden (Actor)
c/o Ellen Drantch-Billet *EDB Management*
11657 La Grange Ave
Los Angeles, CA 90025-5331, USA

Boyd, Cletis L (Clete) (Baseball Player)
2034 20th Avenue Pkwy
Indian Rocks Beach, FL 33785-2967, USA

Boyd, Davis (Oil Can) (Athlete, Baseball Player)
PO Box 8058
Meridian, MS 39303-8058, USA

Boyd, Dennis (Athlete, Baseball Player)
45 Swan St
East Providence, RI 02914-2406, USA

Boyd, Elmo (Athlete, Football Player)
848 Nicklin Ave
Piqua, OH 45356-1714, USA

Boyd, Fred (Athlete, Basketball Player)
10915 Open Trail Rd
Bakersfield, CA 93311-2892, USA

Boyd, Gary (Athlete, Baseball Player)
15308 Haas Ave
Gardena, CA 90249-4239, USA

Boyd, Greg (Baseball Player)
9 Inez Way
Stafford, VA 22554-5515, USA

Boyd, Greg P (Athlete, Football Player)
4021 N 59th St
Phoenix, AZ 85018-4614, USA

Boyd, Herbert W (Inventor, Misc)
PO Box 7318
Rancho Santa Fe, CA 92067-7318, USA

Boyd, James (Athlete, Football Player)
3355 Sweetwater Rd Apt 10204
Lawrenceville, GA 30044-8544, USA

Boyd, Jason (Athlete, Baseball Player)
7962 State Route 140
Edwardsville, IL 62025-6110, USA

Boyd, Jenna (Actor)
c/o Ellen Drantch-Billet *EDB Management*
11657 La Grange Ave
Los Angeles, CA 90025-5331, USA

Boyd, Lance (Stylist)
c/o Staff Member *Art House Management*
1548 16th St
Santa Monica, CA 90404-3309, USA

Boyd, Lynda (Actor)
c/o Michael Greene *Greene & Associates*
1901 Avenue Of The Stars Ste 130
Los Angeles, CA 90067-6030, USA

Boyd, Malcolm (Religious Leader, Writer)
1227 4th St
Santa Monica, CA 90401-1303, USA

Boyd, Malik (Athlete, Football Player)
3635 Mill Run Cir Apt 1518
Indianapolis, IN 46214-5068, USA

Boyd, Paul D (Nobel Prize Laureate)
1033 Somera Rd
Los Angeles, CA 90077-2625, USA

Boyd, Randy (Athlete, Hockey Player)
1769 Blackwillow Dr
Marietta, GA 30066-1954, USA

Boyd, Richard A (Misc)
2100 Gardiner Ln
Louisville, KY 40205-2962, USA

Boyd, Robert (Athlete, Golfer)
828 Robert E Lee Dr
Wilmington, NC 28412-7138, USA

Boyd, Stephen (Athlete, Football Player)
1805 Golf Ridge Dr
Bloomfield Hills, MI 48302-1721, USA

Boyens, Philippa (Writer)
c/o Nick Reed *International Creative Management (ICM-LA)*
10250 Constellation Blvd Fl 7
Los Angeles, CA 90067-6207, USA

Boyer, Blaine (Athlete, Baseball Player)
3672 Chattahoochee Summit Dr SE
Atlanta, GA 30339-3254, USA

Boyer, Brant (Athlete, Football Player)
1683 Old Lake Ln
Kaysville, UT 84037-3231, USA

Boyer, Cloyd (Athlete, Baseball Player)
14528 County Road 210
Jasper, MO 64755, USA

Boyer, Mark (Athlete, Football Player)
21942 Kaneohe Ln
Huntington Beach, CA 92646-7828, USA

Boyer, Verdi (Athlete, Football Player)
300 N Lake Ave Ste 930
Pasadena, CA 91101-4106, USA

Boyer, Wally (Athlete, Hockey Player)
400 Manly St
Midland, ON L4R 3E3, Canada

Boyes, Brad (Athlete, Hockey Player)
42 8th St Apt 3305
Charlestown, MA 02129-4220, USA

Boyett, Lon (Athlete, Football Player)
44361 Nolina Cir
Lancaster, CA 93536-6252, USA

Boyette, Garland (Athlete, Football Player)
4003 E Valley Dr
Missouri City, TX 77459-4322, USA

Boykin, Deral (Athlete, Football Player)
350 Silver Oaks Dr Apt 7
Kent, OH 44240-4165, USA

Boykin, Gerda (Athlete, Golfer)
3019 Colonnade Ct NW
Albuquerque, NM 87107-2961, USA

Boykin, William G (General)
Defense Dept Pentagon
Washington, DC 20301-0001, USA

Boyko, Darren (Athlete, Hockey Player)
1341 Wolseley Ave
Winnipeg, MB R3G 1H8, Canada

Boylan, Eileen (Actor)
c/o Staff Member *Stone Manners Salners Agency (LA)*
9911 W Pico Blvd Ste 1400
Los Angeles, CA 90035-2715, USA

Boylan, Jeanne
c/o Staff Member *WmE2 (WMA-LA)*
1 William Morris Pl
Beverly Hills, CA 90212-4261, USA

Boylan, Jim (Athlete, Football Player)
13155 Portofino Dr
Del Mar, CA 92014-3827, USA

Boyland, Dorian (Athlete, Baseball Player)
15570 SW Cynthia Ln
Beaverton, OR 97007-6867, USA

Boyle, Clune Charlotte (Swimmer)
50 Browns Grv # 31
Scottsville, NY 14546-1302, USA

Boyle, Dan (Athlete, Hockey Player)
18232 Daves Ave
Monte Sereno, CA 95030-3112, USA

Boyle, Danny (Director)
c/o Robert Newman *WmE2 (Endeavor-LA)*
9601 Wilshire Blvd Fl 3
Beverly Hills, CA 90210-5219, USA

Boyle, Jim (Athlete, Football Player)
920 Beechmeadow Ln
Cincinnati, OH 45238-4350, USA

Boyle, Lara Flynn (Actor)
c/o Gina Rugolo-Judd *Rugolo Entertainment*
195 S Beverly Dr Ste 400
Beverly Hills, CA 90212-3044, USA

Boyle, Lisa (Actor, Model)
7336 Santa Monica Blvd # 776
West Hollywood, CA 90046-6616, USA

Boyle, Susan (Musician, Reality TV Star)
5 Riddoch Hill View Blackburn
Bathgate EH47 7LZ, UK

Boyle, T Coraghessan (Writer)
English Dept
Los Angeles, CA 90089-0001, USA

Boyle, Willard S. (Nobel Prize Laureate)
1326 Lower Water St
Halifax, NS B3J 3R3, Canada

Boyles, Harry (Athlete, Baseball Player)
RR 6 Box 17
Eufaula, OK 74432-9153, USA

Boynes, Winford (Athlete, Basketball Player)
8979 Haflinger Way
Elk Grove, CA 95757-3262, USA

Boynton, George (Athlete, Football Player)
917 Sartain Dr
Andrews, TX 79714-3817, USA

Boynton, John (Athlete, Football Player)
203 Pratt St
Pikeville, TN 37367, USA

Boynton, Nick (Athlete, Hockey Player)
3326 N Valencia Ln
Phoenix, AZ 85018-6611, USA

Boynton, Robert M (Doctor, Misc)
6632 Grulla St
Carlsbad, CA 92009-5315, USA

Boynton, Sandra (Artist, Writer)
c/o Staff Member *Simon & Schuster*
1230 Avenue of the Americas Fl CONC1
New York, NY 10020-1586, USA

Boys Like Girls (Music Group)
c/o Staff Member *Primary Talent International (UK)*
The Primary Building 10-11 Jockeys Fields
London WC1R 4BN, UK

Boysaw, Gregory (Athlete, Football Player)
3421 Derby Dr
Jonesboro, AR 72404-7796, USA

boysetsfire (Music Group)
c/o Staff Member *Wind-up Records*
72 Madison Ave Fl 8
New York, NY 10016-8731, USA

Boyz II Men (Music Group)
c/o Joann Mignano *Krupp Kommunications*
59 W 19th St Rm 4C
New York, NY 10011-4245, USA

Bozarth, Marci (Athlete, Golfer)
2929 Buffalo Speedway Unit 1612
Houston, TX 77098-1715, USA

Boze, Marshall (Athlete, Baseball Player)
13139 Windy Lea Ln
Huntersville, NC 28078-2230, USA

Bozek, Steve (Athlete, Hockey Player)
8410 E Whispering Wind Dr
Scottsdale, AZ 85255-2863, USA

Bozilovic, Ivana (Actor)
c/o Jon Orlando *WNWN Media*
348 Hauser Blvd # PH414
Los Angeles, CA 90036-3276, USA

Boznic, Josip Cardinal (Religious Leader)
Kaptol 31 PP 553
Zagreb Hrvatska 10001, CROATIA

Bozo, Laura (Actor)
c/o Staff Member *Telemundo*
2470 W 8th Ave
Hialeah, FL 33010-2000, USA

Bozza, Anthony (Writer)
c/o Richard Abate *3 Arts Entertainment - NY*
49 W 27th St Fl 5
New York, NY 10001-6936, USA

BR5-49 (Music Group, Musician)
c/o Staff Member *Creative Artists Agency (CAA-TN)*
3310 W End Ave Fl 5
Nashville, TN 37203-1028, USA

Braase, Ordell (Athlete, Football Player)
31 Lambourne Rd Unit 307
Towson, MD 21204-2823, USA

Brabham, Daniel (Athlete, Football Player)
42161 Greenfield Xing
Prairieville, LA 70769-6046, USA

Brabham, John A (Jack) (Race Car Driver)
5 Ruxley Lane Ewell
Surrey KT19 0JB, UNITED KINGDOM (UK)

Brabham, Sir Jack (Race Car Driver)
Suite 404 Bag No 1
Robina Town Centre, Queenstown 4230, Australia

Bracco, Lorraine (Actor)
c/o Heather Reynolds *One Entertainment (NY)*
12 W 57th St PH 1
New York, NY 10019-3900, USA

Brace, William F (Geophysicist, Misc, Physicist)
49 Liberty St
Concord, MA 01742-1715, USA

Bracelin, Greg (Athlete, Football Player)
5465 Calumet Ave
La Jolla, CA 92037-7604, USA

Bracewell, Ronald N (Engineer)
PO Box 8780
San Jose, CA 95155-8780, USA

Bracey, Steve (Athlete, Basketball Player)
560 Lincoln Ave
Brooklyn, NY 11208-3256, USA

Bracher, Karl D (Historian, Misc, Politician)
Stationsweg 17
Bonn 53127, GERMANY

Bracht, Stephanie (Athlete, Golfer)
2004 Delancey Dr
Norman, OK 73071-3872, USA

Brack, Kenny (Race Car Driver)
4601 Lyman Dr
Hilliard, OH 43026-1249, USA

Brack, Reginald K Jr (Publisher)
12 Huntzinger Dr
Greenwich, CT 06831-4110, USA

Bracken, Don (Athlete, Football Player)
107 1/2 Malaga Ave
Birmingham, AL 35209-2024, USA

Brackenbury, Curt (Athlete, Hockey Player)
76212 Evergreen Bluff Dr
South Haven, MI 49090-1662, USA

Brackens, Tony (Athlete, Football Player)
193 Private Road 407
Fairfield, TX 75840-6022, USA

Brackett, Griffin (Model)
860 NE 73rd St
Miami, FL 33138-5228

Brackett, M L (Athlete, Football Player)
1216 Monte Vista Dr
Gadsden, AL 35904-3643, USA

Brackins, Charles (Athlete, Football Player)
8418 Bucroft St Apt A
Houston, TX 77029-3986, USA

Bradberry, Allyson (Stylist)
c/o Staff Member *Arlene Wilson Management*
807 N Jefferson St # 200
Milwaukee, WI 53202-8150, USA

Bradberry, Gary (Race Car Driver)
6006 Ball Park Rd
Thomasville, NC 27360-7942, USA

Bradbury, Allyson (Stylist)
c/o Staff Member *Directions USA*
3717 W Market St Ste C
Greensboro, NC 27403-1155, USA

Bradbury, Janette Lane (Actor)
10817 Kling St
Toluca Lake, CA 91602-1488, USA

Bradbury, Ray D (Writer)
10265 Cheviot Dr
Los Angeles, CA 90064-4737, USA

Braddy, Johanna (Actor)
c/o Julian Rosenberg *Tower 10 Entertainment*
412 S Willaman Dr Apt 507
Los Angeles, CA 90048-3990, USA

Brademas, John (Educator)
Presindent's Emeritus Office
New York, NY 10012, USA

Braden, Jeannine (Stylist)
c/o Staff Member *Luxe*
6442 Santa Monica Blvd Ste 200B
Los Angeles, CA 90038-1530, USA

Braden, Vic (Coach, Tennis Player)
22000 Trabuco Canyon Rd
Trabuco Canyon, CA 92678, USA

Bradey, Don (Athlete, Baseball Player)
330 Council Bluff Pkwy
Murfreesboro, TN 37127-8317, USA

Bradford, Barbara Taylor (Writer)
435 E 52nd St # 6
New York, NY 10022-6445, USA

Bradford, Buddy (Athlete, Baseball Player)
6440 Springpark Ave
Los Angeles, CA 90056-2222, USA

Bradford, Chad (Athlete, Baseball Player)
3867 Bill Downing Rd
Raymond, MS 39154-8097, USA

Bradford, Jesse (Actor)
c/o Jason Barrett *Alchemy Entertainment*
7024 Melrose Ave Ste 420
Los Angeles, CA 90038-3394, USA

Bradford, Paul (Athlete, Football Player)
2239 Pulgas Ave
East Palo Alto, CA 94303-1755, USA

Bradford, Richard (Actor)
2511 Canyon Dr
Los Angeles, CA 90068-2415, USA

Bradford, Ronnie (Athlete, Football Player)
985 Allen Lake Ln
Suwanee, GA 30024-4179, USA

Bradford, Sam (Athlete, Football Player)
c/o Tom Condon *CAA - St. Louis*
222 S Central Ave Ste 1008
Saint Louis, MO 63105-3509, USA

Bradford, William (Business Person)
Lincoln Plaza 500 N Akard St
Dallas, TX 75201, USA

Bradfute, Byron (Athlete, Football Player)
939 Moonglow Ave
New Braunfels, TX 78130-6081, USA

Bradlee, Benjamin C (Editor)
3014 N St NW
Washington, DC 20007-3404, USA

Bradley, Alonzo (Athlete, Basketball Player)
1713 Briaroaks Dr
Flower Mound, TX 75028-3482, USA

Bradley, Bert (Athlete, Baseball Player)
300 N Ohio St
Toledo, IL 62468-1142, USA

Bradley, Bob (Coach, Soccer Player)
980 N Michigan Ave Ste 1998
Chicago, IL 60611-7504, USA

Bradley, Brian (Athlete, Hockey Player)
6417 E Maclaurin Dr
Tampa, FL 33647-1171, USA

Bradley, Bruce (Athlete, Misc)
262 Saint Joseph Ave
Long Beach, CA 90803-1720, USA

Bradley, Carlos (Athlete, Football Player)
1316 E Cliveden St
Philadelphia, PA 19119-3948, USA

Bradley, Charles (Athlete, Basketball Player)
10810 Mountshire Cir
Highlands Ranch, CO 80126-7502, USA

Bradley, Christopher (Actor)
c/o Staff Member *Ford/Robert Black Agency*
4032 N Miller Rd Ste 104
Scottsdale, AZ 85251-4572, USA

Bradley, Dave (Athlete, Football Player)
30 Hillside Dr
Lewistown, PA 17044-9307, USA

Bradley, Dick (Cartoonist, Misc)
10176 Corporate Square Dr Ste 200
Saint Louis, MO 63132-2924, USA

Bradley, Doug (Actor)
c/o Elaine Murphy *Elaine Murphy Associates*
50 High St Suite 1
London E11 2RJ, UK

Bradley, Dudley (Athlete, Basketball Player)
9830 Clanford Rd
Randallstown, MD 21133-2508, USA

Bradley, Ed (Athlete, Football Player)
PO Box 1313
Winston Salem, NC 27102-1313, USA

Bradley, Ed (Athlete, Football Player)
206 Mossy Oak Dr
Winston Salem, NC 27127-9234, USA

Bradley, Frank (Baseball Player)
PO Box 516
Benton, LA 71006-0516, USA

Bradley, Fred (Athlete, Baseball Player)
4540 Layman Ave
Pico Rivera, CA 90660-2022, USA

Bradley, Freddie (Athlete, Football Player)
229 S Ventura Rd
Port Hueneme, CA 93041-3368, USA

Bradley, Gordon (Coach, Soccer Player)
15681 Hunton Ln
Haymarket, VA 20169-1733, USA

Bradley, Kathleen (Actor)
11365 Ventura Blvd Ste 100
Studio City, CA 91604-3148, USA

Bradley, Luther (Athlete, Football Player)
19575 Stratford Rd
Detroit, MI 48221-1848, USA

Bradley, Mark (Athlete, Baseball Player)
PO Box 27
Water Valley, KY 42085-0027, USA

Bradley, Michael (Athlete, Basketball Player)
6150 Blackjack Ct N
Punta Gorda, FL 33982-9606, USA

Bradley, Michael (Mike) (Athlete, Golfer)
17914 Burnt Oak Ln
Lithia, FL 33547-4802, USA

Bradley, Milton (Athlete, Baseball Player)
5359 Oak Park Ave
Encino, CA 91316-2627, USA

Bradley, Otha (Athlete, Football Player)
PO Box 59071
Los Angeles, CA 90059-0071, USA

Bradley, Phil (Athlete, Baseball Player)
6950 Seminole Ct
Columbia, MO 65203-9669, USA

Bradley, Rebecca (Athlete, Golfer)
7501 Alderwood Dr
Garland, TX 75044-2521, USA

Bradley, Robert A (Physicist)
2465 S Downing St
Denver, CO 80210-5822, USA

Bradley, Ryan (Athlete, Baseball Player)
3454 Alder Pl
Chino Hills, CA 91709-2005, USA

Bradley, Scott (Athlete, Baseball Player)
43 Chicory Ln
Pennington, NJ 08534-1926, USA

Bradley, Shawn (Athlete, Basketball Player)
PO Box 744
Castle Dale, UT 84513-0744, USA

Bradley, Tom (Athlete, Baseball Player)
4104 Woodberry St
University Park, MD 20782-1169, USA

Bradley, William W (Bill) (Athlete, Basketball Player, Politician)
711 5th Ave Fl 9
New York, NY 10022-3168, USA

Bradley Jr, Harold (Athlete, Football Player)
1302 Asbury Ave
Evanston, IL 60201-4108, USA

Bradshaw (Wrestler)
139 Denny Ln
Athens, TX 75751

Bradshaw, David (Stylist)
c/o Staff Member *Camilla Lowther Managment (CLM Represents)*
30-32 Ericsson Pl
New York, NY 10013, USA

Bradshaw, James A (Athlete, Football Player)
449 Tresham Rd
Gahanna, OH 43230-2224, USA

Bradshaw, John (Actor, Director, Writer)
c/o Victoria Wisdom *Wisdom Literary*
287 S Robertson Blvd Ste 258
Beverly Hills, CA 90211-2810, USA

Bradshaw, Morris (Athlete, Football Player)
82 Steuben Bay
Alameda, CA 94502-6406, USA

Bradshaw, Terry (Athlete, Football Player, Sportscaster)
12221 Merit Dr Ste 70
Dallas, TX 75251-2202

Brady, Beau (Actor)
c/o Darren Gray *Darren Gray Management*
2 Marston Ln Portsmouth
Hampshire PO3 5TW, UK

Brady, Brian (Athlete, Baseball Player)
920 W 23rd St
Odessa, TX 79763-2504, USA

Brady, Charles E (Astronaut)
92 Red Wing Ln
Eastsound, WA 98245-8517, USA

Brady, Doug (Athlete, Baseball Player)
5878 Iron Bridge Rd
Chatham, IL 62629-8014, USA

Brady, Ed (Athlete, Football Player)
5755 White Path Ln
Liberty Twp, OH 45011-1273, USA

Brady, Jeff (Athlete, Football Player)
16411 Burniston Dr
Tampa, FL 33647-2790, USA

Brady, Jim (Athlete, Baseball Player)
1072 Meadow View Ln
Saint Augustine, FL 32092-1055, USA

Brady, Kevin (Congressman, Politician)
301 Cannon Hob
Washington, DC 20515-1701, USA

Brady, Kyle (Athlete, Football Player)
2221 Alicia Ln
Atlantic Beach, FL 32233-5975, USA

Brady, Neil (Athlete, Hockey Player)
125-4300 26 Street Attn Warehouse Manager NE
Calgary, AB T1Y 7H7, Canada

Brady, Nicholas F (Ex-Senator, Politician, Secretary)
1133 Connecticut Ave NW
Washington, DC 20036-4305, USA

Brady, Pat (Cartoonist)
200 Madison Ave
New York, NY 10016-3903, USA

Brady, Patrick (Athlete, Football Player)
8990 Lombardi Rd
Reno, NV 89511-9537, USA

Brady, Patrick H (War Hero)
2809 179th Ave E
Sumner, WA 98391-6419, USA

Brady, Ray (Correspondent)
524 W 57th St
New York, NY 10019-2930, USA

Brady, Robert (Congressman, Politician)
102 Cannon Hob
Washington, DC 20515-0516, USA

Brady, Roscoe O (Misc)
6026 Valerian Ln
Rockville, MD 20852-3410, USA

Brady, Sarah (Activist)
1225 I St NW Ste 1100
Washington, DC 20005-3914, USA

Brady, Tina (Stylist)
58 W Huron St
Chicago, IL 60654-3806, USA

Brady, Tom (Actor)
c/o Stuart Fry *WmE2 (Endeavor-LA)*
9601 Wilshire Blvd Fl 3
Beverly Hills, CA 90210-5219, USA

Brady, Tom (Athlete, Football Player)
c/o Don Yee *Yee & Dubin Sports, LLC*
725 S Figueroa St Ste 3085
Los Angeles, CA 90017-5430, USA

Brady, Wayne (Actor, Comedian, Musician, Producer)
c/o Stacy Mark *WmE2 (Endeavor-LA)*
9601 Wilshire Blvd Fl 3
Beverly Hills, CA 90210-5219, USA

Braeden, Eric (Actor)
c/o Staff Member *Diverse Talent Group*
9911 W Pico Blvd Ste 340W
Los Angeles, CA 90035-2712, USA

Braff, Zach (Actor, Writer)
c/o Sandra Chang *Industry Entertainment Partners*
955 Carrillo Dr Ste 300
Los Angeles, CA 90048-5400, USA

Braga, Alice (Actor)
c/o Will Ward *ROAR (LA)*
9701 Wilshire Blvd Fl 8
Beverly Hills, CA 90212-2008, USA

Braga, Brannon (Writer)
c/o Staff Member *WmE2 (Endeavor-LA)*
9601 Wilshire Blvd Fl 3
Beverly Hills, CA 90210-5219, USA

Braga, Sonia (Actor)
c/o Joe Dapello *Schreck Rose Dapello Adams & Hurwitz*
1790 Broadway Fl 20
New York, NY 10019-1412, USA

Bragan, Bobby (Athlete, Baseball Player, Coach)
3116 W 6th St
Fort Worth, TX 76107-2712, USA

Bragg, Billy (Musician)
6 Bravington Road #6
London W9 3AH, UNITED KINGDOM (UK)

Bragg, Darrell B (Misc)
Vancouver BC V6T 2AZ, CANADA

Bragg, Darren (Athlete, Baseball Player)
163 Patriot Rd
Southbury, CT 06488-1274, USA

Bragg, Donald G (Don) (Athlete, Track Athlete)
554 Mt Dell Dr
Clayton, CA 94517-1503, USA

Bragg, Melvyn (Writer)
12 Hampstead Hill Gardens
London NW3 2PL, UNITED KINGDOM (UK)

Bragg, Mike (Athlete, Football Player)
PO Box 4842
Falls Church, VA 22044-0842, USA

Braggs, Byron (Athlete, Football Player)
19469 Mill Dam Pl
Leesburg, VA 20176-8428, USA

Braggs, Glenn (Athlete, Baseball Player)
28369 Falcon Crest Dr
Canyon Country, CA 91351-5016, USA

Braggs, Stephen (Athlete, Football Player)
120 Power House Rd
Lawndale, NC 28090-7407, USA

Bragnalo, Rick (Athlete, Hockey Player)
515 Christine St E
Thunder Bay, ON P7E 4P3, Canada

Bragonier, Dennis (Athlete, Football Player)
PO Box 1206
Roseville, CA 95678-8206, USA

Braham, Rich (Athlete, Football Player)
19 Miramichi Trl
Morgantown, WV 26508-2928, USA

Brahaney, Thomas F (Tom) (Athlete, Football Player)
17 Winchester Ct
Midland, TX 79705-6360, USA

Brainin, Nobert (Musician)
19 Prowse Ave Busbey Heath
Herts WD2 1JS, UNITED KINGDOM (UK)

Brainville, Ives (Actor)
34 Cours de Vincennes
Paris F-75012, France

Brakes, The (Music Group)
c/o Staff Member *Paradigm (Monterey)*
404 W Franklin St
Monterey, CA 93940-2303, USA

Bramall of Busfield, Edwin N W (Misc)
Westminster
London SW1A 0PW, UNITED KINGDOM (UK)

Bramhall, Mark (Actor)
c/o Alexandra Karrys *Divine Management*
3822 Latrobe St
Los Angeles, CA 90031-1446

Bramlett, John (Athlete, Football Player)
159 Cotton Ridge Cv S
Cordova, TN 38018-7409, USA

Brammell, Abby (Actor)
c/o Robert (Rob) Gomez *Precision Entertainment*
6338 Wilshire Blvd
Los Angeles, CA 90048-5002, USA

Brammer, Mark (Athlete, Football Player)
1680 Amherst St
Buffalo, NY 14214-2002, USA

Branagh, Kenneth (Actor, Director)
c/o Judy Hofflund *Hofflund/Polone*
9465 Wilshire Blvd Ste 420
Beverly Hills, CA 90212-2603, USA

Branca, John G (Attorney, Attorney General, General)
1801 Century Park W
Los Angeles, CA 90067-6409, USA

Branca, Ralph (Athlete, Baseball Player)
88 Biltmore Ave
Rye, NY 10580, USA

Brancaccio, David
2100 Crystal Dr
Arlington, VA 22202-3784, USA

Brancati, Paula (Actor)
c/o Shari Quallenburg 464 King St E
Toronto, ON M5A 1L7, CANADA

Brancato, Al (Athlete, Baseball Player)
108 Green Valley Rd
Upper Darby, PA 19082-1308, USA

Brancato, John D (JD) (Producer, Writer)
c/o Staff Member *Broder Webb Chervin Silbermann Agency, The (BWCS)*
10250 Constellation Blvd
Los Angeles, CA 90067-6200, USA

Brancato Jr, Lillo (Actor)
c/o Craig Shapiro *International Creative Management (ICM-LA)*
10250 Constellation Blvd Fl 7
Los Angeles, CA 90067-6207, USA

Branch, Adrian (Athlete, Basketball Player)
18008 Fence Post Ct
Gaithersburg, MD 20877-3794, USA

Branch, Clifford (Cliff) (Athlete, Coach, Football Coach, Football Player)
2071 Stonefield Ln
Santa Rosa, CA 95403-0952, USA

Branch, Harvey (Athlete, Baseball Player)
4995 Jolly Dr
Memphis, TN 38109-7123, USA

Branch, Michelle (Musician, Songwriter)
c/o Jeff Rabhan *Three Ring Projects*
111 Westwood Pl Ste 101
Brentwood, TN 37027-5057, USA

Branch, Reggie (Athlete, Football Player)
515 San Lanta Cir
Sanford, FL 32771-5903, USA

Branch, Roy (Athlete, Baseball Player)
5322 Terry Ave
Saint Louis, MO 63120-2021, USA

Branch, Vanessa (Actor)
c/o Staff Member *3 Arts Entertainment Inc*
9460 Wilshire Blvd Fl 7
Beverly Hills, CA 90212-2713, USA

Branch, William B (Writer)
53 Cortlandt Ave
New Rochelle, NY 10801-2032, USA

Branco, Antonio (Stylist)
c/o Celebrity Stylist *Bryan Bantry*
900 Broadway Ste 400
New York, NY 10003-1239, USA

Brand, Colette (Skier)
Rigistr 24
Baar 6340, SWITZERLAND

Brand, Daniel (Dan) (Wrestler)
4321 Bridgeview Dr
Oakland, CA 94602-1910, USA

Brand, Elton (Athlete, Basketball Player)
c/o Staff Member *Boston Celtics*
151 Merrimac St
Boston, MA 02114-4714, USA

Brand, Glen (Wrestler)
PO Box 6069
Omaha, NE 68106-0069, USA

Brand, Jolene (Actor)
8321 Beverly Blvd
Los Angeles, CA 90048-2607, USA

Brand, Joshua (Producer)
c/o Staff Member *WmE2 (WMA-LA)*
1 William Morris Pl
Beverly Hills, CA 90212-4261, USA

Brand, Julie (Athlete, Golfer)
7546 Gulf Brook Dr
Remsen, NY 13438-4294, USA

Brand, Myles (Educator)
President's Office
Bloomington, IN 47405, USA

Brand, Neville (Actor)
c/o Staff Member *International Creative Management (ICM-LA)*
10250 Constellation Blvd Fl 7
Los Angeles, CA 90067-6207, USA

Brand, Oscar (Musician, Songwriter, Writer)
141 Baker Hill Rd
Great Neck, NY 11023-1715, USA

Brand, Robert (Designer)
508 W End Ave
New York, NY 10024-4328, USA

Brand, Ron (Athlete, Baseball Player)
4421 Staten Island Dr
Plano, TX 75024-3867, USA

Brand, Russell (Actor, Writer)
c/o Holly Shakoor *42West (LA)*
11400 W Olympic Blvd Ste 1100
Los Angeles, CA 90064-1579, USA

Brand, Steven (Actor)
c/o Brian Medavoy *Jackson-Medavoy Entertainment*
10203 Santa Monica Blvd Fl 4
Los Angeles, CA 90067-6439, USA

Brand, Vance D (Astronaut)
PO Box 273
Edwards, CA 93523-0273, USA

Brandauer, Klaus Maria (Actor)
Paul Lincke Ufer 42-43
Berlin 10999, GERMANY

Brandenburg, Mark (Athlete, Baseball Player)
152 Cottonwood Dr
Coppell, TX 75019-2511, USA

Brandenstein, Daniel C (Astronaut)
15203 Greenleaf Ln
Houston, TX 77062-3672, USA

Brandes, John (Athlete, Football Player)
905 Ashland Ct
Mansfield, TX 76063-3802, USA

Brandi (Model)
23 Watts St
New York, NY 10013, USA

Brandler, Shellylyn (Actor)
c/o Simon Millar *Rumble Media*
1620 Broadway Ste C
Santa Monica, CA 90404-2777, USA

Brandon, Barbara (Cartoonist)
4520 Main St
Kansas City, MO 64111-1876, USA

Brandon, Clark (Actor)
28035 Dorothy Dr Ste 210A
Agoura, CA 91301-2685, USA

Brandon, Darrell (Athlete, Baseball Player)
590 White Cliff Dr
Plymouth, MA 02360-1483, USA

Brandon, Jeb (Actor)
c/o Staff Member *WmE2 (Endeavor-LA)*
9601 Wilshire Blvd Fl 3
Beverly Hills, CA 90210-5219, USA

Brandon, John (Actor)
3350 Barham Blvd
Los Angeles, CA 90068-1404, USA

Brandon, Michael (Actor)
c/o Joel Dean *TalentWorks (LA)*
3500 W Olive Ave Ste 1400
Burbank, CA 91505-5512, USA

Brandon, Michael (Athlete, Football Player)
910 E Green St
Perry, FL 32347-3514, USA

Brands, Tom (Wrestler)
4494 Taft Ave SE
Iowa City, IA 52240-8166, USA

Brands, X (Actor)
17171 Roscoe Blvd # 104
Northridge, CA 91325-4060, USA

Brandt, Hank (Actor)
610 Santa Monica Blvd Ste 202
Santa Monica, CA 90401-1645, USA

Brandt, Jackie (Athlete, Baseball Player)
452 S 78th St Apt 2
Omaha, NE 68114-4547, USA

Brandt, Jim (Athlete, Football Player)
714 Zumbro Dr NW
Rochester, MN 55901-2379, USA

Brandt, Jon (Musician)
509 Hartnell St
Monterey, CA 93940-2825, USA

Brandt, Paul (Musician)
c/o Staff Member *WmE2 (WMA-LA)*
1 William Morris Pl
Beverly Hills, CA 90212-4261, USA

Brandt, Stella (Stylist)
c/o Staff Member *Anyway Productions*
870 Avenue of the Americas
New York, NY 10001-4111, USA

Brandt, Victor (Actor)
733 Seward St PH
Los Angeles, CA 90038-3503, USA

Branduardi, Angelo (Musician)
c/o Faustini Srl. Via Veneto, 18
Pontoglio I-25 037, Italy

Brandy, J C (Actor)
8285 W Sunset Blvd Ste 1
West Hollywood, CA 90046-2420, USA

Brandywine, Marcia (Correspondent)
743 Huntley Dr
Los Angeles, CA 90069-5008, USA

Brannagh, Brigid (Actor)
c/o Adam Levine *Levine Okwu Erickson Management*
9601 Wilshire Blvd Fl 3
Beverly Hills, CA 90210-5219, USA

Brannan, Charles F (Secretary)
3131 E Alameda Ave
Denver, CO 80209-3409, USA

Brannan, Solomon (Athlete, Football Player)
2500 Cascade Rd SW
Atlanta, GA 30311-3228, USA

Brannon, Ronald (Religious Leader)
PO Box 50434
Indianapolis, IN 46250-0434, USA

Branshaw, David (Athlete, Golfer)
16220 Sierra De Avila
Tampa, FL 33613-5221, USA

Branson, Brad (Athlete, Basketball Player)
7419 Cortes Dr
Houston, TX 77083-3617, USA

Branson, Jeff (Athlete, Baseball Player)
10749 Spokane Ct
Union, KY 41091-7160, USA

Branson, Jeff Branson (Actor)
c/o Robert Attermann *Abrams Artists Agency (LA)*
9200 W Sunset Blvd PH 11
Los Angeles, CA 90069-3601, USA

Branson, Jesse (Athlete, Basketball Player)
309 Forest Dr
Graham, NC 27253-4405, USA

Branson, Laura (Stylist)
c/o Staff Member *Judy Inc*
1 Yorkville Ave
Toronto ON M4W 1L1, Canada

Branson, Sir Richard (Business Person)
c/o Staff Member *Virgin Records (UK)*
Kensal House 553-579 Harrow Rd
London W1O 4RH, United Kingdom

Branstad, Terry (Governor)
1007 E Grand Ave
Des Moines, IA 50319-1001, USA

Brant, Marshall (Athlete, Baseball Player)
604 Scotland Dr
Santa Rosa, CA 95409-4419, USA

Brant, Tim (Sportscaster)
77 W 66th St
New York, NY 10023-6201, USA

Brantley, Betsy (Actor)
c/o Staff Member *Mitchell K Stubbs & Assoc (MKS)*
8675 Washington Blvd Ste 203
Culver City, CA 90232-7486, USA

Brantley, Chris (Athlete, Football Player)
257 Hamilton Rd
Teaneck, NJ 07666-6367, USA

Brantley, Cliff (Athlete, Baseball Player)
90 Grandview Ave
Staten Island, NY 10303-2000, USA

Brantley, Jeff (Athlete, Baseball Player)
104 Cherry Laurel Cv
Ridgeland, MS 39157-8643, USA

Brantley, John (Athlete, Football Player)
328 Jefferson Rd
Bishop, GA 30621-1517, USA

Brantley, Mickey (Athlete, Baseball Player)
3095 SW Boxwood Cir
Port Saint Lucie, FL 34953-6971, USA

Brantley, Ollie (Athlete, Baseball Player)
215 S Alabama St
Marianna, AR 72360-2578, USA

Brantley, Rick (Musician)
c/o Staff Member *Paradigm (Monterey)*
404 W Franklin St
Monterey, CA 93940-2303, USA

Brantley, Scot (Athlete, Football Player)
11309 Galleria Dr
Tampa, FL 33618-8748, USA

Branton, Gene (Athlete, Football Player)
7008 Hazelhurst Ct
Tampa, FL 33615-2945, USA

Branyan, Russell (Athlete, Baseball Player)
13400 Osmond Rd
Burton, OH 44021-9519, USA

Brasar, Per-Olov (Athlete, Hockey Player)
Heden 99
Leksand S-79329, Sweden

Brasco, Jim (Athlete, Basketball Player)
225 W Neck Rd
Huntington, NY 11743-2458, USA

Brashares, Ann (Writer)
c/o Jennifer Rudolph Walsh *WmE2 (WMA-NY)*
1 William Morris Pl
Beverly Hills, CA 90212-4261, USA

Brashear, Carl (Misc)
3 Stuttaford Dr
Sandston, VA 23150-1434, USA

Braslow, Paul (Artist)
567 Virginia Dr
Belvedere Tiburon, CA 94920-1336, USA

Brassette, Amy (Actor)
c/o Marv Dauer *Marv Dauer Management*
11661 San Vicente Blvd Ste 104
Los Angeles, CA 90049-5150, USA

Brasseur, Claude (Actor)
20 Ave Rapp
Paris 75007, FRANCE

Brathwaite, Nicholas (Prime Minister)
Saint George's, GRENADA

Bratkowski, Edmund R (Zeke) (Athlete, Coach, Football Player)
224 Anchors Lake Dr N
Santa Rosa Beach, FL 32459-4106, USA

Bratt, Benjamin (Actor)
c/o Staff Member *Dontanville/Frattaroli (D/F)*
270 Lafayette St Ste 402
New York, NY 10012-3327, USA

Bratton, Creed (Musician)
11761 E Speedway Blvd
Tucson, AZ 85748-2017, USA

Bratton, Jason (Athlete, Football Player)
1104 Regal Oak Dr
Longview, TX 75604-2141, USA

Bratton, Joseph K (General)
5902 Blakeford Dr
Windermere, FL 34786-5601, USA

Bratton, William J (Lawyer)
150 S Los Angeles St
Los Angeles, CA 90012, USA

Bratz, Mike (Athlete, Basketball Player)
7503 Tillman Hill Rd
Colleyville, TX 76034-6929, USA

Bratzke, Chad (Athlete, Football Player)
10850 Ruby Ct
Carmel, IN 46032-9303, USA

Brauer, Arik (Artist)
Schillerplatz 3
Vienna 1010, AUSTRIA

Braugher, Andre (Actor)
c/o Jennifer Allen *Viewpoint Inc*
8820 Wilshire Blvd Ste 220
Beverly Hills, CA 90211-2622, USA

Brauman, John (Misc)
849 Tolman Dr
Palo Alto, CA 94305-1025, USA

Braun, Allen (Scientist)
9000 Rockville Pike
Bethesda, MD 20892-0001, USA

Braun, Carl (Athlete, Basketball Player, Coach)
5603 SE Foxcross Pl
Stuart, FL 34997-8044, USA

Braun, Colin (Race Car Driver)
c/o Staff Member *Roush Fenway Racing Team*
4600 Roush Pl NW
Concord, NC 28027-7116, USA

Braun, John (Athlete, Baseball Player)
4711 Westerly Ct
Oceanside, CA 92056-3001, USA

Braun, Lillian Jackson (Writer)
2 Tudor Pl
New York, NY 10017, USA

Braun, Nicholas (Actor)
c/o Staff Member *Levine Okwu Erickson Management*
6363 Wilshire Blvd Ste 300
Los Angeles, CA 90048-5729, USA

Braun, Pinkas (Actor, Director)
Unterdorf 8261
Hemishofen/SH, SWITZERLAND

Braun, Richard L (War Hero)
1912 Whittles Wood Rd
Williamsburg, VA 23185-7697, USA

Braun, Rick (Musician)
c/o Staff Member *APA Talent And Literary Agency (NY)*
45 W 45th St Ste 804
New York, NY 10036-4602, USA

Braun, Ryan (Athlete, Baseball Player)
430 Broad Street Lk
Geneva, WI 53147, USA

Braun, Scott ""Scooter"" (Producer)
c/o Joyce Sevilla *Entertainment Fusion Group*
8899 Beverly Blvd Ste 412
West Hollywood, CA 90048-2431, USA

Braun, Steve (Actor)
c/o Tiffany Kuzon *Evolution Entertainment (LA)*
901 N Highland Ave
Los Angeles, CA 90038-2412, USA

Braun, Steve (Athlete, Baseball Player)
108 Gainsboro Rd
Lawrence Township, NJ 08648-3916, USA

Braun, Tamara (Actor)
c/o Brianne Castillo-Huang *Schiff Company, The*
8440 Warner Dr Ste B1
Culver City, CA 90232-2461, USA

Braun, Wendy (Actor)
c/o Staff Member *House of Representatives, The*
1434 6th St Ste 1
Santa Monica, CA 90401-2527, USA

Braunduardi, Angelo (Musician)
Faustini Srl. Via Veneto, 18
Pontoglio I-25 037, Italy

Braunwald, Eugene (Physicist)
800 Boylston St
Boston, MA 02199-8010, USA

Braver, Rita (Correspondent)
2020 M St NW
Washington, DC 20036-3304, USA

Braverman, Chuck (Director, Producer)
3961 Sepulveda Blvd Ste 206
Culver City, CA 90230-4600, USA

Bravo, Alex (Athlete, Football Player)
2316 Pine Ave
Manhattan Beach, CA 90266-2835, USA

Braxton, Anthony (Composer)
2608 9th St
Berkeley, CA 94710-2550, USA

Braxton, David (Athlete, Football Player)
6406 Donnegal Farm Rd
Charlotte, NC 28270-0875, USA

Braxton, Toni (Musician, Songwriter)
c/o Steve Levine *International Creative Management (ICM-LA)*
10250 Constellation Blvd Fl 7
Los Angeles, CA 90067-6207, USA

Braxton, Tyrone S (Athlete, Football Player)
8155 E Fairmount Dr Unit 171
Denver, CO 80230-6827, USA

Braxton III, Hezekiah (Athlete, Football Player)
12715 Norwood Ln
Fort Washington, MD 20744-6312, USA

Bray, Deanne (Actor)
c/o Sid Craig *Craig Management*
2240 Miramonte Cir E Unit C
Palm Springs, CA 92264-5734, USA

Bray, Kevin (Actor, Director, Producer)
c/o Simon Millar *Rumble Media*
1620 Broadway Ste C
Santa Monica, CA 90404-2777, USA

Brayton, Tyler (Athlete, Football Player)
412 Hunter Ln
Charlotte, NC 28211-3043, USA

Brazadskas, Algirdas (President)
Tumiskiu 30
Vilnius 2016, LITHUANIA

Brazelton, Dewon (Athlete, Baseball Player)
107 Scenic Dr
Tullahoma, TN 37388-5422, USA

Brazelton, T Berry (Doctor)
23 Hawthorne St
Cambridge, MA 02138-4829, USA

Brazen, Randi
10138 Main St
Bellevue, WA 98004-6022, USA

Braziel, Larry (Athlete, Football Player)
831 Netherland Dr
Arlington, TX 76017-6019, USA

Brazil, Jeff (Journalist)
633 N Orange Ave
Orlando, FL 32801-1300, USA

Brazil, John R (Educator)
President S Ofc
Peoria, IL 61625-0001, USA

Brazile Jr, Robert L (Athlete, Football Player)
813 Felder Ave
Mobile, AL 36612-1338, USA

Brazinsky, Sam (Athlete, Football Player)
12 South St
Manville, NJ 08835-1861, USA

Brazzell, Chris (Athlete, Football Player)
1205 Las Palmas Cir
Alice, TX 78332-3169, USA

Bready, Richard L (Business Person)
166 President Ave
Providence, RI 02906-4616, USA

Breaker, Daniel (Actor)
c/o Brian Liebman *Liebman Entertainment*
25 E 21st St PH
New York, NY 10010-6226, USA

Breaking Benjamin (Music Group)
c/o Staff Member *Hollywood Records*
500 S Buena Vista St
Burbank, CA 91521-0002, USA

Breaking Point (Music Group)
c/o Staff Member *Wind-up Records*
72 Madison Ave Fl 8
New York, NY 10016-8731, USA

B-Real (Artist, Musician)
c/o Jack Iannaci *Brass Artists & Associates*
9025 Wilshire Blvd Ste 400
Beverly Hills, CA 90211-1828, USA

Bream, Julian (Musician)
Richmond House 16-20 Regent St
Cambridge CB2 1DB, UNITED KINGDOM (UK)

Bream, Sid (Athlete, Baseball Player)
115 Sable Run
Zelienople, PA 16063-3141, USA

Breathed, Berkeley (Cartoonist)
1150 15th St NW
Washington, DC 20071-0001, USA

Breathwaite, Edward (Writer)
History Dept Mona
Kingston 7, JAMAICA

Breaux, Don (Athlete, Football Player)
19027 Southport Dr
Cornelius, NC 28031-6478, USA

Breaux, Tim (Athlete, Basketball Player)
2401 S Gessner Rd Apt 218
Houston, TX 77063-2051, USA

Breazeale, Jim (Athlete, Baseball Player)
790 County Road 297
Bay City, TX 77414-3644, USA

Breck, Jonathan (Actor)
c/o Staff Member *Vanguard Management Group*
8060 Melrose Ave Fl 4
Los Angeles, CA 90046-7038, USA

Breck, Peter (Actor)
c/o Karin Christopher *Sterling Artists Management Inc*
1836 West 5th Ave #207
Vancouver, BC V6J 1P3, CANADA

Breckenridge, Alex (Actor)
c/o Staff Member *Kritzer Levine Wilkins Entertainment*
11872 La Grange Ave Fl 1
Los Angeles, CA 90025-5283, USA

Breckenridge, Laura (Actor)
c/o Glenn Rigberg *HYPHENATE*
9701 Wilshire Blvd Fl 10
Beverly Hills, CA 90212-2010, USA

Brecker, Randy (Musician)
163 3rd Ave # 206
New York, NY 10003-2523, USA

Brede, Brent (Athlete, Baseball Player)
1891 J Rock Rd
Trenton, IL 62293-2924, USA

Breder, Charles M (Misc)
6275 Manasota Key Rd
Englewood, FL 34223-9258, USA

Breding, Ed (Athlete, Football Player)
126 NW Pritchard
Harlowton, MT 59036, USA

Bredsen, Espen (Skier)
Hellerud Gardsvei 18
Oslo 671, NORWAY

Breech, Jim (Athlete, Football Player)
3189 Princeton Rd # 266
Hamilton, OH 45011-5338, USA

Breeden, Danny (Athlete, Baseball Player)
5111 B Ave
Loxley, AL 36551-4537, USA

Breeden, Hal (Athlete, Baseball Player)
665 Middle Rd S
Leesburg, GA 31763-3442, USA

Breeden, Louis (Athlete, Football Player)
11264 Grooms Rd Ste E
Blue Ash, OH 45242-1418, USA

Breeden, Richard C (Government Official)
1800 M St NW
Washington, DC 20036-5802, USA

Breedlove, Leory (Athlete, Baseball Player)
1910 N 16th St
Orange, TX 77630-3311, USA

Breedlove, N Craig (Race Car Driver)
200 N Front St
Rio Vista, CA 94571-1420, USA

Breedlove, Rod (Athlete, Football Player)
264 New Valley Rd
Conowingo, MD 21918-1609, USA

Breen, Adrian (Athlete, Football Player)
6899 Longview Dr
Liberty Twp, OH 45011-7270, USA

Breen, Bobby (Actor)
10550 NW 71st Pl
Tamarac, FL 33321-2210, USA

Breen, Edward D (Business Person)
273 Corporate Dr # 100
Portsmouth, NH 03801-6807, USA

Breen, George (Swimmer)
425 Pepper Mill Ct
Sewell, NJ 08080-2963, USA

Breen, John G (Business Person)
18800 N Park Blvd
Shaker Heights, OH 44122-1809, USA

Breen, Monica (Producer, Writer)
c/o Ilan Breil *Mosaic Media Group*
9200 W Sunset Blvd Ste 10
Los Angeles, CA 90069-3608, USA

Breen, Patrick (Actor)
232 N Canon Dr
Beverly Hills, CA 90210-5302, USA

Breen, Shelley (Musician)
300 10th Ave S
Nashville, TN 37203-4125, USA

Breen, Stephen (Steve) (Cartoonist)
PO Box 120191
San Diego, CA 92112-0191, USA

Breer, Murle (Athlete, Golfer)
7008 Sand Rd
Savannah, GA 31410-2314, USA

Brees, Drew (Athlete, Football Player)
c/o Tom Condon *CAA - St. Louis*
222 S Central Ave Ste 1008
Saint Louis, MO 63105-3509, USA

Bregel, Jeff (Athlete, Football Player)
15431 Tulsa St Spc 33
Mission Hills, CA 91345-1349, USA

Bregman, Buddy (Actor)
c/o Staff Member *Paul Lane Entertainment*
468 N Camden Dr
Beverly Hills, CA 90210-4507, USA

Bregman, Martin (Producer)
240 E 39th St
New York, NY 10016-7200, USA

Bregman Recht, Tracey (Actor)
7800 Beverly Blvd # 3371
Los Angeles, CA 90036-2112, USA

Brehaut, Jeff (Athlete, Golfer)
1085 Leonello Ave
Los Altos, CA 94024-4914, USA

Breidenbach, Warren (Doctor)
217 E Chestnut St
Louisville, KY 40202-1821, USA

Breiman, Valerie (Director)
c/o Staff Member *Industry Entertainment Partners*
955 Carrillo Dr Ste 300
Los Angeles, CA 90048-5400, USA

Breining, Fred (Athlete, Baseball Player)
2120 Ticonderoga Dr
San Mateo, CA 94402-4045, USA

Breitenbach, Ken (Athlete, Hockey Player)
8 Greenvale Crt Ss 1
Fonthill, ON L0S 1E1, Canada

Breitenstein, Robert (Athlete, Football Player)
4215 We 95th St
Tulsa, OK 74137-2311, USA

Breitenstien, Robert (Athlete, Football Player)
4215 E 95th St
Tulsa, OK 74137-2311, USA

Breitner, Paul (Athlete, Soccer Player)
Eichendorfstrasse 10
Sauerlach, GERMANY 82054

Breitschwerdt, Werner (Business Person)
Mercedesstr 136
Stuttgart 70322, GERMANY

Breland, Mark (Athlete, Boxer)
20514 Heritage Hwy
Denmark, SC 29042-8831, USA

Bremmer, Paul L (Politician, Writer)
c/o Staff Member *Simon & Schuster*
1230 Avenue of the Americas Fl CONC1
New York, NY 10020-1586, USA

Bremmer, Rory
c/o Staff Member *BBC Artist Mail*
PO Box 1116
Belfast BT2 7AJ, United Kingdom

Bremner, Ewen (Actor)
76 Oxford St
London W1N 0AX, UNITED KINGDOM (UK)

Bren, Donald (Business Person, Philanthropist)
2400 Bren Hall University of California
Santa Barbara, CA 93106-0001, USA

Brenan, Gerald (Writer)
Alhaurin El Grande
Malaga, SPAIN

Brendel, Alfred (Musician)
27 W 72nd St
New York, NY 10023-3498, USA

Brendel, Wolfgang (Opera Singer)
Wasagasse 12/1/3
Vienna 1090, AUSTRIA

Brenden, Hallgeir (Skier)
2417 Torberget
NORWAY

Brendi, Pavel (Athlete, Hockey Player)
1400 Edwards Mill Rd
Raleigh, NC 27607-3624, USA

Brendon, Nicholas (Actor)
2666 N Beachwood Dr
Los Angeles, CA 90068-2308, USA

Breneman, Curtis E (Misc)
38 Carlyle Ave
Troy, NY 12180-3104, USA

Brenly, Bob (Athlete, Baseball Player, Coach)
9726 E Laurel Ln
Scottsdale, AZ 85260-5959, USA

Brenly, Robert E (Bob) (Athlete, Basketball Player)
9726 E Laurel Ln
Scottsdale, AZ 85260-5959, USA

Brennaman, Marty (Baseball Player, Sportscaster)
2363 Heather Hill Blvd N
Cincinnati, OH 45244-2666, USA

Brennaman, Thom (Athlete, Baseball Player, Sportscaster)
738 Park Ave
Terrace Park, OH 45174-1021, USA

Brennan, Brian (Athlete, Football Player)
2961 Edgewood Rd
Cleveland, OH 44124-5101, USA

Brennan, Christine (Writer)
1150 15th Ave NW
Washington, DC 20071-0001, USA

Brennan, Dan (Athlete, Hockey Player)
1912 108 Ave
Dawson Creek, BC V1G 2T8, Canada

Brennan, Edward A (Business Person)
433 Amon Carter Blvd
Fort Worth, TX 76155, USA

Brennan, Eileen (Actor)
c/o Jessica Moresco *Unified Management*
4231 W National Ave
Burbank, CA 91505-4022, USA

Brennan, Joseph E (Ex-Governor)
104 Frances St
Portland, ME 04102-2512, USA

Brennan, Kevin (Actor, Comedian)
9560 Wilshire Blvd Ste 500
Beverly Hills, CA 90212-2401, USA

Brennan, Maire (Musician, Songwriter, Writer)
55 Fulham High St
London SW6 3JJ, UNITED KINGDOM (UK)

Brennan, Margaret (Anchor)
c/o Staff Member *CNBC (DC)*
400 N Capitol St NW Ste 850
Washington, DC 20001-1555, USA

Brennan, Melissa (Actor)
6520 Platt Ave # 634
West Hills, CA 91307-3218, USA

Brennan, Mike (Athlete, Football Player)
33660 Fox Rd
Easton, MD 21601-6746, USA

Brennan, Neal (Actor, Comedian)
c/o Gregory McKnight *Creative Artists Agency (CAA-LA)*
2000 Avenue of the Stars Ste 100
Los Angeles, CA 90067-4705, USA

Brennan, Pete (Athlete, Basketball Player)
588-1 Route 23C
Jewett, NY 12444, USA

Brennan, Rich (Athlete, Hockey Player)
14 Reflection Way
South Yarmouth, MA 02664-2045, USA

Brennan, Terrance P (Terry) (Athlete, Coach, Football Player)
1731 Wildberry Dr Unit C
Glenview, IL 60025-1742, USA

Brennan, Tom (Athlete, Baseball Player)
8204 Millbank Dr
Orland Park, IL 60462-1726, USA

Brennan, William (Athlete, Baseball Player)
802 Cottage Hill Dr
Macon, GA 31210-7628, USA

Brenneman, Amy (Actor, Producer)
c/o Connie Tavel *Forward Entertainment*
9255 W Sunset Blvd Ste 805
Los Angeles, CA 90069-3305, USA

Brenneman, John (Athlete, Hockey Player)
247 Radley Rd
Mississauga, ON L5G 2R6, Canada

Brenner, Al (Athlete, Football Player)
698 W Jefferson St
Berea, KY 40403-1431, USA

Brenner, David (Actor, Comedian)
3749 Amber Lantern Cir
Las Vegas, NV 89147-6813, USA

Brenner, Dori (Actor)
210 W 101st St Apt 15C
New York, NY 10025-5040, USA

Brenner, Hoby (Athlete, Football Player)
40 Calle Ameno
San Clemente, CA 92672-2367, USA

Brenner, Lisa (Actor)
7729 Sunset Blvd
Los Angeles, CA 90046, USA

Brenner, Sydney (Nobel Prize Laureate)
10100 N Torrey Pines Rd
La Jolla, CA 92037, USA

Brenner, Teddy (Boxer)
24 W 55th St Apt 9C
New York, NY 10019-5456, USA

Brent, Eve (Actor)
125 S Sycamore Ave
Los Angeles, CA 90036-2938, USA

Bresee, Bobbie (Actor)
PO Box 1222
Hollywood, CA 90078-1222, USA

Breslawsky, Marc C (Business Person)
1 Elmcroft Rd
Stamford, CT 06926-0700, USA

Breslin, Abigail (Actor)
c/o Beth Cannon *Envision Management*
8840 Wilshire Blvd Fl 3
Beverly Hills, CA 90211-2606, USA

Breslin, Jimmy (Journalist)
235 Pinelawn Rd
Melville, NY 11747-4226, USA

Breslin, Spencer (Actor)
c/o Beth Cannon *Envision Management*
8840 Wilshire Blvd Fl 3
Beverly Hills, CA 90211-2606, USA

Breslow, Craig (Athlete, Baseball Player)
26 Finchwood Dr
Trumbull, CT 06611-4040, USA

Breslow, Lester (Physicist)
10926 Verano Rd
Los Angeles, CA 90077-2224, USA

Breslow, Ronald C (Misc)
295 Three Mile Harbor Rd
East Hampton, NY 11937-2014, USA

Bress, Eric (Director, Producer, Writer)
c/o Tobin Babst *United Talent Agency (UTA)*
9560 Wilshire Blvd Fl 5
Beverly Hills, CA 90212-2400, USA

Bressoud, Eddie (Athlete, Baseball Player)
515 Marble Canyon Ln
San Ramon, CA 94582-4830, USA

Brest, Martin (Director, Producer)
c/o John Burnham *International Creative Management (ICM-LA)*
10250 Constellation Blvd Fl 7
Los Angeles, CA 90067-6207, USA

Bretherton, Billy (Reality TV Star)
1201 Linton Rd
Benton, LA 71006-8736, USA

Bretos, Max (Athlete, Soccer Player)
c/o Staff Member *Maxx Sports & Entertainment*
546 5th Ave Fl 6
New York, NY 10036-5000, USA

Brett, George (Athlete, Baseball Player)
6528 Seneca Rd
Mission Hills, KS 66208-1718, USA

Brett, Jonathan (Actor)
9200 W Sunset Blvd Ste 900
Los Angeles, CA 90069-3604, USA

Brettschneider, Carl (Athlete, Football Player)
4649 Bird View Ct
Las Vegas, NV 89129-5326, USA

Breuer, Grit (Athlete, Track Athlete)
Garbsen 30823, GERMANY

Breuer, Jim (Comedian)
c/o Heidi Feigin *United Talent Agency (UTA)*
9560 Wilshire Blvd Fl 5
Beverly Hills, CA 90212-2400, USA

Breuer, Randy (Athlete, Basketball Player)
10481 Misty Morning Ln
Eden Prairie, MN 55347-5023, USA

Breunig, Robert P (Bob) (Athlete, Football Player)
9215 Westview Cir
Dallas, TX 75231-2502, USA

Brew, Dorian (Athlete, Football Player)
3965 Nara Dr
Florissant, MO 63033-3222, USA

Brewer, Albert P (Ex-Governor)
2520 Ashford Pl
Birmingham, AL 35243-2241, USA

Brewer, Billy (Athlete, Baseball Player)
7405 Woodway Dr
Woodway, TX 76712-6153, USA

Brewer, Craig (Director, Producer)
c/o Brad Gross *Brad Gross Agency, The*
161 S Arden Blvd
Los Angeles, CA 90004-3716, USA

Brewer, Derek Stanley (Educator)
English Dept
Cambridge CB2 3AP, UNITED KINGDOM (UK)

Brewer, Dewell (Athlete, Football Player)
950 E Paces Ferry Rd NE Ste 2700
Atlanta, GA 30326-1386, USA

Brewer, Donald (Musician)
PO Box 770850
Orlando, FL 32877-0850, USA

Brewer, Eric (Athlete, Hockey Player)
7396 Stratford Ave
Saint Louis, MO 63130-4137, USA

Brewer, Jamison (Athlete, Basketball Player)
1322 Wind Castle Trl
Indianapolis, IN 46280-2723, USA

Brewer, Jan (Governor)
1700 W Washington St
Phoenix, AZ 85007-2812, USA

Brewer, Jim T (Athlete, Basketball Player, Coach)
1814 S 23rd Ave
Maywood, IL 60153-2810, USA

Brewer, Mike (Athlete, Baseball Player)
40 Amherst Ave
Menlo Park, CA 94025-3802, USA

Brewer, Richard G (Physicist)
730 De Soto Dr
Palo Alto, CA 94303-2806, USA

Brewer, Rodney (Rod) (Athlete, Baseball Player)
2105 Carpathian Dr
Apopka, FL 32712-4711, USA

Brewer, Sean (Athlete, Football Player)
9232 Grangehill Dr
Riverside, CA 92508-9329, USA

Brewer, Tom (Athlete, Baseball Player)
409 State Rd
Cheraw, SC 29520-1621, USA

Brewer, Tony
839 Golden Poppy St
Las Vegas, NV 89110-2858, USA

Brewer, Tony (Athlete, Baseball Player)
659 Wildwood Ln
Palo Alto, CA 94303-3117, USA

Brewington, Jamie (Athlete, Baseball Player)
3370 S Roger Ct
Chandler, AZ 85286-2481, USA

Brewster, Jordana (Actor)
c/o Suzan Bymel *Management 360*
9111 Wilshire Blvd
Beverly Hills, CA 90210-5508, USA

Brewster, Kithe (Stylist)
c/o Staff Member *Creative Exchange Agency*
53 Gansevoort St Ste 3
New York, NY 10014-1414, USA

Brewster, Paget (Actor)
c/o Joanna (Joanie) Burstein *Burstein Company, The*
15304 W Sunset Blvd Ste 208
Pacific Palisades, CA 90272-3656, USA

Brewster, Pete (Athlete, Football Player)
PO Box 183
Peculiar, MO 64078-0183, USA

Brey, Mike (Coach)
Athletic Dept
Notre Dame, IN 46556, USA

Breyer, Stephen G (Judge)
1 1st St NE
Washington, DC 20543-0001, USA

Brezec, Primoz (Athlete, Basketball Player)
10030 Hazelview Dr
Charlotte, NC 28277-2948, USA

Brezina, Bobby (Athlete, Football Player)
1204 Pine Hollow Dr
Friendswood, TX 77546-4634, USA

Brezis, Haim (Mathematician)
18 Rue de la Glaciere
Paris Cedex 13 75640, FRANCE

Brezner, Larry (Producer)
c/o Larry Brezner *Morra Brezner Steinberg & Tenenbaum (MBST) Entertainment*
345 N Maple Dr Ste 200
Beverly Hills, CA 90210-5174, USA

Brian, Frank (Athlete, Basketball Player)
23757 Brian Rd
Zachary, LA 70791-6231, USA

Brice, Alan (Athlete, Baseball Player)
6726 71st St E
Bradenton, FL 34203-7173, USA

Brice, Lee (Musician)
c/o Joey Lee *WmE2 (WMA-TN)*
1600 Division St Ste 300
Nashville, TN 37203-2755, USA

Brice, Pierre (Actor)
c/o Staff Member *Thomas Claasen*
Bismarkstr 22
Itzehoe D-25524, Germany

Brice, William J (Artist)
427 Beloit Ave
Los Angeles, CA 90049-3405, USA

Bricekel, James R (General)
4798 Hanging Moss Ln
Sarasota, FL 34238-4301, USA

Bricekell, Beth (Director)
PO Box 119
Paron, AR 72122-0119, USA

Bricekell, Edie (Musician, Songwriter, Writer)
88 Central Park W
New York, NY 10023-5299, USA

Brickell, Beth (Actor)
3001 N Grant St
Little Rock, AR 72207-2819, USA

Brickell, Edie (Musician)
88 Central Park W
New York, NY 10023-5299, USA

Bricker, Neal S (Physicist)
4240 Piedmont Mesa Rd
Claremont, CA 91711-2332, USA

Brickhouse, Smith N (Religious Leader)
PO Box 472
Independence, MO 64051-0472, USA

Brickley, Andy (Athlete, Hockey Player)
5 Mill River Ln
Hingham, MA 02043-3455, USA

Bricklin, Daniel S (Designer)
300 Bahr Ave
Concord, MA 1742, USA

Brickman, Jim (Composer, Musician, Producer)
c/o Staff Member *International Creative Management (ICM-LA)*
10250 Constellation Blvd Fl 7
Los Angeles, CA 90067-6207, USA

Brickman, Paul (Director)
4116 Holly Knoll Dr
Los Angeles, CA 90027-3222, USA

Brickowski, Frank (Athlete, Basketball Player)
589 7th St
Lake Oswego, OR 97034-2906, USA

Bricusse, Leslie (Composer, Musician)
8730 W Sunset Blvd # 300W
Los Angeles, CA 90069-2210, USA

Bridgeforth, William (Athlete, Baseball Player)
4766 Drakes Branch Rd
Nashville, TN 37218-1436, USA

Bridgeman, Ulysses (Athlete, Basketball Player)
1604 Cherokee Rd Apt 4
Louisville, KY 40205-1349, USA

Bridgers, Sean (Actor)
c/o Darris Hatch *Daris Hatch Management*
10027 Rossbury Pl
Los Angeles, CA 90064-4825, USA

Bridges, Alan J S (Director)
28 High St Shepperton
Middx TW7 9AW, UNITED KINGDOM (UK)

Bridges, Angelica (Actor, Model)
c/o Marv Dauer *Marv Dauer Management*
11661 San Vicente Blvd Ste 104
Los Angeles, CA 90049-5150, USA

Bridges, Beau (Actor)
c/o Samantha Hill *WKT Public Relations (WKT-LA)*
9350 Wilshire Blvd Ste 450
Beverly Hills, CA 90212-3230, USA

Bridges, Bill (Athlete, Basketball Player)
2322 44th St
Santa Monica, CA 90405, USA

Bridges, Jeff (Actor, Producer)
c/o David Schiff *Schiff Company, The*
8440 Warner Dr Ste B1
Culver City, CA 90232-2461, USA

Bridges, Jordan (Actor)
c/o Myrna Jacoby *MJ Management*
130 W 57th St Apt 11A
New York, NY 10019-3311, USA

Bridges, Krista (Actor)
c/o JJ Harris *One Talent Management*
9220 W Sunset Blvd Ste 306
Los Angeles, CA 90069-3503, USA

Bridges, Rocky (Athlete, Baseball Player)
1128 W Shane Dr
Coeur D Alene, ID 83815-9788, USA

Bridges, Todd (Actor)
c/o Staff Member *DVFilmworks*
10850 Wilshire Blvd Ste 350
Los Angeles, CA 90024-4643, USA

Bridges Jr, Roy D (Astronaut, General)
113 William Barksdale
Williamsburg, VA 23185-8211, USA

Bridgewater, Dee Dee (Musician)
Elvirastr 25
Munich 80636, GERMANY

Bridgman, Mel (Athlete, Hockey Player)
211 Concord St # 17
El Segundo, CA 90245-3706, USA

Bridwell, Norman (Writer)
PO Box 869
Edgartown, MA 02539-0869, USA

Brie, Alison (Actor)
c/o Scott Fish *Vital Management Group (VMG)*
5405 Wilshire Blvd # 200
Los Angeles, CA 90036-4203, USA

Brief Smile, A (Music Group)
c/o Staff Member *Paradigm (Monterey)*
404 W Franklin St
Monterey, CA 93940-2303, USA

Briehl, Tom (Athlete, Football Player)
7752 N Via De La Montana
Scottsdale, AZ 85258-3320, USA

Briem, Anita (Actor)
c/o Steve Cohen *United Talent Agency (UTA)*
9560 Wilshire Blvd Fl 5
Beverly Hills, CA 90212-2400, USA

Briere, Daniel (Athlete, Hockey Player)
17 S Hinchman Ave
Haddonfield, NJ 08033-3714, USA

Brierley, Ronald A (Business Person)
21-26 Garlick Hill
London EC4 2AU, UNITED KINGDOM (UK)

Briers, Richard (Actor, Comedian)
c/o Christian Hodell *Hamilton Hodell Ltd*
66-68 Margaret St Fl 5
London W1W 8SR, UK

Brigati, Eddie (Musician, Songwriter, Writer)
32 Ardsley Rd # 201
Montclair, NJ 07042-5002, USA

Briggs, Dan (Athlete, Baseball Player)
231 France St
Sonoma, CA 95476-7141, USA

Briggs, Danny (Athlete, Golfer)
245 Spencer Creek Rd
Franklin, TN 37069-6503, USA

Briggs, Edward S (Admiral)
3648 Lago Sereno
Escondido, CA 92029-7902, USA

Briggs, John (Johnny) (Athlete, Baseball Player)
238 Wall Ave
Paterson, NJ 07504-1016, USA

Briggs, Johnny T (Athlete, Baseball Player)
216 Tom Bell Rd Spc 133
Murphys, CA 95247-9552, USA

Briggs, Kathy (Stylist)
c/o Staff Member *Zenobia Agency Inc*
PO Box 909
Groveland, CA 95321-0909, USA

Briggs, Lance (Athlete, Football Player)
180 Coach Rd
Northfield, IL 60093-3114, USA

Briggs, Paul (Athlete, Football Player)
3309 S Ross St
Santa Ana, CA 92707-3925, USA

Briggs, Raymond R (Cartoonist, Writer)
Underhill Lane Westmeston near Hassocks
Sussex, UNITED KINGDOM (UK)

Briggs, Robert W (Biologist)
480 Rale St
Palo Alto, CA 94301, USA

Briggs, Wilma (Baseball Player)
111 Summit Ave
Wakefield, RI 02879-2228, USA

Briggs of Lewes, Asa (Historian)
Caprons Keere St Lewes
Sussex, UNITED KINGDOM (UK)

Brigham, Jeremy (Athlete, Football Player)
1141 Catalina Dr
Livermore, CA 94550-5928, USA

Bright, Cameron (Actor)
c/o Stephanie Comer *United Talent Agency (UTA)*
9560 Wilshire Blvd Fl 5
Beverly Hills, CA 90212-2400, USA

Bright, Kevin S (Director, Producer, Writer)
c/o Staff Member *International Creative Management (ICM-LA)*
10250 Constellation Blvd Fl 7
Los Angeles, CA 90067-6207, USA

Bright, Leon (Athlete, Football Player)
1183 Dutton Ave
Deland, FL 32720-5011, USA

Bright, Myron H (Judge)
655 1st Ave N Ste 340
Fargo, ND 58102-4952, USA

Brightbill, Susan (Actor, Writer)
c/o Michael Lasker *Mosaic Media Group*
9200 W Sunset Blvd Ste 10
Los Angeles, CA 90069-3608, USA

Brightman, Sarah (Actor, Musician)
Mill Lane
Cookham, Berkshire SL6 9QT, UK

Brigman, D J (Athlete, Golfer)
8304 Calle Soquelle NE
Albuquerque, NM 87113-1771, USA

Briley, Greg (Athlete, Baseball Player)
2170 Sunnybrook Rd
Greenville, NC 27834-1164, USA

Briley, John (Actor, Producer, Writer)
c/o Jack Gilardi *International Creative Management (ICM-LA)*
10250 Constellation Blvd Fl 7
Los Angeles, CA 90067-6207, USA

Brill, Charlie (Actor)
3635 Wrightwood Dr
Studio City, CA 91604-3947, USA

Brill, Francesca (Actor)
Fitzroy Road
London NW1 8TR, UNITED KINGDOM (UK)

Brill, Winston J (Misc)
12529 237th Way NE
Redmond, WA 98053-5618, USA

Brillant, Dany (Actor, Musician)
c/o Laurent Gregoire *Agence Artistique Adequat*
80 Rue D'Amsterdam
Paris 75009, France

Brilz, Darrick (Athlete, Football Player)
3020 Issaquah Pine Lake Rd SE Apt 525
Issaquah, WA 98075-7253, USA

Brimanis, Aris (Athlete, Hockey Player)
12909 Badger Ln
Anchorage, AK 99516-3034, USA

Brimley, Wilford (Actor)
240 Greybull Ave
Greybull, WY 82426-2034, USA

Brimmer, Andrew F (Economist, Government Official)
4400 MacArthur Blvd NW
Washington, DC 20007-2521, USA

Brin, Sergey (Business Person, Engineer, Producer)
c/o Staff Member *Google Inc*
1600 Amphitheatre Pkwy
Mountain View, CA 94043-1351, USA

Brind'amour, Rod (Athlete, Hockey Player)
1153 Four Wheel Dr
Wake Forest, NC 27587-8689, USA

Brindley, Doug (Athlete, Hockey Player)
Caledon Village Ontario Provincial Police
18473 Hurontario St
Caledon Village, ON L0N 1C0, Canada

Bring, Murray H (Business Person)
120 Park Ave
New York, NY 10017-5577, USA

Brink, Andre P (Writer)
English Dept
Rondebosch 7700, SOUTH AFRICA

Brink, Brad (Athlete, Baseball Player)
2628 Surrey Ave
Modesto, CA 95355-4668, USA

Brink, Frank Jr (Physicist)
Pine Run #E1 Ferry & Iron Roads
Doylestown, PA 18901, USA

Brink, Larry (Athlete, Football Player)
13310 Tierra Heights Rd
Redding, CA 96003-7489, USA

Brink, R Alexander (Misc)
8301 Old Sauk Rd Apt 326
Middleton, WI 53562-4394, USA

Brinker, Bob (Business Person, Radio Personality)
5226 E Wagoner Rd
Scottsdale, AZ 85254-7636

Brinker, Christopher (Producer)
c/o David Krintzman *Morris, Yorn, Barnes, Levine, Krintzman, Rubenstein and Kohner*
2000 Ave Of The Stars 3rd Tower Floor NORTH
Los Angeles, CA 90067, USA

Brinker, Nancy (Business Person)
5005 Lbj Fwy Ste 250
Dallas, TX 75244-6125

Brinkley, Christie (Model)
c/o Elliott Mintz *Elliot Mintz Public Relations*
2934 1/2 N Beverly Glen Cir
Los Angeles, CA 90077-1724, USA

Brinkman, Chuck (Athlete, Baseball Player)
11849 County Road C
Bryan, OH 43506-8524, USA

Brinkman, Joe (Athlete, Baseball Player)
10351 NW 70th St
Chiefland, FL 32626-5042, USA

Brinkman, John A (Historian)
1321 E 56th St Apt 4
Chicago, IL 60637-1762, USA

Brinkman, William F (Physicist)
1177 22nd St NW Unit 2C
Washington, DC 20037-1254, USA

Brinkmann, Robert S (Cinematographer)
c/o Ann Murtha 4240 Promenade Way Ste 232
Marina Del Rey, CA 90292, USA

Brino, Lorenzo (Actor)
c/o Wendy Wilke *Media Partners*
636 Acanto St Apt 207
Los Angeles, CA 90049-2128, USA

Brino, Nikolas (Actor)
c/o Wendy Wilke *Media Partners*
636 Acanto St Apt 207
Los Angeles, CA 90049-2128, USA

Brino, Zachary (Actor)
c/o Wendy Wilke *Media Partners*
636 Acanto St Apt 207
Los Angeles, CA 90049-2128, USA

Brinson, Larry (Athlete, Football Player)
300 Cataubaw St
Clemson, SC 28631, USA

Brinster, Ralph L (Biologist)
Veterinary Medicine School
Philadelphia, PA 19104, USA

Brintz, Lisa (Stylist)
c/o Staff Member *Brintz & Associates*
16 Irving St
Newton, MA 02459-1612, USA

Brion, Francoise (Actor)
c/o Staff Member *Cineart*
36 Rue de Ponthieu
Paris F-75008, France

Brion, John (Composer, Musician)
c/o Staff Member *Kraft-Engel Management*
15233 Ventura Blvd Ste 200
Sherman Oaks, CA 91403-2244, USA

Brisbin, David (Actor)
c/o Geneva Bray *GVA Talent Agency Inc*
8981 W Sunset Blvd Ste 101
Los Angeles, CA 90069-1850, USA

Brisco, Jack (Wrestler)
19018 Blake Rd
Odessa, FL 33556-4402, USA

Brisco, Marlin (Athlete, Football Player)
379 Newport Ave Apt 107
Long Beach, CA 90814-7011, USA

Brisco, Valerie (Athlete, Track Athlete)
4341 Starlight Dr
Indianapolis, IN 46239-1473, USA

Briscoe, Brent (Actor)
c/o Robert Enriquez *Red Baron Management*
1600 Rosecrans Ave PMB 4
Manhattan Beach, CA 90266-3708, USA

Briscoe, John (Athlete, Baseball Player)
6815 Casa Loma Ave
Dallas, TX 75214-4003, USA

Briscoe, Mary Beck (Judge)
4839 W 15th St
Lawrence, KS 66049, USA

Brisebois, Danielle (Actor, Musician)
c/o Staff Member *McDaniel Entertainment*
1311 Broadway
Santa Monica, CA 90404-2709, USA

Brisebois, Patrice (Athlete, Hockey Player)
4723 Castle Cir
Broomfield, CO 80023-4079, USA

Brissie, Leland V (Lou) (Athlete, Baseball Player)
1908 White Pine Dr
North Augusta, SC 29841-2147, USA

Brisson, Lance (Actor)
4570 Noeline Way
Encino, CA 91436-2108, USA

Brister, Walter A (Bubby) III (Athlete, Football Player)
139 Fontainbleau Dr
Mandeville, LA 70471-6434, USA

Bristol, Dave (Athlete, Baseball Player, Coach)
1748 Fairview Rd
Andrews, NC 28901-7426, USA

Bristor, John (Athlete, Football Player)
70 Rinehart Ln
Waynesburg, PA 15370-3412, USA

Bristow, Allan (Athlete, Basketball Player)
510 Sand Hill Ct
Marco Island, FL 34145-5859, USA

Bristow, Allan M (Athlete, Basketball Player, Coach)
PO Box 635
Gloucester Point, VA 23062-0635, USA

Britain, Radie (Composer)
PO Box 17
Smithville, IN 47458-0017, USA

Brito, Jorge (Athlete, Baseball Player)
9348 Snake Rd
Athens, AL 35611-8031, USA

Brito, Tilson (Athlete, Baseball Player)
6809 Fishers Farm Ln Unit F1
Charlotte, NC 28277-0334, USA

Britt, Chris (Cartoonist)
1 Copley Plz
Springfield, IL 62701-1927, USA

Britt, James (Athlete, Football Player)
PO Box 371202
Decatur, GA 30037-1202, USA

Britt, Jessie (Athlete, Football Player)
4003 Coltrain Rd
Greensboro, NC 27455-2631, USA

Britt, Michael (Musician)
1222 16th Ave S Ste 23
Nashville, TN 37212-2926, USA

Britt, Tyrone (Athlete, Basketball Player)
4631 Germantown Ave
Philadelphia, PA 19144-3010, USA

Britt, Wayman (Athlete, Basketball Player)
973 Paradise Lake Dr SE
Grand Rapids, MI 49546-3828, USA

Brittain, Michael (Mike) (Athlete, Basketball Player)
2101 Sunset Point Rd Apt 602
Clearwater, FL 33765-1277, USA

Brittany, Morgan (Actor, Model)
3434 Cornell Rd
Agoura Hills, CA 91301-2714, USA

Britten, Roy J (Misc)
101 Dahlia Avenue Ave
Corona del Mar, CA 92625, USA

Brittenham, Harry (Attorney, Attorney General, General)
1801 Century Park W
Los Angeles, CA 90067-6409, USA

Brittenum, John (Athlete, Football Player)
PO Box 3773
Fayetteville, AR 72702-3773, USA

Britton, Benjamin (Inventor)
Fine Arts
Cincinnati, OH 45221-0001, USA

Britton, Bill (Athlete, Golfer)
41 Allen St
Rumson, NJ 07760-1316, USA

Britton, Chris (Athlete, Baseball Player)
7481 NW 11th Ct
Plantation, FL 33313-5913, USA

Britton, Christopher (Actor)
c/o Staff Member *Red Management*
Box 3 415 West Esplanade
North Vancouver, BC V7M 1A6, Canada

Britton, Connie (Actor)
c/o Greg Clark *Untitled Entertainment (LA)*
350 S Beverly Dr Ste 200
Beverly Hills, CA 90212-4819, USA

Britton, Dave (Athlete, Basketball Player)
6321 Old Ox Rd
Dallas, TX 75241-2733, USA

Britton, Jim (Athlete, Baseball Player)
825 Forestwalk Dr
Suwanee, GA 30024-4243, USA

Britton, Tony (Actor)
76 Oxford St
London W1N 0AX, UNITED KINGDOM (UK)

Britz, Greg (Athlete, Hockey Player)
245 Ocean Ave
Marblehead, MA 01945-3700, USA

Britz, Jerilyn (Athlete, Golfer)
415 E Lincoln St Apt 7
Luverne, MN 56156-1643, USA

Brizan, George (Prime Minister)
Botanical Gardens
Saint George's, GRENADA

Brizzolara, Tony (Athlete, Baseball Player)
1638 Princess Cir NE
Atlanta, GA 30345-4160, USA

Broad, Eli (Business Person)
10900 Wilshire Blvd Fl 12
Los Angeles, CA 90024-6548, USA

Broadbent, Jim (Actor)
c/o Staff Member *Independent Talent Group (ITG-UK)*
Oxford House 76 Oxford St
London W1D 1BS, UK

Broadbent, John Edward (Government Official)
1386 Nicola #30
Vancouver BC V6G 2G2, CANADA

Broaddus, J Alfred Jr (Financier)
PO Box 27622
Richmond, VA 23261-7622, USA

Broadhead, James L (Business Person)
700 Universe Blvd
Juno Beach, FL 33408-2657, USA

Broadnax, Jerry (Athlete, Football Player)
2631 Nina Cir
Grand Prairie, TX 75052-5325, USA

Broadway, Lance (Athlete, Baseball Player)
1502 Juneau St
Grand Prairie, TX 75050-3259, USA

Brobeck, John R (Physicist)
224 Vassar Ave
Swarthmore, PA 19081-1634, USA

Broberg, Gus (Athlete, Basketball Player)
208 El Pueblo Way
Palm Beach, FL 33480-3218, USA

Broberg, Pete (Athlete, Baseball Player)
220 Monterey Rd
Palm Beach, FL 33480 3228, USA

Brocail, Doug (Athlete, Baseball Player)
8011 Meadow Vista Dr
Missouri City, TX 77459-5734, USA

Broccoli, Barbara (Producer)
c/o Staff Member *Danjag*
2400 Colorado Ave Suite 310
Santa Monica, CA 90404, USA

Broches, Aron (Attorney, Attorney General, General)
44 Pond St
Wakefield, RI 02879-4009, USA

Brochtrup, William (Bill) (Actor)
1801 Avenue of the Stars Ste 902
Los Angeles, CA 90067-5981, USA

Brochu, Stephane (Athlete, Hockey Player)
6029 Evergreen Ln
Grand Blanc, MI 48439-9643, USA

Brock, Chris (Athlete, Baseball Player)
7684 Markham Bend Pl
Sanford, FL 32771-8107, USA

Brock, Clyde (Athlete, Football Player)
3105 SW 98th Ave
Portland, OR 97225-2924, USA

Brock, Dieter (Athlete, Football Player)
60 Shiloh Rd Attn Athletic
Greeneville, TN 37745-0595, USA

Brock, Greg (Athlete, Baseball Player)
3727 Valley Oak Dr
Loveland, CO 80538-8930, USA

Brock, Lou (Athlete, Baseball Player)
61 Barkley Pl
Saint Charles, MO 63301-4569, USA

Brock, Matt (Athlete, Football Player)
3105 SW 98th Ave
Portland, OR 97225-2924, USA

Brock, Peter (Athlete, Football Player)
29 Canterbury Hill Rd
Topsfield, MA 01983-1521, USA

Brock, Stanley J (Stan) (Athlete, Football Player)
2555 SW 81st Ave
Portland, OR 97225-3839, USA

Brock, Stevie (Actor)
c/o Johnny Wright *Wright Entertainment Group (WEG)*
PO Box 590009
Orlando, FL 32859-0009, USA

Brock, Tarrik (Athlete, Baseball Player)
8111 Fairchild Ave
Winnetka, CA 91306-2012, USA

Brock, Willie (Athlete, Football Player)
3732 NE 70th Ave
Portland, OR 97213-5141, USA

Brock III, William E (Bill) (Ex-Senator, Secretary)
222 Severn Ave Ste 1
Annapolis, MD 21403-2566, USA

Brock Jr, Lou (Athlete, Football Player)
1015 Sandstone Dr
Saint Louis, MO 63146-5031, USA

Brockermeyer, Blake (Athlete, Football Player)
PO Box 789
Wilson, WY 83014-0789, USA

Brockert, Richard C (Misc)
701 E Gude Dr
Rockville, MD 20850-5335, USA

Brockington, John (Athlete, Football Player)
701 B St Ste 1500
San Diego, CA 92101-8170, USA

Brocklander, Fred (Athlete, Baseball Player)
317 Eagles Lndg Ct Apt K
Odenton, MD 21113-5203, USA

Brockovich-Ellis, Erin (Writer)
c/o Staff Member *WmE2 (WMA-LA)*
1 William Morris Pl
Beverly Hills, CA 90212-4261, USA

Broden, Connie (Athlete, Hockey Player)
88 Valecrest Dr
Etobicoke, ON M9A 4P6, Canada

Broder, Samuel (Misc)
4400 Biscayne Blvd
Miami, FL 33137-3212, USA

Broderick, Beth (Actor)
1505 10th St
Santa Monica, CA 90401-2805, USA

Broderick, Ken (Athlete, Hockey Player)
5142 Citation Rd
Niagara Falls, ON L2H 3H7, Canada

Broderick, Len (Athlete, Hockey Player)
216 Inverness Way
Easley, SC 29642-3116, USA

Broderick, Matthew (Actor)
PO Box 10459
Burbank, CA 91510-0459, USA

Broderson, Morris (Artist)
5707 Costello Ave
Valley Glen, CA 91401-4329, USA

Brodeur, Martin (Athlete, Hockey Player)
100 Mountain Ave
West Orange, NJ 07052-4958, USA

Brodeur, Richard (Athlete, Hockey Player)
5007 Angus Dr
Vancouver, BC V6M 3M6, Canada

Brodie, H Keith H (Misc)
63 Beverly Dr
Durham, NC 27707-2223, USA

Brodie, John (Athlete, Football Player, Golfer)
49350 Avenida Fernando
La Quinta, CA 92253-2742, USA

Brodie, Kevin (Actor)
3925 Big Oak Dr Apt 5
Studio City, CA 91604-3800, USA

Brodowski, Dick (Athlete, Baseball Player)
120 Pine St
Manchester, MA 01944-1022, USA

Brodsky, Julian A (Business Person)
1500 Market St
Philadelphia, PA 19102-2109, USA

Brody, Adam (Actor)
c/o Melissa Kates *Viewpoint Inc*
8820 Wilshire Blvd Ste 220
Beverly Hills, CA 90211-2622, USA

Brody, Adrien (Actor)
c/o Jere Douglass *Red Hawk Management*
3940 Laurel Canyon Blvd # 377
Studio City, CA 91604-3709, USA

Brody, Jon Lee (Actor)
c/o Terry Cohen *Cohen Entertainment*
964 Hancock Ave Apt 305
West Hollywood, CA 90069-4091, USA

Brody, Kenneth D (Financier)
450 Park Ave Fl 9
New York, NY 10022-2741, USA

Brody, Lane (Music Group)
PO Box 368
Tujunga, CA 91043-0368, USA

Broecker, Wallace S (Geophysicist, Misc, Physicist)
PO Box 1000
Palisades, NY 10964-8000, USA

Broelsch, Christopher E (Doctor, Misc)
Medical Center Surgery Dept Box 259
Chicago, IL 60690, USA

Brogan, James (Athlete, Basketball Player)
6631 Hollycrest Ct
San Diego, CA 92121-4137, USA

Brogdon, Cindy (Athlete, Basketball Player)
4162 Anson Trl
Suwanee, GA 30024-6753, USA

Broglio, Ernie (Athlete, Baseball Player)
2838 Via Carmen
San Jose, CA 95124-1442, USA

Brogna, Rico (Athlete, Baseball Player)
2 Gate Post Ln
Woodbury, CT 06798-2136, USA

Brohamer, Jack (Athlete, Baseball Player)
39017 Narcissus Dr
Palm Desert, CA 92211-1882, USA

Brohawn, Troy (Athlete, Baseball Player)
1619 Taylors Island Rd
Woolford, MD 21677-1328, USA

Brokaw, Gary (Athlete, Basketball Player)
6614 Augustine Way
Charlotte, NC 28270-0891, USA

Brokaw, Tom (Journalist, Television Host)
c/o Sara Perkowski *NBC Nightly News*
30 Rockefeller Plz Fl 270E
New York, NY 10112-0299, USA

Broken Lizard (Comedian)
c/o Staff Member *United Talent Agency (UTA)*
9560 Wilshire Blvd Fl 5
Beverly Hills, CA 90212-2400, USA

Brolin, James (Actor)
c/o Jeff Wald *Jeff Wald Entertainment*
3000 Olympic Blvd Bldg 2 PMB 1400
Santa Monica, CA 90404-5073, USA

Brolin, Josh (Actor)
c/o Kelly Bush *ID PR (LA)*
7060 Hollywood Blvd Fl 8
Los Angeles, CA 90028-6014, USA

Brolly, Shane (Actor)
c/o Staff Member *Marsh Entertainment*
12444 Ventura Blvd Ste 203
Studio City, CA 91604-2409, USA

Bromberg, David (Musician)
c/o Staff Member *Agency Group Ltd, The (LA)*
1880 Century Park E Ste 711
Los Angeles, CA 90067-1618, USA

Bromell, Loranzo (Athlete, Football Player)
13800 Crowne Hill Ln
Hopkins, MN 55305-2255, USA

Bromley, D Allan (Government Official, Physicist)
3102 23rd St
Lubbock, TX 79410-2123, USA

Bromley, Gary (Athlete, Hockey Player)
3172 Toba Dr
Coquitlam, BC V3B 6A4, Canada

Bromstad, David (Designer)
c/o Ken Slotnick *WmE2 (WMA-NY)*
1325 Avenue of the Americas
New York, NY 10019-6026, USA

Bron, Eleanor (Actor)
c/o Rebecca Blond *Rebecca Blond Associates*
69a Kings Rd
London SW3 4NX, UNITED KINGDOM

Bronars, Edward J (General)
3354 Rose Ln
Falls Church, VA 22042-4031, USA

Bronfman, Charles (Baseball Player, Business Person)
501 N Lake Way
Palm Beach, FL 33480-3520, USA

Bronfman, Yefin (Musician)
40 W 57th St
New York, NY 10019-4001, USA

Bronkey, Jeff (Athlete, Baseball Player)
622 Sunny Brook Dr
Edmond, OK 73034-4224, USA

Bronleewe, Matt (Musician)
1700 Hayes St Ste 304
Nashville, TN 37203-3014, USA

Bronson, Ben (Athlete, Football Player)
13333 West Rd Apt 1717
Houston, TX 77041-6153, USA

Bronson, Oswald P Sr (Educator)
President's Office
Daytona Beach, FL 32114, USA

Bronson, Po (Writer)
1745 Broadway # B1
New York, NY 10019-4368, USA

Bronstad, Jim (Athlete, Baseball Player)
63 One Main Pl
Benbrook, TX 76126-2206, USA

Bronstein, Elizabeth (Producer)
c/o Staff Member *Creative Artists Agency (CAA-LA)*
2000 Avenue of the Stars Ste 100
Los Angeles, CA 90067-4705, USA

Brook, Apple (Actor)
c/o Staff Member *Grays Management & Associates*
Panther House 38 Mount Pleasant
London WC1X 0AP, UK

Brook, Holly (Musician)
c/o Staff Member *Paradigm (Monterey)*
404 W Franklin St
Monterey, CA 93940-2303, USA

Brook, Jayne (Actor)
c/o Leslie Siebert *Gersh (LA)*
9465 Wilshire Blvd Ste 600
Beverly Hills, CA 90212-2612, USA

Brook, Kelly (Actor)
c/o Joan Hyler *Hyler Management*
20 Ocean Park Blvd Unit 25
Santa Monica, CA 90405-3590, USA

Brook, Peter S P (Director)
13 Blvd de Rochechouart
Paris 75009, FRANCE

Brooke, Allison (Music Group, Songwriter, Writer)
6920 W Sunset Blvd
Los Angeles, CA 90028-7010, USA

Brooke, Bob (Athlete, Hockey Player)
15496 Stanbury Curv
Eden Prairie, MN 55347-2433, USA

Brooke, Jonatha (Musician, Songwriter, Writer)
1255 5th Ave Apt 7J
New York, NY 10029-3848, USA

Brooke, Paul (Actor)
c/o Staff Member *Caroline Dawson Assoc.*
125 Gloucester Rd 2nd Floor
London SW7 4TE, UK

Brooke III, Edward W (Ex-Senator, Politician)
727 15th St NW Fl 6
Washington, DC 20005-2168, USA

Brookens, Ike (Athlete, Baseball Player)
1053 Brookens Rd
Fayetteville, PA 17222-9314, USA

Brookens, Tom (Athlete, Baseball Player)
488 Black Gap Rd
Fayetteville, PA 17222-9717, USA

Brooker, Gary (Musician, Songwriter, Writer)
5 Cranley Gardens
London SW7, UNITED KINGDOM (UK)

Brooker, Tommy (Athlete, Football Player)
306 Woodridge Dr
Tuscaloosa, AL 35406-1923, USA

Brookes, Harvey (Physicist)
Aiken Computation Laboratory
Cambridge, MA 2138, USA

Brookes, Peter (Cartoonist)
Editorial Dept 1 Pennington St
London E98 1S5, UNITED KINGDOM (UK)

Brooke-Taylor, Tim (Actor, Comedian)
3 Lonsdale Road
London SW13 9ED, UNITED KINGDOM (UK)

Brookhart, Maurice S (Misc)
Chemistry Dept
Chapel Hill, NC 27514, USA

Brookins, Clarence (Athlete, Basketball Player)
8266 Fayette St
Philadelphia, PA 19150-2002, USA

Brookins, Gary (Cartoonist)
PO Box 85333
Richmond, VA 23293-5333, USA

Brookner, Anita (Writer)
68 Elm Park Gardens #6
London SW10 9PB, UNITED KINGDOM (UK)

Brooks, Aaron (Athlete, Football Player)
6 Viper Ct
Hampton, VA 23666-2277, USA

Brooks, Albert (Actor, Director, Writer)
c/o Robert Lange *Kleinberg Lopez Lange Brisbin and Cuddy*
2049 Century Park E Ste 3180
Los Angeles, CA 90067-3205, USA

Brooks, Amanda (Actor)
c/o Staff Member *Nine Yards Entertainment*
8530 Wilshire Blvd Ste 550
Beverly Hills, CA 90211-3133, USA

Brooks, Angelle (Actor)
c/o Staff Member *Pakula/King & Associates*
9229 W Sunset Blvd Ste 315
Los Angeles, CA 90069-3403, USA

Brooks, Avery (Actor)
c/o Steven Arcieri *Arcieri & Associates Inc*
305 Madison Ave Ste 2315
New York, NY 10165-5015, USA

Brooks, Barrett (Athlete, Football Player)
11 Berkshire Dr Apt 25
Voorhees, NJ 08043-3448, USA

Brooks, Bill (Athlete, Football Player)
1088 Laurelwood
Carmel, IN 46032-8742, USA

Brooks, Bobby D (Athlete, Football Player)
7416 Red Osier Rd
Dallas, TX 75249-1349, USA

Brooks, Bucky (Athlete, Football Player)
1336 Vanagrif Ct
Wake Forest, NC 27587-4479, USA

Brooks, Chet (Athlete, Football Player)
655 Shadyway Dr
Dallas, TX 75232-4821, USA

Brooks, Conrad (Actor)
PO Box 264
Inwood, WV 25428-0264, USA

Brooks, Danny (Musician)
2011 Ferry Ave Apt U19
Camden, NJ 08104-1900, USA

Brooks, David Allen (David A) (Actor)
c/o Staff Member *Candy Entertainment Management*
8981 W Sunset Blvd Ste 310
West Hollywood, CA 90069-1848, USA

Brooks, Derrick (Athlete, Football Player)
2318 Malysa Pl
Pensacola, FL 32504-5905, USA

Brooks, Donnie (Musician)
1817 W Verdugo Ave
Burbank, CA 91506-2149, USA

Brooks, E R (Business Person)
1616 Woodall Rodgers Fwy
Dallas, TX 75202-1234, USA

Brooks, Ed (Athlete, Golfer)
6604 Augusta Rd
Fort Worth, TX 76132-4564, USA

Brooks, Ethan (Athlete, Football Player)
8 Gatewood
Avon, CT 06001-3949, USA

Brooks, Frederick P Jr (Mathematician, Scientist)
413 Granville Rd
Chapel Hill, NC 27514-2723, USA

Brooks, Garth (Actor, Musician, Producer, Songwriter)
c/o Nancy Seltzer *Nancy Seltzer & Associates*
6220 Del Valle Dr
Los Angeles, CA 90048-5306, USA

Brooks, Geraldine (Writer)
c/o Staff Member *Viking Press*
375 Hudson St
New York, NY 10014-3658, USA

Brooks, Golden (Actor)
c/o Mark J. Holder *Zero Gravity Management*
11578 Canton Dr
Studio City, CA 91604-4160, USA

Brooks, Heather (Stylist)
c/o Staff Member *Fifty8 Artists*
58 W Huron St
Chicago, IL 60654-3806, USA

Brooks, Herb (Athlete)
180 Birchwood Ave
Saint Paul, MN 55110-1612

Brooks, Hubert (Hubie) (Athlete, Baseball Player)
15001 Olive St
Hesperia, CA 92345-3306, USA

Brooks, James L (Actor)
c/o Jeff Berg *International Creative Management (ICM-LA)*
10250 Constellation Blvd Fl 7
Los Angeles, CA 90067-6207, USA

Brooks, Jason (Actor)
c/o Staff Member *Commonwealth Talent Group*
PO Box 36514
Los Angeles, CA 90036-0514, USA

Brooks, Jerry (Athlete, Baseball Player)
15152 Mountain View Ln
Frisco, TX 75035-6882, USA

Brooks, Joel (Actor)
c/o Martin Gage *Gage Group, The (LA)*
14724 Ventura Blvd Ste 505
Sherman Oaks, CA 91403-3505, USA

Brooks, John E (Educator)
President's Office
Worcester, MA 1610, USA

Brooks, Jon (Athlete, Football Player)
104 Carver St
Saluda, SC 29138-1514, USA

Brooks, Karen (Musician)
5408 Clearview Ln
Waterford, WI 53185-2950, USA

Brooks, Kevin (Athlete, Football Player)
13410 Preston Rd Apt 360
Dallas, TX 75240-5299, USA

Brooks, Kimberly A (Actor)
c/o Kevin Turner *Coast to Coast Talent Group*
3350 Barham Blvd
Los Angeles, CA 90068-1404, USA

Brooks, Kix (Musician, Songwriter)
PO Box 120669
Nashville, TN 37212-0669, USA

Brooks, Lala (Misc)
PO Box 371371
Las Vegas, NV 89137-1371, USA

Brooks, Lee (Athlete, Football Player)
4206 Bamford Dr
Austin, TX 78731-1355, USA

Brooks, Mark (Athlete, Golfer)
1206 Mistletoe Dr
Fort Worth, TX 76110-1017, USA

Brooks, Mehcad (Actor)
c/o David (Dave) Fleming *Mosaic Media Group*
9200 W Sunset Blvd Ste 10
Los Angeles, CA 90069-3608, USA

Brooks, Mel (Actor, Director)
c/o Staff Member *HarperCollins Publishers*
10 E 53rd St C/O Author Mail Floor 7
New York, NY 10022, USA

Brooks, Meredith (Musician)
1750 Vine St
Los Angeles, CA 90028-5209, USA

Brooks, Michael (Athlete, Basketball Player)
495 Bethany St
San Diego, CA 92114-5539, USA

Brooks, Michael (Athlete, Football Player)
15004 W Georgia Dr
Surprise, AZ 85379-4249, USA

Brooks, Michael (Athlete, Football Player)
30 Pine Tree Dr
Honey Brook, PA 19344-1254, USA

Brooks, Nathan (Boxer)
21274 Ellacott Pkwy Apt M208
Cleveland, OH 44128-6600, USA

Brooks, Perry (Athlete, Football Player)
15010 Plastron Ct
Woodbridge, VA 22193-5846, USA

Brooks, Reggie (Athlete, Football Player)
1701 Portage Ave
South Bend, IN 46616-1919, USA

Brooks, Rich (Athlete, Coach, Football Coach, Football Player)
Athletic
Lexington, KY 40506-0001, USA

Brooks, Richard (Actor)
333 Washington Blvd # 102
Marina Del Rey, CA 90292-5136, USA

Brooks, Robert (Athlete, Football Player)
8611 N 17th Pl
Phoenix, AZ 85020-3320, USA

Brooks, Ross (Athlete, Hockey Player)
196 Old River Rd Apt 215
Lincoln, RI 02865-1133, USA

Brooks, Steve (Athlete, Football Player)
8306 Wilshire Blvd Apt 154
Beverly Hills, CA 90211-2382, USA

Brooks, Terry (Writer)
1540 Broadway
New York, NY 10036-4039, USA

Brooks, Tony (Athlete, Football Player)
19626 Northrop St
Cassopolis, MI 49031-9328, USA

Brooks & Dunn (Music Group, Musician)
c/o Rick Shipp *WmE2 (WMA-TN)*
1600 Division St Ste 300
Nashville, TN 37203-2755, USA

Brooks Jr, Cliff (Athlete, Football Player)
12023 Briar Forest Dr
Houston, TX 77077-3027, USA

Brooks Jr., Mo (Congressman, Politician)
1641 Longworth Hob
Washington, DC 20515-3005, USA

Brophy, Jay (Athlete, Football Player)
260 Graham Rd
Cuyahoga Falls, OH 44223-2256, USA

Brophy, Kevin (Actor)
15010 Hamlin St
Van Nuys, CA 91411-1408, USA

Brophy, Nancy (Athlete, Golfer)
141 Carpenter Ln
Harrisonburg, VA 22801-9777, USA

Brophy, Theodore F (Business Person)
60 Arch St
Greenwich, CT 06830-2507, USA

Brorby, Wade (Judge)
2120 Capitol Ave
Cheyenne, WY 82001-3633, USA

Broshears, Robert (Artist)
8020 NW Holly Rd
Bremerton, WA 98312-9536, USA

Brosius, Scott D (Athlete, Baseball Player)
900 SE Baker St Hhpa Complex Mail Code A440
McMinnville, OR 97128-6808, USA

Broski, David C (Educator)
President's Office
Chicago, IL 60607, USA

Brosky, Albert (Al) (Athlete, Football Player)
2031 Yellow Daisy Ct
Naperville, IL 60563-0234, USA

Brosnan, Jim (Athlete, Baseball Player)
7742 Churchill St
Morton Grove, IL 60053-1805, USA

Brosnan, Pierce (Actor, Producer)
c/o Jennifer Allen *Viewpoint Inc*
8820 Wilshire Blvd Ste 220
Beverly Hills, CA 90211-2622, USA

Bross, Terry (Athlete, Baseball Player)
7952 E Camino Real
Scottsdale, AZ 85255-6136, USA

Brossart, Willie (Athlete, Hockey Player)
9318 Susquehanna Trl
Ashland, VA 23005-3382, USA

Brosseau, Frank (Athlete, Baseball Player)
41 Island Rd
Saint Paul, MN 55127-2635, USA

Brostek, Bern (Athlete, Football Player)
901 N Broadway
Saint Louis, MO 63101-2800, USA

Broten, Aaron (Athlete, Hockey Player)
307 3rd Ave SE
Roseau, MN 56751-1526, USA

Broten, Neal (Athlete, Hockey Player)
N8216 690th St
River Falls, WI 54022-4535, USA

Broten, Paul (Athlete, Hockey Player)
6972 Ashwood Rd Apt 305
Saint Paul, MN 55125-1211, USA

Broth, Ed
c/o Daniel A (Dan) Strone *Trident Media Group LLC*
41 Madison Ave Fl 36
New York, NY 10010-2257, USA

Brothers, Bellamy, The (Musician)
c/o Staff Member *Agency for the Performing Arts (APA-LA)*
405 S Beverly Dr Ste 500
Beverly Hills, CA 90212-4425, USA

Brothers, Dr Joyce (Actor, Doctor)
c/o Monique Moss *Moss Public Relations*
8060 Melrose Ave Fl 4
Los Angeles, CA 90046-7038, USA

Brotherton, John (Actor)
c/o Gabrielle Krengel *Domain Talent*
9229 W Sunset Blvd Ste 710
Los Angeles, CA 90069-3407, USA

Brotman, Jeffrey (Business Person)
999 Lake Dr
Issaquah, WA 98027-8990, USA

Brough, Randi (Actor)
11684 Ventura Blvd # 476
Studio City, CA 91604-2699, USA

Brough Clapp, A Louise (Tennis Player)
1808 Voluntary Rd
Vista, CA 92084-3112, USA

Broughton, Bruce (Composer)
c/o Staff Member *Evolution Music Partners*
1680 Vine St Ste 500
Hollywood, CA 90028-8800, USA

Broughton, Luther (Athlete, Football Player)
PO Box 371
Huger, SC 29450-0371, USA

Broughton, Willie (Athlete, Football Player)
1724 Lacy Ln
Mesquite, TX 75181-1560, USA

Brouhard, Mark (Athlete, Baseball Player)
6289 Jackie Ave
Woodland Hills, CA 91367-1424, USA

Broussard, Ben (Athlete, Baseball Player)
9170 Mapes St
Beaumont, TX 77707-1250, USA

Broussard, Fred (Athlete, Football Player)
9750 False River Rd
New Roads, LA 70760, USA

Broussard, Marc (Musician)
c/o Staff Member *Paradigm (Monterey)*
404 W Franklin St
Monterey, CA 93940-2303, USA

Broussard, Rebecca (Actor)
9911 W Pico Blvd PH PMB A
Los Angeles, CA 90035-2703, USA

Broussard, Steve (Athlete, Football Player)
2024 Shoals View Ct
Lawrenceville, GA 30045-2684, USA

Broussard, Susan (Stylist)
63 Starview Way
San Francisco, CA 94131-1229

Brouwenstyn, Gerada (Actor)
Bachplein 3
Amsterdam NL-1077 GH, The Netherlands

Brouwenstyn, Gerarda (Opera Singer)
3 Bachpiein
Amsterdam, NETHERLANDS

Brow, Scott (Athlete, Baseball Player)
1194 W Remington Dr
Chandler, AZ 85286-6385, USA

Browder, Ben (Actor)
c/o Hank McCann 1321 Londonderry Pl
Los Angeles, CA 90069, USA

Browder, Felix E (Mathematician)
4 Foulet Dr
Princeton, NJ 08540-7638, USA

Brower, Bob (Athlete, Baseball Player)
2703 N Van Buren St
Hutchinson, KS 67502-2017, USA

Brower, James (Jim) (Athlete, Baseball Player)
4644 S Lockwood Ridge Rd
Sarasota, FL 34231-7533, USA

Brower, Jordan
9100 Wilshire Blvd Ste 503E
Beverly Hills, CA 90212-3419

Brower, Jordan Lloyd (Actor)
c/o Beverly Strong *Strong Management*
3532 Hayden Ave
Culver City, CA 90232-2413, USA

Brower, Laurie (Athlete, Golfer)
6001 34th St Spc 170
Lubbock, TX 79407-3106, USA

Brown, A B (Athlete, Football Player)
224 Wesley St
Salem, NJ 08079-1714, USA

Brown, Aaron (Correspondent)
c/o Staff Member *NS Bienstock Inc*
250 W 57th St Ste 333
New York, NY 10107-0302, USA

Brown, Aaron C (Athlete, Football Player)
3312 Russett Dr
Tampa, FL 33618-1308, USA

Brown, Adrian (Baseball Player)
706 Palmetto St
Summit, MS 39666-9323, USA

Brown, Alison (Musician, Songwriter, Writer)
6629 University Ave Ste 206
Middleton, WI 53562-3037, USA

Brown, Allen (Athlete, Football Player)
PO Box 18076
Natchez, MS 39122-8076, USA

Brown, Alton (Chef, Television Host)
c/o Staff Member *Food Network, The*
75 9th Ave
New York, NY 10011-7006, USA

Brown, Alton (Athlete, Baseball Player)
253 Consul Ave
Virginia Beach, VA 23462-3511, USA

Brown, Andre (Athlete, Football Player)
11245 S Emerald Ave
Chicago, IL 60628-4706, USA

Brown, Andy (Athlete, Hockey Player)
6175 S 125 W
Trafalgar, IN 46181, USA

Brown, Arnie (Athlete, Hockey Player)
General Delivery
Woodview, ON K0L 3E0, Canada

Brown, Arnold (Athlete, Football Player)
8763 Stephens Church Rd
Wilmington, NC 28411-7985, USA

Brown, Arthur E Jr (General)
35 Fairway Winds Pl
Hilton Head Island, SC 29928-5547, USA

Brown, Ashley Nicole (Actor)
PO Box 64249
Los Angeles, CA 90064-0249, USA

Brown, Bailey (Judge)
167 N Main St
Memphis, TN 38103-1814, USA

Brown, Bill (Athlete, Football Player)
P.O. Box 8533
Victorville, CA 92392, USA

Brown, Bill (Athlete, Football Player)
9365 Libby Ln
Eden Prairie, MN 55347-4282, USA

Brown, Billy Aaron (Actor)
c/o Staff Member *Stone Manners Salners Agency (LA)*
9911 W Pico Blvd Ste 1400
Los Angeles, CA 90035-2715, USA

Brown, Billy Ray (Athlete, Golfer)
7502 Whitman Ln
Sugar Land, TX 77479-4452, USA

Brown, Blair (Actor)
18 E 53rd St # 140
New York, NY 10022-5202, USA

Brown, Bo (Cartoonist)
3500 W Chester Pike # A210
Newtown Square, PA 19073-4101, USA

Brown, Bob (Athlete, Basketball Player)
7 Charleston St S
Sugar Land, TX 77478-3656, USA

Brown, Bobby (Actor, Dancer, Musician, Producer, Songwriter)
c/o Staff Member *WmE2 (WMA-LA)*
1 William Morris Pl
Beverly Hills, CA 90212-4261, USA

Brown, Bobby (Athlete, Baseball Player)
700 Pleasant Ridge Ct
Chesapeake, VA 23322-2747, USA

Brown, Bobby (Athlete, Baseball Player)
4100 Clarke Ave
Fort Worth, TX 76107-2407, USA

Brown, Booker (Athlete, Football Player)
3354 Arthur Ave
Mojave, CA 93501-1304, USA

Brown, Brant (Athlete, Baseball Player)
1612 Fieldspring Dr
Bakersfield, CA 93311-3542, USA

Brown, Brianna (Actor)
c/o Greg Clark *Untitled Entertainment (LA)*
350 S Beverly Dr Ste 200
Beverly Hills, CA 90212-4819, USA

Brown, Bruce (Photographer)
15550 Calle Real
Gaviota, CA 93117-9729, USA

Brown, Bryan (Actor)
c/o Staff Member *Steve Himber Entertainment*
211 S Beverly Dr Apt S
Beverly Hills, CA 90212-3807, USA

Brown, C Edward (Eddie) (Athlete, Football Player)
3465 Commodore Pt
Knoxville, TN 37922-6566, USA

Brown, Campbell (Correspondent)
c/o Staff Member *CNN (Atlanta)*
1 Cnn Ctr NW
Atlanta, GA 30303-2762, USA

Brown, Candace (Actor)
c/o Judy Orbach *Judy O Productions*
6136 Glen Holly St
Hollywood, CA 90068-2338, USA

Brown, Carlos (Athlete, Football Player)
1106 E Newhall Dr
Fresno, CA 93720-4084, USA

Brown, Cedrick (Athlete, Football Player)
74 Arbor Meadow Dr
Sicklerville, NJ 08081-1754, USA

Brown, Chad (Actor)
c/o Staff Member *Sterling/Winters Company, The*
10877 Wilshire Blvd Fl 15
Los Angeles, CA 90024-4341, USA

Brown, Chadwick (Chad) (Athlete, Football Player)
2827 Holliston Ave
Altadena, CA 91001-2009, USA

Brown, Charles (Athlete, Football Player)
2942 River Rd
Johns Island, SC 29455-8814, USA

Brown, Charles E (Athlete, Football Player)
7317 S Merrill Ave
Chicago, IL 60649-3208, USA

Brown, Charlie (Athlete, Football Player)
3113 Cherry Valley Cir
Fairfield, CA 94534-7510, USA

Brown, Charlie R (Athlete, Football Player)
5226 Washington Pl
Saint Louis, MO 63108-1117, USA

Brown, Chris (Athlete, Football Player)
2869 Acarie Dr
Columbus, OH 43219-6198, USA

Brown, Chris (Musician)
c/o Tammy Brook *FYI Public Relations*
174 5th Ave Ste 400
New York, NY 10010-5935, USA

Brown, Chucky (Athlete, Basketball Player)
102 Balsamwood Ct
Cary, NC 27513-3456, USA

Brown, Cindy (Athlete, Basketball Player)
2 Championship Dr
Auburn Hills, MI 48326-1753, USA

Brown, Clancy (Actor)
3141 Oakdell Ln
Studio City, CA 91604-4218, USA

Brown, Cleophus (Athlete, Baseball Player)
3912 Sharon Church Rd
Pinson, AL 35126-2660, USA

Brown, Clifford (Athlete, Baseball Player)
5104 N 37th St
Tampa, FL 33610-6421, USA

Brown, Cornell (Athlete, Football Player)
1600 Sangloe Pl
Lynchburg, VA 24502-1822, USA

Brown, Corrine (Congressman, Politician)
2336 Rayburn Hob
Washington, DC 20515-2305, USA

Brown, Corwin (Athlete, Football Player)
1124 E 90th St
Chicago, IL 60619-7931, USA

Brown, Courtney (Athlete, Football Player)
1133 Circle Rd
Berea, OH 44017, USA

Brown, Curt (Athlete, Baseball Player)
2921 Landon Dr
Columbus, OH 43209-3257, USA

Brown, Curtis (Athlete, Baseball Player)
3200 Cloudview Dr
Sacramento, CA 95833-2700, USA

Brown, Curtis (Athlete, Football Player)
1035 Lindenwood Ave
Saint Charles, MO 63301-0801, USA

Brown, Curtis (Athlete, Hockey Player)
467 Carroll St
Sunnyvale, CA 94086-6204, USA

Brown, Curtis L Jr (Astronaut)
204 Starrwood
Hudson, WI 54016-7174, USA

Brown, Dale (Writer)
c/o Robert Gottlieb *Trident Media Group LLC*
41 Madison Ave Fl 36
New York, NY 10010-2257, USA

Brown, Dale D (Coach, Sportscaster)
Sports Dept ESPN Plaza 935 Middle St
Bristol, CT 6010, USA

Brown, Dan (Writer)
c/o Staff Member *Doubleday/ RandomHouse*
1745 Broadway
New York, NY 10019-4368, USA

Brown, Daniel G (General)
Deputy CinC US Transportation Command
Scott Air Force Base, IL 62225, USA

Brown, Darrell (Baseball Player)
1323 N Blackwelder Ave
Oklahoma City, OK 73106-2215, USA

Brown, Darryl (Stylist)
c/o Staff Member *Ken Barboza Associates*
115 W 30th St Rm 203
New York, NY 10001-4088, USA

Brown, Dave (Athlete, Hockey Player)
c/o Staff Member *Philadelphia Flyers*
First Union Spectrum 3601 S Broad St, Suite 2
Philadelphia, PA 19148, USA

Brown, David (Producer)
200 W 57th St
New York, NY 10019-3211, USA

Brown, David P (Athlete)
345 Willow Springs Dr
Talent, OR 97540-9682, USA

Brown, Dee (Athlete, Basketball Player)
575 Birnamwood Dr
Suwanee, GA 30024-7577, USA

Brown, Dee (Athlete, Baseball Player)
2626 Balmoral Ct
Kissimmee, FL 34744-8442, USA

Brown, Denise (Misc)
PO Box 3777
Monarch Bay, CA 92629-8777, USA

Brown, Derek (Athlete, Football Player)
13 Four Leaf Mnr
Rexford, NY 12148-1490, USA

Brown, Dermal (Baseball Player)
2626 Balmoral Ct
Kissimmee, FL 34744-8442, USA

Brown, Donald C (Athlete, Football Player)
2797 Union Ave
San Jose, CA 95124-1433, USA

Brown, Donald David (Biologist)
6511 Abbey View Way
Baltimore, MD 21212-1373, USA

Brown, Dorian (Actor)
c/o Staff Member *McKeon-Myones Management*
3500 W Olive Ave Ste 770
Burbank, CA 91505-5527, USA

Brown, Doug (Athlete, Football Player)
PO Box 688
Keno, OR 97627-0688, USA

Brown, Doug (Athlete, Hockey Player)
3188 Bradway Blvd
Bloomfield Hills, MI 48301-2504, USA

Brown, Dustin (Athlete, Hockey Player)
1717 8th St
Manhattan Beach, CA 90266-6320, USA

Brown, Eddie (Athlete, Football Player)
628 Cedar Park Dr
Daytona Beach, FL 32114-5112, USA

Brown, Emil (Athlete, Baseball Player)
2215 W 111th St Apt 303
Chicago, IL 60643-3913, USA

Brown, Eric (Athlete, Football Player)
7566 Lincoln Village Dr
San Antonio, TX 78244-1517, USA

Brown, Errol (Musician)
c/o Staff Member *International Artistes*
Holborn Hall - 4th Floor
London WC1V 7BD, UK

Brown, Faith (Actor)
12 Praed Mews
London W2 1QY, UNITED KINGDOM (UK)

Brown, Foxy (Musician)
c/o Lee Daniels *Lee Daniels Entertainment*
315 W 36th St Rm 1002
New York, NY 10018-6526, USA

Brown, Fred (Athlete, Basketball Player, Coach)
3696 72nd Pl SE
Mercer Island, WA 98040-3353, USA

Brown, Fred (Athlete, Football Player)
1050 Riverbend Club Dr SE
Atlanta, GA 30339-2805, USA

Brown, Fred R (Athlete, Football Player)
4128 Rigel Ave
Lompoc, CA 93436-1248, USA

Brown, Gary (Athlete, Football Player)
5 Crystal Ln
Brentwood, NY 11717-1114, USA

Brown, Gary (Athlete, Football Player)
35401 Saddle Crk
Avon, OH 44011-4917, USA

Brown, Gates (Athlete, Baseball Player)
17206 Santa Barbara Dr
Detroit, MI 48221-2525, USA

Brown, Georg Stanford (Actor)
2565 Greenvalley Rd
Los Angeles, CA 90046-1437, USA

Brown, George (Athlete, Football Player)
4401 Flower Valley Dr
Rockville, MD 20853-1813, USA

Brown, George (Athlete, Basketball Player)
24652 Santa Barbara St
Southfield, MI 48075-2526, USA

Brown, Gordie (Comedian)
c/o Staff Member *WmE2 (WMA-LA)*
1 William Morris Pl
Beverly Hills, CA 90212-4261, USA

Brown, Greg (Athlete, Football Player)
1016 Hartley Ct
Sicklerville, NJ 08081-1109, USA

Brown, Greg (Athlete, Hockey Player)
43 Ladds Way
Scituate, MA 02066-1901, USA

Brown, Hal (Athlete, Baseball Player)
4216 Henderson Rd
Greensboro, NC 27410-4305, USA

Brown, Harold (Secretary)
1800 K St NW # 1800
Washington, DC 20006-2202, USA

Brown, Helen Gurley (Editor, Writer)
1 W 81st St # 22D
New York, NY 10024-6048, USA

Brown, Henry (Actor)
1101 E Pike St Ste 300
Seattle, WA 98122-3938, USA

Brown, Henry (Athlete, Baseball Player)
4075 N 61st St
Milwaukee, WI 53216-1210, USA

Brown, Henry W (War Hero)
2825 Carter Rd Unit 117
Sumter, SC 29150-1733, USA

Brown, Heritage Doris (Athlete, Track Athlete)
Athletic Dept
Seattle, WA 98119, USA

Brown, Himan (Director)
7 Times Sq
New York, NY 10036-6524, USA

Brown, Hubie (Athlete, Basketball Player, Coach)
120 Foxridge Rd NW
Atlanta, GA 30327-4310, USA

Brown, Hyman (Engineer)
Civil Engineering
Fort Collins, CO 80523-0001, USA

Brown, Ivory Lee (Athlete, Football Player)
9931 Brockbank Dr
Dallas, TX 75220-1647, USA

Brown, J B (Athlete, Football Player)
12520 Woodsong Ln
Mitchellville, MD 20721-4224, USA

Brown, J Cristopher (Cris) (Baseball Player)
5015 Brighton Ave
Los Angeles, CA 90062-2434, USA

Brown, J Gordon (Government Official)
Westminister
London SW1A 0AA, UNITED KINGDOM (UK)

Brown, Jackie (Athlete, Baseball Player)
7337 E 136 Rd
Holdenville, OK 74848-6012, USA

Brown, James (Musician)
c/o Rob Heller *WmE2 (WMA-LA)*
1 William Morris Pl
Beverly Hills, CA 90212-4261, USA

Brown, James (Sportscaster)
205 E 67th St
New York, NY 10065-6050, USA

Brown, James (Jim) (Actor, Athlete, Football Player)
c/o Harlan Werner *Sports Placement Service*
330 W 11th St Apt 105
Los Angeles, CA 90015-2230, USA

Brown, James R (General)
18286 Buccaneer Ter
Leesburg, VA 20176-8479, USA

Brown, Jamie (Actor)
c/o Melisa Spamer *Domain Talent*
9229 W Sunset Blvd Ste 710
Los Angeles, CA 90069-3407, USA

Brown, Jamie (Athlete, Baseball Player)
4050 Bailey Acres Cir
Meridian, MS 39305-9263, USA

Brown, Jarvis (Athlete, Baseball Player)
1412 85th St
Kenosha, WI 53143-6420, USA

Brown, Jay W Jr (Financier)
113 King St
Armonk, NY 10504-1611, USA

Brown, Jeff (Athlete, Hockey Player)
800 Tara Oaks Dr
Chesterfield, MO 63005, USA

Brown, Jeremy (Athlete, Baseball Player)
704 Cobb St
Birmingham, AL 35209-6515, USA

Brown, Jerry (Governor, Politician)
State Capitol Fl 1
Sacramento, CA 95814, USA

Brown, Jim (Athlete, Football Player)
2030 N Glenoaks Blvd
Burbank, CA 91504-2835, USA

Brown, Jim Ed (Musician)
5811 Still Hollow Rd
Nashville, TN 37215-4819, USA

Brown, John (Athlete, Basketball Player)
1329 N Florissant Rd
Saint Louis, MO 63135-1153, USA

Brown, John (Athlete, Football Player)
101 Gadshill Pl
Pittsburgh, PA 15237-2341, USA

Brown, Jophrey (Athlete, Baseball Player)
3008 W 81st St
Inglewood, CA 90305-1425, USA

Brown, Judge Joe (Judge)
PO Box 949
Los Angeles, CA 90078-0949, USA

Brown, Julie (Actor, Comedian)
11288 Ventura Blvd # 728
Studio City, CA 91604-3187, USA

Brown, Julie (Downtown) (Entertainer)
c/o Steven Jensen *Independent Group, The*
6363 Wilshire Blvd Ste 115
Los Angeles, CA 90048-5734, USA

Brown, Junior (Musician)
c/o Staff Member *Paradigm (Monterey)*
404 W Franklin St
Monterey, CA 93940-2303, USA

Brown, Kaci (Musician)
c/o Staff Member *Interscope Records (LA) - Main*
2220 Colorado Ave
Santa Monica, CA 90404-3506, USA

Brown, Kale (Actor)
c/o Staff Member *Gage Group, The (LA)*
14724 Ventura Blvd Ste 505
Sherman Oaks, CA 91403-3505, USA

Brown, Katie (Designer, Television Host)
c/o Staff Member *Style Network*
5750 Wilshire Blvd
Los Angeles, CA 90036-3697, USA

Brown, Kedrick (Athlete, Basketball Player)
151 Merrimac St # 1
Boston, MA 02114-4714, USA

Brown, Keith (Athlete, Baseball Player)
6313 Willow Oak Dr
Nashville, TN 37221-3980, USA

Brown, Keith (Athlete, Hockey Player)
8515 Woodland Brooke Trl
Cumming, GA 30028-5048, USA

Brown, Ken (Athlete, Hockey Player)
9300 47 St NW
Edmonton, AB T6B 2P6, Canada

Brown, Ken A (Athlete, Football Player)
1106 Johanna Bay Dr
Midlothian, VA 23114-7116, USA

Brown, Ken J (Athlete, Football Player)
2004 Miramar Blvd
Oklahoma City, OK 73111-1808, USA

Brown, Kenneth J (Misc)
1900 L St NW
Washington, DC 20036-5002, USA

Brown, Kevin (Athlete, Baseball Player)
105 Browns Rdg
Macon, GA 31210-8614, USA

Brown, Kevin (Athlete, Baseball Player)
9201 Ryan Ct
Evansville, IN 47712-5410, USA

Brown, Kevin (Athlete, Baseball Player)
20 McKilt Ct
Sacramento, CA 95835-1334, USA

Brown, Kimberlin Ann (Actor)
c/o Staff Member *Pakula/King & Associates*
9229 W Sunset Blvd Ste 315
Los Angeles, CA 90069-3403, USA

Brown, Kimberly J (Actor)
c/o Staff Member *Gemstone Talent*
27943 Seco Canyon Rd # 212
Santa Clarita, CA 91350-3872, USA

Brown, Koffee (Musician)
481 Eight Ave # 1750
New York, NY 10001

Brown, Kwarne (Athlete, Basketball Player)
601 F St NW
Washington, DC 20004-1605, USA

Brown, Lacey (Musician)
c/o Staff Member *19 Entertainment*
33/32 Ransomes Dock 35-37 Parkgate Rd
London SW11 4NP, UK

Brown, Larry (Athlete, Hockey Player)
5781 Eucalyptus Dr
Garden Valley, CA 95633-9622, USA

Brown, Larry (Athlete, Football Player)
1377 Glencoe Ave
Pittsburgh, PA 15205-4342, USA

Brown, Larry (Athlete, Baseball Player)
13158 La Mirada Cir
Wellington, FL 33414-3997, USA

Brown, Larry (Athlete, Football Player)
12004 Piney Glen Ln
Potomac, MD 20854-1417, USA

Brown, Larry (Athlete, Hockey Player)
21 Landing Dr
Dobbs Ferry, NY 10522-1181, USA

Brown, Lawrence H (Larry) (Athlete, Basketball Player, Coach)
1030 Green Valley Rd
Bryn Mawr, PA 19010-1912, USA

Brown, Lee P (Government Official)
City Hall 901 Bagby St #300
Houston, TX 77002, USA

Brown, Leon (Athlete, Baseball Player)
7537 S La Rosa Dr
Tempe, AZ 85283-4627, USA

Brown, Leonard (Baseball Player)
4411 19th St NE
Washington, DC 20018-3305, USA

Brown, Les (Motivational Speaker)
PO Box 806217
Chicago, IL 60680-4123, USA

Brown, Lewis (Athlete, Basketball Player)
902 E Imperial Hwy
Los Angeles, CA 90059-1622, USA

Brown, Lomas (Athlete, Football Player)
2271 Crystal Dr
Rochester Hills, MI 48309-3753, USA

Brown, Louis (Business Person)
4426B Hugh Howell Rd Ste 200
Tucker, GA 30084-4905, USA

Brown, Mack (Coach)
Athletic Dept
Austin, TX 78712, USA

Brown, Marc (Writer)
PO Box 873
West Tisbury, MA 02575-0873, USA

Brown, Mark (Athlete, Baseball Player)
108 NE 1st Street Ter
Blue Springs, MO 64014-2814, USA

Brown, Mark (Athlete, Football Player)
2761 SW 81st Way
Davie, FL 33328-1617, USA

Brown, Mark N (Astronaut)
80 Earlsgate Rd
Beavercreek, OH 45440-3664, USA

Brown, Marty (Musician)
212 3rd Ave N
Nashville, TN 37201-1626, USA

Brown, Marty (Athlete, Baseball Player)
4425 Bent Tree Blvd
Sarasota, FL 34241-6013, USA

Brown, Marv (Athlete, Football Player)
1204 Irvine Dr
Allen, TX 75013-3654, USA

Brown, Matt (Director)
c/o James Adams *Schreck Rose Dapello Adams & Hurwitz*
1790 Broadway Fl 20
New York, NY 10019-1412, USA

Brown, Max (Actor)
c/o Lena Roklin *Luber Roklin Management*
8530 Wilshire Blvd Ste 550
Beverly Hills, CA 90211-3133, USA

Brown, Melanie (Dancer, Musician)
c/o Wes Stevens *Vox*
6420 Wilshire Blvd Ste 1080
Los Angeles, CA 90048-5539, USA

Brown, Michael (Athlete, Basketball Player)
304 Rays Mill Rd
Aberdeen, NC 28315-3323, USA

Brown, Michael S (Nobel Prize Laureate)
5719 Redwood Ln
Dallas, TX 75209-2421, USA

Brown, Mike (Athlete, Baseball Player)
710 95th Ave N
Naples, FL 34108-2457, USA

Brown, Mike (Astronomer)
Astronomy
Pasadena, CA 91125-0001, USA

Brown, Mike (Coach)
c/o Staff Member *Cleveland Cavaliers*
1 Center Ct
Cleveland, OH 44115-4001, USA

Brown, Mike (Athlete, Baseball Player)
2904 E Minton St
Mesa, AZ 85213-1697, USA

Brown, Myron (Athlete, Basketball Player)
10382 Grubbs Rd
Wexford, PA 15090-9420, USA

Brown, Na (Athlete, Football Player)
PO Box 853
Fletcher, NC 28732-0853, USA

Brown, Norman (Musician)
c/o Staff Member *APA Talent And Literary Agency (NY)*
45 W 45th St Ste 804
New York, NY 10036-4602, USA

Brown, Norman W (Business Person)
101 E Erie St
Chicago, IL 60611-2812, USA

Brown, Norris (Athlete, Football Player)
320 Pinehaven Street Ext
Laurens, SC 29360, USA

Brown, Olivia (Actor)

Brown, Ollie (Athlete, Baseball Player)
8462 Country Club Dr
Buena Park, CA 90621-1421, USA

Brown, Orlando (Actor)
c/o Sharyn Berg *Sharyn Talent Management*
PO Box 18033
Encino, CA 91416-8033, USA

Brown, Oscar (Athlete, Baseball Player)
19113 Gunlock Ave
Carson, CA 90746-2825, USA

Brown, Otto (Athlete, Football Player)
456 Alcorn Ave
Dallas, TX 75217-5833, USA

Brown, Owsley II (Business Person)
850 Dixie Hwy
Louisville, KY 40210-1038, USA

Brown, P J (Athlete, Basketball Player)
1512 Lakeshore Blvd
Slidell, LA 70461-4698, USA

Brown, Patricia (Baseball Player)
821 Solar Ln
Glenview, IL 60025-4464, USA

Brown, Patrick (Misc)
Medical School Biochemistry Dept
Stanford, CA 94305, USA

Brown, Paul (Athlete, Baseball Player)
3617 Highway 75
Holdenville, OK 74848-9421, USA

Brown, Paul (Musician)
c/o Staff Member *Verve Music Group*
1755 Broadway Frnt 3
New York, NY 10019-3743, USA

Brown, Peter (Actor)
5328 Alhama Dr
Woodland Hills, CA 91364-2013, USA

Brown, Philip (Actor)
8721 W Sunset Blvd Ste 200
Los Angeles, CA 90069-2272, USA

Brown, Preston (Athlete, Football Player)
6804 Jones Valley Dr SE
Huntsville, AL 35802-1920, USA

Brown, R Hanbury (Astronomer)
Penton Mewsey
Andover Hants SP11 0RQ, UNITED KINGDOM (UK)

Brown, Ralph (Athlete, Football Player)
9395 Old Post Dr
Rancho Cucamonga, CA 91730-5765, USA

Brown, Randy (Baseball Player)
PO Box 326
Plymouth, FL 32768-0326, USA

Brown, Ray (Athlete, Football Player)
222 Republic Dr
Allen Park, MI 48101-3650, USA

Brown, Raymond (Athlete, Football Player)
4936 Lake Fjord Pass
Marietta, GA 30068-1639, USA

Brown, Reb (Actor)
c/o Staff Member *Gyst Management*
9107 Wilshire Blvd Ste 450
Beverly Hills, CA 90210-5535, USA

Brown, Reggie (Athlete, Football Player)
2242 NW 93rd Ter
Miami, FL 33147-3068, USA

Brown, Reggie D (Athlete, Football Player)
20101 Bentler St
Detroit, MI 48219-1387, USA

Brown, Reggie V (Athlete, Football Player)
1325 Oxford Ln
Union, NJ 07083-5447, USA

Brown, Ricardo (Kurupt) (Actor, Composer, Musician)
c/o Stephen Barnes *Morris, Yorn, Barnes, Levine, Krintzman, Rubenstein and Kohner*
2000 Ave Of The Stars 3rd Tower Floor NORTH
Los Angeles, CA 90067, USA

Brown, Richard (Athlete, Football Player)
5652 Alfred Ave
Westminster, CA 92683-2810, USA

Brown, Richard E (Tex) III (General)
Deputy Cofs for Personnel Hqusaf
Pentagon
Washington, DC 20330-0001, USA

Brown, Rita Mae (Actor, Writer)
PO Box 4671
Charlottesville, VA 22905-4671, USA

Brown, Rob (Athlete, Hockey Player)
5204 84th St
Edmonton, AB T6E 5N8, Canada

Brown, Rob (Actor)
c/o Gabrielle (Gaby) Morgerman *WmE2 (Endeavor-LA)*
9601 Wilshire Blvd Fl 3
Beverly Hills, CA 90210-5219, USA

Brown, Robert (Athlete, Football Player)
2574 US Highway 27 N
Falmouth, KY 41040-7930, USA

Brown, Robert (Athlete, Football Player)
PO Box 211081
Saint Louis, MO 63121-9081, USA

Brown, Robert D (Business Person)
2090 Florence Ave
Cincinnati, OH 45206-2484, USA

Brown, Robert S (Bob) (Athlete, Football Player)
1628 Fairmont Dr
San Leandro, CA 94578-1929, USA

Brown, Roger L (Athlete, Football Player)
9 N Point Dr
Portsmouth, VA 23703-3644, USA

Brown, Ron (Athlete, Football Player)
3961 Via Marisol Apt 331
Los Angeles, CA 90042-4973, USA

Brown, Roosevelt (Athlete)
6551 Thea Ln Apt S17
Columbus, GA 31907-0822

Brown, Roosevelt (Athlete, Baseball Player)
6551 Thea Ln Apt S17
Columbus, GA 31907-0822, USA

Brown, Ruben (Athlete, Football Player)
170 Fox Meadow Ln
Orchard Park, NY 14127-2866, USA

Brown, Rush (Athlete, Football Player)
2425 Cartertown Rd
Clinton, NC 28328-7467, USA

Brown, Samantha (Actor)
c/o Erika Martineau *Brooks Group*
15 W 37th St Rm 1601
New York, NY 10018-5318, USA

Brown, Samuel M (Athlete, Football Player)
25 Franklin Creek Rd N
Savannah, GA 31411-2826, USA

Brown, Sandra (Writer)
1306 W Abram St
Arlington, TX 76013-1703, USA

Brown, Sara (Actor)
6300 Wilshire Blvd Ste 1470
Los Angeles, CA 90048-5200, USA

Brown, Sarah (Actor)
c/o Staff Member *McKeon-Myones Management*
3500 W Olive Ave Ste 770
Burbank, CA 91505-5527, USA

Brown, Scott (Athlete, Baseball Player)
1238 Alton Pierce Rd
Dequincy, LA 70633-4501, USA

Brown, Scott P. (Senator)
359 Dirksen Senate Ofc Building
Washington, DC 20510-0001, USA

Brown, Selwyn (Athlete, Football Player)
3533 Inverrary Blvd W
Lauderhill, FL 33319-7114, USA

Brown, Shane (Athlete, Basketball Player, Coach)
1 Campus View Dr
Vienna, WV 26105-8000, USA

Brown, Shay (Athlete, Misc)
499 Erin Dr
Knoxville, TN 37919, USA

Brown, Sherrod (Senator)
713 Hart Senate Ofc Bldg
Washington, DC 20510-0001, USA

Brown, Sonny (Athlete, Football Player)
825 Shadow Wood Dr
Edmond, OK 73034-7061, USA

Brown, Stan (Athlete, Football Player)
PO Box 533
Benicia, CA 94510-0533, USA

Brown, Stan (Athlete, Basketball Player)
2201 Tremont St
Philadelphia, PA 19115-5041, USA

Brown, Steve (Athlete, Baseball Player)
9626 Cecilwood Dr
Santee, CA 92071-1428, USA

Brown, Susan (Actor)
11931 Addison St
N Hollywood, CA 91607-3106, USA

Brown, T Graham (Musician)
909 Meadowlark Ln
Goodlettsville, TN 37072-2309, USA

Brown, Tarrick (Baseball Player)
18631 Collins St Apt 33
Tarzana, CA 91356-2178, USA

Brown, Terry (Athlete, Football Player)
401 N 6th St
Marlow, OK 73055-1813, USA

Brown, Theotis J (Athlete, Football Player)
9604 W 121st Ter
Overland Park, KS 66213-1691, USA

Brown, Thomas M (Athlete, Football Player)
6024 Approach Rd
Sarasota, FL 34238-5721, USA

Brown, Thomas W (Athlete, Football Player)
27981 Nanticoke Rd
Salisbury, MD 21801-1645, USA

Brown, Thomas Wilson (Actor)
c/o Staff Member *SDB Partners Inc*
1801 Avenue of the Stars Ste 902
Los Angeles, CA 90067-5981, USA

Brown, Timothy D (Tim) (Athlete, Football Player)
1340 Thistlewood Dr
Desoto, TX 75115-7700, USA

Brown, Tina (Talk Show Host, Writer)
c/o Staff Member *Topic A With Tina Brown*
Sylvan Ave Cnbc 900
Englewood Cliffs, NJ 07632-3318, USA

Brown, Tom (Athlete, Football Player)
702 Placid Ct
Gibsonia, PA 15044-8016, USA

Brown, Tom (Athlete, Baseball Player)
27981 Nanticoke Rd
Salisbury, MD 21801-1645, USA

Brown, Tom (Athlete, Baseball Player)
600 Valencia Rd
Venice, FL 34285-2538, USA

Brown, Tom W (Athlete, Football Player)
201 High Point Dr
Waco, TX 76705-1750, USA

Brown, Tommy (Athlete, Baseball Player)
580 S Indigo Rd
Altamonte Springs, FL 32714-3137, USA

Brown, Tony (Athlete, Football Player)
11629 Garrick Ave
Sylmar, CA 91342-6533, USA

Brown, Tracy (Ballerina)
c/o Staff Member *Royal Ballet*
Covent Garden Bow St
London WC2E 9DD, UK

Brown, Trisha (Choreographer, Dancer)
211 W 61st St
New York, NY 10023-7832, USA

Brown, Troy (Athlete, Football Player)
124 Pine Hvn
Barnwell, SC 29812-2817, USA

Brown, Vincent B (Athlete, Football Player)
1615 Thoreau Dr
Suwanee, GA 30024-2090, USA

Brown, W Earl (Actor)
c/o Staff Member *WmE2 (Endeavor-LA)*
9601 Wilshire Blvd Fl 3
Beverly Hills, CA 90210-5219, USA

Brown, Wayne (Athlete, Hockey Player)
50 Montgomerry Blvd
Belleville, ON K8N 1H9, Canada

Brown, Wes (Actor)
c/o Stacy Abrams *Abrams Entertainment*
5225 Wilshire Blvd # Suite 515 PMB 515
Los Angeles, CA 90036, USA

Brown, William D (Bill) (Athlete, Coach, Football Player)
514 Northdale Blvd NW
Minneapolis, MN 55448-3357, USA

Brown, William F (Willie) (Athlete, Coach, Football Player)
27138 Lillegard Ct
Tracy, CA 95304-8866, USA

Brown, Willie (Baseball Player)
3048 Carlow Cir
Tallahassee, FL 32309-3303, USA

Brown, Winston (Baseball Player)
12144 SW 50th St
Cooper City, FL 33330-4476, USA

Brown, Woody (Actor)
11844 Otsego St
Valley Village, CA 91607-3223, USA

Brown, Wren (Actor)
c/o Barry Krost *Barry Krost Management*
9220 W Sunset Blvd Ste 106
West Hollywood, CA 90069-3500, USA

Brown III, Guy (Athlete, Football Player)
2233 Forest Hollow Park
Dallas, TX 75228-7826, USA

Brown Jr, Larry (Athlete, Football Player)
5603 Sycamore Dr
Colleyville, TX 76034-5063, USA

Brownback, Sam (Governor)
300 SW 10th Ave Ste 241S
Topeka, KS 66612-1504, USA

Browne, Anthony (Writer)
c/o Staff Member *Random House Publicity (Toronto)*
1 Toronto St Suite 300
Toronto, ON M5C 2V6, Canada

Browne, Byron (Athlete, Baseball Player)
2831 S 83rd Dr
Tolleson, AZ 85353-7603, USA

Browne, Chris (Cartoonist)
c/o Staff Member *King Features Syndication*
300 W 57th St Fl 15
New York, NY 10019-5238, USA

Browne, E John P (Business Person)
1 Finsbury Circus
London EC2M 7BA, UNITED KINGDOM (UK)

Browne, Gordon (Athlete, Football Player)
25 Harbourside Rd
North Quincy, MA 02171-1555, USA

Browne, Jackson (Musician, Songwriter, Writer)
c/o Donald Miller *Donald Miller Management*
12746 Kling St
Studio City, CA 91604-1125, USA

Browne, Jerry (Athlete, Baseball Player)
274 Memorial Boulevard Attn Coaching Staff E
Hagerstown, MD 21740, USA

Browne, Kale (Actor)
c/o Staff Member *Gage Group, The (LA)*
14724 Ventura Blvd Ste 505
Sherman Oaks, CA 91403-3505, USA

Browne, Leslie (Actor, Ballerina)
2025 Broadway Apt 6F
New York, NY 10023-5038, USA

Browne, Olin (Athlete, Golfer)
9562 SE Sandpine Ln
Hobe Sound, FL 33455-6356, USA

Browne, Secor D (Engineer, Government Official)
2101 L St NW # 207
Washington, DC 20037-1526, USA

Browne, Sylvia (Psychic, Writer)
6000 Hellyer Ave Ste 150
San Jose, CA 95138-1031, USA

Browne, Victor (Actor)
c/o Lara Rosenstock *Lara Rosenstock Management*
8371 Blackburn Ave Apt 1
Los Angeles, CA 90048-4245, USA

Browne, Zachary (Actor)
c/o Staff Member *Iris Burton Agency*
10100 Santa Monica Blvd Ste 1300
Los Angeles, CA 90067-4114, USA

Browner, Jim (Athlete, Football Player)
508 E Sedgwick St
Philadelphia, PA 19119-1326, USA

Browner, Joey (Athlete, Football Player)
2017 Pin Oak Dr
Saint Paul, MN 55122-2327, USA

Browner, Keith (Athlete, Football Player)
1015 Sandoval Ct
Stockton, CA 95206-1896, USA

Browner, Ross (Athlete, Football Player)
7900 Indian Springs Dr
Nashville, TN 37221-1147, USA

Browning, Cal (Athlete, Baseball Player)
111 N Eagle Dr
Ruidoso, NM 88345-6832, USA

Browning, Dominique (Writer)
c/o Staff Member *Curtis Brown Group*
Haymarket House 28 - 29 Haymarket
London SW1Y 4SP, UNITED KINGDOM

Browning, Edmond L (Religious Leader)
5164 Imai Rd
Hood River, OR 97031-9442, USA

Browning, Emily Jane (Actor)
c/o Michael D Aglion *Signpost*
250 S Beverly Dr Ste 201
Beverly Hills, CA 90212-3811, USA

Browning, James R (Judge)
Court Building 95 7th St
San Fransisco, CA 94103, USA

Browning, Kurt (Figure Skater)
175 Bloor St E # 400
Toronto, ON M4W 3R8, CANADA

Browning, Ricou (Actor)
5221 SW 196th Ln
Southwest Ranches, FL 33332-1111, USA

Browning, Ryan (Actor)
9560 Wilshire Blvd Ste 500
Beverly Hills, CA 90212-2401, USA

Browning, Thomas L (Tom) (Athlete, Baseball Player)
1110 Grindstone Ct
Union, KY 41091-8249, USA

Brownlee, Claude (Athlete, Football Player)
2711 Hood St
Columbus, GA 31906-3251, USA

Brownlow, Kevin (Producer)
21 Princess Road
London NW1, UNITED KINGDOM (UK)

Brownmiller, Susan (Activist)
61 Jane St
New York, NY 10014-5107, USA

Brownschidle, Jack (Athlete, Hockey Player)
35 Hidden Pines Ct
East Amherst, NY 14051-1688, USA

Brownson, Mark (Athlete, Baseball Player)
13992 Aster Ave
Wellington, FL 33414-8509, USA

Brownstein, Carrie (Music Group, Musician)
7 Trinity Row
Florence, MA 01062-1931, USA

Brownstein, Michael L (Publisher)
125 Park Ave
New York, NY 10017-5529, USA

Browny, Jann (Musician)
PO Box 158400
Nashville, TN 37215-8400, USA

Broxton, Jonathan (Athlete, Baseball Player)
4751 Rocky Creek Church Rd
Waynesboro, GA 30830-4106, USA

Broyles, Frank F (Coach, Football Player, Sportscaster)
Broyles Athletic Complex
Fayetteville, AR 72701, USA

Brozer, Kim (Athlete, Golfer)
2700 N 16th St
Beaumont, TX 77703-4624, USA

Brubaker, Bruce (Athlete, Baseball Player)
140 Southtown Blvd
Owensboro, KY 42303-7759, USA

Brubaker, Jeff (Athlete, Hockey Player)
1827 Oak Ridge Rd Unit A
Oak Ridge, NC 27310-9865, USA

Brubeck, Dave (Musician)
221 Millstone Rd
Wilton, CT 06897-1218

Brubeck, William H (Government Official)
7 Linden St
Cambridge, MA 02138-5011, USA

Bruce, Aundray (Athlete, Football Player)
1730 Wentworth Dr
Montgomery, AL 36106-2639, USA

Bruce, Bob (Athlete, Baseball Player)
800 E 15th St Unit 207
Plano, TX 75074-5865, USA

Bruce, Bruce (Comedian)
c/o Staff Member *Agency for the Performing Arts (APA-LA)*
405 S Beverly Dr Ste 500
Beverly Hills, CA 90212-4425, USA

Bruce, Christopher (Choreographer)
94 Chiswick High Road
London W4 1SH, UNITED KINGDOM (UK)

Bruce, David (Athlete, Hockey Player)
975 Grand Blvd
Bellingham, WA 98229-2776, USA

Bruce, Ed
1022 16th Ave S
Nashville, TN 37212-2303, USA

Bruce, George (Writer)
c/o Staff Member *Counterpoint*
1919 5th St
Berkeley, CA 94710-1916, USA

Bruce, Isaac I (Athlete, Football Player)
PO Box 550141
Fort Lauderdale, FL 33355-0141, USA

Bruce, Jack (Music Group, Songwriter, Writer)
40 W 57th St # 1800
New York, NY 10019-4001, USA

Bruce, Richard Francis (Editor)
1801 Century Park E Ste 1801
Los Angeles, CA 90067-2320, USA

Bruce, Robert V (Historian)
606 13th Ave SE
Olympia, WA 98501-2313, USA

Bruce, Thomas (Tom) (Swimmer)
122 Sea Terrace Way
Aptos, CA 95003-4521, USA

Bruce, Tom (Athlete, Swimmer)
1750 E Boulder St
Colorado Springs, CO 80909-5724, USA

Brucker, Earle (Athlete, Baseball Player)
629 Mundy Ter
El Cajon, CA 92020-2310, USA

Bruckheimer, Jerry (Director, Producer)
c/o Staff Member *Jerry Bruckheimer Films / Television*
1631 10th St
Santa Monica, CA 90404-3705, USA

Bruckner, Agnes (Actor)
c/o Rich Hueners *Paradigm (LA)*
360 N Crescent Dr
Beverly Hills, CA 90210-4874, USA

Bruckner, Amy (Actor)
c/o Susan Curtis *Curtis Talent Management*
9607 Arby Dr
Beverly Hills, CA 90210-1202, USA

Bruckner, Greg (Athlete, Golfer)
3906 E Potter Dr
Phoenix, AZ 85050-4837, USA

Bruckner, Les (Athlete, Football Player)
1325 Valley View Rd Apt 307
Glendale, CA 91202-4420, USA

Brudzinkski, Robert L (Bob) (Athlete)
1057 Lido Ct
Weston, FL 33326-2903

Brudzinski, Robert L (Bob) (Athlete, Football Player)
1057 Lido Ct
Weston, FL 33326-2903, USA

Brue, Bob (Athlete, Golfer)
5699 N Centerpark Way Apt 422
Milwaukee, WI 53217-4570, USA

Brueckman, Charlie (Athlete, Football Player)
7439 Plott Rd
Charlotte, NC 28215-9440, USA

Bruel, Patrick (Music Group)
20 Ave Rapp
Paris 75007, FRANCE

Brueland, Lowell K (War Hero)
420 La Z Acres Rd
Westminster, SC 29693-5109, USA

Bruen, John D (Business Person, General)
6104 Greenlawn Ct
Springfield, VA 22152-1314, USA

Bruener, Mark (Athlete, Football Player)
26 Commanders Pl
Missouri City, TX 77459, USA

Bruening, Justin (Actor)
c/o Marnie Sparer *Innovative Artists (LA)*
1505 10th St
Santa Monica, CA 90401-2805, USA

Bruestle, Martin (Director)

Bruett, J T (Athlete, Baseball Player)
1437 Woods Creek Dr
Delano, MN 55328-9266, USA

Bruggink, Eric G (Judge)
717 Madison Pl NW
Washington, DC 20439-0001, USA

Bruguera, Sergi (Tennis Player)
C'Escipion 42
Barcelona 8023, SPAIN

Bruhert, Mike (Athlete, Baseball Player)
907 Center Dr
Franklin Square, NY 11010-2005, USA

Bruhin, John (Athlete, Football Player)
6960 Taylors View Ln
Knoxville, TN 37921-2843, USA

Bruhl, Daniel (Actor)
c/o Katrina Bayonas *Kuranda Management*
Santo Angel, 84
Madrid 28043, Spain

Brumback, Charles T (Publisher)
435 N Michigan Ave Fl 7
Chicago, IL 60611-4027, USA

Brumbaugh, Cliff (Athlete, Baseball Player)
216 Moore Ave
New Castle, DE 19720-3559, USA

Brumbly, Charlie (Actor)
c/o Staff Member *DDO Artist Agency (LA)*
6725 W Sunset Blvd Ste 230
Los Angeles, CA 90028-7163, USA

Brumel, Valeryi (Actor)
Louknetzkaya Nab 8
Moscow, Russia

Brumfield, Jackson (Athlete, Football Player)
25644 Highway 25
Franklinton, LA 70438-5126, USA

Brumfield, Jacob D (Athlete, Baseball Player)
7970 Creekstone Way
Riverdale, GA 30274-3929, USA

Brumfield, Scott (Athlete, Football Player)
1150 E 900 S
Spanish Fork, UT 84660-2629, USA

Brumfield-White, Dolores (Baseball Player)
1604 Millcreek Dr
Arkadelphia, AR 71923-3024, USA

Brumley, Duff (Athlete, Baseball Player)
230 Cg Earnest Rd NW
Charleston, TN 37310-6625, USA

Brumley, Mike (Athlete, Baseball Player)
1020 Western Trl
Keller, TX 76248-4924, USA

Brumley, Robert L (Athlete, Football Player)
256 E Sunset Rd
San Antonio, TX 78209-2760, USA

Brumm, Donald D (Don) (Athlete, Football Player)
511 County Road 442
New Franklin, MO 65274-9704, USA

Brumme, Margo (Stylist)
c/o Staff Member *Zenobia Agency Inc*
PO Box 909
Groveland, CA 95321-0909, USA

Brummer, Glenn (Athlete, Baseball Player)
1830 Dalton Dr
Belleville, IL 62226-8207, USA

Brummer, Renate (Astronaut)
325 Broadway St
Boulder, CO 80305-3337, USA

Brummett, Greg (Athlete, Baseball Player)
605 W 10th St
Concordia, KS 66901-4011, USA

Brumwell, Murray (Athlete, Hockey Player)
727 Tabriz Dr
Billings, MT 59105-2809, USA

Brunansky, Thomas A (Tom) (Athlete, Baseball Player)
15444 Harrow Ln
Poway, CA 92064-2374, USA

Brundage, Dewey (Athlete, Football Player)
220 S 400 W
Orem, UT 84058-5329, USA

Brundage, Howard D (Publisher)
RR 2 Box 332-47
Old Lyme, CT 6371, USA

Brundige, Bill (Athlete, Football Player)
2050 Roanoke St
Christiansburg, VA 24073-2510, USA

Brundy, Stan (Athlete, Basketball Player)
4644 Stephen Girard Ave
New Orleans, LA 70126-4756, USA

Brunell, Mark (Athlete, Football Player)
876 Rock Mesa Pt
Castle Rock, CO 80108-7435, USA

Brunelli, Sam (Athlete, Football Player)
1080 Wisconsin Ave NW Apt 104
Washington, DC 20007-6052, USA

Bruner, Jerome S (Misc)
200 Mercer St
New York, NY 10012-1546, USA

Bruner, Michael L (Mike) (Athlete, Swimmer)
339 Garcia Ave
Half Moon Bay, CA 94019-1886, USA

Brunet, Andree Joly (Figure Skater)
2805 Boyne City Rd
Boyne City, MI 49712, USA

Brunet, Bob (Athlete, Football Player)
25001 La Hwy 1032
Denham Springs, LA 70726, USA

Brunetta, Mario (Athlete, Hockey Player)
3874 De L'Hetriere St
Saint-Augustin-De-Desmaures, QC G3A 2X1, Canada

Brunette, Andrew (Athlete, Hockey Player)
2392 Morgan Ave N
Stillwater, MN 55082-1967, USA

Brunette, Justin (Athlete, Baseball Player)
11 Atherton
Irvine, CA 92620-2502, USA

Brunettes, The (Music Group)
c/o Staff Member *Paradigm (Monterey)*
404 W Franklin St
Monterey, CA 93940-2303, USA

Brunetti, Melvin T (Judge)
40 W Liberty St
Reno, NV 89501, USA

Brunetti, Wayne H (Business Person)
1225 17th St
Denver, CO 80202-5534, USA

Bruney, Brian (Athlete, Baseball Player)
c/o Staff Member *Gaylord Sports Management*
13845 N Northsight Blvd Ste 200
Scottsdale, AZ 85260-3609, USA

Bruney, Fred (Athlete, Football Coach, Football Player)
13160 Village Chase Cir
Tampa, FL 33618-8330, USA

Brungardt, Kurt
c/o Daniel A (Dan) Strone *Trident Media Group LLC*
41 Madison Ave Fl 36
New York, NY 10010-2257, USA

Bruni-Sarkozy, Carla (First Lady, Model, Musician)
Palais De L'Elysée 55 Rue Du Faubourg Saint-Honor
Paris F-75008, France

Brunkhorst, Brian (Athlete, Basketball Player)
6182 Brumder Rd
Hartland, WI 53029-9709, USA

Brunner, J Terrance (Misc)
230 N Michigan Ave
Chicago, IL 60601-5906, USA

Brunner, Scott (Athlete, Football Player)
734 14th Ave
Prospect Park, PA 19076-1206, USA

Bruno, Billi (Actor)
c/o Dana Edrick Fletcher *Coast to Coast Talent Group*
3350 Barham Blvd
Los Angeles, CA 90068-1404, USA

Bruno, Chris (Actor)
6500 Wilshire Blvd # 550
Los Angeles, CA 90048-4920, USA

Bruno, Corbucci (Actor)
Via dei Colli della Farnesina #144
Rome I-00194, Italy

Bruno, Dylan (Actor)
c/o Estelle Lasher *Principal Entertainment (LA)*
1964 Westwood Blvd Ste 400
Los Angeles, CA 90025-4695, USA

Bruno, Frank (Athlete, Boxer)
Little Billington Leighton Buzzard
Bedfordshire LU7 9BS, UK

Bruno, Franklin R (Frank) (Boxer)
P O Box 2266 Brentwood
Essex CM15 0AQ, UNITED KINGDOM (UK)

Bruno, Tom (Athlete, Baseball Player)
316 Ft Sully Trl
Pierre, SD 57501-8309, USA

Bruns, George (Athlete, Basketball Player)
16 E Poplar St
Floral Park, NY 11001-3145, USA

Brunsberg, Ario (Athlete, Baseball Player)
883 104th Ln NW
Minneapolis, MN 55433-6542, USA

Brunson, Doyle (Poker Player)
c/o Staff Member *Poker Royalty, LLC*
10789 W Twain Ave Ste 200
Las Vegas, NV 89135-3030, USA

Brunson, Larry (Athlete, Football Player)
6104 E Peakview Pl
Centennial, CO 80111-4326, USA

Brunson, Mike (Athlete, Football Player)
9087 Toast Ave
Las Vegas, NV 89148-4914, USA

Brunson, Will (Athlete, Baseball Player)
13119 Rudys Way
Streetman, TX 75859-7171, USA

Bruntlett, Eric (Athlete, Baseball Player)
1106 Marconi St Apt A
Houston, TX 77019-4261, USA

Brupbacher, Ross (Athlete, Football Player)
200 Pembroke Ln
Lafayette, LA 70508-5616, USA

Bruschi, Tedy (Athlete, Football Player)
31 Jeffrey Dr
North Attleboro, MA 02760-2761, USA

Bruske, Jim (Athlete, Baseball Player)
5242 N Quail Run Pl
Paradise Valley, AZ 85253-7051, USA

Bruskin, Grisha (Artist)
236 W 26th St Rm 705
New York, NY 10001-6789, USA

Bruson, Renato (Opera Singer)
165 W 57th St
New York, NY 10019-2201, USA

Brusstar, Warren (Athlete, Baseball Player)
3320 Redwood Rd
Napa, CA 94558-9544, USA

Brusteln, Robert S (Critic, Educator, Producer)
Loeb Drama Center 64 Brattle St
Cambridge, MA 2138, USA

Brutcher, Len (Baseball Player)
4510 Hallam Hill Ln
Lakeland, FL 33813-1808, USA

Bruton, John G (Prime Minister)
Qomelstown
Dunboyne, County Meath, IRELAND

Bry, Ellen (Actor)
6300 Wilshire Blvd Ste 1470
Los Angeles, CA 90048-5200, USA

Bryan, Alan (Archaeologist)
Archaeology Dept
Edmonton, AB T6G 2J8, CANADA

Bryan, Billy (Athlete, Football Player)
3408 Creekwood Dr
Tuscaloosa, AL 35453, USA

Bryan, Billy (Athlete, Baseball Player)
3001 Hickory Ln
Opelika, AL 36801-2221, USA

Bryan, David (Misc)
248 W 17th St Apt 501
New York, NY 10011-5330, USA

Bryan, Donald S (Misc)
702 Melba St
Adel, GA 31620-1626, USA

Bryan, Dora (Actor)
11 Marine Parade Brighton
Sussex, UNITED KINGDOM (UK)

Bryan, Luke (Musician)
c/o Greg Hill *Red Light Management (Nashville)*
39 Music Sq E
Nashville, TN 37203-4322, USA

Bryan, Mark (Music Group, Musician)
PO Box 5656
Columbia, SC 29250-5656, USA

Bryan, Mary (Athlete, Golfer)
1735 Golf Garden Way
Apopka, FL 32712-2178, USA

Bryan, Rick D (Athlete, Football Player)
15526 S 295th East Ave
Coweta, OK 74429-5550, USA

Bryan, Sabrina (Actor, Dancer)
c/o Julie Colbert *WmE2 (Endeavor-LA)*
9601 Wilshire Blvd Fl 3
Beverly Hills, CA 90210-5219, USA

Bryan, Steve (Athlete, Football Player)
RR 2 Box 332-38
Coweta, OK 74429, USA

Bryan, Walter (Athlete, Football Player)
757 Kenwood Dr
Abilene, TX 79601-5539, USA

Bryan, Zachery Ty (Actor)
c/o Samantha Crisp *Kohner Agency, The*
9300 Wilshire Blvd Ste 555
Beverly Hills, CA 90212-3211, USA

Bryant, Anita (Activist)
PO Box 5331
Sevierville, TN 37864-5331, USA

Bryant, Antonio (Athlete, Football Player)
c/o Staff Member *All Pro Sports and Entertainment*
36 Steele St Ste 100
Denver, CO 80206-5709, USA

Bryant, Bart (Athlete, Golfer)
2205 Rickover Pl
Winter Garden, FL 34787-5401, USA

Bryant, Bonnie (Athlete, Golfer)
8750 SW Liverpool Rd
Arcadia, FL 34269-6896, USA

Bryant, Brad (Golfer)
3407 Bridgefield Dr
Lakeland, FL 33803-5914, USA

Bryant, Brad (Athlete, Golfer)
3407 Bridgefield Dr
Lakeland, FL 33803-5914, USA

Bryant, Charles (Athlete, Football Player)
3110 Lincoln St
Lorain, OH 44052-2715, USA

Bryant, Clark Rosalyn (Athlete, Track Athlete)
3901 Somerset Dr
Los Angeles, CA 90008-1704, USA

Bryant, Derek (Athlete, Baseball Player)
1047 Redwood Dr
Lexington, KY 40511-1133, USA

Bryant, Dez (Athlete, Football Player)
c/o Eugene Parker *Maximum Sports Management*
6435 W Jefferson Blvd # 197
Fort Wayne, IN 46804-6203, USA

Bryant, Domingo (Athlete, Football Player)
19703 Campfield Dr
Katy, TX 77449-6691, USA

Bryant, Don (Athlete, Baseball Player)
270 Stonewell Dr
Saint Johns, FL 32259-8388, USA

Bryant, Edward (Junior) (Athlete, Football Player)
2906 S 102nd St
Omaha, NE 68124-2639, USA

Bryant, Emmette (Athlete, Basketball Player)
P.O. Box 6229
Chicago, IL 11001, USA

Bryant, Fernando (Athlete, Football Player)
2336 Emerald Dr
Jonesboro, GA 30236-5226, USA

Bryant, Gray (Editor)
34 Horatio St
New York, NY 10014-1622, USA

Bryant, Gyude (President)
Executive Mansion Capitol Hill
Monrovia, LIBERIA

Bryant, Hubie (Athlete, Football Player)
4804 Branch Rd
Roanoke, VA 24014-6702, USA

Bryant, Jeff (Athlete, Football Player)
PO Box 362240
Decatur, GA 30036-2240, USA

Bryant, Joe (Athlete, Basketball Player)
1835 N 72nd St
Philadelphia, PA 19151-2311, USA

Bryant, Joshua (Actor)
216 Paseo Del Pueblo Norte Ste M
Taos, NM 87571-5912, USA

Bryant, Joy (Actor)
c/o Brian Young *Untitled Entertainment (LA)*
350 S Beverly Dr Ste 200
Beverly Hills, CA 90212-4819, USA

Bryant, Kevin (Athlete, Football Player)
701 E Church St
Tarboro, NC 27886-4505, USA

Bryant, Kobe (Athlete, Basketball Player)
c/o Rob Pelinka *Landmark Sports Agency*
10990 Wilshire Blvd Ste 1000
Los Angeles, CA 90024-3924, USA

Bryant, Lucas (Actor)
c/o Perry Zimel *Oscars Abrams Zimel & Associates, Inc. (OAZ)*
438 Queen St E
Toronto ON M5A 1T4, CANADA

Bryant, Maeion (Stylist)
c/o Staff Member *Mirror Image Cosmetic Studio*
1708 Whitehead Rd
Baltimore, MD 21207-4021

Bryant, Mark (Athlete, Basketball Player)
3300 Everett Dr
Edmond, OK 73013-7443, USA

Bryant, Ralph (Athlete, Baseball Player)
367 Spruill Bridge Rd
Temple, GA 30179-4568, USA

Bryant, Ray (Music Group, Musician)
7942 W Bell Rd
Glendale, AZ 85308-8708, USA

Bryant, Ron (Baseball Player)
90 Oak St # 1
Westerly, RI 02891-1737, USA

Bryant, Ronald Ray (Baby Bash) (Actor, Musician, Producer)
c/o Staff Member *Sony Music International*
550 Madison Ave Fl 6
New York, NY 10022-3211, USA

Bryant, Steve (Athlete, Football Player)
12618 Laleu Ln
Houston, TX 77071-3735, USA

Bryant, Taman (Athlete, Football Player)
2742 Bryant St
Vineland, NJ 08361-3021, USA

Bryant, Todd (Actor)
9150 Wilshire Blvd Ste 175
Beverly Hills, CA 90212-3450, USA

Bryant, Tony (Athlete, Football Player)
2351 Sombrero Blvd
Marathon, FL 33050-2468, USA

Bryant, Trent (Athlete, Football Player)
4801 S Tiemey Dr
Independence, MO 64055, USA

Bryant, Walter (Athlete, Football Player)
509 Nottingham Rd
Columbia, SC 29210-3719, USA

Bryant, Waymond (Athlete, Football Player)
2440 Covington Dr
Flower Mound, TX 75028-4666, USA

Bryant, Wendell (Athlete, Football Player)
PO Box 888
Phoenix, AZ 85001-0888, USA

Bryars, R Gavin (Composer)
8 Pottery Lane
London W11 4LZ, UNITED KINGDOM (UK)

Bryden, T R (Athlete, Baseball Player)
1021 9th St
Clarkston, WA 99403-2505, USA

Brye, Steve (Athlete, Baseball Player)
255 S Grand Ave Apt 858
Los Angeles, CA 90012-3038, USA

Brylin, Sergei (Athlete, Hockey Player)
32 Robert Dr
Short Hills, NJ 07078-1507, USA

Bryson, Bill (Writer)
c/o Staff Member *Random House Publicity*
1745 Broadway
New York, NY 10019-4368, USA

Bryson, Peabo (Music Group, Musician, Songwriter, Writer)
9200 W Sunset Blvd Ste 900
Los Angeles, CA 90069-3604, USA

Bryson, Peabo (Musician)
c/o Staff Member *Agency for the Performing Arts (APA-LA)*
405 S Beverly Dr Ste 500
Beverly Hills, CA 90212-4425, USA

Bryson, Shawn (Athlete, Football Player)
418 Heatherstone Dr
Franklin, NC 28734-0274, USA

Bryson, William C (Judge)
717 Madison Pl NW
Washington, DC 20439-0001, USA

Bryzgalov, Ilya (Athlete, Hockey Player)
4092 Santa Anita Ln
Yorba Linda, CA 92886-7014, USA

Brzeska, Magdalena (Gymnast)
Porschestr 6
Fellbach 70736, GERMANY

Brzezinski, Mika (Talk Show Host)
30 Rockefeller Plz
New York, NY 10112-0015, USA

Brzezinski, Zbigniew (Educator, Government Official)
1800 K St NW
Washington, DC 20006-2202, USA

Brzezinski, Zbignlew (Educator, Government Official)
1800 K St NW
Washington, DC 20006-2202, USA

B-Side Players (Music Group, Musician)
c/o Staff Member *Skyline Music*
28 Union St
Whitefield, NH 03598-3503, USA

Buacharern, Tym (Stylist)
c/o Staff Member *Karlee Artist Management*
2658 Griffith Park Blvd # 171
Los Angeles, CA 90039-2520, USA

Buanne, Patrizio (Musician)
PO Box 293
Tadworth KT20 5SX, UNITED KINGDOM

Buatta, Mario (Designer)
120 E 80th St
New York, NY 10075-0306, USA

Bubas, Vic (Athlete, Basketball Player, Coach)
133 Robert E Lee Ln
Bluffton, SC 29909-4424, USA

Bubela, Jaime (Athlete, Baseball Player)
14927 Royal Birkdale St
Houston, TX 77095-2812, USA

Bubka, Sergie N (Athlete, Track Athlete)
Vasavagen 13
Solna 171 39, SWEDEN

Bubka, Surgei N (Athlete, Track Athlete)
Vasavagen 13
Solna 171 39, SWEDEN

Bubla, Jiri (Athlete, Hockey Player)
405-1050 Bowron Crt
North Vancouver, BC V7H 2X7, Canada

Buble, Michael (Musician)
c/o Bruce Allen *Bruce Allen Talent*
425 Carrall St Suite 500
Vancouver, BC V6B 6E3, Canada

Bubna, P F (Religious Leader)
P O Box 3500
Colorado Springs, CO 80935, USA

Bucatinsky, Dan (Actor, Producer, Writer)
c/o Staff Member *WmE2 (Endeavor-LA)*
9601 Wilshire Blvd Fl 3
Beverly Hills, CA 90210-5219, USA

Buccellati, Giorgio (Misc)
Near Eastern Languages Dept
Los Angeles, CA 90024, USA

Buccellato, Benedetta (Actor)
Via Giuseppe Pisanelli
Rome 196, ITALY

Bucci, George (Athlete, Basketball Player)
15 Peter Ave
Newburgh, NY 12550-8812, USA

Bucha, Paul W (War Hero)
40 Patriots Point Rd
Mt Pleasant, SC 29464-4377, USA

Buchanan, Bill (Athlete, Baseball Player)
94 Twill Valley Dr
Saint Peters, MO 63376-6566, USA

Buchanan, Bob (Athlete, Baseball Player)
2035 Bever Ave SE
Cedar Rapids, IA 52403-2716, USA

Buchanan, Brian (Athlete, Baseball Player)
8600 El Mirasol Ct
Fort Myers, FL 33967-0521, USA

Buchanan, Charles (Athlete, Football Player)
1715 Windover Dr
Nashville, TN 37218-2410, USA

Buchanan, Edna (Journalist)
PO Box 403556
Miami Beach, FL 33140-1556, USA

Buchanan, Ian (Actor, Model)
3500 W Olive Ave Ste 1400
Burbank, CA 91505-5512, USA

Buchanan, Isobel (Opera Singer)
14 New Burlington St
London W1X 1FF, UNITED KINGDOM (UK)

Buchanan, James M (Nobel Prize Laureate)
Study of Public Choice Center
Fairfax, VA 22030, USA

Buchanan, Jeff (Athlete, Hockey Player)
427 Cedar Ave
Hershey, PA 17033-1624, USA

Buchanan, Jensen (Actor)
10100 Santa Monica Blvd Ste 2500
Los Angeles, CA 90067-4116, USA

Buchanan, Ken (Boxer)
45 Marmion Road Greenfaulds
Cumbemaul G67 4AN, SCOTLAND

Buchanan, Patrick (Pat) (Politician)
1017 Savile Ln
McLean, VA 22101-1830, USA

Buchanan, Phillip (Athlete, Football Player)
6185 Meadowview Cir
Fort Myers, FL 33916-4906, USA

Buchanan, Ray (Athlete, Football Player)
2423 Strand Ave
Lawrenceville, GA 30043-8206, USA

Buchanan, Richard (Athlete, Football Player)
216 Brookwood Ln W
Bolingbrook, IL 60440-5511, USA

Buchanan, Robert S (Astronaut)
3 Lariat Ln
Rolling Hills Estates, CA 90274-4119, USA

Buchanan, Ron (Athlete, Hockey Player)
2007 Harris Rd Unit 911
Clyde, TX 79510, USA

Buchanan, Tim (Athlete, Football Player)
888 Magnolia Ave Apt 1
Pasadena, CA 91106-3700, USA

Buchanan, Tom (Reality TV Star)
3130 Valley Rd
Saltville, VA 24370-4373

Buchanan, Vern (Congressman, Politician)
221 Cannon Hob
Washington, DC 20515-3515, USA

Buchanan, Willie J (Athlete, Football Player)
2742 Mesa Dr
Oceanside, CA 92054-3717, USA

Buchanon, Willie (Athlete, Football Player)
2742 Mesa Dr
Oceanside, CA 92054-3717, USA

Buchberger, Kelly (Athlete, Hockey Player)
c/o Staff Member *Springfield Falcons*
45 Falcons Way
Springfield, MA 01103-1742, USA

Buchbinder, Rudolf (Music Group, Musician)
165 W 57th St
New York, NY 10019-2201, USA

Buchek, Jerry (Athlete, Baseball Player)
19 Par Ln Apt 6
Reeds Spring, MO 65737-7645, USA

Buchel, Lloyd M (Misc)
16296 Rostrata Hill Rd
Poway, CA 92064-1720, USA

Buchel, Marco (Skier)
Ramschwagweg 55
Balzers 9496, SWITZERLAND

Buchheim, Lothar-Gunther (Writer)
Johann-Biersack-Str 23
Feldafing 82340, GERMANY

Buchholz, Christopher (Actor)
c/o Staff Member *TNA The New Agency*
Viale Parioli 41
Roma I-00197, Italy

Buchholz, Clay (Athlete, Baseball Player)
630 King Oaks St
Lumberton, TX 77657-7210, USA

Buchholz, Taylor (Athlete, Baseball Player)
321 Southcroft Rd
Springfield, PA 19064-1353, USA

Buchli, James F (Jim) (Astronaut)
14761A Innerarity Point Rd
Pensacola, FL 32507-8452, USA

Buchwald, Art (Misc, Writer)
4327 Hawthorne St NW # W
Washington, DC 20016-3570, USA

Buck, Detlev (Director)
Goethestr 17
Munich 80336, GERMANY

Buck, Joe (Television Host)
c/o Staff Member *Fox Sports Television Group*
10201 W Pico Blvd Bldg 101
Los Angeles, CA 90064-2606, USA

Buck, John E (Artist)
11229 Cottonwood Rd
Bozeman, MT 59718-9576, USA

Buck, Linda B. (Nobel Prize Laureate)
Basic Sciences Division, 1100 Faiview Ave. North, A3-020 P.O.Box 19024
Seattle, WA 98109-1024, USA

Buck, Mike E (Athlete, Football Player)
321 Fox Den Ct
Destin, FL 32541-4317, USA

Buck, Peter (Music Group, Musician)
170 College Ave
Athens, GA 30601-2805, USA

Buck, Robert T Jr (Director, Misc)
200 Eastern Pkwy
Brooklyn, NY 11238-6052, USA

Buck, Samantha (Actor)
c/o Elise Konialian *Untitled Entertainment (NY)*
322 8th Ave Ste 601
New York, NY 10001-6715, USA

Buck, Scott (Producer)
c/o Ann Blanchard *Creative Artists Agency (CAA-LA)*
9200 W Sunset Blvd Ste 10
Los Angeles, CA 90069-3608, USA

Buckbee, Ed (Misc, Scientist)
47 Revere Way
Huntsville, AL 35801-2847, USA

Buckcherry (Music Group, Musician)
c/o Staff Member *10th Street Entertainment (NY)*
38 W 21st St Rm 300
New York, NY 10010-6979, USA

Buckels, Gary (Athlete, Baseball Player)
3510 E Longridge Dr
Orange, CA 92867-2021, USA

Buckey, Don (Athlete, Football Player)
8809 Audley Cir
Raleigh, NC 27615-3801, USA

Buckey, Jay C Jr (Astronaut)
14 Valley Rd
Hanover, NH 03755-2228, USA

Buckhalter, Joe (Athlete, Basketball Player)
3900 Rose Hill Ave Apt 201A
Cincinnati, OH 45229-1467, USA

Buckingham, Gregory (Greg) (Swimmer)
338 Ridge Rd
San Carlos, CA 94070-4423, USA

Buckingham, Jane (Television Host)
c/o Staff Member *Style Network*
5750 Wilshire Blvd
Los Angeles, CA 90036-3697, USA

Buckingham, Lindsay (Musician)
299 N Saltair Ave
Los Angeles, CA 90049-2912, USA

Buckingham, Lindsey (Music Group, Musician)
c/o Tony Dimitriades *East End Management*
13721B Ventura Blvd
Sherman Oaks, CA 91423-3023, USA

Buckingham, Marcus (Business Person, Writer)
1230 Avenue of the Americas
New York, NY 10020-1513, USA

Buckinghams, The (Music Group)
PO Box 1821
Ojai, CA 93024-1821, USA

Buckland, Jonny (Music Group, Musician)
1650 W 2nd Ave
Vancouver, BC V6J 4R3, CANADA

Buckles, Bradley (Government Official, Misc)
650 Massachusetts Ave NW
Washington, DC 20001-3796, USA

Bucklew, Neil S (Educator)
President's Office
Morgantown, WV 26506, USA

Buckley, A J (Actor)
1505 10th St
Santa Monica, CA 90401-2805, USA

Buckley, Barry (Athlete, Football Player)
26 Forest Notch
Cohasset, MA 02025-1133, USA

Buckley, Betty (Actor, Director, Musician)
3101 W Lancaster Ave
Ft Worth, TX 76107-3042, USA

Buckley, Carol (Misc)
PO Box 393
Hohenwald, TN 38462-0393, USA

Buckley, Curtis (Athlete, Football Player)
2208 Cantura Dr
Mesquite, TX 75181-4653, USA

Buckley, D Terrell (Athlete, Football Player)
10097 Cleary Blvd
Plantation, FL 33324-1065, USA

Buckley, James L (Ex-Senator, Judge)
PO Box 597
Sharon, CT 06069-0597, USA

Buckley, Jean (Baseball Player)
143 Monarch Dr
Fortuna, CA 95540-3451, USA

Buckley, Kathy (Actor)
c/o Staff Member *GVA Talent Agency Inc*
8981 W Sunset Blvd Ste 101
Los Angeles, CA 90069-1850, USA

Buckley, Kevin (Athlete, Baseball Player)
34 Calvin St
Braintree, MA 02184-3814, USA

Buckley, Marcus W (Athlete, Football Player)
7100 Monterrey Dr
Fort Worth, TX 76112-4234, USA

Buckley, Richard E (Conductor)
310 W 55th St Apt 1K
New York, NY 10019-5107, USA

Buckley, Robert (Actor)
c/o Gary Mantoosh *Baker Winokur Ryder Public Relations (BWR-LA)*
9100 Wilshire Blvd Ste 500 PMB WEST
Beverly Hills, CA 90212-3426, USA

Buckley, Travis (Baseball Player)
10020 England Dr
Overland Park, KS 66212-4138, USA

Buckman, James E (Business Person)
9 W 57th St
New York, NY 10019-2701, USA

Buckman, Tom (Athlete, Football Player)
212 Foxford Dr
Keller, TX 76248-2532, USA

Buckner, Betty (Actor)
10643 Riverside Dr
Toluca Lake, CA 91602-2341, USA

Buckner, Bill (Athlete, Baseball Player)
4405 E Wild Horse Ln
Boise, ID 83712-7593, USA

Buckner, Brentson (Athlete, Football Player)
423 Leary Ct
Columbus, GA 31907-5403, USA

Buckner, Cindy (Stylist)
4347 Valley Spring Dr
Westlake Village, CA 91362-4336, USA

Buckner, Cleveland (Athlete, Basketball Player)
19227 S Grandee Ave
Carson, CA 90746-2805, USA

Buckner, Pam (Bowler)
645 Utah St
Reno, NV 89506-8979, USA

Buckner, Shelley (Actor)
c/o Staff Member *Cunningham Escott Slevin & Doherty (CESD-LA)*
10635 Santa Monica Blvd Ste 130
Los Angeles, CA 90025-8306, USA

Buckner, William (Quinn) (Athlete, Basketball Player, Coach)
857 Valencia Blvd
Irving, TX 75039-3057, USA

Bucknor, C B (Athlete, Baseball Player)
46 Midwood St
Brooklyn, NY 11225-5004, USA

Buckson, David P (Ex-Governor)
60 Exchange Dr
Camden Wyoming, DE 19934-4311, USA

Bucshon, Larry (Congressman, Politician)
1123 Longworth Hob
Washington, DC 20515-4601, USA

Bucyk, John (Athlete, Hockey Player)
c/o Staff Member *Boston Bruins*
TD Banknorth Garden 100 Legends Way, Suite 250
Boston, MA 2114, USA

Buczkowski, Bob (Athlete, Football Player)
4515 Northern Pike
Monroeville, PA 15146-2915, USA

Budaj, Peter (Athlete, Hockey Player)
1271 Buffalo Ridge Rd
Castle Pines, CO 80108-8192, USA

Budarin, Nikolai M (Cosmonaut)
Moskovskoi Oblasti
Syvisdny Goroduk 141160, RUSSIA

Budaska, Mark (Athlete, Baseball Player)
15025 W Buttonwood Dr
Sun City West, AZ 85375-5750, USA

Budd, David (Athlete, Basketball Player)
40 N Woodland Ave
Woodbury, NJ 08096-2517, USA

Budd, Frank (Athlete, Football Player, Track Athlete)
138 Dorchester Rd
Mount Laurel, NJ 08054-1408, USA

Budd, Harold (Composer, Misc)
6834 Camrose Dr
Los Angeles, CA 90068 3162, USA

Budd, Julie (Actor, Music Group)
163 Amsterdam Ave # 224
New York, NY 10023-5001, USA

Budd, Pieterse Zola (Athlete, Track Athlete)
General Delivery
Bloemfontein, SOUTH AFRICA

Budde, Brad E (Athlete, Football Player)
5121 W 159th Ter
Stilwell, KS 66085-8956, USA

Budde, Ed (Athlete, Football Player)
5121 W 159th Ter
Stilwell, KS 66085-8956, USA

Budde, Jordan (Producer, Writer)
c/o Ann Blanchard *Creative Artists Agency (CAA-LA)*
9200 W Sunset Blvd Ste 10
Los Angeles, CA 90069-3608, USA

Budde, Ryan (Athlete, Baseball Player)
3109 N Peebly Dr
Oklahoma City, OK 73110-1509, USA

Budden, Joe (Actor)
c/o Staff Member *International Creative Management (ICM-LA)*
10250 Constellation Blvd Fl 7
Los Angeles, CA 90067-6207, USA

Buddie, Mike (Athlete, Baseball Player)
157 Scottsdale Dr
Advance, NC 27006-6933, USA

Buddin, Don (Athlete, Baseball Player)
27 Harvest Ct
Greenville, SC 29601-4409, USA

Budd-Pieterse, Zola (Athlete, Track Athlete)
c/o Staff Member *British Olympic Association*
1 Wandsworth Plain
London SW18 1EH, UK

Buddy, Brandon (Actor)
c/o Jon Simmons *Simmons & Scott Entertainment*
7942 Mulholland Dr
Los Angeles, CA 90046-1225, USA

Budig, Gene (Baseball Player, Educator, President)
5 Sandwedge Ln
Isle Of Palms, SC 29451-2820, USA

Budig, Rebecca (Actor)
13576 Cheltenham Dr
Sherman Oaks, CA 91423-4818, USA

Budka, Frank (Athlete, Football Player)
2637 SW Abel St
Port Saint Lucie, FL 34953-2834, USA

Budko, Walter (Athlete, Basketball Player, Coach)
2525 Pot Spring Rd Unit L703
Lutherville Timonium, MD 21093-2852, USA

Budness, Bill (Athlete, Football Player)
401 Huckle Hill Rd
Bernardston, MA 01337-9423, USA

Budnick, Neil G (Financier)
113 King St
Armonk, NY 10504-1611, USA

Budrewicz, Tom (Athlete, Football Player)
13 Olde Farms Rd
Boxford, MA 01921-1915, USA

Budzinski, Mark (Athlete, Baseball Player)
12005 Foxlawn Ct
Henrico, VA 23233 8900, USA

Bueche, Wendell F (Business Person)
2100 Sanders Rd
Northbrook, IL 60062-6139, USA

Buechele, Steve (Athlete, Baseball Player)
2600 Royal Glen Dr
Arlington, TX 76012-5553, USA

Buechler, John Carl (Director)
12031 Vose St # 19-21
North Hollywood, CA 91605-5752, USA

Buechrle, James (Baseball Player)
Comiskey Park 333 W 35th St
Chicago, IL 60616, USA

Buehler, George (Athlete, Football Player)
63 Tara Rd
Orinda, CA 94563-3116, USA

Buehler, Jud (Athlete, Basketball Player)
4576 South Ln
Del Mar, CA 92014-4139, USA

Buehrle, Mark (Athlete, Baseball Player)
5653 N Ridge Ave
Chicago, IL 60660-5549, USA

Buell, Bebe (Actor)
c/o Ivan Bart *IMG Models (NY)*
825 7th Ave Fl 8
New York, NY 10019-6014, USA

Bueno, Maria (Tennis Player)
Rua Consolagao 3414 #10 Edificio Agustus
Sao Paulo 1001, BRAZIL

Buer, Aaron (Actor)
c/o Staff Member *RPM Talent Agency*
2600 W Olive Ave Fl 5
Burbank, CA 91505-4572, USA

Buerge, Aaron (Reality TV Star)
c/o Staff Member *Maximum Talent*
1873 S Bellaire St Ste 915
Denver, CO 80222-4356, USA

Buerger, Martin J (Misc)
Weston Road
Lincoln, MA 1773, USA

Buerkle, Ann Marie (Congressman, Politician)
1630 Longworth Hob
Washington, DC 20515-2002, USA

Buetow, Bart (Athlete, Football Player)
4152 Kipling St
Wheat Ridge, CO 80033-4147, USA

Buffenbarger, R Thomas (Misc)
9000 Machinists Pl
Upper Marlboro, MD 20772-2675, USA

Buffett, Jimmy (Composer, Musician, Songwriter)
PO Box 3384
Palm Beach, FL 33480-1584, USA

Buffett, Peter (Musician)
c/o Staff Member *Paradigm (Monterey)*
404 W Franklin St
Monterey, CA 93940-2303, USA

Buffett, Warren E (Business Person)
1440 Kiewit Plz
Omaha, NE 68131, USA

Buffington, Harry (Athlete, Football Player)
3306 38th St
Lubbock, TX 79413-2714, USA

Buffkins, Archie Lee (Misc)
Executive
Washington, DC 20566-0001, USA

Buffone, Douglas J (Doug) (Athlete, Football Player)
1272 W Lexington St
Chicago, IL 60607-4110, USA

Bufi, Ylli (Prime Minister)
Keshilli i Ministrave
Tirana, ALBANIA

Bufman, Zev (Producer)
520 Brickett Key Dr # 612
Miami, FL 33131, USA

Buford, Damon J (Athlete, Baseball Player)
791 E Birchwood Pl
Chandler, AZ 85249-3311, USA

Buford, Don (Athlete, Baseball Player)
15412 Valley Vista Blvd
Sherman Oaks, CA 91403-3812, USA

Buford, Maury (Athlete, Football Player)
2901 Sweet Briar St
Grapevine, TX 76051-2651, USA

Bugai, Lynne (Stylist)
746 N McCadden Pl
Los Angeles, CA 90038-3419, USA

Bugel, Joe (Athlete, Football Coach, Football Player)
15517 E Cactus Dr
Fountain Hills, AZ 85268-4123, USA

Bugenhagen, Gary (Athlete, Football Player)
4337 Henneberry Rd
Manlius, NY 13104-8425, USA

Buggs, Dany (Athlete, Football Player)
3186 Evans Mill Rd
Lithonia, GA 30038-2420, USA

Buggs, Wamon (Athlete, Football Player)
1220 Banbury Row
Brentwood, TN 37027-2222, USA

Bugliosi, Vincent T (Writer)
c/o Staff Member *BroadMind Entertainment*
3699 Wilshire Blvd Ste 850
Los Angeles, CA 90010-2737, USA

Bugner, Joe (Boxer)
22 Buckingham St
Surrey Hills, NSW 2010, AUSTRALIA

Buhari, Muhammadu (General, President)
Daura
Katsina State, NIGERIA

Buhner, Jay (Athlete, Baseball Player)
2014 Sandy Coast Cir
League City, TX 77573-6618, USA

Buhrmaster, Robert C (Business Person)
3601 Minnesota Dr Ste 400
Bloomington, MN 55435-6008, USA

Buice, Dewayne (Athlete, Baseball Player)
PO Box 5185
Incline Village, NV 89450-5185, USA

Buie, Drew (Athlete, Football Player)
2815 Eland Dr
Winston Salem, NC 27127-7284, USA

Buitenhuis, Penelope (Director, Writer)
c/o Carl Lieberman *Characters Talent Agency, The (Vancouver)*
1505 W 2nd Ave #200
Vancouver, BC V6H 3Y4, Canada

Bujnoch, Glenn (Athlete, Football Player)
7598 Fairwayglen Dr
Cincinnati, OH 45248-2800, USA

Bujold, Genevieve (Actor)
1327 Ocean Ave Ste J
Santa Monica, CA 90401-1033, USA

Bukaty, Fred (Athlete, Football Player)
10930 Glen Arbor Rd
Kansas City, MO 64114-4959, USA

Buker, Cy (Athlete, Baseball Player)
1711 S Cedar Ave
Marshfield, WI 54449-4937, USA

Bukich, Rudy (Athlete, Football Player)
7910 Ivanhoe Ave Apt 333
La Jolla, CA 92037-4511, USA

Buksar, George (Athlete, Football Player)
33400 N Burr Oak Dr
Solon, OH 44139-5550, USA

Buktenica, Raymond (Actor)
345 N Maple Dr # 302
Beverly Hills, CA 90210-3869, USA

Bukvich, Ryan (Athlete, Baseball Player)
200 Apple Blossom Cir
Brandon, MS 39047-7691, USA

Bulaich, Norman B (Norm) (Athlete, Football Player)
421 Lynndale Ct
Hurst, TX 76054-2725, USA

Bulatovic, Momir (President)
Lenina 2
Belgrade 11070, SERBIA & MONTENEGRO

Bulger, Jason (Athlete, Baseball Player)
1898 Harbour Oaks Dr
Snellville, GA 30078-2316, USA

Bulger, Marc (Athlete, Football Player)
c/o Tom Condon *CAA - St. Louis*
222 S Central Ave Ste 1008
Saint Louis, MO 63105-3509, USA

Bulifant, Joyce (Actor)
3500 W Olive Ave Ste 1470
Burbank, CA 91505-5514, USA

Bull, John S (Astronaut)
PO Box 1106
S Lake Tahoe, CA 96156-1106, USA

Bull, Richard (Actor)
750 N Rush St Apt 1903
Chicago, IL 60611-2581, USA

Bull, Ronald D (Ronnie) (Athlete, Football Player)
15 Redspire Ct
Bolingbrook, IL 60490-3175, USA

Bull, Scott (Athlete, Football Player)
3660 N Front St Ste 3
Fayetteville, AR 72703-5177, USA

Bullard, Louis E (Athlete, Football Player)
3129 Friars Bridge Pass
Franklin, TN 37064-2169, USA

Bullard, Matt (Athlete, Basketball Player)
10 Balmoral Pl
Spring, TX 77382-1343, USA

Bullard, Mike (Athlete, Hockey Player)
1170 Shillington Ave
Ottawa, ON K1Z 7Z4, Canada

Bullet, Scott (Athlete, Baseball Player)
218 Vicky Bullett St
Martinsburg, WV 25404-4511, USA

Bulling, Terry (Bud) (Athlete, Baseball Player)
PO Box 262
Newport, WA 99156-0262, USA

Bullinger, Jim (Athlete, Baseball Player)
2504 Elise Ave
Metairie, LA 70003-1931, USA

Bullinger, Kirk (Athlete, Baseball Player)
3608 David Dr
Metairie, LA 70003-3413, USA

Bullington, Bryan (Athlete, Baseball Player)
20116 Oakwood Dr
Mokena, IL 60448-1395, USA

Bullins, Ed (Writer)
425 Lafayette St
New York, NY 10003-7021, USA

Bullitt, John C (Attorney, Attorney General, General, Government Official)
53 Wall St
New York, NY 10005, USA

Bullmann, Maik (Wrestler)
Postfach 1112
Goldbach 63769, GERMANY

Bulloch, Jeremy (Actor)
10 Birchwood Rd
London SW17 9BQ, UNITED KINGDOM (UK)

Bullock, Bruce (Athlete, Hockey Player)
5226 W Redbird Rd
Phoenix, AZ 85083-6317, USA

Bullock, Eric (Athlete, Baseball Player)
17503 Harwick Ct
Carson, CA 90746-1617, USA

Bullock, J R (Business Person)
3221 N Service Rd
Burlington, ON L7R 3Y8, CANADA

Bullock, Jim J (Actor)
612 Lighthouse Ave # 200
Pacific Grove, CA 93950-2615, USA

Bullock, Jim J (Actor)
c/o Staff Member *Bohemia Group*
1680 Vine St Ste 216
Los Angeles, CA 90028-8829, USA

Bullock, Sandra (Actor, Producer)
c/o Cheryl Maisel *Rogers & Cowan PR (LA)*
Pacific Design Center 8687 Melrose Ave, 7th Floor
West Hollywood, CA 90069, USA

Bullock, Theodore H (Biologist)
Neurosciences
La Jolla, CA 92093-0001, USA

Bullock, Vicki (Athlete, Basketball Player)
100 Hive Dr
Charlotte, NC 28217-4524, USA

Bullocks, Amos (Athlete, Football Player)
17209 Dobson Ave
South Holland, IL 60473-3535, USA

Bullough, Hank (Athlete, Football Player)
4439 Copperhill Dr
Okemos, MI 48864-2067, USA

Bulluck, Keith (Athlete, Football Player)
641 Old Hickory Blvd Unit 301
Brentwood, TN 37027-3949, USA

Bulriss, Mark P (Business Person)
9025 River Rd Ste 400
Indianapolis, IN 46240-6443, USA

Bum, Kim (Actor)
c/o Staff Member *Glory Entertainment*
1-25-5-3F Higashi Azabu Minatoku
Tokyo 106-0044, Japan

Bumbeck, David (Artist)
Drew Lane RD 3
Middleburry, VT 5753, USA

Bumbry, Alonzo B (Al) (Athlete, Baseball Player)
28 Tremblant Ct
Lutherville Timonium, MD 21093-3748, USA

Bumbry, Grace (Opera Singer)
Maximilianstr 22
Munich 80539, GERMANY

Bumgarner, Wayne (Actor)
PO Box 208
Claremont, NC 28610-0208, USA

Bump, Nate (Athlete, Baseball Player)
1106 Cardinal Dr
West Chester, PA 19382-7804, USA

Bumpers, Dale (Ex-Senator)
1050 Connecticut Ave NW
Washington, DC 20036-5303, USA

Bunce, Gregory (Athlete, Basketball Player)
1710 Redwood Way
Upland, CA 91784-1767, USA

Bunce, Larry (Attorney, Basketball Player)
1000 Vintage Ln Apt 338
Mount Vernon, WA 98273-5532, USA

Bunch, Ashli (Athlete, Golfer)
1629 Country Club Dr
Morristown, TN 37814-3316, USA

Bunch, Jarrod (Athlete, Football Player)
1580 Hemlock Dr
Ashtabula, OH 44004-9360, USA

Bunch, Jimmy Castor (Musician)
145 W 57th St
New York, NY 10019-2220, USA

Bunch, Melvin (Athlete, Baseball Player)
12 Tyler Ln
Hooks, TX 75561-7013, USA

Bunch, Sidney (Athlete, Baseball Player)
3285 Towne Village Rd
Antioch, TN 37013-1280, USA

Bund, Karlheinz (Business Person)
Huyssenallee 82-84
Essen Ruhr 45128, GERMANY

Bundchen, Gisele (Model)
c/o Anne Nelson *IMG Models (NY)*
304 Park Ave S # PH
New York, NY 10010, USA

Bundy, Brooke (Actor)
833 N Martel Ave
Los Angeles, CA 90046-7508, USA

Bundy, Laura Bell (Actor, Musician)
c/o Tom Storms *Sanctuary Artist Management (TN)*
54 Music Sq E Ste 300
Nashville, TN 37203-4386, USA

Bungee, Suzanne (Stylist)
c/o Staff Member *Arlene Wilson Management*
807 N Jefferson St # 200
Milwaukee, WI 53202-8150, USA

Bunim, Mary-Ellis (Producer)
c/o Staff Member *Bunim/Murray Productions Inc*
6007 Sepulveda Blvd
Van Nuys, CA 91411-2502, USA

Bunker, Wallace E (Wally) (Athlete, Baseball Player)
330 Coosaw Way Unit 38
Ridgeland, SC 29936-4969, USA

Bunkowsky-Scherbak, Barb (Athlete, Golfer)
8725 Marlamoor Ln
West Palm Beach, FL 33412-1614, USA

Bunnell, John (Actor, Television Host)
c/o Greg Horangic *WmE2 (Endeavor-LA)*
9601 Wilshire Blvd Fl 3
Beverly Hills, CA 90210-5219, USA

Bunnett, Joseph F (Misc)
608 Arroyo Seco
Santa Cruz, CA 95060-3148, USA

Bunnetta, Bill (Bowler)
1176 E San Bruno Ave
Fresno, CA 93710-7109, USA

Bunning, James P D (Jim) (Athlete, Baseball Player, Senator)
4 Fairway Dr
Southgate, KY 41071-3022, USA

Bunny, Lady (Comedian, DJ)
c/o Staff Member *Diva Central Inc*
7510 W Sunset Blvd Ste 1445
Los Angeles, CA 90046-3408, USA

Bunt, Dick (Actor)
11 Irving Pl
Greenlawn, NY 11740-3113, USA

Bunt, Richard (Athlete, Basketball Player)
38 Lawrence Ave
Danbury, CT 06810-5181, USA

Bunting, Eve (Writer)
10 E 53rd St
New York, NY 10022-5244, USA

Bunting, John (Athlete, Football Player)
134 Soundview Dr
Hampstead, NC 28443-2510, USA

Bunting, William (Athlete, Basketball Player)
11000 Pacer Ct
Raleigh, NC 27614-9604, USA

Bunton, Emma (Music Group, Musician)
c/o Jeff Frasco *Creative Artists Agency (CAA-LA)*
2000 Avenue of the Stars Ste 100
Los Angeles, CA 90067-4705, USA

Bunyan, John (Athlete, Football Player)
92 Radburn Rd
Glen Rock, NJ 07452-3417, USA

Bunz, Dan (Athlete, Football Player)
4230 Rocklin Rd Apt 2
Rocklin, CA 95677-2869, USA

Buoniconti, Nicholas A (Nick) (Athlete, Business Person, Football Player)
445 Grand Bay Dr Apt 803
Key Biscayne, FL 33149-1907, USA

Buono, Cara (Actor)
c/o Joanna (Joanie) Burstein *Burstein Company, The*
15304 W Sunset Blvd Ste 208
Pacific Palisades, CA 90272-3656, USA

Buono, Carla (Actor)
25 Sea Colony Dr
Santa Monica, CA 90405-5495, USA

Buraas, Hans-Peter (Skier)
Postboks 3853
Ulleval Hageby, Oslo 805, NORWAY

Burba, Dave (Athlete, Baseball Player)
925 W Juniper Ave
Gilbert, AZ 85233-4258, USA

Burba, Edwin H Jr (General)
256 Montrose Dr
McDonough, GA 30253-4242, USA

Burbach, Bill (Athlete, Baseball Player)
147 Shenandoah Dr
Johnson City, TN 37601-5459, USA

Burbank, Daniel C (Dan) (Astronaut)
3210 Water Elm Way
Houston, TX 77059, USA

Burbidge, E Margaret P (Astronomer)
9500 Astrophysics Ctr
La Jolla, CA 92093-0001, USA

Burbules, Peter G (General)
8287 Chestnut Point Ln
Hayes, VA 23072-3835, USA

Burch, Elliot (Race Car Driver)
12 Hilltop Ave
Middletown, RI 02842-4951, USA

Burch, Jerry (Athlete, Football Player)
3100 Cleburne St
Houston, TX 77004-4501, USA

Burchart, Larry (Athlete, Baseball Player)
5310 E 94th St
Tulsa, OK 74137-4417, USA

Burchfiel, Burrell C (Geophysicist, Misc, Physicist)
9 Robinson Park
Winchester, MA 01890-3717, USA

Burchfield, Don (Athlete, Football Player)
26450 Summer Greens Dr
Bonita Springs, FL 34135-2328, USA

Burchuladze, Paata (Opera Singer)
Piankengasse 7
Vienna 1010, AUSTRIA

Burckhalter, Joseph H (Inventor)
705 Valley Brook Rd
Wilmington, NC 28412-3243, USA

Burd, Steven A (Business Person)
5918 Stoneridge Mall Rd
Pleasanton, CA 94588-3229, USA

Burda, Bob (Athlete, Baseball Player)
5285 S Roanoke
Mesa, AZ 85206-2129, USA

Burden, Ross (Chef)
c/o Staff Member *Roseman Organisation, The*
51 Queen Anne St
London W1G 9HS, UK

Burden, Ticky (Athlete, Basketball Player)
4332 Grove Ave Apt C
Winston Salem, NC 27105-2837, USA

Burden, William A M (Diplomat, Financier)
820 5th Ave
New York, NY 10065-7267, USA

Burdette, Freddie (Athlete, Baseball Player)
PO Box 586
Albany, GA 31702-0586, USA

Burditt, Joyce (Producer, Writer)
c/o Staff Member *WmE2 (Endeavor-LA)*
9601 Wilshire Blvd Fl 3
Beverly Hills, CA 90210-5219, USA

Burdon, Eric (Music Group, Songwriter, Writer)
PO Box 770850
Orlando, FL 32877-0850, USA

Bure, Paval
V100 N. Renfrew St.
Vancouver BC V5K 3N7, CANADA

Bure, Pavel (Athlete, Hockey Player)
7632 Fisher Island Dr
Miami Beach, FL 33109-0780, USA

Bure, Valeri (Athlete, Hockey Player)
237 Monte Grigio Dr
Pacific Palisades, CA 90272-3109, USA

Burega, Bill (Athlete, Hockey Player)
RR 1
Elginburgh, ON K0H 1M0, Canada

Bureker-Stopper, Geraldine (Baseball Player)
2006 SE 41st Ave
Portland, OR 97214-5966, USA

Burfeindt, Betty (Athlete, Golfer)
70 San Simeon Pl
Rancho Mirage, CA 92270-1951, USA

Burford, Christopher W (Chris) (Athlete, Football Player)
1215 Broken Feather Ct
Reno, NV 89511-5350, USA

Burg, Mark (Producer)
c/o Staff Member *Evolution Entertainment (LA)*
901 N Highland Ave
Los Angeles, CA 90038-2412, USA

Burgee, John H (Architect)
Perelanda Farm Skunks Misery Road
Millerton, NY 12546, USA

Burger, Michael (Actor)
c/o Staff Member *Richard De La Font Agency*
3808 W South Park Blvd
Broken Arrow, OK 74011-1261, USA

Burger, Neil (Director)
c/o Staff Member *WmE2 (Endeavor-LA)*
9601 Wilshire Blvd Fl 3
Beverly Hills, CA 90210-5219, USA

Burgere, Andre
67 quai d'Orsay
Paris F-75007, FRANCE

Burgess, Adrian (Mountaineer)
324 G St
Anderson, SC 29625-4147, USA

Burgess, Annie (Athlete)
601 F St NW
Washington, DC 20004-1605

Burgess, Bobby (Actor)
11684 Ventura Blvd # 691
Studio City, CA 91604-2699, USA

Burgess, Christian
33 Gastein Rd
London W6 8LT, ENGLAND

Burgess, Don (Cinematographer)
232 N Canon Dr
Beverly Hills, CA 90210-5302, USA

Burgess, Mitchell (Writer)
c/o Staff Member *Broder Webb Chervin Silbermann Agency, The (BWCS)*
10250 Constellation Blvd
Los Angeles, CA 90067-6200, USA

Burgess, Neil (Engineer)
201 E 5th St Ste 2200
Cincinnati, OH 45202-4113, USA

Burgess, Robert K (Business Person)
33 Bloomfield Hills Pkwy
Bloomfield Hills, MI 48304-2944, USA

Burgess, Ronnie (Athlete, Football Player)
303 Brandymill Blvd
Myrtle Beach, SC 29588-7227, USA

Burgess, Tom (Athlete, Baseball Player)
97 Sunray Ave
London, ON N6P 1C6, Canada

Burgess, Tony (Misc)
119 National Ctr
Reston, VA 22092, USA

Burgess, Warren D (Religious Leader)
475 Riverside Dr
New York, NY 10115-0002, USA

Burghardt, Raymond F (Diplomat)
7 Lang Ha St Ba Dinh
Hanoi, VIETNAM

Burghardt, Walter J (Misc)
19 L St NW
Washington, DC 20001, USA

Burghoff, Gary (Actor)
13701 Riverside Dr Ste 201
Sherman Oaks, CA 91423-2447, USA

Burgi, Richard (Actor)
1019 Baja St
Laguna Beach, CA 92651-3546, USA

Burgin, C David (Editor)
409 13th St
Oakland, CA 94612-2605, USA

Burgio, Danielle (Actor)
c/o Carl Scott *Simmons & Scott Entertainment*
7942 Mulholland Dr
Los Angeles, CA 90046-1225, USA

Burgmeier, Ted (Athlete, Football Player)
861 Scenic Hts
East Dubuque, IL 61025-1041, USA

Burgmeler, Tom (Athlete, Baseball Player)
13118 Walmer St
Leawood, KS 66209-3618, USA

Burgon, Geoffrey (Composer)
8-9 Firth St
London W1V 5TZ, UNITED KINGDOM (UK)

Burham, Daniel (Business Person)
870 Winter St
Waltham, MA 02451-1449, USA

Burham, James B (Financier)
1 Mellon Bank Ctr # 400
Pittsburgh, PA 15258-0001, USA

Burhoe, Ralph Wendell (Misc)
Montgomery Place 5550 S South Shore Dr #715
Chicago, IL 60637, USA

Burich, Bill (Athlete, Baseball Player)
10562 Nobleton Rd
Apple Valley, CA 92308-3308, USA

Burk, Mack (Athlete, Baseball Player)
5710 Glen Pines Dr
Houston, TX 77069-1852, USA

Burk, Scott (Athlete, Football Player)
1330 Castlepoint Cir
Castle Pines, CO 80108-8295, USA

Burka, Vern (Athlete, Football Player)
580 Riviera Cir
Nipomo, CA 93444-8866, USA

Burke, Alfred (Actor)
219 The Plaza 535 Kings St
London SW10 0SZ, USA

Burke, Bernard F (Physicist)
10 Bloomfield St
Lexington, MA 02421-5608, USA

Burke, Billy (Actor)
c/o Ellen Meyer *Ellen Meyer Management*
8899 Beverly Blvd Ste 612
West Hollywood, CA 90048-2429, USA

Burke, Brooke (Actor, Model)
c/o Staff Member *United Talent Agency (UTA)*
9560 Wilshire Blvd Fl 5
Beverly Hills, CA 90212-2400, USA

Burke, Cheryl (Dancer, Reality TV Star)
c/o Susan Madore *Guttman Associates*
118 S Beverly Dr Ste 201
Beverly Hills, CA 90212-3016, USA

Burke, Chris (Actor)
426 S Orange Grove Ave
Los Angeles, CA 90036-3102, USA

Burke, Chris (Athlete, Baseball Player)
15415 Crystal Springs Way
Louisville, KY 40245-5298, USA

Burke, Clement (Clem) (Musician)
32 Court St Ste 1600
Brooklyn, NY 11201-4441, USA

Burke, David (Writer)
c/o Jamie Mandelbaum *Jackoway Tyerman Wertheimer Austen Mandelbaum Morris & Klein*
1925 Century Park E Fl 22
Los Angeles, CA 90067-2701, USA

Burke, Delta (Actor)
c/o Rick Hersh *Celebrity Consultants LLC*
3340 Ocean Park Blvd Ste 1030
Santa Monica, CA 90405-3259, USA

Burke, Don (Athlete, Football Player)
518 Island Ave
Reno, NV 89501-1714, USA

Burke, Ed (Actor)
16717 La Mirada Rd
Los Gatos, CA 95030-4118, USA

Burke, Ernest (Athlete, Baseball Player)
9451 Common Brook Rd Apt 302
Owings Mills, MD 21117-7582, USA

Burke, Hederman Lynn (Swimmer)
26 White Oak Tree Rd
Syosset, NY 11791-1210, USA

Burke, James (Correspondent)
Henley House Terrace Bames
London SW13 0NP, UNITED KINGDOM (UK)

Burke, James D (Director)
Forest Park
Saint Louis, MO 63110-1380, USA

Burke, James E (Business Person)
317 George St # 200
New Brunswick, NJ 08901-2008, USA

Burke, James Lee (Writer)
c/o Staff Member *Random House Publicity (Toronto)*
1 Toronto St Suite 300
Toronto, ON M5C 2V6, Canada

Burke, James Lee (Writer)
1540 Broadway
New York, NY 10036-4039, USA

Burke, Joe (Athlete, Football Player)
7 Maplewood St
Albany, NY 12208-2413, USA

Burke, John (Athlete, Baseball Player)
3490 Westbrook Ln
Highlands Ranch, CO 80129-1527, USA

Burke, John (Athlete, Football Player)
44 Chestnut Ridge Rd
Holmdel, NJ 07733-1437, USA

Burke, John F (Doctor, Educator)
1010 Waltham St Apt 214
Lexington, MA 02421-8062, USA

Burke, Joseph C (Educator)
411 State St
Albany, NY 12203-1003, USA

Burke, Kathy (Actor)
83 Shepperton Road
London N1 3DF, UNITED KINGDOM (UK)

Burke, Kelly H (General)
1006 Cameron St
Alexandria, VA 22314-2427, USA

Burke, Leo (Athlete, Baseball Player)
12916 Woodburn Dr
Hagerstown, MD 21742-2866, USA

Burke, Michael Reilly (Actor)
c/o Staff Member *Paradigm (LA)*
360 N Crescent Dr
Beverly Hills, CA 90210-4874, USA

Burke, Mike (Athlete, Football Player)
1296 E Gibson Rd
Woodland, CA 95776-6378, USA

Burke, Patrick (Athlete, Golfer)
24 Saint Georges Ct
Trabuco Canyon, CA 92679-4926, USA

Burke, Philip (Artist)
335 Buffalo Ave
Niagara Falls, NY 14303-1232, USA

Burke, Randall (Athlete, Football Player)
3420 Chestnut Hill Ln
Lexington, KY 40509-1916, USA

Burke, Robert John (Actor)

Burke, Sarah (Reality TV Star)
c/o Michael (Mike) Esterman
Esterman.Com, LLC
Prefers to be contacted via email
MD, USA

Burke, Shawn (Athlete, Hockey Player)
7175 E Camelback Rd Unit 801
Scottsdale, AZ 85251-1673, USA

Burke, Soloman (Musician)
c/o Staff Member *Coalition Management*
Devonshire House 12 Barley Mow Passage
London W4 4PH, UK

Burke, Steve (Athlete, Football Player)
RR 3 Box 553-F
Austin, TX 78754, USA

Burke, Steve (Athlete, Baseball Player)
1812 Amber Leaf Way
Lodi, CA 95242-4468, USA

Burke, Tim (Athlete, Baseball Player)
12108 W Ida Ln
Littleton, CO 80127-3106, USA

Burke Sr, Jack (Athlete, Golfer)
5602 Glen Pines Dr
Houston, TX 77069-1834, USA

Burket, Harriet (Editor)
700 John Ringling Blvd
Sarasota, FL 34236-1542, USA

Burkett, Chris (Athlete, Football Player)
296 Dover Ln
Madison, MS 39110-9726, USA

Burkett, Jackie (Athlete, Football Player)
929 Lighthouse Rd
Fort Walton Beach, FL 32547-3914, USA

Burkett, John D (Athlete, Baseball Player)
1404 Laurel Ln
Southlake, TX 76092-3573, USA

Burkhalter, Correll (Athlete, Football Player)
221 Robert Owens Rd
Mount Olive, MS 39119-4651, USA

Burkhalter, Edward A Jr (Admiral)
4128 Fort Washington Pl
Alexandria, VA 22304, USA

Burkhard, Jolanda (Stylist)
441 E 12th St Apt 4A
New York, NY 10009-4047, USA

Burkhardt, Francois (Architect)
3 Rue de Venise
Paris 75004, FRANCE

Burkhardt, Lisa (Sportscaster)
4 Pennsylvania Plz
New York, NY 10001, USA

Burkhart, Morgan (Athlete, Baseball Player)
105 Turtle Rock Ct
Saint Charles, MO 63304-7679, USA

Burkholder, JoAnn (Physicist)
Botany
Raleigh, NC 27695-0001, USA

Burkholder, Owen E (Religious Leader)
421 S 2nd St Ste 600
Elkhart, IN 46516-3243, USA

Burkl, Fred A (Misc)
9865 W Roosevelt Rd
Westchester, IL 60154-2767, USA

Burkley, Dennis (Actor)
5145 Costello Ave
Sherman Oaks, CA 91423-1207, USA

Burkman, Roger (Athlete, Basketball Player)
3535 Nanz Ave
Louisville, KY 40207-3717, USA

Burkovich, Shirley (Baseball Player)
67430 Ovante Rd
Cathedral City, CA 92234-8402, USA

Burks, Arthur W (Mathematician)
3445 Vintage Valley Rd
Ann Arbor, MI 48105-2544, USA

Burks, Audra (Athlete, Golfer)
1566 Woodmore Dr
Springfield, IL 62711-6606, USA

Burks, Ellis R (Athlete, Baseball Player)
115 South Ln
Chagrin Falls, OH 44022-1145, USA

Burks, Randy (Athlete, Football Player)
300 Moyer Dr
Broken Bow, OK 74728-1519, USA

Burks, Shawn (Athlete, Football Player)
5752 Nottaway Dr
Baton Rouge, LA 70820-5415, USA

Burks, Steve (Athlete, Football Player)
2568 Mount Tabor Rd
Cabot, AR 72023-9596, USA

Burl, Alex (Athlete, Football Player)
15075 E 43rd Ave
Denver, CO 80239-5147, USA

Burleson, Richard P (Rick) (Athlete, Baseball Player)
241 E Country Hills Dr
La Habra, CA 90631-7623, USA

Burleson, Tom (Athlete, Basketball Player)
PO Box 861
Newland, NC 28657-0861, USA

Burley, Gary (Athlete, Football Player)
514 Bristol Ln
Birmingham, AL 35226-1947, USA

Burley, Nichola
c/o Michael Duff *Troika*
74 Clerkenwell Rd 3rd Floor
London EC1M 5QA, United Kingdom

Burlinson, Tom (Actor)
c/o Staff Member *June Cann Management*
73 Jersey Rd
Woollahra 2025, AUSTRALIA

Burman, George (Athlete, Football Player)
1646 James St
Syracuse, NY 13203-2816, USA

Burn, Scott (Writer)
c/o Staff Member *Creative Artists Agency (CAA-LA)*
2000 Avenue of the Stars Ste 100
Los Angeles, CA 90067-4705, USA

Burnell, Jocelyn Bell (Astronomer)
Physics Dept
Milton Keynes MK7 6AA, UNITED KINGDOM (UK)

Burnell, Max (Athlete, Football Player)
PO Box 1076
Rockwall, TX 75087-1076, USA

Burner, David L (Business Person)
3 Coliseum Centre 2550 West Tyvola Rd
Charlotte, NC 28205, USA

Burnes, Karen (Correspondent)
51 W 52nd St
New York, NY 10019-6119, USA

Burnett, A J (Athlete, Baseball Player)
15208 Jarrettsville Pike
Monkton, MD 21111, USA

Burnett, Bobby (Athlete, Football Player)
657 Kryptonite Dr
Castle Rock, CO 80108-3086, USA

Burnett, Carol (Actor, Comedian)
c/o Bill Robinson *Bill Robinson Management*
PO Box 6284
Malibu, CA 90264-6284, USA

Burnett, Chester (Athlete, Football Player)
2610 Ivanhoe St
Denver, CO 80207-3409, USA

Burnett, David (Stylist)
c/o Staff Member *Agency, The*
1800 Avenue of the Stars Ste 1114
Los Angeles, CA 90067-4201

Burnett, Erin (Correspondent)
c/o Staff Member *CNBC (DC)*
400 N Capitol St NW Ste 850
Washington, DC 20001-1555, USA

Burnett, Howard J (Educator)
President's Office
Washington, PA 15301, USA

Burnett, James E (Government Official)
800 Independence Ave SW
Washington, DC 20594, USA

Burnett, Mark (Producer)
c/o Don Epstein *Greater Talent Network Inc*
437 5th Ave Fl 7
New York, NY 10016-2205, USA

Burnett, Molly (Actor)
c/o Shepard Smith *Archetype*
1608 Argyle Ave
Los Angeles, CA 90028-6408, USA

Burnett, Nancy (Director)
32 Watson St
Unadilla, NY 13849-0735, USA

Burnett, Sean (Athlete, Baseball Player)
14016 Aster Ave
Wellington, FL 33414-2145, USA

Burnett, T-Bone (Musician, Producer, Songwriter)
c/o Staff Member *Paradigm (Monterey)*
404 W Franklin St
Monterey, CA 93940-2303, USA

Burnett, Webbie D (Athlete, Football Player)
5305 San Antonio Ave Apt 128
Orlando, FL 32839-2222, USA

Burnette, Dave (Athlete, Football Player)
4201 Senator St
Texarkana, AR 71854-1528, USA

Burnette, Olivia (Actor)
c/o Staff Member *RPM Talent Agency*
2600 W Olive Ave Fl 5
Burbank, CA 91505-4572, USA

Burnette, Reggie (Athlete, Football Player)
7803 Chasewood Dr
Missouri City, TX 77489-1836, USA

Burnette, Rocky (Musician)
1900 Ave of Stars # 2530
Los Angeles, CA 90067-4301, USA

Burnette, Thomas N Jr (General)
Deputy Cinc US Joint Forces Command
Norfolk, VA 23551-0001, USA

Burnine, Hank (Athlete, Football Player)
1201 W 19th St Apt B112
Higginsville, MO 64037-1472, USA

Burning, Spear (Musician)
13034 231st St
Springfield Gardens, NY 11413-1832, USA

Burnitz, Jeromy (Athlete, Baseball Player)
PO Box 676032
Rancho Santa Fe, CA 92067-6032, USA

Burnley, Benjamin (Musician)

Burnley, James H IV (Secretary)
2300 N St NW
Washington, DC 20037-1122, USA

Burns, Annie (Musician, Songwriter, Writer)
177 Woodland Ave
Westwood, NJ 07675-3218, USA

Burns, Bob (Musician)
12512 Fraser Ave
Granada Hills, CA 91344-1321, USA

Burns, Bob (Athlete, Golfer)
12512 Fraser Ave
Granada Hills, CA 91344-1321, USA

Burns, Britt (Athlete, Baseball Player)
1550 Katy Gap Rd Apt 903
Katy, TX 77494-5872, USA

Burns, Brooke (Actor, Model)
c/o Liza Anderson *Anderson Group Public Relations*
8060 Melrose Ave Fl 4
Los Angeles, CA 90046-7038, USA

Burns, Charles (Artist)
c/o Staff Member *Fantagraphics Books*
7563 Lake City Way NE
Seattle, WA 98115-4218, USA

Burns, Charlie (Athlete, Hockey Player)
7 Fawn Dr
Wallingford, CT 06492-3307, USA

Burns, Christian (Musician)
Crown House 225 Kensington High St
London W8 8SA, UNITED KINGDOM (UK)

Burns, David (Athlete, Basketball Player)
2623 Bainbridge Dr
Dallas, TX 75237-2801, USA

Burns, Edward (Actor, Director)
c/o Alicia Gordon *WmE2 (Endeavor-LA)*
9601 Wilshire Blvd Fl 3
Beverly Hills, CA 90210-5219, USA

Burns, Eileen (Actor)
4000 W 43rd St
New York, NY 10036, USA

Burns, Evers (Athlete, Basketball Player)
7216 Lost Spring Ct
Lanham, MD 20706-3834, USA

Burns, George (Athlete, Golfer)
10459 Prestwick Rd
Boynton Beach, FL 33436-4418, USA

Burns, George (Athlete, Basketball Player)
16 E Poplar St
Floral Park, NY 11001-3145, USA

Burns, Heather (Actor)
c/o Courtney Kivowitz *Schiff Company, The*
8440 Warner Dr Ste B1
Culver City, CA 90232-2461, USA

Burns, James (Athlete, Basketball Player)
2706 Lincoln St
Evanston, IL 60201-2043, USA

Burns, James MacGregor (Historian, Scientist)
High Mowing Bee Hill Road
Williamstown, MA 1267, USA

Burns, Jason (Athlete, Football Player)
8923 S Marshfield Ave
Chicago, IL 60620-4955, USA

Burns, Jeannie (Musician, Songwriter, Writer)
177 Woodland Ave
Westwood, NJ 07675-3218, USA

Burns, Jere (Actor)
c/o Staff Member *International Creative Management (ICM-LA)*
10250 Constellation Blvd Fl 7
Los Angeles, CA 90067-6207, USA

Burns, Jere II (Actor)
1465 Lindacrest Dr
Beverly Hills, CA 90210-2519, USA

Burns, Jerry (Athlete, Football Coach, Football Player)
9520 Viking Dr
Eden Prairie, MN 55344-3825

Burns, Jim (Writer)
c/o Staff Member *Da Capo Press*
44 Farnsworth St Fl 3
Boston, MA 02210-1223, USA

Burns, Keith (Athlete, Football Player)
13572 Heritage Farms Dr
Gainesville, VA 20155-1333, USA

Burns, Ken (Director, Producer)
c/o Staff Member *Florentine Films*
PO Box 613
Walpole, NH 03608-0613, USA

Burns, Kenneth L (Ken) (Director)
Maple Grove Road
Walpole, NH 3608, USA

Burns, Lamont (Athlete, Football Player)
104 Northwood St
Greensboro, NC 27417, USA

Burns, M Anthony (Business Person)
3600 NW 82nd Ave
Doral, FL 33166-6623, USA

Burns, Marie (Musician, Songwriter, Writer)
177 Woodland Ave
Westwood, NJ 07675-3218, USA

Burns, Megan (Actor)
c/o Kathryn Fleming *The Rights House (UK)*
Drury House 34-43 Russell St
London WC2B 5HA, UK

Burns, Mike (Athlete, Football Player)
608 W 103rd St
Los Angeles, CA 90044-4540, USA

Burns, Pat (Coach)
Continental Arena 50 RR 120 N
East Rutherford, NJ 7073, USA

Burns, Patty (Stylist)
c/o Staff Member *Ennis*
119 Braintree St
Boston, MA 02134-1628, USA

Burns, Pete
c/o LIVING 160 Great Portland Street
London, not applicable W1W 5QA, United Kingdom

Burns, Regan (Actor)
c/o Bruce Smith *OmniPop Talent Group*
10700 Ventura Blvd Fl 2
Studio City, CA 91604-3561, USA

Burns, Robert H (Misc)
1015 University Bay Dr
Madison, WI 53705-2250, USA

Burns, Robin (Athlete, Hockey Player)
186 Sherwood Rd
Beaconsfield, QC H9W 2G8, Canada

Burns, Steven (Actor)
c/o Staff Member *Davis Spylios Management*
244 W 54th St Ste 707
New York, NY 10019-5515

Burns, Todd (Athlete, Baseball Player)
PO Box 111
Princeton, AL 35766-0111, USA

Burnside, Pete (Athlete, Baseball Player)
1041 Ridge Rd Unit 210
Wilmette, IL 60091-1569, USA

Burnside, Sheldon (Athlete, Baseball Player)
7519 Wynford Cir
Montgomery, AL 36117-7483, USA

Burnstein, Nanette (Director, Producer)
c/o Scott Greenberg *Creative Artists Agency (CAA-LA)*
2000 Avenue of the Stars Ste 100
Los Angeles, CA 90067-4705, USA

Burpo, George (Athlete, Baseball Player)
8981 E Palms Park Dr
Tucson, AZ 85715-5644, USA

Burr, Bill (Comedian)
c/o Staff Member *WmE2 (WMA-LA)*
1 William Morris Pl
Beverly Hills, CA 90212-4261, USA

Burr, Richard (Senator)
217 Russell Senate Ofc Building
Washington, DC 20510-0001, USA

Burr, Shawn (Athlete, Hockey Player)
1615 River Rd
Saint Clair, MI 48079-3552, USA

Burrell, Garland L Jr (Judge)
5011 St
Sacramento, CA 95814, USA

Burrell, George R (Athlete, Football Player)
129 W Upsal St
Philadelphia, PA 19119-4003, USA

Burrell, John (Athlete, Football Player)
376 Park Lake Dr
Mead, OK 73449-6352, USA

Burrell, Kenneth E (Kenny) (Composer, Musician)
163 3rd Ave # 143
New York, NY 10003-2523, USA

Burrell, Kenny (Musician)
c/o Staff Member *Concord Music Group, Inc*
900 N Rohlwing Rd
Itasca, IL 60143-1161, USA

Burrell, Leroy (Athlete, Track Athlete)
Athletic Dept
Houston, TX 77023, USA

Burrell, Orville (Shaggy) (Musician)
c/o Staff Member *Big Yard Music Group*
PO Box 1060
Valley Stream, NY 11582-1060, USA

Burrell, Pat (Athlete, Baseball Player)
PO Box 1770
Boulder Creek, CA 95006-1770, USA

Burrell, Scott (Athlete, Basketball Player)
331 Evergreen Ave
Hamden, CT 06518-2745, USA

Burrell, Ty (Actor)
c/o Estelle Lasher *Principal Entertainment (LA)*
1964 Westwood Blvd Ste 400
Los Angeles, CA 90025-4695, USA

Burres, Brian (Athlete, Baseball Player)
1420 E Pine St Unit 410
Seattle, WA 98122-8505, USA

Burress, Hedy (Actor)
c/o Jeri Scott *Jeri Scott Management*
211 S Beverly Dr
Beverly Hills, CA 90212-3807, USA

Burridge, Randy (Athlete, Hockey Player)
1911 Nuevo Rd
Henderson, NV 89014-5134, USA

Burright, Larry (Athlete, Baseball Player)
1239 E Palm Dr
Glendora, CA 91741-2347, USA

Burris, Jeffrey L (Jeff) (Athlete, Football Player)
77 Reynolds St
Rock Hill, SC 29730-4368, USA

Burris, Kurt (Buddy) (Athlete, Football Player)
2617 Fairfield Dr
Norman, OK 73072-7024, USA

Burris, Ray (Athlete, Baseball Player)
553 Franklin Dr
Arlington, TX 76011-2243, USA

Burris, Robert H (Misc)
6225 Mineral Point Rd Apt 96
Madison, WI 53705-4574, USA

Burriss, Bo (Athlete, Football Player)
818 Pinemont Dr Apt 38
Houston, TX 77018-1529, USA

Burrough, Junior (Athlete, Basketball Player)
6950 Fernwood Dr Apt A
Charlotte, NC 28211-7210, USA

Burrough, Kenneth O (Ken) (Athlete, Football Player)
7979 Westheimer Rd
Houston, TX 77063-4550, USA

Burroughs, Augusten (Writer)
c/o Christopher Schelling *Ralph Vicinanza, Ltd.*
303 W 18th St
New York, NY 10011-4440, USA

Burroughs, Jeffrey A (Jeff) (Athlete, Baseball Player)
6155 Laguna Ct
Long Beach, CA 90803-4812, USA

Burroughs, Sean (Athlete, Baseball Player)
6155 Laguna Ct
Long Beach, CA 90803-4812, USA

Burroughs, William S (Musician)
PO Box 147
Lawrence, KS 66044-0147, USA

Burrow, Bob (Athlete, Basketball Player)
2228 Oakbranch Cir
Franklin, TN 37064-7407, USA

Burrow, Curtis (Athlete, Football Player)
51 W Cadron Ridge Rd
Greenbrier, AR 72058-9102, USA

Burrow, Ken (Athlete, Football Player)
5371 Dunwoody Club Crk
Atlanta, GA 30360-1363, USA

Burrow, Robert (Athlete, Basketball Player)
2228 Oakbranch Cir
Franklin, TN 37064-7407, USA

Burrowes, Norma E (Opera Singer)
56 Rochester Road
London NW1 9JG, UNITED KINGDOM (UK)

Burrows, Darren E (Actor)
c/o Stephen Hanks *Stephen Hanks Management*
252 N Larchmont Blvd Ste 200
Los Angeles, CA 90004-3754, USA

Burrows, Dave (Athlete, Hockey Player)
c/o Staff Member *Shamrocks Jr A Hockey*
60 Forest St
Parry Sound, ON P2A 2P9, Canada

Burrows, Edwin G (Writer)
198 Madison Ave
New York, NY 10016-4308, USA

Burrows, Eva (Religious Leader)
102 Domain Park 193 Domain Rd
South Yarra, VIC 3141, AUSTRALIA

Burrows, J Stuart (Opera Singer)
Nirvana 35 Saint Fagans Dr Saint Fagans
Cardiff, Wales CF5 6EF, UNITED KINGDOM (UK)

Burrows, James (Director)
c/o Staff Member *Broder Webb Chervin Silbermann Agency, The (BWCS)*
10250 Constellation Blvd
Los Angeles, CA 90067-6200, USA

Burrows, Saffron (Actor)
c/o Staff Member *Premier Model Management*
40-42 Parker St
London WC2B 5PQ, UK

Burrows, Terry (Athlete, Baseball Player)
7019 Burgandy Dr
Lake Charles, LA 70605-0252, USA

Burrus, Harry (Athlete, Football Player)
PO Box 778
Bartow, FL 33831-0778, USA

Burrus, William (Misc)
1300 L St NW
Washington, DC 20005-4107, USA

Burruss, Kandi (Musician, Reality TV Star)
3499 Prince George St
Atlanta, GA 30344-5818, USA

Bursch, Daniel W (Astronaut)
1305 Buena Vista Ave
Pacific Grove, CA 93950-5505, USA

Burshnick, Anthony J (General)
7715 Carrleigh Pkwy
Springfield, VA 22152-1305, USA

Burson, Jim (Athlete, Football Player)
351 Heath Rd
Dawsonville, GA 30534-5603, USA

Burstyn, Ellen (Actor)
PO Box 217
Palisades, NY 10964-0217, USA

Burt, Adam (Athlete, Hockey Player)
34 Smull Ave
Caldwell, NJ 07006-5012, USA

Burt, Jim (Athlete, Football Player)
10 River Farms Ln
Saddle River, NJ 07458-3028, USA

Burtnett, Wellington (Athlete, Hockey Player)
1703 Pouliot Pl
Wilmington, MA 01887-4558, USA

Burton, Albert (Athlete, Football Player)
339 S Dr Martin Luther King Jr Blvd
Daytona Beach, FL 32114-4819, USA

Burton, Amanda (Actor)
c/o Staff Member *Independent Talent Group (ITG-UK)*
Oxford House 76 Oxford St
London W1D 1BS, UK

Burton, Brandie (Athlete, Golfer)
27102 Pleasant Hill Dr
Highland, CA 92346-7214, USA

Burton, Cummy (Athlete, Hockey Player)
348 Howey Dr
Sudbury, ON P3B 1E8, Canada

Burton, Dan (Congressman, Politician)
2308 Raybunn Hob
Washington, DC 20515-0001, USA

Burton, Ed (Actor)
660 W Hile Rd
Norton Shores, MI 49441-5467, USA

Burton, Edward (Athlete, Basketball Player)
660 W Hile Rd
Norton Shores, MI 49441-5467, USA

Burton, Ellis (Athlete, Baseball Player)
15621 Beach Blvd Spc 7
Westminster, CA 92683-7120, USA

Burton, Gary (Musician)
1140 Boylston St
Boston, MA 02215-3631, USA

Burton, Glenn W (Misc)
PO Box 472
Clayton, GA 30525-0012, USA

Burton, Hilarie (Actor)
c/o Meg Mortimer *Principal Entertainment (NY)*
130 W 42nd St Ste 614
New York, NY 10036-7804, USA

Burton, Jake (Skier)
80 Industrial Pkwy
Burlington, VT 05401-5434, USA

Burton, James (Athlete, Football Player)
458 W Altadena Dr
Altadena, CA 91001-4202, USA

Burton, James (Musician)
714 Elvis Presley Ave
Shreveport, LA 71101-3406, USA

Burton, Jeff (Race Car Driver)
15555 Huntersville Concord Rd
Huntersville, NC 28078-6642, USA

Burton, Jim (Athlete, Baseball Player)
6540 Shaftesbury Rd
Charlotte, NC 28270-2839, USA

Burton, Kate (Actor, Musician)
232 N Canon Dr
Beverly Hills, CA 90210-5302, USA

Burton, Lance (Magician)
9775 S Maryland Pkwy Ste F PMB 157
Las Vegas, NV 89183-7123, USA

Burton, Lawrence (Athlete, Football Player)
41 San Gabriel
Rancho Santa Margarita, CA 92688-3127, USA

Burton, Leonard (Athlete, Football Player)
3436 Beech Grove Rd
Memphis, TN 38118-7269, USA

Burton, LeVar (Actor)
13251 Stoneridge Pl
Sherman Oaks, CA 91423-4933, USA

Burton, Nelson (Athlete, Hockey Player)
128 Collington Ct
Arnold, MD 21012-2305, USA

Burton, Nelson Jr (Bowler)
9359 SW Eagles Lndg
Stuart, FL 34997-7969, USA

Burton, Norman (Actor)
3641 Meadville Dr
Sherman Oaks, CA 91403-4312, USA

Burton, Robert G (Publisher)
101 Park Ave
New York, NY 10178-0002, USA

Burton, Ron L (Athlete, Football Player)
PO Box 63125
Colorado Springs, CO 80962-3125, USA

Burton, Shane (Athlete, Football Player)
PO Box 522
Catawba, NC 28609-0522, USA

Burton, Steve (Actor)
4814 Lemore Ave
Sherman Oaks, CA 91403, USA

Burton, Tim (Director, Producer)
c/o Mike Simpson *WmE2 (Endeavor-LA)*
9601 Wilshire Blvd Fl 3
Beverly Hills, CA 90210-5219, USA

Burton, Tony (Actor)
3500 W Olive Ave Ste 1400
Burbank, CA 91505-5512, USA

Burton, Ward (Race Car Driver)
PO Box 519
Halifax, VA 24558-0519, USA

Burton, Warren
c/o Steven Neibert *Imperium 7 Talent Agency*
5455 Wilshire Blvd Ste 1706
Los Angeles, CA 90036-4217, USA

Burton, Willie (Athlete, Basketball Player)
18900 Fleming St
Detroit, MI 48234-1392, USA

Burton Jr, John (Actor)
12711 Ventura Blvd Ste 490
Studio City, CA 91604-2477, USA

Burton-Woody, Patty (Baseball Player)
918 N Walnut St
Steele, MO 63877-1316, USA

Burtt, Dennis (Athlete, Baseball Player)
4691 Brookwillow Cv Apt B
Salt Lake Cty, UT 84117-8042, USA

Burtt, Steve (Athlete, Basketball Player)
200 W 143rd St Apt 12D
New York, NY 10030-1527, USA

Burwell, Barbara (Actor)
1100 Millston Rd
Wayzata, MN 55391-9411, USA

Burwell, Carter (Composer)
PO Box 2040
Amagansett, NY 11930-2040, USA

Burwell, Dick (Athlete, Baseball Player)
7424 N San Manuel Rd
Scottsdale, AZ 85258-3461, USA

Bury, Pol (Artist)
12 Vallee da la Taupe-Perdreauville
Mantes-La-Jolie 78200, FRANCE

Busby, Aretha (Stylist)
c/o Staff Member *Ford Models (Chicago)*
311 W Superior St
Chicago, IL 60654-3548, USA

Busby, Mike (Athlete, Baseball Player)
27399 N 84th Gln
Peoria, AZ 85383-4800, USA

Busby, Paul (Athlete, Baseball Player)
2011 35th Ave
Meridian, MS 39301-2831, USA

Busby, Steve (Athlete, Baseball Player)
2701 Brittany Ln
Grapevine, TX 76051-4302, USA

Busby, Wayne (Athlete, Baseball Player)
287 S Tampa Ave
Orlando, FL 32805-2157, USA

Buscemi, Steve (Actor, Director)
c/o Staff Member *Olive Productions*
161 Avenue of the Americas Fl 11
New York, NY 10013-1205, USA

Busch, Adam (Actor)
c/o Ryan Revel *Benderspink*
5870 W Jefferson Blvd Ste E
Los Angeles, CA 90016-3159, USA

Busch, August A III (Business Person)
1 Busch Pl
Saint Louis, MO 63118-1849, USA

Busch, Charles (Actor, Writer)
c/o Jeff Melnick *Eighth Square Entertainment*
606 N Larchmont Blvd Ste 307
Los Angeles, CA 90004-1309, USA

Busch, Kurt (Race Car Driver)
200 Penske Way
Mooresville, NC 28115-8022

Busch, Kyle (Race Car Driver)
c/o Staff Member *National Association of Stock Car Racing (NASCAR)*
1801 W Speedway Blvd
Daytona Beach, FL 32114-1215, USA

Busch, Mike (Athlete, Baseball Player)
103 E 1st Ave
Donahue, IA 52746-9648, USA

Buscher, Brian (Athlete, Baseball Player)
876 Burnside Dr
Columbia, SC 29209-2505, USA

Buschhorn, Don (Athlete, Baseball Player)
17804 E 26th St S
Independence, MO 64057-1350, USA

Buse, Don (Athlete, Basketball Player)
7300 W State Road 64
Huntingburg, IN 47542-9781, USA

Busemann, Frank (Athlete, Track Athlete)
Borkumstr 13A
Recklinghausen 45665, GERMANY

Buser, Martin (Race Car Driver)
PO Box 520997
Big Lake, AK 99652-0997, USA

Busey, Gary (Actor)
c/o Vicki Roberts *Kismet Talent Agency*
3435 Ocean Park Blvd Ste 107
Santa Monica, CA 90405-3320, USA

Busey, Jake (Actor)
c/o Michael McConnell *Don Buchwald & Associates Inc (LA)*
8619 Washington Blvd
Culver City, CA 90232-7441, USA

Busfield, Timothy (Actor)
435 Locust St Apt 2
San Francisco, CA 94118-5000, USA

Bush
c/o Staff Member *WmE2 (WMA-LA)*
1 William Morris Pl
Beverly Hills, CA 90212-4261, USA

Bush, Barbara P (First Lady, Politician)
10000 Memorial Dr Ste 900
Houston, TX 77024-3412, USA

Bush, Billy (Television Host)
c/o Staff Member *KBIG 104.3 FM*
330 N Brand Blvd Ste 800
Glendale, CA 91203-2318, USA

Bush, Blair (Athlete, Football Player)
16911 SE 32nd Pl
Bellevue, WA 98008-5769, USA

Bush, Dave (Musician)
Ransomes Dock 35-37 Parkgate Road
London SW11 4NP, UNITED KINGDOM (UK)

Bush, David (Athlete, Baseball Player)
PO Box 815
Bridgton, ME 04009-0815, USA

Bush, Dick
8 Grande Parade #16 Plymouth
Devon PL1 3DF, ENGLAND

Bush, Frank (Athlete, Football Player)
110 31st Ave N Apt 504
Nashville, TN 37203-1576, USA

Bush, George W (Ex-President, Politician)
PO Box 259000
Dallas, TX 75225-9000, USA

Bush, Homer (Athlete, Baseball Player)
1402 Exeter Ct
Southlake, TX 76092-4219, USA

Bush, Jeb (Governor) (Ex-Governor, Politician)
629 Altara Ave
Coral Gables, FL 33146-1303, USA

Bush, Jenna (Writer)
1345 S Charles St
Baltimore, MD 21230-4226, USA

Bush, Jim (Coach)
5106 Bounty Ln
Culver City, CA 90230-4302, USA

Bush, Kate (Musician, Songwriter, Writer)
c/o Staff Member *Jukes Productions Ltd*
P.O. Box 13995
London W9 2FL, UK

Bush, Kristian (Musician)
c/o Staff Member *Gail Gellman Management*
23852 Pacific Coast Hwy
Malibu, CA 90265-4876, USA

Bush, Laura (First Lady, Politician)
PO Box 259000
Dallas, TX 75225-9000, USA

Bush, Lauren (Model)
c/o Staff Member *Elite Model Management (NY)*
404 Park Ave S Fl 9
New York, NY 10016-8412, USA

Bush, Randy (Athlete, Baseball Player)
37 Kings Canyon Dr
New Orleans, LA 70131-8611, USA

Bush, Rebeccah (Actor)
c/o Staff Member *Cunningham Escott Slevin & Doherty (CESD-LA)*
10635 Santa Monica Blvd Ste 130
Los Angeles, CA 90025-8306, USA

Bush, Reggie (Football Player)
c/o Jordan Bazant *The Agency Sports and Marketing*
230 Park Ave Rm 851
New York, NY 10169-0927, USA

Bush, Sophia (Actor)
c/o Joan Green *Joan Green Management*
1836 Courtney Ter
Los Angeles, CA 90046-2106, USA

Bush, Walter L (Misc)
5200 Malibu Dr
Minneapolis, MN 55436-1030, USA

Bush, Walter L (Athlete, Hockey Player)
5200 Malibu Dr
Minneapolis, MN 55436-1030, USA

Bush, William Green (Actor)
3500 W Olive Ave Ste 1400
Burbank, CA 91505-5512, USA

Bush Sr, George (Ex-President, President)
10000 Memorial Dr Ste 900
Houston, TX 77024-3412, USA

Bushell, Matt (Actor)
c/o Sandra Joseph *SLJ Management*
833 N Edinburgh Ave Ph 11
Los Angeles, CA 90046-6999, USA

Bushing, Chris (Athlete, Baseball Player)
12830 NW 21st St
Pembroke Pines, FL 33028-2534, USA

Bushinsky, Joseph M (Jay) (Correspondent)
Rehov Hatsafon 5
Savyon 56540, ISRAEL

Bushland, Raymond C (Misc)
200 Concord Plaza Dr
San Antonio, TX 78216-6943, USA

Bushnell, Bill (Director)
2751 Pelham Pl
Los Angeles, CA 90068-2326, USA

Bushnell, Candace (Producer, Writer)
c/o Kevin Crotty *International Creative Management (ICM-LA)*
10250 Constellation Blvd Fl 7
Los Angeles, CA 90067-6207, USA

Bushy, Ronald (Ron) (Musician)
6400 Pleasant Park Dr
Chanhassen, MN 55317-8804, USA

Busick, Steve (Athlete, Football Player)
585 Osage St
Denver, CO 80204-4911, USA

Busino, Orlando (Cartoonist)
12 Shadblow Hill Rd
Ridgefield, CT 06877-5221, USA

Buskas, Rod (Athlete, Hockey Player)
182 Wentworth Dr
Henderson, NV 89074-1049, USA

Buskey, Mike (Athlete, Baseball Player)
3460 Kingsboro Rd Ne Apt 323
Atlanta, GA 30326-3301, USA

Busniuk, Mike (Athlete, Hockey Player)
420 Sycamore Pl
Thunder Bay, ON P7C 1W9, Canada

Busniuk, Ron (Athlete, Hockey Player)
540 Laurentian Dr
Thunder Bay, ON P7C 5J8, Canada

Buss, Jerry H (Business Person)
Staples Center 1111 S Figueroa St
Los Angeles, CA 90015, USA

Busse, Ray (Athlete, Baseball Player)
4265 Lemon St
Cocoa, FL 32926-2148, USA

Bussell, Darcey A (Ballerina)
155 New King's Road
London SW6 4SJ, UNITED KINGDOM (UK)

Bussell, Gerry (Athlete, Football Player)
29 Lockhart Ln
Saint Augustine, FL 32080-6530, USA

Bussey, Barney (Athlete, Football Player)
5059 Park Ridge Ct
West Chester, OH 45069-5552, USA

Bustamante, Carlos (Scientist)
Howard Hughes Medical Institute
Berkeley, CA 94720-0001, USA

Busted (Music Group)
c/o Staff Member *Helter Skelter (UK)*
535 Kings Rd The Plaza
London SW10 0SZ, UNITED KINGDOM (UK)

Buster, Dolly (Adult Film Star)
Am Schornacker 66
Wesel D-46485, Germany

Buster, John E (Misc)
PO Box 2910
Torrance, CA 90509-2910, USA

Bustion, Dave (Athlete, Basketball Player)
706 Tarrant Ct
Gadsden, AL 35901-3150, USA

Butala, Tony (Musician)
PO Box 151
Mc Kees Rocks, PA 15136-0151, USA

Butcher, Clyde (Photographer)
52388 Tamiami Trl E
Chokoloskee, FL 34138, USA

Butcher, Donnie (Athlete, Basketball Player)
1725 Burns Rd
Milford, MI 48381-1215, USA

Butcher, Garth (Athlete, Hockey Player)
1524 Maple Ln
Bellingham, WA 98229-5242, USA

Butcher, Jim (Writer)
ATTN: PUBLICITY DEPT 175 Fifth Avenue
New York, NY 10010, USA

Butcher, John (Athlete, Baseball Player)
820 Woodridge Dr S
Chaska, MN 55318-1266, USA

Butcher, Mike (Athlete, Baseball Player)
324 33rd Ave
East Moline, IL 61244-3124, USA

Butcher, Paul (Actor)
c/o Mitchell Gossett *United Talent Agency (UTA)*
9560 Wilshire Blvd Fl 5
Beverly Hills, CA 90212-2400, USA

Butcher, Rodney (Athlete, Golfer)
7333 Hideaway Trl
New Port Richey, FL 34655-4006, USA

Butcher-Marsh, Mary (Baseball Player)
1119 Cedar St
Carson City, NV 89701-5025, USA

Butera, Sal (Athlete, Baseball Player)
324 Tersas Ct
Lake Mary, FL 32746-5143, USA

Buthelezi, Chief Mangosuthu G (Politician)
Private Bag x741
Pretoria 1, SOUTH AFRICA

Buthelezi, Minister Mangosuthu (Politician)
Parliament St
Cape Town 8000, South Africa

Butkus, Richard J (Dick) (Actor, Athlete, Football Player)
c/o Richard Lewis *Geddes Agency, The*
8430 Santa Monica Blvd Ste 200
Los Angeles, CA 90069-4253, USA

Butler, Adam (Athlete, Baseball Player)
815 Providence Rd
Towson, MD 21286-2964, USA

Butler, Austin (Actor)
c/o Doug Wald *Anonymous Content (AC-LA)*
3531 Hayden Ave
Culver City, CA 90232, USA

Butler, Bernard (Musician)
98 White Lion St
London N1 9PF, UNITED KINGDOM (UK)

Butler, Bill (Athlete, Baseball Player)
141 Buckskin Ln
Berkeley Springs, WV 25411-5519, USA

Butler, Bill C (Cinematographer)
1097 Aviation Blvd
Hermosa Beach, CA 90254-4023, USA

Butler, Bob (Athlete, Football Player)
120 Holly Hills Dr
Mount Sterling, KY 40353-9738, USA

Butler, Brent (Athlete, Baseball Player)
10441 Scotland Farm Rd
Laurinburg, NC 28352-7977, USA

Butler, Brett (Actor, Comedian)
c/o Staff Member *TalentWorks (LA)*
3500 W Olive Ave Ste 1400
Burbank, CA 91505-5512, USA

Butler, Brett M (Athlete, Baseball Player)
4488 E Thomas Rd Unit 2012
Phoenix, AZ 85018-7627, USA

Butler, Caron (Athlete, Basketball Player)
5116 Citation Dr
Racine, WI 53402-2375, USA

Butler, Cecil (Athlete, Baseball Player)
263 Hickory Gap Trl
Dallas, GA 30157-5353, USA

Butler, Charles (Athlete, Basketball Player)
453 Arbor Cir
Youngstown, OH 44505-1915, USA

Butler, Charles W (Athlete, Football Player)
5496 Celestial Dr
Atwater, CA 95301-3165, USA

Butler, Conrad (Actor)
10100 Santa Monica Blvd Ste 2500
Los Angeles, CA 90067-4116, USA

Butler, Dan (Actor)
c/o Staff Member *ATA Management*
12 Desbrosses St
New York, NY 10013-1704, USA

Butler, David (Actor)
c/o Staff Member *The Rights House (UK)*
Drury House 34-43 Russell St
London WC2B 5HA, UK

Butler, Dean (Actor)
1310 Westholme Ave
Los Angeles, CA 90024-5016, USA

Butler, Donald (Athlete, Football Player)
c/o Roosevelt Barnes *Maximum Sports Management*
6435 W Jefferson Blvd # 197
Fort Wayne, IN 46804-6203, USA

Butler, Elbert (Athlete, Basketball Player)
153 Willow Ave
Rochester, NY 14609-1244, USA

Butler, Floyd (Athlete, Football Player)
7354 S Merrill Ave
Chicago, IL 60649-3209, USA

Butler, Gary (Athlete, Football Player)
6660 S Piney Creek Cir
Centennial, CO 80016, USA

Butler, Gary C (Business Person)
1 Adp Blvd
Roseland, NJ 07068-1728, USA

Butler, George L (General)
11122 William Plz
Omaha, NE 68144-1873, USA

Butler, Gerard (Actor)
c/o Alan Siegel *Alan Siegel Entertainment*
345 N Maple Dr Ste 375
Beverly Hills, CA 90210-5174, USA

Butler, Greg (Athlete, Basketball Player)
216 Beverly Rd
Scarsdale, NY 10583-1514, USA

Butler, Jack (Athlete, Football Player)
510 E 11th Ave
Munhall, PA 15120-2004, USA

Butler, James (Athlete, Football Player)
3181 Spring St
Atlanta, GA 30349-2345, USA

Butler, Jerry (Athlete, Hockey Player)
3595 Eldridge Ave
Winnipeg, MB R3R 0L5, Canada

Butler, Jerry (Iceman) (Musician, Songwriter, Writer)
c/o Jeremy Plager *Creative Artists Agency (CAA-LA)*
2000 Avenue of the Stars Ste 100
Los Angeles, CA 90067-4705, USA

Butler, Jerry O (Athlete, Football Player)
17117 Shaker Blvd
Cleveland, OH 44120-1635, USA

Butler, Joe (Musician)
620 16th Ave S
Hopkins, MN 55343-7833, USA

Butler, John (Musician)
c/o Staff Member *Paradigm (Monterey)*
404 W Franklin St
Monterey, CA 93940-2303, USA

Butler, Keith (Athlete, Football Player)
805 Cavan Dr
Cranberry Twp, PA 16066-2333, USA

Butler, Kerry (Actor)
c/o Erica Tuchman *One Entertainment (NY)*
12 W 57th St PH 1
New York, NY 10019-3900, USA

Butler, Kevin (Athlete, Football Player)
3256 Bagley Psge
Duluth, GA 30097-3788, USA

Butler, LeRoy (Athlete, Football Player)
1682 Royalton St
Waupaca, WI 54981-1615, USA

Butler, Lucy (Actor)
c/o Judy Orbach *Judy O Productions*
6136 Glen Holly St
Hollywood, CA 90068-2338, USA

Butler, Martin (Composer)
Music
Princeton, NJ 08544-0001, USA

Butler, Michael (Athlete, Football Player)
3107 Magdalene Forest Ct
Tampa, FL 33618-2509, USA

Butler, Mike (Athlete, Basketball Player)
9900 Woodland Fern Dr Apt D
Lakeland, TN 38002-3809, USA

Butler, Mitchell (Athlete, Basketball Player)
1468 Paseo De Oro
Pacific Palisades, CA 90272-1961, USA

Butler, Paul (Astronomer)
Astronomy
Berkeley, CA 94720-0001, USA

Butler, Ray (Athlete, Football Player)
9700 Leawood Blvd Apt 1307
Houston, TX 77099-2661, USA

Butler, Robert (Director)
650 Club View Dr
Los Angeles, CA 90024-2624, USA

Butler, Robert (Athlete, Football Player)
5567 Naylor Ct
Norcross, GA 30092-2072, USA

Butler, Robert N (Misc)
Geriatrics Dept 1 Levy Plaza
New York, NY 10029, USA

Butler, Robert Olen (Writer)
1009 Concord Rd Apt 230
Tallahassee, FL 32308-6294, USA

Butler, Samuel C (Attorney, Attorney General, General)
825 8th Ave
New York, NY 10019-7416, USA

Butler, Skip (Athlete, Football Player)
1115 Spyglass Dr
Mansfield, TX 76063-4047, USA

Butler, William D (Athlete, Football Player)
200 E Liberty St
Berlin, WI 54923-1223, USA

Butler, William E (Business Person)
Eaton Center 1111 Superior Ave
Cleveland, OH 44114, USA

Butler, William E (Athlete, Football Player)
3030 Cherry Hl
Manhattan, KS 66503-3011, USA

Butler, Yancy (Actor)
c/o Peg Donegan *Framework Entertainment (LA)*
9057 Nemo St Ste C
West Hollywood, CA 90069-5511, USA

Butler-Henderson, Vicki (Actor)
c/o Staff Member *Princess Productions*
Newcombe House 45 Notting Hill Gate
London W11 3LQ, UNITED KINGDOM

Butor, Michael (Writer)
A L'Ecart Lucinges
Bonne 74380, FRANCE

Butsko, Harry (Athlete, Football Player)
4 Milo Cir
Duncannon, PA 17020-9647, USA

Butt, Yondani
450 Fashion Ave Ste 603
New York, NY 10123-0691, USA

Buttafuoco, Joey (Actor)
10835 De Soto Ave
Chatsworth, CA 91311-1547, USA

Buttafuoco, Mary Jo

Butterfield, Alexander P (Government Official)
3410 Brookwood Dr
Fairfax, VA 22030-2009, USA

Butterfield, Betty (Comedian)
c/o Staff Member *Diva Central Inc*
7510 W Sunset Blvd Ste 1445
Los Angeles, CA 90046-3408, USA

Butterfield, Deborah K (Artist)
11229 Cottonwood Rd
Bozeman, MT 59718-9576, USA

Butterfield, G. K. (Congressman, Politician)
2305 Rayburn Hob
Washington, DC 20515-2207, USA

Butterfield, Jack (Misc)
55 Pineridge Dr
Westfield, MA 01085-4544, USA

Butterfield, Jack (Athlete, Hockey Player)
55 Pineridge Dr
Westfield, MA 01085-4544, USA

Butterfly Boucher (Music Group)
c/o Staff Member *Paradigm (Monterey)*
404 W Franklin St
Monterey, CA 93940-2303, USA

Butters, Bill (Athlete, Hockey Player)
12579 Europa Ave N
Saint Paul, MN 55110-5957, USA

Butters, Tom (Athlete, Baseball Player)
4 Turnberry Ct
Durham, NC 27712-9465, USA

Butthole Surfers, The (Music Group, Musician)
c/o Staff Member *Mute Records*
43 Brook Green
London W6 7EF, UK

Buttle, Gregory E (Greg) (Athlete, Football Player)
5 Hollacher Dr
Northport, NY 11768-1552, USA

Button, Richard T (Dick) (Figure Skater, Producer)
765 Park Ave Fl 6B
New York, NY 10021-4271, USA

Butts, Earl (Actor)
2741 N Salisbury St # 2116
West Lafayette, IN 47906-1431, USA

Butts, James (Athlete, Track Athlete)
16950 Belforest Dr
Carson, CA 90746-1113, USA

Butts, Robert (Athlete, Football Player)
108 Circle Dr
Flushing, OH 43977-9738, USA

Butz, David E (Dave) (Athlete, Football Player)
300 Britanna Dr
Swansea, IL 62226-2439, USA

Butzer, Hans E (Architect)
Architecture Division Gould Hall
Norman, OK 73019-0001, USA

Butzner, John D Jr (Judge)
PO Box 2188
Richmond, VA 23218-2188, USA

Buxbaum, Richard M (Attorney, Attorney General, Educator, General)
Boalt Hall
Berkeley, CA 94720-0001, USA

Buxton, Sarah (Actor)
c/o Staff Member *Origin Talent Agency*
4705 Laurel Canyon Blvd Ste 306
Studio City, CA 91607-5940, USA

Buynak, Gordie (Athlete, Hockey Player)
11512 Douglas Lake Rd
Pellston, MI 49769-9105, USA

Buzek, Jerzy (Prime Minister)
Al Ujazdowskie 1/3
Warsaw 00-583, POLAND

Buzhardt, Johnny (Athlete, Baseball Player)
37 Brinton Hite Rd
Prosperity, SC 29127-8237, USA

Buzin, Rich (Athlete, Football Player)
23004 Mastick Rd Apt 216
North Olmsted, OH 44070-3770, USA

Buzolin, Mariah (Actor)
c/o Staff Member *Leslie Allan-Rice Management*
7524 Mulholland Dr
Los Angeles, CA 90046-1239, USA

Buzzi, Ruth (Actor, Comedian)
PO Box 122416
Fort Worth, TX 76121-2416, USA

B*Witched (Music Group)
c/o Staff Member *Concorde Intl Artists Ltd*
101 Shepherds Bush Rd
London W6 7LP, UNITED KINGDOM (UK)

Byars, Betsy C (Writer)
401 Rudder Rdg
Seneca, SC 29678-2035, USA

Byatt, Antonia Susan (A S) (Writer)
37 Rusholme Road
London SW15 3LF, UNITED KINGDOM (UK)

Byce, John (Athlete, Hockey Player)
9701 Hill Creek Dr
Verona, WI 53593-7984, USA

Bychkov, Semyon
71 Symphony Cir
Buffalo, NY 14201-1203, USA

Bye, Karyn (Athlete, Hockey Player)
322 Gandy Dancer Cir
Hudson, WI 54016-8186, USA

Bye, Kermit E (Judge)
657 2nd Ave N
Fargo, ND 58102-4765, USA

Byerly, Bud (Athlete, Baseball Player)
8611 Old Sappington Rd
Saint Louis, MO 63126-2009, USA

Byers, Clinton (Athlete, Basketball Player)
4257 Leewood Rd
Stow, OH 44224-2555, USA

Byers, Ken (Athlete, Football Player)
4650 Willow Hills Ln
Cincinnati, OH 45243-4228, USA

Byers, Lyndon (Athlete, Hockey Player)
20 Guest St Ste 300
Brighton, MA 02135-2040, USA

Byers, Mike (Athlete, Hockey Player)
28 Presidio Dr
Novato, CA 94949-6162, USA

Byers, Nina (Physicist)
Physics Dept
Los Angeles, CA 90024, USA

Byers, Randell (Randy) (Athlete, Baseball Player)
31 Waldens Dr
Bridgeton, NJ 08302-4424, USA

Byers, Scott (Athlete, Football Player)
6060 Buckingham Pkwy Apt 314
Culver City, CA 90230-6825, USA

Byers, Steve (Actor)
c/o Robyn Friedman *Artist Management Inc*
464 King St E
Toronto ON M5A 1L7, CANADA

Byers, Walter (Athlete, Basketball Player)
25707 Aiken Switch Rd
Emmett, KS 66422-9719, USA

Bykovsky, Valeri F (Cosmonaut)
Moskovskoi Oblasti
Syvisdny Goroduk 141160, RUSSIA

Bylsma, Dan (Athlete, Hockey Player)
12637 Broadmoor Pl
Grand Haven, MI 49417-8336, USA

Byman, Bob (Athlete, Golfer)
9325 Eagle Ridge Dr
Las Vegas, NV 89134-6345, USA

Byner, Earnest A (Athlete, Football Player)
850 Stembridge Rd SE
Milledgeville, GA 31061-9527, USA

Byner, John (Actor)
19948 Mayall St
Chatsworth, CA 91311-3522, USA

Bynes, Amanda (Actor, Comedian)
c/o Melissa Raubvogel *Baker Winokur Ryder Public Relations BWR (BWR-NY)*
292 Madison Ave Fl 12
New York, NY 10017-6415, USA

Bynoe, Peter C B (Misc)
Pepsi Center 1000 Chopper Circle
Denver, CO 80204, USA

Bynum, Freddie (Athlete, Baseball Player)
2987 Pope Farm Rd
Stantonsburg, NC 27883-8556, USA

Bynum, Mike (Athlete, Baseball Player)
1811 Fountain View Dr Apt 129
Houston, TX 77057-3056, USA

Bynum, Will (Athlete, Basketball Player)
c/o Brad Ames *Priority Sports & Entertainment - (LA)*
15233 Ventura Blvd Ste 718
Sherman Oaks, CA 91403-2237, USA

Byrd, Benjamin F Jr (Doctor)
4220 Harding Pike # 380
Nashville, TN 37205-2005, USA

Byrd, Boris (Athlete, Football Player)
4411 Lindsey St Apt B
Bowling Green, KY 42101-0518, USA

Byrd, Dan (Actor)
c/o Dan Spilo *Industry Entertainment Partners*
955 Carrillo Dr Ste 300
Los Angeles, CA 90048-5400, USA

Byrd, Darryl (Athlete, Football Player)
138 Mission Dr
East Palo Alto, CA 94303-2752, USA

Byrd, Dennis (Athlete, Football Player)
10757 E 350 Rd
Talala, OK 74080-9689, USA

Byrd, Dennis W (Athlete, Football Player)
105 Gaston Dr
Elizabeth City, NC 27909-8412, USA

Byrd, Dominique (Athlete, Football Player)
c/o Eugene Parker *Maximum Sports Management*
6435 W Jefferson Blvd # 197
Fort Wayne, IN 46804-6203, USA

Byrd, Donald (Musician)
PO Box 2728
Bala Cynwyd, PA 19004-6728, USA

Byrd, Eugene (Actor)
c/o Steve Caserta *Sanders Armstrong Caserta*
2120 Colorado Ave Ste 120
Santa Monica, CA 90404-3561, USA

Byrd, George (Athlete, Football Player)
23 Wayside Rd
Westborough, MA 01581-3620, USA

Byrd, Harry F Jr (Ex-Senator)
2 N Kent St
Winchester, VA 22601-5038, USA

Byrd, Isaac (Athlete, Football Player)
5712 Astra Ave
Saint Louis, MO 63147-1012, USA

Byrd, Israel (Athlete, Football Player)
5712 Astra Ave
Saint Louis, MO 63147-1012, USA

Byrd, Jairus (Athlete, Football Player)
c/o Eugene Parker *Maximum Sports Management*
6435 W Jefferson Blvd # 197
Fort Wayne, IN 46804-6203, USA

Byrd, Jeff (Athlete, Baseball Player)
39376 Opalocka Rd
Boulevard, CA 91905-9682, USA

Byrd, Jim (Athlete, Baseball Player)
511 NW Woodridge Dr
Lawton, OK 73507-2265, USA

Byrd, Jonathan (Athlete, Golfer)
110 Meadow Bark
Saint Simons Island, GA 31522, USA

Byrd, Marlon (Athlete, Baseball Player)
3620 E Hamilton KY
West Palm Beach, FL 33411-6436, USA

Byrd, McArthur (Athlete, Football Player)
10291 Sheldon Rd
Elk Grove, CA 95624-9341, USA

Byrd, Paul (Athlete, Baseball Player)
910 Foxhollow Run
Alpharetta, GA 30004-0977, USA

Byrd, Richard (Athlete, Football Player)
2230 Haley Rd
Terry, MS 39170-8820, USA

Byrd, Robin (Adult Film Star)
PO Box 305
New York, NY 10021-0009, USA

Byrd, Tom (Actor)
14011 Ventura Blvd Ste 213
Sherman Oaks, CA 91423-5222, USA

Byrd, Tracy (Musician)
PO Box 128195
Nashville, TN 37212-8195, USA

Byrd, Vivkey L (Stylist)
PO Box 8
Rock Falls, IL 61071-0008, USA

Byrdak, Tim (Athlete, Baseball Player)
16721 W Seneca Dr
Lockport, IL 60441-4269, USA

Byrds, The (Music Group, Musician)
PO Box 1222
Pleasanton, CA 94566-0122, USA

Byrne, Brendan T (Ex-Governor)
5 Becker Farm Rd
Roseland, NJ 07068-1741, USA

Byrne, Chris (Actor)
c/o Staff Member *Kazarian Spencer Ruskin & Assoc.*
11969 Ventura Blvd Ste 300
Studio City, CA 91604-2619, USA

Byrne, David (Musician, Songwriter)
Maine Road Management 195 Chrystie St #901F
New York, NY 10002, USA

Byrne, Gabriel (Actor)
c/o Tamar Salup *I/D PR (NY)*
150 W 30th St Fl 19
New York, NY 10001-4003, USA

Byrne, Garry (Publisher)
5700 Wilshire Blvd
Los Angeles, CA 90036-3659, USA

Byrne, John (Cartoonist)
1700 Broadway # 700
New York, NY 10019-5905, USA

Byrne, Josh (Actor)
PO Box 64249
Los Angeles, CA 90064-0249, USA

Byrne, Martha
c/o Staff Member *Innovative Artists (LA)*
1505 10th St
Santa Monica, CA 90401-2805, USA

Byrne, Michael (Actor)
18-21 Jermyn St
London SW1Y 6NB, UNITED KINGDOM (UK)

Byrne, Nicky (Musician)
c/o Staff Member *Solo Agency Ltd (UK)*
55 Fulham High St 2nd Floor
London SW6 3JJ, United Kingdom

Byrne, Rhonda (Writer)
c/o Staff Member *Simon & Schuster*
1230 Avenue of the Americas Fl CONC1
New York, NY 10020-1586, USA

Byrne, Rose (Actor)
c/o Robyn Gardiner *RGM Artist Group*
64-76 Kippax St Level 2, Suite 202 & 206
Surry Hills, NSW 2010, Australia

Byrne, Steve (Musician)
c/o Staff Member *Paradigm (Monterey)*
404 W Franklin St
Monterey, CA 93940-2303, USA

Byrne, Thomas J (Tommy) (Athlete, Baseball Player)
1108 Fairway Villas Dr
Wake Forest, NC 27587-5179, USA

Byrnes, Edd (Actor)
PO Box 1623
Beverly Hills, CA 90213-1623, USA

Byrnes, Eric (Athlete, Baseball Player)
c/o Staff Member *WmE2 (WMA-LA)*
1 William Morris Pl
Beverly Hills, CA 90212-4261, USA

Byrnes, Eric (Athlete, Baseball Player)
24404 N 61st Dr
Glendale, AZ 85310-2704, USA

Byrnes, Jim (Actor)
c/o Staff Member *Characters Talent Agency, The (Vancouver)*
1505 W 2nd Ave #200
Vancouver, BC V6H 3Y4, Canada

Byrnes, Kevin P (General)
Hqusa Pentagon
Washington, DC 20310-0001, USA

Byrnes, Marty (Athlete, Basketball Player)
8739 3rd Ave
Pleasant Prairie, WI 53158-4709, USA

Byron, Kari
1268 Missouri St
San Francisco, CA 94107-3310, USA

Byrorn, Don (Musician)
2220 California St
Berkeley, CA 94703-1608, USA

Byrorn, Monty (Musician, Songwriter, Writer)
1204B Cedar Ln
Nashville, TN 37212-5910, USA

Byrum, Curt (Athlete, Golfer)
12441 N 86th St
Scottsdale, AZ 85260-5343, USA

Byrum, John W (Director)
7435 Woodrow Wilson Dr
Los Angeles, CA 90046-1322, USA

Byrum, Tom (Athlete, Golfer)
70 Sierra Oaks Dr
Sugar Land, TX 77479-5724, USA

Bystrom, Marty (Athlete, Baseball Player)
PO Box 89
Geigertown, PA 19523-0089, USA

Bywater, William H (Misc)
1126 16th St NW
Washington, DC 20036-4804, USA

Bzdelik, Jeff (Coach)
Pepsi Center 1000 Chopper Circle
Denver, CO 80204, USA

C

C. Burgess, Michael (Congressman, Politician)
2241 Rayburn Hob
Washington, DC 20515-3212, USA

C. Carney Jr., John (Congressman, Politician)
1429 Longworth Hob
Washington, DC 20515-2302, USA

C. Johnson Jr., Henry (Congressman, Politician)
1427 Longworth Hob
Washington, DC 20515-1503, USA

C. LaTourette, Steven (Congressman, Politician)
2371 Rayburn°Hob
Washington, DC 20515-0001, USA

C. Peters, Gary (Congressman, Politician)
1609 Longworth Hob
Washington, DC 20515-0538, USA

C. Peterson, Collin (Congressman, Politician)
2211 Rayburn Hob
Washington, DC 20515-1317, USA

Caan, James (Actor, Director)
2791 Hutton Dr
Beverly Hills, CA 90210-1215, USA

Caan, James (Business Person)
18 Hanover Sq
London W1S 1HX, UK

Caan, Scott (Actor)
c/o Stacy Boniello *Firm, The*
2049 Century Park E Ste 2550
Los Angeles, CA 90067-3139, USA

Caballe, Monserrat (Opera Singer)
Avenida Madronos 27
Madrid E-28043, Spain

Caballe, Montserrat (Opera Singer)
Via Augusta 59
Barcelona 8006, SPAIN

Caballero, Celestino (Athlete, Boxer)
c/o Jody Kohn *Talent Without Borders*
Prefers to be contacted by telephone
Las Vegas, NV 89145, USA

Caballero, Ralph (Putsy) (Athlete, Baseball Player)
6773 Milne Blvd
New Orleans, LA 70124-2242, USA

Cabana, Robert D (Astronaut)
18315 Cape Bahamas Ln
Houston, TX 77058-3406, USA

Cabas (Musician)
c/o Staff Member *Creative Artists Agency (CAA-LA)*
2000 Avenue of the Stars Ste 100
Los Angeles, CA 90067-4705, USA

Cabel, Barney (Athlete, Basketball Player)
1134 S Main St
Hampstead, MD 21074-2255, USA

Cabell, Enos M (Athlete, Baseball Player)
4103 Frost Lake Ct
Missouri City, TX 77459-2304, USA

Cabibbo, Nicola (Physicist)
Viale Regina Margherita 125
Rome 198, ITALY

Cable, Barney (Athlete, Basketball Player)
1134 S Main St
Hampstead, MD 21074-2255, USA

Cable Guy, The, Larry (Comedian)
c/o J P Williams *Parallel Entertainment*
9420 Wilshire Blvd Ste 250
Beverly Hills, CA 90212-3151, USA

Cabot, Louis W (Business Person)
1775 Massachusetts Ave NW
Washington, DC 20036-2103, USA

Cabot, Meg (Writer)
PO Box 4904
Key West, FL 33041-4904, USA

Cabral, Brian (Athlete, Football Player)
5008 Ellsworth Pl
Boulder, CO 80303-1210, USA

Cabral, Sam A (Misc)
1421 Prince St
Alexandria, VA 22314-2867, USA

Cabranes, Jose A (Judge)
141 Church St
New Haven, CT 06510-2030, USA

Cabrera, John (Actor)
c/o Adam Griffin *Kritzer Levine Wilkins Entertainment*
11872 La Grange Ave Fl 1
Los Angeles, CA 90025-5283, USA

Cabrera, Jolbert (Baseball Player)
c/o Staff Member *Los Angeles Dodgers (LA Dodgers)*
1000 Elysian Park Ave
Los Angeles, CA 90090-1112, USA

Cabrera, Melky (Athlete, Baseball Player)
7912 River Rd
North Bergen, NJ 07047-6271, USA

Cabrera, Miguel (Athlete, Baseball Player)
3255 NE 184th St Apt 12101
North Miami Beach, FL 33160-4990, USA

Cabrera, Orlando (Athlete, Baseball Player)
9248 Scarlette Oak Ave
Fort Myers, FL 33967-5145, USA

Cabrera, Ryan (Musician)
c/o Staff Member *CEG Talent*
251 W 39th St Fl 7
New York, NY 10018-3171, USA

Cabrera, Santiago (Actor)
c/o Suzan Bymel *Management 360*
9111 Wilshire Blvd
Beverly Hills, CA 90210-5508, USA

Caccialanza, Lorenzo (Actor)
PO Box 16758
Beverly Hills, CA 90209-2758, USA

Cacciavillan, Agnostino Cardinal (Religious Leader)
Palazzo Apostolico
Vatican City 120, VATICAN CITY

Cacek, Craig (Athlete, Baseball Player)
909 6th St Apt 3
Santa Monica, CA 90403-2700, USA

Caceres, Edgar (Athlete, Baseball Player)
7501 50th Ter E
Bradenton, FL 34203-7905, USA

Caceres, Kurt (Actor)
c/o Kathy Atkinson *Washington Square Arts (LA)*
1041 N Formosa Ave Lot Bldg
West Hollywood, CA 90046-6703, USA

Cackowski, Liz (Actor, Comedian)
c/o Staff Member *Creative Artists Agency (CAA-LA)*
2000 Avenue of the Stars Ste 100
Los Angeles, CA 90067-4705, USA

Cadaret, Greg (Athlete, Baseball Player)
22636 Bridlewood Ln
Palo Cedro, CA 96073-9567, USA

Cadbury, Adrian (Business Person)
Threadneedle St
London EC2R 8AH, UNITED KINGDOM (UK)

Caddell, Patrick H (Mathematician, Misc)
1625 I St NW
Washington, DC 20006-4061, USA

Cade, Eddie (Athlete, Football Player)
501 W 4th St
Eloy, AZ 85131-2206, USA

Cade, Michael (Actor)

Cade, Mossy (Athlete, Football Player)
1125 E Cordova Ave
Casa Grande, AZ 85122-1114, USA

Cadell, Ava (Actor, Model)
c/o Rick Hersh *Celebrity Consultants LLC*
3340 Ocean Park Blvd Ste 1030
Santa Monica, CA 90405-3259, USA

Cadell, Dr. Ava (Adult Film Star)
9000 W Sunset Blvd Ste 1001
West Hollywood, CA 90069-5802, USA

Cadigan, Dave (Athlete, Football Player)
14416 Katie Rd
Phoenix, MD 21131-1755, USA

Cadile, Jim (Athlete, Football Player)
1746 Dove Ln
Medford, OR 97501-7015, USA

Cadogan, William J (Business Person)
PO Box 1101
Minneapolis, MN 55440-1101, USA

Cadrez, Glenn (Athlete, Football Player)
1174 Chaparral Dr
El Centro, CA 92243-6109, USA

Cady, Sherry (Scientist)
Geology Dept
Portland, OR 97207, USA

Caesar, Shirley (Music Group)
3310 Croasdaile Dr Ste 902
Durham, NC 27705-6806, USA

Caesar, Sid (Actor, Comedian)
c/o Staff Member *Cunningham Escott Slevin & Doherty (CESD-LA)*
10635 Santa Monica Blvd Ste 130
Los Angeles, CA 90025-8306, USA

Caesars, The (Music Group)
c/o Staff Member *Paradigm (Monterey)*
404 W Franklin St
Monterey, CA 93940-2303, USA

Cafagna-Tesoro, Ashley (Actor)
c/o Staff Member *Tesoro Entertainment*
205D N Stephanie St # NO115
Henderson, NV 89074-8060, USA

Cafferata, Hector A Jr (War Hero)
1807 Plum Ln
Venice, FL 34293-2040, USA

Caffery, Terry (Athlete, Hockey Player)
2743 Victoria Park Ave
Scarborough, ON M1T 1A8, Canada

Caffey, Charlotte (Music Group, Musician)
4800 Bryn Mawr Rd
Los Angeles, CA 90027-1109, USA

Caffey, Jason (Athlete, Basketball Player)
PO Box 131
Roswell, GA 30077-0131, USA

Caffie, Joe (Athlete, Baseball Player)
PO Box 1932
Warren, OH 44482-1932, USA

Cagatay, Mustafa (Prime Minister)
60 Cumhuriyet Caddesi
Kyrenia, Cyprus

Cage, Byron (Musician)
c/o Staff Member *Verity Gospel Music Group*
550 Madison Ave Rm 2356
New York, NY 10022-3211, USA

Cage, Michael (Athlete, Basketball Player)
7803 N Via De La Sombre
Scottsdale, AZ 85258-3209, USA

Cage, Nicolas (Actor)
c/o Annett Wolf *WKT Public Relations (WKT-LA)*
9350 Wilshire Blvd Ste 450
Beverly Hills, CA 90212-3230, USA

Cage, Wayne (Athlete, Baseball Player)
1305 Davis Blvd
Ruston, LA 71270-6405, USA

Cagle, Chris (Musician)
c/o Scott McGhee *McGhee Entertainment*
8730 W Sunset Blvd Ste 175
Los Angeles, CA 90069-2246, USA

Cagle, J Douglas (Business Person)
1385 Collier Rd NW
Atlanta, GA 30318-7444, USA

Cagle, Jim (Athlete, Football Player)
745 Sharpshooters Rdg NW
Marietta, GA 30064-4731, USA

Cagle, Johnny (Athlete, Football Player)
1645 Citation Dr
Aiken, SC 29803-5223, USA

Cagle, Yvonne D (Astronaut)
c/o Staff Member *NASA*
2101 Nasa Pkwy Spc Center
Houston, TX 77058-3696, USA

Caglini, Umperto (Actor)
via Don Crocetti #3
Fabriano (Ancona) I-60044, Italy

Cahill, Eddie (Actor)
c/o David Seltzer *Management 360*
9111 Wilshire Blvd
Beverly Hills, CA 90210-5508, USA

Cahill, Erin (Actor)
c/o Cary Anderson *Simmons & Scott Entertainment*
7942 Mulholland Dr
Los Angeles, CA 90046-1225, USA

Cahill, James (Actor)
31 Chambers St Ste 311
New York, NY 10007-4030, USA

Cahill, Katja (Stylist)
c/o Staff Member *Smashbox Beauty*
8549 Higuera St Bldg B
Culver City, CA 90232-2521, USA

Cahill, Laura (Writer)
c/o Staff Member *Broder Webb Chervin Silbermann Agency, The (BWCS)*
10250 Constellation Blvd
Los Angeles, CA 90067-6200, USA

Cahill, Mike (Director, Writer)
c/o George Heller *Apostle Management*
9465 Wilshire Blvd Ste 430
Beverly Hills, CA 90212-2613, USA

Cahill, Teresa M (Opera Singer)
65 Leyland Road
London SE12 8DW, UNITED KINGDOM (UK)

Cahill, Thomas (Writer)
1540 Broadway
New York, NY 10036-4039, USA

Cahill, William (Bill) (Athlete, Football Player)
24328 Crystal Lake Way
Woodinville, WA 98077-9514, USA

Cahn, John W (Misc)
2032 43rd Ave E Apt 18
Seattle, WA 98112-2764, USA

Cahoon, Todd (Actor)
c/o Laura Pallas *Pallas Management*
5301 Bellaire Ave
Valley Village, CA 91607-2329, US

Cahouet, Frank V (Financier)
1 Mellon Bank Center 500 Grant St
Pittsburgh, PA 15219, USA

Caifanes (Music Group)
c/o Staff Member *BMG*
1540 Broadway
New York, NY 10036-4039, USA

Caillat, Colbie (Musician)
c/o Todd Jacobs *WmE2 (Endeavor-LA)*
9601 Wilshire Blvd Fl 3
Beverly Hills, CA 90210-5219, USA

Cain, Carl (Athlete, Basketball Player, Olympic Athlete)
3045 Sun Valley Dr
Pickerington, OH 43147-9090, USA

Cain, Dean (Actor)
c/o Stephen (Steve) Small *Paradigm (LA)*
360 N Crescent Dr
Beverly Hills, CA 90210-4874, USA

Cain, John Paul (Athlete, Golfer)
1404 Avondale St
Sweetwater, TX 79556-2614, USA

Cain, Jonathan (Musician)
160 Spear St Ste 1900
San Francisco, CA 94105-1548, USA

Cain, Les (Athlete, Baseball Player)
31 Cutting Ct
Richmond, CA 94804-4217, USA

Cain, Lynn (Athlete, Football Player)
PO Box 90881
Los Angeles, CA 90009-0881, USA

Cain, Mick (Actor)
7800 Beverly Blvd # 3371
Los Angeles, CA 90036-2112, USA

Caine, Michael (Actor)
c/o Duncan Heath *Independent Talent Group (ITG-UK)*
Oxford House 76 Oxford St
London W1D 1BS, UK

Caio, Francesco (Business Person)
Via G Jervos 77
Ivrea/Truin 10015, USA

Cairns, Eric (Athlete, Hockey Player)
1291 Treeland St
Burlington, ON L7R 3T5, Canada

Cairns, Hugh J F (Biologist)
Wilcote Shipping Norton
Oxon OX7 3EA, UNITED KINGDOM (UK)

Cairns, Leah (Actor)
c/o David M Rudy 815 Moraga Drive
Los angeles, CA 90045, USA

Cairo, Miguel (Athlete, Baseball Player)
209 Highland Woods Dr
Safety Harbor, FL 34695-5437, USA

Calabrese, Gerry (Athlete, Basketball Player)
351 Esplanade Pl
Cliffside Park, NJ 07010-2708, USA

Calabresi, Guido (Judge)
157 Church St
New Haven, CT 06510-2104, USA

Calabro, Deborah (Stylist)
c/o Staff Member *Team*
423 W Broadway Ste 406
Boston, MA 02127-2265, USA

Calabro, Thomas (Actor)
c/o Staff Member *Stone Manners Salners Agency (LA)*
9911 W Pico Blvd Ste 1400
Los Angeles, CA 90035-2715, USA

Calacurcio-Thomas, Aldine (Baseball Player)
5438 Nottingham Dr
Loves Park, IL 61111-3605, USA

Calatrava, Santiago (Architect, Engineer)
Hoschgasse 5
Zurich 8008, SWITZERLAND

Calaway, Mark (The Undertaker) (Athlete, Wrestler)
3722 Eagle Spirit Ct
Fort Collins, CO 80528-9356, USA

Calcavecchia, Mark (Athlete, Golfer)
354 W Riverside Dr
Jupiter, FL 33469-2950, USA

Calder, David (Actor)
1 Winterwell Rd
London SW2 5TB, UK

Calder, Eric (Athlete, Hockey Player)
259 Stanley Dr
Waterloo, ON N2L 1H9, Canada

Calder, Nigel (Writer)
8 The Chase, Furnace Green
Crawley W. Sussex RH10 6HW, UK

Caldera, Rodriguez Rafael (President)
Ave Urdaneta 33-2 Apdo 2060
Caracas 1010, VENEZUELA

Calderon, Leticia (Actor)
c/o Staff Member *Televisa*
Blvd Adolfo Lopez Mateos 232 Colonia
San Angel INN
DF CP 01060, MEXICO

Calderon, Sila Maria (Ex-Governor)
PO Box 9020082
San Juan, PR 00902-0082, USA

Calderon, Wilmer (Actor)
c/o Lena Roklin *Luber Roklin Management*
8530 Wilshire Blvd Ste 550
Beverly Hills, CA 90211-3133, USA

Calderon Fournier, Rafael A (President)
San Jose, COSTA RICA

Caldicott, Helen (Activist, Doctor)
4423 Lehigh Rd # 337
College Park, MD 20740-3127, USA

Caldwell, Adrian (Athlete, Basketball Player)
10990 West Rd Apt 311
Houston, TX 77064-5496, USA

Caldwell, Alan (Athlete, Football Player)
1370 Kerner Rd
Kernersville, NC 27284-8943, USA

Caldwell, Bobby (Musician, Songwriter, Writer)
12702 Landale St
Studio City, CA 91604-1349, USA

Caldwell, Cynthia (Stylist)
PO Box 953
Northampton, MA 01061-0953, USA

Caldwell, Darryl (Athlete, Football Player)
4604 Malinta Ln
Chattanooga, TN 37416-3728, USA

Caldwell, Gail (Journalist)
Editorial Dept 135 W T Morrissey Blvd
Dorchester, MA 2139, USA

Caldwell, Jim (Athlete, Basketball Player)
705 Freedom Ln
Roswell, GA 30075-7911, USA

Caldwell, John (Cartoonist)
c/o Staff Member *King Features Syndication*
300 W 57th St Fl 15
New York, NY 10019-5238, USA

Caldwell, Joseph (Joe) (Athlete, Basketball Player)
15 E Pebble Beach Dr
Tempe, AZ 85282-5127, USA

Caldwell, Kimberly (Musician, Reality TV Star)
c/o Anthony Cordova *Story Road Entertainment*
809 S Bundy Dr Apt 209
Los Angeles, CA 90049-5253, USA

Caldwell, Matt (Musician)
c/o Staff Member *Paradigm (Monterey)*
404 W Franklin St
Monterey, CA 93940-2303, USA

Caldwell, Mike (Athlete, Baseball Player)
1645 Brook Run Dr
Raleigh, NC 27614-9732, USA

Caldwell, Mike (Athlete, Football Player)
646 Robertsville Rd
Oak Ridge, TN 37830-4724, USA

Caldwell, Mike T (Athlete, Football Player)
41621 N Bent Creek Ct
Phoenix, AZ 85086-1903, USA

Caldwell, Philip (Business Person)
200 Vesey St
New York, NY 10285-1000, USA

Caldwell, Ralph W (Athlete, Football Player)
4054 Charlene Dr
Los Angeles, CA 90043-1510, USA

Caldwell, Ravin (Athlete, Football Player)
4415 Johnson St
Fort Smith, AR 72904-4531, USA

Caldwell, Scott (Athlete, Football Player)
1037 Tuskegee St
Grand Prairie, TX 75051-2637, USA

Caldwell, Travis (Actor)
c/o Ellen Meyer *Ellen Meyer Management*
8899 Beverly Blvd Ste 612
West Hollywood, CA 90048-2429, USA

Caldwell, William A (Editor)
Editorial Dept S Summer St
Edgartown, MA 2539, USA

Caldwell, Zoe (Actor)
1501 Broadway
New York, NY 10036-5601, USA

Cale, J J (Music Group, Musician)
PO Box 170429
San Francisco, CA 94117-0429, USA

Cale, John (Music Group, Musician)
12 Rickett St West Brompton
London SW6 1RU, UNITED KINGDOM (UK)

Cale, Paula (Actor)
c/o Staff Member *Morra Brezner Steinberg & Tenenbaum (MBST) Entertainment*
345 N Maple Dr Ste 200
Beverly Hills, CA 90210-5174, USA

Cale, Puala (Actor)
232 N Canon Dr
Beverly Hills, CA 90210-5302, USA

Calero, Enrique (Kiko) (Athlete, Baseball Player)
18 Danson Dr
Saint Peters, MO 63376-4028, USA

Caley, Don (Athlete, Hockey Player)
7127 E Aloe Vera Dr
Scottsdale, AZ 85266-7176, USA

Calfa, Don (Actor)
1910 Holmby Ave Apt 1
Los Angeles, CA 90025-5936, USA

Calfa, Marian (Prime Minister)
Calfa Pravni Kancelar Premyslovska 28
Prague 3 130 00, USA

Calhoun, Bill (Athlete, Basketball Player)
3740 El Cerro View Cir
Reno, NV 89509-5610, USA

Calhoun, Corky (Misc, Yachtsman)
PO Box 1028
Dana Point, CA 92629-5028, USA

Calhoun, David (Athlete, Basketball Player)
17912 Lafayette Dr
Olney, MD 20832-2129, USA

Calhoun, Donald C (Don) (Athlete, Football Player)
1308 N Crestway St
Wichita, KS 67208-2810, USA

Calhoun, Jeff (Athlete, Baseball Player)
10002 Springwood Forest Dr
Houston, TX 77080-6419, USA

Calhoun, Jim (Athlete, Basketball Player, Coach)
PO Box 379
Pomfret Center, CT 06259-0379, USA

Calhoun, Monica (Actor)
1505 10th St
Santa Monica, CA 90401-2805, USA

Cali, Carmen (Athlete, Baseball Player)
5751 Copper Leaf Ln
Naples, FL 34116-6713, USA

Cali, Joseph (Actor)
25630 Edenwild Rd
Monte Nido, CA 91302-2265, USA

Calico, Tyrone (Athlete, Football Player)
3028 Brookview Forest Dr
Nashville, TN 37211-7049, USA

Caliendo, Frank (Actor)
c/o Steve Smooke *Creative Artists Agency (CAA-LA)*
2000 Avenue of the Stars Ste 100
Los Angeles, CA 90067-4705, USA

Califano, Joseph A Jr (Secretary)
633 3rd Ave # 1900
New York, NY 10017-6706, USA

Califano Jr, Joseph A (Government Official)
633 3rd Ave # 1900
New York, NY 10017-6706, USA

Caligiuri, Fred (Athlete, Baseball Player)
100 Baker St
Rimersburg, PA 16248-4324, USA

Calip, Demetrius (Athlete, Basketball Player)
7321 Lennox Ave Unit G5
Van Nuys, CA 91405-6262, USA

Calipari, John (Basketball Player, Coach)
Athletic
Memphis, TN 38152-0001, USA

Call, Anthony (Actor)
134 E 10th St
New York, NY 10021, USA

Call, Brandon (Actor)
5918 Van Nuys Blvd
Van Nuys, CA 91401-3623, USA

Call, Jack (Athlete, Football Player)
PO Box 361
Churchville, MD 21028-0361, USA

Call, Kevin (Athlete, Football Player)
839 Carey Rd
Carmel, IN 46033-9324, USA

Callaghan-Maxwell, Marge (Baseball Player)
203-5748 Rupert St
Vancouver, BC V5R 2K6, CANADA

Callahan, Ben (Athlete, Baseball Player)
1140 Asheford Green Ave NW
Concord, NC 28027-8185, USA

Callahan, Bill (Athlete, Coach, Football Coach, Football Player)
Athletic Dept
Lincoln, NE 68588, USA

Callahan, Bob (Athlete, Football Player)
24055 Paseo Del Lago Unit 102
Laguna Woods, CA 92637-2604, USA

Callahan, John (Actor)
2402 4th St Apt 6
Santa Monica, CA 90405-3664, USA

Callahan, John (Cartoonist)
375 Hudson St
New York, NY 10014-3658, USA

Callan, Cecile (Actor)
8730 W Sunset Blvd Ste 480
Los Angeles, CA 90069-2277, USA

Callan, K (Actor)
4957 Matilija Ave
Sherman Oaks, CA 91423-1921, USA

Callan, Michael (Actor)
1651 Camden Ave Apt 3
Los Angeles, CA 90025-3537, USA

Calland, Lee (Athlete, Football Player)
6624 Windwood Cir
Douglasville, GA 30135-1647, USA

Callaway, Howard H (Bo) (Government Official)
Callaway Gardens
Pine Mountain, GA 31822, USA

Callaway, Liz (Actor, Artist, Voice Over Artist)
c/o Staff Member *Gage Group, The (NY)*
450 7th Ave Ste 207
New York, NY 10123-0207, USA

Callaway, Mickey (Athlete, Baseball Player)
8061 Stonewyck Rd
Germantown, TN 38138-2351, USA

Callaway, Paul Smith (Music Group, Musician)
Mount Saint Alban
Washington, DC 20016, USA

Calle, Paul (Artist)
149 Little Hill Dr
Stamford, CT 06905-2322, USA

Callen, Bryan (Actor, Musician)
c/o Staff Member *Paradigm (Monterey)*
404 W Franklin St
Monterey, CA 93940-2303, USA

Callen, Jones Gloria (Swimmer)
1508 Chafton Rd
Charleston, WV 25314-1603, USA

Callender, Jock (Athlete, Hockey Player)
388 Lear Rd
Avon Lake, OH 44012-2079, USA

Callery, Sean (Composer, Musician)
c/o Staff Member *Gorfaine/Schwartz Agency Inc*
4111 W Alameda Ave Ste 509
Burbank, CA 91505-4171, USA

Callicutt, Ken (Athlete, Football Player)
969 Suchava Dr
White Lake, MI 48386-4558, USA

Callier, Frances (Comedian)
c/o Staff Member *Gekis Management*
4217 Verdugo View Dr
Los Angeles, CA 90065-4317, USA

Callies, Sarah Wayne (Actor)
c/o Alissa Vradenburg *Untitled Entertainment (LA)*
350 S Beverly Dr Ste 200
Beverly Hills, CA 90212-4819, USA

Calligaro, Len (Athlete, Football Player)
303 Taconite St Apt 201
Hurley, WI 54534-1555, USA

Callighen, Brett (Athlete, Hockey Player)
Box 248
Wilcox, SK S0G 5E0, Canada

Calling, The (Music Group)
c/o Staff Member *WmE2 (WMA-LA)*
1 William Morris Pl
Beverly Hills, CA 90212-4261, USA

Callis, James (Actor, Director)
c/o Alan Siegel *Alan Siegel Entertainment*
345 N Maple Dr Ste 375
Beverly Hills, CA 90210-5174, USA

Callner, Marty (Director, Producer)
c/o David Steinberg *Morra Brezner Steinberg & Tenenbaum (MBST) Entertainment*
345 N Maple Dr Ste 200
Beverly Hills, CA 90210-5174, USA

Callow, Simon (Actor)
12/13 Poland St
London WlV 3DE, UNITED KINGDOM (UK)

Calloway, AJ (Television Host)
c/o Michael (Mike) Esterman
Esterman.Com, LLC
Prefers to be contacted via email
MD, USA

Calloway, Chris (Athlete, Football Player)
526 Ralph Mcgill Blvd Ne
Atlanta, GA 30312-1105, USA

Calloway, Ernie (Athlete, Football Player)
4027 Lenox Blvd
Orlando, FL 32811-4107, USA

Calloway, Ron (Athlete, Baseball Player)
3868 Las Colinas Dr
Las Cruces, NM 88012-0693, USA

Callum, Keith Rennie (Actor)
c/o Staff Member *Elizabeth Hodgson Management Group*
1688 Cypress St Suite 405
Vancouver, BC V6J 5J1, Canada

Calmus, Dick (Athlete, Baseball Player)
3823 S 28th West Ave
Tulsa, OK 74107-5452, USA

Calmus, Rocky (Athlete, Football Player)
4131 Trinity Rd
Franklin, TN 37067-7714, USA

Calne, Roy Y (Doctor)
Addenbrooke's Hospital Hills Road
Cambridge CB2 2QQ, UNITED KINGDOM (UK)

Caltabiano, Tom (Comedian)
c/o Staff Member *United Talent Agency (UTA)*
9560 Wilshire Blvd Fl 5
Beverly Hills, CA 90212-2400, USA

Calvaer, Andre J (Engineer)
Blvd Louis Mettewie 270
Molenbeek-Saint-Jean 1080, BELGIUM

Calvert, Ken (Congressman, Politician)
2269 Rayburn Hob
Washington, DC 20515-0005, USA

Calvert, Mark (Athlete, Baseball Player)
908 W Waco St
Broken Arrow, OK 74011-2819, USA

Calvert, Rita (Stylist)
1518 Circle Dr
Annapolis, MD 21409-5831, USA

Calvet, Jacques (Financier)
31 Ave Victor Hugo
Paris 75116, FRANCE

Calvin, John (Actor)
2503 Ware Rd
Austin, TX 78741-5720, USA

Calvin, Mack (Basketball Player)
930 Figueroa Ter Apt 602
Los Angeles, CA 90012-3076, USA

Calvin, Thomas (Athlete, Football Player)
2712 McTavish Ave SW
Decatur, AL 35603-1106, USA

Calvin, William H (Biologist)
Neurobiology
Seattle, WA 98195-0001, USA

Calvo, Paul M (Ex-Governor)
115 Chalen Sando Papa
Hagatna, GU 96910, USA

Calvo-Sotelo, Bustelo Leopoldo (Prime Minister)
Buho 1 Somosaguas
Madrid, SPAIN

Calzaghe, Joe (Boxer)
51 Caerbryn Pentwynmawar Newbridge Gwent
South Wales, UNITED KINGDOM

Camacho, Ernie (Athlete, Baseball Player)
746 Saint Regis Way
Salinas, CA 93905-1642, USA

Camacho, Hector (Macho) (Boxer)
8034 Solitaire Ct
Orlando, FL 32836-6044, USA

Camarda, Charles J (Astronaut)
2386 Sabal Park Ln
League City, TX 77573-0777, USA

Camareno, Joe (Actor)
c/o Staff Member *Conana Caroll & Associates*
6117 Rhodes Ave
N Hollywood, CA 91606-4601, Uninted States

Camarillo, Rich (Athlete, Football Player)
1941 E Clubhouse Dr
Phoenix, AZ 85048-4061, USA

Camastra, Danielle (Actor)
c/o Staff Member *Henderson Hogan Agency (LA)*
850 7th Ave Ste 1003
New York, NY 10019-5230, USA

Cambal, Dennis (Athlete, Football Player)
24 Hedge Row
West Yarmouth, MA 02673-5813, USA

Cambre, Ronald C (Business Person)
9903 W Laurel Pl
Littleton, CO 80127-3900, USA

Cambria, Fred (Athlete, Baseball Player)
12 Iris Ct
Northport, NY 11768-3207, USA

Camby, Marcus (Athlete, Basketball Player)
925 Lincoln St Apt 14G
Denver, CO 80203-2768, USA

Camden, John (Business Person)
Coldgarbour Lane Thorpe
Egham, Surrey TW20 8TD, UNITED KINGDOM (UK)

Camdessus, Michel J (Financier)
700 19th St NW
Washington, DC 20431-0001, USA

Camelia-Romer, Susanne (Prime Minister)
Fort Amsterdam 17
Willemstad, NETHERLANDS ANTILLES

Cameron, Al (Athlete, Hockey Player)
1225 Ormsby Ln NW
Edmonton, AB T5T 6R2, Canada

Cameron, Candance (Actor)
8369 Sausalito Ave # A
Canoga Park, CA 91304-3342, USA

Cameron, Dallas (Athlete, Football Player)
7977 W 12th Ave
Hialeah, FL 33014-3534, USA

Cameron, Dave (Athlete, Coach, Hockey Player)
c/o Staff Member *Mississauga St Michaels Majors*
5500 Rose Cherry Pl
Mississauga, ON L4Z 4B6, Canada

Cameron, David (Designer, Fashion Designer)
Weihburggasse 19
Vienna 1010, AUSTRIA

Cameron, Dean (Actor)
4116 W Magnolia Blvd
Burbank, CA 91505-2782, USA

Cameron, Don R (Educator, Misc)
1201 16th St NW
Washington, DC 20036-3201, USA

Cameron, Duncan (Music Group, Musician)
5200 Old Harding Rd
Franklin, TN 37064-9406, USA

Cameron, Dwayne (Actor)
c/o Scott Karp *Crystal Sky Pictures*
10203 Santa Monica Blvd Ste 500
Los Angeles, CA 90067-6416, USA

Cameron, Glenn S (Athlete, Football Player)
8082 Steeplechase Dr
Palm Beach Gardens, FL 33418-7703, USA

Cameron, James (Director, Producer)
c/o Beth Swofford *Creative Artists Agency (CAA-LA)*
2000 Avenue of the Stars Ste 100
Los Angeles, CA 90067-4705, USA

Cameron, John (Composer)
8-9 Firth St
London W1D 3JB, UK

Cameron, Julia (Writer)
c/o Staff Member *HarperCollins Publishers*
10 E 53rd St C/O Author Mail Floor 7
New York, NY 10022, USA

Cameron, Kenneth D (Astronaut)
Austvagen 13
Vastra Frotunda 42676, SWEDEN

Cameron, Kevin (Athlete, Baseball Player)
26435 S Ivy Ln
Channahon, IL 60410-3341, USA

Cameron, Kirk (Actor)
c/o Staff Member *Mark Craig Productions*
1383 Callens Rd
Ventura, CA 93003-5602, USA

Cameron, Laura (Actor)
8383 Wilshire Blvd # 954
Beverly Hills, CA 90211-2425, USA

Cameron, Mat (Music Group, Musician)
6523 California Ave SW # 348
Seattle, WA 98136-1833, USA

Cameron, Mechelle (Swimmer)
PO Box 2
Calera, AL 35040-0002, CANADA

Cameron, Mike (Athlete, Baseball Player)
615 Champions Dr
Mcdonough, GA 30253-4284, USA

Cameron, Paul (Athlete, Football Player)
29457 Georgetown Ln
Temecula, CA 92591-1896, USA

Cameron, Rhona (Actor)
c/o Staff Member *Jeremy Hicks Associates*
114-115 Tottenham Court Rd
London W1T 5AH, UK

Cameron, Scotty (Golfer)
c/o Gordon Sanborn 333 Bridge St
Fairhaven, MA 2719, USA

Cameron, W Bruce (Writer)
c/o Scott Miller *Trident Media Group LLC*
41 Madison Ave Fl 36
New York, NY 10010-2257, USA

Cameron-Bure, Candace (Actor)
c/o Ford Englerth *Redrock Entertainment Development*
118 S Cordova St Fl 3
Burbank, CA 91505-4610, USA

Camiletti, Rob (Actor)
643 N La Cienega Blvd
Los Angeles, CA 90069-5201, USA

Camille (Stylist)
c/o Staff Member *Campbell Agency, The*
3838 Oak Lawn Ave Ste 900
Dallas, TX 75219-4510, USA

Camilleri, Louis C (Business Person)
120 Park Ave
New York, NY 10017-5577, USA

Camilleri, Terry (Actor)
c/o Christopher Mario Parker *Access LA Talent Management*
2850 Ocean Park Blvd Ste 215
Santa Monica, CA 90405-6206, USA

Camilli, Doug (Athlete, Baseball Player)
4245 61st Ave
Vero Beach, FL 32967-8807, USA

Camilli, Lou (Athlete, Baseball Player)
1314 Sigma Chi Rd NE
Albuquerque, NM 87106-4544, USA

Camilo, Michael (Musician)
300 Mercer St Apt 3J
New York, NY 10003-6732, USA

Camilo, Michel (Music Group, Musician)
590 W End Ave # 6
New York, NY 10024-1722, USA

Caminito, Jerry (Race Car Driver)
PO Box 1486
Jackson, NJ 08527-0486, USA

Cammack, Eric (Athlete, Baseball Player)
605 Remington Dr
Bridge City, TX 77611-2234, USA

Cammalleri, Mike (Athlete, Hockey Player)
43 Stockdale Cres
Richmond Hill, ON L4C 3T1, Canada

Cammermeyer, Margarethe (Activist)
4632 Tompkins Rd
Langley, WA 98260-9695, USA

Cammuso, Frank (Cartoonist)
1725 James St # 1
Syracuse, NY 13206-3201, USA

Camoy, Martin (Economist)
Economic Studies Center
Stanford, CA 94305, USA

Camp, Anna (Actor)
c/o Robert Glennon *Authentic Talent and Literary Management*
45 Main St Ste 1004
Brooklyn, NY 11201-8200, USA

Camp, Colleen (Actor)
473 N Tigertail Rd
Los Angeles, CA 90049-2807, USA

Camp, Dave (Congressman, Politician)
341 Cannon Hob
Washington, DC 20515-1806, USA

Camp, Greg (Composer, Musician)
c/o Staff Member *Creative Artists Agency (CAA-LA)*
2000 Avenue of the Stars Ste 100
Los Angeles, CA 90067-4705, USA

Camp, Jeremy (Musician)
c/o Staff Member *BEC Recordings*
PO Box 12698
Seattle, WA 98111-4698, USA

Camp, John (Journalist)
345 Cedar St
Saint Paul, MN 55101-1004, USA

Camp, Rick (Athlete, Baseball Player)
F P C Montgomery ID # 11973-021
Maxwell Air Force Base
Montgomery, AL 36112, USA

Camp, Steve (Music Group)
2021 21st Ave S Ste 220
Nashville, TN 37212-4348, USA

Campana, Al (Athlete, Football Player)
509 Sexton St
Struthers, OH 44471-1148, USA

Campanella, Joseph (Actor)
4196 Colfax Ave
Studio City, CA 91604-2165, USA

Campaneris, Bert (Athlete, Baseball Player)
PO Box 5096
Scottsdale, AZ 85261-5096, USA

Campanis, Jim (Athlete, Baseball Player)
17082 Cascades Ave
Yorba Linda, CA 92886-4867, USA

Campau, Thomas E (Cinematographer)
2000 S Hammond Lake Rd
West Bloomfield, MI 48324-1816, USA

Campbell, A Kim (Prime Minister)
Kennedy School of Government
Cambridge, MA 2138, USA

Campbell, Alan (Actor)
41 Madison Ave # 3300
New York, NY 10010-2202, USA

Campbell, Allan McCulloch (Biologist)
947 Mears Ct
Stanford, CA 94305-1041, USA

Campbell, Bek David (Beck) (Musician)
c/o John Silva *SAM*
722 Seward St
Los Angeles, CA 90038-3504, USA

Campbell, Ben Nighthorse
456 New Jersey Ave SE
Washington, DC 20003-4038, USA

Campbell, Bill (Athlete, Baseball Player)
133 S Hale St
Palatine, IL 60067-6211, USA

Campbell, Billy (Actor)
c/o Sean Fay *Kritzer Levine Wilkins Entertainment*
11872 La Grange Ave Fl 1
Los Angeles, CA 90025-5283, USA

Campbell, Bruce (Actor, Director, Producer)
c/o Robert Stein *Robert Stein Management*
PO Box 3797
Beverly Hills, CA 90212-0797, USA

Campbell, Bryan (Athlete, Hockey Player)
10895 Tamoron Ln
Boca Raton, FL 33498-6397, USA

Campbell, Carter (Athlete, Football Player)
24834 Winterberry Ln
Plainfield, IL 60585-5685, USA

Campbell, Chad (Athlete, Golfer)
200 Glade Rd
Colleyville, TX 76034-3603, USA

Campbell, Cheryl (Actor)
125 Gloucester Road
London SW7 4TE, UNITED KINGDOM (UK)

Campbell, Christa (Actor)
c/o Staff Member *Origin Talent Agency*
4705 Laurel Canyon Blvd Ste 306
Studio City, CA 91607-5940, USA

Campbell, Christian (Actor)
12533 Woodgreen St
Los Angeles, CA 90066-2723, USA

Campbell, Colin (Soupy) (Athlete, Coach, Hockey Player)
c/o Staff Member *National Hockey League (NHL)*
50 Bay St 11th Floor
Toronto, ON M5J 2X8, Canada

Campbell, Dan (Athlete, Football Player)
PO Box 97
Meridian, TX 76665-0097, USA

Campbell, Darren (Athlete, Track Athlete)
1 Wandsworth Plain
London SW18 1EH, UK

Campbell, Dave (Athlete, Baseball Player)
726 N Dundee Dr
Post Falls, ID 83854-8886, USA

Campbell, Dave (Athlete, Baseball Player)
878 Amidon St
Deltona, FL 32725-7206, USA

Campbell, Dick (Athlete, Football Player)
2557 Nicolet Dr
Green Bay, WI 54311-7225, USA

Campbell, Dick (Athlete, Football Player)
PO Box 198
Jensen Beach, FL 34958-0198, USA

Campbell, Earl C (Athlete, Football Player)
809 Rio Grande St Ste 100
Austin, TX 78701-2233, USA

Campbell, Elden (Athlete, Basketball Player)
17252 Hawthorne Blvd # 493
Torrance, CA 90504, USA

Campbell, Garry (Producer, Writer)
c/o Staff Member *Creative Artists Agency (CAA-LA)*
2000 Avenue of the Stars Ste 100
Los Angeles, CA 90067-4705, USA

Campbell, Gary (Athlete, Football Player)
PO Box 775353
Steamboat Springs, CO 80477-5353, USA

Campbell, Gene (Athlete, Hockey Player)
6149 Sugar Mill Ln
Mound, MN 55364-8624, USA

Campbell, Glen (Musician)
c/o Sanford Brokaw *Brokaw Company, The*
9255 W Sunset Blvd Ste 804
Los Angeles, CA 90069-3305, USA

Campbell, Gregory (Athlete, Hockey Player)
P.O. Box 342
Tillsonburg, ON N4G 4H8, Canada

Campbell, Helen Hannah (Athlete, Baseball Player)
17077 San Mateo St
Fountain Valley, CA 92708-7645, USA

Campbell, Isobel (Music Group, Musician)
7 Trinity Row
Florence, MA 01062-1931, USA

Campbell, James (Jim) (Athlete, Baseball Player)
209 W Seven Pines St
Lamar, SC 29069-8964, USA

Campbell, Jeff (Baseball Player)
4194 San Miguel Ave
San Diego, CA 92113-1842, USA

Campbell, Jeff (Athlete, Football Player)
2601 Berenson Ln
Austin, TX 78746-1963, USA

Campbell, Jennifer Lynn (Actor)
11871 Dubarry Dr
Carmel, IN 46033-8259, USA

Campbell, Jessica (Actor)
8840 Wilshire Blvd # 200
Beverly Hills, CA 90211-2606, USA

Campbell, Jim (Athlete, Baseball Player)
1924 Knollwood Ln
Los Altos, CA 94024-6720, USA

Campbell, Jim (Athlete, Baseball Player)
1671 6th St
Oroville, CA 95965-4057, USA

Campbell, Jim (Athlete, Hockey Player)
32 Lemp Rd
Saint Louis, MO 63122-6947, USA

Campbell, Joe (Athlete, Baseball Player)
1806 Todd Trace Ct
Bowling Green, KY 42103-0916, USA

Campbell, John (Race Car Driver)
823 Allison Dr
Rivervale, NJ 07675-6602, USA

Campbell, John (Congressman, Politician)
1507 Longworth Hob
Washington, DC 20515-4328, USA

Campbell, John W (Athlete, Football Player)
12908 Welcome Ln
Burnsville, MN 55337-3626, USA

Campbell, Joshua (Actor)
c/o Staff Member *Select Artists Ltd (CA-Westside Office)*
1138 12th St Apt 1
Santa Monica, CA 90403-5459, USA

Campbell, Julia (Actor)
1505 10th St
Santa Monica, CA 90401-2805, USA

Campbell, Keith H S (Biologist, Misc)
Roslin Bio Centre
Midlothlan EH25 9PS, SCOTLAND

Campbell, Kevin (Athlete, Baseball Player)
207 Ridout Dr
Des Arc, AR 72040-3335, USA

Campbell, Kim (Prime Minister)
550 S Hope St
Los Angeles, CA 90071-2627

Campbell, L Arthur (Misc, Scientist)
Medical center 1230 York Ave
New York, NY 10021, USA

Campbell, Lamar (Athlete, Football Player)
2511 W 7th St
Chester, PA 19013-2109, USA

Campbell, Larry Joe (Actor)
c/o Geoff Cheddy *Brillstein Entertainment Partners*
9150 Wilshire Blvd Ste 350
Beverly Hills, CA 90212-3453, USA

Campbell, Leslie (Stylist)
4 Coco Pl
Pacific Palisades, CA 90272-4642, USA

Campbell, Lewis B (Business Person)
40 Westminster St
Providence, RI 02903-2525, USA

Campbell, Luther (Musician)
c/o Luther Campbell *Luke Entertainment Group*
Prefers to be contacted via telephone or email
USA

Campbell, Lynn (Stylist)
c/o Staff Member *Montana Artists Agency*
9150 Wilshire Blvd Ste 100
Beverly Hills, CA 90212-3459, USA

Campbell, Marion (Athlete, Football Coach, Football Player)
351 Marsh Point Cir
Saint Augustine, FL 32080-5864, USA

Campbell, Martin (Director)
8942 Wilshire Blvd # 219
Beverly Hills, CA 90211-1908, USA

Campbell, Matthew (Matt) (Athlete, Football Player)
6 Old House Cir
Okatie, SC 29909-7002, USA

Campbell, Michael (Athlete, Golfer)
Sanford Lane
Hurst Berkshire RG10 0SQ, United Kingdom

Campbell, Mike (Athlete, Baseball Player)
4500 36th Ave SW Apt 12
Seattle, WA 98126-2750, USA

Campbell, Mike (Athlete, Football Player)
383 Inverness Dr
Winston Salem, NC 27107-6030, USA

Campbell, Milton (Milt) (Athlete, Football Player, Track Athlete)
3805 Reservoir Dr
Gainesville, GA 30507-7128, USA

Campbell, Naomi (Actor, Model, Music Group)
c/o Vanessa Pereira *Artists Independent Management (LA)*
825 Nowita Pl
Venice, CA 90291-3836, USA

Campbell, Nell (Actor)
P.O. Box 709
Broadway NSW 2007, Australia

Campbell, Nell (Actor)
246 W 14th St
New York, NY 10011-7201, USA

Campbell, Neve (Actor)
c/o Arlene Forster *Forster Entertainment*
12533 Woodgreen St
Los Angeles, CA 90066-2723, USA

Campbell, Nicholas (Actor)
1206 N Orange Grove Ave
West Hollywood, CA 90046-5351, USA

Campbell, Pamela (Stylist)
c/o Staff Member *Artist Untied (LA)*
845 S Mansfield Ave Apt 1
Los Angeles, CA 90036-4979, USA

Campbell, Patrick J (Misc)
101 Constitution Ave NW
Washington, DC 20001-2133, USA

Campbell, Paul (Actor)
c/o Staff Member *ROAR (LA)*
9701 Wilshire Blvd Fl 8
Beverly Hills, CA 90212-2008, USA

Campbell, Rich (Athlete, Football Player)
522 SW McComb Ave
Port Saint Lucie, FL 34953-3811, USA

Campbell, Robert (Architect, Critic)
54 Antrim St
Cambridge, MA 02139-1102, USA

Campbell, Robert H (Business Person)
10 Penn Center 1801 Market St
Philadelphia, PA 19103, USA

Campbell, Ron (Athlete, Baseball Player)
1104 Sweetbriar Ave NW
Cleveland, TN 37311-1657, USA

Campbell, Scott (Athlete, Football Player)
123 Oak Ln
Hershey, PA 17033-1748, USA

Campbell, Scott Michael (Actor)
c/o Danielle Allman-Del *D2 Management*
141 S Barrington Ave
Los Angeles, CA 90049-3368, USA

Campbell, Sonny (Athlete, Football Player)
6250 N Desert Willow Dr
Tucson, AZ 85743-8701, USA

Campbell, Stacy Dean (Musician)
1105-C 16th Avenue Sq
Nashville, TN 37212, USA

Campbell, Tevin (Actor, Musician)
c/o Staff Member *Pyramid Entertainment Group*
377 Rector Pl Apt 21A
New York, NY 10280-1439, USA

Campbell, Tony (Athlete, Basketball Player)
1445 Teaneck Rd
Teaneck, NJ 07666-3627, USA

Campbell, Vivian (Music Group, Musician)
27A Floral St #300
London WC2E 9DQ, UNITED KINGDOM (UK)

Campbell, William (Actor)
21502 Velicata St
Woodland Hills, CA 91364-1905, USA

Campbell, William J (General)
3267 Alex Findlay Pl
Sarasota, FL 34240-8701, USA

Campbell, Woodrow (Athlete, Football Player)
9122 Weymouth Dr
Houston, TX 77031-3034, USA

Campbell Bower, Jamie (Actor)
c/o Warren Zavala *Creative Artists Agency (CAA-LA)*
2000 Avenue of the Stars Ste 100
Los Angeles, CA 90067-4705, USA

Campbell-Martin, Tisha (Actor)
c/o Pearl Wexler *Kohner Agency, The*
9300 Wilshire Blvd Ste 555
Beverly Hills, CA 90212-3211, USA

Campeau, Tod (Athlete, Hockey Player)
5 Rue Victoria E
Salaberry-De-Valleyfield, QC J6T 2L1, Canada

Campedelli, Dominic (Athlete, Hockey Player)
732 Jerusalem Rd
Cohasset, MA 02025-1032, USA

Campen, James (Athlete, Football Player)
PO Box 879
Shingle Springs, CA 95682-0879, USA

Camper, Cardell (Athlete, Baseball Player)
1675 Sera Moon Dr
Beaumont, CA 92223-2049, USA

Campese, David I (Athlete, Misc)
870 Pacific Hwy # 4
Gordon, NSW 2072, AUSTRALIA

Campfield, William (Billy) (Athlete, Football Player)
930 Glenmore Way Apt K
Westerville, OH 43082-9429, USA

Campion, Jane (Director)
c/o Kate Richter *HLA Management*
PO Box 1536
Strawberry Hills 2012, AUSTRALIA

Campisi, Sal (Athlete, Baseball Player)
644 77th Ave
St Pete Beach, FL 33706-1708, USA

Campo, Dave (Coach, Football Coach)
76 Lou Groza Blvd
Berea, OH 44017-1238, USA

Campos, Arsenio (Actor)
c/o Staff Member *Televisa*
Blvd Adolfo Lopez Mateos 232 Colonia San Angel INN
DF CP 01060, MEXICO

Campos, Bruno (Actor)
1801 Avenue of the Stars Ste 902
Los Angeles, CA 90067-5981, USA

Campos, Jorge (Soccer Player)
Col Juarez
Mexico City 6, DF CP 06600, MEXICO

Cam'ron (Musician)
c/o Staff Member *International Creative Management (ICM-LA)*
10250 Constellation Blvd Fl 7
Los Angeles, CA 90067-6207, USA

Canada, Larry (Athlete, Football Player)
17691 Sarah Ln
Country Club Hills, IL 60478-4995, USA

Canada, Ron (Actor)
c/o Christopher (Chris) Wright *Christopher Wright Management*
3207 Winnie Dr
Los Angeles, CA 90068-1439, USA

Canadas, Esther (Actor, Model)
300 Park Ave S # 200
New York, NY 10010-5313, USA

Canadian Brass (Music Group)
c/o Darcy Gregoire *Agency Group Ltd, The (Canada)*
2 Berkeley Street Suite 202
Toronto M5A 4J5, Canada

Canady, James (Jim) (Athlete, Football Player)
303 Sunset Dr
Burnet, TX 78611-9737, USA

Canagata, Bill (Baseball Player)
25 W 132nd St Apt 10R
New York, NY 10037-3205, USA

Canale, George (Athlete, Baseball Player)
7333 Old Mill Rd
Roanoke, VA 24018-6712, USA

Canale, Justin (Athlete, Football Player)
2889 Sky Ridge Dr
Memphis, TN 38127-7415, USA

Canale, Whit (Athlete, Football Player)
2889 Sky Ridge Dr
Memphis, TN 38127-7415, USA

Canalis, Elisabetta (Actor, Model)
c/o Staff Member *Corsa Agency, The*
11704 Wilshire Blvd Ste 204
Los Angeles, CA 90025-1510, USA

Canals-Barrera, Maria (Actor)
c/o Jason Newman *Untitled Entertainment (LA)*
350 S Beverly Dr Ste 200
Beverly Hills, CA 90212-4819, USA

Candaele, Casey (Athlete, Baseball Player)
251 Broad St
San Luis Obispo, CA 93405-2303, USA

Candelaria, John (Athlete, Baseball Player)
3122 Elroy Ave
Pittsburgh, PA 15227-2825, USA

Candeloro, Philippe (Figure Skater)
35 Rue Felicien David
Paris 75016, FRANCE

Candeloro, Philippe (Figure Skater)
42 rue de Louvre
Paris F-75001, FRANCE

Candills, Georges (Architect)
17 Rue Campagne-Premiere
Paris 75014, FRANCE

Candiotti, Thomas C (Tom) (Athlete, Baseball Player)
6061 E Jenan Dr
Scottsdale, AZ 85254-4972, USA

Candlebox (Music Group)
c/o Staff Member *Maverick Recording Co (LA)*
3300 Warner Blvd
Burbank, CA 91505-4632, USA

Canegata, Bill (Athlete, Baseball Player)
307 E 89th St Apt 3J
New York, NY 10128-5008, USA

Caneira, John (Athlete, Baseball Player)
18 Spruce Dr
Naugatuck, CT 06770-4231, USA

Canela, Jencarlos (Actor)
c/o Oswaldo Pisfil *NCM Productions*
10770 NW 66th St Apt 512
Doral, FL 33178-3781, USA

Canella, Guldo (Architect)
Via Revere 7
Milan 20123, ITALY

Canellas, Natalia (Stylist)
c/o Celebrity Stylists *Utopia*
12 W End Ave Fl 2
New York, NY 10023, USA

Canerday, Natalie (Actor)
c/o Staff Member *The Agency Inc*
802 W 8th St
Little Rock, AR 72201-4016, USA

Canet, Guillaume (Actor, Director, Writer)
c/o Robert Newman *WmE2 (Endeavor-LA)*
9601 Wilshire Blvd Fl 3
Beverly Hills, CA 90210-5219, USA

Canete, Ariel (Athlete, Golfer)
1751 Pinnacle Dr Ste 1500
Mc Lean, VA 22102-3833, USA

Canfield, Jack (Business Person, Writer)
PO Box 30880
Santa Barbara, CA 93130-0880, USA

Canfield, Mary Grace (Actor)
13775A Mono Way # 220
Sonora, CA 95370-8813, USA

Canfield, Paul (Physicist)
Physics
Ames, IA 50011-0001, USA

Canfield, William L (Bill) (Cartoonist, Editor)
Editorial Dept ! Star Ledger Plaza
Newark, NJ 7102, USA

Cangelosi, John (Athlete, Baseball Player)
10914 Caribou Ln
Orland Park, IL 60467-7843, USA

Cangemi, Joseph P (Misc)
1409 Mount Ayr Cir
Bowling Green, KY 42103-4708, USA

Canidate, Trung (Athlete, Football Player)
1707 W Clarendon Ave
Phoenix, AZ 85015-5502, USA

Canipe, David (Athlete, Golfer)
505 Oakwood Ave
New Smyrna Beach, FL 32169-2715, USA

Canizales, Gaby (Boxer)
2205 Saint Maria Ave
Laredo, TX 78040, USA

Canizaro, Jay (Athlete, Baseball Player)
2450 Jill Cir
Spring, TX 77388-3581, USA

Canley, Sheldon (Athlete, Football Player)
264 Altair Ave
Lompoc, CA 93436-1424, USA

Cannatella, Trishelle (Reality TV Star)
c/o Staff Member *Bunim/Murray Productions Inc*
6007 Sepulveda Blvd
Van Nuys, CA 91411-2502, USA

Cannava, Anthony (Tony) (Athlete, Football Player)
26 Royall St
Medford, MA 02155-4512, USA

Cannavale, Bobby (Actor)
c/o Peg Donegan *Framework Entertainment (LA)*
9057 Nemo St Ste C
West Hollywood, CA 90069-5511, USA

Cannavino, Joe (Athlete, Football Player)
1600 Brittain Rd
Akron, OH 44310-2796, USA

Canned Heat (Music Group, Musician)
PO Box 3773
San Rafael, CA 94912-3773, USA

Cannell, Stephen J (Producer, Writer)
1220 Hillcrest Ave
Pasadena, CA 91106-4435, USA

Cannida, James (Athlete, Football Player)
4504 Harmony Pl
Rohnert Park, CA 94928-1880, USA

Cannizaro, Andy (Athlete, Baseball Player)
429 Marina Oaks
Mandeville, LA 70471-1567, USA

Cannizzaro, Chris (Athlete, Baseball Player)
13597 Grain Ln
San Diego, CA 92129-2851, USA

Cannon (Stylist)
c/o Staff Member *Oliver Piro Inc*
725 Riverside Dr Apt 3A
New York, NY 10031-2460, USA

Cannon, Ace (Musician)
19948 Mayall St
Chatsworth, CA 91311-3522, USA

Cannon, Billy (Athlete, Football Player)
1640 Sherwood Forest Blvd
Baton Rouge, LA 70815-5458, USA

Cannon, Carey (Actor)
c/o Staff Member *Geddes Agency, The*
8430 Santa Monica Blvd Ste 200
Los Angeles, CA 90069-4253, USA

Cannon, Danny (Producer)
c/o Staff Member *Creative Artists Agency (CAA-LA)*
2000 Avenue of the Stars Ste 100
Los Angeles, CA 90067-4705, USA

Cannon, Dyan (Actor)
1100 Alta Loma Rd Apt 808
West Hollywood, CA 90069-2438, USA

Cannon, Freddy (Musician)
5119 Surfrider Way
Oxnard, CA 93035-1050, USA

Cannon, Freddy (Boom Boom) (Music Group, Songwriter, Writer)
4250 A1A S Unit D11
Saint Augustine, FL 32080-7431, USA

Cannon, Glenn (Actor)
2500 Campus Rd
Honolulu, HI 96822-2217, USA

Cannon, Harold (Actor)
c/o Staff Member *Select Artists Ltd (CA-Valley Office)*
PO Box 4359
Burbank, CA 91503-4359, USA

Cannon, Joe (Soccer Player)
c/o Staff Member *Colorado Rapids Soccer Club*
Pepsi Center 1000 Chopper Circle
Denver, CO 80204-5805, USA

Cannon, Joe (J J) (Athlete, Baseball Player)
3017 Cedarwood Village Ln
Pensacola, FL 32514-6251, USA

Cannon, John (Athlete, Football Player)
2911 W Bay Vista Ave
Tampa, FL 33611-1609, USA

Cannon, Katherine (Actor)
1310 Westholme Ave
Los Angeles, CA 90024-5016, USA

Cannon, Mark (Athlete, Football Player)
2604 Riveroaks Dr
Arlington, TX 76006-3638, USA

Cannon, Nick (Actor, Producer)
c/o Tracy Nguyen *IPR + MKTG*
1515 Broadway Fl 40
New York, NY 10036-8901, USA

Cannon, William A (Billy) (Athlete, Football Player)
176 Shirley Cir
Monterey, LA 71354-4124, USA

Cannon Jr, Billy (Athlete, Football Player)
8857 Sage Hill Rd
Saint Francisville, LA 70775-7168, USA

Cano, Christi (Athlete, Golfer)
PO Box 12792
San Antonio, TX 78212-0792, USA

Cano, Martin (Stylist)
c/o Staff Member *Crews*
828 Clemont Dr NE
Atlanta, GA 30306-3694, USA

Cano, Roberto (Actor)
c/o Staff Member *TV Caracol*
Calle 76 #11 - 35 Piso 10AA
Bogota DC 26484, COLOMBIA

Cano, Robinson (Athlete, Baseball Player)
c/o Team Member *New York Yankees*
Yankee Stadium 161st St & River Ave
Bronx, NY 10451, USA

Canonero, Milena (Designer)
c/o Paul Hook *International Creative Management (ICM-LA)*
10250 Constellation Blvd Fl 7
Los Angeles, CA 90067-6207, USA

Canova, Diana (Actor)
578 Washington Blvd Ste 688
Marina Del Rey, CA 90292-5442, USA

Canseco, Jose (Athlete, Baseball Player, Reality TV Star)
c/o Susan Haber *Haber Entertainment*
434 S Canon Dr Apt 204
Beverly Hills, CA 90212-4501, USA

Canseco, Ozzie (Athlete, Baseball Player)
10833 Wilshire Blvd Apt 525
Los Angeles, CA 90024-4157, USA

Cansino, Athena (Actor)
c/o Victor (Viktor) Kruglov *Victor Kruglov Talent Management*
7461 Beverly Blvd Ste 403
Los Angeles, CA 90036-2774, USA

Cantafio, Jim (Actor)
c/o Laura Lichen *Laura Lichen Management*
PO Box 33051
Granada Hills, CA 91394-3051, USA

Cantaline, Anita (Bowler)
31455 Pinto Dr
Warren, MI 48093-7624, USA

Cantano, Mark (Athlete, Football Player)
9036 Walton St
Indianapolis, IN 46231-1164, USA

Cantey, Charisie (Sportscaster)
77 W 66th St
New York, NY 10023-6201, USA

Cantillo, Jose Pablo (Actor)
c/o Staff Member *New Wave Entertainment (LA)*
2660 W Olive Ave
Burbank, CA 91505-4525, USA

Canton, Denio (Baseball Player)
1330 NW 5th St Apt 5
Miami, FL 33125-4734, USA

Canton, Joanna (Actor)
c/o Staff Member *Liberman/Zerman Management*
252 N Larchmont Blvd Ste 200
Los Angeles, CA 90004-3754, USA

Cantona, Eric (Actor)
60 Bis Ave D'llena
Paris 75783, France

Cantone, Mario (Actor)
c/o Rhonda Price *Gersh (NY)*
41 Madison Ave
New York, NY 10010-2202, USA

Cantone, Vic (Cartoonist, Editor)
238 Blackpool Ct
Ridge, NY 11961-8115, USA

Cantoni, Giulio L (Biologist, Misc)
6938 Blaisdell Rd
Bethesda, MD 20817-3039, USA

Cantor, Andres (Sportscaster)
c/o Staff Member *WmE2 (WMA-LA)*
1 William Morris Pl
Beverly Hills, CA 90212-4261, USA

Cantor, Charles R (Biologist)
11 Bay Street Rd
Boston, MA 2116, USA

Cantor, Eric (Congressman, Politician)
303 Cannon Hob
Washington, DC 20515-1501, USA

Cantoral, Itati (Actor)
c/o Gabriel Blanco *Gabriel Blanco Iglesias (Mexico)*
Rio Balsas 35-32 Colonia Cuauhtemoc
DF 6500, Mexico

Cantrell, Barry (Athlete, Football Player)
142 Underwood Dr
Palatka, FL 32177-8166, USA

Cantrell, Blu (Music Group)
8750 Wilshire Blvd # 300
Beverly Hills, CA 90211-2703, USA

Cantrell, Jerry (Musician)
c/o Michael Moses *Baker Winokur Ryder Public Relations (BWR-LA)*
9100 Wilshire Blvd Ste 500 PMB WEST
Beverly Hills, CA 90212-3426, USA

Cantrell, Lana (Musician)
300 E 71st St
New York, NY 10021-5234, USA

Cantu, Jorge (Athlete, Baseball Player)
5009 S 24th St
McAllen, TX 78503-8936, USA

Cantuniar, Sonia (Stylist)
c/o Staff Member *Artist Untied (LA)*
845 S Mansfield Ave Apt 1
Los Angeles, CA 90036-4979, USA

Cantwell, Maria (Senator)
311 Hart Senate Ofc Building
Washington, DC 20510-0001, USA

Canty, Chris (Athlete, Football Player)
c/o Brad Blank *Brad Blank & Associates*
251 Beacon St Apt 6
Boston, MA 02116-1361, USA

Canup, Robin (Astronomer)
1050 Walnut St Ste 400
Boulder, CO 80302-5143, USA

Canyon, George (Musician)
c/o Staff Member *Paradigm (Monterey)*
404 W Franklin St
Monterey, CA 93940-2303, USA

Cap, Kelly (Athlete, Golfer)
3023 Alcazar Pl Apt 208
Palm Beach Gardens, FL 33410-2878, USA

Capa, Cornell (Photographer)
275 5th Ave
New York, NY 10016-6514, USA

Capalbo, Carmen C (Director, Producer)
500 2nd Ave
New York, NY 10016-8606, USA

Caparulo, John (Comedian)
c/o Staff Member *Brillstein Entertainment Partners*
9150 Wilshire Blvd Ste 350
Beverly Hills, CA 90212-3453, USA

Capasso, Federico (Physicist)
600 Mountain Ave
New Providence, NJ 07974-2008, USA

Capecchi, Mario R (Biologist)
778 E 13800 S
Draper, UT 84020-9714, USA

Capece, Bill (Athlete, Football Player)
867 Hill Roost Rd
Tallahassee, FL 32312-6716, USA

Capel, John (Athlete, Track Athlete)

Capel, Mike (Athlete, Baseball Player)
3901 Northshore Dr
Montgomery, TX 77356-5369, USA

Capellas, Michael (Business Person)
500 Clinton Center Dr
Clinton, MS 39056-5678, USA

Capellino, Ally (Designer, Fashion Designer)
N1R Metropolitan Wharf Wapping Wall
London E1 9SS, UNITED KINGDOM (UK)

Capers, Dom (Athlete, Coach, Football Coach, Football Player)
4400 Post Oak Pkwy Ste 1400
Houston, TX 77027-3440, USA

Capers, Wayne (Athlete, Football Player)
28 Greenlawn Dr
Pittsburgh, PA 15220-2503, USA

Caperton, W Gaston III (Ex-Governor)
President's Office 45 Columbus Ave
New York, NY 10023, USA

Capilla, Doug (Athlete, Baseball Player)
642 Nello Dr Apt 1
Campbell, CA 95008-4746, USA

Capilla, Perez Joaquin (Misc)
Torres de Mixcoac Lomas de Platerce
Mexico City 19, DF, MEXICO

Capitain, Jenny (Stylist)
c/o Staff Member *AFG Management*
62 Chelsea Piers Ste 203
New York, NY 10011-1015, USA

Caplan, Arthur L (Biologist, Misc)
Biomedical Ethics Center
Philadelphia, PA 19104, USA

Caplan, Lizzy (Actor)
c/o Ryan Revel *Benderspink*
5870 W Jefferson Blvd Ste E
Los Angeles, CA 90016-3159, USA

Capleton (Musician)
c/o Staff Member *Agency Group Ltd, The (NY)*
142 W 57th St Fl 6
New York, NY 10019-3300, USA

Caplin, Mortimer M (Government Official)
5610 Wisconsin Ave PH 18E
Bethesda, MD 20815-4442, USA

Capoblanco, Tito (Director, Opera Singer)
711 Penn Ave Ste 800
Pittsburgh, PA 15222-3407, USA

Capodice, John (Actor)
c/o Staff Member *Sharp Talent*
117 N Orlando Ave
Los Angeles, CA 90048-3403, USA

Capon, Edwin G (Religious Leader)
11 Highland Ave
Newtonville, MA 02460-1852, USA

Capone, Warren (Athlete, Football Player)
11999 Longridge Ave Apt 602
Baton Rouge, LA 70816-3923, USA

Caponera, John (Actor, Comedian)
955 Carrillo Dr Ste 100
Los Angeles, CA 90048-5400, USA

Caponetto, Megan (Stylist)
c/o Staff Member *Mel Bryant Management*
611 Broadway Rm 623
New York, NY 10012-2650

Caponi, Donna M (Athlete, Golfer)
2731 Silver River Trl
Orlando, FL 32828-7787, USA

Capp, Dick (Athlete, Football Player)
PO Box 2193
Cary, NC 27512-2193, USA

Cappadona, Robert (Bob) (Athlete, Football Player)
25 Summer St
Watertown, MA 02472-3457, USA

Cappelletti, Gino R M (Athlete, Football Player)
19 Louis Dr
Wellesley Hills, MA 02481-1164, USA

Cappelletti, John (Athlete, Football Player)
28791 Brant Ln
Laguna Beach, CA 92677, USA

Cappleman, William (Bill) (Athlete, Football Player)
1506 Sydney Ln
Lynn Haven, FL 32444-2928, USA

Cappos, Connie (Stylist)
c/o Staff Member *LA Rep*
8312 Utica Dr
Los Angeles, CA 90046-7716, USA

Capps, Lois (Congressman, Politician)
2231 Rayburn Hob
Washington, DC 20515-4321, USA

Capps, Matt (Athlete, Baseball Player)
6348 S Summers Cir
Douglasville, GA 30135-5450, USA

Capps, Thomas E (Business Person)
120 Tredegar St
Richmond, VA 23219-4306, USA

Cappuzzello, George (Athlete, Baseball Player)
2024 Stillwood Pl
Windermere, FL 34786-8329, USA

Capra, Buzz (Athlete, Baseball Player)
15039 W Keswick Pl
Lockport, IL 60441-6251, USA

Capra, Francis (Actor)

Capra, Nick (Athlete, Baseball Player)
300 Town Park Rd
Norman, OK 73072-4538, USA

Capri, Ahna (Actor)
16547 Vanowen St Apt 209
Van Nuys, CA 91406-4710, USA

Capri, Mark (Actor)
225 W 44th St
New York, NY 10036-3964, USA

Capria, Carl (Athlete, Football Player)
9003 Nautical Watch Dr
Indianapolis, IN 46236-9035, USA

Capriati, Jennifer (Tennis Player)
c/o Caroline Smith *Women's Tennis Association (WTA (UK))*
Palliser House Palliser Rd
London W149EB, UK

Caprice (Model, Music Group, Songwriter, Writer)
Business Center Lower Road
London SE16 2XB, UNITED KINGDOM (UK)

Caprice, Frank (Athlete, Hockey Player)
2180 Heron Lake Dr Unit 308
Punta Gorda, FL 33983-6738, USA

Capshaw, Jessica (Actor)
c/o Raj Raghavan *Creative Artists Agency (CAA-LA)*
2000 Avenue of the Stars Ste 100
Los Angeles, CA 90067-4705, USA

Capshaw, Kate (Actor)
c/o Kevin Huvane *Creative Artists Agency (CAA-LA)*
2000 Avenue of the Stars Ste 100
Los Angeles, CA 90067-4705, USA

Captain, Raj (Actor)
951 Munuswamy Salai K K Nagar
Chennai, TN 600 078, INDIA

Capuano, Chris (Athlete, Baseball Player)
10953 E Tusayan Trl
Scottsdale, AZ 85255-8090, USA

Capuano, Dave (Athlete, Hockey Player)
145 Capuano Ave
Cranston, RI 02920-8200, USA

Capuano, Jack (Athlete, Coach, Hockey Player)
c/o Staff Member *Bridgeport Sound Tigers*
600 Main St Ste 1
Bridgeport, CT 06604-5106, USA

Capucill, Terese (Dancer)
440 Lafayette St
New York, NY 10003-6919, USA

Cara, Irene (Actor, Musician)
c/o Betty McCormick *Midwest Talent Management Inc*
4821 Lankershim Blvd Ste F PMB 149
N Hollywood, CA 91601-4572, USA

Carafoli, John F (Stylist)
106 Lexington Ave
New York, NY 10016-8928, USA

Carafotes, Paul (Actor)
8033 W Sunset Blvd # 3554
West Hollywood, CA 90046-2401, USA

Caraman, Alina (Stylist)
c/o Staff Member *Judy Inc*
1 Yorkville Ave
Toronto ON M4W 1L1, Canada

Caramanlis, Costas (Prime Minister)
17 Stissichoros St King George V Ave
Athens, GREECE

Carano, Gina (Crush) (Athlete, Wrestler)
c/o Scott Karp *Crystal Sky Pictures*
10203 Santa Monica Blvd Ste 500
Los Angeles, CA 90067-6416, USA

Carano, Glenn (Athlete, Football Player)
2551 E Lake Ridge Shrs
Reno, NV 89519-5787, USA

Carapella, Alfred (Al) (Athlete, Football Player)
10 Woodlot Rd
Eastchester, NY 10709-1204, USA

Carasco, Joe (King) (Music Group)
2317 Pecan St
Dickinson, TX 77539-4949, USA

Caravello, Joe (Athlete, Football Player)
633 W Palm Ave
El Segundo, CA 90245-2065, USA

Carazo, Odio Rodrigo (Educator, President)
Apdo 199
San Jose, COSTA RICA

Carbajal, Michael (Athlete, Boxer)
PO Box 510
Phoenix, AZ 85001-0510, USA

Carberry, Deirdre (Ballerina)
890 Broadway
New York, NY 10003-1211, USA

Carbo, Bernie (Athlete, Baseball Player)
6352 Woodside Dr S
Theodore, AL 36582-3992, USA

Carbonara, David (Composer, Musician)
c/o Staff Member *Gorfaine/Schwartz Agency Inc*
4111 W Alameda Ave Ste 509
Burbank, CA 91505-4171, USA

Carbonaro, Michael (Actor)
c/o Staff Member *Grapevine Public Relations*
5237 Cahuenga Blvd # 2
N Hollywood, CA 91601-3419, USA

Carbonell, Nestor (Actor)
c/o JB Roberts *Thruline Entertainment*
9250 Wilshire Blvd Ground Fl
Beverly Hills, CA 90212, USA

Carbonneau, Guy (Athlete, Coach, Hockey Player)
c/o Staff Member *Montreal Canadiens*
1275 Rue Saint-Antoine O
Montreal, QB H3C 5L2, Canada

Carcaterra, Lorenzo (Producer, Writer)
c/o Staff Member *Pitt Group, The*
9465 Wilshire Blvd Ste 420
Beverly Hills, CA 90212-2603, USA

Card, Andrew H Jr (Misc, Secretary)
1600 Pennsylvania Ave NW
Washington, DC 20500-0005, USA

Card, Michael (Music Group, Musician)
1143 Dora Whitley Rd
Franklin, TN 37064-4788, USA

Card, Orson Scott (Writer)
PO Box 18184
Greensboro, NC 27419-8184, USA

Cardamone, Richard J (Judge)
10 Broad St
Utica, NY 13501-1233, USA

Cardellini, Linda (Actor)
c/o Pamela Kohl *3 Arts Entertainment Inc*
9460 Wilshire Blvd Fl 7
Beverly Hills, CA 90212-2713, USA

Carden, Joan M (Opera Singer)
596 Saint Kilda Rd # 11
Melbourne, VIC 3004, AUSTRALIA

Cardenal, Jose D (Athlete, Baseball Player)
118 Bridgewater Ct
Bradenton, FL 34212-9302, USA

Cardenas, Leo (Athlete, Baseball Player)
5412 Ravenna St
Cincinnati, OH 45227-1718, USA

Cardich, Augusto (Archaeologist)
Archaeology Dept
La Plata, ARGENTINA

Cardiff, Jack (Cinematographer)
32 Woodland Rise
London N10, UNITED KINGDOM (UK)

Cardigans, The (Music Group)
c/o Staff Member *International Talent Booking (ITB - UK)*
27A Floral St Fl 3 Covent Garden
London WC2E 9, UNITED KINGDOM

Cardille, Lori (Actor)
c/o Tracey Goldblum *Abrams Artists Agency (NY)*
275 7th Ave Fl 26
New York, NY 10001-6708, USA

Cardin, Benjamin L. (Senator)
509 Hart Senate Ofc Building
Washington, DC 20510-0001, USA

Cardin, Claude (Athlete, Hockey Player)
13 Rue Boucher
Sorel-Tracy, QC J3P 1E7, Canada

Cardin, Pierre (Designer, Fashion Designer)
59 Rue du Foubourg-St-Honore
Paris 75008, FRANCE

Cardinahl, Jessika (Actor)
Galerie Am Arkonaplatz Wolliner Str. 11
Berlin D-10435, Germany

Cardinal, Brian (Athlete, Basketball Player)
1680 Lane 105 Lake James
Angola, IN 46703-8533, USA

Cardinal, Conrad (Athlete, Baseball Player)
162 E Hunter Ln
Central, UT 84722-3221, USA

Cardinal, Douglas J (Architect)
7011A Manchester Blvd # 315
Alexandria, VA 22310-3202, USA

Cardinal, Fred (Athlete, Football Player)
1457 Maple St
Barberton, OH 44203-7615, USA

Cardinal, Randy (Baseball Player)
3810 W Verde Way
North Las Vegas, NV 89031-4812, USA

Cardinale, Claudia (Actor)
Via Flaminia Km 77 Prima Porta
Rome 188, ITALY

Cardinalem, Lindsey (Musician)

Cardona, Manolo (Actor)
c/o Nina Shaw *Del Shaw Moonves Tanaka Finkelstein & Lezcano*
2120 Colorado Ave Ste 200
Santa Monica, CA 90404-3561, USA

Cardone, Vivien (Actor)
c/o Staff Member *Persona Management*
40 E 9th St # Suite 11J PMB 11J
New York, NY 10003, USA

Cardos, John Bud (Director)
PO Box 7430
Burbank, CA 91510-7430, USA

Cardosa, Patricia (Director)
c/o Staff Member *International Creative Management (ICM-LA)*
10250 Constellation Blvd Fl 7
Los Angeles, CA 90067-6207, USA

Cardoso, Fernando (Ex-President, Politician)
Rua Formosa, 367 6º andar, Centro
San Paulo 01049-000, Brazil

Cardoso, Patricia (Director)
c/o Rosalie Swedlin *Anonymous Content (AC-LA)*
3531 Hayden Ave
Culver City, CA 90232, USA

Cardoza, Dennis (Congressman, Politician)
2437 Rayburn Hob
Washington, DC 20515-1010, USA

Cardwell, Don (Athlete, Baseball Player)
PO Box 454
Clemmons, NC 27012-0454, USA

Care, Peter (Cinematographer, Director, Writer)
1313 5th St
Santa Monica, CA 90401-1414, USA

Carell, Steve (Actor)
c/o Steve Sauer *Media Four*
8840 Wilshire Blvd Fl 2
Beverly Hills, CA 90211-2606, USA

Carelli, Rick (Race Car Driver)
PO Box 1000
Arvada, CO 80001-1000, USA

Carenard, Brian (Saigon) (Musician)
86-110 Orchard St Ste 2
Hackensack, NJ 07601-4833, USA

Caretto-Brown, Patty (Swimmer)
16079 Mesquite Cir
Santa Ana, CA 92708-1513, USA

Carew, Drew (Actor, Comedian)
955 Carrillo Dr Ste 100
Los Angeles, CA 90048-5400, USA

Carew, Rod (Athlete, Baseball Player)
1171 Via Santiago
Corona, CA 92882 3950, USA

Carey, Clare (Actor)
c/o Steven Jensen *Independent Group, The*
6363 Wilshire Blvd Ste 115
Los Angeles, CA 90048-5734, USA

Carey, Drew (Actor, Comedian)
c/o Rick Messina *Messina Baker/ Entertainment*
955 Carrillo Dr Ste 100
Los Angeles, CA 90048-5400, USA

Carey, Duane G (Astronaut)
5938 Instone Cir
Colorado Springs, CO 80922-1716, USA

Carey, Ezekiel (Music Group)
509 E Ridgecrest Blvd Apt A
Ridgecrest, CA 93555-3959, USA

Carey, George (Religious Leader)
Chancellors Office
Cheltenham GL50 2RH, UNITED KINGDOM

Carey, Marey (Adult Film Star)
19800 Nordhoff Pl
Chatsworth, CA 91311-6607, USA

Carey, Mariah (Musician, Songwriter)
c/o Chris Lighty *Violator Management*
36 W 25th St Fl 11
New York, NY 10010-2752, USA

Carey, Mary (Adult Film Star, Reality TV Star)

Carey, Matthew Thomas (Actor)
c/o Abby Bluestone *Innovative Artists (LA)*
1505 10th St
Santa Monica, CA 90401-2805, USA

Carey, Michelle (Actor)
733 Seward St PH
Los Angeles, CA 90038-3503, USA

Carey, Paul (Athlete, Baseball Player)
5334 Olive Ave
Sarasota, FL 34231-2510, USA

Carey, Peter (Writer)
40 W 57th St # 1800
New York, NY 10019-4001, USA

Carey, Rick (Athlete, Swimmer)
119 Rockland Ave
Larchmont, NY 10538-1430, USA

Carey, Tony (Musician)
BMG Postfach 800149
Munich D-81601, Germany

Carey, Vernon (Athlete, Football Player)
16875 Stratford Ct
Southwest Ranches, FL 33331-1362, USA

Carey Jr, Harry (Actor)
3775 Modoc Rd Apt 43
Santa Barbara, CA 93105-4460, USA

Cargo, David F (Ex-Governor)
6422 Concordia Rd NE
Albuquerque, NM 87111-1228, USA

Carides, Gia (Actor)
397 Riley St
Surrey Hills, NSW 2010, AUSTRALIA

Caridis, Miltiades (Conductor)
Himmelhofgasse 10
Vienna 1130, AUSTRIA

Carillo, Mary (Sportscaster)
822 Boylston St Ste 203
Chestnut Hill, MA 02467-2504, USA

Carimi, Gabe (Football Player)
c/o Gary Uberstine *Premier Sports Management*
1401 Ocean Ave Ste 302
Santa Monica, CA 90401-2161, USA

Cariou, Len (Actor)
c/o Clifford Stevens *Paradigm (NY)*
360 Park Ave S Fl 16
New York, NY 10010-1708, USA

Carithers, William Jr (Physicist)
PO Box 500
Batavia, IL 60510-5011, USA

Carius, Otto (War Hero)
Hauptstr. 77
Herschweiler-Pettersheim 66909, GERMANY

Carkner, Terry (Athlete, Hockey Player)
4 Remington Ln
Malvern, PA 19355-2896, USA

Carl, Harland (Athlete, Football Player)
1419 N Douglas St
Appleton, WI 54914-2517, USA

Carl, Jann (Television Host)
c/o Staff Member *Entertainment Tonight (ET)*
4024 Radford Ave
Studio City, CA 91604-2101, USA

Carl XVI, Gustaf (King)
Kungliga Slottet Slottsbacken
Stockholm 111 30, SWEDEN

Carle, Eric (Artist)
PO Box 485
Northampton, MA 01061-0485, USA

Carlei, Carlo (Director, Writer)
c/o Staff Member *Creative Artists Agency (CAA-LA)*
2000 Avenue of the Stars Ste 100
Los Angeles, CA 90067-4705, USA

Carles Gordo, Ricardo M Cardinal (Religious Leader)
Carrer del Bisbe 5
Barcelona 8002, SPAIN

Carlesimo, Pete J (P J) (Athlete, Basketball Player, Coach, Sportscaster)
1429 Willard Ave W
Seattle, WA 98119-3250, USA

Carlestrom, John E (Astronomer)
5640 S Ellis Ave
Chicago, IL 60637-1433, USA

Carleton, Wayne (Athlete, Hockey Player)
9846 HWY 26 RR 2 LCD
COLLINGWOOD E
Sollingwood, ON L9Y 3Z1, Canada

Carlile, Brandi (Musician)
c/o Staff Member *Paradigm (Monterey)*
404 W Franklin St
Monterey, CA 93940-2303, USA

Carlile, Forbes (Coach, Swimmer)
16 Cross St
Ryde, NSW 2112, AUSTRALIA

Carlin, Brian (Athlete, Hockey Player)
103 Mt Norquay Pk SE
Calgary, AB T2Z 2R3, Canada

Carlin, John W (Ex-Governor)
1208 Wyndham Heights Dr
Manhattan, KS 66503-8676, USA

Carlin, Thomas R (Publisher)
Publisher's Office 345 Cdear
Saint Paul, MN 55101, USA

Carlin, Vidal (Athlete, Football Player)
930 Palm Ave Apt 417
West Hollywood, CA 90069-4080, USA

Carling, William D C (Athlete, Misc, Sportscaster)
22 Suffolk St
London SW1Y 4HG, UNITED KINGDOM (UK)

Carlino, Lewis John (Director, Writer)
991 Oakmont St
Los Angeles, CA 90049-2228, USA

Carlisie, Rick (Basketball Player)
RR 4
Ogdensburg, NY 13669, USA

Carlisle, Belinda (Musician, Songwriter)
c/o Carlos Keyes *Red Entertainment Agency*
16 Penn Plz Ste 824
New York, NY 10001-1809, USA

Carlisle, Cooper (Athlete, Football Player)
2032 Sorrelwood Ct
San Ramon, CA 94582-5004, USA

Carlisle, James B (Ex-Governor)
POB W1644
Saint John's, Antigua

Carlisle, Jennifer (Stylist)
c/o Staff Member *Celestine - CA*
1666 20th St Ste 200B
Santa Monica, CA 90404-3828, USA

Carlisle, Jodi (Actor, Comedian)
c/o Staff Member *International Creative Management (ICM-LA)*
10250 Constellation Blvd Fl 7
Los Angeles, CA 90067-6207, USA

Carlisle, Mary (Actor)
517 N Rodeo Dr
Beverly Hills, CA 90210-3206, USA

Carlisle, Rick (Athlete, Basketball Player, Coach)
Route 4
Ogdensburg, NY 13669, USA

Carlos, Francisco (Cisco) (Athlete, Baseball Player)
6027 N 7th St
Phoenix, AZ 85014-1802, USA

Carlos, John (Athlete, Track Athlete)
68640 Tortuga Rd
Cathedral City, CA 92234-3874, USA

Carlos, Jordan (Musician)
c/o Staff Member *Paradigm (Monterey)*
404 W Franklin St
Monterey, CA 93940-2303, USA

Carlos I, Juan (King)
Madrid 28671, SPAIN

Carlos Moco, Marcolino Jose (Prime Minister)
Luanda, ANGOLA

Carlot, Maxime (Prime Minister)
P O Box 698
Port Vila, VANUATU

Carlson, Amy (Actor)
c/o Darris Hatch *Daris Hatch Management*
10027 Rossbury Pl
Los Angeles, CA 90064-4825, USA

Carlson, Arne H (Ex-Governor)
95 N Marion Ct Unit 136
Punta Gorda, FL 33950-5038, USA

Carlson, Cody (Athlete, Football Player)
3417 Foothill Ter
Austin, TX 78731-5826, USA

Carlson, Dan (Athlete, Baseball Player)
334 N Wickford Cir
Shreveport, LA 71115-2935, USA

Carlson, Dudley L (Admiral)
2300 Wilson Blvd
Arlington, VA 22201-5424, USA

Carlson, Gretchen (Television Host)
c/o Staff Member *Fox News Channel (NY)*
1211 Ave Of The Americas Level C1
New York, NY 10036-8701, USA

Carlson, Jack (Athlete, Hockey Player)
3870 Bridgewater Dr
Saint Paul, MN 55123-2529, USA

Carlson, Jack W (Misc)
1901 K St NW
Washington, DC 20006, USA

Carlson, Jeff (Athlete, Football Player)
3542 Ballastone Dr
Land O Lakes, FL 34638-8067, USA

Carlson, John (Athlete, Golfer)
c/o Jim Lehrman *SFX Golf*
36855 W Main St Ste 200
Purcellville, VA 20132-3561, USA

Carlson, K C (Cartoonist)
1700 Broadway
New York, NY 10019-5905, USA

Carlson, Karen (Actor)
3700 Ventura Canyon Ave
Sherman Oaks, CA 91423-4709, USA

Carlson, Katrina (Actor)
c/o Staff Member *Sara Bennett Agency*
6404 Hollywood Blvd Ste 316
Los Angeles, CA 90028-6244, USA

Carlson, Kelly (Actor)
c/o Margot Klar *Cunningham Escott Slevin & Doherty (CESD-LA)*
10635 Santa Monica Blvd Ste 130
Los Angeles, CA 90025-8306, USA

Carlson, Kent (Athlete, Hockey Player)
58 Branch Tpke Unit 103
Concord, NH 03301-5779, USA

Carlson, Mark (Athlete, Baseball Player)
354 Tall Oak Trl
Tarpon Springs, FL 34688-7711, USA

Carlson, Paulette (Music Group)
250 W 57th St Bldg 1830
New York, NY 10107-0001, USA

Carlson, Richard (Writer)
613 Moore Bldg
University Park, PA 16802-3106

Carlson, Steve (Race Car Driver)
539 Brickl Rd
West Salem, WI 54669-1177, USA

Carlson, Steve (Athlete, Hockey Player)
PO Box 592
Bethpage, NY 11714-0592, USA

Carlson, Stuart (Cartoonist)
4520 Main St
Kansas City, MO 64111-1876, USA

Carlson, Tucker (Television Host)
c/o Staff Member *MSNBC (NJ)*
NBC/One Microsoft Corporation 1 MSNC Plaza
Secaucus, NJ 7094, USA

Carlson, Vanessa (Musician)
c/o Kurt Steffek *Razor & Tie*
PO Box 585
New York, NY 10276-0585, USA

Carlson, Veronica (Actor)
7844 Kavanagh Ct
Sarasota, FL 34240-7906, USA

Carlsson, Arvid (Nobel Prize Laureate)
P O Box 100
Gotheburg 405 30, SWEDEN

Carlsson, Ingvar G (Prime Minister)
Riksdagen
Stockholm 100 12, SWEDEN

Carlton, Carl (Musician)
Oakland
Inkster, MI 48141, USA

Carlton, Larry (Musician)
c/o Staff Member *Paradigm (Monterey)*
404 W Franklin St
Monterey, CA 93940-2303, USA

Carlton, Paul K (General)
1716 Briescrest Dr # 702
Bryan, TX 77802, USA

Carlton, Steven N (Steve) (Athlete, Baseball Player)
555 S Camino Del Rio Ste B2
Durango, CO 81303-6852, USA

Carlton, Vanessa (Musician)
c/o Mitch Rose *Creative Artists Agency (CAA-LA)*
2000 Avenue of the Stars Ste 100
Los Angeles, CA 90067-4705, USA

Carlton, Venessa (Music Group)
410 Park Ave Ste 420
New York, NY 10022-9459, USA

Carlton, Wray (Athlete, Football Player)
29 Pine Ter
Orchard Park, NY 14127-3929, USA

Carlucci, Dave (Music Group)
PO Box 1017
Blackwood, NJ 08012-0837, USA

Carlucci, Frank C
1001 Pennsylvania Ave NW
Washington, DC 20004-2502, USA

Carlucci, Frank C III (Business Person, Secretary)
1001 Pennsylvania Ave NW
Washington, DC 20004-2502, USA

Carlyle, Buddy (Athlete, Baseball Player)
205 Ashmere Ct
Tyrone, GA 30290-2845, USA

Carlyle, Joan H (Opera Singer)
Laundry Cottage Hammer
North Wales SY13 4QX, UNITED KINGDOM (UK)

Carlyle, Randy (Athlete, Coach, Hockey Player)
180 S Lakeview Ave
Anaheim, CA 92807-3606, USA

Carlyle, Robert (Actor)
c/o Jon Rubinstein *Authentic Talent and Literary Management*
45 Main St Ste 1004
Brooklyn, NY 11201-8200, USA

Carmack, Chris (Actor)
c/o Theodore B Gekis *Gekis Management*
4217 Verdugo View Dr
Los Angeles, CA 90065-4317, USA

Carman, Don (Athlete, Baseball Player)
1560 Bluefin Ct
Naples, FL 34102-1576, USA

Carman, Gregory W (Judge)
1 Federal Plz
New York, NY 10278-0001, USA

Carman, Patrick (Writer)
1247 Studebaker Dr
Walla Walla, WA 99362-8845, USA

Carmazzi, Giovanni (Athlete, Football Player)
9401 Cook Riolo Rd
Roseville, CA 95747-9221, USA

Carmel, Leon (duke) (Athlete, Baseball Player)
10 Pheasant Valley Dr
Coram, NY 11727-2320, USA

Carmen, Eric (Music Group, Songwriter, Writer)
1679 S Belvoir Blvd
South Euclid, OH 44121-3773, USA

Carmen, Jeanne (Actor, Model)
PO Box 11812
Newport Beach, CA 92658-5042, USA

Carmen, Julie (Actor)

Carmichael, Al (Athlete, Football Player)
78641 Hampshire Ave
Palm Desert, CA 92211-1960, USA

Carmichael, Greg (Musician)
200 W Superior St Ste 202
Chicago, IL 60654-3554, USA

Carmichael, Ian (Actor)
2-4 Noel St
London W1V 3RB, UNITED KINGDOM (UK)

Carmichael, L Harold (Athlete, Football Player)
38 Birch Ln
Glassboro, NJ 08028-2821, USA

Carmichael, Paul (Athlete, Football Player)
550 Orange Ave Unit 335
Long Beach, CA 90802-7011, USA

Carmichael, Ricky (Motorcycle Racer)
1919 Torrance Blvd Motorcycle Sports 100-4C-3B
Torrance, CA 90501-2722, USA

Carmindy (Stylist, Television Host)
156 5th Ave Ste 420
New York, NY 10010-7794, USA

Carmine, Michael (Cinematographer)
3615 West Dr
Douglaston, NY 11363-1243, USA

Carmine, Robert (Musician)
c/o Staff Member *Geffen Records*
9126 Sunset Blvd
West Hollywood, CA 90069, USA

Carmody, Steve (Athlete, Football Player)
PO Box 119
Jackson, MS 39205-0119, USA

Carmona, Richard H (Government Official, Misc, Physicist)
200 Independence Ave SW
Washington, DC 20201-0004, USA

Carn, Jean (Musician)
PO Box 27641
Philadelphia, PA 19118-0641, USA

Carnahan, Joe (Director)
c/o Staff Member *WmE2 (Endeavor-LA)*
9601 Wilshire Blvd Fl 3
Beverly Hills, CA 90210-5219, USA

Carnahan, Russ (Congressman, Politician)
1710 Longworth Hob
Washington, DC 20515-3206, USA

Carne, Jean (Music Group)
PO Box 27641
Philadelphia, PA 19118-0641, USA

Carne, Judy (Actor, Comedian)
2 Horatio St Apt 10N
New York, NY 10014-1632, USA

Carnegie, Dale (Business Person)
290 Motor Pkwy
Hauppauge, NY 11788-5177, USA

Carnelly, Ray (Athlete, Football Player)
4650 Collier St Apt 135
Beaumont, TX 77706-6999, USA

Carner, Joanne (Athlete, Golfer)
3030 S Ocean Blvd Apt 325
Palm Beach, FL 33480-6610, USA

Carnes, Kim (Music Group, Songwriter, Writer)
1829 Tyne Blvd
Nashville, TN 37215-4701, USA

Carnes, Ryan (Actor)
c/o Jon Simmons *Simmons & Scott Entertainment*
7942 Mulholland Dr
Los Angeles, CA 90046-1225, USA

Carnesale, Albert (Educator)
Chancellor's Office
Los Angeles, CA 90024, USA

Carnesecca, Lou (Athlete, Basketball Player, Coach)
18247 Midland Pkwy
Jamaica, NY 11432-1535, USA

Carnett, Eddie (Athlete, Baseball Player)
RR 1 Box 20C
Ringling, OK 73456-9701, USA

Carnevale, Bernard L (Ben) (Athlete, Basketball Player, Coach)
3055 Larkspur Run
Williamsburg, VA 23185, USA

Carnevale, Mark (Athlete, Golfer)
24 Loggerhead Ln
Ponte Vedra Beach, FL 32082-2581, USA

Carney, John M (Athlete, Football Player)
2950 Wishbone Way
Encinitas, CA 92024-7235, USA

Carney, Keith (Athlete, Hockey Player)
8701 N 55th Pl
Paradise Valley, AZ 85253-2107, USA

Carney, Reeve (Musician)
c/o Staff Member *Paradigm (Monterey)*
404 W Franklin St
Monterey, CA 93940-2303, USA

Carney, Robert (Athlete, Basketball Player)
2 Cypress Pt
Pekin, IL 61554-2620, USA

Carney, Thomas P (General)
9806 Kirktree Ct
Fairfax, VA 22032-1059, USA

Carns, Michael P C (Mike) (General)
966 Coral Dr
Pebble Beach, CA 93953-2503, USA

Caro, Anthony A (Artist, Misc)
111 Frognal Hampstead
London NW3, UNITED KINGDOM (UK)

Caro, Niki (Director, Writer)
c/o Sophy Holodnik *International Creative Management (ICM-LA)*
10250 Constellation Blvd Fl 7
Los Angeles, CA 90067-6207, USA

Caro, Robert A (Writer)
250 W 57th St
New York, NY 10107-0001, USA

Carolan, Brett (Athlete, Football Player)
3218 43rd Ave W
Seattle, WA 98199-2437, USA

Caroline, James C (J C) (Athlete, Football Player)
2501 Stanford Dr
Champaign, IL 61820-7634, USA

Carolla, Adam (Radio Personality, Talk Show Host)
c/o Staff Member *Jackhole Industries*
6834 Hollywood Blvd
Los Angeles, CA 90028-6116, USA

Carollo, Joe (Athlete, Football Player)
4634 Meyer Way
Carmichael, CA 95608-1144, USA

Carolyn, Avelino (Stylist)
c/o Staff Member *CL Avelino & Associates*
152 N Singingwood St Unit 1
Orange, CA 92869-3153, USA

Caron, Jacques (Athlete, Hockey Player)
6426 Moorings Point Cir Unit 201
Lakewood Ranch, FL 34202-1204, USA

Caron, Jason (Athlete, Golfer)
150 Silo Ridge Ln
Vilas, NC 28692-3002, USA

Caron, Leslie (Actor, Dancer)
c/o Staff Member *The Rights House (UK)*
Drury House 34-43 Russell St
London WC2B 5HA, UK

Caron, Roger (Athlete, Football Player)
71 School St
Williamstown, MA 01267-2411, USA

Carothers, Don (Athlete, Football Player)
1405 Cedar Dr
Traverse City, MI 49685-8104, USA

Carothers, Robert L (Educator)
President's Office
Kingston, RI 2881, USA

Carothers, Veronica (Actor)
535 N Heatherstone Dr
Orange, CA 92869-2648, USA

Carpendale, Howard (Actor, Composer)
200 Admirals Cove Blvd
Jupiter, FL 33477-4046, USA

Carpenter, Bob
205 S Princeton Ave
Arlington Heights, IL 60005-1666, USA

Carpenter, Bob (Bobby) (Athlete, Hockey Player)
71 Chestnut St
North Reading, MA 01864-2823, USA

Carpenter, Bobby (Athlete, Football Player)
2396 Andover Rd
Columbus, OH 43221-3744, USA

Carpenter, Bubba (Athlete, Baseball Player)
4601 Saddlebrook Ave
Springdale, AR 72762-0503, USA

Carpenter, Carleton (Actor)
RR 2 Chardavoyne Road
Warwick, NY 10990, USA

Carpenter, Chad (Athlete, Football Player)
21311 S 187th Way
Queen Creek, AZ 85142-3668, USA

Carpenter, Charisma (Actor, Model)
c/o John Carrabino *John Carrabino Management*
5900 Wilshire Blvd Ste 406
Los Angeles, CA 90036-5015, USA

Carpenter, Chris (Athlete, Baseball Player)
809 S Warson Rd
Saint Louis, MO 63124-1258, USA

Carpenter, Cris (Athlete, Baseball Player)
1484 Heritage Pl
Gainesville, GA 30501-1249, USA

Carpenter, Dave (Cartoonist, Editor)
PO Box 520
Emmetsburg, IA 50536-0520, USA

Carpenter, George (War Hero)
1010 Green Hill Dr
Paris, TN 38242-5226, USA

Carpenter, James (Football Player)
c/o Ken Zuckerman *Priority Sports & Entertainment - (LA)*
15233 Ventura Blvd Ste 718
Sherman Oaks, CA 91403-2237, USA

Carpenter, Jennifer (Actor)
c/o Stephanie Ritz *WmE2 (Endeavor-LA)*
9601 Wilshire Blvd Fl 3
Beverly Hills, CA 90210-5219, USA

Carpenter, John (Director)
c/o Jim Wiatt *WmE2 (Endeavor-LA)*
9601 Wilshire Blvd Fl 3
Beverly Hills, CA 90210-5219, USA

Carpenter, John M (Opera Singer)
225 W 34th St Ste 1012
New York, NY 10122-1012, USA

Carpenter, Keion (Athlete, Football Player)
2009 Shin Ct
Buford, GA 30519-6808, USA

Carpenter, Ken (Athlete, Football Player)
20 Necanicum Dr Apt 11
Seaside, Oregon 97138, USA

Carpenter, Kip (Speed Skater)
W375S10897 Prairie Ln
Eagle, WI 53119-1742, USA

Carpenter, Lewis (Lew) (Athlete, Football Player)
1743 Rolling Rapids Dr
New Braunfels, TX 78130-3056, USA

Carpenter, Liz (Activist)
1 Rockefeller Dr
Morrilton, AR 72110-9337, USA

Carpenter, M Scott (Astronaut)
PO Box 3161
Vail, CO 81658-3161, USA

Carpenter, Marj C (Religious Leader)
100 Witherspoon St
Louisville, KY 40202-1396, USA

Carpenter, Mary Chapin (Musician)
c/o Staff Member *Paradigm (Monterey)*
404 W Franklin St
Monterey, CA 93940-2303, USA

Carpenter, Patrick (Race Car Driver)
2015 Peel # 500
Montreal, PQ H3A 1T8, CANADA

Carpenter, Preston (Athlete, Football Player)
2205 W Memphis St
Broken Arrow, OK 74012-4626, USA

Carpenter, Richard (Musician, Songwriter, Writer)
960 Country Valley Rd
Westlake Village, CA 91362-5631, USA

Carpenter, Rob (Athlete, Football Player)
1601 Wheeling Rd NE
Lancaster, OH 43130-8706, USA

Carpenter, Ron (Athlete, Football Player)
1500 Wade Haven Ct
McKinney, TX 75071-5985, USA

Carpenter, Ron (Athlete, Football Player)
1181 Chersonese Round
Mount Pleasant, SC 29464-9544, USA

Carpenter, Russell P (Cinematographer)
232 N Canon Dr
Beverly Hills, CA 90210-5302, USA

Carpenter, Teresa (Journalist)
36 Cooper Sq
New York, NY 10003-7118, USA

Carpenter, W M (Business Person)
36 Knollwood Dr
Rochester, NY 14618-3513, USA

Carpenter, William S (Bill) Jr (Athlete, Football Player)
PO Box 4067
Whitefish, MT 59937-4067, USA

Carper, Thomas R. (Senator)
513 Hart Senate Ofc Building
Washington, DC 20510-0001, USA

Carpin, Frank (Athlete, Baseball Player)
4014 Park Ave
Richmond, VA 23221-1120, USA

Carpinello, James (Actor)
c/o Greg Clark *Untitled Entertainment (LA)*
350 S Beverly Dr Ste 200
Beverly Hills, CA 90212-4819, USA

Carpitella, John J III (Stylist)
1816 Adams Way
Jamison, PA 18929-1797, USA

Carr, Alan (Actor, Writer)
c/o Staff Member *Off The Kerb Productions*
Hammer House, 3rd Fl 113-117 Wardour St
London W1F 0UN, UK

Carr, Antoine (Athlete, Basketball Player)
5724 Croyden Cir
Wichita, KS 67220-3119, USA

Carr, Austin (Athlete, Basketball Player)
4547 Saint Germain Blvd
Cleveland, OH 44128-6205, USA

Carr, Catherine (Cathy) (Swimmer)
409 10th St
Davis, CA 95616-1941, USA

Carr, Charmian (Actor)
PO Box 260584
Encino, CA 91426-0584, USA

Carr, Chuck (Athlete, Baseball Player)
5419 E Greenway St
Mesa, AZ 85205-4360, USA

Carr, Darleen (Actor)
9200 W Sunset Blvd Ste 1125
Los Angeles, CA 90069-3610, USA

Carr, David (Athlete, Football Player)
c/o Jeff Sperbeck *The Novo Agency*
2121 N California Blvd Ste 1025
Walnut Creek, CA 94596-7101, USA

Carr, Eddie (Athlete, Football Player)
7843 Barclay Rd
New Port Richey, FL 34654-6004, USA

Carr, Edwin (Athlete, Football Player)
1908 Scott Rd
Oreland, PA 19075-1519, USA

Carr, Fred (Athlete, Football Player)
6274 S 17th Pl
Phoenix, AZ 85042-4568, USA

Carr, Gene (Athlete, Hockey Player)
PO Box 57258
Sherman Oaks, CA 91413-2258, USA

Carr, Gerald (Astronaut)
49 Maple St Apt 123
Manchester Center, VT 05255-4485, USA

Carr, Gregg (Athlete, Football Player)
4314 Kennesaw Dr
Mountain Brk, AL 35213-3312, USA

Carr, Henry (Athlete, Football Player, Track Athlete)
10037 Riverdale
Redford, MI 48239-1473, USA

Carr, James H (Athlete, Football Player)
13718 Indigo Ln
Fishers, IN 46038-8307, USA

Carr, Jane (Actor)
6200 Mount Angelus Dr
Los Angeles, CA 90042-3526, USA

Carr, Jimmy (Actor)
c/o Staff Member *WmE2 (WMA-LA)*
1 William Morris Pl
Beverly Hills, CA 90212-4261, USA

Carr, Kenneth M (Admiral)
38 Atlantic Ave
Groton, CT 06340-8801, USA

Carr, Kenny (Athlete, Basketball Player)
24421 SW Valley View Rd
West Linn, OR 97068-9632, USA

Carr, Levert (Athlete, Football Player)
169 Brookwood Ln W
Bolingbrook, IL 60440-5508, USA

Carr, Lloyd (Coach)
Athletic Dept
Ann Arbor, MI 48109, USA

Carr, Lydell (Athlete, Football Player)
2217 Harrisburg Ln
Plano, TX 75025-5515, USA

Carr, M L (Basketball Player)
168 Beaver Rd
Weston, MA 02493-1036, USA

Carr, Michael L (M L) (Athlete, Basketball Player, Coach)
168 Beaver Rd
Weston, MA 02493-1036, USA

Carr, Roger D (Athlete, Football Player)
101 Green Forest Dr
Monroe, LA 71203-8860, USA

Carr, Steve (Director, Producer)
c/o Nicole Chabot *PMK/BNC - LA*
8687 Melrose Ave Ste 8
West Hollywood, CA 90069-5746, USA

Carr, Vikki (Actor, Musician)
10370 Michael Todd Ter
Glenview, IL 60025-3747, USA

Carr of Hadley, L Robert (Government Official)
14 North Court Great Peter St
London SW1 3LL, UNITED KINGDOM (UK)

Carrabba, Chris (Musician)
c/o Richard Egan *Hard 8 Management*
1000 Main St Ste 203
Nashville, TN 37206-3626, USA

Carrack, Paul (Musician, Songwriter, Writer)
14724 Ventura Blvd PH
Sherman Oaks, CA 91403-3513, USA

Carradine, Ever (Actor)
c/o Lainie Sorkin Becky *Management 360*
9111 Wilshire Blvd
Beverly Hills, CA 90210-5508, USA

Carradine, Keith (Actor, Musician, Songwriter)
c/o John Bauer *John Bauer Management*
1420 NW Gilman Blvd # 2335
Everett, WA 98207-0001, USA

Carradine, Robert (Actor, Director, Producer)
c/o Staff Member *Marshak/Zachary Company, The*
8840 Wilshire Blvd Fl 1
Beverly Hills, CA 90211-2606, USA

Carragher, Jamie (Soccer Player)
25 Soho Square
London W1D 4FA, UNITED KINGDOM

Carrasco, D J (Athlete, Baseball Player)
2365 Claret Ave
Hanford, CA 93230-8151, USA

Carre, Isabelle (Actor)
c/o Staff Member *Agence Intertalent*
5 Rue Gay Lusac
Paris 75008, France

Carreira, Tony (Composer, Musician)
Rua Helena Felix N 30 4 Esq
Palhais, Charneca Da Caparica 2820-595, Portugal

Carreker, Alphonso (Athlete, Football Player)
5599 Asheforde Ln
Marietta, GA 30068-1851, USA

Carrelas, Gina (Stylist)
c/o Staff Member *Help Me Rhonda*
541 10th St NW # 294
Atlanta, GA 30318-5713, USA

Carrell, Duane (Athlete, Football Player)
6525 Willow Springs Rd
Springfield, IL 62712-9501, USA

Carrell, John (Athlete, Football Player)
2303 Cliffs Edge Dr
Austin, TX 78733-6031, USA

Carreno, J Manuel (Ballerina)
Covent Garden Bow St
London WC2E 9DD, USA

Carreon, Mark (Athlete, Baseball Player)
1034 Hutson Cir
Summit, MS 39666-9152, USA

Carrera, Asia (Adult Film Star)
c/o Staff Member *Atlas Multimedia Inc*
9005 Eton Ave Ste C
Canoga Park, CA 91304-6533, USA

Carrera, Barbara (Actor)
412 N Oakhurst Dr Apt 200
Beverly Hills, CA 90210-4039, USA

Carrera, Carlos (Director)
c/o Staff Member *Creative Artists Agency (CAA-LA)*
2000 Avenue of the Stars Ste 100
Los Angeles, CA 90067-4705, USA

Carreras, Jose (Opera Singer)
c/o Darcy Gregoire *Agency Group Ltd, The (Canada)*
2 Berkeley Street Suite 202
Toronto M5A 4J5, Canada

Carrere, Tia (Actor, Model, Producer)
c/o Gordon Gilbertson *Gilbertson Management*
1334 3rd Street Promenade Ste 201
Santa Monica, CA 90401-1320, USA

Carretto, Joseph A Jr (Astronaut)
4534 E 85th St
Tulsa, OK 74137-1918, USA

Carrey, Jim (Actor, Comedian)
c/o Jimmy Miller *Mosaic Media Group*
9200 W Sunset Blvd Ste 10
Los Angeles, CA 90069-3608, USA

Carrick, Michael (Soccer Player)
25 Soho Square
London W1D 4FA, UNITED KINGDOM

Carrier, Darel (Athlete, Basketball Player)
4224 Glasgow Rd
Oakland, KY 42159-6836, USA

Carrier, George F (Mathematician)
PO Box 5039
Wayland, MA 01778-6039, USA

Carrier, Mark A (Athlete, Football Player)
81 Southern Blvd
Chatham, NJ 07928-1336, USA

Carriere, Jean P J (Writer)
Les Broussanes Domessargues
Ledignan 30350, FRANCE

Carriere, Larry (Athlete, Hockey Player)
94 Dawnbrook Ln
Buffalo, NY 14221-4932, USA

Carriere, Mathieu (Actor)
Friesenstr 53
Cologne 50670, GERMANY

Carrigan, Sam (Athlete, Baseball Player)
607 Sunrise Ave
Alamogordo, NM 88310-4144, USA

Carril, Pete (Athlete, Basketball Player, Coach)
372 Carter Rd
Princeton, NJ 08540-7422, USA

Carrillo, Elpidia (Actor)
11500 W Olympic Blvd Ste 510
Los Angeles, CA 90064-1527, USA

Carrillo, Erick (Actor)
c/o Staff Member *Three Moons Entertainment Inc*
7040F W Sunset Blvd # 206
Los Angeles, CA 90028-7521, USA

Carrillo, Yadhira (Actor)
c/o Staff Member *Televisa*
Blvd Adolfo Lopez Mateos 232 Colonia
San Angel INN
DF CP 01060, MEXICO

Carrington, Alan (Misc)
46 Lakewood Road Chandler's Ford
Hants SO53 1EX, UNITED KINGDOM (UK)

Carrington, Alex (Athlete, Football Player)
c/o Roosevelt Barnes *Maximum Sports Management*
6435 W Jefferson Blvd # 197
Fort Wayne, IN 46804-6203, USA

Carrington, Bob (Athlete, Basketball Player)
PO Box 131301
Carlsbad, CA 92013-1301, USA

Carrington, Chuck (Actor)
c/o Kate Edwards *Grand View Management*
578 Washington Blvd # 688
Marina Del Rey, CA 90292-5442, USA

Carrington, Darren (Athlete, Football Player)
14097 Montfort Ct
San Diego, CA 92128-4283, USA

Carrington, Debbie Lee (Actor)
8147 Tunney Ave
Reseda, CA 91335-1042, USA

Carrington, Paul (Attorney, Educator)
Law School
Durham, NC 27708-0001, USA

Carrington, Peter A R (Government Official)
Manor House Bledlow near Aylesbury
Bucks HP17 9PE, UNITED KINGDOM (UK)

Carrithers, Don (Athlete, Baseball Player)
9367 Sunny Glade Ct
Elk Grove, CA 95758-4208, USA

Carroll, Billy (Athlete, Hockey Player)
239 Station St
Ajax, ON L1S 1S3, Canada

Carroll, Brian (Buckethead) (Musician)
915C W Foothill Blvd Ste 545
Claremont, CA 91711-3304, USA

Carroll, Bruce (Musician, Songwriter, Writer)
2100 W End Ave Ste 1000
Nashville, TN 37203-5240, USA

Carroll, Clay P (Athlete, Baseball Player)
3052 22nd St
Sarasota, FL 34234-8742, USA

Carroll, Diahann (Actor, Musician)
c/o Staff Member *Cunningham Escott Slevin & Doherty (CESD-LA)*
10635 Santa Monica Blvd Ste 130
Los Angeles, CA 90025-8306, USA

Carroll, Earl (Speedo) (Musician)
180 W 78th St
New York, NY 10024, USA

Carroll, Earl W (Misc)
PO Box 239
Hermitage, TN 37076-0239, USA

Carroll, James (Athlete, Football Player)
13880 Stirling Rd
Southwest Ranches, FL 33330-3019, USA

Carroll, Jamey (Athlete, Baseball Player)
503 Dogwood Dr
Wylie, TX 75098-3851, USA

Carroll, Jay (Athlete, Football Player)
117 Homedale Rd
Hopkins, MN 55343-8519, USA

Carroll, Joe (Athlete, Football Player)
4541 Fairfield St
Pittsburgh, PA 15201-2031, USA

Carroll, Joe Barry (Athlete, Basketball Player)
5220 Cascade Rd SW
Atlanta, GA 30331-7358, USA

Carroll, John B (Misc)
2158 Penrose Ln
Fairbanks, AK 99709-6213, USA

Carroll, Kent J (Admiral)
1600 Morganton Rd Unit 30X
Pinehurst, NC 28374-6890, USA

Carroll, Leo (Athlete, Football Player)
34448 Agua Dulce Canyon Rd
Santa Clarita, CA 91390-4668, USA

Carroll, Lester (Les) (Cartoonist)
1715 Ivyhill Loop N
Columbus, OH 43229-5223, USA

Carroll, Madeline (Actor)
c/o Susan Curtis *Curtis Talent Management*
9607 Arby Dr
Beverly Hills, CA 90210-1202, USA

Carroll, Matt (Athlete, Basketball Player)
201 General Hancock Blvd
North Wales, PA 19454-1478, USA

Carroll, Pat (Actor)
c/o Gabrielle Allabashi *Ellis Talent Group*
4705 Laurel Canyon Blvd Ste 300
Valley Village, CA 91607-5901, USA

Carroll, Pete (Athlete, Coach, Football Coach, Football Player)
Heritage Hall
Los Angeles, CA 90089-0001, USA

Carroll, Rocky (Actor)
c/o Staff Member *Innovative Artists (LA)*
1505 10th St
Santa Monica, CA 90401-2805, USA

Carroll, Ron (Ronnie) (Athlete, Football Player)
3320 La Vista Ave
Bay City, TX 77414-2793, USA

Carroll, Sonny (Athlete, Baseball Player)
3311 Lawson St
Richmond, VA 23224-1853, USA

Carroll, Tom (Athlete, Baseball Player)
38572 Pheasant Hill Ln
Hamilton, VA 20158-3302, USA

Carroll, Tom (Tommy) (Athlete, Baseball Player)
304 Sonnet Ct
Peachtree City, GA 30269-3357, USA

Carroll, Wesley (Athlete, Football Player)
11740 SW 102nd St
Miami, FL 33186-2734, USA

Carroll, Willard (Director, Producer, Writer)
c/o Staff Member *Hyperion Pictures*
111 N Maryland Ave # 300
Glendale, CA 91206-4238, USA

Carrot Top (Actor, Comedian)
420 Sylvan Dr
Winter Park, FL 32789-3975, USA

Carruth, Paul (Athlete, Football Player)
373 Brentwood Ave
Trussville, AL 35173-1103, USA

Carruth, Rae (Athlete, Football Player)
12653 Tucker Crossing Ln
Charlotte, NC 28273-4746, USA

Carruthers, Dwight (Athlete, Hockey Player)
9513 W Nelson Dr
Nine Mile Falls, WA 99026-9620, USA

Carruthers, Garrey E (Ex-Governor)
5258 Redman Rd
Las Cruces, NM 88011-7556, USA

Carruthers, James H (Red) (Skier)
8 Malone Ave
Garnerville, NY 10923-1812, USA

Carsey, Marcia L P (Producer)
4024 Radford Ave Bldg 3
Studio City, CA 91604-2101, USA

Carsey, Marcy (Producer)
c/o Staff Member *Carsey-Werner-Mandabach*
16027 Ventura Blvd Ste 600
Encino, CA 91436-2798, USA

Carson, Andre (Congressman, Politician)
425 Cannon Hob
Washington, DC 20515-2301, USA

Carson, Benjamin S (Doctor)
Medical Center
Baltimore, MD 21218, USA

Carson, Carlos A (Athlete, Football Player)
4747 W 150th Ter
Overland Park, KS 66224-3410, USA

Carson, Charlotte (Stylist)
c/o Staff Member *Judy Inc*
1 Yorkville Ave
Toronto ON M4W 1L1, Canada

Carson, Crystal (Actor)
6725 McLennan Ave
Van Nuys, CA 91406-5542, USA

Carson, David (Director)
c/o Chris Simonian *Creative Artists Agency (CAA-LA)*
2000 Avenue of the Stars Ste 100
Los Angeles, CA 90067-4705, USA

Carson, Harold D (Harry) (Athlete, Football Player)
PO Box 852
Westwood, NJ 07675-0852, USA

Carson, Hunter (Actor)
c/o Staff Member *Elkins Entertainment*
8306 Wilshire Blvd Ste 438
Beverly Hills, CA 90211-2382, USA

Carson, James (Jimmy) (Athlete, Hockey Player)
1154 Ridgeway Dr
Rochester, MI 48307-1771, USA

Carson, Jeff (Musician)
2008 Clifton Johnston Ct
Nolensville, TN 37135-9606, USA

Carson, Joanna
400 St Cloud Rd
Los Angeles, CA 90077-3425

Carson, Kern (Athlete, Football Player)
849 45th St
San Diego, CA 92102-3667, USA

Carson, Leonardo (Athlete, Football Player)
9728 Windy Hollow Dr
Irving, TX 75063-5008

Carson, Lisa Nicole (Actor)
c/o Scott Zimmerman *Evolution Entertainment (LA)*
901 N Highland Ave
Los Angeles, CA 90038-2412, USA

Carson, Malcolm (Athlete, Football Player)
PO Box 11847
Birmingham, AL 35202-1847, USA

Carson, Rachelle (Actor)
c/o Staff Member *JC Robbins Management*
113 S Kilkea Dr
Los Angeles, CA 90048-3525, USA

Carson, T C
1505 10th St
Santa Monica, CA 90401-2805, USA

Carson, William H (Willie) (Jockey)
Minster House Bamsley
Cirencester, Glos, UNITED KINGDOM (UK)

Carsten, Peter
Meilenberger Str. 1
Icking-Dorfen G-82057, Germany

Carswell, Diana L (Stylist)
PO Box 7996
McLean, VA 22106-7996, USA

Carswell, Dwayne (Athlete, Football Player)
8202 Abbeyfield Dr
Jacksonville, FL 32277-0966, USA

Carswell, Robert (Athlete, Football Player)
5906 Heritage Walk
Lithonia, GA 30058-3896, USA

Cartagena, Victoria (Actor)
c/o Larry Taube *Principal Entertainment (LA)*
1964 Westwood Blvd Ste 400
Los Angeles, CA 90025-4695, USA

Carter, Aaron (Actor, Musician)
c/o Jane Carter *Spectra Management*
9300 Overseas Hwy
Marathon, FL 33050-3245

Carter, Alex (Actor)
c/o Richard Caplan *Noble Caplan Abrams*
1260 Yonge St 2nd Floor
Toronto, ON M4T 1W6, Canada

Carter, Allen (Athlete, Football Player)
2400 Ridgeview Dr Apt 404
Chino Hills, CA 91709-4378, USA

Carter, Amy (Misc)
1 Woodland Dr
Plains, GA 31780-5466, USA

Carter, Andy (Athlete, Baseball Player)
106 Montgomery Ave
Glenside, PA 19038-8228, USA

Carter, Anson (Athlete, Hockey Player)
820 Haven Oaks Ct NE
Atlanta, GA 30342-4348, USA

Carter, Anthony (Athlete, Football Player)
4314 Danielson Dr
Lake Worth, FL 33467-3628, USA

Carter, Anthony (Athlete, Basketball Player)
3111 Sable Bnd
San Antonio, TX 78259 2638, USA

Carter, Antonio (Athlete, Football Player)
7839 Maple Grove Dr
Lewis Center, OH 43035-9350, USA

Carter, Bernard (Athlete, Football Player)
261 Pinestraw Cir
Altamonte Springs, FL 32714-5416, USA

Carter, Beth (Stylist)
c/o Staff Member *Karlee Artist Management*
2658 Griffith Park Blvd # 171
Los Angeles, CA 90039-2520, USA

Carter, Betsy (Musician)
7561 Brush Lake Rd
North Lewisburg, OH 43060-9649

Carter, Carl (Athlete, Football Player)
3256 Centennial Rd
Forest Hill, TX 76119-7103, USA

Carter, Cheryl (Actor)
10635 Santa Monica Blvd Ste 130
Los Angeles, CA 90025-8306, USA

Carter, Chris (Producer)
c/o Bob Broder *International Creative Management (ICM-LA)*
10250 Constellation Blvd
Los Angeles, CA 90067-6200, USA

Carter, Chris (Athlete, Football Player)
1500 Mill Creek Dr
Desoto, TX 75115-1705, USA

Carter, Clarence (Musician)
1048 Tattnall St
Macon, GA 31201-1537, USA

Carter, Clarence (Athlete, Basketball Player)
900 Legacy Park Dr
Lawrenceville, GA 30043-8715, USA

Carter, Cris (Athlete, Football Player)
2493 NW 46th St
Boca Raton, FL 33431-8432, USA

Carter, Dale (Athlete, Football Player)
10416 Magnolia Heights Cir
Covington, GA 30014-4102, USA

Carter, Darren (Comedian)
c/o Staff Member *WmE2 (WMA-LA)*
1 William Morris Pl
Beverly Hills, CA 90212-4261, USA

Carter, David (Athlete, Football Player)
2401 Long Reach Dr
Sugar Land, TX 77478-4127, USA

Carter, Deana (Musician, Songwriter, Writer)
c/o John Huie *Creative Artists Agency (CAA-TN)*
3310 W End Ave Fl 5
Nashville, TN 37203-1028, USA

Carter, Deanna (Actor, Musician)
c/o John Huie *Creative Artists Agency (CAA-TN)*
3310 W End Ave Fl 5
Nashville, TN 37203-1028, USA

Carter, Dexter A (Athlete, Football Player)
7130 Nesters Dr
Tallahassee, FL 32312-6740, USA

Carter, Donald J (Don) (Bowler)
10331 SW 102nd Ave
Miami, FL 33176-3507, USA

Carter, Dr Jay (Writer)
PO Box 6048
Wyomissing, PA 19610-0048, USA

Carter, Dyshod (Athlete, Football Player)
916 W Carter Rd
Phoenix, AZ 85041-6750, USA

Carter, Elliott C Jr (Composer)
31 W 12th St
New York, NY 10011-8500, USA

Carter, Finn (Actor)
c/o Craig Dorfman *Frontline Management*
5670 Wilshire Blvd Ste 1370
Los Angeles, CA 90036-5679, USA

Carter, Frank (Misc)
608 E Baltimore Pike
Media, PA 19063-1735, USA

Carter, Fred (Athlete, Basketball Player)
2617 Dekalb Pike
Norristown, PA 19401-1838, USA

Carter, Frederick J (Fred) (Baseball Player, Coach)
5070 Parkside Ave # 3500
Philadelphia, PA 19131-4747, USA

Carter, Gary E (Athlete, Baseball Player)
580 Village Blvd Ste 315
West Palm Beach, FL 33409-1953, USA

Carter, Gerald (Athlete, Football Player)
3917 Cheshire Ct
Bryan, TX 77802-4905, USA

Carter, Graydon (Editor)
350 Madison Ave
New York, NY 10017-3700, USA

Carter, Herbert E (Biologist, Educator)
2401 E Cerrada De Promesa
Tucson, AZ 85718-3030, USA

Carter, Hodding III (Government Official)
c/o Staff Member *Random House Publicity (Toronto)*
1 Toronto St Suite 300
Toronto, ON M5C 2V6, Canada

Carter, Howard (Athlete, Basketball Player)
8026 Jefferson Hwy Apt 112
Baton Rouge, LA 70809-1661, USA

Carter, Jack (Actor, Comedian)
1023 Chevy Chase Dr
Beverly Hills, CA 90210-2707, USA

Carter, Jake (Athlete, Basketball Player)
4632 Country Creek Dr Apt 1220
Dallas, TX 75236-1253, USA

Carter, Jay (Musician)
141 Dunbar Ave
Fords, NJ 08863-1551, USA

Carter, Jeff (Athlete, Baseball Player)
4625 River Overlook Dr
Valrico, FL 33596-7878, USA

Carter, Jim (Athlete, Golfer)
12575 N 130th Way
Scottsdale, AZ 85259-3542, USA

Carter, Jim (Athlete, Football Player)
1500 Morning Glory Ln
Wausau, WI 54401-7686, USA

Carter, Jodie (Athlete, Football Player)
5921 Timberview Rd
Little Rock, AR 72204-8559, USA

Carter, Joe (Athlete, Baseball Player)
3000 W 117th St
Leawood, KS 66211-2923, USA

Carter, John (Musician)
2375 E Tropicana Ave # 304
Las Vegas, NV 89119-6564, USA

Carter, John (Athlete, Hockey Player)
27 Country Ln
Sharon, MA 02067-2339, USA

Carter, John Mack (Editor)
959 8th Ave
New York, NY 10019-3737, USA

Carter, Kent (Athlete, Football Player)
18657 Klum Pl
Rowland Heights, CA 91748-4851, USA

Carter, Kevin (Athlete, Football Player)
1070 Vaughn Crest Dr
Franklin, TN 37069-7211, USA

Carter, Ki-Jana (Athlete, Football Player)
1293 NW 121st Ave
Plantation, FL 33323-2441, USA

Carter, Lance (Athlete, Baseball Player)
306 74th Street Ct NW
Bradenton, FL 34209-2220, USA

Carter, Larry (Athlete, Baseball Player)
4305 Wilmette Dr
Denton, TX 76208-4823, USA

Carter, Louis (Athlete, Football Player)
8209 Swamp Rose Pl
Laurel, MD 20724-1963, USA

Carter, Lyle (Athlete, Hockey Player)
Hamilton Ave
Brookfield, NS B0N 1C0, Canada

Carter, Lynda (Actor)
PO Box 59110
Potomac, MD 20859-9110, USA

Carter, M L (Athlete, Football Player)
PO Box 1971
Seaside, CA 93955-1971, USA

Carter, Marshall N (Financier)
225 Franklin St
Boston, MA 02110-2804, USA

Carter, Mel (Musician)
1161 NW 76th Ave
Plantation, FL 33322-5120, USA

Carter, Michael (Actor)
2-4 Noel St
London W1V 3RB, UNITED KINGDOM (UK)

Carter, Michael D (Athlete, Football Player)
901 Red Oak Creek Dr
Red Oak, TX 75154-3615, USA

Carter, Mike (Baseball Player)
12215 Magnolia Crescent Dr Apt D
Roswell, GA 30075-5568, USA

Carter, Mike (Athlete, Football Player)
10705 Celeo Ln
San Jose, CA 95127-2706, USA

Carter, Nathan (Actor)
c/o Norbert Abrams *Noble Caplan Abrams*
1260 Yonge St 2nd Floor
Toronto ON M4T 1W6, Canada

Carter, Nick (Musician, Songwriter)
c/o Kenneth Crear *Wright-Crear Management*
3815 Hughes Ave Fl 3
Culver City, CA 90232-2715, USA

Carter, Pat (Athlete, Football Player)
11321 Cambray Creek Loop
Riverview, FL 33579-3920, USA

Carter, Paula (Bowler)
10331 SW 102nd Ave
Miami, FL 33176-3507, USA

Carter, Perry (Athlete, Football Player)
15719 Sweeney Park Ln
Houston, TX 77084-2281, USA

Carter, Powell F Jr (Admiral)
699 Fillmore St
Harpers Ferry, WV 25425, USA

Carter, Rachel (Misc)
PO Box 1663
Julian, CA 92036-1663, USA

Carter, Rodney (Athlete, Football Player)
4490 Jasmine Dr
Bethlehem, PA 18020-8840, USA

Carter, Ron (Athlete, Basketball Player)
1513 Allegheny Ave
Pittsburgh, PA 15233-1313, USA

Carter, Ronald L (Ron) (Composer, Musician)
35 Clark St Apt A5
Brooklyn, NY 11201-2374, USA

Carter, Rosalynn (First Lady)
451 Freedom Pkwy NE
Atlanta, GA 30307, USA

Carter, Rosana (Opera Singer)
150 5th Ave
New York, NY 10011-4311, USA

Carter, Rubin (Athlete, Coach, Football Player)
PO Box 51537
Albuquerque, NM 87181-1537, USA

Carter, Rubin (Hurricane) (Boxer)
85 King St E # 318
Toronto, ON M5C 1G3, CANADA

Carter, Rublin (Athlete, Football Player)
PO Box 51537
Albuquerque, NM 87181-1537, USA

Carter, Russell (Athlete, Football Player)
216 Lilac Ln
Douglassville, PA 19518-1121, USA

Carter, Sarah (Actor)
c/o Darren Goldberg *Global Creative*
1051 Cole Ave # B
Los Angeles, CA 90038-2601, USA

Carter, Sol (Athlete, Baseball Player)
2402 Gale Pl
El Dorado, AR 71730-3034, USA

Carter, Stephen L (Attorney, Attorney General, General, Writer)
Law School
New Haven, CT 6520, USA

Carter, Steve (Athlete, Baseball Player)
13006 Innisbrook Dr
Beltsville, MD 20705-1196, USA

Carter, Terry (Actor)
244 Madison Ave # 332
New York, NY 10016-2817, USA

Carter, Thomas (Director)
140 N Tigertail Rd
Los Angeles, CA 90049-2706, USA

Carter, Tim (Athlete, Football Player)
4860 26th Ct S
Saint Petersburg, FL 33712-4322, USA

Carter, Tom (Athlete, Golfer)
3787 County Line Rd
Quakertown, PA 18951-2085, USA

Carter, Tom (Athlete, Football Player)
4548 Bristol Ln
Cincinnati, OH 45229-1214, USA

Carter, Tony (Athlete, Football Player)
7839 Maple Grove Dr
Lewis Center, OH 43035-9350, USA

Carter, Vince (Athlete, Basketball Player)
c/o Staff Member *IMG (Cleveland)*
1360 E 9th St Ste 100
Cleveland, OH 44114-1730, USA

Carter, Virgil (Athlete, Football Player)
PO Box 1901
Helendale, CA 92342-1901, USA

Carter III, W Hodding (Government Official)
214 N Columbus St
Alexandria, VA 22314-2412, USA

Carter Jr, James E (Jimmy) (Ex-President, Nobel Prize Laureate, Politician, President)
1 Copenhill Ave NE
Atlanta, GA 30307-1400, USA

Carteris, Gabrielle (Actor)
c/o Jeff Danis *Danis, Panaro, Nist (DPN)*
9201 W Olympic Blvd
Beverly Hills, CA 90212-4605, USA

Carter's Chord (Music Group)
c/o Staff Member *Paradigm (Monterey)*
404 W Franklin St
Monterey, CA 93940-2303, USA

Carthen, Jason (Athlete, Football Player)
3978 Jeanne Dr
Cleveland, OH 44134, USA

Carthon, Maurice (Athlete, Football Player)
2040 E Indigo Dr
Chandler, AZ 85286-4992, USA

Carthy, Eliza (Musician)
c/o Staff Member *Agency Group Ltd, The (NY)*
142 W 57th St Fl 6
New York, NY 10019-3300, USA

Cartwright, Angela (Actor)
c/o Peter Hankwitz *PHP & M, Inc*
9465 Wilshire Blvd Ste 420
Beverly Hills, CA 90212-2603, USA

Cartwright, Bill (Athlete, Basketball Player, Coach)
1839 Wedgewood Ct
Lake Forest, IL 60045-3705, USA

Cartwright, Catherine (Athlete, Golfer)
4505 SE County Road 760
Arcadia, FL 34266-9606, USA

Cartwright, James F (General)
Director Structure Resources Assessment
Hqusmc Navy Sta
Washington, DC 20380-0001, USA

Cartwright, Nancy (Actor)
9420 Reseda Blvd # 572
Northridge, CA 91324-2932, USA

Cartwright, Rock (Athlete, Football Player)
231 Interstate 45 N Apt 21115
Conroe, TX 77304-2326, USA

Cartwright, Veronica (Actor)
c/o Mitch Clem *Shadow Entertainment*
10 Universal City Plz Fl 20
Universal City, CA 91608-1074, USA

Carty, Jay (Athlete, Basketball Player)
5425 Lower Honoapiilani Rd
Lahaina, HI 96761-8766, USA

Carty, Ricardo A J (Rico) (Athlete, Baseball Player)
5 Ens Enriquillo
San Pedro de Macoris, Dominician Republic

Caruana, Patrick P (Sat) (General)
1922 Havemeyer Ln
Redondo Beach, CA 90278-4830, USA

Caruana, Peter R (Politician)
10/3 Irish Town
GIBRALTAR

Caruso, Ann S (Stylist)
69 5th Ave Apt 10A
New York, NY 10003-3008, USA

Caruso, David (Actor)
c/o Jason Weinberg *Untitled Entertainment (LA)*
350 S Beverly Dr Ste 200
Beverly Hills, CA 90212-4819, USA

Caruso, D.J. (Director)
c/o Geyer Kosinski *Media Talent Group*
9200 W Sunset Blvd Ste 550
Los Angeles, CA 90069-3611, USA

Caruso, Mike (Athlete, Baseball Player)
900 N Ocean Blvd Apt E
Pompano Beach, FL 33062-4045, USA

Carver, Brent (Actor, Musician)
1500 Broadway Ste 902
New York, NY 10036-4055, USA

Carver, Dale (Athlete, Football Player)
1328 Vista Ter
Titusville, FL 32780-4343, USA

Carver, Dana (Actor, Comedian)
775 E Blithedale Ave # 501
Mill Valley, CA 94941-1554, USA

Carver, Johnny (Musician)
9 Lucy Ln
Sherwood, AR 72120-3612, USA

Carver, Melvin (Mel) (Athlete, Football Player)
10840 Breaking Rocks Dr
Tampa, FL 33647-3579, USA

Carver, Randall (Actor)
5144 Vineland Ave
North Hollywood, CA 91601-3849, USA

Carver, Shante (Athlete, Football Player)
214 Santa Fe Trl
Irving, TX 75063-4719, USA

Carveth-Dunn, Betty (Baseball Player)
11531 77th Ave
Edmonton, AB T6G 0M2, CANADA

Carvey, Dana (Actor)
c/o Marc Gurvitz *Brillstein Entertainment Partners*
9150 Wilshire Blvd Ste 350
Beverly Hills, CA 90212-3453, USA

Carvilie, C James Jr (Politician)
209 Pennsylvania Ave SE # 800
Washington, DC 20003-1107, USA

Carville, James (Television Host)
424 S Washington St
Alexandria, VA 22314-4100, USA

Cary, Chuck (Athlete, Baseball Player)
484 Bayshore Dr
Miramar Beach, FL 32550-4063, USA

Cary, Diane (Baby Peggy) Serra (Actor)
712 5th Ave
Gustine, CA 95322-1537, USA

Cary, Duane G (Astronaut)
5938 Instone Cir
Colorado Springs, CO 80922-1716, USA

Cary, Scott (Athlete, Baseball Player)
930 Block Rd
Bronson, MI 49028-9251, USA

Cary, W Sterling (Religious Leader)
2344 Vardon Ln
Flossmoor, IL 60422-1363, USA

Cary Brothers (Music Group)
c/o Staff Member *Paradigm (Monterey)*
404 W Franklin St
Monterey, CA 93940-2303, USA

Casablancas, Julian (Musician, Songwriter)
c/o Staff Member *Wiz Kid Management*
123 E 7th St
New York, NY 10009-5747, USA

Casadesus, Jean-Claude (Conductor)
23 Blvd de la Liberte
Lille 59800, FRANCE

Casados, Eloy (Actor)
c/o Michelle Gordon *Michelle Gordon & Assoc*
260 S Beverly Dr Ste 308
Beverly Hills, CA 90212-3814, USA

Casados, Rene (Actor)
c/o Staff Member *Televisa*
Blvd Adolfo Lopez Mateos 232 Colonia San Angel INN
DF CP 01060, MEXICO

Casady, Jack (Musician)
315 S Beverly Dr Ste 407
Beverly Hills, CA 90212-4301, USA

Casale, Jerry (Athlete, Baseball Player)
600 County Ave Apt 408
Secaucus, NJ 07094-2610, USA

Casali, Kim (Cartoonist)
Times-Mirror Square
Los Angeles, CA 90053, USA

Casals, Rosemary (Rosie) (Athlete, Tennis Player)
c/o Staff Member *International Tennis Hall Of Fame*
194 Bellevue Ave
Newport, RI 02840-3586, USA

Casals, Rosemary (Rosie) (Tennis Player)
PO Box 537
Sausalito, CA 94966-0537, USA

Casanega, Ken (Athlete, Football Player)
480 Donald Dr
Hollister, CA 95023-6364, USA

Casanova, Paul (Athlete, Baseball Player)
5370 NW 183rd St
Miami Gardens, FL 33055-2304, USA

Casanova, Raul (Athlete, Baseball Player)
820 NW 87th Ave Apt 313
Miami, FL 33172-3430, USA

Casanova, Thomas H (Tommy) (Athlete, Football Player)
345 Casanova Rd
Crowley, LA 70526-0504, USA

Casares, Ricardo (Rick) (Athlete, Football Player)
4107 Starfish Ln
Tampa, FL 33615-5428, USA

Casbarian, John (Architect)
2370 Rice Blvd Ste 112
Houston, TX 77005-2644, USA

Cascada (Musician)
c/o Frank Ehrlich Varlar 41
D- 48720, Rosendahl, GERMANY

Cascadden, Chad (Athlete, Football Player)
2611 Winsor Dr
Eau Claire, WI 54703-1778, USA

Case, J Scott (Athlete, Football Player)
4930 Price Dr
Suwanee, GA 30024-4186, USA

Case, John (Writer)
1745 Broadway # B1
New York, NY 10019-4368, USA

Case, Pete (Athlete, Football Player)
6960 Driskell Cir
Cumming, GA 30041-4714, USA

Case, Ronald (Ron) (Athlete, Football Player)
6960 Driskell Cir
Cumming, GA 30041-4714, USA

Case, Sharon (Actor)
c/o Jerry Shandrew *Shandrew Public Relations*
1050 S Stanley Ave
Los Angeles, CA 90019-6634, USA

Case, Stephen M (Steve) (Business Person)
1717 Rhode Island Ave NW Fl 7
Washington, DC 20036-3023, USA

Case, Stoney (Athlete, Football Player)
1813 E 49th St
Odessa, TX 79762-4524, USA

Case, Walter Jr (Race Car Driver)
60 Edgecomb Rd
Lisbon Falls, ME 04252-9740, USA

Casel, Nitanju Bolade (Musician)
PO Box 600099
Newtonville, MA 02460-0001, USA

Casella, Max (Actor)
c/o Marcia Hurwitz *Innovative Artists (LA)*
1505 10th St
Santa Monica, CA 90401-2805, USA

Casely-Hayford, Joe (Designer, Fashion Designer)
c/o Staff Member *Joe Casely-Hayford*
128 Shoreditch High Street
London, England E1 6JE, United Kingdom

Casey, Bernie (Athlete, Football Player)
6145 Flight Ave
Los Angeles, CA 90056-1509, USA

Casey, Brent (Stylist)
4312 1st Ave S
Minneapolis, MN 55409-2017, USA

Casey, Dillon (Actor)
c/o Tim Taylor *Luber Roklin Management*
8530 Wilshire Blvd Ste 550
Beverly Hills, CA 90211-3133, USA

Casey, Harry W (Musician)
7530 Loch Ness Dr
Miami Lakes, FL 33014-6014, USA

Casey, John D (Writer)
English Dept
Charlottesville, VA 22903, USA

Casey, Jon (Athlete, Hockey Player)
651 Bluffs View Ct
Eureka, MO 63025-3727, USA

Casey, Kent (Stylist)
c/o Staff Member *Rex Agency, The*
6311 Romaine St
Los Angeles, CA 90038-2617, USA

Casey, Lawrence P. (Actor)
4139 Vanetta Pl
Studio City, CA 91604-2342, USA

Casey, Lee
9300 Wilshire Blvd Ste 555
Beverly Hills, CA 90212-3211

Casey, Maurice F (General)
7017 Union Mill Rd
Clifton, VA 20124-1122, USA

Casey, Paddy (Musician)
c/o Staff Member *Helter Skelter (UK)*
535 Kings Rd The Plaza
London SW10 0SZ, UNITED KINGDOM (UK)

Casey, Paul (Athlete, Golfer)
29167 N 108th St
Scottsdale, AZ 85262-4665, USA

Casey, Peter (Director)
450 N Roxbury Dr Ste 1050
Beverly Hills, CA 90210-4235, USA

Casey, Sean (Athlete, Baseball Player)
271 Trotwood Dr
Pittsburgh, PA 15241-2244, USA

Casey, Tim (Athlete, Football Player)
15901 62nd Ave Nw
Gig Harbor, WA 98332-9098, USA

Casey Jr, Robert P. (Senator)
393 Russell Senate Ofc Building
Washington, DC 20510-0001, USA

Cash, Antoine (Athlete, Football Player)
1400 Lake Polo Dr
Odessa, FL 33556-1787, USA

Cash, Bill (Athlete, Baseball Player)
1715 W Cheltenham Ave
Elkins Park, PA 19027-1048, USA

Cash, Cornelius (Athlete, Basketball Player)
1661 Miami Chapel Rd
Dayton, OH 45417-4527, USA

Cash, David (Dave) (Athlete, Baseball Player)
16308 Birkdale Dr
Odessa, FL 33556-2802, USA

Cash, Keith L (Athlete, Football Player)
9839 Heritage Farm
San Antonio, TX 78245-1217, USA

Cash, Kerry (Athlete, Football Player)
9839 Heritage Farm
San Antonio, TX 78245-1217, USA

Cash, Kevin (Athlete, Baseball Player)
848 Nickajack Rd
Franklin, NC 28734-3605, USA

Cash, Pat (Tennis Player)
281 Clarence St
Sydney NSW 2000, AUSTRALIA

Cash, Rick (Athlete, Football Player)
203 E Benton St
Savannah, MO 64485-1720, USA

Cash, Ron (Athlete, Baseball Player)
5418 Deerbrooke Creek Cir Apt 4
Tampa, FL 33624-4154, USA

Cash, Rosanne (Musician, Songwriter)
c/o Mike Leahy *Concerted Efforts*
PO Box 440326
Somerville, MA 02144-0004, USA

Cash, Sam (Athlete, Basketball Player)
25825 Karisa Cir
Moreno Valley, CA 92551-1968, USA

Cash, Swin (Basketball Player)
2 Championship Dr
Auburn Hills, MI 48326-1753, USA

Cash, Tommy (Musician, Songwriter, Writer)
PO Box 1230
Hendersonville, TN 37077-1230, USA

Cashen, Frank (Athlete, Baseball Player)
7600 Mahogany Run
Port St Lucie, FL 34986-3213, USA

Cashion, Red (Athlete, Football Player)
PO Box 3889
Bryan, TX 77805-3889, USA

Cashman, John Jr (Misc)
PO Box 11889
Lexington, KY 40578-1889, USA

Cashman, Terry (Musician)
15 Engle St
Englewood, NJ 07631-2936, USA

Cashman, Wayne (Athlete, Hockey Player)
5150 NW 80th Avenue Rd
Ocala, FL 34482-2028, USA

Casian, Larry (Athlete, Baseball Player)
1939 Popcorn St NW
Salem, OR 97304-2841, USA

Casiavska, Vera (Gymnast)
SVS Sparta Prague Korunovacni 29
Prague 7, CZECH REPUBLIC

Casida, John E (Misc)
1570 La Vereda Rd
Berkeley, CA 94708-2036, USA

Casillas, Tony (Athlete, Football Player)
6201 Bay Valley Ct
Flower Mound, TX 75022-5573, USA

Casiraghi, Pierlulgi (Soccer Player)
Via Novaro 32
Rome 197, ITALY

Caskey, C Thomas (Biologist, Scientist)
Molecular Genetics Dept
Houston, TX 77030, USA

Caskey, Craig (Athlete, Baseball Player)
17422 Palomino Dr
Bothell, WA 98012-6419, USA

Casner, Ken (Athlete, Football Player)
1808 Laurel Lake Dr
Waco, TX 76710-2829, USA

Casnoff, Philip (Actor)
c/o Darris Hatch *Daris Hatch Management*
10027 Rossbury Pl
Los Angeles, CA 90064-4825, USA

Casnoff, Phillip (Actor)
216 S Plymouth Blvd
Los Angeles, CA 90004-3814, USA

Cason, Aveion (Athlete, Football Player)
3900 48th Ave S
Saint Petersburg, FL 33711-4604, USA

Cason, James (Jim) (Athlete, Football Player)
1002 King Arthur Dr Apt 116
Harlingen, TX 78550-8417, USA

Caspar, Donald L D (Physicist)
PO Box 393
Cataumet, MA 02534-0393, USA

Caspary, Tina (Actor)
11350 Ventura Blvd Ste 206
Studio City, CA 91604-3140, USA

Casper, Billy (Athlete, Golfer)
2561 Stonebury Loop Rd
Springville, UT 84663-3937, USA

Casper, David J (Dave) (Athlete, Football Player)
1525 Alamo Way
Alamo, CA 94507-1502, USA

Casper, Gerhard (Attorney, Educator)
Law School Abbott Way
Stanford, CT 94305, USA

Casper, John H (Astronaut)
4414 Village Corner Dr
Houston, TX 77059-4025, USA

Casper, Robert (Actor)
10635 Santa Monica Blvd Ste 130
Los Angeles, CA 90025-8306, USA

Caspersson, Tobjorn O (Doctor)
Emanuel Birkes Vag 2
Ronninge 14400, SWEDEN

Cass, Christopher (Actor)
PO Box 5597
Santa Monica, CA 90409-5597, USA

Cassaday, Leann (Athlete, Golfer)
542 Orpheus Ave
Encinitas, CA 92024-2660, USA

Cassady, Craig (Athlete, Football Player)
3827 Fairlington Dr
Columbus, OH 43220-4526, USA

Cassady, Howard (Hopalong) (Athlete, Football Player)
539 Severn Ave
Tampa, FL 33606-4045, USA

Cassar, Jon (Producer)
c/o Jeff Benson *Paradigm (LA)*
360 N Crescent Dr
Beverly Hills, CA 90210-4874, USA

Cassara, Frank (Athlete, Football Player)
9113 Brookshire Ave
Downey, CA 90240-2910, USA

Cassaveters, Nick (Actor, Director)
22223 Buena Ventura St
Woodland Hills, CA 91364-5007, USA

Cassavetes, Nick (Actor, Director, Writer)
c/o Staff Member *International Creative Management (ICM-LA)*
10250 Constellation Blvd Fl 7
Los Angeles, CA 90067-6207, USA

Cassel, Jack (Athlete, Baseball Player)
19427 Superior St
Northridge, CA 91324-1646, USA

Cassel, Matt (Athlete, Football Player)
150 Street Of Dreams
Village Of Loch Lloyd, MO 64012-4179, USA

Cassel, Seymour (Actor)
c/o Harry Abrams *Abrams Artists Agency (LA)*
9200 W Sunset Blvd PH 11
Los Angeles, CA 90069-3601, USA

Cassel, Vincent (Actor)
c/o Staff Member *United Talent Agency (UTA)*
9560 Wilshire Blvd Fl 5
Beverly Hills, CA 90212-2400, USA

Cassell, Sam (Athlete, Basketball Player)
6000 Reims Rd Apt 3402
Houston, TX 77036-3054, USA

Cassels, A James H (Misc)
Hamble End Higham Road Barrow Bury Saint Edmunds
Suffolk, UNITED KINGDOM (UK)

Cassels, Andrew (Athlete, Hockey Player)
6550 Lockhart Ln
Dublin, OH 43017-8908, USA

Casserino, Lt Col Frank J (Misc)
2407 Willow Glen Dr
Colorado Springs, CO 80920-1200, USA

Casserta, Bettina (Stylist)
c/o Staff Member *Ford Models (Chicago)*
311 W Superior St
Chicago, IL 60654-3548, USA

Cassese, Tom (Athlete, Football Player)
80 Van Buren St
Port Jefferson Station, NY 11776-3173, USA

Casseus, Gabriel (Actor)
c/o Dan Baron *Agency for the Performing Arts (APA-LA)*
405 S Beverly Dr Ste 500
Beverly Hills, CA 90212-4425, USA

Cassidy (Musician)
c/o Staff Member *J Records (Division of BMG Entertainment)*
745 5th Ave Fl 6
New York, NY 10151-0099, USA

Cassidy, Bill (Congressman, Politician)
1535 Longworth Hob
Washington, DC 20515-1410, USA

Cassidy, Bruce (Athlete, Coach, Hockey Player)
c/o Staff Member *Kingston Frontenacs*
P.O. Box 665 Stn Main
Kingston, ON K7L 4X1, Canada

Cassidy, David (Actor, Musician, Producer)
1536 W 25th St PMB 233
San Pedro, CA 90732-4415, USA

Cassidy, Edward I Cardinal (Religious Leader)
Piazza del S Uffizio 11
Rome 193, ITALY

Cassidy, Elaine (Actor)
c/o Staff Member *International Creative Management (ICM-LA)*
10250 Constellation Blvd Fl 7
Los Angeles, CA 90067-6207, USA

Cassidy, Joanna (Actor)
c/o Bette Smith *Bette Smith Management*
499 N Canon Dr
Beverly Hills, CA 90210-4887, USA

Cassidy, Katie (Actor)
c/o Doreen Wilcox Little *Anonymous Content (AC-LA)*
3531 Hayden Ave
Culver City, CA 90232, USA

Cassidy, Michael (Actor)
c/o Vic Ramos *Vic Ramos Management*
337 E 13th St Apt 6
New York, NY 10003-5852, USA

Cassidy, Patrick (Actor)
1505 10th St
Santa Monica, CA 90401-2805, USA

Cassidy, Ron (Athlete, Football Player)
2214 W 171st St
Torrance, CA 90504-2925, USA

Cassidy, Scott (Athlete, Baseball Player)
4203 Hunting Creek Dr
Clay, NY 13041-8718, USA

Cassidy, Shaun (Actor, Musician)
2661 Quail Valley Rd
Solvang, CA 93463-9613, USA

Cassini, Jack (Athlete, Baseball Player)
24 E Vera Ln
Tempe, AZ 85284-4050, USA

Cassolato, Tony (Athlete, Hockey Player)
576 Camino El Dorado
Encinitas, CA 92024-3820, USA

Casson, Mel (Cartoonist)
c/o Staff Member *King Features Syndication*
300 W 57th St Fl 15
New York, NY 10019-5238, USA

Cast, Edward
4 Bankside Dr Thames Ditton
Surrey, ENGLAND KT7 0AQ, ENGLAND

Cast, PC (Writer)
c/o Sean T. Daily *Hotchkiss & Associates*
611 Broadway Rm 741
New York, NY 10012-2665, USA

Cast, Tricia (Actor)
20 Georgette Rd
Rolling Hills Estates, CA 90274, USA

Casta, Laetitia (Actor)
c/o Staff Member *ArtMedia*
20 avenue Rapp
Paris 75008, France

Castaldi, Debbie (Stylist)
Prefers to be contacted via telephone or email
Los Angeles, CA 90069, USA

Castaneda, Jorge A (Government Official)
Anillo Perferico Sur 3180 #1120
Jardines del Pedregal 1900, MEXICO

Castaneda, Pedro (Actor)
c/o Maggie Woods *Online Talent Group*
Prefers to be contacted via email or telephone
Los Angeles, CA 90069, USA

Castel, Nico (Opera Singer)
4 Adelaide Ln
Washingtonville, NY 10992-1816, USA

Castellaneta, Dan (Actor, Musician, Writer)
c/o Arlene Forster *Forster Entertainment*
12533 Woodgreen St
Los Angeles, CA 90066-2723, USA

Castellini, Clateo (Business Person)
1 Becton Dr
Franklin Lakes, NJ 07417-1815, USA

Castelluccio, Frederico (Actor)
c/o Robyn Ziegler *Robyn Ziegler Management*
30 Irving Pl Fl 6
New York, NY 10003-2303, USA

Caster, Rich (Athlete, Football Player)
41 Lincoln Ct
Rockville Centre, NY 11570-5744, USA

Castete, Jesse (Athlete, Football Player)
302 W Lee St
Sulphur, LA 70663-5440, USA

Castiglia, James (Athlete, Football Player)
24403 Galeano Way
Damascus, MD 20872-2801, USA

Castiglia, Jim (Athlete, Baseball Player)
24403 Galeano Way
Damascus, MD 20872-2801, USA

Castiglione, Joe (Baseball Player, Sportscaster)
100 King Phillips Pathe
Marshfield, MA 02050-5714, USA

Castiglione, Pete (Athlete, Baseball Player)
1320 NE 26th Ter
Pompano Beach, FL 33062-3806, USA

Castilla, Vinny (Athlete, Baseball Player)
7680 Polo Ridge Dr
Littleton, CO 80128-2502, USA

Castille, Jeremiah (Athlete, Football Player)
2904 Kirkcaldy Ln
Birmingham, AL 35242-4117, USA

Castillio, Susie (Actor, Beauty Pageant Winner)
c/o Gordon Gilbertson *Gilbertson Management*
1334 3rd Street Promenade Ste 201
Santa Monica, CA 90401-1320, USA

Castillo, Alberto (Athlete, Baseball Player)
10059 Perfect Dr
Port Saint Lucie, FL 34986-3062, USA

Castillo, Bobby (Athlete, Baseball Player)
316 Calle Amarillo SW
Albuquerque, NM 87121-9300, USA

Castillo, Frank (Athlete, Baseball Player)
9333 N 129th Pl
Scottsdale, AZ 85259-6231, USA

Castillo, Luis (Athlete, Baseball Player)
160 Commodore Dr Apt 816
Plantation, FL 33325-2687, USA

Castillo, Marty (Athlete, Baseball Player)
5005 Catalina Ct
Naples, FL 34112-6993, USA

Castillo, Patricio (Actor)
c/o Staff Member *Televisa*
Blvd Adolfo Lopez Mateos 232 Colonia San Angel INN
DF CP 01060, MEXICO

Castillo, Rafael (De La Ghetto) (Musician)
c/o Staff Member *Baby Records Corp*
R104 Ave Galicia
Carolina, PR 00983-1524, USA

Castillo, Tony (Athlete, Baseball Player)
6402 Silverwood Dr
Huntington Beach, CA 92647-3366, USA

Castillo, Vinicio (Athlete, Baseball Player)
c/o Staff Member *Atlanta Braves*
755 Hank Aaron Dr SW
Atlanta, GA 30315-1120, USA

Castillo Lara, Rosalio Jose Cardinal (Religious Leader)
Palazzo del Governatorato
120, VATICAN CITY

Casting Crowns (Music Group, Musician)
c/o Stacey Jannette *Proper Management*
PO Box 150867
Nashville, TN 37215-0867, USA

Castino, John (Athlete, Baseball Player)
6290 Bluestern Rd S
Hamel, MN 55340, USA

Castle, Don (Athlete, Baseball Player)
24 Country Club Ln
Senatobia, MS 38668, USA

Castle, Eric (Athlete, Football Player)
41984 Cut Off Dr
Lebanon, OR 97355-9120, USA

Castle, Jo Ann (Musician)
1984 State Highway 165
Branson, MO 65616-8936, USA

Castle, John (Actor)
91 Regent St
London W1R 7TB, UNITED KINGDOM (UK)

Castle, Michael N (Congressman, Ex-Governor)
1233 Longworth Hob
Washington, DC 20515-0801, USA

Castle, Nick (Actor, Director, Writer)
c/o Melissa Read *Read Agency*
8033 W Sunset Blvd # 937
Los Angeles, CA 90046-2401, USA

Castle of Blackbum, Barbara A (Government Official)
Westminster
London SW1A 0PW, UNITED KINGDOM (UK)

Castle-Hughes, Keisha (Actor)
c/o Jennifer Rawlings *WmE2 (Endeavor-LA)*
9601 Wilshire Blvd Fl 3
Beverly Hills, CA 90210-5219, USA

Castleman, Albert W Jr (Misc)
425 Hillcrest Ave
State College, PA 16803-3419, USA

Castleman, E Riva (Misc)
11 W 53rd St
New York, NY 10019-5401, USA

Castleman, Foster (Athlete, Baseball Player)
8250 Graves Rd
Cincinnati, OH 45243-3633, USA

Castles, Neil (Race Car Driver)
1525 Stoneyridge Dr
Charlotte, NC 28214-8656, USA

Casto, Kory (Athlete, Baseball Player)
2662 State Highway 111 E
Yoakum, TX 77995-5317, USA

Castonzo, Anthony (Football Player)
c/o Ben Dogra *CAA - St. Louis*
222 S Central Ave Ste 1008
Saint Louis, MO 63105-3509, USA

Castor, Chris (Athlete, Football Player)
206 Connors Cir
Cary, NC 27511-6100, USA

Castor, Kathy (Congressman, Politician)
137 Cannon Hob
Washington, DC 20515-2204, USA

Castrillon Hoyos, Dario Cardinal (Religious Leader)
Calle 33 N 21-18 Bucaramanga
Santander, COLOMBIA

Castro, Bill (Athlete, Baseball Player)
5217 W Harvard Dr
Franklin, WI 53132-8192, USA

Castro, Cristian (Musician)
c/o Staff Member *BMG*
1540 Broadway
New York, NY 10036-4039, USA

Castro, Daniela (Actor)
c/o Staff Member *Televisa*
Blvd Adolfo Lopez Mateos 232 Colonia San Angel INN
DF CP 01060, MEXICO

Castro, David (Actor)
c/o Staff Member *Persona Management*
40 E 9th St # Suite 11J PMB 11J
New York, NY 10003, USA

Castro, Jason (Musician)
c/o Staff Member *Atlantic Recording Corporation*
1290 Avenue of the Americas
New York, NY 10104-0101, USA

Castro, Juan (Athlete, Baseball Player)
7324 W Artie Ave
Peoria, AZ 85383-3291, USA

Castro, Ramon (Athlete, Baseball Player)
1230 Windway Cir
Kissimmee, FL 34744-2552, USA

Castro, Raquel (Actor)
c/o Staff Member *WmE2 (Endeavor-LA)*
9601 Wilshire Blvd Fl 3
Beverly Hills, CA 90210-5219, USA

Castro, Raul H (Diplomat, Ex-Governor)
429 W Crawford St
Nogales, AZ 85621-2507, USA

Castro Ruz, Fidel (President)
Palacio del Gobierno Plaza de Revolucion
Havana, CUBA

Castro Ruz, Raul (Prime Minister)
Plaza de la Revolucion
Havana, CUBA

Castroneves, Helio (Race Car Driver)
c/o Staff Member *Penske Racing South*
200 Penske Way
Mooresville, NC 28115-8022, USA

Castronuova, Cara (Actor, Reality TV Star)
c/o Seth Greenky *Green Key Mgmt (NY)*
251 W 89th St Apt 4A
New York, NY 10024-1713, USA

Catalano, Eduardo F (Architect)
267 Grove St
Cambridge, MA 02138-1013, USA

Catalanotto, Frank (Athlete, Baseball Player)
4 Muffins Mdws
Saint James, NY 11780-1233, USA

Catalino, Ken (Cartoonist, Editor)
5777 W Century Blvd Ste 700
Los Angeles, CA 90045-5652, USA

Catalona, William J (Misc)
Medical School Urology Division
Saint Louis, MO 63110, USA

Catanho, Alcides (Athlete, Football Player)
931 Pennington St Apt 1
Elizabeth, NJ 07202-1584, USA

Catanzaro, Tony (Dancer)
8915 SW 207th St
Cutler Bay, FL 33189-3608, USA

Catchings, Harvey (Athlete, Basketball Player)
17406 Edenwalk
Spring, TX 77379-8513, USA

Catchings, Tamika (Athlete)
125 S Pennsylvania St
Indianapolis, IN 46204-3610

Catchings, Tamika (Basketball Player)
125 S Pennsylvania St
Indianapolis, IN 46204-3610, USA

Cate, Troy (Athlete, Baseball Player)
32499 Via Destello
Temecula, CA 92592-3961, USA

Cater, Danny (Athlete, Baseball Player)
3268 Candlewood Trl
Plano, TX 75023-1320, USA

Cater, Greg (Athlete, Football Player)
19 Warwick Way SE
Rome, GA 30161-4058, USA

Cates, Dariene (Actor)
13340 FM 740
Forney, TX 75126-6802, USA

Cates, Phoebe (Actor)
1636 3rd Ave # 309
New York, NY 10128-3622, USA

Cathcard, Patti (Musician)
PO Box 5501
Beverly Hills, CA 90209-5501, USA

Cathcart, Royal (Athlete, Football Player)
4585 Green Tree Ln
Irvine, CA 92612-2239, USA

Cathcart, Sam (Athlete, Football Player)
370 Las Alturas Rd
Santa Barbara, CA 93103-2179, USA

Cather, Mike (Athlete, Baseball Player)
12215 Magnolia Crescent Dr
Roswell, GA 30075-5568, USA

Catherwood, Mike (Radio Personality, Reality TV Star)
c/o Staff Member *Core Entertainment*
14742 Ventura Blvd Ph
Sherman Oaks, CA 91403, USA

Catledge, Terry (Athlete, Basketball Player)
4667 Market St
Tupelo, MS 38801-8432, USA

Catlett, Mary Jo (Actor)
c/o Nancy Abt *Daniel Hoff Agency*
5455 Wilshire Blvd Ste 1100
Los Angeles, CA 90036-4277, USA

Catlett, Sid (Basketball Player)
3110 Scottish Ave
Suitland, MD 20746-3136, USA

Catlin, Tom (Athlete, Football Player)
22621 NE 25th Way
Sammamish, WA 98074-6413, USA

Cato, Keefe (Athlete, Baseball Player)
98 Maryton Rd
White Plains, NY 10603-2016, USA

Cato, Kelvin (Athlete, Basketball Player)
13607 Winter Creek Ct
Houston, TX 77077-1550, USA

Cato, Robert Milton (Prime Minister)
PO Box 138 Ratho Mill
SAINT VINCENT & GRENADINES

Caton, Jack Joseph (General)
17230 Citronia St
Northridge, CA 91325-1934, USA

Caton Jones, Michael (Director)
c/o Staff Member *WmE2 (WMA-LA)*
1 William Morris Pl
Beverly Hills, CA 90212-4261, USA

Catrow, David (Cartoonist, Editor)
202 N Limestone St
Springfield, OH 45503-4202, USA

Cattage, Bobby (Athlete, Basketball Player)
4838 US Highway 29 S
Auburn, AL 36830-8184, USA

Cattaneo, Peter (Director)
76 Oxford St
London W1N OAX, UNITED KINGDOM (UK)

Cattermole, Paul (Actor)
4 Flitcroft Street
London WC2H 8D, United Kingdom

Catto, Henry E Jr (Diplomat)
110 E Crockett St
San Antonio, TX 78205-2612, USA

Cattrail, Kim (Actor)
c/o Carol Bodie *International Creative Management (ICM-LA)*
10250 Constellation Blvd Fl 7
Los Angeles, CA 90067-6207, USA

Cattrall, Kim (Actor)
89 Gerard Dr
East Hampton, NY 11937-4701, USA

Caubere, Philippe (Actor)
23 Avenue Philippe-Auguste
Paris F-75011, France

Caudill, Bill (Athlete, Baseball Player)
11605 NE 41st St
Kirkland, WA 98033-8742, USA

Caudill, Daniel (Stylist)
c/o Staff Member *Celestine - CA*
1666 20th St Ste 200B
Santa Monica, CA 90404-3828, USA

Cauduro, Eugenia (Actor)
c/o Staff Member *Televisa*
Blvd Adolfo Lopez Mateos 232 Colonia San Angel INN
DF CP 01060, MEXICO

Cauffiel, Jessica (Actor)
c/o Michael Greene *Greene & Associates*
1901 Avenue Of The Stars Ste 130
Los Angeles, CA 90067-6030, USA

Caufield, Jay (Athlete, Hockey Player)
106 Quail Hollow Ln
Wexford, PA 15090-7596, USA

Caulfield, Emma (Actor)
c/o Ellen Drantch-Billet *EDB Management*
11657 La Grange Ave
Los Angeles, CA 90025-5331, USA

Caulfield, Lore (Designer, Fashion Designer)
2228 Cotner Ave
Los Angeles, CA 90064-1802, USA

Caulfield, Maxwell (Actor)
c/o Tim Angle *Don Buchwald & Associates Inc (LA)*
6500 Wilshire Blvd Ste 2200
Los Angeles, CA 90048-4942, USA

Caulkins, Tracy (Athlete, Swimmer)
511 Oman St
Nashville, TN 37203-1234, USA

Causey, Kevin (Athlete, Baseball Player)
3220 St Martins Trl Apt 141
Richmond, VA 23294-4921, USA

Causey, Wayne (Athlete, Baseball Player)
2905 Paynter Dr
Ruston, LA 71270-5242, USA

Causwell, Duane (Athlete, Basketball Player)
3 Pierce Dr
Stony Point, NY 10980-3701, USA

Cauterize (Music Group)
c/o Staff Member *Wind-up Records*
72 Madison Ave Fl 8
New York, NY 10016-8731, USA

Cauthen, Stephen M (Steve) (Misc)
RFD Boone County 167 S Main St
Walton, KY 41094, USA

Cauthen, Steve (Athlete, Jockey)
167 N Main St
Walton, KY 41094-1150, USA

Cavadini, Catherine (Cathy) (Actor)
c/o Staff Member *International Creative Management (ICM-LA)*
10250 Constellation Blvd Fl 7
Los Angeles, CA 90067-6207, USA

Cavaiani, Jon R (War Hero)
10956 Green St Unit 230
Columbia, CA 95310-9742, USA

Cavalera, Max (Musician)
1924 Spring St
Paso Robles, CA 93446-1620, USA

Cavaleri, Ray (Producer)
c/o Staff Member *Cavaleri & Associates*
178 S Victory Blvd Ste 205
Burbank, CA 91502-2881, USA

Cavaliere, Felix (Composer, Musician)
PO Box 253
Audubon, NJ 08106-0253, USA

Cavallari, Kristin (Actor, Reality TV Star)
c/o Susan Calogerakis *Thruline Entertainment*
9250 Wilshire Blvd Ground Fl
Beverly Hills, CA 90212, USA

Cavalli, Carmen (Athlete, Football Player)
6221 Madison Ct
Bensalem, PA 19020-1802, USA

Cavalli, Constanza (Actor)
c/o Gabriel Blanco *Gabriel Blanco Iglesias (Mexico)*
Rio Balsas 35-32 Colonia Cuauhtemoc
DF 6500, Mexico

Cavalli, Roberto (Designer, Fashion Designer)
Via del Cantone 29 Osmannoro Sesto Florentino
Firenze 50019, ITALY

Cavallini, Gino (Athlete, Hockey Player)
6614 Clayton Rd Unit 315
Saint Louis, MO 63117-1602, USA

Cavallini, Paul (Athlete, Hockey Player)
7201 Kingsbury Blvd
Saint Louis, MO 63130-4139, USA

Cavanagh, Megan (Actor)
c/o Staff Member *Framework Entertainment (LA)*
9057 Nemo St Ste C
West Hollywood, CA 90069-5511, USA

Cavanagh, Tom (Actor)
c/o Charles Mastropietro *Dontanville/ Frattaroli (D/F)*
270 Lafayette St Ste 402
New York, NY 10012-3327, USA

Cavanaugh, Christine (Actor)
342 S Cochran Ave # 30
Los Angeles, CA 90036-3320, USA

Cavanaugh, Joe (Athlete, Hockey Player)
25 Nathaniel Green Dr
East Greenwich, RI 02818-2019, USA

Cavanaugh, Matthew A (Matt) (Athlete, Football Player)
8 Barstad Ct
Lutherville Timonium, MD 21093-3501, USA

Cavanaugh, Michael (Actor)
165 W 46th St
New York, NY 10036-2501, USA

Cavanaugh, Page (Musician)
9420 Reseda Blvd
Northridge, CA 91324-2932, USA

Cavaretta, Philip J (Phil) (Athlete, Baseball Player, Coach)
4637 Kellogg Dr SW
Lilburn, GA 30047-4407, USA

Cavazos, Lauro F (Secretary)
173 Annursnac Hill Rd
Concord, MA 01742-5402, USA

Cavazos, Lumi (Actor)
8265 W Sunset Blvd Ste 203
West Hollywood, CA 90046-2470, USA

Cave, Jessie (Actor)
c/o Dallas Smith *United Agents*
12-26 Lexington St
London W1F OLE, UK

Cave, Nick (Musician, Songwriter, Writer)
833 W Chicago Ave Ste 101
Chicago, IL 60642-8408, USA

Caven, Ingrid (Actor)
Parque Pisa C/Exposición, 8, 1° izq
Mairena del Aljarafe 41927, Spain

Cavenall, Ron (Athlete, Basketball Player)
PO Box 450983
Houston, TX 77245-0983, USA

Caver, James (Athlete, Football Player)
10722 Mersington Ave
Kansas City, MO 64137-1870, USA

Caver, Quinton (Athlete, Football Player)
2062 Montclair Manor Dr
Saint Charles, MO 63303-4082, USA

Cavett, Dick (Actor, Writer)
c/o Joanne Nici *Don Buchwald & Associates Inc (NY)*
10 E 44th St Frnt 1
New York, NY 10017-3654

Cavic, Milorad (Mike) (Swimmer)
Swimming Haas Pavilion # 4422
Berkeley, CA 94720-0001, USA

Caviezel, James (Jim) (Actor)
c/o Hildy Gottlieb *International Creative Management (ICM-LA)*
10250 Constellation Blvd Fl 7
Los Angeles, CA 90067-6207, USA

Cavill, Henry (Actor)
c/o Mandi Warren *Viewpoint Inc. - NY*
700 N San Vicente Blvd Ste G910
West Hollywood, CA 90069-5061, USA

Cavness, Grady (Athlete, Football Player)
7007 Roberson Rd
Missouri City, TX 77489-2508, USA

Cavuto, Neil (Television Host)
c/o Staff Member *Fox News Channel (NY)*
1211 Ave Of The Americas Level C1
New York, NY 10036-8701, USA

Cawley, Tucker (Actor)
c/o Adam Berkowitz *Creative Artists Agency (CAA-LA)*
2000 Avenue of the Stars Ste 100
Los Angeles, CA 90067-4705, USA

Cawley, Warren (Rex) (Athlete, Track Athlete)
1655 San Rafael Dr
Corona, CA 92882-6410, USA

Caylor, Lowell (Athlete, Football Player)
403 Woodway Dr
Greer, SC 29651-6869, USA

Cayne, Candis (Actor, Model)
c/o Nikki Weiss *Nikki Weiss & Co.*
754 N La Jolla Ave
Los Angeles, CA 90046-6808, USA

Ce Marco, Cardinal (Religious Leader)
S Marco 318
Venice 30124, ITALY

Ceasar, Andrew (Stylist)
c/o Staff Member *The Montgomery Group*
210 W 29th St Fl 6
New York, NY 10001-5205, USA

Ceaser, Curtis (Athlete, Football Player)
4805 Corley St
Beaumont, TX 77707-4224, USA

Ceballos, Cedric (Athlete, Basketball Player)
3068 FM 1252 W
Kilgore, TX 75662-4830, USA

Ceberano, Kate (Musician)
Kildean Lane
Winchelsea, VIC 3241, AUSTRALIA

Ceccarelli, Art (Athlete, Baseball Player)
63 Hall Dr
Orange, CT 06477-2545, USA

Ceccato, Aldo (Conductor)
Chaunt da Crusch
Zuoz 7524, SWITZERLAND

Cece (Stylist)
c/o Staff Member *Maximum Talent*
1873 S Bellaire St Ste 915
Denver, CO 80222-4356, USA

Cech, Thomas R (Nobel Prize Laureate)
PO Box 215
Boulder, CO 80306-0215, USA

Cechmanek, Roman (Athlete, Hockey Player)
1111 S Figueroa St
Los Angeles, CA 90015-1300, USA

Cecil, Chuck (Radio Personality)
1288 N Bellflower Blvd
Long Beach, CA 90815-4149, USA

Cedano, Roger (Athlete, Baseball Player)
9325 Byron Ave
Surfside, FL 33154-2437, USA

Cedarstrom, Gary (Athlete, Baseball Player)
1610 18th St SE
Minot, ND 58701-6087, USA

Cedeno, Cesar E (Athlete, Baseball Player)
9919 Sagedowne Ln
Houston, TX 77089-4309, USA

Cedeno, Matt (Actor)
c/o Ryan Daly *Zero Gravity Management*
11578 Canton Dr
Studio City, CA 91604-4160, USA

Cedras, Raoul (General)
Panama City, PANAMA

Cefalo, Jimmy (Athlete, Football Player)
6675 Roxbury Ln
Miami Beach, FL 33141-4532, USA

Ceglarski, Leonard (Len) (Athlete, Coach, Hockey Player)
61 Lantern Ln
Duxbury, MA 02332-4915, USA

Ceika, Alex (Athlete, Golfer)
11589 Caldicot Dr
Las Vegas, NV 89138-1541, USA

Celant, Gerwano (Misc)
1971 5th Ave
New York, NY 10128, USA

Celaya, Adolfo (War Hero)
977 Schulman St
Santa Clara, CA 95050, USA

Celeda (Musician)
c/o Staff Member *Diva Central Inc*
7510 W Sunset Blvd Ste 1445
Los Angeles, CA 90046-3408, USA

Celestand, John (Athlete, Basketball Player, Sportscaster)
c/o Staff Member *Maxx Sports & Entertainment*
546 5th Ave Fl 6
New York, NY 10036-5000, USA

Celestin, Oliver (Athlete, Football Player)
635 Hendee St
New Orleans, LA 70114-1409, USA

Celi, AJ (Reality TV Star)
6506 Hollywood Blvd
Los Angeles, CA 90028-6210, USA

Celi, Ari (Actor)
c/o Staff Member *Silver Massetti & Szatmary (SMS) Talent Inc*
8730 W Sunset Blvd Ste 440
Los Angeles, CA 90069-2277, USA

Cellini, Cristina (Stylist)
c/o Staff Member *Artists by Timothy Priano (CA)*
8447 Wilshire Blvd Ste 301
Beverly Hills, CA 90211-3206, USA

Cellins, Art (Basketball Player)
1812 NW 55th Ter
Miami, FL 33142-3044, USA

Cellucci, A Paul (Diplomat, Ex-Governor)
265 Franklin St
Boston, MA 02110-3113, USA

Celmins, Vija (Artist)
49 Crosby St
New York, NY 10012-4464, USA

Celotto, Mario (Athlete, Football Player)
47 Evirel Pl
Oakland, CA 94611-1323, USA

Celtic Woman (Music Group, Musician)
c/o Staff Member *WmE2 (Endeavor-LA)*
9601 Wilshire Blvd Fl 3
Beverly Hills, CA 90210-5219, USA

Cena, John (Actor, Wrestler)
c/o Stacey Pokluda *Baker Winokur Ryder Public Relations (BWR-LA)*
9100 Wilshire Blvd Ste 500 PMB WEST
Beverly Hills, CA 90212-3426, USA

Cenci, John (Athlete, Football Player)
942 Rita Dr
Pittsburgh, PA 15221-3964, USA

Cenker, Robert J (Astronaut)
155 Hickory Corner Rd
East Windsor, NJ 08520-2417, USA

Cennamo, Ralph (Misc)
265 W 14th St
New York, NY 10011-7103, USA

Centers, Larry (Athlete, Football Player)
5023 Stagecoach Way
Grand Prairie, TX 75052-2439, USA

Cepeda, Angie (Actor)
c/o Katrina Bayonas *Kuranda Management*
Santo Angel, 84
Madrid 28043, Spain

Cepeda, Orlando (Athlete, Baseball Player)
2305 Palmer Ct
Fairfield, CA 94534-7550, USA

Cepicky, Matt (Athlete, Baseball Player)
7 Upper Bluffs View Ct
Eureka, MO 63025-3724, USA

Cepicky, Scott (Baseball Player)
1335 Polo Fields Ln
Columbia, TN 38401-7360, USA

Cera, Michael (Actor)
c/o William Mercer *Thruline Entertainment*
9250 Wilshire Blvd Ground Fl
Beverly Hills, CA 90212, USA

Cerami, Anthony (Misc)
Ram Island Dr
Shelter Island, NY 11964, USA

Cerbone, Jason (Actor)
c/o Vera Mihailovich *Forward Entertainment*
9255 W Sunset Blvd Ste 805
Los Angeles, CA 90069-3305, USA

Cerda, Jaime (Athlete, Baseball Player)
2707 Northhill St
Selma, CA 93662-4313, USA

Ceresino, Gordy (Athlete, Football Player)
PO Box 675515
Rancho Santa Fe, CA 92067-5515, USA

Ceresino, Ray (Athlete, Hockey Player)
13282 Ocean Vista Rd
San Diego, CA 92130-1862, USA

Cerezo, Arevalo M Vincio (President)
Avda Elena 20-66
Guatemala City, GUATEMALA

Cerf, Vinton G (Scientist)
3614 Camelot Dr
Annandale, VA 22003-1302, USA

Cerha, Friedrich (Composer, Conductor)
Dorotheergasse 10 PO Box 882
Vienna 1011, AUSTRIA

Cerlan, Paul G (General)
3524 Old Course Ln
Valrico, FL 33596-9219, USA

Cernadas, Segundo (Actor)
c/o Staff Member *Telefe - Argentina*
Pavon 2444 (C1248AAT)
Buenos Aires, ARGENTINA

Cernan, Eugene A. (Astronaut)
c/o Staff Member *St Martins Press*
175 5th Ave
New York, NY 10010-7703, USA

Cerne, Joseph (Joe) (Athlete, Football Player)
408 Prospect Ave
Minneapolis, MN 55419-1263, USA

Cernik, Frantisek (Athlete, Hockey Player)
Arena Ruska 3077/135
Ostraka-Zabreh PSC 700 30, Czech Republic

Cerny, Jobe (Artist, Voice Over Artist)
259 Hazel Ave
Highland Park, IL 60035-3359

Ceron, Laura (Actor)
c/o Michael Greenwald *Don Buchwald & Associates Inc (LA)*
6500 Wilshire Blvd Ste 2200
Los Angeles, CA 90048-4942, USA

Cerone, Rick (Athlete, Baseball Player)
34 Winding Way
Woodland Park, NJ 07424-2669, USA

Cerqua, Marq (Athlete, Football Player)
18800 NE 29th Ave Apt 1122
Miami, FL 33180-2855, USA

Cerrone, Rick (Athlete)
100 Old Palisade Rd
Fort Lee, NJ 07024-7064

Cerruda, Ron (Golfer)
c/o Staff Member *Pro Golfers Association (PGA) Tour*
112 Tpc Blvd
Ponte Vedra Beach, FL 32082, USA

Cerruti, Nino (Designer, Fashion Designer)
3 Place de la Madeleine
Paris 75008, FRANCE

Certo, Tish (Athlete, Golfer)
151 Buffalo Ave Apt 211
Niagara Falls, NY 14303-1200, USA

Cerv, Robert H (Bob) (Athlete, Baseball Player)
805 N 22nd St Apt 1A
Blair, NE 68008-1195, USA

Cervantes, Gary (Actor)
2240 Mardel Ave
Whittier, CA 90601-1532, USA

Cervelli, Francisco (Athlete, Baseball Player)
c/o Team Member *New York Yankees*
Yankee Stadium 161st St & River Ave
Bronx, NY 10451, USA

Cervenka, Exene (Musician)
8901 Melrose Ave # 200
West Hollywood, CA 90069-5605, USA

Cerveris, Michael
c/o Staff Member *Innovative Artists (LA)*
1505 10th St
Santa Monica, CA 90401-2805, USA

Cervi, Al (Athlete, Basketball Player)
177 Dunrovin Ln
Rochester, NY 14618-4815, USA

Cervl, Alfred N (Al) (Basketball Player)
177 Dunrovin Ln
Rochester, NY 14618-4815, USA

Cervl, Valentina (Actor)
20 Ave Rapp
Paris 75007, FRANCE

Cesaire, Aime Ferdinand (Writer)
La Mairie Fort-de-France
Martinique 97200, WEST INDIES

Cesaire, Jacques (Athlete, Football Player)
43 Meadow Pond Dr Apt A
Leominster, MA 01453-4260, USA

Cesare, Billy (Athlete, Football Player)
1655 Hendry Isles Blvd
Clewiston, FL 33440-5825, USA

Cestaro, Alexander (Athlete, Football Player)
289 Devoe Ave
Yonkers, NY 10705-2709, USA

Cetara, Peter (Musician)
c/o Staff Member *MPI Talent Agency*
1801 Avenue of the Stars Ste 1420
Los Angeles, CA 90067-5899, USA

Cetera, Peter (Musician, Songwriter, Writer)
c/o Staff Member *Monterey International (Chicago)*
200 W Superior St Ste 202
Chicago, IL 60654-6422, USA

Cetlinski, Matthew (Matt) (Swimmer)
13121 SE 93rd Terrace Rd
Summerfield, FL 34491-9347, USA

Ceulemans, Raymond
Grote Markt 28
Lier BE-2500, BELGIUM

Cey, Ron (Athlete, Baseball Player)
22714 Creole Rd
Woodland Hills, CA 91364-3925, USA

Chabat, Alain (Actor, Producer)
18, blvd Montmartre
Paris 75009, France

Chaber, Madelyn J (Attorney, Attorney General, General)
101 California St
San Francisco, CA 94111-5802, USA

Chabert, Lacey (Actor)
c/o Aaron Ray *Collective*
8383 Wilshire Blvd Ste 1050
Beverly Hills, CA 90211-2415, USA

Chabon, Michael (Writer)
c/o Staff Member *United Talent Agency (UTA)*
9560 Wilshire Blvd Fl 5
Beverly Hills, CA 90212-2400, USA

Chabot, Herbert L (Judge)
400 2nd St NW
Washington, DC 20217-0001, USA

Chabot, John (Athlete, Coach, Hockey Player)
c/o Staff Member *New York Islanders*
1255 Hempstead Tpke
Uniondale, NY 11553-1260, USA

Chabot, Steve (Congressman, Politician)
2351 Rayburn Hob
Washington, DC 20515-0525, USa

Chabraja, Nicholas D (Business Person)
3190 Fairview Park Dr
Falls Church, VA 22042-4530, USA

Chabria, Renee (Director)
c/o Staff Member *Management 360*
9111 Wilshire Blvd
Beverly Hills, CA 90210-5508, USA

Chace, William E (Educator)
Prisident S Ofc
Atlanta, GA 30322-0001, USA

Chacon, Alex Pineda (Soccer Player)
1010 Rose Bowl Dr
Pasadena, CA 91103, USA

Chacon, Shawn (Athlete, Baseball Player)
7610 W 19th Street Rd
Greeley, CO 80634-8628, USA

Chacurian, Chico (Soccer Player)
96 Stratford Rd
Stratford, CT 06615-7760, USA

Chadha, Gurinder (Director)
c/o Staff Member *International Creative Management (ICM-LA)*
10250 Constellation Blvd Fl 7
Los Angeles, CA 90067-6207, USA

Chadirji, Rifat Kamil (Architect)
28 Troy Court Kensington High St
London W8, UNITED KINGDOM (UK)

Chadli, Bendjedid (President)
Palace Emir Abedelkader
Algiers, ALGERIA

Chadnois, Lynn (Athlete, Football Player)
2048 Walden Ct
Flint, MI 48532-2419, USA

Chadwick, Bill (Athlete, Hockey Player)
PO Box 789
Cutchogue, NY 11935-0789, USA

Chadwick, J Leslie (Les) (Musician)
21A Cliftown Road Southend-on-Sea
Essex SS1 1AB, UNITED KINGDOM (UK)

Chadwick, Jeff (Athlete, Football Player)
23062 Village Dr Apt A
Lake Forest, CA 92630-4955, USA

Chadwick, June (Actor)
610 Santa Monica Blvd Ste 202
Santa Monica, CA 90401-1645, USA

Chadwick, Ray (Athlete, Baseball Player)
607 Gattis St
Durham, NC 27701-2831, USA

Chadwick, William L (Bill) (Misc)
PO Box 501
Cutchogue, NY 11935-0501, USA

Chafee, Lincoln (Governor, Politician)
Office of the Governor 222 State House
Providence, RI 2908, USA

Chafer, Derek (Actor)
Tigris House 256 Edgware Rd
London W2 1DS, UK

Chafetz, Sidney (Artist)
Art Dept
Columbus, OH 43210, USA

Chaffee, Don (Director)
7020 La Presa Dr
Los Angeles, CA 90068-3105, USA

Chaffee, Susan (Suzy) (Skier)
5106 E Woodwind Ln
Anaheim, CA 92807-1239, USA

Chaffetz, Jason (Congressman, Politician)
1032 Longworth Hob
Washington, DC 20515-3819, USA

Chaffey, Pat (Athlete, Football Player)
10415 SW Gardner Ct
Tualatin, OR 97062-7208, USA

Chafin, Bryan (Actor)
c/o Heather Collier *Collier Talent Agency*
2313 Lake Austin Blvd Ste 103
Austin, TX 78703-4545, USA

Chaiken, Ilene (Producer, Writer)
c/o Jen Turner *Wolf Kasteler Van Iden & Associates (NY)*
584 Broadway Rm 310
New York, NY 10012-5246, USA

Chaikin, Carly (Actor)
c/o Andrew Rogers *International Creative Management (ICM-LA)*
10250 Constellation Blvd Fl 7
Los Angeles, CA 90067-6207, USA

Chailly, Riccardo (Conductor)
Royal Concertgebrew Jacob Obrechtstraat 51
Armsterdam, 1071 KJ 41, HOLLAND

Chairmen of the Board (Musician)
c/o Staff Member *The Willis Blume Agency*
PO Box 509
Orangeburg, SC 29116-0509, USA

Chakales, Bob (Athlete, Baseball Player)
8916 River Rd
Richmond, VA 23229-7718, USA

Chakiris, George (Actor, Dancer, Musician)
7266 Clinton St
Los Angeles, CA 90036-1969, USA

Chakraborty, Pramod (Bollywood, Director, Filmmaker, Producer)
Natraj Studios 194 M V Road Andheri (E)
Bombay, MS 400 069, INDIA

Chakravarthi, Vinu (Actor, Bollywood)
63 Apusali St
Chennai, TN 600093, INDIA

Chakravarthy, Dheephan (Actor)
Auroammaa 5/17 Royal Villa 4th Main Road Extn Kottur Gardens
Chennai, TN 600 085, INDIA

Chalayan, Hussein (Designer, Fashion Designer)
71 Endell Road
London WC2 9AJ, UNITED KINGDOM (UK)

Chalenski, Mike (Athlete, Football Player)
225 S Michigan Ave
Kenilworth, NJ 07033-1727, USA

Chalfont, A G (Arthur) (Government Official)
Westminster
London SW1A 0PW, UNITED KINGDOM (UK)

Chalk, Dave (Athlete, Baseball Player)
137 Cross Timbers Trl
Coppell, TX 75019-3731, USA

Chalke, Sarah (Actor)
c/o John Carrabino *John Carrabino Management*
5900 Wilshire Blvd Ste 406
Los Angeles, CA 90036-5015, USA

Chalker, Will (Model)
c/o Staff Member *New York Model Management*
596 Broadway # 701
New York, NY 10012-3396, USA

Challis, Christopher (Cinematographer)
c/o Frances Russell P.O. Box 2587, Winsor Rd
Gerrards Cross SL9 7WZ, UK

Chalmers, Judith (Actor)
23 Eyot Gardens
London W10 5AT, UK

Chalmers, Thea (Stylist)
2459 Mar East St
Tiburon, CA 94920-1203, USA

Chaloner, William G (Misc)
20 Parke Road
London SW13 9NG, UNITED KINGDOM (UK)

Chambaret, Catherine (Stylist)
5015 W 8th St
Los Angeles, CA 90005-3812, USA

Chamberlain, Bill (Athlete, Basketball Player)
1809 Nantuckett Ln Apt 202
Charlotte, NC 28270-3322, USA

Chamberlain, Byron (Athlete, Football Player)
6176 Lake Paddock Dr
Florissant, MO 63033-4721, USA

Chamberlain, Craig (Athlete, Baseball Player)
11292 Los Alamitos Blvd
Los Alamitos, CA 90720-3958, USA

Chamberlain, Dan (Athlete, Football Player)
6356 Puerto Dr
Rancho Murieta, CA 95683-9357, USA

Chamberlain, Jimmy (Actor, Musician)
c/o Staff Member *WmE2 (WMA-LA)*
1 William Morris Pl
Beverly Hills, CA 90212-4261, USA

Chamberlain, Joba (Athlete, Baseball Player)
c/o Team Member *New York Yankees*
Yankee Stadium 161st St & River Ave
Bronx, NY 10451, USA

Chamberlain, John A (Artist)
1315 10th St
Sarasota, FL 34236-3302, USA

Chamberlain, Joseph W (Astronomer)
Space Physics & Astronomy Dept
Houston, TX 77001, USA

Chamberlain, Owen (Nobel Prize Laureate)
882 Santa Barbara Rd
Berkeley, CA 94707-2018, USA

Chamberlain, Richard (Actor)
c/o Staff Member *Diamond Management*
31 Percy St
London W1T 2DD, UK

Chamberlain, Wes (Athlete, Baseball Player)
PO Box 1358
Homewood, IL 60430-0358, USA

Chambers, Al (Athlete, Baseball Player)
1303 N 14th St
Harrisburg, PA 17103-1206, USA

Chambers, Anne Cox (Business Person, Diplomat)
1440 Lake Hearn Dr NE
Atlanta, GA 30319, USA

Chambers, Christina (Actor)
c/o Lena Roklin *Luber Roklin Management*
8530 Wilshire Blvd Ste 550
Beverly Hills, CA 90211-3133, USA

Chambers, Cliff (Athlete, Baseball Player)
815 N Eagle Rd Rm 223
Eagle, ID 83616-5761, USA

Chambers, Emma (Actor)
c/o Staff Member *Conway van Gelder*
8-12 Broadwick St
London W1F 8HW, UK

Chambers, Erin (Actor)
c/o Ted Schachter *Schachter Entertainment*
1157 S Beverly Dr Fl 2
Los Angeles, CA 90035-1119, USA

Chambers, Faune (Actor)
c/o Staff Member *Luber Roklin Management*
8530 Wilshire Blvd Ste 550
Beverly Hills, CA 90211-3133, USA

Chambers, Faune (Actor)
c/o Mara Santino *Luber Roklin Management*
8530 Wilshire Blvd Ste 550
Beverly Hills, CA 90211-3133, USA

Chambers, Jerry (Athlete, Basketball Player)
4135 Don Diablo Dr
Los Angeles, CA 90008-4305, USA

Chambers, Justin (Actor)
c/o Sandra Chang *Industry Entertainment Partners*
955 Carrillo Dr Ste 300
Los Angeles, CA 90048-5400, USA

Chambers, Kasey (Musician)
c/o Staff Member *Paradigm (Monterey)*
404 W Franklin St
Monterey, CA 93940-2303, USA

Chambers, Kirk (Athlete, Football Player)
1294 Lakeview Dr
Provo, UT 84604-2933, USA

Chambers, Lester (Musician)
PO Box 770850
Orlando, FL 32877-0850, USA

Chambers, Lucinda (Stylist)
c/o Staff Member *Art Partner*
145 Hudson St Frnt 2
New York, NY 10013-2122, USA

Chambers, Shawn (Athlete, Hockey Player)
9999 Wood Rdg
Pequot Lakes, MN 56472-3642, USA

Chambers, Tom (Athlete, Basketball Player)
7437 E Via Dona Rd
Scottsdale, AZ 85266-2154, USA

Chambers, Wallace (Wally) (Athlete, Football Player)
1838 Joslin St
Saginaw, MI 48602-1123, USA

Chambers, Willie (Musician)
PO Box 1428
Studio City, CA 91614-0428, USA

Chamblee, Al (Athlete, Football Player)
845 Garrow Rd
Newport News, VA 23608-3387, USA

Chamblee, Brandel (Athlete, Golfer)
6900 E Princess Dr Unit 2157
Phoenix, AZ 85054-4118, USA

Chamblee, Jim (Athlete, Baseball Player)
1408 Broadway St
Denton, TX 76201-2714, USA

Chambliss, Chris (Athlete, Baseball Player)
12755 Wyngate Trl
Alpharetta, GA 30005-7514, USA

Chambliss, Saxby (Senator)
416 Russell Senate Ofc Building
Washington, DC 20510-0001, USA

Chambon, Pierre H (Misc)
BP 163
Illkirch 67404, FRANCE

Champagne, Andre (Athlete, Hockey Player)
6936 E 75th St
Tulsa, OK 74133-3037, USA

Champion, Billy (Athlete, Baseball Player)
240 Triple H Farm Rd
Inman, SC 29349, USA

Champion, Mike (Athlete, Baseball Player)
28952 Modjeska Canyon Rd
Silverado, CA 92676-9779, USA

Champion, Will (Musician)
1650 W 2nd Ave
Vancouver, BC V6J 4R3, CANADA

Champlin, Charles (Critic)
2169 Linda Flora Dr
Los Angeles, CA 90077-1408, USA

Champnella, Eric (Actor, Director, Writer)
c/o Paul Nelson *Mosaic Media Group*
9200 W Sunset Blvd Ste 10
Los Angeles, CA 90069-3608, USA

Champoux, Bob (Athlete, Hockey Player)
8861 Centaurus Way
San Diego, CA 92126-1916, USA

Chan, Ernie (Cartoonist)
4131 Vale Ave
Oakland, CA 94619-2223, USA

Chan, Jackie (Actor, Producer)
c/o Philip Button *WmE2 (Endeavor-LA)*
9601 Wilshire Blvd Fl 3
Beverly Hills, CA 90210-5219, USA

Chan, Johnny (Misc)
c/o Mark Karowe Box 3247
Manhattan Beach, CA 90266, USA

Chan, Jullus (Prime Minister)
PO Box 6030 Boroto
PAPUA NEW GUINEA

Chan, Sy (Misc)
Phnom-Penh
PEOPLE'S REPUBLIC OF KAMPUCHEA

Chance, Bob (Athlete, Baseball Player)
2258 Oakridge Dr
Charleston, WV 25311-1723, USA

Chance, Britton (Misc, Yachtsman)
4014 Pine St
Philadelphia, PA 19104-4132, USA

Chance, Dean (Athlete, Baseball Player)
9505 W Smithville Western Rd
Wooster, OH 44691-9209, USA

Chance, Greyson (Musician)
c/o Guy Oseary *Untitled Entertainment (LA)*
350 S Beverly Dr Ste 200
Beverly Hills, CA 90212-4819, USA

Chance, Larry (Musician)
141 Dunbar Ave
Fords, NJ 08863-1551, USA

Chancellor, Van (Coach)
2 Greenway Plz Ste 400
Houston, TX 77046-0202, USA

Chancey, Robert (Athlete, Football Player)
PO Box 212
Coosada, AL 36020-0212, USA

Chanchez, Hosea (Actor)
c/o Glenn Rigberg *Inphenate*
9701 Wilshire Blvd Fl 10
Beverly Hills, CA 90212-2010, USA

Chandler, Al (Athlete, Football Player)
PO Box 21733
Oklahoma City, OK 73156-1733, USA

Chandler, Ben (Congressman, Politician)
1504 Longworth Hob
Washington, DC 20515-4101, USA

Chandler, Christopher M (Chris) (Athlete, Football Player)
1625 Lugano Ln
Del Mar, CA 92014-4126, USA

Chandler, Donald G (Don) (Athlete, Football Player)
3248 E 93rd St
Tulsa, OK 74137-3639, USA

Chandler, Gene (Athlete, Football Player)
550 Southmoor Cir
Stockbridge, GA 30281-4974, USA

Chandler, Jeff (Boxer)
6242 Horner St
Philadelphia, PA 19144, USA

Chandler, Karl (Athlete, Football Player)
5 Plymouth Rd
Newtown Square, PA 19073-1409, USA

Chandler, Kim (Stylist)
c/o Staff Member *Jam Arts, Inc*
154 W 57th St
New York, NY 10019-3321, USA

Chandler, Kyle (Actor)
c/o Cynthia Pett-Dante *Brillstein Entertainment Partners*
9150 Wilshire Blvd Ste 350
Beverly Hills, CA 90212-3453, USA

Chandler, Mark (Stylist)
c/o Staff Member *Art Department*
48 Greene St Fl 4
New York, NY 10013-2663, USA

Chandler, Thornton (Athlete, Football Player)
8646 Guinevere St
Houston, TX 77029-3357, USA

Chandler, Tyson (Athlete, Basketball Player)
21731 Ventura Blvd Ste 300
Woodland Hills, CA 91364-1851, USA

Chandler, Wesley S (Wes) (Athlete, Football Player)
207 Howard Ave
New Smyrna Beach, FL 32168-8195, USA

Chandler, Wilson (Athlete, Basketball Player)
c/o Chris Luchey *CGL Sports*
885 Woodstock Rd Ste 430-303
Roswell, GA 30075-2277, USA

Chandola, Walter (Photographer)
50 Spring Hill Rd
Annandale, NJ 08801-3505, USA

Chandra, Asha (Actor, Bollywood)
C6/6 Sangeeta Apartments Juhu Santacruz
Mumbai, MS 400049, INDIA

Chandran, S S (Actor)
34A Asumpon Muthuramalingum Street
Rajaji Colony
Chennai, TN 600 092, INDIA

Chandran, Sudha (Actor, Bollywood)
4 Mahant Road Extension 6141250 Vile Parkel E
Mumbai, MS 400057, INDIA

Chandran, T K S (Actor)
D25 Amutham Colony South Boag Road
Chennai, TN 600 017, INDIA

Chandrasekar (Actor)
34 Senthil Nagar Main Road Chinna
Porur Near Valasaravakkam
Chennai, TN 600 116, INDIA

Chandrasekhar, Bhagwat S (Cricketer)
571 31st Cross 4th Block Jayanagar
Bangalore 56011, INDIA

Chandrasekhar, Jay (Comedian)
c/o Staff Member *United Talent Agency (UTA)*
9560 Wilshire Blvd Fl 5
Beverly Hills, CA 90212-2400, USA

Chanel, Tally (Actor, Model)
3349 Cahuenga Blvd W Ste 1
Los Angeles, CA 90068-1379, USA

Chaney, Darrel (Athlete, Baseball Player)
906 Woodbrier
Sautee Nacoochee, GA 30571-5106, USA

Chaney, Don (Athlete, Basketball Player)
2706 Birchmere Ct
Katy, TX 77450-1303, USA

Chaney, John (Coach)
Athletic Dept
Philadelphia, PA 19122, USA

Chaney, John (Athlete, Basketball Player)
1639 Sharp Rd
Baton Rouge, LA 70815-4879, USA

Chang, Christina (Actor)
c/o Myrna Jacoby *MJ Management*
130 W 57th St Apt 11A
New York, NY 10019-3311, USA

Chang, Chun-hsiung (Prime Minister)
1 Chunghsiao East Road Section 1
Taipei, TAIWAN

Chang, Irene (Stylist)
501 Arguello Blvd Apt 302
San Francisco, CA 94118-3252, USA

Chang, Michael (Athlete, Tennis Player)
28562 Oso Pkwy # D343
Rancho Santa Margarita, CA 92688-5595, USA

Chang, Sarah (Musician)
40 W 57th St
New York, NY 10019-4001, USA

Chang-Diaz, Franklin R (Astronaut)
2101 Nasa Pkwy Spc Center
Houston, TX 77058-3607, USA

Changeux, Jean-Pierre G (Biologist)
47 Rue du Four
Paris 75006, FRANCE

Channing, Carol (Actor, Musician)
101 1st St # 443
Los Altos, CA 94022-2750, USA

Channing, Stockard (Actor)
c/o Judy Hofflund *Hofflund/Polone*
9465 Wilshire Blvd Ste 420
Beverly Hills, CA 90212-2603, USA

Chant, Charlie (Athlete, Baseball Player)
7831 Sycamore Ave
Riverside, CA 92504-2632, USA

Chantels, The (Music Group)
c/o Staff Member *Creative Entertainment Associates Inc*
1950 Old Cuthbert Rd Ste J
Cherry Hill, NJ 08034-1439, USA

Chanticleer (Musician)
c/o Staff Member *International Creative Management (ICM-LA)*
10250 Constellation Blvd Fl 7
Los Angeles, CA 90067-6207, USA

Chantos, Heather (Stylist)
c/o Staff Member *Workgroup (Hollywood)*
8491 W Sunset Blvd # 368
West Hollywood, CA 90069-1911, USA

Chantres, Carlos (Baseball Player)
67 Amherst St
Nashua, NH 03064-2561

Chao, Elaine L (Secretary)
200 Constitution Ave NW
Washington, DC 20210-0001, USA

Chao, Rosalind (Actor)
6500 Wilshire Blvd Ste 2200
Los Angeles, CA 90048-4942, USA

Chao, Vic (Actor)
c/o Staff Member *Osbrink Talent Agency*
4343 Lankershim Blvd Ste 100
West Toluca Lake, CA 91602-2705, USA

Chapdelaine, Rene (Athlete, Hockey Player)
662 S Division Rd
Petoskey, MI 49770-8218, USA

Chapelle, Dave (Actor)
c/o Matthew (Matt) Labov *Forefront Media*
5700 Wilshire Blvd Ste 550
Los Angeles, CA 90036-3790, USA

Chapin, Darrin (Athlete, Baseball Player)
328 Portage Easterly Rd
Cortland, OH 44410-9510, USA

Chapin, Doug (Actor, Producer)
1100 Alta Loma Rd Apt 605
West Hollywood, CA 90069-2436, USA

Chapin, Dwight L (Government Official, Publisher)
110 5th St
San Francisco, CA 94103-2918, USA

Chapin, Lauren (Actor)
726 63rd Ave
Vero Beach, FL 32968-9249, USA

Chapin, Schuyler G (Misc)
650 Park Ave
New York, NY 10065-6115, USA

Chapin, Tom (Musician, Songwriter, Writer)
57 Piermont Pl
Piermont, NY 10968-1128, USA

Chaplin, Alexander (Actor)
c/o Tammy Rosen *Sanders Armstrong Caserta*
425 N Robertson Blvd
West Hollywood, CA 90048-1735, USA

Chaplin, Ben (Actor)
c/o Simon Halls *Slate Public Relations*
9000 W Sunset Blvd Ste 915
West Hollywood, CA 90069-5809, USA

Chaplin, Geraldine (Actor, Writer)
c/o Staff Member *WmE2 (WMA-LA)*
1 William Morris Pl
Beverly Hills, CA 90212-4261, USA

Chaplin, Greg (Athlete, Baseball Player)
12426 Glenfield Ave
Tampa, FL 33626-2606, USA

Chaplin, Josephine (Actor)
58 Rue Jean Jacques Rousseau
Paris F-70001, France

Chaplin, Kiera (Actor, Producer)
c/o Staff Member *Creative Artists Agency (CAA-LA)*
2000 Avenue of the Stars Ste 100
Los Angeles, CA 90067-4705, USA

Chaplynsky, Renata (Stylist)
c/o Staff Member *Faucher Artists*
636 Broadway Rm 1218
New York, NY 10012-2624, USA

Chapman, Alvah H Jr (Publisher)
1690 S Bayshore Ln Apt 10A
Miami, FL 33133-4067, USA

Chapman, Beth Nielsen (Musician, Songwriter, Writer)
1222 16th Ave S # 300
Nashville, TN 37212-2926, USA

Chapman, Blair (Athlete, Hockey Player)
2068 Redcoach Rd
Allison Park, PA 15101-3231, USA

Chapman, Bruce K (Government Official)
1201 3rd Ave # 4000
Seattle, WA 98101-3029, USA

Chapman, Clarence (Athlete, Football Player)
14820 Parkside St
Detroit, MI 48238-2155, USA

Chapman, David S (Athlete, Football Player)
789 N Main St
New Martinsville, WV 26155-1414, USA

Chapman, Doug (Athlete, Football Player)
6215 Chesterfield Meadows Dr
Chesterfield, VA 23832-6597, USA

Chapman, Dr Philip K (Astronaut)
11460 E Helm Dr
Scottsdale, AZ 85255-1885, USA

Chapman, Duane (Dog) (Actor, Reality TV Star)
c/o Alan Nevins *Renaissance Literary & Talent*
PO Box 17379
Beverly Hills, CA 90209-3379, USA

Chapman, Gary (Writer)
c/o Staff Member *Northfield Publishing / Moody Publishers*
215 W Locust St
Chicago, IL 60610-3130, USA

Chapman, Georgina (Designer)
601 W 26th St Rm 1425
New York, NY 10001-1160, USA

Chapman, Gil (Athlete, Football Player)
771 Cranford Ave
Westfield, NJ 07090-1308, USA

Chapman, Judith (Actor)
11670 W Sunset Blvd Apt 312
Los Angeles, CA 90049-2069, USA

Chapman, Kelvin (Athlete, Baseball Player)
9301 Laughlin Way
Redwood Valley, CA 95470-6425, USA

Chapman, Kevin (Actor)
c/o Ellen Meyer *Ellen Meyer Management*
8899 Beverly Blvd Ste 612
West Hollywood, CA 90048-2429, USA

Chapman, Lamar (Athlete, Football Player)
18513 N Whitedove Ln
Cleveland, OH 44130-8429, USA

Chapman, Lanei (Actor)
c/o Judy Page *Mitchell K Stubbs & Assoc (MKS)*
8675 Washington Blvd Ste 203
Culver City, CA 90232-7486, USA

Chapman, Leland (Actor, Reality TV Star)
c/o Staff Member *Dog the Bounty Hunter*
235 E 45th St
New York, NY 10017-3305, USA

Chapman, Mark David (Misc)
#81 A 3860 Box 149 Attica Corr. Facility
Attica, NY 14011, USA

Chapman, Mark Lindsay (Actor)
c/o Michael Zanuck *Michael Zanuck Agency*
28035 Dorothy Dr Ste 200
Agoura Hills, CA 91301-2685, USA

Chapman, Michael J (Cinematographer, Director)
505 Sport Hill Rd
Easton, CT 06612-1715, USA

Chapman, Mike (Athlete, Football Player)
8731 Avator Cir
Boerne, TX 78015-4424, USA

Chapman, Nicki (Actor)
c/o Staff Member *Arlington Enterprises Ltd*
1-3 Charlotte St
London W1P 1HD, UNITED KINGDOM (UK)

Chapman, Paul (Actor)
7 Leicester Pl
London WC2H 7RJ, UK

Chapman, Rex (Athlete, Basketball Player)
6014 E Jenan Dr
Scottsdale, AZ 85254-4907, USA

Chapman, Robert F (Judge)
PO Box 253
Linville, NC 28646-0253, USA

Chapman, Steven Curtis (Musician, Songwriter)
PO Box 5010
Brentwood, TN 37024-5010, USA

Chapman, Thomas F (Business Person)
1550 Peachtree St NE
Atlanta, GA 30309-2402, USA

Chapman, Tracy (Musician, Songwriter)
c/o Steven Jensen *The Independent Group*
6363 Wilshire Blvd Ste 115
Los Angeles, CA 90048-5734, USA

Chapman, Travis (Athlete, Baseball Player)
5215 Hickson Rd
Jacksonville, FL 32207-5856, USA

Chapman, Wayne (Athlete, Basketball Player)
3593 Salisbury Dr
Lexington, KY 40510-9742, USA

Chapman, Wes (Ballerina)
890 Broadway
New York, NY 10003-1211, USA

Chapot, Frank (Horse Racer)
1 Ople Rd
Neshanic Station, NJ 8853, USA

Chapoy, Pati (Actor)
c/o Staff Member *TV Azteca*
Periferico Sur 4121 Colonia Fuentes del Pedregal
DF CP 14141, Mexico

Chappas, Harry (Athlete, Baseball Player)
26 SE 1st Ave
Dania, FL 33004-3611, USA

Chappell, Crystal (Actor)
34 Stone Run Rd
Bedminster, NJ 07921-1707, USA

Chappell, Fred D (Writer)
305 Kensington Rd
Greensboro, NC 27403-1732, USA

Chappell, Gregory S (Greg) (Athlete, Cricketer)
60 Jolimont St
Jolimont, VIC 5006, Australia

Chappell, Len (Athlete, Basketball Player)
7624 Chestnut Ln
Waterford, WI 53185-1707, USA

Chappelle, David (Dave) (Actor, Comedian, Producer)
c/o Rick Greenstein *Gersh (LA)*
9465 Wilshire Blvd Ste 600
Beverly Hills, CA 90212-2612, USA

Chapple, Dave (Athlete, Football Player)
5 Kara E
Irvine, CA 92620-1855, USA

Chappuis, Bob (Athlete, Football Player)
4054 Glacier Hills Cir
Ann Arbor, MI 48105-3646, USA

Chapuisat, Stephane (Soccer Player)
Strobeialle
Dortmund 44139, GERMANY

Chapura, Richard (Dick) (Athlete, Football Player)
7853 Saddle Creek Trl
Sarasota, FL 34241-9550, USA

Chara, Zdeno (Athlete, Hockey Player)
343 Commercial St Unit 211-213
Boston, MA 02109-1212, USA

Charan, Raaj N (Actor)
Shri Renuka Mandir 154 Vasudevan Nagar Jaffarkhanpet
Chennai, TN 600 095, INDIA

Charboneau, Joe (Athlete, Baseball Player)
338 Lakeview Ave # B
Sheffield Lake, OH 44054-1718, USA

Charbonneau, Patricia (Actor)
749 1/2 N La Fayette Park Pl
Los Angeles, CA 90026-6559, USA

Charbonneau, Stephane (Athlete, Hockey Player)
1 Wilderness Dr
Voorhees, NJ 08043-3415, USA

Charbonnier, CArole (Athlete, Golfer)
19 Carolina Ave
West Orange, NJ 07052-1804, USA

Charen, Mona (Writer)
c/o Staff Member *HarperCollins Publishers*
10 E 53rd St C/O Author Mail Floor 7
New York, NY 10022, USA

Charette, William R (Doc) (War Hero)
5237 Limberlost Ln
Lake Wales, FL 33898-8866, USA

Charland, Colin (Baseball Player)
1632 Vinewood St
Fort Worth, TX 76112-2948, USA

Charlap, Bill (Musician)
223 1/2 E 48th St
New York, NY 10017, USA

Charlebois, Bob (Athlete, Hockey Player)
318 Duncan Ave
Ottawa, ON K1Z 7G9, Canada

Charles, Annette (Actor)
c/o Staff Member *Coolwaters Productions*
10061 Riverside Dr # 531
Toluca Lake, CA 91602-2560, USA

Charles, Bob (Athlete, Golfer)
5329 Sea Biscuit Rd
Palm Beach Gardens, FL 33418-7818, USA

Charles, Caroline (Designer, Fashion Designer)
56/57 Beauchamp Place
London SW3, UNITED KINGDOM (UK)

Charles, Craig (Actor)
Drury House 34-43 Russell St
London WC2B 5HA, UNITED KINGDOM (UK)

Charles, Daedra (Basketball Player)
Staples Center 111 S Figueroa St
Los Angeles, CA 90015, USA

Charles, Ed (Athlete, Baseball Player)
57 Park Ter E Apt B58
New York, NY 10034-0786, USA

Charles, Frank (Athlete, Baseball Player)
114 Garden Ct
Buffalo, NY 14226-3244, USA

Charles, Gaius (Actor)
c/o Stephen Hirsh *Gersh (LA)*
9465 Wilshire Blvd Ste 600
Beverly Hills, CA 90212-2612, USA

Charles, John (Athlete, Football Player)
5644 Westheimer Rd Apt 164
Houston, TX 77056-4002, USA

Charles, Josh (Actor)
c/o Stephanie Ritz *WmE2 (Endeavor-LA)*
9601 Wilshire Blvd Fl 3
Beverly Hills, CA 90210-5219, USA

Charles, Ken (Athlete, Basketball Player)
621 Putnam Ave
Brooklyn, NY 11221-1601, USA

Charles, RuPaul Andre (Actor, Model, Musician)
332 Bleecker St # F-22
New York, NY 10014-2980, USA

Charles, Suzette
2705 Cricket Hollow Ct
Henderson, NV 89074-1924, USA

Charleson, Leslie (Actor)
4851 Cromwell Ave
Los Angeles, CA 90027-1141, USA

Charlesworth, James H (Misc)
Theology Dept
Princeton, NJ 8540, USA

Charlesworth, Todd (Athlete, Hockey Player)
914 N Brookside Dr
Norton Shores, MI 49441-5365, USA

Charlton, Clifford (Athlete, Football Player)
3708 Carrington Pl
Tallahassee, FL 32303-2041, USA

Charlton, Norm (Athlete, Baseball Player)
312 Estes Dr
Rockport, TX 78382-9758, USA

Charlton, Robert (Bobby) (Soccer Player)
Garthollerton Cleford Road
Ollerton near Knutsford, Cheshire, UNITED KINGDOM (UK)

Charm City Devils (Music Group, Musician)
c/o Staff Member *10th Street Entertainment (NY)*
38 W 21st St Rm 300
New York, NY 10010-6979, USA

Charmila (Actor, Bollywood)
2 7/1 Habibullah Road T Nagar
Chennai, TN 600017, INDIA

Charmoli, Tony (Choreographer, Director)
1271 Sunset Plaza Dr
Los Angeles, CA 90069-1256, USA

Charney, Jordan (Actor)
c/o Staff Member *Leading Artists*
145 W 45th St Rm 1000
New York, NY 10036-4032, USA

Charney, Kim (Actor)
1140 W La Veta Ave
Orange, CA 92868-4225, USA

Charo (Musician)
c/o Staff Member *WmE2 (WMA-LA)*
1 William Morris Pl
Beverly Hills, CA 90212-4261, USA

Charpak, Georges (Nobel Prize Laureate)
2 Rue de Poissy
Paris 75005, FRANCE

Charren, Peggy (Activist)
PO Box 383090
Cambridge, MA 2238, USA

Charron, Guy (Athlete, Hockey Player)
12681 NW 78th Mnr
Parkland, FL 33076-4523, USA

Charron, Paul R (Business Person)
1441 Broadway
New York, NY 10018-1905, USA

Chartier, Dave (Athlete, Hockey Player)
SW 13-19-28 W
Binscarth, MB R0J 0G0, Canada

Chartoff, Melanie (Actor)
1180 S Beverly Dr Ste 301
Los Angeles, CA 90035-1154, USA

Chartoff, Robert (Producer)
PO Box 3628
Granada Hills, CA 91394-0628, USA

Charton, Pete (Athlete, Baseball Player)
104 Hickory Knob Hill Rd
Irmo, SC 29063-9782, USA

Chartraw, Rick (Athlete, Hockey Player)
600 Chaparral Rd
Sierra Madre, CA 91024-1115, USA

Charuhasan (Actor)
37 Maharani Chinnamani Rd
Chennai, TN 600 018, INDIA

Charvet, David (Actor)
c/o Larry Thompson *Larry A Thompson Organization*
9663 Santa Monica Blvd Ste 801
Beverly Hills, CA 90210-4303, USA

Charyk, Joseph V (Business Person)
790 Andrews Ave Apt A302
Delray Beach, FL 33483-7257, USA

Chase, Alison (Director)
PO Box 388
Washington Depot, CT 06794-0388, USA

Chase, Alston (Writer)
c/o Deborah Clarke Grosvenor *The Bohrman Agency*
3141 Ellington Dr
Los Angeles, CA 90068-1738, USA

Chase, Bailey (Actor)
c/o Staff Member *McKeon-Myones Management*
3500 W Olive Ave Ste 770
Burbank, CA 91505-5527, USA

Chase, Barrie (Actor, Dancer)
446 Carroll Canal
Venice, CA 90291-4682, USA

Chase, Chevy (Actor, Comedian, Producer)
c/o Erik Kritzer *Kritzer Levine Wilkins Entertainment*
11872 La Grange Ave Fl 1
Los Angeles, CA 90025-5283, USA

Chase, Daveigh (Actor)
c/o Bonnie Liedtke *Principato/Young Management*
9465 Wilshire Blvd Ste 430
Beverly Hills, CA 90212-2613, USA

Chase, David (Producer)
c/o Staff Member *United Talent Agency (UTA)*
9560 Wilshire Blvd Fl 5
Beverly Hills, CA 90212-2400, USA

Chase, Hayley (Actor)
c/o Staff Member *Bobby Ball Talent Agency*
4116 W Magnolia Blvd Ste 205
Burbank, CA 91505-2700, USA

Chase, John (Athlete, Hockey Player)
170 Broadway Rm 609
New York, NY 10038-4462, USA

Chase, Jonathan (Actor)
c/o Tracy Steinsapir *Main Title Entertainment*
2225 Wilshire Blvd Suite 500
Los Angeles, CA 90036, USA

Chase, Kelly (Athlete, Hockey Player)
16476 Horseshoe Ridge Rd
Chesterfield, MO 63005-4422, USA

Chase, Kristen (Writer)
c/o Staff Member *Adams Media Corporation*
57 Littlefield St Ste 3
Avon, MA 02322-1934, USA

Chase, Leah (Chef, Writer)
c/o Staff Member *Pelican Publishing Company*
1000 Burmaster St
Gretna, LA 70053-2246, USA

Chase, Lorraine (Actor)
c/o Staff Member *Peter Charlesworth & Assoc*
68 Old Brompton Rd
London SW7 3LQ, UK

Chase, Peggy (Stylist)
c/o Staff Member *Team*
423 W Broadway Ste 406
Boston, MA 02127-2265, USA

Chase, Sylvia B (Correspondent)
77 W 66th St
New York, NY 10023-6201, USA

Chasez, Joshua Scott (JC) (Musician)
c/o Eric Podwall *Podwall Entertainment*
710 N Orlando Ave Apt 203
Los Angeles, CA 90069-5549, USA

Chast, Roz (Comedian)
4 Times Sq
New York, NY 10036-6515, USA

Chastain, Brandi (Model, Soccer Player)
1661 University Way
San Jose, CA 95126-1555, USA

Chastain, Jessica (Actor)
c/o Paul Nelson *Mosaic Media Group*
9200 W Sunset Blvd Ste 10
Los Angeles, CA 90069-3608, USA

Chastel, Andre (Writer)
30 Rue de Lubeck
Paris 75116, FRANCE

Chatham, Matt (Athlete, Football Player)
2502 Old Bridge Ln
Bellingham, MA 02019-3124, USA

Chatham, Russell (Artist)
Deep Creek
Livingston, MT 59047, USA

Chatham, Wes (Actor)
c/o Robert Stein *Robert Stein Management*
PO Box 3797
Beverly Hills, CA 90212-0797, USA

Chatman, Charles (Baseball Player)
2024 Clarksdale Ave
Memphis, TN 38108-1313, USA

Chatman, Jesse (Athlete, Football Player)
c/o Eugene Parker *Maximum Sports Management*
6435 W Jefferson Blvd # 197
Fort Wayne, IN 46804-6203, USA

Chatterjee, Moushumi (Actor, Bollywood)
Nibbana annexe 1st Floor Pali Hill
Bandra
Bombay, MS 400 050, INDIA

Chatterji, Basu (Actor, Bollywood, Director, Filmmaker)
Violete Villa 1st Floor West Avenue
Santacruz
Mumbai, MS 400054, INDIA

Chatwin, Justin (Actor)
c/o Theresa Peters *United Talent Agency (UTA)*
9560 Wilshire Blvd Fl 5
Beverly Hills, CA 90212-2400, USA

Chau, François (Actor)

Chaudhry, Mahima (Actor, Bollywood)
D/5 4th Floor Silver View Versova
Andheri
Mumbai, MS 400061, INDIA

Chauvez, Patric (Stylist)
c/o Staff Member *Fifty8 Artists*
58 W Huron St
Chicago, IL 60654-3806, USA

Chauvin, Yves (Nobel Prize Laureate)
1&4 Avenue De Bois-Préau
Rueil-Malmaison F-92852, France

Chauvire, Yvette (Ballerina)
21 Place du Commerce
Paris 75015, FRANCE

Chavarria, Ossie (Athlete, Baseball Player)
3707 Cardiff St
Burnaby, BC V5G 2H1, Canada

Chaves, Richard J (Actor)
c/o Staff Member *Media Artists Group (NY)*
140 E 46th St PH C
New York, NY 10017-2633, USA

Chavez, Anthony (Athlete, Baseball Player)
10569 S Varner Dr
Vail, AZ 85641-2582, USA

Chavez, Eric (Athlete, Baseball Player)
6510 E Bar Z Ln
Paradise Valley, AZ 85253-1873, USA

Chavez, Hugo (President)
Avenida Urdaneta
Caracas 1010, VENEZUELA

Chavez, Julio Cesar (Athlete, Boxer)
c/o Staff Member *Boxing Hall of Fame*
1 Hall of Fame Dr
Canastota, NY 13032-1180, USA

Chavez, Linda (Correspondent)
c/o Staff Member *Fox News Channel (NY)*
1211 Ave Of The Americas Level C1
New York, NY 10036-8701, USA

Chavez, Marga (Actor)
c/o Staff Member *Select Artists Ltd (CA-Valley Office)*
PO Box 4359
Burbank, CA 91503-4359, USA

Chavira, Ricardo Antonio (Actor)
5708 1/2 Hazeltine Ave
Van Nuys, CA 91401-3751, USA

Chavous, Barney L (Athlete, Coach, Football Coach, Football Player)
601 Chavous Rd
Aiken, SC 29803-5031, USA

Chavous, Corey (Athlete, Football Player)
424 Goucher Green Bethel Rd
Gaffney, SC 29340-5910, USA

Chawla, Juhi (Actor, Bollywood)
153 Oxford Tower Yamuna Nagar
Oshiwara Complex Andheri W
Mumbai, MS 400058, INDIA

Chayanne (Actor, Musician)
c/o Steve Chasman *Ace Media*
9200 W Sunset Blvd Ste 10
Los Angeles, CA 90069-3608, USA

Chazov, Yevgeny I (Doctor)
Cherepkovskaya Ul 15-A
Moscow 121552, RUSSIA

Cheadle, Dave (Athlete, Baseball Player)
9556 Bay Front Dr
Norfolk, VA 23518-6314, USA

Cheadle, Don (Actor)
c/o Lenore Zerman *Liberman/Zerman Management*
252 N Larchmont Blvd Ste 200
Los Angeles, CA 90004-3754, USA

Cheaney, Calbert N (Athlete, Basketball Player)
9908 Bentcross Dr
Potomac, MD 20854-4740, USA

Cheatham, Ernie (Athlete, Football Player)
400 Ashton St
Pittsburgh, PA 15207-1786, USA

Cheatham, Maree (Actor)
8787 Shoreham Dr
West Hollywood, CA 90069-2231, USA

Check, Lude (Athlete, Hockey Player)
516-100 Grant Carman Dr
Nepean, ON K2E 8B8, Canada

Checker, Chubby (Musician, Songwriter, Writer)
320 Fayette St # 200
Conshohocken, PA 19428-1960, USA

Checo, Robinson (Baseball Player)
Romulo Bentan Cul #04
Santiago, DOMINICAN REPUBLIC

Cheechoo, Jonathan (Athlete, Hockey Player)
707 Iris Gardens Ct
San Jose, CA 95125-1642, USA

Cheek, James E (Educator)
1201 S Benbow Rd
Greensboro, NC 27406-2115, USA

Cheek, John (Opera Singer)
40 W 57th St
New York, NY 10019-4001, USA

Cheek, Louis (Athlete, Football Player)
545 Woelke Rd
Seguin, TX 78155-9345, USA

Cheek, Molly (Actor)
c/o Staff Member *Pakula/King & Associates*
9229 W Sunset Blvd Ste 315
Los Angeles, CA 90069-3403, USA

Cheeks, Judy (Musician)
50 New Bond St.
London W1S 1RD, UK

Cheeks, Maurica E (Mo) (Athlete, Basketball Player, Coach)
7325 SW Childs Rd
Portland, OR 97224-7713, USA

Cheeks, Maurice (Athlete, Basketball Player)
301 NE 4th St
Oklahoma City, OK 73104-2225, USA

Cheena, Manager (Actor)
No 8 Vivekanandapuram Ist Street West Mambalam
Chennai, TN 600 033, INDIA

Cheesman, Barry (Athlete, Golfer)
2901 Theresa Ln
Sarasota, FL 34239-7008, USA

Cheetwood, Derk (Actor)
c/o Staff Member *Bohemia Group*
1680 Vine St Ste 216
Los Angeles, CA 90028-8829, USA

Cheever, Eddie (Race Car Driver)
1054 S Starwood Dr
Aspen, CO 81611-9706, USA

Cheever, Michael (Athlete, Football Player)
27 Sherwood Dr
Newnan, GA 30263-1134, USA

Cheevers, Gary (Athlete, Hockey Player)
106 Appleton St
North Andover, MA 01845-3138, USA

Cheevers, Gerry (Athlete, Hockey Player)
106 Appleton St
North Andover, MA 01845-3138, USA

Chekamauskas, Vitautas (Architect)
Maironio 6
Vilnius 2600, LITHUANIA

Chelberg, Robert D (General)
Unit 30400 Box R65
Apo, AE 09131-0400, USA

Chelf, Donald (Athlete, Football Player)
7329 Bottle Brush Dr
Spring Hill, FL 34606-7023, USA

Cheli, Giovanni Cardinal (Religious Leader)
Piazza Calisto 16
Rome 153, ITALY

Cheli, Maurizio (Astronaut)
c/o Staff Member *NASA*
2101 Nasa Pkwy Spc Center
Houston, TX 77058-3696, USA

Cheli-Merchez, Marianne (Astronaut)
132 Rue Van Aliard
Bruxelles 1180, BELGIUM

Chelios, Christos K (Chris) (Athlete, Hockey Player)
790 Falmouth Dr
Bloomfield Hills, MI 48304-3308, USA

Chellgren, Paul W (Business Person)
PO Box 15391
Covington, KY 41015-0391, USA

Chelsom, Peter (Actor)
c/o Staff Member *Principato/Young Management*
9465 Wilshire Blvd Ste 430
Beverly Hills, CA 90212-2613, USA

Chemical Brothers (Music Group)
c/o Staff Member *Target Concerts GmbH*
Müllerstrasse 42
München 80469, GERMANY

Chen, Bruce (Athlete, Baseball Player)
114 Dutchfork Creek Trl
Irmo, SC 29063-7834, USA

Chen, Camille (Actor)
c/o Scott Zimmerman *Evolution Entertainment (LA)*
901 N Highland Ave
Los Angeles, CA 90038-2412, USA

Chen, Da (Writer)
c/o Staff Member *Writers and Artists Group Intl (NY)*
360 Park Ave # 16
New York, NY 10022-5909, USA

Chen, Edith (Musician)
165 W 57th St
New York, NY 10019-2201, USA

Chen, Guang Biao (Business Person)
Nanjing
Jiangsu Province, China

Chen, Irvin S Y (Scientist)
Med Center Hematology Dept
Los Angeles, CA 90024, USA

Chen, Joan (Actor, Director)
2601 Filbert St
San Francisco, CA 94123-3215, USA

Chen, Joie (Correspondent)
1050 Techwood Dr NW
Atlanta, GA 30318-5604, USA

Chen, Julie (Reality TV Star, Television Host)
c/o Staff Member *CBS News*
524 W 57th St
New York, NY 10019-2924, USA

Chen, Kaige (Director)
8942 Wilshire Blvd # 219
Beverly Hills, CA 90211-1908, USA

Chen, Lincoln C (Doctor)
302 Dean Rd
Brookline, MA 02445-4141, USA

Chen, Lu (Figure Skater)
54 Baishiqiao Road Haidian District
Beijing 10044, CHINA

Chen, Lynn (Actor)
c/o Staff Member *International Creative Management (ICM-LA)*
10250 Constellation Blvd Fl 7
Los Angeles, CA 90067-6207, USA

Chen, Robert (Musician)
165 W 57th St
New York, NY 10019-2201, USA

Chen, Shui-bian (President)
Chieshshou Hall Chung-King Road
Taipei 100, TAIWAN

Chen, Steve S (Engineer)
1414 W Hamilton Ave
Eau Claire, WI 54701-7252, USA

Chen, Xieyang
105 Hunan Road
Shanghai 200031, CHINA

Chen, Yi (Composer)
Music Dept
Kansas City, MO 64110, USA

Chen, Zuohuang (Conductor)
225 W Douglas Ave
Wichita, KS 67202-3134, USA

Chenery, Penny (Misc)
20 Roberts Ln
Saratoga Springs, NY 12866-2814, USA

Cheney, Lynne V (Government Official)
1150 17th St NW
Washington, DC 20036-4603, USA

Cheney, Richard B (President, Secretary, Vice President)
6613 Madison Dr
McLean, VA 22101, USA

Cheney, Richard B (Dick) (Ex-Vice President, Politician)
1150 17th St NW
Washington, DC 20036-4603, USA

Cheng, Olivia (Actor)
c/o Elena Kirschner *Lucas Talent Inc*
100 W. Pender St Sun Tower, 7th Floor
Vancouver, BC V6B 1R8, Canada

Cheng, Pei-pei (Actor)
c/o Andrew Ooi *Echelon Talent Management*
3674 Oxford St
Vancouver BC V5K 1P3, Canada

Chenier, Phil (Athlete, Basketball Player)
7410 Hindon Cir Unit 301
Windsor Mill, MD 21244-5620, USA

Chennault, Anna (Business Person)
1049 30th St NW
Washington, DC 20007-3823, USA

Chenoweth, Kristin (Actor, Musician)
c/o Dannielle Thomas *Untitled Entertainment (LA)*
350 S Beverly Dr Ste 200
Beverly Hills, CA 90212-4819, USA

Cher (Actor, Director, Musician, Producer)
c/o Lindsay Scott *Lindsay Scott Management*
8899 Beverly Blvd Ste 611
Los Angeles, CA 90048-2429, USA

Chereau, Patrice (Director)
7 Ave Pablo Picasso
Nanterre 9200, FRANCE

Cherestal, Jean-Marie (Prime Minister)
Palais Ministeres
Port-au-Prince, HAITI

Chermayeff, Peter (Architect)
15 E 26th St
New York, NY 10010-1505, USA

Chernin, Peter (Business Person)
1211 Avenue of the Americas
New York, NY 10036-8701, USA

Chernobrovkina, Tatyana A (Ballerina)
B Dimitrovka Str 17
Moscow 103009, RUSSIA

Chernoff, Mike (Athlete, Hockey Player)
1057 Grace St
Moose Jaw, SK S6H 3C2, Canada

Chernomaz, Rich (Athlete, Hockey Player)
6041 Sierra Way
Nanaimo, BC V9V 1R8, Canada

Chernov, Vladimir K (Opera Singer)
165 W 57th St
New York, NY 10019-2201, USA

Chernow, Ron (Writer)
63 Joralemon St
Brooklyn, NY 11201-4003, USA

Cherokee (Adult Film Star)

Cherrelle (Musician)
c/o Staff Member *Associated Booking Corp*
PO Box 2055
New York, NY 10021-0051, USA

Cherri, Agustina (Actor)
c/o Staff Member *Telefe - Argentina*
Pavon 2444 (C1248AAT)
Buenos Aires, ARGENTINA

Cherry, D Richard (Stylist)
220 Renaissance Pkwy NE Apt 1109
Atlanta, GA 30308-2352, USA

Cherry, Deron (Athlete, Football Player)
13800 S Pebblebrook Ln
Greenwood, MO 64034-8216, USA

Cherry, Dick (Athlete, Hockey Player)
Box 346 RR 1
Bath, ON K0H 1G0, Canada

Cherry, Don S (Athlete, Coach, Hockey Player)
P.O. Box 500, STN A, 5H100 Attn: Hockey Night in Canada
Toronto, ON M5W 1E6, Canada

Cherry, Fred V (War Hero)
720 Dale Dr
Silver Spring, MD 20910-4267, USA

Cherry, Je'rod (Athlete, Football Player)
993 Mimosa Dr
Macedonia, OH 44056-2391, USA

Cherry, Joann (Stylist)
14513 Chateau Ln
Burnsville, MN 55306-6474, USA

Cherry, Jonathan (Actor)
c/o Jim Sheasgreen *Look Management*
1529 W 6th Ave #110
Vancouver V6J 1R, CANADA

Cherry, Marc (Producer, Writer)
c/o Andy Patman *Paradigm (LA)*
360 N Crescent Dr
Beverly Hills, CA 90210-4874, USA

Cherry, Mike (Athlete, Football Player)
4106 Central Pl
Texarkana, AR 71854-1617, USA

Cherry, Nena (Musician)
c/o Staff Member *Paradigm (Monterey)*
404 W Franklin St
Monterey, CA 93940-2303, USA

Cherry, Neneh (Musician)
PO Box 1622
London NW10 5TF, UNITED KINGDOM (UK)

Cherry, Rocky (Athlete, Baseball Player)
5624 Gleneagles Dr
Plano, TX 75093-5973, USA

Cherry Poppin' Daddies (Music Group, Musician)
c/o Jim Lenz *Paradise Artists*
PO Box 1821
Ojai, CA 93024-1821, USA

Chertoff, Michael (Attorney, Attorney General, General, Government Official)
10th St & Constitution Ave NW
Washington, DC 20530-0001, USA

Chertok, Jack (Producer)
515 Ocean Ave # 305
Santa Monica, CA 90402-2609, USA

Cherundolo, Charles (Chuck) (Athlete, Football Player)
4230 Simms Rd
Lakeland, FL 33810-0402, USA

Chervyakov, Denis (Athlete, Hockey Player)
21051 Roaming Shores Ter
Ashburn, VA 20147-3208, USA

Chesley, Al (Athlete, Football Player)
2604 32nd St SE
Washington, DC 20020-1448, USA

Chesney, Kenny (Musician)
c/o Dale Morris *Morris Management Group, Inc*
818 19th Ave S
Nashville, TN 37203-3202, USA

Chesnutt, Mark (Musician)
c/o Staff Member *Hoffman Talent Agency*
PO Box 26037
Minneapolis, MN 55426-0037, USA

Chesser, George (Athlete, Football Player)
18 Hialeah St
Starkville, MS 39759-2751, USA

Chesson 3rd, Wes (Athlete, Football Player)
1028 Marlowe Rd
Raleigh, NC 27609-6962, USA

Chester, Colby (Actor)
5670 Wilshire Blvd Ste 820
Los Angeles, CA 90036-5613, USA

Chester, Larry (Athlete, Football Player)
6359 Celtic Dr SW
Atlanta, GA 30331-9414, USA

Chester, Raymond T (Athlete, Football Player)
4722 Grass Valley Rd
Oakland, CA 94605-5622, USA

Chestnut, Cyrus (Musician)
250 W 57th St # 407
New York, NY 10107-0001, USA

Chestnut, Mary Boykin (Educator)
President's Office
Sweet Briar, VA 24595, USA

Chestnut, Morris (Actor)
c/o Brian Wilkins *Kritzer Levine Wilkins Entertainment*
11872 La Grange Ave Fl 1
Los Angeles, CA 90025-5283, USA

Chetry, Kiran (Anchor)
c/o Staff Member *CNN (NY)*
2 Spanish Cove Rd
Larchmont, NY 10538-3815, USA

Chetti, Joseph (Athlete, Football Player)
7 Baur St
West Babylon, NY 11704-3320, USA

Chetwynd, Lionel (Producer, Writer)
c/o Bruce Vinokour *Creative Artists Agency (CAA-LA)*
2000 Avenue of the Stars Ste 100
Los Angeles, CA 90067-4705, USA

Cheung, Maggie (Actor)
c/o Ted Schachter *Schachter Entertainment*
1157 S Beverly Dr Fl 2
Los Angeles, CA 90035-1119, USA

Cheung, Tim (Animator)
c/o Staff Member *DreamWorks SKG*
1000 Flower St
Glendale, CA 91201-3007, USA

Chevalier, Franck (Stylist)
c/o Staff Member *Smashbox Beauty*
8549 Higuera St Bldg B
Culver City, CA 90232-2521, USA

Chevalier, Tracy (Writer)
375 Hudson St
New York, NY 10014-3658, USA

Chevelle (Music Group)
c/o Staff Member *Creative Artists Agency (CAA-LA)*
2000 Avenue of the Stars Ste 100
Los Angeles, CA 90067-4705, USA

Chevrier, Alain (Athlete, Hockey Player)
6857 Rain Forest Dr
Boca Raton, FL 33434, USA

Chew, Geoffrey F (Physicist)
10 Maybeck Twin Dr
Berkeley, CA 94708-2037, USA

Chew Jr, Sam
8075 W 3rd St # 303
Los Angeles, CA 90048-4318, USA

Cheyne, Lori (Stylist)
c/o Staff Member *Creative Talent Columbus*
5864 Nike Dr
Hilliard, OH 43026-8756, USA

Cheyunski, Jim (Athlete, Football Player)
821 W Locust St
Seaford, DE 19973-2122, USA

Chi, Haotian (General)
Jingshanqiq Jie
Beijing, CHINA

Chia, Sandro (Artist)
Castello Romitorio
Montalcino, Siena, ITALY

Chiadel, Dana (Athlete)
5302 Flanders Ave
Kensington, MD 20895-1139, USA

Chiamparino, Scott (Athlete, Baseball Player)
179 Ortega Ave
Mountain View, CA 94040-1439, USA

Chianese, Dominic (Actor)
c/o Brian Liebman *Liebman Entertainment*
25 E 21st St PH
New York, NY 10010-6226, USA

Chiao, Dr Leroy (Astronaut)
2108 Butler Dr
Friendswood, TX 77546-5514, USA

Chiara, Maria (Opera Singer)
165 W 57th St
New York, NY 10019-2201, USA

Chiarello, Michael (Chef)
574 Gateway Dr
Napa, CA 94558-7517, USA

Chiasson, Scott (Athlete, Baseball Player)
3660 N Lake Rd
Erieville, NY 13061-3106, USA

Chiaverini, Darrin (Athlete, Football Player)
6573 Harrow St
Mira Loma, CA 91752-4333, USA

Chicago (Music Group)
c/o Howard Rose *Howard Rose Agency Ltd, The*
9460 Wilshire Blvd Ste 310
Beverly Hills, CA 90212-2710, USA

Chick, Travis (Athlete, Baseball Player)
6713 Circle Dr
Tyler, TX 75703-5930, USA

Chickillo, Anthony (Tony) (Athlete, Football Player)
6920 Spanish Moss Cir
Tampa, FL 33625-6556, USA

Chiechi, Carolyn P (Judge)
400 2nd St NW
Washington, DC 20217-0001, USA

Chieftans, The (Music Group)
c/o Staff Member *International Creative Management (ICM-LA)*
10250 Constellation Blvd Fl 7
Los Angeles, CA 90067-6207, USA

Chiesa, Fabrizio (Producer)
c/o Matt Leipzig *Original Artists (LA)*
9465 Wilshire Blvd Ste 870
Beverly Hills, CA 90212-2610, USA

Chievous, Derrick (Athlete, Basketball Player)
2300 Cherry Ridge Ln
Columbia, MO 65203-5744, USA

Chiffer, Floyd (Athlete, Baseball Player)
4325 Levelside Ave
Lakewood, CA 90712-3752, USA

Chiffons, The (Music Group, Musician)
c/o Staff Member *Lustig Talent Enterprises Inc*
PO Box 770850
Orlando, FL 32877-0850, USA

Chihara, Charles S (Misc)
567 Cragmont Ave
Berkeley, CA 94708-1205, USA

Chihara, Paul (Composer)
3815 W Olive Ave Ste 202
Burbank, CA 91505-4676, USA

Chihuly, Dale P (Artist)
5907 Linden Ave N
Seattle, WA 98103-5845, USA

Chikezie (Musician)

Chikezie, Caroline (Actor)
c/o Jane Lehrer *Jane Lehrer Associates*
100A Chalk Farm Road
London NW1 8EH, UNITED KINGDOM

Chiklis, Michael (Actor, Director, Producer)
c/o Evelyn O'Neill *Management 360*
9111 Wilshire Blvd
Beverly Hills, CA 90210-5508, USA

Child, Jane (Musician)
7095 Hollywood Blvd Ste 747
Los Angeles, CA 90028-8912, USA

Childers, Ambyr (Actor)
c/o Laura Myones *McKeon-Myones Management*
3500 W Olive Ave Ste 770
Burbank, CA 91505-5527, USA

Childers, Ernest (War Hero)
13681 S 308th East Ave
Coweta, OK 74429-5728, USA

Childers, Jason (Athlete, Baseball Player)
417 Aumond Rd
Augusta, GA 30909-3562, USA

Childers, Matt (Athlete, Baseball Player)
417 Aumond Rd
Augusta, GA 30909-3562, USA

Childress, Kallie Flynn (Actor)
c/o TJ Stein *Stein Entertainment Group*
1351 N Crescent Heights Blvd Apt 312
West Hollywood, CA 90046-4549, USA

Childress, Raymond C (Ray) Jr (Athlete, Football Player)
639 Shady Hollow St
Houston, TX 77056-1635, USA

Childress, Richard (R C) (Misc)
PO Box 1189
Welcome, NC 27374-1189, USA

Childress, Rocky (Athlete, Baseball Player)
5 Meadow Glen Ct
Santa Rosa, CA 95404-1845, USA

Childs, Barton (Physicist)
1019 Winding Way
Baltimore, MD 21210-1232, USA

Childs, Billy (Musician)
PO Box 961
Burlington, MA 01803-5961, USA

Childs, Brevard S (Misc)
508 Amity Rd
Bethany, CT 06524-3015, USA

Childs, Charissa (Athlete, Golfer)
25 Green Springs Cir
Columbia, SC 29223-6940, USA

Childs, Clarence (Athlete, Football Player)
1652 Lawrence Cir
Daytona Beach, FL 32117-3942, USA

Childs, David M (Architect)
14 Wall St
New York, NY 10005-2101, USA

Childs, Henry (Athlete, Football Player)
8304 Allman Rd
Lenexa, KS 66219-2705, USA

Chiles, Adrian (Actor)
BBC Television Centre Wood Ln
London W12 7RJ, UK

Chiles, Henry G (Hank) Jr (Admiral)
6436 Pima St
Alexandria, VA 22312-2043, USA

Chiles, Linden (Actor)
2521 Skyline Dr
Topanga, CA 90290, USA

Chiles, Lois (Actor)
c/o Staff Member *Abrams Artists Agency (LA)*
9200 W Sunset Blvd PH 11
Los Angeles, CA 90069-3601, USA

Chiles, Rich (Athlete, Baseball Player)
18147 Mallard St
Woodland, CA 95695-6038, USA

Chilies, Lois (Actor)
c/o Staff Member *Abrams Artists Agency (LA)*
9200 W Sunset Blvd PH 11
Los Angeles, CA 90069-3601, USA

Chi-Lites, The (Music Group)
c/o Staff Member *Universal Attractions*
135 W 26th St Fl 12
New York, NY 10001-6872, USA

Chillar, Brandon (Athlete, Football Player)
1030 Iris Ct
Carlsbad, CA 92011-4823, USA

Chillemi, Connie (Athlete, Golfer)
2701 NE 10th St Apt 705
Ocala, FL 34470-5689, USA

Chilstrom, Ken (Misc)
9120 Belvoir Woods Pkwy Apt 211
Fort Belvoir, VA 22060-2723, USA

Chilton, Gene (Athlete, Football Player)
RR 2 Box 2542
Jacksonville, TX 75766, USA

Chilton, Kevin P (Astronaut)
2555 Talleson Ct
Colorado Springs, CO 80919-4874, USA

Chimes, Terry
21-25 York Rd
Ilford, Essex IG3 8BJ, UK

Chiminello, Bianca (Actor)
c/o Staff Member *Matt Sherman Management*
9107 Wilshire Blvd Ste 225
Beverly Hills, CA 90210-5546, USA

Chin, Tsai (Actor)
c/o Donald Spradlin *Essential Talent Management*
6399 Wilshire Blvd Ste 401
Los Angeles, CA 90048-5716, USA

Chinaglia, Giorgio (Soccer Player)
3-9-1 Via Quartara
Genoa 16148, ITALY

Chinlund, Nick (Actor)
c/o Davien Littlefield *Davien Littlefield Management*
33 W 67th St PH
New York, NY 10023-6224, USA

Chinn, Jerry (Stylist)
5622 Corson Ave S
Seattle, WA 98108-2603, USA

Chinn, Simon (Cinematographer, Producer, Writer)
c/o Paul Stevens *Independent Talent Group (ITG-UK)*
Oxford House 76 Oxford St
London W1D 1BS, UK

Chinnick, Rick (Athlete, Hockey Player)
55 Gregory Dr E
Chatham, ON N7L 2R5, Canada

Chinny, Jayanth (Actor)
67 1st Main Road R A Puram
Chennai, TN 600 028, INDIA

Chiodo, Andy (Athlete, Hockey Player)
17 Fairhaven Dr
Etobicoke, ON M9P 2P8, Canada

Chiodos (Music Group, Musician)
c/o Staff Member *Equal Vision Records*
PO Box 38202
Albany, NY 12203-8202, USA

Chipperfield, Ron (Athlete, Hockey Player)
Box 248
Wilcox, SK S0G 5E0, Canada

Chiranjeevi (Actor, Bollywood)
No. 4 Porur Somasundaram Street T Nagar
Chennai, TN 600017, INDIA

Chishholm-Carrillo, Linda (Athlete, Volleyball Player)
17213 Vose St
Van Nuys, CA 91406-3633, USA

Chisholm, Art (Athlete, Hockey Player)
9 Jefferson Ct
Woburn, MA 01801-4326, USA

Chisholm, Ashleigh (Actor)
c/o Staff Member *Nickelodeon UK*
PO Box 6425
LONDON W1A 6UR, UNITED KINGDOM

Chisholm, Melanie (Musician)
c/o Nancy Phillips *45 Management Ltd*
13 Tottenham Mews
London W1T 4AG, UK

Chism, Tom (Athlete, Baseball Player)
532 W Brookhaven Rd Apt F1
Brookhaven, PA 19015-1824, USA

Chissano, Joaquim A (President)
Avda Julius Nyerere 2000
Maputo, MOZAMBIQUE

Chistov, Stanislaw (Athlete, Hockey Player)
c/o Jay Grossman *S F X Sports (NY)*
220 W 42nd St
New York, NY 10036-7200, USA

Chitalada, Sot (Boxer)
242/19 Moo 10 Sukhumvit Rd
Washington, DC 20210-0001, THAILAND

Chitren, Steve (Athlete, Baseball Player)
10417 Smokemont Ct
Las Vegas, NV 89129-4515, USA

Chittister, Joan D (Misc)
335 E 9th St
Erie, PA 16503, USA

Chittum, Nelson (Nels) (Athlete, Baseball Player)
616 Bonita Pkwy
Hendersonville, TN 37075-4632, USA

Chitwood, Joey, Jr. (Race Car Driver)
800 Speedway Blvd
Joliet, IL 60431, USA

Chitwood, Joey Jr (Race Car Driver)
863 Seddon Cove Way
Tampa, FL 33602-5704, USA

Chiu Wai, Tony Leung (Actor)
c/o Staff Member *WmE2 (Endeavor-LA)*
9601 Wilshire Blvd Fl 3
Beverly Hills, CA 90210-5219, USA

Chivers, Warren (Skier)
Saxtons River, WI 5154, USA

Chlumsky, Anna (Actor)
c/o Cory Richman *Liebman Entertainment*
25 E 21st St PH
New York, NY 10010-6226, USA

Chlupsa, Bob (Athlete, Baseball Player)
55 Willow St
Garden City, NY 11530-6316, USA

Chmerkovskiy, Maksim (Choreographer, Dancer)
c/o Susan Madore *Guttman Associates*
118 S Beverly Dr Ste 201
Beverly Hills, CA 90212-3016, USA

Chmura, Mark W (Athlete, Football Player)
S18W28948 Price Ct
Waukesha, WI 53188-9551, USA

Cho (Actor)
26-A Raja Annamataipuram 2nd Main Rd
Chennai, TN 600 028, INDIA

Cho, Alfred Y (Engineer)
600 Mountain Ave
New Providence, NJ 07974-2008, USA

Cho, Catherine (Musician)
165 W 57th St
New York, NY 10019-2201, USA

Cho, Frank (Cartoonist)
5777 W Century Blvd Ste 700
Los Angeles, CA 90045-5652, USA

Cho, Fujio (Business Person)
1 Toyotacho
Toyota City, Aicji Prefecture 471, JAPAN

Cho, Henry (Actor, Comedian, Writer)
c/o Alex Murray *McDonald-Murray Management*
11846 Ventura Blvd Ste 202
Studio City, CA 91604-2620, USA

Cho, John (Actor)
c/o Rebecca Many Rosenberg *Principato/Young Management*
9465 Wilshire Blvd Ste 430
Beverly Hills, CA 90212-2613, USA

Cho, Margaret (Actor, Comedian)
438 S Serrano Ave
Los Angeles, CA 90020-3670, USA

Cho, Paul (Misc)
Yoida Plaza
Seoul, SOUTH KOREA

Cho, Smith (Actor)
c/o Amy Guenther *Gateway Management Company Inc*
860 Via De La Paz Ste F10
Pacific Palisades, CA 90272-3631, USA

Choate, Don (Athlete, Baseball Player)
9506 Maryann Dr
Fairview Heights, IL 62208-1625, USA

Choate, Jerry D (Business Person)
Allstate Plaza 2775 Sanders Road
Northbrook, IL 60062, USA

Choate, Putt (Athlete, Football Player)
9800 Rockbrook Dr
Dallas, TX 75220-2041, USA

Choate, Randy (Athlete, Baseball Player)
316 Leon Pl
Davis, CA 95616-0236, USA

Chodorow, Marvin (Engineer, Physicist)
6151 Forty Oaks Ln
Paradise, CA 95969-3079, USA

Choi, Edmund (Composer, Musician)
c/o Anita Greenspan *Greenspan Artist Management*
8760 W Sunset Blvd
West Hollywood, CA 90069-2206, USA

Choi, Hee Seop (Athlete, Baseball Player)
14310 SE 29th Cir
Vancouver, WA 98683-7691, USA

Choi, Jane (Stylist)
c/o Staff Member *Montana Artists Agency*
9150 Wilshire Blvd Ste 100
Beverly Hills, CA 90212-3459, USA

Choi, Kathy (Athlete, Golfer)
7912 Beachpoint Cir Apt 18
Huntington Beach, CA 92648-1478, USA

Choi, Kenneth (Actor)
c/o Gail Abbott *Gail Abbott Management*
3019 Hollycrest Dr
Los Angeles, CA 90068-1801, USA

Choi, KJ (Athlete, Golfer)
1360 E 9th St
Cleveland, OH 44114-1737, USA

Choi, Yun (Actor)
c/o Staff Member *Select Artists Ltd (CA-Westside Office)*
1138 12th St Apt 1
Santa Monica, CA 90403-5459, USA

Chojnowska-Liskiewicz, Krystyna (Yachtsman)
Ul Norblina 29 m 50
Gdansk, Oliwa 80 304, POLAND

Chokachi, David (Actor)
c/o Staff Member *Stone Manners Salners Agency (LA)*
9911 W Pico Blvd Ste 1400
Los Angeles, CA 90035-2715, USA

Chokkalinga, Bhavadhar (Actor)
10 Thiruvalluvar Street M G R Nagar
Chennai, TN 600 078, INDIA

Cholodenko, Lisa (Director, Editor, Producer, Writer)
c/o Bart Walker *Cinetic Management*
555 W 25th St Fl 4
New York, NY 10001-5542, USA

Choma, John (Athlete, Football Player)
1544 Carol Ave
Burlingame, CA 94010-5231, USA

Chomet, Sylvain (Director, Writer)
c/o Robert Newman *WmE2 (Endeavor-LA)*
9601 Wilshire Blvd Fl 3
Beverly Hills, CA 90210-5219, USA

Chomsky, A Noam (Linguist)
15 Suzanne Rd
Lexington, MA 02420-1831, USA

Chomsky, Marvin J (Director)
15200 W Sunset Blvd Ste 209
Pacific Palisades, CA 90272-3621

Chon, Justin (Actor)
c/o Staff Member *Abrams Artists Agency (LA)*
9200 W Sunset Blvd PH 11
Los Angeles, CA 90069-3601, USA

Chonacas, Katie (Actor, Model)
c/o Jordyn Borczon *Persona PR*
8840 Wilshire Blvd Ste 109
Beverly Hills, CA 90211-2606, USA

Chones, Jim (Athlete, Basketball Player)
26400 George Zeiger Dr Apt 305
Beachwood, OH 44122-7511, USA

Chong, Rae Dawn (Actor)
c/o David Fox *Myman Abell Fineman Fox Greenspan Light*
11601 Wilshire Blvd Ste 2200
Los Angeles, CA 90025-1758, USA

Chong, Thomas (Tommy) (Actor, Comedian, Writer)
1625 Casale Rd
Pacific Palisades, CA 90272-2717, USA

Chopra, B R (Bollywood, Director)
B R House Juhu Tara Road Santacruz
Mumbai, MS 400049, INDIA

Chopra, Daniel (Athlete, Golfer)
9838 Laurel Valley Dr
Windermere, FL 34786-8911, USA

Chopra, Deepak (Doctor, Writer)
c/o Robert Gottlieb *Trident Media Group LLC*
41 Madison Ave Fl 36
New York, NY 10010-2257, USA

Chopra, Prem (Actor, Bollywood)
144A Nibbana Pali Hill Bandra
Bombay, MS 400 050, INDIA

Chopra, Priyanka (Actor)
1826 Amar Nath Bldg #2 Bhagirath Palace
Delhi 110006, INDIA

Chopra, Ravi (Bollywood, Director, Filmmaker, Producer)
B R House Juhu Tara Road Santacruz
Bombay, MS 400 049, INDIA

Chopra, Uday (Actor)
c/o Staff Member *Yash Raj Films Private Ltd (India)*
17 Vkas Park Jalpankhi Society, Juhu
Mumbai 400 049, India

Chopra, Vidhu Vinod (Bollywood, Director, Filmmaker, Producer)
Bhagtani Krishang, RH1 Plot 16C, Dattatray Road
Santacruz (West), Mumbai 400054, INDIA

Chopra, Yash (Bollywood, Director, Filmmaker, Producer)
Bungalow No. 17 Jalpankhi Soc Vikas Park Juhu Tara Road
Mumbai, MS 400049, INDIA

Chorske, Tom (Athlete, Hockey Player)
23 Cooper Cir
Minneapolis, MN 55436-1316, USA

Chorvat, Scarlett (Actor)
1505 10th St
Santa Monica, CA 90401-2805, USA

Chorzempa, Daniel W (Misc)
Plankengasse 7
Vienna 1010, AUSTRIA

Chou, Collin (Actor)
c/o Tim Kwok *Convergence Entertainment*
9150 Wilshire Blvd Ste 247
Beverly Hills, CA 90212-3429, USA

Chou, Jay (Musician)
c/o Staff Member *BMG*
1540 Broadway
New York, NY 10036-4039, USA

Choudhury, Sarita (Actor)
c/o Kathy Atkinson *Washington Square Arts (LA)*
1041 N Formosa Ave Lot Bldg
West Hollywood, CA 90046-6703, USA

Chouinard, Bobby (Athlete, Baseball Player)
6024 S Paris Pl
Englewood, CO 80111-4152, USA

Chouinard, Guy (Athlete, Hockey Player)
Rm 1564
Ste-Foy, QC G1K 7P4, Canada

Chouinard, Josee (Figure Skater)
c/o Staff Member *IMG (Canada)*
175 Bloor St E S Tower #400
Toronto M4W 3R8, CANADA

Chouinard, Marie (Choreographer, Dancer)
3981 Boul Saint-Laurent
Montreal, PQ H2W 1Y5, CANADA

Choureau, Etchika (Actor)
9 rue du Docteur Blanche
Paris F-75016, France

Chow, Amy (Gymnast)
1190 Dell Ave # 1
Campbell, CA 95008-6614, USA

Chow, China (Actor)
c/o Andy Stabile *Creative Artists Agency (CAA-LA)*
2000 Avenue of the Stars Ste 100
Los Angeles, CA 90067-4705, USA

Chow, Gregory C (Economist)
30 Hardy Dr
Princeton, NJ 08540-1211, USA

Chow, Raymond (Producer)
c/o Staff Member *Golden Harvest Entertainment*
The Peninsula Office Tower 18 Middle Road 16/F Tsim Sha Tsui
Kowloon, Hong Kong

Chow, Stephen (Actor, Director, Writer)
Rm 1201-1204 Sea Bird House 22-28 Wyndham Street
Hong Kong, China

Chow, Steven (Actor)
c/o Alan Grodin *Weissman Wolff Bergman Coleman Silverman Holmes*
9665 Wilshire Blvd Fl 9
Beverly Hills, CA 90212-2316, USA

Chrebet, Wayne (Athlete, Football Player)
147 Heulitt Rd
Colts Neck, NJ 07722-1427, USA

Chretien, J J Jean (Prime Minister)
24 Sussex Dr
Ottawa, ON K1M 0MS, CANADA

Chretien, Jean-Loup (Astronaut, General)
2 Place Maurice Quentin
Paris 75029, FRANCE

Chriqui, Emmanuelle (Actor)
c/o Emily Gerson Saines *Brookside Artists Management (NY)*
250 W 57th St Ste 2303
New York, NY 10107-2399, USA

Chris, Mike (Athlete, Baseball Player)
31257 Corte Alhambra
Temecula, CA 92592-5420, USA

Chrisley, Neil (Athlete, Baseball Player)
280 Myrtle Greens Dr Apt B
Conway, SC 29526-9040, USA

Christ, Chad (Actor)
c/o Brian Liebman *Liebman Entertainment*
25 E 21st St PH
New York, NY 10010-6226, USA

Christ, Dorothy (Baseball Player)
120 E Battell St Apt 108
Mishawaka, IN 46545-6660, USA

Christ, Fred (Athlete, Basketball Player)
2500 Eagle Dr Apt D
Melbourne, FL 32935-3526, USA

Christensen, Anne (Stylist)
c/o Staff Member *Art + Commerce*
531 W 25th St # 4
New York, NY 10001-5593, USA

Christensen, Bruce (Athlete, Baseball Player)
PO Box 178
Moroni, UT 84646-0178, USA

Christensen, Cal (Athlete, Basketball Player)
395 Canal Rd
Waterville, OH 43566-1338, USA

Christensen, Erika (Actor)
c/o Staff Member *Brillstein Entertainment Partners*
9150 Wilshire Blvd Ste 350
Beverly Hills, CA 90212-3453, USA

Christensen, Hayden (Actor)
c/o Staff Member *Todd Shemarya Artists*
2550 Outpost Dr
Los Angeles, CA 90068-2647, USA

Christensen, Helena (Model)
c/o Lene Seested *Panorama Agency*
Ryesgade 103B
CopenHagen DK-2100, Denmark

Christensen, John (Athlete, Baseball Player)
2931 Yuma Dr
Lake Havasu City, AZ 86406-8568, USA

Christensen, Kai (Architect)
100 Vester Voldgade
Copenhagen V 1552, DENMARK

Christensen, McKay (Athlete, Baseball Player)
975 E Alpine Blvd
Alpine, UT 84004-1235, USA

Christensen, Todd (Athlete, Football Player)
991 Sunburst Ln
Alpine, UT 84004-1203, USA

Christensen Jr, Erik (Athlete, Football Player)
308 Sentinel Ln
Newark, DE 19702-8504, USA

Christenson, Gary (Athlete, Baseball Player)
436 E Tremaine Ave
Gilbert, AZ 85234-4624, USA

Christenson, Larry (Athlete, Baseball Player)
1465 Le Boutillier Rd
Malvern, PA 19355-8741, USA

Christenson, Ryan (Athlete, Baseball Player)
100 Lismore Ct
Tyrone, GA 30290-2549, USA

Christenson, Ryan (Athlete, Baseball Player)
100 Lismore Ct
Tyrone, GA 30290-2549, USA

Christian, Andrew (Designer, Fashion Designer)
325 W Cerritos Ave
Glendale, CA 91204-2703, USA

Christian, Ash (Actor, Director, Writer)
c/o Simon Millar *Rumble Media*
1620 Broadway Ste C
Santa Monica, CA 90404-2777, USA

Christian, Bob (Athlete, Football Player)
9450 Lincolnwood Dr
Evanston, IL 60203-1114, USA

Christian, Christina (Actor, Musician)
c/o Allee Newhoff *Elite Model Management*
119 Washington Ave Ste 501
Miami Beach, FL 33139-7228, USA

Christian, Claudia (Actor)
c/o Staff Member *Abrams Artists Agency (LA)*
9200 W Sunset Blvd PH 11
Los Angeles, CA 90069-3601, USA

Christian, David W (Dave) (Athlete, Hockey Player)
1001 State Ave NE
Warroad, MN 56763, USA

Christian, Eddie (Baseball Player)
1126 NE Lija Loop
Portland, OR 97211-1318, USA

Christian, Gabrielle (Actor)
c/o Robert Haas *Innovative Artists (LA)*
1505 10th St
Santa Monica, CA 90401-2805, USA

Christian, Gordon (Athlete, Hockey Player)
604 Lake St NW
Warroad, MN 56763-2123, USA

Christian, Richard (Actor)
c/o Staff Member *Select Artists Ltd (CA-Westside Office)*
1138 12th St Apt 1
Santa Monica, CA 90403-5459, USA

Christian, Roger (Athlete, Hockey Player)
508 Carrol St NW
Warroad, MN 56763, USA

Christian, Shawn (Actor)
c/o Joanna (Joanie) Burstein *Burstein Company, The*
15304 W Sunset Blvd Ste 208
Pacific Palisades, CA 90272-3656, USA

Christian, William (Bill) (Athlete, Hockey Player)
502 Carrol St NW
Warroad, MN 56763, USA

Christian Dior (Designer, Fashion Designer)
St-Anna-Platz 2
Munich 80538, Germany

Christian-Jacque (Director, Writer)
42 Bis Rue De Paris
Boulogne, Billancourt 92100, FRANCE

Christians, F Wilhelm (Financier)
Kobigsallee 51
Dusseldorf, GERMANY

Christiansen, Clay (Athlete, Baseball Player)
7227 Eby Ave
Overland Park, KS 66204-1638, USA

Christiansen, Helena (Actor)
62 Blvd Sebastopol
Paris 75003, FRANCE

Christiansen, Jason (Athlete, Baseball Player)
3428 E Jasmine Cir
Mesa, AZ 85213-3245, USA

Christiansen, Keith (Athlete, Hockey Player)
1023 Timberline Ln
Duluth, MN 55811-4451, USA

Christiansen, Robert S (Bob) (Athlete, Football Player)
2022 Thornhill Dr
Granite Bay, CA 95746-7144, USA

Christianson, Bob (Musician)
c/o Mike Rosen *Working Artists Agency*
13525 Ventura Blvd
Sherman Oaks, CA 91423-3801

Christie, Chris (Governor)
PO Box 1
Trenton, NJ 08625-0001, USA

Christie, Doug (Athlete, Basketball Player)
PO Box 23609
Federal Way, WA 98093-0609, USA

Christie, George
65 Fix Way
Ventura, CA 93001-2526, USA

Christie, Julianna (Actor)
252 N Larchmont Blvd Ste 200
Los Angeles, CA 90004-3754, USA

Christie, Julianne (Actor)
252 N Larchmont Blvd Ste 200
Los Angeles, CA 90004-3754, USA

Christie, Julie (Actor, Model)
c/o Renee Missel *Renee Missel Management*
846 S Wooster St
Los Angeles, CA 90035-1710, USA

Christie, Linford (Athlete, Track Athlete)
107 Sherland Road Twickenham
Middx TW9 4HB, UNITED KINGDOM (UK)

Christie, Lou (Musician)
c/o Staff Member *Dick Fox Entertainment*
1650 Broadway
New York, NY 10019-6833, USA

Christie, Mike (Athlete, Hockey Player)
6093 S Krameria St
Centennial, CO 80111-4273, USA

Christie, Steve (Athlete, Football Player)
PO Box 646
Buffalo, NY 14231-0646, USA

Christie, Tony (Musician)
c/o Staff Member *Chris Davis Management Ltd.*
Tenbury House 36 Teme St, Tenbury Wells
Worcestershire WR15 8AA, UK

Christie, Warren (Actor)
c/o Trina Allen *Play Management*
807 Powell St Suite 220
Vancouver V6A 1H7, Canada

Christie, William (Musician)
2 Rue de Saint-Petersbourg
Paris 75008, FRANCE

Christine, Andrew (Andy) (Cartoonist)
c/o Staff Member *King Features Syndication*
300 W 57th St Fl 15
New York, NY 10019-5238, USA

Christine, Zola (Stylist)
c/o Staff Member *Dossier*
556 S Fair Oaks Ave # 431
Pasadena, CA 91105-2656, USA

Christlieb, Peter (Pete) (Musician)
11761 E Speedway Blvd
Tucson, AZ 85748-2017, USA

Christman, Tim (Athlete, Baseball Player)
1293 Central Ave
Albany, NY 12205-5231, USA

Christmas, Steve (Athlete, Baseball Player)
600 Bentley St
Oviedo, FL 32765-8169, USA

Christo (Javacheff) (Artist)
48 Howard St
New York, NY 10013-3074, USA

Christoff, Steve (Athlete, Hockey Player)
542 Fairview Ave S
Saint Paul, MN 55116-1466, USA

Christon, Shameka (Athlete, Basketball Player)
c/o Staff Member *New York Liberty*
2 Penn Plz Fl 15
New York, NY 10121-1703, USA

Christopher, Dennis (Actor)
5757 Wilshire Blvd Ste 473
Los Angeles, CA 90036-3632, USA

Christopher, Gerald (Actor)
11900 Goshen Ave Apt 203
Los Angeles, CA 90049-6380, USA

Christopher, Gerard
11900 Goshen Ave Apt 203
Los Angeles, CA 90049-6380

Christopher, Gretchen (Musician)
509 E Ridgecrest Blvd # 1A
Ridgecrest, CA 93555-3959, USA

Christopher, Herb (Athlete, Football Player)
PO Box 554
Redan, GA 30074-0554, USA

Christopher, Joe (Athlete, Baseball Player)
PO Box 65240
Baltimore, MD 21209-0240, USA

Christopher, Matt (Writer)
PO Box 2511
Wilton, NY 12831-5511, USA

Christopher, Mike (Athlete, Baseball Player)
8707 Courthouse Rd
Church Road, VA 23833-2712, USA

Christopher, Patrick (Athlete, Basketball Player)
c/o Sam Goldfelder *Excel Sports Management*
9665 Wilshire Blvd Ste 500
Beverly Hills, CA 90212-2312, USA

Christopher, Thom (Actor)
PO Box 16758
Beverly Hills, CA 90209-2758, USA

Christopher, Tyler (Actor)
c/o Ric Beddingfield *Beddingfield Company, The*
13600 Ventura Blvd Ste B
Sherman Oaks, CA 91423-5050, USA

Christopher, William (Actor)
c/o Wes Stevens *Vox*
6420 Wilshire Blvd Ste 1080
Los Angeles, CA 90048-5539, USA

Christopherson, James (Jim) (Athlete, Football Player)
526 Queens Ct
Moorhead, MN 56560-6777, USA

Christy, Brenda (Stylist)
c/o Staff Member *Maximum Talent*
1873 S Bellaire St Ste 915
Denver, CO 80222-4356, USA

Christy, Earl (Athlete, Football Player)
10825 S Prairie Ave
Chicago, IL 60628-3620, USA

Christy, George
170 N Carmelina Ave
Los Angeles, CA 90049-2737

Christy, Greg (Athlete, Football Player)
2 Concord St
Natrona Heights, PA 15065-9732, USA

Christy, James W (Astronomer)
7285 Golden Eagle Dr
Flagstaff, AZ 86004-3254, USA

Christy, Jeff (Athlete, Football Player)
138 Horseshoe Dr
Freeport, PA 16229-1712, USA

Christy, Robert F (Physicist)
1230 Arden Rd
Pasadena, CA 91106-4146, USA

Chryplewicz, Pete (Athlete, Football Player)
17855 Parklane St
Livonia, MI 48152-2726, USA

Chrysostom, Bishop (Religious Leader)
PO Box 519
Libertyville, IL 60048-0519, USA

Chryssa (Artist)
565 Broadway Soho
New York, NY 10012, USA

Chrystal, Bob (Athlete, Hockey Player)
231 Rita St
Winnipeg, MB R3J 2Y3, Canada

Chu, Anna (Stylist)
c/o Staff Member *Artists by Timothy Priano (CA)*
8447 Wilshire Blvd Ste 301
Beverly Hills, CA 90211-3206, USA

Chu, Judy (Congressman, Politician)
1520 Longworth Hob
Washington, DC 20515-4605, USA

Chu, Paul C W (Physicist)
Center for Superconductivity
Houston, TX 77204-0001, USA

Chu, Steven (Nobel Prize Laureate)
4820 Drummond Ave
Chevy Chase, MD 20815-5429, USA

Chubais, Anatoly B (Government Official)
Kitaigorodsky Proyezd 7
Moscow 103074, RUSSIA

Chubin, Steve (Athlete, Basketball Player)
4095 Wilshire Dr
York, PA 17402-4518, USA

Chuck, D (Musician)
1800 Argyle Ave # 408
Los Angeles, CA 90028-5253, USA

Chuck, Wendy (Designer)
c/o Heather Parker *Innovative Artists (LA)*
1505 10th St
Santa Monica, CA 90401-2805, USA

Chuck Wagon Gang
4408 Buffalo Ln
Joshua, TX 76058-5521

Chulack, Christopher (Director, Producer, Writer)
c/o Staff Member *Creative Artists Agency (CAA-LA)*
2000 Avenue of the Stars Ste 100
Los Angeles, CA 90067-4705, USA

Chulk, Vinnie (Athlete, Baseball Player)
10062 SW 223rd Ter
Cutler Bay, FL 33190-1584, USA

Chum, Chuck
733 Trevino Dr
Lady Lake, FL 32159-5575, USA

Chung, Alexa (Musician)
c/o Staff Member *Liz Matthews PR*
83 Charlotte Street
London W1T 4PR, United Kingdom

Chung, Constance Y (Connie) (Correspondent, Journalist)
c/o Alan Berger *Creative Artists Agency (CAA-LA)*
2000 Avenue of the Stars Ste 100
Los Angeles, CA 90067-4705, USA

Chung, Doo Ri (Designer)
c/o Meghan Wood *KCD Worldwide Inc*
450 W 15th St Ste 604
New York, NY 10011-7082, USA

Chung, Eugene (Athlete, Football Player)
109 Surrey Ln
Ponte Vedra Beach, FL 32082-3942, USA

Chung, Jamie (Actor)
c/o Ben Levine *Kritzer Levine Wilkins Entertainment*
11872 La Grange Ave Fl 1
Los Angeles, CA 90025-5283, USA

Chung, Mark (Soccer Player)
2121 Velma Ave
Columbus, OH 43211-2085, USA

Chung, Myung-Whun (Musician)
Postfach 1617
Hanover 30016, GERMANY

Chupack, Cindy
c/o Daniel A (Dan) Strone *Trident Media Group LLC*
41 Madison Ave Fl 36
New York, NY 10010-2257, USA

Church, Charlotte (Musician)
7 Dials Cambridge Bridge Covent Garden
London WC2H 9HU, UNITED KINGDOM (UK)

Church, Eric (Musician)
c/o Cliff Burnstein *Q Prime Inc*
729 7th Ave Ste 1600
New York, NY 10019-6880, USA

Church, Ryan (Athlete, Baseball Player)
625 N 5th St
Lompoc, CA 93436-4809, USA

Church, Sam (Misc)
8315 Lee Hwy # 500
Fairfax, VA 22031-2215, USA

Churches, Brady J (Business Person)
1105 N Market St
Wilmington, DE 19801-1282, USA

Churchill, Caryl (Writer)
60/66 Wardour St
London W1V 4ND, UNITED KINGDOM (UK)

Churchman, Ricky (Athlete, Football Player)
445 Cherry Blossom Loop
Richland, WA 99352-7851, USA

Churchwell, Don (Athlete, Football Player)
1379 George Brown Rd
Lucedale, MS 39452-3364, USA

Churla, Shane (Athlete, Hockey Player)
31826 Scotch Pine Ln
Bigfork, MT 59911-8275, USA

Churn, Chuck (Athlete, Baseball Player)
733 Trevino Dr
Lady Lake, FL 32159-5575, USA

Chute, Robert M (Biologist, Songwriter, Writer)
68 Schellinger Rd
Poland, ME 04274-6142, USA

Chuy, Don (Athlete, Football Player)
11690 Oxnard St
North Hollywood, CA 91606-4878, USA

Chvatal, Cynthia (Producer)
c/o Staff Member *United Talent Agency (UTA)*
9560 Wilshire Blvd Fl 5
Beverly Hills, CA 90212-2400, USA

Chwast, Seymour (Artist)
55 E 9th St Apt 1G
New York, NY 10003-6312, USA

Chychrun, Jeff (Athlete, Hockey Player)
6423 NW 32nd Way
Boca Raton, FL 33496-3396, USA

Chynoweth, Dean (Athlete, Hockey Player)
131 Shawnee Rise SW
Calgary, AB T2Y 2S3, Canada

Chyzowski, Dave (Athlete, Hockey Player)
c/o Staff Member *Kamloops Blazers*
300 Lorne St
Kamloops, BC V2C 1W3, Canada

Ciaffa, Chris
627 N Las Palmas Ave
Los Angeles, CA 90004-1019

Cialini, Julie (Artist, Model)
PO Box 55536
Valencia, CA 91385-0536, USA

Ciampi, Carlo A (Prime Minister)
Palazzo del Quirinale
Rome 187, ITALY

Ciampi, Joe (Coach)
Athletic Dept
Auburn, AL 36831, USA

Ciampl, Joe (Coach)
Athletic Dept
Auburn, AL 36831, USA

Cianfrocco, Archi (Athlete, Baseball Player)
12424 Addax Ct
San Diego, CA 92129-4141, USA

Ciara (Actor, Composer, Musician)
c/o Patti Webster *W&W PR*
476 Union Ave Ste 2
Middlesex, NJ 08846-1968, USA

Ciaramello, Benny (Actor)
c/o Scott Zimmerman *Evolution Entertainment (LA)*
901 N Highland Ave
Los Angeles, CA 90038-2412, USA

Ciardi, Mark (Athlete, Baseball Player)
21 Mitchell Ave
Piscataway, NJ 08854-5560, USA

Cias, Darryl (Athlete, Baseball Player)
12330 Lithuania Dr
Granada Hills, CA 91344-1637, USA

Ciavaglia, Peter (Athlete, Hockey Player)
1137 Carrie Ct
Rochester Hills, MI 48309-3766, USA

Cibrian, Eddie (Actor)
c/o Staff Member *International Creative Management (ICM-LA)*
10250 Constellation Blvd Fl 7
Los Angeles, CA 90067-6207, USA

Cibulkova, Dominika (Athlete, Tennis Player)
1 Progress Plz Ste 1500
Saint Petersburg, FL 33701-4335, USA

Ciccarelli, Dino (Athlete, Hockey Player)
37934 Lakeshore Dr
Harrison Township, MI 48045-2853, USA

Ciccio, Robbin (Stylist)
25 Prince Ave
Winchester, MA 01890-1329, USA

Ciccippio, Joseph
2107 3rd St
Norristown, PA 19401-1930

Ciccolella, Jude (Actor)
c/o Adam Lazarus *Bauman Redanty & Shaul Agency*
5757 Wilshire Blvd Suite 473
Beverly Hills, CA 90212, USA

Ciccolella, Mike (Athlete, Football Player)
8145 Station House Rd
Dayton, OH 45458-2931, USA

Ciccone, Christopher (Designer)
8687 Melrose Ave Ste B230
West Hollywood, CA 90069-5786

Ciccone, Enrico (Athlete, Hockey Player)
c/o Staff Member *Sports Prospects Inc*
77 Rue de Bleury
Rosemere, QC J7A 4L9, Canada

Cicerone, Aldo (Musician)
Dombacher Str 41/III/3
Vienna 1170, AUSTRIA

Cicerone, Ralph J (Scientist)
Earth Science Dept Rowland Hall
Irvine, CA 92717, USA

Cichocki, Chris (Athlete, Hockey Player)
3955 Pine Lake Cir
Stockton, CA 95219-2021, USA

Cichowski, Gene (Chick) (Athlete, Football Player)
3903 Oak Ave
Northbrook, IL 60062-4922, USA

Cichowski, Tom (Athlete, Football Player)
443 N Hill Rd
Kalispell, MT 59901-8107, USA

Cichy, Joe J (Athlete, Football Player)
9806 Island Rd
Bismarck, ND 58503-9261, USA

Cid, Celeste (Actor)
c/o Staff Member *Telefe - Argentina*
Pavon 2444 (C1248AAT)
Buenos Aires, ARGENTINA

Cidre, Cynthia (Producer, Writer)
c/o Ann Blanchard *Creative Artists Agency (CAA-LA)*
2000 Avenue of the Stars Ste 100
Los Angeles, CA 90067-4705, USA

Ciechanover, Aaron (Nobel Prize Laureate)
Taub Building
Haifa 32000, Israel

Cienfuegos, Mauricio (Soccer Player)
1010 Rose Bowl Dr
Pasadena, CA 91103, USA

Cigliuti, Natalia (Actor)
c/o Felicia Sager *Sager Management*
260 S Beverly Dr # 205
Beverly Hills, CA 90212-3805, USA

Cihocki, Al (Athlete, Baseball Player)
43 Cochise Cir
Medford, NJ 08055-9769, USA

Cilento, Diane (Actor)
PO Box 600
Bar Mills, ME 04004-0600, AUSTRALIA

Ciller, Tansu (Prime Minister)
Selanik Cod 40
Kizilay, Ankara, TURKEY

Cilmi, Gabriella (Musician)
c/o David (Dave) Chumbley *Primary Talent International (UK)*
The Primary Building 10-11 Jockeys Fields
London WC1R 4BN, UK

Cimarro, Mario (Actor)
c/o Arlene Forster *Forster Entertainment*
12533 Woodgreen St
Los Angeles, CA 90066-2723, USA

Cimber, Matt (Director, Producer, Writer)
3620 Beverly Glen Blvd # 1A
Sherman Oaks, CA 91423-4403, USA

Cimellaro, Tony (Athlete, Coach, Hockey Player)
c/o Staff Member *Kingston Frontenacs*
P.O. Box 665 Stn Main
Kingston, ON K7L 4X1, Canada

Cimino, Leonardo (Actor)
156 5th Ave Ste 820
New York, NY 10010-7767, USA

Cimino, Michael (Director)
9015 Alto Cedro Dr
Beverly Hills, CA 90210-1804, USA

Cimino, Pete (Athlete, Baseball Player)
14 Fillmore St
Bristol, PA 19007-5415, USA

Cimmo, Leonardo (Actor)
156 5th Ave Ste 820
New York, NY 10010-7767, USA

Cimoli, Gino (Athlete, Baseball Player)
9060 Cook Riolo Rd
Roseville, CA 95747-9239, USA

Cimorelli, Frank (Athlete, Baseball Player)
4759 Lakeside Cir
West Palm Beach, FL 33417-1114, USA

Cincotti, Peter (Musician)
c/o Staff Member *WmE2 (Endeavor-LA)*
9601 Wilshire Blvd Fl 3
Beverly Hills, CA 90210-5219, USA

Cinderella (Music Group, Musician)
6129 S Riverbend Dr
Nashville, TN 37221-3937, USA

Cindric, Ann (Baseball Player)
114 Forest Hills Rd
Pittsburgh, PA 15221-3710, USA

Cindrich, Joe (Athlete, Football Player)
1310 Trinity Dr
Menlo Park, CA 94025-6680, USA

Cindrich, Ralph (Athlete, Football Player)
151 Fort Pitt Blvd Apt 1501
Pittsburgh, PA 15222-1572, USA

Cinematic Sunrise (Music Group, Musician)
c/o Staff Member *Equal Vision Records*
PO Box 38202
Albany, NY 12203-8202, USA

Cineson All-Stars (Music Group)
c/o Staff Member *Paradigm (Monterey)*
404 W Franklin St
Monterey, CA 93940-2303, USA

Cink, Stewart (Athlete, Golfer)
1303 Brunson Way
The Villages, FL 32162-8727, USA

Cintron, Alex (Athlete, Baseball Player)
HC 2 Box 8575
Yabucoa, PR 00767-9599, USA

Cioffi, Charles (Actor)
10100 Santa Monica Blvd Ste 2500
Los Angeles, CA 90067-4116, USA

Ciokey, Janna (Actor)
9255 W Sunset Blvd Ste 710
Los Angeles, CA 90069-3304, USA

Cipa, Larry (Athlete, Football Player)
250 Torrent Ct
Rochester Hills, MI 48307-3871, USA

Cipriani, Frank (Athlete, Baseball Player)
14 Oakhill Dr
Buffalo, NY 14224-4214, USA

Cipriani Thorne, Juan Luis Cardinal (Religious Leader)
Plaza de Armas S/N Apartado 1512
Lima 100, PERU

Circa Survive (Music Group)
c/o Brian Schechter *Riot Squad Management*
335 Cortlandt St Fl 2
Belleville, NJ 07109-3201, USA

Circi, Cristian (Architect)
Carrer de Pujades 63 2-N
Barcelona 8005, SPAIN

Cirella, Joe (Athlete, Hockey Player)
Teranet 600-1 Adelaide St E
Toronto, ON M5C 2V9, Canada

Ciriani, Henri (Architect)
61 Rue Pascal
Paris 75013, FRANCE

Cirillo, Jeff (Athlete, Baseball Player)
PO Box 233
Medina, WA 98039-0233, USA

Cirrincione, Vincent (Producer)
1516 N Fairfax Ave
Los Angeles, CA 90046-2608, USA

Cisar, George (Athlete, Baseball Player)
9026 W 24th St
Riverside, IL 60546-1027, USA

Cisco, Galen (Athlete, Baseball Player)
604 Elmwood Ln
Celina, OH 45822-2966, USA

Cisneros, Evelyn (Ballerina)
455 Franklin St
San Francisco, CA 94102-4438, USA

Cisneros, Evelyo (Ballerina)
455 Franklin St
San Francisco, CA 94102-4438, USA

Cisneros, Henry G (Secretary)
2002 W Houston St
San Antonio, TX 78207-3419, USA

Cisowski, Steve (Athlete, Football Player)
1090 3rd St
Gilroy, CA 95020-5302, USA

Citarella, Ralph (Athlete, Baseball Player)
29 E Sherman Ave
Colonia, NJ 07067-1412, USA

Citro, Ralph (Boxer)
32 N Black Horse Pike
Blackwood, NJ 08012-3093, USA

Citron, Martin (Biologist)
152A 226 Amgen Ctr
Thousand Oaks, CA 91320, USA

Citron, Ralph (Boxer)
32 N Black Horse Pike
Blackwood, NJ 08012-3093, USA

Citterio, Antonio (Architect)
Via Cerva 4
Milan 20122, ITALY

Citti, Christine (Actor)
20 Ave Rapp
Paris 75007, FRANCE

City High (Music Group)
c/o Staff Member *WmE2 (WMA-LA)*
1 William Morris Pl
Beverly Hills, CA 90212-4261, USA

Civiletti, Benjamin R (Attorney, Attorney General, General)
5900 Old Ocean Blvd Apt B3
Boynton Beach, FL 33435-6228, USA

CK, Louis (Actor, Comedian)
c/o Staff Member *United Talent Agency (UTA)*
9560 Wilshire Blvd Fl 5
Beverly Hills, CA 90212-2400, USA

Claar, Brian (Athlete, Golfer)
3987 Lions Paw St
Castle Rock, CO 80104-7768, USA

Clabo, Neal (Athlete, Football Player)
1100 Beaverton Rd
Knoxville, TN 37919-7089, USA

Clabo, Neil (Athlete, Football Player)
1100 Beaverton Rd Apt 1
Knoxville, TN 37919-7089, USA

Clabo, Tyson (Athlete, Football Player)
c/o Chad Speck *Allegiant Athletic Agency*
35 Market Sq Ste 201
Knoxville, TN 37902-1420, USA

Clack, Darryl (Athlete, Football Player)
3891 S Halsted Dr
Chandler, AZ 85286-2612, USA

Clackson, Kim (Athlete, Hockey Player)
342 Thomas Rd
Canonsburg, PA 15317-3534, USA

Claes, Willy (Government Official)
Berkenlaan 23
Hasselt 3500, BELGIUM

Claffey, Norine (Stylist)
915 Sherman Ave Apt 214
Evanston, IL 60202-1736, USA

Claiborne, Chris (Athlete, Football Player)
1000 N Green Valley Pkwy Ste 440-128
Henderson, NV 89074-6170, USA

Claiborne, Craig
30 Park Pl
East Hampton, NY 11937-2407

Clairmont, Patsy (Writer)
PO Box 36
Brighton, MI 48116-0036, USA

Claitt, Rickey (Athlete, Football Player)
5830 Grand Canyon Dr
Orlando, FL 32810-3232, USA

Clampett, Bobby (Athlete, Golfer)
5722 Belmont Valley Ct
Raleigh, NC 27612-6464, USA

Clampi, Cario A (President, Prime Minister)
Palazzo del Quirinale
Rome 187, ITALY

Clampi, Joe (Coach)
Athletic Dept
Auburn, AL 36831, USA

Clancy, Edward B Cardinal (Religious Leader)
Sydney Archdiocese Polding House 276 Pitt St
Sydney, NSW 2000, AUSTRALIA

Clancy, Jim (Athlete, Baseball Player)
177 Lance Dr
Twin Lakes, WI 53181-9635, USA

Clancy, Sam (Athlete, Football Player)
1308 Crest Ln
Oakdale, PA 15071-1748, USA

Clancy, Sean (Athlete, Football Player)
211 Bal Cross Dr
Bal Harbour, FL 33154-1318, USA

Clancy, Terry (Athlete, Hockey Player)
65 Golfdale Rd
Toronto, ON M4N 2B5, Canada

Clancy, Tom (Writer)
PO Box 800
Huntingtown, MD 20639-0800, USA

Clancy Brothers
177 Woodland Ave
Westwood, NJ 07675-3218, US

Clanton, Jimmy (Musician)
4425 Kingwood Dr
Kingwood, TX 77339-3701, USA

Clap Your Hands Say Yeah (Music Group)
c/o Staff Member *Paradigm (Monterey)*
404 W Franklin St
Monterey, CA 93940-2303, USA

Clapinski, Chris (Athlete, Baseball Player)
83328 Wagon Rd
Indio, CA 92203-2837, USA

Clapp, Gordon (Actor)
9300 Wilshire Blvd Ste 555
Beverly Hills, CA 90212-3211, USA

Clapp, Nicholas R (Producer)
PO Box 1019
Borrego Springs, CA 92004-1019, USA

Clapp, Richard (Stubby) (Athlete, Baseball Player)
49 S 4th St Apt 409
Memphis, TN 38103-5222, USA

Clapp, Thomas (Athlete, Football Player)
804 Live Oak St
Metairie, LA 70005-1216, USA

Clapton, Eric (Musician)
c/o Kristin Foster *PMK/BNC Public Relations (PMK-NY)*
622 3rd Ave Fl 8
New York, NY 10017-6707, USA

Clardy, Jon C (Misc)
Chemistry Dept
Ithaca, NY 14853, USA

Clarey, Doug (Athlete, Baseball Player)
2116 Hillhurst Ave
Los Angeles, CA 90027-2004, USA

Claridge, Dennis (Athlete, Football Player)
2621 Calvert St
Lincoln, NE 68502-4935, USA

Clarin, Hans Joachim
Zellerhornstr. 75
Aschau, GERMANY D-83229

Clarizio, Louis (Athlete, Baseball Player)
133 Lela Ln
Schaumburg, IL 60193-1339, USA

Clark, Al (Athlete, Football Player)
PO Box 971
Bogalusa, LA 70429-0971, USA

Clark, Al (Athlete, Baseball Player)
1185 SW 5th Ave
Boca Raton, FL 33432-7140, USA

Clark, Alan (Musician)
16 Lambton Place
London W11 2SH, UNITED KINGDOM (UK)

Clark, Allie (Athlete, Baseball Player)
250 Stevens Ave
South Amboy, NJ 8879, USA

Clark, Anthony (Actor, Comedian)
c/o Mark Rousso *New Wave Entertainment (LA)*
2660 W Olive Ave
Burbank, CA 91505-4525, USA

Clark, Archie (Athlete, Basketball Player)
4268 10th St
Ecorse, MI 48229-1219, USA

Clark, Bernard (Athlete, Football Player)
1506 W Spruce St
Tampa, FL 33607-3513, USA

Clark, Blake (Actor, Writer)
c/o Adrienne McWhorter *Abrams Artists Agency (LA)*
9200 W Sunset Blvd PH 11
Los Angeles, CA 90069-3601, USA

Clark, Bob (Correspondent)
5010 Creston St
Hyattsville, MD 20781-1216, USA

Clark, Bobby (Athlete, Baseball Player)
1030 Perrisito St
Perris, CA 92570-2345, USA

Clark, Brady (Athlete, Baseball Player)
19275 Green Lakes Loop
Bend, OR 97702-1171, USA

Clark, Brett (Athlete, Hockey Player)
8745 Aberdeen Cir
Highlands Ranch, CO 80130-3952, USA

Clark, Brian (Athlete, Football Player)
811 Woodland Forest Dr
Waxhaw, NC 28173-8546, USA

Clark, Bruce (Athlete, Football Player)
1500 W Esplanade Ave Apt 17F
Kenner, LA 70065-5317, USA

Clark, Bryan (Baseball Player)
508 E Clark St
Madera, CA 93638-1662, USA

Clark, Bryan (Athlete, Football Player)
1040 Alder Ln
Naperville, IL 60540-7202, USA

Clark, C Joseph (Joe) (Prime Minister)
707 7th Ave SW # 1300
Calgary, AB T2P 3H6, CANADA

Clark, Candy (Actor)
13935 Hatteras St
Van Nuys, CA 91401-4342, USA

Clark, Carol Hiqgins (Writer)
300 E 56th St
New York, NY 10022-4136, USA

Clark, Cecelia (Stylist)
8036 Hampton Arbor Cir
Chesterfield, VA 23832-1968, USA

Clark, Chris (Athlete, Hockey Player)
160 Pine Tree Ln
South Windsor, CT 06074-3219, USA

Clark, Corinne (Athlete, Baseball Player)
7224 Hawthorn Ave NE
Albuquerque, NM 87113-2084, USA

Clark, Dallas (Athlete, Football Player)
7001 W 56th St
Indianapolis, IN 46254-9725, USA

Clark, Daniel (Actor)
c/o Staff Member *Schachter Entertainment*
1157 S Beverly Dr Fl 2
Los Angeles, CA 90035-1119, USA

Clark, Danny (Athlete, Football Player)
213 Seneca Trl
Bloomingdale, IL 60108-2432, USA

Clark, Dave (Athlete, Baseball Player)
4842 Mayfield Rd W
Collierville, TN 38017-3309, USA

Clark, Derrick (Athlete, Football Player)
430 Sunset Dr Apt 2
Orlando, FL 32805-3305, USA

Clark, Dick (Producer)
c/o Staff Member *Dick Clark Productions*
2900 Olympic Blvd
Santa Monica, CA 90404-4127, USA

Clark, Doran
6399 Wilshire Blvd Ste 414
Los Angeles, CA 90048-5716

Clark, Doug (Athlete, Baseball Player)
106 Piedmont St
Springfield, MA 01104-2042, USA

Clark, Dwight (Athlete, Football Player)
2511 Sedley Rd
Charlotte, NC 28211-3658, USA

Clark, Earl (Swimmer)
1145 NE 126th St Apt 4
North Miami, FL 33161-5027, USA

Clark, Eugenie (Biologist)
1255 N Gulfstream Ave Apt 503
Sarasota, FL 34236-8904, USA

Clark, Gail (Athlete, Football Player)
PO Box 335
Bellefontaine, OH 43311-0335, USA

Clark, Gary (Athlete, Football Player)
PO Box 202
Dublin, VA 24084-0202, USA

Clark, Gene (Musician)
9850 Sandaltoot Rd # 458
Boca Raton, FL 33428, USA

Clark, George W (Physicist)
Physics Dept
Cambridge, MA 2139, USA

Clark, Glen (Athlete, Baseball Player)
5605 Marblehead Dr
Dallas, TX 75232-2356, USA

Clark, Gordie (Athlete)
1 Stratham Grn
Stratham, NH 03885-2341, USA

Clark, Guy (Musician, Songwriter, Writer)
1025 17th Ave S # 200
Nashville, TN 37212-2211, USA

Clark, Harry (Athlete, Football Player)
1121 Patton Dr
Morgantown, WV 26505-3756, USA

Clark, Helen (Prime Minister)
Parliament Buildings
Wellington, NEW ZELAND

Clark, Hilary (Stylist)
c/o Staff Member *Ennis*
119 Braintree St
Boston, MA 02134-1628, USA

Clark, Howie (Athlete, Baseball Player)
14204 439th Ave SE
North Bend, WA 98045-9209, USA

Clark, Jack A (Athlete, Baseball Player)
6541 Scottsdale Way
Frisco, TX 75034-4015, USA

Clark, James (Jim) (Business Person)
PO Box 755
Chicago, IL 60690-0755, USA

Clark, Jerald (Athlete, Baseball Player)
12325 Crisscross Ln
San Diego, CA 92129-3766, USA

Clark, Jermaine (Athlete, Baseball Player)
2 Ute Ct
San Ramon, CA 94583, USA

Clark, Jessie (Athlete, Football Player)
7611 S 9th Way
Phoenix, AZ 85042-6621, USA

Clark, Jim (Athlete, Baseball Player)
659 S Indian Hill Blvd Apt C
Claremont, CA 91711-5486, USA

Clark, Joe
PO Box 96848
Washington, DC 20090-6848

Clark, Joe (Educator)
208 Essex Ave
Newark, NJ 7103, USA

Clark, Kelly (Athlete, Skier)
178 Route 100
West Dover, VT 05356-0725, USA

Clark, Kelvin (Athlete, Football Player)
3812 Evesham Dr
Plano, TX 75025-3818, USA

Clark, Kenneth B (Psychic)
PO Box 126
Hastings On Hudson, NY 10706-0126, USA

Clark, Keon (Basketball Player)
301 W South Temple
Salt Lake City, UT 84101-1216, USA

Clark, Kevin (Athlete, Football Player)
3902 S Chase Way
Denver, CO 80235-3133, USA

Clark, Kevin Alexander (Actor)
c/o Anne Geddes *Geddes Agency, The*
8430 Santa Monica Blvd Ste 200
Los Angeles, CA 90069-4253, USA

Clark, L Hill (Business Person)
100 Stamford Pl
Stamford, CT 06902-6740, USA

Clark, Larry (Filmmaker)
c/o Staff Member *International Creative Management (ICM-LA)*
10250 Constellation Blvd Fl 7
Los Angeles, CA 90067-6207, USA

Clark, Laurel B (Doctor)
4899 Montrose Blvd Apt 1601
Houston, TX 77006-6170, USA

Clark, Leroy (Athlete, Football Player)
5458 Osprey Dr
Houston, TX 77048-1109, USA

Clark, Louis S (Athlete, Football Player)
6144 Kissengen Springs Ct
Jacksonville, FL 32258, USA

Clark, Marcia (Lawyer)
c/o Staff Member *WmE2 (WMA-LA)*
1 William Morris Pl
Beverly Hills, CA 90212-4261, USA

Clark, Mario (Athlete, Football Player)
695 Palisade St Apt 695
Pasadena, CA 91103-2059, USA

Clark, Mark (Athlete, Baseball Player)
18262 E CR 520N
Kilbourne, IL 62655-6628, USA

Clark, Mary Ellen (Swimmer)
117 Blue Hills Rd
Amherst, MA 01002-2221, USA

Clark, Mary Higgins (Writer)
15 Werimus Brook Rd
Saddle River, NJ 07458-3118, USA

Clark, Matt (Actor)
1199 Park Ave Apt 15D
New York, NY 10128-1791, USA

Clark, Mel (Baseball Player)
270 Home Run Dr
West Columbia, WV 25287-8692, USA

Clark, Mel (Athlete, Baseball Player)
270 Home Run Dr
West Columbia, WV 25287-8692, USA

Clark, Micheal (Choreographer, Dancer)
Silk St
London EC2Y 8DS, UNITED KINGDOM

Clark, Mike (Athlete, Football Player)
6909 Bonair Dr Apt C
Tampa, FL 33617-8919, USA

Clark, Mystro (Actor, Comedian)
c/o Staff Member *International Creative Management (ICM-LA)*
10250 Constellation Blvd Fl 7
Los Angeles, CA 90067-6207, USA

Clark, Otey (Athlete, Baseball Player)
207 Parker St
Boscobel, WI 53805-1642, USA

Clark, Perry (Coach)
Athletic Dept
Coral Gables, FL 33124, USA

Clark, Peter B (Publisher)
7675 La Jolla Blvd Unit 203
La Jolla, CA 92037-4747, USA

Clark, Petula (Musician)
15 chemin Rieu Colign
Geneva, SWITZERLAND

Clark, Phil (Athlete, Baseball Player)
112 Hicks Rd
Dawson, GA 39842-4002, USA

Clark, Phil (Athlete, Baseball Player)
9062 Dancy Tree Ct
Orlando, FL 32836-5059, USA

Clark, Phil (Athlete, Football Player)
705 Case St
Evanston, IL 60202-3508, USA

Clark, Richard C (Dick) (Ex-Senator, Politician)
4424 Edmunds St NW # 1070
Washington, DC 20007-1117, USA

Clark, Rickey (Athlete, Baseball Player)
8953 Emerald Waters Ct
Las Vegas, NV 89147-6501, USA

Clark, Robert C (Artist)
34 Monterey Ct
Manhattan Beach, CA 90266-7237, USA

Clark, Ron (Athlete, Baseball Player)
700 Starkey Rd Apt 511
Largo, FL 33771-2344, USA

Clark, Roy (Musician)
3225 S Norwood Ave
Tulsa, OK 74135-5479, USA

Clark, Ryan (Athlete, Football Player)
1236 Camarta Dr
Pittsburgh, PA 15227-3956, USA

Clark, Sedric (Athlete, Football Player)
7819 Chasewood Dr
Missouri City, TX 77489-1836, USA

Clark, Spencer Treat (Actor)
c/o Michael Greenwald *Don Buchwald & Associates Inc (LA)*
6500 Wilshire Blvd Ste 2200
Los Angeles, CA 90048-4942, USA

Clark, Stephen E (Steve) (Swimmer)
29 Martling Rd
San Anselmo, CA 94960-1172, USA

Clark, Susan (Actor)
13400 Riverside Dr Ste 308
Sherman Oaks, CA 91423-2541, USA

Clark, Terry (Athlete, Baseball Player)
1607 E Tam O Shanter St
Ontario, CA 91761-6356, USA

Clark, Tim (Athlete, Golfer)
22400 N 97th St
Scottsdale, AZ 85255-4431, USA

Clark, Tony (Athlete, Baseball Player)
14125 N 65th Ave
Glendale, AZ 85306-3757, USA

Clark, Vernon E (Admiral)
Chief of Naval Operations Hqusn
Pentagon
Washington, DC 20350-0001, USA

Clark, Vinnie (Athlete, Football Player)
8828 Desoto Dr
Cincinnati, OH 45231-4412, USA

Clark, W G (Architect)
4048 E Main St
Charlottesville, VA 22902, USA

Clark, W Ramsey (General)
37 W 12th St Apt 2B
New York, NY 10011-8503, USA

Clark, Wayne (Athlete, Football Player)
14241 Lambeth Way
Tustin, CA 92780-2230, USA

Clark, Wendel (Athlete, Hockey Player)
c/o Staff Member *Toronto Maple Leafs*
Air Canada Centre 400-40 Bay St
Toronto, ON M5J 2X2, Canada

Clark, Wesley K (Wes) (General)
111 Center St
Little Rock, AR 72201-4402, USA

Clark, Will (Adult Film Star)
c/o Staff Member *Diva Central Inc*
7510 W Sunset Blvd Ste 1445
Los Angeles, CA 90046-3408, USA

Clark, William P (Secretary)
4424 Edmunds St NW # 1070
Washington, DC 20007-1117, USA

Clark, William (Will) (Athlete, Baseball Player)
18555 Saint Andrews Ct E
Prairieville, LA 70769-3248, USA

Clark II, Michael (Athlete, Golfer)
4007 Pintail Cir
Rocky Face, GA 30740-8919, USA

Clark-Cole, Dorinda (Musician)
c/o Staff Member *Gospocentric*
421 E Beach Ave
Inglewood, CA 90302-3103, USA

Clarke, Allan (Music Group, Musician)
Hill Farm Hackleton
Northantshire NN7 2DH, UNITED KINGDOM (UK)

Clarke, Angela (Actor)
3930 Weeping Willow Dr
Moorpark, CA 93021-2842, USA

Clarke, Bob (Cartoonist)
7480 Rivershore Dr
Seaford, DE 19973-4328, USA

Clarke, Bobby (Athlete, Hockey Player)
1930 Glenwood Dr
Ocean City, NJ 08226-2611, USA

Clarke, Brian Patrick (Actor)
c/o Staff Member *Orange Grove Group, The*
12178 Ventura Blvd Ste 205
Studio City, CA 91604-2540, USA

Clarke, Darren (Athlete, Golfer)
c/o Andrew ""Chubby"" Chandler *International Sports Management Ltd (ISM UK)*
Cherry Tree Farm Cherry Tree Lane
Rostherne, Cheshire WA14 3RZ, UNITED KINGDOM

Clarke, Elis E I (President)
16 Frederick St
Port of Spain, TRINADAD & TOBAGO

Clarke, Emily (Actor)
c/o Darren Goldberg *Global Creative*
1051 Cole Ave # B
Los Angeles, CA 90038-2601, USA

Clarke, Emmy (Actor)
c/o Darren Goldberg *Global Creative*
1051 Cole Ave # B
Los Angeles, CA 90038-2601, USA

Clarke, Frank (Athlete, Football Player)
6016 Pine Ridge Blvd
McKinney, TX 75070-9518, USA

Clarke, Gary (Actor, Writer)
1113 Heep Run
Buda, TX 78610-5091, USA

Clarke, Gilby (Music Group, Musician)
212 Allen Ave
Allenhurst, NJ 07711-1006, USA

Clarke, Gilmore D (Architect)
480 Park Ave
New York, NY 10022-1613, USA

Clarke, Hagood (Athlete, Football Player)
2500 NE 37th Dr
Fort Lauderdale, FL 33308-6323, USA

Clarke, Hansen (Congressman, Politician)
1319 Longworth Hob
Washington, DC 20515-1305, USA

Clarke, Horace (Athlete, Baseball Player)
PO Box 891
Frederiksted, VI 00841-0891, USA

Clarke, John (Actor)
3000 W Alameda Ave
Burbank, CA 91523-0001, USA

Clarke, Kate (Actor)
c/o JD Sobol 741 N Cahuenga Blvd Ste 101
Los Angeles, CA 90038, USA

Clarke, Ken (Athlete, Football Player)
7610 Willoughby Ct
Alpharetta, GA 30005-3028, USA

Clarke, Kenneth H (Government Official)
Westminster
London SW1A 0AA, UNITED KINGDOM (UK)

Clarke, Lenny (Actor)
c/o Staff Member *Paradigm (LA)*
360 N Crescent Dr
Beverly Hills, CA 90210-4874, USA

Clarke, Martha (Choreographer, Dancer)
130 W 56th St
New York, NY 10019-3962, USA

Clarke, Melinda (Actor)
c/o Michael (Mike) Jelline *United Talent Agency (UTA)*
10250 Constellation Blvd Fl 7
Los Angeles, CA 90067-6207, USA

Clarke, Michael (Music Group, Musician)
9850 Sandalfoot Blvd # 458
Boca Raton, FL 33428-6645, USA

Clarke, Noel (Actor, Director, Writer)
c/o Staff Member *Liz Matthews PR*
83 Charlotte Street
London W1T 4PR, United Kingdom

Clarke, Richard (Lawyer)
1600 Pennsylvania Ave NW
Washington, DC 20500-0005, USA

Clarke, Robert L (Government Official)
711 Louisiana St Ste 2900
Houston, TX 77002-2770, USA

Clarke, Ronald (Ron) (Athlete, Track Athlete)
1 Bay St
Brighton, VIC 3186, USA

Clarke, Sarah (Actor)
c/o Staff Member *Levine Management*
9028 W Sunset Blvd PH 1
Los Angeles, CA 90069-1830, USA

Clarke, Stan (Athlete, Baseball Player)
5333 Sanders Dr
Toledo, OH 43615-6860, USA

Clarke, Stanley (Musician)
c/o Brice Gaeta *Broder Webb Chervin Silbermann Agency, The (BWCS)*
10250 Constellation Blvd
Los Angeles, CA 90067-6200, USA

Clarke, Susanna (Writer)
175 5th Ave
New York, NY 10010-7703, USA

Clarke, Thomas E (Business Person)
1 SW Bowerman Dr
Beaverton, OR 97005-0979, USA

Clark-Sheard, Karen (Musician)
c/o Staff Member *Elektra Records*
75 Rockefeller Plz Fl 17
New York, NY 10019-6927, USA

Clarkson, Adrienne (Ex Governor)
12A Admiral Rd
Ottawa, ON M5R 2L5, Canada

Clarkson, Jeremy (Television Host)
c/o Staff Member *XS Promotions*
57 Fonthill Rd
Aberdeen AB11 6UQ, UNITED KINGDOM (UK)

Clarkson, Kelly (Musician, Songwriter)
c/o Narvel Blackstock *Starstruck Entertainment*
40 Music Sq W
Nashville, TN 37203-3206, USA

Clarkson, Patricia (Actor)
c/o Kevin Huvane *Creative Artists Agency (CAA-LA)*
2000 Avenue of the Stars Ste 100
Los Angeles, CA 90067-4705, USA

Clary, Julian (Actor)
PO Box 976 Swindon
SN5 7HN, UNITED KINGDOM

Clary, Marty (Athlete, Baseball Player)
205 Yorktown Ct
Easley, SC 29642-9042, USA

Clary, Robert (Actor)
10001 Sundial Ln
Beverly Hills, CA 90210-2719, USA

Clasby, Bob (Athlete, Football Player)
8180 E Shea Blvd Unit 1090
Scottsdale, AZ 85260-6572, USA

Clash, Kevin (Artist, Voice Over Artist)
c/o Staff Member *Sesame Workshop*
1 Lincoln Plz Fl 2
New York, NY 10023-7163, USA

Clash, The
268 Camden Rd
London, ENGLAND NW1

Clatworthy, Robert (Artist, Misc)
Moelfre Cynghordy Landovery Dyfed
Wales SA20 OUW, UNITED KINGDOM (UK)

Clatyon, Barry (Artist, Voice Over Artist)
88-90 Crawford St
London W1H 2BS, UNITED KINGDOM (UK)

Claudel, Aurelie (Model)
c/o Staff Member *IMG*
304 Park Ave S Fl 12
New York, NY 10010-4314, USA

Claudel, Philippe (Director, Writer)
c/o Staff Member *ArtMedia*
20 avenue Rapp
Paris 75008, France

Clauser, Francis H (Educator, Engineer)
842 E Villa St
Pasadena, CA 91101-1259, USA

Clauss, Jared (Athlete, Football Player)
215 S 82nd St
West Des Moines, IA 50266-8524, USA

Claussen, Brandon (Athlete, Baseball Player)
2611 N Kentucky Ave Apt 116
Roswell, NM 88201-5870, USA

Clavel, Bernard (Writer)
Albin Michel 22 Rue Huyghens
Paris 75014, FRANCE

Clavier, Christian (Actor)
201 Faubourg Saint Honore
Paris 75008, FRANCE

Clawhammer
PO Box 1519
New Haven, CT 06506-1519

Clawson, John (Athlete, Basketball Player)
30 Eagle Lake Pl Unit 31
San Ramon, CA 94582-4858, USA

Claxton, Craig (Speedy) (Basketball Player)
1001 Broadway
Oakland, CA 94607-4019, USA

Claxton, Paul (Athlete, Golfer)
PO Box 485
Claxton, GA 30417-0485, USA

Clay, Andrew (Actor, Comedian)
9560 Wilshire Blvd # 400
Beverly Hills, CA 90212-2427, USA

Clay, Andrew Dice (Comedian)
c/o Ben Feigin *Anonymous Content (AC-LA)*
3531 Hayden Ave
Culver City, CA 90232, USA

Clay, Bryan (Athlete, Olympic Athlete)
c/o Staff Member *USA Track & Field*
132 E Washington St Ste 800
Indianapolis, IN 46204-3674, USA

Clay, Danny (Athlete, Baseball Player)
5434 Ravine Bluff Ct
Columbus, OH 43231-3157, USA

Clay, Hayward (Athlete, Football Player)
PO Box 234
Snyder, TX 79550-0234, USA

Clay, John (Athlete, Football Player)
1425 Leroy Ave
Saint Louis, MO 63133-1723, USA

Clay, Ken (Athlete, Baseball Player)
4523 60th Street Ct W
Bradenton, FL 34210-2729, USA

Clay, Nicholas
15 Golden Sq # 315
London, ENGLAND W1R 3AG

Clay, Walter (Athlete, Football Player)
2827 Arlington Ave
Pueblo, CO 81003-1315, USA

Clayborn, Adrian (Football Player)
c/o Blake Baratz *The Institute for Athletes*
3600 Minnesota Dr Ste 550
Edina, MN 55435-7925, USA

Clayborn, Raymond D (Ray) (Athlete, Football Player)
20610 Aspen Canyon Dr
Katy, TX 77450-7091, USA

Claybrooks, Devon (Athlete, Football Player)
725 Auburn Pl
Martinsville, VA 24112-4502, USA

Clayderman, Richard (Musician)
P O Box 28286
London N21 3WT, UNITED KINGDOM (UK)

Claydon, Phil (Director)
c/o Jason Burns *United Talent Agency (UTA)*
9465 Wilshire Blvd # 600
Beverly Hills, CA 90212-2612, USA

Clayman, Ralph V (Doctor, Misc)
Surgery Dept 416 S Kingshighway Blvd
Saint Louis, MO 63110, USA

Claypool, James (Athlete, Hockey Player)
302 Paine Farm Rd
Duluth, MN 55804-2632, USA

Claypool, Lee (Music Group, Musician)
3470 19th St
San Francisco, CA 94110-1740, USA

Claypool, Les (Musician)
c/o Staff Member *Paradigm (Monterey)*
404 W Franklin St
Monterey, CA 93940-2303, USA

Clayson, Jane (Correspondent)
c/o Staff Member *CBS Television*
51 W 52nd St
New York, NY 10019-6119, USA

Clayton, Adam (Music Group, Musician)
30-32 Sir John Rogersons Quay
Dublin @, IRELAND

Clayton, Amber (Actor)
c/o Steve Glick *Glick Agency*
1321 7th St Ste 203
Santa Monica, CA 90401-1631, USA

Clayton, Donald D (Misc)
Physic/Astrophysics
Clemson, SC 29634-0001, USA

Clayton, Harvey (Athlete, Football Player)
15303 SW 143rd St
Miami, FL 33196-2879, USA

Clayton, Mark (Athlete, Football Player)
16426 Canyon Chase Dr
Houston, TX 77095-6532, USA

Clayton, Mark (Athlete, Football Player)
9407 Manor Forge Way
Owings Mills, MD 21117-5161, USA

Clayton, Michael (Athlete, Football Player)
8501 Kentucky Derby Dr
Odessa, FL 33556-2446, USA

Clayton, Ralph (Athlete, Football Player)
6356 Selkirk St
Detroit, MI 48211-1836, USA

Clayton, Robert N (Geophysicist, Misc, Physicist)
5201 S Cornell Ave
Chicago, IL 60615, USA

Clayton, Royce (Athlete, Baseball Player)
6035 Murphy Way
Malibu, CA 90265-4490, USA

Clayton, Thomas David (Music Group, Musician)
43 Washington St
Groveland, MA 01834-1142, USA

Cleamons, Jim (Athlete, Basketball Player, Coach)
1426 9th St
Manhattan Bch, CA 90266-6125, USA

Clear, Mark (Athlete, Baseball Player)
12654 S Rene St
Olathe, KS 66062, USA

Clearwater, Keith (Athlete, Golfer)
1077 E Bretonwoods Ln
Orem, UT 84097-8200, USA

Cleary, Danielle (Stylist)
c/o Staff Member *Mark Edward Inc*
325 W 8th St # 1011
New York, NY 10018, USA

Cleary, Jon Stephen (Writer)
23 Ryde Rd
Pymble, NSW 2073, AUSTRALIA

Cleary, Robert (Bob) (Athlete, Hockey Player)
680 South Ave Unit 8
Weston, MA 02493-1192, USA

Cleary, Thomas (Writer)
c/o Staff Member *Random House*
1540 Broadway
New York, NY 10036-4039, USA

Cleary, William J (Bill) Jr (Athlete, Coach, Hockey Player)
27 Kingswood Rd
Auburndale, MA 02466-1013, USA

Cleave, Mary L (Astronaut)
Cadys Ofc 7R86
Washington, DC 20546-0001, USA

Cleaver, Alan (Designer, Fashion Designer)
Via Vallone 11 Monte Conero
Sirolo, ITALY

Cleaver, Emanuel (Congressman, Politician)
1433 Longworth Hob
Washington, DC 20515-0104, USA

Cledwyn of Penrhos (Government Official)
Penmorfa Trearddur Holyhead Gwynedd
Wales, UNITED KINGDOM (UK)

Cleeland, Cam (Athlete, Football Player)
23160 Lanyard Ln
Mount Vernon, WA 98274-8379, USA

Cleese, John (Actor, Comedian, Writer)
c/o Tony Lipp *Anonymous Content (AC-LA)*
3531 Hayden Ave
Culver City, CA 90232, USA

Clef (Music Group, Musician)
83 Riverside Dr
New York, NY 10024-5713, USA

Clegg, Johnny (Music Group, Musician)
c/o Staff Member *Monterey International (Chicago)*
200 W Superior St Ste 202
Chicago, IL 60654-6422, USA

Cleghorne, Ellen (Actor, Comedian)
c/o Frederick Levy *Management 101*
9107 1/2 Cahuenga Blvd
N Hollywood, CA 91601-2920, USA

Cleland, J Maxwell (Max) (Ex-Senator)
340 Mockingbird Ln SE
Smyrna, GA 30082-3729, USA

Clemens, Barry (Athlete, Basketball Player)
3111 Clinton Ave
Cleveland, OH 44113-2973, USA

Clemens, Donella (Religious Leader)
722 N Main St
Newton, KS 67114-1819, USA

Clemens, Doug (Athlete, Baseball Player)
4799 Lower Mountain Rd
New Hope, PA 18938-9454, USA

Clemens, Robert (Bob) (Athlete, Football Player)
2007 Poole Dr NW Ste D
Huntsville, AL 35810-4900, USA

Clemens, Roger (Athlete, Baseball Player)
11535 Quail Hollow Ln
Houston, TX 77024-6508, USA

Clemenson, Christian (Actor)
c/o Mitch Clem *Shadow Entertainment*
10 Universal City Plz Fl 20
Universal City, CA 91608-1074, USA

Clement, Anthony (Athlete, Football Player)
141 Navajo Ln
Opelousas, LA 70570-0324, USA

Clement, Aurore (Actor)
20 Ave Rapp
Paris 75007, FRANCE

Clement, Bill (Athlete, Hockey Player)
9 Channel Nine Ct Attn Hockey Broadcast Dept
Toronto, ON M1S 4B5, Canada

Clement, Jemaine (Actor, Writer)
c/o Jason Heyman *Creative Artists Agency (CAA-LA)*
2000 Avenue of the Stars Ste 100
Los Angeles, CA 90067-4705, USA

Clement, Matt (Athlete, Baseball Player)
143 Milt Miller Rd
Renfrew, PA 16053-9613, USA

Clement, Skip (Athlete, Football Player)
620 Tennis Club Dr Apt 106
Fort Lauderdale, FL 33311-4030, USA

Clement F, Haynsworth Jr (Judge)
111 Boxwood Ln
Greenville, SC 29601-3812, USA

Clemente, Carmine D (Misc, Physicist)
11737 Bellagio Rd
Los Angeles, CA 90049-2158, USA

Clemente, Fransesco (Artist)
684 Broadway
New York, NY 10012-1125, USA

Clements, Dick (Director, Producer, Writer)
c/o Bruce Kaufman *International Creative Management (ICM-LA)*
10250 Constellation Blvd Fl 7
Los Angeles, CA 90067-6207, USA

Clements, John A (Misc, Physicist)
Cardiovascular Institute
San Francisco, CA 94143-0001, USA

Clements, Kim (Writer)
c/o Staff Member *Creative Artists Agency (CAA-LA)*
2000 Avenue of the Stars Ste 100
Los Angeles, CA 90067-4705, USA

Clements, Lennie (Athlete, Golfer)
PO Box 182197
Coronado, CA 92178-2197, USA

Clements, Nate (Athlete, Football Player)
1 Bills Dr
Orchard Park, NY 14127-2237, USA

Clements, Pat (Athlete, Baseball Player)
166 Lazy S Ln
Chico, CA 95928-9112, USA

Clements, Ronald (Director, Producer, Writer)
c/o Staff Member *Creative Artists Agency (CAA-LA)*
2000 Avenue of the Stars Ste 100
Los Angeles, CA 90067-4705, USA

Clements, Suzanne (Designer, Fashion Designer)
48 S Molton St
London W1X 1HE, UNITED KINGDOM (UK)

Clements, Tom (Athlete, Football Player)
220 Heinz St Apt R202
Pittsburgh, PA 15212-5944, USA

Clements, Vincent (Vin) (Athlete, Football Player)
62 Chatham Rd
Berlin, CT 06037-1104, USA

Clements, William P Jr (Ex-Governor)
1901 N Akard St
Dallas, TX 75201-2305, USA

Clemmensen, Scott (Athlete, Hockey Player)
1702 Sterling Dr
Florham Park, NJ 07932-3036, USA

Clemmer, Ronnie (Producer)
c/o Staff Member *Longbow Productions*
4295 N Norway Rd
Lincoln, MI 48742-9645, USA

Clemmons, Ruth (Stylist)
9549 Windy Knoll Dr
Dallas, TX 75243-7561, USA

Clemons, Charlie (Athlete, Football Player)
1973 Bertha Ct
Hampton, GA 30228-4006, USA

Clemons, Chris (Athlete, Baseball Player)
521 Karen Dr
Robinson, TX 76706-5122, USA

Clemons, Craig (Athlete, Football Player)
1517 D Ave NE
Cedar Rapids, IA 52402-5148, USA

Clemons, Duane (Athlete, Football Player)
7512 Dr Phillips Blvd Ste 50-908
Orlando, FL 32819-5420, USA

Clemons, Lance (Athlete, Baseball Player)
4516 Golf Club Ln
Spring Hill, FL 34609-0303, USA

Clendenen, Mike (Athlete, Football Player)
24591 Del Prado Ste 201
Dana Point, CA 92629-3837, USA

Clendenin, Bob (Actor)
c/o Staff Member *Origin Talent Agency*
4705 Laurel Canyon Blvd Ste 306
Studio City, CA 91607-5940, USA

Clennon, David (Actor)

Cleopatra
c/o Staff Member *20th Century Fox*
10201 W Pico Blvd Bldg 103RM PMB 5286
Los Angeles, CA 90064-2651, USA

Clerico, Christian (Business Person, Misc)
116 Bis Ave des Champs Elyees
Paris 75008, FRANCE

Clervoy, Jean-Francois (Misc)
Johnson Space Flight Center 2101 NASA Road 1
Houston, TX 77058, USA

Cleveland, Paul M (Diplomat)
5700 Cricket Pl
Mc Lean, VA 22101-1817, USA

Cleveland, Reggie (Athlete, Baseball Player)
202 Creekview Dr
Anna, TX 75409-3577, USA

Clevenger, Raymond C III (Judge)
717 Madison Pl NW
Washington, DC 20439-0001, USA

Clevenger, Tex (Athlete, Baseball Player)
31727 Country Club Dr
Porterville, CA 93257-9610, USA

Clevlen, Brent (Athlete, Baseball Player)
2405 La Rochelle Dr
Cedar Park, TX 78613-4722, USA

Clexton, Edward W Jr (Admiral)
1000 Bobolink Dr
Virginia Beach, VA 23451-4906, USA

Cliburn, Stan (Athlete, Baseball Player)
727 Nimitz St
Jackson, MS 39209-6118, USA

Cliburn, Stewart (Stew) (Athlete, Baseball Player)
425 William Dr
Pleasant View, TN 37146-7910, USA

Cliburn, Van (Musician)
PO Box 470219
Fort Worth, TX 76147-0219, USA

Cliche, Karen (Actor)
c/o Sandy Martinez *Martinez Creative Management*
7012 St Laurent Blvd Suite 200
Montreal, QC H2S 3E2, Canada

Cliff, Jimmy (Music Group, Songwriter, Writer)
51 Lady Musgrave Rd
Kingston, JAMAICA

Clifford, Chris (Athlete, Hockey Player)
600 Compass Crt
Kingston, ON K7M 8V9, Canada

Clifford, Linda (Music Group)
c/o Staff Member *Diva Central Inc*
7510 W Sunset Blvd Ste 1445
Los Angeles, CA 90046-3408, USA

Clifford, M Richard (Rich) (Astronaut)
3700 Bay Area Blvd
Houston, TX 77058-1160, USA

Clift, Eleanor
1750 Pennsylvania Ave NW Ste 1220
Washington, DC 20006-4504

Clift, William B III (Photographer)
PO Box 6035
Santa Fe, NM 87502-6035, USA

Clifton, Chad (Athlete, Football Player)
346 Heidelberg Ct
Green Bay, WI 54302-4949, USA

Clifton, Greg (Athlete, Football Player)
2717 Botany St
Charlotte, NC 28216-4431, USA

Clifton, Kyle (Athlete, Football Player)
777 S Point Ct
Aledo, TX 76008-4134, USA

Cliks, The (Music Group)
c/o Staff Member *Paradigm (Monterey)*
404 W Franklin St
Monterey, CA 93940-2303, USA

Cline, Bruce (Athlete, Hockey Player)
870 112E Ave
Drummondville, QC J2B 4K6, Canada

Cline, Jackie (Athlete, Football Player)
5935 High Forest Dr
Mc Calla, AL 35111-4205, USA

Cline, Martin J (Educator, Misc)
Med Center Hematology Dept
Los Angeles, CA 90024, USA

Cline, Richard (Cartoonist)
4 Times Sq
New York, NY 10036-6515, USA

Cline, Ty (Athlete, Baseball Player)
37 Wappoo Creek Pl
Charleston, SC 29412-2121, USA

Cline Sr, Tony (Athlete, Football Player)
59 Chestnut Pl
Danville, CA 94506-4542, USA

Cline-Lieberman, Nancy (Athlete, Basketball Player)
2636 Creekway Dr
Carrollton, TX 75010-4227, USA

Clines, Gene (Athlete, Baseball Player)
5303 9th Avenue Dr W
Bradenton, FL 34209-4205, USA

Clinkscale, F Dextor (Athlete, Football Player)
206 Michaux Dr
Greenville, SC 29605-3156, USA

Clinkscales, Joey (Athlete, Football Player)
10207 Shrewsbury Run W
Collierville, TN 38017-8304, USA

Clinkscales, Sherard (Baseball Player)
13688 Oliver Ln
Carmel, IN 46074-8465, USA

Clinton, Bill (Ex-President, Politician)
55 W 125th St
New York, NY 10027-4516, USA

Clinton, Chelsea
15 Old House Ln
Chappaqua, NY 10514, USA

Clinton, George (Musician, Songwriter)
c/o Vasi Vangelos *First Artists Management*
4764 Park Granada Ste 210
Calabasas, CA 91302-3333, USA

Clinton, Hillary Rodham (Ex-First Lady, Ex-Senator, First Lady, Government Official, Politician)
2201 C St NW
Washington, DC 20520-0099, USA

Clinton, Kate (Comedian)
230 W End Ave Apt 10C
New York, NY 10023-3664, USA

Clinton-Davis of Hackney, Stanley C (Government Official)
Westminster
London SW1A 0PW, UNITED KINGDOM (UK)

Clippard, Tyler (Athlete, Baseball Player)
2160 Chianti Pl Unit 118
Palm Harbor, FL 34683-7736, USA

Clippingdale, Steve (Athlete, Hockey Player)
5560 Swordfern Pl
North Vancouver, BC V7R 4T1, Canada

Clique Girlz (Music Group, Musician)
c/o Staff Member *Clique Entertainment Productions*
11 Forest View Ct
Egg Harbor Township, NJ 08234-7132, USA

Clisters, Kim (Tennis Player)
200 Tournament Rd
Ponte Vedra Beach, FL 32082, USA

Clive, John
4 Court Lodge Chelsea
London, ENGLAND SW3 AJA

Cloepfil, Brad (Architect)
910 NW Hoyt St # 200
Portland, OR 97209-3210, USA

Clohessy, Robert (Actor)
6500 Wilshire Blvd Ste 2200
Los Angeles, CA 90048-4942, USA

Cloke, Kristen (Actor)
c/o Staff Member *Mitchell K Stubbs & Assoc (MKS)*
8675 Washington Blvd Ste 203
Culver City, CA 90232-7486, USA

Cloninger, Tony (Athlete, Baseball Player)
PO Box 1500
Denver, NC 28037-1500, USA

Clontz, Brad (Athlete, Baseball Player)
735 Eider Down Ct
Alpharetta, GA 30022-6198, USA

Clooney, George (Actor, Producer)
c/o Stan Rosenfield *Stan Rosenfield & Associates*
2029 Century Park E Ste 1190
Los Angeles, CA 90067-2931, USA

Clooney, Nick (Writer)
4400 Massachusetts Ave NW Rm 330A
Washington, DC 20016-8001, USA

Close, Bill (Basketball Player)
555 Byron St Apt 409
Palo Alto, CA 94301-2038, USA

Close, Charles T (Chuck) (Artist)
20 Bond St
New York, NY 10012-2689, USA

Close, Eric (Actor)
c/o Justin Grey Stone *Untitled Entertainment (LA)*
350 S Beverly Dr Ste 200
Beverly Hills, CA 90212-4819, USA

Close, Glenn (Actor)
c/o Catherine Olim *PMK/BNC Public Relations (PMK-LA)*
8687 Melrose Ave Ste 8
West Hollywood, CA 90069-5746, USA

Close, Joshua (Actor)

Closs, Bill (Athlete, Basketball Player)
10320 W Loyola Dr # 201
Los Altos, CA 94024-6510, USA

Closser, J D (Athlete, Baseball Player)
417 E 1100 N
Alexandria, IN 46001-9025, USA

Closter, Al (Athlete, Baseball Player)
4103 Hickory Rd
Richmond, VA 23235-1437, USA

Closure In Moscow (Music Group, Musician)
c/o Andrew Cook *Run Artist Management*
5753 Cobblestone Dr
Rocklin, CA 95765-4103, USA

Clotet, Lluis (Architect)
Caspe 151
Barcelona 8013, SPAIN

Cloud, Jack M (Athlete, Football Player)
805 Janice Dr
Annapolis, MD 21403 2801, USA

Cloud, Mike (Athlete, Football Player)
62 8th St
Hermosa Beach, CA 90254-4102, USA

Cloude, Ken (Athlete, Baseball Player)
8126 Del Haven Rd
Dundalk, MD 21222-3425, USA

Clough, Gerald W (Educator)
Presidential S Ofc
Atlanta, GA 30332-0001, USA

Clough Jr, Ray W (Engineer)
19800 SW Touchmark Way Apt 280
Bend, OR 97702-3405, USA

Clougherty, Pat (Athlete, Baseball Player)
2002 Langham Ln
Raleigh, NC 27615-5678, USA

Cloutier, Jacques (Athlete, Hockey Player)
12172 Triple Crown Dr
Parker, CO 80134-7747, USA

Clovers, The
1607 Belvidere Rd
Belvidere, NC 27919-9615

Clower, Lee (Stylist)
c/o Staff Member *Sarah Laird Inc*
12 Charles Ln
New York, NY 10014-2526, USA

Clowes, Dan (Artist)
c/o Staff Member *Fantagraphics Books*
7563 Lake City Way NE
Seattle, WA 98115-4218, USA

Clowes, Daniel (Writer)
7563 Lake City Way NE
Seattle, WA 98115-4218, USA

Cluggish, Bob (Athlete, Basketball Player)
270 Lake Seminary Cir
Maitland, FL 32751-3311, USA

Clune, Don (Athlete, Football Player)
322 N Orange St
Media, PA 19063-2308, USA

Clunes, Martin (Actor)
c/o Samira Higham *Independent Talent Group (ITG-UK)*
Oxford House 76 Oxford St
London W1D 1BS, UK

Clunie, Michelle Renee (Actor)
c/o Bernard Kira *Vanguard Management Group*
8060 Melrose Ave Fl 4
Los Angeles, CA 90046-7038, USA

Clutch (Music Group, Musician)
c/o Paul Ryan *Agency Group Ltd, The (UK)*
361-373 City Rd
London EC1V 1PQ, UK

Clutterbuck, Bryan (Athlete, Baseball Player)
2320 Parkwood Ave
Ann Arbor, MI 48104-5110, USA

Clwson, John (Basketball Player)
33 San Ysidro Ct
Danville, CA 94526-1545, USA

Clyburn, Danny (Athlete, Baseball Player)
148 E Brooklyn Ave
Lancaster, SC 29720-3326, USA

Clyde, Ben (Basketball Player)
8356 A St Apt 1
Saint Petersburg, FL 33701, USA

Clyde, David (Athlete, Baseball Player)
7806 Pinehurst Shadows Dr
Humble, TX 77346-1511, USA

Clyde, Tom (Athlete, Baseball Player)
210 Chestnut Ln
Coppell, TX 75019-5390, USA

Clymer, Ben (Athlete, Hockey Player)
2386 Lake View Blvd
Port Charlotte, FL 33948-3612, USA

Clyne, Nikki (Actor)
c/o David Miner *3 Arts Entertainment Inc*
9460 Wilshire Blvd Fl 7
Beverly Hills, CA 90212-2713, USA

CM Punk (Wrestler)
c/o Kerry Rodgerson *World Wrestling Entertainment (WWE)*
1241 E Main St
Stamford, CT 06902-3520, USA

Coachman, Bobby (Baseball Player)
PO Box 44
Cottonwood, AL 36320-0044, USA

Coachman, Davis Alice (Athlete, Track Athlete)
811 Gibson St
Tuskegee, AL 36083-7253, USA

Coachman, Pete (Athlete, Baseball Player)
8795 S County 55 Rd
Cottonwood, AL 36320-3323, USA

Coad, Barbara (Stylist)
7825 Castle Ln
Indianapolis, IN 46256-3215, USA

Coady, Richard (Rich) (Athlete, Football Player)
17106 Spanky Pl
Dallas, TX 75248-1533, USA

Coakley, Dexter (Athlete, Football Player)
1304 Sunset Ridge Cir
Cedar Hill, TX 75104-4541, USA

Coalter, Gary (Athlete, Hockey Player)
Lot 23 Concession 6 Lount Tsp RR1
South River, ON P0A 1X0, Canada

Coan, Bert (Athlete, Football Player)
14517 N US Highway 59
Nacogdoches, TX 75965-9004, USA

Coan, Gil (Athlete, Baseball Player)
PO Box 668
Brevard, NC 28712-0668, USA

Coase, Ronald H (Nobel Prize Laureate)
1111 E 60th St
Chicago, IL 60637-2776, USA

Coasters, The (Music Group, Musician)
2756 N Green Valley Pkwy # 449
Henderson, NV 89014-2120, USA

Coates, Ben (Athlete, Football Player)
123 Lily Green Ct NW
Concord, NC 28027-3395, USA

Coates, Jim (Athlete, Baseball Player)
1098 Oak Hill Rd
Lancaster, VA 22503-4009, USA

Coates, Kim (Actor)
c/o Samantha Crisp *Kohner Agency, The*
9300 Wilshire Blvd Ste 555
Beverly Hills, CA 90212-3211, USA

Coates, Phyllis (Actor)
PO Box 1969
Boyes Hot Springs, CA 95416-1969, USA

Coates, Ray (Athlete, Football Player)
6219 Louis Xiv St
New Orleans, LA 70124-3024, USA

Coates, Sherrod (Athlete, Football Player)
12233 Silveroak Ln
Charlotte, NC 28277-1582, USA

Coates, Steve (Athlete, Hockey Player)
102 Stoney Creek Dr
Egg Harbor Township, NJ 08234-7559, USA

Coats, Dan (Ex-Senator)
1700 Pennsylvania Ave NW
Washington, DC 20006-4700, USA

Coats, Daniel (Senator)
United States Senate SR-493
Washington, DC 20510-0001, USA

Coats, Kristi (Athlete, Golfer)
185 Wildwood Trl
Petal, MS 39465-2681, USA

Coats, Michael L (Astronaut)
3203 Acorn Wood Way
Houston, TX 77059-3175, USA

Cobb, Charles (Athlete, Football Player)
6075 N Forkner Ave
Fresno, CA 93711-1827, USA

Cobb, David (Politician)
c/o Staff Member *The Green Party of the United States*
PO Box 57065
Washington, DC 20037-0065, USA

Cobb, Garry (Athlete, Football Player)
112 Society Hill Blvd
Cherry Hill, NJ 08003-2402, USA

Cobb, Henry N (Architect)
88 Pine St
New York, NY 10005-1801, USA

Cobb, Julie (Actor)
1801 Avenue of the Stars Ste 902
Los Angeles, CA 90067-5981, USA

Cobb, Keith Hamilton (Actor)
c/o Steven Jensen *The Independent Group*
6363 Wilshire Blvd Ste 115
Los Angeles, CA 90048-5734, USA

Cobb, Marvin (Athlete, Football Player)
655 S Flower St Unit 290
Los Angeles, CA 90017-2805, USA

Cobb, Reggie (Athlete, Football Player)
4710 Cambridge St
Sugar Land, TX 77479-3948, USA

Cobb, Trevor (Athlete, Football Player)
1721 Cheston Dr
Houston, TX 77029-2909, USA

Cobbin, James (Athlete, Baseball Player)
121 E Rayen Ave
Youngstown, OH 44503-1620, USA

Cobbs, Bill (Actor, Producer)
c/o Staff Member *Forster Entertainment*
12533 Woodgreen St
Los Angeles, CA 90066-2723, USA

Cobbs, Cedric (Athlete, Football Player)
4710 Fairlee Dr
Little Rock, AR 72209-5218, USA

Cobert, Bob (Composer)
8730 W Sunset Blvd Ste 300
Los Angeles, CA 90069-2276, USA

Cobham, William C (Billy) (Music Group, Musician)
300 Mercer St Apt 3J
New York, NY 10003-6732, USA

Coble, Drew (Athlete, Baseball Player)
205 80th Ave N
Myrtle Beach, SC 29572-4339, USA

Coble, Howard (Congressman, Politician)
2188 Rayburn Hob
Washington, DC 20515-1303, USA

Coblenz, Walter (Director, Producer)
4310 Cahuenga Blvd Unit 401
Toluca Lake, CA 91602-2713, USA

Cobos, Jesus Lopez (Conductor)
1241 Elm St
Cincinnati, OH 45202-7531, USA

Cobra Starship (Music Group)
c/o Jonathan Daniel *Crush Management*
60-62 E 11th St Floor 7
New York, NY 10003, USA

Cobum, Cindy C (Bowler)
7200 Harrison Ave # 7171
Rockford, IL 61112-1017, USA

Cobum, Doris (Bowler)
130 Dalton Dr
Buffalo, NY 14223-2221, USA

Coburn, John G (General)
Commanding General Army Material Command
Alexandria, VA 22333-0001, USA

Coburn, Tom (Senator)
172 Russell Senate Ofc Bldg
Washington, DC 20510-0001, USA

Cocanower, James S (Jaime) (Athlete, Baseball Player)
10777 Gram B Cir
Lowell, AR 72745-8446, USA

Coccioletti, Philip (Actor)
c/o Carmen Lavia *Fifi Oscard Agency*
110 W 40th St Rm 1601
New York, NY 10018-8512, USA

Cochereau, Pierre (Musician)
15 Bis des Ursins
Paris 75004, FRANCE

Cochran, Anita L (Astronomer)
Astronomy Dept
Austin, TX 78712, USA

Cochran, Antonio (Athlete, Football Player)
8433 Manchester Hwy
Woodland, GA 31836-2038, USA

Cochran, Barbara Ann (Skier)
213 Brown Hl W
El Prado, NM 87529, USA

Cochran, Hank (Music Group, Songwriter, Writer)
RR 2 Box 438 Hunter's Lake
Hendersonville, TN 37075, USA

Cochran, John (Correspondent)
5010 Creston St
Hyattsville, MD 20781-1216, USA

Cochran, John (Athlete, Football Player)
1249 Driftwood Dr
De Pere, WI 54115-1813, USA

Cochran, Leslie H (Educator)
Presidential S Ofc
Youngstown, OH 44555-0001, USA

Cochran, Robert (Producer, Writer)
c/o Staff Member *Agency for the Performing Arts (APA-LA)*
405 S Beverly Dr Ste 500
Beverly Hills, CA 90212-4425, USA

Cochran, Russ (Athlete, Golfer)
3 Circle Lake Dr
Paducah, KY 42001-9753, USA

Cochran, Shannon (Actor)
1450 S Robertson Blvd
Los Angeles, CA 90035-3402, USA

Cochran, Thad (Senator)
113 Dirksen Senate Ofc Building
Washington, DC 20510-0001, USA

Cochrane, Dave (Athlete, Baseball Player)
126 Silver Eagle Ln
Mooresville, NC 28117-3703, USA

Cochrane, Glen (Athlete, Hockey Player)
2763 Thompson Dr
Kamloops, BC V2C 4L7, Canada

Cochrane, Rory (Actor)
c/o Beth Holden-Garland *Untitled Entertainment (LA)*
350 S Beverly Dr Ste 200
Beverly Hills, CA 90212-4819, USA

Cockburn, Anna (Stylist)
c/o Staff Member *Management & Production/MAP Inc*
48 Saint Marks Pl Fl 4
New York, NY 10003-8129, USA

Cockburn, Bruce (Musician)
c/o Staff Member *Agency Group Ltd, The (NY)*
142 W 57th St Fl 6
New York, NY 10019-3300, USA

Cocker, Jarvis (Musician, Songwriter)
c/o Staff Member *Paradigm (Monterey)*
404 W Franklin St
Monterey, CA 93940-2303, USA

Cocker, Joe (Musician)
c/o Staff Member *Creative Artists Agency (CAA-LA)*
2000 Avenue of the Stars Ste 100
Los Angeles, CA 90067-4705, USA

Cockerill, Franklin (Biologist, Misc)
200 1st St SW
Rochester, MN 55905-0001, USA

Cockerill, Kay (Athlete, Golfer)
131 Beulah St
San Francisco, CA 94117-2717, USA

Cockrell, Alan (Athlete, Baseball Player)
306 Millstream Ter
Colorado Springs, CO 80905-4217, USA

Cockrell, Kenneth D (Astronaut)
2300 Richmond Ave Apt 350
Houston, TX 77098-3265, USA

Cockroft, Donald L (Don) (Athlete, Football Player)
2418 Dunkeith Dr NW
Canton, OH 44708-1326, USA

Cockroft, Sherman (Athlete, Football Player)
2504 Christopher Ln
Costa Mesa, CA 92626-6750, USA

Cocozza, Elizabeth (Stylist)
c/o Staff Member *Loox Agency*
12 Desbrosses St
New York, NY 10013-1704, USA

Code, Arthur D (Astronomer)
WUPPE Project Astronomy Dept
Madison, WI 53706, USA

Coder, Ron (Athlete, Football Player)
25 N Bryant Ave
Pittsburgh, PA 15202-3346, USA

Codey, Lawrence R (Business Person)
PO Box 1171
Newark, NJ 07101-1171, USA

Codiroli, Chris (Athlete, Baseball Player)
2700 Hillcrest Dr
Cameron Park, CA 95682-9279, USA

Codling, Samantha (Stylist)
c/o Staff Member *Sydney Represents*
280 Mott St
New York, NY 10012-3439, USA

Codrescu, Andrei (Writer)
English
Baton Rouge, LA 70803-0001, USA

Coduri, Camille (Actor)
76 Oxford St
London W1N 0AX, UNITED KINGDOM (UK)

Cody, Bill (Athlete, Football Player)
209 Orleans Dr
Fairhope, AL 36532-4218, USA

Cody, Commander (Musician)
Old Cherry Mountain Road
Jefferson, NH 3583, USA

Cody, Dan (Athlete, Football Player)
104 W 17th St
Ada, OK 74820-7612, USA

Cody, Diablo (Writer)
c/o Sarah Self *Gersh (NY)*
41 Madison Ave
New York, NY 10010-2202, USA

Coe, Barry
PO Box 268
Sun Valley, ID 83353-0268

Coe, David Allan (Musician)
c/o Robert Devine *Maximus Entertainmnet*
6205 Laurel Valley Dr Apt B
Austin, TX 78731-4426, USA

Coe, George (Actor)
c/o Martin Gage *Gage Group, The (LA)*
14724 Ventura Blvd Ste 505
Sherman Oaks, CA 91403-3505, USA

Coe, Sabastian N (Athlete, Track Athlete)
Starswood High Barn Road Effingham
Surrey KT24 5PW, UNITED KINGDOM (UK)

Coe, Sebastian (Athlete, Politician)
One Churchill Place Canary Wharf
London E14 5LN, UK

Coe, Sue (Artist)
527 W 26th St
New York, NY 10001-5503, USA

Coe-Jones, Dawn (Athlete, Golfer)
17319 Emerald Chase Dr
Tampa, FL 33647-3516, USA

Coelen, Chris (Director, Producer, Writer)

Coelho, Paulo (Writer)
Henrique Pechman Av Copacabana 1133
salas 601 / 602
Rio de Janeiro 22070-010, BRAZIL

Coelho, Susie (Actor)
1347 Rossmoyne Ave
Glendale, CA 91207-1852, USA

Coen, Ethan (Director, Writer)
c/o Jim Berkus *United Talent Agency (UTA)*
9560 Wilshire Blvd Fl 5
Beverly Hills, CA 90212-2400, USA

Coen, Joel (Director, Writer)
c/o Jim Berkus *United Talent Agency (UTA)*
9560 Wilshire Blvd Fl 5
Beverly Hills, CA 90212-2400, USA

Coetzee, Gerrie (Boxer)
22 Sydney Rd
Ravenswood, Boksburg 1460, SOUTH AFRICA

Coetzee, John M (Nobel Prize Laureate)
P O Box 92
Rondebosch, Cape Province 7700, SOUTH AFRICA

Coetzer, Amanda (Tennis Player)
1751 Pinnacle Dr Ste 1500
McLean, VA 22102-3833, USA

Cofer, J Michael (Mike) (Athlete, Football Player)
2688 Hollowvale Ln
Henderson, NV 89052-2846, USA

Cofer, Mike (Athlete, Football Player)
110 Bridgestone Cv
Fayetteville, GA 30215-8159, USA

Coffee, Claire (Actor)
c/o Liza Anderson *Anderson Group Public Relations*
8060 Melrose Ave Fl 4
Los Angeles, CA 90046-7038, USA

Coffee, Coena (Stylist)
7815 Queens Ct
Downers Grove, IL 60516-4421, USA

Coffey, Don (Athlete, Football Player)
231 Redfield Dr
Jackson, TN 38305-8534, USA

Coffey, John L (Judge)
E Wisconsin Ave US Courthouse 517
Milwaukee, WI 53202-5370, USA

Coffey, Junior L (Athlete, Football Player)
17228 32nd Ave S Apt E-12
Seatac, WA 98188-4402, USA

Coffey, Kellie (Musician)
c/o Staff Member *WmE2 (WMA-TN)*
1600 Division St Ste 300
Nashville, TN 37203-2755, USA

Coffey, Ken (Athlete, Football Player)
3322 Medinah Ct
Sugar Land, TX 77479-2459, USA

Coffey, Paul
633 Hawthorne St
Birmingham, MI 48009-1650

Coffey, Paul D (Athlete, Hockey Player)
12050 Albion Vaughan Rd
Bolton, ON L7E 1S7, Canada

Coffey, Richard (Athlete, Basketball Player)
4624 Flag Ave N
Minneapolis, MN 55428-4741, USA

Coffey, Scott
143 Wadsworth Ave
Santa Monica, CA 90405-3509

Coffey, Tabatha (Reality TV Star, Stylist)
c/o Staff Member *Bravo (NY)*
30 Rockefeller Plz
New York, NY 10112-0015, USA

Coffey, Todd (Athlete, Baseball Player)
109 Colonel Hampton Ct
Rutherfordton, NC 28139-7804, USA

Coffield, Kelly (Actor)
c/o Staff Member *Innovative Artists (NY)*
235 Park Ave S Fl 7
New York, NY 10003-1404, USA

Coffield, Randy (Athlete, Football Player)
7110 Lake Basin Rd
Tallahassee, FL 32312-6708, USA

Coffin, Edmund (Tad) (Horse Racer)
Strafford, VT 5072, USA

Coffin, Fredrick (Actor)
121 N San Vicente Blvd # A
Beverly Hills, CA 90211-2303, USA

Coffman, Kevin (Athlete, Baseball Player)
313 Kelly Dr
Victoria, TX 77904-1503, USA

Coffman, Mike (Congressman, Politician)
1222 Longworth Hob
Washington, DC 20515-1307, USA

Coffman, Paul (Athlete, Football Player)
14103 E 195th St
Peculiar, MO 64078-9199, USA

Coffman, Vance D (Business Person)
6801 Rockledge Dr
Bethesda, MD 20817-1803, USA

Cofield, Fred (Athlete, Basketball Player)
833 Frederick St
Ypsilanti, MI 48197-5270, USA

Cofield, Tim (Athlete, Football Player)
312 NE Warrington Ct
Lees Summit, MO 64064-1603, USA

Coflin, Hugh (Athlete, Hockey Player)
244 Murphy Dr W
Delta, BC V4M 3P2, Canada

Cogan, Kevin (Race Car Driver)
205 Rocky Point Rd
Palos Verdes Estates, CA 90274-2621, USA

Cogan, Tony (Athlete, Baseball Player)
1483 Gormican Ln
Naples, FL 34110-0921, USA

Cogdill, Gail (Athlete, Football Player)
12922 E 36th Ave
Spokane Valley, WA 99206-8405, USA

Coggin, David (Athlete, Baseball Player)
861 Emerson St
Upland, CA 91784-1227, USA

Coggins, Frank (Athlete, Baseball Player)
2937 Nelson Dr
Duluth, GA 30096-3739, USA

Coggins, Rich (Athlete, Baseball Player)
4095 Fruit St Spc 219
La Verne, CA 91750-2930, USA

Coghill, George (Athlete, Football Player)
307 Chancellor Pl
Fredericksburg, VA 22401-2104, USA

Coghlan, Eamon (Athlete, Track Athlete)
1 Erieview Plaza 1360 East 9th St # 1300
Cleveland, OH 44114, USA

Coghlan, Frank Junior
12522 Argyle Dr
Los Alamitos, CA 90720-4734

Coghlan, Frank (Junior) Jr (Actor)
28506 Ray Ct
Saugus, CA 91350-1244, USA

Cogliano, Andrew (Athlete, Hockey Player)
c/o Staff Member *Edmonton Oilers*
11230 110 St NW
GM, AB T5G 3H7, Canada

Cohan, Chris (Basketball Player, Misc)
1001 Broadway
Oakland, CA 94607-4019, USA

Cohan, Lauren (Actor)
c/o Staff Member *Liberman/Zerman Management*
252 N Larchmont Blvd Ste 200
Los Angeles, CA 90004-3754, USA

Cohan, Robert P (Choreographer)
The Place 17 Dukes Road
London WC1H 9AB, UNITED KINGDOM (UK)

Coheleach, Guy J (Artist)
PO Box 96
Bernardsville, NJ 07924-0096, USA

Cohen, Aaron (Astronaut, Misc)
1310 Essex Grn
College Station, TX 77845-9355, USA

Cohen, Adam (Writer)
c/o Staff Member *Penguin Press HC*
375 Hudson St Bsmt 3
New York, NY 10014-7465, USA

Cohen, Andy (Business Person, Television Host)
c/o Staff Member *Bravo (NY)*
30 Rockefeller Plz
New York, NY 10112-0015, USA

Cohen, Avishai (Music Group, Musician)
2635 Griffith Park Blvd
Los Angeles, CA 90039-2519, USA

Cohen, Ben (Business Person)
30 Community Dr
South Burlington, VT 05403-6809, USA

Cohen, Bruce (Actor, Producer)
c/o Staff Member *Jinks/Cohen Company*
4000 Warner Blvd Bldg 138
Burbank, CA 91522-0001, USA

Cohen, Etan (Director, Producer, Writer)
c/o Jimmy Miller *Mosaic Media Group*
9200 W Sunset Blvd Ste 10
Los Angeles, CA 90069-3608, USA

Cohen, Hy (Athlete, Baseball Player)
35734 Donny Cir
Palm Desert, CA 92211-2695, USA

Cohen, John (Musician, Photographer)
511 W 25th St Rm 73
New York, NY 10001-5561, USA

Cohen, Larry (Director)
2111 Coldwater Canyon Dr
Beverly Hills, CA 90210-1734, USA

Cohen, Leonard N (Musician, Songwriter)
c/o Staff Member *RK Management*
9300 Wilshire Blvd Ste 200
Beverly Hills, CA 90212-3227, USA

Cohen, Linda (Musician)
c/o Staff Member *Greenspan Artist Management*
8760 W Sunset Blvd
West Hollywood, CA 90069-2206, USA

Cohen, Lyor (Producer)
75 Rockefeller Plz
New York, NY 10019-6908, USA

Cohen, Marshall H (Astronomer)
Astronomy
Pasadena, CA 91125-0001, USA

Cohen, Marvin L (Physicist)
10 Forest Ln
Berkeley, CA 94708-1447, USA

Cohen, Mary Ann (Judge)
400 2nd St NW
Washington, DC 20217-0001, USA

Cohen, Matt (Actor)
c/o Sharon Lane *Lane Management Group*
13017 Woodbridge St
Studio City, CA 91604-1431, USA

Cohen, Morris (Engineer)
72 River Park St
Needham Heights, MA 02494-2643, USA

Cohen, Paul J (Mathematician)
755 Santa Ynez St
Stanford, CA 94305-8478, USA

Cohen, Richard M (Journalist, Writer)
c/o Staff Member *The New Press*
38 Greene St Fl 4
New York, NY 10013-2505, USA

Cohen, Rob (Director)
9560 Wilshire Blvd Ste 500
Beverly Hills, CA 90212-2401, USA

Cohen, Robert (Music Group, Musician)
16 Duncan Terrace
London N1 8BZ, UNITED KINGDOM (UK)

Cohen, Sacha Baron (Ali G, Borat, Bruno) (Actor, Producer, Writer)
c/o Matthew (Matt) Labov *Forefront Media*
5700 Wilshire Blvd Ste 550
Los Angeles, CA 90036-3790, USA

Cohen, Sarah (Journalist)
1150 15th St NW
Washington, DC 20071-0001, USA

Cohen, Sasha (Figure Skater)
c/o Staff Member *Champions on Ice*
3500 W 80th St Ste 200
Minneapolis, MN 55431-1090, USA

Cohen, Scott (Actor)
c/o Heather Reynolds *One Entertainment (NY)*
12 W 57th St PH 1
New York, NY 10019-3900, USA

Cohen, Seymour S (Biologist, Misc)
10 Carrot Hill Rd
Woods Hole, MA 02543-1206, USA

Cohen, Sheldon S (Government Official)
5518 Trent St
Chevy Chase, MD 20815-5512, USA

Cohen, Stanley (Nobel Prize Laureate)
Medical Center 1161 21st Ave
Nashville, TN 37232-0001, USA

Cohen, Stanley N (Biologist, Misc)
Medical Center Genetics Dept
Stanford, CA 94305, USA

Cohen, Steve (Business Person)
72 Cummings Ave
Stamford, CT 6902, USA

Cohen, Steve (Actor)
c/o Staff Member *WmE2 (WMA-LA)*
1 William Morris Pl
Beverly Hills, CA 90212-4261, USA

Cohen, Steve (Congressman, Politician)
1005 Longworth Hob
Washington, DC 20515-0701, USA

Cohen, Susan (Stylist)
c/o Staff Member *Judy Inc*
1 Yorkville Ave
Toronto ON M4W 1L1, Canada

Cohen-Tannoudji, Claude K (Nobel Prize Laureate)
38 Rue des Cordelieres
Paris 75013, FRANCE

Cohn, Alfred (Al) (Athlete, Bowler)
85 Odyssey Dr
Tinley Park, IL 60477-4853, USA

Cohn, Bobette (Stylist)
c/o Staff Member *Solo Artists*
2148 Federal Ave
Los Angeles, CA 90025-5327, USA

Cohn, Ethan (Actor)
c/o Darren Goldberg *Global Creative*
1051 Cole Ave # B
Los Angeles, CA 90038-2601, USA

Cohn, Gary (Journalist)
501 N Calvert St
Baltimore, MD 21278-1000, USA

Cohn, Marc (Musician)
c/o Staff Member *The Agency Group*
Vastergatan 23
Malmo 211 21, Sweden

Cohn, Mildred (Biologist, Misc, Physicist)
226 W Rittenhouse Sq
Philadelphia, PA 19103-5768, USA

Cohn, Mindy (Actor)
4343 Lankershim Blvd # 100
West Toluca Lake, CA 91602-2705, USA

Coia, Angelo (Athlete, Football Player)
11 McDermott Pl
Brigantine, NJ 08203-2934, USA

Coia, Arthur A (Misc)
905 16th St NW
Washington, DC 20006-1703, USA

Coifman, Ronald R (Scientist)
11 Hickory Rd
North Haven, CT 6473, USA

Coiro, Rhys (Actor)
c/o Lena Roklin *Luber Roklin Management*
8530 Wilshire Blvd Ste 550
Beverly Hills, CA 90211-3133, USA

Cojocaru, Steven (Correspondent)
c/o Staff Member *Entertainment Tonight (ET)*
4024 Radford Ave
Studio City, CA 91604-2101, USA

Coke, Phil (Athlete, Baseball Player)
c/o Team Member *New York Yankees*
Yankee Stadium 161st St & River Ave
Bronx, NY 10451, USA

Coker, Larry (Coach, Football Coach)
Athletic Dept
Coral Gables, FL 33124, USA

Cokes, Curtis (Boxer)
618 Calcutta Dr
Dallas, TX 75241-1001, USA

Colalillo, Mike (War Hero)
1601 Saint Louis Ave
Duluth, MN 55802-2442, USA

Colalucci, Gianluigi (Artist, Misc)
Vatican City 120, VATICAN CITY

Colangelo, Jerry (Athlete, Basketball Player)
70 E Country Club Dr
Phoenix, AZ 85014-5435, USA

Colangelo, Mike (Athlete, Baseball Player)
5926 Coiner House Pl
Manassas, VA 20112-5485, USA

Colantoni, Enrico (Actor)
11931 Hesby St
Valley Village, CA 91607-3113, USA

Colavito, Rocky (Athlete, Baseball Player)
656 Scenic Dr
Bernville, PA 19506-8257, USA

Colavito, Steve (Athlete, Football Player)
57 Fairview Ct
Nanuet, NY 10954-3230, USA

Colbern, Mike (Athlete, Baseball Player)
5120 E Tano St
Phoenix, AZ 85044-4121, USA

Colbert, Craig (Athlete, Baseball Player)
2042 SE Ladd Ave
Portland, OR 97214-5419, USA

Colbert, Darrell (Athlete, Football Player)
6514 River Bluff Dr
Houston, TX 77085-1306, USA

Colbert, Jim (Athlete, Golfer)
118 Wanish Pl
Palm Desert, CA 92260-7316, USA

Colbert, Nate (Athlete, Baseball Player)
2756 N Green Valley Pkwy
Henderson, NV 89014-2120, USA

Colbert, Rondy (Athlete, Football Player)
5622 Cedarburg Dr
Houston, TX 77048-1821, USA

Colbert, Stephen (Actor, Producer, Writer)
c/o James Dixon *Dixon Talent Agency*
375 Greenwich St Fl 5
New York, NY 10013-2376, USA

Colbert, Steve (Actor, Talk Show Host, Writer)
513 W 54th St
New York, NY 10019-5014, USA

Colbert, Vince (Athlete, Baseball Player)
18071 Blandford Rd
Cleveland, OH 44121-1040, USA

Colborn, James W (Jim) (Athlete, Baseball Player)
2932 Solimar Beach Dr
Ventura, CA 93001-9754, USA

Colborn, Richard (Musician)
7 Trinity Row
Florence, MA 01062-1931, USA

Colbrunn, Greg (Athlete, Baseball Player)
3196 Pignatelli Cres
Mount Pleasant, SC 29466-8060, USA

Colby, Angel (Actor)
62 Chiswick High Rd
London W4 1SY, UK

Colby, Terry (Stylist)
900 Heritage Pl
Decatur, GA 30033-4152, USA

Colchico, Dan (Athlete, Football Player)
5160 Paul Scarlet Dr
Concord, CA 94521-3134, USA

Cold War Kids (Music Group)
c/o Staff Member *Paradigm (Monterey)*
404 W Franklin St
Monterey, CA 93940-2303, USA

Coldplay (Music Group, Musician)
c/o Darin Harmon *3D Management*
1901 Main St Fl 3
Santa Monica, CA 90405-1075, USA

Cole, Alex (Athlete, Baseball Player)
6545 N Stevens Hollow Dr
Chesterfield, VA 23832-8548, USA

Cole, Anne (Designer, Fashion Designer)
6040 Bandini Blvd
Commerce, CA 90040-2905, USA

Cole, Ashley (Athlete, Soccer Player)
c/o Staff Member *Chelsea Football Club*
Stamford Bridge Fulham Road
London SW6 1HS, UNITED KINGDOM

Cole, Bob (Sportscaster)
250 Bloor St E # 805
Toronto, ON M4W 1E6, CANADA

Cole, Bobby (Athlete, Golfer)
204 W 2nd Ave
Windermere, FL 34786-8507, USA

Cole, Bradley (Actor)
c/o Staff Member *The Rights House (UK)*
Drury House 34-43 Russell St
London WC2B 5HA, UK

Cole, Cecil (Baseball Player)
201 N 12th St
Connellsville, PA 15425-2422, USA

Cole, Cheryl (Musician)
c/o Solomon Parker *WmE2 (WMA-UK)*
103 New Oxford St
London WC1A 1DD, UK

Cole, Chris (Athlete, Football Player)
6642 Hudnall Rd
Orange, TX 77632-3589, USA

Cole, Christina (Actor)
c/o Lorrie Bartlett *International Creative Management (ICM-LA)*
10250 Constellation Blvd Fl 7
Los Angeles, CA 90067-6207, USA

Cole, Danton (Athlete, Hockey Player)
7180 Wapiti Way
Saline, MI 48176-9176, USA

Cole, Dave (Athlete, Baseball Player)
10819 Wilcox Dr
Williamsport, MD 21795-1425, USA

Cole, Dick (Athlete, Baseball Player)
3149 Madeira Ave
Costa Mesa, CA 92626-2323, USA

Cole, Emerson (Athlete, Football Player)
1661 Indiana Ave
Toledo, OH 43607-3966, USA

Cole, Erik (Athlete, Hockey Player)
1112 Stone Kirk Dr
Raleigh, NC 27614-7289, USA

Cole, Eunice (Misc)
2420 Pershing Rd
Kansas City, MO 64108-2501, USA

Cole, Ford (Athlete, Football Player)
PO Box 3218
Olympic Valley, CA 96146-3218, USA

Cole, Fred (Athlete, Football Player)
10 Tuscan Rd
Livingston, NJ 07039-2919, USA

Cole, Freddy (Music Group)
11806 N 56th St
Temple Terrace, FL 33617-1652, USA

Cole, George (Actor)
2-19 The Plaza 535 Kings Road
London SW10 0SZ, UNITED KINGDOM (UK)

Cole, Holly (Musician)
41 Britain St # 305
Toronto, ON M5A 1R7, CANADA

Cole, Joanna (Writer)
c/o Staff Member *Scholastic Entertainment*
557 Broadway
New York, NY 10012-3962, USA

Cole, John (Cartoonist)
2828 Pickett Rd
Durham, NC 27705-5613, USA

Cole, Julie Dawn (Actor)
31 Coventry St
London W1V 8AS, UNITED KINGDOM (UK)

Cole, Kenneth (Designer)
601 W 50th St
New York, NY 10019, USA

Cole, Keyshia (Musician)
c/o Manny Halley *Imani Entertainment Group*
Prefers to be contacted via email or telephone
Los Angeles, CA 90028, USA

Cole, Kimberly Lynn (Actor)
36 Longview Ct
Montgomery, AL 36108-2018, USA

Cole, Kyla (Adult Film Star)
Adrian Daskalov Nabrezi SPB 446
Ostrava 70800, CZECH REPUBLIC

Cole, Larry R (Athlete, Football Player)
400 Country Pl
Colleyville, TX 76034-7598, USA

Cole, Lily (Actor, Model)
c/o Staff Member *Storm Model Management*
5 Jubilee Pl 1st Floor
London SW3 3TD, UNITED KINGDOM

Cole, Linzy (Athlete, Football Player)
7700 Creekbend Dr Apt 18
Houston, TX 77071-1728, USA

Cole, Lloyd (Musician)
109B Regents Park Road
London NW1 8UR, UNITED KINGDOM (UK)

Cole, Michael (Actor)
5121 Varna Ave
Sherman Oaks, CA 91423-1526, USA

Cole, Natalie (Actor, Musician)
c/o Julie Colbert *WmE2 (Endeavor-LA)*
9601 Wilshire Blvd Fl 3
Beverly Hills, CA 90210-5219, USA

Cole, Nigel (Director, Writer)
c/o Rosalie Swedlin *Anonymous Content (AC-LA)*
3531 Hayden Ave
Culver City, CA 90232, USA

Cole, Olivia (Actor)
PO Box 59747
Santa Barbara, CA 93150, USA

Cole, P K
32522 Bowman Knoll Dr
Westlake Village, CA 91361-5520, USA

Cole, Paula (Musician)
c/o Staff Member *Paradigm (Monterey)*
404 W Franklin St
Monterey, CA 93940-2303, USA

Cole, Robin (Athlete, Football Player)
9 Brook Ln
Eighty Four, PA 15330-2603, USA

Cole, Stu (Athlete, Baseball Player)
6527 Willow Gate Ln
Charlotte, NC 28215-4014, USA

Cole, Taylor (Actor)
c/o Joanna (Joanie) Burstein *Burstein Company, The*
15304 W Sunset Blvd Ste 208
Pacific Palisades, CA 90272-3656, USA

Cole, Tina (Actor)
778 University Ave
Sacramento, CA 95825-6703, USA

Cole, Tom (Congressman, Politician)
2458 Rayburn Hob
Washington, DC 20515-4323, USA

Cole, Victor (Athlete, Baseball Player)
138 Estonallie Rd
Mercer, TN 38392-7102, USA

Colella, Richard (Rick) (Swimmer)
217 19th Pl
Kirkland, WA 98033-4903, USA

Coleman, Andre (Athlete, Football Player)
7073 Murphy Joy Ln NW
Norcross, GA 30092-6644, USA

Coleman, Catherine G (Cady) (Astronaut)
30 Frank Williams Rd
Shelburne Falls, MA 01370-9724, USA

Coleman, Cosey (Athlete, Football Player)
11901 Northumberland Dr
Tampa, FL 33626-1327, USA

Coleman, Dabney (Actor)
c/o Alexa Pagonas *Michael Black Management*
9701 Wilshire Blvd Fl 10
Beverly Hills, CA 90212-2010, USA

Coleman, Daniel J (Publisher)
224 W 57th St
New York, NY 10019-3212, USA

Coleman, Dave (Athlete, Baseball Player)
4303 Delhi Dr
Dayton, OH 45432-3411, USA

Coleman, Derrick D (Basketball Player)
1st Union Center 3601 South Broad St
Philadelphia, PA 19148, USA

Coleman, Don E (Athlete, Football Player)
424 McPherson Ave
Lansing, MI 48915-1158, USA

Coleman, E C (Basketball Player)
370 E Harmon Ave
Las Vegas, NV 89169-7003, USA

Coleman, Eric (Athlete, Football Player)
2933 Elm St
Denver, CO 80207-2658, USA

Coleman, George E (Musician)
63 E 9th St
New York, NY 10003-6302, USA

Coleman, Greg (Athlete, Football Player)
2313 River Pointe Cir
Minneapolis, MN 55411-4279, USA

Coleman, Harry (Athlete, Football Player)
c/o Michael Harris *Best Sports Consultants LLC.*
1800 John F Kennedy Blvd Ste 300
Philadelphia, PA 19103-7402, USA

Coleman, Jack (Actor)
c/o Steven Levy *Framework Entertainment (LA)*
9057 Nemo St Ste C
West Hollywood, CA 90069-5511, USA

Coleman, Jermaine (Maino) (Musician)
c/o Staff Member *Atlantic Records (NY)*
1290 Avenue of the Americas Fl CONC4
New York, NY 10104-0184

Coleman, Jerry (Athlete, Baseball Player, Coach)
1004 Havenhurst Dr
La Jolla, CA 92037-6803, USA

Coleman, Jospeph H (Joe) (Athlete, Baseball Player)
17851 Eagle View Ln
Cape Coral, FL 33909-3019, USA

Coleman, Karon (Athlete, Football Player)
19503 E 58th Ave
Aurora, CO 80019-2014, USA

Coleman, Kelly (Athlete, Basketball Player)
PO Box 183
Higgins Lake, MI 48627-0183, USA

Coleman, Leonard (Athlete, Football Player)
125 NE 13th Ave
Boynton Beach, FL 33435-3124, USA

Coleman, Lincoln (Athlete, Football Player)
PO Box 496
Seguin, TX 78156-0496, USA

Coleman, Lisa
3575 Cahuenga Blvd W Ste 450
Los Angeles, CA 90068-1364

Coleman, Marco (Athlete, Football Player)
105 Monarch Ct
Saint Augustine, FL 32095-7043, USA

Coleman, Marco D (Athlete, Football Player)
11036 Turnbridge Dr
Jacksonville, FL 32256-2328, USA

Coleman, Marcus (Athlete, Football Player)
1736 Mapleleaf Dr
Wylie, TX 75098-8166, USA

Coleman, Mark (Athlete, Wrestler)
6535 Wilshire Blvd Ste 208
Los Angeles, CA 90048-4963, USA

Coleman, Mary Sue (Educator)
President's Office
Ann Arbor, MI 48109, USA

Coleman, Michael (Mike) (Athlete, Baseball Player)
1053 Mallow Dr
Madison, TN 37115-4219, USA

Coleman, Monique (Actor)
c/o Gina Sorial *Rogers & Cowan PR (LA)*
Pacific Design Center 8687 Melrose Ave, 7th Floor
West Hollywood, CA 90069, USA

Coleman, Monte (Athlete, Football Player)
4700 S Beech St
Pine Bluff, AR 71603-7327, USA

Coleman, Norris (Athlete, Basketball Player)
445 Monument Rd Apt 1007
Jacksonville, FL 32225-6456, USA

Coleman, Oliver (Actor)
c/o Troy Zien *WmE2 (Endeavor-LA)*
9601 Wilshire Blvd Fl 3
Beverly Hills, CA 90210-5219, USA

Coleman, Ornette (Composer, Musician)
200 W Superior St Ste 202
Chicago, IL 60654-3554, USA

Coleman, Paul (Athlete, Baseball Player)
2704 Brentwood Dr
Tyler, TX 75701-5902, USA

Coleman, Ray (Athlete, Baseball Player)
18205 Allora Dr
Edmond, OK 73012-7659, USA

Coleman, Roderick (Rod) (Athlete, Football Player)
6735 Great Water Dr
Flowery Branch, GA 30542-6639, USA

Coleman, Ronnie (Athlete, Football Player)
16039 Williwaw Dr
Houston, TX 77083-5375, USA

Coleman, Sidney (Athlete, Football Player)
299 Highway 39 N Apt A25
De Kalb, MS 39328-9467, USA

Coleman, Sidney R (Physicist)
1 Richdale Ave Unit 12
Cambridge, MA 02140-2610, USA

Coleman, Signy (Actor)
9200 W Sunset Blvd Ste 625
Los Angeles, CA 90069-3609, USA

Coleman, Steve (Athlete, Football Player)
81 W Johnson St
Philadelphia, PA 19144-1937, USA

Coleman, Vincent M (Vince) (Athlete, Baseball Player)
14677 Via Bettona Ste 110
San Diego, CA 92127-4809, USA

Coleman, Walter (Baseball Player)
HC 1 Box 236
New Russia, NY 12964-9705, USA

Coleman, William T Jr (Secretary)
555 13th St NW # 500
Washington, DC 20004-1109, USA

Coleman, Zendaya
c/o Jessie Greene *Monster Talent Management*
6333 W 3rd St Ste 912
Los Angeles, CA 90036-3176, USA

Coleman Jr, Leonard (Baseball Player)
283 3rd St
Beach Haven, NJ 08008-1857, USA

Coles, Bimbo (Athlete, Basketball Player)
203 E Washington St
Lewisburg, WV 24901-1423, USA

Coles, Darnell (Athlete, Baseball Player)
306 Signature Ter
Safety Harbor, FL 34695-5425, USA

Coles, Janet (Athlete, Golfer)
6083 Alumni Gym
Hanover, NH 03755-3501, USA

Coles, Kim (Actor, Comedian)
3483 Woodcliff Rd
Sherman Oaks, CA 91403-5044, USA

Coles, Laveranues (Athlete, Football Player)
2637 Logan Wood Dr
Herndon, VA 20171-4367, USA

Coles, Robert M (Psychic)
75 Mount Auburn St
Cambridge, MA 02138-4960, USA

Colescott, Warrington W (Artist)
RR1
Hollandale, WI 53544, USA

Coletta, Chris (Athlete, Baseball Player)
206 SW 45th St
Cape Coral, FL 33914-5906, USA

Coley, Daryl (Musician)
417 E Regent St
Inglewood, CA 90301-1315, USA

Coley, James (Athlete, Football Player)
111 Pebble Park Rd
Starr, SC 29684-9259, USA

Coley, John Ford (Musician, Songwriter, Writer)
8306 Wilshire Blvd # 981
Beverly Hills, CA 90211-2382, USA

Colfer, Chris (Actor)
c/o Meredith Fine *Coast to Coast Talent Group*
3350 Barham Blvd
Los Angeles, CA 90068-1404, USA

Colgate, Stirling A (Physicist)
422 Estante Way
Los Alamos, NM 87544-3812, USA

Colgrass, Michael C (Composer)
583 Palmerston Ave
Toronto, ON M6G 2P6, CANADA

Colicchio, Tom (Chef, Television Host)
43 E 19th St
New York, NY 10003-1304, USA

Colier, Jason (Basketball Player)
19318 Kristen Pine Dr
Humble, TX 77346-2084, USA

Colin, Charlie (Musician)
80 Main St
Greenwich, CT 6830, USA

Colin, Margaret (Actor)
41 Bradford Ave
Montclair, NJ 07043-1024, USA

Colinet, Stalin (Athlete, Football Player)
3 Mohawk Dr
Framingham, MA 01701-3041, USA

C'Oliveira, Damon (Actor)
c/o Staff Member *LeFeaver Talent Management Ltd*
2 College St #202
Toronto ON M5G 1K3, CANADA

Coll, Stephen W (Journalist)
1150 15th St NW
Washington, DC 20071-0001, USA

Colladay, Martin G (General)
506 Dowding Ct
Bellevue, NE 68005-2409, USA

Collard, Jean-Philippe (Musician)
Paris Cedex 09 75426, USA

Collective Soul (Music Group)
c/o Jordan Feldstein *Career Artist Management*
1100 Glendon Ave Ste 1100
Los Angeles, CA 90024-3515, USA

Collee, John (Writer)
c/o Alex Lerner *Kaplan/Perrone Entertainment*
9744 Wilshire Blvd Ste 300
Beverly Hills, CA 90212-1813, USA

Collen, Phil (Music Group, Musician)
c/o Rod MacSween *International Talent Booking*
1st Floor, Ariel House 74A Charlotte St
London W1T 4QJ, UNITED KINGDOM

Collet, Christopher
8730 W Sunset Blvd Ste 480
Los Angeles, CA 90069-2277

Collett, Elmer (Athlete, Football Player)
PO Box 522
Stinson Beach, CA 94970-0522, USA

Collette, Buddy (Musician)
5532 S Corning Ave
Los Angeles, CA 90056-1303, USA

Collette, Toni (Actor)
c/o Staff Member *Shanahan Management*
Level 3, Berman House 91 Campbell St
Surry Hills NSW 2010, Australia

Colletti, Roseanne (Correspondent)
30 Rockefeller Plz Fl 7
New York, NY 10112-0015, USA

Colletti, Stephen (Reality TV Star)
c/o Leslie Sloane *Baker Winokur Ryder Public Relations BWR (BWR-NY)*
292 Madison Ave Fl 12
New York, NY 10017-6415, USA

Colley, Dana (Musician)
48 Laight St
New York, NY 10013-2156, USA

Colley, Ed (Artist, Cartoonist)
11 Blaisdell Ter
Ipswich, MA 01938-1706, USA

Colley, Kenneth (Actor)
91 Regent St
London W1R 7TB, UNITED KINGDOM (UK)

Colley, Michael C (Admiral)
444 Magnolia Dr
Gulf Shores, AL 36542-4408, USA

Colley, Tom (Athlete, Hockey Player)
71 Dillon Dr
Collingwood, ON L9Y 4S4, Canada

Colley-Lee, Myrna (Designer)
PO Box 5408
Mississippi State, MS 39762-5408

Collie, Bruce (Athlete, Football Player)
9595 Ranch Road 12 Ste 13
Wimberley, TX 78676-5248, USA

Collie, Mark (Actor, Musician, Songwriter, Writer)
2908 Poston Ave
Nashville, TN 37203-1312, USA

Collier, Don
PO Box 1269
Benson, AZ 85602-1269

Collier, James (Athlete, Football Player)
1670 Terral Island Rd
Farmerville, LA 71241-4013, USA

Collier, Lesley F (Ballerina)
c/o Staff Member *Royal Ballet*
Covent Garden Bow St
London WC2E 9DD, UK

Collier, Lou (Athlete, Baseball Player)
7100 S South Shore Dr Apt 203
Chicago, IL 60649-2762, USA

Collier, Mark (Actor)
c/o John Crosby *Crosby/Spilo Management*
1310 N Spaulding Ave
Los Angeles, CA 90046-4010, USA

Collier, Mike (Athlete, Football Player)
528 W Church St Apt B
Hagerstown, MD 21740-4630, USA

Collier, Steve (Athlete, Football Player)
3473 S King Dr # 107
Chicago, IL 60616-4108, USA

Collier, Timothy (Tim) (Athlete, Football Player)
3116 50th St
Dallas, TX 75216-7343, USA

Collingwood, Chris (Musician, Songwriter, Writer)
6404 Wilshire Blvd Ste 505
Los Angeles, CA 90048-5507, USA

Collins, Albin (Athlete, Football Player)
1006 E Bonnie St
Gonzales, LA 70737-4502, USA

Collins, Alfred (Sonny) (Athlete, Football Player)
2455 Cedar Canyon Ct SE
Marietta, GA 30067-6617, USA

Collins, Art (Athlete, Basketball Player)
1812 NW 55th Ter
Miami, FL 33142-3044, USA

Collins, Arthur D Jr (Business Person)
7000 Central Ave NE
Minneapolis, MN 55432-3568, USA

Collins, Bill (Athlete, Hockey Player)
5000 Town Ctr Ste 505
Southfield, MI 48075-1112, USA

Collins, Billy (Writer)
English Dept
New York, NY 10031, USA

Collins, Blake Jeremy
4942 Vineland Ave Ste 200
North Hollywood, CA 91601-5646

Collins, Bobby (Athlete, Football Player)
PO Box 920384
Norcross, GA 30010-0384, USA

Collins, Bootsy (Musician)
8901 Melrose Ave # 200
West Hollywood, CA 90069-5605, USA

Collins, Brett W (Athlete, Football Player)
21275 NW Rock Creek Blvd
Portland, OR 97229-1041, USA

Collins, Bud (Sportscaster)
822 Boylston St Ste 203
Chestnut Hill, MA 02467-2504, USA

Collins, C F (Athlete, Football Player)
21300 Archwood Cir Apt 125
Farmington Hi, MI 48336-4132, USA

Collins, Clifton (Actor)
c/o Will Ward *ROAR (LA)*
9701 Wilshire Blvd Fl 8
Beverly Hills, CA 90212-2008, USA

Collins, David S (Dave) (Athlete, Baseball Player)
92 Lauretta Mae Dr Unit A
Lebanon, OH 45036-2652, USA

Collins, Donald E (Don) (Athlete, Baseball Player)
127 Deerwood Trl
Sharpsburg, GA 30277-2002, USA

Collins, Douglas (Doug) (Athlete, Basketball Player, Coach, Sportscaster)
10040 E Happy Valley Rd Unit 617
Scottsdale, AZ 85255-2355, USA

Collins, Duane E (Business Person)
6035 Parkland Blvd
Cleveland, OH 44124-4186, USA

Collins, Dwight (Athlete, Football Player)
821 12th St
Beaver Falls, PA 15010-4416, USA

Collins, Eileen M (Astronaut)
2024 Pebble Beach Dr
League City, TX 77573-6403, USA

Collins, Francis S (Misc)
31 Center St
Bethesda, MD 20892-0001, USA

Collins, Gary (Actor)
c/o Thomas Richards *Corsa Agency, The*
11704 Wilshire Blvd Ste 204
Los Angeles, CA 90025-1510, USA

Collins, Gary (Athlete, Hockey Player)
1908-1320 Islington Ave
Etobicoke, ON M9A 5C6, Canada

Collins, Gary J (Athlete, Football Player)
221 Lamp Post Ln
Hershey, PA 17033-1881, USA

Collins, George (Athlete, Football Player)
2043 Northside Rd
Perry, GA 31069-2224, USA

Collins, Glen L (Athlete, Football Player)
817 E River Pl
Jackson, MS 39202-3403, USA

Collins, Jack (Actor)
610 Santa Monica Blvd Ste 202
Santa Monica, CA 90401-1645, USA

Collins, Jackie (Writer)
c/o Amy Schiffman *Gersh (LA)*
9465 Wilshire Blvd Ste 600
Beverly Hills, CA 90212-2612, USA

Collins, Jason (Basketball Player)
13120 Constable Ave
Granada Hills, CA 91344-1105, USA

Collins, Javiar (Athlete, Football Player)
2503 S Pennsylvania St
Denver, CO 80210-5722, USA

Collins, Jerome (Athlete, Football Player)
25540 Sova Ln
Warrenville, IL 60555, USA

Collins, Jessica
c/o Rick Ax *Gold Coast Management*
438 S Venice Blvd Apt 5
Venice, CA 90291-4695, USA

Collins, Jim (Athlete, Football Player)
2140 E Oceanfront
Newport Beach, CA 92661-1525, USA

Collins, Joan (Actor)
c/o Barry Krost *Barry Krost Management*
9220 W Sunset Blvd Ste 106
West Hollywood, CA 90069-3500, USA

Collins, Joely (Actor)
c/o Staff Member *TalentWorks (LA)*
3500 W Olive Ave Ste 1400
Burbank, CA 91505-5512, USA

Collins, Judy (Musician, Songwriter, Writer)
PO Box 1296
New York, NY 10025-1296, USA

Collins, Kate (Actor)
1410 York Ave Apt 4D
New York, NY 10021-3401, USA

Collins, Kerry (Athlete, Football Player)
c/o David Dunn *Athletes First, LLC*
3300 Irvine Ave Ste 300
Newport Beach, CA 92660-3108, USA

Collins, Kevin (Athlete, Baseball Player)
9121 Point Charity Dr
Pigeon, MI 48755-9624, USA

Collins, Lauren (Actor)
c/o Steven Kavovit *Thruline Entertainment*
9250 Wilshire Blvd Ground Fl
Beverly Hills, CA 90212, USA

Collins, Lewis
22 Westbere Rd
London, ENGLAND NW2 3SR

Collins, Lily (Actor)
c/o Will Ward *ROAR (LA)*
9701 Wilshire Blvd Fl 8
Beverly Hills, CA 90212-2008, USA

Collins, Lynn (Actor)
c/o Nick Frenkel *3 Arts Entertainment Inc*
9460 Wilshire Blvd Fl 7
Beverly Hills, CA 90212-2713, USA

Collins, Mark (Athlete, Football Player)
2568 Baseline St Apt 155
Highland, CA 92346-2840, USA

Collins, Martha Layne (Educator, Ex-Governor)
921 Taborlake Ct
Lexington, KY 40502-3032, USA

Collins, Marva (Educator)
8035 S Honore St
Chicago, IL 60620-4562, USA

Collins, Michael (Astronaut)
c/o Staff Member *Farrar, Straus and Giroux*
18 W 18th St Fl 7
New York, NY 10011-4675, USA

Collins, Misha (Actor)
c/o Marilyn Szatmary *Silver Massetti & Szatmary (SMS) Talent Inc*
8730 W Sunset Blvd Ste 440
Los Angeles, CA 90069-2277, USA

Collins, Mo (Actor)
c/o Nicole Cataldo *Diverse Talent Group*
9911 W Pico Blvd Ste 340W
Los Angeles, CA 90035-2712, USA

Collins, Patrick (Actor)
c/o Staff Member *Tisherman Gilbert Motley Drozdoski Talent Agency (TGMD)*
6767 Forest Lawn Dr Ste 101
Los Angeles, CA 90068-1050, USA

Collins, Paul (Athlete, Football Player)
1441 Bayshore Dr
Kemah, TX 77565-3045, USA

Collins, Pauline (Actor)
c/o Sarah Camlett *Independent Talent Group (ITG-UK)*
Oxford House 76 Oxford St
London W1D 1BS, UK

Collins, Phil (Musician, Songwriter)
25 Ives St
London SW3 2ND, UK

Collins, Roosevelt (Athlete, Football Player)
3600 Holly St
Denison, TX 75020-3714, USA

Collins, Samuel C (Engineer)
PO Box 441937
Fort Washington, MD 20749-1937, USA

Collins, Shane (Athlete, Football Player)
PO Box 11090
Bozeman, MT 59719-1090, USA

Collins, Shanna (Actor)
c/o Stephanie Simon *Untitled Entertainment (LA)*
350 S Beverly Dr Ste 200
Beverly Hills, CA 90212-4819, USA

Collins, Shawn (Athlete, Football Player)
PO Box 711933
San Diego, CA 92171-1933, USA

Collins, Stephen (Actor)
c/o Beth Cannon *Envision Management*
8840 Wilshire Blvd Fl 3
Beverly Hills, CA 90211-2606, USA

Collins, Susan (Senator)
413 Dirksen Senate Ofc Building
Washington, DC 20510-0001, USA

Collins, Suzanne (Actor)
c/o Tracey Bell *Red Door Actors Management*
21/22 Great Castle St
London W1 G0HZ, UK

Collins, Suzanne (Writer)
c/o Rosemary B. Stimola *Stimola Literary Studio*
308 Livingston Ct
Edgewater, NJ 07020-1611, USA

Collins, Terry (Athlete, Baseball Player, Coach)
40992 Hollydale
Novi, MI 48375-3518, USA

Collins, Terry L (Misc)
PO Box 508
Okemos, MI 48805-0508, USA

Collins, Thomas H (Admiral)
2100 2nd St SW
Washington, DC 20593-0005, USA

Collins, Todd F (Athlete, Football Player)
1279 Collins Rd
New Market, TN 37820-3837, USA

Collins, Todd S (Athlete, Football Player)
26 Cambridge Cir
Victor, NY 14564-1503, USA

Collins, Tony (Athlete, Football Player)
2712 Gulfstream Dr
Miramar, FL 33023-4649, USA

Collinsworth, Cris (Athlete, Football Player, Sportscaster)
c/o Staff Member *Fox Sports*
1211 Avenue of the Americas Ste 302
New York, NY 10036-8799, USA

Collis, Shannon (Actor)
c/o Meredith Fine *Coast to Coast Talent Group*
3350 Barham Blvd
Los Angeles, CA 90068-1404, USA

Collison, Darren (Athlete, Basketball Player)
c/o Bill Duffy *BDA Sports Management (BDA-CA)*
700 Ygnacio Valley Rd Ste 330
Walnut Creek, CA 94596-3838, USA

Collison, Nick (Basketball Player)
351 Elliott Ave W Ste 500
Seattle, WA 98119-4153, USA

Collman, James P (Misc)
794 Tolman Dr
Stanford, CA 94305-1045, USA

Collum, Jackie (Athlete, Baseball Player)
523 11th Ave
Grinnell, IA 50112-2612, USA

Collyard, Bob (Athlete, Hockey Player)
5300 Knox Ave N
Minneapolis, MN 55430-3058, USA

Colman, Booth (Actor)
2160 Century Park E Apt 603
Los Angeles, CA 90067-2214, USA

Colman, Wayne (Athlete, Football Player)
604 N Somerset Ave
Ventnor City, NJ 08406-1551, USA

Colmenares, Grecia (Actor)
c/o Staff Member *Telefe - Argentina*
Pavon 2444 (C1248AAT)
Buenos Aires, ARGENTINA

Colmes, Alan (Correspondent)
c/o Staff Member *Hannity & Colmes*
1211 Avenue of the Americas
New York, NY 10036-8701, USA

Colo, Don (Athlete, Football Player)
7355 E Claremont St
Scottsdale, AZ 85250-5526, USA

Coloma, Marcus (Actor)
c/o Paul Rosicker *Gersh (LA)*
9465 Wilshire Blvd Ste 600
Beverly Hills, CA 90212-2612, USA

Colombini, Aldo (Director, Producer)
PO Box 829
Newbury Park, CA 91319-0829, USA

Colombo, Emilio (Prime Minister)
Via Aurelia
Rome 239, ITALY

Colombo, Marc (Athlete, Football Player)
7219 Marigold Dr
Irving, TX 75063-5509, USA

Colomby, Bobby
1423 Holmby Ave
Los Angeles, CA 90024-5104

Colomby, Scott (Actor)
3172 Dona Susana Dr
Studio City, CA 91604-4356, USA

Colon, Bartolo (Athlete, Baseball Player)
14 Federal St # 1
Passaic, NJ 07055-3209, USA

Colon, Mercedes (Actor)
c/o Jay Schachter *Mavrick Artists Agency*
6100 Wilshire Blvd Ste 550
Los Angeles, CA 90048-5164, USA

Colon, Miriam (Actor)
51 W 52nd St
New York, NY 10019-6119, USA

Colone, Joe (Athlete, Basketball Player)
534 Carter Ave
West Deptford, NJ 08096-1464, USA

Color Me Badd (Music Group, Musician)
PO Box 552113
Carol City, FL 33055-0113, USA

Colorito, Tony (Athlete, Football Player)
17805 SW Cicero Ct
Beaverton, OR 97007-9036, USA

Colpaert, Dick (Athlete, Baseball Player)
47412 Eldon Dr
Shelby Township, MI 48317-2912, USA

Colquitt, Craig (Athlete, Football Player)
1905 Pitts Field Ln
Knoxville, TN 37922-6197, USA

Colquitt, Dustin (Athlete, Football Player)
1905 Pitts Field Ln
Knoxville, TN 37922-6197, USA

Colquitt, Jimmy (Athlete, Football Player)
11722 Hardin Valley Rd
Knoxville, TN 37932-2319, USA

Colson, Charles (Chuck) (Writer)
c/o Staff Member *Simon & Schuster*
1230 Avenue of the Americas Fl CONC1
New York, NY 10020-1586, USA

Colson, Elizabeth F (Misc)
Anthropology
Berkeley, CA 94720-0001, USA

Colson, Loyd A (Athlete, Baseball Player)
309 E Sycamore St
Hollis, OK 73550-1233, USA

Colson, William (Bill) (Editor)
Editorial Dept Time-Life Building
New York, NY 10020, USA

Colston, Tim (Athlete, Football Player)
6804 N 47th St
Tampa, FL 33610-1808, USA

Colt, Marshall (Actor)
1150 Anchorage Ln Unit 612
San Diego, CA 92106-3124, USA

Colter, Jessie (Musician)
2042-A Armacost Ave
Los Angeles, CA 90025, USA

Colter, Steve (Athlete, Basketball Player)
802 E Mountain Sage Dr
Phoenix, AZ 85048-4428, USA

Colteryahn, Lloyd (Athlete, Football Player)
General Delivery
Taylors Island, MD 21669-9999, USA

Colton, Frank B (Inventor)
6402 N 27th St
Phoenix, AZ 85016-8938, USA

Colton, Graham (Musician)
c/o Staff Member *Red Light Management (LA)*
8439 W Sunset Blvd Ste 2
Los Angeles, CA 90069-1925, USA

Colton, Lawrence R (Larry) (Athlete, Baseball Player)
3027 NE 68th Ave
Portland, OR 97213-5215, USA

Colton, Michael (Writer)
c/o Tony Etz *Creative Artists Agency (CAA-LA)*
2000 Avenue of the Stars Ste 100
Los Angeles, CA 90067-4705, USA

Coltraine, Robbie (Actor)
19 Sydney Mews
London SW3 6HL, United Kingdom

Coltrane, Chi
5955 Tuxedo Ter
Los Angeles, CA 90068-2461

Coltrane, Robbie (Actor)
125 Gloucester Road 2nd Fl
London SW7 4TE, UNITED KINGDOM

Coluccio, Bob (Athlete, Baseball Player)
369 Flower St
Costa Mesa, CA 92627-2352, USA

Columbu, Franco (Misc)
2265 Westwood Blvd Ste A
Los Angeles, CA 90064-2050, USA

Columbus, Chris (Director, Producer)
c/o Simon Halls *Slate Public Relations*
9000 W Sunset Blvd Ste 915
West Hollywood, CA 90069-5809, USA

Columbus, Christopher J (Chris) (Director, Writer)
PO Box 3000
Leavesden WD2 7LT, UNITED KINGDOM (UK)

Colunga, Fernando (Actor)
c/o Staff Member *Crossover Agency*
801 SW 3rd Ave Ste 302
Miami, FL 33130-3576, USA

Colussy, Dan A (Business Person)
161 Bears Club Dr
Jupiter, FL 33477-4201, USA

Colville, Alex (Artist)
7LYNWOOD Dr
Wolfville, NS B0P 1XO, Canada

Colvin, James (Jim) (Athlete, Football Player)
1310 Rancho Vista Dr
Mc Kinney, TX 75070-5485, USA

Colvin, John O (Judge)
400 2nd St NW
Washington, DC 20217-0001, USA

Colvin, Roosevelt (Athlete, Football Player)
9340 Sargent Rd
Indianapolis, IN 46256-1128, USA

Colvin, Shawn (Musician, Songwriter)
c/o Staff Member *Paradigm (Monterey)*
404 W Franklin St
Monterey, CA 93940-2303, USA

Colwell, John A (Physicist)
1701 N Beauregard St
Alexandria, VA 22311-1742, USA

Colwell, Rita R (Biologist, Misc)
5110 River Hill Rd
Bethesda, MD 20816-2237, USA

Colwill, Les (Athlete, Hockey Player)
714 20 St N
Lethbridge, AB T1H 3N6, Canada

Colyar, Michael (Actor, Comedian)
1301 S Ogden Dr
Los Angeles, CA 90019-2438, USA

Colyer, Steve (Athlete, Baseball Player)
10 Lakeshores Dr
Saint Charles, MO 63301, USA

Colzie, Jim (Athlete, Baseball Player)
3140 Day Ave
Miami, FL 33133-5111, USA

Comaneci, Nadia (Gymnast)
4421 Hidden Hill Rd
Norman, OK 73072-2899, USA

Combe, Geoff (Athlete, Baseball Player)
743 Tudor Cir
Thousand Oaks, CA 91360-5246, USA

Combes, Willard W (Cartoonist)
1266 Oakridge Dr
Cleveland, OH 44121-1623, USA

Combichrist (Music Group, Musician)
c/o Staff Member *Metropolis Records*
PO Box 974
Media, PA 19063-0974, USA

Combs, Chris (Athlete, Football Player)
3627 Dogwood Ln SW
Roanoke, VA 24015-4503, USA

Combs, Glenn (Athlete, Basketball Player)
3627 Dogwood Ln SW
Roanoke, VA 24015-4503, USA

Combs, Holly Marie (Actor, Producer, Writer)
c/o Martin Berneman *Precision Entertainment*
6338 Wilshire Blvd
Los Angeles, CA 90048-5002, USA

Combs, Jeffrey (Actor)
c/o Leland LaBarre *Bleu, An Entertainment Company*
5225 Wilshire Blvd Ste 336
Los Angeles, CA 90036-4380, USA

Combs, Leroy (Athlete, Basketball Player)
1631 Glenn Bo Dr
Norman, OK 73071-2813, USA

Combs, Patrick D (Pat) (Athlete, Baseball Player)
203 Timber Lake Way
Southlake, TX 76092-7217, USA

Combs, Sean John (P Diddy) (Musician, Producer)
c/o Chris Lighty *Violator Management*
36 W 25th St Fl 11
New York, NY 10010-2752, USA

Comden, Danny (Director)
c/o Ruthanne Secunda *United Talent Agency (UTA)*
9560 Wilshire Blvd Fl 5
Beverly Hills, CA 90212-2400, USA

Comeau, Andy (Actor)
c/o Staff Member *Rugolo Entertainment*
195 S Beverly Dr Ste 400
Beverly Hills, CA 90212-3044, USA

Comeau, Rey (Athlete, Hockey Player)
4 Rue De Cernay
Lorraine, QC J6Z 2Z1, Canada

Comeaux, Darren (Athlete, Football Player)
6313 Kristie Ln
Brusly, LA 70719-2616, USA

Comeaux, John (Athlete, Basketball Player)
PO Box 327
Carencro, LA 70520-0327, USA

Comegys, Dallas (Athlete, Basketball Player)
4330 Wayne Ave
Philadelphia, PA 19140-1745, USA

Comella, Greg (Athlete, Football Player)
90 Fairbanks Ave
Wellesley Hills, MA 02481-5256, USA

Comer, Anjanette (Actor)
6442 Coldwater Canyon Ave Ste 206
Valley Glen, CA 91606-1174, USA

Comer, Francis (Philanthropist)
939 W North Ave Ste 850
Chicago, IL 60642-7145, USA

Comer, James P (Psychic)
Child Study Center 230 S Frontage Road
New Haven, CT 6519, USA

Comer, Steve (Athlete, Baseball Player)
525 Lake Dr Apt 377
Chanhassen, MN 55317-8370, USA

Comer, Wayne (Athlete, Baseball Player)
145 Marcus St
Shenandoah, VA 22849-3917, USA

Comess, Aaron (Musician)
83 Riverside Dr
New York, NY 10024-5713, USA

Comfort, Brad
PO Box 715
Mercer Island, WA 98040-0715

Comi, Paul (Actor)
2395 Ridgeway Rd
San Marino, CA 91108-2116, USA

Comiskey, Chuck (Athlete, Football Player)
2502 Convent Ave
Pascagoula, MS 39567-4517, USA

Comissiona, Sergiu (Conductor)
Karamzininkatu 4
Helsinki 100, FINLAND

Command, Jim (Athlete, Baseball Player)
2136 Cranbrook Dr NE
Grand Rapids, MI 49505-5721, USA

Commodore, Mike (Athlete, Hockey Player)
12017 Fern Dr
Detroit Lakes, MN 56501, USA

Commodores, The (Music Group, Musician)
1920 Benson Ave
Saint Paul, MN 55116-3214, USA

Common (Musician)
c/o Staci Wolfe *Polaris PR*
8135 W 4th St Fl 2
Los Angeles, CA 90048-4415, USA

Commoner, Barry (Misc)
Biology of Natural Systems Center
Flushing, NY 11367, USA

Compagnonl, Deborah (Skier)
Via Frodonfo 3
Santa Catarina Valfurna 2303, ITALY

Compaore, Blaise (President)
Boile Postale 7031
Ouagadougou, BURKINA FASO

Compte, Maurice (Actor)
c/o Brit Reece *PMK/BNC Public Relations (PMK-LA)*
8687 Melrose Ave Ste 8
West Hollywood, CA 90069-5746, USA

Compton, Ann Woodruff (Correspondent)
5010 Creston St
Hyattsville, MD 20781-1216, USA

Compton, Clint (Athlete, Baseball Player)
2609 Wallahatchie Rd
Pike Road, AL 36064-3532, USA

Compton, Denis C S (Cricketer)
245 Blackfriars Road
London SE1 9UX, UNITED KINGDOM (UK)

Compton, Dick (Athlete, Football Player)
3408 Briarcliff Ct S
Irving, TX 75062-3206, USA

Compton, Forrest (Actor)
257 Park Ave S Rm 900
New York, NY 10010-7304, USA

Compton, John G M (Prime Minister)
PO Box 149
Castries, SAINT LUCIA

Compton, Lynn (War Hero)
31736 Saddletree Dr
Westlake Village, CA 91361-4705, USA

Compton, Mike (Athlete, Baseball Player)
8624 Leighton Dr
Tampa, FL 33614-1723, USA

Compton, Ogden (Athlete, Football Player)
13918 Preston Valley Pl
Dallas, TX 75240-4769, USA

Compton, Richard (Actor)
9200 W Sunset Blvd Ste 900
Los Angeles, CA 90069-3604, USA

Compton-Rock, Malaak (Philanthropist)
PO Box 996
Tenafly, NJ 07670-0996, USA

Comrie, Mike (Athlete, Hockey Player)
10800 Wilshire Blvd Apt 203
Los Angeles, CA 90024-4204, USA

Comrie, Paul (Athlete, Business Person, Hockey Player)
16930 114 Avenue Attn The President
NW Ofc OF
Edmonton, AB T5M 3S2, Canada

Comstock, Keith (Athlete, Baseball Player)
9615 E Desert Trl
Scottsdale, AZ 85260-4624, USA

Conacher, Brian (Athlete, Hockey Player)
202-500 Avenue Rd
Toronto, ON M4V 2J6, Canada

Conacher, Jim (Athlete, Hockey Player)
1408 Sandhurst Pl
West Vancouver, BC V7S 2P3, Canada

Conacher, Pat (Athlete, Hockey Player)
18371 W Sweet Acacia Dr
Goodyear, AZ 85338-5295, USA

Conacher, Pete (Athlete, Hockey Player)
3 Conifer Dr
Etobicoke, ON M9C 1X3, Canada

Conant, Kenneth J (Archaeologist)
3 Carlton Vlg # T105
Bedford, MA 1730, USA

Conant, Sean (Actor)
c/o Staff Member *Rising Picture*
PO Box 2
North Hampton, NH 03862-0002, USA

Conatsor, Clint (Athlete, Baseball Player)
26701 Quail Crk Apt 191
Laguna Hills, CA 92656-3010, USA

Conaty, William (Bill) (Athlete, Football Player)
203 Country Club Dr
Moorestown, NJ 08057-3977, USA

Conaway, Christi
334 Huntley Dr
West Hollywood, CA 90048-1919

Conaway, Cristi (Actor)
1759 Old Ranch Rd
Los Angeles, CA 90049-2507, USA

Conaway, Jeff (Actor)
c/o Alexandra Karrys *Divine Management*
3822 Latrobe St
Los Angeles, CA 90031-1446

Conaway, K. Michael (Congressman, Politician)
2430 Rayburn Hob
Washington, DC 20515-3705, USA

Concepcion, David I (Davey) (Athlete, Baseball Player)
Urbanizacion el Castano Botalon 5-D
Maracay, Venezuela

Concepcion, Onix (Athlete, Baseball Player)
1486 Steeplechase Ln
Deltona, FL 32725-4752, USA

Concina, Tommaso (Stylist)
c/o Staff Member *Stockland Martel*
343 E 18th St
New York, NY 10003-2802, USA

Concrete Blonde (Music Group)
16830 Ventura Blvd Ste 501
Encino, CA 91436-1717, USA

Concretes, The (Music Group)
c/o Staff Member *Paradigm (Monterey)*
404 W Franklin St
Monterey, CA 93940-2303, USA

Conde, Ninel (Actor)
c/o Gabriel Blanco *Gabriel Blanco Iglesias (Mexico)*
Rio Balsas 35-32 Colonia Cuauhtemoc
DF 6500, Mexico

Conde, Ramon (Athlete, Baseball Player)
PO Box 57
Juana Diaz, PR 00795-0057, USA

Condit, Garth (Stylist)
c/o Staff Member *Artists by Timothy Priano (NY)*
15 Watts St Fl 6
New York, NY 10013-1677, USA

Condit, Philip M (Business Person)
PO Box 3707
Seattle, WA 98124-2207, USA

Condon, Bill (Director, Writer)
c/o Adam Shulman *Anonymous Content (AC-LA)*
2049 Century Park E Ste 2550
Los Angeles, CA 90067-3139, USA

Condon, Jill (Producer, Writer)
c/o Staff Member *United Talent Agency (UTA)*
9560 Wilshire Blvd Fl 5
Beverly Hills, CA 90212-2400, USA

Condon, Paul (Lawyer)
Metropolitan Police New Scottland Yard
Broadway
London SW1H 0BG, UNITED KINGDOM (UK)

Condon, Tom (Athlete, Football Player)
c/o Staff Member *CAA Sports (LA)*
2000 Avenue of the Stars
Los Angeles, CA 90067-4700, USA

Condra, Julie (Actor)
c/o Staff Member *Gold Coast Management*
438 S Venice Blvd Apt 5
Venice, CA 90291-4695, USA

Condren, Glen (Athlete, Football Player)
8557 N 175th East Ave
Owasso, OK 74055-5638, USA

Condrey, Clay (Athlete, Baseball Player)
412 N 8th St
Navasota, TX 77868-2927, USA

Condron, Christopher M (Financier)
Center 500 Grant St
Pittsburgh, PA 15258-0001, USA

Cone, David B (Athlete, Baseball Player)
303 E 83rd St Apt 6A
New York, NY 10028-4316, USA

Cone, Fred (Athlete, Football Player)
PO Box 1819
Blairsville, GA 30514-1819, USA

Cone Vanderbush, Carin (Swimmer)
116 Washington Rd # B
West Point, NY 10996-1403, USA

Confederate Railroad (Music Group)
PO Box 1547
Goodlettsville, TN 37070-1547, USA

Conforti, Gino (Actor)
12178 Ventura Blvd Ste 205
Studio City, CA 91604-2540, USA

Congdon, Jeff (Athlete, Basketball Player)
505 Highland View Ct
Mesquite, NV 89027-8844, USA

Conger, Harry M (Business Person)
650 California St
San Francisco, CA 94108-2702, USA

Conigliaro, Billy (Athlete, Baseball Player)
501 Cabot St Unit 2
Beverly, MA 01915-2580, USA

Conine, Jeff (Athlete, Baseball Player)
3166 Inverness
Weston, FL 33332-1816, USA

Conjar, Larry (Athlete, Football Player)
542 Sheridan Rd
Evanston, IL 60202-3124, USA

Conkey, Margaret (Archaeologist)
Archaeological Research Facility
Berkeley, CA 94720, USA

Conklin, Cary (Athlete, Football Player)
4695 Savannah Ln
Boise, ID 83714-7424, USA

Conklin, Ty (Athlete, Hockey Player)
2204 Arcadia Dr
Anchorage, AK 99517-1340, USA

Conlan, Shane P (Athlete, Football Player)
521 East Dr
Sewickley, PA 15143-1114, USA

Conlee, John (Musician)
38 Music Sq E Ste 117
Nashville, TN 37203-4334, USA

Conley, Bob (Athlete, Baseball Player)
16A Canton Dr
Whiting, NJ 08759-1977, USA

Conley, Clare D (Editor)
Hemlock Farms
Hawley, PA 18428, USA

Conley, D Eugene (Gene) (Athlete, Basketball Player)
400 Foxboro Blvd Apt 3102
Foxboro, MA 02035-3803, USA

Conley, Darby (Cartoonist)
c/o Staff Member *United Press Media*
PO Box 5610
Cincinnati, OH 45201-5610, USA

Conley, Earl Thomas (Musician, Songwriter, Writer)
657 Baker Rd
Smyrna, TN 37167-4777, USA

Conley, Gene (Athlete, Baseball Player)
400 Foxboro Blvd Apt 3102
Foxboro, MA 02035-3803, USA

Conley, Jack (Actor)
c/o Julia Buchwald *Don Buchwald & Associates Inc (LA)*
6500 Wilshire Blvd Ste 2200
Los Angeles, CA 90048-4942, USA

Conley, Jill
10332 Christine Pl
Chatsworth, CA 91311-1917

Conley, Joe (Actor)
PO Box 6487
Thousand Oaks, CA 91359-6487, USA

Conley, Larry (Athlete, Basketball Player)
5422 Forest Springs Dr
Atlanta, GA 30338-3606, USA

Conley, Michael (Mike) (Athlete, Track Athlete)
Athletic Dept
Fayetteville, AR 72701, USA

COnley, Mike (Athlete, Basketball Player)
3496 Windgarden Cv
Memphis, TN 38125-1732, USA

Conlin, Chris (Athlete, Football Player)
4864 Tropicana Ave
Cooper City, FL 33330-4428, USA

Conlin, Edward (Athlete, Basketball Player)
153 N Mountain Ave
Montclair, NJ 07042-2347, USA

Conlin, Michaela (Actor)
c/o Amanda Glazer *Kohner Agency, The*
9300 Wilshire Blvd Ste 555
Beverly Hills, CA 90212-3211, USA

Conlon, James J
120 W 58th St Apt 8D
New York, NY 10019-2156, USA

Conlon, Marty (Athlete, Basketball Player)
180 Woodbine Dr
East Hampton, NY 11937-1747, USA

Conn, Didi (Actor, Musician)
1901 Avenue of the Stars Ste 1450
Los Angeles, CA 90067-6087, USA

Conn, Richard (Dick) (Athlete, Football Player)
430 Southport Commerce Blvd
Spartanburg, SC 29306-3812, USA

Conn, Terri (Actor)
1268 E 14th St
Brooklyn, NY 11230-5241, USA

Connally, Fritz (Athlete, Baseball Player)
615 Portofino Dr
Arlington, TX 76012-2700, USA

Conneff, Kevin (Musician)
1505 W 2nd Ave # 200
Vancouver, BC V6H 3Y4, CANADA

Connell, Albert (Athlete, Football Player)
3522 Ruth St
Houston, TX 77004-5516, USA

Connell, Chad (Actor)
c/o Marc Hamou *Thruline Entertainment*
9250 Wilshire Blvd Ground Fl
Beverly Hills, CA 90212, USA

Connell, Desmond Cardinal (Religious Leader)
Drumcondra
Dublin 9, IRELAND

Connell, Elizabeth (Opera Singer)
3 Burlingtone Lane Chiswick
London W4 2TH, UNITED KINGDOM (UK)

Connell, Evan S Jr (Writer)
Fort Macy 13 320 Artist Road
Santa Fe, NM 87501, USA

Connell, Jane
905 W End Ave
New York, NY 10025 3530

Connell, Thurman C (Financier)
907 Walnut St
Des Moines, IA 50309-3501, USA

Connelly, Jennifer (Actor)
c/o Risa Shapiro *Schiff Company, The*
8440 Warner Dr Ste B1
Culver City, CA 90232-2461, USA

Connelly, Lynn (Athlete, Golfer)
40 W Elm St Apt 3L
Greenwich, CT 06830-6418, USA

Connelly, Michael (Writer)
3 Center Plz
Boston, MA 02108-2003, USA

Connelly, Mike (Athlete, Football Player)
9352 Creel Creek Dr
Dallas, TX 75228-4132, USA

Connelly, Steve (Athlete, Baseball Player)
1863 Litchfield Ave
Long Beach, CA 90815-3037, USA

Connelly, Wayne (Athlete, Hockey Player)
Site 2 Box 61 RR 2
Swastika, ON P0K 1T0, Canada

Conner, Bart (Gymnast)
4421 Hidden Hill Rd
Norman, OK 73072-2899, USA

Conner, Chris (Actor)
c/o Staff Member *Nine Yards Entertainment*
8530 Wilshire Blvd Ste 550
Beverly Hills, CA 90211-3133, USA

Conner, Clyde (Athlete, Football Player)
510 Valencia Dr
Los Altos, CA 94022-1761, USA

Conner, Darion (Athlete, Football Player)
9553 Prairie Point Rd
Macon, MS 39341-9161, USA

Conner, Dennis
1011 Anchorage Ln
San Diego, CA 92106-3005

Conner, Frank (Golfer)
c/o Staff Member *Pro Golfers Association (PGA) Tour*
112 Tpc Blvd
Ponte Vedra Beach, FL 32082, USA

Conner, Jimmy Dan (Basketball Player)
5009 Old Federal Rd
Louisville, KY 40207-1200, USA

Conner, Jimmy Dan (Athlete, Basketball Player)
5009 Old Federal Rd
Louisville, KY 40207-1200, USA

Conner, Lester (Athlete, Basketball Player)
13836 Coldwater Dr
Carmel, IN 46032-8562, USA

Conners, Dan (Athlete, Football Player)
1032 Chorro St
San Luis Obispo, CA 93401-3223, USA

Connery, Jason (Actor)
c/o Staff Member *Unconditional Entertainment*
3607 W Magnolia Blvd Ste 3
Burbank, CA 91505-2962, USA

Connery, Sean (Actor)
Lyford Cay P.O. Box N-7776
Nassau, The Bahamas

Connery, Vincent L (Misc)
1730 K St NW
Washington, DC 20006, USA

Connes, Alain (Mathematician)
35 Route Chartres
Bures-sur-Yvette 91440, FRANCE

Conney, Terry (Athlete, Baseball Player)
3205 Filbert Ave
Clovis, CA 93611-6050, USA

Connick Jr, Harry (Actor, Musician)
c/o Ann Marie Wilkins *Wilkins Management*
323 Broadway
Cambridge, MA 02139-1801, USA

Conniff, Cal (Skier)
157 Pleasantview Ave
Longmeadow, MA 01106-1021, USA

Connolly, Billy (Actor, Musician, Producer, Writer)
c/o Gene Parseghian *Parseghian Planco LLC*
322 8th Ave Ste 601
New York, NY 10001-6715, USA

Connolly, Dee (Stylist)
c/o Staff Member *Judy Inc*
1 Yorkville Ave
Toronto ON M4W 1L1, Canada

Connolly, Harry (Athlete, Football Player)
22 Sea Breeze Dr Apt B
South Dartmouth, MA 02748-3030, USA

Connolly, Kevin (Actor)
c/o Annick Muller *ID Public Relations (ID-NY)*
150 W 30th St Fl 19
New York, NY 10001-4003, USA

Connolly, Olga Fikotova (Athlete, Track Athlete)
307 Avocado St Apt 4
Costa Mesa, CA 92627-7800, USA

Connolly, Ted (Athlete, Football Player)
1958 F St
Carson City, NV 89706-2209, USA

Connor, Cam (Athlete, Hockey Player)
2716 118 St NW
Edmonton, AB T6J 3P6, Canada

Connor, Chris (Musician)
7942 W Bell Rd Ste C5
Glendale, AZ 85308-8710, USA

Connor, Christopher M (Business Person)
101 W Prospect Ave
Cleveland, OH 44115-1093, USA

Connor, Joseph E (Business Person, Government Official)
United Nations UN Plaza
New York, NY 10021, USA

Connor, Patrick
3 Spring Bank
New Mills nr. Stockport, ENGLAND SK12 4AS

Connor, Ralph (Misc)
9866 W Highwood Ct
Sun City, AZ 85373-1771, USA

Connor, Richard L (Publisher)
400 W 7th St
Fort Worth, TX 76102-4701, USA

Connor, Sarah (Musician)
Postfach 3053
Hannover 30030, GERMANY

Connor, Shannon (Model)
4 Rockage Rd
Warren, NJ 07059-5506

Connors, Bill (Billy) (Athlete, Baseball Player)
3329 Enterprise Rd E
Safety Harbor, FL 34695-5307, USA

Connors, Carol (Songwriter, Writer)
1709 Ferrari Dr
Beverly Hills, CA 90210-1603, USA

Connors, James S (Jimmy) (Tennis Player)
1962 E Valley Rd
Santa Barbara, CA 93108-1428, USA

Connors, Mike (Actor, Producer)
4810 Louise Ave
Encino, CA 91316-3927, USA

Connors, Patrick (Athlete, Baseball Player)
1075 Maricopa Dr
Oshkosh, WI 54904-8116, USA

Connot, Scott (Athlete, Football Player)
PO Box 375
Volga, SD 57071-0375, USA

Connway, Craig (Business Person)
4460 Hacienda Dr
Pleasanton, CA 94588-2761, USA

Conoly, Bill (Athlete, Football Player)
PO Box 35
Brackettville, TX 78832-0035, USA

Conombo, Joseph I (Prime Minister)
2003 Ave de la Liberte BP 613
Dadoya, Ouagadougou, BURKINA FASO

Conover, Lloyd H (Inventor)
5200 Brittany Dr S Apt 304
Saint Petersburg, FL 33715-1523, USA

Conover, Scott (Athlete, Football Player, Sportscaster)
28 Windsor Ter Apt B
Freehold, NJ 07728-3240, USA

Conoway, Christi
PO Box 46515
Los Angeles, CA 90046-0515

Conrad, Barnaby
3530 Pine Valley Dr
Sarasota, FL 34239-4335

Conrad, Bobby Joe (Athlete, Football Player)
148 County Road 3270
Clifton, TX 76634-4678, USA

Conrad, Chris (Athlete, Football Player)
984 Orangewood Dr
Brea, CA 92821-2514, USA

Conrad, David (Actor)
c/o Staff Member *Gersh (LA)*
9465 Wilshire Blvd Ste 600
Beverly Hills, CA 90212-2612, USA

Conrad, Eve Burch
23388 Mulholland Dr
Woodland Hills, CA 91364-2733

Conrad, Kent (Senator)
530 Hart Senate Ofc Building
Washington, DC 20510-0001, USA

Conrad, Kimberly
10236 Charing Cross Rd
Los Angeles, CA 90024-1815

Conrad, Lauren (Actor, Reality TV Star)
c/o Nicole Perez *PMK/BNC Public Relations (PMK-LA)*
Pacific Design Center 8687 Melrose Ave, 7th Floor
West Hollywood, CA 90069, USA

Conrad, Robert (Actor)
3800 Weatherly Cir
Westlake Village, CA 91361-3821, USA

Conrad, Shane
9255 W Sunset Blvd Ste 620
Los Angeles, CA 90069-3303

Conradt, Jody (Athlete, Basketball Player, Coach)
9614 Leaning Rock Cir
Austin, TX 78730-2725, USA

Conran, Jasper A T (Designer, Fashion Designer)
2 Munden St
London W14 0RH, UNITED KINGDOM (UK)

Conran, Philip J (War Hero)
4706 Calle Reina
Santa Barbara, CA 93110-2018, USA

Conran, Terence O (Designer)
22 SHad Thames
London SE1 2YU, UNITED KINGDOM (UK)

Conroy, Craig (Athlete, Hockey Player)
PO Box 549
Henderson Harbor, NY 13651-0549, USA

Conroy, Frances (Actor)
c/o Staff Member *International Creative Management (ICM-LA)*
10250 Constellation Blvd Fl 7
Los Angeles, CA 90067-6207, USA

Conroy, Jeff (Producer)
308 W Verdugo Ave
Burbank, CA 91502-2340, USA

Conroy, Kevin (Actor)
c/o Staff Member *Imperium 7 Talent Agency*
5455 Wilshire Blvd Ste 1706
Los Angeles, CA 90036-4217, USA

Conroy, Pat (Writer)
c/o Marly Rusoff *Marly Rusoff & Associates Inc*
PO Box 524
Bronxville, NY 10708-0524, USA

Conroy, Tim (Athlete, Baseball Player)
109 Moonlight Dr
Monroeville, PA 15146-2028, USA

Conroy, Zack (Actor)
c/o Danielle Quinoa *Innovative Artists (NY)*
235 Park Ave S Fl 7
New York, NY 10003-1404, USA

Considine, John (Actor)
16 1/2 Red Coat Ln
Greenwich, CT 06830-3432, USA

Considine, Paddy (Actor, Writer)
c/o Staff Member *Creative Artists Agency (CAA-LA)*
2000 Avenue of the Stars Ste 100
Los Angeles, CA 90067-4705, USA

Considine, Tim (Actor)
3708 Mountain View Ave
Los Angeles, CA 90066-3112, USA

Consolo, Billy (Athlete, Baseball Player)
3805 Bowsprit Cir
Westlake Village, CA 91361-3815, USA

Conspirator (Music Group)
c/o Staff Member *Paradigm (Monterey)*
404 W Franklin St
Monterey, CA 93940-2303, USA

Constantin, Michel
17 Blvd Bartole Beauvallon
St. Maxime, FRANCE 83120

Constantine, Kevin
5928 Jenny Lind Ct
San Jose, CA 95120-1789

Constantine, Michael (Actor)
6861 Colbath Ave
Van Nuys, CA 91405-4102, USA

Constantine II (King)
4 Linnell Dr Hampstead Way
London NW11, UNITED KINGDOM (UK)

Consuelos, Mark (Actor)
c/o Brian Liebman *Liebman Entertainment*
25 E 21st St PH
New York, NY 10010-6226, USA

Conte, Dino
2325 Fox Hills Dr
Los Angeles, CA 90064-2603, USA

Conte, Lansana (President)
Conakry, GUINEA

Conte, Lou (Choreographer)
1147 W Jackson Blvd
Chicago, IL 60607-2905, USA

Conti, Al
PO Box 701
Portsmouth, RI 02871-0701

Conti, Bill (Composer, Musician)
117 Fremont Pl
Los Angeles, CA 90005-3868, USA

Conti, Jason (Athlete, Baseball Player)
740 N April Dr
Chandler, AZ 85226-1632, USA

Conti, Tom (Actor)
Prince of Wales Coventry St
London W1V 7FE, UNITED KINGDOM(UK)

Contini, Joe (Athlete, Hockey Player)
302 Domville
Arthur, ON N0G 1A0, Canada

Contino, Dick (Music Group, Musician)
3355 Nahatan Way
Las Vegas, NV 89169-3119, USA

Contner, James A (Cinematographer)
3020 Kensington Ave
Richmond, VA 23221-2421, USA

Contorakes, Maria (Stylist)
7160 SW 47th St
Miami, FL 33155-4654, USA

Contostavlos, Tulisa (Model)
c/o Staff Member *Cole Kitchenn Personal Management*
212 Strand
London WC2R 1AP, USA

Contoulis, John (Athlete, Football Player)
404 Champion Cir
Throop, PA 18512-1451, USA

Contours, The
1161 NW 76th Ave
Plantation, FL 33322-5120

Contreras, Jose (Athlete, Baseball Player)
1001 Brickell Bay Dr Ste 1710
Miami, FL 33131-4939, USA

Contreras, Nardi (Athlete, Baseball Player)
5052 Lurgan Rd
Land O Lakes, FL 34638-7653, USA

Contz, Bill (Athlete, Football Player)
106 Grace Dr
Cranberry Twp, PA 16066-2308, USA

Converse, Frank (Actor)
c/o Phil Sutfin *International Creative Management (ICM-LA)*
10250 Constellation Blvd Fl 7
Los Angeles, CA 90067-6207, USA

Converse, Jim (Athlete, Baseball Player)
11865 Cobble Brook Dr
Rancho Cordova, CA 95742-8008, USA

Converse-Roberts, William (Actor)
1505 10th St
Santa Monica, CA 90401-2805, USA

Conway, Billy (Music Group, Musician)
48 Laight St
New York, NY 10013-2156, USA

Conway, Brett (Athlete, Football Player)
630 Virginia Ave NE
Atlanta, GA 30306-3629, USA

Conway, Curtis (Athlete, Football Player)
446 E Phelps St
Gilbert, AZ 85295-2091, USA

Conway, Dave (Athlete, Football Player)
PO Box 278
Buchanan Dam, TX 78609-0278, USA

Conway, Gary (Actor)
11240 Chimney Rock Rd
Paso Robles, CA 93446-7775, USA

Conway, James (General)
Commanding General I Marine Expeditionary Force
Camp Pendleton, CA 92055, USA

Conway, James L (Director, Producer, Writer)
c/o Andrea Simon *Andrea Simon Entertainment*
4230 Woodman Ave
Sherman Oaks, CA 91423-4334, USA

Conway, Jill K (Historian)
65 Commonwealth Ave # 8B
Boston, MA 02116-2304, USA

Conway, John W (Business Person)
1 Crown Way
Philadelphia, PA 19154-4501, USA

Conway, Kevin (Actor)
25 Centurypark W
New York, NY 10023, USA

Conway, Tim (Actor, Comedian)
c/o Staff Member *Lili Ungar Public Relations*
821 Bay St Apt A3
Santa Monica, CA 90405-1330, USA

Conwell, Angell (Actor)
c/o Staff Member *Evolution Entertainment (LA)*
901 N Highland Ave
Los Angeles, CA 90038-2412, USA

Conwell, Easther M (Physicist)
800 Phillips Rd
Webster, NY 14580-9720, USA

Conwell, Ernie (Athlete, Football Player)
13527 SE 268th St
Kent, WA 98042-8033, USA

Conwell, Joseph (Joe) (Athlete, Football Player)
1301 Stoney River Dr
Ambler, PA 19002-1159, USA

Conwell, Tommy (Music Group, Musician)
141 Dunbar Ave
Fords, NJ 08863-1551, USA

Conyers Jr., John (Congressman, Politician)
2426 Rayburn Hob
Washington, DC 20515-2214, USA

Coobar, Abdulmegid (Prime Minister)
Asadu El-Furat St 29 Garden City
Tripoli, LIBYA

Cooder, Ry (Composer, Music Group, Musician)
326 Entrada Dr
Santa Monica, CA 90402-1202, USA

Coody, Charles (Athlete, Golfer)
1555 Oldham Ln
Abilene, TX 79602-4143, USA

Coogan, Dodie
PO Box 413
Palm Springs, CA 92263-0413

Coogan, Keith (Actor)
c/o Drew Elliot *Media Artists Group (NY)*
140 E 46th St PH C
New York, NY 10017-2633, USA

Coogan, Richard
5805 Whitsett Ave Apt 103
Valley Village, CA 91607-1146

Coogan, Steve (Actor, Producer, Writer)
77 Oxford Street
London W1D 2ES, United Kingdom

Cook, A J (Actor)
c/o Jeff Morrone *Jeff Morrone Entertainment*
9350 Wilshire Blvd Ste 224
Beverly Hills, CA 90212-3204, USA

Cook, Aaron (Athlete, Baseball Player)
6113 Liberty Fairfield Rd
Liberty Twp, OH 45011-5114, USA

Cook, Andrea Joy (A.J.) (Actor)
c/o Jeff Morrone *Jeff Morrone Entertainment*
9350 Wilshire Blvd Ste 224
Beverly Hills, CA 90212-3204, USA

Cook, Andy (Athlete, Baseball Player)
3312 Central Ave
Memphis, TN 38111-4402, USA

Cook, Ann T
5412 Riverhills Dr
Temple Terrace, FL 33617-7136, USA

Cook, Anthony (Athlete, Football Player)
203 Grace Hts
Bennettsville, SC 29512-3732, USA

Cook, Barbara (Actor, Musician)
c/o Staff Member *Cunningham Escott Slevin & Doherty (CESD-LA)*
10635 Santa Monica Blvd Ste 130
Los Angeles, CA 90025-8306, USA

Cook, Becket (Stylist)
c/o Staff Member *Celestine - CA*
1666 20th St Ste 200B
Santa Monica, CA 90404-3828, USA

Cook, Bert (Athlete, Basketball Player)
2571 W 5725 S
Roy, UT 84067-1326, USA

Cook, Bob (Athlete, Football Player)
100 Sioux Ct
Hendersonville, TN 37075-4634, USA

Cook, Brian (Basketball Player)
Staples Center 1111 S Figueroa St
Los Angeles, CA 90015, USA

Cook, Carole (Actor, Comedian)
8829 Ashcroft Ave
West Hollywood, CA 90048-2401, USA

Cook, Cliff (Athlete, Baseball Player)
605 E Williamsburg Mnr
Arlington, TX 76014-1145, USA

Cook, Daequan (Basketball Player)
c/o Staff Member *Miami Heat*
1 SE 3rd Ave Ste 2300
Miami, FL 33131-1716, USA

Cook, Dane (Actor)
c/o Brian Volk-Weiss *New Wave Entertainment (LA)*
2660 W Olive Ave
Burbank, CA 91505-4525, USA

Cook, Darwin (Athlete, Basketball Player)
1840 W Avenue J12 Apt 103
Lancaster, CA 93534-4642, USA

Cook, David (Musician)
c/o Michelle Young *19 Entertainment - LA*
9000 W Sunset Blvd Ste 1574
West Hollywood, CA 90069-5817, USA

Cook, Dennis (Athlete, Baseball Player)
3413 Serene Hills Ct
Austin, TX 78738-1230, USA

Cook, Doris (Baseball Player)
1059 Airport Rd
Norton Shores, MI 49441-5101, USA

Cook, Edward J (Athlete, Football Player)
902 Briarwood Ct
Sewell, NJ 08080-3508, USA

Cook, Fielder
180 Central Park S
New York, NY 10019-1562

Cook, Fred (Athlete, Football Player)
4402 Market St
Pascagoula, MS 39567-2224, USA

Cook, Glen (Athlete, Baseball Player)
424 Scarlet Sage Dr
League City, TX 77573-6426, USA

Cook, Jameel (Athlete, Football Player)
PO Box 16293
Sugar Land, TX 77496-6293, USA

Cook, Jason (Actor)
c/o Katie Mason *Luber Roklin Management*
8530 Wilshire Blvd Ste 550
Beverly Hills, CA 90211-3133, USA

Cook, Jeff (Athlete, Basketball Player)
4908 E Doubletree Ranch Rd
Paradise Valley, AZ 85253-1556, USA

Cook, Jeffrey A (Jeff) (Music Group, Musician)
P O Box 35967
Fort Payne, AL 35967, USA

Cook, John (Athlete, Golfer)
9742 Green Island Cv
Windermere, FL 34786-8953, USA

Cook, Judy (Bowler)
7200 Harrison Ave # 7171
Rockford, IL 61112-1017, USA

Cook, Kristy Lee (Musician)
c/o Marty Rendleman *Rendleman Management Group, Inc.*
PO Box 670366
Dallas, TX 75367-0366, USA

Cook, Leigh
9560 Wilshire Blvd # 516
Beverly Hills, CA 90212-2427

Cook, Marv (Athlete, Football Player)
425 Butternut Ln
Iowa City, IA 52246-2782, USA

Cook, Mike (Athlete, Baseball Player)
216 Harlech Way
Charleston, SC 29414-6876, USA

Cook, Norm (Athlete, Basketball Player)
1003 N Logan St
Lincoln, IL 62656-1746, USA

Cook, Paul (Music Group, Musician)
55 Fulham High St
London SW6 3JJ, UNITED KINGDOM(UK)

Cook, Paul M (Business Person)
333 Ravenswood Ave
Menlo Park, CA 94025-3453, USA

Cook, Peter F C (Architect)
54 Compayne Gardens
London NW6 3RY, UNITED KINGDOM(UK)

Cook, Rachael Leigh (Lee) (Actor)
c/o Randy James *James/Levy/Jacobson Management Inc*
3500 W Olive Ave Ste 1470
Burbank, CA 91505-5514, USA

Cook, Rachel Leigh (Actor, Producer)
c/o Staff Member *James/Levy/Jacobson Management Inc*
3500 W Olive Ave Ste 1470
Burbank, CA 91505-5514, USA

Cook, Rashard (Athlete, Football Player)
7882 Gribble St
San Diego, CA 92114-6019, USA

Cook, Richard (Scientist)
4800 Oak Grove Dr
Pasadena, CA 91109-8001, USA

Cook, Robert (Opera Singer)
Quavers 53 Friars Ave Fiem Barnet
London N2O OXG, UNITED KINGDOM(UK)

Cook, Robert (Athlete, Baseball Player)
179 Royal Farm E
Blacklick, OH 43004-9209, USA

Cook, Robert F (Robin) (Government Official)
Westminster
London SW1A 0AA, UNITED KINGDOM(UK)

Cook, Robin (Writer)
4601 Gulf Shore Blvd N # P4
Naples, FL 34103-2221, USA

Cook, Ron (Athlete, Baseball Player)
1918 Franklin Dr
Longview, TX 75601-4111, USA

Cook, Sandra (Stylist)
829 Carolina St
San Francisco, CA 94107-2703, USA

Cook, Stanton R (Publisher)
224 Raleigh Rd
Kenilworth, IL 60043-1209, USA

Cook, Steve (Bowler)
1209 Devonshire Ct
Roseville, CA 95661-5470, USA

Cook, Thomas A (Writer)
1540 Broadway
New York, NY 10036-4039, USA

Cook, Toi (Athlete, Football Player)
11718 Barrington Ct # 805
Los Angeles, CA 90049-2930, USA

Cooke, Amelia (Actor)
c/o Darren Goldberg *Global Creative*
1051 Cole Ave # B
Los Angeles, CA 90038-2601, USA

Cooke, David (Athlete, Basketball Player)
PO Box 270591
San Diego, CA 92198-2591, USA

Cooke, Ed (Athlete, Football Player)
2093 Wake Forest St
Virginia Beach, VA 23451-1421, USA

Cooke, Howard F H (Ex-Governor)
20 Peter Pan Ave
Montego Bay, Saint James, Jamaica

Cooke, Janis (Journalist)
1150 15th St NW
Washington, DC 20071-0001, USA

Cooke, Joe (Athlete, Football Player)
3377 Blackburn St
Dallas, TX 75204-1545, USA

Cooke, John P (Misc)
290 Branchville Rd
Ridgefield, CT 6877, USA

Cooke, Josh (Actor)
c/o Jason Newman *Untitled Entertainment (LA)*
350 S Beverly Dr Ste 200
Beverly Hills, CA 90212-4819, USA

Cooke, Steve (Athlete, Baseball Player)
20709 SW Trails End Dr
Sherwood, OR 97140-2070, USA

Cooke, William (Bill) (Athlete, Football Player)
1851 Hillside Rd
Fairfield, CT 06824-2017, USA

Cooks, Johnie (Athlete, Football Player)
2416 Sun Creek Rd
Starkville, MS 39759-8475, USA

Cooks, Kerry (Athlete, Football Player)
1305 Meadow Creek Dr Apt 111
Irving, TX 75038-7202, USA

Cooks, Rayford (Athlete, Football Player)
1839 Nomas St
Dallas, TX 75212-3806, USA

Cooksey, Danny
9300 Wilshire Blvd Ste 410
Beverly Hills, CA 90212-3228

Cooksey, Dave (Religious Leader)
524 College Ave
Ashland, OH 44805-3703, USA

Cooksey, Patty (Athlete)
700 Central Ave Ofc
Louisville, KY 40208-1212

Cookson, Brent (Athlete, Baseball Player)
1232 Manzanita Dr
Santa Paula, CA 93060-1239, USA

Cookson, Peter
30 Norfolk Rd
Southfield, MA 1259

Cool Breeze
PO Box 470642
San Francisco, CA 94147-0642

Cool kids (Music Group, Musician)
c/o Cara Lewis *WmE2 (WMA-NY)*
1325 Avenue of the Americas
New York, NY 10019-6026, USA

Coolbaugh, Scott (Athlete, Baseball Player)
6708 Carriage Ln
Colleyville, TX 76034-5771, USA

Cooley, Denton (Doctor, Misc)
3014 Del Monte Dr
Houston, TX 77019-3214, USA

Cooley, Ryan (Actor)
c/o Norbert Abrams *Noble Caplan Abrams*
1260 Yonge St 2nd Floor
Toronto ON M4T 1W6, Canada

Cooley, Tonya (Reality TV Star)
c/o Staff Member *Bunim/Murray Productions Inc*
6007 Sepulveda Blvd
Van Nuys, CA 91411-2502, USA

Cooleyb, Chelsea (Beauty Pageant Winner)
c/o Staff Member *Miss Universe Organization, The*
1370 Avenue of the Americas Fl 16
New York, NY 10019-4602, USA

Coolidge, Charles H (War Hero)
1054 Balmoral Dr
Signal Mountain, TN 37377-2904, USA

Coolidge, Charles H Jr (General)
Vice CinC Air Force Material Command
Wright-Patterson Air Force Base, OH 45433, USA

Coolidge, Harold J (Misc)
38 Standley St
Beverly, MA 01915-2020, USA

Coolidge, Jennifer (Actor)
c/o Staff Member *ID PR (LA)*
7060 Hollywood Blvd Fl 8
Los Angeles, CA 90028-6014, USA

Coolidge, Martha (Director)
760 N La Cienega Blvd
Los Angeles, CA 90069-5204, USA

Coolidge, Rita (Music Group)
PO Box 571
Gwynedd Valley, PA 19437-0571, USA

Coolio (Actor, Musician)
c/o Chris Johnston-Davies *Intrigue Management*
25 Spinney Way Needingworth
Cambridgeshire PE27 4SR, United Kingdom

Coombe, George W (Attorney, Attorney General, General)
1 Maritime Plz
San Francisco, CA 94111-3415, USA

Coombs, Danny (Athlete, Baseball Player)
14130 Cleobrook Dr
Houston, TX 77070-3744, USA

Coombs, Pat
5 Wendela Ct Harrow-On-The-Hill
Middlesex, ENGLAND, ENGLAND

Coombs, Philip H (Economist)
617 W Main St
Chester, CT 6412, USA

Coombs, Torrance (Actor)
c/o Danielle Allman-Del *D2 Management*
141 S Barrington Ave
Los Angeles, CA 90049-3368, USA

Coombs-Mueller, Carol
772 Tyrol Dr
Crestline, CA 92325

Coomer, Ron (Athlete, Baseball Player)
7021 Howard Ln
Eden Prairie, MN 55346-3053, USA

Coon, Christopher (Senator)
127A Russell Senate Ofc Building
Washington, DC 20510-0001, USA

Coonce, Ricky (Music Group, Musician)
11761 E Speedway Blvd
Tucson, AZ 85748-2017, USA

Cooney, Gerry (Boxer)
370 North Ave
Fanwood, NJ 07023-1320, USA

Cooney, Joan Ganz (Educator, Misc, Television Host)
1 Lincoln Plz
New York, NY 10023-7129, USA

Cooney, Mark (Athlete, Football Player)
8005 Flower Ct
Arvada, CO 80005-2445, USA

Coonts, Stephen (Writer)
40 Upland Rd
Colorado Springs, CO 80906-4246

Cooper, Adrian (Athlete, Football Player)
3120 Saint Paul St
Denver, CO 80205-4840, USA

Cooper, Alexander (Architect)
311 W 43rd St
New York, NY 10036-6413, USA

Cooper, Alice (Music Group, Songwriter, Writer)
c/o Toby Mamis *Alive Enterprises*
3264 S Kihei Rd
Kihei, HI 96753-9605, USA

Cooper, Amy Levin (Editor)
60 Sutton Pl S # 16C
New York, NY 10022-4168, USA

Cooper, Anderson (Correspondent, Journalist, Television Host)
c/o Staff Member *CNN (NY)*
1 Time Warner Ctr
New York, NY 10019-6038, USA

Cooper, Artis (Athlete, Basketball Player)
5013 Millstone Way
Granite Bay, CA 95746-6126, USA

Cooper, Ashley
194 Bellevue Ave
Newport, RI 02840-3515

Cooper, Bill (Athlete, Football Player)
16056 Greenwood Rd
Monte Sereno, CA 95030-3018, USA

Cooper, Bonnie (Baseball Player)
PO Box 26
Tremont, IL 61568-0026, USA

Cooper, Bradley (Actor)
c/o Nicole Caruso *Wolf Kasteler Van Iden & Associates (NY)*
584 Broadway Rm 310
New York, NY 10012-5246, USA

Cooper, Brian (Athlete, Baseball Player)
346 W Ada Ave
Glendora, CA 91741-4248, USA

Cooper, Camille (Basketball Player)
Madison Square Garden 2 Penn Plaza
New York, NY 10121, USA

Cooper, Carl (Athlete, Golfer)
210 Whispering Mdw
Magnolia, TX 77355-2772, USA

Cooper, Cathy (Stylist)
c/o Staff Member *Mercury Artists*
8460 Higuera St Fl 2
Culver City, CA 90232-2520, USA

Cooper, Cecil C (Athlete, Baseball Player, Coach)
24802 Boulder Lakes Ct
Katy, TX 77494-3900, USA

Cooper, Charles (Actor)
c/o Joel Kleinman *Baier/Kleinman International*
3575 Cahuenga Blvd W Ste 500
Los Angeles, CA 90068-1344, USA

Cooper, Charles G (General)
3410 Barger Dr
Falls Church, VA 22044-1201, USA

Cooper, Chris (Actor)
c/o Staff Member *WKT Public Relations (WKT-LA)*
9350 Wilshire Blvd Ste 450
Beverly Hills, CA 90212-3230, USA

Cooper, Christian
General Delivery
Sun Valley, ID 83353-9999

Cooper, Christin (Skier)
1001 E Hyman Ave
Aspen, CO 81611-2612, USA

Cooper, Daniel L (Admiral)
121 Leisure Ct
Wyomissing, PA 19610-1969, USA

Cooper, Darin (Actor)
c/o Marianne Golan *Marianne Golan Management*
6528 W 6th St
Los Angeles, CA 90048-4716, USA

Cooper, Dave (Artist)
c/o Staff Member *Fantagraphics Books*
7563 Lake City Way NE
Seattle, WA 98115-4218, USA

Cooper, Dominic (Actor)
c/o Joel Lubin *Creative Artists Agency (CAA-LA)*
2000 Avenue of the Stars Ste 100
Los Angeles, CA 90067-4705, USA

Cooper, Don (Athlete, Baseball Player)
2320 Arborfield Ln
Sarasota, FL 34235-1807, USA

Cooper, Duane (Athlete, Basketball Player)
13813 Ocana Ave
Bellflower, CA 90706-2528, USA

Cooper, Earl (Athlete, Football Player)
2224 E Highway 21
Lincoln, TX 78948-6496, USA

Cooper, Eric (Athlete, Baseball Player)
5404 Longview Ct Unit 4
Johnston, IA 50131-2706, USA

Cooper, Gary (Athlete, Baseball Player)
1136 Birch Cir
Alpine, UT 84004-1212, USA

Cooper, Gary (Baseball Player)
402 E Victory Dr
Savannah, GA 31405-2254, USA

Cooper, George (Athlete, Football Player)
1616 Bloomfield Place Dr Apt 141B
Bloomfield Hills, MI 48302-0859, USA

Cooper, Hal (Director)
2651 Hutton Dr
Beverly Hills, CA 90210-1213, USA

Cooper, Imogen (Music Group, Musician)
4 Addison Bridge Place
London W14 8XP, UNITED KINGDOM(UK)

Cooper, James P (Jim) (Athlete, Football Player)
2713 Eastover Dr
Odessa, TX 79762-7830, USA

Cooper, Jeanne (Actor)
8401 Edwin Dr
Los Angeles, CA 90046-1025, USA

Cooper, Jilly (Writer)
c/o Staff Member *Transworld Publishers*
20 Vauxhall Bridge Road
London SW1V 2SA, UK

Cooper, Jim (Congressman, Politician)
1536 Longworth Hob
Washington, DC 20515-4205, USA

Cooper, Joel D (Doctor)
Medical School Surgery Dept
Saint Louis, MO 63110, USA

Cooper, John M (Misc)
182 Western Way
Princeton, NJ 08540-7208, USA

Cooper, Lattie F (Educator)
President S Ofc
Tempe, AZ 85287-0001, USA

Cooper, Leon N (Nobel Prize Laureate)
49 Intervale Rd
Providence, RI 02906-4843, USA

Cooper, Lester I (Producer)
45 Morningside Dr S
Westport, CT 06880-5414, USA

Cooper, Louis (Athlete, Football Player)
200 Gregg Ave
Marion, SC 29571-3824, USA

Cooper, Marcus Ramone (Pleasure P) (Musician)
c/o Staff Member *Atlantic Records (NY)*
1290 Avenue of the Americas Fl CONC4
New York, NY 10104-0184

Cooper, Marilyn (Actor)
315 W 57th St Frnt 4H
New York, NY 10019-3158, USA

Cooper, Mark S (Athlete, Football Player)
6598 S Telluride St
Aurora, CO 80016-3158, USA

Cooper, Matthew T (General)
9326 Fairfax St
Alexandria, VA 22309-3016, USA

Cooper, Minor J (Biologist)
1901 Austin Ave
Ann Arbor, MI 48104-3621, USA

Cooper, Paula (Misc)
534 W 21st St
New York, NY 10011-2812, USA

Cooper, Scott (Actor)
c/o Leland LaBarre *Bleu, An Entertainment Company*
5225 Wilshire Blvd Ste 336
Los Angeles, CA 90036-4380, USA

Cooper, Scott (Athlete, Baseball Player)
7 Fairways Cir Apt F
Saint Charles, MO 63303-3353, USA

Cooper, Stephen (Business Person)
1400 Smith St
Houston, TX 77002-7327, USA

Cooper, Thurlow (Athlete, Football Player)
4350 County Road 115
Glenwood Springs, CO 81601-9020, USA

Cooper, Wayne (Artist)
PO Box 106
Depew, OK 74028-0106, USA

Cooper, Wayne (Athlete, Basketball Player)
5013 Millstone Way
Granite Bay, CA 95746-6126, USA

Cooper, Wilma Lee (Musician)
c/o Staff Member *Charles Rapp Enterprises Inc*
88 Pine St
New York, NY 10005-1801, USA

Cooper, Wima Lee (Musician)
c/o Staff Member *Charles Rapp Enterprises Inc*
88 Pine St
New York, NY 10005-1801, USA

Cooperfield, David (Misc)
c/o Staci Wolfe *Polaris PR*
8135 W 4th St Fl 2
Los Angeles, CA 90048-4415, USA

Cooperwheat, Lee (Designer, Fashion Designer)
14 Cheshire St
London E2 6EH, UNITED KINGDOM (UK)

Coors, William K (Business Person)
1221 Ford St
Golden, CO 80401-1132, USA

Coover, Robert (Writer)
49 George St
Providence, RI 02912-9051, USA

Cope, Derrike (Race Car Driver)
106 Motorsports Rd # C
Mooresville, NC 28115-8258, USA

Cope, Jonathan (Dancer)
Covent Garden Bow St
London WC2E 9DD, UNITED KINGDOM (UK)

Cope, Julian (Musician, Songwriter, Writer)
729 7th Ave Ste 1600
New York, NY 10019-6880, USA

Cope, Kenneth
61-63 Kent House 87 Regent St
London, ENGLAND W1R 7HF

Copeland, Adam (Edge) (Wrestler)
c/o Kerry Rodgerson *World Wrestling Entertainment (WWE)*
1241 E Main St
Stamford, CT 06902-3520, USA

Copeland, Al (Business Person, Race Car Driver)
1001 S Harimaw Ct
Metairie, LA 70001-6233, USA

Copeland, Cyrus
c/o Daniel A (Dan) Strone *Trident Media Group LLC*
41 Madison Ave Fl 36
New York, NY 10010-2257, USA

Copeland, Danny (Athlete, Football Player)
186 Old Newton Rd
Pelham, GA 31779-4043, USA

Copeland, Hollis (Athlete, Basketball Player)
257 Upland Ave
Ewing, NJ 08638-2331, USA

Copeland, Horace (Athlete, Football Player)
4195 Blakemore Pl
Spring Hill, FL 34609-0694, USA

Copeland, Jim (Athlete, Football Player)
1935 Blue Ridge Rd
Charlottesville, VA 22903-1215, USA

Copeland, Joan (Actor)
88 Central Park W
New York, NY 10023-5299, USA

Copeland, John (Athlete, Football Player)
4226 Maxwell Dr
Mason, OH 45040-6504, USA

Copeland, Kenneth (Misc)
PO Box 2908
Fort Worth, TX 76113, USA

Copeland, Kristina (Actor)
1572 W 4th Ave Fl 2
Vancouver, BC V6J1L7, CANADA

Copeland, Lanard (Athlete, Basketball Player)
4115 Pierce Rd
Atlanta, GA 30349-3648, USA

Copeland, Stewart (Composer, Musician)
c/o Derek Power *Derek Power Company*
2695 Montrose Pl
Santa Barbara, CA 93105-2142, USA

Copeland Jr., Zane (Lil Zane) (Musician)
c/o Elayne Rivers *Toonzworld Management*
PO Box 759
New York, NY 10116-0759, USA

Copley, Jeff E
687 State Hwy 194
Kimper, KY 41539, USA

Copley, Sharlto (Actor)
c/o Phillip d'Amecourt *WmE2 (Endeavor-LA)*
9601 Wilshire Blvd Fl 3
Beverly Hills, CA 90210-5219, USA

Copley, Teri (Actor, Model)
13351 Riverside Dr # D513
Sherman Oaks, CA 91423-2542, USA

Copon, Michael (Actor)
c/o Lena Roklin *Luber Roklin Management*
8530 Wilshire Blvd Ste 550
Beverly Hills, CA 90211-3133, USA

Copp, D Harold (Misc)
4755 Belmont Ave
Vancouver, BC V6T 1A8, CANADA

Coppenbarger, Ron (Athlete, Football Player)
7890 James Island Trl
Jacksonville, FL 32256-7355, USA

Coppens, Gus (Athlete, Football Player)
2413 Deerpark Dr
Fullerton, CA 92835-3001, USA

Coppens, Yves (Misc)
4 Rue du Pont-aux-Choux
Paris 75003, FRANCE

Copperfield, David (Magician)
15821 Ventura Blvd Ste 500
Encino, CA 91436-2945, USA

Copping, Allen A (Educator)
President's Office
Baton Rouge, LA 70808, USA

Coppinger, Rocky (Athlete, Baseball Player)
7208 Alto Rey Ave
El Paso, TX 79912-2100, USA

Coppo, Paul (Athlete, Hockey Player)
PO Box 10484
Green Bay, WI 54307-0484, USA

Coppola, Alicia (Actor)
c/o Leslie Allan-Rice *Leslie Allan-Rice Management*
7524 Mulholland Dr
Los Angeles, CA 90046-1239, USA

Coppola, Chris (Actor)
c/o Staff Member *IMG (LA)*
717 N Alta Vista Blvd
Los Angeles, CA 90046-7601, USA

Coppola, Francis Ford (Director)
c/o Staff Member *American Zoetrope*
916 Kearny St
San Francisco, CA 94133-5107, USA

Coppola, Sofia (Actor, Director, Writer)
c/o Bart Walker *Cinetic Management*
555 W 25th St Fl 4
New York, NY 10001-5542, USA

Coppolla, Alicia (Actor)
c/o Jeff Witjas *Agency for the Performing Arts (APA-LA)*
405 S Beverly Dr Ste 500
Beverly Hills, CA 90212-4425, USA

Coquillette, Trace (Athlete, Baseball Player)
5200 Mississippi Bar Dr
Orangevale, CA 95662-5717, USA

Cora, Alex (Athlete, Baseball Player)
F12 Calle 14
Caguas, PR 00727-6935, USA

Cora, Cat (Chef)
c/o Erika Martineau *Brooks Group*
15 W 37th St Rm 1601
New York, NY 10018-5318, USA

Cora, Jose M (Joey) (Athlete, Baseball Player)
F12 Calle 14
Caguas, PR 00727-6935, USA

Corabi, John (Musician)
c/o Staff Member *Union Entertainment Group*
1323 Newbury Rd Ste 104
Thousand Oaks, CA 91320-3679, USA

Coraci, Frank
9701 Wilshire Blvd Ste 1000
Beverly Hills, CA 90212-2010

Coral, The (Music Group)
c/o Staff Member *Paradigm (Monterey)*
404 W Franklin St
Monterey, CA 93940-2303, USA

Corbet, Brady (Actor)
c/o Brian Young *Untitled Entertainment (LA)*
350 S Beverly Dr Ste 200
Beverly Hills, CA 90212-4819, USA

Corbett, Brady (Actor)
c/o Brian Young *Untitled Entertainment (LA)*
350 S Beverly Dr Ste 200
Beverly Hills, CA 90212-4819, USA

Corbett, Doug (Athlete, Baseball Player)
75083 Edwards Rd
Yulee, FL 32097-2660, USA

Corbett, Gene (Athlete, Baseball Player)
1109 S Schumaker Dr Apt 204
Salisbury, MD 21804-9259, USA

Corbett, Gretchen (Actor)
1801 Avenue of the Stars Ste 902
Los Angeles, CA 90067-5981, USA

Corbett, Holly (Stylist)
c/o Staff Member *Bernstein & Andriulli*
58 W 40th St
New York, NY 10018-2658, USA

Corbett, James (Athlete, Football Player)
2723 Marlo Way
Lakeside Park, KY 41017-2121, USA

Corbett, John (Actor)
c/o Steve Lovett *Lovett Management*
1327 Brinkley Ave
Los Angeles, CA 90049-3619, USA

Corbett, Luke R (Business Person)
Kerr-McGee Center
Oklahoma City, OK 73125, USA

Corbett, Michael (Actor)
2665 Charl Pl
Los Angeles, CA 90046-1023, USA

Corbett, Mike (Athlete, Football Player)
41828 Road 600
Ahwahnee, CA 93601-9709, USA

Corbett, Ronnie (Actor, Comedian)
235 Regent St
London W1R 8AX, UNITED KINGDOM (UK)

Corbett, Sherman (Athlete, Baseball Player)
7031 Washita Way
San Antonio, TX 78256-2310, USA

Corbett, Steve (Athlete, Football Player)
3 Wake Robin Rd
Sudbury, MA 01776-1726, USA

Corbett, Tom (Governor, Politician)
Governor S Ofc 225
Harrisburg, PA 17120-0001, USA

Corbin, Archie (Athlete, Baseball Player)
7525 Tram Rd
Beaumont, TX 77713-8723, USA

Corbin, Barry (Actor)
2113 Greta Ln
Fort Worth, TX 76120-5201, USA

Corbin, Ray (Athlete, Baseball Player)
65 Moore St
Franklin, NC 28734-9307, USA

Corbin, Tyrone (Basketball Player)
Madison Square Garden 2 Penn Plaza
New York, NY 10121, USA

Corbin, Tyrone (Athlete, Basketball Player)
652 Edgewood Dr
N Salt Lake, UT 84054-2640, USA

Corbo, Vincent J (Business Person)
Hercules Plaza 1313 North Market St
Wilmington, DE 19894-0001, USA

Corbucci, Bruno
via dei Colli della Farnesia 144
Rome, ITALY

Corbus, William (Athlete, Football Player)
1100 Union St Apt 1100
San Francisco, CA 94109-2019, USA

Corchiani, Chris (Athlete, Basketball Player)
1106 Harvey St
Raleigh, NC 27608-2205, USA

Corcoran, Barbara (Business Person)
226 W 26th St Fl 8
New York, NY 10001-6700, USA

Corcoran, Kevin (Actor)
8617 Balcom Ave
Northridge, CA 91325-3101, USA

Corcoran, Norm (Athlete, Hockey Player)
20 Nickerson Ave
St Catharines, ON L2N 3M4, Canada

Corcoran, Roy (Athlete, Baseball Player)
PO Box 173
Slaughter, LA 70777-0173, USA

Corcoran, Tim (Athlete, Baseball Player)
4349 Friar Cir
La Verne, CA 91750-2718, USA

Cord, Alex (Actor)
c/o Staff Member *Coast to Coast Talent Group*
3350 Barham Blvd
Los Angeles, CA 90068-1404, USA

Cordalis, Costa
Rippoldsauer Str. 32
Freudenstadt, GERMANY D-72250

Corday, Barbara (Business Person)
2011 Cummings Dr
Los Angeles, CA 90027-1728, USA

Corday, Mara (Actor)
PO Box 800393
Valencia, CA 91380-0393

Corddry, Nate (Actor)
c/o Jill McGrath *Abrams Artists Agency (NY)*
275 7th Ave Fl 26
New York, NY 10001-6708, USA

Corddry, Rob (Actor)
c/o Peter Principato *Principato/Young Management*
9465 Wilshire Blvd Ste 430
Beverly Hills, CA 90212-2613, USA

Corder, Roger (Inventor)
Turner St
London E1 2AD, UNITED KINGDOM (UK)

Cordero, Angel T Jr (Jockey)
PO Box 170090
Ozone Park, NY 11417-0090, USA

Cordero, Angelo
PO Box 110090
Cambria Heights, NY 11411-0090

Cordero, Chad (Athlete, Baseball Player)
13305 Noble Pl
Chino, CA 91710-4742, USA

Cordero, Joaquin (Actor)
c/o Staff Member *Televisa*
Blvd Adolfo Lopez Mateos 232 Colonia
San Angel INN
DF CP 01060, MEXICO

Cordero, Wilfredo N (Wil) (Baseball Player)
25844 Kensington Dr
Westlake, OH 44145-1472, USA

Cordes-Elliott, Gloria (Baseball Player)
86 Malone Ave
Staten Island, NY 10306-4110, USA

Cordileone, Lou (Athlete, Football Player)
5312 Mark Ct
Agoura Hills, CA 91301-5200, USA

Cordova, Francisco (Athlete, Baseball Player)
c/o Staff Member *San Diego Padres*
100 Park Blvd
San Diego, CA 92101-7405, USA

Cordova, Jorge (Athlete, Football Player)
23899 Cadenza Dr
Murrieta, CA 92562-2107, USA

Cordova, Marty (Athlete, Baseball Player)
4395 Cameron St Ste C
Las Vegas, NV 89103-3819, USA

Cordovez, Zegers Diego (Educator, Government Official)
Avda 10 Agosta y Carrion
Quito, ECUADOR

Corduner, Allan (Actor)
c/o Staff Member *Conway van Gelder*
8-12 Broadwick St
London W1F 8HW, UK

Corea, Armando (Chick) (Composer, Musician)
10400 Samoa Ave
Tujunga, CA 91042-1921, USA

Corella, Angel
890 Broadway
New York, NY 10003-1211

Corey, Bryan (Athlete, Baseball Player)
7829 E Riverdale Cir
Mesa, AZ 85207-0804, USA

Corey, Elias J (Nobel Prize Laureate)
20 Avon Hill St
Cambridge, MA 02140-3608, USA

Corey, Irwin (Professor) (Actor, Comedian)
c/o Richard Corey *Worlds Foremost Management*
165 W 21st St
New York, NY 10011-3218, USA

Corey, Jill (Musician)
64 Division Ave
Levittown, NY 11756-2999, USA

Corey, Mark (Athlete, Baseball Player)
9321 Cornell Cir
Highlands Ranch, CO 80130-4143, USA

Corey, Mark (Athlete, Baseball Player)
PO Box 113
Austin, PA 16720-0113, USA

Corey, Walt (Athlete, Football Player)
26007 Timber Meadow Dr
Lees Summit, MO 64086-9528, USA

Corgan Jr., Patrick (Billy) (Musician, Songwriter)
c/o John Branigan *WmE2 (Endeavor-LA)*
9601 Wilshire Blvd Fl 3
Beverly Hills, CA 90210-5219, USA

Cori, Carl T (Business Person)
3050 Spruce St
Saint Louis, MO 63103-2530, USA

Cori, Yarckin (Musician)
PO Box 151234
Altamonte Springs, FL 32715-1234, USA

Corigliano, John P (Composer)
365 W End Ave
New York, NY 10024-6511, USA

Corker, Bob (Senator)
Bldg SD-185
Washington, DC 20510-0001, USA

Corker, John (Athlete, Football Player)
825 Martin Luther King Jr Blvd
Baltimore, MD 21201-2306, USA

Corkins, Mike (Athlete, Baseball Player)
3760 Chemehuevi Blvd
Lake Havasu City, AZ 86406-6449, USA

Corkum, Bob (Athlete, Hockey Player)
2 Old County Rd
Veazie, ME 04401-6940, USA

Corley, Al (Actor)
9229 W Sunset Blvd Ste 615
Los Angeles, CA 90069-3419, USA

Corley, Annie (Actor)
c/o Renee Jennett *Renee Jennett Management*
5757 Wilshire Blvd Ste 473
Los Angeles, CA 90036-3632, USA

Corley, Anthony (Athlete, Football Player)
7465 Rodin Ct
Sun Valley, NV 89433-6691, USA

Corley, Kathy (Stylist)
4705 Hazelwood Cir
Nashville, TN 37220-1101, USA

Corley, Ray (Athlete, Basketball Player)
590 Elwood Rd
East Northport, NY 11731-5629, USA

Corley, W Gene (Engineer)
5400 Old Orchard Rd
Skokie, IL 60077-1030, USA

Corman, Avery (Writer)
40 W 57th St # 1800
New York, NY 10019-4001, USA

Corman, Roger W (Actor, Director, Producer, Writer)
c/o Staff Member *New Concorde International*
11600 San Vicente Blvd
Los Angeles, CA 90049-5102, USA

Cormier, Joe (Athlete, Football Player)
9110 La Salle Ave
Los Angeles, CA 90047-3608, USA

Cormier, Lance (Athlete, Baseball Player)
602 Downing St
Lafayette, LA 70506, USA

Cormier, Rheal (Athlete, Baseball Player)
2640 Cody Cir
Park City, UT 84098-6281, USA

Corn, Laura (Writer)
c/o Staff Member *Literary Group International*
330 W 38th St Rm 408
New York, NY 10018-8473, USA

Corneille (Artist)
Cours la Reine
Paris 75008, FRANCE

Corneisen, Rufus (Religious Leader)
415 S Chester Rd
Swarthmore, PA 19081-2303, USA

Cornejo, Mardie (Athlete, Baseball Player)
321 E 3rd St
Wellington, KS 67152-2706, USA

Cornejo, Nate (Athlete, Baseball Player)
1600 N B St
Wellington, KS 67152-4405, USA

Cornelison, Jerry (Athlete, Football Player)
12713 Cedar St
Leawood, KS 66209-1873, USA

Cornelius, Charles (Athlete, Football Player)
12014 Greenway Cir S Apt 103
Royal Palm Beach, FL 33411-2831, USA

Cornelius, Don (Producer)
12685 Mulholland Dr
Beverly Hills, CA 90210-1332, USA

Cornelius, Helen (Musician, Songwriter, Writer)
PO Box 121089
Nashville, TN 37212-1089, USA

Cornelius, James (Business Person)
111 Monument Cir
Indianapolis, IN 46204-5100, USA

Cornelius, Jemalle (Athlete, Football Player)
c/o Chad Speck *Allegiant Athletic Agency*
35 Market Sq Ste 201
Knoxville, TN 37902-1420, USA

Cornelius, Kathy (Athlete, Golfer)
5744 W Del Rio St
Chandler, AZ 85226-6825, USA

Cornelius, Reid (Athlete, Baseball Player)
10117 Hunt Club Ln
Palm Beach Gardens, FL 33418-4568, USA

Cornell, Chris (Musician)
c/o Julie Colbert *WmE2 (Endeavor-LA)*
9601 Wilshire Blvd Fl 3
Beverly Hills, CA 90210-5219, USA

Cornell, Eric A (Nobel Prize Laureate)
PO Box 440
Boulder, CO 80309, USA

Cornell, Harry M Jr (Business Person)
1 Leggett Rd
Carthage, MO 64836-9649, USA

Cornell, Jeff (Athlete, Baseball Player)
1644 SW Jeffrey Cir
Lees Summit, MO 64081-4115, USA

Cornell, Lydia (Actor)
269 S Beverly Dr
Beverly Hills, CA 90212-3851, USA

Cornell, Robert (Bo) (Athlete, Football Player)
200 Congress Ave Unit 24D
Austin, TX 78701-4544, USA

Cornett, Betty Jane (Athlete, Baseball Player)
99 Corbett Ct Apt 410
Pittsburgh, PA 15237-3030, USA

Cornett, Brad (Athlete, Baseball Player)
1704 N Avenue I
Lamesa, TX 79331-3140, USA

Cornett, Leanza (Actor)
c/o Staff Member *WmE2 (Endeavor-LA)*
9601 Wilshire Blvd Fl 3
Beverly Hills, CA 90210-5219, USA

Cornforth, John W (Nobel Prize Laureate)
Saxon Down Cuilfail Lewes
East Sussex BN7 2BE, UNITED KINGDOM (UK)

Cornforth, Mark (Athlete, Hockey Player)
11 Indian Spring Rd
Milton, MA 02186-3716, USA

Cornish, Abbie (Actor)
c/o Hylda Queally *Creative Artists Agency (CAA-LA)*
2000 Avenue of the Stars Ste 100
Los Angeles, CA 90067-4705, USA

Cornish, Frank (Athlete, Football Player)
305 Sheffield Dr
Southlake, TX 76092-7142, USA

Cornish, Frank (Athlete, Football Player)
1024 Inca Dr Apt A
Harvey, LA 70058-4655, USA

Cornish, Nick (Actor)
c/o Robert Stein *Robert Stein Management*
PO Box 3797
Beverly Hills, CA 90212-0797, USA

Cornthwaite, Robert (Actor)
23388 Mulholland Dr # 12
Woodland Hills, CA 91364-2733, USA

Cornutt, Terry (Athlete, Baseball Player)
179 W Hazel St
Roseburg, OR 97471-2211, USA

Cornwell, Fred (Athlete, Football Player)
2107 Windward Ln
Newport Beach, CA 92660-3820, USA

Cornwell, Johnny (Musician)
156 W 56th St # 500
New York, NY 10019-3800, USA

Cornwell, Patricia (Actor, Producer, Writer)
c/o Staff Member *Simon & Schuster*
1230 Avenue of the Americas Fl CONC1
New York, NY 10020-1586, USA

Cornyn, John (Senator)
517 Hart Senate Ofc Bldg
Washington, DC 20510-0001, USA

Corolla, Adam (Actor, Producer, Writer)
c/o Staff Member *Dixon Talent Agency*
375 Greenwich St Fl 5
New York, NY 10013-2376, USA

Corona, Catherine (Stylist)
c/o Staff Member *Maximum Talent*
1873 S Bellaire St Ste 915
Denver, CO 80222-4356, USA

Coronado, Bob (Athlete, Football Player)
1539 Sereno Dr
Vallejo, CA 94589-2726, USA

Corone, Antoni (Actor)
c/o Bonni Allen *Allen - O'leary*
1138 12th St Apt 1
Santa Monica, CA 90403-5459, USA

Coronel, Felipe (Immortal Technique) (Musician)
c/o Staff Member *Viper Records*
230 Mott St
New York, NY 10012-4147, USA

Corr, Andrea (Musician)
c/o Staff Member *Luber Roklin Management*
8530 Wilshire Blvd Ste 550
Beverly Hills, CA 90211-3133, USA

Corr, Caroline (Music Group)
6 Martello Terr Sandycove Dunlaoughaire
Dublin, IRELAND

Corr, Edwin G (Diplomat)
1617 Jenkins Ave
Norman, OK 73072-6508, USA

Corr, Jim (Music Group)
6 Martello Terr Sandycove Dunlaoughaire
Dublin, IRELAND

Corr, Ryan (Actor)
c/o Staff Member *Nickelodeon UK*
PO Box 6425
LONDON W1A 6UR, UNITED KINGDOM

Corr, Sharon (Music Group, Musician)
c/o Staff Member *Solo Agency Ltd (UK)*
55 Fulham High St 2nd Floor
London SW6 3JJ, United Kingdom

Corrado, Fred (Business Person)
2 Paragon Dr
Montvale, NJ 07645-1718, USA

Corrado, Gabriel (Actor)
c/o Staff Member *Telefe - Argentina*
Pavon 2444 (C1248AAT)
Buenos Aires, ARGENTINA

Corral, Frank (Athlete, Football Player)
3900 Main St
Riverside, CA 92522-0001, USA

Corrales, Pat (Athlete, Baseball Player, Coach)
2 W Wesley Rd NW Apt 18
Atlanta, GA 30305-3500, USA

Correa, Charles M (Architect)
Sonmarg Napean Sea Road
Bombay 40006, INDIA

Correa, Edwin (Ed) (Athlete, Baseball Player)
A2 Calle Milagros Cabezas
Carolina, PR 00987-7101, USA

Correal, Charles (Athlete, Football Player)
110 Springbrooke Dr
Venetia, PA 15367-1054, USA

Correale, Pete (Musician)
c/o Staff Member *Monterey International (Chicago)*
200 W Superior St Ste 202
Chicago, IL 60654-6422, USA

Correia, Kevin (Baseball Player)
5844 Riley St Apt 1
San Diego, CA 92110-1789, USA

Correia, Rod (Athlete, Baseball Player)
PO Box 102
Rehoboth, MA 02769-0102, USA

Correll, Alston D (Pete) (Business Person)
133 Peachtree St NE
Atlanta, GA 30303-1804, USA

Correll, Vic (Athlete, Baseball Player)
119 Kentucky Downs
Perry, GA 31069-8514, USA

Corrente, Michael (Actor, Director, Producer)
c/o David Greenblatt *Key Creatives*
1800 N Highland Ave Fl 5
Los Angeles, CA 90028-4523, USA

Correnti, John D (Business Person)
2100 Rexford Rd
Charlotte, NC 28211-3589, USA

Corretja, Alex (Tennis Player)
200 Tournament Rd
Ponte Vedra Beach, FL 32082, USA

Corri, Andrienne (Actor)
c/o Staff Member *Rolf Kruger Management*
205 Chudleigh R
London SE4 1EG, UNITED KINGDOM (UK)

Corridon-Mortell, Marie (Swimmer)
13 Heritage Vlg # A
Southbury, CT 06488-1601, USA

Corrie, Emily (Actor)
c/o Kathryn Fleming *The Rights House (UK)*
Drury House 34-43 Russell St
London WC2B 5HA, UK

Corrigan, E Gerald (Financier, Government Official)
85 Broad St
New York, NY 10004-2434, USA

Corrigan, Kevin (Actor)
c/o Courtney Kivowitz *Schiff Company, The*
8440 Warner Dr Ste B1
Culver City, CA 90232-2461, USA

Corrigan, Mike (Athlete, Hockey Player)
1661 King St
Enfield, CT 06082-6036, USA

Corrigan, Patrick (Cartoonist, Editor)
Editorial Dept 1 Yonge St
Toronto, ON M5E 1E5, CANADA

Corrigan, Robert A (Educator)
President's Office
San Fransisco, CA 94123, USA

Corrigan, Wilfred J (Business Person)
1621 Barber Ln
Milpitas, CA 95035-7455, USA

Corrigan-Maguire, Mairead (Nobel Prize Laureate)
224 Lisburn Road
Belfast BT9 6GB, NORTHERN IRELAND

Corrington, Kip (Athlete, Football Player)
6407 Olympic Ct
Greensboro, NC 27410-8412, USA

Corripio Ahumada, Ernesto Cardinal (Religious Leader)
Apotinar Nieto 40 Col Tetlameyer
Mexico City 4730, MEXICO

Corriveau, Yvon (Athlete, Hockey Player)
396 Willard Ave Apt A2
Newington, CT 06111-2345, USA

Corroface, Georges
1 Rue Guenegaud
Paris, FRANCE F-75006

Corry, Megan (Actor)
c/o Staff Member *Mary Anne Claro Talent Agency*
8600 W Chester Pike Ste 202
Upper Darby, PA 19082-2629, USA

Corsaro, Frank A (Director)
33 Riverside Dr
New York, NY 10023-8012, USA

Corsi, Jim (Athlete, Hockey Player)
785 Rue Maugue
L'Ile-Bizard, QC H9C 2T7, Canada

Corsi, Jim (Athlete, Baseball Player)
6 Edward Cir
Bellingham, MA 02019-2938, USA

Corso, John A (Cinematographer)
241 W 13th St Apt 21
New York, NY 10011-7738, USA

Corson, Dale R (Educator, Physicist)
942 Savage Farm Dr
Ithaca, NY 14850-6515, USA

Corson, Keith D (Business Person)
PO Box 3300
Elkhart, IN 46515-3300, USA

Corson, Shayne (Athlete, Hockey Player)
55 Mill St Bldg 3
Toronto, ON N5A 3C4, Canada

Cort, Barry (Athlete, Baseball Player)
1812 E Okaloosa Ave
Tampa, FL 33604-2032, USA

Cort, Bud (Actor)
c/o Staff Member *Don Buchwald & Associates Inc (NY)*
10 E 44th St Frnt 1
New York, NY 10017-3654

Cortazar, Esteban (Designer, Fashion Designer)
11 1 Northeast 1st St Fl 9
Miami, FL 33132, USA

Cortes, Ron (Journalist)
400 N Broad St
Philadelphia, PA 19130-4015, USA

Cortese, Dan (Actor)
PO Box 4312
Malibu, CA 90264-4312, USA

Cortese, Genevieve (Actor)
c/o Joanna (Joanie) Burstein *Burstein Company, The*
15304 W Sunset Blvd Ste 208
Pacific Palisades, CA 90272-3656, USA

Cortese, Joe (Actor)
100 S Hayworth Ave Apt 201
Los Angeles, CA 90048-3658, USA

Cortese, Valentina (Actor)
Pretta S Erasmo 6
Milan 20121, ITALY

Cortez, Alfonso (Actor)
10635 Santa Monica Blvd Ste 130
Los Angeles, CA 90025-8306, USA

Cortina, George (Stylist)
c/o Celebrity Stylists *Lighthouse Artists Management*
110 Greene St Ste 1102
New York, NY 10012-3824, USA

Cortright, Edgar M Jr (Astronaut, Engineer, Misc)
9701 Calvin Ave
Northridge, CA 91324-1617, USA

Corvino, Anthony (Athlete, Football Player)
299 N Atlantic Ave Apt 304
Cocoa Beach, FL 32931-4305, USA

Corvo (Musician)
c/o Staff Member *Sony Music Miami*
605 Lincoln Rd Ste 700
Miami Beach, FL 33139-2901, USA

Corvo, Joe (Athlete, Hockey Player)
201 E Chestnut St Apt 7D
Chicago, IL 60611-7374, USA

Corwin, Jeff (Actor)
c/o Staff Member *WmE2 (WMA-LA)*
1 William Morris Pl
Beverly Hills, CA 90212-4261, USA

Corwin, Lola (Reality TV Star)
c/o Cindy Osbrink *Osbrink Talent Agency*
4343 Lankershim Blvd Ste 100
West Toluca Lake, CA 91602-2705, USA

Corwin, Norman (Writer)
3551 Ironsdale Pkwy
Los Angeles, CA 90089-0001, USA

Corwin, Sinead (Stylist)
c/o Staff Member *Sydney Represents*
280 Mott St
New York, NY 10012-3439, USA

Coryatt, Quentin J (Athlete, Football Player)
611 Cannon Ln
Sugar Land, TX 77479-5846, USA

Coryell, Larry (Music Group, Musician)
173 Brighton Ave
Boston, MA 02134-2003, USA

Corzine, Dave (Athlete, Basketball Player)
1161 W Hunting Dr
Palatine, IL 60067-6673, USA

Corzine, Lester (Athlete, Football Player)
38423 Nasturtium Way
Palm Desert, CA 92211-5075, USA

Cosbie, Doug (Athlete, Football Player)
4241 Val Verde Rd
Loomis, CA 95650-9474, USA

Cosby, Bill (Actor, Comedian)
PO Box 808
Greenfield, MA 01302-0808, USA

Cosby, Rita (Television Host)
c/o Staff Member *MSNBC (NJ)*
NBC/One Microsoft Corporation 1 MSNC Plaza
Secaucus, NJ 7094, USA

Coscarelli, Don (Director, Producer, Writer)
c/o Staff Member *Starway International*
12021 Wilshire Blvd # 661
Los Angeles, CA 90025-1206, USA

Coscina, Dennis (Athlete, Golfer)
211 Main St
East Windsor, CT 06088-9518, USA

Cose, Ellis (Activist)
10 E 53rd St
New York, NY 10022-5244, USA

Cosey, Ray (Athlete, Baseball Player)
139 Byxbee St
San Francisco, CA 94132-2602, USA

Cosgrave, Liam (Prime Minister)
Beachperk Templeogue County
Dublin, IRELAND

Cosgrove, Daniel (Actor)
c/o Staff Member *James/Levy/Jacobson Management Inc*
3500 W Olive Ave Ste 1470
Burbank, CA 91505-5514, USA

Cosgrove, Mike (Athlete, Baseball Player)
8813 W Corrine Dr
Peoria, AZ 85381-8166, USA

Cosgrove, Miranda (Actor)
c/o Jillian Fowkes *ID Public Relations (ID-LA)*
7080 Hollywood Blvd Fl 8
Los Angeles, CA 90028-6906, USA

Cosic, Dobrica (President)
Knez Mikallove 35
Belgrade, SERBIA-MONTENEGRO

Cosiga, Fransesco (President)
Via Della Dogana Vecchia 29
Rome 186, ITALY

Coslet, Bruce N (Athlete, Coach, Football Coach, Football Player)
1778 Ivy Pointe Ct
Naples, FL 34109-3375, USA

Cosman, Jim (Athlete, Baseball Player)
140 Blackburn Rd
Sewickley, PA 15143, USA

Cosmovici, Cristiano B (Astronaut)
CP 27
Frascati 44, ITALY

Cosner, Don (Athlete, Football Player)
141 NW Carter Farms Ct
Bremerton, WA 98310-2090, USA

Cosper, Kina (Music Group)
PO Box 3172
Beverly Hills, CA 90212-0172, USA

Cosso, Pierre
13 Rue Madeleine Michelis
Neuilly, FRANCE 92200

Cossotto, Fiorenza (Opera Singer)
Via E Filiberto 125
Rome 185, ITALY

Costa, David J (Dave) (Athlete, Football Player)
1732 Latour Ave
Brentwood, CA 94513-4333, USA

Costa, Don
7920 W Sunset Blvd Ste 300
Los Angeles, CA 90046-3300

Costa, Gal (Music Group)
35 Clark St Apt A5
Brooklyn, NY 11201-2374, USA

Costa, Jim (Congressman, Politician)
1314 Longworth Hob
Washington, DC 20515-4908, USA

Costa, Mary (Opera Singer)
3340 Kingston Pike Unit 1
Knoxville, TN 37919-4674, USA

Costa, Paul (Athlete, Football Player)
8017 Kristina Ln
North Richland Hills, TX 76182-8747, USA

Costa-Gavras (Director, Producer, Writer)
c/o Bertrand de Labbey *ArtMedia*
20 avenue Rapp
Paris 75008, France

Costanza, Margaret (Midge) (Government Official)
4518 Agnes Ave
Studio City, CA 91607-4105, USA

Costanzo, Paulo (Actor)
9560 Wilshire Blvd Ste 500
Beverly Hills, CA 90212-2401, USA

Costanzo, Robert (Actor)
3500 W Olive Ave Ste 1400
Burbank, CA 91505-5512, USA

Costas, Bob (Baseball Player, Sportscaster)
c/o Staff Member *WmE2 (Endeavor-LA)*
9601 Wilshire Blvd Fl 3
Beverly Hills, CA 90210-5219, USA

Costas, Carlos
Entenze 332-334 Atico 2a
Barcelona, SPAIN E-08029

Coste, Chris (Athlete, Baseball Player)
3774 Polk St S
Fargo, ND 58104-7595, USA

Costello, Brad (Athlete, Football Player)
402 Boxwood Rd
Bryn Mawr, PA 19010-1222, USA

Costello, Elvis (Musician, Songwriter)
c/o Rebecca Shapiro *Shore Fire Media*
32 Court St Fl 16
Brooklyn, NY 11201-4441, USA

Costello, John (Athlete, Baseball Player)
16614 Willow Glen Dr
Grover, MO 63040-1750, USA

Costello, Mariclare (Actor)
3172 Dona Susana Dr
Studio City, CA 91604-4356, USA

Costello, Mark (Writer)
Law School
New York, NY 10458, USA

Costello, Murray (Athlete, Hockey Player)
105 Kenilworth St
Ottawa, ON K1Y 3Y8, Canada

Costello, Patty (Bowler)
2405 Pittston Ave
Scranton, PA 18505-3213, USA

Costello, Rich (Athlete, Hockey Player)
242 Monarch Bay Dr
Dana Point, CA 92629-3435, USA

Costello, Sean (Actor, Producer)
c/o Staff Member *Concerted Efforts*
PO Box 440326
Somerville, MA 02144-0004, USA

Costello, Sue (Actor)
9560 Wilshire Blvd Ste 500
Beverly Hills, CA 90212-2401, USA

Costello, Thomas (Tom) (Athlete, Football Player)
PO Box 299
Rocky Point, NY 11778-0299, USA

Costello, Vince (Athlete, Football Player)
12300 Perry St
Overland Park, KS 66213-1811, USA

Costelloe, Paul (Designer, Fashion Designer)
Dungannon BT71 7PB, NORTHERN IRELAND

Coster, Nicolas (Actor)
c/o Staff Member *Momentum Talent and Literary Agency*
9401 Wilshire Blvd Ste 501
Beverly Hills, CA 90212-2944, USA

Coster, Ritchie (Actor)
c/o Glenn Daniels *Glenn Daniels Arts Management*
56 Warren St Apt 5E
New York, NY 10007-1097, USA

Coster Waldau, Nikolaj (Actor)
c/o Jill Littman *Impression Entertainment*
9229 W Sunset Blvd Ste 700
West Hollywood, CA 90069-3407, USA

Costin, Simon (Stylist)
c/o Staff Member *Camilla Lowther Managment (CLM Represents)*
30-32 Ericsson Pl
New York, NY 10013, USA

Costle, Douglas M (Educator, Government Official)
Public Health School
Cambridge, MA 2138, USA

Costner, Kevin (Actor, Director)
c/o JJ Harris *One Talent Management*
9220 W Sunset Blvd Ste 306
Los Angeles, CA 90069-3503, USA

Costo, Tim (Athlete, Baseball Player)
3107 Pintail Ln
Signal Mountain, TN 37377-1439, USA

Cota, Chad (Athlete, Football Player)
216 Island Pointe Dr
Medford, OR 97504-9453, USA

Cota, Humberto (Baseball Player)
c/o Staff Member *Pittsburgh Pirates*
PNC Park 115 Federal Street
Pittsburgh, PA 15212, USA

Cotchery, Jerricho (Athlete, Football Player)
79 Carriage Ln
Plainview, NY 11803-1525, USA

Cotchett, Joseph W (Attorney, Attorney General, General)
840 Malcolm Rd
Burlingame, CA 94010-1401, USA

Cote, Alain (Athlete, Hockey Player)
1352 Rue Gabrielle-Roy
Quebec, QC G1Y 3K3, Canada

Cote, David (Business Person)
1900 Richmond Rd
Cleveland, OH 44124, USA

Cote, Sylvain (Athlete, Hockey Player)
1432 Wild Cranberry Ct
Crownsville, MD 21032-2039, USA

Cothran, Jeff (Athlete, Football Player)
5671 Oakview Ter
Liberty Twp, OH 45011-2494, USA

Cothren, Paige (Athlete, Football Player)
1332 Highway 15 S
Woodland, MS 39776-9741, USA

Cotillard, Marion (Actor)
c/o Mara Buxbaum *ID PR (LA)*
7060 Hollywood Blvd Fl 8
Los Angeles, CA 90028-6014, USA

Cotlow, Lewis N (Misc)
132 Lakeshore Dr
North Palm Beach, FL 33408-3677, USA

Cotney, Mark (Athlete, Football Player)
4809 Cheval Blvd
Lutz, FL 33558-5338, USA

Cotorna, D (Actor)
c/o Jeff Golenberg *Collective*
8383 Wilshire Blvd Ste 1050
Beverly Hills, CA 90211-2415, USA

Cotrona, DJ (Actor)
c/o Aron Giannini *Collective*
8383 Wilshire Blvd Ste 1050
Beverly Hills, CA 90211-2415, USA

Cotrubas, Ileana (Opera Singer)
Convent Garden Bow St
London WC2, UNITED KINGDOM(UK)

Cottee, Kay (Yachtsman)
113 Willoughby Rd
Crows Nest, NSW 2065, AUSTRALIA

Cotten, Carole (Stylist)
c/o Staff Member *Zenobia Agency Inc*
PO Box 909
Groveland, CA 95321-0909, USA

Cotterill, Harriet (Stylist)
c/o Staff Member *ESP (London)*
63 Charlotte St. 1st Floor
London W11 4PG, UK

Cottet, Mia (Actor)
c/o David Sweeney *Sweeney Management*
8755 Lookout Mountain Ave
Los Angeles, CA 90046-1861, USA

Cotti, Flavio (President)
Klaraweg 6
Bem 3001, SWITZERLAND

Cottier, Chuck (Athlete, Baseball Player, Coach)
7129 Lake Ballinger Way
Edmonds, WA 98026-8545, USA

Cottier, George Cardinal (Religious Leader)
Piazza Pierro d'Illiria
Rome 193, ITALY

Cottingham, Robert (Artist)
PO Box 604
Newtown, CT 06470-0604, USA

Cotto, Delilah (Actor)
c/o Ivan De Paz *DePaz Management*
2011 N Vermont Ave
Los Angeles, CA 90027-1931, USA

Cotto, Henry (Athlete, Baseball Player)
1141 W Thomas Rd
Phoenix, AZ 85013-4206, USA

Cotto, Miguel (Athlete, Boxer)
c/o Staff Member *Top Rank Inc.*
3908 Howard Hughes Pkwy # 580
Las Vegas, NV 89109, USA

Cotton, Barney (Athlete, Football Player)
2230 Scotch Pine Trl
Lincoln, NE 68512-9512, USA

Cotton, Blaine (Actor)
5118 Vineland Ave # 102
North Hollywood, CA 91601-3814, USA

Cotton, Fearne (Actor)
c/o Staff Member *Rabbit Vocal Management*
27 Poland St 3rd Floor
London W1F 8QW, UK

Cotton, Fest (Athlete, Football Player)
5101 Coulson Dr
Dayton, OH 45417-6034, USA

Cotton, Frank A (Misc)
Twaycliffe Ranch RR 2 Box 230
Bryan, TX 77808, USA

Cotton, James (Musician)
235 W Eugenie St # G PMB 10
Chicago, IL 60614-5774, USA

Cotton, John (Athlete, Basketball Player)
11426 Country Road 4 S
Alamosa, CO 81101-9630, USA

Cotton, Joseph F (Misc)
20 Linda Vista Ave
Atherton, CA 94027-5429, USA

Cotton, Josie (Music Group)
2794 Hume Rd
Malibu, CA 90265-3435, USA

Cotton, Marcus (Athlete, Football Player)
484 Lake Park Ave Apt 280
Oakland, CA 94610-2730, USA

Cotton, Maxwell Perry (Actor)
c/o Matt Fletcher *Greene & Associates*
1901 Avenue Of The Stars Ste 130
Los Angeles, CA 90067-6030, USA

Cotton, Robin (Doctor)
20271 Goldenrod Ln # 120
Germantown, MD 20876-4064, USA

Cottrell, Dana (Athlete, Football Player)
1 Driftwood Ln
North Billerica, MA 01862-1222, USA

Cottrell, Ted (Athlete, Football Player)
135 Spring Meadow Dr Apt 5
Buffalo, NY 14221-8436, USA

Cottrell, William (Bill) (Athlete, Football Player)
39675 Patterson Ln
Solon, OH 44139-6705, USA

Cotts, Neal (Athlete, Baseball Player)
600 N Kingsbury St Apt 1510
Chicago, IL 60654-8124, USA

Couch, Chris (Athlete, Golfer)
307 Johns Creek Pkwy
Saint Augustine, FL 32092-5064, USA

Couch, Tim (Athlete, Football Player)
2110 N Ocean Blvd Apt 28-D
Fort Lauderdale, FL 33305-1947, USA

Couchee, Mike (Athlete, Baseball Player)
3060 N Ridgecrest Unit 155
Mesa, AZ 85207-1080, USA

Coughlan, Marisa (Actor)
c/o Paul Nelson *Mosaic Media Group*
9200 W Sunset Blvd Ste 10
Los Angeles, CA 90069-3608, USA

Coughlin, Bernard J (Educator)
Chancellor S Ofc
Spokane, WA 99258-0001, USA

Coughlin, Kevin
1090 N Euclid Ave
Sarasota, FL 34237-3013

Coughlin, Natalie (Athlete, Olympic Athlete)
c/o Staff Member *Janey Miller Management*
1435 Cherryvale Rd
Boulder, CO 80303-1307, USA

Coughlin, Tom (Coach, Football Coach)
Giants Stadium
East Rutherford, NJ 7073, USA

Coughran, John (Athlete, Basketball Player)
5476 Morningside Dr
San Jose, CA 95138-2244, USA

Coughtry, Marlan (Athlete, Baseball Player)
9113 NE 65th St
Vancouver, WA 98662-4412, USA

Coulier, David (Dave) (Actor)
c/o Geoff Cheddy *Brillstein Entertainment Partners*
9150 Wilshire Blvd Ste 350
Beverly Hills, CA 90212-3453, USA

Coulson, Catherine E (Actor)
1115 Terra Ave
Ashland, OR 97520-3565, USA

Coulson, Christian (Actor)
c/o Staff Member *Artists Rights Group (ARG)*
4 Great Portland St
London W1W 8PA, UNITED KINGDOM (UK)

Coulter, Allen (Director)
c/o Paul Alan Smith *International Creative Management (ICM-LA)*
10250 Constellation Blvd Fl 7
Los Angeles, CA 90067-6207, USA

Coulter, Ann (Writer)
c/o Suzanne Gluck *WmE2 (WMA-NY)*
1325 Avenue of the Americas
New York, NY 10019-6026, USA

Coulter, Art
500 Spanish Fort Blvd Apt 203
Spanish Fort, AL 36527-5008

Coulter, Brian (Music Group, Musician)
2002 Hogback Rd Ste 20
Ann Arbor, MI 48105-9736, USA

Coulter, Catherine (Writer)
PO Box 17
Mill Valley, CA 94942-0017, USA

Coulter, Cher (Stylist)
c/o Staff Member *Luxe*
6442 Santa Monica Blvd Ste 200B
Los Angeles, CA 90038-1530, USA

Coulter, Michael (Cinematographer)
35 Carlton Mansions Randolph Ave
London W9 1NP, UNITED KINGDOM(UK)

Coulter, Phil (Music Group)
24 Upper Mount St
Dublin, IRELAND

Coulter, Tom (Chip) (Athlete, Baseball Player)
718 Trenton St
Toronto, OH 43964-1269, USA

Coulthard, David (Race Car Driver)
Kings Lynn Tottenhill
Norfolk PE32 0PX, UNITED KINGDOM (UK)

Council, Keith (Athlete, Football Player)
4418 Lenox Blvd
Orlando, FL 32811-4541, USA

Counsell, Craig (Athlete, Baseball Player)
992 E Circle Dr
Milwaukee, WI 53217-5361, USA

Counting Crows (Music Group)

Counts, Mel (Athlete, Basketball Player)
1581 Matheny Rd NE
Gervais, OR 97026-8762, USA

Coupland, Douglas (Writer)
c/o Michael Siegel *Michael Siegel & Assoc*
8330 W 3rd St
Los Angeles, CA 90048-4311, USA

Couples, Fred (Athlete, Golfer)
1851 Alexander Bell Dr Ste 410
Reston, VA 20191-4392, USA

Courant, Ernest D (Physicist)
40 W 72nd St # 4I
New York, NY 10023-4119, USA

Couric, Katie (Journalist, Television Host)
c/o Staff Member *CBS News Productions*
524 W 57th St Fl 8
New York, NY 10019-2930, USA

Courier, James S (Jim) Jr (Tennis Player)
9533 Blandford Rd
Orlando, FL 32827-7008, USA

Courier, Jim
1 Erieview Plz # 1300
Cleveland, OH 44114-1738

Cournoyer, Yvan (Athlete, Hockey Player)
c/o Staff Member *Montreal Canadiens*
1275 Rue Saint-Antoine O
Montreal, QB H3C 5L2, Canada

Courreges, Andre (Designer, Fashion Designer)
27 Rue Delabordere
Neuilly-Sur-Seine 92, FRANCE

Court, Alyson (Actor)
c/o Staff Member *Newton-Landry Management*
19 Isabella St
Toronto ON M4Y 1M7, Canada

Court Yard Hounds (Music Group, Musician)
c/o Staff Member *Columbia Records UK*
Bedford House 69-79 Fulham High St
London SW6 3JW, United Kingdom

Courtemanche, Michael (Actor)
c/o Staff Member *Encore Management*
6300 Avenue du Parc bur406
Montreal, QB H2V 4H8, CANADA

Courtenay, Ed (Athlete, Hockey Player)
3107 Firestone Rd
North Charleston, SC 29418, USA

Courtenay, Tom (Actor)
13 Shorts Gardens
London WC2H 9AT, UNITED KINGDOM(UK)

Courtin, Steve (Athlete, Basketball Player)
1109 Grinnell Rd
Wilmington, DE 19803-5125, USA

Courtland, Jerome
1837 Westleigh Dr
Glenview, IL 60025-7611

Courtnall, Geoff (Athlete, Hockey Player)
3265 Beach Dr
Victoria, BC V8R 6L9, Canada

Courtnall, Russ (Athlete, Hockey Player)
c/o Staff Member *Victoria Atom B Hockey*
3651 Shelbourne St
Victoria, BC V8P 4H1, Canada

Courtney, Joe (Congressman, Politician)
215 Cannon Hob
Washington, DC 20515-0702, USA

Courtney, Joel (Actor)
c/o Bonnie Liedtke *Principato/Young Management*
9465 Wilshire Blvd Ste 430
Beverly Hills, CA 90212-2613, USA

Courtney, Patricia (Baseball Player)
8 Eagle Loop Ln
Freedom, NH 03836-5311, USA

Courtney, Thomas W (Tom) (Athlete, Track Athlete)
PO Box 215
Sewickley, PA 15143-0215, USA

Courtright, John (Athlete, Baseball Player)
316 S Roosevelt Ave
Columbus, OH 43209-1829, USA

Courville, Vince (Athlete, Football Player)
5123 Avenue R
Galveston, TX 77551-5282, USA

Cousin, Terry (Athlete, Football Player)
313 Lake Carolina Blvd
Columbia, SC 29229-7549, USA

Cousineau, Tom (Athlete, Football Player)
910 Eaton Ave
Akron, OH 44303-1312, USA

Cousino, Brad (Athlete, Football Player)
10380 Giverny Blvd
Cincinnati, OH 45241-3279, USA

Cousins, Christopher (Actor)
c/o Staff Member *DiSante Frank & Company*
10061 Riverside Dr # 377
Toluca Lake, CA 91602-2560, USA

Cousins, Derryl (Athlete, Baseball Player)
78136 Desert Mountain Cir
Bermuda Dunes, CA 92203-8151, USA

Cousins, Jomo (Athlete, Football Player)
12425 Bramfield Dr
Riverview, FL 33579-7771, USA

Cousins, Ralph W (Admiral)
Leconfield House Curzon St
London W1Y 8JR, UNITED KINGDOM(UK)

Cousins, Robin (Figure Skater)
174-8 N Gower St
London NW1 2NB, UNITED KINGDOM(UK)

Cousteau, Jean-Michel (Oceanographer)
325 Chapala St
Santa Barbara, CA 93101-3407, USA

Cousy, Robert J (Bob) (Athlete, Basketball Player)
427 Salisbury St
Worcester, MA 01609-1266, USA

Coutre, Larry (Athlete, Football Player)
11848 Sunchase Ct
Boca Raton, FL 33498-6814, USA

Coutteure, Ronny
28 Rue Basfroi
Paris, FRANCE 75011

Couture, Randy (Athlete, Wrestler)
4055 W Sunset Rd
Las Vegas, NV 89118-3894, USA

Covay, Don (Music Group, Songwriter, Writer)
PO Box 110002
Cambria Heights, NY 11411-0002, USA

Cover Girls
141 Dunbar Ave
Fords, NJ 08863-1551

Coverdale, David (Music Group, Musician)
c/o Staff Member *Agency for the Performing Arts (APA-LA)*
405 S Beverly Dr Ste 500
Beverly Hills, CA 90212-4425, USA

Coverly, Dave (Cartoonist, Editor)
1900 S Walnut St
Bloomington, IN 47401-7720, USA

Covert, Allen (Actor)
c/o Adam Venit *WmE2 (Endeavor-LA)*
9601 Wilshire Blvd Fl 3
Beverly Hills, CA 90210-5219, USA

Covert, James (Jimbo) (Athlete, Football Player)
2647 Nelson Ct
Weston, FL 33332-1835, USA

Covey, Dr Stephen (Business Person, Writer)
2200 Parkway Blvd MS 411
Salt Lake City, UT 84119-2099, USA

Covey, Richard O (Astronaut)
1155 High Lake Vw
Colorado Springs, CO 80906-8717, USA

Covic, Nebojsa (Prime Minister)
Nemanjina 11
Belgrade 11000, SERBIA

Coville, Bruce
PO Box 6110
Syracuse, NY 13217-6110

Covington, John (Athlete, Football Player)
1305 Kinsale Ct
Locust Grove, GA 30248-2489, USA

Covington, Scott (Athlete, Football Player)
7444 W 81st St
Los Angeles, CA 90045-2304, USA

Covington, Tony (Athlete, Football Player)
11160 S Lakes Dr # C1
Reston, VA 20191-4327, USA

Covington, Warren (Music Group)
1627 Open Field Loop
Brandon, FL 33510-2096, USA

Covington, Wes (Athlete, Baseball Player)
905-10145 119 St NW
Edmonton, AB T5K 1Z2, Canada

Cowan, Billy (Athlete, Baseball Player)
1539 Via Coronel
Palos Verdes Estates, CA 90274-1941, USA

Cowan, Dr. Connell (Writer)
c/o Staff Member *Reece Halsey North*
98 Main St # 704
Tiburon, CA 94920-2517, USA

Cowan, Elliot (Actor)
c/o Laura Berwick *Hofflund/Polone*
9465 Wilshire Blvd Ste 420
Beverly Hills, CA 90212-2603, USA

Cowan, George A (Misc)
1399 Hyde Park Rd
Santa Fe, NM 87501-8943, USA

Cowan, Lawrence (Larry) (Athlete, Football Player)
1456 McCluer Rd
Jackson, MS 39212-6224, USA

Cowan, Liz (Stylist)
c/o Staff Member *Smashbox Beauty*
8549 Higuera St Bldg B
Culver City, CA 90232-2521, USA

Cowan, Ralph Wolfe (Artist)
243 29th St
West Palm Beach, FL 33407-5207, USA

Coward, Herbert (Actor)
1399 Worley Cove Rd
Canton, NC 28716-7069, USA

Cowart, Sam (Athlete, Football Player)
11110 Fallgate Point Ct
Jacksonville, FL 32256-4833, USA

Cowboy Junkies
c/o Staff Member *Paradigm (Monterey)*
404 W Franklin St
Monterey, CA 93940-2303, USA

Cowboy Mouth (Music Group, Musician)
c/o Konrad Leh *Creative Talent Group*
1900 Avenue of the Stars Ste 2475
Los Angeles, CA 90067-4512, USA

Cowell, Simon (Business Person, Judge, Reality TV Star)
c/o Cindi Berger *PMK/BNC Public Relations (PMK-NY)*
622 3rd Ave Fl 8
New York, NY 10017-6707, USA

Cowen, Robert E (Judge)
402 E State St
Trenton, NJ 08608-1507, USA

Cowen, Scott (Educator)
President's Office
New Orleans, LA 70118, USA

Cowen, Wilson (Judge)
717 Madison Pl NW
Washington, DC 20439-0001, USA

Cowen, Zelman (Attorney, Attorney General, Educator, General)
4 Treasury Pl
East Melbourne, VIC 3002, AUSTRALIA

Cowens, Dave (Athlete, Basketball Player)
2600 Center Ave
Fort Lauderdale, FL 33308-7514, USA

Cowher, Bill (Athlete, Football Coach, Football Player)
1225 Briar Patch Ln
Raleigh, NC 27615-6902, USA

Cowhill, William J (Admiral)
9428 Vernon Dr
Great Falls, VA 22066-2227, USA

Cowick, Bruce (Athlete, Hockey Player)
2953 Cressida Crst
Victoria, BC V9B 5W7, Canada

Cowie, Colin (Entertainer)
568 Broadway Sue 705
New York, NY 10012, USA

Cowie, Lennox L (Astronomer)
2600 Campus Rd
Honolulu, HI 96822-2224, USA

Cowley, Joe (Athlete, Baseball Player)
904 Andover Grn
Lexington, KY 40509-2929, USA

Cowlings, Al (Athlete, Football Player)
PO Box 1064
Pacific Palisades, CA 90272-1064, USA

Cowper, Nicola (Actor)
169 Queens Gate #A8
London SW7 5EH, UNITED KINGDOM(UK)

Cowper, Stephen C (Steve) (Ex-Governor)
2301 McGregor Ct
Vienna, VA 22182-5235, USA

Cowsill, Susan (Musician)
c/o Valerie Turner Polishook *V Public Relations LLC*
PO Box 341810
Bethesda, MD 20827-1810, USA

Cox, Alex (Actor, Director)
9560 Wilshire Blvd Ste 500
Beverly Hills, CA 90212-2401, USA

Cox, Billy (Athlete, Football Player)
4227 64th Dr E
Sarasota, FL 34243-7940, USA

Cox, Bobby (Athlete, Baseball Player, Coach)
c/o Staff Member *Atlanta Braves*
755 Hank Aaron Dr SW
Atlanta, GA 30315-1120, USA

Cox, Brian (Actor)
18-21 Jermyn St
London SW1Y 6NB, UNITED KINGDOM (UK)

Cox, Brian (Scientist)
P.O. Box 67130
London SW11 9ET, UK

Cox, Bryan (Athlete, Football Player)
66 Meeker Dr
Florham Park, NJ 07932-1546, USA

Cox, C Jay (Director, Producer, Writer)
c/o Scott Zimmerman *Evolution Entertainment (LA)*
901 N Highland Ave
Los Angeles, CA 90038-2412, USA

Cox, Casey (Athlete, Baseball Player)
2840 La Concha Dr
Clearwater, FL 33762-2203, USA

Cox, Charles C (Government Official)
332 S Michigan Ave
Chicago, IL 60604-4308, USA

Cox, Charlie (Actor)
c/o Nick Frenkel *3 Arts Entertainment Inc*
9460 Wilshire Blvd Fl 7
Beverly Hills, CA 90212-2713, USA

Cox, Chris (Musician)
c/o Staff Member *Diva Central Inc*
7510 W Sunset Blvd Ste 1445
Los Angeles, CA 90046-3408, USA

Cox, Christina (Actor)
3400 W Riverside Dr # 600
Burbank, CA 91505-4669, USA

Cox, Danny (Motivational Speaker, Writer)
17381 Bonner Dr
Tustin, CA 92780-1837, USA

Cox, Danny B (Athlete, Baseball Player)
306 Feagin Mill Rd
Warner Robins, GA 31088-6208, USA

Cox, Darron (Athlete, Baseball Player)
13681 Stuart St
Broomfield, CO 80023-5527, USA

Cox, David R (Doctor, Misc)
Human Genome Center
Stanford, CA 94305, USA

Cox, Deborah (Musician, Songwriter)
c/o Lescelles Stephens *Deco Entertainment*
Prefers to be contacted via email or telephone
Fort Lauderdale, FL, USA

Cox, Emmett R (Judge)
113 Saint Joseph St
Mobile, AL 36602-3606, USA

Cox, Frederick W (Fred) (Athlete, Football Player)
401 E River St
Monticello, MN 55362-9397, USA

Cox, G David (Religious Leader)
PO Box 2420
Anderson, IN 46018-2420, USA

Cox, Glenn (Athlete, Baseball Player)
PO Box 432
Los Molinos, CA 96055-0432, USA

Cox, Harvey G Jr (Educator, Misc)
Divinity School
Cambridge, MA 2140, USA

Cox, Jeff (Athlete, Baseball Player)
2727 E Vanderhoof Dr
West Covina, CA 91791-2247, USA

Cox, Jennifer Elise (Actor)
c/o Lisa DiSante-Frank *DiSante Frank & Company*
10061 Riverside Dr # 377
Toluca Lake, CA 91602-2560, USA

Cox, Jim (Athlete, Baseball Player)
3971 E Barbarita Ave
Gilbert, AZ 85234-3236, USA

Cox, John (Athlete, Football Player)
4227 64th Dr E
Sarasota, FL 34243-7940, USA

Cox, Johnny (Athlete, Basketball Player, Coach)
849 N Main St
Hazard, KY 41701-1345, USA

Cox, Kris (Athlete, Golfer)
2009 Lunenburg Dr
Allen, TX 75013-4708, USA

Cox, Larry (Athlete, Football Player)
10326 Catlett Ln
La Porte, TX 77571-4218, USA

Cox, Lynne (Swimmer)
4141 Ball Rd # 142
Cypress, CA 90630-3465, USA

Cox, Mark (Tennis Player)
Oaks Astead Woods Astead
Surrey KT21 2ER, UNITED KINGDOM(UK)

Cox, Nathalie (Actor)
c/o Chuck James *International Creative Management (ICM-LA)*
10250 Constellation Blvd Fl 7
Los Angeles, CA 90067-6207, USA

Cox, Nikki (Actor)
9560 Wilshire Blvd Ste 500
Beverly Hills, CA 90212-2401, USA

Cox, Paul (Director)
1 Victoria Ave
Albert Park, VIC 3208, AUSTRALIA

Cox, Philip S (Architect)
469 Kent St
Sydney, NSW 2000, AUSTRALIA

Cox, Ralph (Athlete, Hockey Player)
1 Harborside Dr Ste 200S
East Boston, MA 02128-2905, USA

Cox, Richard
9200 W Sunset Blvd Ste 900
Los Angeles, CA 90069-3604

Cox, Richard Ian
8730 W Sunset Blvd Ste 480
Los Angeles, CA 90069-2277

Cox, Robert G (Business Person, Financier)
312 W 1st St
Sanford, FL 32771-1231, USA

Cox, Ronny (Actor)
13948 Magnolia Blvd
Sherman Oaks, CA 91423-1230, USA

Cox, Stephen J (Artist)
154 Barnsbury Road Islington
London N1 0ER, UNITED KINGDOM (UK)

Cox, Steve (Athlete, Baseball Player)
22678 Avenue 188
Strathmore, CA 93267-9680, USA

Cox, Steve (Athlete, Football Player)
1001 E Lakeshore Dr
Jonesboro, AR 72401-4352, USA

Cox, Ted (Athlete, Baseball Player)
3990 E Seward Rd
Guthrie, OK 73044-9854, USA

Cox, Terry (Athlete, Baseball Player)
PO Box 577
Capitan, NM 88316-0577, USA

Cox, Tom (Athlete, Football Player)
2121 S Mill Ave Apt 231
Tempe, AZ 85282-2138, USA

Cox, Tony (Actor)
c/o Staff Member *New Wave Entertainment (LA)*
2660 W Olive Ave
Burbank, CA 91505-4525, USA

Cox, Torrie (Athlete, Football Player)
42 NW 92nd St
Miami Shores, FL 33150-2227, USA

Cox, Veanne (Actor)
c/o Nyle Brenner *Brenner Management*
Prefers to be contacted via telephone or email
CA, USA

Cox, Vera
345 N Maple Dr Ste 397
Beverly Hills, CA 90210-5179

Cox, Warren J (Architect)
1025 Thomas Jefferson St NW
Washington, DC 20007-5201, USA

Cox Arquette, Courteney (Actor)
c/o Cynthia Pett-Dante *Brillstein Entertainment Partners*
9150 Wilshire Blvd Ste 350
Beverly Hills, CA 90212-3453, USA

Coxe, Craig (Athlete, Hockey Player)
45 Rollins Pl
Laguna Niguel, CA 92677-4137, USA

Coyle, Eric (Athlete, Football Player)
397 County Road 26
Longmont, CO 80504-9515, USA

Coyle, Nadine (Actor, Musician)
c/o Julie Colbert *WmE2 (Endeavor-LA)*
9601 Wilshire Blvd Fl 3
Beverly Hills, CA 90210-5219, USA

Coyle, Ross (Athlete, Football Player)
PO Box 68
Blanchard, OK 73010-0068, USA

Coyne, Colleen (Athlete, Hockey Player)
267 Lake Shore Dr
East Falmouth, MA 02536-2701, USA

Coyote, Peter (Actor)
c/o Stephanie Simon *Untitled Entertainment (LA)*
350 S Beverly Dr Ste 200
Beverly Hills, CA 90212-4819, USA

Cozler, Jimmy (Musician, Songwriter, Writer)
745 5th Ave # 600
New York, NY 10151-0099, USA

Cozzarelli, Nicholas R (Biologist)
Biology
Berkeley, CA 94720-0001, USA

Crabb, Claude (Athlete, Football Player)
49851 Wayne St
Indio, CA 92201, USA

Crabbe, Cullen (Cuffy) (Actor)
9437 N 122nd Pl
Scottsdale, AZ 85259-6020, USA

Crable, Bob (Athlete, Football Player)
564 Miami Trace Ct
Loveland, OH 45140-8021, USA

Crabtree, Eric (Athlete, Football Player)
3101 Walnut St # 1
Denver, CO 80205-2326, USA

Crabtree, Michael (Athlete, Football Player)
c/o Eugene Parker *Maximum Sports Management*
6435 W Jefferson Blvd # 197
Fort Wayne, IN 46804-6203, USA

Crabtree, Teresa (Stylist)
c/o Staff Member *Crews*
828 Clemont Dr NE
Atlanta, GA 30306-3694, USA

Crabtree, Tim (Athlete, Baseball Player)
1503 Kingswood Ln
Colleyville, TX 76034-5580, USA

Craddock, Bantz (General)
Commander US Southern Command
Miami
APO, AA 34001, USA

Craddock, Billy Crash
PO Box 428
Portland, TN 37148-0428

Craddock, Billy (Crash) (Musician, Songwriter, Writer)
3007 Old Martinsville Rd
Greensboro, NC 27455, USA

Cradle, Rickey (Athlete, Baseball Player)
1311 Dry Gap Pike
Knoxville, TN 37918-9785, USA

Cradle Of Filth (Music Group, Musician)
c/o Staff Member *In Phase Management*
P O Box 756A
Surbiton KT6 6YZ, UK

Craft, Chris
14919 Village Elm St
Houston, TX 77062-2914

Craft, Jason (Athlete, Football Player)
11688 Amistad Ct
Jacksonville, FL 32256-2925, USA

Craft, Sammi (Actor)
c/o Staff Member *Paradigm (LA)*
360 N Crescent Dr
Beverly Hills, CA 90210-4874, USA

Craft, Terry (Athlete, Baseball Player)
16 Sheldon Ave
Castle Rock, CO 80104-8820, USA

Crafter, Jane (Athlete, Golfer)
317 W Almeria Rd
Phoenix, AZ 85003-1140, USA

Crafts, Hannah (Writer)
c/o Staff Member *Creative Artists Agency (CAA-LA)*
2000 Avenue of the Stars Ste 100
Los Angeles, CA 90067-4705, USA

Cragg, Anthony D (Tony) (Artist)
Adolf-Vorwerk-Str 24
Wuppertal 42287, GERMANY

Craggs, George (Soccer Player)
6223 6th Ave NW
Seattle, WA 98107-2131, USA

Craig, Adam Jamal (Actor)
c/o Christopher Rockwell *Global Creative*
1051 Cole Ave # B
Los Angeles, CA 90038-2601, USA

Craig, Daniel (Actor)
c/o Robin Baum *Slate Public Relations*
9000 W Sunset Blvd Ste 915
West Hollywood, CA 90069-5809, USA

Craig, Demeyune (Athlete, Football Player)
5102 31st Ave
Valley, AL 36854-5214, USA

Craig, Elijah (Actor)
9200 W Sunset Blvd Ste 900
Los Angeles, CA 90069-3604, USA

Craig, Jenny (Doctor, Misc)
5770 Fleet St
Carlsbad, CA 92008-4700, USA

Craig, Jim (Athlete, Hockey Player)
319 1st St W
Saint Petersburg, FL 33715-1706, USA

Craig, Michael (Actor)
Prince of Wales Coventry St
London W1V 7FE, UNITED KINGDOM (UK)

Craig, Mike (Athlete, Hockey Player)
29907 County Road 3
Merrifield, MN 56465-4402, USA

Craig, Neal (Athlete, Football Player)
2231 Crane Ave
Cincinnati, OH 45207-1322, USA

Craig, Paco (Athlete, Football Player)
23668 Marguerite Cir
Moreno Valley, CA 92557-2853, USA

Craig, Pete (Athlete, Baseball Player)
5915 Carmel Ln
Raleigh, NC 27609-3953, USA

Craig, Richard (Inventor)
902 Battelle Blvd
Richland, WA 99354-1793, USA

Craig, Roger (Athlete, Baseball Player, Coach)
16327 Bassett Ct
Ramona, CA 92065-4247, USA

Craig, Roger T (Athlete, Football Player)
271 Vista Verde Way
Portola Valley, CA 94028-8149, USA

Craig, Wendy
29 Roehampton Gate
London, ENGLAND SW15 5JR

Craig, William (Government Official)
23 Annadale Ave
Belfast BT7 3JJ, NORTHERN IRELAND

Craig, William (Bill) (Swimmer)
PO Box 629
Newport Beach, CA 92661-0629, USA

Craig, Yvonne (Actor)
PO Box 827
Pacific Palisades, CA 90272-0827, USA

Craig of Radley, David B (Misc)
Westminster
London SW1A 0PW, UNITED KINGDOM (UK)

Craighead, John (Athlete, Hockey Player)
2595 Barnet Hwy
Coquitlam, BC V3E 1K9, Canada

Craighead, John J (Misc)
5125 Orchard Ave
Missoula, MT 59803-2524, USA

Crain, Jesse (Athlete, Baseball Player)
15 Greenlaw Ct
Sugar Land, TX 77479-2994, USA

Crain, Keith E (Publisher)
1400 Woodbridge St
Detroit, MI 48207-3110, USA

Crain, Rance (Publisher)
360 N Michigan Ave
Chicago, IL 60601-3814, USA

Crain, William (Director)
610 Santa Monica Blvd Ste 202
Santa Monica, CA 90401-1645, USA

Crais, Robert (Writer)
12829 Landale St
Studio City, CA 91604-1352, USA

Cram, Jerry (Athlete, Baseball Player)
33015 Victoria Brooke Ln
Lake Elsinore, CA 92530-5467, USA

Cram, Stephen (Steve) (Athlete, Track Athlete)
General Delivery
Jarrow, UNITED KINGDOM (UK)

Cramer, Douglas
738 Sarbonne Rd
Los Angeles, CA 90077-3302

Cramer, Grant (Actor)
1910 Holmby Ave Apt 1
Los Angeles, CA 90025-5936, USA

Cramer, James (Television Host)
c/o Staff Member *CNBC*
900 Sylvan Ave
Englewood Cliffs, NJ 07632-3312, USA

Cramer, Peggy (Baseball Player)
1160 E Old Andrew Johnson Hwy
Talbott, TN 37877-3103, USA

Cramer, Richard Ben (Journalist, Writer)
400 N Broad St
Philadelphia, PA 19130-4015, USA

Cramps, The (Music Group)
c/o Stormy Shepherd *Leave Home Booking*
1400 Foothill Dr Ste 34
Salt Lake City, UT 84108-2392, USA

Crampton, Barbara (Actor)
6500 Wilshire Blvd # 550
Los Angeles, CA 90048-4920, USA

Crampton, Bruce (Athlete, Golfer)
225 Winter Crest Ln
Severna Park, MD 21146-3104, USA

Cramton, Roger C (Attorney, Attorney General, General)
49 Highgate Cir
Ithaca, NY 14850-1486, USA

Cranberries, The (Music Group)
c/o Staff Member *Creative Artists Agency (CAA-LA)*
2000 Avenue of the Stars Ste 100
Los Angeles, CA 90067-4705, USA

Crandall, Bruce
PO Box 736
Manchester, WA 98353-0736, USA

Crandall, Delmar W (Del) (Athlete, Baseball Player, Coach)
1355 Clear Lake Pl
Brea, CA 92821-2807, USA

Crane, Ben (Athlete, Golfer)
2223 Cedar Elm Ter
Westlake, TX 76262-9028, USA

Crane, Brian (Cartoonist)
2766 Dome Ct
Sparks, NV 89436-4063, USA

Crane, David (Director, Producer, Writer)
c/o Staff Member *Bright Kauffman Crane Productions*
4000 Warner Blvd Bldg 160 PMB 750
Burbank, CA 91522

Crane, Gary (Athlete, Football Player)
6 Greystone
Bentonville, AR 72712-4098, USA

Crane, Horace R (Physicist)
66 Cavanaugh Lake Rd
Chelsea, MI 48118-9732, USA

Crane, John (Writer)
c/o Staff Member *Agency for the Performing Arts (APA-LA)*
405 S Beverly Dr Ste 500
Beverly Hills, CA 90212-4425, USA

Crane, Kenneth G (Director)
6627 Lindenhurst Ave
Los Angeles, CA 90048-4611, USA

Crane, Paul (Athlete, Football Player)
12 N Monterey St
Mobile, AL 36604-1317, USA

Crane, Tony (Actor)
9200 W Sunset Blvd Ste 1125
Los Angeles, CA 90069-3610, USA

Cranston, Bryan (Actor)
c/o Sarah Clossey *United Talent Agency (UTA)*
9560 Wilshire Blvd Fl 5
Beverly Hills, CA 90212-2400, USA

Cranston, Toller (Figure Skater)
1st Clair Ave E # 700
Toronto, ON M4T 2V7, CANADA

Crapo, Mike (Senator)
239 Dirksen Senate
Washington, DC 20510-0001, USA

Crash Test Dummies (Music Group, Musician)
c/o Sandy Rogers *Deep Fried Records*
1146 Lakeshore Rd PO Box 195
Selkirk, ON N0A 1P0, Canada

Crashley, Bart (Athlete, Hockey Player)
61 Buchanan St
Barrie, ON L4M 6B4, Canada

Cravaack, Chip (Congressman, Politician)
508 Cannon Hob
Washington, DC 20515-2210, USA

Craven, Bill (Athlete, Football Player)
4363 N Buckhead Dr NE
Atlanta, GA 30342-3451, USA

Craven, Gemma (Actor)
c/o Jonathan Arun *Jonathan Arun*
Studio 9 33 Stanary St.
London SE11 4AA, UK

Craven, Matt (Actor)
c/o Brad Schenck *Paradigm (LA)*
360 N Crescent Dr
Beverly Hills, CA 90210-4874, USA

Craven, Murray (Athlete, Hockey Player)
2802 Rest Haven Dr
Whitefish, MT 59937, USA

Craven, Ricky (Race Car Driver)
122 Knob Hill Rd
Mooresville, NC 28117-6847, USA

Craven, Wes (Director)
c/o Mike Simpson *WmE2 (Endeavor-LA)*
9601 Wilshire Blvd Fl 3
Beverly Hills, CA 90210-5219, USA

Craver, Aaron (Athlete, Football Player)
821 W Maple St
Compton, CA 90220-1829, USA

Crawford, Bennie (Hank) Jr (Composer, Musician)
7942 W Bell Rd # 51 # C5
Glendale, AZ 85308-8708, USA

Crawford, Bob (Athlete, Hockey Player)
19 Cliff Dr
Avon, CT 06001-3413, USA

Crawford, Brad (Athlete, Football Player)
RR2
Winamac, IL 46996, USA

Crawford, Bryce L Jr (Misc)
3220 Lake Johanna Blvd # 58
Saint Paul, MN 55112-7944, USA

Crawford, Carl (Athlete, Baseball Player)
12515 Silverglen Estates Dr
Houston, TX 77014-2843, USA

Crawford, Carlos (Athlete, Baseball Player)
1605 Martin Luther King Ave E
Bradenton, FL 34208-2801, USA

Crawford, Chace (Actor)
c/o Eric Podwall *Podwall Entertainment*
710 N Orlando Ave Apt 203
Los Angeles, CA 90069-5549, USA

Crawford, Cheyne (Actor)
c/o Amy Slomovits *Flutie Entertainment (LA)*
9320 Wilshire Blvd Ste 202
Beverly Hills, CA 90212-3217, USA

Crawford, Christina (Writer)
7 Springs Farm Sanders Rd
Tensed, ID 83870, USA

Crawford, Cindy (Actor, Model)
c/o Annett Wolf *WKT Public Relations (WKT-LA)*
9350 Wilshire Blvd Ste 450
Beverly Hills, CA 90212-3230, USA

Crawford, Clayne (Actor)
c/o Alex Cole *Elevate Entertainment*
10100 Santa Monica Blvd Ste 300
Los Angeles, CA 90067-4107, USA

Crawford, Ed (Athlete, Football Player)
204 Country Club Rd
Oxford, MS 38655-2606, USA

Crawford, Eric (Congressman, Politician)
1408 Longworth Hob
Washington, DC 20515-3102, USA

Crawford, Fred (Athlete, Basketball Player)
24 W Lawn Dr
Teaneck, NJ 07666-5612, USA

Crawford, Hilton (Athlete, Football Player)
262 Hagen St
Buffalo, NY 14215-3959, USA

Crawford, Jamal (Basketball Player)
1901 W Madison St
Chicago, IL 60612-2459, USA

Crawford, Jennifer (Stylist)
c/o Staff Member *Sydney Represents*
280 Mott St
New York, NY 10012-3439, USA

Crawford, Jerry (Athlete, Baseball Player)
111 9th St E
Saint Petersburg, FL 33715-2204, USA

Crawford, Jim (Athlete, Baseball Player)
4370 E Gemini Pl
Chandler, AZ 85249-5829, USA

Crawford, Joan (Athlete, Basketball Player)
4748 S Harvard Ave Apt 80
Tulsa, OK 74135-3018, USA

Crawford, Joe (Athlete, Baseball Player)
5428 US Highway 50
Hillsboro, OH 45133-7533, USA

Crawford, Johnny (Actor, Musician)
PO Box 1851
Los Angeles, CA 90078-1851, USA

Crawford, Keith (Athlete, Football Player)
RR 5 Box 5008
Palestine, TX 75801, USA

Crawford, Kirsty (Musician)
c/o Zoe Sobol *Rocket Music & Management*
7 Albert Studios
London SW11 4QD, UK

Crawford, Lou (Athlete, Hockey Player)
50 New Gower St
St. John's, NL A1C 1J3, Canada

Crawford, Marc (Athlete, Coach, Hockey Player)
c/o Staff Member *Los Angeles Kings*
1111 S Figueroa St Ste 3100
Los Angeles, CA 90015-1333, USA

Crawford, Michael (Actor, Musician)
c/o Steve Levine *International Creative Management (ICM-LA)*
10250 Constellation Blvd Fl 7
Los Angeles, CA 90067-6207, USA

Crawford, Missy Neville (Stylist)
c/o Staff Member *Elite Model Management/Atlanta*
1708 Peachtree St NW Ste 210
Atlanta, GA 30309-2416, USA

Crawford, Paxton (Athlete, Baseball Player)
536 Highway 92
Plumerville, AR 72127-8875, USA

Crawford, Rachael (Actor)
c/o Staff Member *Coast to Coast Talent Group*
3350 Barham Blvd
Los Angeles, CA 90068-1404, USA

Crawford, Randy (Musician)
911 Park St SW
Grand Rapids, MI 49504-6241, USA

Crawford, Rufus (Jake) (Athlete, Baseball Player)
7900 Shannon Ln
N Richlnd Hls, TX 76180-5735, USA

Crawford, Steve (Athlete, Baseball Player)
6122 E 480
Salina, OK 74365-2496, USA

Crawford, Vernon (Athlete, Football Player)
2001 Gemini St Apt 1305
Houston, TX 77058-2062, USA

Crawford, William J (War Hero)
28520 Country Road 14
Rocky Ford, CO 81067, USA

Crawford-Indri, Marisa (Stylist)
c/o Staff Member *Tricia Joyce Inc*
79 Chambers St Fl 2
New York, NY 10007-1824, USA

Crawley, Pauline (Baseball Player)
68670 Raposa Rd
Cathedral City, CA 92234-8148, USA

Cray, Robert (Musician)
PO Box 170429
San Francisco, CA 94117-0429, USA

Craybas, Jill (Athlete, Tennis Player)
2603 Delaware St
Huntington Beach, CA 92648-2583, USA

Craymer, Judy (Producer)
1634 Broadway
New York, NY 10019-6852, USA

Crayton, Patrick (Athlete, Football Player)
817 La Jolla
Irving, TX 75039-3046, USA

Crazy Mohan (Actor)
5 Chokkalingam Street Mandavelli
Chennai, TN 600 028, INDIA

Creamer, Paula (Athlete, Golfer)
c/o Jay Burton *IMG (Cleveland)*
1360 E 9th St Ste 100
Cleveland, OH 44114-1730, USA

Creamer, Roger W (Writer)
180 E Hartsdale Ave Apt 2E
Hartsdale, NY 10530-3540, USA

Creamer, Timothy J (Astronaut)
5103 Carefree Dr
League City, TX 77573-3195, USA

Crear, Mark (Athlete, Track Athlete)
1751 Pinnacle Dr Ste 1500
McLean, VA 22102-3833, USA

Creavalle, Laura (Misc)
230 Danforth Ave
Toronto ON M4K 1N4, CANADA

Creber, William
140 Hollister Ave Apt 3
Santa Monica, CA 90405-3534

Crecion, Gabe (Athlete, Football Player)
4800 Coyote Wells Cir
Westlake Village, CA 91362-4712, USA

Crede, Joe (Athlete, Baseball Player)
42 Dry Creek Trl
Linn, MO 65051-2617, USA

Creech, Bob (Athlete, Football Player)
6323 Park Ln
Dallas, TX 75225-2108, USA

Creech, Sharon (Writer)
10 E 53rd St
New York

Creech, Wilbur L (General)
20 Quail Run Rd
Henderson, NV 89014-2147, USA

Creed, Clifford Ann (Athlete, Golfer)
240 N Rosemont Dr
Sulphur, LA 70665-7994, USA

Creek, Doug (Athlete, Baseball Player)
12440 Oakview Ct
Newburg, MD 20664-2209, USA

Creekmur, Louis (Lou) (Athlete, Football Player)
7521 SW 1st St
Plantation, FL 33317-3201, USA

Creel, Donna (Stylist)
1188 Meadows Rd
Luthersville, GA 30251, USA

Creel, Gavin (Actor)
c/o Amy Brownstein *Brownstein & Associates Inc*
101 W End Ave Apt 11U
New York, NY 10023-6321, USA

Creel, Keith (Athlete, Baseball Player)
527 Trail Ridge Dr
Duncanville, TX 75116-2433, USA

Creel, Monica (Actor)
c/o Mike Eistenstadt *Amsel, Eisenstadt & Frazier Talent Agency (AEF)*
5055 Wilshire Blvd Ste 860
Los Angeles, CA 90036-6108, USA

Cregar, Bill (Athlete, Football Player)
22 Locust Ct
Spring Lake, NJ 07762-2109, USA

Creighton, Adam (Athlete, Hockey Player)
5202 Spectacular Bid Dr
Wesley Chapel, FL 33544-1576, USA

Creighton, Jim (Athlete, Basketball Player)
5297 S Geneva St
Englewood, CO 80111-6210, USA

Creighton, Joanne V (Educator)
President's Office
South Hadley, MA 1075, USA

Creighton, John D (Publisher)
333 King St E
Toronto, ON M5A 3X5, CANADA

Creighton, John O (Astronaut)
2111 SW 174th St
Burien, WA 98166-3259, USA

Creighton Sr, Dave (Athlete, Hockey Player)
5202 Spectacular Bid Dr
Wesley Chapel, FL 33544-1576, USA

Creme, Lol (Musician)
Heronden Hall Tenferden
Kent, UNITED KINGDOM (UK)

Cremins, Bobby (Coach)
150 Bobby John Rd
Atlanta, GA 30332-0001, USA

Crenkovski, Branko (Prime Minister)
Dame Grueva 6
Skopje 9100, MACEDONIA

Crennel, Carl (Athlete, Football Player)
1501 Dupont St
Conway, PA 15027-1329, USA

Crennel, Romeo (Athlete, Football Coach, Football Player)
80 Cayman Pl
Palm Beach Gardens, FL 33418-8096, USA

Crenshaw, Ander (Congressman, Politician)
440 Cannon Hob
Washington, DC 20515-1504, USA

Crenshaw, Ben (Athlete, Golfer)
PO Box 50568
Austin, TX 78763-0568, USA

Crenshaw, Leon (Athlete, Football Player)
4700 Velpoe Dr
Columbus, GA 31907-6515, USA

Crenshaw, Marshall (Musician)
c/o Staff Member *MCT Management*
520 8th Ave Rm 2205
New York, NY 10018-4160, USA

Crenshaw, Willis (Athlete, Football Player)
21 Carey Dr
Woodstock, NY 12498, USA

Creole, Kid (Musician)
315 S Beverly Dr Ste 407
Beverly Hills, CA 90212-4301, USA

Creskoff, Rebecca (Actor)
c/o Steven Levy *Framework Entertainment (LA)*
9057 Nemo St Ste C
West Hollywood, CA 90069-5511, USA

Crespin, Regine (Opera Singer)
3 Ave Frochet
Paris 75009, FRANCE

Crespino, Robert (Athlete, Football Player)
109 Heatherdown Rd
Decatur, GA 30030-3817, USA

Crespo, Elvis (Musician)
c/o Staff Member *Sony Music Miami*
605 Lincoln Rd Ste 700
Miami Beach, FL 33139-2901, USA

Crespo, Felipe (Athlete, Baseball Player)
80 Calle Arboleda Del Rio
Gurabo, PR 00778-5013, USA

Cressend, Jack (Athlete, Baseball Player)
2409 W Ranch Dr
Friendswood, TX 77546-5579, USA

Cressman, Dave (Athlete, Hockey Player)
200 University Avenue Attn Hockey Program W
Waterloo, ON N2L 3G1, Canada

Cresson, Edith (Prime Minister)
Mairie
Chatellerault Cedex 86018, FRANCE

Creswell, Smiley (Athlete, Football Player)
1 Academy Way
Monroe, WA 98272-2006, USA

Cretler, Jean-Luc (Skier)
153 Ave du Marechal Lereic BP 20
Bourq Saint Maurice 73700, FRANCE

Creutz, Edward C (Physicist)
PO Box 2757
Rancho Santa Fe, CA 92067-2757, USA

Crevalle, Laura
PO Box 557
Old Orchard Beach, ME 04064-0557

Crew, Amanda (Actor)
c/o Vickie Petronio *Play Management*
807 Powell St Suite 220
Vancouver V6A 1H7, Canada

Crew-Cuts, The
29 Cedar St
Cresskill, NJ 07626-2508

Crewdson, John M (Journalist)
435 N Michigan Ave
Chicago, IL 60611-4066, USA

Crewe, Albert V (Physicist)
PO Box 2851
Ruidoso, NM 88355-2851, USA

Crews, David P (Biologist)
Zoology Dept
Austin, TX 78712, USA

Crews, Gina (Reality TV Star)
10103 W State Road 235
Alachua, FL 32615-4946, USA

Crews, Harry E (Writer)
English
Gainesville, FL 32611-0001, USA

Crews, Philip (Misc)
Chemistry Dept
Santa Cruz, CA 99504, USA

Crews, Terry (Actor)
c/o Pamela Kohl *3 Arts Entertainment Inc*
9460 Wilshire Blvd Fl 7
Beverly Hills, CA 90212-2713, USA

Crewson, Wendy (Actor)
438 Queen St E
Toronto, ON M5A 1T4, CANADA

Crha, Jiri (Athlete, Hockey Player)
16390 Braeburn Ridge Trl
Delray Beach, FL 33446-9508, USA

Crialese, Emanuele (Director)
c/o Staff Member *WmE2 (Endeavor-LA)*
9601 Wilshire Blvd Fl 3
Beverly Hills, CA 90210-5219, USA

Cribbins, Barnard (Actor)
Hamm Court
Weybridge, Surrey, UNITED KINGDOM (UK)

Cribbs, Joe S (Athlete, Football Player)
418 Brook Highland Ln
Birmingham, AL 35242-5304, USA

Cribbs, Joshua (Athlete, Football Player)
9333 W Hampton Dr
North Royalton, OH 44133-2884, USA

Cricket Team, Australian (Cricketer)
60 Jolimont St
Jolimont, Victoria 3002, Australia

Cricketts, The
3322 W End Ave # 520
Nashville, TN 37203-1031

Crickhowell of Pont Esgob, Nicholas E (Politician)
4 Henning St
London SW11 3DR, UNITED KINGDOM (UK)

Crider, Melissa (Actor)
c/o Dan Spilo *Industry Entertainment Partners*
955 Carrillo Dr Ste 300
Los Angeles, CA 90048-5400, USA

Crider, Melissa (Actor)
10100 Santa Monica Blvd Ste 2500
Los Angeles, CA 90067-4116, USA

Crier, Catherine (Correspondent, Television Host)
600 3rd Ave
New York, NY 10016-1901, USA

Crile, Susan (Artist)
168 W 86th St
New York, NY 10024-4022, USA

Crim, Chuck (Athlete, Baseball Player)
50039 Golden Horse Dr
Oakhurst, CA 93644-9497, USA

Crimian, Jack (Athlete, Baseball Player)
3012 Green St
Claymont, DE 19703-2026, USA

Cripe, Dave (Athlete, Baseball Player)
1835 Montara Way
San Jacinto, CA 92583-5832, USA

Crippen, Robert L (Astronaut)
781 Harbour Isle Pl
West Palm Beach, FL 33410-4408, USA

Crippen, Susie (Stylist)
c/o Staff Member *Exclusive Artists Mgmt*
7700 W Sunset Blvd Ste 205
Los Angeles, CA 90046-3913, USA

Criqui, Don (Sportscaster)
51 W 52nd St
New York, NY 10019-6119, USA

Criscione, Dave (Athlete, Baseball Player)
87 Hamlet St
Fredonia, NY 14063-2143, USA

Crisman, Joel (Athlete, Football Player)
8823 Creekside Way Apt 1836
Highlands Ranch, CO 80129-1593, USA

Crisostomo, Manny (Journalist, Photographer)
PO Box Dn
Hagatna, GU 96932-7643, USA

Crisp, Covelli (Coco) (Athlete, Baseball Player)
804 N Irena Ave
Redondo Beach, CA 90277-2224, USA

Crisp, Terry A (Athlete, Coach, Hockey Player)
805 Cherry Laurel Ct
Nashville, TN 37215-6173, USA

Crispin, Anne C (Writer)
175 5th Ave
New York, NY 10010-7703, USA

Criss, Charles (Athlete, Basketball Player)
4310 Melanie Ln
Atlanta, GA 30349-2849, USA

Criss, Darren (Actor)
c/o Ricky Rollins *Schumacher Management*
1122 San Vicente Blvd
Santa Monica, CA 90402-2008, USA

Criss, Peter (Musician)
c/o Staff Member *Josselyne Herman & Associates*
345 E 56th St Apt 3B
New York, NY 10022-3745, USA

Crist, Charlie (Attorney)
PO Box 311
Tallahassee, FL 32302-0311, USA

Crist, Chuck (Athlete, Football Player)
PO Box 369
Greenhurst, NY 14742-0369, USA

Crist, George B (General)
51 W 52nd St
New York, NY 10019-6119, USA

Crist, Judith (Journalist)
180 Riverside Dr
New York, NY 10024-1021, USA

Cristal, Linda (Actor)
9129 Hazen Dr
Beverly Hills, CA 90210-1825, USA

Cristofer, Michael (Director, Writer)
c/o Geyer Kosinski *Media Talent Group*
9200 W Sunset Blvd Ste 550
Los Angeles, CA 90069-3611, USA

Cristol, Stanley J (Misc)
1638 W 3rd Ave
Durango, CO 81301-4912, USA

Criswell, Jeff (Athlete, Football Player)
1101 Walnut St
Kansas City, MO 64106-2110, USA

Criswell, Ray (Athlete, Football Player)
2216 Jones Rd
Jacksonville, FL 32220-1210, USA

Critchfield, Charles L (Physicist)
PO Box 993
Los Alamos, NM 87544-0993, USA

Critchfield, Russell (Athlete, Basketball Player)
7 Patches Dr
Chico, CA 95928-4353, USA

Crite, Winston (Athlete, Basketball Player)
8812 Heely Ct
Bakersfield, CA 93311-1923, USA

Critelli, Michael (Business Person)
1 Elmcroft Rd
Stamford, CT 06926-0700, USA

Criter, Ken (Athlete, Football Player)
PO Box 441343
Aurora, CO 80044-1343, USA

Crittenden, Ray (Athlete, Football Player)
4532 Commons Dr
Annandale, VA 22003-4962, USA

Crivello, Anthony (Actor)
c/o Neil Bagg *Don Buchwald & Associates Inc (LA)*
6500 Wilshire Blvd Ste 2200
Los Angeles, CA 90048-4942, USA

Croce, A J
1027 Meade Ave
San Diego, CA 92116-1038, USA

Croce, Pat (Basketball Player, Business Person, Sportscaster)
c/o Staff Member *WmE2 (WMA-LA)*
1 William Morris Pl
Beverly Hills, CA 90212-4261, USA

Croce, Stefania (Athlete, Golfer)
222 W Commack Ave # 208
Winter Park, FL 32789, USA

Crocicchia, James (Athlete, Football Player)
11 Lanesboro Rd
Ladera Ranch, CA 92694-0712, USA

Crocker, Chris (Actor, Reality TV Star)
4040 Vineland Ave Ste 105
Studio City, CA 91604-3350, USA

Crocker, Dillard (Athlete, Basketball Player)
5601 Holiday Park Blvd
North Port, FL 34287-2615, USA

Crocker, Mary Lou (Athlete, Golfer)
1403 Sutton Dr
Carrollton, TX 75006-2943, USA

Crockett, Bobby (Athlete, Football Player)
PO Box 26
Harriet, AR 72639-0026, USA

Crockett, Donald (Ray) (Athlete, Football Player)
1526 Highland Lakes Dr
Keller, TX 76248-3285, USA

Crockett, Gibson (Cartoonist)
4713 Great Oak Rd
Rockville, MD 20853-1607, USA

Crockett, Monte (Athlete, Football Player)
2696 Halleck Dr
Columbus, OH 43209-3220, USA

Crockett, Willis (Athlete, Football Player)
493 Bojo Ella Dr
Douglas, GA 31533-0607, USA

Crockett, Zack (Athlete, Football Player)
6136 NW 120th Ter
Coral Springs, FL 33076-1913, USA

Croel, Mike (Athlete, Football Player)
8305 Lookout Mountain Ave
Los Angeles, CA 90046-1548, USA

Croft, Dwayne (Opera Singer)
165 W 57th St
New York, NY 10019-2201, USA

Crofts, Dash (Musician, Songwriter, Writer)
2756 N Green Valley Pkwy
Henderson, NV 89014-2120, USA

Croghan, Emma-Kate (Director)
500 Oxford St
Bondi Junction, NSW 2022, AUSTRALIA

Croker, Stephen B (Steve) (General)
2 Byford Ct
Chestertown, MD 21620-1642, USA

Croll, Jimmy (Misc)
420 Fair Hill Dr # 1
Elkton, MD 21921-2573, USA

Cromartie, Warren (Athlete, Baseball Player)
c/o Staff Member *Montreal Expos*
4549 Avenue Pierre de Coubertin
Montreal
Quebec H1V 3N7, CANADA

Crombeen, Mike (Athlete, Hockey Player)
817 Foxcroft Blvd
Newmarket, ON L3X 1M8, Canada

Crombie, Jonathan (Actor)
111 Davenport Rd
Toronto, ON M5R 3R3, CANADA

Cromer, D T (Athlete, Baseball Player)
1210 Whitney St
Columbia, SC 29201-4492, USA

Cromer, Tripp (Athlete, Baseball Player)
32 W Tombee Ln
Columbia, SC 29209-0844, USA

Cromwell, James (Actor)
c/o Ro Diamond *SDB Partners Inc*
1801 Avenue of the Stars Ste 902
Los Angeles, CA 90067-5981, USA

Cromwell, Nolan (Athlete, Coach, Football Coach, Football Player)
2624 140th Ave NE
Bellevue, WA 98005-1824, USA

Cron, Chris (Athlete, Baseball Player)
14879 S 43rd Pl
Phoenix, AZ 85044-6788, USA

Cronan, Pete (Athlete, Football Player)
13 Saddle Hill Rd
Hopkinton, MA 01748-1151, USA

Cronbach, Lee J (Educator)
2614 Oregon St
Union City, CA 94587-4320, USA

Crone, Ray (Athlete, Baseball Player)
508 Panorama
Waxahachie, TX 75165-5919, USA

Cronenberg, David (Actor)
c/o Renee Tab *Artist Talent Management*
629 Radcliffe Ave
Pacific Palisades, CA 90272-4332, USA

Cronenweth, Regina
5410 Wilshire Blvd # 227
Los Angeles, CA 90036-4216

Cronin, Eugene (Athlete, Football Player)
2445 37th Ave
Sacramento, CA 95822-3613, USA

Cronin, James W (Nobel Prize Laureate)
5825 S Dorchester Ave
Chicago, IL 60637-1764, USA

Cronin, Kevin (Musician)
9229 W Sunset Blvd Ste 607
Los Angeles, CA 90069-3406, USA

Cronin, Mark (Producer)
c/o Staff Member *Mindless Entertainment*
6565 W Sunset Blvd Ste 301
Los Angeles, CA 90028-7232, USA

Cronin, Rachel (Actor)
c/o Lisa King *King Talent*
303-228 E 4th Ave
Vancouver V5T-1G5, CANADA

Cronin, Shawn (Athlete, Hockey Player)
4163 SE Oakland St
Stuart, FL 34997-5415, USA

Cronnenberg, David (Director)
244 Dupont St # 200
Toronto, ON M5R 1V7, CANADA

Cronyn, Christopher (Producer)
c/o Staff Member *Lichter Grossman Nichols Adler & Goodman*
9200 W Sunset Blvd Ste 1200
Los Angeles, CA 90069-3607, USA

Cronyn, Susan Cooper (Producer, Writer)
c/o Ron Bernstein *International Creative Management (ICM-LA)*
10250 Constellation Blvd Fl 7
Los Angeles, CA 90067-6207, USA

Crook, Edward Jr (Boxer)
4512 Moline Ave
Columbus, GA 31907-6625, USA

Crook & Chase
3201 Dickerson Pike
Nashville, TN 37207-2905

Crooke, Edward A (Business Person)
39 W Lexington St
Baltimore, MD 21201-3910, USA

Croom, Corey (Athlete, Football Player)
414 Lawrence St
Sandusky, OH 44870-2318, USA

Croom, Sylvester (Athlete, Coach, Football Player)
3909 12th St NE
Tuscaloosa, AL 35404-2004, USA

Crooms, Chris (Athlete, Football Player)
810 Landon Springs Ln
Spring, TX 77373-8461, USA

Cropper, Marshall (Athlete, Football Player)
2932 Fort Baker Dr SE
Washington, DC 20020-7222, USA

Crosbie, Annette
c/o Staff Member *Independent Talent Group (ITG-UK)*
Oxford House 76 Oxford St
London W1D 1BS, UK

Crosbie, John C (Politician)
235 Water St
Saint John's NF A1C 5L3, CANADA

Crosby, Alfred W (Historian)
2506 Bowman Ave
Austin, TX 78703-2314, USA

Crosby, Bobby (Athlete, Baseball Player)
11463 Anticost Way
Cypress, CA 90630-5429, USA

Crosby, Bubba (Athlete, Baseball Player)
439 Westmoreland St
Houston, TX 77006-4520, USA

Crosby, Caitlin (Musician)
c/o Gerry Cagle *Crysis Management*
8424 Santa Monica Blvd
West Hollywood, CA 90069-6233, USA

Crosby, Cleveland (Athlete, Football Player)
2703 Sandal Walk
Pearland, TX 77584-3365, USA

Crosby, David (Musician)
c/o Brent Smith *WmE2 (Endeavor-LA)*
9601 Wilshire Blvd Fl 3
Beverly Hills, CA 90210-5219, USA

Crosby, Denise (Actor, Model)
8242 Blackburn Ave
Los Angeles, CA 90048-4216, USA

Crosby, Ed (Athlete, Baseball Player)
6952 Brightwood Ln Apt 9
Garden Grove, CA 92845-2976, USA

Crosby, Elaine (Athlete, Golfer)
2580 Meadowbrook Ln
Jackson, MI 49201-7702, USA

Crosby, Kathryn
508 W Third St
Carson City, NV 89703-4242

Crosby, Kathryn Grant (Actor)
508 W Third St
Carson City, NV 89703-4242, USA

Crosby, Ken (Athlete, Baseball Player)
PO Box 680306
Park City, UT 84068-0306, USA

Crosby, Lucinda (Actor)
4942 Vineland Ave Ste 200
North Hollywood, CA 91601-5646, USA

Crosby, Mark
3500 W Olive Ave Ste 1400
Burbank, CA 91505-5512

Crosby, Mary
3500 W Olive Ave Ste 1400
Burbank, CA 91505-5512

Crosby, Norm (Actor, Comedian)
c/o Staff Member *WmE2 (WMA-LA)*
1 William Morris Pl
Beverly Hills, CA 90212-4261, USA

Crosby, Paul (Musician)
Plaza 535 Kings Road
London SW10 0S, UNITED KINGDOM (UK)

Crosby, Rob
PO Box 121551
Nashville, TN 37212-1551

Crosby, Robbin
8250 Grand View Dr
Los Angeles, CA 90046-1916

Crosby, Sidney (Athlete, Hockey Player)
c/o J P Barry *C A A Hockey*
822 11th Ave SW Suite 204
Calgary, AB T2R 0E5, Canada

Crosby, Sidney (Athlete, Hockey Player)
c/o Pat Brisson *Creative Artists Agency (CAA-LA)*
2000 Avenue of the Stars Ste 100
Los Angeles, CA 90067-4705, USA

Crosby, Steve (Athlete, Coach, Football Coach, Football Player)
2201 W End Ave Attn Footballcoachingstaff
Nashville, TN 37235-0001, USA

Croshere, Austin (Athlete, Basketball Player)
16 Foxglove Way
Dover Foxcroft, ME 4426, USA

Cross, Ben (Actor)
c/o Jeff Goldberg *Jeff Goldberg Management*
817 Monte Leon Dr
Beverly Hills, CA 90210-2629, USA

Cross, Christopher (Musician, Songwriter)
c/o Irving Azoff *Azoff Music Management/ Front Line*
1100 Glendon Ave
Los Angeles, CA 90024-3503, USA

Cross, Cory (Athlete, Hockey Player)
2963 W Bayshore Ct
Tampa, FL 33611, USA

Cross, David (Actor, Comedian)
c/o Staff Member *International Creative Management (ICM-LA)*
10250 Constellation Blvd Fl 7
Los Angeles, CA 90067-6207, USA

Cross, Howard (Athlete, Football Player)
79 Poplar Dr
Paramus, NJ 07652-1357, USA

Cross, Irv (Athlete, Football Player, Sportscaster)
2196 Marion Rd
Saint Paul, MN 55113-3824, USA

Cross, Jeff (Athlete, Basketball Player)
1 Holmes Rd
Dover Foxcroft, ME 04426-3748, USA

Cross, Jeff (Athlete, Football Player)
2715 Walkers Way
Weston, FL 33331-3021, USA

Cross, Joseph (Actor)
1505 10th St
Santa Monica, CA 90401-2805, USA

Cross, Justin (Athlete, Football Player)
10 Longwood Dr
Hampton, NH 03842-1122, USA

Cross, Marcia (Actor)
c/o Howard Green *Framework Entertainment (LA)*
9057 Nemo St Ste C
West Hollywood, CA 90069-5511, USA

Cross, Randall L (Randy) (Athlete, Football Player, Sportscaster)
155 Travertine Trl
Alpharetta, GA 30022-5196, USA

Cross, Roger (Actor)
c/o Staff Member *Silver Massetti & Szatmary (SMS) Talent Inc*
8730 W Sunset Blvd Ste 440
Los Angeles, CA 90069-2277, USA

Cross, Russell (Basketball Player)
190 S Prospect Ave
Elmhurst, IL 60126-3271, USA

Cross, Terry M (Admiral)
Commander US Coast Guard Pacific
Coast Guard Island
Alameda, CA 94501, USA

Crossan, Dave (Athlete, Football Player)
3314 Emory Dr
Winston Salem, NC 27103-1512, USA

Crosse, Liris (Actor, Model)
c/o Staff Member *Cinematic Management*
249 1/2 E 13th St
New York, NY 10003-5602, USA

Crossley, Charlotte (Actor, Musician)
6500 Wilshire Blvd # 550
Los Angeles, CA 90048-4920, USA

Crossley-Holland, Kevin (Writer)
c/o Staff Member *Random House Publicity (Toronto)*
1 Toronto St Suite 300
Toronto, ON M5C 2V6, Canada

Crossman, Doug (Athlete, Hockey Player)
107 Franklin Rd
Glassboro, NJ 08028-2121, USA

Crosswhite, Leon (Athlete, Football Player)
11089 Folkstone Dr
Yukon, OK 73099-8051, USA

Croston, Dave (Athlete, Football Player)
17 Dorchester Rd
Sioux City, IA 51106-9750, USA

Croteau, Gary (Athlete, Hockey Player)
8380 E Hinsdale Ave
Centennial, CO 80112-1905, USA

Crotty, Jim (Athlete, Football Player)
215 S 195th St
Des Moines, WA 98148-2137, USA

Crotty, John (Athlete, Basketball Player)
370 NE Edgewater Dr Apt 404
Stuart, FL 34996-1686, USA

Crouch, Andrae (Musician, Songwriter, Writer)
c/o Staff Member *WmE2 (WMA-LA)*
1 William Morris Pl
Beverly Hills, CA 90212-4261, USA

Crouch, Eric (Athlete, Football Player)
1505 N 138th St
Omaha, NE 68154-3888, USA

Crouch, Lindsay (Actor)
15115 1/2 W Sunset Blvd Ste A
Pacific Palisades, CA 90272-3751, USA

Crouch, Paul (Misc)
PO Box A
Santa Ana, CA 92711-2101, USA

Crouch, Roger K (Astronaut)
Carriage Hill Dr
Laurel, MD 20707, USA

Crouch, Sandra (Musician, Songwriter, Writer)
101 Winners Cir N
Brentwood, TN 37027-5352, USA

Crouch, Terry (Athlete, Football Player)
908 Westlake Dr
Desoto, TX 75115-4142, USA

Crouch, William T (Bill) (Journalist, Photographer)
5660 Valley Oaks Ct
Placerville, CA 95667-9363, USA

Crouch, Zach (Athlete, Baseball Player)
3122 Tory Ln
Sacramento, CA 95827-1915, USA

Croucher, Juan
45 Cayuse Ln
Rancho Palos Verdes, CA 90275-5155

Crouse, Lindsay (Actor)
c/o Christopher Black *Opus Entertainment*
5225 Wilshire Blvd Ste 905
Los Angeles, CA 90036-4353, USA

Croushore, Rick (Athlete, Baseball Player)
4001 Tanglewilde St Apt 101
Houston, TX 77063-5164, USA

Crouthamel, Jake (Athlete, Football Player)
385 Elliott Rd
Centerville, MA 02632-3666, USA

Crouther, Lance (Actor, Producer, Writer)
c/o Ari Greenburg *WmE2 (Endeavor-LA)*
9601 Wilshire Blvd Fl 3
Beverly Hills, CA 90210-5219, USA

Crow, Al (Athlete, Football Player)
6191 Occoquan Forest Dr
Manassas, VA 20112-3034, USA

Crow, Bill (Athlete, Basketball Player)
21300 River Rd # 15
Perris, CA 92570-8390, USA

Crow, Dean (Athlete, Baseball Player)
11507 Wickchester Ln
Houston, TX 77043-4521, USA

Crow, Don (Athlete, Baseball Player)
1554 Brook Dr
Fort Mill, SC 29708-7291, USA

Crow, F Trammell (Business Person)
Trammell Crow Center 2001 Ross Ave
Dallas, TX 75201, USA

Crow, Harian R (Business Person)
Trammell Crow Center 2001 Ross Ave
Dallas, TX 75201, USA

Crow, James F (Misc)
333 W Main St Unit 206
Madison, WI 53703-2778, USA

Crow, John David (Athlete, Coach, Football Coach, Football Player)
5004 Augusta Cir
College Station, TX 77845-8983, USA

Crow, Lindon (Athlete, Football Player)
2869 Riachuelo
San Clemente, CA 92673-4050, USA

Crow, Mark (Athlete, Basketball Player)
501 W Bay St
Jacksonville, FL 32202-4428, USA

Crow, Martin D (Cricketer)
PO Box 109302 New Market
Auckland, NEW ZEALAND

Crow, Sheryl (Musician, Songwriter)
c/o Stephen (Scooter) Weintraub *W Management*
75 E 4th St Frnt 1
New York, NY 10003-0831, USA

Crow, Wayne (Athlete, Football Player)
16561 Fawn St
Truckee, CA 96161-3534, USA

Crowded House, 3 Mitchell Rd
Rose Bay
Sydney, AUSTRALIA NSW 2929, AUSTRALIA

Crowder, Bruce (Athlete, Hockey Player)
7 Nashua Dr
Nashua, NH 3064, USA

Crowder, Channing (Athlete, Football Player)
8921 Southern Orchard Rd N
Davie, FL 33328-6986, USA

Crowder, Corey (Athlete, Basketball Player)
725 Ballard Bridge Rd
Carrollton, GA 30117-9104, USA

Crowder, Keith (Athlete, Hockey Player)
P.O. Box 95 Stn Main
Essex, ON N8M 2Y1, Canada

Crowder, Randy (Athlete, Football Player)
803 Strawberry Ln
Brandon, FL 33511-7533, USA

Crowder, Troy (Athlete, Hockey Player)
103 Panache North Shore Rd
Whitefish, ON P0M 3E0, Canada

Crowe, Cameron (Director, Writer)
c/o Staff Member *Vinyl Films*
5555 Melrose Ave
Los Angeles, CA 90038-3989, USA

Crowe, George (Athlete, Baseball Player)
1955 D O Mills Ct
Gold River, CA 95670-7843, USA

Crowe, James (J.D.) (Musician)
201 S Lexington Ave
Wilmore, KY 40390-1200, USA

Crowe, Martin (Cricketer)
Marylebone Cricket Club Lord's Cricket Ground
London NW8 8QN, UK

Crowe, Mia (Actor, Model)
7336 Santa Monica Blvd # 633
West Hollywood, CA 90046-6616, USA

Crowe, Phil (Athlete, Hockey Player)
PO Box 115
Willow Grove, PA 19090-0115, USA

Crowe, Russell (Actor)
c/o Robin Baum *Slate Public Relations*
9000 W Sunset Blvd Ste 915
West Hollywood, CA 90069-5809, USA

Crowe, Sara
13 Shorts Gdn
London, ENGLAND WC2H 9AT

Crowe, Tonya (Actor)
13030 Mindanao Way Apt 4
Marina Del Rey, CA 90292-6456, USA

Crowe, William J Jr (Admiral, Diplomat)
1615 L St NW Ste 300
Washington, DC 20036-5655, USA

Crowell, Angelo (Athlete, Football Player)
4752 Brompton Dr
Buffalo, NY 14219, USA

Crowell, Craven H Jr (Government Official)
400 W Summit Hill Dr
Knoxville, TN 37902-1401, USA

Crowell, Germane (Athlete, Football Player)
200 Luzelle Dr
Winston Salem, NC 27103-6464, USA

Crowell, James (Jim) (Athlete, Baseball Player)
4003 Sleighbell Ln
Valparaiso, IN 46383-1943, USA

Crowell, John C (Misc)
300 Hot Springs Rd
Montecito, CA 93108-2037, USA

Crowell, Rodney J (Musician, Songwriter, Writer)
c/o Staff Member *Conqueroo*
11271 Ventura Blvd # 552
Studio City, CA 91604-3136, USA

Crowley, Ben (Actor)
c/o Staff Member *Kass & Stokes Management*
9229 W Sunset Blvd Ste 504
Los Angeles, CA 90069-3405, USA

Crowley, Joseph (Congressman, Politician)
2404 Rayburn Hob
Washington, DC 20515-3605, USA

Crowley, Joseph N (Educator)
President S Ofc
Reno, NV 89557-0001, USA

Crowley, Kevin (Actor)
c/o Lorraine Berglund *Lorraine Berglund Management*
11537 Hesby St
North Hollywood, CA 91601-3618, USA

Crowley, Monica (Television Host)
c/o Staff Member *MSNBC (NJ)*
NBC/One Microsoft Corporation 1 MSNC Plaza
Secaucus, NJ 7094, USA

Crowley, Patricia (Actor)
270 N Canon Dr # 1064
Beverly Hills, CA 90210-5323, USA

Crowley, Ted (Athlete, Hockey Player)
41 Westchester Dr
Westwood, MA 02090-2621, USA

Crowley, Terry (Athlete, Baseball Player)
18405 Ensor Farm Ct
Parkton, MD 21120-9685, USA

Crown, David A (Misc)
3344 Twin Lakes Ln
Sanibel, FL 33957-5528, USA

Crown, Lester (Business Person)
222 N La Salle St
Chicago, IL 60601-1003

Crowson, Richard (Cartoonist, Editor)
825 E Douglas Ave
Wichita, KS 67202-3512, USA

Crowton, Gary (Coach, Football Coach)
Athletic Dept
Provo, UT 84602, USA

Croyle, Brodie (Athlete, Football Player)
105 Apple Blossom Dr
Brandon, MS 39047-7443, USA

Croyle, Philip (Athlete, Football Player)
5883 Treetop Ct
San Jose, CA 95123-4346, USA

Crozier, Eric (Athlete, Baseball Player)
3142 Clermont Rd
Columbus, OH 43227-1833, USA

Crozier, Joseph R (Joe) (Athlete, Coach, Hockey Player)
299 Randwood Dr
Buffalo, NY 14221-1444, USA

Crudale, Mike (Athlete, Baseball Player)
141 N Pennsylvania Ave
Belleville, IL 62220-3955, USA

Crudup, Billy (Actor)
c/o Jimmy Darmody *Creative Artists Agency (CAA-LA)*
2000 Avenue of the Stars Ste 100
Los Angeles, CA 90067-4705, USA

Cruikshank, Lucas (Actor)
c/o Evan Weiss *Collective*
8383 Wilshire Blvd Ste 1050
Beverly Hills, CA 90211-2415, USA

Cruikshank, Thomas H (Business Person)
PO Box 192509
Dallas, TX 75219-8521, USA

Cruise, Asia (Musician)
c/o Staff Member *11-16 Entertainment*
10100 Santa Monica Blvd Ste 300
Los Angeles, CA 90067-4107, USA

Cruise, Tom (Actor, Director, Producer)
c/o Amanda Lundberg *42West (NY)*
220 W 42nd St Fl 12
New York, NY 10036-7200, USA

Cruisie, Jennifer (Writer)
285 5th Ave # 470
Brooklyn, NY 11215-2578, USA

Crum, E Denzel (Denny) (Athlete, Basketball Player, Coach)
6901 Routt Rd
Louisville, KY 40299-5243, USA

Crumb, George H (Composer)
240 Kirk Ln
Media, PA 19063-2216, USA

Crumb, Robert (Artist, Cartoonist)
c/o Staff Member *Fantagraphics Books*
7563 Lake City Way NE
Seattle, WA 98115-4218, USA

Crumb, Robert (R) (Cartoonist)
20 Rue du Pont Vieux
Sauve 30610, FRANCE

Crumley Jr, James R (Religious Leader)
108 Castle Church Rd
Chapin, SC 29036-7853, USA

Crumling, Gene (Athlete, Baseball Player)
135 Lisa Cir
York, PA 17406-9323, USA

Crump, Dwayne (Athlete, Football Player)
35708 Marciel Ave
Madera, CA 93636-8414, USA

Crump, Harry (Athlete, Football Player)
9601 Collins Ave PH 201
Bal Harbour, FL 33154-2220, USA

Crumpler, Alge (Athlete, Football Player)
2155 Enclave Mill Dr
Dacula, GA 30019-3290, USA

Crumpler, Carlester (Athlete, Football Player)
12310 NE 92nd St Apt H204
Kirkland, WA 98033-5892, USA

Crusan, Doug (Athlete, Football Player)
6263 Hanover Ct
Fishers, IN 46038-1799, USA

Crutcher, Chris
3405 E Marion Ct
Spokane, WA 99223-7215

Crutcher, Lawrence M (Publisher)
Rockefeller Center
New York, NY 10020, USA

Crutchfield, Dwayne (Athlete, Football Player)
6936 Rebecca Dr
Niagara Falls, NY 14304-3053, USA

Crutchfield, Edward E (Financier)
1 First Union Ctr
Charlotte, NC 28288-0001, USA

Crutzen, Paul J (Nobel Prize Laureate)
J J Becher-Weg 27
Mainz 55128, GERMANY

Cruyff, Johan (Coach, Soccer Player)
Postbus 515
Zeist, AM 3700, NETHERLANDS

Cruz, Alexis (Actor)
c/o Staff Member *Abrams Artists Agency (LA)*
9200 W Sunset Blvd PH 11
Los Angeles, CA 90069-3601, USA

Cruz, Cirilio (Baseball Player)
E8 Calle H
Arroyo, PR 00714-2236, USA

Cruz, Deivi (Baseball Player)
611 Woodward Ave
Detroit, MI 48226-3408, USA

Cruz, Hector (Athlete, Baseball Player)
PO Box 832
Arroyo, PR 00714-0832, USA

Cruz, Henry (Baseball Player)
16 Calle Un W
Fajardo, PR 00738-4706, USA

Cruz, Ivan (Athlete, Baseball Player)
3489 Hartsfield Rd
Jacksonville, FL 32277-1064, USA

Cruz, Jacob (Athlete, Baseball Player)
1582 W Commerce Ave
Gilbert, AZ 85233-4103, USA

Cruz, Juan (Athlete, Baseball Player)
c/o Staff Member *Chicago Cubs*
Wrigley Field 1060 West Addison Street
Chicago, IL 60613, USA

Cruz, Julio (Athlete, Baseball Player)
6599 170th Pl SE
Bellevue, WA 98006-6012, USA

Cruz, Mike (DJ)
c/o Staff Member *Diva Central Inc*
7510 W Sunset Blvd Ste 1445
Los Angeles, CA 90046-3408, USA

Cruz, Monica (Actor)
c/o Antonio Rubial *Kuranda Management*
Santo Angel, 84
Madrid 28043, Spain

Cruz, Penelope (Actor, Model)
c/o Katrina Bayonas *Kuranda Management*
Santo Angel, 84
Madrid 28043, Spain

Cruz, Raymond
8383 Wilshire Blvd # 954
Beverly Hills, CA 90211-2425

Cruz, Smith Martin (Writer)
1745 Broadway # B1
New York, NY 10019-4368, USA

Cruz, Taio (Musician)
c/o Staff Member *Energon Entertainment*
276 5th Ave Rm 704
New York, NY 10001-4527, USA

Cruz, Tommy (Athlete, Baseball Player)
E8 Calle H
Arroyo, PR 00714-2236, USA

Cruz, Valerie (Actor)
c/o Staff Member *Innovative Artists (LA)*
1505 10th St
Santa Monica, CA 90401-2805, USA

Cruz, Wilson
153 San Vicente Blvd Apt 2G
Santa Monica, CA 90402-1507, USA

Cruz Jr, Jose (Athlete, Baseball Player)
2309 Delta Bridge Dr
Pearland, TX 77584-1566, USA

Cruz Sr, Jose D (Athlete, Baseball Player)
2309 Delta Bridge Dr
Pearland, TX 77584-1566, USA

Cruz-Romo, Gilda (Opera Singer)
1315 Lockhill Selma Rd
San Antonio, TX 78213-1915, USA

Crvenkovski, Branko (President)
Skopje, MACEDONIA

Cryder, Robert (Athlete, Football Player)
17411 NE 129th St
Redmond, WA 98052-1323, USA

Crye, John B (Actor, Producer, Writer)
c/o Staff Member *Fewdio*
13348 Reedley St
Panorama City, CA 91402-4061, USA

Cryer, Gretchen (Actor, Songwriter, Writer)
885 W End Ave
New York, NY 10025-3501, USA

Cryer, Jon (Actor)
c/o Connie Tavel *Forward Entertainment*
9255 W Sunset Blvd Ste 805
Los Angeles, CA 90069-3305, USA

Cryer, Suzanne (Actor)
c/o Chris Schmidt *Paradigm (LA)*
360 N Crescent Dr
Beverly Hills, CA 90210-4874, USA

Cryner, Bobby
PO Box 2147
Hendersonville, TN 37077-2147

Crystal, Billy (Actor, Comedian)
c/o Larry Brezner *Morra Brezner Steinberg & Tenenbaum (MBST) Entertainment*
345 N Maple Dr Ste 200
Beverly Hills, CA 90210-5174, USA

Crystal, McClory (Stylist)
c/o Staff Member *ESP (London)*
63 Charlotte St. 1st Floor
London W11 4PG, UK

Crystals (Music Group)
27-L Ambiance Ct
Bardonia, NY 10954-1421, USA

Crystat, Ronald G (Biologist)
435 E 70th St Apt 34B
New York, NY 10021-5351, USA

Csikszentmihalyi, Mihaly (Misc)
5848 S University Ave
Chicago, IL 60637-1554, USA

Csokas, Marton (Actor)
c/o George Freeman *WmE2 (Endeavor-LA)*
9601 Wilshire Blvd Fl 3
Beverly Hills, CA 90210-5219, USA

Csonka, Lawrence R (Larry) (Athlete, Football Player)
37256 Hunter Camp Rd
Lisbon, OH 44432-9464, USA

Cua, Rick (Musician)
1086 Rip Steele Rd
Columbia, TN 38401-7745, USA

Cuaron, Alfonso (Director)
443 Greenwich St Fl 5
New York, NY 10013-1702, USA

Cuban, Mark (Actor, Director)
9100 Wilshire Blvd Ste 500 PMB W
Beverly Hills, CA 90212-3426, USA

Cuban, Mark (Business Person)
c/o Staff Member *Dallas Mavericks*
2500 Victory Ave
Dallas, TX 75219-7601, USA

Cubbage, Mike (Athlete, Baseball Player, Coach)
3349 Carroll Creek Rd
Keswick, VA 22947-9156, USA

Cubitt, David (Actor)
c/o Shelley Browning *Magnolia Entertainment (LA)*
9595 Wilshire Blvd Ste 601
Beverly Hills, CA 90212-2506, USA

Cuccurullo, Waren (Musician)
93A Westbourne Park Villas
London W2 5ED, UNITED KINGDOM (UK)

Cuche, Didier (Skier)
Les Bugnenets
Le Paquier 2058, SWITZERLAND

Cucinotta, Maria Grazia (Actor)
Lundolevere del Melini 10
Rome 192, ITALY

Cuckney, John G (Financier)
1 Comhill
London EC3V 3QR, UNITED KINGDOM (UK)

Cudahy, Richard D (Judge)
219 S Dearborn St
Chicago, IL 60604-1702, USA

Cuddie, Steve (Athlete, Hockey Player)
18 Hill Country Dr
Gormley, ON L0H 1G0, Canada

Cuddy, Jim (Musician)
c/o Staff Member *Agency Group Ltd, The (NY)*
142 W 57th St Fl 6
New York, NY 10019-3300, USA

Cuddyer, Michael (Athlete, Baseball Player)
10240 Washingtonia Palm Way Apt 2024
Fort Myers, FL 33966-6915, USA

Cudi, Kid (Musician)
c/o Drew Elliot *Media Artists Group (NY)*
140 E 46th St PH C
New York, NY 10017-2633, USA

Cudlitz, Michael (Actor)
c/o Rick Ax *Gold Coast Management*
438 S Venice Blvd Apt 5
Venice, CA 90291-4695, USA

Cudmore, Daniel (Actor)
c/o Murray Gibson *Characters Talent Agency, The (Vancouver)*
1505 W 2nd Ave #200
Vancouver, BC V6H 3Y4, Canada

Cuellar, Bobby (Athlete, Baseball Player)
705 E 6th St
Alice, TX 78332-4651, USA

Cuellar, Miguel S (Mike) (Athlete, Baseball Player)
960 English Town Ln Apt 106
Winter Springs, FL 32708-4678, USA

Cueller, Henry (Congressman, Politician)
2463 Rayburn Hob
Washington, DC 20515-4315, USA

Cueto, Al (Athlete, Basketball Player)
5714 Riviera Dr
Coral Gables, FL 33146-2751, USA

Cueto, Bert (Athlete, Baseball Player)
9739 Linksland Dr
Huntersville, NC 28078-2600, USA

Culbertson Jr, Frank L (Astronaut)
15500 Meherrin Dr
Centreville, VA 20120-3733, USA

Culbreath, Jim (Athlete, Football Player)
212 Elder Ave
Lansdowne, PA 19050-3028, USA

Culbreath, Joshua (Josh) (Athlete, Track Athlete)
Athletic Dept
Wilberforce, OH 45384, USA

Culbreth, Feildin (Athlete, Baseball Player)
224 Claiborne Ct
Spartanburg, SC 29301-5345, USA

Culhane, Jim (Athlete, Hockey Player)
1903 W Michigan Ave Attn
Hockeyprogram
Kalamazoo, MI 49008-5200, USA

Culkin, Kieran (Actor)
c/o Emily Gerson Saines *Brookside Artists Management (NY)*
250 W 57th St Ste 2303
New York, NY 10107-2399, USA

Culkin, Macaulay (Actor)
c/o Emily Gerson Saines *Brookside Artists Management (NY)*
250 W 57th St Ste 2303
New York, NY 10107-2399, USA

Culkin, Rory (Actor)
c/o Emily Gerson Saines *Brookside Artists Management (NY)*
250 W 57th St Ste 2303
New York, NY 10107-2399, USA

Cullars, Willie (Athlete, Football Player)
PO Box 172363
Kansas City, KS 66117-1363, USA

Cullen, Barry (Athlete, Hockey Player)
RR 1
Puslinch, ON N0B 2J0, Canada

Cullen, Betsy (Athlete, Golfer)
4144 Greystone Way Apt 707
Sugar Land, TX 77479-3014, USA

Cullen, Brett (Actor)
c/o Melisa Spamer *Domain Talent*
9229 W Sunset Blvd Ste 710
Los Angeles, CA 90069-3407, USA

Cullen, Brian (Athlete, Hockey Player)
386 Ontario St
St Catharines, ON L2R 5L8, Canada

Cullen, Jack (Athlete, Baseball Player)
164 Alexander Ave
Nutley, NJ 07110-1002, USA

Cullen, John (Athlete, Hockey Player)
1002 Legacy Hills Dr
McDonough, GA 30253-8824, USA

Cullen, Kimberly (Actor)
8916 Ashcroft Ave
West Hollywood, CA 90048-2404, USA

Cullen, Matt (Athlete, Hockey Player)
5109 Ste 2
West Fargo, ND 58078, USA

Cullen, Peter (Actor, Voice Over Artist)
c/o Staff Member *Tisherman Gilbert Motley Drozdoski Talent Agency (TGMD)*
6767 Forest Lawn Dr Ste 101
Los Angeles, CA 90068-1050, USA

Cullen, Ray (Athlete, Hockey Player)
20 Sydenham Dr RR 2
Ilderton, ON N0M 2A0, Canada

Cullen, Sean M
10100 Santa Monica Blvd Ste 2500
Los Angeles, CA 90067-4116, USA

Cullen, Tim (Athlete, Baseball Player)
159 W G St
Benicia, CA 94510-3114, USA

Cullens, E Van (Business Person)
1025 W Nasa Blvd
Melbourne, FL 32919-0002, USA

Culler, Glen (Scientist)
100 Burns Pl
Goleta, CA 93117, USA

Culligan, Joe (Writer)
650 NE 126th St
North Miami, FL 33161-4821, USA

Cullimore, Jassen (Athlete, Hockey Player)
5509 S Washington St
Hinsdale, IL 60521-4965, USA

Cullinan, Edward H (Architect)
Wharf 1 Baldwin Terrace
London N1 7RU, UNITED KINGDOM (UK)

Cullity, Dave (Athlete, Football Player)
5420 Jarman St
Colorado Springs, CO 80906-8210, USA

Cullum, Jamie (Musician)
c/o Martin Kirkup *Direct Management Group*
947 N La Cienega Blvd Ste G
Los Angeles, CA 90069-4700, USA

Cullum, Kaitlin (Actor)
c/o Norma Robbins *Abrams Artists Agency (LA)*
9200 W Sunset Blvd PH 11
Los Angeles, CA 90069-3601, USA

Cullum, Kimberly
8916 Ashcroft Ave
Los Angeles, CA 90048-2404

Cullum, Leo (Cartoonist)
2900 Valmere Dr
Malibu, CA 90265-2970, USA

Cullum, Mark E (Cartoonist, Editor)
5401 Forest Acres Dr
Nashville, TN 37220-2100, USA

Culp, Curley (Athlete, Football Player)
16811 Gravesend Rd
Pflugerville, TX 78660-1830, USA

Culp, Jason (Actor, Voice Over Artist)
c/o Staff Member *Random House Publicity (Toronto)*
1 Toronto St Suite 300
Toronto, ON M5C 2V6, Canada

Culp, Ray (Athlete, Baseball Player)
7400 Waterline Rd
Austin, TX 78731-2055, USA

Culp, Stephen (Actor)
c/o Miriam Milgrom *Miriam Milgrom Management*
100 Garden City Plz Ste 300
Garden City, NY 11530-3206, USA

Culp, Steven (Actor)
c/o Miriam Milgrom *Miriam Milgrom Management*
3614 Lankershim Blvd
Los Angeles, CA 90068-1218, USA

Culpepper, Brad (Athlete, Football Player)
136 W Davis Blvd
Tampa, FL 33606-3540, USA

Culpepper, Daunte (Athlete, Football Player)
16730 Berkshire Ct
Southwest Ranches, FL 33331-1331, USA

Culpepper, Ed (Athlete, Football Player)
811 Bluewater Dr
Sun City Center, FL 33573-6245, USA

Culpepper, Robert E (Athlete, Football Player)
811 Bluewater Dr
Sun City Center, FL 33573-6245, USA

Cult, The
c/o Staff Member *Immortal Entertainment*
1620 26th St Ste 1060N
Santa Monica, CA 90404-4037, USA

Cult Jam
PO Box 30284
Brooklyn, NY 11203-0284

Culture Beat
Schleiermacher Str. 2
Darmstadt, GERMANY D-64283

Culver, Curt S (Financier)
250 E Kilbourn Ave
Milwaukee, WI 53202-3102, USA

Culver, George (Athlete, Baseball Player)
5409 Rustic Canyon St
Bakersfield, CA 93306-7315, USA

Culver, John C (Ex-Senator, Politician)
5409 Spangler Ave
Bethesda, MD 20816-1847, USA

Culver, Michael
77 Beak St
London, ENGLAND W1F 9ST

Culver, Molly (Actor)
c/o Staff Member *Stone Manners Salners Agency (LA)*
9911 W Pico Blvd Ste 1400
Los Angeles, CA 90035-2715, USA

Cumberland, John (Athlete, Baseball Player)
19417 Golden Slipper Pl
Lutz, FL 33558-9209, USA

Cumberland Gap
159 Madison Ave Apt 2G
New York, NY 10016-5434

Cumby, George E (Athlete, Football Player)
12090 Cross Fence Trl
Tyler, TX 75706-4239, USA

Cumming, Alan (Actor, Musician)
c/o Jason Weinberg *Untitled Entertainment (LA)*
350 S Beverly Dr Ste 200
Beverly Hills, CA 90212-4819, USA

Cummings, Burton (Musician, Songwriter, Writer)
PO Box 770850
Orlando, FL 32877-0850, USA

Cummings, Dave
4130 La Village Dr # 107
La Jolla, CA 92037

Cummings, Ed (Athlete, Football Player)
237 Schearbrook Ln
Stevensville, MT 59870-6405, USA

Cummings, Erin (Actor)
c/o Nate Bryson *Paradigm (LA)*
360 N Crescent Dr
Beverly Hills, CA 90210-4874, USA

Cummings, Jim (Actor)
c/o Tom Parziali *Visionary Entertainment*
1558 N Stanley Ave
Los Angeles, CA 90046-2711, USA

Cummings, John (Athlete, Baseball Player)
21 Paseo Park
Laguna Niguel, CA 92677, USA

Cummings, Midre (Athlete, Baseball Player)
19525 Morden Blush Dr
Lutz, FL 33558-9084, USA

Cummings, Pat (Athlete, Basketball Player)
9024 Symmes Knoll Ct
Loveland, OH 45140-9330, USA

Cummings, Ralph W (Misc)
228 Muir Brook Pl
Cary, NC 27519-7021, USA

Cummings, Steve (Athlete, Baseball Player)
11010 Sagecrest Ln
Houston, TX 77089-3904, USA

Cummings, Terry (Athlete, Basketball Player)
12820 W Golden Ln
San Antonio, TX 78249-2231, USA

Cummings, Terry (Athlete, Basketball Player)
2855 Candler Rd Ste 9
Decatur, GA 30034-1415, USA

Cummings, Whitney (Actor)
c/o Michael Kives *Creative Artists Agency (CAA-LA)*
2000 Avenue of the Stars Ste 100
Los Angeles, CA 90067-4705, USA

Cummins, Barry (Athlete, Hockey Player)
155 Marsden St
Kimberley, BC V1A 1G8, Canada

Cummins, Gregory Scott (Actor)
1680 Vine St Ste 1016
Los Angeles, CA 90028-8800, USA

Cummins, Peggy (Actor)
17 Brockley Road Bexhill-on-Sea
Sussex TN39 4TT, UNITED KINGDOM (UK)

Cumpsty, Michael (Actor)
c/o Staff Member *Innovative Artists (LA)*
1505 10th St
Santa Monica, CA 90401-2805, USA

Cundall, Teri (Stylist)
222 Alexander Ave
San Rafael, CA 94901-1624, USA

Cundey, Dean R (Cinematographer)
250 S De Lacey Ave Unit 207
Pasadena, CA 91105-4136, USA

Cundieff, Rusty (Actor)
c/o Norman Aladjem *Paradigm (LA)*
360 N Crescent Dr
Beverly Hills, CA 90210-4874, USA

Cunnane, Will (Athlete, Baseball Player)
24636 George Washington Dr
Plainfield, IL 60544-4421, USA

Cunneyworth, Randy (Athlete, Coach, Hockey Player)
c/o Staff Member *Rochester Americans*
1 War Memorial Sq Ste 228
Rochester, NY 14614-2192, USA

Cunniff, Jill (Musician)
2 Penn Plz # 2600
New York, NY 10121-0101, USA

Cunningham, Bennie L (Athlete, Football Player)
PO Box 1086
Seneca, SC 29679-1086, USA

Cunningham, Bill (Musician)
PO Box 8770
Endwell, NY 13762-8770, USA

Cunningham, Bill (Radio Personality)
8044 Montgomery Rd Ste 650
Cincinnati, OH 45236-2959, USA

Cunningham, Carl (Athlete, Football Player)
4471 Saddleworth Cir
Orlando, FL 32826-4123, USA

Cunningham, Doug (Athlete, Football Player)
5060 Harling Pl
Jackson, MS 39211-4731, USA

Cunningham, Gunther (Athlete, Coach, Football Coach, Football Player)
460 Great Circle Rd
Nashville, TN 37228-1404, USA

Cunningham, Jay (Athlete, Football Player)
3617 Farland Rd
Cleveland, OH 44118-3016, USA

Cunningham, Jeffrey M (Publisher)
60 5th Ave
New York, NY 10011-8868, USA

Cunningham, Jennifer (Stylist)
c/o Staff Member *Rex Agency, The*
6311 Romaine St
Los Angeles, CA 90038-2617, USA

Cunningham, Joe (Athlete, Baseball Player)
RR 1 Box 80A
Koshkonong, MO 65692-9526, USA

Cunningham, Katherine (Actor)
c/o Jean-Pierre (JP) Henraux *Shelter Entertainment*
9454 Wilshire Blvd Ste 715
Beverly Hills, CA 90212-2925, USA

Cunningham, Kristan (Actor, Television Host)
c/o Cat Josell *Synergy Management*
22287 Mulholland Hwy Ste 204
Calabasas, CA 91302-5157, USA

Cunningham, Lee (Stylist)
2501 N Commonwealth Ave
Los Angeles, CA 90027-1207, USA

Cunningham, Liam (Actor)
12/13 Poland St
London W1V 3DE, UNITED KINGDOM (UK)

Cunningham, Michael (Writer)
19 Union Sq W
New York, NY 10003-3304, USA

Cunningham, Randall (Athlete, Football Player)
380 E Robindale Rd
Las Vegas, NV 89123-1824, USA

Cunningham, Richard (Athlete, Football Player)
100 Rosewood Ct
Peachtree City, GA 30269-2237, USA

Cunningham, Richie (Athlete, Football Player)
610 Cheyenne Dr
Houma, LA 70360-6060, USA

Cunningham, Sam (Athlete, Football Player)
9316 S 4th Ave
Inglewood, CA 90305-3002, USA

Cunningham, Sean (Director, Producer)
4420 Hayvenhurst Ave
Encino, CA 91436-3248, USA

Cunningham, T J (Athlete, Football Player)
11640 E Walsh Pl
Aurora, CO 80012-3264, USA

Cunningham, Walter (Astronaut)
PO Box 604
Glenn Dale, MD 20769-0604, USA

Cunningham, William J (Billy) (Athlete, Basketball Player, Coach)
31 Front St # 33
Conshohocken, PA 19428-2867, USA

Cuoco, Kaley (Actor)
c/o Andrea Pett-Joseph *Brillstein Entertainment Partners*
9150 Wilshire Blvd Ste 350
Beverly Hills, CA 90212-3453, USA

Cuomo, Andrew

Cuomo, Andrew M (Governor)
Governor of New York State NYS State Capitol Building
Albany, NY 12224, USA

Cuomo, Christopher (Chris) (Correspondent)
c/o Staff Member *Primetime*
147 Columbus Ave
New York, NY 10023-6503, USA

Cuomo, Jerome J (Inventor)
PO Box 218
Yorktown Heights, NY 10598-0218, USA

Cuomo, Mario (Ex-Governor)
787 7th Ave
New York, NY 10019-6018, USA

Cuozzo, Gary S (Athlete, Football Player)
4 Swimming River Rd Ste 4
Lincroft, NJ 07738-1727, USA

Cupp, James N (War Hero)
4904 Aspen Hill Rd
Rockville, MD 20853-3710, USA

Cura, Francesco (Actor)
c/o Staff Member *Origin Talent Agency*
4705 Laurel Canyon Blvd Ste 306
Studio City, CA 91607-5940, USA

Cura, Jose (Opera Singer)
165 W 57th St
New York, NY 10019-2201, USA

Curatola, Vincent (Actor)
c/o Howard Axel *TMT Entertainment Group*
648 Broadway Ste 1002
New York, NY 10012-2348, USA

Curb, Michael (Mike) (Business Person, Composer)
3907 W Alameda Ave # 2
Burbank, CA 91505-4359, USA

Curb, Mike
3907 W Alameda Ave
Burbank, CA 91505-4359

Curbeam, Robert L Jr (Astronaut)
13727 Briaridge Ct
Highland, MD 20777-9539, USA

Curci, Francis (Athlete, Football Player)
14707 Croydon Pl
Tampa, FL 33618-2160, USA

Curcillo, Anthony (Athlete, Football Player)
23887 Corte Emerado
Murrieta, CA 92562-3539, USA

Curcio, Michael (Athlete, Football Player)
165 Lincoln Ave
Hightstown, NJ 08520-4117, USA

Cure, Robert (Athlete, Football Player)
145 Main St
Los Altos, CA 94022-2912, USA

Cure, The (Music Group)
c/o Rick Roskin *Creative Artists Agency (CAA-LA)*
2000 Avenue of the Stars Ste 100
Los Angeles, CA 90067-4705, USA

Cureton, Earl (Athlete, Basketball Player)
7306 Balsam Ct
West Bloomfield, MI 48322-2821, USA

Cureton, Thomas K (Misc)
501 E Washington St
Urbana, IL 61801-4320, USA

Curfman, Shannon (Musician)
200 W Superior St Ste 202
Chicago, IL 60654-3554, USA

Curie-Good, Louise
1317 Delresto Dr
Beverly Hills, CA 90210-2100

Curl, Carolyn (Skier)
405 N Westridge Dr
Idaho Falls, ID 83402-5447, USA

Curl, Robert F Jr (Nobel Prize Laureate)
1824 Bolsover St
Houston, TX 77005-1728, USA

Curlander, Paul J (Business Person)
740 W New Circle Rd
Lexington, KY 40511-1806, USA

Curler, James (Business Person)
222 S 9th St
Minneapolis, MN 55402-3364, USA

Curley, Bill (Athlete, Basketball Player)
377 Autumn Ave
Duxbury, MA 02332-4614, USA

Curley, Edwin M (Misc)
2645 Pin Oak Dr
Ann Arbor, MI 48103-2370, USA

Curley, John J (Publisher)
1100 Wilson Blvd
Arlington, VA 22209-2249, USA

Curley, Marianne (Writer)
43 Nariah Cres
Toormina NSW 2452, AUSTRALIA

Curley, Walter J P Jr (Diplomat, Financier)
885 3rd Ave Ste 1200
New York, NY 10022-4834, USA

Curnen, Monique (Actor)
c/o Sheree Cohen *Kohner Agency, The*
9300 Wilshire Blvd Ste 555
Beverly Hills, CA 90212-3211, USA

Curnin, Thomas F (Attorney, Attorney General, General)
80 Pine St
New York, NY 10005-1702, USA

Curran, Brian (Athlete, Hockey Player)
3600 Vanrick Dr
Kalamazoo, MI 49001-0805, USA

Curran, Brian (Athlete, Coach, Hockey Player)
c/o Staff Member *Quad City Mallards*
1509 3rd Avenue A
Moline, IL 61265-1363, USA

Curran, Charles E (Misc)
Dallas Hall
Dallas, TX 75275-0001, USA

Curran, Kevin (Tennis Player)
5808 Back Ct
Austin, TX 78731-3301, USA

Curran, Mike (Athlete, Hockey Player)
7615 Lanewood Ln N
Maple Grove, MN 55311-2608, USA

Curran, Pat (Athlete, Football Player)
3195 Avenida Magoria
Escondido, CA 92029-7422, USA

Curran, Tony (Actor)
c/o Tammy Rosen *Sanders Armstrong Caserta*
425 N Robertson Blvd
West Hollywood, CA 90048-1735, USA

Currence, Lafayette (Athlete, Baseball Player)
113 Rock Springs Way
Rock Hill, SC 29730-6149, USA

Current, Mike (Athlete, Football Player)
593 Lone Oaks Loop
Silverton, OR 97381-1472, USA

Currey, Francis S (War Hero)
PO Box 515
Selkirk, NY 12158-0515, USA

Currie, Bill (Athlete, Baseball Player)
125 Lakeside Dr SW
Arlington, GA 39813-2344, USA

Currie, Brian (Writer)
c/o David Krintzman *Morris, Yorn, Barnes, Levine, Krintzman, Rubenstein and Kohner*
2000 Ave Of The Stars 3rd Tower Floor NORTH
Los Angeles, CA 90067, USA

Currie, Cherie
10807 Topanga Canyon Blvd
Chatsworth, CA 91311, USA

Currie, Daniel (Dan) (Athlete, Football Player)
6650 W Flamingo Rd Apt 152
Las Vegas, NV 89103-2144, USA

Currie, Gordon (Actor)
c/o Jennifer Goldhar *Characters Talent Agency, The (Toronto)*
1505 W 2nd Ave #200
Vancouver, BC V6H 3Y4, Canada

Currie, Louise (Actor)
1317 Delresto Dr
Beverly Hills, CA 90210-2100, USA

Currie, Malcolm R (Business Person)
PO Box 956
El Segundo, CA 90245-0956, USA

Currie, Nancy J (Astronaut)
403 Cranbrook Ln
League City, TX 77573-1850, USA

Currie, Sondra (Actor)
3951 Longridge Ave
Sherman Oaks, CA 91423-4923, USA

Currie, Tony (Athlete, Hockey Player)
2600-2 Bloor St W
Toronto, ON M4W 3E2, Canada

Currier, William (Athlete, Football Player)
8661 Monticello Rd
Columbia, SC 29203-9706, USA

Currin, James A (Athlete, Football Player)
11770 Thayer Ln
Cincinnati, OH 45249-1566, USA

Currin, Perry (Athlete, Baseball Player)
210 E Sonterra Blvd Apt 815
San Antonio, TX 78258-3956, USA

Currington, Billy (Music Group, Musician)
c/o Staff Member *WmE2 (WMA-TN)*
1600 Division St Ste 300
Nashville, TN 37203-2755, USA

Curris, Constantine W (Educator)
President S Ofc Sikeshall
Clemson, SC 29634-0001, USA

Curry, Adrianne (Model, Reality TV Star)
c/o Phil Viardo *The Viardo Agency*
8484 Wilshire Blvd Ste 220
Beverly Hills, CA 90211-3223, USA

Curry, Alana (Actor)
PO Box 2535
Toluca Lake, CA 91610-0535, USA

Curry, Ann (Television Host)
c/o Staff Member *Today Show, The*
30 Rockefeller Plz
New York, NY 10112-0015, USA

Curry, Bill (Athlete, Coach, Football Coach, Football Player)
2660 Peachtree Rd NW Apt 27H
Atlanta, GA 30305-3680, USA

Curry, Buddy (Athlete, Football Player)
4407 Trestle Way
Buford, GA 30518-6055, USA

Curry, Chad (Stylist)
c/o Staff Member *Seaminx Artist Management*
9234 Peninsula Dr
Dallas, TX 75218-2733, USA

Curry, Craig (Athlete, Football Player)
3210 Amber Forest Dr
Houston, TX 77068-2005, USA

Curry, Dell (Athlete, Basketball Player)
263 Paine Run Rd
Grottoes, VA 24441-5043, USA

Curry, Denise (Athlete, Basketball Player, Coach)
21 Maple Dr
Aliso Viejo, CA 92656-4273, USA

Curry, Don (DC) (Actor, Comedian)
c/o Tony Spires *Full Circle Entertainment*
6320 Canoga Ave Ste 1550
Woodland Hills, CA 91367-2563, USA

Curry, Donald (Athlete, Boxer)
4512 Regal Ridge Dr Apt 2607
Fort Worth, TX 76119-5830, USA

Curry, Dwen (Stylist)
c/o Staff Member *Dawn to Dusk Image Agency*
8306 Wilshire Blvd # 412
Beverly Hills, CA 90211-2382, USA

Curry, Eddy (Athlete, Basketball Player)
17 Magnolia Dr
Purchase, NY 10577-1137, USA

Curry, Eric F (Athlete, Football Player)
PO Box 17321
Jacksonville, FL 32245-7321, USA

Curry, Lucy (Stylist)
c/o Staff Member *Tricia Joyce Inc*
79 Chambers St Fl 2
New York, NY 10007-1824, USA

Curry, Mark (Actor)
c/o Ben Feigin *Anonymous Content (AC-LA)*
3531 Hayden Ave
Culver City, CA 90232, USA

Curry, Mike (Athlete, Basketball Player)
2880 Wells Dr
Augusta, GA 30906-5373, USA

Curry, Roy (Athlete, Football Player)
9045 S Paxton Ave
Chicago, IL 60617-3814, USA

Curry, Stephen (Actor)
c/o Robyn Gardiner *RGM Artist Group*
64-76 Kippax St Level 2, Suite 202 & 206
Surry Hills, NSW 2010, Australia

Curry, Steve (Athlete, Baseball Player)
10725 Obee Rd
Whitehouse, OH 43571-9250, USA

Curry, Tim (Actor)
c/o Jonathan Howard *Innovative Artists (LA)*
1505 10th St
Santa Monica, CA 90401-2805, USA

Curtale, Tony (Athlete, Hockey Player)
7500 Bishop Rd Apt 1311
Plano, TX 75024-5632, USA

Curtin, David S (Journalist)
30 S Prospect St
Colorado Springs, CO 80903-3638, USA

Curtin, David Y (Misc)
870 W 23rd Ave
Eugene, OR 97405-2474, USA

Curtin, Jane T (Actor)
8942 Wilshire Blvd # 219
Beverly Hills, CA 90211-1908, USA

Curtin, John J Jr (Attorney, Attorney General, General)
150 Federal St # 3500
Boston, MA 02110-1713, USA

Curtin, Valerie
15622 Meadowgate Rd
Encino, CA 91436-3431

Curtis, Ben (Actor)
c/o Staff Member *Abrams Artists Agency (NY)*
275 7th Ave Fl 26
New York, NY 10001-6708, USA

Curtis, Ben (Athlete, Golfer)
8959 Bevington Ln
Orlando, FL 32827-7058, USA

Curtis, Chad (Athlete, Baseball Player)
621 Eagle Point Rd
Lake Odessa, MI 48849-9445, USA

Curtis, Cliff (Actor)
c/o Joseph (Joe) Rice *Abrams Artists Agency (LA)*
9200 W Sunset Blvd PH 11
Los Angeles, CA 90069-3601, USA

Curtis, Cuneo Ann E (Swimmer)
35 Golden Hinde Blvd
San Rafael, CA 94903-3816, USA

Curtis, Don (Wrestler)
920 Middleton Rd
Jacksonville, FL 32211-6273, USA

Curtis, Isaac F (Athlete, Football Player)
711 Clinton Springs Ave
Cincinnati, OH 45229-1300, USA

Curtis, J Michael (Mike) (Athlete, Football Player)
5101 River Rd Apt 1803
Bethesda, MD 20816-1574, USA

Curtis, Jack (Athlete, Baseball Player)
4949 Ike Starnes Rd
Granite Falls, NC 28630-8631, USA

Curtis, Jamie Lee (Actor)
c/o Heidi Schaeffer *PMK/BNC Public Relations (PMK-LA)*
8687 Melrose Ave Ste 8
West Hollywood, CA 90069-5746, USA

Curtis, John (Athlete, Baseball Player)
1800 Roundhill Rd Apt 1207
Charleston, WV 25314-1559, USA

Curtis, Kelly (Actor)
651 N Kilkea Dr
Los Angeles, CA 90048-2213, USA

Curtis, Kenneth M (Ex-Governor)
1 Canal Plz Ste 1000
Portland, ME 04101-6407, USA

Curtis, King (Baseball Player)
2538 Beechwood Dr
Vineland, NJ 08361-2932, USA

Curtis, Liane (Actor)
12556 Everglade St
Los Angeles, CA 90066-1818, USA

Curtis, Paul (Athlete, Hockey Player)
150 County Road 322 Unit A
Tuscola, TX 79562-2630, USA

Curtis, Richard (Writer)
c/o Staff Member *The Rights House (UK)*
Drury House 34-43 Russell St
London WC2B 5HA, UK

Curtis, Robin (Actor)
1147 Beverly Hill Dr
Cincinnati, OH 45208-4323, USA

Curtis, Scott (Athlete, Football Player)
31661 Prairie Dunes Ct
Evergreen, CO 80439-5902, USA

Curtis, Todd (Actor)
2046 14th St Apt 10
Santa Monica, CA 90405-1641, USA

Curtis, Tom (Athlete, Football Player)
5433 NW 94th Doral Pl
Doral, FL 33178-2033, USA

Curtola, Bobby (Musician)
720 Spadina Ave # PH2
Toronto, ON M5S 2T9, CANADA

Cusack, Ann (Actor)
1505 10th St
Santa Monica, CA 90401-2805, USA

Cusack, Joan (Actor, Comedian)
c/o Gabrielle (Gaby) Morgerman *WmE2 (Endeavor-LA)*
9601 Wilshire Blvd Fl 3
Beverly Hills, CA 90210-5219, USA

Cusack, John (Actor)
c/o Annett Wolf *WKT Public Relations (WKT-LA)*
9350 Wilshire Blvd Ste 450
Beverly Hills, CA 90212-3230, USA

Cusack, Sinead (Actor)
4 Windmill St.
London W1P 1HF, UNITED KINGDOM (UK)

Cuschieri, Paul (Writer)
c/o Naren Desai *Brillstein Entertainment Partners*
9150 Wilshire Blvd Ste 350
Beverly Hills, CA 90212-3453, USA

Cuse, Carlton (Producer)
c/o Staff Member *WmE2 (WMA-LA)*
1 William Morris Pl
Beverly Hills, CA 90212-4261, USA

Cushenan, Ian (Athlete, Hockey Player)
4014 Dryden Dr
North Olmsted, OH 44070-1928, USA

Cushing, Matt (Athlete, Football Player)
5752 Lyman Ave
Downers Grove, IL 60516-1401, USA

Cushman, David W (Misc)
20 Lake Shore Dr
Princeton Junction, NJ 08550-4906, USA

Cusick, Henry Ian (Actor)
c/o Abi Harris *Ken McReddie Ltd*
11 Connaught Pl
London W2 2ET, UNITED KINGDOM

Cusick, Pete (Athlete, Football Player)
807 Esplanade
Redondo Beach, CA 90277-4734, USA

Cussler, Clive (Writer)
c/o Staff Member *Peter Lampack Agency*
350 5th Ave Ste 5301
New York, NY 10118-5301, United States

Cust, Jack (Athlete, Baseball Player)
9 Club House Dr
Whitehouse Station, NJ 08889-3366, USA

Cutcliffe, David (Coach, Football Coach)
Athletic Dept
University, MS 38677, USA

Cute Is What We Aim For (Music Group)
PO Box 1803
Tampa, FL 33601-1803, USA

Cuthbert, Elisha (Actor)
c/o John Carrabino *John Carrabino Management*
5900 Wilshire Blvd Ste 406
Los Angeles, CA 90036-5015, USA

Cuthbert, Randy (Athlete, Football Player)
6186 Valley Forge Dr
Coopersburg, PA 18036-8803, USA

Cuthbeth, Elizabeth (Betty) (Athlete, Track Athlete)
4/7 Karara Close Halls Head
Mandurah, WA 6210, AUSTRALIA

Cutler, Alexander M (Business Person)
Eaton Center 1111 Superior Ave
Cleveland, OH 44114, USA

Cutler, Bruce (Attorney, Attorney General, General)
41 Madison Ave
New York, NY 10010-2202, USA

Cutler, Jay (Athlete, Football Player)
c/o Bus Cook *Bus Cook Sports, Inc*
1 Willow Bend Dr
Hattiesburg, MS 39402-8552, USA

Cutler, RJ (Director, Producer)
c/o Rowena Arguelles *Creative Artists Agency (CAA-LA)*
2000 Avenue of the Stars Ste 100
Los Angeles, CA 90067-4705, USA

Cutler, Walter L (Diplomat)
1630 Crescent Pl NW
Washington, DC 20009-4004, USA

Cutliffe, Molly (Actor)
PO Box 64249
Los Angeles, CA 90064-0249, USA

Cutrone, Kelly (Business Person, Reality TV Star)
62 Grand St
New York, NY 10013-2245, USA

Cutrufello, Mary (Musician, Songwriter, Writer)
4405 Belmont Park Ter
Nashville, TN 37215-3609, USA

Cutsinger, Gary (Athlete, Football Player)
600 Mountain Dew Rd
Horseshoe Bay, TX 78657-6341, USA

Cutter, Kiki (Skier)
PO Box 1317
Carbondale, CO 81623-1317, USA

Cutter, Lise (Actor)
36 Poplar St
Sag Harbor, NY 11963-1718, USA

Cutter, Slade D (Athlete, Football Player)
9214 River Crescent Dr
Annapolis, MD 21401-7770, USA

Cutts, Don (Athlete, Hockey Player)
PO Box 305
Standard, CA 95373-0305, USA

Cuviello, Peter M (General)
Director Defence Information Systems Agency
Alington, VA 22204, USA

Cuyler, Milt (Athlete, Baseball Player)
962 Lamar Rd
Macon, GA 31210-7109, USA

Cuzzi, Phil (Athlete, Baseball Player)
32 Mapes Ave
Nutley, NJ 07110-1410, USA

Cverko, Andy (Athlete, Football Player)
2650 Brookwood Way Dr Apt 122
Rolling Meadows, IL 60008-2368, USA

Cwiklinski, Stanley (Athlete, Olympic Athlete)
2840 Maple St
San Diego, CA 92104-4940, USA

Cymphonique (Dancer, Musician)
c/o Ben Press *Don Buchwald & Associates Inc (LA)*
8619 Washington Blvd
Culver City, CA 90232-7441, USA

Cypher, John
9229 W Sunset Blvd Ste 315
Los Angeles, CA 90069-3403

Cypher, Jon (Actor)
498 Manzanita Ave
Ventura, CA 93001-2227, USA

Cyphers, Charles
324 E 1st St Ste 300
Los Angeles, CA 90012-3850

Cypress, Tawny
c/o Staff Member *Abrams Artists Agency (NY)*
275 7th Ave Fl 26
New York, NY 10001-6708, USA

Cypress Hill (Music Group)
c/o David Benveniste *Velvet Hammer*
9014 Melrose Ave
West Hollywood, CA 90069-5610, USA

Cyr, Conrad K (Judge)
PO Box 635
Bangor, ME 04402-0635, USA

Cyr, Denis (Athlete, Hockey Player)
9816 N Townsend Dr
Peoria, IL 61615-1388, USA

Cyr, Paul (Athlete, Hockey Player)
5064 Richardson Rd
Port Alberni, BC V9Y 5R8, Canada

Cyrus, Billy Ray (Musician, Songwriter)
c/o Jim Morey *Morey Management Group*
1100 Glendon Ave Ste 1100
Los Angeles, CA 90024-3515, USA

Cyrus, Brandi (Actor)
c/o Staff Member *United Talent Agency (UTA)*
9560 Wilshire Blvd Fl 5
Beverly Hills, CA 90212-2400, USA

Cyrus, Miley (Actor, Musician)
c/o Jason Morey *Morey Management Group*
1100 Glendon Ave Ste 1100
Los Angeles, CA 90024-3515, USA

Czajkowski, Jim (Athlete, Baseball Player)
1648 Rivergate Dr
Sevierville, TN 37862-9321, USA

Czapsky, Stefan (Cinematographer)
RR 3 Box 278
Unadilla, NY 13849, USA

Czemy, Henry (Actor)
438 Queen St E
Toronto, ON M5A 1T4, CANADA

Czerny, Henry (Actor)
c/o Perry Zimel *Oscars Abrams Zimel & Associates, Inc. (OAZ)*
438 Queen St E
Toronto ON M5A 1T4, CANADA

Czrongursky, Jan (Prime Minister)
Nam Slobody 1
Bratislava 81370, SLOVAKIA

Czuchry, Matt (Actor)
c/o Jeff Golenberg *Collective*
8383 Wilshire Blvd Ste 1050
Beverly Hills, CA 90211-2415, USA

Czyz, Bobby (Boxer)
110 Pennsylvania Ave
Flemington, NJ 08822-1202, USA

D

D, Deezer (Actor)
c/o Staff Member *Acme Talent & Literary (LA)*
1400 Atlantic Ave Ste 274
Long Beach, CA 90813-2013, USA

D. Bishop Jr., Sanford (Congressman, Politician)

D. Clarke, Yvette (Congressman, Politician)
1029 Longworth Hob
Washington, DC 20515-2304, USA

D. Dicks, Norman (Congressman, Politician)
2467 Rayburn Hob
Washington, DC 20515-4706, USA

D. Dingell Jr., John (Congressman, Politician)
2328 Rayburn Hob
Washington, DC 20515-2215, USA

D. Hinchey, Maurice (Congressman, Politician)
2431 Rayburn Hob
Washington, DC 20515-3222, USA

D. Lucas, Frank (Congressman, Politician)
2311 Rayburn Hob
Washington, DC 20515-2404, USA

D12 (Music Group)
c/o Staff Member *WmE2 (WMA-NY)*
1325 Avenue of the Americas
New York, NY 10019-6026, USA

D-12 (Musician)
1776 Broadway Fl 15
New York, NY 10019-2002

Da Band (Music Group)
c/o Staff Member *Bad Boy Worldwide Entertainment*
1440 Broadway Fl 16
New York, NY 10018-2320, USA

Da Brat (Musician)
c/o Staff Member *WmE2 (WMA-LA)*
1 William Morris Pl
Beverly Hills, CA 90212-4261, USA

da Silva, Luiz Inacio Lula (Politician)
Setor Comercial Sul - Quadra 2 Bloco C - Nº 256
Edifício Toufic, Brasília DF, CEP: 7, Brazil

Daal, Omar (Athlete, Baseball Player)
3859 E Bellerive Dr
Queen Creek, AZ 85142-3233, USA

Daanen, Jerome (Athlete, Football Player)
1011 S Erie St
De Pere, WI 54115-3109, USA

D'Abaldo, Chris (Musician)
535 Kings Road
London SW10 0S, UNITED KINGDOM (UK)

Daberko, David A (Financier)
National City Center 1900 E 9th St
Cleveland, OH 44114, USA

Dabich, Mike (Athlete, Basketball Player)
464 S Indiana Ave
Hudson, WY 82515, USA

Dabney, Carlton (Athlete, Football Player)
2522 Northumberland Ave
Richmond, VA 23220-1504, USA

D'Abo, Maryam (Actor)
32 Tavistock St
London WC2E 7PB, UNITED KINGDOM (UK)

D'Abo, Olivia (Actor)
c/o Felicia Sager *Sager Management*
260 S Beverly Dr # 205
Beverly Hills, CA 90212-3805, USA

Dacascos, Mark (Actor)
c/o Mary Putnam Greene *MPG Management*
9150 Wilshire Blvd Ste 350
Beverly Hills, CA 90212-3453, USA

Dacquisto, John (Athlete, Baseball Player)
32010 N 20th Ln
Phoenix, AZ 85085-7081, USA

D'Acquisto, John F (Athlete, Baseball Player)
1884 Crossroads St
Chula Vista, CA 91915-2430, USA

Dacruz Policarpo, Jose Cardinal (Religious Leader)
Camo dos Martires da Patria 45
Lisbon 1150, PORTUGAL

Dacus, Don (Actor)
8455 Fountain Ave Unit 512
Los Angeles, CA 90069-2543, USA

Daddario, Alex (Actor)
c/o Jerry Shandrew *Shandrew Public Relations*
1050 S Stanley Ave
Los Angeles, CA 90019-6634, USA

Daddario, Alexandra (Actor)
c/o Donnalyn Carfi *Harvest Talent Management*
124 W 80th St Apt 1
New York, NY 10024-6320, USA

Dade, Paul (Athlete, Baseball Player)
5212 66th Street Ct W
University Place, WA 98467-3337, USA

Dadswell, Doug (Athlete, Hockey Player)
1620 50 Ave SW
Calgary, AB T2T 2V9, Canada

Daehlie, Bjorn (Skier)
Cathinka Guldbergs Veg 64
Holler 2034, NORWAY

Daetweiler, Louella (Baseball Player)
415 S Poplar Ave
Brea, CA 92821-6650, USA

Dafoe, Byron (Athlete, Hockey Player)
15 Perkins Ln
Lynnfield, MA 1940, USA

Dafoe, Willem (Actor)
c/o Frank Frattaroli *Dontanville/Frattaroli (D/F)*
270 Lafayette St Ste 402
New York, NY 10012-3327, USA

Daft, Douglas (Business Person)
1 Coca Cola Plaza 310 North Ave NW
Atlanta, GA 30313, USA

Daft, Kevin (Athlete, Football Player)
13781 Grovesite Dr
Santa Ana, CA 92705, USA

Daggett, Timothy (Tim) (Gymnast)
134 Country Club Dr
East Longmeadow, MA 01028-5807, USA

Daghe, Noelle (Athlete, Golfer)
1300 Tamarac St
Denver, CO 80220-3325, USA

D'agnillo, Ann (Stylist)
c/o Staff Member *Axis Models & Talent*
PO Box 367
Ringwood, NJ 07456-0367, USA

D'Agosto, Nicholas (Nick) (Actor)
c/o Faras Rabadi *Emerald Talent Group*
10 Universal City Plz Fl 20
Universal City, CA 91608-1074, USA

Dagres, Angie (Athlete, Baseball Player)
PO Box 27
Rowley, MA 01969-0027, USA

Dagworthy Prew, Wendy A (Designer, Fashion Designer)
18 Melrose Terrace
London W6, UNITED KINGDOM (UK)

Dahl, Ariene (Actor)
PO Box 116
Sparkill, NY 10976-0116, USA

Dahl, Arlene
PO Box 116
Sparkill, NY 10976-0116

Dahl, Bob (Athlete, Football Player)
363 Elliots Hill Ln
Lexington, VA 24450-7202, USA

Dahl, Christopher (Educator)
President's Office
Genesco, NY 14454, USA

Dahl, Craig (Athlete, Football Player)
309 5th St W
Park River, ND 58270-4322, USA

Dahl, John (Director, Writer)
c/o Jason Spitz *WmE2 (Endeavor-LA)*
9601 Wilshire Blvd Fl 3
Beverly Hills, CA 90210-5219, USA

Dahl, Kevin (Athlete, Hockey Player)
4000 Astoria Way
Avon, OH 44011-3426, USA

Dahl, Lawrence F (Misc)
4817 Woodburn Dr
Madison, WI 53711-1345, USA

Dahl, Sophie (Actor, Model)
c/o Staff Member *Special Artists Agency*
9465 Wilshire Blvd Ste 820
Beverly Hills, CA 90212-2607, USA

Dahlberg, Kenneth H (Ken) (War Hero)
19360 Walden Trl
Wayzata, MN 55391-3548, USA

Dahlen, Ulf (Athlete, Hockey Player)
3909 Wishing Well Ln
Plano, TX 75093-7586, USA

Dahler, Ed (Athlete, Basketball Player)
511 E Tremont St
Hillsboro, IL 62049-1801, USA

Dahlin, Kjell (Athlete, Hockey Player)
Farjestad BK Hockey Club Box 318
Karlstad S-65108, Sweden

Dahllof, Eva (Athlete, Golfer)
419 Glen Crest Dr
Moore, SC 29369-9287, USA

Dahlquist, Chris (Athlete, Hockey Player)
10859 Purdey Rd
Eden Prairie, MN 55347-5236, USA

Dahm, Jaclyn (Actor)
c/o Amy Godsick *Candy Entertainment Management*
8981 W Sunset Blvd Ste 310
West Hollywood, CA 90069-1848, USA

Dahm, Werner K (Misc)
1117 Clubhouse Ave Sw
Huntsville, AL 35802-5016, USA

Dahrendorf, Ralf Gustav
Postfach 5560
Konstanz, GERMANY D-78434

Dai, Ailian (Choreographer, Dancer)
Hua Qiao Gong Yu #2-16 Hua Yuan Cun
Hai Dian, Beijing 100044, CHINA

Dai, Sijie (Writer)
c/o Staff Member *Knopf Publishing Group*
1745 Broadway
New York, NY 10019-4368, USA

Daiches, David (Writer)
22 Belgrave Crescent
Edinburgh EH4 3AL, SCOTLAND

Daigle, Alain (Athlete, Hockey Player)
3510 Rue De Bordeaux
Trois-Rivieres, QC G8Y 3P7, Canada

Daigle, Alexander (Athlete, Hockey Player)
3510 Rue Bordeaux
Trois-Rivieres-Quest, QC G8Y 3P7, Canada

Daigle, Casey (Athlete, Baseball Player)
2607 Wpa Rd
Sulphur, LA 70663-9408, USA

Daigneault, J J (Athlete, Coach, Hockey Player)
c/o Staff Member *Hartford Wolf Pack*
1 Civic Center Plz
Hartford, CT 06103-1504, USA

Dailey, Bill (Athlete, Baseball Player)
5019 Meadow Way
Dublin, VA 24084-5721, USA

Dailey, Bob (Athlete, Hockey Player)
130 7th Ave Apt A
Haddon Heights, NJ 08035-1622, USA

Dailey, Dianne (Athlete, Golfer)
4220 Stonehenge Ln
Lakeland, FL 33813, USA

Dailey, Peter H (Diplomat)
2201 C St NW
Washington, DC 20520-0099, USA

Dailey, Quintin (Athlete, Basketball Player)
4955 Lindell Rd Apt 107
Las Vegas, NV 89118-1371, USA

Daily, Bill (Actor)
1331 Park Ave SW Unit 802
Albuquerque, NM 87102-2855, USA

Daily, Gretchen (Misc)
Ecology Dept
Stanford, CA 94305, USA

Daily, Parker (Religious Leader)
PO Box 191
Springfield, MO 65801-0191, USA

Daingerfield, Michael (Actor)
c/o Staff Member *Kirk Talent Agencies Inc*
70 East 2nd. Ave Suite 301
Vancouver, BC V5T 1B1, Canada

Dainton, Frederick S (Misc)
Fieldside Water Eaton Lane
Kidlington, Oxford OX5 2PR, UNITED KINGDOM (UK)

Daio, Norberto J D C A (Prime Minister)
CP 38
Sao Tome, SAO TOME & PRINCIPE

Dajani, Nadia (Actor)
c/o Tina Thor *TMT Entertainment Group*
648 Broadway Ste 1002
New York, NY 10012-2348, USA

Dal Canton, Bruce (Athlete, Baseball Player)
624 Ray Dr
Carnegie, PA 15106-1808, USA

Daland, Peter (Coach)
14 Chris Ct
Riverhead, NY 11901-1956, USA

Dalbavie, Andre (Composer)
4 Addison Bridge Place
London W14 8XP, UNITED KINGDOM (UK)

Dalberto, Michel (Musician)
13 Blvd Henri Plumof
Vevey 1800, SWITZERLAND

Daldry, Stephen (Director)
Sloane Square
London SW1, UNITED KINGDOM (UK)

Dale, Alan (Actor)
c/o Dan Baron *Agency for the Performing Arts (APA-LA)*
405 S Beverly Dr Ste 500
Beverly Hills, CA 90212-4425, USA

Dale, Bruce (Photographer)
1145 17th St NW
Washington, DC 20036-4707, USA

Dale, Carl (Athlete, Baseball Player)
429 N Walnut Ave
Cookeville, TN 38501-2559, USA

Dale, Carroll W (Athlete, Football Player)
1 College Ave
Wise, VA 24293-4400, USA

Dale, Dick
PO Box 1713
Twentynine Palms, CA 92277-1000, USA

Dale, James Badge (Actor)
c/o Myrna Jacoby *MJ Management*
130 W 57th St Apt 11A
New York, NY 10019-3311, USA

Dale, Jerry (Athlete, Baseball Player)
2112 Middlewood Dr
Maryville, TN 37803-6374, USA

Dale, Jim (Actor)
230 W 56th St # 63B
New York, NY 10019-4306, USA

Dale, Roland (Athlete, Football Player)
128 Bridlewood Dr
Brandon, MS 39047-8410, USA

Dale, William B (Economist, Government Official)
8100 Connecticut Ave Apt 1707
Chevy Chase, MD 20815-2822, USA

Dale & Grace (Music Group)
PO Box 1875
Gretna, LA 70054-1875, USA

Dale Scott, Cynthia (Actor)
c/o Derek Maki *Coolwaters Productions*
10061 Riverside Dr # 531
Toluca Lake, CA 91602-2560, USA

D'Alema, Massima (Prime Minister)
Piazza Colomma 370
Rome 187, ITALY

Dalembert, Samuel (Basketball Player)
1st Union Center 3601 South Broad St
Philadelphia, PA 19148, USA

Dalena, Pete (Athlete, Baseball Player)
4951 N Thorne Ave
Fresno, CA 93704-2935, USA

D'Aleo, Angelo (Musician)
PO Box 12
Far Hills, NJ 07931-0012, USA

Dalesandro, Mark (Athlete, Baseball Player)
1908 Arbor Fields Dr
Plainfield, IL 60586-5729, USA

D'Alesio, Tracy (Stylist)
55 Beverly Rd NE
Atlanta, GA 30309-2645, USA

Dales-Schuman, Stacey (Basketball Player)
MCI Center 601 F St NW
Washington, DC 20004, USA

D'Alessio, Diana (Golfer)
6955 Nunn Rd
Lakeland, FL 33813-3821, USA

D'Alessio, Diana (Athlete, Golfer)
6955 Nunn Rd
Lakeland, FL 33813-3821, USA

Daley, Bud (Athlete, Baseball Player)
922 Moose Dr
Riverton, WY 82501-2537, USA

Daley, Joe (Athlete, Hockey Player)
666 St James St
Winnipeg, MB R3G 3J6, Canada

Daley, John (Golfer)
c/o Staff Member *Pro Golfers Assoc of America (PGA)*
112 Tpc Blvd
Ponte Vedra Beach, FL 32082, USA

Daley, John (Golfer)
10015 E Mountain View Rd Apt 2126
Scottsdale, AZ 85258-5221, USA

Daley, John Francis (Actor)
c/o Staff Member *The Management Company*
2030 Pinehurst Rd
Los Angeles, CA 90068-3732, USA

Daley, Margaret (Stylist)
3054 Braemar Dr
Santa Barbara, CA 93109-1006, USA

Daley, Patrick (Athlete, Hockey Player)
118 Mount Olive Dr
Toronto, ON M9V 2E2, Canada

Daley, Pete (Athlete, Baseball Player)
4019 Calle Mira Monte
Newbury Park, CA 91320-1932, USA

Daley, Richard M (Politician)
City Hall 121 N LaSalle St
Chicago, IL 60602, USA

Daley, Rosle (Chef, Writer)
110 N Carpenter St
Chicago, IL 60607-2104, USA

Daley, William N (Bill) (Secretary)
175 E Houston St
San Antonio, TX 78205-2255, USA

Dalgarno, Alexander (Astronomer)
27 Robinson St
Cambridge, MA 02138-1403, USA

Dalgarno, Brad (Athlete, Hockey Player)
1146 Fairfield Pl
Oakville, ON L6M 2L9, Canada

Dalgilsh, Kenneth M (Kenny) (Coach, Soccer Player)
c/o Staff Member *Liverpool Football Club*
69/71 Anfield Road
Liverpool L4 OTQ, UNITED KINGDOM

Dalheimer, Patrick (Musician)
350 W End Ave Apt 1
New York, NY 10024-6818, USA

Dalhousie, Simon R (Government Official)
Brechin Castle
Brechin DD9 6SH, SCOTLAND

Dali, Tracy (Actor, Model)
PO Box 69541
Los Angeles, CA 90069-0541, USA

Dalian, Susan (Actor)
c/o Staff Member *GVA Talent Agency Inc*
8981 W Sunset Blvd Ste 101
Los Angeles, CA 90069-1850, USA

Dalie, Beatrice (Actor)
20 Ave Rapp
Paris 75007, FRANCE

Dalis, Irene (Opera Singer)
1731 Cherry Grove Dr
San Jose, CA 95125-5512, USA

Dalkas, Nicole (Athlete, Golfer)
288 Green Mountain Dr
Palm Desert, CA 92211-3246, USA

Dalkowski, Steve (Baseball Player)
Walnut Hill Care Center 55 Grand St
New Britain, CT 06052-2021, USA

Dallafior, Ken (Athlete, Football Player)
188 Four Seasons Dr
Lake Orion, MI 48360-2645, USA

Dallas, Matt (Actor)
c/o Katie Rhodes *Untitled Entertainment (LA)*
350 S Beverly Dr Ste 200
Beverly Hills, CA 90212-4819, USA

Dallas Cowboys Cheerleaders
1 Cowboys Pkwy
Irving, TX 75063-4924

Dallesandro, Joe (Actor)
521 W Briar Pl Apt 505
Chicago, IL 60657-4655, USA

Dallimore, Brian (Athlete, Baseball Player)
10531 Haywood Dr
Las Vegas, NV 89135-2850, USA

Dallman, Marty (Athlete, Hockey Player)
3843 Main St
Niagara Falls, ON L2G 6B4, Canada

Dallyn, Stacy (Stylist)
c/o Staff Member *Celestine - CA*
1666 20th St Ste 200B
Santa Monica, CA 90404-3828, USA

Dalm, Jan
Dv de Merwedestraat HI Ambacht
GB 3341, Netherlands

Dalmacci, Ricardo (Actor)
c/o Gabriel Blanco *Gabriel Blanco Iglesias (Mexico)*
Rio Balsas 35-32 Colonia Cuauhtemoc
DF 6500, Mexico

Dalrymple, Clay (Athlete, Baseball Player)
28248 Mateer Rd
Gold Beach, OR 97444-9618, USA

Dalrymple, Gary B (Misc)
1847 NW Hillcrest Dr
Corvallis, OR 97330-1859, USA

Dalrymple, Jack (Governor)
600 E Boulevard Ave Ofc of
Bismarck, ND 58505-0601, USA

Dalton, Audrey (Actor)
22461 Labrusca
Mission Viejo, CA 92692-1325, USA

Dalton, James E (General)
61 Misty Acres Rd
Rolling Hills Estates, CA 90274-5749, USA

Dalton, Kristin (Actor)
c/o Bob McGowan *McGowan Management*
8733 W Sunset Blvd Ste 103
West Hollywood, CA 90069-2241, USA

Dalton, Lacy J (Musician)
820 Cartwright Rd
Reno, NV 89521-7134, USA

Dalton, Lional (Athlete, Football Player)
9858 Clint Moore Rd Ste 128
Boca Raton, FL 33496-1033, USA

Dalton, Mike (Athlete, Baseball Player)
42410 Palm Ave
Fremont, CA 94539-4729, USA

Dalton, Nic (Musician)
c/o Staff Member *Agency Group Ltd, The (NY)*
142 W 57th St Fl 6
New York, NY 10019-3300, USA

Dalton, Nicole (Actor)
c/o Staff Member *Commonwealth Talent Group*
PO Box 36514
Los Angeles, CA 90036-0514, USA

Dalton, Oakley (Athlete, Football Player)
715 Harpertown Ln
Tunnel Hill, IL 62972-3329, USA

Dalton, Timothy (Actor)
c/o Brian Mann *International Creative Management (ICM-LA)*
10250 Constellation Blvd Fl 7
Los Angeles, CA 90067-6207, USA

Daltrey, Roger (Actor, Musician)
Holmhurst Manor Farm Burwash
East Sussex, UK

Daltry, Roger (Actor, Musician)
18-21 Jermyn St
London SW1Y 6NB, UNITED KINGDOM (UK)

Daluiso, Brad (Athlete, Football Player)
13258 Glencliff Way
San Diego, CA 92130-1309, USA

Daly, Cahal Brendan Cardinal (Religious Leader)
Ard Mhacha 23 Rosetta Ave
Belfast BT7 3HG, NORTHERN IRELAND

Daly, Carson (Television Host)
c/o James Dixon *Dixon Talent Agency*
375 Greenwich St Fl 5
New York, NY 10013-2376, USA

Daly, John (Athlete, Golfer)
c/o John Mascatello *SFX World Sports Management*
36855 W Main St Ste 200
Purcellville, VA 20132-3561, USA

Daly, Rad (Actor)
c/o Staff Member *Brady Brannon & Rich*
5670 Wilshire Blvd Ste 820
Los Angeles, CA 90036-5613, USA

Daly, Robert (Baseball Player)
10779 Bellagio Rd
Los Angeles, CA 90077-3731, USA

Daly, Tess (Television Host)
c/o Staff Member *John Noel Management*
10A Belmont St Floor 2
London NW1 8HH, UNITED KINGDOM (UK)

Daly, Tim (Actor, Producer)
c/o Amy Guenther *Gateway Management Company Inc*
860 Via De La Paz Ste F10
Pacific Palisades, CA 90272-3631, USA

Daly, Tyne (Actor)
c/o Staff Member *Raw Talent Management*
545 Veteran Ave
Los Angeles, CA 90024-1915, USA

Daly-Donofrio, Heather (Athlete, Golfer)
414 Long Cove Ct
Ormond Beach, FL 32174-9290, USA

Dam, Kenneth W (Attorney, Attorney General, General, Government Official)
1111 E 60th St
Chicago, IL 60637-2776, USA

Damadian, Raymond V (Inventor)
110 Marcus Dr
Melville, NY 11747-4228, USA

Damageplan (Music Group)
2706 Monterrey St
Arlington, TX 76015-1323, USA

Damanchiah, Godfrey (Actor, Comedian)
c/o Brian Stern *Stern Entertainment Group (Brillstein Entertainment Partners)*
1 William Morris Pl
Beverly Hills, CA 90212-4261, USA

Damas, Bertila (Actor)
PO Box 17193
Beverly Hills, CA 90209-3193, USA

Damasio, Antonio R (Doctor)
Neurology Dept
Iowa City, IA 52242, USA

Damaska, Jack (Athlete, Baseball Player)
252 Blackhawk Rd
Beaver Falls, PA 15010-1404, USA

D'Amato, Lisa (Musician)
c/o Staff Member *Brendan Vaughn*
Prefers to be contact via telephone or email
Los Angeles, CA 90069, USA

D'Amato, Mike (Athlete, Football Player)
7 Lansing Ln
East Northport, NY 11731-5325, USA

DaMatta, Cristiano (Race Car Driver)
50 Tower Pkwy
Lincolnshire, IL 60069, USA

D'Amboise, Jacques (Choreographer, Dancer)
51 W 86th St Apt 702
New York, NY 10024-3618, USA

D'Ambrosio, Dominick (Misc)
3520 W Oklahoma Ave
Milwaukee, WI 53215-4175, USA

Dames, Romi (Actor)
c/o Carlyne Grager *Dramatic Artists Agency*
103 W Alameda Ave Ste 139
Burbank, CA 91502-2253, USA

Dameshek, David (Actor, Writer)
c/o Staff Member *Creative Artists Agency (CAA-LA)*
2000 Avenue of the Stars Ste 100
Los Angeles, CA 90067-4705, USA

Damian, Alexa (Actor)
c/o Staff Member *Televisa*
Blvd Adolfo Lopez Mateos 232 Colonia San Angel INN
DF CP 01060, MEXICO

Damian, Michael (Actor, Musician)
3500 W Olive Ave Ste 1400
Burbank, CA 91505-5512, USA

Damiani, Damiano (Director)
Via Delle Terme Deciane 2
Rome 153, ITALY

Damico, Jeff (Athlete, Baseball Player)
30 Evelyn Ct
Oldsmar, FL 34677-2322, USA

Damico, Jeff (Athlete, Baseball Player)
9567 NE Northtown Loop
Bainbridge Island, WA 98110-3532, USA

D'Amico, Jeff (Baseball Player)
6903 Cedar Ridge Dr N
Pinellas Park, FL 33781-4904, USA

D'Amico, William D (Athlete)
30 Greenwood St
Lake Placid, NY 12946-1214, USA

Damkroger, Maury (Athlete, Football Player)
1722 S 166th Cir
Omaha, NE 68130-1502, USA

Dammerman, Dennis D (Business Person)
3135 Easton Turnpike
Fairfield, CT 06828-0001, USA

Damon, Grey (Actor)
c/o Toni Benson *Third Hill Entertainment*
195 S Beverly Dr Ste 400
Beverly Hills, CA 90212-3044, USA

Damon, Johnny D (Athlete, Baseball Player)
c/o Scott Boras *Boras Corporation*
18 Corporate Plaza Dr
Newport Beach, CA 92660-7901, USA

Damon, Mark (Actor)
2781 Benedict Canyon Dr
Beverly Hills, CA 90210-1024, USA

Damon, Matt (Actor)
c/o Jennifer Allen *Viewpoint Inc*
8820 Wilshire Blvd Ste 220
Beverly Hills, CA 90211-2622, USA

Damon, Stuart (Actor)
387 N Van Ness Ave
Los Angeles, CA 90004, USA

Damon, Una (Actor)
c/o Suzanne DeWalt *Dewalt & Musik Management*
623 N Parish Pl
Burbank, CA 91506-1701, USA

Damone, Vic (Actor, Musician)
2000 S Ocean Blvd
Palm Beach, FL 33480-5205

Damore, John (Athlete, Football Player)
627 Citadel Dr
Westmont, IL 60559-1297, USA

Damphousse, Vincent (Athlete, Hockey Player)
c/o Staff Member *NHL Players Association*
1700-20 Bay St
Toronto, ON M5J 2R8, Canada

Dampier, Erick (Athlete, Basketball Player)
18724 Wainsborough Ln
Dallas, TX 75287-5525, USA

Dampier, Louie (Athlete, Basketball Player)
2808 New Moody Ln
La Grange, KY 40031-9453, USA

Dampler, Erick (Basketball Player)
2635 Sea View Pkwy
Alameda, CA 94502, USA

Dampler, Louie (Basketball Player)
2808 New Moody Ln
La Grange, KY 40031-9453, USA

Damron, Robert (Athlete, Golfer)
6001 Masters Blvd
Orlando, FL 32819-4303, USA

Damus, Mike (Actor)
c/o Staff Member *United Talent Agency (UTA)*
9560 Wilshire Blvd Fl 5
Beverly Hills, CA 90212-2400, USA

Dan, Judith (Stylist)
2751 Monte Mar Ter
Los Angeles, CA 90064-3442, USA

Dana, Bill (Actor, Comedian)
c/o Staff Member *Amsel, Eisenstadt & Frazier Talent Agency (AEF)*
5055 Wilshire Blvd Ste 860
Los Angeles, CA 90036-6108, USA

Dana, Justin (Actor)
13111 Ventura Blvd Ste 102
Studio City, CA 91604-2218, USA

Danare, Malcolm (Actor)
c/o Monique Moss *Moss Public Relations*
8060 Melrose Ave Fl 4
Los Angeles, CA 90046-7038, USA

Danby, Gordon T (Inventor)
126 Sound Rd
Wading River, NY 11792-1058, USA

Dance, Bill (Fisherman)
PO Box 198
Brownsville, TN 38012-0198, USA

Dance, Charies (Actor)
7812 Forsythe St
Sunland, CA 91040-2502, USA

Dance, Charles (Actor)
c/o Susan Smith *Susan Smith Company, The*
1344 N Wetherly Dr
Los Angeles, CA 90069-1817, USA

Dancer, Stanley F (Race Car Driver)
1300 S Ocean Blvd
Pompano Beach, FL 33062-6900, USA

Dancy, Hugh (Actor)
c/o Staff Member *Untitled Entertainment (LA)*
350 S Beverly Dr Ste 200
Beverly Hills, CA 90212-4819, USA

Dancy, John (Correspondent)
Kennedy Government School
Cambridge, MA 2138, USA

Dandenault, Mathieu (Athlete, Hockey Player)
2615 Dorchester Rd
Birmingham, MI 48009-5990, USA

Dando, Evan (Musician)
c/o Staff Member *Good Cop Public Relations*
425 W 13th St # 502
New York, NY 10014-1123, USA

Dandridge, Bob (Athlete, Basketball Player)
1708 Saint Denis Ave
Norfolk, VA 23509-1004, USA

Dandy Warholds, The (Music Group)
c/o Staff Member *Tsunami Entertainment*
2525 Hyperion Ave
Los Angeles, CA 90027-3316, USA

Dandy Warhols (Music Group)
c/o Staff Member *Tsunami Entertainment*
2525 Hyperion Ave
Los Angeles, CA 90027-3316, USA

Dane, Alexandra (Actor)
205 Chudliegh Road
London SE4 1EG, UNITED KINGDOM (UK)

Dane, Eric (Actor)
c/o William Choi *Management 360*
9111 Wilshire Blvd
Beverly Hills, CA 90210-5508, USA

Dane, Paul (Misc)
12105 Ambassador Dr Apt 515
Colorado Springs, CO 80921-3629, USA

Daneker, Pat (Athlete, Baseball Player)
1419 Ritchey St
Williamsport, PA 17701-2640, USA

Danelli, Dino (Musician)
11761 E Speedway Blvd
Tucson, AZ 85748-2017, USA

Danelo, Joe (Athlete, Football Player)
3601 Roxbury St
San Pedro, CA 90731-6440, USA

Danenhauer, Bill (Athlete, Football Player)
10 Kirkby Cir
Bella Vista, AR 72715-2349, USA

Danenhauer, Eldon (Athlete, Football Player)
1030 SW Exmoor Ln
Topeka, KS 66604-1977, USA

Danes, Claire (Actor)
c/o Michael D Aglion *Signpost*
250 S Beverly Dr Ste 201
Beverly Hills, CA 90212-3811, USA

Daneyko, Ken (Athlete, Hockey Player)
11 Combs Hollow Rd
Mendham, NJ 07945-2204, USA

Danforth, Douglas D (Athlete, Baseball Player, Business Person)
8787 Bay Colony Dr Apt 1002
Naples, FL 34108-0784, USA

Danforth, Fred (Artist)
PO Box 828
Middlebury, VT 05753-0828, USA

Danforth, John C (Jack) (Ex-Senator)
799 United Nations Plz
New York, NY 10017-3505, USA

D'Angelo (Musician, Songwriter, Writer)
c/o Staff Member *WmE2 (WMA-LA)*
1 William Morris Pl
Beverly Hills, CA 90212-4261, USA

D'Angelo, Beverly (Actor)
c/o Brian Mann *International Creative Management (ICM-LA)*
10250 Constellation Blvd Fl 7
Los Angeles, CA 90067-6207, USA

D'Angelo, Josephine (Baseball Player)
6141 W Higgins Ave Apt 5A
Chicago, IL 60630-1853, USA

D'Angio, Giulio J (Misc)
& 34th Civic Center Blvd
Philadelphia, PA 19104, USA

Daniel, Brittany (Actor)
c/o Glenn Rigberg *HYPHENATE*
9701 Wilshire Blvd Fl 10
Beverly Hills, CA 90212-2010, USA

Daniel, Chuck (Athlete, Baseball Player)
59 Jilguero Way
Hot Springs Village, AR 71909-6928, USA

Daniel, Elizabeth A (Beth) (Athlete, Golfer)
219 Palm Trl
Delray Beach, FL 33483-5526, USA

Daniel, Eugene (Athlete, Football Player)
PO Box 80345
Baton Rouge, LA 70898-0345, USA

Daniel, Kenny (Athlete, Football Player)
2911 Center Ave
Richmond, CA 94804-3022, USA

Daniel, Robert (Athlete, Football Player)
9860 Scyene Rd Apt 518
Dallas, TX 75227-1951, USA

Daniel, Willie (Athlete, Football Player)
8323 Oktoc Rd
Starkville, MS 39759-6461, USA

Danielpour, Richard (Composer)
2100 Colorado Ave
Santa Monica, CA 90404-3504, USA

Daniels, Anthony (Actor)
c/o Fifi Oscard *Fifi Oscard Agency*
110 W 40th St Rm 1601
New York, NY 10018-8512, USA

Daniels, Antonio (Basketball Player)
351 Elliott Ave W Ste 500
Seattle, WA 98119-4153, USA

Daniels, Bennie (Athlete, Baseball Player)
938 W 156th St
Compton, CA 90220-3504, USA

Daniels, Charlie (Musician, Songwriter, Writer)
14410 Central Pike
Mount Juliet, TN 37122-5800, USA

Daniels, Cheryl (Bowler)
6574 Crest Top Dr
West Bloomfield, MI 48322-2656, USA

Daniels, Clem (Athlete, Football Player)
PO Box 18673
Oakland, CA 94619-0673, USA

Daniels, Dexter (Athlete, Football Player)
518 E Magnolia St
Valdosta, GA 31601-5860, USA

Daniels, Erin (Actor)
c/o Stephen (Steve) Small *Paradigm (LA)*
360 N Crescent Dr
Beverly Hills, CA 90210-4874, USA

Daniels, Fred (Athlete, Baseball Player)
PO Box 6208
Statesville, NC 28687-6208, USA

Daniels, Greg (Actor)
c/o Howard Klein *3 Arts Entertainment Inc*
9460 Wilshire Blvd Fl 7
Beverly Hills, CA 90212-2713, USA

Daniels, Jack (Athlete, Baseball Player)
3001 Galaxy Dr
Evansville, IN 47715-1687, USA

Daniels, Jeff (Actor)
c/o Wendy Morris *Wendy Morris PR*
332 E 84th St Apt 2C
New York, NY 10028-4445, USA

Daniels, Jeff (Athlete, Hockey Player)
5 Henry Johnson Blvd Apt 5
Albany, NY 12210-1316, USA

Daniels, Jenna (Athlete, Golfer)
85140 Amagansett Dr
Fernandina Beach, FL 32034-8711, USA

Daniels, Jerome (Athlete, Football Player)
21831 S 218th St
Queen Creek, AZ 85142-4110, USA

Daniels, Kal (Athlete, Baseball Player)
100 Echo Ln
Warner Robins, GA 31088-7458, USA

Daniels, Kevin (Actor)
c/o Staff Member *Insight*
1134 S Cloverdale Ave
Los Angeles, CA 90019-6737, USA

Daniels, Lee (Director, Producer)
c/o Staff Member *Lee Daniels Entertainment*
315 W 36th St Rm 1002
New York, NY 10018-6526, USA

Daniels, Leshun (Athlete, Football Player)
865 Landsdowne Ave NW
Warren, OH 44485-2227, USA

Daniels, Marquis
c/o Staff Member *Dallas Mavericks*
2500 Victory Ave
Dallas, TX 75219-7601, USA

Daniels, Melvin (Mel) (Athlete, Basketball Player)
19789 Centennial Rd
Sheridan, IN 46069-9789, USA

Daniels, Mitch (Governor)
Office of the Governor Statehouse
Indianapolis, IN 46204-2797, USA

Daniels, Owen (Athlete, Football Player)
5425 Inwood Dr
Houston, TX 77056-4215, USA

Daniels, Phillip (Athlete, Football Player)
1703 Pebble Beach Way
Vernon Hills, IL 60061-4520, USA

Daniels, Scott (Athlete, Hockey Player)
36 Deer Run
Southwick, MA 01077-9523, USA

Daniels, Spencer (Actor)
c/o Staff Member *Stone Manners Salners Agency (LA)*
9911 W Pico Blvd Ste 1400
Los Angeles, CA 90035-2715, USA

Daniels, Susan (Athlete, Golfer)
251 N Lake Blvd
Tahoe City, CA 96145, USA

Daniels, Travis (Athlete, Football Player)
4665 SW 75th Way Unit 104
Davie, FL 33314-4113, USA

Daniels, William (Actor)
12805 Hortense St
Studio City, CA 91604-1124, USA

Daniels, William B (Physicist)
1100 Lovering Ave Apt 1208
Wilmington, DE 19806-3277, USA

Danielsen, Egil (Athlete, Track Athlete)
Roreks Gate 9
Hamar 2300, NORWAY

Danielson, Gary D (Athlete, Football Player)
10112 Magnolia Bnd
Bonita Springs, FL 34135-8109, USA

Danielsson, Bengt F (Misc)
Box 558
Papette, TAHITI

Daniloff, Nicholas (Journalist)
PO Box 892
Chester, VT 05143-0892, USA

Danity Kane (Music Group)
c/o Tammy Brook *FYI Public Relations*
174 5th Ave Ste 400
New York, NY 10010-5935, USA

Danks, John (Athlete, Baseball Player)
702 Oaklands Dr
Round Rock, TX 78681-4029, USA

Danley, Kerwin (Athlete, Baseball Player)
3769 E Libra Pl
Chandler, AZ 85249-5867, USA

Danmeier, Rick (Athlete, Football Player)
4917 Ridge Rd
Minneapolis, MN 55436-1012, USA

Danneels, Godfried Cardinal (Religious Leader)
Aartsbisdom Wollemarkt 15
Mechelen 2800, BELGIUM

Danner, Blythe (Actor)
c/o Tony Lipp *Anonymous Content (AC-LA)*
2000 Avenue of the Stars
Los Angeles, CA 90067-4700, USA

Danner, Christian (Misc)
Viale Europa 72 Strada Bn 1
Cusago 20090, ITALY

Danning, Sybil (Actor, Model)

Danny & The Juniors (Music Group)
PO Box 279
Williamstown, NJ 08094-0279

Dano, Paul Franklin (Actor)
c/o Sandra Chang *Industry Entertainment Partners*
955 Carrillo Dr Ste 300
Los Angeles, CA 90048-5400, USA

Danoff, Bettye (Athlete, Golfer)
1422 Mill St
Gainesville, TX 76240-2514, USA

Dansby, Karlos (Athlete, Football Player)
16850 Stratford Ct
Southwest Ranches, FL 33331-1359, USA

Danson, Ted (Actor)
c/o Keith Addis *Industry Entertainment Partners*
955 Carrillo Dr Ste 300
Los Angeles, CA 90048-5400, USA

Dante, Joe (Director)
c/o Staff Member *Gersh (LA)*
9465 Wilshire Blvd Ste 600
Beverly Hills, CA 90212-2612, USA

Dante, Michael (Actor)
3349 Cahuenga Blvd W Ste 1
Los Angeles, CA 90068-1379, USA

Dante, Peter (Actor)
10460 Charing Cross Rd
Los Angeles, CA 90024-2646, USA

Dantine, Nikki (Actor)
707 N Palm Dr
Beverly Hills, CA 90210-3416, USA

Dantley, Adrian (Athlete, Basketball Player)
9 Barn Ridge Ct
Silver Spring, MD 20906-1105, USA

Danto, Arthur C (Misc)
Philosophy Dept
New York, NY 10024, USA

Danton, Mike (Athlete, Hockey Player)
Fort Dix F C I P.O. Box 1000 #10096-111
Fort Dix, NJ 8640, USA

Dantoni, Mike (Athlete, Basketball Player)
9 Hunter Ln
Rye, NY 10580-1614, USA

D'Antoni, Mike (Athlete, Basketball Player, Coach)
530 Moran Ave
Mullens, WV 25882-1528, USA

Dantzig, George B (Scientist)
2509 Tamalpais Ave
El Cerrito, CA 94530-1561, USA

Dantzig, Rudi Van (Choreographer)
Emma-Straat 27
Amsterdam, NETHERLANDS

Danz, Shirley (Baseball Player)
330 Greystone Dr
Hendersonville, NC 28792-9173, USA

Danza, Tony (Actor)
PO Box 69646
Los Angeles, CA 90069-0646, USA

Danzig
PO Box 884563
San Francisco, CA 94188-4563

Danzig, Frederick P (Editor)
220 E 42nd St
New York, NY 10017-5806, USA

Danziger, Cory (Actor)
c/o Staff Member *Iris Burton Agency*
10100 Santa Monica Blvd Ste 1300
Los Angeles, CA 90067-4114, USA

Danziger, Jeff (Cartoonist, Editor)
Plainfield, VT 5667, USA

Dao, Chloe (Fashion Designer)
6127 Kirby Dr
Houston, TX 77005-3148, USA

Daoud, Ignace Moussa I Cardinal (Religious Leader)
Palazzo del Bramante Via della Conciliazione 34
Rome 193, ITALY

Daoust, Dan (Athlete, Hockey Player)
55 John Stiver Crst
Markham, ON L3R 9B6, Canada

Daphnis, Nassos (Artist)
362 W Broadway
New York, NY 10013-5303, USA

Dapin, Marti (Stylist)
3748 N Sawyer Ave
Chicago, IL 60618-4410, USA

Dapkus-Wolf, Eleanor (Baseball Player)
9150 Mallard Cv
Saint John, IN 46373-9019, USA

Dapolito, Deborah (Stylist)
3731 Folsom St
San Francisco, CA 94110-5653, USA

Dapper, Cliff (Athlete, Baseball Player)
12 Roquedo
Rancho Santa Margarita, CA 92688-2722, USA

Dapper, Marco (Actor, Model)
c/o Steve Himber *Steve Himber Entertainment*
211 S Beverly Dr Apt S
Beverly Hills, CA 90212-3807, USA

Dar Dar, Kirby (Athlete, Football Player)
PO Box 2872
Syracuse, NY 13220-2872, USA

Dara, Olu (Actor)
c/o Staff Member *Monterey International (Chicago)*
200 W Superior St Ste 202
Chicago, IL 60654-6422, USA

D'Arabian, Melissa (Chef)
c/o Josh Bider *WmE2 (WMA-NY)*
1325 Avenue of the Americas
New York, NY 10019-6026, USA

Darabont, Frank (Director, Writer)
c/o Byrdie Lifson Pompan *Creative Artists Agency (CAA-LA)*
2000 Avenue of the Stars Ste 100
Los Angeles, CA 90067-4705, USA

D'Arbanville, Patti (Actor)
c/o Staff Member *Moskowit Agency*
180 Melrose Cir
Tryon, NC 28782-3350, USA

Darboven, Hanne (Artist)
Am Burgberg 26
Hamburg 21079, GERMANY

Darby, Chartric (Athlete, Football Player)
14335 Simonds Rd NE
Kirkland, WA 98034-9201, USA

Darby, Kim (Actor)
c/o Staff Member *Schiowitz Connor Ankrum Wolf*
1680 Vine St Ste 1016
Los Angeles, CA 90028-8800, USA

Darby, Matt (Athlete, Football Player)
501 Sagecreek Ct
Winter Springs, FL 32708-2731, USA

D'Arby, Terence Trent (Musician)
c/o Staff Member *Creative Artists Agency (CAA-LA)*
2000 Avenue of the Stars Ste 100
Los Angeles, CA 90067-4705, USA

D'Arby, Terence Trent (Sananda Maitreya) (Musician)
Sempione 38
Milan 20154, Italy

Darc, Mireille (Actor)
201 Faubourg Saint Honore
Paris 75008, FRANCE

D'Arcangelo, Ildebrando (Opera Singer)
6 Henrietta St
London WC2E 8LA, UNITED KINGDOM (UK)

Darcey, Pete (Athlete, Basketball Player)
17600 N Anderson Rd
Arcadia, OK 73007-7113, USA

Darche, Jean-Philippe (Athlete, Football Player)
9507 W 160th Ter
Stilwell, KS 66085-8127, USA

Darcum, Max (Skier)
PO Box 189
Dillon, CO 80435-0189, USA

D'Arcy (Musician)
500 Molino St Ste 104
Los Angeles, CA 90013-2264, USA

Darcy, Dame (Artist)
c/o Staff Member *Fantagraphics Books*
7563 Lake City Way NE
Seattle, WA 98115-4218, USA

D'Arcy, James (Actor)
c/o Joel Lubin *Creative Artists Agency (CAA-LA)*
2000 Avenue of the Stars Ste 100
Los Angeles, CA 90067-4705, USA

D'Arcy, Margaretta (Writer)
60/66 Wardour St
London W1V 4ND, UNITED KINGDOM (UK)

Darcy, Pat (Athlete, Baseball Player)
535 S Columbus Blvd
Tucson, AZ 85711-4753, USA

D'Arcy James, Brian (Actor)
c/o JB Roberts *Thruline Entertainment*
9250 Wilshire Blvd Ground Fl
Beverly Hills, CA 90212, USA

Darden, Christopher
c/o Staff Member *WmE2 (WMA-LA)*
1 William Morris Pl
Beverly Hills, CA 90212-4261, USA

Darden, Thom (Athlete, Football Player)
637 20th Ave SW
Cedar Rapids, IA 52404-5520, USA

Daredevil (Music Group)
c/o Staff Member *Wind-up Records*
72 Madison Ave Fl 8
New York, NY 10016-8731, USA

Darego, Agbani (Model)
c/o Staff Member *Miss World Ltd*
21 Golden Sq
London W1R 3PA, UNITED KINGDOM (UK)

Darehshori, Nader F (Publisher)
222 Berkeley St
Boston, MA 02116-3748, USA

Darensbourg, Vic (Athlete, Baseball Player)
4151 Abernethy Forest Pl
Las Vegas, NV 89141-4336, USA

Dareus, Marcell (Football Player)
c/o Todd France *France AllPro Athlete Management*
3500 Lenox Rd NE
Atlanta, GA 30326-4228, USA

Darius, Donovin (Athlete, Football Player)
7655 Founders Way
Ponte Vedra Beach, FL 32082-1954, USA

Dark, Al (Athlete, Baseball Player, Coach)
103 Cranberry Way
Easley, SC 29642-3200, USA

Dark, Mike (Athlete, Hockey Player)
741 Wellington St
Sarina, ON N7T 1J3, Canada

Dark Star Orchestra (Music Group)
PO Box 1282
Evanston, IL 60204-1282, USA

Darkins, Chris (Athlete, Football Player)
7 Riverway Unit 610
Houston, TX 77056-1972, USA

Darling, Charles (Chuck) (Athlete, Basketball Player, Olympic Athlete)
8066 S Krameria Way
Centennial, CO 80112-3040, USA

Darling, Devard (Athlete, Football Player)
11410 Via Fontana Ct
Richmond, TX 77406-4598, USA

Darling, Gary (Athlete, Baseball Player)
16609 S 32nd Ln
Phoenix, AZ 85045-1223, USA

Darling, Jennifer (Actor)
13351 Riverside Dr # 427
Sherman Oaks, CA 91423-2542, USA

Darling, Joan (Actor)
PO Box 6700
Tesuque, NM 87574-6700, USA

Darling, Ron (Athlete, Baseball Player)
c/o Staff Member *SportsNet New York*
75 Rockefeller Plz
New York, NY 10019-6908, USA

Darmaatmadja, Julius Riyadi Cardinal (Religious Leader)
Keuskupan Agung Jl Katedral 7
Jakarta 10710, INDONESIA

Darnell, James E Jr (Biologist)
Medical Center 1230 York Ave
New York, NY 10021, USA

Darnton, Robert C (Historian)
975 Memorial Dr Apt 411
Cambridge, MA 02138-5793, USA

Darr, Mike (Athlete, Baseball Player)
1461 Maplebrook Ln
Corona, CA 92881-0704, USA

Darragh, Dan (Athlete, Football Player)
201 Sewickley Ridge Ct
Sewickley, PA 15143-8973, USA

Darren, James (Actor, Musician)
PO Box 1088
Beverly Hills, CA 90213-1088, USA

Darrian, Raquel (Adult Film Star)
49 Eaton Ct
Manhasset, NY 11030-4052

Darrieux, Danielle (Actor)
1 Rue Alfred de Vigny
Paris 75008, FRANCE

Darrow, Barry (Athlete, Football Player)
2406 Chief Victor Camp Rd
Victor, MT 59875-9410, USA

Dart, Iris Rainer (Writer)
938 Coral Dr
Pebble Beach, CA 93953-2503, USA

Darwin, Bobby (Athlete, Baseball Player)
6516 Pleasant Hill Cir
Corona, CA 92880-3015, USA

Darwin, Danny (Athlete, Baseball Player)
11131 Lakecrest Dr
Sanger, TX 76266-3446, USA

Darwin, Jeff (Athlete, Baseball Player)
1010 W Russell Ave
Bonham, TX 75418-2332, USA

Darwin, Matt (Athlete, Football Player)
1103 N Waddill St
Mc Kinney, TX 75069-2963, USA

Darwitz, Natalie (Athlete, Hockey Player)
c/o Staff Member *US Olympic Committee*
1750 E Boulder St
Colorado Springs, CO 80909-5793, USA

Das, Alisha (Actor)
19583 Bowers Dr
Topanga, CA 90290-3102, USA

Das, Nandita (Actor)
c/o Aude Powell *Brunskill Management*
Suite 8A 169 Queen's Gate
London SW7 5HE, United Kingdom

Dascascos, Marc (Actor)
PO Box 1549
Studio City, CA 91614-0549, USA

Dascenzo, Doug (Athlete, Baseball Player)
111 Eastgate Rd
Uniontown, PA 15401-5615, USA

D'Ascoli, Bernard (Musician)
47 Whitehall Park
London N19 3TW, UNITED KINGDOM (UK)

Dash, Damon (Actor, Director, Producer, Writer)
c/o Staff Member *Fortitude*
6500 Wilshire Blvd Ste 2200
Los Angeles, CA 90048-4942, USA

Dash, Julie (Actor, Director, Producer, Writer)
c/o Kimber Wheeler *TalentWorks (LA)*
3500 W Olive Ave Ste 1400
Burbank, CA 91505-5512, USA

Dash, Leon O Jr (Journalist)
1150 15th Ave NW
Washington, DC 20071-0001, USA

Dash, Sam
110 Newlands
Chevy Chase, MD 20015

Dash, Stacey (Actor)
c/o Staff Member *Bleu, An Entertainment Company*
5225 Wilshire Blvd Ste 336
Los Angeles, CA 90036-4380, USA

Dashboard Confessional (Music Group, Musician)
c/o Richard Egan *Hard 8 Management*
1000 Main St Ste 203
Nashville, TN 37206-3626, USA

Daskalakis, Cleon (Athlete, Hockey Player)
752 Main St
Boxford, MA 01921-1127, USA

Dassier, Uwe (Swimmer)
Stolze-Schrey-Str 6
Wilday 15745, GREECE

Dasso, Frank (Athlete, Baseball Player)
1008 NW 85th St Apt 2
Seattle, WA 98117-3356, USA

Dater, Judy L (Photographer)
2430 5th St Ste J
Berkeley, CA 94710-2452, USA

Datsyuk, Pavel (Athlete, Hockey Player)
3166 Rosedale St
Ann Arbor, MI 48108-1884, USA

Dattilo, Bryan (Actor)
c/o Staff Member *Cohen/Thomas Agency*
1888 N Crescent Heights Blvd
Los Angeles, CA 90069-1647, USA

Dattilo, Kristin (Actor)
c/o Jim Hess *Hess Entertainment*
360 N Crescent Dr
Beverly Hills, CA 90210-4874, USA

Datz, Jeff (Athlete, Baseball Player)
4775 Elen Ct
Shingle Springs, CA 95682-9519, USA

Daubach, Brian (Athlete, Baseball Player)
2709 Timberline Dr
Belleville, IL 62226-4933, USA

Daubechies, Ingrid C (Mathematician)
Mathematics
Princeton, NJ 08544-0001, USA

Dauben, William G (Misc)
16820 Woodlake Dr
College Station, TX 77845-8274, USA

Dauer, Rich (Athlete, Baseball Player)
10546 Graymont Ln Unit A
Highlands Ranch, CO 80126-6719, USA

Daugaard, Dennis (Governor, Politician)
500 E Capitol Ave Ofc of
Pierre, SD 57501-5007, USA

Daugherty, Bradley L (Brad) (Athlete, Basketball Player)
62 Willow Farm Rd
Fairview, NC 28730, USA

Daugherty, Doc (Athlete, Baseball Player)
314 Summers Dr
Lancaster, PA 17601-5884, USA

Daugherty, Jack (Athlete, Baseball Player)
20360 N 95th Pl
Scottsdale, AZ 85255-6646, USA

Daugherty, Martha Craig (Judge)
701 Broadway
Nashville, TN 37203-3944, USA

Daughtry, Chris (Musician)
8404 Oakchester Ct
Oak Ridge, NC 27310-9856, USA

Dauline, Marie (Musician)
PO Box 652
New York, NY 10276-0652, USA

Daulton, Darren A (Athlete, Baseball Player)
211 N 3rd St
Arkansas City, KS 67005-2452, USA

Dauplaise, Norman (Jockey)
29 W 36th St # 1000
New York, NY 10018-7907, USA

Daurey, Dana (Actor)
8730 W Sunset Blvd Ste 440
Los Angeles, CA 90069-2277, USA

Dausset, Jean B G (Nobel Prize Laureate)
9 Rue de Villersexel
Paris 75007, FRANCE

Davalillo, Vic (Athlete, Baseball Player)
Calle Trujillo 7 Mariperez Q V
Caracas, Venezuela

Davalos, Alexa (Actor)
c/o Staff Member *Anonymous Content (AC-LA)*
3531 Hayden Ave
Culver City, CA 90232, USA

Davalos, Elyssa
2934 1/2 N Beverly Glen Cir # 53
Los Angeles, CA 90077-1724

Davalos, Richard (Actor)
23388 Mulholland Dr # 28
Woodland Hills, CA 91364-2733, USA

Davanon, Jeff (Athlete, Baseball Player)
2811 Piedmont Ave
Los Alamitos, CA 90720-4244, USA

Davanon, Jerry (Athlete, Baseball Player)
350 Greypine W
Montgomery, TX 77356-8192, USA

Dave, Al (Athlete, Football Player)
5173 Waring Rd Apt 441
San Diego, CA 92120-2705, USA

Davenport, A Nigel (Actor)
5 Ann's Close Kinnerton Street
London SW1, UNITED KINGDOM (UK)

Davenport, Adell (Baseball Player)
1764 Belt Line Rd Apt 155
Garland, TX 75044-6824, USA

Davenport, Charles (Athlete, Football Player)
206 Wapiti Dr
Spring Lake, NC 28390-1530, USA

Davenport, Jack (Actor)
c/o Lorraine Hamilton *Hamilton Hodell Ltd*
66-68 Margaret St Fl 5
London W1W 8SR, UK

Davenport, Jim (Athlete, Baseball Player, Coach)
1016 Hewitt Dr
San Carlos, CA 94070-3601, USA

Davenport, Joe (Athlete, Baseball Player)
10102 Wycliffe St
Santee, CA 92071-1176, USA

Davenport, Lindsay
PO Box 10179
Newport Beach, CA 92658-0179

Davenport, Lindsey (Tennis Player)
PO Box 10179
Newport Beach, CA 92658-0179, USA

Davenport, Madison (Actor)
c/o Erik Kritzer *Kritzer Levine Wilkins Entertainment*
11872 La Grange Ave Fl 1
Los Angeles, CA 90025-5283, USA

Davenport, Najeh (Athlete, Football Player)
1225 NW 103rd Ln
Miami, FL 33147-1412, USA

Davenport, Nigel (Actor)
2 Conduit St
London W1R9TG, UNITED KINGDOM (UK)

Davenport Cabinet (Musician)
c/o Blaze James *Black Sheep Fellowship*
3134 Glenmanor Pl
Los Angeles, CA 90039-1713, USA

Davenport Jr, Guy M (Writer)
621 Sayre Ave
Lexington, KY 40508-2317, USA

Davenport Jr, Wilbur B (Engineer)
1120 Skyline Dr
Medford, OR 97504-8585, USA

Davey, Don (Athlete, Football Player)
212 Ocean Frnt
Neptune Beach, FL 32266, USA

Davey, Mike (Athlete, Baseball Player)
902 W Melinda Ln
Spokane, WA 99203-1363, USA

Davey, Rohan (Athlete, Football Player)
24696 Plank Rd
Slaughter, LA 70777-9703, USA

Davey, Tom (Athlete, Baseball Player)
13125 Andover Dr
Plymouth, MI 48170-8208, USA

Davi, Robert (Actor)
c/o Staff Member *Paradigm (LA)*
360 N Crescent Dr
Beverly Hills, CA 90210-4874, USA

Daviau, Allen (Cinematographer)
2249 Bronson Hill Dr
Los Angeles, CA 90068-2407, USA

Daviault, Ray (Athlete, Baseball Player)
12116 Ontario St E
Pte-Aux-Trembles, Quebec H1B 1L4, Canada

Davich, Jacob (Actor)
c/o Brad Schenck *Paradigm (LA)*
360 N Crescent Dr
Beverly Hills, CA 90210-4874, USA

Davich, Marty (Composer)
530 S Greenwood Ave
Pasadena, CA 91107-5101, USA

David, Andre (Athlete, Baseball Player)
17341 W Banff Ln
Surprise, AZ 85388-7712, USA

David, Charlie (Actor)
205-309 W Cordova St
Vancouver BC V6B 1E5, Canada

David, Craig (Musician)
c/o Cara Lewis *WmE2 (WMA-NY)*
1325 Avenue of the Americas
New York, NY 10019-6026, USA

David, George A L (Business Person)
United Technologies Building
Hartford, CT 6101, USA

David, Hal (Musician)
10430 Wilshire Blvd
Los Angeles, CA 90024-4651, USA

David, John R (Misc)
665 Huntington Ave
Boston, MA 02115-6021, USA

David, Keith (Actor)
c/o Josh Silver *Silver Mine Entertainment*
6705 W Sunset Blvd
Hollywood, CA 90028-7107, USA

David, Larry (Actor, Producer, Writer)
c/o Ariel (Ari) Emanuel *WmE2 (Endeavor-LA)*
9601 Wilshire Blvd Fl 3
Beverly Hills, CA 90210-5219, USA

David, Laurie (Activist)
2934 1/2 N Beverly Glen Cir
Los Angeles, CA 90077-1724, USA

David, Mack
1575 Toledo Cir
Palm Springs, CA 92264-9535

David, Mohato (Prince)
PO Box 524
Maseru, LESOTHO

David, Peter (Actor)
PO Box 239
Bayport, NY 11705-0239, USA

David, Silvana (Stylist)
c/o Staff Member *Rex Agency, The*
6311 Romaine St
Los Angeles, CA 90038-2617, USA

David, Stan (Athlete, Football Player)
502 Baja Cir
Denver City, TX 79323-3747, USA

David, Yuval (Actor, Musician)
c/o Stanzi Stokes *Trio Entertainment Group*
16060 Ventura Blvd # 105-349
Encino, CA 91436-2761, USA

David Bossert, David Bossert (Director, Producer)
c/o Staff Member *Walt Disney Television Animation*
500 S Buena Vista St
Burbank, CA 91521-0007

David Crowder Band (Musician)
c/o Staff Member *Third Coast Artists Agency*
2021 21st Ave S Ste 220
Nashville, TN 37212-4348, USA

David Jr, Edward E (Engineer)
PO Box 435
Bedminster, NJ 07921-0435, USA

Davidoff, Dov (Actor)
c/o Stephanie Davis *3 Arts Entertainment Inc*
9460 Wilshire Blvd Fl 7
Beverly Hills, CA 90212-2713, USA

Davidovich, Bella (Musician)
c/o Staff Member *Columbia Artists Mgmt Inc*
1790 Broadway Fl 6
New York, NY 10019-1537, USA

Davidovich, Lolita (Actor)
c/o Nancy Sanders *Sanders Armstrong Caserta*
2120 Colorado Ave Ste 120
Santa Monica, CA 90404-3561, USA

Davidovsky, Mario (Composer)
Music Dept
Cambridge, MA 2138, USA

Davids, Hollace (Producer)
c/o Staff Member *Universal Pictures*
100 Universal City Plz
Universal City, CA 91608-1085, USA

Davidson, Adam (Actor)
c/o Andrea Simon *Andrea Simon Entertainment*
4230 Woodman Ave
Sherman Oaks, CA 91423-4334, USA

Davidson, Amy (Actor)
c/o Staff Member *Paradigm (LA)*
360 N Crescent Dr
Beverly Hills, CA 90210-4874, USA

Davidson, Ben E (Athlete, Football Player)
4737 Angels Pt
La Mesa, CA 91941-6899, USA

Davidson, Bob (Athlete, Baseball Player)
1420 Bruton Parish Way
Fairfield, OH 45014-4536, USA

Davidson, Bob (Athlete, Baseball Player)
91 Deerwood Dr
Littleton, CO 80127-2626, USA

Davidson, Bruce O (Misc)
RR 842
Unionville, PA 19375, USA

Davidson, Cleatus (Athlete, Baseball Player)
112 Lincoln Ave
Dundee, FL 33838-4394, USA

Davidson, Cotton (Athlete, Football Player)
435 Old Osage Rd
Gatesville, TX 76528-3362, USA

Davidson, Diane Mott (Writer)
c/o Author Mail *Bantam-Dell Publishing (NY)*
1745 Broadway
New York, NY 10019-4368, USA

Davidson, Doug (Actor)
c/o Staff Member *The Young and The Restless*
7800 Beverly Blvd Ste 3305
Los Angeles, CA 90036-2112, USA

Davidson, Eileen (Actor)
11300 W Olympic Blvd Ste 610
Los Angeles, CA 90064-1643, USA

Davidson, Ernest R (Scientist)
5051 50th Ave NE Apt 22
Seattle, WA 98105-2861, USA

Davidson, George A Jr (Business Person)
625 Liberty Ave
Pittsburgh, PA 15222-3120, USA

Davidson, Gordon (Director, Producer)
135 N Grand Ave
Los Angeles, CA 90012-3013, USA

Davidson, Jeff (Motivational Speaker)
3202 Ruffin St
Raleigh, NC 27607-4024, USA

Davidson, Jeff (Athlete, Football Player)
10036 Gristmill Rdg
Eden Prairie, MN 55347-4759, USA

Davidson, Jeremy (Actor)
c/o Matthew Lesher *Insight*
1134 S Cloverdale Ave
Los Angeles, CA 90019-6737, USA

Davidson, Jim (Actor)
c/o Staff Member *International Artistes*
Holborn Hall - 4th Floor
London WC1V 7BD, UK

Davidson, John (Actor, Musician)
c/o Josh Pultz *Douglas Gorman Rothacker & Wilhelm Inc*
1501 Broadway Ste 703
New York, NY 10036-5501, USA

Davidson, John (Athlete, Hockey Player)
6 Briarbrook Trl
Saint Louis, MO 63131-3947, USA

Davidson, Ken (Athlete, Football Player)
1922 Thompson Crossing Dr
Richmond, TX 77406-6707, USA

Davidson, Mark (Athlete, Baseball Player)
996 Old Mountain Rd
Statesville, NC 28677-2082, USA

Davidson, Matthew (Athlete, Golfer)
3 Westminster Pl
Cranbury, NJ 08512-3217, USA

Davidson, Owen (Athlete, Tennis Player)
39 N Lakemist Harbour Pl
Spring, TX 77381-3344, USA

Davidson, Ralph P (Publisher)
494 Harbor Rd
Southport, CT 06890-1319, USA

Davidson, Ronald C (Physicist)
Plasma Physics Laboratory
Princeton, NJ 08544-0001, USA

Davidson, Satch (Athlete, Baseball Player)
2400 Westheimer Rd Apt 209W
Houston, TX 77098-1305, USA

Davidson, Tommy (Actor, Comedian)
c/o Stacy Mark *WmE2 (Endeavor-LA)*
9601 Wilshire Blvd Fl 3
Beverly Hills, CA 90210-5219, USA

Davidtz, Embeth (Actor)
c/o Judy Hofflund *Hofflund/Polone*
9465 Wilshire Blvd Ste 420
Beverly Hills, CA 90212-2603, USA

Davie, Alan (Artist)
Gamels Studio Rush Green
Hertford SG13 7SB, UNITED KINGDOM (UK)

Davie, Donald A (Writer)
4 High St Silverton
Exeter EX5 4JB, UNITED KINGDOM (UK)

Davie, Jerry (Athlete, Baseball Player)
2800 US Highway 17 92 W
Haines City, FL 33844-9391, USA

Davies, Dave (Musician)
29 Ruston Mews
London W11 1RB, UNITED KINGDOM (UK)

Davies, Dennis Russell
Am Wichelshof 24
Bonn 53111, GERMANY

Davies, Gail (Musician)
246 Cherokee Rd
Nashville, TN 37205-1818, USA

Davies, Geralnt Wyn (Actor)
438 Queen St W
Toronto, ON M5A 1T4, CANADA

Davies, Jeremy (Actor)
9560 Wilshire Blvd Ste 500
Beverly Hills, CA 90212-2401, USA

Davies, Kenneth (Athlete, Hockey Player)
370 Williston Way
Pawtucket, RI 02861-4114, USA

Davies, Kyle (Athlete, Baseball Player)
1495 E Lake Rd
McDonough, GA 30252-2615, USA

Davies, Lane (Actor)
906 Black Bass Rd
Cohutta, GA 30710-7809, USA

Davies, Laura (Athlete, Golfer)
1360 E 9th St Ste 100
Cleveland, OH 44114-1730, USA

Davies, Linda (Writer)
Calle Once 286 La Molona
Lima, PERU

Davies, Matt (Artist, Cartoonist, Editor)
1 Gannett Dr
White Plains, NY 10604-3402, USA

Davies, Mike (Architect)
Thames Wharf Rainville Road
London N6 94A, UNITED KINGDOM (UK)

Davies, Paul C W (Mathematician, Physicist)
PO Box 389
Burnside, SA 5066, AUSTRALIA

Davies, Peter (Misc)
Biochemistry Dept
Bronx, NY 10461, USA

Davies, Peter Maxwell (Composer)
50 Hogarth Road
London SW5 OPU, UNITED KINGDOM (UK)

Davies, Raymond D (Ray) (Musician, Songwriter)
29 Ruston Mews
London W11 1RB, UNITED KINGDOM (UK)

Davies, Russel T (Writer)
c/o Lisa Harrison *WmE2 (Endeavor-LA)*
9601 Wilshire Blvd Fl 3
Beverly Hills, CA 90210-5219, USA

Davies, Ryland (Opera Singer)
71 Fairmile Lane Cobham
Surrey KT11 2DG, UNITED KINGDOM (UK)

Davies, Tamara (Actor)
c/o Staff Member *Bauman Redanty & Shaul Agency*
5757 Wilshire Blvd Suite 473
Beverly Hills, CA 90212, USA

Davies, Terence (Director)
c/o Tony Peake *Peake Associates*
14 Grafton Crescent
London NW1 8SL, UK

Davies, Warrick (Actor)
76 Oxford St
London W1N 0AX, UNITED KINGDOM (UK)

Davies, Wyn (Actor)
c/o Staff Member *Screen Actors Guild (SAG-LA)*
5757 Wilshire Blvd
Los Angeles, CA 90036-5810, USA

Davis, A Dano (Business Person)
5050 Edgewood Ct
Jacksonville, FL 32254-3601, USA

Davis, Al (Athlete, Football Coach, Football Player)
300 Mountain Ave
Piedmont, CA 94611-3508, USA

Davis, Alecia (Actor)
c/o Jonathan Clements *Nashville Agency*
PO Box 110909
Nashville, TN 37222-0909, USA

Davis, Allen (Al) (Misc)
1220 Harbor Bay Pkwy
Alameda, CA 94502-6501, USA

Davis, Alvin (Athlete, Baseball Player)
7983 Armagosa Dr
Riverside, CA 92508-8713, USA

Davis, Andra (Athlete, Football Player)
21230 Greenfield Pl
Strongsville, OH 44149-9218, USA

Davis, Andre (Athlete, Football Player)
11407 Jutland Rd
Houston, TX 77048-2631, USA

Davis, Andrew (Director)
c/o Laurence Becsey *Intellectual Property Group (IPG)*
9200 W Sunset Blvd Ste 520
Los Angeles, CA 90069-3507, USA

Davis, Andrew (Misc)
14500 Fiske Dr
Silver Spring, MD 20906-1737, USA

Davis, Andy (Athlete, Football Player)
14500 Fiske Dr
Silver Spring, MD 20906-1737, USA

Davis, Angela Y (Activist, Educator, Politician)
PO Box 99096
Emeryville, CA 94662-9096, USA

Davis, Ann B (Actor)
23315 Eagle Gap
San Antonio, TX 78255-2103, USA

Davis, Anne B (Actor)
c/o Leanna Levy *Cassell-Levy Inc*
843 N Sycamore Ave
Los Angeles, CA 90038-3391, USA

Davis, Anthony (Athlete, Football Player)
8923 Cambridge Ave Apt 2606
Kansas City, MO 64138-5426, USA

Davis, Anthony (Composer, Musician)
115 E 9th St
New York, NY 10003-5414, USA

Davis, Anthony (Athlete, Football Player)
29 Firwood
Irvine, CA 92604-4632, USA

Davis, Antone (Athlete, Football Player)
4016 Norwood Ave
Chattanooga, TN 37415-7112, USA

Davis, Antonio (Basketball Player)
625 Willow Glen Dr
El Paso, TX 79922-2210, USA

Davis, Aree (Actor)
c/o Myrna Lieberman *Myrna Lieberman Management*
3001 Hollyridge Dr
Hollywood, CA 90068-1951, USA

Davis, Arthur (Athlete, Football Player)
8260 SW Woodbridge Ct
Wilsonville, OR 97070-7458, USA

Davis, Bard (Basketball Player)
2703 Ridge Top Ln
Arlington, TX 76006-2729, USA

Davis, Baron (Athlete, Basketball Player)
c/o Staff Member *BDA Sports Management (BDA-CA)*
700 Ygnacio Valley Rd Ste 330
Walnut Creek, CA 94596-3838, USA

Davis, Ben (Athlete, Baseball Player)
416 Homestead Dr
West Chester, PA 19382-8242, USA

Davis, Ben (Athlete, Football Player)
1144 Brandon Rd
Cleveland, OH 44112-3632, USA

Davis, Bennie L (General)
246 Scissortail Trl
Georgetown, TX 78633-4833, USA

Davis, Beryl (Actor)
1870 Caminito Del Cielo
Glendale, CA 91208-3049, USA

Davis, Bill (Athlete, Baseball Player)
6638 Knox Ave S
Minneapolis, MN 55423-2161, USA

Davis, Billy (Athlete, Football Player)
5813 Tautoga Dr
El Paso, TX 79924-5620, USA

Davis, Bob (Athlete, Baseball Player)
PO Box 198
Locust Grove, OK 74352-0198, USA

Davis, Brad (Athlete, Basketball Player)
2703 Ridge Top Ln
Arlington, TX 76006-2729, USA

Davis, Brian (Athlete, Golfer)
4162 Haws Ln
Orlando, FL 32814-6554, USA

Davis, Brian (Athlete, Football Player)
6442 W Park Ave
Chandler, AZ 85226-1146, USA

Davis, Brianne (Actor)
c/o Staff Member *Art Work Entertainment*
5900 Wilshire Blvd Ste 2150
Los Angeles, CA 90036-5021, USA

Davis, Brock (Athlete, Baseball Player)
23759 Heliotrope Way
Moreno Valley, CA 92557-2858, USA

Davis, Buddy (Athlete, Basketball Player)
6582 FM 841
Lufkin, TX 75901-4633, USA

Davis, Butch (Athlete, Baseball Player)
1108 Brucemont Dr
Garner, NC 27529-4505, USA

Davis, Carl (Composer)
99 Church Road Barnes
London SW13 9HL, UNITED KINGDOM (UK)

Davis, Carlos (Stylist)
c/o Staff Member *Mel Bryant Management*
611 Broadway Rm 623
New York, NY 10012-2650

Davis, Carole (Actor)
c/o Judy Orbach *Judy O Productions*
6136 Glen Holly St
Hollywood, CA 90068-2338, USA

Davis, Charles (Athlete, Basketball Player)
615 Main St
Nashville, TN 37206-3603, USA

Davis, Charles (Actor)
c/o Anthony Embry *AE Entertainment Public Relations*
124 Evening Shade Dr
Charleston, SC 29414-9144, USA

Davis, Charles (Chili) (Athlete, Baseball Player)
c/o Team Member *San Francisco Giants*
SBC Park 24 Willie Mays Plaza
San Francisco, CA 94107, USA

Davis, Charles D (Athlete, Football Player)
8935 Aspen Meadow Dr
Houston, TX 77071-3256, USA

Davis, Charles M (Athlete, Football Player)
PO Box 772011
Houston, TX 77215-2011, USA

Davis, Charlie (Athlete, Basketball Player)
302 Heather Ridge Ct
Greensboro, NC 27455-8360, USA

Davis, Chip (Musician)
c/o Staff Member *Brokaw Company, The*
9255 W Sunset Blvd Ste 804
Los Angeles, CA 90069-3305, USA

Davis, Christine (Writer)
PO Box 90125
Portland, OR 97290-0125, USA

Davis, Christopher (Chris) W (Athlete, Football Player)
PO Box 5000
Ogdensburg, NY 13669-5000, USA

Davis, Clarence (Athlete, Football Player)
171 Longleaf St
Pickerington, OH 43147-7940, USA

Davis, Clifton (Actor)
c/o Staff Member *Agency for the Performing Arts (APA-LA)*
405 S Beverly Dr Ste 500
Beverly Hills, CA 90212-4425, USA

Davis, Clive J (Business Person, Producer)
733 3rd Ave Fl 3
New York, NY 10017-3211

Davis, Colin R
39 Huntingdon St
London N1 1BP, UNITED KINGDOM (UK)

Davis, Dale (Baseball Player)
7945 Beaumont Green Pl
Indianapolis, NC 27455-8360, USA

Davis, Dale (Athlete, Basketball Player)
5047 Duxford Dr SE
Smyrna, GA 30082-5059, USA

Davis, Dana (Actor)
c/o Darryl Marshak *Marshak/Zachary Company, The*
8840 Wilshire Blvd Fl 1
Beverly Hills, CA 90211-2606, USA

Davis, Daniel (Actor)
c/o Gary Gersh *Innovative Artists (NY)*
235 Park Ave S Fl 7
New York, NY 10003-1404, USA

Davis, David Brion (Historian, Writer)
783 Lambert Rd
Orange, CT 6477, USA

Davis, David (Dave) (Bowler)
710 Shore Rd
Spring Lake, NJ 07762-1855, USA

Davis, DeRay (Actor)
c/o April Lim *Global Artists Agency*
6253 Hollywood Blvd Apt 508
Los Angeles, CA 90028-8251, USA

Davis, Dexter (Athlete, Football Player)
5054 Vermack Rd
Atlanta, GA 30338-4627, USA

Davis, Dick (Athlete, Baseball Player)
14171 Paso Robles Ct
Victorville, CA 92392-5419, USA

Davis, Dick (Athlete, Football Player)
1626 N 137th St
Omaha, NE 68154-3826, USA

Davis, Domanick (Athlete, Football Player)
5930 Tammy Dr
Manvel, TX 77578-3156, USA

Davis, Don H Jr (Business Person)
777 E Wisconsin Ave Ste 1400
Milwaukee, WI 53202-5317, USA

Davis, Donald (Athlete, Football Player)
739 E 48th St
Los Angeles, CA 90011-4008, USA

Davis, Dorsett (Athlete, Football Player)
605 Rosemary Rd
Cleveland, MS 38732-2048, USA

Davis, Doug (Athlete, Baseball Player)
279 Whites Church Rd
Bloomsburg, PA 17815-7156, USA

Davis, Doug (Athlete, Baseball Player)
1401 N Broadway
Walnut Creek, CA 94596-4696, USA

Davis, Douglas S (Athlete, Football Player)
613 Hitching Post Dr
Brandon, FL 33511-7808, USA

Davis, Dwight (Athlete, Basketball Player)
3231 Woods Canyon Ct
Missouri City, TX 77459-4958, USA

Davis, Ed (Athlete, Basketball Player)
36750 US Highway 19 N # 26-3437
Palm Harbor, FL 34684-1239, USA

Davis, Elizabeth (Musician)
PO Box 310780
Jamaica, NY 11431-0780, USA

Davis, Elliot M (Cinematographer)
1328 Arch St
Berkeley, CA 94708-1825, USA

Davis, Eric (Athlete, Baseball Player)
5334 Collingwood Cir
Calabasas, CA 91302-3137, USA

Davis, Eric W (Athlete, Football Player)
3737 Coyote Cyn
Soquel, CA 95073-3034, USA

Davis, Frenchie (Musician)
c/o Belinda Foster *AWJ Platinum PR*
8350 Wilshire Blvd Ste 200
Beverly Hills, CA 90211-2348, USA

Davis, Gary (Athlete, Football Player)
10750 San Marcos Rd
Atascadero, CA 93422-2126, USA

Davis, Geena (Actor)
c/o Samantha Mast *Rogers & Cowan PR (LA)*
Pacific Design Center 8687 Melrose Ave, 7th Floor
West Hollywood, CA 90069, USA

Davis, Geoff (Congressman, Politician)
1119 Longworth Hob
Washington, DC 20515-0531, USA

Davis, George (Athlete, Baseball Player)
3092 Kimball Ave
Memphis, TN 38114-4070, USA

Davis, Georgia (Stylist)
c/o Staff Member *Loox Agency*
12 Desbrosses St
New York, NY 10013-1704, USA

Davis, Gerry (Athlete, Baseball Player)
2440 Stroebe Island Dr
Appleton, WI 54914-8758, USA

Davis, Glenn (Athlete)
627 Llewelyn Rd
Berwyn, PA 19312-2012, USA

Davis, Glenn A (Athlete, Football Player)
801 Robinson Ave
Barberton, OH 44203-3763, USA

Davis, Glenn E (Athlete, Baseball Player)
27 Cascade Rd
Columbus, GA 31904-2806, USA

Davis, Gray (Ex-Governor)
State Capitol Building
Sacramento, CA 95814, USA

Davis, Greg (Athlete, Football Player)
PO Box 747
Ouray, CO 81427-0747, USA

Davis, H Thomas (Tommy) (Athlete, Baseball Player)
9767 Whirlaway St
Rancho Cucamonga, CA 91737-1643, USA

Davis, Harper (Athlete, Football Player)
1224 Springdale Dr
Jackson, MS 39211-3130, USA

Davis, Harrison (Athlete, Football Player)
6409 Lesser Dr
Greeley, CO 80634-9595, USA

Davis, Harry (Athlete, Basketball Player)
1966 E 75th St
Cleveland, OH 44103-4125, USA

Davis, Hope (Actor)
c/o Perri Kipperman *Kipperman Management*
243 W 72nd St Apt 2
New York, NY 10023-2704, USA

Davis, Hubert (Athlete, Basketball Player)
204 Lancaster Dr
Chapel Hill, NC 27517-3429, USA

Davis, J J (Athlete, Baseball Player)
7302 Forrest Rader Dr
Mint Hill, NC 28227-9830, USA

Davis, Jack (Athlete, Football Player)
3001 Reeder St
Fort Smith, AR 72901-4223, USA

Davis, Jacke (Athlete, Baseball Player)
6806 Castle Pines Ct
Tyler, TX 75703-5890, USA

Davis, James (Athlete, Football Player)
5701 S St Andrews Pl
Los Angeles, CA 90062-2649, USA

Davis, James (Basketball Player)
44 Van Ter
Sparkill, NY 10976-1406, USA

Davis, James B (General)
3600 Wimber Blvd
Palm Harbor, FL 34685, USA

Davis, James O (Doctor)
546 Warren Ave
Saint Louis, MO 63130-4154, USA

Davis, James R (Jim) (Cartoonist)
5440 E Country Rd 450 N
Albany, IN 47320, USA

Davis, Jason (Athlete, Baseball Player)
474 Leatha Ln NW
Cleveland, TN 37312-6522, USA

Davis, Jay (Athlete, Golfer)
2152 S State St
Springfield, IL 62704-4526, USA

Davis, Jeff (Actor)
c/o Staff Member *United Talent Agency (UTA)*
9560 Wilshire Blvd Fl 5
Beverly Hills, CA 90212-2400, USA

Davis, Jeff (Athlete, Football Player)
106 Sycamore Dr
Clemson, SC 29631-2071, USA

Davis, Jerome (Athlete, Football Player)
515 N 4th St
Palatka, FL 32177-3523, USA

Davis, Jerry (Baseball Player)
72 Theresa St
Ewing, NJ 08618-1531, USA

Davis, Jesse (Musician)
100 N Crescent Dr Ste 275
Beverly Hills, CA 90210-5412, USA

Davis, Jill A (Writer)
1745 Broadway # B1
New York, NY 10019-4368, USA

Davis, Jimmy (Athlete, Football Player)
616 Briar Patch Ter
Waxhaw, NC 28173-6822, USA

Davis, Jody (Athlete, Baseball Player)
5631 N 79th St Unit 4
Scottsdale, AZ 85250-6546, USA

Davis, Joel (Athlete, Baseball Player)
651 Grove Park Blvd
Jacksonville, FL 32216-9324, USA

Davis, John (Athlete, Baseball Player)
76871 Castle Ct
Palm Desert, CA 92211-7100, USA

Davis, John (Athlete, Football Player)
901 Forest Pond Dr
Marietta, GA 30068-4420, USA

Davis, John A (Actor, Composer, Director, Producer)
c/o Staff Member *Davis Entertainment*
150 S Barrington Pl
Los Angeles, CA 90049-3306, USA

Davis, Johnny (Athlete, Basketball Player, Coach)
135 W Market St Apt 2D
Indianapolis, IN 46204-2817, USA

Davis, Johnny (Athlete, Football Player)
3726 Ingleside Rd
Shaker Heights, OH 44122-5006, USA

Davis, Jonathan (Musician)
c/o Ian Sales *International Talent Booking*
1st Floor, Ariel House 74A Charlotte St
London W1T 4QJ, UNITED KINGDOM

Davis, Josie (Actor)
10635 Santa Monica Blvd Ste 130
Los Angeles, CA 90025-8306, USA

Davis, Judy (Actor)
c/o Ann Churchill-Brown *Shanahan Management*
Level 3 Berman House
Surry Hills 2010, AUSTRALIA

Davis, Kane (Athlete, Baseball Player)
1558 Noble Rdg
Reedy, WV 25270-9540, USA

Davis, Keith B (Athlete, Football Player)
1343 Marvin Gdns
Lancaster, TX 75134-1684, USA

Davis, Kenneth E (Athlete, Football Player)
1224 Brooklawn Dr
Arlington, TX 76018-2952, USA

Davis, Kim (Athlete, Hockey Player)
14 Shorecrest Dr
Winnipeg, MB R3P 1N2, Canada

Davis, Kristin (Actor, Producer)
c/o David (Dave) Fleming *Mosaic Media Group*
9200 W Sunset Blvd Ste 10
Los Angeles, CA 90069-3608, USA

Davis, Kyle (Athlete, Football Player)
104 Futurity Ln
Weatherford, TX 76087-4606, USA

Davis, L Edward (Religious Leader)
26049 5 Mile Rd
Detroit, MI 48239-3235, USA

Davis, Lamar (Athlete, Football Player)
502 Ashantilly Ave
Saint Simons Island, GA 31522-3609, USA

Davis, Lance (Athlete, Baseball Player)
5845 Old Berkley Rd
Auburndale, FL 33823-8361, USA

Davis, Lee (Director)
232 N Canon Dr
Beverly Hills, CA 90210-5302, USA

Davis, Lee (Athlete, Basketball Player)
5024 Fieldgreen Xing Apt B2
Stone Mountain, GA 30088-3103, USA

Davis, Leonard (Athlete, Football Player)
PO Box 888
Phoenix, AZ 85001-0888, USA

Davis, Linda (Musician)
PO Box 767
Hermitage, TN 37076-0767, USA

Davis, Lorenzo (Athlete, Football Player)
149 Vista Luna Dr
Davie, FL 33325-6929, USA

Davis, Lorne (Athlete, Hockey Player)
236 Frontenac Dr
Regina, SK S4S 4L3, Canada

Davis, Lucy (Actor, Director)
c/o Tammy Rosen *Sanders Armstrong Caserta*
425 N Robertson Blvd
West Hollywood, CA 90048-1735, USA

Davis, Mac (Actor, Musician, Songwriter, Writer)
9100 Wilshire Blvd Ste 1000W
Beverly Hills, CA 90212-3463, USA

Davis, Mark (Athlete, Baseball Player)
1672 E Mountain St
Pasadena, CA 91104-3935, USA

Davis, Mark A (Athlete, Basketball Player)
108 Government Cir # A
Thibodaux, LA 70301-6615, USA

Davis, Mark G (Basketball Player)
3120 Aaron Dr
Chesapeake, VA 23323-2600, USA

Davis, Mark M (Biologist, Misc)
Medical Center Microbiology Dept
Stanford, CA 94305, USA

Davis, Mark W (Athlete, Baseball Player)
8867 E Sierra Pinta Dr
Scottsdale, AZ 85255-9174, USA

Davis, Martha (Musician)
108 E Matilija St
Ojai, CA 93023-2639, USA

Davis, Marv (Butch) (Athlete, Football Player)
700 Ponce De Leon Ave
Clewiston, FL 33440-2413, USA

Davis, Matthew (Actor)
c/o Daniel (Danny) Sussman *Brillstein Entertainment Partners*
9150 Wilshire Blvd Ste 350
Beverly Hills, CA 90212-3453, USA

Davis, Melvyn (Athlete, Basketball Player)
PO Box 29
Suffern, NY 10901-0029, USA

Davis, Michael (Athlete, Basketball Player)
110 W Clay St
Richmond, VA 23220-3913, USA

Davis, Michael A (Athlete, Football Player)
PO Box 23025
Belleville, IL 62223-0025, USA

Davis, Michael L (Athlete, Football Player)
PO Box 614
Beaver Falls, PA 15010-0614, USA

Davis, Mike (Athlete, Baseball Player)
c/o Staff Member *Oakland Athletics*
7000 Coliseum Way Ste 3
Oakland, CA 94621-1992, USA

Davis, Mike (Athlete, Basketball Player)
100 W 92nd St Apt 29E
New York, NY 10025-7546, USA

Davis, Mike (Athlete, Football Player)
37039 N 109th St
Scottsdale, AZ 85262-3582, USA

Davis, Milt (Athlete, Football Player)
3798 Westleigh St
Eugene, OR 97405-1137, USA

Davis, Milton (Composer)
c/o Staff Member *Windswept (LA)*
9320 Wilshire Blvd Ste 200
Beverly Hills, CA 90212-3217, USA

Davis, Monti (Athlete, Basketball Player)
328 Tod Ln
Youngstown, OH 44504-1403, USA

Davis, Musiello
Janette200 Windemere Way
Naples, FL 33999-8125

Davis, N Jan (Astronaut)
4105 Cumberland Pass Apt 814
Fort Worth, TX 76116-0753, USA

Davis, Nathaniel (Diplomat)
1783 Longwood Ave
Claremont, CA 91711-3129, USA

Davis, Odie (Athlete, Baseball Player)
7314 Hidden Hls N
San Antonio, TX 78244-1504, USA

Davis, Oliver (Athlete, Football Player)
1527 Evanston Ct
Marietta, GA 30062-2148, USA

Davis, Paige (Television Host)
c/o Staff Member *WmE2 (WMA-LA)*
1 William Morris Pl
Beverly Hills, CA 90212-4261, USA

Davis, Paschall (Athlete, Football Player)
937 Plumeria Dr
Arlington, TX 76002-2402, USA

Davis, Paul H (Butch) (Athlete, Coach, Football Coach, Football Player)
76 Lou Groza Blvd
Berea, OH 44017-1238, USA

Davis, Phyllis (Actor)
29330 SE Hillyard Dr # D14
Boring, OR 97009-8502, USA

Davis, Preston (Athlete, Football Player)
1282 W 100th Pl
Northglenn, CO 80260-6208, USA

Davis, Ralph (Athlete, Basketball Player)
2624 S Kathwood Cir
Cincinnati, OH 45236-1026, USA

Davis, Rennie (Politician)
905 S Gilpin St
Denver, CO 80209-4520, USA

Davis, Reuben (Athlete, Football Player)
4424 Lystra Rd
Chapel Hill, NC 27517-8854, USA

Davis, Richard (Musician)
6629 University Ave Ste 206
Middleton, WI 53562-3037, USA

Davis, Ricky (Athlete, Basketball Player)
c/o Jeff Schwartz *Excel Sports Management*
9665 Wilshire Blvd Ste 500
Beverly Hills, CA 90212-2312, USA

Davis, Robert T (Bobby) Jr (Athlete, Football Player)
3721 Eaglebrook Dr
Gastonia, NC 28056-8832, USA

Davis, Roger (Athlete, Football Player)
17522 Harvard Ave
Cleveland, OH 44128-1718, USA

Davis, Roger (Actor)
9682 Via Torino
Burbank, CA 91504-1410, USA

Davis, Ron (Athlete, Baseball Player)
11748 N 90th Pl
Scottsdale, AZ 85260-6841, USA

Davis, Ron (Athlete, Basketball Player)
5668 W Evergreen Rd
Glendale, AZ 85302-6026, USA

Davis, Ronald (Ron) (Artist)
PO Box 293
Arroyo Hondo, NM 87513-0293, USA

Davis, Ronald (Ron) (Athlete, Football Player)
4717 Pompton Ln
Chester, VA 23831-4335, USA

Davis, Ross (Athlete, Baseball Player)
8042 Highway 71
Garwood, TX 77442-4158, USA

Davis, Russ (Athlete, Baseball Player)
3351 Crescent Dr
Bessemer, AL 35023-2919, USA

Davis, Russell (Athlete, Football Player)
605 Jones Ferry Rd
Carrboro, NC 27510-2106, USA

Davis, Russell (Athlete, Football Player)
1208 Tanbark Ln E
Jackson, MI 49203-1275, USA

Davis, Russell A (Athlete, Football Player)
4236 Crosswood Dr
Burtonsville, MD 20866-1350, USA

Davis, Russell C (General)
Hqusaf Pentagon
Washington, DC 20310-0001, USA

Davis, Russell S (Russ) (Baseball Player)
3351 Crescent Dr
Hueytown, AL 35023-2919, USA

Davis, Ruth (Baseball Player)
1917 Park Ave
Cheyenne, WY 82007-3395, USA

Davis, Sam (Athlete, Football Player)
423 Edgemont St
Mt Washington, PA 15211-2405, USA

Davis, Sammy (Athlete, Football Player)
4020 Murphy Canyon Rd
San Diego, CA 92123-4407, USA

Davis, Sammy L (War Hero)
3376 N 100th St
Flat Rock, IL 62427, USA

Davis, Spencer
PO Box 1821
Ojai, CA 93024-1821

Davis, Stephen (Athlete, Football Player)
2214 Picardy Meadow Ln
Chesterfield, MO 63017-7134, USA

Davis, Stephen H (Engineer, Mathematician)
2735 Simpson St
Evanston, IL 60201-2029, USA

Davis, Steve (Misc)
10 Western Road Romford
Essex RM1 3JT, UNITED KINGDOM (UK)

Davis, Steve (Athlete, Baseball Player)
6717 Westbury Ct
Benbrook, TX 76132-2700, USA

Davis, Steve (Athlete, Football Player)
295 Dover Rd
Warrenton, VA 20186-2309, USA

Davis, Steve (Athlete, Baseball Player)
6011 86th St
Lubbock, TX 79424-6708, USA

Davis, Storm (Athlete, Baseball Player)
8469 Mizner Cir E
Jacksonville, FL 32217-4326, USA

Davis, Susan (Congressman, Politician)
1526 Longworth Hob
Washington, DC 20515-3305, USA

Davis, Ted (Athlete, Football Player)
5401 Riverbend Dr
Knoxville, TN 37919-8953, USA

Davis, Terrell (Athlete, Football Player)
235 Latimer St
San Diego, CA 92114-4129, USA

Davis, Terry (Athlete, Basketball Player)
2933 Kenmore Rd
Richmond, VA 23225 1429, USA

Davis, Tim (Athlete, Baseball Player)
16161 NW Lakeside Ln
Bristol, FL 32321-3932, USA

Davis, Todd (Actor)
245 S Keystone St
Burbank, CA 91506-2727, USA

Davis, Tommy (Athlete, Baseball Player)
4685 Cavalier Dr
Semmes, AL 36575-4467, USA

Davis, Tracy (Stylist)
c/o Staff Member *Help Me Rhonda*
541 10th St NW # 294
Atlanta, GA 30318-5713, USA

Davis, Travis (Athlete, Football Player)
PO Box 532302
Indianapolis, IN 46253-2302, USA

Davis, Trench (Athlete, Baseball Player)
306 40th Street Cir W
Palmetto, FL 34221-9516, USA

Davis, Troy (Athlete, Football Player)
11861 SW 190th St
Miami, FL 33177-3940, USA

Davis, Truman A (Misc)
303 Ridge St
Alton, IL 62002-6420, USA

Davis, Vernon (Athlete, Football Player)
c/o Todd France *France AllPro Athlete Management*
3500 Lenox Rd NE
Atlanta, GA 30326-4228, USA

Davis, Vicki (Actor)
c/o Staff Member *Innovative Artists (LA)*
1505 10th St
Santa Monica, CA 90401-2805, USA

Davis, Viola (Actor)
c/o Estelle Lasher *Principal Entertainment (LA)*
1964 Westwood Blvd Ste 400
Los Angeles, CA 90025-4695, USA

Davis, W Eugene (Judge)
556 Jefferson St
Lafayette, LA 70501-6950, USA

Davis, Walter (Athlete, Basketball Player)
6549 E Euclid Piace
Centennial, CO 80111-4606, USA

Davis, Warren (Athlete, Basketball Player)
2309 Old Fort Hills Dr
Fort Washington, MD 20744-3937, USA

Davis, Warwick (Actor)
c/o Staff Member *Willow Personal Management*
151 Main St Yaxley
Peterborough PE7 3LD, UK

Davis, Wendell (Athlete, Football Player)
PO Box 76384
Washington, DC 20013-6384, USA

Davis, Wendell (Athlete, Football Player)
180 Rinconada Ave
Palo Alto, CA 94301-3725, USA

Davis, Wendell (Athlete, Football Player)
6831 Kennon St
Shreveport, LA 71119-7519, USA

Davis, William (Actor)
c/o Staff Member *Lucas Talent Inc*
100 W. Pender St Sun Tower, 7th Floor
Vancouver, BC V6B 1R8, Canada

Davis, William D (Willie) (Athlete, Football Player)
7352 Vista Del Mar
Playa Del Rey, CA 90293, USA

Davis, William E (Business Person)
300 Erie Blvd W
Syracuse, NY 13202-4201, USA

Davis, William G (Government Official)
Aetna Tower #3000
Toronto, ON M5K 1N2, CANADA

Davis, William L (Business Person)
77 W Wacker Dr
Chicago, IL 60601-1604, USA

Davis, Willie (Athlete, Baseball Player)
1916 W Victory Blvd
Burbank, CA 91506-1150, USA

Davison, Beverly C (Religious Leader)
PO Box 851
Valley Forge, PA 19482-0851, USA

Davison, Bruce (Actor)
c/o Jean-Pierre (JP) Henraux *Shelter Entertainment*
9454 Wilshire Blvd Ste 715
Beverly Hills, CA 90212-2925, USA

Davison, Fred C (Educator)
1 7th St Ste 502
Augusta, GA 30901-1341, USA

Davison, Michelle
1830 Grace Ave Apt 7
Los Angeles, CA 90028-4881

Davison, Mike (Athlete, Baseball Player)
578 Prospect St NE
Hutchinson, MN 55350-1715, USA

Davison, Peter (Actor)
'Legally Blonde', Savoy Theatre The Strand
London WC2R 0ET, UK

Davison, Sam (Religious Leader)
720 E Kearney St
Springfield, MO 65803-3428, USA

Davison, Scott (Athlete, Baseball Player)
4507 Sharynne Ln
Torrance, CA 90505-3454, USA

Davis-Wrightsil, Clarissa (Basketball Player)
American West Arena 201 E Jefferson St
Phoenix, AZ 85004, USA

Davitian, Ken (Actor)
c/o Tess Finkle *Metro Public Relations*
421 N Sierra Bonita Ave
Los Angeles, CA 90036-2464, USA

Davoli, Andrew (Actor)
c/o Greg Clark *Untitled Entertainment (LA)*
350 S Beverly Dr Ste 200
Beverly Hills, CA 90212-4819, USA

Dawber, Pam (Actor)
c/o Staff Member *Wings Productions Inc*
2236 Encinitas Blvd Ste A
Encinitas, CA 92024-4353

Dawe, Jason (Athlete, Hockey Player)
9077 Drayton Ln
Fort Mill, SC 29707-6484, USA

Dawes, Dominique (Athlete, Gymnast)
129 Ritchie Ave
Silver Spring, MD 20910-5111, USA

Dawes, Joseph (Cartoonist)
20 Church Ct
Closter, NJ 07624-2803, USA

Dawkins, Brian (Athlete, Football Player)
10010 Tavistock Rd
Orlando, FL 32827-7053, USA

Dawkins, C Richard (Biologist)
Museum Parks Road
Oxford OX1 3PW, UNITED KINGDOM (UK)

Dawkins, Dale (Athlete, Football Player)
390 Concord Dr
Bozeman, MT 59715-7100, USA

Dawkins, Darryl (Athlete, Basketball Player)
1708 Glacier Ct
Allentown, PA 18104-1710, USA

Dawkins, Joe (Athlete, Football Player)
9200 S Harvard Blvd
Los Angeles, CA 90047-3801, USA

Dawkins, Johnny (Athlete, Basketball Player)
590 Military Way
Palo Alto, CA 94306-3236, USA

Dawkins, Johnny (Basketball Player)
590 Military Way
Palo Alto, CA 94306-3236, USA

Dawkins, Paul (Athlete, Basketball Player)
PO Box 610010
Dallas, TX 75261-0010, USA

Dawkins, Peter M (Pete) (Business Person, Football Player)
PO Box 218
Rumson, NJ 07760-0218, USA

Dawkins, Sean (Athlete, Football Player)
826 Weichert Dr
Morgan Hill, CA 95037-3785, USA

Dawkins, Travis (Gookie) (Athlete, Baseball Player)
PO Box 81325
Conyers, GA 30013-9325, USA

Dawley, Bill (Athlete, Baseball Player)
2919 Twin Fountains Dr
Houston, TX 77068-3750, USA

Dawley, Joey (Athlete, Baseball Player)
27951 Cactus Ave Unit A
Moreno Valley, CA 92555-3609, USA

Dawley, Joseph W (Joe) (Artist)
13 Wholly St
Cranford, NJ 7016, USA

Dawsey, Lawrence (Athlete, Football Player)
4341 Cheval Blvd
Lutz, FL 33558-5328, USA

Dawson, Andre (Athlete, Baseball Player)
PO Box 431339
Miami, FL 33243-1339, USA

Dawson, Anthony
Via Riccione 6 Fregene
Fiumicino RM, ITALY 50

Dawson, Ashley Taylor (Actor)
c/o Staff Member *Blackburn Sachs Associates*
88-90 Crawford St
London W1H 2BS, UNITED KINGDOM (UK)

Dawson, Buck (Swimmer)
1 Hall of Fame Dr
Fort Lauderdale, FL 33316-1611, USA

Dawson, Dale (Athlete, Football Player)
1710 E Oak Knoll Cir
Davie, FL 33324-6424, USA

Dawson, Dermontti (Athlete, Football Player)
PO Box 712481
San Diego, CA 92171 2481, USA

Dawson, Douglas A (Doug) (Athlete, Football Player)
1 Riverway Ste 900
Houston, TX 77056-1906, USA

Dawson, J Cutler Jr (Admiral)
Commander Striking Fleet Atlantic/2nd Fleet
FPO, AE 8506, USA

Dawson, Jajuan (Athlete, Football Player)
2302 Sun Shadow Ln
Spring, TX 77386-1871, USA

Dawson, Jim (Athlete, Basketball Player)
61 Glendale Ave
Rye, NY 10580-1547, USA

Dawson, Kim (Actor, Producer, Writer)
c/o Staff Member *Skydog Productions*
1000 Universal Studios Plz Bldg 22A
Orlando, FL 32819-7601, USA

Dawson, Lake (Athlete, Football Player)
33228 37th Pl SW
Federal Way, WA 98023-2959, USA

Dawson, Leonard R (Lenny) (Athlete, Football Player, Sportscaster)
1025 W 59th Ter
Kansas City, MO 64113-1335, USA

Dawson, Marco (Athlete, Golfer)
3053 Shoal Creek Village Dr
Lakeland, FL 33803-5425, USA

Dawson, Mike (Athlete, Football Player)
8070 N Highcountry Ave
Tucson, AZ 85741-4624, USA

Dawson, Phil (Athlete, Football Player)
4000 Dunning Ln
Austin, TX 78746-1927, USA

Dawson, Rhett (Athlete, Football Player)
4409 Sacred Arrow Dr
Austin, TX 78735-6363, USA

Dawson, Richard (Actor)
1117 Angelo Dr
Beverly Hills, CA 90210-2703, USA

Dawson, Rosario (Actor)
c/o Evan Hainey *Untitled Entertainment (LA)*
350 S Beverly Dr Ste 200
Beverly Hills, CA 90212-4819, USA

Dawson, Roxann (Actor)
1505 10th St
Santa Monica, CA 90401-2805, USA

Day, Bill (Cartoonist)
495 Union Ave
Memphis, TN 38103-3217, USA

Day, Boots (Athlete, Baseball Player)
1154 Vespasian Way
Chesterfield, MO 63017-3016, USA

Day, Charlie (Actor)
c/o Nick Frenkel *3 Arts Entertainment Inc*
9460 Wilshire Blvd Fl 7
Beverly Hills, CA 90212-2713, USA

Day, Chon (Cartoonist)
127 Main St
Ashaway, RI 02804-2239, USA

Day, Dewon (Athlete, Baseball Player)
1935 Marshall Pl
Jackson, MS 39213-4450, USA

Day, Doris (Actor)
PO Box 1008
Versailles, KY 40383-5008, USA

Day, Eagle (Athlete, Football Player)
262 Eastbrooke St
Jackson, MS 39216-4716, USA

Day, Felicia (Actor)
c/o Meredith Wechter *International Creative Management (ICM-LA)*
10250 Constellation Blvd Fl 7
Los Angeles, CA 90067-6207, USA

Day, Gail (Publisher)
680 N Lake Shore Dr
Chicago, IL 60611-4546, USA

Day, George E (War Hero)
23 Bayshore Dr
Shalimar, FL 32579-2116, USA

Day, Glen (Athlete, Golfer)
25 Valley Estates Ct
Little Rock, AR 72212, USA

Day, Howie (Musician)
c/o Staff Member *Paradigm (Monterey)*
404 W Franklin St
Monterey, CA 93940-2303, USA

Day, Inaya (Musician)
c/o Staff Member *Diva Central Inc*
7510 W Sunset Blvd Ste 1445
Los Angeles, CA 90046-3408, USA

Day, Jason (Actor)
c/o Julio Caro *Caro Entertainment*
3221 Hutchison Ave Ste H
Los Angeles, CA 90034-3298, USA

Day, Jennifer
PO Box 120479
Nashville, TN 37212-0479

Day, Joanne (Stylist)
1105 SW 66th Ave Apt 3321
Portland, OR 97225-6026, USA

Day, Joe (Athlete, Hockey Player)
805 Shoreline Rd
Lake Barrington, IL 60010-3878, USA

Day, Julian (Business Person)
PO Box 8073
Royal Oak, MI 48068-8073, USA

Day, Mary (Misc)
3515 Wisconsin Ave NW
Washington, DC 20016-3010, USA

Day, Matt (Actor)
397 Riley St
Surrey Hills, NSW 2010, AUSTRALIA

Day, Patrick (Pat) (Jockey)
14703 Isleworth Ct
Louisville, KY 40245-5256, USA

Day, Peter R (Scientist)
8200 Tarsier Ave
New Port Richey, FL 34653-6559, USA

Day, Robert (Actor, Director)
8832 Ferncliff Ave NE
Bainbridge Island, WA 98110-2907, USA

Day, Sandra (Stylist)
210 W Brentwood Blvd
Lafayette, LA 70506-6111, USA

Day, Terry (Athlete, Football Player)
PO Box 85
Pickens, MS 39146-0085, USA

Day, Thomas B (Educator)
President S Ofc
San Diego, CA 92182-0001, USA

Day, Zach (Athlete, Baseball Player)
1154 Carolina Trace Rd
West Harrison, IN 47060-9651, USA

Dayan, Isaac (Actor)
c/o Staff Member *TV Caracol*
Calle 76 #11 - 35 Piso 10AA
Bogota DC 26484, COLOMBIA

Daye, Darren (Athlete, Basketball Player)
17 Elderberry
Irvine, CA 92603-3703, USA

Dayett, Brian (Athlete, Baseball Player)
10 Hemlock Terrace Ext
Deep River, CT 06417-1606, USA

Day-George, Lynda (Actor)
10310 Riverside Dr Unit 104
Toluca Lake, CA 91602-2457, USA

Daykin, Anthony (Athlete, Football Player)
5204 Cross Ridge Cir
Woodstock, GA 30188-4381, USA

Day-Lewis, Daniel (Actor)
c/o Gene Parseghian *Parseghian Planco LLC*
322 8th Ave Ste 601
New York, NY 10001-6715, USA

Dayley, Ken (Athlete, Baseball Player)
1300 Windgate Way Ct
Chesterfield, MO 63005-4497, USA

Dayne, Ron (Athlete, Football Player)
2135 Regent St
Madison, WI 53726-3941, USA

Dayne, Taylor (Actor, Musician)
c/o Babette Perry *IMG (LA)*
717 N Alta Vista Blvd
Los Angeles, CA 90046-7601, USA

Days, Drews S III (Educator, Government Official)
Law School
New Haven, CT 6520, USA

Dayton, Jonathan (Director)
1313 5th St
Santa Monica, CA 90401-1414, USA

Dayton, June (Actor)
9200 W Sunset Blvd Ste 1125
Los Angeles, CA 90069-3610, USA

Dayton, Mark (Governor)
130 State Capitol 75 Ofc of
Saint Paul, MN 55155-0001, USA

Daze, Eric (Athlete, Hockey Player)
606 S Washington St
Hinsdale, IL 60521-4439, USA

dc Talk (Music Group, Musician)
c/o Staff Member *True Artist Management*
227 3rd Ave N
Franklin, TN 37064-2504, USa

de Almeida, Joaquim (Actor)
c/o Estelle Lasher *Principal Entertainment (LA)*
1964 Westwood Blvd Ste 400
Los Angeles, CA 90025-4695, USA

De Angelis, Rosemary
817 W End Ave
New York, NY 10025-0139

De Aragon, Maria (Actor)
c/o Staff Member *Coolwaters Productions*
10061 Riverside Dr # 531
Toluca Lake, CA 91602-2560, USA

de Aragow, Maria
1159 10th Ave
San Diego, CA 92101-5509

De Armas, Ana (Actor)
c/o Liz Dalling *Special Artists Agency*
9465 Wilshire Blvd Ste 820
Beverly Hills, CA 90212-2607, USA

De Bello, James (Actor, Musician)
c/o Craig Shapiro *International Creative Management (ICM-LA)*
10250 Constellation Blvd Fl 7
Los Angeles, CA 90067-6207, USA

De Benning, Burr (Actor)
4235 Kingfisher Rd
Calabasas, CA 91302-1842, USA

De Blanc, Jefferson J (Misc)
321 Saint Martin St
Saint Martinville, LA 70582-4531, USA

De Bont, Jan (Director, Producer)
c/o Martin Bauer *Bauer Company, The*
9720 Wilshire Blvd Mezzanine
Beverly Hills, CA 90212, USA

De Bruijn, Inge (Athlete, Olympic Athlete, Swimmer)
Van Ostadestraat 368-2
Amsterdam 1074 XA, NETHERLANDS

de Cordova, Fred (Actor, Director, Producer)
1875 Carla Rdg
Beverly Hills, CA 90210-1936

de Dios, Silvia (Actor)
c/o Staff Member *TV Caracol*
Calle 76 #11 - 35 Piso 10AA
Bogota DC 26484, COLOMBIA

De Eugenia, Coco (Actor)
c/o Nancy Harding *Powerhouse Talent*
PO Box 261939
Encino, CA 91426-1939, USA

De Filipis, Antonio (Stylist)
c/o Staff Member *Blink Management*
421 Washington Ave Ste 202
Miami Beach, FL 33139-6612, USA

de Gruiin, Inge
PO Box 302
Arnhem, NETHERLANDS 6800 AH

De Heer, Rolf (Director, Producer, Writer)
c/o Staff Member *Vertigo Productions Pty Ltd*
3 Butler Dr
Hendon SA 5014, AUSTRALIA

De Jesus, Wanda (Actor)
c/o Bob McGowan *McGowan Management*
8733 W Sunset Blvd Ste 103
West Hollywood, CA 90069-2241, USA

De Jong, Michael
c/o Staff Member *Mark Edward Inc*
325 W 8th St # 1011
New York, NY 10018, USA

de Jongh, John (Governor, Politician)
21-22 Kongens Gade Charlote Amalie
St Thomas, VI

De La Cruz, David (Stylist)
c/o Staff Member *Illusions Management*
129 W 27th St Fl 12
New York, NY 10001-6206, USA

de la Cruz, Melissa (Writer)
c/o Richard Abate *3 Arts Entertainment - NY*
49 W 27th St Fl 5
New York, NY 10001-6936, USA

De La Cruz, Veronica (Television Host)
c/o Staff Member *CNN (Atlanta)*
1 Cnn Ctr NW
Atlanta, GA 30303-2762, USA

De La Fuente, Cristian (Actor, Producer, Writer)

de la Fuente, Marian (Actor)
c/o Staff Member *Telemundo*
2470 W 8th Ave
Hialeah, FL 33010-2000, USA

De La Garza, Alana (Actor)
c/o Jai Khanna *Brillstein Entertainment Partners*
9150 Wilshire Blvd Ste 350
Beverly Hills, CA 90212-3453, USA

De La Hoya, Oscar (Athlete, Boxer)
c/o Staff Member *Leigh Steinberg Enterprises*
1280 Bison Ave
Newport Beach, CA 92660-4258, USA

De La Hoz, Mike (Athlete, Baseball Player)
PO Box 441233
Miami, FL 33144-1233, USA

De la Huerta, Paz (Actor)
c/o Katie Rhodes *Untitled Entertainment (LA)*
350 S Beverly Dr Ste 200
Beverly Hills, CA 90212-4819, USA

De La Maza, Roland (Athlete, Baseball Player)
28533 Silverking Trl
Santa Clarita, CA 91390-5248, USA

de la Reguera, Ana (Actor)
c/o Will Ward *ROAR (LA)*
9701 Wilshire Blvd Fl 8
Beverly Hills, CA 90212-2008, USA

De La Renta, Oscar (Fashion Designer)
550 Seventh Ave Fl 8
New York, NY 10018, USA

De La Rosa, Jo (Actor)
c/o Jack Ketsoyan *EMC / Bowery*
8155 Santa Monica Blvd Ste 200
West Hollywood, CA 90046-4986, USA

De La Soul (Music Group)
2697 Heath Ave
Bronx, NY 10463-7546, USA

De La Tour, Frances (Actor)
c/o Carl Scott *Simmons & Scott Entertainment*
7942 Mulholland Dr
Los Angeles, CA 90046-1225, USA

De Lassus, Christine (Stylist)
c/o Staff Member *Michele Filomeno New York LLC*
515 Greenwich St Ste 503
New York, NY 10013-1097, USA

De Laurentiis, Giada (Chef)
c/o Staff Member *Food Network, The*
75 9th Ave
New York, NY 10011-7006, USA

De Laurentiis, Raffaella (Actor, Producer)
100 Universal City Plz Bungalow 5162
Universal City, CA 91608-1002, USA

de Leon, Miguel (Actor)
c/o Staff Member *Televisa*
Blvd Adolfo Lopez Mateos 232 Colonia San Angel INN
DF CP 01060, MEXICO

de Lesseps, LuAnn (Reality TV Star)
c/o Staff Member *Bravo (NY)*
30 Rockefeller Plz
New York, NY 10112-0015, USA

de Lint, Derek (Actor)
c/o Vanessa Henneman *Features Creative Managment*
76a Entrepotdok
Amsterdam 1018 AD, NETHERLANDS

De Longis, Anthony
PO Box 323
Burbank, CA 91503-0323

De Los Santos, Valerio (Athlete, Baseball Player)
9838 N 119th Pl
Scottsdale, AZ 85259-5069, USA

de Matteo, Drea (Actor)
c/o Evan Hainey *Untitled Entertainment (LA)*
350 S Beverly Dr Ste 200
Beverly Hills, CA 90212-4819, USA

de Mol, John (Producer)
c/o Staff Member *WmE2 (WMA-LA)*
1 William Morris Pl
Beverly Hills, CA 90212-4261, USA

de Molina, Raul (Actor)
c/o Staff Member *Univision*
605 3rd Ave Fl 12
New York, NY 10158-0034, USA

De Munn, Jeffrey (Jeff) (Actor)
c/o Larry Taube *Principal Entertainment (LA)*
1964 Westwood Blvd Ste 400
Los Angeles, CA 90025-4695, USA

De Niro, Robert (Actor)
c/o Stan Rosenfield *Stan Rosenfield & Associates*
2029 Century Park E Ste 1190
Los Angeles, CA 90067-2931, USA

de Pablo, Cote (Actor)
c/o Jason Spire *Inspire Entertainment*
315 7th Ave Apt 17E
New York, NY 10001-6011, USA

De Paul, Lynsey
21A Clifftown Rd
Southend-on-Sea Essex, ENGLAND SSl 1AB

de Ravin, Emilie (Actor)
c/o Darren Goldberg *Global Creative*
1051 Cole Ave # B
Los Angeles, CA 90038-2601, USA

De Rosnay, Tatiana (Writer)
c/o Staff Member *Bazar Forlag*
Hammarby Fabriksvag 25
Stockholm 12033, Sweden

De Rossi, Portia (Actor)
c/o Cari Ross *I/D PR (NY)*
150 W 30th St Fl 19
New York, NY 10001-4003, USA

de Rothschild, David (Producer)
Zetland House 5/25 Scrutton St
London EC2A 4HJ, UK

de Silva, Jorge (Actor)
c/o Staff Member *Televisa*
Blvd Adolfo Lopez Mateos 232 Colonia San Angel INN
DF CP 01060, MEXICO

De Souza, Steven (Producer, Writer)
c/o Alan Gasmer *Alan Gasmer Management Company*
10877 Wilshire Blvd Ste 603
Los Angeles, CA 90024-4348, USA

De Swert, Nico (Stylist)
c/o Staff Member *Bernstein & Andriulli*
58 W 40th St
New York, NY 10018-2658, USA

De Teliga, Louise (Stylist)
c/o Staff Member *LA Rep*
8312 Utica Dr
Los Angeles, CA 90046-7716, USA

de Vasconcelos, Tasha (Actor)
c/o Samira Higham *Independent Talent Group (ITG-UK)*
Oxford House 76 Oxford St
London W1D 1BS, UK

De Voe, Ronald (Musician)
c/o Michael (Mike) Esterman *Esterman.Com, LLC*
Prefers to be contacted via email
MD, USA

De Vries, Peter
170 Cross Hwy
Westport, CT 06880-2841

Dea, Bill (Athlete, Hockey Player)
2636 W Bartlett Way
Queen Creek, AZ 85142-6611, USA

Deacon, Brian
85 Gladstone Rd
London, ENGLAND SW19

Deacon, John (Musician)
367 Windsor Hwy
New Windsor, NY 12553-7900, USA

Deacon, Richard (Artist)
67 Lisson St
London NW1 5DA, UNITED KINGDOM (UK)

Deacon, Terrence (Misc)
Neuroanatomy Dept
Cambridge, MA 2138, USA

Dead Can Dance (Music Group)
c/o Staff Member *WmE2 (WMA-LA)*
1 William Morris Pl
Beverly Hills, CA 90212-4261, USA

Dead, The (Music Group)
c/o Staff Member *Paradigm (Monterey)*
404 W Franklin St
Monterey, CA 93940-2303, USA

Deadmarsh, Adam (Athlete, Hockey Player)
PO Box 262
Metaline Falls, WA 99153-0262, USA

Deadmarsh, Butch (Athlete, Hockey Player)
282 Diamond Dr SE
Calgary, AB T2J 7E2, Canada

deadmau5 (Music Group)
c/o Todd Jacobs *WmE2 (Endeavor-LA)*
9601 Wilshire Blvd Fl 3
Beverly Hills, CA 90210-5219, USA

Deadsy (Music Group)

DeAgostini, Doris (Skier)
6780 Airolo
SWITZERLAND

Deakin, Paul (Musician)
1620 16th Ave S
Nashville, TN 37212-2908, USA

Deakins, Roger (Cinematographer)
8942 Wilshire Blvd # 219
Beverly Hills, CA 90211-1908, USA

Deal, Cot (Athlete, Baseball Player)
9009 N May Ave Apt 164
Oklahoma City, OK 73120-4464, USA

Deal, Ellis (Athlete, Baseball Player)
9009 N May Ave Apt 164
Oklahoma City, OK 73120-4464, USA

Deal, Kelley (Musician)
PO Box 520
Oxford, OH 45056-0520, USA

Deal, Kim (Musician)
c/o Dan Brooks *Key Music Group (Canada)*
227 King St E
Hamilton, Ontario L8N 1B6, Canada

Deal, Lance (Athlete, Track Athlete)
911 Elkay Dr
Eugene, OR 97404-6512, USA

Deal, Nathan (Governor)
203 State Capitol SW
Atlanta, GA 30334-1600, USA

DeAlmeida, Joaquin
2372 Veteran Ave # 102
Los Angeles, CA 90064-2147

Dean, Barry (Athlete, Hockey Player)
315 Marsh St
Maple Creek, SK S0N 1N0, Canada

Dean, Billy (Musician)
c/o Staff Member *Billy Dean Music Group*
PO Box 150889
Nashville, TN 37215-0889, USA

Dean, Christopher (Dancer)
124 Ladies Mile Road Brighton
East Sussex BN1 8TE, UNITED KINGDOM (UK)

Dean, Debby (Stylist)
c/o Celebrity Stylists *Christine Willes Artists Mgmt, Inc.*
11906 Lawler St
Los Angeles, CA 90066-2010, USA

Dean, Eddie (Actor, Musician)
32161 Sailview Ln
Westlake Village, CA 91361-3620, USA

Dean, Fred (Athlete, Football Player)
3911 Whitchurch Dr
Houston, TX 77066-4535, USA

Dean, Fred (Athlete, Football Player)
2411 Highway 3061
Ruston, LA 71270-9626, USA

Dean, Hazel
7 Kentish Town Rd
London, ENGLAND NW1 8N4

Dean, Howard (Politician)
Washington, DC 20003, USA

Dean, Ira (Musician)
6999 E Highway 80
Odessa, TX 79762, USA

Dean, John G (Diplomat)
29 Blvd Jules Sandeau
Paris 75116, FRANCE

Dean, Kevin (Athlete, Hockey Player)
c/o Staff Member *Lowell Devils*
51 S Pearl St
Albany, NY 12207-1527, USA

Dean, Kiley (Musician)
c/o Staff Member *Interscope Records (LA) - Main*
2220 Colorado Ave
Santa Monica, CA 90404-3506, USA

Dean, Laura (Choreographer, Composer)
552 Broadway # 400
New York, NY 10012-3922, USA

Dean, Loren (Actor)
c/o Amy Guenther *Gateway Management Company Inc*
860 Via De La Paz Ste F10
Pacific Palisades, CA 90272-3631, USA

Dean, Mark E (Inventor)
PO Box 218
Yorktown Heights, NY 10598-0218, USA

Dean, Paula (Chef, Television Host)
311 W Congress St
Savannah, GA 31401-2408, USA

Dean, Paula (Actor)
102 W Congress St
Savannah, GA 31401-2508

Dean, Randy (Athlete, Football Player)
1310 E Bay Point Rd
Milwaukee, WI 53217-1405, USA

Dean, Stafford R (Opera Singer)
40 W 57th St
New York, NY 10019-4001, USA

Dean, Ted (Athlete, Football Player)
16474 W Lava Dr
Surprise, AZ 85374-6250, USA

Dean, Tina (Stylist)
c/o Staff Member *Arlene Wilson Management*
807 N Jefferson St # 200
Milwaukee, WI 53202-8150, USA

Dean, Tommy (Athlete, Baseball Player)
PO Box 1014
Iuka, MS 38852-6014, USA

Dean, Vernon (Athlete, Football Player)
9639 W Withers Way Cir
Houston, TX 77065-4905, USA

Dean III, John W (Misc)
9496 Rembert Ln
Beverly Hills, CA 90210-1720, USA

DeAnda, Paula (Musician)
c/o Ed Ocanas *E.D.O. Entertainment*
Prefers to be contact either via telephone or email
TX 78401, USA

Deane, William Patrick (General)
Canberra, ACT 26000, AUSTRALIA

DeAngelis, Barbara (Writer)
c/o Staff Member *St Martins Press*
175 5th Ave
New York, NY 10010-7703, USA

DeAngelis, Beverly (Psychic)
505 S Beverly Dr # 1017
Beverly Hills, CA 90212, USA

Deangelis, Billy (Athlete, Basketball Player)
14 Pickering Dr
Trenton, NJ 08691-2332, USA

Dear and the Headlights (Music Group, Musician)
c/o Brigitte Wright *Brigitte Wright Management*
1674 Broadway Fl 3
New York, NY 10019-5861, USA

Dearden, James (Director)
8942 Wilshire Blvd # 219
Beverly Hills, CA 90211-1908, USA

Deardorff, Jeff (Athlete, Baseball Player)
16823 Rockwell Heights Ln
Clermont, FL 34711-7907, USA

Deardurff-Schmidt, Deena (Swimmer)
742 Murray Dr
El Cajon, CA 92020-5640, USA

DeArmond, Frank (Astronaut)
3086 Ravencrest Cir
Prescott, AZ 86303-5790, USA

D'Eath, Tom (Athlete, Misc)
435 Bay Rd
Mount Dora, FL 32757-4305, USA

Deavenport, Earnest Jr (Business Person)
100 N Eastman Rd
Kingsport, TN 37660-5265, USA

Deaver, Jeffrey (Writer)
1230 Avenue of the Americas
New York, NY 10020-1513, USA

Deaver, Michael K (Government Official)
1025 Thomas Jefferson St NW
Washington, DC 20007-5201, USA

Deb, Debbie (Musician)
c/o Staff Member *Green Light Talent Agency*
PO Box 3172
Beverly Hills, CA 90212-0172, USA

DeBarge, Eldra (El) (Musician)
c/o Staff Member *Geffen Records*
9126 Sunset Blvd
West Hollywood, CA 90069, USA

DeBarge, Kristinia (Musician)
c/o Staff Member *Edmonds Entertainment*
312 W 5th St Apt 815
Los Angeles, CA 90013-1750, USA

Debarr, Denny (Athlete, Baseball Player)
33843 Juliet Cir
Fremont, CA 94555-3452, USA

DeBell, Kristine (Actor)
c/o Ted Elston *Karma Talent Management*
453 S Rexford Dr
Beverly Hills, CA 90212-4711, USA

DeBellevue, Charles B (War Hero)
916 Huntsman Rd
Edmond, OK 73003-3520, USA

DeBello, James (Actor)
c/o Craig Shapiro *International Creative Management (ICM-LA)*
10250 Constellation Blvd Fl 7
Los Angeles, CA 90067-6207, USA

Debenedet, Nelson (Athlete, Hockey Player)
38142 N Vista Dr
Livonia, MI 48152-1066, USA

DeBenning, Burr (Actor)
4235 Kingfisher Rd
Calabasas, CA 91302-1842, USA

DeBerg, Steve (Athlete, Coach, Football Player)
17920 Simms Rd
Odessa, FL 33556-4751, USA

Deblois, Lucien (Athlete, Hockey Player)
c/o Staff Member *Vancouver Canucks*
800 Griffiths Way
Vancouver V6B 6G1, Canada

Debney, John (Composer)
15233 Ventura Blvd Ste 200
Sherman Oaks, CA 91403-2244, USA

DeBoer, Harm E (Business Person)
755 Lee St
Alexander City, AL 35010-2638, USA

DeBoer, Nicole (Actor)
c/o Jeff Witjas *Agency for the Performing Arts (APA-LA)*
405 S Beverly Dr Ste 500
Beverly Hills, CA 90212-4425, USA

DeBoer, Rick (Actor)
510 W Hastings St # 1404
Vancouver, BC V6B 1L8, CANADA

Debol, Dave (Athlete, Hockey Player)
288 Clark St Apt 7
Saline, MI 48176-1247, USA

DeBold, Adolfo J (Doctor, Physicist)
1053 Carling Ave
Ottawa, ON K1Y 4E9, CANADA

DeBorba, Dorothy (Actor)
PO Box 2723
Livermore, CA 94551-2723, USA

DeBorchgrave, Arnaud (Editor)
2141 Wyoming Ave NW
Washington, DC 20008-3916, USA

DeBorda, Dorothy (Actor)
PO Box 2723
Livermore, CA 94551-2723, USA

DeBranges, Louis (Mathematician)
Mathematics Dept
West Lafayette, IN 47907, USA

Debre, Michael (Prime Minister)
20 Rue Jacob
Paris 75006, FRANCE

DeBrunhoff, Laurent (Writer)
527 W 26th St
New York, NY 10001-5503, USA

Debrusk, Louie (Athlete, Hockey Player)
27502 N 84th Dr
Peoria, AZ 85383-3843, USA

DeBurgh, Chris (Musician, Songwriter, Writer)
754 Fulham Road
London, SW6 5SW, UNITED KINGDOM (UK)

Debus, Kim (Stylist)
c/o Celebrity Stylist *Jam Arts, Inc*
154 W 57th St
New York, NY 10019-3321, USA

Deby, Idriss (General, President)
N'Djamena
CHAS

Decambra-Kelley, Lillian (Baseball Player)
250 South St
Somerset, MA 02726-5616, USA

DeCamilli, Pietro V (Biologist)
Medical School Cell Biology Dept
New Haven, CT 6512, USA

DeCarava, Roy (Photographer)
81 Halsey St
Brooklyn, NY 11216-1902, USA

DeCario, Yvonne (Actor)
1483 Golf Course Ln
Nipomo, CA 93444-9307, USA

DeCarl, Nancy
4615 Winnetka
Woodland Hills, CA 91364

Decarlo, Arthur (Athlete, Football Player)
9030 Manordale Ln
Ellicott City, MD 21042-5327, USA

DeCarlo, Mark (Actor)
c/o Staff Member *Lapides Entertainment*
1724 Venture Blvd Ph
Sherman Oaks, CA 92403, USA

DeCasabianca, Carnille (Actor)
20 Ave Rapp
Paris 75007, FRANCE

DeCastelia, F Robert (Athlete, Track Athlete)
PO Box 176
Belconnen, ACT 2616, AUSTRALIA

Deccio, Joan (Stylist)
PO Box 442
Vashon, WA 98070-0442, USA

DeCesare, Carmella (Actor, Model)
c/o Staff Member *Playboy Enterprises Inc*
680 N Lake Shore Dr Ste 115
Chicago, IL 60611-4495, USA

Decinces, Douglas V (Doug) (Athlete, Baseball Player)
124 Riviera Way
Laguna Beach, CA 92651-1012, USA

Deck, William (Athlete, Baseball Player)
6628 N Broad St Apt A
Philadelphia, PA 19126-3222, USA

Decker, Brooklyn (Actor)
c/o Chris Kiely *Marilyn Model Management*
32 Union Sq E PH
New York, NY 10003-3209, USA

Decker, Franz-Paul (Conductor)
266 W 37th St # 2000
New York, NY 10018-6609, USA

Decker, Lori (Stylist)
4912 Midmoor Rd
Monona, WI 53716-2617, USA

Decker, Marty (Athlete, Baseball Player)
1036 Bryn Mawr Dr
Yuba City, CA 95993-9007, USA

Decker, Scott (Business Person)
5030 Riverside Dr
Irving, TX 75039-4336, USA

Decker, Steve (Athlete, Baseball Player)
1024 Laurelridge St NE
Keizer, OR 97303-7208, USA

Deckers, Daphne (Actor)
Hoge Naardenweg 44
Hilversum, AG 1217, NETHERLANDS

DeConcini, Dennis (Ex-Senator, Politician)
6014 Chesterbrook Rd
McLean, VA 22101-3210, USA

Decosmo, Joe (Stylist)
4545 Franklin St
Mantua, OH 44255-9484, USA

DeCosta, Sara (Athlete, Hockey Player)
200 Cowesett Green Dr
Warwick, RI 02886-8570, USA

DeCoster, Roger (Race Car Driver)
1919 Torrance Blvd
Torrance, CA 90501-2722, USA

Decter, Midge (Writer)
120 E 81st St
New York, NY 10028-1428, USA

Dedkov, Anatoli I (Cosmonaut)
Moskovskoi Oblasti
Syvisdny, Goroduk 141160, RUSSIA

Dedler, Karin
Hohenegg 21
Dietmannsried, GERMANY D-87463

Dedmon, Jeff (Athlete, Baseball Player)
21102 Broadwell Ave
Torrance, CA 90502-1636, USA

Dedrick, Jim (Athlete, Baseball Player)
2929 NW Kennedy Ct
Portland, OR 97229-8099, USA

DeDuve, Christian R (Nobel Prize Laureate)
80 Central Park W
New York, NY 10023-5204, USA

Dee, Donald (Don) (Athlete, Basketball Player)
7924 N Pennsylvania Ave
Kansas City, MO 64118-1416, USA

Dee, Donnie (Athlete, Football Player)
4927 Lassen Dr
Oceanside, CA 92056-5478, USA

Dee, Joey (Musician)
PO Box 8770
Endwell, NY 13762-8770, USA

Dee, Ruby (Actor)
PO Box 1318
New Rochelle, NY 10802-1318, USA

Dee, Sally (Athlete, Golfer)
3508 W Barcelona St
Tampa, FL 33629-7010, USA

Deeb, Gary (Critic)
401 N Wabash Ave
Chicago, IL 60611-3546, USA

Deedes of Aldington, William F (Government Official)
New Hayters
Aldington, Kent TN25 7DT, UNITED KINGDOM (UK)

Deedle, Nelson
PO Box 5358
Scottsdale, AZ 85261-5358

Deegan, Bill (Athlete, Baseball Player)
8392 77th Ave
Seminole, FL 33777-4413, USA

Deeley, Cat (Actor)
c/o Todd Diener *Collective*
8383 Wilshire Blvd Ste 1050
Beverly Hills, CA 90211-2415, USA

Dee-Lite (Musician)
428 Cedar St NW
Washington, DC 20012, USA

Deen, Paula (Chef, Television Host)
102 W Congress St
Savannah, GA 31401-2508, USA

Deep Purple (Music Group)
c/o Staff Member *Agency Group Ltd, The (UK)*
361-373 City Rd
London EC1V 1PQ, UK

Deependra Bir, Bikaram Shah Dev (Prince)
Durbeg Marg
Kathmandu, NEPAL

Deer, Ada E (Government Official)
2537 Mutchler Rd
Fitchburg, WI 53711-7011, USA

Deer, Rob (Athlete, Baseball Player)
27030 N 70th Pl
Scottsdale, AZ 85266-8826, USA

Deering, John (Cartoonist)
6701 Westover Dr
Little Rock, AR 72207-3447, USA

Dees, Archie (Athlete, Basketball Player)
4405 N Hillview Dr
Bloomington, IN 47408-9770, USA

Dees, Bowen C (Scientist)
1616 Circa Del Lago Unit C203
San Marcos, CA 92078-5282, USA

Dees, Charlie (Athlete, Baseball Player)
1064 Allison Woods Ct
Lawrenceville, GA 30043-5383, USA

Dees, Morris (Civil Rights Activist, Lawyer)
PO Box 548
Montgomery, AL 36101-0548, USA

Dees, Morris S Jr (Activist)
PO Box 548
Montgomery, AL 36101-0548, USA

Dees, Rick (Actor, Entertainer, Musician, Radio Personality)
3601 W Olive Ave Ste 675
Burbank, CA 91505-4622, USA

Deese, Derrick (Athlete, Football Player)
PO Box 3356
Cerritos, CA 90703-3356, USA

Deezen, Eddie (Actor)
c/o Staff Member *Coolwaters Productions*
10061 Riverside Dr # 531
Toluca Lake, CA 91602-2560, USA

Def Leppard (Music Group, Musician)
c/o Rod MacSween *International Talent Booking*
1st Floor, Ariel House 74A Charlotte St
London W1T 4QJ, UNITED KINGDOM

DeFanti, Tom (Inventor)
Electronic Visualization Labe
Chicago, IL 60607, USA

Default (Music Group)
c/o Staff Member *Agency Group Ltd, The (NY)*
142 W 57th St Fl 6
New York, NY 10019-3300, USA

Defauw, Brad (Athlete, Hockey Player)
14829 120th St
Menahga, MN 56464-3501, USA

Defazio, Dean (Athlete, Hockey Player)
2475 Logan Ave
Oakville, ON L6H 6P3, Canada

DeFazio, Peter (Congressman, Politician)
2134 Rayburn Hob
Washington, DC 20515-3704, USA

DeFelitta, Raymond (Director, Writer)
c/o Gary Ungar *Exile Entertainment*
732 El Medio Ave
Pacific Palisades, CA 90272-3451, USA

DeFer, Kaylee (Actor)
c/o Staff Member *Abrams Artists Agency (LA)*
9200 W Sunset Blvd PH 11
Los Angeles, CA 90069-3601, USA

DeFerran, Gil (Race Car Driver)
524 Royal Plaza Dr
Fort Lauderdale, FL 33301-2518, USA

DeFigueiredo, Rul J P (Engineer)
Intelligent Sensors/Systems Lab
Irvine, CA 92717, USA

DeFina, Barbara (Producer)
School of Arts 513 Dodge Hall, Mail Code 1808, 2960 Broadway
New York, NY 10027, USA

DeFleur, Lois B (Educator)
President's Office
Binghamton, NY 13902, USA

Deford, Frank (Writer)
PO Box 1109
Greens Farms, CT 06838-1109, USA

DeForest, Roy (Artist)
112 Madrone Ave
San Anselmo, CA 94960-2113, USA

DeForrest, Jeff (Sportscaster)
5211 NE 14th Ter
Fort Lauderdale, FL 33334-4907, USA

Defrancesco, Dona (Stylist)
c/o Staff Member *That's a Wrap*
PO Box 693
Shrewsbury, MA 01545-8693, USA

DeFrancisco, Joseph E (Joe) (General)
1201 N Nash St Apt 203
Arlington, VA 22209-3672, USA

DeFranco, Buddy (Musician)
22525 Coral Ave
Panama City, FL 32413-3047, USA

DeFrank, Joe (Race Car Driver)
29 Crescent Hollow Ct
Ramsey, NJ 07446-2661, USA

DeFrantz, Anita (Misc)
1 Olympic Plz
Colorado Springs, CO 80909-5780, USA

DeFreitas, Eric (Bowler)
175 W 12th St
New York, NY 10011-8275, USA

Deftones (Music Group)
c/o David Benveniste *Velvet Hammer*
9014 Melrose Ave
West Hollywood, CA 90069-5610, USA

Deganhardt, Johannes J Cardinal (Religious Leader)
Erzbischofliches Generalvikariat Domplatz 3
Paderborn 33098, GERMANY

DeGarmo, Diana (Musician)
c/o Erica Bines *Headline Talent*
905 Sunset Dr
Fuquay Varina, NC 27526-2189, USA

DeGaspa, Philippe (Publisher)
50 Holly St
Toronto, ON M4S 3B3, CANADA

DeGeneres, Betty (Activist, Writer)
c/o Staff Member *HarperCollins Publishers*
10 E 53rd St C/O Author Mail Floor 7
New York, NY 10022, USA

DeGeneres, Ellen (Actor, Comedian, Talk Show Host)
3500 W Olive Ave Ste 1000
Burbank, CA 91505-5515, USA

DeGennes, Pierre-Gilles (Nobel Prize Laureate)
11 Place Marcelin-Berthelot
Paris 75005, FRANCE

Deger, Vicky (Stylist)
c/o Staff Member *Rex Agency, The*
6311 Romaine St
Los Angeles, CA 90038-2617, USA

Degerick, Mike (Athlete, Baseball Player)
2702 Lake Osborne Dr
Lake Worth, FL 33461-5665, USA

DeGette, Diana (Congressman, Politician)
2335 Rayburn Hob
Washington, DC 20515-4329, USA

Degg, Jakki (Actor, Model)
c/o Staff Member *Jakki Degg.net*
PO Box 3673
Cannock WS12 1WD, UNITED KINGDOM

DeGioia, John (Educator)
President S Ofc
Washington, DC 20057-0001, USA

DeGiorgi, Salvatore Cardinal (Religious Leader)
Corso Vittorio Emanuele 461
Palermo 90134, ITALY

DeGivenchy, Hubert (Designer, Fashion Designer)
3 Avenue George V
Paris 75008, France

Degler, Carl N (Historian, Writer)
907 Mears Ct
Stanford, CA 94305-1041, USA

Degnan, John J (Business Person)
15 Mountainview Rd
Warren, NJ 07059-6711, USA

Degraffenreid, Allen (Athlete, Football Player)
14571 W Lisbon Ln
Surprise, AZ 85379-4760, USA

DeGrate, Tony (Athlete, Football Player)
203 Newport Landing Pl
Round Rock, TX 78665-2856, USA

DeGrate Jr, Donald Earle (DeVante Swing) (Musician)
c/o Staff Member *De Swing Mob Inc / EMI April Music Inc*
c/o EMI Music Publishing 810 7th Avenue
New York, NY 10019, USA

DeGraw, Gavin (Musician)
c/o Jonny (Jon) Podell *Podell Talent Agency LLC*
22 W 21st St Fl 9
New York, NY 10010-7095, USA

Degray, Dale (Athlete, Hockey Player)
c/o Staff Member *Owen Sound Attack*
P.O. Box 1420 Stn Main
Owen Sound, ON N4K 6T5, Canada

Degruttola, Raffaello
c/o Lorraine Berglund *Lorraine Berglund Management*
11537 Hesby St
North Hollywood, CA 91601-3618, USA

Dehaan, Dane (Actor)
c/o Courtney Kivowitz *Schiff Company, The*
8440 Warner Dr Ste B1
Culver City, CA 90232-2461, USA

Dehaan, Kory (Athlete, Baseball Player)
19040 E Superstition Dr
Queen Creek, AZ 85142-6884, USA

DeHaan, Richard W (Religious Leader)
3000 Kraft Ave SE
Grand Rapids, MI 49512-2024, USA

Dehaene, Jean-Luc (Prime Minister)
Berkendallaan 52
Vilvoorde 1800, BELGIUM

Dehart, Rick (Athlete, Baseball Player)
811 NE Wabash Ave
Topeka, KS 66616-1443, USA

DeHaven, Gloria (Actor)
2223 W San Miguel Ave
North Las Vegas, NV 89032-3061, USA

DeHaven, Penny
PO Box 83
Brentwood, TN 37024-0083

DeHavilland, Olivia (Actor)
c/o Staff Member *Douglas Gorman Rothacker & Wilhelm Inc*
1501 Broadway Ste 703
New York, NY 10036-5501, USA

Dehere, Terry (Athlete, Basketball Player)
120 Wayne St
Jersey City, NJ 07302-3406, USA

Dehmelt, Hans G (Nobel Prize Laureate)
1600 43rd Ave E
Seattle, WA 98112-3205, USA

Deidel, Jim (Athlete, Baseball Player)
14312 Wright Way
Broomfield, CO 80023-4045, USA

Deidrick, Casey (Actor)
c/o Jon Simmons *Simmons & Scott Entertainment*
7942 Mulholland Dr
Los Angeles, CA 90046-1225, USA

Deighton, Len
10 Iron Bridge House Bridge Approach
London, ENGLAND NW1 8BD

Deighton, Leonard C (Len) (Writer)
Fairymount Blackrock Dundalk
County Louth, IRELAND

Deisenhofer, Johann (Nobel Prize Laureate)
3860 Echo Brook Ln
Dallas, TX 75229-5221, USA

Deitch, Donna (Director)
8942 Wilshire Blvd # 219
Beverly Hills, CA 90211-1908, USA

Deja (Musician)
c/o Anthony Embry *AE Entertainment Public Relations*
124 Evening Shade Dr
Charleston, SC 29414-9144, USA

Deja, Andreas (Animator)
3494 Berry Dr
Studio City, CA 91604-4152, USA

Deja Vu
1 Touchstone Lane Chard
Somerset, ENGLAND TA20 1RF

DeJager, Cornelis (Astronomer)
Zonnenburg 1
Utrecht, NL 352, NETHERLANDS

Dejdel, Jim (Baseball Player)
14312 Wright Way
Broomfield, CO 80023-4045, USA

Dejean, Mike (Athlete, Baseball Player)
107 Yellowood Dr
West Monroe, LA 71291-9532, USA

Dejesus, Ivan (Athlete, Baseball Player)
14608 Velleux Dr
Orlando, FL 32837-5467, USA

Dejesus, Jose (Baseball Player)
7E6 Villa Del Carmen
Cidra, PR 639, USA

Dejohn, Mark (Athlete, Baseball Player)
24 New Hampshire Dr Apt 1C
New Britain, CT 06052-1166, USA

DeJohnette, Jack (Composer)
Silver Hollow Road
Willow, NY 11201, USA

DeJong, Pierre (Misc)
7000 East Ave
Livermore, CA 94550-9698, USA

DeJordy, Denis E (Athlete, Hockey Player)
472 Chemin Des Patriotes
St-Charles-Sur-Richelieu, QC J0L 2G0, Canada

DeJoria, John Paul (Business Person)
26455 Golden Valley Rd
Santa Clarita, CA 91350-2973, USA

Dejurnett, Charles (Athlete, Football Player)
1355 Heritage Ct
Escondido, CA 92027-3972, USA

DeKierk, Albert (Composer)
Crayenesterlaan
Haarlem 22, NETHERLANDS

DeKierk, Frederik W (Nobel Prize Laureate)
7 Eaton Square
London SW1, UNITED KINGDOM (UK)

DeKieweit, Cornelis W (Historian)
22 Berkeley St
Rochester, NY 14607-2209, USA

Dekker, Thomas (Actor, Director)
c/o Mimi DiTrani *Schiff Company, The*
8440 Warner Dr Ste B1
Culver City, CA 90232-2461, USA

Del Amitri (Music Group, Songwriter, Writer)
c/o Scott Clayton *Creative Artists Agency (CAA-TN)*
3310 W End Ave Fl 5
Nashville, TN 37203-1028, USA

Del Arco, Jonathan (Actor)
c/o Kyle Fritz *Kyle Fritz Management*
6325 Heather Dr
Los Angeles, CA 90068-1633, USA

Del Bello, Jack (Athlete, Football Player)
391 Belfast Ter
Sebastian, FL 32958-5509, USA

del Boca, Andrea (Actor)
c/o Staff Member *Telefe - Argentina*
Pavon 2444 (C1248AAT)
Buenos Aires, ARGENTINA

del Castillo, Eric (Actor)
c/o Staff Member *Televisa*
Blvd Adolfo Lopez Mateos 232 Colonia San Angel INN
DF CP 01060, MEXICO

Del Castillo, Kate (Actor)
c/o Jack Ketsoyan *EMC / Bowery*
8155 Santa Monica Blvd Ste 200
West Hollywood, CA 90046-4986, USA

Del Castillo-Kinney, Ysora (Baseball Player)
1555 W 44th Pl Apt 216C
Hialeah, FL 33012-7837, USA

Del Gaizo, Jim (Athlete, Football Player)
9581 NW 13th St
Plantation, FL 33322-4809, USA

Del Greco, Al (Athlete, Football Player)
1012 Little Turtle Cir
Birmingham, AL 35242-3282, USA

Del Greco, Bobby (Athlete, Baseball Player)
625 Southview Dr
Pittsburgh, PA 15226-2540, USA

Del La Hoya, Daisy (Actor, Model, Reality TV Star)
c/o Michael (Mike) Esterman *Esterman.Com, LLC*
Prefers to be contacted via email
MD, USA

Del Negro, Matthew (Actor)
c/o Adam Lazarus *Bauman Redanty & Shaul Agency*
5757 Wilshire Blvd Suite 473
Beverly Hills, CA 90212, USA

Del Negro, Vinny (Athlete, Basketball Player)
58 Bagnell Dr
Pembroke, MA 02359-2365, USA

Del Piero, Alessandro (Soccer Player)
Piazza Crimea # 7
New York, NY 10131-0001, ITALY

Del Pino, Robin (Stylist)
233 E 77th St Apt 16
New York, NY 10075-2055, USA

Del Regil, Estrellita
PO Box 2004
Beverly Hills, CA 90213-2004

del Rincon, Fernando (Actor)
c/o Staff Member *Univision*
605 3rd Ave Fl 12
New York, NY 10158-0034, USA

Del Rio, Jack (Athlete, Football Coach, Football Player)
1605 Beach Ave
Atlantic Beach, FL 32233-5840, USA

Del Rio, Rebekah (Musician)
2280 Grass Valley Hwy # 138
Auburn, CA 95603-2536, USA

Del Rubio, Millie
PO Box 6923
San Pedro, CA 90734-6923

del Solar, Fernando (Actor)
c/o Staff Member *TV Azteca*
Periferico Sur 4121 Colonia Fuentes del Pedregal
DF CP 14141, Mexico

Del Toro, Benicio (Actor)
c/o Rick Yorn *Yorn Management Group*
2000 Avenue Of The Stars 3rd Tower Floor NORTH
Los Angeles, CA 90067, USA

Del Toro, Guillermo (Director, Writer)
c/o Gary Ungar *Exile Entertainment*
732 El Medio Ave
Pacific Palisades, CA 90272-3451, USA

DeLaBilliere, Peter (General)
25 Copthall Ave
London EC2R 7DR, UNITED KINGDOM (UK)

Delacote, Jacques
Dr Hilbert Maximilianstr 22
Munich 80539, GERMANY

DeLaCruz, Rosie (Model)
300 Park Ave S # 200
New York, NY 10010-5313, USA

DeLaFuente, Joel (Actor)
130 W 42nd St Ste 1906
New York, NY 10036-7902, USA

Delahoussaye, Edward J (Eddie) (Jockey)
1024 S 4th Ave
Arcadia, CA 91006-4218, USA

Delahoussaye, Ryan (Musician)
2002 Hogback Rd Ste 20
Ann Arbor, MI 48105-9736, USA

Delain, Moneca (Actor)
c/o Staff Member *Pacific Artists Management*
1285 W Broadway Suite 685
Vancouver, BC V6H 3X8, Canada

Delaire, Suzy
46 Rue De Varenne
Paris, FRANCE 75007

DeLamielleure, Joseph M (Joe) (Athlete, Football Player)
7818 Ridgeloch Pl
Charlotte, NC 28226-3008, USA

DeLancie, John (Actor)
1313 Brunswick Ave
South Pasadena, CA 91030-3509, USA

Delaney, Don (Athlete, Basketball Player, Coach)
25 High Point Ln
Willoughby, OH 44094-6968, USA

Delaney, F James (Jim) (Athlete, Track Athlete)
3787 Skyfarm Dr
Santa Rosa, CA 95403-0993, USA

Delaney, Jeff (Athlete, Football Player)
215 Village Green Dr
Canonsburg, PA 15317-5423, USA

Delaney, Kim (Actor, Model)
c/o Staff Member *Gersh (LA)*
9465 Wilshire Blvd Ste 600
Beverly Hills, CA 90212-2612, USA

Delaney, Pat
PO Box 273
Tamworth, NH 03886-0273

Delaney, Shelagh (Writer)
11 Jubilee Place
London SW3 3TE, UNITED KINGDOM (UK)

Delaney, Tracie (Stylist)
c/o Staff Member *Judy Inc*
1 Yorkville Ave
Toronto ON M4W 1L1, Canada

Delano, Diane (Actor)
3500 W Olive Ave Ste 1400
Burbank, CA 91505-5512, USA

Delano, Michael (Actor)
c/o Cody Garden *McCarty Agency*
2600 W Olive Ave Fl 5
Burbank, CA 91505-4572, USA

Delano, Robert B (Misc)
225 W Touhy Ave
Park Ridge, IL 60068-4202, USA

Delany, Dana (Actor)
c/o Heidi Schaeffer *PMK/BNC Public Relations (PMK-LA)*
8687 Melrose Ave Ste 8
West Hollywood, CA 90069-5746, USA

DeLap, Tony (Artist)
225 Jasmine Ave
Corona Del Mar, CA 92625-3035, USA

DeLaPuente, Raygada Oscar (Prime Minister)
Urb Corpac Calle 1 Oeste
Lima, S/N, PERU

DelArco, Jonathan (Actor)
8730 W Sunset Blvd Ste 220W
Los Angeles, CA 90069-2275, USA

DeLaria, Lea (Actor)
c/o Diana Doussant *TalentWorks (LA)*
3500 W Olive Ave Ste 1400
Burbank, CA 91505-5512, USA

DeLaRocha, Zack (Musician)
8935 Lindblade St
Culver City, CA 90232-2438, USA

DeLaRosa, Evelyn (Opera Singer)
150 W 55th St
New York, NY 10019-5586, USA

DeLaRosa, Yvonne (Actor)
c/o Staff Member *Heidi Rotbart Management*
1810 Malcolm Ave Apt 207
Los Angeles, CA 90025-7610, USA

Delasin, Dorothy (Athlete, Golfer)
20 Longview Dr
Daly City, CA 94015-4714, USA

Delate, Joseph (Stylist)
c/o Staff Member *Bernstein & Andriulli*
58 W 40th St
New York, NY 10018-2658, USA

DeLatour, David (Actor)
c/o Staff Member *Kass & Stokes Management*
9229 W Sunset Blvd Ste 504
Los Angeles, CA 90069-3405, USA

Delay, Tom (Ex-Congressman, Politician)
242 Cannon Hob
Washington, DC 20515-4322, USA

Delays Delirium (Music Group)
c/o Staff Member *Paradigm (Monterey)*
404 W Franklin St
Monterey, CA 93940-2303, USA

Delcarmen, Manny (Athlete, Baseball Player)
50 Banks St
Brockton, MA 2302, USA

DeLeeuw, Ton (Composer)
Costerusiaan 4
Hilversum, NETHERLANDS

Delehanty, Hugh (Editor)
601 E St NW
Washington, DC 20049-0001, USA

DeLeo, Dean (Musician)
729 7th Ave Ste 1600
New York, NY 10019-6880, USA

DeLeo, Robert (Composer)
729 7th Ave Ste 1600
New York, NY 10019-6880, USA

Deleon, Jose (Baseball Player)
7021 NW 70th St
Parkland, FL 33067-1486, USA

Deleone, Tom (Athlete, Football Player)
PO Box 681472
Park City, UT 84068-1472, USA

Delfino, Carlos Francisco (Basketball Player)
2 Championship Dr
Auburn Hills, MI 48326-1753, USA

Delfino, Majandra (Actor)
c/o Bradley Frank *Platform Public Relations*
2666 N Beachwood Dr
Los Angeles, CA 90068-2308, USA

Delfino, Marieh (Actor)
c/o Amanda Glazer *Kohner Agency, The*
9300 Wilshire Blvd Ste 555
Beverly Hills, CA 90212-3211, USA

Delfs, Andreas (Conductor)
408 Saint Peter St
Saint Paul, MN 55102-1130, USA

Delgado, Carlos J (Athlete, Baseball Player)
9 Repto Ramos
Aguadilla, PR 00603-5944, USA

Delgado, Chiquinquira (Actor)
c/o Gabriel Blanco *Gabriel Blanco Iglesias (Mexico)*
Rio Balsas 35-32 Colonia Cuauhtemoc
DF 6500, Mexico

Delgado, Felix Avila (Cuban Link) (Musician)
c/o Staff Member *Mob Records*
Unit 2A Queens Studios 21 Salusbury Rd
London NW6 6RG, USA

Delgado, Frankie (Actor)
c/o Eric Podwall *Podwall Entertainment*
710 N Orlando Ave Apt 203
Los Angeles, CA 90069-5549, USA

Delgado, Issac (Musician)
568 Broadway # 806
New York, NY 10012-3225, USA

Delguidice, Matt (Athlete, Hockey Player)
25 Church St
North Branford, CT 06471-1418, USA

Delhaven, Robert M (War Hero)
3716 Terrace View Dr
Encino, CA 91436, USA

Delhi, Ganesh (Actor)
No12 62nd Street Ashok Nagar
Chennai, TN 600 083, INDIA

Delhomme, Jake (Athlete, Football Player)
1459 Mills Hwy
Breaux Bridge, LA 70517-7305, USA

Delhoyo, George (Actor)
c/o Staff Member *TalentWorks (LA)*
3500 W Olive Ave Ste 1400
Burbank, CA 91505-5512, USA

D'Elia, Chris (Actor, Writer)
c/o Stephanie Davis *3 Arts Entertainment Inc*
9460 Wilshire Blvd Fl 7
Beverly Hills, CA 90212-2713, USA

D'Elia, Federico (Actor)
c/o Staff Member *Telefe - Argentina*
Pavon 2444 (C1248AAT)
Buenos Aires, ARGENTINA

Delia, Joseph (Athlete, Football Player)
PO Box 19654
Irvine, CA 92623-9654, USA

Deligne, Pierre R (Mathematician)
Math School Einstein Dr
Princeton, NJ 8540, USA

Delilah (Radio Personality)
15260 Ventura Blvd Ste 400
Sherman Oaks, CA 91403-5300, USA

DeLillo, Don (Writer)
57 Rossmore Ave
Bronxville, NY 10708-5615, USA

DeLine, Donald (Producer)
c/o Staff Member *De Line Pictures*
4000 Warner Blvd Bldg 66RM PMB 147
Burbank, CA 91522-0001, USA

Delinsky, Barbara (Writer)
c/o Staff Member *Simon & Schuster*
1230 Avenue of the Americas Fl CONC1
New York, NY 10020-1586, USA

Delisle, Jim (Athlete, Football Player)
S34W32228 Journeys Way
Waukesha, WI 53189-9494, USA

Delizia, Cara (Actor)
6238 De Longpre Ave
Hollywood, CA 90028-8265

Delk, Joan (Athlete, Golfer)
830 Forest Path Ln
Alpharetta, GA 30022-6468, USA

Delk, Tony (Athlete, Basketball Player)
1843 Glenhill Dr
Lexington, KY 40502-2817, USA

Dell, Donald (Athlete, Tennis Player)
5335 Wisconsin Ave NW Ste 850
Washington, DC 20015-2052, USA

Dell, Michael S (Business Person)
1 Dell Way
Round Rock, TX 78682-7000, USA

Dell'Abate, Gary (Producer)
c/o Richard Abate *3 Arts Entertainment - NY*
49 W 27th St Fl 5
New York, NY 10001-6936, USA

DellaCasa-Debeljevic, Lisa (Opera Singer)
Schloss Gottlieben
Thurgau, SWITZERLAND

Dellaero, Jason (Athlete, Baseball Player)
3240 Chapel Creek Cir
Wesley Chapel, FL 33544-7700, USA

Dellanos, Myrka (Actor)
c/o Staff Member *Univision*
605 3rd Ave Fl 12
New York, NY 10158-0034, USA

Dellenbach, Jeff (Athlete, Football Player)
1002 Pine Branch Dr
Weston, FL 33326-2840, USA

Delli Colli, Tomino
Via Pietro Micheli 78
Rome, ITALY I-00197

Dellinger, Dustin (Dusty) (Athlete, Baseball Player)
5203 Grindstone Ln
Granite Falls, NC 28630, USA

Dellinger, Walter (Educator)
Law School
Durham, NC 27706, USA

DelloJolo, Norman (Composer)
PO Box 154
East Hampton, NY 11937-0154, USA

Dellucci, David (Dave) (Athlete, Baseball Player)
18489 Lake Tulip Ave
Baton Rouge, LA 70817-9502, USA

Delo, Ken (Actor)
161 Avondale Dr # 93-8
Branson, MO 65616-3646, USA

Delock, Ivan M (Ike) (Athlete, Baseball Player)
433 Cypress Way E
Naples, FL 34110-1107, USA

Delon, Alain (Actor)
7 Rue Des Battoirs
Genève CH-1 205, Switzerland

Delon, Anthony (Actor)
5 Rue Clement-Marot
Paris 75008, FRANCE

Delon, Nathalie
3 Quai Malaquais
Paris, FRANCE 75006

Delong, Greg (Athlete, Football Player)
4960 Shady Maple Ln
Winston Salem, NC 27106-8704, USA

DeLong, Keith A (Athlete, Football Player)
1850 Greywell Rd
Knoxville, TN 37922-9454, USA

DeLong, Michael P (General)
US Central Command
MacDill Air Force Base, FL 33621, USA

Delong, Nate (Athlete, Basketball Player)
PO Box 485
Hayward, WI 54843-0485, USA

DeLong, Steve C (Athlete, Football Player)
4103 Dyanax St
Chesapeake, VA 23324-1419, USA

DeLonge, Thomas Matthew (Music Group, Musician)
c/o Staff Member *Geffen Records*
9126 Sunset Blvd
West Hollywood, CA 90069, USA

Delonge, Tom (Actor, Musician)
c/o Staff Member *Geffen Records*
9126 Sunset Blvd
West Hollywood, CA 90069, USA

DeLongis, Anthony (Actor)
PO Box 2445
Canyon Country, CA 91386-2445, USA

Deloplaine, Jack (Athlete, Football Player)
215 Montana St
Pittsburgh, PA 15214-1630, USA

Delora, Jennifer (Actor)
9744 Wilshire Blvd Ste 203
Beverly Hills, CA 90212-1812, USA

DeLorenzo, Michael (Actor)
c/o Staff Member *Shelter Entertainment*
9454 Wilshire Blvd Ste 715
Beverly Hills, CA 90212-2925, USA

Delorme, Daniele
16 Rue De Marignan
Paris, FRANCE 75008

Delorme, Gilbert (Athlete, Hockey Player)
2800 Rue Viau Attn Coaching Staff
Montreal, QC H1V 3J3, Canada

Delorme, Ron (Athlete, Hockey Player)
94 Ravine Dr
Port Moody, BC V3H 4T8, Canada

Delors, Jacques L J (Government Official)
19 Blvd de Bercy
Paris 75012, FRANCE

Delparte, Guy (Athlete, Hockey Player)
173 Sandy Hill Rd
South Portland, ME 04106-4029, USA

Delpino, Robert L (Athlete, Football Player)
632 Shadybrook Ln Apt 115
Corona, CA 92879-6547, USA

Delpy, Julie (Actor)
c/o Glenn Rigberg *HYPHENATE*
9701 Wilshire Blvd Fl 10
Beverly Hills, CA 90212-2010, USA

Delsing, Jay (Athlete, Golfer)
14020 Woods Mill Cove Dr
Chesterfield, MO 63017-3434, USA

Delson, Brad (Musician)
c/o Staff Member *Artist Group International (NY)*
150 E 58th St Fl 19
New York, NY 10155-1900, USA

Delta Spirit (Music Group)
c/o Staff Member *Paradigm (Monterey)*
404 W Franklin St
Monterey, CA 93940-2303, USA

DelTredici, David (Composer)
463 West St Apt G121
New York, NY 10014-2029, USA

Deluca, Annette (Athlete, Golfer)
7 Turtle Creek Dr Apt D
Jupiter, FL 33469-1530, USA

DeLuca, Mike (Producer)
10202 W Washington Blvd Astaire Bldg Ste 3028
Culver City, CA 90232, USA

Deluca, Sam (Athlete, Football Player)
42 Shore Rd
Pelham, NY 10803-3612, USA

Deluca, Silvana (Stylist)
c/o Staff Member *Ford Models (Chicago)*
311 W Superior St
Chicago, IL 60654-3548, USA

DeLucas, Lawrence J (Astronaut)
909 19th St S
Birmingham, AL 35205, USA

Delucca, Jerry (Athlete, Football Player)
27 Pulaski St
Peabody, MA 01960-1831, USA

DeLucchi, Michele (Architect)
Via Cenisio 40
Milan 20154, ITALY

DeLucia, Paco (Musician)
278 S Main St # 400
Gloucester, MA 1930, USA

Delucia, Rich (Athlete, Baseball Player)
4 Rick Rd
Reading, PA 19607-9704, USA

Delugg, Milton (Musician)
2740 Claray Dr
Los Angeles, CA 90077-2018, USA

DeLuise, David (Actor)
c/o Ted Schachter *Schachter Entertainment*
1157 S Beverly Dr Fl 2
Los Angeles, CA 90035-1119, USA

Deluise, Michael (Actor)
1186 Corsica Dr
Pacific Palisades, CA 90272-4014, USA

Deluise, Peter (Actor, Director, Producer)
c/o Lee Dinstman *Agency for the Performing Arts (APA-LA)*
405 S Beverly Dr Ste 500
Beverly Hills, CA 90212-4425, USA

Delvecchio, Alexander P (Alex) (Athlete, Hockey Player)
2602 Stoodleigh Dr
Rochester Hills, MI 48309-2836, USA

Delvecchio, Paul (DJ Pauly D) (Reality TV Star)
c/o Amanda Ruisi *AKR Public Relations*
Prefers to be contacted via email or telephone
New York, NY, USA

Del-Vikings, The (Music Group)
PO Box 770850
Orlando, FL 32877-0850, USA

Demaestri, Joe (Athlete, Baseball Player)
50 Fairway Dr
Novato, CA 94949-5904, USA

DeMaiziere, Lothar (Prime Minister)
Am Kupfergraben # 6/6A
New York, NY 10117-0001, GERMANY

Demao, Al (Athlete, Football Player)
16206 Atlantis Dr
Bowie, MD 20716-3839, USA

Demar, Enoch (Athlete, Football Player)
1579 Olympian Cir SW
Atlanta, GA 30310-2440, USA

Demarchelier, Patrick (Photographer)
162 W 21st St
New York, NY 10011-3244, USA

Demarco, Ab Jr (Athlete, Hockey Player)
211 Regal Rd
North Bay, ON P1B 8G4, Canada

DeMarco, Guido (President)
Palace
Valletta, MALTA

DeMarco, Jean (Artist)
Cervaro
Prov-Frosinore 3044, ITALY

Demarco, Robert (Bob) (Athlete, Football Player)
13055 Midfield Ter
Saint Louis, MO 63146-6053, USA

DeMarco, Tony (Boxer)
PO Box 53664
Indianapolis, IN 46253-0664, USA

Demarest, Arthur A (Archaeologist)
Anthropology
Nashville, TN 37235-0001, USA

Demarie, John (Athlete, Football Player)
416 Greenway St
Lake Charles, LA 70605-6828, USA

Demars, Billy (Athlete, Baseball Player)
770 Island Way Apt 305
Clearwater, FL 33767-1824, USA

Demars, Bruce (Admiral)
41 Manters Point Rd
Plymouth, MA 2360, USA

Demartino, Ricci (Stylist)
c/o Staff Member *Cloutier Agency*
2632 La Cienega Ave
Los Angeles, CA 90034-2641, USA

Dembo, Fennis (Athlete, Basketball Player)
430 N Pine St
San Antonio, TX 78202-2850, USA

DeMedeiros, Maria (Actor, Director, Writer)
c/o Staff Member *Alsira García-Maroto Talent Agency*
Calle De Los Invencibles 8 Bajo
Madrid 28019, Spain

DeMenezes, Fradique (President)
Pargo do Povo
Sao Tome, SAO TOME & PRINCIPE

DeMent, Iris (Songwriter, Writer)
c/o Staff Member *Paradigm (Monterey)*
404 W Franklin St
Monterey, CA 93940-2303, USA

DeMent, Jack (Misc)
11325 NE Weidler St # 44
Portland, OR 97220-1950, USA

Dement, Kenneth (Athlete, Football Player)
316 S Kingshighway St
Sikeston, MO 63801-2948, USA

Dementieva, Elena (Tennis Player)
c/o Staff Member *Octagon (VA)*
1751 Pinnacle Dr Ste 1500
McLean, VA 22102-3833, USA

DeMerchant, Paul (Religious Leader)
PO Box 9127
Fort Wayne, IN 46899-9127, USA

Demerit, John (Athlete, Baseball Player)
550 W Walters St
Port Washington, WI 53074-1430, USA

Demery, Larry (Athlete, Baseball Player)
10806 Valverde Dr
Bakersfield, CA 93311-8907, USA

Demeter, Don (Athlete, Baseball Player)
6240 S Country Club Dr
Oklahoma City, OK 73159-1844, USA

Demeter, Steve (Athlete, Baseball Player)
4173 Bentley Dr
North Olmsted, OH 44070-2802, USA

Demetral, Chris (Actor)
c/o Jamie Gold *JMG Management*
18000 Coastline Dr Apt 8
Malibu, CA 90265-5727, USA

Demetriadis, Phoklon (Cartoonist)
3rd September St 174
Athens, GREECE

Demetrios (Religious Leader)
89 E 79th St # 19
New York, NY 10021, USA

Demeulemeester, Ann (Designer, Fashion Designer)
c/o Staff Member *Ann Demeulemeester*
6 Rue Milne Edwards
Paris 75017, France

Demic, Larry (Athlete, Basketball Player)
2551 Via Campo
Montebello, CA 90640-1806, USA

DeMille, Nelson (Writer)
61 Hilton Ave Ste 23
Garden City, NY 11530-2813, USA

Demin, Lev S (Cosmonaut)
Moskovskol Oblasti
Syvisdny Goroduk 141160, RUSSIA

Deming, Peter (Cinematographer)
9150 Wilshire Blvd Ste 220
Beverly Hills, CA 90212-3429, USA

DeMita, L Ciriaco (Prime Minister)
Piazza de Gesu 46
Rome 186, ITALY

Demitra, Pavol (Athlete, Hockey Player)
712 Finch Ct
Chesterfield, MO 63017-1782, USA

Demme, Jonathan (Director, Producer, Writer)
c/o Leslee Dart *42West (NY)*
220 W 42nd St Fl 12
New York, NY 10036-7200, USA

Demmings, Pancho (Actor)
c/o Judy Orbach *Judy O Productions*
6136 Glen Holly St
Hollywood, CA 90068-2338, USA

Demola, Don (Athlete, Baseball Player)
352 Village Dr
Hauppauge, NY 11788-3225, USA

Demon Hunter (Music Group)
c/o Staff Member *Agency Group Ltd, The (NY)*
142 W 57th St Fl 6
New York, NY 10019-3300, USA

DeMont, Rick (Athlete, Swimmer)
84596 Upena St
Waianae, HI 96792-1933, USA

DeMontebello, Philippe L (Misc)
82nd St & 5th Ave
New York, NY 10028, USA

DeMornay, Rebecca (Actor)
c/o Greg Clark *Untitled Entertainment (LA)*
350 S Beverly Dr Ste 200
Beverly Hills, CA 90212-4819, USA

Demoss, Bob (Athlete, Football Player)
117 Knox Dr
West Lafayette, IN 47906-2147, USA

Demps, Will (Athlete)
c/o Staff Member *EAG Sports Management*
12910 Agustin Pl
Playa Vista, CA 90094-2301, USA

Dempsey, Cedric (Misc)
70 W Washington St
Indianapolis, IN 46204, USA

Dempsey, George (Athlete, Basketball Player)
6945 Cedar Ave
Pennsauken, NJ 08109-2713, USA

Dempsey, Mark (Athlete, Baseball Player)
673 W Martindale Rd
Englewood, OH 45322-3043, USA

Dempsey, Michael (Actor)
c/o Vincent Cirrincione *Vincent Cirrincione Associates*
1516 N Fairfax Ave
Los Angeles, CA 90046-2608, USA

Dempsey, Nathan (Athlete, Hockey Player)
c/o Art Breeze *Pro-Rep Entertainment Consulting*
113-276 Midpark Way SE
Calgary, AB T2X 1J6, Canada

Dempsey, Pat (Baseball Player)
10116 Oro Vista Ave
Sunland, CA 91040-3238, USA

Dempsey, Patrick (Actor)
c/o Joanna (Joanie) Burstein *Burstein Company, The*
15304 W Sunset Blvd Ste 208
Pacific Palisades, CA 90272-3656, USA

Dempsey, Rick (Athlete, Baseball Player)
1673 Crown Ridge Ct
Westlake Village, CA 91362-4731, USA

Dempsey, Tanya (Actor)
c/o Dino May *Dino May Management*
6362 Hollywood Blvd
Los Angeles, CA 90028-6323, USA

Dempsey, Thomas (Tom) (Athlete, Football Player)
541 Julius Ave
New Orleans, LA 70121-1613, USA

Dempster, Ryan (Athlete, Baseball Player)
3537 N Greenview Ave
Chicago, IL 60657-1317, USA

Demsetz, Harold (Economist)
Economics Dept
Los Angeles, CA 90024, USA

Demsey, Todd (Athlete, Golfer)
8140 E Arroyo Seco Rd
Scottsdale, AZ 85266-1056, USA

DeMunn, Jeffrey (Actor)
c/o Staff Member *Gersh (LA)*
9465 Wilshire Blvd Ste 600
Beverly Hills, CA 90212-2612, USA

DeMuron, Pierre (Architect)
Rheinschanze 6
Basel 4056, SWITZERLAND

Demus, Jorg (Musician)
Doblinger Hauptstr 77-A/10
Vienna 1190, AUSTRIA

Demuth, Dana (Athlete, Baseball Player)
1156 W Wagner Dr
Gilbert, AZ 85233-7980, USA

Demuth, Richard H (Attorney, Attorney General, Financier, General)
7 Eliot Rd
Lexington, MA 02421-5649, USA

Den, Tagayasu (Choreographer)
Koda Performing Arts Co
Sado Island, JAPAN

Den Herder, Vern W (Athlete, Football Player)
2342 Riviera Rd
Sioux Center, IA 51250-2943, USA

Denard, Michael (Dancer)
Place de l'Opera
Paris 75009, FRANCE

Denberg, Lori Beth (Actor)
c/o Staff Member *Acme Talent & Literary (LA)*
1400 Atlantic Ave Ste 274
Long Beach, CA 90813-2013, USA

Denby-Ashe, Daniela (Actor)

Dench, Judi (Actor)
c/o Gene Parseghian *Parseghian Planco LLC*
322 8th Ave Ste 601
New York, NY 10001-6715, USA

Denebeim, Amy (Stylist)
c/o Staff Member *Artist Untied (LA)*
845 S Mansfield Ave Apt 1
Los Angeles, CA 90036-4979, USA

Denehy, Bill (Athlete, Baseball Player)
2528 Clarinet Dr
Orlando, FL 32837-7033, USA

Denes, Agnes C (Artist)
595 Broadway
New York, NY 10012-3222, USA

Deneuve, Catherine (Actor)
c/o Claire Blondel *ArtMedia*
20 avenue Rapp
Paris 75008, France

Deng, Luol (Athlete, Basketball Player)
3280 Sunset Trl
Northbrook, IL 60062-6332, USA

Denham, Jeff (Congressman, Politician)
1605 Longworth Hob
Washington, DC 20515-1406, USA

Denhardt, David T (Biologist)
Nelson Biological Laboratories
Piscataway, NJ 8855, USA

Denicourt, Marianne (Actor)
20 Ave Rapp
Paris 75007, FRANCE

Denis, Louis (Athlete, Hockey Player)
20051 Country Road 17
Lancaster, ON K0C 1N0, Canada

Denis, Marc (Athlete, Hockey Player)
16336 Burniston Dr
Tampa, FL 33647-2763, USA

Denisof, Alexis (Actor)
c/o Nancy Gates *United Talent Agency (UTA)*
9560 Wilshire Blvd Fl 5
Beverly Hills, CA 90212-2400, USA

Denison, Anthony (Actor)
10100 Santa Monica Blvd Ste 1060
Los Angeles, CA 90067-4151, USA

Denisov, Edison V (Composer)
Studentcheskaia 44/28 #35
Moscow 121165, RUSSIA

Denisse, Francois-Jean (Astronomer)
48 Rue Monsieur Le Prince
Paris 75006, FRANCE

Denisyuk, Yuri N (Engineer)
12 Burzhevaya
Saint Petersburg 199034, RUSSIA

Denker, Henry (Writer)
241 Central Park W
New York, NY 10024-4530, USA

Denkinger, Don (Athlete, Baseball Player)
1980 Kamille Ct
Waterloo, IA 50701-4537, USA

Denman, Brian (Athlete, Baseball Player)
16 Cindy Dr
Buffalo, NY 14221-3002, USA

Denman, David (Actor)
c/o Rebecca (Becca) Kovacik *Hofflund/Polone*
9465 Wilshire Blvd Ste 420
Beverly Hills, CA 90212-2603, USA

Denman, Tony (Actor)
c/o Beverly Strong *Strong Management*
3532 Hayden Ave
Culver City, CA 90232-2413, USA

Dennard, Kenny (Athlete, Basketball Player)
6641 Westchester Ave
Houston, TX 77005-3755, USA

Dennard, Mark (Athlete, Football Player)
4990 Afton Oaks Dr
College Station, TX 77845-7666, USA

Dennard, Preston (Athlete, Football Player)
4545 Greene Ave NW
Albuquerque, NM 87114-4296, USA

Dennehy, Brian (Actor)
c/o Susan Smith *Susan Smith Company, The*
1344 N Wetherly Dr
Los Angeles, CA 90069-1817, USA

Dennehy, Kathleen (Actor)
8281 Melrose Ave Ste 200
Los Angeles, CA 90046-6890, USA

Dennen, Brett (Musician)
c/o Michael McDonald *Mick Management*
35 Washington St
Brooklyn, NY 11201-1028, USA

Dennerlein, Barbara (Musician)
Tsingtauer Str 66
Munich 81827, GERMANY

Dennert-Hill, Pauline (Baseball Player)
415 Clinton St
Owosso, MI 48867-2718, USA

Dennett, Daniel C (Misc)
20 Ironwood Rd
North Andover, MA 01845-2103, USA

Denney, Austin (Athlete, Football Player)
6933 Riverwood Dr
Knoxville, TN 37920-6025, USA

Denney, Kyle (Athlete, Baseball Player)
PO Box 300
Prague, OK 74864-0300, USA

Denney, Mike (Athlete, Football Player)
6419 Oakley St
Philadelphia, PA 19111-5218, USA

Denney, Ryan (Athlete, Football Player)
351 Silver Cir
Alpine, UT 84004-2635, USA

Denning, Blaine (Athlete, Basketball Player)
1283 NW Bentley Cir
Port Saint Lucie, FL 34986-1834, USA

Denning, Hazel M (Writer)
PO Box 64383
Saint Paul, MN 55164-0383

Dennings, Kat (Actor)
c/o Nicole King *Management 360*
9111 Wilshire Blvd
Beverly Hills, CA 90210-5508, USA

Dennis, Cathy (Musician)
Ransomes Gate #32 35-37 Parkgate
London SW11 4NP, UNITED KINGDOM (UK)

Dennis, Clark (Athlete, Golfer)
4117 Sarita Dr
Fort Worth, TX 76109-4743, USA

Dennis, Donna F (Artist)
131 Duane St
New York, NY 10013-3850, USA

Dennis, Gabrielle (Actor)
c/o Staff Member *JC Robbins Management*
113 S Kilkea Dr
Los Angeles, CA 90048-3525, USA

Dennis, Guy (Athlete, Football Player)
PO Box 2500
Hawthorne, FL 32640-2500, USA

Dennis, Jim (Race Car Driver)
1810 Little Mastens Corner Rd
Harrington, DE 19952-3219, USA

Dennis, Mark (Athlete, Football Player)
52 Cambridge Ln
Lincolnshire, IL 60069-3101, USA

Dennis, Mike (Musician)
2011 Ferry Ave Apt U19
Camden, NJ 08104-1900, USA

Dennis, Mike (Athlete, Football Player)
5 Sandalwood Dr
Madison, MS 39110-9249, USA

Dennis, Norm (Athlete, Hockey Player)
1531 Highway 3-B
Fruitvale, BC V0G 1L0, Canada

Dennis, Pamela (Designer, Fashion Designer)
c/o Jerry Shandrew *Shandrew Public Relations*
1050 S Stanley Ave
Los Angeles, CA 90019-6634, USA

Dennison, Bonnie (Actor)
c/o Staff Member *Terrific Talent Associates*
419 Park Ave S Rm 1009
New York, NY 10016-8410, USA

Dennison, Doug (Athlete, Football Player)
2309 Daybreak Trl
Plano, TX 75093-3808, USA

Dennison, Glenn (Athlete, Football Player)
1104 Tucker Ln
Ashton, MD 20861-9766, USA

Dennison, Rick (Athlete, Football Player)
12322 Overcup Dr
Houston, TX 77024-4913, USA

Denny, Christopher (Musician)
c/o Staff Member *Paradigm (Monterey)*
404 W Franklin St
Monterey, CA 93940-2303, USA

Denny, Dorothy (Actor)
15707 La Verida Dr
Victorville, CA 92395-3413, USA

Denny, Floyd W Jr (Misc)
1 Carolina Mdws Apt 308
Chapel Hill, NC 27517-8508, USA

Denny, John (Athlete, Baseball Player)
13225 Fox Glove St
Winter Garden, FL 34787-4716, USA

Denny, Robyn (Artist)
20/30 Wilds Rents #4B
London SE14QG, UNITED KINGDOM (UK)

Denny, Simone (Musician)
c/o Staff Member *Diva Central Inc*
7510 W Sunset Blvd Ste 1445
Los Angeles, CA 90046-3408, USA

Denorfia, Chris (Athlete, Baseball Player)
137 Williamsburg Dr
Southington, CT 06489-3837, USA

DenOuden, Wilernintie (Willy) (Swimmer)
Goudsewagenstraat 23B
Rotterdam, HOLLAND

Densham, Pen (Director)
8942 Wilshire Blvd # 219
Beverly Hills, CA 90211-1908, USA

Densmore, Elizabeth (Actor)
c/o Sharon Lane *Lane Management Group*
13017 Woodbridge St
Studio City, CA 91604-1431, USA

Densmore, John (Musician)
49 Haldeman Rd
Santa Monica, CA 90402-1003, USA

Denson, Al (Athlete, Football Player)
10838 Naples Ct S
Jacksonville, FL 32218-4494, USA

Denson, Autry (Athlete, Football Player)
2585 SW Calder St
Port Saint Lucie, FL 34953-7310, USA

Denson, Drew (Athlete, Baseball Player)
1718 Avonlea Ave
Cincinnati, OH 45237-6110, USA

Denson, Keith (Athlete, Football Player)
28024 Eagle Peak Ave
Canyon Country, CA 91387-3105, USA

Denson, Moses (Athlete, Football Player)
14005 Drake Dr
Rockville, MD 20853-2641, USA

Dent, Bucky (Athlete, Baseball Player, Coach)
8895 Indian River Run
Boynton Beach, FL 33472-2445, USA

Dent, Burnell (Athlete, Football Player)
2904 Essex Ave
La Place, LA 70068-2241, USA

Dent, Catherine (Actor)
c/o Staff Member *Shield, The*
4151 Prospect Ave Bldg A PMB 200
Los Angeles, CA 90027, USA

Dent, Frederick B (Secretary)
221 Montgomery St
Spartanburg, SC 29302, USA

Dent, Jim (Athlete, Golfer)
PO Box 341305
Tampa, FL 33694-1305, USA

Dent, Richard L (Athlete, Coach, Football Coach, Football Player)
4453 RFD
Long Grove, IL 60047-6900, USA

Dent, Robert (Bob) (Athlete, Football Player)
6669 Embarcadero Dr Apt 7
Stockton, CA 95219-3378, USA

Dent, Russell E (Bucky) (Athlete, Baseball Player)
490 Dotterel Rd
Delray Beach, FL 33444-2082, USA

Denton, Derek A (Physicist)
816 Irring Rd
Toorak, VIC 3142, AUSTRALIA

Denton, James (Actor)
c/o John Crosby *Crosby/Spilo Management*
1310 N Spaulding Ave
Los Angeles, CA 90046-4010, USA

Denton, Mona (Baseball Player)
1880 S Newton St
Denver, CO 80219-4503, USA

Denton, Randy (Athlete, Basketball Player)
515 Sunnybrook Rd
Raleigh, NC 27610-2850, USA

Denton, Sandi (Pepa) (Musician)
250 W 57th St
New York, NY 10107-0001, USA

Denvir, John (Athlete, Football Player)
23250 Walker Basin Rd
Caliente, CA 93518-2103, USA

Denzongapa, Danny (Actor, Bollywood)
Dzongrilla 11th Road Juhu
Mumbai, MS, INDIA

Deol, Bobby (Actor, Bollywood)
Plot No 22, 11th Road JVPD Scheme Juhu
Mumbai, MS 400049, INDIA

Deol, Dharmendra (Actor, Bollywood)
Plot No 22 11th Rd Juhu
Mumbai, MS 400049, INDIA

Deol, Sunny (Actor, Bollywood)
Plot No 22 11th Road JVPD Scheme
Mumbai, MS 400026, INDIA

DeOre, Bill (Cartoonist)
Editorial Dept Communications Center
Dallas, TX 75265, USA

Deossie, Steve (Athlete, Football Player)
835 Chestnut St
North Andover, MA 01845-6010, USA

DePalma, Brian R (Director)
c/o Jeff Berg *International Creative Management (ICM-LA)*
10250 Constellation Blvd Fl 7
Los Angeles, CA 90067-6207, USA

Depalo, Jim (Baseball Player)
4727 7th Ave SW
Naples, FL 34119-4039, USA

DePalva, James (Actor)
PO Box 11152
Greenwich, CT 06831-1152, USA

DePandi, Giuliana (Actor)
c/o Staff Member *WmE2 (WMA-LA)*
1 William Morris Pl
Beverly Hills, CA 90212-4261, USA

DePandi, Guiliana (Actor)
c/o Pamela Kohl *3 Arts Entertainment Inc*
9460 Wilshire Blvd Fl 7
Beverly Hills, CA 90212-2713, USA

DePaola, Tomie (Actor, Writer)
c/o Staff Member *Penguin Putnam Books for Young Readers*
345 Hudson St Fl 14
New York, NY 10014-4592

Depardieu, Gerard (Actor)
c/o Amanda Bross *Finch & Partners*
Top Floor 29-37 Heddon St
London W1B 4BR, UNITED KINGDOM

Depardon, Raymond (Photographer)
18 Bis Rue Henri Barbusse
Paris 75005, FRANCE

Departure, Themm (Music Group)
c/o Staff Member *Paradigm (Monterey)*
404 W Franklin St
Monterey, CA 93940-2303, USA

Depaso, Tom (Athlete, Football Player)
2108 Polo Pointe Dr
Vienna, VA 22181-2804, USA

Depastino, Joe (Athlete, Baseball Player)
12853 Sheringham Way
Sarasota, FL 34240-8762, USA

Depaula, Sean (Athlete, Baseball Player)
2 Thomas St
Derry, NH 03038-2988, USA

DePavia, James
PO Box 11152
Greenwich, CT 06831-1152

Depeche Mode (Music Group)
c/o Jonathan Kessler *Baron, Inc*
235 S Westgate Ave
Los Angeles, CA 90049-4205, USA

DePeyer, Gervase
1250 S Washington St Unit 109
Alexandria, VA 22314-4412, USA

Deply, Julie (Actor)
c/o Glenn Rigberg *HYPHENATE*
9701 Wilshire Blvd Fl 10
Beverly Hills, CA 90212-2010, USA

DePortzamparc, Christian (Architect)
Architecte DPLG 1 Rue de L'Aude
Paris 75014, FRANCE

DePoyster, Jerry D (Athlete, Football Player)
PO Box 3029
Rock Springs, WY 82902-3029, USA

Depp, Johnny (Actor, Director)
c/o Robin Baum *Slate Public Relations*
9000 W Sunset Blvd Ste 915
West Hollywood, CA 90069-5809, USA

Depre, Joe (Athlete, Basketball Player)
59 Oneida St
Rochester, NY 14621-4027, USA

DePree, Hopwood (Actor)
c/o Staff Member *ROAR (LA)*
9701 Wilshire Blvd Fl 8
Beverly Hills, CA 90212-2008, USA

DePreist, James A (Conductor)
Konsert AB Kungsgatan 32
Stockholm 11135, SWEDEN

DePrume, Cathryn (Actor)
c/o Staff Member *Flick Commercials*
9057 Nemo St # A
W Hollywood, CA 90069-5511, USA

Dequenne, Emilie (Actor)
c/o Daniele Gain *Cineart*
36 Rue de Ponthieu
Paris F-75008, France

Dequenne, Emilie (Cartoonist)
4888 Loop Central Dr Dept 390
Houston, TX 77081-2227, USA

Derbez, Eugenio (Producer, Writer)
c/o Susan Weaving *WmE2 (WMA-NY)*
1325 Avenue of the Americas
New York, NY 10019-6026, USA

Derbez, Silvia (Actor)
c/o Staff Member *Televisa*
Blvd Adolfo Lopez Mateos 232 Colonia San Angel INN
DF CP 01060, MEXICO

Derby, Dean (Athlete, Football Player)
1682 Corkrum Rd
Walla Walla, WA 99362-8628, USA

Derbyshire, Andrew G (Architect)
4 Sunnyfield Hatfield
Herts AL9 5DX, UNITED KINGDOM (UK)

Derek, Bo (Actor, Model)
PO Box 1940
Santa Ynez, CA 93460-1940, USA

Dereuck, Colleen (Athlete)
4172 Saint Croix St
Boulder, CO 80301, USA

Dergan, Lisa (Actor, Model, Television Host)
c/o Jon Orlando *WNWN Media*
348 Hauser Blvd # PH414
Los Angeles, CA 90036-3276, USA

Deriso, Walter M Jr (Financier)
PO Box 120
Columbus, GA 31902-0120, USA

Derlago, Bill (Athlete, Hockey Player)
2685 Highway 7
Concord, ON L4K 1V8, Canada

Derline, Rodney (Athlete, Basketball Player)
12612 SE 215th St
Kent, WA 98031-2287, USA

Dern, Bruce (Actor)
PO Box 1581
Santa Monica, CA 90406-1581, USA

Dern, Laura (Actor)
c/o Jason Weinberg *Untitled Entertainment (LA)*
350 S Beverly Dr Ste 200
Beverly Hills, CA 90212-4819, USA

Dernesch, Helga (Opera Singer)
Neutorgasse 2/22
Vienna 1013, AUSTRIA

Dernier, Bob (Athlete, Baseball Player)
1242 SW Arbormill Ter
Lees Summit, MO 64082-4165, USA

Deroo, Brian (Athlete, Football Player)
49224 Escalante St
Indio, CA 92201-8850, USA

Derosa, Mark (Athlete, Baseball Player)
58 Avalon Way
Waretown, NJ 08758-2698, USA

DeRosa, William (Misc)
165 W 57th St
New York, NY 10019-2201, USA

DeRosier, David (Physicist)
27 Chesterfield Rd
Newton, MA 02465-2343, USA

Derosier, Michael (Musician)
1250 6th St Ste 401
Santa Monica, CA 90401-1638, USA

Derow, Peter A (Publisher)
PO Box 534
Bedford, NY 10506-0534, USA

Derr, Kenneth T (Business Person)
6001 Bollinger Canyon Rd
San Ramon, CA 94583-2324, USA

Derrick, Edward (Athlete, Baseball Player)
PO Box 158473
Nashville, TN 37215-8473, USA

Derricks, Cleavant (Actor)
480 Burano Ct
Agoura Hills, CA 91377, USA

D'Errico, Donna (Actor, Model)
c/o Mike Arnoldi *Stars For The Stars*
553 N Pacific Coast Hwy # 200
Redondo Beach, CA 90277-2163, USA

Derringer, Rick (Musician)
c/o Steve Peck *Fantasma Productions Inc*
226 Emerald Ln
Palm Beach, FL 33480-3613, USA

Derrington, Jim (Athlete, Baseball Player)
711 Sandlewood Ave
La Habra, CA 90631-7248, USA

Derry, Kathy (Physicist)
PO Box 1656
Laguna Beach, CA 92652-1656, USA

Derryberry, Debi (Actor)
PO Box 2726
Toluca Lake, CA 91610-0726, USA

Dersch, Hans (Swimmer)
7217 E 55th Pl
Tulsa, OK 74145-7704, USA

Dershowitz, Alan M (Educator, Lawyer)
1563 Massachusetts Ave
Cambridge, MA 02138-2903, USA

DeRulo, Jason (Musician)
c/o John Marx *WmE2 (Endeavor-LA)*
9601 Wilshire Blvd Fl 3
Beverly Hills, CA 90210-5219, USA

Dervan, Peter B (Misc)
Chemistry
Pasadena, CA 91125-0001, USA

Derwin, Mark (Actor)
6500 Wilshire Blvd # 550
Los Angeles, CA 90048-4920, USA

Derwinski, Edward J (Secretary)
1800 Diagonal Rd Ste 600
Alexandria, VA 22314-2840, USA

Des Barres, Michael (Actor)
c/o Pam Ellis *Ellis Talent Group*
4705 Laurel Canyon Blvd Ste 300
Valley Village, CA 91607-5901, USA

Des Jardins, Richard (Stylist)
140 7th Ave Apt 2F
New York, NY 10011-1816, USA

Desai, Anita (Writer)
20 Powis Mews
London W11 1JN, UNITED KINGDOM (UK)

Desai, Anoop (Musician)

Desai, Ketan (Bollywood, Director, Producer)
3C Swapnalok Jagmohandas Marg
Bombay, MS 400 026, INDIA

Desailly, Marcel (Soccer Player)
FC Chelsea Stamford Bridge Fulham Road
London SW6 1HS, UNITED KINGDOM (UK)

Desalvo, Matt (Athlete, Baseball Player)
61 Mabel Dr
West Middlesex, PA 16159-2633, USA

deSando, Anthony
PO Box 5617
Beverly Hills, CA 90209-5617

deSantis, Guiseppe
Fiano Romano Via del Commercio 1
Rome, ITALY I-00154

DeSantis, Jaclyn (Actor)
c/o Sarah Fargo *Paradigm (NY)*
360 N Crescent Dr
Beverly Hills, CA 90210-4874, USA

deSantis, Luigi
Via della Villa di Lucina 72
Rome, ITALY I-00145

Desanto, Tom (Producer)
c/o Renee Kurtz *Creative Artists Agency (CAA-LA)*
1 William Morris Pl
Beverly Hills, CA 90212-4261, USA

Descendants, The
4230 Del Rey Ave # 621
Marina Del Rey, CA 90292-5603, USA

Deschaine, Dick (Athlete, Football Player)
205 Cavil Way
De Pere, WI 54115-3775, USA

Deschanel, Caleb (Cinematographer)
812 N Highland Ave
Los Angeles, CA 90038-3417, USA

Deschanel, Emily (Actor)
c/o Lainie Sorkin Becky *Management 360*
9111 Wilshire Blvd
Beverly Hills, CA 90210-5508, USA

Deschanel, Mary Jo (Actor)
844 Chautauqua Blvd
Pacific Palisades, CA 90272-3801, USA

Deschanel, Zooey (Actor)
c/o Sarah Jackson *Seven Summits Pictures & Management*
8906 W Olympic Blvd Ground Floor
Beverly Hills, CA 90211, USA

Descher, Sandra (Actor)
4544 Arcola Ave
Toluca Lake, CA 91602-1517, USA

DesCombes Lesko, Jeneane (Baseball Player)
11227 NE 109th Ln Apt L108
Kirkland, WA 98033-5029, USA

Descombes-Dinehart, Nancy (Baseball Player)
59607 County Road 11
Elkhart, IN 46517-9178, USA

Desert, Alex (Actor)
c/o Katherine Atkinson *Washington Square Arts (LA)*
1041 N Formosa Ave Lot Bldg
West Hollywood, CA 90046-6703, USA

deSeve, Peter (Artist)
25 Park Pl
Brooklyn, NY 11217-3207, USA

Desfor, Max (Journalist)
15115 Interlachen Dr Apt 1018
Silver Spring, MD 20906-5644, USA

Deshales, Jim (Athlete, Baseball Player)
151 N Taylor Point Dr
Spring, TX 77382-1240, USA

DeShields, Delino L (Athlete, Baseball Player)
3399 Kiveton Ct
Norcross, GA 30092-3374, USA

Desiderio, Robert (Actor)
1475 Sierra Vista Dr
Aspen, CO 81611-1044, USA

Desilva, John (Athlete, Baseball Player)
32750 Airport Rd
Fort Bragg, CA 95437-9514, USA

DeSimone, Livio D (Desi) (Business Person)
3M Center
Saint Paul, MN 55144-0001, USA

Desjardins, Eric (Athlete, Hockey Player)
9 Woodglen Ln
Voorhees, NJ 08043-9559, USA

Desjardins, Gerry (Athlete, Hockey Player)
252 Suffolk Pl
London, ON N6G 3S4, Canada

DesJarlais, Scott (Congressman, Politician)
413 Cannon Hob
Washington, DC 20515-3301, USA

Deskins, Donald (Athlete, Football Player)
3240 Pittsview Dr
Ann Arbor, MI 48108-1946, USA

Deskur, Andrzej Maria Cardinal (Religious Leader)
Palazzo S Carlo
120, VATICAN CITY

Deslongchamps, Pierre (Misc)
1884 Rue Des Orioles
Laval, QC H7L 5T8, CANADA

Desman, Shawn (Musician)
c/o Staff Member *BMG*
1540 Broadway
New York, NY 10036-4039, USA

Desmormeaux, Kent (Jockey)
385 W Huntington Dr
Arcadia, CA 91007, USA

Desormeaux, Kent (Jockey)
c/o Staff Member *Jockeys Guild*
103 Wind Haven Dr Ste 200
Nicholasville, KY 40356-8026, USA

Despadovich, Nada
6500 Wilshire Blvd Ste 2200
Los Angeles, CA 90048-4942

Despotopoulos, Johannes (Jan) (Architect)
Anapiron Polemou 7
Athens 11521, GREECE

Des'ree (Musician)
55 Fulham High St
London SW6 3JJ, UNITED KINGDOM (UK)

Dess, Darrell (Athlete, Football Player)
224 Sumner Ave
New Castle, PA 16105-2579, USA

Dessay, Natalie (Opera Singer)
119 W 57th St Ste 1505
New York, NY 10019-2403, USA

Dessens, Elmer (Athlete, Baseball Player)
8547 E Arapahoe Rd Unit J
Greenwood Village, CO 80112-1430, USA

Destiny's Child (Music Group)
c/o Matthew Knowles *Music World Entertainment*
1505 Hadley St
Houston, TX 77002-8927, USA

Destrade, Orestes (Athlete, Baseball Player)
10653 Garda Dr
Trinity, FL 34655-7051, USA

Destri, Jimmy (Misc)
32 Court St Ste 1600
Brooklyn, NY 11201-4441, USA

Desurvive, Emmanuel (Engineer)
Villarceaux Centre
Nozay 91625, FRANCE

Desutter, Wayne (Athlete, Football Player)
4450 Antietam Creek Trl
Leesburg, FL 34748-1203, USA

DeTar, Dean E (War Hero)
7785 Portwood Rd
Azle, TX 76020-5839, USA

Deters, Harold (Athlete, Football Player)
1602 Woods Creek Dr
Garner, NC 27529-4761, USA

DeThe, Guy Blaudin (Biologist)
14 Rue Le Regrattier
Paris 75004, FRANCE

Detherage, Bob (Athlete, Baseball Player)
322 Turf Ln
Carl Junction, MO 64834-9575, USA

Detmer, Amanda (Actor)
c/o John Carrabino *John Carrabino Management*
5900 Wilshire Blvd Ste 406
Los Angeles, CA 90036-5015, USA

Detmer, Koy (Athlete, Football Player)
26730 Rockwall Pkwy
New Braunfels, TX 78132-2652, USA

Detmer, Ty (Athlete, Football Player)
142 Lakota Pass
Austin, TX 78738-6563, USA

Detmers, Maruschka (Actor)
c/o Staff Member *Agence Alvares Correa*
34, Rue Jouffroy D'Abbans
Paris 75017, France

Detorie, Rick (Cartoonist)
5777 W Century Blvd Ste 700
Los Angeles, CA 90045-5652, USA

Detroit, Marcella (Musician, Songwriter, Writer)
40 Langham St #300
London W1N 5RG, UNITED KINGDOM (UK)

Dettlaff, Bill (Athlete, Golfer)
1 Nicklaus Dr
Dearborn, MI 48120-1126, USA

Dettmer, John (Athlete, Baseball Player)
549 Hickory View Ln
Ballwin, MO 63011-1500, USA

Dettore, Tom (Athlete, Baseball Player)
1120 McEwen Ave
Canonsburg, PA 15317-1928, USA

Detweiler, David K (Physicist)
Waverty Heights 1400 Waverty Road #A212
Gladwyne, PA 19035, USA

Detweiler, Ducky (Athlete, Baseball Player)
312 Holt St
Federalsburg, MD 21632-1403, USA

Detweiler, Robert C (Educator)
1450 Ellis Ave
Cambria, CA 93428-5960, USA

Detwiler, Chuck (Athlete, Football Player)
79898 Viento Dr
La Quinta, CA 92253-8811, USA

Deukmejian, C George (Ex-Governor)
5366 E Broadway
Long Beach, CA 90803-3549, USA

Deukmejian, C George (Ex-Governor)
5366 E Broadway
Long Beach, CA 90803-3549, USA

Deutch, Howard (Director)
8942 Wilshire Blvd # 219
Beverly Hills, CA 90211-1908, USA

Deutch, Howie (Actor, Director, Producer, Writer)
c/o Daniel J Talbot *International Creative Management (ICM-LA)*
10250 Constellation Blvd Fl 7
Los Angeles, CA 90067-6207, USA

Deutch, John M (Government Official)
51 Clifton St
Belmont, MA 02478-3353, USA

Deutekom, Cristina (Opera Singer)
Lancasterdreet 41
Dronten, TG 8251, HOLLAND

Deutsch, Dave (Athlete, Basketball Player)
315 Fairmount Rd
Long Valley, NJ 07853-3012, USA

Deutsch, Donny (Television Host)
122 Hudson St Fl 5
New York, NY 10013-2355, USA

Deutsch, Liz (Stylist)
184 W 4th St Apt 8
New York, NY 10014-3883, USA

Deutsch, Patti (Actor)
1040 1st Ave # 1126
New York, NY 10022-2991, USA

Dev, Mukul (Actor, Bollywood)
Karan Apts 5th Floor Yari Road Versova
Mumbai, MS 40061, INDIA

Deva, Prabhu (Actor, Choreographer, Comedian, Dancer, Musician)
68 T T K Road Alwarpet
Chennai, TN 600 018, INDIA

DeValeria, Dennis (Writer)
213 Hillendale Rd
Pittsburgh, PA 15237-1803, USA

Devane, William (Actor)
1505 10th St
Santa Monica, CA 90401-2805, USA

Devarez, Cesar (Athlete, Baseball Player)
35 Arden St Apt B
New York, NY 10040-1318, USA

DeVarona, Donna (Sportscaster, Swimmer)
420 W 45th St # 500
New York, NY 10036-3501, USA

Devaty, Susan (Stylist)
423 Pennsylvania Ave Apt 4
San Francisco, CA 94107-2954, USA

Devaughn, Dennis (Athlete, Football Player)
2416 Clear Field Dr
Plano, TX 75025-5184, USA

DeVaughn, Raheem (Actor, Musician)
c/o Eva Arthur *Universal Attractions*
135 W 26th St Fl 12
New York, NY 10001-6872, USA

Devault, Calvin (Actor)
c/o John Frazier *Amsel, Eisenstadt & Frazier Talent Agency (AEF)*
5055 Wilshire Blvd Ste 860
Los Angeles, CA 90036-6108, USA

Devayani (Actor, Bollywood)
51 Indira Gandhi Street Saligramam
Chennai, TN 600093, INDIA

Devenzio, Dick (Athlete, Basketball Player)
1116 Home Piace
Matthews, NC 28105-6891, USA

Deveraux, Jude (Writer)
1230 Avenue of the Americas
New York, NY 10020-1513, USA

Devereaux, Boyd (Athlete, Hockey Player)
10766 E Palm Ridge Dr
Scottsdale, AZ 85255-1719, USA

Devereaux, Mike (Athlete, Baseball Player)
2236 W Doublegrove St
West Covina, CA 91790-5607, USA

Devgan, Ajay (Actor, Bollywood)
c/o Bunty Bahl *Carving Dreams Entertainment*
304-305, Oberoi Chambers II B Wing, Off New Link Road, Andheri West
Mumbai 400053, INDIA

DeVicenzo, Roberto (Golfer)
5025 Veloz Ave
Tarzana, CA 91356-4514, USA

Devicq, Paula (Actor, Model)
c/o Joanne Horowitz *Joanne Horowitz Management*
9350 Wilshire Blvd Ste 224
Beverly Hills, CA 90212-3204, USA

Deville, CC (Musician)
c/o Michael (Mike) Esterman *Esterman.Com, LLC*
Prefers to be contacted via email
MD, USA

Deville, Michael (Director)
36 Rue Reinhardt
Boulogne 92100, FRANCE

Devine, Adrian (Athlete, Baseball Player)
271 Timber Laurel Ln
Lawrenceville, GA 30043-6504, USA

Devine, Harold (Boxer)
595 Wyckoff Ave
Wyckoff, NJ 07481-1337, USA

Devine, Joey (Athlete, Baseball Player)
932 Chattooga Trce
Suwanee, GA 30024-7672, USA

Devine, Loretta (Actor)
c/o Jonathan Howard *Innovative Artists (LA)*
1505 10th St
Santa Monica, CA 90401-2805, USA

DeVink, Lodewijk J R (Business Person)
201 Tabor Rd
Morris Plains, NJ 07950-2614, USA

Devisree (Actor, Bollywood)
1 Bharathi Apts Bharathi Nagar 3rd Street
T Nagar
Chennai, TN 600017, INDIA

DeVita, Vincent T Jr (Misc)
333 Cedar St
New Haven, CT 06510-3206, USA

DeVito, Danny (Actor, Comedian, Director)
c/o Stan Rosenfield *Stan Rosenfield & Associates*
2029 Century Park E Ste 1190
Los Angeles, CA 90067-2931, USA

Devito, Louie (Athlete, Snowboarder)
c/o Len Evans *Project Publicity*
312 W 53rd St Ste 202
New York, NY 10019-5743, USA

Devitt, John (Swimmer)
46 Beacon Ave
Beacon Hill, NSW 2100, AUSTRALIA

DeVitto, Torrey (Actor)
c/o Matthew Lesher *Insight*
1134 S Cloverdale Ave
Los Angeles, CA 90019-6737, USA

Devliegher, Charles (Chuck) (Athlete, Football Player)
7101 W Beardsley Rd Unit 1201
Glendale, AZ 85308-5695, USA

Devlin, Barry (Director, Writer)

Devlin, Bruce (Athlete, Golfer)
3601 Foot Hills Dr
Weatherford, TX 76087-2239, USA

Devlin, Chris (Athlete, Football Player)
100 Meadow Lark Ln
Boalsburg, PA 16827-1800, USA

Devlin, Dean (Actor, Director, Producer)
1438 N Gower St Ste 24
Los Angeles, CA 90028-8306, USA

Devlin, Joseph (Athlete, Football Player)
3715 Schintzius Rd
Eden, NY 14057-9790, USA

Devlin, Mike (Athlete, Football Player)
48 Shore Rd
Mount Sinai, NY 11766-1420, USA

Devlin, Robert M (Business Person)
2929 Allen Pkwy
Houston, TX 77019-7100, USA

Devlins, The (Music Group)
c/o Staff Member *Paradigm (Monterey)*
404 W Franklin St
Monterey, CA 93940-2303, USA

Devo (Music Group, Musician)
c/o Ian Fintak *Agency Group Ltd, The (LA)*
1880 Century Park E Ste 711
Los Angeles, CA 90067-1618, USA

Devoll, Hal (Athlete, Basketball Player)
8928 Fox Ave
Allen Park, MI 48101-1502, USA

Devon (Adult Film Star)
c/o Staff Member *Atlas Entertainment*
6100 Wilshire Blvd Ste 1170
Los Angeles, CA 90048-5116, USA

Devon, Dayna (Television Host)
c/o Staff Member *Extra (LA)*
1840 Victory Blvd
Glendale, CA 91201-2558, USA

Devore, Doug (Athlete, Baseball Player)
5247 Willow Grove Pl S
Dublin, OH 43017-2116, USA

Devries, Greg (Athlete, Hockey Player)
25 Colonel Winstead Dr
Brentwood, TN 37027-8937, USA

Devries, Jared (Athlete, Football Player)
15342 Lambert Dr
Clear Lake, IA 50428-8637, USA

Devries, Jed (Athlete, Football Player)
2433 W 1425 S
Syracuse, UT 84075-6996, USA

DeVries, William C (Doctor)
7 Snowmound Ct
Rockville, MD 20850-2850, USA

deVry, William (Actor)
c/o Staff Member *House of Representatives, The*
1434 6th St Ste 1
Santa Monica, CA 90401-2527, USA

DeWaart, Edo (Conductor)
Essenlaan 68
Rotterdam 3016, NETHERLANDS

Dewan, Jenna (Actor)
c/o Courtney Knittel *Patricola Lust PR*
9171 Wilshire Blvd Ste 390
Beverly Hills, CA 90210-5515, USA

Dewar, Faber (Designer)
c/o Staff Member *Trading Spaces*
7700 Wisconsin Ave
Bethesda, MD 20814-3578, USA

Dewar, Jane E (Editor)
359 Kent St # 504
Ottawa, ON K2P 0R6, CANADA

Dewar, Susan (Cartoonist)
4520 Main St
Kansas City, MO 64111-1876, USA

Dewberry, Michelle (Reality TV Star)
11 Westway Centre 69 St Marks Road
London W10 6JG, UNITED KINGDOM

Dewese, Mohandas (Kool mo Dee) (Actor)
c/o Staff Member *Identity Talent Agency (ID)*
9107 Wilshire Blvd Ste 500
Beverly Hills, CA 90210-5526, USA

DeWet, Shaun (Model)
c/o Staff Member *Elite Model Management (NY)*
404 Park Ave S Fl 9
New York, NY 10016-8412, USA

Dewey, Duane E (War Hero)
10550 N Forman Rd
Irons, MI 49644-8755, USA

Dewey, Mark (Athlete, Baseball Player)
28150 Rivermont Dr
Meadowview, VA 24361-2822, USA

DeWilde, Edy (Director)
Amsterdam, NETHERLANDS

Dewillis, Jeff (Athlete, Baseball Player)
8918 Wind Side Dr
Houston, TX 77040-3460, USA

DeWinne, Frank (Cosmonaut)
Vilegbaiss Kleine Brogel
Peer, 10W TAC 3990, BELGIUM

DeWitt, Bryce S (Physicist)
Physics Dept
Austin, TX 78712, USA

DeWitt, Doug (Boxer)
2035 Central Ave
Yonkers, NY 10710, USA

DeWitt, Joyce (Actor)
c/o Staff Member *JG Business Management Inc*
PO Box 7309
Santa Monica, CA 90406-7309, USA

Dewitt, Matt (Athlete, Baseball Player)
8015 Vista Twilight Dr
Las Vegas, NV 89123-0725, USA

DeWitt, Rosemarie (Actor)
c/o Troy Nankin *Wishlab*
2438 Canyon Oak Dr
Los Angeles, CA 90068-2428, USA

Dewitt, William O (Baseball Player)
5695 Drake Rd
Cincinnati, OH 45243-3616, USA

DeWitt, Willie (Boxer)
605 N Water St
Burnet, TX 78611-1742, USA

DeWitt-Morette, Cecile (Physicist)
2411 Vista Ln
Austin, TX 78703-2343, USA

Dews, Peter B (Psychic)
280 Newtonville Ave Apt 221
Newtonville, MA 02460-2098, USA

DeWulf, Noureen (Actor)
c/o Tiffany Kuzon *Evolution Entertainment (LA)*
901 N Highland Ave
Los Angeles, CA 90038-2412, USA

DeWyze, Lee (Musician)
c/o Simon Fuller *XIX Entertainment*
33/32 Ransomes Dock 35-37 Parkgate Rd
London SW11 4NP, UK

Dexter, Dex (Stylist)
1133 Broadway Ste 529
New York, NY 10010-8095, USA

Dexter, Mary (Director)
14542 Delaware Dr
Moorpark, CA 93021-3560, USA

Dexter, Pete (Writer)
c/o Author Mail *Doubleday*
1745 Broadway
New York, NY 10019-4368, USA

Dexter, Peter W (Writer)
Editorial Dept 21st & Q Sts
Sacramento, CA 95852, USA

Dey, Susan (Actor)
c/o Staff Member *International Creative Management (ICM-LA)*
10250 Constellation Blvd Fl 7
Los Angeles, CA 90067-6207, USA

Deyette, Alison (Stylist)
c/o Staff Member *Gabler Group*
7 E 14th St Apt 1627
New York, NY 10003-3124, USA

DeYoung, Cliff (Actor)
481 Savona Way
Oak Park, CA 91377-4842, USA

DeYoung, Dennis (Musician)
15941 Harlem Ave
Tinley Park, IL 60477-1609, USA

Dezelan, Frank (Athlete, Baseball Player)
7423 Lighthouse Pt
Pittsburgh, PA 15221-2553, USA

Dezhurov, Vladimir N (Cosmonaut)
Moskovskoi Obtasti
Syvisdny Goroduk 141160, RUSSIA

Dezonie, Hank (Athlete, Basketball Player)
700 Lenox Ave Apt 17D
New York, NY 10039-4518, USA

Dhabhara, Firdaus S (Scientist)
319 Olmsted Rd
Stanford, CA 94305-7702, USA

Dhamu (Actor)
84 Pycrofts Road 36 Adk Mansion
Triplicane
Chennai, TN 600 005, INDIA

Dhanapal (Actor)
8 A G Block Pallaku Maa Nagar Luz
Chennai, TN 600 004, INDIA

Dhanoa, Guddu (Actor)
8A My Little Home 10th Road Jvpd Scheme
Bombay, MS 400 049, INDIA

Dharmasakti, Sanya (Prime Minister)
15 Saukhumvit Road Soi 41
Bangkok, THAILAND

D'Harnoncourt, Anne (Director)
& 25th Franklin Pkwy
Philadelphia, PA 19101, USA

Dhavernas, Caroline (Actor)
c/o Rhonda Price *Gersh (NY)*
41 Madison Ave
New York, NY 10010-2202, USA

Dhawan, David (Director, Filmmaker)
A-15 Sagar Darshan Carter Road Khar
Mumbai, MS 400052, INDIA

Dhoni, Mahendra Singh (Athlete, Cricketer)
c/o Staff Member *IMG (UK)*
Pier House Chiswick
London W4M 3NN, UNITED KINGDOM

Dhue, Laurie (Anchor)
c/o Staff Member *Fox News Channel (NY)*
1211 Ave Of The Americas Level C1
New York, NY 10036-8701, USA

Di Cione, Sevy (Actor)
c/o Cindy Sheffield *The Sheffield Agency*
14020 NW Psge Suite 104
Marina Del Rey, CA 90292, USA

Di Meola, Al (Musician)
c/o Staff Member *Entourage Talent Associates*
133 W 25th St
New York, NY 10001-7206, USA

Di Montezemolo, Luca (Business Person, Race Car Driver)
c/o Staff Member *Jaguar Racing Ltd*
Bradbourne Drive Tilbrook
Milton Keynes MK7 8BJ, United Kingdom

Di Pasquale, James (Composer, Musician)
c/o Staff Member *Gorfaine/Schwartz Agency Inc*
4111 W Alameda Ave Ste 509
Burbank, CA 91505-4171, USA

Di Prima, Denise (Stylist)
c/o Staff Member *L'Agence*
5901 Peachtree Dunwoody Rd NE Ste C60
Atlanta, GA 30328-7155, USA

Di Salvo, Danielle (Stylist)
3243 Harrison St
San Francisco, CA 94110-5212, USA

Dial, Buddy (Athlete, Football Player)
22003 Western Hills Ct
Katy, TX 77450-3828, USA

Diallo, Mmadou (Soccer Player)
CMGI Field 1 Patriot Place
Foxboro, MA 2035, USA

Diamantopoulos, Chris (Actor)
c/o Van Johnson *Van Johnson Company*
350 S Beverly Dr Ste 200
Beverly Hills, CA 90212-4819, USA

Diamini, Barnabas S (Prime Minister)
PO Box 395
Mbabane, SWAZILAND

Diamond, Abel J (Architect)
2 Berkeley St # 600
Toronto, ON M5A 2W3, CANADA

Diamond, Bobby
5309 Comercio Way
Woodland Hills, CA 91364-2030

Diamond, Charles (Athlete, Football Player)
7300 SW 69th Ct
Miami, FL 33143-4420, USA

Diamond, Diane (Television Host)
c/o Staff Member *Court TV*
600 3rd Ave Fl 2
New York, NY 10016-1919, USA

Diamond, Dustin (Actor)
c/o Staff Member *Jack Koshick Presents*
1626 North Prospect Avenue, Suite 1801
Milwaukee WI
53202, USA

Diamond, Jared M (Biologist)
Med School Physiology Dept
Los Angeles, CA 90024, USA

Diamond, Joel (Producer)
3940 Laurel Canyon Blvd Ste 441
Studio City, CA 91604-3709, USA

Diamond, Marian C (Misc)
2583 Virginia St
Berkeley, CA 94709-1108, USA

Diamond, Michael (Mike D) (Musician)
8935 Lindblade St
Culver City, CA 90232-2438, USA

Diamond, Michael T (DJ)
c/o Staff Member *Diva Central Inc*
7510 W Sunset Blvd Ste 1445
Los Angeles, CA 90046-3408, USA

Diamond, Neil (Musician)
c/o Dvora Vener Englefield *42West (LA)*
11400 W Olympic Blvd Ste 1100
Los Angeles, CA 90064-1579, USA

Diamond, Reed (Actor)
c/o David Weise *David Weise and Associates*
16000 Ventura Blvd Ste 600
Encino, CA 91436-2753, USA

Diamond, Seymour (Doctor)
467 W Deming Pl Ste 500
Chicago, IL 60614-2970, USA

Diamond Rio (Music Group)
c/o Staff Member *WmE2 (WMA-TN)*
1600 Division St Ste 300
Nashville, TN 37203-2755, USA

Diamonds, The (Music Group)
561 Keystone Ave # 224
Reno, NV 89503-4304, USA

Diamont, Don (Actor)
125 S Sycamore Ave
Los Angeles, CA 90036-2938, USA

Diana, Rich (Athlete, Football Player)
2 Munson Dr Unit 7
Wallingford, CT 06492-5366, USA

Dias, Ivan Cardinal (Religious Leader)
21 Nathalal Parekh Marg
Mumbai, MS 400001, INDIA

Dias Dos Santos, Fernando da Piedade (Prime Minister)
Council of Ministers
Luanda, ANGOLA

Diaw, Boris (Athlete, Basketball Player)
10430 N 108th Pl
Scottsdale, AZ 85259-4847, USA

Diaz, Aaron (Actor)

Diaz, Arnold (Correspondent)
c/o Staff Member *Shame on You !*
524 W 57th St
New York, NY 10019-2930, USA

Diaz, Cameron (Actor)
c/o Brad Cafarelli *PMK/BNC - LA*
8687 Melrose Ave Ste 8
West Hollywood, CA 90069-5746, USA

Diaz, Carlos (Athlete, Baseball Player)
45236 Ka Hanahou Cir
Kaneohe, HI 96744-3009, USA

Diaz, Carlos (Athlete, Baseball Player)
3037 Homestead Oaks Dr
Clearwater, FL 33759-1626, USA

Diaz, David (Athlete, Boxer)
c/o Staff Member *Top Rank Inc.*
3908 Howard Hughes Pkwy # 580
Las Vegas, NV 89109, USA

Diaz, Einar (Athlete, Baseball Player)
4315 70th Ave E
Ellenton, FL 34222-7329, USA

Diaz, Guillermo (Actor)
c/o Staff Member *Abrams Artists Agency (LA)*
9200 W Sunset Blvd PH 11
Los Angeles, CA 90069-3601, USA

Diaz, Helga (Actor)
c/o Gabriel Blanco *Gabriel Blanco Iglesias (Mexico)*
Rio Balsas 35-32 Colonia Cuauhtemoc
DF 6500, Mexico

Diaz, Izzy (Actor)
c/o Scott Zimmerman *Evolution Entertainment (LA)*
901 N Highland Ave
Los Angeles, CA 90038-2412, USA

Diaz, Jorge (Athlete, Football Player)
10801 Starkey Rd
Seminole, FL 33777-1159, USA

Diaz, Laura (Golfer)
c/o Staff Member *Ladies Pro Golf Association (LPGA)*
100 International Golf Dr
Daytona Beach, FL 32124-1092, USA

Diaz, Lazaro (Athlete, Baseball Player)
13557 Meadow Bay Loop
Orlando, FL 32824-5082, USA

Diaz, Manny (Politician)
3500 Pan American Dr
Miami, FL 33133-5504, USA

Diaz, Mario (Athlete, Baseball Player)
90 Calle Menta
Gurabo, PR 00778-9655, USA

Diaz, Matt (Athlete, Baseball Player)
1124 Afton St
Lakeland, FL 33803-3202, USA

Diaz, Mike (Athlete, Baseball Player)
1113 Everglades Dr
Pacifica, CA 94044-3703, USA

Diaz, Norberto (Actor)
c/o Staff Member *Telefe - Argentina*
Pavon 2444 (C1248AAT)
Buenos Aires, ARGENTINA

Diaz, Robison (Actor)
c/o Staff Member *TV Caracol*
Calle 76 #11 - 35 Piso 10AA
Bogota DC 26484, COLOMBIA

Diaz Balart, Jose (Actor)
c/o Staff Member *Telemundo*
2470 W 8th Ave
Hialeah, FL 33010-2000, USA

Diaz-Balart, Jose (Correspondent)
51 W 52nd St
New York, NY 10019-6119, USA

Diaz-Balart, Mario (Congressman, Politician)
436 Cannon Hob
Washington, DC 20515-3203, USA

Diaz-Infante, David (Athlete, Football Player)
24723 E Park Crescent Dr
Aurora, CO 80016-3190, USA

Diaz-Rahi, Yamila (Model)
23 Watts St
New York, NY 10013, USA

Dibble, Dorne (Athlete, Football Player)
18601 Jamestown Cir
Northville, MI 48168-1834, USA

Dibble, Rob (Athlete, Baseball Player, Television Host)
30020 Trail Creek Dr
Agoura Hills, CA 91301-4041, USA

Dibel, John C (Business Person)
6001 Oak Cyn
Irvine, CA 92618-5200, USA

DiBeliglojoso, Lodovico B (Architect)
2 Via Dei Chiostri
Milan 20121, ITALY

Dibernardo, Rick (Athlete, Football Player)
31942 Via Oso
Trabuco Canyon, CA 92679-3900, USA

DiBiaggio, John A (Educator)
President's Office
Medford, MA 2155, USA

DiBlasio, Raul (Musician)
420 Jefferson Ave
Miami Beach, FL 33139-6503, USA

Diblassio, Raul (Musician)
c/o Staff Member *BMG*
1540 Broadway
New York, NY 10036-4039, USA

DiBona, Craig (Cinematographer)
333 E 66th St Apt 7O
New York, NY 10065-6274, USA

Dibos, Alicia (Athlete, Golfer)
1465 E Putnam Ave Apt 112E
Old Greenwich, CT 06870-1330, USA

Dibra, Bash
c/o Daniel A (Dan) Strone *Trident Media Group LLC*
41 Madison Ave Fl 36
New York, NY 10010-2257, USA

DiCamillo, Brandon (Actor)
c/o Staff Member *Stoic Management*
947 Trinity Ln
King Of Prussia, PA 19406-3603, USA

Dicamillo, Gary T (Business Person)
1001 Saint George Rd
Baltimore, MD 21210-1412, USA

DiCaprio, Leonardo (Actor)
c/o Rick Yorn *Yorn Management Group*
2000 Avenue Of The Stars 3rd Tower Floor NORTH
Los Angeles, CA 90067, USA

DiCenzo, George (Actor)
156 5th Ave Ste 820
New York, NY 10010-7767, USA

Dichter, Misha (Musician)
165 W 57th St
New York, NY 10019-2201, USA

Dicillo, Tom (Cinematographer, Director, Writer)
c/o Jennifer Levine *Untitled Entertainment (LA)*
350 S Beverly Dr Ste 200
Beverly Hills, CA 90212-4819, USA

Dick, Andy (Actor, Comedian)
c/o Michael Green *Collective*
8383 Wilshire Blvd Ste 1050
Beverly Hills, CA 90211-2415, USA

Dick, Douglas (Actor)
604 S Gretna Green Way
Los Angeles, CA 90049-4035, USA

Dick, Ed (Baseball Player)
501 Washington Ave
Ocean Springs, MS 39564-4631, USA

Dickau, Dan (Basketball Player)
190 Marietta St NW
Atlanta, GA 30303-2762, USA

Dickel, Dan (Athlete, Football Player)
970 Maplewood Dr
Coralville, IA 52241-3302, USA

Dickens, Jimmy (Musician)
5010 W Concord Rd
Brentwood, TN 37027-6520, USA

Dickens, Kim (Actor)
c/o Stephen Hirsh *Gersh (LA)*
9465 Wilshire Blvd Ste 600
Beverly Hills, CA 90212-2612, USA

Dickenson, Herb (Athlete, Hockey Player)
240 JERSEYVILLE RD RR 8 STN MAIN
Brantford, ON N3T 5M1, Canada

Dicker, Cintia (Model)
c/o Staff Member *Nova Models Munich*
Siegesstrasse 3
Munich 80802, Germany

Dickerson, Eric (Athlete, Football Player, Sportscaster)
516 Dickerson St
Sealy, TX 77474-4339, USA

Dickerson, Ernest R (Director)
c/o Staff Member *Chasen & Company*
8899 Beverly Blvd Ste 405
Los Angeles, CA 90048-2431, USA

Dickerson, Henry (Athlete, Basketball Player)
3022 Skybrook Ln
Durham, NC 27703-5979, USA

Dickerson, John (Athlete, Baseball Player)
1702 26th St N
Columbus, MS 39701-2606, USA

Dickerson, Kenneth (Athlete, Football Player)
2406 Alabama Ave
Tuskegee Institute, AL 36088-2410, USA

Dickerson, Marty (Athlete, Golfer)
4225 Luzon Way
Sarasota, FL 34241-5728, USA

Dickerson, Sandra (Actor)
Berkeley House Hay Hill
London W1X 7LH, UNITED KINGDOM (UK)

Dickey, Boh A (Business Person)
Safeco Plz
Seattle, WA 98185-0001, USA

Dickey, Charlie (Athlete, Football Player)
1992 Farm Cir
Sandy, UT 84093-6296, USA

Dickey, Curtis (Athlete, Football Player)
1817 Sheehan Ct
Arlington, TX 76012-3777, USA

Dickey, Lynn (Athlete, Football Player)
9220 Pawnee Ln
Leawood, KS 66206-1758, USA

Dickey, R A (Athlete, Baseball Player)
701 Cantrell Ave
Nashville, TN 37215-1022, USA

Dickey, Richard (Athlete, Basketball Player)
1109 Red Maple Dr
Plymouth, IN 46563-3697, USA

Dickey, Wallace (Athlete, Football Player)
220 E Montana Dr
Shiner, TX 77984-6240, USA

Dickinson, Angie (Actor)
1715 Carla Rdg
Beverly Hills, CA 90210-1911, USA

Dickinson, Bruce (Musician)
c/o Staff Member *Agency Group Ltd, The (UK)*
361-373 City Rd
London EC1V 1PQ, UK

Dickinson, David (Actor)
PO Box 229
Bristol BS99 7JN, ENGLAND

Dickinson, Gary (Bowler)
501 Wade Martin Rd
Edmond, OK 73034-6716, USA

Dickinson, Janice (Model, Reality TV Star)
c/o Staff Member *Elite Model Management*
119 Washington Ave Ste 501
Miami Beach, FL 33139-7228, USA

Dickinson, Judy (Athlete, Golfer)
18277 SE Heritage Dr
Jupiter, FL 33469-1439, USA

Dickinson, Parnell (Athlete, Football Player)
1646 Wallace Rd
Lutz, FL 33549-3933, USA

Dickinson, Richard (Athlete, Football Player)
PO Box 166
New Augusta, MS 39462-0166, USA

Dickinson, Steve (Cartoonist)
c/o Staff Member *King Features Syndication*
300 W 57th St Fl 15
New York, NY 10019-5238, USA

Dickman, James B (Journalist)
1471 Peach Creek Dr
Splendora, TX 77372, USA

Dickson, Bob (Athlete, Golfer)
140 Woodlands Creek Dr
Ponte Vedra Beach, FL 32082-3217, USA

Dickson, Chris (Yachtsman)
1 Erieview Plaza 1360 East 9th St # 1300
Cleveland, OH 44114, USA

Dickson, Clarence (Lawyer)
1351 NW 12th St
Miami, FL 33125-1644, USA

Dickson, Jason (Athlete, Baseball Player)
9022 E Helm Dr
Scottsdale, AZ 85260-2704, USA

Dickson, Jennifer (Artist, Photographer)
20 Osborne St
Ottawa, ON K1S 4Z9, CANADA

Dickson, Jim (Athlete, Baseball Player)
90580 Sunset Lake Rd Apt 1
Warrenton, OR 97146-7285, USA

Dickson, John (Athlete, Basketball Player)
4646 Wynmeade Park NE
Marietta, GA 30067-4098, USA

Dickson, Lance (Athlete, Baseball Player)
4615 N Placita Roca Blanca
Tucson, AZ 85718-7476, USA

Dickson, Neil (Actor)
c/o Lorraine Berglund *Lorraine Berglund Management*
11537 Hesby St
North Hollywood, CA 91601-3618, USA

Dickson, Ngila (Designer)
c/o Staff Member *Sandra Marsh Management*
9150 Wilshire Blvd Ste 220
Beverly Hills, CA 90212-3429, USA

Dickson, Paul (Athlete, Football Player)
10841 Little Ave S
Minneapolis, MN 55437-2940, USA

Dicus, Charles (Chuck) (Athlete, Football Player)
852 N Mansfield Ave
Los Angeles, CA 90038-3408, USA

Didier, Bob (Athlete, Baseball Player)
544 SW 335th St
Federal Way, WA 98023-6189, USA

Didier, Clint (Athlete, Football Player)
8770 N Glade Rd
Pasco, WA 99301-8720, USA

Didion, Joan (Writer)
445 Park Ave # 1300
New York, NY 10022-2606, USA

Didion, John (Athlete, Football Player)
48 Elk Ridge Ln
Naselle, WA 98638-8515, USA

Dido (Musician, Songwriter)
c/o Staff Member *Paradigm (NY)*
360 Park Ave S Fl 16
New York, NY 10010-1708, USA

Diduck, Gerald (Athlete, Hockey Player)
3303 Drexel Dr
Dallas, TX 75205-2914, USA

Die Antwoord (Music Group)
c/o Joel Zimmerman *WmE2 (WMA-NY)*
1325 Avenue of the Americas
New York, NY 10019-6026, USA

Diebold, John (Business Person)
41 Peaceable St
Ridgefield, CT 06877-4809, USA

Diehl, David (Athlete, Football Player)
116 Liberty Ridge Trl
Totowa, NJ 07512-1600, USA

Diehl, Digby (Journalist)
788 S Lake Ave
Pasadena, CA 91106-3948, USA

Diehl, Digby R (Journalist)
788 S Lake Ave
Pasadena, CA 91106-3948, USA

Diehl, John (Actor)
c/o Sandi Dudek *Paradigm (LA)*
360 N Crescent Dr
Beverly Hills, CA 90210-4874, USA

Diehl, John A (Athlete, Football Player)
900 S Henry St
Williamsburg, VA 23185-3989, USA

Dieken, Doug H (Athlete, Football Player)
29876 Lake Rd
Bay Village, OH 44140-1276, USA

Diem, Ryan (Athlete, Football Player)
11522 Willow Ridge Dr
Zionsville, IN 46077-7823, USA

Diemecke, Enrique Arturo (Conductor)
266 W 37th St # 2000
New York, NY 10018-6609, USA

Diener, Theodor O (Misc)
11711 Battersea Dr
Beltsville, MD 20705-1552, USA

Dienhart, Mark (Athlete, Football Player)
1944 Bayard Ave
Saint Paul, MN 55116-1216, USA

Dierassi, Carl (Inventor)
2325 Bear Gulch Rd
Redwood City, CA 94062-4405, USA

Dierassi, Issac (Doctor)
2034 Delancey St
Philadelphia, PA 19103-6510, USA

Dierdof, Daniel L (Dan) (Athlete, Football Player, Sportscaster)
13302 Buckland Hall Rd
Saint Louis, MO 63131-1214, USA

Dierdorf, Dan (Athlete, Football Player)
12817 Dubon Ln
Saint Louis, MO 63131-1414, USA

Diering, Chuck (Athlete, Baseball Player)
1 Nob Hill Dr
Saint Louis, MO 63138-1400, USA

Dierker, Larry (Athlete, Baseball Player, Coach)
8318 N Tahoe Dr
Jersey Village, TX 77040-1258, USA

Dierker, Robert R (General)
Deputy Commander Pacific Fleet Camp H M Smith
Honolulu, HI 96861, USA

Dierking, Connie (Athlete, Basketball Player)
5665 Kugler Mill Rd
Cincinnati, OH 45236-2163, USA

Dierking, Scott (Athlete, Football Player)
1862 Wingate Ln
Wheaton, IL 60189-7881, USA

Dierkop, Charles (Actor)
c/o Staff Member *The Actors Studio*
8341 De Longpre Ave
West Hollywood, CA 90069-2601, USA

Diesel (Music Group)
c/o Staff Member *The Harbour Agency*
135 Forbes St
Woolloomooloo NSW 2011, Australia

Diesel, Vin (Actor, Director, Producer)
c/o Stacy O'Neil *Brillstein Entertainment Partners*
9150 Wilshire Blvd Ste 350
Beverly Hills, CA 90212-3453, USA

Dieselboy (DJ, Musician)
c/o Joel Zimmerman *WmE2 (WMA-NY)*
1325 Avenue of the Americas
New York, NY 10019-6026, USA

Dieterich, Chris (Athlete, Football Player)
804 Edisto River Rd
Myrtle Beach, SC 29588-7439, USA

Dietrich, Dena (Actor)
c/o Staff Member *Bauman Redanty & Shaul Agency*
5757 Wilshire Blvd Suite 473
Beverly Hills, CA 90212, USA

Dietrich, Don (Athlete, Hockey Player)
310 Finlay Ave E
Deloraine, MB R0M 0M0, Canada

Dietrich, William A (Bill) (Journalist)
1120 John St
Seattle, WA 98109-5321, USA

Dietrick, Coby (Athlete, Basketball Player)
644 Patterson Ave
San Antonio, TX 78209-5655, USA

Dietzel, Roy (Athlete, Baseball Player)
8421 Coulwood Oak Ln
Charlotte, NC 28214-1165, USA

Difelice, Mike (Athlete, Baseball Player)
3980 Mimosa Pl
Palm Harbor, FL 34685-3674, USA

Diffie, Joe (Musician)
38 Music Sq E Ste 300
Nashville, TN 37203-4304, USA

Diffie, Whitfield (Inventor)
901 San Antonio Rd MS UMTV29-116
Palo Alto, CA 94303-4900, USA

Diffrient, Niels (Designer)
Ridgefield, CT 6877, USA

DiFranco, Ani (Musician, Songwriter, Writer)
c/o Staff Member *Primary Talent International (UK)*
The Primary Building 10-11 Jockeys Fields
London WC1R 4BN, UK

Digby, Marie (Musician)
c/o Staff Member *Nettwerk Management (LA)*
1545 Wilcox Ace Suite 200
Los Angeles, CA 90028, USA

DiGenova, Joseph E (Lawyer)
901 15th St NW # 430
Washington, DC 20005-2327, USA

Diggins, Ben (Athlete, Baseball Player)
4804 E Merrell St
Phoenix, AZ 85018-7876, USA

Diggs, Nail (Athlete, Football Player)
2006 Connonade Dr
Waxhaw, NC 28173-0109, USA

Diggs, Shelton (Athlete, Football Player)
261 Washington Ave Apt 3R
New Rochelle, NY 10801-5967, USA

Diggs, Taye (Actor)
c/o Staff Member *OTaye Productions*
12001 Ventura Pl Ste 340
Studio City, CA 91604-2629, USA

Digiacomo, Curt (Athlete, Football Player)
830 Ida Ave
Solana Beach, CA 92075-2439, USA

Digible Planets (Music Group)
345 N Maple Dr Ste 123
Beverly Hills, CA 90210-5185, USA

DiGregorio, Ernie (Athlete, Basketball Player)
60 Chestnut Ave
Narragansett, RI 02882-6113, USA

Dilauro, Jack (Athlete, Baseball Player)
102 Sea Oats Dr
Panama City Beach, FL 32413-2763, USA

Dilba (Musician)
PO Box 11029
Stockholm 10061, SWEDEN

Dilfer, Trent F (Athlete, Football Player)
15288 Quito Rd
Saratoga, CA 95070-6227, USA

Dilger, Ken (Athlete, Football Player)
10403 Windemere
Carmel, IN 46032-8594, USA

Dilip (Actor)
74 Baskara Colony Virugambakkam
Chennai, TN 600 092, INDIA

Dill, Craig (Athlete, Basketball Player)
10200 Thomas Woods Rd
Saginaw, MI 48609-9512, USA

Dill, Laddie John (Artist)
1625 Electric Ave
Venice, CA 90291-4803, USA

Dill, Terry (Athlete, Golfer)
7003 Western Oaks Blvd
Austin, TX 78749-2229, USA

Dillahunt, Garret (Actor)
c/o Edith Rea *Allman/Rea Management*
9255 W Sunset Blvd Ste 600
West Hollywood, CA 90069-3306, USA

Dillam, Bradford (Actor)
770 Hot Springs Rd
Santa Barbara, CA 93108-1107, USA

Dillane, Stephen (Actor)
10/11 Lower John St #300
London W1R 3PE, UNITED KINGDOM (UK)

Dillard, Alex (Business Person)
1600 Cantrell Rd
Little Rock, AR 72201-1110, USA

Dillard, Annie (Writer)
50 W 29th St
New York, NY 10001-4227, USA

Dillard, Don (Athlete, Baseball Player)
45 Bream Ln
Waterloo, SC 29384-4868, USA

Dillard, Doug (Actor, Musician)
c/o Randy Campbell 340 So Columbus Blvd
Tucson, AZ 857ll-4l38, USA

Dillard, Gordon (Athlete, Baseball Player)
840 Via Manzana
Aromas, CA 95004-9026, USA

Dillard, Harrison H. (Athlete, Olympic Athlete, Track Athlete)
3842 E 147th St
Cleveland, OH 44128-1027, USA

Dillard, Mickey (Athlete, Basketball Player)
224 SW 11th Ave
Dania, FL 33004-3515, USA

Dillard, Phillip (Athlete, Football Player)
c/o Roosevelt Barnes *Maximum Sports Management*
6435 W Jefferson Blvd # 197
Fort Wayne, IN 46804-6203, USA

Dillard, Rodney (Actor, Musician)
c/o Randy Campbell 340 So Columbus Blvd
Tucson, AZ 857ll-4l38, USA

Dillard, Stacey (Athlete, Football Player)
3188 County Road 4220
Annona, TX 75550-4037, USA

Dillard, Steve (Athlete, Baseball Player)
154 Drive 841
Saltillo, MS 38866-9362, USA

Dillard, W Harrison (Athlete, Track Athlete)
3449 Glencairn Rd
Shaker Heights, OH 44122-4801, USA

Dillard, William T Jr (Business Person)
1600 Cantrell Rd
Little Rock, AR 72201-1110, USA

Dille, Bob (Athlete, Basketball Player)
138 Quails Nest Rd Apt 1
Naples, FL 34112-5194, USA

Dillehay, Thomas (Tom) (Misc)
Anthropology
Lexington, KY 40506-0001, USA

Dilleita, Dilleita Mohamed (Prime Minister)
PO Box 2086
Djibouti, DJIBOUTI

Diller, Barry (Business Person)
555 W 18th St
New York, NY 10011-2822, USA

Diller, Phyllis (Actor, Comedian)
163 S Rockingham Ave
Los Angeles, CA 90049-2513, USA

Dillinger, Bob (Athlete, Baseball Player)
15380 Rhododendron Dr
Canyon Country, CA 91387-1851, USA

Dillion, Wayne (Athlete, Hockey Player)
301-1185 Eglinton Ave E
North York, ON M3C 3C6, Canada

Dillman, Bill (Athlete, Baseball Player)
PO Box 5167
Winter Park, FL 32793-5167, USA

Dillman, Bradford (Actor)
770 Hot Springs Rd
Santa Barbara, CA 93108-1107, USA

Dillman, Brooke (Actor)
c/o Staff Member *Domain Talent*
9229 W Sunset Blvd Ste 710
Los Angeles, CA 90069-3407, USA

Dillon, Bobby (Athlete, Football Player)
1289 Morgan Dr
Temple, TX 76502-4245, USA

Dillon, Corey (Athlete, Football Player)
31 Marlboro Rd
Woburn, MA 01801-3427, USA

Dillon, David B (Business Person)
1014 Vine St
Cincinnati, OH 45202-1141, USA

Dillon, Denny (Actor, Comedian)
8942 Wilshire Blvd # 219
Beverly Hills, CA 90211-1908, USA

Dillon, Joe (Athlete, Baseball Player)
200 Farallon Ct
Lincoln, CA 95648-8156, USA

Dillon, Kevin (Actor)
c/o Tiffany Kuzon *Evolution Entertainment (LA)*
901 N Highland Ave
Los Angeles, CA 90038-2412, USA

Dillon, Matt (Actor, Director, Writer)
c/o Staci Wolfe *Polaris PR*
8135 W 4th St Fl 2
Los Angeles, CA 90048-4415, USA

Dillon, Melinda (Actor)
c/o Staff Member *Innovative Artists (LA)*
1505 10th St
Santa Monica, CA 90401-2805, USA

Dillon, Mike (Race Car Driver)
PO Box 30414
Winston Salem, NC 27130-0414, USA

Dillon, Steve (Athlete, Baseball Player)
511 Wateredge Ave
Baldwin, NY 11510-3728, USA

Dilmancheff, Babe (Athlete, Football Player)
3917 Edgehill Dr
Los Angeles, CA 90008-2617, USA

Dilone, Miguel (Athlete, Baseball Player)
Calle El Sol #190
Santiago, Dominican Republic

Dils, Steve (Athlete, Football Player)
10285 Midway Ave
Alpharetta, GA 30022-6028, USA

Dilts, Bucky (Athlete, Football Player)
240 McCaslin Blvd # 101
Louisville, CO 80027-2911, USA

Dilts, Douglas (Athlete, Football Player)
1231 Defoor Ct NW
Atlanta, GA 30318-2973, USA

Dilweg, Anthony (Athlete, Football Player)
5310 S Alston Ave Ste 210
Durham, NC 27713-4381, USA

DiMaggio, John (Actor)
c/o Paul Rosicker *Gersh (LA)*
9465 Wilshire Blvd Ste 600
Beverly Hills, CA 90212-2612, USA

Dimaio, Rob (Athlete, Hockey Player)
c/o Staff Member *Dallas Stars*
2601 Avenue of the Stars Ste 100
Frisco, TX 75034-9016, USA

Dimancheff, Boris (Babe) (Athlete, Football Player)
3917 Edgehill Dr
Los Angeles, CA 90008-2617, USA

Dimarco, Chris (Athlete, Golfer)
3545 Rice Lake Loop
Longwood, FL 32779-3081, USA

Dimas, Trent (Gymnast)
6009 Carmel Ave NE
Albuquerque, NM 87113-1741, USA

Dimbleby, David (Correspondent, Journalist)
14 King St Richmond
Surrey TW9 1NF, UNITED KINGDOM (UK)

DiMeo, Paul (Actor, Reality TV Star)
c/o Staff Member *Extreme Makeover: Home Edition*
Endemol Entertainment USA 9225 Sunset Blvd #1100
Los Angeles, CA 90069, USA

Dimichele, Frank (Athlete, Baseball Player)
812 Tasker St
Philadelphia, PA 19148-1240, USA

Dimitrakos, Niko (Athlete, Hockey Player)
71 Pennsylvania Ave
Somerville, MA 02145-2227, USA

Dimitriades, Alex (Actor)
c/o Staff Member *Shanahan Management*
Level 3 Berman House
Surry Hills 2010, AUSTRALIA

Dimitrova, Ghena (Opera Singer)
40 W 57th St
New York, NY 10019-4001, USA

Dimma, Suzanne (Stylist)
c/o Staff Member *Judy Inc*
1 Yorkville Ave
Toronto ON M4W 1L1, Canada

Dimmel, Mike (Athlete, Baseball Player)
526 Country Ln
Coppell, TX 75019-5129, USA

Dimmick, Thomas (Athlete, Football Player)
204 Broadmoor Blvd
Lafayette, LA 70503-5114, USA

Dimon, James (Jamie) (Business Person)
270 Park Ave
New York, NY 10017-2014, USA

Dimple (Actor, Bollywood)
The Gallop Broad Acres Stud Farm Avan Hali Estate
Bangalore, KA, INDIA

Dimry, Charles (Athlete, Football Player)
611 S Myers St Apt 1
Oceanside, CA 92054-3925, USA

DiMucci, Dion
1650 Broadway Ste 503
New York, NY 10019-6833

Dimuro, Mike (Athlete, Baseball Player)
22594 E Peakview Pl
Aurora, CO 80016-3148, USA

Dimuro, Ray (Athlete, Baseball Player)
9625 N 33rd St
Phoenix, AZ 85028-4919, USA

Dinapoli, Gennaro (Athlete, Football Player)
10 White Oak Farm Rd
Newtown, CT 06470-2501, USA

diNapoli, Marc
8 Rue De Georges-De-Porto-Riche
Paris, FRANCE F-75014

DiNardo, Gerry (Coach, Football Coach)
Athletic Dept
Bloomington, IN 47405, USA

Dinardo, Lenny (Athlete, Baseball Player)
23015 NW 227th Dr
High Springs, FL 32643-9031, USA

Dindal, Mark (Director)
c/o Peter Nichols *Lichter Grossman Nichols Adler & Goodman*
9200 W Sunset Blvd Ste 1200
Los Angeles, CA 90069-3607, USA

Dine, James (Artist)
32 E 57th St
New York, NY 10022-2513, USA

Dineen, Bill (Athlete, Hockey Player)
18 Fairwood Dr
Queensbury, NY 12804-2175, USA

Dineen, Gord (Athlete, Hockey Player)
51 Fitzgerald Rd
Queensbury, NY 12804-1344, USA

Dineen, Kenny (Athlete, Baseball Player)
112 S Ranch St
Santa Maria, CA 93454-5319, USA

Dineen, Kevin (Athlete, Hockey Player)
149 Birdsall Rd
Queensbury, NY 12804-1384, USA

Dineen, Peter (Athlete, Hockey Player)
65 Birch Rd
Lake George, NY 12845-4323, USA

Dineen, William P (Bill) (Coach)
Sawis Center 1401 Clark Ave
Saint Louis, MO 63103, USA

Dinerstein, James (Artist)
20 E 79th St
New York, NY 10075-0106, USA

Dingle, Adrian (Athlete, Football Player)
3228 W Canyon Ave
San Diego, CA 92123-5429, USA

Dingle, Mike (Athlete, Football Player)
512 Menlo Dr
Columbia, SC 29210-6537, USA

Dingman, Chris (Athlete, Hockey Player)
9220 Pine Island Ct
Tampa, FL 33647-2301, USA

Dingman, Craig (Athlete, Baseball Player)
3573 W Del Sienno St
Wichita, KS 67203-4349, USA

Dini, Paul (Actor, Producer, Writer)
c/o Staff Member *United Talent Agency (UTA)*
9560 Wilshire Blvd Fl 5
Beverly Hills, CA 90212-2400, USA

Dinkel, Tom (Athlete, Football Player)
877 Squire Lake Ct
Villa Hills, KY 41017-1362, USA

Dinkeloo, John (Architect)
20 Davis St
Hamden, CT 06517-3501, USA

Dinkins, Byron (Athlete, Basketball Player)
10326 Tallent Ln
Huntersville, NC 28078-5903, USA

Dinkins, Darnell (Athlete, Football Player)
9006 Pembroke Ct
Pittsburgh, PA 15237-6366, USA

Dinkins, Howard (Athlete, Football Player)
5980 Covered Creek Ln
Jacksonville, FL 32277-1447, USA

Dinklage, Peter (Actor)
c/o David Ginsberg *Insight*
1134 S Cloverdale Ave
Los Angeles, CA 90019-6737, USA

Dinnel, Harry (Athlete, Basketball Player)
1427 El Nido Dr
Fallbrook, CA 92028-8697, USA

Dinner, Michael (Director)
c/o Staff Member *Creative Artists Agency (CAA-LA)*
2000 Avenue of the Stars Ste 100
Los Angeles, CA 90067-4705, USA

Dinnigan, Collette (Designer, Fashion Designer)
22-24 Hutchinson St Surry Hls
Sydney, NSW 2010, AUSTRALIA

DioGuardi, Kara (Musician, Reality TV Star, Songwriter)
c/o Stephen Finfer *Arthouse Entertainment*
PO Box 3900
Hollywood, CA 90078-3900, USA

Dion (Musician)
1650 Broadway Ste 503
New York, NY 10019-6833, USA

Dion, Celine (Actor, Musician)
19 Rue Mediterra Dr
Henderson, NV 89011-2011, USA

Dion, Colleen (Actor)
9200 W Sunset Blvd Ste 1125
Los Angeles, CA 90069-3610, USA

Dion, Michel (Athlete, Hockey Player)
33 Mulrain Way
Bluffton, SC 29910-6530, USA

Dion, Terry (Athlete, Football Player)
106 E Libby Rd
Shelton, WA 98584-8132, USA

Dionisi, Stefano (Actor)
Via Giuseppe Pisanelli
Rome 196, ITALY

Dionne, Joseph L (Business Person, Publisher)
1221 Avenue of the Americas
New York, NY 10020-1001, USA

Dionne, Marcel E (Athlete, Hockey Player)
PO Box 2596
Niagara Falls, NY 14302-2596, USA

Diop, DeSagana (Athlete, Basketball Player)
4300 Haddonfield Rd Ste 309
Pennsauken, NJ 08109-3376, USA

Diop, Majhemout (President)
210 HCM Guediawaye
Dakar, SENEGAL

Diorio, Nick (Soccer Player)
273 Clark St
Lemoyne, PA 17043-2010, USA

Diorio, Ron (Athlete, Baseball Player)
2 White Oak Ln
Waterbury, CT 06705-1835, USA

Dipierro, Ramon (Athlete, Football Player)
1750 Brownstone Blvd Apt H
Toledo, OH 43614-1362, USA

Dipietro, Bob (Athlete, Baseball Player)
909 Carriage Hill Dr
Yakima, WA 98908-2414, USA

Dipietro, Rick (Athlete, Hockey Player)
3 Fieldstone Ln
Oyster Bay, NY 11771-3122, USA

Dipino, Frank (Athlete, Baseball Player)
5479 Pebble Beach Dr
Camillus, NY 13031-8651, USA

Dipoto, Jerry (Athlete, Baseball Player)
15130 E Camelview Dr
Fountain Hills, AZ 85268-6405, USA

DiPreta, Tony (Cartoonist)
235 E 45th St
New York, NY 10017-3305, USA

DiPrete, Edward D (Ex-Governor)
686 Reservoir Ave
Cranston, RI 02910-3226, USA

Dirda, Michael (Journalist)
1150 15th St NW
Washington, DC 20071-0001, USA

Dirden, Johnnie (Athlete, Football Player)
1403 S Ulster St
Denver, CO 80231-2744, USA

Director, Kim (Actor)
c/o Rachel Sheedy *Don Buchwald & Associates Inc (NY)*
10 E 44th St Frnt 1
New York, NY 10017-3654

Direnzo, Daniel (Dan) (Athlete, Football Player)
PO Box 958
Albrightsville, PA 18210-0958, USA

Direnzo, Fred (Athlete, Football Player)
5 Togno St
Netcong, NJ 07857-1608, USA

Diresta, John (Actor, Comedian)
c/o Ruthanne Secunda *United Talent Agency (UTA)*
9560 Wilshire Blvd Fl 5
Beverly Hills, CA 90212-2400, USA

Dirie, Waris (Activist, Model)
2-4 Noel Street
London W1V 3RB, UNITED KINGDOM (UK)

Dirk, Robert (Athlete, Hockey Player)
4441 Lee Ave
Groves, TX 77619-6507, USA

Dirnt, Mike (Musician)
c/o Pat Magnarella *Pat's Management Company*
543 Encinitas Blvd Ste 101
Encinitas, CA 92024-3744, USA

Dirt Band, The
PO Box 1915
Aspen, CO 81612-1915

Dirty Pretty Things (Music Group)
c/o Staff Member *Paradigm (Monterey)*
404 W Franklin St
Monterey, CA 93940-2303, USA

Disarcina, Gary (Athlete, Baseball Player)
141 Martingale Ln
Plymouth, MA 02360-3275, USA

Dischinger, Terry (Athlete, Basketball Player)
1730 Oak Ave
Northbrook, IL 60062-5428, USA

Disco, Shanthi (Actor, Bollywood)
19 Habibullah Road T Nagar
Chennai, TN 600017, INDIA

Disco Biscuits, The (Music Group)
c/o Staff Member *Red Light Management (LA)*
8439 W Sunset Blvd Ste 2
Los Angeles, CA 90069-1925, USA

Disel, Vin (Actor, Director)
c/o Stacy Boniello *Firm, The*
2049 Century Park E Ste 2550
Los Angeles, CA 90067-3139, USA

Dishman, Chris E (Athlete, Football Player)
1561 Raymond Rd
Garland, NE 68360-9347, USA

Dishman, Cris (Athlete, Football Player)
5019 Mariposa Cir
Fresno, TX 77545-9219, USA

Dishman, Glenn (Athlete, Baseball Player)
5400 Fairway Dr
San Jose, CA 95127-1609, USA

Dishy, Bob (Actor)
20 E 9th St
New York, NY 10003-5944, USA

Disi, Ursula (Skier)
Krumme Gasse 10A
Ruhpolding 83324, GERMANY

Disi, Uschi (Misc)
Unterer Plattenberg 6
Flossenberg 92696, GERMANY

Disney, Anthea (Editor)
1211 Avenue of the Americas Fl 8
New York, NY 10036-0003, USA

Disney, William (Speed Skater)
1610 Kirk Dr
Lake Havasu City, AZ 86404-2449, USA

DiSpirito, Rocco (Chef, Reality TV Star)
60 E Randolph St # 3203
Chicago, IL 60601-7504, USA

Distaso, Alec (Athlete, Baseball Player)
505 W 7th St Apt 1412
Charlotte, NC 28202-1848, USA

Distefano, Benny (Athlete, Baseball Player)
9911 Murray Lndg
Missouri City, TX 77459-6417, USA

Distel, Sascha
20 rue de Fosses-Saint-Jacques
Paris F-75005, FRANCE

Distler, Natalie (Actor)
c/o Cynthia Booth *Global Artists Agency*
6253 Hollywood Blvd Apt 508
Los Angeles, CA 90028-8251, USA

Disturbed (Music Group, Musician)
c/o Silda Palerm *Warner Bros Records (NY)*
75 Rockefeller Plz
New York, NY 10019-6908, USA

DiSuvero, Mark (Artist)
PO Box 2218
Astoria, NY 11102-0218, USA

Ditka, Mike (Athlete, Coach, Football Coach, Football Player)
161 E Chicago Ave Apt 39F
Chicago, IL 60611-2623, USA

Ditmar, Arthur J (Art) (Athlete, Baseball Player)
6687 Wisteria Dr
Myrtle Beach, SC 29588-6481, USA

Dittmer, Andreas (Athlete)
Fischerbank 5
Neubrandenburg 17033, GERMANY

Dittmer, Edward C (Scientist)
702 Old Mescalero Rd
Tularosa, NM 88352-2525, USA

Dittmer, Jack (Athlete, Baseball Player)
PO Box 98
Elkader, IA 52043-0098, USA

Dityatin, Aleksandr N (Gymnast)
Nevski Prosp 18 #25
Saint Petersburg, RUSSIA

Ditz, Nancy (Athlete, Track Athlete)
524 Moore Rd
Woodside, CA 94062-1109, USA

Diulio, Albert J (Educator)
President's Office
Milwaukee, WI 53233, USA

Diva, Amanda (Television Host)
c/o Michael (Mike) Esterman
Esterman.Com, LLC
Prefers to be contacted via email
MD, USA

Divac, Vlade (Athlete, Basketball Player)
17496 Tramonto Dr
Pacific Palisades, CA 90272-3125, USA

Divina, Luz (DJ)
c/o Len Evans *Project Publicity*
312 W 53rd St Ste 202
New York, NY 10019-5743, USA

Divine, Gary W (Misc)
1016 16th St
Washington, DC 20038, USA

Divine Comedy, The (Music Group)
c/o Staff Member *Paradigm (Monterey)*
404 W Franklin St
Monterey, CA 93940-2303, USA

Divins, Charles (Actor)
c/o Staff Member *Innovative Artists (LA)*
1505 10th St
Santa Monica, CA 90401-2805, USA

Divoff, Andrew (Actor)
c/o Staff Member *Marshak/Zachary Company, The*
8840 Wilshire Blvd Fl 1
Beverly Hills, CA 90211-2606, USA

Diwakar, R R (Writer)
233 Sadashiv Nagar
Bangalore, Karnataka 560006, INDIA

Dix, Drew D (War Hero)
HC 68 Box 70
Mimbres, NM 88049-9347, USA

Dixie Chicks (Music Group)
c/o Simon Renshaw *Strategics Artist Management*
1100 Glendon Ave Ste 1000
Los Angeles, CA 90024-3514, USA

Dixie Cups, The (Music Group)
2535 Noble St
North Las Vegas, NV 89030-3819, USA

Dixieland Rhythm Kings, The
PO Box 12403
Atlanta, GA 30355-2403

Dixit, Madhuri (Actor, Bollywood)
C/O Dr. Shriram Madhav Nene 1390 S Potomac St, Suite 120
Aurora, CO 80012, USA

Dixon, Al (Athlete, Football Player)
120 W 7th St Ste 216
Plainfield, NJ 07060-1629, USA

Dixon, Alan J (Ex-Senator)
7606 Foley Dr
Belleville, IL 62223-2322, USA

Dixon, Alesha (Musician)
c/o Staff Member *Independent Talent Group (ITG-UK)*
Oxford House 76 Oxford St
London W1D 1BS, UK

Dixon, Becky (Sportscaster)
77 W 66th St
New York, NY 10023-6201, USA

Dixon, Cal (Athlete, Football Player)
179 Las Palmas
Merritt Island, FL 32953-2902, USA

Dixon, Cathy (Stylist)
c/o Celebrity Stylist *Jed Root Inc*
61-A Walker St
New York, NY 10013, USA

Dixon, Craig (Athlete, Track Athlete)
10630 Wellworth Ave
Los Angeles, CA 90024-5012, USA

Dixon, D Jeremy (Architect)
41 Shelton St
London WC2H 9HJ, UNITED KINGDOM (UK)

Dixon, David (Athlete, Football Player)
8345 Windsong Dr
Eden Prairie, MN 55344-6764, USA

Dixon, Donna (Actor)
7708 Woodrow Wilson Dr
Los Angeles, CA 90046-1212, USA

Dixon, Dwayne (Athlete, Football Player)
78 Westfield Pl
Athens, OH 45701-3857, USA

Dixon, Floyd (Musician)
1671 Appian Way
Santa Monica, CA 90401-3258, USA

Dixon, Gerald (Athlete, Football Player)
1315 Big Rock Ct
Fort Mill, SC 29708-6950, USA

Dixon, Juan (Basketball Player)
MCI Centre 601 F St NW
Washington, DC 20004, USA

Dixon, Ken (Athlete, Baseball Player)
20 Colony Hill Ct Apt 1A
Halethorpe, MD 21227-2517, USA

Dixon, Leslie (Director, Producer, Writer)
c/o Todd Feldman *Creative Artists Agency (CAA-LA)*
2000 Avenue of the Stars Ste 100
Los Angeles, CA 90067-4705, USA

Dixon, Mark (Athlete, Football Player)
4016 Ivy Ln
Kitty Hawk, NC 27949-4347, USA

Dixon, Randolph C (Randy) (Athlete, Football Player)
9910 Summerlakes Dr
Carmel, IN 46032-9307, USA

Dixon, Robert J (General)
5100 John D Ryan Blvd Apt 2206
San Antonio, TX 78245-3513, USA

Dixon, Rodney (Rod) (Athlete, Track Athlete)
22 Entrican Ave Remuera
Auckland 5, NEW ZEALAND

Dixon, Ronnie (Athlete, Football Player)
1440 W Kemper Rd Apt 510
Cincinnati, OH 45240-1652, USA

Dixon, Scott (Race Car Driver)
7777 Woodland Dr
Indianapolis, IN 46278-1794, USA

Dixon, Sonny (Athlete, Baseball Player)
6624 Lakeside Dr
Charlotte, NC 28215-4059, USA

Dixon, Steve (Athlete, Baseball Player)
6510 Hollow Tree Rd
Louisville, KY 40228-1336, USA

Dixon, Tamecka (Basketball Player)
Staples Center 1111 S Figueroa St
Los Angeles, CA 90015, USA

Dixon, Thomas F (Engineer)
1761 Cuba Island Ln
Hayes, VA 23072-3925, USA

Dixon, Tom (Athlete, Baseball Player)
2945 Delaney St
Orlando, FL 32806-6256, USA

Dixon, Tony (Athlete, Football Player)
4588 Gibson Dr
Bessemer, AL 35022-7045, USA

Dixon, Zachary (Athlete, Football Player)
19365 Hottinger Cir
Germantown, MD 20874-1504, USA

Dizon, Jesse
PO Box 572105
Tarzana, CA 91357-2105, USA

DJ Ashba (Musician)
700 N San Vicente Blvd Ste G410
West Hollywood, CA 90069-5060, USA

DJ Jazzy Jeff (Actor, Musician)
444 N 3rd St
Philadelphia, PA 19123-4107, USA

DJ Mendez (Musician)
c/o Leopoldo Mendez *Macabro Records*
Bolidenvagen 10
Johanneshov 121 63, SWEDEN

DJ Tiesto (Tiësto) (Actor, Musician)
c/o Josh Neuman *The Ascot Club*
55 Washington St Ste 658
Brooklyn, NY 11201-1063, USA

Djalili, Omid (Actor)
c/o Brian Stern *Stern Entertainment Group (Brillstein Entertainment Partners)*
1 William Morris Pl
Beverly Hills, CA 90212-4261, USA

Djodjov Pejoski, Marjan (Designer, Fashion Designer)
c/o Staff Member *Marjan Djodjov Pejoski*
75 Garden Flat Warwick Avenue
London, England W1Y 1DH, United Kingdom

Djokovic, Novak (Athlete, Tennis Player)
c/o Staff Member *Family Sport*
Futog
Novi Sad 21000, Serbia

Djoussouf, Abbass (Prime Minister)
Moroni, BP 421, COMOROS

Djukanovic, Milo (President)
Bul Lenjina 2
Novi Belgrad 11075, SERBIA & MONTENEGRO

Dlouhy, Lukas (Athlete, Tennis Player)
c/o Staff Member *ATP Tour*
201 Atp Tour Blvd
Ponte Vedra Beach, FL 32082-3211, USA

D'Lyn, Shae (Actor)
c/o Miles Levy *James/Levy/Jacobson Management Inc*
3500 W Olive Ave Ste 1470
Burbank, CA 91505-5514, USA

Dmitriev, Artur (Figure Skater)
Luchneksaia Nab 8
Moscow 119871, RUSSIA

Do Amaral, Diogo F (Government Official)
Ave Fontes Perelra de Melo 35 #13A
Lisbon 1050, PORTUGAL

Do Muoi (Politician)
Council of Ministers
Hanoi, VIETNAM

Do Nascimento, Alexandre Cardinal (Religious Leader)
CP 87
Luanda 1230 C, ANGOLA

Doak, Gary (Athlete, Hockey Player)
47 Highland Ave
Lynnfield, MA 01940-1905, USA

Doan, Charles A (Doctor)
4935 Olentangy Blvd
Columbus, OH 43214-2049, USA

Doan, Shane (Athlete, Hockey Player)
9820 E Thompson Peak Pkwy Unit 725
Scottsdale, AZ 85255-6657, USA

Doar, John (Lawyer)
9 E 63rd St
New York, NY 10065-7236, USA

Dobbek, Dan (Athlete, Baseball Player)
4042 SE Yamhill St
Portland, OR 97214-4445, USA

Dobbin, Brian (Athlete, Hockey Player)
5075 Shiloh Line
Petrolia, ON N0N 1R0, Canada

Dobbin, Edmund J (Educator)
President's Office
Villanova, PA 19085, USA

Dobbins, Herb (Athlete, Football Player)
10 Keating Pt
Saint Albert, AB T8N 5W8, Canada

Dobbins, Oliver (Athlete, Football Player)
8187 Omega Way
Summerfield, NC 27358-9418, USA

Dobbs, Greg (Athlete, Baseball Player)
11271 Showdown Ln
Moreno Valley, CA 92557-4816, USA

Dobbs, Leka (Stylist)
c/o Staff Member *Koko Represents*
166 Geary St Ste 1007
San Francisco, CA 94108-5623, USA

Dobbs, Lou (Television Host)
7112 Eagle Ter
West Palm Beach, FL 33412-3101, USA

Dobbs, Mattiwilda (Opera Singer)
1101 S Arlington Ridge Rd
Arlington, VA 22202-1951, USA

Dobek, Michelle (Athlete, Golfer)
292 Chicopee St
Chicopee, MA 01013-1744, USA

Dobelstein, Bob (Athlete, Football Player)
1473 SE Loquat Way
Lake City, FL 32025-6993, USA

Dobie, Alan
Pontus Molash
Kent CT4 8HW, ENGLAND

Dobkin, Alix (Musician)
PO Box 761
Woodstock, NY 12498-0761, USA

Dobkin, David (Director)
3630 Eastham Dr
Culver City, CA 90232-2411, USA

Dobkin, Lawrence
1800 Melhill Way
Los Angeles, CA 90049-2205

Dobkins, Carl Jr (Musician)
7640 Cheviot Rd Apt 212
Cincinnati, OH 45247-4011, USA

Dobler, Conrad F (Athlete, Football Player)
6227 W 126th Ter
Leawood, KS 66209-2530, USA

Dobler, David (Religious Leader)
100 Witherspoon St
Louisville, KY 40202-1396, USA

Dobo, Kata (Actor)
c/o Sara Ramaker *Paradigm (LA)*
360 N Crescent Dr
Beverly Hills, CA 90210-4874, USA

Dobrev, Nina (Actor)
c/o Jeffrey Chassen *Baker Winokur Ryder Public Relations BWR (BWR-NY)*
292 Madison Ave Fl 12
New York, NY 10017-6415, USA

Dobslow, Bill (Musician)
945 Handlebar Rd
Mishawaka, IN 46544-6647, USA

Dobson, Chuck (Athlete, Baseball Player)
4208 Locust St
Kansas City, MO 64110-1017, USA

Dobson, Fefe (Musician)
c/o Staff Member *Island Records*
825 8th Ave Rm C2
New York, NY 10019-7472, USA

Dobson, Helen (Athlete, Golfer)
7638 Eagle Creek Dr
Sarasota, FL 34243-4613, USA

Dobson, James C (Religious Leader)
8605 Explorer Dr
Colorado Springs, CO 80920-1049, USA

Dobson, Kevin (Actor)
c/o Dede Binder-Goldsmith *Defining Artists Agency*
10 Universal City Plz Ste 2000
Universal City, CA 91608-1074, USA

Dobson, Peter (Actor)
1351 N Crescent Heights Blvd Apt 318
West Hollywood, CA 90046-4579, USA

Dockery, Derrick (Athlete, Football Player)
7102 Jack Franzen Dr
Garland, TX 75043-6600, USA

Dockery, John (Athlete, Football Player)
360 Furman St Apt 1208
Brooklyn, NY 11201-4579, USA

Dockett, Darnell (Athlete, Football Player)
2197 E Teakwood Pl
Chandler, AZ 85249-3528, USA

Dockson, Robert R (Financier)
Los Angeles, CA 90069, USA

Dockstader, Frederick J (Misc)
165 W 66th St
New York, NY 10023-6508, USA

Docter, Pete (Actor, Director, Writer)
c/o Staff Member *Pixar Animation Studios*
1200 Park Ave
Emeryville, CA 94608-3677, USA

Doctorow, Cory (Internet Star)
Box 306 456-458
Strand, London WC2R0DZ, UNITED KINGDOM

Doctorow, Edgar Lawrence (E L) (Writer)
c/o Ron Bernstein *International Creative Management (ICM-LA)*
10250 Constellation Blvd Fl 7
Los Angeles, CA 90067-6207, USA

Doda, Carol (Actor, Dancer)
PO Box 387
Fremont, CA 94537-0387, USA

Dodd, Deryl (Musician, Songwriter, Writer)
PO Box 186
Waring, TX 78074-0186, USA

Dodd, Jamie (Actor)
c/o Staff Member *Nikki Bond Management*
Aspect Court 47 Park Square East
Leeds LS1 2NL, United Kingdom

Dodd, Maurice (Cartoonist)
Editorial Dept 1 Canada Square
London E14 5AP, UNITED KINGDOM (UK)

Dodd, Michael T (Mike) (Athlete, Volleyball Player)
960 Knox St Bldg A
Torrance, CA 90502-1086, USA

Dodd, Patty D (Athlete, Volleyball Player)
1017 Manhattan Ave
Manhattan Beach, CA 90266-5452, USA

Dodd, Robert (Athlete, Baseball Player)
3467 Overhill Dr
Frisco, TX 75033-1112, USA

Dodd, Tom (Athlete, Baseball Player)
3735 NE Shaver St
Portland, OR 97212-1871, USA

Dodds, Megan (Actor)
c/o Ron West *Thruline Entertainment*
9250 Wilshire Blvd Ground Fl
Beverly Hills, CA 90212, USA

Dodds, Trevor (Athlete, Golfer)
13103 Beaver Dam Rd
Saint Louis, MO 63131-2109, USA

Dodge, Brooks (Skier)
PO Box C
Jackson, NH 03846-0802, USA

Dodge, Dedrick (Athlete, Football Player)
1109 Bowlin Dr
Locust Grove, GA 30248-7079, USA

Dodge, GeaHrey (Publisher)
Time-Life Building
New York, NY 10020, USA

Dodge, Geoffrey (Publisher)
Time-Life Building
New York, NY 10020, USA

Dodge, Julie (Stylist)
c/o Staff Member *Koko Represents*
166 Geary St Ste 1007
San Francisco, CA 94108-5623, USA

Dodge, Kirk (Athlete, Football Player)
110 Roadrunner Ln
Aliso Viejo, CA 92656-1885, USA

Dodrill, Dale (Athlete, Football Player)
2579 S Independence St
Lakewood, CO 80227-2847, USA

Dodson, Pat (Athlete, Baseball Player)
1034 Hillside Rd
Grove, OK 74344-3514, USA

Dodson, Quintin (Reality TV Star)
4571 Haskell Ave
Encino, CA 91436-3131, USA

Dodson, Richard (Athlete, Football Player)
3095 Siena Dr
Bullhead City, AZ 86442-8458, USA

Doe, Cathy Jeneen (Actor)

Doelling, Fred (Athlete, Football Player)
60 South St
Valparaiso, IN 46383-6445, USA

Doerfling, B J (Stylist)
4045 Liberty Canyon Rd
Agoura Hills, CA 91301-3549, USA

Doerger, Jerome (Athlete, Football Player)
8309 Ridgevalley Ct
Cincinnati, OH 45247-3597, USA

Doering, Chris (Athlete, Football Player)
3843 SW 92nd Ter
Gainesville, FL 32608, USA

Doering, Jason (Athlete, Football Player)
228 Westmont St
West Hartford, CT 06117-2907, USA

Doerr, Robert P (Bobby) (Athlete, Baseball Player)
94449 Territorial Hwy
Junction City, OR 97448-9326, USA

Doerre-Heinig, Katrin (Athlete, Track Athlete)
Westring 53
Erbach 6471, GERMANY

Dog Pschology Center (Misc)
PO Box 1130
Canyon Country, CA 91386-1130, USA

Dog Star (Music Group)
1900 Avenue of the Stars # 1040
Los Angeles, CA 90067-4301, USA

Dogg, Snoop (Actor, Artist, Musician)
c/o Brent Smith *WmE2 (Endeavor-LA)*
9601 Wilshire Blvd Fl 3
Beverly Hills, CA 90210-5219, USA

Doggett, Lloyd (Congressman, Politician)
201 Cannon Hob
Washington, DC 20515-4310, USA

Dogins, Kevin (Athlete, Football Player)
PO Box 342621
Tampa, FL 33694-2621, USA

Doherty, John (Athlete, Baseball Player)
202 Alpine Pl
Tuckahoe, NY 10707-3086, USA

Doherty, Peter C (Nobel Prize Laureate)
67 Madison Ave Apt 417
Memphis, TN 38103-6103, USA

Doherty, Shannen (Actor)
c/o Steven Grossman *Collective*
8383 Wilshire Blvd Ste 1050
Beverly Hills, CA 90211-2415, USA

Dohery, Peter C (Nobel Prize Laureate)
172 Kimbrough Pl Apt 506
Memphis, TN 38104-6724, USA

Dohm, Gaby (Actor)
Wiedenmayerstr 11
Munich 80538, GERMANY

Dohmann, Scott (Athlete, Baseball Player)
1142 Oak Harbor Dr
Morgan City, LA 70380-8043, USA

Dohring, Jason (Actor)
c/o Joel Stevens *Joel Stevens Entertainment*
5627 Allott Ave
Van Nuys, CA 91401-4502, USA

Dohrmann, Angela (Actor)
1505 10th St
Santa Monica, CA 90401-2805, USA

Dohrmann, George (Journalist)
345 Cedar St
Saint Paul, MN 55101-1004, USA

Doi, Takako (Government Official)
2-1-2 Nagatacho Chiyodaku
Tokyo, JAPAN

Doi, Takao (Astronaut)
Tsukuba Space Ctr 2-1-2 Sengern
Tukubashi, Ibaraki, JAPAN

Doig, Jason (Athlete, Hockey Player)
2153 Broderick Ave
Duarte, CA 91010-3508, USA

Doig, Lex (Actor)
8651 Eastlake Dr
Vancouver, BC V5A 4T7

Doig, Lexa (Actor)
c/o Adam Levine *Levine Okwu Erickson Management*
9601 Wilshire Blvd Fl 3
Beverly Hills, CA 90210-5219, USA

Doig, Steve (Athlete, Football Player)
PO Box 206
North Reading, MA 01864-0206, USA

Dokish, Wanita (Athlete, Baseball Player)
403 Todd Farm Rd
Belle Vernon, PA 15012-3869, USA

Dokken, Don (Musician)
9200 W Sunset Blvd Ste 900
Los Angeles, CA 90069-3604, USA

Doktor, Martin (Athlete)
Slinecni 627
Sezemice 533 04, CZECH REPUBLIC

Dolan, Don (Actor)
14228 Emelita St
Van Nuys, CA 91401-4208, USA

Dolan, Ellen (Actor)
10 E 44th St
New York, NY 10017-3601, USA

Dolan, Louise A (Physicist)
Physics
Chapel Hill, NC 27599-0001, USA

Dolan, Michael P (Government Official)
1111 Constitution Ave NW
Washington, DC 20224-0001, USA

Dolan, Tom
1 Olympic Plz
Colorado Springs, CO 80909-5780

Dolbin, Jack (Athlete, Football Player)
1775 Howard Ave
Pottsville, PA 17901-3215, USA

Dolby, David C (War Hero)
PO Box 218
Oaks, PA 19456-0218, USA

Dolby, Raymond M (Ray) (Engineer, Inventor)
100 Potrero Ave
San Francisco, CA 94103-4813, USA

Dolby, Thomas (Musician, Songwriter, Writer)
729 7th Ave Ste 1600
New York, NY 10019-6880, USA

Dolce (Musician)
c/o Staff Member *Diva Central Inc*
7510 W Sunset Blvd Ste 1445
Los Angeles, CA 90046-3408, USA

Dolce, Domenico (Designer, Fashion Designer)
Via Santa Cecilia 7
Milan 20122, ITALY

Dolci, Danilo (Activist, Writer)
Largo Scalia 5 Partinico/Palermo
Sicily, ITALY

Dold, R Bruce (Journalist)
501 N Park Rd # Hse
La Grange Park, IL 60526-5516, USA

Dole, Bob (Politician)
950 F St NW Fl 10
Washington, DC 20004-1439, USA

Dole, Elizabeth H (Politician, Secretary)
c/o Staff Member *WmE2 (WMA-LA)*
1 William Morris Pl
Beverly Hills, CA 90212-4261, USA

Dole, Vincent P (Misc, Scientist)
1230 York Ave
New York, NY 10065-6307, USA

Doleac, Michael (Athlete, Basketball Player)
3212 Matilda St Unit 3212
Miami, FL 33133-5136, USA

Doleman, Christopher J (Chris) (Athlete, Football Player)
1025 Leadenhall St
Alpharetta, GA 30022-8491, USA

Dolenz, Ami (Actor)
1860 Bel Air Rd
Los Angeles, CA 90077-2729, USA

Dolenz, Micky (Actor, Musician)
c/o Staff Member *Grant Management*
1158 26th St # 414
Santa Monica, CA 90403-4698, USA

Dolfini, Monica (Stylist)
c/o Staff Member *Camilla Lowther Managment (CLM Represents)*
30-32 Ericsson Pl
New York, NY 10013, USA

D'Oliveira, Luisa (Actor)
c/o Staff Member *Levine Okwu Erickson Management*
6363 Wilshire Blvd Ste 300
Los Angeles, CA 90048-5729, USA

Doll, Donald (Athlete, Football Player)
32001 Via La Plata
San Juan Capistrano, CA 92675-3817, USA

Dollar, Aubrey (Actor)
c/o Rhonda Price *Gersh (NY)*
41 Madison Ave
New York, NY 10010-2202, USA

Dollar, Linda (Coach)
Athletic Dept
Springfield, MO 65804, USA

Dollard, Christopher Edward (Actor)
3500 W Olive Ave Ste 1400
Burbank, CA 91505-5512, USA

Dollas, Bobby (Athlete, Hockey Player)
c/o Staff Member *Contact Image*
185 rue du Seminaire
Montreal, QC H3C 2A3, Canada

Dollens, Ronald (Business Person)
111 Monument Cir
Indianapolis, IN 46204-5100, USA

Dolley, Jason (Actor)
c/o Nils Larsen *Elements Entertainment*
312 W 5th St Apt 815
Los Angeles, CA 90013-1750, USA

Dollfus, Audouin (Astronomer, Physicist)
77 Rue Albert Perdreaux
92370, Chaville 92370, FRANCE

Dolmayan, John (Musician)
9911 W Pico Blvd # 350
Los Angeles, CA 90035-2703, USA

Dologuele, Anicet Georges (Prime Minister)
Bangui, CENTRAL AFRICAN REPUBLIC

Doman, Brandon (Athlete, Football Player)
1923 N 180 W
Pleasant Grove, UT 84062-4117, USA

Doman, John (Actor)
c/o Staff Member *Peter Strain & Associates Inc (LA)*
5455 Wilshire Blvd Ste 1812
Los Angeles, CA 90036-4268, USA

Domar, Evsey D (Economist)
264 Heaths Bridge Rd
Concord, MA 01742-4921, USA

Dombasle, Arielle (Actor)
5 Rue Clemet Marot
Paris 75008, FRANCE

Dombroski, Paul (Athlete, Football Player)
19122 Beckett Dr
Odessa, FL 33556-2274, USA

Dombrowski, Dave (Baseball Player)
345 Woodridge Rd
Bloomfield Hills, MI 48304-3468, USA

Dombrowski, James M (Jim) (Athlete, Football Player)
220 Evangeline Dr
Mandeville, LA 70471-1874, USA

Domenichelli, Hnat (Athlete, Hockey Player)
1500 Mansell Rd
Alpharetta, GA 30009-4709, USA

Domi, Tie (Athlete, Hockey Player)
1-7357 Woodbine Ave Suite 415
Markham, ON L3R 6L3, Canada

Domi, Tim (Athlete, Hockey Player)
46 Florence St
Ottawa, ON K2P 0W7, Canada

Dominczyk, Dagmara (Actor)
c/o Bill Butler *Industry Entertainment Partners*
955 Carrillo Dr Ste 300
Los Angeles, CA 90048-5400, USA

Dominczyk, Marika (Actor)
c/o Sally Ware *Gersh (NY)*
41 Madison Ave
New York, NY 10010-2202, USA

Domingo, Placido (Musician, Opera Singer)
Zaungergasse 1-3 Tur 16
Vienna 1030, AUSTRIA

Dominguez, Fernandez Adolfo (Designer, Fashion Designer)
Polingono Industrial Calle 4
San Ciprian de Vinas, Ourense 32901, SPAIN

Dominguez, Matt (Athlete, Football Player)
4804 Counts Cv
Austin, TX 78749-3755, USA

Dominik, Andrew (Director, Writer)
c/o Spencer Baumgarten *Creative Artists Agency (CAA-LA)*
2000 Avenue of the Stars Ste 100
Los Angeles, CA 90067-4705, USA

Dominique, Andy (Athlete, Baseball Player)
2016 Lamego Way
El Dorado Hills, CA 95762-7557, USA

Dominis, John (Photographer)
16 Jackson St
East Hampton, NY 11937-2617, USA

Domino, Fats (Musician)
9 Wedgwood Ct
Harvey, LA 70058-7473, USA

Dominy, Charles E (Chuck) (General)
300 Fox Mill Rd
Oakton, VA 22124, USA

Domres, Martin F (Marty) (Athlete, Football Player)
1 South St Ste 2400
Baltimore, MD 21202-3348, USA

Donahue, Aichie G (War Hero)
2402 Lazy Lake Dr
Harlingen, TX 78550-8630, USA

Donahue, Archie G (War Hero)
2402 Lazy Lake Dr
Harlingen, TX 78550-8630, USA

Donahue, Deacon (Athlete, Baseball Player)
150 Weiland Rd # 120
Buffalo Grove, IL 60089-7047, USA

Donahue, Debrah E (Stylist)
873 Broadway Ste 302
New York, NY 10003-1232, USA

Donahue, Elinor (Actor)
78533 Sunrise Mountain Vw
Palm Desert, CA 92211-2403, USA

Donahue, Heather (Actor)
118D S Bevedy Dr # 601
Los Aneles, CA 90035, USA

Donahue, Kenneth (Misc)
245 S Westgate Ave
Los Angeles, CA 90049-4205, USA

Donahue, Mitch (Athlete, Football Player)
3907 Palisades Park Dr
Billings, MT 59102-0133, USA

Donahue, Phil (Talk Show Host)
116 Beachside Ave
Westport, CT 06880-6313, USA

Donahue, Terry (Baseball Player)
215 N 3rd Ave
Saint Charles, IL 60174-2005, USA

Donahue, Thomas R (Misc)
815 L6th St NW
Washington, DC 20006, USA

Donald, Kirkland H (Admiral)
7958 Blandy Rd
Norfolk, VA 23551-2405, USA

Donald, Luke (Athlete, Golfer)
14188 Paradise Point Rd
West Palm Beach, FL 33410-1142, USA

Donald, Mike (Athlete, Golfer)
2400 NW 65th Way
Hollywood, FL 33024-4046, USA

Donaldson, Colby (Actor, Reality TV Star)
c/o Nicole David *WmE2 (Endeavor-LA)*
9601 Wilshire Blvd Fl 3
Beverly Hills, CA 90210-5219, USA

Donaldson, Eugene (Athlete, Football Player)
114 Maud St
Clarksburg, WV 26301-3036, USA

Donaldson, Holly (Stylist)
c/o Staff Member *Team*
423 W Broadway Ste 406
Boston, MA 02127-2265, USA

Donaldson, James (Athlete, Basketball Player)
5601 Natomas Blvd Apt 6104
Sacramento, CA 95835-2261, USA

Donaldson, Jeff (Athlete, Football Player)
4529 Stover St
Fort Collins, CO 80525-3261, USA

Donaldson, John (Athlete, Football Player)
3913 Yates Ct
Charlotte, NC 28215-3955, USA

Donaldson, John (Athlete, Baseball Player)
3913 Yates Ct
Charlotte, NC 28215-3955, USA

Donaldson, Ray (Athlete, Football Player)
3128 Crestwell Dr
Indianapolis, IN 46268-8655, USA

Donaldson, Roger (Director, Producer, Writer)
c/o Martin Spencer *Creative Artists Agency (CAA-LA)*
2000 Avenue of the Stars Ste 100
Los Angeles, CA 90067-4705, USA

Donaldson, Samuel (Sam) (Correspondent)
1125 Crest Ln
McLean, VA 22101-1805, USA

Donaldson, Simon K (Mathematician)
Mathematics Dept
Bristol BS8 1TH, UNITED KINGDOM (UK)

Donan, Holland R (Athlete, Football Player)
212 Valley Vw
Pompton Plains, NJ 07444-2166, USA

Donat, Peter (Actor)
PO Box 441
Wolfville, NS B0P 1X0, CANADA

Donatelli, Clark (Athlete, Hockey Player)
1101 Curtis Corner Rd
Wakefield, RI 02879-1470, USA

Donatelli, Don (Athlete, Football Player)
54846 Seneca Lake Rd
Quaker City, OH 43773-9659, USA

Donath, Helen (Opera Singer)
Bergstr 5
Wedemark 30900, GERMANY

Donato, Ted (Athlete, Hockey Player)
41 Grasshopper Ln
Scituate, MA 02066-1622, USA

Donckers, William (Athlete, Football Player)
8054 S 116th St
Seattle, WA 98178-3842, USA

Done, Kenneth S (Ken) (Artist, Misc)
28 Hopetoun Ave
Mosman, NSW 2088, AUSTRALIA

Donegan, Dan (Musician)
c/o Staff Member *Mitch Schneider Organization, The*
14724 Ventura Blvd Ste 410
Sherman Oaks, CA 91403-3537, USA

Donella, Chad E (Actor)
c/o Staff Member *TalentWorks (LA)*
3500 W Olive Ave Ste 1400
Burbank, CA 91505-5512, USA

Donelly, Tanya (Music Group, Songwriter, Writer)
Plaza 535 Kings Road
London SW10 0S, UNITED KINGDOM (UK)

Donen, Stanley (Director)
c/o Staff Member *La Grange Group, The*
11828 La Grange Ave
Los Angeles, CA 90025-5212, USA

Dong Ghua, Li
rue des O'Euches 10
Moutier 1 CP 359 274, SWITZERLAND

Doniger, Wendy (Historian, Misc)
1319 E 55th St
Chicago, IL 60615-5301, USA

Donlan, Yolande (Actor)
11 Mellina Place
London NW8, UNITED KINGDOM (UK)

Donleavy, James Patrick (J P) (Writer)
Levington Park Mullingar
County Westmeath, IRELAND

Donley, Doug (Athlete, Football Player)
8005 Pullam Cir
Plano, TX 75024-6849, USA

Donlon, Roger H C (War Hero)
2101 Wilson Ave
Leavenworth, KS 66048-4634, USA

Donnahoo, Roger (Athlete, Football Player)
20 Rock Brook Cv
Rossville, GA 30741-5355, USA

Donnalley, Kevin (Athlete, Football Player)
8910 Dove Stand Ln
Charlotte, NC 28226-2671, USA

Donnalley, Rick (Athlete, Football Player)
1796 Danforth Dr
Marietta, GA 30062-5544, USA

Donnan, Jim (Coach, Football Coach)
Athletic
Athens, GA 30602-0001, USA

Donnellan, Declan (Director)
Aveline St
London SW11 5DQ, UNITED KINGDOM (UK)

Donnelley, James R (Business Person)
77 W Wacker Dr
Chicago, IL 60601-1604, USA

Donnelly, Andrew (Actor)
c/o Ruthanne Secunda *United Talent Agency (UTA)*
9560 Wilshire Blvd Fl 5
Beverly Hills, CA 90212-2400, USA

Donnelly, Brendan (Athlete, Baseball Player)
2815 E Arrowhead Trl
Gilbert, AZ 85297-5270, USA

Donnelly, Declan (Actor, Television Host)
c/o Staff Member *Rabbit Vocal Management*
27 Poland St 3rd Floor
London W1F 8QW, UK

Donnelly, George (Athlete, Football Player)
2S530 Beechwood Rd
Glen Ellyn, IL 60137-6955, USA

Donnelly, Gord (Athlete, Coach, Hockey Player)
c/o Staff Member *Hockey Montreal International*
4612 Royal Ave
Montreal, QC H4A 2M8, Canada

Donnelly, Joe
1530 Longworth Hob
Washington, DC 20515-0601, USA

Donnelly, Mike (Athlete, Hockey Player)
18429 Stoneridge Ct
Northville, MI 48168-8571, USA

Donnelly, Rick (Athlete, Football Player)
10408 Buck Brush Rd
Cheyenne, WY 82009-8830, USA

Donnelly, Russell J (Physicist)
2175 Olive St
Eugene, OR 97405-2837, USA

Donnels, Chris (Athlete, Baseball Player)
5 Stone Pne
Aliso Viejo, CA 92656-2131, USA

Donner, Jom J (Director)
Pohjoisranta 12
Helsinki 17 170, FINLAND

Donner, Jorn
Pohjoisranta 12
Helsinki SF-00170, FINLAND

Donner, Lauren Shuler (Producer)
c/o Staff Member *Donners' Company, The*
9465 Wilshire Blvd Ste 420
Beverly Hills, CA 90212-2603, USA

Donner, Richard (Director)
c/o Jim Wiatt *WmE2 (Endeavor-LA)*
9601 Wilshire Blvd Fl 3
Beverly Hills, CA 90210-5219, USA

Donnovan, Elisa (Actor)
8730 W Sunset Blvd Ste 440
Los Angeles, CA 90069-2277, USA

D'Onofrio, Mark (Athlete, Football Player)
295 Harmon Ave
Fort Lee, NJ 07024-4446, USA

D'Onofrio, Vincent (Actor, Producer)
c/o Sam Maydew *Collective*
8383 Wilshire Blvd Ste 1050
Beverly Hills, CA 90211-2415, USA

Donohoe, Amanda (Actor)
Julian House 4 Windmill Street
London W1P 1HF, UNITED KINGDOM (UK)

Donohoe, Michael (Athlete, Football Player)
1110 E Acacia Cir
Litchfield Park, AZ 85340-4528, USA

Donohoe, Peter (Music Group, Musician)
82 Hampton Lane Solihull
West Midlands B91 2RS, UNITED KINGDOM (UK)

Donohue, Jim (Athlete, Baseball Player)
16 Huntleigh Downs
Saint Louis, MO 63131-3416, USA

Donohue, Leon (Athlete, Football Player)
1904 Bechelli Ln
Redding, CA 96002-0132, USA

Donohue, Terry
11918 Laurelwood Dr
Studio City, CA 91604-3749

Donohue, Timothy (Business Person)
2001 Edmund Halley Dr
Reston, VA 20191-3436, USA

Donohue, Tom (Athlete, Baseball Player)
249 Liberty Ave
Westbury, NY 11590-2135, USA

Donoso, Jose (Writer)
Calceite
Province of Teruel, SPAIN

Donovan (Music Group, Songwriter, Writer)
P O Box 1119
London SW9 9JW, UNITED KINGDOM (UK)

Donovan, Alan B (Educator)
President's Office
Oneonta, NY 13820, USA

Donovan, Anne (Athlete, Basketball Player, Coach)
138 Ridge Rd
Nutley, NJ 07110-2137, USA

Donovan, Billy (Athlete, Basketball Player)
8515 SW 31st Ave
Gainesville, FL 32608-2725, USA

Donovan, Brian (Journalist)
235 Pinelawn Rd
Melville, NY 11747-4226, USA

Donovan, Elisa (Actor)
c/o Staff Member *Seven Summits Pictures & Management*
8906 W Olympic Blvd Ground Floor
Beverly Hills, CA 90211, USA

Donovan, Francis R (Frank) (Admiral)
9216 Dellwood Dr
Vienna, VA 22180-6121, USA

Donovan, Harry (Athlete, Basketball Player)
8303 Bayonet Point Ct Apt C
Fredericksburg, VA 22407-2125, USA

Donovan, Jason S (Actor, Music Group)
PO Box 342
South Yarra, VIC 3141, AUSTRALIA

Donovan, Jeffrey (Actor)
c/o Brad Schenck *Paradigm (LA)*
360 N Crescent Dr
Beverly Hills, CA 90210-4874, USA

Donovan, Landon (Athlete, Soccer Player)
18400 Avalon Blvd Ste 200
Carson, CA 90746-2181, USA

Donovan, Martin (Actor)
c/o Gene Parseghian *Parseghian Planco LLC*
322 8th Ave Ste 601
New York, NY 10001-6715, USA

Donovan, Pat (Athlete, Football Player)
113 S Prairiesmoke Cir
Whitefish, MT 59937-8182, USA

Donovan, Raymond J (Misc, Secretary)
PO Box 430
New Vernon, NJ 07976-0430, USA

Donovan, Shean (Athlete, Hockey Player)
11 Mountain Rd
Lexington, MA 02420-1308, USA

Donovan, Tate (Actor)
c/o David DeCamillo *Gersh (LA)*
9465 Wilshire Blvd Ste 600
Beverly Hills, CA 90212-2612, USA

Donovan Jr, Arthur J (Art) (Athlete, Football Player)
8300 Alston Rd
Towson, MD 21204-1914, USA

Donovan (Leich)
PO Box 106
Rochdale OL16 4HW, ENGLAND

Donowho, Ryan (Actor)
c/o Staff Member *Brookside Artists Management (NY)*
250 W 57th St Ste 2303
New York, NY 10107-2399, USA

Doobie Brothers (Music Group)
c/o Staff Member *Paradigm (Monterey)*
404 W Franklin St
Monterey, CA 93940-2303, USA

Doocy, Steve (Television Host)
c/o Staff Member *Fox News Channel (NY)*
1211 Ave Of The Americas Level C1
New York, NY 10036-8701, USA

Doody, Alison (Actor)
46 Albermarle St
London W1X 4PP, UNITED KINGDOM (UK)

Doolan, Wendy (Athlete, Golfer)
3353 Turnberry Dr
Lakeland, FL 33803-5460, USA

Dooley, Jim (Athlete, Football Player)
1350 N Western Ave Apt 212
Lake Forest, IL 60045-1264, USA

Dooley, Paul (Actor)
c/o Marcia Hurwitz *Innovative Artists (LA)*
1505 10th St
Santa Monica, CA 90401-2805, USA

Dooley, Taylor (Actor)
c/o Heather Reynolds *One Entertainment (NY)*
12 W 57th St PH 1
New York, NY 10019-3900, USA

Dooley, Thomas (Athlete, Soccer Player)
20 Via Paquete
San Clemente, CA 92673-6915, USA

Dooley, Vince
PO Box 1472
Athens, GA 30603-1472

Dooley, Vincent J (Vince) (Athlete, Coach, Football Coach, Football Player)
PO Box 1472
Athens, GA 30603-1472, USA

Dooling, Keyon (Basketball Player)
Staples Center 1111 S Figueroa St
Los Angeles, CA 90015, USA

Doolittle, Eliza (Musician)
c/o James Whitting *Coda Music Agency - UK*
229 Shoreditch High St
London E1 6PJ, UK

Doolittle, Melinda (Musician, Reality TV Star)

Doom, Ryan (Actor)
c/o Katie Rhodes *Untitled Entertainment (LA)*
350 S Beverly Dr Ste 200
Beverly Hills, CA 90212-4819, USA

Doornink, Dan (Athlete, Football Player)
402 S 12th Ave
Yakima, WA 98902-3115, USA

Dopazo, Cecilia (Actor)
c/o Staff Member *Telefe - Argentina*
Pavon 2444 (C1248AAT)
Buenos Aires, ARGENTINA

Dope, Edsel (Musician)
c/o Bob Ringe *Survival Management*
30765 Pacific Coast Hwy Ste 325
Malibu, CA 90265-3643, USA

Dopson, John (Athlete, Baseball Player)
3337 Old Gamber Rd
Finksburg, MD 21048-2223, USA

Doran, Bill (Athlete, Baseball Player)
5720 Grand Legacy Dr
Maineville, OH 45039-7757, USA

Doran, Walter F (Admiral)
Chairman Joint Chiefs of Staff Pentagon
Washington, DC 20318-0001, USA

Dorazio, Joyce (Stylist)
c/o Staff Member *Ennis*
119 Braintree St
Boston, MA 02134-1628, USA

Dore, Andre (Athlete, Hockey Player)
73 Betsys Ln
New Canaan, CT 06840-5202, USA

Dore, Daniel (Athlete, Hockey Player)
c/o Staff Member *Boston Bruins*
TD Banknorth Garden 100 Legends Way, Suite 250
Boston, MA 2114, USA

Dore, Jimmy (Comedian)
c/o Staff Member *OmniPop Talent Group*
10700 Ventura Blvd Fl 2
Studio City, CA 91604-3561, USA

Dore, Patricia (Actor)
36 Rue de Ponthieu
Paris 75008, FRANCE

Dore, Ronald Philip (Educator)
157 Surrenden Road Brighton
East Sussex BN1 6ZA, UNITED KINGDOM (UK)

Dorensky, Sergey L (Music Group, Musician)
Bryusov Per 8/10 #75
Moscow 103009, RUSSIA

Dorey, Jim (Athlete, Hockey Player)
105 Aaron Pl
Amherstview, ON K7N 2A1, Canada

Dorff, Stephen (Actor)
c/o David Unger *International Creative Management (ICM-LA)*
10250 Constellation Blvd Fl 7
Los Angeles, CA 90067-6207, USA

Dorfman, Ariel (Writer)
International Studies Center 2122 Campus Dr
Durham, NC 27706, USA

Dorfman, Dan (Correspondent, Misc)
51 W 52nd St
New York, NY 10019-6119, USA

Dorfman, David (Actor)
c/o Wendi Green *Paradigm (LA)*
360 N Crescent Dr
Beverly Hills, CA 90210-4874, USA

Dorfmeister, Michaela (Skier)
Quellensteig
Neusiedl 2763, AUSTRIA

Dorin, Francoise (Actor, Writer)
20 Ave Rapp
Paris 75007, FRANCE

Dorio, Gabriella (Athlete, Track Athlete)
Viale Tialano 70
Rome 196, ITALY

Dorion, Dan (Athlete, Hockey Player)
PO Box 445
Chester, NY 10918-0445, USA

Dority, Douglas R (Misc)
1775 K St NW
Washington, DC 20006-1228, USA

Dorman, Lee (Music Group, Musician)
6400 Pleasant Park Dr
Chanhassen, MN 55317-8804, USA

Dormann, Dana (Athlete, Golfer)
4887 Arlene Pl
Pleasanton, CA 94566-7824, USA

Dormer, Natalie (Actor)
c/o Staff Member *Artists Rights Group (ARG)*
4 Great Portland St
London W1W 8PA, UNITED KINGDOM (UK)

Dorn, Michael (Actor)
c/o Ryan Saul *Metropolitan (MTA)*
4526 Wilshire Blvd
Los Angeles, CA 90010-3801, USA

Dornbrook, Thom (Athlete, Football Player)
5918 Emerald Lakes Dr
Medina, OH 44256-7464, USA

Dorney, Keith R (Athlete, Football Player)
2450 Blucher Valley Rd
Sebastopol, CA 95472-5355, USA

Dornhoefer, Gary (Athlete, Hockey Player)
267 Chestnut Neck Rd
Port Republic, NJ 08241-9701, USA

Doro & Warlock
Postfach 87 21
Dusseldorf D-40086, GERMANY

Dorohoy, Ed (Athlete, Hockey Player)
70 Chown Pl
Victoria, BC V9A 1H5, Canada

Doronina, Tatyana (Actor)
22 Tverskoi Blvd
Moscow 119146, RUSSIA

Dorough, Howie (Musician)
P.O. Box 11069
Palm Day, FL 32911, USA

Dorow, Al (Athlete, Football Player)
1640 Bliss St
Haslett, MI 48840-8273, USA

Dorrell, Karl (Coach, Football Coach)
Athletic Dept
Los Angeles, CA 90024, USA

Dorris, Andrew (Athlete, Football Player)
RR 22 Box 549
Conroe, TX 77303, USA

Dorris, Derek (Athlete, Football Player)
4504 Adobe Dr
Fort Worth, TX 76123-1825, USA

Dorroh, Jefferson D (War Hero)
10032 136th Ave NE
Kirkland, WA 98033-5215, USA

D'Orsay, Brooke (Actor)
c/o Chris Fenton *H2F Entertainment*
644 N Cherokee Ave
Los Angeles, CA 90004-1009, USA

Dorsch, Travis (Athlete, Football Player)
301 Highland Dr
West Lafayette, IN 47906-2405, USA

Dorsen, Norman (Attorney, Attorney General, General)
40 Washington Sq S
New York, NY 10012-1005, USA

Dorsett, Brian (Athlete, Baseball Player)
700 Dobbs Glen St
Terre Haute, IN 47803-2480, USA

Dorsett, Tony (Athlete, Football Player)
5990 Haley Way
Frisco, TX 75034-4878, USA

Dorsett Jr, Anthony (Athlete, Football Player)
3817 Bowser Ave Apt C
Dallas, TX 75219-4385, USA

Dorsey, Christopher (BG) (Musician)
c/o Staff Member *Sosincere Entertainment*
2054 Nostrand Ave Apt 4F
Brooklyn, NY 11210-2526, USA

Dorsey, Eric (Athlete, Football Player)
5 London Ct
Teaneck, NJ 07666-6461, USA

Dorsey, Jacky (Athlete, Basketball Player)
1231 S Teal Estates Cir
Fresno, TX 77545-8652, USA

Dorsey, Jim (Athlete, Baseball Player)
335 Elm St
Seekonk, MA 02771-1724, USA

Dorsey, John (Athlete, Football Player)
425 Arrowhead Dr
Green Bay, WI 54301-2635, USA

Dorsey, Ken (Athlete, Football Player)
7108 Presidio Gln
Lakewood Ranch, FL 34202-5038, USA

Dorsey, Kerris (Actor)
c/o DebraLynn Findon *Discover Inc Management*
11425 Moorpark St
Studio City, CA 91602-2009, USA

Dorsey, Nate (Athlete, Football Player)
6935 Silver Run Dr Apt 202
Tampa, FL 33617-9088, USA

Dorsey, Ron (Athlete, Basketball Player)
3925 Mallard Way
Cumming, GA 30028-4862, USA

Dorsey Brothers Orchestra (Music Group, Musician)
PO Box 643176
Vero Beach, FL 32964-3176, USA

Dorta, Melvin (Athlete, Baseball Player)
1351 Cambridge Ct
Palmyra, PA 17078-9351, USA

Dos Santos, Alexandre J M Cardinal (Religious Leader)
Paco Arquiepiscopal Avenida Eduardo Mondlane
CP Maputo 1448, MOZAMBIQUE

dos Santos Leite, Ricardo Izecson (Kaka) (Athlete, Soccer Player)
c/o Staff Member *Real Madrid*
Avenida De Concha Espina, 1 Estadio Santiago Bernabéu
Madrid 28036, Spain

Doshi, Balkkrishna V (Architect)
Sangath Thaltej Road
Ahmedbad, GJ 380 054, INDIA

Dosien, Mila (Stylist)
c/o Staff Member *Maximum Talent*
1873 S Bellaire St Ste 915
Denver, CO 80222-4356, USA

Doss, Desmond T (War Hero)
372 Valley Creek Rd
Piedmont, AL 36272-7969, USA

Doss, Murphy (Actor)
52 Hospital Road Saidapet
Chennai, TN 600 015, INDIA

Dossey, M.D., Larry (Doctor, Writer)
c/o Author Mail *Bantam-Dell Publishing (NY)*
1745 Broadway
New York, NY 10019-4368, USA

Doster, David (Athlete, Baseball Player)
4123 Sugarhill Run
New Haven, IN 46774-2736, USA

Dosunmu, Andrew (Stylist)
c/o Staff Member *Art Department*
48 Greene St Fl 4
New York, NY 10013-2663, USA

Dotolo, Laura (Stylist)
c/o Staff Member *Art House Management*
1548 16th St
Santa Monica, CA 90404-3309, USA

Dotrice, Roy (Actor)
6 Meadow Lane Leasingham Sleaford
Lincolnshire NG34 8LL, UNITED KINGDOM (UK)

Dotson, Al (Athlete, Football Player)
Coyues 24 Las Playas
Acapulco 39390, Mexico

Dotson, Dewayne (Athlete, Football Player)
PO Box 425
White House, TN 37188-0425, USA

Dotson, Earl (Athlete, Football Player)
1112 Azalea Dr
Longview, TX 75601-3214, USA

Dotson, Richard E (Rich) (Athlete, Baseball Player)
7 Colonel Watson Dr
New Richmond, OH 45157-9002, USA

Dotson, Santana (Athlete, Football Player)
PO Box 79134
Houston, TX 77279-9134, USA

Dotter, Bobby (Race Car Driver)
118 Stutt Rd
Mooresville, NC 28117, USA

Dottley, John (Athlete, Football Player)
PO Box 88
Vicksburg, MS 39181-0088, USA

Doty, Paul M (Biologist, Misc)
130 Mount Auburn St Apt 411
Cambridge, MA 02138-5773, USA

Douaihy, Saliba (Artist)
Vining Road
Windham, NY 12496, USA

Doubleday, Nelson (Baseball Player)
84 Gomez Rd
Hobe Sound, FL 33455-2330, USA

Doucet, Michael (Music Group, Musician)
PO Box 170429
San Francisco, CA 94117-0429, USA

Doucett, Linda (Actor, Model)
c/o Caron Feldman *Feldman Management*
21781 Ventura Blvd
Woodland Hills, CA 91364-1835, USA

Doug, Doug E (Musician)
4024 Radford Ave # 3
Studio City, CA 91604-2101, USA

Dougan, Angel Serafin Seriche (Prime Minister)
Malabo, EQUATORIAL GUINEA

Doughboys (Musician)
Box 5559 Station B
Montreal, QC PQ H3P 4P1, Canada

Dougherty, Dennis A (Misc)
1817 Bushnell Ave
South Pasadena, CA 91030-4905, USA

Dougherty, Ed (Athlete, Golfer)
448 SW Fairway Vis
Port Saint Lucie, FL 34986-2131, USA

Dougherty, Jim (Athlete, Baseball Player)
102 Pinnacle Ct
Kitty Hawk, NC 27949-5911, USA

Dougherty, Joseph (Joe) (Director, Producer, Writer)
c/o Ken Freimann *WmE2 (WMA-LA)*
1 William Morris Pl
Beverly Hills, CA 90212-4261, USA

DOugherty, RObert (Scientist)
864 Flint Rdg
Newport, KY 41076-7112, USA

Dougherty, William A Jr (Admiral)
1505 N Colonial Ct
Arlington, VA 22209-1439, USA

Doughty, Glenn (Athlete, Football Player)
8808 Saint Charles Rock Rd
Saint Louis, MO 63114-4340, USA

Doughty, Kenny (Actor)
c/o Alan Siegel *Alan Siegel Entertainment*
345 N Maple Dr Ste 375
Beverly Hills, CA 90210-5174, USA

Douglas, Aaron (Actor)
c/o Russ Mortensen *Pacific Artists Management*
1285 W Broadway Suite 685
Vancouver, BC V6H 3X8, Canada

Douglas, Anslem (Composer, Entertainer)
2833 Church Ave
Brooklyn, NY 11226-4168, USA

Douglas, Barry (Music Group, Musician)
40 W 57th St
New York, NY 10019-4001, USA

Douglas, Bobby (Coach, Wrestler)
Athletic
Ames, IA 50011-0001, USA

Douglas, Carl (Attorney)
6611 Shenandoah Ave
Los Angeles, CA 90056-2115, USA

Douglas, Carol (Music Group)
250 W 57th St
New York, NY 10107-0001, USA

Douglas, Cathleen (Lawyer)
815 Connecticut Ave NW
Washington, DC 20006-4045, USA

Douglas, Charles (Whammy) (Athlete, Baseball Player)
1711 Catherines Lake Rd
Jacksonville, NC 28540-8755, USA

Douglas, David (Athlete, Football Player)
610 Tennessee St
Spring City, TN 37381-5412, USA

Douglas, Denzil L (Prime Minister)
Government Building
Basseterre, SAINT KITTS & NEVIS

Douglas, Diana (Actor)
c/o Staff Member *Bauman Redanty & Shaul Agency*
5757 Wilshire Blvd Suite 473
Beverly Hills, CA 90212, USA

Douglas, Donna (Actor)
c/o Staff Member *Scott Stander & Associates*
4533 Van Nuys Blvd Ste 401
Sherman Oaks, CA 91403-2950, USA

Douglas, Hugh (Athlete, Football Player)
1 Alltel Stadium Pl
Jacksonville, FL 32202-1917, USA

Douglas, Ileana (Actor)
c/o Staff Member *Baumgarten Management*
406 Wilshire Blvd
Santa Monica, CA 90401-1410, USA

Douglas, Illeana (Actor, Director, Producer)
c/o Geoff Cheddy *Brillstein Entertainment Partners*
9150 Wilshire Blvd Ste 350
Beverly Hills, CA 90212-3453, USA

Douglas, James (Buster) (Athlete, Boxer)
PO Box 342
Johnstown, OH 43031-0342, USA

Douglas, Jay (Athlete, Football Player)
2909 Laurel Cherry Way
The Woodlands, TX 77380-4004, USA

Douglas, Jerry (Actor)
562 Cricketfield Ct
Lake Sherwood, CA 91361-5154, USA

Douglas, John (Athlete, Football Player)
13330 West Rd Apt 1318
Houston, TX 77041-6290, USA

Douglas, Jordy (Athlete, Hockey Player)
5-2727 Portage Ave
Winnipeg, MB R3J 0R2, Canada

Douglas, Katie (Basketball Player)
Mohegan Sun Arena
Uncasville, CT 6382, USA

Douglas, Kirk (Actor, Producer)
141 El Camino Dr
Beverly Hills, CA 90212-2731, USA

Douglas, Kyan (Stylist, Television Host)
c/o Michael Flutie *MFO*
17 Little 12th St Studio W 333
New York, NY 10014, USA

Douglas, Leon (Athlete, Basketball Player)
PO Box 217
Lake Forest, IL 60045-0217, USA

Douglas, Merrill (Athlete, Football Player)
2185 E 3970 S
Salt Lake City, UT 84124-1754, USA

Douglas, Michael (Actor, Director, Producer)
c/o Allen Burry *Further Films*
100 Universal City Plz Bldg 1320-4G
Universal City, CA 91608-1002, USA

Douglas, Nik (Writer)
c/o Staff Member *Simon & Schuster*
1230 Avenue of the Americas Fl CONC1
New York, NY 10020-1586, USA

Douglas, Santiago (Actor)
c/o Charlton Blackburne *A Management Company*
9107 Wilshire Blvd Ste 650
Beverly Hills, CA 90210-5544, USA

Douglas, Sarah (Actor)
c/o Staff Member *Vic Murray Talent*
185 A Latchmere Rd
London SW11 2JZ, UK

Douglas, Sherman (Athlete, Basketball Player)
1330 West Ave Apt 1107
Miami Beach, FL 33139-0905, USA

Douglass, Bobby (Athlete, Football Player)
151 E Laurel Ave Apt 203
Lake Forest, IL 60045-1296, USA

Douglass, Dale (Athlete, Golfer)
6601 E San Miguel Ave
Paradise Valley, AZ 85253-5983, USA

Douglass, Maurice (Athlete, Football Player)
1021 Sunset Dr
Englewood, OH 45322-2252, USA

Douglass, Michael R (Mike) (Athlete, Football Player)
1725 Porterfield Pl
El Cajon, CA 92019-4122, USA

Douglass, Robyn (Actor)
407 S Dearborn St Ste 1675
Chicago, IL 60605-1144, USA

Douglass, Sean (Athlete, Baseball Player)
43956 Johns Ct
Lancaster, CA 93536-8213, USA

Doumit, Ryan (Athlete, Baseball Player)
5232 Ridgeview Dr Loop NE
Moses Lake, WA 98837-8519, USA

Doumit, Sam (Actor)
c/o Staff Member *Baker Winokur Ryder Public Relations (BWR-LA)*
9100 Wilshire Blvd Ste 500 PMB WEST
Beverly Hills, CA 90212-3426, USA

Dourda, Abu Zaid Umar (Prime Minister)
Bab el Aziziya Barracks
Tripoli, LIBYA

Dourdan, Gary (Actor)
c/o Steven Siebert *Lighthouse Entertainment*
9220 W Sunset Blvd Ste 200
West Hollywood, CA 90069-3501, USA

Dourif, Brad (Actor)
c/o Stephen (Steve) LaManna *Innovative Artists (LA)*
1505 10th St
Santa Monica, CA 90401-2805, USA

Douris, Peter (Athlete, Hockey Player)
PO Box 488
York Beach, ME 03910-0488, USA

Douse, Joseph (Athlete, Baseball Player)
16722 Fenmore St
Detroit, MI 48235-3423, USA

Douthitt, Earl (Athlete, Football Player)
8100 Central Ave Apt 211
Cleveland, OH 44104-2173, USA

Dove, Dennis (Athlete, Baseball Player)
144 Kirk Ln
Ocilla, GA 31774-3725, USA

Dove, Eddie (Athlete, Football Player)
1750 Poppy Ave
Menlo Park, CA 94025-5738, USA

Dove, Rita F (Writer)
1757 Lambs Rd
Charlottesville, VA 22901-8911, USA

Dove, Ronnie (Music Group)
c/o Staff Member *Time Machine*
2109 S Wilbur Ave
Walla Walla, WA 99362-9048, USA

Doves (Music Group)
c/o Staff Member *Paradigm (Monterey)*
404 W Franklin St
Monterey, CA 93940-2303, USA

Dovolani, Tony (Choreographer, Dancer)
c/o Tej Bhatia Herring *Rogers & Cowan PR (LA)*
Pacific Design Center 8687 Melrose Ave, 7th Floor
West Hollywood, CA 90069, USA

Dow, Ellen Albertini (Actor)
c/o Juliet Green *Juliet Green Management*
9025 Wilshire Blvd Ste 400
Beverly Hills, CA 90211-1828, USA

Dow, Harley (Athlete, Football Player)
13428 the Sq
Poway, CA 92064-1309, USA

Dow, Peggy (Actor)
2121 S Yorktown Ave
Tulsa, OK 74114-1426, USA

Dow, Tony (Actor)
c/o David Moss *David Moss Company, The*
733 Seward St PH
Los Angeles, CA 90038-3503, USA

Dowd, Jim (Athlete, Hockey Player)
708 New Jersey Ave
Point Pleasant Beach, NJ 08742-2970, USA

Dowd, Maureen (Editor)
c/o Staff Member *The New York Times Company*
229 W 43rd St
New York, NY 10036-3913, USA

Dowdell, Marcus (Athlete, Football Player)
4117 Chateau Blvd Apt A
Kenner, LA 70065-5729, USA

Dowdle, Walter R (Biologist, Misc)
1708 Mason Mill Rd NE
Atlanta, GA 30329-4129, USA

Dowdy, Adam (Athlete, Baseball Player)
3862 S Sage Ct
Chandler, AZ 85248-4137, USA

Dowdy, Steven (Misc, Scientist)
Washington Univesity
Saint Louis, MO 63110, USA

Dowell, Anthony J (Ballerina)
c/o Staff Member *Royal Ballet*
Covent Garden Bow St
London WC2E 9DD, UK

Dowell, Ken (Athlete, Baseball Player)
5221 Helen Way
Sacramento, CA 95822-2868, USA

Dower, John W (Writer)
History Dept
Cambridge, MA 2139, USA

Dowhower, Rod (Athlete, Football Coach, Football Player)
5 Fairway Ct
Dahlonega, GA 30533-7167, USA

Dowle, David (Music Group, Musician)
27A Floral St #300
London WC2E 9DQ, UNITED KINGDOM (UK)

Dowler, Boyd H (Athlete, Football Player)
5309 Creek Heights Dr
Midlothian, VA 23112-6224, USA

Dowling, Brian (Athlete, Football Player)
114 Arboretum Way
Burlington, MA 01803-3827, USA

Dowling, Dave (Athlete, Baseball Player)
2925 Granville Dr
Sparks, NV 89436-7644, USA

Dowling, John E (Biologist, Misc)
135 Charles St
Boston, MA 02114-3275, USA

Dowling, Robert J (Editor, Publisher)
5055 Wilshire Blvd
Los Angeles, CA 90036-6100, USA

Dowling, Timothy (Actor)
c/o Staff Member *WmE2 (Endeavor-LA)*
9601 Wilshire Blvd Fl 3
Beverly Hills, CA 90210-5219, USA

Dowling, Vincent (Director, Writer)
322 E River Rd
Huntington, MA 01050-9645, USA

Down, Lesley-Anne (Actor)
5664 Cahuenga Blvd # 231
North Hollywood, CA 91601-2103, USA

Down, Sarah (Cartoonist)
680 N Lake Shore Dr
Chicago, IL 60611-4546, USA

Downes, Edward (Opera Singer)
Covent Garden
London WC2E 9DD, UNITED KINGDOM (UK)

Downes, Robin Atkin (Actor)
c/o Staff Member *Gordon Agency*
260 S Beverly Dr Ste 308
Beverly Hills, CA 90212-3814, USA

Downey, Bill (Athlete, Basketball Player)
1035 S Moorings Dr
Arlington Heights, IL 60005-3217, USA

Downey, James (Writer)
c/o Staff Member *3 Arts Entertainment Inc*
9460 Wilshire Blvd Fl 7
Beverly Hills, CA 90212-2713, USA

Downey, Jim (Writer)
c/o Staff Member *3 Arts Entertainment Inc*
9460 Wilshire Blvd Fl 7
Beverly Hills, CA 90212-2713, USA

Downey, Robert J (Director)
55 W 900 S
Salt Lake City, UT 84101-2931, USA

Downey, Roma (Actor)
c/o Staff Member *Gersh (LA)*
9465 Wilshire Blvd Ste 600
Beverly Hills, CA 90212-2612, USA

Downey Jr, Robert (Actor)
c/o Alan Nierob *Rogers & Cowan PR (LA)*
Pacific Design Center 8687 Melrose Ave, 7th Floor
West Hollywood, CA 90069, USA

Downie, Leonard Jr (Editor)
1150 15th St NW
Washington, DC 20071-0001, USA

Downing, Alphonso E (Al) (Athlete, Baseball Player)
25343 Silver Aspen Way Apt 735
Valencia, CA 91381-0698, USA

Downing, Brian J (Athlete, Baseball Player)
8095 County Road 135
Celina, TX 75009-2539, USA

Downing, George (Misc, Yachtsman)
3021 Waialae Ave
Honolulu, HI 96816-1505, USA

Downing, Kathryn (Publisher)
2821 Main St
Santa Monica, CA 90405, USA

Downing, Sara (Actor)
c/o Steven Siebert *Lighthouse Entertainment*
9220 W Sunset Blvd Ste 200
West Hollywood, CA 90069-3501, USA

Downing, Walt (Athlete, Football Player)
1141 Durham Cir NW
Massillon, OH 44646-2121, USA

Downs, Dave (Athlete, Baseball Player)
925 E 1050 N
Bountiful, UT 84010-2620, USA

Downs, Gary (Athlete, Football Player)
3953 Balleycastle Ct
Duluth, GA 30097-7368, USA

Downs, Hugh H (Correspondent)
Human Communications Department
Tempe, AZ 85287-0001, USA

Downs, Hugh M (Correspondent, Journalist, Producer)
c/o Rick Hersh *Celebrity Consultants LLC*
3340 Ocean Park Blvd Ste 1030
Santa Monica, CA 90405-3259, USA

Downs, Kelly (Athlete, Baseball Player)
6459 Willow Creek Rd
Morgan, UT 84050-6746, USA

Downs, Lila (Musician)
c/o Bill Traut *Open Door Management*
865 Via De La Paz Ste 365
Pacific Palisades, CA 90272-3618, USA

Downs, Michael (Athlete, Football Player)
1405 Knob Hill Dr
Desoto, TX 75115-5335, USA

Downs, Nicholas (Actor)
c/o Andrew Stawiarski *ADS Management*
269 S Beverly Dr # 441
Beverly Hills, CA 90212-3851, USA

Downs, Robert (Athlete, Football Player)
28024 High Vista Dr
Escondido, CA 92026-7215, USA

Downs, Scott (Athlete, Baseball Player)
6814 Barbrook Rd
Louisville, KY 40258-2668, USA

Dowson, Philip M (Architect)
Piccadilly
London W1V 0DS, UNITED KINGDOM (UK)

Doyen De Montaillou, Jean (Stylist)
c/o Staff Member *Halley Resources*
37 W 20th St Ste 603
New York, NY 10011-3718, USA

Doyle, Allen (Athlete, Golfer)
512 Riverside Dr
Lagrange, GA 30240-9633, USA

Doyle, Brian (Athlete, Baseball Player)
PO Box 9156
Winter Haven, FL 33883-9156, USA

Doyle, Christopher (Cinematographer)
c/o Staff Member *International Creative Management (ICM-LA)*
10250 Constellation Blvd Fl 7
Los Angeles, CA 90067-6207, USA

Doyle, Denny (Athlete, Baseball Player)
PO Box 9156
Winter Haven, FL 33883-9156, USA

Doyle, James H Jr (Admiral)
6200 Oregon Ave NW Apt 420
Washington, DC 20015-1552, USA

Doyle, Jeff (Athlete, Baseball Player)
830 SE Bayshore Cir
Corvallis, OR 97333-3206, USA

Doyle, Patrick (Composer)
18 Rodmarton St
London W1H 3FW, UNITED KINGDOM (UK)

Doyle, Paul (Athlete, Baseball Player)
19361 Brookhurst St Spc 15
Huntington Beach, CA 92646-2949, USA

Doyle, Roddy (Writer)
38A West Road Bromsgrove
Worc B60 2NQ, UNITED KINGDOM (UK)

Doyle & Debbie Show, The (Music Group)
c/o Staff Member *Paradigm (Monterey)*
404 W Franklin St
Monterey, CA 93940-2303, USA

Doyle Kennedy, Maria (Actor)
c/o Ruth Young *United Agents*
12-26 Lexington St
London W1F OLE, UK

Doyle-Childress, Cartha (Baseball Player)
1516 Carowinds Cir
Maryville, TN 37803-7704, USA

Doyne, Cory (Athlete, Baseball Player)
20228 County Line Rd
Lutz, FL 33558-5074, USA

Doyon, Mario (Athlete, Hockey Player)
12530 Windsor Dr
Carmel, IN 46033-3148, USA

Dozier, Buzz (Athlete, Baseball Player)
49 Ashton Ln
South Hadley, MA 01075-2182

Dozier, D J (Athlete, Baseball Player, Football Player)
PO Box 2722
Norfolk, VA 23501-2722, USA

Dozier, James L (General)
2150 Channel Way
North Fort Myers, FL 33917-2514, USA

Dozier, Terry (Athlete, Basketball Player)
521 Sparkleberry Ln
Columbia, SC 29229-8609, USA

Dozier, Tom (Athlete, Baseball Player)
1231 Willow Ave Apt D7
Hercules, CA 94547-1200, USA

Dr Demento (Entertainer)
6102 Pimenta Ave
Lakewood, CA 90712-1042, USA

Dr Dog (Musician)
c/o Staff Member *Paradigm (Monterey)*
404 W Franklin St
Monterey, CA 93940-2303, USA

Dr John (Musician, Songwriter)
c/o Staff Member *Shore Fire Media*
32 Court St Fl 16
Brooklyn, NY 11201-4441, USA

Drabble, Margaret (Writer)
Drury House 34-43 Russell St
London WC2B 5HA, UNITED KINGDOM (UK)

Drabek, Douglas D (Doug) (Athlete, Baseball Player)
15 Ivy Pond Pl
Spring, TX 77381-6326, USA

Drabinsky, Garth H (Producer)
165 Avenue Rd # 600
Toronto, ON M5R 3S4, CANADA

Draffen, Willis (Music Group)
16103 Vista Del Mar Dr
Houston, TX 77083-2309, USA

Draft, Chris (Athlete, Football Player)
970 E Oak St
Anaheim, CA 92805-4138, USA

Draglia, Stacy (Athlete, Track Athlete)
1436 E Lander St
Pocatello, ID 83201-4160, USA

Drago, Billy (Actor)
3800 Barham Blvd Ste 303
Los Angeles, CA 90068-1095, USA

Drago, Richard A (Dick) (Athlete, Baseball Player)
4703 Belle Chase Cir
Tampa, FL 33634-4256, USA

Dragon
122 McEvoy St
Alexandria, NSW 2015, AUSTRALIA

Dragon, Daryl (Musician)
7123 Franktown Rd
Washoe Valley, NV 89704-8531, USA

Drahman, Brian (Athlete, Baseball Player)
46 Mariner Green Dr
Corte Madera, CA 94925-2042, USA

Drahos, Nick (Athlete, Football Player)
3158 State Route 90
Aurora, NY 13026-9741, USA

Drai, Victor (Producer)
10527 Bellagio Rd
Beverly Hills, CA 90210, USA

Draiman, Dave (Musician)
c/o Staff Member *Mitch Schneider Organization, The*
14724 Ventura Blvd Ste 410
Sherman Oaks, CA 91403-3537, USA

Drake (Actor, Musician)
c/o Cortez Bryant *Bryant Management*
555 Washington Ave Ste 240
Miami, FL 33139-6639, USA

Drake, Bebe (Actor)
c/o Staff Member *Baron Entertainment*
13848 Ventura Blvd Ste A
Sherman Oaks, CA 91423-3654

Drake, Betsy (Actor)
10850 Wilshire Blvd Ste 575
Los Angeles, CA 90024-4336, USA

Drake, Dallas (Athlete, Hockey Player)
11472 E Cedar Bay Trl
Traverse City, MI 49684-6841, USA

Drake, Frank D (Astronomer)
Lick Observatory
Santa Cruz, CA 9064, USA

Drake, Jeremy (Astronomer)
Cambridge, MA 2138, USA

Drake, Jerry (Athlete, Football Player)
1893 Colonnade Rd
Cleveland, OH 44112-1567, USA

Drake, Jerry (Athlete, Football Player)
2857 Regal Cir Apt E
Birmingham, AL 35216-4632, USA

Drake, Jessica (Adult Film Star)
c/o Staff Member *Wicked Pictures*
9040 Eton Ave
Canoga Park, CA 91304-1616, USA

Drake, Joe (Athlete, Football Player)
873 University St
San Francisco, CA 94134-1843, USA

Drake, Judith (Actor)
4605 Lankershim Blvd Ste 305
North Hollywood, CA 91602-1875, USA

Drake, Juel D (Misc)
1750 New York Ave NW
Washington, DC 20006-5305, USA

Drake, Larry (Actor)
15260 Ventura Blvd Ste 2100
Sherman Oaks, CA 91403-5360, USA

Drake, Robert (Athlete, Baseball Player)
6046 E Selkirk Cir
Mesa, AZ 85215-7755, USA

Drake, Sammy (Athlete, Baseball Player)
4415 Springdale Dr
Los Angeles, CA 90043-2107, USA

Drake, Solly (Athlete, Baseball Player)
1732 S Corning St
Los Angeles, CA 90035-4302, USA

Drakeford, Tyronne (Athlete, Football Player)
2311 Baron Dekalb Rd
Camden, SC 29020-8224, USA

Drane, Dwight (Athlete, Football Player)
200 NW 107th Ave
Plantation, FL 33324-1700, USA

Dransfeldt, Kelly (Athlete, Baseball Player)
2011 Prairie Rose Dr
Morris, IL 60450-6851, USA

Draper, Charla (Stylist)
5422 S Ingleside Ave
Chicago, IL 60615-5014, USA

Draper, Courtnee
c/o Steve Simon *Landis-Simon Productions Talent Management*
2410 Oakshore Dr
Westlake Village, CA 91361-3416, USA

Draper, E Lynn Jr (Business Person)
1 Riverside Plz
Columbus, OH 43215-2355, USA

Draper, Kris (Athlete, Hockey Player)
3418 Westchester Rd
Bloomfield Hills, MI 48304-2573, USA

Draper, Mike (Athlete, Baseball Player)
18317 Manor Church Rd
Boonsboro, MD 21713-2502, USA

Draper, Polly (Actor)
c/o Staff Member *Innovative Artists (LA)*
1505 10th St
Santa Monica, CA 90401-2805, USA

Draper, Tim (Athlete, Hockey Player)
76 Blackstone Ave
Binghamton, NY 13903-1328, USA

Draper, William H III (Financier)
91 Tallwood Ct
Atherton, CA 94027-6431, USA

Dratch, Rachel (Actor, Comedian)
c/o Tucker Voorhees *Principato/Young Management*
9465 Wilshire Blvd Ste 430
Beverly Hills, CA 90212-2613, USA

Dravecky, David F (Dave) (Athlete, Baseball Player)
19995 Chisholm Trl
Monument, CO 80132-8061, USA

Draven, Jamie (Actor)
c/o Staff Member *Independent Talent Group (ITG-UK)*
Oxford House 76 Oxford St
London W1D 1BS, UK

Draves, Victoria (Vickie) (Athlete, Swimmer)
23842 Shady Tree Cir
Laguna Niguel, CA 92677-1704, USA

Drayton, Charlie (Music Group, Musician)
947 N La Cienega Blvd # 2
Los Angeles, CA 90069-4782, USA

Drayton, Troy (Athlete, Football Player)
601 Ridge St
Steelton, PA 17113-1851, USA

Drdek, John (Writer)
c/o Will Ward *ROAR (LA)*
9701 Wilshire Blvd Fl 8
Beverly Hills, CA 90212-2008, USA

Dream (Music Group)

Dream So Real
PO Box 8061
Athens, GA 30603-8061

Dream Warriors
1505 W 2nd Ave # 200
Vancouver, BC V6H 3Y4, Canada

Dreamstreet (Music Group)
c/o Staff Member *Adonis Productions*
175 Skillman St
Brooklyn, NY 11205-3901, USA

Drechsler, Dave (Athlete, Football Player)
1135 Arabian Farms Rd
Clover, SC 29710-8562, USA

Drechsler, Heike (Athlete, Track Athlete)
Reichenhainer Str 154
Chmnitz 9135, GERMANY

Dreckman, Bruce (Athlete, Baseball Player)
110 N Maple St
Marcus, IA 51035, USA

Drees, Tom (Athlete, Baseball Player)
18638 Bearpath Trl
Eden Prairie, MN 55347-3459, USA

Dreesen, Tom (Actor, Comedian)
14538 Benefit St Unit 301
Sherman Oaks, CA 91403-5507, USA

Dreifort, Darren (Athlete, Baseball Player)
463 Wynola St
Pacific Palisades, CA 90272-4243, USA

Dreifuss, Ruth (President)
Bundeshaus-W Bundesgasse
Beme 3033, SWITZERLAND

Dreilling, Greg (Athlete, Basketball Player)
5952 Willowross Way
Plano, TX 75093-4776, USA

Drell, Persis (Physicist)
Linear Accelerator Center
Stanford, CA 94305, USA

Drell, Sidney D (Physicist)
620 Sand Hill Rd Apt 420D
Palo Alto, CA 94304-2075, USA

Drescher, Fran (Actor)
PO Box 2760
Reston, VA 20195-0760, USA

Drese, Ryan (Athlete, Baseball Player)
311 Oak St Apt 304
Oakland, CA 94607-4605, USA

Dressel, Chris (Athlete, Football Player)
410 Whiskey Hill Rd
Woodside, CA 94062-2571, USA

Dresselhaus, Mildred S (Engineer, Physicist)
1000 Independence Ave SW
Washington, DC 20585-0001, USA

Dressendorfer, Kirk (Athlete, Baseball Player)
1004 Oaklands Dr
Round Rock, TX 78681-4033, USA

Dressler, Doug (Athlete, Football Player)
118 Frostwood Dr
Westwood, CA 96137-9647, USA

Dressler, Rob (Athlete, Baseball Player)
2037 17th Ave
Forest Grove, OR 97116-2709, USA

Drew, B Alvin (Astronaut)
2814 Lighthouse Dr
Houston, TX 77058-4320, USA

Drew, Cameron (Athlete, Baseball Player)
31 Highbridge Rd
Trenton, NJ 08620-9632, USA

Drew, David Jonathan (J D) (Athlete, Baseball Player)
5006 Old US 41 N
Hahira, GA 31632-4405, USA

Drew, Elizabeth H (Publisher)
1350 Avenue of the Americas
New York, NY 10019-4702, USA

Drew, Heather (Athlete, Golfer)
78160 Desert Mountain Cir
Bermuda Dunes, CA 92203-8151, USA

Drew, JD (Athlete, Baseball Player)
c/o Scott Boras *Boras Corporation*
18 Corporate Plaza Dr
Newport Beach, CA 92660-7901, USA

Drew, John (Athlete, Basketball Player)
2303 W Tidwell Rd Apt 3404
Houston, TX 77091-4766, USA

Drew, Larry (Athlete, Basketball Player)
4942 Densmore Ave
Encino, CA 91436-1538, USA

Drew, Sarah (Actor)
c/o Adam Griffin *Kritzer Levine Wilkins Entertainment*
11872 La Grange Ave Fl 1
Los Angeles, CA 90025-5283, USA

Drew, Tim (Athlete, Baseball Player)
5006 Old US 41 N
Hahira, GA 31632-4405, USA

Drew, Urban (War Hero)
451 Neptune Ave
Encinitas, CA 92024-2016, USA

Drewrey, Willie (Athlete, Football Player)
2714 Cheryl Ct
Missouri City, TX 77459-2930, USA

Drexler, Clyde (Basketball Player, Coach)
6442 Coldwater Canyon Ave Ste 206
North Hollywood, CA 91606-1174, USA

Drexler, Clyde (Athlete, Basketball Player)
4045 Piping Rock Ln
Houston, TX 77027-3916, USA

Dreyer, Steve (Athlete, Baseball Player)
6018 Greywood Cir
Johnston, IA 50131-1687, USA

Dreyfus, George (Composer)
3 Grace St
Camberwell, VIC 3124, AUSTRALIA

Dreyfuss, Richard S (Actor, Producer)
PO Box 10459
Burbank, CA 91510-0459, USA

Drickamer, Harry G (Engineer)
1174 Old Racebrook Rd
Woodbridge, CT 06525-1811, USA

Driedger, Florence G (Activist)
3833 Montaigne St
Regina, SK S4S 3J6, CANADA

Drier, David (Congressman, Politician)
233 Cannon Hob
Washington, DC 20515-1308, USA

Driessen, Dan (Athlete, Baseball Player)
97 William Hilton Pkwy
Hilton Head Island, SC 29926-1205, USA

Driest, Burkhard
Alter Militarring 8
Koln 50933, GERMANY

Drinan, Robert F (Educator, Misc)
1507 Isherwood St NE Apt 1
Washington, DC 20002-5564, USA

Drinfeld, Vladimir (Mathematician)
42 Vavilova
ESP-1 Moscow 117966, RUSSIA

Drinkard, Bobby Jon (Reality TV Star)
c/o Staff Member *Mark Burnett Productions*
640 N Sepulveda Blvd
Los Angeles, CA 90049-2108, USA

Drinkwater, Carol (Writer)
c/o Ken McReddie *Ken McReddie Ltd*
11 Connaught Pl
London W2 2ET, UNITED KINGDOM

Drinkwater-Simmons, Maxine (Baseball Player)
18 Belmont Ave
Camden, ME 04843-2028, USA

Driscoll, Edward (Terry) (Athlete, Basketball Player)
PO Box 399
Williamsburg, VA 23187-0399, USA

Driscoll, Jean (Athlete, Motivational Speaker, Olympic Athlete)
8142 Traverse Ct
Montgomery, OH 45242-7224, USA

Driscoll, Jim (Athlete, Baseball Player)
8050 E Indian School Rd
Scottsdale, AZ 85251-2612, USA

Driscoll, John (Actor)
c/o Staff Member *Talented Managers*
65 W 90th St Apt 7G
New York, NY 10024-1509, USA

Driscoll, Peter (Athlete, Hockey Player)
422 N Cypress Dr Apt B
Jupiter, FL 33469-3712, USA

Driskill, Travis (Athlete, Baseball Player)
800 Blue Spring Cir
Round Rock, TX 78681-4047, USA

Driver, Bruce (Athlete, Hockey Player)
21A Crest Ter
Montville, NJ 07045-9370, USA

Driver, Donald (Athlete, Football Player)
1942 Ledgeview Rd
De Pere, WI 54115-9291, USA

Driver, Minnie (Actor)
c/o Jason Weinberg *Untitled Entertainment (LA)*
350 S Beverly Dr Ste 200
Beverly Hills, CA 90212-4819, USA

Driver, William J (Government Official)
215 W Columbia St
Falls Church, VA 22046-3412, USA

D'Rivera, Paquito
2704 Mozart Pl NW
Washington, DC 20009, USA

Drnovsek, Janez (Prime Minister)
Gregorcicova St 20
Ljubljana 61000, SLOVENIA

Drobny, Jaroslav (Actor)
23 Kenilworth Court Lower Richmond Road
London SW15 1EW, United Kingdom

Drogba, Didier (Athlete, Soccer Player)
c/o Staff Member *IMG Artists Worldwide (UK)*
The Light Box 111 Power Road
London W4 5PY, United Kingdom

Drollinger, Ralph (Athlete, Basketball Player)
22831 Market St
Newhall, CA 91321-3605, USA

Dropo, Walter (Walt) (Athlete, Baseball Player)
19 Iverson Rd
Beverly, MA 01915-3717, USA

Drosdick, John G (Business Person)
10 Penn Center 1801 Market St
Philadelphia, PA 19103, USA

Drougas, Tom (Athlete, Football Player)
PO Box 1596
Sun Valley, ID 83353-1596, USA

Droughns, Reuben (Athlete, Football Player)
1405 Huntington St Apt C
Huntingtn Bch, CA 92648-3624, USA

Drouin, Jude (Athlete, Hockey Player)
44479 Maltese Falcon Sq
Ashburn, VA 20147-3886, USA

Droulez, Veronique (Stylist)
c/o Celebrity Stylists *Area 51, Inc.*
104 W 14th St
New York, NY 10011-7329, USA

Drowning Pool (Music Group)
c/o Staff Member *10th Street Entertainment (NY)*
38 W 21st St Rm 300
New York, NY 10010-6979, USA

Drozdov, Darren (Athlete, Football Player)

Drozdova, Margarita S (Ballerina)
Pushkinskaya Str 17
Moscow, RUSSIA

Dru Hill (Music Group)
c/o Staff Member *WmE2 (Endeavor-LA)*
9601 Wilshire Blvd Fl 3
Beverly Hills, CA 90210-5219, USA

Druce, John (Athlete, Hockey Player)
208 Stockton Blvd
Berlin, NJ 08009-7111, USA

Druck, Mirchea (Prime Minister)
Str 31 August 123 #7
Kishinev 277012, MOLDOVA

Druckenmiller, Jim (Athlete, Football Player)
2351 E Aragon Blvd Unit 6
Sunrise, FL 33313-8045, USA

Drucker, Eugene (Music Group, Musician)
3 Burlington Lane Chiswick
London W4 2TH, UNITED KINGDOM (UK)

Drucker, Mort (Cartoonist)
250 W 57th St
New York, NY 10107-0001, USA

Drudge, Matt (Journalist)
1425 Brickell Ave Apt 47C
Miami, FL 33131-3402, USA

Druken, Harold (Athlete, Hockey Player)
16 Shaw Dr
Wayland, MA 01778-3214, USA

Druker, Brian J (Misc)
Cancer Research Center
Portland, OR 97201, USA

Drulia, Stan (Athlete, Hockey Player)
3939 Essex Pl
Fort Gratiot, MI 48059-3762, USA

Drulis, Al (Athlete, Football Player)
5105 N Park Dr Apt 823
Pennsauken, NJ 08109-4668, USA

Drummond, Alice (Actor)
351 E 50th St
New York, NY 10022-7975, USA

Drummond, Jonathan (Jon) (Athlete, Track Athlete)
PO Box 982
Arlington, TX 76004-0982, USA

Drummond, Roscoe (Writer)
6637 MacLean Dr Olde Dominion Sq
McLean, VA 22101, USA

Drummond, Ryan (Actor)
c/o Staff Member *Bobby Ball Talent Agency*
4116 W Magnolia Blvd Ste 205
Burbank, CA 91505-2700, USA

Drummond, Tim (Athlete, Baseball Player)
102 Haldane Ct
La Plata, MD 20646-4308, USA

Drumright, Keith (Athlete, Baseball Player)
1333 W Lindberg St
Springfield, MO 65807-2385, USA

Drungo, Elbert (Athlete, Football Player)
216 Lake Chateau Dr
Hermitage, TN 37076-3072, USA

Drury, Chris (Athlete, Hockey Player)
240 Riverside Blvd Apt 10A
New York, NY 10069-1029, USA

Drury, James (Actor)
12126 Osage Park Dr
Houston, TX 77065-3812, USA

Drury, Ted (Athlete, Hockey Player)
2507 Greenwood Ave
Wilmette, IL 60091-1303, USA

Drury, Ted (Athlete, Hockey Player)
28 Cottage Pl
Trumbull, CT 06611-5227, USA

Druschel, Rick (Athlete, Football Player)
724 Cochran Dr
Greensburg, PA 15601-4610, USA

Drut, Guy J (Athlete, Track Athlete)
Maine
Coulommiers 77120, FRANCE

Dry, Tim (Actor)
c/o Staff Member *Coolwaters Productions*
10061 Riverside Dr # 531
Toluca Lake, CA 91602-2560, USA

Dryburgh, Stuart (Cinematographer)
9150 Wilshire Blvd Ste 220
Beverly Hills, CA 90212-3429, USA

Dryden, Dave (Athlete, Hockey Player)
2257 All Saints Cres
Oakville, ON L6J 5N1, Canada

Dryden, Kenneth (Ken) (Athlete, Hockey Player)
335 W Block Attn Minister Of Social Development
Ottawa, ON K1A 0A6, Canada

Dryer, Fred (Athlete, Football Player)
c/o Staff Member *Fred Dryer Productions*
2934 N Beverly Glen Cir Ste 703
Los Angeles, CA 90077-1724

Drynan, Jeanie (Actor)
c/o Staff Member *Essential Talent Management*
6399 Wilshire Blvd Ste 401
Los Angeles, CA 90048-5716, USA

Drysdale, Cliff (Sportscaster, Tennis Player)
1801 Eastwood Rd # F
Wilmington, NC 28403, USA

Drzewiecki, Ron (Athlete, Football Player)
5977 S 34th St
Milwaukee, WI 53221-4725, USA

D'Souza, Lawrence (Bollywood, Director, Filmmaker, Producer)
302B Red Rose New Link Road Versova Andheri
Bombay, MS 400 058, INDIA

DSquared2 (Fashion Designer)
220 W 19th St Fl 11
New York, NY 10011-4035, USA

Du Prez, John (Composer)
c/o Staff Member *WmE2 (Endeavor-LA)*
9601 Wilshire Blvd Fl 3
Beverly Hills, CA 90210-5219, USA

du Tertre, Celine (Actor)
c/o Staff Member *Harvest Talent Management*
124 W 80th St Apt 1
New York, NY 10024-6320, USA

Du Toit, Elize (Actor)
c/o Vanessa Pereira *Artists Independent Management (LA)*
825 Nowita Pl
Venice, CA 90291-3836, USA

Duany, Andres (Architect)
1023 SW 25th Ave
Miami, FL 33135-4824, USA

DuArt, Louise (Religious Leader, Television Host)
c/o Staff Member *Living the Life*
977 Centerville Tpke
Virginia Beach, VA 23463-1001, USA

Duarte, Marci (Stylist)
c/o Staff Member *Team*
423 W Broadway Ste 406
Boston, MA 02127-2265, USA

Dubbels, Britta (Model)
c/o Staff Member *Ford Models (NY)*
238 E 4th St
New York, NY 10009-7425

Dubble, Curtis (Religious Leader)
1451 Dundee Ave
Elgin, IL 60120-1674, USA

Dube, Gilles (Athlete, Hockey Player)
606-800 Rue De Vimy
Sherbrooke, QC J1J 3N7, Canada

Dube, Joseph (Joe) (Athlete, Wrestler)
8821 Eaton Ave
Jacksonville, FL 32211-0306, USA

Dube, Lucky (Musician)
4856 Haygood Rd Ste 200
Virginia Beach, VA 23455-5349, USA

Dube, Norm (Athlete, Hockey Player)
1590 Rue John-Griffith
Sherbrooke, QC J1J 4L4, Canada

Dubenion, Elbert (Athlete, Football Player)
610 E Walnut St
Westerville, OH 43081-2423, USA

Duberman, Justin (Athlete, Hockey Player)
939 W Madison St Ste 605
Chicago, IL 60607-2567, USA

Dubia, John A (General)
10095 Cover Pl
Fairfax, VA 22030-2494, USA

Dubinbaum, Gail (Opera Singer)
Lincoln Center Plaza
New York, NY 10023, USA

Dubinsky, Steve (Athlete, Hockey Player)
939 Central Ave
Highland Park, IL 60035-3249, USA

Dublinski, James L (Athlete, Football Player)
723 S 900 E
Salt Lake City, UT 84102-3605, USA

Dublinski, Tom (Athlete, Football Player)
15918 E El Lago Blvd
Fountain Hills, AZ 85268-3935, USA

Dubois, Allison
PO Box 7497
Phoenix, AZ 85011-7497, USA

Dubois, Brian (Athlete, Baseball Player)
359 E Ridge St
Braidwood, IL 60408-2095, USA

Dubois, Janet (Actor)
c/o Staff Member *Cunningham Escott Slevin & Doherty (CESD-LA)*
10635 Santa Monica Blvd Ste 130
Los Angeles, CA 90025-8306, USA

Dubois, Jason (Athlete, Baseball Player)
2204 Lord Seaton Cir
Virginia Beach, VA 23454-2923, USA

DuBois, Marta (Actor)
5441 E Beverly Blvd Ste G
Los Angeles, CA 90022-2243, USA

Dubois, Phil (Athlete, Football Player)
405 Speedway Ave
Missoula, MT 59802-5475, USA

Dubose, Brian (Baseball Player)
15336 Oakfield St
Detroit, MI 48227-1532, USA

Dubose, Eric (Athlete, Baseball Player)
326 County Road 8
Gilbertown, AL 36908-2211, USA

DuBose, G Thomas (Misc)
14600 Detroit Ave
Cleveland, OH 44107-4207, USA

DuBose, James (Director, Producer)
c/o Toni Thompson *Toni Thompson PR*
Accepts Calls Only
Los Angeles, CA 90001, USA

Dubose, Jimmy (Athlete, Football Player)
11420 Walker Rd
Thonotosassa, FL 33592-3616, USA

Dubzinski, Walt (Athlete, Football Player)
158 Lovewell St
Gardner, MA 01440-3552, USA

Ducasse, Alain (Chef)
Hotel de Paris
Monte Carlo, MONACO

Ducey, Rob (Athlete, Baseball Player)
699 Richmond Close
Tarpon Springs, FL 34688-8423, USA

Duchesnay, Isamelle (Dancer)
Im Steinach 30
Oberstdorf 87561, GERMANY

Duchesnay, Paul (Figure Skater)
Rossbichstr 2-6
Oberstdorf 87561, GERMANY

Duchesne, Steve (Athlete, Hockey Player)
2104 Cedar Elm Ter
Westlake, TX 76262-9025, USA

Duchin, Peter (Music Group, Musician)
60 E 42nd St # 1625
New York, NY 10165-0006, USA

Duchovny, David (Actor, Producer, Writer)
c/o Melanie Greene *Affirmative Entertainment*
425 N Robertson Blvd
West Hollywood, CA 90048-1735, USA

Duchscherer, Justin (Athlete, Baseball Player)
4700 Green Oaks Dr
Colleyville, TX 76034-4765, USA

DuCille, Michel (Journalist, Photographer)
9571 Pine Meadows Ln
Burke, VA 22015-1550, USA

Duckett, Forey (Athlete, Football Player)
7518 Winona Ave N
Seattle, WA 98103-4838, USA

Duckett, Mahlon (Athlete, Baseball Player)
5325 Old York Rd Apt 611
Philadelphia, PA 19141-2952, USA

Duckett, Richard (Athlete, Basketball Player)
22 Cedar St
Westborough, MA 01581-1606, USA

Duckett, TJ (Athlete, Football Player)
c/o Joel Segal *Lagardere Unlimited - NY*
845 United Nations Plz
New York, NY 10017-3540, USA

Ducksworth, Sheila (Producer)
c/o Staff Member *Creative Artists Agency (CAA-LA)*
2000 Avenue of the Stars Ste 100
Los Angeles, CA 90067-4705, USA

Duckworth, Brandon (Athlete, Baseball Player)
4460 W 6095 S
Salt Lake City, UT 84118-5289, USA

Duckworth, Jim (Athlete, Baseball Player)
3736 Ferrero Way
Redding, CA 96001-0180, USA

Duckworth, Tyler (Reality TV Star)
c/o Len Evans *Project Publicity*
312 W 53rd St Ste 202
New York, NY 10019-5743, USA

Ducsmal, Agnieszka
Al Marchinkowskiego 3
Pozna 61-745, POLAND

Duda, Mark (Athlete, Football Player)
1707 Cherry St
Scranton, PA 18505-3972, USA

Dudamel, Gustavo (Conductor)
c/o Jordi Martin Mont *Van Walsum Management*
The Tower Building 11 York Rd
London SE1 7NX, UK

Dudek, Anne (Actor)
c/o Sandra Chang *Industry Entertainment Partners*
955 Carrillo Dr Ste 300
Los Angeles, CA 90048-5400, USA

Dudek, Joseph A (Joe) (Athlete, Football Player)
31 Ryan Rd
Auburn, NH 03032-3341, USA

Dudek, Mitch (Athlete, Football Player)
1241 Forest Ave
Wilmette, IL 60091-1656, USA

Duden, H Richard (Dick) Jr (Athlete, Football Player)
11 Old Station Rd
Severna Park, MD 21146-4618, USA

Duderstadt, James J (Educator, Government Official)
1800 G St NW
Washington, DC 20006-4403, USA

Dudikoff, Michael (Actor)
c/o Ross Brown *Chartwell Ink Management*
7319 Beverly Blvd Ste 10
Los Angeles, CA 90036-2556, USA

Dudley, Brian (Athlete, Football Player)
6319 London Ave
Rancho Cucamonga, CA 91737-3646, USA

Dudley, Charles (Athlete, Basketball Player)
4032 42nd Ave S
Seattle, WA 98118-1121, USA

Dudley, Chris (Athlete, Basketball Player)
1150 Fairway Rd
Lake Oswego, OR 97034-2818, USA

Dudley, Debra
PO Box 40
Bonnieville, KY 42713-0040

Dudley, James (Baseball Player)
607 Delafield Pl NW
Washington, DC 20011-4054, USA

Dudley, Jaquelin (Biologist, Misc)
Microbiology Dept
Austin, TX 78712, USA

Dudley, Rick (Athlete, Coach, Hockey Player, Misc)
5150 Oakhill Dr
Lewiston, NY 14092-1857, USA

Dudley, Rickey (Athlete, Football Player)
4529 Mahogany Ln
Lewisville, TX 75077-8546, USA

Dudley, William M (Bill) (Athlete, Football Player)
303 Barkley Ct
Lynchburg, VA 24503-4222, USA

Duell, Chad (Actor)
c/o Earl Shank *Earl Shank Management*
520 N Kings Rd Apt 316
West Hollywood, CA 90048-6048, USA

Duenkel Fuldner, Virginia (Swimmer)
2132 NE 17th Ter # 500
Wilton Manors, FL 33305-2414, USA

Duerod, Terry (Athlete, Basketball Player)
6542 Chirrewa St
Westland, MI 48185-2807, USA

Duerson, David R (Dave) (Athlete, Football Player)
2605 Kelly Ln
Highland Park, IL 60035-1654, USA

Dues, Hal (Athlete, Baseball Player)
3932 Amanda Dr
Dickinson, TX 77539-6405, USA

Dueto Voces del Rancho (Musician)
c/o Staff Member *Sony Music Miami*
605 Lincoln Rd Ste 700
Miami Beach, FL 33139-2901, USA

Dufek, Don (Athlete, Football Player)
570 S Maple Rd
Ann Arbor, MI 48103-3837, USA

Dufek, Joe (Athlete, Football Player)
17015 N 7th St Ste 1
Phoenix, AZ 85022-2404, USA

Duff, Haylie (Actor, Composer, Musician)
c/o Adam Cunningham *Robert Thorne Co*
9654 Heather Rd
Beverly Hills, CA 90210-1757, USA

Duff, Hilary (Actor, Model, Musician)
c/o Susan Curtis *Curtis Talent Management*
9607 Arby Dr
Beverly Hills, CA 90210-1202, USA

Duff, Jamal (Athlete, Football Player)
PO Box 20058
Long Beach, CA 90801-3058, USA

Duff, John (Athlete, Football Player)
PO Box 20058
Long Beach, CA 90801-3058, USA

Duff, John B (Educator)
President's Office
Chicago, IL 60605, USA

Duff, John E (Artist, Misc)
7 Doyers St
New York, NY 10013-5112, USA

Duff, Matt (Athlete, Baseball Player)
1701 27th St E
Bradenton, FL 34208-7831, USA

Duff, T Richard (Dick) (Athlete, Hockey Player)
4-7 Elmwood Ave S
Mississauga, ON L5G 3J6, Canada

Duffalo, Jim (Athlete, Baseball Player)
1505 Savannah St
Mesquite, TX 75149-8715, USA

Duffell, Peter
29 Roehampton Gate
London, ENGLAND SW15 5JR

Duffie, John (Athlete, Baseball Player)
177 Lakeside Cir
Douglas, GA 31535-6627, USA

Duffield, David (Business Person)
4460 Hacienda Dr
Pleasanton, CA 94588-2761, USA

Duffner, Mark (Coach, Football Coach)
Athletic Dept
College Park, MD 20740, USA

Duffus, Parris (Athlete, Hockey Player)
8609 Timbermill Pl
Fort Wayne, IN 46804-3411, USA

Duffy, Aimee Anne (DUFFY) (Musician)
c/o Staff Member *Island Records*
825 8th Ave Rm C2
New York, NY 10019-7472, USA

Duffy, Brian (Astronaut)
16410 Heather Bend Ct
Houston, TX 77059-5569, USA

Duffy, Brian (Cartoonist, Editor)
PO Box 957
Des Moines, IA 50306-0957, USA

Duffy, Dorothy (Actor)
Drury House 34-43 Russell St
London WC2B 5HA, UNITED KINGDOM (UK)

Duffy, Frank (Athlete, Baseball Player)
1740 E Silver St
Tucson, AZ 85719-3152, USA

Duffy, James (Business Person)
385 Washington St
Saint Paul, MN 55102-1309, USA

Duffy, JC (Cartoonist)
4520 Main St
Kansas City, MO 64111-1876, USA

Duffy, John (Composer)
2112 Broadway
New York, NY 10023-2105, USA

Duffy, Julia (Actor)
5699 Kanan Rd # 285
Agoura, CA 91301-3358, USA

Duffy, Karen (Actor, Model)
c/o Staff Member *Rebel Entertainment Partners*
5700 Wilshire Blvd Ste 456
Los Angeles, CA 90036-3648, USA

Duffy, Keith (Music Group)
Bushy Park Road 57 Meadowgate
Dublin, IRELAND

Duffy, Matthew (DJ)
c/o Len Evans *Project Publicity*
312 W 53rd St Ste 202
New York, NY 10019-5743, USA

Duffy, Patrick (Actor, Director, Producer)
c/o David Brady *Bx2 Management*
1333 2nd St Ste 620
Santa Monica, CA 90401-4111, USA

Duffy, Roger (Athlete, Football Player)
6509 Lutz Ave NW
Massillon, OH 44646-9512, USA

Duffy, Troy (Actor, Director, Writer)
c/o David Krintzman *Morris, Yorn, Barnes, Levine, Krintzman, Rubenstein and Kohner*
2000 Ave Of The Stars 3rd Tower Floor NORTH
Los Angeles, CA 90067, USA

Dufner, Jason (Athlete, Golfer)
1130 University Blvd
Tuscaloosa, AL 35401-0327, USA

Dufour, Luc (Athlete, Hockey Player)
334 Rue Des Champs-Elysees
Chicoutimi, QC G7H 2V8, Canada

Dufresne, Donald (Athlete, Coach, Hockey Player)
c/o Staff Member *Rimouski Oceanic Hockey Club*
CP 816 Succ A
Rimouski, QC G5L 7C9, Canada

Dugan, Dennis (Actor, Director)
11661 San Vicente Blvd Ste 309
Los Angeles, CA 90049-5111, USA

Dugan, Fred (Athlete, Football Player)
1827 Settlers Dr
Nokomis, FL 34275-1462, USA

Dugan, Jeff (Athlete, Football Player)
13701 Ashcroft Rd
Savage, MN 55378-2374, USA

Dugan, Michael J (General, Misc)
733 3rd Ave
New York, NY 10017-3204, USA

Dugans, Ron (Athlete, Football Player)
1549 Coleman St
Tallahassee, FL 32310-6016, USA

Duggan, Catherine (Athlete, Golfer)
5923 Marilyn Dr
Knoxville, TN 37914-5149, USA

Duggan, Jim (Athlete, Wrestler)
1328 Hornsby Cir
Lugoff, SC 29078-9722, USA

Duggan, Jim (Athlete, Football Player)
1328 Hornsby Cir
Lugoff, SC 29078-9722, USA

Duggar, Michelle (Reality TV Star)
548 Arbor Acres Ave
Springdale, AR 72762-6256, USA

Dugger, John S (Artist)
410 Evelyn Ave Apt 201
Albany, CA 94706-1358, USA

Dugiud, Matthew (Stylist)
c/o Staff Member *Exclusive Artists Mgmt*
7700 W Sunset Blvd Ste 205
Los Angeles, CA 90046-3913, USA

Duguary, Ron (Actor, Athlete, Hockey Player)
982 Ponte Vedra Blvd
Ponte Vedra Beach, FL 32082-4068, USA

Duhamel, Josh (Actor)
c/o John Carrabino *John Carrabino Management*
5900 Wilshire Blvd Ste 406
Los Angeles, CA 90036-5015, USA

Duhart, Paul (Athlete, Football Player)
5 San Jose Dr
Palm Coast, FL 32137-2335, USA

Duhe, Adam J (A J) Jr (Athlete, Football Player)
379 Coconut Cir
Weston, FL 33326-3320, USA

Duhe, John M Jr (Judge)
556 Jefferson St
Lafayette, LA 70501-6950, USA

Duhon, Josh (Actor)
c/o Abby Bluestone *Innovative Artists (LA)*
1505 10th St
Santa Monica, CA 90401-2805, USA

Duhon, Robert (Bobby) (Athlete, Football Player)
4384 Whitewater Creek Rd NW
Atlanta, GA 30327-3958, USA

Duich, Steve (Athlete, Football Player)
PO Box 2
Descanso, CA 91916-0002, USA

Dujardin, Jean (Actor)
c/o Bryna Rifkin *ID PR (LA)*
7060 Hollywood Blvd Fl 8
Los Angeles, CA 90028-6014, USA

Dukakis, Kitty
85 Perry St
Brookline, MA 02446-6935

Dukakis, Michael (Ex-Governor)
Dept. Of Political Science 303 Meserve Hall
Boston, MA 2115, USA

Dukakis, Olympia (Actor)
c/o Gene Parseghian *Parseghian Planco LLC*
322 8th Ave Ste 601
New York, NY 10001-6715, USA

Duke, Annie (Poker Player)
c/o Glen Clarkson *Synergy Management*
22287 Mulholland Hwy Ste 204
Calabasas, CA 91302-5157, USA

Duke, Bill (Director)
7510 W Sunset Blvd # 523
Los Angeles, CA 90046-3408, USA

Duke, Charles
PO Box 310345
New Braunfels, TX 78131-0345

Duke, Charles M Jr (Astronaut, General)
280 Lakeview Blvd
New Braunfels, TX 78130-5200, USA

Duke, Clark (Actor)
c/o Andy Corren *Andy Corren Management*
1545 26th St Ste 200
Santa Monica, CA 90404-3554, USA

Duke, George (Musician)
c/o Staff Member *Associated Booking Corp*
PO Box 2055
New York, NY 10021-0051, USA

Duke, Ken (Athlete, Golfer)
3612 SW Rivers End Way
Palm City, FL 34990-7606, USA

Duke, Norm (Bowler)
10836 Country Road 561A
Clermont, FL 34711, USA

Duke, Patty (Actor)
c/o Mitchell Stubbs *Mitchell K Stubbs & Assoc (MKS)*
8675 Washington Blvd Ste 203
Culver City, CA 90232-7486, USA

Duke, Paul (Athlete, Football Player)
3833 Randall Ridge Rd NW
Atlanta, GA 30327-3105, USA

Duke, Robin (Actor)
c/o Staff Member *Oscars Abrams Zimel & Associates*
438 Queen St. E
Toronto ON M5A 1T4, Canada

Duke, Zach (Athlete, Baseball Player)
2517 County Road 4240
Clifton, TX 76634-5056, USA

Duke Special
c/o Staff Member *Paradigm (Monterey)*
404 W Franklin St
Monterey, CA 93940-2303, USA

Duke Spirit, The (Music Group)
c/o Staff Member *Paradigm (Monterey)*
404 W Franklin St
Monterey, CA 93940-2303, USA

Dukes, Elijah (Athlete, Baseball Player)
1927 Blue Rock Dr Apt 103
Tampa, FL 33612-5252, USA

Dukes, Jamie (Athlete, Football Player)
2553 Northern Oak Dr
Braselton, GA 30517-6059, USA

Dukes, Jan (Athlete, Baseball Player)
959 Helena Dr
Sunnyvale, CA 94087-4126, USA

Dukes, Michael (Athlete, Football Player)
115 N 23rd St
Nederland, TX 77627-5909, USA

Dukes, The (Music Group)
11 Chartfield Sq
London, England SW15, United Kingdom

Dukes, Tom (Athlete, Baseball Player)
325 Monte Vista Rd
Arcadia, CA 91007-6147, USA

Dukes of Dixieland, The
PO Box 56757
New Orleans, LA 70156-6757

Dukochitz, Jonathan (Actor, Musician)
c/o Staff Member *Innovative Artists (LA)*
1505 10th St
Santa Monica, CA 90401-2805, USA

Dulany, Caitlin (Actor)
232 N Canon Dr
Beverly Hills, CA 90210-5302, USA

Dulbecco, Renato (Nobel Prize Laureate)
7525 Hillside Dr
La Jolla, CA 92037-3941, USA

Duley, Ed (Athlete, Football Player)
5219 N Casa Blanca Dr
Paradise Valley, AZ 85253-6201, USA

Dulgan, John (Director)
54A Tite St
London SW3 4JA, UNITED KINGDOM (UK)

Dulhalde, Eduardo (President)
Balcarce 50
Buenos Aires 1064, ARGENTINA

Duliba, Bob (Athlete, Baseball Player)
327 Philadelphia Ave
West Pittston, PA 18643-2146, USA

Dullea, Keir (Actor)
c/o Staff Member *Bret Adams Agency*
448 W 44th St
New York, NY 10036-5220, USA

Dulles, Avery R Cardinal (Misc)
Jesuit Community
Bronx, NY 10458, USA

Dulli, Greg (Music Group)
48 Laight St
New York, NY 10013-2156, USA

Dumars III, Joe (Athlete, Basketball Player)
3499 Franklin Rd
Bloomfield Hills, MI 48302-0960, USA

Dumas, Marlene (Artist)
Tolstraat 94 HS
Amsterdam 1073 BE, The Netherlands

Dumas, Michel (Athlete, Hockey Player)
c/o Staff Member *Chicago Blackhawks*
1901 W Madison St
Chicago, IL 60612-2459, USA

Dumas, Mike (Athlete, Football Player)
6735 Alden Nash Ave SE
Alto, MI 49302-8969, USA

Dumas, Tony (Athlete, Basketball Player)
674 Jay Ct
San Marcos, CA 92069-7393, USA

Dumatrait, Phil (Athlete, Baseball Player)
1412 Stub Oak Ave
Bakersfield, CA 93307-6917, USA

Dumbauld, Jonathan (Athlete, Football Player)
PO Box 728
Canadian, TX 79014-0728, USA

Dumervil, Elvis (Athlete, Football Player)
6115 Trailhead Rd
Highlands Ranch, CO 80130-5328, USA

Dumler, Doug (Athlete, Football Player)
1526 Peterson St
Fort Collins, CO 80524-4130, USA

Dummar, Melvin
Dummar's Restaurant
Gabbs, NV 89409

Dummett, Michael A E (Misc)
54 Park Town
Oxford OX2 6SJ, UNITED KINGDOM (UK)

Dumont, J P (Athlete, Hockey Player)
1512 Kimberleigh Ct
Franklin, TN 37069-7226, USA

Dumont, Sky (Actor)
Leopoldstr 19
Munich 80802, GERMANY

Dumont, Tom (Music Group, Musician)
31652 2nd Ave
Laguna Beach, CA 92651-8244, USA

Dumoulin, Dan (Athlete, Baseball Player)
202 Nancy Dr
Kokomo, IN 46901-5907, USA

Dunagin, Ralph (Cartoonist)
235 E 45th St
New York, NY 10017-3305, USA

Dunaway, Craig (Athlete, Football Player)
1000 Westchester Way
Birmingham, MI 48009-2954, USA

Dunaway, Faye (Actor)
c/o Ben Press *Don Buchwald & Associates Inc (LA)*
8619 Washington Blvd
Culver City, CA 90232-7441, USA

Dunaway, James E (Athlete, Football Player)
170 Mount Carmel Church Rd
Sandy Hook, MS 39478-9793, USA

Dunbar, Bonnie J (Astronaut)
2200 Todville Rd
Seabrook, TX 77586-3005, USA

Dunbar, Dale (Athlete, Hockey Player)
41 Nahant Ave
Winthrop, MA 02152-1514, USA

Dunbar, Huey (Musician)
c/o Staff Member *Sony Music Miami*
605 Lincoln Rd Ste 700
Miami Beach, FL 33139-2901, USA

Dunbar, Matt (Athlete, Baseball Player)
6328 County Donegal Ct
Charlotte, NC 28277-9652, USA

Dunbar, Rockmond (Actor)
c/o Lisa Sorensen *LSPR*
116 W 23rd St Fl 5
New York, NY 10011-2599, USA

Dunbar, Tom (Tommy) (Athlete, Baseball Player)
558 Palm Dr S
Aiken, SC 29803-5450, USA

Dunbar, Vaughn (Athlete, Football Player)
1085 Greatwood Mnr
Alpharetta, GA 30005-7459, USA

Duncan, Andy (Basketball Player)
608 Berry Pi
Marion, VA 24354-4168, USA

Duncan, Angus (Actor)
28035 Dorothy Dr Ste 210A
Agoura, CA 91301-2685, USA

Duncan, Arthur (Dancer)
PO Box 276005
Boca Raton, FL 33427-6005, USA

Duncan, Brian (Athlete, Football Player)
739 Elm St
Graham, TX 76450-3018, USA

Duncan, Charles K (Admiral)
813 1st St
Coronado, CA 92118-1301, USA

Duncan, Charles W Jr (Secretary)
9 Briarwood Ct
Houston, TX 77019-5801, USA

Duncan, Chris (Athlete, Baseball Player)
6547 N Turnberry Dr
Tucson, AZ 85718-2600, USA

Duncan, Cleveland (Cleve) (Music Group)
24210 E East Fork Rd Spc 9
Azusa, CA 91702-6249, USA

Duncan, Courtney (Athlete, Baseball Player)
121 Adalene Ln
Madison, AL 35757-8423, USA

Duncan, Curtis (Athlete, Football Player)
4915 Glen Hollow St
Sugar Land, TX 77479-3804, USA

Duncan, Dan (Business Person)
1100 Louisiana St
Houston, TX 77002-5246, USA

Duncan, Dave (Athlete, Baseball Player)
PO Box 36925
Tucson, AZ 85740-6925, USA

Duncan, David Douglas (Journalist, Photographer)
Castellaras Mouans-Sartoux 6370, FRANCE

Duncan, Dennis (Athlete, Baseball Player)
7650 N Zack Rd
Columbia, MO 65202-9240, USA

Duncan, Iain (Athlete, Hockey Player)
453 Cedarwood Rd
Avon Lake, OH 44012-3141, USA

Duncan, Jamie (Athlete, Football Player)
217 Remi Dr
New Castle, DE 19720-5624, USA

Duncan, Jeff (Athlete, Baseball Player)
825 Lincoln Ln
Frankfort, IL 60423-1087, USA

Duncan, Jeff (Congressman, Politician)
116 Cannon Hob
Washington, DC 20515-0913, USA

Duncan, Ken (Athlete, Football Player)
4 Christina Ave
Camarillo, CA 93012-8102, USA

Duncan, Leslie (Speedy) (Athlete, Football Player)
1607 Porter Way
Stockton, CA 95207-4126, USA

Duncan, Lindsay (Actor)
91 Regent St
London W1R 7TB, UNITED KINGDOM (UK)

Duncan, Mariano (Athlete, Baseball Player)
Ingenio Angelina #137
San Pedro de Macoris, Dominican Republic

Duncan, Melvin (Athlete, Baseball Player)
PO Box 980407
Ypsilanti, MI 48198-0407, USA

Duncan, Meredith (Athlete, Golfer)
244 Arthur Ave
Shreveport, LA 71105-3626, USA

Duncan, Michael Clarke (Actor)
c/o Staff Member *Crosby/Spilo Management*
1310 N Spaulding Ave
Los Angeles, CA 90046-4010, USA

Duncan, Mike (Race Car Driver)
PO Box 21235
Bakersfield, CA 93390-1235, USA

Duncan, Patrick S (Director, Producer, Writer)
c/o David Kanter *Anonymous Content (AC-LA)*
3531 Hayden Ave
Culver City, CA 90232, USA

Duncan, Robert (Astronomer, Misc, Physicist)
Astronomy Dept
Austin, TX 78712, USA

Duncan, Sandy (Actor)
c/o Jim Wilhelm *Douglas Gorman Rothacker & Wilhelm Inc*
1501 Broadway Ste 703
New York, NY 10036-5501, USA

Duncan, Speedy (Athlete, Football Player)
1607 Porter Way
Stockton, CA 95207-4126, USA

Duncan, Tim (Athlete, Basketball Player)
13215 Vista Del Mundo
San Antonio, TX 78216-2250, USA

Duncan, Todd (Motivational Speaker, Writer)
3760 Peachtree Crest Dr Ste A
Duluth, GA 30097-8624, USa

Duncanson, Craig (Athlete, Hockey Player)
935 Ramsey Lake Dr Attn Hockey Program
Sudbury, ON P3E 2C6, Canada

Dundas, Jason (Reality TV Star)
PO Box 128
Surry Hills NSW 2010, AUSTRALIA

Dundas, Rocky (Athlete, Hockey Player)
14 Nantucket Dr
Richmond Hill, ON L4E 3V1, Canada

Dundee, Angelo (Boxer)
5060 Pinnacle Dr
Oldsmar, FL 34677-1926, USA

Dunderstadt, James (Educator)
President's Office
Ann Arbor, MI 48109, USA

Dunegan, Jim (Athlete, Baseball Player)
20246 180th St
New London, IA 52645-8555, USA

Dungey, Merrin (Actor)
c/o Dan Spilo *Industry Entertainment Partners*
955 Carrillo Dr Ste 300
Los Angeles, CA 90048-5400, USA

Dungy, Tony (Athlete, Coach, Football Coach, Football Player)
16604 Villalenda De Avila
Tampa, FL 33613-5200, USA

Dunham, Archie W (Business Person)
600 N Dairy Ashford St
Houston, TX 77079-1100, USA

Dunham, Chip (Cartoonist)
4520 Main St
Kansas City, MO 64111-1876, USA

Dunham, Duane R (Business Person)
1170 8th Ave
Bethlehem, PA 18018-2255, USA

Dunham, Jeff (Comedian)
c/o Staff Member *Levity Entertainment Group*
6701 Center Dr W Ste 1111
Los Angeles, CA 90045-1552, USA

Dunham, John L (Business Person)
611 Olive St
Saint Louis, MO 63101-1711, USA

Dunham, Michael (Mike) (Athlete, Hockey Player)
39 Garfield Rd
Concord, MA 01742-4930, USA

Dunham, Stephen (Actor)
c/o Karen Forman *Domain Talent*
9229 W Sunset Blvd Ste 710
Los Angeles, CA 90069-3407, USA

Dunitz, Jack D (Misc)
Obere Heslibachstr 77
Kusnacht 8700, SWITZERLAND

Dunkie, Nancy (Basketball Player)
Campus Police
Berkeley, CA 94720-0001, USA

Dunkle, Nancy (Athlete, Basketball Player, Olympic Athlete)
1350 Lorawood St
La Habra, CA 90631-7405, USA

Dunlap, Alexander W (Astronaut)
721 Parkside Dr
Woodstock, GA 30188-6057, USA

Dunlap, Carla (Gymnast, Misc)
732 Irvington Ave
Maplewood, NJ 07040-1610, USA

Dunlap, Grant (Athlete, Baseball Player)
1431 Alga Ct
Vista, CA 92081-5016, USA

Dunlap, Page (Athlete, Golfer)
8728 Misty Creek Dr
Sarasota, FL 34241-9561, USA

Dunlap, Robert H (War Hero)
1335 E Broadway
Monmouth, IL 61462-1980, USA

Dunlap, Scott (Athlete, Golfer)
104 Summerour Vale
Duluth, GA 30097-2464, USA

Dunlea, Jennifer (Stylist)
c/o Staff Member *Team*
423 W Broadway Ste 406
Boston, MA 02127-2265, USA

Dunleavy, Mary (Opera Singer)
c/o Staff Member *Columbia Artists Mgmt Inc*
1790 Broadway Fl 6
New York, NY 10019-1537, USA

Dunleavy, Michael J (Mike) (Athlete, Basketball Player, Coach)
127 S Carmelina Ave
Los Angeles, CA 90049-3901, USA

Dunleavy, Mike (Basketball Player)
1001 Broadway
Oakland, CA 94607-4019, USA

Dunleavy Jr, Mike (Athlete, Basketball Player)
127 S Carmelina Ave
Los Angeles, CA 90049-3901, USA

Dunleavy Sr, Mike (Athlete, Basketball Player, Coach)
c/o Warren LeGarie *Warren LeGarie Sports Management*
1108 Masonic Ave
San Francisco, CA 94117-2915, USA

Dunlop, Andy (Music Group, Musician)
21 Heathmans Road
London SW6 4TJ, UNITED KINGDOM (UK)

Dunlop, Blake (Athlete, Hockey Player)
8112 Maryland Ave
Saint Louis, MO 63105-3700, USA

Dunn, Adam (Athlete, Baseball Player)
PO Box 803
Carrollton, KY 41008-0803, USA

Dunn, Andrew W (Cinematographer)
525 Broadway Ste 250
Santa Monica, CA 90401-2419, USA

Dunn, Annie (Stylist)
c/o Staff Member *The Milton Agency (LA)*
6715 Hollywood Blvd Ste 204
Los Angeles, CA 90028-4656, USA

Dunn, Colton (Actor)
c/o Joel Zadak *Principato/Young Management*
9465 Wilshire Blvd Ste 430
Beverly Hills, CA 90212-2613, USA

Dunn, Dave (Athlete, Hockey Player)
1433 Hamilton St
Regina, SK S4R 7V4, Canada

Dunn, Douglas (Writer)
c/o Staff Member *The Rights House (UK)*
Drury House 34-43 Russell St
London WC2B 5HA, UK

Dunn, Gary (Athlete, Football Player)
243 Navajo St
Tavernier, FL 33070-2119, USA

Dunn, Gertie (Baseball Player)
PO Box 88
Chadds Ford, PA 19317-0088, USA

Dunn, Gregory (Publisher)
224 W 57th St
New York, NY 10019-3212, USA

Dunn, Halbert L (Mathematician)
3637 Edelmar Ter
Silver Spring, MD 20906-1765, USA

Dunn, Holly (Actor, Musician)
PO Box 2525
Hendersonville, TN 37077-2525, USA

Dunn, Keldrick (K.D.) (Athlete, Football Player)
1640 Township Ter
McDonough, GA 30252-6813, USA

Dunn, Kevin (Actor)
c/o Steven Siebert *Lighthouse Entertainment*
9220 W Sunset Blvd Ste 200
West Hollywood, CA 90069-3501, USA

Dunn, Mignon (Opera Singer)
5626 N Deer Run Rd
Doylestown, PA 18902-1912, USA

Dunn, Moira (Athlete, Golfer)
15803 Bridgewater Ln
Tampa, FL 33624-1044, USA

Dunn, Nora (Actor, Comedian)
c/o Steven Siebert *Lighthouse Entertainment*
9220 W Sunset Blvd Ste 200
West Hollywood, CA 90069-3501, USA

Dunn, Patricia (Tricia) (Athlete, Hockey Player)
5 Twin Brook Dr
Derry, NH 03038-4358, USA

Dunn, Perry Lee (Athlete, Football Player)
64 Glenway Pl
Brandon, MS 39042-2545, USA

Dunn, Richie (Athlete, Hockey Player)
12229 Clarence Center Rd
Akron, NY 14001-9334, USA

Dunn, Ron (Athlete, Baseball Player)
1161 Husted Ave
San Jose, CA 95125-3633, USA

Dunn, Ronnie (Musician, Songwriter)
PO Box 120669
Nashville, TN 37212-0669, USA

Dunn, Sarah Jayne (Actor)
c/o Michael Ford 3-6 Kenrick Place
London W1U 6HD, UNITED KINGDOM

Dunn, Scott (Athlete, Baseball Player)
1331 Arizona Ash St
San Antonio, TX 78232-3409, USA

Dunn, Shannon (Stylist)
c/o Staff Member *Zenobia Agency Inc*
PO Box 909
Groveland, CA 95321-0909, USA

Dunn, Steve (Athlete, Baseball Player)
484 Broadmoor Dr
Maryville, TN 37803-6575, USA

Dunn, Susan (Opera Singer)
1212 Lancaster Dr
Champaign, IL 61821-7002, USA

Dunn, T R (Athlete, Basketball Player)
1014 19th St SW
Birmingham, AL 35211-3623, USA

Dunn, Todd (Athlete, Baseball Player)
12030 London Lake Dr W
Jacksonville, FL 32258-3317, USA

Dunn, Warrick (Athlete, Football Player)
6016 Beacon Shores St
Tampa, FL 33616-1317, USA

Dunne, Griffin (Actor, Director)
c/o Geyer Kosinski *Media Talent Group*
9200 W Sunset Blvd Ste 550
Los Angeles, CA 90069-3611, USA

Dunne, Mike (Athlete, Baseball Player)
5115 W Ancient Oak Dr
Peoria, IL 61615-2247, USA

Dunne, Robin (Actor)
c/o Chris Fenton *H2F Entertainment*
644 N Cherokee Ave
Los Angeles, CA 90004-1009, USA

Dunne, Roisin (Music Group, Musician)
PO Box 310780
Jamaica, NY 11431-0780, USA

Dunnigan, Frank J (Publisher)
1500 Palisade Ave
Fort Lee, NJ 07024-5337, USA

Dunnigan, T Kevin (Business Person)
8155 Thomas & Betts Blvd
Memphis, TN 38125, USA

Dunning, Debbe (Actor, Model)
c/o Brian McCabe *Venture IAB*
8285 W Sunset Blvd Ste 1
West Hollywood, CA 90046-2420, USA

Dunning, Steve (Athlete, Baseball Player)
35 Prairie
Irvine, CA 92618-8840, USA

Dunphry, Jessica (Actor)
c/o Staff Member *Station3*
1051 Cole Ave
Los Angeles, CA 90038-2601, USA

Dunphy, Jessica (Actor)

Dunphy, Marv (Athlete, Coach, Volleyball Player)
33370 Decker School Rd
Malibu, CA 90265-2344, USA

Dunphy, T J Dermot (Business Person)
Park 80 Plaza E
Saddle Park, NJ 7663, USA

Dunsmore, Barrie (Correspondent)
5010 Creston St
Hyattsville, MD 20781-1216, USA

Dunst, Kirsten (Actor)
c/o Eric Kranzler *Management 360*
9111 Wilshire Blvd
Beverly Hills, CA 90210-5508, USA

Dunst, Kristen (Actor)
8916 Ashcroft Ave
West Hollywood, CA 90048-2404, USA

Dunstan, William (Athlete, Football Player)
PO Box 514
Rancho Mirage, CA 92270-0514, USA

Dunston, Shawon D (Athlete, Baseball Player)
957 Corte Del Sol
Fremont, CA 94539-4925, USA

Dunton, Gary C (Financier)
113 King St
Armonk, NY 10504-1611, USA

Dunwoody, Catherine (Stylist)
c/o Staff Member *Celestine - CA*
1666 20th St Ste 200B
Santa Monica, CA 90404-3828, USA

Dunwoody, Richard (Jockey, Race Car Driver)
14 Saint Maur Road Fulham
London SW6 4DP, UNITED KINGDOM (UK)

Dunwoody, Todd (Athlete, Baseball Player)
1704 King Eider Dr
West Lafayette, IN 47906-6504, USA

Dunye, Cheryl (Actor, Director, Producer, Writer)
c/o Staff Member *Broder Webb Chervin Silbermann Agency, The (BWCS)*
10250 Constellation Blvd
Los Angeles, CA 90067-6200, USA

Dupard, Reggie (Athlete, Football Player)
1316 Green Hills Ct
Duncanville, TX 75137-2842, USA

Duper, Mark (Athlete, Football Player)
1905 Banks Rd
Margate, FL 33063-7713, USA

Dupere, Denis (Athlete, Hockey Player)
185 Weber St S
Waterloo, ON N2J 2B1, Canada

Duplan, Mane (Stylist)
c/o Celebrity Stylist *Frame Representatives*
275 West St
New York, NY 10013, USA

DuPlessis, Christian (Opera Singer)
1 Hinde St
London W1M 5RH, UNITED KINGDOM (UK)

Dupont, Andre (Athlete, Hockey Player)
905 Rue Guilbert
Trois-Rivieres, QC G8T 5V5, Canada

Dupont, Claire (Stylist)
c/o Staff Member *Leyla Basakinci Inc*
681 Lexington Ave Fl 5
New York, NY 10022-2625, USA

Dupont, Jacques (Politician)
Boite Postale 522
Monaco-Cedex 98015, MONACO

Dupont, Jerry (Athlete, Hockey Player)
216 Rosemar Gdns
Richmond Hill, ON L4C 3Z9, Canada

DuPont, Margaret Osborne (Tennis Player)
415 Camino Real Ave
El Paso, TX 79922-2003, USA

Dupont, Norman (Athlete, Hockey Player)
3289 Rue Alfred-De Musset
Laval, QC H7P 0A7, Canada

DuPont, Pierre (Ex-Governor)
601 Pennsylvania Ave NW Ste NW
Washington, DC 20004-2601, USA

DuPont, Pierre S IV (Ex-Governor)
601 Pennsylvania Ave NW Ste NW
Washington, DC 20004-2601, USA

Dupont, Tiffany (Actor)
c/o Leonard Torgan *Collective*
8383 Wilshire Blvd Ste 1050
Beverly Hills, CA 90211-2415, USA

Dupre, Ashley Alexandra (Model)
c/o David Kokakis *The Foundry Media Group*
99 Macdougal St Apt 1
New York, NY 10012-5032, USA

Dupre, Isabel (Stylist)
c/o Staff Member *Bryan Bantry*
900 Broadway Ste 400
New York, NY 10003-1239, USA

Dupree, Billy Joe (Athlete, Football Player)
2512 Springhill Dr
Dallas, TX 75228-4109, USA

Dupree, Donald (Don) (Athlete)
3 Center St
Saranac Lake, NY 12983, USA

Dupree, Marcus (Athlete, Football Player)
274 Davis St
Philadelphia, MS 39350-3431, USA

Dupree, Mike (Athlete, Baseball Player)
2358 E Richmond Ave
Fresno, CA 93720-0438, USA

Dupree, Myron (Athlete, Football Player)
1553 Tadlock Ave
Rocky Mount, NC 27801-3035, USA

Dupri, Jermaine (Musician)
c/o Staff Member *Simon & Schuster*
1230 Avenue of the Americas Fl CONC1
New York, NY 10020-1586, USA

Dupuis, Bob (Athlete, Hockey Player)
446 Algonquin Ave
North Bay, ON P1B 4W5, Canada

Dupuis, Roy (Actor)
3451 Hotel De Ville Montreal
Quebec, Canada H2X 3B5

Duque, Bernardo (Musician)
c/o Gabriel Blanco *Gabriel Blanco Iglesias (Mexico)*
Rio Balsas 35-32 Colonia Cuauhtemoc
DF 6500, Mexico

Duque, Pedro (Astronaut)
1103 Virginia St
South Houston, TX 77587-3945, USA

Durack, David T (Physicist)
815 W Knox St
Durham, NC 27701-1645, USA

Duran, Clarence (Athlete, Football Player)
201 W 54th St
Los Angeles, CA 90037-3803, USA

Duran, Dan (Athlete, Baseball Player)
493 Maxine Ct
Sunnyvale, CA 94086-6338, USA

Duran, Micki (Actor)
c/o Staff Member *DDO Artist Agency (LA)*
6725 W Sunset Blvd Ste 230
Los Angeles, CA 90028-7163, USA

Duran, Roberto (Boxer)
Nuevo Reperto El Carmen
PANAMA

Duran Duran (Music Group)
c/o Staff Member *DD Productions*
93A Westbourne Park Villas
London W2 5ED, UNITED KINGDOM (UK)

Durance, Erica (Actor)
c/o Jeff Palffy *PMG Management*
8826 Burton Way
Beverly Hills, CA 90211-1715, USA

Durand, Kevin (Actor)
c/o Jason Barrett *Alchemy Entertainment*
7024 Melrose Ave Ste 420
Los Angeles, CA 90038-3394, USA

Duranko, Peter (Athlete, Football Player)
417 S Clearfield St
Johnstown, PA 15905-3327, USA

Durant, Graham J (Inventor)
333 Boston Providence Turnpike
Norwood, MA 2062, USA

Durant, Joe (Athlete, Golfer)
PO Box 910
Gulf Breeze, FL 32562-0910, USA

Durant, Kevin (Athlete, Basketball Player)
c/o Aaron Goodwin *Goodwin Sports Management*
Prefers to be contacted via email or telephone
Seattle, WA, USA

Durant, Mike (Athlete, Baseball Player)
9437 Cape Wrath Dr
Dublin, OH 43017-7624, USA

Durante, Viviana P (Ballerina)
20 Bristol Gardens Little Venice
London W9, UNITED KINGDOM (UK)

Durao Barroso, Jose Manuel (Prime Minister)
Rua du Imprensa a Estrela 8
Lisbon 1300, PORTUGAL

Durazo, Erubiel (Athlete, Baseball Player)
1001 W Saint Marys Rd Apt 207
Tucson, AZ 85745-2468, USA

Durbin, Chad (Athlete, Baseball Player)
17918 Jefferson Ridge Dr
Baton Rouge, LA 70817-9535, USA

Durbin, Deanna (Actor, Music Group)
BP 3315
Paris Cedex 03 75123, FRANCE

Durbin, J D (Athlete, Baseball Player)
1913 E Pinto Dr
Gilbert, AZ 85296-3214, USA

Durbin, James (Musician)
c/o Simon Fuller *XIX Entertainment*
33/32 Ransomes Dock 35-37 Parkgate Rd
London SW11 4NP, UK

Durbin, Mike (Bowler)
719 2nd Ave Ste 701
Seattle, WA 98104-1747, USA

Durcal, Rocio (Musician)
c/o Staff Member *BMG*
1540 Broadway
New York, NY 10036-4039, USA

Duren, Clarence (Athlete, Football Player)
201 W 54th St
Los Angeles, CA 90037-3803, USA

Duren, John (Athlete, Basketball Player)
1107 1st St NW
Washington, DC 20001-1304, USA

Durfee, Peter (Athlete, Baseball Player)
4216 Magness Ct
Chico, CA 95973-8507, USA

Durham, Don (Athlete, Baseball Player)
2627 Pennington Bend Rd
Nashville, TN 37214-1107, USA

Durham, Hugh (Basketball Player, Coach)
Athletic Dept
Jacksonville, FL 32211, USA

Durham, Jarrett (Athlete, Basketball Player)
18 McKelvey Ave
Pittsburgh, PA 15218-1454, USA

Durham, Joe (Athlete, Baseball Player)
9715 Mendoza Rd
Randallstown, MD 21133-2530, USA

Durham, Leon (Athlete, Baseball Player)
1553 Williamson Dr
Cincinnati, OH 45240-1549, USA

Durham, Ray (Sugar Ray) (Athlete, Baseball Player)
1815 Lake Dr
Charlotte, NC 28214-8647, USA

Durham, Steve (Athlete, Football Player)
200 Alberta Dr
Woodruff, SC 29388-8610, USA

Duris, Slava (Athlete, Hockey Player)
1-92 Walmer Rd
Toronto, ON M5R 2X7, Canada

Duritz, Adam (Songwriter, Writer)
2220 Colorado Ave
Santa Monica, CA 90404-3506, USA

Durkee, Charlie (Athlete, Football Player)
1210 Danbury Dr
Mansfield, TX 76063-3809, USA

Durkin, Clare (Model)
c/o Staff Member *Ford Models (NY)*
238 E 4th St
New York, NY 10009-7425

Durkin, John A (Ex-Senator)
PO Box 437
Rollinsford, NH 03869-0437, USA

Durko, Sandy (Athlete, Football Player)
2020 Paseo Del Mar
Palos Verdes Estates, CA 90274-2659, USA

Durnbaugh, Bobby (Athlete, Baseball Player)
1638 N Central Dr
Beavercreek, OH 45432-2118, USA

Durning, Charles (Actor)
c/o Judith Moss *Paradigm (LA)*
360 N Crescent Dr
Beverly Hills, CA 90210-4874, USA

Durocher, Jayson (Athlete, Baseball Player)
3997 E Robin Ln
Phoenix, AZ 85050-5416, USA

Durr, Francoise
195 Rue De Lourmel
Paris, FRANCE F-75015

Durr, Jason (Actor)
c/o Staff Member *Ken McReddie Ltd*
11 Connaught Pl
London W2 2ET, UNITED KINGDOM

Durr Browning, Francoise (Tennis Player)
195 Rue de Lourmel
Paris, 75015, FRANCE

Durrance, Samuel T (Astronaut, Astronomer)
770 Kerry Downs Cir
Melbourne, FL 32940-1774, USA

Durrant, Devin (Athlete, Basketball Player)
6239 Pineview Rd
Dallas, TX 75248-3933, USA

Durringer, Annemarie
Hawelgasse 17
Vienna, AUSTRIA 1180

Durrington, Trent (Athlete, Baseball Player)
499 N Canon Dr Apt 400
Beverly Hills, CA 90210-4887, USA

Durslag, Melvin
PO Box 559
Salisbury, NC 28145-0559

Durst, Fred (Musician)
c/o Matt Luber *Luber Roklin Management*
8530 Wilshire Blvd Ste 550
Beverly Hills, CA 90211-3133, USA

Durst, Will (Actor, Comedian)
PO Box 5734
Santa Rosa, CA 95402-5734, USA

Dusay, Debra (Actor)
8281 Melrose Ave Ste 200
Los Angeles, CA 90046-6890, USA

Dusay, Mari (Actor)
320 W 66th St
New York, NY 10023-6304, USA

Dusay, Marj (Actor)
8281 Melrose Ave Ste 200
Los Angeles, CA 90046-6890, USA

Dusbabek, Mark (Athlete, Football Player)
11452 Dona Dorotea Dr
Studio City, CA 91604-4246, USA

Dusek, Brad (Athlete, Football Player)
The 4th Quarter Ranch 8311 Fm 2086
Temple, TX 76501, USA

Dusenberry, Ann (Actor)
1619 San Leandro Ln
Santa Barbara, CA 93108-2637, USA

Duser, Carl (Athlete, Baseball Player)
3021 Cornwall Rd
Bethlehem, PA 18017-3313, USA

Dushku, Eliza (Actor, Producer)
c/o Nicki Fioravante *PMK/BNC - LA*
8687 Melrose Ave Ste 8
West Hollywood, CA 90069-5746, USA

Dushku, Nate (Actor)
c/o Matt Schwartz *Christopher Wright Management*
6100 Wilshire Blvd Ste 1170
Los Angeles, CA 90048-5116, USA

Dusk, Matt (Musician)
c/o Garry Kief *Stiletto Entertainment*
8295 S La Cienega Blvd
Inglewood, CA 90301-1521, USA

Dussault, Jean H (Misc)
2705 Blvd Laurier
Sainte Foy, PQ G1V 4G2, CANADA

Dussault, Nancy (Actor)
c/o Staff Member *The Artists Group Ltd (LA)*
3345 Wilshire Blvd Ste 915
Los Angeles, CA 90010-1820, USA

Dussault, Normand (Athlete, Hockey Player)
103-876 Rue Saint-Francois N
Sherbrooke, QC J1E 3P9, Canada

Dustal, Bob (Athlete, Baseball Player)
625 Marian Ln
Lakeland, FL 33813-1412, USA

Dustrude-Roberson, Beverly (Baseball Player)
2422 Lobelia Dr
Oxnard, CA 93036-6260, USA

Dutch, Deborah (Actor)
850 N Kings Rd # 100
West Hollywood, CA 90069-5442, USA

Dutilleux, Henri (Composer)
12 Rue Saint Louis-en-l'sle
Paris 75004, FRANCE

Dutoit, Charles E
85 Sainte Catherine St W
Montreal, QC H2X 3P4, CANADA

Dutt, Hank (Music Group, Musician)
1235 9th Ave
San Francisco, CA 94122-2306, USA

Dutt, Sanjay (Actor, Bollywood)
58 Smt Nargis Dutt Road Pali Hill Bandra W
Mumbai, MS 400050, INDIA

Dutta, Divya (Actor, Bollywood)
C-17 Nehru Nagar Kishore Kumar Gangulay Marg Juhu Tara Road
Mumbai, MS 400049, INDIA

Dutta, Lara (Beauty Pageant Winner)
c/o Staff Member *Globosport Mumbai Pvt Ltd*
Prime Plaza, 5th Flr, 501, 38 S.V. Rd Santacruz (W).
Mumbai 400 054, India

Dutta, Tanushree (Actor, Bollywood)
c/o Bunty Bahl *Carving Dreams Entertainment*
304-305, Oberoi Chambers II B Wing, Off New Link Road, Andheri West
Mumbai 400053, INDIA

Dutton, Charles S (Actor)
c/o Sherry Marsh *Marsh Entertainment*
12444 Ventura Blvd Ste 203
Studio City, CA 91604-2409, USA

Dutton, John O (Athlete, Football Player)
5706 Moss Creek Trl
Dallas, TX 75252-2380, USA

Dutton, Lawrence (Music Group, Musician)
3 Burlington Lane Chiswick
London W4 2TH, UNITED KINGDOM (UK)

Dutton, Simon (Actor)
Langham House 302/8 Regent St
London W1R 5AL, UNITED KINGDOM (UK)

Duva, Lou (Boxer, Misc)
811 Totowa Rd # 100
Totowa, NJ 07512-1207, USA

Duval, David (Athlete, Golfer)
1000 E Oxford Ln
Englewood, CO 80113-4857, USA

Duval, Dennis (Athlete, Basketball Player)
8105 Verbeck Dr
Manlius, NY 13104-9306, USA

Duval, Helen (Bowler)
50 Silva Ave
Millbrae, CA 94030-2036, USA

Duval, James (Actor)
c/o Ryan Revel *Benderspink*
5870 W Jefferson Blvd Ste E
Los Angeles, CA 90016-3159, USA

Duval, Juliette (Actor)
36 Rue de Ponthieu
Paris 75008, FRANCE

Duval, Mike (Athlete, Baseball Player)
2743 Nature Pointe Loop
Fort Myers, FL 33905-2468, USA

Duvall, Brad (Baseball Player)
438 Sycamore Trl
Woodstock, GA 30189-7423, USA

Duvall, Carol (Television Host)
c/o Staff Member *HGTV/Home & Garden Television*
9721 Sherrill Blvd
Knoxville, TN 37932-3330, USA

DuVall, Clea (Actor)
c/o Sean Elliott *WmE2 (Endeavor-LA)*
9601 Wilshire Blvd Fl 3
Beverly Hills, CA 90210-5219, USA

Duvall, Jed (Correspondent)
5010 Creston St
Hyattsville, MD 20781-1216, USA

Duvall, Robert (Actor)
c/o Steven Arcieri *Arcieri & Associates Inc*
305 Madison Ave Ste 2315
New York, NY 10165-5015, USA

Duvall, Sammy (Skier)
PO Box 871
Windermere, FL 34786-0871, USA

Duvall, Shelley (Actor)
404 Red Bud Trl
Blanco, TX 78606-5070, USA

Duvall-Hero, Camille (Skier)
PO Box 871
Windermere, FL 34786-0871, USA

Duvignaud, Jean (Writer)
28 Rue Saint-Leonard
La Rochelle 1700, FRANCE

Duvillard, Henri (Skier)
Le Monte d'Arbois
Megere 74120, FRANCE

Duwelius, Richard L (Rich) (Athlete, Volleyball Player)
266 Stoddards Wharf Rd
Gales Ferry, CT 06335-1130, USA

Duwez, Pol E (Physicist)
1535 Oakdale St
Pasadena, CA 91106-3552, USA

Dvorak, Miroslav (Athlete, Hockey Player)
Fugnerova 876
Hluboka nad Vitavou 373 41, Czech Republic

Dvorak, Radek (Athlete, Hockey Player)
10342 Lexington Estates Blvd
Boca Raton, FL 33428-4290, USA

Dvorak, Richard (Rick) (Athlete, Football Player)
13587 SE 230 Rd
Spearville, KS 67876-7506, USA

Dvorovenko, Irina (Ballerina)
890 Broadway
New York, NY 10003-1211, USA

Dvorsky, Peter (Opera Singer)
Bradianska Ulica 11
Bratislave SK-811 08, SLOVAKIA

Dwight, Edward Jr (Astronaut)
4022 Montview Blvd
Denver, CO 80207-3713, USA

Dwight, Tim (Athlete, Football Player)
26164 Indigo Dr
Park Rapids, MN 56470-5189, USA

Dworaczyk, Hope (Model)
c/o Liza Anderson *Anderson Group Public Relations*
8060 Melrose Ave Fl 4
Los Angeles, CA 90046-7038, USA

Dwork, Melvin (Designer)
196 Avenue of the Americas
New York, NY 10013-1234, USA

Dworkin, Martin (Biologist, Misc)
2123 Hoyt Ave W
Saint Paul, MN 55108-1314, USA

Dworkins, Lenny (Len) (Cartoonist)
2906 Wilmette Ave
Wilmette, IL 60091-2136, USA

Dworsky, Daniel L (Dan) (Architect, Athlete, Football Player)
9225 Nightingale Dr
Los Angeles, CA 90069-1117, USA

Dwyer, Bil (Comedian, Game Show Host)
c/o Staff Member *OmniPop Talent Group*
10700 Ventura Blvd Fl 2
Studio City, CA 91604-3561, USA

Dwyer, Jim (Athlete, Baseball Player)
825 Hancock Bridge Pkwy
Cape Coral, FL 33990-1236, USA

Dwyer, Karyn (Actor)
438 Queen St E
Toronto, ON M5A 1T4, CANADA

Dwyer, Mary (Athlete, Golfer)
500 Lake View Ave Apt 1C
Highwood, IL 60040-1415, USA

Dyal, Mike (Athlete, Football Player)
426 Shin Oak Way
Kerrville, TX 78028-2097, USA

Dyas, Ed (Athlete, Football Player)
c/o Staff Member *College Football Hall Of Fame*
111 S Saint Joseph St
South Bend, IN 46601-1901, USA

Dybdahl, Thomas (Musician)
c/o Staff Member *Paradigm (Monterey)*
404 W Franklin St
Monterey, CA 93940-2303, USA

Dybzinski, Jerry (Athlete, Baseball Player)
1626 Haywood Pl
Fort Collins, CO 80526-2289, USA

Dychtwald, Ken (Doctor, Misc)
1900 Powell St
Emeryville, CA 94608-1811, USA

Dyck, Ed (Athlete, Hockey Player)
59 Templeby Cres NE
Calgary, AB T1Y 5G3, Canada

Dydek, Malforzata (Margo) (Basketball Player)
1 at and T Center Pkwy
San Antonio, TX 78219-3604, USA

Dye, Cameron (Actor)
13035 Woodbridge St
Studio City, CA 91604-1431, USA

Dye, Ernest (Athlete, Football Player)
580 Bienville Ct
Alpharetta, GA 30004-3157, USA

Dye, Ian (Composer, Musician)
c/o Staff Member *Gorfaine/Schwartz Agency Inc*
4111 W Alameda Ave Ste 509
Burbank, CA 91505-4171, USA

Dye, Jermaine (Athlete, Baseball Player)
6655 N 66th Pl
Paradise Valley, AZ 85253-4340, USA

Dye, Lee (Architect, Golfer)
5500 E Yale Ave
Denver, CO 80222-6925, USA

Dye, Nancy Schrom (Educator)
President's Office
Oberlin, OH 44074, USA

Dyer, Danny (Actor)
c/o Staff Member *International Creative Management (ICM-LA)*
10250 Constellation Blvd Fl 7
Los Angeles, CA 90067-6207, USA

Dyer, David W (Judge)
300 NE 1st Ave
Miami, FL 33132-2126, USA

Dyer, Duffy (Athlete, Baseball Player)
742 W Las Palmaritas Dr
Phoenix, AZ 85021-5545, USA

Dyer, Ellen (Stylist)
c/o Staff Member *Dyer Circumstances*
1406 Lisbon St
Coral Gables, FL 33134-2226, USA

Dyer, Hector (Athlete, Track Athlete)
1620 E Chapman Ave # 214
Fullerton, CA 92831-4016, USA

Dyer, Henry (Athlete, Football Player)
23464 Reames Rd
Zachary, LA 70791-6603, USA

Dyer, Joseph W Jr (Admiral)
Commander Naval Air Systems Command
Patuxent River, MD 20670, USA

Dyer, Ken (Athlete, Football Player)
1151 S Sandstone Ct
Gilbert, AZ 85296-3743, USA

Dyer, Mike (Athlete, Baseball Player)
22392 Manacor
Mission Viejo, CA 92692-1188, USA

Dyer, Wayne W (Writer)
c/o Staff Member *Hay House, Inc*
PO Box 5100
Carlsbad, CA 92018-5100, USA

Dyk, Timothy B (Judge)
717 Madison Pl NW
Washington, DC 20439-0001, USA

Dyke, Charles W (General, Misc)
1330 Connecticut Ave NW
Washington, DC 20036-1704, USA

Dykema, Craig (Athlete, Basketball Player)
10525 Destino St
Bellflower, CA 90706-7125, USA

Dykes, Hart Lee (Athlete, Football Player)
30 Dorothea Ln
Sugar Land, TX 77479-2446, USA

Dykes Bower, John (Music Group, Musician)
4Z Artillery Mansions Westminster
London SW1, UNITED KINGDOM (UK)

Dykhoff, Radhames (Baseball Player)
105 Angelfish Ln
Jupiter, FL 33477-7227, USA

Dykinga, Jack (Journalist, Photographer)
1519 E Tascal Loop
Tucson, AZ 85737-8570, USA

Dykstra, John (Animator, Artist, Cinematographer)
15060 Encanto Dr
Sherman Oaks, CA 91403-4408, USA

Dykstra, Leonard K (Lenny) (Athlete, Baseball Player)
10550 Wilshire Blvd Apt 1203
Los Angeles, CA 90024-7318, USA

Dylan, Bob (Composer, Music Group, Songwriter)
c/o Jeff Kramer *OK Management*
311 N Robertson Blvd # 709
Beverly Hills, CA 90211-1705, USA

Dylan, Jakob (Musician)
c/o Marty Diamond *Paradigm (NY)*
360 Park Ave S Fl 16
New York, NY 10010-1708, USA

Dylan, Jesse (Director)
c/o Nikki Weiss *Nikki Weiss & Co.*
754 N La Jolla Ave
Los Angeles, CA 90046-6808, USA

Dymally, Mervyn M (Misc)
9111 S La Cienega Blvd
Compton, CA 90220, USA

Dyrdek, Rob (Actor, Athlete, Skateboarder)
791 S Mission Rd
Los Angeles, CA 90023-1038, USA

Dysart, Richard (Actor)
654 Copeland Ct
Santa Monica, CA 90405-4416, USA

Dyson, Andre (Athlete, Football Player)
3367 N Shoreline Cir
Layton, UT 84040-7128, USA

Dyson, Freeman J (Physicist, Writer)
105 Battle Road Cir
Princeton, NJ 08540-4904, USA

Dyson, Kevin (Athlete, Football Player)
3109 Chase Point Dr
Franklin, TN 37067-8156, USA

Dyson, Michael Eric (Writer)
English Dept
Chicago, IL 60604, USA

Dystel, Oscar (Publisher)
Springs Purchase Hills Dr
Purchase, NY 10577, USA

Dzau, Victor (Misc, Scientist)
Cardiovascular Medicine Div
Stanford, CA 94305, USA

Dzeliwe (Misc)
Mbabane, SWAZILAND

Dzhanibekov, Vladimir A (Astronaut, General, Misc)
Moskovskoi Oblasti
Syvisdny Goroduk 141160, RUSSIA

Dzhanibelkov, Vladimir
Potchka Kosmon 141 160 Svyosdny Gorodok
Moscow, RUSSIA

Dziedzic, Joe (Athlete, Hockey Player)
2195 Marion Rd
Saint Paul, MN 55113-3805, USA

Dziena, Alexis (Actor)
c/o Adam Schweitzer *International Creative Management (ICM-NY)*
40 W 57th St
New York, NY 10019-4001, USA

Dziura, Jennifer (Comedian)
316 W 39th St Apt 3W
New York, NY 10018-1420, USA

Dzundza, George (Actor)
c/o Glenn Robbins *Raw Talent Management*
545 Veteran Ave
Los Angeles, CA 90024-1915, USA

Dzurlnda, Mikulas (Prime Minister)
Nam Slobody 1
Bratislava 1 81370, SLOVAKIA

E

E 40 (Music Group)
2144 Hills Ave NW # D2
Atlanta, GA 30318-2209, USA

E. Capuano, Michael (Congressman, Politician)
1414 Longworth Hob
Washington, DC 20515-3103, USA

E. Clyburn, James (Congressman, Politician)
2135 Rayburn Hob
Washington, DC 20515-0005, USA

E. Connolly, Gerald (Congressman, Politician)
424 Cannon Hob
Washington, DC 20515-0306, USA

E. Cummings, Elijah (Congressman, Politician)
2235 Rayburn Hob
Washington, DC 20515-0923, USA

E. Deutch, Theodore (Congressman, Politician)
1024 Longworth Hob
Washington, DC 20515-1409, USA

E. Issa, Darrell (Congressman, Politician)
2347 Rayburn Hob
Washington, DC 20515-0915, USA

E. Kildee, Dale (Congressman, Politician)
2107 Rayburn Hob
Washington, DC 20515-2205, USA

E. Latta, Robert (Congressman, Politician)
1323 Longworth Hob
Washington, DC 20515-4704, USA

E. Lungren, Daniel (Congressman, Politician)
2313 Rayburn Hob
Washington, DC 20515-1401, USA

E. Neal, Richard (Congressman, Politician)
2208 Rayburn Hob
Washington, DC 20515-0522, USA

E. Petri, Thomas (Congressman, Politician)
2462 Rayburn Hob
Washington, DC 20515-4906, USA

E. Price, David (Congressman, Politician)
2162 Rayburn Hob
Washington, DC 20515-3304, USA

Eaben, Bill (Athlete, Basketball Player)
12254 Colliers Reserve Dr
Naples, FL 34110-0910, USA

Eackles, Ledell (Athlete, Basketball Player)
9134 Elmgrove Garden Dr
Baton Rouge, LA 70807-4307, USA

Eaddy, Don (Athlete, Baseball Player)
2696 Lake Shore Rd Unit 29
Gilford, NH 03249-7677, USA

Eade, George J (General)
1131 Sunnyside Dr
Healdsburg, CA 95448-3536, USA

Eads, Ora W (Religious Leader)
804 E Hemlock St
La Follette, TN 37766-3758, USA

Eads III, George Coleman (Actor)
c/o Alan Iezman *Shelter Entertainment*
9454 Wilshire Blvd Ste 715
Beverly Hills, CA 90212-2925, USA

Eagan, James (Writer)
c/o Greg Cavic *Creative Artists Agency (CAA-LA)*
2000 Avenue of the Stars Ste 100
Los Angeles, CA 90067-4705, USA

Eagle, Ian (Sportscaster)
51 W 52nd St
New York, NY 10019-6119, USA

Eagleburger, Lawrence S (Secretary)
1450 Owensville Rd
Charlottesville, VA 22901-9582, USA

Eaglen, Jane (Musician, Opera Singer)
c/o Staff Member *Columbia Artists Mgmt Inc*
1790 Broadway Fl 6
New York, NY 10019-1537, USA

Eagles, Mike (Athlete, Hockey Player)
59 Abbott Crt
Fredericton, NB E3B 5V8, Canada

Eagles, The (Music Group)
c/o Irving Azoff *Azoff Music Management/ Front Line*
1100 Glendon Ave
Los Angeles, CA 90024-3503, USA

Eagleson, Alan (Athlete, Hockey Player)
37 Maltland St
Toronto, ON M4Y 1C8, Canada

Eagleton, Thomas (Ex-Senator)
1 Mercantile Ctr
St. Louis, MO 63101, USA

Eagleton, Thomas F (Ex-Senator)
1 Firstar Ctr
Saint Louis, MO 63101, USA

Eagling, Wayne J (Choreographer, Dancer)
Postbus 16486 1001 RN
Amsterdam, Netherlands

Eakes, Bobbie (Actor)
c/o Staff Member *WmE2 (WMA-LA)*
1 William Morris Pl
Beverly Hills, CA 90212-4261, USA

Eakin, Richard R (Educator)
Chancellor's Office
Greenville, NC 27858, USA

Eakin, Thomas C (Business Person)
245 Sandover Dr
Aurora, OH 44202-8774, USA

Eakins, Dallas (Athlete, Hockey Player)
19705 N 84th Way
Scottsdale, AZ 85255-3971, USA

Eakins, Gretchen (Actor)
c/o Mattie Semradek 1438 N Gower St
Bldg 34 2nd Fl
Los Angeles, CA 90027, USA

Eakins, Jim (Athlete, Basketball Player)
2575 Little Cottonwood Rd
Sandy, UT 84092-3469, USA

Eaks, R W (Athlete, Golfer)
15652 N Cabrillo Dr
Fountain Hills, AZ 85268-1615, USA

Ealy, Michael (Actor)
c/o Darryl Taja *Epidemic Pictures*
1635 N Cahuenga Blvd Fl 5
Hollywood, CA 90028-6201, USA

Earl, Glenn (Athlete, Football Player)
838 N Doheny Dr Apt 1207
West Hollywood, CA 90069-4851, USA

Earl, Robin D (Athlete, Football Player)
439 Ferndale Ct
Buffalo Grove, IL 60089-1730, USA

Earl, Roger (Musician)
PO Box 770850
Orlando, FL 32877-0850, USA

Earl, Scott (Athlete, Baseball Player)
8102 Salt Fork Way
Indianapolis, IN 46256-1679, USA

Earle, Acie (Athlete, Basketball Player)
2301 14th Ave
Moline, IL 61265-3203, USA

Earle, Ed (Athlete, Basketball Player)
1940 Burton Ln
Park Ridge, IL 60068-1572, USA

Earle, Steve (Actor, Musician)
c/o Danny Goldberg *Gold Village Entertainment*
37 W 17th St Ste 7W
New York, NY 10011-5525, USA

Earle, Sylvia Alice (Oceanographer)
12812 Skyline Blvd
Oakland, CA 94619-3125, USA

Earles, Jason (Actor)
c/o Dede Binder-Goldsmith *Defining Artists Agency*
10 Universal City Plz Ste 2000
Universal City, CA 91608-1074, USA

Earley, Anthony F Jr (Business Person)
2000 2nd Ave
Detroit, MI 48226-1203, USA

Earley, Bill (Athlete, Baseball Player)
112 Carruthers Pond Dr
Cincinnati, OH 45246-3854, USA

Earley, Liz (Athlete, Golfer)
24 Morton Dr
Buffalo, NY 14226-3338, USA

Earley, Michael M (Business Person)
550 W C St
San Diego, CA 92101-3540, USA

Earley, Quinn (Athlete, Football Player)
PO Box 675752
Rancho Santa Fe, CA 92067-5752, USA

Early, David (Actor)
PO Box 154
Homestead, PA 15120-0154, USA

Early, Gerald L (Writer)
English Dept
Saint Louis, MO 63130, USA

Earnhardt, Jeffrey (Race Car Driver)
c/o Staff Member *Rick Ware Racing*
111 Sunrise Center Dr
Thomasville, NC 27360-4928, USA

Earnhardt, Kerry (Race Car Driver)
PO Box 418
Mooresville, NC 28115-0418, USA

Earnhardt Jr, Dale (Race Car Driver)
1675 Coddle Creek Hwy
Mooresville, NC 28115-8245, USA

Earon, Blaine (Athlete, Football Player)
6640 Lake Run Dr
Flowery Branch, GA 30542-3895, USA

Earp, Mildred (Baseball Player)
PO Box 333
West Fork, AR 72774-0333, USA

Earth Wind & Fire (Music Group)
c/o Damien Smith *Azoff Music Management/Front Line*
1100 Glendon Ave
Los Angeles, CA 90024-3503, USA

Easler, Mike (Athlete, Baseball Player)
3121 Kookaburra Way
North Las Vegas, NV 89084-2310, USA

Easley, Bill (Musician)
328 W 43rd St # 4FW
New York, NY 10036, USA

Easley, Damion (Athlete, Baseball Player)
6420 W Line Dr
Glendale, AZ 85310-5751, USA

Easley, Kenny (Athlete, Football Player)
3906 Kegagie Dr
Norfolk, VA 23518-1500, USA

Easley, Logan (Athlete, Baseball Player)
555 Wildrose Loop
Twin Falls, ID 83301-8247, USA

Easmon, Ricky (Athlete, Football Player)
6605 N Riviera Manor Dr Apt A4
Tampa, FL 33604-6444, USA

Eason, Eric (Actor, Director, Writer)
c/o Simon Millar *Rumble Media*
1620 Broadway Ste C
Santa Monica, CA 90404-2777, USA

Eason, Tony (Athlete, Football Player)
PO Box 340
Walnut Grove, CA 95690-0340, USA

East, Jeff (Actor)
c/o Vaughn Hart *Vaughn Hart & Associates*
12304 Santa Monica Blvd Ste 111
Los Angeles, CA 90025-2586, USA

East, Ron (Athlete, Football Player)
PO Box 2228
Anacortes, WA 98221-8106, USA

East 17
Box 153 Stanmore
Middlesex, ENGLAND HA7 2HF

Easterbrook, Frank (Judge)
111 N Canal St Fl 6
Chicago, IL 60606-7221, USA

Easterbrook, Leslie (Actor)
, CA

Easterbrrok, Frank H (Judge)
111 N Canal St Fl 6
Chicago, IL 60606-7221, USA

Easterday, Deanna (Stylist)
c/o Staff Member *Help Me Rhonda*
541 10th St NW # 294
Atlanta, GA 30318-5713, USA

Easterling, Ray (Athlete, Football Player)
3420 Traylor Dr
Richmond, VA 23235-1750, USA

Easterly, David E (Business Person)
1400 Lake Heam Dr NE
Atlanta, GA 30319, USA

Easterly, Jamie (Athlete, Baseball Player)
1306 Plantation Dr
Crockett, TX 75835-2314, USA

Easterly, Richard (Athlete, Football Player)
206 S Gardenia Ave
Tampa, FL 33609-2506, USA

Eastern Conference Champions (Music Group)
c/o Staff Member *Paradigm (Monterey)*
404 W Franklin St
Monterey, CA 93940-2303, USA

Eastgate, Peter
c/o Staff Member *Poker Royalty, LLC*
10789 W Twain Ave Ste 200
Las Vegas, NV 89135-3030, USA

Eastham, Dean E (Physicist)
281 Bloomingbank Rd
Riverside, IL 60546-2246, USA

Eastin, Steve (Actor)
c/o Staff Member *Agency for the Performing Arts (APA-LA)*
405 S Beverly Dr Ste 500
Beverly Hills, CA 90212-4425, USA

Eastman, John (Attorney, Attorney General, General)
39 W 54th St
New York, NY 10019-5465, USA

Eastman, Kevin (Cartoonist)
8424A Santa Monica Blvd 713
West Hollywood, CA 90069, USA

Eastman, Madeline (Musician)
1450 Southgate Ave Apt 206
Daly City, CA 94015-4021, USA

Eastman, Marilyn (Actor)
138 Hawthome St
Pittsburgh, PA 15218, USA

Eastman, Rodney (Actor)
c/o Justin Evans *The Independent Group*
6363 Wilshire Blvd Ste 115
Los Angeles, CA 90048-5734, USA

Easton, Michael (Actor)
c/o Danielle Allman-Del *D2 Management*
141 S Barrington Ave
Los Angeles, CA 90049-3368, USA

Easton, Micheal (Actor)
c/o Danielle Allman-Del *D2 Management*
141 S Barrington Ave
Los Angeles, CA 90049-3368, USA

Easton, Millard E (Bill) (Coach)
1704 NW Weatherstone Dr
Blue Springs, MO 64015-6317, USA

Easton, Robert
9300 Wilshire Blvd Ste 555
Beverly Hills, CA 90212-3211, USA

Easton, Sheena (Musician)
18136 Califa St
Tarzana, CA 91356-1718, USA

Eastwick, Rawly (Athlete, Baseball Player)
10 River Meadow Dr
West Newbury, MA 01985-1400, USA

Eastwick-Field, Elizabeth (Architect)
Low Farm Low Road Denham Eye
Suffolk IP21 5ET, UNITED KINGDOM

Eastwood, Alison (Actor, Model)
c/o Bob McGowan *McGowan Management*
8733 W Sunset Blvd Ste 103
West Hollywood, CA 90069-2241, USA

Eastwood, Bob (Athlete, Golfer)
PO Box 14769
Haltom City, TX 76117-0769, USA

Eastwood, Clint (Actor, Producer)
c/o Staff Member *Malpaso Productions*
4000 Warner Bros Blvd # 16
Burbank, CA 91522-1100, USA

Eastwood, Kyle (Composer)
c/o Staff Member *Gorfaine/Schwartz Agency Inc*
4111 W Alameda Ave Ste 509
Burbank, CA 91505-4171, USA

Eastwood, Mike (Athlete, Hockey Player)
87 George St Attn Hockey Broadcast Dept
Ottawa, ON K1N 9H7, Canada

Easum, Donald B (Diplomat)
801 W End Ave Apt 3A
New York, NY 10025-5361, USA

Easy, Omar (Athlete, Football Player)
2000 N Bayshore Dr Apt 901
Miami, FL 33137-5121, USA

Eathorne, A J (Athlete, Golfer)
23023 N 25th Pl
Phoenix, AZ 85024-7567, USA

Eaton, Adam (Athlete, Baseball Player)
401 N Angford Dr
Ellensburg, WA 98926-3276, USA

Eaton, Andrew (Producer)
c/o Staff Member *Revolution Films*
9A Dallington St
London EC1V 0BQ, UNITED KINGDOM (UK)

Eaton, Brando (Actor)
c/o Staff Member *Art Work Entertainment*
5900 Wilshire Blvd Ste 2150
Los Angeles, CA 90036-5021, USA

Eaton, Craig (Athlete, Baseball Player)
3307 Baltusrol Ln
Lake Worth, FL 33467-1301, USA

Eaton, Dan L (Doctor)
1 Dna Way
South San Francisco, CA 94080-4918, USA

Eaton, Don (Babtunde) (Composer, Musician)
370 City Road
London EC1V 2QA, UNITED KINGDOM

Eaton, John C (Composer)
4585 N Hartstrait Rd
Bloomington, IN 47404-9318, USA

Eaton, Mark (Basketball Player)
2104 Dayton Ave NE
Renton, WA 98056-2719, USA

Eaton, Mark (Athlete, Hockey Player)
5020 Carnoustie Ct
Presto, PA 15142-1082, USA

Eaton, Mark E (Athlete, Basketball Player)
484 Shepherd Way
Park City, UT 84098-5704, USA

Eaton, Meredith (Actor)
c/o Staff Member *Bresler Kelly & Associates*
11500 W Olympic Blvd Ste 510
Los Angeles, CA 90064-1527, USA

Eaton, Scott (Athlete, Football Player)
3950 W Lake Sammamish Pkwy SE
Bellevue, WA 98008-5836, USA

Eaton, Shirley (Actor)
Upper Saint Martin's Lane
London WC2H PEG, UNITED KINGDOM

Eaton, Tracey (Athlete, Football Player)
PO Box 881
Preston, WA 98050-0881, USA

Eaton, Vic (Athlete, Football Player)
610 Brockton Ln N
Minneapolis, MN 55447-3339, USA

Eatough, Jeff (Athlete, Hockey Player)
2050 Insley Rd
Mississauga, ON L4Y 1P9, Canada

Eave, Gary (Athlete, Baseball Player)
1601 King Ave
Bastrop, LA 71220-4957, USA

Eaves, Jerry (Athlete, Basketball Player)
10 Perch Pl
Greensboro, NC 27455-3437, USA

Eaves, Mike (Athlete, Hockey Player)
3615 Culver Trl
Faribault, MN 55021-7366, USA

Eaves, Murray (Athlete, Hockey Player)
1000 Shumway Ave Attn Coachingstaff
Faribault, MN 55021-4400, USA

Eaves, Patrick (Athlete, Hockey Player)
3615 Culver Trl
Faribault, MN 55021-7366, USA

Ebadi, Shirin (Nobel Prize Laureate)
Enghelab Ave & 16 Azar St
Tehran, IRAN

Ebanks, Selita (Actor, Model)
c/o Staff Member *Full Picture (NY)*
915 Broadway Fl 20
New York, NY 10010-7131, USA

Ebashi, Setsuro (Physicist)
17-503 Nahaizumi Myodaiji
Okazaki 444, JAPAN

Ebben, Bill (Basketball Player)
12254 Colliers Reserve Dr
Naples, FL 34110-0910, USA

Ebebole, Christine (Actor)
c/o Barry McPherson *Agency for the Performing Arts (APA-LA)*
405 S Beverly Dr Ste 500
Beverly Hills, CA 90212-4425, USA

Ebel, David M (Judge)
1929 Stout St
Denver, CO 80294-0003, USA

Ebel, Dino (Athlete, Baseball Player)
c/o Staff Member *Los Angeles Dodgers (LA Dodgers)*
1000 Elysian Park Ave
Los Angeles, CA 90090-1112, USA

Eben, Petr (Composer)
Hamsikova 19
Prague 150 00 Prague 5, CZECH REPUBLIC

Eber, Richard (Athlete, Football Player)
13 Stoney Pt
Laguna Niguel, CA 92677-1000, USA

Eberhard, Al (Athlete, Basketball Player)
203 W Parkway Dr
Columbia, MO 65203-3450, USA

Eberhart, Ralph E (Ed) (General)
Commander US Northen Command
Peterson Air Force Base, CO 80914, USA

Eberharter, Stefan (Athlete, Skier)
Dorfstr 21 6272 Stumm
AUSTRIA

Eberle, Jordan (Athlete, Hockey Player)
c/o Craig Oster *Newport Sports Management*
201 City Centre Dr Suite 400
Mississauga, ON L58 2T4, Canada

Eberle, Markus (Skier)
Unterwestweg 27
Rieztem 87567, GERMANY

Eberle, William D (Business Person)
13 Garland Rd
Concord, MA 01742-2214, USA

Ebersole, Christine (Actor)
c/o Barry McPherson *Agency for the Performing Arts (APA-LA)*
405 S Beverly Dr Ste 500
Beverly Hills, CA 90212-4425, USA

Ebersole, Dick (Business Person)
174 West St # 54
Litchfield, CT 06759-3434, USA

Ebersole, Drew (Actor)
c/o Staff Member *House of Representatives, The*
1434 6th St Ste 1
Santa Monica, CA 90401-2527, USA

Ebersole, John (Athlete, Football Player)
1470 Village Sq
Mount Pleasant, SC 29464-4626, USA

Ebert, Derrin (Athlete, Baseball Player)
6866 Svl Box
Victorville, CA 92395-5174, USA

Ebert, Peter (Musician)
Col di Mura
06010 Lippiano, ITALY

Ebert, Robert D (Physicist)
16 Brewster Rd
Wayland, MA 01778-3704, USA

Ebert, Roger (Actor, Critic, Writer)
108 W Grand Ave
Chicago, IL 60654-5206, USA

Ebertharter, Stefan (Skier)
Dorfstr 21 6272 Stumm
Austria

Eberts, Jake (Producer)
c/o Staff Member *National Geographic Feature Films*
9100 Wilshire Blvd Ste 401E
Beverly Hills, CA 90212-3400, USA

Ebi, Ndudi (Basketball Player)
Target Center 600 1st Ave N
Minneapolis, MN 55403, USA

Ebrahim, Vincent (Actor)
c/o Staff Member *BBC Artist Mail*
PO Box 1116
Belfast BT2 7AJ, United Kingdom

Ebron, Roy (Athlete, Basketball Player)
7100 Virgilian St
New Orleans, LA 70126-2633, USA

Ebsen, Bonnie (Actor)
PO Box 356
Agoura, CA 91376-0356, USA

Eccleston, Christopher (Actor)
c/o Larry Taube *Principal Entertainment (LA)*
1964 Westwood Blvd Ste 400
Los Angeles, CA 90025-4695, USA

Ecclestone, Bernie (Race Car Driver)
6 Prince's Gate
London, England SW7 1QJ, UNITED KINGDOM

Ecclestone, Timothy J (Tim) (Athlete, Hockey Player)
10095 Fairway Village Dr
Roswell, GA 30076-3718, USA

Ecevit, Bulent (Prime Minister)
Or-An Sehri 69/5
Ankara, TURKEY

Echevarria, Angel (Athlete, Baseball Player)
23830 231st Pl SE
Maple Valley, WA 98038-5257, USA

Echeverria Alvarez, Luis (President)
Magnolia 131 San Jeronimo Lidice
Magdalena Contreras, CP 10200, MEXICO

Echikunwoke, Megalyn (Actor)
c/o Ira Belgrade *Ira Belgrade Management*
5850 W 3rd St Ste E
Los Angeles, CA 90036-2836, USA

Echivard, Katia Zimninsky (Stylist)
c/o Staff Member *Zenobia Agency Inc*
PO Box 909
Groveland, CA 95321-0909, USA

Echols, Terry (Athlete, Football Player)
6123 Sissonville Dr
Charleston, WV 25312, USA

Eck, Keith (Athlete, Football Player)
7426 Solano St
Carlsbad, CA 92009-7527, USA

Eckenstahler, Eric (Athlete, Baseball Player)
24250 W Alpine Ct
Lake Villa, IL 60046-8637, USA

Eckersley, Dennis (Athlete, Baseball Player)
6 Macy Ln
Ipswich, MA 01938-1185, USA

Eckert, Robert (Business Person)
333 Continental Blvd
El Segundo, CA 90245-5032, USA

Eckert, Shari (Actor)
PO Box 5761
Sherman Oaks, CA 91413-5761, USA

Eckhart, Aaron (Actor, Producer)
c/o Staci Wolfe *Polaris PR*
8135 W 4th St Fl 2
Los Angeles, CA 90048-4415, USA

Eckholdt, Steven (Actor)
137 N Larchmont Blvd # 138
Los Angeles, CA 90004-3704, USA

Eckhouse, James (Actor, Director)
c/o Tracy Steinsapir *Main Title Entertainment*
2225 Wilshire Blvd Suite 500
Los Angeles, CA 90036, USA

Ecklund, Brad (Athlete, Football Player)
7 Fox Hill Dr
Tabernacle, NJ 08088-9043, USA

Ecko, Marc (Fashion Designer, Producer)
c/o David Schiff *Schiff Company, The*
8440 Warner Dr Ste B1
Culver City, CA 90232-2461, USA

Eckstein, Ashley (Drane)
c/o Kathy Carter *Axiom Management (LA)*
1875 Century Park E # H3600
Los Angeles, CA 90067-2501, USA

Eckstein, David (Athlete, Baseball Player)
6939 Sylvan Woods Dr
Sanford, FL 32771-6435, USA

Eckwood, Jerry (Athlete, Football Player)
496 Pickett Rd
Memphis, TN 38109-7365, USA

Eco, Umberto (Tennis Player)
Piazza Castello 13
Milan, ITALY 20121, ITALY

Econoline Crush
1505 N 2nd Ave # 200
Vancouver, CANADA BC V6H 3Y4

Edberg, Rolf (Athlete, Hockey Player)
Helmerdalsve 4
Farst S-12352, Sweden

Edberg, Stefan (Athlete, Tennis Player)
194 Bellevue Ave
Newport, RI 02840-3515, USA

Eddie, Patrick (Basketball Player)
4424 N 76th St Apt 3
Milwaukee, WI 53218-5336, USA

Eddie X (DJ)
c/o Staff Member *Diva Central Inc*
7510 W Sunset Blvd Ste 1445
Los Angeles, CA 90046-3408, USA

Eddings, Doug (Athlete, Baseball Player)
1405 5th St
Las Cruces, NM 88005-1942, USA

Eddings, Floyd (Athlete, Football Player)
1033 N Cactus Ave Apt 4
Rialto, CA 92376-4005, USA

Eddy, Chris (Athlete, Baseball Player)
47 Winterbury Cir
Wilmington, DE 19808-1429, USA

Eddy, Don (Athlete, Baseball Player)
421 1st St N
Rockwell, IA 50469-1002, USA

Eddy, Nicholas M (Nick) (Athlete, Football Player)
2225 London Cir
Modesto, CA 95356-0731, USA

Eddy, Sonya (Actor)
c/o Staff Member *Marshak/Zachary Company, The*
8840 Wilshire Blvd Fl 1
Beverly Hills, CA 90211-2606, USA

Eddy, Steve (Athlete, Baseball Player)
4491 W Folley Pl
Chandler, AZ 85226-4746, USA

Edelen, Joe (Athlete, Baseball Player)
PO Box 38
Washington, OK 73093-0038, USA

Edelin, Kent (Athlete, Basketball Player)
10950 Clara Barton Dr
Fairfax Station, VA 22039-1431, USA

Edell, Marc Z (Attorney, Attorney General, General)
150 John F Kennedy Pkwy # 1000
Short Hills, NJ 07078-2703, USA

Edelman, Brad M (Athlete, Football Player)
828 Royal St Apt 410
New Orleans, LA 70116-3115, USA

Edelman, Gerald M (Nobel Prize Laureate)
Neurobiology Dept
La Jolla, CA 92037, USA

Edelman, Isidore S (Biologist)
464 Riverside Dr
New York, NY 10027-6822, USA

Edelman, John (Athlete, Baseball Player)
125 Fernwood Rd
Cochranville, PA 19330-1116, USA

Edelman, Marian Wright (Business Person)
25 E St NW
Washington, DC 20001-1522, USA

Edelman, Pawel (Cinematographer)
c/o Staff Member *International Creative Management (ICM-LA)*
10250 Constellation Blvd Fl 7
Los Angeles, CA 90067-6207, USA

Edelman, Randy (Composer, Musician)
c/o Staff Member *Gorfaine/Schwartz Agency Inc*
4111 W Alameda Ave Ste 509
Burbank, CA 91505-4171, USA

Edelstein, Jean (Artist)
48 Brooks Ave
Venice, CA 90291-3226, USA

Edelstein, Lisa (Actor)
c/o Cynthia Campos-Greenberg *Anthem Entertainment*
9595 Wilshire Blvd Ste 900
Beverly Hills, CA 90212-2509, USA

Edelstein, Michael (Producer)
c/o Staff Member *Industry Entertainment Partners*
955 Carrillo Dr Ste 300
Los Angeles, CA 90048-5400, USA

Edelstein, Victor (Designer, Fashion Designer)
3 Stanhope Mews West
London SW7 5RB, UNITED KINGDOM (UK)

Eden, Barbara (Actor)
9816 Denbigh Dr
Beverly Hills, CA 90210-1014, USA

Eden, Harry (Actor)
c/o Peter McGrath *Affirmative Entertainment*
425 N Robertson Blvd
West Hollywood, CA 90048-1735, USA

Eden, Mike (Athlete, Baseball Player)
11531 Forest Hills Dr
Tampa, FL 33612-5121, USA

Eden, Richard (Actor)
1800 Avenue of the Stars Ste 400
Los Angeles, CA 90067-4206, USA

Edenfield, Ken (Athlete, Baseball Player)
12828 Stahl Dr
Knoxville, TN 37934-0868, USA

Edens, Tom (Athlete, Baseball Player)
2033 Quailridge Ct
Clarkston, WA 99403-1787, USA

Eder, Elfriede
Rain 12
Leogang, AUSTRIA 5771

Eder, Linda (Actor)
c/o Staff Member *Agency Group Ltd, The (LA)*
1880 Century Park E Ste 711
Los Angeles, CA 90067-1618, USA

Eder, Richard G (Journalist)
202 W 1st St
Los Angeles, CA 90012-4105, USA

Edestrand, Darryl (Athlete, Hockey Player)
391 Beechwood Ave
London, ON N6J 3J9, Canada

Edgar, David
917 NE 16th Ave Apt 13
Ft Lauderdale, FL 33304-4497

Edgar, David (Dave) (Swimmer)
2633 Middle River Dr Apt 3
Fort Lauderdale, FL 33306-1437, USA

Edgar, Jim (Ex-Governor)
1007 W Nevada St # MC037
Urbana, IL 61801-3812, USA

Edgar, Robert W (Religious Leader)
475 Riverside Dr # 1880
New York, NY 10115-0002, USA

Edge (Musician)
145A Ladbroke Grove
London W10 6HJ, UNITED KINGDOM (UK)

Edge, Butch (Athlete, Baseball Player)
2491 Michelle Dr
Sacramento, CA 95821-2342, USA

Edge, Graeme (Musician)
1222 16th Ave S # 300
Nashville, TN 37212-2926, USA

Edge, Mitzi (Athlete, Golfer)
118 Kings Chapel Rd
Augusta, GA 30907-4002, USA

Edge, Shayne (Athlete, Football Player)
350 SW Legacy Gin
Lake City, FL 32025, USA

Edgerson, Booker (Athlete, Football Player)
68 Union Cmn
Buffalo, NY 14221-7744, USA

Edgerton, Bill (Athlete, Baseball Player)
9700 Fairway Dr
Foley, AL 36535-9334, USA

Edgerton, Joel (Actor)
c/o Ann Churchill-Brown *Shanahan Management*
Level 3 Berman House
Surry Hills 2010, AUSTRALIA

Edgley, Gigi (Actor)
12533 Woodgreen St
Los Angeles, CA 90066-2723, USA

Edgley, Gigi
12533 Woodgreen St
Los Angeles, CA 90066-2723, USA

Edinger, Paul (Athlete, Football Player)
2313 York Pl
Lakeland, FL 33810-4883, USA

Edlen, Bengt (Physicist)
Physics Dept
Lund, SWEDEN

Edler, Dave (Athlete, Baseball Player)
1504 S 34th Ave
Yakima, WA 98902-4808, USA

Edler, Inge G (Doctor)
Cadiology Dept
Lund, SWEDEN

Edler, Lee
1725 K St NW # 1202
Washington, DC 20006-1401

Edlund, David J (Inventor)
PO Box 5339
Bend, OR 97708-5339, USA

Edlund, Richard P (Cinematographer)
2710 Wilshire Blvd
Santa Monica, CA 90403-4706, USA

Edmonds, James P (Jim) (Athlete, Baseball Player)
25 Boulder Vw
Irvine, CA 92603-0409, USA

Edmonds, Kenneth (Babyface) (Musician, Producer)
15030 Ventura Blvd # 710
Sherman Oaks, CA 91403-5470, USA

Edmonds, Louis
250 W 57th St Ste 2317
New York, NY 10107-2306

Edmonds, Tracey E (Producer)
c/o Staff Member *Edmonds Entertainment*
312 W 5th St Apt 815
Los Angeles, CA 90013-1750, USA

Edmondson, Brian (Athlete, Baseball Player)
304 Ridgeview Trce
Canton, GA 30114-7000, USA

Edmondson, James L (Judge)
56 Forsyth St NW
Atlanta, GA 30303-2218, USA

Edmund-Davies, Herbert E (Judge)
5 Gray's Inn Square
London WC1R 5EU, UNITED KINGDOM (UK)

Edmunds, Dave (Musician, Songwriter, Writer)
Main Street Plaza 1000 #303
Voorhees, NJ 8043, USA

Edmunds, Ferrell (Athlete, Football Player)
272 Wilkerson Rd
Danville, VA 24540-0654, USA

Edmunds, Randall (Athlete, Football Player)
2307 Amity Woodlawn Rd
Lincolnton, GA 30817-1910, USA

Edmundson, Gary (Athlete, Hockey Player)
299 N Smith Ave
Corona, CA 92880-1741, USA

Edna, Dame (Actor, Comedian)
c/o Staff Member *PBJ Management*
7 Soho Street
London W1D 3DQ, United Kingdom

Edner, Ashley (Actor)
c/o Nicole Cataldo *Diverse Talent Group*
9911 W Pico Blvd Ste 340W
Los Angeles, CA 90035-2712, USA

Edner, Bobby (Actor)
c/o Kendall Park *JLA Talent Agency*
9151 W Sunset Blvd
West Hollywood, CA 90069-3106, USA

Edney, Leon A (Bud) (Admiral)
1037 Encino Row
Coronado, CA 92118-2813, USA

Edney, Tyus (Athlete, Basketball Player)
1800 S Floyd Ct
La Habra, CA 90631-2058, USA

Edson, Hilary (Actor)
400 S Beverly Dr Ste 216
Beverly Hills, CA 90212-4404, USA

Edson, James (Actor)
c/o Staff Member *Synergy Talent*
13251 Ventura Blvd
Studio City, CA 91604-1838, USA

Eduardo dos Santos, Jose (President)
Palacio do Povo
Luanda, ANGOLA

Edur, Tom (Athlete, Hockey Player)
Puhanga 77
Tallinn 10316, Estonia

Edward (Prince)
Bagshot Park
Surrey, ENGLAND GU19 5PN, UNITED KINGDOM

Edward, John (Psychic, Television Host)
c/o Jill Fritzo *PMK/BNC Public Relations (PMK-NY)*
622 3rd Ave Fl 8
New York, NY 10017-6707, USA

Edwards, Al (Athlete, Football Player)
3225 Arkansas Ave
Kenner, LA 70065-3612, USA

Edwards, Anthony (Actor, Producer)
c/o Steve Lovett *Lovett Management*
1327 Brinkley Ave
Los Angeles, CA 90049-3619, USA

Edwards, Antonio (Athlete, Football Player)
716 2nd St NW
Moultrie, GA 31768-3330, USA

Edwards, Antuan (Athlete, Football Player)
8108 Connestee Dr
McKinney, TX 75070-4820, USA

Edwards, Barbara (Actor, Model)
7767 Hollywood Blvd Apt 202
Los Angeles, CA 90046-2643, USA

Edwards, Bill (Athlete, Basketball Player)
6670 Linzie Ct
Franklin, OH 45005-5373, USA

Edwards, Brad (Athlete, Football Player)
202 Southwood Dr
Columbia, SC 29205-3222, USA

Edwards, Braylon (Athlete, Football Player)
32388 Legacy Pointe Pkwy
Avon Lake, OH 44012-2263, USA

Edwards, Carl (Race Car Driver)
122 Knob Hill Rd
Mooresville, NC 28117-6847, USA

Edwards, Charles C (Physicist)
Keeney Park 10666 N Torrey Pines Road
La Jolla, CA 92037, USA

Edwards, Cid (Athlete, Football Player)
5343 Adobe Falls Rd
San Diego, CA 92120-4403, USA

Edwards, Danny (Athlete, Golfer)
8361 E Evans Rd Ste 106
Scottsdale, AZ 85260-3617, USA

Edwards, Dave (Athlete, Baseball Player)
5059 Quail Run Rd Apt 75
Riverside, CA 92507-6485, USA

Edwards, David (Athlete, Golfer)
5 Champion Pl
Stillwater, OK 74074-1065, USA

Edwards, Dennis (Musician, Opera Singer, Songwriter, Writer)
PO Box 3172
Beverly Hills, CA 90212-0172, USA

Edwards, Don (Music Group, Musician, Songwriter, Writer)
433 S Cuchamas St
Colorado Springs, CO 80903, USA

Edwards, Don (Athlete, Hockey Player)
c/o Staff Member *Saginaw Spirit*
PO Box 6157
Saginaw, MI 48608-6157, USA

Edwards, Doug (Athlete, Basketball Player)
3001 Brookville Dr
Manhattan, KS 66502-8434, USA

Edwards, Dwan (Athlete, Football Player)
8 Norwich Ct
Owings Mills, MD 21117-2262, USA

Edwards, Earl (Athlete, Football Player)
1534 W Saint Thomas Dr
Gilbert, AZ 85233-6534, USA

Edwards, Eddie (Athlete, Football Player)
533 SW 61st Ter
Margate, FL 33068-1717, USA

Edwards, Eric (Cinematographer)
3404 SW Water Ave
Portland, OR 97239-4636, USA

Edwards, Gail
651 N Kilkea Dr
Los Angeles, CA 90048-2213

Edwards, Gareth (Soccer Player)
211 W Rd Nottage
Porthcawl, Mid-Glamorgan CF363RT, WALES

Edwards, Gary (Athlete, Hockey Player)
6818 Pecan Ave
Moorpark, CA 93021-1661, USA

Edwards, Geoff
249 Main
Ilderton, CANADA Ont. N0M 2

Edwards, Glen (Athlete, Football Player)
4115 31st St S
St Petersburg, FL 33712-4049, USA

Edwards, Harry (Activist, Educator)
Sociology
Berkeley, CA 94720-0001, USA

Edwards, Harry T (Judge)
333 Constitution Ave NW
Washington, DC 20001-2804, USA

Edwards, Herm (Athlete, Football Coach, Football Player)
433 Ward Pkwy Unit 1N
Kansas City, MO 64112-2128, USA

Edwards, Howard (Doc) (Athlete, Baseball Player, Coach)
3706 Driftwood Dr
San Angelo, TX 76904-5972, USA

Edwards, James (Basketball Player)
3890 Lakeland Ln
Bloomfield Township, MI 48302-1327, USA

Edwards, James B (Ex-Governor)
100 Venning St
Mount Pleasant, SC 29464-5323, USA

Edwards, Jay (Athlete, Basketball Player)
121 N Washington St Apt 506
Marion, IN 46952-2865, USA

Edwards, Jennifer (Actor)
4123 Saint Clair Ave
Studio City, CA 91604-1608, USA

Edwards, Jesse E (Doctor)
211 2nd St NW Apt 1911
Rochester, MN 55901-3101, USA

Edwards, Joe F Jr (Astronaut)
PO Box 1188
Houston, TX 77251-1188, USA

Edwards, Joel (Athlete, Golfer)
5809 Shoreside Bnd
Irving, TX 75039-3660, USA

Edwards, John (Musician)
3750 Hudson Manor Ter Apt 3AE
Bronx, NY 10463-1167, USA

Edwards, John (Ex-Senator, Politician)
1900 M St NW Ste 500
Washington, DC 20036-3522, USA

Edwards, Johnny (Athlete, Baseball Player)
2511 E Blue Lake Dr
Magnolia, TX 77354-4827, USA

Edwards, Jonathan (Athlete, Track Athlete)
10 Kendall Pl
London, England W1H3AH, United Kingdom

Edwards, Jonathan (Music Group, Songwriter, Writer)
437 Live Oak Loop NE
Albuquerque, NM 87122-1406, USA

Edwards, Kalimba (Athlete)
c/o Staff Member *Detroit Lions*
222 Republic Dr
Allen Park, MI 48101-3650, USA

Edwards, Kalimba (Athlete, Football Player)
6140 Sibling Pine Dr
Durham, NC 27705-7802, USA

Edwards, Kelvin (Athlete, Football Player)
1716 Brookarbor Ct
Arlington, TX 76018-2420, USA

Edwards, Kevin (Athlete, Basketball Player)
821 Reilly Ln
Lake Forest, IL 60045-4915, USA

Edwards, Lena F (Physicist)
821 Woodland Dr
Lakewood, NJ 08701-3038, USA

Edwards, Luke (Actor)
10474 Santa Monica Blvd Ste 380
Los Angeles, CA 90025-6943, USA

Edwards, Marc (Athlete, Football Player)
6426 Autumn Crest Ct
Westerville, OH 43082-8963, USA

Edwards, Mario (Athlete, Football Player)
PO Box 216
Prosper, TX 75078-0216, USA

Edwards, Marshall (Baseball Player)
8948 La Cintura Ct
San Diego, CA 92129-3316, USA

Edwards, Marv (Athlete, Hockey Player)
3277 1st Ave Lot 40
Mims, FL 32754-3136, USA

Edwards, Mike (Athlete, Baseball Player)
11370 Moreno Beach Dr
Moreno Valley, CA 92555-5240, USA

Edwards, Mike (Athlete, Baseball Player)
502 Sharon Ave
Mechanicsburg, PA 17055-6630, USA

Edwards, Paddi
1800 Avenue of the Stars Ste 400
Los Angeles, CA 90067-4206

Edwards, R Lavell (Coach, Football Coach, Football Player)
Athletic Dept
Provo, UT 84602, USA

Edwards, Randy (Athlete, Football Player)
1369 Mountain Park Dr NW
Kennesaw, GA 30152-4780, USA

Edwards, Robert (Athlete, Football Player)
931 Knight Rd
Tennille, GA 31089-4210, USA

Edwards, Robert A (Bob) (Correspondent)
635 Massachusetts Ave NW
Washington, DC 20001-3740, USA

Edwards, Robert G (Physicist)
Duck End Farm Dry Drayton
Cambridge, England CB38DB, United Kingdom

Edwards, Robert J (Editor)
Williamscot House near Banbury
England Oxon OX17 1AE, UNITED KINGDOM

Edwards, Sian (Conductor)
70 Twisden Rd
London, England NW5 1DN, UNITED KINGDOM

Edwards, Stacy (Actor)
10 100 Santa Monica Blvd # 2500
Los Angeles, CA 90067, USA

Edwards, Stephanie (Actor)
c/o Staff Member *Tisherman Gilbert Motley Drozdoski Talent Agency (TGMD)*
6767 Forest Lawn Dr Ste 101
Los Angeles, CA 90068-1050, USA

Edwards, Steve (Composer)
3980 Royal Oak Pl
Encino, CA 91436-3918, USA

Edwards, Teresa (Athlete, Basketball Player)
600 1st Ave N Ste Sky
Minneapolis, MN 55403-1400, USA

Edwards, Theodore (Blue) (Athlete, Basketball Player)
11945 Maria Ester Ct
Charlotte, NC 28277-2303, USA

Edwards, Tommy Lee (Cartoonist)
1700 Broadway
New York, NY 10019-5905, USA

Edwards, Tonya (Basketball Player)
American West Arena 201 E Jefferson St
Phoenix, AZ 85004, USA

Edwards, Troy (Athlete, Football Player)
6835 Foghorn Ln
Grand Prairie, TX 75054-7276, USA

Edwards, Wayne (Athlete, Baseball Player)
9738 Aqueduct Ave
North Hills, CA 91343-2035, USA

Edwards, Williams (Monk) (Athlete, Football Player)
431 W 30th St
Houston, TX 77018-8305, USA

Edwards III, Dixon (Athlete, Football Player)
PO Box 1011
Coppell, TX 75019-1011, USA

Edwards Jr, Charles C (Publisher)
715 Locust St
Des Moines, IA 50309-3703, USA

Eenhoorn, Robert (Athlete, Baseball Player)
Zermilieplaats 15 3068J
Rotterdam, Netherlands

Efron, Zac (Actor)
c/o Gina Hoffman *Baker Winokur Ryder Public Relations (BWR-LA)*
9100 Wilshire Blvd Ste 500 PMB WEST
Beverly Hills, CA 90212-3426, USA

Egan, Christopher (Actor)
c/o George Freeman *WmE2 (Endeavor-LA)*
9601 Wilshire Blvd Fl 3
Beverly Hills, CA 90210-5219, USA

Egan, Dick (Athlete, Baseball Player)
709 Carnoustie Ct
Garland, TX 75044-5054, USA

Egan, Edward M Cardinal (Religious Leader)
1011 1st Ave
New York, NY 10022-4112, USA

Egan, Jennifer (Writer)
1540 Broadway
New York, NY 10036-4039, USA

Egan, John (Johnny) (Athlete, Basketball Player)
2124 Nantucket Dr Apt B
Houston, TX 77057-2906, USA

Egan, John L (Business Person)
130 Wilton Rd
London, England SW1V 1LQ, UNITED KINGDOM

Egan, Kian (Musician)
c/o Staff Member *Solo Agency Ltd (UK)*
55 Fulham High St 2nd Floor
London SW6 3JJ, United Kingdom

Egan, Pat (Athlete, Hockey Player)
40 Cummings Way
Berkeley Heights, NJ 07922-2646, USA

Egan, Peter (Actor)
21 Golden Sq
London, England W1R 3PA, UNITED KINGDOM

Egan, Richard J (Business Person)
35 Parkwood Dr
Hopkinton, MA 01748-1659, USA

Egan, Susan (Actor)
c/o Staff Member *ML Management*
250 W 57th St Frnt 4
New York, NY 10107-0004, USA

Egan, Tom (Athlete, Baseball Player)
184 E Myrna Ln
Tempe, AZ 85284-3118, USA

Egbert, Dave (Television Host)
1329 Southpointe Dr
Red Bluff, CA 96080-5226, USA

Egdahl, Richard H (Doctor)
505 Tremont St Unit 704
Boston, MA 02116-6353, USA

Ege, Julie (Actor)
Upper Saint Martins
London, England WC2H 9EG, UNITED KINGDOM

Eger, David (Athlete, Golfer)
8703 Heydon Hall Cir
Charlotte, NC 28210-6054, USA

Egers, Jack (Athlete, Hockey Player)
24 Zinkann Cres Gd
Wellesley, ON N0B 2T0, Canada

Egerszegi, Kristina
Feszti A. u 4
Budapest, HUNGARY 1032

Egerszegi, Krisztina (Swimmer)
Koer Utca 1/A
1103 Budapest, HUNGARY

Eggar, Samantha (Actor)
c/o Staff Member *Diverse Talent Group*
9911 W Pico Blvd Ste 340W
Los Angeles, CA 90035-2712, USA

Eggby, David (Cinematographer)
c/o Ann Murtha *Murtha Agency*
1025 Colorado Ave Ste B
Santa Monica, CA 90401-2847, USA

Eggeling, Dale (Athlete, Golfer)
8918 Magnolia Chase Cir
Tampa, FL 33647-2219, USA

Eggers, Dave (Writer)
1230 Avenue of the Americas
New York, NY 10020-1513, USA

Eggers, Doug (Athlete, Football Player)
12803 Cedarbrook Ln
Laurel, MD 20708-2449, USA

Eggert, Nicole (Actor)
c/o Staff Member *Identity Talent Agency (ID)*
9107 Wilshire Blvd Ste 500
Beverly Hills, CA 90210-5526, USA

Eggert, Robert J (Economist)
1195 S Bates Rd
Cottonwood, AZ 86326-5415, USA

Eggerth, Marta
Park Dr. No.
Rye, NY 10580

Egglesfield, Colin (Actor)
c/o Colton Gramm *Brillstein Entertainment Partners*
9150 Wilshire Blvd Ste 350
Beverly Hills, CA 90212-3453, USA

Eggleston, William (Photographer)
526 W 26th St Rm 10A
New York, NY 10001-5541, USA

Eggleton, Arthur C (Government Official)
101 Colonel By Dr
Ottawa ON K1A OK2, CANADA

Eggold, Ryan (Actor)
c/o Andy Corren *Andy Corren Management*
1545 26th St Ste 200
Santa Monica, CA 90404-3554, USA

Egielski, Richard
525 B St Ste 1900
San Diego, CA 92101-4495

Egloff, Bruce (Athlete, Baseball Player)
3136 S Emporia Ct
Denver, CO 80231-4739, USA

Egloff, Ron (Athlete, Football Player)
975 Lincoln St # 5G-NT
Denver, CO 80203-2725, USA

Egnew, Danielle (Musician)
15030 Ventura Blvd Ste 843
Sherman Oaks, CA 91403-5470, USA

Egoyan, Atom (Actor)
80 Niagara St
Toronto ON M5V 1C5, CANADA

Ehle, Jennifer (Actor)
c/o Staff Member *International Creative Management (ICM-LA)*
10250 Constellation Blvd Fl 7
Los Angeles, CA 90067-6207, USA

Ehlers, Beth (Actor)
c/o Staff Member *Stone Manners Salners Agency (LA)*
9911 W Pico Blvd Ste 1400
Los Angeles, CA 90035-2715, USA

Ehlers, Edwin (Athlete, Basketball Player)
1236 Wayne St N
South Bend, IN 46615-1036, USA

Ehlers, Tom (Athlete, Football Player)
13898 Layton Rd
Mishawaka, IN 46544-9498, USA

Ehlers, Walter D (War Hero)
8382 Valley View St
Buena Park, CA 90620-2738, USA

Ehlo, Craig (Athlete, Basketball Player)
3323 E 77th Ave
Spokane, WA 99223-1943, USA

Ehrbar, Nicole (Stylist)
c/o Staff Member *Cartier (LA)*
370 N Rodeo Dr
Beverly Hills, CA 90210-5106, USA

Ehrenfeld, Lauren (Stylist)
c/o Staff Member *Celestine - CA*
1666 20th St Ste 200B
Santa Monica, CA 90404-3828, USA

Ehret, Gloria (Athlete, Golfer)
3335 Royal Ln
Dallas, TX 75229-5062, USA

Ehrhoff, Christian (Athlete, Hockey Player)
4517 Carlyle Ct
Santa Clara, CA 95054-3917, USA

Ehrlich, Paul R (Biologist)
Biological Sciences Dept
Stanford, CA 94305, USA

Ehrlich, S Paul Jr (Physicist)
1132 Seaspray Ave
Delray Beach, FL 33483-7140, USA

Ehrman, Bart D (Writer)
125 Saunders Hall Cb University of North Carolina at Chapel Hl # 3225
Chapel Hill, NC 27599-0001, USA

Ehrmann, Joe (Athlete, Football Player)
5 Elmhurst Rd
Baltimore, MD 21210-2216, USA

Eiber, Janet
9300 Wilshire Blvd Ste 410
Beverly Hills, CA 90212-3228

Eichelberger, Charles B (General)
124 Sweetwater Oaks
Peachtree City, GA 30269-2110, USA

Eichelberger, Dave (Athlete, Golfer)
1947 Judd Hillside Rd
Honolulu, HI 96822-2007, USA

Eichelberger, Juan (Athlete, Baseball Player)
14674 Silverset St
Poway, CA 92064-6408, USA

Eichhorn, Lisa (Actor)
c/o Staff Member *Conway van Gelder*
8-12 Broadwick St
London W1F 8HW, UK

Eichhorn, Mark (Athlete, Baseball Player)
147 Norma Ct
Aptos, CA 95003-9789, USA

Eichhorst, Richard (Athlete, Basketball Player)
2701 Sheridan Rd
Saint Louis, MO 63125-4168, USA

Eichorn, Lisa
1501 Broadway Ste 2600
New York, NY 10036-5600

Eick, Dick (Producer, Writer)
100 Universal City Plz Bldg 2372ASTE PMB E
Universal City, CA 91608-1002, USA

Eidem, Erik (Actor, Producer)
c/o Scott Zimmerman *Evolution Entertainment (LA)*
901 N Highland Ave
Los Angeles, CA 90038-2412, USA

Eidson, Jim (Athlete, Football Player)
3116 Purdue Ave
Dallas, TX 75225-7721, USA

Eifrid, Jim (Athlete, Football Player)
2710 Tyler Ave
Fort Wayne, IN 46808-1944, USA

Eigeman, Chris (Actor)
c/o Thomas Cushing *Innovative Artists (LA)*
1505 10th St
Santa Monica, CA 90401-2805, USA

Eigenberg, David (Actor)
c/o Sheree Cohen *Kohner Agency, The*
9300 Wilshire Blvd Ste 555
Beverly Hills, CA 90212-3211, USA

Eighth Wonder
50 Lisson St Unit 1B
London, ENGLAND NW1 5DF

Eigsti, Roger H (Business Person)
Safeco Plz
Seattle, WA 98185-0001, USA

Eikenberry, Jill (Actor)
c/o Wes Stevens *Vox*
6420 Wilshire Blvd Ste 1080
Los Angeles, CA 90048-5539, USA

Eikenes, Adele (Opera Singer)
4 Addison Bridge Pl
London, England W14 8XP, UNITED KINGDOM

Eiland, Dave (Athlete, Baseball Player)
2824 Blue Springs Pl
Wesley Chapel, FL 33544-8746, USA

Eilbacher, Cynthia
PO Box 8920
Universal City, CA 91608

Eilbacher, Lisa (Actor)
4600 Petit Ave
Encino, CA 91436-3216, USA

Eilber, Janet (Actor, Dancer)
344 E 59th St
New York, NY 10022-1593, USA

Eilers, Dave (Athlete, Baseball Player)
602 Perkins Ln
Brenham, TX 77833-4394, USA

Eilers, Pat (Athlete, Football Player)
177 De Windt Rd
Winnetka, IL 60093-3708, USA

Eilts, Hermann F (Diplomat)
PO Box 245
Benton, KS 67017-0245, USA

Einertson, Darrell (Athlete, Baseball Player)
221 Hawthorne Dr
Norwalk, IA 50211-9665, USA

Einziger, Mike (Musician)
c/o Staff Member *ArtistDirect*
9046 Lindblade St
Culver City, CA 90232-2513, USA

Eischeid, Mike (Athlete, Football Player)
306 Auburn St
West Union, IA 52175-1067, USA

Eischen, Joey (Athlete, Baseball Player)
16912 Hawkridge Rd
Lithia, FL 33547-5809, USA

Eisele, Eileen (Stylist)
c/o Staff Member *Ennis*
119 Braintree St
Boston, MA 02134-1628, USA

Eisen, Hal (Actor)
c/o Staff Member *Caldwell Jeffery*
943 Queen St E Fl 2
Toronto ON M4M 1J6, CANADA

Eisen, Herman N (Doctor)
75 Cambridge Pkwy Unit E806
Cambridge, MA 02142-1233, USA

Eisen, Thelma (Baseball Player)
396 Pintoresca Dr
Pacific Palisades, CA 90272-3318, USA

Eisen, Tripp (Music Group)
9100 Wilshire Blvd Ste 400W
Beverly Hills, CA 90212-3464, USA

Eisenberg, Jesse (Actor)
c/o Jennifer Allen *Viewpoint Inc*
8820 Wilshire Blvd Ste 220
Beverly Hills, CA 90211-2622, USA

Eisenberg, Lee B (Editor)
3286 N Park Blvd
Alcoa, TN 37701-3274, USA

Eisenberg, Leon (Doctor)
130 Mount Auburn St Apt 310
Cambridge, MA 02138-5779, USA

Eisenberg, Melvin A (Attorney, Attorney General, Educator, General)
1197 Keeler Ave
Berkeley, CA 94708-1753, USA

Eisenberg, Warren (Business Person)
650 Liberty Ave
Union, NJ 07083-8130, USA

Eisenhauer, Lawrence (Larry) (Athlete, Football Player)
2 Winter St Ste 402B
Waltham, MA 02451-0961, USA

Eisenhauer, Peggy (Designer, Special Effects Designer)
40 W 57th St # 1800
New York, NY 10019-4001, USA

Eisenhauer, Stephen S (Steve) (Athlete, Football Player)
105 Abbey Rd
Winchester, VA 22602-7402, USA

Eisenhooth, John (Athlete, Football Player)
546 Walnut St
Howard, PA 16841, USA

Eisenhower, David
Foxall Lane
Berwyn, PA 19312

Eisenhower, John
27318 Morris Rd
Trappe, MD 21673-1915

Eisenhower, Julie Nixon
Foxall Lane
Berwyn, PA 19312

Eisenhower, Susan
1050 17th St NW Ste 600
Washington, DC 20036-5517

Eisenman, Peter D (Architect)
40 W 25th St
New York, NY 10010-2707, USA

Eisenmann, Ike
6556 Blucher Ave
Van Nuys, CA 91406-6207

Eisenmann, Ike (Actor)
6556 Blucher Ave
Van Nuys, CA 91406-6207, USA

Eisenreich, James M (Jim) (Athlete, Baseball Player)
11 Emerald Shore Dr
Blue Springs, MO 64015-9658, USA

Eisenstein, Michael (Music Group)
155 Avenue of the Americas Rm 700
New York, NY 10013-1507, USA

Eisler, Lloyd
211-800 Montarville
Boucherville, CANADA PQ JYB 125

Eisley, Howard (Athlete, Basketball Player)
20250 Rodeo Ct
Southfield, MI 48075-1285, USA

Eisman, Hy (Cartoonist)
99 Boulevard
Glen Rock, NJ 07452-2003, USA

Eisner, Breck (Director)
c/o Gregory McKnight *Creative Artists Agency (CAA-LA)*
2000 Avenue of the Stars Ste 100
Los Angeles, CA 90067-4705, USA

Eisner, Michael (Business Person)
9401 Wilshire Blvd Ste 760
Beverly Hills, CA 90212-2946, USA

Eitan, Raphael (Admiral, General)
Knesset, Tel-Aviv, ISRAEL

Eitzel, Mark (Music Group, Songwriter, Writer)
7 Trinity Row
Florence, MA 01062-1931, USA

Eizenstat, Stuart E (Diplomat, Government Official)
5610 Wisconsin Ave Apt 603
Chevy Chase, MD 20815-4432, USA

Ejiofor, Chiwetel (Actor)
c/o Christina Papadopoulos *Baker Winokur Ryder Public Relations BWR (BWR-NY)*
292 Madison Ave Fl 12
New York, NY 10017-6415, USA

Ejogo, Carmen (Actor)
Drug House 34-43 Russell St
London WC2B, UNITED KINGDOM (UK)

Ek, Daniel
76 9th Ave PMB 11
New York, NY 10011-4929, USA

Ekberg, Ulf (Musician)
Norrtullsgatan 52
Stockholm 113 45, SWEDEN

Ekberg Anita
Via Aspro N(2 Genzano Di
Roma, ITALY 45

Eker, T Harv (Business Person)
300 N Commercial
Be, WA 98227-5008

Ekland, Britt (Actor)
1888 N Crescent Heights Blvd
Los Angeles, CA 90069-1647, USA

Eklund, A Sigvard (Physicist)
Krapfenwaldgasse 48
Vienna 1190, AUSTRIA

Eklund, Greg (Music Group)
30 Glenn St
White Plains, NY 10603-3254, USA

Eklund, Pelle (Athlete, Hockey Player)
c/o Staff Member *San Jose Sharks*
525 W Santa Clara St
San Jose, CA 95113-1500, USA

Ektaa (Actor, Bollywood)
Sagar Sangeet Opp. Colaba Post Office
Mumbai, MS 400005, INDIA

Ekuban, Ebenezer (Athlete, Football Player)
5391 Moonlight Way
Parker, CO 80134-4535, USA

El, Antwaan Randle (Athlete, Football Player)
c/o Fletcher Smith *Blueprint Sports Group*
221 W Jefferson Ave
Naperville, IL 60540-5355, USA

El Fadil, Siddig (Actor)
5555 Melrose Ave
Los Angeles, CA 90038-3989, USA

El Sitio (Moris y Santiago) (Musician)
c/o Gabriel Blanco *Gabriel Blanco Iglesias (Mexico)*
Rio Balsas 35-32 Colonia Cuauhtemoc
DF 6500, Mexico

Elam, Cleveland (Athlete, Football Player)
722 Brookmont Ave
Salisbury, NC 28146-7293, USA

Elam, Jason (Athlete, Football Player)
3686 Palmer Ridge Dr
Cliffside Park, NJ 7010, USA

Elander, Diane (Stylist)
552 N Las Casas Ave
Pacific Palisades, CA 90272-3310, USA

Elarton, Scott (Athlete, Baseball Player)
52922 Raines Rd
Limon, CO 80828-9029, USA

Elavarasan (Actor)
7 Mahalinga Rd
Chennai, TN 600 034, INDIA

Elba, Idris (DJ Big Driis) (Actor)
c/o Rupert Fowler *ID Public Relations*
Pall Mall Deposit 124-128 Barlby Rd Unit 27A
London W10 6BL, UK

ElBaradei, Mohamed (Nobel Prize Laureate)
Vienna International Centre Wagramer Str. 5
Wien A-1400, Austria

Elbaradel, Mohamed (Government Official)
Wagramserstr
Vienna 1400, AUSTRIA

Eldard, Ron (Actor)
c/o William Choi *Management 360*
9111 Wilshire Blvd
Beverly Hills, CA 90210-5508, USA

Elder, Dave (Athlete, Baseball Player)
2642 High St SW
Conyers, GA 30094-6843, USA

Elder, George (Athlete, Baseball Player)
423 Amethyst Dr
Fruita, CO 81521-8813, USA

Elder, Larry (Actor)
c/o Ariel (Ari) Emanuel *WmE2 (Endeavor-LA)*
9601 Wilshire Blvd Fl 3
Beverly Hills, CA 90210-5219, USA

Elder, Lee E (Athlete, Golfer)
PO Box 667200
Pompano Beach, FL 33066-7200, USA

Elder, Mark P
London Coliseum
London WC2N 4ES, UNITED KINGDOM (UK)

Elders, M Jocelyn (Doctor, Government Official)
Pediatrics Dept
Little Rock, AR 72205, USA

Eldred, Brad (Athlete, Baseball Player)
4182 SW Saint Lucie Ln
Palm City, FL 34990-3830, USA

Eldred, Cal (Athlete, Baseball Player)
1893 Horn Rd
Mount Vernon, IA 52314-9517, USA

Eldredge, Allison (Music Group)
40 W 25th St
New York, NY 10010-2707, USA

Electra, Carmen (Actor, Model)
c/o Stephanie Simon *Untitled Entertainment (LA)*
350 S Beverly Dr Ste 200
Beverly Hills, CA 90212-4819, USA

Electrik Red (Music Group, Musician)
c/o Staff Member *Island Def Jam Music Group*
825 8th Ave Fl 28
New York, NY 10019-7416

Elegant, Robert S (Writer)
Manor House Middle Green near Langley
Bucks SL3 6BS, UNITED KINGDOM (UK)

Eleniak, Erika (Actor, Model)
c/o Danielle Bilodeau *Kirk Talent Agencies Inc*
70 East 2nd. Ave Suite 301
Vancouver, BC V5T 1B1, Canada

Elfman, Bodhi (Actor)
c/o Staff Member *Stone Manners Salners Agency (LA)*
9911 W Pico Blvd Ste 1400
Los Angeles, CA 90035-2715, USA

Elfman, Danny (Composer, Musical Director, Musician)
c/o Richard Kraft *Kraft-Engel Management*
15233 Ventura Blvd Ste 200
Sherman Oaks, CA 91403-2244, USA

Elfman, Jenna (Actor, Model, Producer)
c/o David McIlvain *Brillstein Entertainment Partners*
9150 Wilshire Blvd Ste 350
Beverly Hills, CA 90212-3453, USA

Elfont, Harry (Director, Writer)
c/o Staff Member *WmE2 (WMA-LA)*
1 William Morris Pl
Beverly Hills, CA 90212-4261, USA

Elgart, Larry
2065 Gulf of Mexico Dr
Longboat Key, FL 34228-3202

Elgart, Larry J (Music Group)
2065 Gulf of Mexico Dr
Longboat Key, FL 34228-3202, USA

Elgen, Manfred (Nobel Prize Laureate)
Georg-Dehio-Weg 4
37075 Gottingen, Germany

Eli Young Band (Music Group)
c/o Staff Member *Paradigm (Monterey)*
404 W Franklin St
Monterey, CA 93940-2303, USA

Elia, Bruce (Athlete, Football Player)
7 Grant Ave
Grant, MI 49327, USA

Elia, Lee (Athlete, Baseball Player, Coach)
11613 Innfields Dr
Odessa, FL 33556-5407, USA

Elias, Eliane (Composer, Director, Music Group, Musical Director, Musician)
1282 RR 376
Wappingers Falls, NY 12590, USA

Elias, Homer (Athlete, Football Player)
12250 Walnut Ave
Grant, MI 49327-8695, USA

Elias, Jonathan (Composer, Musician)
c/o Staff Member *Gorfaine/Schwartz Agency Inc*
4111 W Alameda Ave Ste 509
Burbank, CA 91505-4171, USA

Elias, Keith (Athlete, Football Player)
4507 Norma Pl
Toms River, NJ 08755-1097, USA

Elias, Patrick (Composer)
1005 Smith Manor Blvd # 98
West Orange, NJ 07052-4227, USA

Elias, Patrik (Athlete, Hockey Player)
1005 Smith Manor Blvd
West Orange, NJ 07052-4227, USA

Elias, Rosalind (Opera Singer)
Harkness Plaza 61 W 62nd St #6F
New York, NY 10023, USA

Elich, Matt (Athlete, Hockey Player)
276 McKinley Ave
Grosse Pointe Farms, MI 48236-3460, USA

Elie, Mario (Athlete, Basketball Player)
1 Mott Ln
Houston, TX 77024-7315, USA

Eliel, Ernest L (Misc)
345 Carolina Meadows Villa
Chapel Hill, NC 27517-7519, USA

Eliff, Tom (Religious Leader)
901 Commerce St Ste 750
Nashville, TN 37203-3600, USA

Elik, Bo (Athlete, Hockey Player)
1-668 Dean Ave
Oshawa, ON L1H 3E9, Canada

Elinson, Jack (Scientist)
655 Pomander Walk Ave
Teeneck, NJ 07666-1673, USA

Eliopulos, Jim (Athlete, Football Player)
2500 Macero St
Roseville, CA 95747-5000, USA

Eliot, Alison
2 Ironsides # 18
Marina del Rey, CA 90292

Eliot, Darren (Athlete, Hockey Player)
1100 Grayton St
Grosse Pointe Park, MI 48230-1427, USA

Eliot, Jan (Cartoonist)
PO Box 50032
Eugene, OR 97405-0967, USA

Eliot, Sharon (Stylist)
2600 Netherland Ave Apt 2105
Bronx, NY 10463-4820, USA

Elise, Christine (Actor, Writer)
c/o Mara Santino *Luber Roklin Management*
8530 Wilshire Blvd Ste 550
Beverly Hills, CA 90211-3133, USA

Elise, Kimberly (Actor)
c/o Evan Hainey *Untitled Entertainment (LA)*
350 S Beverly Dr Ste 200
Beverly Hills, CA 90212-4819, USA

Elisha, Walter Y (Business Person)
205 N White St
Fort Mill, SC 29715-1654, USA

Elizabeth, Princess
1526 N Beverly Dr
Beverly Hills, CA 90210-2314

Elizabeth, Shannon (Actor, Producer)
c/o Wes Stevens *Vox*
6420 Wilshire Blvd Ste 1080
Los Angeles, CA 90048-5539, USA

Elizondo, Hector (Actor)
c/o Nina Nisenholtz *N2N Entertainment*
1230 Montana Ave Ste 203
Santa Monica, CA 90403-5987, USA

Elk, Jim (Actor)
6442 Coldwater Canyon Ave Ste 206
Valley Glen, CA 91606-1174, USA

Elkes, Joel (Doctor, Psychic)
Psychiatry/Behavioral Sci
Louisville, KY 40292-0001, USA

Elkind, Mortimer M (Physicist)
16925 Hierba Dr
San Diego, CA 92128-2688, USA

Elkington, Steve (Athlete, Golfer)
7010 Kelsey Rae Ct
Houston, TX 77069-1102, USA

Elkins, Hillard (Producer)
1335 N Doheny Dr
Los Angeles, CA 90069-1760, USA

Elkins, Larry
111 S Saint Joseph St
South Bend, IN 46601-1901

Elkins, Larry (Athlete, Football Player)
4407 McArthur Cir
Brownwood, TX 76801-7334, USA

Elkins, Lawrence C (Larry) (Athlete, Football Player)
1 Keats Avenue Norden
Rochdale, Lancestershire OL12 7PZ, UK

Elkins, Mike (Athlete, Football Player)
743 Drifting Wind Run
Dripping Springs, TX 78620-4487, USA

Ell, Erica (Stylist)
c/o Staff Member *Team*
423 W Broadway Ste 406
Boston, MA 02127-2265, USA

Ellard, Henry A (Athlete, Football Player)
4631 E Byrd Ave
Fresno, CA 93725-1640, USA

Ellena, Jack (Athlete, Football Player)
73164 Monterra Cir N
Palm Desert, CA 92260-6616, USA

Ellenbogen, Bill (Athlete, Football Player)
777 Pelham Rd Apt 2G
New Rochelle, NY 10805-1137, USA

Ellenstein, Robert (Actor)
5212 Sepulveda Blvd # 23F
Culver City, CA 90230, USA

Eller, Carl (Athlete, Football Player, Misc)
1035 Washburn Ave N
Minneapolis, MN 55411-3557, USA

Ellerbee, Linda (Correspondent)
c/o Staff Member *Lucky Duck Productions*
96 Morton St Fl 4
New York, NY 10014-3375, USA

Ellerson, Gary (Athlete, Football Player)
S86W18643 Sue Marie Ln
Muskego, WI 53150-8718, USA

Ellett, Dave (Athlete, Hockey Player)
36611 N 51st St
Cave Creek, AZ 85331-8820, USA

Elliman, Donald M Jr (Publisher)
Rockefeller Center
New York, NY 10020, USA

Ellin, Doug (Actor, Director, Producer, Writer)
c/o Stephen (Steve) Levinson *Leverage Management*
3030 Pennsylvania Ave
Santa Monica, CA 90404-4112, USA

Elling, Kurt (Music Group, Musician)
c/o Ted Kurland *Ted Kurland Associates*
173 Brighton Ave
Boston, MA 02134-2003, USA

Ellingsen, Bruce (Athlete, Baseball Player)
5873 Daneland St
Lakewood, CA 90713-1830, USA

Ellingson, Evan (Actor)
c/o Staff Member *Reel Talent Management*
PO Box 491035
Los Angeles, CA 90049-9035, USA

Elliot, Larry (Athlete, Baseball Player)
13010 Caminito Bracho
San Diego, CA 92128-1808, USA

Elliot, Lin (Athlete, Football Player)
540 Lost Hunters Cyn
China Spring, TX 76633-3455, USA

Elliot, Ross
5702 Graves Ave
Encino, CA 91316-1441

Elliot, Stephan
Box 452
Paddington, AUSTRALIA NSW 2021

Elliot, Tony (Athlete, Football Player)
22855 Vasilios Ct
Novi, MI 48374-3520, USA

Elliott, Abby (Actor, Comedian)
c/o Tom Demko *Bauer Company, The*
9465 Wilshire Blvd Ste 420
Beverly Hills, CA 90212-2603, USA

Elliott, Alecia (Actor, Music Group)
PO Box 3075
Muscle Shoals, AL 35662-3075, USA

Elliott, Alison (Actor)
2 Ironsides # 18
Marina del Rey, CA 90292, USA

Elliott, Allison
1505 10th St
Santa Monica, CA 90401-2805

Elliott, Brennan (Actor)
c/o Christopher (Chris) Wright *Christopher Wright Management*
3207 Winnie Dr
Los Angeles, CA 90068-1439, USA

Elliott, Brook (Actor)
c/o Nancy Curtis *Harden-Curtis Associates*
850 7th Ave Ste 903
New York, NY 10019-5438, USA

Elliott, Brooke (Actor)
c/o Jonathan Howard *Innovative Artists (LA)*
1505 10th St
Santa Monica, CA 90401-2805, USA

Elliott, Chalmers (Bump) (Coach, Football Coach, Football Player)
Athletic Dept
Iowa City, IA 52242, USA

Elliott, Chris (Actor, Comedian)
c/o Tom Demko *Bauer Company, The*
9720 Wilshire Blvd Mezzanine
Beverly Hills, CA 90212, USA

Elliott, David James (Actor)
c/o Bob McGowan *McGowan Management*
8733 W Sunset Blvd Ste 103
West Hollywood, CA 90069-2241, USA

Elliott, Dennis (Music Group)
16501 Ventura Blvd Ste 602
Encino, CA 91436-2072, USA

Elliott, DJ (Actor)
c/o Evan Silverberg *Silverberg Management Group (SMG)*
PO Box 572559
Tarzana, CA 91357-2559, USA

Elliott, Donnie (Athlete, Baseball Player)
1206 Bayou Vista Dr
Deer Park, TX 77536-6902, USA

Elliott, Gordon (Chef, Producer)
c/o Staff Member *Follow Productions*
589 8th Ave Fl 12
New York, NY 10018-3086, USA

Elliott, Harry (Athlete, Baseball Player)
9608 Los Coches Rd
Lakeside, CA 92040-4240, USA

Elliott, Herbert (Herb) (Athlete, Track Athlete)
431 St Kilda Rd # 22
Melbourne, VIC 3004, AUSTRALIA

Elliott, Joe (Musician)
c/o Rod MacSween *International Talent Booking*
1st Floor, Ariel House 74A Charlotte St
London W1T 4QJ, UNITED KINGDOM

Elliott, John (Athlete, Football Player)
17 Fieldstone Ln
Oyster Bay, NY 11771-3122, USA

Elliott, John (Athlete, Golfer)
235 Lexington Rd
Glastonbury, CT 06033-1289, USA

Elliott, John (Jumbo) (Athlete, Football Player)
108 Tropical Dr
Victoria, TX 77904-1145, USA

Elliott, Lenvil (Athlete, Football Player)
11579 Wood Oak Ave Apt 2
Richmond, MO 64085-8071, USA

Elliott, Matt (Athlete, Football Player)
7453 Coventry Woods Dr
Dublin, OH 43017-8608, USA

Elliott, Michael (Misc)
45 Larkfield Ewhurst Cranleigh
Surrey GU6 7QU, UNITED KINGDOM (UK)

Elliott, Missy (Actor, Musician, Producer)
c/o Mona Scott-Young *Monami Entertainment*
12 Hillcrest Ave
West Orange, NJ 07052-2404, USA

Elliott, Paul H (Cinematographer)
9150 Wilshire Blvd Ste 220
Beverly Hills, CA 90212-3429, USA

Elliott, Peggy Gordon (Educator)
506 Meadow Creek Dr
Volga, SD 57071-2132, USA

Elliott, Pete3
003 Dunbarton Ave NW
Canton, OH 44708-1818

Elliott, Peter R (Pete) (Athlete, Coach, Football Coach, Football Player)
3003 Dunbarton Ave NW
Canton, OH 44708-1818, USA

Elliott, R Keith (Business Person)
Hercules Plaza 1313 North Market St
Wilmington, DE 19894-0001, USA

Elliott, Randy (Athlete, Baseball Player)
PO Box 834
Somis, CA 93066-0834, USA

Elliott, Robert (Athlete, Basketball Player)
6760 E Fieldstone Ln
Tucson, AZ 85750-2075, USA

Elliott, Sam (Actor)
c/o Iris Grossman *International Creative Management (ICM-LA)*
10250 Constellation Blvd Fl 7
Los Angeles, CA 90067-6207, USA

Elliott, Sean M (Athlete, Basketball Player)
1726 Greystone Rdg
San Antonio, TX 78258-4506, USA

Elliott, Ted (Writer)
c/o Brian Siberell *Creative Artists Agency (CAA-LA)*
2000 Avenue of the Stars Ste 100
Los Angeles, CA 90067-4705, USA

Ellis, Albert (Doctor)
75 W End Ave Apt C14J
New York, NY 10023-7862, USA

Ellis, Alex (Athlete, Basketball Player)
10121 Lone Wolf Dr
Indianapolis, IN 46235-8252, USA

Ellis, Allan (Athlete, Football Player)
4318 Mayfair Ct
Country Club Hills, IL 60478-5132, USA

Ellis, Anita
130 E End Ave
New York, NY 10028-7553

Ellis, Aunjanue (Actor)
c/o Howard Axel *TMT Entertainment Group*
648 Broadway Ste 1002
New York, NY 10012-2348, USA

Ellis, Bo (Athlete, Basketball Player)
516 N 14th St
Milwaukee, WI 53233, USA

Ellis, Bret Easton (Writer)
40 W 57th St # 1800
New York, NY 10019-4001, USA

Ellis, Caroline (Actor)
8060 Saint Clair Ave
North Hollywood, CA 91605-1321, USA

Ellis, Chris (Athlete, Football Player)
c/o Melvin Bratton *DeBartolo Sports and Entertainment*
522 Washington Ave
Pittsburgh, PA 15106, USA

Ellis, Cliff (Basketball Player, Coach)
Athletic Dept
Auburn, AL 36831, USA

Ellis, Dale (Athlete, Basketball Player)
3564 W Hampton Dr NW
Marietta, GA 30064-1775, USA

Ellis, Danny (Athlete, Golfer)
1543 Cherry Lake Way
Lake Mary, FL 32746-1906, USA

Ellis, Dock P (Athlete, Baseball Player)
14042 Jockey Ln
Victorville, CA 92394-7564, USA

Ellis, Don (Bowler)
34 Crestwood Cir
Sugar Land, TX 77478-3914, USA

Ellis, Elmer (Historian)
3300 New Haven Rd # 223
Columbia, MO 65201-5423, USA

Ellis, Gerry (Athlete, Football Player)
250 Cavil Way
De Pere, WI 54115-3772, USA

Ellis, Gregory (Athlete, Football Player)
PO Box 96075
Southlake, TX 76092-0111, USA

Ellis, Harold (Athlete, Basketball Player)
9420 Parkwood Ave
Douglasville, GA 30135-7504, USA

Ellis, Hunter (Actor, Reality TV Star)
c/o Lauren Feeney *Ideal Management*
172 81st St
Brooklyn, NY 11209-3502, United States

Ellis, James R (General)
4213 W Swann Ave
Tampa, FL 33609-4330, USA

Ellis, Janet (Actor)
1/3 Charlotte St
London W1P 1HD, UNITED KINGDOM (UK)

Ellis, Jim (Athlete, Baseball Player)
13608 Avenue 224
Tulare, CA 93274-9304, USA

Ellis, Jimmy (Boxer)
5218 Saint Gabriel Ln
Louisville, KY 40291-1610, USA

Ellis, John (Athlete, Baseball Player)
14 Marina Point Dr
Old Saybrook, CT 06475-2541, USA

Ellis, Joseph J (Writer)
History Dept
South Hadley, MA 1075, USA

Ellis, Kathleen (Kathy) (Swimmer)
3024 Woodshore Ct
Carmel, IN 46033-3643, USA

Ellis, Kenneth (Athlete, Football Player)
13826 Brantley Dr
Baker, LA 70714-4634, USA

Ellis, LaPhonso (Athlete, Basketball Player)
51215 Shannon Brook Ct
Granger, IN 46530-7905, USA

Ellis, Larry R (General)
Deputy Chief of Staff Operations/Plans
Hqusa Pentagon
Washington, DC 20310-0001, USA

Ellis, Leroy (Athlete, Basketball Player)
4818 NE Halsey St
Portland, OR 97213-2166, USA

Ellis, Luther (Athlete, Football Player)
527 Riverside Ave
Mancos, CO 81328, USA

Ellis, M Herbert (Herb) (Music Group)
11806 N 56th St
Temple Terrace, FL 33617-1652, USA

Ellis, Mark (Athlete, Baseball Player)
318 Kinney Ave
Rapid City, SD 57702-2332, USA

Ellis, Mark (Stylist)
c/o Staff Member *Ennis*
119 Braintree St
Boston, MA 02134-1628, USA

Ellis, Mary
54 Eaton Sq
London, ENGLAND SW1 W9BE

Ellis, Maurice (Bo) (Athlete, Basketball Player)
1229 E 158th St
South Holland, IL 60473-1804, USA

Ellis, Michelle (Athlete, Golfer)
4610 N Armenia Ave Apt 225
Tampa, FL 33603-2725, USA

Ellis, Nelsan (Actor)
c/o Emily Gerson Saines *Brookside Artists Management (NY)*
250 W 57th St Ste 2303
New York, NY 10107-2399, USA

Ellis, Osian G (Misc)
90 Chandos Ave
London N20 9DZ, UNITED KINGDOM (UK)

Ellis, Patrick (H J) (Educator)
President S Ofc
Washington, DC 20064-0001, USA

Ellis, Ray (Athlete, Football Player)
4666 E Olney Ave
Gilbert, AZ 85234-7836, USA

Ellis, Rob (Athlete, Baseball Player)
2020 Krislin Dr NE
Grand Rapids, MI 49505-7160, USA

Ellis, Robert (Athlete, Baseball Player)
2066 75th Ave
Baton Rouge, LA 70807-5836, USA

Ellis, Roger (Athlete, Football Player)
196 Blue Heron Lake Cir
Ormond Beach, FL 32174-8153, USA

Ellis, Romallis (Boxer)
2062 San Marco Dr
Ellenwood, GA 30294-1009, USA

Ellis, Ronald J E (Ron) (Athlete, Hockey Player)
c/o Staff Member *Hockey Hall of Fame*
B C E Place 30 Yonge St
Toronto, ON M5E 1X8, Canada

Ellis, Sammy (Athlete, Baseball Player)
12511 Forest Highlands Dr
Dade City, FL 33525-8273, USA

Ellis, Samuel J (Sam) (Baseball Player)
12511 Forest Highlands Dr
Dade City, FL 33525-8273, USA

Ellis, Scott (Director)
301 W 118th St Apt 10I
New York, NY 10026-1078, USA

Ellis, Sedrick (Athlete, Football Player)
c/o Eugene Parker *Maximum Sports Management*
6435 W Jefferson Blvd # 197
Fort Wayne, IN 46804-6203, USA

Ellis, Shuan (Athlete, Football Player)
1000 Fulton Ave
Hempstead, NY 11550-1030, USA

Ellis, Terry (Music Group)
75 Rockefeller Plz # 1200
New York, NY 10019-6908, USA

Ellis Brothers (Music Group, Musician)
PO Box 50221
Nashville, TN 37205-0221, USA

Ellis Jr, Clarence J (Athlete, Football Player)
120 Hights Holw
Fayetteville, GA 30215-5139, USA

Ellis-Bextor, Sophie (Actor, Musician)
c/o Staff Member *Universal Music Ltd (UK)*
22 St Peters Square
London W6 9NW, UNITED KINGDOM

Ellison, Chase (Actor)
c/o Staff Member *Artistry Management*
340 N Camden Dr Ste 302
Beverly Hills, CA 90210-5116, USA

Ellison, David (Actor)
c/o Eddie Michaels *Insignia Public Relations*
1507 20th St Ste D
Santa Monica, CA 90404-3474, USA

Ellison, Faye E (Stylist)
5501 Ewing Cir S
Edina, MN 55410-2366, USA

Ellison, Harlan
PO Box 55548
Sherman Oaks, CA 91413-0548

Ellison, Harlan J (Writer)
PO Box 55548
Sherman Oaks, CA 91413-0548, USA

Ellison, Jason (Athlete, Baseball Player)
3745 248th Ave SE
Issaquah, WA 98029-7717, USA

Ellison, Jennifer (Actor)
c/o Colette Fenlon *Colette Fenlon Management*
2A Eaton Rd West Derby
Liverpool L2 7JJ, UNITED KINGDOM

Ellison, Keith (Congressman, Politician)
1027 Longworth Hob
Washington, DC 20515-2101, USA

Ellison, Larry (Business Person)
500 Oracle Pkwy
Redwood City, CA 94065-1677, USA

Ellison, Lawrence J (Business Person)
500 Oracle Pkwy
Redwood City, CA 94065-1677, USA

Ellison, Pervis (Athlete, Basketball Player)
4602 Kettering Dr NE
Roswell, GA 30075-3190, USA

Ellison, Riki (Athlete, Football Player)
11 Wharf St
Alexandria, VA 22314-3881, USA

Ellison, William H (Willie) (Athlete, Football Player)
3503 Mosley Ct
Houston, TX 77004-4114, USA

Elliss, Luther (Athlete, Football Player)
3760 Evelyn Dr
Salt Lake City, UT 84124-2306, USA

Ellroy, James (Writer)
146 E 19th St
New York, NY 10003-2404, USA

Ellsberg, Daniel (Politician)
90 Norwood Ave
Kensington, CA 94707-1150, USA

Ellsbury, Jacoby (Athlete, Baseball Player)
c/o Scott Boras *Boras Corporation*
18 Corporate Plaza Dr
Newport Beach, CA 92660-7901, USA

Ellsworth, Frank L (Educator)
465 W 23rd St # 15L
New York, NY 10011-2104, USA

Ellsworth, Kiko (Actor)
c/o Staff Member *Psycho Rock Productions*
PO Box 5646
Sherman Oaks, CA 91413-5646, USA

Ellsworth, Percy (Athlete, Football Player)
11261 Fortsville Rd
Drewryville, VA 23844, USA

Ellsworth, Richard C (Dick) (Athlete, Baseball Player)
1099 W Morris Ave
Fresno, CA 93711-2432, USA

Ellsworth, Steve (Athlete, Baseball Player)
546 W Enterprise Ave
Clovis, CA 93619-8356, USA

Ellwood, Paul M Jr (Physicist)
PO Box 270
Bondurant, WY 82922-0270, USA

Ellzey, Charley (Athlete, Football Player)
116 Roosevelt St
Quitman, MS 39355-2018, USA

Elman, Jamie (Actor)
c/o Staff Member *Kohner Agency, The*
9300 Wilshire Blvd Ste 555
Beverly Hills, CA 90212-3211, USA

Elmendorf, Dave (Athlete, Football Player)
17990 FM 1452 W
Normangee, TX 77871-4174, USA

Elmore, Henry (Athlete, Baseball Player)
4311 43rd Pl N
Birmingham, AL 35217-3925, USA

Elmore, Len (Athlete, Basketball Player)
PO Box 22
Highland, MD 20777-0022, USA

Elrod, Jack (Cartoonist)
7240 Hunters Branch Dr NE
Atlanta, GA 30328-1719, USA

Elrod, James (Athlete, Football Player)
10124 S Maplewood Ave
Tulsa, OK 74137-7085, USA

Elrod, Scott (Actor)
c/o Steven Jensen *The Independent Group*
6363 Wilshire Blvd Ste 115
Los Angeles, CA 90048-5734, USA

Els, Ernie (Athlete, Golfer)
c/o Andrew ""Chubby"" Chandler *International Sports Management Ltd (ISM UK)*
Cherry Tree Farm Cherry Tree Lane
Rostherne, Cheshire WA14 3RZ, UNITED KINGDOM

Elshire, Neil (Athlete, Football Player)
2441 NW Torsway St
Bend, OR 97701-8647, USA

Elsna, Hebe (Writer)
162/168 Regent St
London W1R 5TB, UNITED KINGDOM (UK)

Elsner, Hannelore
ZBF Leopoldstr. 19
Munich, GERMANY D-80802

Elson, Francisco (Athlete, Basketball Player)
92 Foxton Dr
San Antonio, TX 78258, USA

Elson, Karen (Model)
9 Rue Scribe
Paris 75009, FRANCE

Elster, Kevin D (Athlete, Baseball Player)
5801 Marshall Dr
Huntington Beach, CA 92649-2727, USA

Elston, Darrell (Athlete, Basketball Player)
2596 W State Road 28
Tipton, IN 46072-9787, USA

Elsworth, Michael (Actor)
PO Box 1243
Wellington, NEW ZEALAND

Elswrit, Richard (Rik) (Music Group)
9850 Sandalwood Blvd # 458
Boca Raton, FL 33428, USA

Elter, Leo (Athlete, Football Player)
13 Emma Dr
Pittsburgh, PA 15223-1201, USA

Elton, Ben (Actor, Comedian)
35 Soho Square
London W1V 5DG, UNITED KINGDOM (UK)

Elvin, Violetta (Ballerina)
Marina di Equa 80066 Seiano
Bay of Naples, ITALY

Elvira
16830 Ventura Blvd Ste 501
Encino, CA 91436-1717, USA

Elway, John A (Athlete, Football Player)
2500 E 1st Ave Ste 101
Denver, CO 80206-5631, USA

Elwes, Cary (Actor)
c/o Staff Member *Kritzer Levine Wilkins Entertainment*
11872 La Grange Ave Fl 1
Los Angeles, CA 90025-5283, USA

Ely, Alexandre (Soccer Player)
5526 N 2nd St
Philadelphia, PA 19120-2904, USA

Ely, Jack (Music Group)
PO Box 53664
Indianapolis, IN 46253-0664, USA

Ely, Joe (Music Group, Songwriter, Writer)
34 N Palm St Ste 100
Ventura, CA 93001-2610, USA

Ely, Larry (Athlete, Football Player)
12190 Waters Edge Ct
Loveland, OH 45140-4828, USA

Ely, Melvin (Basketball Player)
Staples Center 1111 S Figueroa St
Los Angeles, CA 90015, USA

Elynuik, Pat (Athlete, Hockey Player)
143 Aspen Grn
Calgary, AB T3Z 3B9, Canada

Eman, J H A (Henny) (Prime Minister)
Oranjestad, ARUBA

Emanuel, Alphonsia (Actor)
12/13 Poland St
London W1V 2DE, UNITED KINGDOM (UK)

Emanuel, Bert (Athlete, Football Player)
15 Bees Creek Ct
Missouri City, TX 77459-6734, USA

Emanuel, Elizabeth F (Designer, Fashion Designer)
42A Warrington Crescent Maida Vale
London W9 1EP, UNITED KINGDOM (UK)

Emanuel, Frank (Athlete, Football Player)
932 Michele Cir
Dunedin, FL 34698-6132, USA

Emanuel, Rahm (Government Official, Journalist)
c/o Staff Member *White House, The*
1600 Pennsylvania Ave NW
Washington, DC 20500-0004, USA

Embach, Carsten (Athlete)
Grafenrodaer Str 2
Oberhof 98559, GERMANY

Emberg, Kelly (Actor, Model)
PO Box 675401
Rancho Santa Fe, CA 92067-5401, USA

Embery, Joan
. San Diego Zoo
Park Blvd, San Diego 92104

Embrace (Music Group)
c/o Staff Member *Paradigm (Monterey)*
404 W Franklin St
Monterey, CA 93940-2303, USA

Embree, Alan (Athlete, Baseball Player)
61971 Kildonan Ct
Bend, OR 97702-9185, USA

Embree, John (Athlete, Football Player)
431 E Moorehaven Dr
Carson, CA 90746-1150, USA

Embree, Jon (Athlete, Football Player)
9450 Owl Ln
Boulder, CO 80301-5503, USA

Embry, Ethan (Actor)
c/o Brad Schenck *Paradigm (LA)*
360 N Crescent Dr
Beverly Hills, CA 90210-4874, USA

Embry, Wayne (Athlete, Basketball Player, Misc)
1101-211 Queens Quay W
Toronto, Ontario M5J 2M6, Canada

Emburey, John E (Cricketer)
Wantage Road
Northampton NN1 4TJ, UNITED KINGDOM (UK)

Emerick, Kate (Actor)
c/o Matt Sherman *Matt Sherman Management*
9107 Wilshire Blvd Ste 225
Beverly Hills, CA 90210-5546, USA

Emerson, Alice F (Educator)
140 E 62nd St
New York, NY 10065-8124, USA

Emerson, Chris (Actor)
c/o Lorraine Berglund *Lorraine Berglund Management*
11537 Hesby St
North Hollywood, CA 91601-3618, USA

Emerson, David F (Admiral)
211 E 18th St Apt 5O
New York, NY 10003-3627, USA

Emerson, Douglas (Actor)
1450 Belfast Dr
Los Angeles, CA 90069-1327, USA

Emerson, George H (Educator)
President S Ofc
Logan, UT 84322-0001, USA

Emerson, J Martin (Misc)
1501 Broadway
New York, NY 10036-5601, USA

Emerson, Jo Ann (Congressman, Politician)
2230 Rayburn Hob
Washington, DC 20515-1404, USA

Emerson, Keith (Musician)
c/o Staff Member *Carlini Group*
445 Park Ave Fl 9
New York, NY 10022-8632, USA

Emerson, Michael (Actor)
c/o Staff Member *Vanguard Management Group*
8060 Melrose Ave Fl 4
Los Angeles, CA 90046-7038, USA

Emerson, Nelson (Athlete, Hockey Player)
717 33rd St
Manhattan Beach, CA 90266-3425, USA

Emerson, Roy (Athlete, Tennis Player)
2221 Alta Vista Dr
Newport Beach, CA 92660-4128, USA

Emerson Drive (Music Group)
c/o Staff Member *Creative Artists Agency (CAA-TN)*
3310 W End Ave Fl 5
Nashville, TN 37203-1028, USA

Emery, Cal (Athlete, Baseball Player)
4817 S 195th East Ave
Broken Arrow, OK 74014-8068, USA

Emery, John (Athlete)
2001 Union St
San Francisco, CA 94123-4114, USA

Emery, Julie Ann (Actor)
c/o Stacey Bock-McLaughlin *Principal Entertainment (LA)*
1964 Westwood Blvd Ste 400
Los Angeles, CA 90025-4695, USA

Emery, Kenneth O (Oceanographer)
35 Horseshoe Ln
North Falmouth, MA 2556, USA

Emery, Lin (Artist, Misc)
7820 Dominican St
New Orleans, LA 70118-3744, USA

Emery, Oren D (Religious Leader)
6060 Castleway West Dr
Indianapolis, IN 46250-1930, USA

Emery, Ralph (Entertainer)
PO Box 23470
Nashville, TN 37202-3470, USA

Emery, Ray (Athlete, Hockey Player)
1723 Haldimand Road 20
Cayuga, ON N0A 1E0, Canada

Emery, Victor (Athlete)
61 Walton St
London SW 3J, UNITED KINGDOM (UK)

Emick, Jarrod (Actor)
232 N Canon Dr
Beverly Hills, CA 90210-5302, USA

Emilio (Music Group)
209 10th Ave South Cummins Sta # 347
Nashville, TN 37203, USA

Emir of Bahrain
721 5th Ave # 60
New York, NY 10022-2523

Emir of Kuwait
Banyan Palace
Kuwait City, KUWAIT

Emma, David (Athlete, Hockey Player)
193 Eugenia Dr
Naples, FL 34108-2929, USA

Emmanuel (Musician)
532 Colorado Ave
Santa Monica, CA 90401-2408, USA

Emmanuel, Tommy (Musician)
c/o Staff Member *Paradigm (Monterey)*
404 W Franklin St
Monterey, CA 93940-2303, USA

Emme (Model)
c/o Daniel A (Dan) Strone *Trident Media Group LLC*
41 Madison Ave Fl 36
New York, NY 10010-2257, USA

Emmel, Paul (Athlete, Baseball Player)
2989 N Lakeview Dr
Sanford, MI 48657-9105, USA

Emmerich, Noah (Actor, Producer)
c/o Jason Gutman *Gersh (NY)*
41 Madison Ave
New York, NY 10010-2202, USA

Emmerich, Roland (Director, Producer)
c/o Staff Member *Centropolis Entertainment*
1445 N Stanley Ave Fl 3
Los Angeles, CA 90046-4015, USA

Emmerson, Michael (Actor)
c/o Staff Member *Vanguard Management Group*
8060 Melrose Ave Fl 4
Los Angeles, CA 90046-7038, USA

Emmert, Mark (Educator)
President S Ofc
Baton Rouge, LA 70803-0001, USA

Emmerton, Bill (Athlete, Track Athlete)
615 Ocean Ave
Santa Monica, CA 90402-2611, USA

Emmett, John C (Inventor)
Oak House Hatfield Broad Oak Bishop's Stortford
Herts CM22 7HG, UNITED KINGDOM (UK)

Emmons, Howard W (Engineer)
1010 Waltham St Apt 443B
Lexington, MA 02421-8067, USA

Emmons, John (Athlete, Hockey Player)
67589 Rachael Ln
Washington, MI 48095-1844, USA

Emmott, Bill (Editor)
25 Saint James's St
London SW1A 1HG, UNITED KINGDOM (UK)

Emory, Sonny (Musician)
137 N Wetherly Dr Apt 403
Los Angeles, CA 90048-2866, USA

Emotions (Music Group)
c/o Staff Member *Diva Central Inc*
7510 W Sunset Blvd Ste 1445
Los Angeles, CA 90046-3408, USA

Empson, Gay MOrris (Stylist)
c/o Staff Member *Bryan Bantry*
900 Broadway Ste 400
New York, NY 10003-1239, USA

Emtman, Steven C (Steve) (Athlete, Football Player)
19601 S Cheney Spangle Rd
Cheney, WA 99004-9040, USA

En Blanco Y Negro (Music Group)
c/o Staff Member *Sony Music Miami*
605 Lincoln Rd Ste 700
Miami Beach, FL 33139-2901, USA

Ena, Justin (Athlete, Football Player)
2192 E 1630 S
Spanish Fork, UT 84660-6423, USA

Enan, Susan (Musician)
c/o Staff Member *Paradigm (Monterey)*
404 W Franklin St
Monterey, CA 93940-2303, USA

Enberg, Alexander (Actor)
c/o Staff Member *TalentWorks (LA)*
3500 W Olive Ave Ste 1400
Burbank, CA 91505-5512, USA

Enbom, John (Writer)
c/o Staff Member *Creative Artists Agency (CAA-LA)*
2000 Avenue of the Stars Ste 100
Los Angeles, CA 90067-4705, USA

End of Fashion (Music Group)
c/o Staff Member *Paradigm (Monterey)*
404 W Franklin St
Monterey, CA 93940-2303, USA

Endean, Craig (Athlete, Hockey Player)
650 Garnet Rd
Kamloops, BC V2B 6K1, Canada

Endelman, Stephen (Composer, Musician)
c/o Staff Member *Robert Urband & Associates*
8981 W Sunset Blvd Ste 311
W Hollywood, CA 90069-1881, USA

Ender, Grummt Kornelia (Swimmer)
Postfach 420140
Kassel 34070, GERMANY

Enderle, Dick (Athlete, Football Player)
PO Box 69
West Newbury, VT 05085-0069, USA

Enders, Erica (Race Car Driver)
c/o Staff Member *Big Machine Media*
110 E 37th St Fl 4
New York, NY 10016-3029, USA

Enders, Trevor (Athlete, Baseball Player)
25906 Silver Timbers Ln
Katy, TX 77494-0726, USA

Endicott, Bill (Athlete, Baseball Player)
14219 Oak Knoll Rd
Sonora, CA 95370-8822, USA

Endress, Albert (al) (Athlete, Football Player)
5950 Louisville St
Louisville, OH 44641-9461, USA

Endress, Ned (Athlete, Basketball Player)
1632 Highbridge Rd
Cuyahoga Falls, OH 44223-2363, USA

Enevoldsen, Einar (Astronaut, Misc)
103 City Limits Cir
Emeryville, CA 94608-1058, USA

Eng, Chris (Stylist)
4 Stuyvesant Oval # B
New York, NY 10009-2402, USA

Engblom, Brian (Athlete, Hockey Player)
824 Ridgemont Cir
Highlands Ranch, CO 80126-5576, USA

Engel, Albert E (Geophysicist, Physicist)
Scripps Institute Geology
La Jolla, CA 92093-0001, USA

Engel, Albert J (Judge)
110 Michigan St NW
Grand Rapids, MI 49503-2300, USA

Engel, Bob (Athlete, Baseball Player)
3500 Harmony Dr
Bakersfield, CA 93306-1219, USA

Engel, Georgia (Actor)
c/o Staff Member *Peter Strain & Associates Inc (LA)*
5455 Wilshire Blvd Ste 1812
Los Angeles, CA 90036-4268, USA

Engel, Steve (Athlete, Baseball Player)
7854 Kirkland Dr
Cincinnati, OH 45224-1247, USA

Engel, Susan
43A Princess Rd Regents Park
London, ENGLAND NW1 8JS

Engelbart, Douglas C (Scientist)
89 Catalpa Dr
Menlo Park, CA 94027-2167, USA

Engelberger, John (Athlete, Football Player)
1750 Nantucket Cir Apt 238
Santa Clara, CA 95054-3823, USA

Engelberger, Joseph F (Engineer)
15 Durant Ave
Bethel, CT 06801-1901, USA

Engelhard, David H (Religious Leader)
2850 Kalamazoo Ave SE
Grand Rapids, MI 49560-0002, USA

Engelhardt, Thomas A (Tom) (Cartoonist, Editor)
900 N Tucker Blvd
Saint Louis, MO 63101-1069, USA

Engelke, Janice (Stylist)
24 W Cedar Ave
Merchantville, NJ 08109-2320, USA

Engen, D Travis (Business Person)
4 W Red Oak Ln
White Plains, NY 10604-3603, USA

Enger, John (Athlete, Golfer)
c/o Jim Lehrman *SFX Golf*
36855 W Main St Ste 200
Purcellville, VA 20132-3561, USA

Engerman, Stanley L (Economist, Historian)
181 Warrington Dr
Rochester, NY 14618-1122, USA

Engholm, Bjorn (Government Official)
Jurgen-Wallenwever-Str 9
Lubeck, GERMANY

Engibous, Thomas J (Business Person)
PO Box 660199
Dallas, TX 75266-0199, USA

England, Anthony (Astronaut, Geophysicist, Physicist)
7949 Ridgeway Ct
Dexter, MI 48130-9700, USA

England, Audie
6100 Wilshire Blvd Ste 1170
Los Angeles, CA 90048-5116

England, Dan
PO Box 220082
Great Neck, NY 11022-0082

England, Gordon R (Secretary)
Washington, DC 20528, USA

England, Richard (Architect)
26/1 Merchants St
Valletta, MALTA

England, Ty
3322 W End Ave # 520
Nashville, TN 37203-1031

England, Tyler (Music Group)
38 Music Sq E Ste 300
Nashville, TN 37203-4304, USA

Englander, Herold R (Doctor, Scientist)
11502 Whisper Bluff St
San Antonio, TX 78230-3704, USA

Engle, Dave (Athlete, Baseball Player)
5343 Castle Hills Dr
San Diego, CA 92109-1926, USA

Engle, Doug (Baseball Player)
17282 Heiser Rd
Berlin Center, OH 44401-9784, USA

Engle, Eleanor (Baseball Player)
319 W Main St
Camp Hill, PA 17011-6333, USA

Engle, Joe (Astronaut, General)
3280 Cedar Heights Dr
Colorado Springs, CO 80904-4728, USA

Engle, Rick (Athlete, Baseball Player)
6413 Seneca Trl
Mentor, OH 44060-3416, USA

Engle, Robert F (Nobel Prize Laureate)
Stern Business School
New York, NY 10012, USA

Englehart, Robert W (Bob) Jr (Cartoonist, Editor)
Editorial Dept 280 Broad St
Hartford, CT 6105, USA

Englehorn, Shirley (Athlete, Golfer)
849 Shrine Vw
Colorado Springs, CO 80906-8500, USA

Engler, John M (Ex-Governor)
1625 K St NW Ste 900
Washington, DC 20006-1606, USA

Engles, Rick (Athlete, Football Player)
11307 S Vine St
Jenks, OK 74037-2466, USA

English, Alexander (Alex) (Athlete, Basketball Player)
596 Rimer Pond Rd
Blythewood, SC 29016-9448, USA

English, Claude (Athlete, Basketball Player)
14041 Switzer Rd
Overland Park, KS 66221-9735, USA

English, Corri (Actor)
c/o Staff Member *Silver Massetti & Szatmary (SMS) Talent Inc*
8730 W Sunset Blvd Ste 440
Los Angeles, CA 90069-2277, USA

English, Diane (Writer)
c/o Staff Member *Shukovsky/English Entertainment*
15456 Ventura Blvd Ste 200
Sherman Oaks, CA 91403-3020

English, Edmond J (Business Person)
770 Cochituate Rd
Framingham, MA 01701-4666, USA

English, Floyd L (Business Person)
10500 W 153rd St
Orland Park, IL 60462-3071, USA

English, James F Jr (Educator)
31 Potter St
Groton, CT 06340-5734, USA

English, JoJo (Athlete, Basketball Player)
133 Ramblewood Dr
Columbia, SC 29209-4439, USA

English, Joseph T (Doctor)
203 W 12th St
New York, NY 10011-7762, USA

English, Kim (Musician)
c/o Staff Member *Diva Central Inc*
7510 W Sunset Blvd Ste 1445
Los Angeles, CA 90046-3408, USA

English, L Douglas (Doug) (Athlete, Football Player)
4306 Bennedict Ln
Austin, TX 78746-1940, USA

English, Madeline (Athlete, Baseball Player)
55 Clinton St
Everett, MA 02149-4640, USA

English, Michael (Music Group)
209 10th Ave S Ste 302
Nashville, TN 37203-0730, USA

English, Paul (Actor)
19528 Ventura Blvd # 501
Tarzana, CA 91356-2917, USA

English, Ralna (Musician)
PO Box 14522
Scottsdale, AZ 85267-4522, USA

English, Scott (Athlete, Basketball Player)
10740 E Placita Metate
Tucson, AZ 85749-8808, USA

English, Todd (Chef)
c/o Staff Member *Grand Productions*
2811 Champion Rd
Naperville, IL 60564-4958, USA

Engluand, Robert (Actor)
1616 Santa Cruz St
Laguna Beach, CA 92651-3350, USA

Englund, Robert (Actor)
1278 Glenneyre St # 73
Laguna Beach, CA 92651-3103, USA

Engram, Simon (Bobby) (Athlete, Football Player)
1104 Black River Rd
Camden, SC 29020-9720, USA

Engstrom, Ted W (Misc)
919 W Huntington Dr
Arcadia, CA 91007-8811, USA

Engvall, Bill (Actor, Comedian, Producer)
c/o J P Williams *Parallel Entertainment*
9420 Wilshire Blvd Ste 250
Beverly Hills, CA 90212-3151, USA

Enigma (Music Group)
c/o Staff Member *Virgin Records (NY)*
150 5th Ave Fl 7
New York, NY 10011-4372, USA

Enis, Curtis (Athlete, Football Player)
5835 Lostcreek Shelby Rd
Fletcher, OH 45326-9764, USA

Enis, Hunter (Athlete, Football Player)
2521 Marley Rd
Jacksboro, TX 76458-3808, USA

Enke, Fred (Athlete, Football Player)
206 E McMurray Blvd
Casa Grande, AZ 85122-3415, USA

Enke, Werner
Moltkestr. 6
Munich, GERMANY D-80803

Enke-Kania, Karin (Skier)
Tolstoistr 3
Dresden 1326, GERMANY

Enkhbayar, Nambaryn (Prime Minister)
Great Hural
Ulan Bator 12, MONGOLIA

Enlow, Johnny (Religious Leader, Writer)
3434 Pleasantdale Rd
Atlanta, GA 30340-4204, USA

Enn, Hans (Skier)
Hinterglemm 400
Saalbach 5754, AUSTRIA

Ennis, John (Athlete, Baseball Player)
2231 Agate Ct
Simi Valley, CA 93065-1841, USA

Ennis, Ralph (Musician)
2 Kirklake Bank Formby
Liverpool L37 2Y5, UNITED KINGDOM (UK)

Ennis, Ray (Musician)
2 Kirklake Bank Formby
Liverpool L37 2Y5, UNITED KINGDOM (UK)

Ennis Sisters, The (Music Group)
c/o Staff Member *Paradigm (Monterey)*
404 W Franklin St
Monterey, CA 93940-2303, USA

Eno, Brian (Actor)

Eno, Brian (Composer, Musician)
3 Pembridge Mews
London W11 3Eq, UNITED KINGDOM (UK)

Enoch, Russell
43A Princess Rd Regents Park
London, ENGLAND NW1 8JS

Enos, John (Actor)
c/o Lara Rosenstock *Lara Rosenstock Management*
8371 Blackburn Ave Apt 1
Los Angeles, CA 90048-4245, USA

Enos, Lisa (Actor, Producer)
c/o Staff Member *International Creative Management (ICM-LA)*
10250 Constellation Blvd Fl 7
Los Angeles, CA 90067-6207, USA

Enos, Mireille (Actor)
c/o Howard Green *Framework Entertainment (LA)*
9057 Nemo St Ste C
West Hollywood, CA 90069-5511, USA

Enright, George (Athlete, Baseball Player)
3075 Strawflower Way
Lake Worth, FL 33467-1465, USA

Enrique, Luis
c/o Staff Member *Verve Music Group*
1755 Broadway Frnt 3
New York, NY 10019-3743, USA

Enriquez, Jocelyn
1135 Francisco St Apt 7
San Francisco, CA 94109-1075

Ensberg, Morgan (Athlete, Baseball Player)
5535 Memorial Dr Unit F-114
Houston, TX 77007-8021, USA

Ensher, Jason R (Physicist)
Physics
Boulder, CO 80309-0001, USA

Ensign, Michael (Actor)
9200 W Sunset Blvd Ste 1125
Los Angeles, CA 90069-3610, USA

Ensler, Eve (Actor, Producer, Writer)
c/o Staff Member *Little, Brown Book Group*
100 Victoria Embankment
London EC4Y 0DY, UK

Ensley, Frank (Athlete, Baseball Player)
241 Webster Ave
Grambling, LA 71245-3117, USA

Entner, Warren (Music Group)
11761 E Speedway Blvd
Tucson, AZ 85748-2017, USA

Entremont, Philippe
Schwarzenbergplatz 10/7
Vienna, AUSTRIA A-1040

Entremont, Philippe (Musician)
10 Rue de Castuglione
Paris 75001, FRANCE

Entwhistle, John
PO Box 241
Lake Peekskill, NY 10537-0241

Enya (Composer, Musician)
c/o Staff Member *Warner Music Germany GmbH (WMI-Germany)*
Alter Wandrahm 14
Hamburg D - 20457, Germany

Enyart, Terry (Athlete, Baseball Player)
3444 Foxwood Blvd
Wesley Chapel, FL 33543-5155, USA

Enzensberger, Hans M (Writer)
Lindenstr 29
Frankfurt am Maim 60325, GERMANY

Eotvos, Peter (Composer)
Naardeweg 56
Blaircum 1261 BV, NETHERLANDS

Ephraim, Alonzo (Athlete, Football Player)
1713 Five Acre Rd
Dolomite, AL 35061-1038, USA

Ephriam, Mablean (Judge)
c/o Sean Perry *WmE2 (Endeavor-LA)*
9601 Wilshire Blvd Fl 3
Beverly Hills, CA 90210-5219, USA

Ephron, Nora (Director, Producer, Writer)
c/o Amanda Urban *International Creative Management (ICM-NY)*
40 W 57th St
New York, NY 10019-4001, USA

Epic (Artist, Musician)
34 Maple St
London W1 5GD, UNITED KINGDOM (UK)

Eppard, Jim (Athlete, Baseball Player)
23115 153rd Ave
Rapid City, SD 57703-9041, USA

Epperson-Doumani, Brenda (Actor)
11365 Ventura Blvd Ste 100
Studio City, CA 91604-3148, USA

Eppinger, Dale L (War Hero)
4100 Colina Cv
Round Rock, TX 78681-2409, USA

Epple, Maria (Skier)
Gunzesried 3
Blaicach 87544, GERMANY

Epple-Beck, Irene (Skier)
Autmberg 235
Seeg 87637, GERMANY

Eppler, Dieter
Franziskaweg 17
Stuttgart, GERMANY D-70599

Epps, Bobby (Athlete, Football Player)
934 Illinois Ave
Pittsburgh, PA 15221-4718, USA

Epps, Mike (Actor, Comedian)
c/o Niles Kirchner *Niles Ahead Productions*
5441 Bevis Ave
Sherman Oaks, CA 91411-3743, USA

Epps, Omar (Actor, Producer)
c/o Raelle Koota *Anonymous Content (AC-LA)*
3531 Hayden Ave
Culver City, CA 90232, USA

Epps, Phil (Athlete, Football Player)
2920 Benissa
Grand Prairie, TX 75054-5556, USA

Epps, Raymond (Athlete, Basketball Player)
4030 Old Warwick Rd
Richmond, VA 23234-1975, USA

Epstein, Daniel M (Writer)
843 W University Pkwy
Baltimore, MD 21210-2911, USA

Epstein, Gabriel (Architect)
3 Rue Mazet
Paris 75006, FRANCE

Epstein, Jason (Editor)
1745 Broadway # B1
New York, NY 10019-4368, USA

Epstein, Joseph (Educator, Writer)
522 Church St Apt 6B
Evanston, IL 60201-4559, USA

Epstein, Mike (Athlete, Baseball Player)
6384 S Blackhawk Way
Aurora, CO 80016-3112, USA

Erardi, Greg (Athlete, Baseball Player)
42 Westgate Rd
Massapequa Park, NY 11762-1953, USA

Erasure (Music Group)
c/o Jonny (Jon) Podell *Podell Talent Agency LLC*
22 W 21st St Fl 9
New York, NY 10010-7095, USA

Erat, Martin (Athlete, Hockey Player)
4 Crooked Stick Ln
Brentwood, TN 37027-8938, USA

Erautt, Eddie (Athlete, Baseball Player)
7252 Waite Dr
La Mesa, CA 91941-7631, USA

Erb, Christy (Athlete, Golfer)
4043 Country Trl
Bonita, CA 91902-3025, USA

Erb, Donald J (Composer)
2073 Blusestone Rd
Cleveland, OH 44121, USA

Erb, Richard D (Government Official)
700 19th St NW
Washington, DC 20431-0001, USA

Erbe, Kathryn (Actor)
1964 Westwood Blvd Ste 400
Los Angeles, CA 90025-4695, USA

Erburu, Robert F (Business Person, Publisher)
1518 Blue Jay Way
Los Angeles, CA 90069-1215, USA

Erdman, Dennis (Actor, Director, Producer)
c/o Staff Member *International Creative Management (ICM-LA)*
10250 Constellation Blvd Fl 7
Los Angeles, CA 90067-6207, USA

Erdman, Paul E (Writer)
4 Banksville Rd
Greenwich, CT 06831-2745, USA

Erdman, Richard (Actor)
5655 Greenbush Ave
Van Nuys, CA 91401-4513, USA

Erdmann, Susi-Lisa (Athlete)
Karwendelstr 8A
Munich 81369, GERMANY

Erdo, Peter Cardinal (Religious Leader)
Esztergom Magyarirszay 2501, HUNGARY

Erdogan, Recep Tayyip (Prime Minister)
Eski Basbakanlik Bakanliklar
Ankara, TURKEY

Erdos, Todd (Athlete, Baseball Player)
118 Windsor Ct
Cranberry Twp, PA 16066-3216, USA

Erenberg, Richard (Athlete, Football Player)
318 Snowberry Cir
Venetia, PA 15367-1043, USA

Ergen, Charles W (Business Person)
5701 S Santa Fe Dr
Littleton, CO 80120-1813, USA

Erhardt, Ron (Athlete, Football Coach, Football Player)
6400 NW 2nd Ave Apt 221
Boca Raton, FL 33487-3026, USA

Erhardt, Warren R (Publisher)
443 River Rd Ste 104
Highland Park, NJ 08904-1915, USA

Erhuero, Oris (Actor)
c/o Staff Member *Midwest Talent Management Inc*
4821 Lankershim Blvd Ste F PMB 149
N Hollywood, CA 91601-4572, USA

Erias, Bo (Athlete, Basketball Player)
2708 Whitney Ave
Niagara Falls, NY 14301-1432, USA

Eric, B (Music Group, Musician)
1600 Varick St
New York, NY 10013, USA

Eric Kaplan, Bruce (Producer)
c/o Staff Member *WmE2 (WMA-LA)*
1 William Morris Pl
Beverly Hills, CA 90212-4261, USA

Ericks, John (Athlete, Baseball Player)
17000 Oketo Ave
Tinley Park, IL 60477-2630, USA

Erickson, Arthur C (Architect)
1672 W 1st Ave
Vancouver, BC V6J 1G1, CANADA

Erickson, Autry (Athlete, Hockey Player)
22998 De Berry St
Grand Terrace, CA 92313-5585, USA

Erickson, Bryan (Athlete, Hockey Player)
114 3rd St NW Ste A
Roseau, MN 56751-1009, USA

Erickson, Bud (Athlete, Football Player)
14523 165th Pl NE
Woodinville, WA 98072-9037, USA

Erickson, Craig (Athlete, Football Player)
420 N Country Club Dr
Lake Worth, FL 33462-1004, USA

Erickson, Dennis (Athlete, Coach, Football Coach, Football Player)
4949 Centennial Blvd
Santa Clara, CA 95054-1229, USA

Erickson, Don (Athlete, Baseball Player)
1929 Montana Dr
Springfield, IL 62704-4150, USA

Erickson, Emily (Stylist)
PO Box 11121
Oakland, CA 94611-0121, USA

Erickson, Ethan (Actor)
c/o Staff Member *Diverse Talent Group*
9911 W Pico Blvd Ste 340W
Los Angeles, CA 90035-2712, USA

Erickson, Grant (Athlete, Hockey Player)
222 Parks St
Whitewood, SK S0G 5C0, Canada

Erickson, Hal (Athlete, Baseball Player)
2674 Foothill Dr
Ogden, UT 84403-0528, USA

Erickson, Jennifer (Stylist)
c/o Staff Member *Directions USA*
3717 W Market St Ste C
Greensboro, NC 27403-1155, USA

Erickson, Keith (Athlete, Basketball Player, Volleyball Player)
262 18th St
Santa Monica, CA 90402-2404, USA

Erickson, Matt (Athlete, Baseball Player)
1408 S Fidelis St
Appleton, WI 54915-4069, USA

Erickson, Millard J. (Writer)
c/o Staff Member *Crossway Books*
1300 Crescent St
Wheaton, IL 60187-5815, USA

Erickson, Robert (Composer)
Music
La Jolla, CA 92093-0001, USA

Erickson, Roger (Athlete, Baseball Player)
PO Box 235
Sautee Nacoochee, GA 30571-0235, USA

Erickson, Scott (Actor)
501 Chicago Ave
Minneapolis, MN 55415-1517, USA

Erickson, Scott G (Athlete, Baseball Player)
1183 Corral Ave
Sunnyvale, CA 94086-7010, USA

Erickson, Steve (Writer)
1230 Avenue of the Americas
New York, NY 10020-1513, USA

Erickson-Sauer, Louise (Baseball Player)
917 Pleasant Ave
Arcadia, WI 54612-1859, USA

Ericson, John (Actor)
7 Avenida Vista Grande # 310
Santa Fe, NM 87508-9198, USA

Ericsson, Jonathan (Athlete, Hockey Player)
c/o Staff Member *Newport Sports Management*
201 City Centre Dr Suite 400
Mississauga, ON L58 2T4, Canada

Eriksen, Stein (Skier)
7700 Stein Way
Park City, UT 84060-5132, USA

Erikson, Duke (Misc)
1250 6th St Ste 401
Santa Monica, CA 90401-1638, USA

Erikson, Raymond L (Doctor)
25 Shattuck St
Boston, MA 02115-6027, USA

Eriksson, Anders (Athlete, Hockey Player)
2259 Arlington Ave
Columbus, OH 43221-4229, USA

Eriksson, Peter (Athlete, Hockey Player)
V. Storgatan 10
Jonkoping S-55315, Sweden

Eriksson, Roland (Athlete, Hockey Player)
Falkvagen 6
Vasteras S-72223, Sweden

Erin Gray, Erin Gray (Actor)

Erin Gray, Erin Gray (Actor)
c/o Geneva Bray *GVA Talent Agency Inc*
8981 W Sunset Blvd Ste 101
Los Angeles, CA 90069-1850, USA

Erixon, Jan (Athlete, Hockey Player)
Stenbackav 58
Skelleftea S-93142, Sweden

Erkiletian, Lynda (Reality TV Star)
c/o Staff Member *Bravo (NY)*
30 Rockefeller Plz
New York, NY 10112-0015, USA

Erlandson, Eric (Songwriter, Writer)
9560 Wilshire Blvd # 400
Beverly Hills, CA 90212-2427, USA

Erlandson, Tom Sr (Athlete, Football Player)
1045 E Possee Rd
Castle Rock, CO 80108-9312, USA

Erman, John (Director)
c/o Johnnie Planco *Parseghian Planco LLC*
322 8th Ave Ste 601
New York, NY 10001-6715, USA

Ermer, Cal (Athlete, Baseball Player, Coach)
PO Box 3045
Gulf Shores, AL 36547-3045, USA

Ermey, R Lee (Actor)
4348 W Avenue N3
Palmdale, CA 93551-1823, USA

Ermy, R Lee
4348 W Avenue N3
Palmdale, CA 93551-1823, USA

Erna, Sully (Actor, Music Group)
c/o Staff Member *WmE2 (WMA-LA)*
1 William Morris Pl
Beverly Hills, CA 90212-4261, USA

Ernaga, Frank (Athlete, Baseball Player)
50 N Roop St
Susanville, CA 96130-3926, USA

Erni, Hans (Artist)
6045 Meggen
Lucerne, SWITZERLAND

Ernst, Bret (Actor, Comedian)
c/o Joan Green *Joan Green Management*
1836 Courtney Ter
Los Angeles, CA 90046-2106, USA

Ernst, Mark A (Business Person)
4400 Main St
Kansas City, MO 64111-1812, USA

Ernst, Richard R (Nobel Prize Laureate)
Kurlistr 24
Winterthur, SWITZERLAND

Ernster, Paul (Athlete, Football Player)
437 W Division St Apt 904
Chicago, IL 60610-1762, USA

Eroy, Iran (Actor)
c/o Staff Member *Televisa*
Blvd Adolfo Lopez Mateos 232 Colonia San Angel INN
DF CP 01060, MEXICO

Errazuriz Ossa, Francisco J Cardinal (Religious Leader)
Casilla 30D Erasmo Escala 1894
Santiago, CHILE

Errey, Bob (Athlete, Hockey Player)
156 Hickory Heights Dr
Bridgeville, PA 15017-1076, USA

Errico, Melissa (Actor)
c/o Richard Schmenner *Paradigm (LA)*
360 N Crescent Dr
Beverly Hills, CA 90210-4874, USA

Erricson, Charlene (Stylist)
c/o Staff Member *Judy Inc*
1 Yorkville Ave
Toronto ON M4W 1L1, Canada

Erskine, Carl D (Athlete, Baseball Player)
4031 Fallbrook Ln
Anderson, IN 46011-1609, USA

Erskine, Peter (Musician)
1727 Hill St
Santa Monica, CA 90405-4843, USA

Erskine, Ralph (Architect)
Box 156 Gustav III's Vag
Drottningholm 170 11, SWEDEN

Erstad, Darin C (Athlete, Baseball Player)
6230 Doe Creek Cir
Lincoln, NE 68516-6105, USA

Ertel, Mark (Athlete, Basketball Player)
1721 Cloister Dr
Indianapolis, IN 46260-1066, USA

Ertl, Gerhard (Nobel Prize Laureate)
Faradayweg 4-6
Berlin D-14195, Germany

Ertl, Martina (Skier)
Erthofe 17
Lenggries 83661, GERMANY

Ertl, Sue (Athlete, Golfer)
4707 Sabal Key Dr
Bradenton, FL 34203-3126, USA

Eruzione, Michael (Mike) (Athlete, Hockey Player)
1 Sherborn St Floor 7
Boston, MA 2215, USA

Ervin, Janice (Stylist)
2014 Central Ave NE
Minneapolis, MN 55418-4532, USA

Erving, Julius W (Dr J) (Athlete, Basketball Player)
108 Windrush Rd
Winston Salem, NC 27106-2594, USA

Ervins, Ricky (Athlete, Football Player)
20984 Nightshade Pl
Ashburn, VA 20147-4703, USA

Ervolino, Frank (Politician)
107 Delaware Ave
Buffalo, NY 14202-2810, USA

Erwin, Hank
4213th St NE
Leeds, AL 35094

Erwin, Mike (Actor)
c/o Loch Powell *Leverage Management*
3030 Pennsylvania Ave
Santa Monica, CA 90404-4112, USA

Erwin, Terry (Athlete, Football Player)
5596 S Lansing Way
Englewood, CO 80111-4104, USA

Erwitt, Elliott R (Photographer)
88 Central Park W
New York, NY 10023-5299, USA

Erxleban, Russell (Athlete, Football Player)
306 Saddlehorn Dr
Dripping Springs, TX 78620-2740, USA

Erxleben, Russell A (Athlete, Football Player)
306 Saddlehorn Dr
Dripping Springs, TX 78620-2740, USA

Esaki, Leo (Nobel Prize Laureate)
2484 Uenomuro
Tsukuba Ibaraki 305, JAPAN

Esasky, Nick (Athlete, Baseball Player)
1779 Starlight Dr
Marietta, GA 30062-1942, USA

Esau, Len (Athlete, Hockey Player)
809 1st St W
Meadow Lake, SK S9X 1E2, Canada

Escalante, Jaime A (Educator)
6879 14th Ave
Sacramento, CA 95820-3431, USA

Escape (DJ)
c/o Len Evans *Project Publicity*
312 W 53rd St Ste 202
New York, NY 10019-5743, USA

Escarpeta, Arlen (Actor)
c/o Jerry Shandrew *Shandrew Public Relations*
1050 S Stanley Ave
Los Angeles, CA 90019-6634, USA

Esch, Eric (Butterbean) (Boxer)
Rt 13 Box 254
Jasper, MI 35501, USA

Eschbach, Jesse E (Judge)
701 Clematis St
West Palm Beach, FL 33401-5101, USA

Esche, Robert (Athlete, Hockey Player)
800 Calder Ave
Yorkville, NY 13495-1446, USA

Eschelman, Vaughn (Baseball Player)
30106 Falher Dr
Spring, TX 77386-1683, USA

Eschen, Larry (Athlete, Baseball Player)
3649 Garden Blvd
Gainesville, GA 30506-1552, USA

Eschenbach, Christoph
2 Ave D'Alena
Paris, FRANCE 75016

Eschenbach, Christoph (Musician)
Maspalomas Monte Leon 760625
Gran Canaria, SPAIN

Eschenmoser, Albert J (Misc)
Bergstra 9
Kusnacht, ZH 8700, SWITZERLAND

Eschert, Jurgen (Athlete)
Tornowstr 8
Potsdam 1447, GERMANY

Escobar, Kelvim (Athlete, Baseball Player)
1292 Biscaya Dr
Surfside, FL 33154-3316, USA

Escovedo, Pete (Musician)
c/o Victor Pamiroyan PO Box 1741
Alameda, CA 94501, USA

Eshelman, Vaughn (Athlete, Baseball Player)
30106 Falher Dr
Spring, TX 77386-1683, USA

Eshman, Rob (Writer)
c/o Emile Gladstone *International Creative Management (ICM-LA)*
10250 Constellation Blvd Fl 7
Los Angeles, CA 90067-6207, USA

Esiason, Norman J (Boomer) (Athlete, Football Player)
25 Heights Rd
Manhasset, NY 11030-1412, USA

Eskell, Diana
41 Bushgrove Stanmore
Middlesex, ENGLAND HA7 2DY

Eskridge, Jack (Athlete, Basketball Player)
15297 Highway K4
Valley Falls, KS 66088, USA

Esler-Smith, Frank (Misc)
9200 W Sunset Blvd Ste 900
Los Angeles, CA 90069-3604, USA

Esparaza, Michael (Actor)
c/o Carl Scott *Simmons & Scott Entertainment*
7942 Mulholland Dr
Los Angeles, CA 90046-1225, USA

Esparza, Moctesuma (Producer)
c/o Staff Member *International Creative Management (ICM-LA)*
10250 Constellation Blvd Fl 7
Los Angeles, CA 90067-6207, USA

Esparza, Raul (Actor)
c/o Elin McManus-Flack *Elin Flack Management*
435 W 57th St Apt 3M
New York, NY 10019-1724, USA

Esperon, Natalia (Actor)
c/o Staff Member *Televisa*
Blvd Adolfo Lopez Mateos 232 Colonia San Angel INN
DF CP 01060, MEXICO

Espino, Gaby (Actor)
c/o Gabriel Blanco *Gabriel Blanco Iglesias (Mexico)*
Rio Balsas 35-32 Colonia Cuauhtemoc
DF 6500, Mexico

Espinoza, Alvaro (Athlete, Baseball Player)
1157 SW Dalton Ave
Port Saint Lucie, FL 34953-7341, USA

Espinoza, Mark (Actor)
c/o Staff Member *Howard Entertainment*
10850 Wilshire Blvd Ste 1260
Los Angeles, CA 90024-4337, USA

Esposito, Anthony J (Tony) (Athlete, Hockey Player)
418 55th Ave
St Pete Beach, FL 33706-2311, USA

Esposito, Frank (Bowler)
200 N State Rt 17
Paramus, NJ 07652-2902, USA

Esposito, Giancarlo (Actor)
c/o Staff Member *Untitled Entertainment (LA)*
350 S Beverly Dr Ste 200
Beverly Hills, CA 90212-4819, USA

Esposito, Jennifer (Actor)
c/o Katherine Atkinson *Washington Square Arts (LA)*
1041 N Formosa Ave Lot Bldg
West Hollywood, CA 90046-6703, USA

Esposito, Laura (Actor)
232 N Canon Dr
Beverly Hills, CA 90210-5302, USA

Esposito, Mike (Athlete, Football Player)
35 Hampton Towne Est
Hampton, NH 03842-1941, USA

Esposito, Philip A (Phil) (Athlete, Hockey Player)
4003 W Tacon St
Tampa, FL 33629-8544, USA

Esposito, Sammy (Athlete, Baseball Player)
PO Box 1826
Banner Elk, NC 28604-1826, USA

Esposito, Tony
418 55th Ave
St Pete Beach, FL 33706-2311

Espy, A Michael (Mike) (Secretary)
154 Deertrail Ln
Madison, MS 39110-9309, USA

Espy, Cecil (Athlete, Baseball Player)
5480 Encina Dr
San Diego, CA 92114-6307, USA

Esquivel, Laura (Actor, Producer, Writer)
c/o Staff Member *Doubleday/ RandomHouse*
1745 Broadway
New York, NY 10019-4368, USA

Esquivel, Manuel (Prime Minister)
19 King St PO Box 1143
Belize City, BELIZE

Essany, Michael (Actor, Talk Show Host)
c/o Mike Randazzo 139 Concord Circle
Valparaiso, IN 46385, USA

Essegian, Chuck (Athlete, Baseball Player)
15639 Bronco Dr
Canyon Country, CA 91387-4717, USA

Essensa, Bob (Athlete, Hockey Player)
1130 Iroquois Trl
Oxford, MI 48371-6621, USA

Esser, Clarence (Clary) (Athlete, Football Player)
1208 E Central Blvd Apt 4
Orlando, FL 32801-2168, USA

Esser, Mark (Athlete, Baseball Player)
717 S US Highway 1 Apt 708
Jupiter, FL 33477-5915, USA

Essex, David
5 Stratford Saye 20-22 Wellington
Bournemouth Dorset, ENGLAND BG8 8JN

Essex, Myron E (Biologist)
665 Huntington Ave
Boston, MA 02115-6021, USA

Essex, Trai (Athlete, Football Player)
c/o Eugene Parker *Maximum Sports Management*
6435 W Jefferson Blvd # 197
Fort Wayne, IN 46804-6203, USA

Essian, James (Jim) (Athlete, Baseball Player, Coach)
134 Eckford Dr
Troy, MI 48085-4745, USA

Essink, Ron (Athlete, Football Player)
PO Box 265
Hamilton, MI 49419-0265, USA

Esslinger, Hartmut (Designer)
1327 Chesapeake Ter
Sunnyvale, CA 94089-1104, USA

Essman, Susie (Comedian)
c/o Lee Kernis *Brillstein Entertainment Partners*
9150 Wilshire Blvd Ste 350
Beverly Hills, CA 90212-3453, USA

Esswood, Paul L V (Opera Singer)
Jasmine Cottage 42 Ferring Lane
West Sussex BN12 6QT, UNITED KINGDOM (UK)

Estabrook, Mike (Athlete, Baseball Player)
502 Titus Rd
Lambertville, NJ 08530-2235, USA

Estacea, Elizabeth (Musician)
PO Box 691481
Charlotte, NC 28227-7025

Estalella, Bobby (Athlete, Baseball Player)
453 Cinnamon Dr
Kissimmee, FL 34759-5405, USA

Esteban, Samantha (Actor)
c/o Staff Member *James/Levy/Jacobson Management Inc*
3500 W Olive Ave Ste 1470
Burbank, CA 91505-5514, USA

Estefan, Emilio (Business Person, Musician)
420 Jefferson Ave
Miami Beach, FL 33139-6503, USA

Estefan, Gloria (Musician)
c/o Emanuel Nunez *Creative Artists Agency (CAA-LA)*
2000 Avenue of the Stars Ste 100
Los Angeles, CA 90067-4705, USA

Estefan, Lili (Actor)
c/o Staff Member *Univision*
605 3rd Ave Fl 12
New York, NY 10158-0034, USA

Estefan, Manuel A (Educator)
President S Ofc
Chico, CA 95929-0001, USA

Estelle (DJ, Musician)
c/o Tracy Nguyen *IPR + MKTG*
1515 Broadway Fl 40
New York, NY 10036-8901, USA

Estelle, Dick (Athlete, Baseball Player)
2221 Taylor St
Point Pleasant Boro, NJ 08742-3839, USA

Esten, Charles (Actor)
c/o Staff Member *Stone Manners Salners Agency (LA)*
9911 W Pico Blvd Ste 1400
Los Angeles, CA 90035-2715, USA

Estern, Neil (Artist)
432 Cream Hill Rd
West Cornwall, CT 06796-1210, USA

Estes, A Shawn (Athlete, Baseball Player)
6659 E Meadowlark Ln
Paradise Valley, AZ 85253-3620, USA

Estes, Billy Sol
1004 S College St
Brady, TX 76825-5528

Estes, Bob (Athlete, Golfer)
4408 Long Champ Dr Apt 21
Austin, TX 78746-1186, USA

Estes, Ellen (Misc)
Athletic Dept
Stanford, CA 94305, USA

Estes, Howell M Jr (Business Person, General)
7603 Shadywood Rd
Bethesda, MD 20817-2066, USA

Estes, James (Cartoonist)
1103 Callahan St
Amarillo, TX 79106-4201, USA

Estes, Larry (Athlete, Football Player)
115 Alida St
Hammond, LA 70403-9419, USA

Estes, Rob (Actor)
c/o Ron West *Thruline Entertainment*
9250 Wilshire Blvd Ground Fl
Beverly Hills, CA 90212, USA

Estes, Simon L (Opera Singer)
c/o Staff Member *Opera Et Concert*
37, rue de la Chaussée d'Antin
Paris F-75009, France

Estes, Will (Actor)
c/o Jason Barrett *Alchemy Entertainment*
7024 Melrose Ave Ste 420
Los Angeles, CA 90038-3394, USA

Estes, William K (Physicist)
65 Gaston Rd
Morristown, NJ 07960-3418, USA

Esteve-Coll, Elizabeth (Misc)
27 Ursulu St
London SW11 3DW, UNITED KINGDOM (UK)

Estevez, Emilio (Actor, Director)
c/o Scott Melrose *Scott Melrose*
3030 Pennsylvania Ave
Santa Monica, CA 90404-4112, USA

Estevez, Ramon (Actor)
837 Ocean Ave # 101
Santa Monica, CA 90402, USA

Estevez, Renee (Actor)
617 S Olive St Ste 311
Los Angeles, CA 90014-1624, USA

Esthero (Musician)
c/o Staff Member *ArtistDirect*
9046 Lindblade St
Culver City, CA 90232-2513, USA

Estill, Michelle (Athlete, Golfer)
642 Yacavona St
Kent, OH 44240-3318, USA

Estleman, Loren Daniel (Writer)
5552 Walsh Rd
Whitmore Lake, MI 48189-9673, USA

Estock, George (Athlete, Baseball Player)
12137 Clear Harbor Dr
Tampa, FL 33626-2525, USA

Estrada, Charle L (Chuck) (Athlete, Baseball Player)
1289 Manzanita Way
San Luis Obispo, CA 93401-7838, USA

Estrada, Erik (Actor, Producer)
c/o Konrad Leh *Creative Talent Group*
1900 Avenue of the Stars Ste 2475
Los Angeles, CA 90067-4512, USA

Estrada, Erik-Michael (Musician)
c/o PJ Shapiro *Ziffren Brittenham LLP*
1801 Century Park W Fl 7
Los Angeles, CA 90067-6406, USA

estrada, Johnny (Athlete, Baseball Player)
20 Winged Foot Rdg
Newnan, GA 30265-2083, USA

Estrella, Alberto (Actor)
c/o Staff Member *Televisa*
Blvd Adolfo Lopez Mateos 232 Colonia San Angel INN
DF CP 01060, MEXICO

Estrella, Leo (Athlete, Baseball Player)
5462 NW Boydga Ave
Port Saint Lucie, FL 34986-4038, USA

Estrich, Susan (Attorney, Attorney General, General)
9255 Doheny Rd Apt 802
West Hollywood, CA 90069-3206, USA

Estrin, Zack (Writer)
c/o Staff Member *WmE2 (Endeavor-LA)*
9601 Wilshire Blvd Fl 3
Beverly Hills, CA 90210-5219, USA

Eszterhas, Joe (Producer, Writer)
c/o Craig Baumgarten *Baumgarten Management*
406 Wilshire Blvd
Santa Monica, CA 90401-1410, USA

Eszterhas, Joseph A (Writer)
c/o Craig Baumgarten *Baumgarten Management*
406 Wilshire Blvd
Santa Monica, CA 90401-1410, USA

Etaix, Pierre (Actor, Director)
Cirque Fratellini 2 Rue de la Cloture
Paris 75019, France

Etchebarren, Andy (Athlete, Baseball Player)
1488 Vermeer Dr
Nokomis, FL 34275-4470, USA

Etchegaray, Roger Cardinal (Religious Leader)
Piazza San Calisto
Vatican City 120

Etcheverry, Marco (Soccer Player)
14120 Newbrook Dr
Chantilly, VA 20151-2273, USA

Etcheverry, Michel (Actor)
47 Rue du Borrego
Paris 75020, FRANCE

Etcheverry, Sam (Athlete, Football Player)
303 Wexford Ter
Venice, FL 34293-4287, USA

Etebari, Eric (Actor)
c/o Staff Member *Agency for the Performing Arts (APA-LA)*
405 S Beverly Dr Ste 500
Beverly Hills, CA 90212-4425, USA

Etel, Alex (Actor)
c/o Staff Member *International Creative Management (ICM-LA)*
10250 Constellation Blvd Fl 7
Los Angeles, CA 90067-6207, USA

Etharton, Seth (Baseball Player)
16 Saint John
Dana Point, CA 92629-4127, USA

Etheredge, Carlos (Athlete, Football Player)
1231 Tuscumbia Rd
Collierville, TN 38017-3418, USA

Etheridge, Bobby (Athlete, Baseball Player)
118 Portland Rd
Eudora, AR 71640-2174, USA

Etheridge, Joe (Athlete, Football Player)
900 E Bryan St
Kermit, TX 79745-3623, USA

Etheridge, Melissa (Musician, Songwriter, Writer)
c/o Bill Leopold *W.F. Leopold Management*
4425 W Riverside Dr Ste 102
Burbank, CA 91505-4057, USA

Etherton, Seth (Athlete, Baseball Player)
16 Saint John
Dana Point, CA 92629-4127, USA

Ethier, Andre (Athlete, Baseball Player)
c/o Nez Balelo *CAA Sports (LA)*
2000 Avenue of the Stars
Los Angeles, CA 90067-4700, USA

Ethridge, Mark F III (Editor)
5516 Gorham Dr
Charlotte, NC 28226-6414, USA

Etienne, Treva (Actor)
c/o Staff Member *London Flair PR*
7119 W Sunset Blvd # 170
Los Angeles, CA 90046-4411, USA

Etienne-Martin (Artist)
7 Rue du Pot de Fer
Paris 75005, FRANCE

Etrog, Sorel (Artist)
PO Box 67034 23 Yonge St
Toronto, ON M4P 1E0, CANADA

Etsel, Edward (Ed) (Misc)
Athletic Dept
Charlottesville, VA 22906, USA

Etsou-Nzabi-Bamungwabi, Frederic (Religious Leader)
BP 8431
Kinshasa 1, CONGO DEMOCRATIC REPUBLIC

Etter, Bob (Athlete, Football Player)
8609 La Riviera Dr Apt F
Sacramento, CA 95826-1775, USA

Ettinger, Cynthia (Actor)
c/o Dan Barnhardt *Thruline Entertainment*
9250 Wilshire Blvd Ground Fl
Beverly Hills, CA 90212, USA

Ettles, Mark (Athlete, Baseball Player)
3-10 Rose Ave
South Perth, AU 6151, Australia

E-Type (Music Group)
c/o Staff Member *Agency Group Ltd, The (Denmark)*
Slotsgade 2 Fl 2
Copenhagen 2200, DENMARK

Etzel, Gregory A M (War Hero)
7822 Wonder St
Citrus Heights, CA 95610-2422, USA

Etzioni, Amitai W (Activist)
7110 Arran Pl
Bethesda, MD 20817-4771, USA

Etzwiler, Donnell D (Doctor)
7611 Bush Lake Dr
Minneapolis, MN 55438-1695, USA

Eubank, Chris (Boxer)
9 Upper Dr
Hove, East Sussex BN3 6GR, UNITED KINGDOM

Eubank, Karen (Stylist)
c/o Staff Member *Campbell Agency, The*
3838 Oak Lawn Ave Ste 900
Dallas, TX 75219-4510, USA

Eubanks, Bob (Motivational Speaker, Television Host)
74 Queens Garden Dr
Thousand Oaks, CA 91361-5355, USA

Eubanks, Dwight (Reality TV Star, Stylist)
321 Edgewood Ave SE
Atlanta, GA 30312-4003, USA

Eubanks, Kevin (Musician)
c/o Staff Member *NBC Universal (NY)*
30 Rockefeller Plz Fl 270E
New York, NY 10112-0299, USA

Eufemia, Frank (Athlete, Baseball Player)
433 6th Ave
Seaside Heights, NJ 08751-1304, USA

Euhus, Tim (Athlete, Football Player)
3520 SE Shoreline Dr
Corvallis, OR 97333-3208, USA

Eure, Wesley (Actor)
9300 Wilshire Blvd Ste 410
Beverly Hills, CA 90212-3228, USA

Europe (Music Group, Musician)
Box 22036
Stockholm S-10422, Sweden

Eusebio, Tony (Athlete, Baseball Player)
2078 Shannon Lakes Blvd
Kissimmee, FL 34743-3648, USA

Evan & Jaron (Music Group)
c/o Billy Lazarus *United Talent Agency (UTA)*
9560 Wilshire Blvd Fl 5
Beverly Hills, CA 90212-2400, USA

Evancho, Jackie (Musician)
PO Box 11184
Pittsburgh, PA 15237-0484, USA

Evanescence (Music Group)
c/o Kim Estlund *Baker Winokur Ryder Public Relations (BWR-LA)*
9100 Wilshire Blvd Ste 500 PMB WEST
Beverly Hills, CA 90212-3426, USA

Evangelista, Christine (Actor)
c/o Myrna Jacoby *MJ Management*
130 W 57th St Apt 11A
New York, NY 10019-3311, USA

Evangelista, Daniella (Actor)
c/o Steve Chasman *Ace Media*
9200 W Sunset Blvd Ste 10
Los Angeles, CA 90069-3608, USA

Evangelista, Linda (Actor, Model)
c/o Didier Fernandez *DNA Model Management*
555 W 25th St Fl 6
New York, NY 10001-5542, USA

Evanovich, Janet (Writer)
PO Box 5487
Hanover, NH 03755-5487, USA

Evans, Aja (Actor)
c/o Staff Member *Precision Entertainment*
6338 Wilshire Blvd
Los Angeles, CA 90048-5002, USA

Evans, Alice (Actor)
c/o Mary Ellen Mulcahy *Framework Entertainment (LA)*
9057 Nemo St Ste C
West Hollywood, CA 90069-5511, USA

Evans, Andrea (Actor)
8075 W 3rd St # 303
Los Angeles, CA 90048-4318, USA

Evans, Anthony H (Educator)
President's Office
San Bernardino, CA 92407, USA

Evans, Barry (Athlete, Baseball Player)
128 Russell Dr
McDonough, GA 30252-4531, USA

Evans, Bart (Athlete, Baseball Player)
8323 Rolling Hills Dr
Nixa, MO 65714-7392, USA

Evans, Bob (Athlete, Basketball Player)
6631 S New Jersey St
Indianapolis, IN 46227-7326, USA

Evans, Byron (Athlete, Football Player)
1763 E Carter Rd
Phoenix, AZ 85042-5754, USA

Evans, Caryl (Athlete, Hockey Player)
22403 Marjorie Ave
Torrance, CA 90505-2241, USA

Evans, Charlie (Athlete, Football Player)
406 Ozzie St NW
Orting, WA 98360-7405, USA

Evans, Chris (Actor)
c/o Erwin Stoff *3 Arts Entertainment Inc*
9460 Wilshire Blvd Fl 7
Beverly Hills, CA 90212-2713, USA

Evans, Chuck (Athlete, Football Player)
3364 Shady Spring Ln
Mountain View, CA 94040-4581, USA

Evans, Dale (Athlete, Football Player)
8878 N State Highway 5 Unit 3
Camdenton, MO 65020-4599, USA

Evans, Daniel J (Ex-Governor, Ex-Senator)
4000-D NE 41st St
Seattle, WA 98105, USA

Evans, Darrell (Athlete, Baseball Player)
5207 Virtuoso
Irvine, CA 92620-0355, USA

Evans, David (Edge) (Musician)
c/o Keryn Kalpan *Principle Management*
250 W 57th St Ste 2120
New York, NY 10107-0001, USA

Evans, David Mickey (Director)
c/o Gleb Klioner *Schachter Entertainment*
1157 S Beverly Dr Fl 2
Los Angeles, CA 90035-1119, USA

Evans, Demetric (Athlete, Football Player)
3820 Appleton Ln
Flower Mound, TX 75022-2932, USA

Evans, Dick (Writer)
121 Morning Dove Ct
Daytona Beach, FL 32119-8739, USA

Evans, Dick (Athlete, Basketball Player)
4540 Bee Ridge Rd Apt 328
Sarasota, FL 34233-2501, USA

Evans, Dick (Athlete, Football Player)
4540 Bee Ridge Rd Apt 328
Sarasota, FL 34233-2501, USA

Evans, Donald (Athlete, Football Player)
12407 Beauvoir St
Raleigh, NC 27614-7037, USA

Evans, Donald L (Secretary)
14th St & Constitution Ave NW
Washington, DC 20230-0001, USA

Evans, Donna (Actor)
c/o Staff Member *United Stuntwomen's Association*
3518 Cahuenga Blvd W # 206B
Hollywood, CA 90068-1304, USA

Evans, Doug (Athlete, Football Player)
8099 Highway 534
Haynesville, LA 71038-5030, USA

Evans, Dwayne (Athlete)
PO Box 91219
Phoenix, AZ 85066-1219, USA

Evans, Dwight (Athlete, Baseball Player)
c/o Staff Member *Boston Red Sox*
4 Yawkey Way
Boston, MA 02215-3496, USA

Evans, Edward P (Publisher)
PO Box 46
Casanova, VA 20139-0046, USA

Evans, Evans (Actor)
3114 Abington Dr
Beverly Hills, CA 90210-1101, USA

Evans, Faith (Musician)
c/o Staff Member *Little, Brown Book Group*
100 Victoria Embankment
London EC4Y 0DY, UK

Evans, Frank (Athlete, Baseball Player)
PO Box 153
Loachapoka, AL 36865-0153, USA

Evans, George (Cartoonist)
c/o Staff Member *King Features Syndication*
300 W 57th St Fl 15
New York, NY 10019-5238, USA

Evans, Glen (Biologist)
10100 N Torrey Pines Rd
La Jolla, CA 92037, USA

Evans, Greg (Cartoonist)
216 Country Garden Ln
San Marcos, CA 92069-9759, USA

Evans, Harold J (Physicist)
17360 Holy Names Dr Unit 2037
Lake Oswego, OR 97034-5186, USA

Evans, Harold M (Editor)
1745 Broadway # B1
New York, NY 10019-4368, USA

Evans, Heath (Athlete, Football Player)
242 Surfview Dr
Pacific Palisades, CA 90272-2911, USA

Evans, Indiana (Actor)
271 Goulburn St
Darlinghurst, Sydney 2010, AUSTRALIA

Evans, J Handel (Educator)
President S Ofc
San Jose, CA 95192-0001, USA

Evans, J Thomas (Wrestler)
607 S Fir Ct
Broken Arrow, OK 74012-3435, USA

Evans, James B (Jim) (Baseball Player)
1801 Rogge Ln
Austin, TX 78723-3416, USA

Evans, Janet (Swimmer)
c/o Staff Member *Premier Management Group (PMG Sports)*
115 Crescent Commons Dr Ste 250
Cary, NC 27518-8134, USA

Evans, Jay (Athlete, Football Player)
8878 N State Highway 5
Camdenton, MO 65020-4599, USA

Evans, Jerry (Athlete, Football Player)
4139 Ivanhoe Dr
Lorain, OH 44053-1560, USA

Evans, John (Business Person)
1188 Sherbrooke St W
Montreal, PC H3A 3G2, CANADA

Evans, John A (Athlete, Football Player)
PO Box 8501
Raleigh, NC 27695-0001, USA

Evans, John E (Business Person)
701 5th Ave
Des Moines, IA 50391-9997, USA

Evans, John R (Misc)
113 Ave Of Americas
New York, NY 10036, USA

Evans, John V (Ex-Governor)
3975 E Clocktower Ln Apt 229
Meridian, ID 83642-9131, USA

Evans, Josh (Athlete, Football Player)
PO Box 273309
Boca Raton, FL 33427-3309, USA

Evans, Karin
Laubenheimer Str. l
Berlin, GERMANY D-14197

Evans, Kellylee (Musician)
c/o Staff Member *SL Feldman & Associates (Toronto)*
8 Elm St
Toronto, ON M5G 1G7, Canada

Evans, Larry (Athlete, Football Player)
5316 S Broadway Cir Apt 8-208
Englewood, CO 80113-6735, USA

Evans, Lee (Actor, Comedian, Writer)
c/o Staff Member *Off The Kerb Productions*
Hammer House, 3rd Fl 113-117 Wardour St
London W1F 0UN, UK

Evans, Linda (Actor)
PO Box 29
Rainier, WA 98576-0029, USA

Evans, Lynn (Musician)
16207 Mott Dr
Macomb, MI 48044-5650, USA

Evans, Marc (Director)
c/o Jane Villiers *Tessa Sayle Agency*
11 Jubilee Pl
London SW3 3TE, UNITED KINGDOM (UK)

Evans, Marsha Johnson (Admiral)
431 18th St NW
Washington, DC 20006-5310, USA

Evans, Martin J (Misc, Scientist)
Castle Rise 41 Rumney
Cardiff CF3 9BB, WALES

Evans, Mary Beth (Actor, Director)
c/o Michael Bruno *The Michael Bruno Group*
13576 Cheltenham Dr
Sherman Oaks, CA 91423-4818, USA

Evans, Mike (Athlete, Football Player)
1 Hunters Run
Greenville, SC 29615-6050, USA

Evans, Mike (Athlete, Basketball Player)
9931 Cottoncreek Dr
Highlands Ranch, CO 80130-3825, USA

Evans, Murray (Journalist)
1331 Lamar St Ste 1575
Houston, TX 77010-3127, USA

Evans, Natalie (Stylist)
c/o Staff Member *Crews*
828 Clemont Dr NE
Atlanta, GA 30306-3694, USA

Evans, Nicholas (Nick) (Writer)
1540 Broadway
New York, NY 10036-4039, USA

Evans, Norm (Athlete, Football Player)
360 NW Boulder Pl
Issaquah, WA 98027-5645, USA

Evans, Norm E (Athlete, Football Player)
4143 Via Marina
Marina Del Rey, CA 90292-5303, USA

Evans, Raymond R (Ray) (Athlete, Basketball Player, Football Player)
8449 Somerset Dr
Prairie Village, KS 66207-1845, USA

Evans, Reggie (Athlete, Football Player)
2813 Juniper St
Merrifield, VA 22116, USA

Evans, Richard (Sportscaster)
4 Pennsylvania Plz
New York, NY 10001, USA

Evans, Richard Paul (Writer)
PO Box 712137
Salt Lake City, UT 84171-2137, USA

Evans, Rob (Coach)
Athletes
Tempe, AZ 85287-0001, USA

Evans, Robert (Bob/ Bobby) (Actor, Producer, Writer)
c/o Staff Member *Robert Evans Company, The*
5555 Melrose Ave Lubitsch Bldg 117
Los Angeles, CA 90038, USA

Evans, Robert C (Mountaineer)
Ardincaple Capel Curig
Betws-y-Coed, Northern Wales, WALES

Evans, Robert J (Bob) (Producer)
5555 Melrose Ave
Los Angeles, CA 90038-3989, USA

Evans, Robert S (Business Person)
100 Stamford Plz
Stamford, CT 6902, USA

Evans, Ronald E
6134 E Mescal St
Scottsdale, AZ 85254-5419, USA

Evans, Ronald M (Doctor)
10100 N Torrey Pines Rd
La Jolla, CA 92037, USA

Evans, Sara (Musician)
c/o Brenner Van Meter *Modern Management*
1625 Broadway Ste 600
Nashville, TN 37203-3141, USA

Evans, Shaun (Actor)
c/o Jon Rubinstein *Authentic Talent and Literary Management*
45 Main St Ste 1004
Brooklyn, NY 11201-8200, USA

Evans, Thomas (Business Person)
PO Box 7054
Troy, MI 48007-7054

Evans, Tom (Athlete, Baseball Player)
32533 SE 68th St
Issaquah, WA 98027-8729, USA

Evans, Troy (Actor)
PO Box 834
Lakeside, MT 59922-0834, USA

Evans, Vince (Athlete, Football Player)
14084 Bronte Dr
Whittier, CA 90602-2608, USA

Evans, Walker (Race Car Driver)
PO Box 2469
Riverside, CA 92516-2469, USA

Evans, William (Athlete, Basketball Player)
24360 Sandpiper Isle Way Unit 105
Bonita Springs, FL 34134-4933, USA

Evashevski, Forest (Coach, Football Coach)
5820 Clubhouse Dr
Vero Beach, FL 32967-7552, USA

Evason, Dean (Athlete, Hockey Player)
c/o Staff Member *Washington Capitals*
627 N Glebe Rd Ste 850
Arlington, VA 22203-2144, USA

Evastina, Liisa (Actor)
c/o Celia Campbell *Murphy Kidman Edwards*
45 Manchester St
London W1U 7LS, UK

Evdokimova, Eva (Ballerina)
PO Box 1586
New York, NY 10150-1586, USA

Eve (Actor)
c/o Amanda Silverman *42West (NY)*
220 W 42nd St Fl 12
New York, NY 10036-7200, USA

Eve, Alice (Actor)
c/o Alissa Vradenburg *Untitled Entertainment (LA)*
350 S Beverly Dr Ste 200
Beverly Hills, CA 90212-4819, USA

Eve, Diva (Athlete, Wrestler)
c/o Staff Member *World Wrestling Entertainment (WWE)*
1241 E Main St
Stamford, CT 06902-3520, USA

Eve, Trevor J (Actor)
c/o Matthew Lesher *Insight*
1134 S Cloverdale Ave
Los Angeles, CA 90019-6737, USA

Eveland, Dana (Athlete, Baseball Player)
37138 Liana Ln
Palmdale, CA 93551-6237, USA

Evelyn, Lionel (Athlete, Baseball Player)
2508 Edgemere Ave
Far Rockaway, NY 11691-2716, USA

Everclear (Music Group)
c/o Staff Member *Tenth Street Entertainment*
270 Lafayette St Ste 706
New York, NY 10012-3397, USA

Everett, Adam (Athlete, Baseball Player)
4374 Oglethorpe Loop NW
Acworth, GA 30101-9533, USA

Everett, Carl E (Athlete, Baseball Player)
19108 Harborbridge Ln
Lutz, FL 33558-9717, USA

Everett, Chad (Actor)
5472 Island Forest Pl
Westlake Village, CA 91362-5406, USA

Everett, Danny (Athlete)
1801 Ocean Park Blvd Apt 112
Santa Monica, CA 90405-4925, USA

Everett, Jim (Athlete, Football Player)
555 N El Camino Real Ste A445
San Clemente, CA 92672-6740, USA

Everett, Major (Athlete, Football Player)
PO Box 1441
Pine Lake, GA 30072-1441, USA

Everett, Rupert (Actor)
c/o Annett Wolf *WKT Public Relations (WKT-LA)*
9350 Wilshire Blvd Ste 450
Beverly Hills, CA 90212-3230, USA

Everett, Thomas G (Athlete, Football Player)
PO Box 795337
Dallas, TX 75379-5337, USA

Everhard, Nancy (Actor)
11365 Ventura Blvd Ste 100
Studio City, CA 91604-3148, USA

Everhart, Angie (Actor, Producer)
c/o Sheryl Abrams *Global Entertainment Management*
14724 Ventura Blvd PH
Sherman Oaks, CA 91403-3513, USA

Everitt, Leon (Athlete, Baseball Player)
367 Henry Everitt Rd
Marshall, TX 75672-3919, USA

Everitt, Mike (Baseball Player)
12381 Walnut Ridge Ct
Clive, IA 50325-8127, USA

Everitt, Mike (Athlete, Baseball Player)
4215 162nd St
Urbandale, IA 50323-2509, USA

Everitt, Steve (Athlete, Football Player)
17252 Snapper Ln
Summerland Key, FL 33042-3669, USA

Everly Brothers (Musician)
PO Box 3933
Seattle, WA 98124-3933, USA

Evermore (Music Group)
c/o Staff Member *Paradigm (Monterey)*
404 W Franklin St
Monterey, CA 93940-2303, USA

Evers, Bill (Athlete)
PO Box 507
Durham, NC 27702-0507

Evers, Charles (Civil Rights Activist)
1018 Pecan Park Cir
Jackson, MS 39209-6913, USA

Evers, Jackson (Actor)
232 N Crescent Dr Apt 101
Beverly Hills, CA 90210-4827, USA

Evers, Jay (Stylist)
c/o Staff Member *Independent Artists*
448 E Riverdale Ave
Orange, CA 92865-1302, USA

Evers, John (Comedian)
PO Box 169
Mount Airy, NC 27030-0169, USA

Eversgerd, Bryan (Baseball Player, Coach)
PO Box 3496
Davenport, IA 52808-3496, USA

Eversley, Frederick J (Artist)
1110 W Albert Kinney Blvd
Venice, CA 90219, USA

Everson, Corinna (Cory) (Misc)
23705 Vanowen St
West Hills, CA 91307-3030, USA

Everson, Cory (Athlete)
23705 Vanowen St # 209
West Hills, CA 91307-3030

Everson, Mark (Government Official)
111 Constitution Ave NW
Washington, DC 20224-0001, USA

Evert, Christine M (Chris) (Athlete, Tennis Player)
8563 Horseshoe Ln
Boca Raton, FL 33496-1231, USA

Evert, Ray F (Biologist)
810 Woodward Dr
Madison, WI 53704-2238, USA

Every Move A Picture (Music Group)
c/o Staff Member *Paradigm (Monterey)*
404 W Franklin St
Monterey, CA 93940-2303, USA

Everything But The Girl (Music Group, Musician)
c/o Staff Member *High Road Touring*
751 Bridgeway Fl 2
Sausalito, CA 94965-2174, USA

Evey, Dick (Athlete, Football Player)
335 S Springview Rd
Maryville, TN 37801-0977, USA

Evidon, Lisa J (Stylist)
4421 Beard Ave S
Minneapolis, MN 55410-1402, USA

Evigan, Briana (Actor)
c/o Matt Luber *Luber Roklin Management*
8530 Wilshire Blvd Ste 550
Beverly Hills, CA 90211-3133, USA

Evigan, Greg (Actor)
c/o Staff Member *Stone Manners Salners Agency (LA)*
9911 W Pico Blvd Ste 1400
Los Angeles, CA 90035-2715, USA

Evora, Cesar (Actor)
c/o Staff Member *Televisa*
Blvd Adolfo Lopez Mateos 232 Colonia
San Angel INN
DF CP 01060, MEXICO

Evora, Cesaria (Musician)
200 W Superior St Ste 202
Chicago, IL 60654-3554, USA

Evren, Kenan (General, President)
Beyaz Ev Sokak 21
Armutalan, Marmaris, TURKEY

Evron, Ephraim (Government Official)
Tel-Aviv, ISRAEL

Ewald, Esther (Baseball Player)
8455 N Ozanam Ave
Niles, IL 60714-1935, USA

Ewald, Reinhold (Cosmonaut)
Linder Hohe
Cologne 51140, GERMANY

Ewell, Dwight (Actor)
c/o Margrit Polak *Margrit Polak Management*
1954 Hillhurst Ave Ste 405
Los Angeles, CA 90027-2722, USA

Ewell, Kayla (Actor)
c/o Brad Warshaw *Brad Warshaw*
PO Box 931332
Los Angeles, CA 90093-1332, USA

Ewen, Todd (Athlete, Hockey Player)
420 Thunderhead Canyon Dr
Ballwin, MO 63011-1732, USA

Ewing, Barbara (Actor)
Flat 4 1 Candover St
York House, London W1W 7DG, UNITED KINGDOM (UK)

Ewing, Blake
c/o Jeff Morrone *Jeff Morrone Entertainment*
9350 Wilshire Blvd Ste 224
Beverly Hills, CA 90212-3204, USA

Ewing, Lucy (Stylist)
c/o Staff Member *Katy Barker Agency Inc*
6606 10th Ave Apt 3R
Brooklyn, NY 11219-5804, USA

Ewing, Maria L (Opera Singer)
33 Bramerton St
London SW3, UNITED KINGDOM (UK)

Ewing, Patrick (Athlete, Basketball Player)
PO Box 1741
Englewood Cliffs, NJ 07632-1141, USA

Ewing, Reid (Actor)
c/o Justin Grey Stone *Untitled Entertainment (LA)*
350 S Beverly Dr Ste 200
Beverly Hills, CA 90212-4819, USA

Ewing, Sam (Athlete, Baseball Player)
1048 Cedarview Ln
Franklin, TN 37067-4068, USA

Exelby, Garnet (Athlete, Hockey Player)
1182 Saint Louis Pl NE
Atlanta, GA 30306-4834, USA

Exelby, Randy (Athlete, Hockey Player)
10040 E Happy Valley Rd Unit 210
Scottsdale, AZ 85255-2368, USA

Exile
PO Box 1547
Goodlettsville, TN 37070-1547

Exley, Susan (Stylist)
11569 Hartsook St
Valley Village, CA 91601-3614, USA

Expose (Music Group)
c/o Staff Member *Richard Walters Entertainment, Inc*
PO Box 2789
Toluca Lake, CA 91610-0789, USA

Extreme (Music Group, Musician)
c/o Rod MacSween *International Talent Booking*
1st Floor, Ariel House 74A Charlotte St
London W1T 4QJ, UNITED KINGDOM

Eyes, Raymond (Publisher)
375 Lexington Ave
New York, NY 10017-5644, USA

Eyharts, Leopold
49 Rue Desnouttes
Paris 75015, FRANCE

Eyre, Richard (Director)
c/o Staff Member *Creative Artists Agency (CAA-LA)*
2000 Avenue of the Stars Ste 100
Los Angeles, CA 90067-4705, USA

Eyre, Scott (Athlete, Baseball Player)
10739 Round Rock Rd
Charlotte, NC 28277-3469, USA

Eyre, Willie (Athlete, Baseball Player)
PO Box 125
Parowan, UT 84761-0125, USA

Eysenck, Hans J (Misc)
10 Dorchester Dr
London SE24, UNITED KINGDOM (UK)

Eyskens, Mark (Government Official)
Graaf de Grunnelaan
Heverlee 3001, BELGIUM

Eytchison, Ronald M (Admiral)
11 Prentice Ln
Signal Mountain, TN 37377-2081, USA

Ezersky, John (Athlete, Basketball Player)
2564 Walnut Blvd Apt 103
Walnut Creek, CA 94596-4251, USA

Ezinicki, Bill (Athlete, Hockey Player)
166 Ballville Rd
Bolton, MA 01740-1255, USA

Ezor, Blake (Athlete, Football Player)
10622 Salmon Leap St
Las Vegas, NV 89183-4917, USA

Ezra, Derek (Government Official)
2 Salisbury Road Wimbledon
London SW19 4EZ, UNITED KINGDOM (UK)

Ezrin, Bob (Producer)
238 E 2nd Ave Suite 300
Vancouver, BC V5T 1B7, Canada

F

F. Bass, Charles (Congressman, Politician)
2350 Rayburn Hob
Washington, DC 20515-0550, USA

F. Costello, Jerry (Congressman, Politician)
2408 Rayburn Hob
Washington, DC 20515-0922, USA

F. Doyle, Michael (Congressman, Politician)
401 Cannon Hob
Washington, DC 20515-3814, USA

F. Edwards, Donna (Congressman, Politician)
318 Cannon Hob
Washington, DC 20515-3101, USA

F. H. Faleomavaega Jr., Eni (Congressman, Politician)
2422 Rayburn Hob
Washington, DC 20515-5201, USA

F. Lynch, Stephen (Congressman, Politician)
2348 Rayburn Hob
Washington, DC 20515-4611, USA

Fa, Sione (Reality TV Star)
43258 W Chisholm Dr
Maricopa, AZ 85138-1500, USA

Fabac-Bretting, Elizabeth (Baseball Player)
1455 Mesa St
Redding, CA 96001-2310, USA

Fabares, Shelley (Actor)
c/o Staff Member *Innovative Artists (LA)*
1505 10th St
Santa Monica, CA 90401-2805, USA

Fabbricini, Tiziana (Opera Singer)
Via Wrenteggio 31/6
Milan 20146, ITALY

Fabel, Brad (Athlete, Golfer)
247 Windsor Terrace Dr
Nashville, TN 37221-2279, USA

Faber, David (Actor, Writer)
c/o Staff Member *CNBC*
900 Sylvan Ave
Englewood Cliffs, NJ 07632-3312, USA

Faber, Sandra M (Astronomer)
16321 Ridgecrest Ave
Monte Sereno, CA 95030-4139, USA

Fabi, Ted
9350 Castlegate Dr
Indianapolis, IN 46256-1001

Fabian, John M (Astronaut)
100 Shine Rd
Port Ludlow, WA 98365-9274, USA

Fabian, Lara
BP 37
Boussu-1, BELGIUM 7301

Fabian, Lara (Musician, Songwriter, Writer)
1 Place Du Commerce
Nun's Island, PQ H3E 1A2, CANADA

Fabian, Patrick (Actor)
c/o Donald Spradlin *Essential Talent Management*
6399 Wilshire Blvd Ste 401
Los Angeles, CA 90048-5716, USA

Fabini, Jason (Athlete, Football Player)
7106 Nighthawk Dr
Fort Wayne, IN 46835-9395, USA

Fabio (Actor, Model)
c/o Eric Ashenberg *Thor Four LLC*
3000 Olympic Blvd
Santa Monica, CA 90404-5073, USA

Fabiola Moray Aragon, Dona (Royalty)
Laeken-Brussels, BELGIUM

Fabius, Laurent (Misc)
Mairie
Le Grand-Quevilly 76120, FRANCE

Fabray, Nanette (Actor, Musician)
14350 W Sunset Blvd
Pacific Palisades, CA 90272-3935, USA

Fabregas, Francesc (Soccer Player)
Highbury House 75 Drayton Park
London N5 1BU, UNITED KINGDOM

Fabregas, Jorge (Athlete, Baseball Player)
4936 SW 6th St
Coral Gables, FL 33134-1346, USA

Fabulous, Moolah (Wrestler)
101 Moolah Dr
Columbia, SC 29223-3931, USA

Face, Elroy L (Roy) (Athlete, Baseball Player)
608 Della Dr Apt 5F
North Versailles, PA 15137-1518, USA

Facinelli, Peter (Actor)
c/o Randy James *James/Levy/Jacobson Management Inc*
3500 W Olive Ave Ste 1470
Burbank, CA 91505-5514, USA

Faddeyev, Ludwig D (Mathematician, Physicist)
Nab Fontanki 27
Saint Petersburg D11, RUSSIA

Faddis, Jonathan (Jon) (Misc)
PO Box 55
New York, NY 10101-0055, USA

Fadeyechev, Aleksei (Dancer)
Teatralnaya Pl 1
Moscow 103009, RUSSIA

Fadeyechev, Nicolai B (Dancer)
Teatralnaya Pl 1
Moscow 103009, RUSSIA

Fadul, Francisco Jose (Prime Minister)
Prime Minister's Office
Bissau, GUINEA-BISSAU

Faedo, Len (Lenny) (Athlete, Baseball Player)
2920 W Collins St
Tampa, FL 33607-6702, USA

Faerch, Daeg (Actor)
c/o Kieran Maguire *The Arlook Group*
205 S Beverly Dr Ste 209
Beverly Hills, CA 90212-3899, USA

Fagan, Garth (Choreographer)
50 Chestnut St
Rochester, NY 14604-2318, USA

Fagan, John J (Misc)
25 Louisiana Ave NW
Washington, DC 20001-2130, USA

Fagan, Julian (Athlete, Football Player)
208 Mallory Ct
Madison, MS 39110-9038, USA

Fagan, kevin (Cartoonist)
26771 Ashford
Mission Viejo, CA 92692-4106, USA

Fagan, Kevin (Athlete, Football Player)
11441 Camp Dr
Dunnellon, FL 34432-8321, USA

Fagen, Clifford B (Basketball Player)
1021 Royal Saint George Dr
Naperville, IL 60563-2322, USA

Fagen, Donald (Musician, Songwriter, Writer)
9460 Wilshire Blvd Ste 310
Beverly Hills, CA 90212-2710, USA

Fagerbakke, Bill (Actor)
1500 Will Geer Rd
Topanga, CA 90290-4238, USA

Fagg, George G (Judge)
US Courthouse East 1st & Walnut
Des Moines, IA 50309, USA

Faggins, Demarcus (Athlete, Football Player)
3002 Southworth Ln
Manvel, TX 77578-4323, USA

Faggs, Starr H Mae (Athlete, Track Athlete)
10152 Shady Ln
Cincinnati, OH 45215-1322, USA

Fahd bin Ibn, Abdul al-Aziz al Saud (King)
Royal Court
Riyadh, SAUDI ARABIA

Fahey, Bill (Athlete, Baseball Player)
5740 Mona Ln
Dallas, TX 75236-1722, USA

Fahey, Brandon (Athlete, Baseball Player)
5740 Mona Ln
Dallas, TX 75236-1722, USA

Fahey, Damien (Television Host)
c/o Michael (Mike) Esterman
Esterman.Com, LLC
Prefers to be contacted via email
MD, USA

Fahey, Jeff (Actor)
c/o Jeff Goldberg *Jeff Goldberg Management*
817 Monte Leon Dr
Beverly Hills, CA 90210-2629, USA

Fahey, Jim (Athlete, Hockey Player)
PO Box 1518
East Dennis, MA 02641-1518, USA

Fahey, Trevor (Athlete, Hockey Player)
7629 Bayhill Ct
New Port Richey, FL 34654-6100, USA

Fahnhorst, James (Jim) (Athlete, Football Player)
2365 Brockton Ln N
Minneapolis, MN 55447-2043, USA

Fahnhorst, Keith (Athlete, Football Player)
12216 Chadwick Ln
Eden Prairie, MN 55344-3292, USA

Fahr, Alicia (Actor)
c/o Staff Member *Televisa*
Blvd Adolfo Lopez Mateos 232 Colonia San Angel INN
DF CP 01060, MEXICO

Fahr, Jerry (Red) (Athlete, Baseball Player)
343 Bayshore Ct
Suwanee, GA 30024-2969, USA

Fahrberger, Mary Lou (Stylist)
310 Oselka Dr Ste 452
New Buffalo, MI 49117-1096, USA

Faia, Renee (Actor)
c/o Marni Anhalt *Imperium 7 Talent Agency*
5455 Wilshire Blvd Ste 1706
Los Angeles, CA 90036-4217, USA

Fain, Farris
PO Box 1357
Georgetown, CA 95634-1357

Fain, Richard (Athlete, Football Player)
1539 SW 49th Ter
Cape Coral, FL 33914-6976, USA

Faine, Jeff K (Athlete, Football Player)
5644 Commerce Dr Ste A
Orlando, FL 32839-2962, USA

Fainsilber, Adrien (Architect)
7 Rue Salvador Allende
Nanterre 92000, FRANCE

Fair, Terry (Athlete, Football Player)
12910 W Monte Vista Rd
Avondale, AZ 85392-7140, USA

Fairbairn, Bill (Athlete, Hockey Player)
Box 55, Site 30 RR 3 STN Main
Brandon, MB R7A 5Y3, Canada

Fairbairn, Bruce (Actor)
PO Box 59747
Santa Barbara, CA 93150, USA

Fairbank, Richard D (Financier)
1680 Capital One Dr
McLean, VA 22102-3407, USA

Fairbanks, Chuck (Athlete, Football Coach, Football Player)
25191 N 104th Way
Scottsdale, AZ 85255-8179, USA

Fairchild, Barbara (Musician, Songwriter, Writer)
PO Box 5331
Sevierville, TN 37864-5331, USA

Fairchild, Chad (Athlete, Baseball Player)
5704 114th Dr E
Parrish, FL 34219-5821, USA

Fairchild, John (Athlete, Basketball Player)
9801 Chantilly Rd NW
Albuquerque, NM 87114-4402, USA

Fairchild, John B (Publisher)
CHalet Bianchina Talstr GR
Klosters 7250, SWITZERLAND

Fairchild, Morgan (Actor)
PO Box 57593
Sherman Oaks, CA 91413-2593, USA

Fairchild, Paul (Athlete, Football Player)
PO Box 25442
Overland Park, KS 66225-5442, USA

Fairchild, Thomas E (Judge)
111 N Canal St Fl 6
Chicago, IL 60606-7221, USA

Faircloth, Arthur (Athlete, Football Player)
10010 Sandwedge Ct
Fredericksburg, VA 22408-9546, USA

Faircloth, D McLauchlin (Lauch) (Ex-Senator)
813 Beamon St
Clinton, NC 28328, USA

Fairey, Jim (Athlete, Baseball Player)
218 Strawberry Ln
Clemson, SC 29631-1363, USA

Fairey, Shepard
c/o Bradley Frank *Platform Public Relations*
2666 N Beachwood Dr
Los Angeles, CA 90068-2308, USA

Fairley, Nick (Football Player)
c/o Brian E. Overstreet *E.O. Sports Management*
2211 Norfolk St Ste 210
Houston, TX 77098-4055, USA

Fairly, Ronald R (Ron) (Athlete, Baseball Player)
75369 Spyglass Dr
Indian Wells, CA 92210-7650, USA

Fairs, Eric (Athlete, Football Player)
32707 Wales Cir
Fulshear, TX 77441-4250, USA

Faison, Donald (Actor)
c/o Glenn Rigberg *HYPHENATE*
9701 Wilshire Blvd Fl 10
Beverly Hills, CA 90212-2010, USA

Faison, Matthew (Actor)
13701 E Kagel Canyon Rd
Sylmar, CA 91342, USA

Faison, Tiffani (Chef)
c/o Staff Member *Magical Elves Inc*
453 S Spring St Ste
Los Angeles, CA 90013, USA

Faison, William (Earl) (Athlete, Football Player)
2279 Sequoia Dr
Prescott, AZ 86301-4326, USA

Faith, Paloma (Musician)
c/o Olivia Woodward *Curtis Brown Group*
Haymarket House 28 - 29 Haymarket
London SW1Y 4SP, UNITED KINGDOM

Faithfull, Marianne (Actor, Songwriter)
235 Gootscray Rd New Eltham
London SE9 2EL, UNITED KINGDOM (UK)

Faithless (Music Group)
c/o Staff Member *Paradigm (Monterey)*
404 W Franklin St
Monterey, CA 93940-2303, USA

Fakih, Rima (Beauty Pageant Winner)
1370 Avenue of the Americas Fl 16
New York, NY 10019-4602, USA

Fakir, Abdul (Duke) (Music Group)
c/o Staff Member *International Creative Management (ICM-NY)*
40 W 57th St
New York, NY 10019-4001, USA

Falana, Lola (Dancer, Music Group)
217 Seaton Pl NE
Washington, DC 20002-1528, USA

Falcam, Leo A (President)
Palikjr Kolonia
Pohnpei, FM 96941, MICRONESIA

Falcao, Jose Freire Cardinal (Religious Leader)
QL 12-CJ12 Lote 1
Lago Sul, Brasilia DF 71630-325, BRAZIL

Falcao, Jose Friere Cardinal (Religious Leader)
QL 12-CJ 12 Lote 1 Lago Sul
Brasilia DF 71630-325, BRAZIL

Falco, Edie (Actor)
c/o Richie Jackson *Jackson Group Entertainment*
345 W 13th St
New York, NY 10014-1210, USA

Falcone, Ben (Actor)
c/o Staff Member *Parallel Entertainment*
9420 Wilshire Blvd Ste 250
Beverly Hills, CA 90212-3151, USA

Falcone, Pete (Athlete, Baseball Player)
2232 Thornton Ct
Alexandria, LA 71301-5147, USA

Falconi, Irina (Athlete, Tennis Player)
c/o Dan Nagler *South Beach Sports Agency*
770 Claughton Island Dr Apt 1510
Miami, FL 33131-2630, USA

Faldo, Nick (Athlete, Golfer)
18 - 20 Sheet St Windsor
Berkshire SL4 1BG, UK

Falik, Yuri (Composer, Conductor)
Fihlyandsky Prospekt 1 #54
Saint Petersburg 194044, RUSSIA

Falk, David (Lawyer)
5335 Wisconsin Ave NW Ste 960
Washington, DC 20015-2092, USA

Falk, David B (Attorney, Attorney General, General, Misc)
5335 Wisconsin Ave NW Ste 960
Washington, DC 20015-2092, USA

Falk, Paul (Figure Skater)
Sybelstr 21
Dusseldorf 40239, GERMANY

Falk, Randall M (Religious Leader)
5015 Harding Pike
Nashville, TN 37205-2801, USA

Falkenberg, Bob (Athlete, Hockey Player)
7251 190A St NW
Edmonton, AB T5T 5S9, Canada

Falkenborg, Brian (Athlete, Baseball Player)
30223 N 125th Dr
Peoria, AZ 85383, USA

Falkenstein, Claire (Artist)
719 Ocean Front Walk
Venice, CA 90291-3212, USA

Falkner, Keith (Musician)
Low Cottages Ilketshall Saint Margaraet Bungay
Suffolk, UNITED KINGDOM (UK)

Fall, Jim (Actor)
c/o Staff Member *United Talent Agency (UTA)*
9560 Wilshire Blvd Fl 5
Beverly Hills, CA 90212-2400, USA

Fall, Timothy (Actor)
232 N Canon Dr
Beverly Hills, CA 90210-5302, USA

Fall Out Boy (Music Group)
c/o Bob McLynn *Crush Management*
60-62 E 11th St Floor 7
New York, NY 10003, USA

Falldin, Thorbjom (Prime Minister)
As 870 16 Ramvik
Ramvik 870 16, SWEDEN

Fallin, Mary (Governor, Politician)
2300 N Lincoln Blvd Rm 212
Oklahoma City, OK 73105-4801, USA

Fallon, Bob (Athlete, Baseball Player)
1830 SW 81st Ave Apt 4416
North Lauderdale, FL 33068-4253, USA

Fallon, Jimmy (Actor, Comedian, Talk Show Host)
c/o Eric Kranzler *Management 360*
9111 Wilshire Blvd
Beverly Hills, CA 90210-5508, USA

Fallon, Tiffany (Model, Reality TV Star)
c/o Cheryl McLean *Creative Public Relations*
3385 Oak Glen Dr
Los Angeles, CA 90068-1311, USA

Falloon, Pat (Athlete, Hockey Player)
112-155 10th St
Birtle, MB R0M 0C0, Canada

Falls, Mike (Athlete, Football Player)
5831 Secrest Dr
Austin, TX 78759-2416, USA

Faloona, Christopher J (Cinematographer)
138 Via La Soledad
Redondo Beach, CA 90277-6624, USA

Falossi, David (Artist)
377 Geary St
San Francisco, CA 94102-1801, USA

Falteisek, Steve (Athlete, Baseball Player)
12 Verbena Ave
Floral Park, NY 11001-2712, USA

Faltermayer, Harold (Composer)
Wasserburgerlandstrasse 16
Baldham 85598, Germany

Faltings, Gerd (Mathematician)
Mathematics
Princeton, NJ 08544-0001, USA

Faltskog, Agnetha (Musician)
Södra Brobänken 41A
Stockholm 111 49, SWEDEN

Faludi, Susan C (Journalist)
1032 Irving St # 204
San Francisco, CA 94122-2216, USA

Falvey, Justin (Producer)
c/o Staff Member *Dreamworks Television*
100 Universal Plz Bldg 5125
Universal City, CA 91608, USA

Fambrough, Charles (Musician)
Bellvue Broad & Walnut Sts
Philadelphia, PA 19102, USA

Fambrough, Henry (Music Group)
3750 Hudson Manor Ter # 3AG
Bronx, NY 10463-1126, USA

Famiglietti, Mark (Actor)
c/o Robert Stein *Robert Stein Management*
PO Box 3797
Beverly Hills, CA 90212-0797, USA

Famuyiwa, Rick (Director, Writer)
c/o Philip Raskind *WmE2 (Endeavor-LA)*
9601 Wilshire Blvd Fl 3
Beverly Hills, CA 90210-5219, USA

Fancher, Hampton (Director)
262 Old Topanga Canyon Rd
Topanga, CA 90290-3810, USA

Fancy, Richard (Actor)
c/o Paul Kohner *Kohner Agency, The*
9300 Wilshire Blvd Ste 555
Beverly Hills, CA 90212-3211, USA

Faneca, Alan (Athlete, Football Player)
201 Whetherburn Dr
Wexford, PA 15090-8869, USA

Faneyte, Rikkert (Baseball Player)
7408 E Osborn Rd
Scottsdale, AZ 85251-6424, USA

Fang, Lizhi (Activist, Physicist, Politician)
Physics
Tucson, AZ 85721-0001, USA

Fangio, Juan Manuel II (Race Car Driver)
2334 S Broadway
Santa Ana, CA 92707-3250, USA

Fankhauser, Merrell (Composer, Musician)
PO Box 1504
Arroyo Grande, CA 93421-1504, USA

Fankhouser, Scott (Athlete, Hockey Player)
826 Alpine Dr
Jasper, GA 30143-3427, USA

Fann, Al (Actor)
6051 Hollywood Blvd Ste 207
Hollywood, CA 90028-5496, USA

Fanning, Dakota (Actor)
c/o JJ Harris *One Talent Management*
9220 W Sunset Blvd Ste 306
Los Angeles, CA 90069-3503, USA

Fanning, Elle (Actor)
c/o Cindy Osbrink *Osbrink Talent Agency*
4343 Lankershim Blvd Ste 100
West Toluca Lake, CA 91602-2705, USA

Fanning, Jim (Athlete, Baseball Player, Coach)
154 Tiner Ave
Dorchester, ON N0L 1G2, Canada

Fanning, Michael L (Mike) (Athlete, Football Player)
28808 S 4190 Rd
Inola, OK 74036-5276, USA

Fanning, Neil (Actor)
c/o Staff Member *International Casting Service & Associates*
2/218 Crown St (via Kings Lane)
Darlinghurst NSW 2010, Australia

Fanning, Shawn (Business Person)
c/o Staff Member *Roxio Inc*
2830 De La Cruz Blvd
Santa Clara, CA 95050-2619, USA

Fannypack (Music Group)
29 John St Ste 230
New York, NY 10038-4005, USA

Fano, Robert M (Engineer, Scientist)
80 Deaconess Rd Unit 227
Concord, MA 01742-4176, USA

Fanok, Harry (Athlete, Baseball Player)
12373 Old State Rd
Chardon, OH 44024-9560, USA

Fanovich, Frank (Athlete, Baseball Player)
3 Fairgreen Ave
New Smyrna Beach, FL 32168-6112, USA

Fansler, Stan (Athlete, Baseball Player)
32 Bunting Ln
Beckley, WV 25801-3656, USA

Fante, Ricky (Musician)
c/o Staff Member *Virgin Records (NY)*
150 5th Ave Fl 7
New York, NY 10011-4372, USA

Fantetti, Ken (Athlete, Football Player)
1211 SE 175th Pl
Portland, OR 97233-4631, USA

Fanucci, Mike (Athlete, Football Player)
1357 N Tercera Ave
Chandler, AZ 85226-1339, USA

Fanzone, Carmen (Athlete, Baseball Player)
5114 Ranchito Ave
Sherman Oaks, CA 91423-1235, USA

Far East Movement (Music Group, Musician)
c/o Staff Member *Stampede Management*
12530 Beatrice St
Los Angeles, CA 90066-7002, USA

Faracy, Stephanie (Actor)
8765 Lookout Mountain Ave
Los Angeles, CA 90046-1861, USA

Faralla, Lillian (Baseball Player)
102 Antigua Ct
Coronado, CA 92118-3315, USA

Farar, Hassan Abshir (Prime Minister)
People's Palace
Mogadishy, SOMALIA

Farasopoulos, Chris (Athlete, Football Player)
195 Migues Mountain Ln
Aptos, CA 95003-9628, USA

Farbar, Anne (Stylist)
c/o Staff Member *RJ Bennett Represents*
274 1st Ave Apt 8E
New York, NY 10009-1815, USA

Farber, Hap (Athlete, Football Player)
200 Dominican Dr
Madison, MS 39110-8630, USA

Farber, Stacey (Actor)
c/o Yanick Landry *Newton-Landry Management*
19 Isabella St
Toronto ON M4Y 1M7, Canada

Faregalli, Lindy (Bowler)
113 N 5th Ave
Manville, NJ 08835-1201, USA

Farenthold, Blake (Congressman, Politician)
2110 Rayburn Hob
Washington, DC 20515-1306, USA

Farenthold, Frances T (Activist, Educator)
2929 Buffalo Speedway # 18B
Houston, TX 77098-1720, USA

Farentino, Debrah
1505 10th St
Santa Monica, CA 90401-2805

Farentino, James (Actor)
1340 Londonderry Pl
Los Angeles, CA 90069-1335, USA

Fares, Muhammad Ahmed Al (Cosmonaut)
PO Box 1272
Aleppo, SYRIA

Fargas, Antonio (Actor)
733 Seward St PH
Los Angeles, CA 90038-3503, USA

Fargis, Joe (Horse Racer)
PO Box 2168
Middleburg, VA 20118-2168, USA

Fargo, Donna (Musician)
PO Box 210877
Nashville, TN 37221-0877, USA

Fargo, Thomas B (Admiral)
Commander Pacific Fleet Camp H M Smith
Honolulu, HI 96861, USA

Farha (Actor, Bollywood)
308 Dara Villa A B Nair Road Juhu
Mumbai, MS 400049, INDIA

Faries, Paul (Athlete, Baseball Player)
3299 Beechwood Dr
Lafayette, CA 94549-4661, USA

Farina, Battista (Pinin) (Designer)
Via Lesna 78 Turin
Grugliasco 10095, ITALY

Farina, David (Religious Leader)
41 Sherbrooke Rd
Ewing, NJ 08638-2416, USA

Farina, Dennis (Actor)
c/o Amy Guenther *Gateway Management Company Inc*
860 Via De La Paz Ste F10
Pacific Palisades, CA 90272-3631, USA

Farina, Johnny (Music Group)
308 E 6th St Apt 13
New York, NY 10003-8760, USA

Faris, Anna (Actor)
c/o Doug Wald *Anonymous Content (AC-LA)*
3531 Hayden Ave
Culver City, CA 90232, USA

Faris, Sean (Actor)
c/o Dino May *Dino May Management*
6362 Hollywood Blvd
Los Angeles, CA 90028-6323, USA

Faris, Valerie (Director, Producer)
1313 5th St
Santa Monica, CA 90401-1414, USA

Farish, William S (Diplomat)
Grosvenor Square 55 Upper Brook St
London W1A 2LQ, UNITED KINGDOM (UK)

Fariss, Monty (Athlete, Baseball Player)
1015 Waterwood Pkwy Ste C
Edmond, OK 73034-5325, USA

Farkas, Bertalan (Astronaut, Misc)
A Magyar Koztarsasag Kutato Urhajosa Pf 25
Budapest 1885, HUNGARY

Farkas, Ferenc (Composer)
Nagyatai Utca 12
Budapest 1026, HUNGARY

Farkas, Jeff (Athlete, Hockey Player)
284 Patrice Ter
Buffalo, NY 14221-3922, USA

Farley, Bob (Athlete, Baseball Player)
1325 Sycamore Rd
Montoursville, PA 17754-9511, USA

Farley, Carole (Music Group, Opera Singer)
270 Riverside Dr
New York, NY 10025-0132, USA

Farley, Dale (Athlete, Football Player)
RR 8 Box 472
Sparta, TN 38583, USA

Farley, David (Writer)
c/o Staff Member *Morra Brezner Steinberg & Tenenbaum (MBST) Entertainment*
345 N Maple Dr Ste 200
Beverly Hills, CA 90210-5174, USA

Farley, Jenni (JWoww) (Reality TV Star)
c/o Michael (Mike) Esterman
Esterman.Com, LLC
Prefers to be contacted via email
MD, USA

Farley, Lillian
84 Kenneth Ave
Huntington, NY 11743-4929

Farm, Ali (Athlete)
PO Box 160
Berrien Springs, MI 49103-0160

Farman, Melissa (Actor)
c/o Staff Member *Prodigy Talent Group*
Prefers to be contacted by telephone or email
Beverly Hills, CA, USA

Farmer, Art
49 E 96th St
New York, NY 10128-0782

Farmer, Billy (Baseball Player)
18987 E Wilshire Blvd
Jones, OK 73049-5917, USA

Farmer, Danny (Athlete, Football Player)
332 Lorraine Blvd
Los Angeles, CA 90020-4728, USA

Farmer, Dave (Athlete, Football Player)
141 Via Medici
Aptos, CA 95003-5838, USA

Farmer, Ed (Athlete)
333 W 35th St
Chicago, IL 60616-3651

Farmer, Ed (Athlete, Baseball Player)
4581 Camino Del Sol
Calabasas, CA 91302-3836, USA

Farmer, Evan (Actor, Television Host)
c/o Robert Attermann *Abrams Artists Agency (LA)*
9200 W Sunset Blvd PH 11
Los Angeles, CA 90069-3601, USA

Farmer, Gary (Actor)
c/o Staff Member *Gonzo Dr. Records*
PO Box 31096
Santa Fe, NM 87594-1096, USA

Farmer, George (Athlete, Football Player)
332 Lorraine Blvd
Los Angeles, CA 90020-4728, USA

Farmer, George III (Athlete, Football Player)
12422 S Denker Ave
Los Angeles, CA 90047-5339, USA

Farmer, Howard (Athlete, Baseball Player)
1675 W 10th Pl
Gary, IN 46404-1501, USA

Farmer, James (Athlete, Basketball Player)
214 Ashborough Cir
Dothan, AL 36301-1267

Farmer, John Jr (Ex-Governor)
123 Washington St
Newark, NJ 07102-3026, USA

Farmer, Mike (Athlete, Basketball Player, Coach)
2520 Lakeview Dr
Santa Rosa, CA 95405-8657, USA

Farmer, Mimsy (Actor)
36 Rue de Ponthieu
Paris 75008, FRANCE

Farmer, Phillip W (Business Person)
1025 W Nasa Blvd
Melbourne, FL 32919-0002, USA

Farmer, Richard G (Doctor)
9126 Town Gate Ln
Bethesda, MD 20817-4111, USA

Farmiga, Vera (Actor)
c/o Jon Rubinstein *Authentic Talent and Literary Management*
45 Main St Ste 1004
Brooklyn, NY 11201-8200, USA

Farner, Donald S (Biologist, Physicist)
Zoology
Seattle, WA 98195-0001, USA

Farner, Mark (Music Group, Musician)
PO Box 1547
Goodlettsville, TN 37070-1547, USA

Farnham, John (Musician)
Box 6500 St. Kilda Rd.
Central Melbourne, AUSTRALIA 3004

Farnham, John P (Music Group)
663 Victoria St
Abbottsford, VIC 3067, AUSTRALIA

Farnon, Shannon
12743 Milbank St
Studio City, CA 91604-1310

Farnsworth, Jeff (Athlete, Baseball Player)
704 50th Ave W
Bradenton, FL 34207-2683, USA

Farnsworth, Kyle (Athlete, Baseball Player)
1400 Stickley Ave
Kissimmee, FL 34747-4024, USA

Faro, Michele (Stylist)
c/o Staff Member *Art Department*
48 Greene St Fl 4
New York, NY 10013-2663, USA

Farquhar, John W (Doctor)
Med School Disease Prevention Center
Stanford, CA 94305, USA

Farquhar, Marilyn G (Biologist, Misc)
12894 Via Latina
Del Mar, CA 92014-3730, USA

Farquhar, Robert W (Scientist)
Applied Physics Laboratory
Laurel, MD 20723, USA

Farr, Bruce (Architect)
613 Third St
Annapolis, MD 21403-3248, USA

Farr, Diane (Actor)
c/o Josh Katz *United Talent Agency (UTA)*
9560 Wilshire Blvd Fl 5
Beverly Hills, CA 90212-2400, USA

Farr, Dmarco (Athlete, Football Player)
2175 Del Monte Dr
San Pablo, CA 94806-1016, USA

Farr, Felicia (Actor)
1143 Tower Rd
Beverly Hills, CA 90210-2130, USA

Farr, Jaime (Actor)
2316 Delaware Ave Ste 266
Buffalo, NY 14216-2606, USA

Farr, Jamie (Actor)
c/o Robert Malcolm *Artists Group, The (NY)*
1650 Broadway Ste 711
New York, NY 10019-6833, USA

Farr, Jim (Athlete, Baseball Player)
3 Tyndal Ct
Williamsburg, VA 23188-1552, USA

Farr, Kendall (Stylist)
c/o Staff Member *Judy Casey Inc*
114 E 13th St
New York, NY 10003-5329, USA

Farr, Kimberly (Actor)
6767 Forest Lawn Dr Ste 101
Los Angeles, CA 90068-1050, USA

Farr, Mel Jr (Athlete, Football Player)
1650 Emerald Rdg
Marietta, GA 30062-2050, USA

Farr, Melvin (Mel) Sr (Athlete, Football Player)
10550 W 8 Mile Rd
Ferndale, MI 48220-2152, USA

Farr, Michael (Athlete, Football Player)
3950 Paran Rdg NW
Atlanta, GA 30327-3030, USA

Farr, Miller (Athlete, Football Player)
11815 Rowood Dr
Houston, TX 77070-5349, USA

Farr, Norman (Rocky) (Athlete, Hockey Player)
3850 Overton Park Dr W
Fort Worth, TX 76109-3405, USA

Farr, Sam (Congressman, Politician)
1124 Longworth Hob
Washington, DC 20515-4001, USA

Farragut, Ken (Athlete, Football Player)
605 Creek Ln
Flourtown, PA 19031-1114, USA

Farrakhan, Louis (Religious Leader)
734 W 79th St
Chicago, IL 60620-2424, USA

Farrar, Frank L (Ex-Governor)
PO Box 936
Britton, SD 57430-0936, USA

Farrel, Franklin (Athlete, Hockey Player)
89 Notch Hill Rd Apt 223
North Branford, CT 6471, USA

Farrell, Christopher (Musician)
c/o Mike Rosen *Working Artists Agency*
13525 Ventura Blvd
Sherman Oaks, CA 91423-3801

Farrell, Colin (Actor)
c/o Danica Smith *PMK/BNC Public Relations (PMK-LA)*
8687 Melrose Ave Ste 8
West Hollywood, CA 90069-5746, USA

Farrell, John (Athlete, Baseball Player)
PO Box 3519
Clearwater Beach, FL 33767-8519, USA

Farrell, Mike (Actor)
PO Box 6010
Sherman Oaks, CA 91413-6010, USA

Farrell, Paul (Athlete, Football Player)
PO Box 804
Dennis Port, MA 02639-0804, USA

Farrell, Perry (Musician)
c/o Rod MacSween *International Talent Booking*
1st Floor, Ariel House 74A Charlotte St
London W1T 4QJ, UNITED KINGDOM

Farrell, Sean (Athlete, Football Player)
11 Ladoga Ave
Tampa, FL 33606-3803, USA

Farrell, Sharon (Actor)
360 S Doheny Dr
Beverly Hills, CA 90211-3581, USA

Farrell, Shea (Actor)
1180 S Beverly Dr Ste 301
Los Angeles, CA 90035-1154, USA

Farrell, Suzanne (Ballerina)
Education
Washington, DC 20566-0001, USA

Farrell, Terence (Terry) (Architect)
17 Hatton St
London NW8 8PL, UNITED KINGDOM (UK)

Farrell, Terry (Actor)
6500 Wilshire Blvd Ste 2200
Los Angeles, CA 90048-4942, USA

Farrelly, Bobby (Director, Producer, Writer)
c/o David O'Connor *Creative Artists Agency (CAA-LA)*
2000 Avenue of the Stars Ste 100
Los Angeles, CA 90067-4705, USA

Farrelly, Peter (Director, Producer, Writer)
c/o Richard Lovett *Creative Artists Agency (CAA-LA)*
2000 Avenue of the Stars Ste 100
Los Angeles, CA 90067-4705, USA

Farren, Paul (Athlete, Football Player)
21 Gammons Rd
Cohasset, MA 02025-1405, USA

Farrer, Kathy (Athlete, Golfer)
4815 Westgrove Dr Apt 301
Addison, TX 75001-6115, USA

Farrimond, Richard A (Astronaut)
Gunnels Wood Rd Stevenage
Herts SG1 2AS, UNITED KINGDOM (UK)

Farrington, Amy
c/o Staff Member *Meghan Schumacher Management*
13351D Riverside Dr # 387
Sherman Oaks, CA 91423-2508, USA

Farrington, Robert G (Bob) (Race Car Driver)
201 Lake Hinsdale Dr Apt 211
Willowbrook, IL 60527-2688, USA

Farrior, James (Athlete, Football Player)
1004 Summerset Dr
Pittsburgh, PA 15217-2535, USA

Farris, Dionne (Music Group)
c/o Staff Member *Creative Artists Agency (CAA-LA)*
2000 Avenue of the Stars Ste 100
Los Angeles, CA 90067-4705, USA

Farris, Jerome
5th Ave US Courthouse 1010
Seattle, WA 98104-3191, USA

Farris, Joseph (Cartoonist)
68 Sunburst Cir
Fairport, NY 14450-9019, USA

Farris, Rachel (Musician)
c/o Staff Member *Logic House Media*
3123 Traviston Dr
Franklin, TN 37064-6218, USA

Farrish, Dave (Athlete, Hockey Player)
530 S Golden Sky Ln
Anaheim, CA 92807-4749, USA

Farriss, Andrew (Music Group)
8 Hayes St # 1
Neutral Bay, NSW 20891, AUSTRALIA

Farriss, Jon (Music Group, Musician)
8 Hayes St # 1
Neutral Bay, NSW 20891, AUSTRALIA

Farriss, Tim (Music Group, Musician)
8 Hayes St # 1
Neutral Bay, NSW 20891, AUSTRALIA

Farrow, Mallory (Actor)
PO Box 64249
Los Angeles, CA 90064-0249, USA

Farrow, Mia (Actor)
c/o Judy Hofflund *Hofflund/Polone*
9465 Wilshire Blvd Ste 420
Beverly Hills, CA 90212-2603, USA

Farrow, Yvonne (Actor)
8430 Santa Monica Blvd Ste 200
West Hollywood, CA 90069-4253, USA

Farrow-Rapp, Elizabeth (Baseball Player)
401 Quail Run
Metamora, IL 61548-8360, USA

Farulli, Piero (Musician)
Via G D'Annunzio 153
Florence, ITALY

Farwig, Stephanie (Athlete, Golfer)
2110 W Washington St
Phoenix, AZ 85009-5267, USA

Faryniarz, Brett (Athlete, Football Player)
1021 S Patrick Way
Anaheim, CA 92808-1471, USA

Fasano, John (Actor, Director, Producer, Writer)
c/o Craig Baumgarten *Baumgarten Management*
406 Wilshire Blvd
Santa Monica, CA 90401-1410, USA

Fasano, Sal (Athlete, Baseball Player)
905 Catherine Gln
Minooka, IL 60447-4528, USA

Fashoway, Gord (Athlete, Hockey Player)
3131 SE 167th Ave
Portland, OR 97236-1525, USA

Fasman, Gerald D (Biologist)
180 Wells Ave Ste 106
Newton Center, MA 02459-3328, USA

Fass, Horst (Journalist, Photographer)
12 Norwich St
London EC4A, UNITED KINGDOM (UK)

Fassbaender, Brigitte (Opera Singer)
Am Theater
Braunschweig 38100, GERMANY

Fassbender, Michael (Actor)
c/o Connor McCaughan *Troika*
74 Clerkenwell Rd 3rd Floor
London EC1M 5QA, United Kingdom

Fassell, Jim (Athlete, Coach, Football Coach, Football Player)
c/o Tony D. Burton *Don Buchwald & Associates Inc (NY)*
10 E 44th St Frnt 1
New York, NY 10017-3654

Fassero, Jeff (Athlete, Baseball Player)
9841 N 56th St
Paradise Valley, AZ 85253-1108, USA

Fast, Darcy (Athlete, Baseball Player)
2981 Harrison Ave
Centralia, WA 98531-9356, USA

Fast, Darrell (Religious Leader)
PO Box 347
Newton, KS 67114-0347, USA

Fast, Larry (Composer, Musician)
70 Universal City Plz
Universal City, CA 91608-1011, USA

Faszhotz, Jack (Athlete, Baseball Player)
18338 Maries Road 308
Belle, MO 65013-2125, USA

Fatboy Slim (Musician)
c/o David Levy *WmE2 (WMA-UK)*
103 New Oxford St
London WC1A 1DD, UK

Fatefehi, Mario (Athlete, Football Player)
279 W 1360 N
American Fork, UT 84003-2739, USA

Fatel, Mitch (Musician)
c/o Staff Member *Paradigm (Monterey)*
404 W Franklin St
Monterey, CA 93940-2303, USA

Fath, Farah (Actor)
c/o Kurt Patino *Rothman / Patino / Andres Entertainment*
4370 Tujunga Ave Ste 120
Studio City, CA 91604-2763, USA

Fatone, Joey Jr (Dancer, Musician)
c/o Joe Mulvihill *LiveWire Entertainment*
100 Universal Studios Plaza Bldg A Suite 22 PMB 255
Orlando, FL 32819, USA

Fattah, Chaka (Congressman, Politician)
2301 Rayburn Hob
Washington, DC 20515-3802, USA

Faubert, Mario (Athlete, Hockey Player)
356 Ch Du Canal
St-Stanislaus De Kost, QC J0S 1W0, Canada

Fauci, Anthony S (Doctor)
3012 43rd St NW
Washington, DC 20016-3547, USA

Faucon, Bernard (Photographer)
6 Rue Barbanegre
Paris 75019, FRANCE

Faulconer, Martha (Athlete, Golfer)
374 Stratford Dr
Lexington, KY 40503-1813, USA

Faulk, Kevin (Athlete, Football Player)
190 Summer St
South Walpole, MA 02071-1014, USA

Faulk, Marshall (Athlete, Football Player)
6430 Clayton Rd Apt 305
Saint Louis, MO 63117, USA

Faulk, Trev (Athlete, Football Player)
307 Martin Oaks Dr
Lafayette, LA 70501-2507, USA

Faulkner, Alex (Athlete, Hockey Player)
17 Adams Ave
Bishops Falls, NL A0H 1C0, Canada

Faulkner, Chris (Athlete, Football Player)
1596 E 400 S
Tipton, IN 46072-8440, USA

Faulkner, Eric (Musician)
27 Preston Grange Preston Pans E Lothian, SCOTLAND

Faulkner, John (Scientist)
La Jolla, CA 92093, USA

Faumui, Taase (Athlete, Football Player)
1574 Linapuni St
Honolulu, HI 96819-3507, USA

Faure, Maurice H (Government Official)
28 Blvd Raspail
Paris 75007, FRANCE

Fauria, Christian (Athlete, Football Player)
51 Jeffrey Dr
North Attleboro, MA 02760-2761, USA

Fauser, Mark (Actor)
c/o Staff Member *United Talent Agency (UTA)*
9560 Wilshire Blvd Fl 5
Beverly Hills, CA 90212-2400, USA

Fauss, Ted (Athlete, Hockey Player)
6861 Lowell Rd
Rome, NY 13440-1228, USA

Faust, Andre (Athlete, Hockey Player)
250 Heritage Rd
Cherry Hill, NJ 08034-3150, USA

Faust, Chad (Actor)
c/o Evan Hainey *Untitled Entertainment (LA)*
350 S Beverly Dr Ste 200
Beverly Hills, CA 90212-4819, USA

Faust, Paul (Athlete, Football Player)
5522 Highwood Dr W
Minneapolis, MN 55436-1227, USA

Faustino, David (Actor)
c/o Staff Member *Kass & Stokes Management*
9229 W Sunset Blvd Ste 504
Los Angeles, CA 90069-3405, USA

Faut-Eastman, Jean (Baseball Player)
406 Warrington Pl
Rock Hill, SC 29732-7408, USA

Fauts, Dan
4020 Murphy Canyon Rd
San Diego, CA 92123-4407

Fauza, Dario (Doctor, Misc)
25 Shattuck St
Boston, MA 02115-6027, USA

Favell, Doug (Athlete, Hockey Player)
8 Captain Tenbrock Terr
St Catharines, ON L2W 1B2, Canada

Faverty, Hal (Athlete, Football Player)
163 McComb Rd
Sequim, WA 98382-7884, USA

Favier, Jean-Jacques (Misc)
17 Ave des Martys
Grenoble Cedex 38054, FRANCE

Favino, Pierfrancesco (Actor)
c/o Tammy Rosen *Sanders Armstrong Caserta*
425 N Robertson Blvd
West Hollywood, CA 90048-1735, USA

Favor-Hamilton, Suzy
PO Box 120
Indianapolis, IN 46206-0120

Favors, Gregory (Athlete, Football Player)
230 Merritt Dr
Roswell, GA 30076-3936, USA

Favre, Brett L (Athlete, Football Player)
7698A US Highway 98 W
Sumrall, MS 39482-4188, USA

Favreau, Jon (Actor, Writer)
c/o Ina Treciokas *Slate Public Relations*
9000 W Sunset Blvd Ste 915
West Hollywood, CA 90069-5809, USA

Fawcett, Don W (Doctor, Misc)
3710 American Way Apt 325
Missoula, MT 59808-1927, USA

Fawcett, John (Director)
c/o Scott Yoselow *Gersh (NY)*
41 Madison Ave
New York, NY 10010-2202, USA

Fawcett, Sherwood L (Physicist, Scientist)
1852 Riverside Dr # A
Columbus, OH 43212, USA

Faxon Jr, Brad (Athlete, Golfer)
c/o Staff Member *Pro Golfers Association (PGA) Tour*
112 Tpc Blvd
Ponte Vedra Beach, FL 32082, USA

Fay, David B (Golfer)
Golf House Liberty Corner Road
Far Hills, NJ 7931, USA

Fay, Martin (Music Group, Musician)
1505 W 2nd Ave # 200
Vancouver, BC V6H 3Y4, CANADA

Fay, Meagan (Actor)
c/o Staff Member *Paradigm (LA)*
360 N Crescent Dr
Beverly Hills, CA 90210-4874, USA

Fay, Meagen (Actor)
c/o Staff Member *Main Title Entertainment*
2225 Wilshire Blvd Suite 500
Los Angeles, CA 90036, USA

Fay, Peter T (Judge)
99 NE 4th St
Miami, FL 33132-2131, USA

Faydoedeelay (Music Group, Musician)
729 7th Ave Ste 1600
New York, NY 10019-6880, USA

Fayed, Mohamed al- (Business Person)
Craven Cottage Stevenage Road Fulham
London SW6 6HH, UNITED KINGDOM (UK)

Fazande, Jermaine (Athlete, Football Player)
1207 Tanglewood Dr
Westwego, LA 70094-5128, USA

Fazio, Ernie
2310 Royal Oaks Dr
Alamo, CA 94507-2223

Fazio, Ernie (Athlete, Baseball Player)
2310 Royal Oaks Dr
Alamo, CA 94507-2223, USA

Fazio, Foge (Athlete, Football Coach, Football Player)
1704 Wheatland Dr
Coraopolis, PA 15108-9208, USA

Fazio, Tom (Architect, Golfer)
401 N Main St Ste 400
Hendersonville, NC 28792-4915, USA

Fazzini, Enrico (Doctor)
Medical Center 550 1st Ave
New York, NY 10016, USA

Feacher, Ricky (Athlete, Football Player)
1522 Ferman Ave
Cleveland, OH 44109-3642, USA

Feagles, Jeff (Athlete, Football Player)
219 Sunset Ave
Ridgewood, NJ 07450-2420, USA

Feamster, Dave (Athlete, Hockey Player)
1058 S May Valley Dr
Pueblo, CO 81007-5033, USA

Feamster, Tom (Athlete, Football Player)
6403 US Highway 258
Woodland, NC 27897-9622, USA

Fear Before (Music Group, Musician)
c/o Staff Member *Equal Vision Records*
PO Box 38202
Albany, NY 12203-8202, USA

Fearnley-Whittingstall, Hugh (Chef)
c/o Staff Member *BBC Artist Mail*
PO Box 1116
Belfast BT2 7AJ, United Kingdom

Fearon, Douglas T (Doctor, Misc)
Hills Road
Cambridge CB2 2SP, UNITED KINGDOM (UK)

Feasel, Grant (Athlete, Football Player)
7003 Orchard Hill Ct
Colleyville, TX 76034-6623, USA

Feaster, Allison (Basketball Player)
100 Hive Dr
Charlotte, NC 28217-4524, USA

Featherston, Katie (Actor)
c/o Jillian Fowkes *ID Public Relations (ID-LA)*
7080 Hollywood Blvd Fl 8
Los Angeles, CA 90028-6906, USA

Featherstone, Glenn (Athlete, Hockey Player)
8 Larrabee Ave
Danvers, MA 01923-1828, USA

Febles, Carlos (Athlete, Baseball Player, Coach)
45116 Valley Central Way Attn Coachingstaff
Lancaster, CA 93536-1508, USA

Feck, Luke M (Editor)
6880 Worthington Rd
Westerville, OH 43082-9413, USA

Federer, Roger (Athlete, Tennis Player)
1 Erieview Plaza 1360 East 9th St # 1300
Cleveland, OH 44114, USA

Federico, Anthony (Athlete, Football Player)
12306 Van Nuys Blvd
Sylmar, CA 91342-6049, USA

Federko, Bernie (Athlete, Hockey Player)
2219 Devonsbrook Dr
Chesterfield, MO 63005-4519, USA

Federline, Kevin (Actor, Choreographer, Musician)
1777 Westwood Blvd Ste 200
Los Angeles, CA 90024-5607, USA

Federoff, Al (Athlete, Baseball Player)
10150 Mortenview Dr
Taylor, MI 48180-3769, USA

Federov, Sergei (Athlete, Hockey Player)
1865 Huntingwood Ln
Bloomfield Hills, MI 48304-2313, USA

Federspiel, Joe (Athlete, Football Player)
2016 Lakeside Dr
Lexington, KY 40502-3017, USA

Fedewa, Tim (Race Car Driver)
1737 Onondaga Rd
Holt, MI 48842-8600, USA

Fedor, Dave (Athlete, Basketball Player)
4510 Audubon Ave
De Leon Springs, FL 32130-3033

Fedoruk, Paul (Athlete, Hockey Player)
4578 Liam Dr
Frisco, TX 75034-2139, USA

Fedoseyev, Vladimir I
Kachalova 24
Moscow 121069, RUSSIA

Fedotenko, Ruslan (Athlete, Hockey Player)
PO Box 362
Sister Bay, WI 54234-0362, USA

Fedotov, Maxim V (Musician)
Tolbukhin Str 8 #6
Moscow 121596, RUSSIA

Fedyk, Brent (Athlete, Hockey Player)
1204 Shore Club Dr
Saint Clair Shores, MI 48080-1565, USA

Fee, Melinda (Actor)
145 S Fairfax Ave Ste 310
Los Angeles, CA 90036-2176, USA

Feeder (Music Group)
PO Box 2539
London W1A 3HZ, UNITED KINGDOM

Feehery, Gerry (Athlete, Football Player)
5 Sharpless Ln
Media, PA 19063-3931, USA

Feehily, Mark (Musician)
c/o Staff Member *Solo Agency Ltd (UK)*
55 Fulham High St 2nd Floor
London SW6 3JJ, United Kingdom

Feeley, A J (Athlete, Football Player)
19062 Park Ridge St
Weston, FL 33332-2500, USA

Feely, Jay (Athlete, Football Player)
1560 NW 117th Ave
Plantation, FL 33323-2220, USA

Feeney, Joe
32630 Concord Dr
Madison Heights, MI 48071-1110

Fegley, Richard (Photographer)
680 N Lake Shore Dr
Chicago, IL 60611-4546, USA

Feher, George (Physicist)
9500 Gilman Dr
La Jolla, CA 92093-5003, USA

Feher, Raymond (Athlete, Basketball Player)
62 Cool Springs Rd
Signal Mountain, TN 37377-2075, USA

Feherty, David (Athlete, Golfer)
6422 Prestonshire Ln
Dallas, TX 75225-2309, USA

Fehr, Brendan (Actor)
c/o Staff Member *ROAR (LA)*
9701 Wilshire Blvd Fl 8
Beverly Hills, CA 90212-2008, USA

Fehr, Oded (Actor)
c/o Wendy Murphey *IFA Talent Agency*
8730 W Sunset Blvd Ste 490
Los Angeles, CA 90069-2248, USA

Fehr, Rick (Athlete, Golfer)
2869 W Haley Dr
Anthem, AZ 85086-1749, USA

Fehr, Steve (Bowler)
6216 Highcedar Ct
Cincinnati, OH 45233-4871, USA

Fehrenbach, Charles M (Astronomer)
Les Magnanarelles
Lourmarin 84160, FRANCE

Feierabend, Ryan (Athlete, Baseball Player)
366 Windsor Dr
Elyria, OH 44035-1732, USA

Feiffer, Jules (Cartoonist)
PO Box 373
Southampton, NY 11969-0373, USA

Feig, Paul (Actor, Director)
c/o Renee Kurtz *Creative Artists Agency (CAA-LA)*
2000 Avenue of the Stars Ste 100
Los Angeles, CA 90067-4705, USA

Feige, Kevin (Producer)
9242 Beverly Blvd Ste 350
Beverly Hills, CA 90210-3721, USA

Feigenbaum, Armand V (Business Person, Engineer)
23 South St # 250
Pittsfield, MA 1201, USA

Feigenbaum, Edward A (Scientist)
1017 Cathcart Way
Stanford, CA 94305-1048, USA

Feilden, Bernard M (Architect)
Stiffkey Old Hall Wells-next-to-the-Sea
Norfolk NR23 1QJ, UNITED KINGDOM (UK)

Feinberg, Alan (Musician)
3436 Springhill Rd
Lafayette, CA 94549-2535, USA

Feinberg, Wilfred (Judge)
US Courthouse Foley Square
New York, NY 10007, USA

Feingold, Russell (Ex-Senator)
7114 Donna Dr
Middleton, WI 53562-1709, USA

Feinstein, A Richard (Doctor, Physicist)
1760 2nd Ave Apt 32C
New York, NY 10128-5397, USA

Feinstein, Dianne (Politician)
c/o Staff Member *United States Senate (Hart Office)*
316 Hart Senate Ofc Building
Washington, DC 20510-0001, USA

Feinstein, Michael (Music Group, Musician)
4647 Kingswell Ave # 110
Los Angeles, CA 90027-4301, USA

Feitle, Dave (Athlete, Basketball Player)
12255 Highway 62 E
Harrison, AR 72601-7435, USA

Fekete, Gene (Athlete, Football Player)
963 Norway Dr
Columbus, OH 43221-1655, USA

Fekkai, Frederic (Stylist)
444 N Rodeo Dr
Beverly Hills, CA 90210-4502, USA

Felashia
PO Box 31734
Tucson, AZ 85751-1734

Felber, Dean (Music Group, Musician)
P O Box 5456
Columbia, SC 29250, USA

Felch, William C (Doctor, Physicist)
8545 Carmel Valley Rd
Carmel, CA 93923-9556, USA

Feld, Eliot (Choreographer, Dancer)
890 Broadway # 800
New York, NY 10003-1211, USA

Feldenkrais, Moshe (Doctor, Misc)
University of Tel-Aviv Psychology Dept
Tel-Aviv, ISRAEL

Felder, Benny (Athlete, Baseball Player)
5012 N 39th St
Tampa, FL 33610-6628, USA

Felder, Don (Musician)
PO Box 6051
Malibu, CA 90264-6051, USA

Felder, Kenny (Athlete, Baseball Player)
2902 W Amberwood Dr
Phoenix, AZ 85045-2289, USA

Felder, Mike (Athlete, Baseball Player)
322 S 17th St
Richmond, CA 94804-2606, USA

Felder, Raoul Lionel (Attorney, Attorney General, General)
437 Madison Ave
New York, NY 10022-7001, USA

Feldhausen, Paul (Athlete, Football Player)
W137S6949 Clarendon Pl
Muskego, WI 53150-3207, USA

Feldman, Bella (Artist)
12 Summit Ln
Berkeley, CA 94708-2213, USA

Feldman, Ben (Actor)
c/o Michael Baum *Impression Entertainment*
9229 W Sunset Blvd Ste 700
West Hollywood, CA 90069-3407, USA

Feldman, Corey (Actor)
c/o Staff Member *Scott Carlson Entertainment*
5739 Bucknell Ave
Valley Village, CA 91607-1301, USA

Feldman, Ed
7700 Wisconsin Ave
Bethesda, MD 20814-3578

Feldman, Jerome M (Doctor, Physicist)
2744 Sevier St
Durham, NC 27705-5745, USA

Feldman, Michelle (Bowler)
PO Box 713
Skaneateles, NY 13152-0713, USA

Feldman, Myer (Government Official)
1250 Connecticut Ave NW
Washington, DC 20036-2655, USA

Feldman, Sandra (Misc)
555 New Jersey Ave NW
Washington, DC 20001-2029, USA

Feldman, Tamara (Actor)
c/o John Pierce *The Group*
7187 Macapa Dr
Los Angeles, CA 90068-2003, USA

Feldmann, Marc (Doctor, Misc)
Saint Dunstan's Road
London W6 8RP, UNITED KINGDOM (UK)

Feldon, Barbara (Actor, Model)
14 E 74th St
New York, NY 10021-2628, USA

Feldott, Jennifer (Athlete, Golfer)
PO Box 359
Glenn, MI 49416-0359, USA

Feldshuh, Tovah S (Actor)
c/o Staff Member *Brookside Artists Management (NY)*
250 W 57th St Ste 2303
New York, NY 10107 2399, USA

Feldstein, Martin (Economist, Government Official)
147 Clifton St
Belmont, MA 02478-2603, USA

Felici, Angelo Cardinal (Religious Leader)
Piazza della Citta Leonina 9
Rome 193, ITALY

Feliciano, Jose (Musician)
c/o John Reilly *Rogers & Cowan PR (LA)*
Pacific Design Center 8687 Melrose Ave, 7th Floor
West Hollywood, CA 90069, USA

Felipe (Prince)
Palacio de la Zarzuela
Madrid 28080, SPAIN

Felix, Allyson (Athlete, Olympic Athlete)
c/o Staff Member *Octagon (VA)*
7100 Forest Ave Ste 201
Richmond, VA 23226-3742, USA

Felix, Junior (Athlete, Baseball Player)
7545 Treadway Rd
Gresham, SC 29546-4210, USA

Felix the Cat
12020 Chandler Blvd Ste 200
Valley Village, CA 91607-4617

Felke, Petra (Athlete, Track Athlete)
Wollnitzevstr 42
Jena 7749, GERMANY

Feller, Happy (Athlete, Football Player)
4225 Camacho St
Austin, TX 78723-5389, USA

Feller, Jack (Athlete, Baseball Player)
145 Oakwood Dr
Coldwater, MI 49036-8606, USA

Feller, Robert W A (Bob) (Athlete, Baseball Player)
PO Box 157
Gates Mills, OH 44040-0157, USA

Fellowes, Julian (Actor)
c/o Jeremy Barber *United Talent Agency (UTA)*
9560 Wilshire Blvd Fl 5
Beverly Hills, CA 90212-2400, USA

Fellows, Mark (Athlete, Football Player)
PO Box 517
Choteau, MT 59422-0517, USA

Fellows, Ron (Athlete, Football Player)
202 Creekview Dr
Wylie, TX 75098-7481, USA

Felmy, Hansjorg
Berghofen
Eching, GERMANY D-84174

Felsenstein, Lee (Inventor)
1479 Regent St
Redwood City, CA 94061-2821, USA

Felske, John (Athlete, Baseball Player, Coach)
3804 Ridge Rd
Spring Grove, IL 60081-9390, USA

Felsner, Brian (Athlete, Hockey Player)
28376 Lange Rd
Chesterfield, MI 48047-4855, USA

Felsner, Denny (Athlete, Hockey Player)
16094 Haverhill Dr
Macomb, MI 48044-1946, USA

Felt, Richard (Athlete, Football Player)
3993 N 750 E
Provo, UT 84604-4773, USA

Feltham, Denise (Stylist)
c/o Staff Member *Sydney Represents*
280 Mott St
New York, NY 10012-3439, USA

Felton, Dennis (Basketball Player)
Athletic
Athens, GA 30602-0001, USA

Felton, Eric (Athlete, Football Player)
PO Box 1355
Coppell, TX 75019-1355, USA

Felton, John (Musician)
PO Box 1031
Montrose, CA 91021-1031, USA

Felton, Ralph (Athlete, Football Player)
1002 Grant St
Bulger, PA 15019-2225, USA

Felton, Raymond (Athlete, Basketball Player)
15814 Sullivan Ridge Dr
Charlotte, NC 28277-2477, USA

Felton, Terry (Athlete, Baseball Player)
1253 Cordoba Dr
Zachary, LA 70791-6212, USA

Felton, Tom (Actor)
c/o Staff Member *Harry Potter Production*
Leavesden Studios PO Box 3000
Leavesden, Hertfordshire WD2 7LT, UNITED KINGDOM

Feltrin, Tony (Athlete, Hockey Player)
P.O. Box 560
Lake Cowichan, BC V0R 2G0, Canada

Felts, Narvel (Musician, Songwriter, Writer)
2005 Narvel Felts Dr
Malden, MO 63863-1243, USA

Feltsman, Vladimir (Musician)
165 W 57th St
New York, NY 10019-2201, USA

Feltus, Alan E (Artist)
Porziano 68
Assisi PG 6081, ITALY

Feltz, Vanessa (Actor)
c/o Staff Member *XS Promotions*
57 Fonthill Rd
Aberdeen AB11 6UQ, UNITED KINGDOM (UK)

Fem 2 Fem
1122 B St Ste 308
Hayward, CA 94541-4274

Femia, John
1650 Broadway Ste 714
New York, NY 10019-6944

Fencik, J Gary (Athlete, Football Player)
1134 W Schubert Ave
Chicago, IL 60614-1309, USA

Fenech, Edwige (Actor)
Via Giuseppe Pisanelli
Rome 196, ITALY

Fenech, Jeff (Boxer)
PO Box 21
Hardys Bay, NSW 2257, AUSTRALIA

Fenech-Adami, Edward (Prime Minister)
176 Main St
Birkikara, MALTA

Fenenbock, Charles (Athlete, Football Player)
2785 Clipper Ct
Cool, CA 95614-2039, USA

Fenerty, Gill (Athlete, Football Player)
703 Martina Dr NE
Atlanta, GA 30305-2737, USA

Feng, Ying (Ballerina)
3 Taiping St
Beijing 100050, CHINA

Feng-HslungHsu (Engineer)
PO Box 218
Yorktown Heights, NY 10598-0218, USA

Fenimore, Robert D (Bob) (Athlete, Football Player)
1214 S Fairway Dr
Stillwater, OK 74074-1316, USA

Fenley, Bill (Athlete, Basketball Player)
17 Frilham Ln
Manchester, NJ 08759-6636

Fenley, Molissa (Choreographer, Dancer)
59 Walker St # 4
New York, NY 10013-3513, USA

Fenn, John B (Nobel Prize Laureate)
4909 Cary Street Rd
Richmond, VA 23226-1619, USA

Fenn, Sherilyn (Actor)
c/o Cynthia Campos-Greenberg *Anthem Entertainment*
9595 Wilshire Blvd Ste 900
Beverly Hills, CA 90212-2509, USA

Fennema, Carl (Athlete, Football Player)
469 Ena Rd Apt 3105
Honolulu, HI 96815-1727, USA

Fenner, Derrick (Athlete, Football Player)
7533 33rd Ave NW
Seattle, WA 98117-4712, USA

Fenner, Lane (Athlete, Football Player)
412 Labarre Ct
Saint Johns, FL 32259-4024, USA

Fenney, Rick (Athlete, Football Player)
41594 Margarita Rd
Temecula, CA 92591-2922, USA

Fenske, Chuck
3 Tattnall Pl
Hilton Head, SC 29928-3908

Fenton, James (Writer)
34-43 Russell St
London WC2B 5HA, UNITED KINGDOM (UK)

Fenton, Paul (Athlete, Hockey Player)
1020 Sunset Rd
Brentwood, TN 37027-8276, USA

Fenton, Peggy (Baseball Player)
11131 Cottonwood Dr
Palos Hills, IL 60465-2528, USA

Fenwick, Bobby (Athlete, Baseball Player)
51201 Hutchinson Rd
Three Rivers, MI 49093-9029, USA

Fenyves, Dave (Athlete, Hockey Player)
940 Parish Pl
Hummelstown, PA 17036-8986, USA

Feoktistov, Konstantin P (Cosmonaut)
Moskovskoi Oblasti
Syvisdny Goroduk 141160, RUSSIA

Feore, Colm (Actor)
c/o Gayle Abrams *Oscars Abrams Zimel & Associates, Inc. (OAZ)*
438 Queen St E
Toronto ON M5A 1T4, CANADA

Ferarone, Jessica (Actor)
c/o Tiffany Kuzon *Evolution Entertainment (LA)*
901 N Highland Ave
Los Angeles, CA 90038-2412, USA

Feraud, Gianfranco (Designer, Fashion Designer)
25 Rue Saint Honore
Paris 75001, FRANCE

Ferdin, Pamela (Actor)
171 Pier Ave # 453
Santa Monica, CA 90405-5311, USA

Ferdinand, Franz (Musician)
c/o Staff Member *Paradigm (Monterey)*
404 W Franklin St
Monterey, CA 93940-2303, USA

Ferdinand, Marie (Basketball Player)
1 Sbc Center San Antonio
TX, 78219 USA

Ferdinand, Rio (Soccer Player)
c/o Staff Member *Manchester United PLC*
Sir Matt Busby Way Old Trafford
Manchester M160RA, UNITED KINGDOM

Ferdinand, Ron (Cartoonist)
PO Box 1997
Monterey, CA 93942-1997

Ference, Andrew (Athlete, Hockey Player)
1 Devonshire St
Boston, MA 02109-3506, USA

Ference, Brad (Athlete, Hockey Player)
2424 Gold Canyon Dr
San Antonio, TX 78259-3568, USA

Ferentz, Kirk (Coach, Football Coach)
Athletic Dept Iowa City
IA 52242, USA

Fergason, James L (Jim) (Inventor)
145 Garland Dr
Menlo Park, CA 94025-5817, USA

Fergon, Vicki (Athlete, Golfer)
44 Partridge Ln
Aliso Viejo, CA 92656-1701, USA

Fergus, Keith (Athlete, Golfer)
11515 Noblewood Crest Ln
Houston, TX 77082-6814, USA

Fergus, Tom (Athlete, Hockey Player)
2134 Speers Rd
Oakville, ON L6L 2X8, Canada

Ferguson, Alexander C (Alex) (Soccer Player)
Old Trafford
Manchester M16 0RA, UNITED KINGDOM (UK)

Ferguson, Bob (Athlete, Baseball Player)
60 Wyatt Ln
Equality, AL 36026-2633, USA

Ferguson, Charles A (Editor)
123 Walnut St Apt 851
New Orleans, LA 70118-4845, USA

Ferguson, Charley (Athlete, Football Player)
81 Stonecroft Ln
Buffalo, NY 14226-4129, USA

Ferguson, Christopher J (Astronaut)
16111 Park Center Way
Houston, TX 77059-4083, USA

Ferguson, Clarence C Jr (Attorney, Attorney General, Diplomat, General)
Law School
Cambridge, MA 2138, USA

Ferguson, Colin (Actor)
c/o Perry Zimel *Oscars Abrams Zimel & Associates, Inc. (OAZ)*
438 Queen St E
Toronto ON M5A 1T4, CANADA

Ferguson, Craig (Actor, Comedian, Television Host)
7800 Beverly Blvd # 244
Los Angeles, CA 90036-2112, USA

Ferguson, Cullum Cathy (Athlete, Swimmer)
515 Amanda Dr
Bear, DE 19701-1961, USA

Ferguson, Deborah (Stylist)
c/o Staff Member *Judy Inc*
1 Yorkville Ave
Toronto ON M4W 1L1, Canada

Ferguson, Frederick E (War Hero)
106 S Stellar Pkwy
Chandler, AZ 85226-3725, USA

Ferguson, George (Athlete, Hockey Player)
85 Mayfair Dr
Pittsburgh, PA 15228-1164, USA

Ferguson, Jay (Actor)
c/o Robert Marsala *Global Creative*
1051 Cole Ave # B
Los Angeles, CA 90038-2601, USA

Ferguson, Jesse Tyler (Actor)
c/o Jon Rubinstein *Authentic Talent and Literary Management*
45 Main St Ste 1004
Brooklyn, NY 11201-8200, USA

Ferguson, Joe (Athlete, Baseball Player)
11322 River Run Ln
Berlin, MD 21811-3288, USA

Ferguson, Joe (Athlete, Football Player)
12 Mason Ln
Bella Vista, AR 72715-5548, USA

Ferguson, Keith (Athlete, Football Player)
PO Box 19006
Sugar Land, TX 77496-9006, USA

Ferguson, Lorne (Athlete, Hockey Player)
35 Gretna Grn
Kingston, ON K7M 3J3, Canada

Ferguson, Lynda (Actor)
606 N Larchmont Blvd Ste 309
Los Angeles, CA 90004-1309, USA

Ferguson, Nick (Athlete, Football Player)
1114 Arlington Ave SW
Atlanta, GA 30310-3832, USA

Ferguson, Norm (Athlete, Hockey Player)
71 Causeway Dr
Sydney, NS B1L 1C5, Canada

Ferguson, Robert (Athlete, Football Player)
15102 Oldtown Bridge Ct
Sugar Land, TX 77498-1298, USA

Ferguson, Roger W Jr (Economist, Government Official)
Constitution Ave NW
Washington, DC 20551-0001, USA

Ferguson, Sarah (Royalty)
c/o Karen Sellers *International Creative Management (ICM-LA)*
10250 Constellation Blvd Fl 7
Los Angeles, CA 90067-6207, USA

Ferguson, Stacy (Fergie) (Actor, Musician)
c/o William Derella *DAS Communications*
83 Riverside Dr
New York, NY 10024-5713, USA

Ferguson, Thomas A Jr (Business Person)
Newell Center 29 E Stephenson St
Freeport, IL 61032, USA

Ferguson, Vasquero D (Vagas) (Athlete, Football Player)
380 Hub Etchison Pkwy Attn Assistantprincipal
Richmond, IN 47374-5339, USA

Ferguson, Warren J (Judge)
34 Civic Center Plz
Santa Ana, CA 92701-4090, USA

Ferguson, William (Athlete, Football Player)
9433 N Newport Hwy
Spokane, WA 99218-1244, USA

Ferguson-Winn, Mabel (Athlete, Track Athlete)
2575 Steele Rd Apt 206
San Bernardino, CA 92408-3979, USA

Fergusson, Frances D (Educator)
President's Office
Poughkeepsie, NY 12603, USA

Fergus-Thompson, Gordo (Musician)
150 Audley Road Hendon
London NW4 3EG, UNITED KINGDOM (UK)

Ferigno, Lou (Actor)
PO Box 1671
Santa Monica, CA 90406-1671, USA

Ferland, E James (Business Person)
PO Box 1171
Newark, NJ 07101-1171, USA

Ferland, Jodelle (Actor)
c/o Vickie Petronio *Play Management*
807 Powell St Suite 220
Vancouver V6A 1H7, Canada

Ferlinghetti, Lawrence (Publisher, Writer)
261 Columbus Ave
San Francisco, CA 94133-4519, USA

Ferlito, Vanessa (Actor)
c/o Jeff Golenberg *Collective*
8383 Wilshire Blvd Ste 1050
Beverly Hills, CA 90211-2415, USA

Fermin, Felix (Athlete, Baseball Player)
300 S Main St Attn Coachingstaff
Akron, OH 44308-1204, USA

Fernandes, Ron (Athlete, Football Player)
27385 Osmun St
Madison Heights, MI 48071-3335, USA

Fernandez, Adrian (Athlete, Race Car Driver)
6950 Guion Rd # 51
Indianapolis, IN 46268-2576, USA

Fernandez, Alejandro (Musician)
11003 Rooks Rd
Whittier, CA 90601-1624, USA

Fernandez, Alex (Athlete, Baseball Player)
12323 SW 55th St Ste 107
Cooper City, FL 33330-3312, USA

Fernandez, Bernardo (Athlete, Baseball Player)
6701 Dorita Ave Unit 202
Las Vegas, NV 89108-0355, USA

Fernandez, C Sidney (Sid) (Athlete, Baseball Player)
25 Aulike St Apt 218
Kailua, HI 96734-2747, USA

Fernandez, Chico
3322 24th St
Detroit, MI 48208-2412

Fernandez, Chico (Athlete, Baseball Player)
1310 SW 97th Ave
Miami, FL 33174-1384, USA

Fernandez, Chico (Athlete, Baseball Player)
8401 NW 40th Ct
Sunrise, FL 33351-6181, USA

Fernandez, Craig (Director, Writer)
c/o Staff Member *The Gotham Group Inc*
9255 W Sunset Blvd Ste 515
Los Angeles, CA 90069-3308, USA

Fernandez, Ester
Mitla 112 esq. Xola Colonia Narvarte
Mexico DF, MEXICO

Fernandez, Evalina
5911 Allison St
Los Angeles, CA 90022

Fernandez, Ferdinand F (Judge)
125 S Grand Ave
Pasadena, CA 91105-1643, USA

Fernandez, Frank (Athlete, Baseball Player)
37 Coughlan Ave
Staten Island, NY 10310-3149, USA

Fernandez, Gigi (Tennis Player)
4202 E Fowler Ave # 214
Tampa, FL 33620-9951, USA

Fernandez, Giselle (Television Host)
PO Box 498
Quakertown, PA 18951-0498, USA

Fernandez, Jared (Athlete, Baseball Player)
4298 S 4625 W
Salt Lake City, UT 84120-4964, USA

Fernandez, Juan (Actor)
6500 Wilshire Blvd Ste 2200
Los Angeles, CA 90048-4942, USA

Fernandez, Julian (Stylist)
c/o Staff Member *Independent Artists*
448 E Riverdale Ave
Orange, CA 92865-1302, USA

Fernandez, Lisa (Athlete)
1460 Homewood Rd Apt 95B
Seal Beach, CA 90740-4627, USA

Fernandez, Manny (Athlete, Football Player)
1709 Poplar Ridge Rd
Ellaville, GA 31806-5935, USA

Fernandez, Manny (Athlete, Hockey Player)
500 Atlantic Ave Unit 17P
Boston, MA 02210-2254, USA

Fernandez, Mary Jo
133 1st St NE
Saint Petersburg, FL 33701-3307

Fernandez, Mary Joe (Tennis Player)
6040 SW 104th St
Miami, FL 33156-1902, USA

Fernandez, Mervyn (Athlete, Football Player)
2477 Briarwood Dr
San Jose, CA 95125-4918, USA

Fernandez, O Antonio (Tony) (Athlete, Baseball Player)
19232 N Gardenia Ave
Weston, FL 33332-4409, USA

Fernández, Pedro (Musician)
c/o Staff Member *Machete Music*
2220 Colorado Ave
Santa Monica, CA 90404-3506, USA

Fernandez, Pedro (Musician, Songwriter)
PO Box 65948
Los Angeles, CA 90065-0948, USA

Fernandez, Shiloh (Actor)
c/o Justin Grey Stone *Untitled Entertainment (LA)*
350 S Beverly Dr Ste 200
Beverly Hills, CA 90212-4819, USA

Fernandez, Vicente (Musician)
11003 Rooks Rd
Whittier, CA 90601-1624, USA

Ferneyhough, Brian J P (Composer)
848 Allardice Way
Stanford, CA 94305-1056, USA

Fernsten, Eric (Athlete, Basketball Player)
5634 Linden St
Dublin, CA 94568-7704

Ferragamo, Vince (Athlete, Football Player)
6200 E Canyon Rim Rd Ste 204
Anaheim, CA 92807-4315, USA

Ferrante, Orlando (Athlete, Football Player)
1223 Adair St
San Marino, CA 91108-1806, USA

Ferrara, Abel (Director)
8942 Wilshire Blvd # 219
Beverly Hills, CA 90211-1908, USA

Ferrara, Adam (Actor)
697 Middle Neck Rd
Great Neck, NY 11023-1216, USA

Ferrara, Al (Athlete, Baseball Player)
4901 Whitsett Ave Apt 207
Valley Village, CA 91607-3550, USA

Ferrara, Jerry (Actor)
c/o Stephen (Steve) Levinson *Leverage Management*
3030 Pennsylvania Ave
Santa Monica, CA 90404-4112, USA

Ferrara, Laura (Stylist)
c/o Celebrity Stylist *Bryan Bantry*
900 Broadway Ste 400
New York, NY 10003-1239, USA

Ferrare, Cristina (Entertainer, Model)
10727 Wilshire Blvd Apt 1602
Los Angeles, CA 90024-7334, USA

Ferrarese, Don (Athlete, Baseball Player)
15290 Myalon Rd
Apple Valley, CA 92307-4938, USA

Ferrari, Al (Athlete, Basketball Player)
5911 Bristlecone Ct
Saint Louis, MO 63129-2917

Ferrari, Anthony (Athlete, Baseball Player)
17 Bretano Way
Greenbrae, CA 94904-1180, USA

Ferrari, Michael R Jr (Educator)
570 Greenway Dr
Lake Forest, IL 60045-4801, USA

Ferrari, Tina (Dancer, Wrestler)
2901 Las Vegas Blvd S
Las Vegas, NV 89109-1933, USA

Ferrario, Bill (Athlete, Football Player)
116 Hensy Ct
Scranton, PA 18504, USA

Ferraris, Jan (Athlete, Golfer)
7108 N 13th Pl
Phoenix, AZ 85020-5408, USA

Ferraro, Chris (Athlete, Hockey Player)
100 Theresa Blvd
Binghamton, NY 13901-5527, USA

Ferraro, Dave (Bowler)
672 E Chester St
Kingston, NY 12401-1742, USA

Ferraro, Mike (Athlete, Baseball Player, Coach)
5201 Rim View Ln
Las Vegas, NV 89130-3658, USA

Ferraro, Ray (Athlete, Hockey Player)
c/o Staff Member *Rogers Sportsnet*
181 Keefer Pl Suite 221
Vancouver, BC V6B 1W6, Canada

Ferratti, Rebecca (Actor, Model)
10061 Riverside Dr # 721
Toluca Lake, CA 91602-2560, USA

Ferrazzi, Ferruccio (Artist)
Piazza delle Muse Via G G Porro 27
Rome 197, ITALY

Ferrazzi, Pierpaolo (Athlete)
Via del Progresso
Marano Vicenza 36035, ITALY

Ferre, Gianfranco (Designer, Fashion Designer)
Villa Della Spiga 19/A
Milan 20121, ITALY

Ferree, Jim (Athlete, Golfer)
12 Kings Tree Rd
Hilton Head Island, SC 29928-6101, USA

Ferreira, Sky (Musician)
c/o Ron Laffitte *Red Light Management (LA)*
8439 W Sunset Blvd Ste 2
Los Angeles, CA 90069-1925, USA

Ferreira, Tony (Athlete, Baseball Player)
3006 Merrill Ave
Clearwater, FL 33759-3429, USA

Ferreira, Wayne (Tennis Player)
1 Erieview Plaza 1360 East 9th St # 1300
Cleveland, OH 44114, USA

Ferrell, Bob (Athlete, Football Player)
1090 N Shooting Star Dr
Beaumont, CA 92223-8435, USA

Ferrell, Conchata (Actor)
1335 Seward St
Los Angeles, CA 90028-7816, USA

Ferrell, Earl (Athlete, Football Player)
107 E Forest Trl
South Boston, VA 24592-4366, USA

Ferrell, Rachel (Musician)
19800 Cornerstone Sq Apt 415
Ashburn, VA 20147-4250, USA

Ferrell, Rachelle (Musician)
19800 Cornerstone Sq Apt 415
Ashburn, VA 20147-4250, USA

Ferrell, Tyra (Actor)
c/o Staff Member *Gersh (LA)*
9465 Wilshire Blvd Ste 600
Beverly Hills, CA 90212-2612, USA

Ferrell, Will (Actor, Comedian, Producer)
c/o Jimmy Miller *Mosaic Media Group*
9200 W Sunset Blvd Ste 10
Los Angeles, CA 90069-3608, USA

Ferrell Edmonson, Barbara A (Athlete, Track Athlete)
Athletic Dept
Las Vegas, NV 89154, USA

Ferreol, Andrea
10 Ave George V
Paris, FRANCE F-75008

Ferrer, Alex (Judge, Television Host)
4261 Southwest Fwy
Houston, TX 77027-7201, USA

Ferrer, Danay (Musician)
1776 Broadway # 1500
New York, NY 10019-2002, USA

Ferrer, Lupita
861 Stone Canyon Rd
Los Angeles, CA 90077-2911

Ferrer, Miguel (Actor)
c/o Leslie Allan-Rice *Leslie Allan-Rice Management*
7524 Mulholland Dr
Los Angeles, CA 90046-1239, USA

Ferrera, America (Actor)
c/o Jon Rubinstein *Authentic Talent and Literary Management*
45 Main St Ste 1004
Brooklyn, NY 11201-8200, USA

Ferreras, Francisco (Pipin) (Misc)
7548 W Treasure Dr
North Bay Village, FL 33141-4118, USA

Ferrero, Louis P (Business Person)
PO Box 675744
Rancho Santa Fe, CA 92067-5744, USA

Ferrigno, Lou (Actor)
PO Box 1671
Santa Monica, CA 90406-1671, USA

Ferrin, Arnie (Athlete, Basketball Player)
2104 S Barona Rd
Palm Springs, CA 92264-4854, USA

Ferrin, Jennifer (Actor)
c/o Staff Member *As The World Turns*
JC Studios 1268 E 14th St
New York, NY 11230, USA

Ferris, Bob (Athlete, Baseball Player)
18259 Glen Oak Way
Leesburg, VA 20176-3992, USA

Ferris, John (Swimmer)
1961 Klamath River Dr
Rancho Cordova, CA 95670-2910, USA

Ferris, Michael (Mike) (Producer, Writer)
c/o Staff Member *Broder Webb Chervin Silbermann Agency, The (BWCS)*
10250 Constellation Blvd
Los Angeles, CA 90067-6200, USA

Ferris, Pamela
16601 Marquez Ave Unit 405
Pacific Palisades, CA 90272-3263

Ferriss, David M (Boo) (Athlete, Baseball Player)
510 Robinson Dr
Cleveland, MS 38732-2214, USA

Ferriss, Timothy (Tim) (Writer)
c/o Staff Member *Random House Publicity*
1745 Broadway
New York, NY 10019-4368, USA

Ferritor, Daniel E (Educator)
Chancellor's Office
Fayetteville, AR 72701, USA

Ferro, Cindy (Athlete, Golfer)
1901 Brookside Dr
Scotch Plains, NJ 07076-2601, USA

Ferron (Musician, Songwriter, Writer)
4930 Paradise Dr
Tiburon, CA 94920-1060, USA

Ferry, Bryan (Musician, Songwriter, Writer)
c/o Staff Member *Dene Jesmond Entertainment Ltd.*
65 New Cavendish St.
London W1M 7RD, UK

Ferry, Daniel J W (Danny) (Athlete, Basketball Player)
604 Castano Ave
San Antonio, TX 78209-3617, USA

Ferry, David R (Writer)
English Dept
Wellesley, MA 2181, USA

Ferry, John D (Misc)
6175 Mineral Point Rd
Madison, WI 53705-4457, USA

Ferry, Robert (Bob) (Athlete, Basketball Player)
2129 Beach Haven Rd
Annapolis, MD 21409-5744, USA

Fersen, Paul (Athlete, Football Player)
PO Box 4
Dorset, VT 05251-0004, USA

Fersht, Alan R (Misc)
2 Barrow Close
Cambridge CB2 2AT, UNITED KINGDOM (UK)

Fert, Albert (Nobel Prize Laureate)
Unité Mixte De Physique - UMR 137 128 Route Départementale
Palaiseau F-91767, France

Fest, Howard (Athlete, Football Player)
133 Forest Cir
Bandera, TX 78003-4015, USA

Festinger, Leon (Misc)
37 W 12th St
New York, NY 10011-8502, USA

Festinger, Robert (Writer)
c/o Bryan Besser *Verve Talent & Literary Agency, LLC*
9696 Culver Blvd Ste 301
Culver City, CA 90232-2759, USA

Fetchick, Mike (Athlete, Golfer)
4 White Birch Dr
Dix Hills, NY 11746-7720, USA

Fetisov, Viachesiav (Slava) (Athlete, Hockey Player)
65 Avon Dr
Essex Fells, NJ 07021-1717, USA

Fetter, Trevor (Business Person)
13737 Noel Rd Ste 100
Dallas, TX 75240-2017, USA

Fetterhoff, Robert (Religious Leader)
PO Box 386
Winona Lake, IN 46590-0386, USA

Fetters, Mike (Athlete, Baseball Player)
2088 E Mead Pl
Chandler, AZ 85249-3261, USA

Fettig, Jeff M (Business Person)
2000 N State St RR 63
Benton Harbor, MI 49022, USA

Fetting, Katie (Actor)
c/o Ramses Ishak *United Talent Agency (UTA)*
9560 Wilshire Blvd Fl 5
Beverly Hills, CA 90212-2400, USA

Fetting, Ralner (Artist)
Hasenhelde 61
Berlin 61, GERMANY

Fettman, Martin J (Astronaut)
1572 N Saguaro Cliffs Ct
Tucson, AZ 85745-8839, USA

Feuer, Debra
9560 Wilshire Blvd Ste 500
Beverly Hills, CA 90212-2401

Feuerstein, Mark (Actor)
c/o Steven Levy *Framework Entertainment (LA)*
9057 Nemo St Ste C
West Hollywood, CA 90069-5511, USA

Feulner, Edvin J Jr (Misc)
214 Massachusetts Ave NE
Washington, DC 20002-4958, USA

Feustel, Andrew J (Astronaut)
4003 Elm Crest Trl
Houston, TX 77059-3281, USA

Fewx, Gene (Misc)
666 15th St NE
Salem, OR 97301-2616, USA

Fey (Musician)
#1 Chapultapec Lomas
Mexico City 11000, MEXICO

Fey, Michael (Cartoonist)
200 Madison Ave
New York, NY 10016-3903, USA

Fey, Tina (Actor, Comedian)
c/o David Miner *3 Arts Entertainment Inc*
9460 Wilshire Blvd Fl 7
Beverly Hills, CA 90212-2713, USA

Fezler, Forrest (Athlete, Golfer)
6270 Old Water Oak Rd
Tallahassee, FL 32312-3861, USA

Fiala, John (Athlete, Football Player)
12113 268th Dr NE
Duvall, WA 98019-9610, USA

Fiala, Neil (Athlete, Baseball Player)
4709 Woody Terrace Ct
Saint Louis, MO 63129-1683, USA

Fialkowska, Janina (Musician)
7 St George's Ct 131 Putney Bridge Rd
London SW15 2PA, UNITED KINGDOM (UK)

Fiasco, Lupe (Musician)
c/o Cara Lewis *WmE2 (WMA-NY)*
1325 Avenue of the Americas
New York, NY 10019-6026, USA

Fibiger, Jesse (Athlete, Hockey Player)
3336 Ocean Blvd
Victoria, BC V9C 1W6, Canada

Ficca, Dan (Athlete, Football Player)
151 Kansas Ln
Kulpmont, PA 17834-2005, USA

Fichaud, Eric (Athlete, Hockey Player)
191 Rue Charron
Lemoyne, QC J4R 2K6, Canada

Fichtel, Anja
Stauferring 104
Tauberbischofsheim, GERMANY D-97941

Fichter, Mike (Athlete, Baseball Player)
2942 192nd Pl
Lansing, IL 60438-3728, USA

Fichter, Rick T (Cinematographer)
3630 Cabrillo St
San Francisco, CA 94121-3420, USA

Fichtner, Hans J (Scientist)
612 Cleermont Dr SE
Huntsville, AL 35801-1870, USA

Fichtner, Ross (Athlete, Football Player)
46833 Danbridge St
Plymouth, MI 48170-3079, USA

Fichtner, William (Actor)
c/o Andrea Pett-Joseph *Brillstein Entertainment Partners*
9150 Wilshire Blvd Ste 350
Beverly Hills, CA 90212-3453, USA

Fick, Robert (Athlete, Baseball Player)
164 Brodia Way
Walnut Creek, CA 94598-4920, USA

Fiddler, Vern (Athlete, Hockey Player)
9729 Amethyst Ln
Brentwood, TN 37027-3523, USA

Fidler, Mike (Athlete, Hockey Player)
7723 Gleason Rd
Minneapolis, MN 55439-2563, USA

Fidrych, Mark (Athlete, Baseball Player)
260 West St
Northborough, MA 01532-1223, USA

Fiedel, Brad (Composer)
13245 Riverside Dr # 430
Sherman Oaks, CA 91423-5625, USA

Fiedler, Jay (Athlete, Football Player)
25 Russell Rd
Garden City, NY 11530-1947, USA

Fiedler, Jens
Bruno-Granz-Str. 48
Chemnitz, GERMANY D-09122

Fieger, Geoffrey (Attorney, Attorney General, General)
1781 Rathmor Rd
Bloomfield, MI 48304-2144, USA

Field, Arabella (Actor)
8730 W Sunset Blvd Ste 440
Los Angeles, CA 90069-2277, USA

Field, Ayda (Actor)
c/o Staff Member *Brillstein Entertainment Partners*
9150 Wilshire Blvd Ste 350
Beverly Hills, CA 90212-3453, USA

Field, Byron (Actor)

Field, Chelsea (Actor)
15263 Mulholland Dr
Los Angeles, CA 90077-1620, USA

Field, Helen (Opera Singer)
Foresters Hall 25-27 Westow St
London SE19 3RY, UNITED KINGDOM (UK)

Field, Nate (Athlete, Baseball Player)
PO Box 270
Hoisington, KS 67544-0270, USA

Field, Patricia (Stylist)
c/o Ivana Savic *Grant Savic Kopaloff & Associates*
6399 Wilshire Blvd Ste 414
Los Angeles, CA 90048-5716, USA

Field, Sally (Actor)
c/o Judy Hofflund *Hofflund/Polone*
9465 Wilshire Blvd Ste 420
Beverly Hills, CA 90212-2603, USA

Field, Shirley Arin (Actor)
c/o Paul Pearson *Daly Pearson Associates*
586 King's Rd Chelsea
London SW6 2DX, UNITED KINGDOM (UK)

Field, Todd (Actor, Director)
c/o Ariel (Ari) Emanuel *WmE2 (Endeavor-LA)*
9601 Wilshire Blvd Fl 3
Beverly Hills, CA 90210-5219, USA

Fielder, Cecil (Athlete, Baseball Player)
PO Box 495125
Port Charlotte, FL 33949-5125, USA

Fielder, Guyle (Athlete, Hockey Player)
2253 Leisure World
Mesa, AZ 85206-5384, USA

Fielder, Prince (Athlete, Baseball Player)
2080 Shopiere Rd
Beloit, WI 53511-3780, USA

Fielding, Fred F (Attorney, Attorney General, General, Government Official)
7925 Jones Branch Dr Ste 6200
McLean, VA 22102-3376, USA

Fielding, Helen (Writer)
c/o Beth Swofford *Creative Artists Agency (CAA-LA)*
2000 Avenue of the Stars Ste 100
Los Angeles, CA 90067-4705, USA

Fielding, Joy (Writer)
1230 Avenue of the Americas
New York, NY 10020-1513, USA

Fielding, Yvette (Actor)
128 Grove Ln Cheadle Hulme
Cheshire SK8 7ND, UNITED KINGDOM

Fields, Brandon (Athlete, Football Player)
4509 Holt Rd
Sylvania, OH 43560-9795, USA

Fields, Bruce (Athlete, Baseball Player)
20160 Renfrew Rd
Detroit, MI 48221-1334, USA

Fields, Debbi (Business Person)
1290 W 2320 S Ste A
Salt Lake City, UT 84119-1483, USA

Fields, Edgar (Athlete, Football Player)
435 Musket Entry
Roswell, GA 30076-3411, USA

Fields, Freddie
8899 Beverly Blvd Ste 918
Los Angeles, CA 90048-2427

Fields, Harold T Jr (General)
126 Deer Run Strut
Enterprise, AL 36330-7812, USA

Fields, Holly (Actor)
6500 Wilshire Blvd Ste 2200
Los Angeles, CA 90048-4942, USA

Fields, Jitter (Athlete, Football Player)
5776 Kensington Ave
Detroit, MI 48224-2071, USA

Fields, Joseph C (Joe) Jr (Athlete, Football Player)
1 University Pl
Chester, PA 19013-5700, USA

Fields, Kenny (Athlete, Basketball Player)
10624 Crenshaw Blvd Apt 2
Inglewood, CA 90303-2064, USA

Fields, Kim (Actor)
c/o Tracey Mapes *Imperium 7 Talent Agency*
5455 Wilshire Blvd Ste 1706
Los Angeles, CA 90036-4217, USA

Fields, Landry (Athlete, Basketball Player)
c/o Chris Emens *Octagon Home Office*
1751 Pinnacle Dr Fl 15
McLean, VA 22102-3833, USA

Fields, Scott (Athlete, Football Player)
7513 Santa Lucia St
Fontana, CA 92336-3603, USA

Fields, Stephen (Baseball Player)
8306 Wickham Rd
Springfield, VA 22152-1708, USA

Fields, Stephen (Athlete, Baseball Player)
8306 Wickham Rd
Springfield, VA 22152-1708, USA

Fields, Valerie
PO Box 4025
Niagara Falls, NY 14304-8025

Fieldstad, Oivin
Damfaret 59
Bryn-Oslo 6, NORWAY

Fiennes, Joseph (Actor)
c/o Gene Parseghian *Parseghian Planco LLC*
322 8th Ave Ste 601
New York, NY 10001-6715, USA

Fiennes, Ralph (Actor)
c/o Nicole Caruso *Wolf Kasteler Van Iden & Associates (NY)*
584 Broadway Rm 310
New York, NY 10012-5246, USA

Fierek, Wolfgang
Ottobrunner Str. 15
Brunnthal, GERMANY D-85649

Fieri, Guy (Chef, Television Host)
c/o Rebecca Brooks *Brooks Group*
15 W 37th St Rm 1601
New York, NY 10018-5318, USA

Fierstein, Harvey (Actor, Musician, Writer)
c/o Ron Fierstein *RF Entertainment Inc.*
29 Haines Rd
Bedford Hills, NY 10507-1206, USA

Fieser, Louis (Inventor)
58 Medford St
Arlington, MA 02474-3124, USA

Fife, Dan (Danny) (Athlete, Baseball Player)
5854 Misty Hill Dr
Clarkston, MI 48346-3033, USA

Figaro, Cedric (Athlete, Football Player)
205 Staten St
Lafayette, LA 70501-1745, USA

Figga, Mike (Athlete, Baseball Player)
16434 Turnbury Oak Dr
Odessa, FL 33556-2896, USA

Figg-Currier, Cindy (Athlete, Golfer)
109 Blue Jay Dr
Lakeway, TX 78734-5101, USA

Figgins, Chone (Athlete, Baseball Player)
16 San Sovino
Newport Coast, CA 92657-1313, USA

Figgis, Michael (Mike) (Director)
c/o Robert Newman *WmE2 (Endeavor-LA)*
9601 Wilshire Blvd Fl 3
Beverly Hills, CA 90210-5219, USA

Figini, Luigi (Architect)
Via Perone di S Martino 8
Milan, ITALY

Figini, Michela (Skier)
Ariolo
Prato Lavenina 6799, SWITZERLAND

Figlo-Gill, Josephine (Athlete, Baseball Player)
437 N Fork Dr
Lakeland, FL 33809-1426, USA

Figo, Luis (Soccer Player)
Avda Cincha Espina 1
Madrid 28036, SPAIN

Figueras-Dotti, Marta (Athlete, Golfer)
6174 Palomino Cir
Bradenton, FL 34201-2384, USA

Figueroa, Bien (Athlete, Baseball Player)
3272 Addison Ln
Tallahassee, FL 32317-9045, USA

Figueroa, Ed (Athlete, Baseball Player)
A-N15 Calle 41
Santa Juanita, PR 619, USA

Figueroa, Efrain (Actor)
c/o Staff Member *Mitchell K Stubbs & Assoc (MKS)*
8675 Washington Blvd Ste 203
Culver City, CA 90232-7486, USA

Figueroa, Nelson (Athlete, Baseball Player)
14 Clover Ln
Quakertown, PA 18951-3920, USA

Figura, Maria Louisa (Actor)
5716 Cahuenga Blvd
North Hollywood, CA 91601-2105, USA

Figures, Deon (Athlete, Football Player)
1520 S Visalia Ave
Compton, CA 90220-3947, USA

Fikac, Jeremy (Athlete, Baseball Player)
909 Electra
Lakeway, TX 78734-4215, USA

Fike, Dan (Athlete, Football Player)
23479 Wingedfoot Dr
Westlake, OH 44145-4371, USA

Fikrig, Erol (Doctor)
Medical Center Infectious Disease Dept
New Haven, CT 6510, USA

Fila, Ivan (Writer)
c/o David Krintzman *Morris, Yorn, Barnes, Levine, Krintzman, Rubenstein and Kohner*
2000 Ave Of The Stars 3rd Tower Floor NORTH
Los Angeles, CA 90067, USA

Filan, Shane (Musician)
c/o Staff Member *RCA Label Group UK*
9 Derry St
London W8 5HY, UK

Filardi, Peter (Director, Producer, Writer)
c/o Robert Marsala *Global Creative*
1051 Cole Ave # B
Los Angeles, CA 90038-2601, USA

Filarski-Steffes, Helen (Baseball Player)
19623 Damman St
Harper Woods, MI 48225-1753, USA

Filatova, Ludmila P (Opera Singer)
Ryleyevastr 6 #13
Saint Petersburg, RUSSIA

File, Bob (Athlete, Baseball Player)
6412 Riverfront Dr
Palmyra, NJ 08065-2149, USA

File, Sam (Athlete, Baseball Player)
44 Constitution Dr
Chadds Ford, PA 19317-9409, USA

Filer, Tom (Athlete, Baseball Player)
425 Fox Hollow Dr
Feasterville Trevose, PA 19053-2495, USA

Files, Jim (Athlete, Football Player)
6303 Fallstone Rd
Fort Smith, AR 72916-8939, USA

Filicia, Thom (Designer, Television Host)
c/o Staff Member *WmE2 (WMA-LA)*
1 William Morris Pl
Beverly Hills, CA 90212-4261, USA

Filiol, Jalme (Tennis Player)
1025 Thomas Jefferson St NW # 430
Washington, DC 20007-5201, USA

Filion, Herve (Race Car Driver)
18 Evans Ave
Albertson, NY 11507-1902, USA

Filipacchi, Daniel (Publisher)
149-51 Rue Anatole-France
Levallois 92534, FRANCE

Filipchenko, Anatoli N (Cosmonaut, General)
Syvisdny Goroduk 141160, RUSSIA

Filipek, Ron (Athlete, Basketball Player)
933 Hillside Dr
Cookeville, TN 38501-2890, USA

Filippo, Lou
3603 Howard Ave
Los Alamitos, CA 90720-3682

Filippo (Fillipo/Filippo), Fabrizio (Fab) (Actor)
c/o David Lillard *IFA Talent Agency*
8730 W Sunset Blvd Ste 490
Los Angeles, CA 90069-2248, USA

Fill, Shannon (Actor)
260 S Beverly Dr Ste 200
Beverly Hills, CA 90212-3812, USA

Fillion, Nathan (Actor)
c/o Ennis Kamcili *United Talent Agency (UTA)*
9560 Wilshire Blvd Fl 5
Beverly Hills, CA 90212-2400, USA

Fillmore, Greg (Athlete, Basketball Player)
12449 Blueberry Woods Cir E Apt E
Jacksonville, FL 32258-4174

Fillon, Bob (Athlete, Hockey Player)
201-980 Rue Cayer
Saint-Jean-Sur-Richelieu, QC J3A 1N8, Canada

Filner, Bob (Congressman, Politician)
2428 Rayburn Hob
Washington, DC 20515-0551, USA

Filson, Pete (Athlete, Baseball Player)
1034 10th Ave
Folsom, PA 19033-1112, USA

Filter (Music Group)
c/o Staff Member *Warner Bros Records (NY)*
75 Rockefeller Plz
New York, NY 10019-6908, USA

Fimmel, Travis (Actor, Model)
c/o David Seltzer *Management 360*
9111 Wilshire Blvd
Beverly Hills, CA 90210-5508, USA

Fimple, Dennis
3518 Cahuenga Blvd W # 306
Los Angeles, CA 90068-1304

Fimple, Jack (Athlete, Baseball Player)
8012 Cliffrose St
Windsor, CA 95492-9537, USA

Fina, John (Athlete, Football Player)
5180 E Fort Lowell Rd
Tucson, AZ 85712-1309, USA

Finch, Jennie (Athlete, Olympic Athlete)
PO Box 97
La Mirada, CA 90637-0097, USA

Finch, Joel (Athlete, Baseball Player)
68571 Oak Springs Rd
Edwardsburg, MI 49112-9502, USA

Finch, Jon (Actor)
2-4 Noel St
London W1V 3RB, UNITED KINGDOM (UK)

Finch, Karl (Athlete, Football Player)
4408 Copper Crest Ln
Modesto, CA 95355-8970, USA

Finch, Linda (Misc)
211 Switch Oak
Shavano Park, TX 78230-5621, USA

Finch, Tyrone (Comedian)
c/o Staff Member *United Talent Agency (UTA)*
9560 Wilshire Blvd Fl 5
Beverly Hills, CA 90212-2400, USA

Finchem, Timothy W (Athlete, Golfer)
c/o Staff Member *Pro Golfers Association (PGA) Tour*
112 Tpc Blvd
Ponte Vedra Beach, FL 32082, USA

Fincher, Alfred (Athlete, Football Player)
1267 Avenue Du Chateau
Covington, LA 70433-6424, USA

Fincher, David (Director)
c/o Jeff Baron *Anonymous Content (AC-LA)*
3531 Hayden Ave
Culver City, CA 90232, USA

Finck, George C (War Hero)
143 Beaver Ln
Benton, LA 71006-9332, USA

Fincke, E Michael (Mike) (Astronaut)
15819 El Dorado Oaks Dr
Houston, TX 77059-4045, USA

Finckel, David (Musician)
3 Burlington Lane
London W4 2TH, UNITED KINGDOM (UK)

Findlay, Conn F (Athlete, Yachtsman)
1920 Oak Knoll Dr
Belmont, CA 94002-1755, USA

Fine, David (Director, Writer)
c/o Melissa Myers *WmE2 (Endeavor-LA)*
9601 Wilshire Blvd Fl 3
Beverly Hills, CA 90210-5219, USA

Fine, Jeanna
19 Hanover Pl Pmb 313
Hicksville, NY 11801-5103

Fine, Tom (Misc)
2605 Cascade Cove Dr
Little Elm, TX 75068-7603

Fine, Travis (Actor)
200 N Robertson Blvd # 219
Beverly Hills, CA 90211-1769, USA

Fine, Wendy (Stylist)
6232 Tapia Dr Apt A
Malibu, CA 90265-3155, USA

Finfera, Joe (Actor)
c/o Staff Member *Select Artists Ltd (CA-Westside Office)*
1138 12th St Apt 1
Santa Monica, CA 90403-5459, USA

Fingaz, Sticky (Artist, Musician)
c/o David Guc *Vanguard Management Group*
8060 Melrose Ave Fl 4
Los Angeles, CA 90046-7038, USA

Finger Eleven (Music Group)
c/o Staff Member *Wind-up Records*
72 Madison Ave Fl 8
New York, NY 10016-8731, USA

Fingers, Rollie (Athlete, Baseball Player)
PO Box 230729
Las Vegas, NV 89105-0729, USA

Fink, Gerald R (Doctor, Scientist)
40 Alston Rd
West Newton, MA 2465, USA

Fink, Jason (Athlete, Football Player)
2619 Regatta Ln
Davis, CA 95618-6409, USA

Fink, John
1680 Vine St Ste 614
Hollywood, CA 90028-8833

Fink, Mitchell
1835 E Michelle St
West Covina, CA 91791-3942

Fink, Natascha (Athlete, Golfer)
Golfclub Murhof Adriach 54
Frohnleiten A-8130, Austria

Finkbeiner, Kirsten Rowe (Activist)
12011 Bel Red Rd Ste 206
Bellevue, WA 98005-2471, USA

Finkel, Fyvush (Actor)
c/o Dianne Busch *Leading Artists*
145 W 45th St Rm 1000
New York, NY 10036-4032, USA

Finkel, Henry (Hank) (Athlete, Basketball Player)
2 Pocahontas Way
Lynnfield, MA 01940-1042, USA

Finkel, Shelly
310 Madison Ave # 804
New York, NY 10017, USA

Finkelstein, Anita (Stylist)
c/o Staff Member *Elite Model Management/Atlanta*
1708 Peachtree St NW Ste 210
Atlanta, GA 30309-2416, USA

Finkes, Matt (Athlete, Football Player)
5442 Cedar Spgs
Columbus, OH 43228-7200, USA

Finlay, Frank (Actor)
91 Regent St
London W1R 7TB, UNITED KINGDOM (UK)

Finley, Brian (Athlete, Hockey Player)
84 Greenview Ln
Sault Ste Marie, ON P6A 6K9, Canada

Finley, Charles E (Chuck) (Athlete, Baseball Player)
500 McCormick Rd
West Monroe, LA 71291-1921, USA

Finley, David (Opera Singer)
1642 Milvia St Apt 3S
Berkeley, CA 94709-2001, USA

Finley, Gerald H (Opera Singer)
3 Burlington Lane Chiswick
London W4 2TH, UNITED KINGDOM (UK)

Finley, John L (Astronaut)
700 Colonial Rd Ste 120
Memphis, TN 38117-5191, USA

Finley, Karen (Artist)
59 E 4th St Ste 6E
New York, NY 10003-8991, USA

Finley, Margot (Actor)
c/o Staff Member *Pacific Artists Management*
1285 W Broadway Suite 685
Vancouver, BC V6H 3X8, Canada

Finley, Michael (Basketball Player)
2909 Taylor St
Dallas, TX 75226-1909, USA

Finley, Steven (Steve) (Athlete, Baseball Player)
c/o Lew Weitzman *Preferred Artists*
16633 Ventura Blvd Ste 1421
Encino, CA 91436-1885, USA

Finn, Danny (Athlete, Basketball Player)
511 W 25th St Ste 900
New York, NY 10001-5584, USA

Finn, Jim (Athlete, Football Player)
1214 Western Dr
Fair Lawn, NJ 07410-2213, USA

Finn, John (Actor)
c/o Gabrielle Krengel *Domain Talent*
9229 W Sunset Blvd Ste 710
Los Angeles, CA 90069-3407, USA

Finn, John W (War Hero)
10809 Oak Creek Dr
Lakeside, CA 92040-1630, USA

Finn, Neil (Musician, Songwriter, Writer)
c/o Staff Member *WmE2 (WMA-LA)*
1 William Morris Pl
Beverly Hills, CA 90212-4261, USA

Finn, Patrick (Actor)
c/o Staff Member *Brillstein Entertainment Partners*
9150 Wilshire Blvd Ste 350
Beverly Hills, CA 90212-3453, USA

Finn, Steve (Athlete, Hockey Player)
5 De Cheverny St
Blainville, QC J7B 1M7, Canada

Finn, Tim (Musician)
98 Surrey St
Darlinghurst, NSW 2010, AUSTRALIA

Finn, Veronica (Musician)
1776 Broadway # 1500
New York, NY 10019-2002, USA

Finn, William (Composer, Songwriter, Writer)
Music Dept
New York, NY 10012, USA

Finnegan, Christian (Comedian)
c/o Kara Welker *Generate Management*
1545 26th St Ste 200
Santa Monica, CA 90404-3554, USA

Finnegan, Cortland (Athlete, Football Player)
6253 Rivervalley Dr
Nashville, TN 37221-6577, USA

Finneran, Brian (Athlete, Football Player)
1905 Sugarloaf Club Dr
Duluth, GA 30097-7448, USA

Finneran, Gary (Athlete, Football Player)
711 Oak Point Dr
Oak Park, CA 91377-3836, USA

Finneran, John G (Admiral)
2904 N Leisure World Blvd Apt 404
Silver Spring, MD 20906-1394, USA

Finneran, Katie (Actor)
c/o Adena Chawke *Greenlight Management and Production*
13848 Valleyheart Dr
Sherman Oaks, CA 91423-2930, USA

Finneran, Rittenhouse Sharon (Swimmer)
212 Harbor Dr
Santa Cruz, CA 95062-3442, USA

Finnerty, Dan (Actor, Musician)
c/o Staff Member *WmE2 (WMA-LA)*
1 William Morris Pl
Beverly Hills, CA 90212-4261, USA

Finnessey, Shandi (Beauty Pageant Winner)
c/o Staff Member *Miss Universe Organization, The*
1370 Avenue of the Americas Fl 16
New York, NY 10019-4602, USA

Finney, Albert (Actor)
45/51 Whitfield St
London W1P 6AA, UNITED KINGDOM (UK)

Finney, Allison (Athlete, Golfer)
78160 Desert Mountain Cir
Bermuda Dunes, CA 92203-8151, USA

Finney, Tom (Soccer Player)
Deepdale Sir Finney Way
Preston PR1 6RU, UNITED KINGDOM (UK)

Finnie, Linda A (Musician)
16 Golf Course Girvan
Ayrshire KA26 9HW, UNITED KINGDOM (UK)

Finnie, Roger (Athlete, Football Player)
937 NW 58th St
Miami, FL 33127-1321, USA

Finnigan, Jennifer (Actor)
c/o John Carrabino *John Carrabino Management*
5900 Wilshire Blvd Ste 406
Los Angeles, CA 90036-5015, USA

Finnvold, Gar (Athlete, Baseball Player)
1204 NE 4th Ave
Boca Raton, FL 33432-2808, USA

Finsterwald, Dow (Athlete, Golfer)
2772 Fawn Grove Ct
Colorado Springs, CO 80906-3701, USA

Finzer, Dave (Athlete, Football Player)
1435 Kaywood Ln
Glenview, IL 60025-2341, USA

Fiona, Melanie (Musician)
c/o Dennis Ashley *International Creative Management (ICM-LA)*
10250 Constellation Blvd Fl 7
Los Angeles, CA 90067-6207, USA

Fiore, Dave (Athlete, Football Player)
868 Southampton Dr
Palo Alto, CA 94303-3439, USA

Fiore, Kathryn (Actor)
c/o Michael P Levine *Levine Management*
9028 W Sunset Blvd PH 1
Los Angeles, CA 90069-1830, USA

Fiore, Mike (Athlete, Baseball Player)
17 Silver St
Malverne, NY 11565-1116, USA

Fiore, Teri (Stylist)
c/o Staff Member *O'Gorman/Schramm Represents, Inc*
642 Washington St Apt 1A
New York, NY 10014-6327, USA

Fiore, Tony (Athlete, Baseball Player)
19021 Fishermans Bend Dr
Lutz, FL 33558-9754, USA

Fiorentini, Jeff (Athlete, Baseball Player)
4200 Chardonnay Dr
Rockledge, FL 32955-5133, USA

Fiorentino, Peter (Athlete, Hockey Player)
5570 Belmont Ave
Niagara Falls, ON L2H 1J7, Canada

Fiori, Ed (Athlete, Golfer)
50 Burwick St
Sugar Land, TX 77479-2997, USA

Fiori, Fernando (Actor)
c/o Staff Member *Latin World Entertainment Agency (WEA)*
2601 S Bayshore Dr Ste 235
Miami, FL 33133-5432, USA

Fiorillo, Elisbatta (Opera Singer)
165 W 57th St
New York, NY 10019-2201, USA

Fiorito, Jaelle (Actor, Television Host)
c/o Staff Member *Rebel Entertainment Partners*
5700 Wilshire Blvd Ste 456
Los Angeles, CA 90036-3648, USA

Firbank, Ann
76 Oxford St
London, ENGLAND W1N OAX

Fire, Andrew Z. (Nobel Prize Laureate)
3000 Pasteur Dr
Stanford, CA 94305, USA

Firefall
6400 Pleasant Park Dr
Chanhassen, MN 55317-8804

Fireman, Paul B (Business Person)
1895 W J Foster Blvd
Canton, MA 2021, USA

Fireovid, Steve (Athlete, Baseball Player)
1408 Woodstream Dr
Bryan, OH 43506-9049, USA

Fires, Earlie S (Jockey)
16337 Rivervale Ln
Rivervale, AR 72377, USA

Firestone, Andrew (Actor, Reality TV Star)
c/o Staff Member *Paradigm (LA)*
360 N Crescent Dr
Beverly Hills, CA 90210-4874, USA

Firestone, Eddie
303 S Crescent Heights Blvd
Los Angeles, CA 90048-4403

Firestone, Roy (Sportscaster)
257 S Rodeo Dr
Beverly Hills, CA 90212-3803, USA

Firm, The
57A Great Titchfield St
London, ENGLAND W1P 7FL

Firova, Dan (Athlete, Baseball Player)
5115 Coos Bay
Laredo, TX 78041-1963, USA

First, Neal L (Misc)
9437 W Garnette Dr
Sun City, AZ 85373-1732, USA

Firth, Colin (Actor)
c/o Jessica Kolstad *WKT Public Relations (WKT-LA)*
9350 Wilshire Blvd Ste 450
Beverly Hills, CA 90212-3230, USA

Firth, Peter (Actor)
Julian House 4 Windmill St
London W1P 1HF, UNITED KINGDOM (UK)

Fiscella, Nicole (Model)
c/o Staff Member *New York Model Management*
596 Broadway # 701
New York, NY 10012-3396, USA

Fischbach, Ephraim (Physicist)
5821 Farm Ridge Rd
West Lafayette, IN 47906-9492, USA

Fischer, Adam
27 Chancery Lane
London WC2A 1PF, UNITED KINGDOM (UK)

Fischer, Bernard
208 King Rd
Kuna, ID 83634

Fischer, Bill (Athlete, Baseball Player)
139 Upland Dr
Council Bluffs, IA 51503-4823, USA

Fischer, Bill (Athlete, Football Player)
23191 Shady Oak Ln
Estero, FL 33928-4383, USA

Fischer, Edmond H (Nobel Prize Laureate)
5540 NE Windermere Rd
Seattle, WA 98105-2849, USA

Fischer, Ernst Otto (Nobel Prize Laureate)
Munich 81479, GERMANY

Fischer, Hank (Athlete, Baseball Player)
10367 Big Canoe
Big Canoe, GA 30143-5123, USA

Fischer, Heinz (President)
Hofburg Alderstiege
Vienna 1010, AUSTRIA

Fischer, Helmut
Kaiserplatz 5
Munich, GERMANY D-80803

Fischer, Ivan
1 Andrassy Utca 27
Budapest 1061, HUNGARY

Fischer, Jeff (Athlete, Baseball Player)
215 Worth Ct N
West Palm Beach, FL 33405-2751, USA

Fischer, Jenna (Actor)
c/o Michelle Bohan *WmE2 (Endeavor-LA)*
9601 Wilshire Blvd Fl 3
Beverly Hills, CA 90210-5219, USA

Fischer, Lisa (Musician)
3264 S Kihei Rd
Kihei, HI 96753-9605, USA

Fischer, Michael L (Misc)
1330 Broadway Ste 1100
Oakland, CA 94612-2511, USA

Fischer, Patrick (Pat) (Athlete, Football Player)
PO Box 4289
Leesburg, VA 20177-8401, USA

Fischer, Schmidt Birgit (Athlete)
Kuckuckswald 11
Kleinmachnow 14532, GERMANY

Fischer, Stanley (Business Person, Economist)
399 Park Ave Frnt 2
New York, NY 10022-4614, USA

Fischer, Sven (Athlete)
Schillerhoehe 7
Schmalkalden 98574, GERMANY

Fischer, Tiet Jen (Stylist)
c/o Staff Member *Artist Untied (LA)*
845 S Mansfield Ave Apt 1
Los Angeles, CA 90036-4979, USA

Fischer, Todd (Athlete, Baseball Player)
12734 Newtown Rd
Unionville, TN 37180-5004, USA

Fischer, Todd (Athlete, Golfer)
7347 Linwood Ct
Pleasanton, CA 94588-4877, USA

Fischer, Van (Director)
232 N Canon Dr
Beverly Hills, CA 90210-5302, USA

Fischer, Veronika
Glockengiesserwall 3
Hamburg, GERMANY D-20095

Fischer, William A (Moose) (Athlete, Football Player)
1790 Pinnacle Ridge Ln
Colorado Springs, CO 80919-3450, USA

Fischer-Dieskau, Dietrich (Opera Singer)
Hans Einzler Berlin Charlottenstrasse, 55
Berlin D-10117, Germany

Fischerspooner (Music Group)
c/o Staff Member *Paradigm (Monterey)*
404 W Franklin St
Monterey, CA 93940-2303, USA

Fischetti, Brad (Musician)
1776 Roadway Floor 15
New York, NY 10019

Fischetti, Vincent (Biologist)
Medical Center 1230 York Ave
New York, NY 10021, USA

Fischler, Patrick (Actor)
c/o Stewart Strunk *Main Title Entertainment*
2225 Wilshire Blvd Suite 500
Los Angeles, CA 90036, USA

Fischlin, Mike (Athlete, Baseball Player)
1010 Curtright Pl
Greensboro, GA 30642-7432, USA

Fiset, Stephane (Athlete, Hockey Player)
c/o Staff Member *Newport Sports Management*
1042 Charcot Suite 304
Bouchervulle, QC J4B 8R4, Canada

Fish, Ginger (Musician)
c/o Staff Member *Interscope Records (LA) - Main*
2220 Colorado Ave
Santa Monica, CA 90404-3506, USA

Fish, Howard M (General)
15797 Dockside Ct
Tyler, TX 75703-7405, USA

Fish, Matt (Athlete, Basketball Player)
2206 E Lincoln Dr
Phoenix, Arizona 86016, USA

Fishbacher, Siegfried (Magician)
3400 Las Vegas Blvd S
Las Vegas, NV 89109-8923, USA

Fishback, Joe (Athlete, Football Player)
148 Fairoaks Cir
Stockbridge, GA 30281-1189, USA

Fishbone
PO Box 4450
New York, NY 10163-4450

Fishburne, Laurence (Actor)
c/o Helen Sugland *Landmark Artists*
4116 W Magnolia Blvd Ste 101
Burbank, CA 91505-2700, USA

Fishel, Danielle (Actor)
c/o Staff Member *Innovative Artists (LA)*
1505 10th St
Santa Monica, CA 90401-2805, USA

Fishel, John (Athlete, Baseball Player)
329 Marjoram Dr
Columbus, OH 43230-7027, USA

Fisher, Allison (Billiards Player)
9021 Hwy 105
South Boone, NC 28607

Fisher, Anna L (Astronaut)
1912 Elmen St
Houston, TX 77019-6144, USA

Fisher, Bernard (Doctor)
5636 Aylesboro Ave
Pittsburgh, PA 15217-1402, USA

Fisher, Bernard F (War Hero)
4200 W King Rd
Kuna, ID 83634-1610, USA

Fisher, Brian (Athlete, Baseball Player)
3660 S Uravan St
Aurora, CO 80013-3458, USA

Fisher, Bryan (Actor)
c/o Jamie Freed *Paris Hilton Entertainment*
8383 Wilshire Blvd Ste 1050
Beverly Hills, CA 90211-2415, USA

Fisher, Carrie (Actor, Writer)
c/o Staff Member *Creative Artists Agency (CAA-LA)*
2000 Avenue of the Stars Ste 100
Los Angeles, CA 90067-4705, USA

Fisher, Charles (Athlete, Football Player)
PO Box 133
Aliquippa, PA 15001-0133, USA

Fisher, Climie
30 Bridstow Pl
London, ENGLAND W2 5AE

Fisher, Derek (Athlete, Basketball Player)
1888 Century Park E Ste 900
Los Angeles, CA 90067-1735, USA

Fisher, Doug (Athlete, Football Player)
4040 Hancock St Apt 201
San Diego, CA 92110-5109, USA

Fisher, Dunc (Athlete, Hockey Player)
2600 Regina Ave
Regina, SK S4S 0G5, Canada

Fisher, Ed (Athlete, Football Player)
4734 E Redfield Rd
Phoenix, AZ 85032-5520, USA

Fisher, Eddie G (Athlete, Baseball Player)
408 Cardinal Cir S
Altus, OK 73521-1714, USA

Fisher, Elder A (Bud) (Bowler)
7551 Brackenwood Cir N
Indianapolis, IN 46260-5439, USA

Fisher, Evan (Musician)
PO Box 1031
Montrose, CA 91021-1031, USA

Fisher, Frances (Actor)
c/o Tammy Rosen *Sanders Armstrong Caserta*
425 N Robertson Blvd
West Hollywood, CA 90048-1735, USA

Fisher, Fritz (Athlete, Baseball Player)
3703 Barcelona Dr
Toledo, OH 43615-1203, USA

Fisher, Gerry
River Bank Hartsfield Rd.
W. Molesey Surrey, ENGLAND

Fisher, Isla (Actor)
c/o Julie Darmody *Mosaic Media Group*
9200 W Sunset Blvd Ste 10
Los Angeles, CA 90069-3608, USA

Fisher, Jack (Athlete, Baseball Player)
2865 Greenleaf Ct
Bethlehem, PA 18017-3261, USA

Fisher, Jeff (Coach, Football Coach)
215 Ward Cir Ste 200
Brentwood, TN 37027-2306, USA

Fisher, Jeff (Athlete, Football Coach, Football Player)
385 Lake Valley Dr
Franklin, TN 37069-4652, USA

Fisher, Joel (Artist)
PO Box 65
Palisades, NY 10964-0065, USA

Fisher, Joely (Actor)
c/o John Carrabino *John Carrabino Management*
5900 Wilshire Blvd Ste 406
Los Angeles, CA 90036-5015, USA

Fisher, Jules E (Designer)
126 5th Ave
New York, NY 10011-5606, USA

Fisher, Kimberly (Model)
PO Box 69330
West Hollywood, CA 90069-0330

Fisher, Mary (Misc)
866 3rd Ave
New York, NY 10022-6221, USA

Fisher, Matthew (Misc)
39 Croham Road
South Croydon CR2 7HD, UNITED KINGDOM (UK)

Fisher, Maurice (Maury) (Athlete, Baseball Player)
15920 Lucerne Rd
Fredericktown, OH 43019-9531, USA

Fisher, Mimi (Stylist)
c/o Staff Member *Judy Casey Inc*
114 E 13th St
New York, NY 10003-5329, USA

Fisher, Ray (Athlete, Football Player)
RR 2 Box 235
Fairfield, IL 62837-9668, USA

Fisher, Raymond C (Judge)
125 S Grand Ave
Pasadena, CA 91105-1643, USA

Fisher, Red (Writer)
250 Saint Antoine W
Montreal, QC H2Y 3R7, CANADA

Fisher, Rob
45 Montague Rd.
Richmond Surrey, ENGLAND

Fisher, Robert (Business Person)
2 Folsom St
San Francisco, CA 94105-1205, USA

Fisher, Roger (Musician)
1250 6th St Ste 401
Santa Monica, CA 90401-1638, USA

Fisher, Steve (Coach)
Athletic
San Diego, CA 92182-0001, USA

Fisher, Terry Louise
5314 Pacific Ave
Marina Del Rey, CA 90292-7118

Fisher, Thomas L
1844 W Ferry Rd
Naperville, IL 60563-9662, USA

Fisher, Tom (Athlete, Baseball Player)
6515 Lake Suzzanne Cir
Panama City, FL 32404-3418, USA

Fisher, Trisha Leigh
243 Delfern Dr
Los Angeles, CA 90077-3544

Fisher, William F (Astronaut)
1119 Woodland Dr
El Lago, TX 77586-6044, USA

Fisher-Stevens, Lorraine (Baseball Player)
120 Birdsell St
Jackson, MI 49203-4670, USA

Fishman, Jerald G (Business Person)
1 Technology Way
Norwood, MA 02062-2634, USA

Fishman, Jon (Musician)
431 Pine St
Burlington, VT 05401-4726, USA

Fishman, Michael (Actor)
c/o Ryan Glasgow *Bohemia Group*
1680 Vine St Ste 216
Los Angeles, CA 90028-8829, USA

Fisk, Carlton E (Athlete, Baseball Player)
18705 63rd Ave E
Bradenton, FL 34211-7025, USA

Fisk, Pliny III (Architect)
8604 FM 969
Austin, TX 78724-6200, USA

Fisk, Schuyler (Actor)
c/o Staff Member *Fat Dot*
87 Bedford St Apt 1
New York, NY 10014-3769, USA

Fiske, Robert B Jr (Attorney, Attorney General, General)
19 Juniper Rd
Darien, CT 06820-5707, USA

Fisker, Bruce L (General)
9001 Jimson Weed Way
Highlands Ranch, CO 80126-2642, USA

Fitch, Bill (Athlete, Basketball Player, Coach)
627 Nerita St Unit A
Sanibel, FL 33957-6805, USA

Fitch, Val L (Nobel Prize Laureate)
292 Hartley Ave
Princeton, NJ 08540-5656, USA

Fitchner, Bob (Athlete, Hockey Player)
138 Ross Pl
Carman, MB R0G 0J0, Canada

Fites, Donald V (Business Person)
100 NE Adams St
Peoria, IL 61629-0001, USA

Fitgerald, Ann (Stylist)
c/o Staff Member *Team*
423 W Broadway Ste 406
Boston, MA 02127-2265, USA

Fitt of Bell's Hill, Gerald (Government Official)
82 Eaton Square
London SW1, UNITED KINGDOM (UK)

Fittipaldi, Christian (Race Car Driver)
282 Alphaville Barueri
Sao Paulo 64500, BRAZIL

Fittipaldi, Emerson (Race Car Driver)
735 Crandon Blvd Apt 503
Miami, FL 33149-2526, USA

Fitts, Rick
1903 Dracena Dr
Los Angeles, CA 90027-3106

Fitz, Raymond L (Educator)
President's Office
Dayton, OH 45469-0001, USA

Fitzgerald, A Ernest (Government Official, Lawyer)
Pentagon
Washington, DC 20330-0001, USA

Fitzgerald, Brian (Athlete, Baseball Player)
7226 John Taylor Mews
Ruther Glen, VA 22546-4816, USA

Fitzgerald, Caitlin (Actor)
c/o Adam Schweitzer *International Creative Management (ICM-NY)*
40 W 57th St
New York, NY 10019-4001, USA

Fitzgerald, Ed (Athlete, Baseball Player)
431 Christopher St
Folsom, CA 95630-1706, USA

Fitzgerald, Fern (Actor)
10 Universal City Plz Ste 2000
Universal City, CA 91608-1074, USA

FitzGerald, Frances (Writer)
1230 Avenue of the Americas
New York, NY 10020-1513, USA

FitzGerald, Garret (Prime Minister)
30 Palmerston Road
Dublin 6, IRELAND

Fitzgerald, Glenn (Actor)
c/o Sue Leibman *Barking Dog Entertainment*
9 Desbrosses St Fl 2
New York, NY 10013-1701, USA

FitzGerald, Helen (Actor)
9300 Wilshire Blvd Ste 555
Beverly Hills, CA 90212-3211, USA

Fitzgerald, Jack (Actor)
1605 N Cahuenga Blvd # 202
Los Angeles, CA 90028-6201, USA

Fitzgerald, James F (Misc)
1001 Broadway
Oakland, CA 94607-4019, USA

Fitzgerald, John (Athlete, Baseball Player)
1913 Greve Ave Apt 1
Spring Lake, NJ 07762-2354, USA

Fitzgerald, John (Athlete, Football Player)
408 Arborcrest Dr
Richardson, TX 75080-2606, USA

Fitzgerald, Kevin (Misc)
9770 E Alameda Ave
Denver, CO 80247-1301, USA

Fitzgerald, Larry (Athlete, Football Player)
15832 S 22nd St
Phoenix, AZ 85048-4243, USA

Fitzgerald, Marcus (Athlete, Football Player)
c/o Roosevelt Barnes *Maximum Sports Management*
6435 W Jefferson Blvd # 197
Fort Wayne, IN 46804-6203, USA

Fitzgerald, Melissa (Actor)
c/o Staff Member *Geddes Agency, The*
8430 Santa Monica Blvd Ste 200
Los Angeles, CA 90069-4253, USA

Fitzgerald, Mike (Athlete, Baseball Player)
415 Parkview Dr
Rochester, IL 62563-9543, USA

Fitzgerald, Mike (Athlete, Baseball Player)
502 Flint Ave
Long Beach, CA 90814-2039, USA

Fitzgerald, Mosley Benita (Athlete)
14555 Avion Pkwy
Chantilly, VA 20151-1117, USA

FitzGerald, Niali W A (Business Person)
Weena 455
Rotterdam, DK 3000, NETHERLANDS

Fitzgerald, Rusty (Athlete, Hockey Player)
4730 Dodge St
Duluth, MN 55804-1517, USA

Fitzgerald, Tac (Actor)
c/o Staff Member *Iris Burton Agency*
10100 Santa Monica Blvd Ste 1300
Los Angeles, CA 90067-4114, USA

Fitzgerald, Tara (Actor)
125 Gloucester Road
London SW7 4IE, UNITED KINGDOM (UK)

Fitzgerald, Thom (Director)
c/o Gloria Bonelli *Gloria Bonelli & Associates*
Prefers to be contacted via email or telephone
Pine Bush, NY 12566, USA

Fitzgerald, Tom (Athlete, Hockey Player)
3 Samuel Phelps Way
North Reading, MA 01864-2990, USA

Fitzgerald-Leclair, Meryle (Baseball Player)
909 E Hanson Ave
Mitchell, SD 57301-3635, USA

Fitzhugh, Steve (Athlete, Football Player)
1030 Feltl Ct Apt 330
Hopkins, MN 55343-3904, USA

Fitzkee, Scott (Athlete, Football Player)
1611 Grafton Shop Rd
Forest Hill, MD 21050-2535, USA

Fitzmaurice, David J (Misc)
11256 156th St NW
Washington, DC 20005, USA

Fitzmaurice, Michael J (War Hero)
PO Box 178
Hartford, SD 57033-0178, USA

Fitzmaurice, Molly (Stylist)
c/o Staff Member *O'Gorman/Schramm Represents, Inc*
642 Washington St Apt 1A
New York, NY 10014-6327, USA

Fitzmaurice, Shaun (Athlete, Baseball Player)
1911 Normandstone Dr
Midlothian, VA 23113-9669, USA

Fitzmorris, Al (Athlete, Baseball Player)
17512 W 159th Ter
Olathe, KS 66062-4017, USA

Fitzpatrick, Michael (Baseball Player)
262 Lodge Ln
Kalamazoo, MI 49009-9161, USA

Fitzpatrick, Mike (Athlete, Baseball Player)
262 Lodge Ln
Kalamazoo, MI 49009-9161, USA

Fitzpatrick, Rory (Athlete, Hockey Player)
580 Colebrook Dr
Rochester, NY 14617-2009, USA

Fitzpatrick, Ross (Athlete, Hockey Player)
PO Box 459
Hershey, PA 17033-0459, USA

Fitzpatrick, Ryan (Athlete, Football Player)
c/o Jimmy Sexton *SportsTrust Advisors - TN*
1100 Ridgeway Loop Rd Fl 5
Memphis, TN 38120-4053, USA

Fitzpatrick, Sandy (Athlete, Hockey Player)
11250 Lakerim Rd
San Diego, CA 92131-2311, USA

Fitzpatrick, Sonya (Psychic, Writer)
80 Garden Ct Ste 150
Monterey, CA 93940-5389, USA

Fitzsimmons, Greg (Actor)
c/o Kara Welker *Generate Management*
1545 26th St Ste 200
Santa Monica, CA 90404-3554, USA

Fitzsimonds, Roger L (Financier)
777 E Wisconsin Ave
Milwaukee, WI 53202-5302, USA

Fitzwater, Marlin (Government Official)
851 Cedar Dr
Deale, MD 20751-9613, USA

Five for Fighting (Music Group)
c/o Staff Member *Paradigm (NY)*
360 Park Ave S Fl 16
New York, NY 10010-1708, USA

Fix, Oliver (Athlete)
Ringstr 6
Stadtbergen, GERMANY

Fixman, Marshall (Misc)
Chemistry
Fort Collins, CO 80523-0001, USA

Fizer, Marcus (Basketball Player)
129 W Trade St Ste 700
Charlotte, NC 28202-5301, USA

Flach, Ken (Coach, Tennis Player)
Athletic
Nashville, TN 37240-0001, USA

Flach, Thomas (Yachtsman)
Berlin 12439, GERMANY

Flack, Enya (Actor)
c/o Paul Barrutia *The Paradise Group*
PO Box 69451
West Hollywood, CA 90069-0451, USA

Flade, H Kiaus-Dietrich (Cosmonaut)
1 Rond Point M Bellonte
Blagnac Cedex 31707, FRANCE

Flagg, Fannie (Actor, Comedian)
c/o Sally Willcox *Creative Artists Agency (CAA-LA)*
2000 Avenue of the Stars Ste 100
Los Angeles, CA 90067-4705, USA

Flagg, Josh (Business Person, Reality TV Star)
9388 Santa Monica Blvd
Beverly Hills, CA 90210-4885, USA

Flaherty, Harry (Athlete, Football Player)
23 Elizabeth Dr
Oceanport, NJ 07757-1050, USA

Flaherty, Joe
c/o Staff Member *Silver Massetti & Szatmary (SMS-NY)*
145 W 45th St # 1204
New York, NY 10036-4008, USA

Flaherty, John (Athlete, Baseball Player)
17 Joseph Bow Ct
Pearl River, NY 10965-2868, USA

Flaherty, Maureen
PO Box 15967
Long Beach, CA 90815-0967, USA

Flaherty, Stephen (Composer)
c/o Staff Member *Gersh (LA)*
9465 Wilshire Blvd Ste 600
Beverly Hills, CA 90212-2612, USA

Flaherty, Wade (Athlete, Hockey Player)
c/o Art Breeze *Pro-Rep Entertainment Consulting*
113-276 Midpark Way SE
Calgary, AB T2X 1J6, Canada

Flair, Ric (Athlete, Wrestler)
c/o Elaine Gillespie *Gillespie Agency, The*
3007 Millwood Ave
Columbia, SC 29205-1855, USA

Flake, Jeff (Congressman, Politician)
240 Cannon Hob
Washington, DC 20515-1802, USa

Flaman, Ferdinand C (Fernle) (Athlete, Hockey Player)
29 Church St
Westwood, MA 02090-3511, USA

Flame, Penny (Adult Film Star)
19422 Archwood St
Reseda, CA 91335-4903, USA

Flanagan, Barry (Artist)
5E Fawe St
London E14 6PD, UNITED KINGDOM (UK)

Flanagan, Crista (Actor)
c/o Kay Liberman *Liberman/Zerman Management*
252 N Larchmont Blvd Ste 200
Los Angeles, CA 90004-3754, USA

Flanagan, Ed (Athlete, Football Player)
10981 Clayton St
Northglenn, CO 80233-4671, USA

Flanagan, Edward M Jr (General)
Parade Rest 12 Oyster Catcher Road
Beaufort, SC 29907, USA

Flanagan, Fionnula (Actor)
c/o Dick Guttman *Guttman Associates*
118 S Beverly Dr Ste 201
Beverly Hills, CA 90212-3016, USA

Flanagan, Flonnula (Actor)
118 S Beverly Dr
Beverly Hills, CA 90212-3016, USA

Flanagan, Helen (Actor)
c/o Staff Member *Linton Management*
3 The Rock
Greater Manchester BL9 0JP, UNITED KINGDOM

Flanagan, James L (Engineer)
Computer Aids for Industry Center
Piscataway, NJ 8855, USA

Flanagan, Michael K (Mike) (Athlete, Baseball Player)
15010 York Rd
Sparks Glencoe, MD 21152-9669, USA

Flanagan, Mike (Athlete, Football Player)
4631 Waring St
Houston, TX 77027-6217, USA

Flanagan, Shalane (Athlete, Track Athlete)
c/o Staff Member *US Olympic Committee*
1750 E Boulder St
Colorado Springs, CO 80909-5793, USA

Flanagan, Tommy (Actor)
c/o Beth Holden-Garland *Untitled Entertainment (LA)*
350 S Beverly Dr Ste 200
Beverly Hills, CA 90212-4819, USA

Flanery, Bridget
8428 Melrose Pl Ste C
Los Angeles, CA 90069-5300

Flanery, Sean Patrick (Actor)
c/o Jeff Golenberg *Collective*
8383 Wilshire Blvd Ste 1050
Beverly Hills, CA 90211-2415, USA

Flanigan, Jim (Athlete, Football Player)
3820 Sand Bay Point Rd
Sturgeon Bay, WI 54235-8418, USA

Flanigan, Jim (Athlete, Football Player)
4511 Wyandot Trl
Green Bay, WI 54313-6789, USA

Flanigan, Joe (Actor)
c/o John Carrabino *John Carrabino Management*
5900 Wilshire Blvd Ste 406
Los Angeles, CA 90036-5015, USA

Flanigan, Lauren (Opera Singer)
Harkness Plaza 61 W 62nd St #6F
New York, NY 10023, USA

Flanigan, Tom (Athlete, Baseball Player)
114 E 40th St
Covington, KY 41015-1802, USA

Flannery, John (Athlete, Baseball Player)
9002 Scottish Pastures Dr
Austin, TX 78750-3582, USA

Flannery, Kate (Actor)
c/o Kristopher Koller *Seven Summits Pictures & Management*
8906 W Olympic Blvd Ground Floor
Beverly Hills, CA 90211, USA

Flannery, Susan (Actor)
6977 Shepard Mesa Rd
Carpinteria, CA 93013-3134, USA

Flannery, Thomas (Cartoonist, Editor)
911 Dartmouth Glen Way
Baltimore, MD 21212-3247, USA

Flannery, Tim (Athlete, Baseball Player)
715 Hymettus Ave
Encinitas, CA 92024-2148, USA

Flannigan, Maureen (Actor)
3500 W Olive Ave Ste 1400
Burbank, CA 91505-5512, USA

Flaska, Carrie (Actor)
3440 29th St
Astoria, NY 11106-3504, USA

Flatley, Michael (Actor, Dancer)
c/o Staff Member *Creative Artists Agency (CAA-LA)*
2000 Avenue of the Stars Ste 100
Los Angeles, CA 90067-4705, USA

Flatley, Patrick (Pat) (Athlete, Hockey Player)
c/o Staff Member *National Hockey League (NHL)*
50 Bay St 11th Floor
Toronto, ON M5J 2X8, Canada

Flatley, Paul R (Athlete, Football Player)
795 Woods Rd
Richmond, IN 47374-9409, USA

Flatt, Lester
PO Box 647
Hendersonville, TN 37077-0647

Flaum, Joel M (Judge)
219 S Dearborn St
Chicago, IL 60604-1702, USA

Flav, Flavor (Actor, Comedian, Reality TV Star)
c/o Heather Taylor *Alliance Worldwide Communications*
12115 Magnolia Blvd # 137
North Hollywood, CA 91607-2609, USA

Flavell, Richard A (Misc)
Medical Center Immunology Dept
New Haven, CT 6520, USA

Flavin, Jennifer (Model)
30 Beverly Park
Beverly Hills, CA 90210-1546, USA

Flavin, John (Athlete, Baseball Player)
23060 16th St
Newhall, CA 91321-1054, USA

Flavio, Alfaro (Baseball Player)
3240 N Bass Island Rd
West Sacramento, CA 95691-5848, USA

Flay, Bobby (Chef, Television Host)
c/o Jonathan Rosen *WmE2 (WMA-NY)*
1325 Avenue of the Americas
New York, NY 10019-6026, USA

Flchter, Michael (Baseball Player)
8821 Jackson Ct
Munster, IN 46321-2410, USA

Flea (Actor, Musician)
c/o Peter Mensch *Q Prime South*
729 7th Ave Fl 16
New York, NY 10019-6831, USA

Flebotte, Dave (Producer)
c/o Ann Blanchard *Creative Artists Agency (CAA-LA)*
2000 Avenue of the Stars Ste 100
Los Angeles, CA 90067-4705, USA

Fleck, Bela (Composer, Musician)
c/o Ted Kurland *Ted Kurland Associates*
173 Brighton Ave
Boston, MA 02134-2003, USA

Fleck, Jack (Athlete, Golfer)
12006 Edgewater Rd
Fort Smith, AR 72903-5889, USA

Fleckman, Marty (Athlete, Golfer)
26411 Ridgestone Park Ln
Cypress, TX 77433-1279, USA

Fleder, Gary R (Director)
624 Sunset Ave
Venice, CA 90291-2733, USA

Fleeshman, Richard (Actor)
193 Wardour Street
London W1V 3FA, UNITED KINGDOM (UK)

Fleetwood, Ken (Designer, Fashion Designer)
14 Savile Row
London SW1, UNITED KINGDOM (UK)

Fleetwood, Mick (Musician)
c/o Jonathan Todd *Sabre Entertainment*
5737 Kanan Rd # 237
Agoura Hills, CA 91301-1601, USA

Fleigel, Bernie (Athlete, Basketball Player)
21 Granville Rd # 3
Cambridge, MA 02138-6806, USA

Fleischer, Arthur Jr (Attorney, Attorney General, General)
1 New York Plz
New York, NY 10004-1901, USA

Fleischer, Charles
749 N Crescent Heights Blvd
Los Angeles, CA 90046-7001

Fleischer, Daniel (Religious Leader)
6423 Upper 35th St N Unit 1
Saint Paul, MN 55128-2965, USA

Fleischman, Paul (Writer)
PO Box 646
Aromas, CA 95004-0646, USA

Fleischmann, Peter (Director, Producer)
August-Bebel-Str 26-53
Potsdam 14482, GERMANY

Fleisher, Brett (Actor)
c/o Alan Somers *Pure Arts Entertainment*
1925 Century Park E Ste 2320
Los Angeles, CA 90067-2724, USA

Fleisher, Bruce (Athlete, Golfer)
301 Grand Key Ter
Palm Beach Gardens, FL 33418-4628, USA

Fleisher, Leon (Musician)
20 Merrymount Rd
Baltimore, MD 21210-1909, USA

Fleiss, Heidi (Business Person, Reality TV Star)
150 S Highway 160 Ste 4A
Pahrump, NV 89048-2133, USA

Fleiss, Michael (Mike) (Director, Producer)
c/o Staff Member *Next Entertainment*
3300 W Olive Ave Unit 500
Burbank, CA 91505-4665, USA

Fleiss, Noah (Actor)
c/o Ellen Gilbert *Abrams Artists Agency (NY)*
275 7th Ave Fl 26
New York, NY 10001-6708, USA

Fleming, Cory (Athlete, Football Player)
1404 Madison Dr
La Vergne, TN 37086-3996, USA

Fleming, David (Dave) (Athlete, Baseball Player)
37 Laurelwood Ln
Southbury, CT 06488-4657, USA

Fleming, Ed
RD #3Box 261K
Greensbury, PA 15601

Fleming, Eric (Director)
c/o David Krintzman *Morris, Yorn, Barnes, Levine, Krintzman, Rubenstein and Kohner*
2000 Ave Of The Stars 3rd Tower Floor NORTH
Los Angeles, CA 90067, USA

Fleming, Gerry (Athlete, Hockey Player)
c/o Staff Member *Florida Everblades*
11000 Everblades Pkwy
Estero, FL 33928-9412, USA

Fleming, James P (War Hero)
PO Box 487
Manvel, TX 77578-0487, USA

Fleming, John (Congressman, Politician)
416 Cannon Hob
Washington, DC 20515-3220, USA

Fleming, Mac A (Misc)
26555 Evergreen Rd
Southfield, MI 48076-4206, USA

Fleming, Marvin (Marv) (Athlete, Football Player)
909 Howard St
Marina Del Rey, CA 90292-5518, USA

Fleming, Peggy (Athlete, Figure Skater)
c/o Staff Member *IMG*
304 Park Ave S Fl 12
New York, NY 10010-4314, USA

Fleming, Peter E Jr (Attorney, Attorney General, General)
101 Park Ave
New York, NY 10178-0002, USA

Fleming, Reginald S (Reggie) (Athlete, Hockey Player)
352 Duvall Station Rd
Georgetown, KY 40324-9134, USA

Fleming, Renee (Musician, Opera Singer)
c/o Staff Member *IMG (Cleveland)*
1360 E 9th St Ste 100
Cleveland, OH 44114-1730, USA

Fleming, Rhonda (Actor)
10281 Century Woods Dr
Los Angeles, CA 90067-6312, USA

Fleming, Richard C D (Engineer)
1445 Market St
Denver, CO 80202-1731, USA

Fleming, Scott (Government Official)
2750 Shasta Rd
Berkeley, CA 94708-1924, USA

Fleming, Troy (Athlete, Football Player)
PO Box 789
Knoxville, TN 37901-0789, USA

Fleming, Vern (Athlete, Basketball Player)
10713 Brixton Ln
Fishers, IN 46037-8707, USA

Fleming, Wendell H (Mathematician)
9 Dolly Dr
Bristol, RI 02809-1578, USA

Flemming, Catherine
Goethestr. 17
Munich, GERMANY D-80336

Flemming, John (Artist)
1409 Cambronne St
New Orleans, LA 70118-1301, USA

Flemming, William N (Bill) (Sportscaster)
77 W 66th St
New York, NY 10023-6201, USA

Flemyng, Gordon (Director)
1 Albert Road Wilmslow
Cheshire SK9 5HT, UNITED KINGDOM (UK)

Flemyng, Jason (Actor)
18-21 Jermyn St
London SW1Y 6NB, UNITED KINGDOM (UK)

Flemyng, Robert (Actor)
4 Netherbourne Road
London SW4, UNITED KINGDOM (UK)

Flener, Huck (Athlete, Baseball Player)
2186 North Ave
Chico, CA 95926-1430, USA

Flennes, Ranulph T-W (Misc)
Greenlands Exford Minehead
West Sussex, UNITED KINGDOM (UK)

Flerstein, Harvey F (Actor, Musician, Writer)
1479 Carla Ridge Dr
Beverly Hills, CA 90210, USA

Flesch, John (Athlete, Hockey Player)
74101 8th Ave
South Haven, MI 49090-9750, USA

Flesch, Steve (Athlete, Golfer)
PO Box 440
Union, KY 41091-0440, USA

Flessel, Craig (Cartoonist)
40 Camino Alto Apt 2306
Mill Valley, CA 94941-2976, USA

Fletcher, Andrew (Baseball Player)
3282 Kinderhill Ln
Germantown, TN 38138-8210, USA

Fletcher, Andy (Musician)
295 Greenwich St # 109
New York, NY 10007-1049, USA

Fletcher, Andy (Athlete, Baseball Player)
8696 Belmor Crossing Cv
Olive Branch, MS 38654-6362, USA

Fletcher, Betty Binns (Judge)
5th Ave US Courthouse 1010
Seattle, WA 98104-3191, USA

Fletcher, Billy (Athlete, Football Player)
3216 Winners Cir
Germantown, TN 38138-8220, USA

Fletcher, Brendan (Actor)
8447 Wilshire Blvd Ste 200
Beverly Hills, CA 90211-3207, USA

Fletcher, Charles M (Physicist, Scientist)
2 Coastguard Cottages
Newtown PO30 4PA, UNITED KINGDOM (UK)

Fletcher, Chris (Athlete, Football Player)
4818 La Cruz Dr
La Mesa, CA 91941-4489, USA

Fletcher, Cliff (Athlete, Hockey Player)
19980 N 94th Way
Scottsdale, AZ 85255-5576, USA

Fletcher, Darrin (Athlete, Baseball Player)
9146 E 2100 North Rd
Oakwood, IL 61858-6285, USA

Fletcher, Derrick (Athlete, Football Player)
5353 De Soto St Apt 612
Houston, TX 77091-3683, USA

Fletcher, Dexter
1 Kingsway House Albion Rd
London, ENGLAND N16

Fletcher, Diane (Actor)
91 regent St
London W1R 7TB, UNITED KINGDOM (UK)

Fletcher, Guy (Musician)
16 Lambton Place
London W11 2SH, UNITED KINGDOM (UK)

Fletcher, Jamar (Athlete, Football Player)
11063 Worchester Dr
Saint Louis, MO 63136-5828, USA

Fletcher, Louis (Athlete, Football Player)
18898 Shropshire Ct
Leesburg, VA 20176-8493, USA

Fletcher, Louise (Actor)
1520 Camden Ave Apt 105
Los Angeles, CA 90025-3443, USA

Fletcher, Martin (Correspondent)
4001 Nebraska Ave NW
Washington, DC 20016-2733, USA

Fletcher, Paul (Athlete, Baseball Player)
431 Harpold Ave
Ravenswood, WV 26164-1333, USA

Fletcher, Scott B (Athlete, Baseball Player)
300 Birkdale Dr
Fayetteville, GA 30215-2720, USA

Fletcher, Simon (Athlete, Football Player)
2225 S Ensenada St
Aurora, CO 80013-6230, USA

Fletcher, Terrell (Athlete, Football Player)
PO Box 711960
San Diego, CA 92171-1960, USA

Fletcher, Tom (Athlete, Baseball Player)
9287 E 2085 North Rd
Oakwood, IL 61858-6252, USA

Fletcher, Van (Athlete, Baseball Player)
2404 Whitaker Rd
Boonville, NC 27011-9204, USA

Fletcher, William A (Judge)
Courts Building 95 7th St
San Francisco, CA 94103, USA

Fleury, Marc-Andre (Athlete, Hockey Player)
1123 Castletown Ct
Sewickley, PA 15143-8862, USA

Fleury, Theoren (Theo) (Athlete, Hockey Player)
4519 Manhattan Rd SE
Calgary, AB T2G 4B3, Canada

Flichel, Todd (Athlete, Hockey Player)
Bowling Green, OH 43403, USA

Flick, Bob (Musician)
300 Vine St Ste 14
Seattle, WA 98121-1465, USA

Flick, Mick
Sherry Netherlands 5th & 59th
New York, NY 10003

Flick, Tom (Athlete, Football Player)
9718 208th Ave NE
Redmond, WA 98053-5216, USA

Flicker, John (Misc)
President's Office 700 Broadway
New York, NY 10003, USA

Flinelt, Flemming O (Choreographer, Dancer)
Christiansholms Parkv 24
Klampenborg 2930, DENMARK

Flinn, John (Athlete, Baseball Player)
6221 Lake Providence Ln
Charlotte, NC 28277-0565, USA

Flint, George (Athlete, Football Player)
PO Box 2486
Prescott, AZ 86302-2486, USA

Flint, Judson (Athlete, Football Player)
306 Federal St
Farrell, PA 16121-1925, USA

Flint, Keith (Dancer, Musician)
c/o Staff Member *Maverick Recording Co (LA)*
3300 Warner Blvd
Burbank, CA 91505-4632, USA

Flippin, Lucy Lee
1753 S Canfield Ave
Los Angeles, CA 90035-4216

Flitcroft, Garry (Soccer Player)
c/o Staff Member *Blackburn Rovers Football Club*
Ewood Park Blackburn
Lancashire BB2 4JF, UNITED KINGDOM

Flitter, Josh (Actor)
c/o Ellen Gilbert *Abrams Artists Agency (NY)*
275 7th Ave Fl 26
New York, NY 10001-6708, USA

Flobots (Music Group)
c/o Corrie Christopher *Agency for the Performing Arts (APA-LA)*
405 S Beverly Dr Ste 500
Beverly Hills, CA 90212-4425, USA

Flock of Seagulls (Music Group, Musician)
c/o Carlos Keyes *Red Entertainment Agency*
16 Penn Plz Ste 824
New York, NY 10001-1809, USA

Flockhart, Calista (Actor)
c/o Melissa Kates *Viewpoint Inc*
8820 Wilshire Blvd Ste 220
Beverly Hills, CA 90211-2622, USA

Flockhart, Ron (Athlete, Hockey Player)
160 15 St NE
Salmon Arm, BC V1E 1N4, Canada

Floethe, Chris (Baseball Player)
5634 Mount Hood Ct
Martinez, CA 94553-5837, USA

Floetry (Music Group)
c/o Cara Lewis *WmE2 (WMA-NY)*
1325 Avenue of the Americas
New York, NY 10019-6026, USA

Flogging Molly (Music Group, Musician)
c/o Gary Schwindt *Villam Artist Management*
820 Hyperion Ave
Los Angeles, CA 90029-3106, USA

Flood, Ann (Actor)
15 E 91st St
New York, NY 10128-0648, USA

Flood, Staci (Model, Musician)
10950 Ventura Blvd
Studio City, CA 91604-3340, USA

Flor, Claus Peter (Conductor)
16 Duncan Terrace
London N1 8BZ, UNITED KINGDOM (UK)

Flora, Donnie (Stylist)
5805 Hansen Rd
Minneapolis, MN 55436-2401, USA

Flora, Kevin (Athlete, Baseball Player)
25035 Portsmouth
Mission Viejo, CA 92692-2812, USA

Florance, Sheila (Actor)
643 Saint Kikla Rd
Melbourne, VIC 3004, AUSTRALIA

Florek, Dann (Actor)
145 W 45th St # 1204
New York, NY 10036-4008, USA

Florence, Don (Athlete, Baseball Player)
144 Bedford Rd
New Boston, NH 03070-4301, USA

Florence, Tyler (Chef, Television Host)
c/o Staff Member *WmE2 (Endeavor-LA)*
9601 Wilshire Blvd Fl 3
Beverly Hills, CA 90210-5219, USA

Flores, Bill (Congressman, Politician)
1505 Longworth Hob
Washington, DC 20515-3313, USA

Flores, Facusse Carlos (President)
Blvd Juan Pablo II
Tegucigalpa, HONDURAS

Flores, Francisco (President)
Casa Presidencial
San Salvador, El SALVADOR

Flores, Jose (Athlete, Baseball Player)
244 W 109th St Apt 15
New York, NY 10025-2230, USA

Flores, Nikki (Musician)
c/o Staff Member *Sony Music International*
550 Madison Ave Fl 6
New York, NY 10022-3211, USA

Flores, Patrick F (Religious Leader)
2600 W Woodlawn Ave
San Antonio, TX 78228-5122, USA

Flores, Randy (Athlete, Baseball Player)
8230 E Hoverland Rd
Scottsdale, AZ 85255-3908, USA

Flores, Thomas R (Tom) (Athlete, Coach, Football Coach, Football Executive, Football Player)
77741 Cove Pointe Cir
Indian Wells, CA 92210-6101, USA

Flores, Tom
11220 NE 53rd St
Kirkland, WA 98033-7505

Floria, James J (Jim) (Ex-Congressman, Ex-Governor)
80 Wall St Ste 815
New York, NY 10005-3632, USA

Florie, Bryce (Athlete, Baseball Player)
2120 Breezy Point Dr
Mount Pleasant, SC 29466, USA

Florin, Krista (Stylist)
c/o Staff Member *Bulgari (NY)*
730 5th Ave
New York, NY 10019-4105, USA

Florin, Susan (Athlete, Golfer)
1883 Lexington Pl
Tarpon Springs, FL 34688-4965, USA

Florio, Steven T (Publisher)
Publisher's Office 4 Times Square
New York, NY 10036, USA

Florio, Thomas A (Actor)
Publisher's Office 4 Times Square
New York, NY 10036, USA

Flory, Med (Actor)
6044 Ensign Ave
North Hollywood, CA 91606-4905, USA

Flournoy, Craig (Journalist)
Editorial Dept Communications Center
Dallas, TX 75265, USA

Flower, Joseph R (Religious Leader)
1445 N Boonville Ave
Springfield, MO 65802-1894, USA

Flowers, Ben (Athlete, Baseball Player)
130 Beagle Trl
Wilmington, NC 28409-2100, USA

Flowers, Bernard (Athlete, Football Player)
3819 Old Farm Rd
Lafayette, IN 47909-3521, USA

Flowers, Brandon (Musician)

Flowers, Bruce (Athlete, Basketball Player)
276 W Grantley Ave
Elmhurst, IL 60126-2238, USA

Flowers, Charles (Charlie) (Athlete, Football Player)
6170 Mount Brook Way NW
Atlanta, GA 30342, USA

Flowers, Frank E (Director, Writer)
c/o Aleen Keshishian *Brillstein Entertainment Partners*
9150 Wilshire Blvd Ste 350
Beverly Hills, CA 90212-3453, USA

Flowers, Gennifer
4859 Cedar Springs Rd Apt 241
Dallas, TX 75219-1215

Flowers, Richmond (Athlete, Football Player)
3434 Indian Lake Dr
Pelham, AL 35124-2713, USA

Flowers of Queen's Gate, Brian H (Physicist)
53 Athenaeum Road
London N2O 9AL, UNITED KINGDOM (UK)

Floyd, Bobby (Athlete, Baseball Player)
1757 SE Dominic Ave
Port Saint Lucie, FL 34952-5815, USA

Floyd, Bobby Jack (Athlete, Football Player)
2221 Cedar St
Paris, TX 75460-7566, USA

Floyd, C Clifford (Cliff) (Athlete, Baseball Player)
3283 Birch Ter
Davie, FL 33330-1337, USA

Floyd, Carlisie (Composer)
4491 Yoakum Blvd
Houston, TX 77006-5819, USA

Floyd, Eddie (Musician, Songwriter, Writer)
Gables House
Saddlebow Kings Lynn PE34 3AR, UNITED KINGDOM (UK)

Floyd, Eric (Athlete, Football Player)
18047 Sailfish Dr
Lutz, FL 33558-7771, USA

Floyd, Eric (Sleepy) (Athlete, Basketball Player)
3101 Ivy Creek Rd
Gastonia, NC 28056-0301, USA

Floyd, Gavin (Athlete, Baseball Player)
9809 Milano Dr
Trinity, FL 34655-4668, USA

Floyd, George (Athlete, Football Player)
7056 Burlington Pike Attn Facultystaff
Florence, KY 41042-1681, USA

Floyd, Heather (Musician)
300 10th Ave S
Nashville, TN 37203-4125, USA

Floyd, Larry (Athlete, Hockey Player)
3780 Hancock St
San Diego, CA 92110-4340, USA

Floyd, Leslie (Baseball Player)
PO Box 7619
Texarkana, TX 75505-7619, USA

Floyd, Marlene (Athlete, Golfer)
5370 Clubhouse Ln
Hope Mills, NC 28348-9794, USA

Floyd, Ray
PO Box 545957
Surfside, FL 33154-5957

Floyd, Raymond (Athlete, Golfer)
505 S Flagler Dr Ste 910
West Palm Beach, FL 33401-5948, USA

Floyd, Susan
PO Box 5617
Beverly Hills, CA 90209-5617

Floyd, Tim (Coach)
1501 Girod St
New Orleans, LA 70113-3124, USA

Floyd, William (Athlete, Football Player)
7827 Glen Echo Rd N
Jacksonville, FL 32211-6028, USA

Fluegel, Darlanne (Actor)
9255 W Sunset Blvd Ste 1010
Los Angeles, CA 90069-3307, USA

Flueger, Patrick (Actor)
c/o Nancy Kremer *Nancy Kremer Management*
4545 Morse Ave
Studio City, CA 91604-1008, USA

Fluno, Jere D (Business Person)
5500 Howard St
Skokie, IL 60077-2620, USA

Flutie, Darren (Athlete, Football Player)
29 Pine St
Natick, MA 01760-1203, USA

Flutie, Doug (Athlete, Football Player)
22 Chieftain Ln
Natick, MA 01760-6083, USA

Flyleaf (Music Group)
560 Broadway Rm 500
New York, NY 10012-3946, USA

Flynn, Barbara (Actor)
Julian House 4 Windmill St
London W1P 1HF, UNITED KINGDOM (UK)

Flynn, Colleen (Actor)
10390 Santa Monica Blvd Ste 300
Los Angeles, CA 90025-5091, USA

Flynn, Danny (Stylist)
c/o Staff Member *Cloutier Agency*
2632 La Cienega Ave
Los Angeles, CA 90034-2641, USA

Flynn, Don (Athlete, Football Player)
803 E Seattle Pl
Broken Arrow, OK 74012-8112, USA

Flynn, Doug (Athlete, Baseball Player)
2465 Vale Dr
Lexington, KY 40514-1421, USA

Flynn, George W (Misc)
382 Summit Ave
Leonia, NJ 07605-1337, USA

Flynn, Jackie (Comedian)
c/o Staff Member *Don Buchwald & Associates Inc (LA)*
6500 Wilshire Blvd Ste 2200
Los Angeles, CA 90048-4942, USA

Flynn, Julie (Stylist)
c/o Celebrity Stylist *Bernstein & Andriulli*
58 W 40th St
New York, NY 10018-2658, USA

Flynn, Luke (Actor, Producer, Writer)
c/o Kay Liberman *Liberman/Zerman Management*
252 N Larchmont Blvd Ste 200
Los Angeles, CA 90004-3754, USA

Flynn, Mike (Athlete, Basketball Player)
3934 E Battala Ave
Gilbert, AZ 85297-3550, USA

Flynn, Mike (Athlete, Football Player)
1922 Clifden Rd
Catonsville, MD 21228-4838, USA

Flynn, Neil (Actor)
c/o Staff Member *Christopher Wright Management*
3207 Winnie Dr
Los Angeles, CA 90068-1439, USA

Flynn, Raymond L (Diplomat, Politician)
PO Box 1872
Chesapeake, VA 23327-1872, USA

Flynn, Sean (Actor)
c/o Christopher Rockwell *Global Creative*
1051 Cole Ave # B
Los Angeles, CA 90038-2601, USA

Flynn, Tom (Athlete, Football Player)
4008 Holiday Park Dr
Murrysville, PA 15668-8529, USA

Flynn, Vince (Writer)
2316 Delaware Ave # 266
Buffalo, NY 14216-2606, USA

Flynt, Larry (Publisher)
8484 Wilshire Blvd Ste 900
Beverly Hills, CA 90211-3218, USA

Flynville Train (Music Group)
c/o Staff Member *Paradigm (Monterey)*
404 W Franklin St
Monterey, CA 93940-2303, USA

Flythe, Mark (Athlete, Football Player)
505 Pheasant Run
Monmouth Junction, NJ 08852-1929, USA

Fo, Dario (Nobel Prize Laureate)
Via Alessandria 4
Milan 20144, ITALY

Foale, C Michael (Doctor)
2101 Todville Rd # 11
Seabrook, TX 77586, USA

Foale, C Michael (Mike) (Astronaut)
2101 Todville Rd # 11
Seabrook, TX 77586, USA

Fobbs, Brandon
c/o Todd Justice *Marshak/Zachary Company, The*
8840 Wilshire Blvd Fl 1
Beverly Hills, CA 90211-2606, USA

Fodge, Gene (Athlete, Baseball Player)
1505 N Chicago St
South Bend, IN 46628-1421, USA

Foege, William H (Misc)
PO Box 450989
Atlanta, GA 31145-0989, USA

Foeger, Luggi (Skier)
230 S Balsamina Way
Portola Valley, CA 94028-7503, USA

Fogdoe, Tomas (Skier)
Skogsvagen 18
Gallvare 970 02, SWEDEN

Fogel, Robert W (Nobel Prize Laureate)
5321 S University Ave
Chicago, IL 60615-5105, USA

Fogerty, John (Musician, Songwriter)
c/o Daniel Weiner *Paradigm (Monterey)*
404 W Franklin St
Monterey, CA 93940-2303, USA

Fogg, Josh (Athlete, Baseball Player)
4910 S Quincy St
Tampa, FL 33611-3820, USA

Fogg, Kirk (Actor)
c/o Staff Member *Brady Brannon & Rich*
5670 Wilshire Blvd Ste 820
Los Angeles, CA 90036-5613, USA

Foggie, Fred (Athlete, Football Player)
360 Jackson Rd
Inman, SC 29349-9533, USA

Foggs, Edward L (Religious Leader)
PO Box 2420
Anderson, IN 46018-2420, USA

Fogle, Larry (Athlete, Basketball Player)
3 Shafer St
Rochester, NY 14609-4936

Fogleman, Ronald R (Ron) (General)
406 Snowshoe Ln
Durango, CO 81301, USA

Fogler, Dan (Actor, Producer)
c/o Suzan Bymel *Management 360*
9111 Wilshire Blvd
Beverly Hills, CA 90210-5508, USA

Fogler, Eddie (Basketball Player)
Athletic Dept
Columbia, SC 53233, USA

Foglesong, Robert H (Doc) (General)
Vice Chief of Staff Hqusaf Pentagon
Washington, DC 20330-0001, USA

Fogolin Jr, Lee (Athlete, Hockey Player)
352 Lessard Dr NW
Edmonton, AB T6M 1A5, Canada

Foiles, Hank (Athlete, Baseball Player)
4333 Silverleaf Ct
Virginia Beach, VA 23462-5738, USA

Foiles, Lisa (Actor)
C/O Nancy Schmidt Sanford 10 Universal City Plaza #2000
Universal City, CA 91608, USA

Fokin, Vitold P (Prime Minister)
Government Building
Klev, UKRAINE

Folau, Spencer (Athlete, Football Player)
14003 Woodens Ln
Reisterstown, MD 21136-4536, USA

Folco, Peter (Athlete, Hockey Player)
6463 Rue Bannantyne
Verdun, QC H4H 1J8, Canada

Folder-Powell, Rose (Baseball Player)
PO Box 415
Carnation, WA 98014-0415, USA

Folds, Ben (Musician, Songwriter)
c/o Staff Member *International Creative Management (ICM-LA)*
10250 Constellation Blvd Fl 7
Los Angeles, CA 90067-6207, USA

Foley, Christopher (Actor)
c/o Scott Zimmerman *Evolution Entertainment (LA)*
901 N Highland Ave
Los Angeles, CA 90038-2412, USA

Foley, Dave (Comedian)
c/o Matthew (Matt) Labov *Forefront Media*
8500 Melrose Ave Ste 205
West Hollywood, CA 90069-5169, USA

Foley, Dave (Athlete, Football Player)
4500 Redmond Rd
Springfield, OH 45505-1722, USA

Foley, ex-Speaker Tom
601 W 1st Ave # 2W
Spokane, WA 99201-3825

Foley, Gerry (Athlete, Hockey Player)
352 Skead Rd
Garson, ON P3L 1N4, Canada

Foley, Glenn (Athlete, Football Player)
3204 Buxmont Rd
Marlton, NJ 08053-8506, USA

Foley, Jeremy (Actor)
4942 Vineland Ave Ste 103
North Hollywood, CA 91601-5639, USA

Foley, John (Athlete, Basketball Player)
PO Box 143
Barre, MA 01005-0143, USA

Foley, Linda (Misc)
8611 2nd Ave
Silver Spring, MD 20910-3372, USA

Foley, Marv (Athlete, Baseball Player)
10166 Glenmore Ave
Bradenton, FL 34202-4049, USA

Foley, Maurice B (Judge)
400 2nd St NW
Washington, DC 20217-0001, USA

Foley, Mick (Actor, Wrestler)
c/o Elaine Gillespie *Gillespie Agency, The*
3007 Millwood Ave
Columbia, SC 29205-1855, USA

Foley, Robert F (General, War Hero)
200 Stovall St
Alexandria, VA 22332-4013, USA

Foley, Scott (Actor)
c/o Dominique Appel *Baker Winokur Ryder Public Relations (BWR-LA)*
9100 Wilshire Blvd Ste 500 PMB WEST
Beverly Hills, CA 90212-3426, USA

Foley, Steve (Athlete, Football Player)
5555 Dtc Pkwy
Greenwood Village, CO 80111-3005, USA

Foley, Sylvester R Jr (Admiral)
50 Apple Hill Dr
Tewksbury, MA 01876-1140, USA

Foley, Thomas S (Diplomat)
PO Box 1047
Medical Lake, WA 99022-1047, USA

Foley, Tim (Athlete, Football Player)
11093 Lane Park Rd
Tavares, FL 32778-9662, USA

Foley, Tim J (Athlete, Football Player)
2851 Old Clifton Rd
Springfield, OH 45502-9455, USA

Foley, Tom (Athlete, Baseball Player)
5237 Karlsburg Pl
Palm Harbor, FL 34685-3696, USA

Folger, Franklin (Cartoonist)
c/o Staff Member *King Features Syndication*
300 W 57th St Fl 15
New York, NY 10019-5238, USA

Foli, Tim (Athlete, Baseball Player)
525 Timberline Dr
Lenoir City, TN 37772-6934, USA

Foligno, Mike (Athlete, Hockey Player)
c/o Staff Member *Sudbury Wolves*
240 Elgin St
Sudbury, ON P3E 3N6, Canada

Folk, Bill (Athlete, Hockey Player)
2720 Quinn Dr
Regina, SK S4P 2W1, Canada

Folkenberg, Robert S (Religious Leader)
12501 Old Columbia Pike
Silver Spring, MD 20904-6601, USA

Folkers, Rich (Athlete, Baseball Player)
7100 3rd Ave N
Saint Petersburg, FL 33710-7502, USA

Folkins, Lee (Athlete, Football Player)
8749 The Esplanade Apt 13
Orlando, FL 32836-7734, USA

Foll, Tim (Baseball Player)
1003 Hilltop Ln
Kodak, TN 37764-1838, USA

Follesdal, Dagfinn K (Misc)
Staverhagen 7
Slepemdem 1312, NORWAY

Follett, Ken (Writer)
Box 4
Knebworth SG3 6UT, UNITED KINGDOM (UK)

Follows, Megan (Actor)
c/o Perry Zimel *Oscars Abrams Zimel & Associates, Inc. (OAZ)*
438 Queen St E
Toronto ON M5A 1T4, CANADA

Folman, Ari (Director)
c/o Maha Dakhil *Creative Artists Agency (CAA-LA)*
2000 Avenue of the Stars Ste 100
Los Angeles, CA 90067-4705, USA

Folon, Jean-Michel (Artist)
Burcy
Beaumont-du-Gatinais 77890, FRANCE

Folse, John (Chef)
2517 S Philippe Ave
Gonzales, LA 70737-3750, USA

Folsom, Allan R (Writer)
3 Center Plz
Boston, MA 02108-2003, USA

Folsome, Claire (Biologist)
2600 Campus Rd
Honolulu, HI 96822-2224, USA

Foltz, Vern (Athlete, Football Player)
327 Ballard Ave
Baltimore, MD 21220-3605, USA

Fonda, Bridget (Actor)
c/o Staff Member *IFA Talent Agency*
8730 W Sunset Blvd Ste 490
Los Angeles, CA 90069-2248, USA

Fonda, Jane (Actor)
1050 Techwood Dr NW
Atlanta, GA 30318-5604, USA

Fonda, Peter (Actor)
c/o Melody Korenbrot *Block-Korenbrot Public Relations*
North Market Building 110 S Fairfax, Suite 310
Los Angeles, CA 90036, USA

Fondren, Debra Jo (Actor, Model)
PO Box 4351-856
Los Angeles, CA 90078, USA

Foner, Eric (Historian)
606 W 116th St
New York, NY 10027-7011, USA

Fong, Darryl
247 S Beverly Dr # 102
Beverly Hills, CA 90212-3830

Fonoti, Toniu (Athlete, Football Player)
5029 Boomer St Apt D
Kapolei, HI 96707-3674, USA

Fonseca (Musician)
c/o Staff Member *WmE2 (WMA-Miami)*
119 Washington Ave Ste 400
Miami, FL 33139-7202, USA

Fonseca, Adriana (Actor)
c/o Staff Member *Televisa*
Blvd Adolfo Lopez Mateos 232 Colonia San Angel INN
DF CP 01060, MEXICO

Fonseca, Chris (Actor)
1199 Boise Way
Costa Mesa, CA 92626-2704, USA

Fonseca, David (Musician)
c/o Staff Member *Universal Music Publishing Group (Latin)*
420 Lincoln Rd Ste 200
Miami Beach, FL 33139-3014, USA

Fonseca, Lyndsy (Actor)
c/o Felicia Sager *Sager Management*
260 S Beverly Dr # 205
Beverly Hills, CA 90212-3805, USA

Fonsi, Luis
c/o Staff Member *Universal Music Group (UMG - LA)*
2220 Colorado Ave
Santa Monica, CA 90404-3506, USA

Fontaine, Joan (Actor)
c/o Staff Member *Gage Group, The (LA)*
14724 Ventura Blvd Ste 505
Sherman Oaks, CA 91403-3505, USA

Fontaine, Levi (Athlete, Basketball Player)
25 11th Ave
San Mateo, CA 94401-4308

Fontaine, Maurice A (Misc)
25 Rue Pierre Nicole
Paris 75005, FRANCE

Fontana, Tom (Producer, Writer)
c/o Peter Benedek *United Talent Agency (UTA)*
9560 Wilshire Blvd Fl 5
Beverly Hills, CA 90212-2400, USA

Fontana, Wayne (Musician)
PO Box 106
Rochdale OL16 4HW, UNITED KINGDOM (UK)

Fontas, Jon (Athlete, Hockey Player)
38A Worthen Rd Apt 1
Lexington, MA 02421-4821, USA

Fontenot, Albert (Athlete, Football Player)
4919 Gammage St
Houston, TX 77021-3205, USA

Fontenot, Jerry (Athlete, Football Player)
938 Bristol Dr
Deerfield, IL 60015-4843, USA

Fontenot, Joe (Athlete, Baseball Player)
1400 Mall of Georgia Blvd Apt 222
Buford, GA 30519-6596, USA

Fontenot, Ray (Athlete, Baseball Player)
1674 S Crestview Dr
Lake Charles, LA 70605, USA

Fontes, Wayne H (Athlete, Coach, Football Coach, Football Player)
2043 Harbour Watch Cir
Tarpon Springs, FL 34689-2055, USA

Fonteyne, Inge (Stylist)
c/o Staff Member *Agency, The (NY)*
580 Broadway Rm 500
New York, NY 10012-5229, USA

Fonteyne, Val (Athlete, Hockey Player)
5403 52 Ave
Wetaskiwin, AB T9A 0X8, Canada

Fontinato, Lou (Athlete, Hockey Player)
RR 1
Campbellville, ON L0P 1B0, Canada

Fonville, Chad (Athlete, Baseball Player)
2338 Piney Green Rd
Midway Park, NC 28544-1112, USA

Fonville, Charles (Athlete, Track Athlete)
1845 Wintergreen Ct
Ann Arbor, MI 48103-9727, USA

Fonzi, Dolores (Actor)
c/o Staff Member *Kuranda Management*
Santo Angel, 84
Madrid 28043, Spain

Foo, Jon (Actor)
c/o Steve Chasman *Ace Media*
9200 W Sunset Blvd Ste 10
Los Angeles, CA 90069-3608, USA

Foo Fighters (Music Group)
c/o Steve Martin *Nasty Little Man*
110 Greene St Ste 605
New York, NY 10012-3838, USA

Foor, Jim (Athlete, Baseball Player)
2018 Bolsover St
Houston, TX 77005-1616, USA

Foose, Chip (Actor)
17811 Sampson Ln
Huntington Beach, CA 92647-7199, USA

Foot, Michael M (Government Official)
308 Gray's Inn Road
London WC1X 8DY, UNITED KINGDOM (UK)

Foote, Adam (Athlete, Hockey Player)
8080 Tillinghast Dr
Dublin, OH 43017-8841, USA

Foote, Barry (Athlete, Baseball Player)
2588 High Hammock Rd
Johns Island, SC 29455-6121, USA

Foote, Chris (Athlete, Football Player)
1140 Harbin Ridge Ln
Knoxville, TN 37909-2382, USA

Foote, Dan (Cartoonist, Editor)
Editorial Dept Herald Square
Dallas, TX 75202, USA

Foote, Larry (Athlete, Football Player)
7090 Bennington Woods Dr
Pittsburgh, PA 15237-6373, USA

Foote II, Edward T (Educator)
President's Office
Coral Gables, FL 33124, USA

Footman, Dan (Athlete, Football Player)
PO Box 37024
Jacksonville, FL 32236-7024, USA

Foppert, Jesse (Athlete, Baseball Player)
PO Box 150682
San Rafael, CA 94915-0682, USA

For Today (Music Group, Musician)
c/o Shannon Quiggle *Facedown Records*
PO Box 477
Sun City, CA 92586-0477, USA

Foray, June (Actor)
22745 Erwin St
Woodland Hills, CA 91367-3212, USA

Forbert, Steve (Musician, Songwriter, Writer)
743 Center Blvd
Fairfax, CA 94930-1764, USA

Forbes, Brian
Seven Pines Wentworth
Surrey, ENGLAND

Forbes, Bryan (Director, Writer)
Bookshop
Virginia Water, Surrey, UNITED KINGDOM (UK)

Forbes, Dave (Athlete, Hockey Player)
4020 Reserve Pt
Colorado Springs, CO 80904-1043, USA

Forbes, Kristin (Economist, Government Official)
Old Executive Office Bldg
Washington, DC 20500, USA

Forbes, Malcolm S (Steve) Jr (Editor)
60 5th Ave
New York, NY 10011-8868, USA

Forbes, Michelle (Actor)
c/o Laura Berwick *Hofflund/Polone*
9465 Wilshire Blvd Ste 420
Beverly Hills, CA 90212-2603, USA

Forbes, Mike (Athlete, Hockey Player)
547 Waverly Ave
Grand Haven, MI 49417-2127, USA

Forbes, P J (Athlete, Baseball Player)
9017 W Chartwell Cir
Wichita, KS 67205-1445, USA

Forbes, West (Musician)
PO Box 12
Far Hills, NJ 07931-0012, USA

Force, John (Race Car Driver)
22722 Old Canal Rd
Yorba Linda, CA 92887-4602, USA

Ford, Ben (Athlete, Baseball Player)
1717 Applewood Pl NE
Cedar Rapids, IA 52402-3321, USA

Ford, Bette
1801 Avenue of the Stars Ste 902
Los Angeles, CA 90067-5981

Ford, Brian (Athlete, Hockey Player)
51 Dineen Dr Attn Hockey Ofc
Fredericton, NB E3B 5G3, Canada

Ford, Charlie (Athlete, Football Player)
15207 Carol Chase Cir
Missouri City, TX 77489-2316, USA

Ford, Charlotte
25 Sutton Pl S Apt 14N
New York, NY 10022-2456

Ford, Cheryl (Basketball Player)
2 Championship Dr
Auburn Hills, MI 48326-1753, USA

Ford, Chris (Athlete, Basketball Player, Coach)
424 N Vendome Ave
Margate City, NJ 08402-1265, USA

Ford, Clementine (Actor)
c/o Staff Member *Schumacher Management*
1122 San Vicente Blvd
Santa Monica, CA 90402-2008, USA

Ford, Colton (Musician)
c/o Staff Member *Diva Central Inc*
7510 W Sunset Blvd Ste 1445
Los Angeles, CA 90046-3408, USA

Ford, Curt (Athlete, Baseball Player)
6306 Sprig Oak Ct Apt B
Saint Louis, MO 63128-4336, USA

Ford, Dale (Baseball Player)
678 Brethern Church Rd
Jonesborough, TN 37659-3923, USA

Ford, Dale (Athlete, Baseball Player)
678 Brethern Church Rd
Jonesborough, TN 37659-3923, USA

Ford, Dan (Danny) (Athlete, Baseball Player)
1271 Linton Rd
Benton, LA 71006-8736, USA

Ford, Dave (Athlete, Baseball Player)
19523 N Sagamore Rd
Cleveland, OH 44126-1662, USA

Ford, David (Musician)
c/o Staff Member *Paradigm (Monterey)*
404 W Franklin St
Monterey, CA 93940-2303, USA

Ford, Debbie (Motivational Speaker, Writer)
PO Box 8064
La Jolla, CA 92038-8064, USA

Ford, Diane
201 San Vicente Blvd Apt 6
Santa Monica, CA 90402-1579

Ford, Don (Athlete, Basketball Player)
519 W Quinto St Apt B
Santa Barbara, CA 93105-4800, USA

Ford, Doug (Athlete, Golfer)
3737 Gulfstream Rd
Delray Beach, FL 33483-7411, USA

Ford, Edward C (Whitey) (Athlete, Baseball Player)
PO Box 160
Sea Cliff, NY 11579-0160, USA

Ford, Eileen
344 E 59th St
New York, NY 10022-1593

Ford, Eileen (Business Person)
c/o Staff Member *Ford Models (NY)*
238 E 4th St
New York, NY 10009-7425

Ford, Ervin (Baseball Player)
429 Banks St
Greensboro, NC 27401-3105, USA

Ford, Faith (Actor)
c/o Rebecca (Becca) Kovacik *Hofflund/Polone*
9465 Wilshire Blvd Ste 420
Beverly Hills, CA 90212-2603, USA

Ford, Frankie (Musician, Songwriter, Writer)
PO Box 1875
Gretna, LA 70054-1875, USA

Ford, Frederick (Adult Film Star)
c/o Staff Member *Diva Central Inc*
7510 W Sunset Blvd Ste 1445
Los Angeles, CA 90046-3408, USA

Ford, Garrett (Athlete, Football Player)
682 Westview Ave
Morgantown, WV 26505-2418, USA

Ford, Gilbert (Gib) (Athlete, Basketball Player, Coach)
264 Edgemere Way E
Naples, FL 34105-7150, USA

Ford, Harrison (Actor)
P.O. Box 25037
Jackson Hole, WY 83001, USA

Ford, Henry (Athlete, Football Player)
7222 Shannon Rd
Verona, PA 15147-2036, USA

Ford, Henry (Athlete, Football Player)
809 Glendevon Dr
McKinney, TX 75071-6543, USA

Ford, Jack (Correspondent)
51 W 52nd St
New York, NY 10019-6119, USA

Ford, James L (Athlete, Football Player)
2168 College Cir N
Jacksonville, FL 32209-5980, USA

Ford, Kevin A (Astronaut)
1002 Oak Park Ln
Friendswood, TX 77546-3584, USA

Ford, Lew (Athlete, Baseball Player)
2201 Lady Cornwall Dr
Lewisville, TX 75056-5615, USA

Ford, Lita (Actor, Composer, Musician)
c/o Garry Buck *Monterey International*
PO Box 297
Carmel By The Sea, CA 93921-0297, USA

Ford, Matt (Athlete, Baseball Player)
10837 Cypress Glen Dr
Coral Springs, FL 33071-8164, USA

Ford, Melyssa (Model)
c/o Michael (Mike) Esterman
Esterman.Com, LLC
Prefers to be contacted via email
MD, USA

Ford, Mick (Actor)
c/o Staff Member *CDA*
125 Glouchester Rd
London SW7 4TE, UK

Ford, Mike (Athlete, Football Player)
PO Box 100
Detroit, TX 75436-0100, USA

Ford, Phil (Athlete, Basketball Player)
PO Box 90623
Raleigh, NC 27675-0623, USA

Ford, Richard (Writer)
40 W 57th St # 1800
New York, NY 10019-4001, USA

Ford, Robert (Athlete, Basketball Player)
202 Pathway Ln
West Lafayette, IN 47906-2162, USA

Ford, Ruth (Actor)
1 W 72nd St
New York, NY 10023-3486, USA

Ford, Scott (Business Person)
PO Box 96019
Charlotte, NC 28296-0019, USA

Ford, Sherell (Athlete, Basketball Player)
1509 S 6th Ave
Maywood, IL 60153-2014, USA

Ford, T J (Basketball Player)
Bradley Center 1001 N 4th St
Milwaukee, WI 53203, USA

Ford, Ted (Athlete, Baseball Player)
6220 N 11th St Apt 19
McAllen, TX 78504-3275, USA

Ford, Thomas Mikal (Actor)
c/o Staff Member *TalentWorks (LA)*
3500 W Olive Ave Ste 1400
Burbank, CA 91505-5512, USA

Ford, Tom (Designer, Fashion Designer)
845 Madison Ave
New York, NY 10021-4908, USA

Ford, Trent (Actor)
c/o Staff Member *Paradigm (LA)*
360 N Crescent Dr
Beverly Hills, CA 90210-4874, USA

Ford, Wendell H (Ex-Governor, Ex-Senator)
220 Daviess St
Owensboro, KY 42303, USA

Ford, Willa (Musician)
c/o Michael (Mike) Esterman
Esterman.Com, LLC
Prefers to be contacted via email
MD, USA

Ford, William C Jr (Business Person)
American Road
Dearborn, MI 48121, USA

Ford Jr, Gerald R (Ex-President, Politician, President)
40471 Sand Dune Rd
Rancho Mirage, CA 92270-3520, USA

Forde, Brian (Athlete, Football Player)
20225 Bothell Everett Hwy Apt 1131
Bothell, WA 98012-8186, USA

Fordham, Julia (Musician, Songwriter, Writer)
2700 Pennsylvania Ave
Santa Monica, CA 90404-4066, USA

Fordham, Tom (Athlete, Baseball Player)
14559 Miguel Ln
El Cajon, CA 92021-2843, USA

Fordham, Willie (Baseball Player)
3608 Tudor Dr
Harrisburg, PA 17109-1235, USA

Fordyce, Brook (Athlete, Baseball Player)
5 River Crest Ct
Stuart, FL 34996-6515, USA

Foreigner (Music Group)
c/o Staff Member *Creative Artists Agency (CAA-LA)*
2000 Avenue of the Stars Ste 100
Los Angeles, CA 90067-4705, USA

Foreman, Amanda (Actor)
c/o Gregg A Klein *Abrams Artists Agency (LA)*
9200 W Sunset Blvd PH 11
Los Angeles, CA 90069-3601, USA

Foreman, Carol L T (Government Official)
5600 Wisconsin Ave Apt 502
Chevy Chase, MD 20815-4410, USA

Foreman, Chuck (Athlete, Football Player)
9716 Mill Creek Dr
Eden Prairie, MN 55347-4307, USA

Foreman, Deborah (Actor)
PO Box 2305
Big Bear City, CA 92314-2305, USA

Foreman, George (Boxer)
100 N Wilkes Barre Blvd
Wilkes Barre, PA 18702-5253, USA

Foreman, Walter E (Chuck) (Athlete, Football Player)
9716 Mill Creek Dr
Eden Prairie, MN 55347-4307, USA

Foresman, Susan B (Stylist)
2767 N Quincy St
Arlington, VA 22207-5055, USA

Forest, Michael (Actor)
1327 N Vista St Apt 203
Los Angeles, CA 90046-4832, USA

Forester, Bill (Athlete, Football Player)
10448 Stone Canyon Rd Apt 204
Dallas, TX 75230-4879, USA

Forester, Herschel (Athlete, Football Player)
15250 Prestonwood Blvd Apt 230
Dallas, TX 75248-4796, USA

Forester, Nicole (Actor)
c/o Doug Kesten *Paradigm (NY)*
360 Park Ave S Fl 16
New York, NY 10010-1708, USA

Foret, Sarah (Actor)

Forey, Conley (Athlete, Hockey Player)
412-2929 4th Ave W
Vancouver, BC V6K 4T3, Canada

Forget, Guy (Tennis Player)
Rue des Pacs 2
Neuchatel 2000, SWITZERLAND

Forlani, Arnaldo (Prime Minister)
Piazzale Schumann 15
Rome, ITALY

Forlani, Claire (Actor)
c/o Marsha McManus *Principal Entertainment (LA)*
1964 Westwood Blvd Ste 400
Los Angeles, CA 90025-4695, USA

Forman, Al (Baseball Player)
219 W Tateway Rd Apt B
Kitty Hawk, NC 27949-4377, USA

Forman, Al (Athlete, Baseball Player)
115 Acorn Ln
Point Harbor, NC 27964-9604, USA

Forman, Don (Athlete, Basketball Player)
1532 Gormican Ln
Naples, FL 34110-0920, USA

Forman, Milos (Director)
c/o Ariel (Ari) Emanuel *WmE2 (Endeavor-LA)*
9601 Wilshire Blvd Fl 3
Beverly Hills, CA 90210-5219, USA

Forman, Stanley (Journalist, Photographer)
17 Cherry Rd
Beverly, MA 01915-1511, USA

Forman, Tom (Cartoonist)
10544 James Rd
Celina, TX 75009-3744, USA

Formesa, Fern
5018 N 61st Ave
Glendale, AZ 85301-7310

Formia, Osvaldo (Horse Racer)
6501 Winfield Blvd # A10
Margate, FL 33063-7168, USA

Forney, Carl (Athlete, Baseball Player)
169 Ridley St
Marion, NC 28752-4629, USA

Forney, G David Jr (Scientist)
6 Coolidge Hill Rd
Cambridge, MA 02138-5510, USA

Forney, Kynan (Athlete, Football Player)
2046 Skybrooke Ln
Hoschton, GA 30548-6295, USA

Foronjy, Richard (Actor)
c/o Staff Member *House of Representatives, The*
1434 6th St Ste I
Santa Monica, CA 90401-2527, USA

Forrest, Bayard (Athlete, Basketball Player)
300A Squaw Valley Pl
Pagosa Springs, CO 81147-9773, USA

Forrest, Frederic (Actor)
11300 W Olympic Blvd Ste 610
Los Angeles, CA 90064-1643, USA

Forrest, Katherine Virginia (Writer)
PO Box 31613
San Francisco, CA 94131-0613

Forrest, Lili (Designer)
600 Moulton Ave Apt 205
Los Angeles, CA 90031-3485, USA

Forrest, Mark
13266 Bracken St
Arleta, CA 91331-5703

Forrest, Sally (Actor)
1125 Angelo Dr
Beverly Hills, CA 90210-2703, USA

Forrest, Steve (Actor)
2208 Crespi Ln
Westlake Village, CA 91361-1725, USA

Forrestal, Robert P (Financier, Government Official)
1200 Brookhaven Park Pl NE
Atlanta, GA 30319-4565, USA

Forrester, James (Scientist)
8700 Beverly Blvd
West Hollywood, CA 90048-1804, USA

Forrester, Jay W (Inventor)
Management School
Cambridge, MA 2139, USA

Forrester, Patrick G (Astronaut)
3923 Park Circle Way
Houston, TX 77059-3019, USA

Forrester Sisters (Music Group)
c/o Staff Member *Warner Bros Music*
4000 Warner Blvd
Burbank, CA 91522-0002

Forsberg, Fred (Athlete, Football Player)
1727 223rd Ave SE
Sammamish, WA 98075-9570, USA

Forsberg, Peter (Athlete, Hockey Player)
2200-201 Portage Ave Attn Don Baizley
Winnipeg, MB R3B 3L3, Canada

Forsch, Kenneth R (Ken) (Athlete, Baseball Player)
881 S Country Glen Way
Anaheim, CA 92808-2635, USA

Forsch, Robert H (Bob) (Athlete, Baseball Player)
8349 Fair Hill Dr
Weeki Wachee, FL 34613-4069, USA

Forsey, Brock (Athlete, Football Player)
8346 W Sundisk St
Boise, ID 83714-2509, USA

Forslund, Constance (Actor)
165 W 46th St Ste 1109
New York, NY 10036-2516, USA

Forsman, Dan (Athlete, Golfer)
PO Box 1715
Provo, UT 84603-1715, USA

Forst, Bill (Cartoonist)
2320 Byer Rd
Santa Cruz, CA 95062-1949, USA

Forstchen, William (Writer)
c/o Staff Member *Spectrum Literary Agency*
320 Central Park W Ste 1-D
New York, NY 10025-7659, USA

Forster, Brian
16172 Flamstead Dr
Hacienda Heights, CA 91745-3644

Forster, Marc (Director, Producer)
c/o Guymon Cassidy *Management 360*
9111 Wilshire Blvd
Beverly Hills, CA 90210-5508, USA

Forster, Robert (Actor)
c/o Eli Selden *Anonymous Content (AC-LA)*
3531 Hayden Ave
Culver City, CA 90232, USA

Forster, Scott (Athlete, Baseball Player)
901 Sturgis Ln
Ambler, PA 19002-2022, USA

Forster, Terry (Baseball Player)
PO Box 711658
Santee, CA 92072-1658, USA

Forster, William H (General)
10245 Fairfax Dr
Fort Belvoir, VA 22060-2123, USA

Forsyth, Bill (Director)
Drury House 34-43 Russell St
London WC2B 5HA, UNITED KINGDOM (UK)

Forsyth, Bruce (Actor, Comedian)
Kent House Upper Ground
London SE1, UNITED KINGDOM (UK)

Forsyth, Chris (Actor)
c/o Steve Rodriquez *McGowan Management*
8733 W Sunset Blvd Ste 103
West Hollywood, CA 90069-2241, USA

Forsyth, Frederick (Writer)
61-63 Oxbridge Rd Ealing
London W5 5SA, UNITED KINGDOM (UK)

Forsythe, Bill
20 Winton Dr
Glasgow, SCOTLAND G12 0QA

Forsythe, Gerald (Gary) (Motorcycle Race, Motorcycle Racer)
7231 Georgetown Rd
Indianapolis, IN 46268-4126, USA

Forsythe, Gerry
9350 Castlegate Dr
Indianapolis, IN 46256-1001

Forsythe, Rosemary (Actor)
1591 Benedict Canyon Dr
Beverly Hills, CA 90210-2023, USA

Forsythe, William (Actor)
7532 Melba Ave
Canoga Park, CA 91304-5361, USA

Forsythe, William (Choreographer)
Untermainanlage 11
Frankfurt 60311, GERMANY

Fort, Edward B (Educator)
Chancellor S Ofc
Greensboro, NC 27411-0001, USA

Fort-Brescia, Bernardo (Architect)
550 Brickell Ave # 200
Miami, FL 33131, USA

Forte, Deborah (Producer)
c/o Staff Member *Scholastic Entertainment*
557 Broadway
New York, NY 10012-3962, USA

Forte, Fabian
6671 W Sunset Blvd Ste 1502
Los Angeles, CA 90028-7235

Forte, Ike (Athlete, Football Player)
5811 Winchester Dr
Texarkana, TX 75503-4602, USA

Forte, Joseph (Basketball Player)
355 Elmcroft Blvd # 621
Rockville, MD 20850-5662, USA

Forte, Will (Actor, Writer)
c/o Julie Darmody *Mosaic Media Group*
9200 W Sunset Blvd Ste 10
Los Angeles, CA 90069-3608, USA

Fortenberry, Jeff (Congressman, Politician)
1514 Longworth Hob
Washington, DC 20515-0537, USA

Fortier, Claude (Misc)
1014 De Grenoble Sainte-Foy
Quebec, QC G1V 2Z9, CANADA

Fortier, Dave (Athlete, Hockey Player)
150 Kingsmount Blvd
Sudbury, ON P3E 1K9, Canada

Fortier, Laurie (Actor)
c/o Steven Jensen *The Independent Group*
6363 Wilshire Blvd Ste 115
Los Angeles, CA 90048-5734, USA

Fortier, Suzanne (Stylist)
1562 Casale Rd
Pacific Palisades, CA 90272-2714, USA

Fortin, Roman (Athlete, Football Player)
10741 Bell Rd
Duluth, GA 30097-1801, USA

Fortner, Nell (Coach)
Athletic
Auburn, AL 36849-0001, USA

Fortson, Danny (Athlete, Basketball Player)
5601 Hancock Rd
Southwest Ranches, FL 33330-3003, USA

Fortugno, Tim (Athlete, Baseball Player)
3604 Babson Dr
Elk Grove, CA 95758-4576, USA

Fortunato, Don (Athlete, Football Player)
222 Regent Wood Rd
Northfield, IL 60093-2767, USA

Fortunato, Joseph F (Joe) (Athlete, Football Player)
PO Box 934
Natchez, MS 39121-0934, USA

Fortune, Jimmy (Musician)
8747 Highway 304
Hernando, MS 38632-8445, USA

Fortuno, Luis (Governor, Politician)
La Fortaleza
San Juan, PR 901, USA

Foruria, John (Athlete, Football Player)
5603 Edson St
Boise, ID 83705-1852, USA

Forward, Susan (Writer)
c/o Staff Member *HarperCollins Publishers*
10 E 53rd St C/O Author Mail Floor 7
New York, NY 10022, USA

Forzano, Rick (Athlete, Football Coach, Football Player)
3216 Interlaken St
West Bloomfield, MI 48323-1824, USA

Fosbury, Dick
709 Canyon Run Box 1791
Ketchum, ID 83340

Fosnow, Jerry (Athlete, Baseball Player)
369 Caddie Dr
Debary, FL 32713-4512, USA

Foss, Anita (Baseball Player)
2107 Ashland Ave
Santa Monica, CA 90405-6025, USA

Foss, John W II (General)
16 Hampton KY
Williamsburg, VA 23185-5538, USA

Foss, Larry (Athlete, Baseball Player)
4303 E English St
Wichita, KS 67218-1320, USA

Foss, Lukas (Composer, Musician)
1140 5th Ave # 4B
New York, NY 10128-0806, USA

Fossas, Tony (Athlete, Baseball Player)
11302 NW 9th St
Plantation, FL 33325-1501, USA

Fosse, Ray (Athlete, Baseball Player)
PO Box 567
Diablo, CA 94528-0567, USA

Fossey, Brigitte (Actor)
18 Rue Troyon
Paris 75017, FRANCE

Fossum, Casey (Athlete, Baseball Player)
1087 White Bluff Dr
Whitney, TX 76692-2019, USA

Fossum, Michael E (Astronaut)
822 Rolling Run Ct
Houston, TX 77062-2100, USA

Foster, Alan (Athlete, Baseball Player)
10330 Grandview Dr
La Mesa, CA 91941-6844, USA

Foster, Barry (Athlete, Football Player)
1905 Ashton Ct
Colleyville, TX 76034-4401, USA

Foster, Ben (Actor)
c/o Ken Jacobson *Ken Jacobson Management*
Preferred to be contacted by phone
Los Angeles, CA 91367, USA

Foster, Bill (Basketball Player)
Athletic
Blacksburg, VA 24061-0001, USA

Foster, Brendan (Athlete, Track Athlete)
Whitegates 31 Meadowfield Road
Stocksfield, Northumberland, UNITED KINGDOM (UK)

Foster, Corey (Athlete, Hockey Player)
71 Pine Ridge Dr
Arnprior, ON K7S 3G8, Canada

Foster, Coy (Misc)
5486 Glen Lakes Dr
Dallas, TX 75231-4308, USA

Foster, David (Musician, Songwriter)
c/o Marc Johnston *Align Entertainment Group*
200 W 54th St Fl 11
New York, NY 10019-5567, USA

Foster, Deshaun (Athlete, Football Player)
2391 Apple Tree Dr
Tustin, CA 92780-7134, USA

Foster, Dwight (Athlete, Hockey Player)
721 S Livernois Rd
Rochester Hills, MI 48307-2770, USA

Foster, Frank B III (Composer, Musician)
300 Mercer St Apt 3J
New York, NY 10003-6732, USA

Foster, George (Athlete, Baseball Player)
15 E Putnam Ave Apt 320
Greenwich, CT 06830-5424, USA

Foster, George (Athlete, Football Player)
4057 Meadowbrook Dr
Macon, GA 31204-4752, USA

Foster, Jeff (Athlete, Basketball Player)
333 Pickwick Ct
Noblesville, IN 46062-9071, USA

Foster, Jerome (Athlete, Football Player)
18900 Goldwin St
Southfield, MI 48075-7218, USA

Foster, Jodie (Actor, Director)
c/o Jennifer Allen *Viewpoint Inc*
8820 Wilshire Blvd Ste 220
Beverly Hills, CA 90211-2622, USA

Foster, John (Athlete, Baseball Player)
519 Airway Ave
Lewiston, ID 83501-4503, USA

Foster, John (Actor)
c/o Staff Member *Windfall*
3000 W Alameda Ave
Burbank, CA 91523-0001, USA

Foster, Jon (Actor)
c/o Ken Jacobson *Ken Jacobson Management*
3500 W Olive Ave Ste 1470
Burbank, CA 91505-5514, USA

Foster, Kris (Athlete, Baseball Player)
116 Johns Ave
Lehigh Acres, FL 33936-2135, USA

Foster, Larry (Athlete, Baseball Player)
205 W Obell St
Whitehall, MI 49461-1742, USA

Foster, Lawrence T (Conductor)
40 W 57th St # 1800
New York, NY 10019-4001, USA

Foster, Leo (Athlete, Baseball Player)
699 Glensprings Dr
Cincinnati, OH 45246-2129, USA

Foster, Marty (Baseball Player)
319 W 5th Ave
Denver, CO 80204-5118, USA

Foster, Marty (Athlete, Baseball Player)
1718 Arrowhead Dr
Beloit, WI 53511-3808, USA

Foster, Meg (Actor)
c/o Chris Roe *CR Management*
23852 Pacific Coast Hwy Ste 627
Malibu, CA 90265-4876, USA

Foster, Norm (Athlete, Hockey Player)
632 Rewold Dr
Rochester, MI 48307-2233, USA

Foster, Norman R (Architect)
Riverside 3 22 Hester Road
London SW11 4AN, UNITED KINGDOM (UK)

Foster, Radney (Musician, Songwriter, Writer)
c/o Staff Member *WmE2 (WMA-LA)*
1 William Morris Pl
Beverly Hills, CA 90212-4261, USA

Foster, Robert W (Bob) (Boxer)
913 Valencia Dr NE
Albuquerque, NM 87108-1753, USA

Foster, Rod (Athlete, Basketball Player)
1246 Armacost Ave Apt 105
Los Angeles, CA 90025-6432, USA

Foster, Ron (Athlete, Football Player)
17819 Merridy St Apt 117
Northridge, CA 91325-4604, USA

Foster, Roy
650 E 27th Pl N
Tulsa, OK 74106-2409, USA

Foster, Roy (Athlete, Baseball Player)
650 E 27th Pl N
Tulsa, OK 74106-2409, USA

Foster, Roy A (Athlete, Football Player)
12110 Salem Dr
Granada Hills, CA 91344-2351, USA

Foster, Sara (Actor)
c/o Brad Marks *BM Management*
Prefers to be contacted via phone
Los Angeles, CA 90069, USA

Foster, Scott M (Actor)
c/o John Tae Lee *Shapiro/West & Associates*
141 El Camino Dr Ste 205
Beverly Hills, CA 90212-2786, USA

Foster, Scott Michael (Actor)
c/o John Tae Lee *Shapiro/West & Associates*
141 El Camino Dr Ste 205
Beverly Hills, CA 90212-2786, USA

Foster, Steven (Steve) (Athlete, Baseball Player)
1020 Heathrow Dr
Frisco, TX 75034-7806, USA

Foster, Sutton (Actor)
c/o Joe Machota *Creative Artists Agency (CAA-NY)*
162 5th Ave Fl 6
New York, NY 10010-6047, USA

Foster, Todd (Boxer)
303 13th St NW
Great Falls, MT 59404-2213, USA

Foster, William E (Bill) (Coach)
152 Hollywood Dr
Coppell, TX 75019-7302, USA

Foster Jr, John S (Physicist)
1 Space Park Blvd
Redondo Beach, CA 90278-1001, USA

Foster the People (Music Group, Musician)
c/o Staff Member *Star Time Intl*
79 5th Ave Fl 15
New York, NY 10003-3034, USA

Fotiu, Nick (Athlete, Hockey Player)
16 Backus River Rd
East Falmouth, MA 02536-5205, USA

Fou, Ts'ong (Musician)
62 Aberdeen Park
London N5 2BL, UNITED KINGDOM (UK)

Foucault, Steve (Athlete, Baseball Player)
24353 Rolling View Ct
Lutz, FL 33559-8642, USA

Fouch, Allison (Athlete, Golfer)
2949 Oakwood Dr SE
Grand Rapids, MI 49506-4235, USA

Foudy, Judy (Julie) (Model, Soccer Player)
1801 S Prairie Ave
Chicago, IL 60616-1319, USA

Foudy, Julie
1801 S Prairie Ave
Chicago, IL 60616-1319

Fought, John (Athlete, Golfer)
5747 E Via Los Ranchos
Paradise Valley, AZ 85253, USA

Foules, Elbert (Athlete, Football Player)
633 E Ohea St
Greenville, MS 38701-3861, USA

Foulke, Keith C (Athlete, Baseball Player)
4844 W Electra Ln
Glendale, AZ 85310-3833, USA

Foulkes, Llyn (Artist)
6010 Eucalyptus Ln
Los Angeles, CA 90042-1244, USA

Fountain, Pete
237 N Peters St # 400
New Orleans, Los Angeles 71030

Fountain, Peter D (Pete) Jr (Musician)
108 E Matilija St
Ojai, CA 93023-2639, USA

Fountain, Rex
10475 Bellagio Rd
Los Angeles, CA 90077-3818

Fountaine, Jamal (Athlete, Football Player)
245 SW Lincoln St Apt 122
Portland, OR 97201-5083, USA

Fountains of Wayne (Music Group)
c/o Staff Member *Big Hassle*
44 Wall St Ste 2201
New York, NY 10005-2427, USA

Four Aces, The
11761 E Speedway Blvd
Tucson, AZ 85748-2017

Four Freshman, The
PO Box 93534
Las Vegas, NV 89193-3534

Four Freshmen, The (Music Group)
c/o Staff Member *International Ventures*
25115 Avenue Stanford Ste 102
Valencia, CA 91355-4777, USA

Four Lads, The
11761 E Speedway Blvd
Tucson, AZ 85748-2017

Four Non Blondes
PO Box 170545
San Francisco, CA 94117-0545

Fourcade, John (Athlete, Football Player)
2749 Long Branch Dr
Marrero, LA 70072-5856, USA

Fournet, Sid (Athlete, Football Player)
2030 Swamp Fox Rd
Midlothian, VA 23112-5302, USA

Fournier, Brigitte (Opera Singer)
1370 Avenue of the Americas
New York, NY 10019-4602, USA

Fournier, Francine
PO Box 935
Bear, DE 19701-0935, USA

Foust, Nina (Athlete, Golfer)
901 East Dr
Morehead City, NC 28557-3009, USA

Fouts, Dan (Athlete, Football Player)
16820 Varco Rd
Bend, OR 97701-9135, USA

Fowle, Lillia (Stylist)
12918 Valleyheart Dr Apt 5
Studio City, CA 91604-1991, USA

Fowler, Bobby (Athlete, Football Player)
12520 Mexicana Cv
Del Valle, TX 78617-3624, USA

Fowler, Cal (Athlete, Basketball Player)
10121 Godspeed Dr
Ocean City, MD 21842-8854, USA

Fowler, Chris (Sportscaster)
c/o Staff Member *ESPN (Main)*
ESPN Plaza 935 Middle St
Bristol, CT 06010-1001, USA

Fowler, Claudia (Stylist)
2932 Polo Club Rd
Nashville, TN 37221-4344, USA

Fowler, E Michael C (Architect)
Branches Giffords Road
Bienheim RD 3, NEW ZEALAND

Fowler, Jim (Actor)
Mutual of Omaha Mutual of Omaha Plz
Omaha, NE 68175-0001, USA

Fowler, Kevin (Musician)
c/o Staff Member *Paradigm (Monterey)*
404 W Franklin St
Monterey, CA 93940-2303, USA

Fowler, Peggy Y (Business Person)
121 SW Salmon St
Portland, OR 97204-2908, USA

Fowler, Ryan (Athlete, Football Player)
1713 Montclair Blvd
Brentwood, TN 37027-8073, USA

Fowler, Todd (Athlete, Football Player)
10024 FM 3053 N
Kilgore, TX 75662-4721, USA

Fowler, W Wyche Jr (Diplomat, Ex-Senator)
701 A St NE
Washington, DC 20002-6031, USA

Fowler, Willmer (Athlete, Football Player)
517 Lily St
Mansfield, OH 44903-1314, USA

Fowlkes, Alan (Athlete, Baseball Player)
405 Emerald Lake Dr
Lumberton, NC 28358-8022, USA

Fox, Allen (Coach, Tennis Player)
Athletic Dept
Malibu, CA 90265, USA

Fox, Andy (Athlete, Baseball Player)
9087 Tarmac Ct
Fair Oaks, CA 95628-8142, USA

Fox, Bernard (Actor)
6601 Burnet Ave
Van Nuys, CA 91405-4515, USA

Fox, Chad (Athlete, Baseball Player)
6007 Windrose Hollow Ln
Spring, TX 77379-8904, USA

Fox, Charles I (Composer, Conductor)
356 Pine Valley Rd
Hoosick Falls, NY 12090-3859, USA

Fox, Edward (Actor)
25 Maida Ave
London W2, UNITED KINGDOM (UK)

Fox, Emilia (Actor)
125 Glouster Rd
London SW7 4TE, UNITED KINGDOM

Fox, Eric (Athlete, Baseball Player)
PO Box 577198
Modesto, CA 95357-7198, USA

Fox, Everett (Misc)
Jewish Studies Program
Worcester, MA 1610, USA

Fox, George
4950 Yonge St # 2400
Toronto, . CANADA Ont M2N 6K

Fox, Greg (Athlete, Hockey Player)
635 Glendalough Ct
Alpharetta, GA 30004-3056, USA

Fox, Harold (Athlete, Basketball Player)
6511 Wilburn Dr
Capitol Heights, MD 20743-3351, USA

Fox, Jackie
23368 Ostronic Dr
Woodland Hills, CA 91367-6045

Fox, James (Actor)
76 Oxford St
London W1N 0AX, UNITED KINGDOM (UK)

Fox, Jessica (Actor)
Nederlander House 7 Great Russell Street
London
WC1B 3NH UK

Fox, Jim (Athlete, Basketball Player)
4136 N 52nd St
Phoenix, AZ 85018-4402, USA

Fox, Jim (Athlete, Hockey Player)
224 S Juanita Ave # A
Redondo Beach, CA 90277-3438, USA

Fox, John (Athlete, Coach, Football Coach, Football Player)
1 Cantitoe Ln
Englewood, CO 80113-6111, USA

Fox, Jorja (Actor)
c/o Peg Donegan *Framework Entertainment (LA)*
9057 Nemo St Ste C
West Hollywood, CA 90069-5511, USA

Fox, Marye Anne (Misc)
5926 Sagebrush Rd
La Jolla, CA 92037-7039, USA

Fox, Matthew (Religious Leader)
1 Nob Hill Cir
San Francisco, CA 94108-2232, USA

Fox, Matthew (Actor, Director)
c/o William Choi *Management 360*
9111 Wilshire Blvd
Beverly Hills, CA 90210-5508, USA

Fox, Maurice S (Biologist)
983 Memorial Dr Apt 401
Cambridge, MA 02138-5742, USA

Fox, Megan (Actor)
c/o Dominique Appel *Baker Winokur Ryder Public Relations (BWR-LA)*
9100 Wilshire Blvd Ste 500 PMB WEST
Beverly Hills, CA 90212-3426, USA

Fox, Michael J (Actor)
PO Box 4777
New York, NY 10163-4777, USA

Fox, Neil (Actor)
c/o Staff Member *MPC Entertainment*
MPC House 15-16 Maple Mews
London NW6 5UZ, UNITED KINGDOM

Fox, Rick (Actor, Athlete, Basketball Player)
17530 Ventura Blvd Ste 201
Encino, CA 91316-3889, USA

Fox, Samantha (Model, Musician)
PO Box 7834
London NW3 3ZT, UNITED KINGDOM (UK)

Fox, Shayna
6212 Banner Ave
Los Angeles, CA 90038-2802

Fox, Sheldon (Architect)
111 W 57th St
New York, NY 10019-2211, USA

Fox, Spencer (Actor)
c/o Maggie Schuster *J Mitchell Management*
70 W 36th St Rm 1006
New York, NY 10018-8015, USA

Fox, Terry (Athlete, Baseball Player)
2312 Sugar Mill Rd
New Iberia, LA 70563-8648, USA

Fox, Tim (Athlete, Football Player)
10 Longmeadow Dr
Westwood, MA 02090-1079, USA

Fox, Vernon (Athlete, Football Player)
6704 Willow River Ct
Las Vegas, NV 89108-5033, USA

Fox, Vicente (Politician, President)
Patio de Honor 2 Piso
Mexico City DF 06067, MEXICO

Fox, Vivica (Actor)
c/o Lita Richardson *Lita Richardson Entertainment*
4570 Van Nuys Blvd Ste 432
Sherman Oaks, CA 91403-2913, USA

Fox, Wesley L (War Hero)
855 Deercroft Dr
Blacksburg, VA 24060-0272, USA

Fox Brothers
Rt. 6 Bending Chestnut
Franklin, TN 37064

Foxton, Simon (Stylist)
c/o Staff Member *Katy Barker Agency Inc*
6606 10th Ave Apt 3R
Brooklyn, NY 11219-5804, USA

Foxworth, Domonique (Athlete, Football Player)
3533 S Sherwood Rd SE
Smyrna, GA 30082-2833, USA

Foxworth, Robert (Actor)
c/o Chris Schmidt *Paradigm (LA)*
360 N Crescent Dr
Beverly Hills, CA 90210-4874, USA

Foxworthy, Jeff (Actor, Comedian)
c/o J P Williams *Parallel Entertainment*
9420 Wilshire Blvd Ste 250
Beverly Hills, CA 90212-3151, USA

Foxx, Jamie (Actor, Comedian)
c/o Jamie King *King Management*
9229 W Sunset Blvd Ste 830
Los Angeles, CA 90069-3413

Foxx, Shyla (Adult Film Star)
c/o Staff Member *Atlas Multimedia Inc*
9005 Eton Ave Ste C
Canoga Park, CA 91304-6533, USA

Foxx, Tanya
901 W Victoria St Ste G
Compton, CA 90220-5819

Foxx, Virginia (Congressman, Politician)
1230 Longworth Hob
Washington, DC 20515-0547, USA

Foy, Eddie III (Actor)
3003 W Olive Ave
Burbank, CA 91505-4538, USA

Foyle, Adonal (Athlete, Basketball Player)
174 Crestview Dr
Orinda, CA 94563-3922, USA

Foyt IV, A.J. (Race Car Driver)
6803 Coffman Rd
Indianapolis, IN 46268-2561, USA

Foytack, Paul (Athlete, Baseball Player)
1910 Portview Dr
Spring Hill, TN 37174-8249, USA

Frabotta, Don (Actor)
PO Box 962
Douglas, MA 01516-0962, USA

Fradkov, Mikhail (Prime Minister)
Kremlin Staraya Pl 4
Moscow 103132, RUSSIA

Fradon, Dana (Cartoonist)
2 Brushy Hill Rd
Newtown, CT 6470, USA

Fradon, Ramona (Cartoonist)
435 N Michigan Ave Ste 1500
Chicago, IL 60611-4012, USA

Frailing, Ken (Athlete, Baseball Player)
2150 Shadow Oaks Rd
Sarasota, FL 34240-9324, USA

Frain, James (Actor)
c/o Melanie Greene *Affirmative Entertainment*
425 N Robertson Blvd
West Hollywood, CA 90048-1735, USA

Fraiture, Nikolai (Musician)
370 7th Ave # 807
New York, NY 10001-3967, USA

Fraker, William A (Cinematographer)
337 Lorraine Blvd
Los Angeles, CA 90020-4727, USA

Frakes, Jonathan (Actor, Director)
c/o Doug MacLaren *International Creative Management (ICM-LA)*
10250 Constellation Blvd Fl 7
Los Angeles, CA 90067-6207, USA

Fralic, William (Bill) (Athlete, Football Player)
280 Galsworthy Ct
Roswell, GA 30075-6354, USA

Frampton, Peter (Musician, Songwriter)
c/o Nicki Loranger *Vector Management (LA)*
1100 Glendon Ave Ste 2000
Los Angeles, CA 90024-3524, USA

Franca, Celia (Ballerina, Choreographer)
157 King St E
Toronto, ON M5C 1G9, CANADA

France, Brian (Misc)
1801 W Speedway Blvd
Daytona Beach, FL 32114-1215, USA

France, Doug (Athlete, Football Player)
6056 Great Falls Ave
Las Vegas, NV 89110-2709, USA

Francella, Meaghan (Athlete, Golfer)
16 Maywood Ave
Port Chester, NY 10573-2402, USA

Franceschetti, Lou (Athlete, Hockey Player)
72 Orchardcroft Cres
Toronto, ON M3J 1S8, Canada

Franchione, Dennis (Coach, Football Coach)
Athletic
College Station, TX 77843-0001, USA

Franchitti, Dario (Race Car Driver)
7615 Zionsville Rd
Indianapolis, IN 46268-2174, USA

Franci, Jason (Athlete, Football Player)
6410 Hwy 116
Forestville, CA 95436-9401, USA

Francis, Betty (Baseball Player)
11750 S Homan Ave Trlr 19A
Merrionette Park, IL 60803-4513, USA

Francis, Bob (Athlete, Coach, Hockey Player)
23725 N 75th Pl
Scottsdale, AZ 85255-6128, USA

Francis, Clarence (Bevo) (Basketball Player)
18340 Steubenyille Pike Rd
Salineville, OH 43945, USA

Francis, Connie (Actor, Musician)
6413 NW 102nd Ter
Parkland, FL 33076-2357, USA

Francis, Don (Scientist)
1 Dna Way
South San Francisco, CA 94080-4918, USA

Francis, Donna (Stylist)
c/o Staff Member *Bryan Bantry*
900 Broadway Ste 400
New York, NY 10003-1239, USA

Francis, Emile (Athlete, Hockey Player)
7220 Crystal Lake Dr
West Palm Beach, FL 33411-5713, USA

Francis, Emile P (Coach)
7220 Crystal Lake Dr
West Palm Beach, FL 33411-5713, USA

Francis, Fred (Correspondent)
4001 Nebraska Ave NW
Washington, DC 20016-2733, USA

Francis, Genie (Actor)
10990 Wilshire Blvd Ste 1600
Los Angeles, CA 90024-3925, USA

Francis, Harrison (Athlete, Football Player)
207 S Susan Ave
Wagoner, OK 74467-4843, USA

Francis, James (Athlete, Football Player)
2727 Crossview Dr
Houston, TX 77063-4206, USA

Francis, Jeff (Athlete, Baseball Player)
3191 Quitman St
Denver, CO 80212-1457, USA

Francis, Joe (Producer)
c/o Staff Member *Mantra Films*
PO Box 150
Hollywood, CA 90078-0150, USA

Francis, Joe (Athlete, Football Player)
45-570 Kaaluna Pl
Kaneohe, HI 96744-3410, USA

Francis, Paul (Actor)
c/o Staff Member *Gilbertson Management*
1334 3rd Street Promenade Ste 201
Santa Monica, CA 90401-1320, USA

Francis, Ron (Athlete, Hockey Player)
12312 Birchfalls Dr
Raleigh, NC 27614-7900, USA

Francis, Ron (Athlete, Football Player)
3315 Ashton Park Dr
Houston, TX 77082-5307, USA

Francis, Russ (Athlete, Football Player)
800 Putney Rd
Brattleboro, VT 05301-9058, USA

Francis, Steve (Athlete, Basketball Player)
632 Pifer Rd
Houston, TX 77024-5434, USA

Francis, Wally (Athlete, Football Player)
2452 Wilshire Way
Douglasville, GA 30135-8129, USA

Francis, William (Bill) (Musician)
9850 Sandalwood Blvd # 458
Boca Raton, FL 33428, USA

Francisco, Aaron (Athlete, Football Player)
5064 W Geronimo St
Chandler, AZ 85226-4529, USA

Francisco, Don (Television Host)
c/o Staff Member *Univision*
605 3rd Ave Fl 12
New York, NY 10158-0034, USA

Francisco, George J (Misc)
1100 Circle 75 Pkwy SE
Atlanta, GA 30339-3064, USA

Francisco, Pablo (Comedian)
c/o Matt Schuler *Levity Entertainment Group*
6701 Center Dr W Ste 1111
Los Angeles, CA 90045-1552, USA

Franck, George H (Sonny) (Athlete, Football Player)
1209 21st Ave Apt A301
Rock Island, IL 61201-7912, USA

Franck, Martine (Photographer)
Vale Studio 62 Wood Vale
London SE23 3ED, UK

Francke, Martine (Actor)
c/o Staff Member *Agence Artistique Duchesne*
6031 Avenue Du Parc
Montréal, Québec H2V 4H4, Canada

Franckowiak, Mike (Athlete, Football Player)
730 Lake Dornoch Dr
Pinehurst, NC 28374-7124, USA

Francks, Rainbow Sun (Actor)
c/o Staff Member *Sci-FI Channel, The*
100 Universal Plz Bldg 1280/12
Universal City, CA 91608, USA

Franco, Carlos (Athlete, Golfer)
10561 NW 51st St
Doral, FL 33178-3209, USA

Franco, Dave (Actor)
c/o Miles Levy *James/Levy/Jacobson Management Inc*
3500 W Olive Ave Ste 1470
Burbank, CA 91505-5514, USA

Franco, James (Actor)
c/o Miles Levy *James/Levy/Jacobson Management Inc*
3500 W Olive Ave Ste 1470
Burbank, CA 91505-5514, USA

Franco, John A (Athlete, Baseball Player)
111 Helena Rd
Staten Island, NY 10304, USA

Franco, Julio C (Athlete, Baseball Player)
651 NE 23rd Ct
Pompano Beach, FL 33064-5504, USA

Franco, Liliana (Actor)
c/o Staff Member *Eileen O'farrell Personal Management*
11653 Blix St Apt 2
North Hollywood, CA 91602-1051, United States

Franco, Matt (Athlete, Baseball Player)
1008 Clear Sky Pl
Simi Valley, CA 93065-8331, USA

Francoeur, Jeff (Athlete, Baseball Player)
5219 Beech Forest Dr SW
Lilburn, GA 30047-5356, USA

Francois-Poncet, Jean A (Financier, Government Official)
6 Blvd Suchet
Paris 75116, FRANCE

Francona, John P (Tito) (Athlete, Baseball Player)
1109 Penn Ave
New Brighton, PA 15066-1632, USA

Francona, Terry J (Athlete, Baseball Player, Coach)
750 Newton St
Chestnut Hill, MA 02467-2606, USA

Frandsen, Kevin (Athlete, Baseball Player)
2521 Cottle Ave
San Jose, CA 95125-4013, USA

Frangoulis, Mario (Musician)
c/o Staff Member *Sony Music International*
550 Madison Ave Fl 6
New York, NY 10022-3211, USA

Frank, Anthony M (Financier, Government Official)
3800 N Central Ave
Phoenix, AZ 85012-1992, USA

Frank, Barney (Politician)
2252 Rayburn Hob
Washington, DC 20515-2104, USA

Frank, Charles (Actor)
1801 Avenue of the Stars Ste 902
Los Angeles, CA 90067-5981, USA

Frank, Claude (Musician)
165 W 57th St
New York, NY 10019-2201, USA

Frank, Darryl (Producer)
c/o Staff Member *Dreamworks Television*
100 Universal Plz Bldg 5125
Universal City, CA 91608, USA

Frank, Diana (Actor)
1800 Avenue of the Stars Ste 400
Los Angeles, CA 90067-4206, USA

Frank, Donald (Athlete, Football Player)
2039 Weston Green Loop
Cary, NC 27513-2268, USA

Frank, Gary (Actor)
861 S Bundy Dr
Los Angeles, CA 90049-5216, USA

Frank, Howard (Business Person)
3655 NW 87th Ave
Doral, FL 33178-2418, USA

Frank, Jason David (Actor, Comedian)
2 Henrietta St
London WC2E 8PS, UNITED KINGDOM (UK)

Frank, Jerome D (Educator)
818 W 40th St Apt K
Baltimore, MD 21211-2083, USA

Frank, Joanna (Actor)
1274 Capri Dr
Pacific Palisades, CA 90272-4001, USA

Frank, Joe (Entertainer)
1900 Pico Blvd
Santa Monica, CA 90405-1628, USA

Frank, John (Athlete, Football Player)
150 Central Park S Fl 2
New York, NY 10019-1566, USA

Frank, Larry (Race Car Driver)
832 Fork Shoals Rd
Greenville, SC 29605-5832, USA

Frank, Louis A (Astronomer)
Astronomy Dept
Iowa City, IA 52242, USA

Frank, Mike (Athlete, Baseball Player)
1343 W 19th St
Upland, CA 91784-7433, USA

Frank, Neil L (Misc)
1320 S Dixie Hwy
Coral Gables, FL 33146-2926, USA

Frank, Phil (Cartoonist)
500 Turney St
Sausalito, CA 94965-1840, USA

Frank, Robert (Photographer)
745 5th Ave Fl 4
New York, NY 10151-0099, USA

Frank, Scott (Actor, Director, Writer)
c/o Staff Member *Arroyo Films*
50 W Dayton St Apt 308
Pasadena, CA 91105-2094, USA

Frank, Tellis (Athlete, Basketball Player)
4936 Van Noord Ave
Sherman Oaks, CA 91423-2214, USA

Frank-Dummerth, Edna (Baseball Player)
5044 Tealby Ln
Saint Louis, MO 63128-2952, USA

Franke, Robert (Writer)
c/o Allen Fischer *Principato/Young Management*
9465 Wilshire Blvd Ste 430
Beverly Hills, CA 90212-2613, USA

Frankel, Bethenny (Chef, Reality TV Star)
c/o Amanda Silverman *42West (NY)*
220 W 42nd St Fl 12
New York, NY 10036-7200, USA

Frankel, Felice (Artist, Photographer)
Edgerton Center
Cambridge, MA 2139, USA

Franken, Al (Actor, Comedian, Writer)
c/o Staff Member *Creative Artists Agency (CAA-LA)*
2000 Avenue of the Stars Ste 100
Los Angeles, CA 90067-4705, USA

Franken, Steve (Actor)
4727 Wilshire Blvd Ste 333
Los Angeles, CA 90010-3874, USA

Frankenthaler, Helen (Artist)
19 Contentment Island Rd
Darien, CT 06820-6208, USA

Frankl, Peter (Musician)
5 Gresham Gardens
London NW11 8NX, UNITED KINGDOM (UK)

Franklin, Anthony R (Tony) (Athlete, Football Player)
117 Shady Trail St
San Antonio, TX 78232-1313, USA

Franklin, Aretha (Musician)
8450 Linwood St
Detroit, MI 48206-2379, USA

Franklin, Aubrayo (Athlete, Football Player)
105 Lilly Dr
Johnson City, TN 37604, USA

Franklin, Barbara Hackman (Secretary)
1875 Perkins St
Bristol, CT 06010-8910, USA

Franklin, Bobby (Athlete, Football Player)
384 Country Club Dr
Senatobia, MS 38668-6308, USA

Franklin, Bonnie (Actor)
c/o Staff Member *Cunningham Escott Slevin & Doherty (CESD-LA)*
10635 Santa Monica Blvd Ste 130
Los Angeles, CA 90025-8306, USA

Franklin, Byron (Athlete, Football Player)
2613 Singapore Dr
Birmingham, AL 35211-6924, USA

Franklin, Carl M (Director)

Franklin, Diane (Actor)
195 S Beverly Dr Ste 400
Beverly Hills, CA 90212-3044, USA

Franklin, Don
10101 Santa Monica Blvd # 2500
Los Angeles, CA 90067

Franklin, Don (Actor)
10100 Santa Monica Blvd Ste 2500
Los Angeles, CA 90067-4116, USA

Franklin, Farrah (Musician)
8391 Beverly Blvd
Los Angeles, CA 90048-2633, USA

Franklin, Gary
7610 Beverly Blvd # 480820
Los Angeles, CA 90048-9996

Franklin, Howard (Director, Writer)
c/o Staff Member *Agency for the Performing Arts (APA-LA)*
405 S Beverly Dr Ste 500
Beverly Hills, CA 90212-4425, USA

Franklin, Jay (Baseball Player)
2450 Massanutten Ter
Winchester, VA 22601-2774, USA

Franklin, Joe
PO Box 1
Lynbrook, NY 11563-0001

Franklin, John (Actor)
9744 Wilshire Blvd Ste 203
Beverly Hills, CA 90212-1812, USA

Franklin, Jon D (Journalist)
9650 Strickland Rd
Raleigh, NC 27615-1902, USA

Franklin, Kirk (Musician)
c/o Gwendolyn Quinn *GQ Media & Public Relations*
1650 Broadway Ste 1011
New York, NY 10019-6965, USA

Franklin, Larry (Athlete, Football Player)
9390 Afton Grove Rd
Cordova, TN 38018-7519, USA

Franklin, Melissa (Physicist)
Physics Dept
Cambridge, MA 2138, USA

Franklin, Micah (Athlete, Baseball Player)
3948 E Lafayette Ave
Gilbert, AZ 85298-9139, USA

Franklin, Robert (Business Person)
1600-1055 Dunsmuir St
Vancouver, BC V7X 1P1, CANADA

Franklin, Roshawn (Actor)
c/o Staff Member *Freeze Frame Entertainment*
5225 Wilshire Blvd Ste 403
Los Angeles, CA 90036-4348, USA

Franklin, Ryan (Athlete, Baseball Player)
1009 Muirfield Dr
Shawnee, OK 74801-0515, USA

Franklin, Shirley (Politician)
55 Trinity Ave SW
Atlanta, GA 30303-3520, USA

Franklin, Wayne (Athlete, Baseball Player)
15 S Mauldin Ave
North East, MD 21901-4023, USA

Franklin, William (Boxer, Misc)
920 La Sombra Dr
San Marcos, CA 92078-1320, USA

Franklin, Willie (Athlete, Football Player)
PO Box 62
Lake Dallas, TX 75065-0062, USA

Franklyn, Sabina (Actor)
4 Court Lodge 48 Sloane Square
London SW1W 8AT, UNITED KINGDOM (UK)

Frank-Martin, Tobi (Stylist)
4102 Old Topanga Canyon Rd
Calabasas, CA 91302-1860, USA

Franks, Daniel (Bubba) (Athlete, Football Player)
1 Cavil Way
De Pere, WI 54115, USA

Franks, Dennis (Athlete, Football Player)
4 Westmount Ct
Greensboro, NC 27410-2183, USA

Franks, Elvis (Athlete, Football Player)
2147 Rusk St
Beaumont, TX 77701-2525, USA

Franks, Frederick M Jr (General)
5016 Kensington High St
Naples, FL 34105-5636, USA

Franks, Gerold
1745 Camino Palmero St
Los Angeles, CA 90046-2945

Franks, Herman (Athlete, Baseball Player, Coach)
2745 Comanche Dr
Salt Lake City, UT 84108-2810, USA

Franks, Hermine (Baseball Player)
422 Pecor St
Oconto, WI 54153-1800, USA

Franks, Michael (Musician, Songwriter, Writer)
c/o Staff Member *Agency for the Performing Arts (APA-LA)*
405 S Beverly Dr Ste 500
Beverly Hills, CA 90212-4425, USA

Franks, Tommy Ray (General)
4 Star Ranch 15273 North 2280 Rd
Roosevelt, OK 73564, USA

Franks, Trent (Congressman, Politician)
2435 Rayburn Hob
Washington, DC 20515-4318, USA

Frankston, Robert M (Bob) (Designer)
15035 N 73rd St
Scottsdale, AZ 85260-2468, USA

Fransen, Libby (Stylist)
15121 Woodruff Rd
Wayzata, MN 55391-2433, USA

Fransioli, Thomas A (Artist)
55 Dodges Row
Wenham, MA 01984-1627, USA

Franti, Michael (Actor, Composer, Musician)
c/o Jamie Simon *PFA Media NYC*
285 W Broadway Rm 630
New York, NY 10013-0465, USA

Frantz, Adrienne (Actor)
c/o Marnie Sparer *Innovative Artists (LA)*
1505 10th St
Santa Monica, CA 90401-2805, USA

Frantz, Chris (Musician)
3 E 54th St # 1100
New York, NY 10022-3108, USA

Franz, Arthur (Art) (Athlete, Baseball Player)
PO Box 974
El Prado, NM 87529-0974, USA

Franz, Dennis (Actor)
c/o Alisa Adler *Paradigm (LA)*
360 N Crescent Dr
Beverly Hills, CA 90210-4874, USA

Franz, Frederick W (Religious Leader)
25 Columbia Hts
Brooklyn, NY 11201-1300, USA

Franz, Judy R (Physicist)
1 Physics Eclipse
College Park, MD 20740, USA

Franz, Mary (Stylist)
4349 Hillside Rd
Slinger, WI 53086-9798, USA

Franz, Nolan (Athlete, Football Player)
327 31st St
Gulfport, MS 39507-2341, USA

Franz, Rodney T (Rod) (Athlete, Football Player)
1448 Engberg Ct
Carmichael, CA 95608-5812, USA

Franz, Ron (Athlete, Basketball Player)
8590 Beaverwood Dr
Germantown, TN 38138-7715, USA

Franz, Todd (Athlete, Football Player)
16337 Old Ivy Cir
Edmond, OK 73013-3275, USA

Franzen, Johan (Athlete, Hockey Player)
22726 Summer Ln
Novi, MI 48374-3648, USA

Franzen, Jonathan (Writer)
19 Union Sq W
New York, NY 10003-3304, USA

Franzen, Ulrich J (Architect)
975 Park Ave
New York, NY 10028-0323, USA

Frappi, Luigi (Artist)
Via Del Cirone, 6
Bevagna I-06031, Italy

Frasca, Robert J (Architect)
320 SW Oak St Ste 500
Portland, OR 97204-2735, USA

Frascatore, John (Athlete, Baseball Player)
PO Box 1411
Brooksville, FL 34605-1411, USA

Frasconi, Antonio (Artist)
26 Dock Rd
Norwalk, CT 06854-4717, USA

Frase, Paul (Athlete, Football Player)
5150 Palm Valley Rd Ste 210
Ponte Vedra Beach, FL 32082-4631, USA

Fraser, Antonia (Writer)
Haymarket House 28/29 Haymarket
London SW1Y 4SP, UNITED KINGDOM (UK)

Fraser, Brad (Writer)
350 Dupont Ave
Toronto, ON M5R 1V9, CANADA

Fraser, Brendan (Actor)
c/o JoAnne Colonna *Brillstein Entertainment Partners*
9150 Wilshire Blvd Ste 350
Beverly Hills, CA 90212-3453, USA

Fraser, Brooke (Musician)
c/o Jonathan Adelman *Paradigm (NY)*
360 Park Ave S Fl 16
New York, NY 10010-1708, USA

Fraser, Curt (Athlete, Hockey Player)
2205 Whitney Pointe Dr
Chesterfield, MO 63005-4515, USA

Fraser, Dawn (Athlete, Swimmer)
87 Birchgrove Road
Balmain NSW, Australia

Fraser, Douglas (Misc)
8000 E Jefferson Ave
Detroit, MI 48214-3963, USA

Fraser, George MacDonald (Writer)
28/29 Haymarket
London SW1Y 4SP, UNITED KINGDOM (UK)

Fraser, Gretchen
5023 236th Pl SE
Woodinville, WA 98072-8610

Fraser, Hon
MalcolmThurulgoona
Redhill, AUSTRALIA Vic. 3937, AUSTRALIA

Fraser, Honor (Model)
c/o Staff Member *Fam*
boul. Vital Bouhot 30
Neuilly-sur-Seine,Paris 75008, FRANCE

Fraser, Hugh (Actor)
13 Shorts Gardens
London WC2H 9AT, UNITED KINGDOM (UK)

Fraser, Laura (Actor)
c/o Tammy Rosen *Sanders Armstrong Caserta*
425 N Robertson Blvd
West Hollywood, CA 90048-1735, USA

Fraser, Malcolm (Prime Minister)
Thurulgoona
Redhill, VIC 3937, AUSTRALIA

Fraser, Neale (Tennis Player)
21 Bolton Ave
Hampton, VIC 3188, AUSTRALIA

Fraser, Ware Dawn (Swimmer)
403 Darling St
Balmain, NSW 2041, AUSTRALIA

Fraser, Willie (Athlete, Baseball Player)
3 Turano
Laguna Niguel, CA 92677-8927, USA

Frashilla, Fran (Coach)
Athletic
Albuquerque, NM 87131-0001, USA

Frasor, Jason (Athlete, Baseball Player)
15043 Landings Ln
Oak Forest, IL 60452-6011, USA

Fratello, Michael R (Mike) (Athlete, Basketball Player, Coach, Sportscaster)
7642 Fisher Island Dr
Miami Beach, FL 33109-0783, USA

Fratianne, Linda S (Figure Skater)
15691 Borges Ct
Moorpark, CA 93021-3229, USA

Frattare, Lanny (Baseball Player, Sportscaster)
1009 Perry Hwy
Pittsburgh, PA 15237-2108, USA

Frauenfelder, Mark (Internet Star)
13547 Ventura Blvd # 91
Sherman Oaks, CA 91423-3825, USA

Fraumeni, Joseph F Jr (Inventor)
Cancer Etiology Division
Bethesda, MD 20892, USA

Frayn, Michael (Writer)
37A Goldhawk Road
London W12 8QQ, UNITED KINGDOM (UK)

Frazar, Harrison (Athlete, Golfer)
3208 Villanova St
Dallas, TX 75225-4839, USA

Frazer, Liz (Actor)
68 Old Brompton Road #200
London SW7 3LQ, UNITED KINGDOM (UK)

Frazier, Al (Athlete, Football Player)
17240 133rd Avve Apt 12A
Jamaica, NY 11434, USA

Frazier, Albert (Baseball Player)
5749 Copper Hill Ln E
Jacksonville, FL 32218-7311, USA

Frazier, Andre (Athlete, Football Player)
PO Box 40234
Cincinnati, OH 45240-0234, USA

Frazier, Charley (Athlete, Football Player)
4018 Brookston St
Houston, TX 77045-3412, USA

Frazier, Dallas (Musician, Songwriter, Writer)
RR 5 Box 133 Longhollow Pike
Gallatin, TN 37066, USA

Frazier, George (Athlete, Baseball Player)
6886 S Evanston Ave
Tulsa, OK 74136-4554, USA

Frazier, Guy (Athlete, Football Player)
3944 Dickson Ave
Cincinnati, OH 45229-1306, USA

Frazier, Herman (Athlete, Track Athlete)
1024 E Frye Rd Unit 1011
Phoenix, AZ 85048-1988, USA

Frazier, Ian (Writer)
19 Union Sq W
New York, NY 10003-3304, USA

Frazier, Joe (Athlete, Baseball Player, Coach)
519 Fairway Dr
Broken Arrow, OK 74011-8407, USA

Frazier, Kevin (Actor, Television Host)
c/o Staff Member *Entertainment Tonight (ET)*
4024 Radford Ave
Studio City, CA 91604-2101, USA

Frazier, Leslie (Athlete, Football Player)
613 Society Hill Blvd
Cherry Hill, NJ 08003-2430, USA

Frazier, Lisa (Musician)
c/o Staff Member *Diva Central Inc*
7510 W Sunset Blvd Ste 1445
Los Angeles, CA 90046-3408, USA

Frazier, Lou (Athlete, Baseball Player)
1371 N Concord Ave
Chandler, AZ 85225-8624, USA

Frazier, Mavis (Boxer)
2917 N Broad St
Philadelphia, PA 19132-2402, USA

Frazier, Owsley B (Business Person)
850 Dixie Hwy
Louisville, KY 40210-1038, USA

Frazier, Sheila (Actor)
c/o Daniel Hoff *Daniel Hoff Agency*
5455 Wilshire Blvd Ste 1100
Los Angeles, CA 90036-4277, USA

Frazier, Walt (Clyde) (Athlete, Basketball Player)
381 Malcolm X Blvd Ph A
New York, NY 10027-2173, USA

Frazier, Wayne (Athlete, Football Player)
PO Box 413
Brewton, AL 36427-0413, USA

Frazier, Will (Athlete, Basketball Player)
PO Box 380772
Duncanville, TX 75138-0772, USA

Frazier, Willie (Athlete, Football Player)
6203 Bankside Dr
Houston, TX 77096-5608, USA

Frears, Stephen A (Director)
93 Talbot Road
London W2, UNITED KINGDOM (UK)

Freberg, Stanley V (Stan) (Actor, Comedian)
PO Box 3107
Wallingford, CT 06494-3107, USA

Frechette, Peter (Actor)
c/o Staff Member *Don Buchwald & Associates Inc (LA)*
6500 Wilshire Blvd Ste 2200
Los Angeles, CA 90048-4942, USA

Frederic, Dreux (Lil Fizz) (Musician)
c/o Douglas Mark *Mark Music and Media Law*
Prefers to be contacted via telephone
Los Angeles, CA 90069, USA

Frederick, Andrew B (Athlete, Football Player)
7247 Alexander Dr
Dallas, TX 75214-3216, USA

Frederick, Justin (Stylist)
57 Tiffany Ln
Willingboro, NJ 08046-3819, USA

Frederick, Kevin (Athlete, Baseball Player)
20512 N Clarice Ave
Lincolnshire, IL 60069-9618, USA

Fredericks, Frank (Frankie) (Athlete, Track Athlete)
4497 Wimbledon Dr
Provo, UT 84604-5394, USA

Fredericks, Fred (Cartoonist)
PO Box 475
Eastham, MA 02642-0475, USA

Frederickson, Ivan C (Tucker) (Athlete, Football Player)
12414 Indian Rd
North Palm Beach, FL 33408-2539, USA

Frederickson, Rob (Athlete, Football Player)
8312 N 50th St
Paradise Vly, AZ 85253-2005, USA

Frederickson, Scott (Athlete, Baseball Player)
20703 Turning Leaf Lake Ct
Cypress, TX 77433-4612, USA

Fredrickson, George M (Historian)
741 Esplanada Way
Palo Alto, CA 94305-1013, USA

Fredriksson, Gert (Athlete)
Bruunsgat 13
Nykoping 61122, SWEDEN

Fredriksson, Marie (Musician, Songwriter, Writer)
Lilla Nygatan 19
Stockholm 11128, SWEDEN

Free (Actor, Musician)
c/o Damu Bobb *Identity Talent Agency (ID)*
9107 Wilshire Blvd Ste 500
Beverly Hills, CA 90210-5526, USA

Free, Helen M (Inventor)
3752 E Jackson Blvd
Elkhart, IN 46516-5205, USA

Free, Scott (Stylist)
c/o Staff Member *Rex Agency, The*
6311 Romaine St
Los Angeles, CA 90038-2617, USA

Free, World B (Athlete, Basketball Player, Coach)
1131 E County Line Rd
Lakewood, NJ 08701-2115, USA

Freebo
740 N Hayworth Ave
Los Angeles, CA 90046-7142

Freed, Curt R (Biologist)
Health Science Center 4200 E 9th Ave
Denver, CO 80220, USA

Freed, Jack H (Misc)
108 Homestead Cir
Ithaca, NY 14850-6214, USA

Freed, Jill (Stylist)
2112 Iris Ct
Santa Rosa, CA 95404-3224, USA

Freedman, Alix M (Journalist)
200 Liberty St
New York, NY 10281-1003, USA

Freedman, David A (Mathematician)
901 Alvarado Rd
Berkeley, CA 94705-1551, USA

Freedman, Gerald A (Director, Opera Singer)
Lincoln Center Plaza
New York, NY 10023, USA

Freedman, James O (Educator)
President's Office
Hanover, NH 3755, USA

Freedman, Ronald (Activist)
1200 Earhart Rd # 228
Ann Arbor, MI 48105-2768, USA

Freedman, Wendy L (Astronomer)
813 Santa Barbara St
Pasadena, CA 91101-1232, USA

Freeh, LouisFBI
& 9th Pennsylvania Ave NW
Washington, DC 20035

Freehan, William A (Bill) (Athlete, Baseball Player)
6999 Indian Garden Rd
Petoskey, MI 49770-8708, USA

Freel, Ryan (Athlete, Baseball Player)
612 Seabrook Cove Rd
Jacksonville, FL 32211-7184, USA

Freelon, Nnenna (Musician)
173 Brighton Ave
Boston, MA 02134-2003, USA

Freelon, Solomon (Athlete, Football Player)
7214 Towerview Ln
Missouri City, TX 77489-2434, USA

Freeman, Antonio (Athlete, Football Player)
9809 Linden Hill Rd
Owings Mills, MD 21117-6151, USA

Freeman, Arturo (Athlete, Football Player)
1435 Marseille Ct Apt 5402
Weston, FL 33326-4012, USA

Freeman, Bernard (Bun B) (Musician)
c/o Marty Diamond *Paradigm (NY)*
360 Park Ave S Fl 16
New York, NY 10010-1708, USA

Freeman, Bobby (Musician)
PO Box 770850
Orlando, FL 32877-0850, USA

Freeman, Cassidy (Actor)
c/o Janice Lee *MLC PR*
7080 Hollywood Blvd Ste 903
Los Angeles, CA 90028-6936, USA

Freeman, Cathy (Athlete, Track Athlete)
PO Box 700
South Melbourne, VIC 3205, AUSTRALIA

Freeman, Charles W Jr (Diplomat)
1800 K St NW Ste 1010
Washington, DC 20006-2234, USA

Freeman, Crispin (Actor, Writer)
c/o Staff Member *Arlene Thornton & Associates*
12711 Ventura Blvd Ste 490
Studio City, CA 91604-2477, USA

Freeman, Gary (Athlete, Basketball Player)
PO Box 1399
Albany, OR 97321-0548, USA

Freeman, Isaac (Musician)
1025 17th Ave S # 200
Nashville, TN 37212-2211, USA

Freeman, Issac (Fatman Scoop) (Musician)
c/o Staff Member *PhreQuency Entertainment*
1830 South Rd Ste 102 PMB 178
Wappingers Falls, NY 12590-1372, USA

Freeman, J E (Actor)
232 N Canon Dr
Beverly Hills, CA 90210-5302, USA

Freeman, Jennifer Nicole (Actor)
c/o Nils Larsen *Elements Entertainment*
312 W 5th St Apt 815
Los Angeles, CA 90013-1750, USA

Freeman, Jimmy (Athlete, Baseball Player)
4716 E 106th St
Tulsa, OK 74137-6805, USA

Freeman, K Todd (Actor)
c/o Staff Member *Steppenwolf Theatre Co*
758 W North Ave Fl 4
Chicago, IL 60610-1047, USA

Freeman, La Vel (Athlete, Baseball Player)
8941 Laguna Place Way
Elk Grove, CA 95758-5351, USA

Freeman, Martin (Actor)
c/o Jo Yao *United Talent Agency (UTA)*
9560 Wilshire Blvd Fl 5
Beverly Hills, CA 90212-2400, USA

Freeman, Marvin (Athlete, Baseball Player)
20135 Mohawk Trl
Olympia Fields, IL 60461-1135, USA

Freeman, Meg (Stylist)
c/o Staff Member *Jam Arts, Inc*
154 W 57th St
New York, NY 10019-3321, USA

Freeman, Michael WIlliam (Actor)
c/o Scott Zimmerman *Evolution Entertainment (LA)*
901 N Highland Ave
Los Angeles, CA 90038-2412, USA

Freeman, Mike (Athlete, Football Player)
6020 Danny Kaye Dr Apt 1502
San Antonio, TX 78240-1946, USA

Freeman, Mona (Actor)
608 N Alpine Dr
Beverly Hills, CA 90210-3304, USA

Freeman, Morgan (Actor)
c/o Stan Rosenfield *Stan Rosenfield & Associates*
2029 Century Park E Ste 1190
Los Angeles, CA 90067-2931, USA

Freeman, Phil (Athlete, Football Player)
1222 S Stanley Ave
Los Angeles, CA 90019-6617, USA

Freeman, Reggie (Athlete, Football Player)
PO Box 1694
Clewiston, FL 33440-1694, USA

Freeman, Robin (Athlete, Golfer)
115 Chelsea Cir
Palm Desert, CA 92260-4688, USA

Freeman, Rod (Athlete, Basketball Player)
6308 Murray Ln
Brentwood, TN 37027-6210, USA

Freeman, Russ (Athlete, Football Player)
4090 Summit Crossing Dr
Decatur, GA 30034-3542, USA

Freeman, Russell (Writer)
280 Riverside Dr
New York, NY 10025-9010, USA

Freeman, Sandi (Correspondent)
820 1st St NE
Washington, DC 20002-4243, USA

Freeman, Steve (Athlete, Football Player)
PO Box 5308
Mississippi State, MS 39762-5308, USA

Freeman, Yvette (Actor, Musician)
6500 Wilshire Blvd # 550
Los Angeles, CA 90048-4920, USA

Freeman Jr, Al (Actor)
1180 S Beverly Dr Ste 301
Los Angeles, CA 90035-1154, USA

Freeney, Dwight (Athlete, Football Player)
11021 Hintocks Cir
Carmel, IN 46032, USA

Freer, Mark (Athlete, Hockey Player)
823 Linden Rd
Hershey, PA 17033-1735, USA

Freese, Gene (Athlete, Baseball Player)
6504 Glendale St
Metairie, LA 70003-3011, USA

Freese, George (Athlete, Baseball Player)
3341 SW Marigold St
Portland, OR 97219-5309, USA

Freese, Louis (Musician)
c/o Jack Iannaci *Brass Artists & Associates*
9025 Wilshire Blvd Ste 400
Beverly Hills, CA 90211-1828, USA

Fregosi, Jim (Athlete, Baseball Player, Coach)
1092 Copeland Ct
Tarpon Springs, FL 34688-7622, USA

Fregoso, Ramon (Actor)
c/o Staff Member *TV Azteca*
Periferico Sur 4121 Colonia Fuentes del Pedregal
DF CP 14141, Mexico

Frehley, Ace (Musician)
c/o Staff Member *Creative Artists Agency (CAA-LA)*
2000 Avenue of the Stars Ste 100
Los Angeles, CA 90067-4705, USA

Frei, Emil III (Misc)
44 Binney St
Boston, MA 02115-6013, USA

Frei Ruiz-Tagle, Eduardo (President)
Palacio de la Monedo
Santiago, CHILE

Freiberger, Marcus (Athlete, Basketball Player)
985 US Highway 64 W
Mocksville, NC 27028-8427, USA

Freidheim, Cyrus (Business Person)
250 E 5th St
Cincinnati, OH 45202-4119, USA

Freigang, Stephan
Strasse der Jugend 58
Cottbus, GERMANY D-03050

Freilicher, Jane (Artist)
210 11th Ave Rm 801
New York, NY 10001-1224, USA

Freire, Nelson (Musician)
165 W 57th St
New York, NY 10019-2201, USA

Freireich, Emil J (Doctor)
1515 Holcombe Blvd
Houston, TX 77030-4000, USA

Freis, Edward DJ (Doctor)
4515 Willard Ave
Chevy Chase, MD 20815-3622, USA

Freisleben, Dave (Athlete, Baseball Player)
1326 Diamante Dr
Pasadena, TX 77504-1479, USA

Freitas, Jesse (Athlete, Football Player)
1863 Heather Ln
Petaluma, CA 94954-8592, USA

Freitas, Rocky (Athlete, Football Player)
2667 E Manoa Rd
Honolulu, HI 96822-1817, USA

Freitas - CA, Camille (Stylist)
7929 Selma # 7
West Hollywood, CA 90046, USA

Freitas - TX, Camille (Stylist)
12124 Dixfield Dr
Dallas, TX 75218-1224, USA

French, Dawn (Actor, Comedian)
34-43 Russell St
London WC2B 5HA, UNITED KINGDOM (UK)

French, Ernest (Athlete, Football Player)
1004 Moran St
Bay Minette, AL 36507-2443, USA

French, Florence (Stylist)
6414 Pontiac Dr
Indian Head Park, IL 60525-4347, USA

French, Heather (Beauty Pageant Winner)
567 Circle Dr
Maysville, KY 41056-9124, USA

French, Jane (Musician)
c/o Staff Member *Pixie Publishing*
9611 Ross Ave
Montgomery, OH 45242-7123

French, Jim (Athlete, Baseball Player)
PO Box 6452
Chicago, IL 60680-6452, USA

French, Julie (Stylist)
c/o Staff Member *Industry Representation*
448 E Riverdale Ave
Orange, CA 92865-1302, USA

French, Kate (Actor)
c/o Brooklyn Weaver *Energy Entertainment*
999 N Doheny Dr Apt 711
Los Angeles, CA 90069-3151, USA

French, Leigh (Actor)
1850 N Vista St
Los Angeles, CA 90046-2237, USA

French, Marilyn (Writer)
65 Bleecker St # 1200
New York, NY 10012-2420, USA

French, Niki (Musician)
PO Box 89
Edam, ZJ 1135, NETHERLANDS

French, Paige (Actor)
232 N Canon Dr
Beverly Hills, CA 90210-5302, USA

French, Rufus (Athlete, Football Player)
PO Box 10628
Green Bay, WI 54307-0628, USA

French, Sarah (Model, Television Host)
221 Trumbull St
Hartford, CT 06103-1500, USA

French, Susan
110 E 9th St Ste C1005
Los Angeles, CA 90079-6112

Freni, Mirelia (Opera Singer)
31 Sinclair Road
London W14 0NS, UNITED KINGDOM (UK)

Freni, Mirella (Opera Singer)
825 8th Ave
New York, NY 10019-7416, USA

Frenkiel, Richard H (Engineer, Inventor)
WINLAB PO Box 909
Piscataway, NJ 8855, USA

Frentzen, Heinz-Harald (Race Car Driver)
Silverstone Circuit
Northamptonshire NN12 8TN, UNITED KINGDOM (UK)

Freotte, Gus (Athlete, Football Player)
10040 Litzsinger Rd
Saint Louis, MO 63124-1132, USA

Freotte, Mitch (Athlete, Football Player)
445 Reynolds Ave
Kittanning, PA 16201-2713, USA

Frerotte, Gus (Athlete, Football Player)
10040 Litzsinger Rd
Saint Louis, MO 63124-1132, USA

Fresco, Paolo (Business Person)
Corso Marconi # 10/20
New York, NY 10125-0001, ITALY

Fresh, Doug E (Musician)
c/o Reg Reg Askew *Fly Guy Management*
1 W 34th St # 201
New York, NY 10001-3001, USA

Fresh, Mannie (Musician, Producer)
c/o Staff Member *Universal Music Group (UMG - LA)*
2220 Colorado Ave
Santa Monica, CA 90404-3506, USA

Freud, Bella (Designer, Fashion Designer)
48 Rawstorne St
London EC1V 7ND, UNITED KINGDOM (UK)

Freudenthal, Thor (Director)
c/o Peter McHugh *The Gotham Group Inc*
9255 W Sunset Blvd Ste 515
Los Angeles, CA 90069-3308, USA

Freund, Lambert B (Engineer)
3 Palisade Ln
Barrington, RI 02806-3921, USA

Freundlich, Bart (Director, Producer, Writer)
c/o Bart Walker *Cinetic Management*
555 W 25th St Fl 4
New York, NY 10001-5542, USA

Frewer, Matt (Actor)
c/o Carol Gettko *Warren Cowan & Associates PR*
8899 Beverly Blvd Ste 918
Los Angeles, CA 90048-2427, USA

Frey, Christopher
The Toft E. Dean nr. Chichester
Sussex, ENGLAND

Frey, Donald N (Business Person, Engineer)
2758 Sheridan Rd
Evanston, IL 60201-1728, USA

Frey, Glenn (Actor, Musician, Songwriter, Writer)
5020 Brent Knoll Ln
Suwanee, GA 30024-1376, USA

Frey, James (Writer)
c/o Richard Green *Creative Artists Agency (CAA-LA)*
2000 Avenue of the Stars Ste 100
Los Angeles, CA 90067-4705, USA

Frey, James G (Jim) (Athlete, Baseball Player, Coach)
12101 Tullamore Ct Unit 406
Lutherville Timonium, MD 21093-8148, USA

Frey, Lonny (Athlete, Baseball Player)
995 W Woodlawn Dr
Hayden, ID 83835-8810, USA

Frey, Richard (Athlete, Football Player)
11902 Maureens Way
Pinehurst, TX 77362-4017, USA

Frey, Sami
21 Place Des Vosges
Paris, FRANCE F-75003

Frey, Steve (Athlete, Baseball Player)
1414 2nd Street Pike
Southampton, PA 18966-3931, USA

Freyer, Marina (Stylist)
30 Northway
Old Greenwich, CT 06870-2430, USA

Freyndlikh, Alisa B (Actor)
Rubinstein Str 11 #7
Saint Petersburg 191002, RUSSIA

Freytag, Arny (Photographer)
22735 MacFarlane Dr
Woodland Hills, CA 91364-1322, USA

Friberg, Arnold (Artist)
5206 Pinemont Dr
Salt Lake City, UT 84123-4607, USA

Frick, Gottlob (Opera Singer)
Eichelberg-Haus Waldfrieden
Olbronn-Durrn 75248, GERMANY

Frick, Stephen N (Astronaut)
27998 Mercurio Rd
Carmel, CA 93923-8429, USA

Fricke, Janie (Musician)
PO Box 798
Lancaster, TX 75146-0798, USA

Fricker, Brenda (Actor)
c/o Staff Member *IFA Talent Agency*
8730 W Sunset Blvd Ste 490
Los Angeles, CA 90069-2248, USA

Frickle, Ben (Athlete, Football Player)
1323 Alta Vista Ave
Austin, TX 78704-2514, USA

Frickman, Andy (Director)
c/o Staff Member *WmE2 (Endeavor-LA)*
9601 Wilshire Blvd Fl 3
Beverly Hills, CA 90210-5219, USA

Frid, David (Stylist)
c/o Staff Member *Ford Models (Chicago)*
311 W Superior St
Chicago, IL 60654-3548, USA

Friday, Tim (Athlete, Hockey Player)
81 Fisher Rd
Southborough, MA 01772-1004, USA

Friday Jr, Elbert W (Government Official)
1125 East-West Hwy
Silver Spring, MD 20910, USA

Fridell, Squire
15250 Ventura Blvd Ste 200
Sherman Oaks, CA 91403-3215

Fridgen, Dan (Athlete, Hockey Player)
1524 Bouton Rd
Troy, NY 12180-3630, USA

Fridman, Mikhail (Business Person)
1 Arbat St
Moscow 119019, Russia

Fridovich, Irwin (Misc)
3517 Courtland Dr
Durham, NC 27707-5134, USA

Fridriksson, Fridrik T (Director)
Bjarkgata 8
Reykjavik 101, ICELAND

Friebe, Anika
111 E 22nd St Rm 200
New York, NY 10010-5414

Fried, Charles (Educator, Government Official)
Law School
Cambridge, MA 2138, USA

Friede, Mike (Athlete, Football Player)
6943 County Road 56
Johnstown, CO 80534-8237, USA

Friedel, Jacques (Physicist)
2 Rue Jean-Francois Gerbillon
Paris 75006, FRANCE

Friedgen, Ralph (Coach, Football Coach)
Athletic
College Park, MD 20742-0001, USA

Friedlander, Judah (Comedian, Writer)
c/o Josh Lieberman *3 Arts Entertainment Inc*
9460 Wilshire Blvd Fl 7
Beverly Hills, CA 90212-2713, USA

Friedlander, Lee (Artist, Photographer)
44 S Mountain Rd
New City, NY 10956-2315, USA

Friedle, Will (Actor)
c/o Steven Muller *Innovative Artists (LA)*
1505 10th St
Santa Monica, CA 90401-2805, USA

Friedman, Daniel M (Judge)
717 Madison Pl NW
Washington, DC 20439-0001, USA

Friedman, Doug (Athlete, Hockey Player)
36 Surf Rd
Cape Elizabeth, ME 04107-1519, USA

Friedman, Emanuel A (Educator)
330 Brookline Ave
Boston, MA 02215-5400, USA

Friedman, Jeffrey (Misc)
Hughes Medical Institute
New York, NY 10021, USA

Friedman, Jerome I (Nobel Prize Laureate)
75 Greenough St
Brookline, MA 02445-6152, USA

Friedman, Kinky (Politician)
906 1/2 Congress Ave
Austin, TX 78701-2422

Friedman, Lawrence M (Educator, Lawyer)
724 Frenchmans Rd
Palo Alto, CA 94305-1005, USA

Friedman, Lennie (Athlete, Football Player)
1000 Cross Clay Ct
Raleigh, NC 27614-8448, USA

Friedman, Peter (Actor, Musician)
233 Park Ave S # 1000
New York, NY 10003-1606, USA

Friedman, Philip (Writer)
1745 Broadway # B1
New York, NY 10019-4368, USA

Friedman, Sonya
208 Harristown Rd
Glen Rock, NJ 07452-3308

Friedman, Stephen (Financier, Government Official)
1600 Pennsylvania Ave NW
Washington, DC 20500-0005, USA

Friedman, Tom (Artist)
802 De Mun Ave
Clayton, MO 63105-3197, USA

Friedman, Yona (Architect)
33 Blvd Garibaldi
Paris 75015, FRANCE

Friedmann, Phil (Musician)
156 W 56th St # 500
New York, NY 10019-3800, USA

Friel, Anna (Actor)
c/o Abi Harris *Ken McReddie Ltd*
11 Connaught Pl
London W2 2ET, UNITED KINGDOM

Friel, Brian (Writer)
Drumaweir House
Greencastle, County Donegal, IRELAND

Friels, Colin (Actor)
129 Brooke St Woollomooloo
Sydney, NSW 2011, AUSTRALIA

Friend, Lionel (Conductor)
136 Rosendale Road
London SE21 8LG, UNITED KINGDOM (UK)

Friend, Patricia A (Misc)
1275 K St NW # 5
Washington, DC 20005-4083, USA

Friend, Richard H (Misc)
Chemistry Dept
Cambridge, UNITED KINGDOM (UK)

Friend, Robert B (Bob) (Athlete, Baseball Player)
4 Salem Cir
Pittsburgh, PA 15238-2525, USA

Friend, Rupert (Actor)
c/o Boomer Malkin *WmE2 (Endeavor-LA)*
9601 Wilshire Blvd Fl 3
Beverly Hills, CA 90210-5219, USA

Frier, Mike (Athlete, Football Player)
180 Jackson St NE Apt 1615
Atlanta, GA 30312-1358, USA

Fries, Chuck
6922 Hollywood Blvd
Los Angeles, CA 90028-6117

Fries, Donald B (Publisher)
Time-Life Building
New York, NY 10020, USA

Friesen, David (Musician)
11761 E Speedway Blvd
Tucson, AZ 85748-2017, USA

Friesen, Don (Musician)
c/o Staff Member *Paradigm (Monterey)*
404 W Franklin St
Monterey, CA 93940-2303, USA

Friesen, Gil
770 N Bonhill Rd
Los Angeles, CA 90049-2304

Friesen, Jeff (Athlete, Hockey Player)
47 Christopher St
Ladera Ranch, CA 92694-1527, USA

Friesinger, Anni (Speed Skater)
Geilbelweg 24
Fellbach 70736, GERMANY

Friest, Ron (Athlete, Hockey Player)
456 St John St
Windsor, ON N8S 3T7, Canada

Friesz, John (Athlete, Football Player)
1454 E West Pebblestone Ct
Hayden, ID 83835-7999, USA

Frig, Len (Athlete, Hockey Player)
7556 Wynford St
Salt Lake City, UT 84121-5449, USA

Frigid Pink
32885 Northampton Dr
Warren, MI 48093-6164

Frimout, Dirk D (Astronaut)
c/o Staff Member *NASA*
2101 Nasa Pkwy Spc Center
Houston, TX 77058-3696, USA

Frink, Patrick (Athlete, Basketball Player)
13325 S Coleman Rd
Tucson, AZ 85735-2143, USA

Frisbee, Rob (Athlete)
c/o Jerry Shandrew *Shandrew Public Relations*
1050 S Stanley Ave
Los Angeles, CA 90019-6634, USA

Frischman, Daniel
145 S Fairfax Ave Ste 310
Los Angeles, CA 90036-2176

Frischmann, Justine (Musician)
Ransomes Dock 357-37 Parkgate Road
London SW11 4NP, UNITED KINGDOM (UK)

Frisell, William R (Bill) (Musician)
75 Rockefeller Plz
New York, NY 10019-6908, USA

Frishberg, David L (Composer, Musician)
c/o Staff Member *Irvin Arthur Assoc*
1441 3rd Ave Apt 12C
New York, NY 10028-1976, USA

Fritsch, Ted Jr (Athlete, Football Player)
5014 Odins Way
Marietta, GA 30068-1660, USA

Fritsche, Dan (Athlete, Hockey Player)
116 Olentangy Pt
Columbus, OH 43202-1905, USA

Fritsche, Jim (Athlete, Basketball Player)
470 Emerson Ave W
Saint Paul, MN 55118-2034, USA

Fritz, Harold A (War Hero)
1017 W Scottwood Dr
Peoria, IL 61615-1056, USA

Fritz, Larry (Athlete, Baseball Player)
2632 Schrage Ave
Whiting, IN 46394-2117, USA

Fritz, Nikki (Actor)
PO Box 57764
Sherman Oaks, CA 91413-2764, USA

Frizzell, David (Musician)
4694 E Robertson Rd
Cross Plains, TN 37049-4827, USA

Frizzell, John (Composer)
8730 W Sunset Blvd Ste 300
Los Angeles, CA 90069-2276, USA

Frizzelle, William J (Athlete, Football Player)
8001 Tylerton Dr
Raleigh, NC 27613-1557, USA

Frobel, Doug (Athlete, Baseball Player)
37 Willow Crossing Rd
Greensburg, PA 15601-9125, USA

Froboess, Cornelia (Musician)
Kleinholzhausen
Raubling, GERMANY D-83064

Froemming, Bruce (Athlete, Baseball Player)
702 W Haddonstone Pl
Thiensville, WI 53092-5966, USA

Froemming, Bruce N (Baseball Player)
702 W Haddonstone Pl
Thiensville, WI 53092-5966, USA

Froese, Bob (Athlete, Hockey Player)
11701 Clarence Center Rd
Akron, NY 14001-9747, USA

Frohnmayer, David B (Dave) (Educator)
President's Office
Eugene, OR 97403, USA

Frohnmayer, John E (Government Official)
38511 Kelly Rd
Jefferson, OR 97352-9304, USA

Frohwirth, Todd (Athlete, Baseball Player)
S66W24360 Skyline Ave
Waukesha, WI 53189-9254, USA

Froines, John (Activist, Educator)
Public Health School
Los Angeles, CA 90024, USA

Frolov, Alexander (Athlete, Hockey Player)
1467 3rd St
Manhattan Beach, CA 90266-6335, USA

Frolov, Diane (Actor)
c/o Richard Weitz *WmE2 (Endeavor-LA)*
9601 Wilshire Blvd Fl 3
Beverly Hills, CA 90210-5219, USA

Fromherz, Peter (Physicist)
Biophysics Dept
Martinsried, GERMANY

Fromm, Fritz (Misc)
An der Bismarckschule 64
Hannover 30173, GERMANY

Frommelt, Paul (Skier)
Vaduz, LIECHTENSTEIN

Fron, Kenneth (Designer)
333 W North Ave Ste 133
Chicago, IL 60610-1293, USA

Frongillo, John (Athlete, Football Player)
10230 Elmhurst Dr NW
Albuquerque, NM 87114-4617, USA

Froning-O'Meara, Mary (Baseball Player)
417 Bay Hill Dr
Madison, WI 53717-2650, USA

Fronius, Hans (Artist)
Guggenberggasse 18
Perchtoldadorf bel Vienna 2380, AUSTRIA

Frontiere, Dominic
280 S Beverly Dr Ste 411
Beverly Hills, CA 90212-3904

Froom, Mitchell (Misc)
3055 Overland Ave Ste 200
Los Angeles, CA 90034-3431, USA

Frosch, Robert A (Government Official)
18 Heritage Hills Dr PMB A
Somers, NY 10589-3184, USA

Frost, Craig (Misc)
PO Box 770850
Orlando, FL 32877-0850, USA

Frost, Dave (Athlete, Baseball Player)
2206 Ocana Ave
Long Beach, CA 90815-2125, USA

Frost, David (Athlete, Golfer)
4245 N Central Expy Ste 350
Dallas, TX 75205-4570, USA

Frost, David P (Actor, Entertainer, Producer, Writer)
4245 N Central Expy Ste 350
Dallas, TX 75205-4570, USA

Frost, Jo (Actor, Reality TV Star)
3800 Barham Blvd, #210
Los Angeles CA, 90068

Frost, Ken (Athlete, Football Player)
22842 Stinnett Hollow Rd
Athens, AL 35614-3516, USA

Frost, Lindsay (Actor)
c/o Staff Member *Allman/Rea Management*
9255 W Sunset Blvd Ste 600
West Hollywood, CA 90069-3306, USA

Frost, Mark (Writer)
PO Box 1723
North Hollywood, CA 91614-0723, USA

Frost, Nick (Actor)
c/o Tom Drumm *The Safran Company*
8748 Holloway Dr
West Hollywood, CA 90069-2327, USA

Frost, Sadie (Actor)
46 Albermarle St
London W1X 4PP, UNITED KINGDOM (UK)

Frost, Scott (Athlete, Football Player)
99 Thomas Lk
Ashland, NE 68003-9400, USA

Frost, Sir David
BBC Centre Wood Lane
London, ENGLAND W12 7RJ

Froud, Brian (Artist)
c/o Robert Gould *IMAGINOSIS*
2615 Laurel Hill Dr
Eugene, OR 97403-3244, USA

Froud, Wendy (Artist)
c/o Robert Gould *IMAGINOSIS*
2615 Laurel Hill Dr
Eugene, OR 97403-3244, USA

Fruedek, Jacques (Physicist)
2 Rue Jean-Francois Gerbillon
Paris 70006, FRANCE

Fruh, Eugen (Artist)
Romergasse 9
Zurich 8001, SWITZERLAND

Fruhbeck de Burgos, Rafael (Conductor)
Avenida dek Mediterraneo 21
Madrid 28007, SPAIN

Fruhwirth, Amy (Athlete, Golfer)
26431 N 44th Way
Phoenix, AZ 85050-8579, USA

Frusciante, John (Musician)
8942 Wilshire Blvd
Everett, WA 98208, USA

Frutig, Ed (Athlete, Football Player)
9025 Somerset Bay Ln Apt 202
Vero Beach, FL 32963-4015, USA

Fruton, Joseph S (Misc)
123 York St
New Haven, CT 06511-5655, USA

Fry, Arthur L (Inventor)
3M Center Bldg 230-2S
Saint Paul, MN 55144-1001, USA

Fry, Jay (Athlete, Football Player)
PO Box 53
College Corner, OH 45003-0053, USA

Fry, Jerry (Athlete, Baseball Player)
3300 Stanton St
Springfield, IL 62703-4830, USA

Fry, Jordan (Actor)
c/o Carlyne Grager *Dramatic Artists Agency*
103 W Alameda Ave Ste 139
Burbank, CA 91502-2253, USA

Fry, Michael (Cartoonist)
200 Madison Ave
New York, NY 10016-3903, USA

Fry, Robert (Athlete, Football Player)
1604 Bexley Dr
Wilmington, NC 28412-2049, USA

Fry, Scott A (Admiral)
Director Joint Staff Operations Pentagon
Washington, DC 20318-0001, USA

Fry, Stephen J (Actor, Comedian, Writer)
c/o Christian Hodell *Hamilton Hodell Ltd*
66-68 Margaret St Fl 5
London W1W 8SR, UK

Fry, Thornton C (Mathematician)
500 Mohawk Dr
Boulder, CO 80303-3737, USA

Fryar, Irving D (Athlete, Football Player, Sportscaster)
51 Applegate Rd
Jobstown, NJ 08041-2202, USA

Fryce, Trevor (Athlete, Football Player)
20293 E Lake Cir
Centennial, CO 80016-1282, USA

Frydman, Romy (Stylist)
c/o Staff Member *Sarah Laird Inc*
12 Charles Ln
New York, NY 10014-2526, USA

Frye, Jeff (Athlete, Baseball Player)
6833 Lahontan Dr
Fort Worth, TX 76132-5457, USA

Frye, Meno
2713 N Keystone St
Burbank, CA 91504-1602

Frye, Shawn
2713 N Keystone St
Burbank, CA 91504-1602

Frye, Soleil Moon (Actor)
219 N Larchmont Blvd
Los Angeles, CA 90004-3706, USA

Fryer, Bernie (Athlete, Basketball Player)
PO Box 2052
Sequim, WA 98382-4335, USA

Fry-Irvin, Shirley (Tennis Player)
1970 Asylum Ave
West Hartford, CT 06117-3007, USA

Fryling, Victor J (Business Person)
330 Town Center Dr
Dearborn, MI 48126-2738, USA

Fryman, D Travis (Athlete, Baseball Player)
2600 Highway 196
Molino, FL 32577-9502, USA

Fryman, Woodrow T (Woodie) (Athlete, Baseball Player)
RR 1 Box 21
Ewing, KY 41039, USA

Ftorek, Robert B (Robbie) (Athlete, Coach, Hockey Player)
79 Sunset Point Rd
Wolfeboro, NH 03894-4907, USA

Fu, Mingxia (Swimmer)
9 Tiyuguan Road
Bejing, CHINA

Fu Manchu (Music Group, Musician)
c/o Staff Member *Agency for the Performing Arts (APA-LA)*
405 S Beverly Dr Ste 500
Beverly Hills, CA 90212-4425, USA

Fucarino, Frank (Athlete, Basketball Player)
21 Heathcote Ct
Shirley, NY 11967-4423, USA

Fuchs, Joseph L (Publisher)
350 Madison Ave
New York, NY 10017-3700, USA

Fuchs, Leo
609 N Kilkea Dr
Los Angeles, CA 90048-2213

Fuchs, Michael J (Television Host)
1100 Ave Of Americans
New York, NY 10036, USA

Fuchs, Victor R (Economist)
796 Cedro Way
Stanford, CA 94305-1032, USA

Fuchsberger, Joachim (Actor)
Hubertusstr 62
Grunwald 82031, GERMANY

Fudge, Alan (Actor)
c/o Caron Feldman *Feldman Management*
21781 Ventura Blvd
Woodland Hills, CA 91364-1835, USA

Fuente, David I (Business Person)
2200 Germantown Rd
Delray Beach, FL 33445-8223, USA

Fuente, Luis (Dancer)
98 Rue Lepic
Paris 75018, FRANCE

Fuentealba, Victor W (Misc)
4501 Arabia Ave
Baltimore, MD 21214-3306, USA

Fuentes, Alison (Stylist)
c/o Staff Member *Directions USA*
3717 W Market St Ste C
Greensboro, NC 27403-1155, USA

Fuentes, Brian (Athlete, Baseball Player)
1342 El Portal Dr
Merced, CA 95340-0774, USA

Fuentes, Carlos (Writer)
Latin American Studies Dept
Cambridge, MA 2138, USA

Fuentes, Daisy (Entertainer, Model)
c/o Ray McKigney *Shelter Entertainment*
9454 Wilshire Blvd Ste 715
Beverly Hills, CA 90212-2925, USA

Fuentes, Julio M (Judge)
50 Walnut St
Newark, NJ 07102-3551, USA

Fuentes, Mike (Athlete, Baseball Player)
9626 Sycamore Ct
Davie, FL 33328-6768, USA

Fuentes, Rigoberto (Tito) (Athlete, Baseball Player)
61 S Maddux Dr
Reno, NV 89512-1832, USA

Fuentes, Tito
61 S Maddux Dr
Reno, NV 89512-1832

Fuetsch, Herman (Athlete, Basketball Player)
646 Canyon Rd Apt 210
Novato, CA 94947-4355, USA

Fugard, Athol H (Writer)
PO Box 5090 Walmer
Port Elizabeth 6065, SOUTH AFRICA

Fugate, Katherine (Writer)
c/o Bayard Maybank *Hohman Maybank Lieb*
9465 Wilshire Blvd Fl 6
Beverly Hills, CA 90212-2605, USA

Fugees, The
83 Riverside Dr
New York, NY 10024-5713

Fugelsang, John (Actor, Comedian)
c/o Staff Member *WmE2 (WMA-LA)*
1 William Morris Pl
Beverly Hills, CA 90212-4261, USA

Fugere, Joe (Baseball Player)
415 Cinnamon Rdg
Rutherfordton, NC 28139-6876, USA

Fugere, Joe (Athlete, Baseball Player)
415 Cinnamon Rdg
Rutherfordton, NC 28139-6876, USA

Fugett, Jean (Athlete, Football Player)
4801 Westparkway
Baltimore, MD 21229-1336, USA

Fugger, Edward (Biologist)
305 Island View Dr
Penhook, VA 24137-5023, USA

Fugit, Patrick (Actor)
c/o Brett Norensberg *Gersh (LA)*
9465 Wilshire Blvd Ste 600
Beverly Hills, CA 90212-2612, USA

Fuglesang, Christer (Astronaut)
PO Box 555
Bellaire, TX 77402-0555, USA

Fuhr, Grant (Athlete, Hockey Player)
c/o Staff Member *Phoenix Coyotes*
6751 N Sunset Blvd Ste 200
Glendale, AZ 85305-3124, USA

Fuhrman, Isabelle (Actor)
c/o Susie Mains *Trilogy Talent*
13425 Ventura Blvd Fl 2
Sherman Oaks, CA 91423-3974, USA

Fuhrman, Mark (Writer)
PO Box 333
Sagle, ID 83860-0333

Fujisaki, Judge Hiroshi
1705 Main St # Q
Santa Monica, CA 90401

Fujita, Hiroyuki (Engineer)
1-9-14 Senkawa
Toshimaku, Tokyo 171, JAPAN

Fujita, Scott (Athlete, Football Player)
711 Tchoupitoulas St Apt 403
New Orleans, LA 70130-3784, USA

Fujita, Yoshio (Astronomer)
6-21-7 Renkoji
Tamashi 206, JAPAN

Fujiwara, Midori (Stylist)
c/o Staff Member *Judy Inc*
1 Yorkville Ave
Toronto ON M4W 1L1, Canada

Fukuto, Maru (Director)
450 N Roxbury Dr Ste 1050
Beverly Hills, CA 90210-4235, USA

Fukuyarna, Francis (Activist)
Public Policy Dept
Fairfax, VA 22030, USA

Fulcher, Bill (Athlete, Football Player)
18 Eagle Pointe Dr
Augusta, GA 30909-6056, USA

Fulcher, David (Athlete, Football Player)
PO Box 378
Mason, OH 45040-0378, USA

Fulcher, Modriel (Athlete, Football Player)
6010 S Westmoreland Rd Apt 1012
Dallas, TX 75237-2061, USA

Fulchino, Jeff (Athlete, Baseball Player)
6 Beacon Sq
Fairfield, CT 06825-3617, USA

Fuld, Richard S Jr (Financier)
745 7th Ave
New York, NY 10019-6801, USA

Fuld, Sam (Athlete, Baseball Player)
284 Marlberry Cir
Jupiter, FL 33458-2848, USA

Fulford, Cariton W Jr (General)
Deputy CinC US European Command
Stuttgart-Vaihingen Germany
APO, AE 9128, USA

Fulgham, John (Athlete, Baseball Player)
769 Cricklewood Ter
Lake Mary, FL 32746-5310, USA

Fulghum, Robert (Writer)
c/o Staff Member *HarperCollins Publishers*
10 E 53rd St C/O Author Mail Floor 7
New York, NY 10022, USA

Fulghum, Robert (Writer)
1745 Broadway # B1
New York, NY 10019-4368, USA

Fulhage, Scott (Athlete, Football Player)
2340 N Rd
Beloit, KS 67420, USA

Fulks, Robbie (Musician, Songwriter, Writer)
743 Center Blvd
Fairfax, CA 94930-1764, USA

Fuller, Amanda (Actor)
c/o Amy Abell *Innovative Artists (LA)*
1505 10th St
Santa Monica, CA 90401-2805, USA

Fuller, Bob B (Writer)
37 Langton Way
London 5.00E+03, UNITED KINGDOM (UK)

Fuller, Bryan (Writer)
c/o Ari Greenburg *WmE2 (Endeavor-LA)*
9601 Wilshire Blvd Fl 3
Beverly Hills, CA 90210-5219, USA

Fuller, Carl (Athlete, Basketball Player)
8302 Kirkville Dr
Houston, TX 77089-2194, USA

Fuller, Corey (Athlete, Football Player)
1429 Covey Ride St W
Tallahassee, FL 32312-9664, USA

Fuller, Curtis D (Musician)
135 W 50th St # 1915
New York, NY 10020-1201, USA

Fuller, Deiores (Actor, Songwriter, Writer)
3628 Ottawa Cir
Las Vegas, NV 89169-3301, USA

Fuller, Drew (Actor)
c/o Stephanie Simon *Untitled Entertainment (LA)*
350 S Beverly Dr Ste 200
Beverly Hills, CA 90212-4819, USA

Fuller, Jack W (Editor, Publisher)
435 N Michigan Ave
Chicago, IL 60611-4066, USA

Fuller, Jeff (Race Car Driver)
PO Box 3336
Mooresville, NC 28117-3336, USA

Fuller, Jim (Athlete, Baseball Player)
5107 Bur Oak Dr
Pasadena, TX 77505-3028, USA

Fuller, Joe (Athlete, Football Player)
8906 Farnsworth Ave N
Minneapolis, MN 55443-1752, USA

Fuller, John (Athlete, Baseball Player)
31912 Paseo Terraza
San Juan Capistrano, CA 92675-3060, USA

Fuller, Johnny (Athlete, Football Player)
1925 Highland Dr
Salado, TX 76571-5792, USA

Fuller, Kathryn S (Misc)
1250 24th St NW
Washington, DC 20037-1124, USA

Fuller, Kurt (Actor)
c/o Rick Ax *Gold Coast Management*
438 S Venice Blvd Apt 5
Venice, CA 90291-4695, USA

Fuller, Lance
1900 S Longwood Ave
Los Angeles, CA 90016-1408

Fuller, Linda (Activist)
121 Habitat St
Americus, GA 31709-3423, USA

Fuller, Mark (Artist)
90 Universal City Plz
Universal City, CA 91608-1002, USA

Fuller, Marvin D (General)
6799 Patton Dr
Fort Hood, TX 76544-1343, USA

Fuller, Mike (Athlete, Football Player)
4241 Abingdon Trl
Mountain Brk, AL 35243-1737, USA

Fuller, Millard (Activist)
121 Habitat St
Americus, GA 31709-3423, USA

Fuller, Penny (Actor)
12428 Hesby St
North Hollywood, CA 91607-3020, USA

Fuller, Randy (Athlete, Football Player)
2257 Patsy Ln
Columbus, GA 31903-3436, USA

Fuller, Robert (Actor)
PO Box 272
Era, TX 76238-0272, USA

Fuller, Simon (Producer)
c/o Jeff Frasco *Creative Artists Agency (CAA-LA)*
2000 Avenue of the Stars Ste 100
Los Angeles, CA 90067-4705, USA

Fuller, Steve (Athlete, Football Player)
81 Oak Tree Rd
Bluffton, SC 29910-4960, USA

Fuller, Tony (Athlete, Basketball Player)
7400 Old Main
Logan, UT 84322-7400, USA

Fuller, Vem (Athlete, Baseball Player)
155 Ironwood Cir
Aurora, OH 44202-9156, USA

Fuller, Vincent (Athlete, Football Player)
3186 Parthenon Ave Apt J
Nashville, TN 37203-1461, USA

Fuller, William H Jr (Athlete, Football Player)
1014 Fairway Dr
Chesapeake, VA 23320-8200, USA

Fullerton, C Gordon (Astronaut)
44046 28th St W Bldg 4800D
Lancaster, CA 93536-6026, USA

Fullerton, Ed (Athlete, Football Player)
135 Point Vue Dr
Pittsburgh, PA 15237-1883, USA

Fullerton, Fiona (Actor)
2-4 Noel St
London W1V 3RB, UNITED KINGDOM (UK)

Fullerton, Larry (Inventor)
6700 Odyssey Dr NW
Huntsville, AL 35806-3303, USA

Fullington, Darrell (Athlete, Football Player)
1023 W Patrick Cir
Daytona Beach, FL 32117-4565, USA

Fullmer, Brad (Athlete, Baseball Player)
400 S Barrington Ave Apt 202
Los Angeles, CA 90049-6413, USA

Fullmer, Gene (Boxer)
9250 S 2200 W
West Jordan, UT 84088-6405, USA

Fullwood, Brent (Athlete, Football Player)
4002 Maybreeze Rd
Marietta, GA 30066-2734, USA

Fullwood, Troy (Athlete, Baseball Player)
324 Wellington Cir
Smithfield, VA 23430-6282, USA

Fulmer, Phillip (Coach, Football Coach)
Athletic
Knoxville, TN 37996-0001, USA

Fulsher, Sharon (Stylist)
c/o Staff Member *Arlene Wilson Management*
807 N Jefferson St # 200
Milwaukee, WI 53202-8150, USA

Fulton, Bill (Athlete, Baseball Player)
3001 Lexington Ct
Export, PA 15632-9061, USA

Fulton, Eileen (Actor, Musician)
524 W 57th St
New York, NY 10019-2930, USA

Fulton, Fitz
1023 E Avenue J5
Lancaster, CA 93535-4239, USA

Fulton, Fitzhugh Jr (Misc)
1023 E Avenue J # 5
Lancaster, CA 93535-3839, USA

Fulton, Soren (Actor)
c/o Staff Member *Savage Agency*
6212 Banner Ave
Los Angeles, CA 90038-2802, USA

Fultz, Aaron (Athlete, Baseball Player)
PO Box 41
Munford, TN 38058-0041, USA

Fultz, Mike (Athlete, Football Player)
1900 W Foothills Rd
Lincoln, NE 68523-9389, USA

Fumero, David (Actor)
c/o Jerome Martin *Jerome Martin Management*
Prefers to be contacted via telephone
Los Angeles, CA 90024, USA

Fumusa, Dominic (Actor)
c/o Robert Stein *Robert Stein Management*
PO Box 3797
Beverly Hills, CA 90212-0797, USA

Fun Affairs
Flossergasse 7
Munich, GERMANY D-81369

Funaki, Kazuyoshi (Skier)
1-1-1 Jinan Shilbuya-Ku
Tokyo 150, JAPAN

Func, Eric (Composer)
PO Box 1073
Helena, MT 59624-1073, USA

Funchess, Tom (Athlete, Football Player)
1015 Funchess St
Crystal Springs, MS 39059-3017, USA

Fund, John (Writer)
c/o Staff Member *The American Spectator*
1611 N Kent St Ste 901
Arlington, VA 22209-2111, USA

Funderburk, Leonard J (War Hero)
2311 Lathan Rd
Monroe, NC 28112-8023, USA

Funderburk, Mark (Athlete, Baseball Player)
6924 Old Providence Rd
Charlotte, NC 28226-7740, USA

Funderburke, Lawrence (Athlete, Basketball Player)
1688 Meadoway Ct
Blacklick, OH 43004-9759, USA

Funicello, Annette (Actor, Musician)
2502 Zachary Ave
Shafter, CA 93263-9400, USA

Funk, Caribbean (Music Group)
c/o Staff Member *Sony Music Miami*
605 Lincoln Rd Ste 700
Miami Beach, FL 33139-2901, USA

Funk, Elaine (Stylist)
307 W Haven Dr
Arlington Heights, IL 60005-3618, USA

Funk, Frank (Athlete, Baseball Player)
4022 S Alamandas Way
Gold Canyon, AZ 85118-1899, USA

Funk, Fred (Athlete, Golfer)
24729 Harbour View Dr
Ponte Vedra Beach, FL 32082-1509, USA

Funk, Nolan Gerard (Actor)
c/o Katie Rhodes *Untitled Entertainment (LA)*
350 S Beverly Dr Ste 200
Beverly Hills, CA 90212-4819, USA

Funk, Tom (Athlete, Baseball Player)
6952 N Olive St
Kansas City, MO 64118-2876, USA

Funke, Alex (Cinematographer)
1224 21st St Apt A
Santa Monica, CA 90404-1390, USA

Funkmaster Flex (DJ, Musician)
c/o Ron Rivlin *Coast II Coast Entertainment*
8671 Wilshire Blvd Ste 500
Beverly Hills, CA 90211-2943, USA

Funt, Peter
PO Box 827
Monterey, CA 93942-0827

Fuqua, Antoine (Director)
c/o Scott Greenberg *Creative Artists Agency (CAA-LA)*
2000 Avenue of the Stars Ste 100
Los Angeles, CA 90067-4705, USA

Fuqua, John (Athlete, Football Player)
13983 Glastonbury Ave
Detroit, MI 48223-2921, USA

Furay, Richie (Musician)
c/o Staff Member *Agency Group Ltd, The (NY)*
142 W 57th St Fl 6
New York, NY 10019-3300, USA

Furcal, Rafael (Athlete, Baseball Player)
397 Sweet Bay Ave
Plantation, FL 33324-8227, USA

Furey, John (Actor)
c/o Staff Member *Hartig Hilepo Agency Ltd*
54 W 21st St Rm 610
New York, NY 10010-7344, USA

Furgler, Kurt (President)
Dufourstr 34
Saint-Gail 9000, SWITZERLAND

Furian, Mira (Actor)
6410 Blarney Stone Ct
Springfield, VA 22152-2129, USA

Furianetto, Ferruccio (Opera Singer)
Lincoln Center Plaza
New York, NY 10023, USA

Furie, Sidney (Director, Producer, Writer)
c/o Jack Gilardi *International Creative Management (ICM-LA)*
10250 Constellation Blvd Fl 7
Los Angeles, CA 90067-6207, USA

Furjanic, Anthony (Athlete, Football Player)
15220 Cottonwood Ct
Orland Park, IL 60467-7346, USA

Furlan, Mira (Actor)
c/o Chris Roe *CR Management*
23852 Pacific Coast Hwy Ste 627
Malibu, CA 90265-4876, USA

Furlong, Edward (Actor)
c/o Mark Rousso *New Wave Entertainment (LA)*
2660 W Olive Ave
Burbank, CA 91505-4525, USA

Furlong, Shirley (Athlete, Golfer)
6251 S Kimberlee Way
Chandler, AZ 85249-4173, USA

Furmaniak, J J (Athlete, Baseball Player)
184 Nottingham Dr
Bolingbrook, IL 60440-1811, USA

Furmann, Benno (Actor)
c/o Staff Member *Artists Independent Management (UK)*
32 Tavistock St
London WC2E 7PB, UNITED KINGDOM (UK)

Furness, Deborra-Lee (Actor, Director, Producer)
c/o Staff Member *Seed Productions*
10201 W Pico Blvd Bldg 52RM PMB 105
Los Angeles, CA 90064-2606, USA

Furniss, Bruce (Swimmer)
655 S Westford St
Anaheim, CA 92807-3643, USA

Furno, Carlo Cardinal (Religious Leader)
Piazza Della Citta Leonina
Rome 92807, ITALY

Furrer, Will (Athlete, Football Player)
420 Logan Ranch Rd
Georgetown, TX 78628-1211, USA

Furrey, Mike (Athlete, Football Player)
8579 Newbury Ct N
Canton, MI 48187-4444, USA

Furst, Anthony (Athlete, Football Player)
4315 Promenade Ave
Grove City, OH 43123-8267, USA

Furst, Janos K (Conductor)
3 Burlington Lane Chiswick
London W4 2TH, UNITED KINGDOM (UK)

Furst, Nathan (Musician)
c/o Mike Rosen *Working Artists Agency*
13525 Ventura Blvd
Sherman Oaks, CA 91423-3801

Furst, Stephen (Actor, Comedian)
3500 W Olive Ave Ste 1400
Burbank, CA 91505-5512, USA

Furstenfeld, Jeremy (Musician)
2002 Hogback Rd Ste 20
Ann Arbor, MI 48105-9736, USA

Furstenfeld, Justin (Musician)
827 W Hopkins St
San Marcos, TX 78666-4200, USA

Furtado, Nelly (Musician, Songwriter, Writer)
c/o Chris Smith *Chris Smith Management Inc*
21 Camden St 5th Floor
Toronto, ON M5V 1V2, Canada

Furuhashi, Hironshin (Swimmer)
3-9-11 Nozawa Setagayaku
Tokyo, JAPAN

Furukawa, Masaru (Swimmer)
5-5-12 Shinohara Honmachi Nadaku
Kobe, JAPAN

Furukawa, Satoshi (Astronaut)
Tsukuba Space Center 2-1-1 Sengen
Tukuhashi, Ibaraka 305, JAPAN

Furuseth, Ole Christian (Skier)
John Colletts Alle 74
Oslo 854, NORWAY

Fury, Ed (Actor)
6729 Babcock Ave
N Hollywood, CA 91606-1310

Furyk, Jim (Athlete, Golfer)
240 Deer Haven Dr
Ponte Vedra Beach, FL 32082-2107, USA

Fusco, Cosimo (Actor)
Piazzale Di Ponte Milvio 28
Rome 191, Italy

Fusco, Mark (Athlete, Hockey Player)
155 Grove St
Westwood, MA 02090-1027, USA

Fusco, Scott (Athlete, Hockey Player)
87 Turnquist Rd
Bremerton, WA 98312-5766, USA

Fusina, Chuck A (Athlete, Football Player)
1548 King James Dr
Pittsburgh, PA 15237-1588, USA

Fussell, Chris (Athlete, Baseball Player)
3238 N Eastmoreland Dr
Oregon, OH 43616-2933, USA

Futey, Bohdan A (Judge)
717 Madison Pl NW
Washington, DC 20439-0001, USA

Futral, Elizabeth (Opera Singer)
105 Arden St Apt 5G
New York, NY 10040-1119, USA

Futrell, Mary H (Misc)
Education School
Washington, DC 20052-0001, USA

Futter, Ellen V (Educator)
Park Ave West & 79th St
New York, NY 10034, USA

Futterman, Dan (Actor)
232 N Canon Dr
Beverly Hills, CA 90210-5302, USA

Futureheads, The (Music Group)
c/o Staff Member *Paradigm (Monterey)*
404 W Franklin St
Monterey, CA 93940-2303, USA

Fyhrie, Mike (Athlete, Baseball Player)
4 Wellesley Ct
Trabuco Canyon, CA 92679-4725, USA

Fylstra, Daniel (Engineer)
2895 Zanker Rd
San Jose, CA 95134-2101, USA

G

G, Franky (Actor)
c/o Jimmy Darmody *Creative Artists Agency (CAA-LA)*
2000 Avenue of the Stars Ste 100
Los Angeles, CA 90067-4705, USA

G, Kenny (Musician)
c/o Irving Azoff *Azoff Music Management/ Front Line*
1100 Glendon Ave
Los Angeles, CA 90024-3503, USA

G. Bartlett, Roscoe (Congressman, Politician)
2412 Rayburn Hob
Washington, Washington DC, USA

G. Eshoo, Anna (Congressman, Politician)
205 Cannon Hob
Washington, DC 20515-0514, USA

G. Fitzpatrick, Michael (Congressman, Politician)
1224 Longworth Hob
Washington, DC 20515-0553, USA

G. Grimm, Michael (Congressman, Politician)
512 Cannon Hob
Washington, DC 20515-1012, USA

G K (Actor)
11 Shyamala Vadana Street Koyathoppu
Chennai, TN 600 024, INDIA

G Love & Special Sauce (Music Group)
c/o Staff Member *Paradigm (Monterey)*
404 W Franklin St
Monterey, CA 93940-2303, USA

G. McCotter, Thaddeus (Congressman, Politician)
1632 Longworth Hob
Washington, DC 20515-2007, USA

G. Miller, Gary (Congressman, Politician)
2349 Rayburn Hob
Washington, DC 20515-2209, USA

G Ponnambalam (Actor)
10 Dr Subbarray Nagar II Street
Kodambakkam
Chennai, TN 600 024, INDIA

G Unit (Music Group)
c/o Staff Member *Interscope Records (NY)*
1755 Broadway
New York, NY 10019-3743, USA

Gaarder, Jostein (Misc)
Gullkroken 22A
Oslo 377, NORWAY

Gabaldon, Diana (Writer)
10810 N Tatum Blvd # 102-321
Phoenix, AZ 85028-6055, USA

Gabbana, Stefano (Designer, Fashion Designer)
Via Santa Cecilia 7
Milan, 20122 ITALY

Gabbard, Kason (Athlete, Baseball Player)
855 Dogtown Dr
Savannah, TN 38372-3713, USA

Gabbert, Blaine (Football Player)
c/o Tom Condon *CAA - St. Louis*
222 S Central Ave Ste 1008
Saint Louis, MO 63105-3509, USA

Gabel, Seth (Actor)
c/o Christine Tripicchio *WKT Public Relations (WKT-LA)*
9350 Wilshire Blvd Ste 450
Beverly Hills, CA 90212-3230, USA

Gable, Brian (Cartoonist)
67 Riverside Dr Apt 1D
New York, NY 10024-6155, USA

Gable, Daniel M (Danny) (Coach, Wrestler)
RR 2 Box 55
Iowa City, IA 52240, USA

Gable, John Clark
5118 Vineland Ave Ste 102
North Hollywood, CA 91601-3814

Gabler, Bill (Baseball Player)
4443 Mattis Rd
Saint Louis, MO 63128-3136, USA

Gabler, John (Athlete, Baseball Player)
8606 W 81st St
Overland Park, KS 66204-3444, USA

Gabler, William (Gabe) (Athlete, Baseball Player)
3227 Bayshore Pkwy
Arnold, MO 63010-4009, USA

Gabor, William (Athlete, Basketball Player)
101 Ocean Bluffs Blvd Apt 503
Jupiter, FL 33477-7362, USA

Gabor, Zsa Zsa (Actor)
1001 Bel Air Rd
Los Angeles, CA 90077-3011, USA

Gaborik, Marian (Athlete, Hockey Player)
52 Groveland Ter Unit 204
Minneapolis, MN 55403-1118, USA

Gabriel, Ana (Musician)
Peten 117 Col Narvarte
Mexico City 3020, MEXICO

Gabriel, Charles A (General)
International Airport
Newport News, VA 23602, USA

Gabriel, Eric (Stylist)
c/o Staff Member *Rex Agency, The*
6311 Romaine St
Los Angeles, CA 90038-2617, USA

Gabriel, Feliciano (Stylist)
c/o Celebrity Stylist *Camilla Lowther Managment (CLM Represents)*
30-32 Ericsson Pl
New York, NY 10013, USA

Gabriel, Gunter
Vorhelmer Str. 63
Ennigerloh-Enniger, GERMANY D-59320

Gabriel, John (Actor)
130 W 42nd St Ste 1804
New York, NY 10036-7902, USA

Gabriel, Juan (Musician, Songwriter, Writer)
11003 Rooks Rd
Whittier, CA 90601-1624, USA

Gabriel, Michael (Artist)
Dlouha 32
Prague 1 110 00, CZECH REPUBLIC

Gabriel, Peter (Musician, Songwriter)
c/o Staff Member *Real World Records*
Box Mill Box Corsham
Wiltshire SN1 38PN, United Kingdom

Gabriel, Roman
16817 McKee Rd
Charlotte, NC 28278-8406

Gabriel, Seychelle (Actor)
c/o TJ Stein *Stein Entertainment Group*
1351 N Crescent Heights Blvd Apt 312
West Hollywood, CA 90046-4549, USA

Gabriel Jr, Roman I (Athlete, Football Player)
PO Box 4173
Calabash, NC 28467-0373, USA

Gabrielle, Josefina (Actor)
c/o Staff Member *Stone Manners Salners Agency (LA)*
9911 W Pico Blvd Ste 1400
Los Angeles, CA 90035-2715, USA

Gabrielle, Monique (Actor, Model)
2436 N Federal Hwy # 332
Pompano Beach, FL 33064-6854, USA

Gabriels, Ed (Stylist)
c/o Staff Member *Halley Resources*
37 W 20th St Ste 603
New York, NY 10011-3718, USA

Gabrielson, Len (Athlete, Baseball Player)
24230 Hillview Rd
Los Altos, CA 94024-5221, USA

Gacki, Sebastian (Actor)
c/o Staff Member *Lizbell Agency*
216-309 W Cordova St
Vancouver, BC V6B 1E5, USA

Gad, Josh (Actor)
c/o Diane Perez *Zero Gravity Management*
11578 Canton Dr
Studio City, CA 91604-4160, USA

Gaddis, John L (Historian)
Contemporary History Institute Brown House
Athens, OH 45701, USA

Gaddis, Robert (Athlete, Football Player)
1022 Gaddis Rd
Edwards, MS 39066-8007, USA

Gade, Ariel (Actor)
c/o Jennifer Millar *Paradigm (LA)*
9200 W Sunset Blvd PH 11
Los Angeles, CA 90069-3601, USA

Gadinsky, Brian (Producer)
c/o Staff Member *WmE2 (WMA-LA)*
1 William Morris Pl
Beverly Hills, CA 90212-4261, USA

Gadot, Gal (Actor)
c/o Darren Goldberg *Global Creative*
1051 Cole Ave # B
Los Angeles, CA 90038-2601, USA

Gadsby, William A (Bill) (Athlete, Hockey Player)
28765 E Kalong Cir
Southfield, MI 48034-5650, USA

Gadsden, Oronde (Athlete, Football Player)
11241 NW 15th St
Plantation, FL 33323-2433, USA

Gadzhiev, Raul S O (Composer)
Baku, AZERBAIJAN

Gaechter, Mike (Athlete, Football Player)
13 Horizon Pt
Frisco, TX 75034-6840, USA

Gaeta, John (Designer, Special Effects Designer)
c/o Staff Member *International Creative Management (ICM-LA)*
10250 Constellation Blvd Fl 7
Los Angeles, CA 90067-6207, USA

Gaetti, Gary (Athlete, Baseball Player)
2704 Barbara Ln
Houston, TX 77005-3420, USA

Gaff, Brent (Athlete, Baseball Player)
5925 S State Road 9
Albion, IN 46701-9623, USA

Gaffigan, Jim (Actor, Comedian)
c/o Estelle Lasher *Principal Entertainment (LA)*
1964 Westwood Blvd Ste 400
Los Angeles, CA 90025-4695, USA

Gaffney, Derrick T (Athlete, Football Player)
11750 Cherry Bark Dr E
Jacksonville, FL 32218-7674, USA

Gaffney, F Andrew (Drew) (Astronaut)
6613 Chatsworth Pl
Nashville, TN 37205-3955, USA

Gaffney, Jabar (Athlete, Football Player)
7 Messenger St
Plainville, MA 02762-2273, USA

Gaffney, Janice (Athlete, Skier)
8118 Vantage Ave
North Hollywood, CA 91605-1437, USA

Gaffney, Mo (Actor)
c/o Staff Member *Stone Manners Salners Agency (LA)*
9911 W Pico Blvd Ste 1400
Los Angeles, CA 90035-2715, USA

Gaffney, Paul F (Admiral)
President National Defense University
Fort Lesley McNair
Washington, DC 20319-0001, USA

Gaga, Lady (Dancer, Musician)
c/o Amanda Silverman *42West (NY)*
220 W 42nd St Fl 12
New York, NY 10036-7200, USA

Gage, Fred H (Misc)
10110 N Torrey Pines Rd
La Jolla, CA 92037, USA

Gage, Jody (Athlete, Hockey Player)
91 W Forest Dr
Rochester, NY 14624-3755, USA

Gage, Nathaniel L (Educator)
85 Peter Courts Cir
Palo Alto, CA 94305, USA

Gage, Nicholas (Journalist)
37 Nelson St
North Grafton, MA 01536-1424, USA

Gage, Paul (Inventor)
Highway 178 N
Chippewa Falls, WI 55402, USA

Gagliano, Phil (Athlete, Baseball Player)
1095 Crescent Dr
Hollister, MO 65672-4884, USA

Gagliano, Ralph (Athlete, Baseball Player)
1756 Overton Park Ave
Memphis, TN 38112-5344, USA

Gagliano, Robert F (Bob) (Athlete, Football Player)
1064 Dover Ln
Ventura, CA 93001-3808, USA

Gagliardi, John (Coach, Football Coach)
Athletic Dept
Collegeville, MN 56321, USA

Gagne, Eric S (Athlete, Baseball Player)
c/o Scott Boras *Boras Corporation*
18 Corporate Plaza Dr
Newport Beach, CA 92660-7901, USA

Gagne, Greg (Athlete, Baseball Player)
746 Whetstone Hill Rd
Somerset, MA 02726-3702, USA

Gagne, Lynn (Stylist)
1252 Ash St
Winnetka, IL 60093-2106, USA

Gagne, Paul (Athlete, Hockey Player)
Lot 13 Aurora
Iroquois Falls, ON P0K 6K1, Canada

Gagne, Simone (Athlete, Hockey Player)
1167 10th St
Manhattan Beach, CA 90266-6019, USA

Gagner, Dave (Athlete, Coach, Hockey Player)
c/o Staff Member *London Knights*
99 Dundas St
London, ON N6A 6K1, Canada

Gagner, Larry (Athlete, Football Player)
205 W Curtis St
Tampa, FL 33603-3649, USA

Gagnier, Holly (Actor)
6500 Wilshire Blvd # 550
Los Angeles, CA 90048-4920, USA

Gagnon, Andre Philippe
89 Rue Alexandra
Granby, CANADA PQ J2C 2P4

Gago, Jenny (Actor)
c/o Bill Rogin *Bill Rogin Management*
427 N Canon Dr Ste 215
Beverly Hills, CA 90210-4840, USA

Gagosian, Larry (Business Person)
980 Madison Ave PH
New York, NY 10075-1848, USA

Gaidar, Yegor T (Prime Minister)
Gazetny Per 5
Moscow 111024, RUSSIA

Gail, David
c/o Staff Member *Henze Management*
1925 Century Park E Ste 2320
Los Angeles, CA 90067-2724, USA

Gail, Joseph G (Biologist)
107 Bellemore Rd
Baltimore, MD 21210-1314, USA

Gail, Max (Actor)
c/o Laura Pallas *Pallas Management*
5301 Bellaire Ave
Valley Village, CA 91607-2329, US

Gaile, Jeri
880 Hilldale Ave Apt 3
Los Angeles, CA 90069-4921

Gailey, T Chandler (Chan) (Athlete, Coach, Football Coach, Football Player)
176 Rocky Branch Rd
Clarkesville, GA 30523-5602, USA

Gaillard, Bob (Coach)
50 Bonnie Brae Dr
Novato, CA 94949-5851, USA

Gaillard, Eddie (Athlete, Baseball Player)
836 Peppertree Ct
Wellington, FL 33414-4925, USA

Gaillard, Mary Katharine (Physicist)
Physics
Berkeley, CA 94720-0001, USA

Gaiman, Neil (Writer)
c/o Jon Levin *Creative Artists Agency (CAA-LA)*
2000 Avenue of the Stars Ste 100
Los Angeles, CA 90067-4705, USA

Gain, Robert (Bob) (Athlete, Football Player)
11 Nokomis Dr
Eastlake, OH 44095-1943, USA

Gainer, Derrick (Athlete, Football Player)
733 E McDonald Rd
Plant City, FL 33567-3529, USA

Gainer, Jay (Athlete, Baseball Player)
1035 E 8th St
Panama City, FL 32401-3594, USA

Gaines, Ambrose (Rowdy) IV (Swimmer)
6800 Hawaii Kai Dr
Honolulu, HI 96825-1505, USA

Gaines, Bill (Athlete, Basketball Player)
1553 Cypress Bend Dr
Cedar Hill, TX 75104-6918, USA

Gaines, Boyd (Actor, Musician)
c/o Elin McManus-Flack *Elin Flack Management*
435 W 57th St Apt 3M
New York, NY 10019-1724, USA

Gaines, Clark (Athlete, Football Player)
21364 Scara Pl
Broadlands, VA 20148-3602, USA

Gaines, Corey (Athlete, Basketball Player)
3968 Windansea St
Las Vegas, NV 89147-6544, USA

Gaines, Davis
315 W 57th St Frnt 4H
New York, NY 10019-3158

Gaines, Ernest J (Writer)
PO Box 81
Oscar, LA 70762-0081, USA

Gaines, Joe (Athlete, Baseball Player)
77 Anair Way
Oakland, CA 94605-4874, USA

Gaines, Lawrence (Athlete, Football Player)
4963 Cherry Blossom Cir
West Bloomfield, MI 48324-1297, USA

Gaines, Reese (Baseball Player)
Toyota Center 2 E Greenway Plaza
Houston, TX 77046, USA

Gaines, Rowdy
6800 Hawaii Kai Dr
Honolulu, HI 96825-1505

Gaines, Wentford (Athlete, Football Player)
20 Sheffield St
Jersey City, NJ 07305-2813, USA

Gaines, William C (Journalist)
435 N Michigan Ave
Chicago, IL 60611-4066, USA

Gainey, Robert M (Bob) (Athlete, Coach, Hockey Player)
c/o Staff Member *Montreal Canadiens*
1275 Rue Saint-Antoine O
Montreal, QB H3C 5L2, Canada

Gainey, Steve (Athlete, Hockey Player)
PO Box 829
Coppell, TX 75019-0829, USA

Gainey, Ty (Athlete, Baseball Player)
3040 W Market Street Ext
Cheraw, SC 29520-5587, USA

Gainsbourg, Charlotte (Actor)
c/o Frederique Moidon *ArtMedia*
20 avenue Rapp
Paris 75008, France

Gair, Joanne (Stylist)
c/o Staff Member *Mercury Artists*
8460 Higuera St Fl 2
Culver City, CA 90232-2520, USA

Gaiser, George (Athlete, Football Player)
28752 Kalkallo Dr
Boerne, TX 78015-4614, USA

Gaison, Blane (Athlete, Football Player)
45-444 Koa Kahiko St
Kaneohe, HI 96744-2008, USA

Gaitan, Paulina (Actor)
c/o Dar Rollins *International Creative Management (ICM-LA)*
10250 Constellation Blvd Fl 7
Los Angeles, CA 90067-6207, USA

Gaiter, Tony (Athlete, Football Player)
9235 NW 35th Ct
Miami, FL 33147-2829, USA

Gaiters, Bob (Athlete, Football Player)
6909 Knowlton Pl Apt 206
Los Angeles, CA 90045-2036, USA

Gaither, Bill (Musician, Songwriter, Writer)
PO Box 737
Alexandria, IN 46001-0737, USA

Gajan, Hokie (Athlete, Football Player)
213 Cottonwood Ln
Mandeville, LA 70471-2552, USA

Gajarsa, Arthur J (Judge)
717 Madison Pl NW
Washington, DC 20439-0001, USA

Gajdusek, D Carieton (Nobel Prize Laureate)
725 W Lombard St # N460
Baltimore, MD 21201-1009, USA

Gajdusek, Karl (Writer)
c/o Jill McElroy *Management 360*
110 S Fairfax Ave Ste 350
Los Angeles, CA 90036-2165, USA

Gajkowski, Steve (Athlete, Baseball Player)
416 Turner St NE
Olympia, WA 98506-4663, USA

Gakeler, Dan (Athlete, Baseball Player)
3714 Sawgrass Rd
Greensboro, NC 27410-9068, USA

Galabru, Michael
11 Rue Boissiere
Paris, FRANCE F-75116

Galambos, Robert (Misc)
8826 La Jolla Scenic Dr N
La Jolla, CA 92037-1608, USA

Galanos, James (Designer, Fashion Designer)
1316 Sunset Plaza Dr
Los Angeles, CA 90069-1235, USA

Galanos, Mike (Television Host)
1 Time Warner Ctr
New York, NY 10019-6038, USA

Galante, Matt (Baseball Player, Coach)
501 Crawford St Attn Specialassistanttothe
Houston, TX 77002-2113, USA

Galarraga, Andres (Athlete, Baseball Player)
1639 Enclave Cir
West Palm Beach, FL 33411-1862, USA

Galarrage, Andres J P (Baseball Player)
Barrio Nuevo Chapellin Clejon Soledad #5
Caracas, VENEZUELA

Galasso, Bob (Athlete, Baseball Player)
267 Adelaide Rd
Connellsville, PA 15425-6215, USA

Galati, Frank J (Director)
990 Blvd Of The Arts Apt 1003
Sarasota, FL 34236-4877, USA

Galbraith, Clint (Race Car Driver)
PO Box 902
Edwardsville, IL 62025-0902, USA

Galbraith, Scott (Athlete, Football Player)
3700 Plymouth Dr
North Highlands, CA 95660-3312, USA

Galbreath, Harry (Athlete, Football Player)
728 McGraw St
Clarksville, TN 37040-4220, USA

Galbreath, Scott (Athlete, Football Player)
3649 Plymouth Dr
North Highlands, CA 95660-3309, USA

Galbreath, Tony (Athlete, Football Player)
411 W 9th St
Fulton, MO 65251-1178, USA

Galdikas, Birute M F (Misc)
822 Wellesley Ave
Los Angeles, CA 90049-5213, USA

Gale, Ed (Actor)
c/o Cindy Osbrink *Osbrink Talent Agency*
4343 Lankershim Blvd Ste 100
West Toluca Lake, CA 91602-2705, USA

Gale, Greg (Stylist)
c/o Staff Member *Bryan Bantry*
900 Broadway Ste 400
New York, NY 10003-1239, USA

Gale, Joseph H (Judge)
400 2nd St NW
Washington, DC 20217-0001, USA

Gale, Megan (Actor)
c/o Ann Churchill-Brown *Shanahan Management*
Level 3 Berman House
Surry Hills 2010, AUSTRALIA

Gale, Mike (Athlete, Basketball Player)
18003 4th Ave S
Burien, WA 98148-1803, USA

Gale, Rich (Athlete, Baseball Player)
869 Center Park St
Daniel Island, SC 29492-7569, USA

Gale, Robert P (Inventor)
980 Bluegrass Ln
Los Angeles, CA 90049-1433, USA

Galecki, Johnny (Actor)
c/o Ryan Revel *Benderspink*
5870 W Jefferson Blvd Ste E
Los Angeles, CA 90016-3159, USA

Galella, Ronald E (Ron) (Photographer)
12 Nelson Ln
Montville, NJ 07045-9306, USA

Galeotti, Bethany Joy (Actor)
c/o Jill Fritzo *PMK/BNC Public Relations (PMK-NY)*
622 3rd Ave Fl 8
New York, NY 10017-6707, USA

Galer, Robert E (General)
3525 Turtle Creek Blvd Apt 6D
Dallas, TX 75219-5515, USA

Galiena, Anna (Actor)
c/o Dominique Besnehard *ArtMedia*
20 avenue Rapp
Paris 75008, France

Galifianakis, Zach (Actor, Producer, Writer)
c/o Marc Gurvitz *Brillstein Entertainment Partners*
9150 Wilshire Blvd Ste 350
Beverly Hills, CA 90212-3453, USA

Galigher, Ed (Athlete, Football Player)
1465 Paint Mountain Rd
Escondido, CA 92029-5926, USA

Galik, Denise (Actor)
9229 W Sunset Blvd Ste 311
Los Angeles, CA 90069-3403, USA

Galina, Stacy (Actor)
c/o Mark Scroggs *David Shapira & Associates*
193 N Robertson Blvd
Beverly Hills, CA 90211-2103, USA

Galindo, Rudy (Figure Skater)
c/o Staff Member *Champions on Ice*
3500 W 80th St Ste 200
Minneapolis, MN 55431-1090, USA

Gall, Hugues (Opera Singer)
11 Blvd du Theatre
Geneva 1211, SWITZERLAND

Gall, John (Athlete, Baseball Player)
20 Corte Del Sol
Millbrae, CA 94030-2111, USA

Gallacher, Kevin (Soccer Player)
Ewood Park Blackbum
Lancashire BB2 4JF, UNITED KINGDOM (UK)

Gallagher (Misc)
14984 Roan Ct
Wellington, FL 33414-1015, USA

Gallagher, Al (Athlete, Baseball Player)
1810 N Parkwood Dr
Harlingen, TX 78550-8027, USA

Gallagher, Bob (Athlete, Baseball Player)
315 Fair Ave
Santa Cruz, CA 95060-6343, USA

Gallagher, Brian (Misc)
701 N Fairfax St
Alexandria, VA 22314-2058, USA

Gallagher, Bronagh (Actor)
Langham House 302/8 Regent St
London W1R 5AL, UNITED KINGDOM (UK)

Gallagher, Chad (Athlete, Basketball Player)
482 Wynstone Way
Rockton, IL 61072-3434, USA

Gallagher, Dave (Athlete, Baseball Player)
29 Carrs Tavern Rd
Millstone Township, NJ 08510-1505, USA

Gallagher, Dave (Athlete, Football Player)
6105 Horizon Dr
Columbus, IN 47201-1110, USA

Gallagher, David (Actor)
c/o Abby Bluestone *Innovative Artists (LA)*
1505 10th St
Santa Monica, CA 90401-2805, USA

Gallagher, Delia (Anchor)
c/o Staff Member *CNN (LA)*
6430 W Sunset Blvd Ste 300
Hollywood, CA 90028-7906, USA

Gallagher, Doug (Athlete, Baseball Player)
1690 Maple Ln
Fremont, OH 43420-3612, USA

Gallagher, Frank (Athlete, Football Player)
6572 Enclave Dr
Clarkston, MI 48348-4859, USA

Gallagher, Helen (Actor, Musician)
260 W End Ave
New York, NY 10023-3614, USA

Gallagher, John (Religious Leader)
PO Box 551
Presque Isle, ME 04769-0551, USA

Gallagher, Liam (Musician)
54 Linhope St
London NW1 6HL, UNITED KINGDOM (UK)

Gallagher, Mary (Actor)
c/o Michael Greenwald *Don Buchwald & Associates Inc (LA)*
6500 Wilshire Blvd Ste 2200
Los Angeles, CA 90048-4942, USA

Gallagher, Megan (Actor)
6500 Wilshire Blvd Ste 2200
Los Angeles, CA 90048-4942, USA

Gallagher, Mike (Radio Personality)
350 5th Ave Ste 1818
New York, NY 10118-1818, USA

Gallagher, Noel (Musician, Songwriter, Writer)
c/o Staff Member *Ignition Management*
54 Linhope St
London NW1 6HL, UNITED KINGDOM

Gallagher, Patrick (Actor)
c/o Staff Member *Main Title Entertainment*
2225 Wilshire Blvd Suite 500
Los Angeles, CA 90036, USA

Gallagher, Peter (Actor)
c/o John Carrabino *John Carrabino Management*
5900 Wilshire Blvd Ste 406
Los Angeles, CA 90036-5015, USA

Gallagher Jr, Jim (Athlete, Golfer)
PO Box 507
Greenwood, MS 38935-0507, USA

Gallagher-Smith, Jackie (Athlete, Golfer)
193 Paradise Cir
Jupiter, FL 33458-2853, USA

Gallant, Gerard (Athlete, Coach, Hockey Player)
c/o Staff Member *New York Islanders*
1255 Hempstead Tpke
Uniondale, NY 11553-1260, USA

Gallant, Matt (Actor, Television Host)
608 Idaho Ave Unit 8
Santa Monica, CA 90403-2712, USA

Gallant, Mavis (Writer)
14 Rue Jean Ferrandi
Paris 75006, FRANCE

Gallardo, Camillio (Actor)
1505 10th St
Santa Monica, CA 90401-2805, USA

Gallardo, Carlos (Actor)
c/o Michael Henderson *Heresun Management*
4119 W Burbank Blvd
Burbank, CA 91505-2122, USA

Gallardo, Silvana
10637 Burbank Blvd
North Hollywood, CA 91601-2512

Gallatin, Harry J (Athlete, Basketball Player, Coach)
2010 Madison Ave
Edwardsville, IL 62025-2623, USA

Gallegly, Elton (Congressman, Politician)
2309 Rayburn Hob
Washington, DC 20515-3211, USA

Gallego, Gina (Actor)
1800 Avenue of the Stars Ste 400
Los Angeles, CA 90067-4206, USA

Gallego, Mike (Athlete, Baseball Player)
11 Sunningdale
Trabuco Canyon, CA 92679-5103, USA

Gallegos, Gilbert G (Misc)
1410 Donaldson Pike
Nashville, TN 37217, USA

Gallery, Robert (Athlete, Football Player)
3163 20th St
Masonville, IA 50654, USA

Galles, John (Misc)
1156 15th St NW Ste 1100
Washington, DC 20005-1755, USA

Galletti, Carl (Business Person)
PO Box 3934
Sedona, AZ 86340-3934, USA

Galley, Garry (Athlete, Hockey Player)
c/o Staff Member *CBC TV*
P.O. Box 500 STN A, 5H100
Toronto, ON M5W 1E6, Canada

Galliano, John C (Designer, Fashion Designer)
60 Rue D'Avron
Paris 75020, FRANCE

Gallico, Gregory III (Doctor, Inventor)
170 Commonwealth Ave
Boston, MA 02116-2704, USA

Galligan, Zach (Actor, Comedian)
c/o Aine Leicht *Horror & Hilarity*
Prefers to be contacted via telephone
Los Angeles, CA 90067, USA

Gallimore, Jamie (Athlete, Hockey Player)
10931 62 Ave NW
Edmonton, AB T6H 1N3, Canada

Gallison, Joe (Actor)
PO Box 10187
Wilmington, NC 28404-0187, USA

Gallner, Kyle (Actor)
c/o Sarah Shyn *3 Arts Entertainment Inc*
9460 Wilshire Blvd Fl 7
Beverly Hills, CA 90212-2713, USA

Gallo, Carla (Actor)
c/o Stacy Abrams *Abrams Entertainment*
5225 Wilshire Blvd # Suite 515 PMB 515
Los Angeles, CA 90036, USA

Gallo, Frank (Artist)
Art Dept
Urbana, IL 61801, USA

Gallo, George (Director)
c/o Todd Hoffman *International Creative Management (ICM-LA)*
10250 Constellation Blvd Fl 7
Los Angeles, CA 90067-6207, USA

Gallo, Mike (Athlete, Baseball Player)
1415 Christine St
Houston, TX 77017-4003, USA

Gallo, Robert C (Scientist)
Study of Viruses Institute
Baltimore, MD 21228, USA

Gallo, Vincent (Actor, Director)
c/o Danny Goldberg *Gold Village Entertainment*
37 W 17th St Ste 7W
New York, NY 10011-5525, USA

Gallo, William V (Bill) (Boxer, Cartoonist)
1 Mayflower Dr
Yonkers, NY 10710-3801, USA

Gallop, Tom (Actor)
c/o Dan Baron *Agency for the Performing Arts (APA-LA)*
405 S Beverly Dr Ste 500
Beverly Hills, CA 90212-4425, USA

Galloway, David (Athlete, Football Player)
5441 NW 184th St
Miami Gardens, FL 33055-5344, USA

Galloway, Jean (Religious Leader)
1660 Duke St
Alexandria, VA 22314-3473, USA

Galloway, Joey (Athlete, Football Player)
4340 Hanna Hills Dr
Dublin, OH 43016-9518, USA

Gallup II, George H (Mathematician)
Great Road
Princeton, NJ 8540, USA

Galotti, Ronald A (Publisher)
Publisher's Office 4 Times Square
New York, NY 10036, USA

Galston, Arthur W (Biologist)
218 Stearns St
Carlisle, MA 01741-1864, USA

Galvez, Balvino (Athlete, Baseball Player)
3986 SW 190th Ave
Miramar, FL 33029-2726, USA

Galvin, James (Writer)
Writer's Workshop
Iowa City, IA 52242, USA

Galvin, John R (General)
2714 Jodeco Cir
Jonesboro, GA 30236-5329, USA

Galvin, Robert W (Business Person)
1303 E Algonquin Rd
Schaumburg, IL 60196-4041

Galway, James (Musician)
Benzeholzstr 11
Meggen 6045, SWITZERLAND

Galyon, Gregory (Athlete, Football Player)
2352 Monticello Dr
Maryville, TN 37803-7528, USA

Gam, Rita (Actor)
180 W 58th St # 8B
New York, NY 10019-2145, USA

Gamar, Charles D
7660 N 159th Street Ct E
Benton, KS 67017-8926, USA

Gambaccini, Sciascia (Stylist)
c/o Staff Member *Art + Commerce*
531 W 25th St # 4
New York, NY 10001-5593, USA

Gambee, Dave (Athlete, Basketball Player)
6175 SW Arrow Wood Ln
Portland, OR 97223-7261, USA

Gamble, Chris (Athlete, Football Player)
13335 Pierre Reverdy Dr
Davidson, NC 28036-7008, USA

Gamble, David (Athlete, Football Player)
24 Huckleberry Ln
Albany, NY 12205-5036, USA

Gamble, Dick (Athlete, Hockey Player)
1 Vantage Dr
Pittsford, NY 14534-3205, USA

Gamble, Ed (Cartoonist)
1 Riverside Ave
Jacksonville, FL 32202-4917, USA

Gamble, John (Athlete, Baseball Player)
369 Caliente St
Reno, NV 89509-2729, USA

Gamble, Kenny (Ken) (Athlete, Football Player)
4 Algonquin Dr
Wilbraham, MA 01095-2373, USA

Gamble, Kevin (Athlete, Basketball Player)
41 W Huckleberry Rd
Lynnfield, MA 01940-2615, USA

Gamble, Mason (Actor)
9560 Wilshire Blvd Ste 500
Beverly Hills, CA 90212-2401, USA

Gamble, Oscar (Athlete, Baseball Player)
9705 Bent Brook Dr
Montgomery, AL 36117-7445, USA

Gamble, Troy (Athlete, Hockey Player)
12038 Terraza Cove Ln
Houston, TX 77041-6230, USA

Gamboa, Juan Pablo (Actor)
c/o Staff Member *Televisa*
Blvd Adolfo Lopez Mateos 232 Colonia San Angel INN
DF CP 01060, MEXICO

Gambol, Chris (Athlete, Football Player)
PO Box 2154
Glen Ellyn, IL 60138-2154, USA

Gambon, Michael (Actor)
c/o Paul Lyon-Maris *Independent Talent Group (ITG-UK)*
Oxford House 76 Oxford St
London W1D 1BS, UK

Gambon, Michael J (Actor)
40 W 57th St # 1800
New York, NY 10019-4001, USA

Gambon, Sir Michael (Actor)
c/o Staff Member *International Creative Management (ICM-LA)*
10250 Constellation Blvd Fl 7
Los Angeles, CA 90067-6207, USA

Gambrell, Bill (Athlete, Football Player)
341 Osceola Ave
Bogart, GA 30622-1511, USA

Gambrell, David H (Ex-Senator)
3205 Arden Rd NW
Atlanta, GA 30305-1918, USA

Gambril, Don (Coach)
4409 Spring Row
Northport, AL 35473-5231, USA

Gambucci, Andre (Athlete, Coach, Hockey Player)
660 Southpointe Ct
Colorado Springs, CO 80906-3804, USA

Gambucci, Gary (Athlete, Hockey Player)
9241 Yukon Ave S
Minneapolis, MN 55438-1446, USA

Gambucci, Sergio (Athlete, Hockey Player)
4365 Carriage House Vw
Colorado Springs, CO 80906-8702, USA

Gamez, Robert (Athlete, Golfer)
1128 Wilde Dr
Kissimmee, FL 34747-4046, USA

Gammon, Kendall (Athlete, Football Player)
14429 Maple St
Overland Park, KS 66223-1256, USA

Gammons, Peter (Athlete, Baseball Player)
Editorial Dept PO Box 2378
Boston, MA 02107-2378, USA

Gampel, Michele (Stylist)
24617 Stagg St
West Hills, CA 91304-6125, USA

Ganassi, Sonia (Opera Singer)
165 W 57th St
New York, NY 10019-2201, USA

Ganatra, Nisha (Director)
c/o Sheryl Peterson *Agency for the Performing Arts (APA-LA)*
405 S Beverly Dr Ste 500
Beverly Hills, CA 90212-4425, USA

Ganchar, Perry (Athlete, Hockey Player)
8043 Summerhouse Dr W
Dublin, OH 43016-7062, USA

Gand, Gale (Chef, Television Host)
c/o Staff Member *Food Network, The*
75 9th Ave
New York, NY 10011-7006, USA

Gandarillas, Gus (Athlete, Baseball Player)
6320 NW 114th St
Hialeah, FL 33012-2334, USA

Gandee, Sherman (Sonny) (Athlete, Football Player)
1357 Fargo St
Port Charlotte, FL 33952-2315, USA

Gandhi, Sonia (Government Official, Politician)
24 Akbar Rd
New Delhi, New Delhi 110011, INDIA

Gandhimathi (Actor, Bollywood)
59 Saidapet Rd
Chennai, TN 600026, INDIA

Gandler, Markus (Skier)
Sinwell 22
Kitzbuhel 6370, AUSTRIA

Gandolfi, Michael (Model)
c/o Staff Member *Ford Models (NY)*
238 E 4th St
New York, NY 10009-7425

Gandolfini, James (Actor)
c/o Mark Armstrong *Sanders Armstrong Caserta*
2120 Colorado Ave Ste 120
Santa Monica, CA 90404-3561, USA

Gandy, Dylan (Athlete, Football Player)
13161 Haskell Pl
Carmel, IN 46074-8332, USA

Gandy, Mike (Athlete, Football Player)
58 Edwin St
Dorchester Center, MA 02124-2517, USA

Gandy, Wayne L (Athlete, Football Player)
130 Sand Pine Ln
Davenport, FL 33837-5510, USA

Ganellin, C Robin (Inventor)
Chemistry Dept 20 Gordon
London WC1H OAJ, UNITED KINGDOM (UK)

Ganesan, Bhanurekha Gemini (Rekha) (Actor, Bollywood)
c/o Simone Sheffield *Canyon Entertainment*
PO Box 256
Palm Springs, CA 92263-0256, USA

Ganesh, Gemini (Actor)
6 Nungambakkam High Rd
Chennai, TN 600 034, INDIA

Ganev, Tzetzi
1751 N Berendo St # 21
Los Angeles, CA 90027

Gang of Four (Music Group)
c/o Staff Member *Paradigm (Monterey)*
404 W Franklin St
Monterey, CA 93940-2303, USA

Ganga (Actor)
6 S Mada Street Mylapore
Chennai, TN 600 004, INDIA

Gangel, Jamie (Correspondent)
30 Rockefeller Plz
New York, NY 10112-0015, USA

Gann, Mike (Athlete, Football Player)
1479 Ashford Pl NE
Atlanta, GA 30319-1888, USA

Gannascoli, Joseph (Joe) (Actor)
c/o Greg Meyer *Meyer Management Group (MMG)*
1400 Atlantic Ave Ste 274
Long Beach, CA 90813-2013, USA

Gannon, Coleen (Stylist)
c/o Staff Member *Team*
423 W Broadway Ste 406
Boston, MA 02127-2265, USA

Gannon, Richard J (Rich) (Athlete, Football Player, Sportscaster)
3415 University Ave W
Saint Paul, MN 55114-1019, USA

Gansler, Bob (Coach, Soccer Player)
2 Arrowhead Dr
Kansas City, MO 64129-1650, USA

Ganson, Arthur (Artist)
Compton Gallery
Cambridge, MA 2139, USA

Gant, Harry (Race Car Driver)
7531 Millersville Rd
Taylorsville, NC 28681-8946, USA

Gant, Kenneth (Athlete, Football Player)
1820 W 10th St
Lakeland, FL 33805-3308, USA

Gant, Kenneth (Kenny) (Athlete, Football Player)
3906 Carrollwood Place Cir Apt 243
Tampa, FL 33624-3064, USA

Gant, Mtume (Actor)
c/o Maggie Woods *Online Talent Group*
Prefers to be contacted via email or telephone
Los Angeles, CA 90069, USA

Gant, Reuben (Athlete, Football Player)
PO Box 3051
Tulsa, OK 74101-3051, USA

Gant, Robert (Actor)
c/o Brit Reece *PMK/BNC Public Relations (PMK-LA)*
8687 Melrose Ave Ste 8
West Hollywood, CA 90069-5746, USA

Gant, Ronald E (Ron) (Athlete, Baseball Player)
1027 Wellesley Crest Dr
Woodstock, GA 30189-6736, USA

Gantin, Bernardin Cardinal (Religious Leader)
Plazza Pio XII 10
Rome 193, ITALY

Gantner, Jim (Athlete, Baseball Player)
PO Box 156
Eden, WI 53019-0156, USA

Gantos, Jack (Writer)
19 Union Sq W
New York, NY 10003-3304, USA

Gantt, Greg (Athlete, Football Player)
180 Palmer St
Watertown, NY 13601-2344, USA

Gantt, Harvey
Rt. #1 Box 587
Taylorsville, NC 28681

Gantt, Jerry (Athlete, Football Player)
2035 Long Point Trl
Sanford, NC 27332-7449, USA

Ganz, Bruno (Actor)
Keplerstrasse 2
München 81679, GERMANY

Ganzel, Teresa (Actor)
9300 Wilshire Blvd Ste 410
Beverly Hills, CA 90212-3228, USA

Gao, Xiang (Musician)
165 W 57th St
New York, NY 10019-2201, USA

Gao, Xingjian (Nobel Prize Laureate)
Shatin
Hong Kong, CHINA

Gaona, Jessica (Actor)
c/o Staff Member *Abrams Artists Agency (LA)*
9200 W Sunset Blvd PH 11
Los Angeles, CA 90069-3601, USA

Gap Band, The
89 5th Ave Ste 700
New York, NY 10003-3056

Garabaldi, Bob
2143 Oregon Ave
Stockton, CA 95204-4617

Garabedian, Paul R (Mathematician)
110 Bleecker St
New York, NY 10012-2101, USA

Garagiola, Joe (Athlete, Baseball Player)
7433 E Tuckey Ln
Scottsdale, AZ 85250-4640, USA

Garagozzo, Keith (Athlete, Baseball Player)
16 Foxcroft Way
Mount Laurel, NJ 08054-5732, USA

Garai, Romola (Actor)
c/o Billy Lazarus *United Talent Agency (UTA)*
9560 Wilshire Blvd Fl 5
Beverly Hills, CA 90212-2400, USA

Garalczyk, Mark (Athlete, Football Player)
PO Box 27304
Scottsdale, AZ 85255-0138, USA

Garamendi, John (Congressman, Politician)
228 Cannon Hob
Washington, DC 20515-3307, USA

Garan, Ronald J Jr (Astronaut)
2002 Sea Cove Ct
Houston, TX 77058-4228, USA

Garant, Robert Ben (Actor, Director, Producer, Writer)
c/o Joseph Cohen *Creative Artists Agency (CAA-LA)*
2000 Avenue of the Stars Ste 100
Los Angeles, CA 90067-4705, USA

Garas, Kaz (Actor)
10145 N Buchanan Ave
Portland, OR 97203, USA

Garavani, Valentino (Designer, Fashion Designer)
Palazzo Mignanelli Piazza Mignanelli 22
Rome 187, Italy

Garavito, R Michael (Misc)
Biochemistry Dept
East Lansing, MI 48824, USA

Garbacz, Lori (Athlete, Golfer)
777 Albany Post Rd
Briarcliff Manor, NY 10510-2400, USA

Garbage (Music Group)
c/o Staff Member *Creative Artists Agency (CAA-LA)*
2000 Avenue of the Stars Ste 100
Los Angeles, CA 90067-4705, USA

Garbarek, Jan (Musician)
Niels Juels Gate 42
Oslo 257, NORWAY

Garber, H Eugene (Gene) (Athlete, Baseball Player)
771 Stonemill Dr
Elizabethtown, PA 17022-9717, USA

Garber, Terri (Actor)
c/o Maggie Smith *Maggie Smith Management*
6028 Agapanthus Pl
Woodland Hills, CA 91367-7200, USA

Garber, Victor (Actor)
c/o Bill Butler *Industry Entertainment Partners*
955 Carrillo Dr Ste 300
Los Angeles, CA 90048-5400, USA

Garbey, Barbaro (Athlete, Baseball Player)
14094 Woodside St
Livonia, MI 48154-5206, USA

Garbowski, Alex (Athlete, Baseball Player)
100 Oak Ridge Dr
Putnam Valley, NY 10579-1325, USA

Garces, Paula (Actor)
c/o Staff Member *Untitled Entertainment (NY)*
322 8th Ave Ste 601
New York, NY 10001-6715, USA

Garces, Rich (Athlete, Baseball Player)
605 Swigert St
Kerrville, TX 78028-3140, USA

Garcetti, Gil
139 N Cliffwood Ave
Los Angeles, CA 90049-2613, USA

Garci, Jose Luis (Director)
Paseo de la Castellana 109
Madrid 16, SPAIN

Garcia, Adam (Actor)
c/o Peter Safran *The Safran Company*
8748 Holloway Dr
West Hollywood, CA 90069-2327, USA

Garcia, Aimee (Actor)
c/o Jeffrey Chassen *Baker Winokur Ryder Public Relations BWR (BWR-NY)*
292 Madison Ave Fl 12
New York, NY 10017-6415, USA

Garcia, Andrew (Musician)
c/o Simon Fuller *XIX Entertainment*
33/32 Ransomes Dock 35-37 Parkgate Rd
London SW11 4NP, UK

Garcia, Andy (Actor, Musician)
c/o JoAnne Colonna *Brillstein Entertainment Partners*
9150 Wilshire Blvd Ste 350
Beverly Hills, CA 90212-3453, USA

Garcia, Carlos (Athlete, Baseball Player)
5208 William St
Lancaster, NY 14086-9448, USA

Garcia, Danay (Actor)
c/o L Travis Clark PO Box 532
Hollywood, CA 90078, USA

Garcia, Danna (Actor)
c/o Staff Member *Telemundo*
2470 W 8th Ave
Hialeah, FL 33010-2000, USA

Garcia, Danny (Athlete, Baseball Player)
22 Silo Ln
Levittown, NY 11756-3807, USA

Garcia, David (Dave) (Athlete, Baseball Player, Coach)
17842 Avenida Cordillera Unit 28
San Diego, CA 92128-1514, USA

Garcia, Eddie (Athlete, Football Player)
4914 Oreilly Rd
Omro, WI 54963, USA

Garcia, Freddy A (Baseball Player)
Quisquella Qta Etapa M22 #52
La Romana, DOMINICAN REPUBLIC

Garcia, Gonzalo (Stylist)
c/o Staff Member *Mark Edward Inc*
325 W 8th St # 1011
New York, NY 10018, USA

Garcia, Gretchen (Stylist)
c/o Staff Member *Ford Models (Chicago)*
311 W Superior St
Chicago, IL 60654-3548, USA

Garcia, Guillermo (Athlete, Baseball Player)
3806 Shoma Dr
West Palm Beach, FL 33414-4374, USA

Garcia, James (Athlete, Football Player)
999 E Basse Rd Ste 180
San Antonio, TX 78209-1807, USA

Garcia, Jeff (Athlete, Football Player)
30628 Detroit Rd # 294
Westlake, OH 44145-5844, USA

Garcia, Jesus (Actor)
c/o Staff Member *Columbia Artists Mgmt Inc*
1790 Broadway Fl 6
New York, NY 10019-1537, USA

Garcia, Joanna (Actor)
c/o Pamela Kohl *3 Arts Entertainment Inc*
9460 Wilshire Blvd Fl 7
Beverly Hills, CA 90212-2713, USA

Garcia, Jorge (Actor)
c/o Erik Kritzer *Kritzer Levine Wilkins Entertainment*
11872 La Grange Ave Fl 1
Los Angeles, CA 90025-5283, USA

Garcia, Jsu (Actor)
c/o Phyllis Carlyle *Carlyle Productions & Management*
2050 Laurel Canyon Blvd
Los Angeles, CA 90046-2065, USA

Garcia, Juan Carlos (Actor)
c/o Gabriel Blanco *Gabriel Blanco Iglesias (Mexico)*
Rio Balsas 35-32 Colonia Cuauhtemoc
DF 6500, Mexico

Garcia, Karim (Athlete, Baseball Player)
38 Agnew Farm Rd
Armonk, NY 10504-1371, USA

Garcia, Kiko (Athlete, Baseball Player)
526 Trailview Cir
Martinez, CA 94553-3563, USA

Garcia, Leo (Athlete, Baseball Player)
5416 W Sunland Ave
Laveen, AZ 85339-1509, USA

Garcia, Leonardo (Actor)
c/o Staff Member *TV Azteca*
Periferico Sur 4121 Colonia Fuentes del Pedregal
DF CP 14141, Mexico

Garcia, Lilian
1100 Valley Brook Ave
Lyndhurst, NJ 07071-3620, USA

Garcia, Mike (Athlete, Baseball Player)
15892 Lasselle St Unit B
Moreno Valley, CA 92551-4775, USA

Garcia, Nina (Business Person, Designer)
1633 Broadway Fl 44
New York, NY 10019-6708, USA

Garcia, Odalys (Actor)
c/o Staff Member *Univision*
605 3rd Ave Fl 12
New York, NY 10158-0034, USA

Garcia, Pedro (Athlete, Baseball Player)
L4 Parq Del Condado
Caguas, PR 00727-1224, USA

Garcia, Ralph (Athlete, Baseball Player)
7441 Brian Ln
La Palma, CA 90623-1312, USA

Garcia, Ramon (Athlete, Baseball Player)
Hatuey 259 E Oriente Camaguey Arroyo
Havana, Cuba

Garcia, Rich (Baseball Player)
769 Harbor Is
Clearwater Beach, FL 33767-1805, USA

Garcia, Rich (Athlete, Baseball Player)
769 Harbor Is
Clearwater Beach, FL 33767-1805, USA

Garcia, Rodrigo (Director)
c/o Adriana Alberghetti *WmE2 (Endeavor-LA)*
9601 Wilshire Blvd Fl 3
Beverly Hills, CA 90210-5219, USA

Garcia, Russell (Composer)
18558 Citronia # 15
Northridge, CA 91324, USA

Garcia Marquez, Gabriel (Nobel Prize Laureate, Writer)
Pedregal de San Angel
Mexico City, DF, MEXICO

Garciaparra, Nomar (Athlete, Baseball Player)
238 Shawnan Ln
La Habra, CA 90631-8087, USA

Gardeazabal, Marcela (Actor)

Gardell, Billy (Actor)
c/o Nick Nuciforo *Creative Artists Agency (CAA-LA)*
2000 Avenue of the Stars Ste 100
Los Angeles, CA 90067-4705, USA

Gardener, Daryl (Athlete, Football Player)
8925 Legacy Ct Apt 106
Kissimmee, FL 34747-3018, USA

Gardenhire, Ronald C (Ron) (Athlete, Baseball Player, Coach)
585 Country Road B2 E
Saint Paul, MN 55117, USA

Gardin, Ron (Athlete, Football Player)
PO Box 66051
Tucson, AZ 85728-6051, USA

Gardiner, John Eliot (Conductor)
Gore Farm Ashmore
Salisbury, Wilts SP5 5AR, UNITED KINGDOM (UK)

Gardiner, Mike (Athlete, Baseball Player)
26 Read Dr
Hanover, MA 02339-2632, USA

Gardiner, Robert K A (Misc)
PO Box 9274 The Airport
Accra, GHANA

Gardner, Art (Athlete, Baseball Player)
RR 2 Box 41
Walnut Grove, MS 39189, USA

Gardner, Ashley (Actor)
c/o Staff Member *Forster Entertainment*
12533 Woodgreen St
Los Angeles, CA 90066-2723, USA

Gardner, Barry (Athlete, Football Player)
24964 S Willow Brook Trl
Crete, IL 60417-3714, USA

Gardner, Bill (Athlete, Hockey Player)
c/o Staff Member *Chicago Wolves*
2301 Ravine Way
Glenview, IL 60025-7627, USA

Gardner, Brett (Athlete, Baseball Player)
510 Bunch Ford Rd
Holly Hill, SC 29059-8595, USA

Gardner, Carwell (Athlete, Football Player)
9603 Galene Dr
Louisville, KY 40299-3231, USA

Gardner, Chris (Athlete, Baseball Player)
2304 SW Abalon Cir
Port Saint Lucie, FL 34953-5718, USA

Gardner, Christopher (Business Person, Writer)
c/o Rachel Nagler 1345 Avenue of the Americas 30th Fl
New York, NY 10105, USA

Gardner, Cory (Congressman, Politician)
213 Cannon Hob
Washington, DC 20515-0919, USA

Gardner, Dale (Astronaut)
c/o Staff Member *NASA*
2101 Nasa Pkwy Spc Center
Houston, TX 77058-3696, USA

Gardner, Dave (Athlete, Hockey Player)
181 King St S
Waterloo, ON N2J 1P7, Canada

Gardner, David P (Educator)
2121 Sand Hill Rd
Menlo Park, CA 94025-6909, USA

Gardner, Guy S (Astronaut)
PO Box 2730
Gainesville, GA 30503-2730, USA

Gardner, Howard E (Physicist)
Graduate Education School
Cambridge, MA 2138, USA

Gardner, James H (Basketball Player, Coach)
5465 Bromely Dr
Oak Park, CA 91377-4750, USA

Gardner, Jeff (Athlete, Baseball Player)
1850 Boa Vista Cir
Costa Mesa, CA 92626-4701, USA

Gardner, John (Dancer)
890 Broadway
New York, NY 10003-1211, USA

Gardner, Ken (Athlete, Basketball Player)
3795 Hawkeye St
Salt Lake City, UT 84120-3390, USA

Gardner, Lee (Athlete, Baseball Player)
1354 Blue Heron Dr
Highland, MI 48357-3910, USA

Gardner, Lori (Stylist)
c/o Staff Member *Judy Inc*
1 Yorkville Ave
Toronto ON M4W 1L1, Canada

Gardner, Mark (Athlete, Baseball Player)
15216 Mesa View Ave
Friant, CA 93626-9780, USA

Gardner, Martin (Writer)
ATTN: PUBLICITY DEPT 175 Fifth Ave
New York, NY 10010, USA

Gardner, Moe (Athlete, Football Player)
11017 Lorin Way
Duluth, GA 30097-8482, USA

Gardner, Nancy P (Stylist)
2215 W Melrose St # 2
Chicago, IL 60618-6315, USA

Gardner, Paul (Athlete, Hockey Player)
104 Drayton Ct
Franklin, TN 37067-1353, USA

Gardner, Randy (Figure Skater)
4640 Glencoe Ave Apt 6
Marina Del Rey, CA 90292-6388, USA

Gardner, Rob (Athlete, Baseball Player)
727 Via Tripoli
Punta Gorda, FL 33950-6794, USA

Gardner, Rod (Athlete, Football Player)
1883 Executive Dr
Duluth, GA 30096-8922, USA

Gardner, Rulon (Actor)
6791 Brook Forest Dr
Evergreen, CO 80439-6827, USA

Gardner, W Booth (Ex-Governor)
312 N Stadium Way Apt 102
Tacoma, WA 98403-3247, USA

Gardner, Wee Willie (Athlete, Basketball Player)
400 E Van Buren St Ste 300
Phoenix, AZ 85004-2257, USA

Gardner, Wes (Athlete, Baseball Player)
305 Ruth
Benton, AR 72019-2226, USA

Gardner, Wilford R (Physicist)
Natural Resources College
Berkeley, CA 94720-0001, USA

Gardner, William F (Billy) (Athlete, Baseball Player, Coach)
35 Dayton Rd
Waterford, CT 06385-4205, USA

Gardocki, Christopher A (Chris) (Athlete, Football Player)
63 Yorkshire Dr
Hilton Head Island, SC 29928-3368, USA

Gardos, Eva (Director)
c/o Staff Member *International Creative Management (ICM-LA)*
10250 Constellation Blvd Fl 7
Los Angeles, CA 90067-6207, USA

Gare, Danny (Athlete, Hockey Player)
950 Hopkins Rd Apt F
Buffalo, NY 14221-8317, USA

Garelick, Jeremy (Producer)
c/o Staff Member *Principato/Young Management*
9465 Wilshire Blvd Ste 430
Beverly Hills, CA 90212-2613, USA

Garewal, Simi (Actor, Bollywood)
Paviova 6th Floor Little Gibb's Road
Malabar Hill
Bombay, MS 400 006, INDIA

Garfat, Jance (Musician)
9850 Sandalwood Blvd # 458
Boca Raton, FL 33428, USA

Garfield, Allen (Actor)
c/o Brian McCabe *Venture IAB*
3211 Cahuenga Blvd W Ste 104
Los Angeles, CA 90068-1372, USA

Garfield, Andrew (Actor)
c/o Jeff Gollenberg *Collective*
8383 Wilshire Blvd Ste 1050
Beverly Hills, CA 90211-2415, USA

Garfinkel, Jack (Athlete, Basketball Player)
300 Ocean Pkwy Apt 2E
Brooklyn, NY 11218-4078, USA

Garfinkle, David (Producer)
c/o Staff Member *Renegade 83 Entertainment*
5700 Wilshire Blvd Fl 6
Los Angeles, CA 90036-3659, USA

Garfunkel, Art (Actor, Musician)
c/o Staff Member *WmE2 (WMA-LA)*
1 William Morris Pl
Beverly Hills, CA 90212-4261, USA

Garibaldi, Bob (Athlete, Baseball Player)
2143 Oregon Ave
Stockton, CA 95204-4617, USA

Garity, Troy (Actor)
c/o Jason Weinberg *Untitled Entertainment (LA)*
350 S Beverly Dr Ste 200
Beverly Hills, CA 90212-4819, USA

Garland, Beverly (Actor)
4222 Vineland Ave
North Hollywood, CA 91602-3318, USA

Garland, Carrington
8014 Briar Summit Dr
Los Angeles, CA 90046-1127

Garland, George D (Physicist)
5 Mawhiney Ct
Huntsville, ON P0A 1K0, CANADA

Garland, Jon (Athlete, Baseball Player)
2924 Summerwood Dr
Springfield, IL 62712-5865, USA

Garland, Merrick B (Judge)
333 Constitution Ave NW
Washington, DC 20001-2804, USA

Garland, Travis (Musician)
c/o Simon Fuller *XIX Entertainment*
33/32 Ransomes Dock 35-37 Parkgate Rd
London SW11 4NP, UK

Garland, Wayne (Athlete, Baseball Player)
7556 Mossback St
Las Vegas, NV 89123-1581, USA

Garland, Winston (Athlete, Basketball Player)
2304 Cleveland St
Gary, IN 46404-3423, USA

Garlick, Scott (Soccer Player)
555 17th St Ste 3350
Denver, CO 80202-3909, USA

Garlin, Jeff (Actor, Producer)
c/o Staff Member *3 Arts Entertainment Inc*
9460 Wilshire Blvd Fl 7
Beverly Hills, CA 90212-2713, USA

Garlits, Donald G (Big Daddy) (Race Car Driver)
13700 SW 16th Ave
Ocala, FL 34473-3970, USA

Garlock, Bradley (Stylist)
c/o Staff Member *Judy Casey Inc*
114 E 13th St
New York, NY 10003-5329, USA

Garmaker, Dick (Athlete, Basketball Player)
5824 E 11th St
Tulsa, OK 74137, USA

Garman, Mike (Athlete, Baseball Player)
15144 Kings Row Rd
Caldwell, ID 83607-8371, USA

Garman-Hosted, Ann (Baseball Player)
6582 N 100 E
Wawaka, IN 46794-9724, USA

Garmon, Kelvin (Athlete, Football Player)
1424 Creekview Dr
Lewisville, TX 75067-4994, USA

Garn, Stanley M (Misc)
1200 Earhart Rd # 223
Ann Arbor, MI 48105-2768, USA

Garneau, Marc (Astronaut)
6767 Route De Aeroport
Sainte-Hubert, QC J3Y 8Y9, CANADA

Garner, Charlie (Athlete, Football Player)
12944 Royal George Ave
Odessa, FL 33556-5709, USA

Garner, James (Actor)
c/o Bill Robinson *Bill Robinson Management*
PO Box 6284
Malibu, CA 90264-6284, USA

Garner, Jennifer (Actor)
c/o Nicole King *Management 360*
9111 Wilshire Blvd
Beverly Hills, CA 90210-5508, USA

Garner, Kelli (Actor)
c/o John Carrabino *John Carrabino Management*
5900 Wilshire Blvd Ste 406
Los Angeles, CA 90036-5015, USA

Garner, Philip M (Phil) (Athlete, Baseball Player, Coach)
2 Sapling Pl
Spring, TX 77382-2636, USA

Garner, Wendell R (Physicist)
PO Box 650
Branford, CT 06405-0650, USA

Garner, William S (Cartoonist)
495 Union Ave
Memphis, TN 38103-3217, USA

Garnes, Sam (Athlete, Football Player)
7322 S Valdai Cir
Aurora, CO 80016-2311, USA

Garnett, Dave (Athlete, Football Player)
4527 Tyrone Ave
Sherman Oaks, CA 91423-2628, USA

Garnett, Kevin (Athlete, Basketball Player)
c/o Andy Miller *ASM Sports*
920 Undercliff Ave
Edgewater, NJ 07020-1558, USA

Garnett, Scott (Athlete, Football Player)
1637 28th St SE
Puyallup, WA 98372-5188, USA

Garnett, Winfield (Athlete, Football Player)
2029 S 16th Ave
Broadview, IL 60155-3015, USA

Garnica, Ron (Stylist)
c/o Staff Member *Zenobia Agency Inc*
PO Box 909
Groveland, CA 95321-0909, USA

Garofalo, Janeane (Actor)
c/o Kara Welker *Generate Management*
1545 26th St Ste 200
Santa Monica, CA 90404-3554, USA

Garouste, Gerard (Artist)
La Mesangere
Marcilly-sur-Eure 27810, FRANCE

Garpenlov, Johan (Athlete, Hockey Player)
Breviksvagen 133
Tyresso A-13569, Sweden

Garr, Ralph A (Athlete, Baseball Player)
22314 Auburn Canyon Ln
Richmond, TX 77469-5639, USA

Garr, Teri (Terri/Terry) (Actor)
9150 Wilshire Blvd Ste 350
Beverly Hills, CA 90212-3453, USA

Garrahy, J Joseph (Ex-Governor)
63 Starr Dr
Narragansett, RI 02882-3129, USA

Garrard, David (Athlete, Football Player)
10102 Delpoint Ln
Jacksonville, FL 32246-1894, USA

Garrard, Rose (Artist)
105 Carpenters Road #21
London E18, UNITED KINGDOM (UK)

Garreis, Robert M (Geophysicist, Physicist)
Marine Science Dept
Saint Petersburg, FL 33701, USA

Garrelts, Scott (Athlete, Baseball Player)
11070 Ashland Way
Shreveport, LA 71106-9348, USA

Garret, Peter (Musician)
PO Box 249
Maroubra, NSW 2035, Australia

Garrett, Adrian (Athlete, Baseball Player)
PO Box 201
Manchaca, TX 78652-0201, USA

Garrett, Alvin (Athlete, Football Player)
2600 Napoleon Ct
Vestavia, AL 35243-5452, USA

Garrett, Beau (Actor)
c/o Sean Fay *Kritzer Levine Wilkins Entertainment*
11872 La Grange Ave Fl 1
Los Angeles, CA 90025-5283, USA

Garrett, Brad (Actor, Comedian)
c/o Glenn Robbins *Raw Talent Management*
545 Veteran Ave
Los Angeles, CA 90024-1915, USA

Garrett, Carl (Athlete, Football Player)
314 Teal St
Pittsburg, TX 75686-1530, USA

Garrett, Clifton (Athlete, Baseball Player)
7504 Kenicott Ln
Plainfield, IL 60586-4173, USA

Garrett, Dick (Athlete, Basketball Player)
7100 N Park Manor Dr
Milwaukee, WI 53224-4642, USA

Garrett, Drake (Athlete, Football Player)
32600 Concord Dr Apt 724
Madison Heights, MI 48071-1114, USA

Garrett, Jason (Athlete, Football Player)
3656 Maplewood Ave
Dallas, TX 75205-2835, USA

Garrett, Jeremy (Actor)
c/o Staff Member *Paradigm (LA)*
360 N Crescent Dr
Beverly Hills, CA 90210-4874, USA

Garrett, John (Athlete, Hockey Player)
c/o Staff Member *Rogers Sportsnet*
181 Keefer Pl Suite 221
Vancouver, BC V6B 1W6, Canada

Garrett, John (Athlete, Football Player)
1402 Meadow Ln
Southlake, TX 76092-8339, USA

Garrett, Judd (Athlete, Football Player)
900 Meadow Ln
Southlake, TX 76092-8335, USA

Garrett, Kathleen (Actor)
1800 Avenue of the Stars Ste 400
Los Angeles, CA 90067-4206, USA

Garrett, Kenneth (Photographer)
1145 17th St NW
Washington, DC 20036-4707, USA

Garrett, Kenny (Musician)
1915 Cullen Ave
Austin, TX 78757-2435, USA

Garrett, Leif (Actor, Musician)
c/o Barbara Papageorge *Barbara Papageorge Publicity*
790 Amsterdam Ave
New York, NY 10025-5738, USA

Garrett, Len (Athlete, Football Player)
9413 W Tampa Dr
Baton Rouge, LA 70815-8951, USA

Garrett, Lesley (Opera Singer)
Park Offices 121 Dora Road
London SW19 7JT, UNITED KINGDOM (UK)

Garrett, Lila (Director)
1245 Laurel Way
Beverly Hills, CA 90210, USA

Garrett, Michael L (Mike) (Athlete, Football Player)
University of Southern California Athletic Dept
Los Angeles, CA 90089-0001, USA

Garrett, Mike S (Athlete, Football Player)
1040 Dogwood Dr
Greensboro, GA 30642-4827, USA

Garrett, MJ (Reality TV Star)
c/o Michael (Mike) Esterman
Esterman.Com, LLC
Prefers to be contacted via email
MD, USA

Garrett, Pat (Musician, Songwriter, Writer)
PO Box 84
Strausstown, PA 19559-0084, USA

Garrett, Peter (Musician, Politician)
P.O. Box 186
Glebe NSW 2037, Australia

Garrett, Reggie (Athlete, Football Player)
3 Martino Way
Somerset, NJ 08873-4952, USA

Garrett, Rowland (Athlete, Basketball Player)
219 Western Hills Dr
Jackson, MS 39212-3216, USA

Garrett, Scott (Congressman, Politician)
2244 Rayburn Hob
Washington, DC 20515-0921, USA

Garrett, Spencer (Actor)
c/o Erik Kritzer *Kritzer Levine Wilkins Entertainment*
11872 La Grange Ave Fl 1
Los Angeles, CA 90025-5283, USA

Garrett, Wayne (Athlete, Baseball Player)
4331 Linwood St
Sarasota, FL 34232-3905, USA

Garrett, Wilbur E (Editor)
& 17th M Sts
Washington, DC 20036, USA

Garrett, William E (Photographer)
209 Seneca Rd
Great Falls, VA 22066-1108, USA

Garrett III, H Lawrence (Government Official)
RR1 Box 136-18
Boyce, VA 22620, USA

Garrick, Tom (Athlete, Basketball Player)
235 Providence St
West Warwick, RI 02893-2552, USA

Garrido, Gil (Athlete, Baseball Player)
11311 SW 200th St Apt 110D
Miami, FL 33157-8281, USA

Garrido, Norberto (Athlete, Football Player)
15633 Briarbank St
La Puente, CA 91744-1106, USA

Garriott, Owen E (Doctor)
111 Lost Tree Dr SW
Huntsville, AL 35824-1313, USA

Garriott, Owen K (Astronaut)
111 Lost Tree Dr SW
Huntsville, AL 35824-1313, USA

Garris, John (Athlete, Basketball Player)
308 Carroll St
New Bedford, MA 02740-1415, USA

Garris, Kiwane (Athlete, Basketball Player)
23 E Rocket Cir
Park Forest, IL 60466-1613, USA

Garrison, David (Actor)
630 Estrada Redonda
Santa Fe, NM 87506-7942, USA

Garrison, Gary (Athlete, Football Player)
993 N Vulcan Ave Apt 7
Encinitas, CA 92024-1794, USA

Garrison, John (Athlete, Hockey Player)
Old Concord Rd
Lincoln, MA 1773, USA

Garrison, Lane (Actor)
c/o Dannielle Thomas *Untitled Entertainment (LA)*
350 S Beverly Dr Ste 200
Beverly Hills, CA 90212-4819, USA

Garrison, Walt (Athlete, Football Player)
3475 E Hickory Hill Rd
Argyle, TX 76226-3133, USA

Garrison, Webster (Athlete, Baseball Player)
2038 Rue Racine
Marrero, LA 70072-4729, USA

Garrison-Jackson, Zina (Tennis Player)
1701 Hermann Dr Unit 705
Houston, TX 77004-7348, USA

Garrity, Gregg (Athlete, Football Player)
86 Seldom Seen Rd
Bradfordwoods, PA 15015-1320, USA

Garrity, Jack (Athlete, Hockey Player)
1530 Beacon St Apt 1201
Brookline, MA 02446-2640, USA

Garrity, Pat (Athlete, Basketball Player)
85 Harrison Ave
New Canaan, CT 06840-5802, USA

Garron, Larry (Athlete, Football Player)
3 Debra Ln
Framingham, MA 01701-4547, USA

Garror, Leon (Athlete, Football Player)
259 Stocking St
Mobile, AL 36604-1948, USA

Garrum, Larry (Athlete, Hockey Player)
987 Pleasant St
Framingham, MA 01701-8853, USA

Garson, Willie (Actor)
c/o Gladys Gonzalez *John Carrabino Management*
5900 Wilshire Blvd Ste 406
Los Angeles, CA 90036-5015, USA

Garten, Ina (Writer)
1745 Broadway
New York, NY 10019-4368, USA

Garth, Jennie (Actor)
c/o Randy James *James/Levy/Jacobson Management Inc*
3500 W Olive Ave Ste 1470
Burbank, CA 91505-5514, USA

Garth, Leonard I (Judge)
50 Walnut St
Newark, NJ 07102-3551, USA

Gartner, Claus-Theo
Postfach 230313
Essen, GERMANY 45071

Gartner, Mike (Athlete, Hockey Player)
c/o Staff Member *Hockey Hall of Fame*
B C E Place 30 Yonge St
Toronto, ON M5E 1X8, Canada

Garver, Cathy (Actor)
550 Mountain Home Rd
Woodside, CA 94062-2515, USA

Garver, Kathy (Actor)
c/o Staff Member *Morgan Agency, The*
1200 N Doheny Dr
Los Angeles, CA 90069-1723, USA

Garver, Ned F (Athlete, Baseball Player)
1121 Town Line Rd Unit 164
Bryan, OH 43506-8732, USA

Garvey, Steve (Athlete, Baseball Player)
1776 Park Ave
Park City, UT 84060-5148, USA

Garvey-Truhan, Cyndy
13924 Panay Way Apt 309
Marina Del Rey, CA 90292-4124

Garvin, Jerry (Athlete, Baseball Player)
1797 E 700 S
Springville, UT 84663-3241, USA

Garwin, Richard L (Physicist)
1 Christie Pl Unit 402W
Scarsdale, NY 10583-8305, USA

Garwood, William L (Will) (Judge)
903 San Jacinto Blvd
Austin, TX 78701-2449, USA

Gary, Cleveland (Athlete, Football Player)
720 SE Martin Luther King Jr Blvd
Stuart, FL 34994-2368, USA

Gary, Cleveland E (Athlete, Football Player)
1446 SW 169th Ave
Indiantown, FL 37956, USA

Gary, Keith (Athlete, Football Player)
450 Massachusetts Ave NW Apt 903
Washington, DC 20001-6220, USA

Gary, Leonard (Athlete, Basketball Player)
3318 N Decatur Blvd Unit 2086
Las Vegas, NV 89130-3253, USA

Gary, Lorraine (Actor)
1158 Tower Rd
Beverly Hills, CA 90210-2131, USA

Garza, David (Musician)
PO Box 5085
Larkspur, CA 94977-5085, USA

Garza, Emilio M (Judge)
US Courthouse 8200 1-10 W
San Antonio, TX 78230, USA

Garza, Nicole (Actor)
c/o David Rudy *Armada Partners*
815 Moraga Dr
Los Angeles, CA 90049-1633, USA

Garza, Rene (Stylist)
c/o Celebrity Stylist *Oliver Piro Inc*
725 Riverside Dr Apt 3A
New York, NY 10031-2460, USA

Gascoigne, Paul J (Soccer Player)
Holborn Hall 10 Grays Inn Road
London WC1X 8BY, UNITED KINGDOM (UK)

Gascoine, Jill (Actor)
12/13 Poland St
London W1V 3DE, UNITED KINGDOM (UK)

Gascolgne, Sheryl
Stanstead Abbots
Hertfordshire, ENGLAND

Gascon, Elleen (Baseball Player)
249 Trowbridge Rd
Elk Grove Village, IL 60007-3820, USA

Gash, Samuel L (Sam) (Athlete, Football Player)
51180 Park Place Dr
Northville, MI 48167-9112, USA

Gash, Thane (Athlete, Football Player)
201 Whispering Hills Dr
Hendersonville, NC 28792-1213, USA

Gaskill, Brian (Actor)
c/o Marie Mathews *Marie Mathews Management*
8730 W Sunset Blvd Ste 200
Los Angeles, CA 90069-2275, USA

Gaskill, Michael (Stylist)
c/o Celebrity Stylist *Smashbox Beauty*
8549 Higuera St Bldg B
Culver City, CA 90232-2521, USA

Gasol, Pau (Athlete, Basketball Player)
415 S Front St Unit 20
Memphis, TN 38103-6404, USA

Gaspar, Rod (Athlete, Baseball Player)
28771 Peach Blossom
Mission Viejo, CA 92692-1072, USA

Gaspari, Rich (Misc)
PO Box 29
Milltown, NJ 08850-0029, USA

Gass, William H (Writer)
6304 Westminster Pl
Saint Louis, MO 63130-4727, USA

Gassert, Ron (Athlete, Football Player)
11 Sheffield Pl
Southampton, NJ 08088-1306, USA

Gasslyev, Nikolal T (Opera Singer)
Teartainaya Pl 1
Saint Petersburg, RUSSIA

Gassman, Alessandro (Actor)
Lungotevere del Mellini 10
Rome 193, ITALY

Gassner, Dave (Athlete, Baseball Player)
N1376 Woodland Dr
Greenville, WI 54942-8035, USA

Gassoff, Brad (Athlete, Hockey Player)
P.O. Box 85
Wells, BC V0K 2R0, Canada

Gast, Leon (Director, Editor, Producer)
c/o Staff Member *WmE2 (WMA-LA)*
1 William Morris Pl
Beverly Hills, CA 90212-4261, USA

Gasteyer, Ana (Actor, Comedian)
c/o Staff Member *Dontanville/Frattaroli (D/F)*
270 Lafayette St Ste 402
New York, NY 10012-3327, USA

Gastineau, Brittny (Actor, Reality TV Star)
c/o Dana-Lee Schuman *International Creative Management (ICM-LA)*
10250 Constellation Blvd Fl 7
Los Angeles, CA 90067-6207, USA

Gastineau, Lisa (Actor, Reality TV Star)
c/o Staff Member *True Entertainment*
601 W 26th St Rm 1336
New York, NY 10001-1136, USA

Gastineau, Marcus D (Mark) (Athlete, Football Player)
22202 N 48th St
Phoenix, AZ 85054-6171, USA

Gaston, Clarence E (Cito) (Athlete, Baseball Player, Coach)
1454 Woodstream Dr
Oldsmar, FL 34677-4832, USA

Gaston, Hiram (Baseball Player)
18 Burntwood Cres
Winnipeg, AB R2J 3A1, CANADA

Gaston, Michael (Actor)
c/o Lisa Lieberman *Innovative Artists (NY)*
235 Park Ave S Fl 7
New York, NY 10003-1404, USA

Gates, Antonio (Athlete, Football Player)
c/o Staff Member *EAG Sports Management*
12910 Agustin Pl
Playa Vista, CA 90094-2301, USA

Gates, Brent (Athlete, Baseball Player)
4690 Hall St SE
Grand Rapids, MI 49546-3774, USA

Gates, Daryl (Actor)
24876 Sunstar Ln
Dana Point, CA 92629-1930, USA

Gates, David (Musician, Songwriter, Writer)
108 E Matilija St
Ojai, CA 93023-2639, USA

Gates, Gareth (Musician)
c/o Staff Member *19 Entertainment*
33/32 Ransomes Dock 35-37 Parkgate Rd
London SW11 4NP, UK

Gates, Henry Lewis Jr (Educator)
Afro-American Studies Dept
Cambridge, MA 2138, USA

Gates, Joe (Athlete, Baseball Player)
1517 E 19th Ave
Gary, IN 46407-1607, USA

Gates, Josh (Actor)
c/o Noreen Savides *323 Talent Management*
PO Box 3234
Quartz Hill, CA 93586-0234, USA

Gates, Mike (Athlete, Baseball Player)
131 Edgewater Rd
Kooskia, ID 83539-5024, USA

Gates, Robert M (Educator, Government Official)
President S Ofc
College Station, TX 77843-0001, USA

Gates, William H (Bill) (Business Person)
c/o Staff Member *Microsoft Corporation*
1 Microsoft Way
Redmond, WA 98052-8300, USA

Gatewood, Aubrey (Athlete, Baseball Player)
5 Pine Tree Loop
North Little Rock, AR 72116-8313, USA

Gatewood, Les (Athlete, Football Player)
PO Box 414
Kirbyville, TX 75956-0414, USA

Gatewood, Tom (Athlete, Football Player)
101 Cambridge Dr
Nutley, NJ 07110-3913, USA

Gathegi, Edi (Actor)
c/o Mary Ellen Mulcahy *Framework Entertainment (LA)*
9057 Nemo St Ste C
West Hollywood, CA 90069-5511, USA

Gatherum, Dave (Athlete, Hockey Player)
200 Riverview Dr
Thunder Bay, ON P7C 1R5, Canada

Gathright, Joey (Athlete, Baseball Player)
4722 Oak St
Kansas City, MO 64112-2270, USA

Gatlin, Justin (Athlete, Track Athlete)
c/o Staff Member *USA Track & Field*
132 E Washington St Ste 800
Indianapolis, IN 46204-3674, USA

Gatlin, Larry
5100 Harris Ave
Kansas City, MO 64133-2331

Gatlin, Larry W (Musician, Songwriter, Writer)
2821 Bransford Ave
Nashville, TN 37204-3101, USA

Gatling, Chris (Athlete, Basketball Player)
175 Canon Dr
Orinda, CA 94563-2218, USA

Gatti, Jennifer (Actor)
1801 Avenue of the Stars Ste 902
Los Angeles, CA 90067-5981, USA

Gatting, Michael W (Cricketer)
Saint John's Wood Road
London NW8 8QN, UNITED KINGDOM (UK)

Gattison, Kenny (Athlete, Basketball Player)
1204 Northern Lights Dr
Upper Marlboro, MD 20774-6049, USA

Gattorno, Francisco (Actor)
c/o Gabriel Blanco *Gabriel Blanco Iglesias (Mexico)*
Rio Balsas 35-32 Colonia Cuauhtemoc
DF 6500, Mexico

Gatzos, Steve (Athlete, Hockey Player)
166 Charlotte St
Peterborough, ON K9J 2T8, Canada

Gaubatz, Dennis (Athlete, Football Player)
1250 County Road 943
West Columbia, TX 77486-9454, USA

Gaucho, Ronaldinho (Soccer Player)
Avenida Aristides Mailol
Barcelona 8028, SPAIN

Gauci, Miriam (Opera Singer)
Plankengasse 7
Vienna 1010, AUSTRIA

Gaudet, Jim (Athlete, Baseball Player)
3336 Vineville Ave
Macon, GA 31204-2328, USA

Gaudiani, Claire L (Educator)
11 E 1st St Ph 23
New York, NY 10003-9194, USA

Gaudin, Chad (Athlete, Baseball Player)
7612 Stoneleigh Dr
New Orleans, LA 70123-4741, USA

Gaudreau, Rob (Athlete, Hockey Player)
22 Briarbrooke Ln
Cranston, RI 02921-2111, USA

Gaudreault, Armand (Athlete, Hockey Player)
320-5900 3E Av E
Quebec, QC G1H 7N7, Canada

Gaul, Frank (Athlete, Football Player)
3420 Balsam Dr
Westlake, OH 44145-4407, USA

Gaul, Gilbert M (Journalist)
400 N Broad St
Philadelphia, PA 19130-4015, USA

Gaul, Michael (Athlete, Hockey Player)
22 Hampton Gardens Attn Coaching Staff
Pointe-Claire, QC H9S 5B8, Canada

Gault, Bill (Athlete, Football Player)
PO Box 2867
Fredericksburg, TX 78624-1927, USA

Gault, William Campbell (Writer)
481 Mountain Dr
Santa Barbara, CA 93103-1700, USA

Gault, Willie J (Athlete, Football Player)
9201 W Sunset Blvd Ste 406
West Hollywood, CA 90069-3705, USA

Gaultier, Jean Paul (Designer, Fashion Designer)
30, rue du Faubourg St Antoine
Paris 75012, FRANCE

Gaume, Dallas (Athlete, Hockey Player)
4350 Gallaghers Fairway S
Kelowna, BC V1W 4X4, Canada

Gaurav, Kumar (Actor)
Dimple 7 Pali Hill Bandra
Bombay, MS 400 050, INDIA

Gaustad, Paul (Athlete, Hockey Player)
55 Saybrook Pl
Buffalo, NY 14209-1106, USA

Gauthier, Dan (Actor)

Gauthier, Daniel (Athlete, Hockey Player)
17 Rue Nicoud
Charlemagne, QC J5Z 1Z2, Canada

Gauthier, Denis (Athlete, Hockey Player)
11800 N 96th Pl
Scottsdale, AZ 85260-5962, USA

Gauthier, Jean (Athlete, Hockey Player)
415 Av Vinet
Dorval, QC H9S 2M7, Canada

Gauthier, Luc (Athlete, Hockey Player)
c/o Staff Member *Colorado Avalanche*
Pepsi Center 1000 Chopper Cir
Denver, CO 80204, USA

Gauthreaux, Joe (DJ)
c/o Staff Member *Diva Central Inc*
7510 W Sunset Blvd Ste 1445
Los Angeles, CA 90046-3408, USA

Gautier, Dick (Actor)
c/o Staff Member *Beacon Talent Agency*
170 Apple Ridge Rd
Woodcliff Lake, NJ 07677-8149, USA

Gautlier, Jean-Paul (Designer, Fashion Designer)
325 Rue Du Faubaurg St Martin
Paris 75003, FRANCE

Gauvreau, Jocelyn (Athlete, Hockey Player)
19 Rue Le Vasseur
Gatineau, QC J8V 2M8, Canada

Gava, Cassandra (Actor)
1745 Camino Palmero St Apt 210
Los Angeles, CA 90046-2918, USA

Gavankar, Janina (Actor)
c/o Arlene Forster *Forster Entertainment*
12533 Woodgreen St
Los Angeles, CA 90066-2723, USA

Gavaskar, Sunil M (Cricketer)
40 Bhalchandra Road Dadar # A
Bombay, MS 400014, INDIA

Gavey, Aaron (Athlete, Hockey Player)
RR 1
Selkirk, ON N0A 1P0, Canada

Gavilan, Kid
1 Hall of Fame Dr
Canastota, NY 13032-1175

Gavin, Charles E (Chuck) (Athlete, Football Player)
2800 Grape St
Denver, CO 80207-2730, USA

Gavin, Diarmuid (Actor)
c/o Staff Member *John Noel Management*
10A Belmont St Floor 2
London NW1 8HH, UNITED KINGDOM (UK)

Gavin, Erica
c/o Siouxzan Perry *Girlwerks Management*
3395 E Camino Rojos
Palm Springs, CA 92262-5417, USA

Gavin, John (Actor, Diplomat)
2100 Century Park W # 10263
Los Angeles, CA 90067-6900, USA

Gavin, Stewart (Stew) (Athlete, Hockey Player)
1700-320 Bay St
Toronto, ON M5H 4A6, Canada

Gaviria, Trujillo Cesar (President)
& 17th Constitution NW
Washington, DC 20006, USA

Gavitt, Dave (Basketball Player, Misc)
151 Merrimac St # 1
Boston, MA 02114-4714, USA

Gavitt, David (Athlete, Basketball Player)
11 Drowne Pkwy
Rumford, RI 02916-1607, USA

Gavrilov, Andrei V (Musician)
c/o Mark Stephan *Mark Stephan Buhl Artists Management*
Geylinggasse 1
Wien 1130, AUSTRIA

Gavron, Rafi (Actor)
c/o Peter McGrath *Affirmative Entertainment*
425 N Robertson Blvd
West Hollywood, CA 90048-1735, USA

Gay, Billy (Athlete, Football Player)
824 Lisdowney Dr
Lockport, IL 60441-2794, USA

Gay, Brian (Athlete, Golfer)
6809 Valhalla Way
Windermere, FL 34786-5627, USA

Gay, Don
1818 Rodeo Dr
Mesquite, TX 75149-3800

Gay, Everett (Athlete, Football Player)
700 E Johnson St
Waco, TX 76705-3816, USA

Gay, George
588 Charlton Ct NW
Marietta, GA 30064-1451

Gay, Gerald H (Jerry) (Journalist, Photographer)
PO Box 33848
Seattle, WA 98133-0848, USA

Gay, Peter J (Historian)
270 Riverside Dr Apt 8C
New York, NY 10025-5211, USA

Gay, Randall (Athlete, Football Player)
6706 Joyce Dr Apt 3C
Addis, LA 70710-2169, USA

Gay, Rudy (Athlete, Basketball Player)
91 W Galloway Dr
Memphis, TN 38111-6839, USA

Gay, William (Athlete, Football Player)
8200 E Jefferson Ave Apt 804
Detroit, MI 48214-2681, USA

Gaydos, Joey (Actor)
c/o Staff Member *Cunningham Escott Slevin & Doherty (CESD-LA)*
10635 Santa Monica Blvd Ste 130
Los Angeles, CA 90025-8306, USA

Gaydos, Kent (Athlete, Football Player)
1107 Mallard Ct
Granbury, TX 76048-2676, USA

Gaydos Jr, Joey (Actor)
20436 Martinsville Rd
Belleville, MI 48111-8706, USA

Gaydukov, Sergei N (Astronaut, Misc)
Moskovskoi Oblasti
Syvisdny Goroduk 141160, RUSSIA

Gayheart, Rebecca (Actor, Model)
c/o Stephanie Simon *Untitled Entertainment (LA)*
350 S Beverly Dr Ste 200
Beverly Hills, CA 90212-4819, USA

Gayle, Crystal (Actor, Musician)
c/o Staff Member *Webster & Associates PR*
3573 Couchville Pike
Hermitage, TN 37076-4012, USA

Gayle, Shaun (Athlete, Football Player)
PO Box 803887
Chicago, IL 60680-3887, USA

Gaylor, Noel (Admiral)
2111 Mason Hill Dr
Alexandria, VA 22306-2416, USA

Gaylor, Trevor (Athlete, Football Player)
5855 Hammond Dr
Norcross, GA 30071-3412, USA

Gaylord, Frank (Artist)
2844 Vt Route 14 Ste 1
Williamstown, VT 05679-9188, USA

Gaylord, Mitch (Athlete, Gymnast)
c/o Staff Member *WmE2 (WMA-LA)*
1 William Morris Pl
Beverly Hills, CA 90212-4261, USA

Gaylord, Scott
1451 Depew St
Lakewood, CO 80214-2236

Gaylords, The
32630 Concord Dr
Madison Heights, MI 48071-1110

Gaynes, George (Actor)
3344 Campanil Dr
Santa Barbara, CA 93109-1017, USA

Gaynor, Gloria (Music Group, Musician)
c/o Staff Member *Richard De La Font Agency*
3808 W South Park Blvd
Broken Arrow, OK 74011-1261, USA

Gaynor, Mitzi (Actor, Dancer, Musician)
12659 Moorpark St
Studio City, CA 91604-1377, USA

Gayoom, Maumoon Abdul (President)
Orchid Magu
Male 20-05, MALDIVES

Gayson, Eunice (Actor)
7 Leicester Place
London WC2H 7BP, UNITED KINGDOM (UK)

Gayton, Joe (Writer)
c/o David Saunders *Agency for the Performing Arts (APA-LA)*
405 S Beverly Dr Ste 500
Beverly Hills, CA 90212-4425, USA

Gayton, Tony (Writer)
c/o Matt Ochacher *Agency for the Performing Arts (APA-LA)*
405 S Beverly Dr Ste 500
Beverly Hills, CA 90212-4425, USA

Gaze, Andrew (Athlete, Basketball Player)
Australian Basketball Resources P.O. Box 2222
Ivanhoe East 3029, Australia

Gaziano, Frank (Athlete, Football Player)
14 Pinehurst Ln
Falmouth, ME 04105-1161, USA

Gazit, Doron (Artist)
14141 Covello St Bldg 1
Van Nuys, CA 91405-1489, USA

Gazzara, Ben (Actor)
c/o Johnnie Planco *Parseghian Planco LLC*
322 8th Ave Ste 601
New York, NY 10001-6715, USA

Gbagbo, Laurent (President)
Boulevard Clozel
Abidijan, IVORY COAST

Gbaja-Biamila, Akbar (Athlete, Football Player)
1050 Armitage St
Alameda, CA 94502-7931, USA

Geale, Rob (Athlete, Hockey Player)
4167 NW 178th Pl
Portland, OR 97229-7703, USA

Gearan, Mark (Educator, Government Official)
President's Office
Geneva, NY 14456, USA

Gearhart, John (Biologist, Doctor)
Medical Center
Baltimore, MD 21218, USA

Geary, Anthony (Tony) (Actor)
7010 Pacific View Dr
Los Angeles, CA 90068-2038, USA

Geary, Cynthia (Actor)
1041 N Formosa Ave # 200
West Hollywood, CA 90046-6703, USA

Geary, Geoff (Athlete, Baseball Player)
3333 Allen Pkwy Unit 1204
Houston, TX 77019-1842, USA

Geary, Tony
7010 Pacific View Dr
Los Angeles, CA 90068-2038

Geater, Ron (Athlete, Football Player)
3012 Oceanside Ct
Plainfield, IL 60586-5123, USA

Geathers, James (Athlete, Football Player)
200 Tony Dr
Georgetown, SC 29440-2059, USA

Geathers, Robert (Athlete, Football Player)
1 Dab Dr
Georgetown, SC 29440-6059, USA

Gebhard, Bob (Athlete, Baseball Player)
5242 E Otero Pl
Centennial, CO 80122-3889, USA

Gebo, Daniel (Scientist)
Paleontology Dept
De Kalb, IL 60115, USA

Gebrselassie, Haile (Athlete, Track Athlete)
P O Box 3241
Addis Ababa, ETHIOPIA

Geck, Thea (Stylist)
180 Brannan St Apt 227
San Francisco, CA 94107-2052, USA

Gedda, Nicolai (Opera Singer)
Valhallavagen 128
Stockholm 11441, SWEDEN

Geddes, Anne (Photographer)
2 York Street Parnell
Auckland 1001, NEW ZEALAND

Geddes, Bob (Athlete, Football Player)
79251 Tom Fazio Ln S
La Quinta, CA 92253-8031, USA

Geddes, Jane (Athlete, Golfer)
60 Buckingham Dr
Stamford, CT 06902-8310, USA

Geddes, Jim (Athlete, Baseball Player)
6738 Harrisburg London Rd
Orient, OH 43146-9454, USA

Geddes, Ken (Athlete, Football Player)
7702 147th Ave NE
Redmond, WA 98052-4168, USA

Gedman, Rich (Athlete, Baseball Player)
10 Parmenter Rd
Framingham, MA 01701-3019, USA

Gedmintas, Ruta (Actor)
c/o Olivia Homan *United Agents*
12-26 Lexington St
London W1F OLE, UK

Gedney, Chris (Athlete, Football Player)
4881 Excalibur Dr
Syracuse, NY 13215-9303, USA

Gedrick, Jason (Actor)
c/o Staff Member *IFA Talent Agency*
8730 W Sunset Blvd Ste 490
Los Angeles, CA 90069-2248, USA

Gee, E Gordon (Educator)
Chancellor S Ofc
Nashville, TN 37240-0001, USA

Gee, James D (Religious Leader)
4901 Pennsylvania Ave
Joplin, MO 64804-4947, USA

Gee, Prunella (Actor)
1Duchess St #1
London W1N 3DE, UNITED KINGDOM (UK)

Geer, Dennis (Financier)
550 17th St NW
Washington, DC 20429-0001, USA

Geer, Ellen (Actor)
21418 Entrada Rd
Topanga, CA 90290-3539, USA

Geertz, Clifford J (Misc)
Social Science Dept
Princeton, NJ 8540, USA

Geeson, Judy (Actor)
6300 Wilshire Blvd Ste 1470
Los Angeles, CA 90048-5200, USA

Geeson, Sally (Actor)
c/o Staff Member *Michael Summerton Management*
Martin Taylor-Brown Mimosa House, Mimosa St
London SW6 4DS, UK

Gee-Soo, Kim (Actor)
88 Sam-Sung Dong Sambo Building Fl 1
Kang nam gu, Seoul 135 090, Korea

Geffen, Aviv
Bugroashov 26
Tel Aviv, ISRAEL 63342

Geffen, David (Business Person, Producer)
c/o Bert Fields *Greenberg Glusker Fields Claman Machtinger Kinsela*
1900 Avenue of the Stars Ste 2100
Los Angeles, CA 90067-4502, USA

Gegenhuber, John
9171 Wilshire Blvd Ste 441
Beverly Hills, CA 90210-5516

Gehman, Martha
2488 Cheremoya Ave
Los Angeles, CA 90068-3070

Gehring, Frederick W (Mathematician)
1200 Earhart Rd
Ann Arbor, MI 48105-2768, USA

Gehring, Walter J (Doctor, Misc, Scientist)
Hochfeldstr 32
Therwill 4106, SWITZERLAND

Gehringer, Rick (Musician)
c/o Staff Member *Brothers Management Associates Inc*
141 Dunbar Ave
Fords, NJ 08863-1551

Gehrke, Jack (Athlete, Football Player)
5402 Nassau Cir E
Englewood, CO 80113-5134, USA

Gehry, Franko O (Architect)
12541 Beatrice St
Los Angeles, CA 90066-7001, USA

Geiberger, Al (Athlete, Golfer)
73091 Country Club Dr Ste A4
Palm Desert, CA 92260-2338, USA

Geiberger, Brent (Athlete, Golfer)
113 Chelsea Cir
Palm Desert, CA 92260-4688, USA

Geiduschek, E Peter (Biologist)
9500 Gilman Dr
La Jolla, CA 92093-5003, USA

Geier, Philip H Jr (Business Person)
1271 Avenue of the Americas
New York, NY 10020-1300, USA

Geiger, Ken (Journalist, Photographer)
Communications Center
Dallas, TX 75265, USA

Geiger, Matt (Athlete, Basketball Player)
12506 Twin Branch Acres Rd
Tampa, FL 33626-4423, USA

Geiger, Teddy (Musician)
11 Tamarron Way
Pittsford, NY 14534-3347, USA

Geimer, Samantha
4245 Waipua St
Kilauea, HI 96754-5336

Geingob, Hage G (Prime Minister)
Private Bag 13338
Windhoek 9000, NAMIBIA

Geisel, Dave (Athlete, Baseball Player)
4 Blacksmith Ln
Media, PA 19063-4411, USA

Geishert, Vern (Athlete, Baseball Player)
984 N Park St
Richland Center, WI 53581-1428, USA

Geisinger, Justin (Athlete, Football Player)
441 Summit Oaks Dr
Nashville, TN 37221-1317, USA

Geismar, Thomas H (Architect)
1050 Massachusetts Ave
Cambridge, MA 02138-5359, USA

Geiss, Johannes (Physicist)
Physics Instit Sidlerstr 5
Beme 3012, SWITZERLAND

Geissendorfer, Hans
An den Herrenbergen 21a
Neustadt/Aisch, GERMANY D-91413

Geissinger-Harding, Jean (Baseball Player)
539 Hodunk Rd
Coldwater, MI 49036-9273, USA

Geist, Bill (Correspondent)
c/o Staff Member *N.S. Bienstock*
1740 Broadway Fl 24
New York, NY 10019-4315, USA

Geithner, Timothy (Financier, Politician)
1500 Pennsylvania Ave NW
Washington, DC 20220-0001, USA

Gelb, Leslie H (Educator)
58 E 68th St
New York, NY 10065-5953, USA

Gelbaugh, Stan (Athlete, Football Player)
10819 Hob Nail Ct
Potomac, MD 20854-2560, USA

Geldart, Gary (Athlete, Hockey Player)
11 Hiltz Rd
Moncton, NB E1G 2R3, Canada

Geldof, Bob (Actor, Musician)
c/o Rick Shoor *Red Entertainment Agency*
16 Penn Plz Ste 824
New York, NY 10001-1809, USA

Gelfand, Izrael M (Mathematician)
118 N 5th Ave
Highland Park, NJ 08904-2925, USA

Gelfant, Alan (Actor)
5724 W 3rd St Ste 302
Los Angeles, CA 90036-3085, USA

Gelinas, Gratien (Actor, Writer)
316 Girouard St # 207
Oka, QC J0N 1E0, CANADA

Gelinas, Martin (Athlete, Hockey Player)
c/o Staff Member *National Sports Development Ltd*
7475 Flint Rd SE
Calgary, AL T2H 1G3, Canada

Gellar, Sarah Michelle (Actor)
c/o JoAnne Colonna *Brillstein Entertainment Partners*
9150 Wilshire Blvd Ste 350
Beverly Hills, CA 90212-3453, USA

Geller, Glenn (Business Person)
c/o Staff Member *CBS Paramount Network Television*
4024 Radford Ave
Studio City, CA 91604-2190, USA

Geller, Margaret J (Astronomer)
60 Garden St
Cambridge, MA 02138-1516, USA

Geller, Uri (Actor)
c/o Staff Member *Celeb Agents*
77 Oxford St
London ON W1D 2ES, UNITED KINGDOM (UK)

Gell-Mann, Murray (Nobel Prize Laureate)
1399 Hyde Park Rd
Santa Fe, NM 87501-8943, USA

Gelman, Larry (Actor)
5121 Greenbush Ave
Sherman Oaks, CA 91423-1507, USA

Gelman, Michael
7 Lincoln Sq
New York, NY 10023-7219

Gelnar, John (Athlete, Baseball Player)
1811 Suzanne Dr Apt 2
Weatherford, OK 73096-2383, USA

Gemar, Charles D (Astronaut)
7660 N 159th Street Ct E
Benton, KS 67017-8926, USA

Gemma, Giuliano
Via dei Riari 66
Rome, ITALY 165

Gems, Pam (Writer)
60/66 Wardour St
London W1V 4ND, UNITED KINGDOM (UK)

Genaux, Vivicia (Opera Singer)
Harkness Plaza 61 W 62nd St #6F
New York, NY 10023, USA

Gendron, George (Editor)
77 N Washington St
Boston, MA 02114-1908, USA

Gendron, Jean-Guy (Athlete, Hockey Player)
368 Rue De La Corniche
Saint-Nicholas, QC G7A 2Y4, Canada

Generation, The X
184 Glochester Pl
London, ENGLAND NW1

Genesis (Music Group)
c/o Staff Member *Hit and Run Music Ltd*
25 Ives Street South Kensington
London SW3 2ND, United Kingdom

Genet, Sabryn
7800 Beverly Blvd # 3305
Los Angeles, CA 90036-2112

Genitallica (Music Group)
c/o Staff Member *Sony Music Miami*
605 Lincoln Rd Ste 700
Miami Beach, FL 33139-2901, USA

Genovese, Eugene D (Historian)
1487 Shendan Walk NE
Atlanta, GA 30324, USA

Genovese, George (Athlete, Baseball Player)
11474 Erwin St
North Hollywood, CA 91606-4126, USA

Genscher, Hans-Dietrich
Am Kottenforst 16
Wachtberg 3 5307, GERMANY

Gensler, M Arthur Jr (Architect)
550 Keamy St
San Francisco, CA 94108, USA

Gent, Peter (Pete) (Athlete, Football Player)
208 Center St
South Haven, MI 49090, USA

Gentile, Jim (Athlete, Baseball Player)
1016 S Neptune Rd
Edmond, OK 73003-6071, USA

Gentile, Troy (Actor)
c/o Leonard Torgan *Collective*
8383 Wilshire Blvd Ste 1050
Beverly Hills, CA 90211-2415, USA

Gentry, Alvin (Basketball Player, Coach, Misc)
1501 Girod St
New Orleans, LA 70113-3124, USA

Gentry, Bobbie (Music Group)
269 S Beverly Dr # 368
Beverly Hills, CA 90212-3851, USA

Gentry, Curtis (Athlete, Football Player)
3214 Brassfield Rd Apt 3203
Greensboro, NC 27410-9452, USA

Gentry, Dennis (Athlete, Football Player)
916 Queen Elizabeth Dr
Mc Gregor, TX 76657-4000, USA

Gentry, Gary (Athlete, Baseball Player)
301 W Lawrence Ln
Phoenix, AZ 85021-4558, USA

Gentry, Harvey (Athlete, Baseball Player)
109 Eaton Ln
Bristol, TN 37620-2820, USA

Gentry, Montgomery (Music Group)
c/o John Dorris Sr *Hallmark Direction Company*
713 18th Ave S
Nashville, TN 37203-3214, USA

Gentry, Race
2379 Mountain View Dr
Escondido, CA 92027-4951

Gentry, Teddy W (Music Group, Musician)
Fort Payne, AL 35968, USA

Gentry, Troy (Musician)
c/o Staff Member *Hallmark Direction Company*
713 18th Ave S
Nashville, TN 37203-3214, USA

Genzel, Carrie (Actor)
9229 W Sunset Blvd Ste 315
Los Angeles, CA 90069-3403, USA

Genzmer, Harald (Composer)
Eisensteinstr 10
Munich 81679, GERMANY

Geoffrion, Dan (Athlete, Hockey Player)
413 Overall Dr
Brentwood, TN 37027-7649, USA

Geoffripn, Scott (Race Car Driver)
592 Explorer St # B
Brea, CA 92821-3108, USA

George, Alex (Athlete, Baseball Player)
8432 Linden Ln
Prairie Village, KS 66207-1834, USA

George, Alicia (Stylist)
714 N Idlewild St
Memphis, TN 38107-4515, USA

George, Boy (Musician)
1-2 Langham Place
London W1A 3DD, UNITED KINGDOM

George, Cardinal Francis Eugene (Religious Leader)
Palazzo Del S Uffizio LI
Rome 193, ITALY

George, Chris (Athlete, Baseball Player)
428 Kathy Lynn Dr
Pittsburgh, PA 15239-1708, USA

George, Chris (Athlete, Baseball Player)
7703 Goldengrove Dr
Spring, TX 77379-4015, USA

George, Christopher S (Chris) (Baseball Player)
121 E Maranta Rd
Mooresville, NC 28117-6335, USA

George, Ed (Athlete, Football Player)
1220 S Orange Ave
Sarasota, FL 34239-2028, USA

George, Eddie (Athlete, Football Player)
9538 Sanctuary Pl
Brentwood, TN 37027-8498, USA

George, Eddie (Actor)
c/o Peter Schaffer *All Pro Sports and Entertainment*
36 Steele St Ste 100
Denver, CO 80206-5709, USA

George, Edward A J (Financier)
Threadneedle St
London EC2R 8AH, UNITED KINGDOM (UK)

George, Elizabeth (Writer)
c/o Robert Gottlieb *Trident Media Group LLC*
41 Madison Ave Fl 36
New York, NY 10010-2257, USA

George, Eric (Actor)
1964 Westwood Blvd Ste 400
Los Angeles, CA 90025-4695, USA

George, Francis E Cardinal (Religious Leader)
1555 N State Pkwy
Chicago, IL 60610-1613, USA

George, Gotz
Terrassenstr. 32
Berlin, GERMANY D-14129

George, Jason Winston (Actor)
c/o Peter Kiernan *Management 360*
9111 Wilshire Blvd
Beverly Hills, CA 90210-5508, USA

George, Jeffrey S (Jeff) (Athlete, Football Player)
1908 Schwier Ct
Indianapolis, IN 46229-2154, USA

George, Lynda Day
10310 Riverside Dr Unit 104
Toluca Lake, CA 91602-2457

George, Matt (Athlete, Football Player)
24403 Newhall Ave Apt 3
Newhall, CA 91321-2771, USA

George, Melissa (Actor)
c/o Pamela Kohl *3 Arts Entertainment Inc*
9460 Wilshire Blvd Fl 7
Beverly Hills, CA 90212-2713, USA

George, Phyllis (Beauty Pageant Winner, Television Host)
c/o Staff Member *WmE2 (WMA-LA)*
1 William Morris Pl
Beverly Hills, CA 90212-4261, USA

George, Ron (Athlete, Football Player)
15616 Picketts Store Pl
Haymarket, VA 20169-6142, USA

George, Steve (Athlete, Football Player)
5922 W Airport Blvd
Houston, TX 77035-5302, USA

George, Susan (Actor)
1-2 Langham Place
London W1A 3DD, UNITED KINGDOM (UK)

George, Tate (Athlete, Basketball Player)
55 Georgetown Rd
Bristol, CT 06010-5510, USA

George, Terry (Writer)
c/o Ariel (Ari) Emanuel *WmE2 (Endeavor-LA)*
9601 Wilshire Blvd Fl 3
Beverly Hills, CA 90210-5219, USA

George, Tim (Athlete, Football Player)
77 Saddle Ln
Easton, PA 18045-3115, USA

George, Tony (Race Car Driver)
4790 W 16th St
Indianapolis, IN 46222-2550, USA

George, William W (Business Person)
7000 Central Ave NE
Minneapolis, MN 55432-3568, USA

Georgel, Pierre (Misc)
24 Rue Richer
Paris 76009, FRANCE

George-McFaul, Jean (Baseball Player)
2432 Kilkeer Ste 9
N Battleford, SK S9I 3Y5, CANADA

Georges, Anne (Baseball Player)
407 Oak St
Des Plaines, IL 60016-4429, USA

Georgi, Howard (Physicist)
Physics Dept Lyman Laboratory
Cambridge, MA 2138, USA

Georgian, Theodore J (Religious Leader)
P O Box P
Willow Grove, PA 19090, USA

Georgievski, Ljubisa (Ljupco) (Prime Minister)
Dame Grueva 6
Skopje 91000, MACEDONIA

Georgije, Bishop (Religious Leader)
PO Box 519
Libertyville, IL 60048-0519, USA

Gephardt, Richard (Ex-Congressman, Politician)
500 8th St NW
Washington, DC 20004-2131, USA

Geraci, Sonny (Music Group)
27 L Ambiance Ct
Bardonia, NY 10954-1421, USA

Geraghty, Brian (Actor)
c/o Lena Roklin *Luber Roklin Management*
8530 Wilshire Blvd Ste 550
Beverly Hills, CA 90211-3133, USA

Gerard, Bobby (Stylist)
c/o Staff Member *Artists by Timothy Priano (CA)*
8447 Wilshire Blvd Ste 301
Beverly Hills, CA 90211-3206, USA

Gerard, Gil (Actor)
23679 Calabasas Rd # 325
Calabasas, CA 91302-1502, USA

Gerard, Gus (Athlete, Basketball Player)
614 Cypresswood Dr
Spring, TX 77388-5913, USA

Gerard, Jean Shevlin (Diplomat)
22 Blvd Emannanuel Servais
2535, LUXEMBOURG

Gerard, Tara (Reality TV Star)
c/o Michael (Mike) Esterman *Esterman.Com, LLC*
Prefers to be contacted via email
MD, USA

Gerardo (Mejia) (Artist, Music Group)
17337 Ventura Blvd Ste 208
Encino, CA 91316-3992, USA

Gerber, Craig (Athlete, Baseball Player)
4297 N Pershing Ave
San Bernardino, CA 92407-3737, USA

Gerber, H Joseph (Business Person)
83 Gerber Rd W
South Windsor, CT 06074-3230, USA

Gerber, Joel (Judge)
400 2nd St NW
Washington, DC 20217-0001, USA

Gerber, Michael (Business Person, Writer)
2235 Mercury Way Ste 200
Santa Rosa, CA 95407-5472, USA

Gerberding, Julie (Doctor, Government Official, Physicist)
1600 Clifton Rd NE
Atlanta, GA 30329-4018, USA

Gerberman, George (Athlete, Baseball Player)
1501 Michael St
El Campo, TX 77437-9345, USA

Gere, Richard (Actor)
c/o Alan Nierob *Rogers & Cowan PR (LA)*
Pacific Design Center 8687 Melrose Ave, 7th Floor
West Hollywood, CA 90069, USA

Geredine, Tom (Athlete, Football Player)
1155 Woodlands Dr
Kyle, TX 78640-5530, USA

Gerela, Roy (Athlete, Football Player)
3933 Ramrod Frg
Las Cruces, NM 88012-6008, USA

Geren, Bob (Athlete, Baseball Player, Coach)
2710 Bay Canyon Ct
San Diego, CA 92117-6704, USA

Gerena, Samuel (Gringo) (Musician)
c/o Staff Member *Universal Music Publishing Group (Latin)*
420 Lincoln Rd Ste 200
Miami Beach, FL 33139-3014, USA

Gerety, Tom Jr (Educator)
President's Office
Amherst, MA 1002, USA

Gerg, Hilde (Skier)
Brauneck Tolzer Hutte
Lenggries 83661, GERMANY

Gergen, David R (Editor)
31 Ash St
Cambridge, MA 02138-4840, USA

Gergiev, Valery A
Plankengasse 7
Vienna 1010, AUSTRIA

Gerg-Leitner, Michaela (Skier)
Jachenauer Str 26
Lenggries 83661, GERMANY

Gerhardt, Alben (Musician)
165 W 57th St
New York, NY 10019-2201, USA

Gerhardt, Jason (Actor)
C/O Ron Scott 9255 Sunset BlvdSte 803
Los Angeles, CA 90069, USA

Gerhardt, Rusty (Athlete, Baseball Player)
PO Box 426
New London, TX 75682-0426, USA

Gerhart, Ken (Athlete, Baseball Player)
1603 Ashford Ct
Murfreesboro, TN 37129-5888, USA

Gering, Galen (Actor)
c/o Staff Member *Schumacher Management*
1122 San Vicente Blvd
Santa Monica, CA 90402-2008, USA

Gering, Jenna (Actor)
c/o Jonathan Bluman *WmE2 (Endeavor-LA)*
9601 Wilshire Blvd Fl 3
Beverly Hills, CA 90210-5219, USA

Gerlach, Gary (Publisher)
715 Locust St
Des Moines, IA 50309-3703, USA

Gerlach, Jim (Congressman, Politician)
2442 Rayburn Hob
Washington, DC 20515-3011, USA

Germain, Dorothy (Athlete, Golfer)
202 NC Highway 62 W
Randleman, NC 27317-9774, USA

Germain, Eric (Athlete, Hockey Player)
46 Dawes Ave
Hamden, CT 06517-2331, USA

Germain, Paul M (Engineer)
3 Ave de Xhampaubert
Paris 75015, FRANCE

Germain, Stephanie (Producer)
c/o Staff Member *Creative Artists Agency (CAA-LA)*
2000 Avenue of the Stars Ste 100
Los Angeles, CA 90067-4705, USA

German, Aleksei G (Director)
Marsovo Pole 7 #37
Saint Petersburg 191041, RUSSIA

German, Jammi (Athlete, Football Player)
3702 Highland Ave
Fort Myers, FL 33916-6529, USA

German, Lauren (Actor)
c/o Doug Wald *Anonymous Content (AC-LA)*
545 Veteran Ave
Los Angeles, CA 90024-1915, USA

German, William (Editor)
Editorial Dept 901 Mission
San Francisco, CA 94103, USA

Germane, Geoffrey J (Engineer)
Mechanical Engineering Dept
Provo, UT 84602, USA

Germani, Fernando (Music Group, Musician)
Via Delle Terme Decians 11
Rome, ITALY

Germann, Greg (Actor, Director)
c/o Jeff Golenberg *Collective*
8383 Wilshire Blvd Ste 1050
Beverly Hills, CA 90211-2415, USA

Germano, Lisa (Music Group, Musician)
PO Box 35
Pawling, NY 12564-0035, USA

Germany, Reggie (Athlete, Football Player)
246 Haystack Ave
Pataskala, OH 43062-7359, USA

Germany, Willie (Athlete, Football Player)
4401 Pratt St
Omaha, NE 68111-2533, USA

Germar, Manfred (Athlete, Track Athlete)
Alsfelder Str 27
Darmstadt 642889, GERMANY

Germeshausen, Bernhard (Athlete)
Hinter Dem Salon 39
Schwansee 99195, GERMANY

Germond, Jack
1627 K St NW Ste 1100
Washington, DC 20006-1710

Gernander, Ken (Athlete, Hockey Player)
355 Eddy Glover Blvd
New Britain, CT 06053-2411, USA

Gerner, Robert (Doctor, Misc)
Neuropsychiatric Institute
Los Angeles, CA 90024, USA

Gernert, David (Publisher)
136 E 57th St
New York, NY 10022-2707, USA

Gernert, Dick (Athlete, Baseball Player)
1801 Cambridge Ave Apt C12
Reading, PA 19610-2669, USA

Gernhardt, Michael L (Astronaut)
2705 Lighthouse Dr
Houston, TX 77058-4317, USA

Gernon, Bruce (Writer)
c/o Staff Member *Llewellyn Worldwide, LTD*
2143 Wooddale Dr
Saint Paul, MN 55125-2989, USA

Gero, Gary D (Cinematographer)
2 McLaren Ste A
Irvine, CA 92618-2815, USA

Geronimo, Cesar F (Baseball Player)
Tefeda Flo #46
Santo Domingo, DOMINICAN REPUBLIC

Gerrard, Steven (Soccer Player)
Anfield Road Liverpool
Merseyside L4 OTH, UNITED KINGDOM

Gerring, Cathy (Athlete, Golfer)
3328 Tarrant Springs Trl
Fort Wayne, IN 46804-6161, USA

Gersbach, Carl (Athlete, Football Player)
PO Box 433
Devon, PA 19333-0433, USA

Gershon, Gina (Actor)
c/o Risa Shapiro *Schiff Company, The*
8440 Warner Dr Ste B1
Culver City, CA 90232-2461, USA

Gerson, Mark (Photographer)
3 Regal Lane Regent's Park
London NW1 7TH, UNITED KINGDOM (UK)

Gerstell, A Frederick (Business Person)
3200 N San Fernando Rd
Los Angeles, CA 90065-1415, USA

Gerstner V, Jr, Louis (Business Person)
1 N Castle Dr
Armonk, NY 10504-1725, USA

Gertz, Jami (Actor)
c/o Jason Barrett *Alchemy Entertainment*
7024 Melrose Ave Ste 420
Los Angeles, CA 90038-3394, USA

Gerut, Jody (Athlete, Baseball Player)
623 Rochdale Cir
Lombard, IL 60148-4730, USA

Gervais, Ricky (Actor, Director, Producer)
c/o Duncan Hayes *United Agents*
12-26 Lexington St
London W1F OLE, UK

Gervin, Derrick (Athlete, Basketball Player)
1110 Vista Valet Apt 1507
San Antonio, TX 78216-1733, USA

Gervin, George (Athlete, Basketball Player, Coach)
44 Gervin Pass
Spring Branch, TX 78070-6370, USA

Gerwick, Ben C Jr (Architect, Engineer)
5727 Country Club Dr
Oakland, CA 94618-1717, USA

Geschke, Charles (Business Person)
345 Park Ave
San Jose, CA 95110-2704, USA

Gesek, John (Athlete, Football Player)
105 Sand Point Ct
Coppell, TX 75019-5359, USA

Gesinger, Michael (Photographer)
1136 Umatilla Ave
Port Townsend, WA 98368-4809, USA

Gessendorf, Mechthild (Opera Singer)
165 W 57th St
New York, NY 10019-2201, USA

Gessle, Per (Music Group, Musician)
Lilla Nygatan 19
Stockholm 111 28, SWEDEN

Gest, David (Actor, Producer)
c/o Staff Member *Ultra DJ Management*
42 City Business Centre Lower Road
London SE16 2XB, UK

Get Up Kids (Music Group)
c/o Staff Member *Creative Artists Agency (CAA-LA)*
2000 Avenue of the Stars Ste 100
Los Angeles, CA 90067-4705, USA

Getherall, Joey (Athlete, Football Player)
3105 Las Marias Ave
Hacienda Heights, CA 91745-6219, USA

Gethers, Peter (Writer)
c/o Catherine Brackey *International Creative Management (ICM-LA)*
10250 Constellation Blvd Fl 7
Los Angeles, CA 90067-6207, USA

Getliffe, Ray (Athlete, Hockey Player)
18-1200 Riverside Dr
London, ON N6H 5C6, Canada

Gets, Malcolm (Actor)
c/o Lisa Loosemore *Viking Entertainment*
445 W 23rd St Ste 1A
New York, NY 10011-1445, USA

Gettelfinger, Ron (Misc)
800 E Jefferson Ave
Detroit, MI 48214, USA

Gettinger, Ruby (Reality TV Star)
c/o Glenn Rigberg *Inphenate*
9701 Wilshire Blvd Fl 10
Beverly Hills, CA 90212-2010, USA

Gettis, Byron (Athlete, Baseball Player)
6313 Whalen Ave
East Saint Louis, IL 62207-1051, USA

Getty, Andrew
2936 Montcalm Ave
Los Angeles, CA 90046-1304

Getty, Balthazar (Actor)
c/o Jeff Golenberg *Collective*
8383 Wilshire Blvd Ste 1050
Beverly Hills, CA 90211-2415, USA

Getty, Charlie (Athlete, Football Player)
3736 W Morningside St
Springfield, MO 65807-5581, USA

Getty, Gordon
2880 Broadway St
San Francisco, CA 94115-1061

Getz, John (Actor)
4124 Wade St
Los Angeles, CA 90066-5732, USA

Getzlaff, James (Actor)
c/o Staff Member *Douglas Gorman Rothacker & Wilhelm Inc*
1501 Broadway Ste 703
New York, NY 10036-5501, USA

Geyer, Georgie Anne (Editor, Misc)
800 25th St NW
Washington, DC 20037-2208, USA

Geyer, Hugh (Music Group)
2218 Ridge Rd
McKeesport, PA 15135-3037, USA

Geyer, Renee (Actor, Composer)
c/o Staff Member *The Harbour Agency*
135 Forbes St
Woolloomooloo NSW 2011, Australia

Ghadie, Samia (Actor)
Quay Street
Manchester M60 9EA

Ghai, Subhash (Bollywood, Director, Filmmaker, Producer)
12 Cliff Tower Mount Mary Church Road
Bandra W
Mumbai, MS 400050, INDIA

Ghannouchi, Mohamed (Prime Minister)
Place du Gouvernement
Tunis, TUNISIA

Ghattas, Stephenos II Cardinal (Religious Leader)
BP 69 Rue Ibn Sandar
Cairo 11712, EGYPT

Ghauri, Yasmeen (Model)
c/o Staff Member *Next Model Management*
23 Watts St
New York, NY 10013, USA

Ghelfi, Tony (Athlete, Baseball Player)
3414 Geneva Ln
La Crosse, WI 54601-8302, USA

Gheorghiu, Angela (Opera Singer)
2 Rue du Prieure
Nyon 1260, SWITZERLAND

Gheorghiu, Ion A (Artist)
27-29 Emil Pangratti St
Bucharest, ROMANIA

Ghesquiere, Nicolas (Fashion Designer)
11 Avenue Diena
Balenciaga, Paris 75016, UNITED KINGDOM

Ghiardi, John F L (Economist, Government Official)
12 Park Overlook Ct
Bethesda, MD 20817-2720, USA

Ghiglia, Oscar A (Music Group, Musician)
Helfembergstr 14
Basel 4059, SWITZERLAND

Ghigliotti, Marilyn (Actor)
118 S Cordova St Fl 3
Burbank, CA 91505-4610, USA

Ghiorso, Albert (Misc, Scientist)
1 Cyclotron Rd
Berkeley, CA 94720-8099, USA

Ghiuselev, Nicola (Opera Singer)
Villa della Pisana 370/B-2
Rome 163, ITALY

Ghizikis, Phaidon (General, President)
25 Kountouriotou
Pefki 151 21, GREECE

Ghosh, Gautam (Director)
28/1-A Gariahat Road Block 5 # 50
Calcutta, WB 700029, INDIA

Ghosh, Partho (Bollywood, Director, Filmmaker, Producer)
D1 Hawa Apartments Opp Holy Spirit Hospital Mahakali Caves Road Andheri (E)
Bombay, MS 400 093, INDIA

Ghost, Amanda (Musician)
c/o Staff Member *Basina Recording Company*
PO Box 8121
Pittsburgh, PA 15217-0121, USA

Ghostface, Killa (Music Group, Musician)
250 W 57th St
New York, NY 10107-0001, USA

Ghostland Observatory (Music Group)
c/o Staff Member *Paradigm (Monterey)*
404 W Franklin St
Monterey, CA 93940-2303, USA

Ghuman Jr, JB (Actor)
c/o Harry Gold *TalentWorks (LA)*
3500 W Olive Ave Ste 1400
Burbank, CA 91505-5512, USA

Giacconi, Riccardo (Nobel Prize Laureate)
1440 16th St NW # 730
Washington, DC 20036, USA

Giacomarro, Ralph (Athlete, Football Player)
39 Briar Ct
Hamburg, NJ 07419-1214, USA

Giacomin, Edward (Eddie) (Athlete, Hockey Player)
6575 Red Maple Ln
Bloomfield Hills, MI 48301-3225, USA

Giaever, Ivar (Nobel Prize Laureate)
2080 Van Antwerp Rd
Schenectady, NY 12309-1124, USA

Giallombardo, Bob (Athlete, Baseball Player)
7903 Antique Cir
Waxhaw, NC 28173-7858, USA

Giallonardo, Mario (Athlete, Hockey Player)
94 Queen Mary Ave
Burlington, ON L7T 2G7, Canada

Giamatti, Marcus
c/o Mitchell Stubbs *Mitchell K Stubbs & Assoc (MKS)*
8675 Washington Blvd Ste 203
Culver City, CA 90232-7486, USA

Giamatti, Paul (Actor)
c/o Perri Kipperman *Kipperman Management*
243 W 72nd St Apt 2
New York, NY 10023-2704, USA

Giambalvo, Louis (Actor)
c/o Staff Member *Judy Schoen & Associates*
606 N Larchmont Blvd Ste 309
Los Angeles, CA 90004-1309, USA

Giambastiani, Edmund P Jr (Admiral)
Deputy Cno for Resources/Warfare Requirements Hqusn
Washington, DC 20350-0001, USA

Giambi, Jason G (Athlete, Baseball Player)
188 E 78th St Apt 24B
New York, NY 10075-0573, USA

Giambi, Jeremy (Athlete, Baseball Player)
1034 E Belmont Abbey Ln
Claremont, CA 91711-1463, USA

Giambra, Joey (Boxer)
4673 Ashington St
Las Vegas, NV 89147-6068, USA

Giammona, Louie (Athlete, Football Player)
116 Manton St
Philadelphia, PA 19147-5423, USA

Gian, Joey (Musician)
13351D Riverside Dr # 294
Sherman Oaks, CA 91423-2508, USA

Gian, Joseph
8271 Melrose Ave Ste 110
Los Angeles, CA 90046-6800

Gianas, Maria (Stylist)
c/o Staff Member *Ford Models (Chicago)*
311 W Superior St
Chicago, IL 60654-3548, USA

Giancanelli, Hal (Athlete, Football Player)
2227 Portola Ln
Westlake Village, CA 91361-1748, USA

Giancola, Sammi (Reality TV Star)
c/o Sal Bonaventura *CEG Talent*
251 W 39th St Fl 7
New York, NY 10018-3171, USA

Gianelli, John (Athlete, Basketball Player)
28241 Pine Ave
Pinecrest, CA 95364, USA

Giannelli, Ray (Athlete, Baseball Player)
56 E Saltaire Rd
Lindenhurst, NY 11757-6829, USA

Giannini, Andriano (Actor)
c/o Lindy King *United Agents*
12-26 Lexington St
London W1F OLE, UK

Giannini, Giancario (Actor)
Via Salaria 292
Rome 199, ITALY

Giannini, Giancarlo
Via della Giuliana 101
Rome, ITALY I-00195

Gianopoulos, David (Actor)
c/o Staff Member *GVA Talent Agency Inc*
8981 W Sunset Blvd Ste 101
Los Angeles, CA 90069-1850, USA

Gianulias, Nicole (Nikki) (Bowler)
7200 Harrison Ave # 7171
Rockford, IL 61112-1017, USA

Giaquinto, Nick (Athlete, Football Player)
316 3rd Ave
Stratford, CT 06615-7736, USA

Giarraputo, Jack (Producer, Writer)
c/o Staff Member *Happy Madison Productions*
10202 W Washington Blvd Judy Garland Bldg
Culver City, CA 90232, USA

Gibara, Samir (Business Person)
1144 W Market St
Akron, OH 44316-0001, USA

Gibb, Barry (Musician, Songwriter)
c/o Paul Bloch *Rogers & Cowan PR (LA)*
Pacific Design Center 8687 Melrose Ave, 7th Floor
West Hollywood, CA 90069, USA

Gibb, Cynthia (Actor)
c/o Scott Hart *Scott Hart Entertainment*
14622 Ventura Blvd # 746
Sherman Oaks, CA 91403-3600, USA

Gibb, Donald (Actor)
1485 S Beverly Dr
Los Angeles, CA 90035-3021, USA

Gibb, Robin (Musician, Songwriter)
1801 Bay Rd
Miami Beach, FL 33139-1415, USA

Gibberd, Frederick (Architect)
House Marsh Lane Old Harlow
Essex CM17 0NA, UNITED KINGDOM (UK)

Gibbon, Joe (Athlete, Baseball Player)
26 County Road 24142
Newton, MS 39345-8946, USA

Gibbons, Beth (Music Group, Songwriter, Writer)
Saga Center 326 Kensal Road
London W10 5BZ, UNITED KINGDOM (UK)

Gibbons, Billy (Music Group, Musician)
c/o Rick Canny *Sanctuary Artist Management*
8750 Wilshire Blvd Ste 200
Beverly Hills, CA 90211-2707, USA

Gibbons, Brian (Athlete, Baseball Player)
51785 Whitestable Ln
South Bend, IN 46637, USA

Gibbons, Brian (Athlete, Baseball Player)
51788 Whitestable Ln
South Bend, IN 46637-1370, USA

Gibbons, James F (Engineer)
15 Redberry Rdg
Portola Valley, CA 94028-8077, USA

Gibbons, Jay (Athlete, Baseball Player)
6 Spring Forest Ct
Owings Mills, MD 21117-4005, USA

Gibbons, Jim (Athlete, Football Player)
9 Sagewood Ct
Basalt, CO 81621-8314, USA

Gibbons, John (Athlete, Baseball Player, Coach)
3602 Hunters Quail
San Antonio, TX 78230-2052, USA

Gibbons, John D (Prime Minister)
Leeward 5 Leeside Dr
Pembroke HM 05, BERMUDA

Gibbons, Kaye (Writer)
c/o Lynn Pleshette *Lynn Pleshette Literary Agency*
2700 N Beachwood Dr
Los Angeles, CA 90068-1922, USA

Gibbons, Leeza (Entertainer, Producer)
c/o Staff Member *Leeza Gibbons Enterprises (LGE)*
9025 Ashcroft Ave
West Hollywood, CA 90048-1704, USA

Gibbons, Mike (Athlete, Football Player)
9187 Marovelli Forest Dr
Lorton, VA 22079-3452, USA

Gibbons, Tim (Producer)
c/o Staff Member *International Creative Management (ICM-LA)*
10250 Constellation Blvd Fl 7
Los Angeles, CA 90067-6207, USA

Gibbons, Walter (Athlete, Baseball Player)
103 E North St
Tampa, FL 33604-6156, USA

Gibbs, Barry (Athlete, Hockey Player)
11816 12 Ave NW
Edmonton, AB T6J 7E4, Canada

Gibbs, Bob (Congressman, Politician)
329 Cannon Hob
Washington, DC 20515-4607, USA

Gibbs, Connor (Actor)
c/o Geoff Cheddy *Brillstein Entertainment Partners*
9150 Wilshire Blvd Ste 350
Beverly Hills, CA 90212-3453, USA

Gibbs, H Jarrell (Business Person)
Energy Plaza 1601 Bryan St
Dallas, TX 75201, USA

Gibbs, Jerry D (Jake) (Athlete, Baseball Player)
225 Saint Andrews Cir
Oxford, MS 38655-2518, USA

Gibbs, Joe (Athlete, Football Coach, Football Player, Race Car Driver)
13415 Reese Blvd W
Huntersville, NC 28078-7933, USA

Gibbs, L Richard (Cricketer)
276 Republic Park
Peter's Hall EBD, GUYANA

Gibbs, Lawrence B (Government Official)
655 15th St NW Ste 900
Washington, DC 20005-5706, USA

Gibbs, Marla (Actor, Music Group)
c/o Robert Depp *Beverly Hecht Agency*
3500 W Olive Ave Ste 1180
Burbank, CA 91505-4651, USA

Gibbs, Martin (Biologist, Scientist)
5 Arbor Ct
Burlington, MA 01803-3800, USA

Gibbs, Pat (Athlete, Football Player)
4835 Corley St
Beaumont, TX 77707-4224, USA

Gibbs, Patt (Misc)
1275 K St NW Ste 500
Washington, DC 20005-4040, USA

Gibbs, Terri (Musician, Songwriter)
1439 Clary Cut Rd
Appling, GA 30802-2109, USA

Gibbs, Terry (Music Group, Musician)
11761 E Speedway Blvd
Tucson, AZ 85748-2017, USA

Gibbs, Timothy (Actor)
c/o Julia Buchwald *Don Buchwald & Associates Inc (LA)*
6500 Wilshire Blvd Ste 2200
Los Angeles, CA 90048-4942, USA

Gibgot, Adam (Writer)
c/o Adriana Alberghetti *WmE2 (Endeavor-LA)*
9601 Wilshire Blvd Fl 3
Beverly Hills, CA 90210-5219, USA

Giblett, Eloise R (Doctor, Misc)
2518 3rd Ave W
Seattle, WA 98119-2306, USA

Giblin, Robert (Athlete, Football Player)
2818 Reynolds Ln
Port Neches, TX 77651-5410, USA

Gibney, Rebecca (Actor)
128 Rupert St
Collingwood, Vic. 3066, AUSTRALIA

Gibney, Susan (Actor)
c/o Matthew Lesher *Insight*
1134 S Cloverdale Ave
Los Angeles, CA 90019-6737, USA

Gibraltor, Steve (Athlete, Baseball Player)
3651 Asbury St
Dallas, TX 75205-1848, USA

Gibran, Kahill (Artist, Misc)
160 W Canton St
Boston, MA 02118-1216, USA

Gibson, Aaron (Athlete, Football Player)
PO Box 637
Roanoke, IN 46783-0637, USA

Gibson, Antonio (Athlete, Football Player)
2320 Jaguar Dr Apt 502
Bryan, TX 77807-2346, USA

Gibson, Bob (Athlete, Basketball Player)
215 Bellevue Blvd S
Bellevue, NE 68005-2442, USA

Gibson, Bob (Athlete, Baseball Player)
215 Bellevue Blvd S
Bellevue, NE 68005-2442, USA

Gibson, Bob (Athlete, Baseball Player)
260 Sydney Rd
Southampton, PA 18966-2899, USA

Gibson, Charles (Television Host)
c/o Staff Member *ABC News*
77 W 66th St Fl 3
New York, NY 10023-6201, USA

Gibson, Claude (Athlete, Football Player)
47 Gladstone Rd
Asheville, NC 28805-2454, USA

Gibson, Damon (Athlete, Football Player)
4332 Dell Rd Apt J
Lansing, MI 48911-8126, USA

Gibson, Deborah (Actor, Musician)
8491 W Sunset Blvd # 1650
W Hollywood, CA 90069-1911

Gibson, Dennis (Athlete, Football Player)
6900 NE 11th Ct
Ankeny, IA 50023-9300, USA

Gibson, Derrick (Athlete, Football Player)
1220 Harbor Bay Pkwy
Alameda, CA 94502-6501, USA

Gibson, Derrick (Athlete, Baseball Player)
138 Buckeye Loop Rd
Winter Haven, FL 33881-2703, USA

Gibson, Doug (Athlete, Hockey Player)
1220 Cartier Blvd
Peterborough, ON K9H 6S1, Canada

Gibson, Edward G (Astronaut)
1658 S Litchfield Rd
Goodyear, AZ 85338-1509, USA

Gibson, Ellie (Athlete, Golfer)
35705 N 29th Ln
Phoenix, AZ 85086-4219, USA

Gibson, Ernest (Athlete, Football Player)
6518 Paradise Point Rd
Flowery Branch, GA 30542-3144, USA

Gibson, Everett K Jr (Geophysicist, Misc, Physicist)
1015 Trowbridge Dr
Houston, TX 77062-2726, USA

Gibson, Fred (Athlete, Golfer)
2006 Avenel St
Orlando, FL 32828-7813, USA

Gibson, Greg (Baseball Player)
3628 Briarwood Dr
Catlettsburg, KY 41129-9298, USA

Gibson, Greg (Athlete, Baseball Player)
20305 Country Club Dr
Catlettsburg, KY 41129-8602, USA

Gibson, Janice (Athlete, Golfer)
9747 S Granite Ave
Tulsa, OK 74137-4931, USA

Gibson, John (Correspondent)
c/o Staff Member *Fox News Channel (NY)*
1211 Ave Of The Americas Level C1
New York, NY 10036-8701, USA

Gibson, Kelly (Athlete, Golfer)
PO Box 57478
New Orleans, LA 70157-7478, USA

Gibson, Kirk (Athlete, Baseball Player)
33 Sunset Ln
Grosse Pointe Farms, MI 48236-3730, USA

Gibson, Laurie-Anne (Laurieann) (Choreographer)
c/o Stephanie Molina *Rogers & Cowan PR (LA)*
Pacific Design Center 8687 Melrose Ave, 7th Floor
West Hollywood, CA 90069, USA

Gibson, Leah (Actor)
c/o Kim Matuka *Online Talent Group*
Prefers to be contacted via email or telephone
Los Angeles, CA 90069, USA

Gibson, Mel (Actor, Director, Producer)
c/o Alan Nierob *Rogers & Cowan PR (LA)*
Pacific Design Center 8687 Melrose Ave, 7th Floor
West Hollywood, CA 90069, USA

Gibson, Oliver (Athlete, Football Player)
1448 E 52nd St # 406
Chicago, IL 60615-4122, USA

Gibson, Paul (Athlete, Baseball Player)
23421 Water Cir
Boca Raton, FL 33486-8547, USA

Gibson, Quentin H (Biologist, Misc)
5 Carrot Hill Rd
Woods Hole, MA 02543-1205, USA

Gibson, Ralph H (Photographer)
331 W Broadway
New York, NY 10013-2265, USA

Gibson, Reginald W (Judge)
717 Madison Pl NW
Washington, DC 20439-0001, USA

Gibson, Robert L
1709 Shagbark Trl
Murfreesboro, TN 37130-1136, USA

Gibson, Robert L (Hoot) (Astronaut)
1709 Shagbark Trl
Murfreesboro, TN 37130-1136, USA

Gibson, Russ (Athlete)
495 Gardners Neck Rd
Swansea, MA 02777-3131, USA

Gibson, Suzanne (Stylist)
1608 Amberwood Dr Apt 6
South Pasadena, CA 91030-1947, USA

Gibson, Thomas (Actor, Director)
c/o Craig Dorfman *Frontline Management*
5670 Wilshire Blvd Ste 1370
Los Angeles, CA 90036-5679, USA

Gibson, Tom (Athlete, Football Player)
5940 E Sandra Ter
Scottsdale, AZ 85254-9203, USA

Gibson, Tyrese (Actor, Musician, Producer)
c/o Jerome Martin *Jerome Martin Management*
Prefers to be contacted via telephone
Los Angeles, CA 90024, USA

Gick, George (Athlete, Baseball Player)
875 Elston Rd
Lafayette, IN 47909-6322, USA

Gidada, Negasso (President)
P O Box 5707
Addis Ababa, ETHIOPIA

Gideon, Brett (Athlete, Baseball Player)
PO Box 822
Georgetown, TX 78627-0822, USA

Gideon, Jim (Athlete, Baseball Player)
104 Plum Tree Ter Apt 120
Houston, TX 77077-5375, USA

Gideon, Raynold (Actor, Writer)
3524 Multiview Dr
Los Angeles, CA 90068-1222, USA

Gidley, Pamela (Actor)
c/o Tom Harrison *Diverse Talent Group*
9911 W Pico Blvd Ste 340W
Los Angeles, CA 90035-2712, USA

Gidzenko, Yuri P (Astronaut, Misc)
Moskovskoi Oblasti
Syvisdny Goroduk 141160, RUSSIA

Gielen, Michael A (Composer, Conductor)
Postfach 1617
Hanover 30016, GERMANY

Giella, Joseph (Cartoonist)
191 Morris Dr
East Meadow, NY 11554-1317, USA

Gien, Pamela (Actor, Writer)
c/o Heather Schroder *International Creative Management (ICM-NY)*
40 W 57th St
New York, NY 10019-4001, USA

Gienger, Eberhard
Friedrich-Schaal-Str. 53
Tubingen, GERMANY D-72074

Gierasch, Stefan (Actor)
c/o Staff Member *Brandon's Commercials Unlimited*
8383 Wilshire Blvd Ste 850
Beverly Hills, CA 90211-2443, USA

Gierer, Vincent A Jr (Business Person)
100 W Putnam Ave
Greenwich, CT 06830-5342, USA

Gierowski, Stefen (Artist)
Ul Gagarina 15 m 97
Warsaw 00-753, POLAND

Giesler, Jon (Athlete, Football Player)
141 Via Isabela
Jupiter, FL 33458-6925, USA

Giessinger, Andrew (Athlete, Football Player)
1667 Union Ave
Barberton, OH 44203-7644, USA

Gietzen, Pam (Athlete, Golfer)
603 Woodland West Dr
Woodway, TX 76712-3514, USA

Giffin, Lee (Athlete, Hockey Player)
RR 4
Blenheim, ON N0P 1A0, Canada

Gifford, Frank N (Athlete, Football Player, Sportscaster)
300 Main St Ste 802
Stamford, CT 06901-3033, USA

Gifford, Gloria (Actor)
1680 Vine St Ste 1016
Los Angeles, CA 90028-8800, USA

Gifford, Kathie Lee (Correspondent, Entertainer)
c/o Staff Member *Today Show, The*
30 Rockefeller Plz
New York, NY 10112-0015, USA

Giffords, Gabrielle (Congressman, Politician)
1030 Longworth Hob
Washington, DC 20515-0527, USA

Gift, Roland (Actor, Music Group)
1-12 Petonville Road
London N1 9PL, UNITED KINGDOM (UK)

Gigandet, Cam (Actor)
c/o Matt Luber *Luber Roklin Management*
8530 Wilshire Blvd Ste 550
Beverly Hills, CA 90211-3133, USA

Giggie, Bob (Athlete, Baseball Player)
8 Royal Lake Dr Apt 3
Braintree, MA 02184-5457, USA

Gigli, Romeo (Designer, Fashion Designer)
37 W 57th St Ste 900
New York, NY 10019-3411, USA

Gigon, Norm (Athlete, Baseball Player)
2503 Rio Vista Dr
Mahwah, NJ 07430-4506, USA

Gigot, Paul (Journalist)
200 Liberty St
New York, NY 10281-1003, USA

Giguere, Jean-Sebastien (Athlete, Hockey Player)
2066 Port Bristol Cir
Newport Beach, CA 92660-5413, USA

Giguere, Russ (Music Group, Musician)
1924 Spring St
Paso Robles, CA 93446-1620, USA

Giheno, John (President)
Marera Hau
Port Moresby, PAPUA NEW GUINEA

Gil, Ariadna (Actor)
36 Rue de Ponthieu
Paris 75008, FRANCE

Gil, Geronimo (Athlete, Baseball Player)
c/o Staff Member *Baltimore Orioles*
333 W Camden St
Baltimore, MD 21201-2496, USA

Gil, Gilberto (Music Group, Songwriter, Writer)
36 Como St Ramford
Essex RM 7 7DR, UNITED KINGDOM (UK)

Gil, Gus (Athlete, Baseball Player)
2240 SW 42nd Ter
Fort Lauderdale, FL 33317-6618, USA

Gil, R Benjamin (Benji) (Athlete, Baseball Player)
11712 Wild Pear Ln
Fort Worth, TX 76244-8815, USA

Gilbert, Brad
888 17th St NW Ste 1200
Washington, DC 20006-3320

Gilbert, Bradley (Brad) (Tennis Player)
1101 Woodrow Wilson Blvd # 1800
Arlington, VA 22209, USA

Gilbert, Brantley (Musician)
c/o Staff Member *Paradigm (Monterey)*
404 W Franklin St
Monterey, CA 93940-2303, USA

Gilbert, Buddy (Athlete, Baseball Player)
1913 Belcaro Dr
Knoxville, TN 37918-3709, USA

Gilbert, Chris (Athlete, Football Player)
4422 Cypress Creek Pkwy
Houston, TX 77068-3419, USA

Gilbert, Daren (Athlete, Football Player)
13926 Villanova Ave
Chino, CA 91710-7116, USA

Gilbert, David (Cartoonist)
c/o Staff Member *King Features Syndication*
300 W 57th St Fl 15
New York, NY 10019-5238, USA

Gilbert, Ed (Athlete, Hockey Player)
657 Jacksonville Rd
Warminster, PA 18974-1508, USA

Gilbert, Elizabeth (Writer)
c/o Sarah Chalfant *The Andrew Wylie Agency*
250 W 57th St Ste 2114
New York, NY 10107-2114, USA

Gilbert, Elsie
1016 N Orange Grove Ave Apt 4
West Hollywood, CA 90046-6127

Gilbert, Felix (Historian)
918 Bluffwood Dr
Iowa City, IA 52245-3516, USA

Gilbert, Freddie (Athlete, Football Player)
110 Camden Rd
Griffin, GA 30223-1677, USA

Gilbert, Gary (Producer)
c/o Staff Member *Gilbert Films*
8409 Santa Monica Blvd
West Hollywood, CA 90069-4209, USA

Gilbert, Gibby (Athlete, Golfer)
7070 Sunset Mountain Dr
Chattanooga, TN 37421, USA

Gilbert, Gilles (Athlete, Hockey Player)
9964 Rue De La Fariniere
Quebec, QC G2K 1L7, Canada

Gilbert, Greg (Athlete, Coach, Hockey Player)
c/o Staff Member *Toronto Marlies*
100 Princes Blvd
Toronto, ON M6K 3C3, Canada

Gilbert, J Freeman (Geophysicist, Physicist)
780 Kalamath Dr
Del Mar, CA 92014-2630, USA

Gilbert, Joe (Athlete, Baseball Player)
1952 N Bowie St
Jasper, TX 75951, USA

Gilbert, Kenneth A (Music Group, Musician)
23 Cloitre Notre-Dame
Chartres 28000, FRANCE

Gilbert, Lawrence I (Biologist)
857 Fearrington Post
Pittsboro, NC 27312-8503, USA

Gilbert, Lewis (Director, Producer)
19 Blvd de Suisse
Monte Carlo, MONACO

Gilbert, Lewis (Athlete, Football Player)
6331 SW 1st St
Plantation, FL 33317-3407, USA

Gilbert, Mark (Athlete, Baseball Player)
2340 NW 45th St
Boca Raton, FL 33431-8437, USA

Gilbert, Martin J (Historian)
Oxford OX1 4JD, UNITED KINGDOM (UK)

Gilbert, Melissa (Actor)
c/o Jonathan Howard *Innovative Artists (LA)*
1505 10th St
Santa Monica, CA 90401-2805, USA

Gilbert, O'Neill (Athlete, Coach, Football Coach, Football Player)
460 Great Circle Rd
Nashville, TN 37228-1404, USA

Gilbert, Peter (Director)
1505 10th St
Santa Monica, CA 90401-2805, USA

Gilbert, Richard W (Publisher)
715 Locust St
Des Moines, IA 50309-3703, USA

Gilbert, Rodrique G (Rod) (Athlete, Hockey Player)
52 E End Ave Apt 33A
New York, NY 10028-8116, USA

Gilbert, Ronnie (Music Group)
1031 Merced St
Berkeley, CA 94707-2521, USA

Gilbert, S J Sr (Religious Leader)
6717 Centennial Blvd
Nashville, TN 37209-1017, USA

Gilbert, Sara (Actor)
c/o Steven Levy *Framework Entertainment (LA)*
9057 Nemo St Ste C
West Hollywood, CA 90069-5511, USA

Gilbert, Sean (Athlete, Football Player)
7912 Baltusrol Ln
Charlotte, NC 28210-4933, USA

Gilbert, Shawn (Athlete, Baseball Player)
9656 Kathleen Dr
Cypress, CA 90630-4023, USA

Gilbert, Simon (Music Group, Musician)
98 White Lion St
London N1 9PF, UNITED KINGDOM (UK)

Gilbert, Walter (Nobel Prize Laureate)
15 Gray Gdns W
Cambridge, MA 02138-2311, USA

Gilberto, Astrud (Music Group)
530 Howard St Ste 200
San Francisco, CA 94105-3018, USA

Gilberto, Bebel (Music Group)
1 Water Lane Camden Town
London NW1 8NZ, UNITED KINGDOM (UK)

Gilbertson, Harrison (Actor)
c/o Laina Cohn *Laina Cohn Management*
15066 Sutton St
Sherman Oaks, CA 91403-4020, USA

Gilbertson, Keith (Coach, Football Coach)
Athletic
Seattle, WA 98195-0001, USA

Gilbertson, Stan (Athlete, Hockey Player)
2924 Mosswood Dr
Lodi, CA 95242-2051, USA

Gilbreath, Rod (Athlete, Baseball Player)
1438 Ridgeland Way SW
Lilburn, GA 30047-4352, USA

Gilbreth, Bill (Athlete, Baseball Player)
709 Gary Ln
Abilene, TX 79601-5537, USA

Gilbride, Kevin (Athlete, Coach, Football Player)
3400 S Water St
Pittsburgh, PA 15203-2349, USA

Gilburg, Tom (Athlete, Football Player)
29 Valley Rd
Warminster, PA 18974-3738, USA

Gilchrist, Adam (Athlete, Cricketer)
c/o Staff Member *Western Australia Cricket Association*
WACA Ground P.O. Box 6045
East Perth, WA 6892, Australia

Gilchrist, Brent (Athlete, Hockey Player)
200-3200 30 Ave
Vernon, BC V1T 2C5, Canada

Gilchrist, Carlton (Cookie) (Athlete, Football Player)
9248 1st View St
Norfolk, VA 23503-4238, USA

Gilchrist, Jeanne (Baseball Player)
218-67 Miner St
New Westminster, BC V3L 5N5, CANADA

Gilchrist, Keir (Actor)
c/o Willie Mercer *Thruline Entertainment*
9250 Wilshire Blvd Ground Fl
Beverly Hills, CA 90212, USA

Gilchrist, Pual R (Religious Leader)
1862 Century Pl
Atlanta, GA 30345, USA

Gilder, Bob (Athlete, Golfer)
1977 NW Bonney Dr
Corvallis, OR 97330-9161, USA

Gilder, George F (Economist, Writer)
Main Road
Tyringham, MA 1264, USA

Gildon, Jason (Athlete, Football Player)
1562 Barrington Dr
Wexford, PA 15090-9377, USA

Gile, Don (Athlete, Baseball Player)
570 Seahorse Ln
Redwood City, CA 94065-1223, USA

Giles, Bill (Baseball Player)
1755 Cedar Ln
Villanova, PA 19085-2018, USA

Giles, Brian (Athlete, Baseball Player)
4130 Rancho Las Brisas Trl
San Diego, CA 92130-5221, USA

Giles, Curt (Athlete, Hockey Player)
5225 Grandview Sq Apt 402
Minneapolis, MN 55436-1691, USA

Giles, Jimmie (Athlete, Football Player)
10429 Greenmont Dr
Tampa, FL 33626-5306, USA

Giles, Marcus (Athlete, Baseball Player)
2285 Marquand Ct
Alpine, CA 91901-6201, USA

Giles, Nancy (Actor)
12047 178th St
Jamaica, NY 11434-2719, USA

Giles, Sandra
350 N Crescent Dr
Beverly Hills, CA 90210-4847

Giles, Selina (Actor)
Dolphin House 2-5 Manchester St
BN2 1TF, United Kingdom

Giletti, Alain (Figure Skater)
103 Place de L'Eglise
Chamonix 74400, FRANCE

Gilfillan, Jason (Athlete, Baseball Player)
153 Gilfillan Rd
Blacksburg, SC 29702-8521, USA

Gilford, David (Athlete, Golfer)
Andrew Murray 19 Higher Lane
Lymm Cheshire WA13 0AR, United Kingdom

Gilford, Zach (Actor)
c/o Charles Mastropietro *Dontanville/ Frattaroli (D/F)*
270 Lafayette St Ste 402
New York, NY 10012-3327, USA

Gilfry, Rodney (Opera Singer)
165 W 57th St
New York, NY 10019-2201, USA

Gilgorov, Kiro (President)
Skopje, MACEDONIA

Gilhen, Randy (Athlete, Hockey Player)
c/o Staff Member *Manitoba Moose*
260 Hargrave St
Winnipeg, MB R3C 5S5, Canada

Gilhooley, Frank (Athlete, Basketball Player)
5679 Monroe St Unit 607
Sylvania, OH 43560-2715, USA

Gilk, Shelley (Athlete, Golfer)
10537 Toledo Dr N
Minneapolis, MN 55443-5424, USA

Gilkey, Bernard (Athlete, Baseball Player)
11463 Patty Ann Dr
Saint Louis, MO 63146-5453, USA

Gill, George N (Publisher)
525 W Broadway
Louisville, KY 40202-2206, USA

Gill, Hal (Athlete, Hockey Player)
11 Reiling Pond Rd
Lincoln, MA 01773-2311, USA

Gill, Janis (Music Group)
5101 Overton Rd
Nashville, TN 37220-1920, USA

Gill, Johnny (Music Group, Musician, Songwriter, Writer)
4924 Balboa Blvd # 366
Encino, CA 91316-3402, USA

Gill, Kendall (Basketball Player)
c/o Staff Member *Milwaukee Bucks*
1001 N 4th St Ste 1
Milwaukee, WI 53203-1312

Gill, Priya (Actor, Bollywood)
606 Nestle - B 4th Cross Road
Lokhandwala Complex Andheri W
Mumbai, MS 400058, INDIA

Gill, Tanya (Stylist)
c/o Staff Member *Solo Artists*
2148 Federal Ave
Los Angeles, CA 90025-5327, USA

Gill, Thea (Actor)
c/o Cynthia Campos-Greenberg *Anthem Entertainment*
9595 Wilshire Blvd Ste 900
Beverly Hills, CA 90212-2509, USA

Gill, Tim (Business Person, Designer, Engineer)
2215 Market St
Denver, CO 80205-2026, USA

Gill, Todd (Athlete, Hockey Player)
c/o Staff Member *Brockville Braves*
1030 Montrose St
Brockville, ON K6V 7G1, Canada

Gill, Tonya (Athlete, Golfer)
3655 Habersham Rd NE Apt B2229
Atlanta, GA 30305-1142, USA

Gill, Vince (Musician, Songwriter)
c/o Larry Fitzgerald *Fitzgerald Hartley Co (Nashville)*
1908 Wedgewood Ave
Nashville, TN 37212-3733, USA

Gill, William A Jr (Government Official, Misc)
15975 Cove Ln
Dumfries, VA 22025-1412, USA

Gillan, Ian (Musician)
1 Water Lane Camden Town
London NW1 8N2, UNITED KINGDOM (UK)

Gillbreath, Rod (Baseball Player)
1438 Ridgeland Way SW
Lilburn, GA 30047-4352, USA

Gillen, Aidan (Actor)
c/o Leanne Coronel *Coronel Group*
1100 Glendon Ave Fl 17
Los Angeles, CA 90024-3588, USA

Gillen, Don (Athlete, Hockey Player)
618 Forsyth Cres
Saskatoon, SK S7N 4J3, Canada

Giller, Walter
Via Tamporiva 26
Castagnola, SWITZERLAND CH-6976

Gilles, Daniel (Writer)
161 Ave Churchill
Brussels 1180, BELGIUM

Gilles, Tom (Athlete, Baseball Player)
14615 W Southern St
Princeville, IL 61559-9375, USA

Gillespie, Ann (Actor)
7080 Hollywood Blvd Ste 1017
Los Angeles, CA 90028-6937, USA

Gillespie, Charles A Jr (Diplomat)
900 17th St NW Ste 500
Washington, DC 20006-2507, USA

Gillespie, Craig (Director)
c/o Simon Millar *Rumble Media*
1620 Broadway Ste C
Santa Monica, CA 90404-2777, USA

Gillespie, Jack (Athlete, Basketball Player)
600 6th Ave N
Great Falls, MT 59401-2342, USA

Gillespie, Rhondda (Music Group, Musician)
2 Princess Road Saint Leonards-on-Sea
East Sussex TN37 6EL, UNITED KINGDOM (UK)

Gillespie, Robert (Financier)
127 Public Sq
Cleveland, OH 44114-1217, USA

Gillespie, Ronald J (Doctor, Misc)
Chemistry Dept
Hamilton, ON L8S 4M1, CANADA

Gillette (Musician)
c/o Staff Member *Diva Central Inc*
7510 W Sunset Blvd Ste 1445
Los Angeles, CA 90046-3408, USA

Gillette, Anita (Actor)
501 S Beverly Dr Fl 3
Beverly Hills, CA 90212-4520, USA

Gillette, Walker (Athlete, Football Player)
401 N College Dr
Franklin, VA 23851-2401, USA

Gilley, J Wade (Educator)
Presidents Ofc
Knoxville, TN 37996-0001, USA

Gilley, Mickey (Music Group, Songwriter, Writer)
PO Box 1242
Pasadena, TX 77501-1242, USA

Gilliam, Armon (Athlete, Basketball Player)
PO Box 174
South Park, PA 15129-0174, USA

Gilliam, Burton
1427 Tascosa Ct
Allen, TX 75013-1111

Gilliam, Dondre (Athlete, Football Player)
504 Plaza Ct Apt 2A
Aberdeen, MD 21001-2821, USA

Gilliam, Elijah (Baseball Player)
1617 5th Ave N
Birmingham, AL 35203-1953, USA

Gilliam, John (Athlete, Football Player)
4045 Moheb St SW
Atlanta, GA 30331-6418, USA

Gilliam, Jon (Athlete, Football Player)
440 S Walnut Grove Rd
Midlothian, TX 76065-6206, USA

Gilliam, Seth (Actor)
c/o Jason Gutman *Gersh (NY)*
41 Madison Ave
New York, NY 10010-2202, USA

Gilliam, Terry (Actor, Animator, Writer)
Old Hall South Grove Highgate
London N6 6BP, UNITED KINGDOM (UK)

Gilliand, Herman (Baseball Player)
1833 Kern Mountain Way
Antioch, CA 94531-7497, USA

Gilliangham, Gale (Athlete, Football Player)
1605 W River Rd
Little Falls, MN 56345-4155, USA

Gilliatt, Penelope
31 Chester Sq
London, ENGLAND SW1W 9HT

Gillie, Nick (Producer)
c/o Staff Member *Metropolitan (MTA)*
4526 Wilshire Blvd
Los Angeles, CA 90010-3801, USA

Gillies, Ben (Music Group, Musician)
P O Box 281
Sunny Hills, NSW 2010, AUSTRALIA

Gillies, Clark (Athlete, Hockey Player)
17 Pinta Ct
Greenlawn, NY 11740-2314, USA

Gillies, Daniel (Actor, Director, Writer)
c/o Ben Levine *Kritzer Levine Wilkins Entertainment*
11872 La Grange Ave Fl 1
Los Angeles, CA 90025-5283, USA

Gilliford, Paul (Athlete, Baseball Player)
7 Woodland Dr
Malvern, PA 19355-3308, USA

Gilligan, Carol (Educator)
Gender Studies Dept
Cambridge, MA 2138, USA

Gillilan, William J III (Business Person)
PO Box 199000
Dallas, TX 75219-9000, USA

Gilliland, Richard (Actor)
c/o Anthony DeMichele *Beacon Talent Agency*
170 Apple Ridge Rd
Woodcliff Lake, NJ 07677-8149, USA

Gilliland, Robert J (Misc)
PO Box 84
Palm Desert, CA 92261-0084, USA

Gillingwater, Leah (Reality TV Star)
c/o Staff Member *Real World, The*
6007 Sepulveda Blvd
Van Nuys, CA 91411-2502, USA

Gillis, Don (Athlete, Football Player)
4658 Oso Pkwy
Corpus Christi, TX 78413-5269, USA

Gillis, Louis (Baseball Player)
2920 33rd Way N
Birmingham, AL 35207-3720, USA

Gillis, Malcolm (Educator)
President's Office
Houston, TX 77251, USA

Gillis, Mike (Athlete, Hockey Player)
154 Earl St
Kingston, ON K7L 2H2, Canada

Gillis, Tom (Athlete, Golfer)
527 Tanview Dr
Oxford, MI 48371-4769, USA

Gillom, Jennifer (Basketball Player)
c/o Staff Member *LA Sparks*
555 N Nash St
El Segundo, CA 90245-2818, USA

Gillooly (Stone), Jeff
10408 SE 82nd Ave
Portland, OR 97266

Gilman, Alfred G (Nobel Prize Laureate)
10996 Crooked Creek Dr
Dallas, TX 75229-4304, USA

Gilman, Billy (Music Group)
c/o Rodney Essig *Creative Artists Agency (CAA-TN)*
3310 W End Ave Fl 5
Nashville, TN 37203-1028, USA

Gilman, Dorothy (Writer)
321 N Highland Ave
Ossining, NY 10562-2331, USA

Gilman, Kenneth B (Business Person)
3 Limited Parkway P O Box 1600
Columbus, OH 43216, USA

Gilman, Richard H (Publisher)
Publisher's Office 135 W T Morrissey Blvd
Dorchester, MA 2125, USA

Gilman, Sid (Doctor, Misc)
3441 Geddes Rd
Ann Arbor, MI 48105, USA

Gilmartin, Paul (Comedian)
c/o Staff Member *Agency for the Performing Arts (APA-LA)*
405 S Beverly Dr Ste 500
Beverly Hills, CA 90212-4425, USA

Gilmartin, Raymond V (Business Person)
PO Box 100
Whitehouse Station, NJ 08889-0100, USA

Gilmer, Harry V (Athlete, Football Player)
7467 Highway N
O Fallon, MO 63368-7014, USA

Gilmore, Artis (Athlete, Basketball Player)
11043 Turnbridge Dr
Jacksonville, FL 32256-2329, USA

Gilmore, Bryan (Athlete, Football Player)
1908 Fuller Springs Dr
Lufkin, TX 75901-6638, USA

Gilmore, Clarence P (Editor)
6 Adema Way
Old Saybrook, CT 06475-1219, USA

Gilmore, Jimmie Dale (Music Group, Songwriter, Writer)
c/o Staff Member *Concerted Efforts*
PO Box 440326
Somerville, MA 02144-0004, USA

Gilmore, Kenneth O (Editor)
Charles Road
Mount Kisco, NY 10549, USA

Gilmore, Len (Athlete, Baseball Player)
7500 NE 102nd St
Jones, OK 73049-5818, USA

Gilmore, Walt (Athlete, Basketball Player)
257 Benjamin Blvd
Bear, DE 19701-1693, USA

Gilmour, Buddy (Race Car Driver)
50 Merrick Ave Unit 410
East Meadow, NY 11554-1593, USA

Gilmour, David (Music Group, Musician)
c/o Steve Martin *Agency Group Ltd, The (NY)*
142 W 57th St Fl 6
New York, NY 10019-3300, USA

Gilmour, Doug (Athlete, Hockey Player)
c/o Staff Member *Toronto Maple Leafs*
Air Canada Centre 400-40 Bay St
Toronto, ON M5J 2X2, Canada

Gilmour of Craigmillar, Ian (Government Official)
Ferry House Old Isleworth
Middx, UNITED KINGDOM (UK)

Gilmur, Chuck (Athlete, Basketball Player)
PO Box 64290
Tacoma, WA 98464-0290, USA

Gilpin, Peri (Actor)
c/o Scott Henderson *WmE2 (Endeavor-LA)*
9601 Wilshire Blvd Fl 3
Beverly Hills, CA 90210-5219, USA

Gilpin Faust, Drew (Educator)
33 Elmwood Ave
Cambridge, MA 02138-4717, USA

Gilroy, Frank D (Writer)
8 Mangin Rd
Monroe, NY 10950-2203, USA

Gilroy, Tom (Actor, Director, Producer, Writer)
c/o Staff Member *WmE2 (WMA-LA)*
1 William Morris Pl
Beverly Hills, CA 90212-4261, USA

Gilroy, Tony (Director, Writer)
c/o Risa Gertner *Creative Artists Agency (CAA-LA)*
2000 Avenue of the Stars Ste 100
Los Angeles, CA 90067-4705, USA

Gilsig, Jessalyn (Actor)
c/o Steven Levy *Framework Entertainment (LA)*
9057 Nemo St Ste C
West Hollywood, CA 90069-5511, USA

Gilson, Hal (Athlete, Baseball Player)
16013 S Desert Foothills Pkwy Apt 1102
Phoenix, AZ 85048-8441, USA

Gilyard Jr, Clarence (Actor)
24040 Camino Del Avion # A239
Monarch Bay, CA 92629-4005, USA

Gimbel, Norman (Songwriter, Writer)
PO Box 50013
Santa Barbara, CA 93150-0013, USA

Gimbrone, Michael A Jr (Doctor, Misc)
Vascular Pathlogy Dept
Boston, MA 2115, USA

Gimeno, Andres (Tennis Player)
Paseo de la Bnanova 38
Barcelona 6, SPAIN

Gimpel, Erica
c/o Staff Member *Innovative Artists (LA)*
1505 10th St
Santa Monica, CA 90401-2805, USA

Gin Blossoms
PO Box 429094
San Francisco, CA 94142-9094

Gina G (Music Group)
PO Box 1463
Culver City, CA 90232-1463, USA

Ging, Jack (Actor)
48701 San Pedro St
La Quinta, CA 92253-6229, USA

Gingerich, Philip D (Misc, Scientist)
Paleontology Dept
Ann Arbor, MI 48109, USA

Gingras, Gaston (Athlete, Hockey Player)
50 Rue Du Docteur
Pierrefonds, QC H8Z 1L2, Canada

Gingrey, Phil (Congressman, Politician)
442 Cannon Hob
Washington, DC 20515-0106, USA

Gingrich, Newton L (Newt) (Politician)
3110 Maple Dr NE Ste 400
Atlanta, GA 30305-2650, USA

Ginibre, Jean-Louis (Editor)
1633 Broadway
New York, NY 10019-6708, USA

Ginn, Chad (Athlete, Golfer)
c/o Staff Member *Signature Sports Group*
4150 Olson Memorial Hey Suite 110
Minneapolis, MN 55422, USA

Ginn, Hubert (Athlete, Football Player)
16 Egrets Nest Dr
Savannah, GA 31406-4258, USA

Ginn, William H Jr (General)
1002 Priscilla Ln
Alexandria, VA 22308-2645, USA

Ginn Jr, Ted (Athlete, Football Player)
12819 Edmonton Ave
Cleveland, OH 44108-2519, USA

Ginobili, Emanuel (Manu) (Athlete, Basketball Player)
10 Queens Hi
San Antonio, TX 78257, USA

Ginsberg, Joe (Athlete, Baseball Player)
12635 SW Kingsway Cir # D1
Lake Suzy, FL 34269-4585, USA

Ginsberg, Justice Ruth Bader
700 New Hampshire Ave NW
Washington, DC 20037-2407

Ginsburg, Art (Television Host)
1770 NW 64th St Ste 500
Ft Lauderdale, FL 33309-1853, USA

Ginsburg, Douglas H (Judge)
333 Constitution Ave NW
Washington, DC 20001-2804, USA

Ginsburg, Ruth Bader (Judge, Lawyer, Misc)
1 1st St NE
Washington, DC 20543-0001, USA

Ginsburg, William
10100 Santa Monica Blvd Ste 800
Los Angeles, CA 90067-4105, USA

Ginter, Keith (Athlete, Baseball Player)
2907 Maple Ave
Fullerton, CA 92835-2126, USA

Ginter, Matt (Athlete, Baseball Player)
3320 Boonesboro Rd
Winchester, KY 40391-9292, USA

Ginter-Brooker, Susan (Athlete, Golfer)
314 Yorkshire Dr
Greenville, SC 29615-1133, USA

Gintner, Heidi (Stylist)
c/o Staff Member *Zenobia Agency Inc*
PO Box 909
Groveland, CA 95321-0909, USA

Ginzburg, Vitaly L (Nobel Prize Laureate)
Leninsky Prospect 53
Moscow 117924, RUSSIA

Ginzton, Edward L (Business Person, Engineer)
3100 Hansen Way
Palo Alto, CA 94304-1030, USA

Giofriddo, Al
64 Bristol Pl
Goleta, CA 93117-1949

Gioia (Musician)
c/o Staff Member *Diva Central Inc*
7510 W Sunset Blvd Ste 1445
Los Angeles, CA 90046-3408, USA

Giola, Dana (Government Official, Writer)
1100 Pennsylvania Ave NW
Washington, DC 20004-2501, USA

Gionta, Brian (Athlete, Hockey Player)
PO Box 16499
Rochester, NY 14616-0499, USA

Giordano, Michele Cardinal (Religious Leader)
Largo Donnaregina 22
Naples 80138, ITALY

Giordano, Tommy (Athlete, Baseball Player)
176 Riverside Ave
Amityville, NY 11701-3738, USA

Giosia, Nadia (Nadia G) (Chef)
c/o Jason Pinyan *Artist and Brand Management*
8687 Melrose Ave Ste 8
Los Angeles, CA 90069-5746, USA

Giovanni, Joseph (Architect)
140 E 40th St
New York, NY 10016-1701, USA

Giovanni, Nikki E (Writer)
English
Blacksburg, VA 24061-0001, USA

Giovanola, Ed (Athlete, Baseball Player)
1741 Nomark Ct
San Jose, CA 95125-3948, USA

Giovinazzo, Carmine (Actor)
c/o Staff Member *Untitled Entertainment (LA)*
350 S Beverly Dr Ste 200
Beverly Hills, CA 90212-4819, USA

Gipson, Charles (Athlete, Baseball Player)
632 S Earlham St
Orange, CA 92869-5406, USA

Gipsy Kings (Music Group)
c/o Staff Member *Podell Talent Agency LLC*
22 W 21st St Fl 9
New York, NY 10010-7095, USA

Giradeau, Bernard
37 Rue Froidevaux
Paris, FRANCE 75014

Giradelll, Marc (Skier)
9413 Oberegg-Sulzbach
SWITZERLAND

Giraldo, Neil (Musician, Producer)
c/o Staff Member *WmE2 (WMA-LA)*
1 William Morris Pl
Beverly Hills, CA 90212-4261, USA

Girard, Ken (Athlete, Hockey Player)
6-519 Riverside Dr
London, ON N6H 5J3, Canada

Girardi, Joseph E (Joe) (Athlete, Baseball Player)
161st Street And River Avenue Attn Managers Ofc
Bronx, NY 10451, USA

Girardi, Serge (Stylist)
c/o Staff Member *Management + Artists + Organization*
330 W 38th St Ste 1401
New York, NY 10018-8438, USA

Giraudeau, Bernard (Actor)
36 Rue de Ponthieu
Paris 75008, FRANCE

Giri, Tulsi (Prime Minister)
Jawakpurdham
District Dhanuka, NEPAL

Girls Aloud
c/o Staff Member *Concorde Intl Artists Ltd*
101 Shepherds Bush Rd
London W6 7LP, UNITED KINGDOM (UK)

Girls Aloud (Music Group)
72 Black Lion Ln
London W6 9BE, UNITED KINGDOM

Girone, Remo (Actor)
36 Rue de Ponthieu
Paris 75008, FRANCE

Giroux, Bonny (Actor)
c/o Staff Member *Deborah Harry Talent*
408-1917 W 4th Ave
Vancouver, BC V6J 1M7, CANADA

Giroux, Larry (Athlete, Hockey Player)
10 Colleen Dr
Edwardsville, IL 62025-4242, USA

Giscard, d'Estaing Valery (President)
199 Blvd Saint-Germain
Paris 75007, FRANCE

Gish, Annabeth (Actor)
c/o Joan Hyler *Hyler Management*
20 Ocean Park Blvd Unit 25
Santa Monica, CA 90405-3590, USA

Gisler, Mike (Athlete, Football Player)
407 Tampa Dr
Victoria, TX 77904-1649, USA

Gismonti, Egberto (Music Group, Musician)
278 S Main St # 400
Gloucester, MA 1930, USA

Gissell, Chris (Athlete, Baseball Player)
4310 NW 121st Cir
Vancouver, WA 98685-2052, USA

Gissinger, Andy (Athlete, Football Player)
1667 Union Ave
Barberton, OH 44203-7644, USA

Gitai, Yael (Stylist)
c/o Celebrity Stylist *Workgroup (San Francisco)*
450 Linden St
San Francisco, CA 94102-5023, USA

Gitlin, Todd (Historian)
Culture & Communications Dept
New York, NY 10012, USA

Gitomer, Jeffrey (Business Person)
310 Arlington Ave Unit 329
Charlotte, NC 28203-4296, USA

Giudice, Teresa (Reality TV Star)
c/o Michael (Mike) Esterman
Esterman.Com, LLC
Prefers to be contacted via email
MD, USA

Giuffre, Carlo
Via Massimi 45
Rome, ITALY I-00136

Giuffre, James P (Jimmy) (Music Group, Musician)
550 Madison Ave # 1700
New York, NY 10022-3211, USA

Giuliani, Rudolph (Rudy) (Politician)
5 Times Sq
New York, NY 10036-6527, USA

Giuliano, Louis J (Business Person)
4 W Red Oak Ln
White Plains, NY 10604-3603, USA

Giuliano, Tom (Music Group)
6929 N Hayden Rd
Scottsdale, AZ 85250-7978, USA

Giullani, Rudolph W (Misc, Politician)
5 Times Sq
New York, NY 10036-6527, USA

Giuntoli, David (Actor)
c/o Judy Hofflund *Hofflund/Polone*
9465 Wilshire Blvd Ste 420
Beverly Hills, CA 90212-2603, USA

Giuranna, Bruno (Music Group, Musician)
Via Bembo 96
Asolo TV 31011, ITALY

Giusti, David J (Dave) (Athlete, Baseball Player)
524 Clair Dr
Pittsburgh, PA 15241-2013, USA

Givens, Adele (Actor, Comedian)
c/o Staff Member *Gersh (LA)*
9465 Wilshire Blvd Ste 600
Beverly Hills, CA 90212-2612, USA

Givens, Jack (Athlete, Basketball Player, Misc)
9610 Leeside Ct
Windermere, FL 34786-6200, USA

Givens, Robin (Actor)
c/o Darryl Marshak *Marshak/Zachary Company, The*
8840 Wilshire Blvd Fl 1
Beverly Hills, CA 90211-2606, USA

Givins, Brian (Athlete, Baseball Player)
811 Deer Clover Cir
Castle Pines, CO 80108-8202, USA

Givins, Ernest (Athlete, Football Player)
3115 48th Ave S
Saint Petersburg, FL 33712-4344, USA

Gizzi, Claudio (Composer)
Viaile dell Letteratura 30
Rome 100, ITALY

Gladden, Danny (Dan) (Athlete, Baseball Player)
6543 Pinnacle Dr
Eden Prairie, MN 55346-1906, USA

Gladding, Fred (Athlete, Baseball Player)
436 Marsh Pointe Dr
Columbia, SC 29229-7025, USA

Gladieux, Robert (Athlete, Football Player)
802 Arch Ave
South Bend, IN 46601-3204, USA

Gladwell, Malcolm (Business Person, Writer)
410 W 24th St Apt 19A
New York, NY 10011-1309, USA

Glance, Harvey (Athlete, Track Athlete)
2408 Old Creek Rd
Montgomery, AL 36117-2420, USA

Glanville, Brandi (Reality TV Star)
c/o Staff Member *Bravo (LA)*
3000 W Alameda Ave
Burbank, CA 91523-0001, USA

Glanville, Doug (Athlete, Baseball Player)
209 Hillcrest Rd
Raleigh, NC 27605-1719, USA

Glanville, Jerry (Athlete, Coach, Football Coach, Football Player, Sportscaster)
130 Holly Dr
Dawsonville, GA 30534-5727, USA

Glasbergen, Randy (Cartoonist)
c/o Staff Member *King Features Syndication*
300 W 57th St Fl 15
New York, NY 10019-5238, USA

Glaser, Donald A (Nobel Prize Laureate)
Molecular Biology Laboratory
Berkeley, CA 94720-0001, USA

Glaser, Jim (Music Group)
2802 Columbine Pl
Nashville, TN 37204-3104, USA

Glaser, Jon (Actor, Writer)
c/o Staff Member *3 Arts Entertainment Inc*
9460 Wilshire Blvd Fl 7
Beverly Hills, CA 90212-2713, USA

Glaser, Milton (Artist, Misc)
207 E 32nd St
New York, NY 10016-6305, USA

Glaser, Paul Michael (Actor, Director)
c/o Mark Teitelbaum *Teitelbaum Artists Group*
8840 Wilshire Blvd Fl 3
Beverly Hills, CA 90211-2606, USA

Glaser, Rose Mary (Baseball Player)
8929 Long Ln
Cincinnati, OH 45231-5024, USA

Glaser Brothers
91619th Ave
Nashville, TN 37212, US

Glasgow, Brian (Athlete, Football Player)
5 Sage Ct
Bolingbrook, IL 60490-3220, USA

Glasgow, Nesby (Athlete, Football Player)
8402 165th Ave NE Apt 106
Redmond, WA 98052-6648, USA

Glashow, Sheldon Lee (Nobel Prize Laureate)
30 Prescott St
Brookline, MA 02446-4038, USA

Glaspie, April (Diplomat)
2201 C St NW
Washington, DC 20520-0099, USA

Glass, Chip (Athlete, Football Player)
7704 NE 140th St
Kirkland, WA 98034-5360, USA

Glass, David (Baseball Player)
17 Glenbrook
Bentonville, AR 72712-3840, USA

Glass, Gerald (Athlete, Basketball Player)
1123 Tillman Rd
Port Gibson, MS 39150-2890, USA

Glass, Glenn (Athlete, Football Player)
301 Portsmouth Rd
Knoxville, TN 37909-3020, USA

Glass, H Bentley (Biologist)
PO Box 65
East Setauket, NY 11733-0065, USA

Glass, Leland (Athlete, Football Player)
9 Bayou Ct
Sacramento, CA 95831-2403, USA

Glass, Nancy (Journalist)
345 Montgomery Ave
Bala Cynwyd, PA 19004-2801

Glass, Philip (Composer)
c/o Staff Member *Kraft-Engel Management*
15233 Ventura Blvd Ste 200
Sherman Oaks, CA 91403-2244, USA

Glass, Ron (Actor)
c/o Mitchell Stubbs *Mitchell K Stubbs & Assoc (MKS)*
8675 Washington Blvd Ste 203
Culver City, CA 90232-7486, USA

Glass, Todd (Actor)
c/o Alex Murray *McDonald-Murray Management*
8530 Wilshire Blvd Fl 5
Beverly Hills, CA 90211-3122, USA

Glass, William S (Bill) (Athlete, Football Player)
PO Box 761101
Dallas, TX 75376-1101, USA

Glass Tiger
238 Davenport # 126
Toronto, CANADA Ont.M5R 1J

Glasser, Erika (Actor)
c/o Gabriel Blanco *Gabriel Blanco Iglesias (Mexico)*
Rio Balsas 35-32 Colonia Cuauhtemoc
DF 6500, Mexico

Glasser, Ira S (Activist, Attorney, Attorney General, General, Lawyer, Misc)
132 W 43rd St
New York, NY 10036, USA

Glasser, Isabel (Actor)
c/o Kyle Luker *The Group Entertainment*
141 W 28th St Rm 300
New York, NY 10001-6187, USA

Glasser, William (Doctor, Misc)
11633 San Vicente Blvd
Los Angeles, CA 90049-6511, USA

Glassic, Tom (Athlete, Football Player)
1030 S Pine Dr
Bailey, CO 80421-2333, USA

Glassman, Adam (Stylist)
c/o Staff Member *Bryan Bantry*
900 Broadway Ste 400
New York, NY 10003-1239, USA

Glasson, Bill (Athlete, Golfer)
5819 W Villas Ct
Stillwater, OK 74074-2016, USA

Glasvegas (Music Group, Musician)
c/o Ben Winchester *Primary Talent International (UK)*
The Primary Building 10-11 Jockeys Fields
London WC1R 4BN, UK

Glatter, Lesli L (Director)
9560 Wilshire Blvd Ste 500
Beverly Hills, CA 90212-2401, USA

Glatz, Fred (Athlete, Football Player)
224 Perkins Row
Topsfield, MA 01983-1532, USA

Glatzeder, Winfried
Gosslerstrasse 24
Berlin, GERMANY D-12161

Glau, Summer (Actor)
c/o Mimi DiTrani *Schiff Company, The*
8440 Warner Dr Ste B1
Culver City, CA 90232-2461, USA

Glauber, Keith (Athlete, Baseball Player)
20 Highland Ct
Freehold, NJ 07728-9041, USA

Glauber, Roy J. (Nobel Prize Laureate)
17 Oxford St Lyman 331
Cambridge, MA 02138-2933, USA

Glaudini, Lola (Actor, Producer)
c/o Staff Member *Mosaic Media Group*
9200 W Sunset Blvd Ste 10
Los Angeles, CA 90069-3608, USA

Glaus, Troy (Athlete, Baseball Player)
5865 Neal Ave N
Stillwater, MN 55082-2177, USA

Glave, Matthew (Actor)
c/o Staff Member *Innovative Artists (LA)*
1505 10th St
Santa Monica, CA 90401-2805, USA

Glavin, Denis Joseph (Misc)
11 E 1st St
New York, NY 10003-8996, USA

Glavine, Mike (Athlete, Baseball Player)
89 Treble Cove Rd
North Billerica, MA 01862-2215, USA

Glavine, Tom (Athlete, Baseball Player)
920 Hurleston Ln
Alpharetta, GA 30022-6251, USA

Glazer, Jay (Sportscaster)
51 W 52nd St
New York, NY 10019-6119, USA

Glazer, Jonathan (Director, Writer)
c/o David Naylor *David Naylor & Associates*
6535 Santa Monica Blvd
Los Angeles, CA 90038-1407, USA

Glazer, Mitch (Producer)
c/o Staff Member *Creative Artists Agency (CAA-LA)*
2000 Avenue of the Stars Ste 100
Los Angeles, CA 90067-4705, USA

Glazer, Nathan (Activist)
12 Scott St
Cambridge, MA 02138-2016, USA

Glazier, Nancy (Artist)
10688 Haddington Dr
Houston, TX 77043-3229, USA

Glazkov, Yuri N (Astronaut, General, Misc)
Moskovskoi Oblasti
Syvisdny Goroduk 141160, RUSSIA

Glazunov, Ilya S (Artist)
Kamergersky Per 2
Moscow 103009, RUSSIA

Gleason, Andrew M (Mathematician)
110 Larchwood Dr
Cambridge, MA 02138-4639, USA

Gleason, Joanna (Actor)
c/o Vera Mihailovich *Forward Entertainment*
9255 W Sunset Blvd Ste 805
Los Angeles, CA 90069-3305, USA

Gleason, Mary Pat (Actor, Writer)
c/o Tim Stone *Stone Manners Salners Agency (LA)*
9911 W Pico Blvd Ste 1400
Los Angeles, CA 90035-2715, USA

Gleason, Matthew (Stylist)
c/o Staff Member *Pat Bates & Associates*
300 W 12th St
New York, NY 10014-1939, USA

Gleason, Roy (Athlete, Baseball Player)
41770 Margarita Rd Apt 1043
Temecula, CA 92591-1945, USA

Gleason, Tim (Athlete, Hockey Player)
1270 Kenilworth Pl
Clawson, MI 48017-1021, USA

Gleaton, Jerry Don (Athlete, Baseball Player)
3008 Avenue K
Brownwood, TX 76801-6016, USA

Gleeson, Brendan (Actor)
c/o Larry Taube *Principal Entertainment (LA)*
1964 Westwood Blvd Ste 400
Los Angeles, CA 90025-4695, USA

Glemp, Jozef Cardinal (Religious Leader)
Sekretariat Prymasa Kolski Ul Miodowa 17
Warsaw 00 246, POLAND

Glen, John (Director)
1015 Gayley Ave # 300
Los Angeles, CA 90024-3413, USA

Glenn, Aaron (Athlete, Football Player)
30 Commanders Cv
Missouri City, TX 77459-6518, USA

Glenn, Jason (Athlete, Football Player)
15530 Ella Blvd Apt 501
Houston, TX 77090-5309, USA

Glenn, Mike (Athlete, Basketball Player)
3571 Kilpatrick Ln
Snellville, GA 30039-8643, USA

Glenn, Scott (Actor)
c/o Johnnie Planco *Parseghian Planco LLC*
322 8th Ave Ste 601
New York, NY 10001-6715, USA

Glenn, Stanley (Athlete, Baseball Player)
9 Baily Rd
Lansdowne, PA 19050-2817, USA

Glenn, Tarik (Athlete, Football Player)
5216 N Delaware St
Indianapolis, IN 46220-3045, USA

Glenn, Vencie (Athlete, Football Player)
3005 S Leisure World Blvd Apt 811
Silver Spring, MD 20906-8310, USA

Glenn, Wayne E (Misc)
3340 Perimeter Hill Dr
Nashville, TN 37211-4123, USA

Glenn Jr, John H (Astronaut, Ex-Senator)
1947 N College Rd
Columbus, OH 43210-1181, USA

Glennan, Robert E Jr (Educator)
President's Office
Emporia, KS 66801, USA

Glennie, Brian (Athlete, Hockey Player)
4 Curling Rd
Bracebridge, ON P1L 1M6, Canada

Glennie, Evelyn E A (Music Group, Musician)
P O Box 6 Sawtry Huntingdon
Cambs PE17 5WE, UNITED KINGDOM (UK)

Glennie-Smith, Nick (Composer)
15233 Ventura Blvd Ste 200
Sherman Oaks, CA 91403-2244, USA

Glennon, Matt (Athlete, Hockey Player)
59 Beacon Rd
Hull, MA 02045-1457, USA

Gless, Sharon (Actor)
PO Box 48005
Los Angeles, CA 90048-0005, USA

Glick, Alexis (Correspondent)
c/o Staff Member *Fox News Channel (NY)*
1211 Ave Of The Americas Level C1
New York, NY 10036-8701, USA

Glick, Frederick (Freddie) (Athlete, Football Player)
4226 Antlers Ct
Fort Collins, CO 80526-6411, USA

Glick, Gary (Athlete, Football Player)
2801 Middlesborough Ct
Fort Collins, CO 80525-2331, USA

Glickman, Daniel R (Misc, Secretary)
Kennedy Government School
Cambridge, MA 2138, USA

Glidden, Bob (Race Car Driver)
PO Box 183
Whiteland, IN 46184-0183, USA

Glidden, Robert (Educator)
President's Office
Athens, OH 45701, USA

Glidewell, Iain (Judge)
Rough Heys Farm Macclesfield
Cheshire SK11 9PF, UNITED KINGDOM (UK)

Glimcher, Arnold O (Arne) (Artist, Misc)
32 E 57th St
New York, NY 10022-2513, USA

Glimm, James G (Mathematician)
Applied Math
Stony Brook, NY 11794-0001, USA

Glinatsis, George (Athlete, Baseball Player)
13742 W 59th Ave
Arvada, CO 80004-3740, USA

Glisson, Lane (Stylist)
303 11th St
Brooklyn, NY 11215-3910, USA

Glitman, Maynard W (Diplomat)
40 College St Apt 506
Burlington, VT 05401-4488, USA

Glitter, Gary (Music Group, Songwriter, Writer)
1 York St
London W1H 1PZ, UNITED KINGDOM (UK)

Glmble, Johnny (Misc)
6618 Wolfcreek Pall
Austin, TX 78749, USA

Gload, Ross (Athlete, Baseball Player)
23 Harrison Ave
East Hampton, NY 11937-2051, USA

Glockner, Michael
Kaiserslautener Str. 54
Saarbrucken, GERMANY D-66123

Gloden, Fred (Athlete, Football Player)
3821 Andrea Rd
Philadelphia, PA 19154-4211, USA

Gloeckner, Lorry (Athlete, Hockey Player)
11671 King Rd
Richmond, BC V7A 3B5, Canada

Gloor, Danny (Athlete, Hockey Player)
172 Henry
Mitchell, ON N0K 1N0, Canada

Gloriana (Music Group, Musician)
c/o Staff Member *Emblem*
22301 Mulholland Hwy
Calabasas, CA 91302-5140, USA

Glory, New Found (Music Group)
c/o Staff Member *Ellis Industries Inc*
234 Shoreward Dr
Great Neck, NY 11021-2734, USA

Glosson, Clyde (Athlete, Football Player)
5803 Lake Falls Dr
San Antonio, TX 78222-2405, USA

Glouberman, Michael (Producer)
c/o Staff Member *United Talent Agency (UTA)*
9560 Wilshire Blvd Fl 5
Beverly Hills, CA 90212-2400, USA

Glover, Andrew (Athlete, Football Player)
33226 Magnolia Cir
Magnolia, TX 77354-1523, USA

Glover, Bloc (Motorcycle Race, Motorcycle Racer)
13515 Yarmouth Dr
Pickerington, OH 43147-8214, USA

Glover, Brian (Actor)
Manfield House 376/378 Strand
London WC2R OLR, UNITED KINGDOM

Glover, Bruce (Actor)
11449 Woodbine St
Los Angeles, CA 90066-1229, USA

Glover, Chris (Musician)
c/o Staff Member *Paradigm (Monterey)*
404 W Franklin St
Monterey, CA 93940-2303, USA

Glover, Clarence (Athlete, Basketball Player)
811 Lake Forest Pkwy
Louisville, KY 40245-5138, USA

Glover, Crispin (Actor, Director, Producer)
c/o Mark Schulman *3 Arts Entertainment Inc*
9460 Wilshire Blvd Fl 7
Beverly Hills, CA 90212-2713, USA

Glover, Danny (Actor)
PO Box 170069
San Francisco, CA 94117-0069, USA

Glover, Dion (Athlete, Basketball Player)
3691 Seton Hall Way
Decatur, GA 30034-5509, USA

Glover, Donald (Actor, Writer)
c/o Greg Walter *3 Arts Entertainment Inc*
9460 Wilshire Blvd Fl 7
Beverly Hills, CA 90212-2713, USA

Glover, Gary (Athlete, Baseball Player)
19704 Kell Estates Ln
Lutz, FL 33549-4092, USA

Glover, Howie (Athlete, Hockey Player)
15 Wendy Cres
Kitchener, ON N2A 1N0, Canada

Glover, Jane A
130 W 57th St Apt 8G
New York, NY 10019-3311, USA

Glover, John (Actor)
c/o Nevin Dolcefino *Innovative Artists (LA)*
1505 10th St
Santa Monica, CA 90401-2805, USA

Glover, Julian (Actor)
200 Fulham Road
London SW10 9PN, United Kingdom

Glover, Kevin B (Athlete, Football Player)
11553 Manorstone Ln
Columbia, MD 21044-5413, USA

Glover, La'Roi (Athlete, Football Player)
200 Carlyle Lake Dr
Saint Louis, MO 63141-7544, USA

Glover, Lucas (Athlete, Golfer)
105 Annas Pl
Simpsonville, SC 29681-4813, USA

Glover, Richard E (Rich) (Athlete, Football Player)
215 Claremont Ave
Jersey City, NJ 07305-3623, USA

Glover, Stephen (Steve-O) (Actor, Writer)
c/o Tim Curtis *WmE2 (Endeavor-LA)*
9601 Wilshire Blvd Fl 3
Beverly Hills, CA 90210-5219, USA

Glowacki, Janusz (Writer)
845 W End Ave Apt 4B
New York, NY 10025-8436, USA

Gluck, Carol (Historian)
440 Riverside Dr
New York, NY 10027-6828, USA

Gluck, Louise E (Writer)
English Dept
Williamstown, MA 2167, USA

Glueck, Larry (Athlete, Football Player)
10 Cooper Rd
East Falmouth, MA 02536-7413, USA

Glushchenko, Fedor I
1st Prydilnaya Str 11 #5
Moscow 105037, RUSSIA

Glymph, Junior (Athlete, Football Player)
7300 Fontana Dr
Columbia, SC 29209-3248, USA

Glynn, Bill (Athlete, Baseball Player)
6916 51st St
San Diego, CA 92120-1212, USA

Glynn, Brian (Athlete, Hockey Player)
1084 Central Ave Attn Police Dept
Prince Albert, SK S6V 7P3, Canada

Glynn, Carlin (Actor)
1165 5th Ave
New York, NY 10029-6931, USA

Glynn, Ed (Athlete, Baseball Player)
157 San Carlos St
Toms River, NJ 08757-6222, USA

Glynn, Ian M (Misc, Physicist)
Daylesford Conduit Head Road
Cambridge CB3 0EY, UNITED KINGDOM (UK)

Glynn, Robert D Jr (Business Person)
1 Market St
San Francisco, CA 94105-1402, USA

Glynn, Ryan (Athlete, Baseball Player)
1226 Melaleuca Ln
Fort Myers, FL 33901-8847, USA

Gminski, Mike (Athlete, Basketball Player, Sportscaster)
1309 Canterbury Hill Cir
Charlotte, NC 28211-1454, USA

Gnarls Barkley (Music Group)
73 Spring St Rm 504
New York, NY 10012-5802, USA

Gnedovsky, Yuri P (Architect)
Granatny Per 22
Moscow 103001, RUSSIA

Goad, Tim (Athlete, Football Player)
138 Birchwood Dr
Pittsboro, NC 27312-8737, USA

Goalby, Bob (Athlete, Golfer)
904 Briar Hill Rd
Belleville, IL 62223-1133, USA

Gob, Art (Athlete, Football Player)
123 Hiscott Dr
Pittsburgh, PA 15241-1105, USA

Gobble, Jimmy (Athlete, Baseball Player)
150 Lake View Estates Dr
Bristol, TN 37620-1307, USA

Goble, Les (Athlete, Football Player)
21 Dodge Ave
Waverly, NY 14892-9568, USA

Goc, Marcel (Athlete, Hockey Player)
12348 NW 69th Ct
Parkland, FL 33076-3334, USA

Gocke, Justin
6763 Pistachio Pl
Palmdale, CA 93551-1930

Godard, Jean-Luc (Director)
15 Rue du Nord
Roulle 1180, SWITZERLAND

Goday, Dale (Stylist)
55 E 11th St
New York, NY 10003-4603, USA

Godbold, John C (Judge)
PO Box 3038
Montgomery, AL 36109-0038, USA

Godboldo, Dale (Actor)
c/o Joanna (Joanie) Burstein *Burstein Company, The*
15304 W Sunset Blvd Ste 208
Pacific Palisades, CA 90272-3656, USA

Godby, Danny (Athlete, Baseball Player)
RR 2 Box 17A
Chapmanville, WV 25508-9773, USA

Godchaux, Stephen (Producer)
c/o Staff Member *WmE2 (WMA-LA)*
1 William Morris Pl
Beverly Hills, CA 90212-4261, USA

Goddard, Daniel (Actor)
c/o Staff Member *Luber Roklin Management*
8530 Wilshire Blvd Ste 550
Beverly Hills, CA 90211-3133, USA

Goddard, Joe (Athlete, Baseball Player)
304 Ridgepark Dr
Beckley, WV 25801-9593, USA

Goddard, John (Misc, Scientist)
4224 Beulah Dr
La Canada, CA 91011-3826, USA

Goddard, Mark (Actor)
PO Box 778
Middleboro, MA 02346-0778, USA

Godden, Ernie (Athlete, Hockey Player)
31 Rinaldo Rd
Keswick, ON L4P 3X9, Canada

Godecki, Marzena (Actor)
373 Bay Street Port Melbourne
Victoria, Australia 3207

Godfread, Dan (Athlete, Basketball Player)
622 Michigan St
Eagle River, WI 54521-8929, USA

Godfrey, Chris (Athlete, Football Player)
52383 Swanson Dr
South Bend, IN 46635-1067, USA

Godfrey, Paul V (Publisher)
333 King St E
Toronto, ON M5A 3X5, CANADA

Godfrey, Randall (Athlete, Football Player)
4102 Mount Zion Church Rd
Valdosta, GA 31605-6506, USA

Godin, Seth (Business Person, Writer)
PO Box 305
Irvington, NY 10533-0305, USA

Godina, John
PO Box 120
Indianapolis, IN 46204-0120

Godley, Georgina (Designer, Fashion Designer)
42 Bassett Road
London W10 6UL, UNITED KINGDOM (UK)

Godley, Kevin (Music Group, Musician)
Heronden Hall Tenterden
Kent, UNITED KINGDOM (UK)

Godmanis, Ivars (Politician)
Palasta St 1
Riga 1954, LATVIA

Godreche, Judith (Actor, Writer)
c/o Staff Member *Zelig Films*
57 rue Reaumur
Paris 75002, France

Godsmack (Music Group)
c/o John Branigan *WmE2 (Endeavor-LA)*
9601 Wilshire Blvd Fl 3
Beverly Hills, CA 90210-5219, USA

Godsted, Patricia Martin (Stylist)
8931 S Oakley Ave
Chicago, IL 60643-6429, USA

Godwin, Fay S (Photographer)
3-4 Kerby St
London E4N 8TS, UNITED KINGDOM (UK)

Godwin, Gail K (Writer)
PO Box 946
Woodstock, NY 12498-0946, USA

Godwin, Linda M (Astronaut, Physicist)
3801 Eagle View Ct
Columbia, MO 65203-1064, USA

Godynyuk, Alexander (Athlete, Hockey Player)
5670 Vantage Point Rd
Columbia, MD 21044-2612, USA

Goeas, Leo (Athlete, Football Player)
95104 Hiilei Pl
Mililani, HI 96789-1002, USA

Goebel, Brad (Athlete, Football Player)
PO Box 4006
Horseshoe Bay, TX 78657-4006, USA

Goebel, Timothy (Figure Skater)
c/o Staff Member *Champions on Ice*
3500 W 80th St Ste 200
Minneapolis, MN 55431-1090, USA

Goeddeke, George (Athlete, Football Player)
1227 Pinecrest Dr
White Lake, MI 48386-3655, USA

Goegan, Pete (Athlete, Hockey Player)
518 Acadia Crt
Thunder Bay, ON P7C 5B8, Canada

Goehr, Alexander
11 West Rd.
Cambridge, ENGLAND

Goehr, P Alexander (Composer)
Music Faculty 11 West Road
Cambridge, UNITED KINGDOM (UK)

Goel, Jyotin (Actor, Bollywood)
258 Famous Cine Building MAHALAXMI
Bombay, MS 400 011, INDIA

Goellner, Marc-Kevin (Athlete, Tennis Player)
Tennishall Jahnstrasse
Neuss 41464, GERMANY

Goelz, Dave (Gonzo) (Artist, Misc)
117 E 69th St
New York, NY 10021-5004, USA

Goen, Bob (Entertainer)
21767 Plainwood Dr
Woodland Hills, CA 91364, USA

Goerke, Glenn A (Educator)
Presidents Ofc
Houston, TX 77204-0001, USA

Goestenkors, Gail (Basketball Player, Coach)
Athletic
Durham, NC 27708-0001, USA

Goestschi, Renate (Skier)
Schwarzenbach 3
Obdach 8742, AUSTRIA

Goettmann, Georgia
344 E 59th St
New York, NY 10022-1593

Goetz, Bernhard
55 W 14th St
New York, NY 10011-7407

Goetz, Dick (Athlete, Golfer)
4301 Fillbrook Ln
Tyler, TX 75707-5465, USA

Goetz, Eric (Misc, Yachtsman)
15 Broadcommon Rd
Bristol, RI 02809-2721, USA

Goetz, John (Athlete, Baseball Player)
3253 Myddleton Dr
Troy, MI 48084-1274, USA

Goetz, Peter Michael (Actor)
c/o Staff Member *Silver Massetti & Szatmary (SMS) Talent Inc*
8730 W Sunset Blvd Ste 440
Los Angeles, CA 90069-2277, USA

Goetz, Russ (Baseball Player)
937 Fawcett Ave
McKeesport, PA 15132-1409, USA

Goetz, Russ (Athlete, Baseball Player)
937 Fawcett Ave
McKeesport, PA 15132-1409, USA

Goetze-Ackerman, Vicki (Athlete, Golfer)
3621 Sally Parrish Trl
Valrico, FL 33596-8433, USA

Goetzman, Gary (Producer)
c/o Staff Member *Creative Artists Agency (CAA-LA)*
2000 Avenue of the Stars Ste 100
Los Angeles, CA 90067-4705, USA

Goff, Jerry (Athlete, Baseball Player)
3 Oak Valley Dr
Novato, CA 94947-1964, USA

Goff, Mike (Athlete, Football Player)
2225 5th St
Peru, IL 61354-2506, USA

Goff, Willard (Athlete, Football Player)
441 E 10th Ave
Springfield, CO 81073, USA

Goffin, David (Producer)
c/o Staff Member *International Creative Management (ICM-LA)*
10250 Constellation Blvd Fl 7
Los Angeles, CA 90067-6207, USA

Goffin, Gerry (Musician, Songwriter)
9171 Hazen Dr
Beverly Hills, CA 90210-1825, USA

Goffin, Louise (Musician)
c/o Staff Member *Evolution Music Partners*
1680 Vine St Ste 500
Hollywood, CA 90028-8800, USA

Gofourth, Derrel (Athlete, Football Player)
1119 S Woodcrest Dr
Stillwater, OK 74074-1433, USA

Gogan, Kevin (Athlete, Football Player)
4643 286th Ave SE
Fall City, WA 98024-6907, USA

Goganious, Keith (Athlete, Football Player)
4173 Cheswick Ln
Virginia Beach, VA 23455-6560, USA

Gogel, Matt (Athlete, Golfer)
3509 W 68th St
Mission Hills, KS 66208-2142, USA

Goggin, Chuck (Athlete, Baseball Player)
1224 Roundhouse Ln
Alexandria, VA 22314-5908, USA

Goggins, Walton (Actor, Producer)
c/o Darris Hatch *Daris Hatch Management*
10027 Rossbury Pl
Los Angeles, CA 90064-4825, USA

Gogolak, Charlie (Athlete, Football Player)
47 Village Ave Unit 211
Dedham, MA 02026-4233, USA

Gogolak, Peter (Pete) (Athlete, Football Player)
24 Arrowhead Way
Darien, CT 06820-5505, USA

Gogolewski, Bill (Athlete, Baseball Player)
1522 Graham Ave
Oshkosh, WI 54902-2623, USA

Go-Go's, The (Musician)
c/o Bradford Cobb *Direct Management Group*
947 N La Cienega Blvd Ste G
Los Angeles, CA 90069-4700, USA

Goh, Kun (Prime Minister)
77 Sejonh-no Chongnoku
Seoul, SOUTH KOREA

Goh, Michelle (Actor)
c/o Leonard Bonnell *Characters Talent Agency, The (Toronto)*
8 Elm St 2nd Floor
Toronto, ON M5G 1G7, Canada

Goh, Rex (Music Group, Musician)
9200 W Sunset Blvd Ste 900
Los Angeles, CA 90069-3604, USA

Goh Chok Tong (Prime Minister)
Istana Annexe
Singapore 923, SINGAPORE

Goheen, Robert F (Diplomat, Educator)
PO Box 255
Spring Lake, NJ 07762-0255, USA

Gohmert, Louie (Congressman, Politician)
2440 Rayburn Hob
Washington, DC 20515-2508, USA

Gohr, Greg (Athlete, Baseball Player)
77 Scotland Rd
Reading, MA 01867-3323, USA

Goich, Dan (Athlete, Football Player)
PO Box 19068
Las Vegas, NV 89132-0068, USA

Going, Joanna (Actor)
c/o Nevin Dolcefino *Innovative Artists (LA)*
1505 10th St
Santa Monica, CA 90401-2805, USA

Goings, E V (Business Person)
PO Box 2353
Orlando, FL 32802-2353, USA

Goings, Nick (Athlete)
c/o Staff Member *Carolina Panthers*
S Mint St Ericsson Stadium 800
Charlotte, NC 28202-1640, USA

Goings, Nick (Athlete, Football Player)
9603 Sunset Grove Dr
Huntersville, NC 28078-0640, USA

Goitschel-Beranger, Marielle (Skier)
Val Thorens
Saint-Martin de Belleville 73440, FRANCE

Gokey, Danny (Musician)
c/o Staff Member *19 Entertainment - LA*
8560 W Sunset Blvd Ste 9
West Hollywood, CA 90069-2339, USA

Gola, Thomas J (Tom) (Athlete, Basketball Player)
15 Kings Oak Ln
Philadelphia, PA 19115-4008, USA

Gold, Ari (Musician)
c/o Staff Member *Grapevine Public Relations*
5237 Cahuenga Blvd # 2
N Hollywood, CA 91601-3419, USA

Gold, Brandy (Actor)
3500 W Olive Ave Ste 1400
Burbank, CA 91505-5512, USA

Gold, Elon (Actor, Comedian)
c/o Ruthanne Secunda *United Talent Agency (UTA)*
9560 Wilshire Blvd Fl 5
Beverly Hills, CA 90212-2400, USA

Gold, Herbert (Writer)
1051 Broadway # A
San Francisco, CA 94133-4205, USA

Gold, Ian (Athlete, Football Player)
10275 Tradition Pl
Lone Tree, CO 80124-8505, USA

Gold, Jack (Director)
24 Wood Vale
London N1O 3DP, UNITED KINGDOM (UK)

Gold, Jaime (Misc)
11601 Wilshire Blvd Ste 22
Los Angeles, CA 90025-0509, USA

Gold, Jamie (Poker Player)
c/o Staff Member *Buzznation*
233 Wilshire Blvd Ste 400
Santa Monica, CA 90401-1214, USA

Gold, Jimmy
11990 San Vicente Blvd Ste 340
Los Angeles, CA 90049-6608

Gold, Judy (Comedian)
c/o Rick Dorfman *Rick Dorfman Management*
450 W 15th St # 500
New York, NY 10011-7097, USA

Gold, Missy
3500 W Olive Ave Ste 1400
Burbank, CA 91505-5512

Gold, Murray (Musician)
c/o Catherine Manners 18 Broadwick St 4th Fl
London W1F 8HS, UNITED KINGDOM

Gold, Seth (DJ)
c/o Len Evans *Project Publicity*
312 W 53rd St Ste 202
New York, NY 10019-5743, USA

Gold, Todd
c/o Daniel A (Dan) Strone *Trident Media Group LLC*
41 Madison Ave Fl 36
New York, NY 10010-2257, USA

Gold, Tracey (Actor)
c/o Harry Gold *TalentWorks (LA)*
3500 W Olive Ave Ste 1400
Burbank, CA 91505-5512, USA

Goldberg, Adam (Actor)
c/o Nancy Iannios *Nancy Iannios PR*
PO Box 430
Signal Mountain, TN 37377-0430, USA

Goldberg, Bernard (Writer)
c/o Staff Member *HarperCollins Publishers*
10 E 53rd St C/O Author Mail Floor 7
New York, NY 10022, USA

Goldberg, Bill (Athlete, Football Player, Wrestler)
7082 Eagle Mountain Rd
Bonsall, CA 92003-7001, USA

Goldberg, Edward D (Geophysicist, Misc, Physicist)
750 Val Sereno Dr
Encinitas, CA 92024-6919, USA

Goldberg, Eric (Animator)
c/o Ellen Goldsmith-Vein *The Gotham Group Inc*
9255 W Sunset Blvd Ste 515
Los Angeles, CA 90069-3308, USA

Goldberg, Gary David (Actor, Director, Producer, Writer)
c/o Staff Member *UBU Productions*
4024 Radford Ave Bungalow 14
Studio City, CA 91604-2101, USA

Goldberg, Leonard (Producer)
1198 Commerce Dr
Richardson, TX 75081-2307, USA

Goldberg, Lucianne
4 Oak St
Weehawken, NJ 07086-5608

Goldberg, Luella G (Educator)
7019 Tupa Dr
Minneapolis, MN 55439-1643, USA

Goldberg, Marshall (Biggie) (Artist)
222 Bowery
New York, NY 10012-4203, USA

Goldberg, Richard W (Judge)
1 Federal Plz
New York, NY 10278-0001, USA

Goldberg, Stan (Cartoonist)
8 White Birch Ln
Scarsdale, NY 10583-7635, USA

Goldberg, Whoopi (Actor, Comedian, Talk Show Host)
c/o Brad Cafarelli *PMK/BNC - LA*
8687 Melrose Ave Ste 8
West Hollywood, CA 90069-5746, USA

Goldberger, Andi
Bleckenwegen 4
Waldzell, AUSTRIA 4924

Goldberger, Andreas (Skier)
Bleckenwegen 4
Waldzell 4924, AUSTRIA

Goldberger, Marvin L (Educator, Physicist)
7867 La Jolla Vista Dr
La Jolla, CA 92037-3531, USA

Goldblum, Jeff (Actor)
c/o Keith Addis *Industry Entertainment Partners*
955 Carrillo Dr Ste 300
Los Angeles, CA 90048-5400, USA

Golden, Arthur (Writer)
c/o Lynn Pleshette *Lynn Pleshette Literary Agency*
2700 N Beachwood Dr
Los Angeles, CA 90068-1922, USA

Golden, Clyde (Athlete, Baseball Player)
501 N Ocean St Apt 211
Jacksonville, FL 32202-3141, USA

Golden, Harry (Bowler, Misc)
719 2nd Ave Ste 701
Seattle, WA 98104-1747, USA

Golden, Jim (Athlete, Baseball Player)
8630 SW 10th Ave
Topeka, KS 66615-9688, USA

Golden, Kate (Athlete, Golfer)
969 Hunterwood Dr
Jasper, TX 75951-2821, USA

Golden, Kit (Producer)
c/o Staff Member *Manhattan Project*
1775 Broadway Ste 410
New York, NY 10019-1903, USA

Golden, Tim (Athlete, Football Player)
PO Box 278052
Miramar, FL 33027-8052, USA

Golden, William Lee (Music Group, Songwriter, Writer)
PO Box 1795
Hendersonville, TN 37077-1795, USA

Goldens, The
PO Box 1795
Hendersonville, TN 37077-1795

Goldenthal, Elliot (Composer, Musician)
c/o Staff Member *Chasen & Company*
8899 Beverly Blvd Ste 405
Los Angeles, CA 90048-2431, USA

Goldfaden, Ben (Athlete, Basketball Player)
5819 Bounty Cir
Tavares, FL 32778-9293, USA

Goldfinger, Sarah (Actor)
c/o Staff Member *Creative Artists Agency (CAA-LA)*
2000 Avenue of the Stars Ste 100
Los Angeles, CA 90067-4705, USA

Goldfrapp, Alison (Musician)
c/o Staff Member *Mute Records*
43 Brook Green
London W6 7EF, UK

Goldhaber, Maurice (Physicist)
14 Brewster Hill Rd
East Setauket, NY 11733-1426, USA

Goldin, Claudia D (Economist)
Economics Dept
Cambridge, MA 2138, USA

Goldin, Judah (Educator)
3300 Darby Rd
Haverford, PA 19041-1076, USA

Goldin, Nan (Photographer)
334 Bowery
New York, NY 10012-2430, USA

Goldin, Ricky Paull (Actor)
c/o Staff Member *Stone Manners Salners Agency (LA)*
9911 W Pico Blvd Ste 1400
Los Angeles, CA 90035-2715, USA

Golding, Meta (Actor)
c/o Charlton Blackburne *A Management Company*
9107 Wilshire Blvd Ste 650
Beverly Hills, CA 90210-5544, USA

Goldman, Bo (Producer, Writer)
c/o David O'Connor *Creative Artists Agency (CAA-LA)*
2000 Avenue of the Stars Ste 100
Los Angeles, CA 90067-4705, USA

Goldman, Duff (Chef)
2936 Remington Ave
Baltimore, MD 21211-2830, USA

Goldman, Julie (Actor, Comedian)
427 Union St # 3
Brooklyn, NY 11231-5021, USA

Goldman, Les (Athlete, Football Player)
800 E Cypress Creek Rd Ste 203
Fort Lauderdale, FL 33334-3522, USA

Goldman, Matt (Musician)
3900 Las Vegas Blvd S
Las Vegas, NV 89119-1004, USA

Goldman, William (Writer)
445 Park Ave # 1300
New York, NY 10022-2606, USA

Goldoni, Lelia
15459 Wyandotte St
Van Nuys, CA 91406-3334

Goldreich, Peter M (Astronomer)
471 S Catalina Ave
Pasadena, CA 91106-3304, USA

Goldrup, Ray
2383 Broderick
West Jordan, UT 84084

Goldsboro, Bobby (Music Group, Songwriter, Writer)
PO Box 4979
Ocala, FL 34478-4979, USA

Goldsman, Akiva (Director)
c/o Simon Halls *Slate Public Relations*
9000 W Sunset Blvd Ste 915
West Hollywood, CA 90069-5809, USA

Goldsmith, Bethany (Baseball Player)
1000 E Michigan St Apt A
Orlando, FL 32806-4736, USA

Goldsmith, Judy (Activist)
425 13th St NE
Washington, DC 20002-6327, USA

Goldsmith, Kelly (Actor)
c/o Dede Binder-Goldsmith *Defining Artists Agency*
10 Universal City Plz Ste 2000
Universal City, CA 91608-1074, USA

Goldsmith, Paul
1148 Vivian Ln
Munster, IN 46321-2537

Goldsmith, Stephen (Politician)
State House
Indianapolis, IN 46204-2728, USA

Goldspink, Calvin (Actor)
c/o Staff Member *Reel Talent Management*
PO Box 491035
Los Angeles, CA 90049-9035, USA

Goldstein, Allan L (Biologist, Misc, Scientist)
800 25th St NW # 1005
Washington, DC 20037-2208, USA

Goldstein, Avram (Misc)
6466 Bluebird Ave
Longmont, CO 80503-8717, USA

Goldstein, Jenette
3932 Marathon St
Los Angeles, CA 90029-3602

Goldstein, Joseph L (Nobel Prize Laureate)
3831 Turtle Creek Blvd Apt 22B
Dallas, TX 75219-4538, USA

Goldstein, Lonnie (Athlete, Baseball Player)
6799 Granbury Rd Apt 108
Fort Worth, TX 76133-4936, USA

Goldstein, Lori (Stylist)
c/o Staff Member *Art + Commerce*
531 W 25th St # 4
New York, NY 10001-5593, USA

Goldstein, Murray (Misc, Physicist)
1660 L St NW Ste 700
Washington, DC 20036-5638, USA

Goldstine, Herman H (Mathematician, Scientist)
56 Pasture Ln
Bryn Mawr, PA 19010-1764, USA

Goldstone, Jeffrey (Physicist)
77 Massachusetts Ave # 6-313
Cambridge, MA 02139-4301, USA

Goldstone, Ralph (Athlete, Football Player)
4883 Westchester Dr Apt 119
Youngstown, OH 44515-6518, USA

Goldstone, Richard J (Judge)
Constitutional Court Private Bag X32
Braamfontein 2017, SOUTH AFRICA

Goldsworthy, Andrew C (Andy) (Artist, Photographer)
21 Cork St
London W1X 1HB, UNITED KINGDOM (UK)

Goldthwait, Bob (Bobcat) (Actor, Comedian)
c/o Rick Greenstein *Gersh (LA)*
9465 Wilshire Blvd Ste 600
Beverly Hills, CA 90212-2612, USA

Goldup, Glenn (Athlete, Hockey Player)
31 Elizabeth St
Etobicoke, ON M8V 2R9, Canada

Goldup, Hank (Athlete, Hockey Player)
1504-4340 Bloor St W
Etobicoke, ON M9C 2A6, Canada

Goldwasser, Eugene (Biologist, Misc)
5490 S Shore Dr Apt 9N
Chicago, IL 60615-5974, USA

Goldwater Jr, Barry
4401 Connecticut Ave NW PMB 850
Washington, DC 20008-2322, USA

Goldwyn, Tony (Actor, Director)
c/o Peter Levine *Creative Artists Agency (CAA-LA)*
2000 Avenue of the Stars Ste 100
Los Angeles, CA 90067-4705, USA

Goldwyn Jr, Samuel (Producer)
c/o Staff Member *Samuel Goldwyn Company*
9570 W Pico Blvd Ste 400
Los Angeles, CA 90035-1216, USA

Goldy, Purnal (Athlete, Baseball Player)
5231 E Long Ln
Centennial, CO 80122-4013, USA

Golembiewski, Billy (Bowler)
4966 N Wise Rd
Coleman, MI 48618-9658, USA

Golenbock, Peter (Baseball Player, Writer)
849 Jennings Ave N
Saint Petersburg, FL 33704-1142, USA

Golic, Bob (Athlete, Football Player, Sportscaster)
6130 Loch Lomond Ct
Solon, OH 44139-5945, USA

Golic, Mike (Athlete, Football Player)
12110 E Gold Dust Ave
Scottsdale, AZ 85259-5117, USA

Golimowski, David A (Astronomer)
515 Holden Rd
Towson, MD 21286-5637, USA

Golina, Stacy
325 S Swall Dr Apt 502
Los Angeles, CA 90048-3078

Golino, Valeria (Actor, Producer)
c/o Michael (Mike) Jelline *United Talent Agency (UTA)*
10250 Constellation Blvd Fl 7
Los Angeles, CA 90067-6207, USA

Golisano, B Thomas (Business Person)
911 Panorama Trl S
Rochester, NY 14625-2311, USA

Golisano, Tom (Business Person)
911 Panorama Trl S
Rochester, NY 14625-2311, USA

Gollat, Mike (Baseball Player)
2650 Greenlawn Dr
Seven Hills, OH 44131-3623, USA

Golodryga, Bianna (Actor, Anchor)
c/o Staff Member *Good Morning America (NY)*
147 Columbus Ave Fl 6
New York, NY 10023-6503, USA

Golonka, Arlene (Actor)
8730 W Sunset Blvd Ste 480
Los Angeles, CA 90069-2277, USA

Golovin, Tatiana (Athlete, Tennis Player)
c/o Staff Member *Women's Tennis Association (WTA (UK))*
Palliser House Palliser Rd
London W149EB, UK

Golson, Benny (Composer, Music Group, Musician)
223 1/2 E 48th St
New York, NY 10017, USA

Golsteyn, Jerry (Athlete, Football Player)
243 Tadcaster Ct
Raeford, NC 28376-6623, USA

Goltz, Dave (Athlete, Baseball Player)
1009 Stony Brook Mnr
Fergus Falls, MN 56537-4413, USA

Gomes, Jonny (Athlete, Baseball Player)
PO Box 31
Olema, CA 94950-0031, USA

Gomes, Wayne (Athlete, Baseball Player)
5104 W Creek Ct
Suffolk, VA 23435-3523, USA

Gomez (Music Group)
c/o Jason Colton *Red Light Management (VA)*
PO Box 1467
Charlottesville, VA 22902-1467, USA

Gomez, Andres (Tennis Player)
1101 Woodrow Wilson Blvd # 1800
Arlington, VA 22209, USA

Gomez, Carlos (Actor)
c/o Billy Miller *Billy Miller Management*
8322 Ridpath Dr
Los Angeles, CA 90046-7710, USA

Gomez, Chris (Athlete, Baseball Player)
8 Vernal Spg
Irvine, CA 92603-0405, USA

Gomez, Edgar (Eddie) (Music Group, Musician)
PO Box 961
Burlington, MA 01803-5961, USA

Gomez, Hector (Actor)
c/o Staff Member *Televisa*
Blvd Adolfo Lopez Mateos 232 Colonia San Angel INN
DF CP 01060, MEXICO

Gomez, Ian (Actor)
c/o Staff Member *Handprint Entertainment*
1100 Glendon Ave Ste 100
Los Angeles, CA 90024-3593, USA

Gomez, Javier (Actor)
c/o Gabriel Blanco *Gabriel Blanco Iglesias (Mexico)*
Rio Balsas 35-32 Colonia Cuauhtemoc
DF 6500, Mexico

Gomez, Jill (Opera Singer)
16 Milton Park
London N6 5QA, UNITED KINGDOM (UK)

Gomez, Leo (Athlete, Baseball Player)
11760 Frederick Rd
Ellicott City, MD 21042-1032, USA

Gomez, Luis (Athlete, Baseball Player)
676 Chesterfield Dr
Lawrenceville, GA 30044-5624, USA

Gomez, Marga (Comedian)
PO Box 460368
San Francisco, CA 94146-0368, USA

Gomez, Natalie (Actor)
c/o Staff Member *Advance LA*
7904 Santa Monica Blvd Ste 200
West Hollywood, CA 90046-5170

Gomez, Nick (Director)
c/o Staff Member *Evolution Entertainment (LA)*
901 N Highland Ave
Los Angeles, CA 90038-2412, USA

Gomez, Panchito (Actor)
240 N Hollywood Way
Burbank, CA 91505-3431, USA

Gomez, Pat (Athlete, Baseball Player)
2257 Quarry Way
Rocklin, CA 95765-4292, USA

Gomez, Ralph E (Mathematician, Misc)
President's Office 630 5th Ave
New York, NY 10111, USA

Gomez, Randy (Athlete, Baseball Player)
50 Oak St
San Martin, CA 95046-9592, USA

Gomez, Rick (Actor)
c/o Sam Maydew *Collective*
8383 Wilshire Blvd Ste 1050
Beverly Hills, CA 90211-2415, USA

Gomez, Scott (Athlete, Hockey Player)
47 Clarken Dr
West Orange, NJ 07052-3453, USA

Gomez, Selena (Actor)
c/o Brit Reece *PMK/BNC Public Relations (PMK-LA)*
8687 Melrose Ave Ste 8
West Hollywood, CA 90069-5746, USA

Gomez, Wilfredo (Athlete, Boxer)
1 Hall of Fame Dr
Canastota, NY 13032-1175, USA

Gomez-Preston, Reagan (Actor)
c/o Mara Santino *Luber Roklin Management*
8530 Wilshire Blvd Ste 550
Beverly Hills, CA 90211-3133, USA

Gomez-Preston, Reagen (Actor)
c/o Staff Member *Jeff Morrone Entertainment*
9350 Wilshire Blvd Ste 224
Beverly Hills, CA 90212-3204, USA

Gompers, Bill (Athlete, Football Player)
1060 Montego Bay Dr N
Merritt Island, FL 32953-3152, USA

Gompf, Thomas (Tom) (Politician, Swimmer)
2716 Barret Ave
Plant City, FL 33566-9550, USA

Goncalves, Vascos dos Santos (General, Prime Minister)
Ave Estados Unidos da America 86 5 Esq
Lisbon 1700, PORTUGAL

Gonchar, Sergei (Athlete, Hockey Player)
7 Kevin Dr
Sewickley, PA 15143-8523, USA

Gondrezick, Glen (Athlete, Basketball Player)
2008 Sedona Creek Cir
Las Vegas, NV 89128-8213, USA

Gondrezick, Grant (Athlete, Basketball Player)
5906 Etiwanda Ave Unit 19
Tarzana, CA 91356-1649, USA

Gondry, Michel (Director, Writer)
c/o Dan Aloni *Creative Artists Agency (CAA-LA)*
2000 Avenue of the Stars Ste 100
Los Angeles, CA 90067-4705, USA

Gong, Julie (Stylist)
Prefers to be contacted via telephone or email
New York, NY 10012, USA

Gonick, Larry (Cartoonist)
247 Missouri St
San Francisco, CA 94107-2404, USA

Gonnenwein, Wolfgang
Maximilianstr 22
Munich 80539, GERMANY

Gonshaw, Francesca (Actor)
12 D'Arblay St #200
London W1V 3FP, UNITED KINGDOM (UK)

Gonsoulin, Austin (Goose) (Athlete, Football Player)
8062 Indian Blanket
Beaumont, TX 77713-8575, USA

Gonzales, Alberto (Government Official, Judge)
1600 Pennsylvania Ave NW
Washington, DC 20500-0005, USA

Gonzales, Carlos (Cinematographer)
3850 Tracy St
Los Angeles, CA 90027-4610, USA

Gonzales, Dan (Athlete, Baseball Player)
429 W Silvertip Rd
Tucson, AZ 85737-3704, USA

Gonzales, Jaslene (Model)
c/o Lizzie Grubman *Lizzie Grubman Public Relations*
270 Lafayette St Ste 504
New York, NY 10012-0048, USA

Gonzales, Larry (Athlete, Baseball Player)
3800 Bradford St Spc 248
La Verne, CA 91750-3151, USA

Gonzales, Raul (Soccer Player)
Alcala 694 1
Madrid 28019, SPAIN

Gonzales, Rene (Athlete, Baseball Player)
755 E Orangewood Dr
Covina, CA 91723-3620, USA

Gonzalez, Alexander S (Alex) (Athlete, Baseball Player)
7743 SW 119th Ct
Miami, FL 33183-3854, USA

Gonzalez, Ana (Stylist)
2122-A Clinton Ave
Alameda, CA 94501, USA

Gonzalez, Araceli (Actor)
c/o Staff Member *Telefe - Argentina*
Pavon 2444 (C1248AAT)
Buenos Aires, ARGENTINA

Gonzalez, Arthur (Judge)
1 Bowling Grn
New York, NY 10004-1415, USA

Gonzalez, Charles (Congressman, Politician)
1434 Longworth Hob
Washington, DC 20515-0004, USA

Gonzalez, Edith (Actor)
c/o Staff Member *Televisa*
Blvd Adolfo Lopez Mateos 232 Colonia San Angel INN
DF CP 01060, MEXICO

Gonzalez, Fredi (Athlete, Baseball Player, Coach)
2768 Pete Shaw Rd
Marietta, GA 30066-2206, USA

Gonzalez, Gabe (Athlete, Baseball Player)
920 Cerritos Ave
Long Beach, CA 90813-4812, USA

Gonzalez, Hector (Religious Leader)
PO Box 851
Valley Forge, PA 19482-0851, USA

Gonzalez, Jeremi (Athlete, Baseball Player)
1120 N La Salle Dr Apt 14N
Chicago, IL 60610-7609, USA

Gonzalez, Juan (Athlete, Baseball Player)
c/o Staff Member *Texas Rangers*
1000 Ballpark Way Ste 400
Arlington, TX 76011-5170, USA

Gonzalez, Juan A (Baseball Player)
Ext Catoni A9
Vega Baja, PR 693, USA

Gonzalez, Leon (Athlete, Football Player)
4025 Leonnie Rd
Jacksonville, FL 32208-2947, USA

Gonzalez, Luis E (Athlete, Baseball Player)
6026 E Jenan Dr
Scottsdale, AZ 85254-4907, USA

Gonzalez, Macchi Luis (President)
Ave Marisol Lopez
Asuncion, PARAGUAY

Gonzalez, Marquez Felipe (Prime Minister)
Gobefas 31
Madrid 28023, SPAIN

Gonzalez, Mike (Athlete, Baseball Player)
2414 Pine Brook Ct
Deer Park, TX 77536-1518, USA

Gonzalez, Miriam (Actor, Model)
c/o Staff Member *Playboy Productions*
2706 Media Center Dr
Los Angeles, CA 90065-1733, USA

Gonzalez, Nicholas (Actor)
c/o Chuck James *International Creative Management (ICM-LA)*
10250 Constellation Blvd Fl 7
Los Angeles, CA 90067-6207, USA

Gonzalez, Orlando (Athlete, Baseball Player)
12460 NW 11th Ln
Miami, FL 33182-2463, USA

Gonzalez, Pedro (Athlete, Baseball Player)
10 Gen Cabral
San Pedro de Macoris, Dominican Republic

Gonzalez, Phoenix (Actor)
c/o Staff Member *Select Artists Ltd (CA-Westside Office)*
1138 12th St Apt 1
Santa Monica, CA 90403-5459, USA

Gonzalez, Raul (Soccer Player)
Avda Concha Espina 1
Madrid 28036, SPAIN

Gonzalez, Rick (Actor)
c/o Stephanie Nese *Framework Entertainment (LA)*
9057 Nemo St Ste C
West Hollywood, CA 90069-5511, USA

Gonzalez, Susana (Actor)
c/o Staff Member *Televisa*
Blvd Adolfo Lopez Mateos 232 Colonia San Angel INN
DF CP 01060, MEXICO

Gonzalez, Tony (Athlete, Football Player)
c/o Denise White *EAG Sports Management*
12910 Agustin Pl
Playa Vista, CA 90094-2301, USA

Gonzalez, Tony (Athlete, Baseball Player)
8011 SW 196th Ter
Cutler Bay, FL 33189-2103, USA

Gonzalez, Victor (Actor)
c/o Gabriel Blanco *Gabriel Blanco Iglesias (Mexico)*
Rio Balsas 35-32 Colonia Cuauhtemoc
DF 6500, Mexico

Gonzalez Zumarraga, Antonio J Cardinal (Religious Leader)
Apartado 17-01-00106 Called Chile
Quito 1140, ECUADOR

Gonzalo, Julie (Actor)
c/o Sharon Lane *Lane Management Group*
13017 Woodbridge St
Studio City, CA 91604-1431, USA

Goo Goo Dolls (Music Group)
c/o David Levine *WmE2 (Endeavor-LA)*
9601 Wilshire Blvd Fl 3
Beverly Hills, CA 90210-5219, USA

Gooch, Jeff (Athlete, Football Player)
8514 Fawn Creek Dr
Tampa, FL 33626-2323, USA

Good, Andrew (Athlete, Baseball Player)
1433 S Belcher Rd Apt G4
Clearwater, FL 33764-2863, USA

Good, David (Reality TV Star, Writer)
c/o Inna Shamis *AvantGarde Communications Group*
Prefers to be contacted via telephone or email
USA

Good, Hugh W (Religious Leader)
6403 Frame Rd
Elkview, WV 25071-7040, USA

Good, Meagan (Actor)
c/o Evan Hainey *Untitled Entertainment (LA)*
350 S Beverly Dr Ste 200
Beverly Hills, CA 90212-4819, USA

Good, Melanie (Actor)
c/o Staff Member *Bobby Ball Talent Agency*
4116 W Magnolia Blvd Ste 205
Burbank, CA 91505-2700, USA

Good, Michael T (Astronaut)
3874 Cherry Plum Dr
Colorado Springs, CO 80920-2802, USA

Good Charlotte (Music Group)
81 Pondfield Rd # 358
Bronxville, NY 10708-3818, USA

Goodacre, Connick Jill (Model)
323 Broadway
Cambridge, MA 02139-1801, USA

Goodacre, Glenna (Artist, Misc)
1083 5th Ave
New York, NY 10128-0114, USA

Goodall, Caroline (Actor)
34-43 Russell St
London WC2B 5HA, UNITED KINGDOM (UK)

Goodburn, Kelly (Athlete, Football Player)
3710 W 52nd Pl
Roeland Park, KS 66205-2766, USA

Goode, Chris (Athlete, Football Player)
1428 Egret Ln
Birmingham, AL 35214-3410, USA

Goode, David R (Business Person)
3 Commercial Pl
Norfolk, VA 23510-2108, USA

Goode, Irvin (Irv) (Athlete, Football Player)
1030 Schnucks Woodsmill Plz
Chesterfield, MO 63017-0606, USA

Goode, Kerry (Athlete, Football Player)
639 Herron Ct
Fairburn, GA 30213-2398, USA

Goode, Matthew (Actor)
c/o Craig Bankey *WKT Public Relations (WKT-LA)*
9350 Wilshire Blvd Ste 450
Beverly Hills, CA 90212-3230, USA

Goode, Rob (Athlete, Football Player)
2124 Portwood Way
Fort Worth, TX 76179-6633, USA

Goode, Tom (Athlete, Football Player)
9190 Tom Goode Rd
West Point, MS 39773-4487, USA

Goodell, Brian S (Swimmer)
27040 S Ridge Dr
Mission Viejo, CA 92692-5015, USA

Gooden, Drew (Basketball Player)
Waterhouse Center 8701 Maitland Summit Blvd
Orlando, FL 32810, USA

Gooden, Dwight (Athlete, Baseball Player)
3425 E Henry Ave
Tampa, FL 33610-3628, USA

Goodenough, Larry (Athlete, Hockey Player)
3677 Spruce Hill Rd
Ottsville, PA 18942-9508, USA

Goodenough, Ward H (Misc)
3300 Darby Rd Apt 5306
Haverford, PA 19041-7707, USA

Goodeve, Charles P (Misc)
38 Middleway
London NW11, UNITED KINGDOM (UK)

Goodeve, Grant (Actor)
21416 NE 68th Ct
Redmond, WA 98053-2393, USA

Goodfellow, Peter N (Misc, Scientist)
Lincoln Inn Fields
London WC2A 3PX, UNITED KINGDOM (UK)

Goodfriend, Lynda (Actor)
c/o Lynda Goodfriend *Lynda Goodfriend Management*
338 S Beachwood Dr
Burbank, CA 91506-2713, USA

Goodfriend, Lynda (Actor)
338 S Beachwood Dr
Burbank, CA 91506-2713, USA

Gooding, Cuba Jr (Actor)
c/o Michael Rotenberg *3 Arts Entertainment Inc*
9460 Wilshire Blvd Fl 7
Beverly Hills, CA 90212-2713, USA

Gooding, Omar (Actor)
c/o Ericalane Brown *The Kartel Company*
1304 W 2nd St Apt 310
Los Angeles, CA 90026-7011, USA

Goodlatte, Bob (Congressman, Politician)
2240 Rayburn Hob
Washington, DC 20515-4606, USA

Goodlin, Chalmers (Misc)
7620 Red River Rd
West Palm Beach, FL 33411-5812, USA

Goodman, Alfred (Composer)
Bodenstedtstr 31
Munich 81241, GERMANY

Goodman, Allegra (Writer)
375 Hudson St
New York, NY 10014-3658, USA

Goodman, Andre (Athlete, Football Player)
125 Island View Cir
Elgin, SC 29045-9182, USA

Goodman, Brian (Actor)
c/o Paul Santana *Agency for the Performing Arts (APA-LA)*
405 S Beverly Dr Ste 500
Beverly Hills, CA 90212-4425, USA

Goodman, Brian (Athlete, Football Player)
15009 S 14th Pl
Phoenix, AZ 85048-6242, USA

Goodman, Corey S (Biologist, Misc)
Howard Hughes Medical Institute
Molecular/Cell Biology
Berkeley, CA 94720-0001, USA

Goodman, David A. (Writer)
c/o Jon Huddle *United Talent Agency (UTA)*
9560 Wilshire Blvd Fl 5
Beverly Hills, CA 90212-2400, USA

Goodman, Ellen H (Editor, Misc)
Editorial Dept 135 W T Morrissey Blvd
Dorchester, MA 2125, USA

Goodman, Hank (Athlete, Football Player)
2015 Broad St Apt 108
Cranston, RI 02905-3346, USA

Goodman, Harvey (Athlete, Football Player)
2689 County Road 318
Westcliffe, CO 81252-8704, USA

Goodman, Henry
2015 Broad St Apt 108
Cranston, RI 02905-3346, USA

Goodman, Jo (Stylist)
1103 E California Ave
Glendale, CA 91206-3824, USA

Goodman, John (Actor, Musician, Producer)
c/o Bob Gersh *Gersh (LA)*
9465 Wilshire Blvd Ste 600
Beverly Hills, CA 90212-2612, USA

Goodman, John (Athlete, Football Player)
800 E 9th St
Edmond, OK 73034-5407, USA

Goodman, Joseph W (Engineer)
570 University Ter
Los Altos, CA 94022-3587, USA

Goodman, Oscar (Attorney, Attorney General, General)
520 S 4th St
Las Vegas, NV 89101-6520, USA

Goodman, Richard (Producer)
c/o Staff Member *WmE2 (Endeavor-LA)*
9601 Wilshire Blvd Fl 3
Beverly Hills, CA 90210-5219, USA

Goodmann, Terrence (Stylist)
723 E Fairmount Rd
Burbank, CA 91501-1711, USA

Goodnight, James (Jim) (Business Person)
100 Sas Campus Dr
Cary, NC 27513-2414, USA

Goodnoff, Irvin (Cinematographer)
29997 Mulholland Hwy
Agoura Hills, CA 91301-3009, USA

Goodreault, Gene J (Athlete, Football Player)
7 Via Corte
Orinda, CA 94563-2238, USA

Goodrem, Delta (Actor, Musician)
c/o Staff Member *The Harbour Agency*
135 Forbes St
Woolloomooloo NSW 2011, Australia

Goodrich, Dwayne (Athlete, Football Player)
533 Oakcrest Dr
Coppell, TX 75019-4082, USA

Goodrich, Gail (Actor, Athlete, Basketball Player, Sportscaster)
PO Box 4969
Greenwich, CT 06831-0419, USA

Goodrich, Jon (Baseball Player)
123 W Agua Caliente Rd
Sonoma, CA 95476-3340, USA

Goodrich Jr, Gail C (Athlete, Basketball Player)
270 Oceano Dr
Los Angeles, CA 90049-4124, USA

Goodrum, Charles (Athlete, Football Player)
117 Pico Rd
East Palatka, FL 32131, USA

Goodson, Ed (Athlete, Baseball Player)
2330 Cold Springs Ln
Galax, VA 24333-3763, USA

Goodson, James A (War Hero)
37 Carolina Trl
Marshfield, MA 02050-6373, USA

Goodwill, Oliver (Actor)
C/O Marcello Robinson 7920 Sunset Blvd 2nd Fl
Los Angeles, CA 90046, USA

Goodwin, Curtis (Athlete, Baseball Player)
14939 Western Ave
San Leandro, CA 94578-3627, USA

Goodwin, Danny (Athlete, Baseball Player)
1555 Linksview Close
Stone Mountain, GA 30088-3768, USA

Goodwin, Doris Kearns (Historian)
1649 Monument Ln
Concord, MA 1742, USA

Goodwin, Doug (Athlete, Football Player)
245 Grand Ave
Freeport, NY 11520-2403, USA

Goodwin, Ginnifer (Actor)
c/o John Carrabino *John Carrabino Management*
5900 Wilshire Blvd Ste 406
Los Angeles, CA 90036-5015, USA

Goodwin, Hunter (Athlete, Football Player)
PO Box 725
Bellville, TX 77418-0725, USA

Goodwin, Jim (Athlete, Baseball Player)
2613 N Broadway
Saint Louis, MO 63102-1507, USA

Goodwin, Louise (Stylist)
c/o Staff Member *Mel Bryant Management*
611 Broadway Rm 623
New York, NY 10012-2650

Goodwin, Michael (Actor)
8271 Melrose Ave Ste 110
Los Angeles, CA 90046-6800, USA

Goodwin, Ron
Black Nest Cottage Hackford Lane
Brimpton Common, ENGLAND RG7 4RP

Goodwin, Ron (Athlete, Football Player)
3702 Sul Ross St
San Angelo, TX 76904-6229, USA

Goodwin, Tom (Athlete, Baseball Player)
1301 Ardglass Trl
Corinth, TX 76210-3088, USA

Goodwin, Trudie (Actor)
1 Deer Park Rd Merton
London SW19 3TL, ENGLAND

Goody, Joan E (Architect)
334 Boylston St
Boston, MA 02116-3899, USA

Goodyear, Scott (Race Car Driver)
PO Box 589
Carmel, IN 46082-0589, USA

Goolagong Cawley, Evonne F (Tennis Player)
Private Bag 6060
Richmond, SV 3121, AUSTRALIA

Goolagong-Cawley, Evonne (Athlete, Tennis Player)
c/o Staff Member *Ovations*
P.O. Box 1337
Rozelle, NSW 2039, Australia

Goorjian, Michael (Actor)
901 N Highland Ave
Los Angeles, CA 90038-2412, USA

Goosen, Don (Boxer, Misc)
6320 Van Nuys Blvd
Van Nuys, CA 91401-2617, USA

Goosen, Retief (Athlete, Golfer)
14 N Park Sunninghill
Ascot SL59B, United Kingdom

Gopi (Actor)
M3/F Anugraha Colony 3rd Avenue
Ashok Nagar
c, TN 600 083, INDIA

Gopi Krishna, B M (Actor)
14 Soundara Rajan Street T Nagar
Chennai, TN 600 017, INDIA

Goranson, Alicia (Actor)
c/o Staff Member *Paradigm (LA)*
360 N Crescent Dr
Beverly Hills, CA 90210-4874, USA

Gorbachev, Mikhail S (General, Nobel Prize Laureate, Politician, Secretary)
Leningradsky Prospekt 49
Moscow 125468, RUSSIA

Gorbachev, Yuri (Artist)
377 Geary St
San Francisco, CA 94102-1801, USA

Gorbatko, Viktor V (Astronaut, General, Misc)
Moskovskoi Oblasti
Svyisdny Goroduk 141160, RUSSIA

Gorchakova, Galina (Opera Singer)
27 Chancery Lane
London WC2A 1PF, UNITED KINGDOM (UK)

Gordeeva, Ekaterina (Athlete, Figure Skater)
c/o Staff Member *IMG (LA)*
717 N Alta Vista Blvd
Los Angeles, CA 90046-7601, USA

Gordeyev, Vyacheslav M (Ballerina, Choreographer, Dancer)
Tverskaya Str 9 #78
Moscow 103009, RUSSIA

Gordimer, Nadine (Nobel Prize Laureate)
7 Frere Road Parktown
Johannesburg 2193, SOUTH AFRICA

Gordin, Charles (Actor)
187 Chestnut Hill Rd
Wilton, CT 06897-4108, USA

Gordon, Barry (Actor, Music Group)
1912 Kaweah Dr
Pasadena, CA 91105-3604, USA

Gordon, Ben (Athlete, Basketball Player)
c/o Raymond Brothers *International Athlete Management, Inc*
433 N Camden Dr Ste 600
Beverly Hills, CA 90210-4416, USA

Gordon, Bert I (Director)
9640 Arby Dr
Beverly Hills, CA 90210-1202, USA

Gordon, Bridgette (Athlete, Basketball Player)
421 E Chelsea St
Deland, FL 32724-6900, USA

Gordon, Bruce (Actor)
231 Tano Rd # C
Santa Fe, NM 87506-7030, USA

Gordon, Carl
8661 Pine Tree Pl
Los Angeles, CA 90069-1201

Gordon, Carolyn (Stylist)
c/o Staff Member *L'Agence*
5901 Peachtree Dunwoody Rd NE Ste C60
Atlanta, GA 30328-7155, USA

Gordon, Cornell (Athlete, Football Player)
4029 Spring Meadow Cres
Chesapeake, VA 23321-3117, USA

Gordon, Danso (Actor)
c/o Paul Nicholls *Artistry Management*
340 N Camden Dr Ste 302
Beverly Hills, CA 90210-5116, USA

Gordon, Darrien (Athlete, Football Player)
1500 Pecos Dr
Southlake, TX 76092-5933, USA

Gordon, David (Choreographer)
47 Great Jones St Fl 2
New York, NY 10012-1196, USA

Gordon, Dick (Athlete, Football Player)
5017 Anderson Pl
Cincinnati, OH 45227-1601, USA

Gordon, Don
6853 Pacific View Dr
Los Angeles, CA 90068-1831

Gordon, Don (Actor)
4727 Wilshire Blvd Ste 333
Los Angeles, CA 90010-3874, USA

Gordon, Don (Athlete, Baseball Player)
711 Sunset Mountain Dr
Chattanooga, TN 37421-2076, USA

Gordon, Ed (Correspondent)
30 Rockefeller Plz
New York, NY 10112-0015, USA

Gordon, Eve
10100 Santa Monica Blvd Ste 2500
Los Angeles, CA 90067-4116

Gordon, Hannah Taylor (Actor)
4 Old Manor Close Askett
Buckinghamshire HP27 9NA, UNITED KINGDOM (UK)

Gordon, Harold P (Business Person)
1027 Newport Ave
Pawtucket, RI 02861-2539, USA

Gordon, Herold (Athlete, Baseball Player)
8798 Traverse St
Detroit, MI 48213-1158, USA

Gordon, Howard (Producer, Writer)
c/o Rick Rosen *WmE2 (Endeavor-LA)*
9601 Wilshire Blvd Fl 3
Beverly Hills, CA 90210-5219, USA

Gordon, Ira (Athlete, Football Player)
PO Box 3222
Kent, WA 98089-0204, USA

Gordon, Jack (Athlete, Hockey Player)
17-1725 Southmere Cres
Surrey, BC V4A 7A7, Canada

Gordon, Jeff (Race Car Driver)
c/o Jon Edwards *Performance PR Plus*
520 N College St
Charlotte, NC 28202, USA

Gordon, John (Athlete, Football Player)
40 Calle Fresno
San Clemente, CA 92672-9421, USA

Gordon, Keith (Actor, Director, Writer)
c/o Dan Aloni *Creative Artists Agency (CAA-LA)*
2000 Avenue of the Stars Ste 100
Los Angeles, CA 90067-4705, USA

Gordon, Keith (Athlete, Baseball Player)
4601 Thornhurst Dr
Olney, MD 20832-1826, USA

Gordon, Kiowa (Actor)
c/o Ryan Martin *Agency for the Performing Arts (APA-LA)*
405 S Beverly Dr Ste 500
Beverly Hills, CA 90212-4425, USA

Gordon, Lamar (Athlete, Football Player)
5428 N 19th St
Milwaukee, WI 53209-5013, USA

Gordon, Lancaster (Athlete, Basketball Player)
550 Robinhood Rd
Jackson, MS 39206-5403, USA

Gordon, Lawrence (Business Person)
10201 W Pico Blvd
Los Angeles, CA 90064-2606, USA

Gordon, Leo
9977 Wornom Ave
Sunland, CA 91040-1549

Gordon, Lincoln (Diplomat, Economist)
111 Llanfair Rd
Ardmore, PA 19003-3341, USA

Gordon, Mikalah (Musician)
c/o Staff Member *11-16 Entertainment*
10100 Santa Monica Blvd Ste 300
Los Angeles, CA 90067-4107, USA

Gordon, Mike (Musician)
c/o Jason Colton *Red Light Management (VA)*
PO Box 1467
Charlottesville, VA 22902-1467, USA

Gordon, Mike (Athlete, Baseball Player)
35 Longview Rd
Brockton, MA 02301-5637, USA

Gordon, Milton A (Educator)
President's Office
Fullerton, CA 99264, USA

Gordon, Nina (Musician)
c/o Staff Member *Paradigm (Monterey)*
404 W Franklin St
Monterey, CA 93940-2303, USA

Gordon, Pamela (Prime Minister)
Burrows Bldg
Hamilton HM, CX, BERMUDA

Gordon, Phil (Misc)
8075 W 3rd St Ste 500
Los Angeles, CA 90048-4325, USA

Gordon, Richard
1 Craven Hl
London, ENGLAND W2 3EN

Gordon, Richard F Jr (Astronaut)
65 Woodside Dr
Prescott, AZ 86305-5092, USA

Gordon, Robby (Race Car Driver)
10615 Twin Lakes Pkwy
Charlotte, NC 28269-7659, USA

Gordon, Scott (Athlete, Coach, Hockey Player)
c/o Staff Member *Providence Bruins*
1 La Salle Sq
Providence, RI 02903-1888, USA

Gordon, Sean (Model)
c/o Staff Member *IMG*
304 Park Ave S Fl 12
New York, NY 10010-4314, USA

Gordon, Stuart (Director, Producer)
c/o Staff Member *Red Hen Productions*
3607 W Magnolia Blvd Ste L
Burbank, CA 91505-2988, USA

Gordon, Tom (Athlete, Baseball Player)
2006 Lake Lotela Dr
Avon Park, FL 33825-8030, USA

Gordon, William E (Physicist)
PO Box 1892
Houston, TX 77251-1892, USA

Gordon, Zachary (Actor)
c/o Nick Styne *Creative Artists Agency (CAA-LA)*
2000 Avenue of the Stars Ste 100
Los Angeles, CA 90067-4705, USA

Gordon-Levitt, Joey
4024 Radford Ave Bldg 3
Studio City, CA 91604-2101

Gordon-Levitt, Joseph (Actor)
c/o Stephen Huvane *Slate Public Relations*
9000 W Sunset Blvd Ste 915
West Hollywood, CA 90069-5809, USA

Gordy, Berry
878 Stradella Rd
Los Angeles, CA 90077-3310

Gordy, John (Athlete, Football Player)
40 Calle Fresno
San Clemente, CA 92672-9421, USA

Gordy, Walter (Physicist)
2521 Perkins Rd
Durham, NC 27705-1018, USA

Gore, Al (Ex-Senator, Ex-Vice President, Politician)
c/o Staff Member *Current TV*
118 King St Fl 2
San Francisco, CA 94107-5904, USA

Gore, Frank (Athlete, Football Player)
6641 SW 159th Pl
Miami, FL 33193-3633, USA

Gore, Lesley (Musician, Songwriter, Writer)
297101 Kinderkamack Rd # 128
Oradell, NJ 7649, USA

Gore, Martin (Musician)
c/o Staff Member *Mute Records*
43 Brook Green
London W6 7EF, UK

Gore, Michael
15622 Royal Oak Rd
Encino, CA 91436-3906

Gore, Tipper (Politician)
3810 Bedford Ave Ste 250
Nashville, TN 37215-2563, USA

Gore Jr, Albert A (President, Vice President)
312 Lynnwood Blvd
Nashville, TN 37205-2927, USA

Gorecki, Henryk M (Composer)
Ul HA Gornika 4 m 1
Katowice 40-133, POLAND

Gorecki, Rick (Athlete, Baseball Player)
16210 Ridgewood Dr
Homer Glen, IL 60491-8447, USA

Goren, Shlomo (General, Religious Leader)
Chief Rabbinate Hechal Shlomo
Jerusalem, ISRAEL

Gorence, Tom (Athlete, Hockey Player)
120 Hanapepe Loop
Honolulu, HI 96825-2110, USA

Gorenstein, Mark B (Conductor)
Rublevskoye Shosses 28 #25
Moscow 121609, RUSSIA

Goretta, Claude (Director)
10 Tour de Boel
Geneva 1204, SWITZERLAND

Gorgal, Ken (Athlete, Football Player)
304 Spyglass Ln
Vero Beach, FL 32963-4373, USA

Gorham, Christopher (Actor)
c/o Glenn Rigberg *HYPHENATE*
9701 Wilshire Blvd Fl 10
Beverly Hills, CA 90212-2010, USA

Gorham, Eville (Misc)
1933 E River Ter
Minneapolis, MN 55414-3673, USA

Gorie, Dominic L (Astronaut)
13656 Hidden Valley Ln
Salida, CO 81201-9760, USA

Gorillaz (Music Group)
c/o Staff Member *Virgin Records (LA)*
1750 Vine St
Los Angeles, CA 90028-5209, USA

Gorin, Brandon (Athlete, Football Player)
3294 E Morelos Ct
Gilbert, AZ 85295-7636, USA

Gorin, Charles
2617 First Dr
Austin, TX 78731

Gorin, Charlie (Athlete, Baseball Player)
2617 Fiset Dr
Austin, TX 78731-5613, USA

Goring, Robert T (Butch) (Athlete, Hockey Player)
245 W 5th Ave Ste 108
Anchorage, AK 99501-2300, USA

Gorinski, Bob (Athlete, Baseball Player)
221 Kromer Rd
Mount Pleasant, PA 15666-2473, USA

Goris, Eva (Actor)
8942 Wilshire Blvd # 219
Beverly Hills, CA 90211-1908, USA

Gorlin, Alexander (Architect)
137 Varick St
New York, NY 10013-1105, USA

Gorman, Brian (Baseball Player)
PO Box 1208
Somis, CA 93066-1208, USA

Gorman, Brian (Athlete, Baseball Player)
1381 Via Latina Dr
Camarillo, CA 93012-9294, USA

Gorman, Bryan (Athlete, Golfer)
The Auld Course 525 Hunte Pkwy
Chula Vista, CA 91914, USA

Gorman, Burn (Actor)
c/o Staff Member *Luber Roklin Management*
8530 Wilshire Blvd Ste 550
Beverly Hills, CA 90211-3133, USA

Gorman, Cliff
333 W 57th St
New York, NY 10019-3159

Gorman, Joseph T (Business Person)
1900 Richmond Rd
Cleveland, OH 44124, USA

Gorman, Paul F Jr (General)
9175 Batesville Rd
Afton, VA 22920-2620, USA

Gorman, R C (Artist)
PO Box 1258
El Prado, NM 87529-1258, USA

Gorman, Steve (Musician)
c/o Staff Member *Mitch Schneider Organization, The*
14724 Ventura Blvd Ste 410
Sherman Oaks, CA 91403-3537, USA

Gorman, Tom (Tennis Player)
1101 Woodrow Wilson Blvd # 1800
Arlington, VA 22209, USA

Gorman, Tom (Athlete, Baseball Player)
1615 SW 5th Ave
Portland, OR 97201-5403, USA

Gorman-Cahill, Margaret
4216 38th St NW
Washington, DC 20016-2258

Gorme, Eydie (Musician)
944 Pinehurst Dr
Las Vegas, NV 89109-1569, USA

Gormley, Antony (Artist)
13 South Villas
London NW1 9BS, UNITED KINGDOM (UK)

Gorneault, Nick (Athlete, Baseball Player)
94 Seymour Ave
Springfield, MA 01109-1330, USA

Gorney, Karen Lynn (Actor)
Po Box 23-1060
New York, NY 10023, USA

Gorouuch, Edward Lee (Educator)
President's Office
Anchorage, AK 99508, USA

Gorrell, Bob (Cartoonist)
5777 W Century Blvd Ste 700
Los Angeles, CA 90045-5652, USA

Gorrell, Fred (Misc)
501 E Port Au Prince Ln
Phoenix, AZ 85022-3670, USA

Gorris, Marleen (Director, Writer)

Gorski, Tamara (Actor)
18 Gloucester Lane #200
Toronto M4Y 1L5, CANADA

Gorter, Cornelis J (Physicist)
Klobeniersburgwal 29
Amsterdam, NETHERLANDS

Gortman, Shaunzinski (Basketball Player)
100 Hive Dr
Charlotte, NC 28217-4524, USA

Gortner, Marjoe (Actor)
PO Box 356
Sun Valley, ID 83353-0356, USA

Goryl, John (Athlete, Baseball Player, Coach)
528 Dry Run Rd
Monongahela, PA 15063-1223, USA

Gorzelanny, Tom (Athlete, Baseball Player)
208 Shadow Crk
Cranberry Township, PA 16066, USA

Gosar, Paul (Congressman, Politician)
504 Cannon Hob
Washington, DC 20515-4204, USA

Gosger, Jim (Athlete, Baseball Player)
1823 7th St
Port Huron, MI 48060-6301, USA

Goslin, Thomas B Jr (General)
Deputy CinC US Strategic Command
Offutt Air Force Base, NE 68113, USA

Gosling, James (Designer)
2550 Garcia Ave
Mountain View, CA 94043-1109, USA

Gosling, Ryan (Actor)
c/o Carolyn Govers *Artist Management*
1119 Colorado Ave Ste 12
Santa Monica, CA 90401-3009, USA

Gosnell, Raja (Director)
c/o Staff Member *Creative Artists Agency (CAA-LA)*
2000 Avenue of the Stars Ste 100
Los Angeles, CA 90067-4705, USA

Goss, Luke (Actor)
100 Universal Dr Bungalow 7151
Universal City, CA 91608, USA

Goss, Matt (Actor)
c/o Staff Member *Andrew Freedman Public Relations*
9127 Thrasher Ave
Los Angeles, CA 90069-1144, USA

Goss, Porter (Misc)
Office of Public Affairs
Washington, DC 20505-0001

Goss, Robert F (Misc)
1636 Champa St
Denver, CO 80202-2703, USA

Gossage, Gene (Athlete, Football Player)
793 Toby Hill Rd
Westbrook, CT 06498-3502, USA

Gossage, Goose (Athlete, Baseball Player)
303 E 83rd St Apt 6A
New York, NY 10028-4316, USA

Gossage, Rich (Athlete, Baseball Player)
35 Marland Rd
Colorado Springs, CO 80906-4328, USA

Gosselaar, Mark-Paul (Actor)
c/o Staff Member *James/Levy/Jacobson Management Inc*
3500 W Olive Ave Ste 1470
Burbank, CA 91505-5514, USA

Gosselin, Guy (Athlete, Hockey Player)
1946 Valley Ct
Grafton, WI 53024-2808, USA

Gosselin, Jonathan (Reality TV Star)
c/o Mike Heller *Talent Resources*
124 E 36th St Ste A
New York, NY 10016-3402, USA

Gosselin, Kate (Reality TV Star)
c/o Julie May *Media Motion International (MMI)*
15332 Antioch St # 726
Pacific Palisades, CA 90272-3628, 310-459-7310

Gosselin, Mario (Athlete, Hockey Player)
c/o Staff Member *Ecole de Hockey Energie*
70 Rue des Fauvettes
Saint-Basile-Le-Grand, QC J3N 1P4, Canada

Gossett, D Bruce (Athlete, Football Player)
6109 Puerto Dr
Rancho Murieta, CA 95683-9320, USA

Gossett, David (Athlete, Golfer)
4501 Spanish Oaks Club Blvd Unit 9
Austin, TX 78738-6618, USA

Gossett, Jeff (Athlete, Football Player)
6 Lake Forest Ct
Roanoke, TX 76262-5504, USA

Gossett, Robert (Actor)
c/o Staff Member *Leavitt Talent Group*
8255 W Sunset Blvd
West Hollywood, CA 90046-2417, USA

Gossett Jr, Louis (Actor)
c/o Hillard Elkins *Elkins Entertainment*
8306 Wilshire Blvd Ste 438
Beverly Hills, CA 90211-2382, USA

Gossick Crockatt, Sue (Swimmer)
13768 Christian Barrett Dr
Moorpark, CA 93021-2802, USA

Gostkowski, Stephen (Athlete, Football Player)
19 Rhodes Dr
Wrentham, MA 02093-2503, USA

Goswami, Kunal (Director)
47 Jaihind Society 11th N Road Jvpd Scheme S
Bombay, MS 400 049, INDIA

Gotch, Karl
18530 Wayne Rd
Odessa, FL 33556-4739

Gothard, Michael
18 Shirlock Rd
London, ENGLAND NW3 2HS

Gothard, Preston (Athlete, Football Player)
448 Merry Way
Pike Road, AL 36064-2282, USA

Goto, Joji (Stylist)
c/o Staff Member *Ennis*
119 Braintree St
Boston, MA 02134-1628, USA

Gotshalk, Leonard (Athlete, Football Player)
1200 Butler Creek Rd
Ashland, OR 97520-9370, USA

Gott, Jim (Athlete, Baseball Player)
860 La Vina Ln
Altadena, CA 91001-3754, USA

Gott, Karel (Musician)
Nad Bertramkou 18
Prague 160 00, CZECH REPUBLIC

Gottfried, Brian (Tennis Player)
129 Teal Pointe Ln
Ponte Vedra Beach, FL 32082-1937, USA

Gottfried, Gilbert (Actor, Comedian)
c/o Steve Honig *Honig Company, The*
3500 W Olive Ave Ste 300
Burbank, CA 91505-4647, USA

Gotti, Carmine (Reality TV Star)
c/o Staff Member *Growing Up Gotti*
13400 Riverside Dr Ste 300
Sherman Oaks, CA 91423-2546, USA

Gotti, John, Jr (Reality TV Star)
c/o Staff Member *Growing Up Gotti*
13400 Riverside Dr Ste 300
Sherman Oaks, CA 91423-2546, USA

Gotti, Victoria (Actor, Producer, Reality TV Star)
c/o Tammy Brook *FYI Public Relations*
174 5th Ave Ste 400
New York, NY 10010-5935, USA

Gottlieb, Michael (Director)
2436 Washington Ave
Santa Monica, CA 90403-2128, USA

Gottlieb, Robert A (Editor, Publisher)
237 E 48th St
New York, NY 10017-1538, USA

Gottman, John (Writer)
PO Box 15644
Seattle, WA 98115-0644, USA

Gottwald, Lukasz (Dr. Luke) (Producer)
9111 W Sunset Blvd
Los Angeles, CA 90069-3106, USA

Gougeon, Donni (Misc)
1924 Spring St
Paso Robles, CA 93446-1620, USA

Gough, Alfred (Writer)
c/o Renee Kurtz *Creative Artists Agency (CAA-LA)*
1 William Morris Pl
Beverly Hills, CA 90212-4261, USA

Gough, Michael (Actor)
Torleigh Green Lane Ashmore
Salisbury, Wills SP5 5AO, UNITED KINGDOM (UK)

Gough, Tommy (Musician)
141 Dunbar Ave
Fords, NJ 08863-1551, USA

Goulart, Izabel (Actor, Model)
c/o Staff Member *Women Model Management*
199 Lafayette St Fl 7
New York, NY 10012-4281, USA

Gould, Alexander (Actor)
c/o TJ Stein *Stein Entertainment Group*
1351 N Crescent Heights Blvd Apt 312
West Hollywood, CA 90046-4549, USA

Gould, Bob (Athlete, Hockey Player)
3651 Oil Springs Line
Oil Springs, ON N0N 1P0, Canada

Gould, Dana (Actor, Producer, Writer)

Gould, Eileen (Stylist)
31275 Labaya St
Westlake Village, CA 91361, USA

Gould, Elizabeth (Doctor)
Medical Center Neurosciences Dept
Princeton, NJ 08544-0001, USA

Gould, Elliott (Actor)
c/o Jeff Witjas *Agency for the Performing Arts (APA-LA)*
405 S Beverly Dr Ste 500
Beverly Hills, CA 90212-4425, USA

Gould, Hal (Athlete, Baseball Player)
126 Rogers Ave
Millville, NJ 08332-9723, USA

Gould, John (Athlete, Hockey Player)
99 Main St
Beeton, ON L0G 1A0, Canada

Gould, Kelly (Actor)
c/o TJ Stein *Stein Entertainment Group*
1351 N Crescent Heights Blvd Apt 312
West Hollywood, CA 90046-4549, USA

Gould, Lawrence M (Misc)
201 E Rudasill Rd
Tucson, AZ 85704-6024, USA

Gould, Matt Kennedy (Reality TV Star)
c/o Staff Member *WmE2 (WMA-LA)*
1 William Morris Pl
Beverly Hills, CA 90212-4261, USA

Gould, Nolan (Actor)
c/o Jamie Malone *MC Talent Management*
4821 Lankershim Blvd # F329
N Hollywood, CA 91601-4538, USA

Gould, Ronald M (Judge)
5th Ave US Courthouse 1010
Seattle, WA 98104-3191, USA

Gould, Shane
207 Kent St Level 18
Sydney, AUSTRALIA NSW 2000

Gould, Terry (Producer)
c/o Staff Member *Lenhoff & Lenhoff*
830 Palm Ave
West Hollywood, CA 90069-4009

Gould Innes, Shane (Swimmer)
207 Kent St Level 18
Sydney, NSW 2000, AUSTRALIA

Goulding, Ellie
c/o Staff Member *WmE2 (WMA-NY)*
1325 Avenue of the Americas
New York, NY 10019-6026, USA

Goulet, Michael (Athlete, Hockey Player)
1283 Buffalo Ridge Rd
Castle Pines, CO 80108-8192, USA

Goulet, Michel (Athlete, Hockey Player)
1283 Buffalo Ridge Rd
Castle Pines, CO 80108-8192, USA

Goulet, Patrice (Stylist)
c/o Staff Member *Ford Models (Chicago)*
311 W Superior St
Chicago, IL 60654-3548, USA

Goundamani (Actor)
7 Cenatop Ist Cross Street Teynampet
Chennai, TN 600 018, INDIA

Gourley, Roark (Artist)
33151 Paso Dr
South Laguna Beach, CA 92677, USA

Gouveia, Kurt (Athlete, Football Player)
138 Seagrove Ln
Mooresville, NC 28117-8976, USA

Govan, Gerald (Athlete, Basketball Player)
30 Newport Pkwy Apt 2112
Jersey City, NJ 07310-1512, USA

Gove, Jeff (Athlete, Golfer)
21323 31st Ave SE
Bothell, WA 98021-7871, USA

Govedaris, Chris (Athlete, Hockey Player)
325 Brewster Rd
Bristol, CT 06010-5277, USA

Govedaris, David (Athlete, Hockey Player)
3838B Lower Union Rd
Orlando, FL 32814-6508, USA

Govich, Milena (Actor)
c/o Rhonda Price *Gersh (NY)*
41 Madison Ave
New York, NY 10010-2202, USA

Gov't Mule (Music Group)
c/o Staff Member *Paradigm (Monterey)*
404 W Franklin St
Monterey, CA 93940-2303, USA

Gowan, Caroline (Athlete, Golfer)
209 Crescent Ave
Greenville, SC 29605-2814, USA

Gowan, James (Architect)
2 Linden Gardens
London W2 4ES, UNITED KINGDOM (UK)

Gowan, Lawrence (Musician)
c/o Sterling Bacon *TBA Artist Management (Atlanta)*
1111 Alderman Dr Ste 285
Alpharetta, GA 30005-5433, USA

Gowdy, Cornell (Athlete, Football Player)
4611 John St
Suitland, MD 20746-3772, USA

Gowdy, Trey (Congressman, Politician)
1237 Longworth Hob
Washington, DC 20515-0302, USA

Gowell, Larry (Athlete, Baseball Player)
4 Carson St
Auburn, ME 04210-3706, USA

Gower, David I (Cricketer)
6 George St
Nottingham NG1 3BE, UNITED KINGDOM (UK)

Gower, Jessica (Actor)
c/o Jason Newman *Untitled Entertainment (LA)*
350 S Beverly Dr Ste 200
Beverly Hills, CA 90212-4819, USA

Gowers, W Timothy (Mathematician)
16 Mill Lane
Cambridge CB2 1SB, UNITED KINGDOM (UK)

Gowin, Toby (Athlete, Football Player)
1605 Oak Creek Cir
Tyler, TX 75703-0433, USA

Gowon, Yakub (General, President)
38-39 Marina
Lagos 2052, NIGERIA

Gowrie, Earl of (Government Official)
Stag Place
London SW1E 5DS, UNITED KINGDOM (UK)

Gowtham (Actor)
9 Pooram Prakash Rao Road Balaji Nagar
Chennai, TN 600 014, INDIA

Gowthami (Actor, Bollywood)
2-B Syamvilla 2nd Main Road C.I T Colony Mylapore
Chennai, TN 600004, INDIA

Goycoechea, Sergio (Soccer Player)
Via Monte 1366-76
Buenos Aires 1053, ARGENTINA

Goydos, Paul (Athlete, Golfer)
1864 Stearnlee Ave
Long Beach, CA 90815-3040, USA

Goyer, David S (Director, Producer, Writer)

Goyer, Gerry (Athlete, Hockey Player)
205-1963 Durnin Rd
Kelowna, BC V1X 7Y4, Canada

Goyette, J G Philippe (Phil) (Athlete, Hockey Player)
815 38-E Ave
Lachine, QC H8T 2C4, Canada

Goyo, Dakota (Actor)
c/o Steven Kavovit *Thruline Entertainment*
9250 Wilshire Blvd Ground Fl
Beverly Hills, CA 90212, USA

Goyri, Sergio (Actor)
c/o Staff Member *Televisa*
Blvd Adolfo Lopez Mateos 232 Colonia San Angel INN
DF CP 01060, MEXICO

Gozzo, Mauro (Athlete, Baseball Player)
156 Newton St
Berlin, CT 06037-1254, USA

Grabarkewitz, Billy (Athlete, Baseball Player)
2162 Estes Park Rd
Southlake, TX 76092-3835, USA

Grabe, Ronald J (Astronaut)
2652 E Scorpio Pl
Chandler, AZ 85249-5253, USA

Grabeel, Lucas (Actor)
c/o Robert C. Thompson *Group III Management*
16255 Ventura Blvd Ste 625
Encino, CA 91436-2307, USA

Graber, Bill (Athlete, Track Athlete)
PO Box 5019
Upland, CA 91785-5019, USA

Graber, Rod (Athlete, Baseball Player)
4674 Mount Armet Dr
San Diego, CA 92117-4719, USA

Graber, Susan P (Judge)
555 SW Yamhill St
Portland, OR 97204-1303, USA

Grabois, Neil R (Educator)
President's Office
Hamilton, NY 13346, USA

Grabow, John (Athlete, Baseball Player)
258 Clematis Dr
Wexford, PA 15090-7649, USA

Grabowski, James S (Jim) (Athlete, Football Player)
1523 Withorn Ln
Inverness, IL 60067-4367, USA

Grabowski, Jason (Athlete, Baseball Player)
3328 E Franklin Ave
Gilbert, AZ 85295-3401, USA

Grace, Alexis (Musician)

Grace, April (Actor)
c/o Lenore Zerman *Liberman/Zerman Management*
252 N Larchmont Blvd Ste 200
Los Angeles, CA 90004-3754, USA

Grace, Bud (Cartoonist)
PO Box 66
Oakton, VA 22124-0066, USA

Grace, Maggie (Actor)
c/o Darren Goldberg *Global Creative*
1051 Cole Ave # B
Los Angeles, CA 90038-2601, USA

Grace, Mark (Athlete, Baseball Player)
5624 E Via Buena Vis
Paradise Valley, AZ 85253-8129, USA

Grace, Mike (Athlete, Baseball Player)
1156 Buell Ave
Joliet, IL 60435-6809, USA

Grace, Mike (Athlete, Baseball Player)
12791 Big Lake Rd
Davisburg, MI 48350-3419, USA

Grace, Nancy (Lawyer, Television Host)
1 Time Warner Ctr
New York, NY 10019-6038, USA

Grace, Topher (Actor)
c/o Aleen Keshishian *Brillstein Entertainment Partners*
9150 Wilshire Blvd Ste 350
Beverly Hills, CA 90212-3453, USA

Graceland
3765 Elvis Presley Blvd
Memphis, TN 38116-4105

Gracey, James S (Admiral, Business Person)
1 Westin Center 2445 M St NW # 260
Washington, DC 20037, USA

Grach, Eduard D (Musician)
1st Smolensky Per 9 #98
Moscow 113324, RUSSIA

Grachev, Pavel S (General)
Ovchinnikovskaya Nab 18/1
Moscow 113324, RUSSIA

Gracheva, Nadezhda A (Ballerina)
1st Truzhennikov Per 17 #49
Moscow 119121, RUSSIA

Grachvogel, Maria (Designer, Fashion Designer)
c/o Staff Member *Maria Grachvogel*
5 South Molton Street
London, England W11 1LT, United Kingdom

Gracie, Charlie (Musician)
PO Box 53664
Indianapolis, IN 46253-0664, USA

Gracie, Royce (Athlete, Wrestler)
9806 Zackery Ave
Charlotte, NC 28277-2124, USA

Gracin, Joshua (Musician)
c/o Rob Beckham *WmE2 (WMA-TN)*
1600 Division St Ste 300
Nashville, TN 37203-2755, USA

Grad, Harold (Mathematician)
248 Overlook Rd
New Rochelle, NY 10804-3806, USA

Graddy, Sam (Athlete, Football Player)
4792 Brasac Dr
Stone Mountain, GA 30083-5100, USA

Gradin, Thomas (Athlete, Hockey Player)
c/o Staff Member *Vancouver Canucks*
800 Griffiths Way
Vancouver V6B 6G1, Canada

Gradishar, Randy C (Athlete, Football Player)
7628 Pineridge Ter
Castle Pines, CO 80108-8260, USA

Gradison, Ronnie (Athlete, Basketball Player)
6151 Chappellfield Dr
West Chester, OH 45069-6648, USA

Grady, Ellen
150 E Olive Ave Ste 111
Burbank, CA 91502-1849

Grady, James T (Politician)
25 Louisiana Ave NW
Washington, DC 20001-2130, USA

Grady, Wayne (Athlete, Golfer)
PO Box 78
Coolum Beach QLD 4573, Australia

Graeber, Clark (Tennis Player)
411 Harbor Rd
Fairfield, CT 6431, USA

Graelis, Francisco (Pancho) (Cartoonist, Editor)
Editorial Dept 21 Bis Rue Claude Bernard
Paris 75005, FRANCE

Graf, Bianca
Oppenheimstr. 6b
Wolfen, GERMANY D-06766

Graf, Dave (Athlete, Football Player)
1825 Bel Air Ave
Pompano Beach, FL 33062-7672, USA

Graf, Hans
615 Louisiana St
Houston, TX 77002-2715, USA

Graf, Richard (Athlete, Football Player)
6609 Biscayne Blvd
Minneapolis, MN 55436-1703, USA

Graf, Stefanie M (Steffi) (Tennis Player)
8921 Andre Dr
Las Vegas, NV 89148-1405, USA

Graff, Ilena (Actor)
11455 Sunshine Ter
Studio City, CA 91604-3129, USA

Graff, Milt (Athlete, Baseball Player)
1112 Austin Ave
College Station, TX 77845-5136, USA

Graff, Neil (Athlete, Football Player)
PO Box 2696
Sioux Falls, SD 57101-2696, USA

Graff, Randy (Actor)
1501 Broadway Ste 2900
New York, NY 10036-5600, USA

Graff, Todd
547 Hudson St
New York, NY 10014-3290

Graffanino, Tony (Athlete, Baseball Player)
6875 W Cottontail Ln
Peoria, AZ 85383-7090, USA

Graffin, Guillaume (Ballerina)
890 Broadway
New York, NY 10003-1211, USA

Graffman, Gary (Musician)
1726 Locust St
Philadelphia, PA 19103-6107, USA

Grafstein, Bernice (Physicist, Scientist)
1300 York Ave
New York, NY 10065-4805, USA

Grafton, Sue (Writer)
PO Box 41446
Santa Barbara, CA 93140-1446, USA

Gragg, Scott (Athlete, Football Player)
583 Cash Nichols Rd
Stevensville, MT 59870-6625, USA

Graham, Art (Athlete, Football Player)
PO Box 785
South Orleans, MA 02662-0785, USA

Graham, Aubrey (Actor)
c/o Staff Member *Noble Caplan Abrams*
1260 Yonge St 2nd Floor
Toronto ON M4T 1W6, Canada

Graham, Aubrey (Drake) (Actor, Musician)
c/o Cortez Bryant *Bryant Management*
555 Washington Ave Ste 240
Miami, FL 33139-6639, USA

Graham, Bill (Athlete, Football Player)
11013 Sierra Verde Trl
Austin, TX 78759-5129, USA

Graham, Bob (Ex-Senator)
14814 Breckness Pl
Miami Lakes, FL 33016-1458, USA

Graham, Brendan (Musician, Writer)
c/o Staff Member *PeerMusic USA*
2397 Shattuck Ave Ste 202
Berkeley, CA 94704-1567, USA

Graham, Charles P (General)
134 Warbler Way
Georgetown, TX 78633-4804, USA

Graham, Chris (Director)
c/o Simon Millar *Rumble Media*
1620 Broadway Ste C
Santa Monica, CA 90404-2777, USA

Graham, Currie
c/o Vera Mihailovich *Forward Entertainment*
9255 W Sunset Blvd Ste 805
Los Angeles, CA 90069-3305, USA

Graham, Dan (Athlete, Baseball Player)
6444 Little Pine Way
Las Vegas, NV 89108-3420, USA

Graham, Daniel (Athlete, Football Player)
RR 1 60 Washington
Foxboro, MA 2035, USA

Graham, David (Athlete, Golfer)
99 Mountainside Dr
Whitefish, MT 59937-3266, USA

Graham, Derrick (Athlete, Football Player)
203 Pine Hill Rd
West End, NC 27376-8848, USA

Graham, Dirk (Athlete, Coach, Hockey Player)
45 Christine Dr
West Springfield, MA 01089-2220, USA

Graham, Donald E (Publisher)
1150 15th St NW
Washington, DC 20071-0001, USA

Graham, Ed (Musician)
c/o Sue Whitehouse *Whitehouse Management*
PO Box 43829
London NW6 3PJ, UNITED KINGDOM

Graham, Franklin (Religious Leader)
PO Box 3000
Boone, NC 28607-3000, USA

Graham, Gail (Golfer)
Landmark Sport Group 277 Richmond St NW
Toronto, ON M5V 1X1, CANADA

Graham, Gerrit (Actor)
8730 W Sunset Blvd Ste 440
Los Angeles, CA 90069-2277, USA

Graham, Glen (Musician)
9229 W Sunset Blvd Ste 607
Los Angeles, CA 90069-3406, USA

Graham, Greg (Athlete, Basketball Player)
12636 Wolf Run Rd
Noblesville, IN 46060-8001, USA

Graham, Hason (Athlete, Football Player)
140 Shoreline Dr
Fayetteville, GA 30215-4663, USA

Graham, Heather (Actor, Producer)
c/o Risa Shapiro *Schiff Company, The*
8440 Warner Dr Ste B1
Culver City, CA 90232-2461, USA

Graham, Jeff (Athlete, Football Player)
1840 Infirmary Rd
Dayton, OH 45417-5730, USA

Graham, John R (Writer)
Astronomy
Berkeley, CA 94720-0001, USA

Graham, Jorie (Writer)
West Tisbury, MA 2575, USA

Graham, Katerina (Actor)
c/o Jon Simmons *Simmons & Scott Entertainment*
7942 Mulholland Dr
Los Angeles, CA 90046-1225, USA

Graham, Katherine
2920 R St NW
Washington, DC 20007-2920

Graham, Kenny (Athlete, Football Player)
PO Box 7402
Santa Monica, CA 90406-7402, USA

Graham, Kent (Athlete, Football Player)
1001 N Washington St
Wheaton, IL 60187-3857, USA

Graham, Lauren (Actor)
c/o John Carrabino *John Carrabino Management*
5900 Wilshire Blvd Ste 406
Los Angeles, CA 90036-5015, USA

Graham, Lee (Athlete, Baseball Player)
481 Richmond Rd
Cleveland, OH 44143-2745, USA

Graham, Linda (Bowler)
4147 E Seneca Ave
Des Moines, IA 50317-8123, USA

Graham, Loren R (Historian)
7 Francis Ave
Cambridge, MA 02138-2009, USA

Graham, Lou (Athlete, Golfer)
85 Concord Park W
Nashville, TN 37205-4707, USA

Graham, Mal (Athlete, Basketball Player)
122 Christina St
Newton Highlands, MA 02461-1916, USA

Graham, Mikey (Musician)
84A Strand on the Green
London W43 PU, UNITED KINGDOM (UK)

Graham, Parker (Musician)
8901 Melrose Ave # 200
West Hollywood, CA 90069-5605, USA

Graham, Pat (Athlete, Hockey Player)
200-438 University Ave
Toronto, ON M5G 2K8, Canada

Graham, Paul (Athlete, Basketball Player)
5255 N Marshall St
Philadelphia, PA 19120-3134, USA

Graham, Roger (Athlete, Football Player)
10 Ford Ct
Monroe, NY 10950-4946, USA

Graham, Samaria
c/o Steven Jensen *The Independent Group*
6363 Wilshire Blvd Ste 115
Los Angeles, CA 90048-5734, USA

Graham, Stedman (Business Person)
455 N Cityfront Plaza Dr Fl 15
Chicago, IL 60611-5503, USA

Graham, Stephen (Actor)
c/o Ben Levine *Kritzer Levine Wilkins Entertainment*
425 N Robertson Blvd
West Hollywood, CA 90048-1735, USA

Graham, Susan (Opera Singer)
165 W 57th St
New York, NY 10019-2201, USA

Graham, Tommy (Athlete, Football Player)
4084 S Wisteria Way
Denver, CO 80237-1714, USA

Graham, Wayne (Athlete, Baseball Player)
2017 Dryden Rd
Houston, TX 77030-1205, USA

Graham, William B (Business Person)
40 Devonshire Ln
Kenilworth, IL 60043-1205, USA

Graham, William F (Billy) (Religious Leader, Writer)
1 Billy Graham Pkwy
Charlotte, NC 28201-0001, USA

Graham, William R (Government Official)
1110 N Glebe Rd # 620
Arlington, VA 22201-4795, USA

Graham-Douglas, Mary Lou (Baseball Player)
9990 N Hillview Dr
Tucson, AZ 85737-7940, USA

Grahame, John (Athlete, Hockey Player)
4115 English Garden Way
Raleigh, NC 27612-4356, USA

Grahame, Ron (Athlete, Hockey Player)
9000 E Jewell Cir
Denver, CO 80231-3450, USA

Graham-Smith, Francis (Astronomer)
Old School House Henbury
Macclesfield, Cheshire SK11 9PH, UNITED KINGDOM (UK)

Grahe, Joe (Athlete, Baseball Player)
2317 N Wallen Dr
West Palm Beach, FL 33410-2558, USA

Grahn, Nancy
4910 Agnes Ave
Valley Village, CA 91607-3705

Grahn, Nancy Lee (Actor)
c/o Staff Member *Innovative Artists (LA)*
1505 10th St
Santa Monica, CA 90401-2805, USA

Grainger, David W (Business Person)
14441 W Il Route 60
Lake Forest, IL 60045-5203, USA

Grainger, Holliday (Actor)
c/o Connor McCaughan *Troika*
74 Clerkenwell Rd 3rd Floor
London EC1M 5QA, United Kingdom

Gralish, Tom (Journalist, Photographer)
203 E Cottage Ave
Haddonfield, NJ 08033-1824, USA

Gralla, Milton (Publisher)
1515 Broadway
New York, NY 10036-8901, USA

Graman, Alex (Athlete, Baseball Player)
450 E Sunset Dr
Huntingburg, IN 47542-9316, USA

Gramanis, Paul (Athlete, Football Player)
989 Parkview Dr
Tallahassee, FL 32311-1245, USA

Gramatica, Guillermo (Bill) (Athlete, Football Player)
15836 Fishhawk Falls Dr
Lithia, FL 33547-3856, USA

Gramatica, Martin (Athlete, Football Player)
8905 Promise Dr
Tampa, FL 33626-5122, USA

Gramlich, Edward M (Economist, Government Official)
Constitution Aves NW
Washington, DC 20551-0001, USA

Gramly, Tommy (Athlete, Baseball Player)
16485 Red Wood Cir W
McKinney, TX 75071-6198, USA

Gramm, Lou (Musician)
c/o Staff Member *Creative Artists Agency (CAA-LA)*
2000 Avenue of the Stars Ste 100
Los Angeles, CA 90067-4705, USA

Gramm, W Philip (Phil) (Ex-Senator)
1140 Avenue Of The Americas
New York, NY 10036-5803, USA

Gramm, Wendy L (Government Official)
2033 K St NW
Washington, DC 20006-1002, USA

Grammas, Alex (Athlete, Baseball Player, Coach)
4030 Vestview Dr
Vestavia, AL 35242-2554, USA

Grammer, Camille (Actor, Reality TV Star)
c/o Jill Fritzo *PMK/BNC Public Relations (PMK-NY)*
622 3rd Ave Fl 8
New York, NY 10017-6707, USA

Grammer, Kathy (Actor)
1180 S Beverly Dr Ste 301
Los Angeles, CA 90035-1154, USA

Grammer, Kelsey (Actor)
c/o Stan Rosenfield *Stan Rosenfield & Associates*
2029 Century Park E Ste 1190
Los Angeles, CA 90067-2931, USA

Grammer, Spencer (Actor)
c/o Evan Hainey *Untitled Entertainment (LA)*
350 S Beverly Dr Ste 200
Beverly Hills, CA 90212-4819, USA

Gran, Phyllis
200 Madison Ave
New York, NY 10016-3903

Granaderos, Alyson (Stylist)
c/o Staff Member *Montana Artists Agency*
9150 Wilshire Blvd Ste 100
Beverly Hills, CA 90212-3459, USA

Granatelli, Andy (Misc)
1469 Edgecliff Ln
Montecito, CA 93108-2810, USA

Granato, Catherine (Cammi) (Athlete, Hockey Player)
13454 Wood Duck Dr
Plainfield, IL 60585-7766, USA

Granato, Tony (Athlete, Coach, Hockey Player)
1481 Hollow Tree Dr
Pittsburgh, PA 15241-2962, USA

Granby, John (Athlete, Football Player)
11901 Pleasant Ridge Rd Apt 417
Little Rock, AR 72223-2457, USA

Grand, Katie (Stylist)
c/o Staff Member *Camilla Lowther Managment (CLM Represents)*
30-32 Ericsson Pl
New York, NY 10013, USA

Grand Funk Railroad (Musician)
c/o Staff Member *Paradigm (Monterey)*
404 W Franklin St
Monterey, CA 93940-2303, USA

Grand Ole Opry
2804 Opryland Dr
Nashville, TN 37214-1209

Grandberry, Ken (Athlete, Football Player)
108 E Mark Rd
Harker Heights, TX 76548-1224, USA

Grandberry, Omari (Omarion) (Actor)
c/o Guido Giordano *International Creative Management (ICM-LA)*
10250 Constellation Blvd Fl 7
Los Angeles, CA 90067-6207, USA

Grande, Ariana (Actor)
c/o Jennifer Merlino *Untitled Entertainment (LA)*
350 S Beverly Dr Ste 200
Beverly Hills, CA 90212-4819, USA

Grandelius, Everett (Sonny) (Athlete, Football Player)
31531 Robinhood Dr
Beverly Hills, MI 48025-3532, USA

Granderson, Curtis (Athlete, Baseball Player)
20485 Tyler Dr
Lynwood, IL 60411-8706, USA

Granderson, Rufus (Athlete, Football Player)
1717 Paris Ave SE
Grand Rapids, MI 49507-2633, USA

Grandholm, Jim (Athlete, Basketball Player)
211 Spring Park Ave
Sawyer, MI 49125-8353, USA

Grandin, Temple (Scientist)
2918 Silverplume Dr Apt C3
Fort Collins, CO 80526-2402, USA

Grandmaster, Mele-Mel (Musician)
1005 N Alfred St Apt 2
West Hollywood, CA 90069-4757, USA

Grandmont, Jean-Michel (Economist)
55 Blvd de Charonne Les Doukas 23
Paris 75011, FRANCE

Grand-Pierre, Jean-Luc (Athlete, Hockey Player)
4513 Greensbury Dr
New Albany, OH 43054-8678, USA

Grandpre, Mary (Designer)
555 Broadway
New York, NY 10012-3919, USA

Grandy, Fred (Actor)
9417 Spruce Tree Cir
Bethesda, MD 20814-1654, USA

Granger, Charley (Athlete, Football Player)
621 Burbridge St
Port Allen, LA 70767-2128, USA

Granger, Clive W J (Nobel Prize Laureate)
9500 Gilman Dr
La Jolla, CA 92093-5003, USA

Granger, David (Athlete)
61 Broadway # 3100
New York, NY 10006-2701, USA

Granger, Hoyle (Athlete, Football Player)
10611 Cranbrook Rd
Houston, TX 77042-1436, USA

Granger, Jeff (Athlete, Baseball Player)
2905 Glasgow Dr
Arlington, TX 76015-2226, USA

Granger, Kay (Congressman, Politician)
320 CAJ1LLLON
Washington, DC 20515-0001, USA

Granger, Stewart (Athlete, Basketball Player)
54 Boerum St Apt 1G
Brooklyn, NY 11206-2442, USA

Granger, Wayne (Athlete, Baseball Player)
133 Redtail Pl
Winter Springs, FL 32708-5626, USA

Grannis, Paul D (Physicist)
PO Box 500
Batavia, IL 60510-5011, USA

Grant, Alan (Athlete, Football Player)
148 Cisco Rd
Asheville, NC 28805-1311, USA

Grant, Amy (Musician, Songwriter)
c/o Staff Member *The M Collective*
PO Box 273
Franklin, TN 37065-0273, USA

Grant, Beth
2852 Hollyridge Dr
Los Angeles, CA 90068-2321

Grant, Boyd (Coach)
Athletic
Fort Collins, CO 80523-0001, USA

Grant, Brea (Actor)
c/o Nicole Perna *Baker Winokur Ryder Public Relations (BWR-LA)*
9100 Wilshire Blvd Ste 500 PMB WEST
Beverly Hills, CA 90212-3426, USA

Grant, Brian (Athlete, Basketball Player)
24152 SW Petes Mountain Rd
West Linn, OR 97068-4500, USA

Grant, Bud (Athlete, Football Coach, Football Player)
8134 Oakmere Rd
Minneapolis, MN 55438-1333, USA

Grant, Charles (Actor)
6300 Wilshire Blvd Ste 1470
Los Angeles, CA 90048-5200, USA

Grant, Danny (Athlete, Hockey Player)
1163 Route 101
Nasonworth, NB E3C 2C3, Canada

Grant, Darryl (Athlete, Football Player)
6931 Compton Ln
Centreville, VA 20121-5009, USA

Grant, David Marshall (Actor)
c/o Michael Katcher *Creative Artists Agency (CAA-LA)*
2000 Avenue of the Stars Ste 100
Los Angeles, CA 90067-4705, USA

Grant, Deborah (Actor)
17 Broad Ct #12
London WC2B 5QN, UNITED KINGDOM

Grant, Edmond (Eddy) (Musician, Songwriter, Writer)
PO Box 87
Tarporley CW6 9FN, UNITED KINGDOM (UK)

Grant, Faye (Actor)
13000 Brentwood Ter
Los Angeles, CA 90049-4807, USA

Grant, Frank (Athlete, Football Player)
2126 Glencourse Ln
Reston, VA 20191-1315, USA

Grant, Gil (Producer)
c/o Staff Member *Principal Entertainment (LA)*
1964 Westwood Blvd Ste 400
Los Angeles, CA 90025-4695, USA

Grant, Gogi (Musician)
10323 Alamo Ave # 202
Los Angeles, CA 90064, USA

Grant, Harvey (Athlete, Basketball Player)
11802 Woodbrook Ct
Bowie, MD 20721-4102, USA

Grant, Horace (Athlete, Basketball Player)
195 Michael Ln
Arroyo Grande, CA 93420-5323, USA

Grant, Hugh (Actor)
c/o Leslee Dart *42West (NY)*
220 W 42nd St Fl 12
New York, NY 10036-7200, USA

Grant, James T (Mudcat) (Athlete, Baseball Player)
1020 S Dunsmuir Ave
Los Angeles, CA 90019-6754, USA

Grant, Jennifer (Actor)
c/o Mark Teitelbaum *Teitelbaum Artists Group*
8840 Wilshire Blvd Fl 3
Beverly Hills, CA 90211-2606, USA

Grant, John (Athlete, Football Player)
6365 S Harrison Ct
Centennial, CO 80121-3616, USA

Grant, Josh (Athlete, Basketball Player)
3191 S Davis Blvd
Bountiful, UT 84010-5764, USA

Grant, Kate Jennings (Actor)
c/o Tammy Rosen *Sanders Armstrong Caserta*
2120 Colorado Ave Ste 120
Santa Monica, CA 90404-3561, USA

Grant, Lee (Actor, Director)
c/o Joel Dean *TalentWorks (LA)*
3500 W Olive Ave Ste 1400
Burbank, CA 91505-5512, USA

Grant, Leonard (Uncle Murda) (Musician)
c/o Staff Member *Violator Management*
36 W 25th St Fl 11
New York, NY 10010-2752, USA

Grant, Mark (Athlete, Baseball Player)
2837 Via Dieguenos
Alpine, CA 91901-3638, USA

Grant, Martin (Athlete, Hockey Player)
17 Mount View Crt
Collingwood, ON L9Y 5A9, Canada

Grant, Mickie (Actor)
250 W 94th St # 6G
New York, NY 10025-6954, USA

Grant, Orantes (Athlete, Football Player)
5103 Ashford Gables Dr
Atlanta, GA 30338-6780, USA

Grant, Paul (Basketball Player)
Bradley Center 1001 N 4th St
Milwaukee, WI 53203, USA

Grant, Rachel (Actor)
34 South Molton Street
London W1K 5BP, UNITED KINGDOM

Grant, Reginald (Athlete, Football Player)
PO Box 15602
Los Angeles, CA 90015-0602, USA

Grant, Richard E (Actor)
76 Oxford St
London W1N 0AX, UNITED KINGDOM (UK)

Grant, Robert M (Educator)
RR 1 Box 1423
Berlin, NH 3570, USA

Grant, Rodney A. (Actor)
c/o Anne Geddes *Geddes Agency, The*
8430 Santa Monica Blvd Ste 200
Los Angeles, CA 90069-4253, USA

Grant, Steve (Athlete, Football Player)
20134 SW 123rd Dr
Miami, FL 33177-5201, USA

Grant, Susannah (Director, Writer)
c/o Risa Gertner *Creative Artists Agency (CAA-LA)*
2000 Avenue of the Stars Ste 100
Los Angeles, CA 90067-4705, USA

Grant, Tom (Athlete, Baseball Player)
36 Millville Rd
Mendon, MA 01756-1231, USA

Grant, Toni (Misc)
610 S Ardmore Ave
Los Angeles, CA 90005-2322, USA

Grant, Travis (Athlete, Basketball Player)
3314 Pointe Bleue Ct
Decatur, GA 30034-5118, USA

Grant, Wally (Athlete, Hockey Player)
4853 Lone Oak Ct
Ann Arbor, MI 48108-8575, USA

Grant, Wesley (Athlete, Football Player)
3870 Crenshaw Blvd Apt 926
Los Angeles, CA 90008-1837, USA

Grantham, Larry (Athlete, Football Player)
1971 Tissington Dr
Horn Lake, MS 38637-3752, USA

Granville, Billy (Athlete, Football Player)
PO Box 3426
Sugar Land, TX 77487-3307, USA

Grapenthin, Dick (Athlete, Baseball Player)
5040 170th Ave
Linn Grove, IA 51033-8023, USA

Grasmanis, Paul (Athlete, Football Player)
1073 Watkins Creek Dr
Franklin, TN 37067-7830, USA

Grasmick, Lou (Athlete, Baseball Player)
6715 Quad Ave
Rosedale, MD 21237-2406, USA

Grass, Darren (Athlete, Baseball Player, Olympic Athlete)
1086 174th St
Hammond, WI 54015-4831, USA

Grass, Gunter (Nobel Prize Laureate)
Lubeck 23552, GERMANY

Grass, Gunther
Glockengiesserstr. 21
Lubeck D-23552, GERMANY

Grassie, Karen (Actor)
PO Box 913
Pacific Palisades, CA 90272-0913, USA

Grassle, Karen (Actor)
2646 Francisco Way
El Cerrito, CA 94530-1531, USA

Grassroots, The
108 E Matilija St
Ojai, CA 93023-2639

Grata, Enrique (Actor)
c/o Staff Member *Univision*
605 3rd Ave Fl 12
New York, NY 10158-0034, USA

Grate, Carl (Athlete, Football Player)
205 Wind Ship Ln
Woodstock, GA 30189-5286, USA

Grate, Don (Athlete, Basketball Player)
1245 NW 203rd St
Miami, FL 33169-2312, USA

Grate, Don (Athlete, Baseball Player)
1245 NW 203rd St
Miami, FL 33169-2312, USA

Grater, Mark (Athlete, Baseball Player)
1136 Indiana Ave
Monaca, PA 15061-2025, USA

Graterol, Belker (Athlete, Baseball Player)
2301 Lakeland Hills Blvd
Lakeland, FL 33805-2909, USA

Gratham, Larry (Athlete, Football Player)
1971 Tissington Dr
Horn Lake, MS 38637-3752, USA

Gratton, Chris (Athlete, Hockey Player)
8801 Fazio Ct
Tampa, FL 33647-2292, USA

Gratton, Gilles (Athlete, Hockey Player)
20 Av Highlands
Lasalle, QC H8R 3N1, Canada

Gratton, Norm (Athlete, Hockey Player)
2144 De Maricourt St
Montreal, QC H4E 1W1, Canada

Grau, Shirley Ann (Writer)
12 Nassau Dr
Metairie, LA 70005-4434, USA

Grausman, Philip (Artist)
21 Barnes Rd
Washington, CT 06793-1402, USA

Gravel, Maurice R (Mike) (Ex-Senator)
3133 Frontera Way Apt 341
Burlingame, CA 94010-5767, USA

Graveline, Duane E (Astronaut)
494 Pleasant St
Island Pond, VT 05846-9738, USA

Gravelle, Gordon (Athlete, Football Player)
2208 Cordoba Ct
Antioch, CA 94509-5861, USA

Gravelle, Leo (Athlete, Hockey Player)
70 Rue De La Futaie Apt 725
Gatineau, QC J8T 8S2, Canada

Gravelle, Louisa (Stylist)
c/o Staff Member *Solo Artists*
2148 Federal Ave
Los Angeles, CA 90025-5327, USA

Graves, Adam (Athlete, Hockey Player)
c/o Staff Member *New York Rangers*
2 Pennsylvania Plz Rm 2200
New York, NY 10001, USA

Graves, Alex (Producer)
c/o Staff Member *International Creative Management (ICM-LA)*
10250 Constellation Blvd Fl 7
Los Angeles, CA 90067-6207, USA

Graves, Danny (Athlete, Baseball Player)
5041 Rishley Run Way
Mount Dora, FL 32757-8010, USA

Graves, Denyce (Opera Singer)

Graves, Denyce (Opera Singer)
165 W 57th St
New York, NY 10019-2201, USA

Graves, Earl (Athlete, Basketball Player)
123 Random Farms Dr
Chappaqua, NY 10514-1018, USA

Graves, Earl G (Publisher)
130 5th Ave
New York, NY 10011-4306, USA

Graves, Ernest Jr (General)
2328 S Nash St
Arlington, VA 22202-1548, USA

Graves, Harold N Jr (Government Official, Journalist)
4816 Grantham Ave
Chevy Chase, MD 20815-5538, USA

Graves, Hilliard (Athlete, Hockey Player)
100 Simmonds Dr
Dartmouth, NS B3B 1N9, Canada

Graves, Marsharne (Athlete, Football Player)
7544 E Hannibal Cir
Mesa, AZ 85207-4824, USA

Graves, Michael (Architect)
341 Nassau St
Princeton, NJ 08540-4602, USA

Graves, Ray (Athlete, Coach, Football Coach, Football Player)
420 Bay Ave Apt 821
Clearwater, FL 33756-5249, USA

Graves, Richard G (General)
12069 Sage Hollow Cir
Kamas, UT 84036-9348, USA

Graves, Rory (Athlete, Football Player)
7585 Shadow Wood Dr
Jonesboro, GA 30236-7302, USA

Graves, Rupert (Actor)
c/o Barry McPherson *Agency for the Performing Arts (APA-LA)*
405 S Beverly Dr Ste 500
Beverly Hills, CA 90212-4425, USA

Graves, Sam (Congressman, Politician)
1415 Longworth Hob
Washington, DC 20515-2306, USA

Graves, Tom (Athlete, Football Player)
1902 Montclair Ave
Norfolk, VA 23523-2322, USA

Graves, Tom (Congressman, Politician)
1113 Longworth Hob
Washington, DC 20515-0401, USA

Graves, White (Athlete, Football Player)
2610 Birchwood Dr
Monroe, LA 71201-2337, USA

Gravitte, Beau (Actor)
10100 Santa Monica Blvd Ste 2500
Los Angeles, CA 90067-4116, USA

Gray, Alasdair J (Writer)
2 Marchmont Terrace
Glasgow G12 9LT, SCOTLAND

Gray, Alec (Actor)
c/o Delaney Andrews *Strategic Talent Group*
4804 Laurel Canyon Blvd # 149
Valley Village, CA 91607-3717, USA

Gray, Alfred M Jr (General)
6317 Chaucer View Cir
Alexandria, VA 22304-3548, USA

Gray, Billy (Actor)
19612 Grand View Dr
Topanga, CA 90290-3353, USA

Gray, C Boyden (Government Official)
2445 M St NW
Washington, DC 20037-1435, USA

Gray, Coleen (Actor)
2337 Roscomare Rd # 2-112
Los Angeles, CA 90077-1854, USA

Gray, Colleen
2337 Roscomare Rd # 2-112
Los Angeles, CA 90077-1854

Gray, Dave (Athlete, Baseball Player)
PO Box 13861
Ogden, UT 84412-3861, USA

Gray, David (Musician, Songwriter)
c/o Rob Holden *Mondo Management*
26-32 Voltaire Rd #2D
London SW6 6DH, UNITED KINGDOM (UK)

Gray, Dick (Athlete, Baseball Player)
503 S Hampton St
Anaheim, CA 92804-2233, USA

Gray, Dobie (Musician)
3807 Central Pike
Hermitage, TN 37076-3408, USA

Gray, Doug (Musician)
315 S Beverly Dr Ste 407
Beverly Hills, CA 90212-4301, USA

Gray, Duicie (Actor)
31 Coventry St
London W1V 8AS, UNITED KINGDOM (UK)

Gray, Dulcie
44 Brunswick Gardens #2
London W8 4AN, ENGLAND

Gray, D'Wayne (General)
3423 Barger Dr
Falls Church, VA 22044-1202, USA

Gray, Earnest (Athlete, Football Player)
6746 Kirby Oaks Ln
Memphis, TN 38119-8328, USA

Gray, Ed (Basketball Player)
Toyota Center 2 E Greenway Plaza
Houston, TX 77046, USA

Gray, Erin (Actor, Model)
10921 Alta View Dr
Studio City, CA 91604-3904, USA

Gray, F Gary (Director)
c/o Staff Member *Management 360*
9111 Wilshire Blvd
Beverly Hills, CA 90210-5508, USA

Gray, Fred Sr (Attorney, Attorney General, General)
1005 E Lakeshore Dr
Tuskegee, AL 36083-1935, USA

Gray, Gary (Athlete, Basketball Player)
7000 N MO Pac Expy Ste 140
Austin, TX 78731-2627, USA

Gray, Gary G. (Athlete, Baseball Player)
PO Box 98
La Place, LA 70069-0098, USA

Gray, George W (Misc)
Juniper House Furzehill
Wimborne, Dorset BH21 4HD, UNITED KINGDOM (UK)

Gray, Harry B (Misc)
1415 E California Blvd
Pasadena, CA 91106-4101, USA

Gray, Hector (Athlete, Football Player)
751 Dove Ave
Miami Springs, FL 33166-3203, USA

Gray, James (Director, Writer)
c/o Todd Feldman *Creative Artists Agency (CAA-LA)*
2000 Avenue of the Stars Ste 100
Los Angeles, CA 90067-4705, USA

Gray, Jeff (Athlete, Baseball Player)
17634 Esprit Dr
Tampa, FL 33647-2505, USA

Gray, Jim (Actor)
3325 Blair Dr
Los Angeles, CA 90068-1409, USA

Gray, John (Writer)
20 Sunnyside Ave # A130
Mill Valley, CA 94941-1933, USA

Gray, John (Johnny) (Athlete, Baseball Player)
10645 Greenbriar Ct
Boca Raton, FL 33498-1644, USA

Gray, Johnnie (Athlete, Football Player)
220 Short St
Wrightstown, WI 54180-1154, USA

Gray, Ken (Athlete, Football Player)
1114 Willow
Kingsland, TX 78639-3864, USA

Gray, Linda (Actor)
PO Box 5064
Sherman Oaks, CA 91413-5064, USA

Gray, Lorenzo (Athlete, Baseball Player)
2680 E 19th St Apt 1
Signal Hill, CA 90755-1106, USA

Gray, Macy (Musician, Songwriter)
c/o Jim Morey *Morey Management Group*
1100 Glendon Ave Ste 1100
Los Angeles, CA 90024-3515, USA

Gray, Mel (Athlete, Football Player)
137 Winterset Pass
Williamsburg, VA 23188-1758, USA

Gray, Michael
9294 Civic Center Dr
Beverly Hills, CA 90210-3714

Gray, Michael (Stylist)
c/o Staff Member *Artists Management, Inc*
11906 Lawler St
Los Angeles, CA 90066-2010, USA

Gray, Moses (Athlete, Football Player)
1331 Aggie Ln
Indianapolis, IN 46260-4096, USA

Gray, Natalie (Actor, Writer)
c/o Monique Moss *Warren Cowan & Associates PR*
8899 Beverly Blvd Ste 918
Los Angeles, CA 90048-2427, USA

Gray, Nel (Athlete, Football Player)
4507 Skyline Dr
Rockford, IL 61107-3718, USA

Gray, Scott (Cartoonist)
c/o Staff Member *Marvel Entertainment, Inc.*
135 W 50th St Fl 7
New York, NY 10020-1201, USA

Gray, Spaiding (Artist, Writer)
22 Wooster St
New York, NY 10013-2300, USA

Gray, Stuart (Athlete, Basketball Player)
909 Andover Grn
Lexington, KY 40509-2930, USA

Gray, Sylvester (Athlete, Basketball Player)
4929 Bilrae Cir S
Millington, TN 38053-1612, USA

Gray, Tamrya (Actor)
c/o Staff Member *19 Entertainment*
33/32 Ransomes Dock 35-37 Parkgate Rd
London SW11 4NP, UK

Gray, Tamyra (Musician)
c/o Jeff Frasco *Creative Artists Agency (CAA-LA)*
2000 Avenue of the Stars Ste 100
Los Angeles, CA 90067-4705, USA

Gray, Theordore G (Ted) (Athlete, Baseball Player)
401 E Linton Blvd Apt 469
Delray Beach, FL 33483-5086, USA

Gray, Tim (Athlete, Football Player)
6109 Crane St
Houston, TX 77026-4234, USA

Gray, Torrian (Athlete, Football Player)
1045 Roselle Ave
Lakeland, FL 33805-4146, USA

Gray, Vincent (Governor, Politician)
One Judiciary Square 441 Forth St NW
Washington, DC 20001, USA

Gray, William H III (Misc)
500 E 62nd St
New York, NY 10065-8314, USA

Gray Cabey, Noah (Actor)
c/o Blake Bandy *Kritzer Levine Wilkins Entertainment*
11872 La Grange Ave Fl 1
Los Angeles, CA 90025-5283, USA

Graybiel, Ann M (Scientist)
Cognitive Sci Dept
Cambridge, MA 2139, USA

Grayden, Sprague (Actor)
c/o Katie Rhodes *Untitled Entertainment (LA)*
350 S Beverly Dr Ste 200
Beverly Hills, CA 90212-4819, USA

Graydon, Joe
1870 Caminito Del Cielo
Glendale, CA 91208-3049

Graye, Devon (Actor)
c/o Adam Griffin *Kritzer Levine Wilkins Entertainment*
11872 La Grange Ave Fl 1
Los Angeles, CA 90025-5283, USA

Grayer, Jeff (Athlete, Basketball Player)
260 E Ruth Ave
Flint, MI 48505-2749, USA

Grayhm, Steven (Actor, Director, Writer)
c/o Adam Griffin *Kritzer Levine Wilkins Entertainment*
425 N Robertson Blvd
West Hollywood, CA 90048-1735, USA

Graynor, Ari (Actor)
c/o Jill Kaplan *Principal Entertainment (NY)*
130 W 42nd St Ste 614
New York, NY 10036-7804, USA

Graysmith, Robert (Cartoonist, Editor)
901 Mission St
San Francisco, CA 94103-2905, USA

Grayson, C Jackson Jr (Educator, Government Official)
123 N Post Oak Ln
Houston, TX 77024-7715, USA

Grayson, David Lee (Athlete, Football Player)
4012 Ibis St
San Diego, CA 92103-1825, USA

Grayson, Mel (Stylist)
c/o Staff Member *St Rage & Company*
270 N Canon Dr # 1611
Beverly Hills, CA 90210-5323, USA

Grayson Sr, Dave (Athlete, Football Player)
7116 Los Soneto Ct
San Diego, CA 92114-5918, USA

Gray-Stanford, Jason (Actor)
c/o Scott Zimmerman *Evolution Entertainment (LA)*
901 N Highland Ave
Los Angeles, CA 90038-2412, USA

Grazer, Brian (Producer)
c/o Staff Member *Imagine Films Entertainment*
1925 Century Park E Ste 800
Los Angeles, CA 90067-2749, USA

Grazia, Eugene (Athlete, Hockey Player)
2421 NE 49th St
Fort Lauderdale, FL 33308-4788, USA

Graziadei, Michael (Actor)
c/o Amy Abell *Innovative Artists (LA)*
1505 10th St
Santa Monica, CA 90401-2805, USA

Graziani, Ariel (Soccer Player)
3550 Stevens Creek Blvd Ste 200
San Jose, CA 95117-1031, USA

Grazioso, Claudia (Producer, Writer)
c/o Nicole Clemens *International Creative Management (ICM-LA)*
10250 Constellation Blvd Fl 7
Los Angeles, CA 90067-6207, USA

Grazzola, Kenneth E (Publisher)
1221 Avenue of the Americas
New York, NY 10020-1001, USA

Grba, Eli (Athlete, Baseball Player)
106 Fox Run
Florence, AL 35633-1465, USA

Grbac, Elvis (Athlete, Football Player)
17361 Coldwater Trl
Chagrin Falls, OH 44023-1413, USA

Greacen, Bob (Athlete, Basketball Player)
333 Reeder St
Easton, PA 18042-7663, USA

Greason, Bill (Athlete, Baseball Player)
4536 Hillman Dr SW
Birmingham, AL 35221-1816, USA

Greason, Staci
8831 Sunset Blvd # 304
Los Angeles, CA 90069

Greason, William (Baseball Player)
4536 Hillman Dr SW
Birmingham, AL 35221-1816, USA

Great Big Sea (Musician)
733-735 N Main
Ann Arbor, MI 48104-1030

Greaves, Gary (Athlete, Football Player)
8221 SW 176th St
Palmetto Bay, FL 33157-6147, USA

Grebeck, Craig (Athlete, Baseball Player)
27856 Homestead Rd
Laguna Niguel, CA 92677-3763, USA

Grebenshchikov, Boris (Musician)
2 Marata St #3
Saint Petersburg, RUSSIA

Grechko, Georgi M (Cosmonaut)
Moskovskoi Oblasti
Syvisdny Goroduk 141160, RUSSIA

Greco, Buddy (Musician)
5 Monte Verde Way
Palm Desert, CA 92260, USA

Greco, Emilio (Artist)
Viale Cortina d'Ampezzo 132
Rome 135, ITALY

Greco, Juliette (Actor, Musician)
37 Rue Marbeuf
Paris 75008, FRANCE

Greco, Michael (Actor)
c/o Pedro Pinto *Gregg Millard Management*
38 Barton House Sable St
London N1 2AF, UK

Greczyn, Alice (Actor)
c/o Adam Griffin *Kritzer Levine Wilkins Entertainment*
11872 La Grange Ave Fl 1
Los Angeles, CA 90025-5283, USA

Greeley, Andrew
6030 S Ellis Ave
Chicago, IL 60637-2608

Greeley, Andrew M (Andy) (Writer)
6030 S Ellis Ave
Chicago, IL 60637-2608, USA

Green, A C (Athlete, Basketball Player)
904 Silver Spur Rd
Rolling Hills Estates, CA 90274-3800, USA

Green, Adolph
211 Central Park W # 19E
New York, NY 10024-6020

Green, Ahman (Athlete, Football Player)
1750 Limestone Trl
De Pere, WI 54115-7973, USA

Green, A.J. (Football Player)
c/o Tom Condon *CAA - St. Louis*
222 S Central Ave Ste 1008
Saint Louis, MO 63105-3509, USA

Green, Al (Musician)
c/o Staff Member *Shore Fire Media*
32 Court St Fl 16
Brooklyn, NY 11201-4441, USA

Green, Al (Musician, Religious Leader, Songwriter, Writer)
PO Box 456
Millington, TN 38083-0456, USA

Green, Al (Congressman, Politician)
220.1 Rayburn Hob
Washington, DC 20515-0001, USA

Green, Andy (Athlete, Baseball Player)
1025 Lakefront Dr
Lexington, KY 40517-2658, USA

Green, Anthony (Athlete, Football Player)
9611 Wesland Cir
Randallstown, MD 21133-2043, USA

Green, B Eric (Athlete, Football Player)
13131 Luntz Point Ln
Windermere, FL 34786-5802, USA

Green, Barrett (Athlete, Football Player)
1004 Green Pine Blvd Apt D1
West Palm Beach, FL 33409-7013, USA

Green, Barry (Misc)
7615 Zionsville Rd
Indianapolis, IN 46268-2174, USA

Green, Benny (Musician)
211 Thompson St Apt 1D
New York, NY 10012-1335, USA

Green, Boyce (Athlete, Football Player)
18812 Parting Oaks Ln
Davidson, NC 28036-8801, USA

Green, Brian Austin (Actor, Director, Producer)
c/o Tracy Samuels *Interlink Management*
19528 Ventura Blvd
Tarzana, CA 91356-2917, USA

Green, Cee Lo (Artist, Musician)
c/o Cara Lewis *WmE2 (WMA-NY)*
1325 Avenue of the Americas
New York, NY 10019-6026, USA

Green, Charlie (Stylist)
c/o Staff Member *Bryan Bantry*
900 Broadway Ste 400
New York, NY 10003-1239, USA

Green, Charlie (Athlete, Football Player)
255 S Kyrene Rd Unit 214
Chandler, AZ 85226-4460, USA

Green, Chris (Athlete, Baseball Player)
3417 59th Ave W
Bradenton, FL 34210-3525, USA

Green, Chris (Athlete, Football Player)
331 Patio Village Ter
Weston, FL 33326-1622, USA

Green, Cleveland (Athlete, Football Player)
5537 Robinson Road Ext
Jackson, MS 39204-4142, USA

Green, Cornell (Athlete, Football Player)
2106 Trinidad Dr
Dallas, TX 75232-2750, USA

Green, Dallas (Athlete, Baseball Player, Coach)
846 Conowingo Rd
Conowingo, MD 21918-1307, USA

Green, Darrell (Athlete, Football Player)
20998 Rostormel Ct
Ashburn, VA 20147-4780, USA

Green, David (Director)
76 Oxford St
London W1N 0AX, UNITED KINGDOM (UK)

Green, David (Athlete, Baseball Player)
Colinia Managua Grupo H47
Managua, Nicaragua

Green, David E (Misc)
5339 Brody Dr
Madison, WI 53705-5425, USA

Green, David E (Athlete, Football Player)
8311 Pat Blvd
Tampa, FL 33615-1810, USA

Green, David Gordon (Director, Producer, Writer)
c/o Staff Member *The Gotham Group Inc*
9255 W Sunset Blvd Ste 515
Los Angeles, CA 90069-3308, USA

Green, David T (Inventor)
150 Glover Ave
Norwalk, CT 06850-1308, USA

Green, Debbie (Athlete, Volleyball Player)
239 5th St
Seal Beach, CA 90740-6116, USA

Green, Dennis (Athlete, Coach, Football Coach, Football Player)
3930 Torrey Hill Ln
San Diego, CA 92130-1289, USA

Green, Dick (Athlete, Baseball Player)
3924 Ridgemoor Dr
Rapid City, SD 57702-5328, USA

Green, Donnie (Athlete, Football Player)
PO Box 685
Hagerstown, MD 21741-0685, USA

Green, E.G. (Athlete, Football Player)
1504 Whitehall Dr Apt 205
Davie, FL 33324-6608, USA

Green, Eric (Athlete, Football Player)
2306 E Cathy Ct
Gilbert, AZ 85296-3932, USA

Green, Ernie (Athlete, Football Player)
424 Rue Marseille
Dayton, OH 45429-1878, USA

Green, Eva (Actor)
c/o Angharad Wood *Tavistock Wood Management*
32 Tavistock St
London WC2B 5HA, UK

Green, Gary (Athlete, Baseball Player)
939 Kennebec St
Pittsburgh, PA 15217-2604, USA

Green, Gary F (Athlete, Football Player)
16330 Walnut Creek Dr
San Antonio, TX 78247-5636, USA

Green, Gaston (Athlete, Football Player)
2061 Vallejo Dr
Tustin, CA 92782-8619, USA

Green, Gene (Congressman, Politician)
2470 Rayburn Hob
Washington, DC 20515-4327, USA

Green, Gerald (Writer)
88 Arrowhead Trl
New Canaan, CT 06840-3441, USA

Green, Hamilton (Prime Minister)
Plot D Lodge
Georgetown, GUYANA

Green, Harold (Athlete, Football Player)
145 Folk Rd
Blythewood, SC 29016-9031, USA

Green, Howard (Physicist)
Physiology & Biophysics Dept
Boston, MA 2115, USA

Green, Hubert (Athlete, Golfer)
5141 Gulf Dr
Panama City, FL 32408-6903, USA

Green, Hugh (Athlete, Football Player)
4758 Highway 61
Fayette, MS 39069-5422, USA

Green, Jacob (Athlete, Football Player)
4921 Whistling Straits Loop
College Station, TX 77845-3866, USA

Green, Jacquez (Athlete, Football Player)
5102 Madison Lakes Cir W
Davie, FL 33328-4519, USA

Green, Janine (Actor)
c/o David Sweeney *Sweeney Management*
8755 Lookout Mountain Ave
Los Angeles, CA 90046-1861, USA

Green, Jarvis (Athlete, Football Player)
10438 Dunsford Dr
Lone Tree, CO 80124-9796, USA

Green, Jeff (Race Car Driver)
6001 Haas Way Kannapolis Gateway Business Park
Kannapolis, NC 28081, USA

Green, Jeff (Athlete, Basketball Player)
c/o Staff Member *Oklahoma City Thunder*
Two Leadership Square 211 N Robinson Ave, Suite 300
Oklahoma City, OK 73102, USA

Green, Jenna Leigh (Actor)
c/o Aaron Kogan *Sovereign Talent Group*
8421 Wilshire Blvd Ste 200
Beverly Hills, CA 90211-3204, USA

Green, Jessie (Athlete, Football Player)
RR 3 Box 1208
Mount Pleasant, TX 75455, USA

Green, Jimmy (Athlete, Golfer)
1338 Gatewood Dr
Auburn, AL 36830-7702, USA

Green, John (Athlete, Football Player)
1078 Misty Morn Cir
Spring Hill, TN 37174-7404, USA

Green, John M (Johnny) (Athlete, Basketball Player)
9 Susan Ln
Dix Hills, NY 11746-5140, USA

Green, John N (Jack) Jr (Cinematographer)
516 Esplanade Apt E
Redondo Beach, CA 90277-4077, USA

Green, Jordan-Claire (Actor)
c/o Staff Member *Cunningham Escott Slevin & Doherty (CESD-LA)*
10635 Santa Monica Blvd Ste 130
Los Angeles, CA 90025-8306, USA

Green, Kate (Writer)
1540 Broadway
New York, NY 10036-4039, USA

Green, Ken (Athlete, Golfer)
4520 Feivel Rd Apt 56
West Palm Beach, FL 33417-8078, USA

Green, Lamar (Athlete, Basketball Player)
PO Box 490208
Chicago, IL 60649-0208, USA

Green, Lenny (Athlete, Baseball Player)
18693 Sunset St
Detroit, MI 48234-2043, USA

Green, Leonard I (Business Person)
30 Hunter Ln
Camp Hill, PA 17011-2400, USA

Green, Litterial (Athlete, Basketball Player)
1500 N Opdyke Rd
Auburn Hills, MI 48326-2653, USA

Green, Lucinda (Misc)
Appleshaw House Andover
Hants, UNITED KINGDOM (UK)

Green, Mark (Race Car Driver)
345 Marblerock Way
Lexington, KY 40503-6321, USA

Green, Mark A (Athlete, Football Player)
274 Brunswick Dr
Buffalo Grove, IL 60089-6759, USA

Green, Mark J (Activist, Attorney General)
43 E 19th St Fl 3
New York, NY 10003-1304, USA

Green, Maurice Spurgeon (Editor)
Hermitage Twyford House
Hants, UNITED KINGDOM (UK)

Green, Michael (Cinematographer)
11 Stevenson Ln
Upper Saddle River, NJ 07458-2136, USA

Green, Mike (Athlete, Football Player)
15271 Peach St
Chino Hills, CA 91709-2565, USA

Green, Pat (Musician)
c/o Staff Member *WmE2 (WMA-TN)*
1600 Division St Ste 300
Nashville, TN 37203-2755, USA

Green, Patricia (Producer, Writer)
c/o David Greenblatt *Key Creatives*
1800 N Highland Ave Fl 5
Los Angeles, CA 90028-4523, USA

Green, Paul (Athlete, Football Player)
1635 N Formosa Ave Apt 208
Los Angeles, CA 90046-3993, USA

Green, Pumpsie (Athlete, Baseball Player)
2105 Harper St
El Cerrito, CA 94530-1724, USA

Green, Ray (Athlete, Football Player)
180 Dunnemann Ave
Charleston, SC 29403-3510, USA

Green, Rick (Athlete, Hockey Player)
RR 1
Peterborough, ON K9J 6X2, Canada

Green, Rick (Producer)
c/o Glenn Cockburn *Meridian Artists*
2 College St Suite 207
Toronto, ON M5G 1K3, Canada

Green, Rickey (Athlete, Basketball Player)
20584 Tyler Dr
Lynwood, IL 60411-8571, USA

Green, Robin (Writer)
c/o Staff Member *Broder Webb Chervin Silbermann Agency, The (BWCS)*
10250 Constellation Blvd
Los Angeles, CA 90067-6200, USA

Green, Robson (Actor)
c/o Staff Member *Coastal Productions*
25B Broadchare The Quayside
Newcastle-Upon-Tyne NE1 3DQ, UNITED KINGDOM (UK)

Green, Sarah (Producer)
c/o Staff Member *International Creative Management (ICM-LA)*
10250 Constellation Blvd Fl 7
Los Angeles, CA 90067-6207, USA

Green, Scarborough (Athlete, Baseball Player)
2020 Crimson Meadows Dr
O Fallon, MO 63366-4186, USA

Green, Seth (Actor, Comedian, Producer)
c/o Staff Member *Koopman Management*
851 Oreo Pl
Pacific Palisades, CA 90272-2457, USA

Green, Shawn (Athlete, Baseball Player)
1430 Village Way
Santa Ana, CA 92705-4752, USA

Green, Sidney (Basketball Player, Coach)
Athletic Dept
Boca Raton, FL 33431, USA

Green, Skylar (Athlete, Football Player)
3121 Thomas Ave
Dallas, TX 75204-2605, USA

Green, Steve (Athlete, Basketball Player)
942 Round Table Ct
Indianapolis, IN 46260-4923, USA

Green, Suzy (Athlete, Golfer)
26006 Carol Ave
Franklin, MI 48025-1107, USA

Green, Tammie (Athlete, Golfer)
4990 Township Road 147 NE
Somerset, OH 43783-9753, USA

Green, Timothy J (Tim) (Athlete, Football Player, Sportscaster)
1194 Greenfield Ln
Skaneateles, NY 13152-9666, USA

Green, Tom (Actor, Comedian)
c/o Howard Lapides *Core/Lapides Lear Entertainment*
14724 Ventura Blvd PH
Sherman Oaks, CA 91403-3513, USA

Green, Travis (Athlete, Hockey Player)
2 Riverside
Irvine, CA 92602-0903, USA

Green, Trent (Athlete, Football Player)
11223 Hunters Pond Rd
Creve Coeur, MO 63141-7672, USA

Green, Tyler (Athlete, Baseball Player)
536 Championship Dr
Harleysville, PA 19438-2177, USA

Green, Van (Athlete, Football Player)
311 Leta St
Auburndale, FL 33823-4313, USA

Green, Victor (Athlete, Football Player)
3443 Jamont Blvd
Alpharetta, GA 30022-7629, USA

Green, Vivian (Actor)
c/o Staff Member *WmE2 (Endeavor-LA)*
9601 Wilshire Blvd Fl 3
Beverly Hills, CA 90210-5219, USA

Green, Willie (Athlete, Football Player)
152 Farmington Rd
Shelby, NC 28150-8698, USA

Green, Woody (Athlete, Football Player)
702 SE Palmblad Pl
Gresham, OR 97080-1496, USA

Green, Yatil (Athlete, Football Player)
2000 Island Blvd Apt 3002
Aventura, FL 33160-4966, USA

Green Day (Music Group)
c/o John Dehais *Pat's Management Company*
543 Encinitas Blvd Ste 101
Encinitas, CA 92024-3744, USA

Greenaway, Peter (Director)
387B King St
London W6 9NH, UNITED KINGDOM (UK)

Greenberg, Adam (Cinematographer)
232 N Canon Dr
Beverly Hills, CA 90210-5302, USA

Greenberg, Adam (Athlete, Baseball Player)
79 Fernwood Dr
Guilford, CT 06437-2367, USA

Greenberg, Alan C (Financier)
383 Madison Ave
New York, NY 10017-3217, USA

Greenberg, Bernard (Biologist, Scientist)
1463 E 55th Pl
Chicago, IL 60637-1875, USA

Greenberg, Bryan (Actor)
c/o Ellen Meyer *Ellen Meyer Management*
8899 Beverly Blvd Ste 612
West Hollywood, CA 90048-2429, USA

Greenberg, Carl (Journalist)
6001 Canterbury Dr
Culver City, CA 90230-6850, USA

Greenberg, Evan (Business Person)
70 Pine St
New York, NY 10270-0001, USA

Greenberg, Jack (Attorney, Attorney General, Educator, General)
118 Riverside Dr
New York, NY 10024-3708, USA

Greenberg, Maurice R (Business Person)
70 Pine St
New York, NY 10270-0001, USA

Greenberg, Mike (Sportscaster, Television Host)
c/o Lou Oppenheim *Headline Media Management*
888 7th Ave Ste 503
New York, NY 10106-0501, USA

Greenberg, Morton I (Judge)
402 E State St
Trenton, NJ 08608-1507, USA

Greenberg, Peter (Television Host)
c/o Staff Member *Today Show, The*
30 Rockefeller Plz
New York, NY 10112-0015, USA

Greenberg, Robbie S (Cinematographer)
11 Reef St
Marina Del Rey, CA 90292-6725, USA

Greenberg, Ross (Producer, Writer)
c/o Staff Member *Shed Media US*
3800 Barham Blvd Ste 410
Los Angeles, CA 90068-1042, USA

Greenberg, Sarah T (Stylist)
180 W End Ave Apt 17B
New York, NY 10023-4936, USA

Greenberg, Susin Ross (Stylist)
1262 Deerfield Pl
Highland Park, IL 60035-3062, USA

Greenblatt, Stephen J (Writer)
English Dept
Cambridge, MA 2138, USA

Greenblatt, William
30710 Monte Lado Dr
Malibu, CA 90265-3128

Greenburg, Dan (Writer)
323 E 50th St
New York, NY 10022-7901, USA

Greenburg, Paul (Journalist)
5900 Scenic Dr
Little Rock, AR 72207-2833, USA

Greenbush, Rachel Lindsay (Actor)
3500 W Olive Ave Ste 1400
Burbank, CA 91505-5512, USA

Greenbush, Sidney Robin (Actor)
3500 W Olive Ave Ste 1400
Burbank, CA 91505-5512, USA

Greene, A J (Athlete, Football Player)
8401 Castlebay Dr
Charlotte, NC 28277-1879, USA

Greene, Al (Athlete, Baseball Player)
18294 Marlowe St
Detroit, MI 48235-2762, USA

Greene, Ashley (Actor)
c/o Staff Member *McKeon-Myones Management*
3500 W Olive Ave Ste 770
Burbank, CA 91505-5527, USA

Greene, Biloah (Actor)
c/o Vincent Cirrincione *Vincent Cirrincione Associates*
1516 N Fairfax Ave
Los Angeles, CA 90046-2608, USA

Greene, Bob (Fitness Expert)
c/o Tyler Delaney *Westport Entertainment Associates*
1700 Post Rd Ste C15
Fairfield, CT 06824-5726, USA

Greene, Brian (Mathematician, Physicist)
Physics Dept
New York, NY 10027, USA

Greene, Charles E (Charlie) (Athlete, Track Athlete)
PO Box 6938
Lincoln, NE 68506-0938, USA

Greene, Charlie (Athlete, Baseball Player)
10760 S Kendale Blvd
Miami, FL 33176-3459, USA

Greene, David (Actor)
c/o Lenore Zerman *Liberman/Zerman Management*
252 N Larchmont Blvd Ste 200
Los Angeles, CA 90004-3754, USA

Greene, Dawn (Philanthropist)
950 3rd Ave
New York, NY 10022-2705, USA

Greene, Ellen (Musician)
1505 10th St
Santa Monica, CA 90401-2805, USA

Greene, Graham (Actor)
c/o Susan Smith *Susan Smith Company, The*
1344 N Wetherly Dr
Los Angeles, CA 90069-1817, USA

Greene, Jack (Musician)
PO Box 428
Portland, TN 37148-0428, USA

Greene, Jack P (Historian)
1974 Division Rd
East Greenwich, RI 02818-1211, USA

Greene, James
60 Pope's Grove Twickenham
Middlesex, ENGLAND

Greene, Jennifer (Stylist)
c/o Celebrity Stylist *Oliver Piro Inc*
725 Riverside Dr Apt 3A
New York, NY 10031-2460, USA

Greene, Joe (Athlete, Football Player)
PO Box 270953
Flower Mound, TX 75027-0953, USA

Greene, John (Athlete, Football Player)
16351 Rotunda Dr Apt 173
Dearborn, MI 48120-2005, USA

Greene, Julie (Stylist)
c/o Staff Member *Fifty8 Artists*
58 W Huron St
Chicago, IL 60654-3806, USA

Greene, Kenneth E (Ken) (Athlete, Football Player)
5569 Nevil Pt
Brentwood, TN 37027-8281, USA

Greene, Kevin (Athlete, Football Player)
3448 Amber Ln
Green Bay, WI 54311-9003, USA

Greene, Khalil (Athlete, Baseball Player)
102 Banister Ct
Greer, SC 29650-2701, USA

Greene, Leonard M (Inventor)
1010 Greacen Point Rd
Mamaroneck, NY 10543-4609, USA

Greene, Maurice (Athlete, Track Athlete)
c/o Staff Member *Exposure Marketing Group*
348 Hauser Blvd Apt 414
Los Angeles, CA 90036-5590, USA

Greene, Michele (Actor, Musician)
PO Box 382
Skyforest, CA 92385-0382, USA

Greene, Michelle
PO Box 382
Skyforest, CA 92385-0382

Greene, Pat (Writer)
c/o Staff Member *Playscripts, Inc.*
450 Fashion Ave Ste 809
New York, NY 10123-0805, USA

Greene, Shecky (Actor, Comedian)
1642 S La Verne Way
Palm Springs, CA 92264-9296, USA

Greene, Todd (Baseball Player)
725 Pine Leaf Ct
Alpharetta, GA 30022-1026, USA

Greene, Todd (Athlete, Baseball Player)
725 Pine Leaf Ct
Alpharetta, GA 30022-1026, USA

Greene, Tommy (Athlete, Baseball Player)
PO Box 10
Warrington, PA 18976-0010, USA

Greene, Tony (Athlete, Football Player)
9001 Brookville Rd
Silver Spring, MD 20910-1819, USA

Greene, Tony (Athlete, Football Player)
1890 Briarcliff Cir NE Apt D
Atlanta, GA 30329-2574, USA

Greene, Willie (Athlete, Baseball Player)
1044 GA Highway 22 E
Haddock, GA 31033-2360, USA

Greenfield, James L (Journalist)
470 Park Ave Apt 9A
New York, NY 10022-1946, USA

Greenfield, Jeff (Correspondent)
820 1st St NE
Washington, DC 20002-4243, USA

Greenfield, Lauren (Director, Photographer, Producer)
2417 McKinley Ave
Venice, CA 90291-4625, USA

Greenfield, Max (Actor, Producer)
c/o Loch Powell *Leverage Management*
3030 Pennsylvania Ave
Santa Monica, CA 90404-4112, USA

Greenfield-Sanders, Timothy (Artist, Photographer)
821 Broadway Fl 4
New York, NY 10003-4702, USA

Greengard, Paul (Nobel Prize Laureate)
450 E 63rd St Apt 11J
New York, NY 10065-7934, USA

Greengrass, Jim (Athlete, Baseball Player)
232 Talking Rock Creek Pro Rd
Chatsworth, GA 30705-6895, USA

Greengrass, Paul (Director)
c/o Beth Swofford *Creative Artists Agency (CAA-LA)*
2000 Avenue of the Stars Ste 100
Los Angeles, CA 90067-4705, USA

Greenlaw, Jeff (Athlete, Hockey Player)
9213 Colberg Dr
Austin, TX 78749-4151, USA

Greenlaw, Linda (Writer)
c/o Eliot Gunner *Keppler Associates*
4350 Fairfax Dr Ste 700
Arlington, VA 22203-1620, USA

Greenlay, Mike (Athlete, Hockey Player)
c/o Staff Member *Minnesota Wild*
317 Washington St
Saint Paul, MN 55102-1667, USA

Greenlee, David (Actor)
1811 Whitley Ave Apt 800
Los Angeles, CA 90028-4960, USA

Greenspan, Alan (Economist)
1133 Connecticut Ave NW
Washington, DC 20036-4305, USA

Greenspan, Jerry (Athlete, Basketball Player)
291 County Line Rd
Riegelsville, PA 18077-9775, USA

Greenspan, Melissa (Actor)
c/o Jeff Danis *Danis, Panaro, Nist (DPN)*
9201 W Olympic Blvd
Beverly Hills, CA 90212-4605, USA

Greenstein, Jeff (Producer)
c/o Staff Member *International Creative Management (ICM-LA)*
10250 Constellation Blvd Fl 7
Los Angeles, CA 90067-6207, USA

Greenville, Georgina (Model)
188 Rue de Rivoli
Paris 75001, FRANCE

Greenwald, Milton (Misc)
Museum of Paleontology
Berkeley, CA 94720-0001, USA

Greenwalt, T Jack (Misc)
2444 Madison Rd Unit 1501
Cincinnati, OH 45208-1228, USA

Greenway, Chad (Athlete, Football Player)
39448 250th St
Mount Vernon, SD 57363-5005, USA

Greenwell, Michael L (Mike) (Athlete, Baseball Player)
18500 State Road 31
Alva, FL 33920-3016, USA

Greenwood, Bruce (Actor)
c/o Chuck Binder *Binder & Associates*
1465 Lindacrest Dr
Beverly Hills, CA 90210-2519, USA

Greenwood, Colin (Musician)
72 Spring St # 1100
New York, NY 10012-4019, USA

Greenwood, David (Athlete, Basketball Player)
PO Box 746
Chino Hills, CA 91709-0025, USA

Greenwood, Jonny (Musician)
72 Spring St # 1100
New York, NY 10012-4019, USA

Greenwood, L C H (L C) (Athlete, Football Player)
329 S Dallas Ave
Pittsburgh, PA 15208-2627, USA

Greenwood, Lee (Musician, Songwriter)
c/o Roger Neal *Neal Public Relations*
18685 Main St # A-397
Huntington Beach, CA 92648-1723, USA

Greenwood, Michael
Princes Gate1 4 Kingston House E
London, ENGLAND SW7

Greenwood, Morlon (Athlete, Football Player)
3000 Sage Rd Apt 2205
Houston, TX 77056-6327, USA

Greenwood, Norman (Misc)
Chemistry Dept
Leeds, LS2 9JT, UNITED KINGDOM (UK)

Greer, Brian (Athlete, Baseball Player)
307 Bagnall Ave
Placentia, CA 92870-1904, USA

Greer, Brodie
300 S Raymond Ave # II
Pasadena, CA 91105-2620

Greer, David S (Misc)
PO Box G
Providence, RI 02901-1678, USA

Greer, Donovan (Athlete, Football Player)
12023 Bissonnet St Apt 1511
Houston, TX 77099-1451, USA

Greer, Germaine (Writer)
29 Fernshaw Road
London SW10 0TG, UNITED KINGDOM (UK)

Greer, Gordon G (Editor)
1716 Locust St
Des Moines, IA 50309-3038, USA

Greer, Harold E (Hal) (Athlete, Basketball Player)
c/o Staff Member *Naismith Memorial Basketball Hall of Fame*
1000 W Columbus Ave
Springfield, MA 01105-2518, USA

Greer, Howard (Admiral)
2845 Granada Blvd
Coral Gables, FL 33134-6379, USA

Greer, Jim (Athlete, Football Player)
1508 E Sycamore St
Ozark, MO 65721-9436, USA

Greer, Judy (Actor)
c/o Staff Member *Principato/Young Management*
9465 Wilshire Blvd Ste 430
Beverly Hills, CA 90212-2613, USA

Greer, Kenny (Athlete, Baseball Player)
17 Hill St
Cohasset, MA 02025-2218, USA

Greer, Rusty (Athlete, Baseball Player)
4703 Patterson Ln
Colleyville, TX 76034-4507, USA

Greezyn, Alice (Actor)
c/o Staff Member *Windfall*
3000 W Alameda Ave
Burbank, CA 91523-0001, USA

Gregg, Clark (Actor)
c/o Paulette Bartlett *Paulette Bartlett Management*
3000 Olympic Blvd Ste 1364
Santa Monica, CA 90404-5073, USA

Gregg, Forrest (Athlete, Coach, Football Coach, Football Executive, Football Player)
2985 Plaza Azul
Santa Fe, NM 87507-5337, USA

Gregg, John
1/1 Punch St
Mosman, AUSTRALIA NSW 2088

Gregg, Kelly (Athlete, Football Player)
13800 Hollow Glen Rd
Edmond, OK 73013-7278, USA

Gregg, Kevin (Athlete, Baseball Player)
1907 SW Brooklane Dr
Corvallis, OR 97333-1627, USA

Gregg, Randy (Athlete, Hockey Player)
13021 104 Ave NW
Edmonton, AB T5N 0V9, Canada

Gregg, Ricky Lynn (Musician)
1103 Bell Grimes Ln
Nashville, TN 37207-1605, USA

Gregg, Stephen (Writer)
c/o Staff Member *Creative Artists Agency (CAA-LA)*
2000 Avenue of the Stars Ste 100
Los Angeles, CA 90067-4705, USA

Gregg, Stephen R (War Hero)
280 Main St Apt 310
Little Falls, NJ 07424-1375, USA

Gregg, Tommy (Athlete, Baseball Player)
10 Cambridge Ln
Sharpsburg, GA 30277-2462, USA

Gregoire, Chris (Governor, Politician)
PO Box 40002
Olympia, WA 98504-0002, USA

Gregor, Gary (Athlete, Basketball Player)
444 Dove Ridge Rd
Columbia, SC 29223-5589, USA

Gregorian, Vartan (Educator)
President's Office 437 Madison Ave
New York, NY 10022, USA

Gregorio, Rose (Actor)
6500 Wilshire Blvd Ste 2200
Los Angeles, CA 90048-4942, USA

Gregorio, Tom (Athlete, Baseball Player)
66 McArthur Ave
Staten Island, NY 10312-1925, USA

Gregorios, Metropolitan Paulos M (Religious Leader)
PO Box 98
Kottayam, Kerala 686001, INDIA

Gregory, Adam (Actor)
c/o Beverly Strong *Strong Management*
3532 Hayden Ave
Culver City, CA 90232-2413, USA

Gregory, Andre (Actor)
c/o Jeff Hunter *WmE2 (WMA-NY)*
1325 Avenue of the Americas
New York, NY 10019-6026, USA

Gregory, Bettina L (Correspondent)
5010 Creston St
Hyattsville, MD 20781-1216, USA

Gregory, Claude (Athlete, Basketball Player)
14621 Blackburn Rd
Burtonsville, MD 20866-1303, USA

Gregory, Cynthia (Ballerina)
890 Broadway
New York, NY 10003-1211, USA

Gregory, Damian (Athlete, Football Player)
2100 Walmar Dr
Lansing, MI 48917-5104, USA

Gregory, Dick (Activist, Actor, Comedian)
PO Box 3270
Plymouth, MA 02361-3270, USA

Gregory, Dorian (Actor, Television Host)
c/o Staff Member *Creative Management Entertainment Group (CMEG)*
2050 S Bundy Dr Ste 280
Los Angeles, CA 90025-6128, USA

Gregory, Frederick D (Astronaut)
506 Tulip Rd
Annapolis, MD 21403-1326, USA

Gregory, Garland (Athlete, Football Player)
104 Belle Haven Dr
Ruston, LA 71270-2607, USA

Gregory, Glynn (Athlete, Football Player)
7007 Joyce Way
Dallas, TX 75225-1728, USA

Gregory, Jack (Athlete, Football Player)
108 Robertson St
Okolona, MS 38860-1619, USA

Gregory, Jim (Athlete, Hockey Player)
c/o Staff Member *National Hockey League (NHL)*
50 Bay St 11th Floor
Toronto, ON M5J 2X8, Canada

Gregory, Kathy (Cartoonist)
680 N Lake Shore Dr
Chicago, IL 60611-4546, USA

Gregory, Lee (Athlete, Baseball Player)
6456 N Teilman Ave
Fresno, CA 93711-1315, USA

Gregory, Nick (Actor)
c/o Staff Member *Kerin-Goldberg Associates*
155 E 55th St Ste 5D
New York, NY 10022-4038, USA

Gregory, Paul (Actor)
PO Box 415
Desert Hot Springs, CA 92240-0415, USA

Gregory, Philippa (Writer)
c/o Staff Member *Independent Talent Group (ITG-UK)*
Oxford House 76 Oxford St
London W1D 1BS, UK

Gregory, Roberta (Artist)
c/o Staff Member *Fantagraphics Books*
7563 Lake City Way NE
Seattle, WA 98115-4218, USA

Gregory, Stephen (Actor)
64 Thornton Ave
London W4 1QQ, UNITED KINGDOM (UK)

Gregory, William G (Astronaut)
2027 E Freeport Ln
Gilbert, AZ 85234-2829, USA

Gregory, William H (Editor)
1221 Avenue of the Americas
New York, NY 10020-1001, USA

Gregory, William Jr (Athlete, Football Player)
4317 Cityview Dr
Plano, TX 75093-3236, USA

Gregory, Wilton D (Religious Leader)
222 S 3rd St Ofc
Belleville, IL 62220-1916, USA

Gregson, Wallace C (General)
Commanding General Marine Forces Pacific
Camp HM Smith, HI 96861, USA

Gregson-Williams, Harry (Composer, Musician)
c/o Staff Member *Chasen & Company*
8899 Beverly Blvd Ste 405
Los Angeles, CA 90048-2431, USA

Grehl, Michael (Editor)
495 Union Ave
Memphis, TN 38103-3217, USA

Greider, Carol (Nobel Prize Laureate)
725 N Wolfe St Bldg Schoolofmedicine
Baltimore, MD 21205-2105, USA

Greif, Bill (Athlete, Baseball Player)
807 E 31st St
Austin, TX 78705-3205, USA

Greig, John (Athlete, Basketball Player)
2031 218th Pl NE
Sammamish, WA 98074-4049, USA

Greig, Mark (Athlete, Hockey Player)
c/o Art Breeze *Pro-Rep Entertainment Consulting*
113-276 Midpark Way SE
Calgary, AB T2X 1J6, Canada

Greiner, William R (Educator)
President's Office
Buffalo, NY 14221, USA

Greiner-Petter-Memm, Simone (Athlete)
Am Sportplatz 14
Waldau 98667, GERMANY

Greinke, Zack (Athlete, Baseball Player)
8629 Vista Pine Ct
Orlando, FL 32836-6307, USA

Greise, Bob (Athlete)
12044 SE Birkdale Run
Jupiter, FL 33469-1740

Greisen, Chris (Athlete, Football Player)
1710 Arabian Dr
Green Bay, WI 54313-4388, USA

Greisen, Nick (Athlete, Football Player)
12865 Biggin Church Rd S
Jacksonville, FL 32224-7928, USA

Greisinger, Seth (Athlete, Baseball Player)
6460 Overbrook St
Falls Church, VA 22043-1914, USA

Greiss, Gabrielle (Stylist)
c/o Staff Member *Management + Artists + Organization*
330 W 38th St Ste 1401
New York, NY 10018-8438, USA

Greist, Kim (Actor)
1505 10th St
Santa Monica, CA 90401-2805, USA

Grelf, Michael (Director)
PO Box 12039
La Jolla, CA 92039-2039, USA

Grenier, Adrian (Actor)
c/o Stephen (Steve) Levinson *Leverage Management*
3030 Pennsylvania Ave
Santa Monica, CA 90404-4112, USA

Grenier, Gillies (Stylist)
c/o Staff Member *Fifty8 Artists*
58 W Huron St
Chicago, IL 60654-3806, USA

Grenier, Zach (Actor)
c/o Staff Member *Hartig Hilepo Agency Ltd*
54 W 21st St Rm 610
New York, NY 10010-7344, USA

Grennes, Janet (Stylist)
2706 Rosedale Ave
Raleigh, NC 27607-7122, USA

Grentz, Theresa Shank (Coach)
Athletic Dept
Champaign, IL 61820, USA

Greschner, Ron (Athlete, Hockey Player)
PO Box 4513
Greenwich, CT 06831-8513, USA

Gresham, Bob (Athlete, Football Player)
2428 Portstewart Ln
Charlotte, NC 28270-0508, USA

Gretch, Joel (Actor)
c/o Molly Madden *3 Arts Entertainment Inc*
9460 Wilshire Blvd Fl 7
Beverly Hills, CA 90212-2713, USA

Gretsch, Joel (Actor)
c/o David (Dave) Fleming *Mosaic Media Group*
9200 W Sunset Blvd Ste 10
Los Angeles, CA 90069-3608, USA

Gretzky, Wayne (Athlete, Hockey Player)
6436 E Gainsborough Rd
Scottsdale, AZ 85251-1950, USA

Grevey, Kevin (Athlete, Basketball Player)
528 River Bend Rd
Great Falls, VA 22066-2716, USA

Grevioux, Kevin (Actor)
c/o Scott Agostini *WmE2 (Endeavor-LA)*
9601 Wilshire Blvd Fl 3
Beverly Hills, CA 90210-5219, USA

Grey, Alex (Artist)
46 Deer Hill Rd
Wappingers Falls, NY 12590-3911, USA

Grey, Beryl E (Ballerina)
Fernhill Priory Road Forest Row
East Sussex RH18 5JE, UNITED KINGDOM (UK)

Grey, Jennifer (Actor)
c/o Greg Clark *Untitled Entertainment (LA)*
350 S Beverly Dr Ste 200
Beverly Hills, CA 90212-4819, USA

Grey, Joel (Actor)
c/o Nevin Dolcefino *Innovative Artists (LA)*
1505 10th St
Santa Monica, CA 90401-2805, USA

Grey, Sasha (Actor, Adult Film Star)
PO Box 1480
Studio City, CA 91614-0480, USA

Grey, Zena (Actor)
c/o Abby Bluestone *Innovative Artists (LA)*
1505 10th St
Santa Monica, CA 90401-2805, USA

Greyeyes, Michael
3500 W Olive Ave Ste 1400
Burbank, CA 91505-5512

Gribbon, Melissa (Actor)
c/o Dianne Hooper *Starcraft Talent Agency*
PO Box 801390
Santa Clarita, CA 91380-1390, USA

Gribow, Patti
3303 Clerendon Rd
Beverly Hills, CA 90210-1061

Grich, Robert A (Bobby) (Athlete, Baseball Player)
31 Madison Ln
Trabuco Canyon, CA 92679-5012, USA

Grieco, Richard (Actor)
c/o Tracy Quinn *Quinn Management*
17328 Ventura Blvd Ste 416
Encino, CA 91316-3904, USA

Grieder, William (Journalist)
1230 Avenue of the Americas
New York, NY 10020-1513, USA

Griem, Helmut (Actor)
Keplerstr 2
Munich 81679, GERMANY

Grier, David Alan (Actor, Comedian)
c/o Staff Member *ROAR (LA)*
9701 Wilshire Blvd Fl 8
Beverly Hills, CA 90212-2008, USA

Grier, Herbert E (Engineer)
La Jolla, CA 92037, USA

Grier, Marrio (Athlete, Football Player)
826 Almora Dr
Charlotte, NC 28216-3069, USA

Grier, Mike (Athlete, Hockey Player)
72 Stonecrest Dr
Needham, MA 02492-2783, USA

Grier, Pam (Actor)
c/o Harry Gold *TalentWorks (LA)*
3500 W Olive Ave Ste 1400
Burbank, CA 91505-5512, USA

Grier, Roosevelt (Rosey) (Athlete, Football Player)
1250 4th St Fl 6
Santa Monica, CA 90401-1418, USA

Gries, Jonathan (Jon) (Actor, Director, Producer)
c/o Steve Lovett *Lovett Management*
1327 Brinkley Ave
Los Angeles, CA 90049-3619, USA

Griese, Brian (Athlete, Football Player)
17 Polo Club Dr
Denver, CO 80209-3309, USA

Griese, Robert A (Bob) (Athlete, Football Player, Sportscaster)
3195 Ponce De Leon Blvd Apt 412
Coral Gables, FL 33134-6801, USA

Griesemer, John N (Government Official)
RR 2 Box 204B
Springfield, MO 65802, USA

Grieser, Sylvia (Stylist)
c/o Staff Member *Frame Representatives*
275 West St
New York, NY 10013, USA

Grieve, Ben (Athlete, Baseball Player)
6906 Fairway Rd
La Jolla, CA 92037-5619, USA

Grieve, Brent (Athlete, Hockey Player)
1595 16th Ave Suite 602
Richmond Hill, ON L4B 3N9, Canada

Grieve, Pierson M (Business Person)
Ecolab Center 370 Wabasha St N
Saint Paul, MN 55102, USA

Grieve, Tom (Athlete, Baseball Player)
4107 Carnation Dr
Arlington, TX 76016-3922, USA

Griffey, Ken Sr (Athlete, Baseball Player)
1102 Portmoor Way
Winter Garden, FL 34787-4619, USA

Griffey Jr, Ken (Athlete, Baseball Player)
13506 Summerport Village Pkwy PMB 416
Windermere, FL 34786-7366, USA

Griffin, Alfredo (Athlete, Baseball Player)
9731 NW 41st St
Doral, FL 33178-2944, USA

Griffin, Archie M (Athlete, Football Player)
6845 Temperance Point Pl
Westerville, OH 43082-8704, USA

Griffin, Blake (Athlete, Basketball Player)
c/o Jeff Schwartz *Excel Sports Management*
9665 Wilshire Blvd Ste 500
Beverly Hills, CA 90212-2312, USA

Griffin, Bo (Correspondent, Television Host)
c/o Staff Member *Good Day Live*
20th Century Fox Television 10201 Pico Blvd Blg 88 W Rm 29
Los Angeles, CA 90035, USA

Griffin, Cecelia (Stylist)
c/o Staff Member *Punch Artists*
60 E 42nd St Ste 449
New York, NY 10165-0451, USA

Griffin, Cornelius (Athlete, Football Player)
1207 Forestburg Dr
Houston, TX 77038-2122, USA

Griffin, Courtney (Athlete, Football Player)
6302 N Selland Ave
Fresno, CA 93711-0872, USA

Griffin, David
13 Spencer Gdns
London, ENGLAND SW14 7AH

Griffin, Don (Athlete, Football Player)
PO Box 1443
Roswell, GA 30077-1443, USA

Griffin, Doug (Athlete, Baseball Player)
15811 El Soneto Dr
Whittier, CA 90603-1446, USA

Griffin, Eddie (Actor, Comedian, Producer)

Griffin, Eric (Boxer)
PO Box 964
Jasper, TN 37347-0964, USA

Griffin, Forrest (Athlete, Wrestler)
5 E River Park Pl W Ste 203
Fresno, CA 93720-1557, USA

Griffin, Greg (Athlete, Basketball Player)
31300 Auto Center Dr Apt C115
Lake Elsinore, CA 92530-4538, USA

Griffin, James
25 Paulson Dr
Burlington, MA 01803-2819

Griffin, James Bennett (Misc)
5023 Wyandot Ct
Bethesda, MD 20816-2205, USA

Griffin, John W (Athlete, Football Player)
10315 Herons Ridge Dr
Lakeland, TN 38002-8292, USA

Griffin, John-Ford (Athlete, Baseball Player)
7350 Point of Rocks Rd
Sarasota, FL 34242-2641, USA

Griffin, Kathy (Actor, Comedian, Reality TV Star)
c/o Steve Levine *International Creative Management (ICM-LA)*
10250 Constellation Blvd Fl 7
Los Angeles, CA 90067-6207, USA

Griffin, Keith (Athlete, Football Player)
4330 Canada Hills Ct
Waldorf, MD 20602-3106, USA

Griffin, Larry (Athlete, Football Player)
5617 Silchester Ln
Charlotte, NC 28215-5327, USA

Griffin, Leonard (Athlete, Football Player)
PO Box 480
Calhoun, LA 71225-0480, USA

Griffin, Mike (Athlete, Baseball Player)
1620 Grove Ave
Woodland, CA 95695-5149, USA

Griffin, Nikki (Actor)
c/o Staff Member *Agency for the Performing Arts (APA-LA)*
405 S Beverly Dr Ste 500
Beverly Hills, CA 90212-4425, USA

Griffin, Patty (Musician, Songwriter, Writer)
509 Hartnell St
Monterey, CA 93940-2825, USA

Griffin, Paul (Athlete, Basketball Player)
903 Great Tree Dr
San Antonio, TX 78260-7744, USA

Griffin, Ray (Athlete, Football Player)
6058 Medallion Dr W
Westerville, OH 43082-8901, USA

Griffin, Robert P (Ex-Senator, Judge)
PO Box 30052
Lansing, MI 48909-7552, USA

Griffin, Rod L (Writer)
c/o Staff Member *$olvency International Inc*
PO Box 4433
Clearwater, FL 33758-4433, USA

Griffin, Taylor (Athlete, Basketball Player)
c/o Jeff Schwartz *Excel Sports Management*
9665 Wilshire Blvd Ste 500
Beverly Hills, CA 90212-2312, USA

Griffin, Thomas N Jr (General)
9749 S Park Cir
Fairfax Station, VA 22039-2943, USA

Griffin, Timothy (Congressman, Politician)
1232 Longworth Hob
Washington, DC 20515-2108, USA

Griffin, Tom (Athlete, Baseball Player)
13147 Avenida La Valencia
Poway, CA 92064-1905, USA

Griffin, Tony (Actor, Director, Writer)
c/o Staff Member *Merv Griffin Entertainment*
1149 N Gower St
Los Angeles, CA 90038-1801

Griffin, Wade (Athlete, Football Player)
2937 Highway 72
Holly Springs, MS 38635-9512, USA

Griffin, Warren (Warren G) (Actor, Musician)
c/o Johnny Gallo *Artist Representation Group*
9701 Wilshire Blvd Fl 10
Beverly Hills, CA 90212-2010, USA

Griffing, Glynn (Athlete, Football Player)
2318 Irving Pl
Jackson, MS 39211-6133, USA

Griffith, Alan R (Financier)
1 Wall St
New York, NY 10005-2500, USA

Griffith, Andy (Actor, Musician, Producer, Writer)
PO Box 1968
Manteo, NC 27954-1968, USA

Griffith, Bill (Cartoonist)
PO Box 88
Hadlyme, CT 06439-0088, USA

Griffith, Calvin (Baseball Player)
501 Chicago Ave
Minneapolis, MN 55415-1517, USA

Griffith, Darrell (Athlete, Basketball Player)
1300 Leighton Cir
Louisville, KY 40222-5644, USA

Griffith, Emile A (Boxer)
150 Washington St Apt 6J
Hempstead, NY 11550-3133, USA

Griffith, H. Morgan (Congressman, Politician)
1108 Longworth Hob
Washington, DC 20515-3809, USA

Griffith, Howard (Athlete, Football Player)
9152 S Clyde Ave
Chicago, IL 60617-3740, USA

Griffith, James (Business Person)
1835 Dueber Ave SW
Canton, OH 44706-2728, USA

Griffith, Mary A (Activist)
1304 Rudgear Rd
Walnut Creek, CA 94596-5918, USA

Griffith, Melanie (Actor, Producer)
c/o Jason Weinberg *Untitled Entertainment (LA)*
350 S Beverly Dr Ste 200
Beverly Hills, CA 90212-4819, USA

Griffith, Rhiana (Actor)
c/o Staff Member *Darlene Kaplan Entertainment*
4450 Balboa Ave
Encino, CA 91316-4101, USA

Griffith, Robert (Athlete, Football Player)
10433 Wilshire Blvd Apt 801
Los Angeles, CA 90024-4629, USA

Griffith, Thomas Ian (Actor)
9701 Wilshire Blvd Ste 1000
Beverly Hills, CA 90212-2010, USA

Griffith, Thomas Ian (Actor)
c/o Lou Pitt *Pitt Group, The*
9465 Wilshire Blvd Ste 420
Beverly Hills, CA 90212-2603, USA

Griffith, Tom W (Misc)
1448 Duke St # 100
Alexandria, VA 22314-3403, USA

Griffith, Wendy (Religious Leader, Television Host)
c/o Staff Member *CBN News*
977 Centerville Tpke
Virginia Beach, VA 23463-1001, USA

Griffith, Yolanda (Basketball Player)
1 Sports Pkwy
Sacramento, CA 95834-2300, USA

Griffiths, Brian (Baseball Player)
16022 SE Goosehollow Dr
Clackamas, OR 97015-7859, USA

Griffiths, Derrell (Athlete, Baseball Player)
201 E Central Blvd
Anadarko, OK 73005-3431, USA

Griffiths, Isobel
Tower Bridge House St Katharine's Way
London, not applicable E1W 1AA, United Kingdom

Griffiths, Jeremy (Athlete, Baseball Player)
120 Beachdale Dr
Avon Lake, OH 44012-1611, USA

Griffiths, Lucy (Actor)
c/o Larry Taube *Principal Entertainment (LA)*
1964 Westwood Blvd Ste 400
Los Angeles, CA 90025-4695, USA

Griffiths, Nick (Stylist)
c/o Staff Member *Management + Artists + Organization*
330 W 38th St Ste 1401
New York, NY 10018-8438, USA

Griffiths, Phillip A (Mathematician)
Director's Office Olden Lane
Princeton, NJ 8540, USA

Griffiths, Rachel (Actor)
c/o Michael D Aglion *Signpost*
250 S Beverly Dr Ste 201
Beverly Hills, CA 90212-3811, USA

Griffiths, Richard (Actor)
c/o Staff Member *Paradigm (LA)*
360 N Crescent Dr
Beverly Hills, CA 90210-4874, USA

Griffiths, Susan
9300 Wilshire Blvd Ste 410
Beverly Hills, CA 90212-3228

Griggs, Acle (Baseball Player)
820 Newwau Ave SW
Birmingham, AL 35221-3854, USA

Griggs, Andy (Musician)
2813 Azalea Pl
Nashville, TN 37204-3117, USA

Griggs, Hal (Athlete, Baseball Player)
2530 W Tenbrook Way
Tucson, AZ 85741-3782, USA

Griggs, Perry (Athlete, Football Player)
1275 Carlysle Park Dr
Lawrenceville, GA 30044-2242, USA

Griggs, William E (Athlete, Football Player)
18 Summerhill Ln
Medford, NJ 08055-2365, USA

Grigorian, Irina (Figure Skater)
c/o Staff Member *Champions on Ice*
3500 W 80th St Ste 200
Minneapolis, MN 55431-1090, USA

Grigsby, Benji (Baseball Player)
118 Teakwood Dr SW
Huntsville, AL 35801-3453, USA

Grijalva, Lucy (Writer)
PO Box 1634
Benicia, CA 94510-4634

Grijalva, Victor E (Business Person)
277 Park Ave
New York, NY 10172-0003, USA

Grilli, Guido (Athlete, Baseball Player)
250 Sloan Ln
Locust Grove, AR 72550-9000, USA

Grilli, Jason (Athlete, Baseball Player)
9037 Point Cypress Dr
Orlando, FL 32836-5475, USA

Grilli, Steve (Athlete, Baseball Player)
8637 Briar Patch
Baldwinsville, NY 13027-8914, USA

Grillo, Frank
c/o Steven Muller *Innovative Artists (LA)*
1505 10th St
Santa Monica, CA 90401-2805, USA

Grim, Robert (Bob) (Athlete, Football Player)
18 NW Saginaw Ave
Bend, OR 97701-1221, USA

Grimaldi, Dan (Actor)

Grimaud, Helene (Musician)
40 W 57th St
New York, NY 10019-4001, USA

Grimes, Gary
4578 W 165th St
Lawndale, CA 90260-2805

Grimes, Karolyn
PO Box 145
Carnation, WA 98014-0145

Grimes, Martha (Writer)
115 D St SE Apt G6
Washington, DC 20003-1822, USA

Grimes, Paul (Stylist)
c/o Staff Member *Mark Edward Inc*
325 W 8th St # 1011
New York, NY 10018, USA

Grimes, Randy (Athlete, Football Player)
13214 Halifax St
Houston, TX 77015-2829, USA

Grimes, Sally (Stylist)
820 Wenonah Ave
Oak Park, IL 60304-1036, USA

Grimes, Scott (Actor)
c/o Adam Levine *Levine Okwu Erickson Management*
9601 Wilshire Blvd Fl 3
Beverly Hills, CA 90210-5219, USA

Grimes, Shenae (Actor)
c/o Amanda Rosenthal *Amanda Rosenthal Talent Agency*
14 Prince Arthur Ave Suite 206
Toronto, ON M5R 1A9, Canada

Grimes, Tammy (Actor, Musician)
10 E 44th St
New York, NY 10017-3601, USA

Grimes, Tinsley (Actor)
c/o Staff Member *Innovative Artists (LA)*
1505 10th St
Santa Monica, CA 90401-2805, USA

Griminelli, Andrea (Musician)
165 W 57th St
New York, NY 10019-2201, USA

Grimm, Dan (Athlete, Football Player)
2514 Smith Harbour Dr
Denver, NC 28037-8093, USA

Grimm, Russ (Athlete, Coach, Football Coach, Football Player)
3975 Portloe Ter
Fairfax, VA 22033-2245, USA

Grimm, Tim (Actor)
9200 W Sunset Blvd Ste 1125
Los Angeles, CA 90069-3610, USA

Grimshaw, Nicholas T (Architect)
1 Conway St Fitzroy Square
London W1P 5HA, UNITED KINGDOM (UK)

Grimsley, Jason (Athlete, Baseball Player)
13315 Timberwild Ct
Tomball, TX 77375-2939, USA

Grimsley, John (Athlete, Football Player)
3615 Robinson Rd
Missouri City, TX 77459-4313, USA

Grimsley, Ross A (Athlete, Baseball Player)
92 Conewago Ct
Owings Mills, MD 21117-5049, USA

Grimson, Stu (Athlete, Hockey Player)
c/o Staff Member *NHL Players Association*
1700-20 Bay St
Toronto, ON M5J 2R8, Canada

Grimsson, Olafur Ragnar (President)
Sto'marradshusini v/Lackjartog
Reykjavik, ICELAND

Grinberg, Anouk (Actor)
20 Ave Rapp
Paris 75007, FRANCE

Grindenko, Tatyana T (Musician)
Tverskaya Str 31
Moscow 103050, RUSSIA

Grinder, Scott (Baseball Player)
1323 14th Ave N
Birmingham, AL 35204-2712, USA

Grinder, Scott (Athlete, Baseball Player)
1323 14th Ave N
Birmingham, AL 35204, USA

Griner, Paul (Writer)
1745 Broadway # B1
New York, NY 10019-4368, USA

Grinham, Rawley Judy (Swimmer)
103 Green Lane Northwood
Middx HA6 1AP, UNITED KINGDOM (UK)

Grinnell, Alan D (Physicist)
Medical School Lewis Center
Los Angeles, CA 90024, USA

grinnell, todd (Actor)
c/o DEBRA MANNERS *Daniel Hoff Agency*
5455 Wilshire Blvd Ste 1100
Los Angeles, CA 90036-4277, USA

Grinstead, Irish (Musician)
c/o Staff Member *Creative Artists Agency (CAA-LA)*
2000 Avenue of the Stars Ste 100
Los Angeles, CA 90067-4705, USA

Grinstead, LeMisha (Musician)
c/o Staff Member *Creative Artists Agency (CAA-LA)*
2000 Avenue of the Stars Ste 100
Los Angeles, CA 90067-4705, USA

Grinstein, Gerald (Business Person)
Hartsfield International Airport
Atlanta, GA 30320, USA

Grint, Rupert (Actor)
c/o Clair Dobbs *Public Eye Communications*
535 Kings Rd Suite 313 Plaza
London SW10 0SZ, United Kingdom

Grinville, Patrick (Writer)
38 Rue du Faubourg Saint Jacques
Paris 75014, FRANCE

Grisanti, Eugene P (Business Person)
521 W 57th St
New York, NY 10019-2929, USA

Grisdale, John (Athlete, Hockey Player)
A-455 Bromley St
Coquitlam, BC V3K 6N7, Canada

Grise, Pascale (Stylist)
c/o Staff Member *Loox Agency*
12 Desbrosses St
New York, NY 10013-1704, USA

Grisez, Germain (Misc)
Christain Ethics Dept
Emmitsburg, MD 21727, USA

Grisham, John (Writer)
c/o David Gernert *Gernert Company*
136 E 57th St Fl 18
New York, NY 10022-2923, USA

Grishin, Evgenil (Speed Skater)
Skatertny Pl 4
Moscow, RUSSIA

Grishuk, Pasha
Luzhnetskaia nab. 8
Moscow, RUSSIA 119871

Grisman, David (Composer, Musician)
5749 Larryan Dr
Woodland Hills, CA 91367-4041, USA

Grissom, Marquis (Athlete, Baseball Player)
250 Astaire Mnr
Fayetteville, GA 30214-5366, USA

Grissom, Steve (Race Car Driver)
3475 Myer Lee Dr
Winston Salem, NC 27101-6209, USA

Grist, Reri (Opera Singer)
165 W 57th St
New York, NY 10019-2201, USA

Griswold, Sandra (Stylist)
301 Bryant St Apt 401
San Francisco, CA 94107-4172, USA

Grizzard, George (Actor)
400 E 54th St
New York, NY 10022-5164, USA

Grizzard, George (Baseball Player, Basketball Player)
PO Box 288
Bolivar, PA 15923-0288, USA

Groat, Dick (Athlete, Baseball Player, Basketball Player)
320 Beech St
Pittsburgh, PA 15218-1406, USA

Grob, Mike (Athlete, Golfer)
2228 1/2 Grand Ave
Billings, MT 59102-2619, USA

Groban, Josh (Musician, Songwriter)
c/o Cliff Burnstein *Q Prime Inc*
729 7th Ave Ste 1600
New York, NY 10019-6880, USA

Grobell, Werner (Mr Frick) (Misc)
PO Box 7886
Incline Village, NV 89452, USA

Groce, Clifton (Clif) (Athlete, Football Player)
1632 Park Pl
College Station, TX 77840-3123, USA

Groce, Dejuan (Athlete, Football Player)
1443 Oxbow Dr
Cedar Hill, TX 75104-4007, USA

Groce, Ron (Athlete, Football Player)
3624 5th Ave S
Minneapolis, MN 55409-1329, USA

Grocholewski, Zenon Cardinal (Religious Leader)
Palazzo della Congregazioni Piazzo Pio XII #3
Rome 193, ITALY

Grode, Jarrett (Actor)
c/o Ruthanne Secunda *United Talent Agency (UTA)*
9560 Wilshire Blvd Fl 5
Beverly Hills, CA 90212-2400, USA

Grodin, Charles
187 Chestnut Hill Rd
Wilton, CT 06897-4108, USA

Groener, Harry (Actor)
c/o Susan Smith *Susan Smith Company, The*
1344 N Wetherly Dr
Los Angeles, CA 90069-1817, USA

Groening, Matthew (Matt) (Cartoonist)
c/o Michael A Neidorf *Caplan-Groening Family Foundation*
11400 W Olympic Blvd Ste 590
Los Angeles, CA 90064-1574, USA

Groetzinger Jr, Jon (Business Person)
1 American Rd
Cleveland, OH 44144-2301, USA

Grofe Jr, Ferde
18139 Coastline Dr
Malibu, CA 90265-5738, USA

Groff, Angela (Stylist)
c/o Staff Member *Ennis*
119 Braintree St
Boston, MA 02134-1628, USA

Groff, Jonathan (Actor)
c/o Tony Lipp *Anonymous Content (AC-LA)*
3531 Hayden Ave
Culver City, CA 90232, USA

Grogan, John (Writer)
1000 Keystone Industrial Park
Dunmore, PA 18512-1535, USA

Grogan, Steven J (Steve) (Athlete, Football Player)
PO Box 530
Foxboro, MA 02035-0530, USA

Groh, Al (Coach, Football Coach)
Athletic Dept
Charlottesburg, VA 22903, USA

Groh, Gary (Athlete, Golfer)
331 Signe Ct
Lake Bluff, IL 60044-1219, USA

Grohl, Dave (Musician)
c/o Staff Member *RCA Records (LA)*
8750 Wilshire Blvd Fl 2
Beverly Hills, CA 90211-2715, USA

Grollman, Rabbi Earl (Religious Leader, Writer)
c/o Staff Member *Beacon Press*
25 Beacon St
Boston, MA 02108-2892, USA

Groman, William (Athlete, Football Player)
7906 Scherzo Ln
Houston, TX 77040-2529, USA

Gromov, Mikhael L (Mathematician)
91 Rue de la Sante
Paris 75013, FRANCE

Gronberg, Mathias (Athlete, Golfer)
247 Plymouth Rd
West Palm Beach, FL 33405-3324, USA

Gronemeyer, Herbert
Leopoldstr. 19
Munich, GERMANY D-80802

Gronk (Artist)
7525 Beverly Blvd
Los Angeles, CA 90036-2722, USA

Gronman, Tuomas (Athlete, Hockey Player)
66 Mario Lemieux Pl
Pittsburgh, PA 15219-3504, USA

Gronstrand, Jari (Athlete, Hockey Player)
c/o Staff Member *Toronto Maple Leafs*
Air Canada Centre 400-40 Bay St
Toronto, ON M5J 2X2, Canada

Groom, Buddy (Athlete, Baseball Player)
1991 Saint Andrews Dr
Red Oak, TX 75154-5837, USA

Groom, Jerry (Athlete, Football Player)
625 Beach Rd
Sarasota, FL 34242-1948, USA

Groom, Sam (Actor)
8730 W Sunset Blvd Ste 440
Los Angeles, CA 90069-2277, USA

Grootegoed, Matt (Athlete, Football Player)
17302 Destry Cir
Huntington Beach, CA 92647-6135, USA

Gropp, Louis Oliver (Editor)
140 Riverside Dr # 6G
New York, NY 10024-2605, USA

Gros, Earl (Athlete, Football Player)
17424 Airline Hwy Ste 12
Prairieville, LA 70769-3352, USA

Gros, Francois (Misc)
102 Rue de la Tour
Paris 75116, FRANCE

Gros Louis, Kenneth R R (Educator)
President's Office
Bloomington, IN 47405, USA

Grosbard, Ulu (Director)
29 W 10th St
New York, NY 10011-8739, USA

Grosek, Michal (Athlete, Hockey Player)
5 Samba Cir
Sandwich, MA 02563-2597, USA

Gross, Alfred E (Athlete, Football Player)
8227 Grandstaff Dr
Sacramento, CA 95823-5970, USA

Gross, Arye
c/o Paul Greenstone *Paul Greenstone Entertainment*
3008 Sorrelwood Dr
San Ramon, CA 94582-5008, USA

Gross, Charles G (Psychic)
18 E Shore Dr
Princeton, NJ 08540-7412, USA

Gross, David (Comedian)
c/o Staff Member *United Talent Agency (UTA)*
9560 Wilshire Blvd Fl 5
Beverly Hills, CA 90212-2400, USA

Gross, David J. (Nobel Prize Laureate)
Kolm Hall US Santa Barbara
Santa Barbara, CA 93106-0001, USA

Gross, Don (Athlete, Baseball Player)
1299 E Farrand Rd
Clio, MI 48420-9137, USA

Gross, George (Athlete, Football Player)
8 Troyer Ct
Fairhope, AL 36532-3611, USA

Gross, Greg (Athlete, Baseball Player)
802 Hallowell Dr
West Chester, PA 19382-5243, USA

Gross, Henry (Musician)
c/o Pat Horgan *Pat Horgan Talent*
2789 W Main St Ste 5
Wappingers Falls, NY 12590-1524, USA

Gross, Jordan (Athlete, Football Player)
12725 Ninebark Trl
Charlotte, NC 28278-6838, USA

Gross, Kevin (Athlete, Baseball Player)
117 Principia Ct
Claremont, CA 91711-4657, USA

Gross, Kip (Athlete, Baseball Player)
2015 Ridgeview Ct
Redlands, CA 92373-6979, USA

Gross, Lance (Actor)
c/o Sherry Marsh *Marsh Entertainment*
12444 Ventura Blvd Ste 203
Studio City, CA 91604-2409, USA

Gross, Lee (Athlete, Football Player)
871 Holland Rd
Newton, AL 36352-8035, USA

Gross, Mary (Actor, Comedian)
c/o Staff Member *Pakula/King & Associates*
9229 W Sunset Blvd Ste 315
Los Angeles, CA 90069-3403, USA

Gross, Michael (Swimmer)
Paul-Ehrlich-Str 6
Frankfurt/Main 60596, GERMANY

Gross, Michael (Actor)
c/o Staff Member *Silver Massetti & Szatmary (SMS-NY)*
145 W 45th St # 1204
New York, NY 10036-4008, USA

Gross, Paul (Actor)
c/o John S Kelly *Bresler Kelly & Associates*
11500 W Olympic Blvd Ste 510
Los Angeles, CA 90064-1527, USA

Gross, Ricco (Athlete)
Waldbahnstr 34A
Ruhpolding 83324, GERMANY

Gross, Robert A (Physicist)
14 Sunnyside Way
New Rochelle, NY 10804-2109, USA

Gross, Robert (Bob) (Athlete, Basketball Player)
13466 SE Red Rose Ln
Happy Valley, OR 97086-9752, USA

Gross, Terry R (Correspondent)
News Dept Independence Mall W
Philadelphia, PA 19104, USA

Gross, Wayne (Athlete, Baseball Player)
45 Leonard Ct
Danville, CA 94526-1911, USA

Grosscup, Lee (Athlete, Football Player)
703 Atlantic Ave Apt 360
Alameda, CA 94501-8201, USA

Grossfeld, Stanley (Journalist)
Editorial Dept 135 W T Morrissey Blvd
Dorchester, MA 2125, USA

Grossman, Allen R (Writer)
113 Richdale Ave Unit 25
Cambridge, MA 02140-3333, USA

Grossman, Burt (Athlete, Football Player)
1482 Antioch Ave
Chula Vista, CA 91913-1477, USA

Grossman, Judith (Writer)
English Dept
Swannanoa, NC 28778, USA

Grossman, Judith (Athlete, Football Player)
1000 Football Dr
Lake Forest, IL 60045, USA

Grossman, Leslie (Actor)
c/o Staff Member *Metropolitan (MTA)*
4526 Wilshire Blvd
Los Angeles, CA 90010-3801, USA

Grossman, Randy (Athlete, Football Player)
204 Ridge Rd
Pittsburgh, PA 15238-1522, USA

Grossman, Rex (Athlete, Football Player)
115 S Smith Rd
Bloomington, IN 47401, USA

Grossman, Rex (Athlete, Football Player)
115 Meadowbrook Ln
Lake Bluff, IL 60044-1145, USA

Grossman, Robert (Misc)
19 Crosby St
New York, NY 10013-3102, USA

Grosvenor, Gerald Cavendish (Business Person, Royalty)
The Grosvenor Estate Eaton Estate Office
Eccleston, Chester CH49ET, United Kingdom

Grosvenor, Gilbert M (Publisher)
& 17th M NW
Washington, DC 20036, USA

Grote, Jerry (Athlete, Baseball Player)
5807 Babcock Rd # 215
San Antonio, TX 78240-2196, USA

Grote, Jerry C. (Athlete, Basketball Player)
3 Balboa Way
Hot Springs Village, AR 71909-6913, USA

Grotenfelt, Georg E J (Architect)
Kapteeninkatu 20D
Helsinki 140, FINLAND

Grotewold, Jeff (Athlete, Baseball Player)
PO Box 3439
Crestline, CA 92325-3439, USA

Groth, Jeff (Athlete, Football Player)
13824 Driftwood Dr
Carmel, IN 46033-8510, USA

Groth, Johnny (Athlete, Baseball Player)
170 N Ocean Blvd Apt 307
Palm Beach, FL 33480-3931, USA

Grott, Matt (Athlete, Baseball Player)
4714 Rolling Green Dr
Ooltewah, TN 37363-9073, USA

Grottkau, Robert (Athlete, Football Player)
5105 S Muirfield Ln
Spokane, WA 99223-6362, USA

Grouch, Roger K (Astronaut)
Nasa Headquarters
Washington, DC 20546-0001, USA

Groulx, Wayne (Athlete, Hockey Player)
552 Montee De L'Eglise
St-Colomban, QC J5K 2J2, Canada

Grove, Andrew S (Business Person)
2200 Mission College Blvd
Santa Clara, CA 95054-1537, USA

Grover, Gulshan (Actor, Bollywood)
c/o Michael Livingston *Leavitt Talent Group*
8255 W Sunset Blvd
West Hollywood, CA 90046-2417, USA

Groves, George (Athlete, Football Player)
1687 W 900 N
Perrysville, IN 47974-8071, USA

Groves, Napiera Danielle (Actor)
c/o Christine Thomas *Sweet Mud Group*
648 Broadway # 1002
New York, NY 10012-2348, USA

Groves, Philip (Stylist)
c/o Staff Member *Ford Models (Chicago)*
311 W Superior St
Chicago, IL 60654-3548, USA

Groves, Richard H (General)
400 Madison St Apt 1302
Alexandria, VA 22314-1722, USA

Grow, Carol (Actor, Model)
c/o Jon Orlando *WNWN Media*
348 Hauser Blvd # PH414
Los Angeles, CA 90036-3276, USA

Grroms, Charles R (Red) (Artist)
85 Walker St
New York, NY 10013-3523, USA

Grubar, Richard (Athlete, Basketball Player)
1804 Milan Rd
Greensboro, NC 27410-3028, USA

Grubb, John (Athlete, Baseball Player)
6618 Bel Lac Dr
Chester, VA 23831-1431, USA

Grubb, Kevin (Race Car Driver)
5120 Jefferson Davis Hwy
North Chesterfield, VA 23234-2252, USA

Grubb, Robert (Actor)
c/o Staff Member *Shanahan Management*
Level 3 Berman House
Surry Hills 2010, AUSTRALIA

Grubbs, Gary (Actor)
10100 Santa Monica Blvd Ste 2500
Los Angeles, CA 90067-4116, USA

Grubbs, Robert H (Nobel Prize Laureate)
1200 E California Blvd
Pasadena, CA 91125-0001, USA

Gruber, Jonathan (Director, Writer)
c/o Josh Adler *New Wave Entertainment (LA)*
2660 W Olive Ave
Burbank, CA 91505-4525, USA

Gruber, Kelly W (Athlete, Baseball Player)
3300 Bee Cave Rd # 650-227
West Lake Hills, TX 78746-6600, USA

Gruber, Paul (Athlete, Football Player)
PO Box 4239
Edwards, CO 81632-4239, USA

Gruberova, Edita (Opera Singer)
Maximillianstr 22
Munich 80539, GERMANY

Grubman, Allen J (Lawyer)
152 W 57th St
New York, NY 10019-3386, USA

Gruden, John (Athlete, Hockey Player)
1287 Essex Dr
Rochester Hills, MI 48307-3139, USA

Gruden, Jon (Athlete, Coach, Football Coach, Football Player)
709 Guisando De Avila
Tampa, FL 33613-5204, USA

Grudens, Richard
PO Box 344
Stony Brook, NY 11790-0344

Grudzielanek, Mark (Athlete, Baseball Player)
PO Box 1581
Rancho Santa Fe, CA 92067-1581, USA

Gruen, Danny (Athlete, Hockey Player)
RR 1 RPO
South GIllies, ON P0T 2V0, Canada

Gruen, Sara (Writer)
c/o Staff Member *HarperCollins Publishers*
10 E 53rd St C/O Author Mail Floor 7
New York, NY 10022, USA

Gruenberg, Erich (Musician)
80 Northway Hampstead Garden Suburb
London NW11 6PA, UNITED KINGDOM (UK)

Gruffudd, Ioan (Actor)
c/o Stacy O'Neil *Brillstein Entertainment Partners*
9150 Wilshire Blvd Ste 350
Beverly Hills, CA 90212-3453, USA

Grum, Anselm (Religious Leader)
Schweinfurter Strabe 40
Munsterschwarzach, Abtei 97359, GERMANY

Grum, Clifford J (Business Person)
303 S Temple Dr
Diboll, TX 75941-2419, USA

Grumman, Cornelia (Journalist)
435 N Michigan Ave
Chicago, IL 60611-4066, USA

Grummer, Elisabeth (Opera Singer)
Am Schlachtensee 104
Berlin 14163, GERMANY

Grunberg, Greg (Actor)
c/o Susan Calogerakis *Thruline Entertainment*
9250 Wilshire Blvd Ground Fl
Beverly Hills, CA 90212, USA

Grunberg, Peter (Nobel Prize Laureate)
Forschungszentrum
Unternehmenskommunikation
Juelich D-52425, Germany

Grunberg-Manago, Marianne (Misc)
80 Boulevard Pasteur
Paris 75015, FRANCE

Grundfest, Joseph A (Government Official)
Law School
Stanford, CA 94305, USA

Grundhofer, Jerry A (Financier)
777 E Wisconsin Ave
Milwaukee, WI 53202-5302, USA

Grundhofer, John F (Business Person, Financier)
1400 W 94th St
Bloomington, MN 55431-2301, USA

Grundman, Bernie (Musician)
1640 N Gower St
Hollywood, CA 90028-6518, USA

Grundt, Ken (Athlete, Baseball Player)
4814 W Parker Ave
Chicago, IL 60639-1712, USA

Grundy, Hugh (Musician)
PO Box 770850
Orlando, FL 32877-0850, USA

Grune, George V (Publisher)
PO Box 2348
Ponte Vedra Beach, FL 32004-2348, USA

Gruneisen, Sam (Athlete, Football Player)
569 Finsbay Ct
Ocoee, FL 34761-5658, USA

Grunewald, Barbara (Stylist)
2120 W Waveland Ave
Chicago, IL 60618-4923, USA

Grunfeld, Ernie (Athlete, Basketball Player)
10121 Counselman Rd
Potomac, MD 20854-5021, USA

Grunhard, Tim (Athlete, Football Player)
2005 Arno Rd
Mission Hills, KS 66208-2246, USA

Grunsfeld, John M (Astronaut)
PO Box 279
Highland, MD 20777-0279, USA

Grunwald, Al (Athlete, Baseball Player)
21001 Plummer St Spc 11
Chatsworth, CA 91311-0511, USA

Grunwald, Ernie (Actor)
c/o Suzanne (Sue) Wohl *TalentWorks (LA)*
3500 W Olive Ave Ste 1400
Burbank, CA 91505-5512, USA

Grunwald, Henry A (Diplomat, Editor)
62A Barkers Point Rd
Port Washington, NY 11050-1303, USA

Grunwald, Norten
Nyborggade Strandboulevarden 160-162
DK-2100
Copenhagen, DENMARK

Grupo Mania (Music Group)
c/o Staff Member *Sony Music Miami*
605 Lincoln Rd Ste 700
Miami Beach, FL 33139-2901, USA

Grupp, Robert (Athlete, Football Player)
305 Hill Ave
Langhorne, PA 19047-2819, USA

Grushin, Dave
200 W Superior St Ste 202
Chicago, IL 60654-3554

Grushin, Pyotr D (Engineer)
14 Lenisky Prospekt
Moscow, RUSSIA

Grusin, Dave (Composer, Musician)
200 W Superior St Ste 202
Chicago, IL 60654-3554, USA

Grutman, N Roy (Lawyer)
505 Park Ave
New York, NY 10022-1106, USA

Gruttadauria, Mike (Athlete, Football Player)
4250 Swift Rd
Sarasota, FL 34231-6547, USA

Gryboski, Kevin (Athlete, Baseball Player)
127 Castlebrooke Dr
Venetia, PA 15367-1391, USA

Grygiel, George (Athlete, Baseball Player)
451 W Bazille Way
Green Valley, AZ 85614-5270, USA

Grylls, Bear (Television Host)
c/o Michael Foster *The Rights House (UK)*
Drury House 34-43 Russell St
London WC2B 5HA, UK

Grymes, Darrell (Athlete, Football Player)
915 McCleary Ave Apt C
Dayton, OH 45406, USA

Gryp, Bob (Athlete, Hockey Player)
11 Duren Ave
Woburn, MA 01801-5304, USA

Grzanich, Mike (Athlete, Baseball Player)
176 Holliday Trce
Raymond, MS 39154-9569, USA

Grzenda, Joe (Athlete, Baseball Player)
40 Hillcrest Dr
Covington Township, PA 18424-7852, USA

Guadagnino, Kathy Baker (Athlete, Golfer)
1535 SW 4th Cir
Boca Raton, FL 33486-4414, USA

Guadagnino, Vinny (Reality TV Star)
c/o Sal Bonaventura *CEG Talent*
251 W 39th St Fl 7
New York, NY 10018-3171, USA

Guangbiao, Chen (Business Person)
Nanjing, Jiangsu Province, China

Guard, Christopher
76 Oxford St
London, ENGLAND W1N OAX

Guardado, Edward A (Eddie) (Athlete, Baseball Player)
11268 Overlook Pt
Tustin, CA 92782-4314, USA

Guardino, Harry (Actor)
2949 E Via Vaquero Rd
Palm Springs, CA 92262-7941, USA

Guarilia, Gene (Athlete, Basketball Player)
86 Main St
Duryea, PA 18642-1023, USA

Guarini, Justin (Musician)
c/o Jeff Ballard *Jeff Ballard PR*
4814 Lemona Ave
Sherman Oaks, CA 91403-2010, USA

Guarriello, Taimak (Actor)
c/o Staff Member *Chasin Agency, The*
8899 Beverly Blvd Ste 714
Los Angeles, CA 90048-2449, USA

Guaty, Camille (Actor)
c/o Michael Baum *Impression Entertainment*
9229 W Sunset Blvd Ste 700
West Hollywood, CA 90069-3407, USA

Guay, Paul (Athlete, Hockey Player)
34 Kirkbrae Dr
Lincoln, RI 02865-1019, USA

Gubaidulina, Sofia A (Composer)
2D Pugachevskaya 8 Korp 5 #130
Moscow 107061, RUSSIA

Gubanich, Creighton (Athlete, Baseball Player)
240 Hall St
Phoenixville, PA 19460-3511, USA

Gubarev, Aleksei A (Cosmonaut, General)
Moskovskoi Oblasti
Syvisdny Goroduk 141160, RUSSIA

Guber, Peter (Producer)
10202 Washington Blvd # 1070
Culver City, CA 90232-3119, USA

Gubert, Walter A (Financier)
270 Park Ave
New York, NY 10017-2014, USA

Gubicza, Mark (Athlete, Baseball Player)
11808 Macoda Ln
Chatsworth, CA 91311-1271, USA

Gubler, Matthew Gray (Actor, Director, Writer)
c/o Colton Gramm *Brillstein Entertainment Partners*
9150 Wilshire Blvd Ste 350
Beverly Hills, CA 90212-3453, USA

Gucci (Designer, Fashion Designer)
Rembrandt Tower, 1 Amstelplein 1096 HA
Amsterdam, The Netherlands

Gucciardo, Pat (Athlete, Football Player)
2406 Kenmoore Rd
Maumee, OH 43537-1121, USA

Guccione, Chris (Athlete, Baseball Player)
15362 W Iliff Dr
Denver, CO 80228-6443, USA

Guccione, Christopher (Baseball Player)
15362 W Iliff Dr
Denver, CO 80228-6443, USA

Guckel, Henry (Engineer)
Engineering Dept
Madison, WI 53706, USA

Guckert, Elmer (Baseball Player)
900 Lincoln Club Dr
Pittsburgh, PA 15237-5092, USA

Guckert, Elmer (Athlete, Baseball Player)
900 Lincoln Club Dr
Pittsburgh, PA 15237-5092, USA

Gudmundson, Scott (Athlete, Football Player)
11 Guindola Way Apt 268
Hot Springs Village, AR 71909-7128, USA

Guelleh, Ismail Omar (President)
8-10 Ahmed Nessim St
Djibouti, DJIBOUTI

Guennel, Joe (Soccer Player)
835 Front Range Rd
Littleton, CO 80120-4005, USA

Gueno, James (Athlete, Football Player)
6939 General Haig St
New Orleans, LA 70124-4030, USA

Guenther, Johnny (Bowler)
23826 115th Pl W
Woodway, WA 98020-5212, USA

Guerard, Michael E (Chef)
Les Pres d'Eugenie
Eugenie les Bains 40320, FRANCE

Guerard, Stephane (Athlete, Hockey Player)
30 Chemin De L'Artre
Lac Beauport, QC G0A 2C0, Canada

Guerin, Bill (Athlete, Hockey Player)
12 North Rd
Oyster Bay, NY 11771-1904, USA

Guerin, Richie (Athlete, Basketball Player)
1355 Bear Island Dr
West Palm Beach, FL 33409-2042, USA

Guerra, Blanca (Actor)
c/o Staff Member *Televisa*
Blvd Adolfo Lopez Mateos 232 Colonia
San Angel INN
DF CP 01060, MEXICO

Guerra, Eddie (Actor)
c/o Peter Micelli *Creative Artists Agency (CAA-LA)*
2000 Avenue of the Stars Ste 100
Los Angeles, CA 90067-4705, USA

Guerra, Jackie (Comedian)
c/o Staff Member *Brillstein Entertainment Partners*
9150 Wilshire Blvd Ste 350
Beverly Hills, CA 90212-3453, USA

Guerra, Juan Luis (Musician)
c/o Staff Member *EMI Recorded Music (EMI Group - NY)*
150 5th Ave Fl 7
New York, NY 10011-4372, USA

Guerra, Saverio (Actor)
c/o Susan Ferris *Bohemia Group*
1680 Vine St Ste 216
Los Angeles, CA 90028-8829, USA

Guerra, Vida (Actor, Model)
c/o Staff Member *Britto Agency PR*
234 W 56th St PH
New York, NY 10019-4302, USA

Guerrero, Julen (Soccer Player)
Alameda Mazarredo 23
Bilbao 48009, SPAIN

Guerrero, Mario (Athlete, Baseball Player)
Calle Duarte#450
Santo Domingo, Dominican Republic

Guerrero, Pedro (Athlete, Baseball Player)
10720 NW 66th St Apt 408
Doral, FL 33178-3657, USA

Guerrero, Roberto (Race Car Driver)
552 Hillside Ave
Bethlehem, PA 18015-3410, USA

Guerrero, Vladimir (Athlete, Baseball Player)
5160 E Copa De Oro Dr
Anaheim, CA 92807-3639, USA

Guerrero Coles, Lisa (Actor, Sportscaster)
c/o Lorraine Berglund *Lorraine Berglund Management*
11537 Hesby St
North Hollywood, CA 91601-3618, USA

Guerrier, Matt (Athlete, Baseball Player)
5719 E 139th St
Cleveland, OH 44125-4021, USA

Guers, Paul
40 Rue De Buci
Paris, FRANCE 75006

Guess Who
31 Hemlock Pl Winnepeg
Man., CANADA R2H 1L8

Guest, Christopher H (Actor, Director)
c/o Staff Member *Go Film*
51 E 12th St Fl 7
New York, NY 10003-4682, USA

Guest, Cornelia (Model)
1419 Donhill Dr
Beverly Hills, CA 90210-2216, USA

Guest, Douglas (Misc)
Gables Minchinhampton
Gloscester GL6 9JE, UNITED KINGDOM (UK)

Guest, Lance
116 Pinehurst Ave
New York, NY 10033-1755

Guetary, Francois (Actor)
36 Rue de Ponthieu
Paris 75008, FRANCE

Guetta, David (DJ, Musician)
c/o Maria May *International Talent Booking*
1st Floor, Ariel House 74A Charlotte St
London W1T 4QJ, UNITED KINGDOM

Guetterman, Lee (Athlete, Baseball Player)
108 1/2 E Broadway St
Lenoir City, TN 37771-2908, USA

Guevremont, Jocelyn (Athlete, Hockey Player)
4020 SW 84th Ter
Davie, FL 33328-2951, USA

Guffey Jr, John W (Business Person)
2550 W Tyvola Rd
Charlotte, NC 28217-4574, USA

Gugelmin, Mauricio (Race Car Driver)
PO Box 1607
Bellevue, WA 98009-1607, USA

Guggemos, Neal (Athlete, Football Player)
8173 Drexel Ct
Eden Prairie, MN 55347-2189, USA

Guggenheim, Alan (Inventor)
PO Box 5339
Bend, OR 97708-5339, USA

Guggenheim, Marc (Actor)
c/o Eddie Michaels *Insignia Public Relations*
1507 20th St Ste D
Santa Monica, CA 90404-3474, USA

Gugino, Carla (Actor)
c/o Jason Weinberg *Untitled Entertainment (LA)*
350 S Beverly Dr Ste 200
Beverly Hills, CA 90212-4819, USA

Guglielmi, Ralph (Athlete, Football Player)
159 Red Berry Dr
Wallace, NC 28466-2376, USA

Gugliotta, Tom (Athlete, Basketball Player)
992 Wadsworth Dr NW
Atlanta, GA 30318-1654, USA

Gugloitta, Tom (Athlete, Basketball Player)
992 Wadsworth Dr NW
Atlanta, GA 30318-1654, USA

Guice, Jackson (Cartoonist)
1700 Broadway
New York, NY 10019-5905, USA

Guida, Gloria
Via Francesco Denza 48
Rome, ITALY I-00197

Guida, Lou (Misc)
4800 Highway A1A Apt 505
Vero Beach, FL 32963-1224, USA

Guidi, Osvaldo (Actor)
c/o Staff Member *Telefe - Argentina*
Pavon 2444 (C1248AAT)
Buenos Aires, ARGENTINA

Guidinger, Jay (Athlete, Basketball Player)
N39W22702 Grandview Dr
Pewaukee, WI 53072-2735, USA

Guidolin, Aldo (Athlete, Hockey Player)
64 Hilldale Cres
Guelph, ON N1G 4B9, Canada

Guidolin, Bep (Athlete, Hockey Player)
6 Northpark Rd
Barrie, ON L4M 2J3, Canada

Guidoni, Umberto (Astronaut)
15010 Cobre Valley Dr
Houston, TX 77062-2810, USA

Guidry, Kevin (Athlete, Football Player)
4045 W Briarfield St
Lake Charles, LA 70607-3658, USA

Guidry, Mark
1264 Camelot Ln
Lemont, IL 60439-8505

Guidry, N T (Engineer)
23971 Coral Springs Ln
Tehachapi, CA 93561, USA

Guidry, Paul (Athlete, Football Player)
880 Noel Dr
Mount Juliet, TN 37122-1352, USA

Guidry, Ronald A (Ron) (Athlete, Baseball Player)
PO Box 666
Scott, LA 70583-0666, USA

Guiel, Aaron (Athlete, Baseball Player)
18944 69 Ave
Surrey, BC V4N 5K1, Canada

Guilbaut, Jeremy (Actor)
c/o Russ Mortensen *Pacific Artists Management*
1285 W Broadway Suite 685
Vancouver, BC V6H 3X8, Canada

Guilbe, Felix (Baseball Player)
Los Cabos Calle Carambala
Ponce, PR 716, USA

Guilbert, Ann (Actor)
550 Erskine Dr
Pacific Palisades, CA 90272-4247, USA

Guilford, Eric (Athlete, Football Player)
8111 W Wacker Rd Unit 51
Peoria, AZ 85381-4943, USA

Guilfoyle, Paul (Actor)
c/o Donna Massetti *Silver Massetti & Szatmary (SMS) Talent Inc*
8730 W Sunset Blvd Ste 440
Los Angeles, CA 90069-2277, USA

Guill, Juliana (Actor)
c/o Tim Taylor *Luber Roklin Management*
8530 Wilshire Blvd Ste 550
Beverly Hills, CA 90211-3133, USA

Guillaume, Robert (Actor)
c/o Alan David *Alan David Management*
8840 Wilshire Blvd Ste 200
Beverly Hills, CA 90211-2606, USA

Guillem, Sylvie (Ballerina)
c/o Staff Member *Royal Ballet*
Covent Garden Bow St
London WC2E 9DD, UK

Guillemin, Roger C L (Nobel Prize Laureate)
7316 Encelia Dr
La Jolla, CA 92037-5728, USA

Guillemots (Music Group, Musician)
c/o Staff Member *MCT Management*
520 8th Ave Rm 2205
New York, NY 10018-4160, USA

Guillen, Francesca (Actor)
c/o Staff Member *Televisa*
Blvd Adolfo Lopez Mateos 232 Colonia San Angel INN
DF CP 01060, MEXICO

Guillen, Oswaldo J (Ozzie) (Athlete, Baseball Player, Coach)
19462 38th Ct
Golden Beach, FL 33160-2298, USA

Guillerman, John (Director)
309 S Rockingham Ave
Los Angeles, CA 90049-3637, USA

Guillermin, John
309 S Rockingham Ave
Los Angeles, CA 90049-3637

Guillo, Dominque (Actor)
36 Rue de Ponthieu
Paris 75008, FRANCE

Guillory, Bennet
1519 Galaxy Ct
Rohnert Park, CA 94928-5611

Guillory, Sienna (Actor)
c/o Holly Shakoor *42West (LA)*
11400 W Olympic Blvd Ste 1100
Los Angeles, CA 90064-1579, USA

Guinan, Francis
606 N Larchmont Blvd # 309LA
Los Angeles, CA 90004-1321

Guindon, Bob (Athlete, Baseball Player)
437 Marsh Creek Rd
Venice, FL 34292-5314, USA

Guindon, Richard G (Cartoonist)
321 W Lafayette Blvd
Detroit, MI 48226-2703, USA

Guinee, Tim (Actor)
c/o Jonathan Howard *Innovative Artists (LA)*
1505 10th St
Santa Monica, CA 90401-2805, USA

Guiney, Bob (Game Show Host, Reality TV Star)
c/o Anthony Embry *AE Entertainment Public Relations*
124 Evening Shade Dr
Charleston, SC 29414-9144, USA

Guinier, Lani (Educator, Lawyer)
3400 Chestnut St
Philadelphia, PA 19104-6204, USA

Guinn, Skip (Athlete, Baseball Player)
PO Box 911
Stilwell, OK 74960-0911, USA

Guinney, Bob (Reality TV Star)
c/o Kim Jakwerth *Marleah Leslie & Associates PR*
1645 Vine St Apt 712
Los Angeles, CA 90028-8812, USA

Guinta, Frank (Congressman, Politician)
1223 Longworth Hob
Washington, DC 20515-3810, USA

Guirgis, Stephen Adly (Comedian)
c/o Staff Member *Gersh (LA)*
9465 Wilshire Blvd Ste 600
Beverly Hills, CA 90212-2612, USA

Guiry, Thomas (Actor)
c/o Rhonda Price *Gersh (NY)*
41 Madison Ave
New York, NY 10010-2202, USA

Guisewite, Cathy L (Cartoonist)
4039 Camellia Ave
Studio City, CA 91604-3007, USA

Guite, Pierre (Athlete, Hockey Player)
96085 Marsh Lakes Dr
Fernandina Beach, FL 32034-0825, USA

Gujral, Inder Kumar (Prime Minister)
5 Janpath
New Delhi, Delhi 110011, INDIA

Gujral, Namrata
c/o Mike Eistenstadt *Amsel, Eisenstadt & Frazier Talent Agency (AEF)*
5055 Wilshire Blvd Ste 860
Los Angeles, CA 90036-6108, USA

Gulager, Clu (Actor)
320 Wilshire Blvd
Santa Monica, CA 90401-1315, USA

Gulan, Mike (Athlete, Baseball Player)
4409 Fairway Dr
Steubenville, OH 43953-3305, USA

Gulbinowicx, Henryk Roman Cardinal (Religious Leader)
UL Katedraina 11
Wroclaw 50-328, POLAND

Gulbis, Natalie (Athlete, Golfer)
7733 Glenn Ave
Citrus Heights, CA 95610-1508, USA

Guldelli, Giovanni (Actor)
Via Giuseppe Pisanelli
Rome 196, ITALY

Gulden, Brad (Athlete, Baseball Player)
15820 Lundstead Rd
Carver, MN 55315-9702, USA

Guleghina, Maria (Opera Singer)
27 Chancery Lane
London WC2A 1PF, UNITED KINGDOM (UK)

Gulledge, David (Athlete, Football Player)
1064 Inverness Cove Way
Birmingham, AL 35242-4217, USA

Gullett, Donald E (Don) (Athlete, Baseball Player)
196 Kingsway Dr
South Shore, KY 41175, USA

Gulli, Franco (Musician)
165 W 57th St
New York, NY 10019-2201, USA

Gullickson, William L (Bill) (Athlete, Baseball Player)
3 Banchory Ct
Palm Beach Gardens, FL 33418-6811, USA

Gullikson, Tom (Athlete)
8000 Sears Tower
Chicago, IL 60606

Gullit, Ruud (Soccer Player)
Stamford Bridge Fulham Road
London SW6 1HS, UNITED KINGDOM (UK)

Gulliver, Dorothy
28792 Lajos Ln
Valley Center, CA 92082-6107

Gulliver, Glenn (Athlete, Baseball Player)
8123 Cortland Ave
Allen Park, MI 48101-2215, USA

Gulliver, Harold (Editor)
72 Marietta St NW
Atlanta, GA 30303-2804, USA

Gulman, Gary (Musician)
c/o Staff Member *Paradigm (Monterey)*
404 W Franklin St
Monterey, CA 93940-2303, USA

Gulseth, Don (Athlete, Football Player)
100 2nd St SE Apt 202
Minneapolis, MN 55414-2128, USA

Gulyas, Denes (Opera Singer)
Andrassy Utca 22
Budapest 1062, HUNGARY

Gulzar (Bollywood, Songwriter, Writer)
Boskiyana Pali Hill Bandra (W)
Mumbai, MS 400050, INDIA

Guman, Michael D (Mike) (Athlete, Football Player)
3913 Pleasant Ave
Allentown, PA 18103-9773, USA

Gumbel, Bryant C (Correspondent, Television Host)
280 Park Ave Fl 15
New York, NY 10017-1216, USA

Gumbel, Greg (Sportscaster, Television Host)
c/o Staff Member *CBS Television*
51 W 52nd St
New York, NY 10019-6119, USA

Gummer, Henry (Musician)
c/o Matthew Berkson *Undermountain Records*
843 Tipton Ter
Los Angeles, CA 90042-1253, USA

Gummer, Mamie (Actor)
c/o Michelle Benson *42West (NY)*
220 W 42nd St Fl 12
New York, NY 10036-7200, USA

Gummersall, Devon (Actor)
c/o Peg Donegan *Framework Entertainment (LA)*
9057 Nemo St Ste C
West Hollywood, CA 90069-5511, USA

Gump, Scott (Athlete, Golfer)
410 Macchi Ave
Oakland, FL 34787-3058, USA

Gumpert, Dave (Athlete, Baseball Player)
68371 Fleetwood Dr
South Haven, MI 49090-8357, USA

Gumpert, Randy (Athlete, Baseball Player)
49 School St
Douglassville, PA 19518-9777, USA

Gun, Jang Dong (Actor)
152-4-4 Bukit Gembira Condo Off Jalan Kuchai Lama
kuala lumpur, wilayah
persekutuan 58200, Mylasia

Gund, Agnes (Misc)
11 W 53rd St
New York, NY 10019-5401, USA

Gunderman, Robert (Athlete, Football Player)
11 Post Brook Rd S
West Milford, NJ 07480-4518, USA

Gunderson, Eric (Athlete, Baseball Player)
19809 SE 10th St
Camas, WA 98607-7273, USA

Gundi (Actor)
RR1
Roseneath, ON KOK 2XO, CANADA

Gundu, Kalyanam (Actor)
D-1 Block Lloyds Colony Royapettah
Chennai, TN 600 014, INDIA

Gunmuddsson, Petur (Athlete, Basketball Player)
2423 Vibrant Oak
San Antonio, TX 78232-2616, USA

Gunn, Anna (Actor)
c/o Gregg A Klein *Abrams Artists Agency (LA)*
9200 W Sunset Blvd PH 11
Los Angeles, CA 90069-3601, USA

Gunn, James (Actor, Director, Writer)
c/o Peter Safran *The Safran Company*
8748 Holloway Dr
West Hollywood, CA 90069-2327, USA

Gunn, James P (Astronomer)
Astrophysics
Princeton, NJ 08544-0001, USA

Gunn, Lance (Athlete, Football Player)
10600 Arrowhead Dr Ste 225
Fairfax, VA 22030-7306, USA

Gunn, Nathan (Opera Singer)
c/o Staff Member *Opus 3 Artists*
5670 Wilshire Blvd Ste 1790
Los Angeles, CA 90036-5627, USA

Gunn, Richard (Actor)
c/o Chris Henze *Thruline Entertainment*
9250 Wilshire Blvd Ground Fl
Beverly Hills, CA 90212, USA

Gunn, Sean (Actor)
c/o Mitch Clem *Shadow Entertainment*
10 Universal City Plz Fl 20
Universal City, CA 91608-1074, USA

Gunn, Tim (Educator, Reality TV Star, Television Host)
c/o Staff Member *Project Runway*
915 Broadway Fl 20
New York, NY 10010-7131, USA

Gunnell, Sally (Athlete, Track Athlete)
18 Shepherd's Croft Brighton
East Sussex, UNITED KINGDOM (UK)

Gunnels, Riley (Athlete, Football Player)
606 Wesley Ave
Ocean City, NJ 08226-3856, USA

Gunner, Harry (Athlete, Football Player)
3550 Blodgett St Apt 4308C
Houston, TX 77004-6498, USA

Guns N' Roses (Music Group)
c/o Staff Member *Geffen Records*
9126 Sunset Blvd
West Hollywood, CA 90069, USA

Gunter, Dan (Actor)
PO Box 59747
Santa Barbara, CA 93150, USA

Gunther, David (Athlete, Basketball Player)
827 Pleasantview Dr
Auburndale, FL 33823-5870, USA

Guokas Jr, Matt (Athlete, Basketball Player, Coach)
2410 S 19th St
Philadelphia, PA 19145-4226, USA

Guolla, Steve (Athlete, Hockey Player)
733 Spartan Dr
Rochester Hills, MI 48309-2528, USA

Gupta, Neena (Actor)
129 Aram Nagar II Versova Road Andheri
Bombay, MS 400 061, INDIA

Gupta, Raj (Business Person)
100 S Independence Mall W Ste 1A
Philadelphia, PA 19106-2320, USA

Gupta, Sanjay (Correspondent, Doctor)
c/o Staff Member *CNN (Atlanta)*
1 Cnn Ctr NW
Atlanta, GA 30303-2762, USA

Gupta, Sudhir (Misc)
Medicine Dept
Irvine, CA 92717, USA

Gur, Mordechai (General)
25 Mishmeret St Afeka
Tel-Aviv 69694, ISRAEL

Gura, Larry C (Athlete, Baseball Player)
PO Box 94
Litchfield Park, AZ 85340-0094, USA

Gurchenko, Ludmilla M (Actor)
Trekjprudny Per 5/15 #22
Moscow 103001, RUSSIA

Gurdon, John B (Misc)
Magdalene College Master's Cottage
Cambridge CB3 0AG, UNITED KINGDOM (UK)

Guren, Peter (Cartoonist)
5777 W Century Blvd Ste 700
Los Angeles, CA 90045-5652, USA

Gurewitz, Brett (Musician)
c/o Staff Member *WmE2 (WMA-LA)*
1 William Morris Pl
Beverly Hills, CA 90212-4261, USA

Gurganus, Alan (Writer)
1745 Broadway Fl 20
New York, NY 10019-4368, USA

Gurian, Michael (Writer)
417 W 32nd Ave
Spokane, WA 99203-1777, USA

Gurney, Dan (Race Car Driver)
2334 S Broadway
Santa Ana, CA 92707-3250, USA

Gurney, Daniel S (Dan) (Race Car Driver)
2334 S Broadway
Santa Ana, CA 92707-3250, USA

Gurney, Hilda (Horse Racer)
8430 Waters Rd
Moorpark, CA 93021-8715, USA

Gurney, Scott (Actor)
c/o Staff Member *Guttman Associates*
118 S Beverly Dr Ste 201
Beverly Hills, CA 90212-3016, USA

Gurney Jr, Albert R (A R) (Writer)
40 Wellers Bridge Rd
Roxbury, CT 06783-1616, USA

Gurode, Andre (Athlete, Football Player)
PO Box 271835
Flower Mound, TX 75027-1835, USA

Gurry, Kick (Actor)
c/o Robert Stein *Robert Stein Management*
PO Box 3797
Beverly Hills, CA 90212-0797, USA

Gursky, Al (Athlete, Football Player)
54 Securda Rd
Reading, PA 19607-2521, USA

Gurwitch, Annabelle (Actor)
6500 Wilshire Blvd Ste 2200
Los Angeles, CA 90048-4942, USA

Gus Gus (Music Group)
c/o Andrew Curley *International Talent Booking*
1st Floor, Ariel House 74A Charlotte St
London W1T 4QJ, UNITED KINGDOM

Gusarov, Alexei (Athlete, Hockey Player)
1168 Yankee Creek Rd
Evergreen, CO 80439-4108, USA

Gusella, James (Inventor)
25 Shattuck St
Boston, MA 02115-6027, USA

Gusev, Sergei (Athlete, Hockey Player)
16001 Ridley Pl Apt 2-A
Tampa, FL 33647-2050, USA

Gushiken, Koji (Gymnast)
Judo School
Tokyo, JAPAN

Gusmao, Jose Alexandre (Xanana) (President)
Dili, EAST TIMOR

Gustafson, Derek (Athlete, Hockey Player)
3309 NE 165th Ave
Vancouver, WA 98682-8653, USA

Gustafson, Ed (Athlete, Football Player)
6209 Mineral Point Rd Apt 1007
Madison, WI 53705-4555, USA

Gustafson, Kathryn (Architect)
Pier 55 #31101 Alaskan Way
Seattle, WA 98101, USA

Gustafson, Sophie (Athlete, Golfer)
6043 Jamestown Park
Orlando, FL 32819-4435, USA

Gustafson, Steven (Musician)
9200 W Sunset Blvd Ste 900
Los Angeles, CA 90069-3604, USA

Gustafsson, Per (Athlete, Hockey Player)
5605 NE 3rd Ave
Fort Lauderdale, FL 33334-1705, USA

Gustav, H.M. King Carl XVI (Royalty)
Kungl. Slottet
Stockholm SE-111 30, Sweden

Guster (Music Group)
c/o Staff Member *Nettwerk Management (NY)*
345 7th Ave Fl 24
New York, NY 10001-5006, USA

Gutensohn-Knopf, Katrin (Skier)
Oberfeldweg 12
Oberaudorf 83080, GERMANY

Guterman, Lawrence M (Director)
c/o Staff Member *WmE2 (Endeavor-LA)*
9601 Wilshire Blvd Fl 3
Beverly Hills, CA 90210-5219, USA

Guth, Alan H (Physicist)
Physics Dept
Cambridge, MA 2139, USA

Guth, Bucky (Athlete, Baseball Player)
202 Morris Dr
Salisbury, MD 21804-7229, USA

Guthe, Manfred (Cinematographer)
122 Collier St
Toronto, ON M4W 1M3, CANADA

Gutherie, Arlo (Actor, Composer, Musician)
c/o Dora Whitaker *Whitaker Agency, The*
4924 Vineland Ave
N Hollywood, CA 91601-3847, USA

Gutherie, Jeremy (Athlete, Baseball Player)
1004 Clay St
Ashland, OR 97520-3613, USA

Guthrie, Arlo (Musician, Songwriter)
c/o Dora Whitaker *Whitaker Agency, The*
4924 Vineland Ave
N Hollywood, CA 91601-3847, USA

Guthrie, Brett (Congressman, Politician)
308 Cannon Hob
Washington, DC 20515-4701, USA

Guthrie, Janet (Race Car Driver)
PO Box 505
Aspen, CO 81612-0505, USA

Guthrie, Jennifer (Actor)
6500 Wilshire Blvd Ste 2200
Los Angeles, CA 90048-4942, USA

Guthrie, Mark (Athlete, Baseball Player)
3129 Donald Ross Rd E
Sarasota, FL 34240-7628, USA

Gutierrez, Alexander (Stylist)
c/o Staff Member *Workgroup (Hollywood)*
8491 W Sunset Blvd # 368
West Hollywood, CA 90069-1911, USA

Gutierrez, Brock (Athlete, Football Player)
1040 Pueblo Pass
Weidman, MI 48893-9322, USA

Gutierrez, Carlos M (Business Person)
PO Box 3599
Battle Creek, MI 49016-3599, USA

Gutierrez, Diego (Actor)
c/o Staff Member *Creative Artists Agency (CAA-LA)*
2000 Avenue of the Stars Ste 100
Los Angeles, CA 90067-4705, USA

Gutierrez, Franklin (Athlete, Baseball Player)
3180 N Jog Rd Apt 4202
West Palm Bch, FL 33411-7432, USA

Gutierrez, Gustavo (Misc)
Apartado 3090
Lima 100, PERU

Gutierrez, Horacio (Music Group, Musician)
40 W 57th St
New York, NY 10019-4001, USA

Gutierrez, Jackie (Athlete, Baseball Player)
10631 SW 126th Ave
Miami, FL 33186-3744, USA

Gutierrez, Luclo (President)
Garcia Moreno
Quito 1043, ECUADOR

Gutierrez, Ricky (Athlete, Baseball Player)
13803 NW 10th Ct
Pembroke Pines, FL 33028-2350, USA

Gutierrez, Sidney M (Astronaut)
324 Sarah Ln NW
Albuquerque, NM 87114-1026, USA

Gutman, Natalia G (Music Group, Musician)
27 Chancery Lane
London WC2A 1PF, UNITED KINGDOM (UK)

Gutman, Roy W (Journalist)
1349 Windy Hill Rd
McLean, VA 22102-2803, USA

Gutmann, Amy (Educator)
President S Ofc
Princeton, NJ 08544-0001, USA

Gutsche, TorstenHans- (Athlete)
Hans-Marchwitza-Ring 51
Potsdam 14473, GERMANY

Gutschewski, Scott (Basketball Player, Golfer)
20110 Douglas St
Elkhorn, NE 68022-1600, USA

Guttenberg, Steve (Actor)
c/o Staff Member *Binder & Associates*
1465 Lindacrest Dr
Beverly Hills, CA 90210-2519, USA

Gutz, Julie (Baseball Player)
9940 Gappa Rd
Kabetogama, MN 56669-8048, USA

Guy, Buddy (Music Group, Musician)
200 W Superior St Ste 202
Chicago, IL 60654-3554, USA

Guy, Cristy (Stylist)
c/o Staff Member *It's All in the Clothes*
5720 Martway St Apt 102
Mission, KS 66202-3417, USA

Guy, Francois-Frederic (Music Group, Musician)
4 Addison Bridge Place
London W14 8XP, UNITED KINGDOM (UK)

Guy, Jasmine (Actor)
c/o Staff Member *Stone Manners Salners Agency (LA)*
9911 W Pico Blvd Ste 1400
Los Angeles, CA 90035-2715, USA

Guy, Kevan (Athlete, Hockey Player)
10127 Dunsinane Dr
South Jordan, UT 84095-9066, USA

Guy, Louis (Athlete, Football Player)
2127 Sheffield Dr
Jackson, MS 39211-5851, USA

Guy, Melwood (Athlete, Football Player)
128 Clearwater Dr
Ellwood City, PA 16117-3058, USA

Guy, Ray (Athlete, Football Player)
936 Central Rd SW
Thomson, GA 30824-8278, USA

Guy, Sebastien (Actor)
c/o Staff Member *Acme Talent & Literary (LA)*
1400 Atlantic Ave Ste 274
Long Beach, CA 90813-2013, USA

Guy, William L (Ex-Governor)
3330 W Prairiewood Dr S
Fargo, ND 58103-4666, USA

Guyer, Cindy (Actor)
c/o Marta Michaud *Cinematic Management*
249 1/2 E 13th St
New York, NY 10003-5602, USA

Guyer, David B (Misc)
514 2nd St
Owyhee, NV 89832, USA

Guynn, Jack (Financier, Government Official)
1000 Peachtree St NE
Atlanta, GA 30309-3904, USA

Guyon, John C (Educator)
President's Office
Carbondale, IL 62901, USA

Guyot, Paul (Actor, Producer, Writer)
c/o Kathy White *Creative Artists Agency (CAA-LA)*
2000 Avenue of the Stars Ste 100
Los Angeles, CA 90067-4705, USA

Guyton, Myron (Athlete, Football Player)
PO Box 3481
Thomasville, GA 31799-3481, USA

Guzik, John (Athlete, Football Player)
905 Rider Ave
Salinas, CA 93905-1090, USA

Guzman, Alejandra (Musician)
c/o Staff Member *BMG*
1540 Broadway
New York, NY 10036-4039, USA

Guzman, Andrea (Actor)
c/o Staff Member *TV Caracol*
Calle 76 #11 - 35 Piso 10AA
Bogota DC 26484, COLOMBIA

Guzman, Cristian (Athlete, Baseball Player)
10727 Cory Lake Dr
Tampa, FL 33647-2725, USA

Guzman, Jose (Athlete, Baseball Player)
4401 Shadycreek Ln
Colleyville, TX 76034-4729, USA

Guzman, Juan (Athlete, Baseball Player)
176 Dockside Cir
Weston, FL 33327-1100, USA

Guzman, Luis (Actor)
232 N Canon Dr
Beverly Hills, CA 90210-5302, USA

Guzman, Santiago (Baseball Player)
1712 N Douty St
Hanford, CA 93230-2155, USA

Guzy, Carol (Journalist, Photographer)
2145 Fort Scott Dr
Arlington, VA 22202, USA

Gwathmey, Charles (Architect)
475 10th Ave
New York, NY 10018-1120, USA

Gwinn, Mary Ann (Journalist)
1120 John St
Seattle, WA 98109-5321, USA

Gwinn, Ross (Athlete, Football Player)
1736 Washington St
Natchitoches, LA 71457-4926, USA

Gwosdz, Doug (Athlete, Baseball Player)
2108 Rose Rd
Pearland, TX 77581-3844, USA

Gwyn, Marcus (Athlete, Baseball Player)
150 E Elm Cres
Spring, TX 77382-1047, USA

Gwynn, Chris (Athlete, Baseball Player)
10975 Hillside Rd
Rancho Cucamonga, CA 91737-2458, USA

Gwynn, Darrell (Race Car Driver)
4850 SW 52nd St
Davie, FL 33314-5526, USA

Gwynn, Tony (Athlete, Baseball Player)
c/o John Boggs *John Boggs & Associates*
5675 Ruffin Rd Ste 350
San Diego, CA 92123-1398, USA

Gwynn, Tony (Athlete, Baseball Player)
5500 Campanile Dr Attn Headbaseballcoach
San Diego, CA 92182-0001, USA

Gwynn Jr, Tony (Athlete, Baseball Player)
15643 Boulder Ridge Ln
Poway, CA 92064-2172, USA

Gwynne, A Patrick (Architect)
Homewood Esher
Surrey KT10 9JL, UNITED KINGDOM (UK)

Gyanendra (King)
Narayanhiti Durbag Marg
Kathmandu, NEPAL

Gyll, J Soren (Business Person)
Goteborg 405 08, SWEDEN

Gyllenhaal, Jake (Actor)
c/o Evelyn O'Neill *Management 360*
9111 Wilshire Blvd
Beverly Hills, CA 90210-5508, USA

Gyllenhaal, Maggie (Actor)
c/o Courtney Kivowitz *Schiff Company, The*
8440 Warner Dr Ste B1
Culver City, CA 90232-2461, USA

Gyllenhaal, Stephen G (Director, Producer, Writer)
c/o Staff Member *WmE2 (WMA-LA)*
1 William Morris Pl
Beverly Hills, CA 90212-4261, USA

Gyllenhammer, Pehr G (Business Person)
CHU PLC Saint Helen's 1 Undershaft
London EC3P 3DQ, UNITED KINGDOM (UK)

Gym Class Heroes (Music Group)
c/o Bob McLynn *Crush Management*
60-62 E 11th St Floor 7
New York, NY 10003, USA

GZA (Musician)
c/o Staff Member *Agency Group Ltd, The (NY)*
142 W 57th St Fl 6
New York, NY 10019-3300, USA

H

H. Bishop, Timothy (Congressman, Politician)
306 Cannon Hob
Washington, DC 20515-0303, USA

H. Hoyer, Steney (Congressman, Politician)
1705 Longworth Hob
Washington, DC 20515-2005, USA

H. Michaud, Michael (Congressman, Politician)
1724 Longworth Hob
Washington, DC 20515-0509, USA

Ha Jin (Writer)
English
Atlanta, GA 30332-0001, USA

Haag, Rudolf (Physicist)
Waldschmidt Str 4B
Schliersee-Neuhaus 83727, GERMANY

Haag, Ulrika (Stylist)
c/o Staff Member *Wilhelmina Miami Beauty*
927 Lincoln Rd Ste 200
Miami Beach, FL 33139-2618, USA

Haakon (Prince)
Det Kongeligel Slottet Drammensveien 1
Oslo 10, NORWAY

Haas, Andrew T (Misc)
1300 Connecticut Ave NW
Washington, DC 20036-1703, USA

Haas, Carl
500 Tower Pkwy
Lincolnshire, IL 60069-3600

Haas, Dave (Athlete, Baseball Player)
160 E 6th Pl
Mesa, AZ 85201-5068, USA

Haas, Eddie (Athlete, Baseball Player, Coach)
8314 Alpena Way
Louisville, KY 40242-2502, USA

Haas, Ernest (Photographer)
853 7th Ave
New York, NY 10019-5215, USA

Haas, Hunter (Athlete, Golfer)
616 Shady Ln
Southlake, TX 76092-6655, USA

Haas, Jay (Athlete, Golfer)
4 Tuscany Ct
Greer, SC 29650-4021, USA

Haas, Lucas (Actor)
409 N Camden Dr Ste 202
Beverly Hills, CA 90210-4423, USA

Haas, Lukas (Actor)
c/o Jason Weinberg *Untitled Entertainment (LA)*
350 S Beverly Dr Ste 200
Beverly Hills, CA 90212-4819, USA

Haas, Moose (Athlete, Baseball Player)
4351 E Lariat Ln
Phoenix, AZ 85050-8905, USA

Haas, Rachel (Stylist)
c/o Staff Member *Apostrophe (NY)*
527 W 29th St
New York, NY 10001-1342, USA

Haas, Richard J (Artist)
29 Overcliff St
Yonkers, NY 10705-1418, USA

Haas, Robert D (Business Person)
1155 Battery St
San Francisco, CA 94111-1203, USA

Haas, Thomas (Tommy) (Tennis Player)
Schmiritzer Weg
Weiden 92637, GERMANY

Haas, Waltraud
Kuniglberggasse 45
Vienna, AUSTRIA A-1130

Haase, Andy (Athlete, Football Player)
1508 Bon Homme Richard Dr
Fort Collins, CO 80526-9695, USA

Haayer, Adam (Athlete, Football Player)
2362 Stonecrest Path NW
Prior Lake, MN 55372-4006, USA

Habel, Karl (Misc, Scientist)
RR 1 Box 252
Reading, PA 19607, USA

Habel, Sarah (Actor)
c/o Everly Lee *Agency for the Performing Arts (APA-LA)*
405 S Beverly Dr Ste 500
Beverly Hills, CA 90212-4425, USA

Haber, Norman (Inventor)
470 Main Rd
Towaco, NJ 07082-1248, USA

Habermann, Eva
Kuckuchsberg 9
Lutiansee, GERMANY D-22952

Habermas, Jurgen (Misc)
Ringstr 8B
Stamberg 82319, GERMANY

Habib, Brian (Athlete, Football Player)
17235 Sangallo Ln
San Diego, CA 92127-2807, USA

Habib, Munir (Astronaut, Misc)
Moskovskoi Oblasti
Syvisdny Goroduk 141160, RUSSIA

Habibie, Baharuddin Jusuf (President)
15 Jalan Merdeka Utara
Jakarta, INDONESIA

Habiger, Eugene E (Gene) (General)
1000 Independence NW
Washington, DC 20585-0001, USA

Habraken, Nicolaas J (Architect)
63 Wildemislaan
Apeldoom 7313 BD, NETHERLAND

Habscheid, Marc (Athlete, Hockey Player)
6 Sussex Rd
Winchester, MA 01890-3848, USA

Habyan, John (Athlete, Baseball Player)
4 Dorfer Ln
Nesconset, NY 11767-1067, USA

Hachette, Jean-Louis (Publisher)
83 Ave Marceau
Paris 75116, FRANCE

Hachten, William (Athlete, Football Player)
6205 Mineral Point Rd Apt 210
Madison, WI 53705-4577, USA

Hack, Olivia (Actor)
c/o Bonnie Ventis *Clear Talent Group (LA)*
10950 Ventura Blvd
Studio City, CA 91604-3340, USA

Hack, Shelley (Actor, Model)
1208 Georgina Ave
Santa Monica, CA 90402-2120, USA

Hackbart, Dale (Athlete, Football Player)
2541 Cowley Dr
Lafayette, CO 80026-9175, USA

Hacker, Carol (Stylist)
2534 Polk St
San Francisco, CA 94109-1607, USA

Hacker, Rich (Athlete, Baseball Player)
2900 18th Fairway Dr
Belleville, IL 62220-4840, USA

Hackerman, Norman (Scientist)
5842 Westslope Dr
Austin, TX 78731-3633, USA

Hackett, Dino (Athlete, Football Player)
1152 Kearns Hackett Rd
Pleasant Garden, NC 27313-8218, USA

Hackett, D.J. (Athlete, Football Player)
6510 S Delmar Pl
Gilbert, AZ 85298-4061, USA

Hackett, Grant (Swimmer)
PO Box 940
Dickson, ACT 2602, AUSTRALIA

Hackett, Jeff (Athlete, Hockey Player)
c/o Staff Member *Colorado Avalanche*
Pepsi Center 1000 Chopper Cir
Denver, CO 80204, USA

Hackett, Joey (Athlete, Football Player)
1147 Kearns Hackett Rd
Pleasant Garden, NC 27313-8218, USA

Hackett, Martha (Actor)
8899 Beverly Blvd Ste 815
Los Angeles, CA 90048-2452, USA

Hackett, Paul (Politician)
PO Box 43281
Cincinnati, OH 45243-0281, USA

Hackett, Rudy (Athlete, Basketball Player)
10330 Downey Ave Unit 30
Downey, CA 90241-5914, USA

Hackford, Taylor (Director, Producer, Writer)
c/o Stan Rosenfield *Stan Rosenfield & Associates*
2029 Century Park E Ste 1190
Los Angeles, CA 90067-2931, USA

Hackl, Georg (Athlete)
Caftehaus Soamatl Ramsauerstr 100
Berchtesgaden-Engedey 83471, GERMANY

Hackman, Gene (Actor)
c/o Susan Madore *Guttman Associates*
118 S Beverly Dr Ste 201
Beverly Hills, CA 90212-3016, USA

Hackman, Luther (Athlete, Baseball Player)
1406 12th Ave N Apt 16G
Columbus, MS 39701-3602, USA

Hackney, Lisa (Basketball Player, Golfer)
c/o Staff Member *Signature Sports Group*
4150 Olson Memorial Hey Suite 110
Minneapolis, MN 55422, USA

Hackney, Roderick P (Architect)
Saint Peter's House Windmill St
Macclesfield
Cheshire SK11 7HS, UNITED KINGDOM (UK)

Hackwith, Scott (Music Group, Musician, Songwriter, Writer)
156 W 56th St # 500
New York, NY 10019-3800, USA

Hadas, Rachel C (Educator, Writer)
360 Dr Martin Luther King Jr Blvd 520
Hill Hail
Newark, NJ 07102-1801, USA

Haddad, Drew (Athlete, Football Player)
28532 E Brockway Dr
Westlake, OH 44145-5246, USA

Haddix, Margaret (Writer)
c/o Joshua Adams *Adams Literary*
7845 Colony Rd Ste C4
Charlotte, NC 28226-7678, USA

Haddix, Michael (Athlete, Football Player)
614 Fox Run Rd
Sewell, NJ 08080-4254, USA

Haddix, Wayne (Athlete, Football Player)
442 Sand Ridge Dr
Valrico, FL 33594-4057, USA

Haddock, Sherry (Stylist)
115 E 9th St Apt 5G
New York, NY 10003-5416, USA

Haddon, Dayle (Actor, Model)
114 5th Ave
New York, NY 10011-5604, USA

Haddon, Lawrence (Actor)
14950 Sutton St
Sherman Oaks, CA 91403-4018, USA

Haddon, Lloyd (Athlete, Hockey Player)
16806 94 Ave NW
Edmonton, AB T5R 5L5, Canada

Haden, Charles E (Charlie) (Composer, Music Group, Musician)
17609 Ventura Blvd Ste 212
Encino, CA 91316-5125, USA

Haden, Nate (Actor)
c/o Staff Member *Diverse Talent Group*
9911 W Pico Blvd Ste 340W
Los Angeles, CA 90035-2712, USA

Haden, Nick (Athlete, Football Player)
114 Julianna Dr
Coraopolis, PA 15108-3763, USA

Haden, Patrick C (Pat) (Athlete, Football Player, Sportscaster)
1525 Wilson Ave
San Marino, CA 91108-2364, USA

Haden Church, Thomas (Actor)
c/o Jen Turner *Wolf Kasteler Van Iden & Associates (NY)*
584 Broadway Rm 310
New York, NY 10012-5246, USA

Hader, Bill (Actor)
c/o Naomi Odenkirk *Odenkirk Provissiero Entertainment*
650 N Bronson Ave Bldg B145
Los Angeles, CA 90004-1404, USA

Hadfield, Chris A (Astronaut)
638 Shorewood Dr
Kemah, TX 77565, USA

Hadfield, Vic (Athlete, Hockey Player)
438-1011 Upper Middle Rd E
Oakville, ON L6H 5Z9, Canada

Hadid, Zaha (Architect)
10 Bowling Green Lane
London WC1R 0BD, UNITED KINGDOM (UK)

Hadl, John W (Athlete, Football Player)
3700 Quail Creek Ct
Lawrence, KS 66047-2135, USA

Hadlee, Richard J (Cricketer)
PO Box 29186
Christchurch, NEW ZEALAND

Hadley, Brett (Actor)
5070 Woodley Ave
Encino, CA 91436-1411, USA

Hadley, Ron (Athlete, Football Player)
4533 131st Pl SW
Mukilteo, WA 98275-5826, USA

Hadley, Tony (Music Group, Musician)
c/o Staff Member *Shout! Promotions*
P.O. Box 42
Manchester M46 0WX, UK

Hadnot, James (Athlete, Football Player)
5521 48th St Apt 84
Lubbock TX, 79414

Hadnot, Rex (Athlete, Football Player)
2677 Center Court Dr
Weston, FL 33332-1833, USA

Haebler, Ingrid (Music Group, Musician)
420-452 Edgware Road
London W2 1EG, UNITED KINGDOM (UK)

Haechen, Hartmut (Conductor)
16 Ave F D Roosevelt
Paris 75008, FRANCE

Haefner, Ruby (Athlete, Baseball Player)
5305 Redstone Dr
Jacksonville, FL 32210-6754, USA

Haegele, Patricia (Publisher)
959 8th Ave
New York, NY 10019-3737, USA

Haegg, Gunder (Athlete, Track Athlete)
Idrottens Hus
Farsta 12387, SWEDEN

Haendel, Ida (Music Group, Musician)
31 Sinclair Road
London W14 0NS, UNITED KINGDOM (UK)

Haenicke, Diether H (Educator)
President's Office
Kalamazoo, MI 49008, USA

Hafen, Barney (Athlete, Football Player)
1125 Goldenrod Cir
Saint George, UT 84790-7512, USA

Hafer, Fred D (Business Person)
300 Madison Ave
Morristown, NJ 07960-6169, USA

Haffner, Scott (Athlete, Basketball Player)
5062 Sweetwater Dr
Noblesville, IN 46062-7164, USA

Hafner, Dudley H (Misc)
140 Estrada Maya
Santa Fe, NM 87506-8560, USA

Hafner, Travis (Athlete, Baseball Player)
32696 Lake Rd
Avon Lake, OH 44012-1646, USA

Hafstein, Johann (Prime Minister)
Sjalfstaedisflokkurinn Laufasvegi 46
Reykjavik, ICELAND

Hag, Sid (Actor)
6442 Coldwater Canyon Ave Ste 206
Valley Glen, CA 91606-1174, USA

Hagan, Clifford O (Cliff) (Athlete, Basketball Player, Coach)
8839 Lakeside Cir
Vero Beach, FL 32963-4082, USA

Hagan, Glenn (Athlete, Basketball Player)
34 Roth St
Rochester, NY 14621-5320, USA

Hagan, Marianne (Actor)
c/o Scott Zimmerman *Evolution Entertainment (LA)*
901 N Highland Ave
Los Angeles, CA 90038-2412, USA

Hagan, Molly (Actor)
c/o Staff Member *Kohner Agency, The*
9300 Wilshire Blvd Ste 555
Beverly Hills, CA 90212-3211, USA

Hagan, Sarah (Actor)
c/o Staff Member *Mark Robert Management*
2208 Patricia Ave
Los Angeles, CA 90064-2318, USA

Hagar, Sammy (Musician, Songwriter)
c/o Irving Azoff *Azoff Music Management/ Front Line*
1100 Glendon Ave
Los Angeles, CA 90024-3503, USA

Hagee, Michael W (General)
2 Navy Anx
Washington, DC 20380-1775, USA

Hagee, Pastor John (Religious Leader)
PO Box 1400
San Antonio, TX 78295-1400, USA

Hagegard, Hakan (Opera Singer)
Gunnarsbyn
Edane 670 30, SWEDEN

Hageman, Fred (Athlete, Football Player)
4700 Carmel Ct
Lawrence, KS 66047-1842, USA

Hagemeister, Charles C (War Hero)
1908 Canterbury Ct
Leavenworth, KS 66048-6525, USA

Hagen, Alexander
Mittelweg 58
Hamburg, GERMANY D-20149

Hagen, Halvor (Athlete, Football Player)
32 Algonquin Rd
Canton, MA 02021-1202, USA

Hagen, Kevin (Athlete, Baseball Player)
24826 164th Ave SE
Covington, WA 98042-5232, USA

Hager, Bob
4001 Nebraska Ave NW
Washington, DC 20016-2733

Hager, Britt (Athlete, Football Player)
2808 Barton Point Dr
Austin, TX 78733-6352, USA

Hager, Kristen (Actor)
c/o Shelley Browning *Magnolia Entertainment (LA)*
9595 Wilshire Blvd Ste 601
Beverly Hills, CA 90212-2506, USA

Hager, Robert (Correspondent)
4001 Nebraska Ave NW
Washington, DC 20016-2733, USA

Hager Twins
PO Box 1516
Champaign, IL 61824-1516

Hagerstrom, Anastasia (Stylist)
420 Argonaut Ave
San Francisco, CA 94134-3234, USA

Hagerty, Julie (Actor)
c/o Steven Levy *Framework Entertainment (LA)*
9057 Nemo St Ste C
West Hollywood, CA 90069-5511, USA

Hagerty, Michael (Actor)

Haggans, Clark (Athlete, Football Player)
8316 Mount Logan Ct
Las Vegas, NV 89131-1696, USA

Haggard, Merle (Music Group, Songwriter, Writer)
c/o Bobby Roberts *Bobby Roberts Agency*
PO Box 1547
Goodlettsville, TN 37070-1547, USA

Hagge, Marlene (Athlete, Golfer)
PO Box 2212
Palm Desert, CA 92261-2212, USA

Haggerty, Dan (Actor)
2134 62nd Pl SE
Auburn, WA 98092-8027, USA

Haggerty, Jonathan (Athlete, Football Player)
c/o Staff Member *Synergy Sports, Inc.*
14001 Dallas Pkwy Ste 1200
Dallas, TX 75240-7369, USA

Haggerty, Sean (Athlete, Hockey Player)
200 Highland Rd
Rye, NY 10580-1883, USA

Haggerty, Steve (Athlete, Football Player)
3313 E Costilla Ave
Centennial, CO 80122-1849, USA

Haggerty, Tim (Cartoonist)
200 Madison Ave
New York, NY 10016-3903, USA

Haggins, Raymond (Athlete, Baseball Player)
2825 E Lynchburg Ct
Montgomery, AL 36116-3335, USA

Haggis, Paul (Director, Producer, Writer)
c/o Staff Member *Paul Haggis Productions*
9200 W Sunset Blvd Ste 820
Los Angeles, CA 90069-3603, USA

Hagins, Isaac (Ike) (Athlete, Football Player)
1723 Madison Ave
Shreveport, LA 71103-2431, USA

Hagler, Marvin (Boxer)
c/o Valerie Swett *Deutsch Williams*
1 Design Center Pl Ste 600
Boston, MA 02210-2349

Hagman, Larry (Actor)
9950 Sulphur Mountain Rd
Ojai, CA 93023-9374, USA

Hagman, Niklas (Athlete, Hockey Player)
6900 Alderwood Dr
Sarasota, FL 34243-1313, USA

Hagn, Johanna (Athlete)
Behrgasse 6
Elsdorf 50198, GERMANY

Hagner, Meredith (Actor)
c/o James Suskin *James Suskin Management*
2 Charlton St Apt 5K
New York, NY 10014-4970, USA

Hagon, Garrick (Actor)
c/o Staff Member *Coolwaters Productions*
10061 Riverside Dr # 531
Toluca Lake, CA 91602-2560, USA

Hagood, Oksana (Stylist)
c/o Staff Member *Help Me Rhonda*
541 10th St NW # 294
Atlanta, GA 30318-5713, USA

Hague, William MP (Government Official)
Westminster
London SW1A 0AA, UNITED KINGDOM (UK)

Hahn, Beatrice H (Biologist)
Medical School Microbiology
Birmingham, AL 35294-0001, USA

Hahn, Don (Athlete, Baseball Player)
1046 Boise Dr
Campbell, CA 95008-0306, USA

Hahn, Erwin L (Physicist)
69 Stevenson Ave
Berkeley, CA 94708-1732, USA

Hahn, Frank H (Economist)
61 Adams Road
Cambridge CB3 9AD, UNITED KINGDOM (UK)

Hahn, Hilary (Music Group, Musician)
Postfach 1617
Hanover 30016, GERMANY

Hahn, James (Politician)
200 N Spring St
Los Angeles, CA 90012-4801, USA

Hahn, Joseph (Music Group)
9560 Wilshire Blvd # 400
Beverly Hills, CA 90212-2427, USA

Hahn, Kathryn (Actor)
c/o Lindsey Porter *Gersh (NY)*
41 Madison Ave
New York, NY 10010-2202, USA

Hahn, Mary Downing (Writer)
c/o Staff Member *Clarion Books*
215 Park Ave S
New York, NY 10003-1603, USA

Hai, Do Thi (Actor)
c/o Barry McPherson *Agency for the Performing Arts (APA-LA)*
405 S Beverly Dr Ste 500
Beverly Hills, CA 90212-4425, USA

Haid, Charles (Actor)
4376 Forman Ave
Toluca Lake, CA 91602-2944, USA

Haidee, Findlay-Levin (Stylist)
c/o Staff Member *Creative Exchange Agency*
53 Gansevoort St Ste 3
New York, NY 10014-1414, USA

Haig, Sid (Actor)
c/o Staff Member *Kathleen Schultz Associates Talent Agency*
6442 Coldwater Canyon Ave Ste 117
North Hollywood, CA 91606-1184, USA

Haigh, Denise (Athlete, Golfer)
198 Barbados Dr
Jupiter, FL 33458-2920, USA

Haight, Mike (Athlete, Football Player)
105 Windsor Rd
North Liberty, IA 52317-8009, USA

Haignere, Jean-Pierre (Misc)
2Place Maurice Quentin
Paris Cedeux 75039, FRANCE

Haik, Mac (Athlete, Football Player)
11738 Wood Ln
Houston, TX 77024-5129, USA

Hailey, Leisha (Actor, Musician, Songwriter)
c/o Geordie Frey *GEF Entertainment*
122 N Clark Dr Apt 401
West Hollywood, CA 90048-6315, USA

Hailey, Oliver
11747 Canton Pl
Studio City, CA 91604-4166

Haill, Gary H (Athlete, Football Player)
6207 Surflanding Ln
Huntington Beach, CA 92648-7507, USA

Hailston, Earl B (General)
Commanding General Marine Corps Forces Pacific
Camp H M Smith, HI 96861, USA

Haimovitz, Matt (Music Group, Musician)
165 W 57th St
New York, NY 10019-2201, USA

Haine-Daniels, Audrey (Baseball Player)
618 Revere Dr
Bay Village, OH 44140-1971, USA

Haines, Byron (Athlete, Football Player)
16625 1st Ave S Apt 202
Burien, WA 98148-1472, USA

Haines, Emily (Musician)
c/o Staff Member *Paradigm (Monterey)*
404 W Franklin St
Monterey, CA 93940-2303, USA

Haines, John (Athlete, Football Player)
4000 Chamisa Dr
Austin, TX 78730-3310, USA

Haines, Kris (Athlete, Football Player)
1430 N Dearborn St Apt 103
Chicago, IL 60610-1524, USA

Haines, Lee M (Religious Leader)
PO Box 50434
Indianapolis, IN 46250-0434, USA

Haines, Martha (Baseball Player)
2402 Woodhill Ct
Crescent Springs, KY 41017-1243, USA

Haines, Randa (Director)
1429 Avon Park Ter
Los Angeles, CA 90026-2007, USA

Hainsey, Ron (Athlete, Hockey Player)
74 Volpi Rd
Bolton, CT 06043-7551, USA

Hair, Harlod (Athlete, Baseball Player)
1645 W 20th St
Jacksonville, FL 32209-4817, USA

Hair, Harold (Athlete, Baseball Player)
1645 W 20th St
Jacksonville, FL 32209-4817, USA

Haire, John E (Business Person)
92 Hayden Ave
Lexington, MA 02421-7951, USA

Hairi, Gisue (Architect)
18 E 12th St
New York, NY 10003-4458, USA

Hairi, Moigan (Architect)
18 E 12th St
New York, NY 10003-4458, USA

Hairston, Alan (Athlete, Basketball Player)
6120 S 125th St
Seattle, WA 98178-3546, USA

Hairston, Carl (Athlete, Football Player)
1518 Brenland Cir
Virginia Beach, VA 23464-6759, USA

Hairston, Harold (Baseball Player)
542 E 107th St
Cleveland, OH 44108-1432, USA

Hairston, John (Johnny) (Athlete, Baseball Player)
4226 NE 22nd Ave
Portland, OR 97211-5757, USA

Hairston, Scott (Athlete, Baseball Player)
4658 S Banning Dr
Gilbert, AZ 85297-5257, USA

Hairston, Stacey (Athlete, Football Player)
1928 Creeksedge Dr
Columbus, OH 43209-3348, USA

Hairston Jr, Jerry (Athlete, Baseball Player)
6 Austringer Ct
Pikesville, MD 21208-2153, USA

Hairston Sr, Jerry (Athlete, Baseball Player)
7831 W Peace Pipe Rd
Tucson, AZ 85743-5207, USA

Haise, Fred W
14316 Fm 2354 Rd
Baytown, TX 77520, USA

Haise, Fred W Jr (Astronaut, Misc)
14316 Tri City Beach Rd
Baytown, TX 77523-9869, USA

Haise, Jim (Baseball Player)
2425 Albion Ave
Orlando, FL 32833-3981, USA

Haislip, Marcus (Basketball Player)
Bradley Center 1001 N 4th St
Milwaukee, WI 53203, USA

Haitink, Bernard J H (Conductor)
31 Sinclair Road
London W14 0NS, UNITED KINGDOM (UK)

Hajak, Ron
17420 Ventura Blvd # 4
Encino, CA 91316-3846

Hajdu, Richard (Athlete, Hockey Player)
6148 Grieve Rd
Duncan, BC V9L 2H1, Canada

Hajek, Andreas (Athlete)
Weissbundenweg 18
Halle/Saale 6128, GERMANY

Hajek, Dave (Athlete, Baseball Player)
5190 Bitterweed Ln
Colorado Springs, CO 80917-1302, USA

Hajiro, Barney (War Hero)
1642 Hooheke St
Pearl City, HI 96782-2201, USA

Haji-Sheikh, Ali (Athlete, Football Player)
550 S Spinningwheel Ln
Bloomfield Township, MI 48304-1318, USA

Hajt, Bill (Athlete, Hockey Player)
215 Old Lyme Dr
Buffalo, NY 14221-2208, USA

Hakim, Az-Zahir (Athlete, Football Player)
210 Canaan Glen Way SW
Atlanta, GA 30331-8055, USA

Hakkinen, Mikka (Race Car Driver)
Albert Dr Woking
Surrey GU21 5JY, UNITED KINGDOM (UK)

Halama, John (Athlete, Baseball Player)
7615 Fort Hamilton Pkwy
Brooklyn, NY 11228-2325, USA

Haland, Bjoro
Sor-Audnedal, NORWAY N-4520

Halas, John (Animator)
5-7 Kean St
London WC2B 4AT, UNITED KINGDOM (UK)

Halbert, Charles (Athlete, Basketball Player)
100 E Whidbey Ave Apt 35
Oak Harbor, WA 98277-2579, USA

Halbert, David (Business Person)
750 W John Carpenter Fwy Ste 1200
Irving, TX 75039-2507

Halbreich, Kathy (Director, Misc)
725 Vineland Pl
Minneapolis, MN 55403-1139, USA

Haldeman, Charles (Ed) (Financier)
1 Post Office Sq
Boston, MA 02109-2106, USA

Haldorson, Burdette (Burdie) (Athlete, Basketball Player)
2868 Stonewall Hts
Colorado Springs, CO 80909-1735, USA

Hale, Alan (Astronomer)
891 16 Springs Canyon Rd
Cloudcroft, NM 88317-9404, USA

Hale, Alan Spencer
5476 St Paul Rd
Morristown, NJ 7813

Hale, Barbara (Actor)
PO Box 6061-261
Sherman Oaks, CA 91413, USA

Hale, Bob (Athlete, Baseball Player)
616 Overhill Ave
Park Ridge, IL 60068-3455, USA

Hale, Chip (Athlete, Baseball Player)
190 Driftwood Ct
Aptos, CA 95003-5769, USA

Hale, Chris (Athlete, Football Player)
327 E El Sur St
Monrovia, CA 91016-4802, USA

Hale, Dave (Athlete, Football Player)
1204 S Maple St Apt B
Ottawa, KS 66067-3460, USA

Hale, David (Athlete, Hockey Player)
3470 Cortina Dr
Colorado Springs, CO 80918-1814, USA

Hale, Georgina (Actor)
74A St John's Wood High St
London NW8, UNITED KINGDOM (UK)

Hale, John (Athlete, Baseball Player)
2200 Pine St
Bakersfield, CA 93301-3429, USA

Hale, Larry (Athlete, Hockey Player)
795 Chase Ave
Penticton, BC V2A 2H8, Canada

Hale, Lucy (Actor)
c/o Elissa Leeds-Fickman *Reel Talent Management*
PO Box 491035
Los Angeles, CA 90049-9035, USA

Haley, Charles J (Athlete, Football Player)
3787 Royal Cove Dr
Dallas, TX 75229-5237, USA

Haley, Dick (Athlete, Football Player)
5248 Shoreline Cir
Sanford, FL 32771-7168, USA

Haley, Jackie Earle (Actor)
c/o Leslie Allan-Rice *Leslie Allan-Rice Management*
7524 Mulholland Dr
Los Angeles, CA 90046-1239, USA

Haley, Jermaine (Athlete, Football Player)
16806 Heather Knolls Pl
Hamilton, VA 20158-9403, USA

Haley, Katie (Athlete, Golfer)
24312 138th Ave SE
Kent, WA 98042-5168, USA

Haley, Len (Athlete, Hockey Player)
724 Balmer Cres
Elkford, BC V0B 1G0, Canada

Haley, Maria (Financier)
1 Capitol Mall
Little Rock, AR 72201-1049, USA

Haley, Nikki (Governor, Politician)
PO Box 11369
Columbia, SC 29211-1369, USA

Halffter, Cristobal J (Composer, Conductor)
Grillparsestr 24
Hamburg 22085, GERMANY

Halford, Rob (Music Group)
40 W 57th St # 1800
New York, NY 10019-4001, USA

Halfpenny, Jill (Actor)
c/o Staff Member *Talking Heads*
2-4 Noel St
London W1F 8GB, UNITED KINGDOM

Halfvarson, Eric (Opera Singer)
786 Dartmouth St
South Dartmouth, MA 02748-3247, USA

Hali, Tamba (Athlete, Football Player)
13227 Outlook St
Leawood, KS 66209-4022, USA

Haliburton, Ronnie (Athlete, Football Player)
3460 Lake Arthur Dr
Port Arthur, TX 77642-7604, USA

Halicki, Ed (Athlete, Baseball Player)
19605 Paddlewheel Ln
Reno, NV 89521-7850, USA

Halimon, Shaler (Athlete, Basketball Player)
9535 SW Millen Dr
Portland, OR 97224-6510, USA

Halkidis, Bob (Athlete, Hockey Player)
3419 Lake Park Rd
Indian Trail, NC 28079-6561, USA

Halko, Steve (Athlete, Hockey Player)
124 Crystlewood Ct
Morrisville, NC 27560-7569, USA

Hall, Ahmard (Athlete, Football Player)
4541 Winfield Dr
Nashville, TN 37211-8553, USA

Hall, Alaina Reed (Actor)
10636 Rathburn Ave
Northridge, CA 91326-3127, USA

Hall, Albert (Athlete, Baseball Player)
1628 Spaulding Ishkooda Rd
Birmingham, AL 35211-5520, USA

Hall, Amy (Stylist)
c/o Staff Member *Margaret Maldonado Agency*
1100 Glendon Ave Ste 1000
Los Angeles, CA 90024-3514, USA

Hall, Andy (Athlete, Football Player)
28 Hall Cir
Cheraw, SC 29520-3804, USA

Hall, Anthony Michael (Actor)
c/o Staff Member *Morra Brezner Steinberg & Tenenbaum (MBST) Entertainment*
345 N Maple Dr Ste 200
Beverly Hills, CA 90210-5174, USA

Hall, Arsenio (Actor, Musician, Television Host)
c/o Traci Harper *Harper PR*
3940 Laurel Canyon Blvd Ste 1010
Studio City, CA 91604-3709, USA

Hall, Art (Athlete, Football Player)
4601 Bayview Dr
Fort Lauderdale, FL 33308-5333, USA

Hall, Barbara (Producer, Writer)
c/o Chris Harbert *Creative Artists Agency (CAA-LA)*
2000 Avenue of the Stars Ste 100
Los Angeles, CA 90067-4705, USA

Hall, Bill (Athlete, Baseball Player)
169 Arbor Ln
Columbus, MS 39702-9281, USA

Hall, Bobby
20122 Hall Dr
Brooksville, FL 34601

Hall, Bridget (Model)
304 Park Ave S # 1200
New York, NY 10010-4301, USA

Hall, Bruce Michael (Actor)
c/o Jerry Shandrew *Shandrew Public Relations*
1050 S Stanley Ave
Los Angeles, CA 90019-6634, USA

Hall, Bug (Actor)
c/o Laina Cohn *Laina Cohn Management*
15066 Sutton St
Sherman Oaks, CA 91403-4020, USA

Hall, Chad (Athlete, Football Player)
c/o Chad Speck *Allegiant Athletic Agency*
35 Market Sq Ste 201
Knoxville, TN 37902-1420, USA

Hall, Charles (Inventor)
5815 Bennett Valley Rd
Santa Rosa, CA 95404-8565, USA

Hall, Charlie (Athlete, Football Player)
602 Lavaca St
Yoakum, TX 77995-4136, USA

Hall, Cory (Athlete, Football Player)
1202 E Swift Ave
Fresno, CA 93704-3836, USA

Hall, Courtney (Athlete, Football Player)
19912 Enslow Dr
Carson, CA 90746-3028, USA

Hall, Cynthia Holcomb (Judge)
125 S Grand Ave
Pasadena, CA 91105-1643, USA

Hall, Dana (Athlete, Football Player)
9730 Diamond St
Yucaipa, CA 92399-2946, USA

Hall, Dante (Athlete)
c/o Staff Member *Kansas City Chiefs*
1 Arrowhead Dr
Kansas City, MO 64129-1651, USA

Hall, Dante (Athlete, Football Player)
13314 Barbstone Dr
Houston, TX 77044-4957, USA

Hall, Darren (Athlete, Baseball Player)
3508 Castlewood Ct
Flower Mound, TX 75022-7814, USA

Hall, Darryl (Athlete, Football Player)
21013 E Crestline Cir
Centennial, CO 80015-3619, USA

Hall, Daryl (Music Group, Songwriter)
c/o Staff Member *Creative Artists Agency (CAA-LA)*
2000 Avenue of the Stars Ste 100
Los Angeles, CA 90067-4705, USA

Hall, Deangelo (Athlete, Football Player)
5553 Legends Dr
Braselton, GA 30517-4014, USA

Hall, Debi (Actor)
c/o Linda McAlister *Linda McAlister Talent*
100 Oak Ln
Waxahachie, TX 75167-8412, USA

Hall, Deidre (Actor)
1223 Wilshire Blvd # 825
Santa Monica, CA 90403-5400, USA

Hall, Del (Athlete, Hockey Player)
1057 E 6160 S
Salt Lake City, UT 84121-6712, USA

Hall, Delores (Actor, Music Group)
485 Madison Ave
New York, NY 10022-5803, USA

Hall, Delton (Athlete, Football Player)
9 Mystic Ct
Greensboro, NC 27406-5724, USA

Hall, Dick (Athlete, Baseball Player)
403 Plumbridge Ct Unit 403
Lutherville Timonium, MD 21093-8131, USA

Hall, Donald (Writer)
Wilmot, NH 3287, USA

Hall, Donald J (Business Person)
2501 McGee St
Kansas City, MO 64108-2615, USA

Hall, Donald R (Athlete, Football Player)
355 Chestnut Neck Rd
Port Republic, NJ 08241-9703, USA

Hall, Drew (Athlete, Baseball Player)
14125 Dunbritton Ln
Charlotte, NC 28277-1342, USA

Hall, Edward T (Doctor, Writer)
8 Calle Jacinta
Santa Fe, NM 87508-9561, USA

Hall, Ervin (Erv) (Athlete, Track Athlete)
670 Mason Ridge Center Dr
Saint Louis, MO 63141-8573, USA

Hall, Fawn -
1568 Viewsite Dr
Los Angeles, CA 90069-1323

Hall, Galen (Coach, Football Coach, Football Player)
Greenberg Complex
University Park, PA 16802, USA

Hall, Gary C (Engineer)
PO Box 715
Rosamond, CA 93560-0715, USA

Hall, Glenn H (Athlete, Hockey Player)
P.O. Box 2483 Stn Main
Stony Plain, AB T7Z 1X9, Canada

Hall, Greff Kaye (Swimmer)
906 3rd St
Mukilteo, WA 98275-1634, USA

Hall, James E (Jim) (Race Car Driver)
RR 7 Box 640
Midland, TX 79706, USA

Hall, James S (Jim) (Music Group, Musician)
211 Thompson St Apt Ld
New York, NY 10012-1335, USA

Hall, Jeff (Athlete, Football Player)
2201 Lake Ave Apt 205
Knoxville, TN 37916-2814, USA

Hall, Jerry (Actor, Model)
c/o Staff Member *Independent*
2 Henriette St 2nd Floor, Covent Garden
London WC2E 8PS, UK

Hall, Jerry (Doctor, Misc)
Med Center 2300 St NW
Washington, DC 20037, USA

Hall, Jimmie (Athlete, Baseball Player)
8622 Carter Grove Dr
Elm City, NC 27822-7926, USA

Hall, Joe (Athlete, Baseball Player)
961 Peachers Mill Rd
Clarksville, TN 37042-7629, USA

Hall, Joe B (Basketball Player, Coach)
300 W Vine St
Lexington, KY 40507-1621, USA

Hall, John L. (Nobel Prize Laureate)
National Institute Of Standards And Technology
Boulder, CO 80309, USA

Hall, Josh (Athlete, Baseball Player)
3512 Hawkins Mill Rd
Lynchburg, VA 24503-4923, USA

Hall, Kristen (Musician)
c/o Staff Member *Gail Gellman Management*
23852 Pacific Coast Hwy
Malibu, CA 90265-4876, USA

Hall, L Parker (Athlete, Football Player)
4712 Cole Rd
Memphis, TN 38117-4013, USA

Hall, Lani (Music Group)
31930 Pacific Coast Hwy
Malibu, CA 90265-2524, USA

Hall, Lanny (Educator)
President S Ofc
Abilene, TX 79698-0001, USA

Hall, Lemanski (Athlete, Football Player)
2336 Wimbledon Cir
Franklin, TN 37069-1862, USA

Hall, Lloyd M Jr (Religious Leader)
PO Box 1620
Oak Creek, MI 53154, USA

Hall, Michael C (Actor, Producer)
c/o Jon Rubinstein *Authentic Talent and Literary Management*
45 Main St Ste 1004
Brooklyn, NY 11201-8200, USA

Hall, Monty
519 N Arden Dr
Beverly Hills, CA 90210-3507

Hall, Murray (Athlete, Hockey Player)
21-3157 Ontario St
Burlington, ON L7S 1E9, Canada

Hall, Nigel J (Artist)
11 Kensington Park Gardens
London W11 3HD, UNITED KINGDOM (UK)

Hall, Peter R F (Director)
18 Exeter St
London WC2E 7DU, UNITED KINGDOM (UK)

Hall, Philip Baker (Actor)

Hall, Pooch (Actor)
c/o Mark Turner *Abrams Artists Agency (NY)*
9200 W Sunset Blvd PH 11
Los Angeles, CA 90069-3601, USA

Hall, Randy (Athlete, Football Player)
PO Box 447
Genesee, ID 83832-0447, USA

Hall, Reamy (Actor)
c/o Gloria Hinojosa *Amsel, Eisenstadt & Frazier Talent Agency (AEF)*
5055 Wilshire Blvd Ste 860
Los Angeles, CA 90036-6108, USA

Hall, Rebecca (Actor)
c/o Staff Member *Julian Belfrage & Associates*
46 Albemarle St
London W1X 4PP, UK

Hall, Regina (Actor)
c/o Paul Young *Principato/Young Management*
9465 Wilshire Blvd Ste 430
Beverly Hills, CA 90212-2613, USA

Hall, Robert David (Actor)
c/o Cynthia Snyder *Cynthia Snyder Public Relations*
5739 Colfax Ave
N Hollywood, CA 91601-1636, USA

Hall, Robert N (Inventor)
2315 Gurenson Ln
Niskayuna, NY 12309-5908, USA

Hall, Ron (Athlete, Football Player)
14008 NE 162nd St
Kearney, MO 64060-8107, USA

Hall, Samuel (Sam) (Athlete, Swimmer)
5759 Wilcke Way
Dayton, OH 45459-1637, USA

Hall, Sonny (Misc)
80 W End Ave
New York, NY 10023-6301, USA

Hall, Taylor (Athlete, Historian)
4833 Saratoga Blvd # 276
Corpus Christi, TX 78413-2213, USA

Hall, Toby (Athlete, Baseball Player)
3814 Evergreen Oaks Dr
Lutz, FL 33558-5041, USA

Hall, Tom (Athlete, Baseball Player)
3592 Lillian St
Riverside, CA 92504-3609, USA

Hall, Tom (Athlete, Football Player)
PO Box 60441
Longmeadow, MA 01116-0441, USA

Hall, Tom T (Music Group, Songwriter, Writer)
PO Box 1246
Franklin, TN 37065-1246, USA

Hall, Walter (Athlete, Golfer)
271 Orchard Park Dr
Advance, NC 27006-7481, USA

Hall, Willie (Athlete, Football Player)
717 S Hacienda St
Anaheim, CA 92804-2658, USA

Hall, Windlan (Athlete, Football Player)
13609 Pleasant Ln
Burnsville, MN 55337-4547, USA

Hall & Oates (Music Group)
c/o Jonathan Wolfson *Wolfson Public Relations*
22201 Ventura Blvd Ste 207
Woodland Hills, CA 91364-1510, USA

Halla, Brian L (Business Person)
2900 Semiconductor Dr
Santa Clara, CA 95051-0606, USA

Halladay, H Leroy (Roy) (Athlete, Baseball Player)
18509 Council Crest Dr
Odessa, FL 33556-5039, USA

Hallam, John
51 Lansdowne Gdns
London, ENGLAND SW8 2EL

Hallberg, Gary (Athlete, Golfer)
12516 Ventana Mesa Cir
Castle Pines, CO 80108-9147, USA

Halldorson, Dan (Athlete, Golfer)
209 South Rd
Cambridge, IL 61238-1429, USA

Hallen, Bob (Athlete, Football Player)
7052 Rushmore Way
Painesville, OH 44077-2301, USA

Haller, Alan (Athlete, Football Player)
1265 Lobelia Ln
Dewitt, MI 48820-7409, USA

Haller, Bill (Baseball Player)
RR 2 Box 82C
Brownstown, IL 62418-9630, USA

Haller, Bill (Athlete, Baseball Player)
RR 2 Box 82C
Brownstown, IL 62418-9630, USA

Haller, Gordon (Athlete)
16 Thetford Dr
Bella Vista, AR 72715-1508, USA

Haller, Kevin (Athlete, Hockey Player)
c/o Staff Member *Hockey Ministries International*
1100 De La Gauchetiere St W Unit 265 7
Montreal, QC H3B 2S2, Canada

Hallervorden, Dieter
Numberger Str. 33
Berlin, GERMANY D-10777

Hallet, Jim (Athlete, Golfer)
18 Oliver St
South Yarmouth, MA 02664-2902, USA

Hall-Garmes, Ruth (Actor)
432 Alandele Ave
Los Angeles, CA 90036-3153, USA

Halliburton, Jeff (Athlete, Basketball Player)
113 Wake Forest Pl
O Fallon, MO 63368-3786, USA

Hallick, Tom
13900 Tahiti Way Apt 108
Marina Del Rey, CA 90292-6568

Halliday, Nathan (Actor)
c/o Sharon Lane *Lane Management Group*
13017 Woodbridge St
Studio City, CA 91604-1431, USA

Hallier, Lori (Actor)
c/o Richard Lucas *Lucas Talent Inc*
100 W. Pender St Sun Tower, 7th Floor
Vancouver, BC V6B 1R8, Canada

Hallin, Mats (Athlete, Hockey Player)
c/o Staff Member *Chicago Blackhawks*
1901 W Madison St
Chicago, IL 60612-2459, USA

Hallinan, Joseph T (Journalist)
1745 Broadway # B1
New York, NY 10019-4368, USA

Hallion, Tom (Baseball Player)
4040 Ormond Rd
Louisville, KY 40207-2036, USA

Hallion, Tom (Athlete, Baseball Player)
4040 Ormond Rd
Louisville, KY 40207-2036, USA

Hallisay, Brian (Actor)
c/o Justin Grey Stone *Untitled Entertainment (LA)*
350 S Beverly Dr Ste 200
Beverly Hills, CA 90212-4819, USA

Halliwell, Geri (Music Group)
c/o Gina Hoffman *Baker Winokur Ryder Public Relations (BWR-LA)*
9100 Wilshire Blvd Ste 500 PMB WEST
Beverly Hills, CA 90212-3426, USA

Hallman, Tom Jr (Journalist)
1320 SW Broadway
Portland, OR 97201-3411, USA

Hallock, Ty (Athlete, Football Player)
3676 Hunters Way Dr SE
Ada, MI 49301-8351, USA

Hallstrom, Lasse (Director)
c/o Tracey Jacobs *United Talent Agency (UTA)*
9560 Wilshire Blvd Fl 5
Beverly Hills, CA 90212-2400, USA

Hallstrom, Ron (Athlete, Football Player)
PO Box 379
Woodruff, WI 54568-0379, USA

Hallwachs, Hans-Peter
Lindenstr. 9a
Grunwald, GERMANY 83021

Hallworth, Nina & Clare (Stylist)
c/o Staff Member *Artists by Timothy Priano (CA)*
8447 Wilshire Blvd Ste 301
Beverly Hills, CA 90211-3206, USA

Hallyday, Johnny (Actor, Music Group)
6 Rue Daubigny
Paris 75017, FRANCE

Halonen Tarja, Kaarina (President)
Pohjoisesplandi 1
Helsinki 17 170, FINLAND

Halperin, Bertrand I (Physicist)
Physics Dept
Cambridge, MA 2138, USA

Halpern, Daniel (Writer)
9 Mercer St
Princeton, NJ 08540-6807, USA

Halpern, Jack (Misc)
5801 S Dorchester Ave Apt 4A
Chicago, IL 60637-1757, USA

Halpern, James S (Judge)
400 2nd St NW
Washington, DC 20217-0001, USA

Halpern, Jeff (Athlete, Hockey Player)
9212 Sprinklewood Ln
Potomac, MD 20854-2255, USA

Halpin, Brandan Dean (Actor)
c/o Dino May *Dino May Management*
6362 Hollywood Blvd
Los Angeles, CA 90028-6323, USA

Halpin, Luke (Actor)
637 Buoy Ln
Altamonte Springs, FL 32714-7258, USA

Halprin, Lawrence (Architect)
125 E Sir Francis Drake Blvd
Larkspur, CA 94939-1860, USA

Halsell Jr, James D (Astronaut)
257 River Cove Rd
Huntsville, AL 35811-8010, USA

Halstead, Greg (Model, Reality TV Star)
c/o Anthony Embry *AE Entertainment Public Relations*
124 Evening Shade Dr
Charleston, SC 29414-9144, USA

Halstead, Thomas (Stylist)
c/o Staff Member *Zenobia Agency Inc*
PO Box 909
Groveland, CA 95321-0909, USA

Halter, Shane (Athlete, Baseball Player)
2701 W 140th St
Overland Park, KS 66224-3940, USA

Halterman, Aaron (Athlete, Football Player)
522 W Northlane Dr
Bloomington, IN 47404-2205, USA

Haluska, Jim (Athlete, Football Player)
4325 W Cleveland Ave
Milwaukee, WI 53219-3209, USA

Halverson, Dean (Athlete, Football Player)
45971 State Highway 74
Palm Desert, CA 92260-4618, USA

Halward, Doug (Athlete, Hockey Player)
16 Creekstone Pl
Port Moody, BC V3H 4L6, Canada

Ham, Jack R (Athlete, Football Player)
540 Lindbergh Dr
Coraopolis, PA 15108-2750, USA

Ham, Kenneth T (Astronaut)
1315 Falling Leaf Dr
Friendswood, TX 77546-4615, USA

Hamari, Julia (Opera Singer)
Max Brod-Weg 14
Stuttgart 70437, GERMANY

Hamasaki, Ayumi (Actor, Musician)
c/o Staff Member *Avex Entertainment*
3-1-30-7F Minami Aoyama Minato
Tokyo 107-0062, Japan

Hambling, Maggi (Artist)
Westminster Bridge Road
London SE1 7HT, UNITED KINGDOM (UK)

Hambrick, Troy (Athlete, Football Player)
1103 Pinelane Rd
Columbia, SC 29223-1974, USA

Hambright, Roger (Athlete, Baseball Player)
8709 NE 37th Ave
Vancouver, WA 98665-1065, USA

Hamburger, Michael P L (Writer)
45/47 Clerkenwell Green
London EC1R 0HT, UNITED KINGDOM (UK)

Hamed, Nihad (Religious Leader)
25351 Five Mile Rd
Redford Township, MI 48239, USA

Hamed, Prince Naseem (Athlete, Boxer)
Mowbray House Mowbray Street
Stockport, Cheshire SK1 3EJ, UNITED KINGDOM

Hamel, Alan
PO Box 827
Monterey, CA 93942-0827

Hamel, Dean (Athlete, Football Player)
1007 Hawthorne Dr NE
Lenoir, NC 28645, USA

Hamel, Gilles (Athlete, Hockey Player)
1484 Rue Du Mcon
Sherbrooke, QC J1N 1V4, Canada

Hamel, Jean (Athlete, Hockey Player)
5 Rue Lebeau
Asbestos, QC J1T 4L4, Canada

Hamel, Michael A (Astronaut)
HQ AFSPC/DR 150 Vandenburg St#1105
Colorado Springs, CO 80914, USA

Hamel, Pierre (Athlete, Hockey Player)
1613 Beechwood Rd
Yadkinville, NC 27055-6604, USA

Hamel, Veronica (Actor, Model)
c/o Staff Member *Cunningham Escott Slevin & Doherty (CESD-LA)*
10635 Santa Monica Blvd Ste 130
Los Angeles, CA 90025-8306, USA

Hamel, William (Religious Leader)
901 E 78th St
Minneapolis, MN 55420-1334, USA

Hamelin, Bob (Athlete, Baseball Player)
51 Patton Ct SE
Concord, NC 28025-3742, USA

Hamels, Cole (Athlete, Baseball Player)
c/o Jon Orlando *WNWN Media*
348 Hauser Blvd # PH414
Los Angeles, CA 90036-3276, USA

Hamhuis, Dan (Athlete, Hockey Player)
9553 Hampton Reserve Dr
Brentwood, TN 37027-8485, USA

Hamill, Dorothy (Figure Skater)
c/o Rick Hersh 3340 Ocean Park Blvd Ste 3030
Santa Monica, CA 90405, USA

Hamill, Mark (Actor)
20358 Big Rock Dr
Malibu, CA 90265-5306, USA

Hamill, W Pete (Editor, Writer)
8 Whiskey Hill Rd
Wallkill, NY 12589-3421, USA

Hamilton, Allan G (Al) (Athlete, Hockey Player)
2452 115th St NW
Edmonton, AB T6J 3S1, Canada

Hamilton, Anthony (Musician)
c/o Mark Cheatham *Creative Artists Agency (CAA-NY)*
162 5th Ave Fl 6
New York, NY 10010-6047, USA

Hamilton, Arthur Lee (Athlete, Baseball Player)
2243 College Cir N
Jacksonville, FL 32209-5916, USA

Hamilton, Ashley (Actor)
c/o Staff Member *TalentWorks (LA)*
3500 W Olive Ave Ste 1400
Burbank, CA 91505-5512, USA

Hamilton, Ben (Athlete, Football Player)
5240 Golden Ridge Ct
Parker, CO 80134-4546, USA

Hamilton, Bethany (Athlete, Writer)
PO Box 863
Hanalei, HI 96714-0863, USA

Hamilton, Bobby Jr (Race Car Driver)
1435 W Morehead St Ste 190
Charlotte, NC 28208-5291, USA

Hamilton, Charles (Musician)
c/o Staff Member *Violator Management*
36 W 25th St Fl 11
New York, NY 10010-2752, USA

Hamilton, Conrad (Athlete, Football Player)
19619 N 35th Pl
Phoenix, AZ 85050-3938, USA

Hamilton, Darrell (Athlete, Football Player)
22 Sunrise Ct
Randallstown, MD 21133-3629, USA

Hamilton, Darryl (Athlete, Baseball Player)
4721 Southwind Dr
Baton Rouge, LA 70816-4738, USA

Hamilton, Dave (Athlete, Baseball Player)
9464 Cherry Hills Ln
San Ramon, CA 94583-3935, USA

Hamilton, David (Photographer)
41 Blvd du Montpamasse
Paris 75006, FRANCE

Hamilton, Dennis (Athlete, Basketball Player)
1493 E Zion Way
Chandler, AZ 85249-5196, USA

Hamilton, Derek (Actor)
c/o PJ Shapiro *Ziffren Brittenham LLP*
1801 Century Park W Fl 7
Los Angeles, CA 90067-6406, USA

Hamilton, Forestom (Chico) (Composer, Music Group, Musician)
c/o Staff Member *Concerted Efforts*
PO Box 440326
Somerville, MA 02144-0004, USA

Hamilton, George (Actor)
c/o Jeffrey Lane *Jeffrey Lane & Associates*
9255 Doheny Rd Apt 2003
Los Angeles, CA 90069-3224, USA

Hamilton, Guy (Director)
Apartado III
Palma de Mallorca, SPAIN

Hamilton, Harry (Athlete, Football Player)
PO Box 986
Lemont, PA 16851-0986, USA

Hamilton, Jack (Athlete, Baseball Player)
109 Rocky Rd
Ridgedale, MO 65739-9746, USA

Hamilton, James (Athlete, Football Player)
242 McGirt Rd
Hamlet, NC 28345-9124, USA

Hamilton, Jeff (Athlete, Baseball Player)
2485 Golfview Cir
Fenton, MI 48430-9633, USA

Hamilton, Jim (Athlete, Hockey Player)
115 Cutler St
Mc Kees Rocks, PA 15136-3215, USA

Hamilton, Joey (Athlete, Baseball Player)
4035 Wellington Mist Pt
Duluth, GA 30097-2352, USA

Hamilton, Josh (Athlete, Baseball Player)
314 Bluff Ridge Ln
Angier, NC 27501-5840, USA

Hamilton, Keith (Athlete, Football Player)
6 Bonnieview Ln
Towaco, NJ 07082-1289, USA

Hamilton, Laird (Athlete, Producer)
c/o Jane Kachmer *Jane Kachmer Management*
PO Box 2246
Malibu, CA 90265-7246, USA

Hamilton, Laurell K (Writer)
PO Box 270375
Saint Louis, MO 63127-0375, USA

Hamilton, Lee H (Politician)
1300 Pennsylvania Ave NW
Washington, DC 20004-3002, USA

Hamilton, Leonard (Basketball Player, Coach)
Athletic
Tallahassee, FL 32306-0001, USA

Hamilton, Lewis (Race Car Driver)
Corporatec Ltd. 32 St. James°S St
London SW1A 1HD, UK

Hamilton, Linda (Actor)
c/o Bobbie Edrick *Bobbie Edrick*
8955 Norma Pl
Los Angeles, CA 90069-4818, USA

Hamilton, Lisa Gay (Actor)
c/o Stacy Boniello *Firm, The*
2049 Century Park E Ste 2550
Los Angeles, CA 90067-3139, USA

Hamilton, Lynn
1042 S Burnside Ave
Los Angeles, CA 90019-6718

Hamilton, Marcus (Actor)
PO Box 1997
Monterey, CA 93942-1997, USA

Hamilton, Michael (Artist)
2012 N 19th St
Boise, ID 83702-0821, USA

Hamilton, Michael (Athlete, Football Player)
6755 Mira Mesa Blvd # 123-227
San Diego, CA 92121-4392, USA

Hamilton, Milo (Baseball Player, Sportscaster)
2001 Holcombe Blvd Unit 901
Houston, TX 77030-4214, USA

Hamilton, Natasha (Musician)
c/o Staff Member *Concorde Intl Artists Ltd*
101 Shepherds Bush Rd
London W6 7LP, UNITED KINGDOM (UK)

Hamilton, Paula (Actor)
34-43 Russell St
London WC2B 5HA, UNITED KINGDOM (UK)

Hamilton, Ray (Athlete, Football Player)
PO Box 363
Sharon, MA 02067-0363, USA

Hamilton, Richard (Athlete, Basketball Player)
c/o Staff Member *Detroit Pistons*
2 Championship Dr
Auburn Hills, MI 48326-1753, USA

Hamilton, Richard (Artist)
Northend Farm, Northend GB-Henley On Thames
Oxon, UK

Hamilton, Roy Lee (Athlete, Basketball Player)
1644 Del Mar Rd
Oceanside, CA 92057-4910, USA

Hamilton, Ruffin (Athlete, Football Player)
236 Sumac Trl
Woodstock, GA 30188-5154, USA

Hamilton, Scott S (Athlete, Figure Skater)
2451 Hidden River Ln
Franklin, TN 37069-6933, USA

Hamilton, Suzanna (Actor)
46 Albermarie St
London W1X 4PP, UNITED KINGDOM (UK)

Hamilton, Suzy (Athlete, Olympic Athlete)
1014 Beloit Ct
Madison, WI 53705-2233, USA

Hamilton, Todd (Athlete, Golfer)
2004 Rock Dove Ct
Westlake, TX 76262-9076, USA

Hamilton, Tom (Stylist)
1433 W Edgewater Ave
Chicago, IL 60660-4208, USA

Hamilton, Tom (Musician)
PO Box 67039
Chestnut Hill, MA 02467-0001, USA

Hamilton, Victoria (Actor)
c/o Michael Lazo *Untitled Entertainment (LA)*
350 S Beverly Dr Ste 200
Beverly Hills, CA 90212-4819, USA

Hamilton-Klemperer, Kim
44 W 62nd St # 10
New York, NY 10023-7008

Hamiter, Uhuru (Athlete, Football Player)
5737 Hazel Ave
Philadelphia, PA 19143-1910, USA

Hamlin, Brooke (Actor)
c/o Staff Member *Coast to Coast Talent Group*
3350 Barham Blvd
Los Angeles, CA 90068-1404, USA

Hamlin, Denny (Race Car Driver)
215 Overhill Dr Ste A
Mooresville, NC 28117-7037, USA

Hamlin, Eugene (Athlete, Football Player)
26411 24 Mile Rd
Chesterfield, MI 48051-1514, USA

Hamlin, Harry (Actor)
c/o Craig Schneider *Pinnacle Public Relations*
8265 W Sunset Blvd Ste 201
Los Angeles, CA 90046-2470, USA

Hamlin, Ken (Athlete, Baseball Player)
5242 County Road 413
Mc Millan, MI 49853-9266, USa

Hamlin, Shelley (Athlete, Golfer)
4311 W Ardmore Rd
Laveen, AZ 85339-2112, USA

Hamlisch, Marvin (Composer, Conductor)
970 Park Ave # 501
New York, NY 10028-0324, USA

Hamm, Jon (Actor)
c/o Connie Tavel *Forward Entertainment*
9255 W Sunset Blvd Ste 805
Los Angeles, CA 90069-3305, USA

Hamm, Mia (Model, Soccer Player)
PO Box 56
Chapel Hill, NC 27514-0056, USA

Hamm, Morgan (Olympic Athlete)
c/o Sheryl Shade *Shade Global*
10 E 40th St Fl 48
New York, NY 10016-0301, USA

Hamm, Nick (Director)
8942 Wilshire Blvd # 219
Beverly Hills, CA 90211-1908, USA

Hamm, Paul (Athlete, Olympic Athlete)
c/o Sheryl Shade *Shade Global*
10 E 40th St Fl 48
New York, NY 10016-0301, USA

Hamm, Pete (Athlete, Baseball Player)
525 Lockhart Gulch Rd
Scotts Valley, CA 95066-3034, USA

Hamm, Richard L (Religious Leader)
PO Box 1986
Indianapolis, IN 46206-1986, USA

Hammad al-Bassam, Abd al-Mohsin (Cosmonaut)
22 Holland Park
London W11, UNITED KINGDOM (UK)

Hammaker, Atlee (Athlete, Baseball Player)
12740 Manning Ln
Knoxville, TN 37932-1001, USA

Hammarstrom, Inge (Athlete, Hockey Player)
c/o Staff Member *Philadelphia Flyers*
First Union Spectrum 3601 S Broad St, Suite 2
Philadelphia, PA 19148, USA

Hammel, Eugene A (Misc)
2332 Piedmont Ave
Berkeley, CA 94720, USA

Hammel, Penny (Athlete, Golfer)
4786 Orchard Ln
Delray Beach, FL 33445-5306, USA

Hammer (Music Group, Musician)
1500 Broadway Fl 7
New York, NY 10036-4055, USA

Hammer, AJ (Television Host)
1 Time Warner Ctr
New York, NY 10019-6038, USA

Hammer, Armie (Actor)
c/o Megan Moss Pachon *ID Public Relations (ID-LA)*
7080 Hollywood Blvd Fl 8
Los Angeles, CA 90028-6906, USA

Hammer, Jaime (Adult Film Star)
8033 W Sunset Blvd # 535
W Hollywood, CA 90046-2401, USA

Hammer, MC (Actor, Musician, Songwriter)
c/o Jeff Epstein *Universal Attractions*
135 W 26th St Fl 12
New York, NY 10001-6872, USA

Hammer, Victor S (Cinematographer)
PO Box 10788
Marina Del Rey, CA 90295-6788, USA

Hammer Jr, Jan (Composer, Musician)
2 W 45th St Ste 1102
New York, NY 10036-4249, USA

Hammergren, John H (Business Person)
1 Post St
San Francisco, CA 94104-5201, USA

Hammes, Gordon G (Misc)
11 Staley Pl
Durham, NC 27705-2421, USA

Hammett, Kirk (Music Group, Musician)
2505 Divisadero St
San Francisco, CA 94115-1119, USA

Hammink, Geert (Athlete, Basketball Player)
2619 Clementon Park Ct
Orlando, FL 32835-6160, USA

Hammock, Robby (Athlete, Baseball Player)
4200 Chatham View Dr
Buford, GA 30518-4913, USA

Hammon, Becky (Athlete, Basketball Player)
c/o Mike Cound *Sportalents*
Ctra de l'Escladella, 11 El Meu Poblet - Bloc 3E
La Massana, Andorra

Hammon, Jennifer
270 N Canon Dr # 1064
Beverly Hills, CA 90210-5323

Hammond, Albert Jr (Music Group, Musician)
370 7th Ave # 807
New York, NY 10001-3967, USA

Hammond, Beresford (Musician)

Hammond, Beresford (Musician)
c/o Jeff Epstein *Universal Attractions*
135 W 26th St Fl 12
New York, NY 10001-6872, USA

Hammond, Bobby (Athlete, Football Player)
2535 Butler St
East Elmhurst, NY 11369-1628, USA

Hammond, Chris (Athlete, Baseball Player)
908 Old Highway 431
Wedowee, AL 36278-4612, USA

Hammond, Darrell (Actor, Comedian)
c/o Geoff Cheddy *Brillstein Entertainment Partners*
9150 Wilshire Blvd Ste 350
Beverly Hills, CA 90212-3453, USA

Hammond, Donnie (Athlete, Golfer)
1642 Bridgewater Dr
Lake Mary, FL 32746-4103, USA

Hammond, Fred (Music Group)
21421 Hilltop Street Blvd 20
Southfield, MI 48034, USA

Hammond, Gary (Athlete, Football Player)
5321 Seascape Ln
Plano, TX 75093-4121, USA

Hammond, James T (Religious Leader)
PO Box 1568
Dunn, NC 28335-1568, USA

Hammond, Joan H (Opera Singer)
Private Bag 101
Geelong Mail Center, VIC 3221, AUSTRALIA

Hammond, John (Music Group, Musician)
c/o Staff Member *Shore Fire Media*
32 Court St Fl 16
Brooklyn, NY 11201-4441, USA

Hammond, Josh (Actor)
c/o Staff Member *Hines and Hunt Entertainment*
1213 W Magnolia Blvd
Burbank, CA 91506-1829, USA

Hammond, Julie (Athlete, Basketball Player)
2943 S Ulster St
Denver, CO 80231-4170, USA

Hammond, Katherine (Stylist)
c/o Celebrity Stylist *Oliver Piro Inc*
725 Riverside Dr Apt 3A
New York, NY 10031-2460, USA

Hammond, Ken (Athlete, Hockey Player)
38325 McDowell Dr
Solon, OH 44139-4686, USA

Hammond, Kim (Athlete, Football Player)
9 Creek Bluff Run
Flagler Beach, FL 32136-5106, USA

Hammond, L Blaine Jr (Astronaut)
4150 E Donald Douglas Dr # 926
Long Beach, CA 90808-1725, USA

Hammond, Lisa B (Stylist)
c/o Staff Member *Celestine - CA*
1666 20th St Ste 200B
Santa Monica, CA 90404-3828, USA

Hammond, Richard (Actor, Correspondent)
c/o Staff Member *BBC Television Centre*
Incoming Mail Wood Lane
London W12 7RJ, United Kingdom

Hammond, Robert D (General)
219 Del Mesa Carmel
Carmel, CA 93923-7951, USA

Hammond, Steve (Athlete, Baseball Player)
11104 Lake Butler Blvd
Windermere, FL 34786-7808, USA

Hammond, Tom (Sportscaster)
30 Rockefeller Plz
New York, NY 10112-0015, USA

Hammond Jr, Caleb D (Misc, Publisher)
PO Box 194
Mendham, NJ 07945-0194, USA

Hammonds, Jeffrey (Jeff) (Athlete, Baseball Player)
113 Grand Cove Pl
Madison, AL 35758-3034, USA

Hammonds, Tom (Athlete, Basketball Player)
122 Windsor Dr
Crestview, FL 32539-8601, USA

Hammons, David (Artist)
144 W 125th St
New York, NY 10027-4423, USA

Hammons, Roger (Religious Leader)
6403 Frame Rd
Elkview, WV 25071-7040, USA

Hamner, Earl
11575 Amanda Dr
Studio City, CA 91604-4144

Hamnett, Katharine (Designer, Fashion Designer)
202 New North Road
London N1, UNITED KINGDOM (UK)

Hampel, Olaf (Athlete)
Pommenweg 2
Bielefeld 33689, GERMANY

Hampshire, Susan (Actor)
123A Kings Rd
London SW3 4PL, UNITED KINGDOM (UK)

Hampson, Blake (Actor)
c/o Staff Member *Nickelodeon UK*
PO Box 6425
LONDON W1A 6UR, UNITED KINGDOM

Hampson, Justin (Athlete, Baseball Player)
6982 E Frontage Rd
Worden, IL 62097-2604, USA

Hampson, Ted (Athlete, Hockey Player)
4436 Claremore Dr
Minneapolis, MN 55435-4136, USA

Hampson, Thomas (Opera Singer)
Starkfriedgasse 53
Vienna 1180, AUSTRIA

Hampton, Brenda (Producer)
c/o Clifford Gilbert-Lurie *Ziffren Brittenham LLP*
1801 Century Park W Fl 7
Los Angeles, CA 90067-6406, USA

Hampton, Casey (Athlete, Football Player)
105 Conover Rd
Pittsburgh, PA 15208-2601, USA

Hampton, Christopher J (Writer)
2 Kensington Park Gardens
London W11, UNITED KINGDOM (UK)

Hampton, Daniel O (Dan) (Athlete, Football Player)
9191 Falling Waters Dr E
Burr Ridge, IL 60527-0716, USA

Hampton, Ike (Baseball Player)
4415 E Ridge Gate Rd
Anaheim, CA 92807-3507, USA

Hampton, James (Actor)
102 Forest Hill Dr
Roanoke, TX 76262-5522, USA

Hampton, Locksley (Slide) (Music Group, Musician)
2604 Mozart Pl NW
Washington, DC 20009-3601, USA

Hampton, Lorenzo (Athlete, Football Player)
16231 NW 77th Pl
Hialeah, FL 33016-6116, USA

Hampton, Michael W (Mike) (Athlete, Baseball Player)
8601 N 59th Pl
Paradise Valley, AZ 85253-2212, USA

Hampton, Millard (Athlete, Track Athlete)
201 W Mission St
San Jose, CA 95110-1701, USA

Hampton, Ralph C Jr (Religious Leader)
3606 W End Ave
Nashville, TN 37205-2403, USA

Hampton, Rick (Athlete, Hockey Player)
25 Doctors Ln
King City, ON L7B 1G2, Canada

Hampton, Rodney (Athlete, Football Player)
5603 Grand Floral Blvd
Houston, TX 77041-5563, USA

Hamrick, Ray (Athlete, Baseball Player)
349 Saint Andrews Dr
Franklin, TN 37069-7078, USA

Hamrlik, Roman (Athlete, Hockey Player)
56 Alhambra Dr
Oceanside, NY 11572-5425, USA

Hamulack, Tim (Athlete, Baseball Player)
530 Campbell Rd
York, PA 17402-3335, USA

Hamway, Marl (Athlete, Hockey Player)
3758 Loch Bend Dr
Commerce Township, MI 48382-4336, USA

Hamzah (Prince)
Royal Palace
Amman, JORDAN

Han, Suyin (Writer)
37 Montoie
Lausanne 1007, SWITZERLAND

Hanafusa, Hidesaburo (Biologist)
1230 York Ave
New York, NY 10065-6307, USA

Hanauer, Chip (Yachtsman)
2702 NE 88th St
Seattle, WA 98115-3458, USA

Hanauer, Terri
8271 Melrose Ave Ste 110
Los Angeles, CA 90046-6800

Hanburger, Christian (Chris) Jr (Athlete, Football Player)
708 Winter Hill Dr
Apex, NC 27502-1376, USA

Hanbury-Tension, Robin (Scientist)
Cardinham Bodmin
Cornwall PL3O 4DW, UNITED KINGDOM (UK)

Hance Jr, James H (Financier)
100 N Tyron St
Charlotte, NC 28255-0001, USA

Hancken, Buddy (Athlete, Baseball Player)
850 Cactus St
Bridge City, TX 77611-3308, USA

Hancock, Anthony (Athlete, Football Player)
8233 Corteland Dr
Knoxville, TN 37909-2116, USA

Hancock, Eddie (Athlete, Baseball Player)
2104 W 15th St
Pueblo, CO 81003-1126, USA

Hancock, Garry (Athlete, Baseball Player)
2217 Greenhills Dr
Valrico, FL 33596-5215, USA

Hancock, Herbert J (Herbie) (Composer, Musician)
c/o Seth Malasky *Paradigm (NY)*
360 Park Ave S Fl 16
New York, NY 10010-1708, USA

Hancock, John D (Director)
7355 Fail Rd
La Porte, IN 46350-7108, USA

Hancock, John Lee (Director, Producer, Writer)
c/o David O'Connor *Creative Artists Agency (CAA-LA)*
2000 Avenue of the Stars Ste 100
Los Angeles, CA 90067-4705, USA

Hancock, Lee (Athlete, Baseball Player)
8338 Brentwood Blvd
Brentwood, CA 94513-1113, USA

Hancock, Leroy (Athlete, Baseball Player)
2010 Haywood Ave
Forrest City, AR 72335-4518, USA

Hancock, Phillip (Athlete, Golfer)
100 Seascape Dr
Miramar Beach, FL 32550-3919, USA

Hancock, Ryan (Athlete, Baseball Player)
542 Aiden Ridge Dr
Draper, UT 84020-7305, USA

Hancock, Terri (Athlete, Golfer)
115 Devereux Dr
Athens, GA 30606-1634, USA

Hand, Jon T (Athlete, Football Player)
13013 Broad St
Carmel, IN 46032-7226, USA

Hand, Larry (Athlete, Football Player)
4414 Robinhood Rd
Winston Salem, NC 27106-4236, USA

Hand, Norman (Athlete, Football Player)
102 Houmas Pl
Destrehan, LA 70047-3155, USA

Hand, Rich (Athlete, Baseball Player)
3512 Belmont St
Denton, TX 76210-8582, USA

Handelsman, J B (Cartoonist)
4 Times Sq
New York, NY 10036-6515, USA

Handelsman, Walt (Cartoonist, Editor)
235 Pinelawn Rd
Melville, NY 11747-4226, USA

Handford, Martin (Cartoonist)
87 Vauxhall Walk
London SE11 5HU, UNITED KINGDOM (UK)

Handler, Chelsea (Comedian, Television Host)
c/o Stephen Huvane *Slate Public Relations*
9000 W Sunset Blvd Ste 915
West Hollywood, CA 90069-5809, USA

Handler, Daniel (Actor, Writer)
c/o Esther Newberg *International Creative Management (ICM-NY)*
40 W 57th St
New York, NY 10019-4001, USA

Handler, Evan (Actor)
c/o Lenore Zerman *Liberman/Zerman Management*
252 N Larchmont Blvd Ste 200
Los Angeles, CA 90004-3754, USA

Handley, Gene (Athlete, Baseball Player)
393 Hospital Rd # 16
Newport Beach, CA 92663-3501, USA

Handley, Ray (Athlete, Football Coach, Football Player)
PO Box 355
Glenbrook, NV 89413-0355, USA

Handley, Taylor (Actor)
c/o Booh Schut *Booh Schut Company*
11365 Sunshine Ter
Studio City, CA 91604-3141, USA

Handlin, Oscar (Historian)
18 Agassiz St
Cambridge, MA 02140-2802, USA

Handloser, Sandy (Stylist)
752 W End Ave
New York, NY 10025-0148, USA

Handrahan, Vern (Athlete, Baseball Player)
36 Newland Cres
Charlottetown, PE C1A 4H5, Canada

Hands, Terence (Director)
Clwyd Theater Cymru Mold
Flintshire, NORTH WALES

Hands, William A (Bill) (Athlete, Baseball Player)
PO Box 334
Orient, NY 11957-0334, USA

Handsome
9255 W Sunset Blvd Ste 200
Los Angeles, CA 90069-3308

Handy, John (Music Group, Musician)
PO Box 961
Burlington, MA 01803-5961, USA

Handy, John W (General)
Commander-in-Chief Transportation Command
Scott Air Force Base, IL 62225, USA

Handzus, Michal (Athlete, Hockey Player)
33 W Ontario St Apt 37D
Chicago, IL 60654-7771, USA

Hanes, Ken
8281 Melrose Ave Ste 200
Los Angeles, CA 90046-6890

Hanescu, Victor (Athlete, Tennis Player)
c/o Staff Member *SFX Sports Management*
5335 Wisconsin Ave NW Ste 850
Washington, DC 20015-2052, USA

Haney, Chris (Athlete, Baseball Player)
PO Box 135
Barboursville, VA 22923-0135, USA

Haney, Hank (Golfer)
2791 S Stemmons Fwy
Lewisville, TX 75067-4138, USA

Haney, Larry (Athlete, Baseball Player)
PO Box 157
Barboursville, VA 22923-0157, USA

Haney, Lee (Writer)
105 Trail Point Cir
Fayetteville, GA 30214-2633, USA

Haney, Todd (Athlete, Baseball Player)
5404 Pointwood Cir
Waco, TX 76710-1265, USA

Hanfmann, George M A (Archaeologist)
Quincy St Fogg Art Museum 32
Cambridge, MA 02138-3883, USA

Hanft, Ruth S (Scientist)
3340 Brookside Dr
Charlottesville, VA 22901-9566, USA

Hangartner, Geoff (Athlete, Football Player)
805 Park Slope Dr
Charlotte, NC 28209-2049, USA

Hangsleben, Alan (Athlete, Hockey Player)
5760 Little Rd
Lothian, MD 20711-9543, USA

Hanifan, Jim (Athlete, Football Coach, Football Player)
1217 Grey Fox Run
Weldon Spring, MO 63304-0307, USA

Hanin, Roger (Actor)
9 rue du Boccador
Paris 75008, FRANCE

Hankins, Jay (Athlete, Baseball Player)
26509 E Outer Belt Rd
Greenwood, MO 64034-9387, USA

Hankinson, Ben (Athlete, Hockey Player)
1125 Schaeffers Point Rd
Nisswa, MN 56468-8749, USA

Hankinson, Casey (Athlete, Hockey Player)
6615 Parkwood Ln
Minneapolis, MN 55436-1733, USA

Hankinson, Tim (Coach, Soccer Player)
2121 Velma Ave
Columbus, OH 43211-2085, USA

Hanks, Colin (Actor)
c/o Courtney Kivowitz *Schiff Company, The*
8440 Warner Dr Ste B1
Culver City, CA 90232-2461, USA

Hanks, Merton (Athlete, Football Player)
62 Oakland Ave
Bloomfield, NJ 07003-3435, USA

Hanks, Tom (Actor, Producer)
c/o Leslee Dart *42West (NY)*
220 W 42nd St Fl 12
New York, NY 10036-7200, USA

Hanks, Zach (Actor)
c/o Michael Henderson *Heresun Management*
4119 W Burbank Blvd
Burbank, CA 91505-2122, USA

Hankton, Cortez (Athlete, Football Player)
1913 Keswick Ct
Pearland, TX 77581-6535, USA

Hankton, Karl (Athlete, Football Player)
12532 Hennigan Place Ln
Charlotte, NC 28214-1464, USA

Hanley, Bridget
12021 Hesby St
Valley Village, CA 91607-3115

Hanley, Frank (Misc)
1125 17th St NW
Washington, DC 20036-4709, USA

Hanley, Jenny (Actor)
Southbank House Black Prince Road
London SE1 7SJ, UNITED KINGDOM (UK)

Hanley, Kay (Music Group)
c/o Staff Member *Paradigm (Monterey)*
404 W Franklin St
Monterey, CA 93940-2303, USA

Hanley, Richard (Swimmer)
E266 Lake Rd
Ironwood, MI 49938-9736, USA

Hanlon, Edward Jr (General)
Commanding General Marine Combat Development Command
Quantico, VA 22134, USA

Hanlon, Glen (Athlete, Hockey Player)
c/o Staff Member *Washington Capitals*
627 N Glebe Rd Ste 850
Arlington, VA 22203-2144, USA

Hann, Judith
56 Wood Ln
London, ENGLAND W12 7RJ

Hanna, Jack
PO Box 400
Powell, OH 43065-0400

Hanna, Jen (Athlete, Golfer)
9 Zelma Dr
Greenville, SC 29617-7213, USA

Hanna, Jerome (Music Group)
PO Box 12
Far Hills, NJ 07931-0012, USA

Hanna, Preston (Athlete, Baseball Player)
5555 Mayfair Dr
Pensacola, FL 32506-5390, USA

Hannah, Bob (Baseball Player, Coach)
Athletic Dept
Newark, DE 19716, USA

Hannah, Bob (Motorcycle Race, Motorcycle Racer)
13515 Yarmouth Dr
Pickerington, OH 43147-8214, USA

Hannah, Charles A (Charley) (Athlete, Football Player)
PO Box 2671
Lutz, FL 33548-2671, USA

Hannah, Daryl (Actor)
c/o Chuck Binder *Binder & Associates*
1465 Lindacrest Dr
Beverly Hills, CA 90210-2519, USA

Hannah, John (Actor)
c/o Sue Latimer *Artists Rights Group (ARG)*
4 Great Portland St
London W1W 8PA, UNITED KINGDOM (UK)

Hannah, John (Athlete, Football Player)
2407 Hideaway Pl SE
Decatur, AL 35603-5602, USA

Hannah, Travis (Athlete, Football Player)
10807 Lemoli Ave
Inglewood, CA 90303-2023, USA

Hannah, Wayne (Religious Leader)
PO Box 386
Winona Lake, IN 46590-0386, USA

Hannahs, Gerald (Gerry) (Athlete, Baseball Player)
1411 Andover Rdg
Little Rock, AR 72227-3971, USA

Hannam, Ryan (Athlete, Football Player)
10311 Offshore Dr
Irving, TX 75063-5092, USA

Hannan, Dave (Athlete, Hockey Player)
408 Timberlake Dr
Venetia, PA 15367-1394, USA

Hannan, Jacquie (Stylist)
Prefers to be contacted via email

Hannan, Jim (Athlete, Baseball Player)
3907 Cherry Hill Way
Annandale, VA 22003-2220, USA

Hannawald, Sven (Skier)
Im Sabel 4
Trier 54294, GERMANY

Hannelius, Geneveive (Actor)
c/o Karl Hofheinz *Synergy Talent*
13251 Ventura Blvd
Studio City, CA 91604-1838, USA

Hanneman, Craig (Athlete, Football Player)
4350 Gibson Rd NW
Salem, OR 97304-9547, USA

Hanneman, Steve (Actor)
c/o Staff Member *Abrams Artists Agency (LA)*
9200 W Sunset Blvd PH 11
Los Angeles, CA 90069-3601, USA

Hanner, Dave (Athlete, Football Player)
General Delivery
Florence, WI 54121-9999, USA

Hannigan, Alyson (Actor)
c/o Staff Member *Lovett Management*
1327 Brinkley Ave
Los Angeles, CA 90049-3619, USA

Hannigan, Mackenzie (Actor)
c/o Staff Member *Martin Weiss Management*
PO Box 5656
Santa Monica, CA 90409-5656, USA

Hannigan, Pat (Athlete, Hockey Player)
1674 Nigh Rd
Fort Erie, ON L2A 5M4, Canada

Hannigan, Ray (Athlete, Hockey Player)
928 Halo Dr
Troy, MT 59935-9420, USA

Hannity, Sean (Correspondent)
c/o Staff Member *Fox News Channel (NY)*
1211 Ave Of The Americas Level C1
New York, NY 10036-8701, USA

Hannity, Shawn (Talk Show Host)
125 W End Ave Fl 6
New York, NY 10023-6387, USA

Hannon, Tom (Athlete, Football Player)
17398 Roxbury Ave
Southfield, MI 48075-7609, USA

Hannuia, Dick (Coach, Swimmer)
1021 S Westley Dr
Tacoma, WA 98465-1426, USA

Hanrahan, Don (Athlete, Basketball Player)
416 Valley Rd
Cos Cob, CT 06807-1622, USA

Hanrahan, Joel (Athlete, Baseball Player)
4152 River Marsh Dr
Fernandina Beach, Fl 32034, USA

Hanratty, Sammi (Actor)
c/o Linda Henrie *Go Talent Management*
12930 Ventura Blvd Ste 904
Studio City, CA 91604-2200, USA

Hanratty, Terrance R (Terry) (Athlete, Football Player)
31 Gower Rd
New Canaan, CT 06840-6630, USA

Hans, Rollen (Athlete, Basketball Player)
12607 100th Ln NE Apt L156
Kirkland, WA 98034-8830, USA

Hans-Adam II (Prince)
9490 Vaduz
LIECHTENSTEIN

Hansbrough, Tyler (Athlete, Basketball Player)
c/o Jeff Schwartz *Excel Sports Management*
9665 Wilshire Blvd Ste 500
Beverly Hills, CA 90212-2312, USA

Hansch, Theodor W. (Nobel Prize Laureate)
Schelling Strasse 4 / 111
Munchen D-80799, Germany

Hansell, Greg (Athlete, Baseball Player)
1791 W Prescott Dr
Chandler, AZ 85248-4845, USA

Hansen, Beck (Beck) (Musician, Songwriter, Writer)
c/o Staff Member *Nasty Little Man*
110 Greene St Ste 605
New York, NY 10012-3838, USA

Hansen, Bob (Athlete, Baseball Player)
19 N Kelsey Ave
Evansville, IN 47711-6051, USA

Hansen, Bob (Athlete, Basketball Player)
710 36th St
West Des Moines, IA 50265-3166, USA

Hansen, Brian (Athlete, Football Player)
101 W Hazeltine Ln
Sioux Falls, SD 57108-6422, USA

Hansen, Bruce (Athlete, Football Player)
480 N 1100 E
American Fork, UT 84003-1992, USA

Hansen, Chris (Correspondent, Television Host)
c/o Staff Member *Dateline NBC*
30 Rockefeller Plz Fl 270E
New York, NY 10112-0299, USA

Hansen, Courtney (Actor)
c/o Liza Anderson *Anderson Group Public Relations*
8060 Melrose Ave Fl 4
Los Angeles, CA 90046-7038, USA

Hansen, Craig (Athlete, Baseball Player)
1180 Washington St Apt 508
Boston, MA 02118-2154, USA

Hansen, David (Dave) (Athlete, Baseball Player)
9852 Orchard Ln
Villa Park, CA 92861-3105, USA

Hansen, Deborah (Stylist)
PO Box 204
Brookline, MA 2146, USA

Hansen, Don (Athlete, Football Player)
2551 Maple Creek Ct
Snellville, GA 30078-5952, USA

Hansen, Frederick M (Fred) (Athlete, Track Athlete)
201 Vanderpool Ln Apt 12
Houston, TX 77024-6151, USA

Hansen, Gale (Actor)
721 SE 29th Ave
Portland, OR 97214-3027, USA

Hansen, Gunnar (Actor)
PO Box 368
Northeast Harbor, ME 04662-0368, USA

Hansen, Gus (Actor)
c/o Staff Member *Poker Royalty, LLC*
10789 W Twain Ave Ste 200
Las Vegas, NV 89135-3030, USA

Hansen, Jacqueline (Athlete, Track Athlete)
1133 9th St
Santa Monica, CA 90403-5259, USA

Hansen, James E (Physicist, Scientist)
2880 Broadway
New York, NY 10025-7848, USA

Hansen, Jed (Athlete, Baseball Player)
180 SE Cedar Hill Ln
Shelton, WA 98584-7977, USA

Hansen, Lars (Athlete, Basketball Player)
1230 Horn Ave Apt 504
West Hollywood, CA 90069-2175, USA

Hansen, Marcia (Stylist)
2411 Colony Ct
Ann Arbor, MI 48104-6556, USA

Hansen, Mark Victor (Business Person, Motivational Speaker, Writer)
711 W 17th St Ste D2
Costa Mesa, CA 92627-4344, USA

Hansen, Patti (Model)
Redlands W Wittering Chichester
Sussex, UNITED KINGDOM (UK)

Hansen, Peter (Actor)
6500 Wilshire Blvd # 550
Los Angeles, CA 90048-4920, USA

Hansen, Phil (Athlete, Football Player)
24921 N Melissa Dr
Detroit Lakes, MN 56501-7266, USA

Hansen, Rich (Athlete, Hockey Player)
78 Eatons Neck Rd
Northport, NY 11768-1105, USA

Hansen, Rick (Athlete)
520 W 6th Ave Fl 5
Vancouver, BC V5Z 1A1, CANADA

Hansen, Ron (Athlete, Baseball Player)
13602 Alliston Dr
Baldwin, MD 21013-9748, USA

Hansen, Roscoe (Athlete, Football Player)
638 Sooy Ln
Absecon, NJ 08201-1325, USA

Hansis, Van (Actor)
c/o Kathy Kanner *Kanner Entertainment*
30 W 74th St # PH1
New York, NY 10023-2446, USA

Hanson (Music Group)
1045 W 78th St
Tulsa, OK 74132, USA

Hanson, Carl T (Admiral)
900 Birdseye Rd
Orient, NY 11967, USA

Hanson, Curtis (Director, Producer)
c/o David Kramer *United Talent Agency (UTA)*
9560 Wilshire Blvd Fl 5
Beverly Hills, CA 90212-2400, USA

Hanson, Dave (Athlete, Hockey Player)
304 Timberlake Dr
Venetia, PA 15367-1376, USA

Hanson, Erik (Athlete, Baseball Player)
20333 N 83rd Pl
Scottsdale, AZ 85255-3931, USA

Hanson, Isaac (Musician, Songwriter)
c/o Allen Kovac *Tenth Street Entertainment*
270 Lafayette St Ste 706
New York, NY 10012-3397, USA

Hanson, Janet (Stylist)
74 Kensington Ave
Norwood, NJ 07648-1909, USA

Hanson, Jason D (Athlete, Football Player)
27272 Ovid Ct
Franklin, MI 48025-1036, USA

Hanson, Jennifer (Musician)
c/o Staff Member *Creative Artists Agency (CAA-TN)*
3310 W End Ave Fl 5
Nashville, TN 37203-1028, USA

Hanson, Joselio (Athlete, Football Player)
2531 Hudspeth St
Inglewood, CA 90303-2432, USA

Hanson, Stan
PO Box 970
Hotchkiss, CO 81419-0970

Hanson, Taylor (Musician, Songwriter)
c/o Allen Kovac *Tenth Street Entertainment*
270 Lafayette St Ste 706
New York, NY 10012-3397, USA

Hanson, Tracy (Athlete, Golfer)
89 S Atlantic Ave Apt 1403
Ormond Beach, FL 32176-6608, USA

Hanson, William R (Artist)
78 W Notre Dame St
Glens Falls, NY 12801-2721, USA

Hanson, Zachary (Musician, Songwriter)
c/o Allen Kovac *Tenth Street Entertainment*
270 Lafayette St Ste 706
New York, NY 10012-3397, USA

Hanson-Sfingi, Beverly (Athlete, Golfer)
79915 Horseshoe Rd
La Quinta, CA 92253-4309, USA

Hanspard, Byron (Athlete, Football Player)
PO Box 792
Desoto, TX 75123-0792, USA

Hansraj, Jugal (Actor, Bollywood)
14-A Queens Hill Bandra W Apt PALI
Mumbai, MS 400050, INDIA

Hanss, Ted (Scientist)
3025 Boardwalk St
Ann Arbor, MI 48108-3230, USA

Hantla, Robert (Athlete, Football Player)
7815 E Monte Vista Rd
Scottsdale, AZ 85257-2209, USA

Hantuchova, Daniela (Tennis Player)
c/o Staff Member *Women's Tennis Association (WTA (US))*
1 Progress Plz Ste 1500
St Petersburg, FL 33701-4335, USA

Hanuja (Actor, Bollywood)
No 20 Periyar Street Gandhi Nagar
Chennai, TN, INDIA

Hanulak, Chet (Athlete, Football Player)
225 Canal Park Dr Apt 6
Salisbury, MD 21804-7266, USA

Hanzlik, Bill (Athlete, Basketball Player, Coach)
5701 Green Oaks Dr
Greenwood Village, CO 80121-1336, USA

Hape, Patrick (Athlete, Football Player)
105 Sutton Cir
Birmingham, AL 35242-7075, USA

Hapke, Bruce (Misc)
1702 Georgetown Pl
Pittsburgh, PA 15235-4916, USA

Happe, Shannon Bahrke (Athlete, Skier)
c/o Staff Member *US Ski And Snowboard Association*
Box 199
Park City, UT 84060, USA

Harada, Masahiko (Fighting) (Boxer)
2-21-5 Azabu-Juban Minatoku
Tokyo 106, JAPAN

Harald V (King)
Det Kongelige Slott Drammensvelen 1
Oslo 10, NORWAY

Harang, Aaron (Athlete, Baseball Player)
6411 Glenroy St
San Diego, CA 92120-2713, USA

Harbach, Otto
3455 Congress St
Fairfield, CT 06824-2036

Harbaruk, Nick (Athlete, Hockey Player)
32 Groomsport Cres
Scarborough, ON M1T 2K9, Canada

Harbaugh, Gregory J (Astronaut)
1936 Thornwood Ave
Wilmette, IL 60091-1403, USA

Harbaugh, James (jim) (Athlete, Football Player)
111 Carob Way
Coronado, CA 92118-2432, USA

Harbaugh, Robert E (Doctor)
Surgery Dept
Hanover, NH 3756, USA

Harbison, John H (Composer)
479 Franklin St
Cambridge, MA 02139-3115, USA

Harbour, David (Actor)
c/o Meg Mortimer *Principal Entertainment (NY)*
130 W 42nd St Ste 614
New York, NY 10036-7804, USA

Harbo-Weidmann, Claire (Stylist)
476 E Cypress Ave Apt M
Burbank, CA 91501-3230, USA

Harcourt, Ed (Musician)
c/o Staff Member *Paradigm (Monterey)*
404 W Franklin St
Monterey, CA 93940-2303, USA

Hard, Darlene R (Tennis Player)
22924 Erwin St
Woodland Hills, CA 91367-3215, USA

Hardaway, Anfemee (Penny) (Athlete, Basketball Player)
3217 Point Hill Cv
Memphis, TN 38125-8890, USA

Hardaway, Anfernee (Basketball Player)
c/o Team Member *Orlando Magic*
8701 Maitland Summit Blvd
Orlando, FL 32810-5915, USA

Hardaway, Timothy D (Tim) (Athlete, Basketball Player)
10050 SW 62nd Ave
Miami, FL 33156-3378, USA

Hardee, Billy (Athlete, Football Player)
2935 Plantation Rd
Winter Haven, FL 33884-1233, USA

Hardeman, Buddy (Athlete, Football Player)
5711 Heming Ave
Springfield, VA 22151-2714, USA

Hardeman, Don (Athlete, Football Player)
901 S Valley Mills Dr Apt 207-B
Waco, TX 76711-1160, USA

Hardeman, Tami (Stylist)
1921 Brian Way
Decatur, GA 30033-3815, USA

Harden, Bobby (Athlete, Football Player)
5645 NW 117th Ave
Coral Springs, FL 33076-3617, USA

Harden, Marcia Gay (Actor)
242 W 45th St Bernard B
New York, NY 10036-3901, USA

Harden, Michael (Athlete, Football Player)
7150 Leetsdale Dr Apt 315
Denver, CO 80224-1999, USA

Hardenberger, Hahan (Music Group, Musician)
165 W 57th St
New York, NY 10019-2201, USA

Hardesty, Brandon (Actor)
c/o Brandt Joel *WmE2 (Endeavor-LA)*
9601 Wilshire Blvd Fl 3
Beverly Hills, CA 90210-5219, USA

Hardesty Jr, David C (Educator)
President's Office
Morgantown, WV 26506, USA

Hardie, Kate (Actor)
13 Shorts Gardens
London WC2H 9AT, UNITED KINGDOM (UK)

Hardiek, Kevin (Stylist)
c/o Staff Member *Maximum Talent*
1873 S Bellaire St Ste 915
Denver, CO 80222-4356, USA

Hardin, Clifford M (Secretary)
10 Roan Ln
Saint Louis, MO 63124-1479, USA

Hardin, Jerry
3033 Vista Crest Dr
Los Angeles, CA 90068-1824

Hardin, Melora (Actor)
c/o Staff Member *Kohner Agency, The*
9300 Wilshire Blvd Ste 555
Beverly Hills, CA 90212-3211, USA

Hardin, Paul III (Educator)
Chancellor S Ofc
Chapel Hill, NC 27599-0001, USA

Hardin, Ty (Actor)
2210 87street Ct NW
Gig Harbor, WA 98332-7550, USA

Harding, Daniel (Musician)
c/o Staff Member *International Creative Management (ICM-LA)*
10250 Constellation Blvd Fl 7
Los Angeles, CA 90067-6207, USA

Harding, Ian (Actor)
c/o Gina Hoffman *Baker Winokur Ryder Public Relations (BWR-LA)*
9100 Wilshire Blvd Ste 500 PMB WEST
Beverly Hills, CA 90212-3426, USA

Harding, John Wesley (Actor, Composer, Music Group, Songwriter, Writer)
c/o Staff Member *Concerted Efforts*
PO Box 440326
Somerville, MA 02144-0004, USA

Harding, Josh (Athlete, Hockey Player)
1415 Brown St
Regina, SK S4N 5C9, Canada

Harding, Roger (Athlete, Football Player)
1911 Kalakaua Ave Apt 601
Honolulu, HI 96815-1809, USA

Harding, Sarah (Musician)
c/o Sarah Camlett *Independent Talent Group (ITG-UK)*
Oxford House 76 Oxford St
London W1D 1BS, UK

Harding, Tonya (Athlete, Figure Skater)
11805 Bastrop St
Manor, TX 78653-4928, USA

Hardis, Stephen R (Business Person)
Eaton Center 1111 Superior Ave
Cleveland, OH 44114, USA

Hardison, Dee (Athlete, Football Player)
6731 Winthrop Dr
Fayetteville, NC 28311-1072, USA

Hardison, Kadeem (Actor)
19743 Valley View Dr
Topanga, CA 90290-3257, USA

Hardisty, Huntington (Admiral)
1600 Wilson Blvd Ste 900
Arlington, VA 22209-2510, USA

Hardman, Cedrick (Athlete, Football Player)
364 Myrtle St
Laguna Beach, CA 92651-1533, USA

Hardman, Earl
1400 E Carson St
Pittsburgh, PA 15203-1556

Hardnett, Charles (Charlie) (Athlete, Basketball Player, Coach)
1906 Swainsboro Dr
Louisville, KY 40218-2417, USA

Hardrict, Cory (Actor)
c/o Staff Member *Burstein Company, The*
15304 W Sunset Blvd Ste 208
Pacific Palisades, CA 90272-3656, USA

Hardt, Michael (Educator)
English
Durham, NC 27708-0001, USA

Hardtke, Jason (Athlete, Baseball Player)
1538 Bouchard Dr
San Jose, CA 95118-3917, USA

Hardwick, Billy
1576 S White Station Rd
Memphis, TN 38117-7220

Hardwick, Chris (Actor)
c/o Alex Murray *McDonald-Murray Management*
11846 Ventura Blvd Ste 202
Studio City, CA 91604-2620, USA

Hardwick, Gary C (Director, Producer, Writer)
c/o Bruce Kaufman *International Creative Management (ICM-LA)*
10250 Constellation Blvd Fl 7
Los Angeles, CA 90067-6207, USA

Hardwick, Johnny (Artist, Voice Over Artist, Writer)
c/o Staff Member *Creative Artists Agency (CAA-LA)*
2000 Avenue of the Stars Ste 100
Los Angeles, CA 90067-4705, USA

Hardwick, William B (Billy) (Bowler)
1576 S White Station Rd
Memphis, TN 38117-7220, USA

Hardwicke, Catherine (Director)
c/o BeBe Lerner *ID Public Relations (ID-LA)*
7080 Hollywood Blvd Fl 8
Los Angeles, CA 90028-6906, USA

Hardwicke, Edward (Actor)
c/o Staff Member *International Creative Management (ICM-LA)*
10250 Constellation Blvd Fl 7
Los Angeles, CA 90067-6207, USA

Hardy, Adrian (Athlete, Football Player)
7530 Kingsport Blvd
New Orleans, LA 70128-2114, USA

Hardy, Alan (Athlete, Basketball Player)
13841 Gratiot Ave
Detroit, MI 48205-2805, USA

Hardy, Bruce A (Athlete, Football Player)
3310 Pinewalk Dr N Apt 1826
Margate, FL 33063-9341, USA

Hardy, Carroll (Athlete, Baseball Player, Football Player)
1514 Whitehall Dr
Longmont, CO 80504-7971, USA

Hardy, Darrell (Athlete, Basketball Player)
3126 Knoll St
Houston, TX 77080-3011, USA

Hardy, David (Athlete, Football Player)
PO Box 1270
New Waverly, TX 77358-1270, USA

Hardy, Hagood (Composer, Musician)
41 Valleybrook Dr
Don Mills, ON M3B 2S6, CANADA

Hardy, Hugh (Architect)
902 Broadway
New York, NY 10010-6002, USA

Hardy, James (Athlete, Basketball Player)
1682 Lakewood Dr
Salt Lake City, UT 84117-7518, USA

Hardy, James (Athlete, Football Player)
c/o Eugene Parker *Maximum Sports Management*
6435 W Jefferson Blvd # 197
Fort Wayne, IN 46804-6203, USA

Hardy, Jeff (Wrestler)
c/o Kerry Rodgerson *World Wrestling Entertainment (WWE)*
1241 E Main St
Stamford, CT 06902-3520, USA

Hardy, Jim (Athlete, Football Player)
48490 San Vicente St
La Quinta, CA 92253-6253, USA

Hardy, Joe (Athlete, Hockey Player)
1256 ROUTE DE FOSSAMBAULT RR 2
Saint-Augustin-De-Desmaures, QC G3A 1W8, Canada

Hardy, John (Jack) (Athlete, Baseball Player)
1260 NW 192nd Ln
Pembroke Pines, FL 33029-4520, USA

Hardy, Kevin (Athlete, Football Player)
298 Paraiso Dr
Danville, CA 94526-4950, USA

Hardy, Kevin (Athlete, Football Player)
1228 Windsor Harbor Dr
Jacksonville, FL 32225-2651, USA

Hardy, Larry (Athlete, Baseball Player)
7 Jennifer Ct
Roanoke, TX 76262-5402, USA

Hardy, Larry (Athlete, Football Player)
1711 Fairwood Dr
Jackson, MS 39213-7918, USA

Hardy, Mark (Athlete, Hockey Player)
2135 E El Segundo Blvd
El Segundo, CA 90245-4503, USA

Hardy, Matt (Wrestler)
c/o Kerry Rodgerson *World Wrestling Entertainment (WWE)*
1241 E Main St
Stamford, CT 06902-3520, USA

Hardy, Robert (Actor)
Prince of Wales Coventry St
London W1V 7FE, UNITED KINGDOM (UK)

Hardy, Sophie (Doctor)
332 Ave Du Marechal Juin
Boulogne, FRANCE 92100, FRANCE

Hardy, Terry (Athlete, Football Player)
3109 S Rick Dr
Montgomery, AL 36108-3821, USA

Hardy, Tom (Actor)
c/o Clair Dobbs *Public Eye Communications*
535 Kings Rd Suite 313 Plaza
London SW10 0SZ, United Kingdom

Hare, David (Writer)
95 Linden Gardens
London WC2, UNITED KINGDOM (UK)

Hare, Eddie (Athlete, Football Player)
802 Walker School Rd
Sugar Land, TX 77479-5807, USA

Hare, Shawn (Athlete, Baseball Player)
1975 Deer Path Trl
Oxford, MI 48371-6062, USA

Harelik, Mark (Actor)
c/o Staff Member *Gersh (LA)*
9465 Wilshire Blvd Ste 600
Beverly Hills, CA 90212-2612, USA

Haren, Dan (Athlete, Baseball Player)
c/o Joe Urbon *Creative Artists Agency (CAA-NY)*
162 5th Ave Fl 6
New York, NY 10010-6047, USA

Harewood, Dorian (Actor)
c/o Tracy Quinn *Quinn Management*
17328 Ventura Blvd Ste 416
Encino, CA 91316-3904, USA

Hargain, Tony (Athlete, Football Player)
6440 Shady Springs Way
Citrus Heights, CA 95621-3514, USA

Hargan, Steve (Athlete, Baseball Player)
2502 E Morongo Trl
Palm Springs, CA 92264-4839, USA

Harge, Ira (Athlete, Basketball Player)
328 Yucca Dr NW
Albuquerque, NM 87105-1935, USA

Hargesheimer, Alan (Athlete, Baseball Player)
107 N Evanston Ave
Arlington Heights, IL 60004-6617, USA

Hargett, Edd (Athlete, Football Player)
379 County Road 222
Nacogdoches, TX 75965-4806, USA

Hargis, Gary (Athlete, Baseball Player)
157 Gemini St
Lompoc, CA 93436-1244, USA

Hargitay, Mariska (Actor)
c/o Leslie Sloane *Baker Winokur Ryder Public Relations BWR (BWR-NY)*
292 Madison Ave Fl 12
New York, NY 10017-6415, USA

Hargrove, D Michael (Mike) (Athlete, Baseball Player, Coach)
3925 Ramblewood Dr
Richfield, OH 44286-9642, USA

Hargrove, Linda (Coach)
MCI Center 601 E St NW
Washington, DC 20004, USA

Hargrove, Marion
401 Montana Ave # 6
Santa Monica, CA 90403-1303

Hari, Rene (Stylist)
3153 Bloomington Ave
Minneapolis, MN 55407-1717, USA

Harikkala, Tim (Athlete, Baseball Player)
W6132 Everglade Rd
Greenville, WI 54942-8590, USA

Haris, Niki (Musician)
c/o Staff Member *Diva Central Inc*
7510 W Sunset Blvd Ste 1445
Los Angeles, CA 90046-3408, USA

Harker, Al (Athlete, Soccer Player)
409 2nd St
Lafayette Hill, PA 19444-1403, USA

Harker, Susannah
55 Ashburnham Grove Greenwich
London, ENGLAND SW10 8UJ

Harket, Morten (Music Group)
11 Elvaston Place #300
London SW7 5QC, UNITED KINGDOM (UK)

Harkey, Mike (Athlete, Baseball Player)
23930 Strange Creek Dr
Diamond Bar, CA 91765-1144, USA

Harkey, Steve (Athlete, Football Player)
6582 Cherry Tree Ln NE
Atlanta, GA 30328-3319, USA

Harkin, Kenan (Sportscaster)
c/o Staff Member *WmE2 (WMA-LA)*
1 William Morris Pl
Beverly Hills, CA 90212-4261, USA

Harkin, Tom (Senator)
531 Hart Senate Off Bldg
Washington, DC 20510-0001, USA

Harkins, Brett (Athlete, Hockey Player)
4701 Duhme Rd Apt 1D
Saint Petersburg, FL 33708 2801, USA

Harkleroad, Ashley (Tennis Player)
c/o Jill Smoller *WmE2 (Endeavor-LA)*
9601 Wilshire Blvd Fl 3
Beverly Hills, CA 90210-5219, USA

Harkless, Burkley (Athlete, Football Player)
2308 E Windsor Dr
Denton, TX 76209-1447, USA

Harkness, Jerry (Athlete, Basketball Player)
8340 Misty Dr
Indianapolis, IN 46236-9190, USA

Harkness, Ned (Athlete, Hockey Player)
113 Pollet Pl
Rochester, NY 14626-1675, USA

Harkness, Tim (Athlete, Baseball Player)
70 Homefield Sq
Courtice, ON L1E 1L3, Canada

Harlan, Jack R (Scientist)
Agronomy Dept
Urbana, IL 61801, USA

Harlan, Kevin (Sportscaster)
51 W 52nd St
New York, NY 10019-6119, USA

Harlem Globetrotters
400 E Van Buren St Ste 300
Phoenix, AZ 85004-2257

Harley, Steve (Music Group)
19D Pinfold Road
London SW16 2SL, UNITED KINGDOM (UK)

Harlicka, Skip (Athlete, Basketball Player)
2643 Saint Marys St
Raleigh, NC 27609-7644, USA

Harlin, Renny (Director, Producer)
8800 W Sunset Blvd # 400
Los Angeles, CA 90069-2105, USA

Harlock, David (Athlete, Hockey Player)
4714 Oak Hollow Ct
Dexter, MI 48130-9374, USA

Harlow, Larry (Athlete, Baseball Player)
26348 W Burnett Rd
Buckeye, AZ 85396-9239, USA

Harlow, Pat (Athlete, Football Player)
230 W Avenida San Antonio
San Clemente, CA 92672-4356, USA

Harlow, Scott (Athlete, Hockey Player)
117 Cranberry Dr
Halifax, MA 02338-1378, USA

Harlow, Shalom (Model)
c/o Heather Reynolds *One Entertainment (NY)*
12 W 57th St PH 1
New York, NY 10019-3900, USA

Harman, Denham (Biologist)
9817 Hamey Pkwy S
Omaha, NE 68114, USA

Harman, Jane (Congressman, Politician)
2400 Rayburn Hob
Washington, DC 20515-0536, USA

Harman, Jennifer (Misc)
c/o Staff Member *Poker Royalty, LLC*
10789 W Twain Ave Ste 200
Las Vegas, NV 89135-3030, USA

Harman, Katie (Beauty Pageant Winner)
c/o Staff Member *The Miss America Organization*
2 Convention Blvd Ste 1000
Atlantic City, NJ 08401-4137, USA

Harmon, Andrew P (Athlete, Football Player)
1258 Waters Edge Dr
Dayton, OH 45458-3937, USA

Harmon, Chuck (Athlete, Baseball Player)
6035 Ridgeacres Dr Unit A
Cincinnati, OH 45237-4733, USA

Harmon, Clarence (Athlete, Football Player)
PO Box 571
Verona, MS 38879-0571, USA

Harmon, Dan (Writer)
c/o Blair Kohan *United Talent Agency (UTA)*
9560 Wilshire Blvd Fl 5
Beverly Hills, CA 90212-2400, USA

Harmon, Joy (Actor)
9901 Poole Ave
Sunland, CA 91040-1335, USA

Harmon, Kelly (Actor, Model)
13224 Old Oak Ln
Los Angeles, CA 90049-2502, USA

Harmon, Manny -
8350 Santa Monica Blvd
Los Angeles, CA 90069-4393

Harmon, Mark (Actor)
c/o Karen Samfilippo *Image Management PR*
1810 14th St Ste 205
Santa Monica, CA 90404-4662, USA

Harmon, Merle (Sportscaster)
424 E Lamar Blvd Ste 210
Arlington, TX 76011-3606, USA

Harmon, Nigel (Astronaut)
Church Crookham
Aldershot, UNITED KINGDOM (UK)

Harmon, Robert (Director)
c/o Andrew Ruf *Paradigm (LA)*
360 N Crescent Dr
Beverly Hills, CA 90210-4874, USA

Harmon, Ronnie K (Athlete, Football Player)
13022 218th St
Springfield Gardens, NY 11413-1231, USA

Harmon, Terry (Athlete, Baseball Player)
62 Oakwood Dr
Medford, NJ 08055-8824, USA

Harmon, Winsor
c/o Jerry Shandrew *Shandrew Public Relations*
1050 S Stanley Ave
Los Angeles, CA 90019-6634, USA

Harmonica Rascals, The
4585 N River Rd
Zanesville, OH 43701-7768

Harmon-Sehorn, Angie (Actor)
c/o John Carrabino *John Carrabino Management*
5900 Wilshire Blvd Ste 406
Los Angeles, CA 90036-5015, USA

Harms, Alfred G Jr (Admiral)
Chief Education/Training Naval Air Station
Pensacola, FL 32508, USA

Harms, Kristin (Producer)
c/o Staff Member *West Wing, The*
4000 Warner Blvd Trlr 8
Burbank, CA 91522-0001

Harnden, Arthur (Art) (Athlete, Track Athlete)
7218 Pepper Ridge Rd
Corpus Christi, TX 78413-5005, USA

Harnes, Robert (Baseball Player)
833 E Drexel Sq
Chicago, IL 60615-3705, USA

Harness, William E (Opera Singer)
PO Box 328
Washougal, WA 98671-0328, USA

Harney, Paul (Athlete, Golfer)
72 Club Valley Dr
East Falmouth, MA 02536-4223, USA

Harnisch, Peter T (Pete) (Athlete, Baseball Player)
35 Bretwood Dr S
Colts Neck, NJ 07722-2402, USA

Harnois, Elisabeth (Actor)
c/o Ted Schachter *Schachter Entertainment*
1157 S Beverly Dr Fl 2
Los Angeles, CA 90035-1119, USA

Harnoncourt, Nikolaus
38 Piaristangasse
Vienna 1080, AUSTRIA

Harnos, Christine (Actor)
232 N Canon Dr
Beverly Hills, CA 90210-5302, USA

Harnoy, Ofra (Musician)
437 Spadina Road PO Box 23046
Toronto, ON M5P 2W0, CANADA

Harold, Erika (Beauty Pageant Winner)
c/o Staff Member *The Miss America Organization*
2 Convention Blvd Ste 1000
Atlantic City, NJ 08401-4137, USA

Harold, Gale (Actor)
c/o Larry Taube *Principal Entertainment (LA)*
1964 Westwood Blvd Ste 400
Los Angeles, CA 90025-4695, USA

Harout, Magda (Actor)
13452 Vose St
Van Nuys, CA 91405-3416, USA

Harper, Alvin C (Athlete, Football Player)
501 Harry S Truman Dr Apt 109
Upper Marlboro, MD 20774-2061, USA

Harper, Ben (Music Group, Musician, Songwriter, Writer)
c/o Staff Member *Red Light Management (LA)*
8439 W Sunset Blvd Ste 2
Los Angeles, CA 90069-1925, USA

Harper, Bob (Fitness Expert)
c/o Robby Wells *United Entertainment Group*
142 W 57th St Fl 5
New York, NY 10019-3300, USA

Harper, Brian (Athlete, Baseball Player)
8319 E Shetland Trl
Scottsdale, AZ 85258-1343, USA

Harper, Bruce (Athlete, Football Player)
311 Lindbergh Ave
Closter, NJ 07624-2732, USA

Harper, Charles M (Business Person)
6625 State St
Omaha, NE 68152-1633, USA

Harper, Charlie (Athlete, Football Player)
2115 Augusta
McKinney, TX 75070-4301, USA

Harper, Dave (Athlete, Football Player)
4494 Cedar St
Eureka, CA 95503-8901, USA

Harper, Dawn (Athlete, Track Athlete)
c/o Staff Member *HS International Sports Management, Inc.*
9871 Irvine Center Dr
Irvine, CA 92618-4361, USA

Harper, Derek (Athlete, Basketball Player)
301 W 53rd St Apt 14F
New York, NY 10019-5772, USA

Harper, Deveron (Athlete, Football Player)
2749 Huntsville St
Kenner, LA 70062-5124, USA

Harper, Donald D W (Don) (Swimmer)
1765 Lynnhaven Dr
Columbus, OH 43221-1409, USA

Harper, Dwayne (Athlete, Football Player)
104 Cue St
Orangeburg, SC 29115-7593, USA

Harper, Edward J (Composer)
7 Morningside Park
Edinburgh EH10 5HD, SCOTLAND

Harper, Gregg (Congressman, Politician)
307 Cq Nnqn Hob
Washington, DC 20515-0001, USA

Harper, Heather M (Opera Singer)
20 Milverton Road
London NW6 7AS, UNITED KINGDOM (UK)

Harper, Heck
13647 Gaffney Ln Apt 17
Oregon City, OR 97045-8970

Harper, Herschel (Baseball Player)
3302 Hazelwood Dr SW
Atlanta, GA 30311-3038, USA

Harper, Hill (Actor)
c/o Destiny Hill *Destiny Hill*
6253 Hollywood Blvd Apt 501
Los Angeles, CA 90028-8251, USA

Harper, Jessica (Actor, Music Group)
15430 Brownwood Pl
Los Angeles, CA 90077-1609, USA

Harper, John
9700 Kessler Ave
Chatsworth, CA 91311-5503

Harper, Judson M (Engineer)
1818 Westview Rd
Fort Collins, CO 80524-1891, USA

Harper, Mark (Athlete, Football Player)
2162 Albany Ave
Memphis, TN 38108-3011, USA

Harper, Michael (Athlete, Basketball Player)
2387 College Hill Pl
West Linn, OR 97068-1222, USA

Harper, Robert (Actor)
329 N Wetherly Dr Ste 101
Beverly Hills, CA 90211-1674, USA

Harper, Roger (Athlete, Football Player)
1921 Holburn Ave
Columbus, OH 43207-1683, USA

Harper, Roland (Athlete, Football Player)
1391 Westbourne Pkwy
Algonquin, IL 60102-6052, USA

Harper, Ron (Actor)
c/o Staff Member *Tisherman Gilbert Motley Drozdoski Talent Agency (TGMD)*
6767 Forest Lawn Dr Ste 101
Los Angeles, CA 90068-1050, USA

Harper, Ron (Athlete, Basketball Player)
15 Applewood Dr
Upper Saddle, NJ 07458-1002, USA

Harper, Terry (Athlete, Baseball Player)
4225 Jailette Rd
Atlanta, GA 30349-1848, USA

Harper, Terry (Athlete, Hockey Player)
PO Box 5227
El Dorado Hills, CA 95762-0005, USA

Harper, Tess (Actor)
c/o David Guc *Vanguard Management Group*
8060 Melrose Ave Fl 4
Los Angeles, CA 90046-7038, USA

Harper, Tommy (Athlete, Baseball Player)
5 Cow Hill Rd
Sharon, MA 02067-2987, USA

Harper, Travis (Athlete, Baseball Player)
10 Brook Ridge Ln
Morgantown, WV 26508-2542, USA

Harper, Valerie (Actor)
PO Box 7187
Beverly Hills, CA 90212-7187, USA

Harper, Willie M (Athlete, Football Player)
2525 Berryessa Ct
Tracy, CA 95304-5825, USA

Harpring, Matt (Basketball Player)
c/o Staff Member *Utah Jazz*
301 W South Temple
Salt Lake City, UT 84101-1219, USA

Harptones, The
55 W 119th St
New York, NY 10026-1454

Harrah, Colbert D (Toby) (Athlete, Baseball Player, Coach)
316 Leewood Cir
Azle, TX 76020, USA

Harrah, Dennis W (Athlete, Football Player)
925 Rockin One Way
Paso Robles, CA 93446-8433, USA

Harrar, J George (Misc)
125 Puritan Dr
Scarsdale, NY 10583-6734, USA

Harraway, Charlie (Athlete, Football Player)
7961 Megan Hammock Way
Sarasota, FL 34240-8244, USA

Harrell, Anthony (Actor)

Harrell, Billy (Athlete, Baseball Player)
253 Mount Hope Dr
Albany, NY 12202-1017, USA

Harrell, Graham (Athlete, Football Player)
c/o Chad Speck *Allegiant Athletic Agency*
35 Market Sq Ste 201
Knoxville, TN 37902-1420, USA

Harrell, James (Athlete, Football Player)
17826 Crystal Preserve Dr
Lutz, FL 33548-6408, USA

Harrell, James A (Geophysicist, Physicist)
Geology Dept
Toledo, OH 43606, USA

Harrell, John (Athlete, Baseball Player)
756 Erie Cir
Milpitas, CA 95035-3551, USA

Harrell, Justin (Athlete, Football Player)
c/o Eugene Parker *Maximum Sports Management*
6435 W Jefferson Blvd # 197
Fort Wayne, IN 46804-6203, USA

Harrell, Lynn M (Musician)
420 W 45th St
New York, NY 10036-3501, USA

Harrell, Tom (Music Group, Musician)
300 Mercer St Apt 3J
New York, NY 10003-6732, USA

Harrell, Willard (Athlete, Football Player)
8 Scarlet Oak Ct
Lake Saint Louis, MO 63367-2143, USA

Harrell-Doyle, Dorothy (Baseball Player)
68670 Raposa Rd
Cathedral City, CA 92234-8148, USA

Harrelson, Bill (Athlete, Baseball Player)
6900 Kimberly Ave
Bakersfield, CA 93308-3923, USA

Harrelson, Brett (Actor)
9200 W Sunset Blvd Ste 900
Los Angeles, CA 90069-3604, USA

Harrelson, Derrell M (Bud) (Athlete, Baseball Player, Coach)
357 Ridgefield Rd
Hauppauge, NY 11788-2314, USA

Harrelson, Kenneth S (Ken) (Athlete, Baseball Player)
9006 Shawn Park Pl
Orlando, FL 32819-4830, USA

Harrelson, Woody (Actor)
c/o Ina Treciokas *Slate Public Relations*
9000 W Sunset Blvd Ste 915
West Hollywood, CA 90069-5809, USA

Harrer, Tim (Athlete, Hockey Player)
7030 W 113th St
Minneapolis, MN 55438-2446, USA

Harrick, Jim (Basketball Player, Coach)
Pepsi Center 1000 Chopper Circle
Denver, CO 80204, USA

Harriger, Denny (Athlete, Baseball Player)
902 N Water St
Kittanning, PA 16201-1121, USA

Harring, Laura Elena (Actor, Beauty Pageant Winner)
12335 Santa Monica Blvd # 302
Los Angeles, CA 90025-2519, USA

Harrington, Al (Athlete, Basketball Player)
16124 Chancellors Ridge Way
Westfield, IN 46062-7137, USA

Harrington, Bill (Athlete, Baseball Player)
7219 Cleveland School Rd
Garner, NC 27529-8928, USA

Harrington, David (Music Group, Musician)
1235 9th Ave
San Francisco, CA 94122-2306, USA

Harrington, Dennis (Athlete, Golfer)
5668 S Rex Rd Ste 101
Memphis, TN 38119-3829, USA

Harrington, Desmond (Actor)
c/o Stephanie Simon *Untitled Entertainment (LA)*
350 S Beverly Dr Ste 200
Beverly Hills, CA 90212-4819, USA

Harrington, Donald J (Educator)
President S Ofc
Jamaica, NY 11439-0001, USA

Harrington, Jay (Actor)
c/o Abe Hoch *A Management Company*
9107 Wilshire Blvd Ste 650
Beverly Hills, CA 90210-5544, USA

Harrington, Joey (Athlete, Football Player)
222 Republic Dr
Allen Park, MI 48101-3650, USA

Harrington, John (Athlete, Coach, Hockey Player)
PO Box 7277
Collegeville, MN 56321-7277, USA

Harrington, Mike (Mickey) (Athlete, Baseball Player)
135 Scenic Dr
Hattiesburg, MS 39401-8403, USA

Harrington, Othella (Athlete, Basketball Player)
1602 Rika Pt
Houston, TX 77077-3432, USA

Harrington, Padraig (Golfer)
c/o Staff Member *Pro Golfers Association (PGA) Tour*
112 Tpc Blvd
Ponte Vedra Beach, FL 32082, USA

Harrington, Pat
730 Marzella Ave
Los Angeles, CA 90049-2043

Harrington, Pat Jr (Actor)
730 Marzella Ave
Los Angeles, CA 90049-2043, USA

Harrington, Perry (Athlete, Football Player)
1302 Roxbury Ct
Jackson, MS 39211-6367, USA

Harrington, Robert (Race Car Driver)
2609 Woodshade Ave
Kannapolis, NC 28127, USA

Harriott, Ainsley
12 Ogle St
London, ENGLAND W1P 7LG

Harris, Al (Athlete, Football Player)
4200 NW 96th Ave
Coral Springs, FL 33065-1518, USA

Harris, Al (Athlete, Football Player)
12 Stone Ridge Dr
South Barrington, IL 60010-9593, USA

Harris, Alonzo (Candy) (Athlete, Baseball Player)
6948 Lisa Dr
Fontana, CA 92336-5772, USA

Harris, Andy (Congressman, Politician)
506 Callinon Hob
Washington, DC 20515-0001, USA

Harris, Antwan (Athlete, Football Player)
7413 Ray Rd
Raleigh, NC 27613-8801, USA

Harris, Archie (Athlete, Football Player)
17 Hawthorne Ct NE
Washington, DC 20017-1014, USA

Harris, Arlen (Athlete, Football Player)
223 Wellsmont Ct
Saint Charles, MO 63304-2326, USA

Harris, Barbara
159 W 53rd St Apt 12D
New York, NY 10019-6068

Harris, Barbara C (Activist, Religious Leader)
138 Tremont St
Boston, MA 02111-1318, USA

Harris, Barry (DJ, Music Group, Musician)
122 E 57th St # 300
New York, NY 10022-2623, USA

Harris, Bernard A Jr (Astronaut)
3411 Erin Knoll Ct
Houston, TX 77059-3716, USA

Harris, Bill (Critic)
12747 Riverside Dr Apt 208
Valley Village, CA 91607-3303, USA

Harris, Bill (Athlete, Baseball Player)
322 S Reed St
Kennewick, WA 99336-4264, USA

Harris, Billy (Athlete, Baseball Player)
114 Brandywine Cir
Wilmington, NC 28411, USA

Harris, Billy (Athlete, Hockey Player)
171 Forward Pass Rd SW
Pataskala, OH 43062-8520, USA

Harris, Bishop Barbara
138 Tremont St
Boston, MA 02111-1318

Harris, Bo (Athlete, Football Player)
PO Box 52539
Shreveport, LA 71135-2539, USA

Harris, Boyd (Gail) (Athlete, Baseball Player)
9008 Weir St
Manassas, VA 20110-4913, USA

Harris, Brendan (Athlete, Baseball Player)
30 Fox Hollow Ln
Queensbury, NY 12804-1139, USA

Harris, Buddy (Athlete, Baseball Player)
4338 Manayunk Ave
Philadelphia, PA 19128-4926, USA

Harris, Charlaine (Writer)
c/o Joshua Bilmes *JABberwocky Literary Agency*
PO Box 4558
Sunnyside, NY 11104-0558, USA

Harris, Charles (Bubba) (Athlete, Baseball Player)
PO Box 159
Nobleton, FL 34661-0159, USA

Harris, Chris (Athlete, Basketball Player)
100 Oakmont Ln Apt 808
Belleair, FL 33756-1975, USA

Harris, Cliff (Athlete, Football Player)
722 Kentwood Dr
Rockwall, TX 75032-7506, USA

Harris, Corey (Athlete, Football Player)
933 N Tremont St
Indianapolis, IN 46222-3738, USA

Harris, Cristi Ellen
c/o Staff Member *House of Representatives, The*
1434 6th St Ste 1
Santa Monica, CA 90401-2527, USA

Harris, Damian (Director)
8942 Wilshire Blvd # 219
Beverly Hills, CA 90211-1908, USA

Harris, Danielle (Actor, Director)
c/o Felicia Sager *Sager Management*
260 S Beverly Dr # 205
Beverly Hills, CA 90212-3805, USA

Harris, Danneel (Actor)
c/o Jason Newman *Untitled Entertainment (LA)*
350 S Beverly Dr Ste 200
Beverly Hills, CA 90212-4819, USA

Harris, Del (Athlete, Basketball Player, Coach)
1229 Ducks Lndg
Frisco, TX 75033-1616, USA

Harris, Devin (Athlete, Basketball Player)
8 Green Park Dr
Dallas, TX 75248-2798, USA

Harris, Donald (Athlete, Baseball Player)
916 Hubert St
Waco, TX 76704-1936, USA

Harris, Duriel (Athlete, Football Player)
PO Box 334
Bude, MS 39630-0334, USA

Harris, Ed (Actor)
c/o Catherine Olim *PMK/BNC Public Relations (PMK-LA)*
8687 Melrose Ave Ste 8
West Hollywood, CA 90069-5746, USA

Harris, Emmylou (Musician, Songwriter)
c/o Staff Member *Vector Management*
PO Box 120479
Nashville, TN 37212-0479, USA

Harris, Eric (Athlete, Football Player)
498 W Raines Rd
Memphis, TN 38109-4335, USA

Harris, Ernest (Athlete, Baseball Player)
1007 46th Street Ensley
Birmingham, AL 35208 1434, USA

Harris, Estelle (Actor)
c/o Joel Dean *TalentWorks (LA)*
3500 W Olive Ave Ste 1400
Burbank, CA 91505-5512, USA

Harris, Franco (Athlete, Football Player)
200 Chaucer Ct S
Sewickley, PA 15143-8726, USA

Harris, Gail (Baseball Player)
9008 Weir St
Manassas, VA 20110-4913, USA

Harris, Gail Robyn (Actor)
3349 Cahuenga Blvd W Ste 1
Los Angeles, CA 90068-1379, USA

Harris, George (Athlete, Hockey Player)
1467 Miller Dr
Sarnia, ON N7S 3M5, Canada

Harris, Greg (Athlete, Baseball Player)
12613 Richmond Run Ct
Raleigh, NC 27614, USA

Harris, Greg (Athlete, Baseball Player)
PO Box 2665
Orleans, MA 02653-6665, USA

Harris, Henry (Biologist)
South Parks Road
Oxford OX1 3RE, UNITED KINGDOM (UK)

Harris, Hernando (Pep) (Athlete, Baseball Player)
995 Ten Oaks Dr
Lancaster, SC 29720-9039, USA

Harris, Hugh (Athlete, Hockey Player)
150 Sycamore Dr
Carmel, IN 46033-1956, USA

Harris, Ike (Athlete, Football Player)
1025 Lenox Park Blvd NE
Atlanta, GA 30319-5309, USA

Harris, James L (Athlete, Football Player)
9838 Old Baymeadows Rd
Jacksonville, FL 32256-8101, USA

Harris, Jared (Actor)
c/o Amy Guenther *Gateway Management Company Inc*
860 Via De La Paz Ste F10
Pacific Palisades, CA 90272-3631, USA

Harris, Jay (Cartoonist)
c/o Staff Member *King Features Syndication*
300 W 57th St Fl 15
New York, NY 10019-5238, USA

Harris, Jim B (Athlete, Football Player)
3455 Calumet Dr
Shreveport, LA 71107-7407, USA

Harris, Joe (Athlete, Football Player)
4747 River Rd
Ellenwood, GA 30294-1507, USA

Harris, Joe Frank (Ex-Governor)
712 West Ave
Cartersville, GA 30120-3441, USA

Harris, John (Athlete, Hockey Player)
11-4311 20 St
Vernon, BC V1T 4E4, Canada

Harris, John (Athlete, Golfer)
4316 Fremont Ave S
Minneapolis, MN 55409-1721, USA

Harris, John (Athlete, Football Player)
270 NW 120th St
Miami, FL 33168-3525, USA

Harris, John (Athlete, Baseball Player)
7064 Chelsea Dr
Amarillo, TX 79109-6482, USA

Harris, John R (Architect)
24 Devonshire Place
London W1N 2BX, UNITED KINGDOM (UK)

Harris, Jon (Athlete, Football Player)
110 Cedar Ct
Swedesboro, NJ 08085-5054, USA

Harris, Joshua (Actor)
1800 Vine St # 305
Los Angeles, CA 90028-5250, USA

Harris, Julie (Actor)
c/o Staff Member *WmE2 (WMA-LA)*
1 William Morris Pl
Beverly Hills, CA 90212-4261, USA

Harris, Juliette (Actor)
c/o Staff Member *It Girl Public Relations*
5301 Beethoven St Ste 220
Los Angeles, CA 90066-7052, USA

Harris, Katherine
c/o Daniel A (Dan) Strone *Trident Media Group LLC*
41 Madison Ave Fl 36
New York, NY 10010-2257, USA

Harris, Kwame (Athlete, Football Player)
4949 Centennial Blvd
Santa Clara, CA 95054-1229, USA

Harris, Lara (Actor)
c/o Peter Kaiser *Talent House (NY)*
325 W 38th St Rm 605
New York, NY 10018-9642, USA

Harris, Larry (Athlete, Football Player)
41 Alta Ave
Yonkers, NY 10705-1402, USA

Harris, Laura (Actor)
c/o Kami Putnam-Heist *WmE2 (Endeavor-LA)*
9601 Wilshire Blvd Fl 3
Beverly Hills, CA 90210-5219, USA

Harris, Lenny (Athlete, Baseball Player)
7435 N Augusta Dr
Hialeah, FL 33015-2050, USA

Harris, Leon (Correspondent)
1050 Techwood Dr NW
Atlanta, GA 30318-5604, USA

Harris, Leonard (Athlete, Football Player)
1817 Trilogy Park Dr
Hoschton, GA 30548-6237, USA

Harris, Leroy (Athlete, Football Player)
1919 Live Oak St
Savannah, GA 31404-3336, USA

Harris, Lou (Athlete, Football Player)
420 N Fayette St
Alexandria, VA 22314-2229, USA

Harris, Louis (Mathematician)
200 E 66th St # 2004
New York, NY 10065-9175, USA

Harris, Lucious (Athlete, Basketball Player)
1149 W 62nd St
Los Angeles, CA 90044-3733, USA

Harris, M L (Athlete, Football Player)
15589 Apple Valley Rd
Apple Valley, CA 92307-4575, USA

Harris, Major (Athlete, Football Player)
c/o Staff Member *College Football Hall Of Fame*
111 S Saint Joseph St
South Bend, IN 46601-1901, USA

Harris, Marilyn
217 N San Marino Ave
San Gabriel, CA 91775-2909

Harris, Mel (Actor)
c/o Joanna (Joanie) Burstein *Burstein Company, The*
15304 W Sunset Blvd Ste 208
Pacific Palisades, CA 90272-3656, USA

Harris, Meredith Gray (Stylist)
c/o Staff Member *Anyway Productions*
870 Avenue of the Americas
New York, NY 10001-4111, USA

Harris, Moira (Actor)
c/o Staff Member *Creative Artists Agency (CAA-LA)*
2000 Avenue of the Stars Ste 100
Los Angeles, CA 90067-4705, USA

Harris, Naomie (Actor)
c/o Christina Papadopoulos *Baker Winokur Ryder Public Relations BWR (BWR-NY)*
292 Madison Ave Fl 12
New York, NY 10017-6415, USA

Harris, Napoleon (Athlete, Football Player)
c/o Staff Member *EAG Sports Management*
12910 Agustin Pl
Playa Vista, CA 90094-2301, USA

Harris, Neil (Historian)
5555 S Everett Ave
Chicago, IL 60637-5013, USA

Harris, Neil Patrick (Actor)
c/o Booh Schut *Booh Schut Company*
11365 Sunshine Ter
Studio City, CA 91604-3141, USA

Harris, Odie L Jr (Athlete, Football Player)
31 E Mountain Creek Ct
Grand Prairie, TX 75052-5987, USA

Harris, Quentin (Athlete, Football Player)
3013 W Glass Ln
Phoenix, AZ 85041-6366, USA

Harris, Rachael (Comedian)
c/o Peter Principato *Principato/Young Management*
9465 Wilshire Blvd Ste 430
Beverly Hills, CA 90212-2613, USA

Harris, Raymont (Athlete, Football Player)
1144 Aroya Ct
New Albany, OH 43054-9205, USA

Harris, Reggie (Athlete, Baseball Player)
133 Paige St
Waynesboro, VA 22980-7479, USA

Harris, Richard (Athlete, Football Player)
9202 NE 132nd Pl
Kirkland, WA 98034-2634, USA

Harris, Rickie (Athlete, Football Player)
613 Q St NW
Washington, DC 20001-3404, USA

Harris, Robert (Athlete, Football Player)
2711 13th St SW
Lehigh Acres, FL 33976-3114, USA

Harris, Rolf (Entertainer)
c/o Suzanne Westrip *Billy Marsh Associates*
76A Grove End Rd St John's Wood
London NW8 9ND, UK

Harris, Ron (Athlete, Hockey Player)
61 Claude St
Beaconsfield, QC H9W 4G3, Canada

Harris, Ronald W (Ronnie) (Boxer)
1365 Glennview St NE
Canton, OH 44721-1916, USA

Harris, Rosemary (Actor)
76 Oxford St
London W1N 0AX, UNITED KINGDOM (UK)

Harris, Ross
6542 Fulcher Ave
North Hollywood, CA 91606-2717

Harris, Ryan (Athlete, Football Player)
c/o Eugene Parker *Maximum Sports Management*
6435 W Jefferson Blvd # 197
Fort Wayne, IN 46804-6203, USA

Harris, Sam (Actor, Music Group, Writer)
c/o Barry Krost *Barry Krost Management*
9220 W Sunset Blvd Ste 106
West Hollywood, CA 90069-3500, USA

Harris, Samantha (Actor)
c/o David Brady *Bx2 Management*
1333 2nd St Ste 620
Santa Monica, CA 90401-4111, USA

Harris, Sidney (Cartoonist)
302 W 86th St Apt 9A
New York, NY 10024-3154, USA

Harris, Stefon (Misc)
300 Mercer St Apt 3J
New York, NY 10003-6732, USA

Harris, Steve (Musician)
82 Bishop's Bridge Road
London W2 6BB, UNITED KINGDOM (UK)

Harris, Steve (Actor)
c/o Colton Gramm *Brillstein Entertainment Partners*
9150 Wilshire Blvd Ste 350
Beverly Hills, CA 90212-3453, USA

Harris, Steve (Athlete, Basketball Player)
3005 W Fort Worth St
Broken Arrow, OK 74012-3276, USA

Harris, Susan (Producer)
11828 La Grange Ave # 200
Los Angeles, CA 90025-5212, USA

Harris, Ted (Athlete, Hockey Player)
1 Stonegate Ct
Blackwood, NJ 08012-5356, USA

Harris, Thomas (Director, Writer)
c/o Robert (Bob) Bookman *Creative Artists Agency (CAA-LA)*
2000 Avenue of the Stars Ste 100
Los Angeles, CA 90067-4705, USA

Harris, Tim (Athlete, Football Player)
11644 Acacia Ave Apt 17
Hawthorne, CA 90250-2348, USA

Harris, Tim (Athlete, Football Player)
81900 Via La Serena
La Quinta, CA 92253-7882, USA

Harris, Timothy D (Tim) (Athlete, Football Player)
4949 Centennial Blvd
Santa Clara, CA 95054-1229, USA

Harris, Tomas (Writer)
c/o Robert (Bob) Bookman *Creative Artists Agency (CAA-LA)*
2000 Avenue of the Stars Ste 100
Los Angeles, CA 90067-4705, USA

Harris, Tommie (Athlete, Football Player)
1000 Football Dr
Lake Forest, IL 60045, USA

Harris, Tony (Athlete, Football Player)
530 Venice Way Apt 6
Inglewood, CA 90302-2841, USA

Harris, Tyrone (Gene) (Athlete, Baseball Player)
1267 NE 16th Ave
Okeechobee, FL 34972-3066, USA

Harris, Vic (Athlete, Baseball Player)
5420 S Garth Ave
Los Angeles, CA 90056-1116, USA

Harris, Walt (Athlete, Football Player)
4103 Shinault Ln
Olive Branch, MS 38654-8039, USA

Harris, Wendell (Athlete, Football Player)
955 Marilyn Dr
Baton Rouge, LA 70815-4539, USA

Harris, William M (Athlete, Football Player)
2118 Laurel Forest Way
Houston, TX 77014-2452, USA

Harris, Willie (Athlete, Baseball Player)
1176 Willie C Harris Dr
Cairo, GA 39828-3367, USA

Harris, Wilmer (Baseball Player)
441 Tomlinson Rd Apt F3
Philadelphia, PA 19116-3227, USA

Harris, Wood (Actor)
232 N Canon Dr
Beverly Hills, CA 90210-5302, USA

Harris III, James S. (Jimmy Jam) (Composer, Producer)
c/o Staff Member *Flyte Tyme Productions*
PO Box 398045
Edina, MN 55439-8045, USA

Harris Jr, Clifford (TI) (Musician)
c/o Brian Sher *Category 5 Entertainment*
9229 W Sunset Blvd Ste 601
Los Angeles, CA 90069-3406, USA

Harrison, Alvin (Athlete, Track Athlete)
1751 Pinnacle Dr Ste 1500
McLean, VA 22102-3833, USA

Harrison, Bertram C (General)
PO Box 209
Leesburg, VA 20178-0209, USA

Harrison, Bob (Athlete, Baseball Player)
16777 Loch Cir
Noblesville, IN 46060-4482, USA

Harrison, Bob (Athlete, Football Player)
3 Westwind Cir
Stamford, TX 79553-6117, USA

Harrison, Brett (Actor)
c/o Peter Kiernan *Management 360*
9111 Wilshire Blvd
Beverly Hills, CA 90210-5508, USA

Harrison, C Richard (Business Person)
140 Kendrick St
Needham Heights, MA 02494-2739, USA

Harrison, Chris (Actor, Reality TV Star)
c/o Staff Member *Creative Public Relations*
3385 Oak Glen Dr
Los Angeles, CA 90068-1311, USA

Harrison, Chuck (Athlete, Baseball Player)
222 Buckskin Rd
Abilene, TX 79602-4508, USA

Harrison, Dennis (Athlete, Football Player)
1048 Hickory Hollow Rd
Nashville, TN 37221-1139, USA

Harrison, Dwight (Athlete, Football Player)
2265 Buchanan St
Beaumont, TX 77703-2255, USA

Harrison, Glynn (Athlete, Football Player)
485 Huntington Rd Ste 203
Athens, GA 30606-1845, USA

Harrison, Gregory (Actor)
c/o Staff Member *Stone Manners Salners Agency (LA)*
9911 W Pico Blvd Ste 1400
Los Angeles, CA 90035-2715, USA

Harrison, James (Athlete, Football Player)
2525 Matterhorn Dr
Wexford, PA 15090-7963, USA

Harrison, Jane (Stylist)
455 W 23rd St
New York, NY 10011-2148, USA

Harrison, Jenilee (Actor)
19528 Ventura Blvd # 365
Tarzana, CA 91356-2917, USA

Harrison, Jerry (Musician)
3300 Warner Blvd
Burbank, CA 91505-4632, USA

Harrison, Jim (Athlete, Hockey Player)
102-645 Barrera Rd
Kelowna, BC V1W 3C9, Canada

Harrison, Jim (Athlete, Football Player)
4916 Hemphill Dr
San Antonio, TX 78228-3724, USA

Harrison, Kathryn (Writer)
1745 Broadway # B1
New York, NY 10019-4368, USA

Harrison, Linda (Actor)
10370 Ashton Ave
Los Angeles, CA 90024-5365, USA

Harrison, Lisi (Writer)
c/o Richard Abate *3 Arts Entertainment - NY*
49 W 27th St Fl 5
New York, NY 10001-6936, USA

Harrison, Mark (Editor)
250 Saint Antoine St W
Montreal, QC H2Y 2R7, CANADA

Harrison, Martin (Athlete, Football Player)
10624 S Eastern Ave Apt A-251
Henderson, NV 89052-2982, USA

Harrison, Marvin (Athlete, Football Player)
414 Tuvira Ln
Cherry Hill, NJ 08003-2674, USA

Harrison, Matthew (Director)
1180 S Beverly Dr Ste 601
Los Angeles, CA 90035-1158, USA

Harrison, Michael Allen (Composer, Musician)
1610 NE Tillamook St Apt 1
Portland, OR 97212-4464, USA

Harrison, (Mya) Marie (Actor)
c/o Melissa Berger *Melissa Berger Public Relations*
613 N West Knoll Dr Apt C
West Hollywood, CA 90069-5200, USA

Harrison, Nolan (Athlete, Football Player)
2121 N Westmoreland St Apt 543
Arlington, VA 22213-1069, USA

Harrison, Paul (Athlete, Hockey Player)
5-215 Royale St
Timmins, ON P4N 8S7, Canada

Harrison, Randy (Actor, Producer)
c/o Staff Member *Paradigm (LA)*
360 N Crescent Dr
Beverly Hills, CA 90210-4874, USA

Harrison, Reggie (Athlete, Football Player)
1912 Halifax Rd
Woodbridge, VA 22191-2407, USA

Harrison, Robert (Athlete, Basketball Player)
13405 NW Wax Myrtle Trl
Palm City, FL 34990-4826, USA

Harrison, Rodney (Athlete, Football Player)
8 Pasture Brook Ln
North Attleboro, MA 2760, USA

Harrison, Roric (Athlete, Baseball Player)
18662 MacArthur Blvd Ste 200
Irvine, CA 92612-1285, USA

Harrison, Schae
7800 Beverly Blvd # 3371
Los Angeles, CA 90036-2112

Harrison, Tom (Athlete, Baseball Player)
2932 Channing Way
Los Alamitos, CA 90720-4049, USA

Harrison, Tony (Writer)
2 Crescent Grove
London SW4 7AH, UNITED KINGDOM (UK)

Harrison, Tyreo (Athlete, Football Player)
8619 Braun Hill Dr
San Antonio, TX 78254-2301, USA

Harrison, William B Jr (Financier)
270 Park Ave
New York, NY 10017-2014, USA

Harrison, William H (General)
7302 Amber Ln SW
Tacoma, WA 98498-5045, USA

Harrison Breetzke, Joan (Swimmer)
16 Clevedon Road
East London 5201, SOUTH AFRICA

Harris-Stewart, Lusia M (Lucy) (Athlete, Basketball Player)
1002 Cherry St
Greenwood, MS 38930-6506, USA

Harron, Mary (Director, Producer, Writer)
c/o Staff Member *Dontanville/Frattaroli (D/F)*
270 Lafayette St Ste 402
New York, NY 10012-3327, USA

Harrow, Lisa
46 Albermarle St
London, ENGLAND W1X 4PP

Harry (Prince)
Stable Yard Gate
London SW1, UNITED KINGDOM (UK)

Harry, Debbie (Actor, Musician, Songwriter)
c/o Linda Carbone *Covers Media*
138 W 25th St Fl 9
New York, NY 10001-7405, USA

Harry, Deborah (Actor, Musician)
c/o Jason Weinberg *Untitled Entertainment (LA)*
350 S Beverly Dr Ste 200
Beverly Hills, CA 90212-4819, USA

Harry, Emile (Athlete, Football Player)
34 Villa Vista Dr
Brownsville, TX 78520-4649, USA

Harry, Jackee (Actor, Director)
c/o Christopher Barrett *Metropolitan (MTA)*
4526 Wilshire Blvd
Los Angeles, CA 90010-3801, USA

Harryhausen, Ray F (Director)
2 Ilchester Place W Kensington
London W14 8AA, UNITED KINGDOM (UK)

Harsch, Eddie (Musician)
c/o Staff Member *Mitch Schneider Organization, The*
14724 Ventura Blvd Ste 410
Sherman Oaks, CA 91403-3537, USA

Harshman, Jack (Athlete, Baseball Player)
320 Yukon Ter
Georgetown, TX 78633-5098, USA

Harshman, Margo (Actor)

Harshman, Marvel K (Marv) (Athlete, Basketball Player, Coach)
19221 90th Pl NE
Bothell, WA 98011-2253, USA

Hart, Bo (Athlete, Baseball Player)
1815 Portola Dr # A
Santa Cruz, CA 95062-4918, USA

Hart, Bob (Bowler)
5740 Laurel Oak Dr
Suwanee, GA 30024-3370, USA

Hart, Bret
435 Patina Pl SE
Calgary, CANADA Alb T3H 2P

Hart, Christopher
1423 N Martel Ave Apt 4
Los Angeles, CA 90046-4204

Hart, Clinton (Athlete, Football Player)
2894 CR 730
Webster, FL 33597-4084, USA

Hart, Corey
1445 Lambert Close # 300
Montreal, CANADA PQ H3H 1Z5

Hart, Dick (Athlete, Football Player)
273 Oarlock Cir
East Syracuse, NY 13057-3123, USA

Hart, Dolores (Mother Dolores) (Actor)
275 Flanders Rd
Bethlehem, CT 6751, USA

Hart, Doris (Tennis Player)
600 Biltmore Way Apt 306
Coral Gables, FL 33134-7528, USA

Hart, Dorothy
43 Martindale Rd
Asheville, NC 28804-1427

Hart, Doug (Athlete, Football Player)
5018 43rd Ave S
Minneapolis, MN 55417-1617, USA

Hart, Dudley (Athlete, Golfer)
5130 Rockledge Dr
Clarence, NY 14031-2442, USA

Hart, Freddie (Music Group, Musician, Songwriter, Writer)
317 N Kenwood St
Burbank, CA 91505-3446, USA

Hart, Gary W (Ex-Senator, Politician, Writer)
c/o Staff Member *Henry Holt & Company*
175 5th Ave Ste 400
New York, NY 10010-7726, USA

Hart, Gerry (Athlete, Hockey Player)
10 Parkridge Ct
Huntington, NY 11743-3671, USA

Hart, Harold J (Athlete, Football Player)
2004 E Caracas St
Tampa, FL 33610-5025, USA

Hart, Herbert L A (Lawyer)
11 Manor Place
Oxford, UNITED KINGDOM (UK)

Hart, Ian (Actor)
Drury House 34-43 Russell St
London WC2B 5HA, UNITED KINGDOM (UK)

Hart, James V (Director, Producer, Writer)
c/o Jon Levin *Creative Artists Agency (CAA-LA)*
2000 Avenue of the Stars Ste 100
Los Angeles, CA 90067-4705, USA

Hart, James W (Jim) (Athlete, Football Player, Misc)
3141 Dominica Way
Naples, FL 34119-1606, USA

Hart, Jason (Athlete, Baseball Player)
3202 S Westwood Ave
Springfield, MO 65807-5623, USA

Hart, Jeff (Athlete, Golfer)
105 Guanajuato Ct
Solana Beach, CA 92075-2510, USA

Hart, Jeff (Athlete, Football Player)
1307 SE 14th Ave
Canby, OR 97013-6341, USA

Hart, Jim (Athlete, Football Player)
3141 Dominica Way
Naples, FL 34119-1606, USA

Hart, Jim Ray (Athlete, Baseball Player)
17074 Templeton Ln
Lathrop, CA 95330-8634, USA

Hart, Jimmy (Actor, Composer, Wrestler)
c/o Nick Cordasco *Prince Marketing Group*
18 Carillon Cir
Livingston, NJ 07039-2600, USA

Hart, John (Athlete, Baseball Player, Coach)
5205 Latrobe Dr
Windermere, FL 34786-8959, USA

Hart, John R (Correspondent)
40 W 57th St # 1800
New York, NY 10019-4001, USA

Hart, Kevin (Actor, Comedian)
c/o David (Dave) Becky *3 Arts Entertainment Inc*
9460 Wilshire Blvd Fl 7
Beverly Hills, CA 90212-2713, USA

Hart, Leon
3904 Cottontail Ln
Bloomfield, MI 48301-1908

Hart, Linda (Actor)
c/o Staff Member *Gage Group, The (LA)*
14724 Ventura Blvd Ste 505
Sherman Oaks, CA 91403-3505, USA

Hart, Marcy (Athlete, Golfer)
886 Meadowlands Dr
Winston Salem, NC 27107-6026, USA

Hart, Margie
228 S Hudson Ave
Los Angeles, CA 90004-1036

Hart, Mary (Television Host)
150 El Camino Dr Ste 303
Beverly Hills, CA 90212-2738, USA

Hart, Melissa Joan (Actor)
c/o Kieran Maguire *The Arlook Group*
205 S Beverly Dr Ste 209
Beverly Hills, CA 90212-3899, USA

Hart, Mickey (Music Group, Musician)
c/o Staff Member *Agency Group Ltd, The (NY)*
142 W 57th St Fl 6
New York, NY 10019-3300, USA

Hart, Mike (Athlete, Baseball Player)
409 Larkspur Ave
Portage, MI 49002-6243, USA

Hart, Mike (Athlete, Baseball Player)
16552 W Crescent Dr
New Berlin, WI 53151-6514, USA

Hart, Parker T (Diplomat)
4705 Berkeley Ter NW
Washington, DC 20007-1508, USA

Hart, Richard (Athlete, Football Player)
273 Oarlock Cir
East Syracuse, NY 13057-3123, USA

Hart, Roxanne
c/o Staff Member *Seven Summits Pictures & Management*
8906 W Olympic Blvd Ground Floor
Beverly Hills, CA 90211, USA

Hart, Stanley R (Geophysicist, Physicist)
4671 E Madera Vista Rd
Green Valley, AZ 85614-0515, USA

Hart, Terry J (Astronaut)
PO Box V
Hellertown, PA 18055-0218, USA

Hart, Tommy (Athlete, Football Player)
3503 Highland Ave
Redwood City, CA 94062-3109, USA

Harte, Houston H (Publisher)
200 Concord Plaza Dr
San Antonio, TX 78216-6943, USA

Hartenstein, Chuck (Athlete, Baseball Player)
10735 Cassia Dr
Austin, TX 78759-6452, USA

Hartenstine, Michael A (Mike) (Athlete, Football Player)
322 Winchester Ct
Lake Bluff, IL 60044-1930, USA

Harter, Dick (Basketball Player, Coach)
1st Union Center 3601 South Broad St
Philadelphia, PA 19148, USA

Hartgraves, Dean (Athlete, Baseball Player)
1741 S Sierra Vista Dr
Tempe, AZ 85281-6633, USA

Harth, Sidney (Musician)
135 Westland Dr
Pittsburgh, PA 15217-2538, USA

Hartigan, Grace (Artist)
1701 1/2 Eastern Ave
Baltimore, MD 21231-2439, USA

Hartings, Jeff (Athlete, Football Player)
104 Player Ln
Sewickley, PA 15143-7501, USA

Hartler, Vicky (Congressman, Politician)
1023 Longworth Hob
Washington, DC 20515-3701, USA

Hartley, Bob (Athlete, Coach, Hockey Player)
13 S Avenue SE
Atlanta, GA 30315, USA

Hartley, Hal (Director)
39 W 14th St Ste 406
New York, NY 10011-7404, USA

Hartley, Harry J (Educator)
President S Ofc
Storrs, CT 06269-0001, USA

Hartley, Justin (Actor)
c/o Theodore B Gekis *Gekis Management*
4217 Verdugo View Dr
Los Angeles, CA 90065-4317, USA

Hartley, Mariette (Actor)
c/o Judy Milrad 8306 Wilshire Blvd #56
Beverly Hills, CA 90211, USA

Hartley, Mike (Athlete, Baseball Player)
9485 Quail Canyon Rd
El Cajon, CA 92021-6709, USA

Hartley, Nina (Actor, Director, Producer)
9445 De Soto Ave
Chatsworth, CA 91311-4920, USA

Hartley, Shaunya (Stylist)
557 Empire Blvd
Brooklyn, NY 11225-3121, USA

Hartley, Ted
524 N Rockingham Ave
Los Angeles, CA 90049-2640

Hartline, Mary (Actor)
c/o Staff Member *Pierce & Shelly*
13775A Mono Way # 220
Sonora, CA 95370-8813, USA

Hartman, Arthur A (Diplomat)
1615 L St NW
Washington, DC 20036-5610, USA

Hartman, Bob (Athlete, Baseball Player)
2580 18th St Apt 1
Kenosha, WI 53140-4674, USA

Hartman, David
16-00 State Rt 208 # 770
Fair Lawn, NJ 07410-2503

Hartman, George E (Architect)
107 Hesketh St
Chevy Chase, MD 20815-4222, USA

Hartman, J C (Athlete, Baseball Player)
3425 Rosedale St
Houston, TX 77004-6312, USA

Hartman, Kevin (Soccer Player)
1010 Rose Bowl Dr
Pasadena, CA 91103, USA

Hartman, Mike (Athlete, Hockey Player)
PO Box 472405
Charlotte, NC 28247-2405, USA

Hartmann, Frederick W (Editor)
1 Riverside Ave
Jacksonville, FL 32202-4917, USA

Hartmann, Robert T (Government Official)
4129 Estate La Grande Princess # C
Christiansted, VI 00820-4280, USA

Hartnell, Scott (Athlete, Hockey Player)
12632 Manhattan Point Blvd
Crosslake, MN 56442-2113, USA

Hartnett, Josh (Actor)
c/o Jenni Weinman *Patricola Lust PR*
9171 Wilshire Blvd Ste 390
Beverly Hills, CA 90210-5515, USA

Hartog, Jan de (Writer)
45/47 Clerkenwell Green
London EC1R 0HT, UNITED KINGDOM (UK)

Harts, Greg (Athlete, Baseball Player)
829 Humphries St SW
Atlanta, GA 30310-2165, USA

Harts, Shaunard (Athlete, Football Player)
5304 Tamarindo Ln
Elk Grove, CA 95758-6821, USA

Hartsburg, Craig (Athlete, Hockey Player)
c/o Staff Member *Soo Greyhounds Hockey Club*
201-212 Queen Street E
Sault Ste Marie, ON P6A 5X8, Canada

Hartsfield, Henry W
422 Willow Vista Dr
El Lago, TX 77586-6020, USA

Hartsfield, Henry W (Hank) Jr (Astronaut)
422 Willow Vista Dr
El Lago, TX 77586-6020, USA

Hartsfield, Roy (Athlete, Baseball Player, Coach)
159 Preserve Pkwy
Ball Ground, GA 30107-3233, USA

Hartshorn, Lawrence (Athlete, Football Player)
PO Box 1542
Cedar Ridge, CA 95924-1542, USA

Hartsock, Ben (Athlete, Football Player)
2461 Fairway Xing
Dacula, GA 30019-5404, USA

Hartsock, Jeffrey (Jeff) (Athlete, Baseball Player)
1720 Swannanoa Dr
Greensboro, NC 27410-3932, USA

Hartung, Clint (Athlete, Baseball Player)
1003 E Lewis St
Sinton, TX 78387-2726, USA

Hartung, James (Gymnast)
3621 Portia St
Lincoln, NE 68521-1782, USA

Hartwell, Edgerton (Athlete, Football Player)
3830 Galendo Dr
North Las Vegas, NV 89032-0623, USA

Hartwell, Leland H (Lee) (Nobel Prize Laureate)
PO Box 19024
Seattle, WA 98109-1024, USA

Hartwell, Lisa Wu (Reality TV Star)
c/o Staff Member *Bravo (NY)*
30 Rockefeller Plz
New York, NY 10112-0015, USA

Hartwig, Carter (Athlete, Football Player)
13111 Joan St
Stafford, TX 77477-4520, USA

Hartwig, Justin (Athlete, Football Player)
2250 Mary St Apt 117
Pittsburgh, PA 15203-2287, USA

Hartzell, Paul (Athlete, Baseball Player)
367 Santana Hts Unit 4021
San Jose, CA 95128-2025, USA

Hartzog, George B Jr (Government Official)
1643 Chain Bridge Rd
McLean, VA 22101-4329, USA

Haruf, Kent (Writer)
English Dept
Carbondale, IL 62901, USA

Harvey, Anthony (Director)
101 Park Ave # 4300
New York, NY 10178-0002, USA

Harvey, Antonio (Athlete, Basketball Player)
22970 SW Miami Pl
Tualatin, OR 97062-7364, USA

Harvey, Bryan (Athlete, Baseball Player)
1224 Astoria Pkwy
Catawba, NC 28609-8885, USA

Harvey, Buster (Athlete, Hockey Player)
57 Eagle Crt
Fredericton, NB E3B 5Y2, Canada

Harvey, Claude (Athlete, Football Player)
2918 Dragonwick Dr
Houston, TX 77045-4708, USA

Harvey, Cynthia T (Ballerina)
890 Broadway
New York, NY 10003-1211, USA

Harvey, David R (Business Person)
3050 Spruce St
Saint Louis, MO 63103-2530, USA

Harvey, Don
6310 San Vicente Blvd Ste 520
Los Angeles, CA 90048-5421

Harvey, Donnell (Basketball Player)
Waterhouse Center 8701 Maitland Summit Blvd
Orlando, FL 32810, USA

Harvey, Doug (Athlete, Baseball Player)
32398 River Island Dr
Springville, CA 93265-9632, USA

Harvey, Fred
397 Parkhurst Dr
Fredericton, CANADA NB E3B 2K2

Harvey, Guy (Artist)
10408 W State Road 84 Ste 104
Davie, FL 33324-4265, USA

Harvey, H Douglas (Doug) (Athlete, Baseball Player)
32398 River Island Dr
Springville, CA 93265-9632, USA

Harvey, Harry (Educator, Horse Racer)
34 Deep Hollow Ln N
Columbus, NJ 08022-1018, USA

Harvey, James B (Athlete, Football Player)
3685 Clairice Cv
Memphis, TN 38133-0979, USA

Harvey, Jan
169 Queensgate # 8A
London, ENGLAND SW7 5EH

Harvey, Jonathan D (Composer)
3 Queen Square
London WC1N 3AU, UNITED KINGDOM (UK)

Harvey, Ken (Athlete, Football Player)
11600 Great Falls Way
Great Falls, VA 22066-1150, USA

Harvey, Ken (Athlete, Baseball Player)
1065 E 270 S
Santaquin, UT 84655-6700, USA

Harvey, Maurice (Athlete, Football Player)
27 Clark St Apt 4
Pontiac, MI 48342-2079, USA

Harvey, Nancy (Athlete, Golfer)
3134 E Altadena Ave
Phoenix, AZ 85028-1912, USA

Harvey, PJ (Musician)
c/o Staff Member *Island Records*
825 8th Ave Rm C2
New York, NY 10019-7472, USA

Harvey, Polly Jean (P J) (Music Group, Musician, Songwriter, Writer)
Plaza 535 Kings Road
London SW10 0S, UNITED KINGDOM (UK)

Harvey, Richard (Athlete, Football Player)
3414 Baltimore Ave
Pascagoula, MS 39581-4236, USA

Harvey, Steve (Actor, Comedian)
c/o Staff Member *HarperCollins Publishers*
10 E 53rd St C/O Author Mail Floor 7
New York, NY 10022, USA

Harvey, Terry (Baseball Player)
215 Annandale Dr
Cary, NC 27511-6503, USA

Harvey, Todd (Athlete, Hockey Player)
5966 Drytown Pl
San Jose, CA 95120-1710, USA

Harvick, Kevin (Race Car Driver)
PO Box 1189
Welcome, NC 27374-1189, USA

Harville, Chad (Athlete, Baseball Player)
261 Farmington Rd
Savannah, TN 38372-5635, USA

Harvin, Percy (Athlete, Football Player)
c/o Joel Segal *Lagardere Unlimited - NY*
845 United Nations Plz
New York, NY 10017-3540, USA

Harwell, Ernie (Baseball Player, Sportscaster)
41110 Fox Run Apt 211
Novi, MI 48377-4880, USA

Harwell, Steve (Actor, Music Group)
c/o Staff Member *Creative Artists Agency (CAA-LA)*
2000 Avenue of the Stars Ste 100
Los Angeles, CA 90067-4705, USA

Hary, Armin (Athlete, Track Athlete)
Schloss
Diessen/Ammersee 86911, GERMANY

Hase, Dagmar (Swimmer)
Niederndodeleber Str 14
Magdeburg 29110, GERMANY

Hasegawa, Shigetoshi (Athlete, Baseball Player)
110 Newport Center Dr Ste 200
Newport Beach, CA 92660-6973, USA

Hasek, Dominik (Athlete, Hockey Player)
1000 Palladium Dr
Kanata, ON K2V 1A4, Canada

Haselkorn, Robert (Scientist)
5834 S Stony Island Ave
Chicago, IL 60637-2060, USA

Haselman, Bill (Athlete, Baseball Player)
14501 SE 85th St
Newcastle, WA 98059-9218, USA

Haselrig, Carlton (Athlete, Football Player)
386 William Penn Ave
Johnstown, PA 15901-1253, USA

Haseltine, Dan (Music Group)
1700 Hayes St Ste 304
Nashville, TN 37203-3014, USA

Haseltine, William A (Biologist)
9410 Key West Ave
Rockville, MD 20850-3345, USA

Hasen, Irvin H (Cartoonist)
68 E 79th St
New York, NY 10075-0224, USA

Hasenmayer, Don (Athlete, Baseball Player)
721 Golf Dr
Warrington, PA 18976-2053, USA

Hash, Herb (Athlete, Baseball Player)
PO Box 191
Culpeper, VA 22701-0107, USA

Hasham, Josephine (Baseball Player)
575 11th St
Miami, FL 33139, USA

Hashu, Nick (Athlete, Basketball Player)
2514 W Orangethorpe Ave Spc 27
Fullerton, CA 92833-4238, USA

Haskell, Colleen Marie (Actor)
c/o Andy Cohen *Gersh (LA)*
10250 Constellation Blvd Fl 7
Los Angeles, CA 90067-6207, USA

Haskin, Scott (Athlete, Basketball Player)
3078 Roxbury Dr
West Linn, OR 97068-8295, USA

Haskins, Clem (Athlete, Basketball Player, Coach)
2632 Roberts Rd
Campbellsville, KY 42718, USA

Haskins, Dennis (Actor)
c/o Jay Schachter *Mavrick Artists Agency*
6100 Wilshire Blvd Ste 550
Los Angeles, CA 90048-5164, USA

Haskins, Jon (Athlete, Football Player)
4055 Higel Ave
Sarasota, FL 34242-1138, USA

Haskins, Michael D (Admiral)
Inspector General Hqusn Pentagon
Washington, DC 20350-0001, USA

Haskins, Samuel J (Sam) (Photographer)
PO Box 59 Wimbledon
London SW19, UNITED KINGDOM (UK)

Haslam, Bill (Governor, Politician)
State Capitol
Nashville, TN 37243-0001, USA

Haslem, Udonis (Athlete, Basketball Player)
3489 Gulfstream Way
Davie, FL 33328-1354, USA

Hasler, Otmar (Prime Minister)
Regierungsgebaude
Vaduz 9490, USA

Haslett, James D (Jim) (Athlete, Coach, Football Coach, Football Player)
118 Crandon Dr
Saint Louis, MO 63105-3606, USA

Hasluck, Paul M C (Government Official)
2 Adams Rd
Dalkeith, WA 6009, AUSTRALIA

Hass, Robert (Writer)
English
Berkeley, CA 94720-0001, USA

Hassan, Ahmed (Television Host)
5209 Willow Park Ct
Carmichael, CA 95608-5086, USA

Hassan, Fred (Business Person)
1 Giralda Farms
Madison, NJ 07940-1027, USA

Hassan Ibn Talal (Prince)
Royal Palace
Amman, JORDAN

Hassard, Bob (Athlete, Hockey Player)
P.O. Box 580 Stn Main
Stouffville, ON L4A 7Z7, Canada

Hassel, Gerald L (Financier)
1 Wall St
New York, NY 10005-2500, USA

Hasselbach, Harald (Athlete, Football Player)
17919 E Dorado Dr
Centennial, CO 80015-5916, USA

Hasselbeck, Donald W (Don) (Athlete, Football Player)
38 Noon Hill Ave
Norfolk, MA 02056-1145, USA

Hasselbeck, Elisabeth (Reality TV Star, Television Host)
c/o Staff Member *View, The*
320 W 66th St
New York, NY 10023-6304, USA

Hasselbeck, Matt (Athlete, Football Player)
9027 NE 1st St
Bellevue, WA 98004-4814, USA

Hasselbeck, Tim (Athlete, Football Player)
38 Noon Hill Ave
Norfolk, MA 02056-1145, USA

Hasselhoff, David (Actor, Music Group)
c/o Jan McCormack *JSO Management*
1746 S Britain Rd
Southbury, CT 06488-3200, USA

Hasselmo, Nils (Educator)
1200 New York Ave NW # 1200
Washington, DC 20005-3928, USA

Hassenfeld, Alan G (Business Person)
1027 Newport Ave
Pawtucket, RI 02861-2539, USA

Hassett, Joe (Athlete, Basketball Player)
28 Marigold Cir
North Providence, RI 02904-3891, USA

Hassett, Marilyn (Actor)
8905 Rosewood Ave
West Hollywood, CA 90048-2409, USA

Hassey, Ron (Athlete, Baseball Player)
6330 N Calle Tregua Serena
Tucson, AZ 85750-0951, USA

Hassler, Andy (Athlete, Baseball Player)
PO Box 15932
Phoenix, AZ 85060-5932, USA

Hasson, Maurice (Musician)
18 West Heath Court North End Road
London NW11, UNITED KINGDOM (UK)

Hast, Adele (Editor)
60 W Walton St
Chicago, IL 60610-3305, USA

Hastert, Dennis (Ex-Congressman)
27 N River St
Batavia, IL 60510-2666, USA

Hastings, Andre (Athlete, Football Player)
700 N Dobson Rd Unit 37
Chandler, AZ 85224-6940, USA

Hastings, Barry G (Financier)
50 S La Salle St
Chicago, IL 60603-1008, USA

Hastings, Bob (Actor)
620 S Sparks St
Burbank, CA 91506-3034, USA

Hastings, Doc (Congressman, Politician)
1203 Longworth Hob
Washington, DC 20515-3505, USA

Hastings, Don (Actor)
524 W 57th St # 5330
New York, NY 10019-2930, USA

Hastings, Scott (Athlete, Basketball Player)
10210 Ridgegate Cir
Lone Tree, CO 80124-5331, USA

Haston, Kirk (Athlete, Basketball Player)
2600 S Main St
Lobelville, TN 37097, USA

Hasty, James (Athlete, Football Player)
8212 127th Ave SE
Newcastle, WA 98056-9146, USA

Hatalsky, Morris (Athlete, Golfer)
140 S Serenata Dr Unit 111
Ponte Vedra Beach, FL 32082-4585, USA

Hatch, Harold A (General)
8655 White Beech Way
Vienna, VA 22182-5056, USA

Hatch, Henry J (General)
2715 Silkwood Ct
Oakton, VA 22124-1455, USA

Hatch, Monroe W Jr (General)
8210 Thomas Ashleigh Ln
Clifton, VA 20124-2245, USA

Hatch, Orrin (Senator)
104 Hartz Ofc Bldg
Washington, DC 20510-0001, USA

Hatch, Richard (Actor, Reality TV Star)
c/o Michael Kaliski *Omniquest Entertainment (LA)*
1416 N La Brea Ave
Hollywood, CA 90028-7506, USA

Hatchell, Sylvia (Basketball Player)
Athletic Dept
Chapell Hill, NC 27515, USA

Hatcher, Billy (Athlete, Baseball Player)
7079 Shawnee Run Rd
Cincinnati, OH 45243-2521, USA

Hatcher, Chris (Athlete, Baseball Player)
1406 250th St
Audubon, IA 50025-7356, USA

Hatcher, Derian (Athlete, Hockey Player)
567 Chews Landing Rd
Haddonfield, NJ 08033-3843, USA

Hatcher, Kevin (Athlete, Hockey Player)
1225 S Water St
Marine City, MI 48039-3600, USA

Hatcher, Mickey (Athlete, Baseball Player)
9167 E Calle Luna
Gold Canyon, AZ 85118-4689, USA

Hatcher, R Dale (Athlete, Football Player)
906 White Plains Rd
Gaffney, SC 29340-5473, USA

Hatcher, Teri (Actor)
c/o Jeremy Barber *United Talent Agency (UTA)*
9560 Wilshire Blvd Fl 5
Beverly Hills, CA 90212-2400, USA

Hatchett, Derrick (Athlete, Football Player)
7811 Westshire Dr
San Antonio, TX 78227-2760, USA

Hatchett, Joseph W (Judge)
810 Lewis State Bank Building
Tallahassee, FL 32302, USA

Hatchett, Judge Glenda (Judge, Reality TV Star)
c/o Elizabeth Much *Much and House Public Relations*
8075 W 3rd St Ste 500
Los Angeles, CA 90048-4325, USA

Hatchette, Matthew (Athlete, Football Player)
3222 Winding Pine Trl
Longwood, FL 32779-3170, USA

Hatfield, Juliana (Musician, Songwriter)
c/o Staff Member *Concerted Efforts*
PO Box 440326
Somerville, MA 02144-0004, USA

Hatfield, Mark (Ex-Governor, Ex-Senator, Philanthropist, Politician)
414 N Meridian St
Newberg, OR 97132-2697, USA

Hathaway, Amy
c/o Beverly Strong *Strong Management*
3532 Hayden Ave
Culver City, CA 90232-2413, USA

Hathaway, Anne (Actor)
c/o Suzan Bymel *Management 360*
9111 Wilshire Blvd
Beverly Hills, CA 90210-5508, USA

Hathaway, Hilly (Athlete, Baseball Player)
2672 Forest Blvd
Jacksonville, FL 32246-3414, USA

Hathaway, Noah (Actor)
228 Grand Ave
Perryville, MO 63775-1806, USA

Hathaway, Ray (Athlete, Baseball Player)
25 Leisure Mountain Rd
Asheville, NC 28804-1147, USA

Hathaway, William D (Ex-Senator)
6707 Wemberly Way
McLean, VA 22101-1529, USA

Hathcock, Dave (Athlete, Football Player)
417 Rolling Mill Rd
Old Hickory, TN 37138-2137, USA

Hatori, Miho (Music Group)
833 W Chicago Ave Ste 101
Chicago, IL 60642-8408, USA

Hatosy, Shawn (Actor)
c/o Staff Member *Mary Erickson Entertainment*
2122 Hillhurst Ave # A
Los Angeles, CA 90027-2004, USA

Hatsopoulos, George N (Business Person, Engineer)
81 Wyman St PO Box 9046
Waltham, MA 2454, USA

Hatteberg, Scott (Athlete, Baseball Player)
802 Berg Ct NW
Gig Harbor, WA 98335-7709, USA

Hatten, Tom (Actor)
1759 Sunset Plaza Dr
Los Angeles, CA 90069-1311, USA

Hattersley, Roy S G (Government Official)
Westminster
London SW1A 0PW, UNITED KINGDOM (UK)

Hattestad, Stine Lise (Skier)
Sundlia 1B
Nesoya 1315, NORWAY

Hatton, Grady (Athlete, Baseball Player, Coach)
PO Box 97
Warren, TX 77664-0097, USA

Hatton, Noah (Stylist)
c/o Staff Member *Karlee Artist Management*
2658 Griffith Park Blvd # 171
Los Angeles, CA 90039-2520, USA

Hatton, Ricky (Athlete, Boxer)
1231 Bainbridge St
Philadelphia, PA 19147-1805, USA

Hatton, Vernon (Vern) (Athlete, Basketball Player)
PO Box 8405
Lexington, KY 40533-8405, USA

Hau, Lene Vestergaard (Physicist)
Applied Physics Dept
Cambridge, MA 1238, USA

Hauck, Frederick H (Rick) (Astronaut)
2 Redwood Ln
Falmouth, ME 04105-1368, USA

Hauck, Silke 16
Mt. Bundt Verlag K2
Mannheim, GERMANY 69159

Hauck, Tim (Athlete, Football Player)
2410 42nd St
Missoula, MT 59803-1164, USA

Hauer, Brett (Athlete, Hockey Player)
2921 Branch St
Duluth, MN 55812-2340, USA

Hauer, Rutger (Actor)
1601 Cloverfield Blvd Ste 5000N
Santa Monica, CA 90404-4085, USA

Hauerwas, Stanley (Religious Leader)
Divinity School
Durham, NC 27706, USA

Haughey, Chris (Athlete, Baseball Player)
1079 An County Road 446
Palestine, TX 75803-0622, USA

Haught, Gary (Athlete, Baseball Player)
16445 Lynn St
Choctaw, OK 73020-7926, USA

Hauk, A Andrew (Judge, Skier)
312 N Spring St
Los Angeles, CA 90012-4701, USA

Haun, Darla
300 S Raymond Ave Ste 11
Pasadena, CA 91105-2639

Haun, Lindsey (Actor)
c/o Staff Member *Margie Weiner Management*
8205 Santa Monica Blvd Ste 1450
West Hollywood, CA 90046-5967, USA

Hauptman, Herbert A (Nobel Prize Laureate)
637 Downing Ln
Buffalo, NY 14221-8058, USA

Haus, Herman A (Engineer, Scientist)
38 Jeffrey Ter
Lexington, MA 2420, USA

Hauser, Art (Athlete, Football Player)
2816 Walsh Rd
Cincinnati, OH 45208-3426, USA

Hauser, Cole (Actor)
c/o Michael Gruber *After Dark Management Group*
Prefers to be contacted via telephone
Los Angeles, CA 90069, USA

Hauser, Erich (Artist)
Saline 36
Rottweil 78628, GERMANY

Hauser, Tim (Music Group)
c/o Staff Member *The Merlin Company*
16574 Bosque Dr
Encino, CA 91436-3747, USA

Hauser, Wings (Actor)
9450 Chivers Ave
Sun Valley, CA 91352-2654, USA

Hausman, Jerry A (Economist)
Economics Dept
Cambridge, MA 2139, USA

Hausman, Tom (Athlete, Baseball Player)
3165 Westfield Cir
Las Vegas, NV 89121-3332, USA

Hauss, Lenard M (Len) (Athlete, Football Player)
110 Portmere Dr
Jesup, GA 31546-4738, USA

Havelange, Jean M F G (Joao) (Soccer Player)
Ave Rio Branco 89B Conj 602 Centro
Rio de Janiero 20040-004, BRAZIL

Havelange, JoaoRua
Prudente de Marosa 1700 Apto. 1001
Rio de Janeiro, BRAZIL BR 20420-0

Havelid, Niclas (Athlete, Hockey Player)
PO Box 129
Point Roberts, WA 98281-0129, USA

Haven, Annette
PO Box 1244
Sausalito, CA 94966-1244

Haven, James (Actor)
c/o Staff Member *Saffron Management*
9171 Wilshire Blvd Ste 441
Beverly Hills, CA 90210-5516, USA

Havens, Brad (Athlete, Baseball Player)
3227 Eden Trl
Brighton, MI 48114-9185, USA

Havens, Frank B (Athlete)
PO Box 55
Harborton, VA 23389-0055, USA

Havens, Richie (Music Group, Musician, Songwriter, Writer)
177 Woodland Ave
Westwood, NJ 07675-3218, USA

Haverdink, Kevin (Athlete, Football Player)
15844 Prairie Ronde Rd
Schoolcraft, MI 49087-9124, USA

Havers, Nigel (Actor)
c/o John Crosby *Crosby/Spilo Management*
1310 N Spaulding Ave
Los Angeles, CA 90046-4010, USA

Havig, Dennis (Athlete, Football Player)
5964 Old Stilesboro Rd NW
Acworth, GA 30101-4304, USA

Havin, Alexa (Actor)
c/o Staff Member *Mattie Management*
2216 Alcyona Dr
Los Angeles, CA 90068-2805, USA

Havins, Alexa (Actor)
c/o Noreen Konkle *AKA Talent Agency*
6310 San Vicente Blvd Ste 200
Los Angeles, CA 90048-5488, USA

Havlat, Martin (Athlete, Hockey Player)
201 N Westshore Dr Apt 1601
Chicago, IL 60601-7262, USA

Havlicek, John (Athlete, Basketball Player)
24 Beech Rd
Weston, MA 02493-1915, USA

Havlish, Jean (Baseball Player)
PO Box 122
Rockville, MN 56369-0122, USA

Havrilak, Sam (Athlete, Football Player)
1 Trojan Horse Dr
Phoenix, MD 21131-1345, USA

Havrilla, Jo Ann
9751 Old Route 99
McKean, PA 16426-1725

Hawass, Zahi (Writer)
3 Al-Adel Bakr St
Zamalek, Cairo, EGYPT

Hawblitzel, Ryan (Athlete, Baseball Player)
7972 S Four Oaks Pt
Floral City, FL 34436-2623, USA

Hawerchuck, Dale (Athlete, Hockey Player)
RR 5 LCD Main
Orangeville, ON L9W 2Z2, Canada

Hawes, Roy (Athlete, Baseball Player)
PO Box 854
Ringgold, GA 30736-0854, USA

Hawes, Steve (Athlete, Basketball Player)
12620 Interurban Ave S
Tukwila, WA 98168-3314, USA

Hawgood, Greg (Athlete, Hockey Player)
1230 Saint Andrews Way
Kamloops, BC V1S 1S6, Canada

Hawk, A.J. (Athlete, Football Player)
460 N Olden Gln
De Pere, WI 54115-8626, USA

Hawk, John D (War Hero)
3243 Solie Ave
Bremerton, WA 98310-2821, USA

Hawk, Tony (Actor, Athlete, Skateboarder)
1611A S Melrose Dr # 362
Vista, CA 92081-5471, USA

Hawke, Ethan (Actor)
c/o Erwin Stoff *3 Arts Entertainment Inc*
9460 Wilshire Blvd Fl 7
Beverly Hills, CA 90212-2713, USA

Hawke, Jason (Adult Film Star)
c/o Staff Member *Diva Central Inc*
7510 W Sunset Blvd Ste 1445
Los Angeles, CA 90046-3408, USA

Hawke, Robert J L (Prime Minister)
GPO Box 36
Sydney, NSW 2001, AUSTRALIA

Hawkes, Christopher (Archaeologist)
19 Walton St
Oxford OX1 2HQ, UNITED KINGDOM (UK)

Hawkes, John (Actor)
c/o JB Roberts *Thruline Entertainment*
9250 Wilshire Blvd Ground Fl
Beverly Hills, CA 90212, USA

Hawking, Lucy (Writer)
c/o Staff Member *Simon & Schuster*
1230 Avenue of the Americas Fl CONC1
New York, NY 10020-1586, USA

Hawking, Stephen (Physicist, Scientist)
University of Cambridge Applied Math Dept
Cambridge CB3 9EW, UNITED KINGDOM (UK)

Hawkins, Alex (Athlete, Football Player)
215 Bonanza Rd
Denmark, SC 29042-9311, USA

Hawkins, Andy (Athlete, Baseball Player)
P.O. Box 1595
Bruceville, TX 76630, USA

Hawkins, Artrell (Athlete, Football Player)
12166 Peak Dr
Cincinnati, OH 45246-1400, USA

Hawkins, Barbara (Music Group)
PO Box 371371
Las Vegas, NV 89137-1371, USA

Hawkins, Benjamin C (Ben) (Athlete, Football Player)
104 Deforest St
Roslindale, MA 02131-4920, USA

Hawkins, Bill (Athlete, Football Player)
156 Turtle Creek Dr
Jupiter, FL 33469-1547, USA

Hawkins, Brad
47 Music Sq E
Nashville, TN 37203-4324

Hawkins, Chauncey (Loon) (Musician)
c/o Michael (Mike) Esterman
Esterman.Com, LLC
Prefers to be contacted via email
MD, USA

Hawkins, Cornelius (Connie) (Athlete, Basketball Player)
3010 W Colter St Apt 30
Phoenix, AZ 85017-3134, USA

Hawkins, Courtney (Athlete, Football Player)
8305 Gale Rd
Goodrich, MI 48438-9436, USA

Hawkins, Dan (Musician)
c/o Sue Whitehouse *Whitehouse Management*
PO Box 43829
London NW6 3PJ, UNITED KINGDOM

Hawkins, Edwin (Music Group)
2041 Locust St
Philadelphia, PA 19103-5613, USA

Hawkins, Frank (Athlete, Football Player)
2300 Alta Dr
Las Vegas, NV 89107-4616, USA

Hawkins, Heather (Stylist)
8949 Gamesford Dr
Charlotte, NC 28277-5637, USA

Hawkins, Hersey R Jr (Athlete, Basketball Player)
2687 Beacon Hill Dr
West Linn, OR 97068-5614, USA

Hawkins, Jennifer (Actor, Beauty Pageant Winner)
c/o Staff Member *Ovations*
P.O. Box 1337
Rozelle, NSW 2039, Australia

Hawkins, Justin (Musician)
PO Box 40008
London N6 5XT, UNITED KINGDOM

Hawkins, Latroy (Athlete, Baseball Player)
3521 Amberwood Ln
Prosper, TX 75078-9126, USA

Hawkins, Michael Daly (Judge)
230 N 1st
Phoenix, AZ 85025, USA

Hawkins, Mike (Athlete, Football Player)
2320 Bordeaux Dr
Bay City, TX 77414-8512, USA

Hawkins, Paula (Ex-Senator)
1214 N Park Ave
Winter Park, FL 32789-2542, USA

Hawkins, Rip (Athlete, Football Player)
100 Tower Carlile Rd
Devils Tower, WY 82714, USA

Hawkins, Ronnie (Music Group)
59 Berkeley St
Toronto, ON M5A 2W5, CANADA

Hawkins, Rosa (Music Group)
PO Box 371371
Las Vegas, NV 89137-1371, USA

Hawkins, Rowena
PO Box 15277
Chattanooga, TN 37415-0277

Hawkins, Sally (Actor)
c/o Larry Taube *Principal Entertainment (LA)*
1964 Westwood Blvd Ste 400
Los Angeles, CA 90025-4695, USA

Hawkins, Sophie B (Music Group, Musician, Songwriter, Writer)
520 Washington Blvd # 337
Marina del Rey, CA 90292, USA

Hawkins, Thomas (Tommy) (Athlete, Basketball Player)
1745 Manzanita Park Ave
Malibu, CA 90265-3013, USA

Hawkins, Todd (Athlete, Hockey Player)
300 Lamoreaux Dr
Elk Rapids, MI 49629-9737, USA

Hawkins, Wayne (Athlete, Football Player)
3763 Crow Canyon Rd
San Ramon, CA 94582-1472, USA

Hawkins, Wynn (Athlete, Baseball Player)
5326 Cottage Dr
Cortland, OH 44410-9521, USA

Hawkinson, Tim (Artist)
5514 Wilshire Blvd
Los Angeles, CA 90036-3819, USA

Hawks, Steve (Artist)
1101 Hampshire Rd S
Bloomington, MN 55438, USA

Hawksworth, John
24 Cottesmore Gdns # 2
London, ENGLAND W8 5PR

Hawlata, Franz (Opera Singer)
3 Burlington Lane Chiswick
London W4 2TH, UNITED KINGDOM (UK)

Hawley, Frank (Race Car Driver)
County Road 225
Gainesville, FL 32609, USA

Hawley, Sandy (Jockey)
9625 Merrill Rd
Silverwood, MI 48760-9532, USA

Hawley, Steven (Astronaut)
1251 Wescoe Hall Dr Rm 5075
Lawrence, KS 66045-7572, USA

Hawn, Goldie (Actor, Director, Producer)
c/o Alan Nevins *Renaissance Literary & Talent*
PO Box 17379
Beverly Hills, CA 90209-3379, USA

Haworth, Alan (Athlete, Hockey Player)
845 112E Av
Drummondville, QC J2B 4K5, Canada

Haworth, Gord (Athlete, Hockey Player)
845 112E Av
Drummondville, QC J2B 4K5, Canada

Hawpe, Brad (Athlete, Baseball Player)
5917 Lakeside Dr
Fort Worth, TX 76179-6617, USA

Hawpe, David V (Editor)
Editorial Dept 525 Broadway
Louisville, KY 40202, USA

Hawryliw, Neil (Athlete, Hockey Player)
422 Knowles Ave
Winnipeg, MB R2G 1E5, Canada

Hawthorne, Greg (Athlete, Football Player)
1428 E Jefferson Ave
Fort Worth, TX 76104-5714, USA

Hawthorne, Sir Nigel
Febdens Park Cold Christmas Lane
Thundridge Herts, ENGLAND SG12 QUE

Hawthorne, William R (Engineer)
Engineering School
Cambridge CB2 0DS, UNITED KINGDOM (UK)

Hax, Carolyn (Writer)
1150 15th St NW
Washington, DC 20071-0001, USA

Hay, Bill (Athlete, Hockey Player)
4020 Crestview Rd SW
Calgary, AB T2T 2L4, Canada

Hay, Colin (Music Group)
PO Box 125
Round Corner, NSW 2158, AUSTRALIA

Hay, Jim (Athlete, Hockey Player)
2024 NE 76th Ave
Portland, OR 97213-6020, USA

Hay, Louise L (Writer)
PO Box 5100
Carlsbad, CA 92018-5100, USA

Hayaishi, Osamu (Biologist)
1-29 Izumigawacho Shimogamo Sakyoku
Kyoto 606-0807, JAPAN

Hayareet, Haya
Herons Flight Marlow
Buckinghamshire, ENGLAND

Hayashi, Henry
5127 Klump Ave
North Hollywood, CA 91601-3775

Hayashi, Izuo (Engineer)
5-5 Tohkodai Tsukuba
Ibaraki 300-26, JAPAN

Hayashi, Shizuya (War Hero)
1331 Hoowali St
Pearl City, HI 96782-2118, USA

Hayashida, Erica (Athlete, Golfer)
1470 NW 107th Ave Ste R
Doral, FL 33172-2735, USA

Haycox, Marie (Stylist)
337 The Blvd
Glen Rock, NJ 7452, USA

Haydee, Marcia (Ballerina)
Oberer Schlossgarten 6
Stuttgart 70173, USA

Haydel, Hal (Athlete, Baseball Player)
304 Lynwood Dr
Houma, LA 70360-6228, USA

Hayden
431-67 Mowat Ave
Toronto, CANADA Ont. M6K 3

Hayden, Aaron (Athlete, Football Player)
504 Stone Oaks Cv
Collierville, TN 38017-9124, USA

Hayden, Frederick (Biologist)
Med Ctr Microbiology Dept
Charlottesville, VA 22903, USA

Hayden, Gene (Athlete, Baseball Player)
424 W Locust St
Lodi, CA 95240-2018, USA

Hayden, J Michael (Mike) (Ex-Governor, Government Official)
Kansas Dept. Of Wildlife & Parks 1020 S. Kansas, Rm 200
Topeka, KS 66612, USA

Hayden, Jim (Publisher)
400 N Broad St
Philadelphia, PA 19130-4015, USA

Hayden, Leo (Athlete, Football Player)
33 Preston Rd
Columbus, OH 43209-1652, USA

Hayden, Linda (Actor)
1 Duchess St #1
London W1N 3DE, UNITED KINGDOM (UK)

Hayden, Michael (Actor)
3500 W Olive Ave Ste 1400
Burbank, CA 91505-5512, USA

Hayden, Michael V (General)
Director National Security Agency
Fort George C Meade, MD 20755, USA

Hayden, Neil Steven (Publisher)
1755 York Ave Apt 19A
New York, NY 10128-6870, USA

Hayden, Nicky (Athlete, Motorcycle Racer)
419 Medina Rd
Medina, OH 44256-9619, USA

Hayden, Tom (Politician)
152 Wadsworth Ave
Santa Monica, CA 90405-3510, USA

Haydon, Jones Ann (Tennis Player)
85 Westerfield Road Edgloaston
Birmingham 15, UNITED KINGDOM (UK)

Haydon, Nicky (Motorcycle Racer)
c/o Steve Dicterow *International Racers, Inc*
8001 Irvine Center Dr Ste 820
Irvine, CA 92618-2965, USA

Haye, David (Athlete, Boxer)
57 Jackson Rd Bromley
Kent BR2 8NT, UK

Hayek, Julie
5645 Burning Tree Dr
La Canada, CA 91011-2861

Hayek, Nicolas G (Designer)
Seevorstadt 6
Biel 2502, SWITZERLAND

Hayek, Peter (Athlete, Hockey Player)
5644 Upton Ave S
Minneapolis, MN 55410-2623, USA

Hayek, Salma (Actor, Model, Producer)
c/o Evelyn O'Neill *Management 360*
9111 Wilshire Blvd
Beverly Hills, CA 90210-5508, USA

Hayers, Sidney A (Director)
5 Denmark St
London WC2H 8LP, UNITED KINGDOM (UK)

Hayes, Amy (Model, Sportscaster)
641 N Hardin Hts
Harrodsburg, KY 40330-9234, USA

Hayes, Ben (Athlete, Baseball Player)
3501 10th St NE
Saint Petersburg, FL 33704-1605, USA

Hayes, Bill (Actor)
4528 Beck Ave
North Hollywood, CA 91602-1904, USA

Hayes, Bill (Athlete, Baseball Player)
2510 N 57th St
Scottsdale, AZ 85257-1906, USA

Hayes, Billie (Athlete, Football Player)
2876 Avalon St
Riverside, CA 92509-2013, USA

Hayes, Bob
2717 King Cole Dr
Dallas, TX 75216-3430

Hayes, Brian
60 Charlotte St
London, ENGLAND W1P 1LS

Hayes, Charlie (Athlete, Baseball Player)
22503 Holly Creek Trl
Tomball, TX 77377-3656, USA

Hayes, Dade
c/o Daniel A (Dan) Strone *Trident Media Group LLC*
41 Madison Ave Fl 36
New York, NY 10010-2257, USA

Hayes, Darren (Music Group, Musician)
c/o Leonie Messer *Magnolia Music Management Inc*
PO Box 151151
San Rafael, CA 94915-1151, USA

Hayes, Dawn (Stylist)
c/o Staff Member *Dawn to Dusk Image Agency*
8306 Wilshire Blvd # 412
Beverly Hills, CA 90211-2382, USA

Hayes, Denis A (Geophysicist, Misc, Physicist)
PO Box 18237
Washington, DC 20036-8237, USA

Hayes, Dennis C (Engineer, Inventor)
945 E Paces Ferry Rd NE
Atlanta, GA 30326-1179, USA

Hayes, Elvin E (Athlete, Basketball Player)
14 Canaveral Creek Ln
Sugar Land, TX 77479-2724, USA

Hayes, Erinn (Actor)
c/o David Sweeney *Sweeney Management*
8755 Lookout Mountain Ave
Los Angeles, CA 90046-1861, USA

Hayes, Gemma (Musician)
c/o Staff Member *Paradigm (Monterey)*
404 W Franklin St
Monterey, CA 93940-2303, USA

Hayes, Gerald (Athlete, Football Player)
3841 E Windsong Dr
Phoenix, AZ 85048-7916, USA

Hayes, J P (Athlete, Golfer)
740 Camino Real Ave
El Paso, TX 79922-2010, USA

Hayes, Jarvis (Basketball Player)
MCI Center 601 F St NW
Washington, DC 20004, USA

Hayes, Jim (Athlete, Basketball Player)
31 Curley St
Long Beach, NY 11561-2705, USA

Hayes, Jocelyn (Producer)

Hayes, Jonathan (Athlete, Football Player)
1231 Obannon Creek Ln
Loveland, OH 45140-6027, USA

Hayes, Louis S (Music Group, Musician)
PO Box 482
Desoto, TX 75123-0482, USA

Hayes, Mark (Athlete, Golfer)
1014 Saint Andrews Dr
Edmond, OK 73025-2645, USA

Hayes, Mercury (Athlete, Football Player)
138 W Whitney St
Houston, TX 77018-4515, USA

Hayes, Patty (Athlete, Golfer)
3436 Sipsey St
The Villages, FL 32162-6666, USA

Hayes, Ray (Athlete, Football Player)
5000 Laur Rd
North Branch, MI 48461-9782, USA

Hayes, Reggie (Actor)
c/o Staff Member *TalentWorks (LA)*
3500 W Olive Ave Ste 1400
Burbank, CA 91505-5512, USA

Hayes, Robert M (Activist)
105 E 22nd St
New York, NY 10010-5413, USA

Hayes, Sean (Actor)
c/o Staff Member *Principato/Young Management*
9465 Wilshire Blvd Ste 430
Beverly Hills, CA 90212-2613, USA

Hayes, Steve (Athlete, Basketball Player)
2219 N Imperial Path Ln
Spring, TX 77386-2959, USA

Hayes, Von (Athlete, Baseball Player)
435 E Illinois Rd
Lake Forest, IL 60045-2354, USA

Hayes, Wade (Music Group)
40 Music Sq W
Nashville, TN 37203-3206, USA

Hayes, Wendell (Athlete, Football Player)
1935 E 30th St Apt 23
Oakland, CA 94606-3485, USA

Haygood, Clyde (Stylist)
c/o Staff Member *Independent NY*
15 E 30th St Apt 401
New York, NY 10016-7031, USA

Haygood, Herb (Athlete, Football Player)
3103 Browning St
Sarasota, FL 34237-7309, USA

Hayhoe, Bill (Athlete, Football Player)
5146 Santa Anita Dr
Sparks, NV 89436-0801, USA

Haylett, Alice (Athlete, Baseball Player)
243 Pearl Ave
Lakeland, FL 33815-3737, USA

Hayman, David T (Actor, Director)
c/o Staff Member *Independent Talent Group (ITG-UK)*
Oxford House 76 Oxford St
London W1D 1BS, UK

Hayman, Fred (Designer, Fashion Designer)
6946 Wildlife Rd
Malibu, CA 90265-4309, USA

Hayman, Gorgon I (Cinematographer)
54 Lakes Lane Beaconsfield
London HP9 2LB, UNITED KINGDOM (UK)

Hayman, James (Director)
c/o Staff Member *Creative Artists Agency (CAA-LA)*
2000 Avenue of the Stars Ste 100
Los Angeles, CA 90067-4705, USA

Haymond, Alvin (Athlete, Football Player)
2857 Mantis Dr
San Jose, CA 95148-2136, USA

Haynes, Abner (Athlete, Football Player)
1950 FM 489
Oakwood, TX 75855-8409, USA

Haynes, Al (Misc)
4410 S 182nd St
Seatac, WA 98188-4560, USA

Haynes, Betsy (Writer)
5973 Sandhill Cir
The Colony, TX 75056-3678, USA

Haynes, Colton (Actor)
c/o Eric Podwall *Podwall Entertainment*
710 N Orlando Ave Apt 203
Los Angeles, CA 90069-5549, USA

Haynes, Haynes
7200 Sanderling Ct
Carlsbad, CA 92011-5173

Haynes, Heath (Athlete, Baseball Player)
1535 S Carmelina Ave
Los Angeles, CA 90025-3621, USA

Haynes, Jimmy (Athlete, Baseball Player)
516 Riverside Dr
Lagrange, GA 30240-9633, USA

Haynes, Mark (Athlete, Football Player)
8101 E Dartmouth Ave Unit 11
Denver, CO 80231-4258, USA

Haynes, Michael (Athlete, Football Player)
1580 Arbour Glenn Dr
Lawrenceville, GA 30043-7154, USA

Haynes, Mike
8 Morningside Ln
Westport, CT 06880-3815, USA

Haynes, Mike (Athlete, Football Player)
8 Morningside Ln
Westport, CT 06880-3815, USA

Haynes, Reggie (Athlete, Football Player)
2324 Antiqua Ct
Reston, VA 20191-1706, USA

Haynes, Richard (Attorney, Attorney General, General)
2701 Fannin St
Houston, TX 77002-9217, USA

Haynes, Roy O (Musician)
173 Brighton Ave
Boston, MA 02134-2003, USA

Haynes, Todd (Director)
c/o Staff Member *Creative Artists Agency (CAA-LA)*
2000 Avenue of the Stars Ste 100
Los Angeles, CA 90067-4705, USA

Haynes, Verron (Athlete, Football Player)
2500 Northwinds Pkwy Ste 275
Alpharetta, GA 30009-2265, USA

Haynes, Warren (Musician)
c/o Staff Member *Paradigm (Monterey)*
404 W Franklin St
Monterey, CA 93940-2303, USA

Haynes Jr, Cornell (Nelly) (Musician)
c/o Staff Member *Derrty Entertainment*
9648 Olive Blvd # 230
Saint Louis, MO 63132-3002, USA

Haynesworth, Albert (Athlete, Football Player)
c/o Chad Speck *Allegiant Athletic Agency*
35 Market Sq Ste 201
Knoxville, TN 37902-1420, USA

Haynie, Jim
10100 Santa Monica Blvd Ste 2500
Los Angeles, CA 90067-4116

Haynie, Sandra (Athlete, Golfer)
6 Brookfield Ct
Roanoke, TX 76262-5468, USA

Hays, Harold (Athlete, Football Player)
10410 Ravenswood Rd
Granbury, TX 76049-4543, USA

Hays, Kathryn (Actor)
c/o Staff Member *As The World Turns*
JC Studios 1268 E 14th St
New York, NY 11230, USA

Hays, Robert (Actor)
919 Victoria Ave
Venice, CA 90291-3933, USA

Hays, Ronald J (Admiral)
869 Kamoi Pl
Honolulu, HI 96825-1318, USA

Hays, Thomas C (Business Person)
300 Tower Pkwy
Lincolnshire, IL 60069-3640, USA

Haysbert, Dennis (Actor)
c/o Staff Member *Levine Management*
9028 W Sunset Blvd PH 1
Los Angeles, CA 90069-1830, USA

Hayter, David (Writer)
c/o Staff Member *Kaplan/Perrone Entertainment*
9744 Wilshire Blvd Ste 300
Beverly Hills, CA 90212-1813, USA

Hayward, Brian (Athlete, Hockey Player)
7648 E Hollow Oak Rd
Anaheim, CA 92808-1425, USA

Hayward, Brooke
60 E 42nd St Ste 956
New York, NY 10165-0918

Hayward, Charles E (Publisher)
Time-Life Building Rockefeller Center
New York, NY 10020, USA

Hayward, Justin (Musician)
53 High St
Cobham, Surrey KT11 3DP, UNITED KINGDOM (UK)

Hayward, Lazar (Athlete, Basketball Player)
c/o Sam Goldfelder *Excel Sports Management*
9665 Wilshire Blvd Ste 500
Beverly Hills, CA 90212-2312, USA

Hayward, Ray (Athlete, Baseball Player)
5113 Deerhurst Dr
Norman, OK 73072-3882, USA

Hayward, Reggie (Athlete, Football Player)
4651 Swilcan Bridge Ln S
Jacksonville, FL 32224-5621, USA

Hayward, Thomas B (Admiral)
2200 Ross Ave Ste 3800
Dallas, TX 75201-7967, USA

Haywood, Alfred (Athlete, Football Player)
69 Waters Edge Way
Fayetteville, GA 30215-8509, USA

Haywood, Bill (Athlete, Baseball Player)
867 Villa Dr
North Myrtle Beach, SC 29582-2575, USA

Haywood, Spencer (Athlete, Basketball Player)
49447 Plymouth Way
Plymouth, MI 48170-6439, USA

Hayworth, Nan (Congressman, Politician)
1440 Longworth Hob
Washington, DC 20515-0307, USA

Hayworth, Tracy (Athlete, Football Player)
528 Knights Church Rd
Decherd, TN 37324, USA

Hazard, Geoffrey C Jr (Attorney, Attorney General, Educator, General)
2263 California St
San Francisco, CA 94115-2813, USA

Haze, Jonathan
3636 Woodhill Canyon Rd
Studio City, CA 91604-3658

Hazell, Keeley (Actor)
98 De Beauvoir Rd
London N1 4EN, United Kingdom

Hazelton, Major (Athlete, Football Player)
6803 S Crandon Ave
Chicago, IL 60649-1210, USA

Hazen, Maya (Actor)
c/o Adam Griffin *Kritzer Levine Wilkins Entertainment*
11872 La Grange Ave Fl 1
Los Angeles, CA 90025-5283, USA

Hazewood, Drungo (Athlete, Baseball Player)
7991 Westboro Way
Sacramento, CA 95823-4934, USA

Haziza, Shlomi (Artist)
8640 Tamarack Ave
Sun Valley, CA 91352-2504, USA

Hazzard, Johnny (Adult Film Star)
c/o Staff Member *Diva Central Inc*
7510 W Sunset Blvd Ste 1445
Los Angeles, CA 90046-3408, USA

Hazzard, Shirley (Writer)
200 E 66th St
New York, NY 10065-9175, USA

Hazzard, Walt (Athlete, Basketball Player)
1722 Virginia Rd
Los Angeles, CA 90019-5936, USA

Heacock, Raymond L (Engineer)
4800 Oak Grove Dr
Pasadena, CA 91109-8001, USA

Head, Anthony (Actor)
12-13 Poland St
London W1F 8QB, ENGLAND

Head, Anthony Stewart (Actor)
c/o Staff Member *Innovative Artists (LA)*
1505 10th St
Santa Monica, CA 90401-2805, USA

Head, Don (Athlete, Hockey Player)
15240 NE Knott St
Portland, OR 97230-5280, USA

Head, Emily (Actor)
c/o Kate Bryden *Gordon and French*
12-13 Poland St
London W1F 8QB, UNITED KINGDOM (UK)

Head, James W (Scientist)
Geological Sciences
Providence, RI 02912-0001, USA

Head, John (Baseball Player)
12677 Tremblewood Dr
Florissant, MO 63033-4729, USA

Head, Roy (Musician)
2317 Pecan St
Dickinson, TX 77539-4949, USA

Headden, Susan M (Journalist)
307 N Pennsylvania St
Indianapolis, IN 46204-1819, USA

Headen, Andy (Athlete, Football Player)
PO Box 821
Liberty, NC 27298-0821, USA

Headey, Lena (Actor)
c/o Tina Thor *TMT Entertainment Group*
648 Broadway Ste 1002
New York, NY 10012-2348, USA

Headley, Chase (Athlete, Baseball Player)
5243 Avery Woods Ln
Knoxville, TN 37921-5245, USA

Headley, Glenne
8942 Wilshire Blvd
Beverly Hills, CA 90211-1908

Headley, Heather (Actor, Musician)
40 W 56th St Apt 5F
New York, NY 10019-3813, USA

Headley, Shari
11226 178th St
Jamaica, NY 11433-4118

Headly, Glenne (Actor)
c/o Brian Mann *International Creative Management (ICM-LA)*
10250 Constellation Blvd Fl 7
Los Angeles, CA 90067-6207, USA

Headon, Topper (Musician)
c/o Staff Member *Premier Talent*
3 E 54th St # 1100
New York, NY 10022-3108, USA

Headrick, CC (Stylist)
c/o Staff Member *Page.214*
3303 Lee Pkwy Ste 205
Dallas, TX 75219-5145, USA

Headrick, Sherrill (Athlete, Football Player)
5621 S Schilder Dr
River Oaks, TX 76114-3216, USA

Heafner, Vance (Athlete, Golfer)
6212 Godfrey Dr
Raleigh, NC 27612-6717, USA

Heald, Anthony (Actor)
9701 Wilshire Blvd Ste 1000
Beverly Hills, CA 90212-2010, USA

Healey, Danis W (Government Official)
Alfriston
East Sussex BN26 5TT, UNITED KINGDOM (UK)

Healey, Derek E (Composer)
29 Stafford Road Ruislip Gardens
Middx H4A 6PB, UNITED KINGDOM (UK)

Healey, James
415 S Spalding Dr Unit 306
Beverly Hills, CA 90212-4160

Healey, John G (Misc)
322 8th Ave
New York, NY 10001-8001, USA

Healey, Mary (Actor)
c/o Staff Member *Rabbit Vocal Management*
27 Poland St 3rd Floor
London W1F 8QW, UK

Healey, Rich (Athlete, Hockey Player)
1085 Carter Crest Rd NW
Edmonton, AB T6R 2N2, Canada

Healy, Bernadine (Doctor)
430 17th St NW
Washington, DC 20006-5307, USA

Healy, Cornelius T (Misc)
228 S Swarthmore Ave
Ridley Park, PA 19078-1214, USA

Healy, Don (Athlete, Football Player)
3427 Boca Ciega Dr
Naples, FL 34112-6809, USA

Healy, Fran (Music Group)
21 Heathmans Road
London SW6 4TJ, UNITED KINGDOM (UK)

Healy, Fran (Athlete, Baseball Player)
1 Primrose Ln
Holyoke, MA 01040-1523, USA

Healy, Glenn (Athlete, Hockey Player)
c/o Staff Member *The Sports Network*
9 Channel Nine Ct
Toronto, ON M1S 4B5, Canada

Healy, Jane E (Journalist)
633 N Orange Ave
Orlando, FL 32801-1300, USA

Healy, Jeremiah (Writer)
625 Oaks Dr Apt 703
Pompano Beach, FL 33069-3772, USA

Healy, Matthew L. (Matt) (Writer)
c/o Simon Millar *Rumble Media*
1620 Broadway Ste C
Santa Monica, CA 90404-2777, USA

Healy, Patricia (Actor)
9255 W Sunset Blvd Ste 1010
Los Angeles, CA 90069-3307, USA

Heames, Darin (Actor)
c/o Andrew Stawiarski *ADS Management*
269 S Beverly Dr # 441
Beverly Hills, CA 90212-3851, USA

Heaney, Brian (Athlete, Basketball Player)
153 Spinnaker Dr
Halifax, Nova Scotia B3N 3C3, Canada

Heaney, Gerald W (Judge)
Federal Building
Duluth, MN 55802, USA

Heaney, Seamus
3 Queens Sq
London, ENGLAND WC1N 3AU

Heaney, Seamus J (Nobel Prize Laureate)
191 Strand Road
Dublin 4, IRELAND

Heap, Imogen (Musician)
c/o Staff Member *Solar Management*
13 Rosemont Rd
London NW3 6NG, UK

Heap, Joseph (Athlete, Football Player)
410 Laurelleaf Ln
Covington, LA 70433-7203, USA

Heap, Todd (Athlete, Football Player)
4320 N Essex Cir
Mesa, AZ 85207-7167, USA

Heard, Amber (Actor)
c/o Jodi Gottlieb *ID PR (LA)*
7060 Hollywood Blvd Fl 8
Los Angeles, CA 90028-6014, USA

Heard, G Alexander (Educator, Politician, Scientist)
2100 Golf Club Ln
Nashville, TN 37215-1224, USA

Heard, Garfield (Athlete, Basketball Player)
185 Saddle Ridge Way
Fayetteville, GA 30215-8149, USA

Heard, Herman Jr (Athlete, Football Player)
PO Box 938
Broomfield, CO 80038-0938, USA

Heard, Jerry (Athlete, Golfer)
PO Box 429
Central Lake, MI 49622-0429, USA

Heard, John (Actor)
2055 S Sepulveda Blvd
Los Angeles, CA 90025-5621, USA

Hearn, Chick (Misc)
860 Morningside Dr Apt C506
Fullerton, CA 92835-3551, USA

Hearn, Ed (Athlete, Baseball Player)
5737 Theden St
Shawnee, KS 66218-9199, USA

Hearn, George (Actor, Music Group)
211 S Beverly Dr # 211
Beverly Hills, CA 90212-3807, USA

Hearn, J Woodrow (Religious Leader)
PO Box 320
Nashville, TN 37202-0320, USA

Hearn, Kevin (Musician)
c/o Staff Member *Six Shooter Management*
98038, 970 Queen St East
Toronto, ON M4M 1Jo, Canada

Hearn, Thomas K Jr (Educator)
President's Office
Winston Salem, NC 27109, USA

Hearn, Tom (Golfer)
5068 W Plano Pkwy Ste 256
Plano, TX 75093-4441, USA

Hearne, Bill (Music Group, Musician)
PO Box 160236
Nashville, TN 37216-0236, USA

Hearns, Tommy (Boxer)
c/o Staff Member *National Organization of Professional Athletes*
1806 Watermere Ln
Windermere, FL 34786-6121, USA

Hearron, Jeff (Athlete, Baseball Player)
5820 Hill Rd
Powder Springs, GA 30127-4041, USA

Hearst, Amanda Randolph (Model)
c/o Keya Morgan *Keya Morgan Productions*
PO Box 18447
Beverly Hills, CA 90209-4447, USA

Hearst, Donald P (Engineer)
NASA
Hampton, VA 23665, USA

Hearst, Garrison (Athlete, Football Player)
3753 Augusta Hwy
Lincolnton, GA 30817-4402, USA

Hearst, Lydia (Model)
c/o Ryan Brown *Factory PR*
580 Broadway Rm 600
New York, NY 10012-3258, USA

Hearst, Rick (Actor)
6500 Wilshire Blvd # 550
Los Angeles, CA 90048-4920, USA

Hearst, Victoria
865 Comstock Ave
Los Angeles, CA 90024-2572

Hearst Shaw, Patricia C (Patty) (Actor)
110 5th St
San Francisco, CA 94103-2918, USA

Heart (Musician)
c/o Jeff Frasco *Creative Artists Agency (CAA-LA)*
2000 Avenue of the Stars Ste 100
Los Angeles, CA 90067-4705, USA

Heaslip, Mark (Athlete, Hockey Player)
11 Leland Ct
Chevy Chase, MD 20815-4906, USA

Heater, Don (Athlete, Football Player)
8704 Manchester Ave
Kansas City, MO 64138-4167, USA

Heater, Larry (Athlete, Football Player)
3711 Royal Fern Cir
Las Vegas, NV 89115-1257, USA

Heath, Albert (Tootie) (Music Group, Musician)
173 Brighton Ave
Boston, MA 02134-2003, USA

Heath, Bill (Athlete, Baseball Player)
1626 Lake Charlotte Ln
Richmond, TX 77406-7016, USA

Heath, Brandon
c/o Staff Member *Creative Trust, Inc.*
5141 Virginia Way Ste 320
Brentwood, TN 37027-2317, USA

Heath, James E (Jimmy) (Composer, Music Group, Musician)
173 Brighton Ave
Boston, MA 02134-2003, USA

Heath, Kelly (Athlete, Baseball Player)
2249 Portofino Pl Unit 2222
Palm Harbor, FL 34683-7740, USA

Heath, Mike (Athlete, Baseball Player)
8345 Old Town Dr
Tampa, FL 33647-3335, USA

Heath, Shona (Stylist)
c/o Staff Member *Camilla Lowther Managment (CLM Represents)*
30-32 Ericsson Pl
New York, NY 10013, USA

Heath, Tommy (Musician)
c/o JD Sobol *RPM Talent Agency*
2600 W Olive Ave Fl 5
Burbank, CA 91505-4572, USA

Heathcock, Clayton H (Misc)
5235 Alhambra Valley Rd
Martinez, CA 94553-9765, USA

Heathcock, Jeff (Athlete, Baseball Player)
24962 Calle Vecindad
Lake Forest, CA 92630-2105, USA

Heathcote, Bella (Actor)
c/o Brian Medavoy *Jackson-Medavoy Entertainment*
10203 Santa Monica Blvd Fl 4
Los Angeles, CA 90067-6439, USA

Heathcote, Jud (Athlete, Basketball Player, Coach)
5418 S Quail Ridge Cir
Spokane, WA 99223-6391, USA

Heathcott, Mike (Athlete, Baseball Player)
12445 E Saddlehorn Trl
Scottsdale, AZ 85259-6125, USA

Heatherly, Eric (Actor)
c/o Staff Member *The Bazel Group Inc*
4636 Lebanon Pike # 308
Hermitage, TN 37076-1316, USA

Heath-Stubbs, John F A (Writer)
22 Artesian Road
London W2 5AR, UNITED KINGDOM (UK)

Heaton, Neal (Athlete, Baseball Player)
3 Nursery Ct
East Patchogue, NY 11772-6152, USA

Heaton, Patricia (Actor)
c/o CeCe Yorke *True Public Relations*
6725 W Sunset Blvd Ste 470
Los Angeles, CA 90028-7180, USA

Heatwave
6464 W Sunset Blvd Ste 1010
Hollywood, CA 90028-8012

Heaverlo, Dave (Athlete, Baseball Player)
3720 W Lakeshore Dr
Moses Lake, WA 98837-3003, USA

Hebenton, Andy (Athlete, Hockey Player)
3295 SW Sandalwood Ln
Gresham, OR 97080, USA

Hebenton, Clay (Athlete, Hockey Player)
13457 Whitewater Dr
Poway, CA 92064-5227, USA

Hebert, Ashley (Reality TV Star)
240 S 40th St
Philadelphia, PA 19104-3547, USA

Hebert, Bobby (Athlete, Football Player)
724 Crystal St
New Orleans, LA 70124-3608, USA

Hebert, Bud (Athlete, Football Player)
PO Box 250342
Plano, TX 75025-0342, USA

Hebert, Guy (Athlete, Hockey Player)
8 Gleneagles Dr
Newport Beach, CA 92660-4296, USA

Hebert, Johnny (Race Car Driver)
Kettering Hamm Hall Wymondham
Norfolk NR18 7HW, UNITED KINGDOM (UK)

Hebert, Ken (Athlete, Football Player)
7001 Mount Sharp Rd
Wimberley, TX 78676-4245, USA

Hebner, Rich (Richie) (Athlete, Baseball Player)
6 Tetreault Dr
Walpole, MA 02081-2224, USA

Hebron, Vaughn (Athlete, Football Player)
154 Madison Ct
Southampton, PA 18966-2728, USA

Hebson, Bryan (Athlete, Baseball Player)
1151 Fairmont Ln
Auburn, AL 36830-2105, USA

Heche, Anne (Actor)
c/o Jason Weinberg *Untitled Entertainment (LA)*
350 S Beverly Dr Ste 200
Beverly Hills, CA 90212-4819, USA

Hecht, Albie (Producer, Writer)
c/o Staff Member *Spike TV*
1515 Broadway
New York, NY 10036-8901, USA

Hecht, Duvall (Misc)
2910 W Garry Ave
Santa Ana, CA 92704-6510, USA

Hecht, Jessica (Actor)
c/o Staff Member *Innovative Artists (LA)*
1505 10th St
Santa Monica, CA 90401-2805, USA

Hecht, Jochen (Athlete, Hockey Player)
95 Levin Ln
East Amherst, NY 14051-2243, USA

Hechter, Daniel (Designer, Fashion Designer)
4 Ave Ter Hoche
Paris 75008, FRANCE

Hecht-Herskowitz, Gina (Actor)
5930 Foothill Dr
Los Angeles, CA 90068-3524, USA

Heck, Andy (Athlete, Football Player)
221 Deer Haven Dr
Ponte Vedra Beach, FL 32082-2108, USA

Heck, Ralph (Athlete, Football Player)
5575 Howland Ct
Atlanta, GA 30338-2913, USA

Heck, Robert (Athlete, Football Player)
1939 Tarpon Rd
Naples, FL 34102-1565, USA

Hecker, Zvi (Architect)
19 Elzar St
Tel Aviv 65157, ISRAEL

Heckerling, Amy (Director, Producer)
1330 Schuyler Rd
Beverly Hills, CA 90210-2539, USA

Heckler, Margaret M (Secretary)
1401 N Oak St
Arlington, VA 22209-3699, USA

Heckman, James J (Nobel Prize Laureate)
4807 S Greenwood Ave
Chicago, IL 60615-1913, USA

Heckscher, August (Writer)
333 E 68th St
New York, NY 10065-5604, USA

Hector, Johnny (Athlete, Football Player)
525 Caroline St
New Iberia, LA 70560-4913, USA

Hedaya, Dan (Actor)
232 N Canon Dr
Beverly Hills, CA 90210-5302, USA

Hedberg, Anders (Athlete, Hockey Player)
7305 Campeau Dr
Kanata, ON K2K 3M2, Canada

Hedberg, Johan (Athlete, Hockey Player)
c/o Jay Grossman *S F X Sports (NY)*
220 W 42nd St
New York, NY 10036-7200, USA

Hedderick, Herman (Athlete, Basketball Player)
2913 Homestead Dr
Erie, PA 16506-2131, USA

Hedeman, Richard (Tuff) (Misc)
PO Box 224
Morgan Mill, TX 76465-0224, USA

Heder, Jon (Actor, Producer)
c/o Julie Darmody *Mosaic Media Group*
9200 W Sunset Blvd Ste 10
Los Angeles, CA 90069-3608, USA

Hedford, Eric (Music Group, Musician)
PO Box 5908
Portland, OR 97228-5908, USA

Hedges, Clifton
10475 Crosspoint Blvd
Indianapolis, IN 46256-3386

Hedges, Peter (Director, Writer)
c/o Richard Lovett *Creative Artists Agency (CAA-LA)*
2000 Avenue of the Stars Ste 100
Los Angeles, CA 90067-4705, USA

Hedican, Bret (Athlete, Hockey Player)
290 Las Quebradas
Alamo, CA 94507-1732, USA

Hedington, Tim (Producer)
c/o Staff Member *GK Films*
1540 2nd St # 200
Santa Monica, CA 90401-2303, USA

Hedison, Alexandra (Actor)
PO Box 691636
Los Angeles, CA 90069-9636, USA

Hedison, David (Actor)
779 Carissa Dr
Royal Palm Beach, FL 33411-3412, USA

Hedlund, Garrett (Actor)
c/o Cynthia Pett-Dante *Brillstein Entertainment Partners*
9150 Wilshire Blvd Ste 350
Beverly Hills, CA 90212-3453, USA

Hedlund, Mike (Athlete, Baseball Player)
2412 Klinger Rd
Arlington, TX 76016-1143, USA

Hedquist, Julien
c/o Staff Member *IMG*
304 Park Ave S Fl 12
New York, NY 10010-4314, USA

Hedren, Tippi (Actor)
6867 Soledad Canyon Rd
Acton, CA 93510-2221, USA

Hedrick, Jerry L (Misc)
25280 Carlsbad Ave
Davis, CA 95616-9434, USA

Hedrick, Joan D (Writer)
Women's Studies Program 300 Summit St
Hartford, CT 6106, USA

Hedrick, Larry
PO Box 749
Statesville, NC 28687-0749

Heeger, Alan J (Nobel Prize Laureate)
1042 Las Alturas Rd
Santa Barbara, CA 93103-1608, USA

Heenan, Pat (Athlete, Football Player)
10007 Raynor Rd
Silver Spring, MD 20901-2124, USA

Heep, Danny (Athlete, Baseball Player)
18610 Crosstimber
San Antonio, TX 78258-4587, USA

Heera (Actor, Bollywood)
Nungambakkam
Chennai, TN 600034, INDIA

Heeschen, David S (Astronomer)
702 Copa D Oro
Marathon, FL 33050-5406, USA

Heesters, Johannes
Heimgartenstr. 21
Starnberg, GERMANY D-82319

Heeter, Carrie (Inventor)
Communication Technology Lab
East Lansing, MI 48824, USA

Heffern, Meghan (Actor)
c/o Barb Godfrey *Parent Management*
530 Queen St East Toronto
ON M5A 1V2, CANADA

Heffernan, Bert (Athlete, Baseball Player)
130 Eagle Ct
Locust Grove, VA 22508-5432, USA

Heffernan, Dave (Athlete, Football Player)
8101 SW 79th Ter
Miami, FL 33143, USA

Heffernan, Kevin (Actor, Comedian, Producer, Writer)
4000 Warner Blvd Building 139 PMB 102
Burbank, CA 91522, USA

Heffner, Bob (Athlete, Baseball Player)
910 N 12th St
Allentown, PA 18102-1102, USA

Heffner, Kyle (Actor)
c/o Melanie Sharp *Sharp Talent*
117 N Orlando Ave
Los Angeles, CA 90048-3403, USA

Heffron, John (Actor, Comedian)
c/o Peter Rosegarten *Conversation Company*
1044 Northern Blvd Ste 304
Roslyn, NY 11576-1589, USA

Heffron, Richard T (Director)
c/o Staff Member *Shapiro-Lichtman Talent Agency*
1010 Lexington Rd
Beverly Hills, CA 90210-2935, USA

Heflin, Bronson (Athlete, Baseball Player)
PO Box 149112
Nashville, TN 37214-9112, USA

Heflin, Vince (Athlete, Football Player)
5603 Regency Park Ct Apt 3
Suitland, MD 20746-3328, USA

Hefner, Christie (Business Person, Publisher)
680 N Lake Shore Dr
Chicago, IL 60611-4546, USA

Hefner, Hugh (Producer, Publisher)
10236 Charing Cross Rd
Los Angeles, CA 90024-1815, USA

Hefner, Larry (Athlete, Football Player)
1208 Arboretum Dr
Lewisville, NC 27023-8658, USA

Hefner, Lene
15127 Califa St
Van Nuys, CA 91411-3021

Heft, Bob
4098 Green St
Saginaw, MI 48638-6618

Heft, Robert (Bob) (Designer)
PO Box 20404
Saginaw, MI 48602-0404, USA

Hegamin, George (Athlete, Football Player)
1409 S Lamar St Apt 512
Dallas, TX 75215-6827, USA

Hegan, Mike (Athlete, Baseball Player)
7 Wild Turkey Run
Hilton Head Island, SC 29926-1901, USA

Heger, Rene (Actor)
c/o Jerry Shandrew *Shandrew Public Relations*
1050 S Stanley Ave
Los Angeles, CA 90019-6634, USA

Hegerland, Anita
1315 Nesoya
, NORWAY

Heggtveit, Ann Hamilton (Skier)
Grand Isle, VT 5458, USA

Hegland, Jean (Writer)
5450 Mill Creek Rd
Healdsburg, CA 95448-9760, USA

Hegman, Bob (Athlete, Baseball Player)
3529 NW Winding Woods Dr
Lees Summit, MO 64064-1879, USA

Hegman, Mike (Athlete, Football Player)
2958 Suesand Dr
Memphis, TN 38128-5941, USA

Hegyes, Robert (Actor)
c/o Staff Member *Talent Literary Company Productions*
PO Box 252
Metuchen, NJ 08840-0252, USA

Hehn, Sascha
Postfach 100823
Munich, GERMANY D-80082

Heidei, James (Athlete, Football Player)
1425 Wisteria Dr
Vicksburg, MS 39180-4756, USA

Heidelberger, Charles (Misc)
1495 Poppy Peak Dr
Pasadena, CA 91105-2705, USA

Heidemann, Jack (Athlete, Baseball Player)
1816 S Salida Del Sol Cir
Mesa, AZ 85202-5529, USA

Heiden, Beth
PO Box 110
Dollar Bay, MI 49922-0110

Heiden, Elizabeth L (Beth) (Speed Skater)
PO Box 110
Dollar Bay, MI 49922-0110, USA

Heiden, Steve (Athlete, Football Player)
2600 Rushford Vlg
Rushford, MN 55971, USA

Heidmann, Manfred
Borbecker Str. 237
Essen, GERMANY D-45355

Heidt, Mike (Athlete, Hockey Player)
8 Creekside Way
Sprice Grove, AB T7X 3Y7, Canada

Heidt Jr, Horace
4155 Witzel Dr
Sherman Oaks, CA 91423-4613, USA

Heigl, Jennifer (Actor)
8383 Wilshire Blvd # 550
Beverly Hills, CA 90211-2425, USA

Heigl, Katherine (Actor, Model)
c/o Jill Fritzo *PMK/BNC Public Relations (PMK-NY)*
622 3rd Ave Fl 8
New York, NY 10017-6707, USA

Heilbron, Lorna (Actor)
169 Queen's Gate
London SW7 5HE, UNITED KINGDOM (UK)

Heilbroner, Robert L (Economist)
412 W End Ave Apt 3E
New York, NY 10024-5775, USA

Heilman, Aaron (Athlete, Baseball Player)
39W272 Sheldon Ln
Geneva, IL 60134-6045, USA

Heilmeier, Ann (Stylist)
120 Leonard Pl
Dover, NJ 07801-3731, USA

Heim, Val (Athlete, Baseball Player)
PO Box 423
Superior, NE 68978-0423, USA

Heimbold, Charles A Jr (Business Person)
345 Park Ave
New York, NY 10154-0004, USA

Heimburger, Craig (Athlete, Football Player)
311 Flagstone Dr
Belleville, IL 62221-5821, USA

Heimel, Cynthia (Writer)
1230 Avenue of the Americas
New York, NY 10020-1513, USA

Heimlich, Henry J (Doctor, Physicist)
3939 Erie Ave Apt 4060
Cincinnati, OH 45208-1976, USA

Heim-McDaniel, Kay (Baseball Player)
3390 143rd St W
Rosemount, MN 55068-4057, USA

Heimueller, Gorman (Athlete, Baseball Player)
2148 Glen Ave
Riverton, UT 84065-7079, USA

Heimuli, Lakei (Athlete, Football Player)
5385 Baringwood Cir
Salt Lake City, UT 84129-3143, USA

Heine, Jutta (Athlete, Track Athlete)
Blaue Muhle
Burglahr 57614, GERMANY

Heineman, Dave (Governor)
PO Box 94848
Lincoln, NE 68509-4848, USA

Heineman, Ken (Athlete, Football Player)
13012 Fairfield Oaks Rd
Saint Louis, MO 63141-8551, USA

Heinen, Mike (Athlete, Golfer)
4518 E Meadow Ln
Lake Charles, LA 70605-5318, USA

Heinkel, Don (Athlete, Baseball Player)
508 Covington Ave
Birmingham, AL 35206-3057, USA

Heinle, Amelia (Actor)
c/o John Carrabino *John Carrabino Management*
5900 Wilshire Blvd Ste 406
Los Angeles, CA 90036-5015, USA

Heinrich, Martin (Congressman, Politician)
336 Cannon Hob
Washington, DC 20515-3506, USA

Heins, Shawn (Athlete, Hockey Player)
c/o Staff Member *Sports Personnel Services*
125 Lake St W Ste 200
Wayzata, MN 55391-1573, USA

Heinsohn, Thomas W (Tom) (Athlete, Basketball Player, Coach)
15 Hunters Way
Needham Heights, MA 02494-3160, USA

Heintz, Bob (Athlete, Golfer)
2213 Highland Woods Dr
Dunedin, FL 34698-9407, USA

Heintz, Chris (Athlete, Baseball Player)
7128 Wareham Dr
Tampa, FL 33647-1132, USA

Heintzelman, Laura (Stylist)
c/o Staff Member *Ford Models (Chicago)*
311 W Superior St
Chicago, IL 60654-3548, USA

Heintzelman, Tom (Athlete, Baseball Player)
1500 W 8th St Unit 82
Mesa, AZ 85201-3825, USA

Heinz, Bob (Athlete, Football Player)
516 Mansion Ct Unit 502
Santa Clara, CA 95054-4336, USA

Heinz, Rick (Athlete, Hockey Player)
264 Van Allen Gate
Milton, ON L9T 5Y8, Canada

Heinz, W C (Sportscaster, Writer)
1150 Nichols Hill Rd
Dorset, VT 05251-9536, USA

Heinze, Steve (Athlete, Hockey Player)
4659 La Espada Dr
Santa Barbara, CA 93111-1301, USA

Heinzer, Franz (Skier)
Lauenen
Rickenbach/Schwyz 6432, SWITZERLAND

Heise, Bob (Athlete, Baseball Player)
537 Live Oak Dr
Angels Camp, CA 95222, USA

Heise, Jim (Athlete, Baseball Player)
2425 Albion Ave
Orlando, FL 32833-3981, USA

Heiser, Roy (Athlete, Baseball Player)
20185 Apple Tree Ln
Estero, FL 33928-4001, USA

Heiserman, Rick (Athlete, Baseball Player)
17252 Adams St
Omaha, NE 68135-3078, USA

Heiskala, Earl (Athlete, Hockey Player)
982 Ocean Ln
Imperial Beach, CA 91932-2420, USA

Heiss Jenkins, Carol (Figure Skater)
3183 Regency Pl
Westlake, OH 44145-6735, USA

Heisten, Barrett (Athlete, Hockey Player)
5019 A St
Anchorage, AK 99503, USA

Heitmeyer, Jayne
4450 W Lakeside Dr Ste 350
Burbank, CA 91505-4064

Heizer, Miles (Actor)
c/o Staff Member *Stein Entertainment Group*
1351 N Crescent Heights Blvd Apt 312
West Hollywood, CA 90046-4549, USA

Hejduk, Milan (Athlete, Hockey Player)
8651 Sawgrass Dr
Lone Tree, CO 80124-8504, USA

Helberg, Simon (Actor)
c/o Tim Sarkes *Brillstein Entertainment Partners*
9150 Wilshire Blvd Ste 350
Beverly Hills, CA 90212-3453, USA

Held, Archie (Artist, Misc)
1286 Gilman St
Berkeley, CA 94706-2353, USA

Held, Carl
1817 Hillcrest Rd Apt 51
Los Angeles, CA 90068-3150

Held, Franklin (Bud) (Athlete, Track Athlete)
13367 Caminito Mar Villa
Del Mar, CA 92014-3613, USA

Held, Mel (Athlete, Baseball Player)
103 Hogan Ln
Bryan, OH 43506-9161, USA

Held, Paul (Athlete, Football Player)
29055 Blue Moon Dr
Menifee, CA 92584-7302, USA

Held, Richard M (Doctor)
Psychology Dept
Cambridge, MA 2139, USA

Held, Woodie (Athlete, Baseball Player)
28 Aspen Meadows Rd
Dubois, WY 82513, USA

Helde, Annette
8430 Santa Monica Blvd Ste 200
Los Angeles, CA 90069-4253

Heldt, Mike (Athlete, Football Player)
10527 Lake Williams Dr
Odessa, FL 33556-2615, USA

Helem, Carl (Athlete, Basketball Player)
2525 McGurk St
Ashland, KY 41102-4759, USA

Helf, Mark (Stylist)
c/o Celebrity Stylist *Smashbox Beauty*
8549 Higuera St Bldg B
Culver City, CA 90232-2521, USA

Helfand, David (Astronomer)
Astronomer Dept
New York, NY 10027, USA

Helfand, Eric (Athlete, Baseball Player)
7314 Jackson Dr
San Diego, CA 92119-2317, USA

Helfer, Ricki Tigert (Financier)
550 17th St NW
Washington, DC 20429-0001, USA

Helfer, Tricia (Actor)
c/o Gordon Gilbertson *Gilbertson Management*
1334 3rd Street Promenade Ste 201
Santa Monica, CA 90401-1320, USA

Helford, Bruce (Producer, Writer)
c/o Staff Member *United Talent Agency (UTA)*
9560 Wilshire Blvd Fl 5
Beverly Hills, CA 90212-2400, USA

Helgeland, Brian (Director)
c/o Robert Newman *WmE2 (Endeavor-LA)*
9601 Wilshire Blvd Fl 3
Beverly Hills, CA 90210-5219, USA

Helgenberger, Marg (Actor)
c/o Nancy Sanders *Sanders Armstrong Caserta*
2120 Colorado Ave Ste 120
Santa Monica, CA 90404-3561, USA

Helinski, Donald R (Biologist)
Molecular Genetics Ctr
La Jolla, CA 92093-0001, USA

Helix
1505 W 2nd Ave # 200
Vancouver, CANADA BC V6H 3Y4

Hellawell, Keith (Government Official, Lawyer)
Great George St
London SW1A 2AL, UNITED KINGDOM (UK)

Heller, Andre
Singerstr. 8
Vienna, AUSTRIA A-1010

Heller, Daniel M (Attorney, Attorney General, General)
14 NE 1st Ave
Miami, FL 33132-2547, USA

Heller, Jane (Writer)
1014 Ladera Ln
Santa Barbara, CA 93108-1630, USA

Heller, Jeffrey M (Business Person)
5400 Legacy Dr
Plano, TX 75024-3105, USA

Heller, John H (Scientist)
74 Horseshoe Rd
Wilton, CT 06897-3400, USA

Heller, Ron (Athlete, Football Player)
26 W Anapamu St Fl 3
Santa Barbara, CA 93101-3144, USA

Hellerman, Fred (Music Group, Songwriter, Writer)
83 Good Hill Rd
Weston, CT 06883-2802, USA

Hellestrae, Dale (Athlete, Football Player)
11705 E Charter Oak Dr
Scottsdale, AZ 85259-2743, USA

Hellickson, Russell (Russ) (Wrestler)
6893 Lauren Pl
Columbus, OH 43235-2188, USA

Helling, Rick A (Ricky) (Athlete, Baseball Player)
3672 Landings Dr
Excelsior, MN 55331-9709, USA

Hellion
18653 Ventura Blvd # 307
Tarzana, CA 91356-4103

Helliwell, Robert A (Scientist)
2240 Page Mill Rd
Palo Alto, CA 94304, USA

Hellman, Bonnie
1680 Vine St Ste 614
Hollywood, CA 90028-8833

Hellman, Martin E (Inventor)
855 Serra St
Stanford, CA 94305, USA

Hellman, Monte (Director)
8588 Appian Way
Los Angeles, CA 90046-7729, USA

Hellmann, Martina (Athlete, Track Athlete)
Neue Leipziger Str 14
Leipzig 4205, GERMANY

Hellmuth, George F (Architect)
10111 Ingleside Dr
Saint Louis, MO 63124-1246, USA

Hellstrand, Kristoffer (Biologist)
Virology Dept
Goteborg 405 30, SWEDEN

Helluin, Francis (Athlete, Football Player)
3930 Southdown Mandalay Rd
Houma, LA 70360-3001, USA

Hellwig, James (Ultimate Warrior) (Athlete, Wrestler)
43A County Road 119 N
Santa Fe, NM 87506-7101, USA

Hellwig, Jim (Athlete, Wrestler)
43A County Road 119 N
Santa Fe, NM 87506-7101, USA

Hellyer, Paul T (Government Official)
65 Harbour Sq # 506
Toronto, ON M5J 2L4, CANADA

Helm, Darren (Athlete, Hockey Player)
c/o Staff Member *Detroit Red Wings*
600 Civic Center Dr
Detroit, MI 48226-4419, USA

Helm, Levon (Actor, Music Group, Musician)
160 Plochmann Ln
Woodstock, NY 12498-2007, USA

Helm, Peter
1480 S Wild Oaks Dr
Nixa, MO 65714-8269

Helm, Val (Baseball Player)
PO Box 423
Superior, NE 68978-0423, USA

Helmberger, Don V (Misc)
Seismology
Pasadena, CA 91125-0001, USA

Helmer, Frank (Stylist)
c/o Staff Member *Exclusive Artists Mgmt*
7700 W Sunset Blvd Ste 205
Los Angeles, CA 90046-3913, USA

Helmerich, Hans C (Business Person)
Utica & 21st St
Tulsa, OK 74114, USA

Helmerich, Walter H III (Business Person)
Utica & 21st St
Tulsa, OK 74114, USA

Helmerson, Frans (Music Group, Musician)
165 W 57th St
New York, NY 10019-2201, USA

Helmly, James R (General)
US Army Reserves Hqusa Pentagon
Washington, DC 20310-0001, USA

Helmond, Katherine (Actor)
c/o Staff Member *Le Mond/Zetter Management*
3261 Celinda Dr
Carlsbad, CA 92008-2070, USA

Helmreich, Ernst J M (Misc)
Am Hubland
Wurzburg 97074, GERMANY

Helms, Edward (Ed) (Actor, Comedian)
c/o Peter Principato *Principato/Young Management*
9465 Wilshire Blvd Ste 430
Beverly Hills, CA 90212-2613, USA

Helms, L S (Financier)
127 Public Sq
Cleveland, OH 44114-1217, USA

Helms, Susan J (Astronaut)
2101 Nasa Pkwy Spc Center
Houston, TX 77058-3607, USA

Helms, Tommy (Athlete, Baseball Player, Coach)
5427 Bluesky Dr
Cincinnati, OH 45247-7865, USA

Helms, Wes (Athlete, Baseball Player)
9314 Bear Creek Rd
Sterrett, AL 35147-9166, USA

Helmstetter, Shad (Motivational Speaker, Writer)
362 Gulf Breeze Pkwy Ste 104
Gulf Breeze, FL 32561-4492, USA

Helmut
1775 Broadway Ste 433
New York, NY 10019-1903

Helmuth, Phil (Misc)
1101 University Ave
Palo Alto, CA 94301-2239, USA

Helnwein, Gottfried (Artist)
Aul der Burg 2
Burgbrol 56659, GERMANY

Heloise
PO Box 795000
San Antonio, TX 78279-5000

Heloise, (Cruse Evans) (Journalist)
PO Box 795000
San Antonio, TX 78279-5000, USA

Helpern, Joan G (Designer, Fashion Designer)
46 W 56th St # 200
New York, NY 10019-3801, USA

Heltau, Michael (Actor, Music Group)
Sulzweg 11
Vienna 1190, AUSTRIA

Helton, Bill D (Business Person)
1225 17th St
Denver, CO 80202-5534, USA

Helton, Darius (Athlete, Football Player)
5816 Amity Springs Dr
Charlotte, NC 28212-2604, USA

Helton, RJ (Musician)
1400 Market Place Blvd
Cumming, GA 30041-7925, USA

Helton, Todd L (Athlete, Baseball Player)
8720 E 127th Ct
Brighton, CO 80602-8111, USA

Helvin, Marie (Model)
23 Eyot Gardens
London W6 9TN, UNITED KINGDOM (UK)

Hely, Steve (Actor)
c/o Cori Wellins *WmE2 (Endeavor-LA)*
9601 Wilshire Blvd Fl 3
Beverly Hills, CA 90210-5219, USA

Heman, Russ (Athlete, Baseball Player)
5555 Canyon Crest Dr Apt 3D
Riverside, CA 92507-6453, USA

Hemandez, Angel (Baseball Player)
500 Cypress Xing
Wellington, FL 33414-6368, USA

Hemenway, Robert E (Educator)
President S Ofc
Lawrence, KS 66045-0001, USA

Hemingway, Gerardine (Designer, Fashion Designer)
Courtney Road Bldg 201 Wembley
Middx HA9 7PP, UNITED KINGDOM (UK)

Hemingway, Mariel (Actor, Model)
PO Box 2249
Ketchum, ID 83340-2249, USA

Hemingway, Rose (Actor)
c/o Charles Mastropietro *Dontanville/ Frattaroli (D/F)*
270 Lafayette St Ste 402
New York, NY 10012-3327, USA

Hemingway, Toby (Actor)
c/o Carlos Augusto Gonzalez *Gersh (LA)*
9465 Wilshire Blvd Ste 600
Beverly Hills, CA 90212-2612, USA

Hemingway, Wayne (Designer, Fashion Designer)
Courtney Road Bldg 201 Wembley
Middx HA9 7PP, UNITED KINGDOM (UK)

Hemme, Christy (Actor)
c/o Liza Anderson *Anderson Group Public Relations*
8060 Melrose Ave Fl 4
Los Angeles, CA 90046-7038, USA

Hemmens, Heather (Actor)
c/o Stephanie Simon *Untitled Entertainment (LA)*
350 S Beverly Dr Ste 200
Beverly Hills, CA 90212-4819, USA

Hemmer, Bill (Correspondent)
c/o Staff Member *Fox News Channel (NY)*
1211 Ave Of The Americas Level C1
New York, NY 10036-8701, USA

Hemmi, Heini (Skier)
Chalet Bel-Lia
Valbella 7077, SWITZERLAND

Hemming, Lindy (Designer, Stylist)
c/o Robert Arakelian *United Talent Agency (UTA)*
9560 Wilshire Blvd Fl 5
Beverly Hills, CA 90212-2400, USA

Hemmis, Paige (Actor, Reality TV Star)
c/o Staff Member *Extreme Makeover: Home Edition*
Endemol Entertainment USA 9225 Sunset Blvd #1100
Los Angeles, CA 90069, USA

Hemond, Scott (Athlete, Baseball Player)
263 Florida Ave
Dunedin, FL 34698-7530, USA

Hemphill, Bret (Athlete, Baseball Player)
1273 Trehowell Dr
Roseville, CA 95678-6110, USA

Hemphill, Joel (Music Group)
PO Box 144
Goodlettsville, TN 37070-0144, USA

Hemphill, Labreeska (Music Group)
PO Box 144
Goodlettsville, TN 37070-0144, USA

Hemphill, Richard (Baseball Player)
422 Barnes St
Rock Hill, SC 29730-5044, USA

Hempstead, Hessley (Athlete, Football Player)
52900 Winsome Ln
Chesterfield, MI 48051-3723, USA

Hempstone, Smith Jr (Diplomat, Writer)
7611 Fairfax Rd
Bethesda, MD 20814-1313, USA

Hemric, Dick (Athlete, Basketball Player)
1220 7th St NE
North Canton, OH 44720-2116, USA

Hemsley, Nate (Athlete, Football Player)
26 Roberts Pl
Willingboro, NJ 08046-2514, USA

Hemsley, Stephen J (Business Person)
Opus Center 9900 Bren Road E
Minnetonka, MN 55343, USA

Hemsworth, Chris (Actor)
c/o Staff Member *ROAR (LA)*
9701 Wilshire Blvd Fl 8
Beverly Hills, CA 90212-2008, USA

Hemsworth, Liam (Actor)
c/o Will Ward *ROAR (LA)*
9701 Wilshire Blvd Fl 8
Beverly Hills, CA 90212-2008, USA

Hemus, Solly (Athlete, Baseball Player, Coach)
5100 San Felipe St Unit 194E
Houston, TX 77056-3688, USA

Henao, Zulay (Actor)
c/o Jean-Louis Diamonika *One Entertainment (NY)*
12 W 57th St PH 1
New York, NY 10019-3900, USA

Hencken, John F (Athlete, Swimmer)
PO Box 2540
Weaverville, NC 28787-2540, USA

Hendershot, Larry (Athlete, Football Player)
1721 W 6th St
Muncie, IN 47302-2108, USA

Hendershot, Ray (Artist)
1007 Lakeview Ter
Pennsburg, PA 18073-1611, USA

Henderson, Alan (Basketball Player)
190 Marietta St NW
Atlanta, GA 30303-2762, USA

Henderson, Anthony (Krayzie Bone) (Actor, Composer, Musician)
c/o Staff Member *RBC Records*
245 E Olive Ave Ste 300
Burbank, CA 91502-1214, USA

Henderson, Cedric (Athlete, Basketball Player)
PO Box 148
Smyrna, GA 30081-0148, USA

Henderson, Chris (Soccer Player)
2121 Velma Ave
Columbus, OH 43211-2085, USA

Henderson, David (Athlete, Basketball Player)
805 Sweet Hollow Ct
Middletown, DE 19709-8645, USA

Henderson, David L (Dave) (Athlete, Baseball Player)
6004 142nd Ct SE
Bellevue, WA 98006-4901, USA

Henderson, Donald A (Educator, Misc)
3802 Greenway
Baltimore, MD 21218-1825, USA

Henderson, Felicia (Writer)
c/o Scott Schwartz *Vision Art Management*
9465 Wilshire Blvd Ste 870
Beverly Hills, CA 90212-2610, USA

Henderson, Florence (Actor, Music Group)
PO Box 11295
Marina Del Rey, CA 90295-7295, USA

Henderson, Gerald (Athlete, Basketball Player)
185 Birkdale Dr
Blue Bell, PA 19422-3276, USA

Henderson, James A (Business Person)
500 Jackson St
Columbus, IN 47201-6258, USA

Henderson, Jerome (Athlete, Basketball Player)
7441 Zombar Ave
Van Nuys, CA 91406-3338, USA

Henderson, Joe (Athlete, Baseball Player)
525 Agua Clara St
El Paso, TX 79928-9011, USA

Henderson, John (Athlete, Football Player)
1 Alltel Stadium Pl
Jacksonville, FL 32202-1917, USA

Henderson, John (Athlete, Football Player)
18130 19th Ave N
Plymouth, MN 55447-2634, USA

Henderson, Josh (Actor)
c/o Michael Baum *Impression Entertainment*
9229 W Sunset Blvd Ste 700
West Hollywood, CA 90069-3407, USA

Henderson, Julie (Model)
596 Broadway # 701
New York, NY 10012-3396, USA

Henderson, Karen LeCraft (Judge)
333 Constitution Ave NW
Washington, DC 20001-2804, USA

Henderson, Keith (Athlete, Football Player)
PO Box 2754
Cartersville, GA 30120-1696, USA

Henderson, Ken (Athlete, Baseball Player)
200 Winchester Cir Apt D104
Los Gatos, CA 95032-1872, USA

Henderson, Kevin (Athlete, Basketball Player)
2960 Champion Way Apt 2203
Tustin, CA 92782-1238, USA

Henderson, Logan (Musician)
c/o Kimberlin Dalehite *Magnolia Entertainment (LA)*
9595 Wilshire Blvd Ste 601
Beverly Hills, CA 90212-2506, USA

Henderson, Martin (Actor)
c/o Peter Kiernan *Management 360*
9111 Wilshire Blvd
Beverly Hills, CA 90210-5508, USA

Henderson, Murray (Athlete, Hockey Player)
18 Gatehead Rd
North York, ON M2J 2P5, Canada

Henderson, Neale (Athlete, Baseball Player)
PO Box 131251
San Diego, CA 92170-1251, USA

Henderson, Paul (Athlete, Hockey Player)
410-2121 Argentina Rd
Mississauga, ON L5N 2X4, Canada

Henderson, Paul III (Journalist)
1120 John St
Seattle, WA 98109-5321, USA

Henderson, Reuben (Athlete, Football Player)
3918 Hunters Ridge Dr Apt 4
Lansing, MI 48911-1106, USA

Henderson, Richard (Biologist)
Hills Road
Cambridge CB2 2QH, UNITED KINGDOM (UK)

Henderson, Richard (Actor, Musician)

Henderson, Rickey (Athlete, Baseball Player)
10561 Englewood Dr
Oakland, CA 94605-5013, USA

Henderson, Rod (Athlete, Baseball Player)
552 Winter Hill Ln
Lexington, KY 40509-2932, USA

Henderson, Shirley (Actor)
c/o Lorraine Hamilton *Hamilton Hodell Ltd*
66-68 Margaret St Fl 5
London W1W 8SR, UK

Henderson, Steve (Athlete, Baseball Player)
10509 Gretna Green Dr
Tampa, FL 33626-1830, USA

Henderson, Thomas
7 Seafield Ln
Westhampton Beach, NY 11978 2714

Henderson, Thomas (Athlete, Football Player)
8403 Mesa Dr Attn Athletic
Austin, TX 78759-8117, USA

Henderson, Thomas (Athlete, Basketball Player)
6822 Baron Gate Ct
Spring, TX 77379-5094, USA

Henderson, Thomas (Tom) (Athlete, Basketball Player)
14003 Piney Run Ct
Houston, TX 77066-5519, USA

Henderson, Zachary (Athlete, Football Player)
1224 Brentwood Pt
Brentwood, TN 37027-2943, USA

Hendler, Lauri
4034 Stone Canyon Ave
Sherman Oaks, CA 91403-4541

Hendley, Bob (Athlete, Baseball Player)
645 Wimbish Rd
Macon, GA 31210-4328, USA

Hendley, Dick (Athlete, Football Player)
6 Sun Flare Ct
Greer, SC 29650-4419, USA

Hendrick, George (Athlete, Baseball Player)
PO Box 36250
Las Vegas, NV 89133-6250, USA

Hendricks, Barbara (Opera Singer)
420 W 45th St
New York, NY 10036-3501, USA

Hendricks, Christina (Actor)
c/o Ben Levine *Kritzer Levine Wilkins Entertainment*
11872 La Grange Ave Fl 1
Los Angeles, CA 90025-5283, USA

Hendricks, Jon (Music Group)
2737 Edwin Pl
Los Angeles, CA 90046-1031, USA

Hendricks, L H (Baseball Player)
12 Sunset Blvd
Beaufort, SC 29907-1421, USA

Hendricks, Susan (Anchor)
c/o Staff Member *CNN (Atlanta)*
1 Cnn Ctr NW
Atlanta, GA 30303-2762, USA

Hendricks, Theodore P (Ted) (Athlete, Football Player)
165 Sunset Way
Miami Springs, FL 33166-5153, USA

Hendrickson, Darby (Athlete, Hockey Player)
3939 Huntingdon Dr
Hopkins, MN 55305-5112, USA

Hendrickson, Mark (Athlete, Baseball Player)
17289 Dunbar Rd
Mount Vernon, WA 98273-8761, USA

Hendrickson, Steve (Athlete, Football Player)
2558 Miller Ave
Escondido, CA 92029-5704, USA

Hendrix, Elaine (Actor)
1180 S Beverly Dr Ste 601
Los Angeles, CA 90035-1158, USA

Hendrix, Harville (Writer)
c/o Staff Member *Henry Holt & Company*
175 5th Ave Ste 400
New York, NY 10010-7726, USA

Hendrix, John W (General)
Commanding General Army Forces Command
Fort McPherson, GA 30330-0001, USA

Hendrix, Terri (Musician)
PO Box 2340
San Marcos, TX 78667-2340, USA

Hendrix, Tim (Athlete, Football Player)
7251 Hamilton Dr
Midlothian, TX 76065-6974, USA

Hendry, Gloria (Actor)
256 S Robertson Blvd
Beverly Hills, CA 90211-2811, USA

Hendry, Joel (Athlete, Golfer)
c/o Jim Lehrman *SFX Golf*
36855 W Main St Ste 200
Purcellville, VA 20132-3561, USA

Hendry, Ted (Baseball Player)
14740 N 90th Pl
Scottsdale, AZ 85260-2700, USA

Hendry, Ted (Athlete, Baseball Player)
14740 N 90th Pl
Scottsdale, AZ 85260-2700, USA

Hendryx, Nona (Musician)
6201 Sunset Blvd # 329
Hollywood, CA 90028, USA

Hendy, John (Athlete, Football Player)
2120 Brown Ave
Santa Clara, CA 95051-1722, USA

Henenlotter, Frank (Director)
81 Bedford St Apt 6E
New York, NY 10014-5749, USA

Hengel, Dave (Athlete, Baseball Player)
2642 Kingfisher Ln
Lincoln, CA 95648-8753, USA

Hengge, Helga (Mountaineer)
Gabriel-von-Seidl-Str. 31e
Gruenwald D-82031, Germany

Henin-Hardenne, Justine (Tennis Player)
1751 Pinnacle Dr Ste 1500
McLean, VA 22102-3833, USA

Henke, Brad (Actor)
c/o Matt Schwartz *Christopher Wright Management*
930 S Orange Grove Ave
Los Angeles, CA 90036-4457, USA

Henke, Edgar (Athlete, Football Player)
11381 Madrone Ct
Auburn, CA 95602-8380, USA

Henke, Karl (Athlete, Football Player)
1180 Bogota Ct
Oxnard, CA 93035-2608, USA

Henke, Nolan (Athlete, Golfer)
1323 Florida Ave
Fort Myers, FL 33901-7707, USA

Henke, Tom (Athlete, Baseball Player)
6200 Saint Francis Dr
Jefferson City, MO 65101-9292, USA

Henkel, Andrea (Athlete)
Lerchenstr 39
Memmingen 87700, GERMANY

Henkel, Heike (Athlete, Track Athlete)
Tannenbergstr 57
Leverkusen 51373, GERMANY

Henkel, Herbert L (Business Person)
200 Chestnut Ridge Rd
Woodcliff Lake, NJ 07677-7703, USA

Henkin, Louis (Attorney, Attorney General, Educator, General)
460 Riverside Dr
New York, NY 10027-6821, USA

Henle, Gertrude (Scientist)
533 Ott Rd
Bala Cynwyd, PA 19004-2509, USA

Henley, Bob (Athlete, Baseball Player)
11050 Moreland Dr E
Grand Bay, AL 36541-6626, USA

Henley, Carey (Athlete, Football Player)
1611 S Clayton Ave
Chattanooga, TN 37412-1107, USA

Henley, Darryl (Athlete, Football Player)
10178 Woodridge Dr
Rancho Cucamonga, CA 91737-6834, USA

Henley, Don (Music Group, Songwriter)
c/o Irving Azoff *Azoff Music Management/ Front Line*
1100 Glendon Ave
Los Angeles, CA 90024-3503, USA

Henley, Drewe (Actor)
1 Granary Cottages Combpyne, Axminster
Devon EX13 8SX, UK

Henley, Edward T (Misc)
1219 28th St NW
Washington, DC 20007-3362, USA

Henley, Gail (Athlete, Baseball Player)
7338 Alta Vis
La Verne, CA 91750-1115, USA

Henley, Georgie (Actor)
c/o Christian Hodell *Hamilton Hodell Ltd*
66-68 Margaret St Fl 5
London W1W 8SR, UK

Henley, J Smith (Judge)
200 Federal Building
Harrison, AR 72601, USA

Henley, Larry (Composer)
PO Box 335
Brentwood, TN 37024-0335, USA

Henley, Patricia
PO Box 259
Battle Ground, IN 47920-0259

Henley, Robert (Ballerina)
11050 Moreland Dr E
Grand Bay, AL 36541-6626, USA

Henman, Graham (Director)
9200 W Sunset Blvd Ste 900
Los Angeles, CA 90069-3604, USA

Henman, Tim (Tennis Player)
14497 N Dale Mabry Hwy Ste 205 PMB N
Tampa, FL 33618-2047, USA

Henn, Mark (Animator)
PO Box 10200
Lake Buena Vista, FL 32830-0200, USA

Henn, Sean (Athlete, Baseball Player)
3658 Snow Creek Dr
Aledo, TX 76008-3677, USA

Henn, Walter (Architect)
Ramsachleite 13
Mumau 82418, GERMANY

Henneman, Brian (Music Group)
180 Varick St # 800
New York, NY 10014-4606, USA

Henneman, Mike (Athlete, Baseball Player)
806 Lake Creek Dr
McKinney, TX 75070-5590, USA

Hennen, Thomas J (Astronaut)
16315 Cascade Caverns Ln
Houston, TX 77044-1240, USA

Henner, Marilu (Actor)
c/o Rory Rosegarten *Conversation Company*
1044 Northern Blvd Ste 304
Roslyn, NY 11576-1589, USA

Hennessey, Brad (Athlete, Baseball Player)
4811 Brott Rd
Toledo, OH 43613-3279, USA

Hennessey, Tom (Bowler)
157 Forest Brook Ln
Saint Louis, MO 63146-5601, USA

Hennessy, Jill (Actor)
c/o Matt Saver *Matthew Saver Law Offices*
269 N Beverly Dr
Beverly Hills, CA 90210-5317, USA

Hennessy, John (Educator)
President's Office
Stanford, CA 94305, USA

Hennessy, John B (Archaeologist)
497 Old Windsor Rd
Kellyville, NSW 2153, AUSTRALIA

Henney, Daniel (Actor)
c/o Staff Member *WmE2 (WMA-LA)*
1 William Morris Pl
Beverly Hills, CA 90212-4261, USA

Henney, Jane (Government Official)
5600 Fishers Ln
Rockville, MD 20852-1750, USA

Hennig, Shelley (Actor)
c/o Allan Grifka *Alchemy Entertainment*
7024 Melrose Ave Ste 420
Los Angeles, CA 90038-3394, USA

Hennigan, Charley (Athlete, Football Player)
157 Rocking G Farms Rd
Livingston, TX 77351-1226, USA

Hennigan, John (Athlete, Wrestler)
c/o Staff Member *World Wrestling Entertainment (WWE)*
1241 E Main St
Stamford, CT 06902-3520, USA

Hennigan, Mike (Athlete, Football Player)
542 N Washington Ave
Cookeville, TN 38501-2657, USA

Hennigan, Phil (Athlete, Baseball Player)
PO Box 1212
Center, TX 75935-1212, USA

Henning, Dan (Athlete, Football Coach, Football Player)
11205 NW 15th Pl
Pembroke Pines, FL 33026-2601, USA

Henning, John F Jr (Publisher)
80 Willow Rd
Menlo Park, CA 94025-3661, USA

Henning, Larry
7426 43rd Ave SE
Saint Cloud, MN 56304-9579

Henning, Linda (Actor)
10765 Wrightwood Ln
Studio City, CA 91604-3951, USA

Henning, Lorne E (Athlete, Coach, Hockey Player)
18 Coldbrook
Irvine, CA 92604-4649, USA

Henninger, Brian (Athlete, Golfer)
25481 SW Newland Rd
Wilsonville, OR 97070, USA

Henninger, Rick (Athlete, Baseball Player)
98 Park Ln
Pottsboro, TX 75076-3990, USA

Hennings, Chad W (Athlete, Football Player)
6101 Bay Valley Ct
Flower Mound, TX 75022-5575, USA

Henning-Walker, Anne (Speed Skater)
5001 W Portland Dr
Littleton, CO 80128-6409, USA

Hennis, Randy (Athlete, Baseball Player)
1747 Sienna Dr
Melbourne, FL 32934-9030, USA

Henrich, Bobby (Athlete, Baseball Player)
1531 Via Los Coyotes
La Habra, CA 90631-7655, USA

Henrich, Dieter (Misc)
Gerlichstr 7A
Munich 81245, GERMANY

Henrich, Thomas D (Tommy) (Athlete, Baseball Player)
13801 Woodbine Ave
Dayton, OH 45420 2550, USA

Henrich, Tom
1547 Albino Trl
Dewey, AZ 86327

Henrichsen, Brett (DJ)
c/o Len Evans *Project Publicity*
312 W 53rd St Ste 202
New York, NY 10019-5743, USA

Henricks, Jon N (Swimmer)
254 Laurel Ave
Des Plaines, IL 60016-4318, USA

Henricks, Terence T (Tom) (Astronaut)
PO Box 547
Keene, NH 03431-0547, USA

Henrie, David (Actor)
c/o Matt Luber *Luber Roklin Management*
8530 Wilshire Blvd Ste 550
Beverly Hills, CA 90211-3133, USA

Henrik (Prince)
Copenhagen K 1257, DENMARK

Henrikse, Lance (Actor)
c/o Jean-Pierre (JP) Henraux *Shelter Entertainment*
9454 Wilshire Blvd Ste 715
Beverly Hills, CA 90212-2925, USA

Henriksen, Donald (Athlete, Basketball Player)
18160 Cottonwood Rd
Bend, OR 97707-9317, USA

Henrikson, Lance (Actor)
c/o Jeff Witjas *Agency for the Performing Arts (APA-LA)*
405 S Beverly Dr Ste 500
Beverly Hills, CA 90212-4425, USA

Henriques, Sean Paul (Actor, Musician)
c/o Staff Member *WmE2 (WMA-LA)*
1 William Morris Pl
Beverly Hills, CA 90212-4261, USA

Henriquez, Ron (Actor)
4906 College View Ave
Los Angeles, CA 90041-1844, USA

Henry, Albert (Athlete, Basketball Player)
2410 N 52nd St
Philadelphia, PA 19131-1409, USA

Henry, Bill (Athlete, Baseball Player)
47 Oyster Landing Ln
Hilton Head Island, SC 29928-3045, USA

Henry, Bill (Athlete, Baseball Player)
2313 Kilkenny Ln
Deer Park, TX 77536-3955, USA

Henry, Brad (Politician)
State Capitol Bldg #212
Oklahoma City, OK 73105, USA

Henry, Buck (Actor, Writer)
117 E 57th St
New York, NY 10022-2002, USA

Henry, Butch (Athlete, Baseball Player)
12072 Paseo De Amor Ln
El Paso, TX 79936-4499, USA

Henry, Clarence (Forgman) (Music Group, Songwriter, Writer)
3309 Lawrence St
New Orleans, LA 70114-3230, USA

Henry, Conner (Athlete, Basketball Player)
1122 N College Ave
Claremont, CA 91711-3927, USA

Henry, Dale (Attorney, Hockey Player)
8611 Datapoint Dr Apt 43
San Antonio, TX 78229-5922, USA

Henry, David (Actor)
c/o Dallas Smith *United Agents*
12-26 Lexington St
London W1F OLE, UK

Henry, Doug (Athlete, Baseball Player)
2804 Burries Rd
Hartland, WI 53029-8823, USA

Henry, Dwayne (Athlete, Baseball Player)
407 E Hampstead Ct
Middletown, DE 19709-1631, USA

Henry, Geoffrey A (Prime Minister)
PO Box 281
Rarotonga, COOK ISLANDS

Henry, Gloria (Actor)
849 N Harper Ave
Los Angeles, CA 90046-6803, USA

Henry, Gregg (Actor)
8956 Appian Way
Los Angeles, CA 90046-7737, USA

Henry, J J (Athlete, Golfer)
6901 Sanctuary Ln
Fort Worth, TX 76132-7101, USA

Henry, Joe (Athlete, Baseball Player)
220 N 7th St
Lovejoy, IL 62059-6100, USA

Henry, Joe (Music Group, Songwriter, Writer)
509 Hartnell St
Monterey, CA 93940-2825, USA

Henry, John (Baseball Player)
4698 Sanctuary Ln
Boca Raton, FL 33431-5206, USA

Henry, Joseph L (Doctor)
60 Marinita Ave
San Rafael, CA 94901-3431, USA

Henry, Justin (Actor)
c/o Staff Member *Phoenix Organization, The*
1990 S Bundy Dr Ste 630
Los Angeles, CA 90025-6140, USA

Henry, Lenny (Actor)
c/o Staff Member *WmE2 (WMA-LA)*
1 William Morris Pl
Beverly Hills, CA 90212-4261, USA

Henry, Mark (Athlete, Wrestler)
c/o Staff Member *World Wrestling Entertainment (WWE)*
1241 E Main St
Stamford, CT 06902-3520, USA

Henry, Mike (Actor)
10803 Blix St Unit 3
North Hollywood, CA 91602-3822, USA

Henry, Pat (Stylist)
c/o Staff Member *Punch Productions*
11661 San Vicente Blvd Ste 222
Los Angeles, CA 90049-5110, USA

Henry, Pierre (Composer)
32 Rue Toul
Paris 75012, FRANCE

Henry, Piper
1680 Vine St Ste 614
Hollywood, CA 90028-8833

Henry, Robert H (Judge)
PO Box 1767
Oklahoma City, OK 73101-1767, USA

Henry, Ron (Athlete, Baseball Player)
2160 Downing St
Denver, CO 80205-5261, USA

Henry, Thierry (Athlete, Soccer Player)
c/o Nicola Richardson *QVoice*
193-197 High Holborn 4th Floor, Holborn Hall
London WC1V 7BD, UNITED KINGDOM (UK)

Henry, William H Jr (Producer)
Rockefeller Center
New York, NY 10020, USA

Hensarling, Jeb (Congressman, Politician)
129 Cannon Hob
Washington, DC 20515-3501, USA

Hensby, Mark (Athlete, Golfer)
7175 E Camelback Rd Unit 501
Scottsdale, AZ 85251-1296, USA

Hensel, Bruce (Doctor)
17526 Tramonto Dr
Pacific Palisades, CA 90272-3127, USA

Hensel, Robert M (World Record Holder)
138 E 3rd St # A
Oswego, NY 13126-2607, USA

Hensel, Witold (Archaeologist)
Ul Marszalkowska 84/92M
Warsaw 109 00-514, POLAND

Hensilwood, Christopher (Misc, Scientist)
25 Queen Victoria St
Cape Town, SOUTH AFRICA

Henslee, Jimmie (Stylist)
c/o Staff Member *Independent Artists*
448 E Riverdale Ave
Orange, CA 92865-1302, USA

Hensley, Chuck (Athlete, Baseball Player)
259 Bonanza Dr
Erie, CO 80516-8451, USA

Hensley, Clay (Athlete, Baseball Player)
3601 Dogwood Blossom Ct
Pearland, TX 77581-5038, USA

Hensley, Elaine (Stylist)
511 Gun Club Rd
Nashville, TN 37205-3101, USA

Hensley, Jimmy (Race Car Driver)
2570 Horsepasture Price Rd
Ridgeway, VA 24148-3707, USA

Hensley, John (Actor)
c/o Vincent Cirrincione *Vincent Cirrincione Associates*
1516 N Fairfax Ave
Los Angeles, CA 90046-2608, USA

Hensley, Jon (Actor)
c/o Staff Member *Innovative Artists (LA)*
1505 10th St
Santa Monica, CA 90401-2805, USA

Hensley, Kirby J (Religious Leader)
601 3rd St
Modesto, CA 95351-3355, USA

Henson, Brian (Actor, Director, Producer)
c/o Staff Member *Jim Henson Company (LA)*
1416 N La Brea Ave
Hollywood, CA 90028-7506

Henson, Champ (Athlete, Football Player)
PO Box 3
Ashville, OH 43103-0003, USA

Henson, Darrin Dewitt (Actor)
c/o Adam Griffin *Kritzer Levine Wilkins Entertainment*
11872 La Grange Ave Fl 1
Los Angeles, CA 90025-5283, USA

Henson, Drew (Athlete, Baseball Player)
4629 Lorraine Ave
Dallas, TX 75209-6013, USA

Henson, Elden (Actor)
c/o Chuck Binder *Binder & Associates*
1465 Lindacrest Dr
Beverly Hills, CA 90210-2519, USA

Henson, John (Actor, Comedian)
1044 Northem Blvd # 304
Roslyn, NY 11576, USA

Henson, Lisa (Producer)
2400 Riverside Dr
Burbank, CA 91505, USA

Henson, Lou (Basketball Player, Coach)
Athletic Dept
Las Cruces, NM 88033, USA

Henson, Luther (Athlete, Football Player)
5395 Maple Grove Ave
Blanchester, OH 45107-1533, USA

Henson, Taraji P (Actor)
c/o Vincent Cirrincione *Vincent Cirrincione Associates*
1516 N Fairfax Ave
Los Angeles, CA 90046-2608, USA

Henstridge, Natasha (Actor, Model)
c/o David (Dave) Fleming *Mosaic Media Group*
9200 W Sunset Blvd Ste 10
Los Angeles, CA 90069-3608, USA

Hentgen, Pat (Athlete, Baseball Player)
52432 Westcreek Dr
Macomb, MI 48042-2964, USA

Hentoff, Nathan I (Nat) (Critic, Musician)
36 Cooper Sq
New York, NY 10003-7118, USA

Henton, John (Actor)
c/o Staff Member *Gersh (LA)*
9465 Wilshire Blvd Ste 600
Beverly Hills, CA 90212-2612, USA

Hentrich, Craig (Athlete, Football Player)
9130 Old Smyrna Rd
Brentwood, TN 37027-6116, USA

Hentrich, Helmut (Architect)
Dusseldorfer Str 67
Dusseldorf-Oberkassel 40545, GERMANY

Henze, Hans Werner (Composer, Conductor)
Weihergarten 1-5
Mainz 55116, GERMANY

Hepburn, Cassandra (Actor)
c/o Glenn Hughes III *Gem Entertainment Group*
10701 Wilshire Blvd Apt 1202
Los Angeles, CA 90024-4437, USA

Hepler, Bill (Athlete, Baseball Player)
12518 Fort King Rd
Dade City, FL 33525-5609, USA

Heppel, Leon A (Biologist)
Biochemistry Dept
Ithaca, NY 14850, USA

Hepple, Alan (Athlete, Hockey Player)
3804 La Cresta Ave
Oakland, CA 94602-1727, USA

Heppner, Ben (Opera Singer)
165 W 57th St
New York, NY 10019-2201, USA

Herb, Marvin (Business Person)
7400 N Oak Park Ave
Niles, IL 60714-3818

Herbers, Ian (Athlete, Hockey Player)
3124 Wildflower Cir
Saginaw, MI 48603-1357, USA

Herbert, Gary (Governor, Politician)
20 State Capitol
Salt Lake City, UT 84114, USA

Herbert, Holly (Journalist)
4000 Warner Blvd
Burbank, CA 91522-0001, USA

Herbert, James (Writer)
5-8 Lower John St
London W1R 4HA, UNITED KINGDOM (UK)

Herbert, Johnny (Race Car Driver)
Wildbachstr 9
Hinwil 8340, SWITZERLAND

Herbert, Michael K (Editor)
990 Grove St
Evanston, IL 60201-6510, USA

Herbert, Raymond E (Ray) (Athlete, Baseball Player)
9360 Taylors Turn
Stanwood, MI 49346-9686, USA

Herbert, Walter W (Wally) (Scientist)
Catlodge Laggan
Inverness-shire PH20 1AH, UNITED KINGDOM (UK)

Herbert of Hemingford, D Nicholas (Publisher)
Old Rectory Hemingford Abbots
Huntington Cambs PE18 9AN, UNITED KINGDOM (UK)

Herbig, George H (Astronomer)
2680 Woodlawn Dr
Honolulu, HI 96822-1839, USA

Herbig, Gunther
60 Simcoe St # C116
Toronto, ON MJ5 2H5, CANADA

Herbst, William (Astronomer)
Astronomy
Middletown, CT 06459-0001, USA

Herczegh, Gezar G (Judge)
Camegieplein 2
KJ Hague 2517, NETHERLANDS

Herd, Carla
8281 Melrose Ave Ste 200
Los Angeles, CA 90046-6890

Herd, Richard (Actor)
PO Box 56297
Sherman Oaks, CA 91413-1297, USA

Herda, Frank A (War Hero)
PO Box 30967
Cleveland, OH 44130-0914, USA

Heredia, Felix (Athlete, Baseball Player)
PO Box 4842
Hialeah, FL 33014-0842, USA

Heredia, Gil (Athlete, Baseball Player)
4233 E Pontatoc Dr
Tucson, AZ 85718-6154, USA

Heredia, Wilson (Actor)
c/o Sarah Fargo *Paradigm (NY)*
360 N Crescent Dr
Beverly Hills, CA 90210-4874, USA

Heredia, Wilson Jermaine (Actor)
c/o Leanne Coronel *Coronel Group*
9601 Wilshire Blvd Fl 3
Beverly Hills, CA 90210-5219, USA

Herek, Stephen R (Director)
9701 Wilshire Blvd Ste 1000
Beverly Hills, CA 90212-2010, USA

Herera, Sue (Correspondent, Television Host)
c/o Staff Member *CNBC*
900 Sylvan Ave
Englewood Cliffs, NJ 07632-3312, USA

Herger, Wally (Congressman, Politician)
242 Cannon Hob
Washington, DC 20515-4322, USA

Hergert, Joe (Athlete, Football Player)
875 Tater Rd
New Smyrna Beach, FL 32168-9140, USA

Herges, Matt (Athlete, Baseball Player)
21019 N 79th Pl
Scottsdale, AZ 85255, USA

Hergesheimer, Wally (Athlete, Hockey Player)
301B-15 Valhalla Dr
Winnipeg, MB R2G 4G8, Canada

Herincx, Raimund (Opera Singer)
Larkbarrow Shepton Mallet
Somerset BA4 4NR, UNITED KINGDOM (UK)

Herkenhoff, Matt (Athlete, Football Player)
16000 Baywood Ln
Eden Prairie, MN 55346-2409, USA

Herles, Kathleen (Actor)
c/o Shirley Grant *Shirley Grant Management*
PO Box 866
Teaneck, NJ 07666-0866, USA

Herlihy, Tim (Actor, Comedian)
c/o Staff Member *WmE2 (Endeavor-LA)*
9601 Wilshire Blvd Fl 3
Beverly Hills, CA 90210-5219, USA

Herline, Alan (Athlete, Football Player)
610 Post Oak Cir
Brentwood, TN 37027-5189, USA

Herman, Axel (Model)
c/o Celebrity Stylist *Ford Models (NY)*
238 E 4th St
New York, NY 10009-7425

Herman, Bill (Athlete, Basketball Player)
200 Laurel Lake Dr Apt 305
Hudson, OH 44236-2156, USA

Herman, Dave (Athlete, Football Player)
19 Stephens Ln
Valhalla, NY 10595-1601, USA

Herman, David J (Business Person)
Bahnhofplatz 1
Russelsheim 65429, GERMANY

Herman, Jerry (Composer, Musician)
1100 Alta Loma Rd Apt 1508
West Hollywood, CA 90069-2441, USA

Herman, Micah (Director)
c/o Joanna (Joanie) Burstein *Burstein Company, The*
15304 W Sunset Blvd Ste 208
Pacific Palisades, CA 90272-3656, USA

Herman, Pee-Wee (Actor, Comedian)
PO Box 29373
Los Angeles, CA 90029-0373

Hermann, Allen M (Physicist)
2704 Lookout View Dr
Golden, CO 80401-2520, USA

Hermann, Mark (Athlete, Football Player)
8525 Tidewater Dr
Indianapolis, IN 46236-8917, USA

Hermannson, Dustin M (Baseball Player)
9002 E Rimrock Dr
Scottsdale, AZ 85255-9133, USA

Hermannsson, Steingrimur (Prime Minister)
Mavanes 19
Gardaba 210, ICELAND

Hermansen, Chad (Athlete, Baseball Player)
2104 Rhonda Ter
Henderson, NV 89074-0651, USA

Hermanski, Gene (Athlete, Baseball Player)
1 Fairwoods Ct
Homosassa, FL 34446-8239, USA

Hermanson, Dustin (Athlete, Baseball Player)
9002 E Rimrock Dr
Scottsdale, AZ 85255-9133, USA

Hermaszewski, Miroslav (Astronaut, General)
Ul Czeczota 25
Warsaw 02-650, POLAND

Hermeling, Terry (Athlete, Football Player)
717 NW 16th Ave
Portland, OR 97209-2301, USA

Hermida, Jeremy (Athlete, Baseball Player)
3728 Paces Park Cir SE
Smyrna, GA 30080-6874, USA

Hermiston, Michael (Stylist)
c/o Staff Member *Mark Edward Inc*
325 W 8th St # 1011
New York, NY 10018, USA

Hermits s/ Peter Noone, Herman's (Music Group, Musician)
1482 E Valley Rd Ste 515
Montecito, CA 93108-1200, USA

Hermlin, Stephan (Writer)
Hermann-Hesse-Str 39
Berlin 13156, GERMANY

Hermon, John C (Government Official, Lawyer)
Warren Road Donaghadee
County Down, NORTHERN IRELAND

Herms, George (Artist)
357 N La Brea Ave
Los Angeles, CA 90036-2517, USA

Hern, Tom (Actor)
c/o Simon Millar *Rumble Media*
1620 Broadway Ste C
Santa Monica, CA 90404-2777, USA

Hernandez, Adrian (Athlete, Baseball Player)
12821 Darby Ridge Dr
Tampa, FL 33624-4304, USA

Hernandez, Angel (Athlete, Baseball Player)
501 Cypress Xing
Wellington, FL 33414-6369, USA

Hernandez, Carlos (Athlete, Baseball Player)
PO Box 122000
San Diego, CA 92112-2000, USA

Hernandez, David (Musician)

Hernandez, Evelio (Athlete, Baseball Player)
3004 SW 113th Ave
Miami, FL 33165-2228, USA

Hernandez, Genaro (Boxer)
24442 Ferrocarril
Mission Viejo, CA 92691-4027, USA

Hernandez, Guillermo (Willie) (Baseball Player)
PO Box 125
Aguada, PR 00602-0125, USA

Hernandez, Jackie (Athlete, Baseball Player)
13390 NE 7th Ave Apt 103
North Miami, FL 33161-7509, USA

Hernandez, Jay (Actor)
9560 Wilshire Blvd Ste 500
Beverly Hills, CA 90212-2401, USA

Hernandez, Jeremy (Athlete, Baseball Player)
11522 Wistful Vista Way
Porter Ranch, CA 91326-4300, USA

Hernandez, Jose A (Athlete, Baseball Player)
6724 Scimitar Ave
Orlando, FL 32812-3823, USA

Hernandez, Julio (Stylist)
c/o Staff Member *Mercury Artists*
8460 Higuera St Fl 2
Culver City, CA 90232-2520, USA

Hernandez, Keith (Athlete, Baseball Player)
c/o Staff Member *SportsNet New York*
75 Rockefeller Plz
New York, NY 10019-6908, USA

Hernandez, Leo (Athlete, Baseball Player)
1352 SW 75th Ave
Miami, FL 33144-4422, USA

Hernandez, Livan (Athlete, Baseball Player)
560 Gate Ln
Miami, FL 33137-3361, USA

Hernandez, Los Bros (Artist)
c/o Staff Member *Fantagraphics Books*
7563 Lake City Way NE
Seattle, WA 98115-4218, USA

Hernandez, Matt (Athlete, Football Player)
PO Box 682
Eastpointe, MI 48021-0682, USA

Hernandez, Orlando (Athlete, Baseball Player)
1001 Brickell Bay Dr Ste 1710
Miami, FL 33131-4939, USA

Hernandez, Robert J (Business Person)
600 Grant St
Pittsburgh, PA 15219-2702, USA

Hernandez, Roberto (Athlete, Baseball Player)
10764 Woodchase Cir
Orlando, FL 32836-5870, USA

Hernandez, Rodolfo P (War Hero)
5328 Bluewater Place College Lks
Fayetteville, NC 28311, USA

Hernandez, Rudy (Athlete, Baseball Player)
8 Calle Rodriguez Serra
San Juan, PR 00907-1456, USA

Hernandez, Rudy (Athlete, Baseball Player)
PO Box 855
Beloit, WI 53512-0855, USA

Hernandez, Runelvys (Athlete, Baseball Player)
18717 E 24th Street Ct S
Independence, MO 64057-2474, USA

Hernandez, Xavier (Athlete, Baseball Player)
3002 E Autumn Run Cir
Sugar Land, TX 77479-2636, USA

Hernandez Colon, Rafael (Ex-Governor)
P.O. Box 4071
San Juan, PR 902, USA

Herndon, Junior (Athlete, Baseball Player)
1477 Sequoia Ave
Craig, CO 81625-3732, USA

Herndon, Kelly (Athlete, Football Player)
9838 Country Club Cir
Twinsburg, OH 44087-2944, USA

Herndon, Larry (Athlete, Baseball Player)
6149 Brunswick Rd
Arlington, TN 38002-6936, USA

Herndon, Mark J (Music Group, Musician)
RR 1 Box 239A
Mentone, AL 35984, USA

Herndon, Ty (Music Group)
PO Box 121858
Nashville, TN 37212-1858, USA

Heron, Fred (Athlete, Football Player)
3908 Brook Valley Cir
Stockton, CA 95219, USA

Heroux, Yves (Athlete, Hockey Player)
176 Boul Terrebonne
Terrebonne, QC J6W 5R5, Canada

Herr, John C (Scientist)
Med Center Immunology Dept
Charlottesville, VA 22903, USA

Herr, Matt (Athlete, Hockey Player)
1951 Holly Creek Pl
Concord, CA 94521-1550, USA

Herr, Thomas M (Tommy) (Athlete, Baseball Player)
1077 Olde Forge Xing
Lancaster, PA 17601-1738, USA

Herranz Casado, Julian Cardinal (Religious Leader)
Piazza Pio XII #10
Rome 193, ITALY

Herren, James (Athlete, Football Player)
224 Monongahela Ave
Glassport, PA 15045-1319, USA

Herrera, Anthony (Athlete, Football Player)
c/o Chad Speck *Allegiant Athletic Agency*
35 Market Sq Ste 201
Knoxville, TN 37902-1420, USA

Herrera, Carl (Athlete, Basketball Player)
1201 Dulles Ave Apt 6305
Stafford, TX 77477-5730, USA

Herrera, Carolina (Designer, Fashion Designer)
501 Fashion Ave # 1700
New York, NY 10018-5903, USA

Herrera, Caroline (Designer, Fashion Designer)
501 Seventh Ave Fl 17
New York, NY 10018, USA

Herrera, Efren (Athlete, Football Player)
861 Atlanta Ct
Claremont, CA 91711-2515, USA

Herrera, Jaime (Congressman, Politician)
1130 Longworth Hob
Washington, DC 20515-0606, USA

Herrera, Kristin (Actor)
c/o David Eisenberg *Protege Entertainment*
710 E Angeleno Ave
Burbank, CA 91501-2213, USA

Herrera, Pamela (Ballerina)
890 Broadway
New York, NY 10003-1211, USA

Herrera, Silvestre S (War Hero)
7222 W Windsor Blvd
Glendale, AZ 85303-6130, USA

Herriage, Troy (Athlete, Baseball Player)
238 California Ave
Oakdale, CA 95361-2904, USA

Herring, Harold (Athlete, Football Player)
14130 Rosemary Ln Apt 3116
Largo, FL 33774-2916, USA

Herring, Laura
4702 N 36th St
Phoenix, AZ 85018-3423

Herring, Lynn (Actor)
37900 Road 800
Raymond, CA 93653-9714, USA

Herring, Vincent (Composer, Musician)
1906 Chet Atkins Pl Apt 502
Nashville, TN 37212-2122, USA

Herring-James, Katie (Baseball Player)
143 Grouse Ridge Rd
Tamaqua, PA 18252-5442, USA

Herrington, John B (Astronaut)
4367 Bays Water Dr
Colorado Springs, CO 80920-7636, USA

Herrington, John S (Business Person, Secretary)
525 B St
San Diego, CA 92101-4420, USA

Herrman, Ed (Athlete, Baseball Player)
13153 Tobiasson Rd
Poway, CA 92064-4308, USA

Herrmann, Don (Athlete, Football Player)
PO Box 318
Brookside, NJ 07926-0318, USA

Herrmann, Edward (Ed) (Actor)
220 E 23rd St Ste 400
New York, NY 10010-4669, USA

Herrmann, Mark (Athlete, Football Player)
8525 Tidewater Dr
Indianapolis, IN 46236-8917, USA

Herrnstein, John (Athlete, Baseball Player)
603 Seminole Rd
Chillicothe, OH 45601-1547, USA

Herrod, Jeff (Athlete, Football Player)
5518 Southern Mist Dr Apt C
Indianapolis, IN 46237-7336, USA

Herron, Bruce (Athlete, Football Player)
8504 S Calumet Ave
Chicago, IL 60619-6026, USA

Herron, Cindy (Music Group)
75 Rockefeller Plz # 1200
New York, NY 10019-6908, USA

Herron, Denis (Athlete, Hockey Player)
12841 Marsh Pointe Way
West Palm Beach, FL 33418-6973, USA

Herron, Keith (Athlete, Basketball Player)
5374 Chew Ave Apt G2
Philadelphia, PA 19138-2804, USA

Herron, Robert J (Architect)
28-30 Rivington St
London EC2A 3DU, UNITED KINGDOM (UK)

Herron, Tim (Athlete, Golfer)
20440 Linden Rd
Excelsior, MN 55331-9371, USA

Herrscher, Rick (Athlete, Baseball Player)
7714 Marquette St
Dallas, TX 75225-4413, USA

Hersch, Fred (Music Group, Musician)
PO Box 9532
Madison, WI 53715, USA

Hersch, Michael (Composer)
30 W 63rd St Apt 15S
New York, NY 10023-7115, USA

Herschler, E David (Artist)
PO Box 5859
Santa Barbara, CA 93150-5859, USA

Hersh, Earl (Athlete, Baseball Player)
682 Morning Glory Dr
Hanover, PA 17331-7828, USA

Hersh, Kristin (Composer, Music Group, Songwriter, Writer)
c/o Staff Member *Concerted Efforts*
PO Box 440326
Somerville, MA 02144-0004, USA

Hersh, Seymour (Journalist, Writer)
1211 Connecticut Ave NW
Washington, DC 20036-2700, USA

Hershberger, Mike (Athlete, Baseball Player)
2887 Carie Hill Cir NW
Massillon, OH 44646-2362, USA

Hershey, Barbara (Actor)
c/o Jill Littman *Impression Entertainment*
9229 W Sunset Blvd Ste 700
West Hollywood, CA 90069-3407, USA

Hershey, Erin (Actor)
PO Box 16212
Irvine, CA 92623-6212, USA

Hershey, Maralyn
37337 Green Level Rd
Wakefield, VA 23888-2525

Hershey-Reeser, Esther Anne (Baseball Player)
3450 Compass Rd
Gap, PA 17527-9006, USA

Hershiser, Orel L Q (Athlete, Baseball Player)
7163 Helsem Bnd
Dallas, TX 75230-1946, USA

Hershko, Avram (Nobel Prize Laureate)
Taub Building
Haifa 32000, Israel

Herta, Bryan (Race Car Driver)
c/o Gary Herta 3331 Shellbrook Ct
Arlington, TX 76016, USA

Hertel, Rob (Athlete, Football Player)
1707 Camden Pkwy
South Pasadena, CA 91030-4913, USA

Herter, Jason (Athlete, Hockey Player)
PO Box 10367
Fargo, ND 58106-0367, USA

Hertford, Chelsea (Actor)
345 E Tujunga Ave
Burbank, CA 91502-1339, USA

Hertweck, Neal (Athlete, Baseball Player)
111 Leesburg Ln
Troutman, NC 28166-7600, USA

Hertwig, Craig (Athlete, Football Player)
249 Bloomfield St
Athens, GA 30605-1203, USA

Hertz, C Hellmuth (Physicist)
Physics School
Lund, SWEDEN

Hertz, Steve (Athlete, Baseball Player)
10211 SW 96th Ter
Miami, FL 33176-2704, USA

Hertzberg, Daniel (Journalist)
200 Liberty St
New York, NY 10281-1003, USA

Hertzberger, Herman (Architect)
Box 74665
Amsterdam, BR 1070, NETHERLANDS

Hervey, Jason (Actor)
2049 Century Park E Ste 2500
Los Angeles, CA 90067-3127, USA

Hervey, Matt (Athlete, Hockey Player)
4903 E Harvey Way
Long Beach, CA 90808-1603, USA

Herzenberg, Caroline Littlejohn (Physicist)
1700 E 56th St Apt 2707
Chicago, IL 60637-5092, USA

Herzfeld, John (Director)
c/o Staff Member *WmE2 (Endeavor-LA)*
9601 Wilshire Blvd Fl 3
Beverly Hills, CA 90210-5219, USA

Herzfeld, John M (Director)
955 Carrillo Dr Ste 300
Los Angeles, CA 90048-5400, USA

Herzigova, Eva (Model)
c/o Scott Lipps *One Model Management*
42 Bond St Apt 2
New York, NY 10012-2428, USA

Herzlinger, Brian (Director)
c/o Naren Desai *Brillstein Entertainment Partners*
9150 Wilshire Blvd Ste 350
Beverly Hills, CA 90212-3453, USA

Herzner, Uli (Stylist)
c/o Staff Member *Ford Models (Miami)*
311 Lincoln Rd Ste 205
Miami Beach, FL 33139-3150, USA

Herzog, Arthur III (Writer)
4 E 81st St
New York, NY 10028-0235, USA

Herzog, Jacques (Architect)
Rheinschanze 6
Basel 4056, SWITZERLAND

Herzog, Maurice (Mountaineer)
84 Chemin De La Tournette
Chamoinix-Mont-Blanc 74400, FRANCE

Herzog, Roman (Ex-President, Politician, President)
Schloss Bellevue Spreeweg 1
Berlin 10557, GERMANY

Herzog, Werner (Director)
Spiegelgasse 9
Vienna 1010, Austria

Herzog, Whitey (Athlete, Baseball Player, Coach)
9426 Sappington Estates Dr
Saint Louis, MO 63127-1664, USA

Hesburgh, Father Theodore
1320 Hesburgh Library
South Bend, IN 46566

Hesburgh, Theodore M (Educator)
1301 Hesburgh Library
Notre Dame, IN 46556-5629, USA

Heseltine, Michael R D (Government Official)
Thenford House near Banbury
Oxon OX17 2BX, UNITED KINGDOM (UK)

Hesketh, Joe (Athlete, Baseball Player)
202 Glenridge Rd
East Aurora, NY 14052-2625, USA

Heskin, Kam (Actor)
c/o Susan Calogerakis *Thruline Entertainment*
9250 Wilshire Blvd Ground Fl
Beverly Hills, CA 90212, USA

Heslov, Grant (Actor, Director)
c/o Rick Ax *Gold Coast Management*
438 S Venice Blvd Apt 5
Venice, CA 90291-4695, USA

Hess, Bob (Athlete, Hockey Player)
PO Box 598
Chesterfield, MO 63006-0598, USA

Hess, Erika (Skier)
Aeschi
Gratenort 6388, SWITZERLAND

Hess, Ilse
Gailenberg 22
Hindelang/Allgau, GERMANY D-87541

Hess, Jared (Director, Writer)
2644 30th St
Santa Monica, CA 90405-3060, USA

Hess, John B (Business Person)
1185 Avenue of the Americas
New York, NY 10036-2601, USA

Hess, Sandra (Actor)
c/o Chris Henze *Thruline Entertainment*
9250 Wilshire Blvd Ground Fl
Beverly Hills, CA 90212, USA

Hesseman, Howard (Actor)
1505 10th St
Santa Monica, CA 90401-2805, USA

Hessenland, Dagmar
Amsterdamer Str. 3
Munich, GERMANY D-80805

Hession, Therese (Athlete, Golfer)
3871 Stonesthrow Ln
Hilliard, OH 43026-5712, USA

Hessler, Curtis A (Publisher)
Times-Mirror Square
Los Angeles, CA 90053, USA

Hessler, Gordon (Director)
8910 Holly Pl
Los Angeles, CA 90046-1836, USA

Hessler, Robert R (Oceanographer)
Biodiversity Dept
La Jolla, CA 92037, USA

Hest, Ari (Musician)
c/o Staff Member *Paradigm (Monterey)*
404 W Franklin St
Monterey, CA 93940-2303, USA

Hester, Dan (Athlete, Basketball Player)
13846 N Sunset Dr
Fountain Hills, AZ 85268-3173, USA

Hester, Devin (Athlete, Football Player)
c/o Eugene Parker *Maximum Sports Management*
6435 W Jefferson Blvd # 197
Fort Wayne, IN 46804-6203, USA

Hester, Jessie L (Athlete, Football Player)
12813 Pineacre Ct
Wellington, FL 33414-4140, USA

Hester, Paul V (General)
Commander Special Operations Command
Hurlburt Field, FL 32544, USA

Hetfield, James (Musician)
2020 Union St
San Francisco, CA 94123-4103, USA

Hetherington, Eileen M (Doctor)
Psychology Dept Gilmer Hall
Charlottesville, VA, USA

Hetki, Johnny (Athlete, Baseball Player)
4004 Stary Dr
Cleveland, OH 44134-5823, USA

Hetrick, Jennifer (Actor)
c/o Staff Member *AKA Talent Agency*
6310 San Vicente Blvd Ste 200
Los Angeles, CA 90048-5488, USA

Hettema, Dave (Athlete, Football Player)
31 Desert Sky Rd SE
Albuquerque, NM 87123-3983, USA

Hettich, Arthur M (Editor)
180 Montague St Apt 19E
Brooklyn, NY 11201-3620, USA

Hettiger, Julie (Stylist)
c/o Staff Member *JH Creative*
3830 Westerman St
Houston, TX 77005-1138, USA

Hetzel, Eric (Athlete, Baseball Player)
2271 Hetzel Rd
Crowley, LA 70526-8318, USA

Hetzel, Fred (Athlete, Basketball Player)
40290 Iron Liege Ct
Leesburg, VA 20176-7170, USA

Heuga, Jimmie (Skier)
PO Box 686
Avon, CO 81620-0686, USA

Heuring, Lori (Actor)
c/o Holly Shakoor *42West (LA)*
11400 W Olympic Blvd Ste 1100
Los Angeles, CA 90064-1579, USA

Heverly-Williams, Ruth (Baseball Player)
520 Tennis Ave
Ambler, PA 19002-6015, USA

Heward, Jamie (Athlete, Hockey Player)
159 Bentley Dr
Regina, SK S4N 4S7, Canada

Hewett, Christopher
1422 N Sweetzer Ave Apt 110
Los Angeles, CA 90069-1527

Hewett, Howard (Music Group)
6014 N Pointe Pl
Woodland Hills, CA 91367-5500, USA

Hewgley, Claude (Athlete, Football Player)
55 Silvermont Dr
Spring, TX 77382-2007, USA

Hewish, Anthony (Nobel Prize Laureate)
Pryor's Cottage Kingston
Cambridge CB3 7NQ, UNITED KINGDOM (UK)

Hewitt, Angela (Musician)
3436 Springhill Rd
Lafayette, CA 94549-2535, USA

Hewitt, Bob (Tennis Player)
822 Boylston St Ste 203
Chestnut Hill, MA 02467-2504, USA

Hewitt, Christopher (Actor)
154 E 66th St
New York, NY 10065-6643, USA

Hewitt, Heather
6324 Tahoe Dr
Los Angeles, CA 90068-1654

Hewitt, Jennifer Love (Actor)
c/o Danielle Thomas *Untitled Entertainment (LA)*
350 S Beverly Dr Ste 200
Beverly Hills, CA 90212-4819, USA

Hewitt, Martin (Actor)
2396 Fitzgerald Rd
Simi Valley, CA 93065-4938, USA

Hewitt, Paul (Basketball Player, Coach)
Athletic
Atlanta, GA 30332-0001, USA

Hewitt, Peter (Director, Producer, Writer)
c/o Jenne Casarotto *Casarotto Ramsay & Associates Ltd (UK)*
Waverley House 7-12 Noel St
London W1F 8GQ, UK

Hewko, Robert (Athlete, Football Player)
100 Lincoln Rd Apt 634
Miami, FL 33139-2013, USA

Hewlett, David (Actor)
c/o Shelley Browning *Magnolia Entertainment (LA)*
9595 Wilshire Blvd Ste 601
Beverly Hills, CA 90212-2506, USA

Hewlett, Donald
King's Head House Island Wall
Whitstable
Kent, ENGLAND CT5 1EP

Hewlett, Howard (Music Group)
PO Box 3172
Beverly Hills, CA 90212-0172, USA

Hewlett, Mark (Reality TV Star)
c/o Jerry Shandrew *Shandrew Public Relations*
1050 S Stanley Ave
Los Angeles, CA 90019-6634, USA

Hewson, Jack (Athlete, Basketball Player)
114 Tahlequah Ln
Loudon, TN 37774-3143, USA

Hewson, John (Government Official)
10 Spring St # 14
Sydney, NSW 2000, AUSTRALIA

Hextall, Dennis H (Athlete, Hockey Player)
2631 Harvest Hill Dr
Brighton, MI 48114-8299, USA

Hextall, Ronald (Ron) (Athlete, Hockey Player)
570 29th St
Manhattan Beach, CA 90266-2212, USA

Hextall Jr, Brian (Athlete, Hockey Player)
908-6880 Wallace Dr
Brentwood Bay, BC V8M 1N8, Canada

Hey, John D (Economist, Mathematician)
Economics Dept Heslington
York YO1 5DD, UNITED KINGDOM (UK)

Hey, Virginia (Actor)
c/o Michael Henderson *Heresun Management*
4119 W Burbank Blvd
Burbank, CA 91505-2122, USA

Heydeman, Greg (Athlete, Baseball Player)
702 Ramona Ave
Monterey, CA 93940-5430, USA

Heyland, Rob
The Manor Middle Lyttleton
Worcestershire, ENGLAND

Heyman, Arthur B (Art) (Athlete, Basketball Player)
7139 Groveland Farms Rd
Groveland, FL 34736-8992, USA

Heyman, Richard (Biologist)
9393 Towne Centre Dr Ste 100
San Diego, CA 92121-3070, USA

Heymann, C. David (Writer)
c/o Staff Member *Simon & Schuster*
1230 Avenue of the Americas Fl CONC1
New York, NY 10020-1586, USA

Heyward, Cameron (Football Player)
c/o Pat Dye Jr *SportsTrust Advisors - GA*
3340 Peachtree Rd NE Fl 16
Atlanta, GA 30326-1000, USA

Heywood, Anne (Actor)
9966 Liebe Dr
Beverly Hills, CA 90210-1037, USA

Heywood, Ralph (Athlete, Football Player)
2914 State Highway 173 S
Bandera, TX 78003-4602, USA

Hiatt, Andrew (Biologist)
10666 N Torrey Pines Rd
La Jolla, CA 92037-1027, USA

Hiatt, Jack (Athlete, Baseball Player)
715 E 1st St
Coquille, OR 97423-1904, USA

Hiatt, John (Music Group, Musician, Songwriter, Writer)
c/o Staff Member *United Talent Agency (UTA)*
9560 Wilshire Blvd Fl 5
Beverly Hills, CA 90212-2400, USA

Hiatt, Phil (Athlete, Baseball Player)
30 Littleton St
Cantonment, FL 32533-6558, USA

Hiatt, Shana (Actor, Model)
c/o Jerry Shandrew *Shandrew Public Relations*
1050 S Stanley Ave
Los Angeles, CA 90019-6634, USA

Hibbard, Greg (Athlete, Baseball Player)
1957 Arden Landing Cv S
Germantown, TN 38139-5704, USA

Hibbert, Edward (Actor)
14724 Ventura Blvd Ste 505
Sherman Oaks, CA 91403-3505, USA

Hibbs, Jim (Athlete, Baseball Player)
4659 Foothill Rd
Ventura, CA 93003-1903, USA

Hick, Graeme A (Cricketer)
New Road
Worcester, UNITED KINGDOM (UK)

Hick, John H (Religious Leader)
144 Oak Tree Lane Selly Oak
Birmingham B29 6HU, UNITED KINGDOM (UK)

Hickam, Homer H Jr (Writer)
9532 Hemlock Dr SE
Huntsville, AL 35803-1165, USA

Hickcox, Charles B (Charlie) (Swimmer)
8315 E Redfield Rd
Scottsdale, AZ 85260-3535, USA

Hicke, Ernie (Athlete, Hockey Player)
3413 Cimmeron Ct
Rocklin, CA 95677-1502, USA

Hickenbottom, Michael (Wrestler)
c/o Kerry Rodgerson *World Wrestling Entertainment (WWE)*
1241 E Main St
Stamford, CT 06902-3520, USA

Hickenlooper, John (Governor, Politician)
136 State Capitol
Denver, CO 80203-1792, USA

Hickerson, Bryan (Athlete, Baseball Player)
275 S Hunters Rdg
Warsaw, IN 46582-5645, USA

Hickerson, Gene (Athlete)
4471 Nagel Rd
Avon, OH 44011-2735, USA

Hickey, Bo (Athlete, Football Player)
PO Box 1143
New Canaan, CT 06840-1143, USA

Hickey, John Benjamin (Actor)
c/o Sarah Fargo *Paradigm (NY)*
360 N Crescent Dr
Beverly Hills, CA 90210-4874, USA

Hickey, Kevin (Athlete, Baseball Player)
5715 S Mason Ave
Chicago, IL 60638-3606, USA

Hickey, Maurice (Publisher)
65015th St
Denver, CO 80202, USA

Hickey, Pat (Athlete, Hockey Player)
80 Oneida Blvd
Ancaster, ON L9G 4S5, Canada

Hickey, Thomas J (General)
2127 Bobbyber Dr
Vienna, VA 22182-4026, USA

Hickey, William V (Business Person)
Park 80 E
Saddle Brook, NJ 7663, USA

Hickland, Catherine (Actor)
255 W 84th St Apt 2A
New York, NY 10024-4322, USA

Hickman, Dallas (Athlete, Football Player)
6521 E Dreyfus Ave
Scottsdale, AZ 85254-3915, USA

Hickman, Darryl (Actor)
171 Hermosillo Rd
Santa Barbara, CA 93108-2414, USA

Hickman, Dwayne (Actor)
PO Box 17226
Encino, CA 91416-7226, USA

Hickman, Fred (Sportscaster)
1050 Techwood Dr NW
Atlanta, GA 30318-5604, USA

Hickman, Jesse (Athlete, Baseball Player)
1801 Jewel St
Pineville, LA 71360-5156, USA

Hickman, Jim (Athlete, Baseball Player)
PO Box 455
Henning, TN 38041-0455, USA

Hickman, Larry (Athlete, Football Player)
5519 Westchester Dr
Tyler, TX 75703-6009, USA

Hickman, Tracy (Writer)
c/o Staff Member *HarperCollins Publishers*
10 E 53rd St C/O Author Mail Floor 7
New York, NY 10022, USA

Hickox, Edwin (Attorney, Baseball Player)
1721 Baron Ct
Port Orange, FL 32128-6789, USA

Hickox, Edwin (Athlete, Baseball Player)
1721 Baron Ct
Port Orange, FL 32128-6789, USA

Hickox, Marc
10 St Mary St # 308
Toronto, CANADA Ont. M4Y 1

Hickox, Richard S (Conductor)
35 Ellington St
London N7 8PN, UNITED KINGDOM (UK)

Hicks, Adam (Actor)
c/o Mona Loring *MLC PR*
7080 Hollywood Blvd Ste 903
Los Angeles, CA 90028-6936, USA

Hicks, Alex (Athlete, Hockey Player)
7511 E Tailspin Ln
Scottsdale, AZ 85255-4632, USA

Hicks, Betty (Athlete, Golfer)
669 Canyon View Dr
Laguna Beach, CA 92651-2671, USA

Hicks, Buddy (Athlete, Baseball Player)
1526 N Dixie Downs Rd Unit 26
Saint George, UT 84770-4105, USA

Hicks, Catherine (Actor)
c/o Margrit Polak *Margrit Polak Management*
1954 Hillhurst Ave Ste 405
Los Angeles, CA 90027-2722, USA

Hicks, Dan (Music Group)
PO Box 245
Sausalito, CA 94966-0245, USA

Hicks, Dan (Sportscaster)
30 Rockefeller Plz
New York, NY 10112-0015, USA

Hicks, Doug (Athlete, Hockey Player)
8711 138 St NW
Edmonton, AB T5R 0E2, Canada

Hicks, Eric (Athlete, Football Player)
5761 Carriage Hill Dr
Erie, PA 16509-3161, USA

Hicks, Esther (Motivational Speaker, Writer)
PO Box 690070
San Antonio, TX 78269-0070, USA

Hicks, Glenn (Athlete, Hockey Player)
2 Alexis St
Red Deer, AB T4R 3E6, Canada

Hicks, Jerry (Motivational Speaker, Writer)
PO Box 690070
San Antonio, TX 78269-0070, USA

Hicks, Jim (Athlete, Baseball Player)
9331 Portal Dr
Houston, TX 77031-2210, USA

Hicks, Jimmy (Musician)
4110 N Shore Dr
West Palm Beach, FL 33407-3202, USA

Hicks, Joe (Athlete, Baseball Player)
2707 Brookmere Rd
Charlottesville, VA 22901-1106, USA

Hicks, Michele (Actor)
c/o Eric Black *Anonymous Content (AC-LA)*
3531 Hayden Ave
Culver City, CA 90232, USA

Hicks, Michelle (Actor)
c/o Staff Member *Innovative Artists (LA)*
1505 10th St
Santa Monica, CA 90401-2805, USA

Hicks, Robert (Athlete, Football Player)
2544 Hightower Ct NW
Atlanta, GA 30318-7412, USA

Hicks, Scott (Director)
PO Box 824
Kent Town 5071, SOUTH AFRICA

Hicks, Sylvester (Athlete, Football Player)
32 Barrymore Cv
Jackson, TN 38305-6462, USA

Hicks, Taylor (Musician, Reality TV Star)
c/o K. Blaine Johnston *Rogues Gallery*
20 Clinton St Apt C7
New York, NY 10002-1755, USA

Hicks, Thomas O (Baseball Player)
5511 Walnut Hill Ln
Dallas, TX 75229-6610, USA

Hicks, Tom (Athlete, Football Player)
207 Rivershire Ln Apt 106
Lincolnshire, IL 60069-3808, USA

Hicks, Vicki Cheung (Stylist)
2 S Hill Ct
Morristown, NJ 07960-3368, USA

Hicks, W K (Athlete, Football Player)
10149 Kemp Forest Dr
Houston, TX 77080-2509, USA

Hicks, Wayne (Athlete, Hockey Player)
7726 E Buteo Dr
Scottsdale, AZ 85255-4656, USA

Hicks Jr, John C (Athlete, Football Player)
3287 Green Cook Rd
Johnstown, OH 43031-9208, USA

Hidalgo, John (Government Official)
1899 L St NW
Washington, DC 20036-3804, USA

Hiddleston, Tom (Actor)
c/o Jon Rubenstein *Authentic Talent and Literary Management*
45 Main St Ste 1004
Brooklyn, NY 11201-8200, USA

Hide, Herbie (Boxer)
10 Western Road Romford
Essex RM1 3JT, UNITED KINGDOM (UK)

Hide, Raymond (Geophysicist, Physicist)
Jesus College
Oxford OX1 3DW, UNITED KINGDOM (UK)

Hieb, Richard J (Astronaut)
7515 Mission Dr
Lanham Seabrook, MD 20706-2267, USA

Hiebert, Erwin N (Historian)
40 Payson Rd
Belmont, MA 02478-2718, USA

Hiemstra, Ed (Athlete, Football Player)
40 Canyon Dr # B
Heppner, OR 97836-2007, USA

Hier, Marvin (Activist, Religious Leader)
9766 W Pico Blvd
Los Angeles, CA 90035, USA

Hieronymus, Clara W (Journalist)
50 Spring St
Savannah, TN 38372-1454, USA

Hietpas, Joe (Athlete, Baseball Player)
611 E Timberline Dr
Appleton, WI 54913-7104, USA

Hi-Five
PO Box 313030
Jamaica, NY 11431-3030

Higashi, Satoshi (Athlete, Golfer)
45 Higashi-Matsushita-Cho Kanda
Chiyoda-ku
Tokyo 101, Japan

Higdon, Bruce (Cartoonist)
210 Canvasback Ct
Murfreesboro, TN 37130-8855, USA

Higginbotham, Joan E (Astronaut)
1409 Mija Ln
Seabrook, TX 77586-2406, USA

Higginbotham, Patrick E (Judge)
1100 Commerce St
Dallas, TX 75242-1001, USA

Higgins, Al (Producer)
c/o Staff Member *Creative Artists Agency (CAA-LA)*
2000 Avenue of the Stars Ste 100
Los Angeles, CA 90067-4705, USA

Higgins, Brian (Congressman, Politician)
2459 Rayburn Hob
Washington, DC 20515-4311, USA

Higgins, David (Actor)
c/o Ben Feigin *Anonymous Content (AC-LA)*
3531 Hayden Ave
Culver City, CA 90232, USA

Higgins, Dennis (Athlete, Baseball Player)
1123 Boonville Rd
Jefferson City, MO 65109-0621, USA

Higgins, Earle (Athlete, Basketball Player)
29128 Chateau Ct
Farmington Hills, MI 48334-4112, USA

Higgins, J Kenneth (Misc)
PO Box 3707
Seattle, WA 98124-2207, USA

Higgins, Jack (Writer)
September Tide Mont de la Rocque Jersey
Channel Island, UNITED KINGDOM (UK)

Higgins, Jack (Cartoonist, Editor)
59 Waverly Ave
Clarendon Hills, IL 60514-1236, USA

Higgins, John (Coach, Swimmer)
40 Williams Dr
Annapolis, MD 21401-2265, USA

Higgins, Kevin (Athlete, Baseball Player)
10551 Haywood Dr
Las Vegas, NV 89135-2851, USA

Higgins, Mark (Athlete, Baseball Player)
2999 Abbotts Oak Way
Duluth, GA 30097-2193, USA

Higgins, Mike (Athlete, Basketball Player)
137 48th Ave
Greeley, CO 80634-4307, USA

Higgins, Missy (Musician)
c/o Staff Member *EMI Music (Australia)*
PO Box 311
Westwood, MA 02090-0311, Australia

Higgins, Pam (Athlete, Golfer)
5 Pea Pine Ln
Newport Beach, CA 92660, USA

Higgins, Paul (Athlete, Hockey Player)
c/o Staff Member *Toronto Young Nationals Hockey Club*
233-1080 Tapscott Rd
Scarborough, ON M1X 1E7, Canada

Higgins, Robert (Business Person)
1 Federal St
Boston, MA 02110-2012, USA

Higgins, Rod (Athlete, Basketball Player)
743 Mendenhall Ct
Fort Mill, SC 29715-7852, USA

Higgins, Rosalyn (Judge)
Peace Palace
Hague, KJ 2517, NETHERLANDS

Higgins, Scott (Athlete, Baseball Player)
3591 Indian Clover St
Plumas Lake, CA 95961-8740, USA

Higgins, Tim (Athlete, Hockey Player)
c/o Staff Member *Chicago Blackhawks*
1901 W Madison St
Chicago, IL 60612-2459, USA

Higgins, Tom (Athlete, Football Player)
127 Hillgrove Cres SW
Calgary, AB T2V 3K9, Canada

Higginson, Bobby (Athlete, Baseball Player)
2039 Indian Sky Cir
Lakeland, FL 33813-4859, USA

Higginson, John (Doctor)
16 Sundew Rd
Savannah, GA 31411-2955, USA

Higginson, Torri (Actor)
c/o Staff Member *Sci-Fi Channel, The*
100 Universal Plz Bldg 1280/12
Universal City, CA 91608, USA

Higgs, Kenny (Athlete, Basketball Player)
746 Sargent Dr
Owensboro, KY 42301-8332, USA

Higgs, Mark (Athlete, Football Player)
45 NW 156th Ln
Pembroke Pines, FL 33028-1500, USA

High Speed Scene, The (Music Group)
c/o Staff Member *Paradigm (Monterey)*
404 W Franklin St
Monterey, CA 93940-2303, USA

Higham, Scott (Journalist)
1150 15th St NW
Washington, DC 20071-0001, USA

Highman, Charles
4027 Farmouth Dr
Los Angeles, CA 90027-1314

Highmore, Freddie (Actor)
c/o Sue Latimer *Artists Rights Group (ARG)*
4 Great Portland St
London W1W 8PA, UNITED KINGDOM (UK)

Highsmith, Don (Athlete, Football Player)
PO Box 664
Piscataway, NJ 08855-0664, USA

Hightower, John B (Director)
394 Emily Dickinson N
Newport News, VA 23606-1486, USA

Hightower, Rosella (Ballerina, Choreographer, Dancer)
Villa Piege Luiere Parc Florentina Ave Vallauris
Cannes 6400, FRANCE

Highway 101
PO Box 1547
Goodlettsville, TN 37070-1547

Hijuelos, Oscar (Writer)
English Dept 10000 Fulton Ave
Hempstead, NY 11550, USA

Hikaru, Utada (Musician)
c/o Staff Member *Island Records*
825 8th Ave Rm C2
New York, NY 10019-7472, USA

Hiken, Gerald
910 Moreno Ave
Palo Alto, CA 94303-3731

Hil St Soul (Music Group)
c/o Staff Member *Paradigm (Monterey)*
404 W Franklin St
Monterey, CA 93940-2303, USA

Hilario, Maybyner (Nene) (Basketball Player)
Pepsi Center 1000 Chopper Circle
Denver, CO 80204, USA

Hilario, Nene (Athlete, Basketball Player)
c/o Dan Fegan *Lagardere Unlimited - (LA)*
10866 Wilshire Blvd
Los Angeles, CA 90024-4300, USA

Hilbe, Alfred J (Government Official)
9494 Schaan
Garsill 11, LIECHTENSTEIN

Hilbert, Andy (Athlete, Hockey Player)
419 N Michigan Ave
Howell, MI 48843-1505, USA

Hildebrand, John G (Biologist)
629 N Olsen Ave
Tucson, AZ 85719-5136, USA

Hildebrand, Madison (Business Person, Reality TV Star)
29178 Heathercliff Rd
Malibu, CA 90265-4177, USA

Hildebrandt, Dieter
Rollenhagenstr. 3a
Munich, GERMANY D-81739

Hildebrandt, Greg (Cartoonist)
10956 SE Main St
Milwaukie, OR 97222-7644, USA

Hildreth, Eugene A (Doctor)
2000 Cambridge Ave Apt 129
Reading, PA 19610-2741, USA

Hilfiger, Tommy (Designer, Fashion Designer)
601 W 26th St Rm 500
New York, NY 10001-1142, USA

Hilgenberg, Jay W (Athlete, Football Player)
1296 Kimmer Ct
Lake Forest, IL 60045-3669, USA

Hilgenberg, Joel (Athlete, Football Player)
2027 Ridgeway Dr
Iowa City, IA 52245-3239, USA

Hilgenbrinck, Tad (Actor)
c/o Jonathan Howard *Innovative Artists (LA)*
1505 10th St
Santa Monica, CA 90401-2805, USA

Hilgendorf, Tom (Athlete, Baseball Player)
PO Box 124
Camanche, IA 52730-0124, USA

Hilger, Rusty (Athlete, Football Player)
1145 SW 78th Ter
Oklahoma City, OK 73139-2417, USA

Hiljus, Erik (Athlete, Baseball Player)
2253 Demaray Dr
Grants Pass, OR 97527-9147, USA

Hill, A Derek (Artist)
20 John Islip St
London SW1, UNITED KINGDOM (UK)

Hill, Aaron (Actor)
c/o Siri Garber *Platform Public Relations*
2666 N Beachwood Dr
Los Angeles, CA 90068-2308, USA

Hill, Al (Athlete, Hockey Player)
4807 Margaret Ln
Harrisburg, PA 17110-3365, USA

Hill, Anita (Educator)
600 3rd Ave # 200
New York, NY 10016-1901, USA

Hill, Armand (Athlete, Basketball Player)
1626 Laurens Way SW
Atlanta, GA 30311-3718, USA

Hill, Bernard (Actor)
c/o Staff Member *Seven Summits Pictures & Management*
8906 W Olympic Blvd Ground Floor
Beverly Hills, CA 90211, USA

Hill, Bob (Athlete, Basketball Player, Coach)
205 Rio Cordillera
Boerne, TX 78006-5892, USA

Hill, Bobby (Athlete, Baseball Player)
584 Harvard Ave
Santa Clara, CA 95051-6016, USA

Hill, Brendan (Musician)
c/o Staff Member *ArtistDirect*
9046 Lindblade St
Culver City, CA 90232-2513, USA

Hill, Bruce (Athlete, Football Player)
1919 E Citation Ln
Tempe, AZ 85284-4704, USA

Hill, Calvin (Athlete, Football Player)
10300 Walker Lake Dr
Great Falls, VA 22066-3557, USA

Hill, Carolyn (Athlete, Golfer)
5906 Skimmer Point Blvd S
Gulfport, FL 33707-3938, USA

Hill, Cindy (Athlete, Golfer)
2852 NW 8th St
Fort Lauderdale, FL 33311-6637, USA

Hill, Damon G D (Race Car Driver)
PO Box 100 Nelson
Lanscashire BB9 8AQ, UNITED KINGDOM (UK)

Hill, Dan
1407 Mt Pleasant Rd
Toronto, CANADA Ont. M4N 2

Hill, Dan (Music Group, Songwriter, Writer)
1067 Sherwin Rd
Winnipeg, MB R3H 0TB, CANADA

Hill, Daniel W (Dan) (Athlete, Football Player)
171 Montrose Dr
Durham, NC 27707-3929, USA

Hill, Dave (Athlete, Golfer)
3641 Ball Hill Dr
Akron, OH 44333-8305, USA

Hill, Dave (Athlete, Baseball Player)
125 Jenny Lind Dr
Hendersonville, NC 28791-1321, USA

Hill, David H (Athlete, Football Player)
402 Le Grand Dr
Panama City Beach, FL 32413-1324, USA

Hill, David L (Tex) (War Hero)
738 Clayton St
Central, SC 29630-9755, USA

Hill, Derek (Athlete, Football Player)
8939 Gallatin Rd
Pico Rivera, CA 90660-1693, USA

Hill, Donnie (Athlete, Baseball Player)
6 Knob Hl
Laguna Niguel, CA 92677-5903, USA

Hill, Draper (Cartoonist, Editor)
1818 Northbrook Dr
Lancaster, PA 17601-5027, USA

Hill, Dule (Actor)
c/o Katherine Atkinson *Washington Square Arts (LA)*
1041 N Formosa Ave Lot Bldg
West Hollywood, CA 90046-6703, USA

Hill, Dusty (Music Group, Musician)
PO Box 163690
Austin, TX 78716-3690, USA

Hill, Eric (Athlete, Football Player)
5500 Palm Cir
Galveston, TX 77551-5566, USA

Hill, Erica (Television Host)
1 Time Warner Ctr
New York, NY 10019-6038, USA

Hill, Faith (Musician)
c/o Coran Capshaw *Red Light Management (VA)*
PO Box 1467
Charlottesville, VA 22902-1467, USA

Hill, Fred (Athlete, Football Player)
31441 Paseo Riobo
San Juan Capistrano, CA 92675-5524, USA

Hill, Garry (Athlete, Baseball Player)
9602 Willowglen Trl
Charlotte, NC 28215-9767, USA

Hill, Gary (Athlete, Football Player)
6207 Surflanding Ln
Huntington Beach, CA 92648-7507, USA

Hill, Geoffrey W (Writer)
Commonwealth Ave University Professors 745
Boston, MA 02215-1222, USA

Hill, Glenallen (Athlete, Baseball Player)
108 Calvin Pl
Santa Cruz, CA 95060-3124, USA

Hill, Grant (Athlete, Basketball Player)
c/o Jim Tanner *Williams & Connolly*
725 12th St NW
Washington, DC 20005-5901, USA

Hill, Grant (Athlete, Basketball Player)
9600 McCormick Pl
Windermere, FL 34786-8910, USA

Hill, Greg (Athlete, Football Player)
14580 E Beltwood Pkwy
Farmers Branch, TX 75244-3203, USA

Hill, Greg (Athlete, Football Player)
33 Cattail Pond Dr
Frisco, TX 75034-8584, USA

Hill, Greg L (Athlete, Football Player)
33 Cattail Pond Dr
Frisco, TX 75034-8584, USA

Hill, Gregory (Director)
c/o Staff Member *Paul Lane Entertainment*
468 N Camden Dr
Beverly Hills, CA 90210-4507, USA

Hill, Harlon (Athlete, Football Player)
RR 2 Box 276
Killen, AL 35645, USA

Hill, Henry (Writer)
PO Box 1495
Orange, CA 92856-0495, USA

Hill, Ike (Athlete, Football Player)
412 Randolph St
Oak Park, IL 60302-3260, USA

Hill, J D (Athlete, Football Player)
2543 N 53rd Dr
Phoenix, AZ 85035-1910, USA

Hill, Jack (Director, Producer, Writer)
1445 N Fairfax Ave Apt 205
West Hollywood, CA 90046-3927, USA

Hill, James C (Judge)
56 Forsyth St NW
Atlanta, GA 30303-2218, USA

Hill, James T (General)
Commanding General Army Forces Command
Fort McPherson, GA 30330-0001, USA

Hill, J.D. (Athlete, Football Player)
1550 S Yucca St
Chandler, AZ 85286-6859, USA

Hill, Jeremy (Athlete, Baseball Player)
10050 Gooding Dr
Dallas, TX 75229-6209, USA

Hill, Jessie (Music Group, Musician)
1210 Caffin Ave
New Orleans, LA 70117, USA

Hill, Jim (Sportscaster)
77 W 66th St
New York, NY 10023-6201, USA

Hill, Jim (Athlete, Football Player)
4120 Parva Ave
Los Angeles, CA 90027-1365, USA

Hill, John S (Athlete, Football Player)
2005 Boyce Bridge Rd
Creedmoor, NC 27522-8023, USA

Hill, Jonah (Actor)
c/o Matthew (Matt) Labov *Forefront Media*
8500 Melrose Ave Ste 205
West Hollywood, CA 90069-5169, USA

Hill, Julia Butterfly (Misc)
PO Box 3764
Oakland, CA 94609-0764, USA

Hill, Ken (Athlete, Baseball Player)
1360 Shady Oaks Dr
Southlake, TX 76092-4208, USA

Hill, Kenneth (Athlete, Football Player)
121 Hawkins Pl
Boonton, NJ 07005-1127, USA

Hill, Kent (Athlete, Football Player)
630 Hawthorne Pl
Fayetteville, GA 30214-1218, USA

Hill, Kent A (Athlete, Football Player)
630 Hawthorne Pl
Fayetteville, GA 30214-1218, USA

Hill, Kim (Music Group)
PO Box 50358
Nashville, TN 37205-0358, USA

Hill, King (Athlete, Football Player)
7611 Sands Terrace Ln
Spring, TX 77389-2131, USA

Hill, Koyle (Athlete, Baseball Player)
5216 N Valentine Rd
Park City, KS 67219-2718, USA

Hill, Lauryn (Actor, Musician)
c/o Nicole David *WmE2 (Endeavor-LA)*
9601 Wilshire Blvd Fl 3
Beverly Hills, CA 90210-5219, USA

Hill, Madre (Athlete, Football Player)
18 Charleston Ct
Elgin, SC 29045-8521, USA

Hill, Marc (Athlete, Baseball Player)
203 Maple St
Elsberry, MO 63343-1604, USA

Hill, Mike (Athlete, Golfer)
6750 Jefferson Rd
Brooklyn, MI 49230-9717, USA

Hill, Milt (Athlete, Baseball Player)
8401 Avalon Ct
Cumming, GA 30041-5724, USA

Hill, Pat (Football Player)
Athletic
Fresno, CA 93740-0001, USA

Hill, Randal (Athlete, Football Player)
5360 SW 130th Ter
Miramar, FL 33027-5411, USA

Hill, Rich (Athlete, Baseball Player)
17 Spafford Rd
Milton, MA 02186-4408, USA

Hill, Ron (Athlete, Track Athlete)
PO Box 11 Hyde
Cheshire SK14 1RD, UNITED KINGDOM (UK)

Hill, Sean (Athlete, Hockey Player)
2735 E Carob Dr
Chandler, AZ 85286-3118, USA

Hill, Simmie (Athlete, Basketball Player)
1470 Elizabeth Blvd
Pittsburgh, PA 15221-1223, USA

Hill, Steven (Actor)
18 Jill Ln
Monsey, NY 10952-2619, USA

Hill, Susan E (Writer)
Longmoor Farmhouse Ebrington Chipping Campden
Glos GL55 6NW, UNITED KINGDOM (UK)

Hill, Tamia (Musician)
c/o Staff Member *HUFF Events and PR*
325 W 38th St Rm 805
New York, NY 10018-9622, USA

Hill, Terence (Actor)
3 Los Pinos Rd
Santa Fe, NM 87507-4300, USA

Hill, Terrell L (Biologist, Physicist)
5320 Fox Hollow Rd
Eugene, OR 97405-4049, USA

Hill, Thomas (Tom) (Athlete, Track Athlete)
428 Elmcrest Dr
Norman, OK 73071-7053, USA

Hill, Tony (Athlete, Football Player)
729 Forest Bend Dr
Plano, TX 75025-3205, USA

Hill, Tyrone (Baseball Player)
5594 Electric Ave
San Bernardino, CA 92407-2713, USA

Hill, Virgil (Boxer)
1618 Santa Gertrudis Loop
Bismarck, ND 58503-0866, USA

Hill, Virgil L Jr (Admiral)
1000 Glendon Ct
Ambler, PA 19002, USA

Hill, Walter (Director)
836 Greenway Dr
Beverly Hills, CA 90210-3006, USA

Hill, Winston (Athlete, Football Player)
101 Lane Dr
Gladewater, TX 75647-5369, USA

Hill Hearth, Amy
c/o Daniel A (Dan) Strone *Trident Media Group LLC*
41 Madison Ave Fl 36
New York, NY 10010-2257, USA

Hill Smith, Marilyn (Opera Singer)
13 Ardilaun Road Highbury
London N5 2QR, UNITED KINGDOM (UK)

Hillaby, John (Writer)
Lanchesters 102 Fulham Palace Road
London W6 9ER, UNITED KINGDOM (UK)

Hillaker, Harry (Engineer)
1802 Palace Dr
Grand Prairie, TX 75050-2156, USA

Hillan, Patrick (Actor)
11005 Morrison St Apt 206
N Hollywood, CA 91601-3899

Hillary, Edmund P (Mountaineer, Scientist)
278A Remuera Road
Auckland SE2, NEW ZEALAND

Hille, Bertil (Doctor)
10630 Lakeside Ave NE
Seattle, WA 98125-6934, USA

Hille, Einar (Mathematician)
8862 La Jolla Scenic Dr N
La Jolla, CA 92037-1608, USA

Hillebrand, Gerald (Athlete, Football Player)
23 Madison Cir
Davenport, IA 52806-2812, USA

Hillebrecht, Rudolf F H (Architect)
Gneiststr 7
Hanover 30169, GERMANY

Hillegas, Shawn (Athlete, Baseball Player)
870 Rockville Rd
South Fork, PA 15956-3503, USA

Hillel, Shlomo (Government Official)
14 Gelber St
Jerusalem 96755, ISRAEL

Hillen, Bobby (Race Car Driver)
5011 Midlothian Tpke
Richmond, VA 23225, USA

Hillenbrand, Daniel A (Business Person)
700 STATE RR 46 E
Batesville, IN 47006, USA

Hillenbrand, Laura (Writer)
c/o Staff Member *Janklow & Nesbit Associates*
445 Park Ave Fl 13
New York, NY 10022-8628, USA

Hillenbrand, Martin J (Diplomat)
International Trade Security Ctr
Athens, GA 30602-0001, USA

Hillenbrand, Shea (Athlete, Baseball Player)
2614 E Via De Palmas
Gilbert, AZ 85298-2068, USA

Hillenburg, Stephen (Animator, Producer, Writer)
c/o Staff Member *Perry & Neidorf CPA*
9720 Wilshire Blvd Ste 300
Beverly Hills, CA 90212-2015, USA

Hiller, Arthur (Director)
1218 Benedict Canyon Dr
Beverly Hills, CA 90210-2728, USA

Hiller, Jim (Athlete, Coach, Hockey Player)
c/o Staff Member *Chilliwack Bruins*
45323 Hodgins Ave
Chilliwack, BC V2P 8G1, Canada

Hiller, John (Athlete, Baseball Player)
W8085 Becker Dr
Iron Mountain, MI 49801-9385, USA

Hiller, Lee (Journalist)
c/o Staff Member *Artistic Agency*
PO Box 68538
Portland, OR 97268-0538, USA

Hiller, Susan (Artist)
83 Loudoun Road
London NW8 0DL, UNITED KINGDOM (UK)

Hillerman, John (Actor)
12424 Wilshire Blvd
Los Angeles, CA 90025-1052, USA

Hillery, Patrick J (President)
Grasmere Greenfield Road Sutton
Dublin 13, IRELAND

Hilliard, Dalton (Athlete, Football Player)
23 Hermitage Dr
Destrehan, LA 70047-3701, USA

Hilliard, Ike (Athlete, Football Player)
c/o Neil Schwartz *Schwartz & Feinsod*
contact via telephone or email
New York, NY 10603

Hilliard, Issac (Athlete, Football Player)
8240 SW 164th Ter
Palmetto Bay, FL 33157-3653, USA

Hillier, James (Inventor)
22 Arreton Rd # CR31
Princeton, NJ 08540-1402, USA

Hillier, Randy (Athlete, Hockey Player)
308 Brookhaven Ln
Pittsburgh, PA 15241-2582, USA

Hillier, Steve (Music Group, Musician)
2-12 Petonville Road
London N1 9PL, UNITED KINGDOM (UK)

Hillin Jr, Bobby (Race Car Driver)
c/o Staff Member *National Association of Stock Car Racing (NASCAR)*
1801 W Speedway Blvd
Daytona Beach, FL 32114-1215, USA

Hillis, Ali (Actor, Producer)
c/o Staff Member *Pinnacle Public Relations*
8265 W Sunset Blvd Ste 201
Los Angeles, CA 90046-2470, USA

Hillis, Robert (Rib) (Actor)
c/o John Guglielmetti *Continuum Entertainment*
954 3rd Ave Ste 423
New York, NY 10022-2013, USA

Hillis, W Daniel (Danny) (Scientist)
1209 Grand Central Ave
Glendale, CA 91201-2425, USA

Hillman, Avriel (Actor)
PO Box 1234
Rainier, WA 98576-1234, USA

Hillman, Chris (Music Group, Musician, Songwriter, Writer)
433 N Camden Dr Ste 400
Beverly Hills, CA 90210-4408, USA

Hillman, Darnell (Athlete, Basketball Player)
6011 Medora Dr
Indianapolis, IN 46228-1397, USA

Hillman, Dave (Athlete, Baseball Player)
849 Mimosa Dr
Kingsport, TN 37660-2563, USA

Hillman, Eric (Athlete, Baseball Player)
157 Bellaire St
Denver, CO 80220-5632, USA

Hillman, Floyd (Bud) (Athlete, Hockey Player)
28 Cheyenne Crt
Leamington, ON N8H 5E3, Canada

Hillman, Larry (Athlete, Hockey Player)
57 Westland St
St Catharines, ON L2S 3W8, Canada

Hillman, Trey (Athlete, Baseball Player, Coach)
PO Box 419969
Kansas City, MO 64141-6969, USA

Hills, Carla (Secretary)
3125 Chain Bridge Rd NW
Washington, DC 20016-3411, USA

Hills, Roderick M (Business Person, Government Official)
1200 19th St NW
Washington, DC 20036-2402, USA

Hillsong (Musician)
c/o Staff Member *Integrity Music*
1000 Cody Rd S
Mobile, AL 36695-3499, USA

Hillton, Dave (Athlete, Baseball Player)
4910 E Sunnyside Dr
Scottsdale, AZ 85254-4671, USA

Hill-Westerman, Joyce (Baseball Player)
1565 47th Ave
Kenosha, WI 53144-1289, USA

Hilmers, David C (Astronaut)
2846 Bellefontaine St
Houston, TX 77025-1610, USA

Hilmes, Jerome B (General)
4900 Windsor Park
Sarasota, FL 34235-2609, USA

Hilson, Keri (Musician)
c/o Cara Lewis *WmE2 (WMA-NY)*
1325 Avenue of the Americas
New York, NY 10019-6026, USA

Hilton, Barron (Business Person, Philanthropist)
9336 Civic Center Dr
Beverly Hills, CA 90210-3604, USA

Hilton, Fred (Athlete, Basketball Player)
6169 Mourning Dove Dr
Baton Rouge, LA 70817-1107, USA

Hilton, Howard (Athlete, Baseball Player)
106 Redwood Cir
Ventura, CA 93003-3672, USA

Hilton, Janet (Music Group, Musician)
Holly House E Downs Road Bowdon Altrincham
Cheshire WA14 2LH, UNITED KINGDOM (UK)

Hilton, John J (Athlete, Football Player)
3911 S Fairway Dr
Powhatan, VA 23139-7022, USA

Hilton, Kathy
c/o Catherine Saxton *The Saxton Group*
500 5th Ave # 18
New York, NY 10110-0002, USA

Hilton, Nicky (Designer, Heir/Heiress)
3400 S Main St
Los Angeles, CA 90007-4412, USA

Hilton, Paris (Heir/Heiress, Reality TV Star)
c/o Jamie Freed *Paris Hilton Entertainment*
2934 1/2 N Beverly Glen Cir Ste 383
Los Angeles, CA 90077-1724, USA

Hilton, Perez (Entertainer, Writer)
c/o Ben Russo *EMC / Bowery*
8155 Santa Monica Blvd Ste 200
West Hollywood, CA 90046-4986, USA

Hilton, Rick (Business Person)
250 N Canon Dr
Beverly Hills, CA 90210-5322, USA

Hilton, Roy (Athlete, Football Player)
8332 Merrymount Dr
Baltimore, MD 21244-2242, USA

Hilton, Tyler (Actor)
c/o Victoria Blake *Victoria Blake Management*
23622 Calabasas Rd Ste 230
Calabasas, CA 91302-4109, USA

Hilty, Megan (Actor)
c/o Erica Tuchman *One Entertainment (NY)*
12 W 57th St PH 1
New York, NY 10019-3900, USA

Hiltz, Nichole (Actor)
c/o Steve Caserta *Sanders Armstrong Caserta*
2120 Colorado Ave Ste 120
Santa Monica, CA 90404-3561, USA

Hiltzik, Michael A (Journalist)
202 W 1st St
Los Angeles, CA 90012-4105, USA

HIM (Music Group, Musician)
c/o Tim Edwards *Flowerbooking*
1532 N Milwaukee Ave Ste 201
Chicago, IL 60622-6672, USA

Himelstein, Aaron (Actor)
c/o Paul M. Brown *New Wave Entertainment (LA)*
2660 W Olive Ave
Burbank, CA 91505-4525, USA

Himes, Dick (Athlete, Football Player)
615 W Main St
Portland, IN 47371-1708, USA

Himes, James (Congressman, Politician)
119 Cannon Hob
Washington, DC 20515-0501, USA

Himmelfarb, Gertrude (Historian)
2510 Virginia Ave NW
Washington, DC 20037-1902, USA

Himmelman, Peter (Composer, Musician)
230 22nd St
Brentwood, California 94513, USA

Hinault, Bernard (Athlete)
Les Poteries Quessoy
Yffiniac F-22120, France

Hinch, A J (Athlete, Baseball Player)
8415 Avenida De Las Ondas
La Jolla, CA 92037-3026, USA

Hinchliffe, Brett (Athlete, Baseball Player)
37517 Stonegate Cir
Clinton Township, MI 48036-2986, USA

Hinckley Jr, John
2700 Martin Luther King Jr Ave SE
Washington, DC 20032-2601, USA

Hinder (Music Group)
1755 Broadway
New York, NY 10019-3743, USA

Hindle, Art (Actor)
8899 Beverly Blvd # 715
Los Angeles, CA 90048-2412, USA

Hindman, Stan (Athlete, Football Player)
824 Creed Rd
Oakland, CA 94610-1827, USA

Hindmarch, Dave (Athlete, Hockey Player)
3341 Beach Ave
Roberts Creek, BCq V0N 2W2, Canada

Hinds, Aisha (Actor)
c/o Michael Greene *Greene & Associates*
1901 Avenue Of The Stars Ste 130
Los Angeles, CA 90067-6030, USA

Hinds, Ciaran (Actor)
c/o Larry Dalzell *Dalzell & Beresford Ltd*
26 Astwood Mews
London SW7 4DE, UNITED KINGDOM (UK)

Hinds, Cirian (Actor)
c/o Staff Member *WmE2 (Endeavor-LA)*
9601 Wilshire Blvd Fl 3
Beverly Hills, CA 90210-5219, USA

Hinds, Sam (Athlete, Baseball Player)
General Delivery
Fresno, CA 93706-9999, USA

Hinds, Samuel A A (Prime Minister)
Public Buildings
Georgetown, GUYANA

Hinds, William E (Cartoonist)
1301 Spring Oaks Cir
Houston, TX 77055-4703, USA

Hine, Maynard K (Doctor)
1121 W Michigan St
Indianapolis, IN 46202-5211, USA

Hine, Patrick (Misc)
Cox's & Kings 7 Pall Mall
London SW1 5NA, UNITED KINGDOM (UK)

Hiner, Glen H (Business Person)
1 Owens Coming Pkwy
Toledo, OH 43659-0001, USA

Hines, Andre (Athlete, Football Player)
1906 N 44th St
Kansas City, KS 66102-1814, USA

Hines, Cheryl (Actor)
c/o Paul Young *Principato/Young Management*
9465 Wilshire Blvd Ste 430
Beverly Hills, CA 90212-2613, USA

Hines, Deni (Music Group)
49 Hume St # 200
Crows Nest, NSW 2065, AUSTRALIA

Hines, Glen Ray (Athlete, Football Player)
861 N Queen Annes Lace Dr
Fayetteville, AR 72704-5106, USA

Hines, Grainger (Actor, Producer)
c/o Staff Member *Austingrai Productions*
11301 W Olympic Blvd
Los Angeles, CA 90064-1653, USA

Hines, Mimi (Actor)
2540 S Maryland Pkwy
Las Vegas, NV 89109-1627

Hingis, Martina (Tennis Player)
30165 Fairway Dr
Wesley Chapel, FL 33543-4400, USA

Hingorani, Narain G (Engineer)
835 W Big Sand Pl
Oro Valley, AZ 85755-6565, USA

Hings, Donald L (Inventor)
281 Howard Ave
North Burnaby, BC V5B 4Y7, CANADA

Hingsen, Jurgen (Athlete, Track Athlete)
655 Circle Dr
Santa Barbara, CA 93108-1001, USA

Hinkle, Jack (Athlete, Football Player)
2114 Weber Ln
Norristown, PA 19403-3014, USA

Hinkle, Lon (Athlete, Golfer)
PO Box 1347
Bigfork, MT 59911-1347, USA

Hinkle, Marin (Actor)
c/o Staff Member *Innovative Artists (LA)*
1505 10th St
Santa Monica, CA 90401-2805, USA

Hinkle, Robert (Actor)
915 Terrace Dr
Leander, TX 78641-8035, USA

Hinkley, Brent (Actor)
c/o Staff Member *Gage Group, The (LA)*
14724 Ventura Blvd Ste 505
Sherman Oaks, CA 91403-3505, USA

Hinman, Dayle (Misc)
c/o Staff Member *Story House Productions, Inc*
2233 Wisconsin Ave NW Ste 420
Washington, DC 20007-4122, USA

Hinn, Benny (Religious Leader)
PO Box 162000
Irving, TX 75016-2000, USA

Hinnant, Michael (Athlete, Football Player)
43 Ashford Way
Schwenksville, PA 19473-1693, USA

Hinners, Noel (Government Official)
7 Greyswood Ct
Rockville, MD 20854-6149, USA

Hinojosa, Ricardo H (Judge)
PO Box 5007
McAllen, TX 78502-5007, USA

Hinojosa, Ruben (Congressman, Politician)
2262 Rayburn Hob
Washington, DC 20515-0703, USA

Hinojosa, Tish (Music Group, Songwriter, Writer)
PO Box 3304
Austin, TX 78764-3304, USA

Hinote, Dan (Athlete, Hockey Player)
20511 Victoria Dr NW
Elk River, MN 55330-8399, USA

Hinrich, Kirk (Basketball Player)
c/o Staff Member *Chicago Bulls*
1901 W Madison St
Chicago, IL 60612-2459, USA

Hinrichs, Paul (Athlete, Baseball Player)
1982 Brett Dr
Madisonville, KY 42431-9115, USA

Hinse, Andre (Athlete, Hockey Player)
PO Box 237
Fort Cobb, OK 73038-0237, USA

Hinshaw, George (Athlete, Baseball Player)
15125 S Raymond Ave Apt 14
Gardena, CA 90247-3433, USA

Hinske, Eric (Athlete, Baseball Player)
10222 E Southwind Ln Unit 1041
Scottsdale, AZ 85262-4689, USA

Hinsley, Jerry (Athlete, Baseball Player)
4255 Holliday Ln
Las Cruces, NM 88007-5760, USA

Hinson, Jordan (Actor)
c/o Bonnie Liedtke *Principato/Young Management*
9465 Wilshire Blvd Ste 430
Beverly Hills, CA 90212-2613, USA

Hinson, Larry (Athlete, Golfer)
Route 4 Box 397
Douglas, GA 31533, USA

Hinson, Roy (Athlete, Basketball Player)
4272 State Hwy 27
Monmouth Junction, NJ 8852, USA

Hinson, Roy (Athlete, Basketball Player)
8167 Quail Meadow Way
West Palm Beach, FL 33412-1506, USA

Hinterseer, Ernst (Skier)
Hahnenkammstr
Kitzbuhel 6370, AUSTRIA

Hintikka, Jaakko J (Misc)
PO Box 24
Helsinki 14, FINLAND

Hinton, Charles R (Athlete, Football Player)
124 Tanglewood Rd
Natchez, MS 39120-4526, USA

Hinton, Chris (Athlete, Football Player)
374 Citadella Ct
Alpharetta, GA 30022-5336, USA

Hinton, Christopher J (Chris) (Athlete, Football Player)
5136 Falcon Chase Ln
Atlanta, GA 30342, USA

Hinton, Chuck (Athlete, Baseball Player)
6330 16th St NW
Washington, DC 20011-8010, USA

Hinton, Darby (Actor)
1267 Bel Air Rd
Los Angeles, CA 90077, USA

Hinton, Eddie (Athlete, Football Player)
34 Auburn Rdg
Spring Branch, TX 78070-6014, USA

Hinton, James David
2806 Oak Point Dr
Los Angeles, CA 90068

Hinton, Jill (Athlete, Golfer)
9503 Ridgefield Rd
Henrico, VA 23229-3929, USA

Hinton, Rich (Athlete, Baseball Player)
7447 Hawkins Rd
Sarasota, FL 34241-9376, USA

Hinton, S E
8955 Beverly Blvd
West Hollywood, CA 90048-2423, USA

Hinton, Sam (Musician, Songwriter)
1719 Addison St
Berkeley, CA 94703-1501, USA

Hinton of Bankside, Christopher (Engineer, Government Official)
Tiverton Lodge Dulwich Common
London SG2 7EW, UNITED KINGDOM (UK)

Hintz, Donald C (Business Person)
10055 Grogans Mill Rd # 5A
The Woodlands, TX 77380-1059, USA

Hinzo, Tommy (Athlete, Baseball Player)
40798 Camellia Dr
Hemet, CA 92544-2400, USA

Hiort, Esbjonm (Architect)
Parkvej 6
Rungsted Kyst 2960, DENMARK

Hipp, I M (Athlete, Football Player)
27 Underwood Pl
Alexandria, VA 22304-4941, USA

Hipp, Paul (Actor)
c/o Staff Member *Stone Manners Salners Agency (LA)*
9911 W Pico Blvd Ste 1400
Los Angeles, CA 90035-2715, USA

Hipple, Eric (Athlete, Football Player)
7155 Driftwood Dr
Fenton, MI 48430-4304, USA

Hipps, Claude (Athlete, Football Player)
1535 Dartmouth Rd
Columbus, GA 31904-1903, USA

Hipwell, Elizabeth
18 Gramercy Park S
New York, NY 10003-1724

Hirase, Mayumi (Athlete, Golfer)
1360 E 9th St Ste 100
Cleveland, OH 44114-1730, USA

Hirata-Chalfin, Gail (Athlete, Golfer)
15539 Quiet Oak Dr
Chino Hills, CA 91709-4254, USA

Hire, Kathryn P (Kay) (Astronaut)
PO Box 580146
Houston, TX 77258-0146, USA

Hiroshima
1460 4th St Ste 205
Santa Monica, CA 90401-3414

Hirosue, Ryoyo (Actor)
c/o Omiotek Maciej *OmniotComp*
Sowinskiego 27A Grodzisk
Mazowiecki, POLAND

Hirsch, Corey (Athlete, Hockey Player)
c/o Staff Member *Hockey Canada*
2424 University Dr NW
Calgary, AB T2N 3Y9, Canada

Hirsch, David
6255 W Sunset Blvd # 627
Los Angeles, CA 90028-7403

Hirsch, E D Jr (Educator)
Education Dept
Charlottesville, VA 22906, USA

Hirsch, Emile (Actor)
c/o Sam Maydew *Collective*
8383 Wilshire Blvd Ste 1050
Beverly Hills, CA 90211-2415, USA

Hirsch, Hallee (Actor, Musician)
c/o Amy Abell *Innovative Artists (LA)*
1505 10th St
Santa Monica, CA 90401-2805, USA

Hirsch, Judd (Actor)
c/o Joel Rudnick *Paradigm (LA)*
360 N Crescent Dr
Beverly Hills, CA 90210-4874, USA

Hirsch, Laurence E (Business Person)
2728 N Harwood St
Dallas, TX 75201-1516, USA

Hirsch, Lee (Director)
c/o Mark Ross *Paradigm (LA)*
360 N Crescent Dr
Beverly Hills, CA 90210-4874, USA

Hirsch, Leon C (Inventor)
150 Glover Ave
Norwalk, CT 06850-1308, USA

Hirsch, Robert P (Actor)
1 Pl du Palais Bourbon
Paris 75007, FRANCE

Hirsch, Stan
16027 Ventura Blvd Ste 206
Encino, CA 91436-2774

Hirsch, Tom (Athlete, Hockey Player)
8469 Zanzibar Ln N
Osseo, MN 55311-1814, USA

Hirschbeck, John (Baseball Player)
8730 Raintree Run
Youngstown, OH 44514-2987, USA

Hirschbeck, John (Athlete, Baseball Player)
8730 Raintree Run
Youngstown, OH 44514-2987, USA

Hirschbeck, Mark (Baseball Player)
12 Isinglass Ter
Trumbull, CT 06611-4024, USA

Hirschbeck, Mark (Athlete, Baseball Player)
12 Isinglass Ter
Trumbull, CT 06611-4024, USA

Hirschbein, Jonathan (Writer)
c/o Melissa Breaux *Washington Square Arts (LA)*
1041 N Formosa Ave Lot Bldg
West Hollywood, CA 90046-6703, USA

Hirschbiegel, Oliver (Director)
c/o Tobin Babst *United Talent Agency (UTA)*
9560 Wilshire Blvd Fl 5
Beverly Hills, CA 90212-2400, USA

Hirschfeld, Marie (Stylist)
330 Sir Walter Dr
Cheshire, CT 06410-2904, USA

Hirschfelder, David (Composer)
PO Box 567
Crows Nest, NSW 2065, USA

Hirschfielder, Gerald J (Cinematographer)
425 Ashland St
Ashland, OR 97520-3104, USA

Hirschman, Albert O (Economist)
16 Newlin Rd
Princeton, NJ 08540-4916, USA

Hirschmann, Ralph F (Misc)
79 Panorama Crest Ave
Las Vegas, NV 89135-7830, USA

Hirson, Alice (Actor)
PO Box 5597
Santa Monica, CA 90409-5597, USA

Hirst, Damien (Artist)
Saint James's 44 Duke St
London SW1Y 6DD, UNITED KINGDOM (UK)

Hirtz, Dagmar
Jollystr. 14
Munich, GERMANY D-81545

Hirzebruch, Friedrich E P (Mathematician)
Thuringer Allee 127
Saint Augustin 53757, GERMANY

Hisaishi, Joe (Composer, Musician)
c/o Staff Member *Greenspan Artist Management*
8760 W Sunset Blvd
West Hollywood, CA 90069-2206, USA

Hiser, Gene (Athlete, Baseball Player)
1450 Caldwell Ln
Hoffman Estates, IL 60169-1202, USA

Hiskey, Babe (Athlete, Golfer)
4046 Pirates Bch
Galveston, TX 77554-8037, USA

Hisle, Larry E (Athlete, Baseball Player)
312 W Saddleworth Ct
Thiensville, WI 53092-3564, USA

Hislop, Ian (Actor)
c/o Jenne Casarotto *Casarotto Ramsay & Associates Ltd (UK)*
Waverley House 7-12 Noel St
London W1F 8GQ, UK

Hislop, Jamie (Athlete, Hockey Player)
3683 Lakeshore Rd
Kelowna, BC V1W 3K2, Canada

Hisner, Harley (Athlete, Baseball Player)
4411 Park Place Dr Unit 209
Fort Wayne, IN 46845-8609, USA

Hitch, Lew (Athlete, Basketball Player)
PO Box 89
Westmoreland, KS 66549-0089, USA

Hitchcock, Ken (Athlete, Hockey Player)
11118 Valleydale Dr Apt C
Dallas, TX 75230-3351, USA

Hitchcock, Michael (Actor)
c/o Staff Member *Gersh (LA)*
9465 Wilshire Blvd Ste 600
Beverly Hills, CA 90212-2612, USA

Hitchcock, Ray (Athlete, Football Player)
2190 Arcade St
Saint Paul, MN 55109-2572, USA

Hitchcock, Robyn (Musician, Songwriter)
c/o Amanda Howard *Amanda Howard Associates*
21 Berwick St
London W1F 0PZ, UNITED KINGDOM (UK)

Hitchcock, Russell (Musician)
9200 W Sunset Blvd Ste 900
Los Angeles, CA 90069-3604, USA

Hitchcock, Sterling (Athlete, Baseball Player)
255 Yucca Rd
Naples, FL 34102-5318, USA

Hitchins, Christopher
2022 Columbia Rd NW
Washington, DC 20009-1323

Hite, Shere
PO Box 1037
New York, NY 10028-0007

Hite-James, Kathy (Athlete, Golfer)
38651 Nyasa Dr
Palm Desert, CA 92211-7009, USA

Hitt, Joel (Athlete, Football Player)
800 Founders Pointe Blvd
Franklin, TN 37064-0752, USA

Hitt, John C (Educator)
1000 Central Florida Blvd
Orlando, FL 32826-2404, USA

Hitt, Lee (Athlete, Football Player)
4318 N Hall St
Dallas, TX 75219-2731, USA

Hittle, Lloyd (Athlete, Baseball Player)
2031 W Elm St
Lodi, CA 95242-2820, USA

Hitzges, Jennifer (Stylist)
c/o Staff Member *Jed Root Inc*
61-A Walker St
New York, NY 10013, USA

Hix, William (Athlete, Football Player)
5070 White Dr
Batesville, AR 72501-9138, USA

Hjejle, Iben (Actor, Writer)
c/o Staff Member *Kasper Notlev*
Gl. Kongevej 86A 3.Th
Frederiksberg C1850, Denmark

Hjertstedt, Gabriel (Athlete, Golfer)
100 Sawgrass Corners Dr
Ponte Vedra Beach, FL 32082-3567, USA

Hjorth, Maria (Athlete, Golfer)
608 Henley Cir
Davenport, FL 33896-3072, USA

Hlass, I Jerry (Engineer)
NSTL Station, MS 39529, USA

Hnatiuk, Glen (Athlete, Golfer)
8746 Mississippi Run
Weeki Wachee, FL 34613-4046, USA

Hnidy, Shane (Athlete, Hockey Player)
15 Jones Rd
Middleton, MA 01949-1673, USA

Hnilicka, Milan (Athlete, Hockey Player)
1111 S Figueroa St
Los Angeles, CA 90015-1300, USA

Ho, David (Scientist)
455 1st Ave
New York, NY 10016-9102, USA

Ho, Don
PO Box 90039
Honolulu, HI 96825-0039

Ho, Donald T (Don) (Music Group)
277 Lewers St
Honolulu, HI 96815, USA

Ho, Tao (Architect)
Upper Deck North Point West Passenger Ferry Pier
North Point, HONG KONG

Hoag, Charles (Athlete, Basketball Player)
2927 SW Foxcroft Ct # 1
Topeka, KS 66614, USA

Hoag, Jan
855 N Martel Ave
Los Angeles, CA 90046-7561

Hoag, Judith W (Actor)
3500 W Olive Ave Ste 1400
Burbank, CA 91505-5512, USA

Hoag, Peter C (Misc)
3566 Little Rock Dr
Provo, UT 84604, USA

Hoag, Tami (Writer)
1540 Broadway
New York, NY 10036-4039, USA

Hoage, Terrell L (Terry) (Athlete, Football Player)
870 Arbor Rd
Paso Robles, CA 93446-8609, USA

Hoagland, Ashley (Athlete, Golfer)
803 26th Ave W
Palmetto, FL 34221-3576, USA

Hoagland, Edward (Writer)
PO Box 51
Barton, VT 05822-0051, USA

Hoagland, Jimmie L (Jim) (Journalist)
1150 15th St NW
Washington, DC 20071-0001, USA

Hoaglin, Fred (Athlete, Coach, Football Coach, Football Player)
7 Governors Rd
Hilton Head, SC 29928-3018, USA

Hoak, Dick (Athlete, Football Player)
417 Crest View Dr
Greensburg, PA 15601, USA

Hoar, Joseph P (General)
386 13th St
Del Mar, CA 92014-2555, USA

Hoard, Leroy (Athlete, Football Player)
4301 NE 15th Ave
Oakland Park, FL 33334-4712, USA

Hoare, C Antony R (Engineer)
Computing Lab Parks Road
Oxford OX1 3QD, UNITED KINGDOM (UK)

Hoare, Sarajane (Stylist)
c/o Staff Member *Vernon Jolly Inc*
180 Varick St Rm 912
New York, NY 10014-5482, USA

Hoare, Tony
430 Edgware Rd
London, ENGLAND W2 1EG

Hoban, Mike (Athlete, Football Player)
1917 Holly Ave
Darien, IL 60561-3518, USA

Hoban, Russell C (Writer)
6 Musgrave Crescent
London SW6 4PT, UNITED KINGDOM (UK)

Hobart, Nick (Cartoonist)
5632 Indiana Ave
New Port Richey, FL 34652-2333, USA

Hobaugh, Charles O (Astronaut)
2101 Nasa Pkwy Spc Center
Houston, TX 77058-3607, USA

Hobaugh, Ed (Athlete, Baseball Player)
1420 3rd Ave
Ford City, PA 16226-1303, USA

Hobault, John (Scientist)
51 Winster Fax
Williamsburg, VA 23185-5543, USA

Hobbie, Glen (Athlete, Baseball Player)
RR 2 Box 234A
Ramsey, IL 62080-9398, USA

Hobbs, Becky (Musician)
2409 21st Ave S Ste 100
Nashville, TN 37212-5317, USA

Hobbs, Chelsea (Actor)
c/o Sam Maydew *Collective*
8383 Wilshire Blvd Ste 1050
Beverly Hills, CA 90211-2415, USA

Hobbs, Franklin (Fritz) (Misc)
151 E 79th St
New York, NY 10075-0417, USA

Hobbs, Jack (Athlete, Baseball Player)
3 Wade Dr
Cherry Hill, NJ 08034-1741, USA

Hobbs, Rebecca (Actor)
c/o Kathryn Rawlings *Kathryn Rawlings Actors Agency*
4/28 Williamson Ave. Grey Lynn
Auckland, New Zealand

Hobby, Marion (Athlete, Football Player)
708 Nytol Cir
Irondale, AL 35210-2919, USA

Hoblit, Gregory (Director)
c/o David Wirtschafter *WmE2 (Endeavor-LA)*
9601 Wilshire Blvd Fl 3
Beverly Hills, CA 90210-5219, USA

Hobson, Clell L (Butch) (Athlete, Baseball Player, Coach)
6302 Catarata St
Bakersfield, CA 93311-9638, USA

Hobson, J Allan (Scientist)
Sleep Laboratory
Cambridge, MA 2138, USA

Hobson, Jeff (Misc)
32630 Concord Dr
Madison Heights, MI 48071-1110, USA

Hoch, Carin (Athlete, Golfer)
1360 E 9th St Ste 100
Cleveland, OH 44114-1730, USA

Hoch, Danny (Artist)
165 W 57th St
New York, NY 10019-2201, USA

Hoch, Scott (Athlete, Golfer)
8800 Lake Sheen Ct
Orlando, FL 32836-5482, USA

Hochevar, Luke (Athlete, Baseball Player)
2452 Glen Meadow Rd
Knoxville, TN 37909-1092, USA

Hochhuth, Rolf (Writer)
PO Box 661
Alfred, ME 04002-0661, SWITZERLAND

Hochstrasser, Robin M (Misc)
Chemistry Dept
Philadelphia, PA 19104, USA

Hochwald, Bari (Actor)
Via San Gallo, 25
Florence 50129, Italy

Hock, Dee Ward (Business Person)
900 Metro Center Blvd
Foster City, CA 94404-2172, USA

Hocke, Stefan (Skier)
Am Harzwald 3
Oberhof 98558, GERMANY

Hockenberry, Chuck (Athlete, Baseball Player)
1546 Birka Ln
Onalaska, WI 54650-2087, USA

Hockenberry, John (Actor, Correspondent, Writer)
c/o Sally Willcox *Creative Artists Agency (CAA-LA)*
2000 Avenue of the Stars Ste 100
Los Angeles, CA 90067-4705, USA

Hocking, Dennis (Athlete, Baseball Player)
7384 E Villanueva Dr
Orange, CA 92867-6440, USA

Hocking, Justin (Athlete, Hockey Player)
3726 E 52nd Ct
Spokane, WA 99223-8604, USA

Hockney, David (Artist)
7508 Santa Monica Blvd
West Hollywood, CA 90046-6407, USA

Hocott, Brenda (Athlete, Golfer)
261 Cave Ln
San Antonio, TX 78209-2242, USA

Hodder, Kane (Actor)
3701 Senda Calma
Calabasas, CA 91302-3066, USA

Hodder, Kenneth (Religious Leader)
615 Slaters Ln
Alexandria, VA 22314-1112, USA

Hoddinott, Alun (Composer)
64 Gowerton Road Three Crosses
Swansea SA4 3PX, WALES

Hoddle, Glenn (Soccer Player)
16 Lancaster Gate
London W2 3LW, UNITED KINGDOM (UK)

Hodel, Donald P (Secretary)
1801 Sara Dr Ste L
Chesapeake, VA 23320-2647, USA

Hodge, Aldis (Actor)
c/o Matt Luber *Luber Roklin Management*
8530 Wilshire Blvd Ste 550
Beverly Hills, CA 90211-3133, USA

Hodge, Charles E (Charlie) (Athlete, Hockey Player)
27111 25A Ave
Aldergrove, BC V4W 3N4, Canada

Hodge, Daniel A (Dan) (Wrestler)
General Delivery
Perry, OK 73077-9999, USA

Hodge, Douglas (Actor)
c/o Lindy King *United Agents*
12-26 Lexington St
London W1F OLE, UK

Hodge, Ed (Athlete, Baseball Player)
127 Jewell St
Johnson City, TN 37601-5209, USA

Hodge, Edwin (Actor)
c/o Matt Luber *Luber Roklin Management*
8530 Wilshire Blvd Ste 550
Beverly Hills, CA 90211-3133, USA

Hodge, Patricia (Actor)
76 Oxford St
London W1N 0AX, UNITED KINGDOM (UK)

Hodge, Sedrick (Athlete, Football Player)
120 Victoria Pl
Fayetteville, GA 30214-1176, USA

Hodge, Stephanie (Actor)
232 N Canon Dr
Beverly Hills, CA 90210-5302, USA

Hodge, Sue
82 Constance Rd Twickenham
Middlesex A, ENGLAND TW2 7J

Hodge Jr, Kenneth R (Ken) (Athlete, Hockey Player)
1115 Main St
Lynnfield, MA 01940-1030, USA

Hodge Sr, Ken (Athlete, Hockey Player)
13 Longfellow Dr
Newburyport, MA 01950-3325, USA

Hodges, Bill (Basketball Player, Coach)
Athletic Dept
Milledgeville, GA 31061, USA

Hodges, Craig (Athlete, Basketball Player)
67 Elm St
Park Forest, IL 60466-1702, USA

Hodges, Eric (Actor)
3800 W Alameda Ave
Burbank, CA 91505-4300

Hodges, Jean (Stylist)
Prefers to be contacted via telephone or email
Burbank, CA 91501, USA

Hodges, Kevin (Athlete, Baseball Player)
19506 Kuykendahl Rd
Spring, TX 77379-3408, USA

Hodges, Louise
31A St George's Rd Leyton
London, ENGLAND EIO 5RH

Hodges, Mike (Director)
Wesley Farm Durweston Blanford Forum
Dorset DT11 0QG, UNITED KINGDOM (UK)

Hodges, Morris (Baseball Player)
1520 River Haven Ln
Birmingham, AL 35244-1259, USA

Hodges, Morris (Athlete, Baseball Player)
404 Park Lake Ter
Helena, AL 35080-3287, USA

Hodges, Pat (Actor, Musician)
c/o Staff Member *Diva Central Inc*
7510 W Sunset Blvd Ste 1445
Los Angeles, CA 90046-3408, USA

Hodges, Ron (Athlete, Baseball Player)
3190 Rakes Rd
Rocky Mount, VA 24151, USA

Hodges, Trey (Athlete, Baseball Player)
19506 Kuykendahl Rd
Spring, TX 77379-3408, USA

Hodgkin, Howard (Artist)
9/24 Dering St
London W1R 9AA, UNITED KINGDOM (UK)

Hodgman, John (Actor)
c/o Jay Gassner *United Talent Agency (UTA)*
9560 Wilshire Blvd Fl 5
Beverly Hills, CA 90212-2400, USA

Hodgson, James D (Secretary)
28802 Grayfox St
Malibu, CA 90265-4253, USA

Hodgson, Pat (Athlete, Football Player)
816 Commons Park
Statham, GA 30666-2539, USA

Hodo, David (Music Group)
8255 W Sunset Blvd
West Hollywood, CA 90046-2417, USA

Hodson, Kevin (Athlete, Hockey Player)
390 McNabb St Unit 2
Sault Sainte Marie, ON P6B 1, Canada

Hodson, Tom (Athlete, Football Player)
17938 Crossing Blvd
Baton Rouge, LA 70810-3840, USA

Hoebel, Bret (Reality TV Star)
c/o Staff Member *Abrams Artists Agency (LA)*
9200 W Sunset Blvd PH 11
Los Angeles, CA 90069-3601, USA

Hoechlin, Tyler (Actor)
c/o Matt Luber *Luber Roklin Management*
8530 Wilshire Blvd Ste 550
Beverly Hills, CA 90211-3133, USA

Hoeft, Roberta (Stylist)
c/o Staff Member *Ford Models (Chicago)*
311 W Superior St
Chicago, IL 60654-3548, USA

Hoeft, William F (Billy) (Athlete, Baseball Player)
10009 Lost Canyon Dr
Stanwood, MI 49346-9404, USA

Hoekstra, Cecil (Athlete, Hockey Player)
303 St Paul St W
St Catharines, ON L2S 2E8, Canada

Hoelscher, Joel (Athlete, Football Player)
8931 N Star Fort Loramie Rd
Yorkshire, OH 45388-9750, USA

Hoene, Ohil (Athlete, Hockey Player)
1110 Mississippi Ave
Duluth, MN 55811-4920, USA

Hoenig, Michael (Composer, Musician)
c/o Staff Member *Gorfaine/Schwartz Agency Inc*
4111 W Alameda Ave Ste 509
Burbank, CA 91505-4171, USA

Hoenig, Thomas M (Financier, Government Official)
615 W Meyer Blvd
Kansas City, MO 64113-1543, USA

Hoerner, Dick (Athlete, Football Player)
15814 Landmark Dr Apt 9
Whittier, CA 90604-3848, USA

Hoest, Bunny (Cartoonist)
27 Watch Way Lloyd Nck
Huntington, NY 11743, USA

Hoey, George (Athlete, Football Player)
13635 Clermont Ct
Thornton, CO 80602-6965, USA

Hofer, Paul (Athlete, Football Player)
5699 Normandy Pl
Memphis, TN 38120, USA

Hoff, Katie (Athlete, Swimmer)
c/o Staff Member *USA Swimming Association*
1 Olympic Plz
Colorado Springs, CO 80909-5780, USA

Hoff, Marcian E (Ted) Jr (Inventor)
12226 Colina Dr
Los Altos Hills, CA 94024-5299, USA

Hoffa, James P (Misc)
2593 Hounds Chase Dr
Troy, MI 48098-2338, USA

Hoffman, Alan J (Mathematician)
PO Box 218
Yorktown Heights, NY 10598-0218, USA

Hoffman, Alice (Writer)
3 Hurlbut St
Cambridge, MA 02138-1603, USA

Hoffman, Barbara (Baseball Player)
318 E Mill St
Millstadt, IL 62260-1218, USA

Hoffman, Basil (Actor)
26 Aller Ct
Glendale, CA 91206-1701, USA

Hoffman, Bob (Athlete, Football Player)
8200 N Laurelglen Blvd Apt 2112
Bakersfield, CA 93311-2349, USA

Hoffman, Darleane C (Physicist)
1 Cyclotron Rd
Berkeley, CA 94720-8099, USA

Hoffman, Dustin (Actor, Director, Producer)
c/o Kelly Bush *ID PR (LA)*
7060 Hollywood Blvd Fl 8
Los Angeles, CA 90028-6014, USA

Hoffman, Elizabeth (Actor)
5750 Wilshire Blvd # 473
Los Angeles, CA 90036-3697, USA

Hoffman, Elizabeth (Educator)
President S Ofc
Boulder, CO 80309-0001, USA

Hoffman, Glenn E (Athlete, Baseball Player, Coach)
201 S Old Bridge Rd
Anaheim, CA 92808-1326, USA

Hoffman, Guy (Athlete, Baseball Player)
313 Fairway Dr Apt S
Bloomington, IL 61701-8219, USA

Hoffman, Ingrid (Chef, Television Host)
c/o Staff Member *Food Network, The*
75 9th Ave
New York, NY 10011-7006, USA

Hoffman, Jackie (Actor)
c/o Hannah Roth *Don Buchwald & Associates Inc (LA)*
6500 Wilshire Blvd Ste 2200
Los Angeles, CA 90048-4942, USA

Hoffman, Jeffrey A (Astronaut)
2 Ave Gabriel PSC 116/NASA
Paris Cedex 75382, FRANCE

Hoffman, John Robert (Writer)
c/o Rosalie Swedlin *Anonymous Content (AC-LA)*
3531 Hayden Ave
Culver City, CA 90232, USA

Hoffman, Jorg (Swimmer)
Saarmunder Str 74
Potsdam 14478, GERMANY

Hoffman, Kara (Actor)
c/o Rod Baron *Baron Entertainment*
13848 Ventura Blvd Ste A
Sherman Oaks, CA 91423-3654

Hoffman, Marguerite (Business Person, Philanthropist)
1717 N Harwood St
Dallas, TX 75201-2315, USA

Hoffman, Matt (Actor)
c/o Staff Member *Liberation Management*
1412 12th Ave
Los Angeles, CA 90019-4316, USA

Hoffman, Michael (Director)
c/o Doug MacLaren *International Creative Management (ICM-LA)*
10250 Constellation Blvd Fl 7
Los Angeles, CA 90067-6207, USA

Hoffman, Mim (Stylist)
c/o Staff Member *Arlene Wilson Management*
807 N Jefferson St # 200
Milwaukee, WI 53202-8150, USA

Hoffman, Paul Felix (Geophysicist, Physicist)
162 Cypress St
Brookline, MA 02445-6767, USA

Hoffman, Philip Seymour (Actor, Producer)
c/o Staff Member *Cooper's Town Productions*
302A W 12th St # 214
New York, NY 10014-1947, USA

Hoffman, Ray (Athlete, Baseball Player)
14475 Thompson Rd
Alpharetta, GA 30004-6912, USA

Hoffman, Rick (Actor)
c/o Staff Member *Jeff Morrone Entertainment*
9350 Wilshire Blvd Ste 224
Beverly Hills, CA 90212-3204, USA

Hoffman, Robert (Actor, Dancer)
c/o Michael Baum *Impression Entertainment*
9229 W Sunset Blvd Ste 700
West Hollywood, CA 90069-3407, USA

Hoffman, Ted Jr (Bowler)
1568 Tartarian Way
San Jose, CA 95129-4758, USA

Hoffman, Toby (Music Group, Musician)
165 W 57th St
New York, NY 10019-2201, USA

Hoffman, Trevor (Athlete, Baseball Player)
2220 Ocean Frnt
Del Mar, CA 92014, USA

Hoffman, William M (Songwriter, Writer)
190 Prince St
New York, NY 10012-2906, USA

Hoffmann, Christian (Skier)
Frunwald 7
Aigen 4160, AUSTRIA

Hoffmann, Frank N (Nordy) (Athlete, Football Player)
400 N Capitol St NW Apt 327
Washington, DC 20001-1511, USA

Hoffmann, Gaby
8942 Wilshire Blvd
Beverly Hills, CA 90211-1908

Hoffmann, Isabella
6500 Wilshire Blvd Ste 2200
Los Angeles, CA 90048-4942

Hoffmann, Roald (Nobel Prize Laureate)
4 Sugarbush Ln
Ithaca, NY 14850-6326, USA

Hoffmeyer, Bob (Athlete, Hockey Player)
c/o Staff Member *New Jersey Devils*
165 Mulberry St
Newark, NJ 07102-3607, USA

Hofford, Jim (Athlete, Hockey Player)
5 Vanderberg Dr
Fairport, NY 14450-8427, USA

Hoffort, Bruce (Athlete, Hockey Player)
N1778 Hyacinth Ln
Greenville, WI 54942-9005, USA

Hoffs, Susanna (Musician)
1341 W Fullerton Ave # 180
Chicago, IL 60614-2362, USA

Hofheimer, Charlie (Actor)
c/o Abby Bluestone *Innovative Artists (LA)*
1505 10th St
Santa Monica, CA 90401-2805, USA

Hofmann, Al (Race Car Driver)
PO Box 346
Umatilla, FL 32784-0346, USA

Hofmann, Detief (Athlete)
Saarlandstr 164
Karlsruhe 76187, GERMANY

Hofmann, Douglas (Artist)
8602 Saxon Cir
Baltimore, MD 21236-2559, USA

Hofmann, Isabella (Actor)
6500 Wilshire Blvd Ste 2200
Los Angeles, CA 90048-4942, USA

Hofmann, Kenneth (Baseball Player)
1380 Galaxy Way
Concord, CA 94520-4912, USA

Hofschneider, Marco (Actor)
400 S Beverly Dr Ste 216
Beverly Hills, CA 90212-4404, USA

Hofstatter, Peter R (Doctor, Psychic)
Lehmkuhleweg 16
Buxtehude 21614, GERMANY

Hofstetter, Steve (Writer)
c/o David Krintzman *Morris, Yorn, Barnes, Levine, Krintzman, Rubenstein and Kohner*
2000 Ave Of The Stars 3rd Tower Floor NORTH
Los Angeles, CA 90067, USA

Hogaboam, Bill (Athlete, Hockey Player)
1317 Mountainview St
Kelowna, BC V1Y 4M9, Canada

Hogan, Brooke (Musician, Reality TV Star)
2111 Drew St
Clearwater, FL 33765-3215, USA

Hogan, Chris (Actor)
c/o Staff Member *Rugolo Entertainment*
195 S Beverly Dr Ste 400
Beverly Hills, CA 90212-3044, USA

Hogan, Chuck (Writer)
c/o Richard Abate *3 Arts Entertainment - NY*
49 W 27th St Fl 5
New York, NY 10001-6936, USA

Hogan, Craig (Astronomer)
Astronomy
Seattle, WA 98195-0001, USA

Hogan, Darrell (Athlete, Football Player)
14988 Scenic Loop Rd
Helotes, TX 78023-3701, USA

Hogan, Hulk (Actor, Wrestler)
c/o Darren Prince *Prince Marketing Group*
18 Carillon Cir
Livingston, NJ 07039-2600, USA

Hogan, Linda (Writer)
English
Boulder, CO 80309-0001, USA

Hogan, Linda (Actor)
c/o Peter Young *Sovereign Talent Group*
8421 Wilshire Blvd Ste 200
Beverly Hills, CA 90211-3204, USA

Hogan, Marc (Athlete, Football Player)
3761 Colby St
Pittsburgh, PA 15214-2134, USA

Hogan, Michael (Actor)
c/o Jamie Levitt *Lauren Levitt & Associates Inc*
1525 W 8th St 3rd Fl
Vancouver V6J 1T5, British Columbia

Hogan, Mike (Athlete, Football Player)
11 Walton Creek Dr SW
Rome, GA 30165-7228, USA

Hogan, Nick (Actor, Reality TV Star)
c/o Darren Prince *Prince Marketing Group*
18 Carillon Cir
Livingston, NJ 07039-2600, USA

Hogan, Paul (Actor)
18 Marshall Cres
Beacon Hill, NSW 2060, AUSTRALIA

Hogan, Paul (Reality TV Star)
c/o Staff Member *Acme Talent & Literary (LA)*
1400 Atlantic Ave Ste 274
Long Beach, CA 90813-2013, USA

Hogan, Paul (Actor)
c/o Staff Member *Silver Lion Films*
701 Santa Monica Blvd Ste 240
Santa Monica, CA 90401-2625

Hogan, Paul (PJ) (Director, Producer, Writer)
c/o Richard Lovett *Creative Artists Agency (CAA-LA)*
2000 Avenue of the Stars Ste 100
Los Angeles, CA 90067-4705, USA

Hogan, Robert (Actor)
344 W 89th St Apt 1B
New York, NY 10024-2176, USA

Hogan, Terry
130 Willadel Dr
Belleair, FL 33756-1942

Hoganson, Paul (Athlete, Hockey Player)
1070 W Eagle Landing Pl
Tucson, AZ 85737-9230, USA

Hogarth, Freddie
69 St Quentin Ave # 1
London, ENGLAND W10 6PA

Hogdin, Ralph (Athlete, Baseball Player)
3203 Farmington Dr
Greensboro, NC 27407-5703, USA

Hogdon, Marilinda (Stylist)
225 E 9th St # 19-K
New York, NY 10128, USA

Hoge, Merril (Athlete, Football Player)
155 W Maple Ave
Ft Mitchell, KY 41011-2671, USA

Hogeboom, Gary (Athlete, Football Player)
13635 Hofma Ct
Grand Haven, MI 49417-9669, USA

Hogestyn, Drake (Actor)
c/o Staff Member *Hines and Hunt Entertainment*
1213 W Magnolia Blvd
Burbank, CA 91506-1829, USA

Hogg, Christopher A (Business Person)
18 Hanover Square
London W1A 2BB, UNITED KINGDOM (UK)

Hogg, James R (Admiral)
2556 W Main Rd
Portsmouth, RI 02871-1022, USA

Hoggard, Jay (Music Group, Musician)
181 Chrystie St # 300
New York, NY 10002-1275, USA

Hogland, Doug (Athlete, Football Player)
1514 4th St
Tillamook, OR 97141-3426, USA

Hogue, Beniot (Athlete, Hockey Player)
488 Village Oaks Ln
Babylon, NY 11702-3124, USA

Hogue, Linda (Stylist)
5374 Whitehall Pl SE
Mableton, GA 30126-1983, USA

Hogue, Paul (Athlete, Basketball Player)
10195 Ronnie Rd
Cincinnati, OH 45215-1320, USA

Hogue, Stacey
10474 Santa Monica Blvd Ste 380
Los Angeles, CA 90025-6943

Hogwood, Christopher J H (Conductor, Musician)
10 Brookside
Cambridge CB2 1JE, UNITED KINGDOM (UK)

Hohlmayer, Alice (Baseball Player)
5155 Cedarwood Rd Apt 47
Bonita, CA 91902-1946, USA

Hohmann, John (Misc)
1110 E Missouri Ave Ste 200
Phoenix, AZ 85014-2754, USA

Hohn, Bill (Athlete, Baseball Player)
1406 Royal Oak Dr
Blue Bell, PA 19422-2166, USA

Hohn, Robert (Athlete, Football Player)
2624 N 78th St
Lincoln, NE 68507-2965, USA

Hohne, Claus
An der Kiesgrube 3
Holzkirchen, GERMANY D-83607

Hoiles, Chris (Athlete, Baseball Player)
8688 Jerry City Rd
Wayne, OH 43466-9837, USA

Hoisington, Allan (Athlete, Football Player)
71371 Biskra Rd
Rancho Mirage, CA 92270-4251, USA

Hoke, Jon (Athlete, Football Player)
813 Cherokee Rd
Lake Forest, IL 60045-3963, USA

Hoku (Musician)
c/o Staff Member *United Talent Agency (UTA)*
9560 Wilshire Blvd Fl 5
Beverly Hills, CA 90212-2400, USA

Holahan, Dennis
9250 Wilshire Blvd Ste 208
Beverly Hills, CA 90212-3344

Holberg, Fred (Athlete, Basketball Player)
2851 Timberview Trl
Chaska, MN 55318-1113, USA

Holbert, Aaron (Athlete, Baseball Player)
32015 Teague Way
Wesley Chapel, FL 33545-1612, USA

Holbert, Jerry (Cartoonist, Editor)
Editorial Dept 1 Herald St
Roxbury, MA 2118, USA

Holbert, Ray (Athlete, Baseball Player)
13981 W Desert Cove Rd
Surprise, AZ 85379-4329, USA

Holbrook, Bill (Cartoonist)
c/o Staff Member *King Features Syndication*
300 W 57th St Fl 15
New York, NY 10019-5238, USA

Holbrook, Hal (Actor)
c/o Mark Turner *Abrams Artists Agency (NY)*
9200 W Sunset Blvd PH 11
Los Angeles, CA 90069-3601, USA

Holbrook, Karen (Educator)
Ohio State University
Columbus, OH 43210, USA

Holbrook, Sam (Athlete, Baseball Player)
2620 Sungale Ct
Lexington, KY 40513-1463, USA

Holbrook, Terry (Athlete, Hockey Player)
8415 Hendricks Rd
Mentor, OH 44060-2259, USA

Holcomb, Corey (Comedian)
c/o Staff Member *WmE2 (WMA-LA)*
1 William Morris Pl
Beverly Hills, CA 90212-4261, USA

Holcomb, Douglas (Athlete, Basketball Player)
PO Box 331
Lake Ariel, PA 18436-0331, USA

Holcomb, Steven (Athlete, Olympic Athlete)
PO Box 118
Oakley, UT 84055-0118, USA

Holcombe, Ken (Athlete, Baseball Player)
32 Botany Dr
Asheville, NC 28805-1633, USA

Holden, Alexandra (Actor)

Holden, Amanda (Actor)
c/o Melanie Greene *Affirmative Entertainment*
425 N Robertson Blvd
West Hollywood, CA 90048-1735, USA

Holden, Andrew (Stylist)
c/o Staff Member *AFG Management*
62 Chelsea Piers Ste 203
New York, NY 10011-1015, USA

Holden, Gina (Actor)
c/o Staff Member *Collective*
8383 Wilshire Blvd Ste 1050
Beverly Hills, CA 90211-2415, USA

Holden, Henry (Misc)
1140 Bloomfield Ave Ste 220
West Caldwell, NJ 07006-7126, USA

Holden, Jennifer
115 S Topanga Canyon Blvd # 153
Topanga, CA 90290-3160

Holden, Joyce
444 N El Camino Real Spc 89
Encinitas, CA 92024-1313

Holden, Laurie (Actor)
c/o Jason Newman *Untitled Entertainment (LA)*
350 S Beverly Dr Ste 200
Beverly Hills, CA 90212-4819, USA

Holden, Mariean (Actor)
8335 W Sunset Blvd Ste 200
Los Angeles, CA 90069-1534, USA

Holden, Mark (Athlete, Hockey Player)
4827 Spruce Pine Way
North Ridgeville, OH 44039, USA

Holden, Steve (Athlete, Football Player)
1202 N Nevada Way
Mesa, AZ 85203-4323, USA

Holden, Tim (Congressman, Politician)
2417 Rayburn Hob
Washington, DC 20515-3817, USA

Holden, William Wildlife Foundation
PO Box 67981
Los Angeles, CA 90067

Holden-Reid, Kristen (Actor)
c/o Staff Member *Paradigm (LA)*
360 N Crescent Dr
Beverly Hills, CA 90210-4874, USA

Holder, Christopher (Actor)
733 Seward St PH
Los Angeles, CA 90038-3503, USA

Holder, Geoffrey (Actor, Dancer)
565 Broadway
New York, NY 10012-3925, USA

Holderness, Joan (Athlete, Baseball Player)
1037 Summerwind Dr
Crossville, TN 38571-3691, USA

Holderness, Sue
10 Rectory Close Windsor
Berks., ENGLAND SL4 5ER

Holdman, Warrick (Athlete, Football Player)
c/o Fletcher Smith *Blueprint Sports Group*
221 W Jefferson Ave
Naperville, IL 60540-5355, USA

Holdorf, Willi (Athlete, Track Athlete)
Herzogenaurach 91074, GERMANY

Holdridge, David (Athlete, Baseball Player)
39364 N Parisi Cir
San Tan Valley, AZ 85140-5721, USA

Holdsclaw, Chamique (Basketball Player)
MCI Center 601 F St NW
Washington, DC 20004, USA

Holdsworth, Fred (Athlete, Baseball Player)
578 Upland Hills Dr
Chelsea, MI 48118-9650, USA

Hole
150 E 58th St Ste 1900
New York, NY 10155-1901

Holecek, John (Athlete, Football Player)
1828 Prairie St
Glenview, IL 60025-2922, USA

Holgren, Paul H
724 Southwick Cir
Somerdale, NJ 08083-2312, USA

Holiday, Corey (Athlete, Football Player)
302 Oxfordshire Ln
Chapel Hill, NC 27517-6207, USA

Holiday, Debby (Musician)
c/o Staff Member *Diva Central Inc*
7510 W Sunset Blvd Ste 1445
Los Angeles, CA 90046-3408, USA

Holiday, Ron (Athlete, Football Player)
229 Balance Meeting Rd
Peach Bottom, PA 17563-9772, USA

Holik, Bobby (Athlete, Hockey Player)
PO Box 9236
Jackson, WY 83002-9236, USA

Holl, Steven M (Architect)
435 Hudson St Rm 400
New York, NY 10014-3948, USA

Holladay, Robert (Athlete, Football Player)
2369 Timberland Dr NE
Conyers, GA 30207, USA

Holladay, Wilhelmina Cole (Misc)
1250 New York Ave NW
Washington, DC 20005-3970, USA

Holland, Agnieszka (Director, Writer)
1 Rue Alfred de Vigny
Paris 75008, FRANCE

Holland, Al (Athlete, Baseball Player)
3523 Cove Rd NW
Roanoke, VA 24017-1813, USA

Holland, Brad (Athlete, Basketball Player)
1374 Sparrow Rd
Carlsbad, CA 92011-3961, USA

Holland, Darius (Athlete, Football Player)
13972 Meadowbrook Dr
Broomfield, CO 80020-6148, USA

Holland, Dexter (Musician)
31652 2nd Ave
Laguna Beach, CA 92651-8244, USA

Holland, Heinrich D (Geophysicist, Physicist)
14 Rangeley Rd
Winchester, MA 01890-2633, USA

Holland, Jamie L (Athlete, Football Player)
410 Woody Hayes Dr Attn Alumniassociation
Columbus, OH 43210-1104, USA

Holland, Jennifer (Actor)
c/o Jon Simmons *Simmons & Scott Entertainment*
7942 Mulholland Dr
Los Angeles, CA 90046-1225, USA

Holland, Jerry (Athlete, Hockey Player)
115 Douglasbank Pl SE
Calgary, AB T2Z 2J4, Canada

Holland, Joe (Athlete, Basketball Player)
210 Maccorkle Ave SW
Charleston, WV 25303-1507, USA

Holland, John (Athlete, Football Player)
3117 Flagstone Dr
Garland, TX 75044-5882, USA

Holland, John R (Religious Leader)
1910 W Sunset Blvd
Los Angeles, CA 90026-3275, USA

Holland, Johnny (Athlete, Football Player)
3303 Prestwick Sq
Missouri City, TX 77459-2888, USA

Holland, Jools (Music Group)
c/o Staff Member *Miracle Artists*
1 York Street London
England W1U 6PA, United Kingdom

Holland, Josh
4533 Willis Ave
Sherman Oaks, CA 91403-2710

Holland, Juliam M (Jools) (Musician)
Gallery 28 Wood Wharf Horseferry
London SE10 9BT, UNITED KINGDOM (UK)

Holland, Ken (Athlete, Hockey Player)
967 McDonald Dr
Northville, MI 48167-1072, USA

Holland, Paul (Musician)
1924 Spring St
Paso Robles, CA 93446-1620, USA

Holland, Richard (Actor)
453 Frederick St
San Francisco, CA 94117-2719, USA

Holland, Todd (Director)
c/o David Lonner *Oasis Media Group*
8730 W Sunset Blvd Ste 700
Los Angeles, CA 90069-2249, USA

Holland, Wilbur (Athlete, Basketball Player)
538 Georgia Dr
Columbus, GA 31907-5091, USA

Holland, Willa (Actor)
c/o Ellen Meyer *Ellen Meyer Management*
8899 Beverly Blvd Ste 612
West Hollywood, CA 90048-2429, USA

Holland, Willard R Jr (Business Person)
76 S Main St
Akron, OH 44308-1812, USA

Hollander, Dan (Figure Skater)
c/o Staff Member *Champions on Ice*
3500 W 80th St Ste 200
Minneapolis, MN 55431-1090, USA

Hollander, John (Writer)
English Dept
New Haven, CT 6520, USA

Hollander, Lorin (Musician)
40 W 57th St
New York, NY 10019-4001, USA

Hollander, Nicole (Cartoonist)
1440 N Dayton St
Chicago, IL 60642-2644, USA

Hollander, Xaviera
Stadionweg 17
Amsterdam, HOLLAND 1077 RU

Hollander, Zander (Writer)
3805 Yuma St NW
Washington, DC 20016-2213, USA

Hollandsworth, Todd M (Athlete, Baseball Player)
1310 Macalpin Dr
Inverness, IL 60010-6424, USA

Hollas, Donald (Athlete, Football Player)
22015 Gold Leaf Trl
Cypress, TX 77433-4643, USA

Holldobler, Berthold K (Biologist, Writer)
Zoologie II Am Nubland
Wurzburg 97074, GERMANY

Holle, Eric (Athlete, Football Player)
6646 Whitemarsh Valley Walk
Austin, TX 78746-6363, USA

Holle, Gary (Athlete, Baseball Player)
820 5th Ave
Watervliet, NY 12189-3612, USA

Holle, Mabel (Baseball Player)
914 Valley Rd
Lake Forest, IL 60045-2919, USA

Hollein, Hans (Architect)
Eiskellerstr 1
Dusseldorf 40213, GERMANY

Holler, Ed (Athlete, Football Player)
4500 Ivy Hall Dr
Columbia, SC 29206-1229, USA

Holleran, Leslie (Producer)
c/o Staff Member *Laha Films*
115 E 92nd St # 7C
New York, NY 10128-1688, USA

Hollerer, Walter F (Writer)
Heerstr 99
Berlin 14055, GERMANY

Holliday, Charles O (Business Person)
1007 Market St
Wilmington, DE 19801, USA

Holliday, Cheryl (Writer)
c/o Staff Member *United Talent Agency (UTA)*
9560 Wilshire Blvd Fl 5
Beverly Hills, CA 90212-2400, USA

Holliday, Fred (Actor)
4610 Forman Ave
Toluca Lake, CA 91602-1617, USA

Holliday, Jennifer (Actor, Music Group)
W 57th St #1500
New York, NY 10019, USA

Holliday, Kathy
345 N Maple Dr Ste 397
Beverly Hills, CA 90210-5179

Holliday, Kene
9300 Wilshire Blvd Ste 400
Beverly Hills, CA 90212-3210

Holliday, Matt (Athlete, Baseball Player)
216 Jackson St
Denver, CO 80206-5525, USA

Holliday, Polly D (Actor, Music Group)
c/o Staff Member *The Blake Agency*
23441 Malibu Colony Rd
Malibu, CA 90265-4640, USA

Hollie, Doug (Athlete, Football Player)
3917 Midvale Ave
Oakland, CA 94602-3940, USA

Hollier, Dwight (Athlete, Football Player)
5012 Woodview Ln
Matthews, NC 28104-8057, USA

Hollies, The
Hill Farm Hackleton
Northants., ENGLAND NN7 2DH

Holliger, Heinz (Composer, Musician)
Hochstr 51
Basel 4002, SWITZERLAND

Holliman, Earl (Actor)
PO Box 1969
Studio City, CA 91614-0969, USA

Hollimon, Ulysses (Athlete, Baseball Player)
3726 Benton Blvd
Kansas City, MO 64128-2515, USA

Hollings, Ernest (Ex-Senator)
261 Calhoun St Rm 304
Charleston, SC 29401-1378, USA

Hollings, Michael R (Religious Leader)
Saint Mary of Angels Moorhouse Road Bayswater
London W2 5DJ, UNITED KINGDOM (UK)

Hollingsworth, Ben (Actor)
c/o Shelley Browning *Magnolia Entertainment (LA)*
9595 Wilshire Blvd Ste 601
Beverly Hills, CA 90212-2506, USA

Hollingsworth, Shawn (Athlete, Football Player)
6 Broyhill Ct
Stafford, VA 22554-7757, USA

Hollinquest, Lamont (Athlete, Football Player)
13709 S San Pedro St
Los Angeles, CA 90061-2619, USA

Hollins, Damon (Athlete, Baseball Player)
1135 Camellia Ln
Suisun City, CA 94585-3804, USA

Hollins, Dave (Athlete, Baseball Player)
3221 Southwestern Blvd
Orchard Park, NY 14127-1230, USA

Hollins, Jessie (Athlete, Baseball Player)
608 W Stewart St
Willis, TX 77378-9519, USA

Hollins, Lionel (Athlete, Basketball Player, Coach)
7594 Tagg Dr
Germantown, TN 38138-5827, USA

Hollis, Essie (Athlete, Basketball Player)
9102 NW 48th St
Sunrise, FL 33351-5214, USA

Hollis, James (Writer)
1316 Potomac Dr
Houston, TX 77057-1922, USA

Hollis, Michael (Athlete, Football Player)
24 Falling Waters
Oakland, NJ 07436-2341, USA

Hollister, Dave (Actor, Music Group)
c/o Staff Member *Richard De La Font Agency*
3808 W South Park Blvd
Broken Arrow, OK 74011-1261, USA

Hollister, Ken (Athlete, Football Player)
8772 Linksway Dr
Powell, OH 43065-8299, USA

Hollit, Raye (Zapp)
2554 Lincoln Blvd # 638
Venice, CA 90291-5082

Holloman, Laurel (Actor)
c/o Tammy Rosen *Sanders Armstrong Caserta*
425 N Robertson Blvd
West Hollywood, CA 90048-1735, USA

Hollomon, Gus (Athlete, Football Player)
2489 County Road 139
Cameron, TX 76520-3614, USA

Holloway, Brenda (Musician)
145 W 57th St # 1500
New York, NY 10019-2220, USA

Holloway, Brian (Athlete, Football Player)
742 New York Route 43
Stephentown, NY 12168, USA

Holloway, James L III (Admiral)
4800 Fillmore Ave Apt 1058
Alexandria, VA 22311-5076, USA

Holloway, Johnny (Athlete, Football Player)
1500 W 9th St Apt 5
Lawrence, KS 66044-2462, USA

Holloway, Josh (Actor)
c/o Jai Khanna *Brillstein Entertainment Partners*
9150 Wilshire Blvd Ste 350
Beverly Hills, CA 90212-3453, USA

Holloway, Ken (Music Group)
1848 Tyne Blvd
Nashville, TN 37215-4702, USA

Holloway, Matt (Writer)
c/o Staff Member *Nine Yards Entertainment*
8530 Wilshire Blvd Ste 550
Beverly Hills, CA 90211-3133, USA

Holloway, Robin G (Composer)
Music Dept
Cambridge CB2 1TA, UNITED KINGDOM (UK)

Holloway, William J Jr (Judge)
PO Box 1767
Oklahoma City, OK 73101-1767, USA

Hollowell, Matt (Baseball Player)
4851 Chancellor Dr Apt 21
Jupiter, FL 33458-5250, USA

Hollowell, Matt (Athlete, Baseball Player)
4851 Chancellor Dr Apt 21
Jupiter, FL 33458-5250, USA

Hollweg, Ryan (Athlete, Hockey Player)
190 John Olds Dr Apt 212
Manchester, CT 06042-8812, USA

Holly, Buddy Memorial Society
PO Box 6123
Lubbock, TX 79493-6123

Holly, Jeff (Athlete, Baseball Player)
1201 Walnut Ave Apt 57
Tustin, CA 92780-5739, USA

Holly, Lauren (Actor)
c/o Ben Press *Don Buchwald & Associates Inc (LA)*
8619 Washington Blvd
Culver City, CA 90232-7441, USA

Holly, Molly (Wrestler)
c/o Staff Member *World Wrestling Entertainment (WWE)*
1241 E Main St
Stamford, CT 06902-3520, USA

Hollyday, Christopher (Musician)
173 Brighton Ave
Boston, MA 02134-2003, USA

Holm, Celeste (Actor)
88 Central Park W
New York, NY 10023-5299, USA

Holm, Ian (Actor)
Julian House 4 Windmill St
London W1P 1HF, UNITED KINGDOM (UK)

Holm, Jeanne M (General)
2707 Thyme Dr
Edgewater, MD 21037-1120, USA

Holm, Joan (Bowler)
5829 N Magnolia Ave
Chicago, IL 60660-3415, USA

Holm, Peter
1 Rue De Fer Achevel Port Grimaud
Cogolin, FRANCE F- 83310

Holm, Richard H (Misc)
483 Pleasant St Apt 10
Belmont, MA 02478-3266, USA

Holm, Sir Ian
46 Albermarle St
London, ENGLAND W1X 4PP

Holman, Brad (Athlete, Baseball Player)
8006 W Westlawn Cir
Wichita, KS 67212-7305, USA

Holman, Brian (Athlete, Baseball Player)
15821 Parkhill St
Overland Park, KS 66221-2549, USA

Holman, C Ray (Business Person)
675 McDonell Blvd
Saint Louis, MO 63134, USA

Holman, Gary (Athlete, Baseball Player)
PO Box 234265
Encinitas, CA 92023-4265, USA

Holman, Marshall (Athlete, Bowler)
288 Island Pointe Dr
Medford, OR 97504-9453, USA

Holman, Ralph T (Biologist)
3900 Bethel Dr
Saint Paul, MN 55112-6902, USA

Holman, Rodney (Athlete, Football Player)
41460 Herwig Bluff Rd
Slidell, LA 70461-5040, USA

Holman, Scott (Athlete, Baseball Player)
215 Dublin Ct
Brandon, MS 39047-8035, USA

Holman, Scott (Athlete, Football Player)
4 Comiso
Irvine, CA 92614-0224, USA

Holman, Shawn (Athlete, Baseball Player)
105 Edgewood Rd
Sewickley, PA 15143-9681, USA

Holmberg, Mark (Musician)
6404 Wilshire Blvd Ste 505
Los Angeles, CA 90048-5507, USA

Holmberg, Rob (Athlete, Football Player)
316 Coppersmith Ln
Strasburg, PA 17579-1021, USA

Holmes, A M (Writer)
English Dept
New York, NY 10027, USA

Holmes, Ashton (Actor)
c/o Jeff Morrone *Jeff Morrone Entertainment*
9350 Wilshire Blvd Ste 224
Beverly Hills, CA 90212-3204, USA

Holmes, Charlie (Athlete, Hockey Player)
7567 NE Meadowmeer Ln
Bainbridge Island, WA 98110-1223, USA

Holmes, Clayton (Athlete, Football Player)
1142 Hollings Ave
Florence, SC 29506-6725, USA

Holmes, Clint (Music Group)
697 Middle Neck Rd
Great Neck, NY 11023-1216, USA

Holmes, D Brainerd (Business Person, Engineer)
950 Winter St # 4350
Waltham, MA 02451-1424, USA

Holmes, Dame Kelly (Athlete)
17 rue Princesse Florestine BP 359
MC98007, MONACO

Holmes, Darren (Athlete, Baseball Player)
1 Emerald Ct
Arden, NC 28704-9594, USA

Holmes, Earl (Athlete, Football Player)
2978 Stonybrook Ct
Tallahassee, FL 32309-2167, USA

Holmes, JB (Athlete, Golfer)
5175 Latrobe Dr
Windermere, FL 34786-8959, USA

Holmes, Jennifer (Actor)
PO Box 6303
Carmel, CA 93921-6303, USA

Holmes, Jerry (Athlete, Football Player)
107 Chatham Ter
Hampton, VA 23666-4105, USA

Holmes, Katie (Actor)
c/o Ina Treciokas *Slate Public Relations*
9000 W Sunset Blvd Ste 915
West Hollywood, CA 90069-5809, USA

Holmes, Kenneth (Athlete, Football Player)
PO Box 273309
Boca Raton, FL 33427-3309, USA

Holmes, Larry (Boxer)
228 W Canal St
Easton, PA 18042-6244, USA

Holmes, Lester (Athlete, Football Player)
3760 Motor Ave
Los Angeles, CA 90034-6404, USA

Holmes, Louis (Athlete, Hockey Player)
36-17917 68 Ave
Surrey, BC V3S 9C8, Canada

Holmes, Pat (Athlete, Football Player)
221 Mack Hollimon Dr
Kerrville, TX 78028-6628, USA

Holmes, Priest (Athlete, Football Player)
9727 Autumn Arbor
San Antonio, TX 78240, USA

Holmes, Rudell (Athlete, Football Player)
1713 Lisa Ave
Vista, CA 92084-3057, USA

Holmes, Santonio (Athlete, Football Player)
c/o Peter Miller *Jabez Marketing Group*
516 E 2nd St Ste 3
Boston, MA 02127-1438, USA

Holmes, Sherlock Society
221B Baker St
London, ENGLAND W1

Holmes, Susan (Actor, Model)
c/o Jerry Shandrew *Shandrew Public Relations*
1050 S Stanley Ave
Los Angeles, CA 90019-6634, USA

Holmes, Thomas F (Tommy) (Athlete, Baseball Player, Coach)
1850 S Ocean Blvd Apt 309
Pompano Beach, FL 33062-7910, USA

Holmes, Tina (Actor)
c/o Mike Smith *Principal Entertainment (LA)*
1964 Westwood Blvd Ste 400
Los Angeles, CA 90025-4695, USA

Holmes, TJ (Anchor)
1 Cnn Ctr NW
Atlanta, GA 30303-2762

Holmes Norton, Eleanor (Congressman, Politician)
2136 Rayburn Hob
Washington, DC 20515-5100, USA

Holmgren, Janet L (Educator)
President's Office
Oakland, CA 94613, USA

Holmgren, Michael G (Mike) (Athlete, Coach, Football Coach, Football Player)
11220 NE 53rd St
Kirkland, WA 98033-7505, USA

Holmgren, Paul H (Athlete, Coach, Hockey Player)
724 Southwick Cir
Somerdale, NJ 08083-2312, USA

Holmoe, Tom (Athlete, Football Player)
1674 N 1670 W
Provo, UT 84604-7210, USA

Holmquest, Donald L (Astronaut)
205 Princeton Rd
Menlo Park, CA 94025-5217, USA

Holmstrom, Carl (Skier)
1703 E 3rd St Apt 101
Duluth, MN 55812-1743, USA

Holmstrom, Peter (Musician)
PO Box 5908
Portland, OR 97228-5908, USA

Holmstrom, Tomas (Athlete, Hockey Player)
43479 McLean Ct
Novi, MI 48375-4017, USA

Holohan, Pete (Athlete, Football Player)
2945 Curie St
San Diego, CA 92122-4105, USA

Holovak, Michael J (Mike) (Athlete, Football Coach, Football Player)
5051 Sandy Brook Cir
Wimauma, FL 33598-4023, USA

Holroyd, Michael (Writer)
85 Saint Marks Road
London W10 6JS, UNITED KINGDOM (UK)

Holroyd, Scott (Actor)
c/o Christopher (Chris) Wright *Christopher Wright Management*
3207 Winnie Dr
Los Angeles, CA 90068-1439, USA

Holst, Per (Producer)
Rentemestervej 69A
Copenhagen, NV 2400, DENMARK

Holt, Chris (Athlete, Baseball Player)
152 Hollywood Dr
Coppell, TX 75019-7302, USA

Holt, David Lee (Musician)
1620 16th Ave S
Nashville, TN 37212-2908, USA

Holt, Gary (Athlete, Hockey Player)
5820 S Sorrel Ct
Spokane, WA 99224-8298, USA

Holt, Glenn L (Athlete, Football Player)
800 NE 137th St
North Miami, FL 33161-3243, USA

Holt, Issac (Athlete, Football Player)
4028 Fairmont Pl
Birmingham, AL 35207-2732, USA

Holt, Jim (Athlete, Baseball Player)
150 Judge Sharpe Rd
Graham, NC 27253-8202, USA

Holt, Lester (Correspondent)
30 Rockefeller Plz
New York, NY 10112-0015, USA

Holt, Pierce (Athlete, Football Player)
5101 County Road 430
San Angelo, TX 76901-9506, USA

Holt, Robert J (Athlete, Football Player)
1332 Williams Ave
Desoto, TX 75115-3182, USA

Holt, Roger (Athlete, Baseball Player)
804 Hilltop St
Fruitland Park, FL 34731-2061, USA

Holt, Sandrine (Actor)
c/o Jennifer Goldhar *Characters Talent Agency, The (Toronto)*
1505 W 2nd Ave #200
Vancouver, BC V6H 3Y4, Canada

Holt, Torry (Athlete, Football Player)
c/o Mark Lepselter *Maxx Sports & Entertainment*
546 5th Ave Fl 6
New York, NY 10036-5000, USA

Holt Jr, Jack
504 Temple Dr
Harrah, OK 73045, USA

Holt Jr., Rush (Congressman, Politician)
1214 Longworth Hob
Washington, DC 20515-1408, USA

Holtgrave, Vern (Athlete, Baseball Player)
389 N 8th St
Breese, IL 62230-1107, USA

Holt-Kramer, Toni
1229 Santa Monica Blvd
Santa Monica, CA 90404-1705

Holton, A Linwood Jr (Physicist)
64 Francis Ave
Cambridge, MA 02138-1912, USA

Holton, Brian (Athlete, Baseball Player)
3214 Estate Dr
Oakdale, PA 15071-1445, USA

Holton, Mark (Actor)
c/o Staff Member *Gage Group, The (LA)*
14724 Ventura Blvd Ste 505
Sherman Oaks, CA 91403-3505, USA

Holton, Michael (Athlete, Basketball Player, Coach)
5822 NW Redfox Dr
Portland, OR 97229-2657, USA

Holtz, Louis L (Lou) (Athlete, Coach, Football Coach, Football Player)
9209 Cromwell Park Pl
Orlando, FL 32827-7005, USA

Holtz, Mike (Athlete, Baseball Player)
515 Double Dam Rd
Northern Cambria, PA 15714-7404, USA

Holtzman, Elizabeth (Liz) (Misc)
2 Park Ave Rm 2100
New York, NY 10016-9301, USA

Holtzman, Jerome (Baseball Player, Writer)
1225 Forest Ave
Evanston, IL 60202-1409, USA

Holtzman, Kenneth D (Ken) (Athlete, Baseball Player)
256 Waterside Dr
Grover, MO 63040-1632, USA

Holtzman, Wayne H (Doctor)
2500 Barton Creek Blvd Apt 1504
Austin, TX 78735-1622, USA

Holub, Dick (Athlete, Basketball Player)
16159 W Wildflower Dr
Surprise, AZ 85374-5048, USA

Holub, E J (Athlete, Football Player)
2311 S County Road 1120
Midland, TX 79706-4942, USA

Holum, Dianne (Speed Skater)
961 E 1st Ave Apt 605
Broomfield, CO 80020-3724, USA

Holum, Kristin (Speed Skater)
10596 Steele St
Northglenn, CO 80233-6117, USA

Holway, Jerome F (Cinematographer)
448 Spruce Dr
Exton, PA 19341-2020, USA

Holy, Steve (Musician)
c/o Staff Member *Paradigm (Nashville)*
124 12th Ave S Ste 410
Nashville, TN 37203-3170, USA

Holyfield, Evander (Boxer)
794 Evander Holyfield Hwy
Fairburn, GA 30213, USA

Holz, Gordon (Athlete, Football Player)
730 S Plaza Dr Apt 222
Saint Paul, MN 55120-1575, USA

Holzemer, Mark (Athlete, Baseball Player)
10044 MacAlister Trl
Littleton, CO 80129, USA

Holzer, Helmut (Scientist)
2103 Greenwood Pl SW
Huntsville, AL 35802-4462, USA

Holzer, Jenny (Artist)
80 Hewitts Rd
Hoosick Falls, NY 12090, USA

Holzier, James (Actor)
c/o Bob Willems *Champion Entertainment*
2620 Fountain View Dr Ste 220
Houston, TX 77057-7627, USA

Holzinger, Brian (Athlete, Hockey Player)
1005 Ledgemont Dr
Broadview Heights, OH 44147-4021, USA

Holzman, Malcolm (Architect)
902 Broadway
New York, NY 10010-6002, USA

Hom, Aaron (Stylist)
c/o Staff Member *Zenobia Agency Inc*
PO Box 909
Groveland, CA 95321-0909, USA

Homa, Lisa (Stylist)
875 W 81 St
New York, NY 10033, USA

Homan, Dennis (Athlete, Football Player)
1950 Charlotte Ct
Florence, AL 35630-6768, USA

Homeier, Skip (Actor, Director)
75381 Desert Valley Ln
Indian Wells, CA 92210-8316, USA

Homfeld, Conrad (Horse Racer)
11744 Marblestone Ct
Wellington, FL 33414-6041, USA

Honda, Yuka (Music Group)
833 W Chicago Ave Ste 101
Chicago, IL 60642-8408, USA

Honderich, Beland H (Publisher)
1 Yonge St
Toronto, ON M5E 1E6, CANADA

Honderich, John H (Editor)
Editorial Dept 1 Yonge St
Toronto, ON M5E 1E6, CANADA

Honegger, Fritz (President)
Schloss-Str 29
Ruschlidon 8803, SWITZERLAND

Honeycutt, Rick
207 Forrest Rd
Fort Oglethorpe, GA 30742-3706

Honeycutt, Rick (Athlete, Baseball Player)
207 Forrest Rd
Fort Oglethorpe, GA 30742-3706, USA

Honeycutt, Van B (Business Person)
2100 E Grand Ave
El Segundo, CA 90245-5024, USA

Honeycyt (Music Group)
c/o Staff Member *Paradigm (Monterey)*
404 W Franklin St
Monterey, CA 93940-2303, USA

Honeyghan, Lloyd (Boxer)
Park Langley Beckenham
Kent, UNITED KINGDOM (UK)

Honeymoon Suite
1505 W 2nd Ave # 200
Vancouver, CANADA BC V6H 3Y4

Hong, James (Actor)
c/o Carol Weiss *Stage 9 Talent*
1249 Lodi Pl
Los Angeles, CA 90038-1709, USA

Hong Song Nam (Prime Minister)
Pyongyong, NORTH KOREA

Honig, Edwin (Writer)
PO Box 285
Franktown, CO 80116-0285, USA

Honore, Jean Cardinal (Religious Leader)
BP 1117 27 Rue Jules-Simon
Tours Cedex 37011, FRANCE

Hoobastank (Music Group)

Hood, Don (Athlete, Baseball Player)
708 Firestone Dr
Florence, SC 29501-8825, USA

Hood, Estus (Athlete, Football Player)
2105 W Grace St
Kankakee, IL 60901-4590, USA

Hood, Kenneth (Religious Leader)
5799 Bloomfield Ave
Verona, NJ 7044, USA

Hood, Leroy E (Inventor, Scientist)
1441 N 34th St
Seattle, WA 98103-8904, USA

Hood, Robert
1325 W Walnut Hill Ln
Irving, TX 75038-3008, USA

Hoogstratten, Louise
12451 Mulholland Dr
Beverly Hills, CA 90210-1336

Hook, Chris (Athlete, Baseball Player)
30 Northfield Dr
Florence, KY 41042-8924, USA

Hook, Jay (Athlete, Baseball Player)
PO Box 90
Maple City, MI 49664-0090, USA

Hooker, Charles R (Artist)
28 Whippingham Road Brighton
Sussex BN2 3PG, UNITED KINGDOM (UK)

Hooker, Fair (Athlete, Football Player)
3728 Rutherford Ct
Inglewood, CA 90305-2244, USA

Hooks, Jan (Actor)
c/o Staff Member *Innovative Artists (LA)*
1505 10th St
Santa Monica, CA 90401-2805, USA

Hooks, Kevin (Director)
8942 Wilshire Blvd # 219
Beverly Hills, CA 90211-1908, USA

Hooks, Robert (Actor)
145 N Valley St
Burbank, CA 91505-4036, USA

Hooks, Roland (Athlete, Football Player)
3724 Calgary Dr
Reno, NV 89511-6096, USA

Hookstratten, Edward G (Attorney, Attorney General, General)
9536 Wilshire Blvd Ste 500
Beverly Hills, CA 90212-2435, USA

Hoop, Jesca (Musician)
c/o Staff Member *Paradigm (Monterey)*
404 W Franklin St
Monterey, CA 93940-2303, USA

Hooper, Bobby Joe (Athlete, Basketball Player)
825 Ivywood St Apt 4
Dayton, OH 45420-1751, USA

Hooper, Brandon
3003 3rd St Unit 4
Santa Monica, CA 90405-5488

Hooper, C Darrow (Athlete, Track Athlete)
6 Braemore Pl
Dallas, TX 75230-1958, USA

Hooper, Kevin (Athlete, Baseball Player)
2701 Century Dr
Lawrence, KS 66049-2523, USA

Hooper, Tobe
PO Box 5617
Beverly Hills, CA 90209-5617

Hooper, Tom (Director)
c/o Doug MacLaren *International Creative Management (ICM-LA)*
10250 Constellation Blvd Fl 7
Los Angeles, CA 90067-6207, USA

Hoopes, Mitch (Athlete, Football Player)
5000 Murray Blvd Apt F1
Salt Lake City, UT 84123-2674, USA

Hooser, Carroll (Athlete, Basketball Player)
925 Edgefield Trl
Flower Mound, TX 75028-1304, USA

Hooten, Burt
3619 Granby Ct
San Antonio, TX 78217-4653

Hooten, Leon (Athlete, Baseball Player)
461 N 11th St
Coos Bay, OR 97420-1851, USA

Hootie & The Blowfish (Music Group)
c/o Staff Member *Paradigm (Monterey)*
404 W Franklin St
Monterey, CA 93940-2303, USA

Hooton, Burt C (Athlete, Baseball Player)
3619 Granby Ct
San Antonio, TX 78217-4653, USA

Hootselle, Brenda (Stylist)
c/o Staff Member *Talent Plus*
1222 Lucas Ave Ste 300
Saint Louis, MO 63103-1937, USA

Hootselle, Meko (Stylist)
c/o Staff Member *Talent Plus*
1222 Lucas Ave Ste 300
Saint Louis, MO 63103-1937, USA

Hoover, Alice (Baseball Player)
340 Roosevelt Ave
Reading, PA 19605-2337, USA

Hoover, Brad (Athlete, Football Player)
2130 Climbing Rose Ln
Matthews, NC 28104-6232, USA

Hoover, Herbert III
200 S Los Robles Ave # 520
Pasadena, CA 91101-2479

Hoover, Houston (Athlete, Football Player)
1216 Mareed Ave
Yazoo City, MS 39194-2831, USA

Hoover, John (Athlete, Baseball Player)
1615 W Fountain Way
Fresno, CA 93705-3331, USA

Hoover, Paul (Athlete, Baseball Player)
2320 Anderson Rd
Cuyahoga Falls, OH 44221-3620, USA

Hoover, Robert A (Bob) (Misc)
1100 E Imperial Ave
El Segundo, CA 90245-2608, USA

Hoover, Tom (Athlete, Basketball Player)
9 Apple Manor Ln
East Brunswick, NJ 08816-2872, USA

Hoover, Vicky (Stylist)
PO Box 854
Littleton, CO 80160-0854, USA

Hoovler, Skip (Athlete, Football Player)
8249 Broad St SW
Pataskala, OH 43062-7831, USA

Hope, Alec D (Writer)
PO Box 7949
Alice Springs, NT 871, AUSTRALIA

Hope, Jim (Producer)
c/o Staff Member *WmE2 (Endeavor-LA)*
9601 Wilshire Blvd Fl 3
Beverly Hills, CA 90210-5219, USA

Hope, John (Athlete, Baseball Player)
8341 NW 51st St
Lauderhill, FL 33351-4933, USA

Hope, Leslie (Actor)
c/o Lee Wallman *Wallman Public Relations*
10323 Santa Monica Blvd Ste 109
Los Angeles, CA 90025-5056, USA

Hope, Maurice (Boxer)
582 Kingsland Road
London E8, UNITED KINGDOM (UK)

Hope, Tamara (Actor)
c/o Matt Schwartz *Christopher Wright Management*
6100 Wilshire Blvd Ste 1170
Los Angeles, CA 90048-5116, USA

Hopkins, Anthony (Actor)
c/o Paul Bloch *Rogers & Cowan PR (LA)*
Pacific Design Center 8687 Melrose Ave, 7th Floor
West Hollywood, CA 90069, USA

Hopkins, Antony (Composer, Writer)
Woodyard Cottage Ashridge Berkhamsted
Herts HP4 1PS, UNITED KINGDOM (UK)

Hopkins, Bo (Actor)
6628 Ethel Ave
North Hollywood, CA 91606-1018, USA

Hopkins, Bob (Athlete, Basketball Player)
8421 SE 71st St
Mercer Island, WA 98040-5409, USA

Hopkins, Demetrius (Boxer)
c/o Staff Member *Top Rank Inc.*
3908 Howard Hughes Pkwy # 580
Las Vegas, NV 89109, USA

Hopkins, Don (Athlete, Baseball Player)
PO Box 8817
Benton Harbor, MI 49023-8817, USA

Hopkins, Gail (Athlete, Baseball Player)
120 Canterbury Dr
Parkersburg, WV 26104-8048, USA

Hopkins, Gareth (Business Person)
c/o Staff Member *EMI Recorded Music (UK)*
27 Wrights Lane
London W8 5SW, UK

Hopkins, Godfrey T (Photographer)
Wilmington Cottage Wilmington Road Seaford
E Sussex BN25 2EH, UNITED KINGDOM (UK)

Hopkins, Jan (Correspondent)
1050 Techwood Dr NW
Atlanta, GA 30318-5604, USA

Hopkins, Jerry (Athlete, Football Player)
6688 E State Highway 6
Waco, TX 76705-5385, USA

Hopkins, Josh (Actor)
232 N Canon Dr
Beverly Hills, CA 90210-5302, USA

Hopkins, Kaitlin (Actor)
19528 Ventura Blvd # 559
Tarzana, CA 91356-2917, USA

Hopkins, Katherine
215 S La Cienega Blvd PH
Beverly Hills, CA 90211-3322

Hopkins, Larry (Athlete, Hockey Player)
3012 S Fir Ave
Broken Arrow, OK 74012-7496, USA

Hopkins, Linda (Actor, Musician)
2055 Ivar Ave PH
Los Angeles, CA 90068-3918, USA

Hopkins, Michael J (Architect)
27 Broadley Terrace
London NW1 6LG, UNITED KINGDOM (UK)

Hopkins, Stephen
8942 Wilshire Blvd
Beverly Hills, CA 90211-1908

Hopkins, Stephen J (Director)
8942 Wilshire Blvd # 219
Beverly Hills, CA 90211-1908, USA

Hopkins, Sy (Music Group)
PO Box 12
Far Hills, NJ 07931-0012, USA

Hopkins, Tamburo (Athlete, Football Player)
2740 Maitland Crossing Way Apt 2208
Orlando, FL 32810-7130, USA

Hopkins, Telma (Actor, Music Group)
c/o Staff Member *Innovative Artists (LA)*
1505 10th St
Santa Monica, CA 90401-2805, USA

Hopkins, Wesley (Athlete, Football Player)
7412 White Oak Rd
Fairfield, AL 35064-2454, USA

Hoppe, Fred (Artist)
PO Box 42
Milford, NE 68405-0042, USA

Hoppe, Wolfgang (Athlete)
Dieterstedter Str 11
Apolda 99510, GERMANY

Hoppen, Dave (Athlete, Basketball Player)
16341 Webster St
Omaha, NE 68118-2513, USA

Hopper, C Darrow (Athlete, Football Player)
6 Braemore Pl
Dallas, TX 75230-1958, USA

Hopper, John D Jr (General)
Commander Air Education/Training Command
Randolph Air Force Base, TX 78155, USA

Hopper, Norris (Athlete, Baseball Player)
2319 Bonner Bridge Ct
Charlotte, NC 28273-4613, USA

Hopperdeitz, Anna (Actor)
c/o Staff Member *Agentur Fuhrmann*
Lindenstr 8A
Isen-Pemmering 84424, Germany

Hoppock, Doug (Athlete, Football Player)
13212 W 115th St
Shawnee Mission, KS 66210-3540, USA

Hoppus, Cliff (Stylist)
c/o Staff Member *Exclusive Artists Mgmt*
7700 W Sunset Blvd Ste 205
Los Angeles, CA 90046-3913, USA

Hoppus, Mark (Actor, Musician, Producer)
c/o Geyer Kosinski *Media Talent Group*
9200 W Sunset Blvd Ste 550
Los Angeles, CA 90069-3611, USA

Hopson, Dennis (Athlete, Basketball Player)
7229 Donnybrook Dr
Dublin, OH 43017-2403, USA

Horacek, Tony (Athlete, Hockey Player)
71 Clover Pl
Lebanon, PA 17042-9400, USA

Horan, James (Actor)
c/o Staff Member *Angel City Talent*
8318 Kirkwood Dr
Los Angeles, CA 90046-1926, USA

Horan, Machael W (Mike) (Athlete, Football Player)
7235 E La Cumbre Dr
Orange, CA 92869-4464, USA

Horbiger, Christiane
Frankengasse 28
Zurich, SWITZERLAND CH-8001

Horbul, Doug (Athlete, Hockey Player)
2562 Statts
Fruitvale, BC V0G 1L0, Canada

Hordges, Cedrick (Athlete, Basketball Player)
237 W 127th St Apt 28
New York, NY 10027-2901, USA

Hordichuk, Darcy (Athlete, Hockey Player)
1006 Buddleia Ln
Franklin, TN 37067-8610, USA

Horeck, Peter (Athlete, Hockey Player)
P.O. Box 331 Stn B
Sudbury, ON P3E 4P2, Canada

Horecker, Bernard L (Biologist)
16517 Cypress Villa Ln
Fort Myers, FL 33908-7609, USA

Horgan, Joe (Athlete, Baseball Player)
2039 Kellogg Way
Rancho Cordova, CA 95670-2434, USA

Horgan, Patrick (Actor)
201 E 89th St
New York, NY 10128-3421, USA

Horinek, Ramon A (War Hero)
181 National Blvd
Universal City, TX 78148-4444, USA

Horlen, Joel (Athlete, Baseball Player)
3718 Chartwell Dr
San Antonio, TX 78230-3202, USA

Horlock, John H (Educator, Engineer)
2 The Avenue Ampthill
Bedford MK45 2NR, UNITED KINGDOM (UK)

Horn, Don (Athlete, Football Player)
1336 Hazeline Lake Dr
Colorado Springs, CO 80921-4105, USA

Horn, Gyula (Prime Minister)
Kossuth Lajor Ter 1/3
Budepest 1055, HUNGARY

Horn, Joe (Athlete, Football Player)
2408 Shenley Park Ct
Duluth, GA 30097-4961, USA

Horn, Marian Blank (Judge)
717 Madison Pl NW
Washington, DC 20439-0001, USA

Horn, Paul J (Musician)
4601 Leyns Rd
Victoria, BC V8N 3A1, CANADA

Horn, Roy (Magician)
3400 Las Vegas Blvd S
Las Vegas, NV 89109-8923

Horn, Sam (Athlete, Baseball Player)
1305 Narragansett Blvd
Cranston, RI 02905-3825, USA

Horn, Shriley (Music Group)
1007 Towne Ln
Charlottesville, VA 22901-3173, USA

Hornacek, Jeff (Athlete, Basketball Player)
5821 N 37th St
Paradise Valley, AZ 85253-5004, USA

Hornaday, Ron (Race Car Driver)
703 Park Lawn Ct
Kernersville, NC 27284-8967, USA

Hornburg, Hal M (General)
Commander Air Combat Command
Langley Air Force Base, VA 23665, USA

Hornby, Nick (Writer)
60/66 Wardour St
London W1V 4ND, UNITED KINGDOM (UK)

Horne, Donald R (Writer)
53 Grosvenor St Woollahra
Sydney, NSW 2025, AUSTRALIA

Horne, John R (Business Person)
PO Box 1488
Warrenville, IL 60555-7488, USA

Horne, Marilyn (Opera Singer)
315 W 86th St Apt 2D
New York, NY 10024-3108, USA

Horneber, Petra (Misc)
Ringstr 77
Kranzberg 85402, GERMANY

Horneff, Wil (Actor)
c/o Staff Member *Creative Artists Agency (CAA-LA)*
2000 Avenue of the Stars Ste 100
Los Angeles, CA 90067-4705, USA

Horner, Bob (Athlete, Baseball Player)
209 Steeplechase Dr
Irving, TX 75062-3823, USA

Horner, Charles A (General)
2824 Jack Nicklaus Way
Shalimar, FL 32579-2226, USA

Horner, Craig (Actor)
c/o Matt Andrews *Marquee Management*
The Gatehouse 188 Oxford St Studio B
Paddington NSW 2021, Australia

Horner, Freeman V (War Hero)
1501 Doubletree Dr
Columbus, GA 31904-2659, USA

Horner, James (Composer, Musician)
c/o Carri McClure *McClure and Associates Public Relations*
5225 Wilshire Blvd Ste 909
Los Angeles, CA 90036-4353, USA

Horner, John R (Jack) (Scientist)
70 Cougar Dr
Bozeman, MT 59718-8346, USA

Horner, Martina S (Business Person, Educator)
730 3rd Ave
New York, NY 10017-3206, USA

Hornig, Donald F (Misc)
1 Little Pond Cove Rd
Little Compton, RI 02837-1422, USA

Hornsby, Bruce (Musician)
PO Box 3545
Williamsburg, VA 23187-3545, USA

Hornsby, Ron (Athlete, Football Player)
2028 Washington St
Franklinton, LA 70438-2533, USA

Hornsby, Russell (Actor)
c/o Leonard Torgan *Collective*
3301 Exposition Blvd
Santa Monica, CA 90404-5045, USA

Hornung, Paul V (Actor)
Waterfront Plaza #1116 325 West Main St
Louisville, KY 40202, USA

Horovitz, Adam (King Ad-Rock) (Artist, Music Group, Musician)
c/o Staff Member *WmE2 (Endeavor-LA)*
9601 Wilshire Blvd Fl 3
Beverly Hills, CA 90210-5219, USA

Horovitz, Israel A (Writer)
146 W 11th St
New York, NY 10011-8306, USA

Horovitz, Joseph (Composer)
Prince Consort Road
London SW7 2BS, UNITED KINGDOM (UK)

Horowitz, David (Correspondent)
PO Box 49915
Los Angeles, CA 90049-0915, USA

Horowitz, Jerome P (Scientist)
110 E Warren Ave
Detroit, MI 48201-1312, USA

Horowitz, Norman H (Biologist)
2495 Brighton Rd
Pasadena, CA 91104, USA

Horowitz, Paul (Doctor, Physicist)
111 Chilton St
Cambridge, MA 02138-6844, USA

Horowitz, Sari (Journalist)
1150 15th St NW
Washington, DC 20071-0001, USA

Horowitz, Scott J (Astronaut)
5491 Freestyle Way
Park City, UT 84098-7621, USA

Horrocks, Jane (Actor, Music Group)
Drury House 34-43 Russell St
London WC2B 5HA, UNITED KINGDOM (UK)

Horry, Robert (Athlete, Basketball Player)
2618 Sara Ridge Ln
Katy, TX 77450-5374, USA

Horsey, David (Cartoonist, Editor)
c/o Staff Member *King Features Syndication*
300 W 57th St Fl 15
New York, NY 10019-5238, USA

Horsford, Anna Maria (Actor)
PO Box 48082
Los Angeles, CA 90048-0082, USA

Horsley, Lee A (Actor)
c/o Laura Walsh *Central Artists*
3310 W Burbank Blvd # A
Burbank, CA 91505-2230, USA

Horsley, Richard D (Financier)
417 20th St N
Birmingham, AL 35203-3203, USA

Horsman, Vince (Athlete, Baseball Player)
1941 Pinehurst Dr
Clearwater, FL 33763-2228, USA

Horst, Lisa Ann
131 Windover Turn
Lancaster, PA 17601-5331

Horstman, Catherine (Baseball Player)
39018 Desert Greens Dr E
Palm Desert, CA 92260-1403, USA

Horth, Annie (Stylist)
c/o Staff Member *Judy Inc*
1 Yorkville Ave
Toronto ON M4W 1L1, Canada

Horton, Ethan S (Football Player, Sportscaster)
PO Box 30247
Charlotte, NC 28230-0247, USA

Horton, Frank E (Educator)
288 River Ranch Cir
Bayfield, CO 81122-8774, USA

Horton, Greg (Athlete, Football Player)
1053 Lytle St
Redlands, CA 92374-6240, USA

Horton, Jonathan (Athlete, Gymnast, Olympic Athlete)
c/o Staff Member *USA Gymnastics*
Pan American Plz #300 201 S Capitol Ave
Indianapolis, IN 46225, USA

Horton, Lawrence (Athlete, Football Player)
1442 S 13th St
Harrisburg, PA 17104-3107, USA

Horton, Michael (Editor)
c/o Staff Member *Mirisch Agency*
8840 Wilshire Blvd Ste 100
Beverly Hills, CA 90211-2606, USA

Horton, Nathan (Athlete, Hockey Player)
12037 NW 69th Ct
Parkland, FL 33076-3335, USA

Horton, Peter (Actor)
409 Santa Monica Blvd PH
Santa Monica, CA 90401-2232, USA

Horton, Ray (Athlete, Football Player)
8014 Falcon Ct
Gibsonia, PA 15044-6057, USA

Horton, Ricky (Athlete, Baseball Player)
16026 Aston Ct
Chesterfield, MO 63005-4575, USA

Horton, Robert (Actor)
5317 Andasol Ave
Encino, CA 91316-2504, USA

Horton, Tony (Athlete, Fitness Expert, Television Host)
3301 Exposition Blvd Fl 3
Santa Monica, CA 90404-5082, USA

Horton, Willie (Athlete, Baseball Player)
5655 Woodland Pass
Bloomfield Hills, MI 48301-1230, USA

Horton, Willie(baseball)
15124 Warwick St
Detroit, MI 48223-2293

Horvath, Bronco J (Athlete, Hockey Player)
27 Oliver St
South Yarmouth, MA 02664-2901, USA

Horvitz, H Robert (Nobel Prize Laureate)
Biology Dept
Cambridge, MA 2139, USA

Horvitz, Louis J (Director)
c/o Staff Member *Gersh (LA)*
9465 Wilshire Blvd Ste 600
Beverly Hills, CA 90212-2612, USA

Horwitz, Tony (Journalist)
200 Liberty St
New York, NY 10281-1003, USA

Hosbein, Marion (Athlete, Baseball Player)
1347 Cliff Barnes Dr
Kalamazoo, MI 49009-8329, USA

Hosea, Bobby (Actor)
c/o Sara Schedeen *Metropolitan (MTA)*
4526 Wilshire Blvd
Los Angeles, CA 90010-3801, USA

Hosey, Dwayne (Athlete, Baseball Player)
10850 Church St Apt R101
Rch Cucamonga, CA 91730-8050, USA

Hosey, Steve (Athlete, Baseball Player)
2351 W Loma Linda Ave
Fresno, CA 93711-0417, USA

Hosket, William (Bill) (Athlete, Basketball Player)
7461 Worthington Galena Rd
Worthington, OH 43085-6715, USA

Hoskins, Bob (Actor)
60/66 Wardour St
London W1V 4ND, UNITED KINGDOM (UK)

Hoskins, Derrick (Athlete, Football Player)
10491 Road 842
Philadelphia, MS 39350-8204, USA

Hosley, Tim (Athlete, Baseball Player)
112 Elena Dr
Moore, SC 29369-9657, USA

Hosmer, Bradley C (Brad) (General)
PO Box 1128
Cedar Crest, NM 87008-1128, USA

Hospodar, Ed (Athlete, Hockey Player)
37 Greythorne Woods Cir
Wayne, PA 19087-4758, USA

Hoss, Clark (Athlete, Football Player)
5300 Parkview Dr Apt 1078
Lake Oswego, OR 97035-8727, USA

Hossa, Marian (Athlete, Hockey Player)
700 Park Regency Pl NE Apt 905
Atlanta, GA 30326-4208, USA

Hossein, Robert (Actor, Director)
10 Rue du Docteur Roux
Paris 75015, FRANCE

Hosseini, Khaled
c/o Judy Lubershane *Judy Lubershane Agency*
not available
Boston, MA 2101, USA

Hostak, Al (Boxer)
11501 161st Ave SE
Renton, WA 98059-6145, USA

Hostak, Martin (Athlete, Hockey Player)
Ceska Televize odd. kontaktu s divakem
Kavci hory
Praha 4 140 70, Czech Republic

Hostetler, Dave (Athlete, Baseball Player)
3404 Steeplechase Trl
Arlington, TX 76016-2325, USA

Hostetler, David L (Artist)
PO Box 989
Athens, OH 45701-0989, USA

Hostetler, Jeff (Athlete, Football Player)
2032 Magnolia Dr
Morgantown, WV 26508-4467, USA

Hostetter, G Richard (Religious Leader)
1852 Century Plz
Atlanta, GA 30345, USA

Hoston, Ricky (Baseball Player)
16026 Aston Ct
Chesterfield, MO 63005-4575, USA

Hoston, Tony (Baseball Player)
17001 Livorno Dr
Pacific Palisades, CA 90272-3232, USA

Hot Chelle Rae (Music Group)
c/o Staff Member *Jive Records*
550 Madison Ave Fl 6
New York, NY 10022-3211, USA

Hotani, Hirokazu (Engineer)
Biosciences Dept Toyosatodai
Utsunomiya 320, JAPAN

Hotchkiss, Harley (Athlete, Hockey Player)
c/o Staff Member *Calgary Flames*
P.O. Box 1540 Stn M
Calgary, AB T2P 3B9, Canada

Hotchkiss, Rob (Musician)
80 Mason St
Greenwich, CT 06830-5515, USA

Hotchkiss, Rollin D (Doctor, Scientist)
2-4 Rolling Hls
Lenox, MA 01240-2127, USA

Hotchner, Aaron
14 Hillandale Rd
Westport, CT 06880-5225

Hotchner, Aaron Edward (Producer, Writer)
c/o Staff Member *HarperCollins Publishers*
10 E 53rd St C/O Author Mail Floor 7
New York, NY 10022, USA

Hotham, Greg (Athlete, Hockey Player)
40 Ridgeway Ave
Barrie, ON L4N 5L2, Canada

Hottelet, Richard C (Correspondent)
120 Chestnut Hill Rd
Wilton, CT 06897-4608, USA

Hottman, Ken (Athlete, Baseball Player)
9537 2nd Ave
Elk Grove, CA 95624-1936, USA

Hoty, Dee
333 W 56th St
New York, NY 10019-3764

Hou, Ya-Ming (Biologist)
Biology Dept
Cambridge, MA 2139, USA

Houbregs, Robert J (Bob) (Athlete, Basketball Player)
1949 Arena Ct SE
Olympia, WA 98501-6874, USA

Houcke, Sara (Misc)
1313 17th St E
Palmetto, FL 34221-2850, USA

Houda, Doug (Athlete, Hockey Player)
10 Lovell Rd
Lynnfield, MA 01940-1818, USA

Hough, Charlie (Athlete)
2266 Shadetree Cir
Brea, CA 92821-4423

Hough, Charlie (Athlete, Baseball Player)
2266 Shadetree Cir
Brea, CA 92821-4423, USA

Hough, Derek (Dancer, Reality TV Star)
710 N Orlando Ave Apt 203
West Hollywood, CA 90069-5549, USA

Hough, Jim (Athlete, Football Player)
2440 Christian Dr
Chaska, MN 55318-1993, USA

Hough, John (Director)
5 Denmark St
London WC2H 8LP, UNITED KINGDOM (UK)

Hough, Joseph C Jr (Educator)
President's Office
New York, NY 10027, USA

Hough, Julianne (Dancer, Musician)
c/o Brad Cafarelli *PMK/BNC - LA*
8687 Melrose Ave Ste 8
West Hollywood, CA 90069-5746, USA

Hough, Michael A (General)
2 Navy St
Washington, DC 20380-1775, USA

Hough, Mike (Athlete, Hockey Player)
25 Marsh Harbour
Aurora, ON L4G 5Y7, Canada

Hough, Stephen A G (Musician)
12 Penzance Place
London W11 4PA, UNITED KINGDOM (UK)

Houghton, James (Business Person)
Field 36 Spencer Hill Road
Corning, NY 14830, USA

Houghton, John (Physicist)
Chilton
Didcot Oxon OX11 0QX, UNITED KINGDOM (UK)

Houghton, Katherine (Actor)
165 W 46th St
New York, NY 10036-2501, USA

Houghton of Sowerby, Douglas (Government Official)
110 Marsham Court
London SW1, UNITED KINGDOM (UK)

Hougland, William (Bill) (Athlete, Basketball Player)
PO Box 2629
Edwards, CO 81632-2629, USA

Houle, Rejean (Athlete, Hockey Player)
7941 Boul Lasalle
Lasalle, QC H8P 3R1, Canada

Houlemard, Michael (Athlete, Baseball Player)
111 S Orange Grove Blvd Apt 104
Pasadena, CA 91105-1756, USA

Houlton, D J (Athlete, Baseball Player)
2357 N Campus Ave
Upland, CA 91784-1303, USA

Hounsfield, Godfrey N (Nobel Prize Laureate)
15 Crane Park Road Whitton Twickenham
Middx TW2 6DF, UNITED KINGDOM (UK)

Hounsou, Djimon (Actor, Model, Producer)
c/o Peter Safran *The Safran Company*
8748 Holloway Dr
West Hollywood, CA 90069-2327, USA

Hourde, Daniel (Artist)
37, rue Galande
Paris 75005, France

House, Craig (Athlete, Baseball Player)
8845 Patricia Ellen Cv
Memphis, TN 38133-3807, USA

House, David (Dave) (Business Person)
8200 Dixie Rd
Brampton, ON L6T 5P6, CANADA

House, J R (Athlete, Baseball Player)
34 River Ridge Trl
Ormond Beach, FL 32174-4340, USA

House, James
1313 16th Ave S
Nashville, TN 37212-2903

House, Karen Ellot (Journalist)
58 Cleveland Ln
Princeton, NJ 08540-3077, USA

House, Kathryn (Stylist)
c/o Staff Member *Crews*
828 Clemont Dr NE
Atlanta, GA 30306-3694, USA

House, Kevin (Athlete, Football Player)
9724 Mary Robin Dr
Riverview, FL 33569-5572, USA

House, Pat (Athlete, Baseball Player)
2554 W Penick Pointe Ct
Meridian, ID 83646-5182, USA

House, Pat (Athlete, Baseball Player)
2053 S White Pine Ln
Boise, ID 83706-4048, USA

House, Stormy
12334 Gorham Ave
Los Angeles, CA 90049-5206

House, Tom (Athlete, Baseball Player)
603 Ranlett Ave
La Puente, CA 91744-4143, USA

House, Yoanna (Model, Television Host)
c/o Staff Member *Style Network*
5750 Wilshire Blvd
Los Angeles, CA 90036-3697, USA

House of Pain (Music Group)
c/o Staff Member *WmE2 (WMA-LA)*
1 William Morris Pl
Beverly Hills, CA 90212-4261, USA

Householder, Paul (Athlete, Baseball Player)
521 N Swinton Ave
Delray Beach, FL 33444-3969, USA

Houser, Huell
450 N Rossmore Ave # 602
Los Angeles, CA 90004-2406

Houser, Jerry (Actor)
12995 Galewood St
Studio City, CA 91604-4046, USA

Houser, Kevin (Athlete, Football Player)
941 Montclair Cir
Westlake, OH 44145-1445, USA

Houser, Randolph (Randy) (Musician)
c/o Staff Member *Fitzgerald Hartley Co (Nashville)*
1908 Wedgewood Ave
Nashville, TN 37212-3733, USA

Houser, Susan (Stylist)
c/o Staff Member *Independent NY*
15 E 30th St Apt 401
New York, NY 10016-7031, USA

Houshmandzadeh, T J (Athlete, Football Player)
16703 Greenbrook Cir
Cerritos, CA 90703-1188, USA

Housie, Wayne (Athlete, Baseball Player)
16530 Colt Way
Moreno Valley, CA 92555-3303, USA

Housley, Phil (Athlete, Hockey Player)
2877 Itasca Ave S
Lakeland, MN 55043-9742, USA

Housner, George W (Engineer, Misc)
Engineering
Pasadena, CA 91125-0001, USA

Houston (Adult Film Star)
c/o Staff Member *Atlas Multimedia Inc*
9005 Eton Ave Ste C
Canoga Park, CA 91304-6533, USA

Houston, Allan (Athlete, Basketball Player)
350 5th Ave Fl 59
New York, NY 10118-5999, USA

Houston, Andy (Race Car Driver)
c/o Global Performance Co 835 F Williamson Road #36
Mooresville, NC 28117, USA

Houston, Byron (Athlete, Basketball Player)
3108 Birch Ln
Edmond, OK 73034-8249, USA

Houston, Cissy (Music Group, Musician)
2160 N Central Rd
Fort Lee, NJ 07024-7547, USA

Houston, Edwin A (Business Person)
3600 NW 82nd Ave
Doral, FL 33166-6623, USA

Houston, Jarell (J-Boog) (Actor, Musician)
c/o Michael (Mike) Esterman
Esterman.Com, LLC
Prefers to be contacted via email
MD, USA

Houston, Ken (Athlete, Hockey Player)
25 University Dr
Chatham, ON N7L 4V4, Canada

Houston, Kenneth R (Ken) (Athlete, Football Player)
3603 Forest Village Dr
Kingwood, TX 77339-1819, USA

Houston, Marques (Batman) (Actor, Musician)
c/o Tyler Grasham *Agency for the Performing Arts (APA-LA)*
405 S Beverly Dr Ste 500
Beverly Hills, CA 90212-4425, USA

Houston, Marquis (Actor, Musician)

Houston, Penelope (Music Group)
8490 W Sunset Blvd # 403
West Hollywood, CA 90069-1912, USA

Houston, Russell (Artist)
General Delivery
Eagar, AZ 85925-9999, USA

Houston, Thelma (Musician)
2550 Greenvalley Rd
Los Angeles, CA 90046-1438, USA

Houston, Tyler (Athlete, Baseball Player)
325 Pleasant Summit Dr
Henderson, NV 89012-3486, USA

Houston, Wade (Basketball Player, Coach)
Athletic Dept
Knoxville, TN 37901, USA

Houston, Whitney (Musician)
c/o Kirsten Foster *PMK/BNC Public Relations (PMK-NY)*
622 3rd Ave Fl 8
New York, NY 10017-6707, USA

Houston Calls (Music Group)
c/o Staff Member *Drive Thru Records*
5250 Calatrana Dr
Woodland Hills, CA 91364-1811, USA

Houthakker, Hendrik S (Economist)
1 Ivy Pointe Way
Hanover, NH 03755-1407, USA

Hovan, Chris (Athlete, Football Player)
9520 Viking Dr
Eden Prairie, MN 55344-3825, USA

Hove, Andrew C Jr (Financier)
550 17th St NW
Washington, DC 20429-0001, USA

Hovind, David J (Business Person)
777 106th Ave NE
Bellevue, WA 98004-5027, USA

Hoving, Thomas (Director, Editor)
150 E 73rd St
New York, NY 10021-4375, USA

Hovland, Tim (Athlete, Volleyball Player)
431 Main St
El Segundo, CA 90245-3003, USA

Hovley, Steve (Athlete, Baseball Player)
PO Box 655
Oak View, CA 93022-0655, USA

Hovsepian, Vatche (Religious Leader)
1201 Vine St
Los Angeles, CA 90038-1611, USA

Howard, Adina (Musician)
40 W 57th St # 1800
New York, NY 10019-4001, USA

Howard, Adina (Musician)
c/o Staff Member *Diva Central Inc*
7510 W Sunset Blvd Ste 1445
Los Angeles, CA 90046-3408, USA

Howard, Alan (Actor)
46 Albermarle St
London W1X 4PP, UNITED KINGDOM (UK)

Howard, Ann (Opera Singer)
6 Barham Close Weybridge
Surrey KT13 9PR, UNITED KINGDOM (UK)

Howard, Arliss (Actor, Director, Writer)
c/o Gene Parseghian *Parseghian Planco LLC*
322 8th Ave Ste 601
New York, NY 10001-6715, USA

Howard, Ben (Athlete, Baseball Player)
45 Cross Brook Cv
Jackson, TN 38305-3548, USA

Howard, Bob (Athlete, Football Player)
2444 56th St
San Diego, CA 92105-5012, USA

Howard, Brian (Athlete, Basketball Player)
619 Vermont Ave
Fort Walton Beach, FL 32547-3033, USA

Howard, Bruce (Athlete, Baseball Player)
8705 Misty Creek Dr
Sarasota, FL 34241-9562, USA

Howard, Bryce Dallas (Actor)
c/o Peter Kiernan *Management 360*
9111 Wilshire Blvd
Beverly Hills, CA 90210-5508, USA

Howard, Chris (Athlete, Baseball Player)
11 Hawser Ln
Swampscott, MA 01907-1238, USA

Howard, Chris (Athlete, Baseball Player)
8655 Jones Rd Apt 301
Jersey Village, TX 77065-5104, USA

Howard, Clark (Radio Personality, Writer)
1601 W Peachtree St NE
Atlanta, GA 30309-2641, USA

Howard, Clint (Actor)
c/o Tiffany Kuzon *Evolution Entertainment (LA)*
901 N Highland Ave
Los Angeles, CA 90038-2412, USA

Howard, David (Athlete, Baseball Player)
22846 Chesterview Loop Apt 111
Land O Lakes, FL 34639-5343, USA

Howard, David (Athlete, Football Player)
5516 E Rosedale St
Fort Worth, TX 76112-6859, USA

Howard, Desmond (Athlete, Football Player)
7459 Winding Way
Brecksville, OH 44141-1923, USA

Howard, Doug (Athlete, Baseball Player)
8038 Deer Creek Rd
Salt Lake City, UT 84121-5762, USA

Howard, Dwight (Athlete, Basketball Player)
3565 Rice Lake Loop
Longwood, FL 32779-3081, USA

Howard, Eddie (Athlete, Football Player)
1130 E Workman Ave
West Covina, CA 91790-2357, USA

Howard, Frank (Athlete, Baseball Player, Coach)
24178 Lenah Woods Pl
Aldie, VA 20105-2369, USA

Howard, Frank O (Athlete, Baseball Player)
24178 Lenah Woods Pl
Aldie, VA 20105-2369, USA

Howard, Fred (Athlete, Baseball Player)
250 Lake Lulu Dr
Winter Haven, FL 33880-4461, USA

Howard, Gene (Athlete, Football Player)
11051 Lavender Ave
Fountain Valley, CA 92708-2457, USA

Howard, George (Bowler)
8415 Brookwood Dr
Portage, MI 49024-5209, USA

Howard, George (Musician)
PO Box 411197
San Francisco, CA 94141-1197, USA

Howard, Greg (Cartoonist)
3403 W 28th St
Minneapolis, MN 55416-4302, USA

Howard, Greg (Athlete, Basketball Player)
4517 W 16th Pl Apt 2
Los Angeles, CA 90019-5164, USA

Howard, Harry N (Historian)
6508 Greentree Road Bradley Hills Grv
Bethesda, MD 20817, USA

Howard, James Newton (Composer, Musician)
c/o Staff Member *Chasen & Company*
8899 Beverly Blvd Ste 405
Los Angeles, CA 90048-2431, USA

Howard, Jan (Music Group)
c/o Staff Member *Tessier-Marsh Talent*
505 Canton Pass
Madison, TN 37115-5449, USA

Howard, Jeffrey R (Judge)
55 Pleasant St
Concord, NH 03301-3954, USA

Howard, Jim (Athlete, Hockey Player)
518 Hamilton St
Ogdensburg, NY 13669-2714, USA

Howard, Joe (Athlete, Football Player)
2501 Joseph Dr
Clinton, MD 20735-4540, USA

Howard, John W (Prime Minister)
Parliament House
Canbera, ACT 2600, AUSTRALIA

Howard, Josh (Athlete, Basketball Player)
947 Liberty St
Dallas, TX 75204-5503, USA

Howard, Joyce
147 Ocean Avenue Ext
Santa Monica, CA 90402-1211

Howard, Juwan (Athlete, Basketball Player)
11714 Bistro Ln
Houston, TX 77082-2726, USA

Howard, Ken (Actor, Producer, Writer)
c/o Ross Fineman *Fineman Entertainment*
9250 Wilshire Blvd Ste 300
Beverly Hills, CA 90212-3345, USA

Howard, Kyle (Actor)
c/o Steve Himber *Steve Himber Entertainment*
211 S Beverly Dr Apt S
Beverly Hills, CA 90212-3807, USA

Howard, Larry (Athlete, Baseball Player)
4005 Heritage Holw
Georgetown, TX 78628, USA

Howard, Lee (Athlete, Baseball Player)
4650 Dulin Rd Spc 203
Fallbrook, CA 92028-8766, USA

Howard, Leo (Actor)
c/o Emily Urbani *Osbrink Talent Agency*
4343 Lankershim Blvd Ste 100
West Toluca Lake, CA 91602-2705, USA

Howard, Lisa
247 S Beverly Dr # 102
Beverly Hills, CA 90212-3830

Howard, Matt (Athlete, Baseball Player)
37165 Delgado Way
Temecula, CA 92592-8896, USA

Howard, Michael (Government Official)
Westminster
London SW1A 0AA, UNITED KINGDOM (UK)

Howard, Mike (Athlete, Baseball Player)
147 Kehle Rd
Madison, MS 39110-7971, USA

Howard, Miki (Musician)
c/o Mike Gardner *Gardener Entertainment*
5683 Hazelcrest Cir
Westlake Village, CA 91362-5426, USA

Howard, ohn
GPO Box 59
Sydney, AUSTRALIA NSW 2001, AUSTRALIA

Howard, Otis (Athlete, Basketball Player)
231 Manhattan Ave
Oak Ridge, TN 37830-7544, USA

Howard, Paige (Actor)
c/o Meredith Wechter *International Creative Management (ICM-LA)*
10250 Constellation Blvd Fl 7
Los Angeles, CA 90067-6207, USA

Howard, Rance (Actor)
4286 N Clybourn Ave
Burbank, CA 91505-4002, USA

Howard, Rebecca Lynn (Musician)
c/o Staff Member *Paradigm (Monterey)*
404 W Franklin St
Monterey, CA 93940-2303, USA

Howard, Reggie (Athlete, Baseball Player)
4332 Crimson Leaf Cv
Memphis, TN 38125-2905, USA

Howard, Richard (Writer)
23 Waverly Pl Apt 5X
New York, NY 10003-6717, USA

Howard, Robert (Hardcore Holly) (Wrestler)
c/o Kerry Rodgerson *World Wrestling Entertainment (WWE)*
1241 E Main St
Stamford, CT 06902-3520, USA

Howard, Robert L (War Hero)
417 Dixon Dr
Hewitt, TX 76643-3449, USA

Howard, Ron (Actor, Director, Producer, Writer)
c/o Richard Lovett *Creative Artists Agency (CAA-LA)*
2000 Avenue of the Stars Ste 100
Los Angeles, CA 90067-4705, USA

Howard, Ron (Athlete, Football Player)
14701 NE 61st Ct
Redmond, WA 98052-4751, USA

Howard, Ryan (Athlete, Baseball Player)
16543 Clayton Rd
Ballwin, MO 63011-1720, USA

Howard, Sherman (Athlete, Football Player)
5125 Thomas Dr
Richton Park, IL 60471-1639, USA

Howard, Sherri (Athlete, Track Athlete)
14059 Bridle Ridge Rd
Sylmar, CA 91342-1060, USA

Howard, Sherri (Actor)
c/o Michael Henderson *Heresun Management*
4119 W Burbank Blvd
Burbank, CA 91505-2122, USA

Howard, Sherry
14059 Bridle Ridge Rd
Sylmar, CA 91342-1060

Howard, Stephen (Athlete, Basketball Player)
3941 Legacy Dr Ste 204
Plano, TX 75023-8331, USA

Howard, Steven (Athlete, Baseball Player)
4712 Shetland Ave
Oakland, CA 94605-5629, USA

Howard, Susan (Actor)
PO Box 1456
Boerne, TX 78006-1456, USA

Howard, Terrence (Actor)
c/o Jim Toth *Creative Artists Agency (CAA-LA)*
2000 Avenue of the Stars Ste 100
Los Angeles, CA 90067-4705, USA

Howard, Thomas (Athlete, Baseball Player)
822 8th Ave
Middletown, OH 45044-5519, USA

Howard, Tim (Soccer Player)
Sir Matt Busby Way Old Trafford
Manchester M16 0RA, ENGLAND

Howard, Todd (Athlete, Football Player)
1300 Bienville Ave
Ruston, LA 71270-5204, USA

Howard, Traylor (Actor)
c/o John Carrabino *John Carrabino Management*
5900 Wilshire Blvd Ste 406
Los Angeles, CA 90036-5015, USA

Howard, Wilbur (Athlete, Baseball Player)
643 Walston Ln
Houston, TX 77060-5846, USA

Howard, William W Jr (Misc)
11100 Wildlife Center Dr
Reston, VA 20190-5361, USA

Howarth, Elgar (Composer)
27 Cromwell Ave
London N6 5HN, UNITED KINGDOM (UK)

Howarth, Jim (Athlete, Baseball Player)
275 Santini St
Biloxi, MS 39530-2958, USA

Howarth, Judith (Opera Singer)
6 Henrietta St
London WC2E 8LA, UNITED KINGDOM (UK)

Howarth, Roger (Actor)
75 9th Ave Fl 5
New York, NY 10011-7076, USA

Howarth, Thomas (Architect)
230 College St
Toronto, ON M5S 1R1, CANADA

Howatch, Susan (Writer)
29 Femshaw Road
London SW10 0TG, UNITED KINGDOM (UK)

Howatt, Garry (Athlete, Hockey Player)
1275 Sussex Tpke # B
Randolph, NJ 07869-2937, USA

Howe, Adam (Stylist)
c/o Staff Member *Management & Production/MAP Inc*
48 Saint Marks Pl Fl 4
New York, NY 10003-8129, USA

Howe, Arthur (Journalist)
400 N Broad St
Philadelphia, PA 19130-4015, USA

Howe, Brian (Musician)
c/o Samantha Crisp *Kohner Agency, The*
9300 Wilshire Blvd Ste 555
Beverly Hills, CA 90212-3211, USA

Howe, Delles (Athlete, Football Player)
1907 Crescent Dr
Monroe, LA 71202-3023, USA

Howe, G Woodson (Editor)
Editorial Dept World-Herald Square
Omaha, NE 68102, USA

Howe, Garry (Athlete, Football Player)
1159 McCartney St
Pittsburgh, PA 15220-4625, USA

Howe, Gordie (Athlete, Hockey Player)
4935 Fernlee Ave
Royal Oak, MI 48073-1018, USA

Howe, Gordie (Athlete, Hockey Player)
40 Plank Ln
Glastonbury, CT 06033-2523, USA

Howe, Greg (Musician)
7959 Carmel Heights Ave
Las Vegas, NV 89178-3809, USA

Howe, Jonathan T (Admiral)
225 Water St Ste 1510
Jacksonville, FL 32202-5175, USA

Howe, Marie (Writer)
822 Palmer Rd Apt 2A
Bronxville, NY 10708-3317, USA

Howe, Mark S (Athlete, Hockey Player)
106 Barrington Rd
Bloomfield Hills, MI 48302-0602, USA

Howe, Marty (Athlete, Hockey Player)
40 Plank Ln
Glastonbury, CT 06033-2523, USA

Howe, Oscar (Artist)
5900 S Prairie View Ct
Sioux Falls, SD 57108-2003, USA

Howe, Tina (Writer)
333 W End Ave
New York, NY 10023-8128, USA

Howe, Vic (Athlete, Hockey Player)
279 Charles Lutes Rd
Moncton, NB E1G 2R8, Canada

Howe Jr, Arthur H (Art) (Athlete, Baseball Player, Coach)
17214 Calico Peak Way
Cypress, TX 77433-2113, USA

Howe of Aberavon, R E Geoffrey (Government Official)
Cavendish Square Branch 4 Vere St
London W1, UNITED KINGDOM (UK)

Howell, Alex (Cartoonist)
c/o Staff Member *King Features Syndication*
300 W 57th St Fl 15
New York, NY 10019-5238, USA

Howell, Bailey (Athlete, Basketball Player)
4640 S Montgomery St
Starkville, MS 39759-3792, USA

Howell, Brad
Gunterring 21
Hattersheim, GERMANY D-65795

Howell, C Thomas (Actor, Director, Producer, Writer)
c/o Jean-Pierre (JP) Henraux *Shelter Entertainment*
9454 Wilshire Blvd Ste 715
Beverly Hills, CA 90212-2925, USA

Howell, David (Golfer)
c/o Staff Member *International Sports Management Ltd (ISM UK)*
Cherry Tree Farm Cherry Tree Lane
Rostherne, Cheshire WA14 3RZ, UNITED KINGDOM

Howell, Francis C (Misc)
1994 San Antonio Ave
Berkeley, CA 94707-1620, USA

Howell, Henry V (Harry) (Athlete, Hockey Player)
401-49 Robinson St
Hamilton, ON L8P 1Y7, Canada

Howell, Jack (Athlete, Baseball Player)
822 S Lehigh Dr
Tucson, AZ 85710-4741, USA

Howell, Jay (Athlete, Baseball Player)
4560 Colony Pt
Suwanee, GA 30024-3010, USA

Howell, Kanin (Actor)
c/o Brandon Ross *Temptation Management*
1010 S Robertson Blvd Ste 2
Los Angeles, CA 90035-1527, USA

Howell, Kathleen (Engineer)
Aeronautical Engineering Dept
West Lafayette, IN 47907, USA

Howell, Ken (Athlete, Baseball Player)
22090 Buckingham Dr
Farmington Hills, MI 48335-5423, USA

Howell, Margaret (Designer, Fashion Designer)
5 Garden House 8 Battersea Park Road
London SW8, UNITED KINGDOM (UK)

Howell, Mike (Athlete, Football Player)
200 Charlotte St
Monroe, LA 71202-3906, USA

Howell, Pat (Athlete, Football Player)
7692 N Kincaid Ave
Fresno, CA 93711-0363, USA

Howell, Patrick (Pat) (Athlete, Baseball Player)
3081 Lacoste Rd
Mobile, AL 36618-4617, USA

Howell, Roy (Athlete, Baseball Player)
276 El Portal Dr
Pismo Beach, CA 93449-1504, USA

Howell III, Charles (Athlete, Golfer)
5187 Vardon Dr
Windermere, FL 34786-8960, USA

Howells, Anne (Opera Singer)
Milestone Broom Close
Esher Surrey, UNITED KINGDOM (UK)

Howells, Michael (Stylist)
c/o Staff Member *Camilla Lowther Managment (CLM Represents)*
30-32 Ericsson Pl
New York, NY 10013, USA

Howerton, Glenn (Actor)
c/o Nick Frenkel *3 Arts Entertainment Inc*
9460 Wilshire Blvd Fl 7
Beverly Hills, CA 90212-2713, USA

Howes, Sally Ann (Actor, Music Group, Musician)
265 Liverpool Road
London N1 1LX, UNITED KINGDOM (UK)

Howey, Steve (Actor)
c/o Brian Swardstrom *WmE2 (Endeavor-LA)*
9601 Wilshire Blvd Fl 3
Beverly Hills, CA 90210-5219, USA

Howfield, Bobby (Athlete, Football Player)
5529 S Lowell Blvd
Littleton, CO 80123-2840, USA

Howfield, Ian (Athlete, Football Player)
2851 Elk Canyon Ct
Las Vegas, NV 89117-2983, USA

Howison, Ryan (Athlete, Golfer)
245 Barbados Dr
Jupiter, FL 33458-2927, USA

Howitt, Dann (Athlete, Baseball Player)
PO Box 565
Douglas, MI 49406-0565, USA

Howitt, Peter (Director)
c/o Stephen Marks *Evolution Entertainment (LA)*
901 N Highland Ave
Los Angeles, CA 90038-2412, USA

Howland, Ben (Basketball Player, Coach)
Athletic Dept
Los Angeles, CA 90024, USA

Howland, Beth (Actor)
255 Amalfi Dr
Santa Monica, CA 90402-1125, USA

Howland, Chris
Vordersten Buchel 11
Rosrath, GERMANY D-51503

Howle, Paul (Cartoonist)
200 Madison Ave
New York, NY 10016-3903, USA

Howlett, Liam (Composer, Musician)
Jenkins Lane Great Hallinsbury
Essex CM22 7QL, UNITED KINGDOM (UK)

Howley, Chuck (Athlete, Football Player)
26875 FM 47
Wills Point, TX 75169-8266, USA

Howry, Bobby (Athlete, Baseball Player)
24108 N 73rd Ln
Peoria, AZ 85383-3290, USA

Howse, Steven (Layzie Bone) (Actor, Composer, Musician)
c/o Staff Member *Mo Thug West Records*
Prefers to be contacted via email
Los Angeles, CA, USA

Howson, Scott (Athlete, Hockey Player)
c/o Staff Member *Edmonton Oilers*
11230 110 St NW
GM, AB T5G 3H7, Canada

Howze, Leonard Earl (Actor)
c/o Jessica Berlinski *Melissa Prophet Management*
Prefers to be contacted by telephone
CA, USA

Hoy, Peter (Athlete, Baseball Player)
26 Woods Dr
Canton, NY 13617-1061, USA

Hoyda, Dave (Athlete, Hockey Player)
3305 Bahama Dr
Sand Springs, OK 74063-2912, USA

Hoye, James (Athlete, Baseball Player)
12838 Patricia Dr
North Royalton, OH 44133-1024, USA

Hoyem, Steve (Athlete, Football Player)
28 Twilight Blf
Newport Coast, CA 92657-2126, USA

Hoying, Bobby (Athlete, Football Player)
60 Dogwood Dr
Fort Loramie, OH 45845, USA

Hoyland, John (Artist)
41 Charterhouse Square
London EC1M 6EA, UNITED KINGDOM (UK)

Hoyos, Luis Fernando (Actor)
c/o Gabriel Blanco *Gabriel Blanco Iglesias (Mexico)*
Rio Balsas 35-32 Colonia Cuauhtemoc
DF 6500, Mexico

Hoyt, D LaMarr (Athlete, Baseball Player)
1594 Lost Creek Dr
Columbia, SC 29212-2859, USA

Hrabetin, Frank (Athlete, Football Player)
47 Casa Arroyo Ln
Sonoita, AZ 85637, USA

Hrabosky, Alan T (Al) (Athlete, Baseball Player, Sportscaster)
9 Frontenac Estates Dr
Saint Louis, MO 63131-2613, USA

Hrbek, Kent A (Athlete, Baseball Player)
2611 W 112th St
Bloomington, MN 55431-3965, USA

Hrdina, Jiri (Athlete, Hockey Player)
c/o Staff Member *Dallas Stars*
2601 Avenue of the Stars Ste 100
Frisco, TX 75034-9016, USA

Hrdy, Sarah Blaffer (Misc)
Anthropology Dept
Davis, CA 95616, USA

Hrechkosy, Dave (Athlete, Hockey Player)
1352 E 11205 S
Sandy, UT 84092-5006, USA

HRH Prince William (Prince, Royalty)
St James Palace
London SW1A 1BS, UNITED KINGDOM

Hriniak, Walt (Athlete, Baseball Player)
18 Stacy Dr
North Andover, MA 01845-1832, USA

Hrivnak, Gary (Athlete, Football Player)
1508 W Plymouth Dr
Arlington Heights, IL 60004-2847, USA

Hrivnak, Jim (Athlete, Hockey Player)
17819 Bd De Pierrefonds
Pierrefonds, QC H9J 3L1, Canada

Hrkac, Tony (Athlete, Hockey Player)
6904 W Lantern Ln
Mequon, WI 53092-1575, USA

Hrudey, Kelly (Athlete, Hockey Player)
c/o Staff Member *CBC TV*
P.O. Box 500 STN A, 5H100
Toronto, ON M5W 1E6, Canada

Hrycuik, Jim (Athlete, Hockey Player)
1011 Konihowski Rd
Saskatoon, SK S7S 1K5, Canada

Hrymnak, Steve (Athlete, Hockey Player)
Site 15 Comp 125 RR 13 STN P
Thunder Bay, ON P7B 5E4, Canada

Hrynewich, Tim (Athlete, Hockey Player)
1132 North Ln
Norton Shores, MI 49441-4684, USA

Hu, Jintao (President)
1 Zhong Nan Hai
Beijing, CHINA

Hu, Kelly (Actor)
c/o Cheryl McLean *Creative Public Relations*
3385 Oak Glen Dr
Los Angeles, CA 90068-1311, USA

Hu, Qili (Government Official)
23 Taipingqiao St
Beijing 100283, CHINA

Huang, Helen (Musician)
40 W 57th St
New York, NY 10019-4001, USA

Huang, Henry (Biologist, Inventor)
Biology Dept
Saint Louis, MO 63130, USA

Huang, James (Actor)
c/o Staff Member *Cunningham Escott Slevin & Doherty (CESD-LA)*
10635 Santa Monica Blvd Ste 130
Los Angeles, CA 90025-8306, USA

Huang, Motoko (Stylist)
242-06-B Oak Park Dr
Douglaston, NY 11362, USA

Huang, Nina
8007 Highland Trl
Los Angeles, CA 90046-2022

Huang, Ying (Musician)
c/o Staff Member *Sony BMG/Jive Records*
9830 Wilshire Blvd
Beverly Hills, CA 90212-1804, USA

Huard, Bill (Athlete, Hockey Player)
26322 Towne Centre Dr
Foothill Ranch, CA 92610-2473, USA

Huard, Damon (Athlete, Football Player)
9508 NE 18th St
Clyde Hill, WA 98004-2539, USA

Huard, John (Athlete, Football Player)
40 Vista Dr
S Portland, ME 04106-6894, USA

Huarte, John (Athlete, Football Player)
14959 La Cumbre Dr
Pacific Palisades, CA 90272-4457, USA

Huarte, John G (Athlete, Football Player)
8829 S Priest Dr
Tempe, AZ 85284-1905, USA

Hub (Musician)
1325 Avenue of the Americas
New York, NY 10019-6026, USA

Hubbard, Elizabeth
1505 10th St
Santa Monica, CA 90401-2805

Hubbard, Erica (Actor)
c/o Staff Member *Jenny Delaney Management*
3238 Fond Dr
Encino, CA 91436-4206, USA

Hubbard, Glenn (Athlete, Baseball Player)
1515 Kings Xing
Stone Mountain, GA 30087-1914, USA

Hubbard, Gregg (Hobbie) (Music Group, Musician)
5200 Old Harding Rd
Franklin, TN 37064-9406, USA

Hubbard, John (Artist)
Chilcombe House Chilcombe near Bridport
Dorset, UNITED KINGDOM (UK)

Hubbard, Marvin R (Marv) (Athlete, Football Player)
5804 Dawn View Ct
Castro Valley, CA 94552-1803, USA

Hubbard, Mike (Athlete, Baseball Player)
2552 Brookstone Ln
Richmond, VA 23233-6914, USA

Hubbard, Philip (Phil) (Athlete, Basketball Player, Coach)
5130 Pleasant Forest Dr
Centreville, VA 20120-1248, USA

Hubbard, Ray Wylie (Musician)
c/o Staff Member *Davis McLarty Agency*
708 S Lamar Blvd Ste D
Austin, TX 78704-1541, USA

Hubbard, Robert (Athlete, Basketball Player)
353 Piper Rd
West Springfield, MA 01089-1757, USA

Hubbard, Trenidad (Athlete, Baseball Player)
4206 Clearwater Ct
Missouri City, TX 77459-1668, USA

Hubbard, Trent (Baseball Player)
2654 E 77th St
Chicago, IL 60649-4725, USA

Hubbauer, Matt (Athlete, Hockey Player)
c/o Staff Member *Toronto Maple Leafs*
Air Canada Centre 400-40 Bay St
Toronto, ON M5J 2X2, Canada

Hubbell, Frank (Athlete, Football Player)
PO Box 11729
Knoxville, TN 37939-1729, USA

Hubbert, Brad (Athlete, Football Player)
PO Box 360990
Decatur, GA 30036-0990, USA

Hubel, David H (Nobel Prize Laureate)
98 Collins Rd
Waban, MA 02468-2235, USA

Hubenthal, Karl (Cartoonist, Editor)
3901 E Coast Hwy Apt 15
Corona Del Mar, CA 92625-5505, USA

Huber, Anke (Tennis Player)
Dieselstr 10
Karlsdorf-Neuthard 76689, GERMANY

Huber, Jon (Athlete, Baseball Player)
5045 11th Ave NE
Seattle, WA 98105-4344, USA

Huber, Lauren (Stylist)
21 Patricia St
Binghamton, NY 13905-4047, USA

Huber, Robert (Nobel Prize Laureate)
Am Kiopferspitz
Manrinsried 82152, GERMANY

Hubert-Whitten, Janet
10061 Riverside Dr # 204
Toluca Lake, CA 91602-2560

Hubick, Greg (Athlete, Hockey Player)
225 Angus St
Regina, SK S4R 3K5, Canada

Hubka, Gene (Athlete, Football Player)
1065 Marshall St
Milton, PA 17847-7647, USA

Hubley, Season (Actor)
31 Mansfield Ave
Essex Junction, VT 05452-3732, USA

Huchra, John P (Astronomer)
Astronomy Dept
Cambridge, MA 2138, USA

Huck, Fran (Athlete, Hockey Player)
328-2505 11th Ave
Regina, SK S4P 0K6, Canada

Huckabee, Cooper (Actor)
1800 El Cerrito Pl Apt 34
Los Angeles, CA 90068-3743, USA

Huckabee, Mike (Ex-Governor, Politician)
c/o Staff Member *Fox News Channel (NY)*
1211 Ave Of The Americas Level C1
New York, NY 10036-8701, USA

Huckaby, Ken (Athlete, Baseball Player)
4490 S Rio Dr
Chandler, AZ 85249-3382, USA

Huckleby, Harlan (Athlete, Football Player)
7473 Franklin Ridge Way
West Bloomfield, MI 48322-4128, USA

Hucknall, Mick (Musician)
c/o Staff Member *Silentway Managment Ltd*
34 Percy St
London W1T 2DG, UK

Huckstep, Ronald L (Doctor)
108 Sugarloaf Crescent Castlecrag
Syndey, NSW 2068, AUSTRALIA

Hucul, Fred (Athlete, Hockey Player)
4550 N Flowing Wells Rd Unit 226
Tucson, AZ 85705-2387, USA

Hudd, Roy
652 Finchley Rd
London, ENGLAND NW11 7NT

Huddleston, David (Actor)
9200 W Sunset Blvd # 612
Los Angeles, CA 90069-3502, USA

Huddy, Charlie (Athlete, Hockey Player)
c/o Staff Member *Edmonton Oilers*
11230 110 St NW
GM, AB T5G 3H7, Canada

Hudecek, Vaclav (Musician)
Londynska 25
Prague 2 120 00, CZECH REPUBLIC

Hudek, John (Athlete, Baseball Player)
7603 Shady Way Dr
Sugar Land, TX 77479-6284, USA

Hudgens, Dave (Athlete, Baseball Player)
5802 E Windsor Ave
Scottsdale, AZ 85257-1039, USA

Hudgens, Vanessa Anne (Actor)
c/o Evan Hainey *Untitled Entertainment (LA)*
350 S Beverly Dr Ste 200
Beverly Hills, CA 90212-4819, USA

Hudler, Rex (Athlete, Baseball Player)
11745 Riehl Ave
Tustin, CA 92782-3372, USA

Hudlin, Reginald (Actor, Director, Producer, Writer)
c/o Norman Aladjem *Paradigm (LA)*
360 N Crescent Dr
Beverly Hills, CA 90210-4874, USA

Hudner, Thomas J Jr (War Hero)
31 Allen Farm Ln
Concord, MA 01742-2202, USA

Hudson, Bill
7023 Birdview Ave
Malibu, CA 90265-4106

Hudson, Brett (Actor, Producer, Writer)
c/o Staff Member *WmE2 (WMA-LA)*
1 William Morris Pl
Beverly Hills, CA 90212-4261, USA

Hudson, C B Jr (Business Person)
2001 3rd Ave S
Birmingham, AL 35233-2115, USA

Hudson, Charles (Athlete, Baseball Player)
3700 E Highway 85 Apt 6204
Ennis, TX 75119-5391, USA

Hudson, Charles (Charlie) (Athlete, Baseball Player)
32 W Hooker Ave
Coalgate, OK 74538, USA

Hudson, Clifford G (Business Person, Financier)
101 Park Ave
Oklahoma City, OK 73102-7209, USA

Hudson, Dave (Athlete, Hockey Player)
5204 Briar Tree Dr
Dallas, TX 75248-6032, USA

Hudson, Emie (Actor)
5711 Hoback Glen Rd
Hidden Hills, CA 91302-1229, USA

Hudson, Ernie (Actor, Producer)
c/o Darryl Marshak *Marshak/Zachary Company, The*
8840 Wilshire Blvd Fl 1
Beverly Hills, CA 90211-2606, USA

Hudson, Garth (Music Group, Musician)
32 Clayton St
Portland, ME 04103-2250, USA

Hudson, Gary (Actor)
c/o Staff Member *Origin Talent Agency*
4705 Laurel Canyon Blvd Ste 306
Studio City, CA 91607-5940, USA

Hudson, Gordon (Athlete, Football Player)
12498 Falls Creek Rd
Riverton, UT 84065-1915, USA

Hudson, Hal (Athlete, Baseball Player)
422 Sandpiper Dr Apt C
Fort Pierce, FL 34982-5112, USA

Hudson, Haley (Actor)
c/o Staff Member *Weeds*
10880 Wilshire Blvd Ste 1600
Los Angeles, CA 90024-4117, USA

Hudson, Hugh (Director)
c/o Staff Member *International Creative Management (ICM-LA)*
10250 Constellation Blvd Fl 7
Los Angeles, CA 90067-6207, USA

Hudson, James (Doctor)
25 Shattuck St
Boston, MA 02115-6027, USA

Hudson, Jennifer (Actor, Musician)
c/o Irving Azoff *Azoff Music Management/ Front Line*
1100 Glendon Ave
Los Angeles, CA 90024-3503, USA

Hudson, Jesse (Athlete, Baseball Player)
341 Albert Lewis Way
Mansfield, LA 71052-5723, USA

Hudson, Jim (Athlete, Football Player)
3635 Peregrine Falcon Dr
Austin, TX 78746-7438, USA

Hudson, Joe (Athlete, Baseball Player)
123 Queen Anne Ct
Dover, DE 19901-1511, USA

Hudson, John (Athlete, Football Player)
3320 Highway 77
Paris, TN 38242-5495, USA

Hudson, Kate (Actor)
c/o Brad Cafarelli *PMK/BNC - LA*
8687 Melrose Ave Ste 8
West Hollywood, CA 90069-5746, USA

Hudson, Lex (Athlete, Hockey Player)
General Delivery
Flat Rock, NL A0A 3L0, Canada

Hudson, Lou (Athlete, Basketball Player)
2002 Lakeview Dr
Park City, UT 84060-7049, USA

Hudson, Lucy-Jo (Actor)
Quay St
Manchester M60 9EA, ENGLAND

Hudson, Luke (Athlete, Baseball Player)
9912 Aster Cir
Fountain Valley, CA 92708-2309, USA

Hudson, Marvin (Athlete, Baseball Player)
698 Metasville Rd
Washington, GA 30673-2605, USA

Hudson, Oliver (Actor, Producer)

Hudson, Orlando (Athlete, Baseball Player)
PO Box 1888
Darlington, SC 29540-1888, USA

Hudson, Ray (Coach, Soccer Player)
14120 Newbrook Dr
Chantilly, VA 20151-2273, USA

Hudson, Rex (Athlete, Baseball Player)
4704 Spring Meadow Ln
Midland, TX 79705-2966, USA

Hudson, Richard S (Athlete, Football Player)
315 S Wilson St Attn Assistantprincipal
Paris, TN 38242-5053, USA

Hudson, Robert W (Athlete, Football Player)
3408 Dalrock Rd
Rowlett, TX 75088-5538, USA

Hudson, Sally (Skier)
PO Box 2343
Olympic Valley, CA 96146-2343, USA

Hudson, Sid (Athlete, Baseball Player)
PO Box 8637
Waco, TX 76714-8637, USA

Hudson, Timothy A (Tim) (Athlete, Baseball Player)
901 Rocky Hills Dr
Auburn, AL 36830-7222, USA

Hudspeth, Tommy (Athlete, Football Coach, Football Player)
3522 E 71st Pl
Tulsa, OK 74136-5962, USA

Huelskamp, Tim (Congressman, Politician)
126 Cannon Hob
Washington, DC 20515-5401, USA

Huerta, Carlos (Athlete, Football Player)
2980 Howard Hughes Pkwy Suite 550
Las Vegas, NV 89169, USA

Huertas, Jon (Actor, Producer)
c/o Sherry Marsh *Marsh Entertainment*
12444 Ventura Blvd Ste 203
Studio City, CA 91604-2409, USA

Hues, Frankie
2640 NE 135th St Apt 302
North Miami, FL 33181-3540

Hues, Matthias (Actor)
32 rue des Je??neurs
Paris 75002, FRANCE

Huff, Aubrey (Athlete, Baseball Player)
1211 Harbor Island Walk
Baltimore, MD 21230-5461, USA

Huff, Brent (Actor)
c/o Erik Seastrand *WmE2 (Endeavor-LA)*
1 William Morris Pl
Beverly Hills, CA 90212-4261, USA

Huff, Gary E (Athlete, Football Player)
3175 Hawks Landing Dr
Tallahassee, FL 32309-7227, USA

Huff, Kenneth W (Ken) (Athlete, Football Player)
105 Blackford Ct
Durham, NC 27712-9497, USA

Huff, Mike (Athlete, Baseball Player)
PO Box 92385
Southlake, TX 76092-0104, USA

Huff, Robert L (Sam) (Athlete, Football Player, Sportscaster)
8 N Jay St
Middleburg, VA 20118, USA

Huff, Shawn
1505 10th St
Santa Monica, CA 90401-2805

Huffington, Arianna (Journalist, Writer)
c/o Staff Member *Inkwell Management*
521 5th Ave
New York, NY 10175-0003, USA

Huffington, Michael (Ex-Congressman, Politician)
3005 45th St NW
Washington, DC 20016-3528, USA

Huffman, Cady
c/o Alan David *Alan David Management*
8840 Wilshire Blvd Ste 200
Beverly Hills, CA 90211-2606, USA

Huffman, Felicity (Actor)
c/o Staff Member *Desperate Housewives*
2300 W Riverside Dr
Burbank, CA 91506-2976, USA

Huffman, Kerry (Athlete, Hockey Player)
1 Chelsea Ave Apt 313
Long Branch, NJ 07740-8109, USA

Huffman, Logan (Actor)
c/o Tina Thor *TMT Entertainment Group*
648 Broadway Ste 1002
New York, NY 10012-2348, USA

Huffman, Phil (Athlete, Baseball Player)
194 Paxton Rd
Rochester, NY 14617-4657, USA

Huffman, Tim (Athlete, Football Player)
3365 Jubilee Trl
Dallas, TX 75229-3810, USA

Hufnagel, John (Athlete, Football Player)
12859 Biggin Church Rd S
Jacksonville, FL 32224-7928, USA

Hufsey, Billy (Actor)
15415 Muskingum Blvd
Brook Park, OH 44142-2327, USA

Hufstedler, Shirley M (Educator, Secretary)
720 Inverness Dr
La Canada Flintridge, CA 91011-4149, USA

Hug, Procter R Jr (Judge)
400 S Virginia St
Reno, NV 89501-2132, USA

Huggins, Bob (Athlete, Basketball Player, Coach)
207 Beecher Hall
Cincinnati, OH 45221-0001, USA

Hugh, Dianne (Stylist)
55 N Sunset Ave
Freeport, IL 61032-3750, USA

Hughes, Albert (Director, Producer, Writer)
c/o David Wirtschafter *WmE2 (Endeavor-LA)*
9601 Wilshire Blvd Fl 3
Beverly Hills, CA 90210-5219, USA

Hughes, Alfredrick (Athlete, Basketball Player)
5024 S Kildare Ave
Chicago, IL 60632-4543, USA

Hughes, Allen (Director, Producer, Writer)
c/o David Wirtschafter *WmE2 (Endeavor-LA)*
9601 Wilshire Blvd Fl 3
Beverly Hills, CA 90210-5219, USA

Hughes, Bobby (Athlete, Baseball Player)
114 Montreal St
Playa Del Rey, CA 90293-7608, USA

Hughes, Bradley (Athlete, Golfer)
204 Easton Ct
Simpsonville, SC 29680-7627, USA

Hughes, Brent (Athlete, Hockey Player)
2016 Sweetgum Dr
Birmingham, AL 35244-1628, USA

Hughes, Carolyn (Actor, Sportscaster, Television Host)
c/o Staff Member *Fox Sports Television Group*
10201 W Pico Blvd Bldg 101
Los Angeles, CA 90064-2606, USA

Hughes, Danan (Athlete, Football Player)
49 W 19th St
Bayonne, NJ 07002-3609, USA

Hughes, Dave (Hughesy) (Comedian)
c/o Staff Member *Westside Talent*
44 Watton St 1st Floor
Werribee, Victoria 3030, Australia

Hughes, David (Athlete, Football Player)
5307 240th Ave NE
Redmond, WA 98053-2543, USA

Hughes, Dennis (Athlete, Football Player)
360 Beechwood Dr
Athens, GA 30606-4010, USA

Hughes, Eddie (Athlete, Basketball Player)
4253 Deerfield Hills Rd
Colorado Springs, CO 80916-3506, USA

Hughes, Edward Z (Publisher)
60 5th Ave
New York, NY 10011-8868, USA

Hughes, Ernie (Athlete, Football Player)
2116 Camino Brazos
Pleasanton, CA 94566-5811, USA

Hughes, Finola (Actor)
c/o Steven Jensen *Independent Group, The*
6363 Wilshire Blvd Ste 115
Los Angeles, CA 90048-5734, USA

Hughes, Frank (Athlete, Hockey Player)
120 Pruce Ave P O Box 1856
Sparwood, BC V0B 2G0, Canada

Hughes, Frank John (Actor)
c/o Dan Baron *Agency for the Performing Arts (APA-LA)*
405 S Beverly Dr Ste 500
Beverly Hills, CA 90212-4425, USA

Hughes, George (Athlete, Football Player)
1870 E Ocean View Ave
Norfolk, VA 23503-2502, USA

Hughes, Glenn (Musician)
6671 W Sunset Blvd Ste 1585-114
Los Angeles, CA 90028-7116, USA

Hughes, H Richard (Architect)
47 Chiswick Quay
London W4 3UR, UNITED KINGDOM (UK)

Hughes, Howie (Athlete, Hockey Player)
3711 27th Pl W Apt 205
Seattle, WA 98199-2062, USA

Hughes, Irene
500 N Michigan Ave Ste 1039
Chicago, IL 60611-1032

Hughes, Jack (Athlete, Hockey Player)
54 Canal St Fl 5
Boston, MA 02114-2011, USA

Hughes, Jim (Athlete, Baseball Player)
7526 El Manor Ave
Los Angeles, CA 90045-1351, USA

Hughes, John (Athlete, Hockey Player)
317 Laudholm Farm Rd
Wells, ME 04090-4707, USA

Hughes, Karen (Government Official)
2201 C St NW
Washington, DC 20520-0099, USA

Hughes, Kate (Athlete, Golfer)
275 Merlot Ln
Saint Albans, MO 63073-1214, USA

Hughes, Kathleen (Actor)
8818 Rising Glen Pl
Los Angeles, CA 90069-1222, USA

Hughes, Keith (Athlete, Baseball Player)
176 Sycamore Rd
Havertown, PA 19083-3508, USA

Hughes, Keith W (Financier)
PO Box 93
Pittsburg, TX 75686-0093, USA

Hughes, Kim (Athlete, Basketball Player)
2221 Via Cerritos
Palos Verdes Estates, CA 90274-2141, USA

Hughes, Larry (Athlete, Basketball Player)
3 Hanna Ct
Cleveland, OH 44108-1162, USA

Hughes, Mark (Coach)
c/o Staff Member *Blackburn Rovers Football Club*
Ewood Park Blackburn
Lancashire BB2 4JF, UNITED KINGDOM

Hughes, Mervyn G (Cricketer)
90 Jollimant St
Melbourne, VIC 3002, AUSTRALIA

Hughes, Miko (Actor)
53 Sunrise Rd
Superior, MT 59872, USA

Hughes, Pat (Athlete, Football Player)
4 Woodside Dr
Stratham, NH 03885-6549, USA

Hughes, Pat (Athlete, Hockey Player)
8388 Webster Hills Rd
Dexter, MI 48130-9365, USA

Hughes, Phil (Athlete, Baseball Player)
c/o Team Member *New York Yankees*
Yankee Stadium 161st St & River Ave
Bronx, NY 10451, USA

Hughes, Randy (Athlete, Football Player)
17608 Cedar Creek Canyon Dr
Dallas, TX 75252-4966, USA

Hughes, Richard H (Dick) (Athlete, Baseball Player)
PO Box 598
Stephens, AR 71764-0598, USA

Hughes, Robert S F (Critic)
143 Prince St
New York, NY 10012-3113, USA

Hughes, Sarah (Figure Skater)
12 Channel Dr
Great Neck, NY 11024-1212, USA

Hughes, Suzan (Actor)
c/o Staff Member *International Creative Management (ICM-LA)*
10250 Constellation Blvd Fl 7
Los Angeles, CA 90067-6207, USA

Hughes, Terry (Athlete, Baseball Player)
532 Pierpont Avenue Ext
Spartanburg, SC 29303-4100, USA

Hughes, Thomas J Jr (Admiral)
400 Mar Vista Dr Apt 4
Monterey, CA 93940-4359, USA

Hughes, Tom (Athlete, Baseball Player)
610 Kimswick Ct
Deer Park, TX 77536-6139, USA

Hughes, Tyrone C (Athlete, Football Player)
2554 Prairie Hill Dr
Frisco, TX 75033-8361, USA

Hughes, Wendy (Actor)
129 Bourke St Woolloomooloo
Sydney, NSW 2011, AUSTRALIA

Hughes-Fulford, Millie (Astronaut)
Medical Center 4150 Clement St
San Francisco, CA 94121, USA

Hughley, DL (Actor, Comedian)
c/o Staff Member *3 Arts Entertainment Inc*
9460 Wilshire Blvd Fl 7
Beverly Hills, CA 90212-2713, USA

Hugo, Chad (Musician)
c/o Scott Vener *Schiff Company, The*
8440 Warner Dr Ste B1
Culver City, CA 90232-2461, USA

Hugo Boss (Designer, Fashion Designer)
Dieselstrabe 12
Metzingen 72555, Germany

Hugstedt, Petter (Skier)
Kongsberg 3600, NORWAY

Huguenin, G Richard (Inventor)
South Deerfield, MA 1373, USA

Hui, Tammy (Actor)
c/o Lisa King *King Talent*
303-228 E 4th Ave
Vancouver V5T-1G5, CANADA

Huisgen, Rolf (Misc)
Kaulbachstr 10
Munich 80539, GERMANY

Huisman, Justin (Athlete, Baseball Player)
8713 Forest Glen Ct
Saint John, IN 46373-8795, USA

Huisman, Rick (Athlete, Baseball Player)
17W025 Oak Ln
Bensenville, IL 60106-2860, USA

Huismann, Mark (Athlete, Baseball Player)
5751 NW Plantation Ln
Lees Summit, MO 64064-1686, USA

Huizenga, Bill (Congressman, Politician)
1217 Longworth Hob
Washington, DC 20515-4901, USA

Huizenga, H. Wayne (Baseball Player, Business Person)
c/o Staff Member *Miami Dolphins*
7500 SW 30th St
Davie, FL 33314-1020, USA

Huizenga, John R (Scientist)
354 Gravilla St
La Jolla, CA 92037-6006, USA

Hulbert, Mike (Athlete, Golfer)
7770 Apple Tree Cir
Orlando, FL 32819-4686, USA

Hulbig, Joe (Athlete, Hockey Player)
17 Apple Blossom Ln
Stow, MA 01775-1380, USA

Hulce, Tom (Actor)
2305 Stanley Hills Dr
Los Angeles, CA 90046-1533, USA

Hulcher, Janet
9000 Bay Hill Blvd
Orlando, FL 32819-4880, USA

Hulett, Tim (Athlete, Baseball Player)
799 Dumaine Dr
Bossier City, LA 71111-6273, USA

Hull, Bobby (Athlete, Hockey Player)
6916 Lennox Pl
University Park, FL 34201-2256, USA

Hull, Brett A (Athlete, Hockey Player)
3826 Maplewood Ave
Dallas, TX 75205-2829, USA

Hull, Dennis
115 E Maple St
Hinsdale, IL 60521-3730

Hull, Dennis W (Athlete, Hockey Player)
11642 County Rd 29
Roseneath, ON K0K 2X0, Canada

Hull, Don (Misc)
1 Olympic Plz
Colorado Springs, CO 80909-5780, USA

Hull, Gina (Athlete, Golfer)
479 Arricola Ave
Saint Augustine, FL 32080-4520, USA

Hull, J Kent (Athlete, Football Player)
RR 1 Box 5748
Greenwood, MS 38930, USA

Hull, James D (Admiral)
Commander US Coast Guard Atlantic
4131 Crawford St
Portsmouth, VA 23704, USA

Hull, Jody (Athlete, Coach, Hockey Player)
c/o Staff Member *Peterborough Petes*
151 Lansdowne St W
Peterborough, ON K9J 1Y4, Canada

Hull, Mike (Athlete, Football Player)
3809 Vista Azul
San Clemente, CA 92672-4543, USA

Hull, Roger H (Educator)
Chancellor's Office
Schenectady, NY 12308, USA

Hullar, Theodore L (Educator)
7529 S Eliot Ln
Tucson, AZ 85747-9627, USA

Hullet, Jamie (Athlete, Golfer)
1153 Lakeview Dr
Mesquite, TX 75149-5813, USA

Hulme, Denis (Race Car Driver)
CI-6 RDTE Puke
Bay of Plenny, NEW ZEALAND

Hulme, Etta (Cartoonist, Editor)
400 W 7th St
Fort Worth, TX 76102-4701, USA

Hulme, Keri (Writer)
338 Euston Road
London NW1 3BH, UNITED KINGDOM (UK)

Hulse, Cale (Athlete, Hockey Player)
c/o Art Breeze *Pro-Rep Entertainment Consulting*
113-276 Midpark Way SE
Calgary, AB T2X 1J6, Canada

Hulse, David (Athlete, Baseball Player)
1301 Kenwood Dr
San Angelo, TX 76903-7261, USA

Hulse, Russell A (Nobel Prize Laureate)
PO Box 451
Princeton, NJ 08542-0451, USA

Hultgren, Randy (Congressman, Politician)
427 Cannon Hob
Washington, DC 20515-5301, USA

Hultz, Don (Athlete, Football Player)
5078 Pleasant Ridge Rd
Millington, TN 38053-7752, USA

Huly, Jan C (General)
2 Navy St
Washington, DC 20380-1775, USA

Human League (Music Group)
c/o Staff Member *Performers Of the World/ Management Interests Associates (POW/MIA)*
8901 Melrose Ave Fl 2
West Hollywood, CA 90069-5605, USA

Humann, L Philip (Financier)
303 Peachtree St NE
Atlanta, GA 30308-3253, USA

Humayan, Mark S (Doctor)
Wilmer Ophthalmology Institute
Baltimore, MD 21218, USA

Humber, Philip (Athlete, Baseball Player)
PO Box 130788
Tyler, TX 75713-0788, USA

Humbert, John O (Religious Leader)
130 E Washington St
Indianapolis, IN 46204-4605, USA

Humbert, Richard (Athlete, Football Player)
12112 Ashton Park Dr
Glen Allen, VA 23059-7129, USA

Hume, A Britton (Brit) (Correspondent)
3100 N St NW Apt 9
Washington, DC 20007-3427, USA

Hume, Alan
Deanrise Deanwood Rd.
Jordans Bucks., ENGLAND

Hume, Brit (Television Host)
c/o Staff Member *Fox News Channel (DC)*
400 N Capitol St NW Ste 550
Washington, DC 20001-1502, USA

Hume, John (Nobel Prize Laureate)
5 Bayview Terrace
Derry BT48 7EE, NORTHERN IRELAND

Hume, Kirsty (Model)
15, rue Duphot
PAris 75001, FRANCE

Hume, Roger
9 Blenheim St
London, ENGLAND W1Y 9LE

Hume, Stephen (Editor)
2250 Granville St
Vancouver, BC V6H 3G2, CANADA

Hume, Tom (Athlete, Baseball Player)
3810 Redfish Ct
Palmetto, FL 34221-5636, USA

Humenik, Ed (Athlete, Golfer)
4746 SW Hammock Creek Dr
Palm City, FL 34990-7936, USA

Humes, Edward (Journalist)
1230 Avenue of the Americas
New York, NY 10020-1513, USA

Humes, John P (Diplomat)
Forest Mill Road
Mill Neck, NY 11765, USA

Humes, Mary Margaret
PO Box 1168-714
Studio City, CA 91604

Humes, Mary-Margaret (Actor, Model)
6500 Wilshire Blvd # 550
Los Angeles, CA 90048-4920, USA

Humiston, Mike (Athlete, Football Player)
311 N Richhill St
Waynesburg, PA 15370-1224, USA

Humm, David (Athlete, Football Player)
1701 Fairfield Ave
Las Vegas, NV 89102-2809, USA

Hummel, Tim (Athlete, Baseball Player)
1550 Kerr Rd
Whiteford, MD 21160-1318, USA

Hummer, John (Athlete, Basketball Player)
2640 Baker St
San Francisco, CA 94123-3802, USA

Hummes, Claudio Hummes Cardinal (Religious Leader)
Avenida Higienopolis 890 CP 1670
Sao Paulo 01238-908, BRAZIL

Humperdinck, Engelbert (Actor, Musician, Producer)
c/o Arthur Andelson *Kismet Talent Agency*
3435 Ocean Park Blvd Ste 107
Santa Monica, CA 90405-3320, USA

Humphrey, Claude (Athlete, Football Player)
3399 Lord Dunmore Cv
Bartlett, TN 38134-3089, USA

Humphrey, Gordon J (Ex-Senator)
78 Garvin Hill Rd
Chichester, NH 03258-6102, USA

Humphrey, Jay (Athlete, Football Player)
711 Ridgeview Dr
Rockwall, TX 75087-4136, USA

Humphrey, Paul (Athlete, Football Player)
1120 E Davis Dr Apt 515
Terre Haute, IN 47802-4068, USA

Humphrey, Renee
9300 Wilshire Blvd Ste 555
Beverly Hills, CA 90212-3211

Humphrey, Richard (Baseball Player)
21 Midland Dr
Morristown, NJ 07960-5064, USA

Humphrey, Richard (Athlete, Baseball Player)
26 Player Green Pl
Spring, TX 77382-2021, USA

Humphrey, Ryan (Basketball Player)
175 Toyota Plz Ste 150
Memphis, TN 38103-6601, USA

Humphrey, Terry (Athlete, Baseball Player)
7 Oakmont
Trabuco Canyon, CA 92679-4728, USA

Humphreys, Bob (Athlete, Baseball Player)
1803 Oakwood St
Bedford, VA 24523-1217, USA

Humphreys, Mike (Athlete, Baseball Player)
1402 Lost Creek Dr
Desoto, TX 75115-3662, USA

Humphries, Barry (Actor)
5 Soho Square
London W1V 5DE, UNITED KINGDOM (UK)

Humphries, Jay (Athlete, Basketball Player)
22107 N 37th Ter
Phoenix, AZ 85050-8304, USA

Humphries, Kris (Athlete, Basketball Player)
c/o Liza Anderson *Anderson Group Public Relations*
8060 Melrose Ave Fl 4
Los Angeles, CA 90046-7038, USA

Humphries, Rusty (Radio Personality)
225 NE Hillcrest Dr
Grants Pass, OR 97526-3547, USA

Humphries, Stan (Athlete, Football Player)
4100 Chauvin Ln
Monroe, LA 71201-2057, USA

Humphries, Stefan (Athlete, Football Player)
8708 E Redwood Ln
Spokane, WA 99217-9757, USA

Humphry, Derek (Activist)
24828 Norris Ln
Junction City, OR 97448, USA

Hun, Sen (Prime Minister)
Supreme National Council
Phnom Penh, COMBODIA

Hundertwasser, FriedensreichMu
hle Odissenbach
Rapottenstein, AUSTRIA 3911

Hundley, Mandisa (Musician)
c/o Staff Member *The M Collective*
PO Box 273
Franklin, TN 37065-0273, USA

Hundley, Randy (Athlete, Baseball Player)
122 E Forest Ln
Palatine, IL 60067-7443, USA

Hundley, Rod (Hot Rod) (Athlete, Basketball Player, Sportscaster)
1860 Siggard Dr
Salt Lake City, UT 84106-3870, USA

Hundley, Todd (Athlete, Baseball Player)
830 Raleigh Rd
Glenview, IL 60025-4328, USA

Hundt, Reed E (Government Official)
6416 Brookside Dr
Bethesda, MD 20815-6649, USA

Hung, Sammo (Actor)
c/o Staff Member *Innovative Artists (LA)*
1505 10th St
Santa Monica, CA 90401-2805, USA

Hung, William (Musician, Reality TV Star)
c/o Michael (Mike) Esterman
Esterman.Com, LLC
Prefers to be contacted via email
MD, USA

Hunger, Daniela (Swimmer)
Hansastr 190
Berlin 13088, GERMANY

Huniford, James (Architect, Designer)
30 E 67th St
New York, NY 10065-6155, USA

Hunkapiller, Michael (Biologist, Inventor)
850 Lincoln Centre Dr
Foster City, CA 94404-1128, USA

Hunley, Ricky C (Athlete, Football Player)
4435 Circle View Blvd
Los Angeles, CA 90043-1105, USA

Hunnam, Charlie (Actor)
c/o Cynthia Pett-Dante *Brillstein Entertainment Partners*
9150 Wilshire Blvd Ste 350
Beverly Hills, CA 90212-3453, USA

Hunnicutt, Gayle (Actor)
174 Regents Park Road
London NW1, UNITED KINGDOM (UK)

Hunphrey, Bobby (Athlete, Football Player)
4209 Woodbine Ln
Hoover, AL 35226-4122, USA

Hunt, Bobby (Athlete, Football Player)
5928 Bentway Dr
Charlotte, NC 28226-8053, USA

Hunt, Bonnie (Actor, Director, Talk Show Host)
c/o Ariel (Ari) Emanuel *WmE2 (Endeavor-LA)*
9601 Wilshire Blvd Fl 3
Beverly Hills, CA 90210-5219, USA

Hunt, Bryan (Artist)
31 Great Jones St
New York, NY 10012-1178, USA

Hunt, Byron (Athlete, Football Player)
PO Box 281
Rutherford, NJ 07070-0281, USA

Hunt, Cletidus (Athlete, Football Player)
7246 Creek Bend Dr
Memphis, TN 38125-3018, USA

Hunt, Courtney (Director, Writer)
c/o Staff Member *WmE2 (WMA-LA)*
1 William Morris Pl
Beverly Hills, CA 90212-4261, USA

Hunt, Crystal (Actor)
c/o Scott Zimmerman *Evolution Entertainment (LA)*
901 N Highland Ave
Los Angeles, CA 90038-2412, USA

Hunt, Francesca (Actor)
c/o Dallas Smith *United Agents*
12-26 Lexington St
London W1F OLE, UK

Hunt, George (Athlete, Football Player)
40 N Pine Cir
Belleair, FL 33756-1640, USA

Hunt, Helen (Actor)
c/o Stephen Huvane *Slate Public Relations*
9000 W Sunset Blvd Ste 915
West Hollywood, CA 90069-5809, USA

Hunt, Jimmy (Actor)
2279 Lansdale Ct
Simi Valley, CA 93065-2530, USA

Hunt, John (Athlete, Football Player)
145 Fairgreen Trce
Newnan, GA 30265-5541, USA

Hunt, John R (Religious Leader)
5101 N Francisco Ave
Chicago, IL 60625-3676, USA

Hunt, Ken (Athlete, Baseball Player)
268 E 300 N
Morgan, UT 84050-9520, USA

Hunt, Kevin (Athlete, Football Player)
PO Box 612
Londonderry, NH 03053-0612, USA

Hunt, Lamar (Football Executive, Soccer Player, Tennis Player)
1601 Elm St # 2800
Dallas, TX 75201-4701, USA

Hunt, Linda (Actor)
c/o Tim Curtis *WmE2 (Endeavor-LA)*
9601 Wilshire Blvd Fl 3
Beverly Hills, CA 90210-5219, USA

Hunt, Linda (Athlete, Golfer)
6436 Bella Cir Unit 1105
Boynton Beach, FL 33437-5566, USA

Hunt, Marsha (Actor)
13131 Magnolia Blvd
Van Nuys, CA 91423-1528, USA

Hunt, Marsha (Actor, Writer)
c/o Staff Member *D&M Publishers*
2323 Quebec St Suite 201
Vancouver, BC V5T 4S7, Canada

Hunt, Nelson Bunker (Business Person)
Fountain Place 1445 Ross at Field
Dallas, TX 75202-2785, USA

Hunt, Peter (Director, Producer)
c/o Dennis Aspland *Aspland Management*
245 W 55th St Ste 1001
New York, NY 10019-5231, USA

Hunt, R Timothy (Nobel Prize Laureate)
PO Box 123
London WC2A 3PX, UNITED KINGDOM (UK)

Hunt, Randy (Athlete, Baseball Player)
324 Holly Ridge Dr
Montgomery, AL 36109-3904, USA

Hunt, Ray (Business Person)
1900 N Akard St
Dallas, TX 75201-2300

Hunt, Richard
1017 W Lill Ave
Chicago, IL 60614-2205, USA

Hunt, Ronald K (Ron) (Athlete, Baseball Player)
2806 Jackson Rd
Wentzville, MO 63385-4205, USA

Hunt, Sam (Athlete, Football Player)
1708 Eliza St
Nacogdoches, TX 75961-5700, USA

Hunt, Van (Musician)
c/o Staff Member *Creative Artists Agency (CAA-LA)*
2000 Avenue of the Stars Ste 100
Los Angeles, CA 90067-4705, USA

Hunt, Wendy (DJ)
c/o Staff Member *Diva Central Inc*
7510 W Sunset Blvd Ste 1445
Los Angeles, CA 90046-3408, USA

Hunten, Donald M (Astronomer)
10 E Calle Corta
Tucson, AZ 85716-4910, USA

Hunter, Anthony (Athlete, Football Player)
4811 Yarmouth Pl
Cincinnati, OH 45237-5903, USA

Hunter, Anthony R (Tony) (Biologist)
10100 N Torrey Pines Rd
La Jolla, CA 92037, USA

Hunter, Arthur (Art) (Athlete, Football Player)
5540 Yale St
Montclair, CA 91763-2546, USA

Hunter, Billy (Athlete, Baseball Player, Coach)
104 E Seminary Ave
Lutherville Timonium, MD 21093-6127, USA

Hunter, Brian (Athlete, Baseball Player)
31203 NE 49th St
Camas, WA 98607-9671, USA

Hunter, Brian (Athlete, Baseball Player)
12141 Centralia St Unit 219
Lakewood, CA 90715-1565, USA

Hunter, Buddy
14616 Fir Cir
Plattsmouth, NE 68048-5112, USA

Hunter, Buddy (Athlete, Baseball Player)
14616 Fir Cir
Plattsmouth, NE 68048-5112, USA

Hunter, Charlie (Music Group, Musician)
3470 19th St
San Francisco, CA 94110-1740, USA

Hunter, Dale (Athlete, Hockey Player)
c/o Staff Member *London Knights*
99 Dundas St
London, ON N6A 6K1, Canada

Hunter, Dave (Athlete, Hockey Player)
53350 Ran Ge Rd 220
Androssan, AB T8E 6K1, Canada

Hunter, Dorothy (Baseball Player)
2607 Miller Ave NW
Grand Rapids, MI 49544-1948, USA

Hunter, Duncan (Congressman, Politician)
223 Cannon Hob
Washington, DC 20515-0003, USA

Hunter, Holly (Actor)
c/o David Seltzer *Management 360*
9111 Wilshire Blvd
Beverly Hills, CA 90210-5508, USA

Hunter, Ian (Music Group, Musician, Songwriter, Writer)
Plaza 535 Kings Road
London SW10 0S, UNITED KINGDOM (UK)

Hunter, Jack D
22 Hypolita St
Saint Augustine, FL 32084-3606, USA

Hunter, James E (Athlete, Football Player)
5846 Prado Ct
Orchard Lake, MI 48324-2945, USA

Hunter, Jeff (Athlete, Football Player)
3492 Monte Carlo Dr
Augusta, GA 30906-5717, USA

Hunter, Jesse (Music Group, Musician)
1334 Lexington Ave
New York, NY 10128, USA

Hunter, Jim (Skier)
864 Woodpark Way SW
Calgary, AB T2W 2V8, CANADA

Hunter, Jim (Athlete, Baseball Player)
12939 Penshurst Ln
Windermere, FL 34786-6672, USA

Hunter, John (Engineer)
7000 East Ave
Livermore, CA 94550-9698, USA

Hunter, Lauren (Stylist)
c/o Staff Member *Koko Represents*
166 Geary St Ste 1007
San Francisco, CA 94108-5623, USA

Hunter, Les (Athlete, Basketball Player)
8712 W 92nd St
Overland Park, KS 66212-3817, USA

Hunter, Mark (Athlete, Hockey Player)
c/o Staff Member *London Knights*
99 Dundas St
London, ON N6A 6K1, Canada

Hunter, Mellisa (Reality TV Star)
c/o Michael (Mike) Esterman
Esterman.Com, LLC
Prefers to be contacted via email
MD, USA

Hunter, Montgomery (Athlete, Football Player)
411 Washington St
Dover, OH 44622-1938, USA

Hunter, Patrick (Athlete, Football Player)
880 N David Ct
Chandler, AZ 85226-1659, USA

Hunter, Paul (Director, Editor, Writer)
c/o Rob Carlson *WmE2 (Endeavor-LA)*
1 William Morris Pl
Beverly Hills, CA 90212-4261, USA

Hunter, Rachel (Actor, Model)
c/o Chuck Binder *Binder & Associates*
1465 Lindacrest Dr
Beverly Hills, CA 90210-2519, USA

Hunter, Rich (Athlete, Baseball Player)
3820 Agave Ct
Perris, CA 92570-7192, USA

Hunter, Ronald (Actor)
c/o Barbara Price *Kings Highway Entertainment*
14538 Benefit St Unit 103
Sherman Oaks, CA 91403-5504, USA

Hunter, Scott (Athlete, Football Player)
6386 Dolive Ct
Daphne, AL 36526-7159, USA

Hunter, Stephen (Writer)
1150 15th St NW
Washington, DC 20071-0001, USA

Hunter, Steven (Basketball Player)
Waterhouse Center 8701 Maitland Summit Blvd
Orlando, FL 32810, USA

Hunter, Tab (Actor, Writer)
PO Box 50308
Santa Barbara, CA 93150-0308, USA

Hunter, Tim (Director)
c/o Staff Member *Gersh (LA)*
9465 Wilshire Blvd Ste 600
Beverly Hills, CA 90212-2612, USA

Hunter, Tim (Athlete, Coach, Hockey Player)
c/o Staff Member *San Jose Sharks*
525 W Santa Clara St
San Jose, CA 95113-1500, USA

Hunter, Tommy (Musician)
c/o Staff Member *Rocklands Entertainment*
1135 Pasadena Ave S Ste 209
South Pasadena, FL 33707-2855, USA

Hunter, Torii (Athlete, Baseball Player)
PO Box 1357
Prosper, TX 75078-1357, USA

Hunter, Willard (Athlete, Baseball Player)
2562 Poppleton Ave
Omaha, NE 68105-2303, USA

Hunter-Gault, Charlayne (Correspondent)
2700 S Quincy St Ste 250
Arlington, VA 22206-2222, USA

Hunthausen, Raymond G (Religious Leader)
910 Marion St
Seattle, WA 98104-1274, USA

Huntington, Sam (Actor)
c/o Walter Hamada *H2F Entertainment*
644 N Cherokee Ave
Los Angeles, CA 90004-1009, USA

Huntington, Samuel P (Politician)
Olin Institute Political Science Dept
Cambridge, MA 2138, USA

Huntington-Whiteley, Rosie (Actor, Model)
c/o Jeff Speich *Creative Artists Agency (CAA-LA)*
2000 Avenue of the Stars Ste 100
Los Angeles, CA 90067-4705, USA

Huntley, Noah (Actor)
c/o Lindy King *United Agents*
12-26 Lexington St
London W1F OLE, UK

Huntley, Richard (Athlete, Football Player)
6005 Williams Rd Apt A
Charlotte, NC 28215-3606, USA

Huntsman, Stanley H (Coach)
5532 Timbercrest Trl
Knoxville, TN 37909-1837, USA

Huntz, Steve (Athlete, Baseball Player)
3303 Linden Rd Apt 405
Rocky River, OH 44116-4105, USA

Hunyadfi, Steven (Coach, Swimmer)
838 Ridgewood Dr Apt 12
Fort Wayne, IN 46805-5712, USA

Hunyady, Emese (Speed Skater)
Beim Spitzriegel 1/2/9
Baden 2500, AUSTRIA

Hunziker, Terry (Designer)
208 3rd Ave S
Seattle, WA 98104-2608, USA

Huo, Yaobang (General, Secretary)
Zhongguo Gongchan Dang
Beijing, CHINA

Huot, Raymond P (General)
Inspector General Hqusaf Pentagon
Washington, DC 20330-0001, USA

Hupp, Jana Marie (Actor)
c/o Karen Forman *Domain Talent*
9229 W Sunset Blvd Ste 710
Los Angeles, CA 90069-3407, USA

Huppert, Dave (Athlete, Baseball Player)
6732 Stephens Path
Zephyrhills, FL 33542-0652, USA

Huppert, Isabelle (Actor)
20 Ave Rapp
Paris 75007, USA

Huras, Larry (Athlete, Hockey Player)
RR 1 PO
Allenford, ON N0H 1A0, Canada

Hurd, Douglas R (Government Official)
Crosby Court 4 Great Saint Helens
London EC3A 6HA, UNITED KINGDOM (UK)

Hurd, Gale Anne (Producer)
c/o Staff Member *Valhalla Motion Pictures*
3201 Cahuenga Blvd W
Los Angeles, CA 90068-1301, USA

Hurd, Michelle (Actor)
c/o Tina Thor *TMT Entertainment Group*
648 Broadway Ste 1002
New York, NY 10012-2348, USA

Hurd, Molly (Stylist)
c/o Staff Member *Workgroup (Hollywood)*
8491 W Sunset Blvd # 368
West Hollywood, CA 90069-1911, USA

Hurdle, Clinton M (Clint) (Athlete, Baseball Player, Coach)
9068 Sturbridge Pl
Highlands Ranch, CO 80129-2236, USA

Hurford, Peter J (Musician)
Broom House Saint Bernard's Road Saint Albans
Herts AL3 5RA, UNITED KINGDOM (UK)

Hurlburt, Bob (Athlete, Hockey Player)
956 Shadywood Dr
Victoria, BC V8X 4C3, Canada

Hurlbut, Linda (Athlete, Golfer)
24741 Calle Conejo
Calabasas, CA 91302-3009, USA

Hurlbut, Mike (Athlete, Hockey Player)
46 Leo Mar Dr
Fulton, NY 13069-4983, USA

Hurley, Alfred F (Historian)
President's Office
Denton, TX 76203, USA

Hurley, Bobby (Athlete, Basketball Player)
1410 Shoreline Way
Hollywood, FL 33019-5006, USA

Hurley, Chad (Business Person)
901 Cherry Ave
San Bruno, CA 94066-2914, USA

Hurley, Craig (Actor)
c/o Sandie Schnarr *Sandie Schnarr Talent Agency*
5670 Wilshire Blvd Ste 1930
Los Angeles, CA 90036-5603, USa

Hurley, Douglas G (Astronaut)
700 Thomwood Dr
Friendswood, TX 77546, USA

Hurley, Elizabeth (Actor, Model)
c/o Duncan Heath *Independent Talent Group (ITG-UK)*
Oxford House 76 Oxford St
London W1D 1BS, UK

Hurley, Marybeth (Stylist)
c/o Staff Member *Team*
423 W Broadway Ste 406
Boston, MA 02127-2265, USA

Hurn, David (Photographer)
Prospect Cottage Tintem
Gwent, WALES

Hurnick, Ilja (Composer, Musician)
Narodni Trida 35
Prague 1 11000, CZECH REPUBLIC

Hurst, Bill (Athlete, Baseball Player)
15820 SW 88th Ct
Palmetto Bay, FL 33157-2031, USA

Hurst, Bruce (Athlete, Baseball Player)
1080 N Riata St
Gilbert, AZ 85234-3466, USA

Hurst, Geoff (Athlete, Football Player)
c/o Staff Member *The FA*
25 Soho Square
London W1D 4FA, United Kingdom

Hurst, Jackson (Actor)
c/o Staff Member *Lee Peterson and Associates*
78 San Marcos St
Austin, TX 78702-5236, USA

Hurst, James (Athlete, Baseball Player)
1413 Van Pelt Rd
Sebring, FL 33870, USA

Hurst, Jimmy (Athlete, Baseball Player)
901 University Ln
Tuscaloosa, AL 35401-7134, USA

Hurst, Jonathan (Athlete, Baseball Player)
308 Woodburn Creek Rd
Spartanburg, SC 29302-4279, USA

Hurst, Maurice (Athlete, Football Player)
P.O. Box 431068
Dallas, TX 75343, USA

Hurst, Michael (Actor)
218 Richmond Road Grey Lynn
Auckland 2, NEW ZEALAND

Hurst, Pat (Athlete, Golfer)
730 Camino Amigo
Danville, CA 94526-2204, USA

Hurst, Rick (Actor)
1230 Horn Ave Apt 401
West Hollywood, CA 90069-2120, USA

Hurst, Ron (Athlete, Hockey Player)
535 Edgewood Ave
Oshawa, ON L1G 2R7, Canada

Hurst, Ryan (Actor)
c/o Brian Swardstrom *WmE2 (Endeavor-LA)*
9601 Wilshire Blvd Fl 3
Beverly Hills, CA 90210-5219, USA

Hurston, Chuck (Athlete, Football Player)
9360 Prestwick Club Dr
Duluth, GA 30097-2400, USA

Hurt, Frank (Misc)
10401 Connecticut Ave
Kensington, MD 20895-3951, USA

Hurt, John (Actor)
c/o John Crosby *Crosby/Spilo Management*
1310 N Spaulding Ave
Los Angeles, CA 90046-4010, USA

Hurt, Mary Beth (Actor)
1619 Broadway # 900
New York, NY 10019-7412, USA

Hurt, Robert (Congressman, Politician)
1516 Longworth Hob
Washington, DC 20515-0905, USA

Hurt, William (Actor)
c/o Jessica Kolstad *WKT Public Relations (WKT-LA)*
9350 Wilshire Blvd Ste 450
Beverly Hills, CA 90212-3230, USA

Hurtado, Edwin (Baseball Player)
1202 15th Ave N
Lake Worth, FL 33460-1725, USA

Hurtado Larrea, Oswaldo (President)
Suecia 277 y Av Los Shyris
Quito, ECUADOR

Hurwich, Leo M (Doctor)
Psychology Dept
Philadelphia, PA 19104, USA

Hurwicz, Leonid (Economist, Nobel Prize Laureate)
880 527th Cir
Stanchfield, MN 55080-5181, USA

Hurwit, Bruce (Director)
c/o Staff Member *Morra Brezner Steinberg & Tenenbaum (MBST) Entertainment*
345 N Maple Dr Ste 200
Beverly Hills, CA 90210-5174, USA

Hurwitz, Emanuel H (Musician)
25 Dollis Ave
London N3 1DA, UNITED KINGDOM (UK)

Hurwitz, Jerard (Biologist)
1275 York Ave
New York, NY 10065-6007, USA

Hurwitz, Mitchell
c/o Adam Berkowitz *Creative Artists Agency (CAA-LA)*
2000 Avenue of the Stars Ste 100
Los Angeles, CA 90067-4705, USA

Husa, Karel J (Composer)
3417 Foy Glen Ct
Apex, NC 27539-3681, USA

Husain, Mishal (Journalist)
c/o Staff Member *BBC Artist Mail*
PO Box 1116
Belfast BT2 7AJ, United Kingdom

Husaini (Actor)
T 16/2 Kalasethra Colony Besant Nagar
Chennai, TN 600 090, INDIA

Husak, Todd (Athlete, Football Player)
100 N Sepulveda Blvd
El Segundo, CA 90245-4359, USA

Husar, Lubomyr Cardinal (Religious Leader)
Ploscha Sviatoho Jura 5
Lviv 290000, UKRAINE

Husbands, Clifford (Governor)
c/o Private Secretary To The Governor-General Government House
Saint Michael, Barbados

Huscroft, Jamie (Athlete, Hockey Player)
3024 38th St SE
Puyallup, WA 98374-1949, USA

Huselius, Kristian (Athlete, Hockey Player)
1 Panther Pkwy
Sunrise, FL 33323-5315, USA

Husen, Torsten (Educator)
Armfeltsgatan 10
Stockholm 115 34, SWEDEN

Husenov, Surat (Prime Minister)
Baku, AZERBAIJAN

Hush, Lizabeth
4512 Gentry Ave
Valley Village, CA 91607-4117

Huskey, Robert L (Butch) (Athlete, Baseball Player)
PO Box 996
Apache, OK 73006-0996, USA

Husky, Rick
13565 Lucca Dr
Pacific Palisades, CA 90272-2722

Husmann, Ed (Athlete, Football Player)
27266 Orth Ln
Conroe, TX 77385-9087, USA

Huson, Jeff (Athlete, Baseball Player)
10349 Rowlock Way
Parker, CO 80134-9580, USA

Huson, Kimberly (Stylist)
2514 3rd St
Santa Monica, CA 90405-3605, USA

Hussain, Nasir (Director, Filmmaker, Producer)
24 Pali Hill Bandra
Bombay, MS 400 050, INDIA

Hussey, Olivia (Actor)
c/o Staff Member *Richard Schwartz Management*
2934 1/2 N Beverly Glen Cir # 107
Los Angeles, CA 90077-1724, USA

Husted, Dave (Athlete, Bowler)
16231 SE Norma Rd
Portland, OR 97267-5193, USA

Husted, Wayne D (Artist)
Ely Road
Monson, MA 1057, USA

Huston, Anjelica (Actor, Director)
c/o Ina Treciokas *Slate Public Relations*
9000 W Sunset Blvd Ste 915
West Hollywood, CA 90069-5809, USA

Huston, Carol
10100 Santa Monica Blvd Ste 2500
Los Angeles, CA 90067-4116

Huston, Daniel (Danny) (Actor, Director)
c/o Laina Cohn *Laina Cohn Management*
15066 Sutton St
Sherman Oaks, CA 91403-4020, USA

Huston, Geoff (Athlete, Basketball Player)
1960 Ellis Ave
Bronx, NY 10472-5006, USA

Huston, Jack (Actor)
c/o Todd Diener *Collective*
8383 Wilshire Blvd Ste 1050
Beverly Hills, CA 90211-2415, USA

Huston, John (Athlete, Golfer)
1134 Skye Ln
Palm Harbor, FL 34683-1457, USA

Huston, Ron (Athlete, Hockey Player)
238 4th St
Encinitas, CA 92024-3247, USA

Hutch, Jesse (Actor)
c/o Staff Member *Pacific Artists Management*
1285 W Broadway Suite 685
Vancouver, BC V6H 3X8, Canada

Hutcherson, Josh (Actor)
c/o Ric Beddingfield *Beddingfield Company, The*
13600 Ventura Blvd Ste B
Sherman Oaks, CA 91423-5050, USA

Hutcherson, Robert (Bobby) (Musician)
223 1/2 E 48th St
New York, NY 10017, USA

Hutchins, Jason (Athlete, Baseball Player)
2401 Stone Castle Cir
College Station, TX 77845-5494, USA

Hutchins, Mel (Athlete, Basketball Player)
160 Sherri Ln
Oceanside, CA 92054-5327, USA

Hutchins, Paul (Athlete, Football Player)
7251 S South Shore Dr Apt 9F
Chicago, IL 60649-5775, USA

Hutchins, Will (Actor)
PO Box 371
Glen Head, NY 11545-0371, USA

Hutchinson, Andrew (Athlete, Hockey Player)
5860 Printemp Dr
East Lansing, MI 48823-9778, USA

Hutchinson, Anthony (Athlete, Football Player)
124 Bellaire Ct
Bellaire, TX 77401-4219, USA

Hutchinson, Asa (Politician)
1501 N Pierce St Ste 102
Little Rock, AR 72207-5222, USA

Hutchinson, Barbara (Misc)
815 15th St NW
Washington, DC 20005, USA

Hutchinson, Chad (Athlete, Baseball Player)
1388 Elder Ave
Menlo Park, CA 94025-5566, USA

Hutchinson, Clyde A Jr (Misc)
Searle Laboratory Chimestry Dept
Chicago, IL 60637, USA

Hutchinson, Doug (Actor)
9560 Wilshire Blvd Ste 500
Beverly Hills, CA 90212-2401, USA

Hutchinson, Doug (Actor)
c/o Ryan Martin *Agency for the Performing Arts (APA-LA)*
405 S Beverly Dr Ste 500
Beverly Hills, CA 90212-4425, USA

Hutchinson, Frederick E (Educator)
President S Ofc
Orono, ME 04469-0001, USA

Hutchinson, J Maxwell (Architect)
Cavendish Mansions #61 Clerkenwell Road
London EC1R 5DH, UNITED KINGDOM (UK)

Hutchinson, Kieran (Actor)
c/o Adam Levine *Levine Okwu Erickson Management*
9601 Wilshire Blvd Fl 3
Beverly Hills, CA 90210-5219, USA

Hutchinson, Ron (Athlete, Hockey Player)
213 Merlin Ct
Kelowna, BC V1V 1N2, Canada

Hutchinson, Scott (Athlete, Football Player)
726 Forest Glen Ct
Maitland, FL 32751-5109, USA

Hutchinson, Steven (Athlete, Football Player)
16119 Crosby Cove Rd
Wayzata, MN 55391-4528, USA

Hutchison, Dave (Athlete, Hockey Player)
3922 Hamilton Rd
Dorchester, ON N0L 1G2, Canada

Hutchison, Doug (Actor)
c/o Ryan Martin *Agency for the Performing Arts (APA-LA)*
405 S Beverly Dr Ste 500
Beverly Hills, CA 90212-4425, USA

Hutchison, Kay Bailey (Senator)
284 Russell Senate Ofc Building
Washington, DC 20510-0001, USA

Hutchison, Melinda (Stylist)
2913 Toledo Ave S
Saint Louis Park, MN 55416-1926, USA

Huth, Edward J (Doctor, Editor)
1124 Morris Ave
Bryn Mawr, PA 19010-1712, USA

Huth, Gerald (Athlete, Football Player)
5009 Elm Grove Dr
Las Vegas, NV 89130-3639, USA

Huther, Bruce (Athlete, Football Player)
1156 N Bonnie Brae St
Denton, TX 76201-2421, USA

Hutson, Brian (Athlete, Football Player)
6077 Arboretum Dr
Frisco, TX 75034-7270, USA

Hutson, Candace
3500 W Olive Ave Ste 920
Burbank, CA 91505-5514

Hutson, Herb (Athlete, Baseball Player)
7203 W Sugar Tree Ct
Savannah, GA 31410-2414, USA

Hutson, Tracy (Actor, Reality TV Star)
c/o Staff Member *Extreme Makeover: Home Edition*
Endemol Entertainment USA 9225 Sunset Blvd #1100
Los Angeles, CA 90069, USA

Hutt, Peter B (Attorney, Attorney General, General)
1201 Pennsylvania Ave NW
Washington, DC 20004-2401, USA

Hutto, Jim (Athlete, Baseball Player)
1317 John Carroll Dr
Pensacola, FL 32504-7114, USA

Hutton, Anthony (Reality TV Star)
c/o Staff Member *Big Brother (UK)*
Channel 4 Television 124 Horseferry Rd
London SW1P 2TX, UNITED KINGDOM

Hutton, Danny (Music Group, Musician)
2437 Horse Shoe Canyon Rd
Los Angeles, CA 90046-1539, USA

Hutton, Joe (Athlete, Basketball Player)
3008 W 90th St
Minneapolis, MN 55431-2138, USA

Hutton, Lauren (Actor, Model)
c/o Katie Rhodes *Untitled Entertainment (LA)*
350 S Beverly Dr Ste 200
Beverly Hills, CA 90212-4819, USA

Hutton, Mark (Athlete, Baseball Player)
6 Corfu Ct
Westlakes Adelaide, AU 5021, Australia

Hutton, Pascale (Actor)
c/o Ben Levine *Kritzer Levine Wilkins Entertainment*
11872 La Grange Ave Fl 1
Los Angeles, CA 90025-5283, USA

Hutton, Ralph (Swimmer)
312 Main St
Vancouver, BC, CANADA

Hutton, Rif (Actor)
c/o Staff Member *Momentum Talent and Literary Agency*
9401 Wilshire Blvd Ste 501
Beverly Hills, CA 90212-2944, USA

Hutton, Timothy (Actor)
c/o Judy Hofflund *Hofflund/Polone*
9465 Wilshire Blvd Ste 420
Beverly Hills, CA 90212-2603, USA

Hutton, Tommy
18 Huntly Dr
Palm Beach Gardens, FL 33418-6812, USA

Hutton, Tommy (Athlete, Baseball Player)
18 Huntly Dr
Palm Beach Gardens, FL 33418-6812, USA

Hutzler, Brody (Actor)
c/o Staff Member *Pakula/King & Associates*
9229 W Sunset Blvd Ste 315
Los Angeles, CA 90069-3403, USA

Huxhold, Ken (Athlete, Football Player)
8524 Stone Harbor Ave
Las Vegas, NV 89145-5704, USA

Huxley, Andrew F (Nobel Prize Laureate)
Manor Field 1 Vicarage Dr Grantchester
Cambridge CB3 9NG, UNITED KINGDOM (UK)

Huxley, Hugh E (Biologist)
349 Nashawtuc Rd
Concord, MA 01742-1616, USA

Huxley, Laura (Doctor, Writer)
1795 Washington Way
Venice, CA 90291-4701, USA

Huxtable, Ada Louise (Critic)
969 Park Ave
New York, NY 10028-0322, USA

Huyck, Willard (Director)
39 Oakmont Dr
Los Angeles, CA 90049-1901, USA

Hvorostovsky, Dmitri (Opera Singer)
6 Henrietta St
London WC2E 8LA, UNITED KINGDOM (UK)

Hyams, Joe
10375 Wilshire Blvd Apt 4D
Los Angeles, CA 90024-4729

Hyams, Joseph I (Joe) Jr (Writer)
10375 Wilshire Blvd Apt 4D
Los Angeles, CA 90024-4729, USA

Hyams, Peter (Director)
PO Box 10
Basking Ridge, NJ 07920-0010, USA

Hyatt, Fred (Athlete, Football Player)
19350 SE 52nd Pl
Morriston, FL 32668-3968, USA

Hybl, William J (Misc)
1 Olympic Plz
Colorado Springs, CO 80909-5780, USA

Hyche, Heath (Comedian)
c/o Staff Member *Brillstein Entertainment Partners*
9150 Wilshire Blvd Ste 350
Beverly Hills, CA 90212-3453, USA

Hyche, Steve (Athlete, Football Player)
2801 Five Oaks Ln
Vestavia, AL 35243-2621, USA

Hyde, Allan (Actor)
c/o Iris Grossman *International Creative Management (ICM-LA)*
10250 Constellation Blvd Fl 7
Los Angeles, CA 90067-6207, USA

Hyde, Dick (Athlete, Baseball Player)
1506 Cambridge Dr
Champaign, IL 61821-4957, USA

Hyde, Harry
PO Box 291
Harrisburg, NC 28075-0291

Hyde, Jonathan (Actor)
52/53 Poland Place
London W1F 7LX, UNITED KINGDOM (UK)

Hyder, Greg (Athlete, Basketball Player)
16228 Wato Rd Apt A
Apple Valley, CA 92307-7813, USA

Hyde-White, Alex (Actor)
3172 Dona Susana Dr
Studio City, CA 91604-4356, USA

Hyers, Tim (Athlete, Baseball Player)
241 Ridge Rd
Covington, GA 30016-5138, USA

Hyland, Brian (Musician)
PO Box 101
Helendale, CA 92342-0101, USA

Hyland, Robert (Athlete, Football Player)
30 Colonial Rd
White Plains, NY 10605-2212, USA

Hyland, Sarah (Actor)
c/o Richard Konigsberg *RKM*
400 N Mansfield Ave
Los Angeles, CA 90036-2622, USA

Hylton, Thomas J (Journalist)
Editorial Dept Hanover & Kings Sts
Pottstown, PA 19464, USA

Hyman, B D
PO Box 7107
Charlottesville, VA 22906-7107, USA

Hyman, Dick
223 1/2 E 48th St
New York, NY 10017

Hyman, Dorothy
7 Norman Close Barnsley
So. Yorks, ENGLAND S71 244

Hyman, Earle (Actor)
484 W 43rd St Apt 33E
New York, NY 10036-6331, USA

Hyman, Fracaswell (Producer)
c/o Staff Member *WmE2 (WMA-LA)*
1 William Morris Pl
Beverly Hills, CA 90212-4261, USA

Hyman, Kenneth
Sherwood House Tilehouse Lane Denham
Bucks, ENGLAND.

Hyman, Misty (Swimmer)
3826 E Lupine Ave
Phoenix, AZ 85028-2125, USA

Hyman, Misty (Athlete, Swimmer)
3826 E Lupine Ave
Phoenix, AZ 85028-2125, USA

Hyman, Richard R (Dick) (Composer, Musician)
223 1/2 E 48th St
New York, NY 10017, USA

Hymes, Randy (Athlete, Football Player)
8108 Hallmark Dr
N Richlnd Hls, TX 76182-8644, USA

Hymowitz, Kay S. (Writer)
52 Vanderbilt Ave Fl 2
New York, NY 10017-3808, USA

Hynd, Noel
c/o Susan Simons *Broder Webb Chervin Silbermann Agency, The (BWCS)*
10250 Constellation Blvd
Los Angeles, CA 90067-6200, USA

Hynd, Ronald (Ballerina, Choreographer)
Fern Cottage Up Somerton Bury Saint Edmonds
Suffolk IP29 4ND, UNITED KINGDOM (UK)

Hynde, Chrissie (Actor, Musician)
c/o Barbara Skydell *WmE2 (WMA-NY)*
1325 Avenue of the Americas
New York, NY 10019-6026, USA

Hyneman, Jamie (Actor, Special Effects Designer)
1268 Missouri St
San Francisco, CA 94107-3310, USA

Hynes, Dave (Athlete, Hockey Player)
10 Trinity Ct
Wellesley Hills, MA 02481-2505, USA

Hynes, Garry (Director)
Chapel Lane
Galway, IRELAND

Hynes, Samuel (Writer)
Princeton, NJ 8540, USA

Hynes, Tyler (Actor)
201 Laurier Ave E # 202
Ottawa, ON K1N 6P1, CANADA

Hynoski, Henry (Athlete, Football Player)
PO Box 257
Elysburg, PA 17824-0257, USA

Hyre, John (Business Person)
870 High St Ste 104
Worthington, OH 43085-4141, USA

Hysong, Nick (Athlete, Track Athlete)
10424 N 38th St
Phoenix, AZ 85028-4016, USA

Hytner, Nicholas R (Director)
South Bank
London SE1 9PX, UNITED KINGDOM (UK)

Hyzdu, Adam (Athlete, Baseball Player)
7823 E Red Hawk Cir
Mesa, AZ 85207-1167, USA

I

Iacavazzi, Cosmo (Athlete, Football Player)
90 Vine St
Taylor, PA 18517-1225, USA

Iacocca, Lee (Business Person)
867 Boylston St Fl 6
Boston, MA 02116-2774, USA

Iaconelli, Mike (Athlete, Fisherman)
c/o Staff Member *Octagon Outdoors*
916 Loblolly Dr
Lewisville, NC 27023-8613, USA

Iaconio, Frank (Race Car Driver)
250 US Highway 206
Flanders, NJ 07836-9071, USA

Iacono, Paul (Actor)
c/o Wendi Green *Paradigm (LA)*
9200 W Sunset Blvd PH 11
Los Angeles, CA 90069-3601, USA

Iafrate, Al A (Athlete, Hockey Player)
17320 Fairfield St
Livonia, MI 48152-4406, USA

Iakovas, Primate Archbishop (Religious Leader)
31 Park Cir
New York, NY 10021, USA

Ian, Janis (Composer, Musician)
c/o Staff Member *Cooking Vinyl USA*
PO Box 246
Huntington, NY 11743-0246, USA

Iaquaniello, Mike (Athlete, Football Player)
49105 Plum Tree Dr
Plymouth, MI 48170-3263, USA

Iassonga, Dan (Athlete, Baseball Player)
1501 Bailey Farm Ct SW
Marietta, GA 30064-5281, USA

Iassonga, Daniel (Baseball Player)
5950 N 78th St Unit 159
Scottsdale, AZ 85250-6183, USA

Iavaroni, Marcus (Athlete, Basketball Player)
8120 N Via De Lago
Scottsdale, AZ 85258-4211, USA

Ibanez, Raul (Athlete, Baseball Player)
26004 SE 23rd Pl
Sammamish, WA 98075-5947, USA

Ibbetson, Arthur (Cinematographer)
Tanglewood Chalfont Lane Chorley Wood
Herts, UNITED KINGDOM (UK)

Ibers, James A (Misc)
990 N Lake Shore Dr Apt 17C
Chicago, IL 60611-1376, USA

Ibiam, Francis A (Religious Leader)
Ganymede Unwana PO Box 240 Afikpo
Imo State, NIGERIA

Ibn Salman Ibn ' Abd Al-' Aziz Al-Saud (Astronaut, Misc)
PO Box 18368
Riyadh 11415, SAUDI ARABIA

Ibrahim, Abdullah (Dollar Brand) (Composer, Musician)
122 E 57th St # 300
New York, NY 10022-2623, USA

Ibrahim, Barre Mainassara (Misc)
Presidential Palace
Niamey, NIGER

Ibuka, Yaeko (Activist)
Leprosarium
Mount Fuji, JAPAN

Icahn, Carl C (Business Person)
1201 Elm St
Dallas, TX 75270-2002, USA

Ice
11500 W Olympic Blvd Ste 655
Los Angeles, CA 90064-1530

Ice, Vanilla (Musician)
c/o Tommy Quon *TQ Management Agency*
2412 Piedra Dr
Plano, TX 75023-5329, USA

Ice T (Actor, Artist)
3350 Wilshire Blvd Ste 1200
Los Angeles, CA 90010-4708, USA

Icehouse
Box KX-300 Kings Cross
Sydney, AUSTRALIA 2011

Ice-T (Actor, Musician, Producer)
c/o Staff Member *Jorge Hinojosa*
6606 Maryland Dr
Los Angeles, CA 90048-4614, USA

Ichaso, Leon (Director)
c/o Michael Pio *Innovative Artists (LA)*
1505 10th St
Santa Monica, CA 90401-2805, USA

Ickx, Jacky (Race Car Driver)
171 Chaussee de la Hulpe
Brussels 1170, BELGIUM

Idelson, Bill (Actor, Comedian)
710 Brooktree Rd
Pacific Palisades, CA 90272-3901, 90272

Idle, Eric (Actor, Comedian)
c/o Chris Kanarick *ID Public Relations (ID-NY)*
150 W 30th St Fl 19
New York, NY 10001-4003, USA

Idol, Billy (Musician, Songwriter, Writer)
c/o John Marx *WmE2 (WMA-LA)*
1 William Morris Pl
Beverly Hills, CA 90212-4261, USA

Iduarte Foucher, Andres (Writer)
Calle Edimburgo 3 Colonia del Valle
Mexico City, DF 12, MEXICO

Idzlak, Slawomir (Cinematographer)
Ul Wazow 1-Z
Warsaw 01-986, POLAND

Ifans, Rhys (Actor)
9701 Wilshire Blvd Ste 1000
Beverly Hills, CA 90212-2010, USA

Ifeanyi, Israel (Athlete, Football Player)
44733 Ruthron Ave
Lancaster, CA 93536-1431, USA

Ifill, Gwen (Writer)
c/o Staff Member *Doubleday*
1540 Broadway
New York, NY 10036-4039

Iger, Robert A (Business Person)
500 S Buena Vista St
Burbank, CA 91521-0001, USA

Iginla, Jarome (Athlete, Hockey Player)
c/o Donald Meehan *Newport Sports Management*
201 City Centre Dr Suite 400
Mississauga, ON L58 2T4, Canada

Iglesias, Enrique (Musician)
c/o Fernando Giaccardi *Collective*
8383 Wilshire Blvd Ste 1050
Beverly Hills, CA 90211-2415, USA

Iglesias, Gabriel (Actor)
c/o Yvette Shearer *Shearer Public Relations*
1356 Grandview Ave
Glendale, CA 91201-2224, USA

Iglesias, Julio (Musician)
901 Surfside Blvd
Surfside, FL 33154-3107, USA

Iglesias, Julio Jr (Music Group, Musician, Songwriter, Writer)
c/o Doc McGhee *McGhee Entertainment*
8730 W Sunset Blvd Ste 175
Los Angeles, CA 90069-2246, USA

Iglesias, Tuaquin (Athlete, Football Player)
c/o Chad Speck *Allegiant Athletic Agency*
35 Market Sq Ste 201
Knoxville, TN 37902-1420, USA

Ignarro, Louis J (Nobel Prize Laureate)
10833 Le Conte
Los Angeles, CA 90095-3075, USA

Ignasiak, Gary (Athlete, Baseball Player)
3084 Angelus Dr
Waterford, MI 48329-2506, USA

Ignasiak, Mike (Athlete, Baseball Player)
5821 Saline Ann Arbor Rd
Saline, MI 48176-9566, USA

Ignatius, Paul R (Government Official)
3650 Fordham Rd NW
Washington, DC 20016-1906, USA

Ignatius Zakka I Iwas, Patriarch (Religious Leader)
Bab Toma PB 22260
Damascus, SYRIA

Ignizo, Mildred (Bowler)
241 Shore Acres Dr
Rochester, NY 14612-5807, USA

Iguchi, Tadahito (Athlete, Baseball Player)
4211 Tujunga Ave
Studio City, CA 91604-2943, USA

Iguodala, Andre (Athlete, Basketball Player)
c/o Rob Pelinka *Landmark Sports Agency*
10990 Wilshire Blvd Ste 1000
Los Angeles, CA 90024-3924, USA

Igwebuike, Donald (Athlete, Football Player)
14231 Angelton Ter
Burtonsville, MD 20866-2077, USA

Iha, James (Music Group, Musician)
1245 W Glenlake Ave
Chicago, IL 60660-2503, USA

Ihara, Michio (Artist)
63 Wood St
Concord, MA 01742-2225, USA

Ihnacak, Peter (Athlete, Hockey Player)
c/o Staff Member *Toronto Maple Leafs*
Air Canada Centre 400-40 Bay St
Toronto, ON M5J 2X2, Canada

Ihnatowicz, Zbigniew (Architect)
Ul Mokotowska 31 M 15
Warsaw 00-560, POLAND

Ilkin, Tunch (Athlete, Football Player)
2610 Cedarvue Dr
Pittsburgh, PA 15241-2912, USA

Ike, Reverend (Religious Leader)
4140 Broadway
New York, NY 10033-3701, USA

Ikeda, Daisaku (Religious Leader)
32 Shinanomachi Shinjuku
Tokyo 160-8583, JAPAN

Iken, Monica
c/o Staff Member *WmE2 (WMA-LA)*
1 William Morris Pl
Beverly Hills, CA 90212-4261, USA

Ikenberry, Stanley O (Educator)
1 Dupont Cir NW
Washington, DC 20036-1110, USA

Ikeuchi, Hiroyuki (Actor)
c/o Staff Member *LesPros Entertainment*
1-8-1-10F Shimo Meguro Meguro
Tokyo 153-0064, Japan

Ikle, Fred C (Scientist)
7010 Glenbrook Rd
Washington, DC 20014, USA

Ikola, Willard (Athlete, Coach, Hockey Player)
5697 Green Circle Dr Apt 316
Minnetonka, MN 55343-9650, USA

Il Divo (Music Group, Musician)
c/o Meredith Plant *Octagon*
Octagon House 81-83 Fulham High St
London SW6 3JW, UK

Ilavarasi (Actor, Bollywood)
69 Vedawali Street Kannbiran Colony
Chennai, TN 600093, INDIA

Iler, Laura (Stylist)
c/o Staff Member *Marnie Rose Agency*
37 Lower Shad Rd
Pound Ridge, NY 10576-2216, USA

Iler, Robert (Actor)
c/o Maggie Schuster 70 W 36th St Ste 1006
New York, NY 10018

Iley, Barbara (Actor)
10100 Santa Monica Blvd Ste 2500
Los Angeles, CA 90067-4116, USA

Ilg, Ray (Athlete, Football Player)
81 Cross Hill Rd
Wilmot, NH 03287-4501, USA

Ilg, Raymond P (Admiral)
1830 Fountain Dr Unit 1505
Reston, VA 20190-4475, USA

Ilgauskas, Zydrunas (Athlete, Basketball Player)
32654 Lake Rd
Avon Lake, OH 44012, USA

Ilgenfritz, Mark (Athlete, Football Player)
742 Sharp Mountain Crk SE
Marietta, GA 30067-5168, USA

Iliescu, Ion (President)
Calea Victoriei 59-53
Bucharest, ROMANIA

Ilitch, Michael (Athlete, Hockey Player)
237670 Woodlynne Dr
Bingham Farms, MI 48025, USA

Illmann, Margaret (Ballerina)
157 E King St
Toronto, ON M5C 1G9, CANADA

Illsley, John (Musician)
16 Lambton Place
London W11 2SH, UNITED KINGDOM (UK)

Iloilo, Ratu Josefa (President)
PO Box 2513 Suva
Viti Levu, FIJI

Ilsley, Blaise (Athlete, Baseball Player)
2415 Timber Ln
Alpena, MI 49707-1124, USA

Ilyenko, Yuriy G (Cinematographer)
9 Michail Koyzybinksy Str #22
Kiev 252030, UKRAINE

Imada, Ryuji (Athlete, Golfer)
16204 Sierra De Avila
Tampa, FL 33613-5221, USA

Imahara, Grant
1268 Missouri St
San Francisco, CA 94107-3310, USA

Imai, Kenji (Architect)
4-12-28 Kitazawa Setagayaku
Tokyo, JAPAN

Imai, Nobuko (Musician)
Kerkstrat 97
Amsterdam, GD 1017, NETHERLANDS

Iman (Actor, Model)
c/o Cary Berman *WmE2 (Endeavor-LA)*
9601 Wilshire Blvd Fl 3
Beverly Hills, CA 90210-5219, USA

Iman, Ken (Athlete, Football Player)
2 W Thompson Ave
Springfield, PA 19064-2109, USA

Imbert, Bertrand S M (Engineer, Scientist)
50 Rue de Turenne
Paris 75003, FRANCE

Imbert, Peter M (Lawyer)
City Hall Victoria St
London S1E 6QP, UNITED KINGDOM (UK)

Imbrie, Andrew W (Composer)
2625 Rose St
Berkeley, CA 94708-1920, USA

Imbruglia, Natalie (Actor, Musician)
c/o Joanna Milosz *Jm Agency*
143A Chapel St
Prahran VIC 3181, Australia

Imes, Mo'Nique (Actor, Comedian, Television Host)
c/o Terrie Williams *The Terrie Williams Agency*
382 Central Park W Apt 7R
New York, NY 10025-6031, USA

Imhoff, Darrall (Athlete, Basketball Player)
3637 Sterling Woods Dr
Eugene, OR 97408-7201, USA

Imhoff, Darrell (Athlete)
3637 Sterling Woods Dr
Eugene, OR 97408-7201

Imhoff, Gary (Actor)
300 S Raymond Ave
Pasadena, CA 91105-2620, USA

Imhoff, Martin (Athlete, Football Player)
11224 Corte Playa Azteca
San Diego, CA 92124-4135, USA

Imle, John F Jr (Business Person)
2141 Rosecrans Ave
El Segundo, CA 90245-4747, USA

Immelman, Trevor (Athlete, Golfer)
9536 Tavistock Rd
Orlando, FL 32827-7007, USA

Immelt, Jeffrey (Jeff) (Business Person)
705 West Rd
New Canaan, CT 06840-2518, USA

Immerfall, Daniel (Dan) (Speed Skater)
5421 Trempealeau Trl
Madison, WI 53705-4662, USA

Imperato, Carlo
21940 Scallion Dr
Santa Clarita, CA 91350-1636, USA

Imperioli, Michael (Actor)
c/o Tina Thor *TMT Entertainment Group*
648 Broadway Ste 1002
New York, NY 10012-2348, USA

Imus, Don (Radio Personality)
16 West Ave
Darien, CT 06820-4401, USA

IMX (Music Group)
c/o Staff Member *Pyramid Entertainment Group*
377 Rector Pl Apt 21A
New York, NY 10280-1439, USA

Inaba, Carrie Ann (Actor, Choreographer, Dancer)
c/o Nicole Perez *PMK/BNC Public Relations (PMK-LA)*
Pacific Design Center 8687 Melrose Ave, 7th Floor
West Hollywood, CA 90069, USA

Inamori, Kazuo (Business Person)
3-22 Nishi-Shinjuku Shinjuku
Tokyo 163-8003, JAPAN

Inarritu, Alejandro (Actor)
c/o Staff Member *Anonymous Content (AC-LA)*
3531 Hayden Ave
Culver City, CA 90232, USA

Inbal, Eliahu (Conductor)
Bertramstr 8
Frankfurt/Main 60320, GERMANY

Incandella, Sal (Race Car Driver)
5811 W 73rd St
Indianapolis, IN 46278-1743, USA

Incaviglia, Peter J (Pete) (Athlete, Baseball Player)
78 Via Chualar
Monterey, CA 93940-2529, USA

Inclan, Rafael (Actor)
c/o Staff Member *Televisa*
Blvd Adolfo Lopez Mateos 232 Colonia San Angel INN
DF CP 01060, MEXICO

Incubus (Music Group)
c/o Marlene Tsuchii *Creative Artists Agency (CAA-LA)*
2000 Avenue of the Stars Ste 100
Los Angeles, CA 90067-4705, USA

Indelicato, Mark (Actor)
c/o Anne Woodward *ROAR (LA)*
9701 Wilshire Blvd Fl 8
Beverly Hills, CA 90212-2008, USA

Indhu (Actor, Bollywood)
D/o G.K.Ram Kumar 2 Circular Road
United India Colony
Chennai, TN 600024, INDIA

Indiana, Robert (Artist)
Star of Hope
Vinalhaven, ME 4863, USA

Indigo Girls (Music Group)
c/o Staff Member *High Road Touring*
751 Bridgeway Fl 2
Sausalito, CA 94965-2174, USA

Indraja (Actor, Bollywood)
89 Krishna Nagar Virugambakkam
Chennai, TN 600092, INDIA

Indurain, Miguel
Avendia Villava
Pamplona (Navarra), SPAIN E-31013

Infamous Stringdusters, The (Music Group, Musician)
c/o Michael Allenby *The Artist Farm*
100 W South St Apt 1A
Charlottesville, VA 22902-5099, USA

Infante, Lindy (Athlete, Coach, Football Coach, Football Player)
6870 A1AS
Saint Augustine, FL 32080, USA

Infante, To??o (Actor)
c/o Staff Member *Televisa*
Blvd Adolfo Lopez Mateos 232 Colonia San Angel INN
DF CP 01060, MEXICO

Ing, Hout (Government Official)
Phnom Penh, COMBODIA

Ing, Peter (Athlete, Hockey Player)
P.O. Box 300 Stn Main
Niagara Falls, ON L2E 6T3, Canada

Ingarfield Jr, Earl (Athlete, Hockey Player)
619 Mourning Dove Dr
Sarasota, FL 34236-1903, USA

Ingarfield Sr, Earl (Athlete, Hockey Player)
1715 Lakehill Cres S
Lethbridge, AB T1K 3R2, Canada

Inge, Brandon (Athlete, Baseball Player)
832 Upper Scotsborough Way
Bloomfield Hills, MI 48304-3828, USA

Inge, Peter A (Misc)
Westminster
London SW1A 0PW, UNITED KINGDOM (UK)

Ingels, Marty (Actor, Comedian)
c/o Deborah Zucker *Ingels Entertainment Suite One Productions*
16400 Ventura Blvd Ste 335
Encino, CA 91436-2196, USA

Ingelsby, Tom (Athlete, Basketball Player)
1507 Canterbury Ln
Berwyn, PA 19312-1915, USA

Ingersoll, Ralph II (Publisher)
PO Box 1869
Lakeville, CT 06039-1869, USA

Inghram, Mark G (Physicist)
PO Box 771721
Eagle River, AK 99577-1721, USA

Ingle, Doug (Music Group, Musician)
6400 Pleasant Park Dr
Chanhassen, MN 55317-8804, USA

Ingle, John (Actor)
c/o Staff Member *Stone Manners Salners Agency (LA)*
9911 W Pico Blvd Ste 1400
Los Angeles, CA 90035-2715, USA

Ingle, Robert D (Editor)
750 Ridder Park Dr
San Jose, CA 95131-2432, USA

Inglis, Bill (Athlete, Hockey Player)
5709 Ozark Dr
Fort Worth, TX 76131-4004, USA

Inglis, Tim (Athlete, Football Player)
22 Hidden Meadow Dr
Holland, OH 43528-8276, USA

Ingman, Elnar H Jr (War Hero)
W4053 W Silver Lake Rd
Irma, WI 54442-9726, USA

Ingraham, Hubert A (Prime Minister)
Whitfield Center Box CB10980
Nassau, BAHAMAS

Ingraham, Laura (Radio Personality)
c/o Staff Member *XM Satellite Radio Studios*
1500 Eckington Pl NE
Washington, DC 20002-2128, USA

Ingram, A John (Doctor)
4940 Sullivan Woods Cv
Memphis, TN 38117-2011, USA

Ingram, Brian (Athlete, Football Player)
PO Box 110094
Atlanta, GA 30311-0994, USA

Ingram, Garey (Athlete, Baseball Player)
9425 Midland Woods Dr
Midland, GA 31820-7202, USA

Ingram, Jack (Musician)
c/o Staff Member *Capital Sports & Entertainment*
300 W 6th St Ste 2150
Austin, TX 78701-3921, USA

Ingram, James (Music Group, Musician, Songwriter, Writer)
867 S Muirfield Rd
Los Angeles, CA 90005-3836, USA

Ingram, James (Musician)
c/o Staff Member *Agency for the Performing Arts (APA-LA)*
405 S Beverly Dr Ste 500
Beverly Hills, CA 90212-4425, USA

Ingram, Lonnie (Biologist)
Microbiology/Cell Science
Gainesville, FL 32611-0001, USA

Ingram, Mark (Misc)
110 E 55th St Fl 8
New York, NY 10022-4553, USA

Ingram, Mark (Football Player)
c/o Chafie Fields *Lagardere Unlimited - NY*
845 United Nations Plz
New York, NY 10017-3540, USA

Ingram, McKoy (Athlete, Basketball Player)
2301 33rd St
Gulfport, MS 39501-6541, USA

Ingram, Preston (Baseball Player)
174 Douglas St SE
Atlanta, GA 30317-2626, USA

Ingram, Riccardo (Athlete, Baseball Player)
5720 Martin Grove Dr NW
Lilburn, GA 30047-6078, USA

Ingram, Robert (War Hero)
1020 Acapulco Rd
Jacksonville, FL 32216-3287, USA

Ingram, Vernon M (Biologist)
Biochemistry Dept
Cambridge, MA 2139, USA

Ingrao, Pietro (Government Official)
Via Della Vite 13
Rome, ITALY

Ingrassia, Paul J (Journalist)
111 Division Ave
New Providence, NJ 7974, USA

Ink Spots, The
1861 Hickory St SE
Conyers, GA 30013-1647

Inkeles, Alex (Activist)
32 Plaza Dr
Berkeley, CA 94705-2414, USA

Inkster, Juli Simpson (Athlete, Golfer)
23140 Mora Glen Dr
Los Altos, CA 94024-6620, USA

Inman, Bobby Ray (Admiral, Government Official)
701 Brazos St Ste 500
Austin, TX 78701-3232, USA

Inman, Jerry (Athlete, Football Player)
PO Box 1113
Battle Ground, WA 98604-1113, USA

Inman, Joe (Athlete, Golfer)
3599 Tuckers Farm SE
Marietta, GA 30067-5182, USA

Inman, John (Actor)
8 King St
London WC2E 8HN, UNITED KINGDOM (UK)

Inman, John (Athlete, Golfer)
2210 Chase St
Durham, NC 27707-2228, USA

Inmon, Earl (Athlete, Football Player)
38429 Jamestown St
Umatilla, FL 32784-9519, USA

Innauer, Anton (Toni) (Coach, Skier)
Steinbruckstr 8/11
Innsbruck 6024, AUSTRIA

Innes, Laura (Actor)
c/o Troy Nankin *Wishlab*
2438 Canyon Oak Dr
Los Angeles, CA 90068-2428, USA

Inness, Gary (Athlete, Hockey Player)
7 Gowan Rd
Shanty Bay, ON L0L 2L0, Canada

Inniger Jr, Ervin (Athlete, Basketball Player)
311 11th Ave S Apt 101
Fargo, ND 58103-2856, USA

Innis (Musician)
c/o Staff Member *Paradigm (LA)*
360 N Crescent Dr
Beverly Hills, CA 90210-4874, USA

Innis, Jeff (Athlete, Baseball Player)
4920 Woodlong Ln
Cumming, GA 30040-5275, USA

Innis, Roy
800 Riverside Dr Apt 6E
New York, NY 10032-7407

Innis, Roy E A (Activist)
817 Broadway
New York, NY 10003-4709, USA

Inogradov, Pavel (Astronaut, Misc)
Moskovskol Oblasti
Syvisdny Goroduk 141160, RUSSIA

Inoue, Shinya (Biologist, Photographer)
167 Water St
Woods Hole, MA 02543-1031, USA

Inoue, Yuichi (Artist)
Ohkamiyashiki 2475-2 Kurami
Samakawamachi 253-01 Kozagun
Kam, JAPAN

Inouye, Daniel K (Senator, War Hero)
722 Hart Senate Ofc Bldg
Washington, DC 20510-0001, USA

Inouye, Lisa (Actor)
c/o Nick Terzian *Nick Terzian Agency (NTA)*
1445 N Stanley Ave Fl 2
Los Angeles, CA 90046-4015, USA

Insane Clown Posse (Music Group, Musician)
c/o William Dail *Psychopathic Records*
P.O. 332
Royal Oaks, MI 48068, USA

Insko, Delmer M (Del) (Horse Racer)
2360 Fischer Rd
South Beloit, IL 61080-9728, USA

Inslee, Jay (Congressman, Politician)
2329 Rayburn Hob
Washington, DC 20515-3218, USA

Insley, Will (Artist)
231 Bowery
New York, NY 10002-1237, USA

Insolla, Anthony (Editor)
235 Pinelawn Rd
Melville, NY 11747-4226, USA

Inspectah, Deck (Artist)
250 W 57th St
New York, NY 10107-0001, USA

INXS
c/o Michael Moses *Baker Winokur Ryder Public Relations (BWR-LA)*
9100 Wilshire Blvd Ste 500 PMB WEST
Beverly Hills, CA 90212-3426, USA

Inzaghi, Filippo (Soccer Player)
c/o Team Member *AC Milan*
3 Turati Via
Washington, DC 20221-0001, Italy

Iommi, Tony (Musician)
17 Hereford Mansions Hereford Rd
London W2 5BA, UNITED KINGDOM

Ionatana, Ionatana (Prime Minister)
Vaiaku
Funafuti, TUVALU

Iorg, Dane (Athlete, Baseball Player)
5358 W Evergreen Cir
American Fork, UT 84003-9476, USA

Iorg, Garth (Athlete, Baseball Player)
7017 Wyndham Pointe Ln
Knoxville, TN 37931-2566, USA

Ioss, Walter (Photographer)
152 Deforest Rd
Montauk, NY 11954-9619, USA

Iovine, Jimmy (Producer)
c/o Staff Member *Interscope Records (LA) - Main*
2220 Colorado Ave
Santa Monica, CA 90404-3506, USA

Iqbal Rashid, Ian (Director)
c/o Staff Member *United Talent Agency (UTA)*
9560 Wilshire Blvd Fl 5
Beverly Hills, CA 90212-2400, USA

Iraheta, Allison (Musician)

Irani, Aruna (Actor, Bollywood)
603 B Gazdar Apartments Near Juhu Hotel Juhu
Mumbai, MS 400049, INDIA

Irani, Ray R (Business Person)
10889 Wilshire Blvd
Los Angeles, CA 90024-4201, USA

Irbe, Arturs (Athlete, Hockey Player)
10733 Trego Trl
Raleigh, NC 27614-9660, USA

Iredale, Randle W (Architect)
1151 W 8th Ave
Vancouver, BC V6H 1C5, CANADA

Ireland, Dan (Director, Producer, Writer)
c/o Staff Member *Gersh (LA)*
9465 Wilshire Blvd Ste 600
Beverly Hills, CA 90212-2612, USA

Ireland, Kathy (Actor, Business Person, Model)
c/o Danielle Marie Owens *Guttman Associates*
118 S Beverly Dr Ste 201
Beverly Hills, CA 90212-3016, USA

Ireland, Patricia (Misc)
801 Pennsylvania Ave NW Ste 750
Washington, DC 20004-2670, USA

Ireland, Rich (Baseball Player)
181 Glen Dr
Grants Pass, OR 97526-9018, USA

Ireland, Tim (Athlete, Baseball Player)
7324 SW 27th St
Topeka, KS 66614-6001, USA

Iris, Donnie (Music Group, Musician, Songwriter, Writer)
807 Darlington Rd
Beaver Falls, PA 15010-2817, USA

Irish Rovers, The
1505 W 2nd Ave # 200
Vancouver, CANADA BC V6H 3Y4

Irizarry, Vincent (Actor)
c/o Douglas Warner *Warner Artist Management*
2001 Wilshire Blvd Ste 210
Santa Monica, CA 90403-5681, USA

Irobe, Yoshiaki (Financier)
26-6-6 Saginomiya Nakanoku
Tokyo, JAPAN

Iron & Wine (Music Group, Musician)
c/o Rob Challice *Coda Music Agency - UK*
229 Shoreditch High St
London E1 6PJ, UK

Iron Butterfly
PO Box 770850
Orlando, FL 32877-0850

Iron Maiden (Music Group)
c/o Staff Member *EMI Recorded Music (EMI Group - NY)*
150 5th Ave Fl 7
New York, NY 10011-4372, USA

Irons, Gerald (Athlete, Football Player)
30010 E Legends Trail Ct
Spring, TX 77386-2998, USA

Irons, Jeremy (Actor)
c/o Fred Specktor *Creative Artists Agency (CAA-LA)*
2000 Avenue of the Stars Ste 100
Los Angeles, CA 90067-4705, USA

Irons, Max (Actor)
c/o Billy Lazarus *United Talent Agency (UTA)*
9560 Wilshire Blvd Fl 5
Beverly Hills, CA 90212-2400, USA

Irons, Nicholas (Actor)
c/o Michael Emptage 24 Poland St
London W1F 8QL, UNITED KINGDOM

Irons, Robbie (Athlete, Hockey Player)
4227 Cordell Cv
Fort Wayne, IN 46845-8864, USA

Ironside, Michael (Actor, Producer, Writer)
c/o David Ginsberg *Insight*
1134 S Cloverdale Ave
Los Angeles, CA 90019-6737, USA

Irrera, Dom (Actor, Comedian)
c/o Staff Member *Don Buchwald & Associates Inc (LA)*
6500 Wilshire Blvd Ste 2200
Los Angeles, CA 90048-4942, USA

Irsay, Jim (Business Person)
c/o Staff Member *Indianapolis Colts*
7001 W 56th St
Indianapolis, IN 46254-9698, USA

Irvan, Ernie (Race Car Driver)
9939 Troutman Rd
Midland, NC 28107-6751, USA

Irvin, Anthony
1 Olympic Plz
Colorado Springs, CO 80909-5780

Irvin, Byron (Athlete, Basketball Player)
10940 S Parnell Ave
Chicago, IL 60628-3232, USA

Irvin, Cal (Athlete, Baseball Player)
1311 Julian St
Greensboro, NC 27406-2158, USA

Irvin, Daryl (Athlete, Baseball Player)
815 Confederacy Dr
Penn Laird, VA 22846-9633, USA

Irvin, John (Director)
c/o Jack Gilardi *International Creative Management (ICM-LA)*
10250 Constellation Blvd Fl 7
Los Angeles, CA 90067-6207, USA

Irvin, Ken (Athlete, Football Player)
8151 Nesbit Ferry Rd
Atlanta, GA 30350-1009, USA

Irvin, Michael J (Athlete, Football Player)
2339 Aberdeen Bnd
Carrollton, TX 75007-2040, USA

Irvin, Monte (Athlete, Baseball Player)
1815 Enclave Pkwy Apt 6203
Houston, TX 77077-3669, USA

Irvin Jr, LeRoy (Athlete, Football Player)
2905 Ruby Dr Apt C
Fullerton, CA 92831-3249, USA

Irvine, Eddie (Race Car Driver)
Casella Postale 589
Modena 41100, ITALY

Irvine, George (Athlete, Basketball Player)
PO Box 179
Indianola, WA 98342-0179, USA

Irvine, Jeremy (Actor)
c/o Jessica Kolstad *WKT Public Relations (WKT-LA)*
9350 Wilshire Blvd Ste 450
Beverly Hills, CA 90212-3230, USA

Irvine, Paula
23852 Pacific Coast Hwy PMB 195
Malibu, CA 90265-4876

Irvine, Ted (Athlete, Hockey Player)
5-2727 Portage Ave
Winnipeg, MB R3J 0R2, Canada

Irving, Amy (Actor)
1180 S Beverly Dr Ste 601
Los Angeles, CA 90035-1158, USA

Irving, John (Writer)
c/o Robert (Bob) Bookman *Creative Artists Agency (CAA-LA)*
2000 Avenue of the Stars Ste 100
Los Angeles, CA 90067-4705, USA

Irving, John W (Writer)
PO Box 757
Dorset, VT 05251-0757, USA

Irving, Paul H (Attorney, Attorney General, General)
11355 W Olympic Blvd
Los Angeles, CA 90064-1631, USA

Irving, Stu (Athlete, Hockey Player)
93 Hart St
Beverly, MA 01915-2162, USA

Irving, Terry (Athlete, Football Player)
3205 Avenue R 1/2 Apt 2
Galveston, TX 77550-9651, USA

Irwin, Bill (Actor, Writer)
c/o Lisa Loosemore *Viking Entertainment*
445 W 23rd St Ste 1A
New York, NY 10011-1445, USA

Irwin, Bindi (Misc)
Glass House Mountains Tourist Route
Beerwah, Queensland 4519, AUSTRALIA

Irwin, Hale (Athlete, Golfer)
5720 N Saguaro Rd
Paradise Valley, AZ 85253-5237, USA

Irwin, Heath (Athlete, Football Player)
5530 N 115th St
Longmont, CO 80504-8434, USA

Irwin, Ivan (Athlete, Hockey Player)
485 Maple Rd
Ajax, ON L1S 1E4, Canada

Irwin, Jennifer (Actor)
c/o Gayle Abrams *Oscars Abrams Zimel & Associates, Inc. (OAZ)*
438 Queen St E
Toronto ON M5A 1T4, CANADA

Irwin, Malcolm R (Biologist)
4720 Regent St
Madison, WI 53705-4860, USA

Irwin, Mark (Cinematographer)
1522 Olive St
Santa Barbara, CA 93101-1160, USA

Irwin, Paul G (Misc)
2100 L St NW
Washington, DC 20037-1525, USA

Irwin, Robert W (Artist)
32 E 57th St
New York, NY 10022-2513, USA

Irwin, Steven (Athlete, Soccer Player)
Anfield Road Liverpool
Merseyside L4 0TH, UK

Irwin, Tim (Athlete, Football Player)
PO Box 2186
Knoxville, TN 37901-2186, USA

Irwin, Tom
PO Box 5617
Beverly Hills, CA 90209-5617

Irwin-Mellencamp, Elaine (Model)
5072 Stevens Rd
Nashville, IN 47448-9484, USA

Isaac, Oscar (Actor)
c/o Jason Spire *Inspire Entertainment*
315 7th Ave Apt 17E
New York, NY 10001-6011, USA

Isaacks, Levie C (Cinematographer)
6634 Sunnyslope Ave
Van Nuys, CA 91401-1213, USA

Isaacksen, Peter
4635 Placidia Ave
Toluca Lake, CA 91602-1541

Isaacs, Jason (Actor)
c/o Jeff Golenberg *Collective*
8383 Wilshire Blvd Ste 1050
Beverly Hills, CA 90211-2415, USA

Isaacs, Jeremy I (Director)
Covent Garden Bow St
London WC1 7Q4, UNITED KINGDOM (UK)

Isaacs, John (Speed) (Athlete, Basketball Player)
1412 Crotona Ave
Bronx, NY 10456-2217, USA

Isaacs, Susan (Writer)
10 E 53rd St
New York, NY 10022-5244, USA

Isaacson, Julius (Misc)
1815 Franklin Ave
Valley Stream, NY 11581, USA

Isaacson, Walter S (Journalist)
c/o Staff Member *Little, Brown Book Group*
100 Victoria Embankment
London EC4Y 0DY, UK

Isaak, Chris (Actor, Musician, Songwriter)
c/o Howard Kaufman *HK Management (LA)*
10866 Wilshire Blvd Ste 200
Los Angeles, CA 90024-4350, USA

Isaak, Russell (Business Person)
1706 Washington Ave
Saint Louis, MO 63103-1717, USA

Isabel, Margarita (Actor)
c/o Staff Member *TV Azteca*
Periferico Sur 4121 Colonia Fuentes del Pedregal
DF CP 14141, Mexico

Isabelle, Katharine (Actor)
c/o Staff Member *IFA Talent Agency*
8730 W Sunset Blvd Ste 490
Los Angeles, CA 90069-2248, USA

Isabelle, Katherine (Actor)
c/o Staff Member *IFA Talent Agency*
8730 W Sunset Blvd Ste 490
Los Angeles, CA 90069-2248, USA

Isacksen, Peter (Actor)
c/o Staff Member *JWTwo Entertainment*
2425 Olympic Blvd # 200TOWER PMB EAST
Santa Monica, CA 90404-4030, USA

Isaksson, Irma Sara (Musician, Songwriter, Writer)
PO Box 11026
Stockholm 100 61, SWEDEN

Isales, Orlando (Athlete, Baseball Player)
14710 SW 106th Ave
Miami, FL 33176-7791, USA

Isard, Walter (Economist)
3218 Garrett Rd
Drexel Hill, PA 19026-2912, USA

Isbell, Joe Bob (Athlete, Football Player)
1606 Nest Pl
Plano, TX 75093-6030, USA

Isbin, Sharon (Musician)
165 W 57th St
New York, NY 10019-2201, USA

Isbister, Brad (Athlete, Hockey Player)
1818 Lakeview Dr
Fort Wayne, IN 46808-3918, USA

Iscove, Robert (Rob) (Director)
16045 Royal Oak Rd
Encino, CA 91436-3913, USA

Isdell, E Neville (Business Person)
1 Coca-Cola Plaza 310 North Ave NW
Atlanta, GA 30313, USA

Isenbarger, John (Athlete, Football Player)
7808 Somerset Bay Apt C
Indianapolis, IN 46240-3329, USA

Isenhour, Tripp (Athlete, Golfer)
10012 N Fulton Ct
Orlando, FL 32836-3708, USA

Isham, Mark (Composer)
2635 Griffith Park Blvd
Los Angeles, CA 90039-2519, USA

Ishara, B R (Actor, Bollywood)
C36 North Bombay Housing Society Juhu Tara Road
Mumbai, MS 400049, INDIA

Ishibashi, Kanichiro (Business Person)
1 Nagasakacho Azabu Minatoku
Tokyo, JAPAN

Ishida, Jim (Actor)
871 N Vail Ave
Montebello, CA 90640-2432, USA

Ishiguro, Kazuo (Writer)
20 Powis Mews
London W11 1JN, UNITED KINGDOM (UK)

Ishihara, Shintaro (Government Official)
Sanno Grand Building #606 2-14-2
Nagatocho Chiyodaku
Tokyo, JAPAN

Ishii, Kazuhiro (Architect)
4-14-27 Akasaka Minatoku
Tokyo 107, JAPAN

Ishii, Linda (Athlete, Golfer)
2607 E 3rd St
Los Angeles, CA 90033-4124, USA

Ishikawa, Sigeru (Economist)
19-8-4 Chome Kugayama Suginamiku
Tokyo 168-0082, JAPAN

Ishimaru, Akira (Engineer)
2913 165th Pl NE
Bellevue, WA 98008-2137, USA

Ishizaka, Kimishiga (Doctor)
11149 N Torrey Pines Rd
La Jolla, CA 92037-1031, USA

Ishizaka, Teruko (Doctor)
5601 Loch Raven Blvd
Baltimore, MD 21239-2905, USA

Isitt, Debbie (Director)
c/o Nick Marston *Curtis Brown Group*
Haymarket House 28 - 29 Haymarket
London SW1Y 4SP, UNITED KINGDOM

Iskander, Fazil A (Writer)
Krasnoarmeiskaya Str 23 #104
Moscow 125319, RUSSIA

Islas, Claudia (Actor)
c/o Staff Member *TV Azteca*
Periferico Sur 4121 Colonia Fuentes del Pedregal
DF CP 14141, Mexico

Islas, Mauricio (Actor)
c/o Staff Member *Televisa*
Blvd Adolfo Lopez Mateos 232 Colonia San Angel INN
DF CP 01060, MEXICO

Isley, Ronald (Ron) (Musician)
PO Box 261640
Encino, CA 91426-1640, USA

Isley Brothers (Music Group)
c/o Carleen Donovan *Press Here Publicity*
234 W 44th St Ste 1004
New York, NY 10036-3909, USA

Ismail, Ahmed Sultan (Engineer)
43 Ahmed Abdel Aziz St Dokki
Cairo, EGYPT

Ismail, Qadry (Athlete, Football Player)
1506 Sunningdale Way
Bel Air, MD 21015-2101, USA

Ismail, Raghib R (Rocket) (Athlete, Football Player)
7423 Marigold Dr
Irving, TX 75063-5505, USA

Ison, Christopher J (Journalist)
425 Portland Ave
Minneapolis, MN 55488-1511, USA

Isozaki, Arata (Architect)
6-17-9 Adasaka Minatoku
Tokyo 107, JAPAN

Israel, Janine (Stylist)
c/o Staff Member *Celestine - CA*
1666 20th St Ste 200B
Santa Monica, CA 90404-3828, USA

Israel, Steve (Congressman, Politician)
2457 Rayburn Hob
Washington, DC 20515-4313, USA

Israel, Werner (Physicist)
5189 Polson Ter
Victoria, BC V8Y 2C5, CANADA

Isringhausen, Jason (Athlete, Baseball Player)
550 E Lake Rd N
Tarpon Springs, FL 34688-6344, USA

Issel, Daniel P (Dan) (Athlete, Basketball Player, Coach)
4370 Chateau Ridge Ln
Castle Rock, CO 80108-8423, USA

Isselbacher, Kurt J (Doctor)
3 Mcgregor Rd
Woods Hole, MA 02543-1533, USA

Isserlis, Steven (Musician)
12 Penzance Place
London W11 4PA, UNITED KINGDOM (UK)

Ito, Lance (Judge)
210 W Temple St
Los Angeles, CA 90012-3210, USA

Ito, Masayoshi (Government Official)
1-28-3 Chitose-Dai Setagayaku
Tokyo 157, JAPAN

Ito, Midori (Figure Skater)
Kryshi Taaikukan 1-1-1 Shibuyaku
Tokyo 10, JAPAN

Ito, Robert (Actor)
843 N Sycamore Ave
Los Angeles, CA 90038-3316, USA

Itskovich, Anka (Stylist)
c/o Staff Member *Jam Arts, Inc*
154 W 57th St
New York, NY 10019-3321, USA

Itzin, Gregory (Actor)
3172 Dona Susana Dr
Studio City, CA 91604-4356, USA

Iuzzolino, Mike (Athlete, Basketball Player)
1048 New London Dr
Greensburg, PA 15601-1144, USA

Ivanchenkov, Aleksandr S (Astronaut, Misc)
Moskovskoi Oblasti
Syvisdny Goroduk 141160, RUSSIA

Ivanchenkov, Alexander
141 160 Zvezdny Gorodok
Moscow Obl., RUSSIA

Ivanek, Zeljko
145 W 45th St # 1204
New York, NY 10036-4008

Ivanisevic, Goran (Tennis Player)
Alijnoviceva 28
Split 58000, SERBIA & MONTENEGRO

Ivanov, Igor S (Government Official)
Smolenskaya-Sennaya 32/34
Moscow, RUSSIA

Ivanov, Kalina (Actor, Designer)
c/o Sandra Marsh *Sandra Marsh Management*
9150 Wilshire Blvd Ste 220
Beverly Hills, CA 90212-3429, USA

Ivanovic, Ana (Athlete, Tennis Player)
Holeestrasse 86
Basel 4054, Switzerland

Ivens, Teri (Actor)
c/o Stephen Rice *Pantheon Talent*
1801 Century Park E Ste 1910
Los Angeles, CA 90067-2321, USA

Ivens, Terri (Actor)
c/o Staff Member *Kohner Agency, The*
9300 Wilshire Blvd Ste 555
Beverly Hills, CA 90212-3211, USA

Ivers, Eileen (Athlete, Misc)
2100 Colorado Ave
Santa Monica, CA 90404-3504, USA

Iverson, Allen (Athlete, Basketball Player)
c/o Leon Rose *CAA - NJ*
308 Harper Dr Ste 210
Moorestown, NJ 08057-3245, USA

Iverson, Becky (Athlete, Golfer)
4723 Poplar Creek Dr
Madison, WI 53718-2128, USA

Iverson, Duke (Athlete, Football Player)
616 Elm Dr
Petaluma, CA 94952-1838, USA

Iverson, Portia (Religious Leader)
11312 Highway 75
Plattsmouth, NE 68048-8268, USA

Iverson, Willie (Athlete, Basketball Player)
14789 Rosemary St
Detroit, MI 48213-1539, USA

Ivery, Eddie Lee (Athlete, Football Player)
1080 Wrightsboro Rd
Thomson, GA 30824-7500, USA

Ives, J Atwood (Business Person)
201 Rivermoor St
West Roxbury, MA 02132-4905, USA

Ivey, Dana (Actor)
10100 Santa Monica Blvd Ste 2500
Los Angeles, CA 90067-4116, USA

Ivey, James
5856 Dahlia Dr Apt 7
Orlando, FL 32807-3261

Ivey, James B (Jim) (Cartoonist, Editor)
5840 Dahlia Dr Apt 7
Orlando, FL 32807-3251, USA

Ivey, Judith (Actor)
53 W 87th St # 2
New York, NY 10024-3057, USA

Ivey, Phil (Misc)
c/o Staff Member *Kolyma Corporation*
Full Tilt Poker 62 Lloyd G Smith Blvd
Oranjestad, AW, USA

Ivey, Royal (Athlete, Basketball Player)
4601 Flat Rock Rd Unit 618
Philadelphia, PA 19127-2062, USA

Ivie, Mike (Athlete, Baseball Player)
PO Box 1565
Loganville, GA 30052-1565, USA

Ivins, Marsha S (Astronaut)
2811 Timber Briar Cir
Houston, TX 77059-2904, USA

Ivlow, John (Athlete, Football Player)
15238 S Poppy Ln
Plainfield, IL 60544-9201, USA

Ivo, Tommy
247 S Orchard Dr
Burbank, CA 91506-2441

Ivor, Clark (Stylist)
c/o Staff Member *Karlee Artist Management*
2658 Griffith Park Blvd # 171
Los Angeles, CA 90039-2520, USA

Ivory, Elvin (Athlete, Basketball Player)
526 Date Ct
Monrovia, CA 91016-4676, USA

Ivory, Horace O (Athlete, Football Player)
5321 Diaz Ave
Fort Worth, TX 76107-5903, USA

Ivory, James (Athlete, Baseball Player)
3026 Wenonah Park Rd SW
Birmingham, AL 35211-5846, USA

Ivory, James F (Director, Filmmaker, Producer)
18 Patroon St
Claverach, NY 12513, USA

Ivosev, Aleksandra (Misc)
Sluzbeni put Zavoda 5 Careva Cuprija
Belgrad 11030, SERBIA & MONTENEGRO

Iwago, Mitsuaki (Photographer)
Edelhof Daichi Building #2F 8 Honsio-cho Shinjukaku
Tokyo 160, JAPAN

Iwanowski, Mark (Athlete, Football Player)
523 N 12th St
Reading, PA 19604-2718, USA

Iwatani, Yasuko (Stylist)
c/o Staff Member *L'Agence*
5901 Peachtree Dunwoody Rd NE Ste C60
Atlanta, GA 30328-7155, USA

Iwerks, Donald W (Business Person)
4520 W Valerio St
Burbank, CA 91505-1046, USA

Iwerks, Leslie (Director, Producer)
c/o Scott Agostini *WmE2 (Endeavor-LA)*
9601 Wilshire Blvd Fl 3
Beverly Hills, CA 90210-5219, USA

Iyanaga, Shokichi (Mathematician)
12-4 Otsuka 6-Chome Bunkyoku
Tokyo 112-0012, JAPAN

Iyer, Kalpana (Actor, Dancer)
E 43 Geeta Kiran Society J P Road Four Bangalows Andheri
Bombay, MS 400 058, INDIA

Izibor, Laura (Musician)
c/o Staff Member *Paradigm (Monterey)*
404 W Franklin St
Monterey, CA 93940-2303, USA

Izo, George (Athlete, Football Player)
PO Box 325
Alexandria, VA 22313-0325, USA

Izquierdo, Hank (Athlete, Baseball Player)
12458 71st Pl N
West Palm Beach, FL 33412-1438, USA

Izquierdo, Hansel (Athlete, Baseball Player)
8420 SW 154th Circle Ct Apt 515
Miami, FL 33193-1260, USA

Izturis, Cesar (Athlete, Baseball Player)
375 S 3rd St
Burbank, CA 91502-1364, USA

Izzard, Eddie (Actor, Comedian)
c/o Jeff Golenberg *Collective*
8383 Wilshire Blvd Ste 1050
Beverly Hills, CA 90211-2415, USA

Izzo, Larry (Athlete, Football Player)
47 Chancery Pl
The Woodlands, TX 77381-6438, USA

Izzo, Tom (Basketball Player, Coach)
Athletic Dept
East Lansing, MI 48824, USA

J

J. Dold, Robrt

J. Duncan Jr., John (Congressman, Politician)
2207 Rayburn Hob
Washington, DC 20515-2003, USA

J. Fleischmann, Charles (Congressman, Politician)
511 Cannon Hob
Washington, DC 20515-0607, USA

J. Forbes, Randy (Congressman, Politician)
2438 Rayburn Hob
Washington, DC 20515-3518, USA

J. Heck, Joseph (Congressman, Politician)
132 Cannon Hob
Washington, DC 20515-1006, USA

J. Kucinich, Dennis (Congressman, Politician)
2445 Rayburn Hob
Washington, DC 20515-0907, USA

J. Markey, Edward (Congressman, Politician)
2108 Rayburn Hob
Washington, DC 20515-2107, USA

J. Rahall II, Nick (Congressman, Politician)
2307 Rayburn Hob
Washington, DC 20515-4803, USA

Jaa, Tony (Actor)
388 9th Floor Sp Phaholyothin Rd
Building 3B PMB IBM
Payathai, Bangkok 10400, Thailand

Jabali, Warren (Athlete, Basketball Player)
5018 SW 168th Ave
Miramar, FL 33027-4914, USA

Jabe (Stylist)
c/o Staff Member *L'Agence*
5901 Peachtree Dunwoody Rd NE Ste C60
Atlanta, GA 30328-7155, USA

Jablonski, Henryk (President)
Ul Filtrowa 61 m 4
Warsaw 02-056, POLAND

Jablonski, Pat (Athlete, Hockey Player)
4317 Beau Rivage Cir
Lutz, FL 33558-5353, USA

Jabs, Matthias (Musician)
c/o Staff Member *Agency Group Ltd, The (NY)*
142 W 57th St Fl 6
New York, NY 10019-3300, USA

Jace, Michael (Actor)
c/o Craig Dorfman *Frontline Management*
5670 Wilshire Blvd Ste 1370
Los Angeles, CA 90036-5679, USA

Jack, Beau
1 Hall of Fame Dr
Canastota, NY 13032-1175

Jack, Eric (Athlete, Football Player)
425 Concert St
Keokuk, IA 52632-5624, USA

Jack, Jarrett (Athlete, Basketball Player)
c/o Jeff Schwartz *Excel Sports Management*
9665 Wilshire Blvd Ste 500
Beverly Hills, CA 90212-2312, USA

Jack, Lind (Baseball Player)
6132 E Redmont Dr
Mesa, AZ 85215-0878, USA

Jack Davis, Jack Davis (Cartoonist)
c/o Staff Member *Simon & Schuster*
1230 Avenue of the Americas Fl CONC1
New York, NY 10020-1586, USA

Jacke, Chris (Athlete, Football Player)
2120 S Ridge Rd
Green Bay, WI 54304-4327, USA

Jacke, Christoper L (Chris) (Athlete, Football Player)
PO Box 888
Phoenix, AZ 85001-0888, USA

Jackee (Actor)
7250 Franklin Ave Unit 814
Los Angeles, CA 90046-3043, USA

Jacklin, Tony (Golfer, Sportscaster)
8497 Lindrick Ln
Bradenton, FL 34202-4626, USA

Jacklin, Tony (Athlete, Golfer)
8497 Lindrick Ln
Bradenton, FL 34202-4626, USA

Jackman, Barret (Athlete, Hockey Player)
4924 Pershing Pl
Saint Louis, MO 63108-1202, USA

Jackman, Hugh (Actor)
c/o Alan Nierob *Rogers & Cowan PR (LA)*
Pacific Design Center 8687 Melrose Ave, 7th Floor
West Hollywood, CA 90069, USA

Jacks Mannequin (Musician)
c/o Staff Member *Maverick Recording Co (LA)*
3300 Warner Blvd
Burbank, CA 91505-4632, USA

Jackson, Al (Baseball Player)
3221 SE Morningside Blvd
Port Saint Lucie, FL 34952-5919, USA

Jackson, Alan (Musician, Songwriter)
PO Box 121945
Nashville, TN 37212-1945, USA

Jackson, Alfonza (Athlete, Football Player)
2701 Godwin Ln
Pensacola, FL 32526-9047, USA

Jackson, Alfred (Athlete, Football Player)
1811 Kirby Dr
Houston, TX 77019-3415, USA

Jackson, Alphonso (Secretary)
451 7th SW
Washington, DC 20410-0001, USA

Jackson, Alvin N (Al) (Athlete, Baseball Player)
3221 SE Morningside Blvd
Port Saint Lucie, FL 34952-5919, USA

Jackson, Anne (Actor)
90 Riverside Dr
New York, NY 10024-5306, USA

Jackson, Arthur J (War Hero)
1290 E Spring Ct
Boise, ID 83712-8313, USA

Jackson, Barry
29 Rathcoole Ave
London, ENGLAND N8 9LY

Jackson, Betty (Designer, Fashion Designer)
1 Netherwood Place
London W14 0BW, UNITED KINGDOM (UK)

Jackson, Bo (Athlete, Baseball Player)
100 Oak Ridge Dr W
Burr Ridge, IL 60527-6870, USA

Jackson, Bo (Athlete, Football Player)
PO Box 158
Mobile, AL 36601-0158, USA

Jackson, Bobby (Basketball Player)
1 Sports Pkwy
Sacramento, CA 95834-2300, USA

Jackson, Bobby (Athlete, Football Player)
4009 Old Shell Rd Apt E9
Mobile, AL 36608-1385, USA

Jackson, Bobby (Athlete, Football Player)
47 Tippin Dr
Huntington Station, NY 11746-2130, USA

Jackson, Brandon T (Actor, Producer)
c/o Staff Member *ML Management*
250 W 57th St Frnt 4
New York, NY 10107-0004, USA

Jackson, Calvin (Athlete, Football Player)
250 SW 28th Ter
Fort Lauderdale, FL 33312-1285, USA

Jackson, Charles (Athlete, Football Player)
PO Box 888285
Atlanta, GA 30356-0285, USA

Jackson, Cheyenne (Actor)
c/o Pete Sanders *Fifteen Minutes (NY)*
115 W 29th St Fl 8
New York, NY 10001-5069, USA

Jackson, Christine W (Stylist)
368 Penning Rd
Chehalis, WA 98532-9159, USA

Jackson, Chuck (Musician)
225 W 57th St Ste 500
New York, NY 10019-2136, USA

Jackson, Chuck (Athlete, Baseball Player)
15821 SE 175th Pl
Renton, WA 98058-9122, USA

Jackson, Clarence (Athlete, Football Player)
5251 Appleleaf Ct
North Chesterfield, VA 23234-2801, USA

Jackson, Conor (Athlete, Baseball Player)
7301 E 3rd Ave Unit 313
Scottsdale, AZ 85251-4461, USA

Jackson, Dallas (Producer, Writer)
c/o Staff Member *Davis Entertainment*
150 S Barrington Pl
Los Angeles, CA 90049-3306, USA

Jackson, Damian (Athlete, Baseball Player)
1955 Sunset Dr Unit 81
Escondido, CA 92025-6635, USA

Jackson, Danny (Athlete, Baseball Player)
16332 Larsen St
Overland Park, KS 66062-8520, USA

Jackson, Darrell (Athlete, Baseball Player)
PO Box 4424
Downey, CA 90241-1424, USA

Jackson, Darrin (Athlete, Baseball Player)
61 W 15th St Apt 302
Chicago, IL 60605-3415, USA

Jackson, Daryl S (Architect)
161 Hotham St
East Melbourne, VIC 3002, AUSTRALIA

Jackson, Deanna (Basketball Player)
125 S Pennsylvania St
Indianapolis, IN 46204-3610, USA

Jackson, Donald
1080 Brocks
South Pickering ON, CANADA

Jackson, Doris (Musician)
2756 N Green Valley Pkwy
Henderson, NV 89014-2120, USA

Jackson, Earnest (Athlete, Football Player)
PO Box 585
Coraopolis, PA 15108-0585, USA

Jackson, Eddie (Bowler)
3961 Glenmore Ave
Cincinnati, OH 45211-3509, USA

Jackson, Ernie (Athlete, Football Player)
938 Pisgah N
Eads, TN 38028-9799, USA

Jackson, Francis A (Composer, Musician)
Nether Garth East Acklam
Malton North Yorkshire YO17 9RG,
UNITED KINGDOM (UK)

Jackson, Frank (Athlete, Football Player)
5904 Gregory Ln
Allen, TX 75002-6710, USA

Jackson, Gildart (Actor)
c/o Chuck Binder *Binder & Associates*
1465 Lindacrest Dr
Beverly Hills, CA 90210-2519, USA

Jackson, Glenda (Actor)
9-15 Neal St
London WC2H 9PF, UNITED KINGDOM (UK)

Jackson, Grant (Athlete, Baseball Player)
212 Mesa Cir
Pittsburgh, PA 15241-1721, USA

Jackson, Harold (Journalist)
2200 4th Ave N
Birmingham, AL 35203-3802, USA

Jackson, Harold (Athlete, Coach, Football Player)
6144 Flight Ave
Los Angeles, CA 90056-1510, USA

Jackson, Heathermary (Stylist)
c/o Staff Member *Management + Artists + Organization*
330 W 38th St Ste 1401
New York, NY 10018-8438, USA

Jackson, Honor (Athlete, Football Player)
PO Box 1399
Rohnert Park, CA 94927-1399, USA

Jackson, Huson (Architect)
442 Marrett Rd # 101
Lexington, MA 02421-7725, USA

Jackson, James A (Jim) (Athlete, Basketball Player)
17827 Windflower Way
Dallas, TX 75252-5216, USA

Jackson, Janet (Actor, Dancer, Musician)
c/o Stephen Roseberry *Sterling/Winters Company, The*
10877 Wilshire Blvd Fl 15
Los Angeles, CA 90024-4341, USA

Jackson, Jaren (Athlete, Basketball Player)
16813 Hoffman Manor Dr
Silver Spring, MD 20905-5033, USA

Jackson, Jarious (Athlete, Football Player)
2711 Driftwood Dr
Manvel, TX 77578-3240, USA

Jackson, Jeff (Athlete, Hockey Player)
c/o Staff Member *Toronto Maple Leafs*
Air Canada Centre 400-40 Bay St
Toronto, ON M5J 2X2, Canada

Jackson, Jeff (Athlete, Baseball Player)
930 N Martel Ave Apt 107
Los Angeles, CA 90046-6600, USA

Jackson, Jeff (Athlete, Football Player)
1119 Parkview Dr
Griffin, GA 30224-4738, USA

Jackson, Jeremy (Actor, Producer)
c/o Erik Heintz *Insomnia Media Group*
100 Universal City Plaza Drive The Rock
Hudson Bldg Suite G
Universal City, CA 91608, USA

Jackson, Jermaine (Music Group, Musician, Songwriter)
4641 Hayvenhurst Ave
Encino, CA 91436-3251, USA

Jackson, Jermaine (Basketball Player)
190 Marietta St NW
Atlanta, GA 30303-2762, USA

Jackson, Jesse (Activist, Politician, Religious Leader)
400 T St NW
Washington, DC 20001-1809, USA

Jackson, Joe (Business Person)
c/o Staff Member *Paradigm (Monterey)*
404 W Franklin St
Monterey, CA 93940-2303, USA

Jackson, Joe (Athlete, Football Player)
3935 E Greenway Rd Apt 122
Phoenix, AZ 85032-4669, USA

Jackson, Joe M (War Hero)
25320 38th Ave S
Kent, WA 98032-5679, USA

Jackson, John (Athlete, Football Player)
5128 Karrington Dr
Gibsonia, PA 15044-6005, USA

Jackson, John (Athlete, Baseball Player)
PO Box 898
Hodge, LA 71247-0898, USA

Jackson, John David (Boxer)
1022 S State St
Tacoma, WA 98405-3042, USA

Jackson, John (Fabolous) (Musician)
c/o Johnny Gallo *Artist Representation Group*
9701 Wilshire Blvd Fl 10
Beverly Hills, CA 90212-2010, USA

Jackson, John M (Actor)
5555 Melrose Ave Clara Bow # 204
Los Angeles, CA 90038, USA

Jackson, Jonathan (Actor)
c/o David Guillod *Paradigm (LA)*
9560 Wilshire Blvd Fl 5
Beverly Hills, CA 90212-2401, USA

Jackson, Joshua (Actor)
c/o Michael Bircumshaw *Water Street Management*
5225 Wilshire Blvd Ste 615
Los Angeles, CA 90036-4350, USA

Jackson, Kate (Actor)
3200 Oakdell Ln
Studio City, CA 91604-4219, USA

Jackson, Keith (Athlete, Football Player)
1801 Champlin Dr Apt 1707
Little Rock, AR 72223-3987, USA

Jackson, Keith J (Athlete, Football Player)
PO Box 241695
Little Rock, AR 72223-0012, USA

Jackson, Keith M (Sportscaster)
77 W 66th St
New York, NY 10023-6201, USA

Jackson, Ken (Athlete, Baseball Player)
PO Box 613
Waskom, TX 75692-0613, USA

Jackson, Kirby (Athlete, Football Player)
373 Vista Lake Ter
Suwanee, GA 30024-7418, USA

Jackson, Kwame (Business Person, Reality TV Star)
c/o Staff Member *Mark Burnett Productions*
640 N Sepulveda Blvd
Los Angeles, CA 90049-2108, USA

Jackson, La Toya (Model, Musician)
c/o Jeffre Phillips *Ja-Tail Enterprises*
8306 Wilshire Blvd Ste 528
Beverly Hills, CA 90211-2382, USA

Jackson, Larron (Athlete, Football Player)
1750 Saint Charles Ave Apt 229
New Orleans, LA 70130-6740, USA

Jackson, Larry R (Misc)
4949 Oslon Memorial Pkwy
Minneapolis, MN 55422, USA

Jackson, Lauren (Basketball Player)
Key Arena 351 Elliott Ave W #500
Seattle, WA 98119, USA

Jackson, Leshon (Athlete, Football Player)
PO Box 957
Haskell, OK 74436-0957, USA

Jackson, Lillian (Baseball Player)
1050 W Camino Velasquez
Green Valley, AZ 85622-4527, USA

Jackson, Lucious (Luke) (Athlete, Basketball Player)
7711 County Road 511
Rosharon, TX 77583-7286, USA

Jackson, Mannie (Athlete, Basketball Player)
400 E Van Buren St Ste 300
Phoenix, AZ 85004-2257, USA

Jackson, Mark A (Athlete, Basketball Player, Sportscaster)
17 Winmere Pl
Dix Hills, NY 11746-6553, USA

Jackson, Mark A (Athlete, Football Player)
620 Mathews St Apt 202
Fort Collins, CO 80524-3037, USA

Jackson, Marlon
4641 Hayvenhurst Ave
Encino, CA 91436-3251

Jackson, Mel (Actor)
c/o Staff Member *Stone Manners Salners Agency (LA)*
9911 W Pico Blvd Ste 1400
Los Angeles, CA 90035-2715, USA

Jackson, Melvin (Athlete, Football Player)
4345 Enoro Dr
Los Angeles, CA 90008-4870, USA

Jackson, Mervin (Athlete, Basketball Player)
16638 Kildare Ct
Tinley Park, IL 60477-1579, USA

Jackson, Michael (Athlete, Football Player)
14207 128th Pl NE
Kirkland, WA 98034-1575, USA

Jackson, Michelle (Stylist)
c/o Staff Member *Zenobia Agency Inc*
PO Box 909
Groveland, CA 95321-0909, USA

Jackson, Mick (Director)
1349 Berea Pl
Pacific Palisades, CA 90272-2602, USA

Jackson, Mike (Athlete, Baseball Player)
805 11th Ave Apt 2H
Paterson, NJ 07514-1012, USA

Jackson, Mike (Athlete, Baseball Player)
17214 Oak Dale Dr
Spring, TX 77379-8846, USA

Jackson, Milt (Athlete, Football Player)
100 McMindes Ct
Roseville, CA 95747-5853, USA

Jackson, Monte C (Athlete, Football Player)
7646 Westbrook Ave
San Diego, CA 92139-4006, USA

Jackson, Neil (Actor)
c/o Staff Member *IFA Talent Agency*
8730 W Sunset Blvd Ste 490
Los Angeles, CA 90069-2248, USA

Jackson, Nickey (Stylist)
c/o Staff Member *Help Me Rhonda*
541 10th St NW # 294
Atlanta, GA 30318-5713, USA

Jackson, Noah (Athlete, Football Player)
1640 Millburne Rd
Lake Forest, IL 60045-4106, USA

Jackson, O'Shea (Ice Cube) (Actor, Director, Musician)
c/o Jeff Kwatinetz *Prospect Park*
2049 Century Park E Ste 2550
Century City, CA 90067-3139, USA

Jackson, Peter (Director)
c/o Ken Kamins *Key Creatives*
1800 N Highland Ave Fl 5
Los Angeles, CA 90028-4523, USA

Jackson, Phil (Athlete, Basketball Player, Coach)
6413 Ocean Front Walk
Playa Del Rey, CA 90293-7528, USA

Jackson, Phillip (Actor)
c/o Pippa Markham *Markham & Froggatt*
4 Windmill St
London W1T 1HZ, UK

Jackson, Quinton (Rampage) (Athlete, Wrestler)
c/o Staff Member *ROAR (LA)*
9701 Wilshire Blvd Fl 8
Beverly Hills, CA 90212-2008, USA

Jackson, R Graham (Architect)
6200 Savoy Dr
Houston, TX 77036-3300, USA

Jackson, Ralph (Athlete, Basketball Player)
3235 W 111th Pl
Inglewood, CA 90303-2316, USA

Jackson, Randy (Musician, Reality TV Star)
c/o Harriet Sternberg *Harriet Sternberg Management*
4530 Gloria Ave
Encino, CA 91436-2718, USA

Jackson, Randy (Athlete, Baseball Player)
250 Hunnicutt Dr
Athens, GA 30606-1708, USA

Jackson, Randy B (Athlete, Football Player)
747 Musago Run
Lake Mary, FL 32746-2209, USA

Jackson, Randy J (Athlete, Football Player)
4449 Auburn St
Bel Aire, KS 67220-1805, USA

Jackson, Ransom (Baseball Player)
250 Hunnicutt Dr
Athens, GA 30606-1708, USA

Jackson, Rebbie (Music Group, Musician, Songwriter, Writer)
4641 Hayvenhurst Ave
Encino, CA 91436-3251, USA

Jackson, Reggie (Athlete, Baseball Player)
c/o Staff Member *Doubleday/ RandomHouse*
1745 Broadway
New York, NY 10019-4368, USA

Jackson, Richard A (Religious Leader)
5757 N Central Ave
Phoenix, AZ 85012-1315, USA

Jackson, Richard Lee
1815 Butler Ave Apt 120
Los Angeles, CA 90025-5462

Jackson, Richard S (Richie) (Athlete, Football Player)
6000 Kingston Ct
New Orleans, LA 70131-5557, USA

Jackson, Rickey (Athlete, Football Player)
PO Box 655
Pahokee, FL 33476-0655, USA

Jackson, Rickey A (Athlete, Football Player)
325 S Barfield Hwy
Pahokee, FL 33476-1929, USA

Jackson, Ron (Athlete, Baseball Player)
210 Raintree Cir
Kalamazoo, MI 49006-4165, USA

Jackson, Ron (Athlete, Baseball Player)
515 White Rd
Fayetteville, GA 30214-1211, USA

Jackson, Ronald Shannon (Musician)
1128 Broadway # 425
New York, NY 10010, USA

Jackson, Roy Lee (Athlete, Baseball Player)
8269 Lee Road 54
Auburn, AL 36830-8222, USA

Jackson, Ryan (Athlete, Baseball Player)
2335 Alpine Ave
Sarasota, FL 34239-4117, USA

Jackson, Samuel L (Actor)
c/o Eli Selden *Anonymous Content (AC-LA)*
3531 Hayden Ave
Culver City, CA 90232, USA

Jackson, Sasha (Actor)
c/o Ric Beddingfield *Beddingfield Company, The*
13600 Ventura Blvd Ste B
Sherman Oaks, CA 91423-5050, USA

Jackson, Shar (Actor)
c/o Staff Member *It Girl Public Relations*
5301 Beethoven St Ste 220
Los Angeles, CA 90066-7052, USA

Jackson, Sheldon (Athlete, Football Player)
4466 Teresita Ct
Chino, CA 91710-3929, USA

Jackson, Sherry (Actor)
800 N Lucia Ave # A
Redondo Beach, CA 90277-2233, USA

Jackson, Shirley Ann (Educator, Physicist)
President's Office
Troy, NY 12180, USA

Jackson, Sonny (Athlete, Baseball Player)
117 Palm Bay Dr Apt B
Palm Beach Gardens, FL 33418-5790, USA

Jackson, Steve (Athlete, Football Player)
43752 Lees Mill Sq
Leesburg, VA 20176-3821, USA

Jackson, Steve (Athlete, Football Player)
1153 Bergen Pkwy Ste M
Evergreen, CO 80439-9501, USA

Jackson, Steven (Athlete, Football Player)
c/o Eugene Parker *Maximum Sports Management*
6435 W Jefferson Blvd # 197
Fort Wayne, IN 46804-6203, USA

Jackson, Steven R (Randy) (Musician)
c/o Taunya Zilkie *Zilk Inc*
686 S Arroyo Pkwy Ste 300
Pasadena, CA 91105-3233, USA

Jackson, Stonewall (Musician, Songwriter)
6007 Cloverland Dr
Brentwood, TN 37027-7607, USA

Jackson, Stoney (Actor)
3151 Cahuenga Blvd W Ste 310
Los Angeles, CA 90068-1768, USA

Jackson, Thomas Penfield (Judge)
333 Constitution Ave NW
Washington, DC 20001-2804, USA

Jackson, Thomas (Tom) (Athlete, Football Player, Sportscaster)
Sports Dept ESPN Plaza 935 Middle St
Bristol, CT 6010, USA

Jackson, Tim (Athlete, Football Player)
6501 White Oak Dr
Rowlett, TX 75089-7441, USA

Jackson, Tito (Musician)
2467 Taylor Ave
Corona, CA 92882-6980, USA

Jackson, Tony (Athlete, Basketball Player)
1009 Trevey Pt
Lexington, KY 40515-1417, USA

Jackson, Tracy (Athlete, Basketball Player)
10588 Spotted Horse Ln
Columbia, MD 21044-2214, USA

Jackson, Tre (Athlete, Football Player)
680 Harrison Ave
Peekskill, NY 10566-2219, USA

Jackson, Trina (Athlete, Swimmer)
9271 Saltwater Way
Jacksonville, FL 32256-9606, USA

Jackson, Tyoka (Athlete, Football Player)
1 Rams Way
Earth City, MO 63045-1523, USA

Jackson, Tyson (Athlete, Football Player)
c/o Eugene Parker *Maximum Sports Management*
6435 W Jefferson Blvd # 197
Fort Wayne, IN 46804-6203, USA

Jackson, Verdell (Baseball Player)
413 Lincoln St
Venice, IL 62090-1117, USA

Jackson, Vernell (Athlete, Baseball Player)
413 Lincoln St
Venice, IL 62090-1117, USA

Jackson, Vestee (Athlete, Football Player)
2800 S Eastern Ave Apt 410
Las Vegas, NV 89169-1839, USA

Jackson, Victoria (Actor, Comedian)
c/o Kim Dorr *Defining Artists Agency*
10 Universal City Plz Ste 2000
Universal City, CA 91608-1074, USA

Jackson, Victoria (Business Person)
110 S Robertson Blvd
Los Angeles, CA 90048-3208, USA

Jackson, Vincent E (Bo) (Athlete, Baseball Player, Football Player)
PO Box 158
Mobile, AL 36601-0158, USA

Jackson, Wanda (Music Group, Musician)
8200 S Pennsylvania Ave
Oklahoma City, OK 73159-5202, USA

Jackson, Wardell (Athlete, Basketball Player)
PO Box 164142
Columbus, OH 43216-4142, USA

Jackson, Waverly (Athlete, Football Player)
1231 Halifax St
South Hill, VA 23970-2319, USA

Jackson, Wilbur (Athlete, Football Player)
PO Box 1571
Ozark, AL 36361-1571, USA

Jackson, Willie (Athlete, Football Player)
PO Box 12643
Gainesville, FL 32604-0643, USA

Jackson Hoye, Rose (Actor)
c/o Staff Member *Haldeman Business Management*
1137 2nd St Ste 119
Santa Monica, CA 90403-5073, USA

Jackson Lee, Sheila (Congressman, Politician)
2160 Rayburn Hob
Washington, DC 20515-0918, USA

Jacob, Francois (Nobel Prize Laureate)
15 Rue de Conde
Paris 75006, FRANCE

Jacob, Irene (Actor)
1 Rue Alfred du Vigny
Paris 75008, FRANCE

Jacob, John E (Activist)
120 Wall St # 700
New York, NY 10005-3904, USA

Jacob, Katerina (Actor)
Merzstr 14
Munich 81679, USA

Jacob, Ralph (Actor)
c/o Staff Member *Britto Agency PR*
234 W 56th St PH
New York, NY 10019-4302, USA

Jacob, Stanley W (Doctor)
1055 SW Westwood Ct
Portland, OR 97239-2708, USA

Jacobi, Derek G (Actor)
c/o Staff Member *International Creative Management (ICM-LA)*
10250 Constellation Blvd Fl 7
Los Angeles, CA 90067-6207, USA

Jacobs, Allen (Athlete, Football Player)
3050 Tolcate Ln
Salt Lake City, UT 84121-1545, USA

Jacobs, Brandon (Athlete, Football Player)
50 State Rt 120
E Rutherford, NJ 07073-2131, USA

Jacobs, Darlene (Stylist)
c/o Staff Member *Mercury Artists*
8460 Higuera St Fl 2
Culver City, CA 90232-2520, USA

Jacobs, Dave (Athlete, Football Player)
8388 Glen Eagle Dr
Manlius, NY 13104-9445, USA

Jacobs, Forrest (Athlete, Baseball Player)
23073 Lakeview Dr
Millsboro, DE 19966-2881, USA

Jacobs, Fred (Athlete, Basketball Player)
1270 N Ford St Unit 214
Golden, CO 80403-1974, USA

Jacobs, Gillian (Actor)
c/o Jill Kaplan *Principal Entertainment (NY)*
130 W 42nd St Ste 614
New York, NY 10036-7804, USA

Jacobs, Harry (Athlete, Football Player)
108 Lenora Dr
Hamburg, NY 14075-4710, USA

Jacobs, Irwin M (Business Person)
5775 Morehouse Dr
San Diego, CA 92121-1714, USA

Jacobs, Jack H (War Hero)
1 Appold St
London EC2A 2HE, UNITED KINGDOM (UK)

Jacobs, Jake (Athlete, Baseball Player)
2925 Terra Ceia Bay Blvd # 250
Palmetto, FL 34221-5988, USA

Jacobs, Julien I (Judge)
400 2nd St NW
Washington, DC 20217-0001, USA

Jacobs, Katie (Producer, Writer)
c/o Tony Etz *Creative Artists Agency (CAA-LA)*
2000 Avenue of the Stars Ste 100
Los Angeles, CA 90067-4705, USA

Jacobs, Lawrence-Hilton (Actor)
PO Box 67905
Los Angeles, CA 90067-0905, USA

Jacobs, Marc (Designer, Fashion Designer)
403 Bleecker St
New York, NY 10014-2157, USA

Jacobs, Norman J (Publisher)
990 Grove St
Evanston, IL 60201-6510, USA

Jacobs, Proverb (Athlete, Football Player)
4369 Detroit Ave
Oakland, CA 94619-1603, USA

Jacobs, Tim (Athlete, Football Player)
7306 Finns Ln
Lanham, MD 20706-1214, USA

Jacobs, Tim (Athlete, Hockey Player)
6516 County Road 301
Parachute, CO 81635-9122, USA

Jacobs-Badini, Jane (Baseball Player)
1854 4th St
Cuyahoga Falls, OH 44221-3802, USA

Jacobsen, Bucky (Athlete, Baseball Player)
785 W Division Ave
Hermiston, OR 97838-2226, USA

Jacobsen, Casey (Basketball Player)
201 E Jefferson St
Phoenix, AZ 85004-2412, USA

Jacobsen, Peter (Athlete, Golfer)
9400 SW Barnes Rd Ste 550
Portland, OR 97225-6690, USA

Jacobsen, Peter (Athlete, Golfer)
27771 Marina Pointe Dr
Bonita Springs, FL 34134-0762, USA

Jacobsen, Stephanie (Actor)
c/o Christopher Rockwell *Global Creative*
1051 Cole Ave # B
Los Angeles, CA 90038-2601, USA

Jacobsen, Steven C (Engineer)
Engineering Design Center
Salt Lake City, UT 84112, USA

Jacobs-Murk, Janet (Baseball Player)
899 Olentangy Rd
Franklin Lakes, NJ 07417-2811, USA

Jacobson, A Thurl (Geophysicist, Physicist)
7955 W Innsbrook Ct
Boise, ID 83704-4487, USA

Jacobson, D D (Bowler)
8261 Rees St
Playa Del Rey, CA 90293-7823, USA

Jacobson, Herbert L (Diplomat, Journalist)
Apartado 160
Escazu, COSTA RICA

Jacobson, Peter (Actor)
c/o Elizabeth Much *Much and House Public Relations*
8075 W 3rd St Ste 500
Los Angeles, CA 90048-4325, USA

Jacobson, Peter Marc (Actor, Producer, Writer)
c/o Staff Member *New York Nick*
5750 Wilshire Blvd
Los Angeles, CA 90036-3697, USA

Jacobson, Scott (Actor)
c/o Staff Member *Creative Artists Agency (CAA-LA)*
2000 Avenue of the Stars Ste 100
Los Angeles, CA 90067-4705, USA

Jacoby, Billy
PO Box 46324
Los Angeles, CA 90046-0324

Jacoby, Brook (Athlete, Baseball Player)
21825 N Dobson Rd
Scottsdale, AZ 85255-4404, USA

Jacoby, Joe (Athlete, Football Player)
7308 Cedar Run Dr
Warrenton, VA 20187-2212, USA

Jacoby, Laura
PO Box 46324
Los Angeles, CA 90046-0324

Jacoby, Lowell E (Admiral)
Director Defense Intelligence Agency
Washington, DC 20340-0001, USA

Jacoby, Scott (Actor)
PO Box 5569
Sherman Oaks, CA 91413-5569, USA

Jacome, Jason (Athlete, Baseball Player)
5115 N Camino Esplendora
Tucson, AZ 85718-6226, USA

Jacot, Christopher (Actor)
c/o Ted Schachter *Schachter Entertainment*
1157 S Beverly Dr Fl 2
Los Angeles, CA 90035-1119, USA

Jacot, Michele (Skier)
Residence du Brevent
74 Chamonix, FRANCE

Jacott, Carlos (Actor)
c/o JB Roberts *Thruline Entertainment*
9250 Wilshire Blvd Ground Fl
Beverly Hills, CA 90212, USA

Jacox, Kendyl (Athlete, Football Player)
647 Shadyway Dr
Dallas, TX 75232-4821, USA

Jacques, Russell (Artist)
38 Drake St
Newport Beach, CA 92663-4455, USA

Jacquez, Pat (Athlete, Baseball Player)
4430 Annandale Dr
Stockton, CA 95219-1782, USA

Jacquez, Thomas (Tom) (Athlete, Baseball Player)
280 Fell St Apt 410
San Francisco, CA 94102-5174, USA

Jacuzzi, Roy (Business Person)
2121 N California Blvd
Walnut Creek, CA 94596-3572, USA

Jadakiss (Artist, Music Group, Musician)
8942 Wilshire Blvd # 219
Beverly Hills, CA 90211-1908, USA

Jade
c/o Staff Member *Diva Central Inc*
7510 W Sunset Blvd Ste 1445
Los Angeles, CA 90046-3408, USA

Jade, Samantha (Musician)
c/o Staff Member *Jive Records*
550 Madison Ave Fl 6
New York, NY 10022-3211, USA

Jadot, Jean L O (Religious Leader)
Ave de l'Atlantique 71-B-12
Brussels 1150, BELGIUM

Jae, Jana
PO Box 35736
Tulsa, OK 74153

Jaeckel, Barry (Athlete, Golfer)
210 Falcon Cv
Brandon, MS 39047-7733, USA

Jaeckel, Paul (Athlete, Baseball Player)
328 W 7th St
Claremont, CA 91711-4313, USA

Jaeckin, Just (Director)
8 Villa Mequillet
Neuilly/Seine 92200, FRANCE

Jaeger, Andrea (Athlete, Tennis Player)
Silver Lining Ranch 256 Rancho Milagro Way
Hesperus, CO 81326-8750, USA

Jaeger, Jeff T (Athlete, Football Player)
3026 Sahalee Dr W
Sammamish, WA 98074-6304, USA

Jaeger, Sam (Actor)
c/o Steve Dontanville *Dontanville/ Frattaroli (D/F)*
8609 Washington Blvd # 8607
Culver City, CA 90232-7441, USA

Jaenicke, Hannes
Goetherstr. 17
Munich, GERMANY D-80336

Jaffe, Arthur M (Mathematician)
27 Lancaster St
Cambridge, MA 02140-2837, USA

Jaffe, Herold W (Doctor)
1600 Clifton Rd NE
Atlanta, GA 30329-4018, USA

Jaffe, Robert L (Physicist)
Physics Dept
Cambridge, MA 2139, USA

Jaffe, Stanley R (Director, Producer)
10202 Washington Blvd
Culver City, CA 90232-3119, USA

Jaffe, Susan (Ballerina)
890 Broadway
New York, NY 10003-1211, USA

Jaffrey, Saeed (Actor, Bollywood, Comedian)
503 Sejal New Link Road Andheri
Bombay, MS 400 058, INDIA

Jagdeo, Bharrat (Prime Minister)
Brickham New Garden & South Sts
Georgetown, GUYANA

Jagendort, Andre T (Doctor)
455 Savage Farm Dr
Ithaca, NY 14850-6522, USA

Jager, Thomas (Tom) (Swimmer)
745 4th Ave E
Kalispell, MT 59901-5345, USA

Jager, Tom
64 Ramble Wood Blvd
Tijeras, NM 87059-8004

Jagge, Finn Christian (Skier)
Michelets Vei 108
Stabekk 1320, NORWAY

Jagged Edge (Music Group)
c/o Nancy Josephson *WmE2 (Endeavor-LA)*
9601 Wilshire Blvd Fl 3
Beverly Hills, CA 90210-5219, USA

Jagger, Bianca (Actor, Model)
c/o Amanda Bross *Finch & Partners*
Top Floor 29-37 Heddon St
London W1B 4BR, UNITED KINGDOM

Jagger, Jade (Business Person)
752 Pacific St
Brooklyn, NY 11238-3006, USA

Jagger, Mick (Musician)
c/o Fran Curtis *Rogers & Cowan PR (LA)*
Pacific Design Center 8687 Melrose Ave, 7th Floor
West Hollywood, CA 90069, USA

Jagland, Thorbjoern (Prime Minister)
Karl Johans Gate 22
Oslo 26, NORWAY

Jaglom, Henry (Director)
9165 W Sunset Blvd Ste 300
Los Angeles, CA 90069-3195, USA

Jagr, Jaromir (Athlete, Hockey Player)
c/o J P Barry *C A A Hockey*
822 11th Ave SW Suite 204
Calgary, AB T2R 0E5, Canada

Jaguares (Music Group)
c/o Staff Member *BMG*
1540 Broadway
New York, NY 10036-4039, USA

Jaha, John (Athlete, Baseball Player)
12776 SE Geneva Way
Happy Valley, OR 97086-6182, USA

Jahan, Marine (Actor, Dancer)
6300 Wilshire Blvd Ste 1470
Los Angeles, CA 90048-5200, USA

Jaheim (Musician)
100 Evergreen Pt # 402
East Orange, NJ 7018, USA

Jahn, Helmut (Architect)
35 E Wacker Dr
Chicago, IL 60601-2314, USA

Jahn, Robert G (Engineer)
Dept
Princeton, NJ 08544-0001, USA

Jahn, Sigmund (Astronaut, General, Misc)
Fontanestr 35
Strausberg 15344, GERMANY

Jaidah, Ali Mohammed (Government Official)
PO Box 3212
Doha, QATAR

Jaitley, Celina (Actor, Beauty Pageant Winner)
c/o Staff Member *Brillstein Entertainment Partners*
9150 Wilshire Blvd Ste 350
Beverly Hills, CA 90212-3453, USA

Jake Locker, Jake
c/o David Dunn *Athletes First, LLC*
3300 Irvine Ave Ste 300
Newport Beach, CA 92660-3108, USA

Jakel, Bernd (Yachtsman)
Salvador-Allende-Str 48
Berlin 12559, GERMANY

Jakeman, Seth (Musician)
c/o Staff Member *Paradigm (Monterey)*
404 W Franklin St
Monterey, CA 93940-2303, USA

Jakes, Bishop T D (Musician, Writer)
c/o Staff Member *Creative Artists Agency (CAA-LA)*
2000 Avenue of the Stars Ste 100
Los Angeles, CA 90067-4705, USA

Jakes, John (Writer)
445 Meadow Lark Dr
Sarasota, FL 34236-1901, USA

Jakes, T D (Religious Leader)
6777 W Kiest Blvd
Dallas, TX 75236-3006, USA

Jakes, T D (Religious Leader)
1000 Cody Rd S
Mobile, AL 36695-3425, USA

Jakes, Van (Athlete, Football Player)
305 Worthing Ln
McDonough, GA 30253-4244, USA

Jaki, Stanley L (Misc, Physicist)
PO Box 60
New Hope, KY 40052-0060, USA

Jakobs, Marco (Athlete)
Oststr 1B
Unna 59427, GERMANY

Jakobson, Maggie (Actor)
c/o Kesha Williams *Affirmative Entertainment*
425 N Robertson Blvd
West Hollywood, CA 90048-1735, USA

Jakobson, Max (Government Official, Journalist)
Rahapajankatu 3B 17
Helsinki 16 160, FINLAND

Jakopin, John (Athlete, Hockey Player)
57 Samana Dr
Miami, FL 33133-2609, USA

Jakosits, Michael (Misc)
Karlsbergstr 140
Homburg/Saar 66424, GERMANY

Jakovac, JJ (Athlete, Golfer)
c/o Jim Lehrman *SFX Golf*
36855 W Main St Ste 200
Purcellville, VA 20132-3561, USA

Jakowenko, George (Athlete, Football Player)
5 Aberdeen Dr
West Nyack, NY 10994-1301, USA

Jakub, Lisa (Actor)
c/o Nancy LeFeaver *LeFeaver Talent Management Ltd*
2 College St #202
Toronto ON M5G 1K3, CANADA

Jal, Emmanuel (Musician, Writer)
c/o Staff Member *Sonic360, Inc.*
Top Floor East 33 Riding House St.
London W1W 7DZ, UK

Jalal, Farida (Actor, Bollywood)
3B Nandini Unik Housing Society Opp Bon Bon J P Road Andheri
Mumbai, MS 400058, INDIA

Jalbert, Pierre
2642 N Beverly Glen Blvd
Los Angeles, CA 90077-2528

Jamail, Joseph D Jr (Attorney, Attorney General, General)
500 Dallas St Ste 3434
Houston, TX 77002-4802, USA

Jamal, Ahmad (Music Group, Musician)
122 E 57th St # 300
New York, NY 10022-2623, USA

Jambor, Agi (Music Group, Musician)
1616 Bolton St
Baltimore, MD 21217-4316, USA

Jamerson, Dave (Athlete, Basketball Player)
11440 Valley Meadow Dr
Zionsville, IN 46077-9342, USA

James, Aaron (Athlete, Basketball Player)
3057 Orrin Ave
Youngstown, OH 44505-4436, USA

James, Alex (Composer, Musician, Producer)
c/o Staff Member *Parlophone Records*
EMI House 43 Brook Green
London W6 7EF, United Kingdom

James, Anthony (Actor)
1875 Century Park E Ste 2250
Los Angeles, CA 90067-2563, USA

James, Art (Athlete, Baseball Player)
6935 Brown Dr S
Fairburn, GA 30213-3197, USA

James, Bill (Athlete, Baseball Player, Writer)
445 Tennessee St
Lawrence, KS 66044-1376, USA

James, Billy (Athlete, Basketball Player)
12 S Sunset Dr
Lexington, IN 47138-8935, USA

James, Bob (Athlete, Baseball Player)
15844 Cindy Ct
Canyon Country, CA 91387-1881, USA

James, Boney (Musician)
c/o Staff Member *Paradigm (Monterey)*
404 W Franklin St
Monterey, CA 93940-2303, USA

James, Bradley (Actor)
c/o Ruth Young *United Agents*
12-26 Lexington St
London W1F OLE, UK

James, Casey (Musician)
c/o Simon Fuller *XIX Entertainment*
33/32 Ransomes Dock 35-37 Parkgate Rd
London SW11 4NP, UK

James, Charlie (Athlete, Baseball Player)
3303 Tanglewood Way
Fulton, MO 65251-3981, USA

James, Charmayne (Misc)
2100 N State Highway 360 Ste 1207
Grand Prairie, TX 75050-1033, USA

James, Cheryl (Salt) (Musician)
c/o Chris Johnston-Davies *Intrigue Management*
25 Spinney Way Needingworth
Cambridgeshire PE27 4SR, United Kingdom

James, Chris (Athlete, Baseball Player)
1040 County Road 2707
Alto, TX 75925-5915, USA

James, Claudis (Athlete, Football Player)
6767 Presidential Dr
Jackson, MS 39213-2427, USA

James, Cleo (Athlete, Baseball Player)
PO Box 9970
Moreno Valley, CA 92552-1970, USA

James, Clifton (Actor)
500 W 43rd St Apt 25D
New York, NY 10036-4336, USA

James, Clive V L (Journalist, Misc)
Drury House 34-43 Russell St
London WC2B 5HA, UNITED KINGDOM (UK)

James, Craig (Athlete, Football Player)
12714 W FM 455
Celina, TX 75009-3959, USA

James, D Clayton (Historian)
106 Wagon Wheel Trl
Moneta, VA 24121-3328, USA

James, Dalton
303 N Buena Vista St Apt 209
Burbank, CA 91505-3686

James, Danielle (Actor)
c/o Michelle Jannone *Valeo Entertainment*
8265 W Sunset Blvd Ste 103
West Hollywood, CA 90046-2433, USA

James, Delvin (Athlete, Baseball Player)
13355 FM 1878
Nacogdoches, TX 75961-1039, USA

James, Dion (Athlete, Baseball Player)
5 Shelter Point Ct
Sacramento, CA 95831-1415, USA

James, Don (Coach, Football Coach)
7047 Chanticleer Ave SE
Snoqualmie, WA 98065-9785, USA

James, Donald M (Business Person)
1200 Urban Center Dr
Vestavia, AL 35242-2545, USA

James, Duncan (Musician)
c/o Staff Member *Concorde Intl Artists Ltd*
101 Shepherds Bush Rd
London W6 7LP, UNITED KINGDOM (UK)

James, Duncan (Musician)
c/o Staff Member *BMG (UK)*
Bedford House 6979 Fulham High Street
London SW6 3JW, United Kingdom

James, Edgerrin (Athlete, Football Player)
c/o Drew Rosenhaus *Rosenhaus Sports Representation*
6400 Allison Rd
Miami Beach, FL 33141-4540, USA

James, Etta (Musician)
16409 Sally Ln
Riverside, CA 92504-5629, USA

James, G Larry (Athlete, Track Athlete)
Atheletic Dept
Pomona, NJ 8240, USA

James, Geraldine (Actor)
46 Albermarle St
London W1X 4PP, UNITED KINGDOM (UK)

James, Gerry (Athlete, Hockey Player)
3674 Dolphin Dr
Nanoose Bay, BC V9P 9H1, Canada

James, Godfrey
The Shack Western Rd. Pevensey Bay
E. Sussex, ENGLAND

James, Henry (Athlete, Basketball Player)
527 E Leith St
Fort Wayne, IN 46806-1118, USA

James, Jesse (Actor)
1414 S Lamar Blvd
Austin, TX 78704-2388, USA

James, Jessie (Musician)
c/o Staff Member *Island Records*
825 8th Ave Rm C2
New York, NY 10019-7472, USA

James, John (Actor)
PO Box 9
Cambridge, NY 12816-0009, USA

James, John W (Athlete, Football Player)
23108 NE 69th Ave
Melrose, FL 32666-6330, USA

James, Johnny (Athlete, Baseball Player)
6037 E Larkspur Dr
Scottsdale, AZ 85254-4444, USA

James, Joni (Music Group, Musician)
PO Box 7027
Westchester, IL 60154, USA

James, Joshua (Musician)
c/o Brittany Pearce *Fresh and Clean Media*
12701 Venice Blvd
Los Angeles, CA 90066-3705, USA

James, Kate (Model)
199 Lafayette St
New York, NY 10012-4279, USA

James, Kevin (Actor, Comedian)
c/o Jeff Sussman *Jeff Sussman Management*
603 W 115th St # 282
New York, NY 10025-7722

James, Larry D (Astronaut)
USS Space Command
Peterson Air Force Base, CP 80914, USA

James, LeBron (Athlete, Basketball Player)
c/o Keith Estabrook *Estabrook Group LLC*
55 Broad St
New York, NY 10004-2501, US

James, Leela (Musician)
c/o Stephanie Mahler *Creative Artists Agency (CAA-NY)*
162 5th Ave Fl 6
New York, NY 10010-6047, USA

James, Lennie (Actor)
15 Broad Ct Ste 3
London WC2B 5QN, UNITED KINGDOM

James, Lionel (Athlete, Football Player)
199 Woodbury Dr
Sterrett, AL 35147-8144, USA

James, Michael Raymond (Actor)
c/o Mark Armstrong *Sanders Armstrong Caserta*
2120 Colorado Ave Ste 120
Santa Monica, CA 90404-3561, USA

James, Mickie (Athlete, Wrestler)
121 Dogwood Ct
Aylett, VA 23009-4136, USA

James, Mike (Athlete, Baseball Player)
115 Austin Ct
Mary Esther, FL 32569-1396, USA

James, Oliver (Actor, Musician)
c/o Gordon MacDonald *Don Buchwald & Associates Inc (LA)*
8619 Washington Blvd
Culver City, CA 90232-7441, USA

James, Oscar (Stylist)
c/o Staff Member *Ken Barboza Associates*
115 W 30th St Rm 203
New York, NY 10001-4088, USA

James, P D (Writer)
37A Goldhawk Road
London W12 8QQ, UNITED KINGDOM (UK)

James, Paul (Actor, Producer)
c/o Staff Member *HGTV/Home & Garden Television*
9721 Sherrill Blvd
Knoxville, TN 37932-3330, USA

James, Po (Athlete, Football Player)
1421 Sherman St
Hammond, IN 46320-2208, USA

James, Ralph
205 S Arnaz Dr Apt 4
Beverly Hills, CA 90211-2881

James, Rick (Athlete, Baseball Player)
102 Stoney Creek Dr
Florence, AL 35633-1581, USA

James, Robert (Athlete, Football Player)
1511 N Highland Ave
Murfreesboro, TN 37130-2204, USA

James, Robert (Bob) (Music Group, Musician, Songwriter, Writer)
200 W Superior St Ste 202
Chicago, IL 60654-3554, USA

James, Roland (Athlete, Football Player)
19 Spring Ln
Sharon, MA 02067-2240, USA

James, Sheila (Actor)
3201 Pearl St
Santa Monica, CA 90405-3106, USA

James, Sheryl (Journalist)
Editorial Dept 490 1st Ave
Saint Petersburg, FL 33701, USA

James, Skip (Athlete, Baseball Player)
14429 Windsor St
Overland Park, KS 66224-3669, USA

James, Sonny (Music Group, Musician, Songwriter, Writer)
818 18th Ave S
Nashville, TN 37203-6663, USA

James, Steve (Director, Producer, Writer)
c/o Paul Canterna *Seven Summits Pictures & Management*
8906 W Olympic Blvd Ground Floor
Beverly Hills, CA 90211, USA

James, Tommy (Music Group, Musician)
PO Box 4354
Clifton, NJ 07012-8354, USA

James, Tommy (Athlete, Football Player)
1615 Wales Rd NE
Massillon, OH 44646-4167, USA

James, Toran (Athlete, Football Player)
RR 3 Box 14-13
Ahoskie, NC 27910, USA

James, Val (Athlete, Hockey Player)
105 S 32nd St
Wyandanch, NY 11798-2613, USA

James of Holland Park, Phyllis D (Writer)
37A Goldhawk Road
London W12 SQQ, UNITED KINGDOM (UK)

Jameson, Betty (Athlete, Golfer)
1425 S Congress Ave Apt 268
Boynton Beach, FL 33426-6384, USA

Jameson, Elizabeth M (Betty) (Athlete, Golfer)
1425 S Congress Ave Apt 268
Boynton Beach, FL 33426-6384, USA

Jameson, Jenna (Actor, Adult Film Star)
15561 Product Ln Ste D11
Huntington Beach, CA 92649-1301, USA

Jameson, Louise
18-21 Jermyn St
London, ENGLAND SW1Y 6HP

Jameson, Paulene
7 Warrington Gdns
London, ENGLAND W9 2QB

James-Roadman, Charmayne (Misc)
Clayton, NM 88415, USA

Jamieson, Janet (Baseball Player)
6324 212th St SW Trlr 3
Lynnwood, WA 98036-7425, USA

Jamiroquai (Music Group)
c/o Staff Member *Nettwerk Management (LA)*
1545 Wilcox Ace Suite 200
Los Angeles, CA 90028, USA

Jamison, Antawn (Basketball Player)
2909 Taylor St
Dallas, TX 75226-1909, USA

Jamison, Jayne (Publisher)
224 W 57th St
New York, NY 10019-3212, USA

Jamison, Jimi (Musician)
4002 Glendale Dr
Memphis, TN 38128-2408, USA

Jamison, Mae
PO Box 580317
Houston, TX 77258-0317

Jamison, Milo
1231 Tennyson St
Manhattan Beach, CA 90266-6956

Jammeh, Yahya A J J (Misc)
State House
Banjul, GAMBIA

Jammer, Quentin (Athlete, Football Player)
4020 Murphy Canyon Rd
San Diego, CA 92123-4407, USA

Jampolsky, Gerald (Writer)
PO Box 7123
Berkeley, CA 94707-0123

Jan & Dean
221 Main St Ste P
Huntington Beach, CA 92648-8119

Janakaraj (Actor)
8 H D Raja Street Teynampet
Chennai, TN 600 018, INDIA

Janaki, Sowcar (Actor, Bollywood)
13 Cenetop Road 2nd St
Chennai, TN 600018, INDIA

Janaszak, Steve (Athlete, Hockey Player)
42 Montrose Ave
Babylon, NY 11702-2626, USA

Jance, J A (Writer)
1350 Avenue of the Americas
New York, NY 10019-4702, USA

Jancik, Bobby (Athlete, Football Player)
114 5th St SE Apt 501E
Minneapolis, MN 55414-1161, USA

Jancso, Miklos (Director)
Solyom Laszio Utca 17
Budapest II 1022, HUNGARY

Janda, Krystyna (Actor)
Ul Zamoyskiego 20
Warsaw, POLAND

Jande, Marine (Actor)
16 W 22nd St Fl 3
New York, NY 10010-5803

Jane, Jesse (Actor, Adult Film Star)
c/o Staff Member *Media Artists Group (LA)*
8255 W Sunset Blvd
West Hollywood, CA 90046-2417, USA

Jane, Thomas (Actor)
c/o Michael Katcher *Creative Artists Agency (CAA-LA)*
2000 Avenue of the Stars Ste 100
Los Angeles, CA 90067-4705, USA

Janecyl, Bob (Athlete, Hockey Player)
5973 Pheasant View Dr NE
Ada, MI 49301-8648, USA

Janeski, Jerry (Athlete, Baseball Player)
28901 Via Buena Vis
San Juan Capistrano, CA 92675-5554, USA

Janet, Ernest (Athlete, Football Player)
385 Highpoint Ln
Chelan, WA 98816-9579, USA

Janeway, Michael C (Editor)
Fisk Hall
Evanston, IL 60201, USA

Janeway, Richard (Doctor)
1941 Georgia Ave
Winston Salem, NC 27104-3103, USA

Jang, Jeong (Athlete, Golfer)
8749 The Esplanade Apt 33
Orlando, FL 32836-7737, USA

Janik, Doug (Athlete, Hockey Player)
51 Senator Ave
Agawam, MA 01001-2129, USA

Janik, Tom (Athlete, Football Player)
4905 County Road 204
Falls City, TX 78113-3043, USA

Janikowski, Bruce (Athlete, Football Player)
2716 W 112th St
Shawnee Mission, KS 66211-3084, USA

Janis, Byron (Music Group, Musician)
165 W 57th St
New York, NY 10019-2201, USA

Janis, Conrad (Actor, Music Group, Musician)
1434 N Genesee Ave
Los Angeles, CA 90046-3930, USA

Janis, Elizabeth (Actor)
c/o Michael Greenwald *Don Buchwald & Associates Inc (LA)*
6500 Wilshire Blvd Ste 2200
Los Angeles, CA 90048-4942, USA

Janitz, John A (Business Person)
40 Westminster St
Providence, RI 02903-2525, USA

Jankins, Corey (Baseball Player)
456 S Church St Apt J1
Lexington, SC 29072-3342, USA

Jankowska-Cieslak, Jadwiga (Actor)
Ul Mazewiecka 6/8
Warsaw 00-950, POLAND

Jankowski, Gene F (Television Host)
901 15th St NW # 700
Washington, DC 20005-2327, USA

Jankowski, Lou (Athlete, Hockey Player)
1723 19 Ave NW
Calgary, AB T2M 1B4, Canada

Jankowski, Peter (Producer)
c/o Staff Member *Wolf Films Inc (LA)*
100 Universal City Plz Bldg 2252
Universal City, CA 91608-1002, USA

Jannazzo, Izzy (Boxer)
6924 62nd Ave
Flushing, NY 11379-1120, USA

Janney, Allison (Actor)
c/o Chris Henze *Thruline Entertainment*
9250 Wilshire Blvd Ground Fl
Beverly Hills, CA 90212, USA

Janney, Craig H (Athlete, Hockey Player)
4424 N 59th Pl
Phoenix, AZ 85018-3210, USA

Janotta, Howard (Athlete, Basketball Player)
18118 Brookwood Frst
San Antonio, TX 78258-4474, USA

Janov, Arthur (Philanthropist, Psychic)
c/o Staff Member *Reece Halsey North*
98 Main St # 704
Tiburon, CA 94920-2517, USA

Janowicz, Josh (Actor)
c/o Darren Goldberg *Global Creative*
1051 Cole Ave # B
Los Angeles, CA 90038-2601, USA

Janowitz, Gundula (Opera Singer)
3072 Kasten
75, AUSTRIA

Janowitz, Will (Actor)
c/o David Ginsberg *Insight*
1134 S Cloverdale Ave
Los Angeles, CA 90019-6737, USA

Janowski, Marek (Conductor)
3 Burlington Lane Chiswick
London W4 2TH, UNITED KINGDOM (UK)

Janseen, Daniel (Business Person)
33 Rue du Prince Albert
Brussels 1050, BELGIUM

Janseen, Famke (Actor, Model)
c/o Emily Gerson Saines *Brookside Artists Management (NY)*
250 W 57th St Ste 2303
New York, NY 10107-2399, USA

Jansen, Dan (Athlete, Speed Skater)
PO Box 3354
Mooresville, NC 28117-3354, USA

Jansen, Jim (Actor)
c/o Martin Gage *Gage Group, The (LA)*
14724 Ventura Blvd Ste 505
Sherman Oaks, CA 91403-3505, USA

Jansen, Raymond A (Publisher)
235 Pinelawn Rd
Melville, NY 11747-4226, USA

Jansons, Mariss (Conductor)
3 Burlington Lane Chiswick
London W4 2TH, UNITED KINGDOM (UK)

Janssen, Dani
2220 Avenue of the Stars Unit 2803
Los Angeles, CA 90067-5686

Janssen, Famke (Actor, Model)
c/o Emily Gerson Saines *Brookside Artists Management (NY)*
250 W 57th St Ste 2303
New York, NY 10107-2399, USA

Janssen, Frances (Athlete, Baseball Player)
4311 Mayflower Dr
Lafayette, IN 47909-3473, USA

Janssens, Mark (Athlete, Hockey Player)
115 Central Park W Apt 17A
New York, NY 10023-4295, USA

Jantz, Richard (Misc)
Anthropology
Knoxville, TN 37996-0001, USA

Jantzen, Linda (Stylist)
c/o Staff Member *Anyway Productions*
870 Avenue of the Americas
New York, NY 10001-4111, USA

January, Don (Golfer)
4139 Sicily Dr
Frisco, TX 75034-6659, USA

January, Don (Athlete, Golfer)
5006 Village Pl
Dallas, TX 75248-6029, USA

January, Lois (Actor)
PO Box 1233
Beverly Hills, CA 90213-1233, USA

Jany, Alexandre (Alex) (Swimmer)
104 Blvd Livon
Marseille 13007, FRANCE

Janzen, Daniel H (Biologist)
Biology Dept
Philadelphia, PA 19104, USA

Janzen, Edmund (Religious Leader)
8000 W 21st St N
Wichita, KS 67205-1744, USA

Janzen, Lee (Athlete, Golfer)
9088 Point Cypress Dr
Orlando, FL 32836-5476, USA

Janzen, Marty (Athlete, Baseball Player)
14 Fernery Ln
Safety Harbor, FL 34695-5211, USA

Jaqua, Jon (Athlete, Football Player)
34320 McKenzie View Dr
Eugene, OR 97408-9205, USA

Jaquess, Pete (Athlete, Football Player)
631 Cunningham Ln
El Cajon, CA 92019-3504, USA

Jardine, Al
PO Box 36
Big Sur, CA 93920-0036

Jardine, Alan C (Al) (Musician)
PO Box 36
Big Sur, CA 93920-0036, USA

Jarecki, Andrew (Director, Musician, Producer)
c/o Staff Member *Hit the Ground Running Films*
200 W 57th St Ste 1304
New York, NY 10019-3227, USA

Jarman Jr, Claude (Actor)
16 Tamal Vista Ln
Kentfield, CA 94904 1006, USA

Jarmoluk, Mike (Athlete, Football Player)
4546 NW 34th Pl
Ocala, FL 34482-8355, USA

Jarmusch, Jim (Director)
c/o Bart Walker *Cinetic Management*
555 W 25th St Fl 4
New York, NY 10001-5542, USA

Jaroncyk, Ryan (Baseball Player)
2923 Roseann Ave
Escondido, CA 92027-5306, USA

Jarostchuk, Ilia (Athlete, Football Player)
13 Ladyslipper Ln
Stow, MA 01775-4504, USA

Jarreau, Al (Musician)
c/o Staff Member *Agency for the Performing Arts (APA-LA)*
405 S Beverly Dr Ste 500
Beverly Hills, CA 90212-4425, USA

Jarrell, Tom
77 W 66th St
New York, NY 10023-6201

Jarrett, Dale (Race Car Driver)
1510 46th Ave NE
Hickory, NC 28601-8421, USA

Jarrett, Doug (Athlete, Hockey Player)
3486 Maisonneuve Ave
Windsor, ON N9E 1Y8, Canada

Jarrett, Gary (Athlete, Hockey Player)
9662 E Peak View Rd
Scottsdale, AZ 85262-2352, USA

Jarrett, Keith (Composer, Musician)
PO Box 4774
Santa Barbara, CA 93140-4774, USA

Jarrett, Ned (Race Car Driver)
3182 Ninth Tee Dr
Newton, NC 28658-8725, USA

Jarriel, Thomas E (Tom) (Correspondent)
77 W 66th St
New York, NY 10023-6201, USA

Jarrier, Jean-Pierre
17 bd. Larvotto
Monte Carlo, MONACO

Jarryd, Anders (Tennis Player)
Maaneskoldsgatan 37
Lidkoping 531 00, SWEDEN

Jars of Clay (Music Group)
c/o Staff Member *Creative Artists Agency (CAA-LA)*
2000 Avenue of the Stars Ste 100
Los Angeles, CA 90067-4705, USA

Jaru the Damaja (Musician)
1325 Avenue of the Americas
New York, NY 10019-6026, USA

Jaruzelski, Wojciech (General, President)
Ul Klonowa 1
Warsaw 02-001, POLAND

Jarvi, Neeme (Conductor)
PO Box 305
Sea Bright, NJ 07760-0305, USA

Jarvi, Paavo (Conductor)
1241 Elm St
Cincinnati, OH 45202-7531, USA

Jarvis, Bruce (Athlete, Football Player)
4153 Issaquah Pine Lake Rd SE
Sammamish, WA 98075-6243, USA

Jarvis, Curtis (Athlete, Football Player)
401 Albert Dr
Gardendale, AL 35071-2588, USA

Jarvis, Doug (Athlete, Coach, Hockey Player)
c/o Staff Member *Montreal Canadiens*
1275 Rue Saint-Antoine O
Montreal, QB H3C 5L2, Canada

Jarvis, Graham
15351 Via De Las Olas
Pacific Palisades, CA 90272-4648

Jarvis, James (Athlete, Basketball Player)
PO Box 154
Asotin, WA 99402-0154, USA

Jarvis, Katie (Actor)
c/o Billy Lazarus *United Talent Agency (UTA)*
9560 Wilshire Blvd Fl 5
Beverly Hills, CA 90212-2400, USA

Jarvis, Kevin (Athlete, Baseball Player)
1613 Whispering Hills Dr
Franklin, TN 37069-7242, USA

Jarvis, Lucy
171 W 57th St
New York, NY 10019-2203

Jarvis, Martin
2-4 Noel St
London, ENGLAND W1V 3RB

Jarvis, Pat (Athlete, Baseball Player)
4201 Providence Ln
Tucker, GA 30084-2630, USA

Jarvis, Ray (Athlete, Baseball Player)
15 Higgins St Apt 106
Smithfield, RI 02917-4033, USA

Jarvis, Ray (Athlete, Football Player)
19155 Hi View Dr
Brookfield, WI 53045-3684, USA

Jarvis, Wes (Athlete, Hockey Player)
1215 Stellar Dr
Newmarket, ON L3Y 7B8, Canada

Jason, David (Actor)
c/o Staff Member *Lynda Ronan Personal Management*
Hunters House 1 Redcliffe Road
London SW20 9NR, UK

Jason, Harvey
1280 Sunset Plaza Dr
Los Angeles, CA 90069-1245

Jason, Peter (Actor)
c/o Staff Member *Diverse Talent Group*
9911 W Pico Blvd Ste 340W
Los Angeles, CA 90035-2712, USA

Jason, Sybil (Actor)
19200 Salt Lake Pl # Pi
Northridge, CA 91326-2345, USA

Jason & deMarco (Music Group)
c/o Staff Member *RJN Music!*
8033 W Sunset Blvd # 574
West Hollywood, CA 90046-2401, USA

Jasper, Edward (Athlete, Football Player)
110 N Price St
Troup, TX 75789-1429, USA

Jasrai, Puntsagiin (Prime Minister)
Ulan Bator, MONGOLIA

Jaster, Larry (Athlete, Baseball Player)
1105 Mill Creek Dr
Saint Johns, FL 32259-8973, USA

Jastremski, Chet (Swimmer)
1920 E 3rd St
Bloomington, IN 47401-3739, USA

Jastrow, Terry L (Director)
13201 Old Oak Ln
Los Angeles, CA 90049-2501, USA

Jastrow II, Kenneth M (Business Person)
303 S Temple Dr
Diboll, TX 75941-2419, USA

Jata, Paul (Athlete, Baseball Player)
117 Hidden Ridge Ct
Highland Heights, KY 41076-8506, USA

Jathar, Anjali (Actor, Bollywood)
Anand Ashram 1st Floor Building 22
Pandita Rambai Road Gamdevi
Mumbai, MS 400007, INDIA

Jatoi, Ghulan Mustafa (Prime Minister)
18 Khayaban-E-Shamsheer Housing #V
Karachi, PAKISTAN

Jaumotte, Andre (Engineer)
33 Ave jeanne Bte 17
Brussels 1050, BELGIUM

Jauregui, Jessica (Stylist)
c/o Staff Member *Help Me Rhonda*
541 10th St NW # 294
Atlanta, GA 30318-5713, USA

Jauron, Dick M (Athlete, Coach, Football Coach, Football Player)
76 Lou Groza Blvd
Berea, OH 44017-1238, USA

Javan, Ali (Physicist)
12 Hawthorne St
Cambridge, MA 2138, USA

Javed, Miandad Khan (Cricketer)
Gaddafi Stadium
Lahore, PAKISTAN

Javerbaum, David (Writer)
c/o Staff Member *3 Arts Entertainment Inc*
9460 Wilshire Blvd Fl 7
Beverly Hills, CA 90212-2713, USA

Javier, Julian (Athlete, Baseball Player)
P.O. Box 71
San Francisco de Macoris, Dominican Republic

Javier, Stan (Athlete, Baseball Player)
11544 NW 43rd Ter
Doral, FL 33178-4235, USA

Javier Galvan Y Fama (Music Group)
c/o Staff Member *Sony Music Miami*
605 Lincoln Rd Ste 700
Miami Beach, FL 33139-2901, USA

Javierre Ortas, Antonio M Cardinal (Religious Leader)
Via Rusticucci 13
Rome 193, ITALY

Jaworski, Marian Cardinal (Religious Leader)
Ploscha Katedraina 1
29008, UKRAINE

Jaworski, Ronald V (Ron) (Athlete, Football Player, Sportscaster)
18 Brookwood Dr
Medford, NJ 08055-8178, USA

Jax, Garth (Athlete, Football Player)
12014 E Lake Cir
Greenwood Village, CO 80111-5290, USA

Jay, Bob (Athlete, Hockey Player)
25 Winmere Ave
Burlington, MA 01803-4854, USA

Jay, Joey (Athlete, Baseball Player)
7209 Battenwood Ct
Tampa, FL 33615-2023, USA

Jay, Ken (Musician)
9100 Wilshire Blvd Ste 400W
Beverly Hills, CA 90212-3464, USA

Jay, Natalie
6230 Wilshire Blvd Ste 153
Los Angeles, CA 90048-5199

Jay, Peter (Government Official)
Hensington Farmhouse Woodstock
Oxon OX20 1LH, UNITED KINGDOM (UK)

Jay, Ricky (Actor)
1790 Broadway Ste 1000
New York, NY 10019-1412, USA

Jay, Tony (Actor)
c/o Staff Member *Pakula/King & Associates*
9229 W Sunset Blvd Ste 315
Los Angeles, CA 90069-3403, USA

Jay & The Americans
1045 Pomme De Pin Ln
New Port Richey, FL 34655-5627

Jay & The Techniques
4250 Aia S # D-11
St. Augustine, FL 32080-7431

Jayabharathi (Actor, Bollywood)
75 4th Cross Street Loghia Colony
Saligramam
Chennai, TN 600093, INDIA

Jayachitra (Actor, Bollywood)
Lynwood Avenue 9 Lady Madhavan Nair Road Mahalingapuram Gandhi Nagar
Chennai, TN 600093, INDIA

Jayamalini (Actor, Bollywood)
1 1st Mail Road Thirunagar
Chennai, TN 600026, INDIA

Jayanthi (Actor, Bollywood)
873 19th Main Bana Shankari II Stage
Bangalore, KA 500070, INDIA

Jayapradha (Actor, Bollywood)
1 Hindi Prachara Sabha Road T Nagar
Chennai, TN 600017, INDIA

Jayasudha (Actor, Bollywood)
Veenas Colony 9-13 II Street
Chennai, TN 600018, INDIA

Jaymes, Terry (Radio Personality)
c/o Staff Member *The Lex & Terry Morning Radio Network*
11700 Central Pkwy
Jacksonville, FL 32224-2600, USA

Jayne, Billy
8521 Nash Dr
Los Angeles, CA 90046-7705

Jayston, Michael (Actor)
125 Gloucester Road
London SW7 4TE, UNITED KINGDOM (UK)

Jay-Z (Musician, Producer)
255 W 36th St Ste 1501
New York, NY 10018-7757, USA

Jazz Crusaders, The (Music Group)
225 W 57th St Fl 5
New York, NY 10019-2136

Jazzyfatnastees (Music Group)
c/o Staff Member *Paradigm (Monterey)*
404 W Franklin St
Monterey, CA 93940-2303, USA

Jbara, Gregory (Actor)
c/o Marilyn Szatmary *Silver Massetti & Szatmary (SMS) Talent Inc*
8730 W Sunset Blvd Ste 440
Los Angeles, CA 90069-2277, USA

JBJ (Musician)
729 7th Ave Ste 1600
New York, NY 10019-6880, USA

J-Bolt (Producer)
3342 S Sandhill Rd Ste 9-424
Las Vegas, NV 89121-3455, USA

Jean (Royalty)
PB 331
2013, LUXEMBOURG

Jean, Gloria (Actor, Musician)
3844 W Channel Islands Blvd # 166
Oxnard, CA 93035-4001, USA

Jean, Wyclef (Musician)
c/o Staff Member *WmE2 (WMA-LA)*
1 William Morris Pl
Beverly Hills, CA 90212-4261, USA

Jean-Baptiste, Marianne (Actor)
c/o Elise Konialian *Untitled Entertainment (NY)*
322 8th Ave Ste 601
New York, NY 10001-6715, USA

Jeangerard, Robert (Bob) (Athlete, Basketball Player)
1930 Belmont Ave
San Carlos, CA 94070-4731, USA

Jean-Louis, Jimmy (Actor)
c/o Alex Cole *Elevate Entertainment*
10100 Santa Monica Blvd Ste 300
Los Angeles, CA 90067-4107, USA

Jeanmaire, ZiZi (Actor, Ballerina)
20 Blvd Gabes
Marseilles 13008, FRANCE

Jeanrenaud, Joan (Musician)
1235 9th Ave
San Francisco, CA 94122-2306, USA

Jeantot, Philippe (Yachtsman)
Siege: BP 01
Les Sables D'Olonne 85100, FRANCE

Jecha, Ralph (Athlete, Football Player)
717 Vinewood Ave
Willow Springs, IL 60480-1523, USA

Jee, Elizabeth (Actor)
8383 Wilshire Blvd Ste 850
Beverly Hills, CA 90211-2443, USA

Jee, Rupert (Business Person)
213 W 53rd St
New York, NY 10019-5805

Jeelani, Abdul (Athlete, Basketball Player)
W525 State Road 59
Palmyra, WI 53156-9741, USA

Jeetendra (Actor, Bollywood)
Plot No 26 Greater Bombay Co-Op Society Gulmohar Cross Road No 5 JVPD Scheme
Mumbai, MS 400049, INDIA

Jeffcoat, Don (Actor)
c/o Staff Member *House of Representatives, The*
1434 6th St Ste 1
Santa Monica, CA 90401-2527, USA

Jeffcoat, James W (Jim) (Athlete, Football Player)
5135 Summit Hill Dr
Dallas, TX 75287-7537, USA

Jeffcoat, Mike (Athlete, Baseball Player)
4224 Oak Springs Dr
Arlington, TX 76016-4508, USA

Jefferies, Gregg (Athlete, Baseball Player)
7806 Bernal Ave
Pleasanton, CA 94588-7050, USA

Jeffers, Eve Jihan (Actor, Producer)
c/o Amanda Silverman *42West (NY)*
220 W 42nd St Fl 12
New York, NY 10036-7200, USA

Jeffers, Patrick (Athlete, Football Player)
5810 Buckpasser Cv
Austin, TX 78746-1450, USA

Jeffers, Rusty (Athlete)
PO Box 30081
Phoenix, AZ 85046-0081

Jefferson, Al (Athlete, Basketball Player)
c/o Jeff Schwartz *Excel Sports Management*
9665 Wilshire Blvd Ste 500
Beverly Hills, CA 90212-2312, USA

Jefferson, George (Athlete, Track Athlete)
9414 Petit Cir
Ventura, CA 93004-2213, USA

Jefferson, James (Athlete, Football Player)
11220 NE 53rd St
Kirkland, WA 98033-7505, USA

Jefferson, Jesse (Athlete, Baseball Player)
1421 Railroad Ave
Midlothian, VA 23113-4330, USA

Jefferson, John L (Athlete, Football Player)
43590 Merchant Mill Ter
Leesburg, VA 20176-8228, USA

Jefferson, Reggie (Athlete, Baseball Player)
1881 Raymond Tucker Rd
Tallahassee, FL 32311-8793, USA

Jefferson, Richard (Basketball Player)
390 Murray Hill Pkwy
East Rutherford, NJ 07073-2109, USA

Jefferson, Roy (Athlete, Football Player)
8813 Queen Elizabeth Blvd
Annandale, VA 22003-4247, USA

Jefferson, Stan (Athlete, Baseball Player)
2420 Hunter Ave Apt 3E
Bronx, NY 10475-5644, USA

Jefferson, Thad (Athlete, Football Player)
PO Box 1552
Rialto, CA 92377-1552, USA

Jefferson Starship (Music Group)
c/o Staff Member *Mission Control*
15030 Ventura Blvd # 541
Sherman Oaks, CA 91403-5470, USA

Jeffery, Aaron (Actor)
c/o Robert Marsala *Global Creative*
1051 Cole Ave # B
Los Angeles, CA 90038-2601, USA

Jeffires, Haywood (Athlete, Football Player)
2601 Courtyard Ln
Pearland, TX 77584-3000, USA

Jeffory, Dawn (Actor)
PO Box 447
Herndon, VA 20172-0447, USA

Jeffre, Justin (Musician)
83 Riverside Dr
New York, NY 10024-5713, USA

Jeffrey, Arthur F (War Hero)
7305 Englewood Hill Pl
Yakima, WA 98908-1267, USA

Jeffrey, Larry (Athlete, Hockey Player)
35392 Blyth Rd RR 5
Goderich, ON N7A 3Y2, Canada

Jeffrey, Richard C (Misc)
55 Patton Ave
Princeton, NJ 08540-5251, USA

Jeffreys, Anne (Actor)
18915 Nordhoff St Ste 5
Northridge, CA 91324-3790, USA

Jeffreys, Harold (Astronomer)
160 Huntingdon Road
Cambridge CB3 0LB, UNITED KINGDOM (UK)

Jeffries, Chris (Basketball Player)
Air Canada Center 40 Bay St
Toronto, ON M5J 2NB, CANADA

Jeffries, Doug (Adult Film Star)
c/o Staff Member *Diva Central Inc*
7510 W Sunset Blvd Ste 1445
Los Angeles, CA 90046-3408, USA

Jeffries, Herb (Musician)
44489 Town Center Way
Palm Desert, CA 92260-2723, USA

Jeffries, Jared (Basketball Player)
MCI Centre 601 F St NW
Washington, DC 20004, USA

Jeffries, John T (Astronomer)
1652 E Camino Cielo
Tucson, AZ 85718-1105, USA

Jeffries, Willie (Athlete, Football Coach)
c/o Staff Member *College Football Hall Of Fame*
111 S Saint Joseph St
South Bend, IN 46601-1901, USA

Jelen, Ben (Musician)
c/o Staff Member *Maverick Recording Co (LA)*
3300 Warner Blvd
Burbank, CA 91505-4632, USA

Jelesky, Tom (Athlete, Football Player)
9556 W 1160 N
Demotte, IN 46310-9634, USA

Jelic, Chris (Athlete, Baseball Player)
33 Allegheny Ave Apt 5
Cuddy, PA 15031-9763, USA

Jelinek, Elfriede (Nobel Prize Laureate)
c/o Staff Member *Rowohlt Verlag*
Hamburger Strasse 17
Reinbek 21465, Germany

Jelinek, Tomas (Athlete, Hockey Player)
c/o Staff Member *Calgary Flames*
P.O. Box 1540 Stn M
Calgary, AB T2P 3B9, Canada

Jelks, Greg
615 Bay Springs Rd
Centre, AL 35960-1212, USA

Jelks, Greg (Athlete, Baseball Player)
PO Box 501
Slippery Rock, PA 16057-0501, USA

Jelley, Thomas (Athlete, Football Player)
200 Tabernacle Rd
Black Mountain, NC 28711-7733, USA

Jellicoe, George P J R (Government Official)
Tidcombe Manor Tidcombe near Marlborough
Wilts SN8 2SL, UNITED KINGDOM (UK)

Jeltz, Steve (Athlete, Baseball Player)
606 W 28th Pl
Lawrence, KS 66046-4620, USA

Jem (Musician)
c/o Seth Friedman *Red Light Management (LA)*
8439 W Sunset Blvd Ste 2
Los Angeles, CA 90069-1925, USA

Jemison, Antawn (Basketball Player)
MCI Centre 601 F St NW
Washington, DC 20004, USA

Jemison, Eddie (Actor)
c/o Gabrielle Krengel *Domain Talent*
9229 W Sunset Blvd Ste 710
Los Angeles, CA 90069-3407, USA

Jemison, Theodore J (Religious Leader)
1620 White's Creek Pike
Nashville, TN 37207, USA

Jencks, William P (Misc)
11 Revere St
Lexington, MA 02420-4419, USA

Jendresen, Erik (Producer, Writer)
c/o Staff Member *WmE2 (Endeavor-LA)*
9601 Wilshire Blvd Fl 3
Beverly Hills, CA 90210-5219, USA

Jendrick, Megan (Athlete, Swimmer)
1 Olympic Plz
Colorado Springs, CO 80909-5780, USA

Jenes Jr, Theodore G (General)
809 169th Pl SW
Lynnwood, WA 98037-3307, USA

Jeni, Richard (Comedian)
c/o Staff Member *Agency for the Performing Arts (APA-LA)*
405 S Beverly Dr Ste 500
Beverly Hills, CA 90212-4425, USA

Jenifer, Franklyn G (Educator)
President's Office
Richardson, TX 75083, USA

Jenke, Noel (Athlete, Football Player)
17665 Bonnie Ln
Brookfield, WI 53045-7800, USA

Jenkin of Roding, Patrick F (Government Official)
703 Howard House Dolphin Square
London SW1V 3PQ, UNITED KINGDOM (UK)

Jenkins, Alfred le Sesne (Diplomat)
PO Box 586
Front Royal, VA 22630-0013, USA

Jenkins, Andrew (Actor)
c/o Jon Simmons *Simmons & Scott Entertainment*
7942 Mulholland Dr
Los Angeles, CA 90046-1225, USA

Jenkins, Bill (Race Car Driver)
153 Pennsylvania Ave
Malvern, PA 19355-2419

Jenkins, Bill (Grumpy) (Misc)
153 Pennsylvania Ave
Malvern, PA 19355-2419, USA

Jenkins, Carter (Actor)
c/o Mary Sanders *inMomentum Management*
14622 Ventura Blvd # 778
Sherman Oaks, CA 91403-3600, USA

Jenkins, Charlie (Athlete, Track Athlete)
Once RCA Dome Indianapolis
IN, 46225

Jenkins, Cullen (Athlete, Football Player)
49124 Peninsular Dr
Belleville, MI 48111-4966, USA

Jenkins, Daniel (Actor)
8730 W Sunset Blvd Ste 440
Los Angeles, CA 90069-2277, USA

Jenkins, David W (Figure Skater)
5947 S Atlanta Ave
Tulsa, OK 74105-7545, USA

Jenkins, Dean (Athlete, Hockey Player)
244 Fairmount St
Lowell, MA 01852-3708, USA

Jenkins, Don (Athlete, Football Player)
49 W Main St
Frostburg, MD 21532-1640, USA

Jenkins, Don J (War Hero)
3770 Bowling Green Rd
Morgantown, KY 42261-8219, USA

Jenkins, Ed (Athlete, Football Player)
1750 Washington St Ste B1
Boston, MA 02118-1831, USA

Jenkins, Ferguson (Athlete, Baseball Player)
3655 W Anthem Way Ste A109
Anthem, AZ 85086-0430, USA

Jenkins, Fletcher (Athlete, Football Player)
2347 S J St
Tacoma, WA 98405-3831, USA

Jenkins, Geoff (Athlete, Baseball Player)
6683 E Judson Rd
Paradise Valley, AZ 85253-4369, USA

Jenkins, George (Designer, Director)
2402 4th St Apt 10
Santa Monica, CA 90405-3668, USA

Jenkins, Hayes Alan (Figure Skater)
3183 Regency Pl
Westlake, OH 44145-6735, USA

Jenkins, Izel (Athlete, Football Player)
5106 Masters Ln N
Wilson, NC 27896-9136, USA

Jenkins, James (Baseball Player)
630 Malcolm X Blvd
New York, NY 10037-1247, USA

Jenkins, Jay (Young Jezzy) (Musician)
c/o Laura Wright *Avid Exposure*
8721 W Sunset Blvd PH 3
West Hollywood, CA 90069-2273, USA

Jenkins, Jerry B (Writer)
PO Box 80
Wheaton, IL 60187-0080, USA

Jenkins, Kackie (Butch) (Actor)
PO Box 541G
Fairview, NC 28730, USA

Jenkins, Ken (Actor)
c/o Chris Schmidt *Paradigm (LA)*
360 N Crescent Dr
Beverly Hills, CA 90210-4874, USA

Jenkins, Kerry (Athlete, Football Player)
5492 Scout Trace Ln
Birmingham, AL 35244-3912, USA

Jenkins, Kris (Athlete, Football Player)
623 Eagle Rock Ave # 106
West Orange, NJ 07052-2948, USA

Jenkins, Loren (Journalist)
1150 15th St NW
Washington, DC 20071-0001, USA

Jenkins, Lynn (Congressman, Politician)
1122 Longworth Hob
Washington, DC 20515-3209, USA

Jenkins, Marilyn (Baseball Player)
1511 Van Auken St SE
Grand Rapids, MI 49508-2511, USA

Jenkins, Mark (Writer)
c/o Staff Member *HarperCollins Publishers*
10 E 53rd St C/O Author Mail Floor 7
New York, NY 10022, USA

Jenkins, Patty (Director, Writer)
c/o Michael Sugar *Anonymous Content (AC-LA)*
3531 Hayden Ave
Culver City, CA 90232, USA

Jenkins, Paul (Artist)
PO Box 6833
New York, NY 10150-6833, USA

Jenkins, Richard (Actor)
c/o Rhonda Price *Gersh (NY)*
41 Madison Ave
New York, NY 10010-2202, USA

Jenkins, Robert (Athlete, Football Player)
2878 Fieldview Ter
San Ramon, CA 94583-1900, USA

Jenkins, Stephan (Music Group, Musician)
c/o Eric Godtland *Eric Godtland Management*
1040 Mariposa St Ste 200
San Francisco, CA 94107-2520, USA

Jenkins, Tom (Athlete, Golfer)
107 Ranch Road 620 S
Lakeway, TX 78734-3942, USA

Jenner, Brody (Reality TV Star)
c/o Eric Podwall *Podwall Entertainment*
710 N Orlando Ave Apt 203
Los Angeles, CA 90069-5549, USA

Jenner, Bruce (Athlete, Reality TV Star)
c/o Evan Morgenstein *Premier Management Group (PMG Sports)*
115 Crescent Commons Dr Ste 250
Cary, NC 27518-8134, USA

Jenner, Kris (Business Person, Reality TV Star)
4774 Park Granada Ste 5
Calabasas, CA 91302-3355, USA

Jenney, Lucinda
1505 10th St
Santa Monica, CA 90401-2805

Jennings, Bill (Athlete, Baseball Player)
7065 Foxcroft Dr
Saint Louis, MO 63123-1648, USA

Jennings, Brandon (Athlete, Basketball Player)
c/o Bill Duffy *BDA Sports Management (BDA-CA)*
700 Ygnacio Valley Rd Ste 330
Walnut Creek, CA 94596-3838, USA

Jennings, Dave (Athlete, Football Player)
1 Briarcliff Rd
Upper Saddle River, NJ 07458-1401, USA

Jennings, David T (Dave) (Athlete, Football Player)
1 Briarcliff Rd
Upper Saddle River, NJ 07458-1401, USA

Jennings, Delbert O (War Hero)
3701 25th Way SE
Olympia, WA 98501-0909, USA

Jennings, Doug
3030 Canterbury Dr
Boca Raton, FL 33434-3348, USA

Jennings, Doug (Athlete, Baseball Player)
PO Box 812692
Boca Raton, FL 33481-2692, USA

Jennings, Garth (Director)
c/o Frank Wuliger *Gersh (LA)*
9465 Wilshire Blvd Ste 600
Beverly Hills, CA 90212-2612, USA

Jennings, Grant (Athlete, Hockey Player)
PO Box 190434
Anchorage, AK 99519-0434, USA

Jennings, Greg (Athlete, Football Player)
c/o Eugene Parker *Maximum Sports Management*
6435 W Jefferson Blvd # 197
Fort Wayne, IN 46804-6203, USA

Jennings, Jason (Athlete, Baseball Player)
5274 Monterey Dr
Frisco, TX 75034-4087, USA

Jennings, Jonas (Athlete, Football Player)
123 Davis Rd
Fayetteville, GA 30215-4912, USA

Jennings, Keith (Athlete, Football Player)
3424 W Torreys Peak Dr
Superior, CO 80027-4638, USA

Jennings, Keith (Athlete, Basketball Player)
695 Holly Crest Dr
Culpeper, VA 22701-3071, USA

Jennings, Ken (Actor)
c/o Staff Member *JEOPARDY!*
10202 Washington Blvd
Culver City, CA 90232-3119

Jennings, Lyfe (Musician)
c/o Staff Member *Sony/RCA Records*
550 Madison Ave Fl 6
New York, NY 10022-3211, USA

Jennings, Lynn (Athlete, Track Athlete)
17 Cushing Rd
Newmarket, NH 03857-1720, USA

Jennings, Paul C (Engineer)
640 S Grand Ave
Pasadena, CA 91105-2423, USA

Jennings, Richard (Athlete, Football Player)
6499 Park Riviera Way
Sacramento, CA 95831-1053, USA

Jennings, Robert B (Doctor)
Medical Center Pathology Dept
Durham, NC 27710-0001, USA

Jennings, Robert Y (Judge)
61 Bridle Way Grantchester
Cambridge CB3 9NY, UNITED KINGDOM (UK)

Jennings, Robin (Athlete, Baseball Player)
PO Box 981191
Park City, UT 84098-1191, USA

Jennings, Shooter (Musician)
c/o Michael Moses *Baker Winokur Ryder Public Relations (BWR-LA)*
9100 Wilshire Blvd Ste 500 PMB WEST
Beverly Hills, CA 90212-3426, USA

Jennings, Stanford (Athlete, Football Player)
215 Jasmine Way
Alpharetta, GA 30004-4254, USA

Jennings, Will (Musician, Songwriter)
c/o Staff Member *Gorfaine/Schwartz Agency Inc*
4111 W Alameda Ave Ste 509
Burbank, CA 91505-4171, USA

Jenrette, Richard H (Business Person)
67 E 93rd St
New York, NY 10128-1331, USA

Jens, Salome (Actor)
9229 W Sunset Blvd Ste 311
Los Angeles, CA 90069-3403, USA

Jens, Walter (Writer)
Sonnenstr 5
Tubingen, GERMANY

Jensen, Arthur R (Misc)
3330 S Lake Dr
Kelseyville, CA 95451-9042, USA

Jensen, Bob (Athlete, Football Player)
72420 Morningstar Rd
Rancho Mirage, CA 92270-4072, USA

Jensen, David (Athlete, Hockey Player)
65 Cheryl Ln
Holliston, MA 01746-1234, USA

Jensen, David (Athlete, Hockey Player)
19455 Vine Ridge Rd
Excelsior, MN 55331-9173, USA

Jensen, Derrick (Athlete, Football Player)
147 Downing St
Panama City, FL 32413-3650, USA

Jensen, Elwood V (Misc)
Medical Nutrition Dept
Huddinge 141 86, SWEDEN

Jensen, James (Misc)
Geology Dept
Provo, UT 84602, USA

Jensen, Jerry (Athlete, Football Player)
2714 86th St SE
Everett, WA 98208-3548, USA

Jensen, Jim (Athlete, Football Player)
9811 N Oak Knoll Cir
Davie, FL 33324-6406, USA

Jensen, Jim D (Athlete, Football Player)
36205 S Rose Lake Rd
Frazee, MN 56544-8904, USA

Jensen, Karen (Actor)
9363 Wilshire Blvd # 212
Beverly Hills, CA 90210, USA

Jensen, Luke (Tennis Player)
370 Ferry Lndg NW
Atlanta, GA 30328-3539

Jensen, Marcus (Athlete, Baseball Player)
19550 N Grayhawk Dr Unit 1134
Scottsdale, AZ 85255-3987, USA

Jensen, Maren (Actor)
15260 Ventura Blvd Ste 1040
Sherman Oaks, CA 91403-5345

Jensen, Roger W (Ex-Senator)
3542 Pennyroyal Rd
Port Charlotte, FL 33953-4606, USA

Jensen, Ryan (Athlete, Baseball Player)
3059 S Larkspur St
Gilbert, AZ 85295-2034, USA

Jensen, Steve (Athlete, Hockey Player)
24921 Arena Dr
Deerwood, MN 56444-8780, USA

Jensen Jr, James W (Cinematographer)
28853 Garnet Hill Ct
Agoura Hills, CA 91301-2130, USA

Jent, Chris (Athlete, Basketball Player)
445 Retreat Ln W
Powell, OH 43065-9768, USA

Jeong, Ken (Actor)
c/o Brett Carducci *Sovereign Talent Group*
8421 Wilshire Blvd Ste 200
Beverly Hills, CA 90211-3204, USA

Jepsen, Les (Athlete, Basketball Player)
8075 9th Street Way N
Saint Paul, MN 55128-5360, USA

Jeray, Nicole (Athlete, Golfer)
3728 Ridgeland Ave
Berwyn, IL 60402-4020, USA

Jeremiah (Musician)
c/o Staff Member *Siri Music Entertainment*
1324 Lexington Ave
New York, NY 10128-1145, USA

Jeremiah, David E (Admiral)
2898 Melanie Ln
Oakton, VA 22124-1809, USA

Jeremy, Ron (Adult Film Star)
c/o Michael (Mike) Esterman *Esterman.Com, LLC*
Prefers to be contacted via email
MD, USA

Jericho, Chris (Athlete, Wrestler)
c/o Michael Braverman *Braverman/Bloom Company*
14320 Ventura Blvd Ste 632
Sherman Oaks, CA 91423-2717, USA

Jerkens, H Allen (Horse Racer)
9509 242nd St
Floral Park, NY 11001-3906, USA

Jermann, David (Artist)
2 Union St
Sparkill, NY 10976

Jernberg, Sixten (Skier)
Fritidsby 780
Lima 7806, SWEDEN

Jernigan, Tamara E (Tammy) (Astronaut)
4268 Brindisi Pl
Pleasanton, CA 94566-2238, USA

Jernstedt, Ken (War Hero)
911 Pine St
Hood River, OR 97031-1968, USA

Jerusalem, Siegfried (Opera Singer)
Sudring 9
Eckental 90542, GERMANY

Jeruzelski, Wojciech (President)
Al Jerozolimskie 91
Warsaw 02-001, POLAND

Jervey, Travis (Athlete, Football Player)
747 Glossy Ibis Ln
Kiawah Island, SC 29455-5912, USA

Jerzembeck, Mike (Athlete, Baseball Player)
10625 S Hall Dr
Charlotte, NC 28270-0285, USA

Jessamy, Charles (Athlete, Football Player)
1836 S Shenandoah St
Los Angeles, CA 90035-4327, USA

Jessee, Michael A (Financier)
PO Box 990411
Boston, MA 02199-0411, USA

Jessen, Ruth (Athlete, Golfer)
2823 NE Meadow Pl
Lake Forest Park, WA 98155-5348, USA

Jessica (lil mama)Kirkland, Niatia (Musician)
c/o Staff Member *Jive Records*
550 Madison Ave Fl 6
New York, NY 10022-3211, USA

Jessie, Ron (Athlete, Football Player)
202 17th St Apt B
Huntington Beach, CA 92648-8426, USA

Jessie, Tim (Athlete, Football Player)
155 Cedar Ave
Shepherdsville, KY 40165-6465, USA

Jessie J (Musician)
c/o Solomon Parker *WmE2 (WMA-UK)*
103 New Oxford St
London WC1A 1DD, UK

Jessup, Bill (Athlete, Football Player)
13341 Saint Andrews Dr Unit 137D
Seal Beach, CA 90740-4139, USA

Jestadt, Garry (Athlete, Baseball Player)
9875 E Larkspur Dr
Scottsdale, AZ 85260-5145, USA

Jester, Virgil (Athlete, Baseball Player)
8130 Raleigh Pl
Westminster, CO 80031-4317, USA

Jet (Actor)
c/o Staff Member *Creative Artists Agency (CAA-LA)*
2000 Avenue of the Stars Ste 100
Los Angeles, CA 90067-4705, USA

Jeter, Derek (Athlete, Baseball Player)
845 Union Plz
New York, NY 10017-3540, USA

Jeter, Gary M (Athlete, Football Player)
32725 Shadowbrook Dr
Solon, OH 44139-6007, USA

Jeter, John (Athlete, Baseball Player)
113 Bayside Dr
West Monroe, LA 71291-8693, USA

Jeter, Perry (Athlete, Football Player)
772 Lincoln Blvd
Steubenville, OH 43952-3256, USA

Jeter, Robert D (Bob) (Athlete, Football Player)
7147 S Paxton Ave
Chicago, IL 60649-2523, USA

Jeter, Shawn (Athlete, Baseball Player)
4287 Walford St
Columbus, OH 43224-2342, USA

Jeter, Tommy (Athlete, Football Player)
14 Slate Path Dr
Spring, TX 77382-2009, USA

Jeter, Tony (Athlete, Football Player)
71 S Orange Ave
South Orange, NJ 07079-1715, USA

Jethro Tull (Music Group)
c/o Staff Member *WmE2 (WMA-LA)*
1 William Morris Pl
Beverly Hills, CA 90212-4261, USA

Jetsons (Music Group)
5727 Topanga Canyon Blvd Apt 3
Woodland Hills, CA 91367-4847

Jett, Brent W (Astronaut)
2529 Goldsmith St
Houston, TX 77030-1815, USA

Jett, Jack E (Television Host)
c/o Collin Reno *WmE2 (WMA-LA)*
1 William Morris Pl
Beverly Hills, CA 90212-4261, USA

Jett, James (Athlete, Football Player)
PO Box 430
Kearneysville, WV 25430-0430, USA

Jett, Joan (Musician)
c/o Lillian LaSalle *Sweet180*
141 W 28th St Rm 300
New York, NY 10001-6187, USA

Jett, John (Athlete, Football Player)
18521 Northumberland Hwy
Reedville, VA 22539-3412, USA

Jetton, Paul (Athlete, Football Player)
1062 Harmon Hills Rd
Dripping Springs, TX 78620-3642, USA

Jeunet, Jean-Pierre (Director)
8942 Wilshire Blvd # 219
Beverly Hills, CA 90211-1908, USA

Jeung, Peggi (Stylist)
c/o Staff Member *Artist Untied (LA)*
845 S Mansfield Ave Apt 1
Los Angeles, CA 90036-4979, USA

Jevanord, Oystein (Musician)
11 Elvaston Place #300
London SW7 5QC, UNITED KINGDOM (UK)

Jewell, Buddy (Musician)
c/o Staff Member *WmE2 (WMA-TN)*
1600 Division St Ste 300
Nashville, TN 37203-2755, USA

Jewell, Geri (Actor)
c/o Staff Member *Kazarian Spencer Ruskin & Assoc.*
11969 Ventura Blvd Ste 300
Studio City, CA 91604-2619, USA

Jewett, Robert (Athlete, Football Player)
991 N Shore Dr
Springport, MI 49284-9414, USA

Jewison, Norman F (Actor, Director, Producer, Writer)
c/o Staff Member *Yorktown Productions Ltd*
18 Gloucester Ln Floor 5
Toronto ON M4Y 1L5, CANADA

Jewitt-Beckett, Christine (Baseball Player)
PO Box 126
Stewart Valley, SK S0N 2P0, CANADA

Jhabvala, Ruth Prawer (Writer)
400 E 52nd St
New York, NY 10022-6404, USA

Jhene (Musician)

Jhulka, Ayesha (Actor, Bollywood)
102 Tirupati Apartments 7 Bungalows
Versova Andheri W
Mumbai, MS 400061, INDIA

Jia, Li (Misc)
Medical Center Hematology Dept
Durham, NC 27708-0001, USA

Jiahua, Zou (Government Official)
Jhong Nan Hai
Beijing, CHINA

Jiang, Tian (Musician)
165 W 57th St
New York, NY 10019-2201, USA

Jiang, Tiefeng (Artist)
690 Bridgeway
Sausalito, CA 94965-2251, USA

Jiang, Zemin (President)
Zhonganahai
Beijing, CHINA

Jiles, Dwayne (Athlete, Football Player)
3712 Churchill Ct
Plano, TX 75075-6119, USA

Jiles, Pam (Athlete, Track Athlete)
2623 Wisteria St
New Orleans, LA 70122-6041

Jiles, Pamela (Pam) (Athlete, Track Athlete)
2623 Wisteria St
New Orleans, LA 70122-6041, USA

Jillette, Penn (Comedian)
4132 S Rainbow Blvd # 377
Las Vegas, NV 89103-3106, USA

Jillian, Ann (Actor)
PO Box 57739
Sherman Oaks, CA 91413-2739, USA

Jillson, Jeff (Athlete, Hockey Player)
14 Lincoln Dr
North Smithfield, RI 02896-6955, USA

Jimenez, Carlos (Architect)
1116 Willard St
Houston, TX 77006-1238, USA

Jimenez, Flaco (Misc)
4031 Panama Ct
Piedmont, CA 94611-4930, USA

Jimenez, Joe (Athlete, Golfer)
PO Box 1737
Boerne, TX 78006-6737, USA

Jimenez, Manny (Baseball Player)
7080 Central Ave
Lemon Grove, CA 91945-2112, USA

Jimenez, Miguel Angel (Athlete, Golfer)
1751 Pinnacle Dr Ste 1500
Mc Lean, VA 22102-3833, USA

Jimenez, Nicario (Artist)
5531 Teak Wood Dr
Naples, FL 34119-2515, USA

Jimenez, Ubaldo (Athlete, Baseball Player)
c/o Pat Rooney *SFX Baseball*
400 Skokie Blvd Ste 280
Northbrook, IL 60062-7939, USA

Jimenez Pons, Eduardo (Writer)
c/o Gabriel Blanco *Gabriel Blanco Iglesias (Mexico)*
Rio Balsas 35-32 Colonia Cuauhtemoc
DF 6500, Mexico

Jimerson, Charlton (Athlete, Baseball Player)
22048 Betlen Way
Castro Valley, CA 94546-6504, USA

Jiminez, Houston (Athlete, Baseball Player)
30 Buchanan Pl Attn Coachingstaff
Asheville, NC 28801-4243, USA

Jiminez, Miguel (Athlete, Baseball Player)
128 Post Ave
New York, NY 10034-3432, USA

Jimmy Eat World (Music Group)
722 Seward St
Los Angeles, CA 90038-3504

Jin, Svoboda (Director)
Na Balkane 120
Prague 3, CZECH REPUBLIC

Jindal, Bobby (Governor)
PO Box 94004
Baton Rouge, LA 70804-9004, USA

Jindrak, Mark (Wrestler)
2355 Reyer Rd
Auburn, NY 13021

Jinks, Dan (Actor, Producer)
c/o Staff Member *Jinks/Cohen Company*
4000 Warner Blvd Bldg 138
Burbank, CA 91522-0001, USA

Jirsa, Ron (Coach)
Athletic Dept
Athens, GA 30613, USA

Jischke, Martin C (Educator)
President S Ofc
Ames, IA 50011-0001, USA

JJ Grey and Mofro (Music Group, Musician)
c/o Jesse Aratow *Madison House Inc.*
771 Santa Fe Dr Ste 204
Denver, CO 80204-4440, USA

Joanou, Phil (Actor, Director)
c/o Todd Smith *Todd Smith and Associates*
11835 W Olympic Blvd Ste 640E
Los Angeles, CA 90064-5000, USA

Job, Brian (Swimmer)
PO Box 70427
Sunnyvale, CA 94086-0427, USA

Jobe, Brandt (Athlete, Golfer)
2224 King Fisher Dr
Westlake, TX 76262-4815, USA

Jobe, Frank W (Doctor)
501 E Hardy St Ste 200
Inglewood, CA 90301-4057, USA

Jobert, Marlene (Actor)
c/o Staff Member *ArtMedia*
20 avenue Rapp
Paris 75008, France

Jobko, William (Athlete, Football Player)
770 Fawn Ct
Loganville, GA 30052-3270, USA

Jobrani, Maz (Actor)
c/o Mitchell Stubbs *Mitchell K Stubbs & Assoc (MKS)*
8675 Washington Blvd Ste 203
Culver City, CA 90232-7486, USA

Jobs, Steve (Business Person, Producer)
1 Infinite Loop
Cupertino, CA 95014-2083, USA

Joc, Yung (Musician)
c/o Jack Iannaci *Brass Artists & Associates*
9025 Wilshire Blvd Ste 400
Beverly Hills, CA 90211-1828, USA

Jocketty, Walt (Athlete, Baseball Player)
903 Adams Crossing Unit 308
Cincinnati, OH 45202-3573, USA

Jodat, Jim (Athlete, Football Player)
25032 Mammoth Cir
El Toro, CA 92630-2515, USA

Jodie, Brett (Athlete, Baseball Player)
1359 Corley Mill Rd
Lexington, SC 29072-7635, USA

Jodzio, Rick (Athlete, Hockey Player)
31202 Boca Raton Pl
Laguna Niguel, CA 92677-2484, USA

Joe (Musician)
c/o Staff Member *Jive Records*
550 Madison Ave Fl 6
New York, NY 10022-3211, USA

Joe, Billy (Athlete, Football Player)
3964 Butler Springs Way
Hoover, AL 35226-6234, USA

Joe, Cheryl (Stylist)
2312 Colt Rd
Rancho Palos Verdes, CA 90275-6502, USA

Joe, Fat (Actor, Musician)
c/o Drew Elliot *Media Artists Group (NY)*
140 E 46th St PH C
New York, NY 10017-2633, USA

Joe, William (Billy) (Football Player)
Athletic
Tallahassee, FL 32307-0001, USA

Joel, Billy (Musician, Songwriter)
c/o Keri Aylward *Maritime Music*
34 Audrey Ave Unit 5
Oyster Bay, NY 11771-1559, USA

Joel, Katie Lee (Actor)
c/o Jonathan Rosen *WmE2 (WMA-NY)*
1325 Avenue of the Americas
New York, NY 10019-6026, USA

Joel, Richard M (Educator)
President's Office 500 W 185th St
New York, NY 10033, USA

Joelson, Tsianina (Actor)
c/o Sherry Marsh *Marsh Entertainment*
12444 Ventura Blvd Ste 203
Studio City, CA 91604-2409, USA

Joens, Michael (Writer)
c/o Natasha Kern *Natasha Kern Literary Agency*
PO Box 1069
White Salmon, WA 98672-1069, USA

Joey & T (Stylist)
c/o Staff Member *Fred Segal Beauty*
PO Box 5304
Beverly Hills, CA 90209-5304, USA

Joffee, Roland V (Director, Producer)
c/o Craig Baumgarten *Baumgarten Management*
406 Wilshire Blvd
Santa Monica, CA 90401-1410, USA

Jofre, Eder (Boxer)
Alamo de Ministero Rocha Azevedo 373
C Cesar 21-15
Sao Paulo, BRAZIL

Jogia, Avan (Actor)
c/o Alejandra Cristina *Ace PR*
4122 Sunnyslope Ave
Sherman Oaks, CA 91423-4308, USA

Jogis, Chris (Athlete)
7 Birch Rd
Larchmont, NY 10538-1526

Johannesen, Lena (Athlete)
PO Box 325
Culver City, CA 90232-0325

Johannsen, Jake (Actor, Comedian)
c/o Pam Ellis *Ellis Talent Group*
4705 Laurel Canyon Blvd Ste 300
Valley Village, CA 91607-5901, USA

Johannson, John (Athlete, Hockey Player)
38371 US 71
Lake George, MN 56458, USA

Johannsson, Kristian (Opera Singer)
119 W 57th St Ste 1505
New York, NY 10019-2403, USA

Johansen, David (Musician)
c/o Nina Nisenholtz *N2N Entertainment*
1230 Montana Ave Ste 203
Santa Monica, CA 90403-5987, USA

Johansen, Iris (Writer)
c/o Author Mail *Bantam-Dell Publishing (NY)*
1745 Broadway
New York, NY 10019-4368, USA

Johansen, John M (Architect)
821 Broadway
New York, NY 10003-4702, USA

Johansen, Trevor (Athlete, Hockey Player)
6741 N Placita Acebo
Tucson, AZ 85750-1049, USA

Johanson, Donald C (Misc)
Human Origins Institute
Tempe, AZ 85287-0001, USA

Johanson, Erika (Writer)
c/o Gabriel Blanco *Gabriel Blanco Iglesias (Mexico)*
Rio Balsas 35-32 Colonia Cuauhtemoc
DF 6500, Mexico

Johanson, Sue (Talk Show Host)
42 Pardee Ave
Toronto, ON M6K 3H5, CANADA

Johanssen, David
9200 W Sunset Blvd Ste 900
Los Angeles, CA 90069-3604

Johansson, Bjorn (Athlete, Hockey Player)
Stenkulla
Odensbacken S-71593, Sweden

Johansson, Calle (Athlete, Hockey Player)
1708 Mayfair Pl
Crofton, MD 21114-2625, USA

Johansson, Kathy (Model)
PO Box 43351
Tucson, AZ 85733-3351

Johansson, Ove (Athlete, Football Player)
3511 Goodfellow Ln
Amarillo, TX 79121-1613, USA

Johansson, Paul (Actor)
c/o Gordon Gilbertson *Gilbertson Management*
1334 3rd Street Promenade Ste 201
Santa Monica, CA 90401-1320, USA

Johansson, Per-Ulrik (Athlete, Golfer)
18710 SE Pineneedle Ln
Jupiter, FL 33469-1702, USA

Johansson, Scarlett (Actor)
c/o CeCe Yorke *True Public Relations*
6725 W Sunset Blvd Ste 470
Los Angeles, CA 90028-7180, USA

Johjima, Kenji (Athlete, Baseball Player)
2412 109th Ave SE
Bellevue, WA 98004-7332, USA

John, Caspar (Admiral)
Trethewey Mousehole Penzance
Cornwall, UNITED KINGDOM (UK)

John, David D (Misc)
7 Cyncoed Ave
Cardiff CF2 6ST, WALES

John, Elton (Musician, Producer, Songwriter)
c/o Frank Presland *Twenty-First Artists Ltd (UK)*
1 Blythe Rd
London W14 OHG, UK

John, Gottfried (Actor)
Elisabethweg 4
Utting, GERMANY D-86919

John, Tommy (Athlete, Baseball Player)
6202 Seton House Ln
Charlotte, NC 28277-4524, USA

John, Tylyn (Model)
813 Harbor Blvd # 133
W Sacramento, CA 95691-2201

Johnny & The Hurricanes
195 Hannum Ave
Rossford, OH 43460-1109

Johns, Bibi
D-82049
Pullach, GERMANY

Johns, Cindy (Actor)
PO Box 369
Arlington, TX 76004-0369

Johns, Daniel (Musician)
PO Box 281
Sunny Hills, NSW 2010, AUSTRALIA

Johns, Don (Athlete, Hockey Player)
226 Evergreen Dr
Beaconsfield, BC H9W 2A9, Canada

Johns, Doug (Athlete, Baseball Player)
1131 SW 72nd Ave
Plantation, FL 33317-4125, USA

Johns, Freeman (Athlete, Football Player)
906 Sally Cir
Wichita Falls, TX 76301-7230, USA

Johns, Glynis (Actor)
c/o Staff Member *Marshak/Zachary Company, The*
8840 Wilshire Blvd Fl 1
Beverly Hills, CA 90211-2606, USA

Johns, Jasper (Artist)
97 Low Rd # 642
Sharon, CT 06069-2017, USA

Johns, Keith (Athlete, Baseball Player)
PO Box 55066
Little Rock, AR 72215-5066, USA

Johns, Lori (Race Car Driver)
4418 Congressional Dr
Corpus Christi, TX 78413-2624, USA

Johns, Marcus (Actor)
c/o Sharon Lane *Lane Management Group*
13017 Woodbridge St
Studio City, CA 91604-1431, USA

Johns, Milton (Actor)
78 Temple Sheen Rd
London SW14 7RJ, ENGLAND

Johns, Stratford
29 Mostyn Rd Merton Park
London, ENGLAND SW19 3LL

Johnson, Aaron (Athlete, Hockey Player)
3810 Gabrielle Dr
Dublin, OH 43016-7281, USA

Johnson, Aaron Perry (Actor)
c/o Cynthia Pett-Dante *Brillstein Entertainment Partners*
9150 Wilshire Blvd Ste 350
Beverly Hills, CA 90212-3453, USA

Johnson, Abigail (Business Person)
82 Devonshire St # V8C
Boston, MA 02109-3605, USA

Johnson, Adam (Athlete, Baseball Player)
7335 Heritage Palms Estate Dr
Fort Myers, FL 33966-5724, USA

Johnson, Addison (Cartoonist)
c/o Staff Member *King Features Syndication*
300 W 57th St Fl 15
New York, NY 10019-5238, USA

Johnson, Adrian (Athlete, Baseball Player)
8102 Meadville St
Houston, TX 77061-3111, USA

Johnson, Alex (Athlete, Baseball Player)
18425 Bretton Dr
Detroit, MI 48223-1311, USA

Johnson, Alexz (Actor)
c/o Staff Member *WmE2 (WMA-LA)*
1 William Morris Pl
Beverly Hills, CA 90212-4261, USA

Johnson, Allen (Athlete, Track Athlete)
1751 Pinnacle Dr Ste 1500
McLean, VA 22102-3833, USA

Johnson, Alonzo (Athlete, Football Player)
PO Box 134
Stanley, NC 28164-0134, USA

Johnson, Amy Jo (Actor)
c/o Joanna (Joanie) Burstein *Burstein Company, The*
15304 W Sunset Blvd Ste 208
Pacific Palisades, CA 90272-3656, USA

Johnson, Andreas (Musician)
c/o Staff Member *United Stage Artist*
Box 11029
Stockholm S-10061, Sweden

Johnson, Andrew (Athlete, Basketball Player)
1101 Oak Cir
Lansdale, PA 19446-6057, USA

Johnson, Andy (Athlete, Football Player)
PO Box 6828
Athens, GA 30604-6828, USA

Johnson, Anjelah (Actor)
c/o Dave Rath *Generate Management*
1545 26th St Ste 200
Santa Monica, CA 90404-3554, USA

Johnson, Anne-Marie (Actor)
2522 Silver Lake Ter
Los Angeles, CA 90039-2608, USA

Johnson, Anthony (Athlete, Football Player)
752 Peppervine Ave
Jacksonville, FL 32259-5272, USA

Johnson, Anthony (Athlete, Basketball Player)
5162 Inwood Pl
Mableton, GA 30126-7612, USA

Johnson, April (Stylist)
c/o Staff Member *Independent Artists*
448 E Riverdale Ave
Orange, CA 92865-1302, USA

Johnson, Art (Athlete, Baseball Player)
25 Sekelsky Dr
Stratford, CT 06614-1509, USA

Johnson, Arte (Actor, Comedian)
2725 Bottlebrush Dr
Los Angeles, CA 90077-2009, USA

Johnson, Ashley (Actor)
c/o Doreen Wilcox Little *Anonymous Content (AC-LA)*
3531 Hayden Ave
Culver City, CA 90232, USA

Johnson, Avery (Athlete, Basketball Player, Coach)
c/o Staff Member *HarperCollins Publishers*
10 E 53rd St C/O Author Mail Floor 7
New York, NY 10022, USA

Johnson, Bart (Athlete, Baseball Player)
1929 N Newland Ave
Chicago, IL 60707-3308, USA

Johnson, Bart (Actor)
c/o Matt Luber *Luber Roklin Management*
8530 Wilshire Blvd Ste 550
Beverly Hills, CA 90211-3133, USA

Johnson, Batsey L (Designer, Fashion Designer)
498 Fashion Ave Rm 2103
New York, NY 10018-6735, USA

Johnson, Ben (Athlete, Baseball Player)
112 Locksley Dr
Greenwood, SC 29649-9185, USA

Johnson, Betsey (Designer, Fashion Designer)
c/o Staff Member *Betsey Johnson*
498 Seventh Ave Fl 21
New York, NY 10018, USA

Johnson, Beverly (Actor, Model)
c/o Nancy Chaidez *Nancy Chaidez & Associates*
6818 Longridge Ave
North Hollywood, CA 91605-4740, USA

Johnson, Bill (Actor)
c/o Mike Pruitt *Actors Clearinghouse*
501 N 1H35
Austin, TX 78702, USA

Johnson, Bill (Athlete, Baseball Player)
629 Traces Dr
Florence, SC 29501-5823, USA

Johnson, Bill (Athlete, Football Player)
3399 Hartwood Rd
Cleveland Heights, OH 44112-3027, USA

Johnson, Bill (Congressman, Politician)
317 Cannon Hob
Washington, DC 20515-3602, USA

Johnson, Bob (Athlete, Baseball Player)
265 Quari St
Aurora, CO 80011-8339, USA

Johnson, Bob (Athlete, Football Player)
165 Magnolia Ave
Cincinnati, OH 45246-4506, USA

Johnson, Bob (Athlete, Hockey Player)
32361 Hearthstone Rd
Farmington Hills, MI 48334-3438, USA

Johnson, Bob D (Athlete, Baseball Player)
650 Caves Hwy
Cave Junction, OR 97523-9820, USA

Johnson, Bob W (Athlete, Baseball Player)
1474 Barclay St
Saint Paul, MN 55106-1406, USA

Johnson, Brent (Athlete, Hockey Player)
808 N Florida St
Arlington, VA 22205-1153, USA

Johnson, Brian (Musician)
c/o Christopher Dalston *Creative Artists Agency (CAA-LA)*
2000 Avenue of the Stars Ste 100
Los Angeles, CA 90067-4705, USA

Johnson, Brian (Athlete, Baseball Player)
7595 E Placita Vista Del Bosque
Tucson, AZ 85715-3651, USA

Johnson, Brooks (Coach)
Athletic Dept
Stanford, CA 94305, USA

Johnson, Bryce (Actor)
c/o Staff Member *Artists Production Group (APG)*
9348 Civic Center Dr Fl 2
Beverly Hills, CA 90210-3610, USA

Johnson, Buck (Athlete, Basketball Player)
701 Pine Grove Rd
Harvest, AL 35749-9050, USA

Johnson, Butch (Athlete, Football Player)
9719 Red Oakes Dr
Highlands Ranch, CO 80126-3595, USA

Johnson, Calvin
c/o Bus Cook *Bus Cook Sports, Inc*
1 Willow Bend Dr
Hattiesburg, MS 39402-8552, USA

Johnson, Carl (Athlete, Football Player)
8818 S Shannon Dr
Tempe, AZ 85284-3528, USA

Johnson, Carolyn Dawn (Musician, Songwriter)
c/o Staff Member *Creative Artists Agency (CAA-TN)*
3310 W End Ave Fl 5
Nashville, TN 37203-1028, USA

Johnson, Cecil (Athlete, Football Player)
1481 NW 103rd St Apt 260
Miami, FL 33147-1409, USA

Johnson, Chad (Athlete, Football Player)
2899 Juniper Ln
Davie, FL 33330-1349, USA

Johnson, Charles (Athlete, Baseball Player)
12301 NW 7th St
Plantation, FL 33325-1729, USA

Johnson, Charles L (Charley) (Athlete, Football Player)
1660 Boulders Dr
Las Cruces, NM 88011-4054, USA

Johnson, Charles R (Writer)
English Dept
Seattle, WA 98105, USA

Johnson, Charlie W (Athlete, Football Player)
1400 Willow Ave
Louisville, KY 40204-2506, USA

Johnson, Chris (Actor)
c/o Staff Member *Luber Roklin Management*
8530 Wilshire Blvd Ste 550
Beverly Hills, CA 90211-3133, USA

Johnson, Chris (Athlete, Golfer)
6210 W Sunset Rd
Tucson, AZ 85743-9581, USA

Johnson, Chris (Athlete, Football Player)
c/o Denise White *EAG Sports Management*
12910 Agustin Pl
Playa Vista, CA 90094-2301, USA

Johnson, Chuck (Athlete, Football Player)
1203 N Avenue M
Freeport, TX 77541-3611, USA

Johnson, Clark
9560 Wilshire Blvd # 516
Beverly Hills, CA 90212-2427

Johnson, Claude (Juan) (Musician)
27 L Ambiance Ct
Bardonia, NY 10954-1421, USA

Johnson, Clay (Athlete, Basketball Player)
6306 N Strathbury Ave
Kansas City, MO 64151-4331, USA

Johnson, Clemon (Athlete, Basketball Player)
835 N Waukeenah St
Monticello, FL 32344-2119, USA

Johnson, Cliff (Athlete, Baseball Player)
9618 Mediator Pass
Converse, TX 78109-1925, USA

Johnson, Cornelius (Athlete, Football Player)
603 Dale St
Highland Springs, VA 23075-1611, USA

Johnson, Courtney (Misc)
8472 W Granite Dr
Granite Bay, CA 95746-9569, USA

Johnson, Craig (Athlete, Hockey Player)
812 Island Dr Apt A
Alameda, CA 94502-6797, USA

Johnson, Curley (Athlete, Football Player)
5512 Wedgefield Rd
Granbury, TX 76049-4411, USA

Johnson, Curt (Producer, Writer)
c/o Evan Corday *Evolution Entertainment (LA)*
901 N Highland Ave
Los Angeles, CA 90038-2412, USA

Johnson, Curtis (Baseball Player)
PO Box B-188
St Rose, LA 70087, USA

Johnson, Curtis (Athlete, Football Player)
2015 Calumet Ave
Toledo, OH 43607-1608, USA

Johnson, D J (Athlete, Football Player)
3814 Kingsbury Dr
Louisville, KY 40207-4443, USA

Johnson, Dale (Actor)
c/o Staff Member *LA Models/LA Talent Agency*
7700 W Sunset Blvd Ste 203
Los Angeles, CA 90046-3913, USA

Johnson, Dane (Athlete, Baseball Player)
2652 Big Pine Dr
Holiday, FL 34691-8761, USA

Johnson, Dave (Misc)
4207 Lebanon Pike
Hermitage, TN 37076-1200, USA

Johnson, Dave (Athlete, Baseball Player)
3202 Woodhollow Cir
Abilene, TX 79606-4211, USA

Johnson, Dave (Athlete, Baseball Player)
7101 Mount Vista Rd
Kingsville, MD 21087-1728, USA

Johnson, Davey (Athlete, Baseball Player, Coach)
1064 Howell Branch Rd
Winter Park, FL 32789-1004, USA

Johnson, David (Dave) (Athlete, Track Athlete)
PO Box 2713
Azusa, CA 91702, USA

Johnson, David G (Economist)
1700 E 56th St Apt 1306
Chicago, IL 60637-1934, USA

Johnson, David W (Business Person)
1 Campbell Pl
Camden, NJ 08103-1701, USA

Johnson, Demetrios (Athlete, Football Player)
840 Garonne Dr
Ballwin, MO 63021-5656, USA

Johnson, Dennis (Athlete, Football Player)
PO Box 467
Hawthorne, NJ 07507-0467, USA

Johnson, DerMarr (Basketball Player)
201 E Jefferson St
Phoenix, AZ 85004-2412, USA

Johnson, Dick (Athlete, Baseball Player)
704 Novak Ln
Big Rapids, MI 49307-2534, USA

Johnson, Don (Actor)
c/o Justin Grey Stone *Untitled Entertainment (LA)*
350 S Beverly Dr Ste 200
Beverly Hills, CA 90212-4819, USA

Johnson, Don (Athlete, Baseball Player)
1529 NE 21st Ave Apt 205
Portland, OR 97232-1579, USA

Johnson, Don (Athlete, Baseball Player)
3935 King Pl
Cincinnati, OH 45223-2407, USA

Johnson, Dwayne (The Rock) (Actor)
c/o Michael Donkis *Prime*
9696 Culver Blvd Ste 102
Culver City, CA 90232-2734, USA

Johnson, Dwight (Athlete, Football Player)
1812 King Cole Dr
Waco, TX 76705-2753, USA

Johnson, Earl (Bowler)
3625 Woody Ln
Minnetonka, MN 55305-4265, USA

Johnson, Earl (Athlete, Football Player)
340 S Keech St
Daytona Beach, FL 32114-4622, USA

Johnson, Ed (Athlete, Basketball Player)
196 Adobe Ln
Mount Airy, NC 27030-5658, USA

Johnson, Eddie (Athlete, Basketball Player)
PO Box 542
Weirsdale, FL 32195-0542, USA

Johnson, Edward (Eddie) (Athlete, Basketball Player)
6133 N 61st Pl
Paradise Valley, AZ 85253-4209, USA

Johnson, Eric (Actor)
c/o Jai Khanna *Brillstein Entertainment Partners*
9150 Wilshire Blvd Ste 350
Beverly Hills, CA 90212-3453, USA

Johnson, Eric (Musician)
PO Box 5249
Austin, TX 78763-5249, USA

Johnson, Eric (Athlete, Golfer)
893 Chateau Meadows Dr
Eugene, OR 97401-7046, USA

Johnson, Erik (Athlete, Baseball Player)
PO Box 2989
San Ramon, CA 94583-7989, USA

Johnson, Ernest (Athlete, Baseball Player)
3106 Bowdoin St
Des Moines, IA 50313-4613, USA

Johnson, Ernie (Athlete, Baseball Player)
6350 Polo Club Dr
Cumming, GA 30040-6597, USA

Johnson, Ervin (Basketball Player)
Target Center 600 1st Ave N
Minneapolis, MN 55403, USA

Johnson, Essex (Athlete, Football Player)
1633 E Dimondale Dr
Carson, CA 90746-2914, USA

Johnson, Ezra (Athlete, Football Player)
330 Millhaven Lndg
Fayetteville, GA 30215-8179, USA

Johnson, Farnham (Athlete, Football Player)
190 Beech Ave
Winfield, AL 35594-5200, USA

Johnson, Footer (Athlete, Baseball Player)
5001 E Main St
Mesa, AZ 85205-8008, USA

Johnson, Frank (Athlete, Basketball Player, Coach)
4320 N 40th St
Phoenix, AZ 85018-4105, USA

Johnson, Frank (Athlete, Baseball Player)
1151 Cypress Hill Ln
Stockton, CA 95206-6245, USA

Johnson, Gary (Athlete, Baseball Player)
50 Tallwood Ct
Atherton, CA 94027-6432, USA

Johnson, Gary (Athlete, Football Player)
1620 Fullerton St Apt 1314
Shreveport, LA 71107-6415, USA

Johnson, Gary E. (Ex-Governor, Politician)
1623 Connecticut Ave NW Fl 3
Washington, DC 20009-1098, USA

Johnson, Gary L (Athlete, Football Player)
450 Oliver Rd
Haughton, LA 71037-8942, USA

Johnson, Georgann (Actor)
218 Glenroy Pl
Los Angeles, CA 90049-2420, USA

Johnson, George (Athlete, Golfer)
2860 Brookford Ln SW
Atlanta, GA 30331-8119, USA

Johnson, George T (Athlete, Basketball Player)
630 Highland Overlook
Atlanta, GA 30349-3919, USA

Johnson, Graham R (Musician)
83 Fordwych Road
London NW2 3TL, UNITED KINGDOM (UK)

Johnson, Greg (Athlete, Hockey Player)
1186 Sparkle
Rochester Hills, MI 48306-3568, USA

Johnson, Gregory C (Astronaut)
1002 Applewood Dr
Friendswood, TX 77546-5202, USA

Johnson, Hailey Noelle (Actor)
c/o Staff Member *TalentWorks (LA)*
3500 W Olive Ave Ste 1400
Burbank, CA 91505-5512, USA

Johnson, Hansford T (General)
9800 Fredericksburg Rd
San Antonio, TX 78284, USA

Johnson, Harold (Boxer)
6101 Morris St
Philadelphia, PA 19144-3763, USA

Johnson, Haylie (Actor)
c/o Lin Bickelmann *Encore Artists Management*
3815 W Olive Ave Ste 101
Burbank, CA 91505-4674, USA

Johnson, Haynes B (Journalist)
Communications Studies Ctr
Washington, DC 20052-0001, USA

Johnson, Holly (Musician)
PO Box 770850
Orlando, FL 32877-0850, USA

Johnson, Howard (Athlete, Baseball Player)
8597 SE Coconut St
Hobe Sound, FL 33455-2914, USA

Johnson, I Birger (Engineer)
1508 Barclay Pl
Niskayuna, NY 12309-4120, USA

Johnson, Ian (Journalist)
200 Liberty St
New York, NY 10281-1003, USA

Johnson, J Bradley (Brad) (Athlete, Football Player)
1911 Nellie Gray Ct
Athens, GA 30606-8605, USA

Johnson, J J
648 Broadway # 703
New York, NY 10012-2348, USA

Johnson, J Seward (Artist)
2525 Michigan Ave Ste A6
Santa Monica, CA 90404-4031, USA

Johnson, Jack (Musician)
c/o Tom Chauncey *Partisan Arts*
1505 Bridgeway Ste 205
Sausalito, CA 94965-1968, USA

Johnson, James A (Financier)
3900 Wisconsin Ave NW
Washington, DC 20016-2806, USA

Johnson, James E (Johnnie) (War Hero)
Stables Hargate Hall Buxton
Derbyshire SK17 8TA, UNITED KINGDOM (UK)

Johnson, Jamey (Musician)
c/o Staff Member *Webster & Associates PR*
3573 Couchville Pike
Hermitage, TN 37076-4012, USA

Johnson, Jannette (Skier)
PO Box 901
Sun Valley, ID 83353-0901, USA

Johnson, Jason (Athlete, Baseball Player)
18122 Emerald Bay St
Tampa, FL 33647-3315, USA

Johnson, Jason (Athlete, Football Player)
6821 Eagle Pointe Ln Apt 1F
Indianapolis, IN 46254-4453, USA

Johnson, Jay (Actor, Comedian)
c/o Staff Member *WmE2 (WMA-LA)*
1 William Morris Pl
Beverly Hills, CA 90212-4261, USA

Johnson, Jay Kenneth (Actor)
c/o Jeff Morrone *Jeff Morrone Entertainment*
9350 Wilshire Blvd Ste 224
Beverly Hills, CA 90212-3204, USA

Johnson, Jeff (Athlete, Baseball Player)
424 N Hardee St
Durham, NC 27703-2254, USA

Johnson, Jenna (Coach, Swimmer)
PO Box 15016
Knoxville, TN 37901-5016, USA

Johnson, Jerome L (Admiral)
801 S Randolph St
Arlington, VA 22204-1563, USA

Johnson, Jerry (Athlete, Baseball Player)
16670 Espola Rd
Poway, CA 92064-1630, USA

Johnson, Jesse (Athlete, Football Player)
3308 Forest Hill Ave
Richmond, VA 23225-3434, USA

Johnson, Jim (Athlete, Hockey Player)
354 Edward Ave W
Winnipeg, MB R2C 2H8, Canada

Johnson, Jim (Athlete, Hockey Player)
34552 N Scottsdale Rd Suite D8
Scottsdale, AZ 85266, USA

Johnson, Jimmie (Race Car Driver)
4325 Papa Joe Hendrick Blvd
Charlotte, NC 28262-5701, USA

Johnson, Jimmy (Athlete, Football Coach, Football Player)
656 Amaranth Blvd
Mill Valley, CA 94941-2605, USA

Johnson, Jimmy (Cartoonist)
200 Madison Ave
New York, NY 10016-3903, USA

Johnson, Joanna (Actor)
c/o Staff Member *WmE2 (WMA-LA)*
1 William Morris Pl
Beverly Hills, CA 90212-4261, USA

Johnson, Joe (Basketball Player)
c/o Staff Member *Atlanta Hawks*
190 Marietta St NW Ste 405
Atlanta, GA 30303-2717, USA

Johnson, Joe (Athlete, Baseball Player)
14 Evergreen Rd
Plainville, MA 02762-1902, USA

Johnson, Johari (Actor)
3500 W Olive Ave Ste 1400
Burbank, CA 91505-5512, USA

Johnson, John (Athlete, Football Player)
133 Plymouth Dr
Lagrange, GA 30240-8537, USA

Johnson, John (Athlete, Basketball Player)
4751 N 18th St
Milwaukee, WI 53209-6430, USA

Johnson, John (Athlete, Golfer)
236 E Hemlock St
Oxnard, CA 93033-3619, USA

Johnson, John H (Athlete, Football Player)
330 S Michigan Ave Apt 1606
Chicago, IL 60604-4453, USA

Johnson, John Henry (Athlete, Football Player)
4144 W 62nd St
Los Angeles, CA 90043-3613, USA

Johnson, John Henry (Athlete, Baseball Player)
3345 Delna Dr
Sparks, NV 89431-1408, USA

Johnson, Johnny (Athlete, Football Player)
929 Delaware Ave
Santa Cruz, CA 95060-6403, USA

Johnson, Jonathan (Athlete, Baseball Player)
101 Broad Bluff Pt
Irmo, SC 29063-2934, USA

Johnson, Joseph (Athlete, Football Player)
4113 Cherrylaurel Ln
Winston Salem, NC 27106-3574, USA

Johnson, Junior (Race Car Driver)
1100 Glen Oaks Dr
Hamptonville, NC 27020-8279, USA

Johnson, Keith (Athlete, Baseball Player)
PO Box 4122
Park City, UT 84060-4122, USA

Johnson, Ken (Athlete, Baseball Player)
121 Myrtlewood Dr
Pineville, LA 71360-4325, USA

Johnson, Kenneth (Athlete, Football Player)
536 E 169th St
Carson, CA 90746-1105, USA

Johnson, Kenneth (Athlete, Football Player)
1334 NW 42nd St
Miami, FL 33142-4812, USA

Johnson, Kenneth (Athlete, Basketball Player)
1401 N Wheeler Ave
Portland, OR 97227-1831, USA

Johnson, Kenny (Actor)
c/o Josh Katz *United Talent Agency (UTA)*
9560 Wilshire Blvd Fl 5
Beverly Hills, CA 90212-2400, USA

Johnson, Kermit (Athlete, Football Player)
3259 Lincoln Ave
Altadena, CA 91001-4141, USA

Johnson, Kevin (Baseball Player, Sportscaster)
30 Rockefeller Plz
New York, NY 10112-0015, USA

Johnson, Keyshawn (Football Player)
19232 Northfleet Way
Tarzana, CA 91356-5807, USA

Johnson, Kym (Actor)
c/o Siri Garber *Platform Public Relations*
2666 N Beachwood Dr
Los Angeles, CA 90068-2308, USA

Johnson, Lamar (Athlete, Baseball Player)
4105 Sangre Trl
Arlington, TX 76016-2972, USA

Johnson, Lamont (Director)
10100 Santa Monica Blvd Ste 1050
Los Angeles, CA 90067-4143, USA

Johnson, Lance (Athlete, Baseball Player)
5712 Foxfire Rd
Mobile, AL 36618-2653, USA

Johnson, Larry (Athlete, Football Player)
1 Arrowhead Dr
Kansas City, MO 64129-1651, USA

Johnson, Larry (Athlete, Baseball Player)
1905 E Jean St
Tampa, FL 33610-3546, USA

Johnson, Larry D (Basketball Player)
c/o Staff Member *Kansas City Chiefs*
1 Arrowhead Dr
Kansas City, MO 64129-1651, USA

Johnson, Laura
1917 Weepah Way
Los Angeles, CA 90046-7722

Johnson, Laurie (Composer)
Priority House Camp Hill Stanmore
Middx HA7 3JQ, UNITED KINGDOM (UK)

Johnson, Lee (Athlete, Football Player)
1173 McDaniel Ct
Alpine, UT 84004-1231, USA

Johnson, Leon (Athlete, Football Player)
813 Vine Arden Rd
Morganton, NC 28655-2758, USA

Johnson, Leshon (Athlete, Football Player)
PO Box 957
Haskell, OK 74436-0957, USA

Johnson, Lou (Athlete, Baseball Player)
4532 Valley Ridge Ave
Los Angeles, CA 90008-4827, USA

Johnson, Luci Baines
LBJ Ranch
Stonewall, TX 78701

Johnson, Luther (Guitar Jr) (Musician)
c/o Staff Member *Concerted Efforts*
PO Box 440326
Somerville, MA 02144-0004, USA

Johnson, Lynn-Holly (Actor)
178 S Victory Blvd Ste 205
Burbank, CA 91502-2881, USA

Johnson, Magic (Athlete, Basketball Player, Coach)
c/o Darren Prince *Prince Marketing Group*
18 Carillon Cir
Livingston, NJ 07039-2600, USA

Johnson, Manny (Athlete, Football Player)
c/o Chad Speck *Allegiant Athletic Agency*
35 Market Sq Ste 201
Knoxville, TN 37902-1420, USA

Johnson, Marc (Musician)
PO Box 29242
Oakland, CA 94604-9242, USA

Johnson, Margaret (Baseball Player)
625 Country Club Dr SE Apt 1D
Rio Rancho, NM 87124-2265, USA

Johnson, Mark (Boxer)
1204 Howison Pl SW
Washington, DC 20024-4132, USA

Johnson, Mark (Athlete, Baseball Player)
40 Helen Ave
Rye, NY 10580-2447, USA

Johnson, Mark (Athlete, Baseball Player)
109 Mossy Lake Rd
Perry, GA 31069-9217, USA

Johnson, Mark (Athlete, Golfer)
PO Box 2945
Soldotna, AK 99669-2945, USA

Johnson, Mark (Athlete, Hockey Player)
1609 Hidden Hill Dr
Verona, WI 53593-7971, USA

Johnson, Mark Steven (Actor, Director, Writer)
c/o Richard Lovett *Creative Artists Agency (CAA-LA)*
2000 Avenue of the Stars Ste 100
Los Angeles, CA 90067-4705, USA

Johnson, Mark Steven (Director, Writer)
c/o Eddie Michaels *Insignia Public Relations*
1507 20th St Ste D
Santa Monica, CA 90404-3474, USA

Johnson, Marques (Athlete, Basketball Player)
5133 Dawn View Pl
Los Angeles, CA 90043-2006, USA

Johnson, Marvin (Boxer)
5452 Turfway Cir
Indianapolis, IN 46228-2094, USA

Johnson, Marvin M (Engineer)
3055 SE Bison Rd
Bartlesville, OK 74006-7646, USA

Johnson, Maurice (Athlete, Football Player)
112 Mountainview Rd
Mount Laurel, NJ 08054-4729, USA

Johnson, Michael (Musician)
38 Music Sq E Ste 300
Nashville, TN 37203-4304, USA

Johnson, Michael D (Athlete, Track Athlete)
c/o Staff Member *Octagon*
2 Union St Ste 300
Portland, ME 04101-4295, USA

Johnson, Mickey (Athlete, Basketball Player)
3642 W Grenshaw St
Chicago, IL 60624-4207, USA

Johnson, Mike (Athlete, Baseball Player)
27632 N 42nd St
Cave Creek, AZ 85331-6614, USA

Johnson, Mike (Athlete, Baseball Player)
446 23rd Pl
Manhattan Beach, CA 90266-4307, USA

Johnson, Mitchell (Athlete, Football Player)
2764 Unicorn Ln NW
Washington, DC 20015-2234, USA

Johnson, Monica (Writer)
1505 10th St
Santa Monica, CA 90401-2805, USA

Johnson, Monte (Athlete, Football Player)
425 Laurel Chase Ct NW
Atlanta, GA 30327-4655, USA

Johnson, Nate (Athlete, Football Player)
846 W Chestnut St
Freeport, IL 61032-4951, USA

Johnson, Neil (Athlete, Basketball Player)
821 Plymouth Ln
Virginia Beach, VA 23451-5926, USA

Johnson, Nicholas (Lawyer, Writer)
PO Box 1876
Iowa City, IA 52244-1876, USA

Johnson, Nick (Athlete, Baseball Player)
8008 Sacramento St
Fair Oaks, CA 95628-7527, USA

Johnson, Norm (Athlete, Football Player)
400 Peachtree Industrial Blvd Apt 1615
Suwanee, GA 30024-6989, USA

Johnson, Norm (Athlete, Football Player)
8523 NW Anderson Hill Rd
Silverdale, WA 98383-9353, USA

Johnson, Norm (Athlete, Hockey Player)
16427 NE Tillamook St
Portland, OR 97230-5534, USA

Johnson, Norma Holloway (Judge)
333 Constitution Ave NW
Washington, DC 20001-2804, USA

Johnson, Norman (Musician)
PO Box 12
Far Hills, NJ 07931-0012, USA

Johnson, Ollie (Athlete, Basketball Player)
1700 Spring Garden St
Philadelphia, PA 19130-3936, USA

Johnson, Ora J (Religious Leader)
100 Stinson Dr
Poplar Bluff, MO 63901-8736, USA

Johnson, Paul (Athlete, Hockey Player)
1946 Nortonia Ave
Saint Paul, MN 55119-3727, USA

Johnson, Paul (Football Coach)
150 Bobby Dodd Way NW
Atlanta, GA 30332-2500, USA

Johnson, Paul B (Historian)
Coach House Over Stowey near Bridgewater
Somerset TA5 1HA, UNITED KINGDOM (UK)

Johnson, Penny
121 N San Vicente Blvd
Beverly Hills, CA 90211-2303

Johnson, Pete (Athlete, Football Player)
3737 Pendlestone Dr
Gahanna, OH 43230-6005, USA

Johnson, R E (Misc)
1370 Ontario St Ste 1040
Cleveland, OH 44113-1736, USA

Johnson, Rafer L (Actor, Athlete, Track Athlete)
4217 Woodcliff Rd
Sherman Oaks, CA 91403-4339, USA

Johnson, Ralph E (Architect)
330 N Wabash Ave Ste 3600
Chicago, IL 60611-3698, USA

Johnson, Randy (Athlete, Baseball Player)
10645 N Tatum Blvd Ste C200
Phoenix, AZ 85028-3090, USA

Johnson, Raylee (Athlete, Football Player)
3267 Wittman Way
San Diego, CA 92173-2890, USA

Johnson, Raymond Edward
167 Grieb Rd
Wallingford, CT 06492-2511

Johnson, Reed (Athlete, Baseball Player)
30137 Mira Loma Dr
Temecula, CA 92592-2127, USA

Johnson, Rian (Director, Writer)
c/o Brian Dreyfuss *Featured Artists Agency*
6210 Wilshire Blvd Ste 311
Los Angeles, CA 90048-5122, USA

Johnson, Richard K (Actor)
c/o Staff Member *Conway van Gelder*
8-12 Broadwick St
London W1F 8HW, UK

Johnson, Rob (Athlete, Football Player)
26635 Aracena Dr
Mission Viejo, CA 92691-5105, USA

Johnson, Robert (Business Person)
c/o Staff Member *BET - Black EntertainmentTelevision (DC)*
1235 W St NE
Washington, DC 20018-1211, USA

Johnson, Robert L (Business Person)
1900 W Pl NE
Washington, DC 20018-1230, USA

Johnson, Ron (Athlete, Baseball Player)
428 S Maie Ave
Compton, CA 90220-2805, USA

Johnson, Ronald A (Ron) (Athlete, Football Player)
226 Summit Ave
Summit, NJ 07901-2202, USA

Johnson, Rondin (Athlete, Baseball Player)
1025 S 324th Pl
Federal Way, WA 98003-5930, USA

Johnson, Rontrez (Athlete, Baseball Player)
2109 NE 1st St
Cape Coral, FL 33909-2870, USA

Johnson, Roy (Misc)
1125 17th St NW
Washington, DC 20036-4709, USA

Johnson, Russ (Athlete, Baseball Player, Olympic Athlete)
3542 Russell Rd
Green Cove Springs, FL 32043-9498, USA

Johnson, Russell (Actor)
PO Box 1198
Bainbridge Island, WA 98110, USA

Johnson, Sam (Congressman, Politician)
1211 Longworth Hob
Washington, DC 20515-4303, USA

Johnson, Scarlett (Actor)
c/o Duncan Millership *Management 360*
9111 Wilshire Blvd
Beverly Hills, CA 90210-5508, USA

Johnson, Shannon (Basketball Player)
Mohegan Sun Arena
Uncasville, CT 6382, USA

Johnson, Shawn (Athlete, Gymnast, Olympic Athlete)
2210 Park Dr
W Des Moines, IA 50265-5767, USA

Johnson, Sheila (Business Person)
401 9th St NW
Washington, DC 20004-2128, USA

Johnson, Shelly W (Cinematographer)
970 Jimeno Rd
Santa Barbara, CA 93103-2060, USA

Johnson, Sonia (Activist)
3318 2nd St S
Arlington, VA 22204-1709, USA

Johnson, Spencer (Writer)
825 N 1420 E
Orem, UT 84097-5484, USA

Johnson, Stan (Athlete, Baseball Player)
56 Morningside Dr
Daly City, CA 94015-4509, USA

Johnson, Steffond (Athlete, Basketball Player)
10525 Marsh Ln
Dallas, TX 75229-5142, USA

Johnson, Steve (Athlete, Basketball Player)
9715 SW Quail Post Rd
Portland, OR 97219-6363, USA

Johnson, Syl (Musician, Songwriter, Writer)
761 Washington Ave N
Minneapolis, MN 55401-1101, USA

Johnson, Taj
170 N Rexford Dr
Beverly Hills, CA 90210-5406

Johnson, Terry (Athlete, Hockey Player)
400-777 8th Ave Southwest Attn Vice-President Land
Calgary, AB T2P 3R5, Canada

Johnson, Thomas (Athlete, Baseball Player)
1611 Constitution Blvd
Rock Hill, SC 29732-3047, USA

Johnson, Tim (Athlete, Football Player)
6418 Cartmel Ln
Windermere, FL 34786-5423, USA

Johnson, Tim (Athlete, Football Player)
21300 Redskin Park Dr
Ashburn, VA 20147-6100, USA

Johnson, Tim (Athlete, Baseball Player, Coach)
800 Conway Ave
Las Cruces, NM 88005-3744, USA

Johnson, Timothy (Correspondent, Doctor)
c/o Staff Member *Good Morning America (NY)*
147 Columbus Ave Fl 6
New York, NY 10023-6503, USA

Johnson, Tom (Athlete, Baseball Player)
2700 Knox Ave N
Minneapolis, MN 55411-1246, USA

Johnson, Tom (Athlete, Hockey Player)
PO Box 1167
West Falmouth, MA 02574-1167, USA

Johnson, Torrence V (Astronomer)
4800 Oak Grove Dr
Pasadena, CA 91109-8001, USA

Johnson, Tre (Athlete, Football Player)
680 Harrison Ave
Peekskill, NY 10566-2219, USA

Johnson, Undra (Athlete, Football Player)
244 Coventry Dr
Bridgeport, WV 26330-9251, USA

Johnson, Vance (Athlete, Football Player)
PO Box 370781
Denver, CO 80237-0781, USA

Johnson, Vaughan (Athlete, Football Player)
4915 Arendell St Apt 253
Morehead City, NC 28557-2659, USA

Johnson, Vaughan M (Athlete, Football Player)
5800 Airline Dr
Metairie, LA 70003-3876, USA

Johnson, Vicki (Stylist)
8226 Cherokee Cir
Leawood, KS 66206-1130, USA

Johnson, Vickie (Basketball Player)
c/o Staff Member *New York Liberty*
2 Penn Plz Fl 15
New York, NY 10121-1703, USA

Johnson, Vinnie (Athlete, Basketball Player)
5236 Elmgate Dr
Orchard Lake, MI 48324-3017, USA

Johnson, Virginia (Ballerina)
133 W 71st St
New York, NY 10023-3834, USA

Johnson, Virginia E (Doctor)
800 Holland Rd
Ballwin, MO 63021-7230, USA

Johnson, Wallace (Athlete, Baseball Player)
5210 S Campbell Ave
Chicago, IL 60632-1532, USA

Johnson, Walter (Athlete, Football Player)
22361 Rye Rd
Shaker Heights, OH 44122-3041, USA

Johnson, Warren (Race Car Driver)
700 N Price Rd
Sugar Hill, GA 30518-4724, USA

Johnson, Warren C (Misc)
946 Bellclair Rd SE
Grand Rapids, MI 49506, USA

Johnson, Wendy (Race Car Driver)
126 Red Brook Ln
Mooresville, NC 28117-8801, USA

Johnson, William A (Billy White Shoes) (Athlete, Football Player)
3701 Whitney Pl
Duluth, GA 30096-3170, USA

Johnson, William B (Business Person)
4445 Willard Ave Ste 800
Chevy Chase, MD 20815-3699, USA

Johnson, William H (Athlete, Football Player)
522 E Pleasant Grove Rd
Montgomery, AL 36105-6110, USA

Johnson, William L (Athlete, Football Player)
14538 New Hampton Pl
Fort Myers, FL 33912-7010, USA

Johnson, William R (Business Person)
PO Box 57
Pittsburgh, PA 15230-0057, USA

Johnson, William W (Athlete, Football Player)
20 Mohawk Rd
Canton, MA 02021-1254, USA

Johnson, Zach (Athlete, Golfer)
772 Whooping Crane Ct
Sanford, FL 32771-5410, USA

Johnson III, Edward (Business Person)
82 Devonshire St # V8C
Boston, MA 02109-3605, USA

Johnson III, Joseph E (Doctor, Physicist)
2401 Pennsylvania Ave Apt 15C44
Philadelphia, PA 19130-3050, USA

Johnson Jr, Benjamin S (ben) (Athlete, Track Athlete)
2 Saint Clair Ave E # 1500
Toronto, ON M4T 2R1, CANADA

Johnson Jr, Ernie (Sportscaster)
1050 Techwood Dr NW
Atlanta, GA 30318-5604, USA

Johnson Jr, G Griffith (Government Official)
300 Locust Ave
Annapolis, MD 21401-3329, USA

Johnson Jr, Johnnie (Athlete, Football Player)
PO Box 114
La Grange, TX 78945-0114, USA

Johnson Jr, Manuel H (Economist, Government Official)
2099 Pennsylvania Ave NW Ste 950
Washington, DC 20006-6808, USA

Johnson Pucci, Gail (Swimmer)
2132 Ward Dr
Walnut Creek, CA 94596-5731, USA

Johnson-Goodman, Mamie (Peanut) (Athlete, Baseball Player)
618 Southern Ave SE
Washington, DC 20032-3403, USA

Johnson-Noga, Arlene
1923 7th Ave E
Regina, SK S4N 4M7, CANADA

Johnsson, Kim (Athlete, Hockey Player)
5308 Oaklawn Ave
Minneapolis, MN 55424-1309, USA

Johnston, Alastair (Misc)
75490 Fairway Dr
Indian Wells, CA 92210-8423, USA

Johnston, Allen H (Religious Leader)
3 Wymer Terrace PO Box 21
Hamilton, NEW ZELAND

Johnston, Bernie (Athlete, Hockey Player)
715 Central Park Blvd
Port Orange, FL 32127-7555, USA

Johnston, Brian (Athlete, Football Player)
236 Hideaway Ln
Mooresville, NC 28117-8402, USA

Johnston, Bruce (Musician)
8942 Wilshire Blvd # 219
Beverly Hills, CA 90211-1908, USA

Johnston, Daryl (Moose) (Athlete, Football Player)
4414 Woodfin Dr
Dallas, TX 75220-6420, USA

Johnston, Ed (Athlete, Hockey Player)
c/o Staff Member *Pittsburgh Penguins*
66 Mario Lemieux Pl Ste 2
Pittsburgh, PA 15219-3504, USA

Johnston, Freedy (Musician, Songwriter, Writer)
30 Hillcrest Ave
Morristown, NJ 07960-5090, USA

Johnston, Gerald A (Business Person)
PO Box 516
Saint Louis, MO 63166-0516, USA

Johnston, Gerald E (Business Person)
1221 Broadway
Oakland, CA 94612-1837, USA

Johnston, Greg (Athlete, Hockey Player)
c/o Staff Member *Toronto Maple Leafs*
Air Canada Centre 400-40 Bay St
Toronto, ON M5J 2X2, Canada

Johnston, Harold S (Misc)
285 Franklin St
Harrisonburg, VA 22801-4018, USA

Johnston, J Bennett Jr (Ex-Senator)
2099 Pennsylvania Ave NW # 1000
Washington, DC 20006-6800, USA

Johnston, Jamie (Actor)
c/o Norbert Abrams *Noble Caplan Abrams*
1260 Yonge St 2nd Floor
Toronto ON M4T 1W6, Canada

Johnston, Jimmy (Athlete, Golfer)
9 S 12th St Fl 3
Richmond, VA 23219-4032, USA

Johnston, Joe (Director)
c/o Adam Kanter *Creative Artists Agency (CAA-LA)*
2000 Avenue of the Stars Ste 100
Los Angeles, CA 90067-4705, USA

Johnston, Joel (Athlete, Baseball Player)
2 Outpost Ct
North Potomac, MD 20878-4353, USA

Johnston, Joey (Athlete, Hockey Player)
RR 4 Station Delivery Ctr
Peterborough, ON K9J 6X5, Canada

Johnston, John Dennis (Actor)
1801 Avenue of the Stars Ste 902
Los Angeles, CA 90067-5981, USA

Johnston, Ken
6300 Wilshire Blvd # 2110
Los Angeles, CA 90048-5204

Johnston, Kristen (Actor)
c/o Judy Hofflund *Hofflund/Polone*
9465 Wilshire Blvd Ste 420
Beverly Hills, CA 90212-2603, USA

Johnston, Larry (Athlete, Hockey Player)
904 E Liberty St
Milford, MI 48381-2081, USA

Johnston, Levi (Misc)
c/o Rex Lamont Butler *Rex Lamont Butler & Associates*
745 W 4th Ave
Anchorage, AK 99501-2139, USA

Johnston, Lynn (Cartoonist)
4520 Main St
Kansas City, MO 64111-1876, USA

Johnston, Mark (Athlete, Football Player)
5604 Southwest Pkwy Apt 3535
Austin, TX 78735-6278, USA

Johnston, Marshall (Athlete, Hockey Player)
3933 Waville Rd NE
Bemidji, MN 56601-8987, USA

Johnston, Nate (Athlete, Basketball Player)
8870 Fontainebleau Blvd Apt 301
Miami, FL 33172-4427, USA

Johnston, Rex D (Athlete, Baseball Player, Football Player)
15117 Illinois Ave
Paramount, CA 90723-4106, USA

Johnston, Sabrina
c/o Staff Member *Diva Central Inc*
7510 W Sunset Blvd Ste 1445
Los Angeles, CA 90046-3408, USA

Johnston, Tom (Musician)
PO Box 359
Sonoma, CA 95476-0359

Johnston Jr, S K (Business Person)
2500 Windy Ridge Pkwy SE
Atlanta, GA 30339-5677, USA

Johnston McKay, Marry H (Astronaut)
Space Institute
Tullahoma, TN 37388, USA

Johnstone, Jay (Athlete, Baseball Player)
1104 W Magnolia Blvd
Burbank, CA 91506-1812, USA

Johnstone, John (Athlete, Baseball Player)
9330 Clubside Cir Unit 3305
Sarasota, FL 34238-3367, USA

Johnstone, Ross (Athlete, Hockey Player)
508-40 Richview Rd
Etobicoke, ON M9A 5C1, Canada

Johnstone, Tony (Athlete, Golfer)
5335 Wisconsin Ave NW Ste 850
Washington, DC 20015-2052, USA

Johnstone Jr, John W (Business Person)
467 Carter St
New Canaan, CT 06840-5015, USA

Johnston-Forbes, Cathy (Athlete, Golfer)
5104 Lunar Dr
Kitty Hawk, NC 27949-3958, USA

Joiner, Rusty (Actor, Athlete, Model)
c/o Marc Chancer *Origin Talent Agency*
4705 Laurel Canyon Blvd Ste 306
Studio City, CA 91607-5940, USA

Joiner Jr, Charles (Charlie) (Athlete, Coach, Football Coach, Football Player)
16935 W Bernardo Dr Ste 107
San Diego, CA 92127-1635, USA

Jokinen, Olli (Athlete, Hockey Player)
6760 NW 122nd Ave
Parkland, FL 33076-3324, USA

Jolas, Betsy M (Composer)
209 Ave Jaures
Paris 75019, FRANCE

Joli, France (Musician)
c/o Staff Member *Diva Central Inc*
7510 W Sunset Blvd Ste 1445
Los Angeles, CA 90046-3408, USA

Joliceur, David (Musician)
250 W 57th St
New York, NY 10107-0001, USA

Jolie, Angelina (Actor, Philanthropist)
c/o Geyer Kosinski *Media Talent Group*
9200 W Sunset Blvd Ste 550
Los Angeles, CA 90069-3611, USA

Joliot, Pierre A (Biologist)
16 Rue de la Glaciere
Paris 75013, FRANCE

Jolitz, Evan (Athlete, Football Player)
15 Old Kimball Rd
Brooklyn, CT 06234-1414, USA

Jolley, Gordon (Athlete, Football Player)
1459 Navajo Dr
St George, UT 84790-7728, USA

Jolley, Lewis (Athlete, Football Player)
2715 Rosegate Ln
Charlotte, NC 28270-0764, USA

Jolley, Willie (Motivational Speaker)
5711 13th St Nw
Washington, DC 20011-3547, USA

Jolliff, Howie (Athlete, Basketball Player)
2346 Fallen Oak Cir NE
Massillon, OH 44646-4887, USA

Jolly, Allison (Yachtsman)
1275 Seville Ln NE
Saint Petersburg, FL 33704-2424, USA

Jolly, E Grady (Judge)
245 E Capitol St
Jackson, MS 39201-2409, USA

Jolly, Ken (Athlete, Football Player)
159 Bon Aire Dr
Dallas, TX 75218-1034, USA

Jolovitz, Jenna (Actor, Writer)
c/o Staff Member *Creative Artists Agency (CAA-LA)*
2000 Avenue of the Stars Ste 100
Los Angeles, CA 90067-4705, USA

Joltz, Joachim (Engineer)
AM Forsthof 16
Wuppertal 42119, GERMANY

Joly, Frederique (Stylist)
940 1/2 Milwood Ave
Venice, CA 90291-4491, USA

Joly, Greg (Athlete, Hockey Player)
21 McDonald Dr
Queensbury, NY 12804-6426, USA

Joly, Yvan (Athlete, Hockey Player)
16 Hwy 3
Wainfleet, ON L0S 1V0, Canada

Jomdt, L daniel (Business Person)
200 Wilmot Rd
Deerfield, IL 60015-4620, USA

Jomphe, Jean-Francois (Athlete, Hockey Player)
6440 Sky Pointe Dr Ste 140MBB PMB 39
Las Vegas, NV 89131-4047, USA

Jonas, Don (Athlete, Football Player)
1831 Seneca Blvd
Winter Springs, FL 32708-5534, USA

Jonas, Joe (Musician)
c/o Nick Styne *Creative Artists Agency (CAA-LA)*
2000 Avenue of the Stars Ste 100
Los Angeles, CA 90067-4705, USA

Jonas, Kevin (Musician)
c/o Nick Styne *Creative Artists Agency (CAA-LA)*
2000 Avenue of the Stars Ste 100
Los Angeles, CA 90067-4705, USA

Jonas, Nick (Musician)
c/o Nick Styne *Creative Artists Agency (CAA-LA)*
2000 Avenue of the Stars Ste 100
Los Angeles, CA 90067-4705, USA

Jonathan, Stan (Athlete, Hockey Player)
RR 1
Ohsweken, ON N0A 1M0, Canada

Jonathan, Wesley (Actor)
c/o Adrienne McWhorter *Abrams Artists Agency (LA)*
9200 W Sunset Blvd PH 11
Los Angeles, CA 90069-3601, USA

Jones, Aaron (Athlete, Football Player)
7677 Torino Ct
Orlando, FL 32835-8195, USA

Jones, Adam (Athlete, Baseball Player)
c/o Staff Member *Baltimore Orioles*
333 W Camden St
Baltimore, MD 21201-2496, USA

Jones, Al (Athlete, Baseball Player)
1339 Brussels St
San Francisco, CA 94134-2224, USA

Jones, Alex E (Journalist, Radio Personality)
PO Box 19549
Austin, TX 78760-9549, USA

Jones, Alfred (Boxer)
19610 Northbrook Dr
Southfield, MI 48076-5049, USA

Jones, Allen (Artist)
41 Charterhouse Square
London EC1M 6EA, UNITED KINGDOM (UK)

Jones, Andruw (Athlete, Baseball Player)
2931 Grey Moss Pass
Duluth, GA 30097-6274, USA

Jones, Angus T (Actor)
c/o Wendi Green *Paradigm (LA)*
9200 W Sunset Blvd PH 11
Los Angeles, CA 90069-3601, USA

Jones, Anthony (Athlete, Basketball Player)
44 Hempstead Dr
Newark, DE 19702-7711, USA

Jones, Antonia (Actor)
8899 Beverly Blvd Ste 620
Los Angeles, CA 90048-2428, USA

Jones, Ashthon (Musician)
c/o Simon Fuller *XIX Entertainment*
33/32 Ransomes Dock 35-37 Parkgate Rd
London SW11 4NP, UK

Jones, Asjha (Basketball Player)
Mohegan Sun Arena
Uncasville, CT 6382, USA

Jones, Askia (Athlete, Basketball Player)
3160 SW 132nd Ave
Miramar, FL 33027-3868, USA

Jones, Barry (Athlete, Baseball Player)
411 S Morton Ave
Centerville, IN 47330-1429, USA

Jones, Ben (Athlete, Baseball Player)
1323 Tewkesbury Pl NW
Washington, DC 20012-2921, USA

Jones, Ben J (Prime Minister)
Greenville
Saint Andrew's, GRENADA

Jones, Bert (Athlete, Football Player)
PO Box 248
Simsboro, LA 71275-0248, USA

Jones, Bertram H (Bert) (Athlete, Football Player)
PO Box 248
Simsboro, LA 71275-0248, USA

Jones, Bob (Bobby) (Athlete, Baseball Player)
32 Elm St
Rutherford, NJ 07070-1263, USA

Jones, Bobby (Athlete, Basketball Player)
7301 Sardis Rd
Charlotte, NC 28270-6063, USA

Jones, Bobby (Athlete, Baseball Player)
7809 S Oxford Ave
Tulsa, OK 74136-8524, USA

Jones, Bobby (Athlete, Baseball Player)
10222 N Whitney Ave
Fresno, CA 93730-4742, USA

Jones, Booker T (Actor, Musician)
c/o Staff Member *Concerted Efforts*
PO Box 440326
Somerville, MA 02144-0004, USA

Jones, Brad (Athlete, Hockey Player)
c/o Staff Member *International Hockey League*
PO Box 175
Bedford, MI 49020-0175, USA

Jones, Brent M (Athlete, Football Player, Sportscaster)
756 El Pintado Rd
Danville, CA 94526-1407, USA

Jones, Bryn Terfel (Opera Singer)
203 Fidlas Road
Cardiff CF4 5NA, WALES

Jones, Caldwell (Athlete, Basketball Player)
2315 Windsor Ave
Baltimore, MD 21216-3227, USA

Jones, Calvin (Athlete, Baseball Player)
2815 Butterfield Stage Rd
Lewisville, TX 75077-3181, USA

Jones, Carlton (Stylist)
c/o Staff Member *Illusions Management*
129 W 27th St Fl 12
New York, NY 10001-6206, USA

Jones, Carnetta (Actor)
10635 Santa Monica Blvd Ste 130
Los Angeles, CA 90025-8306, USA

Jones, Cedric (Athlete, Football Player)
18 Hollow Wood Ln Apt C
Greenwich, CT 06831-5064, USA

Jones, Charles (Athlete, Basketball Player)
2315 Windsor Ave
Baltimore, MD 21216-3227, USA

Jones, Charles A (Athlete, Basketball Player)
304 Chestnut St
Elizabethtown, KY 42701-9431, USA

Jones, Charles W (Misc)
753 S 8th Ave
Kansas City, KS 66105, USA

Jones, Cherry (Actor)
c/o Scott Henderson *WmE2 (Endeavor-LA)*
9601 Wilshire Blvd Fl 3
Beverly Hills, CA 90210-5219, USA

Jones, Chipper (Athlete, Baseball Player)
c/o Staff Member *Atlanta Braves*
755 Hank Aaron Dr SW
Atlanta, GA 30315-1120, USA

Jones, Chris (Athlete, Baseball Player)
1821 Westward Ho Cir
El Cajon, CA 92021-3721, USA

Jones, Chris (Athlete, Baseball Player)
1312 E Thunderhill Pl
Phoenix, AZ 85048-6200, USA

Jones, Chris T (Athlete, Football Player)
19360 E Country Club Dr
Aventura, FL 33180-4817, USA

Jones, Christopher (Chris) (Actor, Artist)
c/o Sherry Dodd PO Box 15714
Beverly Hills, CA 90209, USA

Jones, Christopher Michael (Actor, Dancer)
c/o Justine Hunt *Hines and Hunt Entertainment*
1213 W Magnolia Blvd
Burbank, CA 91506-1829, USA

Jones, Clarence (Athlete, Baseball Player)
2641 Club Dr
Greensboro, GA 30642-3476, USA

Jones, Claude Earl (Actor)
8285 W Sunset Blvd Ste 1
West Hollywood, CA 90046-2420, USA

Jones, Cleon (Athlete, Baseball Player)
751 Edwards St
Mobile, AL 36610-3334, USA

Jones, Clinton (Athlete, Football Player)
16555 Sherman Way Ste C
Van Nuys, CA 91406-3781, USA

Jones, Cobi (Soccer Player)
501 N Edinburgh Ave
Los Angeles, CA 90048-2309, USA

Jones, Collis (Athlete, Basketball Player)
1217 Argyle Ave
Baltimore, MD 21217-2928, USA

Jones, Courtney J L (Figure Skater)
15-27 Gee St
London EC1V 3RE, UNITED KINGDOM (UK)

Jones, Cullen (Athlete, Olympic Athlete, Swimmer)
c/o Staff Member *Premier Management Group (PMG Sports)*
115 Crescent Commons Dr Ste 250
Cary, NC 27518-8134, USA

Jones, Dahntay (Athlete, Basketball Player)
3247 Wedge Hill Cv
Memphis, TN 38125-8891, USA

Jones, Dalton (Athlete, Baseball Player)
4688 S Dixon Ln
Liberty, MS 39645, USA

Jones, Damon (Athlete, Basketball Player)
c/o Staff Member *Mark Termini Associates*
Prefers to be contacted via telephone
Cleveland, OH, USA

Jones, Damon (Athlete, Football Player)
12690 Copper Springs Rd
Jacksonville, FL 32246-5143, USA

Jones, Dan (Athlete, Football Player)
5150 SW 20th St
Plantation, FL 33317-5410, USA

Jones, Daniel (Writer)
c/o Staff Member *The New York Times Company*
229 W 43rd St
New York, NY 10036-3913, USA

Jones, Dante (Athlete, Football Player)
326 Partridge Run Dr
Duncanville, TX 75137-3133, USA

Jones, Darryl (Musician)
110 W 57th St # 300
New York, NY 10019-3319, USA

Jones, Darryl (Athlete, Baseball Player)
15628 King Dr
Meadville, PA 16335-6546, USA

Jones, Daryll (Athlete, Football Player)
74 Everglade Rd
Daviston, AL 36256-6400, USA

Jones, David A (Business Person)
500 W Main St
Louisville, KY 40202-2946, USA

Jones, David D (Athlete, Football Player)
109 Crawford St
East Orange, NJ 07018-1810, USA

Jones, David (Davy) (Actor, Musician)
PO Box 400
Beavertown, PA 17813-0400, USA

Jones, David (Deacon) (Athlete, Football Player)
715 S Canyon Mist Ln
Anaheim, CA 92808-1433, USA

Jones, Davy (Race Car Driver)
1397 330th St
Adair, IA 50002-8581, USA

Jones, Dax (Athlete, Baseball Player)
10021 W Suddard Pl
Beach Park, IL 60087-1717, USA

Jones, Dean (Actor, Musician)
PO Box 570276
Tarzana, CA 91357-0276, USA

Jones, Denise (Musician)
300 10th Ave S
Nashville, TN 37203-4125, USA

Jones, Dick (Actor)
PO Box 7716
Northridge, CA 91327-7716

Jones, Dickie (Actor)
PO Box 7716
Northridge, CA 91327-7716, USA

Jones, Don (Athlete, Football Player)
8446 Wren Creek Dr
Charlotte, NC 28269-6176, USA

Jones, Donell (Musician)
c/o Ra-Fael Blanco *2R's Entertainment & Media*
601 W 135th St Apt 6E
New York, NY 10031-8304, USA

Jones, Donta (Athlete, Football Player)
6043 Legacy Cir
Charlotte, NC 28277-8116, USA

Jones, Doug (Actor)
c/o John Zander *Zander Magic*
9068 Priscilla St
Downey, CA 90242-4627, USA

Jones, Doug (Athlete, Baseball Player)
129 E Navilla Pl
Covina, CA 91723-3023, USA

Jones, Dwight (Athlete, Basketball Player)
20119 Mayfair Park Ln
Spring, TX 77379-2436, USA

Jones, E Edward (Religious Leader)
777 S R L Thornton Fwy
Dallas, TX 75203-2901, USA

Jones, E Fay (Architect)
619 W Dickson St
Fayetteville, AR 72701-5017, USA

Jones, Earl (Athlete, Track Athlete)
15114 Petoskey Ave
Detroit, MI 48238-2064, USA

Jones, Earl (Athlete, Football Player)
3127 Seiler Ct
Naperville, IL 60565-4424, USA

Jones, Earl (Athlete, Basketball Player)
4601 Saint Barnabas Rd
Temple Hills, MD 20748-1916, USA

Jones, Ed (Athlete, Football Player)
14232 Marsh Ln PMB 282
Addison, TX 75001-3857, USA

Jones, Eddie (Athlete, Basketball Player)
3400 Paddock Rd
Weston, FL 33331-3520, USA

Jones, Eddie (Actor)
14724 Ventura Blvd Ste 505
Sherman Oaks, CA 91403-3505, USA

Jones, Edgar (Athlete, Football Player)
410 Dean St Apt 1
Scranton, PA 18509-1306, USA

Jones, Edith H (Judge)
515 Rusk St
Houston, TX 77002-2600, USA

Jones, Elvin R (Musician)
PO Box 2728
Bala Cynwyd, PA 19004-6728, USA

Jones, Ernest (Athlete, Football Player)
17410 SW 109th Ave
Miami, FL 33157-4042, USA

Jones, Etta
160 Goldsmith Ave
Newark, NJ 07112-2001

Jones, Evan (Actor)
c/o Susan Curtis *Curtis Talent Management*
9607 Arby Dr
Beverly Hills, CA 90210-1202, USA

Jones, Felix (Athlete, Football Player)
c/o Eugene Parker *Maximum Sports Management*
6435 W Jefferson Blvd # 197
Fort Wayne, IN 46804-6203, USA

Jones, Freddie (Actor)
c/o Staff Member *Diamond Management*
31 Percy St
London W1T 2DD, UK

Jones, Freddie (Athlete, Football Player)
5015 E Cheyenne Dr Unit 24
Phoenix, AZ 85044-4314, USA

Jones, Gary (Athlete, Baseball Player)
475 S Westridge Cir
Anaheim, CA 92807-3733, USA

Jones, Gary (Athlete, Football Player)
1410 Ten Mile Dr
Cedar Hill, TX 75104-6239, USA

Jones, Gemma (Actor)
18-21 Jermyn St
London SW1Y 6NB, UNITED KINGDOM (UK)

Jones, George (Athlete, Football Player)
4419 Cleveland Ave Apt 4
San Diego, CA 92116-3911, USA

Jones, George (Musician)
PO Box 680009
Franklin, TN 37068-0009, USA

Jones, Glenn (Musician)
145 W 57th St # 1500
New York, NY 10019-2220, USA

Jones, Gordon (Athlete, Football Player)
18919 Fishermans Bend Dr
Lutz, FL 33558-9756, USA

Jones, Grace (Actor, Model, Musician)
c/o Michael Schweiger 166 Fifth Ave 4th Fl
New York, New York 10010, USA

Jones, Greg (Skier)
PO Box 500
Tahoe City, CA 96145-0500, USA

Jones, Greg (Athlete, Football Player)
2331 S Fenton Dr
Lakewood, CO 80227-3975, USA

Jones, Greg (Athlete, Baseball Player)
14260 Passage Way
Seminole, FL 33776-1001, USA

Jones, Gregory M (Athlete, Football Player)
3203 Kirby Ln
Walnut Creek, CA 94598-3908, USA

Jones, Griff Rhys (Actor, Producer, Writer)
c/o Staff Member *TalkBack Management*
20-21 Newman St
London W1T 1PG, UNITED KINGDOM (UK)

Jones, Grover (Deacon) (Athlete, Baseball Player)
1015 Goldfinch Ave
Sugar Land, TX 77478-3452, USA

Jones, Gwyneth (Opera Singer)
PO Box 556
Hammonton, NJ 08037-0556, SWITZERLAND

Jones, Hal (Baseball Player)
1 S Locust St Apt 126B
Inglewood, CA 90301-5874, USA

Jones, Hal (Athlete, Baseball Player)
1 S Locust St Apt 126B
Inglewood, CA 90301-5874, USA

Jones, Hassan (Athlete, Football Player)
1010 Eldridge St
Clearwater, FL 33755-4205, USA

Jones, Hayes W (Athlete, Track Athlete)
408 Stonewood Dr
Peachtree City, GA 30269-6639, USA

Jones, Henry (Hank) (Musician)
300 Mercer St Apt 3J
New York, NY 10003-6732, USA

Jones, Herita (Stylist)
908 Tipperary Dr
Greensboro, NC 27406-6613, USA

Jones, Homer C (Athlete, Football Player)
416 S Texas St
Pittsburg, TX 75686-1538, USA

Jones, Horace (Athlete, Football Player)
7925 Hobart Ave
Pensacola, FL 32534-4030, USA

Jones, Howard (Musician)
Alexander Road
Aylesbury HP20 2NR, United Kingdom

Jones, Jack (Musician)
c/o Staff Member *International Ventures*
25115 Avenue Stanford Ste 102
Valencia, CA 91355-4777, USA

Jones, Jacque (Athlete, Baseball Player)
347 Saint Rita Ct
San Diego, CA 92113-2092, USA

Jones, James (Athlete, Football Player)
1009 Hunters Creek Dr
Carrollton, TX 75007-1111, USA

Jones, James (Athlete, Football Player)
PO Box 22694
Kansas City, MO 64113-0694, USA

Jones, James (Athlete, Football Player)
9481 Highland Oak Dr Unit 1815
Tampa, FL 33647-2518, USA

Jones, James C (Athlete, Football Player)
1136 S Delano Ct W Apt 715
Chicago, IL 60605-3738, USA

Jones, James Earl (Actor)
263 W End Ave
New York, NY 10023-2612, USA

Jones, James (Jimmy) (Athlete, Basketball Player)
319 Salinas Dr
Henderson, NV 89014-3578, USA

Jones, Jamie (Musician)
9255 W Sunset Blvd Ste 407
Los Angeles, CA 90069-3302, USA

Jones, Janet (Actor)
9100 Wilshire Blvd Ste 1000W
Beverly Hills, CA 90212-3463, USA

Jones, January (Actor)
c/o Paul Nelson *Mosaic Media Group*
9200 W Sunset Blvd Ste 10
Los Angeles, CA 90069-3608, USA

Jones, Jason (Athlete, Baseball Player)
1125 Oakview Dr SE
Smyrna, GA 30080-7917, USA

Jones, Jason (Actor)
c/o Jay Gassner *United Talent Agency (UTA)*
9560 Wilshire Blvd Fl 5
Beverly Hills, CA 90212-2400, USA

Jones, Jeff (Coach)
Athletic Dept
Charlottesville, VA 22903, USA

Jones, Jeff (Athlete, Baseball Player)
2200 Ready Rd
Carleton, MI 48117-9778, USA

Jones, Jeff (Athlete, Baseball Player)
311 White Horse Pike
Haddon Heights, NJ 08035-1704, USA

Jones, Jeffrey (Actor)
7336 Santa Monica Blvd # 691
West Hollywood, CA 90046-6616, USA

Jones, Jenny (Comedian)
c/o Gail Stocker *Gail Stocker Presents*
1025 N Kings Rd Apt 113
Los Angeles, CA 90069-6007, USA

Jones, Jermaine (Athlete, Football Player)
1172 Larry St
Opelousas, LA 70570, USA

Jones, Jerrauld C (Jerry) (Misc)
1 Cowboys Pkwy
Irving, TX 75063-4924, USA

Jones, Jerrell Corron (J-Kwon) (Musician)
c/o Staff Member *So So Def Recordings Inc*
1350 Spring St NW Ste 750
Atlanta, GA 30309-2870, USA

Jones, Jill Marie (Actor)
c/o Peggy Rudman *Identity Talent Agency (ID)*
9107 Wilshire Blvd Ste 500
Beverly Hills, CA 90210-5526, USA

Jones, Jim (Musician)
c/o Gordon MacDonald *Don Buchwald & Associates Inc (LA)*
8619 Washington Blvd
Culver City, CA 90232-7441, USA

Jones, Jimmie (Athlete, Football Player)
2658 Unicorn Ct
Herndon, VA 20171-2425, USA

Jones, Jimmie (Athlete, Football Player)
204 Moss Dr
Cedar Hill, TX 75104-2398, USA

Jones, Jimmy (Athlete, Hockey Player)
12 Aspen Leaf Crt
Aurora, ON L4G 7T3, Canada

Jones, Jimmy (Athlete, Baseball Player)
3054 Newcastle Dr
Dallas, TX 75220-1636, USA

Jones, Joe (Athlete, Football Player)
1413 Scott Ct
Irving, TX 75060-3703, USA

Jones, John E (Athlete, Football Player)
19610 100th Ave NE
Bothell, WA 98011-2318, USA

Jones, John Marshall
1801 Avenue of the Stars Ste 307
Los Angeles, CA 90067-5905

Jones, John Paul (Musician)
49 Portland Road
London W11 4LJ, UNITED KINGDOM (UK)

Jones, Julia (Actor)
c/o Evan Hainey *Untitled Entertainment (LA)*
350 S Beverly Dr Ste 200
Beverly Hills, CA 90212-4819, USA

Jones, Julio (Football Player)
c/o Pat Dye Jr *SportsTrust Advisors - GA*
3340 Peachtree Rd NE Fl 16
Atlanta, GA 30326-1000, USA

Jones, Keith (Athlete, Hockey Player)
c/o Staff Member *Versus Network*
208 Harbor Dr Fl 4
Stamford, CT 06902-7467, USA

Jones, Kelly (Musician)
Home Farm Welfor Newbury
Berkshire RG20 8HR, UNITED KINGDOM (UK)

Jones, Ken (Athlete, Football Player)
4455 Porter Rd
Niagara Falls, NY 14305-3309, USA

Jones, Kenneth V (Actor)
29/33 Berners St
London W1P 4AA, ENGLAND

Jones, Kent (Athlete, Golfer)
5108 Coyote Hill Way NW
Albuquerque, NM 87120-1471, USA

Jones, Kim (Athlete, Football Player)
1396 Madison Ave Apt 150
Loveland, CO 80537-3218, USA

Jones, Kimberly (Lil' Kim) (Actor, Musician, Producer)
c/o Jeff Rabhan *Three Ring Projects*
111 Westwood Pl Ste 101
Brentwood, TN 37027-5057, USA

Jones, L Q (Actor)
2144 1/2 N Cahuenga Blvd
Los Angeles, CA 90068-2708, USA

Jones, Larry (Athlete, Basketball Player)
1442 Cottingham Ct W
Columbus, OH 43209-3144, USA

Jones, LeRoi (Imamu Amiri Baraka) (Writer)
Afro American Studies
Stony Brook, NY 11794-0001, USA

Jones, Levi (Athlete, Football Player)
1449 W Bahia Ct
Gilbert, AZ 85233-5601, USA

Jones, Lolo (Athlete, Olympic Athlete, Track Athlete)
c/o Staff Member *USA Track & Field*
132 E Washington St Ste 800
Indianapolis, IN 46204-3674, USA

Jones, Lyle V (Misc)
RR 7
Pittsboro, NC 27312, USA

Jones, Lynn (Athlete, Baseball Player)
9959 Dicksonburg Rd
Conneautville, PA 16406-1817, USA

Jones, Major (Athlete, Basketball Player)
2475 Brandy Mill Rd
Houston, TX 77067-1275, USA

Jones, Malia (Actor, Athlete)
c/o Michelle Henderson *Henderson & Romo*
100 Universal City Plz # 7152
Universal City, CA 91608-1002, USA

Jones, Mandana (Actor)
19 Denmark Street
London WC2H 8NA, England

Jones, Marcus (Athlete, Football Player)
18701 Pepper Pike
Lutz, FL 33558-5315, USA

Jones, Marcus (Athlete, Baseball Player)
20375 Longbay Dr
Yorba Linda, CA 92887-3250, USA

Jones, Marilyn (Actor)
8383 Wilshire Blvd Ste 923
Beverly Hills, CA 90211-2443, USA

Jones, Marion (Athlete, Track Athlete)
PO Box 3065
Cary, NC 27519-3065, USA

Jones, Marvin (Athlete, Baseball Player)
4134 12th St
Ecorse, MI 48229-1224, USA

Jones, Marvin (Athlete, Football Player)
536 N Biscayne River Dr
Miami, FL 33169-6632, USA

Jones, Marvin M (Athlete, Football Player)
8891 NW 193rd St
Miami, FL 33157, USA

Jones, Maxine (Musician)
75 Rockefeller Plz # 1200
New York, NY 10019-6908, USA

Jones, Merlakia (Basketball Player)
1 Center Ct
Cleveland, OH 44115-4001, USA

Jones, Mick (Musician)
c/o Staff Member *Sanctuary Artist Management (UK)*
Sanctuary House 45-53 Sinclair Road
London W14 0NS, UNITED KINGDOM

Jones, Mick (Musician)
16501 Ventura Blvd Ste 602
Encino, CA 91436-2072, USA

Jones, Mickey (Actor, Musician)
c/o Staff Member *Hervey/Grimes Talent Agency*
10561 Missouri Ave Apt 2
Los Angeles, CA 90025-5940, USA

Jones, Mike (Athlete, Baseball Player)
6761 Atlantic Blvd
Jacksonville, FL 32211-8729, USA

Jones, Mike (Musician)
c/o Staff Member *Warner Bros*
4000 Warner Blvd # 16
Burbank, CA 91522-0002, USA

Jones, Mike A (Athlete, Football Player)
1843 E 76th St
Kansas City, MO 64132-2150, USA

Jones, Nasir (Nas) (Actor, Musician, Producer, Writer)
c/o Staff Member *Richard De La Font Agency*
3808 W South Park Blvd
Broken Arrow, OK 74011-1261, USA

Jones, Nathan (Actor)
c/o Rick Bassman *Cunningham Escott Slevin & Doherty (CESD-LA)*
10635 Santa Monica Blvd Ste 130
Los Angeles, CA 90025-8306, USA

Jones, Nathaniel R (Judge)
425 Walnut St
Cincinnati, OH 45202-3956, USA

Jones, Norah (Musician)
c/o Steve Macklam *Macklam Feldman Mgmt*
1505 W 2nd Ave Suite 200
Vancouver BC V6H 3Y4, Canada

Jones, Odell (Athlete, Baseball Player)
5831 Opal Ave
Palmdale, CA 93552-3967, USA

Jones, Orlando (Actor)
c/o Chuck Jones *Linasea Corp*
8306 Wilshire Blvd Ste 432
Beverly Hills, CA 90211-2382, USA

Jones, Ozell (Athlete, Basketball Player)
1573 Pine Ave
Long Beach, CA 90813-1819, USA

Jones, P J (Race Car Driver)
8431 Georgetown Rd
Indianapolis, IN 46268-5628, USA

Jones, Parnelli (Race Car Driver)
20550 Earl St
Torrance, CA 90503-3012, USA

Jones, Patrick (Actor)
c/o Staff Member *Martin Weiss Management*
PO Box 5656
Santa Monica, CA 90409-5656, USA

Jones, Patti (Stylist)
8231 Campana Dr
Las Vegas, NV 89147-5216, USA

Jones, Peter (Business Person)
Palliser House, Palliser Rd West Kensington
London W14 9EB, UK

Jones, Preston (Athlete, Football Player)
116 Hamilton Dr
Anderson, SC 29621-1558, USA

Jones, Quincy (Actor, Musician, Producer)
c/o Adam Shulman *Anonymous Content (AC-LA)*
3531 Hayden Ave
Culver City, CA 90232, USA

Jones, Randy (Athlete, Baseball Player)
2638 Cranston Dr
Escondido, CA 92025-7338, USA

Jones, Rashida (Actor, Musician)
c/o Andrea Pett-Joseph *Brillstein Entertainment Partners*
9150 Wilshire Blvd Ste 350
Beverly Hills, CA 90212-3453, USA

Jones, Rebecca (Actor)
c/o Gabriel Blanco *Gabriel Blanco Iglesias (Mexico)*
Rio Balsas 35-32 Colonia Cuauhtemoc
DF 6500, Mexico

Jones, Rees (Athlete, Golfer)
10 Belleclaire Pl
Verona, NJ 07044-5106, USA

Jones, Reginald V (Physicist)
8 Queen's Terrace
Aberdeen AB1 1XL, SCOTLAND

Jones, Renee (Actor)
256 S Robertson Blvd # 700
Beverly Hills, CA 90211-2811, USA

Jones, Rich (Athlete, Basketball Player)
101 Luna Way Apt 232
Las Vegas, NV 89145-0187, USA

Jones, Richard T (Actor)
c/o Doug Wald *Anonymous Content (AC-LA)*
545 Veteran Ave
Los Angeles, CA 90024-1915, USA

Jones, Richard Timothy
584 Broadway Rm 1009
New York, NY 10012-5239

Jones, Rick (Athlete, Baseball Player)
6319 Nancy Dr
Jacksonville, FL 32244-2945, USA

Jones, Rickie Lee (Musician, Songwriter, Writer)
476 Broome St Ste 6A
New York, NY 10013-2275, USA

Jones, Ricky (Athlete, Baseball Player)
1832 Brickyard Rd
Comer, GA 30629-3222, USA

Jones, Robert (Athlete, Football Player)
728 Barton Creek Blvd
Austin, TX 78746-4142, USA

Jones, Robert (K C) (Athlete, Basketball Player, Coach)
c/o Staff Member *Naismith Memorial Basketball Hall of Fame*
1000 W Columbus Ave
Springfield, MA 01105-2518, USA

Jones, Robin (Athlete, Basketball Player)
16640 Cynthia Ct
Tinley Park, IL 60477-8209, USA

Jones, Rod (Athlete, Football Player)
1124 Angie Ln
Desoto, TX 75115-3872, USA

Jones, Roger (Athlete, Football Player)
712 Trebor Dr
Goodlettsville, TN 37072-2935, USA

Jones, Ron (Athlete, Hockey Player)
301 Brock St
Coppell, TX 75019-3937, USA

Jones, Ronald (Popeye) (Athlete, Basketball Player)
4004 Sahara Ct
Carrollton, TX 75010-4237, USA

Jones, Rosie (Athlete, Golfer)
4895 High Point Rd NE
Atlanta, GA 30342-2340, USA

Jones, Ross (Athlete, Baseball Player)
1277 Camellia Cir
Weston, FL 33326-3614, USA

Jones, Rulon K (Athlete, Football Player)
3753 E 4100 N
Eden, UT 84310, USA

Jones, Ruppert (Athlete, Baseball Player)
17925 Valle De Lobo Dr
Poway, CA 92064-1021, USA

Jones, Sam (Athlete, Basketball Player)
338 S Hampton Club Way
Saint Augustine, FL 32092-1031, USA

Jones, Sean (Athlete, Football Player)
4602 McKeever Ln
Missouri City, TX 77459-6310, USA

Jones, Selwyn (Athlete, Football Player)
11216 Grimes Ave
Pearland, TX 77584-5524, USA

Jones, Shirley (Actor, Musician)
c/o Staff Member *Gage Group, The (LA)*
14724 Ventura Blvd Ste 505
Sherman Oaks, CA 91403-3505, USA

Jones, Simon (Actor)
1505 10th St
Santa Monica, CA 90401-2805, USA

Jones, Sir Charles
3947 Coxs Ferry Rd
Bolton, MS 39041-9519, USA

Jones, Spike (Athlete, Football Player)
3612 Club Dr NW
Kennesaw, GA 30144-2019, USA

Jones, Stacey (Stylist)
c/o Staff Member *Fifty8 Artists*
58 W Huron St
Chicago, IL 60654-3806, USA

Jones, Stacy (Athlete, Baseball Player)
1777 Ponderosa Rd
Attalla, AL 35954-5653, USA

Jones, Stan (Athlete, Football Player)
1138 Opal St Unit 101
Broomfield, CO 80020-7050, USA

Jones, Star (Actor, Producer, Talk Show Host)
c/o Tamara Houston *Round Table Entertainment*
509 N Fairfax Ave Ste 200
Los Angeles, CA 90036-1733, USA

Jones, Stephen (Lawyer)
PO Box 472
Enid, OK 73702-0472, USA

Jones, Stephen J M (Designer, Fashion Designer)
36 Great Queen St
London WC1E 6BT, UNITED KINGDOM (UK)

Jones, Steve (Musician)
55 Fulham High St
London SW6 3JJ, UNITED KINGDOM (UK)

Jones, Steve (Athlete, Basketball Player)
8303 Quebec Dr
Houston, TX 77096-1034, USA

Jones, Steve (Athlete, Baseball Player)
8116 Kingsdale Dr
Knoxville, TN 37919-7005, USA

Jones, Steve (Football Player)
12774 Fee Fee Rd
Saint Louis, MO 63146-4402, USA

Jones, Steven (Physicist)
Physics Dept
Provo, UT 84602, USA

Jones, Tamala (Actor)
c/o Danielle Allman-Del *D2 Management*
9255 W Sunset Blvd Ste 600
Los Angeles, CA 90069-3306, USA

Jones, Taylor (Cartoonist)
Times-Mirror Square
Los Angeles, CA 90053, USA

Jones, Tebucky (Athlete, Football Player)
PO Box 789
Farmington, CT 06034-0789, USA

Jones, Terry (Animator, Director)
34 Thistlewaite Road
London E5 QQQ, UNITED KINGDOM (UK)

Jones, Terry (Musician)
300 10th Ave S
Nashville, TN 37203-4125, USA

Jones, Thomas D (Astronaut)
2026 Beacon Heights Dr
Reston, VA 20191-4847, USA

Jones, Thomas V (Business Person)
1050 Moraga Dr
Los Angeles, CA 90049-1621, USA

Jones, Tim (Athlete, Baseball Player)
30 Chicot Dr
Maumelle, AR 72113-5801, USA

Jones, Tim (Athlete, Baseball Player)
6049 Roloff Way
Orangevale, CA 95662-4544, USA

Jones, Todd B G (Athlete, Baseball Player)
421 Eagle Pointe Dr
Pell City, AL 35128-7266, USA

Jones, Tom (Musician)
c/o Donna Woodward *Valley Music, Ltd*
Prefers to be contacted via telephone
Oxforshire, England

Jones, Tommy Lee (Actor)
PO Box 966
San Saba, TX 76877-0966, USA

Jones, Tracy (Athlete, Baseball Player)
101 Harbor Green Dr Apt 602
Bellevue, KY 41073-1155, USA

Jones, Trevor (Composer)
46 Ave Road Highgate
London N6 5DR, UNITED KINGDOM (UK)

Jones, Ty (Athlete, Hockey Player)
11803 E 20th Ave
Spokane Valley, WA 99206-7002, USA

Jones, Tyler Patrick (Actor)
400 S Beverly Dr Ste 214
Beverly Hills, CA 90212-4414, USA

Jones, Vaughan F R (Mathematician)
Mathematics
Berkeley, CA 94720-0001, USA

Jones, Victor P (Athlete, Football Player)
17727 Sedona Way
Cornelius, NC 28031-8766, USA

Jones, Victor T (Athlete, Football Player)
PO Box 132241
Dallas, TX 75313-2241, USA

Jones, Vinnie (Actor, Producer)
c/o Ryan Martin *Agency for the Performing Arts (APA-LA)*
405 S Beverly Dr Ste 500
Beverly Hills, CA 90212-4425, USA

Jones, Volus
625 S Griffith Park Dr
Burbank, CA 91506-3001

Jones, Wali (Athlete, Basketball Player)
3160 SW 132nd Ave
Miramar, FL 33027-3868, USA

Jones, Wallace (Wah-Wah) (Athlete, Basketball Player)
512 Chinoe Rd
Lexington, KY 40502-2402, USA

Jones, Walter (Athlete, Football Player)
RR 1 Box 128
Carrolton, AL 35447, USA

Jones, Walter Emanuel (Actor)
1498 W Sunset Blvd
Los Angeles, CA 90026-3471, USA

Jones, Wayne (Actor, Comedian)
206 Belmont Dr
Palatka, FL 32177-6402, USA

Jones, Wesley (Architect)
320 Florida St
San Francisco, CA 94110-1411, USA

Jones, Wilbert (Athlete, Basketball Player)
3360 Idlecreek Way
Decatur, GA 30034-4916, USA

Jones, William A (Dub) (Athlete, Football Player)
904 Glendale Dr
Ruston, LA 71270-2346, USA

Jones, Willie D (Athlete, Football Player)
4440 Hidden Orchard Ln
Indianapolis, IN 46228-3023, USA

Jones Cox, Vena (Business Person)
3707 Warsaw Ave
Cincinnati, OH 45205-1773, USA

Jones Girls, The
PO Box 6010
Sherman Oaks, CA 91413-6010

Jones III, June S (Athlete, Coach, Football Coach, Football Player)
2600 Campus Rd Attn Athletic
Honolulu, HI 96822-2224, USA

Jones III, Samuel L (Actor)
c/o Staff Member *Abrams Artists Agency (LA)*
9200 W Sunset Blvd PH 11
Los Angeles, CA 90069-3601, USA

Jones Jr, James L (General)
Supreme Allied Commander Supreme Headquarters
APO, AE 9705, USA

Jones Jr, Robert Trent (Athlete, Golfer)
1900 S Ocean Dr Apt 1612
Fort Lauderdale, FL 33316-3715, USA

Jones Jr, Roy (Actor, Boxer, Producer, Sportscaster)
c/o Darren Prince *Prince Marketing Group*
18 Carillon Cir
Livingston, NJ 07039-2600, USA

Jones-Doxey, Marilyn (Baseball Player)
6201 Rowena Dr
Palmetto, FL 34221-9337, USA

Jong, Erica
121 Davis Hill Rd
Weston, CT 06883-2015

Jon-Jules, Danny (Actor)
PO Box 1116
Belfast B3Z 7AJ, UK

Jonrowe, Dee Dee (Athlete)
PO Box 272
Willow, AK 99688-0272, USA

Jonsen, Albert R (Doctor)
Med School Medical Ethics
Seattle, WA 98195-0001, USA

Jonson, Johnny (Athlete, Football Player)
PO Box 4283
Mooresville, NC 28117-4283, USA

Jonsson, Hans (Athlete, Hockey Player)
2200-201 Portage Ave Attn Don Baizley
Winnipeg, MB R3B 3L3, Canada

Jonsson, Jorgen (Athlete, Hockey Player)
2000 E Gene Autry Way
Anaheim, CA 92806-6143, USA

Jonze, Spike (Actor, Director)
c/o Staff Member *Dickhouse Productions*
5555 Melrose Ave
Los Angeles, CA 90038-3989, USA

Joop, Wolfgang (Designer, Fashion Designer)
Harvestehuder Weg # 22
Ashburn, VA 20149-0001, GERMANY

Joost, Edwin D (Eddie) (Athlete, Baseball Player)
7021 S Shingle Rd
Shingle Springs, CA 95682-9729, USA

Joost, Henry (Director)
c/o Rowena Arguelles *Creative Artists Agency (CAA-LA)*
2000 Avenue of the Stars Ste 100
Los Angeles, CA 90067-4705, USA

Joosten, Kathryn (Actor)
c/o Gail Abbott *Gail Abbott Management*
2399 Leeward Cir
Westlake Village, CA 91361-3430, USA

Joplin, Josh (Musician)
c/o Staff Member *MCT Management*
520 8th Ave Rm 2205
New York, NY 10018-4160, USA

Jopling, T Michael (Government Official)
Ainderby Hall Thirsk
North Yorks YO7 4HZ, UNITED KINGDOM (UK)

Jorane (Composer, Musician)
c/o Staff Member *Greenspan Artist Management*
8760 W Sunset Blvd
West Hollywood, CA 90069-2206, USA

Jordan, Anthony (Athlete, Football Player)
38 Albemarle St
Rochester, NY 14613-1402, USA

Jordan, Brian (Athlete, Baseball Player)
PO Box 1376
Buford, GA 30515-8376, USA

Jordan, Brian (Athlete, Football Player)
2631 Trailing Ivy Way
Buford, GA 30519-7670, USA

Jordan, Buford (Athlete, Football Player)
11 Acadia St
Kenner, LA 70065-1001, USA

Jordan, Cameron (Cam) (Football Player)
c/o Doug Hendrickson *Octagon Football*
832 Sansome St Fl 1
San Francisco, CA 94111-1558, USA

Jordan, Charles M (Designer)
PO Box 8330
Rancho Santa Fe, CA 92067-8330, USA

Jordan, Claudia (Actor, Television Host)
c/o Laura Wright *Avid Exposure*
8721 W Sunset Blvd PH 3
West Hollywood, CA 90069-2273, USA

Jordan, Curtis (Athlete, Football Player)
5617 Villa Dr
Lubbock, TX 79412-3213, USA

Jordan, Darin (Athlete, Football Player)
44 Connell Dr
Stoughton, MA 02072-3708, USA

Jordan, Don (Boxer)
5100 2nd Ave
Los Angeles, CA 90043-1951, USA

Jordan, Don D (Business Person)
1111 Louisiana St
Houston, TX 77002-5230, USA

Jordan, Eddie (Athlete, Basketball Player, Coach)
150 Berger St
Somerset, NJ 08873-3315, USA

Jordan, Glenn (Director)
9401 Wilshire Blvd Ste 700
Beverly Hills, CA 90212-2944, USA

Jordan, Hamilton (Actor)
355 Lexington Ave Fl 21
New York, NY 10017-6603, USA

Jordan, I King (Educator)
President's Office 800 Florida NW
Washington, DC 20001, USA

Jordan, Jim (Congressman, Politician)
1524 Longworth Hob
Washington, DC 20515-2702, USA

Jordan, Kathy (Tennis Player)
114 Walter Hays Dr
Palo Alto, CA 94303-2923, USA

Jordan, Kevin (Athlete, Baseball Player)
127 Ney St
San Francisco, CA 94112-1642, USA

Jordan, Lamont (Athlete, Football Player)
1407 Alberta Dr
Forestville, MD 20747-1902, USA

Jordan, Larry (Athlete, Football Player)

Jordan, Larry R (General)
Deputy Commander in Chief US Army Europe/7th Army
APO, AE 9014, USA

Jordan, Laura (Actor)
c/o Matthew Lesher *Insight*
1134 S Cloverdale Ave
Los Angeles, CA 90019-6737, USA

Jordan, Le Roy
2425 Burbank St
Dallas, TX 75235-3128

Jordan, Leander (Athlete, Football Player)
5021 Oxfordshire Rd
Waxhaw, NC 28173-7324, USA

Jordan, Lee Roy (Athlete, Football Player)
7710 Caruth Blvd
Dallas, TX 75225-8103, USA

Jordan, Leslie (Actor)
c/o Billy Miller *Billy Miller Management*
8322 Ridpath Dr
Los Angeles, CA 90046-7710, USA

Jordan, Mary (Journalist)
PO Box 60326
Houston, TX 77205-0326, USA

Jordan, Michael (Athlete, Basketball Player)
c/o S.D. Portnoy *F.A.M.E*
Prefers to be contacted via telephone
Washington, DC, USA

Jordan, Montell (Musician)
c/o Staff Member *Richard De La Font Agency*
3808 W South Park Blvd
Broken Arrow, OK 74011-1261, USA

Jordan, Neil (Director, Writer)
c/o Staff Member *WmE2 (WMA-LA)*
1 William Morris Pl
Beverly Hills, CA 90212-4261, USA

Jordan, Neil P (Director)
6 Sorrento Terrace Dalkey
County Dublin, IRELAND

Jordan, Niles (Athlete, Baseball Player)
1114 Metcalf St
Sedro Woolley, WA 98284-1510, USA

Jordan, Patty (Athlete, Golfer)
59 Wildwood Ln
Orchard Park, NY 14127-3713, USA

Jordan, Payton (Coach)
3775 Modoc Rd Apt 264
Santa Barbara, CA 93105-5433, USA

Jordan, Randy (Athlete, Football Player)
2220 Rockingham Loop
College Station, TX 77845-4854, USA

Jordan, Ricardo (Athlete, Baseball Player)
930 SW 10th St
Delray Beach, FL 33444, USA

Jordan, Ricky (Athlete, Baseball Player)
965 Moonlit Way
Folsom, CA 95630-7506, USA

Jordan, Scott (Athlete)
1530 Carroll Dr NW Ste 103
Atlanta, GA 30318-3600, USA

Jordan, Scott (Athlete, Baseball Player)
265 Great Oak Dr
Athens, GA 30605-4504, USA

Jordan, Shelby (Athlete, Football Player)
29208 Posey Way
Rancho Palos Verdes, CA 90275-4629, USA

Jordan, Stanley (Musician)
16845 N 29th Ave # 2000
Phoenix, AZ 85053-3053, USA

Jordan, Steve (Athlete, Football Player)
581 W San Marcos Dr
Chandler, AZ 85225-9555, USA

Jordan, Tom (Athlete, Baseball Player)
2909 S Wyoming Ave
Roswell, NM 88203-2374, USA

Jordan Jr, Vernon E (Civil Rights Activist)
30 Rockefeller Plz # 400
New York, NY 10112-0015, USA

Jordanaires, The
4619 220th Pl
Bayside, NY 11361-3650

Jordanova, Vera (Actor, Model)
c/o Alix Gucovsky *Special Artists Agency*
9465 Wilshire Blvd Ste 820
Beverly Hills, CA 90212-2607, USA

Jorden, Tim (Athlete, Football Player)
11402 N 26th Pl
Scottsdale, AZ 85260, USA

Jordensen, Anker (Prime Minister)
Borgbjergvej 1
Copenhagen, SV 2450, DENMARK

Jordenson, Dale W (Economist)
1010 Memorial Dr Apt 14C
Cambridge, MA 02138-4858, USA

Jordison, Joey (Musician)
c/o Staff Member *Gersh (NY)*
41 Madison Ave
New York, NY 10010-2202, USA

Jorgensen, Bodil (Actor)
c/o Lene Seested *Panorama Agency*
Ryesgade 103B
CopenHagen DK-2100, Denmark

Jorgensen, Mike (Athlete, Baseball Player, Coach)
1820 Harbor Mill Dr
Fenton, MO 63026-2653, USA

Jorgensen, Roger (Athlete, Basketball Player)
642 Woodcrest Dr
Pittsburgh, PA 15205-1520, USA

Jorgensen, Terry (Athlete, Baseball Player)
1493 S Sugar Bush Rd
Luxemburg, WI 54217-9311, USA

Jorginho (Soccer Player)
Rua Levi Carreiro 420
Barra de Tijuca, BRAZIL

Jose, Felix (Athlete, Baseball Player)
6814 W Calumet Cir
Lake Worth, FL 33467-7007, USA

Jose, Jose (Musician)
Melchor Ocampo 309
Mexico City, DF CP 11590, MEXICO

Jose, Lind (Baseball Player)
18 Villa Santa
Dorado, PR 00646-5770, USA

Josefowicz, Leila (Musician)
420 W 45th St
New York, NY 10036-3501, USA

Joseph, Chris (Athlete, Hockey Player)
630 Ched 5204-84th St
Edmonton, AB T6E 5N8, Canada

Joseph, Curtis (Athlete, Hockey Player)
c/o Donald Meehan *Newport Sports Management*
201 City Centre Dr Suite 400
Mississauga, ON L58 2T4, Canada

Joseph, Daryl J (Astronaut)
615 Peachtree Ct
Campbell, CA 95008-6353, USA

Joseph, James (Athlete, Football Player)
1777 Brookhaven Ct
Auburn, AL 36830-7553, USA

Joseph, Jeffrey
400 S Beverly Dr Ste 102
Beverly Hills, CA 90212-4403

Joseph, Stephen (Doctor)
125 Worth St
New York, NY 10013-4006, USA

Joseph, William (Football Player)
Giants Stadium
East Rutherford, NJ 7073, USA

Joseph, William (Musician)
c/o Staff Member *MCT Management*
520 8th Ave Rm 2205
New York, NY 10018-4160, USA

Joseph III, Joseph E (Doctor)
Taubman Center
Ann Arbor, MI 48109, USA

Josephine, Charlotte (Royalty)
Grand Ducal Palace
Luxembourg, LUXEMBOURG

Josephs, Wilfred (Composer)
4 Grand Union Walk Kentish Town Rd
Camden Town
London NW1 9LP, UNITED KINGDOM (UK)

Josephson, Brian D (Nobel Prize Laureate)
Madingley Road
Cambridge CB3 0HE, UNITED KINGDOM (UK)

Josephson, Erland (Actor)
Nybroplan Box 5037
Stockholm 102 41, SWEDEN

Josephson, Karen (Swimmer)
1923 Junction Dr
Concord, CA 94518-3361, USA

Josephson, Lester (Josey) (Athlete, Football Player)
5388 N Genernatas Dr
Tucson, AZ 85704, USA

Josephson, Sarah (Swimmer)
1923 Junction Dr
Concord, CA 94518-3361, USA

Joshi, Indira (Actor)
c/o Staff Member *BBC Artist Mail*
PO Box 1116
Belfast BT2 7AJ, United Kingdom

Joshi, Pallavi (Actor, Bollywood, Talk Show Host)
23 Shefalee Makrand Soc Veer Savarkar Rd Mahim
Bombay, MS 400016, INDIA

Joshua, Larry (Actor)
c/o Judy Orbach *Judy O Productions*
6136 Glen Holly St
Hollywood, CA 90068-2338, USA

Joshua, Von (Athlete, Baseball Player)
20922 E Glen Haven Cir
Northville, MI 48167-2465, USA

Jospin, Lionel R (Prime Minister)
Place Saint Etienne
Toulouse Cedex 31090, FRANCE

Jost, Mike (Athlete, Baseball Player)
14223 E Placita Rancho Loma Alta
Vail, AZ 85641-2036, USA

Jostyn, Jennifer (Actor)
c/o Staff Member *Abrams Artists Agency (LA)*
9200 W Sunset Blvd PH 11
Los Angeles, CA 90069-3601, USA

Joswick, Robert (Athlete, Football Player)
5829 W Orlando Cir
Broken Arrow, OK 74011-1153, USA

Jothilakshmi (Actor, Bollywood)
32 Sarangapani Street T Nagar
Chennai, TN 600017, INDIA

Jothimeena (Actor, Bollywood)
32 Sarangapani Street T Nagar
Chennai, TN 600017, INDIA

Joubert, Beverly (Photographer)
& 17th M Sts NW
Washington, DC 20036, USA

Joubert, Brian (Figure Skater)
35 rue Felicien David
Paris 75016, FRANCE

Joubert, Dereck (Photographer)
& 17th M Sts NW
Washington, DC 20036, USA

Joulwan, George A (General)
1348 19th Rd S
Arlington, VA 22202-1637, USA

Jourdain Jr, Michel (Race Car Driver)
4601 Lyman Dr
Hilliard, OH 43026-1249, USA

Jourdan, Louis (Actor)
1139 Maybrook Dr
Beverly Hills, CA 90210-2717, USA

Journell, Jimmy (Athlete, Baseball Player)
1511 Eastgate Rd
Springfield, OH 45503-2427, USA

Journey (Music Group)
c/o Staff Member *Wizard Promotions Konzertagentur GmbH*
Brühlstr. 37
Frankfurt am Main 60439, Germany

Jovanovich, Peter W (Publisher)
1177 Avenue of the Americas # 1965
New York, NY 10036-2714, USA

Jovanovski, Ed (Athlete, Hockey Player)
5224 NW 27th Ct
Margate, FL 33063-1609, USA

Jovovich, Milla (Actor, Model, Musician)
c/o Jason Weinberg *Untitled Entertainment (LA)*
350 S Beverly Dr Ste 200
Beverly Hills, CA 90212-4819, USA

Jow, Malese (Actor)
c/o Christopher Ledford *Acumen Entertainment Partners*
Prefers to be contacted by telephone or email
CA, USA

Jow, Melise (Actor)
c/o Glenn Hughes III *Gem Entertainment Group*
10701 Wilshire Blvd Apt 1202
Los Angeles, CA 90024-4437, USA

Joy, Kathryn (Stylist)
1679 Penny Ln
Bartlett, IL 60103-7403, USA

Joy, Megan (Musician)

Joyal, Eddie (Athlete, Hockey Player)
6469 Wandermere Dr
San Diego, CA 92120-3214, USA

Joyce, Andrea (Correspondent, Sportscaster)
235 E 45th St
New York, NY 10017-3305, USA

Joyce, Delvin (Athlete, Football Player)
RR 10 Box 111
Martinsville, VA 24112, USA

Joyce, Don (Athlete, Football Player)
5200 Pathways Ave Unit 302
Saint Paul, MN 55110-6556, USA

Joyce, Duane (Athlete, Hockey Player)
143 W Elm St
Pembroke, MA 02359-2136, USA

Joyce, Elaine (Actor)
c/o Staff Member *WmE2 (WMA-LA)*
1 William Morris Pl
Beverly Hills, CA 90212-4261, USA

Joyce, James (Baseball Player)
9785 SW 167th Pl
Beaverton, OR 97007-8705, USA

Joyce, James (Athlete, Baseball Player)
9785 SW 167th Pl
Beaverton, OR 97007-8705, USA

Joyce, Joan (Athlete, Golfer)
20024 Back Nine Dr
Boca Raton, FL 33498-4707, USA

Joyce, John T (Misc)
815 15th St NW
Washington, DC 20005, USA

Joyce, Kevin (Athlete, Basketball Player)
420 W Olive St Apt 9
Long Beach, NY 11561-3128, USA

Joyce, Lisa (Actor)
c/o Staff Member *Stone Manners Salners Agency (LA)*
9911 W Pico Blvd Ste 1400
Los Angeles, CA 90035-2715, USA

Joyce, Matt (Athlete, Football Player)
6330 E Wilshire Dr
Scottsdale, AZ 85257-1122, USA

Joyce, Mike (Athlete, Baseball Player)
2030 Berkshire Pl
Wheaton, IL 60189-8143, USA

Joyce, Tom (Artist)
21 Likely Rd
Santa Fe, NM 87508-5963, USA

Joyce, William (Artist, Writer)
3302 Centenary Blvd
Shreveport, LA 71104-4504, USA

Joyce, William H (Business Person)
39 Old Ridgebury Rd
Danbury, CT 06810-5103, USA

Joyeux, Odette
1 Rue Seguier
Paris, FRANCE 75006

Joyner, Alrederick (Al) (Athlete, Track Athlete)
8560 W Sunset Blvd # 10
West Hollywood, CA 90069-2311, USA

Joyner, Harry (Athlete, Basketball Player)
1100 N Alyssa Cir
Payson, AZ 85541-3371, USA

Joyner, Mark (Business Person, Writer)
7426 Cherry Ave # 210-150
Fontana, CA 92336-4221, USA

Joyner, Michelle (Actor)
10100 Santa Monica Blvd Ste 2500
Los Angeles, CA 90067-4116, USA

Joyner, Tom (Radio Personality)
PO Box 630495
Irving, TX 75063-0128

Joyner, Wally (Athlete, Baseball Player)
516 E 2800 S
Mapleton, UT 84664-4850, USA

Joyner-Kersee, Jacqueline (Jackie) (Athlete, Track Athlete)
Eisenhower Park 1899 Hempstead Turnpike, Suite 400
East Meadow, NY 11554, USA

Jozwiak, Brian J (Athlete, Coach, Football Coach, Football Player)
203 Ruby Lake Ln
Winter Haven, FL 33884-3267, USA

Ju, Ming (Artist)
28 Lane 460 Chih Shan Road Section 2
Taipei, TAIWAN

Juanes (Musician)
c/o Staff Member *Fernan Martinez Communications*
4141 NE 2nd Ave Ste 106C
Miami, FL 33137-3500, USA

Juantorena Danger, Alberto (Athlete, Track Athlete)
Sports City
Havana, CUBA

Juckes, Gordon W (Misc)
1475 Avenue B
Big Pine Key, FL 33043, USA

Judd, Ashley (Actor)
c/o Annett Wolf *WKT Public Relations (WKT-LA)*
9350 Wilshire Blvd Ste 450
Beverly Hills, CA 90212-3230, USA

Judd, Cledus T
22 Harbor Park Dr
Port Washington, NY 11050-4650, USA

Judd, Cris (Actor, Choreographer)
c/o Monica Barkett *Global Artists Agency*
6253 Hollywood Blvd Apt 508
Los Angeles, CA 90028-8251, USA

Judd, Howard L (Misc)
Medical Center Ob-Gyn Dept
Los Angeles, CA 90024, USA

Judd, Jackie (Correspondent)
77 W 66th St
New York, NY 10023-6201, USA

Judd, Mike (Athlete, Baseball Player)
9805 Shadow Rd
La Mesa, CA 91941-4154, USA

Judd, Naomi (Musician)
c/o Julie Colbert *WmE2 (Endeavor-LA)*
9601 Wilshire Blvd Fl 3
Beverly Hills, CA 90210-5219, USA

Judd, Wynonna (Musician)
c/o Mark Itkin *WmE2 (Endeavor-LA)*
9601 Wilshire Blvd Fl 3
Beverly Hills, CA 90210-5219, USA

Juden, Jeff (Athlete, Baseball Player)
85 Proctor St
Salem, MA 01970-2110, USA

Judge, Christopher (Actor, Writer)
c/o Christina King *Pantheon Talent*
1801 Century Park E Ste 1910
Los Angeles, CA 90067-2321, USA

Judge, George (Economist)
Economics
Berkeley, CA 94720-0001, USA

Judge, Mike (Actor, Animator, Producer, Writer)
c/o Michael Rotenberg *3 Arts Entertainment Inc*
9460 Wilshire Blvd Fl 7
Beverly Hills, CA 90212-2713, USA

Judkins, Jeff (Athlete, Basketball Player, Coach)
3471 S 3570 E
Salt Lake City, UT 84109-3243, USA

Judkins, Jeff (Athlete, Basketball Player)
3471 S 3570 E
Salt Lake City, UT 84109-3243, USA

Judson, Howie (Athlete, Baseball Player)
239 Fairway Cir
Winter Haven, FL 33881-8742, USA

Judson, William (Athlete, Football Player)
652 Sinclair Way
Jonesboro, GA 30238-7962, USA

Jue, Bhawoh (Athlete, Football Player)
129 E River Dr
De Pere, WI 54115-3781, USA

Juenger, David (Athlete, Football Player)
5026 132nd Ave E
Parrish, FL 34219-2682, USA

Juergensen, Heather (Actor)
c/o Staff Member *Generate Management*
1545 26th St Ste 200
Santa Monica, CA 90404-3554, USA

Jugnauth, Anerood (Prime Minister)
La Caverne 1
Vacoas, MAURITIUS

Juhl, Finn (Designer)
Chartottenlund 2920, DENMARK

Jules, Gary (Musician)
c/o Staff Member *Paradigm (Monterey)*
404 W Franklin St
Monterey, CA 93940-2303, USA

Julian, Fred (Athlete, Football Player)
730 Strawberry Valley Ave NW
Comstock Park, MI 49321-9600, USA

Julian, Janet (Actor)
3172 Dona Susana Dr
Studio City, CA 91604-4356, USA

Julian, Jonathan (Actor)
c/o Susan Nathe *Nathe & Associates*
8281 Melrose Ave Ste 200
Los Angeles, CA 90046-6823, USA

Julian II, Alexander (Designer, Fashion Designer)
323 Florida Hill Rd
Ridgefield, CT 06877-5205, USA

Julien, Claude (Athlete, Coach, Hockey Player)
c/o Staff Member *Boston Bruins*
TD Banknorth Garden 100 Legends Way, Suite 250
Boston, MA 2114, USA

Julien, Max (Actor)
3580 Avenida Del Sol
Studio City, CA 91604-4018, USA

Julius, DeAnne (Economist)
Threadneedle St
London EC2R 8AH, UNITED KINGDOM (UK)

Jullen, Claude (Coach)
1260 De La Gauchetiere W
Montreal, QC H3B 5E8, CANADA

Juma, Kevin (Athlete, Football Player)
9220 Vancouver Dr NE
Lacey, WA 98516-6038, USA

Jump 5 (Music Group)
c/o Staff Member *Bobby Roberts Agency*
PO Box 1547
Goodlettsville, TN 37070-1547, USA

Jumper, John P (General)
Chief of Staff Hqusaf Pentagon
Washington, DC 20330-0001, USA

Junck, Mary (Publisher)
501 N Calvert St
Baltimore, MD 21278-1000, USA

Juncker, Jean-Claude (Prime Minister)
Hotel de Bourgogne 4 Rue de la Congregation
2910, LUXEMBOURG

Juneau, Joe (Athlete, Hockey Player)
100-2 Rue De Jardin Attn Vice President's Ofc
Port-Rouge, QC G3H 3R7, Canada

Jung, Ernst (Writer)
8815 Lagenensligen/Wiltingen
GERMANY

Jung, Ji-Hoon (Rain) (Actor)
c/o Cho Dong Won *J.tune Entertainment*
2F, M Building 221-5 NonHyunDong GangNamGu
Seoul 135010, Korea

Jung, Richard (Misc)
Waldhofstr 42
Freiburg 71691, GERMANY

Junge, Eric (Athlete, Baseball Player)
89 Clinton St Apt 2R
New York, NY 10002-3889, USA

Junger, Gil (Director, Producer)
c/o Staff Member *Creative Artists Agency (CAA-LA)*
2000 Avenue of the Stars Ste 100
Los Angeles, CA 90067-4705, USA

Junger, Sebastian (Writer)
9560 Wilshire Blvd Ste 500
Beverly Hills, CA 90212-2401, USA

Jungman, Eric (Actor)
c/o Staff Member *Leslie Allan-Rice Management*
7524 Mulholland Dr
Los Angeles, CA 90046-1239, USA

Jungueira, Bruno (Race Car Driver)
2127 Brickell Ave Apt 3105
Miami, FL 33129-2105, USA

Junior, Ester J (E J) (Athlete, Football Player)
911 W Summit St
Bolivar, MO 65613-1021, USA

Junior Balaiya (Actor)
3 Melgai Vaniyagar Street Vadapalani
Chennai, TN 600 026, INDIA

Junior Varsity (Music Group)
346 N Justine St Ste 504
Chicago, IL 60607-1021, USA

Junker, Steve (Athlete, Football Player)
5660 Julmar Dr
Cincinnati, OH 45238-1908, USA

Junkin, Abner (Athlete, Football Player)
5 Lakeside Ln
Newport, AR 72112-3948, USA

Junkin, Joe (Athlete, Hockey Player)
2319 Canby St
Harrisburg, PA 17103-1720, USA

Junkin, Trey (Athlete, Football Player)
300 Wren St
Winnfield, LA 71483-2662, USA

Junor, Daisy (Baseball Player)
402-111 Lockwood Rd
Regina, SK S4S 3G5, CANADA

Juppe, Alain
57 Rue De Varenne
Paris, FRANCE F-75007

Juppe, Alain M (Prime Minister)
Mairie Place Pey-Berland
Bordeaux Cedex 33077, FRANCE

Jur, Jeffrey (Cinematographer)
4438 Wortser Ave
Studio City, CA 91604-1432, USA

Jurak, Ed (Athlete, Baseball Player)
3650 S Walker Ave
San Pedro, CA 90731-6046, USA

Juran, Joseph M (Engineer)
11 River Rd
Wilton, CT 06897-6010, USA

Juran, Nathan (Director, Writer)
197 Desert Lakes Dr
Rancho Mirage, CA 92270-4053, USA

Jurasik, Peter (Actor)
969 1/2 Manzanita St
Los Angeles, CA 90029-3009, USA

Jurevicius, Joe (Athlete, Football Player)
76 Lou Groza Blvd
Berea, OH 44017-1238, USA

Jurewicz, Mike (Athlete, Baseball Player)
13804 Evergreen Ct
Saint Paul, MN 55124-9257, USA

Jurgens, Dan
5033 Green Farms Rd
Edina, MN 55436-1091

Jurgens, Udo
Carmenstr. 25
Zurich, SWITZERLAND CH-8032

Jurgensen, Sonny (Athlete, Football Player)
6963 Greentree Dr
Naples, FL 34108-8528, USA

Jurgensmeier-Carroll, Margaret (Baseball Player)
5245 Rowena Dr
Roscoe, IL 61073-7221, USA

Jurich, Tom (Football Player)
University of Louisville Attn Athletic
Louisville, KY 40292-0001, USA

Juriga, James (Athlete, Football Player)
3001 Easton Pl
Saint Charles, IL 60175-5610, USA

Juriga, Jim (Athlete, Football Player)
3001 Easton Pl
Saint Charles, IL 60175-5610, USA

Jurinac, Sena (Opera Singer)
Opernring 2
Vienna 1010, AUSTRIA

Jurkewicz, Walt (Athlete, Football Player)
5441 Ligurian Dr
San Jose, CA 95138-2325, USA

Jurkovic, John (Athlete, Football Player)
2212 June Dr
Schererville, IN 46375-3079, USA

Jurkovic, Mirko (Athlete, Football Player)
68520 Garver Lake Rd
Edwardsburg, MI 49112-9404, USA

Jurow, Martin
5833 Berkshire Ln
Dallas, TX 75209-2403

Just, Walter (Publisher)
333 W State St
Milwaukee, WI 53203-1305, USA

Just, Ward S (Writer)
36 Ave Junot
Paris, FRANCE

Just Jinger (Music Group)
c/o Staff Member *Paradigm (Monterey)*
404 W Franklin St
Monterey, CA 93940-2303, USA

Justice, David (Athlete, Baseball Player)
18570 Old Coach Way
Poway, CA 92064-6651, USA

Justice, Donald R (Writer)
338 Rocky Shore Dr
Iowa City, IA 52246-3836, USA

Justice, Victoria (Actor)
c/o Shannon Barr *Shannon Barr Public Relations*
3313 N Sepulveda Blvd
Manhattan Beach, CA 90266-3626, USA

Justice, William
3832 Chanson Dr
Los Angeles, CA 90043-1602

Justin, Kerry (Athlete, Football Player)
13331 W Marlette Ct
Litchfield Park, AZ 85340-5377, USA

Justman, Seth (Musician)
652 N Doheny Dr
Los Angeles, CA 90069-5526, USA

Jutze, Skip (Athlete, Baseball Player)
3395 Zephyr Ct
Wheat Ridge, CO 80033-5967, USA

Juvenile (Musician)
c/o Staff Member *International Creative Management (ICM-LA)*
10250 Constellation Blvd Fl 7
Los Angeles, CA 90067-6207, USA

Juzda, Bill (Athlete, Hockey Player)
55 Hazel Dell Ave
Winnipeg, MB R2K 0P3, Canada

K

K Bagyaraj (Actor)
Off 1 Kuppusamy Street T Nagar
Chennai, TN 600 017, INDIA

K Balaji (Actor)
58 Pantheon Road Egmore
Chennai, TN 600 008, INDIA

K Balasing (Actor)
8 6/2 Maddox Street Choolai
Chennai, TN 600 112, INDIA

K Bapaiah (Bollywood, Director)
15 Seethamma Colony 3rd Cross Road
Alwarpet
Madras, TN 600 017, INDIA

K. Davis, Danny (Congressman, Politician)
2159 Rayburn Hob
Washington, DC 20515-2307, USa

K. Hirono, Mazie (Congressman, Politician)
1410 Longworth Hob
Washington, DC 20515-3821, USA

K Prabakaran (Actor)
23-C N Boag Road T Nagar
Chennai, TN 600 017, INDIA

Ka Shing, Li (Business Person)
7/F Cheung Kong Center 2 Queens Road Central
HONG KONG

Kaake, Jeff (Actor)
2533 N Carson St # 3105
Carson City, NV 89706-0242, USA

Kaas, Carmen (Model)
199 Lafayette St # 700
New York, NY 10012-4279, USA

Kaas, Jon H (Psychic)
Psychology
Nashville, TN 37240-0001, USA

Kaas, Patrica (Musician)
3 Rue des Petites-Ecuries
Paris 75010, FRANCE

Kaat, Jim (Athlete, Baseball Player)
PO Box 1130
Port Salerno, FL 34992-1130, USA

Kab, Vyto (Athlete, Football Player)
4 Sugar Hill Rd
Kinnelon, NJ 07405-2137, USA

Kaba, Agim (Actor, Producer)
c/o Adam Griffin *Kritzer Levine Wilkins Entertainment*
11872 La Grange Ave Fl 1
Los Angeles, CA 90025-5283, USA

Kabakov, Ilya (Artist)
525 W 52nd St
New York, NY 10019-5074, USA

Kabat-Zinn, Jon (Writer)
413 S Arthur Ave
Louisville, CO 80027-3013, USA

Kabbah, Ahmad Tejan (President)
State House Independence Ave
Freetown, SIERRA LEONE

Kaberle, Frantisek (Athlete, Hockey Player)
3105 Briar Stream Run
Raleigh, NC 27612-5241, USA

Kabila, Joseph (General, President)
Mont Ngaliema
Kinshaha, CONGO DEMOCRATIC REPUBLIC

Kabua, Imata (President)
Cabinet Building PO Box 2
Majuro, MARSHALL ISLANDS

Kachowski, Mark (Athlete, Hockey Player)
113 Pine Creek Dr
Venetia, PA 15367-1330, USA

Kachur, Ed (Athlete, Hockey Player)
Sawmill Bay Rd
Upsala, ON P0T 2Y0, Canada

Kaci (Musician)
c/o Staff Member *Curb Records (LA)*
3907 W Alameda Ave Ste 104
Burbank, CA 91505-4359

Kaczmarek, Jane (Actor)
c/o Adena Chawke *Greenlight Management and Production*
13848 Valleyheart Dr
Sherman Oaks, CA 91423-2930, USA

Kadafi, Moammar
Bab el Aziziya
Tripoli, LIBYA

Kadanoff, Leo P (Physicist)
5421 S Cornell Ave
Chicago, IL 60615-5646, USA

Kadare, Ismael (Writer)
63 Blvd Saint-Michel
Paris 75005, FRANCE

Kadela, Dave (Athlete, Football Player)
9413 Culross Ct
Dublin, OH 43017-9685, USA

Kadenyuk, Leonld K (Cosmonaut)
Moskovskoi Oblasti
Syvisdny Goroduk 141160, RUSSIA

Kadher, Pakkoda (Actor)
9 Ponmana Semmal Street M G R Nagar
Chennai, TN 600 078, INDIA

Kadish, Michael S (Mike) (Athlete, Football Player)
7941 Sudbury Ln SE
Ada, MI 49301-9356, USA

Kadish, Ronald T (Ron) (General)
Director Missile Defense Agency
Washington, DC 20301-0001, USA

Kadison, Joshua (Musician, Songwriter, Writer)
1265 Electric Ave
Venice, CA 90291-3397, USA

Kadziel, Ron (Athlete, Football Player)
2492 Creek Dr
Park City, UT 84060-6866, USA

Kae-Kazim, Hakeem (Actor)
c/o Staff Member *Rough Diamond Management*
1424 N Kings Rd
West Hollywood, CA 90069-1908, USA

Kaelin, Kato
6404 Wilshire Blvd Ste 950
Los Angeles, CA 90048-5529

Kaelin, Todd (Stylist)
c/o Staff Member *Directions USA*
3717 W Market St Ste C
Greensboro, NC 27403-1155, USA

Kaese, Trent (Athlete, Hockey Player)
1398 Leask Rd
Nanaimo, BC V9X 1P8, Canada

Kaestle, Carl F (Historian)
35 Charlesfield St
Providence, RI 02906-1114, USA

Kafelnikov, Yevgeny A (Tennis Player)
26 Riverside Dr
Rumson, NJ 07760-1048, USA

Kafentzis, Mark (Athlete, Football Player)
15912 134th Avenue Ct E
Puyallup, WA 98374-9647, USA

Kaftan, George (Athlete, Basketball Player)
2591 Lantern Light Way
Manasquan, NJ 08736-2247, USA

Kagan, Daryn (Correspondent)
1050 Techwood Dr NW
Atlanta, GA 30318-5604, USA

Kagan, Daryn
1663 Prince St
Alexandria, VA 22314-2818, USA

Kagan, Daryn (Correspondent)
1579 Monroe Dr NE Ste F-134
Atlanta, GA 30324-5039, USA

Kagan, Henri Boris (Misc)
Institut de Chimie Moleculaire
Orsay 91405, FRANCE

Kagan, Jeremy Paul (Director)
2024 N Curson Ave
Los Angeles, CA 90046-2210, USA

Kagasoff, Daren (Actor)
c/o Janice Lee *MLC PR*
7080 Hollywood Blvd Ste 903
Los Angeles, CA 90028-6936, USA

Kagen, David (Actor)
6457 Firmament Ave
Van Nuys, CA 91406-6219, USA

Kagge, Erling (Skier)
Munkedamsveien 86
Oslo 270, NORWAY

Kahan, Richard (Actor)
c/o Elena Kirschner *Lucas Talent Inc*
100 W. Pender St Sun Tower, 7th Floor
Vancouver, BC V6B 1R8, Canada

Kahane, Jeffrey (Musician)
420 W 45th St
New York, NY 10036-3501, USA

Kahin, Brian (Educator)
Information Infrastructure Project
Cambridge, MA 2138, USA

Kahler, Robert (Athlete, Football Player)
5500 Salem Square Dr N
Palm Harbor, FL 34685-1146, USA

Kahler, Royal (Athlete, Football Player)
13116 Durango Dr
Amarillo, TX 79111-1454, USA

Kahn, Alfred E (Economist, Government Official)
PO Box 6599
Ithaca, NY 14851-6599, USA

Kahn, Joseph (Director, Writer)
c/o Staff Member *HSI Entertainment*
3630 Eastham Dr
Culver City, CA 90232-2411, USA

Kahn, Michael (Editor)
c/o David Gersh *Gersh (LA)*
9465 Wilshire Blvd Ste 600
Beverly Hills, CA 90212-2612, USA

Kahn, Robert E (Scientist)
909 Lynton Pl
McLean, VA 22102-2113, USA

Kahn, Roger (Writer)
280 Marcotte Rd
Kingston, NY 12401-8318, USA

Kahne, Kasey (Race Car Driver)
265 Cayuga Dr
Mooresville, NC 28117-8179

Kahneman, Daniel (Nobel Prize Laureate)
70 E 10th St Ph D
New York, NY 10003-5121, USA

Kai, Teanna (Adult Film Star)
c/o Staff Member *Atlas Multimedia Inc*
9005 Eton Ave Ste C
Canoga Park, CA 91304-6533, USA

Kaif, Katrina (Actor)
3B Dlf Corporate Park 'S' Block Qutab Enclave Phase-III
Gurgaon, Haryana 122002, India

Kaifu, Toshiki (Prime Minister)
Diet
Tokyo 100, JAPAN

Kaimer, Karl (Athlete, Football Player)
3 Kerr Ave
Lavallette, NJ 08735-2138, USA

Kain, Karin A (Dancer)
470 Queens Quay
Toronto, ON M5V 3K4, CANADA

Kain, Khalil (Actor)
c/o Staff Member *Envision Management*
8840 Wilshire Blvd Fl 3
Beverly Hills, CA 90211-2606, USA

Kainer, Don (Athlete, Baseball Player)
1923 Sieber Dr
Houston, TX 77017-6201, USA

Kaiser, A Dale (Misc)
832 Santa Fe Ave
Stanford, CA 94305-1023, USA

Kaiser, Bob (Athlete, Baseball Player)
8 Independence Way
Southampton, NJ 08088-9047, USA

Kaiser, Cecil (Athlete, Baseball Player)
16890 Santa Rosa Dr Apt 1
Detroit, MI 48221-2629, USA

Kaiser, Don (Athlete, Baseball Player)
2901 E 12th St
Ada, OK 74820-7259, USA

Kaiser, George B (Financier)
PO Box 2300
Tulsa, OK 74102-2300, USA

Kaiser, Jason (Athlete, Football Player)
3885 Cheyenne Pl
Sedalia, CO 80135-8931, USA

Kaiser, Jeff (Athlete, Baseball Player)
26227 James Dr
Grosse Ile, MI 48138-2172, USA

Kaiser, Ken (Baseball Player)
56 Holley Sue Ln
Rochester, NY 14626-1170, USA

Kaiser, Ken (Athlete, Baseball Player)
56 Holley Sue Ln
Rochester, NY 14626-1170, USA

Kaiser, Michael (Misc)
Washington, DC 20011, USA

Kaiser, Natasha (Athlete, Track Athlete)
2601 Hickman Rd
Des Moines, IA 50310-6101, USA

Kaiser, Suki (Actor)
c/o Pam Winter *Gary Goddard Agency*
10 St Mary St Suite 305
Toronto, ON M4Y 1P9, Canada

Kaiser, Tim (Producer)
c/o Scott Schwartz *Vision Art Management*
9465 Wilshire Blvd Ste 870
Beverly Hills, CA 90212-2610, USA

Kaiser, Vern (Athlete, Hockey Player)
1275 Kilwinning St
Penticton, BC V2A 4P2, Canada

Kaiser Chiefs (Music Group)
c/o Staff Member *Helter Skelter (UK)*
535 Kings Rd The Plaza
London SW10 0SZ, UNITED KINGDOM (UK)

Kaiserman, William (Designer, Fashion Designer)
29 W 56th St
New York, NY 10019-3986, USA

Kaji, Gautam S (Financier)
2 Seaport Ln Ste 1300
Boston, MA 02210-2058, USA

Kajlich, Bianca (Actor)
c/o Chris Henze *Thruline Entertainment*
9250 Wilshire Blvd Ground Fl
Beverly Hills, CA 90212, USA

Kajol (Actor, Bollywood)
c/o Bunty Bahl *Carving Dreams Entertainment*
304-305, Oberoi Chambers II B Wing, Off New Link Road, Andheri West
Mumbai 400053, INDIA

Kakhidze, Djansug I (Conductor)
Leselidze St 18
Tbilisi 380005, GEORGIA

Kalafat, Ed (Athlete, Basketball Player)
1814 Pinehurst Ave
Saint Paul, MN 55116-2117, USA

Kalafut, Kathy (Stylist)
329 W 55th St Apt 3B
New York, NY 10019-4512, USA

Kalam, A P J Abdul (President)
Bharat ka Rashtrapati Bhavan
New Delhi, New Delhi 110004, INDIA

Kalangis, Ike (Financier)
303 Roma Ave NW
Albuquerque, NM 87102-2219, USA

Kalas, Harry (Sportscaster)
3308 Chatham Pl
Media, PA 19063-4313, USA

Kalas, Todd (Athlete, Baseball Player, Sportscaster)
9417 Cavendish Dr Apt 108
Tampa, FL 33626-5173, USA

Kalashnikov, Mikhail T (Designer, General)
426006 Izhevsk
Udmurtia Republic, RUSSIA

Kalb, Marvin (Correspondent, Educator)
Shorenstein Center 79 JF Kennedy St
Cambridge, MA 2138, USA

Kalem, Toni (Actor)
c/o Joy Gorman *Anonymous Content (AC-LA)*
3531 Hayden Ave
Culver City, CA 90232, USA

Kalember, Patricia (Actor)
1505 10th St
Santa Monica, CA 90401-2805, USA

Kalen, Herbert D (War Hero)
General Delivery
Angel Fire, NM 87710-9999, USA

Kaler, Jamie (Actor)
c/o Sheila Wenzel *Innovative Artists (LA)*
1505 10th St
Santa Monica, CA 90401-2805, USA

Kalichstein, Joseph (Musician)
40 W 57th St
New York, NY 10019-4001, USA

Kalikow, Peter S (Publisher)
101 Park Ave
New York, NY 10178-0002, USA

kalina, Richard (Artist)
44 King St
New York, NY 10014-4960, USA

Kaline, Albert W (Al) (Athlete, Baseball Player)
3613 York Ct
Bloomfield Hills, MI 48301-2058, USA

Kaling, Mindy (Actor)
c/o Tess Finkle *Metro Public Relations*
421 N Sierra Bonita Ave
Los Angeles, CA 90036-2464, USA

Kalinin, Dmitri (Athlete, Hockey Player)
46 Summer Hill Ln
Buffalo, NY 14221-5979, USA

Kalis, Todd A (Athlete, Football Player)
900 Bayview Ct
Cranberry Township, PA 16066-3424, USA

Kalish, Martin (Misc)
853 Broadway
New York, NY 10003-4703, USA

Kalitta, Connie (Race Car Driver)
804 Willow Run Airport
Ypsilanti, MI 48198-0899, USA

Kallaugher, Kevin (Kall) (Cartoonist)
501 N Calvert St
Baltimore, MD 21278-1000, USA

Kallen, Jackie
c/o Daniel A (Dan) Strone *Trident Media Group LLC*
41 Madison Ave Fl 36
New York, NY 10010-2257, USA

Kallen, Kitty (Musician)
35 Winthrop Pl
Englewood, NJ 7631, USA

Kallir, Lilian (Musician)
165 W 57th St
New York, NY 10019-2201, USA

Kallman, Gerhard M (Architect)
939 Boylston St
Boston, MA 02115-3104, USA

Kalloniatis, Anthony (Actor, Comedian, Composer, Director)
c/o Barry Katz *New Wave Entertainment (LA)*
2660 W Olive Ave
Burbank, CA 91505-4525, USA

Kallur, Anders (Athlete, Hockey Player)
Utsiktsvagen 14
Falun S-79131, Sweden

Kalman, Rudolf E (Mathematician)
Zurich 8092, SWITZERLAND

Kalmanir, Thomas (Athlete, Football Player)
425 E Shelldrake Cir
Fresno, CA 93730-1230, USA

Kalmbach, Herbert
1056 Santiago Dr
Newport Beach, CA 92660-5728

Kalplan, Deborah (Director, Writer)
c/o Staff Member *WmE2 (WMA-LA)*
1 William Morris Pl
Beverly Hills, CA 90212-4261, USA

Kalpokas, Donald (Prime Minister)
PO Box 110
Port Vila, VANUTA

Kalu, Ndukwe (Athlete, Football Player)
1910 Quail Hollow Dr
Fresno, TX 77545, USA

Kalule, Ayub (Boxer)
Bagsvaert 12
Copenhagen 2880, DENMARK

Kalyagin, Aleksander A (Actor)
1905 Goda Str 3 #91
Moscow 123100, RUSSIA

Kamal, Gray (Musician)
1325 Avenue of the Americas
New York, NY 10019-6026, USA

Kamali, Norma (Designer, Fashion Designer)
11 W 56th St
New York, NY 10019-3902, USA

Kamana III, John (Athlete, Football Player)
2319 Kapahu St
Honolulu, HI 96813-1433, USA

Kamano, Stacy (Actor)
c/o Staff Member *AKA Talent Agency*
6310 San Vicente Blvd Ste 200
Los Angeles, CA 90048-5488, USA

Kamarck, Martin A (Financier)
850 3rd Ave Fl 9
New York, NY 10022-7770, USA

Kamb, Alexander (Misc)
300 Alberta Way
Hillsborough, CA 94010-7148, USA

Kamen, Dean (Inventor)
15 W Wind Dr
Bedford, NH 03110-5610, USA

Kamenshek, Dottie (Baseball Player)
314 Longview Pl
Thousand Oaks, CA 91360-2019, USA

Kamensky, Valeri (Athlete, Hockey Player)
5 Stonehedge Dr S
Greenwich, CT 06831-3219, USA

Kamesh, Kamala (Actor, Bollywood)
4F 3rd Block Shanthi Towers 88
Arcotroad Vadapalani
Chennai, TN 600026, INDIA

Kamieniecki, Scott (Athlete, Baseball Player)
7800 Somerhill Ln
Clarkston, MI 48348-4383, USA

Kamin, Blair (Critic)
435 N Michigan Ave
Chicago, IL 60611-4066, USA

Kaminir, Lisa (Actor)
14241 N Maple Dr # 207
Sherman Oaks, CA 1423, USA

Kaminski, Janusz Z (Cinematographer)
23801 Calabasas Rd Ste 2004
Calabasas, CA 91302-1565, USA

Kaminski, Kevin (Athlete, Hockey Player)
135 Arnould Blvd
Lafayette, LA 70506-6213, USA

Kaminski, Larry (Athlete, Football Player)
31423 State Highway 3 NE
Poulsbo, WA 98370-9373, USA

Kaminski, Marek (Misc)
Ul Dickmana 14/15
Gdansk 80-339, POLAND

Kaminsky, Walter (Misc)
Martin-Luther-King Platz 6
Hamburg 20146, GERMANY

Kaminsky, Yan (Athlete, Hockey Player)
4842 Wildrose Ct NW
Kennesaw, GA 30152-7752, USA

Kamisar, Yale (Educator, Lawyer)
2910 Daleview Dr
Ann Arbor, MI 48105-9684, USA

Kamm, Brian (Athlete, Golfer)
479 Barnette Rd
Bluff City, TN 37618-4143, USA

Kammen, Michael G (Historian)
History Dept McGraw Hall
Ithaca, NY 14853, USA

Kammerer, Carl (Athlete, Football Player)
6941 Brooks Rd
Highland, MD 20777-9540, USA

Kamoze, Ini (Musician)
250 W 57th St
New York, NY 10107-0001, USA

Kampa, Robert (Athlete, Football Player)
2001 Jennifer Dr
Aptos, CA 95003-2840, USA

Kampelman, Max M (Diplomat, Government Official)
3131 Connecticut Ave NW Apt 2811
Washington, DC 20008-5030, USA

Kampman, Aaron (Athlete, Football Player)
3999 Chicora Wood Pl
Jacksonville, FL 32224-7694, USA

Kamprad, Ingvar (Business Person)
Box 200
Odakra 26035, Sweden

Kamu, Okko T
Calle Mozart 7 Rancho Domingo
Benalmedina Pueblo 29369, SPAIN

Kan, Yuet Wai (Misc)
20 Yerba Buena Ave
San Francisco, CA 94127-1544, USA

Kanaga (Actor)
33 1st Mall Road R A Puram
Chennai, TN 600028, INDIA

Kanakaredes, Melina (Actor)
c/o Bill Butler *Industry Entertainment Partners*
955 Carrillo Dr Ste 300
Los Angeles, CA 90048-5400, USA

Kanal, Brooke (Stylist)
1 Blackberry Ln
Framingham, MA 01701-3710, USA

Kanal, Tony (Musician, Songwriter, Writer)
31652 2nd Ave
Laguna Beach, CA 92651-8244, USA

Kanaly, Steve (Actor)
4663 Grand Ave
Ojai, CA 93023-9309, USA

Kanamori, Hiroo (Physicist)
Geophysics
Pasadena, CA 91125-0001, USA

Kanan, Sean
c/o Kim Matuka *Online Talent Group*
Prefers to be contacted via email or telephone
Los Angeles, CA 90069, USA

Kananln, Roman G (Architect)
13/14 1 Brestkaya Str
Moscow 125190, RUSSIA

Kancheli, Giya A (Georgy) (Composer)
Tovstonogov Str 6
Tbilisi 380064, GEORGIA

Kandel, Eric R (Nobel Prize Laureate)
9 Sigma Pl
Bronx, NY 10471-1215, USA

Kander, John H (Composer)
8730 W Sunset Blvd Ste 300
Los Angeles, CA 90069-2276, USA

Kane (Wrestler)
c/o Kerry Rodgerson *World Wrestling Entertainment (WWE)*
1241 E Main St
Stamford, CT 06902-3520, USA

Kane, Abigail (Stylist)
c/o Staff Member *Crews*
828 Clemont Dr NE
Atlanta, GA 30306-3694, USA

Kane, Andy (Handy Andy) (Actor)
c/o Staff Member *David Anthony Promotions*
PO Box 286 Warrington
Cheshire WA2 8GA, UNITED KINGDOM

Kane, Big Daddy (Musician)
c/o Ron Rivlin *Coast II Coast Entertainment*
8671 Wilshire Blvd Ste 500
Beverly Hills, CA 90211-2943, USA

Kane, Carol (Actor)
c/o Wes Stevens *Vox*
6420 Wilshire Blvd Ste 1080
Los Angeles, CA 90048-5539, USA

Kane, Chelsea (Actor, Musician)
c/o Margot Menzel *Evolution Entertainment (LA)*
901 N Highland Ave
Los Angeles, CA 90038-2412, USA

Kane, Christian (Actor)
c/o Marsha McManus *Principal Entertainment (LA)*
1964 Westwood Blvd Ste 400
Los Angeles, CA 90025-4695, USA

Kane, John C (Business Person)
7000 Cardinal Pl
Dublin, OH 43017-1091, USA

Kane, Khalil (Actor)
c/o Staff Member *Envision Management*
8840 Wilshire Blvd Fl 3
Beverly Hills, CA 90211-2606, USA

Kane, Lorie (Athlete, Golfer)
101-5397 Eglinton Ave W
Etobicoke, Ontario M9C 5K6, Canada

Kane, Nick (Musician)
1620 16th Ave S
Nashville, TN 37212-2908, USA

Kane, Patrick (Athlete, Hockey Player)
c/o Pat Brisson *Creative Artists Agency (CAA-LA)*
2000 Avenue of the Stars Ste 100
Los Angeles, CA 90067-4705, USA

Kane, Richard (Athlete, Football Player)
2525 Greensboro Pt
Reno, NV 89509-5708, USA

Kane Elson, Marion (Swimmer)
4669 Badger Rd
Santa Rosa, CA 95409-2632, USA

Kanell, Danny (Athlete, Football Player)
4632 Sea Grape Dr
Lauderdale By The Sea, FL 33308-3524, USA

Kanellis, Maria (Actor, Wrestler)
c/o Jessica Cohen *JCPR*
9903 Santa Monica Blvd Ste 983
Beverly Hills, CA 90212-1671, USA

Kaneshiro, Takeshi (Actor)
c/o Staff Member *WmE2 (Endeavor-LA)*
9601 Wilshire Blvd Fl 3
Beverly Hills, CA 90210-5219, USA

Kanew, Jeffery R (Director)
c/o Staff Member *Directors Guild of America*
7920 W Sunset Blvd
Los Angeles, CA 90046-3347, USA

Kang, Dong-Suk (Musician)
47 Whitehall Park
London N19 3TW, UNITED KINGDOM (UK)

Kang, Jimin (Athlete, Golfer)
8539 E Cactus Wren Cir
Scottsdale, AZ 85266-1332, USA

Kang, Sung (Actor)
c/o Scott Schachter *International Creative Management (ICM-LA)*
10250 Constellation Blvd Fl 7
Los Angeles, CA 90067-6207, USA

Kang, Tim (Actor)
c/o Anna Liza Recto *Vincent Cirrincione Associates*
1516 N Fairfax Ave
Los Angeles, CA 90046-2608, USA

Kangas-Brody, Jennifer (Athlete, Golfer)
6275 Knob Bend Dr
Grand Blanc, MI 48439-7459, USA

Kango, Mayuri (Actor, Bollywood)
21 Kala Pathar Gokul Paradise Thakur Complex Kandivili E
Mumbai, MS 400101, INDIA

Kanicki, James (Athlete, Football Player)
4590 Schramling Rd
Pierpont, OH 44082-9712, USA

Kanievska, Marek (Director)
8942 Wilshire Blvd # 219
Beverly Hills, CA 90211-1908, USA

Kanin, Fay (Writer)
653 Palisades Beach Rd
Santa Monica, CA 90402-2605, USA

Kann, Donald (Stylist)
414 NW Breezy Point Loop
Port St Lucie, FL 34986-2667, USA

Kann, Peter R (Business Person, Journalist, Publisher)
200 Liberty St
New York, NY 10281-1003, USA

Kann, Stan
570 N Rossmore Ave
Los Angeles, CA 90004-2465

Kannadasan, Vishali (Actor, Bollywood)
2 9/1 Ist Cross Street Chinmaya Nagar
Chennai, TN 600011, INDIA

Kannaiah, Ennathe (Actor)
RP Block No8 Llyods Colony Royapet
Chennai, TN 600 014, INDIA

Kanne, Michael S (Judge)
PO Box 1340
Lafayette, IN 47902-1340, USA

Kannegiesser, Gordon (Gord) (Athlete, Hockey Player)
312 Main St
Mattawa, ON P0H 1V0, Canada

Kannegiesser, Sheldon (Athlete, Hockey Player)
32214 Oakshore Dr
Westlake Village, CA 91361-3810, USA

Kannenberg, Bernd (Athlete, Track Athlete)
Sportschule
Sonthofen/Aligau 87527, GERMANY

Kannokada, Melanie (Actor, Bollywood)
c/o Asal Masomi *Asal Masomi Public Relations*
6320 Canoga Ave Ste 1513
Woodland Hills, CA 91367-2526, USA

Kanouse, Lyle (Actor)
c/o Staff Member *Gage Group, The (LA)*
14724 Ventura Blvd Ste 505
Sherman Oaks, CA 91403-3505, USA

Kanovitz, Howard (Artist)
20 Tyrone Dr
East Hampton, NY 11937-1443, USA

Kansas (Music Group)
c/o Staff Member *Creative Artists Agency (CAA-LA)*
2000 Avenue of the Stars Ste 100
Los Angeles, CA 90067-4705, USA

Kansch, Heather (Artist)
Knowle Rundlerohy Newton Abbot
Devon TQ12 2PJ, UNITED KINGDOM (UK)

Kanter, Paul (Musician)
315 S Beverly Dr Ste 407
Beverly Hills, CA 90212-4301, USA

Kantor, Michael (Mickey) (Secretary)
1117 San Vicente Blvd
Santa Monica, CA 90402-2007, USA

Kantor, Secy
5019 Klingle St NW
Washington, DC 20016-2653, USA

Kantrowitz, Adrian (Doctor)
70 Gallogly Rd
Lake Angelus, MI 48326-1227, USA

Kantrowitz, Arthur R (Physicist)
4 Downing Rd
Hanover, NH 03755-1902, USA

Kanwaljit (Actor, Bollywood)
B-1001 Abhishek Apts Juhu Versova Link Road 4 Bungalows Andheri (W)
Mumbai, MS 400053, INDIA

Kanwar, Anita (Actor, Bollywood)
501A Anisha Apartments Yari Road
Versova Andheri
Mumbai, MS 400061, INDIA

Kanwar, Raj (Bollywood, Director, Filmmaker, Producer)
6 Mewawala House Next To Arrow Studio Vakola Masjid Santacruz E
Building HAIDERY
Bombay, MS 400 055, INDIA

Kao, Archie (Actor)
c/o Tim Kwok *Convergence Entertainment*
9150 Wilshire Blvd Ste 247
Beverly Hills, CA 90212-3429, USA

Kao, Charles K (Engineer, Nobel Prize Laureate)
1 Harbour Road #1708, Wen Chai
Hong Kong, China

Kapadia, Asif (Actor, Director, Writer)
c/o Robert (Bob) Bookman *Creative Artists Agency (CAA-LA)*
2000 Avenue of the Stars Ste 100
Los Angeles, CA 90067-4705, USA

Kapadia, Dimple (Actor, Bollywood)
201-A Vastu Rd Juhu Bldg MILITARY
Mumbai, MS 400049, INDIA

Kapanen, Sami (Athlete, Hockey Player)
12 Breckenridge Dr
Shamong, NJ 08088-8226, USA

Kapele, John (Athlete, Football Player)
45-543 Paleka Rd
Kaneohe, HI 96744-3413, USA

Kapellusch, Kim (Stylist)
30528 Yosemite Dr
Castaic, CA 91384-3735, USA

Kapelos, John (Actor)
c/o Staff Member *McCabe Group, The*
3211 Cahuenga Blvd W Ste 104
Los Angeles, CA 90068-1372, USA

Kapioitas, John (Business Person)
1111 Westchester Ave
West Harrison, NY 10604-3525, USA

Kaplan, Bonnie (Stylist)
7033 N Kedzie Ave Apt 1411
Chicago, IL 60645-2851, USA

Kaplan, Gabriel
9551 Hidden Valley Rd
Beverly Hills, CA 90210-1311

Kaplan, Jonathan S (Director)
4323 Ben Ave
Studio City, CA 91604-1704, USA

Kaplan, Justin (Writer)
16 Francis Ave
Cambridge, MA 02138-2010, USA

Kaplan, Ken (Athlete, Football Player)
8313 N Fremont Ave
Tampa, FL 33604-2707, USA

Kaplan, Marvin (Actor)
PO Box 1522
Burbank, CA 91507-1522, USA

Kaplan, Nathan O (Misc)
8587 La Jolla Scenic Dr N
La Jolla, CA 92037-2142, USA

Kaplan, Steven (Actor)
c/o Ellen Gilbert *Abrams Artists Agency (LA)*
9200 W Sunset Blvd PH 11
Los Angeles, CA 90069-3601, USA

Kapler, Gabe (Athlete, Baseball Player)
30375 Morning View Dr
Malibu, CA 90265-3618, USA

Kaplon, Al (Actor)
2899 Agoura Rd Ste 172
Westlake Village, CA 91361-3218, USA

Kaplow, Herbert E (Correspondent)
211 N Van Buren St
Falls Church, VA 22046-3654, USA

Kaplowitz, Ralph (Athlete, Basketball Player)
27110 Grand Central Pkwy Apt 1B
Floral Park, NY 11005-1201, USA

Kapnek, Emily (Actor)
c/o Staff Member *Creative Artists Agency (CAA-LA)*
2000 Avenue of the Stars Ste 100
Los Angeles, CA 90067-4705, USA

Kapono, Jason (Basketball Player)
c/o Staff Member *Miami Heat*
1 SE 3rd Ave Ste 2300
Miami, FL 33131-1716, USA

Kapoor, Anil (Actor, Bollywood)
c/o Staff Member *International Creative Management (ICM-LA)*
10250 Constellation Blvd Fl 7
Los Angeles, CA 90067-6207, USA

Kapoor, Anish (Artist)
33 Coleherne Road
London SW10, UNITED KINGDOM (UK)

Kapoor, Karishma (Actor, Bollywood)
2B Excellency 1101/1201 4th Cross Road
Lokhandwala Complex Andheri W
Mumbai, MS 400048, INDIA

Kapoor, Karisma (Actor, Bollywood)
2B Excellency 1101 1201 4th Cross Road
Lokhandwala Complex
Bombay, MS 400 058, INDIA

Kapoor, Kunal (Actor)
c/o Staff Member *Globosport Mumbai Pvt Ltd*
Prime Plaza, 5th Flr, 501, 38 S.V. Rd
Santacruz (W).
Mumbai 400 054, India

Kapoor, Rajiv (Actor, Bollywood, Director, Filmmaker, Producer)
R K Studios Chembur
Bombay, MS 400 071, INDIA

Kapoor, Ranbir (Actor, Bollywood)
c/o Staff Member *Globosport Mumbai Pvt Ltd*
Prime Plaza, 5th Flr, 501, 38 S.V. Rd
Santacruz (W).
Mumbai 400 054, India

Kapoor, Randhir (Actor, Bollywood, Director, Producer)
R K Studios Chembur
Bombay, MS 400 071, INDIA

Kapoor, Ravi (Actor)
c/o Matthew Lesher *Insight*
1134 S Cloverdale Ave
Los Angeles, CA 90019-6737, USA

Kapoor, Rishi (Actor, Bollywood)
27 Krishna Raj Pali Hill Bandra
Mumbai, MS 400058, INDIA

Kapoor, Sanjay (Actor, Bollywood)
18 Arjun Magnum Bungalows
Lokhandwala Complex Andheri W
Mumbai, MS 400053, INDIA

Kapoor, Shakti (Actor, Bollywood, Comedian)
Palm Beach 7th Floor Gandhigram Road Juhu
Bombay, MS 400 049, INDIA

Kapoor, Shammi (Actor, Bollywood)
2 Blue Heaven Malabar Hill Mt Pleasant Rd
Mumbai, MS 400006, INDIA

Kapoor, Shashi (Actor, Bollywood)
112 Atlas Apartments Harkness Rd
Bombay, MS 400 006, INDIA

Kapor, Mitchell D (Engineer)
177 Post St Ste 900
San Francisco, CA 94108-4712, USA

Kapp, Joseph (Joe) (Athlete, Coach, Football Coach, Football Player)
PO Box 1973
Los Gatos, CA 95031-1973, USA

Kapp Horner, Alex (Actor, Producer)
c/o Staff Member *T&A Pictures*
15233 Ventura Blvd Fl 9
Sherman Oaks, CA 91403-2250, USA

Kappu, Satyen (Actor, Bollywood)
201 Canvera J P Road Versova Andheri
Bombay, MS 400 061, INDIA

Kapriski, Valerie
10 Ave George V
Paris, FRANCE F-75008

Kaprisky, Valerie (Actor)
20 Ave Rapp
Paris 75007, FRANCE

Kapter, Alex (Athlete, Football Player)
2508 Haymarket St
Thousand Oaks, CA 91362-5322, USA

Kaptur, Marcy (Congressman, Politician)
2186 Rayburn Hob
Washington, DC 20515-1502, USA

Kapture, Mitzi (Actor)
c/o Rod Baron *Baron Entertainment*
13848 Ventura Blvd Ste A
Sherman Oaks, CA 91423-3654

Kapur, Shekhar (Actor, Bollywood, Director, Filmmaker, Producer)
42 Sheetal A B Nair Road Juhu
Bombay, MS 400 049, INDIA

Kapur, Steve (Apache Indian) (Musician)
c/o Staff Member *Mission Control Artists Agency*
Unit 3 City Business Centre St Olav's Court, Lower Road
London SE16 2XB, UNITED KINGDOM (UK)

Karabin, Ladislav (Athlete, Hockey Player)
5742 Sunberry Cir
Fort Pierce, FL 34951-3117, USA

Karageorghis, Vassos (Misc)
28 Sofoulis St
Nicosia, CYPRUS

Karamanov, Alemdar S (Composer)
Voykova Str 2 #4
Simferopol, Crimea, UKRAINE

Karamatic, George (Athlete, Football Player)
982 Donald Way
Santa Maria, CA 93455-5019, USA

Karan, Amara (Actor)
c/o Ciara Parkes *Public Eye Communications*
535 Kings Rd Suite 313 Plaza
London SW10 0SZ, United Kingdom

Karan, Donna (Designer, Fashion Designer)
550 Seventh Ave
NY 10018, USA

Karapati, Gyorgy (Misc)
II Liva Utca 1
Budapest 1025, HUNGARY

Karath, Kym (Actor)
40 Halsey Dr
Old Greenwich, CT 06870-1226, USA

Karathanasis, Sotirios K (Scientist)
25 Shattuck St
Boston, MA 02115-6027, USA

Karatz, Bruce E (Business Person)
10990 Wilshire Blvd
Los Angeles, CA 90024-3913, USA

Karbacher, Bernd
Hufnagelstrasse 13
Munich, GERMANY D-80686

Karchner, Matt (Athlete, Baseball Player)
401 E 2nd St
Berwick, PA 18603-4801, USA

Kardashian, Khloe (Actor)
c/o Staff Member *Agency for the Performing Arts (APA-LA)*
405 S Beverly Dr Ste 500
Beverly Hills, CA 90212-4425, USA

Kardashian, Kim (Actor, Reality TV Star)
c/o Jill Fritzo *PMK/BNC Public Relations (PMK-NY)*
622 3rd Ave Fl 8
New York, NY 10017-6707, USA

Kardashian, Kourtney (Reality TV Star)
c/o Jill Fritzo *PMK/BNC Public Relations (PMK-NY)*
622 3rd Ave Fl 8
New York, NY 10017-6707, USA

Kardashian, Rob
c/o Staff Member *Commercial Talent Agency*
9255 W Sunset Blvd Ste 505
West Hollywood, CA 90069-3301, USA

Kardashian Jr, Robert (Actor, Reality TV Star)
c/o Lance Klein *WmE2 (Endeavor-LA)*
9601 Wilshire Blvd Fl 3
Beverly Hills, CA 90210-5219, USA

Karelskaya, Rimma K (Ballerina)
Teatralnaya Pi 1
Moscow 103009, RUSSIA

Karen, Ehrisman (Stylist)
1243 Redfield Rd
Naperville, IL 60563-0440, USA

Karen, James
4455 Los Feliz Blvd Apt 807
Los Angeles, CA 90027-2138

Karieva, Bernara (Ballerina)
28 M K Otaturk St
Tashkent 700029, UZBEKISTAN

Karim, Reef (Actor)
c/o Staff Member *Daris Hatch Management*
10027 Rossbury Pl
Los Angeles, CA 90064-4825, USA

Karim-Lamrani, Mohammed (Prime Minister)
Anfa Superieur
Casablanca 21300, MOROCCO

Karimov, Islam M (President)
Uzbekistansky Prosp 45
Tashkent, UZBEKISTAN

Karin, Anna (Actor)
7080 Hollywood Blvd Ste 1017
Los Angeles, CA 90028-6937, USA

Karina, Anna (Actor)
20 Ave Rapp
Paris 75007, FRANCE

Kariya, Paul (Athlete, Hockey Player)
2493 Aquasanta
Tustin, CA 92782-1104, USA

Karkovice, Ron (Athlete, Baseball Player)
272 Celebration Blvd
Kissimmee, FL 34747-5082, USA

Karl, George (Coach)
10936 N Port Washington Rd
Mequon, WI 53092-5031, USA

Karl, George (Athlete, Basketball Player)
245 S Krameria St
Denver, CO 80224-1044, USA

Karl, Jan
5555 Melrose Ave # L
Los Angeles, CA 90038-3989

Karl, Scott (Athlete, Baseball Player)
6446 Lilium Ln
Carlsbad, CA 92011-2793, USA

Karlander, Al (Athlete, Hockey Player)
4940 Deer Ridge Dr N
Carmel, IN 46033-8904, USA

Karle, Isabelia (Misc)
6304 Lakeview Dr
Falls Church, VA 22041-1309, USA

Karle, Jerome (Nobel Prize Laureate)
6304 Lakeview Dr
Falls Church, VA 22041-1309, USA

Karlen, John (Actor)
PO Box 1195
Santa Monica, CA 90406-1195, USA

Karlin, Ben (Producer, Writer)
c/o Staff Member *3 Arts Entertainment Inc*
9460 Wilshire Blvd Fl 7
Beverly Hills, CA 90212-2713, USA

Karlin, Fred
1187 Coast Village Rd # 1-339
Montecito, CA 93108-2737

Karlin, Samuel (Mathematician)
Mathematics Dept
Stanford, CA 94305, USA

Karling, John S (Misc)
West Lafayette, IN 47906, USA

Karlis, Rich (Athlete, Football Player)
194 S Lafayette St
Denver, CO 80209-2522, USA

Karloff, Sara
PO Box 2424
Rancho Mirage, CA 92270-1087

Karlson, Phil
3094 Patricia Ave
Los Angeles, CA 90064-4534

Karlsson, Lena (Musician)
6404 Wilshire Blvd # 807
Los Angeles, CA 90048-5501, USA

Karlstad, Geir (Speed Skater)
Hamarveien 5A
Fjellhamar 1472, NORWAY

Karlzen, Mary (Musician, Songwriter, Writer)
155 Avenue of the Americas Rm 700
New York, NY 10013-1507, USA

Karmanos Jr, Peter (Business Person)
1 Campus Martius
Detroit, MI 48226-5000, USA

Karmazin, Mike (Athlete, Football Player)
100 Morris St
Revere, MA 02151-1017, USA

Karmi, Ram (Architect)
17 Kaplan St
Tel Aviv 64734, ISRAEL

Karmi-Melamede, Ada (Architect)
17 Kaplan St
Tel Aviv 64734, ISRAEL

Karn, Richard (Actor)
c/o Staff Member *Stone Manners Salners Agency (LA)*
9911 W Pico Blvd Ste 1400
Los Angeles, CA 90035-2715, USA

Karnad, Girish (Actor)
Silver Cascade Mount Mary Road Bandra
Bombay, MS 400 050, INDIA

Karnes, David K (Ex-Senator)
1650 Farnam St
Omaha, NE 68102-2104, USA

Karnes, Jay (Actor)
c/o Jonathan Howard *Innovative Artists (LA)*
1505 10th St
Santa Monica, CA 90401-2805, USA

Karnofsky, Sonny (Athlete, Football Player)
14801 Nevar Ct
Rancho Murieta, CA 95683-9553, USA

Karnow, Stanley (Historian)
10850 Spring Knoll Dr
Potomac, MD 20854-1550, USA

Karnuth, Jason (Athlete, Baseball Player)
2822 Helding Park Ct
Katy, TX 77494-8522, USA

Karol, Scott (Producer)
c/o Staff Member *Crystal Sky Pictures*
10203 Santa Monica Blvd Ste 500
Los Angeles, CA 90067-6416, USA

Karolyi, Bela (Coach)
478 Forest Service 200 Rd
Huntsville, TX 77340, USA

Karon, Jan (Writer)
7060 Esmont Farm
Esmont, VA 22937-1818, USA

Karp, Richard M (Scientist)
Dept
Seattle, WA 98195-0001, USA

Karp, Ryan (Athlete, Baseball Player)
1 Winterberry Ln
Medway, MA 02053-6209, USA

Karpatkin, Rhonda H (Publisher)
101 Truman Ave
Yonkers, NY 10703-1044, USA

Karpinski, Keith (Athlete, Football Player)
9461 Clewley Rd
Lachine, MI 49753-9683, USA

Karpluk, Erin (Actor)
c/o Staff Member *ROAR (LA)*
9701 Wilshire Blvd Fl 8
Beverly Hills, CA 90212-2008, USA

Karplus, Martin (Misc)
Chemistry Dept
Cambridge, MA 2138, USA

Karpov, Anatoly (Misc)
Prechistenka 10
Moscow, RUSSIA

Karpowich, Ed (Athlete, Football Player)
PO Box 177
Fallon, NV 89407-0177, USA

Karr, Mary (Writer)
English
Syracuse, NY 13244-0001, USA

Karras, Alexander G (Alex) (Actor, Athlete, Football Player)
7943 Woodrow Wilson Dr
Los Angeles, CA 90046-1215, USA

Karras, John (Athlete, Football Player)
123 Acacia Cir Apt 612
Indian Head Park, IL 60525-9098, USA

Karras, Louis (Athlete, Football Player)
904 Tulip Cir
Weston, FL 33327-2450, USA

Karras, Ted (Athlete, Football Player)
1122 N Shelby St
Gary, IN 46403-1447, USA

Karros, Eric P (Athlete, Baseball Player)
41 Sausalito Cir W
Manhattan Beach, CA 90266-7234, USA

Karsay, Steve (Athlete, Baseball Player)
1861 Post Oak Pl
Westlake, TX 76262-4808, USA

Karslake, Betty L (Stylist)
1253 Andrews Ave
Lakewood, OH 44107-2403, USA

Karstens, George (Athlete, Football Player)
9425 Kingston Dr
Bradenton, FL 34210-1830, USA

Karstens, Jeff (Athlete, Baseball Player)
7280 Jamacha Rd
San Diego, CA 92114-3013, USA

Kartheiser, Vincent (Actor)
c/o Evan Hainey *Untitled Entertainment (LA)*
350 S Beverly Dr Ste 200
Beverly Hills, CA 90212-4819, USA

Kartz, Keith (Athlete, Football Player)
19232 E Hinsdale Ln
Centennial, CO 80016-2147, USA

Karusseit, Ursula (Actor)
Rasa Luxemburg Platz
Berlin 10178, GERMANY

Karvan, Claudia (Actor, Musician)
c/o Robyn Gardiner *RGM Artist Group*
64-76 Kippax St Level 2, Suite 202 & 206
Surry Hills, NSW 2010, Australia

Kar-Wai, Wong (Director)
21/F Park Commercial Centre No. 180
Tung Lo Wan Rd.
Hong Kong, China

Karwales, Jack (Athlete, Football Player)
1116 Church St
Glenview, IL 60025-2929, USA

Karyo, Tcheky (Actor)
c/o Staff Member *Current Entertainment*
9200 W Sunset Blvd Ste 10
Los Angeles, CA 90069-3608, USA

Karzai, Hamid (Prime Minister)
Shar Rahi Sedarat
Kabul, AFGHANISTAN

Kasabian, Kamera (Musician)
c/o Staff Member *Paradigm (Monterey)*
404 W Franklin St
Monterey, CA 93940-2303, USA

Kasabov, Anton (Actor)
c/o Scott Karp *Crystal Sky Pictures*
10203 Santa Monica Blvd Ste 500
Los Angeles, CA 90067-6416, USA

Kasarova, Vesselina (Opera Singer)
165 W 57th St
New York, NY 10019-2201, USA

Kasatkina, Natalya R (Ballerina, Choreographer)
Saint Karietny Riad H 5/10 B 37
Moscow 103006, RUSSIA

Kasatonov, Alexei (Athlete, Hockey Player)
153 Eagle Rock Way
Montclair, NJ 07042-1621, USA

Kasay, John (Athlete, Football Player)
8812 Covey Rise Ct
Charlotte, NC 28226-2649, USA

Kasch, Cody (Actor)
c/o Staff Member *International Creative Management (ICM-LA)*
10250 Constellation Blvd Fl 7
Los Angeles, CA 90067-6207, USA

Kasch, Max (Actor)
c/o Staff Member *Abrams Artists Agency (LA)*
9200 W Sunset Blvd PH 11
Los Angeles, CA 90069-3601, USA

Kasdan, Lawrence (Actor, Director, Producer, Writer)
c/o Staff Member *Kasdan Pictures*
PO Box 17578
Beverly Hills, CA 90209-3578, USA

Kasem, Casey (Actor, Entertainer)
138 N Mapleton Dr
Los Angeles, CA 90077-3536, USA

Kasem, Jean (Actor)
138 N Mapleton Dr
Los Angeles, CA 90077-3536, USA

Kasem, Kerri (Actor)
c/o Steve Rohr *Lexicon Public Relations*
1901 Avenue of the Stars Fl 2
Los Angeles, CA 90067-6001, USA

Kaser, Helmut A (Misc)
Hitzigweg 11
Zurich 8032, SWITZERLAND

Kash, Daniel (Actor, Director)
c/o Staff Member *Coolwaters Productions*
10061 Riverside Dr # 531
Toluca Lake, CA 91602-2560, USA

Kasha, Al (Composer, Musician)
458 N Oakhurst Dr Apt 102
Beverly Hills, CA 90210-5701, USA

Kashanchi, Ashkan (Actor, Bollywood)
c/o Asal Masomi *Asal Masomi Public Relations*
6320 Canoga Ave Ste 1513
Woodland Hills, CA 91367-2526, USA

Kashkashian, Kim (Musician)
c/o Staff Member *Musicians Corporate Management*
PO Box 825
Highland, NY 12528-0825, USA

Kashthuri (Actor, Bollywood)
4 Kashthuri Ranga Rd
Chennai, TN 600018, INDIA

Kasich, John (Governor, Politician)
Vern Riffe Ctr 77 S High St Fl 30
Columbus, OH 43215-6108, USA

Kaskade (DJ, Music Group)
c/o Joel Zimmerman *WmE2 (WMA-NY)*
1325 Avenue of the Americas
New York, NY 10019-6026, USA

Kaskey, Raymond J (Artist)
3804 38th St
Brentwood, MD 20722-1707, USA

Kasko, Eddie (Athlete, Baseball Player, Coach)
32 Major Ginter Ct
Richmond, VA 23227-3349, USA

Kasl, Dr. Charlotte (Writer)
PO Box 1302
Lolo, MT 59847-1302, USA

Kasner, Sherrie (Stylist)
c/o Staff Member *Solo Artists*
2148 Federal Ave
Los Angeles, CA 90025-5327, USA

Kason, Corinne (Actor)
7095 Hollywood Blvd Ste 1006
Los Angeles, CA 90028-8912, USA

Kasovitz, Mathieu (Actor)
36 Rue De Ponthieu
Paris, FRANCE 75008

Kasparaitis, Darius (Athlete, Hockey Player)
PO Box 130
Armonk, NY 10504-0130, USA

Kasparaltis, Darius
170 Fairway Landings Dr
Canonsburg, PA 15317-9567

Kasparov, Garri (Misc)
Luzhnetskaya 8
Moscow 119270, RUSSIA

Kasper, Steve (Athlete, Coach, Hockey Player)
6 Swan Ln
Andover, MA 01810-2844, USA

Kasper, Walter Cardinal (Religious Leader)
Via dell Erba 1
Rome 193, ITALY

Kasperek, Dick (Athlete, Football Player)
PO Box 99
Glenn, MI 49416-0099, USA

Kaspszyk, Jacek (Conductor)
Pl Teatrainy 1
Warsaw 00-077, POLAND

Kasrashvili, Makvala (Opera Singer)
Teatralnaya Pl 1
Moscow 103009, RUSSIA

Kass, Carmen (Model)
Rue Jean Mermoz
Paris 75008, FRANCE

Kass, Danny (Skier)
4315 NE Laurelhurst Pl
Portland, OR 97213-1665, USA

Kass, Leon R (Misc)
1150 17th St NW # AE1
Washington, DC 20036-4603, USA

Kass, Patricia
B.P. 203
Illkirch, FRANCE F-06700

Kassebaum, Nancy Landon (Ex-Senator)
Unit 45004 Box 200
Apo, AP 96337-5004, USA

Kassebaum-Baker, Nancy (Ex-Senator)
PO Box 8
Huntsville, TN 37756-0008, USA

Kassell, Brad (Athlete, Football Player)
20117 Rancho Cielo Ct
Lago Vista, TX 78645-6046, USA

Kassell, Carl (Correspondent)
635 Massachusetts Ave NW
Washington, DC 20001-3740, USA

Kassir, John (Actor)
c/o Vincent Cirrincione *Vincent Cirrincione Associates*
1516 N Fairfax Ave
Los Angeles, CA 90046-2608, USA

Kassorla, Irene C (Doctor)
908 N Roxbury Dr
Beverly Hills, CA 90210-3020, USA

Kassovitz, Mathieu (Actor, Director, Producer)
18 Rue Du Fbg Du Temple
Paris 75011, France

Kassulke, Karl O (Athlete, Football Player)
3030 McCarthy Rdg
Eagan, MN 55121-1907, USA

Kastelic, Ed (Athlete, Hockey Player)
1839 W Muirwood Dr
Phoenix, AZ 85045-1773, USA

Kasyanov, Mikhail M (Prime Minister)
Kremlin Staraya Pl 4
Moscow 103132, RUSSIA

Kaszycki, Mike (Athlete, Hockey Player)
9 Shore Blvd
St Catharines, ON L2N 5T9, Canada

Kata, Matt (Athlete, Baseball Player)
1711 Westend Pl
Round Rock, TX 78681-2252, USA

Katchik, Joe (Athlete, Football Player)
25 Forty Oaks Rd
Whitehouse Station, NJ 08889-3121, USA

Katchor, Ben (Cartoonist)
3 Center Plz
Boston, MA 02108-2003, USA

Kate, Lauren (Writer)
PO Box 461514
Los Angeles, CA 90046-9514, USA

Kates, Kimberley (Actor)
116 S Gardner St
Los Angeles, CA 90036-2718, USA

Kates, Kimberly
3500 W Olive Ave Ste 1400
Burbank, CA 91505-5512

Kates, Robert W (Misc)
1081 Bar Harbor Rd
Trenton, ME 04605-6017, USA

Kathadi, Ramamurthi (Actor)
4 Krishna Avenue C V Raman Rd
Chennai, TN 600 006, INDIA

Katic, Stana (Actor)
c/o Toni Benson *Third Hill Entertainment*
195 S Beverly Dr Ste 400
Beverly Hills, CA 90212-3044, USA

Katims, Jason (Producer)
c/o Staff Member *Creative Artists Agency (CAA-LA)*
2000 Avenue of the Stars Ste 100
Los Angeles, CA 90067-4705, USA

Katims, Milton (Conductor, Musician)
8001 Sand Point Way NE
Seattle, WA 98115-8112, USA

Katin, Peter R (Musician)
Top Farm Parish Lane Hedgerley
Bucks SL2 3JH, UNITED KINGDOM (UK)

Katkaveck Sr, Leo (Athlete, Basketball Player)
507 W Queen St
Edenton, NC 27932-1751, USA

Katona, Kerry (Actor)
c/o Staff Member *Random House Group Limited*
The Book Service Limited 20 Vauxhall Bridge Road
London SW1V 2SA, United Kingdom

Katrina & The Waves
45 Belvoir Rd Cambridge
Cambridgeshire, ENGLAND CB4 1JH

Katritzky, Alan R (Misc)
1221 SW 21st Ave
Gainesville, FL 32601-8417, USA

Katsav, Moshe (Politician, President)
3 Hanassi
Jerusalem 92188, ISRAEL

Katsoudas, Stella (Musician, Songwriter, Writer)
2002 Hogback Rd Ste 20
Ann Arbor, MI 48105-9736, USA

Katt, Nicky (Actor)
c/o John Carrabino *John Carrabino Management*
5900 Wilshire Blvd Ste 406
Los Angeles, CA 90036-5015, USA

Katt, William (Actor)
5860 Le Sage Ave
Woodland Hills, CA 91367-5902, USA

Kattan, Chris (Comedian)
c/o Staff Member *3 Arts Entertainment Inc*
9460 Wilshire Blvd Fl 7
Beverly Hills, CA 90212-2713, USA

Kattan, Mohammed Imad (Architect)
PO Box 950846
Amman 11195, JORDAN

Katy B (Musician)
c/o Tom Schroeder *Coda Music Agency - UK*
229 Shoreditch High St
London E1 6PJ, UK

Katz, Alex (Artist)
435 W Broadway
New York, NY 10012-5902, USA

Katz, Cindy
1680 Vine St Ste 1016
Los Angeles, CA 90028-8800, USA

Katz, Donald L (Engineer)
2011 Washtenaw Ave
Ann Arbor, MI 48104, USA

Katz, Douglas J (Doug) (Admiral)
1530 Gordon Cove Dr
Annapolis, MD 21403-5004, USA

Katz, Harold (Misc)
1st Union Center 3601 South Broad St
Philadelphia, PA 19148, USA

Katz, Hilda (Artist)
915 W End Ave Apt 5D
New York, NY 10025-3503, USA

Katz, Jonathan (Actor, Animator, Comedian, Producer, Writer)
c/o Staff Member *President Street Productions*
137 5th Ave Fl 9
New York, NY 10010-7140, USA

Katz, Michael (Misc)
200 E 57th St Apt 11K
New York, NY 10022-2867, USA

Katz, Omri (Actor)
23679 Calabasas Rd # 333
Calabasas, CA 91302-1502, USA

Katz, Richard (Actor)
c/o Kirsten Wright *Amanda Howard Associates*
21 Berwick St
London W1F 0PZ, UNITED KINGDOM (UK)

Katz, Ross (Producer)
c/o Staff Member *United Talent Agency (UTA)*
9560 Wilshire Blvd Fl 5
Beverly Hills, CA 90212-2400, USA

Katz, Samuel L (Misc)
1917 Wildcat Creek Rd
Chapel Hill, NC 27516-9786, USA

Katz, Simon (Musician)
Chapel 26A Munster St
London SW6 4EN, UNITED KINGDOM (UK)

Katz, Tonnie L (Editor)
625 N Grand Ave
Santa Ana, CA 92701-4347, USA

katz, Vera (Politician)
1221 SW 4th Ave # 340
Portland, OR 97204-1900, USA

Katzenberg, Jeffrey (Business Person)
c/o Staff Member *DreamWorks SKG*
1000 Flower St
Glendale, CA 91201-3007, USA

Katzenmayer, Travis (Baseball Player)
1128 N Mountain Rd
Mesa, AZ 85207-2408, USA

Katzenmoyer, Andy (Athlete, Football Player)
859 W Main St
Westerville, OH 43081-1224, USA

Katzur, Klaus (Swimmer)
Robert-Siewart-Str 76
Chemnitz 912, GERMANY

Kauffman, Marta (Producer, Writer)
c/o Staff Member *Bright Kauffman Crane Productions*
4000 Warner Blvd Bldg 160 PMB 750
Burbank, CA 91522

Kaufman, Adam (Actor)
c/o Steven Levy *Framework Entertainment (LA)*
9057 Nemo St Ste C
West Hollywood, CA 90069-5511, USA

Kaufman, Avy (Actor)
c/o Rick Kurtzman *Creative Artists Agency (CAA-LA)*
2000 Avenue of the Stars Ste 100
Los Angeles, CA 90067-4705, USA

Kaufman, Bob (Ajax) (Athlete, Basketball Player)
1677 Rivermist Dr SW
Lilburn, GA 30047-2451, USA

Kaufman, Charlie (Writer)
c/o Staff Member *United Talent Agency (UTA)*
9560 Wilshire Blvd Fl 5
Beverly Hills, CA 90212-2400, USA

Kaufman, Curt (Athlete, Baseball Player)
308 Hillway Dr
Glenwood, IA 51534-1210, USA

Kaufman, Dan S (Misc)
Medical School Hematology Dept
Madison, WI 53706, USA

Kaufman, Donald (Writer)
c/o Staff Member *United Talent Agency (UTA)*
9560 Wilshire Blvd Fl 5
Beverly Hills, CA 90212-2400, USA

Kaufman, Henry (Financier)
25 Bank St 30th Floor
London E14 5LE, United Kingdom

Kaufman, Joan (Baseball Player)
1111 Crystal Spg
San Antonio, TX 78258-6909, USA

Kaufman, Moises (Director)
c/o Patty Detroit *Todd Smith and Associates*
10250 Constellation Blvd Fl 7
Los Angeles, CA 90067-6207, USA

Kaufman, Napolean (Athlete, Football Player)
72 Incline Green Ln
Alamo, CA 94507-2334, USA

Kaufman, Napoleon (Athlete, Football Player)
1913 Via Di Salemo
Pleasanton, CA 94566, USA

Kaulitz, Bill (Musician)
c/o Staff Member *Universal Music Deutschland*
Stralauer Allee 1
Berlin 10245, Germany

Kausalya (Actor)
15 A-2 Akshar Palace Rd
Bangalore, KA 52, INDIA

Kaushal, Kamini (Actor, Bollywood, Dancer)
B2 Anita Mt Pleasant Road Malabar Hill
Bombay, MS 400 006, INDIA

Kaushik, Satish (Actor, Bollywood, Comedian, Director, Filmmaker)
1/124 Park View Zakaria Agadi Nagar
Yari Road Versova Andheri
Bombay, MS 400 061, INDIA

Kavana (Musician)
19 S Molton Ln Mayfair
London, England W1K 5LE

kavanaugh, Kenneth W (Ken) (Athlete, Football Player)
4907 Palm Aire Dr
Sarasota, FL 34243-3718, USA

Kavandi, Janet L (Astronaut)
3907 Park Circle Way
Houston, TX 77059-3019, USA

Kavelaars, Ingrid (Actor)
c/o Staff Member *Silver Massetti & Szatmary (SMS-NY)*
145 W 45th St # 1204
New York, NY 10036-4008, USA

Kaveri (Actor, Bollywood)
114 4th Street New Britania Nagar
Chennai, TN 600087, INDIA

Kaviya (Actor, Bollywood)
Santhi Apts Kumaran Colony 9th Street
Chennai, TN 600026, INDIA

Kavner, Julie (Actor)
c/o Paul Martino *International Creative Management (ICM-NY)*
40 W 57th St
New York, NY 10019-4001, USA

Kavovit, Andrew (Actor)
c/o Staff Member *TalentWorks (LA)*
3500 W Olive Ave Ste 1400
Burbank, CA 91505-5512, USA

Kawakubo, Rei (Designer, Fashion Designer)
5-11-5 Minamiaoyana Minatoku
Tokyo, JAPAN

Kawalerowicz, Jersy (Director, Writer)
Ul Marconich 5m 21
Warsaw 02-954, POLAND

Kawawa, Rashidi M (Prime Minister)
Dar es Salaam
TANZANIA

Kay, Alan C (Engineer)
1209 Grand Capital Ave
Glendale, CA 91201, USA

Kay, Charles
18 Epple Rd
London, ENGLAND SW6

Kay, Dianne (Actor)
1565 Calle Del Estribo
Pacific Palisades, CA 90272-2009, USA

Kay, Jason (Jay) (Musician)
c/o Staff Member *WmE2 (WMA-LA)*
1 William Morris Pl
Beverly Hills, CA 90212-4261, USA

Kay, John (Musician)
2211 Norfolk St Ste 760
Houston, TX 77098-4033, USA

Kay, Lisa (Actor)
c/o Jeremy Conway *Conway van Gelder*
8-12 Broadwick St
London W1F 8HW, UK

Kay, Peter (Actor)
c/o Staff Member *McIntyre Management Ltd*
35 Soho Sq 2nd Floor
London W1D 3QX, UK

Kay, Vanessa (Actor)
c/o Staff Member *Comedy Central (LA)*
2049 Century Park E Ste 4170
Los Angeles, CA 90067-3216, USA

Kay, William H (Athlete, Football Player)
4266 Waterston Courtyard
Evans, GA 30809-5036, USA

Kaye, Davie A
1044 Ironwork Pass
Vancouver BC V6H 3P1, CANADA

Kaye, Jonathan (Athlete, Golfer)
328 W El Camino Dr
Phoenix, AZ 85021-5525, USA

Kaye, Jonathan (Stylist)
c/o Staff Member *Katy Barker Agency Inc*
6606 10th Ave Apt 3R
Brooklyn, NY 11219-5804, USA

Kaye, Judy (Actor, Musician)
448 W 44th St
New York, NY 10036-5205, USA

Kaye, Justin (Athlete, Baseball Player)
3580 Yorba Linda Dr
Las Vegas, NV 89122-4714, USA

Kaye, Lila
47 Courtfield Rd # 9
London, ENGLAND SW7 4DB

Kaye, Melvina
PO Box 6085
Burbank, CA 91510-6085

Kaye, Thorsten (Actor)
c/o Staff Member *International Creative Management (ICM-LA)*
10250 Constellation Blvd Fl 7
Los Angeles, CA 90067-6207, USA

Kaye, Tony (Misc)
9 Hillgate St
London W8 7SP, UNITED KINGDOM (UK)

Kayleigh, Layla (Actor, Television Host)
c/o Staff Member *United Talent Agency (UTA)*
9560 Wilshire Blvd Fl 5
Beverly Hills, CA 90212-2400, USA

Kaysen, Carl (Economist)
975 Memorial Dr Apt 209
Cambridge, MA 02138-5793, USA

Kayser, Elmer L (Historian)
2921 34th St NW
Washington, DC 20008-3510, USA

Kaz (Artist)
c/o Staff Member *Fantagraphics Books*
7563 Lake City Way NE
Seattle, WA 98115-4218, USA

Kazan, Lainie (Actor, Musician)
9903 Santa Monica Blvd # 283
Beverly Hills, CA 90212-1671, USA

Kazan, Zoe (Actor)
c/o Michelle Benson *42West (NY)*
220 W 42nd St Fl 12
New York, NY 10036-7200, USA

Kazankina, Tatyana (Athlete, Track Athlete)
Hoshimina St 111211
Saint Petersburg, RUSSIA

Kazanski, Ted (Athlete, Baseball Player)
1544 Dormie Dr
Gladwin, MI 48624-8104, USA

Kazarnovskaya, Lubov Y (Opera Singer)
Hohenbergstr 50
Vienna 1120, AUSTRIA

Kazer, Beau
139-A N San Fernando Rd
Burbank, CA 91502

Kazmaier, Dick
261 Park Ln
Concord, MA 01742-1621

Kazmaier Jr, Richard W (Dick) (Athlete, Football Player)
24 Dockside Ln # 29
Key Largo, FL 33037-5267, USA

KC & The Sunshine Band (Music Group)
c/o Staff Member *WmE2 (WMA-LA)*
1 William Morris Pl
Beverly Hills, CA 90212-4261, USA

K-Ci & JoJo (Music Group)
c/o Staff Member *Devour*
3575 Cahuenga Blvd W Ste 254
Los Angeles, CA 90068-1341, USA

Ke Quan, Jonathan (Actor)

Kea, Clarence (Athlete, Basketball Player)
9175 Jennifer St
Beaumont, TX 77707-2727, USA

Keach, James (Actor)
c/o Staff Member *Catfish Productions*
23852 Pacific Coast Hwy Ste 313
Malibu, CA 90265-4876, USA

Keach, Stacy (Actor)
101 N Robertson Blvd Ste 200
Beverly Hills, CA 90211-2191, USA

Keady, Gene (Coach)
Mackey Arena
West Lafayette, IN 47907, USA

Keagan, Carrie (Television Host)
c/o Staff Member *No Good TV (NGTV)*
9944 Santa Monica Blvd
Beverly Hills, CA 90212-1607, USA

Keaggy, Phil (Musician)
c/o Staff Member *Street Level Artists Agency*
107 E Center St
Warsaw, IN 46580-2841, USA

Keagle, Greg (Athlete, Baseball Player)
11 Wolcott Dr
Horseheads, NY 14845-1012, USA

Kealey, Steve (Athlete, Baseball Player)
1080 1700 Ave
Abilene, KS 67410-6321, USA

Kean, Jane
c/o Staff Member *Pierce & Shelly*
13775A Mono Way # 220
Sonora, CA 95370-8813, USA

Kean, Laurel (Athlete, Golfer)
25280 Ojibway Ct
Punta Gorda, FL 33983-6069, USA

Kean, Thomas H (Ex-Governor)
360 W 31st St Rm 1501
New York, NY 10001-2727, USA

Keanan, Staci (Actor)
c/o Jennifer Goodwin *PMK/BNC - LA*
8687 Melrose Ave Ste 8
West Hollywood, CA 90069-5746, USA

Keane (Musician)
c/o Staff Member *Island Records*
825 8th Ave Rm C2
New York, NY 10019-7472, USA

Keane, Dolores (Musician)
Caherlistrane, Galway, IRELAND

Keane, Glen (Animator)
500 S Buena Vista St
Burbank, CA 91521-0001, USA

Keane, James
612 Lighthouse Ave # 220
Pacific Grove, CA 93950-2615

Keane, James P (Athlete, Football Player)
5016 W Oakwood Dr
McHenry, IL 60050-4941, USA

Keane, John M (Jack) (General)
Vice Chief of Staff Hqusa Pentagon
Washington, DC 20310-0001, USA

Keane, Katie Amanda (Actor)
c/o Paul Bennett *PB Management*
6523 W 6th St
Los Angeles, CA 90048-4715, USA

Keane, Kerrie (Actor)
1801 Avenue of the Stars Ste 902
Los Angeles, CA 90067-5981, USA

Keane, Roy M (Soccer Player)
Sunderland Stadium Park
Manchester, Tyne & Wear SR5 1SU, UNITED KINGDOM (UK)

Keane, Sean (Misc)
1505 W 2nd Ave # 200
Vancouver, BC V6H 3Y4, CANADA

Keans, Doug (Athlete, Hockey Player)
240 Dartmouth Ave
Spring Hill, FL 34606-5435, USA

Kear, David (Misc)
34 W End
Ohope, NEW ZELAND

Kearney, Bob (Athlete, Baseball Player)
4155 Elizabeth Dr
Stevensville, MI 49127-9530, USA

Kearney, Jim (Athlete, Football Player)
7340 Leavenworth Rd
Kansas City, KS 66109-1226, USA

Kearney, Mat (Musician)
c/o Staff Member *First Company Management*
504 Autumn Springs Ct Ste A8
Franklin, TN 37067-8277, USA

Kearney, Tim (Athlete, Football Player)
2144 Dartmouth Gate Ct
Ballwin, MO 63011-5436, USA

Kearns, Austin (Athlete, Baseball Player)
719 Haverhill Dr
Lexington, KY 40503-3426, USA

Kearns, Dennis M (Athlete, Hockey Player)
1292 Esquimalt Ave
West Vancouver, BC V7T 1K3, Canada

Kearns, Michael (Athlete, Basketball Player)
PO Box 263
Monroe, NC 28111-0263, USA

Kearns, Thomas (Athlete, Football Player)
121 Bay Colony Dr
Fort Lauderdale, FL 33308-2024, USA

Kearns, Thomas (Athlete, Basketball Player)
101 W 79th St Apt 15A
New York, NY 10024-6479, USA

Kearse, Amalya L (Judge)
US Courthouse Foley Square
New York, NY 10007, USA

Kearse, Jevon (Athlete, Football Player)
3750 Madison Ave
Fort Myers, FL 33916-1218, USA

Keathley, George (Director)
4949 Cherry St
Kansas City, MO 64110-2229, USA

Keating, Bill (Athlete, Football Player)
4810 S Lafayette Ln
Englewood, CO 80113-7011, USA

Keating, Charles (Actor)
10 E 44th St
New York, NY 10017-3601, USA

Keating, Chris (Athlete, Football Player)
741 Canton Ave
Milton, MA 02186-3121, USA

Keating, Dominic (Actor)
c/o Staff Member *Shelter Entertainment*
9454 Wilshire Blvd Ste 715
Beverly Hills, CA 90212-2925, USA

Keating, Paul (Royalty)
31 Bligh St Level 2
Sydney 2000, AUSTRALIA

Keating, Paul J (Prime Minister)
Bushy Park Road 57 Meadowbank
Dublin, IRELAND

Keating, Ronan (Musician)
c/o Amanda Bross *Finch & Partners*
Top Floor 29-37 Heddon St
London W1B 4BR, UNITED KINGDOM

Keating, Ronan (Musician)
Bushy Park Rd 57 Meadowbank
Dublin, IRELAND

Keating, Thomas A (Athlete, Football Player)
3725 W St NW
Washington, DC 20007-1714, USA

Keatley, Greg (Athlete, Baseball Player)
140 Rockridge Ct
Lexington, SC 29072-7970, USA

Keaton, Curtis (Athlete, Football Player)
246 Briarcliff Dr
Kannapolis, NC 28081-7155, USA

Keaton, Diane (Actor, Director, Producer)
c/o Adam Venit *WmE2 (Endeavor-LA)*
9601 Wilshire Blvd Fl 3
Beverly Hills, CA 90210-5219, USA

Keaton, Joshua (Josh) (Actor)
c/o Brian Wilkins *Kritzer Levine Wilkins Entertainment*
11872 La Grange Ave Fl 1
Los Angeles, CA 90025-5283, USA

Keaton, Michael (Actor, Director, Producer)
c/o Paul Bloch *Rogers & Cowan PR (LA)*
Pacific Design Center 8687 Melrose Ave, 7th Floor
West Hollywood, CA 90069, USA

Keats, Donald H (Composer)
Music School
Denver, CO 80208-0001, USA

Keats, Ele (Actor)
c/o Rob D'Avola *Rob DAvola & Associates*
9107 Wilshire Blvd Ste 450
Beverly Hills, CA 90210-5535, USA

Keb Mo (Musician, Songwriter, Writer)
200 W Superior St Ste 202
Chicago, IL 60654-3554, USA

Kebbel, Arielle (Actor)
c/o Martin Berneman *Precision Entertainment*
6338 Wilshire Blvd
Los Angeles, CA 90048-5002, USA

Kebbell, Toby (Actor)
c/o Samantha Mast *Rogers & Cowan PR (LA)*
Pacific Design Center 8687 Melrose Ave, 7th Floor
West Hollywood, CA 90069, USA

Kebede, Liya (Model)
c/o Staff Member *IMG Models (NY)*
304 Park Ave S # PH
New York, NY 10010, USA

Kebich, Vyacheslau F (Prime Minister)
K Marksa Str 38 Dom Urada
Minsk 220016, BELARUS

Keck, Donald B (Inventor)
2877 Chequers Cir
Big Flats, NY 14814-9610, USA

Kecman, Dan (Athlete, Football Player)
16413 Fox Valley Ter
Rockville, MD 20853-3220, USA

Keczmer, Don (Athlete, Hockey Player)
PO Box 1203
Brentwood, TN 37024-1203, USA

Kedah (King)
Istana Anak Bukit
Alor Setar, Kedah Darul Aman, MALAYSIA

Keddie, Asher (Actor)
c/o Staff Member *Shanahan Management*
Level 3, Berman House 91 Campbell St
Surry Hills NSW 2010, Australia

Kedes, Maureen (Actor)
6767 Forest Lawn Dr Ste 101
Los Angeles, CA 90068-1050, USA

Kee, Lee Shau (Business Person)
72-76/F, Two International Finance Centre
8 Finance Street, Central
Hong Kong

Keeble, Jerry (Athlete, Football Player)
PO Box 367
Dunnigan, CA 95937-0367, USA

Keeble, John (Musician)
729 7th Ave Ste 1600
New York, NY 10019-6880, USA

Keedy, Pat (Athlete, Baseball Player)
6308 Mountainview Cir
Gardendale, AL 35071-2088, USA

Keefe, Adam (Athlete, Basketball Player)
15933 Alcima Ave
Pacific Palisades, CA 90272-2405, USA

Keefe, Mike (Cartoonist)
PO Box 1709
Denver, CO 80201-1709, USA

Keefe, Sheldon (Athlete, Hockey Player)
c/o Staff Member *Pembroke Lumber Kings*
P.O. Box 92 Stn Main
Pembroke, ON K8A 6X1, Canada

Keefer, Don (Actor)
4146 Allott Ave
Sherman Oaks, CA 91423-4302, USA

Keeffe, Bernard (Conductor)
153 Honor Oak Road
London SE23 3RN, UNITED KINGDOM (UK)

Keegan, Andrew (Actor)
c/o Barry McPherson *Agency for the Performing Arts (APA-LA)*
405 S Beverly Dr Ste 500
Beverly Hills, CA 90212-4425, USA

Keegan, John (Historian)
Manor House Kilmington near Warminster
Wilts BA12 6RD, UNITED KINGDOM (UK)

Keehne, Virginya (Actor)
125 S Sycamore Ave
Los Angeles, CA 90036-2938, USA

Keel Jr, Alton G (Business Person, Diplomat)
2891 S River Rd
Stanardsville, VA 22973-2416, USA

Keeler, Don
24000 Jensen Dr
West Hills, CA 91304-3011

Keeler, William H Cardinal (Religious Leader)
3211 4th St NE
Washington, DC 20017-1104, USA

Keeley, Robert V (Diplomat)
3814 Livingston St NW
Washington, DC 20015-2803, USA

Keeling, Alexandra (Stylist)
c/o Staff Member *Artists by Timothy Priano (CA)*
8447 Wilshire Blvd Ste 301
Beverly Hills, CA 90211-3206, USA

Keeling, Charles D (Musician)
9500 Gilman Dr
La Jolla, CA 92093-5004, USA

Keeling, Harold (Athlete, Basketball Player)
6707 Broad Oaks Dr
Richmond, TX 77406-7629, USA

Keeling, Rex (Athlete, Football Player)
PO Box 680026
Fort Payne, AL 35968-1601, USA

Keelor, Greg (Musician)
c/o Staff Member *ArtistDirect*
9046 Lindblade St
Culver City, CA 90232-2513, USA

Keen, Robert Earl (Musician, Songwriter)
PO Box 2186
Bandera, TX 78003-2186, USA

Keen, Sam (Writer)
16331 Norrbom Rd
Sonoma, CA 95476-4783, USA

Keena, Monica (Actor)
c/o Sarah Fargo *Paradigm (NY)*
360 N Crescent Dr
Beverly Hills, CA 90210-4874, USA

Keenan, Joseph D (Misc)
2727 29th St NW
Washington, DC 20008-5505, USA

Keenan, Larry (Athlete, Hockey Player)
132 Gordon Dr
North Bay, ON P1B 8B2, Canada

Keenan, Maynard James (Musician)
c/o Staff Member *Virgin Records (NY)*
150 5th Ave Fl 7
New York, NY 10011-4372, USA

Keenan, Mike (Misc)
550 NE 21st Ave Apt 13
Deerfield Beach, FL 33441-3809, USA

Keene, Bob (Football Player)
W Laurel Lane
Etowah, NC 28729, USA

Keene, Donald L (Educator)
Language Dept Kent Hall
New York, NY 10027, USA

Keene, Tommy (Musician, Songwriter, Writer)
PO Box 107
Sunbury, NC 27979-0107, USA

Keene Cherot, Kyera (Actor)
c/o Staff Member *Creative Artists Agency (CAA-LA)*
2000 Avenue of the Stars Ste 100
Los Angeles, CA 90067-4705, USA

Keenen, Mary Jo
9200 W Sunset Blvd Ste 1130
Los Angeles, CA 90069-3606

Keener, Catherine (Actor)
c/o Staff Member *ID Public Relations (ID-LA)*
7080 Hollywood Blvd Fl 8
Los Angeles, CA 90028-6906, USA

Keener, Jeff (Athlete, Baseball Player)
2107 Dewey St
Murphysboro, IL 62966-2451, USA

Keener, Joe (Athlete, Baseball Player)
16915 Glendower Ave
North Edwards, CA 93523-3515, USA

Keenlyside, Simon (Opera Singer)
165 W 57th St
New York, NY 10019-2201, USA

Keeny Jr, Spurgeon M (Misc)
3600 Albemarle St NW
Washington, DC 20008, USA

Keerthana, K (Actor, Bollywood)
71 A Kamarajar Salai R A Puram
Chennai, TN 600028, INDIA

Keeslar, Matt (Actor)
c/o Staff Member *Stone Manners Salners Agency (LA)*
9911 W Pico Blvd Ste 1400
Los Angeles, CA 90035-2715, USA

Keesling, Barbara (Writer)
c/o Staff Member *Random House Publicity*
1745 Broadway
New York, NY 10019-4368, USA

Keeton, Durwood (Athlete, Football Player)
1372 Diamond Gate Pl
El Paso, TX 79936-7841, USA

Keeton, Rickey (Athlete, Baseball Player)
3433 Stathem Ave
Cincinnati, OH 45211-5723, USA

Keezer, Geoff (Misc)
PO Box 2728
Bala Cynwyd, PA 19004-6728, USA

Kegel, Oliver (Athlete)
Am Bogen 23
Berlin 13589, GERMANY

Keggi, Caroline (Athlete, Golfer)
807 Westlake Dr
Ormond Beach, FL 32174-1476, USA

Kehoe, Rick (Athlete, Hockey Player)
1027 Highland Dr
Canonsburg, PA 15317-5227, USA

Keibler, Stacy (Actor, Wrestler)
c/o Leslie Grossnickle *Untitled Entertainment (LA)*
350 S Beverly Dr Ste 200
Beverly Hills, CA 90212-4819, USA

Keightley, David N (Historian)
History
Berkeley, CA 94720-0001, USA

Keillor, Garrison E (Correspondent, Writer)
480 Cedar St
Saint Paul, MN 55101-2217, USA

Keim, Jenny (Swimmer)
1 Hall of Fame Dr
Fort Lauderdale, FL 33316-1611, USA

Keisler, Randy (Athlete, Baseball Player)
312 Hawk Dr
Slidell, LA 70461-3111, USA

Keita, Ibrahaim Boubakar (Prime Minister)
BP97
Bamako, MALI

Keita, Salif (Composer, Musician)
278 S Main St # 400
Gloucester, MA 1930, USA

Keitel, Harvey (Actor)
c/o Staff Member *Goatsingers, The*
443 Greenwich St # 4B
New York, NY 10013-1702, USA

Keith, Louis (Doctor)
333 E Superior St # 476
Chicago, IL 60611-2654, USA

Keith, Penelope (Actor)
66 Berkeley House Hay Hill
London SW3, UNITED KINGDOM (UK)

Keith, Toby (Musician)
PO Box 8739
Rockford, IL 61126-8739, USA

Keith Rennie, Callum (Actor)
c/o Elizabeth Hodgson *Elizabeth Hodgson Management Group*
1688 Cypress St Suite 405
Vancouver, BC V6J 5J1, Canada

Keithley, Gary (Athlete, Football Player)
1801 W Westhill Dr
Cleburne, TX 76033-5952, USA

Kekalainen, Jarmo (Athlete, Hockey Player)
525 Delaford Ct
Canton, MI 48188-6262, USA

Kekich, Mike (Athlete, Baseball Player)
4942 Kokopelli Dr NE
Rio Rancho, NM 87144-0850, USA

Kelcher, Louie J (Athlete, Football Player)
10204 Carlotta Cv
Austin, TX 78733-1542, USA

Keleti, Agnes (Misc)
Matanya 42902, ISRAEL

Kelis (Musician)
c/o Jeff Rabhan *Three Ring Projects*
111 Westwood Pl Ste 101
Brentwood, TN 37027-5057, USA

Kelis, Kid 'N Play (Music Group)
1650 Broadway Ste 508
New York, NY 10019-6833, USA

Kelker-Kelly, Robert (Actor)
4704 Whitsett Ave
Studio City, CA 91604-1140, USA

Kell, Ayla (Actor)
c/o Scott Zimmerman *Evolution Entertainment (LA)*
901 N Highland Ave
Los Angeles, CA 90038-2412, USA

Kell, Everett (Skeeter) (Athlete, Baseball Player)
PO Box 10113
Conway, AR 72034-0001, USA

Kellagher, Bill (Athlete, Football Player)
17254 Valley Dr
Lewes, DE 19958-4035, USA

Kellan (Stylist)
c/o Staff Member *Igroup + Ridecreative*
315 W 39th St Rm 908
New York, NY 10018-3954, USA

Kellar, Mark (Athlete, Football Player)
3537 W Fuller St
Edina, MN 55410-2361, USA

Kellaway, Roger (Composer)
520 E 81st St PH PMB C
New York, NY 10028-7095, USA

Kelleher, Erhard (Misc)
Sudliche Munchneustr 6A
Grunwald 82031, GERMANY

Kelleher, Herbert D (Business Person)
144 Thelma Dr
San Antonio, TX 78212-2516, USA

Kelleher, Mick (Athlete, Baseball Player)
1451 Alamo Pintado Rd
Solvang, CA 93463-9757, USA

Keller, Bill (Athlete, Basketball Player)
14602 Scarborough Ln
Noblesville, IN 46062-9729, USA

Keller, Cord (Producer)
c/o Staff Member *Innovative Artists (LA)*
1505 10th St
Santa Monica, CA 90401-2805, USA

Keller, Dustin (Athlete, Football Player)
c/o Roosevelt Barnes *Maximum Sports Management*
6435 W Jefferson Blvd # 197
Fort Wayne, IN 46804-6203, USA

Keller, Gary (Athlete, Basketball Player)
220 Estado Way NE
Saint Petersburg, FL 33704-3752, USA

Keller, Hal (Athlete, Baseball Player)
241 Madrona Ter
Sequim, WA 98382-6804, USA

Keller, Jason (Race Car Driver)
177 Knob Hill Rd
Mooresville, NC 28117-6847, USA

Keller, Joseph B (Mathematician)
820 Sonoma Ter
Stanford, CA 94305-1072, USA

Keller, Joyce (Psychic, Radio Personality, Television Host, Writer)
600 Harbor Blvd Unit 905
Weehawken, NJ 07086-6748, USA

Keller, Kris (Athlete, Baseball Player)
1074 Gallant Fox Cir
Jacksonville, FL 32218, USA

Keller, Larry (Athlete, Football Player)
3050 Bluebonnet Blvd
Brenham, TX 77833-9046, USA

Keller, Leonard B (War Hero)
821 Woodland Dr
Rockford, IL 61108-3831, USA

Keller, Martha (Actor)
Munich 81679, GERMANY

Keller, Marthe (Actor)
c/o Laurent Gregoire *Agence Artistique Adequat*
80 Rue D'Amsterdam
Paris 75009, France

Keller, Mary Page (Actor)
c/o Staff Member *Silver Massetti & Szatmary (SMS) Talent Inc*
8730 W Sunset Blvd Ste 440
Los Angeles, CA 90069-2277, USA

Keller, Melissa (Actor)
c/o Margie Weiner *Margie Weiner Management*
8205 Santa Monica Blvd Ste 1450
West Hollywood, CA 90046-5967, USA

Keller, Ralph (Athlete, Hockey Player)
1099 W Governor Rd
Hummelstown, PA 17036-9236, USA

Keller, Rita (Baseball Player)
6410 Westchester St
Portage, MI 49024-3276, USA

Keller, Ron (Athlete, Baseball Player)
PO Box 3267
Cashiers, NC 28717-3267, USA

Keller, Thomas (Chef)
6540 Washington St
Yountville, CA 94599-1315, USA

Kellerman, Ernie (Athlete, Football Player)
408 Fairway Vw
Chagrin Falls, OH 44023-6718, USA

Kellerman, Faye (Writer)
357 W 20th St
New York, NY 10011-3379, USA

Kellerman, Jonathan S (Writer)
357 W 20th St
New York, NY 10011-3379, USA

Kellerman, Max (Actor, Sportscaster)
c/o Staff Member *I, Max*
10201 W Pico Blvd Bldg 101
Los Angeles, CA 90064-2606, USA

Kellerman, Sally (Actor)
c/o Chuck Binder *Binder & Associates*
1465 Lindacrest Dr
Beverly Hills, CA 90210-2519, USA

Kellermeyer, Doug (Athlete, Football Player)
1028 Daisy Ave
Carlsbad, CA 92011-4820, USA

Kelley, Alexis (Stylist)
c/o Staff Member *Montana Artists Agency*
9150 Wilshire Blvd Ste 100
Beverly Hills, CA 90212-3459, USA

Kelley, Allen (Al) (Athlete, Basketball Player)
5900 Longleaf Dr
Lawrence, KS 66049-5801, USA

Kelley, Bill (Athlete, Football Player)
6446 US Highway 69 S
Lone Oak, TX 75453-2242, USA

Kelley, Brian (Athlete, Football Player)
98 Constitution Way
Basking Ridge, NJ 07920-2961, USA

Kelley, David E (Producer, Writer)
c/o Staff Member *David E Kelley Productions*
1600 Rosecrans Ave # 4B
Manhattan Beach, CA 90266-3708, USA

Kelley, Dean (Athlete, Basketball Player)
5900 Longleaf Dr
Lawrence, KS 66049-5801, USA

Kelley, Donald R (Historian)
45 Jefferson Ave
New Brunswick, NJ 08901-1737, USA

Kelley, Dwight (Athlete, Football Player)
1006 Clubview Blvd N
Columbus, OH 43235-1222, USA

Kelley, Earl A (Athlete, Basketball Player)
5900 Longleaf Dr
Lawrence, KS 66049-5801, USA

Kelley, Gaynor N (Business Person)
710 Bridgeport Ave
Shelton, CT 06484-4750, USA

Kelley, Gordon (Athlete, Football Player)
3101 S Ocean Blvd Apt 126
Highland Beach, FL 33487-2573, USA

Kelley, Harold H (Psychic)
21634 Rambla Vista St
Maliby, CA 90265, USA

Kelley, Jack (Athlete, Hockey Player)
PO Box 538
Oakland, ME 04963-0538, USA

Kelley, John A (Marathon) (Athlete, Track Athlete)
136 Cedar Hill Rd
East Dennis, MA 2641, USA

Kelley, Jon (Television Host)
c/o Staff Member *Extra (LA)*
1840 Victory Blvd
Glendale, CA 91201-2558, USA

Kelley, Josh (Musician)
c/o Debbie Wilson *Wilspro Management*
P.O. Box 9
Point Pleasant, NY 10001, USA

Kelley, Kevin (Athlete, Baseball Player)
1311 Quarterpath Ct
Richmond, TX 77406-6502, USA

Kelley, Kitty (Writer)
1228 Eton Ct NW
Washington, DC 20007-3240, USA

Kelley, Malcolm David (Actor)
c/o Nelson Parks *ESI Network*
6399 Wilshire Blvd Ste 300
Los Angeles, CA 90048-5706, United States

Kelley, Manon (Adult Film Star)
PO Box 315
Bellmore, NY 11710-0315, USA

Kelley, Mike (Artist)
2472 Eastman Ave # 35-36
Ventura, CA 93003-7709, USA

Kelley, Nathalie (Actor)
c/o Megan Silverman *WmE2 (Endeavor-LA)*
9601 Wilshire Blvd Fl 3
Beverly Hills, CA 90210-5219, USA

Kelley, Paul X (General)
1600 N Oak St Apt 1619
Arlington, VA 22209-2769, USA

Kelley, Rich (Athlete, Basketball Player)
314 Raymundo Dr
Woodside, CA 94062-4129, USA

Kelley, Ryan (Actor)
c/o Beverly Strong *Strong Management*
9350 Wilshire Blvd Ste 224
Beverly Hills, CA 90212-3204, USA

Kelley, Sheila (Actor, Producer)
524 Lorraine Blvd
Los Angeles, CA 90020-4732, USA

Kelley, Shelia (Actor)
524 Lorraine Blvd
Los Angeles, CA 90020-4732, USA

Kelley, Steve (Cartoonist)
350 Camino De La Reina
San Diego, CA 92108-3003, USA

Kelley, Thomas G (War Hero)
600 Washington St Ste 1100
Boston, MA 02111-1704, USA

Kelley, Tom (Athlete, Baseball Player)
710 11th Ave S
North Myrtle Beach, SC 29582-3754, USA

Kelley, William G (Business Person)
1105 N Market St
Wilmington, DE 19801-1282, USA

Kellin, Kevin (Athlete, Football Player)
12500 Capri Cir N Apt 302
Treasure Island, FL 33706-4972, USA

Kellman, Barnet (Director)
c/o Staff Member *Jackoway Tyerman Wertheimer Austen Mandelbaum Morris & Klein*
1925 Century Park E Fl 22
Los Angeles, CA 90067-2701, USA

Kellner, Catherine (Actor)
c/o Michael Lazo *Untitled Entertainment (LA)*
350 S Beverly Dr Ste 200
Beverly Hills, CA 90212-4819, USA

Kellner, Deborah (Actor)
c/o Jessica (Pilch) Samuel *Sanders Armstrong Caserta*
2120 Colorado Ave Ste 120
Santa Monica, CA 90404-3561, USA

Kellogg, Clark (Athlete, Basketball Player, Sportscaster)
5423 Medallion Dr E
Westerville, OH 43082-8691, USA

Kellogg, Jeffrey (Baseball Player)
22900 Cherry Hill Ct
Mattawan, MI 49071-9562, USA

Kellogg, Jeffrey (Athlete, Baseball Player)
22900 Cherry Hill Ct
Mattawan, MI 49071-9562, USA

Kellogg, Mike (Athlete, Football Player)
7497 Tabor St
Arvada, CO 80005-3283, USA

Kellogg, Vivian (Athlete, Baseball Player)
9145 Olcott Lk
Jackson, MI 49201-7832, USA

Kellogg, William S (Business Person)
N56W17000 Ridgewood Dr
Menomonee Falls, WI 53051-5660, USA

Kellogg Jr, Allan J (War Hero)
250 Lihau St
Kailua, HI 96734, USA

Kellum, Marv (Athlete, Football Player)
235 Jamaica Ave
Pittsburgh, PA 15229-1748, USA

Kelly, Aaron (Musician)
c/o Simon Fuller *XIX Entertainment*
33/32 Ransomes Dock 35-37 Parkgate Rd
London SW11 4NP, UK

Kelly, Annesse (Bowler)
2912 Cape Verde Ln
Las Vegas, NV 89128-7236, USA

Kelly, Arvesta (Athlete, Basketball Player)
1040 Oxford St N
Saint Paul, MN 55103-1246, USA

Kelly, Barbara
5 Kidderpore Ave
London, ENGLAND NW3 7SX

Kelly, Bob (Athlete, Baseball Player)
9 Mohawk Dr
Niantic, CT 6357, USA

Kelly, Bob (Athlete, Hockey Player)
10 Peyton Ct
Marlton, NJ 08053-4700, USA

Kelly, Brendan (Actor)
c/o Staff Member *Allman/Rea Management*
9255 W Sunset Blvd Ste 600
West Hollywood, CA 90069-3306, USA

Kelly, Brendon John (Actor)
c/o Toni Scheinbaum *C3 Management Group*
4555 Matilija Ave
Sherman Oaks, CA 91423-2918, USA

Kelly, Brian (Athlete, Football Player)
939 Harbour Bay Dr Apt 5102
Tampa, FL 33602-5738, USA

Kelly, Bryan (Athlete, Baseball Player)
5400 Cub Lake Dr
Apopka, FL 32703-1946, USA

Kelly, Chris
21/22 Poland St
London, ENGLAND W1V 3DD

Kelly, Clinton
c/o Staff Member *The Learning Channel (TLC)*
10100 Santa Monica Blvd Ste 1500
Los Angeles, CA 90067-4117, USA

Kelly, Colleen (Stylist)
c/o Staff Member *Directions USA*
3717 W Market St Ste C
Greensboro, NC 27403-1155, USA

Kelly, Dale (Baseball Player)
3417 Quail Meadows Dr
Santa Maria, CA 93455-2477, USA

Kelly, Daniel-Hugh (Actor)
1505 10th St
Santa Monica, CA 90401-2805, USA

Kelly, David (Actor)
535 King Street The Plz # 219
London, ENGLAND SW10 0SZ

Kelly, David Patrick (Actor)
c/o Staff Member *Paradigm (LA)*
360 N Crescent Dr
Beverly Hills, CA 90210-4874, USA

Kelly, Dean Lennox (Actor)
c/o Staff Member *Scott Marshall Partners Ltd*
15 Little Portland St 2nd Floor
London W1W 8BW, UK

Kelly, Diva Kelly (Athlete, Wrestler)
c/o Staff Member *World Wrestling Entertainment (WWE)*
1241 E Main St
Stamford, CT 06902-3520, USA

Kelly, Donald P (Business Person)
701 Harger Rd Ste 190
Oak Brook, IL 60523-1490, USA

Kelly, Eamon M (Educator)
3122 Octavia St
New Orleans, LA 70125-4936, USA

Kelly, Elisworth (Artist)
PO Box 1708
Chatham, NY 12037, USA

Kelly, Ellison (Athlete, Football Player)
110 Eglinton Ave W
Toronto, ON M4R 1A3, Canada

Kelly, Henry
10 Clorane Gdns
London, ENGLAND NW3 7PR

Kelly, James E (Jim) (Athlete, Football Player)
1961 Wehrle Dr Ste 5
Buffalo, NY 14221-8460, USA

Kelly, James M (Jim) (Astronaut)
403 S Northfield St
Mediapolis, IA 52637-9702, USA

Kelly, Jean Louisa (Actor)
c/o Staff Member *Levine Okwu Erickson Management*
6363 Wilshire Blvd Ste 300
Los Angeles, CA 90048-5729, USA

Kelly, Jeff (Athlete, Football Player)
6437 Munke Rd
La Grange, TX 78945-5836, USA

Kelly, Jerry (Athlete, Golfer)
531 Farwell Dr
Madison, WI 53704-6027, USA

Kelly, Joanne (Actor)
c/o Joanna (Joanie) Burstein *Burstein Company, The*
15304 W Sunset Blvd Ste 208
Pacific Palisades, CA 90272-3656, USA

Kelly, John (Musician)
6920 W Sunset Blvd
Los Angeles, CA 90028-7010, USA

Kelly, John D (Athlete, Football Player)
816 NE 18th Ave Apt 4
Fort Lauderdale, FL 33304-3005, USA

Kelly, John H (Diplomat)
1808 Over Lake Dr SE Ste D
Conyers, GA 30013-6608, USA

Kelly, Kenny (Athlete, Baseball Player)
1318 Louisiana St
Plant City, FL 33563-5828, USA

Kelly, Kevin (Baseball Player)
1311 Quarterpath Ct
Richmond, TX 77406-6502, USA

Kelly, Leonard P (Red) (Athlete, Hockey Player)
30 Dunvegan Rd
Toronto, ON M4V 2P6, Canada

Kelly, Leroy (Athlete, Football Player)
91 Club House Dr
Willingboro, NJ 08046-3418, USA

Kelly, Lisa Robin (Actor)
c/o Dan Baron *Agency for the Performing Arts (APA-LA)*
405 S Beverly Dr Ste 500
Beverly Hills, CA 90212-4425, USA

Kelly, Malcolm (Athlete, Football Player)
c/o Chad Speck *Allegiant Athletic Agency*
35 Market Sq Ste 201
Knoxville, TN 37902-1420, USA

Kelly, Mark E (Astronaut)
2121 Barrington Dr
League City, TX 77573, USA

Kelly, Megyn (Correspondent)
c/o Staff Member *Fox News Channel (NY)*
1211 Ave Of The Americas Level C1
New York, NY 10036-8701, USA

Kelly, Michael (Actor)
c/o Brian Liebman *Liebman Entertainment*
25 E 21st St PH
New York, NY 10010-6226, USA

Kelly, Mike (Athlete, Baseball Player)
8490 S Maple Ave
Tempe, AZ 85284-2244, USA

Kelly, Mike (Athlete, Football Player)
7941 David Kenney Farm Rd
Huntersville, NC 28078-8730, USA

Kelly, Minka (Actor)
c/o Nicole King *Management 360*
9111 Wilshire Blvd
Beverly Hills, CA 90210-5508, USA

Kelly, Moira (Actor)
c/o Troy Nankin *Wishlab*
2438 Canyon Oak Dr
Los Angeles, CA 90068-2428, USA

Kelly, Morgan (Actor)
c/o Tina Petro *Epic Talent*
3451 St. Laurent #400
Montreal QC H2X 2T6, Canada

Kelly, Pat (Athlete, Baseball Player)
10 Murray St
Bangor, PA 18013, USA

Kelly, Pat (Athlete, Baseball Player)
6748 Friendship Dr
Sarasota, FL 34241-5757, USA

Kelly, Paul (Musician, Songwriter)
c/o Staff Member *Paradigm (Monterey)*
404 W Franklin St
Monterey, CA 93940-2303, USA

Kelly, Raymond (Misc)
1 Police Plz
New York, NY 10038-1403, USA

Kelly, Richard (Rich) (Director, Writer)
c/o John Campisi *Creative Artists Agency (CAA-LA)*
2000 Avenue of the Stars Ste 100
Los Angeles, CA 90067-4705, USA

Kelly, Robert (Athlete, Football Player)
5380 N 750 E
Hamlet, IN 46532-9531, USA

Kelly, Robert (R Kelly) (Artist, Musician, Songwriter, Writer)
c/o Derrel McDavid *Winkler & McDavid, Ltd*
308 Madison St
Oak Park, IL 60302-4110, USA

Kelly, Roberto (Athlete, Baseball Player)
PO Box 3746
Augusta, GA 30914-3746, USA

Kelly, Roz
5161 Riverton Ave Apt 105
North Hollywood, CA 91601-3943

Kelly, Ryan (Actor)
c/o Staff Member *Ambition Talent*
439 Wellington St. W. Suite 204
Toronto, ON M5V 1E7, Canada

Kelly, Scott J (Astronaut)
2121 Barrington Dr
League City, TX 77573, USA

Kelly, Thomas (Athlete, Football Player)
14524 La Mesa Dr
La Mirada, CA 90638-4026, USA

Kelly, Thomas (Athlete, Basketball Player)
1850 Eucalyptus Hill Rd
Santa Barbara, CA 93108-1829, USA

Kelly, Tom (Athlete, Baseball Player, Coach)
1643 Currie St N
Saint Paul, MN 55119-7160, USA

Kelly, Van (Athlete, Baseball Player)
11 Beauregard Dr
Spencer, NC 28159-1957, USA

Kelly III, Thomas J (Journalist)
PO Box 2208 Sanatoga Branch
Pottstown, PA 19464, USA

Kelly Jr, Thomas J (Biologist)
1275 York Ave
New York, NY 10065-6007, USA

Kelm, Larry (Athlete, Football Player)
67 Driftoak Cir
The Woodlands, TX 77381-6632, USA

Kelman, Arthur (Misc)
175 1st St S Apt 2001
Saint Petersburg, FL 33701-4531, USA

Kelman, James (Writer)
Weidenfeld-Nicolson Upper Saint Martin's Lane
London WC2H 9EA, UNITED KINGDOM (UK)

Kelser, Gregory (Athlete, Basketball Player)
30400 Forest Dr
Franklin, MI 48025-1598, USA

Kelsey, David (Actor)
c/o Staff Member *Select Artists Ltd (CA-Westside Office)*
1138 12th St Apt 1
Santa Monica, CA 90403-5459, USA

Kelsey, Frances O (Misc)
5600 Fishers Ln
Rockville, MD 20852-1750, USA

Kelso, Ben (Athlete, Basketball Player)
1877 Midchester Dr
West Bloomfield, MI 48324-1138, USA

Kelso, Bill (Athlete, Baseball Player)
114 NE 50th Ct Apt 1021
Kansas City, MO 64118-4520, USA

Kelso, Mark (Athlete, Football Player)
897 Luther Rd
East Aurora, NY 14052-9764, USA

Kelso II, Frank B (Admiral)
7794 Turlock Rd
Springfield, VA 22153-2331, USA

Kelton, David (Athlete, Baseball Player)
515 Riverside Dr
Lagrange, GA 30240-9635, USA

Kelvin (Stylist)
c/o Staff Member *Smashbox Beauty*
8549 Higuera St Bldg B
Culver City, CA 90232-2521, USA

Kem (Music Group)
c/o Staff Member *Paradigm (Monterey)*
404 W Franklin St
Monterey, CA 93940-2303, USA

Kemal, Yashar (Writer)
PK14 Basinkoy
Istanbul, TURKEY

Kemmerer, Beatrice (Baseball Player)
6437 Carter St
Bremen, IN 46506-4306, USA

Kemmerer, Russ (Athlete, Baseball Player)
6335 Colebrook Dr
Indianapolis, IN 46220-4205, USA

Kemp, Gary (Musician)
729 7th Ave Ste 1600
New York, NY 10019-6880, USA

Kemp, Jeff (Athlete, Football Player)
22101 NE 66th Pl
Redmond, WA 98053-2337, USA

Kemp, Jeremy (Actor)
12/13 Poland St
London W1V 3DE, UNITED KINGDOM (UK)

Kemp, Martin (Musician)
Business Center Lower Road
London SE16 2XB, UNITED KINGDOM (UK)

Kemp, Matt (Athlete, Baseball Player)
c/o Staff Member *Los Angeles Dodgers (LA Dodgers)*
1000 Elysian Park Ave
Los Angeles, CA 90090-1112, USA

Kemp, Ross (Actor)
BBC Elstree Centre Clarendon Road
Borehamwood, Herts UK WD6 1JF

Kemp, Shawn T (Athlete, Basketball Player)
51297 Stratford Dr
Elkhart, IN 46514-9113, USA

Kemp, Steve (Athlete, Baseball Player)
1428 Colony Plz
Newport Beach, CA 92660-6362, USA

Kemper, Ellie (Actor)
c/o Liz Mahoney *ID Public Relations (ID-LA)*
7080 Hollywood Blvd Fl 8
Los Angeles, CA 90028-6906, USA

Kemper, Victor J (Cinematographer)
232 N Canon Dr
Beverly Hills, CA 90210-5302, USA

Kemper II, David W (Financier)
1000 Walnut St
Kansas City, MO 64106-2145, USA

Kempf, Cecil J (Admiral)
831 Olive Ave
Coronado, CA 92118-2525, USA

Kempf, Florian (Athlete, Football Player)
8039 Pine Rd Apt 1
Philadelphia, PA 19111-1808, USA

Kempinska, Charles (Athlete, Football Player)
925 State St
Natchez, MS 39120-3577, USA

Kempner, Walter (Misc)
1505 Virginia Ave
Durham, NC 27705-3118, USA

Kempton, Tim (Athlete, Basketball Player)
16223 W Cambridge Ave
Goodyear, AZ 85395-2084, USA

Ken, Baird (Athlete, Hockey Player)
Lot 4 Berry Bay
White Lake, MB R0B 1M0, Canada

Kenady, Chris (Athlete, Hockey Player)
5042 Tuxedo Blvd
Mound, MN 55364-9254, USA

Kenan, Sean
77 W 66th St
New York, NY 10023-6201

Kendal, Felicity (Actor)
Chatto & Linnit Prince of Wales Coventry St
London W1V 7FE, UNITED KINGDOM (UK)

Kendall, A Bruce (Yachtsman)
6 Pedersen Place Bucklands Beach
Auckland, NEW ZELAND

Kendall, Barbara (Yachtsman)
82B Great South Road
Auckland, NEW ZELAND

Kendall, Donald M (Business Person)
Anderson Hill Road
Purchase, NY 10577, USA

Kendall, Fred (Athlete, Baseball Player)
57575 Johnston Rd
Anza, CA 92539-9646, USA

Kendall, Jason (Athlete, Baseball Player)
11730 Stonehenge Ln
Los Angeles, CA 90077-1302, USA

Kendall, Jeannie (Musician)
2802 Columbine Pl
Nashville, TN 37204-3104, USA

Kendall, Pete (Athlete, Football Player)
PO Box 888
Phoenix, AZ 85001-0888, USA

Kendall, Skip (Athlete, Golfer)
8406 Kemper Ln
Windermere, FL 34786-5318, USA

Kendall, Tom (Race Car Driver)
1394 Broadway Ave
Braselton, GA 30517-2909, USA

Kendall, Tony
Via G. Talombini 12
Rome, ITALY 156

Kenders, Al (Athlete, Baseball Player)
8744 Matilija Ave
Panorama City, CA 91402-3320, USA

Kendler, Bob (Misc)
4101 Dempster St
Skokie, IL 60076-2152, USA

Kendrena, Ken (Baseball Player)
4235 Stone Mountain Dr
Chino Hills, CA 91709-6155, USA

Kendrick, Alex (Producer)
c/o Staff Member *Sherwood Pictures*
2201 Whispering Pines Rd
Albany, GA 31707-2421, USA

Kendrick, Anna (Actor)
c/o Lisa Perkins *Fifteen Minutes (LA)*
8436 W 3rd St Ste 650
Los Angeles, CA 90048-4131, USA

Kendrick, Frank (Athlete, Basketball Player)
8355 Providence Dr
Fishers, IN 46038-5233, USA

Kendrick, Rodney (Composer, Musician)
410 W 53rd St Apt 128C
New York, NY 10019-5693, USA

Keneally, Thomas M (Writer)
24 Serpentine
Bilgola Beach, NSW 2107, AUSTRALIA

Keneley, Matt (Athlete, Football Player)
25142 Sandia Ct
Laguna Hills, CA 92653-5606, USA

Kener, Kira (Adult Film Star)
3599 Cahuenga Blvd W
Los Angeles, CA 90068-1397, USA

Kenerson, John (Athlete, Football Player)
4949 S Cottage Grove Ave Apt 602
Chicago, IL 60615-2647, USA

Kenilorea, Peter (Prime Minister)
Kalala House PO Box 535 Honiara
Guadacanal, SOLOMON ISLANDS

Kenn, Michael L (Mike) (Athlete, Football Player)
360 Bardolier
Alpharetta, GA 30022-5129, USA

Kenna, E Douglas (Doug) (Athlete, Business Person, Football Player)
111 S Saint Joseph St
South Bend, IN 46601-1901, USA

Kenna, Edward (War Hero)
121 Coleraine Rd
Hamilton, VIC 3300, AUSTRALIA

Kennan, Brian (Musician)
PO Box 770850
Orlando, FL 32877-0850, USA

Kennard, George (Athlete, Football Player)
13852 N 45th Pl
Phoenix, AZ 85032-5527, USA

Kennard, William (Bill) (Government Official)
1001 Pennsylvania Ave NW
Washington, DC 20004-2502, USA

Kenne, Leslie F (General)
Deputy Cofs for Warfighting Integration
Hqusa Pentagon
Washington, DC 20310-0001, USA

Kennedy, Adam (Athlete, Baseball Player)
5025 Windhill Dr
Riverside, CA 92507-0615, USA

Kennedy, Alan D (Business Person)
PO Box 2353
Orlando, FL 32802-2353, USA

Kennedy, Allan (Stylist)
c/o Staff Member *Katy Barker Agency Inc*
6606 10th Ave Apt 3R
Brooklyn, NY 11219-5804, USA

Kennedy, Anthony M (Judge)
1 1st St NE
Washington, DC 20543-0001, USA

Kennedy, Claudia J (General)
c/o Staff Member *WmE2 (WMA-NY)*
1325 Avenue of the Americas
New York, NY 10019-6026, USA

Kennedy, Coenelia G (Judge)
231 W Lafayette Blvd
Detroit, MI 48226-2700, USA

Kennedy, Cortez (Athlete, Football Player)
121 Gary Lynn Dr
Osceola, AR 72370-1709, USA

Kennedy, D James (Religious Leader)
5554 N Federal Hwy
Fort Lauderdale, FL 33308-3209, USA

Kennedy, Dan (Business Person, Writer)
5818 N 7th St # 103
Phoenix, AZ 85014-5806, USA

Kennedy, David M (Historian)
History Dept
Stanford, CA 94305, USA

Kennedy, David M (Secretary)
3838 Ruth Dr
Salt Lake City, UT 84124-2327, USA

Kennedy, Dean (Athlete, Hockey Player)
General Delivery
Pincher Creek, AB T0K 1W0, Canada

Kennedy, Donald (Educator)
International Studies Institute
Stanford, CA 94305, USA

Kennedy, Dwayne (Comedian)
c/o Rick Messina *Messina Baker/ Entertainment*
955 Carrillo Dr Ste 100
Los Angeles, CA 90048-5400, USA

Kennedy, Ethel (Misc)
1367 Connecticut Ave NW Ste 200
Washington, DC 20036-1859, USA

Kennedy, Eugene (Athlete, Basketball Player)
8218 Westrock Dr
Dallas, TX 75243-6524, USA

Kennedy, Forbes (Athlete, Hockey Player)
20 Oakland Dr
Charlottetown, PA C1C 1P4, Canada

Kennedy, George (Actor)
c/o Rick Hersh *Celebrity Consultants LLC*
3340 Ocean Park Blvd Ste 1030
Santa Monica, CA 90405-3259, USA

Kennedy, Ian (Athlete, Baseball Player)
c/o Team Member *New York Yankees*
Yankee Stadium 161st St & River Ave
Bronx, NY 10451, USA

Kennedy, James C (Business Person)
1400 Lake Hearn Dr NE
Atlanta, GA 30319-1464, USA

Kennedy, Jamie (Actor, Producer, Writer)
c/o Stephen (Steve) Small *Paradigm (LA)*
360 N Crescent Dr
Beverly Hills, CA 90210-4874, USA

Kennedy, Jim (Athlete, Baseball Player)
13940 SW Lisa Ln
Beaverton, OR 97005-4315, USA

Kennedy, Jimmy (Athlete, Football Player)
901 N Broadway
Saint Louis, MO 63101-2800, USA

Kennedy, Joe (Athlete, Basketball Player)
201 43rd St
Virginia Beach, VA 23451-2503, USA

Kennedy, Joe (Athlete, Baseball Player)
10880 Highway 67 Spc 116
Lakeside, CA 92040-1455, USA

Kennedy, Joey D (Joe) Jr (Journalist)
1635 11th Pl S
Birmingham, AL 35205-5907, USA

Kennedy, John (Athlete, Baseball Player)
2 Rodney Rd
Peabody, MA 01960-3517, USA

Kennedy, John Milton (Actor)
5711 Reseda Blvd # 204
Tarzana, CA 91356-2201, USA

Kennedy, Junior (Athlete, Baseball Player)
6601 Eucalyptus Dr Spc 215
Bakersfield, CA 93306-6844, USA

Kennedy, Kathleen (Producer)
c/o Staff Member *United Talent Agency (UTA)*
9560 Wilshire Blvd Fl 5
Beverly Hills, CA 90212-2400, USA

Kennedy, Ken (Wrestler)
c/o Kerry Rodgerson *World Wrestling Entertainment (WWE)*
1241 E Main St
Stamford, CT 06902-3520, USA

Kennedy, Kenoy (Athlete, Football Player)
16275 O Conner Ave
Forney, TX 75126-7572, USA

Kennedy, Kevin (Athlete, Baseball Player, Coach, Television Host)
c/o Staff Member *Fox Sports*
1211 Avenue of the Americas Ste 302
New York, NY 10036-8799, USA

Kennedy, Lee (Business Person)
1550 Peachtree St NE
Atlanta, GA 30309-2402, USA

Kennedy, Leon Isaac (Actor)
859 N Hollywood Way # 384
Burbank, CA 91505-2814, USA

Kennedy, Lincoln (Athlete, Football Player)
PO Box 920431
Norcross, GA 30010-0431, USA

Kennedy, M Peter (Figure Skater)
7650 SE 41st St
Mercer Island, WA 98040-3437, USA

Kennedy, Mike (Athlete, Hockey Player)
402-3000 Manitoba St
Etobicoke, ON M8Y 4G6, Canada

Kennedy, Mimi (Actor)
c/o Todd Justice *Marshak/Zachary Company, The*
8840 Wilshire Blvd Fl 1
Beverly Hills, CA 90211-2606, USA

Kennedy, Nigel (Musician)
Regency House 1-4 Warwick St
London W1R 5WB, UNITED KINGDOM (UK)

Kennedy, Page (Actor)
c/o Judy Page *Mitchell K Stubbs & Assoc (MKS)*
8675 Washington Blvd Ste 203
Culver City, CA 90232-7486, USA

Kennedy, Paul M (Historian)
409 Humphrey St
New Haven, CT 06511-3710, USA

Kennedy, Randall L (Educator, Lawyer)
Law School
Cambridge, MA 2138, USA

Kennedy, Ray F (Business Person)
21001 Van Born Rd
Taylor, MI 48180-1340, USA

Kennedy, Robert F Jr (Lawyer)
N Broadway Fl 78
White Plains, NY 10601-2319, USA

Kennedy, Robert H (Athlete, Football Player)
4906 N 76th Pl
Scottsdale, AZ 85251-1507, USA

Kennedy, Ryan (Actor)
c/o Lesa Kirk *Kirk Talent Agencies Inc*
70 East 2nd. Ave Suite 301
Vancouver, BC V5T 1B1, Canada

Kennedy, T Lincoin (Athlete, Football Player)
3917 Spring Garden Pl Apt 1
Spring Valley, CA 91977, USA

Kennedy, Ted (Athlete, Hockey Player)
Physically unable to sign autographs

Kennedy, Terrence E (Terry) (Athlete, Baseball Player)
333 N Pennington Dr Unit 23
Chandler, AZ 85224-8266, USA

Kennedy, Theodore S (Teeder) (Athlete, Hockey Player)
22 Lakeside Pl W
Port Colbome, ON L3K 6B1, Canada

Kennedy, William (Athlete, Basketball Player)
9927 Galleon Dr
West Palm Beach, FL 33411-1807, USA

Kennedy, William J (Writer)
Washington Ave
Albany, NY 12210-2205, USA

Kennedy, William J (Athlete, Football Player)
21423 Archwood Cir
Farmington Hills, MI 48336-4113, USA

Kennedy, X Joseph (X J) (Writer)
22 Revere St
Lexington, MA 02420-4424, USA

Kennedy Schlossberg, Caroline (Writer)
111 5th Ave Fl 12
New York, NY 10003-1005, USA

Kennedy-Powell, Kathleen (Judge)
110 N Grand Ave
Los Angeles, CA 90012-3014, USA

Kenner, Ellen (Radio Personality, Talk Show Host)
PO Box 440
North Scituate, RI 02857-0440, USA

kenner, Kevin (Musician)
165 W 57th St
New York, NY 10019-2201, USA

Kennerly, David Hume (Journalist)
1015 18th St
Santa Monica, CA 90403-4435, USA

Kenney, Art (Athlete, Baseball Player)
3 Timber Ln
North Reading, MA 01864-3016, USA

Kenney, Jerry (Athlete, Baseball Player)
1980 Harrison Ave
Beloit, WI 53511-3048, USA

Kenney, Stephen F (Steve) (Athlete, Football Player)
1105 Silver Oaks Ct
Raleigh, NC 27614-9359, USA

Kenney, William P (Athlete, Football Player)
13450 E State Route 150
Kansas City, MO 64149-1243, USA

Kennibrew, Dee Dee (Musician)
PO Box 371371
Las Vegas, NV 89137-1371, USA

Kenniff, Sean (Doctor)
6 Madison Ln # 2
Carle Place, NY 11514-1064, USA

Kennison, Eddie (Athlete, Football Player)
1 Arrowhead Dr
Kansas City, MO 64129-1651, USA

Kenny, Shannon (Actor)
c/o Joanna (Joanie) Burstein *Burstein Company, The*
15304 W Sunset Blvd Ste 208
Pacific Palisades, CA 90272-3656, USA

Kenny, Shirley Strum (Educator)
President S Ofc
Stony Brook, NY 11794-0001, USA

Kenny, Tom (Actor, Musician, Writer)
c/o Kara Welker *Generate Management*
1545 26th St Ste 200
Santa Monica, CA 90404-3554, USA

Kenny, Yvonne (Opera Singer)
3 Burlington Lane Chiswick
London W4 2TH, UNITED KINGDOM (UK)

Kenny G (Musician)
c/o Staff Member *Richard De La Font Agency*
3808 W South Park Blvd
Broken Arrow, OK 74011-1261, USA

Kenon, Larry (Athlete, Basketball Player)
25057 Toutant Beauregard Rd
San Antonio, TX 78255-3402, USA

Kenseth, Matt (Race Car Driver)
4101 Roush Pl NW
Concord, NC 28027-8196, USA

Kensing, Logan (Athlete, Baseball Player)
2-8 W Bandera Rd
Boerne, TX 78006, USA

Kensit, Patsy (Actor, Musician)
14 Lambton Place Nottinghill
London W11 2SH, UNITED KINGDOM (UK)

Kent, Allegra (Ballerina)
c/o Staff Member *Sanford J Greenburger Associates Inc*
55 5th Ave
New York, NY 10003-4301, USA

Kent, Arthur (Correspondent)
2184 Torringford St
Torrington, CT 06790-2540, USA

Kent, (Edward G N P Patrick) (Misc)
York House Saint James's Place
London SW1, UNITED KINGDOM (UK)

Kent, Heather Paige
c/o Justin Grey Stone *Untitled Entertainment (LA)*
350 S Beverly Dr Ste 200
Beverly Hills, CA 90212-4819, USA

Kent, Jean (Actor)
2-4 Noel St
London W1V 3RB, UNITED KINGDOM (UK)

Kent, Jeff (Athlete, Baseball Player)
550 Chaparral Ct
Altadena, CA 91001-3859, USA

Kent, Joey (Athlete, Football Player)
6409 Eric St NW
Huntsville, AL 35810-1605, USA

Kent, Jonathan (Director)
76 Oxford St
London W1N 0AX, UNITED KINGDOM (UK)

Kent, Julie (Ballerina)
890 Broadway
New York, NY 10003-1211, USA

Kent, Marjorie
1169 Mary Cir
La Verne, CA 91750-4210

Kent, Peter (Misc)
43 Trinity Court Gray's Inn Road
London WC1, UNITED KINGDOM (UK)

Kent, Steve (Athlete, Baseball Player)
3118 Minthorn Dr
Killeen, TX 76542-1932, USA

Kentner, Louis (Musician)
1 Mallord St
London SW3, UNITED KINGDOM (UK)

Kentucky Headhunters
PO Box 1895
Glasgow, KY 42142-1895, USA

Kenty, Hilmer (Boxer)
19260 Bretton Dr
Detroit, MI 48223-1364, USA

Kenville, Bill (Athlete, Basketball Player)
59 Crary Ave
Binghamton, NY 13905-3828, USA

Kenworthy, Dick (Athlete, Baseball Player)
3707 E 106th Ter
Kansas City, MO 64137-1710, USA

Kenya, Wendi (Actor)
409 N Camden Dr Ste 205
Beverly Hills, CA 90210-4423, USA

Kenyon, Mel (Race Car Driver)
2645 S 25 W
Lebanon, IN 46052-9748, USA

Kenzle, Leila (Actor)
c/o Staff Member *Agency for the Performing Arts (APA-LA)*
405 S Beverly Dr Ste 500
Beverly Hills, CA 90212-4425, USA

Kenzo (Designer, Fashion Designer)
3 Place des Victories
Paris 75001, FRANCE

Keobouphan, Sisavat (Prime Minister)
Vientiane, LAOS

Keoghan, Phil (Television Host)
c/o Staff Member *International Creative Management (ICM-LA)*
10250 Constellation Blvd Fl 7
Los Angeles, CA 90067-6207, USA

Keohane, Nannerl O (Educator)
President's Office
Durham, NC 27706, USA

Keoke, Kimo (Actor)
612 1/2 N Spaulding Ave
Los Angeles, CA 90036-1838, USA

Keon, David M (Dave) (Athlete, Hockey Player)
115 Brackenwood Rd
Palm Beach Gardens, FL 33418-9065, USA

Keough, Donald R (Financier)
200 Galleria Pkwy SE Ste 970
Atlanta, GA 30339-5945, USA

Keough, Harry J (Coach, Soccer Player)
21 N Old Orchard Ave Apt 123
Saint Louis, MO 63119-2668, USA

Keough, Joe (Athlete, Baseball Player)
110 Binham Hts
Shavano Park, TX 78249-2056, USA

Keough, Lainey (Designer, Fashion Designer)
42 Dawson St
Dublin 2, IRELAND

Keough, Marty (Athlete, Baseball Player)
6874 E Nightingale Star Cir
Scottsdale, AZ 85266-7044, USA

Keough, Matt (Athlete, Baseball Player)
12 Shire
Trabuco Canyon, CA 92679-4907, USA

Kepcher, Carolyn (Reality TV Star)
c/o Staff Member *The Apprentice*
725 5th Ave
New York, NY 10022-2519, USA

Keppinger, Jeff (Athlete, Baseball Player)
1321 Center Dr
Auburn, GA 30011-3318, USA

Kepshire, Kurt (Athlete, Baseball Player)
4 Stonebridge Rd
Oxford, CT 06478-1164, USA

Ker, Crawford (Athlete, Football Player)
214 Harbor View Ln
Largo, FL 33770-4007, USA

Ker, Joshua (Athlete, Football Player)
2927 Lakeshore Dr
Muskegon, MI 49441, USA

Kerbow, Randall (Athlete, Football Player)
3803 Crystal Falls Dr
Missouri City, TX 77459-4249, USA

Kercher, Dick (Athlete, Football Player)
3205 May Cir SE
Rio Rancho, NM 87124-7402, USA

Kercheval, Ken (Actor)
11935 Kling St Apt 10
Valley Village, CA 91607-5406, USA

Kercheval, Ralph (Athlete, Football Player)
1220 Richmond Rd
Lexington, KY 40502-1614, USA

Kerdyk, Tracy (Athlete, Golfer)
441 Valencia Ave Apt 401
Coral Gables, FL 33134-5782, USA

Kerekorian, Kirk (Business Person)
2500 Broadway
Santa Monica, CA 90404-3065, USA

Kerekou, Mathieu A (General, President)
Boite Postale
Cotonou 2020, BENIN

Keresztes, K Sandor (Architect)
Fo Utca 44/50
Budapest 1011, HUNGARY

Kerfeld, Charlie (Athlete, Baseball Player)
PO Box 1666
Gig Harbor, WA 98335-3666, USA

Kerkorian, Kirk (Business Person)
150 S Rodeo Dr Ste 250
Beverly Hills, CA 90212-2417, USA

Kerkovich, Rob (Actor)
c/o Lorraine Berglund *Lorraine Berglund Management*
11537 Hesby St
North Hollywood, CA 91601-3618, USA

Kerley, James (Television Host)
c/o Mark Morrissey And Associates 45 Oxford St
Bondi Junction NSW 2022

Kern, Bill (Athlete, Baseball Player)
625 W Green St
Allentown, PA 18102-1601, USA

Kern, Ericca
3972 Barranca Pkwy # J-321
Irvine, CA 92606-1204

Kern, Geof (Photographer)
1355 Conant St
Dallas, TX 75207-6005, USA

Kern, Jim (Athlete, Baseball Player)
6009 Amberwood Ct
Arlington, TX 76016-1001, USA

Kern, Joey (Actor)
c/o Staff Member *Paradigm (LA)*
360 N Crescent Dr
Beverly Hills, CA 90210-4874, USA

Kern, Rex W (Athlete, Football Player)
2816 Avenida De Autlan
Camarillo, CA 93010-7471, USA

Kernaghan, Lee (Musician)
c/o Stephen White *Stephen White Management*
7 Kingslangley Rd
Greenwich, NSW 2065, Australia

Kernek, George (Athlete, Baseball Player)
16423 Cotton Gin Ave
Wayne, OK 73095-3172, USA

Kerner, Gabriele (Nena) (Musician)
C/O EAS Beethofenstrasse, 53
Hamburg D-22083, Germany

Kerner, Ian (Writer)
c/o Staff Member *HarperCollins Publishers*
10 E 53rd St C/O Author Mail Floor 7
New York, NY 10022, USA

Kerns, Joanna (Actor)
c/o Sean Freidin *International Creative Management (ICM-LA)*
10250 Constellation Blvd Fl 7
Los Angeles, CA 90067-6207, USA

Kerns, Sandra
620 Resolano Dr
Pacific Palisades, CA 90272-3032

Kerns Jr, David V (Engineer)
Electrical Engineering
Nashville, TN 37235-0001, USA

Kerr, Alan (Athlete, Hockey Player)
101-697 Wade Avenue Attn President's W Ofc
Penticton, BC V2A 1V6, Canada

Kerr, Allen (Musician)
419 Carrington St
Adelaide, SA 5000, AUSTRALIA

Kerr, Brook (Actor)
c/o Martin Berneman *Precision Entertainment*
6338 Wilshire Blvd
Los Angeles, CA 90048-5002, USA

Kerr, Cristie (Athlete, Golfer)
8367 SW 137th Ave
Miami, FL 33183-4045, USA

Kerr, Edward
9701 Wilshire Blvd Fl 10
Beverly Hills, CA 90212-2010

Kerr, Graham (Chef, Writer)
1020 N Sunset Dr
Camano Island, WA 98282-6665, USA

Kerr, John G (Actor)
2975 Monterey Rd
San Marino, CA 91108-1735, USA

Kerr, Judy (Actor)
4139 Tujunga Ave
Studio City, CA 91604-3065, USA

Kerr, Kristen (Actor)
c/o Steven Jensen *Independent Group, The*
6363 Wilshire Blvd Ste 115
Los Angeles, CA 90048-5734, USA

Kerr, Miranda (Model)
c/o Ursula Hufnagl *Chic Management*
36 Jersey Road
Woollahra NSW 2025, AUSTRALIA

Kerr, Pat (Designer, Fashion Designer)
200 Wagner Pl
Memphis, TN 38103-3617, USA

Kerr, Philip (Writer)
20 John St
London WC1N 2DR, UNITED KINGDOM (UK)

Kerr, Reg (Athlete, Hockey Player)
2291 Birchwood Ln
Northfield, IL 60093-3103, USA

Kerr, Steve (Athlete, Basketball Player)
PO Box 1964
Rancho Santa Fe, CA 92067-1964, USA

Kerr, Tim (Athlete, Coach, Hockey Player)
2528 Dune Dr
Avalon, NJ 8202, USA

Kerr, William T (Business Person)
1716 Locust St
Des Moines, IA 50309-3038, USA

Kerr Jr, Donald M (Physicist)
1241 Cave St
La Jolla, CA 92037-3602, USA

Kerrey, J Robert (Bob) (Ex-Governor, War Hero)
278 W 4th St
New York, NY 10014-2468, USA

Kerrick, Donald L (General)
Deputy Assistant National Security Agency
Fort George C Meade, MD 20755, USA

Kerrigan, Joseph T (Joe) (Athlete, Baseball Player, Coach)
450 Forest Ln
North Wales, PA 19454-2478, USA

Kerrigan, Marguerite (Baseball Player)
12179 94th St
Largo, FL 33773-4306, USA

Kerrigan, Nancy (Figure Skater)
40 Salem St # 101
Lynnfield, MA 01940-2673, USA

Kerrigan, Pamela (Athlete, Golfer)
3205 Tuckers Ln
Hingham, MA 02043-1567, USA

Kerrigan, Ryan (Football Player)
c/o David Dunn *Athletes First, LLC*
3300 Irvine Ave Ste 300
Newport Beach, CA 92660-3108, USA

Kerry, Alexandra (Actor)
c/o Staff Member *TalentWorks (LA)*
3500 W Olive Ave Ste 1400
Burbank, CA 91505-5512, USA

Kerry, Bob (Ex-Senator)
7602 Pacific St
Omaha, NE 68114-5428, USA

Kerry, John (Politician)
19 Louisburg Sq
Boston, MA 02108-1202, USA

Kerry, Teresa Heinz (Misc)
1101 Pennsylvania Ave NW Ste 350
Washington, DC 20004-2532, USA

Kersee, Bob
1034 S Brentwood Blvd # 1530
Saint Louis, MO 63117-1223

Kersey, Jerome (Athlete, Basketball Player)
24140 SW Petes Mountain Rd
West Linn, OR 97068-4500, USA

Kersey, Merritt (Athlete, Football Player)
17 Ballance Mill Rd
Nottingham, PA 19362-9507, USA

Kersey, Paul (Actor)
c/o Staff Member *TalentWorks (LA)*
3500 W Olive Ave Ste 1400
Burbank, CA 91505-5512, USA

Kersh, David (Musician)
PO Box 223
Shiner, TX 77984-0223, USA

Kershaw, Clayton (Athlete, Baseball Player)
c/o Staff Member *Los Angeles Dodgers (LA Dodgers)*
1000 Elysian Park Ave
Los Angeles, CA 90090-1112, USA

Kershaw, Doug (Musician)
RR 1 Box 34285 Weld County Road 47
Eaton, CO 80615, USA

Kershaw, Sammy (Musician)
c/o Richard De La Font *Richard De La Font Agency*
3808 W South Park Blvd
Broken Arrow, OK 74011-1261, USA

Kersten, Wally (Athlete, Football Player)
4604 Longfellow Ave
Minneapolis, MN 55407-3638, USA

Kertesz, Imre (Nobel Prize Laureate)
Acte Sud Paris 18 Rue Séguier
Paris 75 006, France

Kerwin, Brian (Actor)
c/o Staff Member *Paradigm (LA)*
360 N Crescent Dr
Beverly Hills, CA 90210-4874, USA

Kerwin, Irene (Baseball Player)
610 W Albany Ave
Peoria, IL 61604-1506, USA

Kerwin, Joseph P (Astronaut)
10411 River Rd
College Station, TX 77845-6719, USA

Kerwin, Lance (Actor)
26331 Osborne Ln
Homeland, CA 92548-9653, USA

Kerwin, Larkin (Physicist)
2166 Bourboniere Park
Sillery, QC G1T 1B4, CANADA

Kerwin, Tom (Athlete, Basketball Player)
283 Salter Path Rd Unit 114
Atlantic Beach, NC 28512-6178, USA

Keseday, Robert (Athlete, Football Player)
57 Linden Ave
Park Ridge, NJ 07656-1254, USA

Keselowski, Brad (Race Car Driver)
c/o John Caponigro *Sports Management Network, Inc.*
1668 S Telegraph Rd Ste 200
Bloomfield Hills, MI 48302-0016, USA

Keser, Dean (Athlete, Football Player)
202 Rod Cir
Middletown, MD 21769-7826, USA

Keshishian, Alek (Director, Writer)
c/o Aleen Keshishian *Brillstein Entertainment Partners*
9150 Wilshire Blvd Ste 350
Beverly Hills, CA 90212-3453, USA

Kesner, Jillian (Actor)
11360 Brill Dr
Studio City, CA 91604-3103, USA

Kessel Jr, Phil (Athlete, Hockey Player)
14 Turnwood Cir
Verona, WI 53593-7942, USA

Kessell, Rick (Athlete, Hockey Player)
60 Underhill Dr
North York, ON M3A 2J7, Canada

Kessell, Simone (Actor)
c/o Will Ward *ROAR (LA)*
9701 Wilshire Blvd Fl 8
Beverly Hills, CA 90212-2008, USA

Kessinger, Donald E (Don) (Athlete, Baseball Player, Coach)
1306 Pelican Loop
Oxford, MS 38655-7344, USA

Kessinger, Keith (Athlete, Baseball Player)
4517 Clubhouse Dr
Jonesboro, AR 72401-8153, USA

Kessinger, Ted (Athlete, Football Player)
612 N Washington St
Lindsborg, KS 67456-1516, USA

Kessler, Alice & Ellen
Nymphenburger Str. 86
Munich, GERMANY D-80636

Kessler, David A (Doctor, Writer)
c/o Phyllis Parsons *The Parsons Company*
1738 Almond Ave
Walnut Creek, CA 94596-4308, USA

Kessler, Glenn (Producer, Writer)
c/o Staff Member *Creative Artists Agency (CAA-LA)*
2000 Avenue of the Stars Ste 100
Los Angeles, CA 90067-4705, USA

Kessler, Ron (Writer)
c/o Staff Member *Trident Media Group LLC*
41 Madison Ave Fl 36
New York, NY 10010-2257, USA

Kessler, Stephen
1120 S Ridgeley Dr
Los Angeles, CA 90019-2528

Kessler, Todd (Producer, Writer)
c/o Staff Member *Creative Artists Agency (CAA-LA)*
2000 Avenue of the Stars Ste 100
Los Angeles, CA 90067-4705, USA

Kester, Rick (Athlete, Baseball Player)
PO Box 623
Gardnerville, NV 89410-0623, USA

Kestner, Boyd (Actor)
1801 Century Park E Ste 1801
Los Angeles, CA 90067-2320, USA

Ketchum, Dave
2318 Waterby St
Westlake Village, CA 91361-1834

Ketchum, Hal (Musician)
602 Wayside Dr
Wimberley, TX 78676-5151

Ketchum, Howard (Engineer)
3800 Washington Rd
West Palm Beach, FL 33405-0905, USA

Ketchum, Rai (Musician, Songwriter, Writer)
602 Wayside Dr
Wimberley, TX 78676-5151, USA

Ketola, Veli-Pekka (Athlete, Hockey Player)
Talikkalankuja 6
Pori 28300, Finland

Ketola-Lacamera, Helen (Baseball Player)
907 New York St
Edgewater, FL 32132-2373, USA

Ketter, Kerry (Athlete, Hockey Player)
3259 Majestic Dr
Courtenay, BC V9N 9X4, Canada

Ketterle, Wolfgang (Nobel Prize Laureate)
25 Bellingham Dr
Brookline, MA 2446, USA

Kettle, Roger (Cartoonist)
c/o Staff Member *King Features Syndication*
300 W 57th St Fl 15
New York, NY 10019-5238, USA

Keves, Gyorgy (Architect)
Keves es Epitesztarsai Rt Melinda Utca 21
Budapest 1121, HUNGARY

Key, Jimmy (Athlete, Baseball Player)
128 Talavera Pl
Palm Beach Gardens, FL 33418-6221, USA

Key, Keegan Michael (Actor)
c/o Joel Zadak *Principato/Young Management*
9465 Wilshire Blvd Ste 430
Beverly Hills, CA 90212-2613, USA

Key, Larry (Athlete, Football Player)
9661 60th St N Attn
Churchadministrations
Pinellas Park, FL 33782-3206, USA

Key, Sean (Athlete, Football Player)
4637 Chapel Creek Dr
Plano, TX 75024-6852, USA

Key, Ted (Cartoonist)
108 Chesley Dr
Media, PA 19063-1712, USA

Key, Wade (Athlete, Football Player)
PO Box 857
Hondo, TX 78861-0857, USA

Keyes, Alan (Politician)
PO Box 83759
Gaithersburg, MD 20883-3759, USA

Keyes, Daniel (Writer)
222 NW 69th St
Boca Raton, FL 33487-2389, USA

Keyes, Leroy (Athlete, Football Player)
6156 Pleasant Ave
Pennsauken, NJ 08110-3537, USA

Keyes, Robert W (Engineer)
PO Box 218
Yorktown Heights, NY 10598-0218, USA

Keyfitz, Nathan (Mathematician)
61 Mill Rd
North Hampton, NH 03862-2320, USA

Keymah, T'Keyah Crystal (Actor)
121 N San Vicente Blvd
Beverly Hills, CA 90211-2303, USA

Keynes, Skander (Actor)
c/o Brian Swardstrom *WmE2 (Endeavor-LA)*
9601 Wilshire Blvd Fl 3
Beverly Hills, CA 90210-5219, USA

Keys, Alicia (Actor, Musician, Songwriter)
c/o Will Botwin *Red Light Management (NY)*
44 Wall St Fl 22
New York, NY 10005-2401, USA

Keys, Ronald E (General)
Commander in Chief Allied Forces South
Europe Box 1 PSC 813
FPO, AE 9620, USA

Keys, Rudy (Athlete, Basketball Player)
4308 Ludi Mae Ct
Charlotte, NC 28227-6638, USA

Keyser, Brian (Athlete, Baseball Player)
11983 Cypress Links Dr
Fort Myers, FL 33913-8404, USA

Keyser, Joan (Stylist)
8008 Taylor Rd
Victor, NY 14564-9126, USA

Keyser, Richard L (Business Person)
14441 W Il Route 60
Lake Forest, IL 60045-5203, USA

Keyser Jr, F Ray (Ex-Governor)
814 E Keller Ct
Hernando, FL 34442-3373, USA

Keysey, Ken
Rt. 8 Box 477
Pleasant Hill, OR 97401

Keyworth, Jon (Athlete, Football Player)
1722 E Ridgefield Rd
Spanish Fork, UT 84660-8477, USA

Khabibulin, Nikolai (Athlete, Hockey Player)
6451 E El Maro Cir
Paradise Valley, AZ 85253-2622, USA

Khajag, Barsamian (Religious Leader)
630 2nd Ave
New York, NY 10016-4806, USA

Khaled, DJ (Musician)
c/o Staff Member *5W Public Relations (NY)*
888 7th Ave # 12
New York, NY 10106-0001, USA

Khali, Simbi (Actor)
1505 10th St
Santa Monica, CA 90401-2805, USA

Khalifa, Sam (Baseball Player)
741 E 6th St
Tucson, AZ 85719-5003, USA

Khalifa, Sam (Athlete, Baseball Player)
1050 N Camino Seco Apt 1044
Tucson, AZ 85710-1770, USA

Khalifa, Sheikh Hamad bin Isa al (Misc)
Manama, BAHARIN

Khalifa, Sheikh Khalifa bin Sulman al (Prime Minister)
Government House
Manama, BAHARIN

Khalifa, Wiz (Musician)
c/o Peter Schwartz *Agency Group Ltd, The (NY)*
142 W 57th St Fl 6
New York, NY 10019-3300, USA

Khalifa-al-Thani, Hamad Bin (Prime Minister, Prince)
PO Box 923
Doha, QATAR

Khalil, Christel (Actor)
c/o Meredith Fine *Coast to Coast Talent Group*
3350 Barham Blvd
Los Angeles, CA 90068-1404, USA

Khalil, Cristel (Actor)

Khamenei, Hojatolislam Sayyed Ali (President)
Teheran, IRAN

Khamtai, Siphandon (Prime Minister)
Council of Ministers
Vientiane, LAOS

Khan, Aamir (Actor, Bollywood)
c/o Staff Member *WmE2 (Endeavor-LA)*
9601 Wilshire Blvd Fl 3
Beverly Hills, CA 90210-5219, USA

Khan, Abdulla (Actor)
2 0/1 Arch Bishop Avenue Boat Club Rd
Chennai, TN 600 018, INDIA

Khan, Ali Akbar (Composer)
121 Jordan St
San Rafael, CA 94901-3919, USA

Khan, Alia (Designer)
40 E 34th St Rm 1719
New York, NY 10016-4504, USA

Khan, Amjad Ali (Composer)
3 Sadhna Enclave Panchsheel Park
New Delhi, New Delhi 110 017, INDIA

Khan, Ayub (Actor, Bollywood)
Xavier House 2nd Floor St Peter Colony
Bandra (W)
Mumbai, MS 400050, INDIA

Khan, Chaka (Actor, Musician)
c/o Jeff Frasco *Creative Artists Agency (CAA-LA)*
2000 Avenue of the Stars Ste 100
Los Angeles, CA 90067-4705, USA

Khan, Farah (Director)
c/o Staff Member *Indya.com Portal Pvt Ltd.*
Embassy Point, 3rd Floor 150, Infantry Road
Bangalore, Karnataka 560001, India

Khan, Fardeen (Actor, Bollywood)
Sunshine Jassawala Wadi Juhu Road Juhu
Mumbai, MS 400049, INDIA

Khan, Feroz (Actor, Bollywood, Director, Filmmaker, Producer)
Sunshine Jussawala Wadi Juhu Church Road
Mumbai, MS 400049, INDIA

Khan, Gulam Ishaq (Ex-President, President)
3B University Town Jamrud Road
Peshawar, PAKISTAN

Khan, Inamullah (Religious Leader)
D26 Block 8 Gulshan-E_Iqbal
Karachi 75300, PAKISTAN

Khan, Jemima (Heir/Heiress, Journalist)
c/o Staff Member *AP Watt Ltd*
20 John St
London WC1N 2DR, UK

Khan, Kader (Actor, Bollywood)
102 Raj Kamal 2nd Hasnabad Lane
Santacruz
Mumbai, MS 400054, INDIA

Khan, Niazi Imran (Cricketer)
29 Shah Jamai
Lahore 546000, PAKISTAN

Khan, Prince Sadruddin Aga
Collonge-Bellerive,
SWITZERLAND CH-1245

Khan, Princess Yasmin
146 Central Park W
New York, NY 10023-6297

Khan, Salman (Actor, Bollywood)
3 Galaxy Apartments Bt Road Bandstand
Bandra, Bombay 400 050, India

Khan, Sanjay (Actor, Bollywood, Director, Producer)
Sanjay House 11 Silver Beach A B Nair Road Juhu
Bombay, MS 400 049, INDIA

Khan, Shahbaaz (Actor, Bollywood)
GB6 Agha Khan Baug Versova Andheri
Bombay, MS 400 061, INDIA

Khan, Shahrukh (Actor, Bollywood)
c/o Staff Member *Red Chillies Entertainment*
Lokhandwala, Andheri (West)
Mumbai, Maharashtra, India

Khan, Sohail (Actor, Bollywood, Director, Producer)
4 Coral Reef 55 Chimbai Road Bandra W
Mumbai, MS 400050, INDIA

Khan, The Aga IV
Aiglemont
Gouvieux, FRANCE F-60270

Khanh, Emanuelle (Designer, Fashion Designer)
45 Ave Victor Hugo
Paris 75116, FRANCE

Khanna, Akshaye (Actor, Bollywood)
13/C Elplaza Little Gibs Road Malabar Hl
Mumbai, MS 400026, INDIA

Khanna, Amit (Actor, Bollywood)
301 Sea Star Near Holiday Inn Balraj Sahni Marg
Mumbai, MS 400049, INDIA

Khanna, Mukesh (Actor, Bollywood, Director)
3 Parijat 95 Marine Dr
Bombay, MS 400 002, INDIA

Khanna, Rahul (Actor, Bollywood)
12/18 V P Road C.P Tank Mumbai 4
Mumbai, MS 400004, INDIA

Khanna, Rajesh (Actor, Bollywood)
Ashirwad 2 Carter Road Bandra
Bombay, MS 400 050, INDIA

Khanna, Rinke (Actor, Bollywood)
201-A Vastu Rd Juhu Bldg MILITARY
Mumbai, MS 400049, INDIA

khanna, Twinkle (Actor, Bollywood)
Samudra Mahal Birla Lane Juhu
Mumbai, MS 400049, INDIA

Khanna, Vinod (Actor, Bollywood)
11 Palazo 13th Wiaa Malabar Hl Flr BEHIND
Mumbai, MS 400006, INDIA

Khanzadian, Vahan (Opera Singer)
3604 Broadway Apt 2N
New York, NY 10031-3200, USA

Kharbanda, Kulbhushan (Actor)
501 Silver Cascade Mount Mary Road Bandra
Bombay, MS 400 050, INDIA

Kharin, Sergei (Athlete, Hockey Player)
3306 N Riverwood Dr
Twin Lake, MI 49457-9789, USA

Khariton, Yuli B (Physicist)
Arsamas 16
Nizhy Novgorog Region, RUSSIA

Khashoggi, Adnan
Box 6
Riyadh, SAUDI ARABIA

Khashoggi, Adnan M (Business Person)
La Baraka
Marbella, SPAIN

Khatami, Mohammad (Politician, President)
Dr Ali Shariati Ave
Teheran, IRAN

Khavin, Vladimir Y (Architect)
Mayakovsky Square 1
Moscow 103001, RUSSIA

Khayat, Edward (Eddie) (Athlete, Coach, Football Coach, Football Player)
7813 Haydenberry Cv
Nashville, TN 37221-4675, USA

Khayat, Robert (Educator)
Chancellor's Office
University, MS 38677, USA

Khayat, Robert (Athlete, Football Player)
PO Box 667
Oxford, MS 38655-0667, USA

Kheel, Theodore W (Misc)
280 Park Ave
New York, NY 10017-1216, USA

Kher, Anupam (Actor, Bollywood)
402 Marina Juhu Tara Road Juhu Bch
Mumbai, MS 400049, INDIA

Khitty (Actor)
E3 Sea Brook Apartments 4th C'Ward Road Valmigi Nagar Thiruvanmiyur
Chennai, TN 600 041, INDIA

Khmylev, Yuri (Athlete, Hockey Player)
8236 Oakway Ln
Buffalo, NY 14221-2871, USA

Khokhlov, Boris (Dancer)
Myaskovsky St 11-13 #102
Moscow 121019, USA

Khondji, Darius (Cinematographer)
8942 Wilshire Blvd # 219
Beverly Hills, CA 90211-1908, USA

Khorana, Har Gobind (Nobel Prize Laureate)
3 Birch Hill Rd
Stow, MA 01775-1308, USA

Khorkina, Svetlana (Gymnast, Olympic Athlete)
Lujnetskaya Nabereynaya 8
Moscow 119270, RUSSIA

Khotan (Musician)
c/o Gabriel Blanco *Gabriel Blanco Iglesias (Mexico)*
Rio Balsas 35-32 Colonia Cuauhtemoc
DF 6500, Mexico

Khouna, Sheikh El Afia Quid Mohamed (Prime Minister)
Nouakchott, MAURITANIA

Khouri, Callie (Writer)
c/o Byrdie Lifson Pompan *Creative Artists Agency (CAA-LA)*
2000 Avenue of the Stars Ste 100
Los Angeles, CA 90067-4705, USA

Khourl, Callie (Director)
8942 Wilshire Blvd # 219
Beverly Hills, CA 90211-1908, USA

Khrennikov, Tikhon N (Composer)
Plotnikov Per 10/28 #19
Moscow 121200, RUSSIA

Khristenko, Viktor (Prime Minister)
Kremlin Staraya Pl 4
Moscow 103132, RUSSIA

Khristich, Dmitri (Athlete, Hockey Player)
5002 N Convent Ln Apt E
Philadelphia, PA 19114-3125, USA

Khruschev, Sergei
PO Box 1948
Providence, RI 02912-1948

Khush, Gurdev S (Scientist)
PO Box 933
Manila 1099, PHILLIPINES

Khvorostovsky, Dimitri A (Opera Singer)
Mosfilmovskaya 26 #5
Moscow, RUSSIA

Kiana (Talk Show Host)
935 Middle St
Bristol, CT 06010-1000

Kiarostaml, Abbas (Director)
247 Centre St # 200
New York, NY 10013-3216, USA

Kibaki, Mwai (President)
Harambee House Harambee Ave
Nairobi, KENYA

Kibler, John (Athlete, Baseball Player)
2701 El Camino Real # 205
Palo Alto, CA 94306-1713, USA

Kibrick, Anne (Educator)
130 Seminary Ave # 312
Auburndale, MA 02466-2651, USA

Kibrick, Sidney
10490 Wilshire Blvd Apt 1901
Los Angeles, CA 90024-4649

Kichel III, Walter (Editor)
1291 Avenue of the Americas
New York, NY 10019-6021, USA

Kickinger, Roland (Actor)
c/o Staff Member *Coralie Jr Theatrical Agency*
907 S Victory Blvd
Burbank, CA 91502-2430, USA

Kid Rock (Musician)
c/o Ken Levitan *Vector Management*
PO Box 120479
Nashville, TN 37212-0479, USA

Kidd, Billy
2305 Mount Werner Cir
Steamboat Springs, CO 80487-9023

Kidd, Dylan (Director)
c/o Staff Member *Creative Artists Agency (CAA-LA)*
2000 Avenue of the Stars Ste 100
Los Angeles, CA 90067-4705, USA

Kidd, Ian (Athlete, Hockey Player)
2512 E 7th St
Duluth, MN 55812-1406, USA

Kidd, Jason (Athlete, Basketball Player)
c/o Jeff Schwartz *Excel Sports Management*
9665 Wilshire Blvd Ste 500
Beverly Hills, CA 90212-2312, USA

Kidd, Jodie (Model)
c/o Staff Member *IMG*
304 Park Ave S Fl 12
New York, NY 10010-4314, USA

Kidd, John (Athlete, Football Player)
4204 Moorland Dr
Midland, MI 48640-1906, USA

Kidd, Sue (Baseball Player)
51 17th St
Logansport, IN 46947-2842, USA

Kidd, Warren (Athlete, Basketball Player)
313 River Rd
Harpersville, AL 35078-7014, USA

Kidd, William W (Billy) (Skier)
2305 Mount Werner Cir
Steamboat Springs, CO 80487-9023, USA

Kidder, Margot (Actor)
c/o Staff Member *Coolwaters Productions*
10061 Riverside Dr # 531
Toluca Lake, CA 91602-2560, USA

Kidder Lee, Barbara (Skier)
1308 W Highland Ave
Phoenix, AZ 85013-2425, USA

Kidjo, Angelique (Musician)
c/o Staff Member *Red Light Management (LA)*
8439 W Sunset Blvd Ste 2
Los Angeles, CA 90069-1925, USA

Kidman, Nicole (Actor, Producer)
c/o Geyer Kosinski *Media Talent Group*
9200 W Sunset Blvd Ste 550
Los Angeles, CA 90069-3611, USA

Kiecker, Dana (Athlete, Baseball Player)
4104 Prairie Ridge Rd
Saint Paul, MN 55123-1625, USA

Kiedis, Anthony (Musician)
c/o Jason Weinberg *Untitled Entertainment (LA)*
350 S Beverly Dr Ste 200
Beverly Hills, CA 90212-4819, USA

Kiefer, Adolph G (Coach, Swimmer)
42125 N Hunt Club Rd
Wadsworth, IL 60083-9264, USA

Kiefer, Mark (Athlete, Baseball Player)
11822 Old Fashion Way
Garden Grove, CA 92840-2117, USA

Kiefer, Nicolas (Athlete, Tennis Player)
c/o Staff Member *ATP Tour*
201 Atp Tour Blvd
Ponte Vedra Beach, FL 32082-3211, USA

Kiefer, Steve (Athlete, Baseball Player)
12389 Cloudburst Trl
Moreno Valley, CA 92555-5426, USA

Kiehl, Marina (Skier)
Hermie-Bland Str 11
Munich 81545, GERMANY

Kiehl, Stuart (Cinematographer)
4193 Concord Ave
Santa Rosa, CA 95407-6507, USA

Kiel, John (Athlete, Football Player)
12100 Pebblepointe Pass
Carmel, IN 46033-9678, USA

Kiel, Richard (Actor)
c/o Steve (Sr) Stevens *The Stevens Group*
14011 Ventura Blvd Ste 201
Sherman Oaks, CA 91423-5216, USA

Kielty, Bob (Bobby) (Athlete, Baseball Player)
22870 San Joaquin Dr E
Canyon Lake, CA 92587-7830, USA

Kiely, John (Athlete, Baseball Player)
84 Brown St
Brockton, MA 02301-1006, USA

Kiely, Mark
9255 W Sunset Blvd Ste 620
Los Angeles, CA 90069-3303

Kier, Miss Lady (Musician)
P.O. Box 32805
London, England N1 5WP, United Kingdom

Kier, Udo (Actor)
c/o Richard Schwartz *Richard Schwartz Management*
2934 1/2 N Beverly Glen Cir # 107
Los Angeles, CA 90077-1724, USA

Kiermayer, Susanne (Misc)
Amthofplatz 5
Kirchberg 94259, GERMANY

Kieschnick, Brook (Baseball Player)
201 Evans Ave
San Antonio, TX 78209-3721, USA

Kieschnick, Brooks (Athlete, Baseball Player)
122 Tuttle Rd
San Antonio, TX 78209-6143, USA

Kiesel, Theresia (Athlete, Track Athlete)
Stifterstr 24
Truan 4050, AUSTRIA

Kiewel, Jeff (Athlete, Football Player)
637 Industrial Park Rd
Evans, GA 30809, USA

Kiffin, Irv (Athlete, Basketball Player)
1441 Trellis Ln
Pembroke Pines, FL 33026-3250, USA

Kiggens, Lisa (Athlete, Golfer)
1504 Club View Dr
Bakersfield, CA 93309-3541, USA

Kightlinger, Laura (Actor, Comedian, Producer, Writer)
c/o David Martin *Avalon Management*
8332 Melrose Ave Fl 2
Los Angeles, CA 90069-5420, USA

Kihn, Greg (Musician)
55 Santa Clara Ave Ste 120
Oakland, CA 94610-1375, USA

Kiick, James F (Jim) (Athlete, Football Player)
2900 S University Dr Apt 9112
Davie, FL 33328-1409, USA

Kikuchi, Rinko (Actor)
c/o Staff Member *Creative Artists Agency (CAA-LA)*
2000 Avenue of the Stars Ste 100
Los Angeles, CA 90067-4705, USA

Kikutake, Kiyonori (Architect)
1-11-15 Otsuka
Bunkyoku, Tokyo, JAPAN

Kilar, Wojciech (Composer)
Ul Ksciuszki 165
Katowice 40-524, POLAND

Kilbey, Steven (Musician)
101 Chamberlayne Road
London NW10 3ND, UNITED KINGDOM (UK)

Kilborn, Craig (Talk Show Host)
c/o Shani Rosenzweig *United Talent Agency (UTA)*
9560 Wilshire Blvd Fl 5
Beverly Hills, CA 90212-2400, USA

Kilbourne, Wendy (Actor)
9300 Wilshire Blvd Ste 410
Beverly Hills, CA 90212-3228, USA

Kilburn, Terry (Actor)
Oakland University Walton & Squirrel
Rochester, MI 48063, USA

Kilcher, Jewel (Musician, Songwriter)
c/o Irving Azoff *Azoff Music Management/ Front Line*
1100 Glendon Ave
Los Angeles, CA 90024-3503, USA

Kilcher, Q'Orianka (Actor)
c/o Carlyne Grager *Dramatic Artists Agency*
103 W Alameda Ave Ste 139
Burbank, CA 91502-2253, USA

Kiley, Ariel (Actor)
c/o Gene Parseghian *Parseghian Planco LLC*
322 8th Ave Ste 601
New York, NY 10001-6715, USA

Kilgallon, Robert D (Scientist)
662 Park Ave
Meadville, PA 16335-1743, USA

Kilgore, Al (Cartoonist)
21655 113th Dr
Queens Village, NY 11429-2617, USA

Kilgore, Jon (Athlete, Football Player)
2422 Glen Oaks Ct NE
Atlanta, GA 30345-3928, USA

Kilgus, Paul (Athlete, Baseball Player)
2102 Smallhouse Rd
Bowling Green, KY 42104-3266, USA

Kilguss-Crall, Annette (Stylist)
4438 Ethel Ave
Studio City, CA 91604-1409, USA

Kilian, Thomas J (Business Person)
PO Box 1957
Carmel, IN 46082-1957, USA

Kilius, Marika (Figure Skater)
Postfach 201151
Dreieich 63271, GERMANY

Kilkenny, Mike (Athlete, Baseball Player)
274 Holland St W
Bradford, ON L3Z 1J1, Canada

Kill Hannah (Music Group, Musician)
c/o Staff Member *In De Goot Entertainment*
119 W 23rd St Ste 609
New York, NY 10011-2594, USA

Killeen, Denise (Athlete, Golfer)
803 Golden Wood Trce
Canton, GA 30114-6572, USA

Killeen, Evans (Athlete, Baseball Player)
PO Box 885
Westhampton Beach, NY 11978-0885, USA

Killens, Terry (Athlete, Football Player)
5665 Water Spring Way
Mason, OH 45040-7319, USA

Killett, Charlie (Athlete, Football Player)
PO Box 573
Paris, TN 38242-0573, USA

Killinger, Kerry K (Financier)
1201 3rd Ave
Seattle, WA 98101-3029, USA

Killip, Christopher D (Photographer)
24 Quincy St
Cambridge, MA 02138-3804, USA

Killorin, Pat (Athlete, Football Player)
8304 Partridgeberry Dr
Baldwinsville, NY 13027-8946, USA

Killum, Ernie (Athlete, Basketball Player)
710 Pennybrook Ln
Stone Mountain, GA 30087-5917, USA

Killy, Jean-Claude (Skier)
Villa Les 13 Chemin Bellefontaine
Cologny-GE 1223, SWITZERLAND

Kilmer, Val (Actor)
c/o David Unger *International Creative Management (ICM-LA)*
10250 Constellation Blvd Fl 7
Los Angeles, CA 90067-6207, USA

Kilmer, William O (Billy) (Athlete, Football Player)
1853 Monte Carlo Way Apt 36
Coral Springs, FL 33071-7829, USA

Kilmore, Chris (Musician)
c/o Staff Member *ArtistDirect*
9046 Lindblade St
Culver City, CA 90232-2513, USA

Kilner, Kevin (Actor)
1505 10th St
Santa Monica, CA 90401-2805, USA

Kilpatrick, Carl (Athlete, Basketball Player)
10517 23rd Street Ct E
Edgewood, WA 98372-1595, USA

Kilpatrick, Eric
6330 Simpson Ave Apt 3
North Hollywood, CA 91606-3427

Kilpatrick, Kwame (Politician)
2 Woodward Ave
Detroit, MI 48226-3437, USA

Kilrain, Susan L (Astronaut)
625 Cedar Ln
Virginia Bch, VA 23452-1805, USA

Kilrea, Brian (Athlete, Coach, Hockey Player)
2192 Saunderson Dr
Ottawa, ON K1G 2G4, Canada

Kilroy, Bucko (Athlete, Football Player)
89 South St
Foxboro, MA 02035-1714, USA

Kilts, James M (Business Person)
Prudential Tower Building
Boston, MA 2199, USA

Kilzer, Louis C (Lon) (Journalist)
425 Portland Ave
Minneapolis, MN 55488-1511, USA

Kim, Anthony (Athlete, Golfer)
c/o Clarke Jones *IMG (Cleveland)*
1360 E 9th St Ste 100
Cleveland, OH 44114-1730, USA

Kim, Byung-Hyun (Athlete, Baseball Player)
4601 E Skyline Dr Apt 1302
Tucson, AZ 85718-1661, USA

Kim, Daniel Dae (Actor)
c/o Steven Siebert *Lighthouse Entertainment*
9220 W Sunset Blvd Ste 200
West Hollywood, CA 90069-3501, USA

Kim, Jacqueline (Actor)
1505 10th St
Santa Monica, CA 90401-2805, USA

Kim, Jaegwon (Misc)
Philosophy
Providence, RI 02912-0001, USA

Kim, Nelli V (Gymnast)
2480 Cobblehill Alocove # A
Woodbury, MN 55125, USA

Kim, Peter S (Misc)
9 Cambridge Ctr
Cambridge, MA 02142-1401, USA

Kim, Stephan Sou-hwan Cardinal (Religious Leader)
Archbishop's House 2 Ka 1 Myong Dong Chungku
Seoul 100, SOUTH KOREA

Kim, Yoon-jin (Actor)
c/o Staff Member *WmE2 (WMA-LA)*
1 William Morris Pl
Beverly Hills, CA 90212-4261, USA

Kim, Young Sam (President)
Sangdo-dong 7-6 Tongjakku
Seoul, SOUTH KOREA

Kim, Young Uck (Musician)
165 W 57th St
New York, NY 10019-2201, USA

Kim, Yunjin (Actor)
c/o Alex Chaice *Global Creative*
1051 Cole Ave # B
Los Angeles, CA 90038-2601, USA

Kimball, Bobby (Musician)
297101 Kinderkamack Rd # 128
Oradell, NJ 7649, USA

Kimball, Bruce (Athlete, Football Player)
41 Spring Rd
Rye, NH 03870-2449, USA

Kimball, Cheyenne (Musician)

Kimball, Dick (Coach)
1540 Waltham Dr
Ann Arbor, MI 48103-5631, USA

Kimball, Toby (Athlete, Basketball Player)
6859 Avenida Ave
La Jolla, CA 92037, USA

Kimball, Ward
1685 La Vista Pl
Pasadena, CA 91103-1127

Kimball, Warren F (Historian)
2540 Otter Ln
Johns Island, SC 29455-6104, USA

Kimball-Purdham, Mary Ellen (Baseball Player)
PO Box 9
Irons, MI 49644-0009, USA

Kimber, William (Athlete, Football Player)
7801 Point Meadows Dr Unit 3102
Jacksonville, FL 32256-9145, USA

Kimble, Bo (Athlete, Basketball Player)
100 Poe Ct
North Wales, PA 19454-4430, USA

Kimble, Darin (Athlete, Hockey Player)
1202 27th St
Granite City, IL 62040-3431, USA

Kimble, Warren (Artist)
RR 3Box 1038
Brandon, VT 5733, USA

Kimbrough, Charles (Actor, Musician)
255 Amalfi Dr
Santa Monica, CA 90402-1125, USA

Kimbrough, Elbert (Athlete, Football Player)
45340 Medicine Bow Ct
Fremont, CA 94539-6639, USA

Kimbrough, Stan (Athlete, Basketball Player)
3922 Elm Ave
Cincinnati, OH 45236-3908, USA

Kimbrough, Will (Musician)
164 Dove Creek Rd
Frankfort, KY 40601-8945, USA

Kimery, James L (Misc)
405 W 34th St
Kansas City, MO 64111, USA

Kimm, Bruce (Athlete, Baseball Player, Coach)
3168 121st St
Amana, IA 52203-8046, USA

Kimmel, Jerry (Athlete, Football Player)
1411 Colesville Rd
Harpursville, NY 13787-1430, USA

Kimmel, Jimmy (Comedian, Television Host, Writer)
6834 Hollywood Blvd Ste 600
Hollywood, CA 90028-6135, USA

Kimmelman, Jamie (Stylist)
c/o Staff Member *Mel Bryant Management*
611 Broadway Rm 623
New York, NY 10012-2650

Kimmins, Kenneth (Actor)
c/o Joanna (Joanie) Burstein *Burstein Company, The*
15304 W Sunset Blvd Ste 208
Pacific Palisades, CA 90272-3656, USA

Kims of Comedy (Comedian)
c/o Staff Member *Paradigm (Monterey)*
404 W Franklin St
Monterey, CA 93940-2303, USA

Kimura, Doreen (Psychic)
211 Madison Ave
Toronto, ON M5R 2S6, CANADA

Kimura, Kazuo (Designer)
2-2 Cenba Chuo Higashiku
Osaka 541, JAPAN

Kimura, Motoo (Biologist)
Yata 1 111 Mishima
Shizuokaken 411, JAPAN

Kinard, Billy (Athlete, Football Player)
PO Box 680944
Fort Payne, AL 35968-1610, USA

Kinard, Terry (Athlete, Football Player)
PO Box 1780
Conyers, GA 30012-7954, USA

Kincaid, Aron (Actor)
3350 Barham Blvd
Los Angeles, CA 90068-1404, USA

Kincaid, Jamaica (Writer)
College Road
North Bennington, VT 5257, USA

Kinchen, Brian (Athlete, Football Player)
19052 E Pinnacle Cir
Baton Rouge, LA 70810-7996, USA

Kinchen, Todd W (Athlete, Football Player)
5854 Menlo Dr
Baton Rouge, LA 70808-5047, USA

Kinchla, Chan (Musician)
c/o Staff Member *ArtistDirect*
9046 Lindblade St
Culver City, CA 90232-2513, USA

Kincses, Veronika (Opera Singer)
Andrassy Ulca 22
Budapest 1061, HUNGARY

Kind, Danielle (Actor)
Take One Talent Management Inc PO Box 20019
Ottawa K1N 9N5, CANADA

Kind, Richard (Actor)
c/o Arlene Forster *Forster Entertainment*
12533 Woodgreen St
Los Angeles, CA 90066-2723, USA

Kind, Ron (Congressman, Politician)
1406 Longworth Hob
Washington, DC 20515-4903, USA

Kind, Roslyn (Actor, Musician)
13707 Riverside Dr # 201
Sherman Oaks, CA 91423, USA

Kindall, Jerry (Athlete, Baseball Player)
7220 E Grey Fox Ln
Tucson, AZ 85750-1377, USA

Kinder, Melvyn (Psychic)
1951 San Ysidro Dr
Beverly Hills, CA 90210-1555, USA

Kinder, Melvyn (Writer)
c/o Staff Member *Random House*
1540 Broadway
New York, NY 10036-4039, USA

Kinder, Richard D (Business Person)
500 Dallas St Ste 1000
Houston, TX 77002-4718, USA

Kinderman, Keith (Athlete, Football Player)
5837 Bradfordville Rd
Tallahassee, FL 32309-6613, USA

Kindig, Howard (Athlete, Football Player)
8740 Bayside Ave
Baton Rouge, LA 70806-7947, USA

Kindle, Greg (Athlete, Football Player)
7606 Heron Park Ct
Humble, TX 77396-2222, USA

Kindler, Klaus
Am Berg 6
Schwietenkirchen, GERMANY D-85301

Kindrachuk, Orest (Athlete, Hockey Player)
106 Meeshaway Trl
Medford, NJ 08055-1402, USA

Kindred, David A (Writer)
72 Marietta St NW
Atlanta, GA 30303-2804, USA

Kiner, Ralph M (Athlete, Baseball Player, Sportscaster)
19 Doubling Rd
Greenwich, CT 06830-4845, USA

Kiner, Steve (Athlete, Football Player)
112 N Ole Hickory Trl
Carrollton, GA 30117-3509, USA

King, Adrienne (Actor)
c/o Aine Leicht *Horror & Hilarity*
Prefers to be contacted via telephone
Los Angeles, CA 90067, USA

King, Alan (Actor, Producer, Writer)
c/o Lisa Gallant *International Creative Management (ICM-LA)*
10250 Constellation Blvd Fl 7
Los Angeles, CA 90067-6207, USA

King, Albert (Athlete, Basketball Player)
88 Sturbridge Cir
Wayne, NJ 07470-8402, USA

King, Alton (Athlete, Baseball Player)
8226 Esper St
Detroit, MI 48204-3120, USA

King, Angelo (Athlete, Football Player)
2922 W Royal Ln Apt 2090
Irving, TX 75063-6235, USA

King, BB (Musician)
c/o Staff Member *Solters & Digney*
1680 Vine St Ste 1105
Hollywood, CA 90028-8844, USA

King, Ben E (Musician)
PO Box 1097
Teaneck, NJ 07666-1097, USA

King, Benjamin (Actor)
c/o Peter Principato *Principato/Young Management*
9465 Wilshire Blvd Ste 430
Beverly Hills, CA 90212-2613, USA

King, Bernard (Athlete, Basketball Player)
307 Jupiter Hills Dr
Duluth, GA 30097-5900, USA

King, Bernard (Athlete, Football Player)
1708 N State Road 7 Attn Athletic
Hollywood, FL 33021-4507, USA

King, Betsy (Athlete, Golfer)
7418 E Alta Sierra Dr
Scottsdale, AZ 85266-1887, USA

King, Billie Jean (Athlete, Tennis Player)
101 W 79th St
New York, NY 10024-6474, USA

King, Cammie (Actor)
511 Cypress St
Fort Bragg, CA 95437-5417, USA

King, Cammie Conlon
c/o Staff Member *Pierce & Shelly*
13775A Mono Way # 220
Sonora, CA 95370-8813, USA

King, Candie (Athlete, Golfer)
2673 Saleroso Dr
Rowland Heights, CA 91748-4364, USA

King, Carlos (Athlete, Football Player)
107 S Corncrib Ct
Cary, NC 27513-5407, USA

King, Carole (Musician)
c/o Daniel Weiner *Paradigm (Monterey)*
404 W Franklin St
Monterey, CA 93940-2303, USA

King, Carolyn Dineen (Judge)
515 Rusk St
Houston, TX 77002-2600, USA

King, Cheryl (Actor)
843 N Sycamore Ave
Los Angeles, CA 90038-3316, USA

King, Chick (Athlete, Baseball Player)
4036 Highway 54
Paris, TN 38242-6335, USA

King, Claude (Musician)
9 Lucy Ln
Sherwood, AR 72120-3612, USA

King, Clyde E (Athlete, Baseball Player, Coach)
103 Stratford Rd
Goldsboro, NC 27534-8971, USA

King, Colbert (Journalist)
1150 15th St NW
Washington, DC 20071-0001, USA

King, Curtis (Athlete, Baseball Player)
2538 Beechwood Dr
Vineland, NJ 08361-2932, USA

King, Dan (Athlete, Basketball Player)
4320 Hickoryview Dr
Louisville, KY 40299-5824, USA

King, Dana (Correspondent)
524 W 57th St
New York, NY 10019-2930, USA

King, David A (Misc)
Masters Lodge Downing College
Cambridge CB2 1DQ, UNITED KINGDOM (UK)

King, David J (Athlete, Football Player)
4177 Chapel Lake Dr
Decatur, GA 30034-3568, USA

King, Dennis (Artist)
108 Andrew Ct
Mount Shasta, CA 96067-9660, USA

King, Derek (Athlete, Hockey Player)
34 Maple Ave
Northport, NY 11768-1935, USA

King, Dexter Scott (Misc)
449 Auburn Ave NE
Atlanta, GA 30312, USA

King, Don (Business Person)
501 Fairway Dr
Deerfield Beach, FL 33441-1865, USA

King, Don (Misc)
968 Pinehurst Dr
Las Vegas, NV 89109-1569, USA

King, Donald W (Athlete, Football Player)
1621 Fox Hall Rd
Savannah, GA 31406-5005, USA

King, Ed (Athlete, Football Player)
405 River Oak Way
Phenix City, AL 36867-1306, USA

King, Ed (Athlete, Football Player)
9903 North Blvd
Cleveland, OH 44108-3429, USA

King, Eric (Athlete, Baseball Player)
1063 Stanford Dr
Simi Valley, CA 93065-4952, USA

King, Erik (Actor)
c/o Joanna (Joanie) Burstein *Burstein Company, The*
15304 W Sunset Blvd Ste 208
Pacific Palisades, CA 90272-3656, USA

King, Evelyn (Musician)
c/o JD Sobol *RPM Talent Agency*
2600 W Olive Ave Fl 5
Burbank, CA 91505-4572, USA

King, Ezell (Athlete, Baseball Player)
PO Box 321154
Houston, TX 77221-1154, USA

King, Francis H (Writer)
19 Gordon Place
London W8 4JE, UNITED KINGDOM (UK)

King, Frank (Baseball Player)
415 E Rhinehill Rd SE
Atlanta, GA 30315-7403, USA

King, G Stephen (Athlete, Football Player)
45 Chipping Stone Rd
North Attleboro, MA 02760-4485, USA

King, Gayle (Correspondent, Editor)
c/o Tyler Delaney *Westport Entertainment Associates*
1700 Post Rd Ste C15
Fairfield, CT 06824-5726, USA

King, Gordon (Athlete, Football Player)
2641 Highwood Dr
Roseville, CA 95661-7916, USA

King, Gordon D (Athlete, Football Player)
2641 Highwood Dr
Roseville, CA 95661-7916, USA

King, Graham (Producer)
c/o Joy Fehily *Prime*
9696 Culver Blvd Ste 102
Culver City, CA 90232-2734, USA

King, Hal (Athlete, Baseball Player)
828 Geneva Dr
Oviedo, FL 32765-9503, USA

King, Hogue Maxine (Mick) (Swimmer)
PO Box 155
Usaf Academy, CO 80840-0155, USA

King, Horace (Athlete, Football Player)
884 Fairburn Rd NW
Atlanta, GA 30331-3341, USA

King, Jaime (Actor)
c/o Brad Cafarelli *PMK/BNC - LA*
8687 Melrose Ave Ste 8
West Hollywood, CA 90069-5746, USA

King, James A (Opera Singer)
165 W 57th St
New York, NY 10019-2201, USA

King, James B (Editor)
1120 John St
Seattle, WA 98109-5321, USA

King, James C (General)
Director National Imagery/Mapping Agency
Chantilly, VA 22021, USA

King, Jean
5510 Cahuenga Blvd
North Hollywood, CA 91601-2919

King, Jeff (Misc)
PO Box 48
Denali National Park, AK 99755-0048, USA

King, Jeff (Athlete, Baseball Player)
50401 Highway 278
Wisdom, MT 59761-9703, USA

King, Jim (Athlete, Baseball Player)
720 Stokenbury Rd
Elkins, AR 72727-3214, USA

King, Joe (Athlete, Football Player)
373 Boyd Rd
Hallsville, TX 75650-7003, USA

King, Jonathan
1 Wyndham Yard
London, ENGLAND W1H 1AR

King, Kaki (Musician)
c/o Staff Member *Paradigm (Monterey)*
404 W Franklin St
Monterey, CA 93940-2303, USA

King, Kathryn (Katie) (Athlete, Hockey Player)
3 Birchwood Rd
Salem, NH 03079-3407, USA

King, Kent Masters (Actor)
c/o Richard Schwartz *Richard Schwartz Management*
2934 1/2 N Beverly Glen Cir # 107
Los Angeles, CA 90077-1724, USA

King, Kevin (Athlete, Baseball Player)
RR 1 Box 107
Braggs, OK 74423-9739, USA

King, Kris (Athlete, Hockey Player)
c/o Staff Member *National Hockey League (NHL)*
50 Bay St 11th Floor
Toronto, ON M5J 2X8, Canada

King, Lamar (Athlete, Football Player)
1453 Browning Dr
Essex, MD 21221-4337, USA

King, Lamnar (Athlete, Football Player)
1453 Browning Dr
Essex, MD 21221-4337, USA

King, Larry (Journalist, Talk Show Host)
c/o Geyer Kosinski *Media Talent Group*
9200 W Sunset Blvd Ste 550
Los Angeles, CA 90069-3611, USA

King, Linden (Athlete, Football Player)
1130 S Flower St Apt 416
Los Angeles, CA 90015-2144, USA

King, Loyd (Athlete, Basketball Player)
118 Wilde Brook Dr
Asheville, NC 28806-1052, USA

King, Mark (Musician)
P.O. Box 23
Sandown PO36 9QL, UK

King, Mary-Claire (Misc)
Medical School Genetics
Seattle, WA 98195-0001, USA

King, Maurice (Athlete, Basketball Player)
6207 E 108th St
Kansas City, MO 64134-2530, USA

King, Mervyn A (Economist)
Threadneedle St
London EC2R 8AH, UNITED KINGDOM (UK)

King, Michael (Business Person)
c/o Staff Member *King World Productions Inc (LA)*
2401 Colorado Ave Ste 110
Santa Monica, CA 90404-3577

King, Michael (Business Person)
12400 Wilshire Blvd
Los Angeles, CA 90025-1019, USA

King, Michael Patrick (Producer, Writer)
c/o Simon Halls *Slate Public Relations*
9000 W Sunset Blvd Ste 915
West Hollywood, CA 90069-5809, USA

King, Michel Patrick (Director)
c/o Simon Halls *Slate Public Relations*
9000 W Sunset Blvd Ste 915
West Hollywood, CA 90069-5809, USA

King, Morgana (Actor, Musician)
330 W 56th St Apt 18M
New York, NY 10019-4222, USA

King, Nellie (Athlete, Baseball Player)
3890 Bigelow Blvd Apt 405
Pittsburgh, PA 15213-1158, USA

King, Patsy
6/70 Hawksburn Road Yarra S
Victoria, AUSTRALIA 3141

King, Perry (Actor)
3647 Wrightwood Dr
Studio City, CA 91604-3947, USA

King, Phillip (Artist)
14A Clifford St
London W1X 1RF, UNITED KINGDOM (UK)

King, R Stacey (Athlete, Basketball Player)
5340 RFD
Long Grove, IL 60047-9744, USA

King, Ray (Athlete, Baseball Player)
14870 W Encanto Blvd Unit 1046
Goodyear, AZ 85395-6605, USA

King, Reggie (Athlete, Basketball Player)
600 N 81st Ter
Kansas City, KS 66112-2518, USA

King, Regina (Actor)
c/o John Carrabino *John Carrabino Management*
5900 Wilshire Blvd Ste 406
Los Angeles, CA 90036-5015, USA

King, Richard L (Business Person)
250 Parkcenter Blvd
Boise, ID 83706-3940, USA

King, Roger (Business Person)
12400 Wilshire Blvd
Los Angeles, CA 90025-1019, USA

King, Shaun (Athlete, Football Player)
1646 41st St S
Saint Petersburg, FL 33711-2710, USA

King, Shawn Southwick (Actor)
c/o Staff Member *WmE2 (WMA-LA)*
1 William Morris Pl
Beverly Hills, CA 90212-4261, USA

King, Stephen (Writer)
1390 Hammond St
Bangor, ME 4401, USA

King, Steve (Congressman, Politician)
1131 Longworth Hob
Washington, DC 20515-1008, USA

King, Steven (Athlete, Hockey Player)
55 Chestnut Dr
East Greenwich, RI 02818-2102, USA

King, Ted (Actor, Musician)
c/o Staff Member *Paradigm (LA)*
360 N Crescent Dr
Beverly Hills, CA 90210-4874, USA

King, Thea (Musician)
16 Milverton Road
London NW6 7AS, UNITED KINGDOM (UK)

King, Thomas J (Tom) (Government Official)
Westminster
London SW1A 0AA, UNITED KINGDOM (UK)

King, Tom (Athlete, Basketball Player)
4930 Sea Watch Dr
Fernandina Beach, FL 32034-5741, USA

King, Vania (Athlete, Tennis Player)
c/o John Tobias *Lagardere Unlimited - (D.C.)*
5335 Wisconsin Ave NW Ste 850
Washington, DC 20015-2052, USA

King, W David (Coach)
PO Box 1540 Station M
Calgary, AB T2P 3B9, CANADA

King, Wayne (Athlete, Hockey Player)
129 Seventh St
Midland, ON L4R 3Y9, Canada

King, Zalman (Director)
308 Alta Ave
Santa Monica, CA 90402-2730, USA

King III, Martin Luther (Activist)
191 Peachtree St NE Ste 3300
Atlanta, GA 30303-1740, USA

King Jr, Woodie (Producer)
417 Convent Ave
New York, NY 10031-4213, USA

King Kong (Actor)
77 Sastri Street Kaveri Nagar Saidapet
Chennai, TN 600 015, INDIA

King Sisters
10275 S 2505 E
Sandy, UT 84092-4464

Kingdom, Roger (Athlete, Track Athlete)
146 S Fairmount St Apt 1
Pittsburgh, PA 15206-3580, USA

Kingery, Ellsworth (Athlete, Football Player)
501 Auburn Ave
Monroe, LA 71201-5303, USA

Kingery, Mike (Athlete, Baseball Player)
51923 298th St
Grove City, MN 56243-4305, USA

Kingery, Wayne (Athlete, Football Player)
1045 Walters St Apt 411
Lake Charles, LA 70607-4686, USA

Kinglsey, Ben (Actor)
76 Oxford St
London W1N 0AX, UNITED KINGDOM (UK)

Kingman, Brian (Athlete, Baseball Player)
8825 5th Ave
Hesperia, CA 92345-3645, USA

Kingman, Dave (Athlete, Baseball Player)
PO Box 209
Glenbrook, NV 89413-0209, USA

Kingrea, Richard O (Athlete, Football Player)
102 N Bayview St
Fairhope, AL 36532-2505, USA

Kings Norton, (Harold R Cox) (Engineer, Scientist)
Westcote House Chipping Campden
Glos, UNITED KINGDOM (UK)

Kings of Convenience (Music Group)
c/o Staff Member *Paradigm (Monterey)*
404 W Franklin St
Monterey, CA 93940-2303, USA

Kings of Leon (Music Group, Musician)
c/o Andy Mendelson *Vector Management - New York*
113 E 55th St
New York, NY 10022-3502, USA

Kingsale, Gene (Athlete, Baseball Player)
105 Angelfish Ln
Jupiter, FL 33477-7227, USA

Kingsley, Ben (Actor)
c/o Christina Papadopoulos *Baker Winokur Ryder Public Relations BWR (BWR-NY)*
292 Madison Ave Fl 12
New York, NY 10017-6415, USA

Kingsley, Patricia
371 Alma Real Dr
Pacific Palisades, CA 90272-4416

Kingsmen, The
1720 N Ross St
Santa Ana, CA 92706-3605

Kingsriter, Doug (Athlete, Football Player)
3118 Saint Johns Dr
Dallas, TX 75205-2938, USA

Kingston, Alex (Actor)
c/o Lorrie Bartlett *International Creative Management (ICM-LA)*
10250 Constellation Blvd Fl 7
Los Angeles, CA 90067-6207, USA

Kingston, Jack (Congressman, Politician)
2372 Rayburn Hob
Washington, DC 20515-0605, USA

Kingston, Kenny
11561 Dona Dorotea Dr
Studio City, CA 91604-4250

Kingston, Mark
47 Courtfield Rd # 9
London, ENGLAND SW7 4DB

Kingston, Maxine Hong (Writer)
English
Berkeley, CA 94720-0001, USA

Kingston, Sean (Musician)
c/o Zach Katz *Beluga Heights Management*
10323 Santa Monica Blvd Ste 111
Los Angeles, CA 90025-5056, USA

Kingston Trio, The
9410 S 46th St
Phoenix, AZ 85044-7512

Kinkade, Mike (Athlete, Baseball Player)
3005 SE Spyglass Dr
Vancouver, WA 98683-3704, USA

Kinkade, Thomas (Artist)
900 Lightpost Way
Morgan Hill, CA 95037-2869, US

Kinkel, Klaus (Government Official)
Adenauerallee 101
Bonn 53113, GERMANY

Kinks, The
29 Ruston Mews
London, ENGLAND W11 1RB

Kinley, Heather (Musician)
1211 S Highland Ave
Los Angeles, CA 90019-1734, USA

Kinley, Jennifer (Musician)
1211 S Highland Ave
Los Angeles, CA 90019-1734, USA

Kinleys (Music Group)
PO Box 128501
Nashville, TN 37212-8501, USA

Kinley's, The
PO Box 128501
Nashville, TN 37212-8501

Kinmont, Boothe Jill (Skier)
310 Sunland Dr RR1 Box 11
Bishop, CA 93514, USA

Kinmont, Jill
310 Sunland Dr
Bishop, CA 93514-7002

Kinmont, Kathleen (Actor)
9929 Sunset Blvd # 310
Los Angeles, CA 90069, USA

Kinnamon, Bill (Baseball Player)
1010 Spencer Ave
Clearwater, FL 33756-4535, USA

Kinnamon, Bill (Athlete, Baseball Player)
1010 Spencer Ave
Clearwater, FL 33756-4535, USA

Kinnan, Timothy A (General)
US Military Representative NATO Blvd Leopold III
Brussels 1110, BELGIUM

Kinnear, Dominic (Coach)
3550 Stevens Creek Blvd Ste 200
San Jose, CA 95117-1031, USA

Kinnear, Greg (Actor, Comedian)
c/o Leslie Sloane *Baker Winokur Ryder Public Relations BWR (BWR-NY)*
292 Madison Ave Fl 12
New York, NY 10017-6415, USA

Kinnear III, James W (Business Person)
PO Box 120
Stamford, CT 06904-0120, USA

Kinnebrew, Larry (Athlete, Football Player)
216 Kingston Ave NE
Rome, GA 30161-5628, USA

Kinney, Dallas (Journalist)
13010 Silver Sands Dr
Fort Myers, FL 33913-6934, USA

Kinney, Dennis (Athlete, Baseball Player)
125 Olde Towne Way Unit 1
Myrtle Beach, SC 29588-1314, USA

Kinney, Kathy (Actor)
c/o Billy Miller *Billy Miller Management*
8322 Ridpath Dr
Los Angeles, CA 90046-7710, USA

Kinney, Matt (Athlete, Baseball Player)
12 Owens Way
Hermon, ME 04401-0878, USA

Kinney, Steve (Athlete, Football Player)
1714 Merrill Loop
San Jose, CA 95124-5814, USA

Kinney, Taylor (Actor)
c/o Geneva Bray *GVA Talent Agency Inc*
8981 W Sunset Blvd Ste 101
Los Angeles, CA 90069-1850, USA

Kinney, Terry (Actor)
232 N Canon Dr
Beverly Hills, CA 90210-5302, USA

Kinnock, Neil G (Government Official)
200 Rue de Loi
Brussels 1049, BELGIUM

Kinnunen, Mike (Athlete, Baseball Player)
5818 McKinley Pl N
Seattle, WA 98103-5711, USA

Kinscherf, Carl (Athlete, Football Player)
18 Jackson Ave
Gladstone, NJ 07934-2117, USA

Kinsella, Brian (Athlete, Hockey Player)
1408 Longfellow Dr
Temperance, MI 48182-9296, USA

Kinsella, John P (Swimmer)
PO Box 3067
Sumas, WA 98295-3067, USA

Kinsella, Thomas (Writer)
Killalane Laragh
County Wicklow, IRELAND

Kinsella, W P
PO Box 3067
Sumas, WA 98295-3067, USA

Kinsella, William Patrick (W P) (Writer)
1952-152A St # 216
Surrey, BC V4A 9T2, CANADA

Kinser, Steve (Race Car Driver)
280 E Smithville Rd
Bloomington, IN 47401-9251, USA

Kinsey, Angela (Actor)
c/o Staff Member *Jenny Delaney Management*
3238 Fond Dr
Encino, CA 91436-4206, USA

Kinsey, James L (Misc)
Natural Sciences School
Houston, TX 77005, USA

Kinshofer-Guthlein, Christa (Skier)
Munchnerstr 44
Rosenheim 83026, GERMANY

Kinski, Nastassja (Actor, Model)
c/o Staff Member *Artists Independent Management (LA)*
825 Nowita Pl
Venice, CA 90291-3836, USA

Kinsler, Ian (Athlete, Baseball Player)
3516 Greenbrier Dr
Dallas, TX 75225-5003, USA

Kinsman, Brent (Actor)
c/o Staff Member *AKA Talent Agency*
6310 San Vicente Blvd Ste 200
Los Angeles, CA 90048-5488, USA

Kinsman, Shane (Actor)
c/o Staff Member *AKA Talent Agency*
6310 San Vicente Blvd Ste 200
Los Angeles, CA 90048-5488, USA

Kintner, William R (Scientist)
3508 Market St
Philadelphia, PA 19104-3311, USA

Kinzer, Matt (Athlete, Baseball Player)
6717 Sweetbrier Dr
Fort Wayne, IN 46814-4564, USA

Kinzer, Matt (Athlete, Football Player)
6717 Sweetbrier Dr
Fort Wayne, IN 46814-4564, USA

Kinzinger, Adam (Congressman, Politician)
1218 Longworth Hob
Washington, DC 20515-2901, USA

KioKio (DJ)
c/o Staff Member *Diva Central Inc*
7510 W Sunset Blvd Ste 1445
Los Angeles, CA 90046-3408, USA

Kiper Jr, Mel (Sportscaster)
Sports Dept ESPN Plaza 935 Middle St
Bristol, CT 6010, USA

Kipketer, Wilson (Athlete, Track Athlete)
Atletik Forbund Idraettens Hus Brondby Stadion 20
Brondby 2605, DENMARK

Kiplinger, Austin H (Publisher)
Montevideo 1680 River Road
Poolesville, MD 20837, USA

Kipp, Fred (Athlete, Baseball Player)
6613 W 126th Ter
Leawood, KS 66209-2599, USA

Kipper, Bob (Athlete, Baseball Player)
117 Tuscany Way
Greer, SC 29650-4070, USA

Kipper, Thornton (Athlete, Baseball Player)
4680 W Geronimo St
Chandler, AZ 85226-5306, USA

Kiprusoff, Miikka (Athlete, Hockey Player)
c/o Staff Member *Octagon Sports Representation*
7400 Metro Blvd Ste 280
Minneapolis, MN 55439-2363, USA

Kiraly, Charles F (Karch) (Athlete, Coach, Volleyball Player)
c/o Staff Member *Simon & Schuster*
1230 Avenue of the Americas Fl CONC1
New York, NY 10020-1586, USA

Kirby, Bruce (Actor)
629 N Orlando Ave Apt 3
West Hollywood, CA 90048-2193, USA

Kirby, Durwood (Writer)
PO Box 3454
Fort Myers, FL 33918-3454, USA

Kirby, Jack (Athlete, Football Player)
PO Box 206
Los Olivos, CA 93441-0206, USA

Kirby, Jim (Athlete, Baseball Player)
520 Lohman Rd
Mount Juliet, TN 37122-4005, USA

Kirby, Luke (Actor)
c/o Kish Igbal *Gary Goddard Agency*
10 St Mary St Suite 305
Toronto, ON M4Y 1P9, Canada

Kirby, Pete
PO Box 1734
Madison, TN 37116-1734

Kirby, Ronald H (Architect)
PO Box 337 Melville
Johannesburg 2109, SOUTH AFRICA

Kirby, Terry (Athlete, Football Player)
113 Kirby Ln
Tabb, VA 23693-2532, USA

Kirby, Wayne (Athlete, Baseball Player)
320 Kenya Rd
Las Vegas, NV 89123-1169, USA

Kirby, Will (Reality TV Star)
c/o Staff Member *Metropolitan (MTA)*
4526 Wilshire Blvd
Los Angeles, CA 90010-3801, USA

Kirchbach, Gunar (Athlete)
Georgi-Dobrowoiski-Ste 10
Furstenwalde 15517, GERMANY

Kirchenbauer, Bill
3800 Barham Blvd
Los Angeles, CA 90068-1054

Kirchhoff, Ulrich (Misc)
Hoven 258
Rosendahl 48720, GERMANY

Kirchiro, Bill (Athlete, Football Player)
9889 Fleming Ave
Bethesda, MD 20814-2145, USA

Kirchner, Mark (Athlete)
Haruptstr 74A
Scheibe-Alsbach 98749, GERMANY

Kirchschlager, Angelika (Opera Singer)
161 W 61st St Apt 17E
New York, NY 10023-7460, USA

Kirgo, George (Actor, Writer)
178 N Carmelina Ave
Los Angeles, CA 90049-2737, USA

Kiriazis, Nick (Actor)
c/o Staff Member *Pakula/King & Associates*
9229 W Sunset Blvd Ste 315
Los Angeles, CA 90069-3403, USA

Kirilenko, Maria (Tennis Player)
c/o Staff Member *Women's Tennis Association (WTA (US))*
1 Progress Plz Ste 1500
St Petersburg, FL 33701-4335, USA

Kirk, Bill (Athlete, Baseball Player)
300 W Lemon St
Lititz, PA 17543-2311, USA

Kirk, Claude R Jr (Ex-Governor)
1180 Gator Trl
West Palm Beach, FL 33409-2043, USA

Kirk, James (Actor)
c/o Tyman Stewart *Characters Talent Agency, The (Vancouver)*
8 Elm St 2nd Floor
Toronto, ON M5G 1G7, Canada

Kirk, Justin (Actor)
c/o Lainie Sorkin Becky *Management 360*
9111 Wilshire Blvd
Beverly Hills, CA 90210-5508, USA

Kirk, Ken (Athlete, Football Player)
202 Milford St Apt 201
Tupelo, MS 38801-4691, USA

Kirk, Rahsaan Roland (Musician)
9229 W Sunset Blvd Ste 900
Los Angeles, CA 90069-3410, USA

Kirk, Thomas B (Physicist)
2 Center St
Upton, NY 11973-9700, USA

Kirk Jr, Walton (Walt) (Athlete, Basketball Player)
3730 Pennsylvania Ave Apt 302
Dubuque, IA 52002-3785, USA

Kirkby, Emma (Musician)
54A Leamington Road Villas
London W11 1HT, UNITED KINGDOM (UK)

Kirkconnell, Clare
PO Box 63
Rutherford, CA 94573-0063

Kirkeby, Per (Artist)
545 Broadway
New York, NY 10012-3921, USA

Kirkland, Gelsey (Ballerina)
500 Mount Tailac Ct
Roseville, CA 95747-8028, USA

Kirkland, Levon (Athlete, Football Player)
18200 Town Harbour Rd
Cornelius, NC 28031-7775, USA

Kirkland, Lori (Producer)
c/o Staff Member *Luber Roklin Management*
8530 Wilshire Blvd Ste 550
Beverly Hills, CA 90211-3133, USA

Kirkland, Mike (Musician)
300 Vine St Ste 14
Seattle, WA 98121-1465, USA

Kirkland, Sally (Actor)

Kirkland, Wilber (Athlete, Basketball Player)
127 Kimberwick Cir
Glenmoore, PA 19343-1124, USA

Kirkland, Willie (Athlete, Baseball Player)
19374 Northrop St
Detroit, MI 48219-5500, USA

Kirkman, Rick (Cartoonist)
c/o Staff Member *King Features Syndication*
300 W 57th St Fl 15
New York, NY 10019-5238, USA

Kirkpatrick, Chris (Actor, Musician)
c/o Staff Member *Good Guy Entertainment*
3733 Oakfield Dr
Sherman Oaks, CA 91423-4430, USA

Kirkpatrick, David (Director, Producer)
c/o Staff Member *Plymouth Rock Studios*
444 Long Pond Rd
Plymouth, MA 02360-2610, USA

Kirkpatrick, Ed (Athlete, Baseball Player)
24791 Via Larga
Laguna Niguel, CA 92677-1933, USA

Kirkpatrick, Maggie (Actor)
PO Box 1509
Darlinghurst, NSW 1300, AUSTRALIA

Kirkpatrick, Ralph (Musician)
Old Quarry
Guilford, CT 6437, USA

Kirkreit, Daron (Athlete, Baseball Player)
161 Steeplechase Cir
Sanford, FL 32771-9540, USA

Kirkup, James (Writer)
BM-Box 2780
London WC1V 6XX, UNITED KINGDOM (UK)

Kirkwood, Craig (Actor)
c/o Staff Member *Levine Management*
9028 W Sunset Blvd PH 1
Los Angeles, CA 90069-1830, USA

Kirkwood, Don (Athlete, Baseball Player)
455 W Elmwood Ave
Clawson, MI 48017-1231, USA

Kirllenko, Andrei (Basketball Player)
Delta Center 301 W South Temple
Salt Lake City, UT 84101, USA

Kirner, Gary (Athlete, Football Player)
3507 Senasac Ave
Long Beach, CA 90808-2847, USA

Kirouac, Lou (Athlete, Football Player)
3630 Chattahoochee Ct
Duluth, GA 30096-3210, USA

Kirrane, John (Jack) (Athlete, Hockey Player)
3 Country Rd
Chestnut Hill, MA 02467-2912, USA

Kirrene, Joe (Athlete, Baseball Player)
2557 Kilpatrick Ct
San Ramon, CA 94583-1726, USA

Kirschke, Travis (Athlete, Football Player)
10196 Crooked Stick Trl
Lone Tree, CO 80124-8510, USA

Kirschner, Carl (Educator)
President's Office
New Brunswick, NJ 8093, USA

kirschner, David (Actor)
c/o Staff Member *WmE2 (WMA-LA)*
1 William Morris Pl
Beverly Hills, CA 90212-4261, USA

Kirschstein, Ruth L (Doctor)
9000 Rockville Pike
Bethesda, MD 20892-0001, USA

Kirsebom, Vendela (Model)
c/o Staff Member *Ford Models (NY)*
238 E 4th St
New York, NY 10009-7425

Kirshbaum, Laurence J (Publisher)
Time-Life Building Rockefeller Center
New York, NY 10020, USA

Kirshbaum, Ralph (Musician)
165 W 57th St
New York, NY 10019-2201, USA

Kirshner, Mia (Actor)
c/o Daniel (Danny) Sussman *Brillstein Entertainment Partners*
9150 Wilshire Blvd Ste 350
Beverly Hills, CA 90212-3453, USA

Kirstein, Adam (Stylist)
c/o Staff Member *Judy Inc*
1 Yorkville Ave
Toronto ON M4W 1L1, Canada

Kirszenstein, Szewinska Irena (Athlete, Track Athlete)
Ul Bagno 5m 80
Warsaw 00-112, POLAND

Kirton, Mark (Athlete, Hockey Player)
251 N Service Rd W
Oakville, ON L6M 3E7, Canada

Kisabaka, Lisa (Athlete, Track Athlete)
Franz-Hitze-Str 22
Leverkusen 51372, GERMANY

Kiselak, Mike (Athlete, Football Player)
316 Cimarron Trl
Irving, TX 75063-4598, USA

Kiser, Garland (Athlete, Baseball Player)
267 Carr Dr
Blountville, TN 37617-4608, USA

Kiser, Terry (Actor)
1505 10th St
Santa Monica, CA 90401-2805, USA

Kishida, Kyoko
7-5-34-801 Akasada Miatuku
Tokyo, JAPAN

Kishlansky, Mark A (Historian)
History Dept
Cambridge, MA 2138, USA

Kisio, Kelly (Athlete, Hockey Player)
c/o Staff Member *Calgary Hitmen*
P.O. Box 1420 Stn Main
Calgary, AB T2P 3B9, Canada

Kison, Bruce E (Athlete, Baseball Player)
1403 Riverside Cir
Bradenton, FL 34209, USA

Kisor, Henry (Writer)
2800 Harrison St
Evanston, IL 60201-1218, USA

KISS (Music Group)
c/o Doc McGhee *McGhee Entertainment*
8730 W Sunset Blvd Ste 175
Los Angeles, CA 90069-2246, USA

Kissane, James (Athlete, Basketball Player)
6 Mellen Ln
Wayland, MA 01778-2015, USA

Kissell, Ed (Athlete, Football Player)
40 Sebbins Pond Dr
Bedford, NH 03110-6630, USA

Kissell, Larry (Congressman, Politician)
1632 Longworth Hob
Washington, DC 20515-2007, USA

Kissel-Lafser, Audrey (Baseball Player)
9506 Port Dr
Affton, MO 63123-6530, USA

Kissin, Evgeni I (Musician)
31 Sinclair Rd
London W14 0NS, UNITED KINGDOM (UK)

Kissinger, Henry A (Nobel Prize Laureate, Secretary)
350 Park Ave
New York, NY 10022-6022, USA

Kissling, Conny (Skier)
Hubel
Messen 3254, SWITZERLAND

Kistler, Darci (Ballerina)
Lincoln Center Plaza
New York, NY 10023, USA

Kitaen, Tawny (Actor)
5670 Wilshire Blvd Ste 820
Los Angeles, CA 90036-5613, USA

Kitaj, R B (Artist)
6 Albermarle St
London W1, UNITED KINGDOM (UK)

Kitano, Takeshi (Actor, Director)
5-4-14 Akasaka Minataku
Tokyo 107-0052, JAPAN

Kitaro (Composer, Musician)
1140, AUSTRIA

Kitayenko, Dmitri G (Conductor)
Chalet Kalimor
Botterens 1652, SWITZERLAND

Kitbunchu, M Michael Cardinal (Religious Leader)
122 Soi Naaksuwan Thanon Nonsi
Yannawa
Bangkok 10120, THAILAND

Kitchen, Curtis (Athlete, Basketball Player)
343 19th Ave
Seattle, WA 98122-5735, USA

Kitchen, Michael (Actor)
76 Oxford St
London W1N 0AX, UNITED KINGDOM (UK)

Kitchen, Mike (Athlete, Coach, Hockey Player)
c/o Staff Member *Florida Panthers*
1 Panther Pkwy
Sunrise, FL 33323-5315, USA

Kitchens, Bobbie (Stylist)
PO Box 3352
Pasadena, CA 91109, USA

Kite, Greg (Athlete, Basketball Player)
3060 Seigneury Dr
Windermere, FL 34786-8353, USA

Kite, Tom (Athlete, Golfer)
907 Terrace Mountain Dr
West Lake Hills, TX 78746-2730, USA

Kithune, Robert K U (Admiral)
1597 Haleloke St
Hilo, HI 96720-1571, USA

Kitna, Jon (Athlete, Football Player)
18898 Bella Vista Ct
Northville, MI 48168-3534, USA

Kitsch, Taylor (Actor)
c/o Katie Rhodes *Untitled Entertainment (LA)*
350 S Beverly Dr Ste 200
Beverly Hills, CA 90212-4819, USA

Kitson, Syd (Athlete, Football Player)
7232 Horizon Dr
West Palm Beach, FL 33412-3027, USA

Kitt, A J (Skier)
2437 N Franklin Ave
Louisville, CO 80027-1216, USA

Kittel, Charles (Physicist)
Physics
Berkeley, CA 94720-0001, USA

Kittinger Jr, Joseph W (Joe) (Misc)
608 Mariner Way
Altamonte Springs, FL 32701-5434, USA

Kittle, Ronald D (Ron) (Athlete, Baseball Player)
PO Box 1998
Valparaiso, IN 46384-1998, USA

Kittles, Kerry (Athlete, Basketball Player)
PO Box 641
Franklin Lakes, NJ 07417-0641, USA

Kittles, Tory (Actor)
c/o Matt Luber *Luber Roklin Management*
8530 Wilshire Blvd Ste 550
Beverly Hills, CA 90211-3133, USA

Kitzhaber, John (Governor, Politician)
900 Court St NE
Salem, OR 97301-4042, USA

Kiyoko, Hayley (Actor)
c/o Staff Member *AKA Talent Agency*
6310 San Vicente Blvd Ste 200
Los Angeles, CA 90048-5488, USA

Kiyosaki, Kim (Business Person, Writer)
4330 N Civic Center Plz Ste 100
Scottsdale, AZ 85251-3529, USA

Kiyosaki, Robert T (Business Person, Writer)
4330 N Civic Center Plz Ste 100
Scottsdale, AZ 85251-3529, USA

Kizer, Carolyn A (Writer)
English Dept
Tucson, AZ 85271, USA

Kizim, Leonid D (Cosmonaut)
Russian Space Forces
Saint Petersburg, RUSSIA

Kjer, Bodil (Actor)
Vestre Pavilion Frydenlund Frydenlund Alle 19
Vedbaek 2950, DENMARK

Kjus, Lasse (Athlete, Skier)
LK International AG Gewerbestr. 11
Cham 6330, Switzerland

Klabunde, Charles S (Artist)
68 W 3rd St
New York, NY 10012-1029, USA

Klages, Fred (Athlete, Baseball Player)
10510 Six Pines Dr
Spring, TX 77380-0904, USA

Klammer, Franz (Skier)
Mooswald 22
Fresach/Ktn 9712, AUSTRIA

Klaplisch, Cedric (Director)
36 Rue de Ponthieu
Paris 75008, FRANCE

Klares, John (Athlete, Bowler)
867 N Lamb Blvd Spc 223
Las Vegas, NV 89110-2337, USA

Klas, Eri (Conductor)
Nurme 54
Tallinn 16, ESTONIA

Klasnic, John (Athlete, Football Player)
924 Highland Ave
McKeesport, PA 15133-3920, USA

Klass, Beverly (Athlete, Golfer)
PO Box 244364
Boynton Beach, FL 33424-4364, USA

Klassen, Danny (Athlete, Baseball Player)
28925 N 11th Pl
Scottsdale, AZ 85262, USA

Klassen, Ralph (Athlete, Hockey Player)
826 Avenue C N
Saskatoon, SK S7L 1J8, Canada

Klatt, Trent (Athlete, Hockey Player)
267 SW 12th Ave
Grand Rapids, MN 55744-3487, USA

Klattenhoff, Diego (Actor)
c/o Francis Okwu *Levine Okwu Erickson Management*
6363 Wilshire Blvd Ste 300
Los Angeles, CA 90048-5729, USA

Klaus, Bobby (Athlete, Baseball Player)
10661 Gabacho Dr
San Diego, CA 92124-1404, USA

Klaus, Deita (Actor)
c/o Staff Member *Digigraphics/Dream Girl World*
4650 Libbit Ave
Encino, CA 91436-2122, USA

Klaus, Vaclav (Politician, President)
c/o Staff Member *Kancelar Prezidenta Republiky (Czech Republic)*
Hradecek
Prague 1 119 08, Czech Republic

Klausing, Chuck (Coach, Football Coach)
2115 Lazor St
Indiana, PA 15701-3463, USA

Klausner, Richard D (Biologist)
31 Center Dr
Bethesda, MD 20892-0001, USA

Klawitter, Tom (Athlete, Baseball Player)
605 Foxglove Ln
Whitewater, WI 53190-2665, USA

Klaxons (Music Group)
c/o Staff Member *Paradigm (Monterey)*
404 W Franklin St
Monterey, CA 93940-2303, USA

Klebba, Martin (Actor)
c/o Staff Member *The Stevens Group*
14011 Ventura Blvd Ste 201
Sherman Oaks, CA 91423-5216, USA

Klebe, Giselher (Composer)
Bruchstr 16
Detmold 32756, GERMANY

Kleber, Karen (Stylist)
150 E 18th St Apt 4H
New York, NY 10003-2447, USA

Klecko, Joseph E (Joe) (Athlete, Football Player)
105 Stella Ln
Aston, PA 19014-2741, USA

Klee, Ken (Athlete, Hockey Player)
78 W Ranch Trl
Morrison, CO 80465-9503, USA

Klees, Christian (Misc)
Schutzenweg 26
Eutin 23701, GERMANY

Kleihues, Josef P (Architect)
Schlickweg 4
Berlin 14129, GERMANY

Klein, Alex (Misc)
165 W 57th St
New York, NY 10019-2201, USA

Klein, Calvin (Designer, Fashion Designer)
c/o Staff Member *Calvin Klein Inc*
200 Madison Ave
New York, NY 10016-3903, USA

Klein, Chris (Actor)
c/o Cynthia Pett-Dante *Brillstein Entertainment Partners*
9150 Wilshire Blvd Ste 350
Beverly Hills, CA 90212-3453, USA

Klein, Danny (Musician)
652 N Doheny Dr
Los Angeles, CA 90069-5526, USA

Klein, David (Misc)
9000 Rockville Pike
Bethesda, MD 20892-0001, USA

Klein, Edward
c/o Staff Member *St Martins Press*
175 5th Ave
New York, NY 10010-7703, USA

Klein, Emilee (Athlete, Golfer)
3535 Lebon Dr Apt 4111
San Diego, CA 92122-6400, USA

Klein, George (Biologist)
Kottlavagen 10
Lidingo 181 61, SWEDEN

Klein, Herbert G (Government Official, Publisher)
350 D Ave
San Diego, CA 92118-1331, USA

Klein, Jennifer (Producer)
c/o Carlos Goodman *Bloom Hergott Diemer Rosenthal Laviolette & Feldman*
150 S Rodeo Dr Fl 3
Beverly Hills, CA 90212-2410, USA

Klein, Jenny
201 S Capitol Ave Ste 430
Indianapolis, IN 46225-1026

Klein, Jess (Musician, Songwriter, Writer)
177 Woodland Ave
Westwood, NJ 07675-3218, USA

Klein, Joe (Journalist, Writer)
251 W 57th St
New York, NY 10019-1802, USA

Klein, Joel (Educator, Government Official, Lawyer)
Chancellor's Office 110 Livingston St
Brooklyn, NY 11201, USA

Klein, Jonathan (Business Person)
c/o Staff Member *CNN (NY)*
1 Time Warner Ctr
New York, NY 10019-6038, USA

Klein, Lawrence R (Nobel Prize Laureate)
1400 Waverly Rd Apt B35
Gladwyne, PA 19035-1260, USA

Klein, Lester A (Doctor)
10666 N Torrey Pines Rd
La Jolla, CA 92037-1027, USA

Klein, Marci (Director, Producer, Writer)
c/o Jeffrey Jacobs *Creative Artists Agency (CAA-LA)*
2000 Avenue of the Stars Ste 100
Los Angeles, CA 90067-4705, USA

Klein, Naomi (Producer, Writer)
PO Box 67746 280 Spadina Ave
Toronto, ON M5T3BO, CANADA

Klein, Perry (Athlete, Football Player)
30760 Broad Beach Rd
Malibu, CA 90265-2613, USA

Klein, Richard J (Athlete, Football Player)
RR 1 Box 33
Tower Hill, IL 62571-9711, USA

Klein, Robert (Actor, Musician)
c/o Rory Rosegarten *Conversation Company*
1044 Northern Blvd Ste 304
Roslyn, NY 11576-1589, USA

Klein, Robert O (Bob) (Athlete, Football Player)
15263 Friends St
Pacific Palisades, CA 90272-4606, USA

Klein Borkow, Dana (Producer)
c/o Staff Member *WmE2 (WMA-LA)*
1 William Morris Pl
Beverly Hills, CA 90212-4261, USA

Kleindienst, Richard
3103 W Crestview Dr
Prescott, AZ 86305-5001

Kleine, Joe (Athlete, Basketball Player)
53 Hickory Hills Cir
Little Rock, AR 72212-2766, USA

Kleine, Joseph (Joe) (Baseball Player)
4819 Stony Ford Dr
Dallas, TX 75287-7214, USA

Kleinendorst, Scot (Athlete, Hockey Player)
35387 Lake St
Cohasset, MN 55721-2160, USA

Kleinert, Harold E (Doctor)
225 Abraham Flexner Way
Louisville, KY 40202-1882, USA

Kleinfeld, Andrew J (Judge)
Courthouse Square 250 Cushman St
Fairbanks, AK 99701, USA

Kleinman, Arthur M (Psychic)
Anthropology Dept
Cambridge, MA 2138, USA

Kleinrock, Leonard (Scientist)
318 N Rockingham Ave
Los Angeles, CA 90049-2636, USA

Kleinsasser, Jim (Athlete, Football Player)
5955 3rd St SE
Carrington, ND 58421-8804, USA

Kleinsmith, Bruce (Cartoonist)
PO Box 1083
San Juan Bautista, CA 95045-1083, USA

Kleiser, Randal (Director)
3050 Runyon Canyon Rd
Los Angeles, CA 90046-1347, USA

Kleisinger, Terry (Athlete, Hockey Player)
37 Elisia Dr
Moose Jaw, SK S6j 1G9, Canada

Klemm, Adrian (Athlete, Football Player)
2931 Plaza Del Amo Unit 114
Torrance, CA 90503-9331, USA

Klemm, Jay (Athlete, Baseball Player)
1605 Airy Hill Ct Unit D
Crofton, MD 21114-2723, USA

Klemm, Jay (Athlete, Baseball Player)
47 Choctaw Ridge Rd
Branchburg, NJ 08876-5441, USA

Klemm, Jon (Athlete, Hockey Player)
400 61st St
Willowbrook, IL 60527-1806, USA

Klemmer, John (Musician)
10548 Clearwood Ct
Los Angeles, CA 90077-2019, USA

Klemp, Cardinal Jozef
Kolski U1Miodowa 17
Warsaw, POLAND PL-00-583

Klemperer, William (Misc)
53 Shattuck Rd
Watertown, MA 02472-1310, USA

Klemt, Becky (Lawyer)
PO Box 1285
Laramie, WY 82073-1285, USA

Klensch, Elsa
1050 Techwood Dr NW
Atlanta, GA 30318-5604

Kleppe, Thomas S (Secretary)
8300 Burdette Rd Apt 568
Bethesda, MD 20817-2834, USA

Klesko, Ryan A (Athlete, Baseball Player)
c/o Staff Member *San Diego Padres*
100 Park Blvd
San Diego, CA 92101-7405, USA

Klesla, Rotislav (Athlete, Hockey Player)
9425 E Desert Village Dr
Scottsdale, AZ 85255-6095, USA

Klett, Peter (Musician)
11410 NE 124th St # 627
Kirkland, WA 98034-4399, USA

Kleven, Jay (Athlete, Baseball Player)
118 Via Bolsa
San Lorenzo, CA 94580-3311, USA

Klever, Rocky (Athlete, Football Player)
3829 W 42nd Ave
Anchorage, AK 99517-2752, USA

Kley Minnis, Chaney (Actor)
c/o Staff Member *Foundation Management*
100 N Crescent Dr Ste 323
Beverly Hills, CA 90210-5403, USA

Klick, Jim (Athlete, Football Player)
4001 E Lake Estates Dr
Davie, FL 33328-3072, USA

Klicullen, Bob (Athlete, Football Player)
400 E Division St
Pilot Point, TX 76258-4510, USA

Kliks, Rudolf R (Architect)
Ul Kuibysheva 6
Moscow, RUSSIA

Klim, Michael (Swimmer)
177 Bridge Rd
Richmond, VIC 3121, AUSTRALIA

Klima, Petr (Athlete, Hockey Player)
1000 Forest Ln
Bloomfield Hills, MI 48301-4112, USA

Klimchock, Lou (Athlete, Baseball Player)
8876 S Myrtle Ave
Tempe, AZ 85284-3178, USA

Klimek, Tony (Athlete, Football Player)
17730 Brook Hill Dr
Orland Park, IL 60467-7524, USA

Klimke, Reiner (Misc)
Krumme Str 3
Munster 48143, GERMANY

Klimkowski, Ron (Athlete, Baseball Player)
117 Candy Ln
Syosset, NY 11791-4911, USA

Klimuk, Pyotr I (Cosmonaut)
Moskovskoi Oblasti
Syvisdny Goroduk 141160, RUSSIA

Kline, Bobby (Athlete, Baseball Player)
6656 31st Way S
Saint Petersburg, FL 33712-5404, USA

Kline, Jeff (Producer, Writer)
c/o Staff Member *WmE2 (Endeavor-LA)*
9601 Wilshire Blvd Fl 3
Beverly Hills, CA 90210-5219, USA

Kline, John (Congressman, Politician)
2439 Rayburn Hob
Washington, DC 20515-3001, USA

Kline, John
2439 Rayburn Hob
Washington, DC 20515-3001, USA

Kline, Kevin D (Actor)
c/o Judy Hofflund *Hofflund/Polone*
9465 Wilshire Blvd Ste 420
Beverly Hills, CA 90212-2603, USA

Kline, Owen (Actor)
c/o Staff Member *WmE2 (WMA-LA)*
1 William Morris Pl
Beverly Hills, CA 90212-4261, USA

Kline, Richard (Actor)
c/o Harry Gold *TalentWorks (LA)*
3500 W Olive Ave Ste 1400
Burbank, CA 91505-5512, USA

Kline, Steve (Athlete, Baseball Player)
PO Box 1525
Chelan, WA 98816-1525, USA

Kline, Steve (Athlete, Baseball Player)
258 Trutt Rd
Winfield, PA 17889-9304, USA

Kline-Randall, Maxine (Baseball Player)
3751 Milnes Rd
Hillsdale, MI 49242-9313, USA

Klingbeil, Chuck (Athlete, Football Player)
51977 Bootjack Rd
Lake Linden, MI 49945-9765, USA

Klingenbeck, Scott (Athlete, Baseball Player)
6230 Kincora Ct
Cincinnati, OH 45233-4458, USA

Klingler, David (Athlete, Football Player)
2206 Shelby Park Dr
Katy, TX 77450-6600, USA

Klingman, Lynzee (Actor)
c/o Staff Member *United Talent Agency (UTA)*
9560 Wilshire Blvd Fl 5
Beverly Hills, CA 90212-2400, USA

Klink, Joe (Athlete, Baseball Player)
188 Bermuda Petrel Ct
Daytona Beach, FL 32119-1393, USA

Klinsmann, Jurgen (Soccer Player)
3419 Via Lido # 600
Newport Beach, CA 92663-3908, USA

Klitbo, Cynthia (Actor)
c/o Staff Member *Televisa*
Blvd Adolfo Lopez Mateos 232 Colonia San Angel INN
DF CP 01060, MEXICO

Klitschko, Wladimir (Actor, Athlete, Boxer)
Borselstr.28 Haus I
Hamburg 22765, Germany

Kllesmet, Robert B (Misc)
815 16th St NW # 307
Washington, DC 20006-4101, USA

Klosowski, Dolores (Baseball Player)
14254 Farnsworth Dr
Sterling Heights, MI 48312-4352, USA

Kloss, Ilana (Athlete, Tennis Player)
1776 Broadway Ste 600
New York, NY 10019-2002, USA

Klosterman, Bruce (Athlete, Football Player)
14194 Deerfield Ct
Dubuque, IA 52003-9414, USA

Klotz, H Louis (Red) (Athlete, Basketball Player, Coach)
114 S Osborne Ave
Margate City, NJ 08402-2530, USA

Klotz, Irving M (Misc)
1500 Sheridan Rd Unit 7D
Wilmette, IL 60091-1844, USA

Klotz, John S (Athlete, Football Player)
729 E 25th St
Chester, PA 19013-5229, USA

Klous, Patricia (Actor)
2539 Benedict Canyon Dr
Beverly Hills, CA 90210-1020, USA

Kloves, Steve (Director, Writer)
c/o David O'Connor *Creative Artists Agency (CAA-LA)*
2000 Avenue of the Stars Ste 100
Los Angeles, CA 90067-4705, USA

Klueh, Duane (Athlete, Basketball Player)
9011 US Highway 98 W
Destin, FL 32550-7254, USA

Kluer, Duane (Athlete, Basketball Player, Coach)
252 Francis Avenue Ct
Terre Haute, IN 47804-5101, USA

Klug, Aaron (Nobel Prize Laureate)
70 Cavendish Ave
Cambridge CB1 40T, UNITED KINGDOM (UK)

Kluger, Richard (Writer)
c/o Staff Member *Random House Publicity*
1745 Broadway
New York, NY 10019-4368, USA

Klugh, Earl (Musician)
c/o Staff Member *Richard De La Font Agency*
3808 W South Park Blvd
Broken Arrow, OK 74011-1261, USA

Klugman, Jack (Actor)
22548 Pacific Coast Hwy
Malibu, CA 90265-5053, USA

Klum, Heidi (Model, Producer)
c/o Sara Jane Lieb *Full Picture (NY)*
568 Broadway Rm 603
New York, NY 10012-3260, USA

Klutka, Nick (Athlete, Football Player)
1050 Rosemont Dr
Van Wert, OH 45891-2640, USA

Klutts, Mickey (Athlete, Baseball Player)
6136 Maple Ave
Lake Isabella, CA 93240-9706, USA

Kluttz, Lonnie (Athlete, Basketball Player)
183 Greenwing Ln
Saint Matthews, SC 29135-8168, USA

Kluzak, Gord (Athlete, Hockey Player)
770 Boylston St Apt 18L
Boston, MA 02199-7700, USA

Klymaxx (Music Group)
c/o Staff Member *Diva Central Inc*
7510 W Sunset Blvd Ste 1445
Los Angeles, CA 90046-3408, USA

Klymkiw, Julius (Athlete)
66 Buttercup Ave
Winnipeg, MB R2V 2S5, Canada

Klyn, Vincent
4200 Ocean View Dr
Malibu, CA 90265-2822

Klyszewski, Waclaw (Architect)
Ul Gomoslaska 16m 15A
Warsaw 00-432, POLAND

Kmak, Joe (Athlete, Baseball Player)
1021 Hatteras Ct
Foster City, CA 94404-3546, USA

Kmetko, Steve
5670 Wilshire Blvd Ste 200
Los Angeles, CA 90036-5657

K'naan (Music Group, Musician)
c/o Aaron Schubert *Paquin Entertainment Agency*
468 Stradbrook Ave
Winnipeg, Manitoba R3L 0J9, Canada

Knackert, Brent (Athlete, Baseball Player)
16802 Leafwood Cir
Huntington Beach, CA 92647-4851, USA

Knafelc, Gary (Athlete, Football Player)
2147 Burley Ave
Clermont, FL 34711-5744, USA

Knafelc, Greg (Athlete, Football Player)
612 Chantilly Rue
Green Bay, WI 54301-1432, USA

Knape, Lindberg Ulrike (Swimmer)
Drostvagen 7
Karlskoga 691 33, SWEDEN

Knapp, Charles B (Educator)
1333 New Hampshire Ave NW
Washington, DC 20036-1500, USA

Knapp, Chris (Athlete, Baseball Player)
788 Rich Dr
Oviedo, FL 32765-6447, USA

Knapp, Cleon T (Publisher)
10100 Santa Monica Blvd Ste 2000
Los Angeles, CA 90067-4134, USA

Knapp, Jennifer (Musician)
c/o Staff Member *Creative Artists Agency (CAA-TN)*
3310 W End Ave Fl 5
Nashville, TN 37203-1028, USA

Knapp, John W (Educator, General)
Superintendent's Office
Lexington, VA 24450, USA

Knapp, Lindsay (Athlete, Football Player)
5018 Bruce Ave
Minneapolis, MN 55424-1318, USA

Knapp, Sebastian (Actor)
c/o Lorraine Berglund *Lorraine Berglund Management*
11537 Hesby St
North Hollywood, CA 91601-3618, USA

Knapp, Stefan (Artist)
Sandhills Godalming
Surrey, UNITED KINGDOM (UK)

Knaus, William (Doctor)
Medical Ctr
Washington, DC 20052-0001, USA

Knauss, Hans (Skier)
Fastenberg 60
Schladming 8970, AUSTRIA

Kneale, R Bryan C (Artist)
10A Muswell Road
London N10 2BG, UNITED KINGDOM (UK)

Knebel, John A (Secretary)
1418 Labumum St
McLean, VA 22101, USA

Knepper, Robert (Actor)
c/o Ben Levine *Kritzer Levine Wilkins Entertainment*
11872 La Grange Ave Fl 1
Los Angeles, CA 90025-5283, USA

Knepper, Robert W (Bob) (Athlete, Baseball Player)
3010 Hightower Pl Apt 219
Fairfax, VA 22031-1296, USA

Kness, Richard M (Opera Singer)
240 Central Park S Apt 16M
New York, NY 10019-1460, USA

Kneuer, Cameo (Misc)
2554 Lincoln Blvd # 640
Venice, CA 90291-5082, USA

Knicely, Alan (Athlete, Baseball Player)
PO Box 433
Dayton, VA 22821-0433, USA

Knickle, Rick (Athlete, Hockey Player)
192 Martinwood Way NE
Calgary, AB T3J 3H8, Canada

Knief, Gayle (Athlete, Football Player)
1825 SE Birchwood Cir
Waukee, IA 50263-8194, USA

Knight, Andrew S B (Editor, Publisher)
PO Box 495 Virginia St
London W1 9XY, UNITED KINGDOM (UK)

Knight, Beverley (Musician)
c/o Staff Member *International Talent Booking (ITB - UK)*
27A Floral St Fl 3 Covent Garden
London WC2E 9, UNITED KINGDOM

Knight, Billy (Athlete, Basketball Player)
1051 Bluffhaven Way NE
Atlanta, GA 30319-4818, USA

Knight, Brandon (Baseball Player)
PO Box 1685
Ventura, CA 93002-1685, USA

Knight, Brevin (Athlete, Basketball Player)
3226 Bedford Ln
Germantown, TN 38139-8043, USA

Knight, Brian (Baseball Player)
1123 Stuart St
Helena, MT 59601-2138, USA

Knight, Brian (Athlete, Baseball Player)
1123 Stuart St
Helena, MT 59601-2138, USA

Knight, C Ray (Athlete, Baseball Player, Coach)
PO Box 129
Auburn, AL 36831-0129, USA

Knight, Charles F (Business Person)
8000 W Florissant Ave # 41000
Saint Louis, MO 63136-1414, USA

Knight, Chris (Musician, Songwriter, Writer)
1018 17th Ave S Ste 12
Nashville, TN 37212-2219, USA

Knight, Christopher (Actor)
c/o Staff Member *Venture IAB*
3211 Cahuenga Blvd W Ste 104
Los Angeles, CA 90068-1372, USA

Knight, Curt (Athlete, Football Player)
7230 Rio Flora Pl
Downey, CA 90241-2030, USA

Knight, David (Athlete, Football Player)
3801 Porter St Nw Apt 301
Washington, DC 20016-2947, USA

Knight, Douglas M (Educator)
773 Greenwood Ave
Glencoe, IL 60022-1514, USA

Knight, Gladys (Musician)
3221 La Mirada Ave
Las Vegas, NV 89120-3011, USA

Knight, Jean (Musician)
PO Box 1875
Gretna, LA 70054-1875, USA

Knight, Jonathan (Musician)
c/o Staff Member *Interscope Records (LA) - Main*
2220 Colorado Ave
Santa Monica, CA 90404-3506, USA

Knight, Jordan (Musician)
c/o Tracy Nguyen *IPR + MKTG*
1515 Broadway Fl 40
New York, NY 10036-8901, USA

Knight, Marion (Suge) (Actor, Musician, Producer)
c/o Staff Member *Acme Talent & Literary (LA)*
1400 Atlantic Ave Ste 274
Long Beach, CA 90813-2013, USA

Knight, Michael E
1344 Lexington Ave
New York, NY 10128-1507, USA

Knight, Negele (Athlete, Basketball Player)
18624 N 4th Ave
Phoenix, AZ 85027-5665, USA

Knight, Paul (Producer)
c/o Anthony Jones *United Agents*
12-26 Lexington St
London W1F OLE, UK

Knight, Phil (Business Person)
1 SW Bowerman Dr
Beaverton, OR 97005-0979, USA

Knight, Robert M (Bobby) (Athlete, Basketball Player, Coach)
8003 County Road 6910
Lubbock, TX 79407-5760, USA

Knight, Ron (Athlete, Basketball Player)
1426 Ellsmere Ave
Los Angeles, CA 90019-3800, USA

Knight, Scott (Stylist)
c/o Staff Member *Artists by Timothy Priano (CA)*
8447 Wilshire Blvd Ste 301
Beverly Hills, CA 90211-3206, USA

Knight, Shirley (Actor)
c/o Martin Gage *Gage Group, The (LA)*
14724 Ventura Blvd Ste 505
Sherman Oaks, CA 91403-3505, USA

Knight, Sterling (Actor)
c/o Christopher Rockwell *Global Creative*
1051 Cole Ave # B
Los Angeles, CA 90038-2601, USA

Knight, Steve (Writer)
c/o Staff Member *Creative Artists Agency (CAA-LA)*
2000 Avenue of the Stars Ste 100
Los Angeles, CA 90067-4705, USA

Knight, Steve (Athlete, Football Player)
4503 Bevington Ln Apt A
Indianapolis, IN 46240-4478, USA

Knight, Summer
PO Box 9786
Marina Del Rey, CA 90295-2186

Knight, Toby (Athlete, Basketball Player)
106 Claywood Dr
Brentwood, NY 11717-5724, USA

Knight, Tom (Athlete, Football Player)
PO Box 888
Phoenix, AZ 85001-0888, USA

Knight, TR (Actor)
c/o Staff Member *Gersh (LA)*
9465 Wilshire Blvd Ste 600
Beverly Hills, CA 90212-2612, USA

Knight, Travis (Athlete, Basketball Player)
3159 Millcreek Rd
Pleasant Grove, UT 84062-8790, USA

Knight, Trevor (Adult Film Star)
c/o Staff Member *Diva Central Inc*
7510 W Sunset Blvd Ste 1445
Los Angeles, CA 90046-3408, USA

Knight, Wayne (Actor)
c/o Staff Member *Agency for the Performing Arts (APA-LA)*
405 S Beverly Dr Ste 500
Beverly Hills, CA 90212-4425, USA

Knight, Wendi (Adult Film Star)
c/o Staff Member *Atlas Multimedia Inc*
9005 Eton Ave Ste C
Canoga Park, CA 91304-6533, USA

Knightley, Keira (Actor)
c/o Will Ward *WmE2 (Endeavor-LA)*
9601 Wilshire Blvd Fl 3
Beverly Hills, CA 90210-5219, USA

Knightlinger, Lauren (Actor)
c/o Peter Principato *Principato/Young Management*
9465 Wilshire Blvd Ste 430
Beverly Hills, CA 90212-2613, USA

Knighton, Zachary (Actor)
c/o Nick Frenkel *3 Arts Entertainment Inc*
9460 Wilshire Blvd Fl 7
Beverly Hills, CA 90212-2713, USA

Knights, Dave (Musician)
195 Sandycombe Road
Kew TW9 2EW, UNITED KINGDOM (UK)

Knisley, Sam (Athlete, Basketball Player)
14808 Hanover Pike
Upperco, MD 21155-9735, USA

Knobbs, Brian
14804 58th St
North Clearwater, FL 34620

Knoblauch, E Charles (Chuck) (Athlete, Baseball Player)
101 Westcott St Unit 1105
Houston, TX 77007-7048, USA

Knoedler, Justin (Athlete, Baseball Player)
136 N State St
Springfield, IL 62702-4843, USA

Knoff, Kurt (Athlete, Football Player)
11121 Bluestem Ln
Eden Prairie, MN 55347-4732, USA

Knoll, Andrew H (Misc)
36 Oxford St Apt 26
Cambridge, MA 02138-1957, USA

Knoll, Jozsef (Misc)
Pharmacology Dept
Budapest 1089, HUNGARY

Knoop, Bobby (Athlete, Baseball Player)
2543 E Mountain Sky Ave
Phoenix, AZ 85048-9516, USA

Knopf, Sascha (Actor, Model)
c/o Bradley Frank *Platform Public Relations*
2666 N Beachwood Dr
Los Angeles, CA 90068-2308, USA

Knopfler, David (Musician)
16 Lambton Place
London W11 2SH, UNITED KINGDOM (UK)

Knopfler, Mark (Musician)
37 Ruston Mews
London W11 1RB, UNITED KINGDOM (UK)

Knopoff, Leon (Physicist)
Geophysics Institute
Los Angeles, CA 90024, USA

Knopper, Steve (Writer)
3445 W Moncrieff Pl
Denver, CO 80211-3161, USA

Knorr, Micah (Athlete, Football Player)
2127 Bluebell
Forney, TX 75126-6353, USA

Knorr, Randy (Athlete, Baseball Player)
12134 Bishopsford Dr
Tampa, FL 33626-1319, USA

Knostman, Richard (Dick) (Athlete, Basketball Player)
346 Crestone Ave
Salida, CO 81201-1521, USA

Knott, Eric (Athlete, Baseball Player)
1107 Hyacinth Ave
Sebring, FL 33875-8059, USA

Knott, Jon (Athlete, Baseball Player)
4250 Vicenza Dr Unit A
Venice, FL 34293-0714, USA

Knotts, Gary (Athlete, Baseball Player)
18 Covey St
Decatur, AL 35603-6021, USA

Knowles, Beyonce (Actor, Musician)
c/o Yvette Noel-Schure *Schure Media*
16 Skyline Dr # 594
Montville, NJ 07045-9422, USA

Knowles, Darold (Athlete, Baseball Player)
1515 Whisper Wind Ln
Oldsmar, FL 34677-5133, USA

Knowles, Harry (Internet Star)
PO Box 180011
Austin, TX 78718-0011, USA

Knowles, Jeremy R (Misc)
67 Francis Ave
Cambridge, MA 02138-1911, USA

Knowles, Miki & Gregg (Stylist)
1740 Anzle Ave
Winter Park, FL 32789-4002, USA

Knowles, Rodney (Athlete, Basketball Player)
3592 Island Dr
N Topsail Beach, NC 28460-8202, USA

Knowles, Solange (Actor, Musician)
c/o Staff Member *Creative Artists Agency (CAA-LA)*
2000 Avenue of the Stars Ste 100
Los Angeles, CA 90067-4705, USA

Knowles, William S (Nobel Prize Laureate)
PO Box 71
Kelly, WY 83011-0071, USA

Knowlton, Steve R (Skier)
6600 E Hampden Ave # 210
Denver, CO 80224-3045, USA

Knox, Bill (Athlete, Football Player)
7836 Forest Ave
Gary, IN 46403-2139, USA

Knox, Chuck (Athlete, Football Coach, Football Player)
11220 NE 53rd St
Kirkland, WA 98033-7505, USA

Knox, John (Athlete, Baseball Player)
3701 W Oak Shores Dr
Crossroads, TX 76227-2606, USA

Knox, Kenny (Athlete, Golfer)
3813 Dills Rd
Monticello, FL 32344-4699, USA

Knox, Terence (Actor)
c/o Lin Bickelmann *Encore Artists Management*
3815 W Olive Ave Ste 101
Burbank, CA 91505-4674, USA

Knox-Johnson, Robin (Yachtsman)
26 Sefton St Putney
London SW15, UNITED KINGDOM (UK)

Knoxville, Johnny (Actor)
c/o Sean Robinson *LW1*
7257 Beverly Blvd Ste 200
Los Angeles, CA 90036-2567, USA

Knuble, Mike (Athlete, Hockey Player)
2107 San Lu Rae Dr SE
Grand Rapids, MI 49506-3425, USA

Knudsen, Arthur G (Skier)
5111 Wright Ave # 104
Racine, WI 53406-4543, USA

Knudsen, Erik (Actor)
c/o Staff Member *Burstein Company, The*
15304 W Sunset Blvd Ste 208
Pacific Palisades, CA 90272-3656, USA

Knudsen, Kurt (Athlete, Baseball Player)
5155 Patti Jo Dr
Carmichael, CA 95608-0968, USA

Knudson, Mark (Athlete, Baseball Player)
881 W 100th Ave
Northglenn, CO 80260-6255, USA

Knudson, Thomas J (Journalist)
Editorial Dept 21st & Q Sts
Sacramento, CA 95852, USA

Knudson Jr, Alfred G (Misc)
7701 Burholme Ave
Philadelphia, PA 19111-2437, USA

Knussen, S Oliver (Composer)
12 Penzance Place
London W11 4PA, UNITED KINGDOM (UK)

Knuth, Donald E (Scientist)
Computer Sciences Dept Gates Building
Stanford, CA 94305, USA

Koart, Matt (Athlete, Football Player)
122 Sonora Ave
Danville, CA 94526-3834, USA

Koba, Jeff
8899 Beverly Blvd # 705
Los Angeles, CA 90048-2412

Koback, Nick (Athlete, Baseball Player)
71 Hopmeadow St Apt 9A-1
Weatogue, CT 06089-9635, USA

Kobasew, Chuck (Athlete, Hockey Player)
4112 36th Ave
Osoyoos, BC V0H 1V0, Canada

Kobashigawa, Yeiki (War Hero)
85 Mill St # 120
Waianae, HI 96792, USA

Kobayashi, Makoto (Nobel Prize Laureate)
6 Ichibancho, Chiyoda-ku
Tokyo 102-8471, Japan

Kobel, Kevin (Athlete, Baseball Player)
7650 E Williams Dr Unit 1072
Scottsdale, AZ 85255-4810, USA

Kober, Jeff (Actor)
4544 Ethel Ave
Studio City, CA 91604-1002, USA

Koblik, Steven (Educator)
1151 Oxford Rd
San Marino, CA 91108-1218, USA

Koblitz, Karen (Artist)
2919 Tilden Ave
Los Angeles, CA 90064-4013, USA

Koch, Aaron (Athlete, Football Player)
1 Alltel Stadium Pl
Jacksonville, FL 32202-1917, USA

Koch, Alan (Athlete, Baseball Player)
1714 Pebble Creek Dr
Prattville, AL 36066-7206, USA

Koch, Bill
PO Box 1011
Kula, HI 96790-1011

Koch, Billy (Athlete, Baseball Player)
2577 Hobblebrush Dr
North Port, FL 34289-4305, USA

Koch, Carin (Athlete, Golfer)
2000 Auburn Dr Ste 330
Beachwood, OH 44122-4327, USA

Koch, Charles S (Business Person)
655 15th St NW Ste 825
Washington, DC 20005-5718, USA

Koch, David (Business Person)
459 Columbus Ave # 216
New York, NY 10024-5129, USA

Koch, Desmond (Des) (Athlete, Football Player, Track Athlete)
23296 Gilmore St
Canoga Park, CA 91307-3426, USA

Koch, Ed (Artist)
1211 NW Ogden Ave
Bend, OR 97701-1513, USA

Koch, Edward I (Politician)
1290 Avenue of the Americas
New York, NY 10104-0101, USA

Koch, Gary (Athlete, Golfer)
2934 W Lawn Ave
Tampa, FL 33611-1647, USA

Koch, Gregory M (Greg) (Athlete, Football Player)
5983 E Division Rd
Logansport, IN 46947-7972, USA

Koch, James V (Educator)
Presidential S Ofc
Norfolk, VA 23529-0001, USA

Koch, Marianne
Am Hohenberg 27
Tutzing, GERMANY D-82327

Koch, Pete (Athlete, Football Player)
866 W 16th St
Newport Beach, CA 92663-2802, USA

Koch, Peter (Actor)
c/o Staff Member *Fly Trap, The*
900 E 1st St
Los Angeles, CA 90012-4032, USA

Koch, Stacey (Stylist)
52 Bow St
Concord, MA 01742-1701, USA

Koch, William (Bill) (Skier)
PO Box 115
Ashland, OR 97520-0004, USA

Koch, William I (Bill) (Business Person, Yachtsman)
1601 Forum Pl
West Palm Beach, FL 33401-8101, USA

Koch Jr, Howard (Producer)
8530 Wilshire Blvd Ste 450
Beverly Hills, CA 90211-3115, USA

Kochan, Dieter (Athlete, Hockey Player)
2005 Spruce Ln
Houghton, MI 49931-2721, USA

Kocharian, Robert (President, Prime Minister)
Marshal Bagramian Prosp # 19
Memphis, TN 37501-0001, ARMENIA

Kocherga, Anatoli I (Opera Singer)
Gogolevskaya 37/2/47
Kiev 254053, RUSSIA

Kochi, Jay K (Misc)
4372 Faculty Ln
Houston, TX 77004-6601, USA

Kochman, Roger (Athlete, Football Player)
521 Beverly Blvd
Upper Darby, PA 19082-3615, USA

Kocourek, Dave (Athlete, Football Player)
1170 Cara Ct
Marco Island, FL 34145-4518, USA

Kocsis, Zoltan (Composer, Musician)
Narcisa Ulca 29
Budapest 1126, HUNGARY

Kocur, Joe (Athlete, Hockey Player)
c/o Staff Member *Detroit Red Wings*
600 Civic Center Dr
Detroit, MI 48226-4419, USA

Kodba, Joe (Athlete, Football Player)
4287 Latifee Ct
Swartz Creek, MI 48473-1710, USA

Kodes, Jan (Tennis Player)
Na Berance 18
Prague 6/Dejvioe 160 00, CZECH REPUBLIC

Kodjoe, Boris (Actor, Model)
c/o Maani Golesorkhi *Bluestone Entertainment*
5639 Vista Del Monte Ave
Van Nuys, CA 91411-3356, USA

Koecher, Dick (Athlete, Baseball Player)
3310 Grand Cypress Dr Apt 102
Naples, FL 34119-7979, USA

Koechner, David (Actor, Writer)
c/o John Elliott *Mosaic Media Group*
9200 W Sunset Blvd Ste 10
Los Angeles, CA 90069-3608, USA

Koegel, Pete (Athlete, Baseball Player)
301 the Birches
Saugerties, NY 12477-5249, USA

Koegel, Warren (Athlete, Football Player)
1273 N Fraser St
Georgetown, SC 29440-2853, USA

Koehler, Horst (Financier, President)
Spreeweg 1
Berlin 10557, Germany

Koelle, George B (Misc)
3300 Darby Rd Apt 3310
Haverford, PA 19041-7701, USA

Koelling, Brian (Athlete, Baseball Player)
20230 Augusta Dr
Lawrenceburg, IN 47025-7370, USA

Koen, Karleen (Writer)
1745 Broadway # B1
New York, NY 10019-4368, USA

Koenekamp, Fred (Cinematographer)
9222 Corbin Ave # 402
Northridge, CA 91324-2409, USA

Koenig, Brad (Model)
c/o Staff Member *Ford Models (NY)*
238 E 4th St
New York, NY 10009-7425

Koenig, Walter (Actor)
PO Box 4395
North Hollywood, CA 91617-0395, USA

Koepfer, Karl (Athlete, Football Player)
2017 Waters Edge Dr
Westlake, OH 44145-6603, USA

Koepke, Andreas
441 Av Du Prado B P 124
Marseilles Cedex 08, FRANCE F-13267

Koepp, David (Director, Writer)
c/o Richard Lovett *Creative Artists Agency (CAA-LA)*
2000 Avenue of the Stars Ste 100
Los Angeles, CA 90067-4705, USA

Koester, Helmut H K E (Misc)
12 Flintlock Rd
Lexington, MA 02420-1704, USA

Koetter, Dirk (Coach, Football Coach)
Athletes
Tempe, AZ 85287-0001, USA

Koffler, Pamela (Producer)
c/o Staff Member *Killer Films (US)*
526 W 26th St Rm 715
New York, NY 10001-5524, USA

Kofler, Matt (Athlete, Football Player)
12520 Heatherton Ct Unit 2
San Diego, CA 92128-5123, USA

Kofoed, Bart (Athlete, Basketball Player)
10161 Foxhall Dr
Charlotte, NC 28210-7846, USA

Kogan, Pavel L (Conductor, Musician)
Bryusov Per 8/10
Moscow 103009, RUSSIA

Kogan, Theo (Actor, Musician)
300 Park Ave S # 200
New York, NY 10010-5313, USA

Kogen, Jay (Producer)
c/o Staff Member *WmE2 (Endeavor-LA)*
9601 Wilshire Blvd Fl 3
Beverly Hills, CA 90210-5219, USA

Koger, Gene (Athlete, Baseball Player)
285 Koger Rd
Reidsville, NC 27320-9555, USA

Kohan, David (Producer)
c/o Staff Member *KoMut Entertainment*
300 Television Plz
Burbank, CA 91505, USA

Kohde-Kilsch, Claudia (Tennis Player)
Elsa-Brandstrom-Str 22
Saarbrucken 66119, GERMANY

Kohl, Ernest (Musician)
c/o Staff Member *Diva Central Inc*
7510 W Sunset Blvd Ste 1445
Los Angeles, CA 90046-3408, USA

Kohl, Helmut (Politician)
85 Maurestr
New York, NY 10117-0001, GERMANY

Kohlbrand, Joe (Athlete, Football Player)
3709 Indian River Dr
Cocoa, FL 32926-8705, USA

Kohler, Jurgen (Soccer Player)
Postfach 100509
Dortmund 44005, GERMANY

Kohlhaas, Jeannette (Athlete, Golfer)
6287 Battlegate Rd
Jacksonville, FL 32258-9424, USA

Kohli, Armaan (Actor, Bollywood)
44 Union Park Chembur
Mumbai, MS 400071, INDIA

Kohli, Raj Kumar (Bollywood, Director, Filmmaker, Producer)
Behind Lido Cinema Juhu Road
Bombay, MS 400 049, INDIA

Kohlmeier, Ryan (Athlete, Baseball Player)
301 Vine St
Cottonwood Falls, KS 66845-9812, USA

Kohlsaat, Peter (Cartoonist)
420 N 5th St Ste 707
Minneapolis, MN 55401-1372, USA

Kohn, A Eugene (Architect)
570 Park Ave Apt 11C
New York, NY 10065-7343, USA

Kohn, Alfie (Writer)
c/o Staff Member *Houghton Mifflin Company (Trade Division)*
222 Berkeley St Adult Editorial Floor 8
Boston, MA 02116-3764, USA

Kohn, Joseph J (Mathematician)
32 Sturges Way
Princeton, NJ 08540-5335, USA

Kohn, Walter (Nobel Prize Laureate)
236 La Vista Grande
Santa Barbara, CA 93103-2819, USA

Kohn-Stevenson, Perri (Stylist)
5651 Willis Ave
Van Nuys, CA 91411-3326, USA

Kohoutek, Lubos (Astronomer)
Corthumstr 5
Hamburg 21029, GERMANY

Kohrs, Bob (Athlete, Football Player)
2910 E Nance St
Mesa, AZ 85213-1647, USA

Koib, Thomas Claudia A (Coach, Swimmer)
Athletic Dept
Stanford, CA 94305, USA

Koirala, manicha (Actor, Bollywood)
302 Beachwood Towers Yari Road Versova
Andheri (W), Mumbai 400061, India

Koiv, Kerli (Musician)
c/o Staff Member *Island Def Jam Music Group*
825 8th Ave Fl 28
New York, NY 10019-7416

Koivu, Saku (Athlete, Hockey Player)
2200-201 Portage Ave
Winnipeg, MB R3B 3L3, Canada

Koizumi, Junichiro (Prime Minister)
1-6-1 Negatoicho
Chiyodaku, Tokyo 100, JAPAN

Kojac, George (Swimmer)
33 Arboles Del Norte
Fort Pierce, FL 34951-2877, USA

Kojis, Don (Athlete, Basketball Player)
8186 Commercial St
La Mesa, CA 91942-2926, USA

Kok Oudegeest, Mary (Swimmer)
Izarra
Alava, SPAIN

Kokkonen, Elissa Lee (Musician)
165 W 57th St
New York, NY 10019-2201, USA

Kokonin, Vladimir (Opera Singer)
Teatralnaya Pl 1
Moscow 103009, RUSSIA

Kokosalaki, Sophia (Designer, Fashion Designer)
c/o Staff Member *Sophia Kokosalaki*
3/138 Long Acre Convent Garden
London, England, United Kingdom

Kokotakis, Nick
9229 W Sunset Blvd Ste 315
Los Angeles, CA 90069-3403

Kola, Joey (Comedian)
c/o Staff Member *WmE2 (WMA-LA)*
1 William Morris Pl
Beverly Hills, CA 90212-4261, USA

Kolakowski, Leszek (Misc)
77 Hamilton Road
Oxford OX2 7QA, UNITED KINGDOM (UK)

Kolanko, Mary Lou (Baseball Player)
6811 N Himes Ave
Tampa, FL 33614-4031, USA

Kolanos, Krys (Athlete, Hockey Player)
43 Lake Sundance Pl SE
Calgary, AB T2J 2S9, Canada

Kolb, Brandon (Athlete, Baseball Player)
2043 Pin Oak Pl
Danville, CA 94506-2119, USA

Kolb, Danny (Athlete, Baseball Player)
PO Box 700
Walnut, IL 61376-0700, USA

Kolb, Gary (Athlete, Baseball Player)
5143 Hopewell Dr
Charleston, WV 25313-1784, USA

Kolb, Jon (Athlete, Football Player)
1775 McDowell St
Sharon, PA 16146-3857, USA

Kolber, Suzy (Sportscaster)
Sports Dept ESPN Plaza 935 Middle St
Bristol, CT 6010, USA

Kolbert, Kathryn (Lawyer)
120 Wall St
New York, NY 10005-3904, USA

Kolden, Scott
293 N State College Blvd Apt 1025
Orange, CA 92868-5703

Kole, Karen (Stylist)
c/o Staff Member *The Docherty Agency - OH*
2044 Euclid Ave
Cleveland, OH 44115-2282, USA

Kole, Warren (Actor)
c/o Staff Member *D/F Management*
8609 Washington Blvd # 8607
Culver City, CA 90232-7441, USA

Kolehmainen, Mikko (Athlete)
Poppelitie 18
Mikkeli 50130, FINLAND

Kolen, Mike (Athlete, Football Player)
1613 Manchester Ln
Vestavia, AL 35243-4862, USA

Kolesar, Robert (Athlete, Football Player)
5003 Lincoln Ave
Cleveland, OH 44134-1866, USA

Kolinsky, Sue (Producer)
c/o Staff Member *Innovative Artists (LA)*
1505 10th St
Santa Monica, CA 90401-2805, USA

Kollar, Bill (Athlete, Football Player)
1 Rams Way
Earth City, MO 63045-1523, USA

Kollas, Konstantinos V (Prime Minister)
124 Vassil Sophias St Ampelokipi
Athens, GREECE

Kollek, Mayor Teddy
22 Jaffa Rd.
Jerusalem, ISRAEL

Koller, Dagmar
Naglergasse 2
Vienna, AUSTRIA A-1010

Koller, William C (Misc)
Medical School Neurology
Kansas City, KS 66160-0001, USA

Kollner, Eberhard (Cosmonaut)
An der Trainierbahn 7
Neuenhagen 115366, GERMANY

Kollo, Rene (Opera Singer)
Maximillianstr 22
Munich 80539, GERMANY

Kolm, Henry V (Engineer)
Weir Meadow Road
Wayland, MA 1778, USA

Kolnik, Juraj (Athlete, Hockey Player)
HC Geneve-Servette Chemin de la Graviere 4
Les Acasias CH-1227, Switzerland

Kolodner, Richard D (Scientist)
44 Binney St
Boston, MA 02115-6013, USA

Kolodziewjski, Chris (Athlete, Football Player)
1123 Sandalwood Dr
Lawrenceville, GA 30043-4621, USA

Kolpakova, Irina A (Ballerina)
890 Broadway
New York, NY 10003-1211, USA

Kolstad, Dean (Athlete, Hockey Player)
15492 Brooklodge Rd
Hickory Corners, MI 49060-9740, USA

Kolstad, Hal (Athlete, Baseball Player)
15149 Bel Escou Dr
San Jose, CA 95124-5032, USA

Kolsti, Paul (Cartoonist)
Editorial Dept Communications Center
Dallas, TX 75265, USA

Kolta, Lajos (Cinematographer, Director)
c/o Staff Member *Gersh (LA)*
9465 Wilshire Blvd Ste 600
Beverly Hills, CA 90212-2612, USA

Kolvenbach, Peter-Hans (Religious Leader)
Borgo Santo Spirito 5 CP 6139
Rome 195, ITALY

Kolzig, Olaf (Athlete, Hockey Player)
9900 Meriden Rd
Potomac, MD 20854-4312, USA

Komadoski, Neil (Athlete, Hockey Player)
240 Big Sky Dr
Saint Charles, MO 63304-7170, USA

Komal (Royalty)
Narayanhiti Durbag Marg
Kathmandu, NEPAL

Koman, Bill (Athlete, Football Player)
5 Upper Ladue Rd
Saint Louis, MO 63124-1677, USA

Koman, Michael (Writer)
c/o Staff Member *International Creative Management (ICM-LA)*
10250 Constellation Blvd Fl 7
Los Angeles, CA 90067-6207, USA

Komarkova, Vera (Misc)
INSTAAR
Boulder, CO 80302, USA

Komarniski, Zenith (Athlete, Hockey Player)
3773 18 St NW
Edmonton, AB T6T 1S5, Canada

Komenich, Kim (Journalist)
111 Cornelia Ave
Mill Valley, CA 94941-4812, USA

Komenich, Nadia (Gymnast)
PO Box 720217
Norman, OK 73070-4166, USA

Kometani, Pam (Athlete, Golfer)
4342 Kilauea Ave
Honolulu, HI 96816-5113, USA

Komine, Shane (Athlete, Baseball Player)
641 8th Ave
Honolulu, HI 96816-2109, USA

Kominsky, Cheryl (Bowler)
7200 Harrison Ave # 7171
Rockford, IL 61112-1017, USA

Komisarek, Mike (Athlete, Hockey Player)
37 Wagon Wheel Ln
Dix Hills, NY 11746-5025, USA

Komleva, Gabriela T (Ballerina)
Fontanka River 116 #34
Saint Petersburg 198005, RUSSIA

Komlos, Peter (Musician)
Torokvesz Ulca 94
Budapest 1025, HUNGARY

Komminsk, Brad (Athlete, Baseball Player)
688 Fallside Ln
Westerville, OH 43081-5003, USA

Kompara, John (Athlete, Football Player)
13030 Coldwater Loop
Clermont, FL 34711-8014, USA

Konare, Alpha Oumar (President)
BP
Bamako, MALI

Koncak, Jon (Athlete, Basketball Player)
PO Box 10040
Jackson, WY 83002-0040, USA

Koncar, Mark (Athlete, Football Player)
447 N Alpine Blvd
Alpine, UT 84004-1264, USA

Konchalovsky, Andrei (Director, Producer, Writer)

Kondakova, Elena V (Cosmonaut)
Ulica Lenina 4A
Kallningrad 141070, USA

Kondia, Tom (Athlete, Basketball Player)
3517 Cleveland Ave
Brookfield, IL 60513-1103, USA

Kondratiyeva, Maria V (Ballerina)
Teatralnaya Pt1
Moscow 103009, RUSSIA

Kondria, John (Athlete, Football Player)
599 Collier Rd
Uniontown, PA 15401-6877, USA

Konerko, Paul (Athlete, Baseball Player)
8053 E Leaning Rock Rd
Scottsdale, AZ 85266-1645, USA

Konian, Desiree (Stylist)
c/o Staff Member *Artists by Timothy Priano (CA)*
8447 Wilshire Blvd Ste 301
Beverly Hills, CA 90211-3206, USA

Konieczny, Doug (Athlete, Baseball Player)
9503 Dundalk St
Spring, TX 77379-4314, USA

Konik, George (Athlete, Hockey Player)
1027 Savannah Rd
Saint Paul, MN 55123-1543, USA

Koniszewski, John (Athlete, Football Player)
207 Eleanor St
Peckville, PA 18452-1205, USA

Konitz, Lee (Musician)
1282 RR 376
Wappingers Falls, NY 12590, USA

Konner, Lawrence (Larry) (Writer)
c/o Tom Strickler *WmE2 (Endeavor-LA)*
9601 Wilshire Blvd Fl 3
Beverly Hills, CA 90210-5219, USA

Kononenko, Oleg D (Cosmonaut)
Moskovskoi Oblasti
Syvisdny Goroduk 141160, RUSSIA

Konopasek, Ed (Athlete, Football Player)
2336 Meadowledge Ct
De Pere, WI 54115-8690, USA

Konowalchuk, Steve (Athlete, Hockey Player)
27493 254th Pl SE
Maple Valley, WA 98038-2042, USA

Konrad, Dorothy
10650 Missouri Ave Apt 2
Los Angeles, CA 90025-4815

Konrad, John H (Astronaut)
PO Box 92919
Los Angeles, CA 90009-2919, USA

Konrad, Rob (Athlete, Football Player)
6600 N Andrews Ave Ste 130
Fort Lauderdale, FL 33309-2188, USA

Konroyd, Steve (Athlete, Hockey Player)
317 S Park Ave
Hinsdale, IL 60521-4638, USA

Konsalik, Heinz
Aegidienberg
Bad Honnef, GERMANY D-53604

Konstantinidis, Aris (Architect)
4 Vasilissis Sofias Blvd
Athens 106 74, GREECE

Konstantinov, Vladimir (Athlete, Hockey Player)
6782 Enclave
West Bloomfield, MI 48322-1399, USA

Kontos, Chris (Athlete, Hockey Player)
40 Beck Blvd
Penetanguishene, ON L9M 1E1, Canada

Konuszewski, Dennis (Athlete, Baseball Player)
3054 Yorkshire Dr
Bay City, MI 48706-9244, USA

Konyukhov, Fedor F (Misc)
Studeniy Proyezd 7
Moscow 129282, RUSSIA

Konz, Kenny (Athlete, Football Player)
12787 Greenbower St NE
Alliance, OH 44601-8862, USA

Kooks, The (Music Group)
c/o Staff Member *Paradigm (Monterey)*
404 W Franklin St
Monterey, CA 93940-2303, USA

Kool & The Gang (Music Group)
c/o Staff Member *J Bird Entertainment Agency*
4905 S Atlantic Ave
Ponce Inlet, FL 32127-7311, USA

Koolhaas, Rem (Architect)
Heer Bokelweg 149
Rotterdam 3032, NETHERLANDS

Koolhoven, Martin (Director)
c/o Daniel Koefoed *Montecatini Management*
Teerketelsteeg 1
Amsterdam 1012 TB, The Netherlands

Koonce, Graham (Athlete, Baseball Player)
2474 Pimlico Pl
Alpine, CA 91901-3952, USA

Koons, Jeff (Artist)
600 Broadway
New York, NY 10012-3206, USA

Koontz, Dean (Writer)
PO Box 9529
Newport Beach, CA 92658-9529, USA

Koop, C Everett (Doctor)
3 Ivy Pointe Way
Hanover, NH 03755-1407, USA

Kooper, Al (Musician)
550 Madison Ave # 1700
New York, NY 10022-3211, USA

Koopman, A Ton G M (Conductor)
Meerweg 23
BC Bussu 1405, NETHERLANDS

Koopmans-Kint, Cor (Swimmer)
Pacific Sands C'Van Park
Nambucca Heads, NSW 2448, AUSTRALIA

Kooser, Ted (Writer)
1820 Branched Oak Rd
Garland, NE 68360-9303, USA

Koosman, Jerry (Athlete, Baseball Player)
2483 State Road 35
Osceola, WI 54020-4216, USA

Kopacz, George (Athlete, Baseball Player)
14150 Somerset Ct
Orland Park, IL 60467-1142, USA

Kopay, Dave (Athlete, Football Player)
100 W Highland Dr Apt 102
Seattle, WA 98119-3503, USA

Kopell, Bernie (Actor)
19413 Olivos Dr
Tarzana, CA 91356-4403, USA

Kopeloff, Eric (Director)
c/o Staff Member *WmE2 (WMA-LA)*
1 William Morris Pl
Beverly Hills, CA 90212-4261, USA

Kopelson, Arnold (Producer)
901 N Roxbury Dr
Beverly Hills, CA 90210-3019, USA

Koper, Herbert (Athlete, Basketball Player)
11707 Rushmore
Oklahoma City, OK 73162-1636, USA

Kopervas, Gary (Cartoonist)
c/o Staff Member *King Features Syndication*
300 W 57th St Fl 15
New York, NY 10019-5238, USA

Kopicki, Joe (Athlete, Basketball Player)
47608 Cheryl Ct
Shelby Township, MI 48315-4708, USA

Kopins, Karen (Actor)
145 S Fairfax Ave Ste 310
Los Angeles, CA 90036-2176, USA

Kopit, Arthur (Writer)
207 W 106th St Apt 7D
New York, NY 10025-3696, USA

Kopitar, Anze (Athlete, Hockey Player)
c/o Staff Member *Los Angeles Kings*
1111 S Figueroa St Ste 3100
Los Angeles, CA 90015-1333, USA

Koplitz, Howie (Athlete, Baseball Player)
623 Boyd St
Oshkosh, WI 54901-4634, USA

Koplitz, Lynne (Actor)
c/o Staff Member *Paradigm (Monterey)*
404 W Franklin St
Monterey, CA 93940-2303, USA

Koplove, Mike (Athlete, Baseball Player)
3235 Chaucer St
Philadelphia, PA 19145-5841, USA

Kopp, Jeff (Athlete, Football Player)
9409 Hannahs Mill Dr Apt 403
Owings Mills, MD 21117-6855, USA

Kopp, Wendy (Misc)
315 W 36th St # 6
New York, NY 10018-6404, USA

Koppel, Ted (Correspondent)
10701 Ardnave Pl
Potomac, MD 20854-1261, USA

Koppelman, Chaim (Artist)
141 Wooster St Apt 6C
New York, NY 10012-3182, USA

Koppelman, Charles (Business Person)
c/o Staff Member *Martha Stewart Living Omnimedia Inc*
11 W 42nd St Fl 25
New York, NY 10036-8002, USA

Kopper, Hilmar (Financier)
Taunusanlage 12
Frankfurt/Main 60325, GERMANY

Koppes, Peter (Musician)
101 Chamberlayne Road
London NW10 3ND, UNITED KINGDOM (UK)

Koppikar, Isha (Actor)
c/o Staff Member *Canyon Entertainment*
PO Box 256
Palm Springs, CA 92263-0256, USA

Kopple, Barbara J (Director)
155 Avenue of the Americas
New York, NY 10013-1507, USA

Kopra, Timothy L (Astronaut)
4912 Cross Creek Ln
League City, TX 77573-6267, USA

Koprowski, Hilary (Biologist)
334 Fairhill Rd
Wynnewood, PA 19096-1804, USA

Koptchak, Sergei (Opera Singer)
Harkness Plaza 61 W 62nd St #6F
New York, NY 10023, USA

Korab, Jerry (Athlete, Hockey Player)
3000 Washington Blvd # 4
Bellwood, IL 60104-1946, USA

Koralek, Paul G (Architect)
7 Chalcot Road #1
London NW1 8LH, UNITED KINGDOM (UK)

Korcheck, Steve (Athlete, Baseball Player)
6424 98th St E
Bradenton, FL 34202-9769, USA

Kord, Kazimierz (Conductor)
Ul Jasna 5
Warsaw 00-950, POLAND

Korda, Maria
304 N Screenland Dr
Burbank, CA 91505-3805

Korda, Michael V (Writer)
1230 Avenue of the Americas
New York, NY 10020-1513, USA

Korda, Petr (Tennis Player)
4909 61st Avenue Dr W
Bradenton, FL 34210-4041, USA

Korec Jan, Chryzostom Cardinal (Religious Leader)
Biskupstvo Nitra PP 46A
Nitra 95050, SLOVAKIA

Koreeda, Hirokazu (Director)
3-2 5F Maruyamacho
Shibuya, Tokyo 150-0044, JAPAN

Koren, Edward B (Cartoonist)
4 Times Sq
New York, NY 10036-6515, USA

Koren, Steve (Producer, Writer)
c/o Staff Member *Creative Artists Agency (CAA-LA)*
2000 Avenue of the Stars Ste 100
Los Angeles, CA 90067-4705, USA

Korf, Mia (Actor)
10100 Santa Monica Blvd Ste 2500
Los Angeles, CA 90067-4116, USA

Korince, George (Athlete, Baseball Player)
710-610 Lake St
St Catharines, ON L2N 5T1, Canada

Korjus, Tapio (Athlete, Track Athlete)
Lapua, FINLAND

Korman, Maxime Carlot (Prime Minister)
PO Box 110
Port Vila, VANUATU

Kormann, Peter (Gymnast)
1 Olympic Plz
Colorado Springs, CO 80909-5780, USA

Korn (Music Group)
c/o Mark Philips *Prospect Park*
2049 Century Park E Ste 2550
Century City, CA 90067-3139, USA

Korn, Jim (Athlete, Hockey Player)
19670 Sweetwater Curv
Excelsior, MN 55331-8113, USA

Kornberg, Arthur (Nobel Prize Laureate)
365 Golden Oak Dr
Portola Valley, CA 94028-7732, USA

Kornberg, Hannah (Actor)
c/o Holly Williams *Williams Unlimited*
5010 Buffalo Ave
Sherman Oaks, CA 91423-1414

Kornberg, Roger D. (Nobel Prize Laureate)
299 Campus Dr Dept of
Stanford, CA 94305-5101, USA

Kornet, Frank (Athlete, Basketball Player)
9580 Stanton Rd
Lantana, TX 76226-7304, USA

Korney, Mike (Athlete, Hockey Player)
2565 Departure Bay Rd
Nanaimo, BC V9S 3W2, Canada

Kornheiser, Tony (Sportscaster, Writer)
1150 15th St NW
Washington, DC 20071-0001, USA

Koroll, Cliff (Athlete, Hockey Player)
23W569 Glendale Ter
Roselle, IL 60172-3541, USA

Koromzay, Alix (Actor)
334 Vernon Ave
Venice, CA 90291-2637, USA

Koronka, John (Athlete, Baseball Player)
17320 Palm Dr
Montverde, FL 34756-3254, USA

Korpan, Richard (Business Person)
100 Central Ave
Saint Petersburg, FL 33701-3324, USA

Kors, Michael (Designer, Fashion Designer)
11 W 42nd St
New York, NY 10036-8002, USA

Kors, R J (Athlete, Football Player)
956 Gardenia Way
Corona Del Mar, CA 92625-1546, USA

Korsantiya, Alexander (Musician)
165 W 57th St
New York, NY 10019-2201, USA

Kortas, Ken (Athlete, Football Player)
466 Brooks Ln
Simpsonville, KY 40067-7419, USA

Korte, Steven J (Athlete, Football Player)
5640 Oslo Ln
Park City, UT 84098-7708, USA

Korvald, Lars (Prime Minister)
Vinkelgaten 6
Mjondalen 3050, NORWAY

Korver, Kelvin (Athlete, Football Player)
16800 Pella Rd
Adams, NE 68301-7755, USA

Korver, Kyle (Athlete, Basketball Player)
c/o Jeff Schwartz *Excel Sports Management*
9665 Wilshire Blvd Ste 500
Beverly Hills, CA 90212-2312, USA

Kosar Jr, Bernie J (Athlete, Football Player)
8744 Estada Cir
Hollywood, FL 33024-8741, USA

Kosberg, Robert (Producer, Writer)
1438 N Gower St Ste 10
Hollywood, CA 90028-8306, USA

Kosc, Greg (Baseball Player)
3465 Hunting Run Rd
Medina, OH 44256-8200, USA

Kosc, Greg (Athlete, Baseball Player)
3465 Hunting Run Rd
Medina, OH 44256-8200, USA

Kosco, Andy (Athlete, Baseball Player)
10324 Springfield Rd
Youngstown, OH 44514-3158, USA

Kosens, Terry (Athlete, Football Player)
69 Lumur Dr
Sayville, NY 11782-1605, USA

Koshalek, Richard (Director)
250 S Grand Ave
Los Angeles, CA 90012-3007, USA

Koshansky, Joe (Athlete, Baseball Player)
13314 Point Pleasant Dr
Fairfax, VA 22033-3507, USA

Koshiba, Masatoshi (Nobel Prize Laureate)
7-3-1 Hongo
Nunkyoku, Tokyo 113-8654, JAPAN

Koshiro IV, Matsumoto (Actor, Dancer)
12-15-4 Ginza
Chuoku, Tokyo 104, JAPAN

Koshland Jr, Daniel E (Misc)
76 Plaza Dr
Berkeley, CA 94705-2432, USA

Kosins, Gary (Athlete, Football Player)
PO Box 340072
Dayton, OH 45434-0072, USA

Koski, Bill (Athlete, Baseball Player)
1120 Valencia Ct
Modesto, CA 95350-4665, USA

Koski, Tony (Athlete, Basketball Player)
143 King James Dr
South Dennis, MA 2260, USA

Koskie, Corey (Athlete, Baseball Player)
161 Primrose Ln
Hamel, MN 55340-3603, USA

Koskoff, Sarah (Actor)
c/o Cliff Roberts *WmE2 (Endeavor-LA)*
9601 Wilshire Blvd Fl 3
Beverly Hills, CA 90210-5219, USA

Koslo, Paul (Actor)
c/o Noreen Savides *323 Talent Management*
PO Box 3234
Quartz Hill, CA 93586-0234, USA

Koslofski, Kevin (Athlete, Baseball Player)
1910 Shore Oak Dr
Decatur, IL 62521-5563, USA

Koslow, Lauren (Actor)
c/o John Crosby *Crosby/Spilo Management*
1310 N Spaulding Ave
Los Angeles, CA 90046-4010, USA

Kosmalski, Len (Athlete, Basketball Player)
404 Washington Ave PH 8
Miami Beach, FL 33139-6606, USA

Kosner, Edward A (Editor)
1790 Broadway Ste 1300
New York, NY 10019-1412, USA

Koss, Johann Olav (Speed Skater)
Dagaliveien 21
Oslo 387, NORWAY

Koss, John C (Inventor)
4129 N Port Washington Rd
Milwaukee, WI 53212-1029, USA

Koss, Stein (Athlete, Football Player)
5219 N Casa Blanca Dr Apt 31
Paradise Valley, AZ 85253-6201, USA

Kostadinova, Stefka (Athlete, Track Athlete)
Rue Anghel Kantchev 4
Sofia 1000, BULGARIA

Kostelic, Janica (Skier)
Trg Sportova 11
Zagreb 1000, CROATIA

Koster, Steven J (Cinematographer)
26881 Goya Cir
Mission Viejo, CA 92691-6108, USA

Kostiuk, Mike (Athlete, Football Player)
24663 Beierman Ave
Warren, MI 48091-1716, USA

Kostner, Isolde (Skier)
General Delivery
Hortisei BZ, ITALY

Kostro, Frank (Athlete, Baseball Player)
3161 S Jasmine Way
Denver, CO 80222-7627, USA

Kosugi, Kane (Actor)
c/o Lou Pitt *Pitt Group, The*
9465 Wilshire Blvd Ste 420
Beverly Hills, CA 90212-2603, USA

Kosuth, Joseph (Artist)
591 Broadway
New York, NY 10012-3211, USA

Kotarski, Mike (Athlete, Baseball Player)
11466 Bronzedale Dr
Oakton, VA 22124-2123, USA

Kotb, Hoda (Anchor, Television Host)
c/o Staff Member *Today Show, The*
30 Rockefeller Plz
New York, NY 10112-0015, USA

Kotcheff, W Theodore (Ted) (Director)
13451 Firth Dr
Beverly Hills, CA 90210-1118, USA

Kotchman, Casey (Athlete, Baseball Player)
8442 125th Ct
Seminole, FL 33776-3200, USA

Koteas, Elias (Actor)
c/o Staff Member *WmE2 (Endeavor-LA)*
9601 Wilshire Blvd Fl 3
Beverly Hills, CA 90210-5219, USA

Koterba, Jeff (Cartoonist)
Editorial Dept 14th & Dodge St Wichita
Omaha, NE 68102, USA

Kotero, Apollonia (Actor, Model)
c/o Staff Member *Mary Grady Agency (MGA)*
4400 Coldwater Canyon Ave Ste 135
Studio City, CA 91604-5038, USA

Kotil, Ariene (Baseball Player)
13045 S 70th Ct
Palos Heights, IL 60463-2107, USA

Kotite, Richard E (Rich) (Athlete, Coach, Football Coach, Football Player)
241 Fanning St
Staten Island, NY 10314-5309, USA

Kotlarek, Gene (Skier)
4910 Walking Horse Pt
Colorado Springs, CO 80923-1110, USA

Kotlarek, George (Skier)
330 N Arlington Ave Apt 512
Duluth, MN 55811-5127, USA

Kotlayakov, Vladimir M (Geophysicist, Physicist)
Staromonetny per 29
Moscow 109017, RUSSIA

Kotsay, Mark (Athlete, Baseball Player)
2947 Flint Ridge Ct
Reno, NV 89511-5327, USA

Kotsonis, Ieronymous (Religious Leader)
Hatzichristou 8
Athens 402, Greece 53212, USA

Kotsopoulos, Chris (Athlete, Hockey Player)
1713 Midnight Ln
Stroudsburg, PA 18360-7771, USA

Kottke, Leo (Musician, Songwriter)
c/o Staff Member *Paradigm (Monterey)*
404 W Franklin St
Monterey, CA 93940-2303, USA

Kotto, Yaphet (Actor, Director, Producer, Writer)
c/o Staff Member *Diverse Talent Group*
9911 W Pico Blvd Ste 340W
Los Angeles, CA 90035-2712, USA

Kotto, Yaphet F (Actor)
c/o Nicole Green *Rival Agency, The*
9157 W Sunset Blvd Ste 212
W Hollywood, CA 90069-3167, USA

Kotulak, Ronald (Editor)
435 N Michigan Ave
Chicago, IL 60611-4066, USA

Kotzky, Alex S (Cartoonist)
20317 56th Ave
Oakland Gardens, NY 11364-1641, USA

Kouchner, Bernard (Doctor)
8 Ave de Segur
Paris 75350, USA

Koudelka, Josef (Photographer)
Moreland Bldgs 23 Old St
London EC1V 9HL, UNITED KINGDOM (UK)

Koufax, Sandy (Athlete, Baseball Player)
c/o Harlan Werner *Sports Placement Service*
330 W 11th St Apt 105
Los Angeles, CA 90015-2230, USA

Kounen, Jan (Actor, Director, Producer, Writer)
c/o Robert Newman *WmE2 (Endeavor-LA)*
9601 Wilshire Blvd Fl 3
Beverly Hills, CA 90210-5219, USA

Kournikova, Anna (Athlete, Tennis Player)
c/o Staff Member *Octagon (VA)*
7100 Forest Ave Ste 201
Richmond, VA 23226-3742, USA

Kouzmanoff, Kevin (Athlete, Baseball Player)
28606 Evergreen Manor Dr
Evergreen, CO 80439-8387, USA

Kovacevich, Richard M (Financier)
420 Montgomery St
San Francisco, CA 94104-1207, USA

Kovacevich, Stephen (Conductor, Musician)
4 Addison Bridge Place
London W14 8XP, UNITED KINGDOM (UK)

Kovach, Bill (Editor)
Nieman Fellows Program
Cambridge, MA 2138, USA

Kovacic, Ernst (Musician)
14 Kensington Court
London W8 5DN, UNITED KINGDOM (UK)

Kovacic-Ciro, Zdravko (Misc)
JP Kamova 57
Rijeka 51000, SERBIA & MONTENEGRO

Kovack, Nancy (Actor)
27 Oakmont Dr
Los Angeles, CA 90049-1901, USA

Kovacs, Andras (Director)
Magyar Jakobinusok Ter 2/3
Budapest 1122, HUNGARY

Kovacs, Denes (Musician)
Iranyi Utca 12
Budapest V, HUNGARY

Kovacs, Mijou (Actor)
c/o Staff Member *JFPM*
11 rue Chanez Paris Cedex 16
Paris 75781, FRANCE

Kovai, Anuradha (Actor)
2 23rd Street Amirtha Apartments
Nanganallur
Chennai, TN 600 061, INDIA

Kovai, Sarala (Actor, Bollywood)
80 Nevkatesh Nagar I Street Dhasaratha Puram
Chennai, TN 600093, INDIA

Kovalchick-Roark, Dorothy (Golfer)
112 Maridale Dr
West Monroe, LA 71291-2350, USA

Kovalchuk, Ilja (Athlete, Hockey Player)
2900 Pharr Court South NW Apt 2419
Atlanta, GA 30305-4971, USA

Kovalenko, Alexei (Athlete, Hockey Player)
1 Trimont Ln Apt 2000A
Pittsburgh, PA 15211-1279, USA

Kovalenok, Vladimir S (Cosmonaut, General)
3 Ap 22 Hovanskaya St
Moscow 129515, RUSSIA

Kovalev, Alexei (Athlete, Hockey Player)
36 Reichert Cir
Westport, CT 06880-2643, USA

Kovalevsky, Jean (Astronomer)
Villa La Padovane 8 Rue Saint Michael
Saint-Antoine, Grasse 6130, FRANCE

Kovatch, John P (Athlete, Football Player)
619 Willowglen Rd
Santa Barbara, CA 93105-2437, USA

Kove, Martin (Actor)
c/o Michael Kaliski *Omniquest Entertainment (LA)*
1416 N La Brea Ave
Hollywood, CA 90028-7506, USA

Kovic, Ronald L (War Hero)
507 N Lucia Ave
Redondo Beach, CA 90277-3009, USA

Kowal, Charles T (Astronomer)
Homewood Campus
Baltimore, MD 21218, USA

Kowalczyk, Ed (Musician)
350 W End Ave Apt 1
New York, NY 10024-6818, USA

Kowalczyk, Jozef (Religious Leader)
Al Ch Szucha 12 #163
Warsaw 00-582, POLAND

Kowalczyk, Paula (Stylist)
37 W 85th St Apt 1C
New York, NY 10024-4128, USA

Kowalczyk, Walt (Athlete, Football Player)
144 W Maryknoll Rd
Rochester Hills, MI 48309-1938, USA

Kowalkowski, Robert (Athlete, Football Player)
2410 Correll Dr
Lake Orion, MI 48360-2258, USA

Kowalkowski, Scott (Athlete, Football Player)
3995 Kelsey Rd
Lake Orion, MI 48360-2516, USA

Kowalski, Ted (Musician)
PO Box 1031
Montrose, CA 91021-1031, USA

Kowitz, Brian (Athlete, Baseball Player)
1657 Bullock Cir
Owings Mills, MD 21117-1609, USA

Koy, Ernie (Athlete, Football Player)
PO Box 6
Kenney, TX 77452-0006, USA

Koy, Ted (Athlete, Football Player)
3501 Williams Dr
Georgetown, TX 78628-2421, USA

Koyama, Debbie (Athlete, Golfer)
118 Tranquila Dr
Camarillo, CA 93012-5174, USA

Koz, Dave (Musician)
c/o Staff Member *Agency for the Performing Arts (APA-LA)*
405 S Beverly Dr Ste 500
Beverly Hills, CA 90212-4425, USA

Kozak, Don (Athlete, Hockey Player)
1510 E Beacon Dr
Gilbert, AZ 85234-2674, USA

Kozak, Harley Jane (Actor)
21336 Colina Dr
Topanga, CA 90290, USA

Kozak, Julie (Journalist)
4000 Warner Blvd
Burbank, CA 91522-0001, USA

Kozak, Les (Athlete, Hockey Player)
1072 Kimbro Dr
Baton Rouge, LA 70808-6042, USA

Kozak, Scott (Athlete, Football Player)
18617 S Grasle Rd
Oregon City, OR 97045-8898, USA

Kozakov, Mikhail M (Actor, Director)
B Nikitskaya Str 17
Moscow 103009, RUSSIA

Kozar, Al (Athlete, Baseball Player)
5966 Bay Hill Cir
Lake Worth, FL 33463-6569, USA

Kozeev, Konstantin (Cosmonaut)
Moskovskoi Oblasti
Syvisdny Goroduk 141160, RUSSIA

Kozelko, Tom (Athlete, Basketball Player)
6200 Peninsula Dr
Traverse City, MI 49686-1916, USA

Kozena, Magdalena (Opera Singer)
Narodni Divadio Dvorakova 11
Brno 60000, CZECH REPUBLIC

Kozer, Sarah (Actor)
c/o Ric Tanner 8383 Wilshire Blvd #510
Beverly Hills, CA 90211, USA

Kozinski, Alex (Judge)
125 S Grand Ave
Pasadena, CA 91105-1643, USA

Kozlicki, Ron (Athlete, Basketball Player)
5002 Hidden Branches Dr
Atlanta, GA 30338-3910, USA

Kozlov, Viktor (Athlete, Hockey Player)
363 Merlin Way
Plantation, FL 33324-2165, USA

Kozlov, Vyacheslav (Athlete, Hockey Player)
4240 Irma Ct
Atlanta, GA 30327-3713, USA

Kozlova, Anna (Swimmer)
c/o Staff Member *Premier Management Group (PMG Sports)*
115 Crescent Commons Dr Ste 250
Cary, NC 27518-8134, USA

Kozlova, Valentina (Ballerina)
Lincoin Center Plaza
New York, NY 10023, USA

Kozlowski, Ben (Athlete, Baseball Player)
9083 Briarwood Dr
Seminole, FL 33772-2810, USA

Kozlowski, Brian (Athlete, Football Player)
61 E Shore Dr
Niantic, CT 06357-3833, USA

Kozlowski, Christine (Beauty Pageant Winner)
PO Box 742
Vicksburg, MS 39181-0742, USA

Kozlowski, Glen (Athlete, Football Player)
18095 W Timber Ln
Grayslake, IL 60030-1936, USA

Kozlowski, Linda (Actor)
18 Marshall Cres
Beacon Hill, NSW 2060, AUSTRALIA

Kozlowski, Mike (Athlete, Football Player)
563 N 2430 W
Provo, UT 84601-7278, USA

Kozol, Jonathan (Writer)
PO Box 145
Byfield, MA 01922-0145, USA

Kraatz, Victor (Figure Skater)
300 Alumni Rd
Newington, CT 06111-1868, USA

Kraayeveld, Dave (Athlete, Football Player)
10515 124th Ave NE
Kirkland, WA 98033-4628, USA

Krabbe, Jeroen (Actor)
Van Eeghaustraat 107
Amsterdam, EZ 1071, NETHERLANDS

Krabbe, Katrin
Jahnstadion Schwedenstr. 25
Neubrandenburg, GERMANY D-17033

Krabbe-Zimmermann, Katrin (Athlete, Track Athlete)
Dorfstr 9
Pinnow 17091, GERMANY

Krackow, Jurgen (Business Person)
Schumannstr 100
Dusseldorf 40237, GERMANY

Kraemer, Joe (Athlete, Baseball Player)
3212 NE 401st Cir
La Center, WA 98629-5241, USA

Kraft, Chris
14919 Village Elm St
Houston, TX 77062-2914

Kraft, Christopher C (Chris) Jr (Misc)
14919 Village Elm St
Houston, TX 77062-2914, USA

Kraft, Craig A (Artist)
931 R St NW
Washington, DC 20001-4109, USA

Kraft, Greg (Athlete, Golfer)
14820 Rue De Bayonne Apt 302
Clearwater, FL 33762-3029, USA

Kraft, Leo A (Composer)
45 Hill Park Ave # 219
Great Neck, NY 11021-3774, USA

Kraft, Lindsey (Actor)
c/o Matt Sherman *Matt Sherman Management*
9107 Wilshire Blvd Ste 225
Beverly Hills, CA 90210-5546, USA

Kraft, Robert (Football Executive)
c/o Staff Member *New England Patriots*
Gillette Stadium One Patriots Pl
Foxboro, MA 02035-1388, USA

Kraft, Robert (Composer)
4722 Noeline Ave
Encino, CA 91436-2106, USA

Kraft, Robert P (Physicist)
Lick Observatory
Santa Cruz, CA 95064, USA

Kraft, Ryan (Athlete, Hockey Player)
16219 Hawthorn Path
Lakeville, MN 55044-7573, USA

Kragen, Greg (Athlete, Football Player)
301 Livoma Heights Rd
Alamo, CA 94507, USA

Kragen, Ken
240 Baroda
Los Angeles, CA 90077

Krahl, Jim (Athlete, Football Player)
514 Rolling Mill Dr
Sugar Land, TX 77498-3072, USA

Krainev, Vladimir V (Musician)
Walderseestr 100
Hanover, GERMANY

Krainin, Julian (President)
25211 Summerhill Ln
Stevenson Ranch, CA 91381-2262, USA

Krajicek, Richard (Tennis Player)
1751 Pinnacle Dr Ste 1500
McLean, VA 22102-3833, USA

Krakau, Merv (Athlete, Football Player)
706 Prairie St
Guthrie Center, IA 50115-1711, USA

Krake, Skip (Athlete, Hockey Player)
5401 37 St
Lloydminster, AB T9V 1T8, Canada

Krakoski, Joe (Athlete, Football Player)
1359 Garden Wall Cir
Reston, VA 20194-1979, USA

Krakowski, Jane (Actor, Musician)
c/o Bill Butler *Industry Entertainment Partners*
955 Carrillo Dr Ste 300
Los Angeles, CA 90048-5400, USA

Krall, Diana (Musician)
c/o Sam Feldman *Macklam Feldman Mgmt*
1505 W 2nd Ave Suite 200
Vancouver BC V6H 3Y4, Canada

Krall, Gerald (Athlete, Football Player)
9236 Mandell Rd
Perrysburg, OH 43551-3913, USA

Kraly, Steve (Athlete, Baseball Player)
12 Davis Ave
Johnson City, NY 13790-3007, USA

Kramarsky, David (Director, Producer)
1630 Berkeley St Apt 1
Santa Monica, CA 90404-4134, USA

Kramer, Barry (Athlete, Basketball Player)
101 Deanna Ct
Schenectady, NY 12309-1333, USA

Kramer, Billy J (Musician)
27 L Ambiance Ct
Bardonia, NY 10954-1421, USA

Kramer, Chris (Actor)
c/o Deb Dillistone *Lucas Talent Inc*
100 W. Pender St Sun Tower, 7th Floor
Vancouver, BC V6B 1R8, Canada

Kramer, Clare (Actor)
c/o Darren Goldberg *Global Creative*
1051 Cole Ave # B
Los Angeles, CA 90038-2601, USA

Kramer, Eric Allen (Actor)
c/o Steve Rodriquez *McGowan Management*
8733 W Sunset Blvd Ste 103
West Hollywood, CA 90069-2241, USA

Kramer, Erik (Athlete, Football Player)
5950 Kingham Ct
Agoura Hills, CA 91301-4436, USA

Kramer, Gerald L (Jerry) (Athlete, Football Player)
11768 W Chinden Ridge Dr
Boise, ID 83714-1028, USA

Kramer, Jack
48900 Avenida El Nido
La Quinta, CA 92253-6232

Kramer, Jana (Actor)
c/o Katie Rhodes *Untitled Entertainment (LA)*
350 S Beverly Dr Ste 200
Beverly Hills, CA 90212-4819, USA

Kramer, Jim (Writer)
c/o Staff Member *3 Arts Entertainment Inc*
9460 Wilshire Blvd Fl 7
Beverly Hills, CA 90212-2713, USA

Kramer, Joel (Athlete, Basketball Player)
3817 E Highland Ave
Phoenix, AZ 85018-3619, USA

Kramer, Joel R (Editor)
425 Portland Ave
Minneapolis, MN 55488-1511, USA

Kramer, Joey (Musician)
4 Brussels St
Worcester, MA 01610-2904, USA

Kramer, John A (Jack) (Tennis Player)
48900 Avenida El Nido
La Quinta, CA 92253-6232, USA

Kramer, Kent (Athlete, Football Player)
200 Troon Rd
McKinney, TX 75070-6783, USA

Kramer, Kyle (Athlete, Football Player)
821 Orchard Ln
Beavercreek Township, OH 45434-7216, USA

Kramer, Larry (Activist, Writer)
119 W 24th St
New York, NY 10011-1913, USA

Kramer, Paul
20023 Bernist Ave
Torrance, CA 90503-2103

Kramer, Randy (Athlete, Baseball Player)
143 Camino Pacifico
Aptos, CA 95003-5886, USA

Kramer, Ronald J (Ron) (Athlete, Football Player)
PO Box 473
Fenton, MI 48430-0473, USA

Kramer, Stepfanie (Actor, Director, Writer)
c/o Mark Teitelbaum *Teitelbaum Artists Group*
8840 Wilshire Blvd Fl 3
Beverly Hills, CA 90211-2606, USA

Kramer, Steve
1126 N Hollywood Way # 203-A
Burbank, CA 91505-2527

Kramer, Thomas (Tommy) (Athlete, Football Player)
16650 Huebner Rd Apt 1717
San Antonio, TX 78248-2322, USA

Kramer, Tom (Athlete, Baseball Player)
10665 Hamilton Ave
Cincinnati, OH 45231-1703, USA

Kramer, Wayne (Musician)
8901 Melrose Ave # 200
West Hollywood, CA 90069-5605, USA

Kramer-Hartman, Ruth (Golfer)
1100 Limekiln Rd
Limekiln, PA 19535, USA

Kramnik, Vladmir (Misc)
Luchnetskaya 8
Moscow 119270, RUSSIA

Kranek, Ernst
623 W Chino Canyon Rd
Palm Springs, CA 92262-2701

Kranepool, Ed (Athlete, Baseball Player)
177 High Pond Dr
Jericho, NY 11753-2806, USA

Krantz, Judith (Writer)
166 Groverton Pl
Los Angeles, CA 90077-3732, USA

Kranz, Eugene (Gene) (Scientist)
1108 Shady Oak Ln
Dickinson, TX 77539-3327, USA

Kranz, Fran (Actor)
c/o Rebecca (Becca) Kovacik *Hofflund/Polone*
9465 Wilshire Blvd Ste 420
Beverly Hills, CA 90212-2603, USA

Kranz, Ken (Athlete, Football Player)
N57W24143 N Sycamore Cir
Sussex, WI 53089-5160, USA

Krapek, Karl (Business Person)
United Technologies Building
Hartford, CT 6101, USA

Krasinski, John (Actor)
c/o Carrie Byalick *I/D PR (NY)*
150 W 30th St Fl 19
New York, NY 10001-4003, USA

Krasniqi, Luan (Boxer)
Oschlewg 10
Rottweil 78628, GERMANY

Krasnoff, Eric (Business Person)
2200 Northem Blvd
Greenvale, NY 11548, USA

Krasny, Yuri (Artist)
1612 17th St Ofc Bldg
Denver, CO 80202-1204, USA

Kratch, Bob (Athlete, Football Player)
10685 County Road 24
Watertown, MN 55388-9324, USA

Kratochvilova, Jarmila (Athlete, Track Athlete)
Goleuv Jenikov
582 82, CZECH REPUBLIC

Kratt, Chris (Cinematographer, Director, Producer, Television Host, Writer)

Kratt, Martin (Cinematographer, Director, Producer, Television Host, Writer)

Kratzert, Bill (Athlete, Golfer)
7470 Founders Way
Ponte Vedra Beach, FL 32082-1914, USA

Kraulis, Andrew (Actor)
c/o Staff Member *Amanda Rosenthal Talent Agency*
14 Prince Arthur Ave Suite 206
Toronto, ON M5R 1A9, Canada

Kraus, Daniel (Athlete, Basketball Player)
10101 Governor Warfield Pkwy Unit 222
Columbia, MD 21044-3322, USA

Kraus, Peter
Kaiserplatz 7
Munich, GERMANY D-80803

Krause, Brian (Actor)
c/o Leland LaBarre *Bleu, An Entertainment Company*
5225 Wilshire Blvd Ste 336
Los Angeles, CA 90036-4380, USA

Krause, Chester L (Publisher)
700 E State St
Iola, WI 54990-0001, USA

Krause, Dieter (Athlete)
Karl-Marx-Allee 21
Berlin 1017, GERMANY

Krause, Larry (Athlete, Football Player)
N9169 Mill Rd
Summit Lake, WI 54485-9717, USA

Krause, Nick (Actor)
c/o Rebecca Many Rosenberg *Principato/ Young Management*
9465 Wilshire Blvd Ste 430
Beverly Hills, CA 90212-2613, USA

Krause, Paul J (Athlete, Football Player)
18099 Judicial Way N
Lakeville, MN 55044-7105, USA

Krause, Peter (Actor)
c/o Peter Levine *Creative Artists Agency (CAA-LA)*
2000 Avenue of the Stars Ste 100
Los Angeles, CA 90067-4705, USA

Krause, Richard M (Misc)
4000 Cathedral Ave NW Apt 134B
Washington, DC 20016-5235, USA

Kraushaar, Sitke (Athlete)
Friedr-Ludwig-Jahn-Str 34
Sonneberg 2692, GERMANY

Kraushaar, William L (Physicist)
27 Stoney Creek Rd
Scarborough, ME 04074-8385, USA

Krauss, Alison (Musician)
c/o Staff Member *Shore Fire Media*
32 Court St Fl 16
Brooklyn, NY 11201-4441, USA

Krauss, Lawrence M (Physicist)
Physics Dept
Cleveland, OH 44106, USA

Krausse, Lew (Athlete, Baseball Player)
12811 NE 186th St
Holt, MO 64048-8956, USA

Krausse, Stefan (Athlete)
Kart-Zink-Str 2
Ilmenau 96883, GERMANY

Krauthammer, Charles (Writer)
1150 15th St NW
Washington, DC 20071-0001, USA

Kravchuk, Igor (Athlete, Hockey Player)
300 Chemin De La Riviere Rouge
Harrington, QC J8G 2S7, Canada

Kravec, Ken (Athlete, Baseball Player)
6752 Taeda Dr
Sarasota, FL 34241-9152, USA

Kravitch, Phyllis A (Judge)
56 Forsyth St NW
Atlanta, GA 30303-2218, USA

Kravits, Jason
6310 San Vicente Blvd Ste 520
Los Angeles, CA 90048-5421

Kravitz, Danny (Athlete, Baseball Player)
8810 Route 487
Dushore, PA 18614-8040, USA

Kravitz, Lenny (Musician, Songwriter)
c/o Steve Sherr *The Artists Organization*
212 Marine St Unit 307
Santa Monica, CA 90405-6514, USA

Kravitz, Zoe (Actor)
c/o Jillian Neal *Untitled Entertainment (LA)*
350 S Beverly Dr Ste 200
Beverly Hills, CA 90212-4819, USA

Krawczyk, Ray (Athlete, Baseball Player)
67 Cloudcrest
Aliso Viejo, CA 92656-1323, USA

Krawitz, Jan (Filmmaker)
Bldg l20 Stanford University
Stanford, CA 94305-2050, USA

Krayzelburg, Lenny (Swimmer)
1751 Pinnacle Dr Ste 1500
McLean, VA 22102-3833, USA

Kreamcheck, John (Athlete, Football Player)
2508 N Villa Ln
McHenry, IL 60051-2975, USA

Krebbs, John (Race Car Driver)
Diamond Ridge 3232 Amoruso Way
Roseville, CA 95747, USA

Krebs, Edwin G (Nobel Prize Laureate)
1630 43rd Ave E Apt 12
Seattle, WA 98112-6211, USA

Krebs, Robert D (Business Person)
2650 Lou Menk Dr
Fort Worth, TX 76131-2830, USA

Krebs, Susan (Actor)
6019 Buffalo Ave Apt A
Van Nuys, CA 91401-3043, USA

Kredel, Elmar Maria (Religious Leader)
Obere Karolinenstra 5
Bamber 96033, GERMANY

Kregel, Kevin R (Astronaut)
2601 Bay Shore Dr
Seabrook, TX 77586-1690, USA

Krehbiel, Frederick A (Business Person)
2222 Wellington Ct
Lisle, IL 60532-3831

Krehbiel, John Hammond (Business Person)
2222 Wellington Ct
Lisle, IL 60532-3831

Kreider, Steve (Athlete, Football Player)
350 Harrow Ln
Blue Bell, PA 19422-3110, USA

Kreischer, Bert (Musician)
c/o Staff Member *Paradigm (Monterey)*
404 W Franklin St
Monterey, CA 93940-2303, USA

Kreitling, Richard (Athlete, Football Player)
12121 Vonn Rd
Largo, FL 33774-3401, USA

Krejc, Otomar
Kubisova 26
Praha 8 CZ-18200, Czech Republic

Krejci, David (Athlete, Hockey Player)
c/o Staff Member *Boston Bruins*
TD Banknorth Garden 100 Legends Way, Suite 250
Boston, MA 2114, USA

Kreklow, Wayne (Athlete, Basketball Player)
4001 S Old Mill Creek Rd
Columbia, MO 65203-9635, USA

krels, Jason (Soccer Player)
14800 Quorum Dr Ste 300
Dallas, TX 75254-1442, USA

Krementz, Jill (Photographer)
620 Sagg Main St
Sagaponack, NY 11962, USA

Kremer, Andrea (Sportscaster)
Sports Dept ESPN Plaza 935 Middle St
Bristol, CT 6010, USA

Kremer, Gidon (Musician)
40 W 57th St
New York, NY 10019-4001, USA

Kremer, Howard (Comedian)
c/o Staff Member *International Creative Management (ICM-LA)*
10250 Constellation Blvd Fl 7
Los Angeles, CA 90067-6207, USA

Kremer, Ken (Athlete, Football Player)
6116 Double Eagle Ct
Kansas City, MO 64152-4970, USA

Kremers, James (Jimmy) (Athlete, Baseball Player)
6209 W Orlando St
Broken Arrow, OK 74011-1264, USA

Kremmel, Jim (Athlete, Baseball Player)
524 W 18th Ave
Spokane, WA 99203-2011, USA

Kremser, Karl (Athlete, Football Player)
301 W Glenview Dr
Salisbury, NC 28147-7227, USA

Krenchicki, Wayne (Athlete, Baseball Player)
2524 Hawthorne Dr
Beloit, WI 53511-2338, USA

Krenk, Mitch (Athlete, Football Player)
1822 4th Ave
Nebraska City, NE 68410-1822, USA

Krens, Thomas (Misc)
1071 5th Ave
New York, NY 10128-0112, USA

Krentz, Dale (Athlete, Hockey Player)
71 Lodge Pl
Sylvan Lake, AB T4S 2N2, Canada

Krenwinkel, Patricia
#W8314 Bed #MA11U CA Inst. for Women16756 Chino Corona
Frontera, CA 91720

Krenz, Jan (Composer, Conductor)
Ul Jasna 5
Warsaw, POLAND

Krenzel, Craig (Athlete, Football Player)
10174 Jerome Rd
Dublin, OH 43017-7606, USA

Kreppel, Paul
14300 Killion St
Sherman Oaks, CA 91401-5108

Kreps, David M (Economist)
Graduate Business School
Stanford, CA 94305, USA

Kreps, Juanita M (Secretary)
1407 W Pettigrew St
Durham, NC 27705, USA

Krerowicz, Mark (Athlete, Football Player)
1425 Luscombe Dr
Toledo, OH 43614-2618, USA

Kresa, Kent (Business Person)
1840 Century Park E
Los Angeles, CA 90067-2101, USA

Kresge, Chris (Athlete, Golfer)
834 Trailwood Dr
Apopka, FL 32712-3217, USA

Kresge, Cliff (Athlete, Golfer)
c/o Jim Lehrman *SFX Golf*
36855 W Main St Ste 200
Purcellville, VA 20132-3561, USA

Kreskin (Misc)
444 2nd St
Pitcaim, PA 15140, USA

Kress, Chuck (Athlete, Baseball Player)
1705 Pine St Apt 104
Sandpoint, ID 83864-2044, USA

Kress, Nathan (Actor)
c/o Donna Jeanne Goheen *Young Performers Management*
14431 Ventura Blvd # 506
Sherman Oaks, CA 91423-2606, USA

Kressley, Carson (Stylist, Television Host)
c/o Jason Weinberg *Untitled Entertainment (LA)*
350 S Beverly Dr Ste 200
Beverly Hills, CA 90212-4819, USA

Kretchmer, Arthur (Editor)
680 N Lake Shore Dr
Chicago, IL 60611-3057, USA

Kretschmann, Thomas (Director)
c/o Staff Member *United Talent Agency (UTA)*
9560 Wilshire Blvd Fl 5
Beverly Hills, CA 90212-2400, USA

Kretschmer, Christina (Stylist)
c/o Staff Member *Ennis*
119 Braintree St
Boston, MA 02134-1628, USA

Kreuger, Rick (Athlete, Baseball Player)
4664 Sheldon Ct
Hudsonville, MI 49426-7810, USA

Kreuk, Kristin (Actor)
c/o Russ Mortensen *Pacific Artists Management*
1285 W Broadway Suite 685
Vancouver, BC V6H 3X8, Canada

Kreuter, Chad (Athlete, Baseball Player)
5800 SW 85th St
Miami, FL 33143-8224, USA

Kreutz, Olin (Athlete, Football Player)
1373 Honokahua St
Honolulu, HI 96825-3024, USA

Kreutzer, Frank (Athlete, Baseball Player)
921 Windwhisper Ln
Annapolis, MD 21403-3486, USA

Kreutzmann, Bill (Musician)
PO Box 1073
San Rafael, CA 94915-1073, USA

Kreuzer, Lisa
Bavariaring 32
Munich, GERMANY D-80336

Kreviazuk, Chantal (Musician, Songwriter)
c/o Staff Member *Paradigm (Monterey)*
404 W Franklin St
Monterey, CA 93940-2303, USA

Krevis, Al (Athlete, Football Player)
1 Springbrook Rd
Auburn, MA 01501-3114, USA

Krevlazuk, Chantel
1505 W 2nd Ave # 200
Vancouver, CANADA BC V6H 3Y4

Kribel, Joel (Athlete, Golfer)
26254 N 46th St
Phoenix, AZ 85050-8510, USA

Kricfalusi (Kricfaluci), John K (Actor, Animator, Director, Writer)
c/o Staff Member *Rough Draft Korea*
Kyejin B/D, 425-7 Togok-dong, Kannam-Gu
Seoul 135-270, Korea

Krick, Jaynie (Baseball Player)
1522 Azalea Dr
Arlington, TX 76013-3609, USA

Krickstein, Aaron (Tennis Player)
7559 Fairmont Ct
Boca Raton, FL 33496-5902, USA

Krieg, Arthur M (Misc)
Medical College Immunology Dept
Iowa City, IA 52242, USA

Krieger, Robbie (Musician, Songwriter, Writer)
3011 Ledgewood Dr
Los Angeles, CA 90068-1959, USA

Krier, Leon (Architect)
16 Belsize Park
London NW3, UNITED KINGDOM (UK)

Kriewald, Doug (Athlete, Football Player)
5031 Snow Mesa Dr
Fort Collins, CO 80528-8590, USA

Kriewaldt, Clint (Athlete, Football Player)
2705 Beacon Hill Dr Apt 104
Auburn Hills, MI 48326-3755, USA

Krige, Alice (Actor)
2875 Barrymore Dr
Malibu, CA 90265-2959, USA

Krikalev, Sergei K (Cosmonaut)
Moskovskoi Oblasti
Syvisdny Goroduk 141160, RUSSIA

Krimm, John (Athlete, Football Player)
320 11th Ave S Apt 339
Nashville, TN 37203-4070, USA

Kring, Tim (Writer)
c/o Richard Abate *3 Arts Entertainment - NY*
49 W 27th St Fl 5
New York, NY 10001-6936, USA

Kripke, Eric (Director, Producer, Writer)
c/o Staff Member *Principato/Young Management*
9465 Wilshire Blvd Ste 430
Beverly Hills, CA 90212-2613, USA

Kripke, Saul A (Misc)
Philosophy
Princeton, NJ 08544-0001, USA

Krisher, Bill (Athlete, Football Player)
5915 Over Downs Dr
Dallas, TX 75230-4044, USA

Krishnamurthy, Suchithra (Actor, Bollywood)
402A Leela Apartments Cuerpark Co-Op Society Yari Road Andheri W
Mumbai, MS 400061, INDIA

Krishnan, Ramya (Actor, Bollywood)
7 Lakshmi Sri Street Janaki Nagar
Chennai, TN 600087, INDIA

Kriss, Gerard A (Astronomer)
Astronomy Dept
Baltimore, MD 21218, USA

Kristel, Sylvia (Actor)
2400 Whitman Pl
Los Angeles, CA 90068-2464, USA

Kristen, Marta (Actor)
c/o Joel Kleinman *Baier/Kleinman International*
3575 Cahuenga Blvd W Ste 500
Los Angeles, CA 90068-1344, USA

Kristiansen, Ingrid (Athlete, Track Athlete)
Nils Collett Vogts Vei 51B
Oslo, 765, NORWAY

Kristiansen, Kjeld Kirk (Business Person, Educator)
Billund 7190, DENMARK

Kristien, Dale
691 Country Club Dr
Burbank, CA 91501-1121

Kristina Sisco, Kristina (Actor)
c/o Staff Member *Cohen/Thomas Agency*
1888 N Crescent Heights Blvd
Los Angeles, CA 90069-1647, USA

Kristof, Kathy M (Writer)
202 W 1st St
Los Angeles, CA 90012-4105, USA

Kristoff, Joe (Bowler)
4290 Meadowview Ct
Columbus, OH 43224-1927, USA

Kristofferson, Kris (Actor, Musician, Songwriter)
c/o Steve Chasman *Ace Media*
9200 W Sunset Blvd Ste 10
Los Angeles, CA 90069-3608, USA

Kristol, Irving (Editor, Scientist)
1112 16th St NW
Washington, DC 20036-4823, USA

Kristol, William
6625 Jill Ct
McLean, VA 22101-1613

Krivda, Rick (Athlete, Baseball Player)
112 Dolores Dr
Irwin, PA 15642-5519, USA

Krivokrasov, Sergei (Athlete, Hockey Player)
99 SE Mizner Blvd Apt 729
Boca Raton, FL 33432-5046, USA

Kriwet, Heinz (Business Person)
August-Thyssen-Str 1
Dusseldorf 40211, GERMANY

Krizmanich, Jack (Actor)
c/o Mara Santino *Luber Roklin Management*
8530 Wilshire Blvd Ste 550
Beverly Hills, CA 90211-3133, USA

Kroeger, Gary (Actor, Comedian)
10474 Santa Monica Blvd Ste 380
Los Angeles, CA 90025-6943, USA

Kroell, Ronnie (Actor, Model)
c/o Dino May *Dino May Management*
6362 Hollywood Blvd
Los Angeles, CA 90028-6323, USA

Kroemer, Herbert (Nobel Prize Laureate)
Electrical/Computer Eng Dept
Santa Barbara, CA 93106-0001, USA

Kroes, Doutzen (Model)
c/o Staff Member *Paparazzi Model Management*
Singel 512-2
AZ 1017, THE NETHERLANDS

Krofft, Marty (Actor, Producer)
c/o CBS Studio Center 4024 Radford Ave
Studio City, CA 91604, USA

Krofft, Sid (Misc)
7710 Woodrow Wilson Dr
Los Angeles, CA 90046-1212, USA

Kroft, Steve (Correspondent)

Krogh, Sandy (Stylist)
14 Haggerston Aisle
Irvine, CA 92603-5732, USA

Krohn, Jonathan (Writer)
15335 Little Stone Way
Alpharetta, GA 30004-6901, USA

Krol, John Cardinal
222 N 17th St
Philadelphia, PA 19103-1202

Kroll, Alexander S (Alex) (Athlete, Football Player)
581 Whalley Rd
Charlotte, VT 05445-9531, USA

Kroll, Gary (Athlete, Baseball Player)
9038 E 40th St
Tulsa, OK 74145-3713, USA

Kroll, Lucien (Architect)
Ave Louis Berlaimont 20 Boite 9
Brussels 1160, BELGIUM

Kroll, Robert L (Athlete, Football Player)
P.O. Box 8563
Maitland, FL 32751, USA

Kroll, Sylvio
Tranitzer Str. 8
Cottbus, GERMANY D-03048

Krom, Tommy (Athlete, Basketball Player)
519 Briar Hill Rd
Louisville, KY 40206-3009, USA

Kromm, Bob (Coach)
600 Civic Center Dr
Detroit, MI 48226-4408, USA

Kromm, Richard (Rich) (Athlete, Coach, Hockey Player)
1935 Cheyenne Dr
Evansville, IN 47715-7044, USA

Kronberger, Petra (Skier)
Ellmautal 37
Pfarrwerfen 5452, AUSTRIA

Krone, Julie (Jockey)
100 Broadway # 700
New York, NY 10005-1983, USA

Kroner, Gary (Athlete, Football Player)
7330 Buckingham Ct
Boulder, CO 80301-6409, USA

Kronwall, Niklas (Athlete, Hockey Player)
22235 Picadilly Cir
Novi, MI 48375-4796, USA

Krook, Kevin (Athlete, Hockey Player)
216 20 St
Cold Lake, AB T9M 1E2, Canada

Kroon, Marc (Athlete, Baseball Player)
12617 N 56th Pl
Scottsdale, AZ 85254-4259, USA

Kropfelder, Nicholas (Soccer Player)
13803 Lighthouse Ave
Ocean City, MD 21842-4565, USA

Kropp, Tom (Athlete, Basketball Player)
1811 W 41st St
Kearney, NE 68845-8286, USA

Kross, David (Actor)
c/o Staff Member *Julian Belfrage & Associates*
46 Albemarle St
London W1X 4PP, UK

Kroto, Harold W (Nobel Prize Laureate)
Chemistry Dept Falmer
Brighton BN1 9QJ, UNITED KINGDOM (UK)

Krsnich, Rocky (Athlete, Baseball Player)
5701 W 92nd St
Overland Park, KS 66207-2442, USA

KRS-One (Musician)
c/o Sasha Brookner *Heliocentric Public Relations*
5535 Westlawn Ave Apt 256
Los Angeles, CA 90066-7098, USA

Krstic, Nenad (Basketball Player)
390 Murray Hill Pkwy
East Rutherford, NJ 07073-2109, USA

Kruckei, Marie (Baseball Player)
52128 Woodridge Dr
South Bend, IN 46635-1053, USA

Kruczek, Mike (Athlete, Football Player)
4028 Gilder Rose Pl
Winter Park, FL 32792-9416, USA

Krueger, Anne O (Economist)
Economics Dept
Stanford, CA 94305, USA

Krueger, Bill (Athlete, Baseball Player)
30132 SE Redmond Fall City Rd
Fall City, WA 98024-7104, USA

Krueger, Charles A (Charlie) (Athlete, Football Player)
44 Regency Dr
Clayton, CA 94517-1729, USA

Krueger, James G (Misc)
Medical Center 1230 York Ave
New York, NY 10021, USA

Krueger, Kurt
1221 La Collina Dr
Beverly Hills, CA 90210-2633

Krueger, Robert C (Bob) (Diplomat, Ex-Senator)
2201 C St NW
Washington, DC 20522-0099, USA

Krueger, Rolf (Athlete, Football Player)
PO Box 638
Wallis, TX 77485-0638, USA

Krug, Chris (Athlete, Baseball Player)
40695 Posada Ct
Palm Desert, CA 92260-2317, USA

Krug, Gene (Athlete, Baseball Player)
1327 Baylor Dr
Colorado Springs, CO 80909-3301, USA

Krug, Manfred
Rankestr. 9
Berlin, GERMANY D-10789

Kruger, Christiane
Waldschmidtstr. 16
Starnberg, GERMANY 82319

Kruger, Diane (Actor, Model)
c/o Abi Harris *Ken McReddie Ltd*
11 Connaught Pl
London W2 2ET, UNITED KINGDOM

Kruger, Hardy (Actor)
PO Box 2450
Palm Springs, CA 92263-2450, USA

Kruger, Mike
Gorch-Fock-Kehre 9
Quickborn, GERMANY D-25451

Kruger, Pit (Actor)
Geleitstr 10
Frankfurt/Main 60599, GERMANY

Krugman, Paul R (Economist)
70 Lambert Dr
Princeton, NJ 08540-2319, USA

Kruk, John (Athlete, Baseball Player)
935 Middle St Attn Baseballbroadcast
Bristol, CT 06010-1000, USA

Krukow, Mike (Athlete, Baseball Player)
6094 Madbury Ct
San Luis Obispo, CA 93401-8244, USA

Krulicki, Jim (Athlete, Hockey Player)
35 Primrose Path
Kitchener, ON N2E 2R2, Canada

Krulwich, Robert (Correspondent)
524 W 57th St
New York, NY 10019-2930, USA

Krumholtz, David (Actor)
c/o Jeff Golenberg *Collective*
8383 Wilshire Blvd Ste 1050
Beverly Hills, CA 90211-2415, USA

Krumrie, Tim (Football Player)
c/o Staff Member *Kansas City Chiefs*
1 Arrowhead Dr
Kansas City, MO 64129-1651, USA

Krupa, Joanna (Actor)
c/o Tom Harrison *Diverse Talent Group*
9911 W Pico Blvd Ste 340W
Los Angeles, CA 90035-2712, USA

Krupa, Joe (Athlete, Football Player)
PO Box 1356
North Riverside, IL 60546-0756, USA

Krupp, Uwe (Athlete, Hockey Player)
3716 the Strand
Manhattan Beach, CA 90266-3244, USA

Kruschen, Jack
PO Box 10143
Canoga Park, CA 91309-1143

Kruse, Earl J (Misc)
1125 17th St NW
Washington, DC 20036-4709, USA

Kruse, Martin (Religious Leader)
Prinz-Friedrrich-Leopold-Str 14
Berlin 14219, GERMANY

Krushelnyski, Mike (Athlete, Hockey Player)
PO Box 834
Cohoes, NY 12047-0834, USA

Krusiec, Michelle (Actor)
c/o Jennifer Wiley *Framework Entertainment (NY)*
129 W 27th St Fl 12
New York, NY 10001-6206, USA

Kruskal, Martin D (Mathematician)
60 Littlebrook Rd N
Princeton, NJ 08540-4062, USA

Krygier, Todd (Athlete, Hockey Player)
23946 Wintergreen Cir Apt 13
Novi, MI 48374-3681, USA

Krynzel, Dave (Athlete, Baseball Player)
4065 E Woodland Dr
Appleton, WI 54911, USA

Krypreos, Nick (Athlete, Hockey Player)
9209 Copenhaver Dr
Potomac, MD 20854-3016, USA

Kryskow, Dave (Athlete, Hockey Player)
58 Sandstone Ridge Cres
Okotoks, AB T1S 1P9, Canada

Krystkowiak, Larry (Athlete, Basketball Player)
2343 Dallin St
Salt Lake City, UT 84109-1524, USA

Krzyzewski, Michael W (Mike) (Athlete, Basketball Player, Coach)
4406 W Cornwallis Rd
Durham, NC 27705-8126, USA

Ksionzyk, John (Athlete, Football Player)
1106 Washington St
Olean, NY 14760-2128, USA

KT Tunstall (Musician)
c/o Simon Banks *SB Management*
The Homestead Cottage 111 Church Rd
London SW13 9HL, UK

Kuba, Filip (Athlete, Hockey Player)
17216 Emerald Chase Dr
Tampa, FL 33647-2780, USA

Kubala, Ray (Athlete, Football Player)
5 Meandering Way
Round Rock, TX 78664-9619, USA

Kuban, Bob (Musician)
17626 Lasiandra Dr
Chesterfield, MO 63005-4912, USA

Kubasov, Valeri N (Cosmonaut)
Moskovskoi Oblasti
Syvisdny Goroduk 141160, RUSSIA

Kubasov, Valery
141-160 Svyossdy Gorodok
Potchta Kosmonavtov, RUSSIA

Kubek, Anthony C (Tony) (Athlete, Baseball Player, Sportscaster)
121 E Water St Apt 120
Appleton, WI 54911-5775, USA

Kubel, Jason (Athlete, Baseball Player)
39529 Willowvale Rd
Palmdale, CA 93551, USA

Kubenka, Jeff (Athlete, Baseball Player)
6935 FM 957
Schulenburg, TX 78956-5091, USA

Kuberski, Robert (Athlete, Football Player)
13 Forwood Dr
Marcus Hook, PA 19060-1215, USA

Kuberski, Steve (Athlete, Basketball Player)
91 Lawson Rd
Winchester, MA 01890-3153, USA

Kubiak, Gary (Athlete, Coach, Football Coach, Football Player)
PO Box 37415
Houston, TX 77237-7415, USA

Kubiak, Leo (Athlete, Basketball Player)
2638 N Prestwick Way
Lecanto, FL 34461-6902, USA

Kubiak, Ted (Athlete, Baseball Player)
11956 Bernardo Plaza Dr
San Diego, CA 92128-2538, USA

Kubik, Brad (Athlete, Football Player)
11114 W 144th Ter
Overland Park, KS 66221-8052, USA

Kubin, Larry (Athlete, Football Player)
315 Cannery Ln
Forest Hill, MD 21050-3066, USA

Kubina, Pavel (Athlete, Hockey Player)
1145 81st St S
Saint Petersburg, FL 33707-2726, USA

Kubinski, Tim (Athlete, Baseball Player)
384 Santa Maria Ave
San Luis Obispo, CA 93405-2140, USA

Kubiszyn, Jack (Athlete, Baseball Player)
2306 University Blvd
Tuscaloosa, AL 35401-1580, USA

Kubski, Gil (Athlete, Baseball Player)
4542 Scenario Dr
Huntington Beach, CA 92649-2221, USA

Kucan, Milan (President)
Erjavcera 17
Ljubljana 61000, SOLVENIA

Kucek, Jack (Athlete, Baseball Player)
8220 Blue Heron Ln
Canfield, OH 44406-9134, USA

Kucera, Frantisek (Athlete, Hockey Player)
Sportovni Centrum Letnany Tupolevova ul. 699
Praha Letnany 9, Czech Republic

Kuchar, Matt (Athlete, Golfer)
121 Plantation Cir
Ponte Vedra Beach, FL 32082-3921, USA

Kuchma, Leonid D (President)
Bankova Str 11
Kiev 252011, UKRAINE

Kuchta, Frank (Athlete, Football Player)
5021 Fairlawn Rd
Lyndhurst, OH 44124-1124, USA

Kucinich, Dennis
12217 Milan Ave
Cleveland, OH 44111-4550

Kucinich, Dennis J (Misc)
14518 Drake Rd
Cleveland, OH 44136-7932, USA

Kucks, Johnny (Athlete, Baseball Player)
15 Oakland St
Hillsdale, NJ 07642-1846, USA

Kuczek, Steve (Athlete, Baseball Player)
4 Stephen Rd
Schenectady, NY 12302-5815, USA

Kuczenski, Bruce (Athlete, Basketball Player)
135 Southshire Dr
Southington, CT 06489-4224, USA

Kuczynski, Betty (Bowler)
4515 Prescott Ave
Lyons, IL 60534-1960, USA

Kudelka, James A (Choreographer, Dancer)
470 Queens Quay W
Toronto, ON M5V 3K4, CANADA

Kudelski, Bob (Athlete, Hockey Player)
93 Copperleaf Dr
Cody, WY 82414-6700, USA

Kuder, Mary (Artist)
539 Navahopi Rd
Sedona, AZ 86336-4007, USA

Kudlow, Lawrence (Television Host)
Sylvan Ave Cnbc 900
Englewood Cliffs, NJ 07632-3318, USA

Kudoh, Youki (Actor)
c/o Vincent Cirrincione *Vincent Cirrincione Associates*
1516 N Fairfax Ave
Los Angeles, CA 90046-2608, USA

Kudrna, Julius (Athlete)
Sekaninova 36
Prague 2 120 00, CZECH REPUBLIC

Kudrow, Lisa (Actor)
c/o Jennifer Allen *Viewpoint Inc*
8820 Wilshire Blvd Ste 220
Beverly Hills, CA 90211-2622, USA

Kuebler, David (Opera Singer)
36 Station Road
London SE20 7BQ, UNITED KINGDOM (UK)

Kuechenberg, Robert J (Bob) (Athlete, Football Player)
2519 SW 30th Ter
Fort Lauderdale, FL 33312-4729, USA

Kuechenberg, Rudy (Athlete, Football Player)
2928 SE 20th Ave
Cape Coral, FL 33904-4019, USA

Kuehl, Karl (Athlete, Baseball Player, Coach)
PO Box 17017
Fountain Hills, AZ 85269-7017, USA

Kuehl, Ryan (Athlete, Football Player)
10409 Masters Ter
Potomac, MD 20854-3862, USA

Kuehn, Art (Athlete, Football Player)
19520 NE 185th St
Woodinville, WA 98077-5403, USA

Kuehn, Enrico (Athlete)
An der Schiessstatte 4
Berchtesgaden 83471, GERMANY

Kuehne, Hank (Athlete, Golfer)
11117 Green Bayberry Dr
Palm Beach Gardens, FL 33418-1511, USA

Kuehne, Kelli (Athlete, Golfer)
7211 Oakbluff Dr
Dallas, TX 75254-2736, USA

Kuerten, Gustavo (Tennis Player)
1751 Pinnacle Dr Ste 1500
McLean, VA 22102-3833, USA

Kuester, John (Athlete, Basketball Player)
105 Carnoustie Way
Media, PA 19063-1858, USA

Kufeldt, James (Business Person)
5050 Edgewood Ct
Jacksonville, FL 32254-3601, USA

Kufuor, John Agyekum (President)
Castle PO Box 1627
Accra, GHANA

Kugler, Pete (Athlete, Football Player)
9984 Whitetail Ln
Littleton, CO 80127-6104, USA

Kuhaulua, Fred (Athlete, Baseball Player)
89-203 Ualakahiki Pl
Waianae, HI 96792-3937, USA

Kuhaulua, Jesse (Wrestler)
4-6-4 Higashi Komagata Ryogoku
Tokyo, JAPAN

Kuhlman, Ron (Actor)
5738 Willis Ave
Van Nuys, CA 91411-3327, USA

Kuhlmann, Kathleen M (Opera Singer)
G Paris 54 Ave Marceau
Paris 75008, FRANCE

Kuhlmann-Wilsdorf, Doris (Physicist)
Materials Science Dept
Charlottesville, VA 22901, USA

Kuhn, Gustav (Conductor)
6343 Ere
AUSTRIA

Kuhn, Kenny (Athlete, Baseball Player)
280 Panoramic Hwy
Mill Valley, CA 94941-2631, USA

Kuhn, Stephen L (Steve) (Composer, Musician)
2608 9th St
Berkeley, CA 94710-2550, USA

Kuhweide, Wilhelm
10031 E Buckskin Trl
Scottsdale, AZ 85255-2338

Kuiper, Duane (Athlete, Baseball Player)
3665 Deer Trail Dr
Danville, CA 94506-6021, USA

Kukoc, Toni (Athlete, Basketball Player)
1830 Hybernia Dr
Highland Park, IL 60035-5500, USA

Kukulowicz, Adolph (Athlete, Hockey Player)
1342 Sea Lovers Ln RR 5
Gabriola, BC V0R 1X5, Canada

Kukunoor, Nagesh

Kulak, Stu (Athlete, Hockey Player)
1086 Forestbrook Dr
Penticton, BC V2A 2G3, Canada

Kulbacki, Joseph (Athlete, Football Player)
9419 S Hill Rd
Boston, NY 14025, USA

Kuleshov, Valery (Musician)
c/o Staff Member *Musicians Corporate Management*
PO Box 825
Highland, NY 12528-0825, USA

Kulich, Vladimir (Actor)
c/o Jeff Goldberg *Jeff Goldberg Management*
817 Monte Leon Dr
Beverly Hills, CA 90210-2629, USA

Kulikov, Viktor G (Misc)
Myasnitskaya Str 37
Moscow 10100, RUSSIA

Kulka, Konstanty A (Musician)
Ul Jasna 5
Warsaw 00-007, POLAND

Kulkarni, Mamta (Actor, Bollywood)
D Wing 7th Floor 701 RC Complex
Versova Yari Road
Mumbai, MS 400061, INDIA

Kulkarni, Shrinivas R (Astronomer)
Astronomy
Pasadena, CA 91125-0001, USA

Kulpa, Ronald (Athlete, Baseball Player)
1958 Parkland Woods Dr
Maryland Heights, MO 63043-4701, USA

Kumanyika, Shiriki K (Misc)
Nutrition/Dietetics Dept
Chicago, IL 60607, USA

Kumar, Akshay (Actor, Bollywood)
203 A Wing Benzer Lokhandwala Complex Andheri W
Mumbai, MS 400053, India

Kumar, Ashok (Actor, Bollywood)
47 Union Park Chembur
Mumbai, MS 400071, INDIA

Kumar, Dilip (Actor, Bollywood)
34/B Palli Hill Nargis Dutt Road Bandra W
Mumbai, MS 400050, INDIA

Kumar, Kiran (Actor)
Jeevan Kiran S V Road Bandra
Bombay, MS 400 050, INDIA

Kumar, Manoj (Actor, Director, Filmmaker, Producer)
Lakshmi Villa Grount Floor-45 Tagore Road Santacruz (W)
Bombay, MS 400 054, INDIA

Kumar, Mehul (Bollywood, Director, Filmmaker, Producer)
302 Atlantic J P Road Seven Bangalows Andheri
Bombay, MS 400 061, INDIA

Kumar, Mohan (Bollywood, Director, Filmmaker)
Prem Sagar 'B' Linking Road Khar
Bombay, MS 400 052, INDIA

Kumar, Rajendra (Actor, Bollywood, Director, Filmmaker, Producer)
Dimple 7 Pali Hill Bandra
Bombay, MS 400 050, INDIA

Kumar, Sanjay (Business Person)
1 CA Plz
Islandia, NY 11749-5305, USA

Kumar, Sarath (Actor)
16 Rajamannaar Saalai Thyagaraya Nagar
Chennai, TN 600 017, INDIA

Kumaratunga, Chandrika B (President)
Republic Square Sri Jayewardenepura Kotte
SRI LANKA

Kumbernuss, Astrid (Athlete, Track Athlete)
Schwedenstr 25
Neubrandenburg 17033, GERMANY

Kumble, Roger (Actor, Director, Writer)
c/o David Kramer *United Talent Agency (UTA)*
9560 Wilshire Blvd Fl 5
Beverly Hills, CA 90212-2400, USA

Kume, Mike (Athlete, Baseball Player)
6810 Woodard Rd
Andover, OH 44003-9638, USA

Kumerow, Eric (Athlete, Football Player)
736 Fairview Ln
Bartlett, IL 60103-4566, USA

Kumin, Maxine W (Writer)
Joppa Road
Warner, NH 3278, USA

Kummer, Glenn F (Business Person)
3125 Myers St
Riverside, CA 92503-5527, USA

Kump, Ernest J (Architect)
Villa Boecklin Jupiterstr 15
Zurich 8032, SWITZERLAND

Kumpel, Mark (Athlete, Hockey Player)
22 Oceanwood Dr
Scarborough, ME 04074-8755, USA

Kundera, Milan (Writer)
5 Rue Sebastien-Bottin
Paris 75007, FRANCE

Kundla, John A (Athlete, Basketball Player, Coach)
909 Main St NE Apt 208
Minneapolis, MN 55413-1854, USA

Kunerth, Mark J (Producer, Writer)
c/o Ted Chervin *International Creative Management (ICM-LA)*
10250 Constellation Blvd Fl 7
Los Angeles, CA 90067-6207, USA

Kunes, Ellen (Editor)
224 W 57th St # 900
New York, NY 10019-3212, USA

Kung, Hans (Misc)
Waldhauserstr 23
Tubingen 72076, GERMANY

Kung, Patrick C (Misc)
119 4th Ave
Needham, MA 02494-2725, USA

Kunis, Mila (Actor)
c/o Susan Curtis *Curtis Talent Management*
9607 Arby Dr
Beverly Hills, CA 90210-1202, USA

Kunitz, Matt (Producer)
c/o Staff Member *WmE2 (WMA-LA)*
1 William Morris Pl
Beverly Hills, CA 90212-4261, USA

Kunkel, Jeff (Athlete, Baseball Player)
4921 County Road 605
Burleson, TX 76028-1155, USA

Kunkel, Louis M (Misc)
300 Longwood Ave
Boston, MA 02115-5724, USA

Kunkel-Huff, Anna (Baseball Player)
9220 E Fairway Blvd Apt C136
Sun Lakes, AZ 85248-6579, USA

Kunnert, Kevin (Athlete, Basketball Player)
8286 SW Wilderland Ct
Portland, OR 97224-7646, USA

Kunstmann, Doris
Alexander Lamonstrasse 9
Munich, GERMANY D-81679

Kuntar, Les (Athlete, Hockey Player)
9721 SW 89th Loop
Ocala, FL 34481-5577, USA

Kuntz, Murray (Athlete, Hockey Player)
4571 Sugar Maple Dr
Gloucester, ON K1V 1R7, Canada

Kuntz, Rusty (Athlete, Baseball Player)
10102 W 152nd Ter
Overland Park, KS 66221-2709, USA

Kunz, George J (Athlete, Football Player)
8215 Bermuda Rd
Las Vegas, NV 89123-2213, USA

Kunz, Lee (Athlete, Football Player)
4096 Youngfield St
Wheat Ridge, CO 80033-3862, USA

Kunze, Terry (Athlete, Basketball Player)
6931 Halifax Ave N
Minneapolis, MN 55429-1373, USA

Kunzel, Erich Jr (Conductor)
825 S Lazelle St
Columbus, OH 43206-2021, USA

Kunzu, Hari (Writer)
375 Hudson St
New York, NY 10014-3658, USA

Kuok Hock Nien, Robert (Business Person)
No.1 Kim Seng Promenade #07-01 Great World City
237994, Singapore

Kupchak, Mitch (Athlete, Basketball Player)
361 Fordyce Rd
Los Angeles, CA 90049-2009, USA

Kupcinet, Kari (Actor)
1660 Mill Trl
Highland Park, IL 60035-1502, USA

Kupec, C J (Athlete, Basketball Player)
6448 River Run
Columbia, MD 21044-6022, USA

Kupfer, Carl (Misc)
9000 Rockville Pike
Bethesda, MD 20892-0001, USA

Kupfer, Harry (Director)
5557 Behrenstr
New York, NY 10117-0001, GERMANY

Kupferberg, Sabine (Ballerina)
Scheldoldoekshaven 60
Gravenhage, EN 2511, NETHERLANDS

Kuplowsky, Winn (Stylist)
c/o Staff Member *Judy Inc*
1 Yorkville Ave
Toronto ON M4W 1L1, Canada

Kupp, Craig (Athlete, Football Player)
609 S 31st Ave
Yakima, WA 98902-4009, USA

Kupp, Jacob (Jake) (Athlete, Football Player)
4801 Snowmountain Rd
Yakima, WA 98908-2848, USA

Kupper, William P Jr (Publisher)
1221 Avenue of the Americas
New York, NY 10020-1001, USA

Kupperman, Joel (Actor)
115 E 9th St Apt 15E
New York, NY 10003-5421, USA

Kuranari, Tadashi (Government Official)
2-18-12 Daita Setangayaku
Tokyo 155, JAPAN

Kurant, Willy (Cinematographer)
800 S Robertson Blvd Ste 6
Los Angeles, CA 90035-1635, USA

Kuras, Ellen M (Cinematographer)
54 Summit St
Nyack, NY 10960-3726, USA

Kurasov, Georgy (Artist)
4/2 Inzenernaja St
Saint Petersburg 191011, RUSSIA

Kureishi, Hanif (Writer)
81 Comeragh Road
London W14 9HS, UNITED KINGDOM (UK)

Kurek, Ralph (Athlete, Football Player)
2913 N Burling St Apt 3
Chicago, IL 60657-6553, USA

Kurgan, Barbara (Stylist)
c/o Staff Member *Tricia Joyce Inc*
79 Chambers St Fl 2
New York, NY 10007-1824, USA

Kurisko, Jamie (Athlete, Football Player)
337 Hill Ave
Montgomery, NY 12549-2052, USA

Kuriyama, Chiaki (Actor)
c/o Staff Member *Crystal Sky Pictures*
10203 Santa Monica Blvd Ste 500
Los Angeles, CA 90067-6416, USA

Kurkova, Karolina (Model)
c/o Paul Bloch *Rogers & Cowan PR (LA)*
Pacific Design Center 8687 Melrose Ave, 7th Floor
West Hollywood, CA 90069, USA

Kurland, Robert A (Bob) (Athlete, Basketball Player)
1024 Kings Crown Dr
Sanibel, FL 33957-4910, USA

Kurlander, Tom
1801 Avenue of the Stars Ste 902
Los Angeles, CA 90067-5981

Kurnick, Howie (Athlete, Football Player)
2339 Bretton Dr
Cincinnati, OH 45244-3729, USA

Kurokawa, Kisho (Architect)
Aoyama Building #11F 1-2-3 Kita Aoyama
Minatoku, Tokyo, JAPAN

Kurosaki, Ryan (Athlete, Baseball Player)
2024 Fairmont Dr
Benton, AR 72015-3163, USA

Kurrasch, David B (Business Person)
31482 Paseo Campeon
San Juan Capo, CA 92675-1828, USA

Kurrat, Kiaus-Dieter (Athlete, Track Athlete)
Am Hochwald 30 28460
Klemmachow 1453, GERMANY

Kurri, Jarri (Athlete, Hockey Player)
c/o Staff Member *Hockey Hall of Fame*
B C E Place 30 Yonge St
Toronto, ON M5E 1X8, Canada

Kurt, Gary (Athlete, Hockey Player)
P.O. Box 3070
Cambridge, ON N3H 5M1, Canada

Kurtag, Gyorgy (Composer)
Lihego V3
Veroce 2621, HUNGARY

Kurtenbach, Orland J (Athlete, Hockey Player)
14066 29A Ave
Surrey, BC V4P 2J8, Canada

Kurth, Wallace (Wally) (Actor, Musician)
2143 N Valley Dr
Manhattan Beach, CA 90266-2247, USA

Kurtis, Bill (Television Host)
c/o Staff Member *Kurtis Productions*
400 W Erie St Ste 500
Chicago, IL 60654-5741, USA

Kurtis, Dalene (Actor)
c/o Juliette Harris *It Girl Public Relations*
5301 Beethoven St Ste 220
Los Angeles, CA 90066-7052, USA

Kurtz, Hal (Athlete, Baseball Player)
511 Flat Iron Square Rd
Church Hill, MD 21623-1269, USA

Kurtz, Swoosie (Actor)
c/o Konrad Leh *Creative Talent Group*
1900 Avenue of the Stars Ste 2475
Los Angeles, CA 90067-4512, USA

Kurtzberg, Joanne (Physicist)
Medical Ctr
Durham, NC 27708-0001, USA

Kurtzman, Alex (Producer)
c/o BeBe Lerner *ID Public Relations (ID-LA)*
7080 Hollywood Blvd Fl 8
Los Angeles, CA 90028-6906, USA

Kurtzman, Katy (Actor, Director)
c/o Staff Member *Lynn Production & Mgmt*
20411 Chapter Dr
Woodland Hills, CA 91364-5612, USA

Kurvers, Tom (Athlete, Hockey Player)
11328 Stratton Ave
Eden Prairie, MN 55344-4419, USA

Kurylenko, Olga (Actor)
c/o Joel Lubin *Creative Artists Agency (CAA-LA)*
2000 Avenue of the Stars Ste 100
Los Angeles, CA 90067-4705, USA

Kuryluk, Merve (Athlete, Hockey Player)
63 Alexandra Ave
Yorkton, SK S3N 2J6, Canada

Kurys, Sophie (Baseball Player)
8301 E Fairmount Ave
Scottsdale, AZ 85251-4835, USA

Kurz, Sabina (Stylist)
c/o Staff Member *Bryan Bantry*
900 Broadway Ste 400
New York, NY 10003-1239, USA

Kurzweil, Raymond (Inventor)
411 Waverley Oaks Rd
Waltham, MA 02452-8448, USA

Kusama, Karyn (Director)
9701 Wilshire Blvd Ste 1000
Beverly Hills, CA 90212-2010, USA

Kusatsu, Clyde (Actor)
10100 Santa Monica Blvd Ste 2500
Los Angeles, CA 90067-4116, USA

Kush, Rod (Athlete, Football Player)
45 Willow Point Dr
Ashland, NE 68003-9408, USA

Kushboo (Actor, Bollywood)
2 0/1 Arch Bshap Mithyas Ave Boat Club Rd
Chennai, TN 600018, INDIA

Kushell, Lisa (Actor)
c/o Staff Member *Abrams Artists Agency (LA)*
9200 W Sunset Blvd PH 11
Los Angeles, CA 90069-3601, USA

Kushner, Dale (Athlete, Hockey Player)
632 River Oak Ct
Salisbury, MD 21801-5366, USA

Kushner, Harold S (Writer)
145 Hartford St
Natick, MA 01760-3125

Kushner, Robert E (Artist)
724 5th Ave
New York, NY 10019-4106, USA

Kushner, Tony (Writer)
c/o Staff Member *Creative Artists Agency (CAA-LA)*
2000 Avenue of the Stars Ste 100
Los Angeles, CA 90067-4705, USA

Kuske, Kevin (Athlete)
An der Schlessstatte 4
Berchtesgaden 83471, GERMANY

Kusnitz, Jared (Actor)
c/o TJ McMurdo *McMurdo Management & Associates*
1616 N Fuller Ave Apt 313
Los Angeles, CA 90046-3587, USA

Kusnyer, Art (Athlete, Baseball Player)
6598 Taeda Dr
Sarasota, FL 34241-9145, USA

Kusturica, Emir (Actor, Director, Musician, Writer)
Largo VIII Marzo, 9
Parma 43100, ITALY

Kutcher, Ashton (Actor, Producer)
c/o Stephanie Simon *Untitled Entertainment (LA)*
350 S Beverly Dr Ste 200
Beverly Hills, CA 90212 4819, USA

Kutcher, Randy (Athlete, Baseball Player)
3016 Purple Sage Ln
Palmdale, CA 93550-7972, USA

Kuti, Fela (Musician)
PO Box 170429
San Francisco, CA 94117-0429, USA

Kutless (Musician)
c/o Staff Member *WmE2 (WMA-TN)*
1600 Division St Ste 300
Nashville, TN 37203-2755, USA

Kutner, Malcom J (Mal) (Athlete, Football Player)
4121 Mojave Dr
Granbury, TX 76049-5253, USA

Kutner, Rob (Writer)
c/o Staff Member *Kaplan Stahler Agency*
8383 Wilshire Blvd Ste 923
Beverly Hills, CA 90211-2443, USA

Kutsugeras, Kelle (Stylist)
c/o Staff Member *Celestine - CA*
1666 20th St Ste 200B
Santa Monica, CA 90404-3828, USA

Kuttner, Robert (Writer)
c/o Staff Member *Chelsea Green Publishing*
85 N Main St Ste 120
White River Junction, VT 05001-7135, USA

Kuttner, Stephan G (Historian)
2270 Le Conte Ave # 601
Berkeley, CA 94709, USA

Kutty, Padmini (Actor, Bollywood)
33 1st Street Kamdar Nagar
Nungambakkam
Chennai, TN 600034, INDIA

Kutyna, Donald J (General)
4818 Kenyon Ct
Colorado Springs, CO 80917-3615, USA

Kutyna, Marty (Athlete, Baseball Player)
2255 NW 14th St
Delray Beach, FL 33445-2610, USA

Kutz, Mae
140 Buckingham Ct
Goodlettsville, TN 37072-2146

Kutzler, Jerry (Athlete, Baseball Player)
8415 27th Ave
Kenosha, WI 53143-6232, USA

Kuykendall, Fulton (Athlete, Football Player)
1497 Rucker Cir
Woodstock, GA 30188-2133, USA

Kuykendall, John W (Educator)
President's Office
Davidson, NC 28036, USA

Kuzava, Bob (Athlete, Baseball Player)
1118 Vinewood St
Wyandotte, MI 48192-4945, USA

Kuziel, Bob (Athlete, Football Player)
3375 Walnut Dr
Ellicott City, MD 21043-4351, USA

Kuzman, John (Athlete, Football Player)
201 Arbor Vw
Pompton Plains, NJ 07444-1522, USA

Kuznetsoff, Alexel (Musician)
165 W 57th St
New York, NY 10019-2201, USA

Kuzyk, Mimi (Actor)
1180 S Beverly Dr Ste 301
Los Angeles, CA 90035-1154, USA

Kvasha, Oleg (Athlete, Hockey Player)
22 Bluff Rd
Glen Cove, NY 11542-1778, USA

Kvitova, Petra (Athlete, Tennis Player)
c/o Staff Member *Women's Tennis Association (WTA (UK))*
Palliser House Palliser Rd
London W149EB, UK

Kwalick, Thaddeus J (Ted) (Athlete, Football Player)
755 Purdue Ct
Santa Clara, CA 95051-5527, USA

Kwan, Jennie (Actor)
1505 10th St
Santa Monica, CA 90401-2805, USA

Kwan, Michelle (Figure Skater)
c/o Staff Member *Champions on Ice*
3500 W 80th St Ste 200
Minneapolis, MN 55431-1090, USA

Kwan, Nancy (Actor)
252 7th Ave Apt 9P
New York, NY 10001-7340, USA

Kwanten, Ryan (Actor)
c/o Orly Adelson *Orly Adelson Management*
2900 Olympic Blvd
Santa Monica, CA 90404-4127, USA

Kwapis, Ken (Comedian, Director, Producer)
c/o Staff Member *In Cahoots*
4024 Radford Ave Bldg 2EDITORIAL PMB 7
Studio City, CA 91604-2101, USA

Kwasniewski, Aleksander (President)
Ul Wiejska 4/8
Warsaw 00-902, POLAND

Kweli, Talib (Musician)
c/o Steve Levine *International Creative Management (ICM-LA)*
10250 Constellation Blvd Fl 7
Los Angeles, CA 90067-6207, USA

Kweli, Talieb (Musician)
c/o Steve Levine *International Creative Management (ICM-LA)*
10250 Constellation Blvd Fl 7
Los Angeles, CA 90067-6207, USA

Kweller, Ben (Musician)
c/o Staff Member *Paradigm (Monterey)*
404 W Franklin St
Monterey, CA 93940-2303, USA

Kwiatkowski, Joel (Athlete, Hockey Player)
2020 Tall Pines Dr SE
Grand Rapids, MI 49546-7923, USA

Kwoh, Yik San (Engineer)
PO Box 1428
Long Beach, CA 90801-1428, USA

Kwolek, Stephanie L (Inventor)
312 Spalding Rd
Wilmington, DE 19803-2422, USA

Kwon, Boa (Musician)
c/o Staff Member *Creative Artists Agency (CAA-LA)*
2000 Avenue of the Stars Ste 100
Los Angeles, CA 90067-4705, USA

Kwouk, Burt (Actor)
31 Percey St
London W1T 2DD, UNITED KINGDOM (UK)

Kyle, Aaron (Athlete, Football Player)
8544 Townley Rd Apt 2M
Huntersville, NC 28078-1868, USA

Kyle, David L (Business Person)
PO Box 871
Tulsa, OK 74102-0871, USA

Kyles, Cedric (The Entertainer) (Actor, Comedian, Producer, Writer)
c/o Eric Rhone *Visions Management Group*
11469 Olive Blvd # 230
Saint Louis, MO 63141-7108, USA

Kyles, Whitney (Stylist)
c/o Staff Member *Dawn to Dusk Image Agency*
8306 Wilshire Blvd # 412
Beverly Hills, CA 90211-2382, USA

Kylian, Jiri (Dancer)
Scheldeldoekshaven 60
Gravenhage, EN 2511, NETHERLANDS

Kyo, Machiko (Actor)
6-35 JinguMae Shibuyaku
Tokyo, JAPAN

Kypreos, Nick (Athlete, Hockey Player)
c/o Staff Member *Rogers Sportsnet (Toronto)*
9 Channel Nine Crt
Toronto, ON M1S 4B5, Canada

Kysar, Jeff (Athlete, Football Player)
570 June St
Rialto, CA 92376-5729, USA

Kyte, Jim (Athlete, Hockey Player)
226 Sherwood Dr
Ottawa, ON K1Y 3V8, Canada

L

L. Berman, Howard (Congressman, Politician)
2221 Rayburn Hob
Washington, DC 20515-0528, USA

L. Boswell, Leonard (Congressman, Politician)
1026 Longworth Hob
Washington, DC 20515-4319, USA

L. Braley, Bruce (Congressman, Politician)
1727 Longworth Hob
Washington, DC 20515-1007, USA

L. Delauro, Rosa (Congressman, Politician)
2413 Rayburn Hob
Washington, DC 20515-0512, USA

L. Ellmers, Renee (Congressman, Politician)
1533 Longworth Hob
Washington, DC 20515-3302

L. Engel, Eliot (Congressman, Politician)
2161 Rayburn Hob
Washington, DC 20515-2206, USA

L. Fudge, Marcia (Congressman, Politician)
1019 Longworth Hob
Washington, DC 20515-3012, USA

L. Hanna, Richard (Congressman, Politician)
319 Cajimon Hob
Washington, DC 20515-0001, USA

L. Hastings, Alcee (Congressman, Politician)
2353 Rayburn Hob
Washington, DC 20515-3811, USA

L. Jackson Jr., Jesse (Congressman, Politician)
2419 Rayburn Hob
Washington, DC 20515-1302, USA

L. Mica, John (Congressman, Politician)
2187 Rayburn Hob
Washington, DC 20515-4609, USA

L. Noem, Kristi (Congressman, Politician)
226 Cannon Hob
Washington, DC 20515-3818, USA

L. Owens, William (Congressman, Politician)
431 Cannon Hob
Washington, DC 20515-1603, USA

La Coste??a, Banda (Music Group)
c/o Staff Member *BMG*
1540 Broadway
New York, NY 10036-4039, USA

La Fong, Michelle
3855 Shore Pkwy Apt 1D
Brooklyn, NY 11235-1053

La Frenais, Ian (Director, Producer, Writer)
c/o Bruce Kaufman *International Creative Management (ICM-LA)*
10250 Constellation Blvd Fl 7
Los Angeles, CA 90067-6207, USA

La Lanne, Jack
430 Quintana Rd # 151
Morro Bay, CA 93442-1937

La Lanne, Jack (Athlete)
430 Quintana Rd
Morro Bay, CA 93442-1937, USA

La Ley (Music Group)
c/o Staff Member *United Talent Agency (UTA)*
9560 Wilshire Blvd Fl 5
Beverly Hills, CA 90212-2400, USA

La Mura, Mark
6399 Wilshire Blvd Ste 414
Los Angeles, CA 90048-5716

La Oreja de Van Gogh (Music Group)
c/o Staff Member *Sony Music Miami*
605 Lincoln Rd Ste 700
Miami Beach, FL 33139-2901, USA

La Placa, Alison (Actor)
c/o Staff Member *Marshak/Zachary Company, The*
8840 Wilshire Blvd Fl 1
Beverly Hills, CA 90211-2606, USA

La Rosa, Linda (Stylist)
c/o Staff Member *Ford Models (Chicago)*
311 W Superior St
Chicago, IL 60654-3548, USA

La Roux (Musician)
c/o Marty Diamond *Paradigm (NY)*
360 Park Ave S Fl 16
New York, NY 10010-1708, USA

La Rue, Danny
57 Gr Cumberland Pl
London, ENGLAND W1M 7LJ

La Rue, Eva (Actor, Television Host)
c/o Marv Dauer *Marv Dauer Management*
11661 San Vicente Blvd Ste 104
Los Angeles, CA 90049-5150, USA

La Rue, Florence
4300 Louise Ave
Encino, CA 91316-3916

La Scala, Nancy (Actor)
c/o Victor (Viktor) Kruglov *Victor Kruglov Talent Management*
7461 Beverly Blvd Ste 403
Los Angeles, CA 90036-2774, USA

Laakso, Eric (Athlete, Football Player)
300 N Palm Aire Dr Apt 707
Pompano Beach, FL 30690, USA

Laaksonen, Antti (Athlete, Hockey Player)
9225 Red Oak Dr
Victoria, MN 55386-4515, USA

Laatasi, Kamuta (Prime Minister)
Vaiaku
Funafuti, TUVALU

Laaveg, Paul (Athlete, Football Player)
PO Box 2134
Leesburg, VA 20177-7529, USA

Labaff, Ernie (Misc)
3362 Hollenberg Dr
Bridgeton, MO 63044-2432, USA

Labandeira, Josh (Athlete, Baseball Player)
2166 W Cricklewood Ct
Porterville, CA 93257-6270, USA

L'Abbe, Moe (Athlete, Hockey Player)
63 Green Acres
Morin-Heights, QC J0R 1H0, Canada

LaBeef, Sleepy (Musician)
14469 E Highway 264
Lowell, AR 72745-9212, USA

LaBelle, Patti (Musician)
c/o Patti Webster *W&W PR*
476 Union Ave Ste 2
Middlesex, NJ 08846-1968, USA

Labelle, Rob (Actor)
c/o Staff Member *Elizabeth Hodgson Management Group*
1688 Cypress St Suite 405
Vancouver, BC V6J 5J1, Canada

LaBeouf, Shia (Actor)
c/o John Crosby *Crosby/Spilo Management*
1310 N Spaulding Ave
Los Angeles, CA 90046-4010, USA

Labeque, Katia (Musician)
165 W 57th St
New York, NY 10019-2201, USA

Labeque, Marielle (Musician)
165 W 57th St
New York, NY 10019-2201, USA

Laber, Honey Jeanne (Stylist)
235 W 102nd St Apt 10D
New York, NY 10025-8429, USA

Labeyrie, Antoine (Astronomer)
Saint-Michael Observatolre
FRANCE

Labine, Tyler (Actor)
c/o Jason Heyman *Creative Artists Agency (CAA-LA)*
2000 Avenue of the Stars Ste 100
Los Angeles, CA 90067-4705, USA

Labiosa, David (Actor)
c/o Daryl Kane *Guinan Management*
4942 Vineland Ave Ste 111
North Hollywood, CA 91601-5641, USA

Labonte, Bobby (Race Car Driver)
PO Box 358
Trinity, NC 27370-0358, USA

Labonte, Terry (Race Car Driver)
1100 Clodfelter Rd
Winston Salem, NC 27107-8806, USA

Laborde, Alden J (Business Person)
63 Oriole St
New Orleans, LA 70124-4517, USA

Labossiere, Gord (Athlete, Hockey Player)
114 RUE DE FAUBOURG RR 5 RPO
Saint-Ferreol-Les-Neiges, QC G0A 3R0, Canada

Labounty, Matt (Athlete, Football Player)
360 W 17th Ave
Eugene, OR 97401-3859, USA

Labovitch, Max (Athlete, Hockey Player)
22 Ashbury Bay
Winnipeg, MB R2V 2T4, Canada

Laboy, Travis (Athlete, Football Player)
517 Brennan Ln
Franklin, TN 37067-6237, USA

Labraaten, Dan (Athlete, Hockey Player)
Byrviken 303
Leksand S-79392, Sweden

Labrador, Honey (Actor, Television Host)
c/o Staff Member *Last Bastion Entertainment*
5226 Parkglen Ave
Los Angeles, CA 90043-1030, USA

Labre, Yvon (Athlete, Hockey Player)
7812 Tilmont Ave
Parkville, MD 21234-5539, USA

LaBute, Neil (Director, Writer)
c/o Brad Gross *Brad Gross Agency, The*
161 S Arden Blvd
Los Angeles, CA 90004-3716, USA

Labyorteaux, Matthew (Actor)
10808 Hartsook St
N Hollywood, CA 91601-3914, USA

Labyorteaux, Patrick (Actor)
c/o Kim Dorr *Defining Artists Agency*
10 Universal City Plz Ste 2000
Universal City, CA 91608-1074, USA

Lacefield, Reggie (Athlete, Basketball Player)
674 Old School House Rd
Middletown, DE 19709-9690, USA

Lacey, Bob (Athlete, Baseball Player)
1717 20th St Nw Apt 308
Washington, DC 20009-1114, USA

Lacey, Chonn (Athlete, Football Player)
1314 W Ontario St
Philadelphia, PA 19140-5220, USA

Lacey, Deborah (Actor)
1801 Ave of Stars Ste 1250
Los Angeles, CA 90067-5817, USA

Lacey, Jeff (Boxer)
33 Divan Way
Wayne, NJ 07470-5201, USA

Lach, Elmer J (Athlete, Hockey Player)
89 Bayview Ave
Pointe Claire, QC M9S 5C4, Canada

Lachance, Michael (Mike) (Race Car Driver)
183 Sweetmans Ln
Englishtown, NJ 7726, USA

Lachance, Scott (Athlete, Hockey Player)
15 Meadow View Ln
Andover, MA 01810-4759, USA

LaChapelle, David (Artist, Photographer)
601 W 26th St Rm 1420
New York, NY 10001-1136, USA

Lachapelle, Sean (Athlete, Football Player)
9860 Izilda Ct
Sacramento, CA 95829-8167, USA

LaChappelle, Sean P (Athlete, Football Player)
9860 Izilda Ct
Sacramento, CA 95829-8167, USA

Lachemann, Marcel E (Athlete, Baseball Player, Coach)
529 Fieldview Pl
Arroyo Grande, CA 93420-3510, USA

Lachemann, Rene G (Athlete, Baseball Player, Coach)
7500 E Boulders Pkwy Unit 66
Scottsdale, AZ 85266-1212, USA

Lacher, Blaine (Athlete, Hockey Player)
55 Sierra Pl SW
Medicine Hat, AB T1B 4X7, Canada

Lachey, Drew (Musician, Television Host)
c/o Staff Member *The Artists Group*
2049 Century Park E # 4060
Los Angeles, CA 90067-3101, USA

Lachey, James M (Jim) (Athlete, Football Player)
1445 Roxbury Rd Apt G
Columbus, OH 43212-3211, USA

Lachey, Nick (Musician)
c/o Colton Gramm *Brillstein Entertainment Partners*
9150 Wilshire Blvd Ste 350
Beverly Hills, CA 90212-3453, USA

Lachhiman, Gurung (War Hero)
Village Dahakhani Village Development Conmelle
Ward 4, Chitwan, NEPAL

Lachowicz, Al (Athlete, Baseball Player)
1000 Sunset Bay Ct
Granbury, TX 76048-1239, USA

Lachter, Sylvia (Stylist)
136 W 24th St
New York, NY 10011-1908, USA

Lacina, Corbin (Athlete, Football Player)
40 Sunny Side Ln
Sunfish Lake, MN 55118-4718, USA

Lackey, Brad (Race Car Driver)
35 Monument Plz
Pleasant Hill, CA 94523, USA

Lackey, John (Athlete, Baseball Player)
10 Shore Walk
Newport Coast, CA 92657-2158, USA

Laclavere, Georges (Physicist)
53 Ave de Breteuil
Paris 75007, FRANCE

Laclotte, Michel R (Director)
10 Bis Rue du Pre-aux-Clerc
Paris 75007, FRANCE

Lacock, Pete (Athlete, Baseball Player)
10019 Mackey Cir
Overland Park, KS 66212-3461, USA

Lacombe, Henri (Oceanographer)
20 Bis Ave de Lattre de Tassigny
Bourg-la-Reine 92340, FRANCE

Lacorte, Frank (Athlete, Baseball Player)
1667 El Dorado Dr
Gilroy, CA 95020-3754, USA

Lacoss, Mike (Athlete, Baseball Player)
PO Box 44033
Lemon Cove, CA 93244-0033, USA

Lacoste, Catherine (Golfer)
Calle B6 #4 El Soto de la Moraleja
Alcobendas
Madrid, SPAIN

Lacroix, Andre J (Athlete, Hockey Player)
6770 Oakwood Dr
Oakland, CA 94611-1152, USA

LaCroix, Christian
73 Rue Du Faubourg-St -Honore
Paris, FRANCE F-75008

Lacroix, Christian M M (Designer, Fashion Designer)
73 Rue du Faubourg Saint Honore
Paris 75008, FRANCE

Lacrosse, Dave (Athlete, Football Player)
1712 Harmon Rd
Conshohocken, PA 19428-1205, USA

Lacy, Alan (Business Person)
3333 Beverly Blvd
Hoffman Estates, IL 60179-0001, USA

Lacy, Edgar (Athlete, Basketball Player)
215 6th St Apt D
West Sacramento, CA 95605-2767, USA

Lacy, Kerry (Athlete, Baseball Player)
124 County Road 713
Higdon, AL 35979-6123, USA

Lacy, Lee (Athlete, Baseball Player)
6310 Neveda Ave Apt E420
Woodland Hills, CA 91367, USA

Lacy Clay Jr., William (Congressman, Politician)
2418 Rayburn Hob
Washington, DC 20515-1702, USA

Ladd, Carol (Stylist)
2867 SW Montgomery Dr
Portland, OR 97201-1634, USA

Ladd, Cheryl (Actor)
PO Box 1329
Santa Ynez, CA 93460-1329, USA

Ladd, David (Actor)
9212 Hazen Dr
Beverly Hills, CA 90210-1827, USA

Ladd, Diane (Actor)
3860 Grand Ave
Ojai, CA 93023-8350, USA

Ladd, Ernie (Athlete, Football Player)
106 Jackson St
Franklin, LA 70538-5431, USA

Ladd, Jim (Radio Personality, Writer)
3321 S La Cienega Blvd
Los Angeles, CA 90016-3114, USA

Ladd, Jordan (Actor)
c/o Staff Member *Kritzer Levine Wilkins Entertainment*
11872 La Grange Ave Fl 1
Los Angeles, CA 90025-5283, USA

Ladd, Margaret (Actor)
c/o Staff Member *Abrams Artists Agency (LA)*
9200 W Sunset Blvd PH 11
Los Angeles, CA 90069-3601, USA

Ladd, Pete (Athlete, Baseball Player)
239 Town Farm Rd
New Gloucester, ME 04260-4438, USA

Ladd Jr, Alan
c/o Staff Member *Ladd Company, The*
9255 W Sunset Blvd Ste 620
West Hollywood, CA 90069 3303, USA

Laden, Nina B
6750 26th Ave NW
Seattle, WA 98117-5828, USA

Laderman, Exra (Composer)
Music School
New Haven, CT 6520, USA

Ladewig, Marion (Bowler)
7200 Harrison Ave # 7171
Rockford, IL 61112-1017, USA

Ladin, Eric (Actor)
c/o Staff Member *Main Title Entertainment*
2225 Wilshire Blvd Suite 500
Los Angeles, CA 90036, USA

Lady Antebellum (Music Group)
c/o Daniel Miller *Borman Entertainment (TN)*
4322 Harding Pike Ste 429
Nashville, TN 37205-2661, USA

Ladygo, Pete (Athlete, Football Player)
708 Summit Ave Apt 1
Hagerstown, MD 21740-6485, USA

Ladysmith Black Mambazo (Musician)
326 Ridge Rd Unit D
Cedar Grove, NJ 07009-1636, USA

Laettner, Christian (Athlete, Basketball Player)
1225 Church Rd
Angola, NY 14006-8831

LaFave, Debra
2220 Nichols Rd
Lithia, FL 33547-2230, USA

Laffer, Arthur (Doctor)
5375 Exec Sq # 330
La Jolla, CA 92037, USA

Laffer, Arthur B (Economist)
24255 Pacific Coast Hwy
Malibu, CA 90263-0001, USA

Lafferty, James (Actor)
c/o Eric Nelson *Paceline Entertainment*
6840 Firmament Ave
Van Nuys, CA 91406-5103, USA

Laffite, Jacques
Technopole de la Nievre
Magny Cours, FRANCE F-58470

Laffitte, Havana (Stylist)
c/o Staff Member *Art Department*
48 Greene St Fl 4
New York, NY 10013-2663, USA

Lafforgue, Laurent (Mathematician)
Mathematics Dept
Bures-sur-Yvette 91440, FRANCE

LaFleur, Art (Actor)
c/o Joel King *Pakula/King & Associates*
9229 W Sunset Blvd Ste 315
Los Angeles, CA 90069-3403, USA

Lafleur, David (Athlete, Football Player)
3900 Thompson Rd
Sulphur, LA 70665-8901, USA

Lafleur, Greg (Athlete, Football Player)
2911 Rene Beauregard Ave
Baton Rouge, LA 70820-5712, USA

Lafleur, Guy D (Athlete, Hockey Player)
14 Place Du Molin
L'lle-Bizard, QC H9E 1N2, Canada

Lafley, Alan G (Business Person)
1 Procter and Gamble Plz
Cincinnati, OH 45202-3315, USA

Lafontaine, Oskar (Government Official)
Postfach 101833
Saarbrucken 66018, GERMANY

LaFontaine, Patrick (Pat) (Athlete, Hockey Player)
3 Beach Dr
Lloyd Harbor, NY 11743-9766, USA

Laforest, Pete (Athlete, Baseball Player)
2523 E Chester Dr
Chandler, AZ 85286-1366, USA

LaFosse, Robert (Choreographer)
Lincoln Center Plaza
New York, NY 10023, USA

Lafrancois, Roger (Athlete, Baseball Player)
64 Aspinook St
Jewett City, CT 06351-1802, USA

LaFrentz, Raef (Athlete, Basketball Player)
PO Box 220
Adel, IA 50003-0220, USA

Lafton, James D (Athlete, Football Player)
15487 Mesquite Tree Trl
Poway, CA 92064-2286, USA

Laga, Mike (Athlete, Baseball Player)
148 Maple Ridge Rd
Florence, MA 01062-9749, USA

Laga'aia, Jay (Actor)
PO Box 446
Auckland, NEW ZEALAND

Lagarde, Tom (Athlete, Basketball Player)
3809 E Greensboro Chapel Hill Rd
Snow Camp, NC 27349-9841, USA

Lagasse, Emeril (Chef, Television Host)
839 Saint Charles Ave
New Orleans, LA 70130-3739, USA

Lagattuta, Bill (Correspondent)
7800 Beverly Blvd
Los Angeles, CA 90036-2112, USA

Lagedrost, Kelly (Athlete, Golfer)
10011 Kimbrough Dr
Brooksville, FL 34601-5260, USA

Lageman, Jeff (Athlete, Football Player)
2907 Forest Cir
Jacksonville, FL 32257-5617, USA

Lagerberg, Bengt (Musician)
Gotabergs Gatan 2
Gothenburg 400 14, SWEDEN

Lagerfeld, Karl (Designer, Fashion Designer)
29-31 Rue Cambon
Paris 75001, France

Lagerfelt, Caroline (Actor)
8730 W Sunset Blvd Ste 480
Los Angeles, CA 90069-2277, USA

Laghi, Pio Cardinal (Religious Leader)
Piazza Pio XII 3
Rome 193, ITALY

Lago, David (Actor)
c/o Mark Robert *Mark Robert Management*
2208 Patricia Ave
Los Angeles, CA 90064-2318, USA

Lagod, Chet (Athlete, Football Player)
1053 Restoration Dr
Chattanooga, TN 37421-8340, USA

Lagoo, Shreeram (Actor, Bollywood)
3 Gold Mist 36 Carter Road Bandra
Bombay, MS 400 050, INDIA

Lagos, Richard (President)
Palacio de la Monedo
Santiago, CHILE

Lagrand, Morris (Athlete, Football Player)
4419 Ellenwood Ave
Saint Louis, MO 63116-1521, USA

LaGravenese, Richard (Director, Producer, Writer)
c/o Staff Member *Writers Co-Op*
4000 Warner Blvd Bldg 1
Burbank, CA 91522-0001, USA

Lagrossa, Stephanie (Reality TV Star)
3400 Beacon Ave S
Seattle, WA 98144-6702, USA

Lagrow, Lerrin (Athlete, Baseball Player)
12271 E Turquoise Ave
Scottsdale, AZ 85259-5105, USA

Laguardia, Ernesto (Actor)
c/o Gabriel Blanco *Gabriel Blanco Iglesias (Mexico)*
Rio Balsas 35-32 Colonia Cuauhtemoc
DF 6500, Mexico

Laguna, Frederica de (Misc)
S Bryn Mawr Ave Quadrangle 10
Bryn Mawr, PA 19010-2195, USA

Laguna, Ismael (Boxer)
Entrega General
PANAMA

LaHaye, Tim (Writer)
PO Box 80
Wheaton, IL 60187-0080, USA

Lahbib, Simone (Actor)
c/o Staff Member *Ken McReddie Ltd*
11 Connaught Pl
London W2 2ET, UNITED KINGDOM

Lahey, Pat (Athlete, Football Player)
13 Old Hunt Rd
Northfield, IL 60093-1074, USA

Lahiri, Jhumpa (Writer)
222 Berkeley St # 700
Boston, MA 02116-3748, USA

Lahood, Mike (Athlete, Football Player)
1416 N Autumn Ln
Peoria, IL 61604-4605, USA

Lahoud, Joe (Athlete, Baseball Player)
90 Tinker Hill Rd
New Preston Marble Dale,
CT 06777-1415, USA

Lahould, Emile (President)
Baabda
Beirut, LEBANON

Lahti, Christine (Actor, Director)
c/o David Seltzer *Management 360*
9111 Wilshire Blvd
Beverly Hills, CA 90210-5508, USA

Lahti, Jeff (Athlete, Baseball Player)
4632 Tyler Dr
Hood River, OR 97031-9742, USA

Lai, Francis (Composer)
23 Rue Franklin
Paris 75016, FRANCE

Laidlaw, Scott (Athlete, Football Player)
28 Colonel Winstead Dr
Brentwood, TN 37027-8936, USA

Lail, Leah (Actor)
c/o Staff Member *Diverse Talent Group*
9911 W Pico Blvd Ste 340W
Los Angeles, CA 90035-2712, USA

Laimbeer, Bill (Athlete, Basketball Player)
470 Gray Ct
Marco Island, FL 34145-1939, USA

Laine, Cleo (Musician)
53 Cambridge Mansions
London SW11 4RX, UNITED KINGDOM (UK)

Laine, Dame Cleo
The Old Rectory Wavendon
Milton Keynes, ENGLAND MK17 8LT

Laine, Sarah (Actor)
c/o Eric Black *Anonymous Content (AC-LA)*
3531 Hayden Ave
Culver City, CA 90232, USA

Laingen, L Bruce (Diplomat)
5627 Old Chester Rd
Bethesda, MD 20814-1035, USA

Laird, Bruce (Athlete, Football Player)
1405 Margarette Ave
Towson, MD 21286-1550, USA

Laird, Gerald (Athlete, Baseball Player)
8891 Mac Alpine Rd
Garden Grove, CA 92841-2321, USA

Laird, Melvin R (Business Person, Secretary)
1730 Rhode Island Ave NW Ste 406
Washington, DC 20036-3134, USA

Laird, Peter (Cartoonist, Writer)
PO Box 486
Northampton, MA 01061-0486, USA

Laird, Ron
4706 Diane Dr
Ashtabula, OH 44004-4636

Laird, Ronald (Ron) (Athlete, Track Athlete)
4706 Diane Dr
Ashtabula, OH 44004-4636, USA

Laithwaite, Eric R (Engineer)
Electrical Engineering Dept
London SW7 2BT, UNITED KINGDOM (UK)

Laitman, Jeffrey (Misc)
Anatomy Dept 1 Lavy Place
New York, NY 10029, USA

LaJoie, Jon (Comedian)
c/o Trevor Engelson *Underground Management*
447 S Highland Ave
Los Angeles, CA 90036-3530, USA

LaJoie, Randy (Race Car Driver)
195 Jones Rd
Spartanburg, SC 29307-5448, USA

Lajole, Bill (Baseball Player)
456 Yacht Harbor Dr
Osprey, FL 34229-9744, USA

Lake, Carnell A (Athlete, Football Player)
PO Box 55048
Irvine, CA 92619-5048, USA

Lake, Don (Actor, Writer)
c/o Gayle Divine *Divine Management*
3822 Latrobe St
Los Angeles, CA 90031-1446

Lake, Greg (Musician)
9 Hillgate St
London W8 7SP, UNITED KINGDOM (UK)

Lake, James A (Biologist)
Molecular Biology Institute
Los Angeles, CA 90024, USA

Lake, Oliver E (Musician)
PO Box 2728
Bala Cynwyd, PA 19004-6728, USA

Lake, Ricki (Actor, Talk Show Host)
c/o Josh Sabarra *Breaking News PR*
9601 Wilshire Blvd Ste 1106
Beverly Hills, CA 90210-5213, USA

Lake, Sanoe (Actor)
c/o Staff Member *Luber Roklin Management*
8530 Wilshire Blvd Ste 550
Beverly Hills, CA 90211-3133, USA

Lake, Steve (Athlete, Baseball Player)
7402 N 177th Ave
Waddell, AZ 85355-9320, USA

Laker, Fredrick A (Business Person)
Princess Tower West Sunrise Box F207
Freeport
Grand Bahamas, BAHAMAS

Laker, Jim (Cricketer)
Oak End 9 Portlinscale Road Putney
London SW15, UNITED KINGDOM (UK)

Laker, Tim (Athlete, Baseball Player)
673 Azure Hills Dr
Simi Valley, CA 93065-5518, USA

Lakes, Gary (Opera Singer)
40 W 57th St
New York, NY 10019-4001, USA

Lakes, Roland (Athlete, Football Player)
2334 20th St
San Pablo, CA 94806-3508, USA

Lakin, Christine (Actor)
c/o Amy Abell *Innovative Artists (LA)*
1505 10th St
Santa Monica, CA 90401-2805, USA

Lakner, Yehoshua (Composer)
Postfach 7851
Luceme 7 6000, SWITZERLAND

Lakoue, Enoch Devant (Prime Minister)
Bangui, CENTRAL AFRICAN REPUBLIC

Lakshmi, Padma (Actor)
c/o Christina Papadopoulos *Baker Winokur Ryder Public Relations BWR (BWR-NY)*
292 Madison Ave Fl 12
New York, NY 10017-6415, USA

Lalaine (Actor)
c/o Beverly Strong *Strong Management*
3532 Hayden Ave
Culver City, CA 90232-2413, USA

Laliberte, Guy (Misc)
8400 2nd Ave
Montreal, QC H1Z 4M6, CANADA

LaLiberte, Nicole (Actor)
c/o Allan Mindel *Framework Entertainment (LA)*
9057 Nemo St Ste C
West Hollywood, CA 90069-5511, USA

Laliberte-Bourque, Andree (Director)
1 Ave Wolfe-Montcalm
Quebec, QC G1R 5H3, CANADA

Lalime, Patrick (Athlete, Hockey Player)
1401 Clark Ave
Saint Louis, MO 63103-2700, USA

Lalitha, Devi (Actor, Bollywood)
23 Karaneeswar Koil Street Saidapet
Chennai, TN 600015, INDIA

Lally, Bob (Athlete, Football Player)
1635 242nd Pl
Harbor City, CA 90710-1758, USA

Lalonde, Donny
2554 Lincoln Blvd # 729
Venice, CA 90291-5082

Lalonde, Larry (Musician)
3470 19th St
San Francisco, CA 94110-1740, USA

Lama, Dalai (Nobel Prize Laureate, Religious Leader)
Thekchen Choeling PO McLeod Ganj
Himachai, Pradesh, INDIA

Lamabe, Jack (Athlete, Baseball Player)
16224 Antietam Ave
Baton Rouge, LA 70817-3148, USA

Lamacchia, Al (Athlete, Baseball Player)
13515 Vista Bonita
San Antonio, TX 78216-2203, USA

Lamar, Dwight (Bo) (Athlete, Basketball Player)
103 Claire St
Lafayette, LA 70507-4803, USA

LaMarr, Phil (Actor, Comedian)
c/o Staff Member *Sanders Armstrong Caserta*
2120 Colorado Ave Ste 120
Santa Monica, CA 90404-3561, USA

Lamas, A J (Actor)
c/o Ryan Daly *Zero Gravity Management*
11578 Canton Dr
Studio City, CA 91604-4160, USA

Lamb, Allan J (Cricketer)
4 Saint Giles St #400
Northampton NN1 1JB, UNITED KINGDOM (UK)

Lamb, Brad (Athlete, Football Player)
6460 Chase Dr
Mentor, OH 44060-3606, USA

Lamb, David (Baseball Player)
821 Jensen St
Livermore, CA 94550-3630, USA

Lamb, John (Athlete, Baseball Player)
PO Box 2
Sharon, CT 06069-0002, USA

Lamb, Mike (Athlete, Baseball Player)
17 Meadow Wood Dr
Trabuco Canyon, CA 92679-4737, USA

Lamb, Ray (Athlete, Baseball Player)
3 Corte Tallista
San Clemente, CA 92673-6863, USA

Lamb, Wally (Writer)
c/o Staff Member *HarperCollins Publishers*
10 E 53rd St C/O Author Mail Floor 7
New York, NY 10022, USA

Lamb Jr, Willis E (Nobel Prize Laureate)
315 Red Rock Dr
Sedona, AZ 86351-9534, USA

Lamb Of God (Music Group, Musician)
c/o Larry Mazer *Entertainment Services Unlimited*
Main Street Plaza 1000 #303
Vorhees, NJ 8043, USA

Lamberg, Adam (Actor)
c/o Stephanie Davis *3 Arts Entertainment Inc*
9460 Wilshire Blvd Fl 7
Beverly Hills, CA 90212-2713, USA

Lambert, Adam (Musician)
c/o Staff Member *19 Entertainment - LA*
8560 W Sunset Blvd Ste 9
West Hollywood, CA 90069-2339, USA

Lambert, Christophe (Actor)
9 Ave Trempley C/Lui
Geneva 1209, SWITZERLAND

Lambert, Christopher (Actor, Producer, Writer)
c/o Gerry Harrington *Brillstein Entertainment Partners*
9150 Wilshire Blvd Ste 350
Beverly Hills, CA 90212-3453, USA

Lambert, Dion (Athlete, Football Player)
11157 Sunburst St
Lake View Terrace, CA 91342-6628, USA

Lambert, Frank (Athlete, Football Player)
9009 Lyndon Lakes Pl
Louisville, KY 40242-4538, USA

Lambert, Jerry
PO Box 25371
Charlotte, NC 28229-5371

Lambert, John (Athlete, Basketball Player)
884 Dolphin Dr
Danville, CA 94526-1826, USA

Lambert, John H (Jack) (Athlete, Football Player)
318 Gaiser Rd
Worthington, PA 16262-4810, USA

Lambert, L W
Rt. #1
Olin, NC 28860, USA

Lambert, Mary M (Director)
8942 Wilshire Blvd # 219
Beverly Hills, CA 90211-1908, USA

Lambert, Miranda (Musician)
c/o Simon Renshaw *Strategics Artist Management*
1100 Glendon Ave Ste 1000
Los Angeles, CA 90024-3514, USA

Lambert, Phyllis (Architect)
1920 Rue Baile
Montreal, QC H3H 2S6, CANADA

Lambert, Sheila (Basketball Player)
100 Hive Dr
Charlotte, NC 28217-4524, USA

Lamberti, Pasquale (Athlete, Football Player)
8 Wellington Ave
Everett, MA 02149-1818, USA

Lambiel, Stephane (Figure Skater)
c/o Staff Member *Art on Ice Production*
Siewerdtstrasse 95
Zurich CH-8050, SWITZERLAND

Lamborn, Doug (Congressman, Politician)
437 Cannon Hob
Washington, DC 20515-1902, USA

Lambrecht, Dietrich R (Engineer)
11 Rathenaustr
Dayton, OH 45470-0001, GERMANY

Lambro, Phillip (Composer)
1888 Century Park E # 10
Los Angeles, CA 90067-1702, USA

Lambros, Andy
9310 Topanga Canyon Blvd # 125
Chatsworth, CA 91311-5713

Lambsdorff, Otto (Government Official)
Strasschensweg 7
Bon 53113, GERMANY

Lamelin, Stephanie (Actor)
c/o Katie Mason *Luber Roklin Management*
8530 Wilshire Blvd Ste 550
Beverly Hills, CA 90211-3133, USA

Lamkin, Kathy (Actor)
c/o Linda McAlister *Linda McAlister Talent*
100 Oak Ln
Waxahachie, TX 75167-8412, USA

Lamm, Julie
PO Box B
Aspen, CO 81612-7402

Lamm, Richard D (Ex-Governor)
Public Policy Ctr
Denver, CO 80208-0001, USA

Lamm, Robert (Musician)
115 West Rd
Winchester Center, CT 06098-2301, USA

Lammers, Esmee (Director, Writer)
Entrepotdok 76A
Amsterdam, AD 101, NETHERLANDS

Lammons, Pete (Athlete, Football Player)
5006 E Fallen Bough Dr
Houston, TX 77041-7887, USA

Lamonica, Darryl (Athlete, Football Player)
8796 N 6th St
Fresno, CA 93720-1711, USA

Lamonica, Roberto de (Artist)
Rua Anibal de Mendanca 180 AP 202
Rio de Janeiro, RJ ZC-37, BRAZIL

Lamont, Gene W (Athlete, Baseball Player, Coach)
5194 Siesta Woods Dr
Sarasota, FL 34242-1457, USA

Lamont, Norman S H (Government Official)
5 Stanhope Gate
London W1Y 5LA, UNITED KINGDOM (UK)

Lamontagne, Donald A (General)
Commander Air University
Maxwell Air Force Base, AL 36112, USA

LaMontagne, Ray (Musician)
c/o Staff Member *Paradigm (Monterey)*
404 W Franklin St
Monterey, CA 93940-2303, USA

Lamorte, Gina (Stylist)
c/o Staff Member *Axis Models & Talent*
PO Box 367
Ringwood, NJ 07456-0367, USA

LaMorte, Robia (Actor)
c/o Rob D'Avola *Rob DAvola & Associates*
9107 Wilshire Blvd Ste 450
Beverly Hills, CA 90210-5535, USA

Lamott, Anne (Activist, Writer)
c/o Staff Member *Steven Barclay Agency*
12 Western Ave
Petaluma, CA 94952-2907, USA

LaMotta, Jake (Boxer)
400 E 57th St
New York, NY 10022-3019, USA

Lamoureux, Robert
29 Bd D'Aulteuil
Bologne, FRANCE 92100

Lamp, Dennis (Athlete, Baseball Player)
30824 La Miranda Unit 228
Rancho Santa Margarita, CA 92688-5812, USA

Lamp, Jeff (Athlete, Basketball Player)
4971 Credit River Dr
Savage, MN 55378-4610, USA

Lampa, Rachael
25 Music Sq W
Nashville, TN 37203-3205

Lampanelli, Lisa (Actor, Producer, Writer)
c/o Sonya Rosenfeld *Creative Artists Agency (CAA-LA)*
2000 Avenue of the Stars Ste 100
Los Angeles, CA 90067-4705, USA

Lampard, Frank (Soccer Player)
Stamford Bridge Fulham Road
London SW6 1HS, UNITED KINGDOM

Lampard, Keith (Athlete, Baseball Player)
6124 Highway 6 N
Houston, TX 77084-1304, USA

Lamparski, Richard (Writer)
4202 Calle Real Apt 245
Santa Barbara, CA 93110-4081, USA

Lampert, Edward S (Business Person)
200 Greenwich Ave
Greenwich, CT 06830-2506

Lampert, Zohra (Actor)
6500 Wilshire Blvd Ste 2200
Los Angeles, CA 90048-4942, USA

Lamphear, Dan (Athlete, Football Player)
669 Bent Ridge Ln
Barrington, IL 60010-6604, USA

Lampkin, Tom (Athlete, Baseball Player)
3810 SE 153rd Ct
Vancouver, WA 98683-5313, USA

Lampley, Jim (Sportscaster)
c/o Staff Member *Crystal Spring Productions*
9713 Santa Monica Blvd Ste 214
Beverly Hills, CA 90210-4229, USA

Lampley, Jimmy (Athlete, Basketball Player)
3197 Balsam Cv
Memphis, TN 38127-7483, USA

Lamplugh, Ian (Baseball Player)
1830 Fairburn Dr
Victoria, BC V8N 1P9, CANADA

Lamplugh, Ian (Athlete, Baseball Player)
1830 Fairburn Dr
Victoria, BC V8N 1P9, Canada

Lampson, Butler W (Engineer)
16011 NE 36th Way
Redmond, WA 98052-6301, USA

Lampton, Michael (Astronaut)
Space Science Laboratory
Berkeley, CA 94720-0001, USA

Lanbros, Andy
9040 Topanga Canyon Blvd # 200
West Hills, CA 91304-1435

Lancaster, Amber
c/o Cindy Guagenti *Baker Winokur Ryder Public Relations (BWR-LA)*
9100 Wilshire Blvd Ste 500 PMB WEST
Beverly Hills, CA 90212-3426, USA

Lancaster, Les (Athlete, Baseball Player)
PO Box 1105
Dothan, AL 36302-1105, USA

Lancaster, Neal (Athlete, Golfer)
6 Quail Run
Smithfield, NC 27577, USA

Lancaster, Penny (Actor)
c/o Staff Member *Special Artists Agency*
9465 Wilshire Blvd Ste 820
Beverly Hills, CA 90212-2607, USA

Lancaster, Sarah (Actor)
c/o Amanda Glazer *Kohner Agency, The*
9300 Wilshire Blvd Ste 555
Beverly Hills, CA 90212-3211, USA

Lance, Bert
PO Box 637
Calhoun, GA 30703-0637

Lance, Dirk (Musician)
c/o Staff Member *ArtistDirect*
9046 Lindblade St
Culver City, CA 90232-2513, USA

Lance, Gary (Athlete, Baseball Player)
212 Sunset Cir
Prosperity, SC 29127-8426, USA

Lance, Leonard (Congressman, Politician)
426 Cannon Hob
Washington, DC 20515-3813, USA

Lancelotti, Rick (Athlete, Baseball Player)
5190 Thompson Rd
Clarence, NY 14031-1127, USA

Land, Tammi
c/o Staff Member *Osbrink Talent Agency*
4343 Lankershim Blvd Ste 100
West Toluca Lake, CA 91602-2705, USA

Landa, Sonny (Stylist)
c/o Staff Member *Manifest Artist Management*
1975 E Sunrise Blvd Ste 412
Fort Lauderdale, FL 33304-1408, USA

Landaker, Dave (Baseball Player)
3593 Buffum St
Simi Valley, CA 93063-3215, USA

Landau, Irvin (Editor)
101 Truman Ave
Yonkers, NY 10703-1044, USA

Landau, Jacob (Artist)
2 Pine Dr
Roosevelt, NJ 08555-7011, USA

Landau, Jon (Director, Producer, Writer)
c/o Staff Member *LightStorm Entertainment*
919 Santa Monica Blvd
Santa Monica, CA 90401-2704

Landau, Juliet (Actor)
PO Box 2792
Hollywood, CA 90078-2792

Landau, Martin (Actor)
c/o Rona Menashe *Guttman Associates*
118 S Beverly Dr Ste 201
Beverly Hills, CA 90212-3016, USA

Landeau, Aleksia (Actor)
c/o Staff Member *Metropolitan (MTA)*
4526 Wilshire Blvd
Los Angeles, CA 90010-3801, USA

Landecker, John Records
180 N Stetson Ave Ste Prudential
Chicago, IL 60601-6710

Lander, Benjamin (Educator)
President's Office
Washington, DC 20016, USA

Lander, David L (Actor)
c/o Staff Member *Arlene Thornton & Associates*
12711 Ventura Blvd Ste 490
Studio City, CA 91604-2477, USA

Lander, Natalie (Actor)
c/o Scott Zimmerman *Evolution Entertainment (LA)*
901 N Highland Ave
Los Angeles, CA 90038-2412, USA

Landers, Amy (Actor)
c/o Staff Member *Badgley-Connor-King*
9229 W Sunset Blvd Ste 311
Los Angeles, CA 90069-3403, USA

Landers, Andy (Coach)
Athletic
Athens, GA 30602-0001, USA

Landers, Audrey (Actor, Musician)
4048 Las Palmas Way
Sarasota, FL 34238-4530, USA

Landers, Judy (Actor)
6300 Wilshire Blvd Ste 1470
Los Angeles, CA 90048-5200, USA

Landers, Kristy (Actor)
c/o Gregory (Greg) Redlitz *Robert Thorne Co*
9654 Heather Rd
Beverly Hills, CA 90210-1757, USA

Landers, Robert (Athlete, Golfer)
PO Box 497
Azle, TX 76098-0497, USA

Landes, David S (Historian)
1010 Memorial Dr Apt 11E
Cambridge, MA 02138-4856, USA

Landes, Michael (Actor)
c/o Chris Andrews *Creative Artists Agency (CAA-LA)*
2000 Avenue of the Stars Ste 100
Los Angeles, CA 90067-4705, USA

Landesberg, Sylven (Athlete, Basketball Player)
c/o Jeff Schwartz *Excel Sports Management*
9665 Wilshire Blvd Ste 500
Beverly Hills, CA 90212-2312, USA

Landestoy, Rafael (Athlete, Baseball Player)
3121 SW 140th Ave
Miami, FL 33175-6504, USA

Landeta, Sean (Athlete, Football Player)
PO Box 422
Manhasset, NY 11030-0422, USA

Landey, Nina (Actor)
c/o Staff Member *Bauman Redanty & Shaul Agency*
5757 Wilshire Blvd Suite 473
Beverly Hills, CA 90212, USA

Landgrebe, Ludrun
Goethstr. 17
Munich, GERMANY D-80336

Landham, Sonny (Actor)

Landi, Sal (Actor)
c/o Craig Mobbs *AKA Talent Agency*
6310 San Vicente Blvd Ste 200
Los Angeles, CA 90048-5488, USA

Landig, Rhea (Stylist)
c/o Staff Member *Perrella Management*
330 W 38th St Rm 1407
New York, NY 10018-8435, USA

Landis, Bill (Athlete, Baseball Player)
525 E Sycamore Dr
Hanford, CA 93230-1443, USA

Landis, Floyd (Athlete)
3530 Grand Ave Ste 4
Oakland, CA 94610-2036, USA

Landis, Jim (Athlete, Baseball Player)
203 Alchemy Way
Napa, CA 94558-7214, USA

Landis, John D (Director)
c/o Abram Nalibotsky *Gersh (LA)*
9465 Wilshire Blvd Ste 600
Beverly Hills, CA 90212-2612, USA

Lando, Joe (Actor)
c/o Staff Member *Metropolitan (MTA)*
4526 Wilshire Blvd
Los Angeles, CA 90010-3801, USA

Landon, Howard C R (Writer)
Chateau de Foncoussieres Rabastens
Tarn 81800, FRANCE

Landon, Jennifer (Actor)
c/o Jamie Freed *Paris Hilton Entertainment*
8383 Wilshire Blvd Ste 1050
Beverly Hills, CA 90211-2415, USA

Landon, Tina (Actor, Choreographer)
c/o Staff Member *McDonald/Selznick Assoc (MSA)*
1611A N El Centro Ave
Hollywood, CA 90028, USA

Landon Jr, Michael (Actor, Director, Producer, Writer)
6401 Chesebro Rd
Agoura Hills, CA 91301-1803, USA

Landreaux, Ken (Athlete, Baseball Player)
1510 N Siesta Ave
La Puente, CA 91746-1151, USA

Landres, Paul
5343 Amestoy Ave
Encino, CA 91316-2613

Landreth, Larry (Athlete, Baseball Player)
116 St Vincent St S
Stratford, ON N5A 2W8, Canada

Landrieu, Mary (Senator)
724 Hart Senate Ofc Building
Washington, DC 20510-0001, USA

Landrieu, Moon (Secretary)
4301 S Prieur St
New Orleans, LA 70125-5125, USA

Landrith, Hobie (Athlete, Baseball Player)
1462 Nome Ct
Sunnyvale, CA 94087-4264, USA

Landrum, Bill (Athlete, Baseball Player)
840 Silver Point Rd
Chapin, SC 29036-7963, USA

Landrum, Ced (Athlete, Baseball Player)
2425 Hillview Dr
Fort Worth, TX 76119-2722, USA

Landrum, Joe (Athlete, Baseball Player)
715 Sharpe Rd
Columbia, SC 29203-9347, USA

Landrum, Mike (Athlete, Football Player)
88 Raybourn Rd
Sumrall, MS 39482-3926, USA

Landrum, Tito (Athlete, Baseball Player)
160 W 66th St Apt 39H
New York, NY 10023-6564, USA

Landry, Ali (Actor, Model)
c/o Staff Member *Reel Talent Management*
PO Box 491035
Los Angeles, CA 90049-9035, USA

Landry, Gregory P (Greg) (Athlete, Coach, Football Coach, Football Player)
133 Melanie Ln
Troy, MI 48098-1707, USA

Landsberger, Mark (Athlete, Basketball Player)
1702 8th Ave SE
Saint Cloud, MN 56304-2104, USA

Landsburg, Valerie (Actor)
22745 Chamera Ln
Topanga, CA 90290-4006, USA

Landsee, Robert (Athlete, Football Player)
PO Box 628128
Middleton, WI 53562-8128, USA

Landy, Bernard (Government Official)
885 Grand Allee Est
Quebec, QC GLA 1A2, CANADA

Landzaat, Andre
7500 Devista Dr
Los Angeles, CA 90046-1712

Lane, Abbe (Actor, Musician)
500 Bel Air Rd
Los Angeles, CA 90077-3817, USA

Lane, Barry (Athlete, Golfer)
1360 E 9th St Ste 100
Cleveland, OH 44114-1730, USA

Lane, Cristy (Musician)
PO Box 654
Madison, TN 37116-0654, USA

Lane, Diane (Actor)
c/o Joan Hyler *Hyler Management*
20 Ocean Park Blvd Unit 25
Santa Monica, CA 90405-3590, USA

Lane, Dick (Athlete, Baseball Player)
2717 Legend Dr
Las Vegas, NV 89134-8829, USA

Lane, Garcia (Athlete, Football Player)
902 Wabash Ave
Youngstown, OH 44502-2063, USA

Lane, Jason (Athlete, Baseball Player)
8930 Oak Grove Ave
Sebastopol, CA 95472-2460, USA

Lane, Jerome (Athlete, Basketball Player)
1500 Marion Ave Apt 509
Akron, OH 44313-7628, USA

Lane, John R (Jack) (Misc)
151 3rd St
San Francisco, CA 94103-3107, USA

Lane, Johnny
5048 Casa Dr
Tarzana, CA 91356-4422

Lane, Kenneth Jay (Designer, Fashion Designer)
20 W 37th St
New York, NY 10018-7479, USA

Lane, Lilas (Actor)
c/o Peter Himberger *Impact Artists Group LLC*
42 Hamilton Ter
New York, NY 10031-6403, USA

Lane, MacArthur (Athlete, Football Player)
3238 Knowland Ave
Oakland, CA 94619-2630, USA

Lane, Malcolm D (Misc)
5607 Roxbury Pl
Baltimore, MD 21209-4501, USA

Lane, Marvin (Marv) (Athlete, Baseball Player)
40164 Gulliver Dr
Sterling Heights, MI 48310-1729, USA

Lane, Mary (Stylist)
1069 Sea Palms West Dr
Saint Simons Island, GA 31522-5224, USA

Lane, Max (Athlete, Football Player)
79 Bond St
Gloucester, MA 01930-4925, USA

Lane, Melvin B (Publisher)
99 Tallwood Ct
Menlo Park, CA 94027-6431, USA

Lane, Mike (Cartoonist)
501 N Calvert St
Baltimore, MD 21278-1000, USA

Lane, Nathan (Actor, Musician)
c/o Simon Halls *Slate Public Relations*
9000 W Sunset Blvd Ste 915
West Hollywood, CA 90069-5809, USA

Lane, Skip (Athlete, Business Person, Football Player)
14 Roosevelt Rd
Westport, CT 06880-6840, USA

Lane Jr, Lawrence W (Diplomat, Publisher)
3000 Sand Hill Rd # 215
Menlo Park, CA 94025-7113, USA

Lane of St Ippollitts, Geoffrey D (Judge)
Strand
London WC2A 2LL, UNITED KINGDOM (UK)

Lanegan, Mark (Musician)
535 Kings Road
London SW1O 0S, UNITED KINGDOM (UK)

Laneuville, Eric (Actor)
5138 W Slauson Ave
Los Angeles, CA 90056-1641, USA

Laney, James T (Diplomat, Educator)
2015 Grand Prix Dr NE
Atlanta, GA 30345-3931, USA

Lang, Andrew (Athlete, Basketball Player)
1048 Woodruff Plantation Pkwy SE
Marietta, GA 30067-9106, USA

Lang, Antonio (Athlete, Basketball Player)
2255 Barretts Ln
Mobile, AL 36617-2734, USA

Lang, Belinda (Actor)
91 Regent St
London W1R 7TB, UNITED KINGDOM (UK)

Lang, Chip (Athlete, Baseball Player)
132 Westminster Dr
Pittsburgh, PA 15229-3165, USA

Lang, Don (Athlete, Baseball Player)
701 N Montgomery St # 22
Ojai, CA 93023-1844, USA

Lang, Ed (Photographer)
16255 Ventura Blvd Ste 515
Encino, CA 91436-2310, USA

Lang, Gene (Athlete, Football Player)
11526 Azalea Trce
Gulfport, MS 39503-8398, USA

Lang, George C (War Hero)
3786 Clark St
Seaford, NY 11783-2101, USA

Lang, Helmut (Designer, Fashion Designer)
819 Washington St
New York, NY 10014-1405, USA

Lang, Jack (Government Official)
Mairie
Blois 41000, FRANCE

Lang, Jack (Writer)
4 Barry Dr
E Northport, NY 11731-1307, USA

Lang, Jonny (Musician)
761 Washington Ave N
Minneapolis, MN 55401-1101, USA

Lang, June (Actor)
12756 Kahlenberg Ln
North Hollywood, CA 91607-2919, USA

Lang, Katherine Kelly (Actor, Model)
7800 Beverly Blvd Ste 3371
Los Angeles, CA 90036-2112, USA

Lang, KD (Actor, Musician)
c/o Larry Wanagas *Bumstead Productions Ltd.*
P.O. Box 158 Station E
Toronto, ON M6H 4E2, Canada

Lang, Kenard (Athlete, Football Player)
1781 Oakbrook Dr
Longwood, FL 32779-3168, USA

Lang, Lang (Musician)
c/o Staff Member *Columbia Artists Mgmt Inc*
1790 Broadway Fl 6
New York, NY 10019-1537, USA

Lang, Le-Lo (Athlete, Football Player)
19436 E Maplewood Pl
Aurora, CO 80016-3868, USA

Lang, Pearl (Choreographer, Dancer)
382 Central Park W
New York, NY 10025-6054, USA

Lang, Stephen (Actor)
c/o Susan Calogerakis *Thruline Entertainment*
9250 Wilshire Blvd Ground Fl
Beverly Hills, CA 90212, USA

Langbo, Arnold G (Business Person)
PO Box 3599
Battle Creek, MI 49016-3599, USA

Langdon, Brooke
1180 S Beverly Dr Ste 608
Los Angeles, CA 90035-1158

Langdon, Harry (Photographer)
PO Box 16816
Beverly Hills, CA 90209-2816, USA

Langdon, Michael
34 Arnham Ct. Grand Ave.
Hove E. Sussex, ENGLAND

Langdon, Sue Ane (Actor)
4618 Park Mirasol
Calabasas, CA 91302-1731, USA

Lange, Allison
3500 W Olive Ave Ste 1400
Burbank, CA 91505-5512

Lange, Andre (Athlete)
An der Schiessstatte 4
Berchtesgaden 83471, GERMANY

Lange, Andrew (Astronomer)
Astronomy
Berkeley, CA 94720-0001, USA

Lange, Artie (Actor)
c/o Richard Abate *3 Arts Entertainment - NY*
49 W 27th St Fl 5
New York, NY 10001-6936, USA

Lange, Bonnie
PO Box 3827
Beverly Hills, CA 90212-0827

Lange, Detective Tom
12021 Wilshire Blvd # 846
Los Angeles, CA 90025-1206

Lange, Dick (Athlete, Baseball Player)
39744 Salvatore Dr
Sterling Heights, MI 48313-5165, USA

Lange, Jessica (Actor)
c/o Jason Weinberg *Untitled Entertainment (LA)*
350 S Beverly Dr Ste 200
Beverly Hills, CA 90212-4819, USA

Lange, Niklaus (Actor)
c/o Staff Member *Schumacher Management*
1122 San Vicente Blvd
Santa Monica, CA 90402-2008, USA

Lange, Ted (Actor)
c/o Staff Member *Schiowitz Connor Ankrum Wolf*
1680 Vine St Ste 1016
Los Angeles, CA 90028-8800, USA

Lange, Thomas (Athlete)
57 Domhof
Farmville, VA 23909-0001, GERMANY

Langehorne, Reggie (Athlete, Football Player)
12260 Smiths Neck Rd
Carrollton, VA 23314-3802, USA

Langella, Frank (Actor)
c/o Toni Howard *International Creative Management (ICM-LA)*
10250 Constellation Blvd Fl 7
Los Angeles, CA 90067-6207, USA

Langen, Christoph (Athlete)
16 BC Onterhaching Ottobrunner St
Cheyenne, WY 82008-0001, GERMANY

Langencamp, Reather (Actor)
156 F St SE
Washington, DC 20003-2603, USA

Langenkamp, Heather (Actor)
c/o Harrison Cheung *Harrison Cheung & Associates*
11617 Natrona Dr
Austin, TX 78759-4123, USA

Langer, AJ (Actor)
c/o Staff Member *Valeo Entertainment*
8265 W Sunset Blvd Ste 103
West Hollywood, CA 90046-2433, USA

Langer, Alois A (Inventor)
111 Saddlebrook Dr
Harrison City, PA 15636-1413, USA

Langer, Bernhard (Athlete, Golfer)
3667 Princeton Pl
Boca Raton, FL 33496-2711, USA

Langer, James J (Jim) (Athlete, Football Player)
14280 Wolfram St NW
Ramsey, MN 55303-4563, USA

Langer, James S (Physicist)
1130 Las Canoas Ln
Santa Barbara, CA 93105-2331, USA

Langer, Robert (Doctor)
Chem Engineer Dept
Cambridge, MA 2139, USA

Langer, Robert S (Engineer, Inventor)
Engineering Dept
Cambridge, MA 2139, USA

Langerhans, Ryan (Athlete, Baseball Player)
PO Box 1026
Round Rock, TX 78680-1026, USA

Langevin, Dave (Athlete, Hockey Player)
1090 W Circle Ct
Saint Paul, MN 55118-4148, USA

Langevin, Jim (Politician)
181 Knight St Ste A
Warwick, RI 02886-1296, USA

Langford, Jevon (Athlete, Football Player)
1 Paul Brown Stadium
Cincinnati, OH 45202-3418, USA

Langford, John (Engineer)
9950 Wakeman Dr
Manassas, VA 20110-2702, USA

Langford, Rick (Athlete, Baseball Player)
8330 9th Avenue Ter NW
Bradenton, FL 34209-9678, USA

Langham, C Antonio (Athlete, Football Player)
PO Box 232
Town Creek, AL 35672-0232, USA

Langham, Franklin (Athlete, Golfer)
PO Box 3428
Peachtree City, GA 30269-7428, USA

Langham, Michael (Director)
Drama Division 144 W 66th St
New York, NY 10023, USA

Langham, Wallace (Actor)
10264 Rochester Ave
Los Angeles, CA 90024-5331, USA

Langham, Wally (Actor)
c/o Josh Katz *United Talent Agency (UTA)*
9560 Wilshire Blvd Fl 5
Beverly Hills, CA 90212-2400, USA

Langkow, Daymond (Athlete, Hockey Player)
P.O. Box 1540 Station M
Calgary, AB T2P 3B9, Canada

Langley, Roger (Skier)
Broad St
Barre, MA 1005, USA

Langlois, Lisa (Actor)
c/o Staff Member *Leavitt Talent Group*
8255 W Sunset Blvd
West Hollywood, CA 90046-2417, USA

Langlois, Paul (Musician)
219 Dufferin St # 309B
Toronto, ON M5K 3J1, CANADA

Langlois Jr, Albert (Athlete, Hockey Player)
2473 Crest View Dr
Los Angeles, CA 90046-1406, USA

Langone, Kenneth (Business Person)
375 Park Ave Ste 2205
New York, NY 10152-2201, USA

Langone, Stefano (Musician)
c/o Simon Fuller *XIX Entertainment*
33/32 Ransomes Dock 35-37 Parkgate Rd
London SW11 4NP, UK

Langston, J William (Doctor)
2444 Moorpark Ave
San Jose, CA 95128, USA

Langston, Mark E (Athlete, Baseball Player)
56 Golden Eagle
Irvine, CA 92603-0309, USA

Langston, Murray (Actor, Comedian)
PO Box 4734
Santa Rosa, CA 95402-4734, USA

Langton, Brooke (Actor)
c/o Mark Measures *Abrams Artists Agency (LA)*
9200 W Sunset Blvd PH 11
Los Angeles, CA 90069-3601, USA

Langton, Brooke (Actor)
1180 S Beverly Dr Ste 601
Los Angeles, CA 90035-1158, USA

Langway, Rod C (Athlete, Hockey Player)
30 Yonge St
Toronto, ON M5E 1X8, Canada

Lanier, Chris (Artist)
c/o Staff Member *Fantagraphics Books*
7563 Lake City Way NE
Seattle, WA 98115-4218, USA

Lanier, Harold C (Hal) (Athlete, Baseball Player, Coach)
3270 Countryside View Dr
Saint Cloud, FL 34772-7050, USA

Lanier, Jaron (Engineer)
200 Business Park Dr
Armonk, NY 10504-1700, USA

Lanier, Lorenzo (Rimp) (Athlete, Baseball Player)
4515 E Frontenac Dr
Cleveland, OH 44128-5004, USA

Lanier, Willie E (Athlete, Football Player)
2911 E Brigstock Rd
Midlothian, VA 23113-3905, USA

Lanier Jr, Robert J (Bob) (Athlete, Basketball Player, Coach)
8316 N Steven Rd
Milwaukee, WI 53223-3355, USA

Lanker, Brian (Journalist)
1993 Kimberly Dr
Eugene, OR 97405-5849, USA

Lankford, Frank (Athlete, Baseball Player)
104 Lakeview Ave NE
Atlanta, GA 30305-3725, USA

Lankford, James (Congressman)
509 Cannon Hob
Washington, DC 20515-4207, USA

Lankford, Kim (Actor)
6071 Highway 64
Bloomfield, NM 87413-9551, USA

Lankford, Paul (Athlete, Football Player)
3838 Biggin Church Rd W
Jacksonville, FL 32224-7984, USA

Lankford, Ray (Athlete, Baseball Player)
1520 Lake Whitney Dr
Windermere, FL 34786-6041, USA

Lanois, Daniel (Actor, Musician)
c/o Staff Member *Paradigm (Monterey)*
404 W Franklin St
Monterey, CA 93940-2303, USA

Lanphear, Dan (Athlete, Football Player)
669 Bent Ridge Ln
Barrington, IL 60010-6604, USA

LanSala, James (Misc)
5025 Wisconsin Ave NW
Washington, DC 20016-4113, USA

Lansbury, Angela (Actor, Musician)
c/o Tim Curtis *WmE2 (Endeavor-LA)*
9601 Wilshire Blvd Fl 3
Beverly Hills, CA 90210-5219, USA

Lansbury, David (Actor)
6500 Wilshire Blvd Ste 2200
Los Angeles, CA 90048-4942, USA

Lansdale, Joe R
199 County Road 508
Nacogdoches, TX 75961-0170, USA

Lansford, Alex (Athlete, Football Player)
PO Box 905
Lampasas, TX 76550-0007, USA

Lansford, Carney (Athlete, Baseball Player)
43736 Pocahontas Rd
Baker City, OR 97814-8173, USA

Lansford, Jody (Athlete, Baseball Player)
5730 San Lorenzo Dr
San Jose, CA 95123-2967, USA

Lansford, Mike (Athlete, Football Player)
6200 E Canyon Rim Rd Ste 205
Anaheim, CA 92807-4340, USA

Lansing, Mike (Athlete, Baseball Player)
9691 Sun Meadow St
Highlands Ranch, CO 80129-6925, USA

Lansing, Sherry L (Producer)
10741 Levico Way
Los Angeles, CA 90077-1918, USA

Lanter, Matt (Actor)
c/o Faras Rabadi *Emerald Talent Group*
10 Universal City Plz Fl 20
Universal City, CA 91608-1074, USA

Lantz, Stu (Athlete, Basketball Player)
5270 Mount Burnham Dr
San Diego, CA 92111-3948, USA

Lanus, Valentino (Actor)
c/o Angel Hidalgo *Angel Hidalgo Management*
Gral Mendez #3 Int. C001 Col
Ampliacion Daniel Garza
Mexico City 11830, MEXICO

Lanvin, Bernard (Designer, Fashion Designer)
22 Rue du Faubourg Saint Honore
Paris 70008, FRANCE

Lanz, David (Musician)
4650 N Port Washington Rd
Milwaukee, WI 53212-1077, USA

Lanza, Charles (Athlete, Football Player)
19 Snowberry Ct
Cockeysville, MD 21030-1954, USA

Lanza, Suzanne
345 N Maple Dr Ste 397
Beverly Hills, CA 90210-5179

Laoretti, Larry (Athlete, Golfer)
10567 SW Whooping Crane Way
Palm City, FL 34990-7806, USA

LaPage, Paul (Governor)
1 State House Sta Ofc of
Augusta, ME 04333-0001, USA

LaPaglia, Anthony (Actor)
c/o Jennifer Allen *Viewpoint Inc*
8820 Wilshire Blvd Ste 220
Beverly Hills, CA 90211-2622, USA

LaPaglia, Jonathan
1505 10th St
Santa Monica, CA 90401-2805

Lapaine, Daniel (Actor)
409 Santa Monica Blvd
Santa Monica, CA 90401-2232, USA

Lapalme, Paul (Athlete, Baseball Player)
167 Smith St
Leominster, MA 01453-2155, USA

Laperriere, J Jacques H (Athlete, Coach, Hockey Player)
1983 Nice Chomedey Est
Laval, QC H7S 1G5, Canada

Lapham, Bill (Athlete, Football Player)
136 S 52nd St
West Des Moines, IA 50265-2895, USA

Lapham, Dave (Athlete, Football Player)
8254 Sunfish Ln
Maineville, OH 45039-8978, USA

Lapham, Lewis H (Editor)
666 Broadway
New York, NY 10012-2317, USA

Lapidus, Alan (Architect)
43 W 61st St
New York, NY 10023-7607, USA

Lapidus, Edmond (Ted) (Designer, Fashion Designer)
66 Blvd Maurice-Barres
Neuilly-sur-Seine 92200, FRANCE

Lapierre, Dominique (Historian)
Les Bignoles
Ramatuelle 83350, FRANCE

Lapin, Kathy (Stylist)
1440 Wilmot Rd
Deerfield, IL 60015-2068, USA

Lapine, James E (Director, Writer)
c/o Staff Member *Judi Farkas Management*
116 N Mansfield Ave
Los Angeles, CA 90036-3021, USA

Lapira, Liza (Actor)
c/o Eric Nelson *Paceline Entertainment*
6840 Firmament Ave
Van Nuys, CA 91406-5103, USA

Lapka, Myron (Athlete, Football Player)
4129 Gertrude St
Simi Valley, CA 93063-2925, USA

Lapka, Ted (Athlete, Football Player)
1700 Robin Ln Apt 127
Lisle, IL 60532-4157, USA

LaPlaca, Alison (Actor)
1614 Argyle Ave
Hollywood, CA 90028-6408, USA

LaPlanche, Rosemary (Actor)
13914 Hartsook St
Sherman Oaks, CA 91423-1210, USA

LaPlante, Lynda (Writer)
1745 Broadway # B1
New York, NY 10019-4368, USA

Lapli, John (General)
Box 252
Honiara, GUADACANAL SOLOMON ISLANDS

Lapoint, Dave (Athlete, Baseball Player)
11704 Stonewood Gate Dr
Riverview, FL 33579-4025, USA

Lapointe, Guy
4568 E Des Bousquets
Augustin, CANADA PQ 6A3 1C4

Laport, Osvaldo (Actor)
c/o Staff Member *Telefe - Argentina*
Pavon 2444 (C1248AAT)
Buenos Aires, ARGENTINA

LaPorte, Danny (Race Car Driver)
949 Via Del Monte
Palos Verdes Estates, CA 90274-1615, USA

Laposata, Joseph S (General)
20 Massachusetts
Washington, DC 20529-2099, USA

Lapotaire, Jane (Actor)
92 Oxford Gardens #C
London W10, UNITED KINGDOM (UK)

Lappalainen, Markku (Musician)
8920 W Sunset Blvd # 200
Los Angeles, CA 90069-1812, USA

Lappas, Steve (Coach)
Athletic Dept
Villanova, PA 19085, USA

Lappe, Frances Moore (Writer)
989 Market St
San Francisco, CA 94103-1708, USA

Laprade, Edgar (Athlete, Hockey Player)
12 Shuniah St
Thunder Bay, ON P7A 2Y8, Canada

LaPraed, Ronald (Ron) (Musician)
1920 Benson Ave
Saint Paul, MN 55116-3214, USA

Laquer, Walter (Historian)
1800 K St NW
Washington, DC 20006-2202, USA

Lara, Brian C (Cricketer)
PO Box 616
Saint John's, ANTIGUA

Lara, Claude Autant
66 Rue Lepic
Paris, FRANCE 75018

Lara, Joe (Actor)
c/o Peter Giagni *Peter Giagni Management*
8981 W Sunset Blvd Ste 103
West Hollywood, CA 90069-1850, USA

Laragh, John H (Doctor, Educator)
435 E 70th St
New York, NY 10021-5342, USA

Laraki, Azeddine (Prime Minister)
Mace Rd Kilo 6
Annapolis, MD 21411-0001, SAUDI ARABIA

Laraway, Jack (Athlete, Football Player)
5250 Fox Hollow Dr Apt 530
Naples, FL 34104-5191, USA

Lardner Jr, George (Journalist)
1150 15th St NW
Washington, DC 20071-0001, USA

Lardon, Brad (Athlete, Golfer)
17334 Sioux Springs Dr
College Station, TX 77845-4589, USA

Lardy, Henry A (Misc)
1829 Thorstrand Rd
Madison, WI 53705-1052, USA

Laredo, Jaime (Musician)
31 Sinclair Road
London W14 0NS, UNITED KINGDOM (UK)

Laredo, Ruth (Musician)
40 W 57th St
New York, NY 10019-4001, USA

Larena, John (Designer)
c/o Staff Member *Mirisch Agency*
8840 Wilshire Blvd Ste 100
Beverly Hills, CA 90211-2606, USA

Laresca, Vincent (Actor)
c/o Brandy Gold *TalentWorks (LA)*
3500 W Olive Ave Ste 1400
Burbank, CA 91505-5512, USA

Larese, York (Athlete, Basketball Player)
22 Grove Pl Unit 15
Winchester, MA 01890-3863, USA

Large, Kiersten (Stylist)
c/o Staff Member *Solo Artists*
2148 Federal Ave
Los Angeles, CA 90025-5327, USA

Large, Storm (Musician)
444 Park Ave S PH
New York, NY 10016-7321, USA

Largent, Steve (Athlete, Football Player)
1400 16th St NW Ste 600
Washington, DC 20036-2225, USA

Larionov, Igor (Athlete, Hockey Player)
600 Civic Center Dr
Detroit, MI 48226-4408, USA

Lark, Maria (Actor)
c/o Staff Member *Frontier Booking International*
1560 Broadway Ste 1110
New York, NY 10036-1537, USA

Larkin, Andy (Athlete, Baseball Player)
2844 E Flower St
Gilbert, AZ 85298-5754, USA

Larkin, Barry (Athlete, Baseball Player)
5410 Osprey Isle Ln
Orlando, FL 32819-4015, USA

Larkin, Barry L (Baseball Player)
3348 Brinton Trl
Cincinnati, OH 45241-4811, USA

Larkin, Gene (Athlete, Baseball Player)
9496 Abbott Ct
Eden Prairie, MN 55347-2817, USA

Larkin, Pat (Athlete, Baseball Player)
23400 Canzonet St
Woodland Hills, CA 91367-6013, USA

Larkin, Patty (Musician, Songwriter, Writer)
6629 University Ave Ste 206
Middleton, WI 53562-3037, USA

Larkin, Sheila
9229 W Sunset Blvd Ste 311
Los Angeles, CA 90069-3403

Larkin, Stephen (Athlete, Baseball Player)
9178 Solon Dr
Cincinnati, OH 45242-4616, USA

Larmore, Jennifer (Opera Singer)
40 W 57th St
New York, NY 10019-4001, USA

Larner, Stevan (Cinematographer)
1209 Ballard Canyon Rd
Solvang, CA 93463-9716, USA

Laro, David (Judge)
400 2nd St NW
Washington, DC 20217-0001, USA

Larocca, Greg (Athlete, Baseball Player)
14 Tinker Rd
Bedford, NH 03110-4429, USA

Laroche, Adam (Athlete, Baseball Player)
1735 E Oak St
Fort Scott, KS 66701-1841, USA

Laroche, Dave (Athlete, Baseball Player)
815 W 18th St
Fort Scott, KS 66701-3400, USA

LaRoche, Philippe (Skier)
Lac Beauport, QC G0A 20Q, CANADA

LaRocque, Gene R (Government Official)
5015 Macomb St NW
Washington, DC 20016-2609, USA

Laroque, Michele (Actor)
20 Ave Rapp
Paris 75007, FRANCE

LaRosa, Julius (Musician)
67 Sycamore Ln
Irvington, NY 10533-1933, USA

Larose, Claude D (Athlete, Hockey Player)
5060 NW 54th St
Coconut Creek, FL 33073-3713, USA

Larose, Dan (Athlete, Football Player)
4873 N Raymond Rd
Luther, MI 49656-9503, USA

Larose, John (Athlete, Baseball Player)
99 Roland St
Cumberland, RI 02864-5515, USA

Larose, Vic (Athlete, Baseball Player)
2908 E Sylvia St
Phoenix, AZ 85032-7135, USA

Larouch, Pierre
116 Lancaster Ave
Pittsburgh, PA 15228-2354

LaRouche, Lyndon
15820 Round Top Ln
Round Hill, VA 20141-2052

Larouche, Pierre (Athlete, Hockey Player)
112 Vanderbilt Dr
Pittsburgh, PA 15243-1323, USA

LaRouche Jr, Lyndon H (Politician)
18520 Round Top Ln
Round Hill, VA 20141-2052, USA

Larrieux, Amel (Musician)
2114 Pico Blvd # B
Santa Monica, CA 90405-1718, USA

Larroquette, John (Actor)
c/o Staff Member *Brillstein Entertainment Partners*
9150 Wilshire Blvd Ste 350
Beverly Hills, CA 90212-3453, USA

Larry, Wendy (Coach)
Athletic
Norfolk, VA 23529-0001, USA

Larry Sanitsky, Larry Sanitsky (Producer)
c/o Nancy Josephson *WmE2 (Endeavor-LA)*
9601 Wilshire Blvd Fl 3
Beverly Hills, CA 90210-5219, USA

Larsen, Art (Tennis Player)
203 Lorraine Blvd
San Leandro, CA 94577-2724, USA

Larsen, Blaine (Musician)
c/o Staff Member *Paradigm (Monterey)*
404 W Franklin St
Monterey, CA 93940-2303, USA

Larsen, Bruce (Editor)
2250 Granville St
Vancouver, BC V6H 3G2, CANADA

Larsen, Don (Athlete, Baseball Player)
PO Box 2863
Hayden Lake, ID 83835-2863, USA

Larsen, Gary L (Athlete, Football Player)
4317 San Juan St NE
Lacey, WA 98516-6277, USA

Larsen, Libby (Composer)
2205 Kenwood Pkwy
Minneapolis, MN 55405-2329, USA

Larsen, Paul E (Religious Leader)
5101 N Francisco Ave
Chicago, IL 60625-3676, USA

Larsen, Ralph S (Business Person)
1 Johnson and Johnson Plz
New Brunswick, NJ 08933-0001, USA

Larson, Brandon (Athlete, Baseball Player)
8922 Rich Way
San Antonio, TX 78251-2971, USA

Larson, Brie (Actor)
c/o Anne Woodward *ROAR (LA)*
9701 Wilshire Blvd Fl 8
Beverly Hills, CA 90212-2008, USA

Larson, Charles R (Chuck) (Admiral)
1840 Century Park E
Los Angeles, CA 90067-2101, USA

Larson, Dan (Athlete, Baseball Player)
797 Oxen St
Paso Robles, CA 93446-4656, USA

Larson, Darrell
8380 Melrose Ave Ste 207
Los Angeles, CA 90069-5498

Larson, Gary (Cartoonist)
4520 Main St
Kansas City, MO 64111-1876, USA

Larson, Gerald (Jerry Lacy) (Actor)
c/o Staff Member *Sutton Barth & Vennari Inc*
145 S Fairfax Ave Ste 310
Los Angeles, CA 90036-2176, USA

Larson, Greg (Athlete, Football Player)
PO Box 393
Nisswa, MN 56468-0393, USA

Larson, Jack (Actor)
449 N Skyewiay Rd
Los Angeles, CA 90049-2844, USA

Larson, Jay (Musician)
c/o Staff Member *Paradigm (Monterey)*
404 W Franklin St
Monterey, CA 93940-2303, USA

Larson, Jill (Actor)
1505 10th St
Santa Monica, CA 90401-2805, USA

Larson, Kent (Adult Film Star)
c/o Staff Member *Diva Central Inc*
7510 W Sunset Blvd Ste 1445
Los Angeles, CA 90046-3408, USA

Larson, Kurt (Athlete, Football Player)
N57W35564 Misty Ter
Oconomowoc, WI 53066-2410, USA

Larson, Lance (Swimmer)
41 Balboa Cvs
Newport Beach, CA 92663-3226, USA

Larson, Lyndon (Athlete, Football Player)
4117 E Encanto St
Mesa, AZ 85205-5121, USA

Larson, Paul (Athlete, Football Player)
3718 W Harding Rd
Turlock, CA 95380-9217, USA

Larson, Peter N (Business Person)
1 N Field Ct
Lake Forest, IL 60045-4810, USA

Larson, Reed
14334 Fairway Dr
Eden Prairie, MN 55344-1955

Larson, Rick (Congressman, Politician)
108 Cannon Hob
Washington, DC 20515-0914, USA

Larson, Sarah (Model)
c/o Kenya Knight *Nous Model Management*
117 N Robertson Blvd
Los Angeles, CA 90048-3101, USA

Larson, Shana (Producer, Writer)
c/o Lucy Stille *Paradigm (LA)*
360 N Crescent Dr
Beverly Hills, CA 90210-4874, USA

Larson, William H (Athlete, Football Player)
1365 Redwood Dr
Windsor, CO 80550-4603, USA

Larson, Wolf (Actor)
10600 Holman Ave Apt 1
Los Angeles, CA 90024-5931, USA

Larson-Pessolano, Becky (Athlete, Golfer)
121 Manor Ct
Springfield, MA 01118-2449, USA

Larsson, Dean (Athlete, Golfer)
1751 Pinnacle Dr Ste 1500
Mc Lean, VA 22102-3833, USA

Larsson, Lars-Eric
Master Ernsts gata 6A
Helsingborg, SWEDEN S-25435

Larsson, Magnus
Pier House Strand on the Green Chiswick
London, ENGLAND W4

Larter, Al
6100 Wilshire Blvd Ste 1170
Los Angeles, CA 90048-5116

Larter, Ali (Actor)
c/o Michael Bircumshaw *Water Street Management*
5225 Wilshire Blvd Ste 615
Los Angeles, CA 90036-4350, USA

LaRue, Chi Chi (Director, DJ)
c/o Staff Member *Diva Central Inc*
7510 W Sunset Blvd Ste 1445
Los Angeles, CA 90046-3408, USA

LaRue, Florence (Actor, Musician)
10877 Wilshire Blvd # 15
Los Angeles, CA 90024-4341, USA

Larue, Jason (Athlete, Baseball Player)
3237 Hawthorne
Spring Branch, TX 78070-6424, USA

Larue, Renee (Adult Film Star)
c/o Staff Member *Atlas Multimedia Inc*
9005 Eton Ave Ste C
Canoga Park, CA 91304-6533, USA

LaRussa, Tony (Athlete, Baseball Player, Coach)
c/o Staff Member *Saint Louis Cardinals (St Louis Cardinals)*
700 Clark St
Saint Louis, MO 63102-1727, USA

LaRusso, Vincent
419 Park Ave S Rm 1009
New York, NY 10016-8410

Lary, Frank S (Athlete, Baseball Player)
11813 Baseball Dr
Northport, AL 35475-4908, USA

Lary, R Yale (Athlete, Football Player)
6366 Lansdale Rd
Fort Worth, TX 76116-1622, USA

Las Ketchup (Music Group)
c/o Staff Member *Sony Music Miami*
605 Lincoln Rd Ste 700
Miami Beach, FL 33139-2901, USA

LaSalle, Denise (Musician)
PO Box 9267
Jackson, MS 39286-9267, USA

LaSalle, Eriq (Actor, Director)
PO Box 2369
Beverly Hills, CA 90213-2369, USA

Lasardo, Robert (Actor)
c/o Staff Member *Silver Massetti & Szatmary (SMS) Talent Inc*
8730 W Sunset Blvd Ste 440
Los Angeles, CA 90069-2277, USA

Lascher, David (Actor)
c/o Staff Member *Vanguard Management Group*
8060 Melrose Ave Fl 4
Los Angeles, CA 90046-7038, USA

LaScola, Judith (Artist)
317 Sutter St
San Francisco, CA 94108-4301, USA

Lash, Bill (Skier)
17438 Bothell Way NE Unit C305
Bothell, WA 98011-1965, USA

Lash, Jim (Athlete, Football Player)
597 Van Everett Ave
Akron, OH 44306-2418, USA

Lashar, Tim (Athlete, Football Player)
4056 Nicole Pl
Norman, OK 73072-1758, USA

Lashay, Gia (Adult Film Star)
PO Box 70741
Sunnyvale, CA 94086-0741, USA

Lasher, Fred (Athlete, Baseball Player)
N9596 County Road K
Merrillan, WI 54754-8038, USA

Lasker, Deedee (Athlete, Golfer)
1665 Chamisal Ct
Carlsbad, CA 92011-5031, USA

Lasker, Greg (Athlete, Football Player)
2521 Yeoman Ln
West Lafayette, IN 47906-0617, USA

Laskey, Bill (Athlete, Baseball Player)
PO Box 1556
Burlingame, CA 94011-1556, USA

Laskey, Bill (Athlete, Football Player)
PO Box 734
Leland, MI 49654-0734, USA

Laskey, Frank (Athlete, Football Player)
584 Battle Branch Vista Dr
Franklin, NC 28734-8548, USA

Laskin, Melissa (Stylist)
c/o Staff Member *Celestine - CA*
1666 20th St Ste 200B
Santa Monica, CA 90404-3828, USA

Laskowski, John (Athlete, Basketball Player)
7425 N Canyon Ct
Bloomington, IN 47404-8968, USA

Lasky, Scott (Sportscaster)
c/o Staff Member *Maxx Sports & Entertainment*
546 5th Ave Fl 6
New York, NY 10036-5000, USA

Laslavic, Jim (Athlete, Football Player)
648 A Ave
Coronado, CA 92118-2205, USA

Lasorda, Tommy (Athlete, Baseball Player, Coach)
c/o Staff Member *WmE2 (WMA-LA)*
1 William Morris Pl
Beverly Hills, CA 90212-4261, USA

Lassally, Walter (Cinematographer)
6 Ladbroke Gardens
London W11 2PT, UNITED KINGDOM (UK)

Lasse, Richard S (Athlete, Football Player)
111 Windcrest Ct
Beaver Falls, PA 15010-1178, USA

Lasser, Louise (Actor, Comedian)
200 E 71st St Apt 20C
New York, NY 10021-0472, USA

Lasseter, John (Animator, Director)
c/o Staff Member *Pixar Animation Studios*
1200 Park Ave
Emeryville, CA 94608-3677, USA

Lassetter, Don (Athlete, Baseball Player)
PO Box 326
Lyon, MS 38645-0326, USA

Lassez, Sarah (Actor)
1505 10th St
Santa Monica, CA 90401-2805, USA

Lassic, Derrick (Athlete, Football Player)
353 Shawnee Indian Ct
Suwanee, GA 30024, USA

Lassick, Sydney
2734 Bellevue Ave
Los Angeles, CA 90026-3882

Lassiter, Amanda (Basketball Player)
Target Center 600 1st Ave N
Minneapolis, MN 55403, USA

Lassiter, Isaac (Athlete, Football Player)
2812 Rawson St
Oakland, CA 94619-3348, USA

Lassiter, Kwamie (Athlete, Football Player)
1222 W Sunrise Pl
Chandler, AZ 85248-3741, USA

Last, James (Musician)
Schone Aussicht 16
Hamburg 22085, GERMANY

Laster, Danny B (Scientist)
PO Box 166
Clay Center, NE 68933-0166, USA

Laswell, Greg (Musician)
c/o Jena Vuylsteke *Vanguard Records*
11400 W Olympic Blvd Ste 1450
Los Angeles, CA 90064-1649, USA

Laszlo, Andrew (Cinematographer)
15838 Magnolia Blvd
Encino, CA 91436-1513, USA

Lateef (Music Group, Musician)
c/o Staff Member *Madison House Inc.*
771 Santa Fe Dr Ste 204
Denver, CO 80204-4440, USA

Lateef, Yusef (Composer, Musician)
10635 Santa Monica Blvd
Los Angeles, CA 90025-8300, USA

Latham, Bill (Athlete, Baseball Player)
211 Magnolia St
Trussville, AL 35173-1307, USA

Latham, Chris (Athlete, Baseball Player)
6331 Buzz Aldrin Dr
Las Vegas, NV 89149-1389, USA

Latham, David (Astronomer)
Astronomy Dept
Cambridge, MA 2138, USA

Latham, Jim (Composer)
c/o John Tempereau *Soundtrack Music Assoc*
1460 4th St Ste 308
Santa Monica, CA 90401-3483, USA

Latham, Jody (Actor)
c/o Lindy King *United Agents*
12-26 Lexington St
London W1F OLE, UK

Latham, Louise (Actor)
300 Hot Springs Rd
Santa Barbara, CA 93108-2037, USA

Latham, Tom (Congressman, Politician)
2217 Rayburn Hob
Washington, DC 20515-4904, USA

Lathan, Sanaa (Actor)
c/o Philip Grenz *WmE2 (Endeavor-LA)*
9601 Wilshire Blvd Fl 3
Beverly Hills, CA 90210-5219, USA

Lathan, Stan (Director, Producer, Writer)
c/o Staff Member *Simmons Lathan Media Group*
6100 Wilshire Blvd Ste 1111
Los Angeles, CA 90048-5198, USA

Lathiere, Bernard (Business Person)
5 Ave de Villiers
Paris 75017, FRANCE

Lathon, Lamar L (Athlete, Football Player)
3711 Poplar Springs Dr
Missouri City, TX 77459-6722, USA

Latifah, Queen (Actor, Musician)
c/o Amanda Silverman *42West (NY)*
220 W 42nd St Fl 12
New York, NY 10036-7200, USA

Latimer, Don (Athlete, Football Player)
562 S Kalispell Way
Aurora, CO 80017-2112, USA

Latimore (Musician)
1048 Tattnall St
Macon, GA 31201-1537, USA

Latimore, Joseph
1505 10th St
Santa Monica, CA 90401-2805

Latin, Jerry (Athlete, Football Player)
5253 Linden Rd Apt 10316
Rockford, IL 61109-5854, USA

Latman, Barry (Athlete, Baseball Player)
2726 Shelter Island Dr P O Box 519
San Diego, CA 92106, USA

Latortue, Gerard (Prime Minister)
Palais Ministeres
Port-au-Prince, HAITI

LaTourette, John E (Educator)
218 S Deerview Cir
Prescott, AZ 86303-5705, USA

Lattanzi, Chloe (Musician)
c/o Staff Member *Innovative Artists (NY)*
235 Park Ave S Fl 7
New York, NY 10003-1404, USA

Lattimore, Brian (Athlete, Football Player)
1790 Santa Blas Walk Apt 503
Saint Louis, MO 63138-1950, USA

Lattimore, Kenny (Actor)
c/o Sara Ramaker *Paradigm (LA)*
360 N Crescent Dr
Beverly Hills, CA 90210-4874, USA

Lattin, David (Athlete, Basketball Player)
8230 Twin Tree Ln
Houston, TX 77071-2918, USA

Lattisaw, Stacy (Musician)
PO Box 27641
Philadelphia, PA 19118-0641, USA

Lattlmore, Kenny (Musician)
4465 Don Milagro Dr
Los Angeles, CA 90008-2831, USA

Lattner, John J (Johnny) (Athlete, Football Player)
1700 Riverwoods Dr Apt 503
Melrose Park, IL 60160-1617, USA

Lattner, Johnny
933 Wenonah Ave
Oak Park, IL 60304-1810

Latzke, Paul (Athlete, Football Player)
1123 Escalona Dr
Santa Cruz, CA 95060-3303, USA

Lau, Andy (Actor, Producer)
c/o Staff Member *Focus Films*
18/F, Futura Plaza 111-113 How Ming St
Kwun Tong, Kowloon, Hong Kong

Lauda, Andreas-Nikolaus (Niki) (Race Car Driver)
San Costa de Baix Santa Eulalia
Ibiza, SPAIN

Lauda, Niki
San Costa de Baix
Santa Eularia des Riu (Ibiza),
SPAIN E-07840

Lauder, Leonard A (Business Person)
767 5th Ave
New York, NY 10153-0023, USA

Lauder, Ronald (Business Person)
767 5th Ave
New York, NY 10153-0023, USA

Laudner, Tim (Athlete, Baseball Player)
PO Box 10
Hamel, MN 55340-0010, USA

Lauen, Michel (Athlete, Hockey Player)
7605 Edinborough Way Apt 6214
Minneapolis, MN 55435-5827, USA

Lauer, Andrew (Actor)
3018 3rd St
Santa Monica, CA 90405-5410, USA

Lauer, Andy (Actor)
c/o Andrea Pett-Joseph *Brillstein Entertainment Partners*
9150 Wilshire Blvd Ste 350
Beverly Hills, CA 90212-3453, USA

Lauer, Bonnie (Athlete, Golfer)
525 Via Laguna Vis
San Luis Obispo, CA 93405-4757, USA

Lauer, Martin (Athlete, Track Athlete)
Hardstr 41
Lauf 77886, GERMANY

Lauer, Matt (Correspondent)
c/o Staff Member *Today Show, The*
30 Rockefeller Plz
New York, NY 10112-0015, USA

Lauer, Tod R (Astronomer)
6471 N Tierra De Las Catalinas
Tucson, AZ 85718-2163, USA

Laufenberg, Brandon (Athlete, Football Player)
5917 Azalea Ln
Dallas, TX 75230-3403, USA

Laughlin, John (Actor)
13116 Albers St
Sherman Oaks, CA 91401-6002, USA

Laughlin, Robert B (Nobel Prize Laureate)
Physics Dept
Stanford, CA 94305, USA

Laughlin, Teresa (TC) (Actor, Designer)
8 Larchmont Ave
Larchmont, NY 10538-4220, USA

Laughlin, Thomas R (Tom) (Actor, Director)
PO Box 840
Moorpark, CA 93020-0840, USA

Laughlin, Tom (Actor)
PO Box 840
Moorpark, CA 93020-0840, USA

Laukkanen, Janne (Athlete, Hockey Player)
401 Channelside Dr
Tampa, FL 33602-5400, USA

Lauper, Cyndi (Musician, Songwriter)
c/o Lisa Barbaris *So What Management*
890 W End Ave Apt 1A
New York, NY 10025-3520, USA

Laurance, Ashley (Actor)
c/o Leland LaBarre *Bleu, An Entertainment Company*
5225 Wilshire Blvd Ste 336
Los Angeles, CA 90036-4380, USA

Laurance, Dale (Business Person)
10889 Wilshire Blvd
Los Angeles, CA 90024-4201, USA

Laurance, Matthew (Actor)
1951 Hillcrest Rd
Los Angeles, CA 90068-3116, USA

Laure, Carole (Actor, Musician)
36 Rue de Ponthieu
Paris 75008, FRANCE

Laurel, Rich (Athlete, Basketball Player)
706 Antelope Way
Kissimmee, FL 34759-4212, USA

Lauren, Joy (Actor)
c/o Mary Sanders *inMomentum Management*
14622 Ventura Blvd # 778
Sherman Oaks, CA 91403-3600, USA

Lauren, Ralph (Designer, Fashion Designer)
650 Madison Ave
New York, NY 10022-1029, USA

Lauren, Tammy (Actor)
14724 Ventura Blvd Ste 505
Sherman Oaks, CA 91403-3505, USA

Laurent, Melanie (Actor, Writer)
c/o Cecile Felsenberg *UBBA*
6 rue de Braque
Paris 75003, France

Laurente, Dennis (Boxer)
c/o Staff Member *Top Rank Inc.*
3908 Howard Hughes Pkwy # 580
Las Vegas, NV 89109, USA

Laurents, Arthur (Writer)
608 Northville Tpke
Riverhead, NY 11901-4717, USA

Laurer, Joanie (Chyna) (Actor, Wrestler)
c/o Michael (Mike) Esterman
Esterman.Com, LLC
Prefers to be contacted via email
MD, USA

Lauria, Dan (Actor)
c/o Harry Gold *TalentWorks (LA)*
3500 W Olive Ave Ste 1400
Burbank, CA 91505-5512, USA

Lauricella, Francis E (Hank) (Athlete, Football Player)
1200 S Clearview Pkwy Ste 1166
Harahan, LA 70123-2378, USA

Lauridsen, Morten (Composer, Musician)
Music Dept
Los Angeles, CA 90089-0001, USA

Laurie, Greg (Religious Leader)
6115 Arlington Ave
Riverside, CA 92504-1911, USA

Laurie, Harry (Athlete, Basketball Player)
540 Bramhall Ave Apt 3
Jersey City, NJ 07304-2323, USA

Laurie, Hugh (Actor, Comedian)
c/o Christian Hodell *Hamilton Hodell Ltd*
66-68 Margaret St Fl 5
London W1W 8SR, UK

Laurie, Piper (Actor)
2118 Wilshire Blvd # 931
Santa Monica, CA 90403-5704, USA

Laurita, Jacqueline (Reality TV Star)
c/o Staff Member *Bravo (NY)*
30 Rockefeller Plz
New York, NY 10112-0015, USA

Lauro, Lindore (Athlete, Football Player)
3213 Lexington Dr
New Castle, PA 16105-1113, USA

Lautenberg, Frank (Senator)
506 Hart Senate Ofc Bldg
Washington, DC 20510-0001, USA

Lautenschlaeger, Fred (Athlete, Football Player)
612 Breton Pl
Arnold, MD 21012-1536, USA

Lauter, Ed (Actor)
9165 W Sunset Blvd Ste 202
Los Angeles, CA 90069-3195, USA

Lauterbur, Paul C (Nobel Prize Laureate)
2702 Holcomb Dr
Urbana, IL 61802-7777, USA

Lauterstein, Alex (DJ)
c/o Staff Member *Diva Central Inc*
7510 W Sunset Blvd Ste 1445
Los Angeles, CA 90046-3408, USA

Lautner, Georges C (Director)
9 Chemin des Basses Ribes
Grasse 6130, FRANCE

Lautner, Taylor (Actor)
c/o Peter Kiernan *Management 360*
9111 Wilshire Blvd
Beverly Hills, CA 90210-5508, USA

Lauzerique, George (Athlete, Baseball Player)
601 Oleaster Ave
Wellington, FL 33414-8197, USA

Lavalliere, Mike (Athlete, Baseball Player)
216 81st St W
Bradenton, FL 34209-2154, USA

Lave, Lester B (Economist)
1008 Devonshire Rd
Pittsburgh, PA 15213-2914, USA

Laveikin, Aleksandr I (Cosmonaut)
Moskovskoi Oblasti
Syvisdny Goroduk 141160, RUSSIA

Lavelle, Gary (Athlete, Baseball Player)
1100 Worthington Ct
Virginia Beach, VA 23464-5855, USA

Lavelle, James (DJ, Musician)
c/o Joel Zimmerman *WmE2 (WMA-NY)*
1325 Avenue of the Americas
New York, NY 10019-6026, USA

Lavender, Jay (Producer)
c/o Staff Member *Principato/Young Management*
9465 Wilshire Blvd Ste 430
Beverly Hills, CA 90212-2613, USA

Lavender, Joseph (Athlete, Football Player)
1215 Alma St
Glendale, CA 91202-2014, USA

Laventhol, Henry L (Hank) (Artist)
445 Heritage Hls Unit F
Somers, NY 10589-1941, USA

Laver, Rodney G (Rod) (Tennis Player)
PO Box 4798
Hilton Head Island, SC 29938-4798, USA

Lavery, Sean (Dancer)
Lincoln Center Plaza
New York, NY 10023, USA

Lavi, Daliah (Actor)
134 W Wainman Ave
Asheboro, NC 27203-5639, GERMANY

Lavigne, Avril (Musician, Songwriter)
c/o Nicole Perna *Baker Winokur Ryder Public Relations (BWR-LA)*
9100 Wilshire Blvd Ste 500 PMB WEST
Beverly Hills, CA 90212-3426, USA

Lavin, Bernice E (Business Person)
2525 Armitage Ave
Melrose Park, IL 60160-1125, USA

Lavin, Leonard H (Business Person)
2525 Armitage Ave
Melrose Park, IL 60160-1125, USA

Lavin, Linda (Actor, Musician)
c/o Staff Member *Lavin Entertainment Group*
411 S Front St
Wilmington, NC 28401-5011, USA

Lavin, TJ (Athlete, Television Host)
c/o Staff Member *Dragon Talent*
8444 Wilshire Blvd PH
Beverly Hills, CA 90211-3200, USA

Laviolette, Peter (Athlete, Coach, Hockey Player)
10303 Town Center Blvd
Voorhees, NJ 08043-2683, USA

Lavoine, Marc (Actor)
c/o Staff Member *ArtMedia*
20 avenue Rapp
Paris 75008, France

Lavon, Peaches (Musician)
c/o Janice Gaffney *Butterscotch Castle*
535 Geary St Apt 612
San Francisco, CA 94102-1635, USA

LaVoo, George (Director, Producer, Writer)
c/o Jon Rubinstein *Authentic Talent and Literary Management*
45 Main St Ste 1004
Brooklyn, NY 11201-8200, USA

LaVorgna, Adam (Actor)
c/o Beverly Strong *Strong Management*
9350 Wilshire Blvd Ste 224
Beverly Hills, CA 90212-3204, USA

Lavoy, Robert (Athlete, Basketball Player)
613 Wood Rd
Seffner, FL 33584-5446, USA

Lavrosky, Mikhail L (Ballerina)
Voznesesenky Per 16/4 #7
Moscow 103009, RUSSIA

Lavrov, Kyrill Y (Actor)
Michurinskaya 1 #36
Saint Petersburg 197046, RUSSIA

Law, Bernard F Cardinal (Religious Leader)
Saint Mary Major Basilica
120, VATICAN CITY

Law, Jude (Actor)
c/o Rick Yorn *Yorn Management Group*
2000 Avenue Of The Stars 3rd Tower Floor NORTH
Los Angeles, CA 90067, USA

Law, Ron (Baseball Player)
3 Mountainview Rd
Greenwood Village, CO 80111-1736, USA

Law, Rudy (Athlete, Baseball Player)
PO Box 1320
Hawthorne, CA 90251-1320, USA

Law, Ty (Athlete, Football Player)
10862 Hawks Vista St
Plantation, FL 33324-8206, USA

Law, Vance (Athlete, Baseball Player)
1682 N 1950 W
Provo, UT 84604-1177, USA

Law, Vern (Athlete, Baseball Player)
1718 N 1050 W
Provo, UT 84604-1159, USA

Lawford, Christopher (Actor)
c/o Christine Holder *Zero Gravity Management (II)*
5225 Wilshire Blvd Ste 600
Los Angeles, CA 90036-4351, USA

Lawler, Jerry
415 Saint Nick Dr
Memphis, TN 38117-4115

Lawler, Kate (Reality TV Star)
c/o Staff Member *Channel 4 Television Corporation*
124 Horseferry Road
London SW1P 2

Lawler, Steve (DJ, Musician)
c/o Joel Zimmerman *WmE2 (WMA-NY)*
1325 Avenue of the Americas
New York, NY 10019-6026, USA

Lawless, Burton (Athlete, Football Player)
2035 Oak Glen Dr
Mc Gregor, TX 76657-3455, USA

Lawless, Lucy (Actor)
c/o Alex Martinetti *Fifteen Minutes (LA)*
8436 W 3rd St Ste 650
Los Angeles, CA 90048-4131, USA

Lawless, Tom (Athlete, Baseball Player)
16619 Evergreen Forest Dr
Ballwin, MO 63011-1879, USA

Lawn, John C (Lawyer)
Yankee Stadium 161st St & River Ave
Bronx, NY 10451, USA

Lawrence, Andrew (Actor)
c/o Staff Member *Kass & Stokes Management*
9229 W Sunset Blvd Ste 504
Los Angeles, CA 90069-3405, USA

Lawrence, Bill (Writer)
c/o Staff Member *Broder Webb Chervin Silbermann Agency, The (BWCS)*
10250 Constellation Blvd
Los Angeles, CA 90067-6200, USA

Lawrence, Braxton Janice (Basketball Player)
1 Center Ct
Cleveland, OH 44115-4001, USA

Lawrence, Brian (Athlete, Baseball Player)
RR 3 Box 120
Linden, TX 75563, USA

Lawrence, Carol (Actor)
12337 Ridge Cir
Los Angeles, CA 90049-1183, USA

Lawrence, Cynthia (Opera Singer)
119 W 57th St Ste 1505
New York, NY 10019-2403, USA

Lawrence, David Jr (Publisher)
1 Herald Plz
Miami, FL 33132-1609, USA

Lawrence, Don (Athlete, Football Player)
12620 Cedar St
Shawnee Mission, KS 66209-3167, USA

Lawrence, Donald (Stylist)
c/o Lara Funod *Bernstein & Andriulli*
58 W 40th St
New York, NY 10018-2658, USA

Lawrence, Francis (Director)
c/o David Naylor *David Naylor & Associates*
6535 Santa Monica Blvd
Los Angeles, CA 90038-1407, USA

Lawrence, Francis (Actor)
c/o Gretchen Rush *Hansen, Jacobson, Teller, Hoberman, Newman, Warren & Richman*
450 N Roxbury Dr Fl 8
Beverly Hills, CA 90210-4222, USA

Lawrence, Francis L (Educator)
President's Office
New Brunswick, NJ 8903, USA

Lawrence, Henry (Athlete, Football Player)
401 17th St W
Palmetto, FL 34221-3257, USA

Lawrence, James (Loz) (Musician)
PO Box 33
Pontypool, Gwent NP4 6YU, UNITED KINGDOM (UK)

Lawrence, Jennifer (Actor)
c/o Liz Mahoney *ID Public Relations (ID-LA)*
7080 Hollywood Blvd Fl 8
Los Angeles, CA 90028-6906, USA

Lawrence, Jim (Athlete, Baseball Player)
225 Haddington St
Caledonia, ON N3W 1G1, Canada

Lawrence, Joe (Athlete, Baseball Player)
4358 Poydras St
Lake Charles, LA 70605-4400, USA

Lawrence, Joseph (Joey) (Actor)
c/o Mark Rousso *New Wave Entertainment (LA)*
2660 W Olive Ave
Burbank, CA 91505-4525, USA

Lawrence, Kent (Athlete, Football Player)
150 Charter Ct
Athens, GA 30605-4628, USA

Lawrence, Linda
4926 Commonwealth Ave
La Canada, CA 91011-2514

Lawrence, Marjie
13 Glenhurst Ave
London, ENGLAND NW5

Lawrence, Martin (Actor, Comedian)
c/o Sam Maydew *Collective*
8383 Wilshire Blvd Ste 1050
Beverly Hills, CA 90211-2415, USA

Lawrence, Matthew (Actor)
c/o Robbie Kass *Kass & Stokes Management*
9229 W Sunset Blvd Ste 504
Los Angeles, CA 90069-3405, USA

Lawrence, Nigel (Musician)
c/o Staff Member *Paradigm (Monterey)*
404 W Franklin St
Monterey, CA 93940-2303, USA

Lawrence, Patricia
33 St Luke's St
London, ENGLAND SW3

Lawrence, Richard D (General)
7301 Valbum Dr
Austin, TX 78731, USA

Lawrence, Robert S (Physicist)
4000 N Charles St Apt 1112
Baltimore, MD 21218-1737, USA

Lawrence, Rolland (Athlete, Football Player)
317 Sugarcreek Dr
Franklin, PA 16323-5641, USA

Lawrence, Russell
7800 Beverly Blvd # 3305
Los Angeles, CA 90036-2112

Lawrence, Sean (Athlete, Baseball Player)
336 S Poplar Ave
Elmhurst, IL 60126-3565, USA

Lawrence, Sharon (Actor, Producer)
c/o David Lust *Patricola Lust PR*
9171 Wilshire Blvd Ste 390
Beverly Hills, CA 90210-5515, USA

Lawrence, Steve (Musician)
944 Pinehurst Dr
Las Vegas, NV 89109-1569, USA

Lawrence, Tracy (Musician, Songwriter)
c/o Staff Member *WmE2 (WMA-TN)*
1600 Division St Ste 300
Nashville, TN 37203-2755, USA

Lawrence, Vicki (Actor, Musician)
6000 Lido Ln
Long Beach, CA 90803-4105, USA

Lawrence, Wendy B (Astronaut)
14675 Lee Rd
Chantilly, VA 20151-1708, USA

Laws, Hubert
1078 S Ogden Dr
Los Angeles, CA 90019-6501

Laws, Mary Jane (Stylist)
921 Lawn Cir
Western Springs, IL 60558-2262, USA

Laws, Ronnie (Musician)
c/o Staff Member *Pyramid Entertainment Group*
377 Rector Pl Apt 21A
New York, NY 10280-1439, USA

Lawson, Ana Maria (Beauty Pageant Winner)
PO Box 59064
Potomac, MD 20859-9064, USA

Lawson, Bianca (Actor)
c/o Staff Member *Luber Roklin Management*
8530 Wilshire Blvd Ste 550
Beverly Hills, CA 90211-3133, USA

Lawson, Denis (Actor, Director, Writer)
c/o Staff Member *Yakety Yak*
8-A Bloomsbury Sq
London WC1A 2NE, UNITED KINGDOM (UK)

Lawson, Doyle (Musician)
c/o Staff Member *Paradigm (Monterey)*
404 W Franklin St
Monterey, CA 93940-2303, USA

Lawson, Josh (Actor, Writer)
c/o Gabriel Cohen *Management 360*
9111 Wilshire Blvd
Beverly Hills, CA 90210-5508, USA

Lawson, Kara (Basketball Player)
c/o Staff Member *Sacramento Monarchs*
1 Sports Pkwy
Sacramento, CA 95834-2300, USA

Lawson, Ken (Ken L) (Actor)
c/o Staff Member *Agency West Entertainment*
6255 W Sunset Blvd Ste 908
Hollywood, CA 90028-7410, USA

Lawson, Leigh (Actor)
34-43 Russell St
London WC2B 5HA, UNITED KINGDOM (UK)

Lawson, Maggie (Actor)
c/o Ellen Meyer *Ellen Meyer Management*
8899 Beverly Blvd Ste 612
West Hollywood, CA 90048-2429, USA

Lawson, Nigella (Chef, Writer)
c/o Staff Member *Uitgeverij Contact*
Portbus 218
Amsterdam 1000 AE, The Netherlands

Lawson, Richard (Actor)
8840 Wilshire Blvd # 200
Beverly Hills, CA 90211-2606, USA

Lawson, Richard L (General)
6910 Clifton Rd
Clifton, VA 20124-1524, USA

Lawson, Steve (Athlete, Baseball Player)
PO Box 5630
Brookings, OR 97415-0120, USA

Lawson, Twiggy (Actor, Model)
c/o Maureen Vincent *United Agents*
12-26 Lexington St
London W1F OLE, UK

Lawson, William (Baseball Player)
8800 E McClellan St
Tucson, AZ 85710-4419, USA

Lawson, William (Athlete, Baseball Player)
8800 E McClellan St
Tucson, AZ 85710-4419, USA

Lawson of Blaby, Nigel (Government Official)
32 Sutherland Walk
London SE17, UNITED KINGDOM (UK)

Lawston, Marlene (Actor)
c/o Victoria Kress *Don Buchwald & Associates Inc (NY)*
10 E 44th St Frnt 1
New York, NY 10017-3654

Lawton, Jared (Stylist)
c/o Staff Member *Loox Agency*
12 Desbrosses St
New York, NY 10013-1704, USA

Lawton, Jonathan (J.F.) (Writer)
c/o Sara Bottfeld *Industry Entertainment Partners*
955 Carrillo Dr Ste 300
Los Angeles, CA 90048-5400, USA

Lawton, Liam (Musician)
86 Haddington Rd Ballsbridge, Dublin 4
IRELAND

Lawton, Marcus (Athlete, Baseball Player)
110 Connie Dr
Gulfport, MS 39503-3254, USA

Lawton, Mary (Cartoonist)
901 Mission St
San Francisco, CA 94103-2905, USA

Lawton, Matthew (Matt) (Athlete, Baseball Player)
27264 Bethel Rd
Saucier, MS 39574-9020, USA

Lawton, Robert B (Educator)
President's Office
Los Angeles, CA 90045, USA

Lawwill, Theodore (Misc)
PO Box 44
Fort Myers Beach, FL 33931-1281, USA

Lax, John (Athlete, Hockey Player)
3 Greendale Ln
Harwich, MA 2645, USA

Lax, Melvin (Physicist)
12 High St
Summit, NJ 07901-2413, USA

Lax, Peter D (Mathematician)
251 Mercer St
New York, NY 10012-1110, USA

Laxalt, Paul D (Ex-Governor, Ex-Senator)
4312 Victoria Ln
Alexandria, VA 22304-7400, USA

Laxamana, ROn (Stylist)
c/o Staff Member *Blink Management*
421 Washington Ave Ste 202
Miami Beach, FL 33139-6612, USA

Laxmikant, Berde (Actor, Bollywood)
105 Nirakar B-Wing 1st Complex Yari Road Versova Andheri Floor KALYAN
Bombay, MS 400061, INDIA

Laxton, Bill (Athlete, Baseball Player)
261 Mansion Ave
Audubon, NJ 08106-1529, USA

Laxton, Brett (Athlete, Baseball Player)
823 Sonora Cir
Evans, GA 30809-4292, USA

Lay, Donald P (Judge)
316 Robert St N
Saint Paul, MN 55101-1495, USA

Layden, Frank (Athlete, Basketball Player, Coach)
241 N Vine St Apt 1204W
Salt Lake City, UT 84103-1938, USA

Layevska, Anna (Actor)
c/o Staff Member *Cesar Carrera*
C/ Isabel Serrano, 12
Madrid 28029, Spain

Layman, Jason (Athlete, Football Player)
163 New Center Rd
Sevierville, TN 37876-2167, USA

Layne, Hillis (Hilly) (Athlete, Baseball Player)
101 Woodcliff Cir
Signal Mountain, TN 37377-3142, USA

Layne, Jerry (Baseball Player)
2323 Cypress Gardens Blvd
Winter Haven, FL 33884-2120, USA

Layne, Jerry (Athlete, Baseball Player)
2323 Cypress Gardens Blvd
Winter Haven, FL 33884-2120, USA

Layne, Shontelle (Musician)
c/o Carl Sturken *SRC - Street Records Corporation*
Universal - Motown 1755 Broadway New Media
New York, NY 10019, USA

Layton, Dennis (Athlete, Basketball Player)
872 S 14th St
Newark, NJ 07108-1320, USA

Layton, Les (Athlete, Baseball Player)
6424 Washington St Spc 76
Yountville, CA 94599-9461, USA

Lazar, Danny (Athlete, Baseball Player)
8444 Oakwood Ave
Munster, IN 46321-1915, USA

Lazar, Laurence (Religious Leader)
2522 Grey Tower Rd
Jackson, MI 49201-9120, USA

Lazard, Justin
9350 Wilshire Blvd Ste 324
Beverly Hills, CA 90212-3206

Lazarev, Alexander N
39 Taderna ROad #2
London SW10 0PY, UNITED KINGDOM (UK)

Lazaroff, Barbara
805 N Sierra Dr
Beverly Hills, CA 90210-2644

Lazarus, Lisa (Actor, Beauty Pageant Winner)
c/o Michael (Mike) Esterman
Esterman.Com, LLC
Prefers to be contacted via email
MD, USA

Lazarus, Mell (Cartoonist)
5777 W Century Blvd Ste 700
Los Angeles, CA 90045-5652, USA

Lazarus, Shelly (Business Person)
309 W 49th St
New York, NY 10019-7316, USA

Lazear, Edward P (Economist)
277 Old Spanish Trl
Portola Valley, CA 94028-8129, USA

Lazenby, George (Actor)
c/o Staff Member *Hervey/Grimes Talent Agency*
10561 Missouri Ave Apt 2
Los Angeles, CA 90025-5940, USA

Lazetich, Bill (Athlete, Football Player)
3840 Rimrock Rd Apt 2100
Billings, MT 59102-0153, USA

Lazetich, Pete (Athlete, Football Player)
185 Martin St
Reno, NV 89509-2827, USA

Lazier, Buddy (Race Car Driver)
9375 Whitley Dr
Indianapolis, IN 46240-1349, USA

Lazlo, Viktor
56 Rue De Lisbonne
Paris, FRANCE F-75008

Lazorko, Jack (Athlete, Baseball Player)
1360 Meandering Way
Rockwall, TX 75087-2309, USA

Lazuktin, Alexander I (Cosmonaut)
Moskovskoi Oblasti
Syvisdny Goroduk 141160, RUSSIA

Lazure, Gabrielle (Actor)
36 Rue de Ponthieu
Paris 75008, FRANCE

Le, Cung (Actor)
c/o Scott Karp *Crystal Sky Pictures*
10203 Santa Monica Blvd Ste 500
Los Angeles, CA 90067-6416, USA

Le Bon, Yasmin (Model)
c/o Staff Member *Ford Models (NY)*
238 E 4th St
New York, NY 10009-7425

Le Duc, Anh (General, President)
Hoang Hoa Tham
Hanoi, VIETNAM

Le Mat, Paul (Actor)
6300 Wilshire Blvd Ste 1460
Los Angeles, CA 90048-5200, USA

Le May Doan, Catriona (Speed Skater)
1 City Centre Dr Ste 301
Mississauga, ON L5B 1M2, CANADA

Le Prevost, Nicholas
43A Princess Rd Regents Park
London, ENGLAND NW1 8JS

Le Prevost, Nigel
43A Princess Rd
London, ENGLAND W1

Le Rosa, Stefan (Actor)
c/o Staff Member *Nickelodeon UK*
PO Box 6425
LONDON W1A 6UR, UNITED KINGDOM

Le Tigre (Music Group)
c/o Tom Sarig 27 W 24th St Ste 404
New York, NY 10010, USA

Le Vert
110-112 Lantoga Rd # D
Wayne, PA 19087

Lea, Charles W (Charlie) (Athlete, Baseball Player)
3064 Mistwood Cv S
Collierville, TN 38017-8921, USA

Lea, Nicholas (Actor)
c/o Adam Levine *Levine Okwu Erickson Management*
9601 Wilshire Blvd Fl 3
Beverly Hills, CA 90210-5219, USA

Leabu, Tristan Lake (Actor)
c/o Tracy Dwyer 7700 Sunset Blvd
Los Angeles, CA 90046, USA

Leach, Henry C (Admiral)
Wonston Lea
Winchester, Hants SO21 3LS, UNITED KINGDOM (UK)

Leach, Jalal (Athlete, Baseball Player)
3718 Phillip Island Rd
West Sacramento, CA 95691-5939, USA

Leach, Penelope (Misc)
3 Tanza Lane
London NW3 2UA, UNITED KINGDOM (UK)

Leach, Reggie (Athlete, Hockey Player)
906 Clydesdale Dr
Bear, DE 19701-2205, USA

Leach, Rick (Athlete, Baseball Player)
593 Layman Creek Cir
Grand Blanc, MI 48439-1384, USA

Leach, Robin (Entertainer, Producer, Television Host)
c/o Staff Member *Diverse Talent Group*
9911 W Pico Blvd Ste 340W
Los Angeles, CA 90035-2712, USA

Leach, Rosemary (Actor)
51 Maida Vale
London W9 1SD, UNITED KINGDOM (UK)

Leach, Sheryl (Animator)
300 E Bethany Dr
Allen, TX 75002-3802, USA

Leach, Terry (Athlete, Baseball Player)
2135 SW Locks Rd
Stuart, FL 34997-7011, USA

Leachman, Cloris (Actor)
c/o George Englund *George Englund Jr Management*
11661 San Vicente Blvd Ste 609
Los Angeles, CA 90049-5114, USA

Leadbetter, Kelly (Athlete, Golfer)
14729 Augustine Rd
Orlando, FL 32832-6520, USA

Leader, George M (Ex-Governor)
1528 Sand Hill Rd
Hummelstown, PA 17036-9704, USA

Leader, Tom (Architect)
537 Golden Gate Ave
Richmond, CA 94801-3709, USA

Leadon, Bernie (Musician)
4405 Belmont Park Ter
Nashville, TN 37215-3609, USA

Leaf, Alexander (Physicist)
100 Newbury Ct Apt 5515
Concord, MA 01742-4167, USA

Leaf, Ryan (Athlete, Football Player)
8111 Barstow Dr
Amarillo, TX 79118-8111, USA

League, Brandon (Athlete, Baseball Player)
708 Shenandoah Ridge Rd
Wausau, WI 54403-9173, USA

Leah, Rachelle (Actor, Athlete)
c/o Ivo Fischer *WmE2 (Endeavor-LA)*
9601 Wilshire Blvd Fl 3
Beverly Hills, CA 90210-5219, USA

Leahy, Bob (Athlete, Football Player)
2701 Rosedale Dr
Monroe, LA 71201-3068, USA

Leahy, Pat (Baseball Player)
1350 Dazet Rd
Yakima, WA 98908-9600, USA

Leahy, Patrick (Senator)
433 Russell Senate Ofc Bldg
Washington, DC 20510-0001, USA

Leahy, Patrick J (Pat) (Athlete, Football Player)
717 Chamblee Ln
Saint Louis, MO 63141-7324, USA

Leak, Jennifer (Actor)
PO Box 2219
Amagansett, NY 11930-2219, USA

Leak, Justice (Actor)
c/o Staff Member *People Store*
645 Lambert Dr NE
Atlanta, GA 30324-4125, USA

Leake, Brett (Comedian)
3561 Leatherwood Ln
Maidens, VA 23102-2025, USA

Leakes, NeNe (Reality TV Star)
c/o Eva Arthur *Universal Attractions*
135 W 26th St Fl 12
New York, NY 10001-6872, USA

Leakey, Meave G (Biologist)
PO Box 24926
Nairobi, KENYA

Leakey, Richard E F (Biologist)
PO Box 24926
Nairobi, KENYA

Leaks, Manny (Athlete, Basketball Player)
9912 North Blvd
Cleveland, OH 44108-3430, USA

Leaks Jr, Roosevelt (Athlete, Football Player)
11525 Glen Falloch Ct
Austin, TX 78754-5807, USA

Leal, Sharon (Actor, Musician)
c/o Scott Wexler *Brillstein Entertainment Partners*
9150 Wilshire Blvd Ste 350
Beverly Hills, CA 90212-3453, USA

Leandros, Vicky
Postfach 31 28
Kiel, GERMANY D-24030

LeAnn, Summer (Actor)
c/o Rebecca Wood *Triple Threat*
7070 W Sunset Blvd Ste 126
Los Angeles, CA 90028-7521, USA

Leannette (Stylist)
c/o Staff Member *Ken Barboza Associates*
115 W 30th St Rm 203
New York, NY 10001-4088, USA

Lear, Evelyn (Opera Singer)
414 Sailboat Cir
Weston, FL 33326-1506, USA

Lear, Harold (Athlete, Basketball Player)
11321 E Sunnyside Dr
Scottsdale, AZ 85259-3119, USA

Lear, Norman M (Director, Producer, Writer)
c/o Staff Member *Act III Productions*
100 N Crescent Dr Ste 250
Beverly Hills, CA 90210-5451, USA

Learned, Michael (Actor)
1600 N Beverly Dr
Beverly Hills, CA 90210-2316, USA

Leary, Denis (Actor, Comedian, Producer, Writer)
c/o Heidi Slan *42West (LA)*
11400 W Olympic Blvd Ste 1100
Los Angeles, CA 90064-1579, USA

Leary, Tim (Athlete, Baseball Player)
1766 Michael Ln
Pacific Palisades, CA 90272-2037, USA

Leatherdale, Douglas W (Business Person)
385 Washington St
Saint Paul, MN 55102-1309, USA

Leaud, Jean-Pierre (Actor)
20 Ave Rapp
Paris 75007, FRANCE

Leavell, Allen (Athlete, Basketball Player)
7007 Windy Pines Dr
Spring, TX 77379-4733, USA

Leavell, Chuck (Musician)
665 Charlane Dr
Dry Branch, GA 31020-5256, USA

Leavelle, James
1221 Colonel Dr Apt 403
Garland, TX 75043-7906, USA

Leavenworth, Scotty (Actor)
c/o Susan Curtis *Curtis Talent Management*
9607 Arby Dr
Beverly Hills, CA 90210-1202, USA

Leaves (Music Group)
c/o Staff Member *Paradigm (Monterey)*
404 W Franklin St
Monterey, CA 93940-2303, USA

Leavitt, Michael O (Ex-Governor)
299 S Main St Ste 2300
Salt Lake City, UT 84111-2299, USA

Leavitt, Phil (Musician)
PO Box 1031
Montrose, CA 91021-1031, USA

Leavy, Edward (Judge)
555 SW Yamhill St
Portland, OR 97204-1303, USA

Lebadang (Artist)
303 E Wacker Dr
Chicago, IL 60601-5212, USA

LeBaron, Edward W (Eddie) Jr (Athlete, Football Player)
7524 Pineridge Ln
Fair Oaks, CA 95628-4854, USA

LeBeau, Becky
9461 Charleville Blvd # 602
Beverly Hills, CA 90212-3017

LeBeau, C Richard (Dick) (Athlete, Coach, Football Player)
10405 Stone Ct
Montgomery, OH 45242-5128, USA

LeBeauf, Sabrina (Actor)
11 Asbury Rd
Asheville, NC 28804-2701, USA

Lebedev, Valentin V (Cosmonaut)
Moskovskoi Oblasti
Syvisdny Goroduk 141160, RUSSIA

LeBel, B Harper (Athlete, Football Player)
3379 Scadlock Ln
Sherman Oaks, CA 91403-4914, USA

LeBel, Robert (Bob) (Misc)
25 Rue Saint Pierre
Cite de Chambly, QC J3L 1L7, CANADA

Leber, Ben (Athlete, Football Player)
4457 35th Ave S
Minneapolis, MN 55406-3840, USA

Lebis, Attilo (Choreographer, Dancer)
120 Rue Lyon
Paris 75012, FRANCE

LeBlanc, Christian LeBlanc (Actor)
c/o Staff Member *The Young and The Restless*
7800 Beverly Blvd Ste 3305
Los Angeles, CA 90036-2112, USA

LeBlanc, Matt (Actor)
c/o Michael Rotenberg *3 Arts Entertainment Inc*
9460 Wilshire Blvd Fl 7
Beverly Hills, CA 90212-2713, USA

Lebo, Jeff (Athlete, Basketball Player)
500 Hidden Lake Way
Santa Rosa Beach, FL 32459-0200, USA

Leboeuf, Laurence (Actor)
c/o Karen Benzakein 1445 Lambert Closse
Montreal H3H 1Z5, CANADA

LeBoeuf, Raymond W (Business Person)
1 Ppg Pl
Pittsburgh, PA 15272-0001, USA

LeBon, Simon (Musician, Songwriter, Writer)
c/o Staff Member *DD Productions*
93A Westbourne Park Villas
London W2 5ED, UNITED KINGDOM (UK)

Lebowitz, Fran (Writer)
1745 Broadway # B1
New York, NY 10019-4368, USA

Lebowitz, Joel L (Mathematician)
Mathematics Dept
New Brunswick, NJ 8903, USA

Leboyer, Frederick (Physicist)
136 E 57th St
New York, NY 10022-2707, USA

LeBrock, Kelly (Actor, Model)
PO Box 57593
Sherman Oaks, CA 91413-2593, USA

Lebron, Juan (Baseball Player)
PO Box 242
Arroyo, PR 00714-0242, USA

LeBrun, Christopher M (Artist)
6 Albermarle St
London W1X 4BY, UNITED KINGDOM (UK)

Lecaine, Bill (Athlete, Hockey Player)
10484 Tracewood Cir
Highlands Ranch, CO 80130-8893, USA

LeCarre, John (Writer)
9 Gainsborough Gardens
London NW3 1BJ, UNITED KINGDOM (UK)

LeCavalier, Vincent (Athlete, Hockey Player)
c/o Staff Member *Tampa Bay Lightning*
401 Channelside Dr
Tampa, FL 33602-5400, USA

Lechter, Sharon L (Writer)
4330 N Civic Center Plz
Scottsdale, AZ 85251-3528, USA

Leckner, Eric (Athlete, Basketball Player)
608 27th St
Manhattan Beach, CA 90266-2231, USA

Leckonby, William (Athlete, Football Player)
1311 Santee Mill Rd
Bethlehem, PA 18017-1111, USA

LeClair, James M (Jim) (Athlete, Football Player)
32 4th Ave NE
Mayville, ND 58257-1226, USA

Leclair, Jim (Athlete, Football Player)
600 Plymouth Way
Burlingame, CA 94010-2733, USA

LeClerc, Jean (Actor)
19 W 44th St Ste 1500
New York, NY 10036-6101, USA

Leclerc, Roger (Athlete, Football Player)
257 Elm St
Agawam, MA 01001-2444, USA

LeClere, Jennifer
5601 Navigation Blvd
Houston, TX 77011-1105

LeClezio, Jean-Marie (Writer)
5 Rue Sebastien-Bottin
Paris 75007, USA

Lecomte, Benoit (Swimmer)
3005 S Lamar Blvd # D109-353
Austin, TX 78704-8864, USA

Leconte, Henri (Tennis Player)
Pier House Strand-on-Green
Chiswick, London W4 3NN, UNITED KINGDOM (UK)

Leconte, Patrice (Director, Writer)
c/o Staff Member *ArtMedia*
20 avenue Rapp
Paris 75008, France

Lecoultre, Francine (Stylist)
1918 N Main St Apt 204
Los Angeles, CA 90031-2498, USA

Lecount, Terry (Athlete, Football Player)
1288 Branchfield Ct
Riverdale, GA 30296-2148, USA

Lecroy, Matt (Athlete, Baseball Player)
11314 Cedar Pointe Dr N
Hopkins, MN 55305-2987, USA

Ledbetter, Monte (Athlete, Football Player)
340 Sawgrass Dr
Valdosta, GA 31602-1477, USA

Ledee, Ricky (Athlete, Baseball Player)
PO Box 22024
Hilton Head Island, SC 29925-2024, USA

Leder, Mimi (Director)
c/o Sara Bottfeld *Industry Entertainment Partners*
955 Carrillo Dr Ste 300
Los Angeles, CA 90048-5400, USA

Leder, Philip (Scientist)
4000 Jones Bridge Road
Chevy Chase MD, 20815

Lederberg, Joshua (Nobel Prize Laureate)
President's Office 1230 York Ave
New York, NY 10021, USA

Lederman, Leon M (Nobel Prize Laureate)
3101 S Dearborn St
Chicago, IL 60616-2852, USA

Ledesma, Aaron (Athlete, Baseball Player)
2446 Douglas St
Union City, CA 94587-1865, USA

Ledford, Brandy (Actor)
c/o Leonard Bonnell *Characters Talent Agency, The (Toronto)*
8 Elm St 2nd Floor
Toronto, ON M5G 1G7, Canada

Ledford, Frank F Jr (General)
PO Box 760549 San Antonio
TX, 78245 USA

Ledford, Judith
11365 Ventura Blvd Ste 100
Studio City, CA 91604-3148

Ledley, Robert S (Inventor)
17000 Melbourne Dr
Laurel, MD 20707-2796, USA

Ledoyen, Virginie (Actor, Model)
c/o Beatrice Hall *ArtMedia*
20 avenue Rapp
Paris 75008, France

Leduc-Alverson, Noella (Baseball Player)
5 Leonard Ave
Leonardo, NJ 07737-1536, USA

Ledyard, Courtney (Athlete, Football Player)
419 Miller Ave
Freeport, NY 11520-6112, USA

Lee, Alexondra (Actor)
c/o Staff Member *Loeb & Loeb (Office 1)*
10100 Santa Monica Blvd Ste 2200
Los Angeles, CA 90067-4120, USA

Lee, Andy (Radio Personality, Television Host)
Level 15 50 Goulburn St
Sidney, NSW 2000, Australia

Lee, Andy Scott (Musician)
c/o Staff Member *DCM International & Dance Crazy Management*
Suite 3, 294-296 Nether St Finchley
London N3 1RJ, UK

Lee, Ang (Director, Producer, Writer)
c/o Simon Halls *Slate Public Relations*
9000 W Sunset Blvd Ste 915
West Hollywood, CA 90069-5809, USA

Lee, Anthonia W (Amp) (Athlete, Football Player)
1306 Plum Cir
Chipley, FL 32428-1111, USA

Lee, Barbara (Congressman, Politician)
2267 Rayburn Hob
Washington, DC 20515-4202, USA

Lee, Bertram M (Misc)
Pepsi Center 1000 Chopper Circle
Denver, CO 80204, USA

Lee, Beverly (Musician)
PO Box 100
Clifton, NJ 07015-0100, USA

Lee, Bill (Athlete, Baseball Player)
305 Common View Dr
Craftsbury, VT 05826-9779, USA

Lee, Bob (Athlete, Baseball Player)
PO Box 1589
Lake Havasu City, AZ 86405-1589, USA

Lee, Bobby (Actor)
c/o Staff Member *Gersh (LA)*
9465 Wilshire Blvd Ste 600
Beverly Hills, CA 90212-2612, USA

Lee, Brandon (Adult Film Star)
c/o Staff Member *Diva Central Inc*
7510 W Sunset Blvd Ste 1445
Los Angeles, CA 90046-3408, USA

Lee, Brenda (Musician)
c/o Staff Member *Paradigm (Monterey)*
404 W Franklin St
Monterey, CA 93940-2303, USA

Lee, Briana (Adult Film Star)
8033 W Sunset Blvd # 851
W Hollywood, CA 90046-2401, USA

Lee, Butch (Athlete, Basketball Player)
6616 Bluestone Ct
Charlotte, NC 28212-6431, USA

Lee, Carl (Athlete, Football Player)
1 Stonegate Dr
Hurricane, WV 25526-9217, USA

Lee, Carlos (Athlete, Baseball Player)
1400 N 11th Ave
Melrose Park, IL 60160-3524, USA

Lee, Catherine J (Artist)
PO Box 132
Condon, OR 97823-0132, USA

Lee, Chang-Rae (Writer)
40 W 57th St # 1800
New York, NY 10019-4001, USA

Lee, Charles R (Business Person)
1255 Corporate Dr
Irving, TX 75038-2562, USA

Lee, Christopher (Congressman, Politician)
1711 Longworth Hob
Washington, DC 20515-1201, USA

Lee, Christopher F C (Actor)
c/o Jean Diamond *Diamond Management*
31 Percy St
London W1T 2DD, UK

Lee, Cliff (Athlete, Baseball Player)
c/o Darek Braunecker *Braunecker Sports Counseling*
226 Trelon Cir
Little Rock, AR 72223-3920, USA

Lee, Clyde (Athlete, Basketball Player)
1118 Crater Hill Dr
Nashville, TN 37215-4510, USA

Lee, Corey (Athlete, Baseball Player)
278 Lancashire Run
Smithfield, NC 27577-8025, USA

Lee, C.S. (Actor, Director)
c/o Andrew Tetenbaum *ATA Management*
12 Desbrosses St
New York, NY 10013-1704, USA

Lee, David (Director, Writer)
450 N Roxbury Dr Ste 1050
Beverly Hills, CA 90210-4235, USA

Lee, David (Athlete, Baseball Player)
56 Terrace Dr
Pittsburgh, PA 15205-4312, USA

Lee, David (Athlete, Basketball Player)
2580 Rampart Ter
Reno, NV 89519-8361, USA

Lee, David A (Athlete, Football Player)
2518 N Waverly Dr
Bossier City, LA 71111-5940, USA

Lee, David H (Astronomer, Writer)
233 Spring St
New York, NY 10013-1522, USA

Lee, David L (Business Person)
Wessex House 45 Reid St
Hamilton, HM 12, Bermuda

Lee, David M (Nobel Prize Laureate)
Physics Dept Clark Hall
Ithaca, NY 14853, USA

Lee, Denise (Actor)
c/o Terry Loftis *Verve Communications Group*
325 N Saint Paul St Ste 2360
Dallas, TX 75201-3824, USA

Lee, Derek (Athlete, Baseball Player)
8834 Liatris Dr
Frankfort, IL 60423-1742, USA

Lee, Derek (Athlete, Baseball Player)
3576 Brittany Way
El Dorado Hills, CA 95762-3952, USA

Lee, Derek
5230 Hyland Hills Ave Unit 1311
Sarasota, FL 34241-7154, USA

Lee, Dickey (Musician)
27 L Ambiance Ct
Bardonia, NY 10954-1421, USA

Lee, Don (Athlete, Baseball Player)
9101 E Palm Tree Dr
Tucson, AZ 85710-8626, USA

Lee, Doug (Athlete, Basketball Player)
10770 Procyon St
Las Vegas, NV 89141-8844, USA

Lee, Dwight (Athlete, Football Player)
PO Box 480397
New Haven, MI 48048-0397, USA

Lee, Edward (Writer)
PO Box 540298
Orlando, FL 32854-0298, USA

Lee, Edward (Athlete, Football Player)
1781 Verbena St NW
Washington, DC 20012-1048, USA

Lee, Eugene (Actor)
c/o Vincent Cirrincione *Vincent Cirrincione Associates*
1516 N Fairfax Ave
Los Angeles, CA 90046-2608, USA

Lee, Eunice (Musician)
165 W 57th St
New York, NY 10019-2201, USA

Lee, Geddy (Musician)
1505 W 2nd Ave # 200
Vancouver, BC V6H 3Y4, CANADA

Lee, Grandma (Actor, Comedian)
626 Staffordshire Dr
Jacksonville, FL 32225, USA

Lee, Gregory (Athlete, Basketball Player)
8077 Wild Flower Way
San Diego, CA 92120-1622, USA

Lee, H Douglas (Educator)
President's Office
Deland, FL 32720, USA

Lee, Harper (Writer)
353 Lexington Ave Rm 1500
New York, NY 10016-0941, USA

Lee, Homer & The Braschler's
PO Box 1408
Branson, MO 65615-1408

Lee, Howard V (War Hero)
529 King Arthur Dr
Virginia Beach, VA 23464-2235, USA

Lee, Jack R (Athlete, Football Player)
6306 Mid Pines Dr
Houston, TX 77069-1346, USA

Lee, James Kyson (Actor)
c/o Staff Member *Kass & Stokes Management*
9229 W Sunset Blvd Ste 504
Los Angeles, CA 90069-3405, USA

Lee, Jared B (Cartoonist)
2942 Hamilton Rd
Lebanon, OH 45036-8857, USA

Lee, Jason (Actor, Producer, Writer)
c/o Gay Ribisi *Ribisi Entertainment*
3278 Wilshire Blvd Apt 702
Los Angeles, CA 90010-1425, USA

Lee, Jason Scott (Actor)
c/o Cynthia Shelton-Droke *Sweet Mud Group*
648 Broadway # 1002
New York, NY 10012-2348, USA

Lee, Jeahette (Billiards Player)
1751 Pinnacle Dr Ste 1500
McLean, VA 22102-3833, USA

Lee, Jeanette (Billiards Player)
c/o Arlene dela Cruz dela Cruz *Octagon (VA)*
1751 Pinnacle Dr Ste 1500
McLean, VA 22102-3833, USA

Lee, Jenny (Athlete, Golfer)
c/o Staff Member *Ladies Pro Golf Association (LPGA)*
100 International Golf Dr
Daytona Beach, FL 32124-1092, USA

Lee, Joe (Business Person)
5900 Lake Ellenor Dr
Orlando, FL 32809-4634, USA

Lee, Jon (Actor, Musician)
c/o Staff Member *McLean-Williams Management*
Gainsborough House 81 Oxford St
London W1D 2EU, UK

Lee, Jonna (Actor)
8721 W Sunset Blvd Ste 103
Los Angeles, CA 90069-2271, USA

Lee, Julia (Actor)
c/o Staff Member *Privilege Talent Agency*
PO Box 260860
Encino, CA 91426-0860, USA

Lee, Kathy
204 Rivers Edge Ln
Sevierville, TN 37862-5213

Lee, Keith (Athlete, Basketball Player)
11653 Metz Pl
Eads, TN 38028-6912, USA

Lee, Kuan Yew (Prime Minister)
Istana Annexe Istana
Singapore 923, SINGAPORE

Lee, Kurk (Athlete, Basketball Player)
2745 Scarborough Cir
Windsor Mill, MD 21244-8024, USA

Lee, Larry (Athlete, Football Player)
PO Box 3889
Highland Park, MI 48203-0889, USA

Lee, Laura
155 N Beverwyck Pmb 245
Lake Hiawatha, NJ 7034

Lee, Laurie Ann (Baseball Player)
19528 Cohasset St
Reseda, CA 91335-2436, USA

Lee, Lela (Actor)
c/o Marilyn Szatmary *Silver Massetti & Szatmary (SMS) Talent Inc*
8730 W Sunset Blvd Ste 440
Los Angeles, CA 90069-2277, USA

Lee, Leron (Athlete, Baseball Player)
8150 Warren Ct
Granite Bay, CA 95746-9576, USA

Lee, London
1650 Broadway Ste 1410
New York, NY 10019-6957

Lee, Malcolm D (Actor, Director, Writer)
c/o Adam Kanter *Creative Artists Agency (CAA-LA)*
2000 Avenue of the Stars Ste 100
Los Angeles, CA 90067-4705, USA

Lee, Mark (Athlete, Baseball Player)
130 N Rosemont St
Amarillo, TX 79106-5214, USA

Lee, Mark (Athlete, Baseball Player)
3580 Brunswick Dr
Colorado Springs, CO 80920-7338, USA

Lee, Mark (Athlete, Football Player)
14120 NE 183rd St Unit 233
Woodinville, WA 98072-7073, USA

Lee, Mark C (Astronaut)
79 S Player Crest Cir
Spring, TX 77382-1809, USA

Lee, Michele (Actor)
c/o Irvin Arthur *Park Ave Talent*
1560 Broadway Ste 1100
New York, NY 10036-1537, USA

Lee, Michelle (Actor)
c/o Michael Henderson *Heresun Management*
4119 W Burbank Blvd
Burbank, CA 91505-2122, USA

Lee, Mike (Athlete, Baseball Player)
1790 Calmin Dr
Fallbrook, CA 92028 1303, USA

Lee, Min-ho (Actor)
c/o Staff Member *Starhaus Entertainment*
L#601 Hill B/D 563-4 Shinsa-dong,
Kangnam-gu,
Seoul, Korea

Lee, Natasha (Actor, Dancer, Model)
c/o Staff Member *Don Capo Entertainment*
Ste 5 South Bank Terrace Surbiton
Surrey KT6 6DG, UNITED KINGDOM (UK)

Lee, Raphael C (Doctor)
Engineering Dept
Cambridge, MA 2139, USA

Lee, Reggie (Actor)
c/o Adam Griffin *Kritzer Levine Wilkins Entertainment*
11872 La Grange Ave Fl 1
Los Angeles, CA 90025-5283, USA

Lee, Rex (Actor)
c/o Marc Hamou *Thruline Entertainment*
9250 Wilshire Blvd Ground Fl
Beverly Hills, CA 90212, USA

Lee, Robert M (Athlete, Football Player)
363 Parker Ave
San Francisco, CA 94118-4235, USA

Lee, Robinne (Actor)
c/o Darren Goldberg *Global Creative*
1051 Cole Ave # B
Los Angeles, CA 90038-2601, USA

Lee, Rock (Athlete, Basketball Player)
4616 Blackfoot Ave
San Diego, CA 92117-6230, USA

Lee, Ron (Athlete, Basketball Player)
35788 Woodridge Ct
Farmington Hills, MI 48335-2206, USA

Lee, Ronnie (Athlete, Football Player)
139 Shady Trl
Mc Gregor, TX 76657-3768, USA

Lee, RonReaco
c/o Brett Carella *Lab, The*
5540 Hollywood Blvd # 200
Hollywood, CA 90028-6808, USA

Lee, Russell (Athlete, Basketball Player)
1457 Smokehouse Ln
Stone Mountain, GA 30088-3312, USA

Lee, Ruta (Actor)
2623 Laurel Canyon Blvd
Los Angeles, CA 90046-1106, USA

Lee, Sammy (Doctor)
16537 Harbour Ln
Huntington Beach, CA 92649-2105, USA

Lee, Samuel (Sammy) (Coach)
16537 Harbour Ln
Huntington Beach, CA 92649-2105, USA

Lee, Sandra (Chef, Television Host)
c/o Staff Member *Food Network, The*
75 9th Ave
New York, NY 10011-7006, USA

Lee, Shannon (Actor)
c/o John Elias *Three Twins Entertainment, Inc*
PO Box 100210
Staten Island, NY 10310-0210, USA

Lee, Sheryl (Actor)
c/o Daniel (Danny) Sussman *Brillstein Entertainment Partners*
9150 Wilshire Blvd Ste 350
Beverly Hills, CA 90212-3453, USA

Lee, Spike (Director, Producer)
c/o Evelyn Santana *Bazan Entertainment*
4 Rainbow Ter
West Orange, NJ 07052-5023, USA

Lee, Stan (Cartoonist, Publisher)
1440 S Sepulveda Blvd # 114
Los Angeles, CA 90025-3458, USA

Lee, Steven (Television Host)
c/o Staff Member *Travel Channel*
1 Discovery Pl
Silver Spring, MD 20910-3354, USA

Lee, Sung Hi (Actor)
c/o Staff Member *TalentWorks (LA)*
3500 W Olive Ave Ste 1400
Burbank, CA 91505-5512, USA

Lee, Terry (Athlete, Baseball Player)
4650 Wendover St
Eugene, OR 97404-1348, USA

Lee, Tommy (Musician)
c/o David Weise *David Weise and Associates*
16000 Ventura Blvd Ste 600
Encino, CA 91436-2753, USA

Lee, Tony (Actor)
c/o Dave Phillips *Edmonds Management*
1635 N Cahuenga Blvd Fl 5
Los Angeles, CA 90028-6201, USA

Lee, Travis (Athlete, Baseball Player)
PO Box 231081
Encinitas, CA 92023-1081, USA

Lee, Tsung-Dao (Nobel Prize Laureate)
25 Claremont Ave
New York, NY 10027-6813, USA

Lee, Vernon R (Religious Leader)
4621 W Hillsboro St
El Dorado, AR 71730-6768, USA

Lee, Vincent (Baseball Player)
3228 Avondale Ave
Baltimore, MD 21215-4702, USA

Lee, Wayne (Engineer)
4800 Oak Grove Dr
Pasadena, CA 91109-8001, USA

Lee, William Gregory (Actor)
c/o Jeff Witjas *Agency for the Performing Arts (APA-LA)*
405 S Beverly Dr Ste 500
Beverly Hills, CA 90212-4425, USA

Lee, Willie James (Athlete, Baseball Player)
400 5th Way
Birmingham, AL 35214-5706, USA

Lee, Yuan T (Nobel Prize Laureate)
Academy Sinica Nankang
Taipei 11529, TAIWAN

Lee, Zeph (Athlete, Football Player)
7417 1/2 S Normandie Ave
Los Angeles, CA 90044-2468, USA

Lee Fincher, Stephen (Congressman, Politician)
1118 Longworth Hob
Washington, DC 20515-1011, USA

Leech, Beverly
9150 Wilshire Blvd Ste 175
Beverly Hills, CA 90212-3450

Leech, Richard (Opera Singer)
59 E 54th St
New York, NY 10022-4211, USA

Leede, Ed (Athlete, Basketball Player)
307 Roca Pl
Castle Rock, CO 80108-9020, USA

Lee-Dries, Dolores (Baseball Player)
HC 78 Box 125X
Deming, NM 88030-9805, USA

Lee-Harmon, Annabelle (Baseball Player)
960 Senate St
Costa Mesa, CA 92627-3332, USA

Leek, Gene (Athlete, Baseball Player)
731 Palmer St
Nipomo, CA 93444-9572, USA

Leek, Sybil (Misc)
RR 9W
Englewood Cliffs, NJ 7632, USA

Leen, Bill (Musician)
2100 W End Ave Ste 1000
Nashville, TN 37203-5240, USA

Leeper, Dave (Athlete, Baseball Player)
23997 Kaleb Dr
Corona, CA 92883-9385, USA

Leerhsen, Erica (Actor)
c/o Staff Member *Kritzer Levine Wilkins Entertainment*
11872 La Grange Ave Fl 1
Los Angeles, CA 90025-5283, USA

Leese, Howard (Musician)
219 2st Ave N # 333
Seattle, WA 98109, USA

Leestma, David C (Astronaut)
4314 Lake Grove Dr
Seabrook, TX 77586-4114, USA

Leetch, Brian J (Athlete, Hockey Player)
c/o Staff Member *PuckAgency LLC*
810 7th Ave Fl 11
New York, NY 10019-5818, USA

Leetsma, David C
2101 Nasa Pkwy
Houston, TX 77058-3607, USA

Leetzow, Max (Athlete, Football Player)
6590 S Williams Cir E
Centennial, CO 80121-2737, USA

Leeuwenburg, Jay (Athlete, Football Player)
6268 S Coventry Ln W
Littleton, CO 80123-6756, USA

Leeves, Jane (Actor)
c/o Molly Madden *3 Arts Entertainment Inc*
9460 Wilshire Blvd Fl 7
Beverly Hills, CA 90212-2713, USA

Lefcourt, Peter (Actor)
c/o Staff Member *Creative Artists Agency (CAA-LA)*
2000 Avenue of the Stars Ste 100
Los Angeles, CA 90067-4705, USA

Lefebvre, Jim (Athlete, Baseball Player, Coach)
10160 E Whispering Wind Dr
Scottsdale, AZ 85255-3007, USA

Lefebvre, Joe (Athlete, Baseball Player)
10 Shore View Dr
Bow, NH 03304-4116, USA

Lefevre, Rachelle (Actor)
c/o Pearl Hanan *Pearl Hanan Management*
7775 W Sunset Blvd Ste 118
Los Angeles, CA 90046-3911, USA

Lefferts, Craig (Athlete, Baseball Player)
40820 N Laurel Valley Way
Anthem, AZ 85086-1850, USA

Leflore, Ron (Athlete, Baseball Player)
6263 93rd Ter N Apt 4206
Pinellas Park, FL 33782-4640, USA

Leforce Jr, Clyde (Athlete, Football Player)
715 Spring Ln
Bristow, OK 74010-1846, USA

Lefton, Jacqui (Stylist)
c/o Staff Member *Susan Price Inc*
333 Hudson St Rm 1002
New York, NY 10013-1028, USA

Leftwich, Phil (Athlete, Baseball Player)
15819 S 31st St
Phoenix, AZ 85048-7775, USA

Legace, Jean-Guy (Athlete, Hockey Player)
126 Casa Grande Ln
Santa Rosa Beach, FL 32459-3162, USA

LeGault, Lance (Actor)
c/o Staff Member *Tisherman Gilbert Motley Drozdoski Talent Agency (TGMD)*
6767 Forest Lawn Dr Ste 101
Los Angeles, CA 90068-1050, USA

Legend, John (Actor, Musician)
c/o Gary Gersh *The Artists Organization*
212 Marine St Unit 307
Santa Monica, CA 90405-6514, USA

Legett, Earl (Athlete, Football Player)
PO Box 1204
Raymond, MS 39154-1204, USA

Legette, Burnie (Athlete, Football Player)
1118 Doyle Pl
Colorado Springs, CO 80915-2327, USA

Legette, Tyrone (Athlete, Football Player)
1304 Hancock St
Columbia, SC 29205-4850, USA

Legg, Greg (Athlete, Baseball Player)
412 Jenna Kay Dr
Archbald, PA 18403-1583, USA

Leggat, Ashley (Actor)
c/o Staff Member *Walt Disney Co, The (Buena Vista Motion Picture Group)*
500 S Buena Vista St Ink And Paint Building Rm 230
Burbank, CA 91521-

Leggatt, Ian (Athlete, Golfer)
9726 E Mountain Spring Rd
Scottsdale, AZ 85255-6640, USA

Legge, Michael (Actor)
c/o Staff Member *Hatton McEwan*
3 Chocolate Studios 7 Shepherdess Place
London N1 7LJ, UK

Leggero, Natasha (Actor)
c/o Geoff Cheddy *Brillstein Entertainment Partners*
9150 Wilshire Blvd Ste 350
Beverly Hills, CA 90212-3453, USA

Leggett, Anthony J (Nobel Prize Laureate)
607 W Pennsylvania Ave
Urbana, IL 61801-4818, USA

Leggett, Jay (Actor, Producer, Writer)
c/o Lenore Zerman *Liberman/Zerman Management*
252 N Larchmont Blvd Ste 200
Los Angeles, CA 90004-3754, USA

Legien, Waldemar (Athlete)
Ul Grottgera 10
Bytom 41-902, POLAND

Legler, Tim (Athlete, Basketball Player)
275 82nd St
Stone Harbor, NJ 08247-1707, USA

Legorreta, Vilchis Ricardo (Architect)
#285A C Lomas Reforma
Mexico City 11020, MEXICO

Legrand, Michel (Composer, Musician)
c/o Staff Member *Kraft-Engel Management*
15233 Ventura Blvd Ste 200
Sherman Oaks, CA 91403-2244, USA

Legrande, Larry (Athlete, Baseball Player)
1331 Leon St NW
Roanoke, VA 24017-6011, USA

Legree, Lance (Athlete, Football Player)
4697 N Highway 52
Saint Stephen, SC 29479, USA

Legris, Manuel C (Ballerina)
8 Rue Scribe
Paris 75009, FRANCE

LeGros, James (Actor)
8730 W Sunset Blvd Ste 490
Los Angeles, CA 90069-2248, USA

LeGuin, Ursula K (Writer)
PO Box 10541
Portland, OR 97296-0541, USA

Leguizamo, John (Actor, Comedian, Producer)
c/o Jeff Golenberg *Collective*
8383 Wilshire Blvd Ste 1050
Beverly Hills, CA 90211-2415, USA

Legwand, David (Athlete, Hockey Player)
26310 S Offshore Dr
Harrison Township, MI 48045-1553, USA

Lehane, Dennis (Writer)
341 Kerrville South Dr
Kerrville, TX 78028-8770, USA

Lehew, Jim (Athlete, Baseball Player)
3086 Fairview Rd
Grantsville, MD 21536-2239, USA

Lehman, I Robert (Scientist)
895 Cedro Way
Palo Alto, CA 94305-1002, USA

Lehman, Jeffrey (Educator)
President's Office
Ithaca, NY 14853, USA

Lehman, Ken (Athlete, Baseball Player)
3463 Renee Dr
Sedro Woolley, WA 98284-8812, USA

Lehman, Kristen (Actor)
c/o Perry Zimel *Oscars Abrams Zimel & Associates, Inc. (OAZ)*
438 Queen St E
Toronto ON M5A 1T4, CANADA

Lehman, Manny (DJ)
c/o Len Evans *Project Publicity*
312 W 53rd St Ste 202
New York, NY 10019-5743, USA

Lehman, Tom (Athlete, Golfer)
9820 E Thompson Peak Pkwy Unit 704
Scottsdale, AZ 85255-6656, USA

Lehmann, Edie (Actor)
24844 Malibu Rd
Malibu, CA 90265-4617, USA

Lehmann, Erich L (Misc)
Education Testing Service
Princeton, NJ 08541-0001, USA

Lehmann, Karl Cardinal (Religious Leader)
PF 1560 Bischofsplatz 2
Mainz 55116, GERMANY

Lehmann, Michael (Director, Producer)
c/o Staff Member *Industry Entertainment Partners*
955 Carrillo Dr Ste 300
Los Angeles, CA 90048-5400, USA

Lehmberg, Stanford E (Historian)
1005 Calle Largo
Santa Fe, NM 87501-1068, USA

Lehmkuhl, Reichen (Model, Reality TV Star, Writer)
c/o Mara Santino *Luber Roklin Management*
8530 Wilshire Blvd Ste 550
Beverly Hills, CA 90211-3133, USA

Lehn, Jean Marie
21 Rue D'Oslo
Strasbourg, FRANCE F-67000

Lehn, Jean-Marie P (Nobel Prize Laureate)
4 Rue Blaise Pascal
Strasbourg 67008, FRANCE

Lehne, Fredric (Actor)
c/o Staff Member *Bauman Redanty & Shaul Agency*
5757 Wilshire Blvd Suite 473
Beverly Hills, CA 90212, USA

Lehninger, Albert L (Misc)
15020 Tanyard Rd
Sparks, MD 21152-9752, USA

Lehr, John (Actor, Producer, Writer)
c/o Staff Member *WmE2 (WMA-LA)*
1 William Morris Pl
Beverly Hills, CA 90212-4261, USA

Lehr, Justin (Athlete, Baseball Player)
6015 Nagel St
La Mesa, CA 91942-3109, USA

Lehrer, Jim (Journalist)
3620 27th St S
Arlington, VA 22206-2350, USA

Lehrer, Robert I (Biologist)
Med Center Hematology Dept
Los Angeles, CA 90024, USA

Lehrman, Logan (Actor)
c/o Joseph (Joe) Rice *Abrams Artists Agency (LA)*
9200 W Sunset Blvd PH 11
Los Angeles, CA 90069-3601, USA

Lehtinen, Dexter (Attorney, Attorney General, General, Government Official)
155 S Miami Ave
Miami, FL 33130-1617, USA

Lehtinen, Jere (Athlete, Hockey Player)
622 Stratford Ln
Coppell, TX 75019-6129, USA

Leiba, Freddie (Stylist)
c/o Staff Member *Bryan Bantry*
900 Broadway Ste 400
New York, NY 10003-1239, USA

Leibel, Rudolph (Misc)
464 Riverside Dr # 95
New York, NY 10027-6822, USA

Leibman, Ron (Actor)
c/o Staff Member *Agency for the Performing Arts (APA-LA)*
405 S Beverly Dr Ste 500
Beverly Hills, CA 90212-4425, USA

Leibovitz, Annie (Artist, Photographer)
c/o Staff Member *Doubleday/ RandomHouse*
1745 Broadway
New York, NY 10019-4368, USA

Leibovitz, Mitchell G (Business Person)
3111 W Allegheny Ave
Philadelphia, PA 19132-1116, USA

Leibowitz, Barry (Athlete, Basketball Player)
3900 Galt Ocean Dr Apt 912
Ft Lauderdale, FL 33308-6630, USA

Leibrandt, Charlie (Athlete, Baseball Player)
1235 Stuart Rdg
Alpharetta, GA 30022-6364, USA

Leicester, Jon (Athlete, Baseball Player)
PO Box 1269
Valley Center, CA 92082-1269, USA

Leick, Hudson (Actor)
c/o Staff Member *Geddes Agency, The*
8430 Santa Monica Blvd Ste 200
Los Angeles, CA 90069-4253, USA

Leifer, Carol (Actor, Comedian)
c/o Howard Klein *3 Arts Entertainment Inc*
9460 Wilshire Blvd Fl 7
Beverly Hills, CA 90212-2713, USA

Leiferkus, Sergei P (Opera Singer)
5 The Paddocks Abberbury Rd
Iffley, Oxford OX4 4ET, UNITED KINGDOM (UK)

Leifheit, Sylvia (Model)
Treppendorfer Weg 13
Berlin 12527, GERMANY

Leigeb, Brian (Football Player)
c/o Team Member *Oakland Raiders*
1220 Harbor Bay Pkwy
Alameda, CA 94502-6570, USA

Leigh, Barbara (Actor)
9320 Wilshire Blvd Ste 302
Beverly Hills, CA 90212-3218, USA

Leigh, Charlie (Athlete, Football Player)
PO Box 12931
Albany, NY 12212-2931, USA

Leigh, Chyler (Actor)
c/o Joanna (Joanie) Burstein *Burstein Company, The*
15304 W Sunset Blvd Ste 208
Pacific Palisades, CA 90272-3656, USA

Leigh, Danni (Musician)
c/o Bridget Bauer *Bismeaux Productions*
PO Box 463
Austin, TX 78767-0463, USA

Leigh, Jennifer Jason (Actor)
c/o Greg Clark *Untitled Entertainment (LA)*
350 S Beverly Dr Ste 200
Beverly Hills, CA 90212-4819, USA

Leigh, Mike (Director)
9 Greek St Soho
London W1D 4DQ, UNITED KINGDOM (UK)

Leigh, Mitch (Composer)
29 W 57th St # 1000
New York, NY 10019-3406, USA

Leigh, Regina (Musician)
909 Meadowlark Ln
Goodlettsville, TN 37072-2309, USA

Leighton, GB (Musician)
c/o Staff Member *Paradigm (Monterey)*
404 W Franklin St
Monterey, CA 93940-2303, USA

Leighton, Laura (Actor)
c/o Paul Santana *Agency for the Performing Arts (APA-LA)*
405 S Beverly Dr Ste 500
Beverly Hills, CA 90212-4425, USA

Leija, James (Jesse) (Athlete, Boxer)
154 Octavia Pl
San Antonio, TX 78214-1236, USA

Leiker, Tony (Athlete, Football Player)
411 E 21st St
Hays, KS 67601-2805, USA

Leimkuehler, Paul (Business Person, Skier)
351 Darbys Run
Bay Village, OH 44140-2968, USA

Leinart, Matt (Football Player)

Leiper, Dave (Athlete, Baseball Player)
13082 N 103rd St
Scottsdale, AZ 85260-7272, USA

Leister, John (Athlete, Baseball Player)
304 Devon Dr
Saint Louis, MI 48880-9427, USA

Leisure, David (Actor)
26807 Fairlain Dr
Valencia, CA 91355-4961, USA

Leitch, Donovan
8794 Lookout Mountain Ave
Los Angeles, CA 90046-1859

Leitch, Matthew (Actor)
c/o Colleen Schlegel *Frontline Management*
5670 Wilshire Blvd Ste 1370
Los Angeles, CA 90036-5679, USA

Leiter, Alois T (Al) (Athlete, Baseball Player)
161st Street And River Avenue Attn Broadcast Dept
Bronx, NY 10451, USA

Leiter, Mark (Athlete, Baseball Player)
121 Carriage Way
Forked River, NJ 08731-5843, USA

Leith, Emmett N (Engineer)
4028 Oella Ct
San Jose, CA 95124-4832, USA

Leitner, Patric-Fritz (Athlete)
An der Schiessstatte 4
Berchtesgaden 83471, GERMANY

Leitso, Tyron (Actor)
c/o Deb Dillistone *Lucas Talent Inc*
100 W. Pender St Sun Tower, 7th Floor
Vancouver, BC V6B 1R8, Canada

Leitzel, Joan (Educator)
President's Office
Lincoln, NE 68588, USA

Leius, Scott (Athlete, Baseball Player)
12620 42nd Pl N
Minneapolis, MN 55442-2344, USA

Lekakis, Paul (Musician)
c/o Staff Member *Diva Central Inc*
7510 W Sunset Blvd Ste 1445
Los Angeles, CA 90046-3408, USA

Lekang, Anton (Skier)
47 Pratt St
Winsted, CT 06098-2025, USA

Lelbrandt, Charlie (Athlete, Baseball Player)
1235 Stuart Rdg
Alpharetta, GA 30022-6364, USA

Lelliott, Jeremy (Actor)
c/o Joan Green *Joan Green Management*
1836 Courtney Ter
Los Angeles, CA 90046-2106, USA

Lelong, Pierre J (Mathematician)
9 Place de Rungis
Paris 75013, FRANCE

LeLouch, Claude (Director)
15 Ave Hoche
Paris 75008, FRANCE

Lemaire, Jacques G (Athlete, Coach, Hockey Player)
PO Box 1207
Palmetto, FL 34220-1207, USA

Lemaire, Pascale (Stylist)
c/o Elizabeth Centenari *T.H.E. Artist Agency*
1207 Potomac St NW
Washington, DC 20007-3212, USA

Lemanczyk, Dave (Athlete, Baseball Player)
24 Lehigh Ct
Rockville Centre, NY 11570-2016, USA

Lemaster, Denny (Athlete, Baseball Player)
1909 Indian Rd
Lincolnton, GA 30817-3805, USA

Lemaster, Frank (Athlete, Football Player)
PO Box 159
Birchrunville, PA 19421-0159, USA

Lemaster, Johnnie (Athlete, Baseball Player)
PO Box 943
Paintsville, KY 41240-0943, USA

Lemay, Dick (Athlete, Baseball Player)
1741 N Holland Ln
Wichita, KS 67212-6242, USA

LeMay-Doan, Michelle (Speed Skater)
277 Richmond St W
Toronto, ON M5V 1X1, CANADA

Lembeck, Michael (Actor, Director)
23852 Pacific Coast Hwy # 355
Malibu, CA 90265-4876, USA

Lemche, Kris (Actor)
c/o Brian Wilkins *Kritzer Levine Wilkins Entertainment*
11872 La Grange Ave Fl 1
Los Angeles, CA 90025-5283, USA

Lemelson, Jerome H (Inventor)
48 Parkside Dr
Princeton, NJ 08540-4813, USA

LeMesurier, John (Actor)
56 Barron's Keep
London W14, UNITED KINGDOM (UK)

Lemieux, Claude (Athlete, Hockey Player)
6008 N Saguaro Rd
Paradise Valley, AZ 85253-4223, USA

Lemieux, Jocelyn (Athlete, Hockey Player)
1123 Sandhurst Ct
Buffalo Grove, IL 60089-6822, USA

Lemieux, Joseph H (Business Person)
1 Seagate
Toledo, OH 43604-1442, USA

LeMieux, Kathryn (Cartoonist)
c/o Staff Member *King Features Syndication*
300 W 57th St Fl 15
New York, NY 10019-5238, USA

Lemieux, Mario (Athlete, Hockey Player)
630 Academy Ave
Sewickley, PA 15143-1172, USA

Lemieux, Raymond U (Misc)
7602 119th St
Edmonton, AB T6G 1W3, CANADA

Lemke, Anthony (Actor)
c/o Jennifer Goldhar *Characters Talent Agency, The (Toronto)*
1505 W 2nd Ave #200
Vancouver, BC V6H 3Y4, Canada

Lemke, Cheryl (Television Host)
300 Interstate North Pkwy SE
Atlanta, GA 30339-2403

Lemke, Mark A (Athlete, Baseball Player)
3 Olena Dr
Whitesboro, NY 13492-2103, USA

Lemme, Steve (Comedian)
c/o Staff Member *United Talent Agency (UTA)*
9560 Wilshire Blvd Fl 5
Beverly Hills, CA 90212-2400, USA

Lemmerman, Bruce (Athlete, Football Player)
621 Silverado Way
Eagle Point, OR 97524-9011, USA

Lemmon, Chris (Actor)
80 Murray Dr
South Glastonbury, CT 06073-2435, USA

Lemmons, Kasi (Actor, Director)
c/o Frank Wuliger *Gersh (LA)*
9465 Wilshire Blvd Ste 600
Beverly Hills, CA 90212-2612, USA

Lemoine, Tobe (Stylist)
533 Malden Ave
La Grange Park, IL 60526-5514, USA

Lemon, Chet (Athlete, Baseball Player)
38150 Timberlane Dr
Umatilla, FL 32784-9302, USA

Lemon, Don (Correspondent, Journalist)
c/o Staff Member *CNN (Atlanta)*
1 Cnn Ctr NW
Atlanta, GA 30303-2762, USA

Lemon, Meadow (Meadowlark) (Actor, Athlete, Basketball Player)
6501 E Greenway Pkwy Ste 1206
Scottsdale, AZ 85254-2065, USA

Lemon, Peter C (War Hero)
6245 Viewfield Hts
Colorado Springs, CO 80919-3747, USA

Lemon Jelly (Music Group)
c/o Staff Member *Paradigm (Monterey)*
404 W Franklin St
Monterey, CA 93940-2303, USA

Lemonds, Dave (Athlete, Baseball Player)
1501 Aringill Ln
Matthews, NC 28104-8049, USA

Lemongelio, Mark (Baseball Player)
13437 S 47th St
Phoenix, AZ 85044-4833, USA

Lemonheads
1775 Broadway Ste 433
New York, NY 10019-1903

Lemons, Abe
4314 Saint Thomas Dr
Oklahoma City, OK 73120-8320

Lemos, Richie (Boxer)
18658 Klum Pl
Rowland Heights, CA 91748-4850, USA

Lemper, Ute (Actor, Dancer, Musician)
40 Rue de la Folie Regnault
Paris 75011, FRANCE

Lenarcic, Spela (Stylist)
c/o Staff Member *Michele Filomeno New York LLC*
515 Greenwich St Ste 503
New York, NY 10013-1097, USA

Lenard, Michael B (Misc)
1 Olympic Plz
Colorado Springs, CO 80909-5780, USA

Lenard, Voshon (Athlete, Basketball Player)
22694 Nottingham Ln
Southfield, MI 48033-3393, USA

Lendl, Ivan (Athlete, Tennis Player)
400 5 1/2 Mile Rd
Goshen, CT 06756-1032, USA

Lenehan, Nancy (Actor)
c/o Meghan Schumacher *Meghan Schumacher Management*
13351D Riverside Dr # 387
Sherman Oaks, CA 91423-2508, USA

Lenfant, Claude J M (Physicist)
PO Box 65278
Vancouver, WA 98665-0010, USA

Lengies, Vanessa (Actor)
c/o Joanna (Joanie) Burstein *Burstein Company, The*
15304 W Sunset Blvd Ste 208
Pacific Palisades, CA 90272-3656, USA

Lenhardt, Don (Athlete, Baseball Player)
1513 Timberlake Manor Pkwy
Chesterfield, MO 63017-5582, USA

Lenich, Bill (Athlete, Football Player)
545 Bambury Way
Kirkwood, MO 63122-1142, USA

Lenihan, Brian J (Government Official)
24 Park View Castleknock
County Dublin, IRELAND

Leningrad CowboysBMG Ariola
Steinhauser Str. 3
Munich, GERMANY D-81677

Lenk, Maria (Swimmer)
Rua Cupertino Durao 16 Leblon
Rio de Janeiro 22441, BRAZIL

Lenk, Thomas (Artist)
Gemeinde Braunsbach
Schloss Tierberg 7176, GERMANY

Lenk, Tom (Actor)
c/o Bernard Kira *Vanguard Management Group*
8060 Melrose Ave Fl 4
Los Angeles, CA 90046-7038, USA

Lenkaitis, William E (Athlete, Football Player)
26 Rose Court Way
East Walpole, MA 02032-1185, USA

Lenkin, Elysha (Stylist)
c/o Staff Member *Mark Edward Inc*
325 W 8th St # 1011
New York, NY 10018, USA

Lennie, Angus (Actor)
15 Pembroke Gardens
London W8, UNITED KINGDOM (UK)

Lennix, Harry (Actor)
c/o Staff Member *Creative Artists Agency (CAA-LA)*
2000 Avenue of the Stars Ste 100
Los Angeles, CA 90067-4705, USA

Lennon, Cynthia (Artist, Writer)
c/o Staff Member *Crown Publicity*
1745 Broadway Frnt 3
New York, NY 10019-4343, USA

Lennon, Diane (Musician)
1984 State Highway 165
Branson, MO 65616-8936, USA

Lennon, Janet (Musician)
1984 State Highway 165
Branson, MO 65616-8936, USA

Lennon, Julian (Musician, Songwriter)
30 Ives St
London SW3 2ND, UNITED KINGDOM (UK)

Lennon, Kathy (Musician)
Overlook Dr #10
Branson, MO 65616, USA

Lennon, Patrick (Athlete, Baseball Player)
60 Meister Blvd
Freeport, NY 11520-5938, USA

Lennon, Peggy (Musician)
1984 State Highway 165
Branson, MO 65616-8936, USA

Lennon, Richard G (Religious Leader)
2121 Commonwealth Ave
Boston, MA 02135-3101, USA

Lennon, Sean (Musician)
1 W 72nd St
New York, NY 10023-3486, USA

Lennon, Thomas (Actor, Producer, Writer)
c/o Peter Principato *Principato/Young Management*
9465 Wilshire Blvd Ste 430
Beverly Hills, CA 90212-2613, USA

Lennon Sisters
1984 State Highway 165
Branson, MO 65616-8936

Lennox, Annie (Musician)
c/o Staff Member *19 Entertainment*
33/32 Ransomes Dock 35-37 Parkgate Rd
London SW11 4NP, UK

Lennox, Kai (Actor)
c/o Gabrielle Allabashi *Ellis Talent Group*
4705 Laurel Canyon Blvd Ste 300
Valley Village, CA 91607-5901, USA

Lennox, William Jr (Educator, General)
US Military Academy
West Point, NY 10996, USA

Lenny, Rick H. (Business Person)
100 Crystal A Dr
Hershey, PA 17033-9524, USA

Leno, Jay (Actor, Comedian, Talk Show Host)
c/o Dick Guttman *Guttman Associates*
118 S Beverly Dr Ste 201
Beverly Hills, CA 90212-3016, USA

Lenoir, William B (Astronaut)
MS
Washington, DC 20546-0001, USA

Lenox, Adriane (Actor)
c/o Staff Member *Leading Artists*
145 W 45th St Rm 1000
New York, NY 10036-4032, USA

Lenska, Rula (Actor, Model)
586A Kings Road
London SW6 2DX, UNITED KINGDOM (UK)

Lentine, Jim (Athlete, Baseball Player)
1066 Calle Del Cerro Unit 1411
San Clemente, CA 92672-6075, USA

Lenton, Lisbeth (Athlete, Olympic Athlete)
Unit 12/7 Beissel Street
Canberra, Belconnen 2617, AUSTRALIA

Lentz, Leary (Athlete, Basketball Player)
1309 Whispering Pines Dr
Houston, TX 77055-6854, USA

Lenz, Kay (Actor)
5916 Filaree Hts
Malibu, CA 90265-3721, USA

Lenz, Kim (Musician, Songwriter, Writer)
5000 Oak Bluff Ct
Atlanta, GA 30350-1069, USA

Lenz, Nicole (Actor)
c/o Staff Member *Kazarian Spencer Ruskin & Assoc.*
11969 Ventura Blvd Ste 300
Studio City, CA 91604-2619, USA

Lenz, Rick (Actor)
12955 Calvert St
Van Nuys, CA 91401-3206, USA

Lenzi, Mark (Misc)
207 Westwood Dr
Greenville, NC 27834-5015, USA

Leo, Chuck (Athlete, Football Player)
33 Holcroft Rd W
Rochester, NY 14612-5519, USA

Leo, Melissa (Actor)
c/o Jason Weinberg *Untitled Entertainment (LA)*
350 S Beverly Dr Ste 200
Beverly Hills, CA 90212-4819, USA

Leon
1180 S Beverly Dr Ste 608
Los Angeles, CA 90035-1158

Leon, Carlos
4519 Cockerham Dr
Los Angeles, CA 90027-1223

Leon, Eddie (Athlete, Baseball Player)
5285 N Strada De Rubino
Tucson, AZ 85750-6043, USA

Leon, Kenny (Actor, Business Person, Director)
659 Auburn Ave NE Apt 257
Atlanta, GA 30312-1981, USA

Leon, Lourdes (Lola) (Actor)
c/o Liz Rosenberg *Warner Bros Records (NY)*
75 Rockefeller Plz
New York, NY 10019-6908, USA

Leon, Melina (Musician)
c/o Staff Member *Sony Music Miami*
605 Lincoln Rd Ste 700
Miami Beach, FL 33139-2901, USA

Leon, Sarah (Stylist)
5990 NW 31st Ave
Fort Lauderdale, FL 33309-2208, USA

Leon, Valerie (Actor)
2 Conduit St
London, W1R 9TG, UNITED KINGDOM (UK)

Leonard, Bill (Athlete, Football Player)
928 Meadow Ln
Schenectady, NY 12309-6529, USA

Leonard, Bob (Slick) (Athlete, Basketball Player, Coach)
1241 Hillcrest Dr
Carmel, IN 46033-2343, USA

Leonard, Dennis P (Athlete, Baseball Player)
4102 SW Evergreen St
Blue Springs, MO 64015-9713, USA

Leonard, Elmore (Writer)
2192 Yarmouth Rd
Bloomfield Village, MI 48301-2339, USA

Leonard, Gary (Athlete, Basketball Player)
2406 Ridgefield Rd
Columbia, MO 65203-1532, USA

Leonard, James (Athlete, Football Player)
RR 332 Box 349
Mullica Hill, NY 10862, USA

Leonard, Jeffrey (Athlete, Baseball Player)
205 Redfield Pkwy Suite Attn Manager's Ofc 201
Reno, NV 89509, USA

Leonard, Joanne (Photographer)
Art Dept
Ann Arbor, MI 48109, USA

Leonard, Joe (Motorcycle Race, Motorcycle Racer, Race Car Driver)
PO Box 194
Novi, MI 48376-0194, USA

Leonard, Joshua (Actor)
c/o Laina Cohn *Laina Cohn Management*
15066 Sutton St
Sherman Oaks, CA 91403-4020, USA

Leonard, Justin (Athlete, Golfer)
7048 Turtle Creek Ln
Dallas, TX 75205-1263, USA

Leonard, Mark (Athlete, Baseball Player)
22042 Hibiscus Dr
Cupertino, CA 95014-0109, USA

Leonard, Pauline (Stylist)
c/o Staff Member *Cloutier Agency*
2632 La Cienega Ave
Los Angeles, CA 90034-2641, USA

Leonard, Robert Sean (Actor)
c/o Scott Henderson *WmE2 (Endeavor-LA)*
9601 Wilshire Blvd Fl 3
Beverly Hills, CA 90210-5219, USA

Leonard, Sugar Ray (Athlete, Boxer)
c/o Christopher Barrett *Metropolitan (MTA)*
4526 Wilshire Blvd
Los Angeles, CA 90010-3801, USA

Leonard, Wayne (Business Person)
10055 Grogans Mill Rd # 5A
The Woodlands, TX 77380-1059, USA

Leonard-Linehan, Rhoda (Baseball Player)
84 Bruce Rd
Norwood, MA 02062-3103, USA

Leone, Sunny (Adult Film Star)
c/o Staff Member *Vivid Entertainment*
3599 Cahuenga Blvd W # 400
Los Angeles, CA 90068-1397, USA

Leonetti, Jean-Baptiste (Director)
c/o Jerome Duboz *WmE2 (Endeavor-LA)*
9601 Wilshire Blvd Fl 3
Beverly Hills, CA 90210-5219, USA

Leonetti, John R (Cinematographer)
3822 Calle Ariana
San Clemente, CA 92672-4502, USA

Leonetti, Matthew (Cinematographer)
1362 Bella Oceana Vis
Pacific Palisades, CA 90272-2359, USA

Leong, Page (Actor)
1925 Century Park E Ste 750
Los Angeles, CA 90067-2708, USA

Leonhard, Dave (Athlete, Baseball Player)
87 Corning St
Beverly, MA 01915-3732, USA

Leonhart, William (Diplomat)
119 Oak Ter
Lake Bluff, IL 60044-2717, USA

Leoni, Tea (Actor, Producer)
c/o Jimmy Miller *Mosaic Media Group*
9200 W Sunset Blvd Ste 10
Los Angeles, CA 90069-3608, USA

Leonidas, Stephanie (Actor)
c/o Andrew Rogers *International Creative Management (ICM-LA)*
10250 Constellation Blvd Fl 7
Los Angeles, CA 90067-6207, USA

Leonov, Aleksei A (Cosmonaut, General)
Acad Sakharov Prospect 12
Moscow 107078, RUSSIA

Leonskaja, Elisabeth (Musician)
165 W 57th St
New York, NY 10019-2201, USA

Leopold, Bobby (Athlete, Football Player)
801 Beckleymeade Ave Apt 1116
Dallas, TX 75232-5225, USA

Leopold, Tom (Comedian)
c/o Staff Member *Gersh (LA)*
9465 Wilshire Blvd Ste 600
Beverly Hills, CA 90212-2612, USA

LeParmentier, Richard (Actor)
12A Russel St
Bath BA1 2QF, UK

Lepchenko, Varvara (Athlete, Tennis Player)
1362 Doe Trail Rd
Allentown, PA 18104-2053, USA

Lepcio, Ted (Athlete, Baseball Player)
263 Greenlodge St
Dedham, MA 02026-6400, USA

LePelley, Guernsey (Cartoonist, Editor)
35 Saint Germain St
Boston, MA 02115-3216, USA

LePichon, Xavier (Geophysicist, Physicist)
24 Rue Lhomond
Paris 75005, FRANCE

Lepore, Amanda (Actor, Model)
c/o Staff Member *Grapevine Public Relations*
5237 Cahuenga Blvd # 2
N Hollywood, CA 91601-3419, USA

Leppard, Raymond J
32 E Washington St Ste 600
Indianapolis, IN 46204-3513, USA

Lepperd, Thomas (Baseball Player)
5962 Wistful Vista Dr
West Des Moines, IA 50266-2864, USA

Lepperd, Thomas (Athlete, Baseball Player)
5962 Wistful Vista Dr
West Des Moines, IA 50266-2864, USA

Leppert, Don (Athlete, Baseball Player)
317 Sunrise Cay Apt 201
Naples, FL 34114-9650, USA

Leppert, Don (Athlete, Baseball Player)
1630 Epping Forest Dr
Southaven, MS 38671-8849, USA

Lepsis, Matt (Athlete, Football Player)
6787 Trailing Oaks Dr
Frisco, TX 75034-5883, USA

Lerach, William (Bill) (Attorney, Attorney General, General)
1600 Broadway # 1800
San Diego, CA 92101-5715, USA

L'Erario, Joe
7700 Wisconsin Ave
Bethesda, MD 20814-3578

Lerch, Randy (Athlete, Baseball Player)
19490 Monterey St
Morgan Hill, CA 95037-2606, USA

Lerche, Sondre (Musician)
c/o Staff Member *Paradigm (Monterey)*
404 W Franklin St
Monterey, CA 93940-2303, USA

Lerchen, George (Athlete, Baseball Player)
354 E Rose Ave
Garden City, MI 48135-2645, USA

Lerew, Anthony (Athlete, Baseball Player)
6 Summer Dr
Dillsburg, PA 17019-9544, USA

Lerman, Logan (Actor)
c/o Kami Putnam-Heist *WmE2 (Endeavor-LA)*
9601 Wilshire Blvd Fl 3
Beverly Hills, CA 90210-5219, USA

Lerner, Harriet (Writer)
c/o Staff Member *HarperCollins Publishers*
10 E 53rd St C/O Author Mail Floor 7
New York, NY 10022, USA

Lerner, Michael (Actor)
1505 10th St
Santa Monica, CA 90401-2805, USA

LeRoux, Francois (Opera Singer)
3 Burlington Lane Chiswick
London W4 2TH, UNITED KINGDOM (UK)

Leroux, Nicolette (Athlete, Golfer)
4786 Orchard Ln
Delray Beach, FL 33445-5306, USA

Leroy, Emarlos (Athlete, Football Player)
10135 Gate Pkwy N
Jacksonville, FL 32246-4400, USA

LeRoy, Gloria (Actor)
13775A Mono Way # 220
Sonora, CA 95370-8813, USA

Leroy, Philippe
77 Rue Pigalle
Paris, FRANCE F-75009

Lersch, Barry (Athlete, Baseball Player)
967 S Ivory Cir Apt D
Aurora, CO 80017-3055, USA

Les, Jim (Athlete, Basketball Player)
4030 Shadybrooke Ct
Granite Bay, CA 95746-8839, USA

Lesane, Jimmy (Athlete, Football Player)
3629 Coronado Rd
Baltimore, MD 21244-3848, USA

Lesar, David (Business Person)
Lincoln Plaza 500 N Akard St
Dallas, TX 75201, USA

Leschin, Luisa (Producer, Writer)
c/o Staff Member *WmE2 (WMA-LA)*
1 William Morris Pl
Beverly Hills, CA 90212-4261, USA

Lesh, Phil (Musician)
c/o Staff Member *Paradigm (Monterey)*
404 W Franklin St
Monterey, CA 93940-2303, USA

Leshana, David C (Educator)
8246 E Hoverland Rd
Scottsdale, AZ 85255-3908, USA

Lesher, Brian (Athlete, Baseball Player)
217 Vassar Dr
Newark, DE 19711-3158, USA

Leshnock, Don (Athlete, Baseball Player)
289 Carlin Ct W
Columbus, OH 43230-1608, USA

Leskanic, Curt (Athlete, Baseball Player)
2032 Alaqua Dr
Longwood, FL 32779-3116, USA

Leskanich, Katrina (& the Waves) (Music Group, Musician)
c/o Staff Member *International Artists Holland*
PO Box 32
West Wardsboro, VT 05360-0032, The Netherlands

Lesko, Matthew (Writer)
C/O Kim McCoy 1555 N Dearborn Pkwy Fl25
Chicago, IL 60610, USA

Lesley, Brad (Athlete, Baseball Player)
5235 Kester Ave Apt 207
Sherman Oaks, CA 91411-4076, USA

Leslie, Aleen
1700 Lexington Rd
Beverly Hills, CA 90210-2810

Leslie, Ed (Actor, Wrestler)
c/o Nick Cordasco *Prince Marketing Group*
18 Carillon Cir
Livingston, NJ 07039-2600, USA

Leslie, Fred W (Astronaut)
2038 Springhouse Rd SE
Huntsville, AL 35802-1890, USA

Leslie, Joan (Actor)
2228 N Catalina St
Los Angeles, CA 90027-1127, USA

Leslie, Lisa (Athlete, Basketball Player, Model)
c/o Lynn Jeter *Lynn Jeter & Associates*
3699 Wilshire Blvd Ste 850
Los Angeles, CA 90010-2737, USA

Leslie, Robbie (DJ)
c/o Staff Member *Diva Central Inc*
7510 W Sunset Blvd Ste 1445
Los Angeles, CA 90046-3408, USA

Leslie, Ryan (Musician)
c/o Chris Chambers *The Chamber Group*
416 W 13th St Ste 105
New York, NY 10014-1179, USA

Lesnar, Brock (Athlete, Wrestler)
c/o Staff Member *UFC*
PO Box 26959
Las Vegas, NV 89126-0959, USA

Lesnie, Andrew (Cinematographer)
c/o Wayne Fitterman *United Talent Agency (UTA)*
9560 Wilshire Blvd Fl 5
Beverly Hills, CA 90212-2400, USA

L'esperance, Carrie (Stylist)
c/o Staff Member *Zenobia Agency Inc*
PO Box 909
Groveland, CA 95321-0909, USA

Lesseos, Mimi (Actor, Athlete)
2484 Vista Del Monte Dr
Acton, CA 93510-1899, USA

Lessin, Leslie (Stylist)
c/o Staff Member *Katy Barker Agency Inc*
6606 10th Ave Apt 3R
Brooklyn, NY 11219-5804, USA

Lessing, Doris M (Writer)
c/o Staff Member *Hoffmann und Campe Verlag GmbH*
Harvestehuder Weg # 42
Ashburn, VA 20149-0001, Germany

Lester, Adrian (Actor)
c/o William Baylock *Seven Summits Pictures & Management*
8906 W Olympic Blvd Ground Floor
Beverly Hills, CA 90211, USA

Lester, Darrell G (Athlete, Football Player)
3721 Echo Trl
Fort Worth, TX 76109-3432, USA

Lester, Ketty (Actor, Musician)
5931 Comey Ave
Los Angeles, CA 90034-2213, USA

Lester, Mark (Actor)
1 Carlton St Cheltenham
Glou GLS2 6AG, UNITED KINGDOM (UK)

Lester, Mark L (Director)
17268 Camino Yatasto
Pacific Palisades, CA 90272, USA

Lester, Richard (Dick) (Director)
c/o Staff Member *Creative Artists Agency (CAA-LA)*
2000 Avenue of the Stars Ste 100
Los Angeles, CA 90067-4705, USA

Lester, Ronnie (Athlete, Basketball Player)
PO Box 2187
Manhattan Beach, CA 90267-2187, USA

Lester, Tim (Athlete, Football Player)
1160 Bream Dr
Alpharetta, GA 30004-4411, USA

Lester, Tom
c/o Gary Moore *Gary Moore Management*
55 Karen Dr
Greenville, SC 29607-1207, USA

Lester of Herne Hill, Anthony P (Attorney, Attorney General, General)
Blackstone House Temple
London EC4Y 9BW, UNITED KINGDOM (UK)

Lesure, James (Actor)
c/o Vincent Cirrincione *Vincent Cirrincione Associates*
1516 N Fairfax Ave
Los Angeles, CA 90046-2608, USA

Letarte, Pierre (Cinematographer)
551 W Pinacle
Albercom, QC J0E 1B0, CANADA

Letbetter, R Steve (Business Person)
1111 Louisiana St
Houston, TX 77002-5230, USA

Leterrier, Louis (Director)
c/o Guymon Casady *Management 360*
9111 Wilshire Blvd
Beverly Hills, CA 90210-5508, USA

Letlow, W R (Russ) (Athlete, Football Player)
1876 Thelma Dr
San Luis Obispo, CA 93405-6238, USA

Letner, Robert (Athlete, Football Player)
6515 Patty Ln
Harrison, TN 37341-6987, USA

Leto, Jared (Actor)
c/o Jason Weinberg *Untitled Entertainment (LA)*
350 S Beverly Dr Ste 200
Beverly Hills, CA 90212-4819, USA

Letowski, Trevor (Athlete, Hockey Player)
3612 Lion Ridge Ct
Raleigh, NC 27612-4235, USA

Letscher, Matt (Actor)
c/o Nancy Sanders *Sanders Armstrong Caserta*
2120 Colorado Ave Ste 120
Santa Monica, CA 90404-3561, USA

Letsie III (King)
PO Box 524
Maseru, LESOTHO

Lett, Clifford (Athlete, Basketball Player)
7067 Rampart Way
Pensacola, FL 32505-3478, USA

Lett, Leon (Athlete, Football Coach, Football Player)
308 Warhawk Way
Monroe, LA 71209-0001, USA

Letterle, Daniel (Actor)
c/o Geordie Frey *GEF Entertainment*
122 N Clark Dr Apt 401
West Hollywood, CA 90048-6315, USA

Letterman, David (Comedian, Talk Show Host)
1697 Broadway Fl 11
New York, NY 10019-5904, USA

Lettermen, The
9255 W Sunset Blvd Ste 407
Los Angeles, CA 90069-3302

Letts, Tracy (Actor, Writer)
c/o Staff Member *Dewalt & Musik Management*
623 N Parish Pl
Burbank, CA 91506-1701, USA

Leung, Ken (Actor)
c/o Paul Hilepo *Hartig Hilepo Agency Ltd*
54 W 21st St Rm 610
New York, NY 10010-7344, USA

Leuwerik, Ruth
Zuccalistr. 31
Munich, GERMANY D-80639

Levane, Andrew (Athlete, Basketball Player)
26 Dolphin Grn Apt H2E
Port Washington, NY 11050-3164, USA

Levangie, Gigi (Writer)
c/o David Lubliner *WmE2 (WMA-LA)*
1 William Morris Pl
Beverly Hills, CA 90212-4261, USA

LeVay, Simon (Scientist)
970 Palm Ave
West Hollywood, CA 90069-4072, USA

Levchenko, Alexander
141 Sryosdny Gorodok
Potchta Kosmonavtov, RUSSIA

Level 42 (Music Group, Musician)
c/o Guy Richard *Agency Group Ltd, The (LA)*
1880 Century Park E Ste 711
Los Angeles, CA 90067-1618, USA

Levellers (Music Group)
c/o Staff Member *Paradigm (Monterey)*
404 W Franklin St
Monterey, CA 93940-2303, USA

Levene, Ben (Artist)
Piccadilly
London W1V 2LP, UNITED KINGDOM (UK)

Levene, Keith (Musician)
c/o Staff Member *Taang! Records*
3830 5th Ave
San Diego, CA 92103-3141, USA

Levenick, Dave (Athlete, Football Player)
8570 SW Sea Captain Dr
Stuart, FL 34997-9122, USA

Levens, Dorsey (Athlete, Football Player)
2070 Meadowsweet Dr
Green Bay, WI 54313-5447, USA

Levenseller, Mike (Athlete, Football Player)
1570 SW Wadleigh Dr
Pullman, WA 99163-2049, USA

Levenstein, John (Comedian)
c/o Staff Member *International Creative Management (ICM-LA)*
10250 Constellation Blvd Fl 7
Los Angeles, CA 90067-6207, USA

Leveque, Michel (Politician)
BP 522
Monaco Cedex 98015, MONACO

Lever, Johny (Actor, Bollywood, Comedian)
151/152 Oxford Tower Yamuna Nagar
Lokhandwala Complex Andheri
Bombay, MS 400 058, INDIA

Lever, Lafayette (Athlete, Basketball Player)
2001 Club Center Dr Apt 3111
Sacramento, CA 95835-1405, USA

Levering, Kate (Actor)
c/o Staff Member *Forward Entertainment*
9255 W Sunset Blvd Ste 805
Los Angeles, CA 90069-3305, USA

Leverington, Shelby
1801 Avenue of the Stars Ste 1250
Los Angeles, CA 90067-5817

Leveritt, Mara (Writer)
c/o Staff Member *St Martins Press*
175 5th Ave
New York, NY 10010-7703, USA

Levert, Eddie (Musician)
c/o Staff Member *Associated Booking Corp*
PO Box 2055
New York, NY 10021-0051, USA

Levesque, Joanna (JoJo) (Musician)
c/o Brian Bunnin *International Creative Management (ICM-LA)*
10250 Constellation Blvd Fl 7
Los Angeles, CA 90067-6207, USA

Levesque, Paul (Triple H) (Athlete, Wrestler)
c/o Kerry Rodgerson *World Wrestling Entertainment (WWE)*
1241 E Main St
Stamford, CT 06902-3520, USA

Levet, Thomas (Athlete, Golfer)
108 Via Quantera
Palm Beach Gardens, FL 33418-6217, USA

Levi, Wayne (Athlete, Golfer)
2809 Tiburon Blvd E Apt 101
Naples, FL 34109-3674, USA

Levi, Yoel
27 Chancery Lane
London WC2A 1PF, UNITED KINGDOM (UK)

Levi, Zachary (Actor)
c/o Tej Bhatia Herring *Rogers & Cowan PR (LA)*
Pacific Design Center 8687 Melrose Ave, 7th Floor
West Hollywood, CA 90069, USA

LeVias, Jerry (Athlete, Football Player)
3322 Chris Dr
Houston, TX 77063-6230, USA

Levi-Montalcini, Rita (Nobel Prize Laureate)
Piazzale Aldo Moro 7
Rome 185, ITALY

Levin, Amy Colvin (Stylist)
c/o Staff Member *Maximum Talent*
1873 S Bellaire St Ste 915
Denver, CO 80222-4356, USA

Levin, Drake (Musician)
108 E Matilija St
Ojai, CA 93023-2639, USA

Levin, Harvey (Journalist)
c/o Staff Member *NS Bienstock Inc*
250 W 57th St Ste 333
New York, NY 10107-0302, USA

Levin, Mark (Radio Personality, Talk Show Host)
7201 W Lake Mead Blvd
Las Vegas, NV 89128-8347, USA

Levin, Richard C (Educator)
President's Office
New Heaven, CT 6520, USA

Levin, Tony (Musician)
c/o Val Wolfe *Agency Group Ltd, The (LA)*
1880 Century Park E Ste 711
Los Angeles, CA 90067-1618, USA

Levine, Adam (Musician)
c/o Carleen Donovan *Press Here Publicity*
138 W 25th St Ste 900
New York, NY 10001-7470, USA

Levine, Alan (Al) (Athlete, Baseball Player)
10916 E Paradise Dr
Scottsdale, AZ 85259-7007, USA

Levine, Arnold (Biologist, Educator)
President's Office 1230 York Ave
New York, NY 10021, USA

Levine, David (Artist)
161 Henry St
Brooklyn, NY 11201-2500, USA

Levine, Ellen R (Editor)
959 8th Ave
New York, NY 10019-3737, USA

Levine, Jack (Artist)
333 Rector Pl Apt 1109
New York, NY 10280-1220, USA

Levine, James
301 Massachusetts Ave
Boston, MA 02115-4557, USA

Levine, Jerry
1505 10th St
Santa Monica, CA 90401-2805

Levine, Jonathan (Director)
c/o Ragna Nervik *The Ragna Nervik Company*
Prefers to be contacted via telephone
Los Angeles, CA, USA

Levine, Ken (Writer)
c/o Staff Member *Broder Webb Chervin Silbermann Agency, The (BWCS)*
10250 Constellation Blvd
Los Angeles, CA 90067-6200, USA

Levine, Michael (Business Person)
1180 S Beverly Dr Ste 301
Los Angeles, CA 90035-1154, USA

Levine, Philip (Writer)
4549 N Van Ness Blvd
Fresno, CA 93704-3727, USA

Levine, Rachmiel (Misc)
614 Walnut St
Newton, MA 02460-2462, USA

Levine, S Robert (Business Person)
PO Box 5005
Rochester, NH 3866, USA

Levine, Samm (Actor, Producer)
c/o Leonard Torgan *Collective*
8383 Wilshire Blvd Ste 1050
Beverly Hills, CA 90211-2415, USA

Levine, Samuel A (Actor)
c/o Staff Member *Badgley-Connor-King*
9229 W Sunset Blvd Ste 311
Los Angeles, CA 90069-3403, USA

Levine, Seymour (Biologist)
1515 Shasta Dr Apt 3103
Davis, CA 95616-6686, USA

Levine, Sol (Activist)
30 Powell St
Brookline, MA 02446-3921, USA

Levine, Ted (Actor)
c/o Robbi Kass *RK Management*
9300 Wilshire Blvd Ste 200
Beverly Hills, CA 90212-3227, USA

Levingston, Cliff (Basketball Player)
Pepsi Center 1000 Chopper Circle
Denver, CO 80204, USA

Levingstone, Ken (Government Official)
Westminster
London SW1A 0AA, UNITED KINGDOM (UK)

Levinsohn, Gary (Producer)
c/o Staff Member *Mutual Film Company*
650 N Bronson Ave Bldg Clinton
Los Angeles, CA 90004-1404, USA

Levinson, Barry (Actor, Director, Producer, Writer)
c/o Carol Goll *International Creative Management (ICM-LA)*
10250 Constellation Blvd Fl 7
Los Angeles, CA 90067-6207, USA

Levinson, Chris (Writer)
c/o Staff Member *WmE2 (Endeavor-LA)*
9601 Wilshire Blvd Fl 3
Beverly Hills, CA 90210-5219, USA

Levinson, Jay Conrad (Business Person, Writer)
3700 S Westport Ave # 2994
Sioux Falls, SD 57106-6360, USA

Levinson, Sanford V (Attorney, Attorney General, Educator, General)
3410 Windsor Rd
Austin, TX 78703-2248, USA

Levinthal, Cyrus (Biologist)
Biological Sciences Dept
New York, NY 10027, USA

Levis, Jesse (Athlete, Baseball Player)
1219 Highland Ave
Fort Washington, PA 19034-1605, USA

Levis, Patrick (Actor)
c/o Staff Member *Defining Artists Agency*
10 Universal City Plz Ste 2000
Universal City, CA 91608-1074, USA

Levi-Strauss, Claude (Misc)
2 Rue des Marronniers
Paris 75016, FRANCE

Levitas, Andrew (Actor)
c/o Justin Grey Stone *Untitled Entertainment (LA)*
350 S Beverly Dr Ste 200
Beverly Hills, CA 90212-4819, USA

Levitt, Arthus Jr (Financier, Government Official)
1001 Pennsylvania Ave NW
Washington, DC 20004-2502, USA

Levitt, Chad (Athlete, Football Player)
104 Towanda Ave
Melrose Park, PA 19027-2932, USA

Levitt, Gene
9200 W Sunset Blvd PH 25
Los Angeles, CA 90069-3601

Levitt, George (Misc)
82 Via Del Corso
Palm Beach Gardens, FL 33418-3773, USA

Levrault, Allen (Athlete, Baseball Player)
PO Box 1316
Westport, MA 02790-0694, USA

Levy, David (Government Official)
Knesset Kiryat Ben Gurion
Jerusalem 91950, ISRAEL

Levy, David H (Astronomer)
Palomar Mountain
Mount Palomar, PA 92060, USA

Levy, Ed (Baseball Player)
2471 SW 82nd Ave Apt 209
Davie, FL 33324-5795, USA

Levy, Eugene (Actor, Director)
c/o Ben Feigin *Anonymous Content (AC-LA)*
3531 Hayden Ave
Culver City, CA 90232, USA

Levy, Kenneth (Business Person)
160 Rio Robles
San Jose, CA 95134-1813, USA

Levy, Leonard W (Historian)
1025 Timberline Ter
Ashland, OR 97520-3436, USA

Levy, Mariana (Actor)
c/o Staff Member *Televisa*
Blvd Adolfo Lopez Mateos 232 Colonia San Angel INN
DF CP 01060, MEXICO

Levy, Marv (Coach, Football Coach, Football Player)
2800 N Lake Shore Dr Apt 1516
Chicago, IL 60657-6269, USA

Levy, Marvin David (Composer)
130 W 56th St
New York, NY 10019-3962, USA

Levy, Michael R (Publisher)
PO Box 1569
Austin, TX 78767-1569, USA

Levy, Peter (Cinematographer)
8942 Wilshire Blvd # 219
Beverly Hills, CA 90211-1908, USA

Levy, Richard C (Business Person, Inventor)
c/o Staff Member *Penguin Group*
90 Eglinton Ave E #700
Toronto, Ontario M4P 2Y3, CANADA

Levy, Sara (Stylist)
c/o Staff Member *Crews*
828 Clemont Dr NE
Atlanta, GA 30306-3694, USA

Levy, Shawn (Actor, Director)
c/o Amanda Lundberg *42West (NY)*
220 W 42nd St Fl 12
New York, NY 10036-7200, USA

Levy, William (Actor)
c/o Reina Rojas *Reina Rojas Management*
13345 NW 13th St
Pembroke Pines, FL 33028-2716, USA

Lewallyn, Dennis (Athlete, Baseball Player)
2900 Breckenridge Dr
Pensacola, FL 32526-2903, USA

Lewis, Aaron (Musician)
75 Rockefeller Plz
New York, NY 10019-6908

Lewis, Al (Grandpa) (Actor)
PO Box 277
New York, NY 10044-0205, USA

Lewis, Albert R (Athlete, Football Player)
3532 Macedonia Rd
Centreville, MS 39631-3634, USA

Lewis, Allen (Government Official)
Beaver Lodge Mom PO Box 1076
Castries, Sanit Lucia, WEST INDIES

Lewis, Ananda (Actor)
c/o Staff Member *Britto Agency PR*
234 W 56th St PH
New York, NY 10019-4302, USA

Lewis, Andrew L (Drew) (Business Person, Secretary)
PO Box 70
Lederach, PA 19450-0070, USA

Lewis, Anthony (Writer)
Editorial Dept 2 Faneuil Hall
Boston, MA 2109, USA

Lewis, Barbara (Musician)
PO Box 300488
Fern Park, FL 32730-0488, USA

Lewis, Bernard (Historian)
Near Eastern Studies
Princeton, NJ 08544-0001, USA

Lewis, Bill (Coach, Football Coach)
Athletic
Atlanta, GA 30332-0001, USA

Lewis, Blake (Musician)

Lewis, Bob (Athlete, Basketball Player)
63910 E Squash Blossom Ln
Tucson, AZ 85739-1264, USA

Lewis, Bobby (Musician)
PO Box 770850
Orlando, FL 32877-0850, USA

Lewis, Brooke (Actor)
c/o Staff Member *Coolwaters Productions*
10061 Riverside Dr # 531
Toluca Lake, CA 91602-2560, USA

Lewis, Buddy (Athlete, Baseball Player)
3635 Brentwood Dr
Gastonia, NC 28056-6667, USA

Lewis, Carl (Actor, Athlete)
c/o Cat Stone *Stone Management*
121 Ave Of The Stars # 3000
Los Angeles, CA 90067, USA

Lewis, Charlotte (Athlete, Basketball Player)
2814 N Sheridan Rd
Peoria, IL 61604-2716, USA

Lewis, Clea (Actor)
1659 S Highland Ave
Los Angeles, CA 90019-5540, USA

Lewis, Colby (Athlete, Baseball Player)
14800 Orchard Crest Ave
Bakersfield, CA 93314-9280, USA

Lewis, Crystal (Musician)
PO Box 150867
Nashville, TN 37215-0867, USA

Lewis, D D (Athlete, Football Player)
1624 Northcrest Dr
Plano, TX 75075-8749, USA

Lewis, Damian (Actor)
Julian House 4 Windmill St
London W1P 1HF, UNITED KINGDOM (UK)

Lewis, Damione (Athlete, Football Player)
9601 Gato Del Sol Ct
Waxhaw, NC 28173-0113, USA

Lewis, Dan (Athlete, Football Player)
460 S Park St
Detroit, MI 48215-4108, USA

Lewis, Darren (Athlete, Football Player)
641 Seabeach Rd
Dallas, TX 75232-4842, USA

Lewis, Darren (Athlete, Baseball Player)
2212 Rosemount Ln
San Ramon, CA 94582-5719, USA

Lewis, Dave (Athlete, Coach, Hockey Player)
22583 Heatherbridge Ln
Northville, MN 48167, USA

Lewis, Dave (Athlete, Football Player)
14015 Tahiti Way Apt 111
Marina Del Rey, CA 90292-6507, USA

Lewis, David Levering (Writer)
History Dept
East Rutherford, NJ 8903, USA

Lewis, David R (Athlete, Football Player)
406 142nd St
Ocean City, MD 21842-5602, USA

Lewis, Dawnn (Actor)
c/o Staff Member *Gage Group, The (LA)*
14724 Ventura Blvd Ste 505
Sherman Oaks, CA 91403-3505, USA

Lewis, Emmanuel (Manny) (Actor)
c/o Michael (Mike) Esterman
Esterman.Com, LLC
Prefers to be contacted via email
MD, USA

Lewis, Frank (Athlete, Football Player)
118 Presque Isle Dr
Houma, LA 70363-3828, USA

Lewis, Freddie (Athlete, Basketball Player)
4122 Illinois Ave NW
Washington, DC 20011-5950, USA

Lewis, Garry (Athlete, Football Player)
1000 Alcorn Dr Apt 737
Lorman, MS 39096-7500, USA

Lewis, Gary (Musician)
701 Barlin Ct
Nashville, TN 37221-3453, USA

Lewis, Gary W (Athlete, Football Player)
10 N Farm Road 144
Mount Pleasant, TX 75455-8809, USA

Lewis, Geoffrey (Actor, Writer)
c/o Joel Stevens *Joel Stevens Entertainment*
5627 Allott Ave
Van Nuys, CA 91401-4502, USA

Lewis, Glenn (Musician)
c/o Staff Member *Creative Artists Agency (CAA-LA)*
2000 Avenue of the Stars Ste 100
Los Angeles, CA 90067-4705, USA

Lewis, Huey (Actor, Musician)
c/o Bob Brown *Bob Brown Management*
PO Box 779
Mill Valley, CA 94942-0779, USA

Lewis, J L (Athlete, Golfer)
2504 Orleans Dr
Cedar Park, TX 78613-4727, USA

Lewis, Jamal (Athlete, Football Player)
PO Box 1416
Randallstown, MD 21133-1410, USA

Lewis, Jason (Actor)
c/o Alissa Vradenburg *Untitled Entertainment (LA)*
350 S Beverly Dr Ste 200
Beverly Hills, CA 90212-4819, USA

Lewis, Jazsmin
c/o Dan Spilo *Industry Entertainment Partners*
955 Carrillo Dr Ste 300
Los Angeles, CA 90048-5400, USA

Lewis, Jeff (Designer, Reality TV Star)
c/o Nicole Perez *PMK/BNC Public Relations (PMK-LA)*
Pacific Design Center 8687 Melrose Ave, 7th Floor
West Hollywood, CA 90069, USA

Lewis, Jeff (Athlete, Football Player)
RR 2 Box 189
Greentop, MO 63546-9730, USA

Lewis, Jenifer (Actor)
c/o Arnold M Preston *Preston Entertainment Inc*
8033 W Sunset Blvd # 7250
Los Angeles, CA 90046-2401

Lewis, Jenna (Reality TV Star)
c/o Juliette Harris *It Girl Public Relations*
5301 Beethoven St Ste 220
Los Angeles, CA 90066-7052, USA

Lewis, Jensen (Athlete, Baseball Player)
1278 W 9th St Apt 928
Cleveland, OH 44113-1079, USA

Lewis, Jermaine (Athlete, Football Player)
1751 Pinnacle Dr Ste 1500
McLean, VA 22102-3833, USA

Lewis, Jerry (Actor, Comedian, Director)
1701 Waldman Ave
Las Vegas, NV 89102-2428, USA

Lewis, Jerry (Congressman, Politician)
2112 Rayburn Hob
Washington, DC 20515-0541, USA

Lewis, Jerry Lee (Musician)
1595 Malone Rd
Nesbit, MS 38651-9310, USA

Lewis, Jim (Athlete, Baseball Player)
5062 Big Rock St
Jackson, MI 49201-8126, USA

Lewis, Jim (Athlete, Baseball Player)
5311 Hansel Ave Apt D12
Orlando, FL 32809-3415, USA

Lewis, John (Congressman, Politician)
343 Cannon Hob
Washington, DC 20515-1005, USA

Lewis, Johnny (Athlete, Baseball Player)
810 Tara Cir
Cantonment, FL 32533-9700, USA

Lewis, Johnny (Actor)
c/o Ryan Martin *Agency for the Performing Arts (APA-LA)*
405 S Beverly Dr Ste 500
Beverly Hills, CA 90212-4425, USA

Lewis, Jon Peter (Musician, Reality TV Star)
PO Box 533
Newbury Park, CA 91319-0533, USA

Lewis, Judy
71359 Cypress Dr
Rancho Mirage, CA 92270-3553

Lewis, Juliette (Actor)
c/o Brandy Lewis *BL Management*
3940 Laurel Canyon Blvd Ste 612
Studio City, CA 91604-3709, USA

Lewis, Karen (Writer)
c/o James Sarnoff *The Sarnoff Company Inc*
10 Universal City Plz Ste 2000
Universal City, CA 91608-1074, USA

Lewis, Kenneth D (Financier)
100 N Tryon St
Charlotte, NC 28202-2135, USA

Lewis, Kevin (Athlete, Football Player)
4417 Roy St
Orlando, FL 32812-7350, USA

Lewis, Lennox (Boxer)
57 Fonthill Road
Aberdeen AB11 6UQ, UNITED STATES

Lewis, Leona (Actor, Musician)
c/o Sarah Weinstein *Sony Music Entertainment*
555 Madison Ave
New York, NY 10022-3301, USA

Lewis, Marcedes (Athlete, Football Player)
3725 Bouton Dr
Lakewood, CA 90712-3822, USA

Lewis, Marcia
700 New Hampshire Ave NW
Washington, DC 20037-2407

Lewis, Mark (Athlete, Baseball Player)
1753 Cleveland Ave
Hamilton, OH 45013-5114, USA

Lewis, Mark (Athlete, Football Player)
PO Box 11021
Spring, TX 77391-1021, USA

Lewis, Marvin (Coach, Football Coach)
1 Paul Brown Stadium
Cincinnati, OH 45202-3418, USA

Lewis, Mary (Christianni Brand) (Writer)
88 Maida Vale
London W9, UNITED KINGDOM (UK)

Lewis, Matthew (Actor)
c/o Sarah Spear *Curtis Brown Ltd*
Hay Market House 28-29 Hay Market
London SW1Y 4SP, UK

Lewis, Michael (Writer)
500 5th Ave
New York, NY 10110-0002, USA

Lewis, Mike (Athlete, Football Player)
3350 Blodgett St
Houston, TX 77004-6305, USA

Lewis, Mike (Athlete, Basketball Player)
490 Windsor Park Rd
Kernersville, NC 27284-7013, USA

Lewis, Mo (Athlete, Football Player)
22012 Gardner Dr
Alpharetta, GA 30009-2186, USA

Lewis, Monica (Musician)
1100 Alta Loma Rd Apt 16A
Los Angeles, CA 90069-2441, USA

Lewis, Peter B (Business Person)
32854 Sorrento Ln
Avon Lake, OH 44012-2386, USA

Lewis, Phill (Actor)
c/o Gregg A Klein *Abrams Artists Agency (LA)*
9200 W Sunset Blvd PH 11
Los Angeles, CA 90069-3601, USA

Lewis, Ralph (Athlete, Basketball Player)
3004 Maryannes Ct
North Wales, PA 19454-2024, USA

Lewis, Ramsey (Composer, Musician)
c/o Ted Kurland *Ted Kurland Associates*
173 Brighton Ave
Boston, MA 02134-2003, USA

Lewis, Rashard (Basketball Player)
351 Elliott Ave W Ste 500
Seattle, WA 98119-4153, USA

Lewis, Ray (Athlete, Football Player)
c/o David Dunn *Athletes First, LLC*
3300 Irvine Ave Ste 300
Newport Beach, CA 92660-3108, USA

Lewis, Richard (Actor, Comedian)
c/o Mike Eistenstadt *Amsel, Eisenstadt & Frazier Talent Agency (AEF)*
5055 Wilshire Blvd Ste 860
Los Angeles, CA 90036-6108, USA

Lewis, Richard J (Producer)
c/o Carel Cutler *International Creative Management (ICM-LA)*
10250 Constellation Blvd Fl 7
Los Angeles, CA 90067-6207, USA

Lewis, Richie (Athlete, Baseball Player)
13209 E County Road 700 S
Losantville, IN 47354-9514, USA

Lewis, Robert (Athlete, Basketball Player)
3656 Bay Dr
Edgewater, MD 21037-4143, USA

Lewis, Ron (Athlete, Football Player)
5812 Geranium Rd
Jacksonville, FL 32209-2416, USA

Lewis, Scott (Athlete, Baseball Player)
2584 Fairway Dr
Costa Mesa, CA 92627-1312, USA

Lewis, Shaznay (Musician)
c/o Staff Member *Concorde Intl Artists Ltd*
101 Shepherds Bush Rd
London W6 7LP, UNITED KINGDOM (UK)

Lewis, Sherman (Athlete, Football Player)
45822 Bristol Cir
Novi, MI 48377-3900, USA

Lewis, Terry (Stylist)
c/o Celebrity Stylist *Oliver Piro Inc*
725 Riverside Dr Apt 3A
New York, NY 10031-2460, USA

Lewis, Tim (Athlete, Football Player)
2938 Major Ridge Trl
Duluth, GA 30097-4985, USA

Lewis, Vaughan A (Prime Minister)
1 Riverside Road
Castries, SAINT LUCIA

Lewis, Vicki (Actor, Comedian)
c/o Staff Member *Stone Manners Salners Agency (LA)*
9911 W Pico Blvd Ste 1400
Los Angeles, CA 90035-2715, USA

Lewis, Victor (Musician)
130 W 28th St
New York, NY 10001-6151, USA

Lewis III, Leo (Athlete, Football Player)
10116 Ivywood Ct
Eden Prairie, MN 55347-4543, USA

Lewit-Nirenberg, Julie (Publisher)
350 Madison Ave
New York, NY 10017-3700, USA

Ley, Terry (Athlete, Baseball Player)
2955 SE Custer Rd
Prineville, OR 97754-9424, USA

Leyden, Paul (Actor)
c/o Rhonda Price *Gersh (NY)*
41 Madison Ave
New York, NY 10010-2202, USA

Leygue, Louis Georges (Artist)
6 Rue de Docteur Blanche
Paris 75016, FRANCE

Leyland, James R (Jim) (Athlete, Baseball Player, Coach)
261 Tech Rd
Pittsburgh, PA 15205-1734, USA

Leyritz, James J (Jim) (Baseball Player)
495 Vinegarten Dr
Cincinnati, OH 45255-5204, USA

Leyritz, Jim (Athlete, Baseball Player)
9875 Ridge Trce
Davie, FL 33328-7100, USA

Leyton, John (Actor, Musician)
53 Keyes House Dolphin Square
London SW1V 3NA, UNITED KINGDOM (UK)

Leyva, Nicholas T (Nick) (Athlete, Baseball Player, Coach)
1098 Tilghman Rd
Chesterbrook, PA 19087-5878, USA

Lezak, Jason (Athlete, Swimmer)
c/o Evan Morgenstein *Premier Management Group (PMG Sports)*
115 Crescent Commons Dr Ste 250
Cary, NC 27518-8134, USA

Lezcano, Carlos (Athlete, Baseball Player)
415 W Boxelder Pl
Chandler, AZ 85225-7114, USA

Lezcano, Sixto (Athlete, Baseball Player)
7828 Bardmoor Hill Cir
Orlando, FL 32835-8158, USA

LFO (Musician)
1776 Broadway Fl 15
New York, NY 10019-2002

L'Hermitte, Thierry (Actor)
13 Rue Yves-Toudic
Paris 75010, France

Li, Frederick (Biologist)
44 Binney St
Boston, MA 02115-6013, USA

Li, Gong (Actor, Model)
c/o Julie Moore *The J-Line Group Inc*
8671 Wilshire Blvd Fl 4
Beverly Hills, CA 90211-2926, USA

Li, Jet (Actor)
c/o Steve Chasman *Ace Media*
9200 W Sunset Blvd Ste 10
Los Angeles, CA 90069-3608, USA

Li, Ka-shing (Business Person)
Rooms 1712 - 1716, 17th Floor,
Hopewell Centre 183 Queen's Road East
Hong Kong, Hong Kong

Li, Keyu (Designer, Fashion Designer)
21 Gong-Jian Hutong Di An-Men
Beijing 100009, CHINA

Li, Lanqing (Government Official)
Zhong Nan Hai
Beijing, CHINA

Li, Peng (President)
Zhong Nan Hai
Beijing, CHINA

Li, Yiyun (Writer)
c/o Richard Abate *3 Arts Entertainment - NY*
49 W 27th St Fl 5
New York, NY 10001-6936, USA

Liacouras, Peter J (Educator)
President's Office
Philadelphia, PA 19122, USA

Liaklev, Reidar (Speed Skater)
2770 Jaren
NORWAY

Liars (Music Group)
c/o David T Viecelli *Billions Corporation, The*
3522 W Armitage Ave
Chicago, IL 60647-3603, USA

Liars Inc (Music Group)
c/o Staff Member *Foodchain Records*
6464 W Sunset Blvd Ste 920
Los Angeles, CA 90028-8011, USA

Libano Christo, Carlos A (Activist, Writer)
Rua Atibaia 420
Sao Paulo 01235-010, BRAZIL

Liber, Jon (Baseball Player)
2805 Churchbell Ct
Mobile, AL 36695-2528, USA

Liberace, Dora
1775 E Tropicana Ave
Las Vegas, NV 89119-6529

Libertini, Richard (Actor)
2313 McKinley Ave
Venice, CA 90291-4623, USA

Liberty, Richard
225 SW 6th St
Dania, FL 33004-3943

Libeskind, Daniel (Architect)
Windscheidstr 18
Berlin 10627, GERMANY

Liboiron, Landon (Actor)
c/o Kimberlin Dalehite *Magnolia Entertainment (LA)*
9595 Wilshire Blvd Ste 601
Beverly Hills, CA 90212-2506, USA

Libran, Frankie (Athlete, Baseball Player)
100 Calle Principe Apt 1
Mayaguez, PR 00680-3403, USA

Libutti, Frank (General, Misc)
Police Plaza
New York, NY 10038, USA

Licad, Cecile (Musician)
165 W 57th St
New York, NY 10019-2201, USA

Lichfield, Earl of (Photographer)
133 Oxford Gardens
London, W10 6NE, UNITED KINGDOM (UK)

Licht, Jeremy (Actor)
4355 Clybourn Ave
Toluca Lake, CA 91602-2906, USA

Licht, Louis (Scientist)
3017 Valley View Ln NE
North Liberty, IA 52317-9538, USA

Lichtenberg, Byron K (Astronaut)
5701 Impala South Rd
Athens, TX 75752-6053, USA

Lichtenberger, H W (Business Person)
39 Old Ridgebury Rd
Danbury, CT 06810-5103, USA

Lichtenstein, Harvey (Music Group)
30 Lafayette Ave
Brooklyn, NY 11217-1430, USA

Lichti, Todd (Athlete, Basketball Player)
2331 Holly View Dr
Martinez, CA 94553-3375, USA

Lichtwardt, Nancy (Stylist)
3114 NE 36th Ave
Portland, OR 97212-2838, USA

Lick, Dennis A (Athlete, Football Player)
6140 S Knox Ave
Chicago, IL 60629-5424, USA

Lickert, John (Athlete, Baseball Player)
PO Box 279
North Scituate, RI 02857-0279, USA

Lickliter, Frank (Athlete, Golfer)
846 S Main St
Franklin, OH 45005-2731, USA

Licon, Jeffrey (Actor)
c/o Katie Mason *Luber Roklin Management*
8530 Wilshire Blvd Ste 550
Beverly Hills, CA 90211-3133, USA

Lidback, Jenny (Athlete, Golfer)
1130 Graystone Xing
Alpharetta, GA 30005-7436, USA

Liddell, Chuck (Iceman) (Athlete, Wrestler)
c/o Staff Member *UFC*
PO Box 26959
Las Vegas, NV 89126-0959, USA

Liddell, Dave (Athlete, Baseball Player)
2631 Preakness Way
Norco, CA 92860-4201, USA

Liddy, Edward M (Business Person)
Allstate Plaza 2775 Sanders Road
Northbrook, IL 60062, USA

Liddy, G Gordon (Actor)
9112 Riverside Dr
Fort Washington, MD 20744-6863, USA

Lidge, Brad (Athlete, Baseball Player)
447 N Gate Stone
Houston, TX 77007-8341, USA

Lidov, Arthur (Artist)
Pleasant Ridge Rd
Poughquag, NY 12570, USA

Lidstrom, Nicklas (Athlete, Hockey Player)
47725 Bellagio Dr
Northville, MI 48167-9803, USA

Liebensteuin, Todd (Athlete, Football Player)
4486 Chain O Lakes Rd
Eagle River, WI 54521-8856, USA

Lieber, Jon (Athlete, Baseball Player)
3060 Isle of Palms Dr W
Mobile, AL 36695-2576, USA

Lieber, Larry (Cartoonist)
c/o Staff Member *King Features Syndication*
300 W 57th St Fl 15
New York, NY 10019-5238, USA

Lieber, Paul (Actor)
c/o Margrit Polak *Margrit Polak Management*
1954 Hillhurst Ave Ste 405
Los Angeles, CA 90027-2722, USA

Lieber, Rob (Writer)
c/o Staff Member *International Creative Management (ICM-LA)*
10250 Constellation Blvd Fl 7
Los Angeles, CA 90067-6207, USA

Lieberman, Andrea (Stylist)
c/o Staff Member *Margaret Maldonado Agency*
1100 Glendon Ave Ste 1000
Los Angeles, CA 90024-3514, USA

Lieberman, Joseph I (Senator)
706 Hart Senate
Washington, DC 20510-0001, USA

Lieberman, Wendy
PO Box 5617
Beverly Hills, CA 90209-5617

Lieberman, William S (Misc)
5th Ave & 82nd St
New York, NY 10028, USA

Liebert, Ottmar (Musician)
10123 Camarillo St
Toluca Lake, CA 91602-1601, USA

Lieberthal, Michael S (Mike) (Athlete, Baseball Player)
1740 Larkfield Ave
Westlake Village, CA 91362-4245, USA

Liebeskind, John (Doctor)
Surgery Dept
Los Angeles, CA 90024, USA

Liebesman, Jonathan (Director)
c/o David Gardner *Principato/Young Management*
9465 Wilshire Blvd Ste 430
Beverly Hills, CA 90212-2613, USA

Liebman, David (Musician)
1541 Brislin Rd
Stroudsburg, PA 18360-7689, USA

Liebowitz, Fran
205 W 57th St
New York, NY 10019-2105

Liebrich, Barbara (Athlete, Baseball Player)
16608 N 51st St
Scottsdale, AZ 85254-1063, USA

Liefeld, Rob (Artist, Cartoonist)
1942 University Ave Ste 305
Berkeley, CA 94704-1244, USA

Liefer, Jeff (Athlete, Baseball Player)
1116 W Bay Ave
Newport Beach, CA 92661-1017, USA

Lien, Chan (Prime Minister)
1 Chunghsiano East Road Sec 1
Taipei, TAIWAN

Lien, Jennifer (Actor)
c/o Staff Member *Abrams Artists Agency (LA)*
9200 W Sunset Blvd PH 11
Los Angeles, CA 90069-3601, USA

Lienas, Winston (Baseball Player)
Apartado #92
Santiago Dominican Republic

Lienhard, Bill (Athlete, Basketball Player)
1320 Lawrence Ave
Lawrence, KS 66049-2938, USA

Lienhard, William (Bill) (Athlete, Basketball Player)
1320 Lawrence Ave
Lawrence, KS 66049-2938, USA

Liepa, Andris (Ballerina)
Bryusov Per 17 #12
Moscow 103009, RUSSIA

Liepa, Ilsa (Ballerina)
Bryusov Per 17 #12
Moscow 103009, RUSSIA

Liepmann, Hans W (Engineer, Physicist)
55 Haverstock Rd
La Canada-Flintridge, CA 91011, USA

Lietzke, Bruce (Athlete, Golfer)
PO Box 177
Larue, TX 75770-0177, USA

Life On Repeat (Music Group, Musician)
c/o Steve Taylor *Anthem Artist Management*
9048 Woodland Trl
Alpharetta, GA 30009-8758, USA

Lifehouse (Music Group)
c/o Staff Member *Creative Artists Agency (CAA-TN)*
3310 W End Ave Fl 5
Nashville, TN 37203-1028, USA

Lifeson, Alex (Musician)
1505 W 2nd Ave # 200
Vancouver, BC V6H 3Y4, CANADA

Lifford, Tina (Actor)
c/o Nancy Sanders *Sanders Armstrong Caserta*
2120 Colorado Ave Ste 120
Santa Monica, CA 90404-3561, USA

Lifvendahl, Harold R (Publisher)
633 N Orange Ave
Orlando, FL 32801-1300, USA

Ligarde, Sebastian (Actor)
c/o Staff Member *Televisa*
Blvd Adolfo Lopez Mateos 232 Colonia San Angel INN
DF CP 01060, MEXICO

Light, John (Actor)
c/o Arlene Forster *Forster Entertainment*
12533 Woodgreen St
Los Angeles, CA 90066-2723, USA

Light, Judith (Actor)
c/o Bob Gersh *Gersh (LA)*
9465 Wilshire Blvd Ste 600
Beverly Hills, CA 90212-2612, USA

Lightfoot, Gordon (Musician, Songwriter, Writer)
c/o Staff Member *Early Morning Productions, Inc.*
1365 Yonge St Suite 207
Toronto, ON M4T 2P7, Canada

Lightfoot, Leonard
446 S Orchard Dr
Burbank, CA 91506-2738

Lightner, Candy (Activist)
22653 Pacific Coast Hwy # 289
Malibu, CA 90265-5096, USA

Ligon, Bill (Athlete, Basketball Player)
PO Box 1432
Gallatin, TN 37066-1432, USA

Ligon, Tom
227 Waverly Pl
New York, NY 10014-2407

Ligouri, James A (Educator)
President's Office
New Rochelle, NY 10801, USA

Ligtenberg, Kerry (Athlete, Baseball Player)
9274 Albright Ct
Inver Grove Heights, MN 55077-4546, USA

Likens, Gerie E (Biologist)
PO Box AB
Millbrook, NY 12545-0129, USA

Likens, Peter W (Educator)
President's Office
Bethlehem, PA 18015, USA

Lil' Cease (Musician)
250 W 57th St
New York, NY 10107-0001, USA

Lil' J (Actor, Musician, Television Host)
c/o Staff Member *Thruline Entertainment*
9250 Wilshire Blvd Ground Fl
Beverly Hills, CA 90212, USA

Lil Jon (Musician)
c/o David Wirtschafter *WmE2 (Endeavor-LA)*
9601 Wilshire Blvd Fl 3
Beverly Hills, CA 90210-5219, USA

Lil Wayne (Musician)
c/o Cortez Bryant *Bryant Management*
555 Washington Ave Ste 240
Miami, FL 33139-6639, USA

Liles, Kevin (Business Person)
512 Fashion Ave Rm 4100
New York, NY 10018-4741, USA

Lilienfeld, Abraham M (Biologist)
3203 Old Post Dr
Pikesville, MD 21208-3212, USA

Lilja, George (Athlete, Football Player)
8 Driftwood Dr
Warren, PA 16365-3380, USA

Liljeberg, Rebecka (Actor)
Kolbäcksgränd 33
Bagarmossen 12846, Sweden

Lill, John R (Musician)
31 Sinclair Road
London W14 0NS, UNITED KINGDOM (UK)

Lillard, Bill (Bowler)
5418 Imogene St
Houston, TX 77096-2206, USA

Lillard, Bill (Athlete, Baseball Player)
1690 Quiet Oaks Dr
Arroyo Grande, CA 93420-5685, USA

Lillard, Mathew (Actor, Director, Producer)

Lillard, Matthew (Actor, Producer)
c/o Melissa Kates *Viewpoint Inc*
8820 Wilshire Blvd Ste 220
Beverly Hills, CA 90211-2622, USA

Lillee, Dennis K (Cricketer)
PO Box 158
Byron Bay, NSW 2481, AUSTRALIA

Lilley, Chris (Actor)
c/o Sharne MacDonald PO Box 128
Surry Hills NSW 2010, AUSTRALIA

Lilley, James R (Diplomat)
2801 New Mexico Ave NW Apt 407
Washington, DC 20007-3929, USA

Lillien, Lisa (Writer)
c/o Bill Stankey *Westport Entertainment Associates*
1700 Post Rd Ste C15
Fairfield, CT 06824-5726, USA

Lilliquist, Derek (Athlete, Baseball Player)
226 10th Ave
Vero Beach, FL 32962-2819, USA

Lillis, Bob (Athlete, Baseball Player, Coach)
5107 Cherry Tree Ln
Orlando, FL 32819-3848, USA

Lillis, Charles M (Business Person)
188 Inverness Dr W
Englewood, CO 80112-5205, USA

Lillix (Music Group)
c/o Staff Member *Bruce Allen Talent*
425 Carrall St Suite 500
Vancouver, BC V6B 6E3, Canada

Lilly, Evangeline (Actor)
c/o David Miner *3 Arts Entertainment Inc*
9460 Wilshire Blvd Fl 7
Beverly Hills, CA 90212-2713, USA

Lilly, Kristine (Athlete, Soccer Player)

Lilly, Robert L (Bob) (Athlete, Football Player)
3310 Drexel Dr
Dallas, TX 75205-2915, USA

Lilly, Ted (Athlete, Baseball Player)
1305 W Waveland Ave
Chicago, IL 60613-3720, USA

Lilly, Theodore (Baseball Player)
PO Box 257
Bass Lake, CA 93604-0257, USA

Lillywhite, Verl (Athlete, Football Player)
1828 N Barkley
Mesa, AZ 85203-2702, USA

Lily, Morgan (Actor)
c/o Casey Crawford *Origin Talent Agency*
4705 Laurel Canyon Blvd Ste 306
Studio City, CA 91607-5940, USA

Lim, Kwan Hi
1660 Piikoi St
Honolulu, HI 96822-2719

Lim, Siew-Ai (Athlete, Golfer)
304 Morning Sun Dr
Birmingham, AL 35242-2912, USA

Lima, Adriana (Actor, Model)
c/o Chris Kiely *Marilyn Model Management*
32 Union Sq E PH
New York, NY 10003-3209, USA

Lima, Devin
8750 Wilshire Blvd
Beverly Hills, CA 90211-2703

Lima, Jose (Athlete, Baseball Player)
8012 Wiles Rd # 7
Coral Springs, FL 33067-2072, USA

Lima, Luis (Opera Singer)
1950 Redondela Dr
Rancho Palos Verdes, CA 90275-1028, USA

Liman, Doug (Director, Producer, Writer)
c/o Adam Kanter *Creative Artists Agency (CAA-LA)*
2000 Avenue of the Stars Ste 100
Los Angeles, CA 90067-4705, USA

Limato, Ed
456 S Plymouth Blvd
Los Angeles, CA 90020-4708

Limbaugh, Rush (Radio Personality)
PO Box 420058
Palm Coast, FL 32142-0058, USA

Limbrick, Garrett (Athlete, Football Player)
PO Box 472
Hempstead, TX 77445-0472, USA

Lime, Yvonne (Actor)
6135 E McDonald Dr
Paradise Valley, AZ 85253-5222, USA

Limelighters, The
11761 E Speedway Blvd
Tucson, AZ 85748-2017

Limelights
11761 E Speedway Blvd
Tucson, AZ 85748-2017

Limos, Tiffany (Actor)
c/o Staff Member *Paradigm (LA)*
360 N Crescent Dr
Beverly Hills, CA 90210-4874, USA

Lin, Bridget (Actor)
8 Fei Ngo Shan Road Kowloon
Hong Kong, CHINA

Lin, Ching-Hsia (Actor)
196 Chunghua Road 10/F Sec 1
Taipei, TAIWAN

Lin, Cho-Laing
5404 John Dreaper Dr
Houston, TX 77056-4231

Lin, Cho-Liang (Musician)
60 Lincoln Center Plz
New York, NY 10023-6500, USA

Lin, Justin (Director)
c/o Rowena Arguelles *Creative Artists Agency (CAA-LA)*
2000 Avenue of the Stars Ste 100
Los Angeles, CA 90067-4705, USA

Lin, Maya Ying (Architect, Artist)
120 E 75th St # 6A
New York, NY 10021-3240, USA

Lin, Ting Ting (Stylist)
c/o Staff Member *Jed Root Inc*
61-A Walker St
New York, NY 10013, USA

Lin, Tsung-Yi (Misc)
6287 MacDonald St
Vancouver, BC V6N 1E7, CANADA

Lin, Yu Ping (Athlete, Golfer)
1450 Subtropic Dr
La Habra Heights, CA 90631-8073, USA

Lincicome, Brittany (Athlete, Golfer)
7971 Idlewild Ln
Seminole, FL 33777-3108, USA

Lincoln, Andrew (Actor)
c/o Staff Member *Independent Talent Group (ITG-UK)*
Oxford House 76 Oxford St
London W1D 1BS, UK

Lincoln, Howard (Baseball Player)
6 Holly Hill Dr
Mercer Island, WA 98040-5326, USA

Lincoln, Jeremy (Athlete, Football Player)
71 Broadway Apt 20A
New York, NY 10006-2612, USA

Lincoln, Keith P (Athlete, Football Player)
550 SE Crestview St
Pullman, WA 99163-2257, USA

Lincoln, Lar Park
8899 Beverly Blvd Ste 510
Los Angeles, CA 90048-2449

Lincoln, Michael (Mike) (Athlete, Baseball Player)
8269 Moss Oak Ave
Citrus Heights, CA 95610-0763, USA

Lind, DeDe
PO Box 1712
Boca Raton, FL 33429-1712

Lind, Don L (Astronaut)
51 N 376 E
Smithfield, UT 84335-1111, USA

Lind, Jack (Athlete, Baseball Player)
6132 E Redmont Dr
Mesa, AZ 85215-0878, USA

Lind, Joan (Athlete)
240 Euclid Ave
Long Beach, CA 90803-6020, USA

Lind, Jose (Athlete, Baseball Player)
18 Brisas Del Plata
Dorado, PR 00646-5123, USA

Lind, Juha (Athlete, Hockey Player)
1260 De La Gauchetiere W
Montreal, QC H3B 5E8, Canada

Lind, Marshall L (Educator)
Chancellor's Office
Janeau, AK 99801, USA

Lind, Sarah (Actor)
c/o Staff Member *Lucas Talent Inc*
100 W. Pender St Sun Tower, 7th Floor
Vancouver, BC V6B 1R8, Canada

Lindahl, David (Business Person)
75 Old High St
Whitman, MA 02382-1143

Lindahl, George III (Business Person)
PO Box 1330
Houston, TX 77251-1330, USA

Lindahl, Virgil (Athlete, Football Player)
3022 W 19th St
Greeley, CO 80634-5707, USA

Lindbeck, Assar (Economist)
50 Ostermalmsgatan
Stockholm 114 26, SWEDEN

Lindbeck, Em (Athlete, Baseball Player)
210 Hillcrest Dr
Kewanee, IL 61443-3424, USA

Lindberg, Chad (Actor)
c/o Staff Member *Michael Black Management*
9701 Wilshire Blvd Fl 10
Beverly Hills, CA 90212-2010, USA

Lindbergh, Reeve (Writer)
1230 Avenue of the Americas Fl 11
New York, NY 10020-1513, USA

Lindelind, Liv (Model)
PO Box 1029
Frazier Park, CA 93225-1029, USA

Lindell, Heather (Actor)
c/o Alan Ellsweig *Shadow Entertainment*
10 Universal City Plz Fl 20
Universal City, CA 91608-1074, USA

Lindell, Rian (Athlete, Football Player)
712 NE 157th Ct
Vancouver, WA 98684-8734, USA

Lindelof, Damon (Producer, Writer)
c/o Ted Miller *Creative Artists Agency (CAA-LA)*
2000 Avenue of the Stars Ste 100
Los Angeles, CA 90067-4705, USA

Lindeman, Jim (Athlete, Baseball Player)
2278 S Scott St
Des Plaines, IL 60018-3147, USA

Linden, Hal (Actor)
c/o Staff Member *Stone Manners Talent & Literary (NY)*
900 Broadway Ste 803
New York, NY 10003-1229, USA

Linden, Todd (Athlete, Baseball Player)
7825 NW Anderson Hill Rd
Silverdale, WA 98383-9313, USA

Linden, Walt (Athlete, Baseball Player)
4432 Harvey Ave
Western Springs, IL 60558-1645, USA

Lindenlaub, Karl W (Cinematographer)
3021 Nichols Canyon Rd
Los Angeles, CA 90046-1242, USA

Lindenmann, Tony (Bowler)
35096 Jefferson Ave Apt 216
Harrison Township, MI 48045-3275, USA

Linder, Kate (Actor)
c/o Sandra Siegal *Siegal Company, The*
9025 Wilshire Blvd Ste 400
Beverly Hills, CA 90211-1828, USA

Lindes, Hal (Musician)
16 Lambton Place
London W11 2SH, UNITED KINGDOM (UK)

Lindh, Hilary (Skier)
PO Box 33036
Juneau, AK 99803-3036, USA

Lindholm, Ingvar
Hringe Hages Vag 33
Ronninge, SWEDEN 14400

Lindhome, Riki (Actor, Director, Writer)
c/o Mary Ellen Mulcahy *Framework Entertainment (LA)*
9057 Nemo St Ste C
West Hollywood, CA 90069-5511, USA

Lindig, Bill M (Business Person)
1390 Enclave Pkwy
Houston, TX 77077-2025, USA

Lindlar, Renate (Stylist)
c/o Staff Member *Bransch*
131 Varick St Rm 1006
New York, NY 10013-1453, USA

Lindley, Christina (Model)
114 Rhine Dr
Madison, TN 37115-3561, USA

Lindley, Leta (Athlete, Golfer)
104 Alegria Way
Palm Beach Gardens, FL 33418-1722, USA

Lindner, Carl (Baseball Player)
8455 Shawnee Run Rd
Cincinnati, OH 45243-3312, USA

Lindner, William G (Misc)
80 W End Ave
New York, NY 10023-6301, USA

Lindo, Delroy (Actor)
c/o Brian Swardstrom *WmE2 (Endeavor-LA)*
9601 Wilshire Blvd Fl 3
Beverly Hills, CA 90210-5219, USA

Lindon, Vincent (Actor)
20 Ave Rapp
Paris 75007, FRANCE

Lindquist, Susan L (Biologist)
9 Cambridge Cir
Cambridge, MA 2142, USA

Lindros, Eric (Athlete, Hockey Player)
411 Glencaim Ave
Toronto, ON M5N 1V4, Canada

Lindroth, Eric (Misc)
13151 Dufresne Pl
San Diego, CA 92129-2383, USA

Lindsay, Everett (Athlete, Football Player)
10416 Whitestone Rd
Raleigh, NC 27615-1236, USA

Lindsay, Jack (Writer)
56 Maids Causeway
Cambridge, UNITED KINGDOM (UK)

Lindsay, Mark (Musician, Songwriter, Writer)
27 L Ambiance Ct
Bardonia, NY 10954-1421, USA

Lindsay, Mort
6970 Fernhill Dr
Malibu, CA 90265-4239

Lindsay, R B Theodore (Ted) (Athlete, Hockey Player)
2598 Invitational Dr
Oakland, MI 48363-2453, USA

Lindsay, Robert (Actor, Musician)
c/o Christian Hodell *Hamilton Hodell Ltd*
66-68 Margaret St Fl 5
London W1W 8SR, UK

Lindsey, Bill (Athlete, Baseball Player)
1317 Winterberry Dr
Reidsville, NC 27320-7154, USA

Lindsey, Dale (Athlete, Football Player)
4020 Murphy Canyon Rd
San Diego, CA 92123-4407, USA

Lindsey, Doug (Athlete, Baseball Player)
2410 Silver Spur Ln
Leander, TX 78641-7883, USA

Lindsey, George (Actor)
c/o Staff Member *Richard De La Font Agency*
3808 W South Park Blvd
Broken Arrow, OK 74011-1261, USA

Lindsey, James E (Athlete, Football Player)
1165 E Joyce Blvd
Fayetteville, AR 72703-5183, USA

Lindsey, Rodney (Rod) (Athlete, Baseball Player)
610 Comanchee Dr Lot 43
Opelika, AL 36804-6500, USA

Lindsey, Steven W (Astronaut)
3217 W Yarrow Cir
Superior, CO 80027-6021, USA

Lindsey, Tracy
651 N Kilkea Dr
Los Angeles, CA 90048-2213

Lindsley, Blake (Actor)
3500 W Olive Ave Ste 1400
Burbank, CA 91505-5512, USA

Lindsley, Donald B (Physicist)
517 11th St
Santa Monica, CA 90402-2901, USA

Lindstrand, Per (Misc)
Maesbury Road
Oswestry, Shropshire SY10 8HA, UNITED KINGDOM (UK)

Lindstrom, Charlie (Chuck) (Athlete, Baseball Player)
PO Box 486
Atlanta, IL 61723-0486, USA

Lindstrom, Chris (Athlete, Football Player)
70 Dudley Hill Rd
Dudley, MA 01571-5924, USA

Lindstrom, David (Dave) (Athlete, Football Player)
13209 Woodson St
Overland Park, KS 66209-3817, USA

Lindstrom, Jack (Cartoonist)
200 Madison Ave
New York, NY 10016-3903, USA

Lindstrom, Jon (Actor)
c/o Staff Member *Gilbertson Management*
1334 3rd Street Promenade Ste 201
Santa Monica, CA 90401-1320, USA

Lindvall, Angela (Actor, Model)
c/o Brett Norensberg *Gersh (LA)*
9465 Wilshire Blvd Ste 600
Beverly Hills, CA 90212-2612, USA

Lindvall, Olle (Doctor)
Medical Cell Research Dept
Lund 23362, SWEDEN

Lindwall, Raymond R (Cricketer)
3 Wentworth Court Endeavour St Mt Ommaney
Brisbane, QLD 4074, AUSTRALIA

Line, Bill (Athlete, Football Player)
6048 Plumas St Apt E
Reno, NV 89519-6024, USA

Line, Lorie (Musician)
PO Box 400
Mound, MN 55364-0400, USA

Linebrink, Scott (Athlete, Baseball Player)
PO Box 28
Walburg, TX 78673-0028, USA

Lineger, Jerry (Astronaut)
c/o Staff Member *Washington Speakers Bureau*
1663 Prince St
Alexandria, VA 22314-2818, USA

Lineker, Gary W (Soccer Player)
6 Saint George St
Nottingham NG1 3BE, UNITED KINGDOM (UK)

Linenger, Jerry M (Astronaut)
550 S Stony Point Rd
Suttons Bay, MI 49682-9575, USA

Lines, Dick (Athlete, Baseball Player)
1716 Pebble Beach Ln
Lady Lake, FL 32159-2238, USA

Liney, John (Cartoonist)
c/o Staff Member *King Features Syndication*
300 W 57th St Fl 15
New York, NY 10019-5238, USA

Ling (Model)
304 Park Ave S # 1200
New York, NY 10010-4301, USA

Ling, Bai (Actor)
c/o Matt Luber *Luber Roklin Management*
8530 Wilshire Blvd Ste 550
Beverly Hills, CA 90211-3133, USA

Ling, Lisa (Correspondent, Journalist)
c/o Henry Reisch *WmE2 (WMA-NY)*
1325 Avenue of the Americas
New York, NY 10019-6026, USA

Ling, Sergei S (Prime Minister)
Pl Nezavisimosti
Minsk 220010, BELARUS

Lingenfelter, Bob (Football Player)
53144 865 Rd
Plainview, NE 68769-2505, USA

Lingenfelter, Steve (Athlete, Basketball Player)
17378 Ithaca Ct
Lakeville, MN 55044-8742, USA

Lingmerth, Goran (Athlete, Football Player)
624 Enfield Ct
Delray Beach, FL 33444-1749, USA

Lingner, Adam (Athlete, Football Player)
70 Stoughton Ln
Orchard Park, NY 14127-2084, USA

Linhart, Anton (Athlete, Football Player)
13 Summer Run Ct
Timonium, MD 21093-4346, USA

Linhart, Carl (Athlete, Baseball Player)
2647 Delmar Ave
Granite City, IL 62040-3439, USA

Linhart, Toni (Athlete, Football Player)
13 Summer Run Ct
Lutherville Timonium, MD 21093-4346, USA

Liniak, Cole (Athlete, Baseball Player)
PO Box 235625
Encinitas, CA 92023-5625, USA

Linke, Paul (Actor)
139 S Beverly Dr Ste 225
Beverly Hills, CA 90212-3028, USA

Linkert, Lo (Artist, Cartoonist)
9541 Lenore Dr
Garden Grove, CA 92841-4925, USA

Linklater, Hamish (Actor)
c/o Leanne Coronel *Coronel Group*
1100 Glendon Ave Fl 17
Los Angeles, CA 90024-3588, USA

Linklater, Hamish (Actor)
c/o Hildy Gottlieb *International Creative Management (ICM-LA)*
10250 Constellation Blvd Fl 7
Los Angeles, CA 90067-6207, USA

Linklater, Richard (Director, Producer, Writer)
PO Box 13351
Austin, TX 78711-3351, USA

Linkletter, John A (Editor)
224 W 57th St
New York, NY 10019-3212, USA

Linkletter, Nicole (Model)
c/o Staff Member *Ford Models (NY)*
238 E 4th St
New York, NY 10009-7425

Linley, Cody (Actor)
c/o Staff Member *Reel Talent Management*
PO Box 491035
Los Angeles, CA 90049-9035, USA

Linn, Jack (Athlete, Football Player)
6250 Half Mile Rd
Theodore, AL 36582-2721, USA

Linn, Richard (Judge)
717 Madison Pl NW
Washington, DC 20439-0001, USA

Linn, Teri Ann (Actor)
145 S Fairfax Ave Ste 310
Los Angeles, CA 90036-2176, USA

Linn-Baker, Mark (Actor)
27702 Fairweather St
Canyon Country, CA 91351-2925, USA

Linne, Aubrey (Athlete, Football Player)
4606 Lanham St
Midland, TX 79705-3213, USA

Linne, Larry (Athlete, Football Player)
6861 Pumpkin Ridge Dr
Windsor, CO 80550-7015, USA

Linnehan, Richard M (Astronaut)
16802 Hartwood Way
Houston, TX 77058-2305, USA

Linney, Laura (Actor)
c/o Aleen Keshishian *Brillstein Entertainment Partners*
9150 Wilshire Blvd Ste 350
Beverly Hills, CA 90212-3453, USA

Linnin, Chris (Athlete, Football Player)
1037 Purple Sage Loop
Castle Rock, CO 80104-7846, USA

Linowitz, Sol M (Diplomat)
2230 California St NW # 4B
Washington, DC 20008-3936, USA

Linsalata, Joe (Baseball Player)
4017 Washington St
Hollywood, FL 33021-7349, USA

Linsalata, Joe (Athlete, Baseball Player)
4017 Washington St
Hollywood, FL 33021-7349, USA

Linseman, Ken (Athlete, Hockey Player)
1070 Ocean Blvd
Hampton, NH 03842-1500, USA

Linskey, Mike (Baseball Player)
18826 Polo Meadow Dr
Humble, TX 77346-8121, USA

Linson, Art (Director, Producer)
4000 Warner Blvd
Burbank, CA 91522-0001, USA

Lintel, Michelle (Actor)
c/o John Paradise *The Paradise Group*
PO Box 69451
West Hollywood, CA 90069-0451, USA

Linteris, Gregory T (Astronaut)
Fire Science Division
Gaithersburg, MD 20899-0001, USA

Linton, Doug (Athlete, Baseball Player)
201 Ellison St
Rochester, NY 14609-4047, USA

Lintz, Larry (Athlete, Baseball Player)
PO Box 231854
Sacramento, CA 95823-0414, USA

Linville, Joanne (Actor)
345 N Maple Dr # 302
Beverly Hills, CA 90210-3869, USA

Linz, Alex D (Actor)
1505 10th St
Santa Monica, CA 90401-2805, USA

Linz, Phil (Athlete, Baseball Player)
20 Rocky Rapids Rd
Stamford, CT 06903-3131, USA

Linzy, Frank (Athlete, Baseball Player)
38947 E 151st St S
Coweta, OK 74429-8550, USA

Lioeanjie, Rene (Misc)
1150 17th St NW
Washington, DC 20036-4603, USA

Lionetti, Donald M (General)
4517 W Rosemere Rd
Tampa, FL 33609-4209, USA

Lions, Jacques-Louis (Mathematician)
7 Rue Paul Barruel
Paris 75015, USA

Lions, Pierre-Louis (Mathematician)
Place Marechal Lattre-de-Tessigny
Paris 75775, FRANCE

Liotta, Ray (Actor)
c/o Beth Holden-Garland *Untitled Entertainment (LA)*
350 S Beverly Dr Ste 200
Beverly Hills, CA 90212-4819, USA

Lioutas, Tommy (Actor)
c/o Norbert Abrams *Noble Caplan Abrams*
1260 Yonge St 2nd Floor
Toronto ON M4T 1W6, Canada

Lipa, Elisabeta (Athlete)
Str Reconstructiei 1 #78
Bucharest, ROMANIA

Lipetri, Angelo (Athlete, Baseball Player)
150 Yoakum Ave
Farmingdale, NY 11735-5034, USA

Lipinski, Ann Marie (Journalist)
435 N Michigan Ave
Chicago, IL 60611-4066, USA

Lipinski, Daniel (Congressman, Politician)
1717 Longworth Hob
Washington, DC 20515-1901, USA

Lipinski, Tara (Actor, Figure Skater)
c/o Tracy Quinn *Quinn Management*
17328 Ventura Blvd Ste 416
Encino, CA 91316-3904, USA

Lipman, Maureen (Actor, Writer)
c/o Staff Member *Talking Concepts*
19 Bird Street Lichfield
Staffordshire WS13 6PW, UNITED KINGDOM

Lipnicki, Jonathan (Actor)
c/o Jason Egenberg *United Talent Agency (UTA)*
9560 Wilshire Blvd Fl 5
Beverly Hills, CA 90212-2400, USA

Lipovsek, Marjana (Opera Singer)
Rutistr 52
Zurich-Gockhausen 8044, SWITZERLAND

Lippard, Stephen J (Misc)
975 Memorial Dr Apt 602
Cambridge, MA 02138-5803, USA

Lippett, Ronnie (Athlete, Football Player)
PO Box 1338
Easton, MA 02334-1338, USA

Lippincott, Philip E (Business Person)
Campbell Place
Cemden, NJ 8103, USA

Lipporien, Paavo Tapio (Prime Minister)
Snellmaninkatu 1
Helsinki 170, FINLAND

Lipps, Lisa (Adult Film Star)
69 Moonlight Rd
Mound House, NV 89706-7048, USA

Lipset, Seymour M (Misc)
900 N Stafford St Apt 2131
Arlington, VA 22203-1850, USA

Lipsett, Mortimer B (Physicist)
9000 Rockville Pike
Bethesda, MD 20892-0001, USA

Lipshutz, Bruce H (Misc)
Chemistry Dept
Santa Barbara, CA 93106-0001, USA

Lipski, Bob (Athlete, Baseball Player)
1 Snook St
Scranton, PA 18505-2865, USA

Lipson, D Herbert (Publisher)
1500 Walnut St
Philadelphia, PA 19102-3523, USA

Lipton, Bruce (Motivational Speaker)
2574 Pine Flat Rd
Santa Cruz, CA 95060-9497, USA

Lipton, Holly (Musician)
c/o Staff Member *Charles Rapp Enterprises Inc*
88 Pine St
New York, NY 10005-1801, USA

Lipton, James (Actor, Producer, Television Host)
c/o Staff Member *James Lipton Productions*
120A E 23rd St Fl 3A
New York, NY 10010-4516, USA

Lipton, Martin (Attorney, Attorney General, General)
51 W 52nd St
New York, NY 10019-6119, USA

Lipton, Peggy (Actor, Writer)
c/o Staff Member *St Martins Press*
175 5th Ave
New York, NY 10010-7703, USA

Lipton, Robert (Actor)
c/o Staff Member *Judy Fox Personal Talent Management*
Prefers to be contacted via telephone
Los Angeles, CA 90069, USA

Liquor, Shirley Q (Comedian)
c/o Staff Member *Diva Central Inc*
7510 W Sunset Blvd Ste 1445
Los Angeles, CA 90046-3408, USA

Liquori, Martin (Marty) (Athlete, Sportscaster, Track Athlete)
2915 NW 58th Blvd
Gainesville, FL 32606-8517, USA

Liquori, Marty
2915 NW 58th Blvd
Gainesville, FL 32606-8517

Liriano, Nelson (Athlete, Baseball Player)
801 Shipyard Dr
Wilmington, DE 19801-5154, USA

Lis, Joe (Athlete, Baseball Player)
PO Box 1599
Newburgh, IN 47629-1599, USA

Lisa, Mona
8860 Corbin Ave # 185
Northridge, CA 91324-3309

Lisbe, Mike (Writer)
c/o Brian Sher *Category 5 Entertainment*
10250 Constellation Blvd Fl 7
Los Angeles, CA 90067-6207, USA

Lisch, Russell (Athlete, Football Player)
206 Country Club Ln
Belleville, IL 62223-1910, USA

Liscio, Patti (Golfer)
7803 Glenneagle Dr
Dallas, TX 75248-2335, USA

Liscio, Tony (Athlete, Football Player)
10348 Trailcliff Dr
Dallas, TX 75238-1556, USA

Lisi, Rick (Athlete, Baseball Player)
1207 N Wren Dr
Rogers, AR 72756-1952, USA

Lisi, Virna (Actor)
Via di Filomarino 4
Rome, ITALY

Lisin, Vladimir (Business Person)
2, pl. Metallurgov
Lipetsk 398040, Russia

Lisitsa, Valentina (Musician)
165 W 57th St
New York, NY 10019-2201, USA

Liska, Stephen (Actor)
c/o Larry Metzger *Grant Savic Kopaloff & Associates*
6399 Wilshire Blvd Ste 414
Los Angeles, CA 90048-5716, USA

Liskov, Barbara H (Engineer)
Computer Sci Lab
Cambridge, MA 2139, USA

Liss, Joe (Actor)
c/o Scott Howard *Howard Entertainment*
10850 Wilshire Blvd Ste 1260
Los Angeles, CA 90024-4337, USA

Lissie (Musician)
c/o Staff Member *Paradigm (Monterey)*
404 W Franklin St
Monterey, CA 93940-2303, USA

Lissner, Stephane (Opera Singer)
2 Rue Eduouard Colonne
Paris 75001, FRANCE

List, Peyton (Actor)
c/o Abby Bluestone *Innovative Artists (LA)*
1505 10th St
Santa Monica, CA 90401-2805, USA

Listach, Pat (Athlete, Baseball Player)
6030 Durande Dr
Baton Rouge, LA 70820-5421, USA

Lister, Alton (Athlete, Basketball Player)
5413 Kirkridge Pl
Garland, TX 75044-4633, USA

Lister Jr, Tommy (Tiny Zeus) (Actor)
c/o Staff Member *Cindy Cowan Entertainment*
8265 W Sunset Blvd Ste 205
West Hollywood, CA 90046-2470, USA

Listopad, Ed (Athlete, Football Player)
6719 Roberts Ave
Dundalk, MD 21222-1053, USA

Listowel, Earl of (William F Hare) (Government Official)
10 Downshire Hill
London NW3, UNITED KINGDOM (UK)

Lithgow, John (Actor)
c/o Mandi Warren *Viewpoint Inc. - NY*
Prefers to be contacted via telephone
New York, NY 10012, USA

Littell, Mark (Athlete, Baseball Player)
27358 N 88th Ln
Peoria, AZ 85383-4853, USA

Littenberg, Barbara (Architect)
131 E 66th St Apt 1B
New York, NY 10065-6147, USA

Litterell, Brian (Musician)
9100 Wilshire Blvd Ste 100W
Beverly Hills, CA 90212-3435, USA

Little, Anthony (Gordine) (Musician)
27 L Ambiance Ct
Bardonia, NY 10954-1421, USA

Little, Big Tiny
3985 W Taft Dr
Spokane, WA 99208-4870

Little, Bryan (Athlete, Baseball Player)
4766 Tiffany Park Cir
Bryan, TX 77802-5822, USA

Little, Chad (Race Car Driver)
5400 Little Pkwy
Sherrills Ford, NC 28673-9114, USA

Little, Charles L (Misc)
14600 Detroit Ave
Cleveland, OH 44107-4207, USA

Little, Dwight H (Director)
c/o Robert Lazar *International Creative Management (ICM-LA)*
10250 Constellation Blvd Fl 7
Los Angeles, CA 90067-6207, USA

Little, Eric (Choreographer)
11135 Knott Ave Ste C
Cypress, CA 90630-5139, USA

Little, Everett (Athlete, Football Player)
5219 Kingsbury St
Houston, TX 77021-3724, USA

Little, Floyd D (Athlete, Football Player)
PO Box 24839
Federal Way, WA 98093-1839, USA

Little, George (Athlete, Football Player)
1805 Powers St
McKeesport, PA 15132-5150, USA

Little, Jack (Athlete, Football Player)
PO Box 23528
Waco, TX 76702-3528, USA

Little, Jeff (Athlete, Baseball Player)
5711 W Camper Rd
Genoa, OH 43430-9300, USA

Little, Larry C (Athlete, Coach, Football Player)
14761 SW 169th Ln
Miami, FL 33187-1745, USA

Little, Leonard (Athlete, Football Player)
c/o Chad Speck *Allegiant Athletic Agency*
35 Market Sq Ste 201
Knoxville, TN 37902-1420, USA

Little, Mark (Athlete, Baseball Player)
28014 Moss Fern Dr
Katy, TX 77494-3240, USA

Little, Milton (Musician)
6606 Solitary Ave
Las Vegas, NV 89110, USA

Little, Rich (Actor, Comedian)
c/o David Martin *David Martin Management*
13849 Riverside Dr
Sherman Oaks, CA 91423-2426, USA

Little, Robert A (Chef)
49 Firth St
London W1V 5TE, UNITED KINGDOM (UK)

Little, Sally (Athlete, Golfer)
3210 S Ocean Blvd Apt 702
Highland Beach, FL 33487-2597, USA

Little, Scott (Athlete, Baseball Player)
1321 Rosebud Dr
Jackson, MO 63755-1086, USA

Little, Steven (Musician)
3 E 54th St # 1100
New York, NY 10022-3108, USA

Little, Tasmin E (Musician)
31 Sinclair Road
London W14 0NS, UNITED KINGDOM (UK)

Little, Tawny
5515 Melrose Ave
Los Angeles, CA 90038-3149

Little, Tawny Godin (Beauty Pageant Winner, Entertainer)
17941 Sky Park Cir Ste F
Irvine, CA 92614-4375, USA

Little, Tony
12750 59th Way N
Clearwater, FL 33760-3906, USA

Little, W Grady (Athlete, Baseball Player, Coach)
13115 Odell Heights Dr
Mint Hill, NC 28227-4390, USA

Little, William (Athlete, Baseball Player)
4889 Horn Lake Rd
Memphis, TN 38109-6625, USA

Little Anthony (Gourdine)
27 L Ambiance Ct
Bardonia, NY 10954-1421

Little Big Town (Music Group)
c/o Risha Rodgers *WmE2 (WMA-TN)*
1600 Division St Ste 300
Nashville, TN 37203-2755, USA

Little Eva
1161 NW 76th Ave
Plantation, FL 33322-5120

Little JJ (Actor)
c/o Charles King *WmE2 (Endeavor-LA)*
9601 Wilshire Blvd Fl 3
Beverly Hills, CA 90210-5219, USA

Little Man Tate (Music Group)
c/o Staff Member *Paradigm (Monterey)*
404 W Franklin St
Monterey, CA 93940-2303, USA

Little Ones, The (Music Group)
c/o Jason Colton *Red Light Management (VA)*
PO Box 1467
Charlottesville, VA 22902-1467, USA

Little Richard (Musician)
c/o Dick Alen *WmE2 (Endeavor-LA)*
9601 Wilshire Blvd Fl 3
Beverly Hills, CA 90210-5219, USA

Little River Band
9850 Sandalfoot Blvd # 458
Boca Raton, FL 33428-6645

Littlefield, John (Athlete, Baseball Player)
1935 Ramar Rd
Bullhead City, AZ 86442-6949, USA

Littlefield, John (Actor)
c/o Judy Orbach *Judy O Productions*
6136 Glen Holly St
Hollywood, CA 90068-2338, USA

Littlefield, Warren (Producer)
815 Brooktree Rd
Pacific Palisades, CA 90272-3904, USA

Littleford, Beth (Actor)
c/o Karen Forman *Domain Talent*
9229 W Sunset Blvd Ste 710
Los Angeles, CA 90069-3407, USA

Littlejohn, Dennis (Athlete, Baseball Player)
6813 Klamath Way Apt D
Bakersfield, CA 93309-7899, USA

Littler, Gene (Athlete, Golfer)
PO Box 1949
Rancho Santa Fe, CA 92067-1949, USA

Littles, Gene (Athlete, Basketball Player)
6421 E Beck Ln
Scottsdale, AZ 85254-2005, USA

Littleton, Harvey K (Artist)
RR 1 Box 843
Spruce Pine, NC 28777, USA

Littleton, Larry (Athlete, Baseball Player)
1076 Dunbarton Trce NE
Atlanta, GA 30319-2674, USA

Littleton, Wes (Athlete, Baseball Player)
30085 Clear Water Dr
Canyon Lake, CA 92587-7455, USA

Littman, Jonathan (Producer)
c/o Staff Member *Creative Artists Agency (CAA-LA)*
2000 Avenue of the Stars Ste 100
Los Angeles, CA 90067-4705, USA

Litton, Andrew
Media House 3 Burlington Lane
London W4 2TH, UNITED KINGDOM (UK)

Litton, Drew (Cartoonist, Editor)
Editorial Dept 400 W Colfax Ave
Denver, CO 80204, USA

Litton, Greg (Athlete, Baseball Player)
22 Hillbrook Way
Pensacola, FL 32503-2850, USA

Littrell, Brian (Musician)
c/o Johnny Wright *Wright Entertainment Group (WEG)*
PO Box 590009
Orlando, FL 32859-0009, USA

Littrell, Gary L (War Hero)
4302 Belle Vista Dr
St Pete Beach, FL 33706-3825, USA

Littrell, Jack (Athlete, Baseball Player)
46 Pleasant Railway
Taylorsville, KY 40071-6755, USA

Litwhiler, Danny (Athlete, Baseball Player)
1099 N McMullen Booth Rd Apt 124
Clearwater, FL 33759-3452, USA

Litzinger, Elin (Stylist)
2333 Hidalgo Ave
Los Angeles, CA 90039-3633, USA

Liu, Lucy (Actor)
c/o Mary Ellen Mulcahy *Framework Entertainment (LA)*
9057 Nemo St Ste C
West Hollywood, CA 90069-5511, USA

Liu, Matthew Stephen
10635 Santa Monica Blvd Ste 130
Los Angeles, CA 90025-8306

Liu, Nancy
9057-C Nemo St
W. Hollywood, CA 90069

Liuget, Corey (Football Player)
c/o Tony Fleming *Impact Sports - LA*
11331 Ventura Blvd Ste 1A
Studio City, CA 91604-3147, USA

Liukin, Nastia (Athlete, Gymnast, Olympic Athlete)
c/o Staff Member *Premier Management Group (PMG Sports)*
115 Crescent Commons Dr Ste 250
Cary, NC 27518-8134, USA

Liut, Mike (Athlete, Hockey Player)
26011 German Mill Rd
Franklin, MI 48025-1139, USA

Livage, Jacques (Misc)
11 Place M Berthelot
Paris Cedex 05 75231, FRANCE

Live (Music Group)
c/o Staff Member *Paradigm (Monterey)*
404 W Franklin St
Monterey, CA 93940-2303, USA

Lively, Blake (Actor)
c/o Jason Weinberg *Untitled Entertainment (LA)*
350 S Beverly Dr Ste 200
Beverly Hills, CA 90212-4819, USA

Lively, Bud (Athlete, Baseball Player)
8605 Esslinger Ct SE
Huntsville, AL 35802-3640, USA

Lively, Eric (Actor)
c/o Justin Grey Stone *Untitled Entertainment (LA)*
350 S Beverly Dr Ste 200
Beverly Hills, CA 90212-4819, USA

Lively, Penelope M (Writer)
5-8 Lower John Street
London W1R 4HA, UNINTED KINGDOM

Lively, Robyn (Actor)
c/o Staff Member *Innovative Artists (LA)*
1505 10th St
Santa Monica, CA 90401-2805, USA

Livermore, Ann (Business Person)
300 Hanover St
Palo Alto, CA 94304, USA

Livers, Virgil (Athlete, Football Player)
313 Clearview Ave
Bowling Green, KY 42101-3613, USA

Living Colour
6201 Sunset Blvd # 329
Hollywood, CA 90028

Livingston, Andrew (Athlete, Football Player)
650 E Century Ave
Gilbert, AZ 85296-1118, USA

Livingston, Barry (Actor)
11310 Blix St
North Hollywood, CA 91602-1209, USA

Livingston, Bruce (Athlete, Football Player)
511 25th Ave W
Bradenton, FL 34205-8264, USA

Livingston, Cliff (Athlete, Football Player)
4682 Deer Forest Ave
Las Vegas, NV 89139-7642, USA

Livingston, Dale (Athlete, Football Player)
748 Lowell Rd
Luxemburg, WI 54217-9283, USA

Livingston, James E (General, War Hero)
3146 Pignatelli Cres
Mt Pleasant, SC 29466-8059, USA

Livingston, Julia Bassett (Stylist)
7206 Strawberry Rd
Summerfield, NC 27358-7205, USA

Livingston, Mike (Athlete, Football Player)
8181 Monrovia St
Shawnee Mission, KS 66215-2728, USA

Livingston, Robert L Jr (Politician)
499 S Capitol St SW Ste 600
Washington, DC 20003-4037, USA

Livingston, Ron (Actor)
1180 S Beverly Dr Ste 601
Los Angeles, CA 90035-1158, USA

Livingston, Shaun (Basketball Player)
Staples Center 1111 S Figueroa St
Los Angeles, CA 90015, USA

Livingston, Stanley (Actor)
PO Box 1782
Studio City, CA 91614-0782, USA

Livingston, Warren (Athlete, Football Player)
308 E Malibu Dr
Tempe, AZ 85282-5304, USA

Livingstone, Bob (Athlete, Football Player)
1625 Bluebird Ln
Munster, IN 46321-3322, USA

Livingstone, Scott (Athlete, Baseball Player)
3504 Sunrise Ranch Rd
Southlake, TX 76092-2082, USA

Livinston (Actor)
45 Thackers Street Pursawakkam
Chennai, TN 600 084, INDIA

Lizalde, Enrique (Actor)
c/o Staff Member *Televisa*
Blvd Adolfo Lopez Mateos 232 Colonia San Angel INN
DF CP 01060, MEXICO

Lizarazo, Carolina (Actor)
c/o Gabriel Blanco *Gabriel Blanco Iglesias (Mexico)*
Rio Balsas 35-32 Colonia Cuauhtemoc
DF 6500, Mexico

Lizaso, Saul (Actor)
c/o Staff Member *Televisa*
Blvd Adolfo Lopez Mateos 232 Colonia San Angel INN
DF CP 01060, MEXICO

Ljungberg, Fredrik (Model, Soccer Player)
c/o Noelle Keshishian *PMK/BNC Public Relations (PMK-LA)*
8687 Melrose Ave Ste 8
West Hollywood, CA 90069-5746, USA

LL Cool J (Actor, Musician)
c/o Chris Lighty *Violator Management*
36 W 25th St Fl 11
New York, NY 10010-2752, USA

Llaca, Patricia (Actor)
c/o Staff Member *TV Azteca*
Periferico Sur 4121 Colonia Fuentes del Pedregal
DF CP 14141, Mexico

Llamosa, Carlos (Soccer Player)
CMGI Field 1 Patriot Place
Foxboro, MA 2035, USA

Llenas, Winston (Athlete, Baseball Player)
Apartado #92
Santiago, Dominican Republic

Llewellyn, John A (Astronaut)
4202 E Fowler Ave
Tampa, FL 33620-9951, USA

Llewellyn, Robert (Actor, Writer)
c/o Maureen Vincent *United Agents*
Drury House 34-43 Russell St
London WC2B 5HA, UK

Llewelyn, Doug
8075 W 3rd St # 303
Los Angeles, CA 90048-4318

Llewelyn-Bowen, Laurence (Actor, Designer)
c/o Staff Member *Fresh Partners LTD*
Centre Square Hardwicks Way
Wandsworth SW18 4AW, UK

Llitch, Michael (Athlete, Baseball Player, Business Person, Hockey Player)
c/o Staff Member *Detriot Tigers*
Comerica Park 2100 Woodward Ave
Detroit, MI 48201 - 34, USA

Llosa, Mario Vargas (Writer)
Las Magnolias 295 6 Piso
Barranco, Lima 4, PERU

Lloyd, Arroyn (Actor)
c/o Michael Bircumshaw *Water Street Management*
5225 Wilshire Blvd Ste 615
Los Angeles, CA 90036-4350, USA

Lloyd, Charles (Composer, Musician)
300 Mercer St Apt 3J
New York, NY 10003-6732, USA

LLoyd, Cher (Musician)
c/o Staff Member *Hackford Jones PR*
19 Nassau St
London W1W 7AF, UK

Lloyd, Christopher (Actor)
PO Box 491246
Los Angeles, CA 90049-9246, USA

Lloyd, Clive H (Cricketer)
Harefield Dr
Wilmslow, Cheshire SK9 1NJ, UNITED KINGDOM (UK)

Lloyd, Dave (Athlete, Football Player)
24432 County Road 3107
Gladewater, TX 75647-8842, USA

Lloyd, Earl (Athlete, Basketball Player, Coach)
PO Box 1976
Crossville, TN 38558-1976, USA

Lloyd, Emily Ann (Actor)
c/o Staff Member *United Talent Agency (UTA)*
9560 Wilshire Blvd Fl 5
Beverly Hills, CA 90212-2400, USA

Lloyd, Eric (Actor)
c/o Mark Schumacher *Schumacher Management*
1122 San Vicente Blvd
Santa Monica, CA 90402-2008, USA

Lloyd, Geoffrey E R (Misc)
2 Prospect Row
Cambridge CB1 1DU, UNITED KINGDOM (UK)

Lloyd, Georgina (Writer)
1540 Broadway
New York, NY 10036-4039, USA

Lloyd, Graeme (Athlete, Baseball Player)
455 Oceanview Ave
Palm Harbor, FL 34683-1816, USA

Lloyd, Jake (Actor)
4343 Lankershim Blvd # 100
North Hollywood, CA 91602-2705, USA

Lloyd, Lewis (Athlete, Basketball Player)
1038 N Pallas St
Philadelphia, PA 19104-1221, USA

Lloyd, Madison (Actor)
4343 Lankershim Blvd # 100
North Hollywood, CA 91602-2705, USA

Lloyd, Norman (Actor)
c/o Staff Member *Marion Rosenberg Office, The*
PO Box 69826
Los Angeles, CA 90069-0826, USA

Lloyd, Robert A (Opera Singer)
67B Fortis Green
London SE1 9HL, UNITED KINGDOM (UK)

Lloyd, Sabrina (Actor)
c/o Rachel Sheedy *Don Buchwald & Associates Inc (NY)*
10 E 44th St Frnt 1
New York, NY 10017-3654

Lloyd, Sam (Actor)
c/o Staff Member *Heidi Rotbart Management*
1810 Malcolm Ave Apt 207
Los Angeles, CA 90025-7610, USA

Lloyd, Scott (Athlete, Basketball Player)
6838 Alexander Dr
Dallas, TX 75214-3208, USA

Lloyd, Sue (Actor)
31 Coventry St
London W1V 8AS, UNITED KINGDOM (UK)

Lloyd, Tony (Athlete, Baseball Player)
6536 Cherokee Dr
Fairfield, AL 35064-1703, USA

Lloyd, Walt (Cinematographer)
22287 Mulholland Hwy # 393
Calabasas, CA 91302-5157, USA

Llyod, Tony (Baseball Player)
6536 Cherokee Dr
Fairfield, AL 35064-1703, USA

LMFAO (Music Group)
c/o Staff Member *Polydor Records*
364-366 Kensington High St
London W14 8NS, UK

Lo, Ismael (Musician)
5-7 Rue Paul Bert
Saint Ouen 93400, FRANCE

Lo Bianco, Tony
c/o Staff Member *Artists Only Management*
10203 Santa Monica Blvd
Los Angeles, CA 90067-6405, USA

Loach, Ken C (Director)
c/o Staff Member *Sixteen Films*
187 Wardour St Floor 2
London W1F 8ZB, ENGLAND

Loach, Kenneth (Ken) (Director)
7 Denmark St
London WC2H 8LS, UNITED KINGDOM (UK)

Loaf, Meat (Actor, Musician, Producer)
c/o Irving Azoff *Azoff Music Management/ Front Line*
1100 Glendon Ave
Los Angeles, CA 90024-3503, USA

Loaiza, Esteban A (Athlete, Baseball Player)
1404 Lands End Ct
Southlake, TX 76092-4224, USA

Loar, John (Producer)
c/o Staff Member *Red Bird Cinema*
PO Box 826
Danville, CA 94526-0826, USA

Lobdell, Erinn (Reality TV Star)
2472 N Bremen St
Milwaukee, WI 53212-3036, USA

Lobdell, Frank (Artist)
Pier 70
San Francisco, CA 94102, USA

Lobel, Bruno
Ramering 4
Heldenstein, GERMANY 84431

Lobenstein, William (Athlete, Football Player)
3272 Deerfield Rd
Deerfield, WI 53531-9733, USA

LoBiondo, Frank (Congressman, Politician)
2427 Rayburn Hob
Washington, DC 20515-0524, USA

Lobkowicz, Nicholas (Misc)
Eichstatt 85071, GERMANY

Lobo, Rebecca (Athlete, Basketball Player)
PO Box 734
Granby, CT 06035-0734, USA

Loc, Tone
7932 Hillside Ave
Los Angeles, CA 90046-2122

Loc, Tone (Music Group)
c/o Staff Member *Universal Attractions*
135 W 26th St Fl 12
New York, NY 10001-6872, USA

Local, Ivars Godmanis (Prime Minister)
Brivibus Bluv 36
Riga, PDP 226170, LATVIA

Locane, Amy (Actor)
c/o Staff Member *Don Buchwald & Associates Inc (LA)*
6500 Wilshire Blvd Ste 2200
Los Angeles, CA 90048-4942, USA

Locatelli, Paul L (Educator)
President S Ofc
Santa Clara, CA 95053-0001, USA

Loceff, Michael (Producer)
c/o Staff Member *Luber Roklin Management*
8530 Wilshire Blvd Ste 550
Beverly Hills, CA 90211-3133, USA

Locher, Dick
435 N Michigan Ave
Chicago, IL 60611-4066

Locher, Richard (Dick) (Cartoonist, Editor)
435 N Michigan Ave
Chicago, IL 60611-4066, USA

Lochhead, Kenneth C (Artist)
35 Wilton Cres
Ottawa, ON K1S 2T4, CANADA

Lochmueller, Robert (Athlete, Basketball Player)
18 William Tell Blvd
Tell City, IN 47586-2030, USA

Lochner, Philip R Jr (Business Person, Government Official)
75 Rockefeller Plz
New York, NY 10019-6908, USA

Lochner, Rudi
Hofreitstr. 15
Schonau, GERMANY D-83471

Lock, Don (Athlete, Baseball Player)
11725 W Alderny Ct Unit 42
Wichita, KS 67212-6510, USA

Lockbaum, Gordie (Athlete, Football Player)
35 Brookshire Rd
Worcester, MA 01609-1251, USA

Locke, Bobby (Athlete, Baseball Player)
194 Eighty Acres Rd
Dunbar, PA 15431-2274, USA

Locke, Bruce (Actor)
5670 Wilshire Blvd Ste 820
Los Angeles, CA 90036-5613

Locke, Charlie (Chuck) (Athlete, Baseball Player)
1560 Haven Hills Rd
Poplar Bluff, MO 63901-2749, USA

Locke, Kimberley (Actor, Musician)
PO Box 45378
Los Angeles, CA 90045-0378, USA

Locke, Larry (Baseball Player)
155 Eighty Acres Rd Apt 2
Dunbar, PA 15431-2275, USA

Locke, Ron (Athlete, Baseball Player)
11140 Caravel Cir Apt 102
Fort Myers, FL 33908-3996, USA

Locke, Sonda (Actor)
c/o Staff Member *David Shapira & Associates*
193 N Robertson Blvd
Beverly Hills, CA 90211-2103, USA

Locke, Sondra (Actor)
7465 Hillside Ave
Los Angeles, CA 90046-2228, USA

Locke, Spencer (Actor)
c/o Sharon Lane *Lane Management Group*
13017 Woodbridge St
Studio City, CA 91604-1431, USA

Locke, Tembi (Actor)
c/o Bob McGowan *McGowan Management*
8733 W Sunset Blvd Ste 103
West Hollywood, CA 90069-2241, USA

Locker, Bob (Athlete, Baseball Player)
1561 Rancho View Rd
Lafayette, CA 94549-2236, USA

Lockerman, Brad
300 S Raymond Ave Ste 11
Pasadena, CA 91105-2639

Lockett, Kevin (Athlete, Football Player)
1319 W Xyler St
Tulsa, OK 74127-2717, USA

Lockhart, Anne (Actor)
c/o Linda McAlister *Linda McAlister Talent*
100 Oak Ln
Waxahachie, TX 75167-8412, USA

Lockhart, Eugene (Athlete, Football Player)
2215 High Country Dr
Carrollton, TX 75007-1701, USA

Lockhart, Ian (Athlete, Basketball Player)
Q25 Calle Excelsa
Yauco, PR 00698-3172, USA

Lockhart, James
105 Woodcock Hl
Harrow, Middx HA3 0JJ, UNITED KINGDOM (UK)

Lockhart, June (Actor)
c/o Staff Member *Agency for the Performing Arts (APA-LA)*
405 S Beverly Dr Ste 500
Beverly Hills, CA 90212-4425, USA

Lockhart, Keith
Massachusetts Ave Symphony Hall 301
Boston, MA 02115-4511, USA

Lockhart, Keith (Athlete, Baseball Player)
3330 McKinley Point Dr
Dacula, GA 30019-1599, USA

Lockhart, Paul S (Astronaut)
3142 Pleasant Cove Ct
Houston, TX 77059-3232, USA

Lockington, David
3436 Springhill Rd
Lafayette, CA 94549-2535, USA

Locklear, Gene (Athlete, Baseball Player)
1811 Penasco Rd
El Cajon, CA 92019-3708, USA

Locklear, Heather (Actor)
c/o Daniel (Danny) Sussman *Brillstein Entertainment Partners*
9150 Wilshire Blvd Ste 350
Beverly Hills, CA 90212-3453, USA

Locklin, Stu (Athlete, Baseball Player)
532 Carfax Pl SW
Albuquerque, NM 87121-2273, USA

Lockwood, Gary (Actor)
1065 E Loma Alta Dr
Altadena, CA 91001-1507, USA

Lockwood, Scott (Athlete, Football Player)
1995 E Coalton Rd Apt 44-103
Superior, CO 80027-4428, USA

Lockwood, Skip (Athlete, Baseball Player)
47 John Druce Ln
Wrentham, MA 02093-1390, USA

Locorriere, Dennis (Musician)
P.O. Box 4444
Worthing BN11 3WJ, SUSSEX

Loder, Anne Marie (Actor)
c/o Jamie Levitt *Lauren Levitt & Associates Inc*
1525 W 8th St 3rd Fl
Vancouver V6J 1T5, British Columbia

Loder, Kevin (Athlete, Basketball Player)
505 W 4th St
Mishawaka, IN 46544-1818, USA

Loder, Kurt (Journalist, Television Host)
c/o Staff Member *MTV News*
1515 Broadway Fl 29
New York, NY 10036-8901, USA

Lodge, David
8 Sydney Rd.
Richmond Surrey, ENGLAND

Lodge, David John (Writer)
English Dept
Birmingham B15 2TT, UNITED KINGDOM (UK)

Lodge, Roger (Actor, Television Host)
c/o Michelle Bega *Rogers & Cowan PR (LA)*
Pacific Design Center 8687 Melrose Ave, 7th Floor
West Hollywood, CA 90069, USA

Lodigiani, Dario (Athlete, Baseball Player)
745 Lathrop St
Napa, CA 94558-5117, USA

Lodish, Harvey F (Biologist)
195 Fisher Ave
Brookline, MA 02445-5706, USA

Lodish, Mike (Athlete, Football Player)
1150 Trailwood Path
Bloomfield Hills, MI 48301-1742, USA

Loduca, Paul (Athlete, Baseball Player)
207 Bentley Mnr
Shavano Park, TX 78249-2020, USA

Loe, Harald A (Doctor)
9000 Rockville Pike
Bethesda, MD 20892-0001, USA

Loe, Kameron (Athlete, Baseball Player)
20132 Marilla St
Chatsworth, CA 91311-5421, USA

Loeb, Jerome T (Business Person)
611 Olive St
Saint Louis, MO 63101-1711, USA

Loeb, Lisa (Musician, Songwriter)
c/o Alix Gucovsky *Special Artists Agency*
9465 Wilshire Blvd Ste 820
Beverly Hills, CA 90212-2607, USA

Loeb, Marshall R (Editor)
41 E 72nd St
New York, NY 10021-4122, USA

Loebsak, David (Congressman, Politician)
1527 Longworth Hob
Washington, DC 20515-4316, USA

Loehr, Bet (Actor)
c/o Staff Member *Coast to Coast Talent Group*
3350 Barham Blvd
Los Angeles, CA 90068-1404, USA

Loehr, Bret (Actor)
c/o Staff Member *Coast to Coast Talent Group*
3350 Barham Blvd
Los Angeles, CA 90068-1404, USA

Loengard, John (Photographer)
20 W 86th St
New York, NY 10024-3604, USA

Loepfe, Richard (Athlete, Football Player)
9301 N 76th St
Milwaukee, WI 53223-1074, USA

Loes, Billy (Athlete, Baseball Player)
3636 N Campbell Ave Apt 6111
Tucson, AZ 85719-1550, USA

Loewen, Adam (Athlete, Baseball Player)
12302 N 136th Pl
Scottsdale, AZ 85259-2311, USA

Loewen, James W (Historian)
History
Washington, DC 20064-0001, USA

Loewer, Carlton (Athlete, Baseball Player)
PO Box 3590
Alpine, WY 83128-0590, USA

Lofgren, Nils (Musician, Songwriter, Writer)
8012 Old Georgetown Rd
Bethesda, MD 20814-2427, USA

Lofgren, Zoe (Congressman, Politician)
1401 Longworth Hob
Washington, DC 20515-4005, USA

Loftin, Lennie (Actor)
c/o Scott Zimmerman *Evolution Entertainment (LA)*
901 N Highland Ave
Los Angeles, CA 90038-2412, USA

Lofton, Cirroc (Actor)
c/o Staff Member *Innovative Artists (LA)*
1505 10th St
Santa Monica, CA 90401-2805, USA

Lofton, Fred C (Religious Leader)
601 50th St NE
Washington, DC 20019-5450, USA

Lofton, James (Athlete, Baseball Player)
14103 Cerise Ave Apt 18
Hawthorne, CA 90250-8843, USA

Lofton, James D (Athlete, Football Player)
13177 Via Mesa Dr
San Diego, CA 92129-2287, USA

Lofton, Kenny (Athlete, Baseball Player)
PO Box 68473
Tucson, AZ 85737-8473, USA

Logan, Chuck (Athlete, Football Player)
2526 Lawndale Ave
Evanston, IL 60201-1158, USA

Logan, Daniel (Actor)
c/o Staff Member *Entertainment Legends Management*
1100 Irvine Blvd # 66
Tustin, CA 92780-3529, USA

Logan, David R (Athlete, Football Player)
5875 S Dry Creek Ct
Greenwood Village, CO 80121-1709, USA

Logan, Dick (Athlete, Football Player)
475 Chapple Hill Dr NE
North Canton, OH 44720-1775, USA

Logan, Don (Publisher)
Time-Life Building Rockefeller Center
New York, NY 10020, USA

Logan, Ernie (Athlete, Football Player)
609 Francis Ct
Spring Lake, NC 28390-3006, USA

Logan, Exavier (Nook) (Athlete, Baseball Player)
19410 Creek Bend Dr
Spring, TX 77388-3095, USA

Logan, Jack (Musician)
1325 Avenue of the Americas
New York, NY 10019-6026, USA

Logan, James K (Judge)
PO Box 790
Olathe, KS 66051-0790, USA

Logan, Jerry (Athlete, Football Player)
1624 Hillcrest Dr
Graham, TX 76450-4702, USA

Logan, John (Producer, Writer)
c/o David O'Connor *Creative Artists Agency (CAA-LA)*
2000 Avenue of the Stars Ste 100
Los Angeles, CA 90067-4705, USA

Logan, John (Johnny) (Athlete, Baseball Player)
6115 W Cleveland Ave
Milwaukee, WI 53219-2653, USA

Logan, Marc (Athlete, Football Player)
409 Asbury Ln
Lexington, KY 40511-1619, USA

Logan, Melissa (Musician)
924 Jefferson St SE # 101
Olympia, WA 98501, USA

Logan, Phyllis
47 Courtfield Rd # 9
London, ENGLAND SW7 4DB

Logan, Randy (Athlete, Football Player)
330 W Fornance St
Norristown, PA 19401-2906, USA

Logan, Rayford W (Historian)
3001 Veazey Ter NW
Washington, DC 20008-5400, USA

Logano, Joey (Race Car Driver)
c/o Staff Member *Joe Gibbs Racing*
13415 Reese Blvd W
Huntersville, NC 28078-7933, USA

Loges, Stephan (Opera Singer)
4 Addison Bridge Place
London W14 8XP, UNITED KINGDOM (UK)

Loggia, Robert (Actor)
c/o Steve Lovett *Lovett Management*
1327 Brinkley Ave
Los Angeles, CA 90049-3619, USA

Loggins, Kenny (Musician, Songwriter, Writer)
c/o Steve Moir *Moir / Borman Entertainment*
1250 6th St Ste 401
Santa Monica, CA 90401-1638, USA

Logue, Donal (Actor)
c/o Perri Kipperman *Kipperman Management*
243 W 72nd St Apt 2
New York, NY 10023-2704, USA

Logue, Karina (Actor)
c/o Justin Evans *The Independent Group*
6363 Wilshire Blvd Ste 115
Los Angeles, CA 90048-5734, USA

Loh, John M (Mike) (General)
125 Captaine Graves
Williamsburg, VA 23185-8906, USA

Lohan, Ali (Actor)
c/o Glenn Gulino *G2 Entertainment LLC*
1 Columbus Pl Apt S25E
New York, NY 10019-8208, USA

Lohan, Lindsay (Actor)
c/o Jason Weinberg *Untitled Entertainment (LA)*
350 S Beverly Dr Ste 200
Beverly Hills, CA 90212-4819, USA

Lohan, Sinead (Musician, Songwriter, Writer)
Merchant's Court 24 Merchant's Quay
Dublin, IRELAND

Lohaus, Brad (Athlete, Basketball Player)
55 Tartan Dr
North Liberty, IA 52317-8002, USA

Lohman, Alison (Actor)
c/o Nicole King *Management 360*
9111 Wilshire Blvd
Beverly Hills, CA 90210-5508, USA

Lohmann, Katie (Actor)
c/o Giovanni Elmore *WNWN Media*
348 Hauser Blvd # PH414
Los Angeles, CA 90036-3276, USA

Lohr, Aaron (Actor)
c/o Beth Rosner *Beth Rosner Management*
15 Stuyvesant Oval
New York, NY 10009-2011, USA

Lohr, Bob (Athlete, Golfer)
8225 Breeze Cove Ln
Orlando, FL 32819-5078, USA

Lohrke, Jack (Athlete, Baseball Player)
2817 Lucena Dr
San Jose, CA 95132-2244, USA

Lohse, Kyle (Athlete, Baseball Player)
8613 E Artisan Pass
Scottsdale, AZ 85266-1643, USA

Loiola, Jose (Athlete, Volleyball Player)
1135 23rd St
Manhattan Beach, CA 90266-2927, USA

Loisel, John S (War Hero)
464 Rs County Road 3378
Emory, TX 75440-8024, USA

Loiselle, Rich (Athlete, Baseball Player)
560 Timber Dr
Harvard, IL 60033-7823, USA

Lokanc, Joe (Athlete, Football Player)
2666 E 73rd St Apt SE
Chicago, IL 60649-2798, USA

Loken, Kristanna (Actor)
c/o Staff Member *International Creative Management (ICM-LA)*
10250 Constellation Blvd Fl 7
Los Angeles, CA 90067-6207, USA

Lokey, Lorey (Business Person)
44 Montgomery St Fl 39
San Francisco, CA 94104-4812, USA

Lokoloko, Tore (Ex-Governor)
P.O. Box 5622
Boroko, NCD, Papua New Guinea

Lolich, Michael S (Mickey) (Athlete, Baseball Player)
6252 Robin Hl
Washington, MI 48094-2186, USA

Lolich, Ron (Athlete, Baseball Player)
7055 SW Dogwood Pl
Portland, OR 97225-1571, USA

Lolita
Grossgmain
, AUSTRIA #NAME?

Lollar, Tim (Athlete, Baseball Player)
16626 W Bayaud Dr
Golden, CO 80401-6577, USA

Lollobrigida, Gina (Actor)
Via Appia Antica 223
Rome 178, ITALY

Lom, Herbert (Actor)
2-4 Noel St
London W1V 3RB, UNITED KINGDOM (UK)

Loman, Doug (Athlete, Baseball Player)
25 Lincoln St
Bakersfield, CA 93305-3412, USA

Lomas, Mark (Athlete, Football Player)
PO Box 17781
Irvine, CA 92623-7781, USA

Lomasney, Steve (Athlete, Baseball Player)
7 Arnold Rd
Peabody, MA 01960-5203, USA

Lomax, Melanie
5900 Wilshire Blvd
Los Angeles, CA 90036-5013

Lomax, Michael (Educator)
500 E 62nd St
New York, NY 10065-8314, USA

Lomax, Neil V (Athlete, Football Player)
13060 Knaus Rd
Lake Oswego, OR 97034-1551, USA

Lombard, George (Athlete, Baseball Player)
2275 Rhinehill Rd SE
Atlanta, GA 30315-7413, USA

Lombard, Karina (Actor, Model)
1209 N Orange St
Wilmington, DE 19801-1120, USA

Lombard, Louise (Actor)
c/o Lena Roklin *Luber Roklin Management*
8530 Wilshire Blvd Ste 550
Beverly Hills, CA 90211-3133, USA

Lombardi, John V (Educator)
President S Ofc
Gainesville, FL 32611-0001, USA

Lombardi, Leigh (Actor)
c/o Staff Member *Abrams Artists Agency (NY)*
275 7th Ave Fl 26
New York, NY 10001-6708, USA

Lombardi, Louis (Actor)
c/o Erik Kritzer *Kritzer Levine Wilkins Entertainment*
11872 La Grange Ave Fl 1
Los Angeles, CA 90025-5283, USA

Lombardi, Phil (Athlete, Baseball Player)
26440 Brooks Cir
Stevenson Ranch, CA 91381-1417, USA

Lombardo, John (Musician)
9200 W Sunset Blvd Ste 900
Los Angeles, CA 90069-3604, USA

Lombardozzi, Domenick (Actor)
c/o Michael Garnett *Leverage Management*
3030 Pennsylvania Ave
Santa Monica, CA 90404-4112, USA

Lombardozzi, Steve (Athlete, Baseball Player)
12404 Hall Shop Rd
Fulton, MD 20759-9746, USA

Lomma, Jonathan
1120 S Washington Ave
Scranton, PA 18505-1532

Lommi, Tony (Musician)
3305 Lobban Pl
Charlottesville, VA 22903-7069, USA

Lomon, Kevin (Athlete, Baseball Player)
13397 Morris Loop
Cameron, OK 74932-2173, USA

Lonborg, James R (Jim) (Athlete, Baseball Player)
498 First Parish Rd
Scituate, MA 02066-3201, USA

Lonchakov, Yuri V (Cosmonaut)
Moskovskoi Oblasti
Syvisdny Goroduk 141160, RUSSIA

London, Antonio (Athlete, Football Player)
404 SW Atlantic St
Tullahoma, TN 37388-4409, USA

London, Carolyn (Producer)
c/o Staff Member *Bankable Productions*
226 W 26th St Fl 4
New York, NY 10001-6700, USA

London, Irving M (Physicist)
77 Massachusetts Ave
Cambridge, MA 02139-4301, USA

London, Jason (Actor)
c/o Staff Member *Levine Okwu Erickson Management*
6363 Wilshire Blvd Ste 300
Los Angeles, CA 90048-5729, USA

London, Jeremy (Actor, Director, Producer)
c/o Jean-Pierre (JP) Henraux *Shelter Entertainment*
9454 Wilshire Blvd Ste 715
Beverly Hills, CA 90212-2925, USA

London, Lauren (Actor)
c/o Staff Member *WmE2 (WMA-LA)*
1 William Morris Pl
Beverly Hills, CA 90212-4261, USA

London, Lisa (Actor, Model)
8949 W Sunset Blvd Ste 201
Los Angeles, CA 90069-1806, USA

London, Michael (Producer)
c/o Staff Member *Groundswell Productions / Michael Landon Productions*
11925 Wilshire Blvd Ste 310
Los Angeles, CA 90025-6649, USA

London, Rick (Cartoonist)
c/o Staff Member *Artistic Licensing Agency*
240 Central Ave Apt 224
Hot Springs, AR 71901-3541, USA

London, Stacy (Reality TV Star, Television Host)
c/o Staff Member *The Learning Channel (TLC)*
10100 Santa Monica Blvd Ste 1500
Los Angeles, CA 90067-4117, USA

Loneker, Keith (Athlete, Football Player)
56 W Lincoln Ave
Roselle Park, NJ 07204-1358, USA

Lonergan, Kenneth (Writer)
c/o Staff Member *WmE2 (WMA-LA)*
1 William Morris Pl
Beverly Hills, CA 90212-4261, USA

Lonestar (Music Group)
c/o Gary Borman *Moir / Borman Entertainment*
1250 6th St Ste 401
Santa Monica, CA 90401-1638, USA

Lonetto, Sarah (Baseball Player)
26560 Burg Rd Apt 132
Warren, MI 48089-3594, USA

Loney, James (Athlete, Baseball Player)
c/o Joe Urbon *Creative Artists Agency (CAA-NY)*
162 5th Ave Fl 6
New York, NY 10010-6047, USA

Long, Anthony A (Educator)
1088 Tevlin St
Albany, CA 94706-2467, USA

Long, Bill (Athlete, Baseball Player)
145 Dale Hollow Dr Apt 4
Erlanger, KY 41018-4069, USA

Long, Billy (Congressman, Politician)
1541 Longworth Hob
Washington, DC 20515-3806, USA

Long, Bishop Eddie (Religious Leader)
6400 Woodrow Rd
Lithonia, GA 30038-2437, USA

Long, Bob (Athlete, Football Player)
PO Box 245
Ashland, PA 17921-0245, USA

Long, Bob (Athlete, Baseball Player)
3646 Willow Lake Cir
Chattanooga, TN 37419-1459, USA

Long, Bob (Athlete, Football Player)
3695 Stonebrook Ct
Brookfield, WI 53005-2265, USA

Long, Bob (Athlete, Football Player)
1413 W Via De La Gloria
Green Valley, AZ 85622-5007, USA

Long, Carl (Athlete, Baseball Player)
401 Duggins Dr
Kinston, NC 28501-8211, USA

Long, Charles F (Chuck) II (Athlete, Football Player)
2425 N MacArthur Blvd
Oklahoma City, OK 73127-1605, USA

Long, Chris (Athlete, Football Player)
c/o Steve Rosner *16W Marketing LLC*
75 Union Ave
Rutherford, NJ 07070-1212, USA

Long, Chuck (Athlete, Football Coach, Football Player)
5500 Campanile Dr
San Diego, CA 92182-0001, USA

Long, Dallas (Athlete, Track Athlete)
PO Box 355
Whitefish, MT 59937-0355, USA

Long, Dave (Athlete, Football Player)
4890 W Spoonbill Dr
Tucson, AZ 85742-9547, USA

Long, David L (Publisher)
Rockefeller Center
New York, NY 10020, USA

Long, Dennis (Denny) (Soccer Player)
RR 5
Poplar Bluff, MO 63901, USA

Long, Elizabeth Valk (Business Person)
1 Strawberry Ln
Orrville, OH 44667-1241, USA

Long, Grant (Athlete, Basketball Player)
8501 Morton Taylor Rd
Belleville, MI 48111-5313, USA

Long, Howie (Actor, Football Player, Sportscaster)
c/o Jack Gilardi *International Creative Management (ICM-LA)*
10250 Constellation Blvd Fl 7
Los Angeles, CA 90067-6207, USA

Long, Jackie
c/o Tammy Brook *FYI Public Relations*
174 5th Ave Ste 400
New York, NY 10010-5935, USA

Long, Jeoff (Athlete, Baseball Player)
11 Flower Ct
Lakeside Park, KY 41017-2102, USA

Long, Joan D (Producer)
La Burrage Place
Lindfield, NSW 2070, AUSTRALIA

Long, Joey (Athlete, Baseball Player)
5541 Kiser Lake Rd
Conover, OH 45317-9643, USA

Long, John (Athlete, Basketball Player)
11976 Hunt St
Romulus, MI 48174-3830, USA

Long, Justin (Actor)
c/o Paul Young *Principato/Young Management*
9465 Wilshire Blvd Ste 430
Beverly Hills, CA 90212-2613, USA

Long, Mark (Reality TV Star)
c/o Staff Member *MTV Networks (LA)*
2600 Colorado Ave
Santa Monica, CA 90404-3519

Long, Matthew (Matt) (Actor)
c/o Robert Glennon *Authentic Talent and Literary Management*
45 Main St Ste 1004
Brooklyn, NY 11201-8200, USA

Long, Mel (Athlete, Football Player)
837 Imani Cir
Toledo, OH 43604-8425, USA

Long, Nia (Actor)
c/o Priscilla Moralez *One Talent Management*
9220 W Sunset Blvd Ste 306
Los Angeles, CA 90069-3503, USA

Long, Richard (Artist)
Lower Failand
Bristol BS8 3SL, UNITED KINGDOM (UK)

Long, Rien (Athlete, Football Player)
460 Great Circle Rd
Nashville, TN 37228-1404, USA

Long, Robert (Misc)
Paleontology Museum
Berkeley, CA 94720-0001, USA

Long, Robert M (Business Person)
PO Box 3827
Walnut Creek, CA 94598-0827, USA

Long, Ryan (Athlete, Baseball Player)
3102 Winchester Ranch Trl
Katy, TX 77493-4400, USA

Long, Scott (Actor, Reality TV Star)
c/o Staff Member *Big Brother*
4146 Lankershim Blvd Ste 300
North Hollywood, CA 91602-2878, USA

Long, Shelley (Actor)
PO Box 45530
Los Angeles, CA 90045-0530, USA

Long, Terrance (Athlete, Baseball Player)
3433 Cross Creek Dr
Montgomery, AL 36116-3648, USA

Long, Tim (Athlete, Football Player)
112 Towns Walk Dr
Athens, GA 30606-7986, USA

Long, William Ivey (Designer)
40 W 57th St # 1800
New York, NY 10019-4001, USA

Longdon, Johnny
5401 W Palmer Dr
Banning, CA 92220-5149

Longet, Claudine (Actor)
6000 E Hopkins
Aspen, CO 81611, USA

Longfield, William (Business Person)
730 Central Ave
New Providence, NJ 07974-1139, USA

Longhi, Rick (Stylist)
2041 W Carroll Ave
Chicago, IL 60612-1630, USA

Longley, Clint (Athlete, Football Player)
13602 Camino De Oro Ct
Corpus Christi, TX 78418-6910, USA

Longley, Luc (Athlete, Basketball Player)
500 Marquette Ave NW Ste 400
Albuquerque, NM 87102-5308, USA

Longmire, Tony (Athlete, Baseball Player)
1700 E Tabor Ave Apt A8
Fairfield, CA 94533-2801, USA

Longmuir, Alan (Musician)
27 Preston Grange Preston Pans E
Lothian, SCOTLAND

Longmuir, Derek (Musician)
27 Preston Grange Preston Pans E
Lothian, SCOTLAND

Longo, Cody (Actor)
c/o Mara Santino *Luber Roklin Management*
8530 Wilshire Blvd Ste 550
Beverly Hills, CA 90211-3133, USA

Longo, Lenny (Musician)
PO Box 1644
Dickinson, TX 77539-1644, USA

Longo, Robert (Artist)
224 Centre St
New York, NY 10013-3619, USA

Longo, Tom (Athlete, Football Player)
2 Donna Ln
Wayne, NJ 07470-2711, USA

Longo, Tony
24 Westwind St
Marina Del Rey, CA 90292-7135

Longoria, Eva (Actor)
c/o Liza Anderson *Anderson Group Public Relations*
8060 Melrose Ave Fl 4
Los Angeles, CA 90046-7038, USA

Longoria, Evan (Athlete, Baseball Player)
c/o Staff Member *Tampa Bay Devil Rays*
Tropicana Field 1 Tropicana Drive
Saint Petersburg, FL 33705, USA

Longuet-Higgins, H Christopher (Misc)
Exper Psych Lab
Falmer, Brighton BN1 9QG, UNITED KINGDOM (UK)

Long-View (Music Group)
c/o Staff Member *Paradigm (Monterey)*
404 W Franklin St
Monterey, CA 93940-2303, USA

Longwell, Ryan (Athlete, Football Player)
17570 Bearpath Trl
Eden Prairie, MN 55347-3488, USA

Lonneke (Model)
379 W Broadway # 502
New York, NY 10012-5121, USA

Lonnett, Joe (Athlete, Baseball Player)
126 Duncan Cir
Beaver, PA 15009-9660, USA

Lonow, Claudia (Comedian)
c/o Staff Member *International Creative Management (ICM-LA)*
10250 Constellation Blvd Fl 7
Los Angeles, CA 90067-6207, USA

Lonsbrough, Porter Anita (Swimmer)
6 Rivendell Gardens Tettendall
Wolverhampton WV6 8SY, UNITED KINGDOM (UK)

Lonsdale, Gordon (Cinematographer, Director)
4513 W 10600 N
Highland, UT 84003-9552, USA

Lonsdale, Laurie (Writer)
49 Lighthouse St
Whitby, Ontario L1N 9R9, CANADA

Lonsdale, Michael
25 Rue De General-Foy
Paris, FRANCE F-75008

Look, Bruce
4298 Maitland Rd
Williamsburg, MI 49690-9575, USA

Look, Bruce (Athlete, Baseball Player)
4298 Maitland Rd
Williamsburg, MI 49690-9575, USA

Look, Dean (Athlete, Baseball Player)
80 Victorian Hills Dr
Okemos, MI 48864-3160, USA

Look, Dean Z (Athlete, Football Player)
80 Victorian Hills Dr
Okemos, MI 48864-3160, USA

Lookinland, Mike (Actor)
PO Box 9968
Salt Lake City, UT 84109-0968, USA

Loomis, Rod
5114 Vineland Ave
Valley Vlg, CA 91601-3814

Loon (Musician)
c/o Michael (Mike) Esterman
Esterman.Com, LLC
Prefers to be contacted via email
MD, USA

Looney, Brian (Athlete, Baseball Player)
188 Romulus Rd
Cheshire, CT 06410-3535, USA

Looney, Donald L (Don) (Athlete, Football Player)
PO Box 3103
Midland, TX 79702-3103, USA

Looney, Shelley (Athlete, Hockey Player)
31 Beaman Ln
North Falmouth, MA 02556-2823, USA

Looney, William R III (General)
Commander Electronic Systems Center
Hanscom Air Force Base, MA 1731, USA

Looper, Aaron (Athlete, Baseball Player)
1405 Manchester Dr
Shawnee, OK 74804-2327, USA

Looper, Braden (Athlete, Baseball Player)
16253 Wynncrest Ridge Ct
Chesterfield, MO 63005-6724, USA

Loose, A Mohan (Actor)
15A/4 Kesavaperumal East St
Chennai, TN 600 004, INDIA

Loose, John W (Business Person)
Houghton Park
Corning, NY 14831-0001, USA

Looseleaf, Victoria
144 S Doheny Dr Apt 304
Los Angeles, CA 90048-2939

Lopardo, Frank (Opera Singer)
7 Suzanne B Ct
Massapequa, NY 11758-7300, USA

Lopasky, William (Athlete, Football Player)
Huntsville Ceasetown Rd
Dallas, PA 18612, USA

Lopata, Stan (Athlete, Baseball Player)
2239 Leisure World
Mesa, AZ 85206-5384, USA

Lopert, Tanya (Actor)
36 Rue de Pnthieu
Paris 75008, FRANCE

Lopes, David E (Davey) (Athlete, Baseball Player, Coach)
309 San Elijo St
San Diego, CA 92106-3455, USA

Lopes, Lisa
1505 10th St
Santa Monica, CA 90401-2805

Lopez, Adamari (Actor)
c/o Staff Member *Telemundo*
2470 W 8th Ave
Hialeah, FL 33010-2000, USA

Lopez, Albie (Athlete, Baseball Player)
1019 S Roles Dr
Gilbert, AZ 85296-8606, USA

Lopez, Areliano Oswaldo (General, President)
Servico Aereo de Honduras Apdo 129
Tegucigalpa, DC, HONDURAS

Lopez, Arturo (Athlete, Baseball Player)
706 S Cherry Grove Ave Apt 304
Annapolis, MD 21401-4253, USA

Lopez, Danny (Little Red) (Boxer)
16531 Aquamarine Ct
Chino Hills, CA 91709-4644, USA

Lopez, Feliciano (Athlete, Tennis Player)
1360 E 9th St Ste 100
Cleveland, OH 44114-1730, USA

Lopez, Felipe (Athlete, Baseball Player)
2142 Walden Park Cir Apt 204
Kissimmee, FL 34744-6338, USA

Lopez, George (Actor, Comedian, Producer, Talk Show Host)
c/o Ina Treciokas *Slate Public Relations*
9000 W Sunset Blvd Ste 915
West Hollywood, CA 90069-5809, USA

Lopez, Hector (Athlete, Baseball Player)
11415 Faldo Ct
Hudson, FL 34667, USA

Lopez, Israel (Cachao) (Musician)
c/o Staff Member *Paradigm (Monterey)*
404 W Franklin St
Monterey, CA 93940-2303, USA

Lopez, Javier (Athlete, Baseball Player)
1002 Capistrano Ct
College Station, TX 77845-7920, USA

Lopez, Javy (Athlete, Baseball Player)
3475 Oak Valley Rd NE Apt 1530
Atlanta, GA 30326-1292, USA

Lopez, Jennifer (Actor, Musician)
c/o Benny Medina *The Medina Company*
Prefers to be contact via telephone
Los Angeles, CA 90024, USA

Lopez, Luis (Athlete, Baseball Player)
636 40th St
Brooklyn, NY 11232-3108, USA

Lopez, Luis (Athlete, Baseball Player)
1701 Pleasant Run Rd
Carrollton, TX 75006-7537, USA

Lopez, Lynda (Television Host)
c/o Staff Member *Style Network*
5750 Wilshire Blvd
Los Angeles, CA 90036-3697, USA

Lopez, Marga (Actor)
c/o Staff Member *Televisa*
Blvd Adolfo Lopez Mateos 232 Colonia
San Angel INN
DF CP 01060, MEXICO

Lopez, Maria (Judge)
c/o Staff Member *Rebel Entertainment Partners*
5700 Wilshire Blvd Ste 456
Los Angeles, CA 90036-3648, USA

Lopez, Mario (Actor, Television Host)
c/o Mark Schulman *3 Arts Entertainment Inc*
9460 Wilshire Blvd Fl 7
Beverly Hills, CA 90212-2713, USA

Lopez, Mickey (Athlete, Baseball Player)
17430 SW 117th Ave
Miami, FL 33177-2203, USA

Lopez, Nancy (Athlete, Golfer)
2308 Tara Dr
Albany, GA 31721-9111, USA

Lopez, Raul (Basketball Player)
Delta Center 301 W South Temple
Salt Lake City, UT 84101, USA

Lopez, Robert S (Historian)
41 Richmond Ave
New Haven, CT 06515-2013, USA

Lopez, Rodrigo (Baseball Player)
Oriole Park 333 W Camden St
Baltimore, MD 21201, USA

Lopez, Sal (Actor, Musician)
c/o Ivan De Paz *DePaz Management*
2011 N Vermont Ave
Los Angeles, CA 90027-1931, USA

Lopez, Sergi (Actor)
c/o Staff Member *International Creative Management (ICM-LA)*
10250 Constellation Blvd Fl 7
Los Angeles, CA 90067-6207, USA

Lopez, Steven (Athlete)
P.O. Bix 678
Sugarland, TX 77487, USA

Lopez, Trini (Actor, Musician)
1139 Abrigo Rd
Palm Springs, CA 92262-4101, USA

Lopez Rodriguez, Nicolas de J Cardinal (Religious Leader)
Santo Domingo, AP 186, DOMINICAN REPUBLIC

Lopez Tarso, Ignacio (Actor)
c/o Staff Member *Televisa*
Blvd Adolfo Lopez Mateos 232 Colonia
San Angel INN
DF CP 01060, MEXICO

Lopez Trujillo, Alfonso Cardinal (Religious Leader)
Arzobispado Calle 57 N 48-28
Medellin, COLUMBIA

Lopez-Alegria, Michael E (Astronaut)
1919 Tangle Press Ct
Houston, TX 77062, USA

Lopez-Cobos, Jesus
1 Clarendon Ct
Charlbury, Oxon OX7 3PS, UNITED KINGDOM (UK)

Lopez-Garcia, Antonio (Artist)
6 Albermarle St
London W1, UNITED KINGDOM (UK)

Loquasto, Santo (Designer)
10100 Santa Monica Blvd Ste 2500
Los Angeles, CA 90067-4116, USA

Lorant, Stefan
215 W Mountain Rd
Lenox, MA 1240

Lorca, Valeria (Actor)
c/o Staff Member *Telefe - Argentina*
Pavon 2444 (C1248AAT)
Buenos Aires, ARGENTINA

Lorch, George A (Business Person)
313 W Liberty St
Lancaster, PA 17603-2798, USA

Lorch, Karl (Athlete, Football Player)
92-861 Palailai St
Kapolei, HI 96707-1239, USA

Lord, Albert L (Business Person)
11600 American Dream Way
Reston, VA 20190-4758, USA

Lord, Lance W (General)
Commander US Space Command
Peterson Air Force Base, CO 80914, USA

Lord, M G (Cartoonist, Editor)
235 Pinelawn Rd
Melville, NY 11747-4226, USA

Lord, Marjorie (Actor)
1110 Maytor Pl
Beverly Hills, CA 90210-2600, USA

Lord, Peter (Animator, Director)
Gas Ferry Road
Bristol BS1 6UN, UNITED KINGDOM (UK)

Lord, Walter
116 E 68th St
New York, NY 10065-5955

Lord, Winston (Diplomat)
740 Park Ave
New York, NY 10021-4251, USA

Lords, Traci
c/o Staff Member *Juliet Green Management*
9025 Wilshire Blvd Ste 400
Beverly Hills, CA 90211-1828, USA

Loree, Brad (Actor)
c/o Brenda Wong *TalentCo*
111 Water St #308
Vancouver BC V6B 1A7, CANADA

Loren, Josie (Actor)
c/o Scott Wine *Osbrink Talent Agency*
4343 Lankershim Blvd Ste 100
West Toluca Lake, CA 91602-2705, USA

Loren, Sophia (Actor)
c/o Leonard Hirshan *Leonard Hirshan Management*
9171 Wilshire Blvd Ste 400
Beverly Hills, CA 90210-5516, USA

Loren, Veronica (Actor)
c/o Staff Member *International Artists PR & Talent Management*
3010 Wilshire Blvd # 594
Los Angeles, CA 90010-1103, USA

Lorentz, Jim (Athlete, Hockey Player)
2555 Staley Rd
Grand Island, NY 14072-2040, USA

Lorenz, Edward N (Scientist)
Earth Sciences Dept
Cambridge, MA 2139, USA

Lorenz, Lee (Cartoonist)
PO Box 131
Easton, CT 06612-0131, USA

Lorenz, Robert (Producer)
c/o Staff Member *Malpaso Productions*
4000 Warner Bros Blvd # 16
Burbank, CA 91522-1100, USA

Lorenzen, Fred (Race Car Driver)
64 E Elm St Apt 4
Chicago, IL 60611-1019, USA

Lorenzo, Blas (Actor)
PO Box 2127
Los Angeles, CA 90078-2127

Lorenzo, Francisco (Boxer)
c/o Staff Member *Top Rank Inc.*
3908 Howard Hughes Pkwy # 580
Las Vegas, NV 89109, USA

Lorenzoni, Andrea (Astronaut)
Via B Vergine del Carmelo 168
Rome 144, ITALY

Loretta, Mark (Athlete, Baseball Player)
7844 Sendero Angelica
San Diego, CA 92127-2553, USA

Lorey, Dean (Writer)
121 Saddlebow Rd
Bell Canyon, CA 91307-1033

Loria, Christopher (Gus) (Astronaut)
102 Sea Mist Dr
League City, TX 77573-6928, USA

Loria, Jeffrey (Baseball Player)
44 Cocoanut Row Unit 407-B
Palm Beach, FL 33480-4069, USA

Lorick, Tony (Athlete, Football Player)
349 Burney Ln
Kerrville, TX 78028-8074, USA

Loring, Gloria (Actor, Musician)
PO Box 1243
Cedar Glen, CA 92321-1243, USA

Loring, John R (Artist)
621 Avon Rd
West Palm Bch, FL 33401-7803, USA

Loring, Lynn (Actor)
4910 Petit Ave
Encino, CA 91436-1131, USA

Loriod, Yvonne (Musician)
7 Rue de Richepanse
Paris 75008, FRANCE

Lorius, Claude (Scientist)
Rue Moliere
Saint-Martin d'Heres 38402, FRANCE

Lorraine, Andrew (Athlete, Baseball Player)
10436 E Acoma Dr
Scottsdale, AZ 85255-1711, USA

Lorre, Chuck
c/o Staff Member *Chuck Lorre Productions*
4000 Warner Blvd Bldg 136
Burbank, CA 91522-0001, USA

Lorring, Joan
345 E 68th St
New York, NY 10065-5656

Lorscheider, Aloisio Cardinal (Religious Leader)
Guna Metropolitana CP 05 Tone Basilica
Aparecida, SP 12570-000, BRAZIL

Lorthridge, Ryan (Athlete, Basketball Player)
PO Box 68693
Jackson, MS 39286-8693, USA

Lortie, Louis (Musician)
3436 Springhill Rd
Lafayette, CA 94549-2535, USA

Los, Marinus (Misc)
4201 Quakerbridge Rd
Princeton Junction, NJ 08550-5205, USA

Los Lagos, Banda (Music Group)
c/o Staff Member *Sony Music Miami*
605 Lincoln Rd Ste 700
Miami Beach, FL 33139-2901, USA

Los Lobos (Music Group)
c/o Staff Member *Paradigm (Monterey)*
404 W Franklin St
Monterey, CA 93940-2303, USA

Los Lonely Boys (Music Group)
PO Box 162045
Austin, TX 78716-2045, USA

Los Mauricios (Writer)
c/o Staff Member *Gabriel Blanco Iglesias (Colombia)*
Dg 127A #20-36 Conjunto Plenitud, Apto 132
Bogota, Colombia

Los Rabanes (Music Group)
c/o Staff Member *Sony Music Miami*
605 Lincoln Rd Ste 700
Miami Beach, FL 33139-2901, USA

Los Sementales de Nuevo Leon (Music Group)
c/o Staff Member *Sony Music Miami*
605 Lincoln Rd Ste 700
Miami Beach, FL 33139-2901, USA

Los Super Reyes (Music Group, Musician)
c/o Staff Member *Warner Music International (WMI-USA)*
75 Rockefeller Plz
New York, NY 10019-6908, USA

Losch, Jack (Athlete, Football Player)
1606 Kaiser Ave
Williamsport, PA 17702-7015, USA

Loscutoff, James (Jim) (Athlete, Basketball Player, Coach)
166 Jenkins Rd
Andover, MA 01810-2304, USA

Losier, Michael (Writer)
605 827 Fairfield Rd
Victoria, British Columbia V8V 5B2, Canada

Lost Boys
1775 Broadway Ste 433
New York, NY 10019-1903

Lostprophets (Music Group)
c/o Staff Member *Sony Music International*
550 Madison Ave Fl 6
New York, NY 10022-3211, USA

Lothamer, Ed (Athlete, Football Player)
14545 W 183rd St
Olathe, KS 66062-9192, USA

Lott, Felicity A (Opera Singer)
Plankengasse 7
Vienna 1010, AUSTRIA

Lott, John (Athlete, Football Player)
14 E Oakwood Hills Dr
Chandler, AZ 85248-6200, USA

Lott, Pixie (Musician)
c/o Staff Member *Mercury Records UK*
1 Sussex Pl
London W6 9XS, UK

Lott, Ronald M (Ronnie) (Sportscaster)
PO Box 900
Beverly Hills, CA 90213-0900, USA

Lott, Ronnie (Athlete, Football Player)
11342 Canyon View Cir
Cupertino, CA 95014-4838, USA

Lott, Thomas (Athlete, Football Player)
PO Box 940585
Plano, TX 75094-0585, USA

Lott, Trent (Senator)
3100 Pascagoula St
Pascagoula, MS 39567-4215, USA

Lotti, Helmut
Bevrijdingstraat 39
Turnhout, BELGIUM 2300

Lotz, Anne Graham (Religious Leader)
3246 Lewis Farm Rd
Raleigh, NC 27607-6723, USA

Louboutin, Christian (Designer)
306 W 38th St Fl 3
New York, NY 10018-2927, USA

Louchiey, Corey (Athlete, Football Player)
8 Misty Creek Ln
Greenville, SC 29611-7718, USA

Loucks, Scott (Athlete, Baseball Player)
1801 Viola Dr
Sierra Vista, AZ 85635-2149, USA

Loucks, Vernon R Jr (Business Person)
1 Baxter Pkwy
Deerfield, IL 60015-4625, USA

Louden, Stephanie (Athlete, Golfer)
621 Verbena Ln
Frisco, TX 75034-8849, USA

Louderback, Tom (Athlete, Football Player)
PO Box 6879
Oakland, CA 94603-0879, USA

Loudon, Rodney (Physicist)
3 Gaston Street Bergholt E
Colchester, Essex CO7 6SD, UNITED KINGDOM (UK)

Louganis, Greg (Athlete, Swimmer)
c/o Evan Morgenstein *PMG Sports*
700 Evanvale Ct
Cary, NC 27518-2806, USA

Loughery, Kevin (Athlete, Basketball Player, Coach)
4474 Club Dr NE
Atlanta, GA 30319-1122, USA

Loughlin, Kimerley (Stylist)
1445 N Harlem Ave Apt A
Oak Park, IL 60302-1273, USA

Loughlin, Lori (Actor)
c/o Joanna (Joanie) Burstein *Burstein Company, The*
15304 W Sunset Blvd Ste 208
Pacific Palisades, CA 90272-3656, USA

Loughlin, Mary Anne (Correspondent)
1050 Techwood Dr NW
Atlanta, GA 30318-5604, USA

Loughran, James
34 Cleveden Dr
Glasgow G12 0RX, SCOTLAND

Louis, Clercine (Stylist)
1080 E 57th St
Brooklyn, NY 11234-2508, USA

Louis, Jin Luxian (Religious Leader)
Shesshan Catholic Seminary
Beijing, CHINA

Louis, Murray (Choreographer, Dancer)
375 W Broadway
New York, NY 10012-4324, USA

Louisa, Maria (Model)
23 Watts St
New York, NY 10013, USA

Louis-Dreyfus, Julia (Actor, Comedian)
c/o Judy Hofflund *Hofflund/Polone*
9465 Wilshire Blvd Ste 420
Beverly Hills, CA 90212-2603, USA

Louis-Dreyfus, Robert L M (Business Person)
Adi Dassier Str 2
Herzogenaurach 91702, GERMANY

Louise, Tina (Actor, Musician)
c/o Michael Einfeld *Michael Einfeld Management*
10630 Moorpark St Unit 101
Toluca Lake, CA 91602-2797, USA

Louiso, Todd (Actor)
8730 W Sunset Blvd Ste 440
Los Angeles, CA 90069-2277, USA

Louisy, C Pearlette (Governor)
Government House Morne Fortune
Castries, Saint Lucia,, West Indies

Loukas, Angelo (Athlete, Football Player)
1535 Robin Rd
Bannockburn, IL 60015-1852, USA

Loun, Don (Athlete, Baseball Player)
9095 Wexford Dr
Vienna, VA 22182-2152, USA

Lounge, John
555 Forge River Rd # 150
Webster, TX 77598-4369, USA

Lounge, John M (Mike) (Astronaut)
4002 Park Thicket
Houston, TX 77058-1222, USA

Lourdusamy, D Simon Cardinal (Religious Leader)
Palazzo dei Convertendi 64 Via della Conciliazione
Rome 193, ITALY

Lourie, Alan D (Judge)
717 Madison Pl NW
Washington, DC 20439-0001, USA

Louris, Gary (Musician, Songwriter, Writer)
1222 16th Ave S # 300
Nashville, TN 37212-2926, USA

Lousma, Jack R (Astronaut)
2722 Roseland Dr
Ann Arbor, MI 48103-2137, USA

Loutty, All (Prime Minister)
29 Ahmed Hesmat St Zamalek
Cairo, EGYPT

Louvier, Alain (Composer)
53 Ave Victor Hugo
Boulogne-Billancourt 92100, FRANCE

Louvin, Charlie (Musician, Songwriter)
111 Justice Hollow Rd
Wartrace, TN 37183-3410, USA

Loux, Shane (Athlete, Baseball Player)
3105 E Sparrow Pl
Chandler, AZ 85286-5612, USA

Lovano, Joe (Composer)
278 S Main St # 400
Gloucester, MA 1930, USA

Lovato, Demi (Actor)
c/o Tracy Brennan *Creative Artists Agency (CAA-LA)*
2000 Avenue of the Stars Ste 100
Los Angeles, CA 90067-4705, USA

Love, Alexis
PO Box 491205
Los Angeles, CA 90049-9205

Love, Ben H (Misc)
Boy Scouts of America 1327 Anne Court
Cedar Park, TX 78613-4022, USA

Love, Courtney (Musician, Songwriter)
c/o Jonathan Daniel *Crush Management*
60-62 E 11th St Floor 7
New York, NY 10003, USA

Love, Darlene (Actor, Musician)
437 5th Ave
New York, NY 10016-2205, USA

Love, Duval (Athlete, Football Player)
8985 Yuba River Ave
Fountain Valley, CA 92708-6346, USA

Love, Faizon (Actor)
c/o Paula Rosenberg *ICA Talent*
818 12th St Apt 9
Santa Monica, CA 90403-1727, USA

Love, Gael (Editor)
1790 Broadway
New York, NY 10019-1412, USA

Love, Ian (Musician)
c/o Staff Member *Paradigm (Monterey)*
404 W Franklin St
Monterey, CA 93940-2303, USA

Love, Kevin (Athlete, Basketball Player)
c/o Jeff Schwartz *Excel Sports Management*
9665 Wilshire Blvd Ste 500
Beverly Hills, CA 90212-2312, USA

Love, Loni (Actor, Comedian)
c/o Staff Member *Power Entertainment*
9100 Wilshire Blvd Ste 700
Beverly Hills, CA 90212-3423, USA

Love, Michael D (Mike) (Musician)
PO Box 7800
Incline Village, NV 89452, USA

Love, Mike
24563 Ebelden Ave
Santa Clarita, CA 91321-3745

Love, Patricia (Writer)
c/o Author Mail *Bantam-Dell Publishing (NY)*
1745 Broadway
New York, NY 10019-4368, USA

Love, Randy (Athlete, Football Player)
2202 Fairlands Dr
Garland, TX 75040-1158, USA

Love, Sean (Athlete, Football Player)
121 Hunter St
Tamaqua, PA 18252-2405, USA

Love, Stan (Athlete, Basketball Player)
1950 Egan Way
Lake Oswego, OR 97034-2728, USA

Love, Stanley G (Astronaut)
4315 Indian Sunrise Ct
Houston, TX 77059-5582, USA

Love & Rockets (Music Group)
4 The Lakes Bushey
Hertfordshire WD2 1HS, UK

Love III, Davis (Athlete, Golfer)
100 Brunswick Ave
Saint Simons Island, GA 31522-2605, USA

Lovelace, Vance (Athlete, Baseball Player)
5608 12th Ave S
Tampa, FL 33619-3756, USA

Lovelady, Edwin (Athlete, Football Player)
2707 Glenwood Pkwy
Chattanooga, TN 37404-1712, USA

Loveless, Patty (Musician, Songwriter)
c/o Staff Member *WmE2 (Endeavor-LA)*
9601 Wilshire Blvd Fl 3
Beverly Hills, CA 90210-5219, USA

Lovell, A C Bernard (Astronomer)
Quinta Swettenham near Congleton
Cheshire, UNITED KINGDOM (UK)

Lovell, Jacqueline (Actor)
c/o Staff Member *Martin and Donalds*
2131 Hollywood Blvd Ste 304
Hollywood, FL 33020-6751, USA

Lovell, James A, Jr (Astronaut)
PO Box 49
Lake Forest, IL 60045-0049, USA

Lovell, Jim (Astronaut, Writer)
c/o Staff Member *Cunningham Escott Slevin & Doherty (CESD-LA)*
10635 Santa Monica Blvd Ste 130
Los Angeles, CA 90025-8306, USA

Lovell, Marilyn
7840 Torreyson Dr
Los Angeles, CA 90046-1229

Lovellette, Clyde E (Athlete, Basketball Player)
8 Woodspoint Cir
North Manchester, IN 46962-9123, USA

Lovelock, James E (Inventor, Scientist)
Coombe Mill Saint Giles-on-Heath
Launceston, Cornwall PL 15 9RY, UNITED KINGDOM (UK)

Lovemark, Jaime (Athlete, Golfer)
16449 La Via Feliz
Rancho Santa Fe, CA 92067, USA

Lover, Seth (Engineer, Inventor)
4 Village Dr
Saint Louis, MO 63146-5346, USA

Loverboy
1505 W 2nd St # 200
Vancouver, CANADA BC V6H 3Y4

Loverne, David (Athlete, Football Player)
2307 Amber Falls Dr
Rocklin, CA 95765-4200, USA

Lovetere, John (Athlete, Football Player)
PO Box 2901
Lebanon, TN 37088-2901, USA

Lovett, Lyie (Musician, Songwriter, Writer)
1016 17th Ave S # 1
Nashville, TN 37212-2202, USA

Lovett, Lyle (Musician)
c/o Staff Member *Paradigm (Monterey)*
404 W Franklin St
Monterey, CA 93940-2303, USA

Lovett, Ruby (Musician)
PO Box 378
Canton, NY 13617, USA

Lovett, Steve (Actor)
c/o Steve Lovett *Lovett Management*
1327 Brinkley Ave
Los Angeles, CA 90049-3619, USA

Loviglio, Jay (Athlete, Baseball Player)
23 3rd Ave
East Islip, NY 11730-2015, USA

Loville, Derek (Athlete, Football Player)
11707 E Estrella Ave
Scottsdale, AZ 85259-5018, USA

Lovin' Spoonful
35 White Birch Rd
Ridgefield, CT 06877-5620, USA

Lovine, Vicki
c/o Daniel A (Dan) Strone *Trident Media Group LLC*
41 Madison Ave Fl 36
New York, NY 10010-2257, USA

Loving, Candy (Actor, Model)
c/o Staff Member *Playboy Enterprises Inc*
680 N Lake Shore Dr Ste 115
Chicago, IL 60611-4495, USA

Lovins, Amory B (Physicist)
220 Cody Ln
Basalt, CO 81621-9106, USA

Lovitz, Jon (Actor, Comedian, Producer, Writer)
c/o Jason Shapiro *United Talent Agency (UTA)*
9560 Wilshire Blvd Fl 5
Beverly Hills, CA 90212-2400, USA

Lovrich, Pete (Athlete, Baseball Player)
19626 Beechnut Dr
Mokena, IL 60448-9333, USA

Lovullo, Torey (Athlete, Baseball Player)
16825 Bajio Rd
Encino, CA 91436-3522, USA

Lovuolo, Frank (Athlete, Football Player)
6 Pleasant Ct
Binghamton, NY 13905-1516, USA

Low, Francis E (Physicist)
7102 Plantation Ln
Rockville, MD 20852-4421, USA

Low, G David (Astronaut)
21839 Atlantic Blvd
Sterling, VA 20166-6850, USA

Low, Stephen (Diplomat)
2855 Tilden St NW
Washington, DC 20008-3820, USA

Low Stars (Music Group)
c/o Staff Member *Paradigm (Monterey)*
404 W Franklin St
Monterey, CA 93940-2303, USA

Lowder, Kyle (Actor)
c/o Michael P Levine *Levine Management*
9028 W Sunset Blvd PH 1
Los Angeles, CA 90069-1830, USA

Lowdermilk, R Kirk (Athlete, Football Player)
9475 Apollo Rd NE
Kensington, OH 44427, USA

Lowe, Barry
31S Audley St
London, ENGLAND W1

Lowe, Chad (Actor)
c/o David Rose *Innovative Artists (LA)*
1505 10th St
Santa Monica, CA 90401-2805, USA

Lowe, Chan (Cartoonist, Editor)
200 E Olas Blvd
Fort Lauderdale, FL 33301, USA

Lowe, Cortland (Athlete, Golfer)
713 Taylor Ridge Rd
Winston Salem, NC 27106-5075, USA

Lowe, Crystal (Actor, Model)
8 Elm St
Toronto, ON M5G 1G&, CANADA

Lowe, Derek C (Athlete, Baseball Player)
724 Irolo St
Los Angeles, CA 90005-2331, USA

Lowe, Gary (Athlete, Football Player)
16940 Lauderdale Ave
Beverly Hills, MI 48025-5549, USA

Lowe, Kevin (Athlete, Coach, Hockey Player)
11230 110th St
Edmonton, AB T5G 3H7, Canada

Lowe, Lloyd (Athlete, Football Player)
8805 Deerwood Dr
Rowlett, TX 75088-4809, USA

Lowe, Nick (Musician, Songwriter, Writer)
307 7th Ave Rm 807
New York, NY 10001-6066, USA

Lowe, Paul (Athlete, Football Player)
3906 Marine View Ave
San Diego, CA 92113-4331, USA

Lowe, Rob (Actor)
c/o David McIlvain *Brillstein Entertainment Partners*
9150 Wilshire Blvd Ste 350
Beverly Hills, CA 90212-3453, USA

Lowe, Sean (Athlete, Baseball Player)
802 Oak Dr
Mesquite, TX 75149-4028, USA

Lowe, Sidney (Athlete, Basketball Player, Coach)
2631 Wallingford Rd
Winston Salem, NC 27101-1923, USA

Lowe, Stephanie (Athlete, Golfer)
2004 Delancey Dr
Norman, OK 73071-3872, USA

Lowe, Woodrow (Athlete, Coach, Football Player)
510 12th St
Midfield, AL 35228-2421, USA

Loweecey, Alice (Writer)
c/o Staff Member *Midnight Ink*
2143 Wooddale Dr
Woodbury, MN 55125-2989, USA

Lowell, Carey (Actor)
c/o Sue Leibman *Barking Dog Entertainment*
9 Desbrosses St Fl 2
New York, NY 10013-1701, USA

Lowell, Charlie (Musician)
1700 Hayes St Ste 304
Nashville, TN 37203-3014, USA

Lowell, Christopher (Designer, Television Host)
c/o Staff Member *Christopher Lowell Inc*
11845 W Olympic Blvd Ste 645W
Los Angeles, CA 90064-5065, USA

Lowell, Michael A (Mike) (Athlete, Baseball Player)
620 Santurce Ave
Coral Gables, FL 33143-6360, USA

Lowell, Scott
6500 Wilshire Blvd Ste 2200
Los Angeles, CA 90048-4942

Lowenstein, Evan (Actor, Musician)
c/o Ruthanne Secunda *United Talent Agency (UTA)*
9560 Wilshire Blvd Fl 5
Beverly Hills, CA 90212-2400, USA

Lowenstein, Jaron (Actor, Musician)
c/o Ruthanne Secunda *United Talent Agency (UTA)*
9560 Wilshire Blvd Fl 5
Beverly Hills, CA 90212-2400, USA

Lowenstein, John (Athlete, Baseball Player)
7017 Via Locanda Ave
Las Vegas, NV 89131-0114, USA

Lowenstein, Louis (Attorney, Attorney General, Educator, General)
5 Oak Ln
Larchmont, NY 10538-3917, USA

Lowery, Nick (Athlete, Football Player)
30616 W 98th St
De Soto, KS 66018-9311, USA

Lowery, Steve (Athlete, Golfer)
1073 Royal Mile
Birmingham, AL 35242-6061, USA

Lowery, Terrell (Athlete, Baseball Player)
3565 Antigua Pl
West Sacramento, CA 95691-5822, USA

Lown, Bernard (Doctor)
21 Longwood Ave
Brookline, MA 02446-5239, USA

Lown, Turk (Athlete, Baseball Player)
1106 Van Buren St
Pueblo, CO 81004-2832, USA

Lowndes, Jessica (Actor)
c/o Jeff Witjas *Agency for the Performing Arts (APA-LA)*
405 S Beverly Dr Ste 500
Beverly Hills, CA 90212-4425, USA

Lowrey, Dawn (Stylist)
412 N Coast Hwy PMB 221
Laguna Beach, CA 92651-1674, USA

Lowry, Lois (Writer)
205 Brattle St
Cambridge, MA 02138-3345, USA

Lowry, Mark
PO Box 1405
Hendersonville, TN 37077-1405, USA

Lowry, Noah (Athlete, Baseball Player)
181 N Encinal Ave
Ojai, CA 93023-2119, USA

Lowry, Shanti (Actor)

Loy, Frank E (Misc)
11 Dupont Cir NW
Washington, DC 20036-1207, USA

Loy, James M (Admiral, Government Official)
400 7th St SW
Washington, DC 20590, USA

Loynd, Mike (Athlete, Baseball Player)
19 Randall Dr
Short Hills, NJ 07078-1957, USA

Lozada, Johnny (Actor)
c/o Staff Member *Televisa*
Blvd Adolfo Lopez Mateos 232 Colonia San Angel INN
DF CP 01060, MEXICO

Lozado, Willie (Athlete, Baseball Player)
3032 Shagbark Trl
Sellersburg, IN 47172-9117, USA

Lozano, Conrad (Musician)
3575 Cahuenga Blvd W Ste 450
Los Angeles, CA 90068-1364, USA

Lozano, Ignacio E Jr (Editor)
700 S Flower St Ste 3000
Los Angeles, CA 90017-4217, USA

Lozano, Karyme (Actor)
c/o Ivan De Paz *DePaz Management*
2011 N Vermont Ave
Los Angeles, CA 90027-1931, USA

Lozano, Silvia (Choreographer)
31 Esq Con Riva Palacio
Mexico City, DF, MEXICO

Lozano Barragan, Javier Cardinal (Religious Leader)
Via Conciliazione 3
Rome 193, ITALY

Lu, Amy (Stylist)
c/o Staff Member *Judy Inc*
1 Yorkville Ave
Toronto ON M4W 1L1, Canada

Lu, Cindy (Actor)
c/o Kim Matuka *Online Talent Group*
Prefers to be contacted via email or telephone
Los Angeles, CA 90069, USA

Lu, Edward T (Ed) (Astronaut)
18222 Bal Harbour Dr
Houston, TX 77058-4311, USA

Lu, Lisa
1737 N Orange Grove Ave
Los Angeles, CA 90046-2131

Lu, Qihui (Artist)
100-301 398 Xin-Pei Road
Xin-Zuan, Shanghai, CHINA

Lu Yu, Chen (Talk Show Host, Television Host)
c/o Staff Member *Phoenix TV / HongKong Shenzhen*
No. 2-6 Dai King St Tai Po Industrial Estate
Tai Po, N. T. Hong Kong

Lualdi, Antonella
via Cassia Antica 35
Rome, ITALY

Lubanski, Ed (Bowler)
5326 Christi Dr
Warren, MI 48091-4195, USA

Lubbers, Ruud F M (Prime Minister)
Lambertweg 4
Rotterdam, RA 3062, NETHERLANDS

Lubchenco, Jane (Biologist)
Marine Biology Dept
Corvallis, OR 97331, USA

Lubezki, Emmanuel (Cinematographer)
c/o Julia Kole *Jacob & Kole Agency, The*
522 Wilshire Blvd Ste H
Santa Monica, CA 90401-1445, USA

Lubich, Bronko (Wrestler)
3146 Whitemarsh Cir
Dallas, TX 75234-2239, USA

Lubich, Silvia Chiara (Misc)
306 Via Di Frascati
Rocca di Papa, RM 40, ITALY

Lubin, Arthur
5737 Newcastle Ave
Encino, CA 91316-1054

Lubin, Steven (Musician)
School of Arts
Purchase, NY 10577, USA

Lubischer, Steve (Athlete, Football Player)
6 Fiore Ct
Oceanport, NJ 07757-1405, USA

Lublin, Nancy (Business Person)
24 Union Sq E Fl 4 # 32
New York, NY 10003-3201, USA

Lubotsky, Mark (Musician)
Overtoom 329 III
Amsterdam, JM 1054, NETHERLANDS

Lubovitch, Lar (Choreographer, Dancer)
229 W 42nd St Fl 8
New York, NY 10036-7205, USA

Lubratich, Steve (Athlete, Baseball Player)
24 Sackett Rd
Lee, NH 03861-6616, USA

Lubs, Herbert A (Scientist)
5133 SW 71st Pl
Miami, FL 33155-5639, USA

Lubys, Bronislovas (Prime Minister)
Tuo-Vaizganto 2
Vilnius, LITHUANIA

Luc, Tone (Actor, Musician)
1650 Broadway Ste 508
New York, NY 10019-6833, USA

Lucado, Max (Religious Leader, Writer)
19595 W 1H 10
San Antonio, TX 78257-9506

Lucaro, Carlos (Judge)
1929 Stout St
Denver, CO 80294-0003, USA

Lucas, Aubrey K (Educator)
President S Ofc
Hattiesburg, MS 39406-0001, USA

Lucas, Cornel (Photographer)
57 Addison Road
London W148JJ, UNITED KINGDOM (UK)

Lucas, Craig (Director, Producer, Writer)
c/o Staff Member *Gersh (LA)*
9465 Wilshire Blvd Ste 600
Beverly Hills, CA 90212-2612, USA

Lucas, Erin (Actor, Reality TV Star)
c/o Staff Member *Creative Management Entertainment Group (CMEG)*
2050 S Bundy Dr Ste 280
Los Angeles, CA 90025-6128, USA

Lucas, Gary (Athlete, Baseball Player)
1511 High St
Rice Lake, WI 54868-1874, USA

Lucas, George (Business Person, Director, Producer)
c/o Staff Member *LucasFilm Ltd*
5858 Lucas Valley Rd
Nicasio, CA 94946-9703, USA

Lucas, Geralyn (Writer)
1349 Lexington Ave
New York, NY 10128-1511, USA

Lucas, Isabel (Actor)
c/o Staff Member *Schiff Company, The*
8440 Warner Dr Ste B1
Culver City, CA 90232-2461, USA

Lucas, Jerry (Athlete, Basketball Player)
1825 Santa Rita Rd
Templeton, CA 93465-9322, USA

Lucas, Jessica (Actor)
c/o Staff Member *Thruline Entertainment*
9250 Wilshire Blvd Ground Fl
Beverly Hills, CA 90212, USA

Lucas, John (Athlete, Basketball Player)
21 Pin Oak Estates Ct
Bellaire, TX 77401-4225, USA

Lucas, Josh (Actor)
c/o Nicole Caruso *Wolf Kasteler Van Iden & Associates (NY)*
584 Broadway Rm 310
New York, NY 10012-5246, USA

Lucas, Ken (Athlete, Football Player)
1108 Stamps Cv
Cleveland, MS 38732-4014, USA

Lucas, Matt (Actor, Producer, Writer)
c/o Kevin McLaughlin *Baker Winokur Ryder Public Relations (BWR-LA)*
9100 Wilshire Blvd Ste 500 PMB WEST
Beverly Hills, CA 90212-3426, USA

Lucas, Maurice (Athlete, Basketball Player, Coach)
5691 Bonita Rd
Lake Oswego, OR 97035-3217, USA

Lucas, Michael (Adult Film Star, Director)
589 8th Ave Fl 2
New York, NY 10018-3097, USA

Lucas, Ray (Athlete, Football Player)
44 Harrison Ave # 2
Harrison, NJ 07029-1331, USA

Lucas, Richard J (Richie) (Athlete, Football Player)
1238 Old Boalsburg Rd
State College, PA 16801-6152, USA

Lucas, Robert E Jr (Nobel Prize Laureate)
5448 S East View Park Apt 3
Chicago, IL 60615-5929, USA

Lucas, William (Government Official)
Constitution & 10th NW
Washington, DC 20530, USA

Lucca, Lou (Baseball Player)
10211 Willow Bend Cir Apt 1B
Charlotte, NC 28210-8424, USA

Lucchesi, Frank (Athlete, Baseball Player, Coach)
4703 Mill Creek Dr
Colleyville, TX 76034-3646

Lucchesini, Andrea (Musician)
1133 Broadway Ste 1025
New York, NY 10010-7985, USA

Lucci, Mike (Athlete, Football Player)
3184 Middlebelt Rd
West Bloomfield, MI 48323-1937, USA

Lucci, Susan (Actor)
c/o Fran Curtis *Rogers & Cowan PR (NY)*
919 3rd Ave Fl 18
New York, NY 10022-3902, USA

Lucci, Vince Sr (Bowler)
1182 Queens Way
West Chester, PA 19382, USA

Luce, Derrel (Athlete, Football Player)
4112 Green Oak Dr
Waco, TX 76710-1440, USA

Luce, Henry III (Publisher)
Mill Hill Road
Mill Neck, NY 11765, USA

Luce, Lew (Athlete, Football Player)
850 Symphony Isles Blvd
Ruskin, FL 33572-2764, USA

Luce, R Duncan (Misc)
20 Whitman Ct
Irvine, CA 92617-4057, USA

Luce, Richard N (Government Official)
London SW1A 0PW, UK

Luce, William (Bill) (Writer)
PO Box 370
Depoe Bay, OR 97341-0370, USA

Lucebert (Artist, Writer)
Boendermakerhof 10
Bergen N-H, TB 1861, NETHERLANDS

Lucero (Musician)
c/o Staff Member *Sony Music Miami*
605 Lincoln Rd Ste 700
Miami Beach, FL 33139-2901, USA

Lucey, Dorothy (Actor, Correspondent, Television Host)
c/o Staff Member *Good Day Live*
20th Century Fox Television 10201 Pico Blvd Blg 88 W Rm 29
Los Angeles, CA 90035, USA

Luchko, Klara S (Actor)
Kotelmicheskaya Nab 1/15 Korp B #308
Moscow 109240, RUSSIA

Luchsinger, Susie (Musician)
406 W 10th St
Atoka, OK 74525-2804, USA

Lucic, Milan (Athlete, Hockey Player)
c/o Staff Member *Boston Bruins*
TD Banknorth Garden 100 Legends Way, Suite 250
Boston, MA 2114, USA

Lucid, Shannon W (Astronaut, Physicist)
1622 Gunwale Rd
Houston, TX 77062-4538, USA

Lucier, Lou (Athlete, Baseball Player)
7 Jaclyn Rae Dr
Millbury, MA 01527-3372, USA

Lucille Bliss, Lucille Bliss (Actor, Voice Over Artist)
673 Center St # 4A
Costa Mesa, CA 92627-2708, USA

Lucin, Arthur
5737 Newcastle Ave
Encino, CA 91316-1054

Lucio, Shannon (Actor)
c/o Justin Grey Stone *Untitled Entertainment (LA)*
350 S Beverly Dr Ste 200
Beverly Hills, CA 90212-4819, USA

Luck, Frank (Athlete)
Lerchenweg 9
Springstille 98587, GERMANY

Luckenbill, Laurence
PO Box 330
Georgetown, CT 06829-0330

Luckenbill, Theodore (Athlete, Basketball Player)
302 N 7th St
Crockett, TX 75835-1620, USA

Luckhurst, Mick (Athlete, Football Player)
103 Pierrepont Isle
Duluth, GA 30097-5908, USA

Luckinbill, Laurence (Actor)
RR 3 Flintlock Ridge Rd
Katonah, NY 10536, USA

Luckinbill, Lawrence (Actor)
PO Box 330
Georgetown, CT 06829-0330, USA

Luckinbill, Thad (Actor)
c/o Marnie Sparer *Innovative Artists (LA)*
1505 10th St
Santa Monica, CA 90401-2805, USA

Lucking, William (Actor)
c/o Staff Member *Twentieth Century Artists*
15760 Ventura Blvd Ste 700
Encino, CA 91436-3016, USA

Luckovich, Mike (Cartoonist, Editor)
72 Marietta St NW
Atlanta, GA 30303-2804, USA

Lucky, Lillian (Baseball Player)
243 Owens St
Niles, MI 49120-4150, USA

Lucky, Mike (Athlete, Football Player)
4156 N Morning Dove Cir
Mesa, AZ 85207-1194, USA

Lucky, Robert W (Engineer)
48 Gillespie Ave
Fair Haven, NJ 07704-3309, USA

Luczo, Stephen J (Business Person)
920 Disc Dr
Scotts Valley, CA 95066-4544, USA

Ludacris (Actor, Musician, Producer)
c/o Chaka Zulu *Disturbing Tha Peace*
1451 Woodmont Ln NW
Atlanta, GA 30318-2866, USA

Ludaker, Dave (Baseball Player)
3593 Buffum St
Simi Valley, CA 93063-3215, USA

Luddy, Barbara
119 Sultan Ave
Capitol Heights, MD 20743-1954

Luder, Owen H (Architect)
2 Smith Square
London SW1P 3H5, UNITED KINGDOM (UK)

Ludes, John T (Business Person)
300 Tower Pkwy
Lincolnshire, IL 60069-3640, USA

Luding-Rothenburger, Christa (Speed Skater)
Pieschener Allee 1
Dresden 1067, GERMANY

Ludlum, Robert (Actor)
c/o Ben Smith *International Creative Management (ICM-LA)*
10250 Constellation Blvd Fl 7
Los Angeles, CA 90067-6207, USA

Ludwick, Eric (Athlete, Baseball Player)
10183 Whispy Willow Way
Las Vegas, NV 89135-2089, USA

Ludwick, Ryan (Athlete, Baseball Player)
10183 Whispy Willow Way
Las Vegas, NV 89135-2089, USA

Ludwig, Alexander (Actor)
c/o Guido Giordano *International Creative Management (ICM-LA)*
10250 Constellation Blvd Fl 7
Los Angeles, CA 90067-6207, USA

Ludwig, Christa (Opera Singer)
162 Chemin du Santon
Mougins 6250, FRANCE

Ludwig, George H (Physicist)
215 Aspen Trl
Winchester, VA 22602-1404, USA

Ludwig, Ken (Writer)
c/o Peter Franklin *WmE2 (WMA-NY)*
1325 Avenue of the Americas
New York, NY 10019-6026, USA

Luebber, Steve (Athlete, Baseball Player)
3302 Moorhead Dr
Joplin, MO 64804-5323, USA

Luebbers, Larry (Athlete, Baseball Player)
844 Isaac Shelby Cir E
Frankfort, KY 40601-8806, USA

Luebbert, Eric (Stylist)
c/o Staff Member *Talent Plus*
1222 Lucas Ave Ste 300
Saint Louis, MO 63103-1937, USA

Lueck, Bill (Athlete, Football Player)
5206 N 134th Dr
Litchfield Park, AZ 85340-9425, USA

Luecken, Rick (Athlete, Baseball Player)
2902 Fontana Dr
Houston, TX 77043-1305, USA

Luetkemeyer, Blaine (Congressman, Politician)
1740 Longworth Hob
Washington, DC 20515-3503, USA

Luft, Joey (Actor)
108 E Matilija St
Ojai, CA 93023-2639

Luft, Lorna (Actor, Musician)
c/o Garry Kief *Stiletto Entertainment*
8295 S La Cienega Blvd
Inglewood, CA 90301-1521, USA

Lugar, Richard (Senator)
7841 Old Dominion Dr
McLean, VA 22102-2425, USA

Lugavere, Max (Television Host)
c/o Rob Levy *Untitled Entertainment (LA)*
350 S Beverly Dr Ste 200
Beverly Hills, CA 90212-4819, USA

Lugbill, Jon (Athlete)
7432 Alban Station Blvd Ste B232
Springfield, VA 22150-2321, USA

Luger, Lex
52B49 Uford Hwy
Atlanta, GA 30340

Lugo, Julio (Athlete, Baseball Player)
12622 Lady Jane Ct
Houston, TX 77044-4910, USA

Lugosi Jr, Bela
520 N Central Ave Ste 800
Glendale, CA 91203-3962, USA

Luhn, Nolan (Athlete, Football Player)
1400C Zillock Rd
San Benito, TX 78586, USA

Luhrmann, Baz (Director, Producer)
c/o Staff Member *Bazmark Inq (AUS)*
PO Box 430 Kings Cross
NSW 2011, AUSTRALIA

Lui, Stephen
10635 Santa Monica Blvd Ste 130
Los Angeles, CA 90025-8306

Luisi, Caesar (Actor)
c/o Christopher Smith *Paradigm (LA)*
360 N Crescent Dr
Beverly Hills, CA 90210-4874, USA

Luisi, James
22562 Seaver Ct
Santa Clarita, CA 91350-1389

Lujack, John C (Johnny) (Athlete, Football Player)
3700 N Harrison St
Davenport, IA 52806-5905, USA

Lujan, Ben Ray (Congressman, Politician)
330 Cannon Hob
Washington, DC 20515-4302, USA

Lujan, Fernando (Actor)
c/o Staff Member *TV Azteca*
Periferico Sur 4121 Colonia Fuentes del Pedregal
DF CP 14141, Mexico

Lujan, Manuel Jr (Secretary)
PO Box 3727
Albuquerque, NM 87190-3727, USA

Lukachyk, Robert (Rob) (Athlete, Baseball Player)
100 High St
Woodbridge, NJ 07095-3018, USA

Lukas, D Wayne (Coach)
5242 Katella Ave # 103
Los Alamitos, CA 90720-2820, USA

Lukashenko, Aleksandr (President)
JK Marks St 38
Minsk 220016, BELARUS

Lukasiewicz, Mark (Athlete, Baseball Player)
8035 Fir Dr
Clay, NY 13041-8646, USA

Lukather, Steve (Musician)
34 N Palm St
Ventura, CA 93001-2600, USA

Luke (Musician)
1800 Argyle Ave # 408
Los Angeles, CA 90028-5253, USA

Luke, Derek (Actor)
c/o Lisa Kasteler *WKT Public Relations (WKT-LA)*
9350 Wilshire Blvd Ste 450
Beverly Hills, CA 90212-3230, USA

Luke, John A Jr (Business Person)
299 Park Ave
New York, NY 10171-0002, USA

Luke, Matt (Athlete, Baseball Player)
5262 Eucalyptus Hill Rd
Yorba Linda, CA 92886-4209, USA

Luke, Steve (Athlete, Football Player)
812 Bluffview Dr
Columbus, OH 43235-1728, USA

Luken, Tom (Athlete, Football Player)
8036 Cast A Way
Mason, OH 45040-8365, USA

Lukens, Max L (Business Person)
3900 Essex Ln
Houston, TX 77027-5133, USA

Lukens, Susan (Stylist)
5200 Knox Ave S
Minneapolis, MN 55419-1042, USA

Luker, Rebecca (Actor)
c/o Staff Member *WmE2 (WMA-LA)*
1 William Morris Pl
Beverly Hills, CA 90212-4261, USA

Luketic, Robert (Actor)
c/o Paul Nelson *Mosaic Media Group*
9200 W Sunset Blvd Ste 10
Los Angeles, CA 90069-3608, USA

Lukin, Matt (Musician)
7 Trinity Row
Florence, MA 01062-1931, USA

Lukkarinen, Marjut (Skier)
Lohja, FINLAND

Lula da Silva, Luis Ignacio (President)
Praca dos 3 Poderas
Brasilia, DF 70 150, BRAZIL

Lulabel & Scottie
PO Box 171132
Nashville, TN 37217-8132

Lulu (Actor, Musician)
101 Shepherds Bush Concorde House
London W6 7LP, UNITED KINGDOM (UK)

Lum, Hadrien (Stylist)
c/o Staff Member *Judy Inc*
1 Yorkville Ave
Toronto ON M4W 1L1, Canada

Lum, Mike (Athlete, Baseball Player)
3476 Cochise Dr SE
Atlanta, GA 30339-4324, USA

Lumbly, Carl (Actor)
c/o Karen Forman *Domain Talent*
9229 W Sunset Blvd Ste 710
Los Angeles, CA 90069-3407, USA

Lumenti, Ralph (Athlete, Baseball Player)
9 Tomaso Rd
Milford, MA 01757-2224, USA

Lumley, Joanna (Actor)
c/o Staff Member *Conway van Gelder*
8-12 Broadwick St
London W1F 8HW, UK

Lumley, John L (Physicist)
743 Snyder Hill Rd
Ithaca, NY 14850-8708, USA

Lumme, Jyrki (Athlete, Hockey Player)
40 Bay St
Toronto, ON M5J 2K2, Canada

Lumpe, Jerry (Athlete, Baseball Player)
732 S Pearson Dr
Springfield, MO 65809-1613, USA

Lumpkin, Elgin (Ginuwine) (Musician)
c/o Michael Irving *Emancipated Talent*
215 Clinton St
Brooklyn, NY 11201, USA

Lumpp, Raymond (Ray) (Athlete, Basketball Player)
21 Hewlett Dr
East Williston, NY 11596-2003, USA

Lumsden, David J
Melton House
Soham, Cambridgeshire, UNITED KINGDOM (UK)

Luna, Barbara (Actor)
18026 Rodarte Way
Encino, CA 91316-4370, USA

Luna, Diego (Actor)
c/o Brandon Liebman *WmE2 (Endeavor-LA)*
9601 Wilshire Blvd Fl 3
Beverly Hills, CA 90210-5219, USA

Luna-Hill, Betty (Baseball Player)
19887 Red Feather Rd
Apple Valley, CA 92307-5514, USA

Lunar, Fernando (Athlete, Baseball Player)
3125 Zuni Pl
Alamogordo, NM 88310-4029, USA

Lunatics, St (Musician)
c/o Staff Member *Team Lunatics (MO)*
4246 Forest Park Ave Ste 2C
Saint Louis, MO 63108-2811, USA

Lund, Bill (Athlete, Football Player)
77 S Franklin St
Chagrin Falls, OH 44022-3212, USA

Lund, Don (Athlete, Baseball Player)
1200 Earhart Rd
Ann Arbor, MI 48105-2768, USA

Lund, Gordon (Gordy) (Athlete, Baseball Player)
1602 S Harvard Ave
Arlington Heights, IL 60005-3517, USA

Lund, Katia (Director)
c/o Sandra Lucchesi *Gersh (LA)*
9465 Wilshire Blvd Ste 600
Beverly Hills, CA 90212-2612, USA

Lunday, James (Actor)
c/o Staff Member *The Learning Channel (TLC)*
10100 Santa Monica Blvd Ste 1500
Los Angeles, CA 90067-4117, USA

Lunday, Kenneth (Athlete, Football Player)
1419 W Locust St
Durant, OK 74701-3458, USA

Lundberg, Anders (Misc)
Physiology Dept Box 33033
Goteborg 40 033, SWEDEN

Lundeen, George (Artist)
328 E 4th St
Loveland, CO 80537, USA

Lunden, Joan (Correspondent, Producer)
c/o Bill Stankey *Westport Entertainment Associates*
1700 Post Rd Ste C15
Fairfield, CT 06824-5726, USA

Lundgren, Dolph (Actor)
c/o Craig Baumgarten *Baumgarten Management*
406 Wilshire Blvd
Santa Monica, CA 90401-1410, USA

Lundgren, Terry (Business Person)
151 W 34th St
New York, NY 10001-2101, USA

Lundholm, Mark (Actor, Comedian)
c/o Staff Member *WmE2 (WMA-LA)*
1 William Morris Pl
Beverly Hills, CA 90212-4261, USA

Lundi, Monika
Viktoriastr. 24
Munich, GERMANY D-80803

Lundquist, Dave (Athlete, Baseball Player)
714 12th Ave NE
Hickory, NC 28601-2707, USA

Lundquist, David (Athlete, Baseball Player)
PO Box 1268
Hickory, NC 28603-1268, USA

Lundquist, Gus (Misc)
5100 John D Ryan Blvd Apt 616
San Antonio, TX 78245-3535, USA

Lundquist, Steve (Swimmer)
PO Box 1545
Stockbridge, GA 30281-8545, USA

Lundquist, Verne (Sportscaster)
30 Rockefeller Plz
New York, NY 10112-0015, USA

Lundqvist, Alex (Model)
c/o Staff Member *Boss Models*
80 8th Ave
New York, NY 10011-5126, USA

Lundqvist, Henrik (Athlete, Hockey Player)
c/o Staff Member *New York Rangers*
2 Pennsylvania Plz Rm 2200
New York, NY 10001, USA

Lundstedt, Tom (Athlete, Baseball Player)
9813 Brookside Ln
Ephraim, WI 54211, USA

Lundy, Carmen (Musician)
223 1/2 E 48th St
New York, NY 10017, USA

Lundy, Jessica (Actor)
c/o Staff Member *Metropolitan (MTA)*
4526 Wilshire Blvd
Los Angeles, CA 90010-3801, USA

Lundy, Lamar (Athlete, Football Player)
825 S 11th St
Richmond, IN 47374-6334, USA

Lundy, Victor A (Architect)
701 Mulberry Ln
Bellaire, TX 77401-3805, USA

Luner, Jaime (Actor)
427 N Canon Dr Ste 215
Beverly Hills, CA 90210-4840, USA

Luner, Jamie (Actor)
c/o Martin Berneman *Precision Entertainment*
6338 Wilshire Blvd
Los Angeles, CA 90048-5002, USA

Lunghi, Cherie (Actor)
8A Bloomsbury Square
London WC1A 2NE, UNITED KINGDOM

Lunka, Zoltan (Boxer)
Weinheimer Str 2
Schriesheim 69198, GERMANY

Lunke, Hilary (Athlete, Golfer)
11701 Broad Oaks Dr
Austin, TX 78759-3713, USA

Lunn, Bob (Athlete, Golfer)
PO Box 1495
Woodbridge, CA 95258-1495, USA

Lunney, Glenn (Scientist)
1150 Gemini St
Houston, TX 77058-2708, USA

Lunsford, Scott (Actor)
c/o Robert Yaffee *Infinity Management*
7923 Hollywood Blvd
Los Angeles, CA 90046-2611, USA

Lunsford, Trey (Athlete, Baseball Player)
3955 Nail Rd
Southaven, MS 38672-6739, USA

Luongo, Roberto (Athlete, Hockey Player)
7280 Lemon Grass Dr
Parkland, FL 33076-3950, USA

Lupberger, Edwin A (Business Person)
10055 Grogans Mill Rd # 5A
The Woodlands, TX 77380-1059, USA

Lupica, Mike (Writer)
87 Bald Hill Rd
New Canaan, CT 06840-2404, USA

Luplow, Al (Athlete, Baseball Player)
4250 Lakecress Dr E
Saginaw, MI 48603-1687, USA

Lupo, Benedetto (Musician)
Dombacher Str 41/III/3
Vienna 1170, AUSTRIA

Lupo, Frank (Producer, Writer)
c/o Stephen Marks *Evolution Entertainment (LA)*
901 N Highland Ave
Los Angeles, CA 90038-2412, USA

LuPone, Patti (Actor, Musician)
c/o Gary Gersh *Innovative Artists (NY)*
235 Park Ave S Fl 7
New York, NY 10003-1404, USA

Luppi, Daniele (Composer, Musician)
c/o Staff Member *Greenspan Artist Management*
8760 W Sunset Blvd
West Hollywood, CA 90069-2206, USA

Lupu, Radu (Musician)
3 Clarendon Ct
Charlbury, Oxon 0X7 3PS, UNITED KINGDOM (UK)

Lupus, Peter (Actor)
2401 S 24th St # 110
Phoenix, AZ 85034-6806, USA

Lurie, Alison (Writer)
English Dept
Ithaca, NY 14850, USA

Lurie, Ranan R (Cartoonist, Editor)
PO Box 698
Greenwich, CT 06836-0698, USA

Lurie, Rod (Director)
c/o Staff Member *WmE2 (Endeavor-LA)*
9601 Wilshire Blvd Fl 3
Beverly Hills, CA 90210-5219, USA

Lurtsema, Bob (Athlete, Football Player)
16920 Judicial Rd
Lakeville, MN 55044-8975, USA

Lusader, Scott (Athlete, Baseball Player)
4169 Bold Mdws
Oakland Township, MI 48306-4701, USA

Luse, Bernadette (Athlete, Golfer)
2528 Reading Dr
Orlando, FL 32804-4938, USA

Lush, Mike (Athlete, Football Player)
910 Rebecca Ln
Orefield, PA 18069-8842, USA

Lusha, Masiela (Actor, Producer)
7046 Hollywood Blvd
Los Angeles, CA 90028-6008, USA

Lusis, Janis (Athlete, Track Athlete)
Vesetas 8-3
Riga, 1013, LATVIA

Lusk, Herbert (Athlete, Football Player)
71 Palomar Real
Campbell, CA 95008-4206, USA

Lusk, Jacob (Musician)
c/o Simon Fuller *XIX Entertainment*
33/32 Ransomes Dock 35-37 Parkgate Rd
London SW11 4NP, UK

Lusteg, Booth (Athlete, Football Player)
18297 NW 6th St
Pembroke Pines, FL 33029-3677, USA

Lustig, Aaron (Actor)
c/o Staff Member *House of Representatives, The*
1434 6th St Ste 1
Santa Monica, CA 90401-2527, USA

Lustig, William (Producer)
15016 Marble Dr
Sherman Oaks, CA 91403-4521, USA

Lustiger, Jean-Marie Cardinal (Religious Leader)
Maison Dioceine 8 Rue de la Ville-l'Eveque
Paris 75008, FRANCE

Lusztig, George (Mathematician)
106 Grant Ave
Newton, MA 02459-1347, USA

Lutes, Eric (Actor)
c/o Kate Edwards *Grand View Management*
578 Washington Blvd # 688
Marina Del Rey, CA 90292-5442, USA

Luther, Bobbi Sue (Actor, Model)
c/o Staff Member *Urge Artists*
9107 Wilshire Blvd Ste 500
Beverly Hills, CA 90210-5526, USA

Luther, Ed (Athlete, Football Player)
30486 Le Prt
Laguna Niguel, CA 92677-5537, USA

Luther, Tina (Stylist)
580 Andrieux St
Sonoma, CA 95476-7327, USA

Lutt, Jorg-UweProf
Mensing-Str 17
Flensburg D-24937, GERMANY

Luttig, J Michael (Judge)
200 S Washington St
Alexandria, VA 22314-5405, USA

Luttrell, Rachel (Actor)
c/o Staff Member *Silver Massetti & Szatmary (SMS) Talent Inc*
8730 W Sunset Blvd Ste 440
Los Angeles, CA 90069-2277, USA

Lutz, Bob (Tennis Player)
101 Via Ensueno
San Clemente, CA 92672-2456, USA

Lutz, Joe (Athlete, Baseball Player)
1411 Quail Dr
Sarasota, FL 34231-3563, USA

Lutz, Joleen (Actor)
733 Seward St PH
Los Angeles, CA 90038-3503, USA

Lutz, Kellan (Actor)
c/o Nicole Perna *Baker Winokur Ryder Public Relations (BWR-LA)*
9100 Wilshire Blvd Ste 500 PMB WEST
Beverly Hills, CA 90212-3426, USA

Lutz, Mark (Actor)
c/o Nancy LeFeaver *LeFeaver Talent Management Ltd*
2 College St #202
Toronto ON M5G 1K3, CANADA

Lutz, Robert A (Business Person)
3600 Green Ct Ste 720
Ann Arbor, MI 48105-1570, USA

Lutz, Robin (Stylist)
11409 Frances Green Dr
North Potomac, MD 20878-4256, USA

Luuloa, Keith (Athlete, Baseball Player)
30905 Young Dove St
Menifee, CA 92584-8358, USA

LuValle, James (Athlete, Track Athlete)
1174 Los Altos Ave Apt 160
Los Altos, CA 94022-1062, USA

Luvana, Carmen (Adult Film Star)
9445 De Soto Ave
Chatsworth, CA 91311-4920, USA

Lüvland, Rolf (Composer, Musician)
c/o Staff Member *Continental Artist Management AS*
Sandakerveien 24 D, F2
Oslo N-0473, Norway

Luxon, Benjamin M (Opera Singer)
Relubbus Lane Saint Hillary
Penzance, Cornwall TR20 9DS, UNITED KINGDOM (UK)

Luyendyk, Arie (Race Car Driver)
12494 N 116th St
Scottsdale, AZ 85259-2704, USA

Luyties, Ricci (Athlete, Volleyball Player)
9500 Gilman Dr # Mc
La Jolla, CA 92093-5004, USA

Luz, Franc
606 N Larchmont Blvd Ste 309
Los Angeles, CA 90004-1309

Luzhkov, Yuri M (Politician)
Tverskaya Str 13
Moscow 103032, RUSSIA

Luzi, Mario (Writer)
Via Belle Riva 20
Florence 50136, ITALY

Luzinski, Ryan (Athlete, Baseball Player)
25680 Streamlet Ct
Bonita Springs, FL 34135-7829, USA

Lyakhov, Vladimir A (Cosmonaut)
Moskovskoi Oblasti
Syvisdny, Goroduk 141160, RUSSIA

Lyden, Mitch (Athlete, Baseball Player)
227 Shore Ct
Lauderdale By The Sea, FL 33308-5030, USA

Lydon, James (Jimmy) (Actor)
3538 Lomacitas Ln
Bonita, CA 91902-1105, USA

Lydon, John (Johnny Rotten) (Musician)
31962 Pacific Coast Hwy
Malibu, CA 90265-2506, USA

Lydon, Malcolm (Astronaut)
1429 Jaudon Rd
Dover, FL 33527, USA

Lydy, Scott (Athlete, Baseball Player)
4278 S Leoma Ln
Chandler, AZ 85249-4782, USA

Lye, Mark (Athlete, Golfer)
285 Grande Way Apt 1406
Naples, FL 34110-6491, USA

Lyfe (Musician)
c/o Staff Member *Sony/RCA Records*
550 Madison Ave Fl 6
New York, NY 10022-3211, USA

Lyle, Garry (Athlete, Football Player)
222 Beach Dr NE
Saint Petersburg, FL 33701-3414, USA

Lyle, Jarrod (Athlete, Golfer)
c/o Jim Lehrman *SFX Golf*
36855 W Main St Ste 200
Purcellville, VA 20132-3561, USA

Lyle, Kami (Musician, Songwriter, Writer)
2814 12th Ave S Ste 202
Nashville, TN 37204-2513, USA

Lyle, Sandy (Athlete, Golfer)
4905 Duck Creek Ln
Ponte Vedra Beach, FL 32082-3023, USA

Lyle, Sparky (Athlete, Baseball Player)
17 Signal Hill Dr
Voorhees, NJ 08043-2948, USA

Lyles, A C
2115 Linda Flora Dr
Los Angeles, CA 90077-1408, USA

Lyles, Leonard (Athlete, Football Player)
2315 Cross Hill Rd
Louisville, KY 40206-2809, USA

Lyles, Lester (Athlete, Football Player)
6315 14th St NW
Washington, DC 20011-8003, USA

Lyles, Lester L (Les) (General)
Commander Air Material Command
Wright-Patterson Air Force Base, OH 45433, USA

Lyman, Arthur
508 Kaanini St
Hilo, HI 96720-2751

Lyman, Dorothy
c/o Staff Member *Stone Manners Salners Agency (LA)*
9911 W Pico Blvd Ste 1400
Los Angeles, CA 90035-2715, USA

Lyman, Richard W (Educator)
Education School
Stanford, CA 94305, USA

Lymon, Frankie
1650 Broadway Ste 508
New York, NY 10019-6833

Lympany, Moura (Musician)
8 Bristol Gardens
London W9 2JG, UNITED KINGDOM (UK)

Lyn, Mai
190 W Kern Ave
Mc Farland, CA 93250-1349

Lynch, Allen J (War Hero)
438 Belle Plaine Ave
Gurnee, IL 60031-2902, USA

Lynch, Claire
1 Camp St
Cambridge, MA 02140-1103

Lynch, Cynthia (Athlete, Wrestler)
4205 Bridlepath Pl
Louisville, KY 40245-1971, USA

Lynch, Dan (Cartoonist, Editor)
600 W Main St
Fort Wayne, IN 46802-1408, USA

Lynch, David (Director)
PO Box 93158
Los Angeles, CA 90093-0158, USA

Lynch, Ed (Athlete, Baseball Player)
7832 E Parkview Ln
Scottsdale, AZ 85255-2704, USA

Lynch, Edele (Musician)
55 Drury Lane Covent Garden
London WC2B 5SQ, UNITED KINGDOM (UK)

Lynch, Evanna

Lynch, Evanna (Actor)
c/o Ricky Rollins *Schumacher Management*
1122 San Vicente Blvd
Santa Monica, CA 90402-2008, USA

Lynch, Holly (Actor)
c/o Scott Karp *Crystal Sky Pictures*
10203 Santa Monica Blvd Ste 500
Los Angeles, CA 90067-6416, USA

Lynch, James E (Jim) (Athlete, Football Player)
1009 W 67th St
Kansas City, MO 64113-1916, USA

Lynch, Jane (Actor)
c/o Gabrielle Krengel *Domain Talent*
9229 W Sunset Blvd Ste 710
Los Angeles, CA 90069-3407, USA

Lynch, Jennifer (Director, Producer)
1894 El Cerrito Pl
Los Angeles, CA 90068-3781, USA

Lynch, Jerry (Athlete, Baseball Player)
3527 S Sherwood Rd SE
Smyrna, GA 30082-2833, USA

Lynch, Jessica (War Hero)
c/o Gregory Lynch RR #1
Palestine, WV 26160-9801, USA

Lynch, Jessica (Beauty Pageant Winner)
c/o Staff Member *Miss New York City Scholarship Organization*
35 E 19th St Fl 2
New York, NY 10003-1313, USA

Lynch, John (Football Player)
c/o Staff Member *Denver Broncos*
13655 Broncos Pkwy
Englewood, CO 80112 4151, USA

Lynch, John (Governor)
107 N Main St Ofc of
Concord, NH 03301-4951, USA

Lynch, John Carroll (Actor)
c/o James Suskin *James Suskin Management*
2 Charlton St Apt 5K
New York, NY 10014-4970, USA

Lynch, Keavy (Musician)
55 Drury Lane Covent Garden
London WC2B 5SQ, UNITED KINGDOM (UK)

Lynch, Kelly (Actor, Model)
c/o Staff Member *Crestview Entertainment*
521 Montana Ave
Santa Monica, CA 90403-1313, USA

Lynch, Peg
304 11th St Box 339
Becket, MA 1223

Lynch, Peter S (Financier)
27 State St
Boston, MA 02109-2706, USA

Lynch, Richard (Actor)
1910 Holmby Ave Apt 1
Los Angeles, CA 90025-5936, USA

Lynch, Sandra L (Judge)
McCormack Federal Building
Boston, MA 2109, USA

Lynch, Shane (Musician)
Bushy Park Road 57 Meadowbank
Dublin, IRELAND

Lynch, Stephen (Comedian)
c/o Staff Member *WmE2 (WMA-LA)*
1 William Morris Pl
Beverly Hills, CA 90212-4261, USA

Lynch, Thomas C (Admiral)
751 Eagle Farm Rd
Villanova, PA 19085-2035, USA

Lynche, Michael (Musician)
c/o Simon Fuller *XIX Entertainment*
33/32 Ransomes Dock 35-37 Parkgate Rd
London SW11 4NP, UK

Lynde, Janice (Actor)
c/o David Moore *Moore Artist's Management*
310 Washington Blvd Ste 117
Marina Del Rey, CA 90292-5149, USA

Lynden-Bell, Donald (Astronomer)
MAdingley Road
Cambridge CB3 0HA, UNITED KINGDOM (UK)

Lyndon, Frank (Musician)
PO Box 12
Far Hills, NJ 07931-0012, USA

Lynds, Roger (Astronomer)
Tucson, AZ 85726, USA

Lyne, Adrian
9876 Beverly Grove Dr
Beverly Hills, CA 90210-2120

Lyngstad, Anni-Frida (Musician, Songwriter, Writer)
Sodra Brobaeken 41A Skeppsholmen
Stockholm 111 49, Sweden

Lynley, Carol (Actor)
3349 Cahuenga Blvd W Ste 1
Los Angeles, CA 90068-1379, USA

Lynn, Anthony (Athlete, Football Player)
1508 Brook Ln
Celina, TX 75009-2279, USA

Lynn, Bari (Stylist)
c/o Staff Member *Mel Bryant Management*
611 Broadway Rm 623
New York, NY 10012-2650

Lynn, Betty (Actor)
PO Box 141
Mount Airy, NC 27030-0141, USA

Lynn, Cheryl (Actor, Musician)
PO Box 667
Smithtown, NY 11787-0667, USA

Lynn, Frederic M (Fred) (Athlete, Baseball Player)
7336 El Fuerte St
Carlsbad, CA 92009-6409, USA

Lynn, Ginger (Adult Film Star)
c/o Staff Member *Atlas Multimedia Inc*
9005 Eton Ave Ste C
Canoga Park, CA 91304-6533, USA

Lynn, Greg (Architect)
Architecture School
Los Angeles, CA 90024, USA

Lynn, James T (Secretary)
6901 Radnor Rd
Bethesda, MD 20817-6328, USA

Lynn, Johnnie (Athlete, Football Player)
238 Hidden Dr
Blackwood, NJ 08012-4432, USA

Lynn, Jonathan (Director)
c/o Mike Marcus *Echo Lake Productions*
421 S Beverly Dr Fl 8
Beverly Hills, CA 90212-4408, USA

Lynn, Loretta (Musician, Songwriter)
44 Hurricane Mills Rd
Hurricane Mills, TN 37078-2147, USA

Lynn, Meredith Scott (Actor)
1180 S Beverly Dr Ste 601
Los Angeles, CA 90035-1158, USA

Lynn, Salomon Janet (Figure Skater)
PO Box 1026
Haymarket, VA 20168-8026, USA

Lynn, Therese
PO Box 6057
Hoboken, NJ 07030-7201

Lynn, Vera (Actor, Musician)
Ditchling, Sussex, UNITED KINGDOM (UK)

Lynn Chadwick, Aimee (Actor)
c/o Melanie Sharp *Sharp Talent*
117 N Orlando Ave
Los Angeles, CA 90048-3403, USA

Lynne, Bobbe
22732 Foothill Rd # 6
Hayward, CA 94541

Lynne, Gillian (Choreographer, Dancer)
18 Rutland St Knightsbridge
London SW7 1EF, UNITED KINGDOM (UK)

Lynne, Gloria (Musician)
330 W 56th St Apt 18M
New York, NY 10019-4222, USA

Lynne, Shelby (Musician, Songwriter, Writer)
c/o Staff Member *WmE2 (WMA-LA)*
1 William Morris Pl
Beverly Hills, CA 90212-4261, USA

Lynskey, Melanie (Actor)
c/o Susan Smith *Susan Smith Company, The*
1344 N Wetherly Dr
Los Angeles, CA 90069-1817, USA

Lynyrd Skynyrd (Music Group)
c/o Staff Member *Vector Management*
PO Box 120479
Nashville, TN 37212-0479, USA

Lyon, Brandon (Athlete, Baseball Player)
526 W 8th S
Preston, ID 83263-1459, USA

Lyon, Sue (Actor)
1244 Havenhurst Dr
West Hollywood, CA 90046-4911, USA

Lyon, William (Business Person, General)
36 Executive Park Ste 200
Irvine, CA 92614-4717, USA

Lyonne, Natasha (Actor, Producer)
c/o Tammy Rosen *Sanders Armstrong Caserta*
425 N Robertson Blvd
West Hollywood, CA 90048-1735, USA

Lyons, Barry (Athlete, Baseball Player)
1079 Frank P Corso St
Biloxi, MS 39530-1922, USA

Lyons, Bill (Athlete, Baseball Player)
811 Tomahawk
Heyworth, IL 61745-9309, USA

Lyons, Brooke (Actor)
c/o Staff Member *Burstein Company, The*
15304 W Sunset Blvd Ste 208
Pacific Palisades, CA 90272-3656, USA

Lyons, Curt (Athlete, Baseball Player)
124 Virginia Dr
Richmond, KY 40475-8631, USA

Lyons, David (Actor)
c/o Annabelle Sheehan *RGM Artist Group*
64-76 Kippax St Level 2, Suite 202 & 206
Surry Hills, NSW 2010, Australia

Lyons, Elena (Actor)
c/o Brian McCabe *Venture IAB*
8285 W Sunset Blvd Ste 1
West Hollywood, CA 90046-2420, USA

Lyons, Hersh (Athlete, Baseball Player)
7900 Dunbarton Ave
Los Angeles, CA 90045-1035, USA

Lyons, James A Jr (Admiral)
2189 Creeks Edge Dr
Virginia Bch, VA 23451-6805, USA

Lyons, Jeffrey
205 W 57th St
New York, NY 10019-2105

Lyons, Lamar (Athlete, Football Player)
3726 Bluff Pl
San Pedro, CA 90731-7006, USA

Lyons, Marty (Athlete, Football Player)
8 White Pine Ct
Smithtown, NY 11787-1199, USA

Lyons, Mitchell W (Mitch) (Athlete, Football Player)
8344 Woodcrest Dr NE
Rockford, MI 49341-8507, USA

Lyons, Phyllis
9171 Wilshire Blvd Ste 441
Beverly Hills, CA 90210-5516

Lyons, Robert F (Actor)
1801 Ave of Stars Ste 1250
Los Angeles, CA 90067-5817, USA

Lyons, Steve (Athlete, Baseball Player)
8196 E Del Platino Dr
Scottsdale, AZ 85258-1718, USA

Lyons, Thomas L (Athlete, Football Player)
2814 Drummond Pt SE
Atlanta, GA 30339-5332, USA

Lysacek, Evan (Figure Skater)
555 N Nash St
El Segundo, CA 90245-2818, USA

Lysander, Rick (Athlete, Baseball Player)
12667 Gaillon Ct
San Diego, CA 92128-6179, USA

Lysiak, Tom (Athlete, Hockey Player)
1050 Cedar Grove Rd
Buckhead, GA 30625-1818, USA

Lyst, John H (Editor)
307 N Pennsylvania St
Indianapolis, IN 46204-1819, USA

Lythgoe, Nigel (Producer)
c/o Staff Member *19 Entertainment*
33/32 Ransomes Dock 35-37 Parkgate Rd
London SW11 4NP, UK

Lytle, Jason
c/o Staff Member *Paradigm (Monterey)*
404 W Franklin St
Monterey, CA 93940-2303, USA

Lytle, Matt (Athlete, Football Player)
4602 Irish Creek Rd
Bernville, PA 19506-8346, USA

Lytle, Rob (Athlete, Football Player)
1829 Buckland Ave
Fremont, OH 43420-3503, USA

Lyttle, Jim (Athlete, Baseball Player)
751 Camino Lakes Cir
Boca Raton, FL 33486-6961, USA

Lyttle, Kevin (Musician)
c/o Michael (Mike) Esterman
Esterman.Com, LLC
Prefers to be contacted via email
MD, USA

Lytton, Louisa (Actor)
Milton Keynes Theatre Marlborough Gate
Central Milton Keynes MK9 3NZ, United Kingdom

Lyubimov, Alexey B (Musician)
Klimentovskiy Per 9 #12
Moscow, RUSSIA

Lyubimov, Yuri P (Actor, Director)
Chkalova Str 76
Moscow, RUSSIA

Lyubshin, Stanislav A (Actor)
#171
Moscow 117571, RUSSIA

M

M, Banumathi (Actor, Bollywood)
15 Poes Road 4th St
Chennai, TN 600018, INDIA

M. Bilirakis, Gus (Congressman, Politician)
407 Cannon Hob
Washington, DC 20515-3901, USA

M. Christensen, Donna (Congressman, Politician)
1510 Longworth Hob
Washington, DC 20515-5501, USA

M. Grijalva, Raul (Congressman, Politician)
1511 Longworth Hob
Washington, DC 20515-4330, USA

M. Hall, Ralph (Congressman, Politician)
2405 Rayburn Hob
Washington, DC 20515-4304, USA

M. Honda, Michael (Congressman, Politician)
1713 Longworth Hob
Washington, DC 20515-0515, USA

M. Landry, Jeffrey (Congressman, Politician)
206 Cannon Hob
Washington, DC 20515-3801, USA

M. Levin, Sander (Congressman, Politician)
1236 Longworth Hob
Washington, DC 20515-2503, USA

M. Lowey, Nita (Congressman, Politician)
2365 Rayburn Hob
Washington, DC 20515-2308, USA

M. Lumis, Cynthia (Congressman, Politician)
113 Cannon Hob
Washington, DC 20515-3512, USA

M. Payne, Donald (Congressman, Politician)
2310 Rayburn Hob
Washington, DC 20515-0505, USA

M2M (Music Group)
c/o Staff Member *Creative Artists Agency (CAA-LA)*
2000 Avenue of the Stars Ste 100
Los Angeles, CA 90067-4705, USA

Ma, Tzi (Actor)
526 N Larchmont Blvd # 201
Los Angeles, CA 90004-1300

Ma, Yo-Yo (Musician)
c/o Staff Member *Shore Fire Media*
32 Court St Fl 16
Brooklyn, NY 11201-4441, USA

Maarleveld, John (Athlete, Football Player)
42 Carlton Pl
Rutherford, NJ 07070-1120, USA

Maas, Alex
6962 Wildlife Rd
Malibu, CA 90265-4309

Maas, Bill (Athlete, Football Player)
653 NE Shoreline Dr
Lees Summit, MO 64064-1382, USA

Maas, Kevin (Athlete, Baseball Player)
PO Box 21019
Castro Valley, CA 94546-9019, USA

Maas, William T (Bill) (Athlete, Football Player)
PO Box 2175
Lees Summit, MO 64063-7175, USA

Maathai, Wangari (Activist)
PO Box 67545
Nairobi, KENYA

Maazel, Lorin V (Conductor, Musician)
10 Lincoln Center Plz
New York, NY 10023-6912, USA

Mabe, Manabu (Artist)
Rua das Canjeranas 321 Jabaquara
Sao Paulo, SP, BRAZIL

Mabius, Eric (Actor)
c/o Geordie Frey *GEF Entertainment*
122 N Clark Dr Apt 401
West Hollywood, CA 90048-6315, USA

Mably, Luke (Actor)
c/o Stephanie Ritz *WmE2 (Endeavor-LA)*
9601 Wilshire Blvd Fl 3
Beverly Hills, CA 90210-5219, USA

Mabon, Lee (Athlete, Baseball Player)
2084 Vollintine Ave
Memphis, TN 38107-4700, USA

Mabra, Ron (Athlete, Football Player)
155 Thornton Ct
Fayetteville, GA 30214-3830, USA

Mabrey, Sunny (Actor)
c/o Chris Schmidt *Paradigm (LA)*
360 N Crescent Dr
Beverly Hills, CA 90210-4874, USA

Mabrey, Vicki (Correspondent, Journalist)
c/o Staff Member *Nightline*
1717 Desales St NW
Washington, DC 20036-4401, USA

Mabry, John (Athlete, Baseball Player)
715 Bellerive Manor Dr
Saint Louis, MO 63141-6084, USA

Mac, Fleetwood (Music Group)
c/o Staff Member *Agency for the Performing Arts (APA-LA)*
405 S Beverly Dr Ste 500
Beverly Hills, CA 90212-4425, USA

Mac Mohan (Actor)
Gulam Cottage Four Bungalows Andheri
Bombay, MS 400 058, INDIA

Mac Quayle (DJ)
c/o Staff Member *Diva Central Inc*
7510 W Sunset Blvd Ste 1445
Los Angeles, CA 90046-3408, USA

Macafee, Ken (Athlete, Football Player)
241 Fox Hill Rd
Needham, MA 02492-2752, USA

MacAfee Sr, Ken (Athlete, Football Player)
26 W Elm Ter
Brockton, MA 02301-3629, USA

Macapagal-Arroyo, Gloria (President)
JP Laurel St
Metro Manila 100, PHILIPPINES

MacArthur, Ellen (World Record Holder)
Whitegates Arctic Rd
Cowes, Isle of Wight PO31 7PG, UNITED KINGDOM

MacArthur, Robb (Reality TV Star)
c/o Staff Member *Boy Meets Boy*
299 Queen Street West
Toronto ON M5V 2Z5, Canada

Macat, Julio G (Cinematographer)
232 N Canon Dr
Beverly Hills, CA 90210-5302, USA

Macauley, Ed (Athlete, Basketball Player)
1312 Autumn Wood Cir
Ballwin, MO 63011-4211, USA

Macauley, Edward C (Easy Ed) (Athlete, Basketball Player)
1312 Autumn Wood Cir
Ballwin, MO 63011-4211, USA

MacAvoy, Paul W (Economist)
6 Mechanic St
Woodstock, VT 05091-1316, USA

MacBeth, Lois
4095 Athenian Way
Los Angeles, CA 90043-1617

Macc, Willie (Actor)
c/o Charles Belk 8939 S Sepulveda Blvd 110-240
Los Angeles, CA 90045, USA

Maccarone, Sam (Director)
c/o David Krintzman *Morris, Yorn, Barnes, Levine, Krintzman, Rubenstein and Kohner*
2000 Ave Of The Stars 3rd Tower Floor NORTH
Los Angeles, CA 90067, USA

Macchio, Ralph (Actor)
c/o Rob Levy *Untitled Entertainment (LA)*
350 S Beverly Dr Ste 200
Beverly Hills, CA 90212-4819, USA

MacCormac, Richard C (Architect)
9 Heneage St
London E1 5LJ, UNITED KINGDOM (UK)

Maccormack, Frank (Athlete, Baseball Player)
2 Schmidts Pl
Secaucus, NJ 07094-4110, USA

MacCormack, Jean F (Educator)
President's Office
Boston, MA 2125, USA

MacCready, Paul B (Engineer)
222 E Huntington Dr
Monrovia, CA 91016-8006, USA

MacDermid, Paul (Athlete, Hockey Player)
81 Lakeland Dr
Sauble Beach, ON N0H 2G0, Canada

MacDermot, Galt (Composer)
12 Silver Lake Rd
Staten Island, NY 10301-3013, USA

MacDiarmid, Alan G (Nobel Prize Laureate)
635 Drexel Ave
Drexel Hill, PA 19026-3816, USA

Macdissi, Peter (Actor)
c/o Melissa Stone *42West (LA)*
11400 W Olympic Blvd Ste 1100
Los Angeles, CA 90064-1579, USA

MacDonald, Adam (Actor)
c/o Staff Member *Characters Talent Agency, The (Vancouver)*
1505 W 2nd Ave #200
Vancouver, BC V6H 3Y4, Canada

MacDonald, Ann-Marie (Writer)
c/o Staff Member *Simon & Schuster*
1230 Avenue of the Americas Fl CONC1
New York, NY 10020-1586, USA

Macdonald, Bob (Athlete, Baseball Player)
522 Harbor Grove Cir
Safety Harbor, FL 34695-4977, USA

MacDonald, C Parker (Athlete, Hockey Player)
3 Miller Rd
Northford, CT 06472-1424, USA

MacDonald, Jeffrey (Doctor)
#00131-177 Fed Corr Inst 27072 Ballston
Sheridan, OR 97378, USA

MacDonald, Julien (Designer, Fashion Designer)
c/o Staff Member *Julien MacDonald*
Haydens Place 247A Portobello Road
London, England W11 1LT, United Kingdom

MacDonald, Kelly (Actor)
c/o Emily Yomtobian *PMK/BNC Public Relations (PMK-LA)*
8687 Melrose Ave Ste 8
West Hollywood, CA 90069-5746, USA

MacDonald, Mark (Athlete, Football Player)
19178 Echo Ln
Farmington, MN 55024-9184, USA

Macdonald, Norm (Actor, Comedian)
c/o Marc Gurvitz *Brillstein Entertainment Partners*
9150 Wilshire Blvd Ste 350
Beverly Hills, CA 90212-3453, USA

MacDonald, Ryan
10801 Connecticut Ave
Kensington, MD 20895-2134

Macdougal, Mike (Athlete, Baseball Player)
2429 N Travis
Mesa, AZ 85207-2539, USA

MacDowell, Andie (Actor)
c/o Risa Shapiro *Schiff Company, The*
8440 Warner Dr Ste B1
Culver City, CA 90232-2461, USA

Macek, Don (Athlete, Football Player)
3615 Monte Real
Escondido, CA 92029-7911, USA

Macfadyen, Matthew (Actor)
c/o Hylda Queally *Creative Artists Agency (CAA-LA)*
2000 Avenue of the Stars Ste 100
Los Angeles, CA 90067-4705, USA

MacFarlane, Luke (Actor)
c/o Bonnie Bernstein *International Creative Management (ICM-NY)*
40 W 57th St
New York, NY 10019-4001, USA

Macfarlane, Mike (Athlete, Baseball Player)
7421 Woodside Dr
Stockton, CA 95207-1554, USA

MacFarlane, Seth (Actor, Director)
c/o John Jacobs *Smart Entertainment*
9595 Wilshire Blvd Ste 900
Beverly Hills, CA 90212-2509, USA

MacGowan, Shane (Musician)
Chapel Place Rivington St
London EC2A 3DQ, UNITED KINGDOM (UK)

MacGraw, Ali (Actor)
c/o Laina Cohn *Laina Cohn Management*
15066 Sutton St
Sherman Oaks, CA 91403-4020, USA

MacGregor, Ian K (Government Official)
Castleton House Lochgilphead
Argyll, SCOTTLAND

MacGregor, Jeff (Actor, Writer)
c/o Katherine Herring *HarperCollins Publishers*
10 E 53rd St C/O Author Mail Floor 7
New York, NY 10022, USA

MacGregor, Joanna C (Musician)
165 W 57th St
New York, NY 10019-2201, USA

MacGregor, Katherine (Actor)
1900 Vine St Apt 306
Los Angeles, CA 90068-3979, USA

Macha, Kenneth H (Ken) (Athlete, Baseball Player, Coach)
6934 Berkshire Dr
Export, PA 15632-8946, USA

Macha, Mike (Athlete, Baseball Player)
PO Box 3844
Victoria, TX 77903-3844, USA

Machado, Justina (Actor)
c/o Danielle Allman-Del *D2 Management*
141 S Barrington Ave
Los Angeles, CA 90049-3368, USA

Machado, Mario
5750 Briarcliff Rd
Los Angeles, CA 90068-3633

Machado, Robert (Athlete, Baseball Player)
9095 Misty Creek Dr
Sarasota, FL 34241-8581, USA

Macharski, Franciszak Cardinal (Religious Leader)
Ul Franciszkanska 3
Krakow 31-004, POLAND

Machel, Graca (Activist)
1800 Massachusetts Ave NW Ste 400
Washington, DC 20036-1218, USA

Machemer, Dave (Athlete, Baseball Player)
2159 Alpine Ct
Stevensville, MI 49127-9554, USA

Machida, Lyoto (Athlete, Boxer)
c/o Staff Member *UFC*
PO Box 26959
Las Vegas, NV 89126-0959, USA

Machover, Tod (Composer)
Media Laboratory
Cambridge, MA 2139, USA

Macht, Gabriel (Actor)
c/o Staff Member *Management 360*
9111 Wilshire Blvd
Beverly Hills, CA 90210-5508, USA

Macht, Stephen (Actor)
248 S Rodeo Dr
Beverly Hills, CA 90212-3804, USA

Macias, Eduardo R (Director)
c/o Gabriel Blanco *Gabriel Blanco Iglesias (Mexico)*
Rio Balsas 35-32 Colonia Cuauhtemoc
DF 6500, Mexico

Macias, Jose (Athlete, Baseball Player)
c/o Staff Member *Montreal Expos*
4549 Avenue Pierre de Coubertin
Montreal
Quebec H1V 3N7, CANADA

Macinnis, Allan (Athlete, Hockey Player)
1132 Highland Pointe Dr
Saint Louis, MO 63131-1408, USA

MacIntosh, Craig (Cartoonist)
3403 W 28th St
Minneapolis, MN 55416-4302, USA

MacIntosh, Sir Cameron
1 Bedford Sq
London, ENGLAND WC1B 3RA

MacIntyre, Colin (Musician)
c/o Staff Member *Paradigm (Monterey)*
404 W Franklin St
Monterey, CA 93940-2303, USA

Macintyre, Marguerite (Actor)
c/o Donna Massetti *Silver Massetti & Szatmary (SMS) Talent Inc*
8730 W Sunset Blvd Ste 440
Los Angeles, CA 90069-2277, USA

MacIntyre, Scott (Musician)

Macio (Musician)
c/o Staff Member *Paradigm (Monterey)*
404 W Franklin St
Monterey, CA 93940-2303, USA

Macionis, John (Swimmer)
2600 Barracks Rd Apt 246
Charlottesville, VA 22901-4216, USA

Mack, Allison (Actor)
c/o Sheila Wenzel *Innovative Artists (LA)*
1505 10th St
Santa Monica, CA 90401-2805, USA

Mack, Cedric (Athlete, Football Player)
116 Chestnut St
Lake Jackson, TX 77566-5526, USA

Mack, Connie (Congressman, Politician)
804 Nicholas Pkwy E Ste 1
Cape Coral, FL 33990-2811, USA

Mack, J Kevin (Athlete, Football Player)
7402 Greatwood Lake Dr
Sugar Land, TX 77479-6302, USA

Mack, Lonnie (Musician)
59 Parsons St
West Newton, MA 02465-2137, USA

Mack, Quinn (Athlete, Baseball Player)
2228 Maple Rose Dr
Las Vegas, NV 89134-0187, USA

Mack, Rico (Athlete, Football Player)
1200 R D Mack Rd
Statham, GA 30666-3140, USA

Mack, Sam (Athlete, Basketball Player)
8142S S Prairie Park Pl
Chicago, IL 60619, USA

Mack, Shane (Athlete, Baseball Player)
35324 Marsh Ln
Wildomar, CA 92595-9019, USA

Mack, Thomas (Tom) (Athlete, Football Player)
6268 N Willard Ave
San Gabriel, CA 91775-2548, USA

Mack, Tony (Baseball Player)
8214 E McDonald Dr
Scottsdale, AZ 85250-6218, USA

Mack, Tremain (Athlete, Football Player)
3604 Rock Creek Dr
Tyler, TX 75707-1634, USA

Mack, Warner (Musician)
2260 E Apple Ave
Muskegon, MI 49442-4369, USA

Mack, William (Athlete, Football Player)
51910 N Shoreham Ct
South Bend, IN 46637-1357, USA

Mackall, Michelle (Athlete, Golfer)
2057 Oxford Ave
Cardiff By The Sea, CA 92007-1719, USA

Mackanin, Pete (Athlete, Baseball Player, Coach)
11563 E Bronco Trl
Scottsdale, AZ 85255-8243, USA

Mackay, David (Director)
232 N Canon Dr
Beverly Hills, CA 90210-5302, USA

Mackay, Harvey (Writer)
2100 Elm St SE
Minneapolis, MN 55414-2533, USA

Mackbee, Earsell (Athlete, Football Player)
9742 Russell Ave S
Minneapolis, MN 55431-2469, USA

Macke, Richard C (Admiral)
1887 Alaweo St
Honolulu, HI 96821-1343, USA

MacKenney, Tamara
4935 Parkers Mill Rd
Lexington, KY 40513-9760

Mackenroth, Jack (Designer, Reality TV Star)
c/o Steve Le Vine *Grapevine Public Relations*
5237 Cahuenga Blvd # 2
N Hollywood, CA 91601-3419, USA

MacKenzie, Benjamin (Actor)
c/o Staff Member *Management 360*
9111 Wilshire Blvd
Beverly Hills, CA 90210-5508, USA

Mackenzie, Brock (Athlete, Golfer)
c/o Jim Lehrman *SFX Golf*
36855 W Main St Ste 200
Purcellville, VA 20132-3561, USA

MacKenzie, Eric (Athlete, Baseball Player)
2002 James E
Bright Grove, ON N0N 1C0, Canada

Mackenzie, Gordy (Athlete, Baseball Player)
36535 Micro Racetrack Rd
Fruitland Park, FL 34731-5163, USA

MacKenzie, J C
3500 W Olive Ave Ste 1400
Burbank, CA 91505-5512, USA

Mackenzie, Jeremy J G (General)
Chelsea
London Sw3 4SR, UNITED KINGDOM (UK)

MacKenzie, John L (Director)
8942 Wilshire Blvd # 219
Beverly Hills, CA 90211-1908, USA

Mackenzie, Ken (Athlete, Baseball Player)
15 Fair St
Guilford, CT 06437-2601, USA

MacKenzie, Patch
3500 W Olive Ave Ste 1400
Burbank, CA 91505-5512

MacKenzie, Peter (Actor)

Mackenzie, Warren (Artist)
8695 68th St N
Stillwater, MN 55082-7310, USA

Mackenzie, Will (Athlete, Golfer)
35 Laurel Oaks Cir
Jupiter, FL 33469-2757, USA

Mackerras, A Charles M
10 Hamilton Terrace
London NW8 9UG, UNITED KINGDOM (UK)

Mackey, Cindy (Athlete, Golfer)
1190 Millstone Run
Bogart, GA 30622-3062, USA

Mackey, George W (Mathematician)
25 Coolidge Hill Rd
Cambridge, MA 02138-5509, USA

Mackey, John (Athlete, Football Player)
1198 Pacific Coast Hwy Apt D506
Seal Beach, CA 90740-6251, USA

Mackey, Kyle (Athlete, Football Player)
PO Box 156
Arp, TX 75750-0156, USA

Mackey, Malcolm (Athlete, Basketball Player)
504 Hemphill Ave
Chattanooga, TN 37411-2910, USA

Mackey, Rick (Misc)
5938 Four Mile Rd
Nanana, AK 99760, USA

Macki, Debra (Stylist)
c/o Sandie Torres *Lily Artist Management*
PO Box 610
Southborough, MA 01772-0610, USA

Mackie, Anthony (Actor)
c/o Jason Spire *Inspire Entertainment*
315 7th Ave Apt 17E
New York, NY 10001-6011, USA

Mackie, Bob (Fashion Designer)
230 Park Ave # 303
New York, NY 10169-0005, USA

MacKinney, Steven (Stylist)
c/o Staff Member *Katy Barker Agency Inc*
6606 10th Ave Apt 3R
Brooklyn, NY 11219-5804, USA

MacKinnon, Catherine (Lawyer)
Law School
Ann Arbor, MI 48109, USA

MacKinnon, Gillies (Director)
c/o Patty Detroit *Todd Smith and Associates*
10250 Constellation Blvd Fl 7
Los Angeles, CA 90067-6207, USA

MacKinnon, Roderick (Nobel Prize Laureate)
545 W End Ave
New York, NY 10024-2713, USA

Mackintosh, Cameron A (Producer)
1 Bedford Sq
London WC1B 3RA, UNITED KINGDOM (UK)

Mackintosh, Steven (Actor)
c/o Staff Member *Yakety Yak*
8-A Bloomsbury Sq
London WC1A 2NE, UNITED KINGDOM (UK)

Macklin, David (Actor)
5410 Wilshire Blvd # 227
Los Angeles, CA 90036-4216, USA

Macklin, Rudy (Athlete, Basketball Player)
9336 Jefferson Hwy
Baton Rouge, LA 70809-2474, USA

Macknowski, John (Athlete, Basketball Player)
1920 Garnet Ln
Dandridge, TN 37725-4428, USA

Macknowski, Stephen (Athlete)
462 Kimball Ave
Yonkers, NY 10704-2329, USA

Mackovic, John (Athlete, Football Coach, Football Player)
114 Rancho Del Sol
Camino, CA 95709-9318, USA

Mackrides, William (Athlete, Football Player)
23 Roberts Rd
Newtown Square, PA 19073-2011, USA

MacLachian, Kyle (Actor)
955 Carrillo Dr Ste 300
Los Angeles, CA 90048-5400, USA

MacLachlan, Janet
1919 Taft Ave
Los Angeles, CA 90068-3620

MacLachlan, Kyle (Actor)
c/o David Seltzer *Management 360*
9111 Wilshire Blvd
Beverly Hills, CA 90210-5508, USA

MacLachlan, Patricia (Writer)
21 Unquomonk Rd
Williamsburg, MA 01096-9718, USA

MacLaine, Shirley (Actor, Writer)
PO Box 25962
Munds Park, AZ 86017-5962, USA

MacLane, Saunders (Mathematician)
5401 Westbard Ave Unit 115
Bethesda, MD 20816-1424, USA

MacLean, Bonnie (Artist)
PO Box 103
Buckingham, PA 18912-0103, USA

MacLean, Don (Athlete, Basketball Player)
216 Los Padres Dr
Thousand Oaks, CA 91361-1333, USA

MacLean, Doug (Coach)
330 Tucker Dr
Worthington, OH 43085-3030, USA

MacLean, Steven G (Astronaut)
6767 Route De Aeroport
Saint-Hubert, QC J3Y 8Y9, CANADA

MacLean-Ross, Lucella (Baseball Player)
401-5107 47th St
Lloydminster, AB T9V 0G1, CANADA

MacLeish, Rick (Athlete, Hockey Player)
5612 Bay Ave
Ocean City, NJ 08226-1000, USA

Maclennan, Robert A R (Government Official)
74 Abingdon Villas
London W8 6XB, UNITED KINGDOM (UK)

Macleod, Bill (Athlete, Baseball Player)
14 Heritage Way
Marblehead, MA 01945-2332, USA

MacLeod, Gavin (Actor)
70070 Frank Sinatra Dr Apt 7
Rancho Mirage, CA 92270-2538, USA

MacLeod, John (Athlete, Basketball Player, Coach)
4610 E Fanfol Dr
Phoenix, AZ 85028-5206, USA

MacLeod, Lewis (Actor)
c/o Staff Member *Hobsons International*
62 Chiswick High Road
London W4 1SY, United Kingdom

Macleod, Tom (Athlete, Football Player)
RR 5 Box 431
Spokane, WA 99208, USA

Maclin, Lonnie (Athlete, Baseball Player)
9635 Meeks Blvd
Saint Louis, MO 63132-1507, USA

MacMahon, Brian (Misc)
89 Warren St
Needham, MA 02492-3115, USA

MacMahon, Julian (Actor)

MacMillan, Shannon (Soccer Player)
Athletic Dept
Portland, OR 97203, USA

MacMurray, William (Engineer)
200 Deer Run Dr
Schaghticoke, NY 12154-3607, USA

MacNabb, B Gordon (Engineer)
1406 Praine Ave
Cheyenne, WY 82009, USA

Macnee, Patrick (Actor)
PO Box 1853
Rancho Mirage, CA 92270-1081, USA

MacNeil, Bernie (Athlete, Hockey Player)
1014 Cunningham Rd
Kingston, ON K7L 4V3, Canada

MacNeil, Cornell H (Opera Singer)
165 W 57th St
New York, NY 10019-2201, USA

MacNeil, Robert (Correspondent, Writer)
c/o Staff Member *Penguin Press HC*
375 Hudson St Bsmt 3
New York, NY 10014-7465, USA

MacNichol, Peter (Actor)
8942 Wilshire Blvd # 219
Beverly Hills, CA 90211-1908, USA

MacNicol, Peter (Actor)
c/o Ron West *Thruline Entertainment*
9250 Wilshire Blvd Ground Fl
Beverly Hills, CA 90212, USA

Macomber, Debbie (Writer)
c/o Irene Goodman *Irene Goodman Literary Agency*
27 W 24th St Ste 700B
New York, NY 10010-4105, USA

Macomber, Dick (Jockey)
6720 NW 28th Ter
Fort Lauderdale, FL 33309-1320, USA

Macomber, George B H (Skier)
1 Design Center Pl Ste 600
Boston, MA 02210-2349, USA

Macosko, Anna (Athlete, Golfer)
304 Earl Dr
Kerrville, TX 78028-7019, USA

MacPhail, Andy (Baseball Player)
12403 Hunters Gln
Owings Mills, MD 21117-1040, USA

Macphail, Lee (Athlete, Baseball Player)
4474 N Ocean Blvd Apt 6A
Delray Beach, FL 33483, USA

Macphail, Lee (Athlete, Baseball Player)
33 Wildwood Rd
Scarsdale, NY 10583-7436, USA

Macpherson, Daniel (Actor)
c/o Staff Member *Morrissey Management*
77 Glebe Point Road
Sydney NSW 2037, AUSTRALIA

MacPherson, Dick (Athlete, Football Coach, Football Player)
6202 the Hamlet
Jamesville, NY 13078-9785, USA

MacPherson, Duncan I (Cartoonist, Editor)
Editorial Dept 1 Yonge St
Toronto, ON M5E 1E6, CANADA

Macpherson, Elle (Model)
c/o Michael McConnell *Don Buchwald & Associates Inc (LA)*
6500 Wilshire Blvd Ste 2200
Los Angeles, CA 90048-4942, USA

Macpherson, Harry (Athlete, Baseball Player)
971 Bay Vista Blvd
Englewood, FL 34223-2405, USA

Macpherson, Wendy (Bowler)
PO Box 93433
Henderson, NV 89009-3433, USA

MacQuitty, Jonathan (Inventor)
2465 E Bayshore Rd Ste 348
Palo Alto, CA 94303-3227, USA

Macrae, Scott (Athlete, Baseball Player)
1164 Forest Brook Ct
Marietta, GA 30068-2827, USA

MacRae, Sheila (Actor, Musician)
666 W End Ave Apt 10H
New York, NY 10025-1448, USA

MacTavish, Craig (Athlete, Coach, Hockey Player)
3 Quail Hollow Ct
Voorhees, NJ 08043-2800, USA

Maculan, Tim (Actor)
c/o Christopher Black *Opus Entertainment*
5225 Wilshire Blvd Ste 905
Los Angeles, CA 90036-4353, USA

Macwhorter, Keith (Athlete, Baseball Player)
75 Martin St
Rehoboth, MA 02769-2114, USA

Macy, Bill (Actor)
10130 Angelo Cir
Beverly Hills, CA 90210-2701, USA

Macy, Geoffrey W (Astronomer)
Integrative Planetary Science Ctr
Berkeley, CA 94720-0001, USA

Macy, Kyle (Athlete, Basketball Player)
3320 Overbrook Dr
Lexington, KY 40502-3352, USA

Macy, William H (Actor)
c/o Peter Levine *Creative Artists Agency (CAA-LA)*
2000 Avenue of the Stars Ste 100
Los Angeles, CA 90067-4705, USA

Maczuzak, John (Athlete, Football Player)
9070 Lucia Ln
Irwin, PA 15642-4913, USA

Madadian, Andy (Actor, Bollywood)
c/o Staff Member *Cherokee Productions*
8491 W Sunset Blvd # 277
Los Angeles, CA 90069-1911, USA

Madball (Musician)
c/o Paul Gourlie *Agency Group Ltd, The (LA)*
1880 Century Park E Ste 711
Los Angeles, CA 90067-1618, USA

Maddalena, Julie (Actor)
c/o Staff Member *Tisherman Gilbert Motley Drozdoski Talent Agency (TGMD)*
6767 Forest Lawn Dr Ste 101
Los Angeles, CA 90068-1050, USA

Maddaloni, Martin J (Misc)
901 Massachusetts Ave NW
Washington, DC 20001-4307, USA

Madden, Benji (Musician)
c/o Staff Member *Creative Artists Agency (CAA-LA)*
2000 Avenue of the Stars Ste 100
Los Angeles, CA 90067-4705, USA

Madden, D S (Religious Leader)
4605 N State Line Ave
Texarkana, TX 75503-2916, USA

Madden, Dave (Actor)
1009 Flora Parke Dr
Saint Johns, FL 32259-4255, USA

Madden, David (Writer)
US Civil War Ctr
Baton Rouge, LA 70803-0001, USA

Madden, Diane (Dancer)
211 W 61st St
New York, NY 10023-7832, USA

Madden, Joel (Musician)
c/o Brian Greenbaum *Creative Artists Agency (CAA-LA)*
2000 Avenue of the Stars Ste 100
Los Angeles, CA 90067-4705, USA

Madden, John (Director)
c/o Jenne Casarotto *Casarotto Ramsay & Associates Ltd (UK)*
Waverley House 7-12 Noel St
London W1F 8GQ, UK

Madden, John E (Athlete, Football Coach, Football Player, Sportscaster)
5955 Coronado Ln
Pleasanton, CA 94588-8518, USA

Madden, John P (Director)
52/53 Poland Place
London W1F 7LX, UNITED KINGDOM (UK)

Madden, Mike (Athlete, Baseball Player)
4733 Frankfort Way
Denver, CO 80239-5922, USA

Madden, Morris (Athlete, Baseball Player)
105 Jennings St
Laurens, SC 29360-3317, USA

Madden, Steve (Designer)
5216 Barnett Ave
Long Island City, NY 11104-1018, USA

Maddix, Raydell (Athlete, Baseball Player)
3724 E North Bay St
Tampa, FL 33610-7959, USA

Maddock, Robert (Athlete, Football Player)
3541 Geranium Ave
Corona Del Mar, CA 92625-1673, USA

Maddon, Joe (Athlete, Baseball Player, Coach)
2560 N Lindsay Rd Unit 32
Mesa, AZ 85213-1520, USA

Maddow, Rachel (Actor, Journalist, Radio Personality)
c/o Staff Member *MSNBC (DC)*
400 N Capitol St NW Ste 850
Washington, DC 20001-1555, USA

Maddox, Elliott (Athlete, Baseball Player)
980 Coral Ridge Dr Apt 104
Coral Springs, FL 33071-4148, USA

Maddox, Garry (Athlete, Baseball Player)
312 Wynne Ln
Penn Valley, PA 19072-1338, USA

Maddox, Jerry (Athlete, Baseball Player)
20647 Thundersky Cir
Riverside, CA 92508-3177, USA

Maddox, Mark (Athlete, Football Player)
1020 E Mountain Vista Dr
Phoenix, AZ 85048-1904, USA

Maddox, Robert (Athlete, Football Player)
7612 Colson Dr
Louisville, KY 40220-3358, USA

Maddux, Greg (Athlete, Baseball Player)
36 Innisbrook Ave
Las Vegas, NV 89113-1225, USA

Maddux, Mike (Athlete, Baseball Player)
3172 N Rainbow Blvd Unit 225
Las Vegas, NV 89108-4534, USA

Maddy, Penelope Jo (Misc)
Philosophy Dept
Irvine, CA 92717, USA

Madekwe, Ashley (Actor)
c/o Jeff Golenberg *Collective*
8383 Wilshire Blvd Ste 1050
Beverly Hills, CA 90211-2415, USA

Mader, Gunther (Skier)
Am Brenner # 28
Hartford, CT 06156-0001, AUSTRIA

Mader, Rebecca (Actor)
c/o Paul Nelson *Mosaic Media Group*
9200 W Sunset Blvd Ste 10
Los Angeles, CA 90069-3608, USA

Maderos, George (Athlete, Football Player)
12 Spinnaker Way
Chico, CA 95926-1627, USA

Madfai, Kahtan al (Architect)
22 Vassileos Constantinou
Athens 11635, GREECE

Madhavi (Actor, Bollywood)
21/C Neha Ave Juhu Tara Rd
Mumbai, MS 400049, INDIA

Madhoo (Actor, Bollywood)
Krishna Kutir Sagarika Society Juhu Tara Road
Bombay, MS 400049, INDIA

Madhubala (Actor, Bollywood)
Krishna Kutir 1 Juhu Tara Road
Mumbai, MS 400049, INDIA

Madi, Ferenc (President)
Egyetem Ter 1-3
Budapest 1364, HUNGARY

Madigan, Amy (Actor)
c/o Staff Member *Industry Entertainment Partners*
955 Carrillo Dr Ste 300
Los Angeles, CA 90048-5400, USA

Madigan, John W (Business Person, Publisher)
435 N Michigan Ave Ste 1800
Chicago, IL 60611-4030, USA

Madigan, Kathleen (Comedian)
c/o Staff Member *Gersh (LA)*
9465 Wilshire Blvd Ste 600
Beverly Hills, CA 90212-2612, USA

Madigan, Martha (Photographer)
Philadelphia, PA 19126, USA

Madigan, Sam (Athlete, Football Player)
3685 Heron Ridge Ln
Weston, FL 33331-3711, USA

Madio, James (Actor)
c/o Melisa Spamer *Domain Talent*
9229 W Sunset Blvd Ste 710
Los Angeles, CA 90069-3407, USA

Madison, Bailee (Actor)
c/o Chris Rossi *Rossi Public Relations (RPR)*
4705 Laurel Canyon Blvd Ste 306
Studio City, CA 91607-5940, USA

Madison, Holly (Model, Reality TV Star)
c/o Jason Verona *Marc Entertainment*
9903 Santa Monica Blvd # 523
Beverly Hills, CA 90212-1671, USA

Madison, Martha (Actor)
c/o Jason Egenberg *United Talent Agency (UTA)*
9560 Wilshire Blvd Fl 5
Beverly Hills, CA 90212-2400, USA

Madison, Sarah Danielle (Actor)
c/o Connie Tavel *Forward Entertainment*
9255 W Sunset Blvd Ste 805
Los Angeles, CA 90069-3305, USA

Madison, Scotty (Athlete, Baseball Player)
5397 Thornapple Ln NW
Acworth, GA 30101-7886, USA

Madkins, Gerald (Athlete, Basketball Player)
528 W 8th St
Merced, CA 95341-6023, USA

Madlock, Bill (Athlete, Baseball Player)
1565 Calle Del Estribo
Pacific Palisades, CA 90272-2009, USA

Madoff, Bernard (Bernie) (Business Person)
PO Box 999
Butner, NC 27509-0999, USA

Madonna (Actor, Dancer, Musician, Songwriter)
c/o Jason Weinberg *Untitled Entertainment (LA)*
350 S Beverly Dr Ste 200
Beverly Hills, CA 90212-4819, USA

Madrazo, Ignacio N (Doctor)
Av Paseo de la Reforma #476 1er Piso
Col Juarez CP, DF 6698, MEXICO

Madrid, Alex (Athlete, Baseball Player)
PO Box 1974
Saint Johns, AZ 85936-1974, USA

Madritsch, Bobby (Athlete, Baseball Player)
8628 Linder Ave
Burbank, IL 60459-2928, USA

Madrugada (Music Group)
c/o Staff Member *Paradigm (Monterey)*
404 W Franklin St
Monterey, CA 93940-2303, USA

Madsen, Loren (Artist)
426 Broome St
New York, NY 10013-3251, USA

Madsen, Michael (Actor)
c/o Chuck Binder *Binder & Associates*
1465 Lindacrest Dr
Beverly Hills, CA 90210-2519, USA

Madsen, Virgina (Actor)
c/o Katie Rhodes *Untitled Entertainment (LA)*
350 S Beverly Dr Ste 200
Beverly Hills, CA 90212-4819, USA

Madsen, Virginia (Actor)
c/o Katie Rhodes *Untitled Entertainment (LA)*
350 S Beverly Dr Ste 200
Beverly Hills, CA 90212-4819, USA

Madson, Michael (Actor)
9100 Wilshire Blvd Ste 100W
Beverly Hills, CA 90212-3435, USA

Madson, Ryan (Athlete, Baseball Player)
75 Mullen Dr
Sicklerville, NJ 08081-1300, USA

Madura, Ricardo (President)
Blvd Juan Pablo II
Tegucigalpa, HONDURAS

Maduro, Calvin (Athlete, Baseball Player)
793 Springdale Dr
Millersville, MD 21108-1435, USA

Mae, Vanessa (Actor, Musician)
c/o Staff Member *Agency Group Ltd, The (UK)*
361-373 City Rd
London EC1V 1PQ, UK

Maegte, Richard L (Dick) (Athlete, Football Player)
4047 Aberdeen Way
Houston, TX 77025-2305, USA

Maestri, Hector (Athlete, Baseball Player)
581 SW 89th Ct
Miami, FL 33174-2338, USA

Maestro, Mia (Actor)
c/o Pamela Kohl *3 Arts Entertainment Inc*
9460 Wilshire Blvd Fl 7
Beverly Hills, CA 90212-2713, USA

Maffay, Peter
Klenzestr. 1
Tutzing, GERMANY D-82327

Maffett, Debra
1525 McGavock St
Nashville, TN 37203

Maffett, Debra Sue (Debbie) (Beauty Pageant Winner)
1525 McGavock St
Nashville, TN 37203, USA

Maffia, Roma (Actor)
c/o Staff Member *Stone Manners Salners Agency (LA)*
9911 W Pico Blvd Ste 1400
Los Angeles, CA 90035-2715, USA

Magadan, Dave (Athlete, Baseball Player)
3733 Johnathon Ave
Palm Harbor, FL 34685-3605, USA

Magallanes, Ever (Athlete, Baseball Player)
17597 W Aster Dr
Surprise, AZ 85388-5656, USA

Magaw, John W (Government Official, Lawyer)
400 7th St SW
Washington, DC 20590, USA

Magaziner, Henry J (Architect)
1504 South St
Philadelphia, PA 19146-1636, USA

Magee, Alex (Athlete, Football Player)
c/o Roosevelt Barnes *Maximum Sports Management*
6435 W Jefferson Blvd # 197
Fort Wayne, IN 46804-6203, USA

Magee, Andrew (Andy) (Athlete, Golfer)
6100 E Huntress Dr
Paradise Valley, AZ 85253-4217, USA

Magee, Dave (Race Car Driver)
5S350 Deer Ridge Path
Big Rock, IL 60511-9777, USA

Magee, Wendell (Athlete, Baseball Player)
6500 Muskogee Cv
Leeds, AL 35094-3868, USA

Maggard, Amy (Stylist)
c/o Staff Member *Creative Talent Columbus*
5864 Nike Dr
Hilliard, OH 43026-8756, USA

Maggard, Dave (Athlete, Track Athlete)
Athletic
Houston, TX 77204-0001, USA

Maggart, Brandon (Actor)
8730 W Sunset Blvd Ste 480
Los Angeles, CA 90069-2277

Maggart, Garett (Actor)
c/o Staff Member *SDB Partners Inc*
1801 Avenue of the Stars Ste 902
Los Angeles, CA 90067-5981, USA

Maggert, Jeff (Athlete, Golfer)
62 W Bracebridge Cir
Spring, TX 77382-2539, USA

Maggette, Corey (Basketball Player)
Staples Center 1111 S Figueroa St
Los Angeles, CA 90015, USA

Magic Numbers, The (Music Group)
c/o Staff Member *Paradigm (Monterey)*
404 W Franklin St
Monterey, CA 93940-2303, USA

Magill, Frank J (Judge)
657 2nd Ave N
Fargo, ND 58102-4765, USA

Magilton, Gerald E (Jerry) (Astronaut)
100 Campus Dr
Newtown, PA 18940-1784, USA

Maginnes, John (Athlete, Golfer)
612 Topwater Ln
Greensboro, NC 27455-3458, USA

Magistretti, Vico (Architect)
Via Conservatorio 20
Milan, ITALY

Magliozzi, Ray (Television Host)
c/o Staff Member *Car Talk Plaza*
Harvard St Apt 3500
Cambridge, MA 02138-4117, USA

Magliozzi, Tom (Actor, Television Host)
c/o Staff Member *Car Talk Plaza*
Harvard St Apt 3500
Cambridge, MA 02138-4117, USA

Magnante, Mike (Athlete, Baseball Player)
5305 Via Quinto
Newbury Park, CA 91320-6937, USA

Magnus, Edie (Correspondent)
30 Rockefeller Plz
New York, NY 10112-0015, USA

Magnus, Robert (General)
2 Navy St
Washington, DC 20380-0001, USA

Magnus, Sandra H (Sandy) (Astronaut)
3477 Vinings North Trl SE
Smyrna, GA 30080-4581, USA

Magnus, Siobhan (Musician)
c/o Simon Fuller *XIX Entertainment*
33/32 Ransomes Dock 35-37 Parkgate Rd
London SW11 4NP, UK

Magnuson, Ann
1317 Maltman Ave
Los Angeles, CA 90026-6224

Magnussen, Karen
2852 Thorndiff Dr
N. Vancouver BC, CANADA V7R 285

Magoon, Bob (Misc)
1688 Meridian Ave
Miami Beach, FL 33139-2710, USA

Magowan, Peter (Baseball Player)
2100 Washington St
San Francisco, CA 94109-2845, USA

Magrane, Joe (Athlete, Baseball Player)
705 Guisando De Avila
Tampa, FL 33613-5204, USA

Magrann, Tom (Athlete, Baseball Player)
910 N 31st Ct
Hollywood, FL 33021-5509, USA

Magri, Charles G (Charlie) (Boxer)
345 Bethnal Green Road Bethnal Green
London E2 6LG, UNITED KINGDOM (UK)

Magrini, Pete (Athlete, Baseball Player)
2402 Rancho Cabeza Dr
Santa Rosa, CA 95404-2326, USA

Magro, Ronnie (Fist Pump) (Reality TV Star)
c/o Matt Cohen *IAG Entertainment & Sports*
5189 Argonne Ct
San Diego, CA 92117-1054, USA

Magruder, Chris (Athlete, Baseball Player)
1740 Leisure Ln
Yakima, WA 98908-9224, USA

Magsamen, Sandra (Artist, Writer)
557 Broadway
New York, NY 10012-3962, USA

Maguire, Adrian E (Jockey)
42 Portman Square
London W1H 0EM, UNITED KINGDOM (UK)

Maguire, Gregory (Writer)
1350 Avenue of the Americas
New York, NY 10019-4702, USA

Maguire, Les (Musician)
21A Cliftown Road Southend-on-Sea
Essex SS1 1AB, UNITED KINGDOM (UK)

Maguire, Paul L (Athlete, Football Player, Sportscaster)
707 Ocean Blvd
Isle Of Palms, SC 29451-2136, USA

Maguire, Richard W (Cinematographer)
605 Summer Mesa Dr
Las Vegas, NV 89144-1502, USA

Maguire, Sean (Actor)
c/o Staff Member *The Management Company*
2030 Pinehurst Rd
Los Angeles, CA 90068-3732, USA

Maguire, Tobey (Actor)
c/o Kelly Bush *ID PR (LA)*
7060 Hollywood Blvd Fl 8
Los Angeles, CA 90028-6014, USA

Maguson, Keith A (Athlete, Hockey Player)
265 King Muir Rd
Lake Forest, IL 60045-2034, USA

Magyar, Derek (Actor)
c/o Staff Member *Wilkins Management*
12200 W Olympic Blvd Ste 400
Los Angeles, CA 90064-1047, USA

Mahaffey, Arthur (Art) (Athlete, Baseball Player)
PO Box 1212
Allentown, PA 18105-1212, USA

Mahaffey, John (Athlete, Golfer)
594 Sawdust Rd Unit 229
Spring, TX 77380-2215, USA

Mahaffey, Randy (Athlete, Basketball Player)
25 Berkeley Rd
Avondale Estates, GA 30002-1468, USA

Mahaffey, Valerie (Actor)
c/o Steven Muller *Innovative Artists (LA)*
1505 10th St
Santa Monica, CA 90401-2805, USA

Mahaffey, Valerio
121 N San Vicente Blvd
Beverly Hills, CA 90211-2303

Mahal, Taj (Musician, Songwriter, Writer)
c/o Staff Member *Red Light Management (LA)*
8439 W Sunset Blvd Ste 2
Los Angeles, CA 90069-1925, USA

Mahalingam, Gemini (Actor)
47 Harrington Rd
Chennai, TN 600 031, INDIA

Mahan, Art (Athlete, Baseball Player)
418 Glenmore Ave
Elkins Park, PA 19027-1841, USA

Mahan, Hunter (Athlete, Golfer)
24 Lake View Dr
Trabuco Canyon, CA 92679-5119, USA

Mahan, Larry
PO Box 41
Camp Verde, TX 78010-0041

Mahan, Lawrence (Larry) (Rodeo Rider)
PO Box 119
Sunset, TX 76270-0119, USA

Maharidge, Date D (Writer)
Communications Dept
Stanford, CA 94305, USA

Maharis, George (Actor)
9401 Wilshire Blvd Ste 700
Beverly Hills, CA 90212-2944, USA

Mahay, Ron (Athlete, Baseball Player)
13177 E Cochise Rd
Scottsdale, AZ 85259-5304, USA

Maher, Bill (Talk Show Host)
c/o Marc Gurvitz *Brillstein Entertainment Partners*
9150 Wilshire Blvd Ste 350
Beverly Hills, CA 90212-3453, USA

Maher, Sean
c/o Staff Member *Gersh (LA)*
9465 Wilshire Blvd Ste 600
Beverly Hills, CA 90212-2612, USA

Maheswari (Actor, Bollywood)
9 N Ave Sree Nagar Colony Saidapet
Chennai, TN 600015, INDIA

Maheu, Robert (Government Official, Misc)
2140 Vista Famosa Ct
Las Vegas, NV 89123-4304, USA

Mahindra, Anan (Business Person)
Mahindra Towers G.M. Bhosale Marg, Worli
Mumbai 400 018, India

Mahlberg, Greg (Athlete, Baseball Player)
5100 N Placita Del Lazo
Tucson, AZ 85750-1535, USA

Mahler, Mickey (Athlete, Baseball Player)
7911 Quirt St
San Antonio, TX 78227-2636, USA

Mahogany, Kevin (Actor, Musician)
173 Brighton Ave
Boston, MA 02134-2003, USA

Maholm, Paul (Athlete, Baseball Player)
518 Village Green Blvd W
Mars, PA 16046-4816, USA

Mahomes, Patrick (Baseball Player)
PO Box 1025
Lindale, TX 75771-1025, USA

Mahon, Sean (Actor)
c/o Staff Member *McCabe Group, The*
3211 Cahuenga Blvd W Ste 104
Los Angeles, CA 90068-1372, USA

Mahoney, Brian (Athlete, Basketball Player)
96 Greystone Rd
Rockville Centre, NY 11570-4515, USA

Mahoney, David L (Business Person)
1 Post St
San Francisco, CA 94104-5201, USA

Mahoney, Jim (Athlete, Baseball Player)
345 Hawthorne Ave # 2
Hawthorne, NJ 07506-1244, USA

Mahoney, John (Actor)
c/o Staff Member *International Creative Management (ICM-NY)*
40 W 57th St
New York, NY 10019-4001, USA

Mahoney, Marle (Baseball Player)
207 Birdsall St
Houston, TX 77007-8107, USA

Mahoney, Mike (Athlete, Baseball Player)
4412 98th St
Urbandale, IA 50322-1362, USA

Mahony, Cardinal Roger
1531 W 9th St
Los Angeles, CA 90012

Mahood, Beverly (Musician)
c/o Staff Member *Paquin Entertainment Agency*
468 Stradbrook Ave
Winnipeg, Manitoba R3L 0J9, Canada

Mahorn, Rick (Athlete, Basketball Player)
3091 Mapleridge Ct
Rochester Hills, MI 48309-4505, USA

Mahovlich, Francis W (Frank) (Athlete, Hockey Player)
2-954 Ave Rd
Toronto, ON M5P 2K8, Canada

Mahre, Phil
PO Box 100
Park City, UT 84060-0100, USA

Mahre, Phillip (Phil) (Skier)
70 Roza View Dr
Yakima, WA 98901-9390, USA

Mahre, Steve (Athlete, Skier)
1041 Red Sky Dr
Yakima, WA 98903-9309, USA

Maida, Adam J Cardinal (Religious Leader)
1234 Washington Blvd
Detroit, MI 48226-1894, USA

Maida, Raine (Musician)
c/o Staff Member *Paradigm (Monterey)*
404 W Franklin St
Monterey, CA 93940-2303, USA

Maiden-Naccarato, Jeanne (Bowler)
1 N Stadium Way Apt 4
Tacoma, WA 98403-3154, USA

Maier, Hermann (Skier)
Reitdorf 116
Flachau 5542, AUSTRIA

Maier, Pat (Stylist)
c/o Staff Member *Arlene Wilson Management*
807 N Jefferson St # 200
Milwaukee, WI 53202-8150, USA

Maier, Pauline R (Historian)
60 Larchwood Dr
Cambridge, MA 02138-4639, USA

Maier, Sepp (Soccer Player)
Anzing 84405, GERMANY

Mailhouse, Robert (Actor)
1623 N Dillon St
Los Angeles, CA 90026-1203, USA

Mailinvaud, Edmond (Economist)
42 Ave de Saxe
Paris 75007, FRANCE

Maillard, Carol (Musician)
PO Box 600099
Newtonville, MA 02460-0001, USA

Maiman, Theodore H (Ted) (Inventor)
15A Alberni St
Vancouver, BC V6G 3N7, CANADA

Maine, John (Athlete, Baseball Player)
129 Richards Ferry Rd
Fredericksburg, VA 22406-4812, USA

Maines, Natalie (Musician)
c/o Simon Renshaw *Strategics Artist Management*
1100 Glendon Ave Ste 1000
Los Angeles, CA 90024-3514, USA

Maire, Annie (Stylist)
c/o Staff Member *Ford Models (Miami)*
311 Lincoln Rd Ste 205
Miami Beach, FL 33139-3150, USA

Mairena, Oswaldo (Athlete, Baseball Player)
160 E 6th Pl
Mesa, AZ 85201-5068, USA

Maisel, Jay (Photographer)
190 Bowery
New York, NY 10012-4203, USA

Maisel, Lucian (Actor)
c/o Marc Hamou *Thruline Entertainment*
9250 Wilshire Blvd Ground Fl
Beverly Hills, CA 90212, USA

Maisel, Sherman J (Economist)
2164 Hyde St
San Francisco, CA 94109-1701, USA

Maisenberg, Olega (Musician)
In Der Gugl 9
Klostemeuburg, AUSTRIA

Maisky, Mischa M (Musician)
165 W 57th St
New York, NY 10019-2201, USA

Maisonneuve, Brian (Soccer Player)
2121 Volman Ave
Columbus, OH 43211, USA

Majdarzavyn, Ganzorig (Cosmonaut)
Peace Ave 54B
Ulan Bator 51, MONGOLIA

Majerle, Dan (Athlete, Basketball Player)
4534 E Oregon Ave
Phoenix, AZ 85018-1718, USA

Majerus, Rick (Basketball Player, Coach)
ESPN Plaza 935 Middle St
Bristol, CT 6010, USA

Majewski, Gary (Athlete, Baseball Player)
1103 Chamboard Ln
Houston, TX 77018-3212, USA

Majewski, Val (Athlete, Baseball Player)
890 Oakley Dr
Freehold, NJ 07728-8237, USA

Majoli, Iva (Tennis Player)
27 Framingham Ln
Pittsford, NY 14534-1047, USA

Major, Clarence L (Writer)
English Dept Voorhies Hall
Davis, CA 95616, USA

Major, John (Prime Minister)
8 Stuckley Road
Huntingdon, Cambs, UNITED KINGDOM (UK)

Majoras, Deborah (Government Official)
Pennsylvania Ave & 6th St NW
Washington, DC 20580, USA

Majorino, Tina (Actor)
c/o Sarah Lum *Leverage Management*
3030 Pennsylvania Ave
Santa Monica, CA 90404-4112, USA

Majors, Austin
3940 Laurel Canyon Blvd # 177
Studio City, CA 91604-3709

Majors, John I (Johnny) (Athlete, Coach, Football Coach, Football Player)
4207 Beechwood Rd
Knoxville, TN 37920-6011, USA

Majors, Lee (Actor)
c/o David Shapira *David Shapira & Associates*
193 N Robertson Blvd
Beverly Hills, CA 90211-2103, USA

MajorSundararajan (Actor)
9 Pooram Prakash Rao Street Balaji Nagar Royapeta
Chennai, TN 600 014, INDIA

Majumder, Shaun (Musician)
c/o Staff Member *Paradigm (Monterey)*
404 W Franklin St
Monterey, CA 93940-2303, USA

Makarov, Askold A (Dancer)
Plutalova Str 18-4
Saint Petersburg 197136, RUSSIA

Makarov, Sergei (Athlete, Hockey Player)
4072 Teale Ave
San Jose, CA 95117-3432, USA

Makarova, Inna V (Actor)
Ukrainian Blvd 11
Moscow 121059, RUSSIA

Makarova, Natalia R (Ballerina)
119 W 57th St Ste 1505
New York, NY 10019-2403, USA

Make Good Your Escape (Music Group)
c/o Staff Member *Paradigm (Monterey)*
404 W Franklin St
Monterey, CA 93940-2303, USA

Makhalina, Yufia (Ballerina)
1 Pl Iskusstr
Saint Petersburg 190000, RUSSIA

Makings, Elizabeth (Athlete, Golfer)
10063 E San Bernardo Dr
Scottsdale, AZ 85258-5665, USA

Makinson, Jessica (Comedian)
c/o Staff Member *OmniPop Talent Group*
10700 Ventura Blvd Fl 2
Studio City, CA 91604-3561, USA

Makk, Karoly (Director)
Hanoczy Jeno Utca 15
Budapest 1022, HUNGARY

Makkena, Wendy (Actor)
c/o Staff Member *Schumacher Management*
1122 San Vicente Blvd
Santa Monica, CA 90402-2008, USA

Mako (Actor)
6477 Peppertree Ln
Somis, CA 93066-9758, USA

Mako, C Gene (Tennis Player)
430 S Burnside Ave Apt Mc
Los Angeles, CA 90036-5319, USA

Makowski, Tom (Athlete, Baseball Player)
6686 Omphalius Rd
Colden, NY 14033-9763, USA

Maksimoya, Yekaterina S (Ballerina)
Teatrainsya Pl 1
Moscow 103009, RUSSIA

Maksudian, Mike (Athlete, Baseball Player)
12148 E San Simeon Dr
Scottsdale, AZ 85259-6049, USA

Maksymiuk, Jerzy
Hoza 5A m 13
Warsaw 00-528, POLAND

Malach-Webb, Kay (Baseball Player)
3257 Louisville Rd
Louisville, TN 37777-3732, USA

Malahide, Patrick (Actor)
76 Oxford St
London W1N 0AX, UNITED KINGDOM (UK)

Malakar, Sanjaya (Musician, Reality TV Star)
c/o Staff Member *SUM Company*
10736 Jefferson Blvd # 140
Culver City, CA 90230-4933, USA

Malakhov, Vladimir (Athlete, Hockey Player)
10225 Collins Ave Apt 302
Bal Harbour, FL 33154-1400, USA

Malakian, Daron (Musician)
9911 W Pico Blvd # 350
Los Angeles, CA 90035-2703, USA

Malandrino, Catherine (Designer, Fashion Designer)
468 Broome St
New York, NY 10013-2611, USA

Malandro, Kristina (Actor)
2518 Cardigan Ct
Los Angeles, CA 90077-1337, USA

Malanowski-Marlowe, Jean (Baseball Player)
100 Smallacombe Dr # 205-24
Scranton, PA 18508-2650, USA

Malaska, Mark (Athlete, Baseball Player)
3823 Cumberland Dr
Youngstown, OH 44515-4610, USA

Malatesta, Romina Herrera (Stylist)
c/o Staff Member *Michele Filomeno New York LLC*
515 Greenwich St Ste 503
New York, NY 10013-1097, USA

Malavoy, Christopher
9 Sq De Montsouris
Paris, FRANCE F-75014

Malaysia Vasudevan (Actor)
5 Kaman Street Sfi Apts 6-B Samiyar Matt
Chennai, TN 600 024, INDIA

Malchow, Tom
1 Olympic Plz
Colorado Springs, CO 80909-5780

Malco, Romany (Actor)
c/o Staff Member *Mosaic Media Group*
9200 W Sunset Blvd Ste 10
Los Angeles, CA 90069-3608, USA

Malcolm, George J (Musician)
99 Wimbledon Hill Road
London SW19 4BE, UNITED KINGDOM (UK)

Malcomson, Paula (Actor, Producer)
c/o Sean Fay *Kritzer Levine Wilkins Entertainment*
11872 La Grange Ave Fl 1
Los Angeles, CA 90025-5283, USA

Maldacena, Juan (Physicist)
Physics Dept
Cambridge, MA 2138, USA

Maldini, Paolo (Coach, Soccer Player)
3 Turati Via
Washington, DC 20221-0001, ITALY

Maldonado, Candy (Athlete, Baseball Player)
HC 2 Box 16800
Arecibo, PR 00612-9396, USA

Maleeva, Katerina (Tennis Player)
Mladostr 1 #45 NH 14
Sofia 1174, BULGARIA

Maleeva-Fragniere, Manuela (Tennis Player)
Bourg-Dessous 28
La Tour de Peitz 1814, SWITZERLAND

Malek, Rami (Actor)
c/o Kyle Fritz *Kyle Fritz Management*
6325 Heather Dr
Los Angeles, CA 90068-1633, USA

Malenchenko, Yuri I (Cosmonaut)
Moskovskoi Oblasti
Syvisdny Goroduk 141160, RUSSIA

Maler, Jim (Athlete, Baseball Player)
5132 SW 129th Ter
Miramar, FL 33027-5839, USA

Malerba, Franco E (Astronaut)
Via Cantore 10
Genova 16149, ITALY

Malerba, Luigi
Via Tro Millina 31
Rome, CA ITALY

Maley, David (Athlete, Hockey Player)
800 Embedded Way
San Jose, CA 95138-1074, USA

Malhotra, Harmesh (Bollywood, Director, Filmmaker, Producer)
32A Sunset Heights 59 Pali Hill Nargis Dutt Road Bandra
Bombay, MS 400 050, INDIA

Malick, Terrence (Director, Producer)
c/o Roeg Sutherland *Creative Artists Agency (CAA-LA)*
2000 Avenue of the Stars Ste 100
Los Angeles, CA 90067-4705, USA

Malick, Wendie (Actor, Model)
c/o Nevin Dolcefino *Innovative Artists (LA)*
1505 10th St
Santa Monica, CA 90401-2805, USA

malicki-Sanchez, Keram (Actor)
c/o Tiffany Kuzon *Evolution Entertainment (LA)*
901 N Highland Ave
Los Angeles, CA 90038-2412, USA

Malicky, Neal (Educator)
President's Office
Berea, OH 44017, USA

Malielegaoi, Tuilaepa Sailele (Prime Minister)
PO Box L1861
Vailima, Apia, SAMOA

Malige, Didier (Stylist)
c/o Staff Member *Mercury Artists*
8460 Higuera St Fl 2
Culver City, CA 90232-2520, USA

Malik, Art (Actor)
18 Sydney Mews
London SW3 6HL, UNITED KINGDOM (UK)

Malil, Shelley (Actor)
c/o Mark Measures *Abrams Artists Agency (LA)*
9200 W Sunset Blvd PH 11
Los Angeles, CA 90069-3601, USA

Malina, Josh
2262 Cloverfield Blvd
Santa Monica, CA 90405-1821

Malina, Joshua (Actor, Producer)
c/o David Ginsberg *Insight*
1134 S Cloverdale Ave
Los Angeles, CA 90019-6737, USA

Malinger, Ross
6212 Banner Ave
Los Angeles, CA 90038-2802

Malingri, Micaela (Stylist)
c/o Staff Member *Artist Untied (LA)*
845 S Mansfield Ave Apt 1
Los Angeles, CA 90036-4979, USA

Malini, Hema (Actor, Bollywood)
17 Jai Hind Society 12th Road Juhu Scheme
Mumbai, MS 400049, INDIA

Malinosky, Tony (Athlete, Baseball Player)
PO Box 1835
Lancaster, CA 93539-1835, USA

Maliponte, Adrianna (Opera Singer)
35 Darer
London W1, UNITED KINGDOM (UK)

Malizia, Mike (Athlete, Golfer)
570 SE Southwood Trl
Stuart, FL 34997-6367, USA

Malkan, Matthew A (Astronomer)
Steward Observatory
Tucson, AZ 85721-0001, USA

Malkhov, Vladimir (Ballerina)
890 Broadway
New York, NY 10003-1211, USA

Malkin, Evgenl (Athlete, Hockey Player)
66 Mario Lemieux Pl
Pittsburgh, PA 15219-3504, USA

Malkin, Laurence (Writer)
c/o Josh Kesselman *Jericho Entertainment*
2121 Avenue of the Stars Ste 2900
Los Angeles, CA 90067-5057

Malkin, Michelle (Correspondent)
c/o Staff Member *Creators Syndicate*
5777 W Century Blvd Ste 700
Los Angeles, CA 90045-5652, USA

Malkmus, Bobby (Athlete, Baseball Player)
400 Wallingford Ter
Union, NJ 07083-7328, USA

Malkovich, John (Actor)
c/o Liz Mahoney *ID Public Relations (ID-LA)*
7080 Hollywood Blvd Fl 8
Los Angeles, CA 90028-6906, USA

Mallary, Robert (Artist)
PO Box 97
Conway, MA 01341-0097, USA

Mallea, Eduardo (Writer)
Posadas 1120
Buenos Aires, ARGENTINA

Mallet, W George (Actor, Ex-Governor)
c/o Staff Member *Guiding Light*
51 W 52nd St Bsmt 1
New York, NY 10019-6188, USA

Mallett, Jerry (Athlete, Baseball Player)
4070 Cascade Trl
Mc Gregor, TX 76657-4102, USA

Mallette, Alfred J (General)
7040 Quail Hill Rd
Charlotte, NC 28210-5104, USA

Mallette, Brian (Athlete, Baseball Player)
3012 Gilder Rd
Glenwood, GA 30428-2202, USA

Malley, Kenneth C (Admiral)
136 Riverside Rd
Edgewater, MD 21037-1405, USA

Mallick, Dan (Misc)
42045 Tilton Dr
Quartz Hill, CA 93536-7321, USA

Mallicoat, Rob (Athlete, Baseball Player)
10406 Great Plains Ln
Houston, TX 77064-7113, USA

Mallinger, John (Athlete, Golfer)
2020 N Beverly Plz
Long Beach, CA 90815-2882, USA

Mallon, Meg (Athlete, Golfer)
5105 N Ocean Blvd Apt C
Boynton Beach, FL 33435-7087, USA

Mallory, Carole (Actor)
2300 5th Ave
New York, NY 10037-1610, USA

Mallory, Glynn C Jr (General)
19221 Heather Frst
San Antonio, TX 78258-3820, USA

Mallory, Larry (Athlete, Football Player)
1911 Stonebrook Dr
Arlington, TX 76012-5707, USA

Mallory, Sheldon (Athlete, Baseball Player)
21353 Old North Church Rd
Frankfort, IL 60423-3016, USA

Malloy, Bob (Athlete, Baseball Player)
1904 San Carlos Ave
Allen, TX 75002-2626, USA

Malloy, Dan (Governor, Politician)
210 Capitol Ave
Hartford, CT 06106-1535, USA

Malloy, Edward A (Educator)
President's Office
Notre Dame, IN 46556, USA

Malloy, Marty (Athlete, Baseball Player)
PO Box 1644
Chiefland, FL 32644-1644, USA

Malloy, Matt (Actor)
c/o Mark A. Schlegel *Cornerstone Talent Agency*
37 W 20th St
New York, NY 10011-3706, USA

Malloy, Robert (Pete Hamil) (Actor, Writer)
c/o Staff Member *International Creative Management (ICM-LA)*
10250 Constellation Blvd Fl 7
Los Angeles, CA 90067-6207, USA

Malloy, Tommy
1687 Amsterdam Ave Merrick
LI, NY 11566

Malloys, The (Music Group)
c/o Staff Member *Creative Artists Agency (CAA-LA)*
2000 Avenue of the Stars Ste 100
Los Angeles, CA 90067-4705, USA

Malo, Raul (Musician, Songwriter, Writer)

Maloff, Sam (Designer)
PO Box 8051
Rancho Cucamonga, CA 91701-0051, USA

Malone, Arthur L (Art) (Athlete, Football Player)
1619 E Carmen St
Tempe, AZ 85283-4145, USA

Malone, Beverly L (Misc)
Maryland Ave SW
Washington, DC 20002, USA

Malone, Brendan (Coach)
125 S Pennsylvania St
Indianapolis, IN 46204-3610, USA

Malone, Chuck (Athlete, Baseball Player)
310 Liberty St
Marked Tree, AR 72365-2209, USA

Malone, Dorothy (Actor)
PO Box 7287
Dallas, TX 75209-0287, USA

Malone, Jeff (Athlete, Basketball Player)
415 Lee Road 313
Smiths Station, AL 36877-3168, USA

Malone, Jena (Actor)
c/o Allison Band *Gersh (LA)*
9465 Wilshire Blvd Ste 600
Beverly Hills, CA 90212-2612, USA

Malone, John (Business Person)
12300 Liberty Blvd
Englewood, CO 80112-7009

Malone, Karl (Actor, Athlete, Basketball Player, Producer)
105 W Charter St
Farmerville, LA 71241-2841

Malone, Karl (Athlete, Basketball Player)
105 W Charter St
Farmerville, LA 71241-2841, USA

Malone, Moses (Athlete, Basketball Player)
310 S Keswick Ct
Sugar Land, TX 77478-3952, USA

Malone, Patricia (Business Person)
c/o Staff Member *Gucci America*
50 Hartz Way
Secaucus, NJ 07094-2420, USA

Malone, Shannon (Actor, Television Host)
c/o Jerry Shandrew *Shandrew Public Relations*
1050 S Stanley Ave
Los Angeles, CA 90019-6634, USA

Maloney, Jim (Athlete, Baseball Player)
7027 N Teilman Ave Unit 102
Fresno, CA 93711-0589, USA

Maloney, Sean (Athlete, Baseball Player)
244 Pheasant Run
Saunderstown, RI 02874-2033, USA

Maloof, Adrienne (Business Person, Reality TV Star)
c/o Shaila Arora *Arora/Wasserman Entertainment Media*
23679 Calabasas Rd Ste 633
Calabasas, CA 91302-1502, USA

Maloof, Gavin (Business Person)
c/o Staff Member *Sacramento Kings*
1 Sports Pkwy
Sacramento, CA 95834-2301

Maloof, Mary Lou Metzger (Musician)
5100 Stern Ave
Sherman Oaks, CA 91423-1244, USA

Malouf, Kerry (Stylist)
c/o Staff Member *Mercury Artists*
8460 Higuera St Fl 2
Culver City, CA 90232-2520, USA

Malrena, Oswaldo (Baseball Player)
160 E 6th Pl
Mesa, AZ 85201-5068, USA

Maltbie, Roger (Athlete, Golfer)
179 Longmeadow Dr
Los Gatos, CA 95032-5655, USA

Maltin, Leonard (Correspondent)
c/o Staff Member *Entertainment Tonight (ET)*
4024 Radford Ave
Studio City, CA 91604-2101, USA

Maltz, Rachel (Stylist)
c/o Staff Member *Ford Models (Chicago)*
311 W Superior St
Chicago, IL 60654-3548, USA

Malubay, Ramiele (Musician)

Maly, Arturo (Actor)
c/o Staff Member *Telefe - Argentina*
Pavon 2444 (C1248AAT)
Buenos Aires, ARGENTINA

Malzone, Frank (Athlete, Baseball Player)
16 Aletha Rd
Needham, MA 02492-4302, USA

Mamas & The Papas, The
61 Purchase St Ste 2
Rye, NY 10580-3059

Mambo, Kevin
3500 W Olympic Blvd # 1400
Burbank, CA 91505

Mamet, David (Actor, Director, Producer, Writer)
c/o Jeff Berg *International Creative Management (ICM-LA)*
10250 Constellation Blvd Fl 7
Los Angeles, CA 90067-6207, USA

Mamoa, Jason (Actor)
c/o Jeff Witjas *Agency for the Performing Arts (APA-LA)*
405 S Beverly Dr Ste 500
Beverly Hills, CA 90212-4425, USA

Mana (Music Group)
c/o Staff Member *Creative Artists Agency (CAA-LA)*
2000 Avenue of the Stars Ste 100
Los Angeles, CA 90067-4705, USA

Manahan, Austin (Athlete, Baseball Player)
4827 E Estevan Rd
Phoenix, AZ 85054-6194, USA

Manatt, Charles T
4814 Woodway Ln NW
Washington, DC 20016-3243, USA

Manchester, Melissa (Musician)
c/o Staff Member *Columbia Artists Mgmt Inc*
1790 Broadway Fl 6
New York, NY 10019-1537, USA

Mancina, Mark (Actor)
c/o Staff Member *Gorfaine/Schwartz Agency Inc*
4111 W Alameda Ave Ste 509
Burbank, CA 91505-4171, USA

Mancini, Ray
12524 Indianapolis St
Los Angeles, CA 90066-1512

Mancuso, Nick (Actor)
c/o Joel Dean *TalentWorks (LA)*
3500 W Olive Ave Ste 1400
Burbank, CA 91505-5512, USA

Mancuso Jr, Frank (Producer)
c/o Staff Member *FGM Entertainment*
201 N Canon Dr # 328
Beverly Hills, CA 90210

Mandan, Robert
16700 Celtic St
Granada Hills, CA 91344-5109

Mandarich, Tony (Athlete, Football Player)
12767 E Altadena Dr
Scottsdale, AZ 85259-3418, USA

Mandel, Howie (Comedian, Game Show Host, Television Host)
c/o Michael Rotenberg *3 Arts Entertainment Inc*
9460 Wilshire Blvd Fl 7
Beverly Hills, CA 90212-2713, USA

Mandel, Johnny
28946 Cliffside Dr
Malibu, CA 90265-4212

Mandel, Loring
555 W 57th St Ste 1230
New York, NY 10019-2925

Mandela, N Winnie Madikizela (Activist)
Orlando West Soweto
Johannesburg, SOUTH AFRICA

Mandela, Nelson (Politician)
Private Bag X70000
Houghton 2041, South Africa

Mandelbaum, Michael (Writer)
387 Park Ave S
New York, NY 10016-8810, USA

Manders, Hal (Athlete, Baseball Player)
PO Box 340
Dallas Center, IA 50063-0340, USA

Mandich, Dan (Athlete, Hockey Player)
24275 County Road 57
Bovey, MN 55709-6006, USA

Mandich, Jim (Athlete, Football Player)
16101 Aberdeen Way
Miami Lakes, FL 33014-6566, USA

Mandrell, Barbara (Musician)
PO Box 620
Hendersonville, TN 37077-0620, USA

Mandrell, Louise (Actor)
c/o Staff Member *Morris Management Group, Inc*
818 19th Ave S
Nashville, TN 37203-3202, USA

Mandvi, Aasif (Actor)
c/o Lillian LaSalle *LaSalle Holland*
141 W 28th St Rm 300
New York, NY 10001-6187, USA

Mandylor, Costas (Actor)
c/o Staff Member *Evolution Entertainment (LA)*
901 N Highland Ave
Los Angeles, CA 90038-2412, USA

Mandylor, Louis (Actor)
c/o Erik Kritzer *Kritzer Levine Wilkins Entertainment*
11872 La Grange Ave Fl 1
Los Angeles, CA 90025-5283, USA

Mane, Gucci (Musician)
c/o Nick Carcaterra *Susan Blond Inc (NY)*
50 W 57th St Fl 14
New York, NY 10019-3914, USA

Mane, Tyler (Actor)
c/o Lesa Kirk *Open Entertainment*
Prefers to be contacted via telephone
Los Angeles, CA 90069, USA

Maneche, Daria (Stylist)
c/o Staff Member *Ennis*
119 Braintree St
Boston, MA 02134-1628, USA

Manelona, Jesse (Athlete, Football Player)
c/o Chad Speck *Allegiant Athletic Agency*
35 Market Sq Ste 201
Knoxville, TN 37902-1420, USA

Manetti, Larry (Actor)
4615 Winnetka
Woodland Hills, CA 91364

Manganiello, Joe (Actor)
c/o Colleen Schlegel *Frontline Management*
5670 Wilshire Blvd Ste 1370
Los Angeles, CA 90036-5679, USA

Mangelsdorff, AlbertEmil-
Claar-Str. 23
Frankfurt/Main, GERMANY 60322

Manges, Mark (Athlete, Football Player)
13199 Fifth Ave
Cumberland, MD 21502-5567, USA

Mangieri, Dino (Athlete, Football Player)
108 Lamport Blvd
Staten Island, NY 10305-3629, USA

Mangione, Chuck (Musician)
476 Hampton Blvd
Rochester, NY 14612-4227

Mangold, James Allen (Director, Producer, Writer)
c/o Bo Morrison *Block-Korenbrot Public Relations*
North Market Building 110 S Fairfax, Suite 310
Los Angeles, CA 90036, USA

Mangual, Angel (Baseball Player)
1406 R Del Valle
Ponce, PR 728, USA

Mangual, Pepe (Athlete, Baseball Player)
2325 Calle Tabonuco
Ponce, PR 00716-2712, USA

Mangum, John (Athlete, Football Player)
150 Sherwood Ln
Brandon, MS 39042, USA

Mangum, John (Athlete, Football Player)
508 10th Ave SE
Magee, MS 39111-3820, USA

Mangum, Jonathan (Actor)
c/o Staff Member *Shapiro/West & Associates*
141 El Camino Dr Ste 205
Beverly Hills, CA 90212-2786, USA

Mangum, Kris (Athlete, Football Player)
9 Mossy Oak Pt
Petal, MS 39465-2703, USA

Manheim, Camryn (Actor, Producer)
c/o Peg Donegan *Framework Entertainment (LA)*
9057 Nemo St Ste C
West Hollywood, CA 90069-5511, USA

Maniaci, Joe (Athlete, Football Player)
3215 Rankin Ave
Windsor, ON N9E 3C2, Canada

Manic Street Preachers (Music Group)
c/o Staff Member *Paradigm (Monterey)*
404 W Franklin St
Monterey, CA 93940-2303, USA

Manigault-Stallworth, Omarosa (Actor, Reality TV Star)

Manilow, Barry (Composer, Musician, Producer)
c/o Garry Kief *Stiletto Entertainment*
8295 S La Cienega Blvd
Inglewood, CA 90301-1521, USA

Manis, Randy (Producer)
c/o Staff Member *Killer Films (US)*
526 W 26th St Rm 715
New York, NY 10001-5524, USA

Manisha, Koirala (Actor, Bollywood)
302 Beachwood Towers Yari Road
Versova Andher W
Mumbai, MS 400061, INDIA

Manjia, Nicki (Musician)
c/o Staff Member *Motown Records (NY)*
1755 Broadway Fl 7
New York, NY 10019-3743, USA

Mankell, Henning (Writer)
c/o Staff Member *Leopard förlag AB*
S:t Paulsgatan 11
Stockholm 118 46, Sweden

Mankiewicz, Frank
The Wyoming Columbia Rd. NW
Washington, DC 20009

Mankiewicz, Tom
10850 Wilshire Blvd Ste 730
Los Angeles, CA 90024-4325

Mankiller, Wilma P (Activist)
c/o Staff Member *Cherokee Nation*
PO Box 948
Tahlequah, OK 74465-0948, USA

Mankowitz, Wolf
Ahakista County Cork
Kilcrohane, IRELAND 11

Mankowski, Phil (Athlete, Baseball Player)
2280 Southwestern Blvd
Buffalo, NY 14224-4423, USA

Manley, Elizabeth (Figure Skater)
74830 Velie Way Ste A
Palm Desert, CA 92260-7954, USA

Manley, Leon (Athlete, Football Player)
1207 Knollpark Cir
Austin, TX 78758-3815, USA

Manlikova, Hana
Vymolova 8
Prague 5 15000, Czech Republic

Mann, Aimee (Musician)
59 W 19th St Ste 4A
New York, NY 10011-4228, USA

Mann, Almee (Musician, Songwriter, Writer)
511 Avenue of the Americas # 197
New York, NY 10011-8436, USA

Mann, Art (Producer, Television Host)
122 Hudson St Fl 5
New York, NY 10013-2355, USA

Mann, Barry (Composer)
1010 Laurel Way
Beverly Hills, CA 90210-2305, USA

Mann, Carol (Athlete, Golfer)
6 Cape Chestnut Dr
Spring, TX 77381-2978, USA

Mann, Catherine
9417 Spruce Tree Cir
Bethesda, MD 20814-1654

Mann, Charles (Athlete, Football Player)
1518 Night Shade Ct
Vienna, VA 22182-7301, USA

Mann, David W (Religious Leader)
10550 S 200 W
Columbia City, IN 46725-9618, USA

Mann, Dick (Motorcycle Race, Motorcycle Racer)
13515 Yarmouth Dr
Pickerington, OH 43147-8214, USA

Mann, Errol (Athlete, Football Player)
5521 Bonanza Pl
Missoula, MT 59808-9386, USA

Mann, Gabriel (Actor)
c/o Van Johnson *Van Johnson Company*
10250 Constellation Blvd Ste 2320
Los Angeles, CA 90067-6256, USA

Mann, Garbriel (Actor)
9560 Wilshire Blvd Ste 500
Beverly Hills, CA 90212-2401, USA

Mann, H Thompson (Athlete, Swimmer)
23 Pleasant St Apt 501
Newburyport, MA 01950-2634, USA

Mann, Jim (Athlete, Baseball Player)
197 N Franklin St
Holbrook, MA 02343-1111, USA

Mann, Johnny (Composer, Conductor)
78516 Gorman Ln
Indio, CA 92203, USA

Mann, Kelly (Athlete, Baseball Player)
1335 Franklin St Apt 4
Santa Monica, CA 90404-2629, USA

Mann, Leslie (Actor)
c/o Jodi Gottlieb *ID PR (LA)*
7060 Hollywood Blvd Fl 8
Los Angeles, CA 90028-6014, USA

Mann, Manfred (Misc)
43 Brook Green
London W6 7EF, UNITED KINGDOM (UK)

Mann, Marvin L (Business Person)
740 W New Circle Rd
Lexington, KY 40511-1806, USA

Mann, Michael K (Actor, Director, Producer, Writer)
c/o Staff Member *Forward Pass Inc*
12233 W Olympic Blvd Ste 340
Los Angeles, CA 90064-1039

Mann, Monroe (Actor, Producer, Writer)
c/o Staff Member *Loco Dawn Films, LLC*
499 Seventh Avenue 12th Floor NORTH
New York, NY 10018, USA

Mann, Robert (Athlete, Football Player)
515 SW Hampton Ct
Port Saint Lucie, FL 34986-2022, USA

Mann, Robert W (Engineer)
85 Murray Ave
Port Washington, NY 11050-3527, USA

Mann, Shelley I (Swimmer)
1301 S Scott St # 638S
Arlington, VA 22204-6205, USA

Mann, Terrence V (Actor)
c/o Steve Stone *Cornerstone Talent Agency*
37 W 20th St
New York, NY 10011-3706, USA

Manners, Miss
1651 Harvard St NW
Washington, DC 20009-3702

Mannheim Steamroller (Music Group)
9120 Mormon Bridge Rd
Omaha, NE 68152-1937, USA

Manning, Archie (Athlete, Football Player)
639 Loyola Ave Fl 8
New Orleans, LA 70113-3125, USA

Manning, Danny (Athlete, Basketball Player)
205 Running Ridge Rd
Lawrence, KS 66049-2180, USA

Manning, Ed (Athlete, Basketball Player)
5112 Meridian Ln
Keller, TX 76244-5916, USA

Manning, Eli (Athlete, Football Player)
1500 Hudson St Fl 10
Hoboken, NJ 07030-5590, USA

Manning, Jane (Opera Singer)
2 Wilton Square
London N1, UNITED KINGDOM (UK)

Manning, Jim (Athlete, Baseball Player)
41 Fox Run Dr
Weaverville, NC 28787-8307, USA

Manning, Peyton (Athlete, Football Player)
c/o Tom Condon *CAA - St. Louis*
222 S Central Ave Ste 1008
Saint Louis, MO 63105-3509, USA

Manning, Richard E (Rick) (Athlete, Baseball Player)
12151 New Market
Chesterland, OH 44026-2041, USA

Manning, Rob (Engineer)
4800 Oak Grove Dr
Pasadena, CA 91109-8001, USA

Manning, Taryn (Actor, Musician)
c/o Van Johnson *Van Johnson Company*
350 S Beverly Dr Ste 200
Beverly Hills, CA 90212-4819, USA

Manning, Wade (Athlete, Football Player)
5133 Malaya St
Denver, CO 80249-8548, USA

Mannion, Pace (Athlete, Basketball Player)
4190 Achilles Dr
Salt Lake City, UT 84124-3266, USA

Mannix, Ernie (Actor, Composer, Musician)
c/o Staff Member *Greenspan Artist Management*
8760 W Sunset Blvd
West Hollywood, CA 90069-2206, USA

Manno, Bob (Athlete, Hockey Player)
5643 Peer St
Niagara Falls, ON L2G 1W8, Canada

Manoa, Tim (Athlete, Football Player)
15332 Howe Rd
Cleveland, OH 44136-5324, USA

Manoff, Dinah (Actor)
1505 10th St
Santa Monica, CA 90401-2805, USA

Manon, Julio (Athlete, Baseball Player)
4726 15th Ave S
Saint Petersburg, FL 33711-2328, USA

Manoogian, Richard A (Business Person)
2100 Van Born Rd
Taylor, MI 48180, USA

Manor, Brison (Athlete, Football Player)
285 Spruce St
Bridgeton, NJ 08302-3347, USA

Manorama (Actor, Bollywood)
5 Neelagandan Street T Nagar
Chennai, TN 600017, INDIA

Manos, Sam (Athlete, Football Player)
1424 E Normandy Blvd
Deltona, FL 32725-8408, USA

Manoukian, Don (Athlete, Football Player)
5405 Mae Anne Ave
Reno, NV 89523-1813, USA

Manowar (Music Group)
Prefers to be contacted via email

Manrique, Fred (Baseball Player)
1775 SW 2nd Ave
Boca Raton, FL 33432-7230, USA

Mansell, Kevin (Business Person)
N56W17000 Ridgewood Dr
Menomonee Falls, WI 53051-5660, USA

Mansell, Nigel (Race Car Driver)
Brands Hatch
Longfield, Kent DA3 8NG, UNITED KINGDOM (UK)

Manser, Michael J (Architect)
Morton House Chiswick Mall
London W4 2PS, UNITED KINGDOM (UK)

Mansfield, Mike (Ex-Senator, Senator)
1101 Pennsylvania Ave NW Ste 900
Washington, DC 20004-2514, USA

Mansfield, Peter (Nobel Prize Laureate)
Physics Dept
Nottingham NG7 2RD, UNITED KINGDOM (UK)

Mansfield, Von (Athlete, Football Player)
3600 W 203rd St
Olympia Fields, IL 60461-1025, USA

Mansfield-Kelley, Marie (Baseball Player)
9 Eastland Rd
Jamaica Plain, MA 02130-4616, USA

Mansholt, Sicco L (Government Official)
Oosteinde 16
Wapserveen, HB 8351, NETHERLANDS

Manson, Charles (Misc)
PO Box 3476
Corcoran, CA 93212-3476, USA

Manson, Dave (Athlete, Hockey Player)
211 Cowboys Pkwy
Irving, TX 75063-5931, USA

Manson, Marilyn (Musician)
c/o Tony Cuilla *Ciulla Management*
1509 N Crescent Heights Blvd Ste 4
West Hollywood, CA 90046-2425, USA

Manson, Shirley (Musician)
c/o Staff Member *Untitled Entertainment (LA)*
350 S Beverly Dr Ste 200
Beverly Hills, CA 90212-4819, USA

Mansour, Nicole (Actor)

Mansouri, Lotfi (Actor)
301 Van Ness Ave
San Francisco, CA 94102-4509, USA

Mant, Cathy (Athlete, Golfer)
326 Broadmoor Way
McDonough, GA 30253-4291, USA

Mantee, Paul (Actor)
9057 Nemo St # A
West Hollywood, CA 90069-5511, USA

Mantegna, Joe (Actor, Producer, Writer)
c/o Jack Gilardi *International Creative Management (ICM-LA)*
10250 Constellation Blvd Fl 7
Los Angeles, CA 90067-6207, USA

Mantei, Matt (Athlete, Baseball Player)
4709 Chicago Path
Stevensville, MI 49127-9356, USA

Mantel, Hillary M (Writer)
79 Saint Martin's Lane
London WC2N 4AA, UNITED KINGDOM (UK)

Mantello, Joe (Director)
c/o Staff Member *Creative Artists Agency (CAA-LA)*
2000 Avenue of the Stars Ste 100
Los Angeles, CA 90067-4705, USA

Mantenuto, Michael (Actor)
c/o Kim Hodgert *Creative Artists Agency (CAA-LA)*
2000 Avenue of the Stars Ste 100
Los Angeles, CA 90067-4705, USA

Mantha, Mo
8423 Tally Ho Rd
Lutherville, MD 21093-4725

Mantha, Moe (Athlete, Hockey Player)
1538 Scio Ridge Rd
Ann Arbor, MI 48103-8991, USA

Manthey, Jerri (Actor)
PO Box 801507
Valencia, CA 91380-1507

Manthra (Actor, Bollywood)
5-A Block 2 Vijay Shanti Apts Arcot Road Vadapalani
Chennai, TN 600026, INDIA

Mantilla, Felix (Athlete, Baseball Player)
6973 N Tacoma St
Milwaukee, WI 53224-4759, USA

Mantis, Nick (Athlete, Basketball Player)
2344 Autumn Dr
Crown Point, IN 46307, USA

Mantley, John
4121 Longridge Ave
Sherman Oaks, CA 91423-4335

Manto, Jeff (Athlete, Baseball Player)
725 Radcliffe St
Bristol, PA 19007-5223, USA

Mantooth, Randolph (Actor)
c/o Staff Member *Stone Manners Salners Agency (LA)*
9911 W Pico Blvd Ste 1400
Los Angeles, CA 90035-2715, USA

Mantranga, Jonah (Musician)
c/o Staff Member *Paradigm (Monterey)*
404 W Franklin St
Monterey, CA 93940-2303, USA

Mantreola, Patricia
c/o Staff Member *BMG*
1540 Broadway
New York, NY 10036-4039, USA

Mantzoukas, Jason (Actor)
c/o Christie Smith *Mosaic Media Group*
9200 W Sunset Blvd Ste 10
Los Angeles, CA 90069-3608, USA

Manucci, Dan (Athlete, Football Player)
1208 W Sand Dune Dr
Gilbert, AZ 85233-5615, USA

Manuel, Barry (Athlete, Baseball Player)
805 Oak St
Mamou, LA 70554-2715, USA

Manuel, Charles F (Chuck) (Baseball Player)
2931 Plantation Rd
Winter Haven, FL 33884-1233, USA

Manuel, Charlie (Athlete, Baseball Player, Coach)
2931 Plantation Rd
Winter Haven, FL 33884-1233, USA

Manuel, Jay (Reality TV Star, Television Host)
c/o Staff Member *Bankable Productions*
226 W 26th St Fl 4
New York, NY 10001-6700, USA

Manuel, Jerry (Athlete, Baseball Player, Coach)
5556 Ridge Park Dr
Loomis, CA 95650-9400, USA

Manuel, Lionel (Athlete, Football Player)
827 E Cedar Dr
Chandler, AZ 85249-3319, USA

Manuel, Robert (Actor)
La Maison du Buisson 22-26 Rue Jules Regnier
Plaisir 78370, FRANCE

Manuelidis, Laura (Misc)
Neuropathology Dept
New Haven, CT 6520, USA

Manumaleuna, Brandon (Athlete, Football Player)
1218 Koleeta Dr
Harbor City, CA 90710-1824, USA

Manusky, Greg (Athlete, Football Player)
17133 Castello Cir
San Diego, CA 92127-2803, USA

Manville, Dick (Athlete, Baseball Player)
1436 Lake Francis Dr
Apopka, FL 32712-2007, USA

Manwaring, Kirt (Baseball Player)
20 Prospect Rdg
Horseheads, NY 14845-7988, USA

Manwaring, Kurt D (Athlete, Baseball Player)
20 Prospect Rdg
Horseheads, NY 14845-7988, USA

Manz, Wolfgang (Musician)
Pasteuralle 55
Hanover 30655, GERMANY

Manza, Ralph
550 Hygeia Ave
Encinitas, CA 92024-2601

Manzanero, Armando (Musician)
Paz Soidan 170 Of 903
San Isidro, Lima 27, PERU

Manzanillo, Josias (Athlete, Baseball Player)
274 Kennebec St
Mattapan, MA 02126-1106, USA

Manzarek, Ray (Musician)
1801 Century Park E Ste 2160
Los Angeles, CA 90067-2343, USA

Manzi, Catello (Horse Racer)
1 Hickory Ln
Freehold, NJ 07728-1588, USA

Manzo, Caroline (Business Person, Reality TV Star)
c/o Sal Bonaventura *CEG Talent*
251 W 39th St Fl 7
New York, NY 10018-3171, USA

Manzo, Dina (Business Person, Reality TV Star)
c/o Staff Member *Bravo (NY)*
30 Rockefeller Plz
New York, NY 10112-0015, USA

Manzo, Joe (Athlete, Football Player)
121 Riverside Ave Apt 1006
Medford, MA 02155-4649, USA

Manzoni, Giacomo (Composer)
Viale Papiniano 31
Milan 20123, ITALY

Manzullo, Donald (Congressman, Politician)
2228 Rayburn Hob
Washington, DC 20515-1316, USA

Mapes, Cliff
PO Box 872
Pryor, OK 74362-0872

Maples, Marla (Actor)
c/o Jonathan Todd *Sabre Entertainment*
5737 Kanan Rd # 237
Agoura Hills, CA 91301-1601, USA

Mapother, William (Actor)
c/o Brian Medavoy *Jackson-Medavoy Entertainment*
10203 Santa Monica Blvd Fl 4
Los Angeles, CA 90067-6439, USA

Mar, Marcela (Actor)
c/o Luis Balaguer *Latin World Entertainment Agency (WEA)*
2601 S Bayshore Dr Ste 235
Miami, FL 33133-5432, USA

Mara, Adele (Actor, Dancer)
1928 Mandeville Canyon Rd
Los Angeles, CA 90049-2225, USA

Mara, Kate (Actor)
c/o Kenneth (Kenny) Goodman *Schiff Company, The*
8440 Warner Dr Ste B1
Culver City, CA 90232-2461, USA

Mara, Ratu Sir Kamisese K T (President)
11 Ballery Road
Suva, FIJI

Mara, Rooney (Actor)
c/o Steve Caserta *Sanders Armstrong Caserta*
2120 Colorado Ave Ste 120
Santa Monica, CA 90404-3561, USA

Marachuk, Steve
568 Hana Hwy
Paia, HI 96779-8133

Maradona, Diego (Athlete, Soccer Player)
Brandsen 805
Capital Federal 1161, ARGENTINA

Marak, Paul (Athlete, Baseball Player)
1211 Comanche Trl
Alamogordo, NM 88310-4010, USA

Maramorosch, Karl (Scientist)
1050 George St
New Brunswick, NJ 08901-1012, USA

Marangi, Gary (Athlete, Football Player)
26 Morton St
Port Jefferson Station, NY 11776-4013, USA

Maraniss, David (Journalist)
1150 15th St NW
Washington, DC 20071-0001, USA

Marasca, Dana (Stylist)
c/o Staff Member *Celestine - CA*
1666 20th St Ste 200B
Santa Monica, CA 90404-3828, USA

Maratos, Terry (Actor)
c/o Staff Member *Cage Group, The*
14724 Ventura Blvd Ste 505
Sherman Oaks, CA 91403-3505

Maratos-Flier, Elfetheria (Doctor)
1 Joslin Pl
Boston, MA 02215-5306, USA

Marber, Patrick (Writer)
2 Saint Charles Place
London W10 6EG, UNITED KINGDOM (UK)

Marble, Roy (Athlete, Basketball Player)
1355 Wagon Wheel Ln
Grand Blanc, MI 48439-4863, USA

Marbury, Joseph (Athlete, Baseball Player)
1472 21st St N
Birmingham, AL 35234-2708, USA

Marbury, Rendon (Athlete, Baseball Player)
1472 21st St N
Birmingham, AL 35234-2708, USA

Marbury, Stephon (Athlete, Basketball Player)
2940 W 31st St Apt 4G
Brooklyn, NY 11224-1734, USA

Marbut, Robert G (Publisher)
100 NE Loop # 1400
San Antonio, TX 78216, USA

Marc, Alessandra (Opera Singer)
165 W 57th St
New York, NY 10019-2201, USA

Marceau, Sophie (Actor)
20 Ave Rapp
Paris 75007, FRANCE

Marcelino, Mario
1418 N Highland Ave # 102
Los Angeles, CA 90028-7611

March, Forbes (Actor)
c/o Staff Member *Innovative Artists (LA)*
1505 10th St
Santa Monica, CA 90401-2805, USA

March, Jane (Actor, Model)
5 Jubilee Place #100
London SW3 3TD, UNITED KINGDOM (UK)

March, Joan
Whale Rock Ranch Rd.
Ojai, CA 93023

March, Little Peggy (Musician)
1161 NW 76th Ave
Plantation, FL 33322-5120, USA

March, Peggy
1161 NW 76th Ave
Plantation, FL 33322-5120

March, Stephanie (Actor)
c/o Erica Tarin *ID Public Relations (ID-LA)*
7080 Hollywood Blvd Fl 8
Los Angeles, CA 90028-6906, USA

Marchand, Guy
40 Rue Francois Ler
Paris, FRANCE F-75008

Marchant, Kenny (Congressman, Politician)
1110 Longworth Hob
Washington, DC 20515-3401, USA

Marchette, Josh
6500 Wilshire Blvd Ste 2200
Los Angeles, CA 90048-4942

Marchetti, Gino J (Athlete, Football Player)
324 Devon Way
West Chester, PA 19380-6825, USA

Marchetti, Leo V (Misc)
5615 Belair Rd
Baltimore, MD 21206-3619, USA

Marchibroda, Ted (Athlete, Football Player)
90 Orchard Point Dr
Weems, VA 22576-2648, USA

Marchinko, Jhoni (Producer)
c/o Staff Member *United Talent Agency (UTA)*
9560 Wilshire Blvd Fl 5
Beverly Hills, CA 90212-2400, USA

Marchiol, Ken (Athlete, Football Player)
6489 S Olathe St
Centennial, CO 80016-1052, USA

Marchionne, Sergio (Business Person)
250 Nizza Via
New York, NY 10126-0001, ITALY

Marchisano, Francesco Cardinal (Religious Leader)
Plazza Cancelleria 1
Rome 186, ITALY

Marchlewski, Frank (Athlete, Football Player)
428 Toledo Dr
Lower Burrell, PA 15068-3315, USA

Marchuk, Guri I (Mathematician)
Gubkin Str 8
Mascow 117333, RUSSIA

Marchuk, Yevhen K (Prime Minister)
Verkovna Rada M Hrushevskoho Str 5
Kiev 252008, UKRAINE

Marciano, David (Actor)
c/o Staff Member *Don Buchwald & Associates Inc (LA)*
6500 Wilshire Blvd Ste 2200
Los Angeles, CA 90048-4942, USA

Marciano, Rob (Anchor)
c/o Staff Member *CNN (Atlanta)*
1 Cnn Ctr NW
Atlanta, GA 30303-2762, USA

Marcikic, Ivan (Inventor, Physicist)
24 Rue du General Dufour
Geneva 1211, SWITZERLAND

Marcil, Vanessa (Actor)
c/o Adena Chawke *Greenlight Management and Production*
13848 Valleyheart Dr
Sherman Oaks, CA 91423-2930, USA

Marcinkevicius, Iustinus M (Writer)
#6
Vilnius 232055, LITHUANIA

Marcinyshyn, Dave (Athlete, Hockey Player)
36 Doucette Pl
St. Albert, AB T8N 6S6, Canada

Marcis, Dave (Race Car Driver)
PO Box 645
Skyland, NC 28776-0645, USA

Marciulionis, Sarunas (Athlete, Basketball Player)
Raitininku Street 4 Attn: Management Office
Vilnius 2051, Lithuania

Marco, Gian (Musician)
c/o Staff Member *Creative Artists Agency (CAA-LA)*
2000 Avenue of the Stars Ste 100
Los Angeles, CA 90067-4705, USA

Marcol, Czeslaw C (Chester) (Athlete, Football Player)
PO Box 466
Dollar Bay, MI 49922-0466, USA

Marcontell, Ed (Athlete, Football Player)
PO Box 884
Rusk, TX 75785-0884, USA

Marcos (Musician)
75 Rockefeller Plz
New York, NY 10019-6908, USA

Marcos, Imelda
Leyte Providencia Dept
Tolosa Leyte, PHILIPPINES

Marcotte, Don (Athlete, Hockey Player)
12 Cote St
Amesbury, MA 01913-3804, USA

Marcovicci, Andrea (Actor, Musician)
1640 E 48th St # 14U
New York, NY 10017, USA

Marcucci, Bob
PO Box 1559
Santa Ynez, CA 93460-1559

Marcum, Art (Writer)
c/o Staff Member *Nine Yards Entertainment*
8530 Wilshire Blvd Ste 550
Beverly Hills, CA 90211-3133, USA

Marcum, Shaun (Athlete, Baseball Player)
1413 Jill Ln
Excelsior Springs, MO 64024-9790, USA

Marcus, Bernard (Business Person)
2455 Paces Ferry Road 22nd SE Bldg C
Atlanta, GA 30339, USA

Marcus, Jurgen
Pestalozzistr. 23a
Munich, GERMANY D-80469

Marcus, Ken (Photographer)
6916 Melrose Ave
Los Angeles, CA 90038-3306, USA

Marcus, Rudolph A (Nobel Prize Laureate)
331 S Hill Ave
Pasadena, CA 91106-3405, USA

Marcus, Ruth B (Misc)
311 Saint Ronan St
New Haven, CT 06511-2328, USA

Marcus, Trula M (Actor)
1800 Avenue of the Stars Ste 400
Los Angeles, CA 90067-4206, USA

Marcy, Geoffrey (Astronomer)
Astronomy Dept
San Francisco, CA 94132, USA

Mardall, Cyril L (Architect)
5 Boyne Terrace Mews
London W11 3LR, UNITED KINGDOM (UK)

Marden, Brice (Artist)
6 Saint Lukes Pl
New York, NY 10014-3974, USA

Marder, Barry
c/o Daniel A (Dan) Strone *Trident Media Group LLC*
41 Madison Ave Fl 36
New York, NY 10010-2257, USA

Marderian, Greg (Athlete, Football Player)
10133 Crebs Ave
Northridge, CA 91324-1304, USA

Mardones, Benny (Musician)
PO Box 410
Utica, NY 13503-0410, USA

Mare, Olindo (Athlete, Football Player)
106 Wescoe Dr
Mooresville, NC 28117-6713, USA

Maree, Sydney (Athlete, Track Athlete)
2 Braxton Rd
Bryn Mawr, PA 19010-1029, USA

Maren, Elizabeth (Actor)
PO Box 90010
San Diego, CA 92169-2010, USA

Maren, Jerry (Actor)
PO Box 90010
San Diego, CA 92169-2010

Marentette, Leo (Athlete, Baseball Player)
33606 Beechwood St
Westland, MI 48185-3002, USA

Margal, Albert M (Prime Minister)
8 Hornsey Rise Gardens
London N19, UNITED KINGDOM (UK)

Margalit, Israela (Musician)
165 W 57th St
New York, NY 10019-2201, USA

Margarita, Henry R (Athlete, Football Player)
4 Drury Ln
Stoneham, MA 02180-3205, USA

Margeot, Jean Cardinal (Religious Leader)
Bonne Terre
Vacoas, MAURITIUS

Margera, Brandon (Bam) (Actor, Producer, Writer)
c/o Kevin McLaughlin *Baker Winokur Ryder Public Relations (BWR-LA)*
9100 Wilshire Blvd Ste 500 PMB WEST
Beverly Hills, CA 90212-3426, USA

Margera, Vincent (Actor)
c/o Michael (Mike) Esterman
Esterman.Com, LLC
Prefers to be contacted via email
MD, USA

Margerum, Ken (Athlete, Football Player)
494 Riverview Dr
Capitola, CA 95010-2778, USA

Margison, Richard (Opera Singer)
352 7th Ave
New York, NY 10001-5012, USA

Margo, Philip (Musician)
19948 Mayall St
Chatsworth, CA 91311-3522, USA

Margoliash, Emmanuel (Scientist)
554 Oakdale Ave
Glencoe, IL 60022-2043, USA

Margolin, Phillip (Writer)
c/o Jean V Naggar *Jean Naggar Literary Agency*
216 E 75th St Ste 1E
New York, NY 10021-2921, USA

Margolin, Stuart (Actor)
Box 478
Ganges, BC V0S 1E0, CANADA

Margolis, Cindy (Actor, Model)
c/o Glenn Gulino *G2 Entertainment LLC*
1 Columbus Pl Apt S25E
New York, NY 10019-8208, USA

Margolis, Lawrence S (Judge)
717 Madison Pl NW
Washington, DC 20439-0001, USA

Margolyes, Miriam (Actor)
c/o Staff Member *The Rights House (UK)*
Drury House 34-43 Russell St
London WC2B 5HA, UK

Margon, Bruce H (Astronomer)
PO Box 351580
Seattle, WA 98195-1580, USA

Margoneri, Joe (Athlete, Baseball Player)
341 Turkeytown Rd
West Newton, PA 15089-1850, USA

Margot, Sandra (Athlete, Wrestler)
PO Box 1168
Studio City, CA 91614-0168, USA

Margoyles, Miriam (Actor)
34-43 Russell St
London WC2B 5HA, UNITED KINGDOM (UK)

Margrave, John L (Misc)
4511 Verone St
Bellaire, TX 77401-5513, USA

Margrethe II (Royalty)
Copenhgen K 1257, DENMARK

Margulies, Donald (Writer)
English Dept
New Haven, CT 6520, USA

Margulies, James H (Jimmy) (Cartoonist, Editor)
150 River St
Hackensack, NJ 07601-7110, USA

Margulies, Julianna (Actor)
c/o Annick Muller *ID Public Relations (ID-NY)*
150 W 30th St Fl 19
New York, NY 10001-4003, USA

Margulis, Lynn (Biologist)
2 Cummington St
Boston, MA 02215-2425, USA

Mariago, Cesare
19 788 Citadel Dr # 120
Pt. Coquitlam, CANADA BC V3C 6G

Mariam, Mengistu Haile (President)
PO Box 1536 Gunhill Enclave
Harare, ZIMBABWE

Mariategui, Sandro (Prime Minister)
Ave Ramirez Gaston 375
Miraflores, Lima, PERU

Marichal, Juan (Athlete, Baseball Player)
9458 NW 54th Doral Circle Ln
Doral, FL 33178-2048, USA

Marie, Ann (Actor)
1608 N Cahuenga Blvd # 354
Hollywood, CA 90028-6202, USA

Marie, Aurelius J B L (President)
Zicack
Portsmouth, DOMINICA

Marie, Constance (Actor)
c/o Staff Member *Kass & Stokes Management*
9229 W Sunset Blvd Ste 504
Los Angeles, CA 90069-3405, USA

Marie, Lisa (Actor, Model)
c/o Staff Member *WmE2 (WMA-LA)*
1 William Morris Pl
Beverly Hills, CA 90212-4261, USA

Marie, Princess (Royalty)
Vaduz 9490, LIECHTENSTEIN

Marie, Rose (Actor)
c/o Leanna Levy *Cassell-Levy Inc*
843 N Sycamore Ave
Los Angeles, CA 90038-3391, USA

Marienthal, Eli (Actor)
c/o Lisa Gallant *International Creative Management (ICM-LA)*
10250 Constellation Blvd Fl 7
Los Angeles, CA 90067-6207, USA

Marienthal, Eric (Musician)
15030 Ventura Blvd # 710
Sherman Oaks, CA 91403-5470, USA

Marillion (Musician)
c/o Staff Member *Paradigm (Monterey)*
404 W Franklin St
Monterey, CA 93940-2303, USA

Marilyn
33-34 Cleveland St
London, ENGLAND W1

Marimow, William K (Journalist)
7117 E Rancho Vista Dr Unit 3002
Scottsdale, AZ 85251-1356, USA

Marin, Christian
27 Rue De Richelieu
Paris, FRANCE F-75001

Marin, Jack (Athlete, Basketball Player)
3909 Regent Rd
Durham, NC 27707-5311, USA

Marin, Maguy (Choreographer)
Place Salvador Allende
Creteil 94000, FRANCE

Marin, Mindy (Director)
c/o Jeremy Plager *Creative Artists Agency (CAA-LA)*
2000 Avenue of the Stars Ste 100
Los Angeles, CA 90067-4705, USA

Marin, Nole (Stylist)
c/o Staff Member *Bernstein & Andriulli*
58 W 40th St
New York, NY 10018-2658, USA

Marin, Richard (Stylist)
c/o Staff Member *Cloutier Agency*
2632 La Cienega Ave
Los Angeles, CA 90034-2641, USA

Marin, Richard A (Cheech) (Actor, Comedian)
c/o Ben Feigin *Anonymous Content (AC-LA)*
3531 Hayden Ave
Culver City, CA 90232, USA

Marin, Rosario (Government Official, Writer)
1340 E McWood St
West Covina, CA 91790-5320, USA

Marinaro, Ed (Athlete, Football Player)
1466 N Doheny Dr
Los Angeles, CA 90069-1143, USA

Marini, Gilles (Actor, Model)
c/o Vikram Dhawer *Authentic Talent and Literary Management*
45 Main St Ste 1004
Brooklyn, NY 11201-8200, USA

Marinin, Maxim (Figure Skater)
c/o Staff Member *Champions on Ice*
3500 W 80th St Ste 200
Minneapolis, MN 55431-1090, USA

Marino, Cathy (Athlete, Golfer)
6313 Willowdale Dr
Plano, TX 75093-7802, USA

Marino, Dan (Football Player)
c/o Staff Member *Miami Dolphins*
7500 SW 30th St
Davie, FL 33314-1020, USA

Marino, Ken (Actor)
8730 W Sunset Blvd Ste 490
Los Angeles, CA 90069-2248, USA

Marino, Stephen (Athlete, Golfer)
PO Box 3760
Jupiter, FL 33469-1012, USA

Marino, Tom (Congressman, Politician)
410 Cannon Hob
Washington, DC 20515-4402, USA

Marinovich, Marv (Athlete, Football Player)
1/2 Santa Margarita Pkwy
Rancho Santa Margarita, CA 92688, USA

Marinovich, Todd (Athlete, Football Player)
132 E Balboa Blvd
Newport Beach, CA 92661-1118, USA

Marinus, Martin
Postbus 724
AS Gouda, THE NETHERLANDS 2800

Mario (Musician)
c/o Staff Member *J Erving Group*
555 Whitehall St SW Ste N
Atlanta, GA 30303-3721, USA

Mario, Ernest (Business Person)
1950 Charleston Rd
Mountain View, CA 94043-1218, USA

Marion, Brock (Athlete, Football Player)
10 NW 42nd St
Ocala, FL 34475-1503, USA

Marion, Frank (Athlete, Football Player)
27416 SW 143rd Ave
Homestead, FL 33032-8867, USA

Marion, Fred (Athlete, Football Player)
10032 Oak Quarry Dr
Orlando, FL 32832-5645, USA

Marion, Martin W (Marty) (Athlete, Baseball Player)
8 Forcee Ln
Saint Louis, MO 63124-1245, USA

Marion, Shawn (Athlete, Basketball Player)
2500 Northwinds Pkwy
Alpharetta, GA 30009-2243, USA

Mariotti, Ray (Editor)
Editorial Dept 166 E Riverside
Austin, TX 78704, USA

Maris, Ada
10100 Santa Monica Blvd Ste 2500
Los Angeles, CA 90067-4116

Marisol (Artist)
40 W 57th St
New York, NY 10019-4001, USA

Mariucci, Steve (Athlete, Coach, Football Coach, Football Player)
222 Republic Dr
Allen Park, MI 48101-3650, USA

Mariye, Lily (Director, Writer)
c/o Staff Member *Bauman Redanty & Shaul Agency*
5757 Wilshire Blvd Suite 473
Beverly Hills, CA 90212, USA

Mark, Albert J (Beauty Pageant Winner)
1325 Broadway
Atlantic City, NJ 8401, USA

Mark, Bruce (Artist, Ballerina, Director)
19 Clarendon St
Boston, MA 02116-6107, USA

Mark, Greg (Athlete, Football Player)
2920 Washington St
Miami, FL 33133-3825, USA

Mark, Hans M (Educator, Government Official, Physicist)
1715 Scenic Dr
Austin, TX 78703, USA

Mark, Marky
63 Pilgrim Rd
Braintree, MA 02184-6003

Mark, Mary Ellen (Photographer)
143 Prince St
New York, NY 10012-3113, USA

Mark, Reuben (Business Person)
300 Park Ave
New York, NY 10022-7402, USA

Mark, Robert (Government Official, Lawyer)
Esher
Surrey KT10 8LU, UNITED KINGDOM (UK)

Mark Green, Mark
PO Box 3453
Dana Point, CA 92629-8453, USA

Markakis, Nick (Athlete, Baseball Player)
1140 Fairbanks Dr
Lutherville Timonium, MD 21093-3974, USA

Markaryants, Vladimir S (Government Official)
Yerevan, ARMENIA

Markbreit, Jerry (Athlete, Football Player)
9739 Keystone Ave
Skokie, IL 60076-1136, USA

Markell, Jack (Governor, Politician)
Legislative Hall William Penn St Fl 2
Dover, DE 19901, USA

Marken, William R (Editor)
80 Willow Rd
Menlo Park, CA 94025-3661, USA

Marker, Laurie (Biologist, Scientist)
PO Box 2496
Alexandria, VA 22301-0496, USA

Marker, Steve (Musician)
1250 6th St Ste 401
Santa Monica, CA 90401-1638, USA

Markey, Lucille P (Misc)
18 La Gorce Circle Lane La Gorce Is
Miami Beach, FL 33141, USA

Markham, Dale (Athlete, Football Player)
891 Tower Hill Dr
Milton, WI 53563-1843, USA

Markham, Monte (Actor)
PO Box 607
Malibu, CA 90265-0607, USA

Markie, Biz (Actor, Musician)
c/o Ron Rivlin *Coast II Coast Entertainment*
8671 Wilshire Blvd Ste 500
Beverly Hills, CA 90211-2943, USA

Markland, Jeff (Athlete, Football Player)
1331 W Cinnabar Ave
Phoenix, AZ 85021-2251, USA

Markle, C Wilson (Engineer)
26 Scho St
Toronto, ON M5T 1Z7, CANADA

Markle, Meghan (Actor)
c/o Pearl Servat *PMK/BNC Public Relations (PMK-LA)*
8687 Melrose Ave Ste 8
West Hollywood, CA 90069-5746, USA

Markle, Peter F (Director)
7510 W Sunset Blvd # 509
Los Angeles, CA 90046-3408, USA

Markov, Danny (Athlete, Hockey Player)
17875 Collins Ave Apt 3402
Sunny Isles Beach, FL 33160-2718, USA

Markovich, Mark (Athlete, Football Player)
400 W Thousand Oaks Dr
Peoria, IL 61615-1394, USA

Markowitz, Barry (Cinematographer)
225 W 83rd St Apt 20G
New York, NY 10024-4964, USA

Markowitz, Harry M (Nobel Prize Laureate)
1010 Turquoise St Ste 245
San Diego, CA 92109-1266, USA

Markowitz, Michael (Artist)
3747 23rd St
San Francisco, CA 94114-3407, USA

Markowitz, Robert (Director, Producer)
11521 Amanda Dr
Studio City, CA 91604-4144, USA

Marks, Chandler
PO Box 184
Franklin, TN 37065-0184

Marks, John (Athlete, Hockey Player)
2733 47th St S Apt 205
Fargo, ND 58104-8539, USA

Marks, Paul A (Biologist)
25680 Military Rd
Watertown, NY 13601-5222, USA

Markstein, Gary (Cartoonist, Editor)
333 W State St
Milwaukee, WI 53203-1305, USA

Markwart, Nevin (Athlete, Hockey Player)
210 Cushing Hill Rd
Hanover, MA 02339-1192, USA

Marlatt, Harvey (Athlete, Basketball Player)
10145 Lakeview Dr
Atlanta, MI 49709-9224, USA

Marler, Serena (Stylist)
c/o Staff Member *Team*
423 W Broadway Ste 406
Boston, MA 02127-2265, USA

Marley, Damian (Musician)
c/o Staff Member *Red Light Management (LA)*
8439 W Sunset Blvd Ste 2
Los Angeles, CA 90069-1925, USA

Marley, Ziggy (Musician, Songwriter)
Jack's Hill
Kingston, JAMAICA

Marlin, Sterling (Race Car Driver)
995 Mahon Rd
Columbia, TN 38401-8808, USA

Marling, Laura (Musician)
c/o Linda Carbone *Covers Media*
138 W 25th St Fl 9
New York, NY 10001-7405, USA

Marlow, Jean
32 Exeter Rd
London, ENGLAND NW2

Marlowe, Scott
6399 Wilshire Blvd Ste 414
Los Angeles, CA 90048-5716

Marm, Walter J Jr (War Hero)
PO Box 2017
Fremont, NC 27830-1217, USA

Marmolejo, Sylvia (Stylist)
1052 S Burnside Ave
Los Angeles, CA 90019-6718, USA

Marnay, Audrey (Actor)
c/o Elisabeth Simpson *Agence Elisabeth Simpson*
62 Boulevard Du Montparnasse
Paris 75015, FRANCE

Marnie, Larry (Coach, Football Coach)
Athletes
Tempe, AZ 85287-0001, USA

Marohn, William D (Business Person)
2000 N State St RR 63
Benton Harbor, MI 49022, USA

Marolewski, Fred (Athlete, Baseball Player)
15705 W Waterford Ln
Manhattan, IL 60442-8160, USA

Maron, Marc (Comedian)
c/o Staff Member *United Talent Agency (UTA)*
9560 Wilshire Blvd Fl 5
Beverly Hills, CA 90212-2400, USA

Marone, Lou (Athlete, Baseball Player)
10851 Carbet Pl
San Diego, CA 92124-2042, USA

Maroney, Daniel V Jr (Misc)
5025 Wisconsin Ave NW
Washington, DC 20016-4113, USA

Maroney, Kelli (Actor, Producer)
c/o Staff Member *Bohemia Group*
1680 Vine St Ste 216
Los Angeles, CA 90028-8829, USA

Maroon 5 (Music Group)
c/o Jordan Feldstein *Career Artist Management*
1100 Glendon Ave Ste 1100
Los Angeles, CA 90024-3515, USA

Maroth, Mike (Athlete, Baseball Player)
2333 Pesaro Cir
Ocoee, FL 34761-5006, USA

Marotte, Carl
438 Queen E
Toronto, CANADA Ont. M5A 1

Marotte, J Gilles (Athlete, Hockey Player)
1759 Notre Dameo
Victoriaville, QC G6A 7M4, Canada

Maroulis, Constantine (Musician)
c/o Paul Reisman *Abrams Artists Agency (NY)*
275 7th Ave Fl 26
New York, NY 10001-6708, USA

Marquand, Christian
45 Rue De Bellechasse
Paris, FRANCE F-75007

Marquardt, Bridget (Model, Reality TV Star)
10236 Charing Cross Rd
Los Angeles, CA 90024-1815, USA

Marques, Maria Elena
Nubes 723 Pedregal
Mexico DF, MEXICO

Marquette, Chris (Actor)
c/o Holly Williams *Williams Unlimited*
5010 Buffalo Ave
Sherman Oaks, CA 91423-1414

Marquez, Alfonso (Baseball Player)
4102 S Skyline Ct
Gilbert, AZ 85297-9668, USA

Marquez, Alfonso (Athlete, Baseball Player)
29 Pasto Rico
Rancho Santa Margarita, CA 92688-2992, USA

Marquez, Raul -
14611 Maisemore Rd
Houston, TX 77015-1772

Marquis, Bob (Athlete, Baseball Player)
5786 Townhouse Ln
Beaumont, TX 77707-1838, USA

Marquis, Jason (Athlete, Baseball Player)
300 Vogel Ave
Staten Island, NY 10309-2905, USA

Marr, Aileen (Stylist)
c/o Staff Member *Kramer + Kramer*
156 5th Ave Ste 415
New York, NY 10010-7774, USA

Marraccini, Matt (Actor)
c/o Cynthia Campos-Greenberg *Anthem Entertainment*
9595 Wilshire Blvd Ste 900
Beverly Hills, CA 90212-2509, USA

Marrero, Connie (Athlete, Baseball Player)
129 Gordon St
Perth Amboy, NJ 08861-4658, USA

Marrero, Eli (Athlete, Baseball Player)
10230 SW 64th St
Miami, FL 33173-2807, USA

Marriner, Neville
Raine St
London E1 9RG, UNITED KINGDOM (UK)

Marriott, Craig (Actor)
c/o Staff Member *Nickelodeon UK*
PO Box 6425
LONDON W1A 6UR, UNITED KINGDOM

Marriott, Evan (Reality TV Star)
c/o Michael (Mike) Esterman *Esterman.Com, LLC*
Prefers to be contacted via email
MD, USA

Marriott, J Willard Jr (Business Person)
10400 Fernwood Rd
Bethesda, MD 20817-1102, USA

Marriott, Richard E (Business Person)
10400 Fernwood Rd
Bethesda, MD 20817-1102, USA

Marro, Anthony J (Editor)
235 Pinelawn Rd
Melville, NY 11747-4226, USA

Marron, Donald B (Financier)
375 Park Ave Fl 11
New York, NY 10152-1199, USA

Marrone, Doug (Athlete, Football Player)
150 Bobby Dodd Way NW Attn Athletic
Atlanta, GA 30332-2500, USA

Marrow, Tracy (Ice T) (Musician)
c/o Staff Member *United Talent Agency (UTA)*
9560 Wilshire Blvd Fl 5
Beverly Hills, CA 90212-2400, USA

Marryshow, Bryan (Stylist)
c/o Staff Member *Jam Arts, Inc*
154 W 57th St
New York, NY 10019-3321, USA

Mars, Bruno (Musician)
c/o Sara Newkirk *WmE2 (Endeavor-LA)*
9601 Wilshire Blvd Fl 3
Beverly Hills, CA 90210-5219, USA

Mars, Jacqueline (Business Person)
6885 Elm St
McLean, VA 22101-6031, USA

Mars, John (Business Person)
6885 Elm St
McLean, VA 22101-6031, USA

Mars Jr, Forrest E (Business Person)
6885 Elm St
McLean, VA 22101-6031, USA

Marsalis, Branford (Composer, Musician)
323 Broadway
Cambridge, MA 02139-1801, USA

Marsalis, James (Athlete, Football Player)
101 Royal Oak Ln
Kathleen, GA 31047-2149, USA

Marsalis, Wynton (Composer, Musician)
c/o Staff Member *Creative Artists Agency (CAA-LA)*
2000 Avenue of the Stars Ste 100
Los Angeles, CA 90067-4705, USA

Marsan, Edward (Eddie) (Actor)
c/o Marsha McManus *Principal Entertainment (LA)*
1964 Westwood Blvd Ste 400
Los Angeles, CA 90025-4695, USA

Marschall, Marita (Actor)
Lamontstr 9
Munich 81679, GERMANY

Marsden, Bernie (Musician)
27A Floral St #300
London WC2E 9DQ, UNITED KINGDOM (UK)

Marsden, Freddie (Musician)
21A Cliftown Road Southend-on-Sea
Essex SS1 1AB, UNITED KINGDOM (UK)

Marsden, Gerald (Gerry) (Musician)
21A Cliftown Rd Southend-on-Sea
Essex SS1 1AB, UNITED KINGDOM (UK)

Marsden, James (Actor)
c/o Andrea Pett-Joseph *Brillstein Entertainment Partners*
9150 Wilshire Blvd Ste 350
Beverly Hills, CA 90212-3453, USA

Marsden, Jason (Actor)
c/o Staff Member *Cunningham Escott Slevin & Doherty (CESD-LA)*
10635 Santa Monica Blvd Ste 130
Los Angeles, CA 90025-8306, USA

Marsden, Matthew (Actor)
c/o Paul Nelson *Mosaic Media Group*
9200 W Sunset Blvd Ste 10
Los Angeles, CA 90069-3608, USA

Marsden, Roy (Actor)
2-4 Noel St
London W1V 3RB, UNITED KINGDOM (UK)

Marsh, Brad (Athlete, Hockey Player)
1000 Palladium Dr
Kanata, ON K2V 1A4, Canada

Marsh, Carol
7 Leicester Pl # 100
London, ENGLAND WC2H 7B1

Marsh, Frank (Athlete, Baseball Player)
304 Bay Shore Ave Apt 426
Mobile, AL 36607-2059, USA

Marsh, Gary (Athlete, Hockey Player)
1871 Cardiff Crst
Courtenay, BC V9N 3Z5, Canada

Marsh, Graham (Athlete, Golfer)
29 Commerce Drive P O Box 300
Rogina, Queensland 4226, Australia

Marsh, Graham (Golfer)
112 Pga Tour Blvd
Ponte Vedra Beach, FL 32082-3046, USA

Marsh, Henry (Athlete, Track Athlete)
Bountiful, UT 84010, USA

Marsh, Jean (Actor)
c/o Staff Member *Diamond Management*
31 Percy St
London W1T 2DD, UK

Marsh, Jodie (Model)
c/o Staff Member *Page 3*
News International Newspapers Ltd 1 Virginia St
London E98 1XY, UNITED KINGDOM

Marsh, Julian (DJ)
c/o Staff Member *Diva Central Inc*
7510 W Sunset Blvd Ste 1445
Los Angeles, CA 90046-3408, USA

Marsh, Kym (Musician)
c/o Staff Member *Safe Management*
111 Guildford Rd Lightwater
Surrey GU18 5RA, UNITED KINGDOM (UK)

Marsh, Linda (Actor)
170 W End Ave Apt 22P
New York, NY 10023-5414, USA

Marsh, Little Peggy
8236 NW 9th St
Plantation, FL 33324-1208

Marsh, Marian (Actor)
PO Box 1
Palm Desert, CA 92261-0001, USA

Marsh, Michael (Mike) (Athlete, Track Athlete)
2425 Holly Hall St Apt 152
Houston, TX 77054-3996, USA

Marsh, Mike
2847 Indian Trail Dr
Missouri City, TX 77489

Marsh, Miles L (Business Person)
1919 S Broadway
Green Bay, WI 54304-4905, USA

Marsh, Randy (Baseball Player)
3023 Winterbourne Rd
Edgewood, KY 41017-9683, USA

Marsh, Randy (Athlete, Baseball Player)
3023 Winterbourne Rd
Edgewood, KY 41017-9683, USA

Marsh, Robert T (Business Person, General)
6659 Avignon Blvd
Falls Church, VA 22043-1724, USA

Marsh, Thomas (Tom) (Athlete, Baseball Player)
9140 Summerfield Rd
Temperance, MI 48182-9757, USA

Marsh of Mannington, Richard W (Government Official)
Westminster
London SW1A 0PW, UNITED KINGDOM (UK)

Marshall, Albert L (Ben) (Athlete, Hockey Player)
9603 166th Street Ct E
Puyallup, WA 98375-2203, USA

Marshall, Amanda (Actor)
1505 W 2nd Ave # 200
Vancouver, BC V6H 3Y4, CANADA

Marshall, Amanda (Musician)
c/o Rob Light *Creative Artists Agency (CAA-LA)*
2000 Avenue of the Stars Ste 100
Los Angeles, CA 90067-4705, USA

Marshall, Amanda (Musician)
c/o Staff Member *Creative Artists Agency (CAA-LA)*
2000 Avenue of the Stars Ste 100
Los Angeles, CA 90067-4705, USA

Marshall, Arthur (Athlete, Football Player)
2918 Crosscreek Rd
Hephzibah, GA 30815-6547, USA

Marshall, Barry J (Scientist)
Nedlands, WA 6009, AUSTRALIA

Marshall, Brandon (Athlete, Football Player)
c/o Harlan Werner *Sports Placement Service*
330 W 11th St Apt 105
Los Angeles, CA 90015-2230, USA

Marshall, Brian (Musician)
1776 Broadway Ste 430
New York, NY 10019-2002, USA

Marshall, Burchard (Athlete, Baseball Player)
60 Crouch Ave Apt C12B
Norwich, CT 06360-7329, USA

Marshall, Carolyn M (Religious Leader)
204 N Newlin St
Veedersburg, IN 47987-1358, USA

Marshall, Chan (Cat Power) (Actor, Composer, Musician)
c/o Staff Member *Matador Records (NY)*
304 Hudson St Rm 701
New York, NY 10013-1012, USA

Marshall, Charles (Athlete, Football Player)
4605 Preston Bend Dr
Arlington, TX 76016-1970, USA

Marshall, Clarence (Athlete, Baseball Player)
27642 Susan Beth Way Unit I
Santa Clarita, CA 91350-1797, USA

Marshall, Dale Rogers (Educator)
President's Office
Norton, MA 2766, USA

Marshall, Dave (Athlete, Baseball Player)
4802 E Centralia St
Long Beach, CA 90808-1312, USA

Marshall, David (Athlete, Football Player)
2740 Towne Village Dr
Duluth, GA 30097-7614, USA

Marshall, Donny (Athlete, Basketball Player)
410 N 63rd St
Seattle, WA 98103-5526, USA

Marshall, Donyell (Athlete, Basketball Player)
55 Ridgecreek Trl
Chagrin Falls, OH 44022-2379, USA

Marshall, Ed (Athlete, Football Player)
4828 Delwood St Apt 2
Corpus Christi, TX 78413-5178, USA

Marshall, F Ray (Secretary)
PO Box Y
Austin, TX 78713-8925, USA

Marshall, Frank W (Filmmaker, Producer)
650 N Bronson Ave # 100
Los Angeles, CA 90004-1404, USA

Marshall, Garry K (Actor, Director)
c/o Michelle Bega *Rogers & Cowan PR (LA)*
Pacific Design Center 8687 Melrose Ave, 7th Floor
West Hollywood, CA 90069, USA

Marshall, James (Actor)
1833 Rutgers Dr
Thousand Oaks, CA 91360-5021, USA

Marshall, James L (Jim) (Athlete, Football Player)
7151 York Ave S Apt 519
Minneapolis, MN 55435-4465, USA

Marshall, Jim (Athlete, Baseball Player, Coach)
19700 N 76th St Apt 1119
Scottsdale, AZ 85255-4787, USA

Marshall, Jim C (Athlete, Football Player)
5258 Brookleigh Dr
Jackson, MS 39272-6009, USA

Marshall, Keith (Athlete, Baseball Player)
334 Beckwith Rd
Pine City, NY 14871, USA

Marshall, Ken (Actor)
345 N Maple Dr # 302
Beverly Hills, CA 90210-3869, USA

Marshall, Kris (Actor)
c/o Claire Maroussas *Independent Talent Group (ITG-UK)*
Oxford House 76 Oxford St
London W1D 1BS, UK

Marshall, Larry (Athlete, Football Player)
4605 SW Hickory Ln
Blue Springs, MO 64015-4524, USA

Marshall, Leonard (Athlete, Football Player)
PO Box 272016
Boca Raton, FL 33427-2016, USA

Marshall, Margaret A (Opera Singer)
Woodside Main St
Gargunnock, Stirling FKS 3BP, SCOTLAND

Marshall, Michael A (Mike) (Athlete, Baseball Player)
1280 W Desert Sun Dr Attn Manager's Ofc
Yuma, AZ 85365, USA

Marshall, Michael G (Mike) (Athlete, Baseball Player)
38324 Jendral Ave
Zephyrhills, FL 33542-7830, USA

Marshall, Mike
4436 Plum St
Zephyrhills, FL 33542-7846

Marshall, Patricia
969 Hilgard Ave Apt 401
Los Angeles, CA 90024-3078

Marshall, Paula (Actor)
c/o Nevin Dolcefino *Innovative Artists (LA)*
1505 10th St
Santa Monica, CA 90401-2805, USA

Marshall, Penny (Actor, Director)
c/o Staff Member *Parkway Productions*
7095 Hollywood Blvd Ste 1009
Hollywood, CA 90028-8912, USA

Marshall, Peter (Television Host)
16714 Oak View Dr
Encino, CA 91436-3238, USA

Marshall, Rob (Director)
2644 30th St
Santa Monica, CA 90405-3060, USA

Marshall, Scott (Actor, Director)
c/o Staff Member *Creative Artists Agency (CAA-LA)*
2000 Avenue of the Stars Ste 100
Los Angeles, CA 90067-4705, USA

Marshall, Theda (Athlete, Baseball Player)
708 E Phillips Dr N
Littleton, CO 80122-2864, USA

Marshall, Tom (Athlete, Basketball Player)
9548 Mariners Cove Ln
Fort Myers, FL 33919-4592, USA

Marshall, Tony (Stylist)
c/o Staff Member *Directions USA*
3717 W Market St Ste C
Greensboro, NC 27403-1155, USA

Marshall, Vester (Athlete, Basketball Player)
2204 1st Ave Apt 201
Seattle, WA 98121-1600, USA

Marshall, W W (Bones) (General, War Hero)
1517 Ehupua Pl
Honolulu, HI 96821-1468, USA

Marshall, Whit (Athlete, Football Player)
57 Putnam Dr Nw
Atlanta, GA 30342-4411, USA

Marshall, Wilber B (Athlete, Football Player)
3016 E Main St
Mims, FL 32754-3924, USA

Marshall, Willard
204 Main St
Fort Lee, NJ 07024-5702

Marshall Green, Logan (Actor)
c/o Nick Frenkel *3 Arts Entertainment Inc*
9460 Wilshire Blvd Fl 7
Beverly Hills, CA 90212-2713, USA

Marshall of Knightsbridge, Colin M (Business Person)
Heathrow Airport Hounslow
Middx TW6 2JA, UNITED KINGDOM (UK)

Marshall Tucker Band
100 W Putnam Ave
Greenwich, CT 06830-5342

Marsonek, Sam (Athlete, Baseball Player)
712 Welton Rd
Lutz, FL 33548-5039, USA

Marsters, James (Actor)
c/o Staff Member *Steve Himber Entertainment*
211 S Beverly Dr Apt S
Beverly Hills, CA 90212-3807, USA

Marston, Joshua (Director, Writer)
c/o Cliff Roberts *WmE2 (Endeavor-LA)*
1 William Morris Pl
Beverly Hills, CA 90212-4261, USA

Marston, Natalie Elizabeth (Actor)
c/o Shepard Smith *Archetype*
1608 Argyle Ave
Los Angeles, CA 90028-6408, USA

Marston, Nathanial (Actor)
c/o Staff Member *Donegan Entertaiment*
129 W 27th St
New York, NY 10001-6206, USA

Marston, Nathaniel (Actor)
c/o Staff Member *One Life to Live*
56 E 66th St
New York, NY 10065-6538, USA

Marta, Lynn (Actor)
c/o Staff Member *Bobby Ball Talent Agency*
4116 W Magnolia Blvd Ste 205
Burbank, CA 91505-2700, USA

Marte, Judy (Actor)
c/o Michael Cooper *Creative Artists Agency (CAA-LA)*
1 William Morris Pl
Beverly Hills, CA 90212-4261, USA

Martel, Arlene (Actor)
2109 S Wilbur Ave
Walla Walla, WA 99362-9048, USA

Martell, Donna
PO Box 3335
Granada Hills, CA 91394-0335

Martemucci, Anna (Director)
c/o Chad Hamilton *Anonymous Content (AC-LA)*
3531 Hayden Ave
Culver City, CA 90232, USA

Martens, Wilfried (Prime Minister)
16 Rue de la Victoire
Brussels 1060, BELGIUM

Martensen, Gayle (Stylist)
c/o Staff Member *Independent Artists*
448 E Riverdale Ave
Orange, CA 92865-1302, USA

Martha, Paul (Athlete, Football Player)
110 Riding Trail Ln
Pittsburgh, PA 15215-1500, USA

Marti, Benita (Actor)
c/o Staff Member *Select Artists Ltd (CA-Valley Office)*
PO Box 4359
Burbank, CA 91503-4359, USA

Martika (Musician)
2409 21st Ave S Ste 100
Nashville, TN 37212-5317, USA

Martin, Aaron (Athlete, Football Player)
3605 Seth Ct
Springdale, MD 20774-5408, USA

Martin, Agnes B (Artist)
414 Placilas Rd
Taos, NM 87571, USA

Martin, Al (Athlete, Baseball Player)
15251 S 50th St Apt 2054
Phoenix, AZ 85044-9117, USA

Martin, Alastair B (Misc)
630 5th Ave
New York, NY 10111-0100, USA

Martin, Albert C (Architect)
811 W 7th St Ste 800
Los Angeles, CA 90017-3419, USA

Martin, Amos (Athlete, Football Player)
2605 Bradford Commons Dr Unit 103
Louisville, KY 40299-6189, USA

Martin, Andrea (Actor)
c/o Staff Member *Innovative Artists (LA)*
1505 10th St
Santa Monica, CA 90401-2805, USA

Martin, Ann (Correspondent)
News Dept 6121 Sunset Blvd
Los Angeles, CA 90028, USA

Martin, Ann M (Writer)
c/o Staff Member *Scholastic Entertainment*
557 Broadway
New York, NY 10012-3962, USA

Martin, Babe (Athlete, Baseball Player)
114 N Holloway Rd
Ballwin, MO 63011-3205, USA

Martin, Barri (Stylist)
c/o Staff Member *Seaminx Artist Management*
9234 Peninsula Dr
Dallas, TX 75218-2733, USA

Martin, Billy (Musician)
c/o Brian Greenbaum *Creative Artists Agency (CAA-LA)*
2000 Avenue of the Stars Ste 100
Los Angeles, CA 90067-4705, USA

Martin, Billy (Athlete, Football Player)
PO Box 2969
Cumming, GA 30028-6513, USA

Martin, Blanche (Athlete, Football Player)
1621 Stoney Point Dr
Lansing, MI 48917-1409, USA

Martin, Boyce F Jr (Judge)
601 W Broadway
Louisville, KY 40202-2284, USA

Martin, Brian (Athlete)
777 San Antonio Rd Apt 132
Palo Alto, CA 94303-4858, USA

Martin, Casey
PO Box 109601
Palm Beach Gardens, FL 33410-9601

Martin, Casey (Athlete, Golfer)
2727 Leo Harris Pkwy Attn Athletic
Eugene, OR 97401-8835, USA

Martin, Chris (Musician)
c/o Darin Harmon *3D Management*
1901 Main St Fl 3
Santa Monica, CA 90405-1075, USA

Martin, Chris (Actor)
c/o Barry McPherson *Agency for the Performing Arts (APA-LA)*
405 S Beverly Dr Ste 500
Beverly Hills, CA 90212-4425, USA

Martin, Chris (Athlete, Football Player)
c/o Jeff Lynch *Sports Management Worldwide*
1100 NW Glisan St Ste 2B
Portland, OR 97209-3064, USA

Martin, Christy (Boxer)
PO Box 1782
Apopka, FL 32704-1782, USA

Martin, Cuonzo (Athlete, Basketball Player)
4315 Thistlewood Way
Knoxville, TN 37919-7884, USA

Martin, Curtis (Athlete, Football Player)
1000 Fulton Ave
Hempstead, NY 11550-1030, USA

Martin, Dave (Chef)
c/o Staff Member *Magical Elves Inc*
453 S Spring St Ste
Los Angeles, CA 90013, USA

Martin, Dave (Athlete, Football Player)
9306 E Berry Ave
Greenwood Village, CO 80111-3509, USA

Martin, David (Correspondent)
2020 M St NW
Washington, DC 20036-3304, USA

Martin, Deana (Actor)
c/o Jeffrey Lane *Jeffrey Lane & Associates*
9255 Doheny Rd Apt 2003
Los Angeles, CA 90069-3224, USA

Martin, Demetri (Actor, Comedian)
c/o Jason Heyman *Creative Artists Agency (CAA-LA)*
2000 Avenue of the Stars Ste 100
Los Angeles, CA 90067-4705, USA

Martin, Denise B (Editor)
Editorial Dept Time-Life Building
New York, NY 10020, USA

Martin, Don (Athlete, Coach, Football Coach, Football Player)
1220 Harbor Bay Pkwy Attn Coachingstaff
Alameda, CA 94502-6501, USA

Martin, Doug (Athlete, Golfer)
1406 Meadowlake Way
Union, KY 41091-7118, USA

Martin, Duane (Actor)
c/o Pearl Wexler *Kohner Agency, The*
9300 Wilshire Blvd Ste 555
Beverly Hills, CA 90212-3211, USA

Martin, Ed (Baseball Player)
6666 Brookmont Ter Apt 407
Nashville, TN 37205-4622, USA

Martin, Ed F (Actor)
c/o Steven Neibert *Imperium 7 Talent Agency*
5455 Wilshire Blvd Ste 1706
Los Angeles, CA 90036-4217, USA

Martin, Edward H (Admiral)
729 Guadalupe Ave
Coronado, CA 92118-2314, USA

Martin, Eric (Athlete, Football Player)
111 Windfall Pl
Clinton, MS 39056-6072, USA

Martin, Eric Band
PO Box 5952
San Francisco, CA 94101

Martin, Gene (Athlete, Baseball Player)
133 Winchester Dr
Leesburg, GA 31763-5064, USA

Martin, George (Athlete, Football Player)
50 Cheshire Ln
Ringwood, NJ 07456-2743, USA

Martin, George C (Engineer)
900 University St Apt 5P
Seattle, WA 98101-2728, USA

Martin, Greg (Musician)
212 3rd Ave N Ste 301
Nashville, TN 37201-1632, USA

Martin, Gregory S (General)
US Air Forces Europe Ramstein Air Base
APO, AE 9094, USA

Martin, Helen
1440 N Fairfax Ave Apt 109
West Hollywood, CA 90046-3939

Martin, Henry R (Cartoonist)
1382 Newtown Langhorne Rd # G206
Newtown, PA 18940-2418, USA

Martin, J C (Athlete, Baseball Player)
112 Oakmont Ct
Advance, NC 27006-7097, USA

Martin, Jacques (Coach)
1 Panther Pkwy
Sunrise, FL 33323-5315, USA

Martin, James G (Ex-Governor)
Bank of America Corporate Center 201 N Tryon St
Charlotte, NC 28202, USA

Martin, Jeanne
613 N Linden Dr
Beverly Hills, CA 90210-3223

Martin, Jennifer (Stylist)
c/o Staff Member *Zenobia Agency Inc*
PO Box 909
Groveland, CA 95321-0909, USA

Martin, Jerry (Athlete, Baseball Player)
109 Chelton Ct
Columbia, SC 29212-8522, USA

Martin, Jesse L (Actor)
c/o Bob McGowan *McGowan Management*
8733 W Sunset Blvd Ste 103
West Hollywood, CA 90069-2241, USA

Martin, Joe (Cartoonist)
C/O Neatly Chiseled Features 1870 Loramoor Lane
Lake Geneva, WI 53147, USA

Martin, John (Athlete, Baseball Player)
2037 SW Stratford Way
Palm City, FL 34990-2033, USA

Martin, John H (Educator)
3930 Rca Blvd # 3240
Palm Beach Gardens, FL 33410-4267, USA

Martin, Judith (Miss Manners) (Journalist)
1651 Harvard St NW
Washington, DC 20009-3702, USA

Martin, Justin (Actor)
c/o Ellen Meyer *Ellen Meyer Management*
8899 Beverly Blvd Ste 612
West Hollywood, CA 90048-2429, USA

Martin, Kellie (Actor)
c/o William Mercer *Thruline Entertainment*
9250 Wilshire Blvd Ground Fl
Beverly Hills, CA 90212, USA

Martin, Kelvin (Athlete, Football Player)
608 Guadalupe Rd
Keller, TX 76248-7337, USA

Martin, Kenyon (Athlete, Basketball Player)
924 Bentwater Pkwy
Cedar Hill, TX 75104-8269, USA

Martin, Larue (Athlete, Basketball Player)
1236 Harvest Ln
University Park, IL 60484-3320, USA

Martin, LeRoy (Government Official, Lawyer)
Superintendent's Office
Chicago, IL 60602, USA

Martin, Lynn M (Secretary)
171 Willabay Dr
Williams Bay, WI 53191-9673, USA

Martin, Madeleine (Actor)
c/o Jill Fritzo *PMK/BNC Public Relations (PMK-NY)*
622 3rd Ave Fl 8
New York, NY 10017-6707, USA

Martin, Maria (Actor)
c/o Staff Member *Select Artists Ltd (CA-Valley Office)*
PO Box 4359
Burbank, CA 91503-4359, USA

Martin, Mark (Race Car Driver)
1900 Seclusion Dr
Port Orange, FL 32128-6826, USA

Martin, Marsha P (Financier)
1501 Farm Credit Dr
McLean, VA 22102-5000, USA

Martin, Meaghan Jette (Actor)
c/o Myrna Lieberman *Myrna Lieberman Management*
3001 Hollyridge Dr
Hollywood, CA 90068-1951, USA

Martin, Medeski (Musician)
c/o Staff Member *Paradigm (Monterey)*
404 W Franklin St
Monterey, CA 93940-2303, USA

Martin, Mike (Athlete, Baseball Player)
704 Waterfalls Ave
Las Vegas, NV 89128, USA

Martin, Millicent (Actor, Musician)
2-4 Noel St
London W1V 3RB, UNITED KINGDOM (UK)

Martin, Morrie (Athlete, Baseball Player)
1786 Pottery Rd
Washington, MO 63090-4189, USA

Martin, Nicole (Stylist)
c/o Staff Member *Fifty8 Artists*
58 W Huron St
Chicago, IL 60654-3806, USA

Martin, Norberto (Athlete, Baseball Player)
PO Box 6756
Helena, MT 59604-6756, USA

Martin, Paul (Government Official)
140 O'Connor St
Ottawa, ON K1A 0G5, CANADA

Martin, Paul (Athlete, Baseball Player)
1529 33rd St
San Diego, CA 92102-1609, USA

Martin, Phil (Athlete, Basketball Player)
6937 Vineridge Dr
Dallas, TX 75248-5553, USA

Martin, Preston (Financier, Government Official)
1130 N Lake Shore Dr Apt 4E
Chicago, IL 60611-1048, USA

Martin, R Bruce (Misc)
Chemistry Dept
Charlottesville, VA 22903, USA

Martin, Ray (Billiards Player)
11-05 Cadmus Pl
Fair Lawn, NJ 07410-2122, USA

Martin, Ray (Athlete, Baseball Player)
383 Adams St
Quincy, MA 02169-1703, USA

Martin, Renie (Athlete, Baseball Player)
509 Little Eagle Ct
Valrico, FL 33594-3973, USA

Martin, Ricky (Musician)
5130 N Bay Rd
Miami Beach, FL 33140-2009, USA

Martin, Rod (Athlete, Football Player)
PO Box 2315
Manhattan Beach, CA 90267-2315, USA

Martin, Roland (Correspondent)
c/o Staff Member *CNN (Atlanta)*
1 Cnn Ctr NW
Atlanta, GA 30303-2762, USA

Martin, Ronald D (Editor)
72 Marietta St NW
Atlanta, GA 30303-2804, USA

Martin, Rudolf (Actor)
c/o Amanda Glazer *Kohner Agency, The*
9300 Wilshire Blvd Ste 555
Beverly Hills, CA 90212-3211, USA

Martin, Rudolph (Actor)
c/o Staff Member *Treusch/Erickson Associates*
8955 Norma Pl
Los Angeles, CA 90069-4818, USA

Martin, Sandy (Actor)
1875 Century Park E Ste 2250
Los Angeles, CA 90067-2563, USA

Martin, Sir George
Lynhurst Road Hampstead
London, ENGLAND NW3 5NG

Martin, Slater (Athlete, Basketball Player)
4119 Placid St
Houston, TX 77022-4127, USA

Martin, Steve (Actor, Comedian, Producer, Writer)
c/o Alan Nierob *Rogers & Cowan PR (LA)*
Pacific Design Center 8687 Melrose Ave, 7th Floor
West Hollywood, CA 90069, USA

Martin, Susan (Stylist)
307 W Tremont Ave Ste C
Charlotte, NC 28203-4977, USA

Martin, Sylvia Wene (Bowler)
2701 Clark Towers Ct Apt 125
Las Vegas, NV 89102-5855, USA

Martin, Todd (Athlete, Tennis Player)
156 Coach Lamp Way
Ponte Vedra Beach, FL 32082-1904, USA

Martin, Tom (Athlete, Baseball Player)
8001 Surf Dr
Panama City, FL 32408-8530, USA

Martin, Tony (Actor, Musician)
10724 Wilshire Blvd Apt 1406
Los Angeles, CA 90024-4473, USA

Martin, Tony (Athlete, Football Player)
1198 B Green Rd
Boston, GA 31626 2010, USA

Martin, Victor Hugo (Actor)
c/o Staff Member *TV Azteca*
Periferico Sur 4121 Colonia Fuentes del Pedregal
DF CP 14141, Mexico

Martin, Wayne (Athlete, Football Player)
25 Chateau Mouton Dr
Kenner, LA 70065-1902, USA

Martin Chase, Deborah (Debra) (Producer)
c/o Staff Member *WmE2 (WMA-LA)*
1 William Morris Pl
Beverly Hills, CA 90212-4261, USA

Martindale, Kate (Stylist)
c/o Staff Member *Cloutier Agency*
2632 La Cienega Ave
Los Angeles, CA 90034-2641, USA

Martindale, Margo (Actor)
c/o Andrew Freedman *Andrew Freedman Public Relations*
9127 Thrasher Ave
Los Angeles, CA 90069-1144, USA

Martindale, Wink (Entertainer, Musician)
5744 Newcastle Ln
Calabasas, CA 91302-3117, USA

Martine, Suzanne (Stylist)
92 Grove St
New York, NY 10014-3548, USA

Martines, Alessandra (Actor)
c/o Francois-Xavier Molin *ArtMedia*
20 avenue Rapp
Paris 75008, France

Martinez, A (Actor)
PO Box 6387
Malibu, CA 90264-6387, USA

Martinez, Alfredo (Athlete, Baseball Player)
2346 Thomas St
Los Angeles, CA 90031-2820, USA

Martinez, Ana Maria (Opera Singer)
151 W 51st St # 17E
New York, NY 10019-6019, USA

Martinez, Anais (Musician)
5820 Canoga Ave Ste 300
Woodland Hills, CA 91367-6533, USA

Martinez, Angela (Television Host)
c/o Staff Member *Abrams Artists Agency (LA)*
9200 W Sunset Blvd PH 11
Los Angeles, CA 90069-3601, USA

Martinez, Angie (Musician)
395 Hudson St Fl 7
New York, NY 10014-7452, USA

Martinez, Billy Joe (Actor)
c/o Linda McAlister *Linda McAlister Talent*
100 Oak Ln
Waxahachie, TX 75167-8412, USA

Martinez, Buck (Athlete, Baseball Player, Coach)
10315 Long Beach Blvd
Long Beach Township, NJ 08008-3135, USA

Martinez, Carmelo (Athlete, Baseball Player)
32 Brisas Del Plata
Dorado, PR 00646-5118, USA

Martinez, Chito (Athlete, Baseball Player)
1205 Oak Creek Dr
Collierville, TN 38017-2651, USA

Martinez, Constantino (Tino) (Athlete, Baseball Player)
324 Blanca Ave
Tampa, FL 33606-3630, USA

Martinez, Daniel J (Artist)
Studio Art Dept
Irvine, CA 92717, USA

Martinez, Dave (Athlete, Baseball Player)
3315 Enterprise Rd E
Safety Harbor, FL 34695-5307, USA

Martinez, Edgar (Athlete, Baseball Player)
3036 249th Ave SE
Sammamish, WA 98075-9421, USA

Martinez, Fred (Baseball Player)
2346 Thomas St
Los Angeles, CA 90031-2820, USA

Martinez, Greg (Athlete, Baseball Player)
1596 Palora Ave
Las Vegas, NV 89169-2504, USA

Martinez, J Dennis (Athlete, Baseball Player)
9400 SW 63rd Ct
Miami, FL 33156-1817, USA

Martinez, Jorge (Actor)
c/o Staff Member *Telefe - Argentina*
Pavon 2444 (C1248AAT)
Buenos Aires, ARGENTINA

Martinez, Jose (Athlete, Baseball Player)
14601 SW 33rd Ct
Miramar, FL 33027-3729, USA

Martinez, Natalie (Actor)
c/o Sean Fay *Kritzer Levine Wilkins Entertainment*
11872 La Grange Ave Fl 1
Los Angeles, CA 90025-5283, USA

Martinez, Olivier (Actor)
c/o Staff Member *Parseghian Planco LLC*
322 8th Ave Ste 601
New York, NY 10001-6715, USA

Martinez, Patrice (Actor)
c/o Staff Member *Select Artists Ltd (CA-Valley Office)*
PO Box 4359
Burbank, CA 91503-4359, USA

Martinez, Pedro (Athlete, Baseball Player)
3029 Birkdale
Weston, FL 33332-1813, USA

Martinez, Pedro A (Baseball Player)
186 Fairmount Ave
Hyde Park, MA 02136-3506, USA

Martinez, Ramon J (Athlete, Baseball Player)
3029 Birkdale
Weston, FL 33332-1813, USA

Martinez, Robert (Bob) (Ex-Governor)
100 N Tampa St Ste 4100
Tampa, FL 33602-3642, USA

Martinez, Rosealee (Stylist)
c/o Staff Member *Team*
423 W Broadway Ste 406
Boston, MA 02127-2265, USA

Martinez, Silvio (Athlete, Baseball Player)
8321 Cornish Ave Apt 2
Elmhurst, NY 11373-3753, USA

Martinez, Susana (Governor)
State Capitol 300 Old Santa Fe Trl
Santa Fe, NM 87501, USA

Martinez, Tippy (Athlete, Baseball Player)
1524 Dellsway Rd
Towson, MD 21286-5901, USA

martinez, Victor (Athlete, Baseball Player)
6201 Maypine Farm Blvd
Cleveland, OH 44143-4508, USA

Martinez Somalo, Eduardo Cardinal (Religious Leader)
Piazza Pio XII 3
Rome 193, ITALY

Martini, Carlo Maria Cardinal (Religious Leader)
Palazzo Arcivescovile Piazza Fontana 2
Milan 20122, ITALY

Martini, Max (Actor, Director)
c/o Vera Mihailovich *Forward Entertainment*
9255 W Sunset Blvd Ste 805
Los Angeles, CA 90069-3305, USA

Martinkovic, John (Athlete, Football Player)
1001 Ernst Dr
Green Bay, WI 54304-2205, USA

Martino, Frank D (Misc)
1655 W Market St
Akron, OH 44313-7004, USA

Martino, Pat (Composer, Musician)
2318 S 16th St
Philadelphia, PA 19145-4310, USA

Martino, Renato R Cardinal (Religious Leader)
Piazzo S Calisto 16
Vatican City 120, VATICAN CITY

Martins, Joao Carlos (Musician)
c/o Staff Member *Musicians Corporate Management*
PO Box 825
Highland, NY 12528-0825, USA

Martins, Nilas (Ballerina, Dancer, Director)
c/o Staff Member *New York City Ballet*
20 Lincoln Center Plz
New York, NY 10023-6913, USA

Martinson, Leslie
2288 Coldwater Canyon Dr
Beverly Hills, CA 90210-1756

Martinson, Lestie H (Director)
2288 Coldwater Canyon Dr
Beverly Hills, CA 90210-1756, USA

Martlin, Marlee (Actor)
10340 Santa Monica Blvd
Los Angeles, CA 90025-6904, USA

Marton, Eva (Opera Singer)
Maximilianstr 22
Munich 80539, GERMANY

Marton, Katalin (Kati) (Writer)
c/o Amanda Urban *International Creative Management (ICM-NY)*
40 W 57th St
New York, NY 10019-4001, USA

Martone, Lino (Musician)
c/o Gabriel Blanco *Gabriel Blanco Iglesias (Mexico)*
Rio Balsas 35-32 Colonia Cuauhtemoc
DF 6500, Mexico

Marts, Lonnie (Athlete, Football Player)
13650 Bromley Point Dr
Jacksonville, FL 32225-2635, USA

Marty, Martin E (Religious Leader)
175 E Delaware Pl Apt 8508
Chicago, IL 60611-7750, USA

Marty, Mike (Coach, Football Coach)
901 N Broadway
Saint Louis, MO 63101-2800, USA

Martyn, Bob (Athlete, Baseball Player)
PO Box 778
Pacific City, OR 97135-0778, USA

Martz, Gary (Athlete, Baseball Player)
525 Sage Hills Dr
Wenatchee, WA 98801-2466, USA

Martz, Mike (Athlete, Football Coach, Football Player)
222 Republic Dr
Allen Park, MI 48101-3650, USA

Martz, Randy (Athlete, Baseball Player)
211 HI Pointe Pl
East Alton, IL 62024-1641, USA

Martzke, Rudy (Writer)
1000 Wilson Blvd
Arlington, VA 22209-2230, USA

Maruk, Dennis (Athlete, Hockey Player)
2624 Garfield Ave
Minneapolis, MN 55408-1331, USA

Marusha
Kaiser-Friedrich-Str. 41
Berlin, GERMANY D-10627

Marusin, Yury M (Opera Singer)
Teatralnaya Pl 1
Saint Petersburg, RUSSIA

Maruskin, Chelsea (Stylist)
c/o Staff Member *Art House Management*
1548 16th St
Santa Monica, CA 90404-3309, USA

Maruyama, Karen (Actor)
c/o Staff Member *Halpern Management*
PO Box 5042
Santa Monica, CA 90409-5042, USA

Maruyama, Shigeki (Athlete, Golfer)
15210 Antelo Pl
Los Angeles, CA 90077-1634, USA

Marvaso, Tommy (Athlete, Football Player)
2 W Melrose St
Chevy Chase, MD 20815-4244, USA

Marve, Eugene (Athlete, Football Player)
4510 S Cameron Ave
Tampa, FL 33611-2223, USA

Marvel, Elizabeth (Actor)
c/o Robert Glennon *Authentic Talent and Literary Management*
45 Main St Ste 1004
Brooklyn, NY 11201-8200, USA

Marvelettes, The (Music Group)
9936 Majorca Pl
Boca Raton, FL 33434-3714, USA

Marx, Gilda (Designer, Fashion Designer)
11755 Exposition Blvd
Los Angeles, CA 90064-1338, USA

Marx, Greg (Athlete, Football Player)
18721 Jamestown Cir
Northville, MI 48168-3532, USA

Marx, Gyorgy (Physicist)
Fehervari Utca 119
Budapest 1119, HUNGARY

Marx, Jeffrey A (Journalist)
Editorial Dept Main & Midland
Lexington, KY 40507, USA

Marx, Melissa (Stylist)
c/o Staff Member *Axis Models & Talent*
PO Box 367
Ringwood, NJ 07456-0367, USA

Marx, Richard (Musician, Songwriter)
c/o Staff Member *Marleah Leslie & Associates PR*
1645 Vine St Apt 712
Los Angeles, CA 90028-8812, USA

Marx, Timothy (Producer)
c/o Staff Member *International Creative Management (ICM-LA)*
10250 Constellation Blvd Fl 7
Los Angeles, CA 90067-6207, USA

Mary Mary (Music Group)
c/o Richard De La Font *Richard De La Font Agency*
3808 W South Park Blvd
Broken Arrow, OK 74011-1261, USA

Maryland, Russell (Athlete, Football Player)
1330 Eagle Bnd
Southlake, TX 76092-9406, USA

Marzano, John (Athlete, Baseball Player)
1224 S 11th St
Philadelphia, PA 19147-5032, USA

Marzich, Andy (Bowler)
25141 Whitespring
Mission Viejo, CA 92692-2871, USA

Marzio, Peter C (Director)
PO Box 6826
Houston, TX 77265-6826, USA

Marzoli, Andrea (Misc)
2455 Ridge Rd
Berkeley, CA 94709-1211, USA

Mas, Adrian (Actor)
c/o Gabriel Blanco *Gabriel Blanco Iglesias (Mexico)*
Rio Balsas 35-32 Colonia Cuauhtemoc
DF 6500, Mexico

Masak, Ron (Actor)
5440 Shirley Ave
Tarzana, CA 91356-2941, USA

Masakayan, Liz (Athlete, Volleyball Player)
2864 Palomino Cir
La Jolla, CA 92037-7066, USA

Masako, Princess (Royalty)
1-1 Chiyoda-ku
Tokyo, JAPAN

Masaoka, Onan (Athlete, Baseball Player)
1323 Auwae Rd
Hilo, HI 96720-6906, USA

Mascaras, Mil
200 W 16th St # 10
New York, NY 10011-6165

Masco, Judit
Paseo De Gracia 67 Pral. IA
Barcelona, SPAIN 8008

Mascolo, Joseph (Actor)
c/o Staff Member *Bold and The Beautiful, The*
7800 Beverly Blvd # 3371
Los Angeles, CA 90036-2112

Mase (Musician)
c/o Staff Member *Interscope Records (NY)*
1755 Broadway
New York, NY 10019-3743, USA

Masekela, Hugh (Musician)
c/o Staff Member *Opus 3 Artists*
5670 Wilshire Blvd Ste 1790
Los Angeles, CA 90036-5627, USA

Masekela, Sal (Television Host)
c/o Staff Member *ROAR (LA)*
9701 Wilshire Blvd Fl 8
Beverly Hills, CA 90212-2008, USA

MaShay, Pepper (Actor, Musician)
c/o Staff Member *Diva Central Inc*
7510 W Sunset Blvd Ste 1445
Los Angeles, CA 90046-3408, USA

Mashburn, Jamal (Athlete, Basketball Player)
5625 Pine Tree Dr
Miami Beach, FL 33140-2149, USA

Mashburn, Jesse (Athlete, Track Athlete)
8520 S Pennsylvania Ave
Oklahoma City, OK 73159-5226, USA

Mashkov, Vladimir L (Actor)
Chaokygina Str 12A
Moscow, RUSSIA

Mashore, Clyde (Athlete, Baseball Player)
590 Valmore Pl
Brentwood, CA 94513-6909, USA

Mashore, Damon (Athlete, Baseball Player)
1538 W Rush Rd
Eagle, ID 83616-3630, USA

Masiello, Tony (Politician)
65 Niagara Sq
Buffalo, NY 14202-3313, USA

Masire, Q Ketumile J (President)
PO Box 70
Gaborone, BOTSWANA

Maskawa, Toshihide (Nobel Prize Laureate)
Motoyama,Kamigamo, Kita-Ku
Kyoto-City 603-8555, Japan

Maske, Henry (Boxer)
Hochstadenstr 1-3
Cologne 50674, GERMANY

Maslansky, Paul (Director, Filmmaker, Producer)
10866 Wilshire Blvd Ste 1000
Los Angeles, CA 90024-4684, USA

Masloff, Sophie (Politician)
414 Grant St
Pittsburgh, PA 15219-2409, USA

Maslow, Emilie (Stylist)
c/o Staff Member *Celestine - CA*
1666 20th St Ste 200B
Santa Monica, CA 90404-3828, USA

Maslow, James (Actor, Musician)
c/o Liza Anderson *Anderson Group Public Relations*
8060 Melrose Ave Fl 4
Los Angeles, CA 90046-7038, USA

Maslowski, Matt (Athlete, Football Player)
22281 Destello
Mission Viejo, CA 92691-1525, USA

Mason, Anthony (Athlete, Basketball Player)
1512 Palisade Ave Apt 2A
Fort Lee, NJ 07024-5309, USA

Mason, B John (Misc)
64 Christchurch Road East Sheen
London SW14, UNITED KINGDOM (UK)

Mason, Birny Jr (Engineer)
6 Island Dr
Rye, NY 10580-4306, USA

Mason, Bobbie Ann (Writer)
PO Box 518
Lawrenceburg, KY 40342-0518, USA

Mason, Brent (Musician)
54 Music Sq E Ste 300
Nashville, TN 37203-4386, USA

Mason, Dave (Musician, Songwriter)
3130 E Ojai Ave
Ojai, CA 93023-9319, USA

Mason, Dave (Athlete, Football Player)
960 Springfield Dr
De Pere, WI 54115-7661, USA

Mason, Debbi (Stylist)
c/o Staff Member *Bryan Bantry*
900 Broadway Ste 400
New York, NY 10003-1239, USA

Mason, Derrick (Athlete, Football Player)
2402 Long Ridge Rd
Reisterstown, MD 21136-5679, USA

Mason, Desmond (Basketball Player)
Bradley Center 1001 N 4th St
Milwaukee, WI 53203, USA

Mason, Don (Athlete, Baseball Player)
8 Fawn Rd
South Yarmouth, MA 02664-1808, USA

Mason, Glen (Coach, Football Coach)
Athletic Dept
Minneapolis, MN 55455, USA

Mason, Hank (Athlete, Baseball Player)
5004 W Leyburn Ct Apt 102
Henrico, VA 23228-4852, USA

Mason, Jackie (Actor, Comedian)
146 W 57th St # 68D
New York, NY 10019-3301, USA

Mason, James Appreciation Society
PO Box 3552
London, ENGLAND SWl9 3QH

Mason, Jim (Athlete, Baseball Player)
11410 Queens Way
Theodore, AL 36582-8312, USA

Mason, Larry B (War Hero)
826 Cinebar Rd
Cinebar, WA 98533-9732, USA

Mason, Laurence (Actor)
c/o Mara Santino *Luber Roklin Management*
8530 Wilshire Blvd Ste 550
Beverly Hills, CA 90211-3133, USA

Mason, Lindsey (Athlete, Football Player)
8665 Ritchboro Rd
District Heights, MD 20747-2658, USA

Mason, Marilyn
27 Glen Oak Ct
Medford, OR 97504-7671

Mason, Marlyn (Actor, Musician)
27 Glen Oak Ct
Medford, OR 97504-7671, USA

Mason, Marsha (Actor)
c/o Alexa Pagonas *Michael Black Management*
9701 Wilshire Blvd Fl 10
Beverly Hills, CA 90212-2010, USA

Mason, Mike (Athlete, Baseball Player)
2711 Piper Ridge Ln
Excelsior, MN 55331-7803, USA

Mason, Monica (Ballerina)
Convent Garden Bow St
London WC2, UNITED KINGDOM (UK)

Mason, Nick (Musician)
370 City Road
London EC1V 2QA, UNITED KINGDOM (UK)

Mason, Roger (Athlete, Baseball Player)
4587 Stover Rd
Bellaire, MI 49615-9046, USA

Mason, Ron (Coach)
Athletic Dept
East Lansing, MI 48224, USA

Mason, Stephen (Musician)
1700 Hayes St Ste 304
Nashville, TN 37203-3014, USA

Mason, Stephen (Musician, Songwriter, Writer)
1776 Broadway # 1500
New York, NY 10019-2002, USA

Mason, Steve (Musician)
370 City Road
London EC1V 2QA, UNITED KINGDOM (UK)

Mason, Sully
4043 Irving Pl
Culver City, CA 90230

Mason, Tom (Actor)
870 Heights Pl
Oyster Bay, NY 11771-1122, USA

Mason, Tommy (Athlete, Football Player)
240 S Orange Acres Dr
Anaheim, CA 92807-3617, USA

Mason, Vince (Musician)
250 W 57th St
New York, NY 10107-0001, USA

Mason, Willy (Musician)
c/o Staff Member *Paradigm (Monterey)*
404 W Franklin St
Monterey, CA 93940-2303, USA

Mason Dixon
PO Box 214
Flint, TX 75762-0214

Mason of Barnsley, Roy (Government Official)
12 Victoria Ave Barnsley
South Yorks S7O 2BH, UNITED KINGDOM (UK)

Masri, Tahir Nashat (Prime Minister)
PO Box 5550
Amman, JORDAN

Mass, Jochen (Race Car Driver)
RTL-Sportredaktion
Cologne 50570, GERMANY

Mass, Marychris (Stylist)
1903 SE Umatilla St
Portland, OR 97202-7324, USA

Mass, Wayne (Athlete, Football Player)
71 Eagle Vw
Durango, CO 81303-6686, USA

Massa, Felipe (Race Car Driver)
c/o Staff Member *Jaguar Racing Ltd*
Bradbourne Drive Tilbrook
Milton Keynes MK7 8BJ, United Kingdom

Massa, Gordon (Athlete, Baseball Player)
8255 Bonanza Ln
Cincinnati, OH 45255-2504, USA

Massari, Lea
Viale Parioli 59
Rome, ITALY I-00197

Massaro, Ashley (Wrestler)
c/o Kerry Rodgerson *World Wrestling Entertainment (WWE)*
1241 E Main St
Stamford, CT 06902-3520, USA

Masse, Bill (Baseball Player)
2501 Amherst Ct Apt 25A
Boynton Beach, Fl 33436-9017, USA

Massen, Osa
10501 Wilshire Blvd Unit 704
Los Angeles, CA 90024-6321

Massenburg, Tony (Athlete, Basketball Player)
13265 Tony Ln
Stony Creek, VA 23882-3209, USA

Masset, Andrew
11635 Huston St
Valley Village, CA 91601-4315

Masset, Nick (Athlete, Baseball Player)
14575 W Mountain View Blvd Unit 11107
Surprise, AZ 85374-8674, USA

Massevitch, Alla G (Astronomer)
6 Pushkurev Per #4
Moscow 103045, RUSSIA

Massey, Debbie (Athlete, Golfer)
PO Box 116
Cheboygan, MI 49721-0116, USA

Massey, Kyle (Actor)
Creekmoor Ln POB 6811
Riverdale, GA 30296, USA

Massey, Robert (Athlete, Football Player)
6746 Terry Ln
Charlotte, NC 28215-3672, USA

Massey, Vincent (Misc)
Biochemistry Dept
Ann Arbor, MI 48109, USA

Massey, Walter E (Educator, Physicist)
President's Office 830 Westview Dr SW
Atlanta, GA 30314, USA

Massie, Robert K (Writer)
52 W Clinton Ave
Irvington, NY 10533-2130, USA

Massimino, Michael J (Astronaut)
15814 Elk Park Ln
Houston, TX 77062-4775, USA

Massimino, Rollie (Coach)
18578 SE Ferland Ct
Jupiter, FL 33469-1775, USA

Massive Attack (Music Group)
c/o Staff Member *Paradigm (Monterey)*
404 W Franklin St
Monterey, CA 93940-2303, USA

Massoglia, Chris (Actor)
c/o Sandra Chang *Industry Entertainment Partners*
955 Carrillo Dr Ste 300
Los Angeles, CA 90048-5400, USA

Mast, Dick (Athlete, Golfer)
15831 Tower View Dr
Clermont, FL 34711-9381, USA

Mast, Rick (Race Car Driver)
390 E Midland Trl
Lexington, VA 24450-5703, USA

Mastan, Abbas (Director, Producer)
B/8 Juhu Tara Road
Mumbai 400059, India

Masteller, Dan (Athlete, Baseball Player)
159111 Aldersyde Dr
Shaker Heights, OH 44120, USA

Masters, Ben (Actor)
c/o Staff Member *Silver Massetti & Szatmary (SMS) Talent Inc*
8730 W Sunset Blvd Ste 440
Los Angeles, CA 90069-2277, USA

Masters, Billy (Athlete, Football Player)
501 SW Silverspur Cir
Lees Summit, MO 64081-2482, USA

Masters, Geoff (Tennis Player)
De Lorain St
Wavell Heights, QLD 4012, AUSTRALIA

Masters, Margie (Athlete, Golfer)
8440 E Hazeltine Ln
Tucson, AZ 85710-7161, USA

Masters, Norm (Athlete, Football Player)
2249 Chestnut Dr
Bloomfield Hills, MI 48304-2107, USA

Masterson, Christopher (Chris) Kennedy (Actor)
c/o Staff Member *United Talent Agency (UTA)*
9560 Wilshire Blvd Fl 5
Beverly Hills, CA 90212-2400, USA

Masterson, Connie (Athlete, Golfer)
4004 Island Bay Cir
Sanford, FL 32771-6344, USA

Masterson, Danny (Actor, Producer)
c/o Jenni Weinman *Patricola Lust PR*
9171 Wilshire Blvd Ste 390
Beverly Hills, CA 90210-5515, USA

Masterson, Fay (Actor)
c/o Francis Okwu *Levine Okwu Erickson Management*
6363 Wilshire Blvd Ste 300
Los Angeles, CA 90048-5729, USA

Masterson, Forrest (Athlete, Football Player)
310 W Broad St
Louisville, OH 44641-1314, USA

Masterson, Lisa (Talk Show Host)
1333 Ocean Ave
Santa Monica, CA 90401-1023, USA

Masterson, Mary Stuart (Actor)
c/o John Carrabino *John Carrabino Management*
5900 Wilshire Blvd Ste 406
Los Angeles, CA 90036-5015, USA

Masterson, Peter (Director, Producer, Writer)
1165 5th Ave # 15A
New York, NY 10029-6931, USA

Masterson, Sean (Actor, Writer)
c/o Melanie Truhett *Messina Baker/ Entertainment*
955 Carrillo Dr Ste 100
Los Angeles, CA 90048-5400, USA

Masterson, Valerie (Opera Singer)
13 Ardilaun Road
London N5 2QR, UNITED KINGDOM (UK)

Masterson, Walt (Athlete, Baseball Player)
2600 Croasdaile Farm Pkwy Apt A158
Durham, NC 27705-1340, USA

Maston, Le'shai (Athlete, Football Player)
7856 Overridge Dr
Dallas, TX 75232-4316, USA

Mastracchio, Richard A
1910 Hillside Oak Ln
Houston, TX 77062-3663, USA

Mastracchio, Richard A (Rick) (Astronaut)
4410 Pine Blossom Trl
Houston, TX 77059-3144, USA

Mastrangelo, Carlo (Musician)
PO Box 12
Far Hills, NJ 07931-0012, USA

Mastrantonio, Mary Elizabeth (Actor, Musician)
8942 Wilshire Blvd # 219
Beverly Hills, CA 90211-1908, USA

Mastrogiacomo, Gina (Actor)
9229 W Sunset Blvd Ste 315
Los Angeles, CA 90069-3403, USA

Mastroianni, Chiara (Actor)
34-43 Russell St
London WC2B 5HA, UNITED KINGDOM (UK)

Mastrov, Mark (Sportscaster)
c/o Staff Member *WmE2 (WMA-LA)*
1 William Morris Pl
Beverly Hills, CA 90212-4261, USA

Masui, Yoshio (Biologist)
32 Iverton Cres
North York, ON M3B 2V2, CANADA

Masur, Kurt
Augustusplatz 8
Leipzig 4109, GERMANY

Masur, Richard (Actor)
10340 Santa Monica Blvd
Los Angeles, CA 90025-6904, USA

Mata, Victor (Athlete, Baseball Player)
161st Street And River Avenue Attn Latin Maerican Coordinator
Bronx, NY 10451, USA

Mata'aho (Royalty)
PO Box 6
Nuku'alofa, TONGA

Matalin, Mary (Journalist, Talk Show Host, Writer)
424 S Washington St
Alexandria, VA 22314-4100, USA

Matalon-Degni, Francine (Stylist)
260 Riverside Dr Apt 5A
New York, NY 10025-5257, USA

Matamoros, Kristi (Stylist)
c/o Staff Member *Rex Agency, The*
6311 Romaine St
Los Angeles, CA 90038-2617, USA

Matarazzo, Heather (Actor)
c/o Kieran Maguire *The Arlook Group*
205 S Beverly Dr Ste 209
Beverly Hills, CA 90212-3899, USA

Matarazzo, Len (Athlete, Baseball Player)
2715 Carlisle St
New Castle, PA 16105-1714, USA

Matchbox 20 (Music Group)
c/o Staff Member *Creative Artists Agency (CAA-LA)*
2000 Avenue of the Stars Ste 100
Los Angeles, CA 90067-4705, USA

Matchett, Kari (Actor)
c/o Staff Member *Brillstein Entertainment Partners*
9150 Wilshire Blvd Ste 350
Beverly Hills, CA 90212-3453, USA

Matchetts, John (Athlete, Hockey Player)
2415 N Chelton Rd
Colorado Springs, CO 80909-1350, USA

Matchick, Tom (Athlete, Baseball Player)
7700 Pilliod Rd
Holland, OH 43528-8077, USA

Matenopoulos, Debbie (Actor, Producer)
c/o Staff Member *Fifteen Minutes (LA)*
8436 W 3rd St Ste 650
Los Angeles, CA 90048-4131, USA

Mateo, Guillermo (Athlete, Baseball Player)
c/o Staff Member *Montreal Expos*
4549 Avenue Pierre de Coubertin
Montreal
Quebec H1V 3N7, CANADA

Matesa, Zlatko (Prime Minister)
Jordanovac 71
Zagreb 41000, CROATIA

Matheny, Jim (Athlete, Football Player)
16 San Bernardino Ave
Ventura, CA 93004-1131, USA

Matheny, Mike (Athlete, Baseball Player)
2034 Joes Way
Chesterfield, MO 63005-6545, USA

Mather, Chuck (Athlete, Football Player)
10725 Thatcher Way
Duluth, GA 30097-5711, USA

Mather, John C. (Nobel Prize Laureate)
Office of Public Affairs Code 443
Greenbelt, MD 20771-0001, USA

Mather, Paul (Stylist)
c/o Staff Member *Creative Exchange Agency*
53 Gansevoort St Ste 3
New York, NY 10014-1414, USA

Mathers, Frank (Athlete, Hockey Player)
32 Oakglade Dr
Hummelstown, PA 17036-9516, USA

Mathers, Jerry (Actor)
10 Universal City Plz Ste 2000
Universal City, CA 91608-1074, USA

Mathers, Marshall (Eminem) (Actor, Musician, Producer)
c/o Paul Rosenberg *Goliath Artists*
151 Lafayette St Rm 6
New York, NY 10013-3617, USA

Matherson, Tim (Actor, Director)
246 Miramar Ave
Montecito, CA 93108-2628, USA

Matheson, Chris (Writer)
c/o Rima Greer *Above the Line Agency*
468 N Camden Dr Ste 200
Beverly Hills, CA 90210-4507, USA

Matheson, Jim (Congressman, Politician)
2434 Rayburn Hob
Washington, DC 20515-0305, USA

Matheson, Richard C. (Producer)
c/o Jon Karas *Infinity Management*
7923 Hollywood Blvd
Los Angeles, CA 90046-2611, USA

Matheson, Tim (Actor, Director)
c/o Michael Nilon *Creative Artists Agency (CAA-LA)*
2000 Avenue of the Stars Ste 100
Los Angeles, CA 90067-4705, USA

Mathews, Byron (Baseball Player)
557 Golfwood Dr
Ballwin, MO 63021-6316, USA

Mathews, F David (Secretary)
6050 Mad River Rd
Dayton, OH 45459-1508, USA

Mathews, Greg (Athlete, Baseball Player)
8327 Gannon Ave
Saint Louis, MO 63132-5029, USA

Mathews, Harlan (Senator)
420 Hunt Club Rd
Nashville, TN 37221-4310, USA

Mathews, Nelson (Athlete, Baseball Player)
211 E Crestview Dr
Columbia, IL 62236-1203, USA

Mathews, Ray (Athlete, Football Player)
PO Box 108
Harrisville, PA 16038-0108, USA

Mathews, Sheila
21554 Pacific Coast Hwy
Malibu, CA 90265-5207

Mathews, T J (Athlete, Baseball Player)
211 E Crestview Dr
Columbia, IL 62236-1203, USA

Mathews, Terry (Athlete, Baseball Player)
1132 Belgard Bnd
Boyce, LA 71409-9216, USA

Mathias, Bob (Athlete)
7469 E Pine Ave
Fresno, CA 93737-9520

Mathias, Buster Jr (Boxer)
4409 Carol Ave SW
Wyoming, MI 49519-4519, USA

Mathias, Carl (Athlete, Baseball Player)
567 Long Ln
Oley, PA 19547-9009, USA

Mathias, Charles McC Jr (Financier, Senator)
3808 Leland St
Chevy Chase, MD 20815-4902, USA

Mathias, William (Composer)
Y Graigwen Cadnant Road Menai Bridge
Anglesey, Gwynedd LL59, WALES

Mathieson, John (Director)
c/o Spyros Skouras *The Skouras Agency*
1149 3rd St Ste 300
Santa Monica, CA 90403-7201, USA

Mathieu, Georges V A (Artist)
125 Ava de Makakoff
Paris 75116, FRANCE

Mathieu, Mireille
12 Rue Du Bois De Boulogne
Neuilly, FRANCE F-92200

Mathieu, Philip (Musician)
5 Loblolly Ct Ste Executive
Pinehurst, NC 28374-9349, USA

Mathilde, Princess (Royalty)
Rue de Brederode
Brussels 1000, BELGIUM

Mathis, Alonzo (Gorilla Zoe) (Musician)
c/o Staff Member *Atlantic Records (NY)*
1290 Avenue of the Americas Fl CONC4
New York, NY 10104-0184

Mathis, Bill (Athlete, Football Player)
1699 Lauda Dr
Mt Pleasant, SC 29464-9780, USA

Mathis, Clint (Soccer Player)
1 Harmon Plz # 300
Secaucus, NJ 07094-2803, USA

Mathis, Edith (Opera Singer)
14 Kensington Court
London W8 5DN, UNITED KINGDOM (UK)

Mathis, Jeff (Athlete, Baseball Player)
4420 Spring Valley Dr
Marianna, FL 32448-5414, USA

Mathis, Johnny (Musician)
c/o David Snyder *WmE2 (Endeavor-LA)*
9601 Wilshire Blvd Fl 3
Beverly Hills, CA 90210-5219, USA

Mathis, Judge Greg (Judge)
PO Box 152
Palisades, NY 10964-0152, USA

Mathis, Ron (Athlete, Baseball Player)
2922 Kismet Ln
Houston, TX 77043-1322, USA

Mathis, Samantha (Actor)
c/o Courtney Kivowitz *Schiff Company, The*
8440 Warner Dr Ste B1
Culver City, CA 90232-2461, USA

Mathis, Terance (Athlete, Football Player)
3415 Camellia Ln
Suwanee, GA 30024-5348, USA

Mathis Jr, Buster
4409 Carol Ave SW
Wyoming, MI 49519-4519, USA

Mathison, Cameron (Actor)
c/o Marcia Hurwitz *Innovative Artists (LA)*
1505 10th St
Santa Monica, CA 90401-2805, USA

Mathison, Camerson (Actor)
c/o Staff Member *Innovative Artists (LA)*
1505 10th St
Santa Monica, CA 90401-2805, USA

Mathison, Melissa (Writer)
655 Macculloch Dr
Los Angeles, CA 90049-2024, USA

Matias, John (Athlete, Baseball Player)
98-1616 Hoolauae St
Aiea, HI 96701-1801, USA

Matiko, Marie (Actor)
c/o Staff Member *Sovereign Talent Group*
8421 Wilshire Blvd Ste 200
Beverly Hills, CA 90211-3204, USA

Matine-Coburn, Persia (Stylist)
Prefers to be contacted via telephone or email
CA, USA

Matisyahu (Musician)
c/o Don Van Cleave *The Artists Organization*
212 Marine St Unit 307
Santa Monica, CA 90405-6514, USA

Matkevich, Mark (Actor)
c/o Staff Member *Glasser/Black Management*
283 Cedarhurst Ave
Cedarhurst, NY 11516-1671, USA

Matlack, Jon (Athlete, Baseball Player)
192 Cleveland Rd
Johnsburg, NY 12843-2802, USA

Matlack-Sagrati, Ruth (Baseball Player)
925 Rock Hill Rd
Quakertown, PA 18951-3215, USA

Matlin, Marlee (Actor, Producer)
c/o Lisa Perkins *Fifteen Minutes (LA)*
8436 W 3rd St Ste 650
Los Angeles, CA 90048-4131, USA

Matlock, Glen (Musician)
55 Fulham High St
London SW6 3JJ, UNITED KINGDOM (UK)

Matlock, Jack F Jr (Diplomat)
940 Princeton Kingston Rd
Princeton, NJ 08540-4128, USA

Matlock, John (Athlete, Football Player)
127 Seagrape Dr Apt 102
Jupiter, FL 33458-7885, USA

Matola, Sharon (Misc)
PO Box 1787
Belize City, BELIZE

Matondkar, Urmila (Actor, Bollywood)
93/14 Sanman, Lokhandwala Road
Andheri (W)
Bombay 400058, India

Matorin, Vladimir A (Opera Singer)
#53
Moscow 103045, RUSSIA

Matos, Francisco (Athlete, Baseball Player)
970 W University Pkwy Attn Coachingstaff
Orem, UT 84058-6735, USA

Matos, Julius (Athlete, Baseball Player)
13200 NE 7th Ave
North Miami, FL 33161-7500, USA

Matranga, Dave (Athlete, Baseball Player)
303 N Park Ln
Orange, CA 92867-7642, USA

Matricaria, Ronald (Business Person)
1 Lillehei Plz
Saint Paul, MN 55117-1761, USA

Matsch, Richard P (Judge)
1929 Stout St
Denver, CO 80294-0003, USA

Matsik, George A (Business Person)
10 Longs Peak Dr
Broomfield, CO 80021-2510, USA

Matson, April (Actor)
c/o Jennifer Millar *Paradigm (LA)*
9200 W Sunset Blvd PH 11
Los Angeles, CA 90069-3601, USA

Matson, J Randel (Randy) (Athlete, Track Athlete)
1002 Park Pl
College Station, TX 77840-3008, USA

Matson, Pat (Athlete, Football Player)
987 Village Circle Dr
Greenwood, IN 46143-8465, USA

Matson, Randy
1002 Park Pl
College Station, TX 77840-3008

Matsos, Arch (Athlete, Football Player)
1410 Coventry Close St
East Lansing, MI 48823-2419, USA

Matsuda, Naomi (Actor)
c/o Staff Member *AKA Talent Agency*
6310 San Vicente Blvd Ste 200
Los Angeles, CA 90048-5488, USA

Matsuda, Seiko (Actor, Musician)
1741 Ivar Ave
Los Angeles, CA 90028-5105, USA

Matsui, Hideki (Athlete, Baseball Player)
845 United Nations Plz Apt 52C
New York, NY 10017-3536, USA

Matsui, Kaz (Athlete, Baseball Player)
229 N Almont Dr
Beverly Hills, CA 90211-1615, USA

Matsui, Keiko (Musician)
173 Brighton Ave
Boston, MA 02134-2003, USA

Matsui, Kosei (Artist)
Ibaraki-ken Kasama-shi
Kasama 350, JAPAN

Matsukisa, Nobuyaki (Nobu) (Chef)
c/o Staff Member *Verve Entertainment*
5900 Wilshire Blvd Ste 1720
Los Angeles, CA 90036-5021, USA

Matsumoto, Shigeharu (Writer)
11-16 Roppongi Minatuku
Tokyo, JAPAN

Matsushita, Hiro (Race Car Driver)
14772 Ridgeboro Pl
Tustin, CA 92780-6666, USA

Matsuzaka, Daisuke (Athlete, Baseball Player)
c/o Scott Boras *Boras Corporation*
18 Corporate Plaza Dr
Newport Beach, CA 92660-7901, USA

Matta, del Meskin (Religious Leader)
Deir el Makarios Monastery
Cairo, EGYPT

Matte, Thomas R (Tom) (Athlete, Football Player)
11309 Old Carriage Rd
Glen Arm, MD 21057-9422, USA

Mattea, Kathy (Actor, Musician)
PO Box 1776
Orem, UT 84059-1776, USA

Mattei, Frank (Musician)
PO Box 1017
Turnersville, NJ 08012-0837, USA

Mattek-Sands, Bethanie (Athlete, Tennis Player)
c/o Staff Member *CMPR*
2121 Rosecrans Ave Ste 3375
El Segundo, CA 90245-4767, USA

Matter, Niall (Actor)
c/o Trina Allen *Play Management*
807 Powell St Suite 220
Vancouver V6A 1H7, Canada

Mattes, Eva (Actor)
1C Neurieder St
San Diego, CA 92152-0001, GERMANY

Mattes, Ron (Athlete, Football Player)
1718 Moreland Wood Trl NW
Concord, NC 28027-8093, USA

Mattes, Troy (Athlete, Baseball Player)
2932 Lexington St
Sarasota, FL 34231-6118, USA

Mattesich, Rudi (Skier)
Troy, VT 5868, USA

Matteson, Troy (Athlete, Golfer)
6518 Old Shadburn Ferry Rd
Buford, GA 30518-1138, USA

Matthes, Roland (Swimmer)
Luitpoldstr 35A
Marktheidenfeld 97828, GERMANY

Matthes, Ulrich (Actor)
Kuno-Fischer-Str 14
Berlin 14057, GERMANY

Matthew, Catriona (Athlete, Golfer)
Pier House Strand on the Green Chiswick
London W4 3NN, United Kingdom

Matthews, Alvin (Athlete, Football Player)
19541 Diablo Dr
Pflugerville, TX 78660-5088, USA

Matthews, Amy (Stylist)
c/o Staff Member *Crews*
828 Clemont Dr NE
Atlanta, GA 30306-3694, USA

Matthews, Bill (Athlete, Football Player)
32 Olde Farm Rd
South Easton, MA 02375-1438, USA

Matthews, Bo (Athlete, Football Player)
10053 Vine Ct
Thornton, CO 80229-2385, USA

Matthews, Bruce R (Athlete, Football Player)
6423 Oilfield Rd
Sugar Land, TX 77479-9603, USA

Matthews, Cerys (Musician)
c/o Staff Member *Agency Group Ltd, The (UK)*
361-373 City Rd
London EC1V 1PQ, UK

Matthews, Chris (Television Host)
c/o Staff Member *MSNBC (DC)*
400 N Capitol St NW Ste 850
Washington, DC 20001-1555, USA

Matthews, Dakin (Actor)
c/o Staff Member *McCabe Group, The*
3211 Cahuenga Blvd W Ste 104
Los Angeles, CA 90068-1372, USA

Matthews, Dave (Music Group, Musician)
c/o David Lillard *IFA Talent Agency*
8730 W Sunset Blvd Ste 490
Los Angeles, CA 90069-2248, USA

Matthews, DeLane (Actor)
5500 Wilshire Blvd # 2200
Los Angeles, CA 90036-3802, USA

Matthews, Gary N (Athlete, Baseball Player)
1542 W Jackson Blvd
Chicago, IL 60607-5304, USA

Matthews, Ian (Musician)
11846 Balboa Blvd # 204
Granada Hills, CA 91344-2753, USA

Matthews, Keith (Astronomer)
Astronomy
Pasadena, CA 91125-0001, USA

Matthews, Liesel (Actor)
c/o Staff Member *Creative Artists Agency (CAA-LA)*
2000 Avenue of the Stars Ste 100
Los Angeles, CA 90067-4705, USA

Matthews, Mike (Athlete, Baseball Player)
976 Spirea
Howell, MI 48843-6872, USA

Matthews, Pat Stanley (Actor)
210 Stanton St
Walla Walla, WA 99362-2058, USA

Matthews, Rachel (Stylist)
c/o Staff Member *Judy Inc*
1 Yorkville Ave
Toronto ON M4W 1L1, Canada

Matthews, Robert C O (Economist)
CB2 1TL, UNITED KINGDOM (UK)

Matthews, Ross (Correspondent)

Matthews, Shane (Athlete, Football Player)
8608 SW 38th Ave
Gainesville, FL 32608-8694, USA

Matthews, Vincent (Vince) (Athlete, Track Athlete)
6755 193rd Ln
Fresh Meadows, NY 11365-4034, USA

Matthews, W Clay Jr (Athlete, Football Player)
6068 Canterbury Dr
Agoura Hills, CA 91301-4131, USA

Matthews Jr, Gary (Athlete, Baseball Player)
4653 Willens Ave
Woodland Hills, CA 91364-3812, USA

Matthies, Nina (Athlete, Coach, Volleyball Player)
24255 Pacific Coast Hwy
Malibu, CA 90263-0001, USA

Matthiessen, Peter (Writer)
Bridge Lane
Sagaponack, NY 11962, USA

Mattiace, Len (Athlete, Golfer)
12803 Hunt Club Rd N
Jacksonville, FL 32224-7654, USA

Mattiello, Matthew (Stylist)
c/o Staff Member *Perrella Management*
330 W 38th St Rm 1407
New York, NY 10018-8435, USA

Mattila, Karita M (Opera Singer)
45B Croxley Road
London W9 3HJ, UNITED KINGDOM (UK)

Mattingly, Don (Athlete, Baseball Player)
7601 Newburgh Rd
Evansville, IN 47715-4527, USA

Mattingly, Mack F (Senator)
4315 10th St East Bch
Saint Simons Island, GA 31522, USA

Mattingly, Thomas K II (Admiral, Astronaut)
1501 Quail St # 102
Newport Beach, CA 92660-2726, USA

Mattox, Gus (Adult Film Star)
c/o Staff Member *Diva Central Inc*
7510 W Sunset Blvd Ste 1445
Los Angeles, CA 90046-3408, USA

Mattson, Riley (Athlete, Football Player)
3900 SW 75th Ave
Portland, OR 97225-2731, USA

Mattson, Robin (Actor)
7772 Torreyson Dr
Los Angeles, CA 90046-1227, USA

Mattson-Baumgart, Jacqueline (Baseball Player)
4814 W Fillmore Dr
West Allis, WI 53219-2364, USA

Mattsson, Helena (Actor)
c/o Liza Anderson *Anderson Group Public Relations*
8060 Melrose Ave Fl 4
Los Angeles, CA 90046-7038, USA

Matula, Rick (Athlete, Baseball Player)
1817 Chapel Heights Dr
Wharton, TX 77488-4459, USA

Matuszak, Marv (Athlete, Football Player)
3054 Mill Grove Ter
Dacula, GA 30019-5019, USA

Matuszek, Len (Athlete, Baseball Player)
10326 Deerfield Rd
Cincinnati, OH 45242-5105, USA

Matuza, Albert (Athlete, Football Player)
131 Paul Rd
Morrisville, PA 19067-4855, USA

Matvichuk, Richard (Athlete, Hockey Player)
2104 Falcon Pass
Westlake, TX 76262-4805, USA

Matz, Johanna
Opernring 4
Vienna, AUSTRIA 1010

Matzdorf, Pat (Athlete, Track Athlete)
1252 Bainbridge Dr
Naperville, IL 60563-2065, USA

Mauban, Maria
4 Sq Vitruve
Paris, FRANCE 75020

Mauch, Billy & Bobby
538 W Northwest Hwy Unit C
Palatine, IL 60067-8695

Mauch, Billy (Bill) (Actor)
538 W Northwest Hwy Unit C
Palatine, IL 60067-8695, USA

Mauck, Carl (Athlete, Football Player)
160 W Commerce Ct
Gilbert, AZ 85233-4418, USA

Mauer, Joe (Athlete, Baseball Player)
671 Lexington Pkwy N
Saint Paul, MN 55104-2025, USA

Maugham, R H (Religious Leader)
PO Box 35000
Colorado Springs, CO 80935-3500, USA

Maughan, Deryck (Financier)
980 Great West Rd
Brentford, Middlesex TW8 9GS, United Kingdom

Maulden, Jerry L (Business Person)
10055 Grogans Mill Rd # 5A
The Woodlands, TX 77380-1059, USA

Mauldin, William H (Cartoonist)
150 E 35th St
New York, NY 10016-4102

Maule, Brad (Actor)
c/o Hank Hedland *Opus Entertainment*
5225 Wilshire Blvd Ste 905
Los Angeles, CA 90036-4353, USA

Maumenee, Alfred E (Misc)
1700 Hillside Rd
Stevenson, MD 21153-0662, USA

Maura, Carmen (Actor)
Calle Fuencarral 17
Madrid 28004, SPAIN

Maurer, Andy (Athlete, Football Player)
30 Perrydale Ave
Medford, OR 97501-2037, USA

Maurer, Dave (Athlete, Baseball Player)
6845 Lake Harrison Cir
Chanhassen, MN 55317-4589, USA

Maurer, Rob (Athlete, Baseball Player)
3114 E Gum St
Evansville, IN 47714-2614, USA

Maurer, Robert D (Inventor)
2572 W 28th Ave
Eugene, OR 97405-1456, USA

Mauresmo, Amelie (Amy) (Tennis Player)
2 rue du chemin vert
Clichy 92110, FRANCE

Maurey, Nicole (Actor)
6 Square De Caustiglione BP 9005
Le Chesnay F-78150, FRANCE

Mauriac, Claude (Writer)
24 Quai de Bethune
Paris 75004, FRANCE

Maurice, Ann (Actor)
c/o Lucy Inskip *House Doctor Network*
Gladstone Forge, Gladstone Ln Cold Ash
Berkshire RG18 9PR, UK

Maurice, Paul (Athlete, Hockey Player)
205 Calm Winds Ct
Cary, NC 27513-3579, USA

Mauriello, Julianna Rose (Actor)
c/o Nancy Carson *Carson-Adler Agency*
250 W 57th St Ste 2030
New York, NY 10107-2013, USA

Mauriello, Ralph (Athlete, Baseball Player)
4241 Persimmon St
Moorpark, CA 93021-3515, USA

Maurier, Claire
Il rue de la Montague-le-Breuil
Epinay Orge, FRANCE 91360

Maurin, Laurence (Skier)
PO Box 1980
West Bend, WI 53095-7980, USA

Mauroy, Pierre (Prime Minister)
17-19 Rue Voltaire
Lille 59800, FRANCE

Maurstad, Toralv (Actor, Director)
Storlingsgt 15
Osto 1, NORWAY

Mauser, Tim (Athlete, Baseball Player)
114 Shadow Creek Ln
Aledo, TX 76008-3111, USA

Mauti, Rich (Athlete, Football Player)
304 Plantation Dr
Mandeville, LA 70471-1502, USA

Mauz, Henry H (Hank) Jr (Admiral)
1608 Viscaino Rd
Pebble Beach, CA 93953-3303, USA

Maven, Max
PO Box 1298
La Mesa, CA 91944-1298

Mavericks, The (Music Group)
c/o Staff Member *Asgard Promotions*
125 Parkway
London NW1 7PS, United Kingdom

Mavraides, Menil (Athlete, Football Player)
651 Varnum Ave
Lowell, MA 01854-2129, USA

Mawae, Kevin J (Athlete, Football Player)
3704A Estes Rd
Nashville, TN 37215-1729, USA

Mawby, Russell G (Misc)
1 Michigan Ave E
Battle Creek, MI 49017-4005, USA

Max, Peter (Artist)
37 W 65th St
New York, NY 10023-6610, USA

Maxa, Rudy (Radio Personality, Television Host)
PO Box 65066
Saint Paul, MN 55165-0066, USA

Maxcy, Brian (Athlete, Baseball Player)
982 Cobble Creek Dr
Birmingham, AL 35226-2867, USA

Maxey, Caty (Designer)
c/o Staff Member *Mirisch Agency*
8840 Wilshire Blvd Ste 100
Beverly Hills, CA 90211-2606, USA

Maxey, Marlon (Athlete, Basketball Player)
9013 S Blackstone Ave
Chicago, IL 60619-7909, USA

Maxey, Virginia
16414 Pick Pl
Riverside, CA 92504-5645

Maxi, Fumihiko (Architect)
5-16-22 Higashi Gotanda Shinagawaku
Tokyo, JAPAN

Maxie, Brett (Athlete, Football Player)
10251 Blue Palm St
Plantation, FL 33324-8262, USA

Maxie, Larry (Athlete, Baseball Player)
296 Verdugo Way
Upland, CA 91786-7138, USA

Maximova, Ekaterina (Ballerina)
Teatralnaya Pi 1
Moscow 103009, RUSSIA

Maxson, Alvin (Athlete, Football Player)
17377 E Adriatic Pl
Aurora, CO 80013-4191, USA

Maxson, Robert (Educator)
President S Ofc
Long Beach, CA 90840-0001, USA

Maxvill, Dal (Athlete, Baseball Player)
1115 Eagle Creek Rd
Chesterfield, MO 63005-6606, USA

Maxwell, Arthur E (Oceanographer)
PO Box 31249
Santa Fe, NM 87594-1249, USA

Maxwell, Cedric (Cornbread) (Athlete, Basketball Player)
151 Tremont St Apt 25R
Boston, MA 02111-1123, USA

Maxwell, Charlie (Athlete, Baseball Player)
730 Mapleview Dr
Paw Paw, MI 49079-1185, USA

Maxwell, Dobie (Comedian)
333 W North Ave # 343
Chicago, IL 60610-1293, USA

Maxwell, Frank (Politician)
260 Madison Ave
New York, NY 10016-2401, USA

Maxwell, Ian (Publisher)
Eaton Terrace
London SW1, UNITED KINGDOM (UK)

Maxwell, Jacqui (Actor)
c/o Karen Goldberg *HYPHENATE*
9701 Wilshire Blvd Fl 10
Beverly Hills, CA 90212-2010, USA

Maxwell, Jason (Athlete, Baseball Player)
406 Hicks Rd
Nashville, TN 37221-2002, USA

Maxwell, Julie (Writer)
c/o Staff Member *Rogers, Coleridge & White Ltd.*
20 Powis Mews
London W11 1JN, UK

Maxwell, Kevin F H (Publisher)
Hill Burn Hailey near Wallingford
Oxford OX10 6AD, UNITED KINGDOM (UK)

Maxwell, Kim (Stylist)
3450 Mission Ridge Cir
Atlanta, GA 30339-3503, USA

Maxwell, Robert D (War Hero)
1001 SE 15th St Unit 44
Bend, OR 97702-2351, USA

Maxwell, Ronald F (Director, Writer)
c/o Staff Member *Phoenix Organization, The*
1990 S Bundy Dr Ste 630
Los Angeles, CA 90025-6140, USA

Maxwell, Tommy (Athlete, Football Player)
1634 Rockview Dr
Granbury, TX 76049-5733, USA

Maxwell, Vernon (Athlete, Basketball Player)
2601 NW 23rd Blvd Apt 170
Gainesville, FL 32605-5954, USA

May, Alan (Athlete, Hockey Player)
c/o Staff Member *Boston Bruins*
TD Banknorth Garden 100 Legends Way, Suite 250
Boston, MA 2114, USA

May, Arthur (Architect)
111 W 57th St
New York, NY 10019-2211, USA

May, Bob (Athlete, Golfer)
420 Grand Augusta Ln
Las Vegas, NV 89144-4300, USA

May, Briane (Musician, Songwriter, Writer)
Old Bakehouse 16A High St Barnes
London SW13, UNITED KINGDOM (UK)

May, Carlos (Athlete, Baseball Player)
6102 Amherst Pl
Matteson, IL 60443-1988, USA

May, Darrell (Athlete, Baseball Player)
747 Minthorne Rd
Rogue River, OR 97537-9692, USA

May, Dave (Athlete, Baseball Player)
2011 Chipmunk Ct
Bear, DE 19701-2754, USA

May, David (Actor)
c/o Staff Member *Cunningham Escott Slevin & Doherty (CESD-LA)*
10635 Santa Monica Blvd Ste 130
Los Angeles, CA 90025-8306, USA

May, Deborah (Actor)
1180 S Beverly Dr Ste 301
Los Angeles, CA 90035-1154, USA

May, Deems (Athlete, Football Player)
3922 Ayscough Rd
Charlotte, NC 28211-3470, USA

May, Derrick (Athlete, Baseball Player)
2 Jaymar Blvd
Newark, DE 19702-2877, USA

May, Don (Athlete, Basketball Player)
1128 Colwick Dr
Dayton, OH 45420-2206, USA

May, Donald
733 Seward St
Los Angeles, CA 90038-3503

May, Elaine (Actor, Director, Writer)
c/o Staff Member *WmE2 (WMA-LA)*
1 William Morris Pl
Beverly Hills, CA 90212-4261, USA

May, Joe (Misc)
General Delivery
Thorne Bay, AK 99919-9999, USA

May, Lee (Baseball Player)
2272 4th Place Cir NE # NE
Center Point, AL 35215-3808, USA

May, Lee A (Baseball Player)
5593 Hill Dale Dr
Cincinnati, OH 45213, USA

May, Mark E (Football Player, Sportscaster)
c/o Staff Member *ESPN (Main)*
ESPN Plaza 935 Middle St
Bristol, CT 06010-1001, USA

May, Mathilda (Actor)
20 Ave Rapp
Paris 75007, FRANCE

May, Milt (Athlete, Baseball Player)
4581 Riverview Blvd
Bradenton, FL 34209-1961, USA

May, Ralphie (Actor, Comedian, Producer, Writer)

May, Rudy (Athlete, Baseball Player)
8090 N Augusta St
Fresno, CA 93720-2031, USA

May, Scott (Athlete, Baseball Player)
1630 Raven Cir Unit H
Estes Park, CO 80517-9477, USA

May, Scott G (Athlete, Basketball Player)
2001 E Hillside Dr
Bloomington, IN 47401-6203, USA

May, Suzanne (Actor)
c/o Staff Member *Frontline Management*
5670 Wilshire Blvd Ste 1370
Los Angeles, CA 90036-5679, USA

May, Torsten (Boxer)
Hans-Bockler-Str 163
Hurth 50354, GERMANY

Mayaki, Ibrahim Hassane (Prime Minister)
State House
Niamey, NIGER

Mayall, John (Composer, Musician)
200 W Superior St Ste 202
Chicago, IL 60654-3554, USA

Mayall, Rik (Actor, Comedian)
169 Queen's Gale
London SW7 5HE, UNITED KINGDOM (UK)

Mayasich, John E (Athlete, Hockey Player)
2250 Riverwood Pl
Saint Paul, MN 55104-5646, USA

Mayberry, Jermane (Athlete, Football Player)
2208 Court Del Rey
Round Rock, TX 78681-2247, USA

Mayberry, John C (Athlete, Baseball Player)
11115 W 121st Ter
Overland Park, KS 66213-1945, USA

Mayberry, Lee (Athlete, Basketball Player)
4115 E 36th St N
Tulsa, OK 74115-1709, USA

Mayberry, Tony (Athlete, Football Player)
15704 Cochester Rd
Tampa, FL 33647-1100, USA

Maybury, John (Director)
c/o Staff Member *WmE2 (Endeavor-LA)*
9601 Wilshire Blvd Fl 3
Beverly Hills, CA 90210-5219, USA

Maydan, Dan (Business Person)
3050 Bowers Ave
Santa Clara, CA 95054-3201, USA

Mayer, Chip
4601 Willis Ave Apt 210
Sherman Oaks, CA 91403-2623, USA

Mayer, Christian (Skier)
Siedlerweg 18
Finkelstein 9884, AUSTRIA

Mayer, Ed (Athlete, Baseball Player)
440 Oakland Ave
Corte Madera, CA 94925, USA

Mayer, Gene (Tennis Player)
115 South St
Glen Dale, MD 20769, USA

Mayer, H Robert (Judge)
717 Madison Pl NW
Washington, DC 20439-0001, USA

Mayer, John (Musician, Songwriter, Writer)
c/o Michael McDonald *Mick Management*
35 Washington St
Brooklyn, NY 11201-1028, USA

Mayer, Joseph E (Physicist)
2345 Via Siena
La Jolla, CA 92037-3933, USA

Mayer, Martin J (Admiral)
116 Lake View Pkwy
Suffolk, VA 23435-2659, USA

Mayer, P Augustin Cardinal (Religious Leader)
Ecclesia Dei
Vatican City 120, VATICAN CITY

Mayer, Phil
Rt. 9 Box 715-M
Yakima, WA 98901

Mayer, Travis (Skier)
37050 Williams St
Steamboat Springs, CO 80487, USA

Mayes, Alonzo (Athlete, Football Player)
3000 SE 56th St
Oklahoma City, OK 73135-1620, USA

Mayes, David (Athlete, Football Player)
3018 Kingsley Rd
Shaker Heights, OH 44122-2816, USA

Mayes, Derrick (Athlete, Football Player)
4425 Brown Rd
Indianapolis, IN 46226-3147, USA

Mayes, Rueben (Athlete, Football Player)
2953 Lord Byron Pl
Eugene, OR 97408-4638, USA

Mayes, Wendell
1504 Bel Air Rd
Los Angeles, CA 90077-3022

Mayfair, Billy (Athlete, Golfer)
PO Box 25844
Scottsdale, AZ 85255-0114, USA

Mayfield, Corey (Athlete, Football Player)
210 Tournament Rd
Tyler, TX 75702-6649, USA

Mayfield, Jeremy (Athlete, Race Car Driver)
PO Box 3998
Mooresville, NC 28117-3998, USA

Mayhew, Lauren (Actor)
c/o David Eisenberg *Protege Entertainment*
710 E Angeleno Ave
Burbank, CA 91501-2213, USA

Mayhew, Patrick B B (Government Official)
Westminster
London SW1A 0PW, UNITED KINGDOM (UK)

Maynard, Andrew (Boxer)
3922 Fairmont Ave
Bethesda, MD 20814, USA

Maynard, Brad (Athlete, Football Player)
13225 Mattock Chase
Carmel, IN 46033-8643, USA

Maynard, Mimi (Actor)
9229 W Sunset Blvd Ste 311
Los Angeles, CA 90069-3403, USA

Mayne, Brent (Athlete, Baseball Player)
1863 Parkglen Cir
Costa Mesa, CA 92627-4506, USA

Mayne, D Roger (Photographer)
Colway Manor Colway Lane
Lyme Regis, Dorset DT7 3HD, UNITED KINGDOM (UK)

Mayne, Kenny (Sportscaster)
Sports Dept ESPN Plaza 935 Middle St
Bristol, CT 6010, USA

Mayne, Thomas (Architect)
2041 Colorado Ave
Santa Monica, CA 90404-3415, USA

Maynor, Asa
PO Box 1641
Beverly Hills, CA 90213-1641

Maynor, Stephanie (Athlete, Golfer)
5205 Bordeaux Cv
Ellicott City, MD 21043-7086, USA

Mayo, Jackie (Athlete, Baseball Player)
450 Boardman Poland Rd
Youngstown, OH 44512 4906, USA

Mayock, Michael (Athlete, Football Player)
607 Georges Ln
Ardmore, PA 19003-1905, USA

Mayor, Michel (Astronomer)
Geneva Observatory
Geneva, SWITZERLAND

Mayor, Zaragoza Federico (Government Official)
7 Place de Fonteroy
Paris 75352, FRANCE

Mayotte, Timothy S (Tim) (Tennis Player)
2665 S Bayshore Dr # 602
Miami, FL 33133-5448, USA

Mayron, Melanie (Actor, Director)
1435 N Ogden Dr
Los Angeles, CA 90046-3906, USA

Mays, Alvoid (Athlete, Football Player)
3903 Cape Vista Dr
Bradenton, FL 34209-6725, USA

Mays, Damon (Athlete, Football Player)
12705 N 57th Dr
Glendale, AZ 85304-1884, USA

Mays, Jayma (Actor)
c/o Steven Levy *Framework Entertainment (LA)*
9057 Nemo St Ste C
West Hollywood, CA 90069-5511, USA

Mays, Jeryn (Actor)
28318 Birdie St
Moreno Valley, CA 92555-6358, USA

Mays, Joe (Athlete, Baseball Player)
10314 Riverbank Ter
Bradenton, FL 34212-5256, USA

Mays, Lyle (Musician)
173 Brighton Ave
Boston, MA 02134-2003, USA

Mays, Rueben
7306 172nd St SW
Edmonds, WA 98026-5121

Mays, Willie (Athlete, Baseball Player)
51 Mount Vernon Ln
Atherton, CA 94027-3036, USA

Maysey, Matt (Athlete, Baseball Player)
1415 Canter Cir
Bourbonnais, IL 60914-4593, USA

May-Treanor, Misty (Athlete, Volleyball Player)
2892 N Bellflower Blvd Ste 482
Long Beach, CA 90815-1125, USA

Mayweather Jr., Floyd (Athlete, Boxer)
4720 Laguna Vista St
Las Vegas, NV 89147-6043, USA

Mazach, John J (Admiral)
1137 Quail Roost Ct
Virginia Beach, VA 23451-3879, USA

Mazar, Debi (Actor)
c/o Peg Donegan *Framework Entertainment (LA)*
9057 Nemo St Ste C
West Hollywood, CA 90069-5511, USA

Mazarella, Jacqueline (Actor)
c/o Tony Martinez *GVA Talent Agency Inc*
8981 W Sunset Blvd Ste 101
Los Angeles, CA 90069-1850, USA

Mazaroski, William S (Bill) (Baseball Player)
RR 6 Box 130
Greensburg, PA 15601, USA

Mazeroski, Bill (Athlete, Baseball Player)
281 Walton Tea Room Rd
Greensburg, PA 15601-6406, USA

Maznicki, Frank (Athlete, Football Player)
2 Coaches Ct
West Warwick, RI 2893, USA

Mazor, Stanley (Stan) (Inventor)
3031 Tisch Way
San Jose, CA 95128-2541, USA

Mazowiecki, Tadeusz (Prime Minister)
Sejm RP Ul Qiekska 4/6/8
Warsaw 00-902, POLAND

Mazur, Jay J (Misc)
275 7th Ave Fl 11
New York, NY 10001-6708, USA

Mazur, John (Athlete, Football Coach, Football Player)
672 Cornwallis Dr
Mount Laurel, NJ 08054-3217, USA

Mazur, Monet (Actor)
c/o Marsha McManus *Principal Entertainment (LA)*
1964 Westwood Blvd Ste 400
Los Angeles, CA 90025-4695, USA

Mazursky, Paul (Director)
c/o Larry Shapiro *Nine Yards Entertainment*
8530 Wilshire Blvd Ste 550
Beverly Hills, CA 90211-3133, USA

Mazza, Valeria (Model)
8/10 Via Revere
Milan 20123, ITALY

Mazzanti, Geno (Athlete, Football Player)
4188 E Highway 82
Lake Village, AR 71653-6057, USA

Mazzanti, Jerry (Athlete, Football Player)
1712 S Lakeshore Dr
Lake Village, AR 71653-1573, USA

Mazzara, Glen (Producer)
c/o Staff Member *Creative Artists Agency (CAA-LA)*
2000 Avenue of the Stars Ste 100
Los Angeles, CA 90067-4705, USA

Mazzarello, Marcelo (Actor)
c/o Staff Member *Telefe - Argentina*
Pavon 2444 (C1248AAT)
Buenos Aires, ARGENTINA

Mazzello, Joseph (Actor)
46691 Mission Blvd # 536
Fremont, CA 94539-7994

Mazzetti, Tim (Athlete, Football Player)
2609 W 118th St
Leawood, KS 66211-3035, USA

Mazzie, Marin (Actor, Musician)
233 Park Ave S # 1000
New York, NY 10003-1606, USA

Mazzilli, Lee L (Athlete, Baseball Player, Coach)
67 Stonehedge Dr S
Greenwich, CT 06831-3220, USA

Mazzo, Kay (Ballerina)
144 W 66th St
New York, NY 10023, USA

Mazzola, Anthony T (Editor)
1790 Broadway
New York, NY 10019-1412, USA

Mba, Casimir Oye (Prime Minister)
Boile Postale 546
Libreville, GABON

Mbasogo, Teodoro Obiang Nguema (President)
Malabo, EQUATORIAL GUINEA

Mbatha-Raw, Gugu (Actor)
c/o Meg Mortimer *Principal Entertainment (NY)*
130 W 42nd St Ste 614
New York, NY 10036-7804, USA

Mbeki, Thabo (President)
Union Buildings
Pretoria 1, SOUTH AFRICA

Mbenga, D J (Athlete, Basketball Player)
6112 Winton St
Dallas, TX 75214-2636, USA

M'Bow, Amadou-Mahtar (Government Official)
BP 5276
Dakar-Fann, SENEGAL

McAdams, Carl (Athlete, Football Player)
HC 82 Box 526
Atoka, OK 74525, USA

McAdams, Rachel (Actor)
c/o Shelley Browning *Magnolia Entertainment (LA)*
9595 Wilshire Blvd Ste 601
Beverly Hills, CA 90212-2506, USA

McAdoo, Robert A (Bob) (Athlete, Basketball Player, Coach)
20970 Via Alamanda Apt 1
Boca Raton, FL 33428-1335, USA

McAfee, Ken
8 Deerfield Dr
Medfield, MA 02052-1318

McAillister-Morton, Susie (Athlete, Golfer)
40241 Club View Dr
Rancho Mirage, CA 92270-3527, USA

McAleese, Mary P (President)
Baile Athe Cliath 8
Dublin, IRELAND

McAleese, Peter (Producer)
c/o Lisa Helsing Lenhoff *Lenhoff & Lenhoff*
830 Palm Ave
West Hollywood, CA 90069-4009

McAleney, Ed (Athlete, Football Player)
981 Shore Rd
Cape Elizabeth, ME 04107-1908, USA

McAlister, Chris (Athlete, Football Player)
259 W Duarte Rd Apt H
Monrovia, CA 91016, USA

McAlister, James E (Athlete, Football Player, Track Athlete)
155 Glorieta St
Pasadena, CA 91103-3018, USA

McAllister, Deuce (Football Player)
c/o Staff Member *Philadelphia Eagles*
1 Novacare Way
Philadelphia, PA 19145-5996

McAlpine, Donald M (Cinematographer)
377 Placer Creek Ln
Henderson, NV 89014-4560, USA

McAnally, Ernie (Athlete, Baseball Player)
1800 Fairway N
Mount Pleasant, TX 75455-6714, USA

McAnally, Mac (Musician, Songwriter)
c/o Staff Member *Paradigm (Monterey)*
404 W Franklin St
Monterey, CA 93940-2303, USA

McAnany, Jim (Athlete, Baseball Player)
1723 Cochran St Apt G
Simi Valley, CA 93065-2174, USA

McAndrew, Jamie (Athlete, Baseball Player)
9620 E Diamond Rim Dr
Scottsdale, AZ 85255-3330, USA

McAndrew, Jim (Athlete, Baseball Player)
9620 E Diamond Rim Dr
Scottsdale, AZ 85255-3330, USA

McAndrew, Tracey (Nell) (Actor, Model)
c/o Staff Member *Adult Model SEM Group*
98 Cockfosters Rd Barnet
Hertfordshirt EN4 0DP, UNITED KINGDOM

McArdle, Andrea (Actor, Musician)
14 Shady Glen Ct
New Rochelle, NY 10805-1806, USA

McArdle, John (Athlete, Baseball Player)
6640 Lynford St
Philadelphia, PA 19149-2124, USA

McArthur, Alex (Actor)
9443 Hillrose St
Sunland, CA 91040-1716, USA

McArthur, Kevin (Athlete, Football Player)
3817 Meredith Ln
Mesquite, TX 75180-5017, USA

McArthur, William S (Bill) Jr (Astronaut)
2512 Mountain Falls Ct
Friendswood, TX 77546-5592, USA

McAuley, Alphonso (Actor)
c/o David (Dave) Fleming *Mosaic Media Group*
9200 W Sunset Blvd Ste 10
Los Angeles, CA 90069-3608, USA

McAuley, Jordan (Business Person, Writer)
8721 Santa Monica Blvd # 431
Los Angeles, CA 90069-4507, USA

McAuliffe, Callan (Actor)
c/o Nicholas Bogner *Affirmative Entertainment*
425 N Robertson Blvd
West Hollywood, CA 90048-1735, USA

McAuliffe, Dennis P (General)
9160 Belvoir Woods Pkwy
Fort Belvoir, VA 22060-2703, USA

McAuliffe, Dick (Athlete, Baseball Player)
32 Worthington Dr
Farmington, CT 06032-1493, USA

McAvoy, James (Actor)
c/o Meredith O'Sullivan *42West (LA)*
11400 W Olympic Blvd Ste 1100
Los Angeles, CA 90064-1579, USA

McAvoy, Tom (Athlete, Baseball Player)
2 Clinton Ct
Stillwater, NY 12170-1306, USA

McBain, Diane (Actor)
PO Box 1377
Lake Dallas, TX 75065-1377, USA

McBath, Mike (Athlete, Football Player)
5044 Sailwind Cir
Orlando, FL 32810-1839, USA

McBean, Al (Baseball Player)
PO Box 4475
St Thomas, VI 801, USA

McBee, Rives (Athlete, Golfer)
1504 Canyon Oaks Dr
Irving, TX 75061-2116, USA

McBeth, Marcus (Athlete, Baseball Player)
211 Wilson Rd
Enoree, SC 29335-3729, USA

McBratney, Sam (Writer)
c/o Staff Member *HarperCollins Publishers*
10 E 53rd St C/O Author Mail Floor 7
New York, NY 10022, USA

McBrayer, Jack
c/o Jo Yao *United Talent Agency (UTA)*
9560 Wilshire Blvd Fl 5
Beverly Hills, CA 90212-2400, USA

McBride, Bake (Athlete, Baseball Player)
4077 Reliant Cir
Owensboro, KY 42301-0024, USA

McBride, Chi (Actor)
c/o Sam Maydew *Collective*
8383 Wilshire Blvd Ste 1050
Beverly Hills, CA 90211-2415, USA

McBride, Danny (Actor)
c/o Lindsay Williams *The Gotham Group Inc*
9255 W Sunset Blvd Ste 515
Los Angeles, CA 90069-3308, USA

McBride, Jeff
4185 Paradise Rd # 2081
Las Vegas, NV 89169-6501

McBride, Jon A (Astronaut)
1018 Kanawha Blvd E Ste 901
Charleston, WV 25301-2800, USA

McBride, Justin (Misc)
101 W Riverwalk
Pueblo, CO 81003-3243, USA

McBride, Ken (Athlete, Baseball Player)
3446 Cypress Cir
Westlake, OH 44145-4409, USA

McBride, Macay (Athlete, Baseball Player)
2100 Woodward Ave Attn Autographsforacause
Detroit, MI 48201-3470, USA

McBride, Martina (Musician)
c/o Jake Basden *Big Machine Records*
1219 16th Ave S
Nashville, TN 37212-2901, USA

McBride, Oscar (Athlete, Football Player)
PO Box 247
Chiefland, FL 32644-0247, USA

McBride, Patricia (Ballerina)
150 W End Ave
New York, NY 10023-5702, USA

Mcbride, Susan (Writer)
8712 Garden Ct
Brentwood, MO 63144-1830, USA

McBride, Turk (Athlete, Football Player)
c/o Eugene Parker *Maximum Sports Management*
6435 W Jefferson Blvd # 197
Fort Wayne, IN 46804-6203, USA

McBride, William J (Misc)
Gorse Lodge Ballyclare
County Antrim BT39 9DE, NORTHERN IRELAND

McBroom, Amanda (Musician, Songwriter, Writer)
167 Fairview Rd
Ojai, CA 93023-9537, USA

McCabe, Bryan (Athlete, Hockey Player)
c/o Staff Member *Toronto Maple Leafs*
Air Canada Centre 400-40 Bay St
Toronto, ON M5J 2X2, Canada

McCabe, Frank (Athlete, Basketball Player)
6712 N White Fir Dr
Edwards, IL 61528-9424, USA

McCabe, Joe (Athlete, Baseball Player)
3932 E 79th St
Indianapolis, IN 46240-3458, USA

McCabe, John (Musician)
8/9 Firth St
London W1V 5TZ, UNITED KINGDOM (UK)

McCabe, Marcia
1990 Broadway Ansonia Sta Box 417
. New York, NY 10023

McCabe, Patrick (Writer)
Macmillan Books 25 Eckkeston Place
London SW1W 9NF, UNITED KINGDOM (UK)

McCabe, Zia (Musician)
PO Box 5908
Portland, OR 97228-5908, USA

McCafferty, Donald F (Don) Jr (Coach, Football Coach)
167 E Shore Rd
Halesite, NY 11743-1128, USA

McCaffery, Marcia (Stylist)
629 Cole Ranch Rd
Encinitas, CA 92024-6523, USA

McCaffrey, Barry R (General)
506 Crown View Dr
Alexandria, VA 22314-4806, USA

McCaffrey, Mike (Athlete, Football Player)
341 W Muncie Ave
Fresno, CA 93711-6036, USA

McCain, Bob (Athlete, Football Player)
606 1/2 W Henry St
Greenwood, MS 38930-5325, USA

McCain, Edwin (Songwriter, Writer)
PO Box 1267
Decatur, GA 30031-1267, USA

McCain, John (Politician)
241 Russell Senate Ofc Bldg
Washington, DC 20510-0001, USA

McCain, Meghan
241 Russell Senate Ofc Bldg
Washington, DC 20510-0001, USA

McCall, Brett (Stylist)
c/o Staff Member *Seaminx Artist Management*
9234 Peninsula Dr
Dallas, TX 75218-2733, USA

McCall, Brian (Athlete, Baseball Player)
550 Tremont Ave
Greensburg, PA 15601-4263, USA

McCall, Davina (Actor)
c/o Staff Member *John Noel Management*
10A Belmont St Floor 2
London NW1 8HH, UNITED KINGDOM (UK)

McCall, Don (Athlete, Football Player)
16830 Kingsbury St Apt 131
Granada Hills, CA 91344-6465, USA

McCall, John (Athlete, Baseball Player)
8043 E Ragweed Dr
Tucson, AZ 85710-8580, USA

McCall, Larry (Athlete, Baseball Player)
370 Justice Ridge Rd
Candler, NC 28715-9576, USA

McCall, Mitzi (Actor)
c/o Staff Member *Cunningham Escott Slevin & Doherty (CESD-LA)*
10635 Santa Monica Blvd Ste 130
Los Angeles, CA 90025-8306, USA

McCall, Reese (Athlete, Football Player)
4913 Richard M Scrushy Pkwy
Fairfield, AL 35064-1454, USA

McCall, Robert T (Artist)
4816 E Moonlight Way
Paradise Valley, AZ 85253-2926, USA

McCall Smith, Alexander (Writer)
c/o Staff Member *Random House*
1540 Broadway
New York, NY 10036-4039, USA

McCallany, Holt (Actor)
c/o David (Dave) Fleming *Mosaic Media Group*
9200 W Sunset Blvd Ste 10
Los Angeles, CA 90069-3608, USA

McCallister, Blaine (Athlete, Golfer)
1878 Epping Forest Way S
Jacksonville, FL 32217-2670, USA

McCallum, David (Actor)
Caprice House 3 New Burlington St
London W1X 1FE, UNITED KINGDOM (UK)

McCallum, John
1740 Pittwater Rd
Bayview, AUSTRALIA NSW 2104

McCallum, Napoleon (Athlete, Football Player)
314 Doe Run Cir
Henderson, NV 89012-2700, USA

McCambridge, Mercedes (Astronaut)
210932 Pleasant Park Dr
Conifer, CO 80433, USA

McCament, Randy (Athlete, Baseball Player)
17338 N Del Webb Blvd
Sun City, AZ 85373-1951, USA

McCandless, Bruce (Astronaut)
21852 Pleasant Park Rd
Conifer, CO 80433-6802, USA

McCanlies, Tim (Director, Producer, Writer)
c/o Lindsay Williams *The Gotham Group Inc*
9255 W Sunset Blvd Ste 515
Los Angeles, CA 90069-3308, USA

McCann, Brendan (Athlete, Basketball Player)
3599 Shinnecock Ln
Green Cove Springs, FL 32043-8028, USA

McCann, Brian (Athlete, Baseball Player)
2782 Norwood Way
Duluth, GA 30096-3664, USA

McCann, Chuck (Actor, Comedian)
2941 Briar Knoll Dr
Los Angeles, CA 90046-1122, USA

McCann, Kate (Stylist)
c/o Staff Member *Marnie Rose Agency*
37 Lower Shad Rd
Pound Ridge, NY 10576-2216, USA

McCann, Les (Composer, Musician)
4031 Panama Ct
Piedmont, CA 94611-4930, USA

McCann, Lila (Musician)
c/o Rick Shipp *WmE2 (WMA-TN)*
1600 Division St Ste 300
Nashville, TN 37203-2755, USA

McCann, Michelle
1200 Singer Dr
Riviera Beach, FL 33404-2765

McCann, Tim (Director)
c/o Jennifer Konawal *Gersh (NY)*
41 Madison Ave
New York, NY 10010-2202, USA

McCants, Keith (Athlete, Football Player)
5323 Forest Park Dr
Mobile, AL 36618-2421, USA

McCants, Mel (Athlete, Basketball Player)
6404 Somis Way
Sacramento, CA 95828-1523, USA

McCants, Rashad (Athlete, Basketball Player)
c/o Jeff Schwartz *Excel Sports Management*
9665 Wilshire Blvd Ste 500
Beverly Hills, CA 90212-2312, USA

McCardell, Keenan (Athlete, Football Player)
4918 Newpoint Dr
Fresno, TX 77545-9200, USA

McCarren, Larry (Athlete, Football Player)
520 W Chickadee Ln
Green Bay, WI 54313-5039, USA

McCarrick, Theodore E Cardinal (Religious Leader)
5001 Eastern Ave
Washington, DC 20017, USA

McCarroll, Jay (Fashion Designer)
c/o Nancy Kane *Kane & Associates*
319 N Venice Blvd
Venice, CA 90291-4598, USA

McCarron, Chris
PO Box 861
Sierra Madre, CA 91025-0861

McCarron, Christopher (Chris) (Jockey)
318 N Terrace View Dr
Monrovia, CA 91016-1570, USA

McCarron, Douglas J (Misc)
101 Connecticut Ave NW
Washington, DC 20001, USA

McCarron, Scott (Athlete, Golfer)
78225 Calle Cadiz
La Quinta, CA 92253-2911, USA

McCarry, Charles (Writer)
1745 Broadway # B1
New York, NY 10019-4368, USA

McCartan, Jack (Athlete, Hockey Player)
15504 Almond Ln
Eden Prairie, MN 55347-2554, USA

McCarter, Andre (Athlete, Basketball Player)
3257 Kibbe Ct
Lawrenceville, GA 30044-3263, USA

McCarter, Willie (Athlete, Basketball Player)
1123 Buckingham St Sw
Wyoming, MI 49509-2832, USA

McCarter Sisters
PO Box 121551
Nashville, TN 37212-1551

McCarthy, Andrew (Actor)
c/o Emily Gerson Saines *Brookside Artists Management (NY)*
250 W 57th St Ste 2303
New York, NY 10107-2399, USA

McCarthy, Bill (Athlete, Football Player)
1640 Walnut Ave
Winter Park, FL 32789-2036, USA

McCarthy, Carolyn (Congressman, Politician)
2346 Rayburn Hob
Washington, DC 20515-3507, USA

McCarthy, Dennis (Composer)
15233 Ventura Blvd Ste 200
Sherman Oaks, CA 91403-2244, USA

McCarthy, Dennis M (General)
2 Navy St
Washington, DC 20380-0001, USA

McCarthy, Donald W (Astronomer)
University of Arizona
Tucson, AZ 85721-0001, USA

McCarthy, Greg (Athlete, Baseball Player)
56 Wakelee Avenue Ext
Shelton, CT 06484-3954, USA

McCarthy, Jenny (Actor)
150 S Rodeo Dr # 300
Beverly Hills, CA 90212-2408, USA

McCarthy, John (Scientist)
Computer Science Dept
Stanford, CA 94305, USA

McCarthy, John (Athlete, Basketball Player)
1350 Union Rd Apt 2F
West Seneca, NY 14224-2940, USA

McCarthy, Julianna (Actor)
6500 Wilshire Blvd # 550
Los Angeles, CA 90048-4920, USA

McCarthy, Kevin (Congressman, Politician)
326 Cannon Hob
Washington, DC 20515-0529, USA

McCarthy, Lin
233 N Swall Dr
Beverly Hills, CA 90211-1712

McCarthy, Mary Frances (Educator, Writer)
English Dept
Washington, DC 20017, USA

McCarthy, Melissa (Actor)
c/o Christian Donatelli *Schiff Company, The*
8440 Warner Dr Ste B1
Culver City, CA 90232-2461, USA

McCarthy, Nobu
9229 W Sunset Blvd Ste 311
Los Angeles, CA 90069-3403

McCarthy, Norma
818385 Mead Lane Slu Box 9063
Victorville, CA 92392

McCarthy, Shawn (Athlete, Football Player)
300 N Lakeshore Rd
Payson, AZ 85541-6220, USA

McCarthy, Tim (Stylist)
c/o Staff Member *Judy Inc*
1 Yorkville Ave
Toronto ON M4W 1L1, Canada

McCarthy, Timothy
8686 Butterfield Ln
Orland Park, IL 60462-1492

McCarthy, Tom (Director)
c/o Rhonda Price *Gersh (NY)*
41 Madison Ave
New York, NY 10010-2202, USA

McCarthy, Tom (Athlete, Baseball Player)
PO Box 38
Limington, ME 04049-0038, USA

McCarthy, Tony (Songwriter, Writer)
29/33 Berners Road
London W1P 4AA, UNITED KINGDOM (UK)

McCartney, Jesse (Musician)
c/o Nicole Perna *Baker Winokur Ryder Public Relations (BWR-LA)*
9100 Wilshire Blvd Ste 500 PMB WEST
Beverly Hills, CA 90212-3426, USA

McCartney, Paul (Musician, Songwriter)
c/o Scott Rodger *Quest Management*
36 Warple Way Unit 1D
London W3 0RG, UK

McCartney, Stella (Designer, Fashion Designer)
The Larches, Farm Hill Furze Road
Bishampton, Pershore WR10 2NA, UNITED KINGDOM (UK)

McCarty, Chris
9105 Carmelita Ave Apt 101
Beverly Hills, CA 90210-3543

McCarty, Darren (Athlete)
c/o Staff Member *Detroit Red Wings*
600 Civic Center Dr
Detroit, MI 48226-4419, USA

McCarty, David (Athlete, Baseball Player)
110 Waldo Ave
Piedmont, CA 94611-3943, USA

McCarty, Mary (Baseball Player)
9455 N Genesee Rd
Mount Morris, MI 48458-9734, USA

McCarty, Mickey (Athlete, Football Player)
4803 Mistletoe Rd
Pasadena, TX 77505-2144, USA

McCarty, Walter (Athlete, Basketball Player)
5 Stratford Way
Lincoln, MA 01773-2813, USA

McCarver, J Timothy (Tim) (Athlete, Baseball Player, Sportscaster)
5825 Riegels Harbor Rd
Sarasota, FL 34242-1779, USA

McCarver, Shonna
13280 Northwest Fwy # F-252
Houston, TX 77040-6029

McCarver, Tim (Baseball Player)
5825 Riegels Harbor Rd
Sarasota, FL 34242-1779, USA

McCary, Michael (Musician)
10675 Santa Monica Blvd
Los Angeles, CA 90025-4807, USA

McCashin, Constance (Actor)
66 Fountain St
West Newton, MA 02465-3023, USA

McCaskill, Kirk E (Athlete, Baseball Player)
PO Box 451
Rancho Santa Fe, CA 92067-0451, USA

McCatty, Steve (Athlete, Baseball Player)
1075 Woodbriar Dr
Oxford, MI 48371-6069, USA

McCauley, Barry (Opera Singer)
598 Ridgewood Rd
Oradell, NJ 07649-2104, USA

McCauley, William F (Admiral)
570 Margarita Ave
Coronado, CA 92118, USA

McCay, Peggy (Actor)
2714 Carmar Dr
Los Angeles, CA 90046-1009, USA

McChesney, Robert (Bob) (Writer)
311 W University Ave Ste 301
Champaign, IL 61820-3941, USA

McChrystal, Stanley A (General)
9999 Joint Staff Pentagon
Washington, DC 20318-0001, USA

McCkorkle, Kevin (Actor)
c/o Peter Himberger *Impact Artists Group LLC*
42 Hamilton Ter
New York, NY 10031-6403, USA

McClain, Cady (Actor)
c/o Marnie Sparer *Innovative Artists (LA)*
1505 10th St
Santa Monica, CA 90401-2805, USA

McClain, Charly (Musician)
PO Box 198888
Nashville, TN 37219-8888, USA

McClain, China Anne (Actor)
c/o Wendi Green *Paradigm (LA)*
9200 W Sunset Blvd PH 11
Los Angeles, CA 90069-3601, USA

McClain, Dewey (Athlete, Football Player)
1032 Flagg Way
Lawrenceville, GA 30044-3354, USA

McClain, Eugene (Athlete, Baseball Player)
828 W 8th St
Chester, PA 19013-3712, USA

McClain, Joe (Athlete, Baseball Player)
1370 Milligan Hwy
Johnson City, TN 37601-5518, USA

McClain, Katrina (Athlete, Basketball Player)
1208 Wimbee Dr
Charleston, SC 29407-6639, USA

McClain, Scott (Athlete, Baseball Player)
660 Golden Gate Pt Apt 61
Sarasota, FL 34236-6645, USA

McClain, Ted (Athlete, Basketball Player)
104 Eaton Ct
Nashville, TN 37218-1003, USA

McClairen, Jack (Cy) (Coach, Football Coach)
1337 Idlewild Dr
Daytona Beach, FL 32114-1614, USA

McClanahan, Brent (Athlete, Football Player)
1100 Sayword Ct
Bakersfield, CA 93312-5750, USA

McClanahan, Randy (Athlete, Football Player)
8107 W Via Del Sol
Peoria, AZ 85383-2142, USA

McClanahan, Robert (Rob) (Athlete, Hockey Player)
1462 Hunter Dr
Wayzata, MN 55391-9658, USA

McClard, Bill (Athlete, Football Player)
149 N Pleasant Ridge Dr
Rogers, AR 72756-0702, USA

McClarnon, Zahn (Actor)
c/o Gloria Hinojosa *Amsel, Eisenstadt & Frazier Talent Agency (AEF)*
5055 Wilshire Blvd Ste 860
Los Angeles, CA 90036-6108, USA

McClary, Thomas (Tom) (Musician)
1920 Benson Ave
Saint Paul, MN 55116-3214, USA

McClatchy, Kevin (Baseball Player)
350 S Highland Ave Apt 1
Pittsburgh, PA 15206-3955, USA

McCleary, Norris (Athlete, Football Player)
115 Ferguson Dr
Kings Mountain, NC 28086-9727, USA

McCleery, Finnis D (War Hero)
616 N Jackson St
San Angelo, TX 76901-2520, USA

McClellan, Mike (Athlete, Football Player)
1801 Longbranch Ct
Arlington, TX 76012-5723, USA

McClellan, Paul (Athlete, Baseball Player)
1648 Andover Ln
Lincoln, CA 95648-8454, USA

McClellan, Scott (Government Official, Writer)
c/o Staff Member *Public Affairs*
250 W 57th St Ste 1321
New York, NY 10107-1318

McClelland, David C (Psychic)
81 Washington Ave
Cambridge, MA 02140-2716, USA

McClelland, Melissa (Musician)
c/o Staff Member *Paradigm (Monterey)*
404 W Franklin St
Monterey, CA 93940-2303, USA

McClelland, Tim (Baseball Player)
5405 Woodland Ave
West Des Moines, IA 50266-7259, USA

McClelland, Tim (Athlete, Baseball Player)
5405 Woodland Ave
West Des Moines, IA 50266-7259, USA

McClendon, Lloyd (Athlete, Baseball Player, Coach)
1082 Mission Hills Ct
Chesterton, IN 46304-9605, USA

McClendon, Reiley (Actor)
c/o Staff Member *Kritzer Levine Wilkins Entertainment*
11872 La Grange Ave Fl 1
Los Angeles, CA 90025-5283, USA

McClendon, Sarah
3133 Connecticut Ave NW Apt 215
Washington, DC 20008-5105

McClendon, Skip (Athlete, Football Player)
16844 Forrer St
Detroit, MI 48235, USA

McClendon, Willie (Athlete, Football Player)
575 Cativo Dr SW
Atlanta, GA 30311-2107, USA

McClintock, Eddie (Actor)
c/o Ric Beddingfield *Beddingfield Company, The*
13600 Ventura Blvd Ste B
Sherman Oaks, CA 91423-5050, USA

McClintock, Jessica (Designer, Fashion Designer)
1400 16th St
San Francisco, CA 94103-5110, USA

McClintock, Tom (Congressman, Politician)
428 Cannon Hob
Washington, DC 20515-4308, USA

McClinton, Curtis (Athlete, Football Player)
1020 N Rutland St
Wichita, KS 67206-3823, USA

McClinton, Delbert (Musician)
c/o Staff Member *Alligator Records*
PO Box 60234
Chicago, IL 60660-0234, USA

McCloskey, J Michael (Misc)
85 2NS St # 200
San Francisco, CA 94105, USA

McCloskey, Jack (Basketball Player)
Target Center 600 1st Ave N
Minneapolis, MN 55403, USA

McCloskey, Jim (Activist)
221 Witherspoon St
Princeton, NJ 08542-3240, USA

McCloskey, Leigh
6032 Philip Ave
Malibu, CA 90265-3747

McCloskey, Leigh J (Actor)
6032 Philip Ave
Malibu, CA 90265-3747, USA

McCloskey, Mike (Athlete, Football Player)
108 Summer Ridge Dr
Lansdale, PA 19446-6707, USA

McCloskey, Rep (Politician)
580 Mountain Home Rd
Woodside, CA 94062-2515

McCloskey, Robert J (Diplomat)
84 Old Black Point Rd
Niantic, CT 06357-2833, USA

McCloskey-Rogers, Gloria (Baseball Player)
PO Box 512
Macon, MO 63552-0512, USA

McCloud, George (Athlete, Basketball Player)
19501 W Country Club Dr Apt 1603
Aventura, FL 33180-2478, USA

McCloud, Tyrus (Athlete, Football Player)
2850 NW 8th St
Pompano Beach, FL 33069-2139, USA

McCloughan, Dave (Athlete, Football Player)
2225 W 46th St
Loveland, CO 80538-1456, USA

McCloughan, Kent (Athlete, Football Player)
2241 Woody Creek Cir
Loveland, CO 80538-5333, USA

McClung, Seth (Athlete, Baseball Player)
13588 Park Blvd
Seminole, FL 33776-3432, USA

McClure, Bob (Athlete, Baseball Player)
3834 SE Fairway E
Stuart, FL 34997-6120, USA

McClure, Bryton (Actor)
c/o Jeff Witjas *Agency for the Performing Arts (APA-LA)*
405 S Beverly Dr Ste 500
Beverly Hills, CA 90212-4425, USA

McClure, Donald S (Misc)
23 Hemlock Cir
Princeton, NJ 08540-5405, USA

McClure, Kandyse (Actor)
c/o Richard Lucas *Lucas Talent Inc*
100 W. Pender St Sun Tower, 7th Floor
Vancouver, BC V6B 1R8, Canada

McClure, Lisi (Stylist)
388 NE 88th St
El Portal, FL 33138-3105, USA

McClure, Marc
1420 Beaudry Blvd
Glendale, CA 91208-1708

McClure, Molly
12456 Ventura Blvd Ste 1
Studio City, CA 91604-2484

McClure, Tane (Actor)
3349 Cahuenga Blvd W Ste 1
Los Angeles, CA 90068-1379, USA

McClurg, Edie
9229 W Sunset Blvd Ste 315
Los Angeles, CA 90069-3403

McClurkin, Donnie (Musician)
c/o Staff Member *The Alliance Agency*
1035 Bates Ct
Hendersonville, TN 37075-8864, USA

McCole Bartusiak, Skye (Actor)
c/o Mitchell Gossett *United Talent Agency (UTA)*
9560 Wilshire Blvd Fl 5
Beverly Hills, CA 90212-2400, USA

McColister, Antoine (Ace Hood) (Musician)
c/o Staff Member *Island Def Jam Records*
2220 Colorado Ave
Santa Monica, CA 90404-3506, USA

McColl, Bill (Football Player)
5166 Chelsea St
La Jolla, CA 92037-7908, USA

McColl, Peggy (Writer)
1 Stafford Rd Suite 312
NePean, Ontario K2H 1B9, Canada

McCollough, Cynthia (Stylist)
c/o Staff Member *Mark Edward Inc*
325 W 8th St # 1011
New York, NY 10018, USA

McCollum, Andy (Athlete, Football Player)
3933 Autumn Farms Dr
Pacific, MO 63069-2517, USA

McCollum, Betty (Congressman, Politician)
1714 Longworth Hob
Washington, DC 20515-2203, USA

McColm, Matt (Actor)
c/o Bob Read *ReBar Management*
10061 Riverside Dr # 722
Toluca Lake, CA 91602-2560

McColms, Matt (Actor)
c/o Staff Member *Agency for the Performing Arts (APA-LA)*
405 S Beverly Dr Ste 500
Beverly Hills, CA 90212-4425, USA

McComas, Brian (Musician)
c/o Staff Member *Leon Medica Management*
187 Hidden Lake Rd
Hendersonville, TN 37075-5528, USA

McComb, Jeremy (Musician)
c/o Staff Member *Paradigm (Monterey)*
404 W Franklin St
Monterey, CA 93940-2303, USA

McComb, Joanne (Baseball Player)
105 Nottingham Rd
Bloomsburg, PA 17815-3021, USA

McConathy, John (Athlete, Basketball Player)
2320 Belmont Blvd
Bossier City, LA 71111-2427, USA

McConaughey, Matthew (Actor)
c/o Alan Nierob *Rogers & Cowan PR (LA)*
Pacific Design Center 8687 Melrose Ave, 7th Floor
West Hollywood, CA 90069, USA

McConkey, Phil (Athlete, Football Player)
1856 Viking Way
La Jolla, CA 92037-3354, USA

McConnell, Harden M (Misc)
Chemistry Dept
Stanford, CA 94305, USA

McConnell, John P (Business Person)
1205 Dearborn Dr
Columbus, OH 43085-4769, USA

McConnell, Page (Musician)
c/o Staff Member *Paradigm (Monterey)*
404 W Franklin St
Monterey, CA 93940-2303, USA

McConnell, Robert M G (Rob) (Musician)
11761 E Speedway Blvd
Tucson, AZ 85748-2017, USA

McConnell, Sam (Athlete, Baseball Player)
301 McKinley St
Middletown, OH 45042-3256, USA

McConnell-Serio, Suzie (Athlete, Basketball Player)
2590 Rossmoor Dr
Pittsburgh, PA 15241-2584, USA

McConville, Frank (Misc)
25510 Kelly Rd
Roseville, MI 48066-4932, USA

McCoo, Marilyn (Actor, Musician)
PO Box 7905
Beverly Hills, CA 90212-7905, USA

McCook, John (Actor)
10245 Briarwood Dr
Los Angeles, CA 90077-2521, USA

McCool, Bill (Athlete, Baseball Player)
9250 SE 121st Loop
Summerfield, FL 34491-9477, USA

McCool, Michelle (Wrestler)
c/o Kerry Rodgerson *World Wrestling Entertainment (WWE)*
1241 E Main St
Stamford, CT 06902-3520, USA

McCord, Alex (Reality TV Star)
c/o Staff Member *Bravo (NY)*
30 Rockefeller Plz
New York, NY 10112-0015, USA

McCord, AnnaLynne (Actor)
c/o Gary Mantoosh *Baker Winokur Ryder Public Relations (BWR-LA)*
9100 Wilshire Blvd Ste 500 PMB WEST
Beverly Hills, CA 90212-3426, USA

McCord, Bob (Athlete, Hockey Player)
11540 Donley Dr
Parker, CO 80138-8027, USA

McCord, Clinton (Athlete, Baseball Player)
1821 Knowles St
Nashville, TN 37208-2438, USA

McCord, Darris (Athlete, Football Player)
6160 W Surrey Rd
Bloomfield Hills, MI 48301-1661, USA

McCord, Gary (Athlete, Golfer)
5318 E Desert Vista Rd
Paradise Valley, AZ 85253-3365, USA

McCord, Keith (Athlete, Basketball Player)
1609 Five Acre Rd
Dolomite, AL 35061-1036, USA

McCord, Kent
c/o Staff Member *Tisherman Gilbert Motley Drozdoski Talent Agency (TGMD)*
6767 Forest Lawn Dr Ste 101
Los Angeles, CA 90068-1050, USA

McCord, Quentin (Athlete, Football Player)
1902 Greenleaf Dr
Lexington, KY 40505-2325, USA

McCorkle, Kevin (Actor)
c/o Staff Member *Impact Artists Group LLC*
42 Hamilton Ter
New York, NY 10031-6403, USA

McCormack, Catherine (Actor)

McCormack, Don (Athlete, Baseball Player)
866 Glenfield Dr
Palm Harbor, FL 34684-3218, USA

McCormack, Eric (Actor)
c/o Leanne Coronel *Coronel Group*
1100 Glendon Ave Fl 17
Los Angeles, CA 90024-3588, USA

McCormack, Mary (Actor)
PO Box 67335
Los Angeles, CA 90067-0335, USA

McCormack, Mike (Athlete, Football Coach, Football Player)
30720 229th Pl SE
Black Diamond, WA 98010-1295, USA

McCormack, Patty (Actor)
c/o Staff Member *House of Representatives, The*
1434 6th St Ste 1
Santa Monica, CA 90401-2527, USA

McCormack, Will (Actor)
c/o Greg Clark *Untitled Entertainment (LA)*
350 S Beverly Dr Ste 200
Beverly Hills, CA 90212-4819, USA

McCormick, Carolyn (Actor)
11500 W Olympic Blvd Ste 510
Los Angeles, CA 90064-1527, USA

McCormick, John (Athlete, Football Player)
2615 Oak Dr Unit 34
Lakewood, CO 80215-7168, USA

McCormick, Kelly
PO Box 250
Seal Beach, CA 90740-0250

McCormick, Maureen (Actor, Musician)
c/o Debra Goldfarb *Rebel Entertainment Partners*
5700 Wilshire Blvd Ste 456
Los Angeles, CA 90036-3648, USA

McCormick, Mike (Athlete, Baseball Player)
10 Sawgrass Pl
Pinehurst, NC 28374-7114, USA

McCormick, Pat (Swimmer)
PO Box 250
Seal Beach, CA 90740-0250, USA

McCormick, Richard (Educator)
President's Office
East Rutherford, NJ 8903, USA

McCormick, Tim (Athlete, Basketball Player)
2500 Leroy Ln
West Bloomfield, MI 48324-2234, USA

McCormick, Tom (Athlete, Football Player)
397 Wehmeyer Loop
Mountain Home, AR 72653-6656, USA

McCormick, Walter (Athlete, Football Player)
2150 N Peppertree Ct
Visalia, CA 93291-8878, USA

McCorvey, Norma
12730 Thomas Sumter St
San Antonio, TX 78233-4630

McCouch, Grayson
c/o Dan Baron *Agency for the Performing Arts (APA-LA)*
405 S Beverly Dr Ste 500
Beverly Hills, CA 90212-4425, USA

McCourt, James (Actor, Television Host)
c/o Staff Member *Princess Productions*
Newcombe House 45 Notting Hill Gate
London W11 3LQ, UNITED KINGDOM

McCourt, Malachy (Actor, Writer)
c/o Marc Bass *Beacon Talent Agency*
170 Apple Ridge Rd
Woodcliff Lake, NJ 07677-8149, USA

McCoury, Del (Musician)
c/o Staff Member *Paradigm (Monterey)*
404 W Franklin St
Monterey, CA 93940-2303, USA

McCovey, Willie (Athlete, Baseball Player)
PO Box 620342
Redwood City, CA 94062-0342, USA

McCowen, Sir Alec
3 Goodwin's Ct St Martin's Ln
London, ENGLAND WG2

McCoy, Benny (Athlete, Baseball Player)
PO Box 611
Rockford, MI 49341-0611, USA

McCoy, Charlie (Musician)
PO Box 50455
Nashville, TN 37205-0455, USA

McCoy, Colt (Athlete, Football Player)
c/o Jordan Bazant *The Agency Sports and Marketing*
230 Park Ave Rm 851
New York, NY 10169-0927, USA

McCoy, Dave (Misc)
PO Box 24
Mammoth Lakes, CA 93546-0024, USA

McCoy, Gerald (Athlete, Football Player)
c/o Kelli Masters *Kelli Masters Management*
100 N Broadway Ste 1700
Oklahoma City, OK 73102-9211, USA

McCoy, John B (Financier)
3400 NW John Olsen Pl
Hillsboro, OR 97124-5808, USA

McCoy, Larry (Athlete, Baseball Player)
5758 Highway 139
Greenway AR, 72430 USA

McCoy, Larry (Baseball Player)
5758 Highway 139
Greenway, AR 72430-7045, USA

McCoy, LisaRaye (Actor)
c/o Staff Member *The Forum Entertainment Group*
10940 Wilshire Blvd Ste 1600
Los Angeles, CA 90024-3910, USA

McCoy, Mark
7120 Hawthorn Ave Apt 18
Los Angeles, CA 90046-3280

McCoy, Matt (Actor)
1180 S Beverly Dr Ste 301
Los Angeles, CA 90035-1154, USA

McCoy, Mike (Athlete, Football Player)
2224 Cotton Gin Row
Jefferson, GA 30549-8819, USA

McCoy, Neal (Musician)
c/o Joey Lee *WmE2 (WMA-TN)*
1600 Division St Ste 300
Nashville, TN 37203-2755, USA

McCoy, Rosero (Choreographer)
c/o Tim O'Brien *Clear Talent Group (LA)*
10950 Ventura Blvd
Studio City, CA 91604-3340, USA

McCoy, Sandra (Actor)
c/o Staff Member *Metropolitan (MTA)*
4526 Wilshire Blvd
Los Angeles, CA 90010-3801, USA

McCoy, Sonya (Stylist)
c/o Staff Member *Mark Edward Inc*
325 W 8th St # 1011
New York, NY 10018, USA

McCoy, Tony (Athlete, Football Player)
PO Box 616382
Orlando, FL 32861-6382, USA

McCracken, Jeff
15760 Ventura Blvd Ste 1730
Encino, CA 91436-3048

McCracken, Paul (Athlete, Basketball Player)
914 Westwood Blvd Apt 256
Los Angeles, CA 90024-2905, USA

McCracken, Paul W (Economist, Government Official)
2564 Hawthorne Rd
Ann Arbor, MI 48104, USA

McCracken, Quinton (Athlete, Baseball Player)
11308 E Autumn Sage Dr
Scottsdale, AZ 85255-8949, USA

McCrane, Paul (Actor)
5670 Wilshire Blvd Ste 820
Los Angeles, CA 90036-5613, USA

McCrary, Darius (Actor)
c/o Stephen Rice *Diverse Talent Group*
9911 W Pico Blvd Ste 340W
Los Angeles, CA 90035-2712, USA

McCrary, Joel (Actor)
c/o Holly Shelton *Precision Entertainment*
6338 Wilshire Blvd
Los Angeles, CA 90048-5002, USA

McCrary, Michael (Athlete, Football Player)
9907 Chase Hill Ct
Vienna, VA 22182-1427, USA

McCrary, Prentice (Athlete, Football Player)
5414 E Dolphin Cir
Mesa, AZ 85206-2225, USA

McCraw, Tommy (Athlete, Baseball Player)
3142 SE Monte Vista Ct
Port Saint Lucie, FL 34952-6062, USA

McCray, Bobby (Athlete, Football Player)
c/o Staff Member *EAG Sports Management*
12910 Agustin Pl
Playa Vista, CA 90094-2301, USA

McCray, Nikki (Athlete, Basketball Player)
4278 Fox Hills Dr
Louisville, TN 37777-5105, USA

McCray, Rodney (Athlete, Baseball Player)
4111 Center Gate Blvd
Sarasota, FL 34233-1520, USA

McCray, Rodney (Athlete, Basketball Player)
33 Bonita Vista Rd
Mount Vernon, NY 10552-1301, USA

McCready, Mindy (Musician)
c/o Staff Member *Iconic Records, LLC*
61 Jackson St Unit F
Denver, CO 80206-5580, USA

McCreary, Scotty (Musician)
c/o Simon Fuller *XIX Entertainment*
33/32 Ransomes Dock 35-37 Parkgate Rd
London SW11 4NP, UK

McCreary, Tex
PO Box 405
Mill Neck, NY 11765-0405

McCrills, John W (Writer)
17 Depot St
Newport, NH 03773-1533, USA

McCrindle, Andrea (Stylist)
c/o Staff Member *Judy Inc*
1 Yorkville Ave
Toronto ON M4W 1L1, Canada

McCrory, Glenn (Boxer)
Holborn 35 Station Road
County Durham, UNITED KINGDOM (UK)

McCrory, Helen (Actor)
c/o Clair Dobbs *Public Eye Communications*
535 Kings Rd Suite 313 Plaza
London SW10 0SZ, United Kingdom

McCrory, Milton (Milt) (Boxer)
19244 Bretton Dr
Detroit, MI 48223-1364, USA

McCrudden, Ian (Actor)
c/o Josh Silver *Silver Mine Entertainment*
6705 W Sunset Blvd
Hollywood, CA 90028-7107, USA

McCullers, Lance (Athlete, Baseball Player)
3309 Hoedt Ro
Tampa, FL 33618, USA

McCulley, Michael J (Astronaut)
365 Private Road 652
Bay City, TX 77414-2451, USA

McCullin, Donald (Don) (Photographer)
Holly Hill House Batcombe Shepton Mallet
Somerset BA4 6BL, UNITED KINGDOM (UK)

McCulloch, Ed (Race Car Driver)
136 W Jordan Ave
Clovis, CA 93611-3536, USA

McCulloch, Frank W (Educator, Lawyer)
5604 Kirkside Dr
Chevy Chase, MD 20815-7112, USA

McCulloch, Nan (Stylist)
200 Broken Lance Pl
Alpharetta, GA 30022-5716, USA

McCulloch (McCullough), Bruce (Actor)

McCullough, Bob (Athlete, Football Player)
2225 Deerfield Ln
Helena, MT 59601-8643, USA

McCullough, Colleen (Writer)
PO Box 333
Norfolk Island, NSW 2899, AUSTRALIA

McCullough, David (Actor)
c/o Staff Member *Creative Artists Agency (CAA-LA)*
2000 Avenue of the Stars Ste 100
Los Angeles, CA 90067-4705, USA

McCullough, David (Writer)
445 Park Ave # 1300
New York, NY 10022-2606, USA

McCullough, Earl (Athlete, Football Player, Track Athlete)
2108 Santa Fe Ave
Long Beach, CA 90810-3546, USA

McCullough, Julian (Musician)
c/o Staff Member *Paradigm (Monterey)*
404 W Franklin St
Monterey, CA 93940-2303, USA

McCullough, Julie (Actor)
c/o Hillard Elkins *Elkins Entertainment*
8306 Wilshire Blvd Ste 438
Beverly Hills, CA 90211-2382, USA

McCullough, Kimberly
9229 W Sunset Blvd Ste 315
Los Angeles, CA 90069-3403

McCullough, Mike (Athlete, Golfer)
6334 E Evening Glow Dr
Scottsdale, AZ 85266-7339, USA

McCullough, Shanna
7920 Alabama Ave
Canoga Park, CA 91304-4907

McCullough, Wayne (Athlete, Boxer)
5535 Chicory Falls Ct
Las Vegas, NV 89148-4656, USA

McCullum, Sam (Athlete, Football Player)
7701 88th Pl SE
Mercer Island, WA 98040-5746, USA

McCully, Kilmer (Doctor)
Pathology Dept Davis Park
Providence, RI 2908, USA

McCumber, Josh (Athlete, Golfer)
2121 Sea Hawk Dr
Ponte Vedra Beach, FL 32082-1683, USA

McCumber, Mark (Athlete, Golfer, Sportscaster)
527 Le Master Dr
Ponte Vedra Beach, FL 32082-2312, USA

McCune, Lisa (Actor)
c/o Staff Member *RGM Artist Group*
64-76 Kippax St Level 2, Suite 202 & 206
Surry Hills, NSW 2010, Australia

McCurdy, Cindy (Golfer)
18 Cottage Dr
Newnan, GA 30265-5513, USA

McCurdy, Jennette (Actor)
c/o Chris Huvane *Management 360*
9111 Wilshire Blvd
Beverly Hills, CA 90210-5508, USA

McCurry, Jeff (Athlete, Baseball Player)
9015 Linkmeadow Ln
Houston, TX 77025-4122, USA

McCurry, Margaret (Architect)
444 N Wells St
Chicago, IL 60654-4501, USA

McCurry, Mike (Journalist, Politician)
1050 Techwood Dr NW
Atlanta, GA 30318-5604, USA

McCusker, Jim (Athlete, Football Player)
209 N Main St
Jamestown, NY 14701-5209, USA

McCutcheon, Darwin (Athlete, Hockey Player)
PO Box 2909
Avon, CO 81620-2909, USA

McCutcheon, Dayton (Athlete, Football Player)
901 Golden Springs Dr # F-G
Diamond Bar, CA 91765-1181, USA

McCutcheon, Lawrence (Athlete, Football Player)
19981 Weems Ln
Huntington Beach, CA 92646-3835, USA

McCutcheon, Linda (Publisher)
Director's St NW Ofc 601
Washington, DC 20049-0001, USA

McCutcheon, Martine (Musician)
34-43 Russell St
London WC2B 5HA, UNITED KINGDOM (UK)

McDaniel, James (Actor)
c/o Craig Shapiro *International Creative Management (ICM-LA)*
10250 Constellation Blvd Fl 7
Los Angeles, CA 90067-6207, USA

McDaniel, Jeremy (Athlete, Football Player)
124 Derby Park Ave
New Bern, NC 28562-7054, USA

McDaniel, John (Cinematographer, Musician, Producer)
c/o Glenn Daniels *Glenn Daniels Arts Management*
56 Warren St Apt 5E
New York, NY 10007-1097, USA

McDaniel, John (Athlete, Football Player)
586 Janney Rd
Ohatchee, AL 36271-5213, USA

McDaniel, Lecharls (Athlete, Football Player)
12844 Starwood Ln
San Diego, CA 92131-4210, USA

McDaniel, Lindy
Rt. #2 Box 353A
Hollis, OK 73550

McDaniel, Lyndall D (Lindy) (Athlete, Baseball Player)
1095 Meadow Hill Dr
Lavon, TX 75166-1262, USA

McDaniel, Randall C (Athlete, Football Player)
20405 Manor Rd
Excelsior, MN 55331-9470, USA

McDaniel, Terry (Athlete, Baseball Player)
10326 N Central St
Kansas City, MO 64155-3527, USA

McDaniel, Terry (Athlete, Football Player)
730 Shenandoah
Cedar Hill, TX 75104-1242, USA

McDaniel, Xavier (Athlete, Basketball Player)
2 Oakmist Ct
Blythewood, SC 29016-8707, USA

McDaniels, Darryl (Darryl M) (Music Group, Musician)
2409 21st Ave S Ste 100
Nashville, TN 37212-5317, USA

McDavid, Ray (Athlete, Baseball Player)
1245 Market St Apt 1348
San Diego, CA 92101-7358, USA

McDermott, Alice (Writer)
19 Union Sq W
New York, NY 10003-3304, USA

McDermott, Brian
27 Upper Berkeley St
London, ENGLAND W1

McDermott, Charlie (Actor)
c/o Adam Griffin *Kritzer Levine Wilkins Entertainment*
11872 La Grange Ave Fl 1
Los Angeles, CA 90025-5283, USA

McDermott, Dean (Actor)
c/o Gleb Klioner *Schachter Entertainment*
1157 S Beverly Dr Fl 2
Los Angeles, CA 90035-1119, USA

McDermott, Dylan (Actor, Director)
c/o Geyer Kosinski *Media Talent Group*
9200 W Sunset Blvd Ste 550
Los Angeles, CA 90069-3611, USA

McDermott, Edward A (Government Official)
Lake House South 875 E Camino Real
Boca Raton, FL 33432, USA

McDermott, Jim (Congressman, Politician)
1035 Longworth Hob
Washington, DC 20515-4707, USA

McDermott, R Terrance (Terry) (Speed Skater)
5078 Chain Bridge Rd
Bloomfield Hills, MI 48304-3727, USA

McDermott, Shane
200 W 57th St Ste 900
New York, NY 10019-3211

McDermott, Terry (Athlete, Baseball Player)
7205 Sunlight Peak Dr NE
Rio Rancho, NM 87144-7508, USA

McDevitt, Danny (Athlete, Baseball Player)
1145 River Cove Rd
Social Circle, GA 30025-4878, USA

McDiarmid, Ian (Actor)
Wood Lane
London W12 7RJ, UNITED KINGDOM (UK)

McDill, Allen (Athlete, Baseball Player)
244 Richwoods Rd
Arkadelphia, AR 71923-8836, USA

McDivitt, James
9146 Cherry Ave
Rapid City, MI 49676-8624

McDivitt, James A (Jim) (Astronaut, General)
3530 E Calle Puerta De Acero
Tucson, AZ 85718-6000, USA

McDole, Ron (Athlete, Football Player)
2083 Lockes Mill Rd
Berryville, VA 22611-3931, USA

McDonagh, John Michael (Director, Writer)
c/o Jeremy Barber *United Talent Agency (UTA)*
9560 Wilshire Blvd Fl 5
Beverly Hills, CA 90212-2400, USA

McDonagh, Martin (Director, Writer)
c/o Staff Member *The Rod Hall agency*
6th Floor Fairgate House 78 New Oxford Street
London WC1A 1HB, United Kingdom

McDonald, Alvin B (Ab) (Athlete, Hockey Player)
419 Thompson Dr
Winnipeg, MB R3J 3E7, Canada

McDonald, Audra (Actor, Musician)
c/o Staff Member *Parseghian Planco LLC*
322 8th Ave Ste 601
New York, NY 10001-6715, USA

McDonald, Ben (Athlete, Baseball Player)
8780 Henderson Rd
Denham Springs, LA 70726-6705, USA

McDonald, Bruce (Director, Producer)
c/o Bill Douglass *Paradigm (LA)*
360 N Crescent Dr
Beverly Hills, CA 90210-4874, USA

McDonald, Christopher
c/o Daniel (Danny) Sussman *Brillstein Entertainment Partners*
9150 Wilshire Blvd Ste 350
Beverly Hills, CA 90212-3453, USA

McDonald, Country Joe (Musician)
PO Box 7054
Berkeley, CA 94707-0054, USA

McDonald, Darnell (Athlete, Football Player)
13551 Bentley Cir
Woodbridge, VA 22192-4336, USA

McDonald, Darnell (Athlete, Baseball Player)
542 W Windsor Ave Frnt
Phoenix, AZ 85003-1062, USA

McDonald, Dave (Athlete, Baseball Player)
2545 SE 3rd St
Pompano Beach, FL 33062-5401, USA

McDonald, David L (Admiral)
PO Box 45214
Jacksonville, FL 32232-5214, USA

McDonald, Devon (Athlete, Football Player)
425 E 25th St
Paterson, NJ 07514-2306, USA

McDonald, Donzell (Athlete, Baseball Player)
3225 Scranton St
Aurora, CO 80011-1827, USA

McDonald, Forrest (Historian)
PO Box 155
Coker, AL 35452-0155, USA

McDonald, Glenn (Athlete, Basketball Player)
2135 Vuelta Grande Ave
Long Beach, CA 90815-3562, USA

McDonald, Jiggs (Sportscaster)
8331 Arborfield Ct
Fort Myers, FL 33912-4684, USA

McDonald, Jim (Athlete, Baseball Player)
PO Box 995
Brea, CA 92822-0995, USA

McDonald, Joe
17337 Ventura Blvd Ste 208
Encino, CA 91316-3992

McDonald, John (Athlete, Baseball Player)
3546 Michigan Ave
Cincinnati, OH 45208-1410, USA

McDonald, Keith (Athlete, Baseball Player)
5162A E Greensboro Ln
Anaheim, CA 92807, USA

McDonald, Kevin Hamilton (Actor, Writer)

McDonald, Lanny (Athlete, Hockey Player)
2424 University NW
Calgary, AB T2N 3Y9, Canada

McDonald, Michael H (Musician, Songwriter, Writer)
c/o Staff Member *WmE2 (WMA-LA)*
1 William Morris Pl
Beverly Hills, CA 90212-4261, USA

McDonald, Michael James (Actor, Director, Writer)
c/o Staff Member *3 Arts Entertainment Inc*
9460 Wilshire Blvd Fl 7
Beverly Hills, CA 90212-2713, USA

McDonald, Mike (Athlete, Football Player)
1067 E Angeleno Ave
Burbank, CA 91501-1420, USA

McDonald, Miriam (Actor)
c/o Brantley Brown *Schachter Entertainment*
1157 S Beverly Dr Fl 2
Los Angeles, CA 90035-1119, USA

McDonald, Paul (Athlete, Football Player)
1815 Tradewinds Ln
Newport Beach, CA 92660-3810, USA

McDonald, Ramos (Athlete, Football Player)
5901 Whitney Ln
Texarkana, TX 75503-4519, USA

McDonald, Ricardo (Athlete, Football Player)
425 E 25th St
Paterson, NJ 07514-2306, USA

McDonald, Richie (Musician)
PO Box 128648
Nashville, TN 37212, USA

McDonald, Thomas F (Tommy) (Athlete, Football Player)
537 W Valley Forge Rd
King Of Prussia, PA 19406-1568, USA

McDonald, Tim (Athlete, Attorney, Football Player)
10851 N Maple Ave
Fresno, CA 93730-3501, USA

McDonell, R Terry (Editor)
1290 Avenue of the Americas
New York, NY 10104-0111, USA

McDonnell, Bob (Governor, Politician)
E Broad St State Capitol 1111
Richmond, VA 23219-1887, USA

McDonnell, John F (Business Person)
PO Box 516
Saint Louis, MO 63166-0516, USA

McDonnell, Mary (Actor)
c/o Perri Kipperman *Kipperman Management*
243 W 72nd St Apt 2
New York, NY 10023-2704, USA

McDonnell, Patrick (Cartoonist)
c/o Staff Member *King Features Syndication*
300 W 57th St Fl 15
New York, NY 10019-5238, USA

McDonough, Mary (Actor)
6858 Cantaloupe Ave
Van Nuys, CA 91405-4148, USA

McDonough, Neal (Actor)
c/o JJ Harris *One Talent Management*
9220 W Sunset Blvd Ste 306
Los Angeles, CA 90069-3503, USA

McDonough, Neil (Actor)
1180 S Beverly Dr Ste 601
Los Angeles, CA 90035-1158, USA

McDonough, Sean (Sportscaster)
77 W 66th St
New York, NY 10023-6201, USA

McDonough, William (Architect)
410 E Water St
Charlottesville, VA 22902-5276, USA

McDonough, William J (Financier)
1666 K St NW
Washington, DC 20006-2801, USA

McDorman, Jake (Actor)
c/o Elissa Leeds-Fickman *Reel Talent Management*
PO Box 491035
Los Angeles, CA 90049-9035, USA

McDormand, Frances (Actor)
c/o Brian Swardstrom *WmE2 (Endeavor-LA)*
9601 Wilshire Blvd Fl 3
Beverly Hills, CA 90210-5219, USA

McDormond, Frances
333 W End Ave Apt 12C
New York, NY 10023-8132

McDougal, Bob (Athlete, Football Player)
PO Box 430119
Miami, FL 33243-0119, USA

McDougal, Mike (Athlete, Hockey Player)
2892 Tanglewood Dr
Kimball, MI 48074-1535, USA

McDougal, Susan
350 S Grand Ave Ste 3900
Los Angeles, CA 90071-3410

McDougald, Gil
10 Warren Ave
Spring Lake, NJ 07762-1216

McDougald, Gilbert J (Gil) (Athlete, Baseball Player)
2005 Mill Pond Ct
Wall Township, NJ 07719-3660, USA

McDougale, Stockar (Athlete, Football Player)
15 Bradford Ct
Dearborn, MI 48126-4170, USA

McDougall, Charles (Writer)
c/o Staff Member *Industry Entertainment Partners*
955 Carrillo Dr Ste 300
Los Angeles, CA 90048-5400, USA

McDougall, Ian (Producer)
c/o Staff Member *Gersh (LA)*
9465 Wilshire Blvd Ste 600
Beverly Hills, CA 90212-2612, USA

McDougall, Marshall (Athlete, Baseball Player)
213 Bell Branch Ln
Saint Johns, FL 32259-4438, USA

McDougall, Walter A (Historian)
History Dept
Philadelphia, PA 19104, USA

McDowell, Bubba (Athlete, Football Player)
6353 Richmond Ave
Houston, TX 77057-5964, USA

McDowell, Frank (Doctor)
100 N Kalaheo Ave Apt F
Kailua, HI 96734-2306, USA

McDowell, Jack (Athlete, Baseball Player)
2875 Calle Rancho Vis
Encinitas, CA 92024-6672, USA

McDowell, Malcolm (Actor)
c/o Staff Member *Dontanville/Frattaroli (D/F)*
270 Lafayette St Ste 402
New York, NY 10012-3327, USA

McDowell, Oddibe (Athlete, Baseball Player)
5240 SW 18th St
West Park, FL 33023-3157, USA

McDowell, Roger (Athlete, Baseball Player)
2690 Pete Shaw Rd
Marietta, GA 30066-2224, USA

McDowell, Ronnie (Musician)
c/o Bobby Roberts *Bobby Roberts Agency*
PO Box 1547
Goodlettsville, TN 37070-1547, USA

McDowell, Samuel E (Sam) (Athlete, Baseball Player)
12902 Brown Bark Trl
Clermont, FL 34711-7646, USA

McDuffie, George (Athlete, Football Player)
819 Independence Rd
Toledo, OH 43607-2529, USA

McDuffie, Otis J (O J) (Athlete, Football Player)
1333 NW 121st Ave
Plantation, FL 33323-2438, USA

McDuffie, Robert (Musician)
165 W 57th St
New York, NY 10019-2201, USA

McDyess, Antonio (Athlete, Basketball Player)
979 County Road 473
Meridian, MS 39301-9636, USA

McEldowney, Brooke (Cartoonist)
200 Madison Ave
New York, NY 10016-3903, USA

McElhenney, Rob (Actor)
c/o Nick Frenkel *3 Arts Entertainment Inc*
9460 Wilshire Blvd Fl 7
Beverly Hills, CA 90212-2713, USA

McElhenny, Hugh (Athlete, Football Player)
3013 Via Venezia
Henderson, NV 89052-3802, USA

McElhone, Natascha (Actor)
c/o Christina Papadopoulos *Baker Winokur Ryder Public Relations BWR (BWR-NY)*
292 Madison Ave Fl 12
New York, NY 10017-6415, USA

McElhorne, Natascha (Artist)
c/o Staff Member *International Creative Management (ICM-LA)*
10250 Constellation Blvd Fl 7
Los Angeles, CA 90067-6207, USA

McElligott, Sarah (Actor)
c/o Monica Barkett *Global Artists Agency*
6253 Hollywood Blvd Apt 508
Los Angeles, CA 90028-8251, USA

McElmury, Jim (Athlete, Hockey Player)
9122 78th St S
Cottage Grove, MN 55016-2211, USA

McElroy, Chuck (Athlete, Baseball Player)
1049 Nederland Ave
Port Arthur, TX 77640-4338, USA

McElroy, Hugh (Athlete, Football Player)
3899 Fonville Ave
Beaumont, TX 77705-2207, USA

McElroy, Reggie (Athlete, Football Player)
19397 Joplin Rd
Lebanon, MO 65536-6903, USA

McElroy, Vann (Athlete, Football Player)
524 Private Road 4450
Uvalde, TX 78801-1194, USA

McElwain, Jason (Sportscaster)
c/o Staff Member *WmE2 (WMA-LA)*
1 William Morris Pl
Beverly Hills, CA 90212-4261, USA

McEnaney, Will (Athlete, Baseball Player)
1055 SW 3rd St
Boca Raton, FL 33486-4553, USA

McEnery, Peter (Actor)
76 Oxford St
London W1N 0AX, UNITED KINGDOM (UK)

McEnroe, John (Athlete, Tennis Player)
211 Central Park W
New York, NY 10024-6020, USA

McEntee, Gerald W (Politician)
1625 L St NW
Washington, DC 20036-5665, USA

McEntire, Reba (Musician)
c/o Narvel Blackstock *Starstruck Entertainment*
40 Music Sq W
Nashville, TN 37203-3206, USA

McEwan, Geraldine (Actor)
Langham House 302/8 Regent St
London W1R 5AL, UNITED KINGDOM (UK)

McEwan, Ian R (Writer)
15 Park Town
Oxford OX2 6SN, UNITED KINGDOM (UK)

McEwen, Bruce S (Scientist)
1230 York Ave
New York, NY 10065-6307, USA

McEwen, Craig (Athlete, Football Player)
1610 Hilton Head Ct Apt 1265
El Cajon, CA 92019-4578, USA

McEwen, Mark (Correspondent)
51 W 52nd St
New York, NY 10019-6119, USA

McEwen, Tom (Writer)
202 S Parker St
Tampa, FL 33606-2308, USA

McEwing, Joe (Athlete, Baseball Player)
630 Deerbrook Dr
Yardley, PA 19067-4537, USA

McFadden, Cynthia (Correspondent, Journalist, Television Host)
c/o Staff Member *Nightline*
1717 Desales St NW
Washington, DC 20036-4401, USA

McFadden, Daniel L (Nobel Prize Laureate)
41 Southampton Ave
Berkeley, CA 94707-2034, USA

McFadden, Davenia (Actor)
c/o Felicia Sager *Sager Management*
260 S Beverly Dr # 205
Beverly Hills, CA 90212-3805, USA

McFadden, Gates (Actor)
c/o Marcia Hurwitz *Innovative Artists (LA)*
1505 10th St
Santa Monica, CA 90401-2805, USA

McFadden, Leon (Athlete, Baseball Player)
8617 S 10th Ave
Inglewood, CA 90305-2346, USA

McFadden, Paul (Athlete, Football Player)
7395 Christopher Dr
Youngstown, OH 44514-2563, USA

McFadden-Rusynyk, Betty Jean (Baseball Player)
7267 W 130th St
Parma, OH 44130-7814, USA

McFadin, Bud
1467 Albrecht Rd
Victoria, TX 77905-2613

McFadin, Lewis P (Bud) (Athlete, Football Player)
647 Springwood
Victoria, TX 77905-2580, USA

McFadyen, Angus (Actor)
c/o Douglas Urbanski *Douglas Management Group*
9713 Little Santa Monica Blvd
Beverly Hills, CA 90210, USA

McFarland, Anthony (Athlete, Football Player)
7733 Still Lakes Dr
Odessa, FL 33556-2262, USA

McFarland, Jim (Athlete, Football Player)
5102 S 90th St
Lincoln, NE 68526-9627, USA

McFarland, Kay (Athlete, Football Player)
7394 S Monaco St
Centennial, CO 80112-1528, USA

McFarland, Kirsten (Writer)
c/o Staff Member *International Creative Management (ICM-LA)*
10250 Constellation Blvd Fl 7
Los Angeles, CA 90067-6207, USA

McFarlane, Andrew (Actor)
c/o Staff Member *Jeff Morrone Entertainment*
9350 Wilshire Blvd Ste 224
Beverly Hills, CA 90212-3204, USA

McFarlane, Robert C (Government Official)
2010 Prospect St NW
Washington, DC 20037, USA

McFarlane, Todd (Cartoonist)
PO Box 12230
Tempe, AZ 85284-0038, USA

McFayden, Brian (Actor)
c/o Babette Perry *IMG (LA)*
717 N Alta Vista Blvd
Los Angeles, CA 90046-7601, USA

McFeeley, William S (Historian, Writer)
35 Concord Ave Apt 2
Cambridge, MA 02138-2342, USA

McFerrin, Bobby (Actor, Songwriter, Writer)
826 Broadway # 400
New York, NY 10003-4826, USA

Mcfly (Music Group)
c/o Staff Member *Universal Music Group (UMG - LA)*
2220 Colorado Ave
Santa Monica, CA 90404-3506, USA

McG (Director, Producer)
8739 W Sunset Blvd
West Hollywood, CA 90069-2205, USA

McGaffigan, Andy (Athlete, Baseball Player)
6243 Forestwood Dr E
Lakeland, FL 33811-2402, USA

McGahee, Willis (Athlete, Football Player)
1 Bills Dr
Orchard Park, NY 14127-2237, USA

McGahern, John (Writer)
3 Queen Square
London WC1N 3AU, UNITED KINGDOM (UK)

McGahey, James C (Misc)
25510 Kelly Rd
Roseville, MI 48066-4932, USA

McGann, Michelle (Athlete, Golfer)
1200 Singer Dr
Riviera Beach, FL 33404-2765, USA

McGann, Paul (Actor)
12/13 Poland St
London W1V 3DE, UNITED KINGDOM (UK)

McGarity, Vernon (War Hero)
6901 Andrews Rd
Bartlett, TN 38135-3010, USA

McGarity, Wane (Athlete, Football Player)
4622 Lavender Ln
San Antonio, TX 78220-2511, USA

McGarrahan, Scott (Athlete, Football Player)
6636 W William Cannon Dr
Austin, TX 78735-8529, USA

McGarrigle, Anne (Composer, Musician)
c/o Staff Member *Concerted Efforts*
PO Box 440326
Somerville, MA 02144-0004, USA

McGarrigle, Kate (Composer, Musician)
c/o Staff Member *Concerted Efforts*
PO Box 440326
Somerville, MA 02144-0004, USA

McGarry, John (Athlete, Football Player)
5725 S Woodlawn Ave
Chicago, IL 60637-1602, USA

McGarry, Kelly (Actor)
c/o Staff Member *Heresun Management*
4119 W Burbank Blvd
Burbank, CA 91505-2122, USA

McGarry, Steve (Cartoonist)
200 Madison Ave
New York, NY 10016-3903, USA

McGaugh, James L (Biologist)
2327 Aralia St
Newport Beach, CA 92660-4135, USA

McGauley, Diane (Stylist)
36 Marguerite Ave
Mill Valley, CA 94941-1019, USA

McGaw, Patrick (Actor)
8265 W Sunset Blvd Ste 200
West Hollywood, CA 90046-2470, USA

McGeady, Sister Mary Rose (Activist)
460 W 41st St
New York, NY 10036-6801, USA

McGee, Ben (Athlete, Football Player)
35 Castle Cv
Jackson, MS 39212-3448, USA

McGee, Henry
19 Sydney Mews
London, ENGLAND SW3 6HL

McGee, Michael B (Mike) (Athlete, Football Player)
2 Medical Park Rd Ste 502
Columbia, SC 29203-6876, USA

McGee, Pamela (Pam) (Basketball Player)
Staples Center 1111 S Figueroa St
Los Angeles, CA 90015, USA

McGee, Stephen (Athlete, Football Player)
c/o Staff Member *Dallas Cowboys*
1 Cowboys Pkwy
Irving, TX 75063-4999

McGee, Tim (Athlete, Football Player)
4226 Maxwell Dr
Mason, OH 45040-6504, USA

McGee, Tony (Athlete, Football Player)
170 Tana Dr
Fayetteville, GA 30214-7539, USA

McGee, Trina (Actor)
c/o Stephen Rice *Pantheon Talent*
1801 Century Park E Ste 1910
Los Angeles, CA 90067-2321, USA

McGee, William M (Max) (Athlete, Football Player)
510 Locust Hills Dr
Wayzata, MN 55391-1968, USA

McGee, Willie D (Athlete, Baseball Player)
65 Pleasant Knoll Ct
Alamo, CA 94507-1264, USA

McGeever, John (Athlete, Football Player)
3479 Norwich Dr
Vestavia, AL 35243-2128, USA

McGegan, Nicholas (Conductor)
170 E 61st St # 5N
New York, NY 10065-8551, USA

McGehee, Kevin (Athlete, Baseball Player)
131 Hood Rd
Pollock, LA 71467-3617, USA

McGeorge, Missie (Athlete, Golfer)
1836 Willow Springs Ct
Haslet, TX 76052-2856, USA

McGeorge, Rich (Athlete, Football Player)
2200 Trail Wood Dr
Durham, NC 27705-1305, USA

McGhee, Carla (Athlete, Basketball Player)
6345 Tahoe Dr
Atlanta, GA 30349-4052, USa

McGhee, George C (Government Official)
12 Eastman St
Saint Augustine, FL 32084-0325, USA

McGhee-Anderson, Kathleen (Producer)
c/o Staff Member *Creative Artists Agency (CAA-LA)*
2000 Avenue of the Stars Ste 100
Los Angeles, CA 90067-4705, USA

McGiffin, Carol (Actor, Talk Show Host)
c/o Staff Member *ITV Network*
200 Gray's Inn Rd
London, CA WC1X 8HF, United Kingdom

McGilberry, Randy (Athlete, Baseball Player)
2110 Foxford St
Cantonment, FL 32533-6851, USA

McGill, Billy (Athlete, Basketball Player)
5129 W 58th Pl
Los Angeles, CA 90056-1601, USA

McGill, Bruce (Actor)
c/o Scott Manners *Stone Manners Salners Agency (LA)*
9911 W Pico Blvd Ste 1400
Los Angeles, CA 90035-2715, USA

McGill, Bryant (Writer)
11C Lower Dorset St
Dubline 1, IRELAND

McGill, Everett (Actor)
c/o Staff Member *WmE2 (WMA-LA)*
1 William Morris Pl
Beverly Hills, CA 90212-4261, USA

McGill, Jill (Athlete, Golfer)
3765 Carmel View Rd Unit 3
San Diego, CA 92130-3565, USA

McGill, Karmeeleyah (Athlete, Football Player)
1626 N Greenwood Ave
Clearwater, FL 33755, USA

McGill, Mike (Athlete, Football Player)
8930 Louis Ct
Saint John, IN 46373-9708, USA

McGill, Paul (Actor)
c/o Jill Fritzo *PMK/BNC Public Relations (PMK-NY)*
622 3rd Ave Fl 8
New York, NY 10017-6707, USA

McGill, William J (Educator)
2624 Costebelle Dr
La Jolla, CA 92037-3516, USA

McGillin, Howard (Actor)
c/o Staff Member *Cunningham Escott Slevin & Doherty (CESD-LA)*
10635 Santa Monica Blvd Ste 130
Los Angeles, CA 90025-8306, USA

McGillis, Kelly (Actor, Producer)
c/o Staff Member *David Williams Management*
9614 W Olympic Blvd Apt F
Beverly Hills, CA 90212-3761, USA

McGinest, Willie (Athlete, Football Player)
2211 Easy Ave
Long Beach, CA 90810-3534, USA

McGinley, John C (Actor)
1505 10th St
Santa Monica, CA 90401-2805, USA

McGinley, Ted (Actor)
c/o Mark Teitelbaum *Teitelbaum Artists Group*
8840 Wilshire Blvd Fl 3
Beverly Hills, CA 90211-2606, USA

McGinn, Bernard J (Misc)
5702 Kenwood Ave
Chicago, IL 60637, USA

McGinn, Dan (Athlete, Baseball Player)
1309 S 189th Ct
Omaha, NE 68130-2842, USA

McGinnis, Dave (Athlete, Coach, Football Coach, Football Player)
PO Box 888
Phoenix, AZ 85001-0888, USA

McGinnis, George (Athlete, Basketball Player)
11245 Marlin Rd
Indianapolis, IN 46239-8400, USA

McGinnis, Joe (Writer)
445 Park Ave # 1300
New York, NY 10022-2606, USA

McGinnis, Russ (Athlete, Baseball Player)
15444 Artesian Spring Rd
San Diego, CA 92127-5736, USA

McGinnis, Susan (Television Host)
c/o Staff Member *CBS News*
524 W 57th St
New York, NY 10019-2924, USA

McGinty, Damian (Actor)
c/o Paul Lyttle *SRP Media*
Prefers to be contacted via telephone or email
Los Angeles, CA, USA

McGinty, John J III (War Hero)
51 Barbara Ln
Hudson, NH 03051-3769, USA

McGirt, James (Buddy) (Boxer)
195 Suffolk Ave
Brentwood, NY 11717-4205, USA

McGlinchy, Kevin (Athlete, Baseball Player)
10 West St
Malden, MA 02148-5311, USA

McGlockin, Jon (Athlete, Basketball Player)
5281 State Rd # 83
Heartland, WI 53029, USA

McGlockton, Chester (Athlete, Football Player)
6930 S Perth St
Aurora, CO 80016-2340, USA

McGlothin, Pat (Athlete, Baseball Player)
1454 Kenesaw Ave
Knoxville, TN 37919-7749, USA

McGlynn, Dennis (Race Car Driver)
PO Box 843
Dover, DE 19903-0843, USA

McGlynn, Dick (Athlete, Hockey Player)
17 Butternut Ave
Peabody, MA 01960-4603, USA

McGlynn, Pat (Musician)
27 Preston Grange Preston Pans E
Lothian, SCOTLAND

McGoon, Dwight C (Doctor)
840 9th Ave SW
Rochester, MN 55902-6314, USA

McGovern, Elizabeth (Actor)
c/o Staff Member *Anonymous Content (AC-LA)*
3531 Hayden Ave
Culver City, CA 90232, USA

McGovern, George S (Politician, Senator)
Via delle Terme di Carachkka
Rome 100, ITALY

McGovern, Jim (Athlete, Golfer)
900 Amaryllis Ave
Oradell, NJ 07649-1302, USA

McGovern, Maureen (Actor, Musician)
c/o Jennifer Howe 12087 Evergreen St NW
Minneapolis, MN 55448, USA

McGovern, Rob (Athlete, Football Player)
419 E 57th St Apt 2D
New York, NY 10022-3176, USA

McGowan, Alistair (Actor)
c/o Oriana Elia *MF Management Limited*
Drury House 34-43 Russell St
London WC2B 5HA, UK

McGowan, Charles E (Religious Leader)
1852 Century Pl NE
Atlanta, GA 30345-4305, USA

McGowan, Dustin (Athlete, Baseball Player)
PO Box 1281
Ludowici, GA 31316-1281, USA

McGowan, Pat (Athlete, Golfer)
PO Box 88
Southern Pines, NC 28388-0088, USA

McGowan, Rose (Actor)
c/o Oren Segal *Media Talent Group*
9200 W Sunset Blvd Ste 550
Los Angeles, CA 90069-3611, USA

McGrady, Michael (Actor)
c/o Staff Member *Main Title Entertainment*
2225 Wilshire Blvd Suite 500
Los Angeles, CA 90036, USA

McGrady, Tracy (Athlete, Basketball Player)
6004 Cartmel Ln
Windermere, FL 34786-5406, USA

McGrath, Alister (Writer)
c/o Staff Member *HarperCollins Publishers*
10 E 53rd St C/O Author Mail Floor 7
New York, NY 10022, USA

McGrath, Doug (Director)
c/o Staff Member *International Creative Management (ICM-LA)*
10250 Constellation Blvd Fl 7
Los Angeles, CA 90067-6207, USA

McGrath, Douglas (Actor, Director, Writer)
c/o Staff Member *Creative Artists Agency (CAA-LA)*
2000 Avenue of the Stars Ste 100
Los Angeles, CA 90067-4705, USA

McGrath, Eugene R (Business Person)
4 Irving Pl
New York, NY 10003-3502, USA

McGrath, James (Scientist)
Genetics Dept
New Haven, CT 6520, USA

McGrath, Jeremy (Motorcycle Race, Motorcycle Racer)
13515 Yarmouth Dr
Pickerington, OH 43147-8214, USA

McGrath, Judy (Business Person)
c/o Staff Member *MTV Networks (LA)*
2600 Colorado Ave
Santa Monica, CA 90404-3519

McGrath, Mark (Musician, Television Host)
c/o John Marx *WmE2 (Endeavor-LA)*
9601 Wilshire Blvd Fl 3
Beverly Hills, CA 90210-5219, USA

McGrath, Mike (Bowler)
738 Colusa Ave
El Cerrito, CA 94530-3313, USA

McGraw, Harold W Jr (Publisher)
1221 Avenue of the Americas
New York, NY 10020-1001, USA

McGraw, Jay (Writer)
c/o Staff Member *The Dr. Phil Show*
5555 Melrose Ave Mae W Bldg
Los Angeles, CA 90038, USA

McGraw, Melinda (Actor)
c/o Staff Member *McKeon-Myones Management*
3500 W Olive Ave Ste 770
Burbank, CA 91505-5527, USA

McGraw, Mike (Athlete, Football Player)
P.O. Box 529
Medicine Bow, WY 82328, USA

McGraw, Phil (Dr. Phil) (Doctor, Talk Show Host)
c/o Staff Member *The Dr. Phil Show*
5555 Melrose Ave Mae W Bldg
Los Angeles, CA 90038, USA

McGraw, Robin (Writer)
c/o Staff Member *Peteski Productions Inc*
137 N Larchmont Blvd # 705
Los Angeles, CA 90004-3704, USA

McGraw, Thurman (Athlete, Football Player)
749 Sandpiper Pt
Fort Collins, CO 80525-3111, USA

McGraw, Tim (Musician)
c/o Coran Capshaw *Red Light Management (VA)*
PO Box 1467
Charlottesville, VA 22902-1467, USA

McGraw, Tom (Athlete, Baseball Player)
11300 NE 379th St
La Center, WA 98629-4307, USA

McGraw III, Harold W (Business Person, Publisher)
1221 Avenue of the Americas
New York, NY 10020-1001, USA

McGregor, Ewan (Actor)
c/o Nanci Ryder *Baker Winokur Ryder Public Relations (BWR-LA)*
9100 Wilshire Blvd Ste 500 PMB WEST
Beverly Hills, CA 90212-3426, USA

McGregor, Gilbert (Athlete, Basketball Player)
3700 Orleans Ave Apt 4411
New Orleans, LA 70119-4854, USA

McGregor, Keli (Athlete, Baseball Player, Football Player, President)
14776 W Byers Pl
Golden, CO 80401-5170, USA

McGregor, Maurice (Doctor)
687 Pine Ave W
Montreal, QC H3A 1A1, CANADA

McGregor, Scott H (Athlete, Baseball Player)
1514 Providence Rd
Towson, MD 21286-1523, USA

McGrew, Larry (Athlete, Football Player)
PO Box 2623
Berkeley, CA 94702-0623, USA

McGrew, Reggie (Athlete, Football Player)
1247 Lakeside Dr Apt 2039
Sunnyvale, CA 94085-1008, USA

McGriff, Elton (Athlete, Basketball Player)
4011 Shoreline Dr
Dallas, TX 75233-3709, USA

McGriff, Frederick S (Fred) (Athlete, Baseball Player)
16314 Millan De Avila
Tampa, FL 33613-1089, USA

McGriff, Hershel (Race Car Driver)
Green Valley, AZ 85622, USA

McGriff, Lee (Athlete, Football Player)
3501 W University Ave Ste A
Gainesville, FL 32607-2465, USA

McGriff, Tery (Athlete, Baseball Player)
2905 Langston Dr
Fort Pierce, FL 34946-1180, USA

McGriff, Travis (Athlete, Football Player)
5910 NW 19th Pl
Gainesville, FL 32605-3246, USA

McGriggs, Lamar (Athlete, Football Player)
1209-115 Main St E
Hamilton, ON L8N 1G5, Canada

McGruder, Aaron (Cartoonist)
4520 Main St
Kansas City, MO 64111-1876, USA

McGuane III, Thomas F (Writer)
410 S 3rd Ave
Bozeman, MT 59715-5251, USA

McGuinn, Martin G (Financier)
Center 500 Grant St
Pittsburgh, PA 15258-0001, USA

McGuinn, Roger (Musician)
c/o Staff Member *Shore Fire Media*
32 Court St Fl 16
Brooklyn, NY 11201-4441, USA

McGuire, Allie
4 Tanglewood Ln
Winchester, MA 01890-3376

McGuire, Betty (Actor)
733 Seward St PH
Los Angeles, CA 90038-3503, USA

McGuire, Bill (Athlete, Baseball Player)
17209 L St
Omaha, NE 68135, USA

McGuire, Christine (Musician)
100 Rancho Cir
Las Vegas, NV 89107-4600, USA

McGuire, Dorothy (Musician)
100 Rancho Cir
Las Vegas, NV 89107-4600, USA

McGuire, Kevin E (Athlete, Basketball Player)
20 Blue Jay Ln
North Oaks, MN 55127-2015, USA

Mcguire, Maeve
c/o Staff Member *Gage Group, The (LA)*
14724 Ventura Blvd Ste 505
Sherman Oaks, CA 91403-3505, USA

McGuire, Mickey (Athlete, Baseball Player)
1521 Middle Park Dr
Dayton, OH 45414-1500, USA

McGuire, Patricia A (Educator)
President's Office
Washington, DC 20017, USA

McGuire, Phyllis (Musician)
7373 N Scottsdale Rd Ste A130
Scottsdale, AZ 85253-3522, USA

McGuire, Richard J (Dick) (Athlete, Basketball Player, Coach)
17 Redwood Dr
Dix Hills, NY 11746-7727, USA

McGuire, Ryan (Athlete, Baseball Player)
171 Great Lawn
Irvine, CA 92620-3832, USA

McGuire, Walter E (Gene) (Athlete, Football Player)
3229 Country Club Dr
Lynn Haven, FL 32444-5125, USA

McGuire, Willard H (Misc)
1201 16th St NW
Washington, DC 20036-3201, USA

McGuire, William Biff (Actor)
1443 Pandora Ave
Los Angeles, CA 90024-5164, USA

McGuire, William W (Business Person)
Opus Center 9900 Bren Road E
Minnetonka, MN 55343, USA

McGuire Sisters (Music Group)
c/o Stan Scottland *Stan Scottland Entertainment*
157 E 57th St Apt 18B
New York, NY 10022-2115, USA

McGuire-Leveque, Sarah (Athlete, Golfer)
2433 S 15th St
Springfield, IL 62703-3644, USA

McGwire, Mark (Athlete, Baseball Player)
PO Box 165
East Irvine, CA 92650-0165, USA

McHale, Christina (Athlete, Tennis Player)
c/o Staff Member *Women's Tennis Association (WTA (US))*
1 Progress Plz Ste 1500
St Petersburg, FL 33701-4335, USA

Mchale, Joel (Actor, Television Host)
c/o James Dolin *Sonesta Entertainment*
150 Ocean Park Blvd Unit 423
Santa Monica, CA 90405-3574, USA

McHale, John (Athlete, Baseball Player)
2269 NE Ginger Ter
Jensen Beach, FL 34957-6704, USA

McHale, Kevin (Actor)
c/o Jamie Malone *MC Talent Management*
4821 Lankershim Blvd # F329
N Hollywood, CA 91601-4538, USA

McHale, Kevin E (Athlete, Basketball Player)
20 Blue Jay Ln
Saint Paul, MN 55127-2015, USA

McHattie, Stephen (Actor)
c/o Christopher (Chris) Wright *Christopher Wright Management*
3207 Winnie Dr
Los Angeles, CA 90068-1439, USA

McHattle, Stephen (Actor)
1505 W 2nd Ave # 200
Vancouver, BC V6H 3Y4, CANADA

McHenry, Donald F (Diplomat)
Foreign Service School
Washington, DC 20057-0001, USA

McHenry, Vance (Athlete, Baseball Player)
2396 Brown St
Durham, CA 95938-9620, USA

McHugh, Heather (Writer)
PO Box 35330
Seattle, WA 98195-0001, USA

McIlhenny, Don (Athlete, Football Player)
8505 Edgemere Rd Apt 101
Dallas, TX 75225-3520, USA

McIlvaine, Jim (Athlete, Basketball Player)
W5639 Anokijig Ln
Plymouth, WI 53073-2879, USA

McInerney, Jay (Actor, Writer)
c/o Doug MacLaren *International Creative Management (ICM-LA)*
10250 Constellation Blvd Fl 7
Los Angeles, CA 90067-6207, USA

McInnis, Hugh (Athlete, Football Player)
290 Rockwell Church Rd NE
Winder, GA 30680-3039, USA

Mcinnis, Jeffrey (Athlete, Basketball Player)
3404 Lazy Day Ln
Charlotte, NC 28269-0144, USA

McInnis, Marty (Athlete, Hockey Player)
21 Peter Hobart Dr
Hingham, MA 02043-3751, USA

McIntosh, Bill (Athlete, Golfer)
5263 SW Bimini Cir N
Palm City, FL 34990-1246, USA

Mcintosh, Bradley (Actor, Musician)
c/o Becky Thompson *Action Talent International*
Moray House 23 - 31 Great Titchfield Street
London W1W 7PA, United Kingdom

McIntosh, Joe (Athlete, Baseball Player)
9120 SE 54th St
Mercer Island, WA 98040-5148, USA

McIntosh, Tim (Athlete, Baseball Player)
1815 S Talbott Pl
Waynesboro, VA 22980-2250, USA

McIntyre, Guy (Athlete, Football Player)
257 Arrowhead Way
Hayward, CA 94544-6649, USA

McIntyre, Joe (Actor)
c/o Gina Rugolo-Judd *Rugolo Entertainment*
195 S Beverly Dr Ste 400
Beverly Hills, CA 90212-3044, USA

McIntyre, Joey (Musician)
520 W 43rd St
New York, NY 10036-4304, USA

McIntyre, Melissa (Actor)
c/o Dani De Lio 20 Carlton St #123
Toronto, ON M5B 2H5, CANADA

McIntyre, Mike (Congressman, Politician)
2133 Rayburn Hob
Washington, DC 20515-2102, USA

McIntyre, Secedrick (Athlete, Football Player)
4801 Tannery Ave
Tampa, FL 33624-4533, USA

McIver, Everett (Athlete, Football Player)
1205 Avignon Dr SW
Conyers, GA 30094-8406, USA

McIvor, Richard (Athlete, Football Player)
PO Box 148
Fort Davis, TX 79734-0002, USA

McJulien, Paul (Athlete, Football Player)
12111 Gibbens Rd
Baton Rouge, LA 70807-1602, USA

McKagan, Duff (Musician)
c/o Ian Sales *International Talent Booking*
1st Floor, Ariel House 74A Charlotte St
London W1T 4QJ, UNITED KINGDOM

McKagen, Duff
8647 Edwin Dr
Los Angeles, CA 90046-1047

McKay, Adam (Actor, Director, Writer)
c/o Jimmy Miller *Mosaic Media Group*
9200 W Sunset Blvd Ste 10
Los Angeles, CA 90069-3608, USA

McKay, Bob (Athlete, Football Player)
4110 Bluffridge Dr
Austin, TX 78759-7354, USA

McKay, Cody (Athlete, Baseball Player)
7830 S Yarrow St
Littleton, CO 80128-5492, USA

McKay, Dave (Athlete, Baseball Player)
9702 E La Posada Cir
Scottsdale, AZ 85255-3716, USA

McKay, David S (Scientist)
2101 Nasa Pkwy Spc Center
Houston, TX 77058-3607, USA

McKay, Gardner (Actor, Director, Writer)
1040 Lunalilo St PH 2
Honolulu, HI 96822-5712, USA

McKay, Heather (Athlete)
48 Nesbitt Dr
Toronto, ON M4W 2G3, CANADA

McKay, John (Athlete, Football Player)
4110 Bluffridge Dr
Austin, TX 78759-7354, USA

McKay, Mhairi (Athlete, Golfer)
898 W Ashbourne Dr
Eagle, ID 83616-6433, USA

McKay, Nellie (Actor)
c/o Staff Member *Kid Logic*
156 Liberty St Apt 12
Little Ferry, NJ 07643-1768, USA

McKay, Peggy (Actor)
8811 Wonderland Ave
Los Angeles, CA 90046-1851, USA

McKean, Jim (Athlete, Baseball Player)
740 Sand Pine Dr NE
Saint Petersburg, FL 33703-3181, USA

McKean, Michael (Actor, Comedian)
c/o Harriet Sternberg *Harriet Sternberg Management*
4530 Gloria Ave
Encino, CA 91436-2718, USA

McKee, Bonnie (Musician)
15353 SE 49th Pl
Bellevue, WA 98006-3652, USA

McKee, Frank S (Misc)
5 Gateway Ctr
Pittsburgh, PA 15222, USA

McKee, Gina (Actor)
8 Silver Place
London W1R 3LJ, UNITED KINGDOM (UK)

McKee, Kinnaird R (Admiral)
7100 Wheeler Park Cir
Easton, MD 21601-8448, USA

McKee, Lonette (Actor)
c/o Keith Perkins 545 8th Ave Ste 401
New York, NY 10018, USA

McKee, Lucky (Director)
9300 Wilshire Blvd Ste 555
Beverly Hills, CA 90212-3211, USA

McKee, Maria (Musician)
449 Trollingwood Rd # A
Haw River, NC 27258-8750, USA

McKee, Rogers (Athlete, Baseball Player)
409 Forest Hill Dr
Shelby, NC 28150-5520, USA

McKee, Susan (Stylist)
c/o Staff Member *Clutts Agency, The*
1400 Turtle Creek Blvd # 171
Dallas, TX 75207-3337, USA

McKee, Theodore A (Judge)
601 Market St
Philadelphia, PA 19106-1737, USA

McKee, Todd (Actor)
316 N Flores St
Los Angeles, CA 90048-2610, USA

McKeehan, Pat
PO Box 486
Louisville, TN 37777-0486

McKeel, Walt (Athlete, Baseball Player)
7669 NC Highway 58 N
Stantonsburg, NC 27883-8635, USA

McKeever, Marlin (Athlete, Football Player)
4000 E 2nd St
Long Beach, CA 90803-5223, USA

McKellar, Danica (Actor)
c/o Andrew Edwards *Wishlab*
2438 Canyon Oak Dr
Los Angeles, CA 90068-2428, USA

McKellen, Ian (Actor)
c/o Chris Andrews *Creative Artists Agency (CAA-LA)*
2000 Avenue of the Stars Ste 100
Los Angeles, CA 90067-4705, USA

McKeller, Keith (Athlete, Football Player)
1972 Waccamaw Path
Winston Salem, NC 27127-9433, USA

McKelvey, Rob (Athlete, Golfer)
1814 Duke Rd
Atlanta, GA 30341-4853, USA

McKenna, Alex (Actor)
c/o Staff Member *Grey Media Group*
16848 Charmel Ln
Pacific Palisades, CA 90272-2216, USA

McKenna, Aline Brosh (Writer)
c/o Todd Feldman *Creative Artists Agency (CAA-LA)*
2000 Avenue of the Stars Ste 100
Los Angeles, CA 90067-4705, USA

McKenna, Andrew J (Business Person)
1 McDonald's Plaza 1 Kroc Dr
Oak Brook, IL 60523, USA

McKenna, David (Dave) (Musician)
11761 E Speedway Blvd
Tucson, AZ 85748-2017, USA

McKenna, Kevin (Athlete, Basketball Player)
15387 Nicholas St
Omaha, NE 68154-3712, USA

McKenna, Paul (Motivational Speaker)
c/o Staff Member *United Agents*
12-26 Lexington St
London W1F OLE, UK

McKenna, T P (Actor)
28 Claverley Grove
London N3 2DH, UNITED KINGDOM (UK)

McKenna, Virginia (Actor)
8 Buckfast Ct
Runcorn, Cheshire WA7 1QJ, UNITED KINGDOM (UK)

McKenney, Donald H (Don) (Athlete, Hockey Player)
16 Edgewater Dr
Norton, MA 02766-2123, USA

McKennitt, Loreena (Musician)
c/o Staff Member *Quinlan Road*
P.O. Box 933
Stratford, Ontario N5A 7M3, Canada

McKennitt, Lorena (Musician, Songwriter, Writer)
PO Box 933
Stratford, ON N5A 7M3, CANADA

McKennon, Keith R (Business Person)
6079 N Paradise View Dr
Paradise Valley, AZ 85253-3828, USA

McKenzie, Andrew (Misc)
265 W 14th St
New York, NY 10011-7103, USA

McKenzie, Benjamin (Actor)
c/o David Seltzer *Management 360*
9111 Wilshire Blvd
Beverly Hills, CA 90210-5508, USA

McKenzie, Constance
3360 Barham Blvd
Los Angeles, CA 90068-1473

McKenzie, Dan P (Misc)
Madingley Rise Madingley Road
Cambridge CB3 0EZ, UNITED KINGDOM (UK)

McKenzie, Forrest (Athlete, Basketball Player)
2516 S Laurelwood
Santa Ana CA, 92704 USA

McKenzie, Jacqueline (Actor)
c/o Brett Carella *Lab, The*
5540 Hollywood Blvd # 200
Hollywood, CA 90028-6808, USA

McKenzie, Jim (Athlete, Hockey Player)
135 Technology Dr Ste 401
Canonsburg, PA 15317-9519, USA

McKenzie, Julia
Kingston Richmond Park
Surrey, ENGLAND

McKenzie, Kevin (Ballerina)
890 Broadway
New York, NY 10003-1211, USA

McKenzie, Melanie (Stylist)
430 E 65th St Apt 2D
New York, NY 10065-7160, USA

McKenzie, Raleigh (Athlete, Football Player)
715 Huntsman Pl
Herndon, VA 20170-3160, USA

McKenzie, Reggie (Athlete, Football Player)
411 Carta Rd
Knoxville, TN 37914-3619, USA

McKenzie, Reginald (Reggie) (Athlete, Football Player)
1849 Campau Farms Cir
Detroit, MI 48207-5167, USA

McKenzie, Roger (Stylist)
c/o Staff Member *Tapestry Creative Management, Inc*
274 W 132nd St Apt 3
New York, NY 10027-7809, USA

McKenzie, Stan (Athlete, Basketball Player)
8316 Governor Grayson Way
Ellicott City, MD 21043-3450, USA

McKenzie, Vashti (Religious Leader)
1714 Madison Ave # 16
Baltimore, MD 21217-3750, USA

McKeon, Doug (Actor)
c/o Raymond Miller *Archetype*
1608 Argyle Ave
Los Angeles, CA 90028-6408, USA

McKeon, Joel (Athlete, Baseball Player)
1901 Pierce St Apt 7
Hollywood, FL 33020-4047, USA

McKeon, John A (Jack) (Athlete, Baseball Player, Coach)
1529 Charleigh Ct
Elon, NC 27244-9770, USA

McKeon, Lindsey (Actor)
c/o Robbie Kass *Kass & Stokes Management*
9229 W Sunset Blvd Ste 504
Los Angeles, CA 90069-3405, USA

McKeon, Matt (Soccer Player)
2 Arrowhead Dr
Kansas City, MO 64129-1650, USA

McKeon, Nancy (Actor)
PO Box 6778
Burbank, CA 91510-6778, USA

McKeown, Bob (Correspondent)
51 W 52nd St
New York, NY 10019-6119, USA

McKeown, Les
27 Preston Grange Preston Pans
E. Lothian, SCOTLAND

McKeown, Leslie (Les) (Music Group, Musician)
PO Box 106
Rochdale, OL 16 4HW, UNITED KINGDOM (UK)

McKeown, M Margaret (Judge)
5th Ave US Courthouse 1010
Seattle, WA 98104-3191, USA

McKernan, John R Jr (Ex-Governor)
210 6th Ave Fl 33
Pittsburgh, PA 15222-2602, USA

McKey, Derrick (Athlete, Basketball Player)
8 Woodard Pl
Zionsville, IN 46077-8189, USA

McKibben, Mike (Athlete, Football Player)
2523 Forest Brook Dr
Upper Saint Clair, PA 15241-2586, USA

McKibbin, Nikki (Actor, Musician)
c/o JD Sobol *RPM Talent Agency*
2600 W Olive Ave Fl 5
Burbank, CA 91505-4572, USA

McKidd, Kevin (Actor)
c/o Peter Kiernan *Management 360*
9111 Wilshire Blvd
Beverly Hills, CA 90210-5508, USA

McKie, Aaron (Athlete, Basketball Player)
328 Coral St
Lancaster, PA 17603-5171, USA

McKiernan, David (General)
Commanding General 3rd Army
Fort McPherson, GA 30330-0001, USA

McKinley, Dennis (Athlete, Football Player)
150 McKinley Rd
Mc Cool, MS 39108-4220, USA

McKinley, John (Misc)
952 Bloomfield Village Blvd
Auburn Hills, MI 48326-3572, USA

McKinley, Robin (Writer)
21 W 26th St
New York, NY 10010-1003, USA

McKinley-Uselmann, Therese (Baseball Player)
1644 N Greenwood Ave
Park Ridge, IL 60068-1215, USA

McKinnely, Phil (Athlete, Football Player)
585 Edgehill Pl
Alpharetta, GA 30022-7006, USA

McKinney, Carlton (Athlete, Basketball Player)
310 E 4th Ave
Nixon, TX 78140-2939, USA

Mckinney, Frank (Business Person)
PO Box 388
Boynton Beach, FL 33425-0388, USA

McKinney, Gil (Actor)
c/o Steven Levy *Framework Entertainment (LA)*
9057 Nemo St Ste C
West Hollywood, CA 90069-5511, USA

McKinney, Greg
1800 Avenue of the Stars Ste 400
Los Angeles, CA 90067-4206

McKinney, Jack (Athlete, Basketball Player, Coach)
300 Lincoln Rd
King Of Prussia, PA 19406-1840, USA

McKinney, Kurt
9200 W Sunset Blvd Ste 1130
Los Angeles, CA 90069-3606

McKinney, Mark (Actor)
c/o Staff Member *WmE2 (WMA-LA)*
1 William Morris Pl
Beverly Hills, CA 90212-4261, USA

McKinney, Odis (Athlete, Football Player)
23126 Collins St
Woodland Hills, CA 91367-4225, USA

McKinney, Rich (Athlete, Baseball Player)
2495 E Peterson Rd
Troy, OH 45373-7790, USA

McKinney, Royce (Athlete, Football Player)
1930 N Beech Daly Rd
Dearborn Heights, MI 48127-3462, USA

McKinney, Steve (Athlete, Football Player)
2403 Crown Ct
College Station, TX 77845-2006, USA

McKinney, Tamara
4935 Parkers Mill Rd
Lexington, KY 40513-9760

McKinnie, Bryant (Athlete, Football Player)
15821 Porchlight Ln
Eden Prairie, MN 55347-3576, USA

McKinnie, Silas (Athlete, Football Player)
22875 Summer House Ct Apt 205
Novi, MI 48375-4582, USA

McKinnney, Kurt (Actor)
5003 Tilden Ave Unit 206
Sherman Oaks, CA 91423-1747, USA

McKinnney, Richard (Rick) (Athlete)
549 E Silver Creek Rd
Gilbert, AZ 85296-1150, USA

McKinnney, Tamara (Skier)
4935 Parkers Mill Rd
Lexington, KY 40513-9760, USA

McKinnon, Bruce (Cartoonist, Editor)
Editorial Dept PO Box 610
Halifax, NS B3J 2T2, CANADA

McKinnon, Dan (Athlete, Hockey Player)
610 E River Dr
Warroad, MN 56763, USA

McKinnon, Dennis (Athlete, Football Player)
1016 Adams St
North Chicago, IL 60064-1227, USA

McKinnon, Ray (Actor)
606 N Larchmont Blvd Ste 309
Los Angeles, CA 90004-1309, USA

McKinnon, Ronald (Athlete, Football Player)
1603 Grand Oaks Dr
Bessemer, AL 35022-7237, USA

McKinny, Laura Hart
3224 Nottingham Rd
Winston Salem, NC 27104-1839

Mckinzie, Gordon (Engineer)
PO Box 3707
Seattle, WA 98124-2207, USA

McKissock, Gary S (General)
2 Navy St
Washington, DC 20380-0001, USA

McKnight, Brian (Musician, Songwriter)
c/o Ann Gurrola *Marleah Leslie & Associates PR*
1645 Vine St Apt 712
Los Angeles, CA 90028-8812, USA

McKnight, Clarence E Jr (General)
1624 Linway Park Dr
McLean, VA 22101-4149, USA

McKnight, Ira (Baseball Player)
8417 Laurel Valley Dr
Indianapolis, IN 46250-3906, USA

McKnight, James (Athlete, Football Player)
16705 Berkshire Ct
Southwest Ranches, FL 33331-1331, USA

McKnight, Jeff (Athlete, Baseball Player)
3296 Highway 92 W
Bee Branch, AR 72013-8937, USA

McKnight, Joe (Athlete, Football Player)
c/o Roosevelt Barnes *Maximum Sports Management*
6435 W Jefferson Blvd # 197
Fort Wayne, IN 46804-6203, USA

McKnight, Steven L (Biologist)
8513 Swananoah Rd
Dallas, TX 75209-2839, USA

McKnight, Ted (Athlete, Football Player)
10236 Cedarbrooke Ln
Kansas City, MO 64131-4210, USA

McKnight, Tom (Athlete, Golfer)
2 Willingham Ct
Okatie, SC 29909-3120, USA

McKnight, Tony (Athlete, Baseball Player)
406 Dundee Rd
Texarkana, AR 71854-9768, USA

McKuen, Rod (Musician, Songwriter, Writer)
PO Box 2783
Los Angeles, CA 90051-0783, USA

McKyer, Tim (Athlete, Football Player)
12333 McAllister Park Dr
Charlotte, NC 28277-2503, USA

McLachlan, Craig
Box 176
Potts Point, AUSTRALIA NSW 2011

McLachlan, Sarah (Musician, Songwriter)
c/o Terry McBride *Nettwerk Productions*
1650 W 2nd Ave
Vancouver BC V6J 4R3, CANADA

McLafferty, Fred W (Scientist)
103 Needham Pl
Ithaca, NY 14850-2120, USA

McLagien, Andrew V (Director)
PO Box 1056
Friday Harbor, WA 98250-1056, USA

McLaglen, Andrew (Director)
PO Box 1056
Friday Harbor, WA 98250-1056, USA

McLain, Dennis D (Denny) (Athlete, Baseball Player)
4432 Golf View Dr
Brighton, MI 48116-9187, USA

McLain, Kevin (Athlete, Football Player)
2551 State St Ste 222
Carlsbad, CA 92008-1682, USA

McLane, Drayton (Baseball Player)
100 N Apache Dr
Temple, TX 76504-2863, USA

McLane, James P (Jimmy) Jr (Swimmer)
85 Pinckney St
Boston, MA 02114-4303, USA

McLaren, John (Athlete, Baseball Player, Coach)
PO Box 4100
Seattle, WA 98194-0100, USA

McLaren, Richard (Photographer)
580 Paseo Miramar
Pacific Palisades, CA 90272-3022, USA

McLaren, Sally
28 Berkeley Sq
London, ENGLAND W1X 6HD

McLaughlin, Ann Dore (Secretary)
2100 M St NW
Washington, DC 20037-1207, USA

McLaughlin, Audrey (Government Official)
House of Commons
Ottawa, ON K1A 0A6, CANADA

McLaughlin, Bo (Athlete, Baseball Player)
536 N Grand
Mesa, AZ 85201-5031, USA

McLaughlin, Byron (Baseball Player)
7030 Alamitos Ave
San Diego, CA 92154-4764, USA

McLaughlin, Carol (Musician)
165 W 57th St
New York, NY 10019-2201, USA

McLaughlin, Joey (Athlete, Baseball Player)
1611 S Troost Ave
Tulsa, OK 74120-6615, USA

McLaughlin, John (Government Official)
Deputy Director S Ofc
Washington, DC 20505-0001, USA

McLaughlin, John (Athlete, Football Player)
6038 Marina Pointe Ct Apt 207
Tampa, FL 33635, USA

McLaughlin, John J (Television Host)
1717 Rhode Island Ave NW Ste 640
Washington, DC 20036-3025, USA

McLaughlin, Mike (Race Car Driver)
PO Box 45
Waterloo, NY 13165-0045, USA

McLean, AJ (Actor, Musician)
c/o Eric Podwall *Podwall Entertainment*
710 N Orlando Ave Apt 203
Los Angeles, CA 90069-5549, USA

McLean, Barney (Athlete, Skier)
9555 W 59th Ave Apt 303
Arvada, CO 80004-5396, USA

McLean, Constance (Stylist)
24572 Harbor View Dr Unit A
Dana Point, CA 92629-1749, USA

McLean, Deborah (Stylist)
c/o Staff Member *Zenobia Agency Inc*
PO Box 909
Groveland, CA 95321-0909, USA

McLean, Don (Musician, Songwriter, Writer)
c/o Jim Lenz *Paradise Artists*
PO Box 1821
Ojai, CA 93024-1821, USA

McLean, Greg (Director)
c/o Staff Member *WmE2 (Endeavor-LA)*
9601 Wilshire Blvd Fl 3
Beverly Hills, CA 90210-5219, USA

McLean, James (Athlete, Golfer)
c/o Jim Lehrman *SFX Golf*
36855 W Main St Ste 200
Purcellville, VA 20132-3561, USA

McLean, Rene (Musician)
122 E 57th St # 300
New York, NY 10022-2623, USA

McLean, Sally (Actor, Producer)
c/o Staff Member *Salmac Management*
PO Box 526
Mt Martha VIC 3934, AUSTRALIA

McLean, Scott (Athlete, Football Player)
375 Bear Ln
Lake Placid, FL 33852-4411, USA

McLeary, Marty (Athlete, Baseball Player)
2120 Long Meadow Dr
Spring Hill, TN 37174-7129, USA

Mclellan, Zoe (Actor)
c/o Mandi Warren *Viewpoint Inc. - NY*
700 N San Vicente Blvd Ste G910
West Hollywood, CA 90069-5061, USA

McLemore, Dana (Athlete, Football Player)
2908 Fairman St
Lakewood, CA 90712-3634, USA

McLemore, LaMonte (Musician)
10877 Wilshire Blvd # 15
Los Angeles, CA 90024-4341, USA

McLemore, Mark (Athlete, Baseball Player)
533 S White Chapel Blvd
Southlake, TX 76092-7316, USA

McLemore, Mark (Athlete, Baseball Player)
7965 Eagle View Ln
Granite Bay, CA 95746-7333, USA

McLemore, McCoy (Athlete, Basketball Player)
11100 Braesridge Dr Apt 1621
Houston, TX 77071-2134, USA

McLendon-Covey, Wendi (Actor)
c/o Ben Feigin *Anonymous Content (AC-LA)*
3531 Hayden Ave
Culver City, CA 90232, USA

McLeod, George (Athlete, Basketball Player)
834 Greenpark Dr
Houston, TX 77079-4502, USA

McLeod, Robert D (Athlete, Football Player)
600 Spring Creek Rd
Brenham, TX 77833-8159, USA

McLerie, Allyn Ann (Actor, Dancer)
3344 Campanil Dr
Santa Barbara, CA 93109-1017, USA

McLish, Cal (Athlete, Baseball Player)
639 Timber Ln
Edmond, OK 73034-4631, USA

Mclntyre, Donald C (Opera Singer)
Foxhill Farm Jackass Lane Keston Bromley
Kent BR2 6AN, UNITED KINGDOM (UK)

McLouth, Nate (Athlete, Baseball Player)
218 Glenn Canyon Dr SE
Caledonia, MI 49316, USA

McMahan, Jack (Athlete, Baseball Player)
131 Forest View Cir
Hot Springs National Park,
AR 71913-6557, USA

McMahon, Art (Athlete, Football Player)
PO Box 292
Reading, MA 01867-0492, USA

McMahon, James R (Jim) (Athlete, Football Player)
22431 N Violetta Dr
Scottsdale, AZ 85255-4428, USA

McMahon, Jenna (Actor)
PO Box 5033
Carmel By The Sea, CA 93921-5033, USA

McMahon, Julian (Actor, Producer)
c/o Will Ward *ROAR (LA)*
9701 Wilshire Blvd Fl 8
Beverly Hills, CA 90212-2008, USA

McMahon, Mike (Athlete, Football Player)
313 Oak Grove Ct
Wexford, PA 15090-9570, USA

McMahon, Shane (Wrestler)
c/o Kerry Rodgerson *World Wrestling Entertainment (WWE)*
1241 E Main St
Stamford, CT 06902-3520, USA

McMahon, Stephanie (Wrestler)
c/o Kerry Rodgerson *World Wrestling Entertainment (WWE)*
1241 E Main St
Stamford, CT 06902-3520, USA

McMahon Jr, Vincent (Vince) K (Business Person)
47 Hurtingham Dr
Greenwich, CT 6831, USA

McMakin, John (Athlete, Football Player)
PO Box 863
Anacortes, WA 98221-0863, USA

McMann, Harry (Stylist)
408 N Lakewood Ave
Baltimore, MD 21224-1112, USA

McManus, Don (Actor)
c/o Staff Member *Principal Entertainment (LA)*
1964 Westwood Blvd Ste 400
Los Angeles, CA 90025-4695, USA

McManus, Jim (Athlete, Baseball Player)
2352 Hopkins Mill Rd
Duluth, GA 30096-4524, USA

McManus, Michelle (Musician)

McManus, Rove (Actor, Talk Show Host)
c/o Staff Member *Token*
1st Floor 274 Brunswick St
Fitzroy, Victoria 3065, Australia

McMartin, John (Actor, Musician)
1180 S Beverly Dr Ste 301
Los Angeles, CA 90035-1154, USA

McMath, Jimmy (Athlete, Baseball Player)
3321 22nd St
Tuscaloosa, AL 35401-5203, USA

McMenamin, Mark (Misc)
Geology Dept
South Hadley, MA 1075, USA

McMichael, Greg (Athlete, Baseball Player)
240 Parkside Club Ct
Duluth, GA 30097-7847, USA

McMichael, Steve D (Athlete, Football Player)
1268 Holiday Dr
Somonauk, IL 60552-9639, USA

McMichen, Robert S (Misc)
PO Box 157
Colorado Springs, CO 80901-0157, USA

McMillan, Audray (Athlete, Football Player)
1230 Hahlo St
Houston, TX 77020-7340, USA

McMillan, Caroline (Athlete, Golfer)
5101 N Casa Blanca Dr Unit 206
Paradise Valley, AZ 85253-6987, USA

McMillan, Caroline (Athlete, Golfer)
7525 E Phantom Way
Scottsdale, AZ 85255-4622, USA

McMillan, Eddie (Athlete, Football Player)
6204 222nd St SW
Mountlake Terrace, WA 98043-2530, USA

McMillan, Erik (Athlete, Football Player)
17209 Chesterfield Airport Rd # 308
Chesterfield, MO 63005-1423, USA

McMillan, Ernie (Athlete, Football Player)
14816 Sycamore Manor Ct
Chesterfield, MO 63017-5535, USA

McMillan, Nate (Athlete, Basketball Player, Coach)
3525 Ghiglieri Ct
West Linn, OR 97068-3686, USA

McMillan, Susan Carpenter
1744 Oak Ln
San Marino, CA 91108-1021

McMillan, Terry (Writer)
PO Box 2408
Danville, CA 94526-7408, USA

McMillan, Tommy (Athlete, Baseball Player)
712 Spring Lake Rd
Thomasville, GA 31792-8605, USA

McMillan, William (Bill) (Misc)
1930 Sandstone Vista Ln
Encinitas, CA 92024-4247, USA

McMillen, C Thomas (Tom) (Athlete, Basketball Player)
4100 Fairfax Dr Ste 1150
Arlington, VA 22203-1666, USA

McMillian, Audray G (Athlete, Football Player)
4015 Brightwood St
Missouri City, TX 77459-1814, USA

McMillian, Jim (Athlete, Basketball Player)
1790 Polo Rd
Winston Salem, NC 27106-4541, USA

McMillian, Michael (Actor)
c/o Abby Bluestone *Innovative Artists (LA)*
1505 10th St
Santa Monica, CA 90401-2805, USA

McMillin, James R (Athlete, Football Player)
7985 Westview Dr
Lakewood, CO 80214-4541, USA

McMillon, Billy (Athlete, Baseball Player)
1516 Lost Creek Dr
Columbia, SC 29212-2859, USA

McMonagle, Donald R (Astronaut)
7737 E Shadow Vista Ct
Tucson, AZ 85750-0742, USA

McMorris, Cathy (Congressman, Politician)
2421 Rayburn Hob
Washington, DC 20515-2902, USA

McMorris, Jerry (Baseball Player)
PO Box 217
Timnath, CO 80547-0217, USA

McMullen, Curtis T (Mathematician)
Science Center
Cambridge, MA 2138, USA

McMullen, Kathy (Athlete, Golfer)
526 Harrison St
Emmaus, PA 18049-2314, USA

McMullen, Ken (Athlete, Baseball Player)
10 Estaban Dr
Camarillo, CA 93010-1610, USA

McMurray, Jamie (Race Car Driver)
c/o Staff Member *Ganassi Racing*
8500 Westmoreland Dr NW
Concord, NC 28027-7571, USA

McMurray, Sam
11500 W Olympic Blvd Ste 510
Los Angeles, CA 90064-1527

McMurray, W Grant (Religious Leader)
PO Box 1059
Independence, MO 64051-0559, USA

McMurtry, Craig (Athlete, Baseball Player)
2835 Bottoms East Rd
Troy, TX 76579-3008, USA

McMurtry, James (Musician, Songwriter, Writer)
751 Bridgeway # 300
Sausalito, CA 94965-2102, USA

McMurtry, Larry (Writer)
PO Box 552
Archer City, TX 76351-0552, USA

McNab, Mercedes (Actor)
c/o Jason Egenberg *United Talent Agency (UTA)*
9560 Wilshire Blvd Fl 5
Beverly Hills, CA 90212-2400, USA

McNabb, Dexter (Athlete, Football Player)
1449 Pat Tillman St
De Pere, WI 54115-7529, USA

McNabb, Donovan (Athlete, Football Player)
c/o Fletcher Smith *Blueprint Sports Group*
221 W Jefferson Ave
Naperville, IL 60540-5355, USA

McNair, Kelly (Actor)
c/o Staff Member *GVA Talent Agency Inc*
8981 W Sunset Blvd Ste 101
Los Angeles, CA 90069-1850, USA

McNair, Sylvia (Opera Singer)
Plankengasse 7
Vienna 1010, AUSTRIA

McNally, Kevin (Actor)
c/o Mark A. Schlegel *Cornerstone Talent Agency*
37 W 20th St
New York, NY 10011-3706, USA

McNally, Stephen (Ste) (Musician)
Crown House 225 Kensington High St
London W8 8SA, UNITED KINGDOM (UK)

McNally, Terrence (Writer)
c/o Jonathan Lomma *WmE2 (Endeavor-LA)*
9601 Wilshire Blvd Fl 3
Beverly Hills, CA 90210-5219, USA

McNamara, Bob (Athlete, Football Player)
4909 Prescott Cir
Edina, MN 55436-1011, USA

McNamara, Bob (Athlete, Baseball Player)
4764 Dalea Pl
Oceanside, CA 92057-6136, USA

McNamara, Brian (Actor)
c/o Staff Member *Pathway Entertainment*
1739 Berkeley St Ste 110C
Santa Monica, CA 90404-4155, USA

McNamara, Eileen (Journalist)
Editorial Dept 135 W T Morrissey Blvd
Dorchester, MA 2125, USA

McNamara, Jim (Baseball Player)
15317 Surrey House Way
Centreville, VA 20120-1196, USA

McNamara, John (Athlete, Baseball Player, Coach)
1206 Beech Hill Rd
Brentwood, TN 37027-5530, USA

McNamara, John F (Athlete, Baseball Player)
15317 Surrey House Way
Centreville, VA 20120-1196, USA

McNamara, Julianne L (Actor, Gymnast)
2236 Encinitas Blvd Ste A
Encinitas, CA 92024-4353, USA

McNamara, Julie (Business Person)
c/o Staff Member *CBS Paramount Network Television*
4024 Radford Ave
Studio City, CA 91604-2190, USA

McNamara, Melissa (Athlete, Golfer)
1940 S Florence Pl
Tulsa, OK 74104-6112, USA

McNamara, William (Actor)
c/o Frederick Levy *Management 101*
9107 1/2 Cahuenga Blvd
N Hollywood, CA 91601-2920, USA

McNamee, Joe (Athlete, Basketball Player)
521 S Eliseo Dr
Greenbrae, CA 94904-2920, USA

McNanie, Sean (Athlete, Football Player)
14915 Rancho Real
Del Mar, CA 92014-4213, USA

McNaught, Erin (Beauty Pageant Winner)
c/o Ursula Hufnagl *Chic Management*
36 Jersey Road
Woollahra NSW 2025, AUSTRALIA

McNaught, Judith (Writer)
1230 Avenue of the Americas
New York, NY 10020-1513, USA

McNaughton, John D (Director)
1370 N Milwaukee Ave
Chicago, IL 60622-9107, USA

McNaughton, Robert F Jr (Scientist)
2218 Burdett Ave Apt 316
Troy, NY 12180-2491, USA

McNeal, Donald (Don) (Athlete, Football Player)
3311 Toledo Plz
Coral Gables, FL 33134-6483, USA

McNeal, Krista (Beauty Pageant Winner)
12708 Northrup Hwy # 101
Bellevue, WA 98005, USA

McNealey, Christopher (Athlete, Basketball Player)
30 Shady Oak Ct
Danville, CA 94506-6145, USA

McNealy, Rusty (Athlete, Baseball Player)
3301 Bozeman St
Sacramento, CA 95838-4105, USA

McNealy, Scott G (Business Person)
901 San Antonio Rd
Palo Alto, CA 94303-4900, USA

McNeeley, Big Jay (Misc)
PO Box 1967
Studio City, CA 91614-0967, USA

McNeely, Jeff (Athlete, Baseball Player)
405 Everette St
Monroe, NC 28112-5622, USA

McNeely, Tom (Artist)
9 Blythwood Gardens
Toronto, ON M4N 3L2, Canada

McNeice, Ian (Actor)
c/o Renee Jennett *Renee Jennett Management*
5757 Wilshire Blvd Ste 473
Los Angeles, CA 90036-3632, USA

McNeil, Clifton (Athlete, Football Player)
1001 Westbury Dr Apt 98
Mobile, AL 36609-3336, USA

McNeil, Emanuel (Athlete, Football Player)
15335 Park Row Apt 402
Houston, TX 77084-2893, USA

McNeil, Frederick A (Fred) (Athlete, Football Player)
9667 W Olympic Blvd Apt 5
Beverly Hills, CA 90212-3745, USA

McNeil, Freeman (Athlete, Football Player)
PO Box 62
Greenlawn, NY 11740-0062, USA

McNeil, Kate (Actor)
1743 N Dillon St
Los Angeles, CA 90026-1113, USA

McNeil, Lori (Tennis Player)
1 Erieview Plaza 1360 East 9th St # 1300
Cleveland, OH 44114, USA

McNeil, Ryan (Athlete, Football Player)
4702 Avenue Q
Fort Pierce, FL 34947-7049, USA

McNeill, Fred (Athlete, Football Player)
3556 S Van Ness Ave
Los Angeles, CA 90018-4350, USA

McNeill, Robert (Athlete, Basketball Player)
1318 Wooded Way
Bryn Mawr, PA 19010-1781, USA

McNeill, Rod (Athlete, Football Player)
1048 S Magnolia Ave
West Covina, CA 91791-3730, USA

McNeill, W Donald (Don) (Tennis Player)
2165 15th Ave
Vero Beach, FL 32960-3435, USA

McNeish, Richard (Archaeologist)
1 Woodland Rd
Andover, MA 01810-2111, USA

McNell, Rufus (Baseball Player)
205 Heard St
Kinston, NC 28501-5850, USA

McNerney, David H (War Hero)
PO Box 475
Crosby, TX 77532-0475, USA

McNerney, Jerry (Congressman, Politician)
1210 Longworth Hob
Washington, DC 20515-1311, USA

McNerney, Moisette (Stylist)
1214 E Clarendon St
Arlington Heights, IL 60004-5050, USA

McNertney, Gerald (Jerry) (Athlete, Baseball Player)
584 193rd St
Ames, IA 50010, USA

McNett, Wendy (Stylist)
c/o Sydney Oliver *Oliver Piro Inc*
725 Riverside Dr Apt 3A
New York, NY 10031-2460, USA

McNichol, Brian (Athlete, Baseball Player)
15725 E Palisades Blvd
Fountain Hills, AZ 85268-3626, USA

McNichol, Kristy (Actor)
c/o Staff Member *Good Guy Entertainment*
3733 Oakfield Dr
Sherman Oaks, CA 91423-4430, USA

McNorton, Bruce (Athlete, Football Player)
PO Box 672
Bloomfield Hills, MI 48303-0672, USA

McNown, Cade (Athlete, Football Player)
7540 Kentwood Ct
Gilroy, CA 95020-4741, USA

McNulty, Bill (Athlete, Baseball Player)
12210 172nd St E Apt G101
Puyallup, WA 98374-8825, USA

McNulty, Carl (Athlete, Basketball Player)
212 Westmoreland Dr E
Kokomo, IN 46901-5155, USA

McPartlin, Ant (Television Host)
c/o Kevin McLaughlin *Baker Winokur Ryder Public Relations (BWR-LA)*
9100 Wilshire Blvd Ste 500 PMB WEST
Beverly Hills, CA 90212-3426, USA

McPartlin, Ryan (Actor)
c/o Miles Levy *James/Levy/Jacobson Management Inc*
3500 W Olive Ave Ste 1470
Burbank, CA 91505-5514, USA

McPartlnad, Marian M (Musician)
223 1/2 E 48th St
New York, NY 10017, USA

McPeak, Holly (Athlete, Volleyball Player)
1400 the Strand
Manhattan Beach, CA 90266-4731, USA

McPeak, Merrill A (Tony) (General)
123 Furnace St
Lake Oswego, OR 97034-3954, USA

McPhail, Coleman (Athlete, Football Player)
104 Flagstone Ct
Chapel Hill, NC 27517-8381, USA

McPhee, John A (Writer)
475 Drakes Corner Rd
Princeton, NJ 08540-7516, USA

McPhee, Katharine (Musician, Reality TV Star)
c/o Jason Weinberg *Untitled Entertainment (LA)*
350 S Beverly Dr Ste 200
Beverly Hills, CA 90212-4819, USA

McPherson, Charles (Misc)
300 Mercer St Apt 3J
New York, NY 10003-6732, USA

McPherson, Dallas (Athlete, Baseball Player)
307 Swaim St
Randleman, NC 27317-2033, USA

McPherson, Don (Athlete, Football Player)
360 Huntington Ave
Boston, MA 02115-5005, USA

McPherson, Harry C Jr (Government Official)
10213 Montgomery Ave
Kensington, MD 20895-3325, USA

McPherson, James M (Historian)
15 Randall Rd
Princeton, NJ 08540-3609, USA

McPherson, John (Cartoonist)
4520 Main St
Kansas City, MO 64111-1876, USA

McPherson, M Peter (Educator)
President's Office
East Lansing, MI 48824, USA

McPherson, Miles (Athlete, Football Player)
11360 Mandrake Pt
San Diego, CA 92131-3766, USA

McQuagg, Sam (Race Car Driver)
8886 Hamilton Rd
Midland, GA 31820, USA

McQuarrie, Christopher (Director, Producer)
c/o Ken Kamins *Key Creatives*
1800 N Highland Ave Fl 5
Los Angeles, CA 90028-4523, USA

McQuarters, R W (Athlete, Football Player)
1548 E 54th St N
Tulsa, OK 74126-2811, USA

McQueen, Chad (Actor)
c/o Staff Member *MSI Entertainment*
5900 Wilshire Blvd Ste 2250
Los Angeles, CA 90036-5025, USA

McQueen, Cozell (Athlete, Basketball Player)
100 E Charing Cross
Cary, NC 27513-3024, USA

McQueen, Mike (Athlete, Baseball Player)
6623 Lost Horizon Dr
Austin, TX 78759-6191, USA

McQueen, Steve R (Director, Writer)
c/o Maha Dakhil *Creative Artists Agency (CAA-LA)*
2000 Avenue of the Stars Ste 100
Los Angeles, CA 90067-4705, USA

McQueen, Steven R (Actor)
c/o Risa Shapiro *Schiff Company, The*
8440 Warner Dr Ste B1
Culver City, CA 90232-2461, USA

McQueeney, Barbara (Stylist)
c/o Staff Member *Campbell Agency, The*
3838 Oak Lawn Ave Ste 900
Dallas, TX 75219-4510, USA

McQuilken, Kim (Athlete, Football Player)
1050 Techwood Dr NW
Atlanta, GA 30318-5604, USA

McRae, Bennie (Athlete, Football Player)
532 W 143rd St Apt 63
New York, NY 10031-6518, USA

McRae, Brian (Athlete, Baseball Player)
519 Sand Crane Ct
Saint Louis, Bradenton FL, 34212

McRae, Charles (Athlete, Football Player)
601 Self Hollow Rd
Rockford, TN 37853-3411, USA

McRae, Donyale (Stylist)
c/o Staff Member *Montana Artists Agency*
9150 Wilshire Blvd Ste 100
Beverly Hills, CA 90212-3459, USA

McRae, Frank (Actor)
8840 Wilshire Blvd Fl 1
Beverly Hills, CA 90211-2606, USA

McRae, Harold O (Hal) (Athlete, Baseball Player, Coach)
519 Sand Crane Ct
Bradenton, FL 34212-6203, USA

McRae, Tom (Musician)
c/o Staff Member *Paradigm (Monterey)*
404 W Franklin St
Monterey, CA 93940-2303, USA

McRaney, Gerald (Actor)
c/o Geoffrey Brandt *Course Management*
15159 Greenleaf St
Sherman Oaks, CA 91403-4008, USA

McReynolds, Jesse (Musician)
PO Box 1385
Gallatin, TN 37066-1385, USA

McReynolds, Kevin (Athlete, Baseball Player)
2 Country Pl
Roland, AR 72135-9763, USA

McReynolds, Madison (Actor)
c/o Bonnie Ventis *Clear Talent Group (LA)*
10950 Ventura Blvd
Studio City, CA 91604-3340, USA

McRoy, Spike (Athlete, Golfer)
742 Mira Vista Dr SE
Huntsville, AL 35802-3220, USA

McShane, Ian (Actor)
c/o Staff Member *McShane Productions*
New Bridge Street House 30 New Bridge St
London EC4V 6BJ, UNITED KINGDOM (UK)

McShane, Jamie (Actor)
c/o Staff Member *Select Artists Ltd (CA-Westside Office)*
1138 12th St Apt 1
Santa Monica, CA 90403-5459, USA

McShane, Jennifer (Jenny) (Actor)
c/o Laura Pallas *Pallas Management*
5301 Bellaire Ave
Valley Village, CA 91607-2329, US

McShane, Michael (Actor)
c/o Maureen Vincent *United Agents*
Drury House 34-43 Russell St
London WC2B 5HA, UK

McShann, James C (Jay) (Musician)
718 Schwarz Rd
Lawrence, KS 66049-4506, USA

McSorley, Gerard (Actor)
c/o Staff Member *Insight*
1134 S Cloverdale Ave
Los Angeles, CA 90019-6737, USA

McSorley, Marty (Athlete, Hockey Player)
3301 the Strand
Hermosa Beach, CA 90254-2053, USA

McSwain, Chuck (Athlete, Football Player)
PO Box 603
Caroleen, NC 28019-0603, USA

McSwain, Rod (Athlete, Football Player)
5393 Stonewood Dr
Hickory, NC 28602-5578, USA

McSweeney, Alex
c/o Staff Member *EastEnders*
1 Mortimer St
London W1T 3JA, UNITED KINGDOM

McTeer, Janet (Actor)
1741 Ivar Ave
Los Angeles, CA 90028-5105, USA

McTeer Jr, Robert D (Financier, Government Official)
601 Pennsylvania Ave NW Ste NW
Washington, DC 20004-2601, USA

McTeigue, James (Director)
c/o Lawrence Mattis *Circle of Confusion LLC (NY)*
10723 71st Rd # 300
Forest Hills, NY 11375-4707, USA

McTiernan, John C (Director)
9100 Wilshire Blvd Ste 100W
Beverly Hills, CA 90212-3435, USA

McVay, John (Athlete, Football Coach, Football Player)
7300 Sierra Dr
Phoenix, AZ 85044, USA

McVeigh, John (Athlete, Football Player)
3240 Spanish River Dr
Pompano Beach, FL 33062-6810, USA

McVicar, Daniel (Actor)
1704 Oak St
Santa Monica, CA 90405-4804, USA

McVie, Christine (Actor, Musician)
c/o Staff Member *Sugaroo! LLC*
3650 Helms Ave
Culver City, CA 90232-2417, USA

McVie, John (Musician, Songwriter, Writer)
21731 Ventura Blvd Ste 300
Woodland Hls, CA 91364-1851, USA

McVie, Tom (Athlete, Hockey Player)
1 Fleet St
Boston, MA 02136-2015, USA

McWashington, Shawn (Athlete, Football Player)
3400 S King St
Seattle, WA 98144-2653, USA

McWethy, John F (Correspondent)
4850 Meredith Way Apt 304
Boulder, CO 80303-9105, USA

McWhirter, Jillian (Actor)
PO Box 6308
Beverly Hills, CA 90212-1308, USA

McWilliam, Edward (Artist)
8A Holland Villas Road
London W14 8DP, UNITED KINGDOM (UK)

McWilliams, Brian (Misc)
1188 Franklin St
San Francisco, CA 94109-6800, USA

McWilliams, David (Football Executive, Football Player)
Athletic Dept
Austlin, TX 78712, USA

McWilliams, Eric (Athlete, Basketball Player)
798 Hearst Way
Corona, CA 92882-6396, USA

McWilliams, Fleming (Musician)
119 Pebble Creek Rd
Franklin, TN 37064-5525, USA

McWilliams, John (Athlete, Football Player)
4540 E Blue Spruce Ln
Gilbert, AZ 85298-4637, USA

McWilliams, Larry (Athlete, Baseball Player)
4102 Beckley Ct
Colleyville, TX 76034-4670, USA

McWilliams, Robert H (Judge)
1929 Stout St
Denver, CO 80294-0003, USA

MDO (Music Group)
c/o Staff Member *Sony Music Miami*
605 Lincoln Rd Ste 700
Miami Beach, FL 33139-2901, USA

Me First And The Gimme Gimmes (Music Group)
c/o Staff Member *Fat Wreck Chords*
PO Box 193690
San Francisco, CA 94119-3690, USA

Meacham, Bobby (Athlete, Baseball Player)
20610 Prince Creek Dr
Katy, TX 77450-4908, USA

Meacham, Jon (Editor, Writer)
c/o Staff Member *Royce Carlton*
866 United Nations Plz Rm 587
New York, NY 10017-1880, USA

Meacham, Mildred (Baseball Player)
4027 Winedale Ln
Charlotte, NC 28205-4524, USA

Meacham, Rusty (Athlete, Baseball Player)
1906 Eden Glen Ln
Pearland, TX 77581-1700, USA

Mead, Amber (Actor)
c/o Courtney Kivowitz *Schiff Company, The*
8440 Warner Dr Ste B1
Culver City, CA 90232-2461, USA

Mead, Charlie (Athlete, Baseball Player)
7482 Svl Box
Victorville, CA 92395-5157, USA

Mead, John (Athlete, Football Player)
10567 Westwood Dr Unit 2
Sister Bay, WI 54234-9030, USA

Mead, Matt (Governor, Politician)
200 W 24th St
Cheyenne, WY 82001-3642, USA

Mead, Richelle (Writer)
c/o Staff Member *Kensington Publishing Corp.*
119 W 40th St
New York, NY 10018-2500, USA

Mead, Shepherd (Writer)
53 Rivermead Court
London SW6 3RY, UNITED KINGDOM (UK)

Meade, Carl J (Astronaut)
5711 Bienveneda Ter
Palmdale, CA 93551-1189, USA

Meade, Glenn (Writer)
175 5th Ave
New York, NY 10010-7703, USA

Meade, Julia
101O Fifth Ave
New York, NY 10021

Meade, Robin (Television Host)
100 International Blvd NW
Atlanta, GA 30303, USA

Meaden, Deborah (Business Person, Talk Show Host)
Moortown Lane Curry Rivel
Langport, Somerset TA10 0AB, United Kingdom

Meador, Eddle D (Ed) (Athlete, Football Player)
1135 Padgetts Hill Rd
Natural Bridge, VA 24578-4147, USA

Meador, Vaughn
1096 Middle Two Rock Rd
Petaluma, CA 94952-3601

Meadows, Bernard W (Artist)
34 Belsize Grove
London NW3, UNITED KINGDOM (UK)

Meadows, Brian (Athlete, Baseball Player)
208 Palos Verdes Dr
Troy, AL 36079-1701, USA

Meadows, Jayne (Actor)
16185 Woodvale Rd
Encino, CA 91436-3448, USA

Meadows, Louie (Athlete, Baseball Player)
110 Heavens Ln
Maysville, NC 28555-9479, USA

Meadows, Stephen (Actor)
1760 Courtney Ave
Los Angeles, CA 90046-2103, USA

Meadows, Tim (Actor, Comedian)
c/o Geoff Cheddy *Brillstein Entertainment Partners*
9150 Wilshire Blvd Ste 350
Beverly Hills, CA 90212-3453, USA

Meads, Dave (Athlete, Baseball Player)
3220 Cypress Way
Santa Rosa, CA 95405-7512, USA

Meads, Johnny (Athlete, Football Player)
9419 Pine Lilly Ct
Navarre, FL 32566-2865, USA

Meagher, Mary T (Swimmer)
404 Vanderwall
Peachtree City, GA 30269-3335, USA

Meals, Gerald (Baseball Player)
2164 Shamrock Arbor Dr
Salem, OH 44460-7639, USA

Meals, Gerry (Athlete, Baseball Player)
2164 Shamrock Arbor Dr
Salem, OH 44460-7639, USA

Meaney, Colm (Actor)
11921 Laurel Hills Rd
Studio City, CA 91604-3726, USA

Meaney, Kevin (Actor, Comedian)
36 High St
Tarrytown, NY 10591-6226, USA

Means, Natrone J (Athlete, Football Player)
14602 Greenpoint Ln
Huntersville, NC 28078-2624, USA

Means, Russell (Activist)
444 Crazy Horse Dr
Porcupine, SD 57772, USA

Means, Winslow (Athlete, Basketball Player)
1336 Arch St
Zanesville, OH 43701-5714, USA

Meara, Anne (Actor, Comedian)
c/o Staff Member *Innovative Artists (LA)*
1505 10th St
Santa Monica, CA 90401-2805, USA

Meares, Pat (Athlete, Baseball Player)
8405 E Bridlewood St
Wichita, KS 67206-4408, USA

Mears, Casey (Race Car Driver)
4400 Papa Joe Hendrick Blvd
Charlotte, NC 28262-5703, USA

Mears, Derek (Actor)
c/o Staff Member *Kazarian Spencer Ruskin & Assoc.*
11969 Ventura Blvd Ste 300
Studio City, CA 91604-2619, USA

Mears, Gary (Musician)
12170 Country Road 215
Tyler, TX 75707, USA

Mears, Roger Sr (Race Car Driver)
PO Box 520
Terrell, NC 28682-0520, USA

Mears, Walter R (Journalist)
2021 K St NW
Washington, DC 20006-1003, USA

Mecchi, Irene (Actor)
c/o Staff Member *WmE2 (Endeavor-LA)*
9601 Wilshire Blvd Fl 3
Beverly Hills, CA 90210-5219, USA

Meche, Gil (Athlete, Baseball Player)
PO Box 932
Scott, LA 70583-0932, USA

Mechlowicz, Scott (Actor)
c/o Eric Kranzler *Management 360*
9111 Wilshire Blvd
Beverly Hills, CA 90210-5508, USA

Mechoso, Julio Oscar (Actor)
c/o Staff Member *Gage Group, The (LA)*
14724 Ventura Blvd Ste 505
Sherman Oaks, CA 91403-3505, USA

Meciar, Vladimir (Prime Minister)
Urad Vlady SR Nam Slobody 1
Bratislava 81370, SLOVAKIA

Mecir, Jim (Athlete, Baseball Player)
21219 W Creekside Dr
Kildeer, IL 60047-7847, USA

Mecir, Miloslav (Tennis Player)
Julova 1
Bratislava 83101, CZECH REPUBLIC

Mecklenburg, Karl (Football Player)
6372 S Zenobia Ct
Littleton, CO 80123-6740, USA

Medak, Peter (Director)
c/o Jon Brown *Ensemble Entertainment*
10474 Santa Monica Blvd Ste 380
Los Angeles, CA 90025-6943, USA

Medaris, J Bruce (General)
Po Box 415
Fem Park, FL 32751, USA

Medavoy, Mike (Producer)
c/o Staff Member *Phoenix Pictures*
10202 W Washington Blvd Frankovich Bldg
Culver City, CA 90232, USA

Medcalf, Kim (Actor)
2-4 Noel St
London W1V 3RB, UNITED KINGDOM (UK)

Medders, Brandon (Athlete, Baseball Player)
9732 Charolais Dr
Tuscaloosa, AL 35405-9771, USA

Meddick, Jim (Cartoonist)
200 Madison Ave
New York, NY 10016-3903, USA

Meddine, Raya (Actor)
c/o Audrey Caan *Audrey Caan Management*
8665 Burton Way Apt 520
Los Angeles, CA 90048-3995, USA

Medearis, Angela Shelf (Chef, Writer)
c/o Staff Member *Diva Productions, Inc*
PO Box 91625
Austin, TX 78709-1625, USA

Medeiros, Glenn (Musician)
PO Box 8
Lawai, HI 96765-0008, USA

Medgyessy, Peter (Prime Minister)
Kossuth Lajos Ter 1-3
Budapest 1055, HUNGARY

Mediate, Rocco (Athlete, Golfer)
8425 NE 12th St
Medina, WA 98039-3906, USA

Medich, George (Doc) (Athlete, Baseball Player)
3007 Woodfield Dr
Aliquippa, PA 15001-1163, USA

Medieros-Baker, Deborah (Stylist)
c/o Staff Member *Ken Barboza Associates*
115 W 30th St Rm 203
New York, NY 10001-4088, USA

Medina, Benny (Producer)
c/o Staff Member *Handprint Entertainment*
1100 Glendon Ave Ste 100
Los Angeles, CA 90024-3593, USA

Medina, Luis (Athlete, Baseball Player)
16630 S Mountain Stone Trl
Phoenix, AZ 85048-2081, USA

Medina, Patricia (Actor)
10787 Wilshire Blvd Apt 1503
Los Angeles, CA 90024-4475, USA

Medina, Rafael (Baseball Player)
18322 NW 68th Ave
Hialeah, FL 33015-3423, USA

Medina Estevez, Jorge Arturo Cardinal (Religious Leader)
Vatican City 120, VATICAN CITY

Medley, Bill (Musician)
c/o Staff Member *WmE2 (WMA-LA)*
1 William Morris Pl
Beverly Hills, CA 90212-4261, USA

Medley, Charles R O (Artist)
Charterhouse Charterhouse Square
London EC1M 6AN, UNITED KINGDOM (UK)

Medlock, Mark (Musician)
Postfach 206143
Berlin 13537, GERMANY

Medrano, Frank (Actor)
c/o Kate Ward *Ward Agency*
1617 N El Centro Ave Ste 15
Hollywood, CA 90028-6429, USA

Medress, Henry (Musician)
141 Dunbar Ave
Fords, NJ 08863-1551, USA

Medved, Aleksandr V (Wrestler)
Skatertny p 4
Moscow, RUSSIA

Medved, Michael (Radio Personality, Writer)
c/o Staff Member *Greater Talent Network Inc*
437 5th Ave Fl 7
New York, NY 10016-2205, USA

Medved, Ron (Athlete, Football Player)
6615 239th Ave E
Buckley, WA 98321-9422, USA

Medvedev, Zhores A (Biologist)
4 Osborn Gardens
London NW7 1DY, UNITED KINGDOM (UK)

Medvin, Scott (Athlete, Baseball Player)
673 Lynbrook Ave
Tonawanda, NY 14150-7309, USA

Medwin, Michael (Actor)
76 Oxford St
London W1N 0AX, UNITED KINGDOM (UK)

Mee, Darnell (Athlete, Basketball Player)
2005 Westland Dr SW Apt 1201
Cleveland, TN 37311-8180, USA

Meehan, Kim (Stylist)
c/o Staff Member *Walter Schupfer Management Corp*
413 W 14th St Ste 3
New York, NY 10014-1097, USA

Meehan, Patrick (Congressman, Politician)
613 Cannon Hob
Washington, DC 20515-0003, USA

Meehan, Thomas E (Musician, Writer)
Brook House Obtuse Road
Newtown, CT 6470, USA

Meehl, Paul E (Misc)
1544 E River Ter
Minneapolis, MN 55414-3646, USA

Meek, Heidi (Stylist)
c/o Celebrity Stylist *Cloutier Agency*
2632 La Cienega Ave
Los Angeles, CA 90034-2641, USA

Meek, Jeffrey
c/o Anne Geddes *Geddes Agency, The*
8430 Santa Monica Blvd Ste 200
Los Angeles, CA 90069-4253, USA

Meek Millz (Musician)
c/o Staff Member *Grand Hustle*
541 10th St NW PMB 161
Atlanta, GA 30318-5713, USA

Meeke, Brent (Athlete, Hockey Player)
11331 Whitetail Run St NW
Bolivar, OH 44612-9230, USA

Meeker, Howie (Athlete, Hockey Player, Sportscaster)
979 Dickenson Way
Parksville, BC V9P 1Z7, Canada

Meeks, Aaron (Actor)
c/o Staff Member *Showtime Networks (LA)*
10880 Wilshire Blvd Ste 1600
Los Angeles, CA 90024-4117, USA

Meeks, Bob (Athlete, Football Player)
2223 S Quentin Way Apt 201
Aurora, CO 80014-6323, USA

Meeks, Bryant (Athlete, Football Player)
3484 Ga Highway 19 S
Dublin, GA 31021-7344, USA

Meeler, Phil (Athlete, Baseball Player)
102 Pine St
Knightdale, NC 27545-9443, USA

Meely, Cliff (Athlete, Basketball Player)
3240 Iris Ave Apt 204
Boulder, CO 80301-1969, USA

Meena (Actor, Bollywood)
58 Second Street Venkatesh Nagar
Chennai, TN 600093, INDIA

Meents, Scott (Athlete, Basketball Player)
4231 155th Pl SE
Bellevue, WA 98006-2579, USA

Meese (Music Group)
c/o Staff Member *Red Light Management (LA)*
8439 W Sunset Blvd Ste 2
Los Angeles, CA 90069-1925, USA

Meese, Edwin III (Attorney, Attorney General, General)
1075 Spring Hill Rd
McLean, VA 22102-2304, USA

Meester, Brad (Athlete, Football Player)
7644 Chipwood Ln
Jacksonville, FL 32256-2338, USA

Meester, Leighton (Actor)
c/o Loch Powell *Leverage Management*
3030 Pennsylvania Ave
Santa Monica, CA 90404-4112, USA

Meeuwsen, Terry (Religious Leader, Television Host)
c/o 700 Club *Christian Broadcasting Network (CBN)*
977 Centerville Tpke
Virginia Beach, VA 23463-1001, USA

Meggysey, Dave (Athlete, Football Player)
1024 Linden St
Oakland, CA 94607-2728, USA

Megrew, Mike (Athlete, Baseball Player)
25 Karen Dr
Hope Valley, RI 02832-1267, USA

Meher, Bill (Comedian, Correspondent)
9200 W Sunset Blvd Ste 900
Los Angeles, CA 90069-3604, USA

Mehl, Lance A (Athlete, Football Player)
44920 Kacsmar Estates Dr
Saint Clairsville, OH 43950-9454, USA

Mehra, Prakash (Bollywood, Director, Filmmaker, Producer)
30 Sumeet Bangalow 11th Road Jvpd Scheme
Bombay, MS 400 049, INDIA

Mehra, Smirti (Athlete, Golfer)
4038 Greystone Dr
Clermont, FL 34711-7197, USA

Mehrabian, Robert (Educator)
President's Office
Pittsburgh, PA 15213, USA

Mehregany, Mehran (Engineer)
Electrical Engineer Dept
Cleveland, OH 44106, USA

Mehringer, David M (Astronomer)
Astronomy Dept
Champaign, IL 61820, USA

Mehta, Shailesh J (Business Person)
201 Mission St
San Francisco, CA 94105-1851, USA

Mehta, Sujata (Actor, Bollywood)
56 Dev Chhaya Tardeo Haji Ali Road Tardeo
Bombay, MS 400 034, INDIA

Mehta, Ved (Writer)
139 E 79th St
New York, NY 10075-0324, USA

Mehta, Zubin (Conductor)
1 Huberman St
Tel Aviv 61112, ISRAEL

Mehta (Metha) Saltzman, Deepa (Director, Editor, Producer, Writer)
421 S Beverly Dr Fl 8
Beverly Hills, CA 90212-4408, USA

Meier, Dave (Athlete, Baseball Player)
523 W Stuart Ave
Fresno, CA 93704-1430, USA

Meier, Richard A (Architect)
475 10th Ave
New York, NY 10018-1120, USA

Meier, Shad (Athlete, Football Player)
4001 Skyline Dr
Nashville, TN 37215-2318, USA

Meier, Waltraud (Opera Singer)
Bayreuth 95445, GERMANY

Meiko (Musician)
c/o Michael Moses *Baker Winokur Ryder Public Relations (BWR-LA)*
9100 Wilshire Blvd Ste 500 PMB WEST
Beverly Hills, CA 90212-3426, USA

Meilinger, Steve (Athlete, Football Player)
719 Camino Rd
Lexington, KY 40502-2776, USA

Meineke, Don (Athlete, Basketball Player)
329 Silvertree Ct
Dayton, OH 45459-4441, USA

Meinhold, Carl (Athlete, Basketball Player)
5 Courtleigh Pl
Reading, PA 19606-2941, USA

Meinwald, Jerrold (Misc)
Chemistry Dept
Ithaca, NY 14853, USA

Meirelles, Fernando (Director, Producer)
c/o Staff Member *WmE2 (Endeavor-LA)*
9601 Wilshire Blvd Fl 3
Beverly Hills, CA 90210-5219, USA

Meirelles, Priscilla (Model)
8 San Manuel St Capitol
Pasig City, Metro Manila 1603, PHILIPPINES

Meisel, Stephen (Photographer)
1271 Avenue of the Americas
New York, NY 10020-1300, USA

Meiselas, Susan (Photographer)
256 Mott St
New York, NY 10012-3482, USA

Meisner, Greg (Athlete, Football Player)
512 Brighton Ct
Greensburg, PA 15601-9693, USA

Meisner, Joachim Cardinal (Religious Leader)
Marzellenstr 32
Cologne 50668, GERMANY

Meisner, Randy (Musician)
3706 Eureka Dr
Studio City, CA 91604-3104, USA

Meissner, Kimmie (Figure Skater)
105 E Main St
Newark, DE 19716-0799, USA

Meja (Musician)
Norrtullsgatan 51
Stockholm 113 45, SWEDEN

Mejdani, Rexhep (President)
Keshilli i Ministrave
Tirana, ALBANIA

Mejia, Hipolito (President)
Calle Moises Garcia
Santo Domingo, DOMINICAN REPUBLIC

Mejia, Jorge Maria Cardinal (Religious Leader)
Biblioteca Apostolica Vaticina
Vatican City 120, VATICAN CITY

Mejia, Paul R (Ballerina, Choreographer)
6848 Green Oaks Rd
Fort Worth, TX 76116, USA

Mejias, Roman (Athlete, Baseball Player)
27325 Terrytown Rd
Sun City, CA 92586-5220, USA

Mekka, Eddie (Actor)
129 W Wilson St Ste 202
Costa Mesa, CA 92627-1586, USA

Melamld, Aleksandr (Artist)
31 Mercer St
New York, NY 10013-2541, USA

Melancon, Mei (Actor)
c/o Lena Roklin *Luber Roklin Management*
8530 Wilshire Blvd Ste 550
Beverly Hills, CA 90211-3133, USA

Melander, Jon (Athlete, Football Player)
8255 Kelzer Pond Dr
Victoria, MN 55386-4500, USA

Melanie (Musician, Songwriter, Writer)
53 Baymont St # 5
Clearwater Beach, FL 33767-1705, USA

Melato, Mariangela (Actor)
Via Giuseppe Pisanelli
Rome 196, ITALY

Melcher, John (Senator)
2519 Wylie Ave
Missoula, MT 59802-3260, USA

Melchionni, Bill (Athlete, Basketball Player)
720 Bay Tree Ct
Naples, FL 34108-3429, USA

Melchionni, Gary (Athlete, Basketball Player)
1040 Grandview Blvd
Lancaster, PA 17601-5108, USA

Melchior, Ib (Writer)
8228 Marmont Ln
Los Angeles, CA 90069-1624, USA

Melchoir, Tracy Lindsay
c/o Michael Bruno *The Michael Bruno Group*
13576 Cheltenham Dr
Sherman Oaks, CA 91423-4818, USA

Meldgaard, Gitte (Stylist)
c/o Staff Member *Mercury Artists*
8460 Higuera St Fl 2
Culver City, CA 90232-2520, USA

Mele, Sam (Athlete, Baseball Player, Coach)
340 Adams St
Quincy, MA 02169-1702, USA

Melendez, A J (Musician)

Melendez, John (Musician)
c/o Staff Member *Paradigm (Monterey)*
404 W Franklin St
Monterey, CA 93940-2303, USA

Melendez, John (Actor, Writer)
c/o Staff Member *Chapter 2 Productions*
3500 W Olive Ave Ste 300
Burbank, CA 91505-4647, USA

Melendez, Kiki (Musician)
c/o Staff Member *Paradigm (Monterey)*
404 W Franklin St
Monterey, CA 93940-2303, USA

Melendez, Lisette (Musician)
250 W 57th St
New York, NY 10107-0001, USA

Melendez, Ron
12533 Woodgreen St
Los Angeles, CA 90066-2723

Meler, Dave (Baseball Player)
523 W Stuart Ave
Fresno, CA 93704-1430, USA

Meler, Raymond (Photographer)
532 Broadway
New York, NY 10012-3939, USA

Melhuse, Adam (Athlete, Baseball Player)
245 Almond St
San Luis Obispo, CA 93405-2301, USA

Melinda (Artist)
120 E Flamingo Rd
Las Vegas, NV 89109-4574, USA

Mellanby, Scott (Athlete, Hockey Player)
2548 Town and Country Ln
Saint Louis, MO 63131-1121, USA

Mellekas, John (Athlete, Football Player)
498 Broadway
Newport, RI 02840-1440, USA

Mellen, Polly (Stylist)
c/o Staff Member *Art + Commerce*
531 W 25th St # 4
New York, NY 10001-5593, USA

Mellenby, Scott (Athlete, Hockey Player)
2548 Town and Country Ln
Saint Louis, MO 63131-1121, USA

Mellencamp, John (Musician, Songwriter)
PO Box 6777
Bloomington, IN 47407-6777, USA

Mellers, Wilfrid H (Composer, Writer)
Oliver Sheldon House 17 Aldwark
York YO1 2BX, UNITED KINGDOM (UK)

Melles, Carl
Grunbergstr 4
Vienna 1130, AUSTRIA

Melling, O R (Writer)
C/O Geraldine Whlean 26 Wolfe Tone Square E
Bray, Co Wicklow, IRELAND

Mellinkoff, Sherman M (Educator, Physicist)
Med Center 10833 Leconte Ave
Los Angeles, CA 90095-0001, USA

Mello, Craig C. (Nobel Prize Laureate)
373 Plantation St Ste 219
Worcester, MA 01605-2377, USA

Mello, Jim (Athlete, Football Player)
5133 E Emerald Cir
Mesa, AZ 85206-2870, USA

Mello, Tamara (Actor)
c/o Brandy Gold *TalentWorks (LA)*
3500 W Olive Ave Ste 1400
Burbank, CA 91505-5512, USA

Mellons, Ken (Musician)
c/o Staff Member *Buddy Lee Attractions Inc*
38 Music Sq E Ste 300
Nashville, TN 37203-4304, USA

Mellor, John W (Economist)
801 Pennsylvania Ave NW Apt PH18
Washington, DC 20004-2672, USA

Mellor, Thomas (Tom) (Athlete, Hockey Player)
48 4th Ave
Weymouth, MA 02188-3710, USA

Melnick, Bruce E (Astronaut)
PO Box 21233
Kennedy Space Center, FL 32815-0233, USA

Melnick, Daniel (Producer)
1123 Sunset Hills Rd
Los Angeles, CA 90069-1756, USA

Melniker, Benjamin (Producer)
123 W 44th St # 10-K
New York, NY 10036-4089, USA

Melnikov, Vitaly V (Director)
Svetianovsky Proyezd 105 #20
Saint Petersburg 195269, RUSSIA

Melnyk, Steve (Athlete, Golfer)
5015 Pirates Cove Rd
Jacksonville, FL 32210-8309, USA

Meloan, Jonathan (Athlete, Baseball Player)
8017 Lichtenauer Dr
Lenexa, KS 66219-2037, USA

Melody (Musician)
c/o Staff Member *Sony Music Miami*
605 Lincoln Rd Ste 700
Miami Beach, FL 33139-2901, USA

Meloff, Chris (Athlete, Hockey Player)
8568 NW 52nd Pl
Coral Springs, FL 33067-2839, USA

Meloni, Christopher (Actor)
c/o Melissa Raubvogel *Baker Winokur Ryder Public Relations BWR (BWR-NY)*
292 Madison Ave Fl 12
New York, NY 10017-6415, USA

Melrose, Barry J (Athlete, Coach, Hockey Player)
935 Middle St
Bristol, CT 06010-1000, USA

Melroy, Pamela A (Astronaut)
920 N Barton St
Arlington, VA 22201-1910, USA

Melton, Bill (Athlete, Baseball Player)
333 E 35th St
Chicago, IL 60616-3951, USA

Melton, Dave (Athlete, Baseball Player)
72 Cherry Ridge Ct
San Jose, CA 95136-3635, USA

Melton, Sid (Actor)
17212 Midwood Dr
Granada Hills, CA 91344-2452, USA

Meltzer, Allan L (Economist)
Economics Dept
Pittsburgh, PA 15260, USA

Melua, Katie (Musician)
c/o Rob Zifarelli *Agency Group Ltd, The (Canada)*
2 Berkeley Street Suite 202
Toronto M5A 4J5, Canada

Meluskey, Mitch (Athlete, Baseball Player)
26 Meadowbrook Rd
Yakima, WA 98903-9505, USA

Melvill, Michael W (Astronaut)
24120 Jacaranda Dr
Tehachapi, CA 93561-8309, USA

Melvin, Bob (Athlete, Baseball Player, Coach)
5637 E Canyon Ridge North Dr
Cave Creek, AZ 85331-9319, USA

Melvin, Donnie
45 Overlook Ter
New York, NY 10033-2218

Melvin, Murray
Plaza 535 Kings Road
London SW10 OSZ, UNITED KINGDOM (UK)

Melvin, Rachel (Actor)
c/o Anne Woodward *ROAR (LA)*
9701 Wilshire Blvd Fl 8
Beverly Hills, CA 90212-2008, USA

Melvoin, Wendy (Actor)
c/o Rick Jacobellis *First Artists Management*
4764 Park Granada Ste 210
Calabasas, CA 91302-3333, USA

Melzack, Ronald (Misc)
51 Banstead Rd
Montreal, QC H4X 1P1, CANADA

Member, Tim (Athlete, Football Player)
3410 Grant St
Vancouver, WA 98660-1823, USA

Members, Swollen (Music Group, Musician)
c/o Staff Member *Agency Group Ltd, The (LA)*
1880 Century Park E Ste 711
Los Angeles, CA 90067-1618, USA

Meminger, Dean (Athlete, Basketball Player)
45 W 139th St Apt 16E
New York, NY 10037-1411, USA

Memmel, Chellsie (Athlete, Gymnast, Olympic Athlete)
PO Box 510474
New Berlin, WI 53151-0474, USA

Men, Baha (Music Group)
1776 Broadway Fl 15
New York, NY 10019-2002

Men Women & Children (Music Group)
c/o Staff Member *Paradigm (Monterey)*
404 W Franklin St
Monterey, CA 93940-2303, USA

Menafee, Cornell (Athlete, Football Player)
403 Elm Ct
Opelika, AL 36801-6423, USA

Menaker, Mitchell G
5062 Isleworth Country Club Dr
Windermere, FL 34786-8920, USA

Menand, Louis (Historian, Writer)
4 Times Sq
New York, NY 10036-6515, USA

Menard, Marc (Actor)
10 - 206 East 6th Ave
Vancouver, BC V5T 1J8, CANADA

Menard, Renry W (Misc)
Geology
La Jolla, CA 92093-0001, USA

Mench, Kevin (Athlete, Baseball Player)
11 Brookridge Ln
Newark, DE 19711-2952, USA

Menchu Tum, Rigoberta (Nobel Prize Laureate)
UN Plaza
New York, NY 10017, USA

Mencia, Carlos (Actor)
c/o Tim Sarkes *Brillstein Entertainment Partners*
9150 Wilshire Blvd Ste 350
Beverly Hills, CA 90212-3453, USA

Mendenhall, John (Athlete, Football Player)
PO Box 532
Cullen, LA 71021-0532, USA

Mendenhall, Ken (Athlete, Football Player)
1708 S Rankin St
Edmond, OK 73013-5128, USA

Mendes, Eva (Actor)
c/o David Seltzer *Management 360*
9111 Wilshire Blvd
Beverly Hills, CA 90210-5508, USA

Mendes, Sam (Director)
c/o Simon Halls *Slate Public Relations*
9000 W Sunset Blvd Ste 915
West Hollywood, CA 90069-5809, USA

Mendez, Lazaro (DJ Laz) (Radio Personality)
194 NW 187th St
Miami, FL 33169-4050, USA

Mendez, Lucia (Actor)
c/o Staff Member *TV Azteca*
Periferico Sur 4121 Colonia Fuentes del Pedregal
DF CP 14141, Mexico

Mendler, Bridgit (Actor)
c/o Elaine Lively *Elaine Entertainment*
Prefers to be contacted via telephone
Northridge, CA 91324, USA

Mendonca, Albert (Stylist)
c/o Staff Member *Celestine - CA*
1666 20th St Ste 200B
Santa Monica, CA 90404-3828, USA

Mendoza, Dayana (Beauty Pageant Winner)
c/o Staff Member *Miss Universe Organization, The*
1370 Avenue of the Americas Fl 16
New York, NY 10019-4602, USA

Mendoza, Jessica (Athlete)
2801 NE 50th St
Oklahoma City, OK 73111-7203, USA

Mendoza, June (Artist)
34 Inner Park Road
London SW19 6DD, UNITED KINGDOM (UK)

Mendoza, Linda (Director)
c/o Staff Member *Creative Artists Agency (CAA-LA)*
2000 Avenue of the Stars Ste 100
Los Angeles, CA 90067-4705, USA

Mendoza, Mike (Athlete, Baseball Player)
14207 S 20th St
Phoenix, AZ 85048-4519, USA

Mendoza, Minnie (Athlete, Baseball Player)
701 Samuel Adams Cir SW
Concord, NC 28027-0134, USA

Mendoza, Ramiro (Athlete, Baseball Player)
18706 Pepper Pike
Lutz, FL 33558-5303, USA

Mendoza, Reynol (Baseball Player)
2408 2nd St
Eagle Pass, TX 78852-4119, USA

Mendoza, Zuleyka Rivera (Beauty Pageant Winner)
c/o Richie Walls *International Talent Agency (ITA)*
10 Nbc Universal Studios Plz Floor 20
Universal City, CA 91608, USA

Mendte, Larry
330 Bob Hope Dr
Burbank, CA 91505-4751

Menechino, Frank (Athlete, Baseball Player)
522 Arlene St
Staten Island, NY 10314-3818, USA

Menedez, Steven (Stylist)
c/o Staff Member *Artists by Timothy Priano (CA)*
8447 Wilshire Blvd Ste 301
Beverly Hills, CA 90211-3206, USA

Menendez, Erik
1878449 Csp-Sac # 290066
Represa, CA 95671-0001, USA

Menendez, Lyle
#1887106 CCI-Box 1031
Tehachapi, CA 93581, USA

Menendez, Tony (Athlete, Baseball Player)
18730 NW 48th Ct
Miami Gardens, FL 33055-2536, USA

Meneses, Alex (Actor)
c/o Cindy Schultzel-Ambers *Art/Work Entertainment*
5900 Wilshire Blvd Ste 2150
Los Angeles, CA 90036-5021, USA

Meneses, Antonio (Musician)
165 W 57th St
New York, NY 10019-2201, USA

Menew (Music Group, Musician)
c/o Staff Member *REDCORE MUSIC GROUP*
520 8th Ave Rm 2001
New York, NY 10018-4166, USA

Menez, Bernard
119 Blvd De Grenelle
Paris, FRANCE 75015

Mengatti, John
8322 Beverly Blvd # 200
Los Angeles, CA 90048-2600

Mengelt, John (Athlete, Basketball Player)
1270 Breckenridge Ct
Lake Forest, IL 60045-3875, USA

Mengers, Sue
938 Bel Air Rd
Los Angeles, CA 90077-3010

Menhart, Paul (Athlete, Baseball Player)
725 Kelsall Dr
Richmond Hill, GA 31324-7707, USA

Menheer-Zoromapal, Marie (Baseball Player)
8871 Lake Marion Creek Rd
Haines City, FL 33844-2004, USA

Menichetti, Roberto (Designer, Fashion Designer)
3 Loc Monteleto
Gubbio, ITALY

Menke, Andrea (Stylist)
c/o Staff Member *Ford Models (Miami)*
311 Lincoln Rd Ste 205
Miami Beach, FL 33139-3150, USA

Menke, Denis (Athlete, Baseball Player)
1246 Berkshire Ln
Tarpon Springs, FL 34688-7626, USA

Menken, Alan (Composer)
670 W End Ave Apt 8A
New York, NY 10025-7327, USA

Mennea, Pietro (Athlete, Track Athlete)
Via Cassia 1041
Rome 189, ITALY

Menneron, Laurence (Stylist)
c/o Staff Member *Fifty8 Artists*
58 W Huron St
Chicago, IL 60654-3806, USA

Meno, Chorepiscopus John (Religious Leader)
771 Cedarwood Ct
Stanley, NC 28164-6846, USA

Menon, Krishnan (Actor)
c/o Jai Khanna *Brillstein Entertainment Partners*
9150 Wilshire Blvd Ste 350
Beverly Hills, CA 90212-3453, USA

Menon, Mambillikalathil G K (Physicist)
C-63 Tarang Apts Mother Dairy Road
Patparganj, Delhi 110092, INDIA

Menounos, Maria (Actor, Correspondent)

Mensah, Peter (Actor)
c/o Cheri Barner *Artist Management*
1119 Colorado Ave Ste 12
Santa Monica, CA 90401-3009, USA

Menshov, Vladimir V (Actor, Director)
3D Tverskaya-Yamskaya 52
Moscow 125047, RUSSIA

Mentez, Chris (Musician)
6671 W Sunset Blvd Ste 1502
Los Angeles, CA 90028-7235, USA

Menudo
2895 Biscayne Blvd # 455
Miami, FL 33137-4537

Menzel, Idina (Actor, Musician)
c/o Heather Reynolds *One Entertainment (NY)*
12 W 57th St PH 1
New York, NY 10019-3900, USA

Menzel, Jiri (Director)
Kratky Film Jindrisska 34
Prague 1 112 07, CZECH REPUBLIC

Menzies, Peter G Jr (Cinematographer)
903 Tahoe Blvd # 802
Incline Village, NV 89451, USA

Meola, Eric (Photographer)
535 Greenwich St
New York, NY 10013-1004, USA

Meola, Tony (Soccer Player)
488 Forest St
Kearny, NJ 07032-3623, USA

Meoli, Christian (Actor)
c/o Brian McCabe *Venture IAB*
8285 W Sunset Blvd Ste 1
West Hollywood, CA 90046-2420, USA

Meoli, Rudy (Athlete, Baseball Player)
8150 E Oak Ridge Cir
Anaheim, CA 92808-1941, USA

Meraz, Alex (Actor)
c/o Jeb Brandon *Kritzer Levine Wilkins Entertainment*
11872 La Grange Ave Fl 1
Los Angeles, CA 90025-5283, USA

Merbold, Ulf (Astronaut)
Am Sonnenhang 4
Siegburg 53721, GERMANY

Mercado, Orlando (Athlete, Baseball Player)
PO Box 1465
Arecibo, PR 00613-1465, USA

Mercado, Syesha (Musician)

Mercante, Arthur (Referee)
596 Pacing Way
Westbury, NY 11590-6677, USA

Merced, Orlando (Athlete, Baseball Player)
5323 S Fort Ave
Springfield, MO 65810-2784, USA

Mercein, Chuck (Athlete, Football Player)
746 Mamaroneck Ave Apt 1320
Mamaroneck, NY 10543-1989, USA

Mercer, Marian (Actor, Musician)
5250 Colodny Dr Apt 13
Agoura Hills, CA 91301-2657, USA

Mercer, Mark (Athlete, Baseball Player)
10607 Penn Ave S
Minneapolis, MN 55431-3445, USA

Mercer, Mike (Athlete, Football Player)
64463 McGrath Rd
Bend, OR 97701-8830, USA

Mercer, Ron (Basketball Player)
Alamodome 1 SBC Center
San Antonio, TX 78219, USA

Mercer, Toby (Artist)
316 E Reserve Dr
Kalispell, MT 59901-6647, USA

Merchant, Andy (Athlete, Baseball Player)
108 Bates Lake Rd
Malcolm, AL 36556, USA

Merchant, Natalie (Musician, Songwriter, Writer)

Merchant, Stephen (Actor, Director, Producer, Writer)
c/o Staff Member *WmE2 (Endeavor-LA)*
9601 Wilshire Blvd Fl 3
Beverly Hills, CA 90210-5219, USA

Mercker, Kent (Athlete, Baseball Player)
8690 Hawick Ct N
Dublin, OH 43017-9618, USA

Merckx, Eddy (Athlete)
s'Herenweg 11
Meise 1860, Belgium

Mercurio, Nicole (Actor)
1505 10th St
Santa Monica, CA 90401-2805, USA

Mercurio, Paul (Actor, Musician)
53-55 Brisbane St Surreyhills
Sydney, NSW 2010, AUSTRALIA

Mercurio, Steven
165 W 57th St
New York, NY 10019-2201, USA

Mercurio, Tara (Actor)
c/o Aaron Ray *Collective*
8383 Wilshire Blvd Ste 1050
Beverly Hills, CA 90211-2415, USA

Mercy Me (Music Group, Musician)
c/o Scott Bickell *Brickhouse Entertainment*
106 Mission Ct Ste 1202
Franklin, TN 37067-6484, USA

Meredith, Cla (Athlete, Baseball Player)
14722 Swift Water Rd
Chesterfield, VA 23838-6139, USA

Meredith, James H (Misc)
929 Meadowbrook Rd
Jackson, MS 39206-5945, USA

Meredith, Richard (Athlete, Hockey Player)
6520 Ridgeview Dr
Edina, MN 55439-1235, USA

Meredith, William (Writer)
PO Box 1498
New London, CT 6320, USA

Meridith, Ron (Athlete, Baseball Player)
308 Via Promesa
San Clemente, CA 92673-6820, USA

Merigan Jr, Thomas C (Scientist)
620 Sand Hill Rd Apt 214E
Palo Alto, CA 94304-2608, USA

Merila, Mark (Athlete, Baseball Player)
3730 Union Terrace Ln N
Minneapolis, MN 55441-2425, USA

Merisola, Linda (Stylist)
3702 E Shangri La Rd
Phoenix, AZ 85028-2817, USA

Meritano, Lorena (Actor)
c/o Gabriel Blanco *Gabriel Blanco Iglesias (Mexico)*
Rio Balsas 35-32 Colonia Cuauhtemoc
DF 6500, Mexico

Meriweather, Joe C (Athlete, Basketball Player)
5316 NW 84th Ter
Kansas City, MO 64154-1445, USA

Meriweather, Lee (Actor, Beauty Pageant Winner)
12139 Jeanette Pl
Granada Hills, CA 91344-2336, USA

Meriwether, Chick (Baseball Player)
2409 Seifried St
Nashville, TN 37208-1344, USA

Meriwether, Chuck (Athlete, Baseball Player)
2409 Seifried St
Nashville, TN 37208-1344, USA

Meriwether, Lee (Actor)
c/o Scott Stander *Scott Stander & Associates*
4533 Van Nuys Blvd Ste 401
Sherman Oaks, CA 91403-2950, USA

Meriwether, Porter (Athlete, Basketball Player)
8137 S Saint Lawrence Ave
Chicago, IL 60619-5007, USA

Merkens, Guido (Athlete, Football Player)
2301 S Millbend Dr Apt 405
Spring, TX 77380-1754, USA

Merkerson, S Epatha (Actor)
c/o Jillian Fowkes *ID Public Relations (ID-LA)*
7080 Hollywood Blvd Fl 8
Los Angeles, CA 90028-6906, USA

Merkin, Daphne (Writer)
c/o Staff Member *The New York Times Company*
229 W 43rd St
New York, NY 10036-3913, USA

Merkosky, Glenn (Athlete, Hockey Player)
113 Farr Ln
Queensbury, NY 12804-1996, USA

Merle, Carole (Skier)
Chalet La Calette
Super-Sauze 4400, FRANCE

Merletti, Lewis C (Lawyer)
76 Lou Groza Blvd
Berea, OH 44017-1238, USA

Merlin, Jan (Actor)
347 N California St
Burbank, CA 91505-3508, USA

Merlo, James L (Athlete, Football Player)
1547 E Starpass Dr
Fresno, CA 93730-3448, USA

Merloni, Lou (Athlete, Baseball Player)
207 Quail Run
Marshfield, MA 02050-2066, USA

Merlyn-Rees, Merlyn (Government Official)
Westminster
London SW1A 0PW, UNITED KINGDOM (UK)

Mero, Rena (Sable) (Athlete, Model, Wrestler)
c/o Staff Member *Identity Talent Agency (ID)*
9107 Wilshire Blvd Ste 500
Beverly Hills, CA 90210-5526, USA

Meron, Neil (Producer)
c/o Staff Member *WmE2 (WMA-LA)*
1 William Morris Pl
Beverly Hills, CA 90212-4261, USA

Merovich, Pete (Soccer Player)
831 Maplewood Dr
Pittsburgh, PA 15234-2540, USA

Merow, James F (Judge)
717 Madison Pl NW
Washington, DC 20439-0001, USA

Merrells, Jason (Actor)
c/o Nicola Richardson *QVoice*
193-197 High Holborn 4th Floor, Holborn Hall
London WC1V 7BD, UNITED KINGDOM (UK)

Merrick, Dawn
8281 Melrose Ave Ste 200
Los Angeles, CA 90046-6890

Merrifield, R Bruce (Nobel Prize Laureate)
43 Mezzine Dr
Cresskill, NJ 7626, USA

Merrill, Carl (Stump) (Athlete, Baseball Player, Coach)
18 Merrymeeting Dr
Topsham, ME 04086-1839, USA

Merrill, Casey (Athlete, Football Player)
78395 Avenue 41
Indio, CA 92203-1008, USA

Merrill, Catherine (Artist)
1456 Florida St
San Francisco, CA 94110-4812, USA

Merrill, Dina (Actor)
405 E 54th St Apt 12A
New York, NY 10022-5159, USA

Merrill, Edward W (Engineer)
90 Somerset St
Belmont, MA 02478-2010, USA

Merrill, John O (Architect)
101 Gardner Pl
Colorado Springs, CO 80906-3314, USA

Merrill, Mark (Athlete, Football Player)
782 Mimosa Ln
New Brighton, MN 55112-2520, USA

Merriman, Brent (Athlete, Baseball Player)
551 W Scott Ave
Gilbert, AZ 85233 3265, USA

Merriman, Randy
PO Box 70025
Houston, TX 77270-0025

Merriman, Ryan (Actor)
c/o Beth Holden-Garland *Untitled Entertainment (LA)*
350 S Beverly Dr Ste 200
Beverly Hills, CA 90212-4819, USA

Merriman, Shawne (Athlete, Football Player)
c/o David Dunn *Athletes First, LLC*
3300 Irvine Ave Ste 300
Newport Beach, CA 92660-3108, USA

Merritt, Chris (Opera Singer)
352 7th Ave
New York, NY 10001-5012, USA

Merritt, David (Athlete, Football Player)
357 Prospect St
Nutley, NJ 07110-2240, USA

Merritt, Gilbert S (Judge)
701 Broadway
Nashville, TN 37203-3944, USA

Merritt, Jack N (General)
2425 Wilson Blvd
Arlington, VA 22201-3326, USA

Merritt, James J (Jim) (Athlete, Baseball Player)
2777 Blue Spruce Dr
Hemet, CA 92545-8701, USA

Merritt, Lloyd (Athlete, Baseball Player)
4703 Wlld Iris Dr Apt 301
Myrtle Beach, SC 29577, USA

Merritt, Tift (Musician)
c/o Staff Member *Red Light Management (LA)*
8439 W Sunset Blvd Ste 2
Los Angeles, CA 90069-1925, USA

Merriweather, Mike (Athlete, Football Player)
PO Box 8351
Stockton, CA 95208-0351, USA

Merrow, Susan (Misc)
85 2nd St Ste 200
San Francisco, CA 94105-3456, USA

Merson, Michael (Government Official)
Ave Appia
Geneva 27 1211, SWITZERLAND

Merten, Lauri (Athlete, Golfer)
1010 Del Harbour Dr
Delray Beach, FL 33483-6510, USA

Mertens, Alan (Misc)
150 Gasoline Alley Rd
Indianapolis, IN 46222, USA

Mertens, Jerry (Athlete, Football Player)
465 Woodside Dr
Woodside, CA 94062-2375, USA

Merton, Robert C (Nobel Prize Laureate)
Business School
Boston, MA 2163, USA

Mertz, Edwin T (Misc)
1504 Via Della Scala
Henderson, NV 89052-4128, USA

Mertz, Francis J (Educator)
President's Office
Teaneck, NJ 7666, USA

Merullo, Lennie (Athlete, Baseball Player)
159 Summer Ave
Reading, MA 01867-2825, USA

Merullo, Matt (Athlete, Baseball Player)
8 Fox Run Rd
Madison, CT 06443-2052, USA

Merwin, John D (Ex-Governor)
PO Box 1029
Hudson, OH 44236-6229, USA

Merwin, William Stanley (Writer)
285 Madison Ave
Madison, NJ 07940-1006, USA

Merz, Curt (Athlete, Football Player)
1111 W Seminole St
Springfield, MO 65807-2551, USA

Merz, Suzanne (Sue) (Athlete, Hockey Player)
5 Douglas Dr
Greenwich, CT 06831-3612, USA

Mesa, Carlos (President)
Palacio de Gobierno Plaza Murilla
La Paz, BOLIVIA

Mesa, Jose (Athlete, Baseball Player)
1204 NW 24th Pl
Cape Coral, FL 33993-4897, USA

Meschery, Tom (Athlete, Basketball Player)
1216 Versailles Ave
Alameda, CA 94501-5453, USA

Meselson, Matthew S (Misc)
Fairchild Biochemistry Laboratories
Cambridge, MA 2138, USA

Mesereau, Thomas (Lawyer)
1875 Century Park E
Los Angeles, CA 90067-2501, USA

Meseroll, Mark (Athlete, Football Player)
450 Roger Dr
Salisbury, NC 28147-8878, USA

Mesguich, Daniel (Actor, Director)
17-21 Rue Duret
Paris 75116, FRANCE

Mesic, Stipe (President)
Pantovcak 241
Zagreb 10000, CROATIA

Mesina Stanley, Dianne (Producer)
c/o Staff Member *United Talent Agency (UTA)*
9560 Wilshire Blvd Fl 5
Beverly Hills, CA 90212-2400, USA

Mesner, Bruce (Athlete, Football Player)
6881 Lions Head Ln
Boca Raton, FL 33496-5955, USA

Mesnil Du Buisson, Robert (Archaeologist)
Chateau de Champobert Par Exmes
Orne 61310, FRANCE

Mesquida, Roxane (Actor)
c/o Elisabeth Simpson *Agence Elisabeth Simpson*
62 Boulevard Du Montparnasse
Paris 75015, FRANCE

Messager, Annette (Artist)
146 Blvd Camelinat
Colombier-Fontaine 92240, FRANCE

Messenger, Melinda (Model)
2-3 Golden Square
London W1R 3AD, UNITED KINGDOM (UK)

Messenger, Randy (Athlete, Baseball Player)
455 Market St Ste 2240
San Francisco, CA 94105-2446, USA

Messer, Dale (Athlete, Football Player)
5449 N Brooks Ave
Fresno, CA 93711-2914, USA

Messer, Thomas M (Misc)
1105 Park Ave
New York, NY 10128-1200, USA

Messerschmid, Ernst (Astronaut)
Pfaffenwaldring 31
Stuttgart 70569, GERMANY

Messerschmidt, J Alexander (Andy) (Baseball Player)
200 Lagunita Dr
Soquel, CA 95073-9594, USA

Messersmith, Andy (Athlete, Baseball Player)
200 Lagunita Dr
Soquel, CA 95073-9594, USA

Messi, Lionel (Athlete, Soccer Player)
Av. Aristides Maillol S/n
Barcelona 8028, SPAIN

Messier, Mark (Athlete, Hockey Player)
45 Birchwood Dr
Greenwich, CT 06831-3311, USA

Messina, Chris (Actor)
c/o Jon Rubinstein *Authentic Talent and Literary Management*
45 Main St Ste 1004
Brooklyn, NY 11201-8200, USA

Messina, Jim (Musician)
c/o Staff Member *Agency for the Performing Arts (APA-LA)*
405 S Beverly Dr Ste 500
Beverly Hills, CA 90212-4425, USA

Messina, Jo Dee (Musician, Songwriter)
c/o Tom Storms *Sanctuary Artist Management (TN)*
54 Music Sq E Ste 300
Nashville, TN 37203-4386, USA

Messing, Debra (Actor)
c/o Molly Madden *3 Arts Entertainment Inc*
9460 Wilshire Blvd Fl 7
Beverly Hills, CA 90212-2713, USA

Messner, Heinrich (Heini) (Skier)
11 Huebenweg
Hartford, CT 06150-0001, AUSTRIA

Messner, Johnny (Actor)
c/o Staff Member *McKeon-Myones Management*
3500 W Olive Ave Ste 770
Burbank, CA 91505-5527, USA

Messner, Reinhold (Mountaineer)
Schloss Juval
Kastelbell, Tschars 39040, ITALY

Mestrik, Frank (Athlete, Football Player)
730 Eagles Mere Ct
Alpharetta, GA 30005-4233, USA

Meszaros, Maria (Director)
Lumumba Utca 174
Budapest 1149, HUNGARY

Metallica (Music Group)
c/o Cliff Burnstein *Q Prime Inc*
729 7th Ave Ste 1600
New York, NY 10019-6880, USA

Metcalf, Eric Q (Athlete, Football Player)
5112 S Fountain St
Seattle, WA 98178-2114, USA

Metcalf, John (Writer)
128 Lewis St
Ottawa, ON K2P 0S7, CANADA

Metcalf, Joseph III (Admiral)
4658 Charleston Ter NW
Washington, DC 20007-1900, USA

Metcalf, Laurie (Actor)
1650 N Halsted St
Chicago, IL 60614-5518, USA

Metcalf, Mark (Actor)
c/o Staff Member *Peter Strain & Associates Inc (LA)*
5455 Wilshire Blvd Ste 1812
Los Angeles, CA 90036-4268, USA

Metcalf, Shelby (Coach)
Athletic
College Station, TX 77843-0001, USA

Metcalf, Terrance R (Terry) (Athlete, Football Player)
5112 S Fountain St
Seattle, WA 98178-2114, USA

Metcalf, Tom (Athlete, Baseball Player)
1390 Wisconsin River Dr
Port Edwards, WI 54469-1042, USA

Metcalf, Travis (Athlete, Baseball Player)
409 John Doy Ct
Lawrence, KS 66049-4257, USA

Metcalfe, Burt
11800 Brookdale Ln
Studio City, CA 91604-4203

Metcalfe, Jesse (Actor)
c/o Beth Holden-Garland *Untitled Entertainment (LA)*
350 S Beverly Dr Ste 200
Beverly Hills, CA 90212-4819, USA

Metcalfe, Mike (Athlete, Baseball Player)
9 Cottage Pl
Ashland, NH 03217-4370, USA

Metcalfe, Robert M (Scientist)
1000 Winter St Ste 3350
Waltham, MA 02451-1437, USA

Metesh, Bernice (Baseball Player)
1210 Kelly Ave
Joliet, IL 60435-4251, USA

Metheny, Pat (Musician)
c/o Ted Kurland *Ted Kurland Associates*
173 Brighton Ave
Boston, MA 02134-2003, USA

Metheny, Patrick B (Pat) (Composer, Musician)
173 Brighton Ave
Boston, MA 02134-2003, USA

Metrano, Art (Actor)
131 N Croft Ave Apt 402
Los Angeles, CA 90048-3472, USA

Metric (Music Group)
c/o Staff Member *Paradigm (Monterey)*
404 W Franklin St
Monterey, CA 93940-2303, USA

Metro, Charlie (Athlete, Baseball Player, Coach)
7890 Indiana St
Arvada, CO 80007-7123, USA

Metro Station (Music Group, Musician)
c/o Staff Member *Sony Music Entertainment*
555 Madison Ave
New York, NY 10022-3301, USA

Metrolis, Norma (Baseball Player)
175 Sea Dunes Dr
Melbourne Beach, FL 32951-3313, USA

Mette-Marit, Princess (Royalty)
Slottet Drammensvein 1
Oslo 10, NORWAY

Metwally, Omar (Actor)
c/o James Suskin *James Suskin Management*
2 Charlton St Apt 5K
New York, NY 10014-4970, USA

Metzelaars, Pete (Athlete, Football Player)
292 Point Carpenter Rd
Fort Mill, SC 29707-6875, USA

Metzenbaum, Howard M (Senator)
1424 16th St NW
Washington, DC 20036-2211, USA

Metzger, Clarence (Butch) (Athlete, Baseball Player)
641 Rivergate Way
Sacramento, CA 95831-3345, USA

Metzger, Henry (Misc)
PO Box 1641
Center Harbor, NH 03226-1641, USA

Metzger, Roger (Athlete, Baseball Player)
3560 Bluebonnet Blvd
Brenham, TX 77833-7180, USA

Metzig, Bill (Athlete, Baseball Player)
221 Chuck Wagon Rd
Lubbock, TX 79404-1903, USA

Metzler, Jim
6300 Wilshire Blvd # 2110
Los Angeles, CA 90048-5204

Metzner, Evyan (Stylist)
c/o Staff Member *Jed Root Inc*
61-A Walker St
New York, NY 10013, USA

Meulens, Hensley (Athlete, Baseball Player)
501 W Maryland St Attn Coachingstaff
Indianapolis, IN 46225-1041, USA

Meunier-Lebouc, Patricia (Athlete, Golfer)
110 Dalena Way
Palm Beach Gardens, FL 33418-1739, USA

Mewes, Jason (Actor)
c/o Andrew Weitz *WmE2 (Endeavor-LA)*
9601 Wilshire Blvd Fl 3
Beverly Hills, CA 90210-5219, USA

Mey, Reinhard
Sigismundkorso 63
Berlin, GERMANY D-13465

Mey, Uwe-Jens (Speed Skater)
Vulkanstr 22
Berlin 10367, GERMANY

Meyer, Alejandra (Actor)
c/o Staff Member *Televisa*
Blvd Adolfo Lopez Mateos 232 Colonia San Angel INN
DF CP 01060, MEXICO

Meyer, Armin H (Diplomat)
6624 Rannoch Rd
Bethesda, MD 20817-5411, USA

Meyer, Bess
PO Box 5617
Beverly Hills, CA 90209-5617

Meyer, Bob (Athlete, Baseball Player)
24446 Caswell Ct
Laguna Niguel, CA 92677-7008, USA

Meyer, Breckin (Actor)
c/o Ashley Franklin *Thruline Entertainment*
8383 Wilshire Blvd Ste 1050
Beverly Hills, CA 90211-2415, USA

Meyer, Brian (Athlete, Baseball Player)
33 Bank St
Medford, NJ 08055-2635, USA

Meyer, Dan (Athlete, Baseball Player)
11540 Marsh Creek Rd
Clayton, CA 94517-9759, USA

Meyer, Daniel J (Business Person)
2090 Florence Ave
Cincinnati, OH 45206-2484, USA

Meyer, Debbie
PO Box 2076
Carmichael, CA 95609-2076

Meyer, Dina (Actor)
c/o Stephen (Steve) LaManna *Innovative Artists (LA)*
1505 10th St
Santa Monica, CA 90401-2805, USA

Meyer, Edgar (Composer, Musician)
c/o Staff Member *Studio Art Concert Agency*
Viale Della Resistenza # 9
Suffield, CT 06080-0001, Italy

Meyer, Edward C (General)
1101 S Arlington Ridge Rd Apt 1116
Arlington, VA 22202-1929, USA

Meyer, Gregory (Stylist)
c/o Staff Member *Halley Resources*
37 W 20th St Ste 603
New York, NY 10011-3718, USA

Meyer, Jerome J (Business Person)
26600 SW Parkway Ave
Wilsonville, OR 97070-9246, USA

Meyer, Joey (Athlete, Baseball Player)
392 Kaimake Loop
Kailua, HI 96734-2019, USA

Meyer, John (Athlete, Football Player)
2123 Lost Dauphin Rd
De Pere, WI 54115-1607, USA

Meyer, Joyce (Religious Leader)
PO Box 655
Fenton, MO 63026-0655, USA

Meyer, Karl H (Misc)
642 Wyndham Rd
Teaneck, NJ 07666-1825, USA

Meyer, Lawrence H (Economist, Government Official)
Constitution NW
Washington, DC 20551-0001, USA

Meyer, Nicholas (Director, Producer, Writer)
c/o Alan Gasmer *Alan Gasmer Management Company*
10877 Wilshire Blvd Ste 603
Los Angeles, CA 90024-4348, USA

Meyer, Robert K (Misc)
3 Rawlings Pl
Fadden, ACT 2904, AUSTRALIA

Meyer, Ron (Athlete, Football Player)
628 18th St
Windom, MN 56101-1102, USA

Meyer, Ron (Business Person, Producer)
c/o Staff Member *NBC Universal (LA)*
100 Universal City Plz
Universal City, CA 91608-1002, USA

Meyer, Scott (Athlete, Baseball Player)
9311 E Calle De Valle Dr
Scottsdale, AZ 85255-4303, USA

Meyer, Stephenie (Writer)
c/o Jodi Reamer *Writers House*
21 W 26th St
New York, NY 10010-1083, USA

Meyer Reyes, Deborah E (Debbie) (Swimmer)
PO Box 2076
Carmichael, CA 95609-2076, USA

Meyerowitz, Elliot M (Biologist)
Biology
Pasadena, CA 91125-0001, USA

Meyerowitz, Joel (Photographer)
817 W End Ave
New York, NY 10025-0139, USA

Meyer-Petrovic, Anna (Baseball Player)
1125 N Nema Ave
Tucson, AZ 85712-4723, USA

Meyerriecks, Jeffrey (Director, Musical Director)
5 Loblolly Ct
Pinehurst, NC 28374-9349, USA

Meyers, Anne Akiko (Musician)
40 W 57th St
New York, NY 10019-4001, USA

Meyers, Ari (Actor)
c/o Holly Lebed *Holly Lebed Personal Management*
10535 Wilshire Blvd Apt 808
Los Angeles, CA 90024-4556, USA

Meyers, Augie (Musician)
2137 Zercher Rd
San Antonio, TX 78209-1122, USA

Meyers, Chad (Athlete, Baseball Player)
816 Summit Ridge Dr
Papillion, NE 68046-8096, USA

Meyers, David (Dave) (Director)
c/o Ramses Ishak *United Talent Agency (UTA)*
9560 Wilshire Blvd Fl 5
Beverly Hills, CA 90212-2400, USA

Meyers, David (Dave) (Athlete, Basketball Player)
40629 Carmelita Cir
Temecula, CA 92591-1609, USA

Meyers, Josh (Comedian)
c/o Staff Member *WmE2 (WMA-LA)*
1 William Morris Pl
Beverly Hills, CA 90212-4261, USA

Meyers, Krystal (Musician)
605 Moss Ln
Franklin, TN 37064-5230, USA

Meyers, Nancy (Director)
c/o Jeff Berg *International Creative Management (ICM-LA)*
10250 Constellation Blvd Fl 7
Los Angeles, CA 90067-6207, USA

Meyers, Patricia (Athlete, Golfer)
2784 Moran Dr
Waldorf, MD 20601-2604, USA

Meyers, Seth (Actor, Comedian)
c/o Tim Sarkes *Brillstein Entertainment Partners*
9150 Wilshire Blvd Ste 350
Beverly Hills, CA 90212-3453, USA

Meyers-Drysdale, Ann (Athlete, Basketball Player, Sportscaster)
6621 Doral Dr
Huntington Beach, CA 92648-6129, USA

Meyerson, Martin (Educator)
2016 Spruce St
Philadelphia, PA 19103-6524, USA

Meyfarth, Ulrike
Friedensweg 59
Wesseling, GERMANY D-50389

Meyfarth, Ulrike Nasse (Athlete, Track Athlete)
Buschweg 53
Odenthal 51519, GERMANY

Meyjes, Menno (Director, Producer, Writer)
c/o Gabi Morgerman *WmE2 (WMA-LA)*
1 William Morris Pl
Beverly Hills, CA 90212-4261, USA

Meysel, Inge
Sudstrand 13
Bullenhausen, GERMANY D-21217

Mezentseva, Galina (Ballerina)
1 Ploshchad Iskusstr
Saint Petersburg, RUSSIA

Mezzogiorno, Giovanna (Actor)
c/o Estelle Lasher *Principal Entertainment (LA)*
1964 Westwood Blvd Ste 400
Los Angeles, CA 90025-4695, USA

Mfume, Kweisi (Misc)
President's Office P.O. Box 1557
Baltimore, MD 21203-1557, USA

MGMT (Music Group)
c/o Staff Member *Columbia Records (NY) - Main*
550 Madison Ave
New York, NY 10022-3211

Miadich, Bart (Athlete, Baseball Player)
17841 Hillside Dr
Lake Oswego, OR 97034-7525, USA

Mialik, Larry (Athlete, Football Player)
100 Wisconsin Ave Apt 900
Madison, WI 53703-4169, USA

Miami Sound Machine
6205 Bird Rd
Miami, FL 33155-4823

Miano, Rich (Athlete, Football Player)
7168 Makaa St
Honolulu, HI 96825-3103, USA

Micech, Phil (Athlete, Football Player)
3029 N 91st St
Milwaukee, WI 53222-4620, USA

Miceli, Dan (Danny) (Athlete, Baseball Player)
1712 Cottonwood Creek Pl
Lake Mary, FL 32746-4407, USA

Miceli, Joe
189 Vanderbilt Ave
Brentwood, NY 11717-2518

Micell, Justine (Actor)
6500 Wilshire Blvd Ste 2200
Los Angeles, CA 90048-4942, USA

Micelotta, Mickey (Athlete, Baseball Player)
2035 E Warm Springs Rd Unit 1007
Las Vegas, NV 89119-0454, USA

Michael (King)
Villa Serena 77 Chemin Louis-Degallier
Versoix-Geneva 1290, SWITZERLAND

Michael, Alum E (Government Official)
Cardiff Bay
Cardiff CF99 1NA, WALES

Michael, Archbishop (Religious Leader)
358 Mountain Rd
Englewood, NJ 07631-3727, USA

Michael, Bob (Politician)
1029 N Glenwood Ave
Peoria, IL 61606-1007

Michael, Eugene R (Gene) (Misc)
49 Union Ave
Upper Saddle River, NJ 07458-2024, USA

Michael, ex-King
77 Chemin Louis Degallier
Versoix, SWITZERLAND 1290

Michael, Gene (Athlete, Baseball Player, Coach)
49 Union Ave
Upper Saddle River, NJ 07458-2024, USA

Michael, George (Musician, Songwriter)
c/o Michael Lippman *Lippman Entertainment*
23586 Calabasas Rd Ste 208
Calabasas, CA 91302-1361, USA

Michael, Gregory (Actor)
c/o Mitchell Gossett *United Talent Agency (UTA)*
9560 Wilshire Blvd Fl 5
Beverly Hills, CA 90212-2400, USA

Michael, Kevin (Musician)
c/o Staff Member *Paradigm (Monterey)*
404 W Franklin St
Monterey, CA 93940-2303, USA

Michael, Prince & Princess of Kent
Kensington Palace
London, ENGLAND W8 5AF

Michael, Thomas (Actor, Producer, Writer)

Michael Carroll, Jason (Musician)
c/o Staff Member *Creative Artists Agency (CAA-TN)*
3310 W End Ave Fl 5
Nashville, TN 37203-1028, USA

Michaels, Al
47 W 66th St
New York, NY 10023-6201

Michaels, Alan R (Al) (Sportscaster)
77 W 66th St
New York, NY 10023-6201, USA

Michaels, Beverly
11921 Weddington St
North Hollywood, CA 91607-2853

Michaels, Bret (Musician, Reality TV Star)
c/o Howard Kaufman *HK Management (LA)*
10866 Wilshire Blvd Ste 200
Los Angeles, CA 90024-4350, USA

Michaels, Eugene H (Misc)
15825 Shady Grove Rd
Rockville, MD 20850-4008, USA

Michaels, Fern (Writer)
1006 S Main St
Summerville, SC 29483-4231, USA

Michaels, Gianna (Adult Film Star)
7 - 9 Clifford St Unit 101
York, Yorkshire YO1 9RA, UK

Michaels, James W (Editor)
60 5th Ave
New York, NY 10011-8868, USA

Michaels, Jason (Athlete, Baseball Player)
5019 Avenue Avignon
Lutz, FL 33558-2826, USA

Michaels, Jillian (Fitness Expert, Reality TV Star)
c/o Amie Yavor *Creative Artists Agency (CAA-LA)*
2000 Avenue of the Stars Ste 100
Los Angeles, CA 90067-4705, USA

Michaels, Lori (Musician)
352 7th Ave Rm 202
New York, NY 10001-5012, USA

Michaels, Lorne (Producer, Writer)
c/o Staff Member *Broadway Video Entertainment*
5555 Melrose Ave Dressing Room Bldg 105
Los Angeles, CA 90038-3197

Michaels, Louis A (Lou) (Athlete, Football Player)
69 Grace St
Swoyersville, PA 18704-3040, USA

Michaels, Marilyn
185 W End Ave
New York, NY 10023-5539

Michaels, Mia (Choreographer)
c/o Tim O'Brien *Clear Talent Group (LA)*
10950 Ventura Blvd
Studio City, CA 91604-3340, USA

Michaels, Shawn (Wrestler)
7700 Bloomington Ave
Minneapolis, MN 55423-4660, USA

Michaels, Tammy Lynn (Actor)
c/o Marcel Pariseau *True Public Relations*
6725 W Sunset Blvd Ste 470
Los Angeles, CA 90028-7180, USA

Michaels, Walter (Walt) (Athlete, Coach, Football Coach, Football Player)
282 Michaels Rd
Shickshinny, PA 18655-4142, USA

Michaelsen, Kari (Actor)
11365 Ventura Blvd Ste 100
Studio City, CA 91604-3148, USA

Michaelson, Ingrid (Musician)
c/o Patrick Confrey *Sunshine, Sachs & Associates*
149 5th Ave Fl 7
New York, NY 10010-6824, USA

Michalak, Chris (Athlete, Baseball Player)
1108 Mockingbird Ln
Keller, TX 76248-2903, USA

Michaleczewski, Dariusz (Boxer)
Am Stadtrand 27
Hamburg 22047, GERMANY

Michalik, Art (Athlete, Football Player)
33400 Gafford Rd
Wildomar, CA 92595-8293, USA

Michalka, Aly (Actor, Musician)
c/o Jeff Kwatinetz *Prospect Park*
2049 Century Park E Ste 2550
Century City, CA 90067-3139, USA

Michalka, Amanda (Musician)
c/o Staff Member *Lynda Goodfriend Management*
338 S Beachwood Dr
Burbank, CA 91506-2713, USA

Michals, Duane (Photographer)
109 E 19th St
New York, NY 10003-9603, USA

Micheaux, Larry (Athlete, Basketball Player)
2914 Calender Lake Dr
Missouri City, TX 77459-3920, USA

Micheaux, Nicki (Actor)
c/o Charlton Blackburne *A Management Company*
9107 Wilshire Blvd Ste 650
Beverly Hills, CA 90210-5544, USA

Micheel, Shaun (Athlete, Golfer)
1267 Dubray Lake Cir
Collierville, TN 38017-3952, USA

Michel, Alex (Reality TV Star)
PO Box 46605
Los Angeles, CA 90046-0605, USA

Michel, F Curtis (Astronaut)
2101 University Blvd
Houston, TX 77030-1218, USA

Michel, Hartmut (Nobel Prize Laureate)
Heinrich-Hoffmann-Str 7
Frankfort 60528, GERMANY

Michel, Jean-Louis (Oceanographer, Scientist)
Center de Toulon
La Seyne dur Mer, Toulon 83500, FRANCE

Michel, Mike (Athlete, Football Player)
378 Drexel Ave
Ventura, CA 93003-2329, USA

Michel, Paul R (Judge)
717 Madison Pl NW
Washington, DC 20439-0001, USA

Michele, Chrisette (Musician)
c/o Staff Member *Selverne & Co.*
3450 Cahuenga Blvd W Apt 906
Los Angeles, CA 90068-1594, USA

Michele, Lea (Actor, Musician)
c/o Jason Weinberg *Untitled Entertainment (LA)*
350 S Beverly Dr Ste 200
Beverly Hills, CA 90212-4819, USA

Michele, Lisa (Stylist)
c/o Staff Member *Ennis*
119 Braintree St
Boston, MA 02134-1628, USA

Michele, Michael (Actor)
c/o Staff Member *A Management Company*
9107 Wilshire Blvd Ste 650
Beverly Hills, CA 90210-5544, USA

Micheler, Elisabeth (Athlete)
Gruntenstr 45
Augsburg 86163, GERMANY

Michell, Keith (Actor)
Prince of Wales Coventry St
London W1V 7FE, UNITED KINGDOM (UK)

Michell, Roger (Director)
Paramount House 162 Wardour
London, W1V 3AT, UNITED KINGDOM (UK)

Michelle, Candice (Actor, Model)
c/o Jerry Donato *Abraxas Talent Agency*
4260 Troost Ave Apt 1
Studio City, CA 91604-2882, USA

Michelle, Sheley (Actor)
c/o Mike Simpson *WmE2 (Endeavor-LA)*
9601 Wilshire Blvd Fl 3
Beverly Hills, CA 90210-5219, USA

Michelmore, Guy
72 Goldsmith Ave
London, ENGLAND W3 6HN

Michelmore, Lawrence (Government Official)
4924 Sentinel Dr
Bethesda, MD 20816-3590, USA

Michels, John (Athlete, Football Player)
4544 Alveo Rd
La Canada Flintridge, CA 91011-3703, USA

Michels, John (Athlete, Football Player)
39 Meadow Brook Pl
Spring, TX 77382-1234, USA

Michels, Rinus (Coach, Football Coach)
Hotel Breitenbacher Hof H-Heine-Allee 36
Dusseldorf 40213, GERMANY

Michener, Charles D (Misc)
1706 W 2nd St
Lawrence, KS 66044-1016, USA

Michibata, Jessica (Model)
c/o Staff Member *The Tanabe Agency*
2-21-4 Aobadai Meguro
Tokyo 153-0042, JAPAN

Michie, Donald (Scientist)
6 Inveralmond Grove Cramond
Edinburg EH4 6RA, SCOTLAND

Michiko (Royalty)
Imperial Palace 1-1 Chiyoda-ku
Tokyo 100, JAPAN

Michnik, Adam (Editor)
Czerha 8/10
Warsaw 732, POLAND

Michos, Anastas N (Cinematographer)
232 N Canon Dr
Beverly Hills, CA 90210-5302, USA

Mickal, Abe (Athlete, Football Player, Physicist)
774 Topaz St
New Orleans, LA 70124-3624, USA

Mickell, Darren (Athlete, Football Player)
9250 Chelsea Dr
Miramar, FL 33025-3803, USA

Mickelson, Ed (Athlete, Baseball Player)
1532 Charlemont Dr
Chesterfield, MO 63017-4604, USA

Mickelson, Phil (Athlete, Golfer)
c/o Steve Loy *Gaylord Sports Management*
13845 N Northsight Blvd Ste 200
Scottsdale, AZ 85260-3609, USA

Mickens, Glenn (Athlete, Baseball Player)
5920 Kini Pl
Kapaa, HI 96746-8938, USA

Mickey, Joey (Athlete, Football Player)
6213 Canyon Dr
Oklahoma City, OK 73105-6415, USA

Middendorf, Dave (Athlete, Football Player)
PO Box 525
Port Orchard, WA 98366-0525, USA

Middendorf, J William II (Diplomat, Secretary)
565 W Main Rd
Little Compton, RI 02837-1131, USA

Middendorf, Tracy (Actor)
PO Box 480410
Los Angeles, CA 90048-1410, USA

Middle of the Road
18 Irvine Dr. Linwood
Refrewshire, ENGLAND

Middlebrook, Jason (Athlete, Baseball Player)
3309 Glenview Ave
Austin, TX 78703-1446, USA

Middlebrooks, Charley (Baseball Player)
528 Rigby St NE
Marietta, GA 30060-1703, USA

Middlebrooks, Willie (Athlete, Football Player)
2050 Camelot Dr
Allen, TX 75013-3016, USA

Middleton, Dave (Football Player)
Too Ill To Sign Autographs
USA

Middleton, Kate (Princess, Royalty)
St James Palace
London SW1A 1BS, UNITED KINGDOM

Middleton, Mike (Model)
Ebersberger Str 9
Munich 81679, GERMANY

Middleton, Rick (Athlete, Hockey Player)
PO Box 1161
Hampton, NH 03843-1161, USA

Middleton, Terdell (Athlete, Football Player)
1893 Prospect St
Memphis, TN 38106-7645, USA

Middleton-Gentry, Ruth (Baseball Player)
28 Grandview Hts
Hamilton, IN 46742, USA

Midkiff, Dale (Actor)
c/o John Frazier *Amsel, Eisenstadt & Frazier Talent Agency (AEF)*
5055 Wilshire Blvd Ste 860
Los Angeles, CA 90036-6108, USA

Midler, Bette (Actor, Musician)
c/o Ken Sunshine *Sunshine, Sachs & Associates*
149 5th Ave Fl 7
New York, NY 10010-6824, USA

Midnight Fish
Samlandstr. 32
Munich, GERMANY D-81825

Midnight Oil
Box 186 Glebe
Sydney, AUSTRALIA NSW 2037

Midon, Raul (Musician)
c/o Barry Dickins *International Talent Booking*
1st Floor, Ariel House 74A Charlotte St
London W1T 4QJ, UNITED KINGDOM

Midori (Musician)
850 7th Ave Ste 705
New York, NY 10019-5438, USA

Miechur, Thomas F (Misc)
2500 Brickvale Dr
Elk Grove Village, IL 60007-6800, USA

Mieczko, A J (Athlete, Hockey Player)
295 Central Park W Apt 9G
New York, NY 10024-3023, USA

Mielke, Gary (Athlete, Baseball Player)
1718 Orchid Dr S
North Mankato, MN 56003-1435, USA

Mientkiewicz, Doug (Athlete, Baseball Player)
125 Bayview Isle Dr
Islamorada, FL 33036-3308, USA

Mierkowicz, Ed (Athlete, Baseball Player)
7530 Macomb St Apt 1A
Grosse Ile, MI 48138-1522, USA

Mieske, Matt (Athlete, Baseball Player)
2199 E Bombay Rd
Midland, MI 48642-8351, USA

Mieszkowski, Ed (Athlete, Football Player)
10251 S Spaulding Ave
Evergreen Park, IL 60805-3761, USA

Mieto, Juha (Skier)
Mieto, FINLAND

Miggins, Larry (Athlete, Baseball Player)
2405 Kingston St
Houston, TX 77019-6603, USA

Mighty Clouds of Joy
PO Box 570815
Tarzana, CA 91357-0815

Mighty Mighty Bosstones (Music Group)
c/o Staff Member *Paradigm (Monterey)*
404 W Franklin St
Monterey, CA 93940-2303, USA

Migliazzo, Paul (Athlete, Football Player)
605 W 68th Ter
Kansas City, MO 64113-1954, USA

Mignola, Mike (Cartoonist)
c/o Staff Member *Dark Horse Entertainment*
1438 N Gower St Box Bldg 23 PMB 200
Hollywood, CA 90028, USA

Miguel, Luis (Musician)
c/o Jeremy Norkin *WmE2 (WMA-Miami)*
119 Washington Ave Ste 400
Miami, FL 33139-7202, USA

Mihaly, Andras (Composer)
Verhalom Ter 9B
Budapest II 1025, HUNGARY

Mihm, Chris (Basketball Player)
1 Center Ct
Cleveland, OH 44115-4001, USA

Mihok, Dash (Actor)
c/o Staff Member *Untitled Entertainment (LA)*
350 S Beverly Dr Ste 200
Beverly Hills, CA 90212-4819, USA

Mikan, Larry (Athlete, Basketball Player)
891 Carmona Ct
Chula Vista, CA 91910-8012, USA

Mike Rizzo, Mike (DJ)
c/o Staff Member *Diva Central Inc*
7510 W Sunset Blvd Ste 1445
Los Angeles, CA 90046-3408, USA

Mikel, Liz (Actor)
c/o Terry Loftis *Verve Communications Group*
325 N Saint Paul St Ste 2360
Dallas, TX 75201-3824, USA

Mikell, George
23 Shuttleworth Rd
London, ENGLAND SW11

Mike-Mayer, Istvan (Steve) (Athlete, Football Player)
681 Lincoln Ave
Glen Rock, NJ 07452-2519, USA

Mike-Mayer, Nicholas (Nick) (Athlete, Football Player)
681 Lincoln Ave
Glen Rock, NJ 07452-2519, USA

Mikeska, Russ (Athlete, Football Player)
100 Spirit Run
Eatonton, GA 31024-5035, USA

Mikhalchenko, Alla A (Ballerina)
Malaya Gruzinskaya St 12/18
Moscow 123242, RUSSIA

Mikhalkov, Nikita (Director)
Maly Kozikhinksy Per 4 #16-17
Moscow 103001, RUSSIA

Mikhalkov-Konchalovsky, Andrei S (Director)
Malaya Gruzinskaya 28 #130
Moscow 123557, RUSSIA

Miki, Minouri (Composer)
1-11-6 Higashi Nogawa Komae-shi
Tokyo 201, JAPAN

Mikita, Valerie (Actor)
c/o Staff Member *The Stevens Group*
14011 Ventura Blvd Ste 201
Sherman Oaks, CA 91423-5216, USA

Mikkelsen, A Verner (Vern) (Athlete, Basketball Player, Golfer)
17715 Breconville Rd
Wayzata, MN 55391-3303, USA

Mikkelsen, Mads (Actor)
c/o Theresa Peters *United Talent Agency (UTA)*
9560 Wilshire Blvd Fl 5
Beverly Hills, CA 90212-2400, USA

Miklich, William (Athlete, Football Player)
Highway 106
Dousman, WI 53118, USA

Miklos, Arpad (Adult Film Star)
c/o Staff Member *Diva Central Inc*
7510 W Sunset Blvd Ste 1445
Los Angeles, CA 90046-3408, USA

Miko, Izabella (Actor)
c/o Kesha Williams *Affirmative Entertainment*
425 N Robertson Blvd
West Hollywood, CA 90048-1735, USA

Mikolajewski, Pete (Athlete, Football Player)
2520 Singing Vista Way
El Cajon, CA 92019-2740, USA

Miksis, Al (Athlete, Basketball Player)
522 E Algonquin Rd Apt 203
Schaumburg, IL 60173-3801, USA

Mikulski, Barbara (Senator)
212 W Main St Ste 200
Salisbury, MD 21801-5106, USA

Mikva, Abner J (Judge)
442 New Jersey Ave SE
Washington, DC 20003-4008, USA

Mikvy, Bill (Athlete, Basketball Player)
586 Linton Hill Rd
Newtown, PA 18940-1204, USA

Milacki, Bob (Athlete, Baseball Player)
1873 Martinique Dr
Lake Havasu City, AZ 86406-9218, USA

Milan, Don (Athlete, Football Player)
1709 Sawmill Rd
Minden, NV 89423-7052, USA

Milandro, Kristina
2518 Cardigan Ct
Los Angeles, CA 90077-1337

Milani, Denise
60027 Via St
Cathedral City, CA 92234, USA

Milano, Alyssa (Actor)
c/o Jason Barrett *Alchemy Entertainment*
7024 Melrose Ave Ste 420
Los Angeles, CA 90038-3394, USA

Milano, Fred (Musician)
PO Box 12
Far Hills, NJ 07931-0012, USA

Milbourne, Larry (Athlete, Baseball Player)
747 Yale Ter
Vineland, NJ 08360-5818, USA

Milbrett, Tiffeny (Soccer Player)
1801 S Prairie Ave
Chicago, IL 60616-1319, USA

Milburn, Darryl (Athlete, Football Player)
270 E Harding St
Baton Rouge, LA 70802-7323, USA

Milburn, Glyn (Athlete, Football Player)
515 S Kihei Rd Apt C502
Kihei, HI 96753-7585, USA

Milbury, Mike (Athlete, Coach, Hockey Player)
PO Box 405
Needham, MA 02494-0010, USA

Milchan, Arnon (Producer)
c/o Staff Member *New Regency Productions*
10201 W Pico Blvd Bldg 12
Los Angeles, CA 90064-2606, USA

Milchin, Mike (Athlete, Baseball Player)
13118 Bellaria Cir
Windermere, FL 34786-7401, USA

Miledi, Ricardo (Biologist)
9 Gibbs Ct
Irvine, CA 92617-4032, USA

Miles, Aaron (Athlete, Baseball Player)
1716 San Jose Dr
Antioch, CA 94509-4217, USA

Miles, Carl (Athlete, Baseball Player)
3710 S Lenoir St
Columbia, MO 65201-5463, USA

Miles, Darius (Basketball Player)
1 Center Ct
Cleveland, OH 44115-4001, USA

Miles, Don (Athlete, Baseball Player)
22335 Baneberry Rd
Magnolia, TX 77355-3548, USA

Miles, Eddie (Athlete, Football Player)
8575 Atlas Cir
Inver Grove Heights, MN 55077-3639, USA

Miles, Jim (Athlete, Baseball Player)
635D Highway 6 E
Batesville, MS 38606-3005, USA

Miles, Joanna (Actor)
2062 Vine St
Los Angeles, CA 90068-3928, USA

Miles, John (Baseball Player)
4130 Treehouse Dr
San Antonio, TX 78222-3510, USA

Miles, John R (Jack) (Writer)
3568 Mountain View Ave
Pasadena, CA 91107-4616, USA

Miles, John W (Geophysicist, Physicist, Scientist)
16800 Academy Dr # 30
Palos Verdes Peninsula, CA 90274-3975, USA

Miles, Mark (Athlete, Tennis Player)
200 Tournament Players Rd
Ponte Vedra Beach, FL 32082, USA

Miles, Paige (Musician)
c/o Simon Fuller *XIX Entertainment*
33/32 Ransomes Dock 35-37 Parkgate Rd
London SW11 4NP, UK

Miles, Sarah (Actor)
Chithurst Manor Trotton near Petersfield
Hants GU31 5EU, UNITED KINGDOM (UK)

Miles, Sylvia (Actor)
c/o Staff Member *Agency for the Performing Arts (APA-LA)*
405 S Beverly Dr Ste 500
Beverly Hills, CA 90212-4425, USA

Miles, Vera (Actor)
PO Box 1599
Palm Desert, CA 92261-1599, USA

Miles-Clark, Jearl (Athlete, Track Athlete)
University of Florida Athletic Dept
Gainsville, FL 32604, USA

Miley, Dave (Athlete, Baseball Player, Coach)
7111 N Coarsey Dr
Tampa, FL 33604-5258, USA

Milhoan, Michael (Actor)
c/o Staff Member *Sanders Armstrong Caserta*
2120 Colorado Ave Ste 120
Santa Monica, CA 90404-3561, USA

Milian, Christina (Actor)
c/o Carmen Milian *Milian Management*
16830 Ventura Blvd Ste 501
Encino, CA 91436-1717, USA

Milian, Marilyn (Judge, Television Host)
401 5th Ave
New York, NY 10016-3317, USA

Milicevic, Ivana (Actor, Model)
c/o Staff Member *One Talent Management*
9220 W Sunset Blvd Ste 306
Los Angeles, CA 90069-3503, USA

Milinchik, Joe (Athlete, Football Player)
16 N Forrest Dr
Thomasville, NC 27360-8971, USA

Militello, Sam (Athlete, Baseball Player)
3217 W Saint John St
Tampa, FL 33607-2127, USA

Militzok, Nathan (Athlete, Basketball Player)
78 Blue Lagoon
Laguna Beach, CA 92651-4216, USA

Milius, John F (Director, Writer)
888 Linda Flora Dr
Los Angeles, CA 90049-1629, USA

Milken, Michael R (Financier, Philanthropist)
4543 Tara Dr
Encino, CA 91436-3217, USA

Milla, Roger (Soccer Player)
BP 1116
Yaounde, CAMEROON

Millan, Cesar (Television Host)
c/o Tony Angellotti *Angellotti Company*
12423 Ventura Ct
Studio City, CA 91604-2417, USA

Millan, Felix (Athlete, Baseball Player)
G16 Calle Camarero
Carolina, PR 00987-8523, USA

Millar, Jeffrey L (Jeff) (Cartoonist)
1301 Spring Oaks Cir
Houston, TX 77055-4703, USA

Millar, Kevin (Athlete, Baseball Player)
14200 Flat Top Ranch Rd
Austin, TX 78732-2483, USA

Millar, Miles (Writer)
c/o Staff Member *Millar/Gough Ink*
3800 Barham Blvd Ste 503
Los Angeles, CA 90068-1042, USA

Millard, Keith (Athlete, Football Player)
3739 Oakhurst Way
Dublin, CA 94568-8834, USA

Millbern, David (Actor)
c/o Staff Member *Barry Krost Management*
9220 W Sunset Blvd Ste 106
West Hollywood, CA 90069-3500, USA

Millcic, Darko (Basketball Player)
2 Championship Dr
Auburn Hills, MI 48326-1753, USA

Milledge, Lastings (Athlete, Baseball Player)
11114 Sailbrooke Dr
Riverview, FL 33579-7074, USA

Millegan, Eric (Actor)
c/o Peter Young *Sovereign Talent Group*
8421 Wilshire Blvd Ste 200
Beverly Hills, CA 90211-3204, USA

Millen, Corey (Athlete, Hockey Player)
4651 Reka Dr Unit 4
Anchorage, AK 99508-3686, USA

Millen, Hugh (Athlete, Football Player)
6836 Cascade Ave SE
Snoqualmie, WA 98065-9725, USA

Miller, Aaron David (Writer)
c/o Staff Member *Random House*
1540 Broadway
New York, NY 10036-4039, USA

Miller, Alan (Journalist)
202 W 1st St
Los Angeles, CA 90012-4105, USA

Miller, Alan (Athlete, Football Player)
3118 Erie Dr
Orchard Lake, MI 48324-1512, USA

Miller, Alice (Athlete, Golfer)
2 Log Church Rd
Wilmington, DE 19807-1724, USA

Miller, Allan (Actor)
1501 Broadway Ste 703
New York, NY 10036-5501, USA

Miller, Allison (Actor)
c/o Staff Member *Beth Goldstein Management*
4433 Colbath Ave Apt 34
Sherman Oaks, CA 91423-3527, USA

Miller, Andre (Basketball Player)
Pepsi Center 1000 Chopper Circle
Denver, CO 80204, USA

Miller, Andrew (Athlete, Baseball Player)
2100 Woodward Ave Attn Autographsforacause
Detroit, MI 48201-3470, USA

Miller, Anthony (Athlete, Basketball Player)
1083 Superior St
Benton Harbor, MI 49022-5310, USA

Miller, Ben (Actor, Producer)
c/o Staff Member *Independent Talent Group (ITG-UK)*
Oxford House 76 Oxford St
London W1D 1BS, UK

Miller, Bennett (Director)
c/o Bryan Lourd *Creative Artists Agency (CAA-LA)*
2000 Avenue of the Stars Ste 100
Los Angeles, CA 90067-4705, USA

Miller, Bill (Athlete, Football Player)
701 Belden Ct
St Augustine, FL 32086-6821, USA

Miller, Bill (Athlete, Baseball Player)
PO Box 2681
Aptos, CA 95001-2681, USA

Miller, Billy (Athlete, Football Player)
465 Cosmos Ct
Westlake, CA 91362, USA

Miller, Billy (Actor)
c/o Staff Member *James/Levy/Jacobson Management Inc*
3500 W Olive Ave Ste 1470
Burbank, CA 91505-5514, USA

Miller, Bob (Athlete, Baseball Player)
1702 Keim Trl
Saint Charles, IL 60174-5827, USA

Miller, Bob (Athlete, Baseball Player)
1202 Andover Cir
Commerce Town, MI 48390-2249, USA

Miller, Bode (Skier)
63 Eastern Valley Rd
Franconia, NH 3580, USA

Miller, Brad (Basketball Player)
1 Sports Pkwy
Sacramento, CA 95834-2300, USA

Miller, Brad (Congressman, Politician)
1127 Longworth Hob
Washington, DC 20515-3219, USA

Miller, Bruce (Athlete, Baseball Player)
2126 Parkland Dr
Fort Wayne, IN 46825-3929, USA

Miller, Buddy (Musician)
5000 Oak Bluff Ct
Atlanta, GA 30350-1069, USA

Miller, C Arden (Doctor)
350 Carolina Meadows Villa
Chapel Hill, NC 27517-7549, USA

Miller, C Ray (Religious Leader)
302 Lake St
Huntington, IN 46750-1264, USA

Miller, Calvin (Athlete, Football Player)
1602 Fairfield Dr
Stillwater, OK 74074-2331, USA

Miller, Carl (Athlete, Football Player)
PO Box 773
Crowley, TX 76036-0773, USA

Miller, Charles D (Business Person)
150 N Orange Grove Blvd
Pasadena, CA 91103-3534, USA

Miller, Cheryl D (Athlete, Basketball Player, Coach)
3206 Ellington Dr
Los Angeles, CA 90068-1741, USA

Miller, Chris (Athlete, Football Player)
2760 Chuckanut St
Eugene, OR 97408-4737, USA

Miller, Chris (Director)
c/o Joy Fehily *Prime*
9696 Culver Blvd Ste 102
Culver City, CA 90232-2734, USA

Miller, Christa (Actor)
c/o Jill Littman *Impression Entertainment*
9229 W Sunset Blvd Ste 700
West Hollywood, CA 90069-3407, USA

Miller, Christine Cook (Judge)
717 Madison Pl NW
Washington, DC 20439-0001, USA

Miller, Coco (Basketball Player)
MCI Center 601 F St NW
Washington, DC 20004, USA

Miller, Corey (Athlete, Football Player)
2528 Crofton Way
Columbia, SC 29223-2299, USA

Miller, Corky (Athlete, Baseball Player)
1115 7th St
Calimesa, CA 92320-1013, USA

Miller, Damian (Athlete, Baseball Player)
N1276 Wuensch Rd
La Crosse, WI 54601-2655, USA

Miller, Dan (Musician)
7380 W Sand Lake Rd # 350
Orlando, FL 32819-5248, USA

Miller, Darrell (Athlete, Baseball Player)
21159 Via Alisa
Yorba Linda, CA 92887-2510, USA

Miller, David (Cartoonist)
167 Tremont St
Rehoboth, MA 02769-2818, USA

Miller, Denise (Actor, Producer)
c/o Richard Sindell *Bob Waters Agency*
9301 Wilshire Blvd Ste 300
Beverly Hills, CA 90210-6119, USA

Miller, Dennis (Actor, Comedian)
c/o Brad Grey *Brillstein Entertainment Partners*
9150 Wilshire Blvd Ste 350
Beverly Hills, CA 90212-3453, USA

Miller, Denny (Actor)
9612 Gavin Stone Ave
Las Vegas, NV 89145-8626, USA

Miller, Dyar (Athlete, Baseball Player)
8816 Admirals Bay Dr
Indianapolis, IN 46236-9292, USA

Miller, Eddie (Athlete, Baseball Player)
1819 Alfreda Blvd
San Pablo, CA 94806-4715, USA

Miller, Eddie (Athlete, Football Player)
1503 Summerwood Dr
Clarkston, GA 30021-3096, USA

Miller, Elizabeth C (Doctor, Educator)
1822 Masters Ln
Madison, WI 53719-4440, USA

Miller, Eugene A (Financier)
500 Woodward Ave
Detroit, MI 48226-3407, USA

Miller, Frank (Actor, Writer)
c/o Staff Member *Shapiro-Lichtman Talent Agency*
1010 Lexington Rd
Beverly Hills, CA 90210-2935, USA

Miller, Frank (Cartoonist)
10956 SE Main St
Milwaukie, OR 97222-7644, USA

Miller, Fred (Athlete, Football Player)
7143 Sawmill Trl
Houston, TX 77040-1830, USA

Miller, Fred D (Athlete, Football Player)
4535 Black Rock Rd
Upperco, MD 21155-9544, USA

Miller, Gabrielle (Actor)
c/o Staff Member *Corner Gas*
PO Box 9 Station O
Scarborough, ON M4A 2M9, CANADA

Miller, George A (Doctor)
PO Box 228
Spring Lake, NJ 07762-0228, USA

Miller, George D (General)
20 Phillips Pond Rd
Natick, MA 01760-5643, USA

Miller, George T (Kennedy) (Director)
30 Orwell St King's Cross
Sydney, NSW 2011, AUSTRALIA

Miller, Glenn Birthplace Society
PO Box 61
Clarinda, IA 51632-0061

Miller, Glenn (Orchestra)
605 Crescent Executive Ct # 300
Lake Mary, FL 32746-2100

Miller, Glenn Society
18 Crendon St
High Wycombe, Bucks. ENGLAND

Miller, Harvey R (Attorney, Attorney General, General)
797 5th Ave
New York, NY 10065-8401, USA

Miller, J Ronald (Religious Leader)
21116 Washington Pkwy
Frankfort, IL 60423-3112, USA

Miller, James C III (Government Official)
1250 H St NW
Washington, DC 20005-3952, USA

Miller, Jamir (Athlete, Football Player)
331 Grenadine Way
Hercules, CA 94547-2048, USA

Miller, Janet (Stylist)
107 Shoreline Dr
Rancho Mirage, CA 92270-5813, USA

Miller, Jarod (Scientist, Talk Show Host)
c/o Staff Member *NS Bienstock Inc*
250 W 57th St Ste 333
New York, NY 10107-0302, USA

Miller, Jeff
1301 Spring Oaks Cir
Houston, TX 77055-4703

Miller, Jeff (Congressman, Politician)
2416 Rayburn Hob
Washington, DC 20515-1301, USA

Miller, Jeffrey W (Stylist)
c/o Staff Member *Art Department*
48 Greene St Fl 4
New York, NY 10013-2663, USA

Miller, Jeremy (Actor)
1812 W Burbank Blvd
Burbank, CA 91506-1315, USA

Miller, Jerry (Admiral)
750 9th St NW # 4300
Washington, DC 20560-0011, USA

Miller, Jim (Athlete, Football Player)
PO Box 863
Ripley, MS 38663-0863, USA

Miller, Jody (Musician)
PO Box 413
Blanchard, OK 73010-0413, USA

Miller, Joel McKinnon (Actor)
c/o Michael Greene *Greene & Associates*
1901 Avenue Of The Stars Ste 130
Los Angeles, CA 90067-6030, USA

Miller, John (Correspondent)
77 W 66th St
New York, NY 10023-6201, USA

Miller, John (Athlete, Baseball Player)
5105 River Ave Apt A
Newport Beach, CA 92663-2415, USA

Miller, John (Athlete, Baseball Player)
13443 Old Annapolis Rd
Mount Airy, MD 21771-7732, USA

Miller, Johnny (Athlete, Football Player)
94 Beach St
Revere, MA 02151-5006, USA

Miller, Johnny (Athlete, Golfer)
PO Box 2260
Napa, CA 94558-0060, USA

Miller, Johnny Lee (Actor)
c/o Staff Member *IFA Talent Agency*
8730 W Sunset Blvd Ste 490
Los Angeles, CA 90069-2248, USA

Miller, Jon (Baseball Player, Sportscaster)
201 Nevada Ave
Moss Beach, CA 94038-9615, USA

Miller, Jonathan (Director)
63 Gloucester Crescent
London NW1, UNITED KINGDOM (UK)

Miller, Jonny Lee (Actor)
c/o Ina Treciokas *Slate Public Relations*
9000 W Sunset Blvd Ste 915
West Hollywood, CA 90069-5809, USA

Miller, Josh (Athlete, Football Player)
16 Summer Heights Dr
Franklin, MA 02038-2365, USA

Miller, Joyce D (Misc)
1710 Broadway Frnt 3
New York, NY 10019-5254, USA

Miller, Julie (Musician, Songwriter, Writer)
5000 Oak Bluff Ct
Atlanta, GA 30350-1069, USA

Miller, Justin (Athlete, Baseball Player)
2646 Dalemead St
Torrance, CA 90505-7027, USA

Miller, Justin (Athlete, Football Player)
c/o Eugene Parker *Maximum Sports Management*
6435 W Jefferson Blvd # 197
Fort Wayne, IN 46804-6203, USA

Miller, Keith (Athlete, Baseball Player)
190 Water St # 2
Milford, MI 48381-1869, USA

Miller, Keith (Athlete, Baseball Player)
1831 W Alamosa Dr
Terrell, TX 75160-0811, USA

Miller, Keith H (Ex-Governor)
3705 Arctic Blvd
Anchorage, AK 99503-5774, USA

Miller, Kelly (Basketball Player)
125 S Pennsylvania St
Indianapolis, IN 46204-3610, USA

Miller, Kenny
5312 Eagle Lake Dr
Palm Beach Gardens, FL 33418-1539

Miller, Kristen (Actor)
409 N Camden Dr Ste 202
Beverly Hills, CA 90210-4423, USA

Miller, Kurt (Athlete, Baseball Player)
1511 Iroquois Cir
Carrollton, TX 75007-6264, USA

Miller, Lajos (Opera Singer)
Balogh Adam Utca 28
Budapest 1026, HUNGARY

Miller, Larry (Actor, Comedian)
c/o Staff Member *Brillstein Entertainment Partners*
9150 Wilshire Blvd Ste 350
Beverly Hills, CA 90212-3453, USA

Miller, Larry (Athlete, Baseball Player)
3205 E Desert Cove Ave
Phoenix, AZ 85028-2735, USA

Miller, Larry (Athlete, Football Player)
3 Cour De La Reine
Palos Hills, IL 60465-2405, USA

Miller, Lemmie (Athlete, Baseball Player)
4503 Interstate Blvd Attn Coachingstaff
Loves Park, IL 61111-5700, USA

Miller, Lennox (Athlete, Track Athlete)
2120 Pinecrest Dr
Altadena, CA 91001-2121, USA

Miller, Lenore (Misc)
30 E 29th St
New York, NY 10016-7925, USA

Miller, Linda G
242 Conway Ave
Los Angeles, CA 90024-2602, USA

Miller, M Lynn (Stylist)
434 Bronxville Rd
Bronxville, NY 10708-1116, USA

Miller, Marisa (Actor, Model)
c/o Zoe Lee *Cartel Management*
665 Lillian Way
Los Angeles, CA 90004-1107, USA

Miller, Mark (Musician)
5200 Old Harding Rd
Franklin, TN 37064-9406, USA

Miller, Mark (Athlete, Football Player)
6020 Poling Rd
Elida, OH 45807-9492, USA

Miller, Mark Thomas (Actor)
2554 Lincoln Blvd # 124
Venice, CA 90291-5082, USA

Miller, Marvin J (Director)
211 E 70th St Apt 32G
New York, NY 10021-5210, USA

Miller, Matt (Athlete, Baseball Player)
3203 61st St
Lubbock, TX 79413-5519, USA

Miller, Matt (Athlete, Football Player)
15 Highgate Cir
Ithaca, NY 14850-1429, USA

Miller, Michael (Athlete, Football Player)
2337 Kellar Ave
Flint, MI 48504-7102, USA

Miller, Mike (Athlete, Basketball Player)
9107 W 32nd St
Sioux Falls, SD 57106-4848, USA

Miller, Mildred (Opera Singer)
PO Box 110108
Pittsburgh, PA 15232-0608, USA

Miller, Mulgrew (Musician)
3725 Farmersville Rd
Easton, PA 18045-2300, USA

Miller, Nate (Boxer)
1214 Allengrove St
Philadelphia, PA 19124-2904, USA

Miller, Nicole J (Designer, Fashion Designer)
780 Madison Ave
New York, NY 10065-6108, USA

Miller, Norm (Athlete, Baseball Player)
43 Columbia Crest Pl
Spring, TX 77382-1331, USA

Miller, Oliver (Athlete, Basketball Player)
2912 S Meadow Dr
Fort Worth, TX 76133-7214, USA

Miller, Omar Benson (Actor)
c/o Stephen Tenenbaum *Morra Brezner Steinberg & Tenenbaum (MBST) Entertainment*
345 N Maple Dr Ste 200
Beverly Hills, CA 90210-5174, USA

Miller, Paul (Athlete, Baseball Player)
252 Redbud Ln
Batavia, IL 60510-3623, USA

Miller, Penelope Ann (Actor)
c/o Greg Clark *Untitled Entertainment (LA)*
350 S Beverly Dr Ste 200
Beverly Hills, CA 90212-4819, USA

Miller, Percy (Master P) (Actor, Musician)
c/o Adam Robinson *Releve Entertainment*
6255 W Sunset Blvd Ste 923
Los Angeles, CA 90028-7410, USA

Miller, Percy (Romeo) (Musician)
c/o Shannon Barr *Shannon Barr Public Relations*
3313 N Sepulveda Blvd
Manhattan Beach, CA 90266-3626, USA

Miller, Peter North (Business Person)
Dawson House 5 Jewry St
London EC3N 2EX, UNITED KINGDOM (UK)

Miller, Randy (Athlete, Baseball Player)
22523 Oak Mist Ln
Katy, TX 77494-2256, USA

Miller, Raymond (Ray) (Athlete, Baseball Player, Coach)
PO Box 41
New Athens, OH 43981-0041, USA

Miller, Reginald W (Reggie) (Athlete, Basketball Player)
3785 Puerco Canyon Rd
Malibu, CA 90265-4551, USA

Miller, Renee (Stylist)
1200 W Monroe St Apt 510
Chicago, IL 60607-2553, USA

Miller, Rick (Athlete, Baseball Player)
12790 Silverthorn Ct
Bonita Springs, FL 34135-2452, USA

Miller, Robert M (Athlete, Football Player)
8208 Rattalee Lake Rd
Clarkston, MI 48348-1736, USA

Miller, Robert N (Red) (Athlete, Coach, Football Coach, Football Player)
3841 S Narcissus Way
Denver, CO 80237-1239, USA

Miller, Rod (Athlete, Baseball Player)
413 Cabarton Rd
Cascade, ID 83611-5004, USA

Miller, Ron (Athlete, Football Player)
6392 Washington
Youngville, CA 94599, USA

Miller, Ryan (Athlete, Hockey Player)
700 Walbert Dr
E Lansing, MI 48823, USA

Miller, Scott (Athlete, Football Player)
26432 Charford Way
Lake Forest, CA 92630-6520, USA

Miller, Shannon (Athlete, Gymnast)
505 Lancaster St Apt 10AB
Jacksonville, FL 32204-4136, USA

Miller, Shawn (Athlete, Football Player)
3070 W Old Highway Rd
Morgan, UT 84050-9307, USA

Miller, Sienna (Actor)
c/o Scott Melrose *Scott Melrose*
Prefers to be contacted via email or telephone
CA, USA

Miller, Stanley L (Misc)
Chemistry
La Jolla, CA 92093-0001, USA

Miller, Stephanie (Comedian, Television Host)
3400 W Olive Ave Ste 550
Burbank, CA 91505-5544, USA

Miller, Steve (Musician, Songwriter)
PO Box 12680
Seattle, WA 98111-4680, USA

Miller, Stu (Athlete, Baseball Player)
3701 Ocaso Ct
Cameron Park, CA 95682-8961, USA

Miller, Stuart L (Stu) (Baseball Player)
3701 Ocaso Ct
Cameron Park, CA 95682-8961, USA

Miller, Tangi (Actor)
c/o Staff Member *Releve Entertainment*
6255 W Sunset Blvd Ste 923
Los Angeles, CA 90028-7410, USA

Miller, Terry (Athlete, Football Player)
9015 W 2nd Ave
Stillwater, OK 74074-6775, USA

Miller, Tom (Athlete, Football Player)
430 Grant St Apt 240
De Pere, WI 54115-2161, USA

Miller, Tracie (Stylist)
c/o Staff Member *Help Me Rhonda*
541 10th St NW # 294
Atlanta, GA 30318-5713, USA

Miller, Travis (Athlete, Baseball Player)
269 Lakengren Dr
Eaton, OH 45320-2943, USA

Miller, Trever (Athlete, Baseball Player)
24155 Hideout Trl
Land O Lakes, FL 34639-8111, USA

Miller, Ty (Actor)
c/o Staff Member *Tedesco Management*
Prefers to be contacted via telephone
Los Angeles, CA 90069, USA

Miller, Valarie Rae
3500 W Olive Ave Ste 1400
Burbank, CA 91505-5512

Miller, Von (Football Player)
c/o David Dunn *Athletes First, LLC*
3300 Irvine Ave Ste 300
Newport Beach, CA 92660-3108, USA

Miller, Wade (Athlete, Baseball Player)
12 Woods Way
Reading, PA 19610-1199, USA

Miller, Warren (Photographer)
505 Pier Ave
Hermosa Beach, CA 90254-3822, USA

Miller, Wentworth (Actor)
c/o Eryn Brown *Industry Entertainment Partners*
955 Carrillo Dr Ste 300
Los Angeles, CA 90048-5400, USA

Miller, Wiley (Artist, Cartoonist)
8 Granite Heights Rd
Kennebunkport, ME 04046-5262, USA

Miller, William (Athlete, Baseball Player)
PO Box 2681
Aptos, CA 95001-2681, USA

Miller, Willie T (Athlete, Football Player)
308 Martin Dr
Birmingham, AL 35215-1180, USA

Miller, Zell (Government Official)
303 Peachtree St NE Ste 5300
Atlanta, GA 30308-3265, USA

Millett, Kate (Writer)
20 Old Overlook Rd
Poughkeepsie, NY 12603-6220, USA

Millett, Lewis L (War Hero)
1816 S Figueroa St # 700
Los Angeles, CA 90015-3422, USA

Millette, Joe (Athlete, Baseball Player)
759 Solana Dr
Lafayette, CA 94549-5206, USA

Millhauser, John (Stylist)
c/o Staff Member *Exclusive Artists Mgmt*
7700 W Sunset Blvd Ste 205
Los Angeles, CA 90046-3913, USA

Millhauser, Steven (Writer)
235 Caroline St
Saratoga Springs, NY 12866-3505, USA

Milligan, Dustin (Actor)
c/o Deb Dillistone *Lucas Talent Inc*
100 W. Pender St Sun Tower, 7th Floor
Vancouver, BC V6B 1R8, Canada

Milligan, Randy (Athlete, Baseball Player)
6905 Real Princess Ln
Gwynn Oak, MD 21207-4577, USA

Millionaire, Tony (Artist)
c/o Staff Member *Fantagraphics Books*
7563 Lake City Way NE
Seattle, WA 98115-4218, USA

Millionaires (Music Group)
c/o Jonathan Daniel *Crush Management*
60-62 E 11th St Floor 7
New York, NY 10003, USA

Millman, Dan (Writer)
PO Box 6148
San Rafael, CA 94903-0148, USA

Millo, Aprile E (Opera Singer)
165 W 57th St
New York, NY 10019-2201, USA

Milloy, Lawyer (Athlete, Football Player)
1 Bills Dr
Orchard Park, NY 14127-2237, USA

Mills, Alan (Athlete, Baseball Player)
1811 Bellgrove St
Lakeland, FL 33805-2523, USA

Mills, Alley (Actor)
444 Carroll Canal
Venice, CA 90291-4682, USA

Mills, Bill (Athlete, Baseball Player)
4344 Commercial St
Port Charlotte, FL 33953-5945, USA

Mills, Billy (Athlete, Track Athlete)
c/o Staff Member *Billy Mills Speakers Bureau, The*
7760 Winding Way # 723
Fair Oaks, CA 95628-5735, USA

Mills, Brad (Athlete, Baseball Player)
4746 W Buena Vista Ct
Visalia, CA 93291-9112, USA

Mills, Chris (Athlete, Basketball Player)
2223 Camden Ave
Los Angeles, CA 90064-1905, USA

Mills, Curtis (Athlete, Track Athlete)
328 Lake St
Lufkin, TX 75904, USA

Mills, Dick (Athlete, Baseball Player)
10345 E Desert Cove Ave
Scottsdale, AZ 85260-6304, USA

Mills, Donna (Actor)
c/o Staff Member *Darlene Kaplan Entertainment*
4450 Balboa Ave
Encino, CA 91316-4101, USA

Mills, Eddie (Actor)
c/o Staff Member *Peter Strain & Associates Inc (LA)*
5455 Wilshire Blvd Ste 1812
Los Angeles, CA 90036-4268, USA

Mills, Erie (Opera Singer)
801 W 18th St # 20
New York, NY 10033, USA

Mills, Ernie (Athlete, Football Player)
5763 NE 34th St
Silver Springs, FL 34488-1887, USA

Mills, Frank (Composer, Musician)
PO Box 1282
Peterborough, ON K9L 7H5, CANADA

Mills, Hayley (Actor)
c/o Alan Willig *Don Buchwald & Associates Inc (NY)*
10 E 44th St Frnt 1
New York, NY 10017-3654

Mills, Heather (Activist)
1 Soho Square
London, W1V 6BQ, ENGLAND

Mills, John Henry (Athlete, Football Player)
755 Bahia Cir
Ocala, FL 34472-8831, USA

Mills, Jordan
6500 Wilshire Blvd Ste 2200
Los Angeles, CA 90048-4942

Mills, Judson (Actor)
c/o Dino May *Dino May Management*
6362 Hollywood Blvd
Los Angeles, CA 90028-6323, USA

Mills, Juliet (Actor, Writer)
442 Montana Cir
Ojai, CA 93023-1621, USA

Mills, Kyle (Writer)
c/o Staff Member *Vanguard Press*
387 Park Ave S Fl 12
New York, NY 10016-8802, USA

Mills, Leigh Ann (Athlete, Golfer)
1919 W Carmen St
Tampa, FL 33606-1225, USA

Mills, Mary (Athlete, Golfer)
310 S Ocean Blvd Apt 106
Boca Raton, FL 33432-6207, USA

Mills, Mike (Musician)
c/o Staff Member *International Creative Management (ICM-LA)*
10250 Constellation Blvd Fl 7
Los Angeles, CA 90067-6207, USA

Mills, Noah (Actor, Model)
c/o Tiffany Kuzon *Evolution Entertainment (LA)*
901 N Highland Ave
Los Angeles, CA 90038-2412, USA

Mills, Pete (Football Player)
27 Langfield Dr
Buffalo, NY 14215-3321, USA

Mills, Samuel D (Sam) Jr (Athlete, Football Player)
9 Precedent Pl
Manalapan, NJ 07726-8670, USA

Mills, Stephanie (Actor, Musician)
1995 Broadway # 501
New York, NY 10023-5882, USA

Mills, Terry (Basketball Player)
125 S Pennsylvania St
Indianapolis, IN 46204-3610, USA

Mills, William M (Billy) (Athlete, Track Athlete)
7760 Winding Way
Fair Oaks, CA 95628-5735, USA

Mills, Zach (Actor)
c/o Judy Savage *Savage Agency*
6212 Banner Ave
Los Angeles, CA 90038-2802, USA

Millsaps, Knox (Engineer)
323 NW 24th St
Gainesville, FL 32607-2693, USA

Millwood, Kevin A (Athlete, Baseball Player)
1204 Suncast Ln Ste 2
El Dorado Hills, CA 95762-9665, USA

Milmoe, Caroline (Actor)
41 S King St
Manchester M2 6DE, UNITED KINGDOM (UK)

Milne, Brian (Football Player)
15314 Willy Rd
Union City, PA 16438-8504, USA

Milner, Anthony F D (Composer)
147 Heythorp St Southfields
London SW18 5BT, UNITED KINGDOM (UK)

Milner, Brian (Athlete, Baseball Player)
11825 Elko Ln
Fort Worth, TX 76108-4783, USA

Milner, Brian (Baseball Player)
536 N Grand
Mesa, AZ 85201-5031, USA

Milner, Eddie (Athlete, Baseball Player)
491 Stambaugh Ave
Columbus, OH 43207-2565, USA

Milner, Martin (Actor)
3106 Azahar St
Carlsbad, CA 92009-8362, USA

Milnes, Sherrill E (Opera Singer)
266 W 37th St # 2000
New York, NY 10018-6609, USA

Milnor, John W (Mathematician)
3 Laurel Ln
Setauket, NY 11733-1615, USA

Milo, Sandra
Viale Liegi 42
Rome, ITALY I-00198

Milonakis, Andy (Actor)
c/o Jeff Golenberg *Collective*
8383 Wilshire Blvd Ste 1050
Beverly Hills, CA 90211-2415, USA

Milongo, Andre (Prime Minister)
Brazzaville, CONGO REPUBLIC

Milos, Sofia (Actor)
PO Box 173
Beverly Hills, CA 90213-0173, USA

Milow, Keith (Artist)
32 W 20th St
New York, NY 10011-4207, USA

Milsap, Ronnie (Musician, Songwriter)
c/o Staff Member *Buddy Lee Attractions Inc*
38 Music Sq E Ste 300
Nashville, TN 37203-4304, USA

Milsome, Doug (Cinematographer)
PO Box 1156
Studio City, CA 91614-0156, USA

Milstead, Charles (Football Player)
14414 Sandalin Dr
Cypress, TX 77429-1861, USA

Milstead, Rod (Athlete, Football Player)
11815 Brookeville Landing Ct
Bowie, MD 20721-4502, USA

Milstein, Elliott (Educator)
President's Office
Washington, DC 20016, USA

Milteer, Lee (Business Person, Writer)
2100 Thoroughgood Rd
Virginia Beach, VA 23455-4015, USA

Milton, DeLisha (Basketball Player)
Staples Center 1111 S Figueroa St
Los Angeles, CA 90015, USA

Milton, Eric (Athlete, Baseball Player)
1133 Asquith Dr
Arnold, MD 21012-2153, USA

Milva
9 Via Gabrio Serbelloni
Milan, ITALY I-20122

Mimbs, Michael (Athlete, Baseball Player)
2761 Mimbs Rd
Alamo, GA 30411-2502, USA

Mimoun, Alain (Athlete, Track Athlete)
27 Ave Edouard-Jenner
Champigny-sur-Marne 94500, FRANCE

Mims (Musician)
c/o Michael Schweiger *CEG Talent*
251 W 39th St Fl 7
New York, NY 10018-3171, USA

Mims, Madeline Manning (Athlete, Track Athlete)
7477 E 48th St # 83-4
Tulsa, OK 74145-6679, USA

Min, Gao (Misc)
9 Tuyuguan
Beijing, CHINA

Minaj, Nicki (Musician)
c/o Gee Roberson *Hip Hop Since 1978*
1290 Avenue of the Americas Fl 26
New York, NY 10104-0101, USA

Minarcin, Rudy (Athlete, Baseball Player)
1037 1st St
Vandergrift, PA 15690-1007, USA

Minarik, Henry (Athlete, Football Player)
1001 N Linda Ln
Lake City, MI 49651-9227, USA

Minaya, Omar Minaya (Business Person)
33 Dimas Ct
Harrington Park, NJ 07640-1604, USA

Mincer, Jacob (Economist)
448 Riverside Dr
New York, NY 10027-6819, USA

Mincher, Don (Athlete, Baseball Player)
5605 Criner Rd SE
Huntsville, AL 35802-1858, USA

Minchey, Nate (Athlete, Baseball Player)
1212 Ramble Creek Dr
Pflugerville, TX 78660-2155, USA

Mincy, Charles (Athlete, Football Player)
2227 W 24th St Apt 7
Los Angeles, CA 90018-1944, USA

Mincy, Purnell (Baseball Player)
127 W 96th St Apt 160
New York, NY 10025-6427, USA

Mindel, Lee F (Architect)
56 W 22nd St Fl 12
New York, NY 10010-7279, USA

Mindell, Earl (Writer)
PO Box 5100
Carlsbad, CA 92018-5100

Mindless Behavior (Music Group)
c/o Troy Carter *Atom Factory/Coalition Media Group*
10351 Washington Blvd
Culver City, CA 90232-3149, USA

Minds, Simple (Music Group)
c/o Staff Member *Solo Agency Ltd (UK)*
55 Fulham High St 2nd Floor
London SW6 3JJ, United Kingdom

Minear, Tim (Director, Writer)
c/o Lawrence Shuman *Shuman Company*
3815 Hughes Ave Fl 4
Culver City, CA 90232-2715, USA

Minehan, Cathy E (Financier, Government Official)
600 Atlantic Ave
Boston, MA 02210-2211, USA

Miner, Roger J (Judge)
445 Broadway Ste 414
Albany, NY 12207-2926, USA

Miner, Steve (Director)
1137 2nd St Ste 103
Santa Monica, CA 90403-5069, USA

Minervini, Craig (Athlete, Baseball Player)
229 Cameron Dr
Weston, FL 33326-3515, USA

Mineta, Norman Y (Secretary)
400 7th St SW
Washington, DC 20590, USA

Minetto, Craig (Athlete, Baseball Player)
1809 Lakeshore Dr
Lodi, CA 95242-4230, USA

Ming, Tsai (Chef)
1180 Avenue of the Americas # 1200
New York, NY 10036-8401, USA

Ming, Yao (Athlete, Basketball Player)
18923 Crescent Bay Dr
Houston, TX 77094-3329, USA

Ming Wang, Chien (Athlete, Baseball Player)
c/o Team Member *New York Yankees*
Yankee Stadium 161st St & River Ave
Bronx, NY 10451, USA

Mingenbach, Louise (Designer)
c/o Wayne Fitterman *United Talent Agency (UTA)*
9560 Wilshire Blvd Fl 5
Beverly Hills, CA 90212-2400, USA

Minghella, Max (Actor)
c/o Tony Lipp *Anonymous Content (AC-LA)*
2000 Avenue of the Stars
Los Angeles, CA 90067-4700, USA

Ming-Na, Wen (Actor)
c/o Troy Nankin *Wishlab*
2438 Canyon Oak Dr
Los Angeles, CA 90068-2428, USA

Mingo, Gene (Athlete, Football Player)
5701 E Colorado Ave
Denver, CO 80224-2102, USA

Mingori, Steve (Athlete, Baseball Player)
8841 N Congress Ave Apt 637
Kansas City, MO 64153-1914, USA

Mingus, Charles
484 W 43rd St Apt 43S
New York, NY 10036-6327

Minh, Tran (Choreographer, Dancer)
2014 NE 47th Ave
Portland, OR 97213-2016, USA

Miniefield, Kevin (Athlete, Football Player)
1030 Lakehurst Dr
Waukegan, IL 60085-8232, USA

Minisi, Anthony S (Skip) (Athlete, Football Player)
300 Continental Ln
Paoli, PA 19301-2043, USA

Mink, Rep (Politician)
PO Box 50144
Honolulu, HI 96850-5544

Minka (Adult Film Star)
8635 W Sahara Ave # 564
Las Vegas, NV 89117-5858, USA

Minkoff, Rob (Director, Producer)
c/o Rand Holston *Creative Artists Agency (CAA-LA)*
2000 Avenue of the Stars Ste 100
Los Angeles, CA 90067-4705, USA

Minnelli, Liza (Actor, Musician, Producer)
c/o Liz Rosenberg *Warner Bros Records (NY)*
75 Rockefeller Plz
New York, NY 10019-6908, USA

Minnick, Don (Athlete, Baseball Player)
215 Bernard Rd
Rocky Mount, VA 24151-2243, USA

Minniear, Randy (Athlete, Football Player)
6506 Loon Dr
Nineveh, IN 46164-9119, USA

Minniefield, Dick (Athlete, Basketball Player)
10902 Little Gap Ct
Sugar Land, TX 77498-0946, USA

Minnifield, Frank (Athlete, Football Player)
4809 Chaffey Ln
Lexington, KY 40515-1166, USA

Minnillo, Vanessa (Actor, Television Host)
c/o Melissa Raubvogel *Baker Winokur Ryder Public Relations BWR (BWR-NY)*
292 Madison Ave Fl 12
New York, NY 10017-6415, USA

Minogue, Dannii (Actor, Musician)
c/o Melissa LeGear *Melissa LeGear Management*
329 Montague St
Albert Park, Victoria 3206, Australia

Minogue, Kylie (Actor, Musician)
c/o Allsion MacGregor *Terry Blamey Management*
PO Box 13196
London SW6 4WF, UNITED KINGDOM (UK)

Minor, Blas (Athlete, Baseball Player)
7139 Dean St
Winton, CA 95388-9766, USA

Minor, Claudie (Athlete, Football Player)
730 17th St Ste 520
Denver, CO 80202-3539, USA

Minor, Damon (Athlete, Baseball Player)
413 N Chautauqua St
Sedan, KS 67361-1123, USA

Minor, Greg (Athlete, Basketball Player)
13814 Bluebird Park Rd
Windermere, FL 34786-3113, USA

Minor, Kory (Athlete, Football Player)
1402 W Farlington St
West Covina, CA 91790-3354, USA

Minor, Lincoln (Athlete, Football Player)
720 Carrollwood Village Dr
Gretna, LA 70056-6001, USA

Minor, Mark (Athlete, Basketball Player)
5693 Muldoon Ct
Dublin, OH 43016-4334, USA

Minor, Rickey (Director, Musical Director)
c/o Staff Member *WmE2 (WMA-LA)*
1 William Morris Pl
Beverly Hills, CA 90212-4261, USA

Minor, Ronald R (Religious Leader)
4901 Pennsylvania Ave
Joplin, MO 64804-4947, USA

Minor, Ryan (Athlete, Baseball Player)
5727 Cairn Ct
Salisbury, MD 21801-2340, USA

Minor, Shane (Musician)
838 N Doheny Dr Apt 302
West Hollywood, CA 90069-4849, USA

Minor, Susie (Stylist)
1544 Michigan Ave
Miami, FL 33139-3310, USA

Minor, Travis (Athlete, Football Player)
PO Box 1635
Hallandale, FL 33008-1635, USA

Minoso, Minnie (Basketball Player, Coach)
c/o Jim Stocchero 25449 W Ruff St
Plainfield, IL 60585, USA

Minoso, Minnle (Athlete, Baseball Player)
3700 N Lake Shore Dr Apt 303
Chicago, IL 60613-4244, USA

Minow, Newton N (Government Official)
179 E Lake Shore Dr # 15W
Chicago, IL 60611-1340, USA

Minshall, Jim (Athlete, Baseball Player)
615 Manatee Ave
Ellenton, FL 34222-2249, USA

Minshew, Alicia (Actor)
c/o Seth Greenky *Green Key Mgmt (NY)*
251 W 89th St Apt 4A
New York, NY 10024-1713, USA

Minsky, Marvin L (Scientist)
Computer Sci Dept
Cambridge, MA 2139, USA

Mint Condition (Musician)
c/o Staff Member *Green Light Talent Agency*
PO Box 3172
Beverly Hills, CA 90212-0172, USA

Minter, Barry (Athlete, Football Player)
2626 Garcitas Crk
Richmond, TX 77406-1961, USA

Minter, Cedric (Athlete, Football Player)
5653 E Bay Trail Ct
Boise, ID 83716-7031, USA

Minter, Kelly (Actor)
c/o John Ly *John Ly Agency*
PO Box 2607
Toluca Lake, CA 91610-0607, USA

Minter, Kristin (Actor)
c/o Charles Silver *Silver Massetti & Szatmary (SMS) Talent Inc*
8730 W Sunset Blvd Ste 440
Los Angeles, CA 90069-2277, USA

Minter, Mike (Athlete, Football Player)
3661 Richwood Cir
Kannapolis, NC 28081-6704, USA

Minter, Patricia (Stylist)
2056 W Belle Plaine Ave
Chicago, IL 60618-3040, USA

Mintoff, Dominic (Prime Minister)
Olives Xintill St
Tarxien, MALTA

Minton, Greg (Athlete, Baseball Player)
690 N Muleshoe Rd
Apache Junction, AZ 85119-9868, USA

Minton, Yvonne F (Opera Singer)
26 Wadham Road
London SW15 2LR, UNITED KINGDOM (UK)

Mintz, Shiomo (Musician)
40 W 57th St
New York, NY 10019-4001, USA

Mintz, Steve (Athlete, Baseball Player)
128 Forest Hills Dr
Leland, NC 28451-9744, USA

Mintz-Plasse, Christopher (Actor)
c/o Josh Katz *United Talent Agency (UTA)*
9560 Wilshire Blvd Fl 5
Beverly Hills, CA 90212-2400, USA

Minutelli, Gino (Athlete, Baseball Player)
3305 Foxtrot Ct
Spring Hill, TN 37174-7116, USA

Miou-Miou (Actor)
20 Ave Rapp
Paris 75008, FRANCE

Mir, Isabelle (Athlete, Skier)
Saint-Lary 65170, France

Mira, George (Athlete, Football Player)
19225 SW 128th Ct
Miami, FL 33177-4222, USA

Mirabella, Paul (Athlete, Baseball Player)
125 Jenks Rd
Morristown, NJ 07960-8701, USA

Mirabelli, Doug (Athlete, Baseball Player)
9788 Edgewood Ave
Traverse City, MI 49685-8173, USA

Miracles, The
141 Dunbar Ave
Fords, NJ 08863-1551

Miranda, Christianne (Musician, Songwriter, Writer)
c/o Staff Member *Kult Records*
38 W 36th St Fl 3
New York, NY 10018-8078, USA

Miranda, Lin-Manuel (Actor)
c/o Brian Liebman *Liebman Entertainment*
25 E 21st St PH
New York, NY 10010-6226, USA

Miranda, Patricia (Wrestler)
Stanford University Arrillaga Family Sports Center
Stanford, CA 94305-6150, USA

Miranda, Willie
5502 Whitwood Rd
Baltimore, MD 21206-3748

Mirchoff, Beau (Actor)
c/o Scott Fish *Vital Management Group (VMG)*
5225 Wilshire Blvd Ste 303
Los Angeles, CA 90036-4347, USA

Mirer, Rick
11220 NE 53rd St
Kirkland, WA 98033-7505

Miriciolu, Nelly (Opera Singer)
53 Midhurst Ave Muswell Hill
London N10, UNITED KINGDOM (UK)

Mirikitani, Janice (Writer)
330 Ellis St
San Francisco, CA 94102-2735, USA

Mirisch, Walter M (Producer)
647 Warner Ave
Los Angeles, CA 90024-2566, USA

Mirkerevic, Dragen (Prime Minister)
Vojvode Putnkia 3
Sarajevo 71000, BOSNIA & HERZEGOVINA

Mirkin, David (Actor, Director)
c/o David Gersh *Gersh (LA)*
9465 Wilshire Blvd Ste 600
Beverly Hills, CA 90212-2612, USA

Mirnyi, Max (Athlete, Tennis Player)
c/o Staff Member *ATP Tour*
201 Atp Tour Blvd
Ponte Vedra Beach, FL 32082-3211, USA

Mironov, Boris (Athlete, Hockey Player)
2 Penn Plz
New York, NY 10121-0101, USA

Mironov, Dmitri (Athlete, Hockey Player)
2000 E Gene Autry Way
Anaheim, CA 92806-6143, USA

Mironov, Yevgeniy V (Actor)
Chaokygina Str 12A
Moscow, RUSSIA

Mirra, Dave (Athlete)
12100 W Olympic Blvd Ste 400
Los Angeles, CA 90064-1052, USA

Mirren, Helen (Actor, Director, Producer)
c/o Melissa Sun *Stan Rosenfield & Associates*
2029 Century Park E Ste 1190
Los Angeles, CA 90067-2931, USA

Mirrlees, James A (Nobel Prize Laureate)
Economics Dept
Cambridge CB2 1TQ, UNITED KINGDOM (UK)

Mirza, Dia (Actor)
G-41, Saket
New Delhi 110017, India

Mirza, Sania (Athlete, Tennis Player)
c/o Staff Member *Globosport India Pvt Ltd*
G-41, Saket
New Dehli 110017, India

Mirzoev, Akbar (Prime Minister)
Dushaube, TAJIKISTAN

Misaka, Walt (Athlete, Basketball Player)
173 Aruba Dr
Saratoga Springs, UT 84045-5115, USA

Misch, Patrick (Athlete, Baseball Player)
725 N Dobson Rd Apt 255
Chandler, AZ 85224-9110, USA

Mischak, Bob (Athlete, Football Player)
73 Brookwood Rd Unit 12
Orinda, CA 94563-3310, USA

Mischka, Badgley (Designer, Fashion Designer)
525 Seventh Ave Fl 14
New York, NY 10018, USA

Mischke, Carl H (Religious Leader)
1034 Buena Vista Dr
Sun Prairie, WI 53590-2031, USA

Misersky, Antje (Athlete)
Grenzgraben 3A
Stutzerbach 98714, GERMANY

Misiano, Christopher (Director)
c/o Staff Member *Creative Artists Agency (CAA-LA)*
2000 Avenue of the Stars Ste 100
Los Angeles, CA 90067-4705, USA

Misiano, Vincent (Director)
c/o Staff Member *Creative Artists Agency (CAA-LA)*
2000 Avenue of the Stars Ste 100
Los Angeles, CA 90067-4705, USA

Mison, Tom (Actor)
c/o Ben Mison 32 St Johns Rd
Woking GU21 7SA, GB

Misraki, Paul
35 Av Bugeaud
Paris, FRANCE F-75116

Miss Teen USA
6420 Wilshire Blvd
Los Angeles, CA 90048-5502

Missick, Dorian (Actor)
c/o Myrna Jacoby *MJ Management*
130 W 57th St Apt 11A
New York, NY 10019-3311, USA

Missing Persons
11935 Laurel Hills Rd
Studio City, CA 91604-3726

Misterek, Hope (Stylist)
10812 Forbes Creek Dr Apt V307
Kirkland, WA 98033-5078, USA

Mistler, John (Athlete, Football Player)
3111 E Desert Flower Ln
Phoenix, AZ 85048-8331, USA

Mistral, Fernanda (Actor)
c/o Staff Member *Telefe - Argentina*
Pavon 2444 (C1248AAT)
Buenos Aires, ARGENTINA

Mistry, Jimi (Actor)
c/o Staff Member *WmE2 (Endeavor-LA)*
9601 Wilshire Blvd Fl 3
Beverly Hills, CA 90210-5219, USA

Misuraca, Mike (Athlete, Baseball Player)
2203 Kingsbridge Ct
San Dimas, CA 91773-3723, USA

Miszak, Anna Cepinska (Beauty Pageant Winner)
c/o Staff Member *Miss World Ltd*
21 Golden Sq
London W1R 3PA, UNITED KINGDOM (UK)

Mitchell, Aaron (Athlete, Football Player)
1701 Broadway Attn Athleticdept
Seattle, WA 98122-2413, USA

Mitchell, Andrea (Correspondent)
2710 Chain Bridge Rd NW
Washington, DC 20016-3404, USA

Mitchell, Betsy (Swimmer)
1 Lyman Cir
Cleveland, OH 44122-2110, USA

Mitchell, Beverley (Actor)
c/o Barry McPherson *Agency for the Performing Arts (APA-LA)*
405 S Beverly Dr Ste 500
Beverly Hills, CA 90212-4425, USA

Mitchell, Beverly (Actor)
c/o Staff Member *Forster Entertainment*
12533 Woodgreen St
Los Angeles, CA 90066-2723, USA

Mitchell, Billy (Misc)
4799 Hollywood Blvd
Hollywood, FL 33021-6503, USA

Mitchell, Bobby (Athlete, Baseball Player)
13887 Torrey Bella Ct
San Diego, CA 92129-4628, USA

Mitchell, Bobby (Athlete, Golfer)
435 Wimbish Dr
Danville, VA 24541-5823, USA

Mitchell, Bobby (Athlete, Football Player)
450 Blue Beech Way
Chesapeake, VA 23320-3812, USA

Mitchell, Bobby (Athlete, Baseball Player)
8697 Tiogawoods Dr
Sacramento, CA 95828-5116, USA

Mitchell, Brian (Actor)
5307B Wilkinson Ave Unit 20
Valley Village, CA 91607-2464, USA

Mitchell, Brian K (Football Player)
c/o Staff Member *Maxx Sports & Entertainment*
546 5th Ave Fl 6
New York, NY 10036-5000, USA

Mitchell, Brian Stokes (Actor, Musician)
243 W 98th St Apt 5C
New York, NY 10025-5566, USA

Mitchell, Charlie (Athlete, Baseball Player)
5017 Hasty Dr
Nashville, TN 37211-5345, USA

Mitchell, Craig (Athlete, Baseball Player)
PO Box 174
Elk, CA 95432-0174, USA

Mitchell, Dale (Athlete, Football Player)
2156 Stone Castle
Fallbrook, CA 92028-4489, USA

Mitchell, Darryl (Actor)
c/o Staff Member *Forster Entertainment*
12533 Woodgreen St
Los Angeles, CA 90066-2723, USA

Mitchell, Daryl (Chill) (Actor)
c/o Jenny Delaney *Jenny Delaney Management*
3238 Fond Dr
Encino, CA 91436-4206, USA

Mitchell, Don (Actor)
4139 S Cloverdale Ave
Los Angeles, CA 90008-1034, USA

Mitchell, Donald (Athlete, Football Player)
5620 Minner Dr
Beaumont, TX 77708-4515, USA

Mitchell, Eddy
40 Av Sainte Foy
Neuilly, FRANCE 92200

Mitchell, Edgar D (Astronaut)
PO Box 540037
Greenacres, FL 33454-0037, USA

Mitchell, Elizabeth (Actor)
c/o Ben Levine *Kritzer Levine Wilkins Entertainment*
11872 La Grange Ave Fl 1
Los Angeles, CA 90025-5283, USA

Mitchell, Elvis (Producer, Radio Personality, Writer)
1900 Pico Blvd
Santa Monica, CA 90405-1628, USA

Mitchell, Freddie (Athlete, Football Player)
PO Box 23901
Tampa, FL 33623-3901, USA

Mitchell, George J (Politician, Senator)
1251 Avenue of the Americas
New York, NY 10020-1104, USA

Mitchell, Harris A (War Hero)
2701 Dees St
San Marcos, TX 78666-5074, USA

Mitchell, Helen (Stylist)
c/o Staff Member *Judy Casey Inc*
114 E 13th St
New York, NY 10003-5329, USA

Mitchell, Jack (Photographer)
1413 Live Oak St
New Smyrna Beach, FL 32168-7740, USA

Mitchell, Jeff (Athlete, Football Player)
14747 Ballantyne Country Club Dr
Charlotte, NC 28277-2716, USA

Mitchell, Jessie (Baseball Player)
1964 Cherry Ave
Birmingham, AL 35214-1802, USA

Mitchell, Jim H (Athlete, Football Player)
120 Twin Creek Ter
Forest, VA 24551-1328, USA

Mitchell, Jim R (Athlete, Football Player)
1655 Centerview Dr Apt 222
Duluth, GA 30096-7696, USA

Mitchell, John (Athlete, Baseball Player)
5017 Hasty Dr
Nashville, TN 37211-5345, USA

Mitchell, John Cameron (Actor, Director)
c/o Richie Jackson *Jackson Group Entertainment*
345 W 13th St
New York, NY 10014-1210, USA

Mitchell, Joni (Musician)

Mitchell, Keith (Athlete, Baseball Player)
731 S 42nd St
San Diego, CA 92113-1813, USA

Mitchell, Keith C (Prime Minister)
Ministerial Complex 6th Fl Botanical Gardens
Saint George's, GRENADA

Mitchell, Kel (Actor)
c/o Staff Member *Nine Yards Entertainment*
8530 Wilshire Blvd Ste 550
Beverly Hills, CA 90211-3133, USA

Mitchell, Ken (Athlete, Football Player)
4313 Cityview Dr
Plano, TX 75093-3236, USA

Mitchell, Kenneth (Actor)
c/o Stephen (Steve) Small *Paradigm (LA)*
360 N Crescent Dr
Beverly Hills, CA 90210-4874, USA

Mitchell, Kevin (Athlete, Baseball Player)
3869 Ocean View Blvd
San Diego, CA 92113-1736, USA

Mitchell, Kevin (Athlete, Football Player)
c/o Roosevelt Barnes *Maximum Sports Management*
6435 W Jefferson Blvd # 197
Fort Wayne, IN 46804-6203, USA

Mitchell, Kim (Musician)
41 Britain St # 305
Toronto, ON M5A 1R7, Canada

Mitchell, Larry (Athlete, Baseball Player)
1040 Preston Ave
Charlottesville, VA 22903-2109, USA

Mitchell, Leland (Athlete, Basketball Player)
Route 5 Box 4
Starksville, MS 39759, USA

Mitchell, Leona (Opera Singer)
165 W 57th St
New York, NY 10019-2201, USA

Mitchell, Leroy (Athlete, Football Player)
6598 N Pinewood Dr
Parker, CO 80134-6356, USA

Mitchell, Lydell D (Athlete, Football Player)
702 Reservoir St
Baltimore, MD 21217-4632, USA

Mitchell, Lynne (Stylist)
c/o Staff Member *Crews*
828 Clemont Dr NE
Atlanta, GA 30306-3694, USA

Mitchell, Mack (Athlete, Football Player)
1200 Maynard St
Diboll, TX 75941-2602, USA

Mitchell, Michael (Actor)
c/o Abby Bluestone *Innovative Artists (LA)*
1505 10th St
Santa Monica, CA 90401-2805, USA

Mitchell, Mike (Director)
c/o Gregory McKnight *Creative Artists Agency (CAA-LA)*
2000 Avenue of the Stars Ste 100
Los Angeles, CA 90067-4705, USA

Mitchell, Mike (Athlete, Basketball Player)
3986 Flakes Mill Rd
Decatur, GA 30034-5829, USA

Mitchell, Murray (Athlete, Basketball Player)
401 Northshore Blvd Apt 905
Portland, TX 78374-3807, USA

Mitchell, Paul (Athlete, Baseball Player)
23 Carr Rd
Berlin, MA 01503-1116, USA

Mitchell, Pete (Athlete, Football Player)
100 Paddock Pl
Ponte Vedra Beach, FL 32082-3957, USA

Mitchell, Radha (Actor)
c/o Rick Ax *Gold Coast Management*
438 S Venice Blvd Apt 5
Venice, CA 90291-4695, USA

Mitchell, Rick (DJ)
c/o Staff Member *Diva Central Inc*
7510 W Sunset Blvd Ste 1445
Los Angeles, CA 90046-3408, USA

Mitchell, Robert (Baseball Player)
2009 Elmwood Ave
Tampa, FL 33605-6625, USA

Mitchell, Roger (Director, Producer)
c/o Beth Swofford *Creative Artists Agency (CAA-LA)*
2000 Avenue of the Stars Ste 100
Los Angeles, CA 90067-4705, USA

Mitchell, Roger (Athlete, Football Player)
500 E Chaminade Dr
Hollywood, FL 33021-5853, USA

Mitchell, Roland (Athlete, Football Player)
PO Box 5701
Lake Charles, LA 70606-5701, USA

Mitchell, Roscoe E Jr (Composer, Musician)
6629 University Ave Ste 206
Middleton, WI 53562-3037, USA

Mitchell, Russ (Correspondent, Television Host)
c/o Staff Member *CBS News Productions*
524 W 57th St Fl 8
New York, NY 10019-2930, USA

Mitchell, Sam (Athlete, Basketball Player, Coach)
73 Smokerise Pt
Peachtree City, GA 30269-4068, USA

Mitchell, Sasha (Actor)
9057 A Nemo St # A
West Hollywood, CA 90069, USA

Mitchell, Scott (Athlete, Football Player)
5060 Franklin Rd
Bloomfield Hills, MI 48302-2614, USA

Mitchell, Shareen (Actor)
9255 W Sunset Blvd Ste 710
Los Angeles, CA 90069-3304, USA

Mitchell, Sharon
1122 White Rock Dr
Dixon, IL 61021-9049

Mitchell, Shirley
10635 Santa Monica Blvd Ste 130
Los Angeles, CA 90025-8306

Mitchell, Steve (Actor)
c/o Staff Member *Select Artists Ltd (CA-Westside Office)*
1138 12th St Apt 1
Santa Monica, CA 90403-5459, USA

Mitchell, Susan (Writer)
English Dept
Boca Raton, FL 33431, USA

Mitchell, Todd (Athlete, Basketball Player)
4134 Emmajean Rd
Toledo, OH 43607-1015, USA

Mitchell, Tom (Athlete, Football Player)
1421 SW 49th Ter
Cape Coral, FL 33914-6934, USA

Mitchell, Vernessa (Musician)
c/o Staff Member *Diva Central Inc*
7510 W Sunset Blvd Ste 1445
Los Angeles, CA 90046-3408, USA

Mitchell, Warren
28 Sheldon Ave
London, ENGLAND N6

Mitchison, N Avrion (Biologist)
14 Belitha Villas
London N1 1PD, UNITED KINGDOM (UK)

Mitchum, Carrie (Actor)
1501 Main St Ste 204
Venice, CA 90291-3699, USA

Mithun, Chakraborty (Actor, Bollywood)
Monarch Hotel
Ooty, TN, INDIA

Mitinger, Bob (Athlete, Football Player)
2147 E College Ave
State College, PA 16801-7204, USA

Mitra, Rhona (Actor)
c/o Jason Weinberg *Untitled Entertainment (LA)*
350 S Beverly Dr Ste 200
Beverly Hills, CA 90212-4819, USA

Mitre, Sergio (Athlete, Baseball Player)
1707 Summer Sky St
Chula Vista, CA 91915-1846, USA

Mitrione, Matt (Athlete, Football Player)
729 Toddsbury Ln
Richmond, IN 47374-7152, USA

Mitrov, Miliana (Stylist)
c/o Staff Member *Perrella Management*
330 W 38th St Rm 1407
New York, NY 10018-8435, USA

Mitsotakis, Constantine (Prime Minister)
1 Aravantinou St
Athens 106 74, GREECE

Mitsoula, Jana (Actor)
c/o Dylan Thomas Collingwood #300 - 100 West Pender St
Vancouver, BC V6B 1R8, CANADA

Mitta, Aleksander N (Director)
Malaya Gruzinskaya Str 28 #105
Moscow 123557, RUSSIA

Mittal, Lakshmi (Business Person)
15th Floor Hofplein 20
Rotterdam 3032, NETHERLANDS

Mitte, RJ (Actor)
c/o Addison Witt *Witt Management*
255 S Grand Ave Apt 1505
Los Angeles, CA 90012-3043, USA

Mittermaier, Rosi
Winklmoosalm
Reit im Winkl, GERMANY D-83242

Mittermaier-Neureuther, Rosi (Skier)
Winkelmoosalm
Reit Im Winkel 83242, GERMANY

Mittermayer, Tatjana (Skier)
Bucha 2A
Lenggries, GERMANY

Mitterwald, George (Athlete, Baseball Player)
5314 Kenyon Rd
Orlando, FL 32810-1714, USA

Mitts, Heather (Soccer Player)
18400 Avalon Blvd Ste 500
Carson, CA 90746-2183, USA

Mitz, Alonzo (Athlete, Football Player)
2609 NE 4th St Apt 216
Renton, WA 98056-4053, USA

Mitzelfeld, Jim (Journalist)
969 N Lebanon St
Arlington, VA 22205-1455, USA

Mivelaz, Betty (Bowler)
6671 Shadygrove St
Tujunga, CA 91042-3348, USA

Mix, Bryant (Athlete, Football Player)
37 Greenwood Plantation Rd
Natchez, MS 39120-8946, USA

Mix, Ronald J (Ron) (Athlete, Football Player)
2317 Caminito Recodo
San Diego, CA 92107-1529, USA

Mix, Steve (Athlete, Basketball Player)
25743 Willowbend Rd
Perrysburg, OH 43551-9787, USA

Mix Master Mike (DJ)
c/o Staff Member *Agency Group Ltd, The (UK)*
361-373 City Rd
London EC1V 1PQ, UK

Mixon, Billy (Athlete, Football Player)
4145 Woodvale St
Jackson, MS 39211-6541, USA

Mixon, Ken (Athlete, Football Player)
3225 E Quayside Dr
Hollywood, FL 33026-3788, USA

Mixson, J Wayne (Ex-Governor)
2219 Demeron Rd
Tallahassee, FL 32308-0943, USA

Miyamura, Hiroshi H (War Hero)
1905 Mossman Ave
Gallup, NM 87301-4831, USA

Miyazaki, Hayao (Animator)
1-4-25 Kajinocho
Koganeishi 184, JAPAN

Miyazawa, Kiichi (Prime Minister)
6-34-1 Jingu-Mae Shibuyaku
Tokyo 150, JAPAN

Mize, John D (War Hero)
112 Sunset Dr
Belmond, IA 50421-1733, USA

Mize, Larry (Athlete, Golfer)
PO Box 1748
Fortson, GA 31808-1748, USA

Mize, Ola L (War Hero)
211 Hartwood Dr
Gadsden, AL 35901-6228, USA

Mize, Ola Lee
311 W Hartwood Dr
Gadsden, AL 35906-6220, USA

Mizerak, Steve (Billiards Player)
140 Alfred St
Edison, NJ 08820-3839, USA

Mizerock, John (Athlete, Baseball Player, Coach)
1189 Leasure Run Rd
Rochester Mills, PA 15771-7507, USA

Mizrahi, Isaac (Fashion Designer, Television Host)
475 10th Ave Fl 4
New York, NY 10018-9723, USA

Mizrahie, Barbara (Athlete, Golfer)
6440 Park Lake Cir
Boynton Beach, FL 33437-3228, USA

Mkapa, Benjamin William (President)
State House PO Box 9120
Dar es Salaam, TANZANIA

Mlicki, Dave (Athlete, Baseball Player)
5350 Reserve Dr
Dublin, OH 43017-8404, USA

Mlkvy, Bill (Basketball Player)
586 Linton Hill Rd
Newtown, PA 18940-1204, USA

Mmahat, Kevin (Athlete, Baseball Player)
5500 Erlanger Rd
Kenner, LA 70065-1534, USA

Mnookin, Robert H (Attorney, Attorney General, Educator, General)
10 Follen St
Cambridge, MA 02138-3503, USA

Mnouchkine, Ariane (Director)
Cartoucherie
Paris 75012, FRANCE

Moakler, Shanna (Actor, Model, Reality TV Star)
c/o Lizzie Grubman *Lizzie Grubman Public Relations*
270 Lafayette St Ste 504
New York, NY 10012-0048, USA

Moates, Dave (Athlete, Baseball Player)
7906 4th Ave W
Bradenton, FL 34209-3254, USA

Moats, David (Journalist)
PO Box 668
Rutland, VT 05702-0668, USA

Mobb Deep (Music Group)
c/o Staff Member *Interscope Records (NY)*
1755 Broadway
New York, NY 10019-3743, USA

Mobley, Cuttino (Athlete, Basketball Player)
c/o Staff Member *Britto Agency PR*
234 W 56th St PH
New York, NY 10019-4302, USA

Mobley, Mary Ann (Actor, Beauty Pageant Winner)
2751 Hutton Dr
Beverly Hills, CA 90210-1215, USA

Mobley, Rudy (Athlete, Football Player)
RR 3
Ahoskie, NC 27910, USA

Mobley, Singor (Athlete, Football Player)
2123 US Highway 80 E
Mesquite, TX 75150-5549, USA

Mobley, William H (Educator)
4312 Ravine Ridge Trl
Austin, TX 78746-1283, USA

Moby (Actor, Composer, Musician)
c/o Staff Member *Mute Records*
43 Brook Green
London W6 7EF, UK

Moceanu, Dominique (Gymnast)
4676 McLeod Rd
Orlando, FL 32811, USA

Mochrie, Colin (Actor)
385 Adelaide St W
Toronto, ON M5V 1S4, CANADA

Mochrie, Dottie (Athlete, Golfer)
15 Blazing Star Trl
Landrum, SC 29356-3305, USA

Mockett, Cathy (Athlete, Golfer)
1601 Antigua Way
Newport Beach, CA 92660-4345, USA

Mocumbi, Pascoal (Prime Minister)
Avenida Julius Nyerere 1780
Maputo, MOZAMBIQUE

Moczynski, Betty (Baseball Player)
5209 Lakeside Dr
Greendale, WI 53129-1924, USA

Modano, Mike (Athlete, Hockey Player)
6424 Mimosa Ln
Dallas, TX 75230-5137, USA

Modell, Arthur B (Football Executive)
Ravens Stadium 11001 Russell St
Baltimore, MD 21230, USA

Modell, Frank (Cartoonist)
115 Three Mile Crse
Guilford, CT 06437-2522, USA

Modern Talking
56200 Hoehr-Grenzhausen
, GERMANY

Modernaires, The
11761 E Speedway Blvd
Tucson, AZ 85748-2017

Modine, Matthew (Actor, Director, Producer)
c/o Elise Konialian *Untitled Entertainment (NY)*
322 8th Ave Ste 601
New York, NY 10001-6715, USA

Modrow, Hans (Prime Minister)
Frankfurter Tor 6
Berlin 10243, GERMANY

Modrzejewski, Robert J (War Hero)
4725 Oporto Ct
San Diego, CA 92124-2446, USA

Modugno, Lori (Stylist)
c/o Staff Member *Stockland Martel*
343 E 18th St
New York, NY 10003-2802, USA

Modzelewski, Ed (Athlete, Football Player)
PO Box 4207
Sedona, AZ 86340-4207, USA

Modzelewski, Richard B (Dick) (Athlete, Football Player)
1 Pier Pt
New Bern, NC 28562-8820, USA

Moe (Music Group)
c/o Staff Member *Paradigm (Monterey)*
404 W Franklin St
Monterey, CA 93940-2303, USA

Moe, Douglas E (Doug) (Athlete, Basketball Player)
13 Arnold Palmer
San Antonio, TX 78257-1722, USA

Moe, Thomas S (Tommy) (Skier)
1556 Hidden Ln
Anchorage, AK 99501-4916, USA

Moe, Tommy
2138 Churchill Dr
Anchorage, AK 99517-1389

Moegle, Dick (Athlete, Football Player)
4047 Aberdeen Way
Houston, TX 77025-2305, USA

Moehler, Brian (Athlete, Baseball Player)
269 Woodlawn Dr NE
Marietta, GA 30067-4017, USA

Moe-Humphreys, Karen (Swimmer)
505 Augusta Dr
Moraga, CA 94556-3004, USA

Moeller, Chad (Athlete, Baseball Player)
11058 E Raintree Dr
Scottsdale, AZ 85255-1809, USA

Moeller, Dennis (Inventor)
25 Cobbie Ridge Dr
Chapel Hill, NC 27516, USA

Moeller, Dennis (Athlete, Baseball Player)
24979 Constitution Ave Apt 536
Valencia, CA 91381-1735, USA

Moeller, Edward (Athlete, Basketball Player)
1011 Kelton Cottage Way
Morrisville, NC 27560-7031, USA

Moeller, Joe (Athlete, Baseball Player)
1505 Avenida De Nogales
San Clemente, CA 92672-9464, USA

Moeller, Ralf (Actor)
c/o Chuck Binder *Binder & Associates*
1465 Lindacrest Dr
Beverly Hills, CA 90210-2519, USA

Moeller, Ron (Athlete, Baseball Player)
7355 Appleridge Ct
Cincinnati, OH 45247-5055, USA

Moeller, Walter L (Stylist)
7420 Cove Dr
Cary, IL 60013-1717, USA

Moellering, John H (General)
50130 Manly
Chapel Hill, NC 27517-8565, USA

Moennig, Katherine (Actor)
c/o Peg Donegan *Framework Entertainment (LA)*
9057 Nemo St Ste C
West Hollywood, CA 90069-5511, USA

Moesta-Anderson, Rebecca (Writer)
PO Box 767
Monument, CO 80132-0767, USA

Moffat, Donald (Actor)
c/o Staff Member *Jenny Delaney Management*
3238 Fond Dr
Encino, CA 91436-4206, USA

Moffat, Katherine (Kitty) (Actor)
8285 W Sunset Blvd Ste 1
West Hollywood, CA 90046-2420, USA

Moffat, Steven (Writer)
c/o Charlie Ferraro *United Talent Agency (UTA)*
9560 Wilshire Blvd Fl 5
Beverly Hills, CA 90212-2400, USA

Moffatt, Henry K (Mathematician, Physicist)
6 Banhams Close
Cambridge CB4 1HX, UNITED KINGDOM (UK)

Moffatt, John
59A Warrington St
London, ENGLAND W9

Moffatt, Katy (Musician, Songwriter, Writer)
PO Box 334
O Fallon, IL 62269-0334, USA

Moffet, Jane (Athlete, Baseball Player)
501 Tidewater Ave
Rio Grande, NJ 08242-2807, USA

Moffett, D W (Actor)
9460 Wilshire Blvd Ste 700
Beverly Hills, CA 90212-2713, USA

Moffett, James R (Business Person)
1615 Poydras St
New Orleans, LA 70112-1254, USA

Moffett, Randy
110 Lakeover Dr
Athens, GA 30607-2046

Moffett, Tim (Athlete, Football Player)
115 County Road 213
Oxford, MS 38655-8855, USA

Moffitt, Randy (Athlete, Baseball Player)
1725 Baltic Ave
Prescott, AZ 86301-6501, USA

Mofford, Rose (Ex-Governor)
330 W Maryland Ave Unit 104
Phoenix, AZ 85013-1340, USA

Mogae, Festus G (President)
State House Private Bag 001
Gaborone, BOTSWANA

Mogenburg, Dietmar (Athlete, Track Athlete)
Alter Garfen 34
Leverkusen 51371, GERMANY

Mogilevsky, Evgeny (Musician)
165 W 57th St
New York, NY 10019-2201, USA

Mogilny, Alexander (Athlete, Hockey Player)
801 6th St SW
Calgary, AB T2P 3V8, Canada

Mohacsi, Mary (Bowler)
15445 Sunset St
Livonia, MI 48154-3215, USA

MoHair (Music Group)
c/o Staff Member *Paradigm (Monterey)*
404 W Franklin St
Monterey, CA 93940-2303, USA

Mohammed VI (King)
Rabat, MOROCCO

Mohan (Actor, Bollywood)
8 Mylai Ranganathan Street T Nagar
Chennai, TN 600017, INDIA

Mohler, Mike (Athlete, Baseball Player)
1627 S Shirley Ave
Gonzales, LA 70737-3917, USA

Mohler, R Albert
2825 Lexington Rd Ofc of
Louisville, KY 40206-2997, USA

Mohmand, Abdul Ahad (Cosmonaut)
Moskovkoi Oblasti
Syvlsdny Goroduk 141160, RUSSIA

Mohoney, J Daniel (Judge)
40 Foley Sq
New York, NY 10007-1502, USA

Mohoney, John (Actor)
8942 Wilshire Blvd # 219
Beverly Hills, CA 90211-1908, USA

Mohoney, Roger (Cartoonist)
c/o Staff Member *King Features Syndication*
300 W 57th St Fl 15
New York, NY 10019-5238, USA

Mohony, Roger Cardinal (Religious Leader)
3424 Wilshire Blvd
Los Angeles, CA 90010-2263, USA

Mohorcic, Dale (Athlete, Baseball Player)
15501 Rockside Rd
Maple Heights, OH 44137-3948, USA

Mohr, Chris (Athlete, Football Player)
PO Box 1232
Thomson, GA 30824-1232, USA

Mohr, Dustan (Athlete, Baseball Player)
103 Parkwood Dr
Hattiesburg, MS 39402-2217, USA

Mohr, Jay (Actor, Comedian)
c/o Barry Katz *New Wave Entertainment (LA)*
2660 W Olive Ave
Burbank, CA 91505-4525, USA

Mohr, Todd (Musician)
1658 York St
Denver, CO 80206-1410, USA

Mohri, Mamoru (Astronaut)
2-1-2 Sengen Tukubashi
Ibaraki 305, JAPAN

Moine, Marc Forne (President)
Casa de la Valle
Andorra la Vella, ANDORRA

Moir, Richard (Actor)
PO Box 1509
Darlinghurst, NSW 1300, AUSTRALIA

Moisan, Bill (Athlete, Baseball Player)
PO Box 41
Newton, NH 03858-0041, USA

Moiseyev, Igor A (Choreographer, Director)
20 Triumfalnaya Pl
Moscow, RUSSIA

Mojsiejenko, Ralf (Athlete, Football Player)
11334 Baldwin Rd
Bridgman, MI 49106-9727, USA

Mojslejenko, Ralf (Athlete, Football Player)
11334 Baldwin Rd
Bridgman, MI 49106-9727, USA

Mok, Karen (Actor)
c/o Staff Member *Creative Artists Agency (CAA-LA)*
2000 Avenue of the Stars Ste 100
Los Angeles, CA 90067-4705, USA

Mok, Ken (Director, Producer)
c/o Steve Wohl *Paradigm (LA)*
360 N Crescent Dr
Beverly Hills, CA 90210-4874, USA

Mokeski, Paul (Athlete, Basketball Player)
4004 Crestwood Dr
Carrollton, TX 75007-1645, USA

Mokri, Amir (Cinematographer)
c/o Staff Member *Montana Artists Agency*
9150 Wilshire Blvd Ste 100
Beverly Hills, CA 90212-3459, USA

Mokrzynski, Jerzy (Architect)
Ul Marszalkowska 140 m 18
Warsaw 00 061, POLAND

Mokus (Stylist)
c/o Staff Member *Mokus de Barcza*
53 E 96th St Apt 5C
New York, NY 10128-0816, USA

Mol, Gretchen (Actor)
c/o John Carrabino *John Carrabino Management*
5900 Wilshire Blvd Ste 406
Los Angeles, CA 90036-5015, USA

Molale, Brandon (Actor)
c/o Staff Member *DDC Entertainment*
1009 N Redondo Ave
Manhattan Beach, CA 90266-6122, USA

Molden, Alex (Athlete, Football Player)
2083 Wellington Dr
West Linn, OR 97068-3663, USA

Moldofsky, Philip J (Scientist)
7701 Burholme Ave
Philadelphia, PA 19111-2437, USA

Mole, Fenton (Athlete, Baseball Player)
738 Glen Eagle Ct
Danville, CA 94526-6209, USA

Moler, Jason (Athlete, Baseball Player)
2918 Ranch Road 620 N Apt 281
Austin, TX 78734-2269, USA

Molina, Alfred (Actor)
c/o Joan Hyler *Hyler Management*
20 Ocean Park Blvd Unit 25
Santa Monica, CA 90405-3590, USA

Molina, Gabe (Athlete, Baseball Player)
1620 Coronado Pkwy S Apt 6102
Denver, CO 80229-8052, USA

Molina, Islay (Izzy) (Athlete, Baseball Player)
369 Atwater St
Port Charlotte, FL 33954-2904, USA

Molina, Jose (Athlete, Baseball Player)
c/o Team Member *New York Yankees*
Yankee Stadium 161st St & River Ave
Bronx, NY 10451, USA

Molina, Mario J (Nobel Prize Laureate)
PO Box 12406
La Jolla, CA 92039-2406, USA

Molina, Yadier (Athlete, Baseball Player)
7150 N Terra Vista Dr
Peoria, IL 61614-1360, USA

Molinaro, Al (Actor)
1530 Arboles Dr
Glendale, CA 91207-1204, USA

Molinaro, Bob (Athlete, Baseball Player)
1 Harbourside Dr Apt 2312
Delray Beach, FL 33483-5170, USA

Molitor, Paul L (Athlete, Baseball Player, Coach)
c/o Staff Member *John Boggs & Associates*
5675 Ruffin Rd Ste 350
San Diego, CA 92123-1398, USA

Molko, Brian (Musician)
c/o Rod MacSween *International Talent Booking*
1st Floor, Ariel House 74A Charlotte St
London W1T 4QJ, UNITED KINGDOM

Moll, Georgia
229A V Pineta Sacchetti
Rome, CA ITALY

Moll, John L (Engineer)
4111 Old Trace Rd
Palo Alto, CA 94306-3728, USA

Moll, Kurt (Opera Singer)
Voigtelstr 22
Cologne 50933, GERMANY

Moll, Richard (Actor)
1119 Amalfi Dr
Pacific Palisades, CA 90272-4031, USA

Molla, Jordi (Actor)
Calle Segre 14
Madrid 28002, SPAIN

Moller, Andreas (Soccer Player)
Postfach 100509
Dortmund 44005, GERMANY

Moller, Frank (Athlete)
Weissenseer Weg 51-55
Berlin 13051, GERMANY

Moller, Gunnar
6 Cloverdale Rd
London, ENGLAND NW2

Moller, Hans (Artist)
2207 W Allen St
Allentown, PA 18104-4327, USA

Moller, Paul (Engineer, Inventor)
1222 Research Park Dr
Davis, CA 95618-4849, USA

Moller-Gladisch, Silke (Athlete, Track Athlete)
Lange Str 6
Rostock 18055, GERMANY

Mollo-Christiansen, Erik L (Oceanographer)
10 Barberry Rd
Lexington, MA 02421-8026, USA

Molloy, Bryan B (Inventor)
7948 Beaumont Green Pl
Indianapolis, IN 46250-1663, USA

Molloy, Irene
PO Box 5617
Beverly Hills, CA 90209-5617

Molloy, Matt (Musician)
1505 W 2nd Ave # 200
Vancouver, BC V6H 3Y4, CANADA

Moloney, Janel (Actor)
c/o Staff Member *Gersh (LA)*
9465 Wilshire Blvd Ste 600
Beverly Hills, CA 90212-2612, USA

Moloney, Michael (Actor, Reality TV Star)
c/o Staff Member *Extreme Makeover: Home Edition*
Endemol Entertainment USA 9225 Sunset Blvd #1100
Los Angeles, CA 90069, USA

Moloney, Paddy (Musician)
1505 W 2nd Ave # 200
Vancouver, BC V6H 3Y4, CANADA

Moloney, Rich (Athlete, Baseball Player)
125 Mallard Way
Waltham, MA 02452-8117, USA

Molyneux, Juan Pablo (Architect)
29 E 69th St
New York, NY 10021-4952, USA

Mom Rajawong, Sirikit Kitiyarara (Royalty)
Chirtalad a Villa
Bangkok, Thailand

Momaday, N Scott (Writer)
English
Tucson, AZ 85721-0001, USA

Momoa, Jason (Actor)
c/o Jeff Witjas *Agency for the Performing Arts (APA-LA)*
405 S Beverly Dr Ste 500
Beverly Hills, CA 90212-4425, USA

Momolu-Briggs, Korto (Fashion Designer)
200 E 3rd St
Little Rock, AR 72201-1608, USA

Momsen, Robert (Athlete, Football Player)
4730 Glendale Ave Apt 102
Toledo, OH 43614-1974, USA

Momsen, Taylor (Musician)
c/o William Derella *DAS Communications*
83 Riverside Dr
New York, NY 10024-5713, USA

Mon, Randy (Stylist)
179 Arbor St
San Francisco, CA 94131-2920, USA

Monacelli, Amieto (Bowler)
719 2nd Ave Ste 701
Seattle, WA 98104-1747, USA

Monaco, Kelly (Actor)
c/o Alejandra Cristina *Ace PR*
4122 Sunnyslope Ave
Sherman Oaks, CA 91423-4308, USA

Monaco, Ray (Athlete, Football Player)
950 Smith St
Providence, RI 02908-2717, USA

Monaghan, Dominic (Actor)
c/o Jeff Raymond *Rogers & Cowan PR (LA)*
Pacific Design Center 8687 Melrose Ave, 7th Floor
West Hollywood, CA 90069, USA

Monaghan, Kris (Athlete, Golfer)
54 Golf Course Dr
Ranchos De Taos, NM 87557-7914, USA

Monaghan, Marjorie
2109 S Wilbur Ave
Walla Walla, WA 99362-9048, USA

Monaghan, Michelle (Actor)
c/o Frank Frattaroli *Dontanville/Frattaroli (D/F)*
270 Lafayette St Ste 402
New York, NY 10012-3327, USA

Monaghan, Thomas L
3001 Earhart
Ann Arbor, MI 48106, USA

Monaghan, Tom (Business Person)
PO Box 373
Ann Arbor, MI 48106-0373, USA

Monahan, Dan (Actor)
c/o Helene Sokol *Cuzzins Management*
499 N Canon Dr
Beverly Hills, CA 90210-4887, USA

Monahan, David (Actor, Director)
c/o Staff Member *Metropolitan (MTA)*
4526 Wilshire Blvd
Los Angeles, CA 90010-3801, USA

Monahan, Pat (Musician)
80 Mason St
Greenwich, CT 06830-5515, USA

Monahan, Shane (Athlete, Baseball Player)
624 Stickley Oak Way
Woodstock, GA 30189-3781, USA

Monan, J Donald (Educator)
President's Office
Chestnut Hill, MA 2167, USA

Monbouquette, William C (Bill) (Athlete, Baseball Player)
46 Doonan St
Medford, MA 02155-1333, USA

Monchak, Alex (Al) (Athlete, Baseball Player)
7414 8th Ave W
Bradenton, FL 34209-3425, USA

Moncrief, Sidney (Athlete, Basketball Player)
4110 S Lake Dr Unit 141
Saint Francis, WI 53235-5953, USA

Moncrieff, Karen (Actor)
c/o Brad Gross *Brad Gross Agency, The*
161 S Arden Blvd
Los Angeles, CA 90004-3716, USA

Mond, Philip (Photographer)
PO Box 8906
Fort Lauderdale, FL 33310-8906, USA

Mondale, Walter F (President, Senator, Vice President)
50 S 6th St Ste 1500
Minneapolis, MN 55402-1498, USA

Monday, Rick (Athlete, Baseball Player)
811 Gayfeather Ln
Vero Beach, FL 32963-2048, USA

Monday, Robert J (Rick) (Baseball Player, Sportscaster)
811 Gayfeather Ln
Vero Beach, FL 32963-2048, USA

Mondesi, Raul (Athlete, Baseball Player)
1169 Old Phillips Rd
Glendale, CA 91207-1153, USA

Monds, Wonderful (Athlete, Baseball Player)
665 NW Fairhaven Dr
Port St Lucie, FL 34983-1079, USA

Monduzzi, Dino Cardinal (Religious Leader)
Via Monfe della Farina 64
Rome 186, ITALY

Moneo, J Fafael (Architect)
Calle Mino 5
Madrid 28002, SPAIN

Monet, Daniella (Actor)
c/o Staff Member *Elaine Entertainment*
Prefers to be contacted via telephone
Northridge, CA 91324, USA

Money, Don (Athlete, Baseball Player)
282 Old Forest Rd
Vineland, NJ 08360-1667, USA

Money, Eddie (Musician)
c/o Josh Humiston *Agency for the Performing Arts (APA-LA)*
405 S Beverly Dr Ste 500
Beverly Hills, CA 90212-4425, USA

Money, Eric (Athlete, Basketball Player)
457 S Harvard Ave
Tucson, AZ 85710-4630, USA

Money, John W (Misc)
2104 E Madison St
Baltimore, MD 21205-2337, USA

Money, Ken (Astronaut)
1133 Sheppard Ave W # 2000
Downsview, ON M3M 3B9, CANADA

Moneyham, Bill (Baseball Player)
5731 White Crane Rd
Merced, CA 95340-8573, USA

Monfort, Avery (Athlete, Football Player)
PO Box 84
Twain Harte, CA 95383-0084, USA

Monge, Sid (Athlete, Baseball Player)
10 Lilah Ln
Reading, MA 01867-1075, USA

Monger, Matt (Athlete, Football Player)
1306 N Douglas Dr
Claremore, OK 74017-4623, USA

Monheim, Annett (Stylist)
c/o Staff Member *Streeters*
560 Broadway Rm 203
New York, NY 10012-3945, 212-219-9566

Monheit, Jane (Musician)
c/o Cynthia B. Herbst *American International Artists*
356 Pine Valley Rd
Hoosick Falls, NY 12090-3859, USA

Monica (Musician)
c/o Cara Lewis *WmE2 (WMA-NY)*
1325 Avenue of the Americas
New York, NY 10019-6026, USA

Monicelli, Mario (Director)
Via del Babuino 135
Rome 137, ITALY

Monin, Clarence V (President)
1370 Ontario St
Cleveland, OH 44113-1744, USA

Moniz, Karletta (Stylist)
903 Pine St Apt 30
San Francisco, CA 94108-2942, USA

Moniz, Wendy (Actor)
c/o Nancy Sanders *Sanders Armstrong Caserta*
2120 Colorado Ave Ste 120
Santa Monica, CA 90404-3561, USA

Monk, Arthur (Art) (Athlete, Football Player, Sportscaster)
10896 Lake Windermere Dr
Great Falls, VA 22066-1528, USA

Monk, Debra (Actor)
315 W 57th St Frnt 4H
New York, NY 10019-3158, USA

Monk, Meredith J (Choreographer, Composer)
131 Varick St
New York, NY 10013-1410, USA

Monk, Quincy (Athlete, Football Player)
104 White Oak Blvd Apt 104
Jacksonville, NC 28546-4539, USA

Monk, Sophie (Actor)
c/o Jenni Weinman *Patricola Lust PR*
9171 Wilshire Blvd Ste 390
Beverly Hills, CA 90210-5515, USA

Monk Jr, Thelonious
173 Brighton Ave
Boston, MA 02134-2003, USA

Monkees, The (Music Group)
c/o Staff Member *Primary Talent International (UK)*
The Primary Building 10-11 Jockeys Fields
London WC1R 4BN, UK

Monreal Luque, Alberto (Government Official)
Eurotabac Monte Esquinza 28
Madrid 28010, SPAIN

Monroe, A L (Mike) (Misc)
1750 New York Ave NW
Washington, DC 20006-5301, USA

Monroe, Betty (Actor)
c/o Staff Member *TV Azteca*
Periferico Sur 4121 Colonia Fuentes del Pedregal
DF CP 14141, Mexico

Monroe, Craig (Athlete, Baseball Player)
4123 Lynn Dr
Texarkana, TX 75503-2816, USA

Monroe, Earl (Athlete, Basketball Player)
113 W 88th St
New York, NY 10024-2401, USA

Monroe, Larry (Athlete, Baseball Player)
725 N Hundley St
Hoffman Estates, IL 60169-4559, USA

Monroe, Meredith (Musician)
c/o Ame Van Iden *PMK/BNC Public Relations (PMK-LA)*
8687 Melrose Ave Ste 8
West Hollywood, CA 90069-5746, USA

Monroe, Mircea (Actor)
c/o Tiffany Kuzon *Evolution Entertainment (LA)*
901 N Highland Ave
Los Angeles, CA 90038-2412, USA

Monroe, Zach (Athlete, Baseball Player)
1 Sandalwood Ln
Bartonville, IL 61607-2145, USA

Monson, Dan (Basketball Player, Coach)
Bierman Athletic Building
Minneapolis, MN 55455, USA

Monsters, The (Music Group)
c/o Staff Member *Paradigm (Monterey)*
404 W Franklin St
Monterey, CA 93940-2303, USA

Mont, Tommy (Athlete, Football Player)
15414 W Sky Hawk Dr
Sun City, AZ 85375-6511, USA

Montag, Holly (Reality TV Star)
c/o Anna Babbitt *New Wave Entertainment (LA)*
2660 W Olive Ave
Burbank, CA 91505-4525, USA

Montagnier, Luc (Scientist)
25 Rue du Docteur
Paris Cedux 15 75015, FRANCE

Montague, Diana (Opera Singer)
91 Saint Martin's Lane
London WC2, UNITED KINGDOM (UK)

Montague, Ed (Athlete, Baseball Player)
1521 Cherrywood Dr
San Mateo, CA 94403-3903, USA

Montague, John (Athlete, Baseball Player)
52 Northshore Cir
Dadeville, AL 36853-4275, USA

Montague, Lee (Actor)
18-21 Jermyn St
London SW1Y 6NB, UNITED KINGDOM (UK)

Montague-Smith, Patrick W (Editor)
197 Park Road Kingston-upon-Thames
Surrey, UNITED KINGDOM (UK)

Montalban, Paolo (Actor)
c/o Staff Member *Innovative Artists (LA)*
1505 10th St
Santa Monica, CA 90401-2805, USA

Montalbano, Chuck (Athlete, Golfer)
4725 Farmdale Ave
North Hollywood, CA 91602-1109, USA

Montalvo, Rafael (Athlete)
PO Box 661
Fishkill, NY 12524-0661, USA

Montana, Claude (Designer, Fashion Designer)
131 Rue Saint-Denis
Paris 75001, FRANCE

Montana, Joe (Athlete, Football Player)
c/o Staff Member *Henry Holt & Company*
175 5th Ave Ste 400
New York, NY 10010-7726, USA

Montanez, Phillip (Stylist)
c/o Staff Member *Clutts Agency, The*
1400 Turtle Creek Blvd # 171
Dallas, TX 75207-3337, USA

Montanez, Willie (Athlete, Baseball Player)
HC 5 Box 52020
Caguas, PR 00725-9201, USA

Montano, Sumalee (Actor)
c/o Kim Dorr *Defining Artists Agency*
10 Universal City Plz Ste 2000
Universal City, CA 91608-1074, USA

Montazeri, Ayatollah Hussein Ali (Religious Leader)
Qom, IRAN

Monte, Chante
c/o Staff Member *WmE2 (WMA-NY)*
1325 Avenue of the Americas
New York, NY 10019-6026, USA

Montefusco, John (Athlete, Baseball Player)
1 Oakdale Dr Apt 3D
Middletown, NJ 07748-2124, USA

Monteiro, Antonio M (President)
Cia de la Republica
Sao Tiago Praia, CAPE VERDE

Monteith, Cory (Actor)
c/o Melissa Fonzino *Viewpoint Inc*
8820 Wilshire Blvd Ste 220
Beverly Hills, CA 90211-2622, USA

Monteith, Kelly
PO Box 11669
Knoxville, TN 37939-1669

Monteleone, Rich (Athlete, Baseball Player)
441 Lucerne Ace
Tampa, FL 33606, USA

Montermini, Andrea (Race Car Driver)
434 E Main St
Brownsburg, IN 46112-1419, USA

Montero, Gabriela (Musician)
c/o Staff Member *Paradigm (Monterey)*
404 W Franklin St
Monterey, CA 93940-2303, USA

Montero, Pablo (Actor)
c/o Staff Member *Televisa*
Blvd Adolfo Lopez Mateos 232 Colonia
San Angel INN
DF CP 01060, MEXICO

Monterola, Pablo (Musician)
c/o Staff Member *BMG*
1540 Broadway
New York, NY 10036-4039, USA

Montevecchi, Liliane (Musician)
8899 Beverly Blvd Ste 620
Los Angeles, CA 90048-2428, USA

Montez, Chris
6671 W Sunset Blvd Ste 1502
Hollywood, CA 90028-7235

Montgomerie, Colin S (Athlete, Golfer)
1360 E 9th St Ste 100
Cleveland, OH 44114-1730, USA

Montgomery, Alton (Athlete, Football Player)
441 N 9th St
Griffin, GA 30223-2506, USA

Montgomery, Anthony (Actor)
c/o Jerry Shandrew *Shandrew Public Relations*
1050 S Stanley Ave
Los Angeles, CA 90019-6634, USA

Montgomery, Belinda (Actor)
280 S Beverly Dr Ste 400
Beverly Hills, CA 90212-3904, USA

Montgomery, Bob (Athlete, Baseball Player)
2 Parkway Dr
Saugus, MA 01906-1957, USA

Montgomery, Chuck (Actor)
c/o Staff Member *Don Buchwald & Associates Inc (LA)*
6500 Wilshire Blvd Ste 2200
Los Angeles, CA 90048-4942, USA

Montgomery, Cleo (Athlete, Football Player)
404 Dakota Trl
Irving, TX 75063-4547, USA

Montgomery, David (Photographer)
11 Edith Grove #B
London SW10, UNITED KINGDOM (UK)

Montgomery, Delmonico (Athlete, Football Player)
3011 Pecan Way Ct
Richmond, TX 77406-6902, USA

Montgomery, Dorothy (Baseball Player)
2621 Berkley Dr
Chattanooga, TN 37415-5701, USA

Montgomery, Eddie (Musician)
c/o Staff Member *Hallmark Direction Company*
713 18th Ave S
Nashville, TN 37203-3214, USA

Montgomery, Grady (Baseball Player)
11904 Fort Washington Rd
Fort Washington, MD 20744-5908, USA

Montgomery, James P (Jim) (Athlete, Coach, Swimmer)
1537 Bella Vista Dr
Dallas, TX 75218-3510, USA

Montgomery, Jeff (Athlete, Baseball Player)
3701 W 140th St
Overland Park, KS 66224-8406, USA

Montgomery, John Michael (Musician)
c/o John Dorris Sr *Hallmark Direction Company*
713 18th Ave S
Nashville, TN 37203-3214, USA

Montgomery, John W (Misc)
2 Rue de Rome
Starsbourg 67000, FRANCE

Montgomery, Lisa Kennedy (Actor)
10202 Washington Blvd
Culver City, CA 90232-3119, USA

Montgomery, Marv (Athlete, Football Player)
1509 S Macon St
Aurora, CO 80012-5140, USA

Montgomery, Melba (Musician)
2802 Columbine Pl
Nashville, TN 37204-3104, USA

Montgomery, Mike (Basketball Player, Coach)
1001 Broadway
Oakland, CA 94607-4019, USA

Montgomery, Mike (Athlete, Football Player)
4224 High Star Ln
Dallas, TX 75287-6624, USA

Montgomery, Monique (Stylist)
1756 Marin Ave
Berkeley, CA 94707-2206, USA

Montgomery, Monty (Athlete, Baseball Player)
807 Corn Tassel Trl
Martinsville, VA 24112-5601, USA

Montgomery, Poppy (Actor)
c/o Peg Donegan *Framework Entertainment (LA)*
9057 Nemo St Ste C
West Hollywood, CA 90069-5511, USA

Montgomery, Ray (Athlete, Baseball Player)
2 Whynwood Rd
Simsbury, CT 06070-3030, USA

Montgomery, Steve (Athlete, Baseball Player)
13731 Mercado Dr
Del Mar, CA 92014-3415, USA

Montgomery, Wilbert (Athlete, Football Player)
45990 Tournament Dr
Northville, MI 48168-8498, USA

Montgomery Jr, Dan (Actor)
c/o Karyn Spencer *Peter Strain & Associates Inc (LA)*
5455 Wilshire Blvd Ste 1812
Los Angeles, CA 90036-4268, USA

Montiel, Fernando (Boxer)
c/o Staff Member *Top Rank Inc.*
3908 Howard Hughes Pkwy # 580
Las Vegas, NV 89109, USA

Montiel, H Pierre
102 W 73rd St
New York, NY 10023-3047, USA

Montler, Mike (Athlete, Football Player)
479 Tiara Vista Dr
Grand Junction, CO 81507-8716, USA

Montminy, Marc R (Scientist)
10100 N Torrey Pines Rd
La Jolla, CA 92037, USA

Montoya, Al (Athlete, Hockey Player)
2 Penn Plz
New York, NY 10121-0101, USA

Montoya, Juan Pablo (Race Car Driver)
8500 Westmoreland Dr NW
Concord, NC 28027-7571, USA

Montoyo, Jose Carlos (Charlie) (Athlete, Baseball Player)
438 Summer Sails Dr
Valrico, FL 33594-8021, USA

Montreuil, Allan (Athlete, Baseball Player)
2016 Laurel Ave
Gretna, LA 70056-5232, USA

Montross, Eric (Athlete, Basketball Player)
4668 S NC Highway 150
Lexington, NC 27295-8026, USA

Montsho, Este (Musician)
1325 Avenue of the Americas
New York, NY 10019-6026, USA

Montvidas, Edgaras (Opera Singer)
4 Addison Bridge Place
London W14 8XP, USA

Montville, Leigh (Writer)
Editorial Dept 135 WT Morrissey Blvd
Dorchester, MA 2125, USA

Monty, Harry
1600 N Bronson Ave Apt 17
Hollywood, CA 90028-6598

Monty Q (DJ)
c/o Staff Member *Diva Central Inc*
7510 W Sunset Blvd Ste 1445
Los Angeles, CA 90046-3408, USA

Monzikova, Anya (Actor)
c/o Greg Meyer *Meyer Management Group (MMG)*
1901 Avenue of the Stars Ste 365
Century City, CA 90067-6025, USA

Moock, Joe (Athlete, Baseball Player)
12432 Pecos Ave
Greenwell Springs, LA 70739-3039, USA

Moodie, Janice (Athlete, Golfer)
10746 Woodchase Cir
Orlando, FL 32836-5870, USA

Moody, Eric (Athlete, Baseball Player)
336 Gleneagle Cir
Irmo, SC 29063-8432, USA

Moody, Keith M (Athlete, Football Player)
4632 Riverview Ct
Tracy, CA 95377-8288, USA

Moody, Lynne (Actor)
c/o Lorraine Berglund *Lorraine Berglund Management*
11537 Hesby St
North Hollywood, CA 91601-3618, USA

Moody, Micky (Musician)
27A Floral St #300
London WC2E 9DQ, UNITED KINGDOM (UK)

Moody, Orville (Athlete, Golfer)
9221 Chesapeake Ln
McKinney, TX 75071-6039, USA

Moody, Ritchie (Baseball Player)
1321 Orchardview Ct
Dayton, OH 45458-9682, USA

Moody, Ron (Actor)
28 Berkeley Square
London W1X 6HD, UNITED KINGDOM (UK)

Moody-Luckhurst, Terri (Athlete, Golfer)
103 Pierrepont Isle
Duluth, GA 30097-5908, USA

Moodysson, Lukas (Director)
Hantverkaregatan 12
Malmo 21155, Sweden

Moog, Andy (Athlete, Hockey Player)
530 Rolling Hills Rd
Coppell, TX 75019-4049, USA

Moomaw, Donn D (Athlete, Football Player)
3124 Corda Dr
Los Angeles, CA 90049-1104, USA

Moon, Lynne (Stylist)
9629 Carnegie Dr
Dallas, TX 75228-3603, USA

Moon, Philip
449 N Highland Ave
Los Angeles, CA 90036-2627

Moon, Sun Myung (Religious Leader)
4 W 43rd St
New York, NY 10036-7408, USA

Moon, Wallace W (Wally) (Athlete, Baseball Player)
702 Ellen Lee Ct
Bryan, TX 77802-1146, USA

Moon, Wally
3801 E Crest Dr Apt 6401
Bryan, TX 77802-5715

Moon, Warren (Athlete, Football Player)
PO Box 22388
Houston, TX 77227-2388, USA

Moon Zombie, Sherrie (Actor)
8491 W Sunset Blvd # 125
West Hollywood, CA 90069-1911, USA

Mooney, Debra (Actor)
c/o Mike Smith *Principal Entertainment (LA)*
1964 Westwood Blvd Ste 400
Los Angeles, CA 90025-4695, USA

Mooney, Ed (Athlete, Football Player)
4105 63rd St
Lubbock, TX 79413-5023, USA

Mooney, Harold A (Biologist)
2625 Ramona St
Palo Alto, CA 94306-2315, USA

Mooney, John (Musician)
Midtown Plaza 1300 Baxter St #405
Charlotte, NC 28204, USA

Mooney, Michael J (Educator)
President's Office
Portland, OR 97219, USA

Mooney, Michael P (Mike) (Athlete, Football Player)
4801 Diane Ave
Mount Airy, MD 21771-8923, USA

Mooney, Peter (Actor)
c/o Fisher Pence *3 Arts Entertainment Inc*
9460 Wilshire Blvd Fl 7
Beverly Hills, CA 90212-2713, USA

Mooneyhan, Bill (Athlete, Baseball Player)
5731 White Crane Rd
Atwater, CA 95301-8573, USA

Moonsammy, Camille (Stylist)
c/o Staff Member *Pat Bates & Associates*
300 W 12th St
New York, NY 10014-1939, USA

Moonves, Leslie (Business Person, Producer)
51 W 52nd St
New York, NY 10019-6119, USA

Moordyukova, Nonna V (Actor)
Rublevskoye Shosse 34 Korp 2 #549
Moscow 121609, RUSSIA

Moore, Abra (Musician)
16830 Ventura Blvd Ste 501
Encino, CA 91436-1717, USA

Moore, Andre (Athlete, Basketball Player)
12137 S Justine St
Chicago, IL 60643-5443, USA

Moore, Ann S (Publisher)
Publisher's Office Time & Life Building
New York, NY 10020, USA

Moore, Archie (Athlete, Baseball Player)
201 Courtland Rd
Indiana, PA 15701-3202, USA

Moore, Arthur (Misc)
1750 New York Ave NW
Washington, DC 20006-5305, USA

Moore, Balor (Athlete, Baseball Player)
901 W Viejo Dr
Friendswood, TX 77546-5836, USA

Moore, Barry (Athlete, Baseball Player)
6702 Conifer Cir
Indian Trail, NC 28079-7588, USA

Moore, Benjamin (Artist)
3123 39th Pl S
Seattle, WA 98144, USA

Moore, Bill (Billy) (Athlete, Baseball Player)
10849 Mirador Dr
Rancho Cucamonga, CA 91737-6991, USA

Moore, Billie (Athlete, Basketball Player, Coach)
2247 Meadow Ln
Fullerton, CA 92831-2122, USA

Moore, Bob (Athlete, Baseball Player)
2500 Wellington Rd
Los Angeles, CA 90016-3034, USA

Moore, Bobby (Athlete, Baseball Player)
3703 Hyde Park Ave
Cincinnati, OH 45209-2321, USA

Moore, Brad (Athlete, Baseball Player)
3135 Challenger Point Dr
Loveland, CO 80538-7222, USA

Moore, Brandon (Athlete, Football Player)
15010 S 47th St
Phoenix, AZ 85044-6889, USA

Moore, Brent (Athlete, Football Player)
137 Wild Horse Valley Dr
Novato, CA 94947-3615, USA

Moore, Bud (Race Car Driver)
PO Box 2916
Spartanburg, SC 29304-2916, USA

Moore, Calvin C (Mathematician)
1408 Eagle Point Ct
Lafayette, CA 94549-2328, USA

Moore, Chante (Musician, Songwriter)
1350 Spring St NW Ste 700
Atlanta, GA 30309-2874, USA

Moore, Chante
c/o Staff Member *Creative Artists Agency (CAA-LA)*
2000 Avenue of the Stars Ste 100
Los Angeles, CA 90067-4705, USA

Moore, Charlie (Athlete, Baseball Player)
342 County Road 276
Cullman, AL 35057-4976, USA

Moore, Chessie
PO Box 1516
Palatka, FL 32178-1516

Moore, Chris (Producer)
c/o Staff Member *LivePlanet*
11150 Santa Monica Blvd Ste 1200
Los Angeles, CA 90025-3386, USA

Moore, Christina (Actor)
c/o Paul Rosicker *Gersh (LA)*
9465 Wilshire Blvd Ste 600
Beverly Hills, CA 90212-2612, USA

Moore, Christopher (Chris) (Director, Producer)
c/o Staff Member *WmE2 (Endeavor-LA)*
9601 Wilshire Blvd Fl 3
Beverly Hills, CA 90210-5219, USA

Moore, Christopher (Lil Twist) (Musician)
c/o Cortez Bryant *Bryant Management*
555 Washington Ave Ste 240
Miami, FL 33139-6639, USA

Moore, Christy (Musician)
c/o Paul Charles *Asgard Promotions*
125 Parkway
London NW1 7PS, United Kingdom

Moore, Corwin (Writer)
c/o Staff Member *Creative Artists Agency (CAA-LA)*
2000 Avenue of the Stars Ste 100
Los Angeles, CA 90067-4705, USA

Moore, Darryl (Athlete, Football Player)
503 High St
Minden, LA 71055-3698, USA

Moore, Dave (Football Player)
c/o Team Member *Tampa Bay Buccaneers*
1 Bucaneer Pl
Tampa, FL 33607, USA

Moore, Demi (Actor)
c/o Jason Weinberg *Untitled Entertainment (LA)*
350 S Beverly Dr Ste 200
Beverly Hills, CA 90212-4819, USA

Moore, Derland P (Athlete, Football Player)
1917 Madison St
Mandeville, LA 70448-5840, USA

Moore, Derrick (Athlete, Football Player)
3164 Jackson Creek Dr
Stockbridge, GA 30281-5688, USA

Moore, Dick (Cartoonist)
1560 Broadway
New York, NY 10036-1537, USA

Moore, Dickie
150 W End Ave Apt 26C
New York, NY 10023-5743

Moore, Dorothy (Musician)
13531 Clairmont Way Unit 8
Oregon City, OR 97045-4249, USA

Moore, Earl
215 W End Blvd
Winston-Salem, NC 27101-1203

Moore, Eric P (Athlete, Football Player)
2225 Lindsay Ln
Florissant, MO 63031-5626, USA

Moore, Gary (Athlete, Baseball Player)
7985 Roundrock Rd
Dallas, TX 75248-5341, USA

Moore, George E (Doctor)
12048 Black Hawk Dr
Conifer, CO 80433-7137, USA

Moore, Gwen (Congressman, Politician)
2245 Rayburn Hob
Washington, DC 20515-2001, USA

Moore, Henry (Athlete, Football Player)
2200 Pleasure Dr
Benton, AR 72019-6365, USA

Moore, Herman J (Athlete, Football Player)
265 Mount Hermon Cir
Danville, VA 24540-5227, USA

Moore, J Jeremy (General)
Cox's & King's Branch 7 Pall Mall
London SW1, UNITED KINGDOM (UK)

Moore, Jackie (Musician)
508 Honey Lake Ct
Danville, CA 94506-1237, USA

Moore, Jackie (Athlete, Baseball Player, Coach)
2721 Laurel Valley Ln
Arlington, TX 76006-4019, USA

Moore, Jacqueline (Wrestler)
15030 Ventura Blvd Ste 525
Sherman Oaks, CA 91403-5470, USA

Moore, James E Jr (General)
18940 Joaquin Ct
Salinas, CA 93908-9609, USA

Moore, Jeffrey B (Athlete, Football Player)
4055 Delgate Cv
Memphis, TN 38125-2718, USA

Moore, Jerald (Athlete, Football Player)
1806 Sabine Ln
Richmond, TX 77406-7940, USA

Moore, Jerry (Athlete, Football Player)
401 Ivory Dr
Little Rock, AR 72205-2640, USA

Moore, Jesse W (Engineer)
Boulder Industrial Park
Boulder, CO 80306, USA

Moore, Joe
2410 Memorial Dr # 3C
Bryan, TX 77802-2851

Moore, Joel David (Actor)
11271 Ventura Blvd Ste 434
Studio City, CA 91604-3136, USA

Moore, John (Director, Producer, Writer)
c/o Rowena Arguelles *Creative Artists Agency (CAA-LA)*
2000 Avenue of the Stars Ste 100
Los Angeles, CA 90067-4705, USA

Moore, John A (Biologist)
11522 Tulane Ave
Riverside, CA 92507-6649, USA

Moore, John W (Educator)
President S Ofc
Terre Haute, IN 47809-0001, USA

Moore, Julianne (Actor)
c/o Evelyn O'Neill *Management 360*
9111 Wilshire Blvd
Beverly Hills, CA 90210-5508, USA

Moore, Junior (Athlete, Baseball Player)
3728 Wall Ave
Richmond, CA 94804-3346, USA

Moore, Kelvin (Athlete, Baseball Player)
75 Stoney Point Ter
Covington, GA 30014-7070, USA

Moore, Kelvin (Athlete, Football Player)
1564 W 110th Pl
Los Angeles, CA 90047-4915, USA

Moore, Ken (Athlete, Football Player)
7497 SE Jamestown Ter
Hobe Sound, FL 33455-5879, USA

Moore, Kenya (Actor)
c/o Staff Member *Cunningham Escott Slevin & Doherty (CESD-LA)*
10635 Santa Monica Blvd Ste 130
Los Angeles, CA 90025-8306, USA

Moore, Kerwin (Athlete, Baseball Player)
26592 Stanford Dr W
Southfield, MI 48033-2272, USA

Moore, Leonard E (Lenny) (Athlete, Football Player)
8815 Stonehaven Rd
Randallstown, MD 21133-4223, USA

Moore, Leroy (Athlete, Football Player)
842 Golf Dr Apt 201
Pontiac, MI 48341-2385, USA

Moore, Lorrie (Writer)
English Dept
Madison, WI 53706, USA

Moore, Lucille (Baseball Player)
6450 Miami Cir
South Bend, IN 46614-6480, USA

Moore, Malcolm A S (Scientist)
1275 York Ave
New York, NY 10065-6007, USA

Moore, Mandy (Actor, Musician)
c/o Jon Leshay *Storefront Entertainment*
647 N Martel Ave Ste 102
Los Angeles, CA 90036-1930, USA

Moore, Manfred (Athlete, Football Player)
1672 Buckingham Rd
Los Angeles, CA 90019-5903, USA

Moore, Marcus (Athlete, Baseball Player)
PO Box 5144
Richmond, CA 94805-0144, USA

Moore, Mary (Baseball Player)
4225 Lake Grove Ct
White Lake, MI 48383-1528, USA

Moore, Mary Tyler (Actor)
c/o Erica Tarin *ID Public Relations (ID-LA)*
7080 Hollywood Blvd Fl 8
Los Angeles, CA 90028-6906, USA

Moore, McNeil (Athlete, Football Player)
3150 Canterbury Ln
Port Neches, TX 77651-6217, USA

Moore, Melanie
3500 W Olive Ave Ste 920
Burbank, CA 91505-5514

Moore, Melba (Actor, Musician)
1017 O St NW # B
Washington, DC 20001-4229, USA

Moore, Melissa Anne (Actor)
PO Box 55
Versailles, KY 40383-0055, USA

Moore, Michael (Director)
c/o Ariel (Ari) Emanuel *WmE2 (Endeavor-LA)*
9601 Wilshire Blvd Fl 3
Beverly Hills, CA 90210-5219, USA

Moore, Michael K (Mike) (Prime Minister)
154 Rue Lausanne
Geneva 21 1211, SWITZERLAND

Moore, Michael (Mike) (Attorney, Attorney General, General)
PO Box 220
Jackson, MS 39205-0220, USA

Moore, Mike (Athlete, Baseball Player)
1472 E Calle De Caballos
Tempe, AZ 85284-2406, USA

Moore, Mindy (Athlete, Golfer)
36 Black Hickory Way
Ormond Beach, FL 32174-5704, USA

Moore, Moulty (Athlete, Football Player)
5781 S Sable Cir
Margate, FL 33063-5697, USA

Moore, Nathanlel (Nat) (Athlete, Football Player)
20041 E Oakmont Dr
Hialeah, FL 33015-2048, USA

Moore, Otis (Baseball Player)
2923 178th Dr Apt 3
Hammond, IN 46323-3245, USA

Moore, Patrick (Astronomer, Writer)
Farthings 39 West St
Selsey, Sussex PO20 9AAD, UNITED KINGDOM (UK)

Moore, Patrick (Athlete, Golfer)
4638 E Dartmouth St
Mesa, AZ 85205-6324, USA

Moore, Rachel (Actor, Model)
c/o Staff Member *WNWN Media*
348 Hauser Blvd # PH414
Los Angeles, CA 90036-3276, USA

Moore, Ralph (Musician)
135 W 50th St # 1915
New York, NY 10020-1201, USA

Moore, Red (Baseball Player)
2450 Perry Blvd NW
Atlanta, GA 30318-8809, USA

Moore, Richard (Actor)
2-4 Noel St
London W1V 3RB, UNITED KINGDOM (UK)

Moore, Richard W (Dickie) (Athlete, Hockey Player)
4955 Clemin Saint Francois
Saint Laurent, QC 1P3, Canada

Moore, Rob (Athlete, Football Player)
1 River Pl Apt 2306
New York, NY 10036-4379, USA

Moore, Robert A (Athlete, Football Player)
1906 E Gate Dr
Stone Mountain, GA 30087-1947, USA

Moore, Robert R (Athlete, Football Player)
20 Sally Ann Rd
Orinda, CA 94563-3525, USA

Moore, Roger (Actor, Director)
c/o Tom Chasin *Chasin Agency, The*
8899 Beverly Blvd Ste 714
Los Angeles, CA 90048-2449, USA

Moore, Ron (Athlete, Football Player)
5730 Oakwood St
Spencer, OK 73084, USA

Moore, Ronald D (Producer, Writer)
c/o Brett Loncar *Creative Artists Agency (CAA-LA)*
2000 Avenue of the Stars Ste 100
Los Angeles, CA 90067-4705, USA

Moore, Sam (Musician)
7119 E Shea Blvd # 109-436 PMB 109-436
Scottsdale, AZ 85254-6107, USA

Moore, Scotty (Musician)
5340 Simpkins Rd
Whites Creek, TN 37189-9061, USA

Moore, Shawn (Athlete, Football Player)
573 Brookfield Dr
Centreville, MD 21617-2397, USA

Moore, Shemar (Actor)
c/o Charlton Blackburne *A Management Company*
9107 Wilshire Blvd Ste 650
Beverly Hills, CA 90210-5544, USA

Moore, Stephen (Actor)
Royal National Theatre South Bank
London SE1 9PX, UK

Moore, Tamara
American West Arena 201 E Jefferson St
Phoenix, AZ 85004, USA

Moore, Terry (Actor)
c/o Budd Burton Moss *Burton Moss*
10533 Strathmore Dr
Los Angeles, CA 90024-2540, USA

Moore, Toby (Actor)
c/o Staff Member *Sanders Armstrong Caserta*
2120 Colorado Ave Ste 120
Santa Monica, CA 90404-3561, USA

Moore, Tom (Athlete, Football Player)
1038 Forest Harbor Dr
Hendersonville, TN 37075-9649, USA

Moore, Tommy (Athlete, Baseball Player)
329 Mountainview Dr
Hurst, TX 76054-3018, USA

Moore, Tracy (Athlete, Basketball Player)
12116 E 37th Pl
Tulsa, OK 74146-3104, USA

Moore, Trey (Athlete, Baseball Player)
5128 Bellerive Bend Dr
College Station, TX 77845-4477, USA

Moore, Vanessa (Stylist)
c/o Staff Member *Art Department*
48 Greene St Fl 4
New York, NY 10013-2663, USA

Moore, W Edward C (Biologist)
1607 Boxwood Dr
Blacksburg, VA 24060-1952, USA

Moore, Zeke (Athlete, Football Player)
3422 Prudence Dr
Houston, TX 77045-5718, USA

Moore Capito, Shelley (Congressman, Politician)
2443 Rayburn Hob
Washington, DC 20515-4705, United States

Moore Jr, Charles (Athlete, Track Athlete)
10 Barclay St
New York, NY 10007-2708, USA

Moore (Paxson), Melanie Deanne (Actor)
c/o Melisa Spamer *Domain Talent*
9229 W Sunset Blvd Ste 710
Los Angeles, CA 90069-3407, USA

Moorehead, Emery (Athlete, Football Player)
1005 Sussex Dr
Northbrook, IL 60062-3328, USA

Moorehouse, Adrian
St. Helier Bradford Rd. Bringley
W. York., ENGLAND BD16 1PA

Moorer, Allison (Actor, Musician, Songwriter, Writer)
1107 17th Ave S
Nashville, TN 37212-2203, USA

Moorer, Llana (MC Lyte) (Musician)
PO Box 691394
Los Angeles, CA 90069-9394, USA

Moore-Warner, Eleanor (Baseball Player)
2172 Kinney Ave NW
Grand Rapids, MI 49534-1160, USA

Moore-Watkins, Pauline (Actor)
4077 Sunset Dr Apt 202
Lake Oswego, OR 97035-4391, USA

Mooring, John (Athlete, Football Player)
1901 Pat Booker Rd
Universal City, TX 78148-3438, USA

Moorman, Mo (Athlete, Football Player)
9641 Shelbyville Rd
Simpsonville, KY 40067-6506, USA

Moorse, Kiki (Musician)
924 Jefferson St SE # 101
Olympia, WA 98501, USA

MOP (Music Group)
c/o Staff Member *Interscope Records (NY)*
1755 Broadway
New York, NY 10019-3743, USA

Mora, Danny (Actor)
c/o Staff Member *Acme Talent & Literary (LA)*
1400 Atlantic Ave Ste 274
Long Beach, CA 90813-2013, USA

Mora, Gene (Cartoonist)
200 Madison Ave
New York, NY 10016-3903, USA

Mora, Melvin (Athlete, Baseball Player)
2316 Willow Vale Dr
Fallston, MD 21047-1502, USA

Mora, Philippe (Director)
9255 W Sunset Blvd Ste 901
Los Angeles, CA 90069-3306, USA

Mora, Sergio (Reality TV Star)
c/o Staff Member *The Contender*
3000 W Alameda Ave # 5366
Burbank, CA 91523-0001, USA

Mora Gramunt, Gabriel (Architect)
Passtage Sant Felip 12 Bis
Barcelona 8006, SPAIN

Mora Jr, James E (Jim) (Coach, Football Coach)
c/o Bob LaMonte *Professional Sports Representation*
2425 Manzanita Ln
Reno, NV 89509-7027, 775-828-1864

Morabito, Rocky (Journalist, Photographer)
3036 Gilmore St
Jacksonville, FL 32205, USA

Morabito, Tim (Athlete, Football Player)
PO Box 152
Garnerville, NY 10923-0152, USA

Moraga, David (Athlete, Baseball Player)
608 Peach Ct
Fairfield, CA 94534-1522, USA

Morahan, Christopher T (Director)
Devil's Punchbowl Thursley
Godalming, Surrey GU8 6NS, UNITED KINGDOM (UK)

Morales, Esai (Actor)
c/o Jai Khanna *Brillstein Entertainment Partners*
9150 Wilshire Blvd Ste 350
Beverly Hills, CA 90212-3453, USA

Morales, Esal (Actor)
7527 Woodrow Wilson Dr
Los Angeles, CA 90046-1324, USA

Morales, Jerry (Athlete, Baseball Player, Coach)
2400 E Capitol Street Attn Coaching Staff NE
Washington, DC 20003, USA

Morales, Jose M (Athlete, Baseball Player)
17411 Fosgate Rd
Montverde, FL 34756-3002, USA

Morales, Kendry (Athlete, Baseball Player)
c/o Staff Member *Los Angeles Dodgers (LA Dodgers)*
1000 Elysian Park Ave
Los Angeles, CA 90090-1112, USA

Morales, Natalie (Correspondent)
c/o Staff Member *NBC Universal (NY)*
30 Rockefeller Plz Fl 270E
New York, NY 10112-0299, USA

Morales, Natalie (Actor)
c/o Vincent Nastri *Bleecker Street Entertainment*
853 Broadway Ste 1214
New York, NY 10003-4717, USA

Morales, P Pablo (Swimmer)
Athletic Dept
Lincoln, NE 68588, USA

Morales, Pedro (Athlete, Wrestler)
118 Willery St
Woodbridge, NJ 96712, USA

Morales, Rich (Athlete, Baseball Player)
1650 Rosita Rd
Pacifica, CA 94044-4431, USA

Morales, Willie (Athlete, Baseball Player)
5001 W Camino Del Desierto
Tucson, AZ 85745-9119, USA

Moran, Al (Athlete, Baseball Player)
34134 Banbury St
Farmington Hills, MI 48331-2216, USA

Moran, Bill (Athlete, Baseball Player)
200 Shore Dr
Portsmouth, VA 23701-1241, USA

Moran, Billy (Athlete, Baseball Player)
PO Box 82
Luthersville, GA 30251-0082, USA

Moran, Carl (Baseball Player)
200 Shore Dr
Portsmouth, VA 23701-1241, USA

Moran, Ian (Athlete, Hockey Player)
427 Bay Rd
Duxbury, MA 02332-5228, USA

Moran, John (Religious Leader)
PO Box 9127
Fort Wayne, IN 46899-9127, USA

Moran, Nick (Actor)
c/o Staff Member *Diverse Talent Group*
9911 W Pico Blvd Ste 340W
Los Angeles, CA 90035-2712, USA

Moran, Pauline
275 Kensington Rd
London, ENGLAND SW1 6BY

Moran, Richard J (Rich) (Athlete, Football Player)
7252 Mimosa Dr
Carlsbad, CA 92011-5149, USA

Moran, Sean (Athlete, Football Player)
13577 W 84th Dr
Arvada, CO 80005-5825, USA

Moran, Tommy (Actor)
c/o Staff Member *Creative Artists Agency (CAA-LA)*
2000 Avenue of the Stars Ste 100
Los Angeles, CA 90067-4705, USA

Moran, Tony (DJ)
c/o Len Evans *Project Publicity*
312 W 53rd St Ste 202
New York, NY 10019-5743, USA

Morandini, Mickey (Athlete, Baseball Player)
1045 Walker Pass
Chesterton, IN 46304-3473, USA

Moranis, Rick (Actor)
c/o Staff Member *WmE2 (WMA-LA)*
1 William Morris Pl
Beverly Hills, CA 90212-4261, USA

Morante, Laura (Actor)
Via Giuseppe Pisanelli
Rome 196, ITALY

Morasca, Jenna (Reality TV Star)
6027 Belle Terre Ct
Bridgeville, PA 15017-3459, USA

Morast, Daniel J (Misc)
634 N Falmouth Hwy
North Falmouth, MA 02556-9998, USA

Morath, Max (Musician)
1186 N 56th St
Tampa, FL 33617, USA

Morauta, Mekere (Prime Minister)
Marea Haus Walgani
Port Moresby, PAPUA NEW GUINEA

Moravec, Ivan (Musician)
3436 Springhill Rd
Lafayette, CA 94549-2535, USA

Morceli, Noureddine (Athlete, Track Athlete)
3 Rue Mohamed Belouizdad
Algiers, ALGERIA

Morcott, Southwood J (Business Person)
PO Box 1000
Toledo, OH 43697-1000, USA

Mordashov, Alexei (Business Person)
2/3 Klara Tsetkin St
Moscow RU-127299, Russia

Mordecai, Mike (Athlete, Baseball Player)
10 Cross Creek Ln
Dothan, AL 36303-9320, USA

Mordillo, Guillermo (Cartoonist)
8 Oberweg
Cheyenne, WY 82008-0001, GERMANY

Mordkovitch, Lydia (Musician)
25B Belsize Ave
London NW3 3BL, UNITED KINGDOM (UK)

More, Camilla (Actor)
477 S Robertson Blvd # 204
Beverly Hills, CA 90211, USA

Moreau, Doug (Athlete, Football Player)
5875 Highland Rd
Baton Rouge, LA 70808-6559, USA

Moreau, Jeanne (Actor)
5 Rue Clemont Marot
Paris 75008, FRANCE

Moreau, Marguerite (Actor)
c/o Heather Reynolds *One Entertainment (NY)*
12 W 57th St PH 1
New York, NY 10019-3900, USA

Moreau, Sylvie
11 Av Corentin Cariou
Paris, FRANCE 75019

Morehead, Dave (Athlete, Baseball Player)
13872 Glenmere Dr
Santa Ana, CA 92705-2812, USA

Moreino, Joe (Athlete, Football Player)
25 Gemini Dr
East Providence, RI 02914-4081, USA

Moreira, Airto (Musician)
PO Box 29242
Oakland, CA 94604-9242, USA

Morejon, Dan (Athlete, Baseball Player)
22625 SW 207th Ave
Miami, FL 33170-4846, USA

Moreland, Keith (Athlete, Baseball Player)
4209 Hidden Canyon Cv
Austin, TX 78746-1256, USA

Morelli, Oscar (Actor)
c/o Staff Member *Televisa*
Blvd Adolfo Lopez Mateos 232 Colonia San Angel INN
DF CP 01060, MEXICO

Morello, Tom (Musician)
8935 Lindblade St
Culver City, CA 90232-2438, USA

Morelos, Lisette (Actor)
c/o Staff Member *Televisa*
Blvd Adolfo Lopez Mateos 232 Colonia San Angel INN
DF CP 01060, MEXICO

Moreno, Arturo "'Arte"' (Business Person)
c/o Staff Member *Los Angeles Angels Of Anaheim*
2000 E Gene Autry Way
Anaheim, CA 92806-6143, USA

Moreno, Azucar (Music Group)
c/o Staff Member *Sony Music Miami*
605 Lincoln Rd Ste 700
Miami Beach, FL 33139-2901, USA

Moreno, Catalina Sandino (Actor)
c/o Staff Member *Creative Artists Agency (CAA-LA)*
2000 Avenue of the Stars Ste 100
Los Angeles, CA 90067-4705, USA

Moreno, Isabel (Actor)
c/o Gabriel Blanco *Gabriel Blanco Iglesias (Mexico)*
Rio Balsas 35-32 Colonia Cuauhtemoc
DF 6500, Mexico

Moreno, Jaime (Race Car Driver)
252 Montclaire Cir
Weston, FL 33326, USA

Moreno, Jaime (Musician)
1 Harmon Plz # 300
Secaucus, NJ 07094-2803, USA

Moreno, Jose Elias (Actor)
c/o Staff Member *Televisa*
Blvd Adolfo Lopez Mateos 232 Colonia San Angel INN
DF CP 01060, MEXICO

Moreno, Lea
4739 Lankershim Blvd
North Hollywood, CA 91602-1803

Moreno, Moses (Athlete, Football Player)
11627 Lakeside Ave
Lakeside, CA 92040-1614, USA

Moreno, Orber (Athlete, Baseball Player)
4833 Kingston Cir
Kissimmee, FL 34746-5102, USA

Moreno, Rita (Actor)
7027 Devon Way
Berkeley, CA 94705-1722, USA

Moresco, Robert (Actor, Director, Producer, Writer)
c/o Chris Silbermann *International Creative Management (ICM-LA)*
10250 Constellation Blvd Fl 7
Los Angeles, CA 90067-6207, USA

Moresco, Tim (Athlete, Football Player)
2413 Pond Rd
Duluth, GA 30096-6002, USA

Moret, Rogelio (Roger) (Athlete, Baseball Player)
HC 1 P.O. Box 5225
Guaynabo, PR 971, USA

Moretti, Fabrizio (Musician)
370 7th Ave # 807
New York, NY 10001-3967, USA

Moretz, Chloe (Actor)
c/o Pamela Kohl *3 Arts Entertainment Inc*
9460 Wilshire Blvd Fl 7
Beverly Hills, CA 90212-2713, USA

Morey, Bill (Actor)
11365 Ventura Blvd Ste 100
Studio City, CA 91604-3148, USA

Morfogen, George (Actor)
c/o Staff Member *Gersh (LA)*
9465 Wilshire Blvd Ste 600
Beverly Hills, CA 90212-2612, USA

Morgado, Arnold (Athlete, Football Player)
1750 Kaahumanu St Apt 53-C
Pearl City, HI 96782, USA

Morgan, Angelique (Reality TV Star)
c/o Anthony Embry *AE Entertainment Public Relations*
124 Evening Shade Dr
Charleston, SC 29414-9144, USA

Morgan, Barbara R (Astronaut)
2996 S Rookery Ln
Boise, ID 83706-5484, USA

Morgan, Bill (Writer)
c/o Staff Member *Da Capo Press*
44 Farnsworth St Fl 3
Boston, MA 02210-1223, USA

Morgan, Bobby (Athlete, Baseball Player)
3004 Stonybrook Rd
Oklahoma City, OK 73120-5716, USA

Morgan, Brit (Actor)
c/o Jessica Cohen *JCPR*
9903 Santa Monica Blvd Ste 983
Beverly Hills, CA 90212-1671, USA

Morgan, Chad (Actor)
c/o Staff Member *Silver Massetti & Szatmary (SMS) Talent Inc*
8730 W Sunset Blvd Ste 440
Los Angeles, CA 90069-2277, USA

Morgan, Craig (Musician)
c/o Staff Member *WmE2 (WMA-TN)*
1600 Division St Ste 300
Nashville, TN 37203-2755, USA

Morgan, Dan (Athlete, Football Player)
21214 SE 40th Pl
Sammamish, WA 98075-7284, USA

Morgan, Debbi (Actor)
c/o Elissa Leeds-Fickman *Reel Talent Management*
PO Box 491035
Los Angeles, CA 90049-9035, USA

Morgan, Debelah (Musician)
83 Riverside Dr
New York, NY 10024-5713, USA

Morgan, Derrick (Athlete, Football Player)
26826 Morgan Run
Westlake, OH 44145-7404, USA

Morgan, Donald M (Cinematographer)
15826 Mayall St
North Hills, CA 91343-1415, USA

Morgan, Elaine
24 Aberford Rd. Mt. Ash
Glamorgan, ENGLAND

Morgan, Frank (Musician)
PO Box 961
Burlington, MA 01803-5961, USA

Morgan, Gil (Athlete, Golfer)
PO Box 806
Edmond, OK 73083-0806, USA

Morgan, Glen (Director, Producer, Writer)
c/o Staff Member *WmE2 (Endeavor-LA)*
9601 Wilshire Blvd Fl 3
Beverly Hills, CA 90210-5219, USA

Morgan, James C (Business Person)
3050 Bowers Ave
Santa Clara, CA 95054-3201, USA

Morgan, James N (Economist)
1217 Bydding Rd
Ann Arbor, MI 48103-3103, USA

Morgan, Jane (Musician)
27740 Pacific Coast Hwy
Malibu, CA 90265-4341, USA

Morgan, Jaye P (Actor, Musician)
1185 La Grange Ave
Newbury Park, CA 91320-5316, USA

Morgan, Jeffrey Dean (Actor)
c/o Robert (Rob) Gomez *Precision Entertainment*
6338 Wilshire Blvd
Los Angeles, CA 90048-5002, USA

Morgan, Joe (Athlete, Baseball Player, Coach)
15 Oak Hill Dr
Walpole, MA 02081-2713, USA

Morgan, Joseph (Actor)
c/o Richard Konigsberg *RKM*
400 N Mansfield Ave
Los Angeles, CA 90036-2622, USA

Morgan, Katie (Actor)
18663 Ventura Blvd Ste 703
Tarzana, CA 91356-4162, USA

Morgan, Kevin (Athlete, Baseball Player)
205 Yearling Rd Lot 10
Duson, LA 70529-3118, USA

Morgan, Lewis R (Judge)
25 Elmtree Dr
Sharpsburg, GA 30277-1946, USA

Morgan, Lorrie (Actor, Musician)
c/o Staff Member *Webster & Associates PR*
3573 Couchville Pike
Hermitage, TN 37076-4012, USA

Morgan, Marabel (Writer)
1300 NW 167th St
Miami, FL 33169-5787, USA

Morgan, Mia (Stylist)
c/o Staff Member *Ford Models (Chicago)*
311 W Superior St
Chicago, IL 60654-3548, USA

Morgan, Michael (Scientist)
183 Euston Road
London NW1 2BE, UNITED KINGDOM (UK)

Morgan, Michele (Actor, Musician)
5 Rue Jacques Dulud
Neuillysur-Seine 92200, FRANCE

Morgan, Michelle (Actor)
c/o Staff Member *Levine Okwu Erickson Management*
6363 Wilshire Blvd Ste 300
Los Angeles, CA 90048-5729, USA

Morgan, Mike (Athlete, Football Player)
14383 Carey Rd
Baker, LA 70714, USA

Morgan, Mike (Athlete, Baseball Player)
PO Box 681130
Park City, UT 84068-1130, USA

Morgan, Mike (Cartoonist)
5777 W Century Blvd Ste 1700
Los Angeles, CA 90045-5671, USA

Morgan, Munden (Athlete, Basketball Player)
149 Windrush Rd
Winston Salem, NC 27106-2593, USA

Morgan, Peter (Director, Producer, Writer)
c/o Jeremy Barber *United Talent Agency (UTA)*
9560 Wilshire Blvd Fl 5
Beverly Hills, CA 90212-2400, USA

Morgan, Piers (Reality TV Star, Television Host)
c/o John Ferriter *Octagon Entertainment*
8687 Melrose Ave Ste 7
West Hollywood, CA 90069-5721, USA

Morgan, Quincy (Athlete, Football Player)
4654 N Jupiter Rd Apt 1411
Garland, TX 75044-8820, USA

Morgan, Robert B (Senator)
101 E Front St
Lillington, NC 27546-6683, USA

Morgan, Shelly Taylor (Actor)
9229 W Sunset Blvd Ste 315
Los Angeles, CA 90069-3403, USA

Morgan, Sonja (Reality TV Star)
c/o Staff Member *Bravo (NY)*
30 Rockefeller Plz
New York, NY 10112-0015, USA

Morgan, Stanley D (Athlete, Football Player)
PO Box 383048
Germantown, TN 38183-3048, USA

Morgan, Tracy (Actor, Comedian)
c/o David (Dave) Becky *3 Arts Entertainment Inc*
9460 Wilshire Blvd Fl 7
Beverly Hills, CA 90212-2713, USA

Morgan, Trevor (Actor)
c/o Beverly Strong *Strong Management*
3532 Hayden Ave
Culver City, CA 90232-2413, USA

Morgan, W Jason (Misc)
Geophysic
Princeton, NJ 08544-0001, USA

Morgan, Walter (Athlete, Golfer)
15536 Fishermans Rest Ct
Cornelius, NC 28031-7646, USA

Morgan, Walter T J (Misc)
57 Woodbury Dr Sutton
Surrey, UNITED KINGDOM (UK)

Morgan, William N (Architect)
1945 Beach Ave
Atlantic Beach, FL 32233-5936, USA

Morganna (Entertainer, Model)
PO Box 20281
Columbus, OH 43220-0281, USA

Morgenstern, Maia (Actor)
c/o Catherine Davray *Catherine Davray Agency*
16 bis rue de l'Abbe de l'Epee
Paris 75005, FRANCE

Morgenthau, Robert M (Attorney, Attorney General, General)
1085 Park Ave
New York, NY 10128-1168, USA

Morgridge, John P (Business Person)
170 W Tasman Dr
San Jose, CA 95134-1700, USA

Morhardt, Moe (Athlete, Baseball Player)
219 Spencer Hill Rd
Winsted, CT 06098-2214, USA

Mori, Barbara (Actor)
c/o Eric Rovner *WmE2 (WMA-Miami)*
119 Washington Ave Ste 400
Miami, FL 33139-7202, USA

Mori, Hanae (Designer, Fashion Designer)
17-19 Ave Montaigne
Paris, 75008, FRANCE

Mori, Yoshiro (Prime Minister)
1-6-1 Nagatoicho Chiyodaku
Tokyo 100, JAPAN

Moriarty, Evelyn
6251 Coldwater Canyon Ave Unit 102
North Hollywood, CA 91606-3001

Moriarty, Michael (Actor)
200 W 58th St Apt 3B
New York, NY 10019-1477, USA

Moriarty, Mike (Athlete, Baseball Player)
5 E Oleander Dr
Mount Laurel, NJ 08054-3601, USA

Moriarty, Phillip (Phil) (Coach)
12 Vista De Laguna
Fort Pierce, FL 34951-2826, USA

Moriarty, Tom (Athlete, Football Player)
28800 Fairmount Blvd
Cleveland, OH 44124-4542, USA

Moriarty-Gentile, Cathy (Actor)
c/o Brian Liebman *Liebman Entertainment*
25 E 21st St PH
New York, NY 10010-6226, USA

Morimoto, Masaharu
105 Hudson St
New York, NY 10013-2331

Morin, Alan (Athlete, Golfer)
139 Jay Ct
Royal Palm Beach, FL 33411-1723, USA

Morin, Jim (Cartoonist, Editor)
Editorial Dept Herald Plaza
Miami, FL 33101, USA

Morin, Lee M E (Astronaut)
10 Marys Creek Ln
Friendswood, TX 77546-3492, USA

Morin, Milt (Athlete, Football Player)
45 N Maple St # B
Hadley, MA 01035-9768, USA

Morison, Patricia (Actor, Musician)
125 S Sycamore Ave
Los Angeles, CA 90036-2938, USA

Morissette, Alanis (Musician, Songwriter, Writer)

Moritz, Brett (Athlete, Football Player)
613 Cameron Ridge Ct
Parkton, MD 21120-8906, USA

Moritz, Louisa
405 S Cliffwood Ave
Los Angeles, CA 90049-3827

Moriyama, Raymond (Architect)
32 Daveport Rd
Toronto, ON 1H3, CANADA

Mork, Truis (Musician)
12 Penzance Place
London W11 4PA, UNITED KINGDOM (UK)

Morkis, Dorothy (Horse Racer)
17 Farm St
Dover, MA 02030-2303, USA

Morlan, John (Athlete, Baseball Player)
3290 Belgreen Dr
Grove City, OH 43123-8297, USA

Morland, David (Athlete, Golfer)
5531 Oxford Moor Blvd
Windermere, FL 34786-7012, USA

Morley, Joanne (Athlete, Golfer)
Pier House Strand on the Ocean Chiswick
London W4 3NN, United Kingdom

Morley, Lawrence W (Geophysicist, Physicist)
90 Hemlock St
Saint Thomas, ON N5R 1X9, CANADA

Morley, Malcolm (Artist)
32 E 57th St
New York, NY 10022-2513, USA

Morley, W I (Editor)
369 York St
London, ON N6A 4G1, UNITED KINGDOM (UK)

Morman, Alvin (Athlete, Baseball Player)
117 Philadelphia Dr
Rockingham, NC 28379-8607, USA

Mormon, Russ (Athlete, Baseball Player)
3209 S Mark Twain Ave
Blue Springs, MO 64015-1127, USA

Morneau, Justin (Athlete, Baseball Player)
1829 Forestview Ln N
Minneapolis, MN 55441-4105, USA

Mornell, Sara
9300 Wilshire Blvd Ste 555
Beverly Hills, CA 90212-3211

Mornhinweg, Marty (Athlete, Football Coach, Football Player)
3507 Trevi Ct
Philadelphia, PA 19145-5759, USA

Morning After Girls, The (Music Group)
c/o Staff Member *Paradigm (Monterey)*
404 W Franklin St
Monterey, CA 93940-2303, USA

Morningstar, Darren (Athlete, Basketball Player)
1515 W Ingomar Rd
Pittsburgh, PA 15237-1644, USA

Morningwood (Music Group)
Bad Moon PR 19 B All Saints Rd
London W11 1HE, UNITED KINGDOM

Moroder, Giorgio (Composer)
1880 Century Park E Ste 900
Los Angeles, CA 90067-1610, USA

Morogiello, Dan (Athlete, Baseball Player)
99 Distillery Rd
Whitehouse Station, NJ 08889-3005, USA

Moronko, Jeff (Athlete, Baseball Player)
3903 Bartons Ct
Sugar Land, TX 77479-1941, USA

Moroski, Mike (Athlete, Football Player)
1214 Pine Ln
Davis, CA 95616-1700, USA

Morozov, Akexei (Athlete, Hockey Player)
66 Mario Lemieux Pl
Pittsburgh, PA 15219-3504, USA

Morozov, Vladimir M (Opera Singer)
Mariinsky Theater Reatralnaya 1
Saint Petersburg, RUSSIA

Morphet, David
101 Honor Oak Rd
London, ENGLAND SE23 3LB

Morphine
48 Laight St
New York, NY 10013-2156

Morrall, Earl (Athlete, Football Player)
2751 68th St SW
Naples, FL 34105-7235, USA

Morrell, David (Writer)
c/o Staff Member *Vanguard Press*
387 Park Ave S Fl 12
New York, NY 10016-8802, USA

Morretti, Tobias (Actor)
Ordensmeisterstr 15-16
Berling 12099, GERMANY

Morrey, Charles B Jr (Mathematician)
210 Yale Ave
Kensington, CA 94708-1014, USA

Morrice, Norman A (Ballerina, Choreographer)
Covent Garden Bow St
London WC2E 9DD, UNITED KINGDOM (UK)

Morricone, Ennio (Composer)
Viale delle Letteratura #30
Rome 144, ITALY

Morris, Ashley Austin (Actor)
c/o Rob Kolker *Red Letter Entertainment*
437 W 48th St Apt D
New York, NY 10036-1285, USA

Morris, Betty (Bowler)
225 Lemming Dr
Reno, NV 89523-9662, USA

Morris, Byron (Bam) (Athlete, Football Player)
251 NE 4th St
Cooper, TX 75432-1833, USA

Morris, Charles R. (Writer)
1333 H St NW Fl 10
Washington, DC 20005-4703, USA

Morris, Chris (Athlete, Basketball Player)
3097 Milford Chase SW
Marietta, GA 30008-6883, USA

Morris, Colleen
8271 Melrose Ave Ste 110
Los Angeles, CA 90046-6800

Morris, Danny (Athlete, Baseball Player)
6527 Rhode Island Ave
Hammond, IN 46323-1923, USA

Morris, Desmond (Doctor)
78 Danbury Rd
Oxford, ENGLAND

Morris, Desmond J (Biologist, Writer)
20 Vauxhall Bridge Road
London SW1V 2SA, UNITED KINGDOM (UK)

Morris, Dick (Misc)
64 Twin Lakes Rd
South Salem, NY 10590-1009, USA

Morris, Donnie Joe (Athlete, Football Player)
1414 NW 13th Ave
Amarillo, TX 79107-1604, USA

Morris, Doug (Business Person)
c/o Staff Member *Universal Music Group (UMG - LA)*
2220 Colorado Ave
Santa Monica, CA 90404-3506, USA

Morris, Dwaine (Athlete, Football Player)
4002 Kilkenny Dr
Baton Rouge, LA 70814-7525, USA

Morris, Edmund (Educator, Writer)
222 Central Park S # 14A
New York, NY 10019-1408, USA

Morris, Errol (Director)
c/o Staff Member *Block-Korenbrot Public Relations*
North Market Building 110 S Fairfax, Suite 310
Los Angeles, CA 90036, USA

Morris, Eugene (Athlete, Football Player)
11315 SW 243rd Ter
Homestead, FL 33032-7125, USA

Morris, Gary (Musician)
PO Box 176
Chromo, CO 81128-0176, USA

Morris, Hal (Athlete, Baseball Player)
6138 Payne Stewart Dr
Windermere, FL 34786-8936, USA

Morris, Heather (Actor)
c/o Jennifer Merlino *Untitled Entertainment (LA)*
350 S Beverly Dr Ste 200
Beverly Hills, CA 90212-4819, USA

Morris, Isaiah (Athlete, Basketball Player)
4308 W Cermak Rd
Chicago, IL 60623-2901, USA

Morris, Jack (Athlete, Baseball Player)
7993 100th St N
Saint Paul, MN 55110-1445, USA

Morris, James P (Opera Singer)
111 W 57th St
New York, NY 10019-2211, USA

Morris, Jan (Writer)
Trefan Morys Llanystumdwy
Criccieth, Gwymedd, WALES

Morris, Jason (Athlete)
16 Gail St
Chelmsford, MA 01824-3510, USA

Morris, Jenny (Musician)
PO Box 537
Randwick, NSW 2031, AUSTRALIA

Morris, Jim (Athlete, Baseball Player)
156 Edinburgh Rd
San Angelo, TX 76901-9501, USA

Morris, John (Athlete, Baseball Player)
5538 E Paradise Ln
Scottsdale, AZ 85254-1165, USA

Morris, John (Athlete, Baseball Player)
2645 Elm Dr
North Bellmore, NY 11710-1303, USA

Morris, Johnny (Athlete, Football Player)
753 Shoreline Rd
Lake Barrington, IL 60010-3825, USA

Morris, Jon (Athlete, Football Player)
Berkley Court
Bluffton, SC 29910-4839, USA

Morris, Julian (Actor)
c/o Jai Khanna *Brillstein Entertainment Partners*
9150 Wilshire Blvd Ste 350
Beverly Hills, CA 90212-3453, USA

Morris, Kathryn (Actor)
c/o David (Dave) Fleming *Mosaic Media Group*
9200 W Sunset Blvd Ste 10
Los Angeles, CA 90069-3608, USA

Morris, Keith (Musician)
8942 Wilshire Blvd # 219
Beverly Hills, CA 90211-1908, USA

Morris, Lamorne (Actor)
c/o Staff Member *11-16 Entertainment*
10100 Santa Monica Blvd Ste 300
Los Angeles, CA 90067-4107, USA

Morris, Larry (Artist)
105 N Union St # 4
Alexandria, VA 22314-3217, USA

Morris, Lawrence C (Larry) (Athlete, Football Player)
4737 Upper Berkshire Rd
Flowery Branch, GA 30542-3692, USA

Morris, Marianne (Athlete, Golfer)
4013 Lisa Ln
Middletown, OH 45042-2832, USA

Morris, Mark W (Choreographer)
3 Lafayette Ave # 504
Brooklyn, NY 11217-1415, USA

Morris, Matt (Athlete, Baseball Player)
397 Old Jupiter Beach Rd
Jupiter, FL 33477-5034, USA

Morris, Matt (Musician)
c/o Staff Member *WmE2 (Endeavor-LA)*
9601 Wilshire Blvd Fl 3
Beverly Hills, CA 90210-5219, USA

Morris, Mitch (Actor)
c/o Benjamin Tappan *Tappan Entertainment*
8324 Fountain Ave Apt C
Los Angeles, CA 90069-2916, USA

Morris, Nathan (Musician)
c/o Staff Member *Southpaw Entertainment*
1710 N Fuller Ave Apt 323
Los Angeles, CA 90046-3064, USA

Morris, Oswald (Ossie) (Cinematographer)
Holbrook Church St Fontmell Magna
Shaftesbury SP7 0NY, UNITED KINGDOM (UK)

Morris, Phil (Actor)
704 Strand
Manhattan Beach, CA 90266, USA

Morris, Reginald H (Cinematographer)
255 Bambaugh Cir # 308
Scarborough, ON M1W 3T6, CANADA

Morris, Robert (Artist)
Art Dept
New York, NY 10021, USA

Morris, Ronald (Ron) (Athlete, Track Athlete)
330 S Reese Pl
Burbank, CA 91506-2724, USA

Morris, Sarah Ann (Actor)
c/o Staff Member *TalentWorks (LA)*
3500 W Olive Ave Ste 1400
Burbank, CA 91505-5512, USA

Morris, Sarah Jane (Actor)
c/o Melissa Stone *42West (LA)*
11400 W Olympic Blvd Ste 1100
Los Angeles, CA 90064-1579, USA

Morris, Seth Irvin (Architect)
2 Waverly Ct
Houston, TX 77005-1842, USA

Morris, Shellee
6117 Highway 135
Lake City, AR 72437-8851

Morris, Wanya (Musician)
c/o Staff Member *Creative Artists Agency (CAA-LA)*
2000 Avenue of the Stars Ste 100
Los Angeles, CA 90067-4705, USA

Morris, Warren (Athlete, Baseball Player)
1215 Wilshire Dr
Alexandria, LA 71303-3141, USA

Morris, Wayna (Musician)
c/o Staff Member *Southpaw Entertainment*
1710 N Fuller Ave Apt 323
Los Angeles, CA 90046-3064, USA

Morris, Wayne (Athlete, Football Player)
5715 Old Ox Rd
Dallas, TX 75241-2118, USA

Morris, Wingerter Pam (Swimmer)
PO Box 14381
New Bern, NC 28561-4381, USA

Morrison, Adam (Athlete, Basketball Player)
c/o Team Member *Los Angeles (LA) Lakers*
555 N Nash St
El Segundo, CA 90245-2818, USA

Morrison, Allan E (Athlete, Football Player)
PO Box 777935
Henderson, NV 89077-7935, USA

Morrison, Christopher (Mink) (Director)
c/o Staff Member *International Creative Management (ICM-LA)*
10250 Constellation Blvd Fl 7
Los Angeles, CA 90067-6207, USA

Morrison, Dan (Athlete, Baseball Player)
13120 Plantation Ter
Seminole, FL 33776-2430, USA

Morrison, Darryl (Athlete, Football Player)
703 Brigadier Ct SE
Leesburg, VA 20175-4450, USA

Morrison, Don (Athlete, Football Player)
PO Box 432
Wolfe City, TX 75496-0432, USA

Morrison, Dwight (Athlete, Basketball Player)
6112 E Singletree St
Apache Junction, AZ 85119-9548, USA

Morrison, Felton (Baseball Player)
3860 N Bouvier St
Philadelphia, PA 19140-3528, USA

Morrison, Fred (Athlete, Football Player)
38189 Greywalls Dr
Murrieta, CA 92562-3058, USA

Morrison, Ian (Scotty) (Misc)
Kennisis Lake RR 1 PO Box 314
Haliburton, ON K0M 1S0, CANADA

Morrison, James (Actor)
c/o Mitch Clem *Shadow Entertainment*
10 Universal City Plz Fl 20
Universal City, CA 91608-1074, USA

Morrison, Jennifer (Actor)
c/o John Carrabino *John Carrabino Management*
5900 Wilshire Blvd Ste 406
Los Angeles, CA 90036-5015, USA

Morrison, Jim (Baseball Player)
8715 11th Avenue Pl NW
Bradenton, FL 34209-9661, USA

Morrison, Kirk (Athlete, Football Player)
c/o Staff Member *EAG Sports Management*
12910 Agustin Pl
Playa Vista, CA 90094-2301, USA

Morrison, Mark (Musician)
1290 Avenue of the Americas
New York, NY 10104-0101, USA

Morrison, Matthew (Actor)
c/o Evelyn Karamanos *WKT Public Relations (WKT-LA)*
9350 Wilshire Blvd Ste 450
Beverly Hills, CA 90212-3230, USA

Morrison, Mike (Athlete, Basketball Player)
113 Rivanna Ln
Greenville, SC 29607-5488, USA

Morrison, Patricia (Musician)
P.O. Box 400
Chichester, West Sussex PO20 7YE, Great Britian

Morrison, Robert S (Bob) (Business Person)
Quaker Tower PO Box 049001
Chicago, IL 60604, USA

Morrison, Shelley (Actor)
1209 S Alfred St
Los Angeles, CA 90035-2569, USA

Morrison, Stacy (Editor)
c/o Staff Member *Redbook Magazine*
300 W 57th St
New York, NY 10019-3741, USA

Morrison, Temuera (Actor)
c/o Joseph (Joe) Rice *Abrams Artists Agency (LA)*
9200 W Sunset Blvd PH 11
Los Angeles, CA 90069-3601, USA

Morrison, Temuera (Actor)
c/o Staff Member *Abrams Artists Agency (LA)*
9200 W Sunset Blvd PH 11
Los Angeles, CA 90069-3601, USA

Morrison, Toni (Nobel Prize Laureate, Writer)
c/o Staff Member *International Creative Management (ICM-LA)*
10250 Constellation Blvd Fl 7
Los Angeles, CA 90067-6207, USA

Morrison, Van (Musician, Songwriter)
c/o Staff Member *Universal Music Group (UMG - LA)*
1620 Euclid St
Santa Monica, CA 90404-3724, USA

Morrison-Gamberdella, Ester (Baseball Player)
3179 Pleasant Creek Rd
Rogue River, OR 97537-9803, USA

Morrissette, Billy (Actor, Director, Writer)
c/o Brian Inerfeld *Protocol Entertainment (LA)*
9336 Washington Blvd
Culver City, CA 90232-2628, USA

Morrissey, Bill (Musician, Songwriter, Writer)
c/o Staff Member *Creative Artists Agency (CAA-LA)*
2000 Avenue of the Stars Ste 100
Los Angeles, CA 90067-4705, USA

Morrissey, David (Actor)
c/o Melanie Greene *Affirmative Entertainment*
425 N Robertson Blvd
West Hollywood, CA 90048-1735, USA

Morrissey, Jim (Athlete, Football Player)
48 Fox Trl
Lincolnshire, IL 60069-4012, USA

Morrissey, Neil (Actor)
c/o Staff Member *International Creative Management (ICM-LA)*
10250 Constellation Blvd Fl 7
Los Angeles, CA 90067-6207, USA

Morrissey, Steven Patrick (Actor, Composer, Music Group, Songwriter, Writer)
c/o Staff Member *Universal Music Group (UMG - LA)*
2220 Colorado Ave
Santa Monica, CA 90404-3506, USA

Morrone, Joe (Coach, Football Coach)
Athletic
Storrs Mansfield, CT 06269-0001, USA

Morrow, Bobby
18512 Minor Rd
San Benito, TX 78586-7039

Morrow, Bobby Joe (Athlete, Track Athlete)
8003 North Holw Apt 604
San Antonio, TX 78240-2386, USA

Morrow, Bruce (Cousin Brucie) (Radio Personality)
c/o Staff Member *SIRIUS Satellite Radio*
1221 Avenue of the Americas Fl 19
New York, NY 10020-1011, USA

Morrow, Bruce (Cousin Brucie) (Entertainer, Radio Personality)
1221 Avenue of the Americas
New York, NY 10020-1001, USA

Morrow, Harold (Athlete, Football Player)
3390 US Highway 82
Maplesville, AL 36750-5112, USA

Morrow, Joshua (Actor)
c/o Marv Dauer *Marv Dauer Management*
11661 San Vicente Blvd Ste 104
Los Angeles, CA 90049-5150, USA

Morrow, Kenneth (Ken) (Athlete, Hockey Player)
6732 NW Monticello Dr
Kansas City, MO 64152-5703, USA

Morrow, Mari (Actor)
c/o David Ziff *Cunningham Escott Slevin & Doherty (CESD-LA)*
10635 Santa Monica Blvd Ste 130
Los Angeles, CA 90025-8306, USA

Morrow, Rob (Actor)
c/o Judy Hofflund *Hofflund/Polone*
9465 Wilshire Blvd Ste 420
Beverly Hills, CA 90212-2603, USA

Morse, Cathy (Athlete, Golfer)
6228 Celadon Cir
West Palm Beach, FL 33418-1436, USA

Morse, Cheryl (Stylist)
c/o Staff Member *Team*
423 W Broadway Ste 406
Boston, MA 02127-2265, USA

Morse, David (Musician)
9200 W Sunset Blvd Ste 900
Los Angeles, CA 90069-3604, USA

Morse, David (Actor)
1040 1st Ave # 1126
New York, NY 10022-2991, USA

Morse, David E (Publisher)
Publisher's Office 1 Norway St
Boston, MA 2115, USA

Morse, Helen (Actor)
147 King St # A
Sydney, NSW 2000, AUSTRALIA

Morse, John (Athlete, Golfer)
9291 17 Mile Rd
Marshall, MI 49068-9755, USA

Morse, Mike (Athlete, Baseball Player)
417 NW 97th Ave
Plantation, FL 33324-7075, USA

Morse, Natalie (Actor)
52/53 Poland Place
London W1F 7LX, UNITED KINGDOM (UK)

Morse, Philip M (Physicist)
126 Wildwood St
Winchester, MA 01890-2308, USA

Morse, Ray
1845 NW Garfield Ave
Corvallis, OR 97330-2535

Morse, Robert (Actor)
13830 Davana Ter
Sherman Oaks, CA 91423-4216, USA

Morse, Steve (Athlete, Football Player)
3913 FM 359 Rd
Richmond, TX 77406-9685, USA

Mortensen, Chris (Sportscaster)
Sports Dept ESPN Plaza 935 Middle St
Bristol, CT 6010, USA

Mortensen, J D (Doctor)
5060 Amelia Earhart Dr
Salt Lake City, UT 84116-2800, USA

Mortensen, Viggo (Actor)
c/o Lynn Rawlins *Rawlins Company*
Prefers to be contacted via telephone or email
CA 91301, USA

Mortier, Gerard (Opera Singer)
Hofstallgasse 1
Salzburg 5020, AUSTRIA

Mortimer, Barrett Angela (Tennis Player)
Oaks Coombe Hill
Kingston-on-Thames, Surrey, UNITED KINGDOM (UK)

Mortimer, Emily (Actor)
c/o Aleen Keshishian *Brillstein Entertainment Partners*
9150 Wilshire Blvd Ste 350
Beverly Hills, CA 90212-3453, USA

Mortimer, John (Stylist)
c/o Staff Member *Seaminx Artist Management*
9234 Peninsula Dr
Dallas, TX 75218-2733, USA

Mortimer, Kenneth P (Educator)
President's Office
Honolulu, HI 96822, USA

Mortimer, Tinsley (Reality TV Star)
c/o Jan Planit *Planit Management*
11 E 26th St
New York, NY 10010-1402, USA

Mortita, Pat (Noriyuki) (Actor)
6399 Wilshire Blvd # 444
Los Angeles, CA 90048-5703, USA

Mortola, Alessandra (Stylist)
c/o Staff Member *Artist Untied (LA)*
845 S Mansfield Ave Apt 1
Los Angeles, CA 90036-4979, USA

Morton, Alicia (Actor)
c/o Staff Member *WmE2 (WMA-LA)*
1 William Morris Pl
Beverly Hills, CA 90212-4261, USA

Morton, Bruce A (Correspondent)
820 1st St NE
Washington, DC 20002-4243, USA

Morton, Craig (Athlete, Football Player)
9850 N 73rd St Unit 2037
Scottsdale, AZ 85258-1032, USA

Morton, Guy (Athlete, Baseball Player)
567 Femdale Ave
Vermilion, OH 44089, USA

Morton, Joe (Actor)
605 N Larchont Blvd # 309
Los Angeles, CA 90004, USA

Morton, John (Athlete, Football Player)
39991 Purmice Dr
Cassel, CA 96016, USA

Morton, Johnnie (Athlete, Football Player)
2911 Oakwood Ln
Torrance, CA 90505-7121, USA

Morton, Kevin (Athlete, Baseball Player)
26 Glen Ave
Norwalk, CT 6850, USA

Morton, Kristopher (Colt) (Athlete, Baseball Player)
3245 Santa Barbara Dr
Wellington, FL 33414-7267, USA

Morton, Richard (Athlete, Basketball Player)
1111 Gilman Ave
San Francisco, CA 94124-3622, USA

Morton, Samantha (Actor)
c/o Troy Nankin *Wishlab*
2438 Canyon Oak Dr
Los Angeles, CA 90068-2428, USA

Morukov, Boris V (Cosmonaut)
Moskovskoi Oblasti
Syvisdny Goroduk 141160, RUSSIA

Morze, Frank (Athlete, Football Player)
P.O. Box 9097
Incline Village, NV 89452, USA

Mosbacher, Robert A (Secretary)
712 Main St Ste 2200
Houston, TX 77002-3206, USA

Moschen, Michael (Artist)
PO Box 178
Cornwall Bridge, CT 06754-0178, USA

Moschitta Jr, John
11601 Dunstan Way Apt 206
Los Angeles, CA 90049-4300, USA

Moschitto, Ross (Athlete, Baseball Player)
1633 SW Harbour Isles Cir
Port St Lucie, FL 34986-3405, USA

Moscow, David (Actor)
c/o Robert Stein *Robert Stein Management*
PO Box 3797
Beverly Hills, CA 90212-0797, USA

Mosebar, Donald H (Don) (Athlete, Football Player)
1713 Walnut Ave
Manhattan Beach, CA 90266-5016, USA

Moseby, Lloyd (Athlete, Baseball Player)
9140 Los Lagos Cir S
Granite Bay, CA 95746-5842, USA

Moseley, Bill (Actor)
c/o Peter Young *Sovereign Talent Group*
8421 Wilshire Blvd Ste 200
Beverly Hills, CA 90211-3204, USA

Moseley, Dustin (Athlete, Baseball Player)
2305 E Lakeview
Benton, AR 72015-2598, USA

Moseley, Jonny (Skier)
167 Trinidad Dr
Tiburon, CA 94920-1037, USA

Moseley, Mark (Athlete, Football Player)
7250 Middle Rd
Middletown, VA 22645-2121, USA

Moseley, Roy
152 Ivor Ct Gloucester Pl
London, ENGLAND NW1

Moseley, T Michael (Buzz) (General)
Vice Cheif of Staff Hqusaf Pentagon
Washington, DC 20330-0001, USA

Moseley, William (Actor)
c/o Rupert Fowler *ID Public Relations*
Pall Mall Deposit 124-128 Barlby Rd Unit 27A
London W10 6BL, UK

Moselle, Dominic (Athlete, Football Player)
2019 Hammond Ave
Superior, WI 54880-2751, USA

Moser, Barry (Misc)
115 Pantry Rd
North Hatfield, MA 1066, USA

Moser, Casey (Athlete, Baseball Player)
15050 N 27th Dr
Phoenix, AZ 85053-4908, USA

Moser, Donald B (Don) (Editor)
900 Jefferson SW
Washington, DC 20560-0004, USA

Moser, Rick (Athlete, Football Player)
1616 Esplanada Ave Apt 10
Redondo Beach, CA 90277, USA

Moser, Thomas (Opera Singer)
6 Henrietta St
London WC2E 8LA, UNITED KINGDOM (UK)

Moser-Proll, Annemarie (Skier)
#92
Kleinari 115 5602, AUSTRIA

Moses, Albert
15 Overstone Rd
Harpenden Herts., ENGLAND AL5 5PN

Moses, Billy E
409 N Camden Dr Ste 202
Beverly Hills, CA 90210-4423, USA

Moses, Ed (Athlete)
c/o Staff Member *Premier Management Group (PMG Sports)*
115 Crescent Commons Dr Ste 250
Cary, NC 27518-8134, USA

Moses, Edwin (Track Athlete)
1184 Daventry Way NE
Atlanta, GA 30319-4547, USA

Moses, Haven C (Athlete, Football Player)
1140 Cherokee St Unit 640
Denver, CO 80204-3684, USA

Moses, Jerry (Athlete, Baseball Player)
9 Court Ln
Ipswich, MA 01938-3027, USA

Moses, John (Athlete, Baseball Player)
21322 N 83rd St
Scottsdale, AZ 85255-6472, USA

Moses, Kim (Producer)
c/o Staff Member *WmE2 (WMA-LA)*
1 William Morris Pl
Beverly Hills, CA 90212-4261, USA

Moses, Lincoln E (Mathematician)
Medical Center Statistics Dept
Stanford, CA 94305, USA

Moses, Mark (Actor)
c/o Suzanne (Sue) Wohl *TalentWorks (LA)*
3500 W Olive Ave Ste 1400
Burbank, CA 91505-5512, USA

Moses, Rick (Actor, Musician)
19919 Redwing St
Woodland Hills, CA 91364-2620, USA

Moses, Robert (Bob) (Activist, Educator)
99 Bishop Richard Allen Dr
Cambridge, MA 02139-3428, USA

Moses, William R. (Actor, Producer)
c/o Richard Caplan *Noble Caplan Abrams*
1260 Yonge St 2nd Floor
Toronto, ON M4T 1W6, Canada

Moses, Yolanda T (Educator)
President's Office
New York, NY 10031, USA

Mosher, Gregory D (Director, Producer)
c/o Patrick Herold *Helen Merrill Ltd*
730 5th Ave Frnt 3A
New York, NY 10019-4149, USA

Moshinsky, Elijah (Opera Singer)
28 Kidbrooke Groove
London SE3 0LG, UNITED KINGDOM (UK)

Mosimann, Anton (Chef)
11B W Halkin St
London SW1X 8JL, UNITED KINGDOM (UK)

Mosisilli, Pakalitha (Prime Minister)
Military Council PO Box 527
Maseru 100, LESOTHO

Moskau, Paul (Athlete, Baseball Player)
5041 N Apache Hills Trl
Tucson, AZ 85750-5912, USA

Mosko, Lisa (Stylist)
c/o Staff Member *De Facto*
15 W 26th St Fl 5
New York, NY 10010-1028, USA

Moskow, Michael (Financier, Government Official)
230 S La Salle St
Chicago, IL 60604-1404, USA

Moskowitz, Robert (Artist)
81 Leonard St
New York, NY 10013-3436, USA

Mosler, John (Athlete, Football Player)
12604 Cambridge Rd
Leawood, KS 66209-1327, USA

Mosley, Brian (Actor)
Saga Court S Heath G Missenden
Bucks HP16 9QQ, UNITED KINGDOM (UK)

Mosley, J Brooke (Religious Leader)
1604 Foulkeways
Gwynedd, PA 19436-1033, USA

Mosley, Max R (Race Car Driver)
2 Chermin Blandonnet
Geneva 1215, SWITZERLAND

Mosley, Michael (Actor)
c/o Laurie Smith *Smith Talent Group*
14 Minetta St Fl 1
New York, NY 10012-1205, USA

Mosley, Mike (Athlete, Football Player)
109 Heritage Hill Rd
Wimberley, TX 78676-5632, USA

Mosley, Norm (Athlete, Football Player)
1056 53rd St S
Birmingham, AL 35222-4038, USA

Mosley, Roger E (Actor)
4470 W Sunset Blvd # 107-342
Los Angeles, CA 90027-6302, USA

Mosley, Russ (Athlete, Football Player)
5577 Cherry Tree Cir
Blytheville, AR 72315-3862, USA

Mosley, Sugar Shane (Boxer)
c/o Larry O. Williams Jr. *Williams Talent Agency*
550 W Regent St Apt 223
Inglewood, CA 90301-1038, USA

Mosley, Walter (Writer)
c/o Bruce Miller *Washington Square Arts (NY)*
310 Bowery Fl 2
New York, NY 10012-2861, USA

Mosoke, Kintu (Prime Minister)
PO Box 341
Kampala, UGANDA

Mosquera, Julio (Athlete, Baseball Player)
1419 Stone Creek Dr
Tarpon Springs, FL 34689-3045, USA

Moss, Carrie-Anne (Actor)
c/o Staff Member *WmE2 (WMA-LA)*
1 William Morris Pl
Beverly Hills, CA 90212-4261, USA

Moss, Cynthia (Misc)
Mara Road PO Box 48177
Nairobi, KENYA

Moss, Damian (Athlete, Baseball Player)
1877 GA Highway 19 S
Dublin, GA 31021-1480, USA

Moss, Eddie (Athlete, Football Player)
15404 Eagle Estates Ln
Florissant, MO 63034-1616, USA

Moss, Elisabeth (Actor)
c/o Gay Ribisi *Ribisi Entertainment*
3278 Wilshire Blvd Apt 702
Los Angeles, CA 90010-1425, USA

Moss, Elza (Religious Leader)
6403 Frame Rd
Elkview, WV 25071-7040, USA

Moss, Eric Owen (Architect)
8557 Higuera St
Culver City, CA 90232-2535, USA

Moss, Geoffrey (Cartoonist)
315 E 68th St
New York, NY 10065-5692, USA

Moss, Jon
64 Knighton Park Rd
London, ENGLAND SE26 5RL

Moss, Kate (Model)
c/o Staff Member *Storm Model Management*
5 Jubilee Pl 1st Floor
London SW3 3TD, UNITED KINGDOM

Moss, Les (Athlete, Baseball Player, Coach)
420 Tullis Ave
Longwood, FL 32750-5535, USA

Moss, Paige (Actor)
c/o Staff Member *Marshak/Zachary Company, The*
8840 Wilshire Blvd Fl 1
Beverly Hills, CA 90211-2606, USA

Moss, Perry (Athlete, Football Player, Golfer)
5660 S Lakeshore Dr Apt 505
Shreveport, LA 71119-4038, USA

Moss, Perry (Athlete, Basketball Player)
165 Columbia Dr
Amherst, MA 01002-3107, USA

Moss, Randy (Athlete, Football Player)
c/o Greg Barnett *Lagardere Unlimited - Miami*
235 Park Ave S Fl 6
New York, NY 10003-1405, USA

Moss, Roland (Athlete, Football Player)
411 Camelot Dr
Salisbury, NC 28144-9416, USA

Moss, Ronn (Actor)
2401 Nottingham Ave
Los Angeles, CA 90027-1036, USA

Moss, Santana (Athlete, Football Player)
18619 SW 50th Ct
Miramar, FL 33029-6245, USA

Moss, Shirley (Artist)
PO Box 18104
Anaheim, CA 92817-8104, USA

Moss, Stirling (Race Car Driver)
46 Shephard St
London W1Y 8JN, UNITED KINGDOM (UK)

Moss, Tegan (Actor)
c/o Tyman Stewart *Characters Talent Agency, The (Vancouver)*
8 Elm St 2nd Floor
Toronto, ON M5G 1G7, Canada

Moss, Zefross (Athlete, Football Player)
126 Kensington Dr
Madison, AL 35758-7844, USA

Mossbauer, Rudolf L (Nobel Prize Laureate)
Stumpflingstr 6A
Grunwald 82031, GERMANY

Mosser, Jonell (Musician)
PO Box 304
Bomoseen, VT 05732-0304, USA

Mossi, Don (Athlete, Baseball Player)
23250 Canyon Ln
Caldwell, ID 83607-7709, USA

Mossman, Doug
999 Kalapaki St
Honolulu, HI 96825-2707

Most, Don (Actor)
6643 Buttonwood Ave
Agoura, CA 91301, USA

Mostardo, Rich (Athlete, Football Player)
3376 Summit Rd
Ravenna, OH 44266-9015, USA

Mosteller, Frederick (Mathematician)
Statistics Dept
Cambridge, MA 2138, USA

Mostert, Dutch (Artist)
93696 Mallard Ln
North Bend, OR 97459-8407, USA

Mostow, George D (Mathematician)
300 Audubon Ct
New Haven, CT 06510-1203, USA

Mostow, Jonathan (Director)
9830 Wilshire Blvd
Beverly Hills, CA 90212-1804, USA

Mostowicz, Jeanette (Stylist)
41 Koclas Dr
Netcong, NJ 07857-1214, USA

Mota, Andres (Athlete, Baseball Player)
PO Box 2820
Toluca Lake, CA 91610-0820, USA

Mota, Andy (Athlete, Baseball Player)
9068 NW 50th Ct
Coral Springs, FL 33067-1933, USA

Mota, Guillermo (Athlete, Baseball Player)
c/o Staff Member *Los Angeles Dodgers (LA Dodgers)*
1000 Elysian Park Ave
Los Angeles, CA 90090-1112, USA

Mota, Jose (Athlete, Baseball Player)
PO Box 2820
Toluca Lake, CA 91610-0820, USA

Mota, Manny (Athlete, Baseball Player)
PO Box 2820
Toluca Lake, CA 91610-0820, USA

Mota, Ross (Athlete, Track Athlete)
R Teatro 194 4 Esq
Porto 4100, PORTUGAL

Mote, Bobby (Rodeo Rider)
20840 NW Kachina Ave
Redmond, OR 97756-8626, USA

Mote, Kelley (Athlete, Football Player)
41121 Ocean View Dr
Avon, NC 27915, USA

Moten, Mike (Athlete, Football Player)
706 Loomis Ave
Daytona Beach, FL 32114-4724, USA

Mother Mother (Music Group)
c/o Staff Member *Paradigm (Monterey)*
404 W Franklin St
Monterey, CA 93940-2303, USA

Mothersbaugh, Mark (Composer, Musician)
c/o Staff Member *Greenspan Artist Management*
8760 W Sunset Blvd
West Hollywood, CA 90069-2206, USA

Motion, Andrew (Writer)
English Dept
Norwich NR4 7TJ, UNITED KINGDOM (UK)

Motion City Soundtrack (Music Group)
2336 W Belmont Ave
Chicago, IL 60618-6423, USA

Motley, Darryl (Athlete, Baseball Player)
10800 W 65th St
Shawnee, KS 66203-3810, USA

Motley Crue (Music Group)
c/o Staff Member *10th Street Entertainment (NY)*
38 W 21st St Rm 300
New York, NY 10010-6979, USA

Motooka, Jackie (Stylist)
1516 W Edgewater Ave
Chicago, IL 60660-4211, USA

Motorhead (Music Group)
98 Puddleton Cres Poole
Dorset, ENGLAND, United Kingdom

Mott, John C (Athlete, Football Player)
PO Box 992
Hamilton, MT 59840-0992, USA

Mott, Steve (Athlete, Football Player)
7018 N Highfield Dr
Birmingham, AL 35242-7239, USA

Mott, Stewart R (Politician)
515 Madison Ave
New York, NY 10022-5403, USA

Motta, Dick (Athlete, Basketball Player, Coach)
423 Highway 89
Fish Haven, ID 83287-5109, USA

Mottau, CHristine (Stylist)
c/o Staff Member *Judy Casey Inc*
114 E 13th St
New York, NY 10003-5329, USA

Mottau, Mike (Athlete, Hockey Player)
46 Oxbow Ln
Summit, NJ 07901-2216, USA

Mottelson, Ben R (Nobel Prize Laureate)
Nordita Blegdamsvei 17
Copenhagen 2100, DENMARK

Mottola, Chad (Athlete, Baseball Player)
6479 Lake Pembroke Pl
Orlando, FL 32829-7620, USA

Mottola, Greg (Director, Writer)
c/o Staff Member *United Talent Agency (UTA)*
9560 Wilshire Blvd Fl 5
Beverly Hills, CA 90212-2400, USA

Mottola, Thomas (Tommy) (Business Person)
c/o Staff Member *Mottola Company, The*
745 5th Ave # 800
New York, NY 10151-0099, USA

Motton, Curt (Athlete, Baseball Player)
19903 Quiet Valley Ct
Parkton, MD 21120-8917, USA

Motulsky, Amo G (Scientist)
4347 53rd Ave NE
Seattle, WA 98105-4938, USA

Motz, Diana Gribbon (Judge)
101 W Lombard St
Baltimore, MD 21201-2605, USA

Motzfeldt, Jonathan (Prime Minister)
PO Box 1015
Nuuk 3900, GREENLAND

Mouawad, Jerry (Director)
17 SE 8th Ave
Portland, OR 97214-1239, USA

Mould, Bob (Musician, Songwriter, Writer)
c/o Staff Member *High Road Touring*
751 Bridgeway Fl 2
Sausalito, CA 94965-2174, USA

Moulder-Brown, John
193 Wardour St
London, ENGLAND W1V 3FA

Mouli (Actor, Bollywood)
12 Srinivasa Ave
Chennai, TN 600028, INDIA

Moulton, Alexander E (Engineer)
Hall Bradford-on-Avon
Wilts BA15 1AJ, UNITED KINGDOM (UK)

Moulton, Sara (Chef, Television Host)
c/o Staff Member *Grand Productions*
2811 Champion Rd
Naperville, IL 60564-4958, USA

Mounce, Tony (Athlete, Baseball Player)
237 Cotton Bayou Ln
Kenner, LA 70065-6620, USA

Mounsey, Tara (Athlete, Hockey Player)
24 E Sugar Ball Rd
Concord, NH 03301-5803, USA

Mounsey, Yvonne (Ballerina)
1711 Stewart St
Santa Monica, CA 90404-4021, USA

Mount, Anson (Actor)
1325 Avenue of the Americas
New York, NY 10019-6026, USA

Mount, Rick (Athlete, Basketball Player)
904 Hopkins Rd
Lebanon, IN 46052-1436, USA

Mount, Thomas H (Tom) (Producer)
c/o Staff Member *Mount Film Company*
9245 Cordell Dr
Los Angeles, CA 90069-1753, USA

Mountcastle Jr, Vernon B (Misc)
6605 Walnutwood Cir
Baltimore, MD 21212-1214, USA

Mourning, Alonzo (Athlete, Basketball Player)
3525 Anchorage Way
Miami, FL 33133-5923, USA

Mouse, Mickey Club
PO Box 10200
Lake Buena Vista, FL 32830-0200

Mouskouri, Nana J (Musician, Songwriter)
12 Rue Gitenberg
Boulogne 92000, FRANCE

Moussier, Sabine (Actor)
c/o Staff Member *Televisa*
Blvd Adolfo Lopez Mateos 232 Colonia San Angel INN
DF CP 01060, MEXICO

Moustaki, Georges (Musician)
20 Rue des Fosses-Saint-Jacques
Paris 75005, FRANCE

Mouton, James (Athlete, Baseball Player)
4710 Lakeside Meadow Ct
Missouri City, TX 77459-1630, USA

Mouton, Leslie (Journalist)
1333 Northland Dr
Mendota Heights, MN 55120-1345

Mouton, Lyle (Athlete, Baseball Player)
4101 Auston Way
Palm Harbor, FL 34685-4014, USA

Moverman, Oren (Director)
c/o Staff Member *WmE2 (WMA-LA)*
1 William Morris Pl
Beverly Hills, CA 90212-4261, USA

Movessian, Victoria (Viki) (Athlete, Hockey Player)
17 Webb St
Lexington, MA 02420-2219, USA

Movita
2766 Motor Ave
Los Angeles, CA 90064-3436

Mowat, Farley M (Writer)
18 King St
Port Hope, ON L1A 2R4, CANADA

Mowatt, Ezekial (Athlete, Football Player)
245 Prospect Ave Apt 2B
Hackensack, NJ 07601-2571, USA

Mower, Patrick (Actor)
c/o Staff Member *Burnett Granger & Assoc*
Prince of Wales Theatre 31 Coventy St
London W1D 6AS, UNITED KINGDOM (UK)

Mowerson, Robert (Swimmer)
2601 Kenzie Ter Apt 324
Minneapolis, MN 55418-4239, USA

Mowrey, Caitlin (Actor)

Mowrey, Dude (Musician)
2802 Columbine Pl
Nashville, TN 37204-3104, USA

Mowry, Tahj (Actor)
c/o Jason Egenberg *United Talent Agency (UTA)*
9560 Wilshire Blvd Fl 5
Beverly Hills, CA 90212-2400, USA

Mowry, Tamera (Actor, Producer)
c/o Tracy Steinsapir *Main Title Entertainment*
2225 Wilshire Blvd Suite 500
Los Angeles, CA 90036, USA

Mowry, Tia (Actor)
c/o Adam Griffin *Kritzer Levine Wilkins Entertainment*
11872 La Grange Ave Fl 1
Los Angeles, CA 90025-5283, USA

Moxness, Barbara (Athlete, Golfer)
5512 Mirror Lakes Dr
Minneapolis, MN 55436-2037, USA

Moyer, Jamie (Athlete, Baseball Player)
2426 32nd Ave W
Seattle, WA 98199-3202, USA

Moyer, Ken (Athlete, Football Player)
3896 Magma Ct
Mason, OH 45040-2896, USA

Moyer, Paul (Correspondent)
12742 Highwood St
Los Angeles, CA 90049-2624, USA

Moyer, Stephen (Actor)
c/o Lena Roklin *Luber Roklin Management*
8530 Wilshire Blvd Ste 550
Beverly Hills, CA 90211-3133, USA

Moyers, Bill D (Correspondent)
c/o Staff Member *HarperCollins Publishers*
10 E 53rd St C/O Author Mail Floor 7
New York, NY 10022, USA

Moyet, Alison (Musician)
2-12 Petonville Road
London N1 9PL, UNITED KINGDOM (UK)

Moyle, Allan (Director, Writer)
c/o Staff Member *Wisdom Literary*
287 S Robertson Blvd Ste 258
Beverly Hills, CA 90211-2810, USA

Moynahan, Bridget (Actor, Model)
c/o Andrea Pett-Joseph *Brillstein Entertainment Partners*
9150 Wilshire Blvd Ste 350
Beverly Hills, CA 90212-3453, USA

Moynihan, Bobby (Actor, Comedian)
c/o Staff Member *Odenkirk Provissiero Entertainment*
650 N Bronson Ave Bldg B145
Los Angeles, CA 90004-1404, USA

Moynihan, Christopher (Actor)
c/o Ron West *Thruline Entertainment*
9250 Wilshire Blvd Ground Fl
Beverly Hills, CA 90212, USA

Moynihan, Colin B (Government Official)
Crown Reach 16 Grosvenor Road
London SW1V 3JV, UNITED KINGDOM (UK)

Moyroud, Louis M (Inventor)
7667 Park Lane Rd
Lake Worth, FL 33449-6728, USA

Mozo, Rebecca (Actor)
c/o Staff Member *Insight*
1134 S Cloverdale Ave
Los Angeles, CA 90019-6737, USA

Mphahele, Ezekiel (Writer)
5444 Zone 5 Pimville
Johannesburg, SOUTH AFRICA

Mraz, Jason (Musician, Songwriter)
PO Box 69A36
Los Angeles, CA 90069-0047, USA

Mrazovich, Chuck (Athlete, Basketball Player)
7260 W 12th Ave
Hialeah, FL 33014-4618, USA

Mrkonic, George (Athlete, Football Player)
5712 Lowell St
Shawnee Mission, KS 66202-2248, USA

Mrosko, Robert (Athlete, Football Player)
2874 Coleridge Rd
Cleveland, OH 44118-3544, USA

Mroudjae, Ali (Prime Minister)
BP 58 Rond Point Gobadjou
Moroni, COMOROS

Msuya, Cleopa D (Prime Minister)
PO Box 980
Dodoma, TANZANIA

Mswati III (King)
PO Box 1
Mbabane, SWAZILAND

Mu'all, Sheikh Rashid bin Ahmed al (Politician)
Umm Al Quwain
UNITED ARAB EMIRATES

Mubarak, Muhammad Hosni (General, President)
Abdeen
Cairo, EGYPT

Muccino, Gabriele (Director)
c/o Simon Halls *Slate Public Relations*
9000 W Sunset Blvd Ste 915
West Hollywood, CA 90069-5809, USA

Mucha, Barb (Athlete, Golfer)
5922 Crystal View Dr
Orlando, FL 32819-4207, USA

Muchlinski, Mike (Athlete, Baseball Player)
3908 243rd Pl SE Unit Q301
Bothell, WA 98021-6918, USA

Mucke, Manuela (Athlete)
Charlottenstr 13
Berlin 10315, GERMANY

Muckensturm, Jerry (Athlete, Football Player)
4209 Hickory Ln
Jonesboro, AR 72401-8430, USA

Muckler, John (Coach)
1000 Palladium Dr
Kanata, ON K2V 1A4, CANADA

Mudcrutch (Music Group)
c/o Staff Member *Warner Bros Records (LA)*
PO Box 6868
Burbank, CA 91510-6868, USA

Mudd, Howard E (Athlete, Coach, Football Player)
311 W Walnut St
Indianapolis, IN 46202-3163, USA

Mudd, Jodie (Athlete, Golfer)
3512 Mildred Dr
Louisville, KY 40216-4341, USA

Mudd, Roger
7167 Old Dominion Dr
McLean, VA 22101-2705

Mudd, Roger H (Correspondent)
7167 Old Dominion Dr
McLean, VA 22101-2705, USA

Mudge-Cato, Nancy (Baseball Player)
23019 County Road 1
Elk River, MN 55330-9437, USA

Mudra, Darrell (Coach, Football Coach)
424 Tiger Hammock Rd
Crawfordville, FL 32327-1470, USA

Mudrock, Phil (Athlete, Baseball Player)
2548 E 6600 S
Salt Lake City, UT 84121-2346, USA

Mudvayne (Music Group)
c/o Chuck Toler *Anger Management*
6907 University Ave # 199
Middleton, WI 53562-2767, USA

Muehlheuser, Frank (Athlete, Football Player)
780 County Road 579
Pittstown, NJ 08867-5152, USA

Muelhaupt Jr, Chuck (Athlete, Football Player)
4111 Tonawanda Dr
Des Moines, IA 50312-2911, USA

Muelier, Charles W (Business Person)
1901 Chouteau Ave
Saint Louis, MO 63103-3003, USA

Mueller, Bill (Athlete, Baseball Player)
570 W Canyon Way
Chandler, AZ 85248-5123, USA

Mueller, Don (Athlete, Baseball Player)
12102 Autumn Lakes Dr
Maryland Heights, MO 63043-4909, USA

Mueller, George E (Engineer)
3760 Carillon Pt
Kirkland, WA 98033-7455, USA

Mueller, Les (Athlete, Baseball Player)
PO Box 294
Millstadt, IL 62260-0294, USA

Mueller, Vance (Athlete, Football Player)
8141 Damico Dr
El Dorado Hills, CA 95762-5482, USA

Mueller, Willard (Willie) (Athlete, Baseball Player)
2320 Tolbert Ln
West Bend, WI 53090-1234, USA

Mueller-Bajda, Dolores (Baseball Player)
2913 N Linder Ave
Chicago, IL 60641-4812, USA

Mueller-Stahl, Armin (Actor)
Ordensmeisterstr. 15-16
Berlin, GERMANY D-12099

Muellner, William (Athlete, Football Player)
727 Sherwood Rd
La Grange Park, IL 60526-1545, USA

Muench, David (Photographer)
PO Box 30500
Santa Barbara, CA 93130-0500, USA

Muetterties, Earl L (Misc)
Chemistry
Berkeley, CA 94720-0001, USA

Muetzelfeldt, Bruno (Religious Leader)
150 Rt de Femey
Geneva 20 1211, SWITZERLAND

Muffett, Billy (Athlete, Baseball Player)
1145 Finks Hideaway Rd
Monroe, LA 71203-2425, USA

Mugabe, Robert G (President)
Munhumutapa Bldg Samora Machel Ave
Harare, ZIMBABWE

Mugler, Thierry (Designer, Fashion Designer)
4-6 Rue Aux Ours
Paris 75003, FRANCE

Muhammad, Elijah
7351 S Stony Island Ave
Chicago, IL 60649-3106

Muhammad, Muhsin (Athlete, Football Player)
c/o Staff Member *Golden Peak Sports & Entertainment LLC*
11352 Haswell Dr
Parker, CO 80134-7548, USA

Muhammad, Wallace D (Religious Leader)
7351 S Stony Island Ave
Chicago, IL 60649-3106, USA

Muir, Roger
10 Drewid Hill Ave
Methuen, MA 1844

Muir DeGraad, Karen (Swimmer)
Ozwatini
Natal, SOUTH AFRICA

Muirhead, Brian (Astronomer, Scientist)
4800 Oak Grove Dr
Pasadena, CA 91109-8001, USA

Muirsheil of Kilmacolm, Viscount (Government Official)
Knapps Kilmacolm
Renfrewshire, SCOTLAND

Muise, Andi (Model)

Muise, Andi (Model)
c/o Staff Member *Premier Model Management*
40-42 Parker St
London WC2B 5PQ, UK

Mujica, Aylin (Actor)
c/o Staff Member *TV Azteca*
Periferico Sur 4121 Colonia Fuentes del Pedregal
DF CP 14141, Mexico

Mukaddam, Ali (Actor)
c/o Yanick Landry *Edward G Agency*
19 Isabella St
Toronto ON M4Y 1M7, CANADA

Mukai, Chiaki Naito (Astronaut)
15836 Seahorse Dr # 253
Houston, TX 77062-6222, USA

Mukhamedov, Irek J (Ballerina)
Covent Garden Bow St
London WC2E 9DD, UNITED KINGDOM (UK)

Mukherjee, Bharati (Writer)
130 Rivoli St
San Francisco, CA 94117-4341, USA

Mukherjee, Hrishikesh (Bollywood, Director, Filmmaker, Producer)
123A Anupama Carter Road Bandra
Bombay, MS 400 050, INDIA

Mukherjee, Rani (Actor, Bollywood)
B/405 Shakti Apartments Kaylan Complex
Yari Road Versova
Mumbai, MS 400061, INDIA

Mulari, Tarja (Speed Skater)
Vanhan Mankkaantie 33
Espoo 2180, FINDLAND

Mularkey, Mike (Athlete, Football Coach, Football Player)
1713 SE 7th St
Philadelphia, PA 19145, USA

Mulcahy, Anne
800 Long Ridge Rd
Stamford, CT 06902-1227, USA

Mulcahy, J Patrick (Business Person)
Checkerboard Sq
Saint Louis, MO 63164-0001, USA

Mulcahy, Russell (Director)
c/o Staff Member *Agency for the Performing Arts (APA-LA)*
405 S Beverly Dr Ste 500
Beverly Hills, CA 90212-4425, USA

Muldaur, Maria (Musician, Songwriter, Writer)
PO Box 680006
Charlotte, NC 28216-0001, USA

Mulder, Karen (Model)
c/o Staff Member *Elite Model Management (NY)*
404 Park Ave S Fl 9
New York, NY 10016-8412, USA

Mulder, Mark (Athlete, Baseball Player)
10295 E Cholla St
Scottsdale, AZ 85260-6038, USA

Muldoon, Leslie L (Doctor)
Neurology Dept
Portland, OR 97201, USA

Muldoon, Patrick (Actor, Model)
11030 Ventura Blvd Ste 3
Studio City, CA 91604-3571, USA

Muldoon, Paul B (Writer)
Creative Writing Program
Princeton, NJ 08544-0001, USA

Muldowney, Dominic J (Composer)
Music Dept South Bank
London SE1 1PX, UNITED KINGDOM (UK)

Mulgrew, Kate (Actor)
c/o Lisa Loosemore *Viking Entertainment*
445 W 23rd St Ste 1A
New York, NY 10011-1445, USA

Mulhern, Matt (Actor)
3500 W Olive Ave Ste 1400
Burbank, CA 91505-5512, USA

Mulhern, Sinead (Opera Singer)
4 Addison Bridge Place
London W14 8XP, UNITED KINGDOM (UK)

Mulholland, Terry (Athlete, Baseball Player)
11655 N 18th Pl
Phoenix, AZ 85020-1319, USA

Mulis, Kary B (Nobel Prize Laureate)
2519 Avenida De La Palaya
La Jolla, CA 92037, USA

Mulitalo, Edwin (Athlete, Football Player)
110 Santa Barbara Ave
Daly City, CA 94014-1045, USA

Mulkerin, Ted (Writer)
c/o Staff Member *WmE2 (Endeavor-LA)*
9601 Wilshire Blvd Fl 3
Beverly Hills, CA 90210-5219, USA

Mulkey, Chris (Actor)
10100 Santa Monica Blvd Ste 2500
Los Angeles, CA 90067-4116, USA

Mulkey-Robertson, Kim (Basketball Player, Coach)
Athletic Dept
Waco, TX 76798, USA

Mull, Martin (Actor)
338 S Chadbourne Ave
Los Angeles, CA 90049-3709, USA

Mullady, Tom (Athlete, Football Player)
2855 Crooked Oak Dr
Germantown, TN 38138-7614, USA

Mullally, Megan (Actor, Musician)
c/o Dannielle Thomas *Untitled Entertainment (LA)*
350 S Beverly Dr Ste 200
Beverly Hills, CA 90212-4819, USA

Mullan, Peter (Writer)
c/o Staff Member *International Creative Management (ICM-LA)*
10250 Constellation Blvd Fl 7
Los Angeles, CA 90067-6207, USA

Mullane, Richard M (Mike) (Astronaut)
1301 Las Lomas Rd NE
Albuquerque, NM 87106-4527, USA

Mullaney, Mark (Athlete, Football Player)
17448 Frondell Ct
Eden Prairie, MN 55347-3416, USA

Mullavey, Greg (Actor)
1818 Thayer Ave Apt 303
Los Angeles, CA 90025-4965, USA

Mullavy, Greg
1818 Thayer Ave Apt 303
Los Angeles, CA 90025-4965

Mullen, Bill (Stylist)
c/o Staff Member *Art + Commerce*
531 W 25th St # 4
New York, NY 10001-5593, USA

Mullen, Ford (Moon) (Athlete, Baseball Player)
20505 Marine Dr Unit 3
Stanwood, WA 98292-7852, USA

Mullen, Josep P (Joey) (Athlete, Hockey Player)
126 Fieldgate Dr
Pittsburg, PA 15241, USA

Mullen, Larry Jr (Musician)
30-32 Sir John Rogerson Quay
Dublin 2, IRELAND

Mullen, Michael G (Admiral)
Vice Chief of Naval Operations Hqusn Pentagon
Washington, DC 20350-0001, USA

Mullen, Nicole (Musician)
c/o Staff Member *Word Records*
25 Music Sq W
Nashville, TN 37203-3205, USa

Mullen, Rodney (Skateboarder)
c/o Staff Member *HarperCollins Publishers*
10 E 53rd St C/O Author Mail Floor 7
New York, NY 10022, USA

Mullen, Scott (Athlete, Baseball Player)
73 Walling Grove Rd
Beaufort, SC 29907-1067, USA

Mullen, Tom (Athlete, Football Player)
107 Greenbriar Ridge Ct
Saint Louis, MO 63122-3355, USA

Muller, Egon (Motorcycle Race, Motorcycle Racer)
Dorfstr 17
Rodenbek, Kiel 24247, GERMANY

Muller, Elisabeth
. Feld 14
Sempach/Lu, SWITZERLAND 6204

Muller, Gerd (Soccer Player)
Neuestr 21
Munich 81479, GERMANY

Muller, Herta (Writer)
c/o Staff Member *Henry Holt & Company*
175 5th Ave Ste 400
New York, NY 10010-7726, USA

Muller, Jennifer (Choreographer, Dancer)
131 W 24th St
New York, NY 10011-1942, USA

Muller, Jorg (Race Car Driver)
Fassoldshof 1
Mainleus 95336, GERMANY

Muller, K ALex (Nobel Prize Laureate)
Saumerstr 4
Ruschlikon 8803, SWITZERLAND

Muller, Lisel (Writer)
PO Box 25053
Baton Rouge, LA 70894-5053, USA

Muller, Marcia (Writer)
Warner Books 1271 6th Ave
New York, NY 10020, USA

Muller, Michel (Actor, Writer)
c/o Celine Kamina *UBBA*
6 rue de Braque
Paris 75003, France

Muller, Peter (Architect)
PO Box 545
Essex Junction, VT 05453-0545, AUSTRALIA

Muller, Peter (Skier)
Haldenstr 18
Adliswil 8134, SWITZERLAND

Muller, Richard S (Engineer)
Sensor Acutator Ctr
Berkeley, CA 94720-0001, USA

Muller, Robby (Cinematographer)
PO Box 1156
Studio City, CA 91614-0156, USA

Muller, Robert (Misc)
Pennsylvania NW
Washington, DC 20535-0001, USA

Muller, Steven (Educator)
919 18th St NW Ste 800
Washington, DC 20006-5509, USA

Muller-Stahl, Armin (Actor)
Gartenweg 31
Sierksdorf 23730, GERMANY

Muller-Westernhagen, Marius
Mittelweg 69
Hamburg, GERMANY D-20149

Mulley of Manor Park, Frederick W (Government Official)
Westminster
London SW1A 0PW, UNITED KINGDOM (UK)

Mulligan, Carey (Actor)
c/o Jessica Kolstad *WKT Public Relations (WKT-LA)*
9350 Wilshire Blvd Ste 450
Beverly Hills, CA 90212-3230, USA

Mulligan, Gerry (Writer)
c/o Staff Member *3 Arts Entertainment Inc*
9460 Wilshire Blvd Fl 7
Beverly Hills, CA 90212-2713, USA

Mulligan, Richard C (Biologist)
11 Sumner Rd
Cambridge, MA 02138-3025, USA

Mulligan, Sean (Athlete, Baseball Player)
24474 Eastgate Dr
Diamond Bar, CA 91765-4626, USA

Mulligan, Wayne (Athlete, Football Player)
2410 the Haul Over
Johns Island, SC 29455-6103, USA

Mulliken, William (Bill) (Swimmer)
4216 N Keeler Ave
Chicago, IL 60641-2271, USA

Mullin, Chris (Baseball Player)
116 Laurelwood Dr
Danville, CA 94506-1408, USA

Mullin, Christopher P (Chris) (Athlete, Basketball Player)
116 Laurelwood Dr
Danville, CA 94506-1408, USA

Mullin, J Stanley (Skier)
333 S Hope St
Los Angeles, CA 90071-1406, USA

Mulliniks, Rance (Athlete, Baseball Player)
2614 S Peppertree St
Visalia, CA 93277-5507, USA

Mullins, Eric (Athlete, Football Player)
3249 Parkwood Dr
Houston, TX 77021-1136, USA

Mullins, Fran (Athlete, Baseball Player)
9226 Ritenour Ct
Lone Tree, CO 80124-8971, USA

Mullins, Gerry (Athlete, Football Player)
PO Box 523
Saxonburg, PA 16056-0523, USA

Mullins, Greg (Athlete, Baseball Player)
PO Box 443
Florahome, FL 32140-0443, USA

Mullins, Jeffrey (Jeff) (Athlete, Basketball Player)
8866 N Sea Oaks Way Apt 202
Vero Beach, FL 32963-4195, USA

Mullins, Larry (Model)
30-32 Sir John Rogerson's Quarry
Dublin, IRELAND

Mullins, Shawn (Musician, Songwriter, Writer)
751 Bridgeway # 300
Sausalito, CA 94965-2102, USA

Mullova, Viktoria Y (Musician)
27 Chancery Lane
London WC2A 1PF, UNITED KINGDOM (UK)

Mulloy, Gardner (Tennis Player)
800 NW 9th Ave
Miami, FL 33136-3006, USA

Mulroney, Dermot (Actor)
c/o Stephen Huvane *Slate Public Relations*
9000 W Sunset Blvd Ste 915
West Hollywood, CA 90069-5809, USA

Mulroney, Kieran
6100 Wilshire Blvd Ste 1170
Los Angeles, CA 90048-5116

Mulroney, M Brian (Prime Minister)
47 Forden Cres
Westmount, QC H3Y 2Y5, CANADA

Muluzi, Bakili (President)
Private Bag 301 Capitol City
Lilongwe 3, MALAWI

Mulva, James J (Business Person)
600 N Dairy Ashford St
Houston, TX 77079-1100, USA

Mulvaney, Mick (Congressman, Politician)
1004 Longworth Hob
Washington, DC 20515-1703, USA

Mulvey, Grant (Athlete, Hockey Player)
70 E Scott St Apt 706
Chicago, IL 60610-2392, USA

Mulvey, Peter (Musician)
c/o Staff Member *Young / Hunter Management*
350 Massachusetts Ave # 230
Arlington, MA 02474-6713, USA

Mulvhill, Robert (Athlete, Basketball Player)
322 North Ave E Apt 3
Cranford, NJ 07016-2472, USA

Mulvihill, Kristen (Stylist)
c/o Staff Member *Sarah Laird Inc*
12 Charles Ln
New York, NY 10014-2526, USA

Mulvoy, Mark (Editor, Publisher)
Rockefeller Center
New York, NY 10020, USA

Mumba, Samantha (Actor, Musician)
1 Sussex Place
London W6 9XT, UNITED KINGDOM (UK)

Mumford, David B (Mathematician)
65 Milton St
Milton, MA 02186-2322, USA

Mumley, Nick (Athlete, Football Player)
1432 Audubon Dr
Columbus, IN 47203-1432, USA

Mumphord, Lloyd (Athlete, Football Player)
2316 Mumphord St
Victoria, TX 77901-7750, USA

Mumphrey, Jerry (Athlete, Baseball Player)
7709 FM 850
Tyler, TX 75705-2135, USA

Mumy, Bill (Actor)
11333 Moorpark St PO Box 433
Studio City, CA 91602, USA

Mumy, Billy (Actor)
11333 Moorpark St PO Box 433
Studio City, CA 91602, USA

Mumy, Liliana (Actor)
c/o Meredith Fine *Coast to Coast Talent Group*
3350 Barham Blvd
Los Angeles, CA 90068-1404, USA

Muna, Solomon Tandeng (Prime Minister)
PO Box 15 Mbengwi Mono Division
North West Province, CAMEROON

Munchak, Michael A (Mike) (Athlete, Football Player)
9155 Saddlebow Dr
Brentwood, TN 37027-6060, USA

Muncrief, Kevin (Athlete, Golfer)
939 S Flood Ave
Norman, OK 73069-4504, USA

Mundae, Misty (Actor)
PO Box 447
Ringwood, NJ 07456-0447

Mundell, Robert A (Nobel Prize Laureate)
35 Claremont Ave
New York, NY 10027-6815, USA

Mundie, Craig (Business Person)
Waggener Edstrom Worldwide - Rapid Response Team Three Centerpointe Drive, Suite 300
Lake Oswego, OR 97035

Mundy, Carl E Jr (General)
9308 Ludgate Dr
Alexandria, VA 22309-2740, USA

Muni, Craig (Athlete, Hockey Player)
9291 Via Cimato Dr
Clarence Center, NY 14032-9152, USA

Munitz, Barry A (Educator)
400 Golden Shore St
Long Beach, CA 90802, USA

Muniz, Frankie (Actor)
c/o Michael Rotenberg *3 Arts Entertainment Inc*
9460 Wilshire Blvd Fl 7
Beverly Hills, CA 90212-2713, USA

Muniz, Manuel (Athlete, Baseball Player)
PO Box 6301
Caguas, PR 00726-6301, USA

Munk, Chris (Athlete, Basketball Player)
14 Hillview Ct
San Francisco, CA 94124-2487, USA

Munk, Peter (Business Person)
200 Bay St
Toronto, ON M5J 2J3, CANADA

Munk, Walter H (Geophysicist, Physicist)
9530 La Jolla Shores Dr
La Jolla, CA 92037-1138, USA

Munn, Allison (Actor)
c/o Steve Caserta *Sanders Armstrong Caserta*
2120 Colorado Ave Ste 120
Santa Monica, CA 90404-3561, USA

Munn, Olivia (Actor, Talk Show Host)
c/o David (Dave) Fleming *Mosaic Media Group*
9200 W Sunset Blvd Ste 10
Los Angeles, CA 90069-3608, USA

Munninghoff, Scott (Athlete, Baseball Player)
866 Laverty Ln
Cincinnati, OH 45230-3558, USA

Munos, Maria (Television Host)
c/o Staff Member *Entertainment Tonight (ET)*
4024 Radford Ave
Studio City, CA 91604-2101, USA

Munoz, Bobby (Athlete, Baseball Player)
9040 NW 20th St
Pembroke Pines, FL 33024-3211, USA

Munoz, M Anthony (Athlete, Football Player, Sportscaster)
6529 Irwin Simpson Rd
Mason, OH 45040-9285, USA

Munoz, Mike (Athlete, Baseball Player)
1000 Carroll Meadows Ct
Southlake, TX 76092-3830, USA

Munoz, Oscar (Athlete, Baseball Player)
14161 Leaning Pine Dr
Hialeah, FL 33014-2512, USA

Munro, Alice (Writer)
PO Box 1133
Clinton, ON N0M 1L0, CANADA

Munro, Caroline (Admiral)
PO Box 2589
London W1A 3NQ, UNITED KINGDOM (UK)

Munro, Dana G (Diplomat)
PO Box 317
Media, PA 19063-0317, USA

Munro, Glen (Stylist)
c/o Staff Member *Judy Inc*
1 Yorkville Ave
Toronto ON M4W 1L1, Canada

Munro, Lochlyn (Actor)
8942 Wilshire Blvd # 219
Beverly Hills, CA 90211-1908, USA

Munro, Peter (Athlete, Baseball Player)
4311 Westmoreland St
Little Neck, NY 11363-1943, USA

Munroe, George (Athlete, Basketball Player)
870 United Nations Plz Apt 13E
New York, NY 10017-1824, USA

Munsel, Patrice (Opera Singer)
PO Box 472
Schroon Lake, NY 12870-0472, USA

Munsey, Nelson (Athlete, Football Player)
12190 Cuyamaca College Dr E Unit 1212
El Cajon, CA 92019-4353, USA

Munson, Eric (Athlete, Baseball Player)
5550 Wilshire Blvd Apt 314
Los Angeles, CA 90036-4858, USA

Munson, Jeanne L (Stylist)
2248 41st St
Astoria, NY 11105-1762, USA

Munson, John (Musician)
509 Hartnell St
Monterey, CA 93940-2825, USA

Munter, Scott (Athlete, Baseball Player)
13024 Jessie Ave
Omaha, NE 68164-1375, USA

Muntyan, Mikhail (Opera Singer)
16 N Iorga Str #13
Chisnau 277012, MOLDOVA

Muppets, The
c/o Staff Member *Jim Henson Company (LA)*
1416 N La Brea Ave
Hollywood, CA 90028-7506

Mura, Steve (Athlete, Baseball Player)
31892 Old Oak Rd
Trabuco Canyon, CA 92679-3245, USA

Murad, Ferid (Nobel Prize Laureate)
2121 W Holcombe Blvd
Houston, TX 77030-3303, USA

Murad, Raza (Actor, Bollywood)
B 104 Mayfair Raviraj Oberoi Complex Near Lakxmi Industrial Estate New Link Road Andheri
Bombay, MS 400 058, INDIA

Muradov, Sakhat A (Government Official)
17 Gogol St
Ashkhabad 744017, TURKENISTAN

Murakami, Masanori (Athlete, Baseball Player)
1-4-15-1506 Nisho Ohi Shinagawa-Ku
Tokyo 140-0015, Japan

Murakami, Ryu (Writer)
2-12-21 Otowa Bunkyoku
Tokyo 112-8001, JAPAN

Murali (Actor, Bollywood)
3-77th St
Chennai, TN 600083, INDIA

Muraliyev, Amangeldy (Prime Minister)
Ul Perromayskaya 57
Bishkek, KYRGYZSTAN

Muransky, Ed (Athlete, Football Player)
16221 Villarreal De Avila
Tampa, FL 33613-1083, USA

Muratova, Kira G (Director)
Proletarsjy Blvd 14B #15
Odessa 270015, RUSSIA

Murayama, Makio (Scientist)
5010 Benton Ave
Bethesda, MD 20814-2804, USA

Murayama, Tomiichi (Prime Minister)
3-2-2 Chiyomachi Oita
Oita 870, JAPAN

Murchison, Ira (Athlete, Track Athlete)
10113 S Sangamon St
Chicago, IL 60643-2228, USA

Murchison, Lee (Athlete, Football Player)
1976 E Mariposa Rd
Stockton, CA 95205-7736, USA

Murciano, Jr, Enrique (Actor)
c/o Ilene Feldman *IFA Talent Agency*
8730 W Sunset Blvd Ste 490
Los Angeles, CA 90069-2248, USA

Murdoch, Murray (Athlete, Hockey Player)
190 Dessa Dr
Hamden, CT 06517-2108, USA

Murdoch, Robert J (Bob) (Athlete, Coach, Hockey Player)
410 11th Ave S
Cranbrook, BC V1C 2P9, Canada

Murdoch, Rupert (Publisher)
1211 Avenue of the Americas
New York, NY 10036-8701, USA

Murdoch, Sarah (Actor)
c/o Staff Member *WmE2 (Endeavor-LA)*
9601 Wilshire Blvd Fl 3
Beverly Hills, CA 90210-5219, USA

Murdoch, Stuart (Musician, Songwriter, Writer)
7 Trinity Row
Florence, MA 01062-1931, USA

Murdock, David H (Business Person)
10900 Wilshire Blvd Ste 1600
Los Angeles, CA 90024-6538, USA

Murdock, George (Actor)
5733 Sunfield Ave
Lakewood, CA 90712-1823, USA

Murdock, George P (Doctor)
Wynnewood Plaza #107
Wynnewood, PA 19096, USA

Murdock, Guy (Athlete, Football Player)
106 Medinah Ln
Tower Lakes, IL 60010-1350, USA

Murdock, Shirley (Musician)
1319 5th Ave N
Nashville, TN 37208-2725, USA

Muresan, Georghe (Actor, Basketball Player)
390 Murray Hill Pkwy
East Rutherford, NJ 07073-2109, USA

Murff, Red (Athlete, Baseball Player)
5401 Hollytree Dr Apt 1301
Tyler, TX 75703-3467, USA

Muris, Timothy (Government Official)
Pennsylvania Ave & 6th St NW
Washington, DC 20580, USA

Muris, Timothy J (Educator, Government Official)
Law School
Fairfax, VA 22030, USA

Murphey, Michael Martin (Musician, Songwriter, Writer)
PO Box 450
Ranchos De Taos, NM 87557-0450, USA

Murphy, Ben (Actor)
2690 Rambla Pacifico
Malibu, CA 90265-3423, USA

Murphy, Bill (Athlete, Football Player)
6411 SW 25th St
Miramar, FL 33023-2829, USA

Murphy, Billy (Athlete, Baseball Player)
5309 66th Avenue Ct W
University Place, WA 98467-2231, USA

Murphy, Bob (Baseball Player, Sportscaster)
220 Coral Cay Ter
Palm Beach Gardens, FL 33418-4003, USA

Murphy, Bob (Athlete, Golfer)
12005 Dunes Rd
Boynton Beach, FL 33436-5508, USA

Murphy, Brian
265 Liverpool Rd
London, ENGLAND N1 1LX

Murphy, Calvin J (Athlete, Basketball Player)
8218 Cliffshire Ct
Houston, TX 77083-6526, USA

Murphy, Carolyn (Model)
c/o Staff Member *IMG (NY)*
432 W 45th St Fl 5
New York, NY 10036-3503, USA

Murphy, Caryle M (Journalist)
1150 15th St NW
Washington, DC 20071-0001, USA

Murphy, Charles Q (Actor)
c/o Lorrie Bartlett *International Creative Management (ICM-LA)*
10250 Constellation Blvd Fl 7
Los Angeles, CA 90067-6207, USA

Murphy, Charles S (Government Official)
100 Bluff View Dr Apt 503C
Belleair Bluffs, FL 33770-1376, USA

Murphy, Cillian (Actor)
c/o Craig Bankey *WKT Public Relations (WKT-LA)*
9350 Wilshire Blvd Ste 450
Beverly Hills, CA 90212-3230, USA

Murphy, Dale (Athlete, Baseball Player)
467 Aspen Ridge Ln
Alpine, UT 84004-1223, USA

Murphy, Dan (Athlete, Baseball Player)
19661 Symeron Rd
Apple Valley, CA 92307-4736, USA

Murphy, Danny (Actor)
c/o Staff Member *Kazarian Spencer Ruskin & Assoc.*
11969 Ventura Blvd Ste 300
Studio City, CA 91604-2619, USA

Murphy, Danny (Athlete, Baseball Player)
5030 Champion Blvd Apt 6226
Boca Raton, FL 33496-2473, USA

Murphy, David Lee (Musician)
c/o Staff Member *Agency for the Performing Arts (APA-LA)*
405 S Beverly Dr Ste 500
Beverly Hills, CA 90212-4425, USA

Murphy, Diana E (Judge)
300 S 4th St
Minneapolis, MN 55415-1320, USA

Murphy, Dick (Athlete, Baseball Player)
6890 Connie Dr
Avon, IN 46123-8532, USA

Murphy, Donna (Actor, Musician)
250 W 57th St Ste 2303
New York, NY 10107-2399, USA

Murphy, Dwayne (Athlete, Baseball Player)
1811 S Karen Dr
Chandler, AZ 85286-6350, USA

Murphy, Ed (Basketball Player, Coach)
Smith Coliseum
University, MS 38677, USA

Murphy, Eddie (Actor, Comedian)
c/o Arnold Robinson *Rogers & Cowan PR (LA)*
Pacific Design Center 8687 Melrose Ave, 7th Floor
West Hollywood, CA 90069, USA

Murphy, Erin (Actor)
c/o Staff Member *James/Levy/Jacobson Management Inc*
3500 W Olive Ave Ste 1470
Burbank, CA 91505-5514, USA

Murphy, Lawrence T (Larry) (Athlete, Hockey Player)
927 S Bates St
Birmingham, MI 48009-1974, USA

Murphy, Mark (Athlete, Football Player)
935 N Broadway
De Pere, WI 54115-2607, USA

Murphy, Mark H (Musician)
1450 Southgate Ave Apt 206
Daly City, CA 94015-4021, USA

Murphy, Mark S (Athlete, Football Player)
3699 Myersville Rd
Uniontown, OH 44685-7561, USA

Murphy, Mary (Athlete, Golfer)
11218 Winterwood Dr
Indianapolis, IN 46235-6821, USA

Murphy, Mary (Choreographer, Reality TV Star)
3580 5th Ave
San Diego, CA 92103-5017, USA

Murphy, Michael (Actor)
c/o Gayle Abrams *Oscars Abrams Zimel & Associates, Inc. (OAZ)*
438 Queen St E
Toronto ON M5A 1T4, CANADA

Murphy, Michael Martin
4077 State Hwy 68
Rancho de Taos, NM 87557

Murphy, Michael R (Judge)
125 S State St
Salt Lake City, UT 84138-1102, USA

Murphy, Mike (Athlete, Coach, Hockey Player)
317 15th St
Manhattan Beach, CA 90266-4605, USA

Murphy, Peter (Musician)

Murphy, Raymond D (War Hero)
4677 Sutton St NW
Albuquerque, NM 87114-4239, USA

Murphy, Reg (Editor, Publisher)
1145 17th St NW
Washington, DC 20036-4707, USA

Murphy, Richard W (Diplomat)
16 Sutton Pl # 9A
New York, NY 10022-3179, USA

Murphy, Rob (Athlete, Baseball Player)
44 S Sewalls Point Rd
Stuart, FL 34996-6728, USA

Murphy, Roisin (Musician)
c/o Staff Member *Spectrum / Envy*
139 N Hamilton Dr Apt 4
Beverly Hills, CA 90211-2218, USA

Murphy, Ron (Athlete, Basketball Player)
14800 Hanover Pike
Upperco, MD 21155-9735, USA

Murphy, Rosemary (Actor)
220 E 73rd St
New York, NY 10021-4319, USA

Murphy, Ryan (Director, Producer, Writer)
c/o Simon Halls *Slate Public Relations*
9000 W Sunset Blvd Ste 915
West Hollywood, CA 90069-5809, USA

Murphy, Sean (Athlete, Golfer)
1004 June Pl
Lovington, NM 88260-4521, USA

Murphy, Terry (Entertainer)
3575 Cahuenga Blvd W Ste 600
Los Angeles, CA 90068-1345, USA

Murphy, Tim (Congressman, Politician)
322 Cannon Hob
Washington, DC 20515-4602, USA

Murphy, Tod (Athlete, Basketball Player)
23 Parsons Hill Rd
Wenham, MA 01984-1823, USA

Murphy, Tom (Athlete, Baseball Player)
26561 Via Sacramento
Capistrano Beach, CA 92624-1337, USA

Murphy, Troy (Basketball Player)
404 W Mountain Rd
Sparta, NJ 07871-3532, USA

Murphy-O'Connor, Cormac Cardinal (Religious Leader)
Ambrosden Ave
London SW1P 1QJ, UNITED KINGDOM (UK)

Murray, Albert L (Writer)
45 W 132nd St
New York, NY 10037-3101, USA

Murray, Andy (Athlete, Tennis Player)
c/o Staff Member *ACE Group*
21 Quayside William Morris Way
London SW6 2UZ, UK

Murray, Anne (Musician)
Box 69030 12 St. Clair Ave East
Toronto, ON M4T 1K0, CANADA

Murray, Anne (Opera Singer)
Sebastianplatz 3
Munich 80331, GERMANY

Murray, Bill (Actor, Comedian)
c/o David Nochimson *Ziffren Brittenham LLP*
1801 Century Park W Fl 7
Los Angeles, CA 90067-6406, USA

Murray, Brain Doyle (Actor)
9200 W Sunset Blvd Ste 1125
Los Angeles, CA 90069-3610, USA

Murray, Bruce C (Scientist)
4800 Oak Grove Dr
Pasadena, CA 91109-8001, USA

Murray, Bryan C (Athlete, Hockey Player)
2215 NE 32nd Ave
Fort Lauderdale, FL 33305-1856, USA

Murray, Calvin (Athlete, Baseball Player)
17434 Courtney Pine Cir
Spring, TX 77379-8505, USA

Murray, Chad Michael (Actor)
c/o JoAnne Colonna *Brillstein Entertainment Partners*
9150 Wilshire Blvd Ste 350
Beverly Hills, CA 90212-3453, USA

Murray, Chad Micheal (Actor)
c/o JoAnne Colonna *Brillstein Entertainment Partners*
9150 Wilshire Blvd Ste 350
Beverly Hills, CA 90212-3453, USA

Murray, Charles A (Scientist)
1150 17th St NW
Washington, DC 20036-4603, USA

Murray, Charles P Jr (War Hero)
5906 Northridge Rd
Columbia, SC 29206-4336, USA

Murray, Cherry A (Business Person, Physicist)
700 Mountain Ave
New Providence, NJ 07974-1208, USA

Murray, Chris (Misc)
PO Box 218
Yorktown Heights, NY 10598-0218, USA

Murray, Dale (Athlete, Baseball Player)
RR 2 Box 1850
Yorktown, TX 78164, USA

Murray, Dan (Athlete, Baseball Player)
14200 N May Ave Apt 814
Oklahoma City, OK 73134-5026, USA

Murray, Dan (Athlete, Football Player)
9 Washington Rd
Ogdensburg, NJ 07439-1036, USA

Murray, Dave (Musician)
82 Bishop's Bridge Road
London W2 6BB, UNITED KINGDOM (UK)

Murray, David K (Musician)
300 Mercer St Apt 3J
New York, NY 10003-6732, USA

Murray, Devon (Actor)
PO Box 814 Maynooth
Co. Kildare, IRELAND

Murray, Don (Actor)
1201 La Patera Canyon Rd
Goleta, CA 93117-1548, USA

Murray, Doug (Cartoonist)
10 E 40th St # 900
New York, NY 10016-0200, USA

Murray, Eddie C (Athlete, Baseball Player)
15609 Bronco Dr
Canyon Country, CA 91387-4717, USA

Murray, Edward P (Eddie) (Athlete, Football Player)
1070 Forest Bay Dr
Waterford, MI 48328-4284, USA

Murray, Glenn (Athlete, Baseball Player)
41 W End St
Manning, SC 29102-2021, USA

Murray, Heath (Athlete, Baseball Player)
2605 Greenlawn Dr
Troy, OH 45373-4362, USA

Murray, Iain (Yachtsman)
75490 Fairway Dr
Indian Wells, CA 92210-8423, USA

Murray, Jaime (Actor)
c/o Lena Roklin *Luber Roklin Management*
8530 Wilshire Blvd Ste 550
Beverly Hills, CA 90211-3133, USA

Murray, James D (Biologist)
PO Box 352420
Seattle, WA 98195-2420, USA

Murray, Jasmine (Musician)

Murray, Joe (Athlete, Football Player)
12900 Ridgemoor Dr
Prospect, KY 40059-8195, USA

Murray, Joel
PO Box 5617
Beverly Hills, CA 90209-5617

Murray, John E Jr (Educator)
President S Ofc
Pittsburgh, PA 15282-0001, USA

Murray, Jonathan (Producer)
c/o Staff Member *Bunim/Murray Productions Inc*
6007 Sepulveda Blvd
Van Nuys, CA 91411-2502, USA

Murray, Joseph E (Nobel Prize Laureate)
108 Abbott Rd
Wellesley Hills, MA 02481-6104, USA

Murray, Keith (Artist, Musician)
250 W 57th St
New York, NY 10107-0001, USA

Murray, Ken (Athlete, Basketball Player)
24 Berkeley Heights Park
Bloomfield, NJ 07003-4803, USA

Murray, Larry (Athlete, Baseball Player)
3200 Round Hill Dr
Hayward, CA 94542-2122, USA

Murray, Margaret (Baseball Player)
1320 S Desert Meadows Cir Apt 3109
Green Valley, AZ 85614-1832, USA

Murray, Matt (Athlete, Baseball Player)
109 Greenwood Ave
Swampscott, MA 01907-2124, USA

Murray, Michael (Musician)
4436 Zeller Rd
Columbus, OH 43214-2620, USA

Murray, Neil (Musician)
27A Floral St #300
London WC2E 9DQ, UNITED KINGDOM (UK)

Murray, Peg (Actor)
800 Lighthouse Rd
Southold, NY 11971-2301, USA

Murray, Rich (Athlete, Baseball Player)
435 E 108th St
Los Angeles, CA 90061-2507, USA

Murray, Sean (Actor)
c/o Al Onorato *Unified Management*
4231 W National Ave
Burbank, CA 91505-4022, USA

Murray, Terence R (Terry) (Athlete, Hockey Player)
3601 S Broad St
Philadelphia, PA 19148-5250, USA

Murray, Timothy V (Architect)
444 Springfield Rd
Ottawa, ON K1M 0K4, CANADA

Murray, Tracy (Athlete, Basketball Player)
2419 Tour Edition Dr
Henderson, NV 89074-8301, USA

Murray, Ty (Rodeo Rider)
1660 Private Rd # 1213
Stephenville, TX 76401, USA

Murray of Epping Forest, Lionel (Len) (Misc)
29 Crescent Loughton
Essex 1G10 4PY, UNITED KINGDOM (UK)

Murray-Leslie, Alex (Musician)
924 Jefferson St SE # 101
Olympia, WA 98501, USA

Murrey, Dorie (Athlete, Basketball Player)
230 NE 178th St
Shoreline, WA 98155-3500, USA

Murro, Noam (Director)
c/o Staff Member *Management 360*
9111 Wilshire Blvd
Beverly Hills, CA 90210-5508, USA

Murtagh, Kate (Actor)
5104 Greenbush Ave
Sherman Oaks, CA 91423-1508, USA

Murton, Matt (Athlete, Baseball Player)
545 N Dearborn St Apt 2011
Chicago, IL 60654-5835, USA

Murukarni, Masanori (Baseball Player)
1-4-15-1506 Nisho Ohi Shinagawaku
Tokyo 140-0015, JAPAN

Musa, Said (Prime Minister)
East Bloc
Belmopan, BELIZE

Musabayev, Talgat A (Cosmonaut)
Moskovskoi Oblasti
Syvisdny Goroduk 141160, RUSSIA

Musante, Tony (Actor)
38 Bedford St
New York, NY 10014-4413, USA

Musberger, Brent
47 W 66th St
New York, NY 10023-6201

Musburger, Brent (Sportscaster)
286 Locha Dr
Jupiter, FL 33458-7733, USA

Muscarello, Carl
720 NW 71st Ave
Plantation, FL 33317-1125

Muse (Music Group)
c/o Cliff Burnstein *Q Prime Inc*
729 7th Ave Ste 1600
New York, NY 10019-6880, USA

Muse, William V (Educator)
President S Ofc
Auburn University, AL 36849-0001, USA

Muser, Tony (Athlete, Baseball Player, Coach)
11222 Martha Ann Dr
Los Alamitos, CA 90720-2956, USA

Museveni, Yoweri K (President)
PO Box 7108
Kampala, UGANDA

Musgrave, Bill (Athlete, Football Player)
15703 Portico Dr
Wayzata, MN 55391-4534, USA

Musgrave, F Story (Astronaut)
8572 Sweetwater Trl
Kissimmee, FL 34747-1519, USA

Musgrave, Mandy (Actor)
c/o Adam Levine *Levine Okwu Erickson Management*
9601 Wilshire Blvd Fl 3
Beverly Hills, CA 90210-5219, USA

Musgrave, R Kenton (Judge)
1 Federal Plz
New York, NY 10278-0001, USA

Musgrave, Spain (Athlete, Football Player)
9727 Mount Pisgah Rd Apt 811
Silver Spring, MD 20903-2011, USA

Musgrave, Ted (Race Car Driver)
175 Lakeside Dr E
Port Orange, FL 32128-6620, USA

Musgrave, Thea (Composer)
PO Box 2580
Norfolk, VA 23501-2580, USA

Musgraves, Dennis (Athlete, Baseball Player)
17100 N Highway 124
Centralia, MO 65240-3830, USA

Musgrove, Spain (Athlete, Football Player)
2350 Deckman Ln
Silver Spring, MD 20906-2266, USA

Musharraf, Parvez (President)
Aiwan-e-Sadr Mall & Mayo Roads
Islamabad, PAKISTAN

Mushok, Mike (Musician)
c/o Staff Member *Agency Group Ltd, The (UK)*
361-373 City Rd
London EC1V 1PQ, UK

Musi, Angelo (Athlete, Basketball Player)
930 Montgomery Ave Apt T2
Bryn Mawr, PA 19010-3036, USA

Musial, Stan (Athlete, Baseball Player)
1650 Des Peres Rd Ste 125
Saint Louis, MO 63131-1899, USA

Music, The (Music Group)
c/o Staff Member *Paradigm (Monterey)*
404 W Franklin St
Monterey, CA 93940-2303, USA

Musiol, Bogdan (Athlete)
Talstr 50
Zella-Mehlis 98544, GERMANY

Musiq (Musician)
825 8th Ave # 2700
New York, NY 10019-7416, USA

Musiq Soulchild (Music Group)
c/o Staff Member *Paradigm (Monterey)*
404 W Franklin St
Monterey, CA 93940-2303, USA

Musker, John (Animator, Director)
c/o Staff Member *Creative Artists Agency (CAA-LA)*
2000 Avenue of the Stars Ste 100
Los Angeles, CA 90067-4705, USA

Musonge, Pater Mafani (Prime Minister)
Yaounde, BP 1057, CAMEROON

Mussa, Michael (Economist)
700 19th St NW
Washington, DC 20431-0001, USA

Musselman, Jeff (Athlete, Baseball Player)
1842 Port Tiffin Pl
Newport Beach, CA 92660-7121, USA

Musselman, Ron (Athlete, Baseball Player)
5313 Autumn Dr
Wilmington, NC 28409-5701, USA

Musselwhite, Charlie (Musician)
c/o Kevin Morrow *Morrow Management*
5003 Westpark Dr Unit 102
Valley Village, CA 91601-3612, 818-985-8592

Musser, Neal (Athlete, Baseball Player)
6140 NW Gaylord Ter
Port Saint Lucie, FL 34986-3766, USA

Mussill, Barney (Athlete, Baseball Player)
912 Moorland Dr
Grosse Pointe Woods, MI 48236-1131, USA

Mussina, Mike (Athlete, Baseball Player)
1302 Spruce St
Montoursville, PA 17754-2116, USA

Musso, John (Athlete, Football Player)
242 E 3rd St
Hinsdale, IL 60521-4221, USA

Musso, Mitchel (Actor)
c/o Elissa Leeds-Fickman *Reel Talent Management*
PO Box 491035
Los Angeles, CA 90049-9035, USA

Mussolini, Alessandra (Government Official)
Chamber of Deputies
Rome 100, ITALY

Must (Music Group)
c/o Staff Member *Wind-up Records*
72 Madison Ave Fl 8
New York, NY 10016-8731, USA

Mustafa, Isaiah (Actor)
c/o Siri Garber *Platform Public Relations*
2666 N Beachwood Dr
Los Angeles, CA 90068-2308, USA

Mustaine, Dave (Musician)
838 N Doheny Dr Apt 302
West Hollywood, CA 90069-4849, USA

Mustalov, Abdulkhashim M (Prime Minister)
Tashkent 700008, UZBEKISTAN

Mustan, Abbas (Actor, Bollywood)
119 Haveliwala Building 1st R Rd Floor E
Mumbai, MS 400003, INDIA

Muster, Brad (Athlete, Football Player)
2017 Stony Oak Ct
Santa Rosa, CA 95403-0912, USA

Muster, Thomas (Tennis Player)
370 Felter Ave
Hewlett, NY 11557-1132, USA

Mustin, Henry C (Admiral)
2347 S Rolfe St
Arlington, VA 22202-1544, USA

Musto, Michael (Writer)
36 Cooper Sq
New York, NY 10003-7118

Mustonen, Olli (Composer, Musician)
120 W 58th St Apt 8D
New York, NY 10019-2156, USA

Mutchie, Marjorie Ann
1169 Mary Cir
La Verne, CA 91750-4210

Mutchnick, Max (Producer)
c/o Staff Member *KoMut Entertainment*
300 Television Plz
Burbank, CA 91505, USA

Muteba II, Ronald Muwenda (King)
Kampala, UGANDA

Muth, Ellen (Actor)
c/o Barbara Gale *Envoy Entertainment*
2637 Centinela Ave Apt 8
Santa Monica, CA 90405-3162, USA

Muth, Rene (Coach)
Athletic Dept
University Park, PA 16802, USA

Muthu, Kumari (Actor)
A-6 53 South West Boag Road T Nagar
Chennai, TN 600 017, INDIA

Muti, Ornella (Actor)
c/o Staff Member *Agentur Reuter*
Feldbrunnenstr. 50
Hamburg 20148, Germany

Muti, Riccardo
Via Corti Alle Mura 25
Ravenna 48100, ITALY

Muti, Richard
via Corti alle Mura 25
Ravenna, ITALY 48100

Mutis, Jeff (Athlete, Baseball Player)
630 E Wyoming St
Allentown, PA 18103-3536, USA

Mutombo, Dikembe (Athlete, Basketball Player)
c/o Staff Member *Houston Rockets*
Toyota Center 1510 Polk St
Houston, TX 77003-5028, USA

Mutscheller, Jim (Athlete, Football Player)
12350 Rosslare Ridge Rd Unit 102
Lutherville Timonium, MD 21093-8233, USA

Mutschler, Carlfried (Architect)
E7 7
Mannheim 68159, GERMANY

Mutter, Anne-Sophie (Musician)
Effnerstr 48
Munich 81925, GERMANY

Mutter, Carol A (General)
PO Box 1907
Woodbridge, VA 22195-1907, USA

Muxworthy, Jake (Actor)
c/o Staff Member *United Talent Agency (UTA)*
9560 Wilshire Blvd Fl 5
Beverly Hills, CA 90212-2400, USA

Muzorewa, Abel T (Religious Leader)
PO Box 353 Borrowdale
Harare, ZIMBABWE

Mwine, Ntare (Actor)
c/o August Kammer *TalentWorks (LA)*
3500 W Olive Ave Ste 1400
Burbank, CA 91505-5512, USA

Mwinyi, Ali Hassam (President)
State House PO Box 9120
Dar es Salaam, TANZANIA

My Chemical Romance (Music Group)
c/o Matt Galle *Paradigm (NY)*
360 Park Ave S Fl 16
New York, NY 10010-1708, USA

Mya (Actor, Musician)
c/o Gina Hoffman *Baker Winokur Ryder Public Relations (BWR-LA)*
9100 Wilshire Blvd Ste 500 PMB WEST
Beverly Hills, CA 90212-3426, USA

Myer, Steve (Athlete, Football Player)
23709 S Harmony Way
Sun Lakes, AZ 85248-6022, USA

Myers, A Maurice (Business Person)
1001 Fannin St
Houston, TX 77002-6706, USA

Myers, Anne M (Religious Leader)
1451 Dundee Ave
Elgin, IL 60120-1674, USA

Myers, Barton (Architect)
9348 Civic Center Dr
Beverly Hills, CA 90210-3624, USA

Myers, Billie
PO Box 12198
Miami, FL 33101-2198

Myers, Brett (Athlete, Baseball Player)
385 Summerset Dr
Saint Johns, FL 32259-8885, USA

Myers, Cynthia (Actor, Model)
PO Box 10
Llano, CA 93544-0010, USA

Myers, Dale D (Engineer)
7835 Rush Rose Dr Unit 214
Carlsbad, CA 92009-6830, USA

Myers, Danny (Race Car Driver)
PO Box 1189
Welcome, NC 27374-1189, USA

Myers, Dee Dee (Actor, Writer)
c/o Ari Greenburg *WmE2 (Endeavor-LA)*
9601 Wilshire Blvd Fl 3
Beverly Hills, CA 90210-5219, USA

Myers, Donnie (Stylist)
c/o Staff Member *De Facto*
15 W 26th St Fl 5
New York, NY 10010-1028, USA

Myers, Frank (Athlete, Football Player)
6603 Spring Branch Dr
Krum, TX 76249-7022, USA

Myers, Greg (Athlete, Baseball Player)
7917 Brasado Way
Riverside, CA 92508-8719, USA

Myers, Jack (Athlete, Football Player)
25 Biltmore Ln
Menlo Park, CA 94025-6686, USA

Myers, Jack D (Physicist)
1291 Scaife Hall
Pittsburgh, PA 15261-2012, USA

Myers, Jimmy (Athlete, Baseball Player)
2824 NW 159th St
Edmond, OK 73013-1234, USA

Myers, Lisa (Correspondent)
4001 Nebraska Ave NW
Washington, DC 20016-2733, USA

Myers, Margaret J (Dee Dee) (Government Official)
1233 20th St NW Ste 302
Washington, DC 20036-2482, USA

Myers, Mike (Actor, Comedian)
c/o Ina Treciokas *Slate Public Relations*
9000 W Sunset Blvd Ste 915
West Hollywood, CA 90069-5809, USA

Myers, Mike (Athlete, Baseball Player)
337 High Ridge Way
Castle Pines, CO 80108-3422, USA

Myers, Norman (Scientist)
Upper Meadow Old Road Headington
Oxford OX3 8SZ, UNITED KINGDOM (UK)

Myers, Pete (Athlete, Basketball Player)
PO Box 101242
Chicago, IL 60610-8903, USA

Myers, Randy (Athlete, Baseball Player)
15525 NE Caples Rd
Brush Prairie, WA 98606-8504, USA

Myers, Reginald R (War Hero)
PO Box 803
Annandale, VA 22003-0803, USA

Myers, Richard (Scientist)
Human Genome Center
Stanford, CA 94305, USA

Myers, Richard B (Dick) (General)
Chairman Joint Chiefs of Staff Pentagon
Washington, DC 20318-0001, USA

Myers, Richie (Athlete, Baseball Player)
521 Pony Trl
Mount Shasta, CA 96067-9063, USA

Myers, Robert (Bob) (Athlete)
c/o Staff Member *SFX Sports Management*
5335 Wisconsin Ave NW Ste 850
Washington, DC 20015-2052, USA

Myers, Rochelle (Writer)
3827 California St
San Francisco, CA 94118-1501, USA

Myers, Roderick (Rod) (Athlete, Baseball Player)
1816 S 3rd St
Conroe, TX 77301-5131, USA

Myers, Rodney (Rod) (Athlete, Baseball Player)
229 E Tanya Rd
Phoenix, AZ 85086-9253, USA

Myers, Russell (Cartoonist)
435 N Michigan Ave Ste 1500
Chicago, IL 60611-4012, USA

Myers, Tikalsky Linda (Skier)
RR 5 Box 2651
Santa Fe, NM 87506, USA

Myers, Tom (Athlete, Football Player)
6015 Rapid Creek Ct
Kingwood, TX 77345-1954, USA

Myers, Walter Dean (Photographer)
555 Broadway
New York, NY 10012-3919, USA

Myers Jr, Harry J (Publisher)
46 W Ranch Trl
Morrison, CO 80465-9504, USA

Myerson, Bess (Actor, Beauty Pageant Winner, Lawyer)
3 E 71st St Apt 9A
New York, NY 10021-4168, USA

Myerson, Harvey (Attorney, Attorney General, General)
425 Park Ave
New York, NY 10022-3506, USA

Myerson, Jacob M (Diplomat, Economist)
2 Rue Lucien-Gaulard
Paris 75018, FRANCE

Myette, Aaron (Athlete, Baseball Player)
14277 101A Ave
Surrey, BC V0B 2G2, Canada

Myhre, Wencke
Im Vendla 22
Nesoya, NORWAY N-1315

Myles, Alannah (Musician)
1 Water Lane Camden Town
London NW1 8N2, UNITED KINGDOM (UK)

Myles, Eve (Actor)
BBC Television Centre
Cardiff, Wales, UNITED KINGDOM

Myles, Sophia (Actor)
c/o Christian Hodell *Hamilton Hodell Ltd*
66-68 Margaret St Fl 5
London W1W 8SR, UK

Myre, Philippe (Phil) (Athlete, Hockey Player)
101 Rue Dugas
Joliette, QC J6E 4G7, Canada

Myrick, Bob (Athlete, Baseball Player)
32 Troon
Hattiesburg, MS 39401-8629, USA

Myrick, Daniel (Director)
2700 Colorado Ave
Santa Monica, CA 90404-3553, USA

Myrin, Arden (Actor)
c/o Steve Caserta *Sanders Armstrong Caserta*
2120 Colorado Ave Ste 120
Santa Monica, CA 90404-3561, USA

Myron, Vicki (Writer)
c/o Staff Member *Grand Central Publishing*
237 Park Ave C/O Author Mail Author's Name
New York, NY 10017, USA

Myrow, Brian (Athlete, Baseball Player)
713 Lottie Ln
Saginaw, TX 76179-2010, USA

Myrtle, Chip (Athlete, Football Player)
6010 S Lima Way
Englewood, CO 80111-5813, USA

Mysen, Bjorn O (Misc)
5221 Broad Branch Rd
Washington, DC 20015, USA

Myslinski, Tom (Athlete, Football Player)
105 Old Markham Pl
Chapel Hill, NC 27514-5230, USA

Myss, Caroline (Motivational Speaker)
61-63 Uxbridge Road
London W5 5SA, United Kingdom

Mysterio, Rey (Wrestler)
c/o Kerry Rodgerson *World Wrestling Entertainment (WWE)*
1241 E Main St
Stamford, CT 06902-3520, USA

Mystic (Music Group, Musician)
c/o Staff Member *General Entertainment*
PO Box 91868
Atlanta, GA 30364-1868, USA

Mystics
The88 Anador St.
Staten Island, NY 10303

Mystikal (Musician)
c/o Staff Member *International Creative Management (ICM-LA)*
10250 Constellation Blvd Fl 7
Los Angeles, CA 90067-6207, USA

N

N Chandra (Bollywood, Director, Filmmaker, Producer)
Ankush 1 Belscot Units Lokhandwala Complex Andheri Linking Road Andheri
Bombay, MS 400 058, INDIA

N. Cicilline, David (Congressman, Politician)
128 Cannon Hob
Washington, DC 20515-1102, USA

Na, Li (Athlete, Tennis Player)
c/o Max Eisenbud *IMG (Cleveland)*
1360 E 9th St Ste 100
Cleveland, OH 44114-1730, USA

Nabe, Ricky (Actor)
c/o Staff Member *Envision Management*
8840 Wilshire Blvd Fl 3
Beverly Hills, CA 90211-2606, USA

Naber, Jofin P (Swimmer)
PO Box 50107
Pasadena, CA 91115-0107, USA

Naber, John
PO Box 50107
Pasadena, CA 91115-0107

Nabers, Drayton Jr (Business Person)
2801 Highway 280 S
Birmingham, AL 35223-2490, USA

Nabholz, Chris (Athlete, Baseball Player)
2030 W Market St
Pottsville, PA 17901-1917, USA

Nabokov, Evgeni (Athlete, Hockey Player)
525 W Santa Clara St
San Jose, CA 95113-1520, USA

Nabors, Jim (Actor, Musician)
P.O. Box 6364
Honolulu, HI 96816, USA

Nabors, Richard (Athlete, Football Player)
1625 Brighton Ct
Beaumont, TX 77706-3220, USA

Naccarato, Vin (Musician)
PO Box 12
Far Hills, NJ 07931-0012, USA

Nachamkin, Boris (Athlete, Basketball Player)
350 E 62nd St Apt 5J
New York, NY 10065-8261, USA

Nachmansohn, David (Misc)
560 Riverside Dr
New York, NY 10027-3202, USA

Nacincik, John (Athlete, Basketball Player)
2815 Garrett Rd
White Hall, MD 21161-9737, USA

Nackret, Petra (Stylist)
c/o Staff Member *Ford Models (Miami)*
311 Lincoln Rd Ste 205
Miami Beach, FL 33139-3150, USA

Nada Surf (Music Group)
c/o Staff Member *Paradigm (Monterey)*
404 W Franklin St
Monterey, CA 93940-2303, USA

Nadal, Rafael (Athlete, Tennis Player)
c/o Staff Member *ATP Tour*
201 Atp Tour Blvd
Ponte Vedra Beach, FL 32082-3211, USA

Nadel, Barbara (Writer)
c/o Staff Member *St Martins Press*
175 5th Ave
New York, NY 10010-7703, USA

Nader, Michael (Actor)
28 E 10th St
New York, NY 10003-6201, USA

Nader, Ralph (Activist)
1600 20th St NW
Washington, DC 20009-1001, USA

Nadiadwala, Firoz (Actor, Bollywood)
c/o Jai Khanna *Brillstein Entertainment Partners*
9150 Wilshire Blvd Ste 350
Beverly Hills, CA 90212-3453, USA

Nadiya (Actor, Bollywood)
A Block Door No 23 Anna Nagar
Chennai, TN 600102, INDIA

Nadon, Branden (Actor)
1118 Homer St 228
Vancouver, BC V6B 6L5, CANADA

Nady, Xavier (Athlete, Baseball Player)
11320 Wild Meadow Pl
San Diego, CA 92131-4224, USA

Naehring, Tim (Athlete, Baseball Player)
7300 Pinehurst Dr
Cincinnati, OH 45244-3272, USA

Naeole, Chris (Athlete, Football Player)
1314 Charter Ct E
Jacksonville, FL 32225-2658, USA

Nafziger, Dana A (Athlete, Football Player)
251 El Dorado Way
Pismo Beach, CA 93449-1535, USA

Nagahama, Kazu (Actor)
c/o Staff Member *Ology Entertainment*
9151 W Sunset Blvd
West Hollywood, CA 90069-3106, USA

Nagakura, Saburo (Misc)
2-7-13 Higashicho Kichijoji
Musashino, Tokyo 1800002, JAPAN

Nagano, Kent G
4 Addison Bridge Place
London W14 8XP, UNITED KINGDOM (UK)

Nagao, Tomoaki (Nigo) (Business Person, Producer)
2-9-9 Sendagaya Shibuyaku
Tokyo 151-0051, Japan

Nagarjuna (Actor, Bollywood)
29 Kasturi Rangan Rd Alwarpet
Madras, TN 600018, INDIA

Nagashima, Shigeo (Baseball Player)
3-29-19 Denenchofu Ohtaku
Tokyo 145, JAPAN

Nagel, Craig (Athlete, Football Player)
222 Woodcrest Dr
Loveland, OH 45140-7772, USA

Nagel, Sidney R (Physicist)
4913 S Kimbark Ave
Chicago, IL 60615-2954, USA

Nagel, Steven R (Astronaut)
3801 Eagle View Ct
Columbia, MO 65203-1064, USA

Nagel, Thomas (Misc)
40 Washington Sq S
New York, NY 10012-1005, USA

Nagelson, Russ (Rusty) (Athlete, Baseball Player)
4 Carriage Ct
Little Rock, AR 72211-2280, USA

Nageotte, Clint (Athlete, Baseball Player)
4703 Spokane Ave Apt 1
Cleveland, OH 44144-4309, USA

Nagesh (Actor)
127 St Marys Rd
Chennai, TN 600 018, INDIA

Naghma (Actor, Bollywood)
23 A Kalpak Aspen 1st Cross Road
Bandra Floor PERRY
Bombay, MS 400 050, INDIA

Nagl, Miriam (Athlete, Golfer)
2120 Harbourside Dr Unit 616
Longboat Key, FL 34228-4261, USA

Nagle, Browning (Athlete, Football Player)
1153 Willow Bend Cv
Collierville, TN 38017-3479, USA

Nagler, Gern (Athlete, Football Player)
16190 NW Birdie Ln
Portland, OR 97229-8727, USA

Nagma (Actor, Bollywood)
43 lind Street Navarathna Gardens
Ekkaduthangal
Chennai, TN 600017, INDIA

Nagra, Parminder (Actor)
c/o Michael Foster *The Rights House (UK)*
Drury House 34-43 Russell St
London WC2B 5HA, UK

Nagy, Charles (Athlete, Baseball Player)
60 Robin Rd
Westbury, NY 11590-1104, USA

Nagy, Mike (Athlete, Baseball Player)
8 Indian Trl
Bronx, NY 10465-3813, USA

Nagy, Stanislaw Cardinal (Religious Leader)
Via Casale S Piov 20
Rome 126, ITALY

Nagy, Steve (Athlete, Baseball Player)
2205 NE Ridgewood Dr
Poulsbo, WA 98370-8529, USA

Nahan, Stu (Sportscaster)
11274 Canton Dr
Studio City, CA 91604-4154, USA

Naharin, Ohad (Choreographer)
Scheldeldoekshaven 60
Gravenhage, EN 2511, NETHERLANDS

Nahorodny, Bill (Athlete, Baseball Player)
1948 Rainbow Dr
Clearwater, FL 33765-3564, USA

Naifeh, Steven W (Writer)
335 Sumter St SE
Aiken, SC 29801-4661, USA

Nail, Jimmy
76 Oxford St
London, ENGLAND W1N 0AX

Naimoli, Vincent (Baseball Player)
16616 Villalenda De Avila
Tampa, FL 33613-5200, USA

Naipaul, V S (Nobel Prize Laureate)
29 Fernshaw Road
London SW10 0TG, UNITED KINGDOM (UK)

Nair, Mira (Director)
c/o Staff Member *Mirabai Films*
27 W 24th St Ste 403
New York, NY 10010-3287, USA

Naisbitt, John (Writer)
Spittelauer Platz 5A3A
Vienna 1090, AUSTRIA

Naish, Bronwen (Musician)
Gamdolbenmaen Gwunedd
North Wales LL5 9AX, WALES

Najarian, John S (Doctor)
Health Center Surgery Dept
Minneapolis, MN 55455, USA

Najee (Musician)
1995 Broadway # 501
New York, NY 10023-5882, USA

Najera, Eduardo (Basketball Player)
c/o Staff Member *Dallas Mavericks*
2500 Victory Ave
Dallas, TX 75219-7601, USA

Najera, Rick (Actor)
c/o Michelle Grant *Grant Management*
1158 26th St # 414
Santa Monica, CA 90403-4698, USA

Najimy, Kathy (Actor, Comedian)
c/o Leigh Brillstein *International Creative Management (ICM-LA)*
10250 Constellation Blvd Fl 7
Los Angeles, CA 90067-6207, USA

Nakajiim, Tadashi (Astronomer)
Astronomy
Pasadena, CA 91125-0001, USA

Nakajima, Tommy (Athlete, Golfer)
c/o Staff Member *IMG (Tokyo)*
8-18 Moto-Akasaka 1-chome, Minato-ku
Tokyo 107, JAPAN

Nakama, Keo (Swimmer)
1344 9th Ave
Honolulu, HI 96816-2615, USA

Nakasone, Yasuhiro (Prime Minister)
3-22-7 Kamikitazawa Setagayaku
Tokyo, JAPAN

Naked, Bif (Musician)
PO Box 779
New Hope, PA 18938-0779, USA

Nalder, Eric C (Journalist)
1120 John St
Seattle, WA 98109-5321, USA

Nalen, Thomas (Athlete, Football Player)
PO Box 4864
Englewood, CO 80155-4864, USA

Nalick, Anna (Musician)
23586 Calabasas Rd Ste 208
Calabasas, CA 91302-1361, USA

Nalinikanth (Actor)
413 29th Street 6th Sector
Chennai, TN 600 078, INDIA

Nall, Benita Krista (Actor)
c/o Staff Member *Main Title Entertainment*
2225 Wilshire Blvd Suite 500
Los Angeles, CA 90036, USA

Nall, N Anita (Swimmer)
PO Box 872505
Tempe, AZ 85287-0001, USA

Nalle, Karen Dotrice (Actor)
12751 Evanston St
Los Angeles, CA 90049-3710, USA

Nam, Leonardo (Actor)
c/o Staff Member *Overbrook Entertainment*
450 N Roxbury Dr Fl 4
Beverly Hills, CA 90210-4218, USA

Namaliu, Rabbie L (Prime Minister)
PO Box 6655 National Capital District
Boroko, PAPUA NEW GUINEA

Namath, Joseph W (Joe) (Actor, Athlete, Football Player)
c/o Harlan Werner *Sports Placement Service*
330 W 11th St Apt 105
Los Angeles, CA 90015-2230, USA

Nambiar, M N (Actor)
4 6th Street Gopalapuram
Chennai, TN 600 086, INDIA

Nambu, Yoichiro (Nobel Prize Laureate, Physicist)
5640 S Ellis Ave # 29
Chicago, IL 60637-1433, USA

Na-Ming
9903 Santa Monica Blvd # 575
Beverly Hills, CA 90212-1671

Namtchylak, Sainkho (Actor, Composer)
c/o Staff Member *Concerted Efforts*
PO Box 440326
Somerville, MA 02144-0004, USA

Nance, John J (Writer)
4512 S 8th St
Tacoma, WA 98405-1208, USA

Nance, Shane (Athlete, Baseball Player)
3403 Harbour Breeze Ln
Pearland, TX 77584-7958, USA

Nance, Todd (Musician)
400 Foundry St
Athens, GA 30601-2623, USA

Nancy, Ted L
c/o Daniel A (Dan) Strone *Trident Media Group LLC*
41 Madison Ave Fl 36
New York, NY 10010-2257, USA

Nankin, Jenna (Stylist)
c/o Staff Member *Workgroup (San Francisco)*
450 Linden St
San Francisco, CA 94102-5023, USA

Nanne, Louis V (Lou) (Athlete, Hockey Player)
6982 Tupa Dr
Edina, MN 55439-1641, USA

Nanni, Gianna
Carmenstr. 12
Zurich, SWITZERLAND CH-8032

Nantucket
250 N Kepler Rd Deland
FL, CA 33724

Nantz, Jim (Sportscaster)
51 W 52nd St
New York, NY 10019-6119, USA

Napier, Charles (Actor)
c/o Staff Member *Bauman Redanty & Shaul Agency*
5757 Wilshire Blvd Suite 473
Beverly Hills, CA 90212, USA

Napier, Hugo
2207 N Beachwood Dr
Los Angeles, CA 90068-2903

Napier, James (Actor)
c/o Grahame Dunster *Auckland Actors*
PO Box 56460 Dominion Road
Auckland, NEW ZEALAND

Napier, John (Designer)
16-18 Douglas St
London SW1P 4PB, UNITED KINGDOM (UK)

Napier, Wilfrid F Cardinal (Religious Leader)
154 Gordon Road
Greyville 4023, SOUTH AFRICA

Naples, Al (Athlete, Baseball Player)
99 Nickerson Rd
Orleans, MA 02653-3314, USA

Napoles, Jose (Boxer)
Cerrada De Tizapan 9-303 Ediciov
Codigo Postel
Suffield, CT 06080-0001, MEXICO

Napoli, Mike (Athlete, Baseball Player)
c/o Staff Member *Los Angeles Dodgers (LA Dodgers)*
1000 Elysian Park Ave
Los Angeles, CA 90090-1112, USA

Naponic, Robert (Athlete, Football Player)
10807 Timberglen Dr
Houston, TX 77024-6808, USA

Naragon, Hal (Athlete, Baseball Player)
1521 Hagey Dr
Barberton, OH 44203-7724, USA

Narain, Nicole (Actor)
8033 W Sunset Blvd # 224
West Hollywood, CA 90046-2401

Naranjo, Gonzola (Cholly) (Athlete, Baseball Player)
15600 SW 80th St Apt 212
Miami, FL 33193-2669, USA

Naranjo, Monica (Musician)
c/o Staff Member *Sony Music Miami*
605 Lincoln Rd Ste 700
Miami Beach, FL 33139-2901, USA

Narasimhan, V L (Actor)
9-6 L I C Staff Quarters K K Nagar
Chennai, TN 600 078, INDIA

Nardini, Thomas (Tom) (Actor)
139 Beach Ave
Madison, CT 06443-2854, USA

Narducci, Katherine
2843 Waterbury Ave
Bronx, NY 10461-6150

Narducci, Tim (Musician)
9560 Wilshire Blvd # 400
Beverly Hills, CA 90212-2427, USA

Narita, Hiro (Cinematographer)
2262 Magnolia Ave
Petaluma, CA 94952-1631, USA

Narita, Richard
8831 Sunset Blvd # 304
Los Angeles, CA 90069

Narizzano, Silvio (Cas) (Director)
55 Park Lane
London W1Y 3DD, UNITED KINGDOM (UK)

Narleski, Ray (Athlete, Baseball Player)
1183 Chews Landing Rd
Clementon, NJ 08021-2805, USA

Narron, Jerry (Athlete, Baseball Player, Coach)
304 Ashworth Dr
Goldsboro, NC 27530-5563, USA

Narron, Sam (Athlete, Baseball Player)
101 Mill Pl
Goldsboro, NC 27534-8933, USA

Naruhito (Royalty)
1-1 Chiyoda Chiyoda-ku
Tokyo, JAPAN

Narveson, Chris (Athlete, Baseball Player)
4927 Whitner Dr
Wilmington, NC 28409-2085, USA

Narz, Jack (Television Host)
1906 Beverly Pl
Beverly Hills, CA 90210, USA

NAS (Musician)
c/o Staff Member *Richard De La Font Agency*
3808 W South Park Blvd
Broken Arrow, OK 74011-1261, USA

Nasclemento, Milton (Musician, Songwriter, Writer)
Av A Lombardi 800
Rio de Janeiro 22 640-000, BRAZIL

Naseeruddin, Shah (Actor, Bollywood)
204 Sand Pebbles Perry X Road Bandra
Mumbai, MS 400050, INDIA

Nash, Charles F (Cotton) (Athlete, Baseball Player, Basketball Player)
600 Summershade Cir
Lexington, KY 40502-2723, USA

Nash, David (Artist)
Capel Rhiw Blanau Flestiniog
Gwynedd Wales LL41 3NT, WALES

Nash, Graham W (Musician, Songwriter, Writer)
709 E Colorado Blvd Ste 220
Pasadena, CA 91101-2125, USA

Nash, Jamia Simone (Actor)
c/o Staff Member *Carson-Adler Agency*
250 W 57th St Ste 2030
New York, NY 10107-2013, USA

Nash, Jim (Athlete, Baseball Player)
4383 White Surrey Dr NW
Kennesaw, GA 30144-5106, USA

Nash, Joe (Athlete, Football Player)
59 Walpole St Unit 307
Canton, MA 02021-1875, USA

Nash, John F Jr (Nobel Prize Laureate)
Economics Department Fine Hall
Princeton, NJ 08544-0001, USA

Nash, Kate (Musician)

Nash, Keisha
344 E 59th St
New York, NY 10022-1593

Nash, Kevin (Wrestler)
c/o Andrew Stawiarski *ADS Management*
269 S Beverly Dr # 441
Beverly Hills, CA 90212-3851, USA

Nash, Leigh (Musician)
c/o Staff Member *Paradigm (Monterey)*
404 W Franklin St
Monterey, CA 93940-2303, USA

Nash, Niecy (Actor, Television Host)
c/o E Brian Dobbins *Principato/Young Management*
9465 Wilshire Blvd Ste 430
Beverly Hills, CA 90212-2613, USA

Nash, Noreen (Actor)
719 N Maple Dr
Beverly Hills, CA 90210-3480, USA

Nash, Richard
19323 Oxnard St
Tarzana, CA 91356-1122

Nash, Rick (Athlete, Hockey Player)
c/o Staff Member *Columbus Blue Jackets*
200 W Nationwide Blvd Unit 1
Columbus, OH 43215-2564, USA

Nash, Robert (Athlete, Basketball Player)
659 Kahiau Loop
Honolulu, HI 96821-2539, USA

Nash, Steve (Athlete, Basketball Player)
c/o Bill Duffy *BDA Sports Management (BDA-CA)*
700 Ygnacio Valley Rd Ste 330
Walnut Creek, CA 94596-3838, USA

Nash, Terius (The-Dream) (Musician)
c/o Staff Member *Island Def Jam Music Group*
825 8th Ave Fl 28
New York, NY 10019-7416

Naslund, Markus (Athlete, Hockey Player)
154 Earl St
Kingston, ON K7L 2H2, Canada

Naslund, Mats (Athlete, Hockey Player)
6963 Progressona
Switzerland

Naslund, Ron (Athlete, Hockey Player)
2600 Cheyenne Cir
Minnetonka, MN 55305-2309, USA

Nasr, Seyyed Hossein (Misc)
Gelman Library
Washington, DC 20052-0001, USA

Nasser, Jacques A (Business Person)
1st National Plz
Chicago, IL 60607, USA

Nasser M (Actor)
245 Guhan Street Kamakoti Nagar
Valasarawakkam
Chennai, TN 600 087, INDIA

Nastase, Ilie (Tennis Player)
Calea Plevnei 14
Bucarest, HUNGARY

Nastu, Phil (Athlete, Baseball Player)
52 Stratfield Pl
Bridgeport, CT 06606-4002, USA

Nat, Marie-Jose (Actor)
c/o Laurent Gregoire *Agence Artistique Adequat*
80 Rue D'Amsterdam
Paris 75009, France

Natal, Bob (Athlete, Baseball Player)
3913 Cockrill Dr
McKinney, TX 75070-2413, USA

Natali, Vincenzo (Director)
c/o Philip Raskind *WmE2 (Endeavor-LA)*
9601 Wilshire Blvd Fl 3
Beverly Hills, CA 90210-5219, USA

Natalicio, Diana S (Educator)
University of Texas at El Paso President S Ofc
El Paso, TX 79968-0001, USA

Natalie (Musician)
c/o Staff Member *Motown Records (NY)*
1755 Broadway Fl 7
New York, NY 10019-3743, USA

Nater, Swen (Athlete, Basketball Player)
3590 Wetherbee Ln
Enumclaw, WA 98022-6421, USA

Nath, Alok (Actor, Bollywood)
901 Skydeck Oshiwara Complex Off New Link Road Andheri
Mumbai, MS 400061, INDIA

Nathan, Amy (Stylist)
99 El Camino Real
Berkeley, CA 94705-2423, USA

Nathan, David G (Physicist)
44 Binney St
Boston, MA 02115-6013, USA

Nathan, Joe (Athlete, Baseball Player)
19066 Vogel Farm Rd
Eden Prairie, MN 55347-4199, USA

Nathan, Joseph A (Business Person)
1 Campus Martius
Detroit, MI 48226-5000, USA

Nathan, S R (President)
Orchard Road Istana
Singapore 922, SINGAPORE

Nathan, Tony C (Athlete, Coach, Football Coach, Football Player)
15110 Dunbarton Pl
Miami Lakes, FL 33016-1415, USA

Nathaniel (Popp), Bishop (Religious Leader)
2522 Grey Tower Rd
Jackson, MI 49201-9120, USA

Nathanson, Jeff (Writer)
c/o Staff Member *United Talent Agency (UTA)*
9560 Wilshire Blvd Fl 5
Beverly Hills, CA 90212-2400, USA

Nathanson, Roy (Musician)
122 E 57th St # 300
New York, NY 10022-2623, USA

Nathman, John B (Admiral)
Commander Naval Air Force Pacific NAS North Island
San Diego, CA 92135, USA

Nation, Joey (Athlete, Baseball Player)
2125 N Roff Ave
Oklahoma City, OK 73107-2749, USA

Natividad, Kitten (Actor)
c/o Siouxzan Perry *Girlwerks Management*
3395 E Camino Rojos
Palm Springs, CA 92262-5417, USA

Natkin, Robert (Artist)
24 Mark Twain Ln
West Redding, CT 06896-2227, USA

Naton, Pete (Athlete, Baseball Player)
4136 Split Rock Rd
Camillus, NY 13031-8704, USA

Natowich, Andrew (Athlete, Football Player)
24 Lexington Ave
Brattleboro, VT 05301-6626, USA

Natsios, Andrew (Government Official)
320 21st NW
Washington, DC 20523-0002, USA

Natt, Calvin (Athlete, Basketball Player)
25201 E Indore Dr
Aurora, CO 80016-2189, USA

Natter, Robert J (Admiral)
Commander Atlantic Fleet
Norfolk, VA 23551-0001, USA

Nattiel, Ricky (Athlete, Football Player)
835 NW 119th St
Gainesville, FL 32606-0449, USA

Natural (Musician)
PO Box 5097
Bellingham, WA 98227-5097, USA

Naude, C F Beyers (Religious Leader)
26 Hoylake Road
Greenside 2193, SOUTH AFRICA

Naudet, Jules (Producer)
c/o Staff Member *WmE2 (WMA-LA)*
1 William Morris Pl
Beverly Hills, CA 90212-4261, USA

Nauert, Paul (Baseball Player)
1201 Steeple Run
Lawrenceville, GA 30043-6354, USA

Nauert, Paul (Athlete, Baseball Player)
1201 Steeple Run
Lawrenceville, GA 30043-6354, USA

Naughton, David (Actor)
c/o Steven Neibert *Imperium 7 Talent Agency*
5455 Wilshire Blvd Ste 1706
Los Angeles, CA 90036-4217, USA

Naughton, James (Actor)
c/o Staff Member *Brookside Artists Management (NY)*
250 W 57th St Ste 2303
New York, NY 10107-2399, USA

Naughton, Laurie (Actor)
c/o Bruce Smith *OmniPop Talent Group*
10700 Ventura Blvd Fl 2
Studio City, CA 91604-3561, USA

Naughton, Naturi (Musician)
c/o Matt Luber *Luber Roklin Management*
8530 Wilshire Blvd Ste 550
Beverly Hills, CA 90211-3133, USA

Naulis, Willie (Basketball Player)
13900 Hawthome Blvd
Hawthome, CA 90250, USA

Naulls, Willie (Athlete, Basketball Player)
435 Loring Ave
Los Angeles, CA 90024-2642, USA

Naulty, Dan (Athlete, Baseball Player)
23705 Via Del Rio
Yorba Linda, CA 92887-2717, USA

Nauman, Bruce L (Artist)
4630 Rising Hill Rd
Altadena, CA 91001-3748, USA

Naumenko, Gregg (Athlete, Hockey Player)
2 E Erie St Apt 2006
Chicago, IL 60611-3170, USA

Naumoff, Paul (Athlete, Football Player)
7783 Fenway Rd
New Albany, OH 43054-9690, USA

Naum-Parker, Dorothy (Baseball Player)
2620 Bridlecreek Ln
Galesburg, IL 61401-5547, USA

Nause, Martha (Athlete, Golfer)
13206 Patterson Trl
Minocqua, WI 54548, USA

Nauta, Kate (Actor)
c/o Ben Press *Don Buchwald & Associates Inc (LA)*
8619 Washington Blvd
Culver City, CA 90232-7441, USA

Nava, Gregory (Director)
8942 Wilshire Blvd
Beverly Hills, CA 90211-1908, USA

Navaira, Emilio (Musician)
c/o Staff Member *WmE2 (WMA-LA)*
1 William Morris Pl
Beverly Hills, CA 90212-4261, USA

Naval, Deepti (Actor, Bollywood)
603 Oceanic Seven Bungalows Versova Andheri
Mumbai, MS 400061, INDIA

Navarez, Alfred (Musician)
9255 W Sunset Blvd Ste 407
Los Angeles, CA 90069-3302, USA

Navarro, Dave (Musician)
c/o Larissa Friend *Larissa Friend Management*
Prefers to be contacted via telephone
Los Angeles, CA 90069, USA

Navarro, Dioner (Athlete, Baseball Player)
13243 Pike Lake Dr
Riverview, FL 33579-4039, USA

Navarro, Emilio (Baseball Player)
97 Calle Torre
Ponce, PR 00730-3655, USA

Navarro, Guillermo J (Cinematographer)
800 S Robertson Blvd Ste 6
Los Angeles, CA 90035-1635, USA

Navarro, Jaime (Athlete, Baseball Player)
8100 Oak Park Rd
Orlando, FL 32819-3266, USA

Navarro, Juan Carlos (Athlete, Basketball Player)
10545 S Ashglen Cir
Collierville, TN 38017-3660, USA

Navarro, Tito (Athlete, Baseball Player)
556 Calle Creuz
San Juan, PR 00923-1826, USA

Navas, Bibiana (Actor)
c/o Gabriel Blanco *Gabriel Blanco Iglesias (Mexico)*
Rio Balsas 35-32 Colonia Cuauhtemoc
DF 6500, Mexico

Navasky, Victor S (Editor, Publisher)
33 W 67th St
New York, NY 10023-6224, USA

Navayne, Kevin (Actor)
c/o Talon Outlaw *Outlaw Management Group*
9777 Wilshire Blvd
Beverly Hills, CA 90212-1910, USA

Navies, Hannibal (Athlete, Football Player)
2356 Bransley Pl
Duluth, GA 30097-4336, USA

Navis, Hannibal (Athlete, Football Player)
4616 Rustling Woods Dr
Denver, NC 28037-5600, USA

Navon, Itzhak (President)
Hakiria
Jerusalem, ISRAEL

Navratilova, Martina (Tennis Player)
W Red Oak Ln Usta National Headquarters 70
White Plains, NY 10604-3622, USA

Naylor, Gloria (Writer)
PO Box 89559
Honolulu, HI 96830-7559, USA

Naymenko, Gregg (Athlete)
2695 E Katella Ave
Anaheim, CA 92806-5904

Nayyar, Kunal (Actor)
c/o Jason Kim *Lovett Management*
1327 Brinkley Ave
Los Angeles, CA 90049-3619, USA

Nazam, Hisham (Government Official)
Riyadh, SAUDI ARABIA

Nazarbayev, Nursultan A (President)
Pl Respublik
Astana 480091, KAZAKHSTAN

Nazarian, Sam (Business Person)
8000 Beverly Blvd
Los Angeles, CA 90048-4504, USA

Ndayizeye, Domitien (President)
Bujumbura, BURUNDI

Ndegeocello, Me'Shell (Musician)
509 Hartnell St
Monterey, CA 93940-2825, USA

Ndegeocello, Michelle (Musician)
c/o Staff Member *Paradigm (Monterey)*
404 W Franklin St
Monterey, CA 93940-2303, USA

Ndimira, Pascal Firmin (Prime Minister)
Bujumbura, BURUNDI

N'Dour, Youssou (Musician)
Nonnengasse 15
Fulda 36037, GERMANY

N'Dour, Youssou (Musician)
c/o Staff Member *Nonesuch Records*
75 Rockefeller Plz Fl 8
New York, NY 10019-6908, USA

Neagle, Denny (Athlete, Baseball Player)
16254 Sandstone Dr
Morrison, CO 80465-2163, USA

Neal, Blaine (Athlete, Baseball Player)
256 Dowdy Dr
Gibbstown, NJ 08027-1175, USA

Neal, Craig (Athlete, Basketball Player)
9205 Tanoan Dr NE
Albuquerque, NM 87111-5828, USA

Neal, Curley (Athlete, Basketball Player)
1275 Regency Pl
Lake Mary, FL 32746-4339, USA

Neal, Diane (Actor)

Neal, Doris (Baseball Player)
1212 Stoeber Ave Rear
Sarasota, FL 34232-2136, USA

Neal, Dylan (Actor)
c/o Sara Schedeen *Metropolitan (MTA)*
4526 Wilshire Blvd
Los Angeles, CA 90010-3801, USA

Neal, Edwin (Actor)
501 W Powell Ln
Austin, TX 78753-5978, USA

Neal, Elise (Actor)
c/o Vincent Cirrincione *Vincent Cirrincione Associates*
1516 N Fairfax Ave
Los Angeles, CA 90046-2608, USA

Neal, Fred (Curly) (Basketball Player)
PO Box 915415
Longwood, FL 32791-5415, USA

Neal, James (Athlete, Basketball Player)
803 Medora Dr
Greer, SC 29650-4751, USA

Neal, James F (Attorney, Attorney General, General)
3rd National Bank Building 800
Nashville, TN 37219, USA

Neal, Lloyd (Athlete, Basketball Player)
905 NE Mariners Loop
Portland, OR 97211-1574, USA

Neal, Lorenzo (Athlete, Football Player)
777 S Orange Ave
Fresno, CA 93702-3401, USA

Neal, Mike (Athlete, Football Player)
c/o Roosevelt Barnes *Maximum Sports Management*
6435 W Jefferson Blvd # 197
Fort Wayne, IN 46804-6203, USA

Neal, Philip M (Business Person)
150 N Orange Grove Blvd
Pasadena, CA 91103-3534, USA

Neal, Scott (Actor)
c/o Staff Member *Jonathan Altaras Assoc Ltd*
11 Garrick Street Covent Garden
London WC2E 9AT, UNITED KINGDOM (UK)

Neal, T Daniel (Dan) (Athlete, Football Player)
711 Homestead Blvd
Louisville, KY 40207-3630, USA

Neale, Gary L (Business Person)
801 E 86th Ave
Merrillville, IN 46410-6271, USA

Nealon, Kevin (Actor, Comedian)
c/o Marc Gurvitz *Brillstein Entertainment Partners*
9150 Wilshire Blvd Ste 350
Beverly Hills, CA 90212-3453, USA

Nealy, Eddie (Athlete, Basketball Player)
702 Lightstone Dr
San Antonio, TX 78258-2305, USA

Neame, Christopher (Actor)
3172 Dona Susana Dr
Studio City, CA 91604-4356, USA

Near, Holly (Actor, Musician, Songwriter, Writer)
PO Box 236
Ukiah, CA 95482-0236, USA

Nearing, Merna (Baseball Player)
21079 W Good Hope Rd Apt D-1
Lannon, WI 53046-9770, USA

Neary, Martin G J (Musician)
2 Little Cloister Westminster Abbey
London SW1P 3PL, UNITED KINGDOM (UK)

Neary, Robert (Actor, Director)
c/o Lin Bickelmann *Encore Artists Management*
3815 W Olive Ave Ste 101
Burbank, CA 91505-4674, USA

Nebel, Dorothy Hoyt (Skier)
5340 Balfor Dr
Virginia Beach, VA 23464-2441, USA

Neblett, Carol (Opera Singer)
180 W End Ave
New York, NY 10023-4902, USA

Nebout, Claire (Actor)
20 Ave Rapp
Paris 75007, FRANCE

Necciai, Ron (Athlete, Baseball Player)
PO Box 704
Anna Maria, FL 34216-0704, USA

Nechaev, Victor (Athlete, Hockey Player)
1806 Twin Palms Dr
San Marino, CA 91108-2555, USA

Nechkov, Anne McLaughlin (Stylist)
559 Fieldstream Blvd
Orlando, FL 32825-7206, USA

Neck, Tommy (Athlete, Football Player)
2107 Marie Pl
Monroe, LA 71201-3413, USA

Ned, Derrick (Athlete, Football Player)
421 S Iberville Ave
Gonzales, LA 70737-3547, USA

Nedeljakova, Barbara (Actor)
c/o Robert Depp 3500 W Olive Ave Ste 1180
Burbank, CA 91505, USA

Nedney, Joe (Athlete, Football Player)
121 Lauren Cir
Scotts Valley, CA 95066-3836, USA

Nedomansky, Vaclav (Athlete, Hockey Player)
57 Crest Verde Ln
Rolling Hills Estates, CA 90274, USA

Nedorost, Vaclav (Athlete, Hockey Player)
1 Panther Pkwy
Sunrise, FL 33323-5315, USA

Nedved, Petr (Athlete, Hockey Player)
11230 110th St
Edmonton, AB T5G 3H7, Canada

Needham, Connie (Actor)
126 Laurent
Newport Beach, CA 92660-8302, USA

Needham, Hal (Director)
PO Box 46609
Los Angeles, CA 90046-0609, USA

Needham, James J (Business Person)
1500 Brecknock Rd Apt 103
Greenport, NY 11944-3119, USA

Needham, Tracey (Actor)
c/o Tony Chargin *Ovation Management*
12028 National Blvd
Los Angeles, CA 90064-3542, USA

Needham, Tracy
9229 W Sunset Blvd Ste 311
Los Angeles, CA 90069-3403

Needleman, Jacob (Misc)
841 Wawona Ave
Oakland, CA 94610-1250, USA

Neel, Troy (Athlete, Baseball Player)
PO Box 1582
El Campo, TX 77437-1582, USA

Neelu (Actor)
G-5 Madhuram Flats Ururalagat Kuppam
5th Avenue Besant Nagar
Chennai, TN 600 090, INDIA

Neely, Cam (Athlete, Hockey Player)
76 Davison Dr
Lincoln, MA 01773-2216, USA

Neely, Gina (Television Host)
585 S Cooper St
Memphis, TN 38104-5358, USA

Neely, Patrick (Pat) (Television Host)
5700 Mount Moriah Rd
Memphis, TN 38115-1623, USA

Neely, Ralph E (Athlete, Football Player)
6943 Sperry St
Dallas, TX 75214-2855, USA

Neely Jr, Mark E (Historian)
198 Madison Ave
New York, NY 10016-4308, USA

Neeman, Cal (Athlete, Baseball Player)
93 Champagne Dr
Lake Saint Louis, MO 63367-1604, USA

Ne'eman, Yuval (Physicist)
Physics/Astronomy Dept
Tel-Aviv 69978, ISRAEL

Neeson, Liam (Actor)
c/o Alan Nierob *Rogers & Cowan PR (LA)*
Pacific Design Center 8687 Melrose Ave, 7th Floor
West Hollywood, CA 90069, USA

Nef, John U (Historian)
2726 N St NW
Washington, DC 20007-3323, USA

Nef, Sonia (Skier)
Halten 345
Grub 9035, SWITZERLAND

Neff, Bob (Athlete, Football Player)
2 Crestview
Athens, TX 75751-2932, USA

Neff, Francine I (Government Official)
PO Box 1498
Pena Blanca, NM 87041-1498, USA

Neff, Lucas (Actor)
c/o Jason Weinberg *Untitled Entertainment (LA)*
350 S Beverly Dr Ste 200
Beverly Hills, CA 90212-4819, USA

Neff, William D (Psychic)
2080 Hideaway Ct
Morris, IL 60450-9601, USA

Negishi, Takashi (Economist)
2-10-5-301 Motoazabu Minatoku
Tokyo 106, JAPAN

Negoesco, Stephen (Coach)
Athletic Dept
San Francisco, CA 94117, USA

Negray, Ron (Athlete, Baseball Player)
587 W Nimisila Rd
Akron, OH 44319-4616, USA

Negreanu, Daniel (Actor)
PO Box 416
Las Vegas, NV 89125-0416, USA

Negri Sembilan, Yang Di-Pertuan Besar (President)
Serembam, MALAYSIA

Negron, Chuck (Musician)
c/o Staff Member *Mitch Schneider Organization, The*
14724 Ventura Blvd Ste 410
Sherman Oaks, CA 91403-3537, USA

Negron, Taylor
8447 Wilshire Blvd Ste 206
Beverly Hills, CA 90211-3207

Negroponte, John D (Diplomat)
2201 C St NW
Washington, DC 20520-0099, USA

Negroponte, Nicholas (Engineer)
69 Mount Vernon St
Boston, MA 02108-1330, USA

Negus, Fred (Athlete, Football Player)
435 W Starin Rd
Whitewater, WI 53190-1133, USA

Nehamas, Alexander (Misc)
Philosophy
Princeton, NJ 08544-0001, USA

Nehemiah, Renaldo (Athlete, Football Player)
1751 Pinnacle Dr Ste 1500
Mc Lean, VA 22102-3833, USA

Neher, Erwin (Nobel Prize Laureate)
Domane 11
Bovenden 37120, GERMANY

Nehmer, Meinhard (Athlete)
Vamkevitz
Altenkirchen 18556, GERMANY

Neibauer, Gary (Athlete, Baseball Player)
146 Delta Ave
Bismarck, ND 58504-6655, USA

Neibhors, William (Athlete, Football Player)
1904 Chippendale Dr SE
Huntsville, AL 35801-1309, USA

Neid, Silvia (Soccer Player)
Betramstr 18
Frankfurt/Main 60320, GERMANY

Neidert, John (Athlete, Football Player)
4731 Placid Cir
Sarasota, FL 34231-6486, USA

Neidich, Charles (Musician)
111 W 57th St
New York, NY 10019-2211, USA

Neidlinger, Jim (Athlete, Baseball Player)
139 Sunset Dr
Burlington, VT 05408-1910, USA

Neiger, Al (Athlete, Baseball Player)
213 Pinehurst Rd
Wilmington, DE 19803-3125, USA

Neighbors, William (Billy) (Football Player)
1904 Chippendale Dr SE
Huntsville, AL 35801-1309, USA

Neil, Andrew F (Editor)
PO Box 584
London SW7 3QY, UNITED KINGDOM (UK)

Neil, Hildegarde (Actor)
5 Spring St
London W2 3RA, UNITED KINGDOM (UK)

Neil, Ray (Baseball Player)
250 N Wells Ave Apt 511
Benton Harbor, MI 49022-7735, USA

Neil, Vince (Composer, Musician)
c/o Darren Prince *Prince Marketing Group*
18 Carillon Cir
Livingston, NJ 07039-2600, USA

Neil, Warden (Stylist)
367 N Laurel Ave
Los Angeles, CA 90048-2313, USA

Neill, Mary Gardner (Director)
Volunteer Park
Seattle, WA 98112, USA

Neill, Mike (Athlete, Baseball Player)
17 Cape May Pt
Greensboro, NC 27455-1363, USA

Neill, Noel (Actor)
4421 N Bear Canyon Rd
Tucson, AZ 85749-9649

Neill, Rolfe (Publisher)
600 S Tryon St
Charlotte, NC 28202-1842, USA

Neill, Sam (Actor)
c/o Ann Churchill-Brown *Shanahan Management*
Level 3 Berman House
Surry Hills 2010, AUSTRALIA

Neill, Ve (Stylist)
306254 Hasley Canyon Rd
Castaic, CA 91384, USA

Neill, William M (Athlete, Football Player)
19 Nicholas Dr
Butler, NJ 07405-2742, USA

Neils, Steve (Athlete, Football Player)
1329 Waterford Rd
Woodbury, MN 55125-2366, USA

Neilson-Bell, Sandra (Swimmer)
3101 Mistyglen Cir
Austin, TX 78746-7811, USA

Neiman, LeRoy (Artist)
c/o Gail Parenteau *Parenteau Guidance*
132 E 35th St # 3J
New York, NY 10016-3892, USA

Neinas, Charles M (Chuck) (Misc)
5344 Westridge Dr
Boulder, CO 80301-6501, USA

Neis, Reagan Dale (Actor)
c/o Susan Curtis *Curtis Talent Management*
9607 Arby Dr
Beverly Hills, CA 90210-1202, USA

Neison, Chuck (Athlete, Baseball Player)
8681 Carriage Hill Draw
Savage, MN 55378-2366, USA

Neizvestny, Ernst I (Artist)
81 Grand St
New York, NY 10013-2256, USA

Nelkin, Stacey
2770 Hutton Dr
Beverly Hills, CA 90210-1216

Nelligan, Kate (Actor)
c/o Gary Gersh *Innovative Artists (NY)*
235 Park Ave S Fl 7
New York, NY 10003-1404, USA

Nellis, William J (Physicist)
7000 East Ave
Livermore, CA 94550-9698, USA

Nellssen, Roelof J (Financier, Government Official)
PO Box 552
AN Laren 1250, NETHERLANDS

Nelms, Michael (Mike) (Athlete, Football Player)
10411 James Monroe Hwy
Culpeper, VA 22701-8028, USA

Nelsen, Bill (Athlete, Football Player)
13512 Dornoch Dr
Orlando, FL 32828-8802, USA

Nelson
15003 Greenleaf St
Sherman Oaks, CA 91403-4006

Nelson, Al (Athlete, Football Player)
660 Boas St Apt 918
Harrisburg, PA 17102-1323, USA

Nelson, Andy (Athlete, Football Player)
12251 Manor Rd
Glen Arm, MD 21057-9542, USA

Nelson, Bill (Athlete, Football Player)
PO Box 9235
Pahrump, NV 89060-9235, USA

Nelson, Bob (Baseball Player)
18110 Langford Ln
Forney, TX 75126-8173, USA

Nelson, Bry (Athlete, Baseball Player)
11 Campden Hill Rd
Sherwood, AR 72120-6536, USA

Nelson, Cailin (Physicist)
7000 East Ave
Livermore, CA 94550-9698, USA

Nelson, Charles L (Athlete, Football Player)
3028 162nd Pl SE
Mill Creek, WA 98012-7848, USA

Nelson, Charlie (Athlete, Baseball Player, Olympic Athlete)
4448 N 24th Way
Phoenix, AZ 85016-4974, USA

Nelson, Colette (Fitness Expert, Model)
PO Box 1122
Seaford, NY 11783-0078, USA

Nelson, Cordner (Misc)
4341 Starlight Dr
Indianapolis, IN 46239-1473, USA

Nelson, Craig Richard (Actor)
3172 Dona Susana Dr
Studio City, CA 91604-4356, USA

Nelson, Craig T (Actor)
c/o Connie Tavel *Forward Entertainment*
9255 W Sunset Blvd Ste 805
Los Angeles, CA 90069-3305, USA

Nelson, Cynthia (Cindy) (Skier)
PO Box 1699
Vail, CO 81658-1699, USA

Nelson, Darrin (Athlete, Football Player)
215 Marianne Ct
Mountain View, CA 94040-3283, USA

Nelson, Dave (Athlete, Baseball Player)
12213 Clubhouse Dr
Lakewood Ranch, FL 34202-2098, USA

Nelson, David (Stylist)
c/o Staff Member *Clutts Agency, The*
1400 Turtle Creek Blvd # 171
Dallas, TX 75207-3337, USA

Nelson, David A (Judge)
425 Walnut St
Cincinnati, OH 45202-3904, USA

Nelson, Deborah (Journalist)
1120 John St
Seattle, WA 98109-5321, USA

Nelson, Dennis (Athlete, Football Player)
6098 E 2370 St
Kewanee, IL 61443-8529, USA

Nelson, Derrie (Athlete, Football Player)
7790 S Marian Rd
Hastings, NE 68901-7564, USA

Nelson, Dick (Athlete, Baseball Player)
102 N Maple St
Enfield, CT 06082-3958, USA

Nelson, Donald A (Nellie) (Basketball Player, Coach)
2909 Taylor St
Dallas, TX 75226-1909, USA

Nelson, Dorothy W (Judge)
125 S Grand Ave
Pasadena, CA 91105-1643, USA

Nelson, Drew (Actor)
c/o Staff Member *Select Artists Ltd (CA-Westside Office)*
1138 12th St Apt 1
Santa Monica, CA 90403-5459, USA

Nelson, Ed (Athlete, Football Player)
4568 Peeples Rd
Oak Ridge, NC 27310-9763, USA

Nelson, Gene (Athlete, Baseball Player)
PO Box 946
Dade City, FL 33526-0946, USA

Nelson, George D (Astronaut)
1200 New York Ave NW Ste 100
Washington, DC 20005-3929, USA

Nelson, Gunnar
13030 Valleyheart Dr Apt 105
Studio City, CA 91604-1960

Nelson, Jameer (Athlete, Basketball Player)
c/o Staff Member *Cornerstone Management*
944 County Line Rd
Bryn Mawr, PA 19010-2502, USA

Nelson, James E (Religious Leader)
536 Sheridan Rd
Wilmette, IL 60091-2891, USA

Nelson, Jamie (Athlete, Baseball Player)
PO Box 5646
Princeton, WV 24740-5646, USA

Nelson, Janet (Stylist)
311 N Robertson Blvd # 777
Beverly Hills, CA 90211-1705, USA

Nelson, Jeff (Athlete, Baseball Player)
5846 Pine Brook Farm Rd
Sykesville, MD 21784-8679, USA

Nelson, Jeff (Athlete, Baseball Player)
11462 Claymont Cir
Windermere, FL 34786-5317, USA

Nelson, Jerry E (Astronomer, Physicist)
Astronomy
Berkeley, CA 94720-0001, USA

Nelson, Jimmy
10404 Greenhaven Pkwy
Brecksville, OH 44141-1625

Nelson, Joe (Athlete, Baseball Player)
1816 San Antonio Ave
Alameda, CA 94501-4125, USA

Nelson, John Allen (Actor)
c/o Cynthia Booth *Global Artists Agency*
6253 Hollywood Blvd Apt 508
Los Angeles, CA 90028-8251, USA

Nelson, John R (Misc)
1111 Hermann Dr Unit 19A
Houston, TX 77004-6930, USA

Nelson, John W
Monckebergallee 41
Hanover 30453, GERMANY

Nelson, Judd (Actor)
c/o Jean-Pierre (JP) Henraux *Shelter Entertainment*
9454 Wilshire Blvd Ste 715
Beverly Hills, CA 90212-2925, USA

Nelson, Judith (Opera Singer)
2600 Buena Vista Way
Berkeley, CA 94708-1930, USA

Nelson, Karl (Athlete, Football Player)
10 Grand St
Westwood, NJ 07675-1644, USA

Nelson, Kent C (Business Person)
55 Glenlake Pkwy NE
Atlanta, GA 30328-3474, USA

Nelson, Kirsten (Actor)
c/o Staff Member *Meghan Schumacher Management*
13351D Riverside Dr # 387
Sherman Oaks, CA 91423-2508, USA

Nelson, Kristin (Stylist)
15150 Blanco Rd Apt 3206
San Antonio, TX 78232-3314, USA

Nelson, Larry (Athlete, Golfer)
421 Oakmont Cir SE
Marietta, GA 30067-4819, USA

Nelson, Lee (Athlete, Football Player)
23 Lindley Ave NW
Marietta, GA 30064-2185, USA

Nelson, Marilyn Carison (Business Person)
PO Box 59159
Minneapolis, MN 55459-8200, USA

Nelson, Mary (Baseball Player)
4222 Katrina Ln
San Antonio, TX 78222-2712, USA

Nelson, Matthew
12344 Moorpark St Unit 4
Studio City, CA 91604-1277

Nelson, Mel (Athlete, Baseball Player)
27420 Fisher St
Highland, CA 92346-3251, USA

Nelson, Prince Rogers (Prince) (Actor, Director, Musician)
c/o Staff Member *Marshall Arts Ltd*
P.O. Box 66142
London NW1W 8PA, UK

Nelson, Ralph A (Misc)
611 W Park St
Urbana, IL 61801-2500, USA

Nelson, Richard (Baseball Player)
104 Montgomery Ln
Perryville, AR 72126-8114, USA

Nelson, Ricky (Baseball Player)
2599 E Desert Broom Pl
Chandler, AZ 85286-2464, USA

Nelson, Rob (Athlete, Baseball Player)
312 Alta Vista Ave
South Pasadena, CA 91030-3502, USA

Nelson, Robert L (Athlete, Football Player)
14711 Copperfield Pl
Wayzata, MN 55391-2503, USA

Nelson, Roger (Athlete, Baseball Player)
4113 Limerick Dr
Lake Wales, FL 33859-5748, USA

Nelson, Ron (Athlete, Basketball Player)
1550 Eagle Ridge Ln NE
Albuquerque, NM 87122-1187, USA

Nelson, Scott (Baseball Player)
800 Sara Dr
Coshocton, OH 43812-8813, USA

Nelson, Scott (Athlete, Baseball Player)
800 Sara Dr
Coshocton, OH 43812-8813, USA

Nelson, Shane (Athlete, Football Player)
559 Carmel Dr
Sandia, TX 78383-5678, USA

Nelson, Terry (Athlete, Football Player)
3393 Highway 51 N
Arkadelphia, AR 71923-8584, USA

Nelson, Tex (Athlete, Baseball Player)
10830 Wallbrook Dr
Dallas, TX 75238-2943, USA

Nelson, Thomas G (Judge)
550 W Fort St
Boise, ID 83724-0201, USA

Nelson, Tim Blake (Actor, Director)
c/o Amy Guenther *Gateway Management Company Inc*
860 Via De La Paz Ste F10
Pacific Palisades, CA 90272-3631, USA

Nelson, Tracy (Actor)
c/o James Kellem *JKA Talent*
12725 Ventura Blvd Ste H
Studio City, CA 91604-2437, USA

Nelson, William (Bill) (Astronaut, Senator)
200 E Gaines St
Tallahassee, FL 32399-6502, USA

Nelson, Willie (Musician, Songwriter)
12400 W Highway 71 Ste 350
Bee Cave, TX 78738-6500, USA

Nelson Jr, J Bryon (Golfer)
PO Box 5
Roanoke, TX 76262-0005, USA

Nelson-Walker, Doris (Baseball Player)
7887 N 16th St Unit 129
Phoenix, AZ 85020-4453, USA

Nemchinov, Sergei (Athlete, Hockey Player)
53 Walker Ave
Rye, NY 10580-1219, USA

Nemcova, Petra (Model)
c/o Michael Samonte *Sunshine, Sachs & Associates - LA*
8409 Santa Monica Blvd
West Hollywood, CA 90069-4209, USA

Nemec, Corin (Actor)
859 N Hollywood Way # 104
Burbank, CA 91505-2814, USA

Nemecek, Bohumil (Boxer)
V Zahradkach 30
Usti Nad Labem 400 00, CZECH REPUBLIC

Nemechek, Joe (Race Car Driver)
1035 Mecklenburg Hwy
Mooresville, NC 28115-7853, USA

Nemelka, Richard (Athlete, Basketball Player)
6108 S 1300 E
Salt Lake City, UT 84121, USA

Nemeth, Miklos (Prime Minister)
1 Exchange Square
London EC2A 2EH, UNITED KINGDOM (UK)

Nemov, AlekseiRGF
Lujnetskaya Nabereunaya 8
Moscow, RUSSIA 119.27

Nemov, Alexei (Gymnast)
Lujnetskaya Nabereynaya 8
Moscow 119270, RUSSIA

Nen, Dick (Athlete, Baseball Player)
48 Via Barcaza
Trabuco Canyon, CA 92679-4831, USA

Nen, Robb (Athlete, Baseball Player)
8 S View
Trabuco Canyon, CA 92679-5376, USA

Nenez, Clemente (Baseball Player)
6433 Blackberry Pl
Riverside, CA 92505-2205, USA

Nennerman, Richard A (Editor)
PO Box 992
East Brunswick, NJ 08816-0992, USA

Nenninger, Eric (Actor)
c/o Lena Roklin *Luber Roklin Management*
8530 Wilshire Blvd Ste 550
Beverly Hills, CA 90211-3133, USA

Nepoleon (Actor)
1 2/5 Sandilya Apartments Jagathambal Colony II Street Royapettah
Chennai, TN 600 014, INDIA

Nepote, Jean (Lawyer)
26 Rue Armengaud 92210 Saint-Cloud
Hauts-de-Seine, FRANCE

N*E*R*D (Music Group)
c/o Staff Member *Paradigm (Monterey)*
404 W Franklin St
Monterey, CA 93940-2303, USA

NERD (Music Group)
c/o Amanda Silverman *42West (NY)*
220 W 42nd St Fl 12
New York, NY 10036-7200, USA

Nerette, Joseph (Judge, President)
Chief Justice's Office
Port-au-Prince, HAITI

Neri, Francesca (Actor)
c/o Philip Button *WmE2 (Endeavor-LA)*
9601 Wilshire Blvd Fl 3
Beverly Hills, CA 90210-5219, USA

Nerl, Manuel (Artist)
212 3rd Ave S
Seattle, WA 98104-2608, USA

Nerl Vela, Rodolfo (Astronaut)
Playa Copacabana 131 Col Marte
Mexico City, DF 8830, MEXICO

Nerlove, Marc L (Economist)
Agricultural/Resource Economics
College Park, MD 20742-0001, USA

Nerman, Maxens (Actor)
62, Rue des Grands Champs
75020, PARIS

Nero, Franco (Actor)
c/o Camilla Fluxman-Pines *Muse Management*
1541 Ocean Ave Ste 200
Santa Monica, CA 90401-2104, USA

Nero, Haley (Actor)
c/o Staff Member *Charlie's Talent Agency*
1350 Old Skokie Rd Ste 202
Highland Park, IL 60035-3058, USA

Nero, Peter (Musician)
202 Hidden Acres Ln
Media, PA 19063-1666, USA

Nerud, John (Misc)
19 Pound Hollow Rd
Glen Head, NY 11545-2209, USA

Nery, Carl (Athlete, Football Player)
239 Ryan Dr
Pittsburgh, PA 15220-1915, USA

Nesbit, Jamar (Athlete, Football Player)
4083 Richmond Park Dr E
Jacksonville, FL 32224-2223, USA

Nesbitt, James (Actor)
c/o Staff Member *Yakety Yak*
8-A Bloomsbury Sq
London WC1A 2NE, UNITED KINGDOM (UK)

Nesbitt-Wisham, Mary (Baseball Player)
PO Box 194
Hollister, FL 32147-0194, USA

Neserovic, Radoslav (Basketball Player)
Alamodome 1 SBC Center
San Antonio, TX 78219, USA

Neshek, Pat (Athlete, Baseball Player)
PO Box 43127
Minneapolis, MN 55443-0127, USA

Nesher, Avi (Director)
232 N Canon Dr
Beverly Hills, CA 90210-5302, USA

Nesic, Alex (Actor)
c/o Staff Member *Principato/Young Management*
9465 Wilshire Blvd Ste 430
Beverly Hills, CA 90212-2613, USA

Nesmith, Michael (Mike) (Musician)
8 Harris Ct Ste C1
Monterey, CA 93940-5715, USA

Nespral, Charo (Stylist)
c/o Staff Member *Illusions Management*
129 W 27th St Fl 12
New York, NY 10001-6206, USA

Nespral, Jackie (Correspondent)
30 Rockefeller Plz
New York, NY 10112-0015, USA

Ness, Norman F (Physicist)
980 Cooper St Unit 403
Venice, FL 34285-3535, USA

Ness, Rick (Musician)
2 Penn Plz # 2600
New York, NY 10121-0101, USA

Nessen, Ronald H (Ron) (Correspondent, Government Official)
6409 Walhonding Rd
Bethesda, MD 20816-2264, USA

Nesterenko, Eric (Athlete, Hockey Player)
2395 Bald Mountain Rd
Vail, CO 81657-5842, USA

Nesterenko, Evgeny Y (Opera Singer)
Fruzenskaya Nab 24 Korp 1 #178
Moscow 119146, RUSSIA

Nestorowicz, Victoria (Actor)
c/o Staff Member *Noble Caplan Abrams*
1260 Yonge St 2nd Floor
Toronto, ON M4T 1W6, Canada

Netherland, Joseph H (Business Person)
200 E Randolph St
Chicago, IL 60601-6436, USA

Netherton, Tom (Musician)
1801 Exeter Rd
Germantown, TN 38138-2934, USA

Netolicky, Bob (Athlete, Basketball Player)
12123 Windpointe Pass
Carmel, IN 46033-9520, USA

Netravali, Arun N (Engineer)
10 Byron Ct
Westfield, NJ 07090-2250, USA

Nett, Robert B (War Hero)
23326 Cibolo Vis
San Antonio, TX 78261-2639, USA

Nettles, Doug (Athlete, Football Player)
13105 Quail Creek Ct
Silver Spring, MD 20904-3588, USA

Nettles, Graig (Athlete, Baseball Player)
4255 Parris Dr
Lenoir City, TN 37772-3947, USA

Nettles, Jennifer (Musician)
c/o Gail Gellman *Gail Gellman Management*
23852 Pacific Coast Hwy
Malibu, CA 90265-4876, USA

Nettles, Jim (Athlete, Baseball Player)
4632 N Darien Dr
Tacoma, WA 98407-1212, USA

Nettles, Jim (Athlete, Football Player)
3817 Mandeville Canyon Rd
Los Angeles, CA 90049-1027, USA

Nettles, John (Actor)
265 Liverpool Road
London N1 1LX, UNITED KINGDOM (UK)

Nettles, Morris (Athlete, Baseball Player)
551 1/2 San Juan Ave
Venice, CA 90291-5643, USA

Neu, Mike (Athlete, Baseball Player)
406 Fraga Ct
Martinez, CA 94553-6812, USA

Neubert, Keith
10000 Santa Monica Blvd # 305
Los Angeles, CA 90067

Neufeld, Elizabeth F (Misc)
Medical School Biology Dept
Los Angeles, CA 90024, USA

Neufeld, Ray (Athlete, Hockey Player)
3919 Henderson Hwy
Winnipeg, MB R2G 1P4, Canada

Neufeld, Ryan (Athlete, Football Player)
625 Spring Hill Dr
Morgan Hill, CA 95037-4814, USA

Neugebauer, Marcia (Physicist)
7519 S Eliot Ln
Tucson, AZ 85747-9627, USA

Neugebauer, Nick (Athlete, Baseball Player)
101 S Sahuaro Dr
Gilbert, AZ 85233-5927, USA

Neugebauer, Randy (Congressman, Politician)
1424 Kibgwirth Hob
Washington, DC 20515-0001, USA

Neuharth, Allen H (Publisher)
1101 Wilson Blvd
Arlington, VA 22209-2211, USA

Neuhaus, Max (Artist, Composer)
350 5th Ave Ste 3304
New York, NY 10118-3304, USA

Neuhaus, Richard J (Religious Leader)
152 Madison Ave
New York, NY 10016-5424, USA

Neuhauser, Duncan V B (Misc)
2655 N Park Blvd
Cleveland Heights, OH 44106-3622, USA

Neuheisel, Richard (Rick) (Athlete, Coach, Football Coach, Football Player)
3601 Winding Creek Rd
Sacramento, CA 95864-1530, USA

Neumann, Liselotte (Athlete, Golfer)
11003 Muirfield Dr
Rancho Mirage, CA 92270-1431, USA

Neumann, Wolfgang (Opera Singer)
Maximilianstr 22
Munich 80539, GERMANY

Neumark, Julie
900 E 1st St Apt 314
Los Angeles, CA 90012-4039

Neumeier, Dan (Athlete, Baseball Player)
N2635 County Road V
Lodi, WI 53555-1568, USA

Neumeier, John (Choreographer)
54 Caspar-Voght-Str
Washington, DC 20535-0001, GERMANY

Neuner, Doris (Athlete)
6024 Innsbruck
AUSTRIA

Neuwelt, Edward A (Misc)
Neurology Dept
Portland, OR 97201, USA

Neuwirth, Bebe (Actor)
c/o Risa Shapiro *Schiff Company, The*
8440 Warner Dr Ste B1
Culver City, CA 90232-2461, USA

Nevett, Elijah (Athlete, Football Player)
931 30th St N
Bessemer, AL 35020-3565, USA

Nevil, Bobbie
20 Manchester Sq
London W1M 5AE, ENGLAND

Neville, Aaron (Musician)
c/o Jay Wilson *Elevation Group Inc.*
360 17th St Ste 200
Oakland, CA 94612-3340, USA

Neville, Arthel (Correspondent, Television Host)
1840 Victory Blvd
Glendale, CA 91201-2558, USA

Neville, Bill (Cartoonist)
506 Oakdale Rd
Jamestown, NC 27282-9214, USA

Neville, John (Actor, Director)
139 Winnett Ave
Toronto, ON M6C 3L7, CANADA

Neville, Katherine (Writer)
PO Box 788
Warrenton, VA 20188-0788, USA

Neville, Robert C (Misc)
Theology School
Boston, MA 2215, USA

Neville, Thomas O (Athlete, Football Player)
PO Box 11175
Montgomery, AL 36111-0175, USA

Nevin, Brooke (Actor)
c/o Suzanne (Sue) Wohl *TalentWorks (LA)*
3500 W Olive Ave Ste 1400
Burbank, CA 91505-5512, USA

Nevin, Kaleigh (Actor)
c/o Mary Swinton LL7 45 Charles St E
Toronto, ON M4Y 1S2, CANADA

Nevin, Phil (Athlete, Baseball Player)
18795 Heritage Dr
Poway, CA 92064-6643, USA

Nevins, Claudette (Actor)
3500 W Olive Ave Ste 1400
Burbank, CA 91505-5512, USA

Nevins, Sheila (Business Person, Producer)
c/o Staff Member *Home Box Office (HBO-LA)*
2500 Broadway Ste 400
Santa Monica, CA 90404-3176, USA

Nevinson, Nancy
23 Mill Close Fishbourne
Chichester, ENGLAND

Nevitt, Chuck (Athlete, Basketball Player)
3124 Cartwright Dr
Raleigh, NC 27612-2113, USA

New Boyz (Music Group, Musician)
c/o Staff Member *Genuine Music Group*
11271 Ventura Blvd Ste 225
Studio City, CA 91604-3136, USA

New Edition (Music Group)
c/o Staff Member *International Creative Management (ICM-LA)*
10250 Constellation Blvd Fl 7
Los Angeles, CA 90067-6207, USA

New Grass Revival
PO Box 128037
Nashville, TN 37212-8037

New Kids on the Block (NKOTB) (Music Group)
c/o Staff Member *Interscope Records (LA) - Main*
2220 Colorado Ave
Santa Monica, CA 90404-3506, USA

New Order (Music Group, Musician)
c/o Staff Member *Warner Bros Records (NY)*
75 Rockefeller Plz
New York, NY 10019-6908, USA

New Radicals
c/o Staff Member *MCA Records (LA)*
2220 Colorado Ave
Santa Monica, CA 90404-3506, 310-865-4500

New Rascals, The
PO Box 1821
Ojai, CA 93024-1821

New Riders of the Purple Sage
PO Box 3773
San Rafael, CA 94912-3773

New Song (Music Group)
c/o Staff Member *VanLiere-Wilcox*
251 2nd Ave S
Franklin, TN 37064-2659, USA

New York Yankees
& 161st Riv
Bronx, NY 10451, USA

Newark, Samantha (Musician)
c/o Arlene Thornton *Arlene Thornton & Associates*
12711 Ventura Blvd Ste 490
Studio City, CA 91604-2477, USA

Newbern, George (Actor)
c/o Paul Kohner *Kohner Agency, The*
9300 Wilshire Blvd Ste 555
Beverly Hills, CA 90212-3211, USA

Newberry, Jeremy (Athlete, Football Player)
1225 Almondwood Dr
Antioch, CA 94509-5170, USA

Newberry, Thomas (Tom) (Athlete, Football Player)
224 Tarpon St
Tavernier, FL 33070-2534, USA

Newbigging, William (Publisher)
10006 101st St
Edmonton, AB T5J 2S6, CANADA

Newbill, Ivano (Athlete, Basketball Player)
3877 6th Ave
Los Angeles, CA 90008-1918, USA

Newborn, Ira (Composer)
15233 Ventura Blvd Ste 200
Sherman Oaks, CA 91403-2244, USA

Newbrough, Ashley (Actor)
c/o William Mercer *Thruline Entertainment*
9250 Wilshire Blvd Ground Fl
Beverly Hills, CA 90212, USA

Newburn, George
PO Box 5617
Beverly Hills, CA 90209-5617

Newcomb, Gerry (Artist)
7029 17th Ave NW
Seattle, WA 98117-5551, USA

Newcomb, Jonathan (Publisher)
35 Pierrepont St
Brooklyn, NY 11201-3359, USA

Newcomb, Mike (Radio Personality)
4927 E Palo Brea Ln
Cave Creek, AZ 85331-5995, USA

Newcombe, Don (Athlete, Baseball Player)
4510 Murietta Ave Unit 201
Sherman Oaks, CA 91423-5447, USA

Newcombe, John (Athlete, Tennis Player)
325 Mission Valley Rd
New Braunfels, TX 78132-3629, USA

Newcomer, Carrie (Musician)
PO Box 5653
Bloomington, IN 47407-5653, USA

Newell, Horner E (Physicist)
2567 Nicky Ln
Alexandria, VA 22311-1311, USA

Newell, James
15023 Cranbrook Ave
Hawthorne, CA 90250-8476

Newell, Mike (Actor, Director, Producer)
c/o Staff Member *50 Cannon Entertainment*
Oxford House 76 Oxford St
London W1D 1BS, UNITED KINGDOM (UK)

Newell, Peter F (Pete) (Athlete, Basketball Player, Coach)
16078 Via Viajera
Rancho Santa Fe, CA 92091-4328, USA

Newell, Tom (Athlete, Baseball Player)
9525 Cordoba Blvd
Sparks, NV 89441-5569, USA

Newfield, Heidi (Musician)
c/o Staff Member *Red Light Management (LA)*
8439 W Sunset Blvd Ste 2
Los Angeles, CA 90069-1925, USA

Newfield, Marc (Athlete, Baseball Player)
5591 Selkirk Dr
Huntington Beach, CA 92649-4830, USA

Newgard, Christopher (Misc)
Biochemistry Dept
Dallas, TX 75237, USA

Newhan, David (Athlete, Baseball Player)
2678 Harvest Crest Ln
Corona, CA 92881-3572, USA

Newhart, Bob (Actor, Comedian)
c/o Staff Member *Monarch Entertainment Group*
16000 Ventura Blvd Ste 800
Encino, CA 91436-2759, USA

Newhauser, Don (Athlete, Baseball Player)
321 Sheryl Dr
Deltona, FL 32738-8441, USA

Newhouse, Bob
6847 Truxton Dr
Dallas, TX 75231-5717

Newhouse, Donald E (Publisher)
950 W Fingerboard Rd
Staten Island, NY 10305-1453, USA

Newhouse, Fred
816 Bantry Way
Benicia, CA 94510-3804

Newhouse, Fredrick (Fred) (Athlete, Track Athlete)
3003 Pine Lake Trl
Houston, TX 77068-1435, USA

Newhouse, Robert F (Athlete, Football Player)
6847 Truxton Dr
Dallas, TX 75231-5717, USA

Newhouse Jr, Samuel I (Publisher)
950 W Fingerboard Rd
Staten Island, NY 10305-1453, USA

Newkirk, Scott (Stylist)
c/o Staff Member *Art Department*
48 Greene St Fl 4
New York, NY 10013-2663, USA

Newkirk (Anastacia), Anastacia (Musician)
c/o Lisa Braude *Braude Management Inc*
PO Box 7249
San Diego, CA 92167-0249, USA

Newland, Bob (Athlete, Football Player)
3895 Vine Maple St
Eugene, OR 97405-4494, USA

Newlin, Mike (Athlete, Basketball Player)
1414 Horseshoe Dr
Sugar Land, TX 77478-3464, USA

Newman, Al (Athlete, Baseball Player)
3676 Wyndcrest Dr
Elko, MN 55020-9736, USA

Newman, Alan (Al) (Athlete, Baseball Player)
24 Rice Ln
Dry Prong, LA 71423-8742, USA

Newman, Alec (Actor)
c/o Laina Cohn *Laina Cohn Management*
15066 Sutton St
Sherman Oaks, CA 91403-4020, USA

Newman, Anthony (Conductor, Musician)
40 W 57th St
New York, NY 10019-4001, USA

Newman, Barry (Actor)

Newman, Edward K (Ed) (Athlete, Football Player)
10100 SW 140th St
Miami, FL 33176-6685, USA

Newman, James H (Astronaut)
18583 Martinique Dr
Houston, TX 77058-4213, USA

Newman, Jeff (Athlete, Baseball Player, Coach)
10133 N 103rd St
Scottsdale, AZ 85258-4953, USA

Newman, Jimmy C (Musician, Songwriter, Writer)
RR2
Christiana, TN 37037, USA

Newman, Johnny (Basketball Player)
2909 Taylor St
Dallas, TX 75226-1909, USA

Newman, Jon O (Judge)
450 Main St
Hartford, CT 06103-3025, USA

Newman, Kevin (Correspondent)
77 W 66th St
New York, NY 10023-6201, USA

Newman, Kyle (Director)
c/o Staff Member *United Talent Agency (UTA)*
9560 Wilshire Blvd Fl 5
Beverly Hills, CA 90212-2400, USA

Newman, Laraine (Actor, Comedian)
c/o Staff Member *TalentWorks (LA)*
3500 W Olive Ave Ste 1400
Burbank, CA 91505-5512, USA

Newman, Loraine (Comedian)
c/o Staff Member *TalentWorks (LA)*
3500 W Olive Ave Ste 1400
Burbank, CA 91505-5512, USA

Newman, Nanette (Actor)
Seven Pines Wentworth
Surrey GU25 4QP, UNITED KINGDOM (UK)

Newman, Nell (Business Person)
246 Post Rd E
Westport, CT 06880-3615, USA

Newman, Oscar (Architect)
66 Clover Dr
Great Neck, NY 11021-1030, USA

Newman, Pauline (Judge)
717 Madison Pl NW
Washington, DC 20439-0001, USA

Newman, Phyllis (Actor, Musician)
c/o Judy Katz *Judy Katz PR*
250 W 57th St
New York, NY 10107-0001, USA

Newman, Randy (Musician, Songwriter)
c/o Staff Member *Paradigm (Monterey)*
404 W Franklin St
Monterey, CA 93940-2303, USA

Newman, Ray (Athlete, Baseball Player)
1260 Malibu Ln
Myrtle Beach, SC 29577-6342, USA

Newman, Rebecca (Stylist)
5 N Ridge Rd
Westport, CT 06880-2235, USA

Newman, Ryan (Actor)
c/o Gladys Gonzalez *John Carrabino Management*
5900 Wilshire Blvd Ste 406
Los Angeles, CA 90036-5015, USA

Newman, Ryan (Race Car Driver)
PO Box 500
Mooresville, NC 28115-0500, USA

Newman, Terence (Athlete, Football Player)
1 Cowboys Pkwy
Irving, TX 75063-4924, USA

Newman, Thomas (Composer)
c/o Staff Member *Chasen & Company*
8899 Beverly Blvd Ste 405
Los Angeles, CA 90048-2431, USA

Newman, Thomas (Actor)
c/o Staff Member *Chasen & Company*
8899 Beverly Blvd Ste 405
Los Angeles, CA 90048-2431, USA

Newmar, Julie (Actor)
204 S Carmelina Ave
Los Angeles, CA 90049-3952, USA

Newmark, Craig
354 Shotwell St
San Francisco, CA 94110-1325, USA

Newmark, Dave (Athlete, Basketball Player)
545 Pierce St Apt 2301
Albany, CA 94706-1065, USA

Newsboys (Music Group, Musician)
PO Box 5010
Brentwood, TN 37024-5010, USA

Newsom, David (Actor)
1505 10th St
Santa Monica, CA 90401-2805, USA

Newsom, David D (Diplomat)
500 Crestwood Dr Unit 2504
Charlottesville, VA 22903-4883, USA

Newsom, Gavin (Politician)
400 S Van Ness Ave
San Francisco, CA 94103-3630, USA

Newsome, Billy (Athlete, Football Player)
PO Box 2001
Shreveport, LA 71166-2001, USA

Newsome, Harry (Athlete, Football Player)
531 Manor Rd
Cheraw, SC 29520, USA

Newsome, Ozzie (Athlete, Football Player)
6 Padonia Woods Ct
Cockeysville, MD 21030-1744, USA

Newsome, Timothy A (Athlete, Football Player)
7005 Quartermile Ln
Dallas, TX 75248-1447, USA

Newsome, Vince (Athlete, Football Player)
5308 Woodnote Ln
Columbia, MD 21044-5707, USA

Newson, Warren (Athlete, Baseball Player)
13232 Padre Ave
Keller, TX 76244-4326, USA

Newsted, Jason (Musician)
205 Alamo View Pl
Walnut Creek, CA 94595-2600, USA

Newton, Becki (Actor)
c/o Nicole King *Management 360*
9111 Wilshire Blvd
Beverly Hills, CA 90210-5508, USA

Newton, Ben (Actor)
c/o Staff Member *Sasha Leslie Management*
34 Pember Rd
London NW10 5LS, UNITED KINGDOM

Newton, Bill (Athlete, Basketball Player)
105 Brixworth Ln Apt 6
Nashville, TN 37205-2089, USA

Newton, C M (Athlete, Basketball Player, Coach)
9160 Enterprise Ave NE
Tuscaloosa, AL 35406-1042, USA

Newton, Cam (Athlete, Football Player)
c/o Bus Cook *Bus Cook Sports, Inc*
1 Willow Bend Dr
Hattiesburg, MS 39402-8552, USA

Newton, Christopher (Director)
22 Prideaux St
Niagara-on-the-Lake, ON L0S 1J0, CANADA

Newton, John Haymes (Actor)
c/o Staff Member *Pakula/King & Associates*
9229 W Sunset Blvd Ste 315
Los Angeles, CA 90069-3403, USA

Newton, Jon (Business Person)
2929 Allen Pkwy
Houston, TX 77019-7100, USA

Newton, Juice (Musician, Songwriter, Writer)
4321 Reyes Dr
Tarzana, CA 91356-5127, USA

Newton, Nate (Athlete, Football Player)
1921 White Oak Clearing
Southlake, TX 76092-6929, USA

Newton, Robert L (Athlete, Football Player)
11500 NE 76th St Apt A-353
Vancouver, WA 98662-3901, USA

Newton, Roger (Scientist)
695 Kms Place 3621 South State St
Ann Arbor, MI 48108, USA

Newton, Thandie (Actor)
c/o Jillian Fowkes *ID Public Relations (ID-LA)*
7080 Hollywood Blvd Fl 8
Los Angeles, CA 90028-6906, USA

Newton, Tom (Athlete, Football Player)
169 Park Rd
Rochester, NY 14622-1217, USA

Newton, Wayne (Actor, Musician)
3422 Happy Ln
Las Vegas, NV 89120-2904, USA

Newton-John, Olivia (Actor, Musician, Producer)
PO Box 2710
Malibu, CA 90265-7710, USA

Nex, Kristin (Stylist)
3589 Military Ave
Los Angeles, CA 90034-6103, USA

Ney, Edward N (Business Person, Diplomat)
230 Park Ave S
New York, NY 10003-1528, USA

Neyelova, Marina M (Actor)
Potapovsky Per 12
Moscow 117333, RUSSIA

Ne-Yo (Musician)
c/o Reynell Hay *Compound Entertainment*
PO Box 93303
Atlanta, GA 30377-0303, USA

Neyra, Gianella (Actor)
c/o Staff Member *Telefe - Argentina*
Pavon 2444 (C1248AAT)
Buenos Aires, ARGENTINA

Nezelek, Andy (Athlete, Baseball Player)
5707 Long Cove Rd
Midlothian, VA 23112-2450, USA

Nezhat, Camran (Misc)
5555 Peachtree Dunwoody Rd NE
Atlanta, GA 30342-1772, USA

Ngata, Haoti (Athlete, Football Player)
c/o Staff Member *Baltimore Ravens*
1 Winning Dr
Owings Mills, MD 21117-4776, USA

Nguema, Tedoro Obiang (President)
Malabo
EQUATORIAL GUINEA

Nguyen, Dat (Athlete, Football Player)
3610 Spears Rd
Houston, TX 77066-4117, USA

Nguyen, Dustin (Actor)
1051 S Dunsmuir Ave
Los Angeles, CA 90019-6755, USA

Nguyen, Long (Stylist)
Prefers to be contacted via telephone or email

Nguyen, Navia (Actor)
c/o Michael Greenwald *Don Buchwald & Associates Inc (LA)*
6500 Wilshire Blvd Ste 2200
Los Angeles, CA 90048-4942, USA

Nguyen, Scotty (Misc)
c/o Staff Member *Poker Royalty, LLC*
10789 W Twain Ave Ste 200
Las Vegas, NV 89135-3030, USA

Niarchos, Philip (Philanthropist)
645 Madison Ave Ste 2200
New York, NY 10022-1010, USA

Nicaud, Philippe
104 Rue Des Sablons
Mareil-Marly, FRANCE 78750

Niccol, Andrew (Director, Producer, Writer)
c/o Richard Green *Creative Artists Agency (CAA-LA)*
2000 Avenue of the Stars Ste 100
Los Angeles, CA 90067-4705, USA

Nichol, Joseph McGinty (McG) (Musician, Producer, Writer)
c/o Staff Member *Wonderland Sound and Vision*
8739 W Sunset Blvd
W Hollywood, CA 90069-2205, USA

Nicholas, Alison (Athlete, Golfer)
Badgar Farm House
Badgar near Wolverhampton WV6 7IS, United Kingdom

Nicholas, Denise (Actor)
932 S Longwood Ave
Los Angeles, CA 90019-1752, USA

Nicholas, Don (Athlete, Baseball Player)
12311 Chase St
Garden Grove, CA 92845-2109, USA

Nicholas, Eric (Writer)
c/o Staff Member *Gersh (LA)*
9465 Wilshire Blvd Ste 600
Beverly Hills, CA 90212-2612, USA

Nicholas, Henry (Misc)
330 W 42nd St # 1905
New York, NY 10036-6902, USA

Nicholas, J D (Musician)
1920 Benson Ave
Saint Paul, MN 55116-3214, USA

Nicholas, Peter M (Business Person)
1 Boston Scientific Pl
Natick, MA 01760-1536, USA

Nicholas, Stephen (Athlete, Football Player)
c/o Chad Speck *Allegiant Athletic Agency*
35 Market Sq Ste 201
Knoxville, TN 37902-1420, USA

Nicholas, Thomas Ian (Actor)
4343 Lankershim Blvd # 100
North Hollywood, CA 91602-2705, USA

Nicholas Jr, Nicholas J (Publisher)
1000 SW Broadway # 1850
Portland, OR 97205-3035, USA

Nicholas(Smisko), Bishop (Religious Leader)
312 Garfield St
Johnstown, PA 15906-2122, USA

Nicholls, Craig (Musician)
17 Holdsworth St
Newton, NSW 2042, AUSTRALIA

Nicholls, Paul (Actor)
c/o Staff Member *IFA Talent Agency*
8730 W Sunset Blvd Ste 490
Los Angeles, CA 90069-2248, USA

Nichols, Austin (Actor)
c/o Joan Green *Joan Green Management*
1836 Courtney Ter
Los Angeles, CA 90046-2106, USA

Nichols, Bobby (Athlete, Golfer)
8681 Glenlyon Ct
Fort Myers, FL 33912-2408, USA

Nichols, Carl (Athlete, Baseball Player)
901 E Artesia Blvd
Compton, CA 90221-5356, USA

Nichols, Dorothy L (Financier)
1501 Farm Credit Dr
McLean, VA 22102-5000, USA

Nichols, Dr. Michael (Writer)
c/o Staff Member *Guilford Press*
72 Spring St
New York, NY 10012-4019, USA

Nichols, Hamilton J (Athlete, Football Player)
11015 Kirkmead Dr
Houston, TX 77089-3116, USA

Nichols, Joe (Musician)
c/o Larry Murray *Triple 8 Management*
1611 W 6th St
Austin, TX 78703-5059, USA

Nichols, John (Writer)
c/o Staff Member *The New Press*
38 Greene St Fl 4
New York, NY 10013-2505, USA

Nichols, Kenwood C (Business Person)
1 Champion Plz
Stamford, CT 06921-0001, USA

Nichols, Kyra (Ballerina)
133 W 71st St
New York, NY 10023-3834, USA

Nichols, Larry (Designer)
139 Main St
Cambridge, MA 02142-1530, USA

Nichols, Lorrie (Bowler)
1251 Lexington Dr
Algonquin, IL 60102-2065, USA

Nichols, Marisol (Actor)
c/o Jill Littman *Impression Entertainment*
9229 W Sunset Blvd Ste 700
West Hollywood, CA 90069-3407, USA

Nichols, Mark (Athlete, Football Player)
5905 Penn Station Ln
Bakersfield, CA 93311-9016, USA

Nichols, Mike (Comedian, Director)
594 Broadway Rm 706
New York, NY 10012-3257, USA

Nichols, Nichelle (Actor)
c/o Jeffrey Leavitt *Leavitt Talent Group*
8255 W Sunset Blvd
West Hollywood, CA 90046-2417, USA

Nichols, Pamela (Stylist)
PO Box 585
North San Juan, CA 95960-0585, USA

Nichols, Peter R (Writer)
211 Piccadilly
London W1V 9LD, UNITED KINGDOM (UK)

Nichols, Rachel (Actor)
c/o Peter Kiernan *Management 360*
9111 Wilshire Blvd
Beverly Hills, CA 90210-5508, USA

Nichols, Reid (Athlete, Baseball Player)
1 Brewers Way Attn Cir
Milwaukee, WI 53214-3655, USA

Nichols, Rod (Athlete, Baseball Player)
1570 Elk Trail Dr
Helena, MT 59601-9633, USA

Nichols, Stephen (Actor)
11664 National Blvd # 116
Los Angeles, CA 90064-3802, USA

Nicholson, Bruce
PO Box 2573
Georgetown, SC 29442-2573

Nicholson, Dave (Athlete, Baseball Player)
15316 Lakepoint Dr
Benton, IL 62812-4676, USA

Nicholson, Jack (Actor)
c/o Sandy Bresler *Bresler Kelly & Associates*
11500 W Olympic Blvd Ste 510
Los Angeles, CA 90064-1527, USA

Nicholson, Jim (Government Official, Secretary)
412 Russell Senate Ofc Building
Washington, DC 20510-0001, USA

Nicholson, Jim (Athlete, Football Player)
91-845 Kauwili St
Ewa Beach, HI 96706-2854, USA

Nicholson, Julianne (Actor)
c/o Courtney Kivowitz *Schiff Company, The*
8440 Warner Dr Ste B1
Culver City, CA 90232-2461, USA

Nicholson, Kathrin
9057-A Nemo St
W. Hollywood, CA 90069

Nichting, Chris (Athlete, Baseball Player)
7151 Gracely Dr
Cincinnati, OH 45233-1019, USA

Nickel, Elbert (Athlete, Football Player)
453 McKell Rd
Chillicothe, OH 45601-1535, USA

Nickel Creek (Music Group)
c/o Staff Member *WmE2 (WMA-TN)*
1600 Division St Ste 300
Nashville, TN 37203-2755, USA

Nickelback (Music Group)
c/o John Greenberg *Union Entertainment Group*
1323 Newbury Rd Ste 104
Thousand Oaks, CA 91320-3679, USA

Nickerson, Camilla (Stylist)
c/o Staff Member *Art + Commerce*
531 W 25th St # 4
New York, NY 10001-5593, USA

Nickerson, Denise (Actor)
c/o Frann Harrison 6853 S. Ivy Way 7-301
Centennial, CO 80112, USA

Nickerson, Hardy O (Athlete, Football Player)
8716 Longview Club Dr
Waxhaw, NC 28173-6696, USA

Nickerson Jr, Donald A (Religious Leader)
815 2nd Ave
New York, NY 10017-4503, USA

Nickla, Ed (Athlete, Football Player)
21 Ida Ln
North Babylon, NY 11703-1403, USA

Nicklaus, Gary
112 Tpc Blvd
Ponte Vedra Beach, FL 32082

Nicklaus, Jack (Athlete, Golfer)
11780 US Highway 1 Ste 500
North Palm Beach, FL 33408-3042, USA

Nickle, Doug (Athlete, Baseball Player)
19440 Victoria Ct
Sonoma, CA 95476-3829, USA

Nicks, John A W (Misc)
13211 Brooks Dr # A
Baldwin Park, CA 91706, USA

Nicks, Orlando (Athlete, Basketball Player)
10200 Yosemite Ln
Indianapolis, IN 46234-9821, USA

Nicks, Regina (Musician)
909 Meadowlark Ln
Goodlettsville, TN 37072-2309, USA

Nicks, Stevie (Musician, Songwriter)
c/o Liz Rosenberg *Warner Bros Records (NY)*
75 Rockefeller Plz
New York, NY 10019-6908, USA

Nickson, Julia (Actor)
8306 Wilshire Blvd # 438
Beverly Hills, CA 90211-2382, USA

Nicol, Steve (Coach, Football Coach)
CMGI Field 1 Patriot Place
Foxboro, MA 2035, USA

Nicolaou, Kyriacos Costa (Misc)
10550 N Torrey Pines Rd
La Jolla, CA 92037-1000, USA

Nicole
Im Pfarrwittum 1
Nohfelden, GERMANY D-66625

Nicole, Britt (Musician)
c/o Amy Fogleman *Creative Trust, Inc.*
5141 Virginia Way Ste 320
Brentwood, TN 37027-2317, USA

Nicole, Elizabeth (Stylist)
c/o Staff Member *Zenobia Agency Inc*
PO Box 909
Groveland, CA 95321-0909, USA

Nicole, Kaylan (Adult Film Star)
9800D Topanga Canyon Blvd # 3252
Chatsworth, CA 91311-4005, USA

Nicolet, Aurele (Musician)
Postfach 1617
Hanover 30016, GERMANY

Nicolet, Danielle (Actor)
c/o Lena Roklin *Luber Roklin Management*
8530 Wilshire Blvd Ste 550
Beverly Hills, CA 90211-3133, USA

Nicoletti Susi
Goethegasse
Vienna, AUSTRIA 1 A-1010

Nicol-Fox, Helen (Baseball Player)
432 E Cornell Dr
Tempe, AZ 85283-1908, USA

Nicollier, Claude (Astronaut)
18710 Martinique Dr
Houston, TX 77058-4218, USA

Nicolucci, Guy (Writer)
c/o Staff Member *Gersh (LA)*
9465 Wilshire Blvd Ste 600
Beverly Hills, CA 90212-2612, USA

Nicora, Attilio Cardinal (Religious Leader)
Palazzo Apostolico
120, VATICAN CITY

Nicosia, Steve (Athlete, Baseball Player)
190 Northshore Xing
Dallas, GA 30157-1641, USA

Nieberg, Lars (Misc)
Gestit Waldershausen
Homberg 35315, GERMANY

Nied, David (Athlete, Baseball Player)
211 Masters Ln
Midlothian, TX 76065-7209, USA

Niedenfuer, Tom (Athlete, Baseball Player)
3933 Losillias Dr
Sarasota, FL 34238-4537, USA

Nieder, William H (Bill) (Athlete, Track Athlete)
PO Box 310
Mountain Ranch, CA 95246-0310, USA

Niederhoffer, Victor (Misc)
757 3rd Ave
New York, NY 10017-2013, USA

Niedermayer, Scott (Athlete, Hockey Player)
49 Belcourt Dr
Newport Beach, CA 92660-4214, USA

Niedernhuber, Barbara (Athlete)
Schwarzeckstr 58
Ramsau 83486, GERMANY

Niehaus, Dave (Sportscaster)
PO Box 4100
Seattle, WA 98194-0100, USA

Niehaus, David (Athlete, Baseball Player)
18406 NW Montreux Dr
Issaquah, WA 98027-7817, USA

Niehaus, Lennie (Composer)
6404 Wilshire Blvd Ste 1225
Los Angeles, CA 90048-5550, USA

Niehaus, Ralph (Athlete, Football Player)
7219 E Nathan St
Mesa, AZ 85207-0822, USA

Niehaus, Steve (Athlete, Football Player)
114 Siebenthaler Ave
Cincinnati, OH 45215-3716, USA

Niekro, Lance (Athlete, Baseball Player)
3822 Cheverly Dr E
Lakeland, FL 33813-1203, USA

Niekro, Phil (Athlete, Baseball Player)
6382 Nichols Rd
Flowery Branch, GA 30542-2619, USA

Niel, Steve (Actor)
c/o Laura Walsh *Central Artists*
3310 W Burbank Blvd # A
Burbank, CA 91505-2230, USA

Nielsen, Brigitte (Actor, Model)
c/o Staff Member *M&G Entertainment*
19360 Rinaldi St # 517
Porter Ranch, CA 91326-1607, USA

Nielsen, Connie (Actor)
c/o Estelle Lasher *Principal Entertainment (LA)*
1964 Westwood Blvd Ste 400
Los Angeles, CA 90025-4695, USA

Nielsen, Gifford (Athlete, Football Player)
10 Sarahs Cv
Sugar Land, TX 77479-2449, USA

Nielsen, Jerry (Athlete, Baseball Player)
4631 Kewanee St
Fair Oaks, CA 95628-6219, USA

Nielsen, Lonnie (Athlete, Golfer)
6 Marlwood Ln
Palm Beach Gardens, FL 33418-6805, USA

Nielsen, Rick (Musician)
509 Hartnell St
Monterey, CA 93940-2825, USA

Nielsen, Scott (Athlete, Baseball Player)
2898 Valley View Ave
Salt Lake City, UT 84117-5550, USA

Niemann, Randy (Athlete, Baseball Player)
1585 SW Harbour Isles Cir
Port Saint Lucie, FL 34986-3403, USA

Niemann, Richard (Athlete, Basketball Player)
7911 Stanford Ave
Saint Louis, MO 63130-3613, USA

Niemann-Stirnemann, Gunda (Speed Skater)
Postfach 503
Erfurt 99010, GERMANY

Niemeyer, Paul V (Judge)
101 W Lombard St
Baltimore, MD 21201-2605, USA

Niemi, Lisa (Actor)
c/o Staff Member *Atria Books*
1230 Avenue of the Americas
New York, NY 10020-1513, USA

Niemiec-Konwinski, Dolly (Baseball Player)
1821 Spring Meadow Ct SE
Caledonia, MI 49316-9154, USA

Nieminen, Toni (Skier)
vesijarvenkatu 74
Lahti 15140, FINLAND

Nierman, Leonardo (Artist)
Amsterdam 43 PH
Mexico City 11 DF, MEXICO

Nies, Eric (Actor, Model, Reality TV Star)
c/o Staff Member *Bunim/Murray Productions Inc*
6007 Sepulveda Blvd
Van Nuys, CA 91411-2502, USA

Nieto, Adriana (Actor)
c/o Staff Member *Televisa*
Blvd Adolfo Lopez Mateos 232 Colonia San Angel INN
DF CP 01060, MEXICO

Nieto, Tom (Athlete, Baseball Player)
22446 Eagles Watch Dr
Land O Lakes, FL 34639-6759, USA

Nieuwendyk, Joe (Athlete, Hockey Player)
11784 NW 69th Pl
Parkland, FL 33076-3322, USA

Nieves, Juan (Athlete, Baseball Player, Coach)
333 W 35th St Attn Coachingstaff
Chicago, IL 60616-3651, USA

Nieves, Melvin (Athlete, Baseball Player)
6131 7 Lks W
West End, NC 27376-9320, USA

Nigam, Anjul (Actor)
c/o Lisa DiSante-Frank *DiSante Frank & Company*
10061 Riverside Dr # 377
Toluca Lake, CA 91602-2560, USA

Nigam, Sonu (Musician)
c/o Linda Jones *The Mass Appeal*
3940 Laurel Canyon Blvd Unit 447
Studio City, CA 91604-3709, USA

Nigh, George P (Ex-Governor)
2946 NW 160th St
Edmond, OK 73013-1464, USA

Nighswander, Nicholas (Athlete, Football Player)
PO Box 46
Burgoon, OH 43407-0046, USA

Nightingale, Maxine
c/o Staff Member *Diva Central Inc*
7510 W Sunset Blvd Ste 1445
Los Angeles, CA 90046-3408, USA

Nighy, Bill (Actor)
c/o Chris Andrews *Creative Artists Agency (CAA-LA)*
2000 Avenue of the Stars Ste 100
Los Angeles, CA 90067-4705, USA

Nigro, Lynn (Stylist)
c/o Staff Member *Judy Casey Inc*
114 E 13th St
New York, NY 10003-5329, USA

Nihalani, Govind (Director, Filmmaker, Producer)
139 Aradhana Behind Bhavishya Nidhi
Bandra E
Bombay, MS 400 051, INDIA

Niinimaa, Janne (Athlete, Hockey Player)
2200-201 Portage Ave
Winnipeg, MB R3B 3L3, Canada

Nikkanen, Kurt (Musician)
165 W 57th St
New York, NY 10019-2201, USA

Nikko (Stylist)
c/o Staff Member *Cloutier Agency*
2632 La Cienega Ave
Los Angeles, CA 90034-2641, USA

Niklas, Jan
Konigsberger Str. 20
Munich, GERMANY D-81927

Niklason, Laura A (Engineer)
Durham, NC 27706, USA

Nikolishin, Andrei (Athlete, Hockey Player)
105 Bloomfield Ave
Hartford, CT 06105-1007, USA

Niland, John H (Athlete, Football Player)
16058 Chalfont Ct
Dallas, TX 75248-3547, USA

Niles, John (Composer, Musician)
PO Box 222
West Linn, OR 97068-0222, USA

Niles, Nicholas H (Publisher)
1212 N Lindbergh Blvd
Saint Louis, MO 63132, USA

Niles, Prescott (Musician)
PO Box 35
Pawling, NY 12564-0035, USA

Niles, Thomas M T (Diplomat)
101 C By Dr
Ottawa, ON K1A 0K2, CANADA

Nilsen, Reed (Athlete, Football Player)
1078 S 1400 W
Salt Lake City, UT 84104-3233, USA

Nilsmark, Catrin (Athlete, Golfer)
187 Commodore Dr
Jupiter, FL 33477-4007, USA

Nilsson, David (Dave) (Athlete, Baseball Player)
24615 S 182nd Pl
Gilbert, AZ 85298-5804, USA

Nilsson, Inger
Box 12710
Stockholm, SWEDEN 11294

Nilsson, Lennart (Photographer)
201 E 50th St
New York, NY 10022-7703, USA

Nimmo, Dirk (Actor)
125 Gloucester Road
London SW7 4TE, UNITED KINGDOM (UK)

Nimmons, Ernest (Baseball Player)
500 Pine Hollow Blvd
Lorain, OH 44055-3003, USA

Nimoy, Leonard (Actor, Director, Photographer)
c/o Tim Curtis *WmE2 (Endeavor-LA)*
9601 Wilshire Blvd Fl 3
Beverly Hills, CA 90210-5219, USA

Nimphius, Kurt (Athlete, Basketball Player)
750 Dry Creek Rd
Sedona, AZ 86336-3621, USA

Nimri, Najwa (Actor, Musician)
c/o Staff Member *Kuranda Management*
Santo Angel, 84
Madrid 28043, Spain

Nimziki, Joe (Director)
10100 Santa Monica Blvd Ste 2500
Los Angeles, CA 90067-4116, USA

Nine Black Alps (Music Group)
c/o Staff Member *Paradigm (Monterey)*
404 W Franklin St
Monterey, CA 93940-2303, USA

Nine Inch Nails (NIN) (Music Group)
c/o Jim Guerinot *Rebel Waltz Inc*
31652 2nd Ave
Laguna Beach, CA 92651-8244, USA

Ninedays (Music Group)
c/o Staff Member *Epic Records Group*
550 Madison Ave Fl 6
New York, NY 10022-3211, USA

Nininger, Harvey H (Misc)
PO Box 420
Sedona, AZ 86339-0420, USA

Nininger, Susan (Stylist)
c/o Tom Marquardt *International Creative Management (ICM-LA)*
10250 Constellation Blvd Fl 7
Los Angeles, CA 90067-6207, USA

Ninowski, Jim (Athlete, Football Player)
2715 Melcombe Cir Apt 302
Troy, MI 48084-3453, USA

Nipar, Yvette (Actor)
9300 Wilshire Blvd Ste 410
Beverly Hills, CA 90212-3228, USA

Nipp, Maury (Athlete, Football Player)
631 E Michelle St
West Covina, CA 91790-5146, USA

Nipper, Al (Athlete, Baseball Player)
401 White Birch Valley Ct
Chesterfield, MO 63017-2457, USA

Nippert, Dustin (Athlete, Baseball Player)
102 Martin Ln
Morgantown, WV 26501-4520, USA

Nippert, Merlin (Athlete, Baseball Player)
1015 N Michigan Ave
Mangum, OK 73554-1820, USA

Nirenberg, Louis (Mathematician)
221 W 82nd St
New York, NY 10024-5406, USA

Nirenberg, Marshall W (Nobel Prize Laureate)
10005 Gary Rd
Potomac, MD 20854-4110, USA

Nirmala, Sister (Religious Leader)
54A Lower Circular Rd
Kolkata, WB 700016, INDIA

Nirosha (Actor, Bollywood)
3 Paul Appasamy Street T Nagar
Chennai, TN 600017, INDIA

Nisbet, Robert A (Activist, Historian)
6131 Purple Aster Ln NE
Albuquerque, NM 87111-8082, USA

Nisby, John (Athlete, Football Player)
6339 Saint Andrews Dr
Stockton, CA 95219-1861, USA

Nischwitz, Ron (Athlete, Baseball Player)
17 S Saint Clair St Ste 330
Dayton, OH 45402-2178, USA

Nishizawa, Junichi (Engineer, Inventor)
Kawauchi Aobaku
Sendai 9800862, JAPAN

Nishizuka, Yasutomi (Physicist)
7-5-1 Kusunokichochuoki
Kobe 650-0017, JAPAN

Nishkian, Byron (Skier)
150 4th St PH
San Francisco, CA 94103-3048, USA

Niskanen Jr, William A (Economist, Government Official)
1000 Massachusetts Ave NW # 6
Washington, DC 20001-5401, USA

Nispel, Marcus (Director)
c/o Staff Member *WmE2 (Endeavor-LA)*
9601 Wilshire Blvd Fl 3
Beverly Hills, CA 90210-5219, USA

Nissalke, Tom (Athlete, Basketball Player, Coach)
3075 Kennedy Dr Apt 406
Salt Lake City, UT 84108-2200, USA

Nissen, Steve (Doctor)
817 Hanover Rd
Gates Mills, OH 44040-9602, USA

Nithya (Actor, Bollywood)
37 Palayakaran St
Chennai, TN 600024, INDIA

Nitkowski, C J (Athlete, Baseball Player)
205 Townsend Ln
Alpharetta, GA 30004-2553, USA

Nitsirk (Stylist)
c/o Staff Member *Igroup + Ridecreative*
315 W 39th St Rm 908
New York, NY 10018-3954, USA

Nittmann, David (Artist)
PO Box 19065
Boulder, CO 80308-2065, USA

Nittmo, Bjorn (Athlete, Football Player)
201 E Jefferson St
Phoenix, AZ 85004-2412, USA

Nitty Gritty Dirt Band (Music Group)
c/o Staff Member *Paradigm (Monterey)*
404 W Franklin St
Monterey, CA 93940-2303, USA

Nitzkowski, Monte (Coach)
7041 Seal Cir
Huntington Beach, CA 92648-3035, USA

Niven, Barbara
10926 Bluffside Dr Unit 26
Studio City, CA 91604-3347, USA

Niven, Kip (Actor)
9000 W Sunset Blvd Ste 801
Los Angeles, CA 90069-5808, USA

Niven, Laurence (Larry) (Writer)
11874 Macoda Ln
Chatsworth, CA 91311-1271, USA

Niven Jr, David
1457 Blue Jay Way
Los Angeles, CA 90069-1212, USA

Nivola, Alessandro (Actor)
c/o William Choi *Management 360*
9111 Wilshire Blvd
Beverly Hills, CA 90210-5508, USA

Niwa, Gail (Musician)
1416 Hinman Ave
Evanston, IL 60201-5324, USA

Niwano, Nikkyo (Religious Leader)
Rissho Kosel-Kai 2-11-1 Wada Suginamiku
Tokyo 166, JAPAN

Nix, Doyle (Athlete, Football Player)
710 E 4th St
Weatherford, TX 76086-1844, USA

Nix, Dyron (Athlete, Basketball Player)
1425 Juneau Way
Grayson, GA 30017-2915, USA

Nix, Emery (Athlete, Football Player)
RR 4 Box 385
Blanco, TX 78606, USA

Nix, Garth (Writer)
77 - 85 Fulham palace road
London W12 8ER, UNITED KINGDOM

Nix, John L (Athlete, Football Player)
2278 Lindsey Ct
Fallbrook, CA 92028-5304, USA

Nix, Kent (Athlete, Football Player)
2732 Colonial Pkwy
Fort Worth, TX 76109-1211, USA

Nix, Laynce (Athlete, Baseball Player)
6401 Chadbourn Hwy
Chadbourn, NC 28431-1613, USA

Nix, Matt (Writer)
c/o Staff Member *WmE2 (Endeavor-LA)*
9601 Wilshire Blvd Fl 3
Beverly Hills, CA 90210-5219, USA

Nixey, Troy (Director)
c/o Gary Ungar *Exile Entertainment*
732 El Medio Ave
Pacific Palisades, CA 90272-3451, USA

Nixon, Agnes (Producer, Writer)
774 Conestoga Rd
Bryn Mawr, PA 19010-1257, USA

Nixon, Cynthia (Actor)
c/o Emily Gerson Saines *Brookside Artists Management (NY)*
250 W 57th St Ste 2303
New York, NY 10107-2399, USA

Nixon, Derek Lee (Actor, Producer, Writer)
c/o Staff Member *Mark Robert Management*
2208 Patricia Ave
Los Angeles, CA 90064-2318, USA

Nixon, Donell (Baseball Player)
2681 Mount Olive Rd
Whiteville, NC 28472-6863, USA

Nixon, Gary (Motorcycle Race, Motorcycle Racer)
2408 Carroll Mill Rd
Phoenix, MD 21131-1104, USA

Nixon, Jay (Governor)
PO Box 720
Jefferson City, MO 65102-0720, USA

Nixon, Jeff (Athlete, Football Player)
549 Linwood Ave
Buffalo, NY 14209-1403, USA

Nixon, Kimberley (Actor)
c/o Larry Taube *Principal Entertainment (LA)*
1964 Westwood Blvd Ste 400
Los Angeles, CA 90025-4695, USA

Nixon, Marni (Actor, Musician)
9200 W Sunset Blvd Ste 900
Los Angeles, CA 90069-3604, USA

Nixon, Norm (Athlete, Basketball Player)
3623 Hayden Ave
Culver City, CA 90232-2458, USA

Nixon, Otis (Athlete, Baseball Player)
1304 Morningside Park Dr
Alpharetta, GA 30022-6664, USA

Nixon, Russ (Athlete, Baseball Player, Coach)
4265 N Tee Pee Ln
Las Vegas, NV 89129-2628, USA

Nixon, Sam (Musician)
c/o Staff Member *QVoice*
193-197 High Holborn 4th Floor, Holborn Hall
London WC1V 7BD, UNITED KINGDOM (UK)

Nixon, Torran (Athlete, Football Player)
PO Box 308
Colfax, CA 95713-0308, USA

Nixon, Trot (Athlete, Baseball Player)
1023 Ocean Ridge Dr
Wilmington, NC 28405-5287, USA

Niyazov, Saparmurad (President)
Karl Marx Str 24
Ashkabad 744017, TURKMENISTAN

Nizhalgal, Raviee (Actor)
4 Sriram Nagar North St
Chennai, TN 600 018, INDIA

Niziolek, Robert (Athlete, Football Player)
206 W Brome Ave
Lafayette, CO 80026-1738, USA

Niznik, Stephanie (Actor)
c/o Staff Member *Niad Management*
15030 Ventura Blvd Bldg 19STE PMB 860
Sherman Oaks, CA 91403-5470, USA

Noah, Joakim (Athlete, Basketball Player)
c/o Staff Member *Blackwave Media Group*
220 W 42nd St Fl 5
New York, NY 10036-7200, USA

Noah, John (Athlete, Hockey Player)
3315 W Prairiewood Dr S
Fargo, ND 58103-4666, USA

Noah, Max W (General)
820 Arcturus-On-Potomac
Alexandria, VA 22308, USA

Noah, Trevor (Comedian)
c/o Matthew Blake *Creative Artists Agency (CAA-LA)*
2000 Avenue of the Stars Ste 100
Los Angeles, CA 90067-4705, USA

Noah, Yannick (Athlete, Coach, Musician, Tennis Player)
230 Central Park S
New York, NY 10019-1409, USA

Noakes, Michael (Artist)
146 Hamilton Terrace Saint John's Wood
London NW8 9UX, UNITED KINGDOM (UK)

Nobel, Ben (Actor)
c/o Bella Grundy *King Talent (Toronto)*
36 Tiverton Ave
Toronto ON M4M, Canada

Nobile, Leo (Athlete, Football Player)
109 Cottonwood Ct
Coraopolis, PA 15108-2605, USA

Nobilo, Frank (Athlete, Golfer)
10209 Atterbury Ct
Orlando, FL 32827-7041, USA

Nobis, Thomas H (Tommy) Jr (Athlete, Football Executive, Football Player)
40 S Battery Placa NE
Atlanta, GA 30342, USA

Noble, Adrian K (Director)
Barbican Theater
London EC2Y 8BQ, UNITED KINGDOM (UK)

Noble, Brandon (Athlete, Football Player)
173 Magnolia Dr
Chester Springs, PA 19425-3631, USA

Noble, Brian D (Athlete, Football Player)
2400 Luberon Dr
Henderson, NV 89044-0360, USA

Noble, Chuck (Athlete, Basketball Player)
3585 W Beechwood Ave Ste 106
Fresno, CA 93711-0600, USA

Noble, James (Actor)
113 Ledgebrook Dr
Norwalk, CT 06854-1070, USA

Noble, John (Actor)
c/o Nicolas Bernheim *Seven Summits Pictures & Management*
8906 W Olympic Blvd Ground Floor
Beverly Hills, CA 90211, USA

Noble, Karen (Athlete, Golfer)
36 Edgewood Rd
Chatham, NJ 07928-2002, USA

Noble, Reginald (Redman) (Musician)
c/o Greg Weiss *Vanguard Management Group (NY)*
220 5th Ave PH West
New York, NY 10001-7745, USA

Noble, Ross (Actor, Comedian)
c/o Staff Member *Real Talent Management (UK)*
24 Goodge St
London W1T 2QF, UNITED KINGDOM

Noble, Samantha (Actor)
c/o David Rudy *Armada Partners*
815 Moraga Dr
Los Angeles, CA 90049-1633, USA

Noblitt, Niles L (Business Person)
PO Box 587
Warsaw, IN 46581-0587, USA

Noboa, Gustavo (Educator, President)
Garcia Moreno, Quito 1043, ECUADOR

Noboa, Junior (Athlete, Baseball Player)
PO Box 2095
Phoenix, AZ 85001-2095, USA

Noce, Paul (Athlete, Baseball Player)
942 W Maumee St
Adrian, MI 49221-1916, USA

Nock, George (Athlete, Football Player)
1025 Nine North Dr Ste H
Alpharetta, GA 30004-3951, USA

Nodell, Mart (Cartoonist)
117 Lake Irene Dr
West Palm Beach, FL 33411-2266, USA

Noe, Vergilius Cardinal (Religious Leader)
Piazza della Citta Leonina 1
Rome 193, ITALY

Noel, Alyson (Writer)
14 Monarch Bay Plz # 186
Monarch Beach, CA 92629-3424, USA

Noel, Chris (Actor)
2120 Dock St
West Palm Beach, FL 33401-7558, USA

Noel, Philip W (Ex-Governor)
20403 Wildcat Run Dr
Estero, FL 33928-2014, USA

Nofsinger, Terry (Athlete, Football Player)
21 Windsor Ct
Bountiful, UT 84010-8079, USA

Noguchi, Soichi (Astronaut)
2101 Nasa Pkwy Spc Center
Houston, TX 77058-3607, USA

Noguchi, Thomas (Doctor)
1110 Avoca Ave
Pasadena, CA 91105-3405, USA

Nogulich, Natalia (Actor)
11841 Kiowa Ave Apt 7
Los Angeles, CA 90049-6016

Nogulich, Natalija (Actor)
11841 Kiowa Ave Apt 7
Los Angeles, CA 90049-6016, USA

Noji, Minae (Actor)
c/o Steven Jensen *The Independent Group*
6363 Wilshire Blvd Ste 115
Los Angeles, CA 90048-5734, USA

Nojima, Minoru (Musician)
PO Box 515
New York, NY 10023, USA

Nokelainen, Petteri (Athlete, Hockey Player)
c/o Staff Member *Boston Bruins*
TD Banknorth Garden 100 Legends Way, Suite 250
Boston, MA 2114, USA

Nokes, Matt (Athlete, Baseball Player)
2033 San Elijo Ave Apt 503
Cardiff By The Sea, CA 92007-1726, USA

Nolan, Christopher (Writer)
c/o Stuart Manashil *Creative Artists Agency (CAA-LA)*
2000 Avenue of the Stars Ste 100
Los Angeles, CA 90067-4705, USA

Nolan, Coleen (Actor)
c/o Staff Member *Urban Associates*
Prefers to be contacted via email or telephone
London, UK

Nolan, Deanna (Basketball Player)
2 Championship Dr
Auburn Hills, MI 48326-1753, USA

Nolan, Gary (Athlete, Baseball Player)
97 Acacia Ave
Oroville, CA 95966-3658, USA

Nolan, Graham
162 Godfrey Ter
East Aurora, NY 14052-2040

Nolan, Joe (Athlete, Baseball Player)
9515 Alix Dr
Saint Louis, MO 63123-7101, USA

Nolan, Jonathan (Writer)
c/o Keya Khayatian *United Talent Agency (UTA)*
9560 Wilshire Blvd Fl 5
Beverly Hills, CA 90212-2400, USA

Nolan, Kathleen (Actor)
c/o Staff Member *House of Representatives, The*
1434 6th St Ste 1
Santa Monica, CA 90401-2527, USA

Nolan, Owen (Athlete, Hockey Player)
3402 Crestmoor Dr
Saint Paul, MN 55125-5032, USA

Nolan, Ted (Athlete, Coach, Hockey Player)
269 Queen St E
Sault Sainte Marie, ON P6A 1Y9, Canada

Nolan, Thomas B (Scientist)
2219 California St NW
Washington, DC 20008-3917, USA

Nolan, Tom
1335 N Ontario St
Burbank, CA 91505-1910

Noland, Kenneth C (Artist)
PO Box 359
Port Clyde, ME 04855-0359, USA

Nolasco, Amaury (Actor)
c/o Evan Hainey *Untitled Entertainment (LA)*
350 S Beverly Dr Ste 200
Beverly Hills, CA 90212-4819, USA

Nold, Dick (Athlete, Baseball Player)
715 Athens St
San Francisco, CA 94112-3513, USA

Nolen, Paul (Athlete, Basketball Player)
480 Pecan Dr
Burleson, TX 76028-6308, USA

Noles, Dickie (Athlete, Baseball Player)
20 Dougherty Blvd Apt I2
Glen Mills, PA 19342-1141, USA

Nolfi, George (Director)
c/o David Wirtschafter *WmE2 (Endeavor-LA)*
9601 Wilshire Blvd Fl 3
Beverly Hills, CA 90210-5219, USA

Nolin, Gena Lee (Actor)
c/o David Rose *Innovative Artists (LA)*
1505 10th St
Santa Monica, CA 90401-2805, USA

Noll, Chuck (Athlete, Football Coach)
c/o Staff Member *Keppler Associates*
4350 Fairfax Dr Ste 700
Arlington, VA 22203-1620, USA

Nolte, Claudia (Government Official)
Mulgarten 28
Ilmenau 98693, GERMANY

Nolte, Eric (Athlete, Baseball Player)
23885 Noelle Ave
Murrieta, CA 92562-2258, USA

Nolte, Nick (Actor, Producer)
c/o Angharad Wood *Tavistock Wood Management*
32 Tavistock St
London WC2B 5HA, UK

Nolting, Paul F (Religious Leader)
620 E 50th St
Loveland, CO 80538-1838, USA

Nomellini, Leo
520 Saint Claire Dr
Palo Alto, CA 94306-3050

Nomina, Tom (Athlete, Football Player)
20509 County Road 3
Berthoud, CO 80513-8043, USA

Nomo, Hideo (Athlete, Baseball Player)
10380 Wilshire Blvd Apt 202
Los Angeles, CA 90024-4741, USA

Nomura, Masayasu (Biologist)
74 Whitman Ct
Irvine, CA 92617-4066, USA

Nool, Erki (Athlete, Track Athlete)
Regati 1
Tallinn 11911, ESTONIA

Noonan, Brian (Athlete, Hockey Player)
262 W Eggleston Ave
Elmhurst, IL 60126-3822, USA

Noonan, Chris (Director)
c/o Craig Gering *Creative Artists Agency (CAA-LA)*
2000 Avenue of the Stars Ste 100
Los Angeles, CA 90067-4705, USA

Noonan, Danny (Athlete, Football Player)
1 Cowboys Pkwy
Irving, TX 75063-4924, USA

Noonan, John T Jr (Judge)
Court Building 95 7th St
San Francisco, CA 94103, USA

Noonan, Karl (Athlete, Football Player)
7149 Oxford Hunt Dr
Stanley, NC 28164-6803, USA

Noonan, Katie (Musician)
c/o Staff Member *The Harbour Agency*
135 Forbes St
Woolloomooloo NSW 2011, Australia

Noonan, Patrick F (Misc)
3553 Hamlet Pl
Chevy Chase, MD 20815-4822, USA

Noonan, Peggy (Writer)
10 E 53rd St
New York, NY 10022-5244, USA

Noonan, Robert W Jr (General)
Hqusa Pentagon
Washington, DC 20310-0001, USA

Noonan, Timothy J (Business Person)
30 Hunter Ln
Camp Hill, PA 17011-2400, USA

Noone, Kathleen (Actor)
130 W 42nd St Ste 1804
New York, NY 10036-7902, USA

Noone, Nora Jane (Actor)
c/o Staff Member *Independent Talent Group (ITG-UK)*
Oxford House 76 Oxford St
London W1D 1BS, UK

Noone, Peter (Actor, Musician)
9265 Robin Dr
Los Angeles, CA 90069-1146, USA

Noor, Queen
Baab al-Salem Palace
Amman, JORDAN

Noor Al-Hussein (Royalty)
Amman, JORDAN

Noppenberg, John (Athlete, Football Player)
7350 SW 89th St Apt 816
Miami, FL 33156-7731, USA

Norcross, Clayton
951 Galloway St
Pacific Palisades, CA 90272-3850

Nordbrook, Tim (Athlete, Baseball Player)
70 Open Gate Ct
Nottingham, MD 21236-1681, USA

Nordenberg, Mark A (Educator)
President S Ofc
Pittsburgh, PA 15261-0001, USA

Nordenstrom, Bjorn (Doctor)
Radiology Dept
Stockholm, SWEDEN

Nordhagen, Wayne (Athlete, Baseball Player)
5538 Baker Pl
Stevenson Ranch, CA 91381, USA

Nordheim, Arne (Composer)
Wergelandsveien 2
Oslo 167, NORWAY

Nordlander, Mattias (Musician)
6404 Wilshire Blvd Ste 505
Los Angeles, CA 90048-5507, USA

Nordli, Odvar (Prime Minister)
Sanveien 4
Ottestad 2312, NORWAY

Nordling, Jeffrey (Actor)
c/o Dan Baron *Agency for the Performing Arts (APA-LA)*
405 S Beverly Dr Ste 500
Beverly Hills, CA 90212-4425, USA

Nordmann, Robert (Athlete, Basketball Player)
631 E Sherwood Rd
Williamston, MI 48895-9436, USA

Nordquist, Helen (Baseball Player)
PO Box 474
Alton, NH 03809-0474, USA

Nordquist, Mark (Athlete, Football Player)
3495 Seacrest Dr
Carlsbad, CA 92008-2039, USA

Nordsieck, Kenneth H (Astronaut)
Space Astronomy Laboratory
Madison, WI 53706, USA

Nordstrom, Christy (Stylist)
1517 NE 107th St
Seattle, WA 98125-6517, USA

Noren, Irv (Athlete, Baseball Player, Basketball Player)
3154 Camino Crest Dr
Oceanside, CA 92056-3613, USA

Noren, Lars (Writer)
Ostermalmsgatan 33
Stockholm 11426, SWEDEN

Norgard, Erik C (Athlete, Football Player)
404 Winterthur Way
Highlands Ranch, CO 80129-5662, USA

Noriander, John (Basketball Player)
801 9th St N Apt 102
Virginia, MN 55792-2393, USA

Noriega, Carlos I (Astronaut)
4630 Silhouette Dr
Katy, TX 77493-8099, USA

Noriega, Danny (Musician, Reality TV Star)

Noriega, Victor (Actor)
c/o Staff Member *Televisa*
Blvd Adolfo Lopez Mateos 232 Colonia San Angel INN
DF CP 01060, MEXICO

Norman, Chris (Musician)
PO Box 28286
London N21 3WT, UNITED KINGDOM (UK)

Norman, ChrisNL-
Venlo, THE NETHERLANDS 5902 MA

Norman, Dan (Athlete, Baseball Player)
430 McBroom Ave
Barstow, CA 92311-5538, USA

Norman, Edie Jo (Bowler)
3544 Mariner Blvd
Spring Hill, FL 34609-2487, USA

Norman, Fred (Athlete, Baseball Player)
5921 Monnett Rd
Julian, NC 27283-9187, USA

Norman, Greg (Athlete, Golfer)
2041 Vista Pkwy Ste Level
West Palm Bch, FL 33411-6758, USA

Norman, Jessye (Musician)
PO Box South
Crugers, NY 10521, USA

Norman, Joe (Athlete, Football Player)
1526 Saunders Dr
Wooster, OH 44691-1558, USA

Norman, Ken (Athlete, Basketball Player)
19020 Kedzie Ave
Homewood, IL 60430-4359, USA

Norman, Les (Athlete, Baseball Player)
1401 Dogwood Dr
Greenwood, MO 64034-8671, USA

Norman, Marsha (Writer)
275 7th Ave # 2600
New York, NY 10001-6708, USA

Norman, Michael (Astronomer, Physicist)
Astronomy Dept
La Jolla, CA 90293, USA

Norman, Monty (Composer)
29/33 Berners St
London W1P 4AA, UNITED KINGDOM (UK)

Norman, Nelson (Athlete, Baseball Player)
6135 Long Key Ln
Boynton Beach, FL 33472-2369, USA

Norman, Pettis (Athlete, Football Player)
1430 Bar Harbor Cir
Dallas, TX 75232-3010, USA

Norman, Steve (Musician)
729 7th Ave Ste 1600
New York, NY 10019-6880, USA

Norman, Todd (Athlete, Football Player)
27517 Via Montoya
San Juan Capistrano, CA 92675-5364, USA

Norodom Sihanouk, Prince Samdech Preah (King)
Phnom Penh, CAMBODIA

Norona, David (Actor)
c/o Staff Member *Kohner Agency, The*
9300 Wilshire Blvd Ste 555
Beverly Hills, CA 90212-3211, USA

Norrington, Roger A C
Bergstr 22
Salzburg 5020, AUSTRIA

Norris, Aaron (Director, Producer)
2450 Colorado Ave Ste 400 PMB E
Santa Monica, CA 90404-3575, USA

Norris, Alan E (Judge)
85 Marconi Blvd
Columbus, OH 43215-2823, USA

Norris, Chuck (Actor, Producer, Writer)
3 Fountain Manor Dr
Greensboro, NC 27405-8052, USA

Norris, Darran (Actor)
c/o Staff Member *International Creative Management (ICM-LA)*
10250 Constellation Blvd Fl 7
Los Angeles, CA 90067-6207, USA

Norris, David Owen (Musician)
Aughton Rise Collingbourne
Kingston Wilts SN8 3SA, UNITED KINGDOM (UK)

Norris, Duane (Stylist)
c/o Staff Member *Elite Model Management/Atlanta*
1708 Peachtree St NW Ste 210
Atlanta, GA 30309-2416, USA

Norris, James R Jr (Misc)
5735 S Ellis Ave
Chicago, IL 60637-1403, USA

Norris, Jim (Athlete, Baseball Player)
6375 Oak Hollow Dr
Burleson, TX 76028-2839, USA

Norris, John (Journalist, Television Host)
c/o Staff Member *MTV News*
1515 Broadway Fl 29
New York, NY 10036-8901, USA

Norris, Michele (Correspondent)
5010 Creston St
Hyattsville, MD 20781-1216, USA

Norris, Mike (Athlete, Baseball Player)
407 Perkins St Apt 105B
Oakland, CA 94610-4763, USA

Norris, Paul J (Business Person)
7500 Grace Dr
Columbia, MD 21044-4009, USA

Norris, Terry (Boxer)
968 Pinehurst Dr
Las Vegas, NV 89109-1569, USA

Norris, Tim (Athlete, Golfer)
1604 Little Kitten Ave
Manhattan, KS 66503-7500, USA

Norris, William A (Judge)
312 N Spring St
Los Angeles, CA 90012-4701, USA

Norseth, Mike (Athlete, Football Player)
9774 Jameson Point Cv
Sandy, UT 84092-4200, USA

Norstrom, Mattias (Athlete, Hockey Player)
3516 Amherst Ave
Dallas, TX 75225-7419, USA

North, Andy (Athlete, Golfer)
3289 High Point Rd
Madison, WI 53719-4911, USA

North, Billy (Athlete, Baseball Player)
5523 106th Ave NE
Kirkland, WA 98033-7413, USA

North, Chandra (Model)
c/o Staff Member *Storm Model Management*
5 Jubilee Pl 1st Floor
London SW3 3TD, UNITED KINGDOM

North, Douglass C (Nobel Prize Laureate)
7569 Homestead Rd
Benzonia, MI 49616-9520, USA

North, Heather (Actor)
12996 Galewood St
Studio City, CA 91604-4045, USA

North, J J
PO Box 614
Bloomfield, NJ 07003-0614, USA

North, Jay (Actor)
290 NE 1st Ave
Lake Butler, FL 32054-1202, USA

North, Oliver L (General, Government Official, Television Host)
c/o Staff Member *Fox News Channel (NY)*
1211 Ave Of The Americas Level C1
New York, NY 10036-8701, USA

North, Peter (Adult Film Star)
c/o Staff Member *Vivid Entertainment*
3599 Cahuenga Blvd W # 400
Los Angeles, CA 90068-1397, USA

Northam, Jeremy (Actor)
c/o Chris Andrews *Creative Artists Agency (CAA-LA)*
2000 Avenue of the Stars Ste 100
Los Angeles, CA 90067-4705, USA

Northcutt, Dennis (Athlete, Football Player)
17038 River Birch Ct
Canyon Country, CA 91387-6949, USA

Northey, Scott (Athlete, Baseball Player)
9920 Bankside Dr
Roswell, GA 30076-3735, USA

Northrop, Wayne (Actor)
37900 Road 800
Raymond, CA 93653-9714, USA

Northrup, Jim (Athlete, Baseball Player)
29508 Southfield Rd Ste 205
Southfield, MI 48076-2022, USA

Northrup, Wayne
21919 Canon Dr
Topanga, CA 90290-4336

Northrup, MD, Christiane (Writer)
PO Box 199
Yarmouth, ME 04096-0199

Northtrip, Richard A (Misc)
2500 Brickvale Dr
Elk Grove Village, IL 60007-6800, USA

Northway, Douglas (Doug) (Swimmer)
3239 E 3rd St
Tucson, AZ 85716-4231, USA

Norton, Bryan (Athlete, Golfer)
3816 W 65th St
Mission Hills, KS 66208-1738, USA

Norton, Corin (Actor)
c/o Staff Member *Bruce Heller and Associates*
3272 Motor Ave Suites F&G
Los Angeles, CA 90034-3772, USA

Norton, Edward (Actor)
c/o Cynthia Swartz *42West (NY)*
220 W 42nd St Fl 12
New York, NY 10036-7200, USA

Norton, Gale (Secretary)
1849 C St NW
Washington, DC 20240-0001, USA

Norton, Graham (Actor)
c/o Melanie Rockcliffe *Troika*
74 Clerkenwell Rd 3rd Floor
London EC1M 5QA, United Kingdom

Norton, Greg (Athlete, Baseball Player)
11130 Eliot Ct
Denver, CO 80234-4682, USA

Norton, James A (Athlete, Football Player)
2550 S Ellsworth Rd Unit 13
Mesa, AZ 85209-1198, USA

Norton, James C (Athlete, Football Player)
PO Box 495997
Garland, TX 75049-5997, USA

Norton, James J (Misc)
1900 L St NW
Washington, DC 20036-5002, USA

Norton, Jeff (Athlete, Hockey Player)
1701 E Las Olas Blvd Apt 1
Fort Lauderdale, FL 33301-2441, USA

Norton, Jerry (Athlete, Football Player)
6901 Chevy Chase Ave
Dallas, TX 75225-2416, USA

Norton, Peter (Designer)
225 Arizona Ave # 200W
Santa Monica, CA 90401-1243, USA

Norton, Phil (Athlete, Baseball Player)
677 County Road 3772
Queen City, TX 75572-7947, USA

Norton, Richard (Actor)
c/o Ray Cavaleri *Cavaleri & Associates*
178 S Victory Blvd Ste 205
Burbank, CA 91502-2881, USA

Norton, Rick (Athlete, Football Player)
901 W Mahoney St
Plant City, FL 33563-4435, USA

Norton, Tom (Athlete, Baseball Player)
4900 Southwood Dr
Sheffield Lake, OH 44054-1559, USA

Norton, Virginia (Bowler)
11706 Mindanao St
Cypress, CA 90630-5662, USA

Norton Jr, Ken (Athlete, Football Player)
135 Union Jack Mal
Marina Del Rey, CA 90292, USA

Norvell, Jay (Athlete, Football Player)
2166 Clinton Ave
Alameda, CA 94501-4945, USA

Norville, Deborah (Television Host)
c/o Rick Hersh *Celebrity Consultants LLC*
3340 Ocean Park Blvd Ste 1030
Santa Monica, CA 90405-3259, USA

Norvind, Nailea (Actor)
c/o Staff Member *Televisa*
Blvd Adolfo Lopez Mateos 232 Colonia
San Angel INN
DF CP 01060, MEXICO

Norwich, Craig (Athlete, Hockey Player)
11448 Welters Way
Eden Prairie, MN 55347-2848, USA

Norwood, Brandy (Actor, Musician)
c/o Everly Lee *Agency for the Performing Arts (APA-LA)*
405 S Beverly Dr Ste 500
Beverly Hills, CA 90212-4425, USA

Norwood, Jerious (Football Player)
c/o Staff Member *Atlanta Falcons*
4400 Falcon Pkwy
Flowery Branch, GA 30542-3176, USA

Norwood, Ray J (Actor, Musician)
c/o Staff Member *Defining Artists Agency*
10 Universal City Plz Ste 2000
Universal City, CA 91608-1074, USA

Norwood, Robin (Writer)
c/o Staff Member *Simon & Schuster*
1230 Avenue of the Americas Fl CONC1
New York, NY 10020-1586, USA

Norwood, Scott (Athlete, Football Player)
42923 Shelbourne Sq
Chantilly, VA 20152-2097, USA

Norwood, Willie (Athlete, Baseball Player)
225 Gunsmoke Dr
Diamond Bar, CA 91765-1257, USA

Norwood, Willie (Athlete, Basketball Player)
414 W 122nd St Apt B
Los Angeles, CA 90061-1314, USA

Nosbusch, Desiree
Mohrengasse 18
Hohenems, AUSTRIA A-6845

Nosek, Randy (Athlete, Baseball Player)
15485 Knobhill Dr
Linden, MI 48451-8716, USA

Noseworthy, Jack
955 Carrillo Dr Ste 300
Los Angeles, CA 90048-5400

Nossal, Gustav J V (Doctor)
46 Fellows St
Kew, VIC 3101, AUSTRALIA

Nosseck, Noel (Director)
1435 San Ysidro Dr
Beverly Hills, CA 90210-2108, USA

Nossek, Joe (Athlete, Baseball Player)
630 Sunrise Dr
Amherst, OH 44001-1659, USA

Notaro, Phyllis (Bowler)
20284 Brant Angota Rd
Angola, NY 14006, USA

Notebaert, Richard (Business Person)
1801 California St
Denver, CO 80202-2658, USA

Noth, Christopher (Actor)
c/o Nancy Sanders *Sanders Armstrong Caserta*
2120 Colorado Ave Ste 120
Santa Monica, CA 90404-3561, USA

Nothstein, Marty
1 Olympic Plz
Colorado Springs, CO 80909-5780

Notkins, Abner L (Scientist)
9000 Rockville Pike
Bethesda, MD 20892-0001, USA

Notley, Alice (Writer)
c/o Staff Member *Wesleyan University Press*
215 Long Ln
Middletown, CT 06457-4073, USA

Noto, Lucio A (Business Person)
3225 Gallows Rd
Fairfax, VA 22037-0001, USA

Nott, John W F (Government Official)
32 Hampstead High St
London NW3 1QD, UNITED KINGDOM (UK)

Nottebohm, Andreas (Artist)
Mentzstr 44
Mulheim An Der Ruhr, GERMANY

Nottingham, Don (Athlete, Football Player)
PO Box 459
Belleview, FL 34421-0459, USA

Nottingham, Robert
4348 Coldwater Canyon Ave Apt B
Studio City, CA 91604-5016

Nouri, Michael (Actor)

Noury, Alain
Soyans s/Crest
, FRANCE 26400

Nouvel, Jean (Architect)
10 Cite d'Angouleme
Paris 75011, FRANCE

Nova, Heather
Box 3704
London, ENGLAND W4 4ZN

Nova, Nikki (Actor)
4331 E Baseline Rd # PO
Gilbert, AZ 85234-2961, USA

Novack, K J (Business Person)
22000 Aol Way
Dulles, VA 20166-9302, USA

Novack, William
3 Ashton Ave
Newton, MA 02459-1526

Novak, BJ (Actor, Comedian)
c/o Kevin McLaughlin *Baker Winokur Ryder Public Relations (BWR-LA)*
9100 Wilshire Blvd Ste 500 PMB WEST
Beverly Hills, CA 90212-3426, USA

Novak, David C (Business Person)
1441 Gardiner Ln
Louisville, KY 40213-1914, USA

Novak, Jack (Athlete, Football Player)
308 River Chase Ct
Georgetown, TX 78628-5314, USA

Novak, John R (Inventor)
101 Wood Ave S
Iselin, NJ 08830-2703, USA

Novak, Kim (Actor)
13777 Agate Rd
Eagle Point, OR 97524-6567, USA

Novak, Michael (Misc)
1150 17th St NW
Washington, DC 20036-4603, USA

Novak, Pablo (Actor)
c/o Staff Member *Telefe - Argentina*
Pavon 2444 (C1248AAT)
Buenos Aires, ARGENTINA

Novak, Popper Ilona (Swimmer)
II Orso Utca 23
Budapest, HUNGARY

Novakovic, Bojana (Actor)
c/o Suzan Bymel *Management 360*
9111 Wilshire Blvd
Beverly Hills, CA 90210-5508, USA

Novarina, Maurice P J (Architect)
52 Rue Raynouard
Paris 75116, FRANCE

Novelli, William (Misc)
601 E St NW
Washington, DC 20049-0001, USA

Novello, Antonia C (Misc)
2700 Virginia Ave NW # 501
Washington, DC 20037-1909, USA

Novello, Antonia C (Government Official)
1616 Foss Ave
Orlando, FL 32814-6732, USAs

Novello, Don
PO Box 245
Fairfax, CA 94978-0245

Novello, Don (Fr Guido Sarducci) (Actor, Comedian)
82 Cumberland Ave
Verona, NJ 07044-2105, USA

Noveskey, Matt (Musician)
2002 Hogback Rd Ste 20
Ann Arbor, MI 48105-9736, USA

Novoa, Rafael (Actor)
c/o Staff Member *TV Caracol*
Calle 76 #11 - 35 Piso 10AA
Bogota DC 26484, COLOMBIA

Novoa, Rafael (Athlete, Baseball Player)
3420 N 47th Way
Phoenix, AZ 85018-6014, USA

Novosel, Michael J (War Hero)
10 Doral Dr
Shalimar, FL 32579-1612, USA

Novoselic, Krist (Activist, Musician)
6930 Carroll Ave Ste 610
Takoma Park, MD 20912-4498, USA

Novoselsky, Brent (Athlete, Football Player)
405 Marvins Way
Buffalo Grove, IL 60089-6419, USA

Novotna, Jana (Tennis Player)
7834 Montvale Way
McLean, VA 22102-2028, USA

Novotny, Dave (Musician)
535 Kings Road
London SW10 0S, UNITED KINGDOM (UK)

Nowak, Lisa M (Astronaut)
17123 Parsley Hawthome Ct
Houston, TX 77059, USA

Nowak, Peter (Coach, Soccer Player)
14120 Newbrook Dr
Chantilly, VA 20151-2273, USA

Nowatzke, Tom (Athlete, Football Player)
6900 Whitmore Lake Rd
Whitmore Lake, MI 48189-9363, USA

Nowell, Peter C (Biologist)
9 Foxcroft Ln
Media, PA 19063-4818, USA

Nowicki, Tom (Actor)
c/o Staff Member *Davis Management*
4111 Lankershim Blvd
Studio City, CA 91602-2828

Nowitzki, Dirk (Athlete, Basketball Player)
5311 Byron Ave
Dallas, TX 75205-2846, USA

Nowra, Louis (Writer)
Level 18 Plaza 11 500 Oxford St
Bondi Junction, NSW 2011, AUSTRALIA

Noxon, Marti (Writer)
c/o Staff Member *WmE2 (Endeavor-LA)*
9601 Wilshire Blvd Fl 3
Beverly Hills, CA 90210-5219, USA

Noyce, Phillip (Director)
c/o Steve Rabineau *United Talent Agency (UTA)*
9560 Wilshire Blvd Fl 5
Beverly Hills, CA 90212-2400, USA

Noyd, R Allen (Religious Leader)
1294 Rutledge Rd
Transfer, PA 16154-2226, USA

Noyes, Albert Jr (Misc)
5102 Fairview Dr
Austin, TX 78731-5426, USA

Noyori, Ryoji (Nobel Prize Laureate)
135-417 Shinden Umemoricho
Nisshin, Aichi 470-0132, JAPAN

Nozieres, Philippe P G F (Physicist)
15 Route d Saint Nizier
Seyssins 38180, FRANCE

Nri, Cyril (Actor)
1 Deer Park Road Merton
London SW19 3TL, UK

Nsengiyremeye, Dismas (Prime Minister)
Kigali, RWANDA

Nsibanbi, Apolo (Prime Minister)
International Conference Center
Kampala, UGANDA

Ntombi (Royalty)
PO Box 1
Lobamba, SWAZILAND

Ntoutoume, Jean-Francois (Prime Minister)
BP 546
Libreville, GABON

Nuami, Sheikh Humaid bin Rashid an- (King, Royalty)
PO Box 1
Ajman, UNITED ARAB EMIRATES

Nubla, Malou (Journalist)
855 Battery St
San Francisco, CA 94111-1503, USA

Nucci, Danny (Actor)
3500 W Olive Ave Ste 1400
Burbank, CA 91505-5512, USA

Nucci, Leo (Opera Singer)
40 W 57th St
New York, NY 10019-4001, USA

Nuckolls, Sara (Stylist)
c/o Staff Member *Celestine - CA*
1666 20th St Ste 200B
Santa Monica, CA 90404-3828, USA

Nugent, Eddie
PO Box 1266
New York, NY 10150-1266

Nugent, Nelle (Producer)
234 W 44th St Ste 1005
New York, NY 10036-3909, USA

Nugent, Ted (Musician)
4008 W Michigan Ave
Jackson, MI 49202-1829, USA

Nujoma, Sam S (President)
State House Mugabe Ave
Windhoek 9000, NAMIBIA

Numan, Gary (Musician, Songwriter, Writer)
86 Staines Road Wraysbury
N Staines, Middlesex TW19 5A, UNITED KINGDOM (UK)

Numeroff, Laura Joffe (Writer)
c/o Staff Member *HarperCollins Publishers*
10 E 53rd St C/O Author Mail Floor 7
New York, NY 10022, USA

Numminen, Teppo (Athlete, Hockey Player)
3422 E Palo Verde Dr
Paradise Valley, AZ 85253-5015, USA

Nunes, Devin (Congressman, Politician)
1013 Longworth Hob
Washington, DC 20515-0004, USA

Nunez, Abraham (Baseball Player)
2505 Fox Hollow Dr
Pittsburgh, PA 15237-3833, USA

Nunez, Chris (Reality TV Star)
c/o Adena Chawke *Greenlight Management and Production*
13848 Valleyheart Dr
Sherman Oaks, CA 91423-2930, USA

Nunez, Edwin (Athlete, Baseball Player)
2618 E Locust Dr
Chandler, AZ 85286-2721, USA

Nunez, Jorge (Musician)

Nunez, Miguel Angel Jr (Actor)
c/o Patricia (Patty) Woo *Patty Woo Management*
3500 W Olive Ave Ste 1400
Burbank, CA 91505-5512, USA

Nunez, Oscar (Actor)
c/o Bruce Smith *OmniPop Talent Group*
10700 Ventura Blvd Fl 2
Studio City, CA 91604-3561, USA

Nunez, Victor (Director)
9300 Wilshire Blvd Ste 555
Beverly Hills, CA 90212-3211, USA

Nunez, Vladimir (Athlete, Baseball Player)
18053 SW 139th Pl
Miami, FL 33177-2792, USA

Nunley, Frank (Athlete, Football Player)
2131 Mulberry Cir
San Jose, CA 95125-4647, USA

Nunley, Jeremy (Athlete, Football Player)
1595 Little Hurricane Rd
Winchester, TN 37398-4229, USA

Nunn, Howie (Athlete, Baseball Player)
204 S Depot St
Pilot Mountain, NC 27041-8528, USA

Nunn, Sam (Ex-Senator, Senator)
75 14th St NE Unit 4810
Atlanta, GA 30309-7623, USA

Nunn, Samuel A (Sam) (Senator)
75 14th St NE Unit 4810
Atlanta, GA 30309-7623, USA

Nunn, Teri (Musician)
6404 Wilshire Blvd Ste 505
Los Angeles, CA 90048-5507, USA

Nunn, Trevor R (Director)
South Bank
London SE1 9PX, UNITED KINGDOM (UK)

Nunnally, Jon (Athlete, Baseball Player)
36550 Chester Rd Apt 504
Avon, OH 44011-1098, USA

Nunnari, Talmadge (Athlete, Baseball Player)
7101 Joy St Apt A8
Pensacola, FL 32504-6480, USA

Nunnelee, Alan (Congressman, Politician)
1432 Longworth Hob
Washington, DC 20515-1505, USA

Nunnery, R B (Athlete, Football Player)
3276 Claude Smith Rd
Magnolia, MS 39652-9534, USA

Nurding, Louise (Actor)
42 Colwith Rd
London, ENGLAND W6 9EY

Nurse, Paul M (Nobel Prize Laureate)
Cell Cycle Control Lab
Herts EN6 3LD, UNITED KINGDOM (UK)

Nussbaum, Danny (Actor)
18-21 Jermyn St
London SW1Y 6NB, UNITED KINGDOM (UK)

Nussbaum, Joe (Actor, Director, Writer)
c/o Adriana Alberghetti *WmE2 (Endeavor-LA)*
9601 Wilshire Blvd Fl 3
Beverly Hills, CA 90210-5219, USA

Nussbaum, Karen (Misc)
231 W Wisconsin Ave Apt 900
Milwaukee, WI 53203-2306, USA

Nussbaum, Martha C (Misc)
111 E 60th St
Chicago, IL 60637-2105, USA

Nussiein-Volhard, Christiane (Nobel Prize Laureate)
Spenmannstr 35/III
Tubingen 72076, GERMANY

Nussmeier, Doug (Athlete, Football Player)
28493 SW Meadows Loop
Wilsonville, OR 97070-6779, USA

Nutini, Paolo (Musician)
Electric Lighting Station 46 Kensington Ct
Londo W8 5DA, UNITED KINGDOM

Nutt, Dennis (Athlete, Basketball Player)
704 Magnolia Dr
Arkadelphia, AR 71923-4109, USA

Nutt, Jim (Artist)
1035 Greenwood Ave
Wilmette, IL 60091-1753, USA

Nutter, Alice (Musician)
PO Box 1151
London W3 8ZJ, UNITED KINGDOM (UK)

Nutter, David (Director)
c/o Staff Member *Genrebend Productions*
233 Wilshire Blvd Ste 700
Santa Monica, CA 90401-1207, USA

Nutting, Ed (Athlete, Football Player)
607 Ashford Pkwy
Atlanta, GA 30338-5534, USA

Nutting, Wallace H (General)
6 Schooner Way
Saco, ME 04072-2153, USA

Nutzie, Futzie (Artist, Cartoonist)
PO Box 325
Aromas, CA 95004-0325, USA

Nuwer, Hank (Journalist, Writer)
PO Box 31
Fairland, IN 46126-0031, USA

Nuyen, France (Actor)
c/o Budd Burton Moss *Burton Moss*
10533 Strathmore Dr
Los Angeles, CA 90024-2540, USA

Nuzorewa, Abel Tendekayi (Prime Minister)
40 Charter Road
Harare, ZIMBABWE

Nwosu, Julius (Athlete, Basketball Player)
12436 Vance Jackson Rd Apt 1122
San Antonio, TX 78230-5992, USA

Nyad, Diana (Sportscaster, Swimmer)
151 E 86th St
New York, NY 10028-2106, USA

Nyberg, Frederik (Skier)
Kaptensgatan 2C
Froson 832 00, SWEDEN

Nyberg, Karen L (Astronaut)
1848 Lake Landing Dr
League City, TX 77573-7781, USA

Nye, Bill (Actor, Talk Show Host)
4742 42nd Ave SW # 143
Seattle, WA 98116-4553, USA

Nye, Blaine (Athlete, Football Player)
702 Marshall St Ste 200
Redwood City, CA 94063-1823, USA

Nye, Erie (Business Person)
Energy Plaza 1601 Bryan St
Dallas, TX 75201, USA

Nye, Flora (Stylist)
c/o Staff Member *Stockland Martel*
343 E 18th St
New York, NY 10003-2802, USA

Nye, Naomi Shihab (Writer)
c/o Staff Member *HarperCollins Children's Books*
1350 Avenue of the Americas
New York, NY 10019-4702, USA

Nye, Rich (Athlete, Baseball Player)
7510 W North Ave
Elmwood Park, IL 60707-4140, USA

Nye, Robert (Writer)
Thomfield Kingsland
Ballinghassig, County Cork, IRELAND

Nye, Ryan (Athlete, Baseball Player)
3319 Golf Course Dr
Alma, AR 72921-8601, USA

Nyers, Dick (Athlete, Football Player)
4055 N Riverside Dr
Columbus, IN 47203-1118, USA

Nyers, Rezso (Secretary)
Ozgida Utca 22/A
Budapest 1025, HUNGARY

Nygaard, Richard L (Judge)
1st National Bank State St Building 717
Erie, PA 16501, USA

Nyland, William L (General)
2 Navy St
Washington, DC 20380-1775, USA

Nyman, Chris (Athlete, Baseball Player)
1700 Happy Creek Rd
Front Royal, VA 22630-6438, USA

Nyman, Jerry (Athlete, Baseball Player)
76 Sundance Ln
Afton, WY 83110, USA

Nyman, Michael L (Composer, Musician)
PO Box 430
High Wycombe HP13 5QT, UNITED KINGDOM (UK)

Nyman, Nyls (Athlete, Baseball Player)
PO Box 236
Susanville, CA 96130-0236, USA

Nyquist, Ryan (Athlete)
c/o Staff Member *Familie, The*
1545 Faraday Ave
Carlsbad, CA 92008-7449, USA

Nystrom, Bob (Athlete, Hockey Player)
475 Berry Hill Rd
Oyster Bay, NY 11771, USA

Nystrom, Joakim (Tennis Player)
Torsgatan 194
Skellefteaa 931 00, SWEDEN

Nystrom, Lee (Athlete, Football Player)
18411 Priory Ave
Minnetonka, MN 55345-2459, USA

Nystrom, Lene (Actor)
c/o Staff Member *Lindberg Management*
Lavendelstraede 5-7 Baghuset 4.sal
Copenhagen K DK-1462, Denmark

Nyvell, Vic (Athlete, Football Player)
P.O. Box 159C
Kilgore, TX 75663, USA

N'Zinga, Naila (Stylist)
c/o Staff Member *Stockland Martel*
343 E 18th St
New York, NY 10003-2802, USA

O

O, Karen (Musician)
249 Metropolitan Ave
Brooklyn, NY 11211-4009, USA

O, Tommy (Director)
c/o Staff Member *WmE2 (WMA-LA)*
1 William Morris Pl
Beverly Hills, CA 90212-4261, USA

O. Matsui, Doris (Congressman, Politician)
222 Cannon Hob
Washington, DC 20515-3517, USA

O' Sullivan, Thaddeus (Director)
c/o Anthony Jones *United Agents*
Drury House 34-43 Russell St
London WC2B 5HA, UK

O Town
7380 W Sand Lake Rd # 350
Orlando, FL 32819-5248

Oak Ridge Boys, The (Music Group)
88 New Shackle Island Rd
Hendersonville, TN 37075-2393, USA

Oakes, Don (Athlete, Football Player)
101 Aftons Meadow Rd
Vinton, VA 24179-9701, USA

Oakes, James L (Judge)
PO Box 696
Brattleboro, VT 05302-0696, USA

Oakes, Summer Rayne (Model)
59 Grand St
Brooklyn, NY 11249-4110, USA

Oakley, Charles (Basketball Player)
MCI Centre 601 F St NW
Washington, DC 20004, USA

OAR (Music Group)
c/o Dave Roberge *Red Light Management (NY)*
44 Wall St Fl 22
New York, NY 10005-2401, USA

Oasis
54 Linhope St
London, ENGLAND NW1 6HL

Oates, Adam R (Athlete, Hockey Player)
1480 S County Rd
Osterville, MA 02655-1544, USA

Oates, Bart S (Athlete, Football Player, Sportscaster)
2 Silverbrook Rd
Morristown, NJ 07960-8003, USA

Oates, John (Musician, Songwriter)
c/o Staff Member *Doyle-Kos Entertainment*
1 Penn Plz Ste 2107
New York, NY 10119-2107, USA

Oates, Joyce Carol (Writer)
English Dept
Princeton, NJ 8540, USA

Oats, Carleton (Athlete, Football Player)
10605 E Coralbell Ave
Mesa, AZ 85208-7442, USA

Oatway, Devin
10635 Santa Monica Blvd Ste 130
Los Angeles, CA 90025-8306

Obama, Barack (Politician, President)
1600 Pennsylvania Ave NW
Washington, DC 20500-0005, USA

Obama, Michelle (First Lady)
1600 Pennsylvania Ave NW
Washington, DC 20500-0005, USA

Obando, Bravo Miguel Cardinal (Religious Leader)
Arzobispado Apartado 3050
Managua, NICARAGUA

Obando, Sherman (Athlete, Baseball Player)
7037 Coral Cove Dr
Orlando, FL 32818-2866, USA

O'Bannon, Dan (Director)
c/o Staff Member *Agency for the Performing Arts (APA-LA)*
405 S Beverly Dr Ste 500
Beverly Hills, CA 90212-4425, USA

O'Bannon, Ed (Basketball Player)
11930 Agnes St
Cerritos, CA 90703-6902, USA

O'Bannon, Ed (Athlete, Basketball Player)
1387 Minuet St
Henderson, NV 89052-6454, USA

O'Bard, Ronnie (Athlete, Football Player)
27121 Puerta Del Oro
Mission Viejo, CA 92691-4421, USA

Obasanjo, Olusegun (General, President)
State House Ribadu Road Ikoyi
Lagos, NIGERIA

Obato, Gyo (Architect)
1 Metropolitan Sq Ste 600
Saint Louis, MO 63102-2733, USA

Obee, Duncan (Athlete, Football Player)
4488 283rd St
Toledo, OH 43611-1864, USA

Obeid, Atef (Prime Minister)
PO Box 191 1 Majlis El-Shaab St
Cairo, EGYPT

Obeidallah, Dean (Comedian)
400 E 59th St
New York, NY 10022-2342, USA

Obeidat, Ahmad Abdul-Majeed (Prime Minister)
PO Box 926544
Amman, JORDAN

Oben, Roman (Athlete, Football Player)
11476 Creekstone Ln
San Diego, CA 92128-6325, USA

Oberding, Mark (Basketball Player)
4131 Cliff Oaks St
San Antonio, TX 78229-3536, USA

Oberg, Margo (Misc)
RR 1 Box 73 Koloa
Kaui, HI 96756, USA

Oberg, Tom (Athlete, Football Player)
280 Avery St
Ashland, OR 97520-2202, USA

Oberholser, Arron (Golfer)
c/o Staff Member *Pro Golfers Association (PGA) Tour*
112 Tpc Blvd
Ponte Vedra Beach, FL 32082, USA

Oberkfell, Ken (Athlete, Baseball Player)
1335 W Welsford Dr
Spring, TX 77386-2599, USA

Oberlin, David W (Government Official)
800 Independence Ave SW # 814
Washington, DC 20591-0001, USA

Obermeyer, Klaus F (Designer, Fashion Designer)
115 Aspen Airport Business Ctr
Aspen, CO 81611-2502, USA

Obermueller, Wes (Athlete, Baseball Player)
7031 27th Ave
Newhall, IA 52315-9600, USA

Oberoi, Vivek (Actor, Bollywood)
5 Kartar Kunj Golden Beach Ruia Park
Juhu
Mumbai, MS 400 0049, INDIA

O'Berry, Mike (Athlete, Baseball Player)
5977 S Fork Dr
Hoover, AL 35244-5466, USA

Oberst, Conner
c/o Brian Young *Untitled Entertainment (LA)*
350 S Beverly Dr Ste 200
Beverly Hills, CA 90212-4819, USA

Oberst, Conor
PO Box 1235
Chapel Hill, NC 27514-1235, USA

Oberto, Fabricio (Athlete, Basketball Player)
230 W Superior St Ste 510
Chicago, IL 60654-3584, USA

O'Boyle, Maureen (Entertainer)
30 Rockefeller Plz # 820E
New York, NY 10112-0015, USA

Obradors, Jacqueline (Actor)
c/o Todd Eisner *Agency for the Performing Arts (APA-LA)*
405 S Beverly Dr Ste 500
Beverly Hills, CA 90212-4425, USA

O'Bradovich, Ed (Athlete, Football Player)
235 N Smith St Apt 207
Palatine, IL 60067-8503, USA

Obradovich, James R (Jim) (Athlete, Football Player)
2601 Morningside Dr
Lomita, CA 90717, USA

Obradovich, Jim (Athlete, Baseball Player)
1133 Bryants Camp Rd
Lancaster, KY 40444-7032, USA

Obraztsova, Elena V (Opera Singer)
Teatralnaya Pl 1
Moscow 103009, RUSSIA

Obregon, Alejandro (Artist)
Apartado Aereo 37
Barranquilla, COLOMBIA

Obregon, Ana (Actor)
9300 Wilshire Blvd Ste 555
Beverly Hills, CA 90212-3211, USA

O'Brian, Hugh (Actor)
31255 Cedar Valley Dr Ste 327
Westlake Village, CA 91362-7140, USA

O'Brian, Richard (Actor)
27 Floral St
London C2E 9DP, UNITED KINGDOM (UK)

O'Brian-Cooke, Penny (Baseball Player)
307-1335 E 27th St
North Vancouver, BC V7J 1S6, CANADA

O'Brien, Austin (Actor)
232 N Canon Dr
Beverly Hills, CA 90210-5302, USA

O'Brien, Bill (Athlete, Football Player)
1253 Flamingo
Wixom, MI 48393-1506, USA

O'Brien, Bob (Athlete, Baseball Player)
2303 E Acacia Ave Apt 148
Fresno, CA 93726-0302, USA

O'Brien, Brian (Physicist)
PO Box 166
Woodstock, CT 06281-0166, USA

O'Brien, Carl (Cubby) (Actor)
2530 Independence Ave Apt 2J
Bronx, NY 10463-6236, USA

O'Brien, Cathy (Athlete, Track Athlete)
19 Foss Farm Rd
Durham, NH 03824-2927, USA

O'Brien, Charlie (Athlete, Baseball Player)
4932 E 38th Pl
Tulsa, OK 74135-5529, USA

O'Brien, Conan (Comedian, Talk Show Host)
c/o Gavin Polone *Hofflund/Polone*
9465 Wilshire Blvd Ste 420
Beverly Hills, CA 90212-2603, USA

O'Brien, Conor Cruise (Diplomat, Writer)
Whitewater Howth Summit
Dublin, IRELAND

O'Brien, Cubby
2839 N Surrey Dr
Carrollton, TX 75006-4800

O'Brien, Dan (Athlete, Baseball Player)
8223 Forest Hills Blvd
Dallas, TX 75218-4410, USA

O'Brien, Dave (Athlete, Football Player)
304 Newbury St # 349
Boston, MA 02115-2839, USA

O'Brien, David (Athlete, Football Player)
61 Colony Rd
Jupiter, FL 33469-3507, USA

O'Brien, Ed (Musician)
72 Spring St # 1100
New York, NY 10012-4019, USA

O'Brien, Eddie (Athlete, Baseball Player)
522 Alder St Apt 101
Edmonds, WA 98020-3494, USA

O'Brien, Edna (Writer)
52 Knightsbridge
London SW1X 7JP, UNITED KINGDOM (UK)

O'Brien, Emily (Actor)
c/o Beverly Strong *Strong Management*
9350 Wilshire Blvd Ste 224
Beverly Hills, CA 90212-3204, USA

O'Brien, G Dennis (Educator)
PO Box 510
Middlebury, VT 05753-0510, USA

O'Brien, George H Jr (War Hero)
2001 Douglas Ave
Midland, TX 79701-4059, USA

O'Brien, Gregory M (Educator)
Chancellor S Ofc
New Orleans, LA 70148-0001, USA

O'Brien, Jim (Basketball Player, Coach)
1 Union Center 3601 South Broad St
Philadelphia, PA 19148, USA

O'Brien, Jim (Athlete, Football Player)
413 Bethany St
Thousand Oaks, CA 91360-2025, USA

O'Brien, John (Writer)
2 Columbine Placa
Delran, NJ 8075, USA

O'Brien, John T (Johnny) (Athlete, Baseball Player)
2405 N 75th St
Seattle, WA 98103-4959, USA

O'Brien, Keith M P Cardinal (Religious Leader)
113 Whitehouse Loan
Edinburgh EH9 1BB, SCOTLAND

O'Brien, Kenneth J (Ken) Jr (Athlete, Football Player)
201 Manhattan Ave
Manhattan Beach, CA 90266-6439, USA

O'Brien, M Vincent (Coach, Horse Racer)
Ballydoyle House Cashel
County Tipperary, IRELAND

O'Brien, Margaret (Actor)
14840 Valerio St
Van Nuys, CA 91405-1819, USA

O'Brien, Mark (Business Person)
33 Bloomfield Hills Pkwy
Bloomfield Hills, MI 48304-2944, USA

O'Brien, Maureen (Actor)
Primrose Hill Studios Fitzroy Road
London NW1 8TR, UNITED KINGDOM (UK)

O'Brien, Miles (Television Host)
c/o Staff Member *CNN (NY)*
1 Time Warner Ctr
New York, NY 10019-6038, USA

O'Brien, Pat (Sportscaster, Television Host)
c/o Steven Simon *Prince Marketing Group*
18 Carillon Cir
Livingston, NJ 07039-2600, USA

O'Brien, Pete (Athlete, Baseball Player)
5509 Montclair Dr
Colleyville, TX 76034-5028, USA

O'Brien, Peter
397 Riley St
Surry Hills, AUSTRALIA NSW 2010

O'Brien, Richard (Composer, Songwriter, Writer)
1 Elm Grove Hildenborough
Tonbridge Kent TN11 9HE, UNITED KINGDOM (UK)

O'Brien, Ron (Coach)
80450 Overseas Hwy Apt 401
Islamorada, FL 33036-3751, USA

O'Brien, Scott (Athlete, Football Player)
12690 Overlook Mountain Dr
Charlotte, NC 28216-6726, USA

O'Brien, Soledad (Correspondent, Television Host)
c/o Staff Member *CNN (Atlanta)*
1 Cnn Ctr NW
Atlanta, GA 30303-2762, USA

O'Brien, Syd (Athlete, Baseball Player)
10189 Hemlock St
Rancho Cucamonga, CA 91730-3023, USA

O'Brien, Thomas H (Financier)
1 Pnc Center 249 5th Ave
Pittsburgh, PA 15222, USA

O'Brien, Thomas M (Financier)
185 W 23rd St
Bronx, NY 10463, USA

O'Brien, Tim (Athlete, Track Athlete)
17 Partride Ln
Boxford, MA 1921, USA

O'Brien, Tina (Actor)
c/o Martin Spencer *Creative Artists Agency (CAA-LA)*
2000 Avenue of the Stars Ste 100
Los Angeles, CA 90067-4705, USA

O'Brien, Trever (Actor)
c/o Faras Rabadi *Emerald Talent Group*
10 Universal City Plz Fl 20
Universal City, CA 91608-1074, USA

O'Brien, Trevor (Actor)
c/o Staff Member *Abrams Artists Agency (LA)*
9200 W Sunset Blvd PH 11
Los Angeles, CA 90069-3601, USA

O'Brien, W Parry (Athlete, Track Athlete)
3415 Alginet Dr
Encino, CA 91436, USA

O'Bryan, Sean (Actor)
c/o Staff Member *Alan Siegel Entertainment*
345 N Maple Dr Ste 375
Beverly Hills, CA 90210-5174, USA

Obst, Lynda (Producer)
c/o Staff Member *Lynda Obst Productions*
5555 Melrose Ave Rm 210
Los Angeles, CA 90038-3996

O'Callahan, John (Athlete, Football Player)
361A La Perle Ln
Costa Mesa, CA 92627-3757, USA

O'Callahan, John (Jack) (Athlete, Hockey Player)
101 Linden Ave
Glencoe, IL 60022-2144, USA

Ocampo Uria, Adriana C (Scientist)
300 E St SW
Washington, DC 20456, USA

O'Caroll, Sinead (Musician)
55 Drury Lane Covent Garden
London WC2B 5SQ, UNITED KINGDOM (UK)

Ocasek, Ric (Musician, Songwriter, Writer)
75 Rockefeller Plz
New York, NY 10019-6908, USA

Occhipinti, Andrea (Actor)
Via Giuseppe Pisanelli
Rome 196, ITALY

Ocean, Billy (Musician)
32 Willesden Lane
London NW6 7ST, UNITED KINGDOM (UK)

Ocean Colour Scene (Music Group)
c/o Staff Member *Paradigm (Monterey)*
404 W Franklin St
Monterey, CA 93940-2303, USA

Oceansize (Music Group)
c/o Staff Member *Paradigm (Monterey)*
404 W Franklin St
Monterey, CA 93940-2303, USA

Ochirbat, Punsalmaagiyn (President)
Olympic St 14
Ulan Bator, MONGOLIA

Ochman, Wieslaw (Opera Singer)
Ul Miaczynska 46B
Warsaw 02-637, POLAND

Ochoa, Alex (Athlete, Baseball Player)
8325 NW 158th Ter
Hialeah, FL 33016-6604, USA

Ochoa, Ellen (Astronaut)
4515 Sterling Wood Way
Houston, TX 77059-3153, USA

Ochoa, Lorena (Golfer)
c/o Alejandro Ochoa 413 Interamerica Blvd Ste 14 #222
Laredo, TX 78045, USA

Ochoa, Raymond (Actor)
c/o Robin Spitzer *Origin Talent Agency*
4705 Laurel Canyon Blvd Ste 306
Studio City, CA 91607-5940, USA

Ochoa, Ryan (Actor)
c/o Kelly Marie Smith *Brilliant Public Relations*
6260 W 3rd St Apt 425
Los Angeles, CA 90036-7610, USA

Ochocinco, Chad (Athlete, Football Player)
c/o Drew Rosenhaus *Rosenhaus Sports Representation*
6400 Allison Rd
Miami Beach, FL 33141-4540, USA

Ockels, Wubbo (Astronaut)
Postbus 299
Noordwijk, AG 2200, NETHERLANDS

O'Connell, Charlie (Actor)
c/o Staff Member *Artistry Management*
340 N Camden Dr Ste 302
Beverly Hills, CA 90210-5116, USA

O'Connell, Deirdre (Actor)
c/o Martin Berneman *Precision Entertainment*
6338 Wilshire Blvd
Los Angeles, CA 90048-5002, USA

O'Connell, Jerry (Actor)
c/o Michael Rotenberg *3 Arts Entertainment Inc*
9460 Wilshire Blvd Fl 7
Beverly Hills, CA 90212-2713, USA

O'Connell, Maura (Musician)
4222 Lindawood Dr
Nashville, TN 37215-3208, USA

O'Connell, Patricia (Hitchcock)
3835 E Thousand Oaks Blvd # 435
Westlake Village, CA 91362-3637

O'Conner, Tom
1 The Stiles Ormskirk
Lancashire, ENGLAND L39 3QG

O'Connolly, James (Director)
61 Edith Grove
London SW10, UNITED KINGDOM (UK)

O'Connolly, James (Astronaut)
1305 Lafayette Dr
Alexandria, VA 22308-1107, USA

O'Connor, Bill (Athlete, Football Player)
1905-40 Richview Rd
Toronto, ON M9A 5C1, Canada

O'Connor, Brian (Athlete, Baseball Player)
3054 Inwood Dr
Cincinnati, OH 45241-3101, USA

O'Connor, Bryan D (Astronaut)
2615 Gadsby Pl
Alexandria, VA 22311-4929, USA

O'Connor, Derrick (Actor)
c/o Staff Member *Markham & Froggatt*
4 Windmill St
London W1T 1HZ, UK

O'Connor, Des
23 Eyot Gdns
London, ENGLAND W6 9TR

O'Connor, Edmund F (General)
1169 Ironsides Ave
Melbourne, FL 32940-6735, USA

O'Connor, Frances (Actor)
c/o Staff Member *Creative Artists Agency (CAA-LA)*
2000 Avenue of the Stars Ste 100
Los Angeles, CA 90067-4705, USA

O'Connor, Gavin (Director)
9560 Wilshire Blvd Ste 500
Beverly Hills, CA 90212-2401, USA

O'Connor, Glynnis (Actor)
c/o Staff Member *Bauman Redanty & Shaul Agency*
5757 Wilshire Blvd Suite 473
Beverly Hills, CA 90212, USA

O'Connor, J Dennis (Educator)
Provost S Ofc
Washington, DC 20560-0001, USA

O'Connor, Jack (Athlete, Baseball Player)
PO Box 430
Yucca Valley, CA 92286-0430, USA

O'Connor, Mark (Musician)
5749 Lanyan Dr
Woodland Hills, CA 91367, USA

O'Connor, Martin J (Religious Leader)
Palazzo San Carlo
Vatican City 120, VATICAN CITY

O'Connor, Maryanne (Basketball Player)
60 Romanock Pl
Fairfield, CT 06825-7240, USA

O'Connor, Maryanne (Athlete, Basketball Player)
60 Romanock Pl
Fairfield, CT 06825-7240, USA

O'Connor, Michael (Athlete, Baseball Player)
c/o Staff Member *Washington Nationals*
1500 S Capitol St SE
Washington, DC 20003-3599, USA

O'Connor, Patrick (Actor)
c/o Staff Member *Select Artists Ltd (CA-Westside Office)*
1138 12th St Apt 1
Santa Monica, CA 90403-5459, USA

O'Connor, Patrick D (Pat) (Director)
76 Oxford St
London W1N 0AX, UNITED KINGDOM (UK)

O'Connor, Renee (Actor)
c/o Staff Member *Grant Management*
1158 26th St # 414
Santa Monica, CA 90403-4698, USA

O'Connor, Sandra Day (Judge)
PO Box 8795
Williamsburg, VA 23187-8795, USA

O'Connor, Sinead (Musician, Songwriter)
c/o Staff Member *Paradigm (Monterey)*
404 W Franklin St
Monterey, CA 93940-2303, USA

O'Connor, Thom (Artist)
Moss Road
Voorheesville, NY 12186, USA

O'Connor, Tim (Actor)
PO Box 458
Nevada City, CA 95959-0458, USA

O'Connor, Zeke (Athlete, Football Player)
222 Jarvis St
Toronto, ON M5B 2B8, Canada

O'Conor, John (Musician)
165 W 57th St
New York, NY 10019-2201, USA

O'Day, Alan (Musician, Songwriter)
c/o Ken Kaufman *Hollywood RPM Entertainment*
4732 Park Granada Unit 223
Calabasas, CA 91302-1534, USA

O'Day, Aubrey (Musician)
c/o Tammy Brook *FYI Public Relations*
174 5th Ave Ste 400
New York, NY 10010-5935, USA

O'Day, George (Yachtsman)
6 Turtle Ln
Dover, MA 02030-2053, USA

ODB (Musician)
250 W 57th St
New York, NY 10107-0001, USA

Oddsson, David (Prime Minister)
Stjo'maaroshusio
Reykjavik 150, ICELAND

Odegard, Vickie (Golfer)
112 Ashford Dr
Bridgeport, WV 26330-1138, USA

Odelein, Lyle (Athlete, Hockey Player)
12569 Winding Hollow Ln
Frisco, TX 75033-3497, USA

Odelein, Selmar (Athlete, Hockey Player)
Farm
Quill Lake, SK S0A 3E0, Canada

O'Dell, Billy (Athlete, Baseball Player)
225 Odell Rd
Newberry, SC 29108-9250, USA

Odell, Bob H (Athlete, Coach, Football Coach, Football Player)
911 Stenton Pl
Ocean City, NJ 08226-4343, USA

Odell, Deborah (Actor)
c/o Staff Member *Characters Talent Agency, The (Vancouver)*
1505 W 2nd Ave #200
Vancouver, BC V6H 3Y4, Canada

O'Dell, Jennifer (Actor)
c/o Scott Hart *Scott Hart Entertainment*
14622 Ventura Blvd # 746
Sherman Oaks, CA 91403-3600, USA

O'Dell, Nancy (Television Host)
c/o Staff Member *Fifteen Minutes (LA)*
8436 W 3rd St Ste 650
Los Angeles, CA 90048-4131, USA

Odell, Noel E (Mountaineer, Scientist)
5 Dean Court
Cambridge, UNITED KINGDOM (UK)

O'Dell, Stewart (Athlete, Football Player)
3532 State Road 144
Mooresville, IN 46158, USA

O'Dell, Tawni (Writer)
375 Hudson St
New York, NY 10014-3658, USA

O'Dell, Tony
417 N Griffith Park Dr
Burbank, CA 91506-2031

Oden, Derrick (Athlete, Football Player)
1805 S Barkley Dr
Mobile, AL 36606-1151, USA

Oden, Greg
c/o Staff Member *BDA Sports Management (BDA-CA)*
700 Ygnacio Valley Rd Ste 330
Walnut Creek, CA 94596-3838, USA

Oden, Songul (Actor)
c/o Gaye Sokmen *Gaye Sökmen Talent Agency*
Karanfil Caddesi Yolal Sokak Ic Levent No:3
Istanbul 34330, Turkey

Odenkirk, Bob (Actor)
c/o Tim Sarkes *Brillstein Entertainment Partners*
9150 Wilshire Blvd Ste 350
Beverly Hills, CA 90212-3453, USA

Odermatt, Robert A (Architect)
140 Camino Don Miguel
Orinda, CA 94563-1710, USA

Odessa, Devon (Actor)
c/o Staff Member *Vincent Cirrincione Associates*
1516 N Fairfax Ave
Los Angeles, CA 90046-2608, USA

Odjig, Daphne (Artist)
102 Foresbrook Pl
Penticton, BC V2A 7N4, CANADA

Odle, Phil (Athlete, Football Player)
691 W 650 S
Orem, UT 84058-6065, USA

Odom, Cliff (Athlete, Football Player)
6708 Marthas Vineyard Dr
Arlington, TX 76001-5508, USA

Odom, Jason (Athlete, Football Player)
11506 Joshuas Bend Dr
Tampa, FL 33612-5071, USA

Odom, John Lee (Blue Moon) (Athlete, Baseball Player)
10343 Slater Ave Apt 204
Fountain Valley, CA 92708-4783, USA

Odom, Lamar (Athlete, Basketball Player)
c/o Jeff Schwartz *Excel Sports Management*
9665 Wilshire Blvd Ste 500
Beverly Hills, CA 90212-2312, USA

Odom, Steve (Athlete, Football Player)
1482 Lincoln St
Berkeley, CA 94702-1247, USA

Odomes, Nathaniel B (Nate) (Athlete, Football Player)
900 Quail Creek Dr
Columbus, GA 31907-6536, USA

Odoms, Riley M (Athlete, Football Player)
834 1/2 Staffordshire Rd
Stafford, TX 77477, USA

O'Donahue, Pat (Athlete, Football Player)
1524 Wheeler Rd Unit D
Madison, WI 53704-7048, USA

O'Donis, Colby (Musician)
c/o Juliette Harris *It Girl Public Relations*
5301 Beethoven St Ste 220
Los Angeles, CA 90066-7052, USA

O'Donnell, Andrew (Athlete, Basketball Player)
3310 Lincoln Ave
Allentown, PA 18103-7917, USA

O'Donnell, Annie (Actor)
6404 Wilshire Blvd Ste 950
Los Angeles, CA 90048-5529, USA

O'Donnell, Charles (Chuck) (Bowler)
7354 Forest Haven Est
Saint Louis, MO 63123-2101, USA

O'Donnell, Chris (Actor)
c/o Jason Weinberg *Untitled Entertainment (LA)*
350 S Beverly Dr Ste 200
Beverly Hills, CA 90212-4819, USA

O'Donnell, George (Athlete, Baseball Player)
70 Crusaders Rd
Springfield, IL 62704-5207, USA

O'Donnell, James Michael (Baseball Player)
204 N Diamond St
Clifton Heights, PA 19018-1507, USA

O'Donnell, Joe (Athlete, Football Player)
447 Bodley Cres
Milan, MI 48160-1206, USA

O'Donnell, John J (Misc)
1625 Massachusetts Ave NW
Washington, DC 20036-2212, USA

O'Donnell, Keir (Actor)
c/o Tom Parziali *Visionary Entertainment*
1558 N Stanley Ave
Los Angeles, CA 90046-2711, USA

O'Donnell, Lawrence (Producer, Writer)
c/o Ariel (Ari) Emanuel *WmE2 (Endeavor-LA)*
9601 Wilshire Blvd Fl 3
Beverly Hills, CA 90210-5219, USA

O'Donnell, Mark (Writer)
202 Riverside Dr Apt 8E
New York, NY 10025-7280, USA

O'Donnell, Neil K (Athlete, Football Player)
PO Box 403
New Vernon, NJ 07976-0403, USA

O'Donnell, Rosie (Actor, Comedian, Talk Show Host)
c/o Cindi Berger *PMK/BNC Public Relations (PMK-NY)*
622 3rd Ave Fl 8
New York, NY 10017-6707, USA

O'Donnell, William (Bill) (Horse Racer)
569 Penn Est
East Stroudsburg, PA 18301-9062, USA

O'Donoghue, John (Athlete, Baseball Player)
5246 Far Oak Cir
Sarasota, FL 34238-3304, USA

O'Donoghue, John (Athlete, Baseball Player)
10107 Summerfield Dr
Denham Springs, LA 70726-1583, USA

O'Donoghue, Neil (Athlete, Football Player)
1118 Flushing Ave
Clearwater, FL 33764-4906, USA

O'Donohue, Jessica (Actor)
c/o Dan Cotoia *Letnom Management*
1776 Broadway Fl 9
New York, NY 10019-2002, USA

O'Dowd, Anna Mae (Baseball Player)
3000 Carefree Blvd Apt E-15
Fort Myers, FL 33917-7135, USA

O'Dowd, Chris (Actor)
c/o Nick Frenkel *3 Arts Entertainment Inc*
9460 Wilshire Blvd Fl 7
Beverly Hills, CA 90212-2713, USA

O'Driscoll, Martha (Actor)
22 Indian Creek Island Rd
Indian Creek Village, FL 33154-2904, USA

Odrowski, Gerry (Athlete, Hockey Player)
Box 126
Trout Creek, Ontario P0H 2L0, Canada

Oduber, Nelson O (Prime Minister)
Cumana 84
Oranjestad, ARUBA

Oe, Kenzaburo (Nobel Prize Laureate)
585 Seijo-Machi Setagayaku
Tokyo, JAPAN

Oechsle, Jennifer (Stylist)
5934 Vicksburg Ln
Indianapolis, IN 46254-5099, USA

Oedekerk, Steve (Actor, Director, Producer, Writer)
26162 Calle Roberto
San Juan Capo, CA 92675-3014, USA

Oefelein, William A (Astronaut)
1205 Hawkhill Dr
Friendswood, TX 77546-7811, USA

Oelkers, Bryan (Athlete, Baseball Player)
3404 Taylor Ave
Bridgeton, MO 63044-3055, USA

Oenish, Dean (Doctor)
900 Bridgeway # 204
Sausalito, CA 94965-2100, USA

Oester, Ron (Athlete, Baseball Player)
3780 9 Mile Tobasco Rd
Cincinnati, OH 45255-5232, USA

Oetiker, Phil (Cinematographer)
422 10th St
Brooklyn, NY 11215-4009, USA

Oettinger, Anthony G (Mathematician)
65 Elizabeth Rd
Belmont, NY 11215, USA

Of Monaco, Prince Albert II (Royalty)
Palouis De Monaco Boite Postal 518
Monte Carlo 98015, Monaco

Of Monaco, Princess Stephanie (Royalty)
Palais Grimaldi 2 Boulevard De Moulins
Monte Carlo 98015, Monaco

of Wales, Prince Charles (Prince, Royalty)
St. James' Palace
London SW1, UK

O'Farrill, Orlando (Baseball Player)
Villa Rafaela Herrera Casa A-30
Managua, NICARAGUA

Offerdahl, John A (Athlete, Football Player)
2749 NE 37th Dr
Fort Lauderdale, FL 33308-6326, USA

Offerman, Jose (Athlete, Baseball Player)
10720 Moorpark St
North Hollywood, CA 91602-2723, USA

Office, Rowland (Athlete, Baseball Player)
1028 Lake Glen Way
Sacramento, CA 95822-3224, USA

Offishall, Kardinal (Musician)
c/o Staff Member *MCA Records (LA)*
2220 Colorado Ave
Santa Monica, CA 90404-3506, 310-865-4500

Offspring (Music Group)
c/o Staff Member *Epitaph Records*
2798 W Sunset Blvd
Los Angeles, CA 90026-2102, USA

Ogato, Sadako (Government Official)
CP 2500
Geneva 2 1211, SWITZERLAND

Ogden, Bud (Athlete, Basketball Player)
3324 S 4th St
Springfield, IL 62703-4619, USA

Ogden, Joanne (Baseball Player)
200 1/2 W Cypress St
Glendale, CA 91204-2660, USA

Ogden, Jonathan (Jon) (Athlete, Football Player)
9 Jenner Ct
Owings Mills, MD 21117-1260, USA

Ogden, Margaret (Writer)
4621 N 28th St
Tacoma, WA 98407-4617, USA

Ogden, Ray (Athlete, Football Player)
188 Anderson Dr
Brunswick, GA 31520-1610, USA

Ogea, Chad (Athlete, Baseball Player)
3233 Plantation Ct
Baton Rouge, LA 70820-5753, USA

Ogi, Adolf (President)
Bundesiause-Nord Kochergasse 10
Berne 3003, SWITZERLAND

Ogier, Bulle (Actor)
20 Ave Rapp
Paris 75007, FRANCE

Ogier, Maurice (Baseball Player)
6118 N Fawnlake Dr
Katy, TX 77493-8035, USA

Ogier, Vivian (Stylist)
c/o Staff Member *Talent Plus*
1222 Lucas Ave Ste 300
Saint Louis, MO 63103-1937, USA

Ogilvie, Kelvin K (Educator)
Po Box 307
Canning, NS B0P 1X0, CANADA

Ogilvie, Lana (Model)
17 Little West 12th St Ste 333
New York, NY 10014-1315, USA

Ogilvy, Geoff (Golfer)
c/o Staff Member *Pro Golfers Association (PGA) Tour*
112 Tpc Blvd
Ponte Vedra Beach, FL 32082, USA

Ogilvy, Ian (Actor)
46 Albermarle St
London W1X 4PP, UNITED KINGDOM (UK)

Ogle, Brett (Golfer)
1751 Pinnacle Dr Ste 1500
Mc Lean, VA 22102-3833, USA

Oglesby, Randy (Actor)

Oglive, Benjamin A (Ben) (Athlete, Baseball Player)
1012 E Sandpiper Dr
Tempe, AZ 85283-2021, USA

O'Grady, Gail (Actor)
c/o Alan Iezman *Shelter Entertainment*
9454 Wilshire Blvd Ste 715
Beverly Hills, CA 90212-2925, USA

O'Grady, Scott
3519 Wallingford Ave N Apt 2
Seattle, WA 98103-9057, USA

O'Grady, Sean (Boxer)
PO Box 9
Bay City, MI 48707-0009, USA

Ogrin, David (Athlete, Golfer)
1927 Club Xing
New Braunfels, TX 78130-2453, USA

Ogrodnick, John (Athlete, Hockey Player)
37034 Aldgate Ct
Farmington Hills, MI 48335-5402, USA

Ogunleye, Adewale (Athlete, Football Player)
19113 NW 23rd Ct
Pembroke Pines, FL 33029-5336, USA

Oh, Sadaharu (Baseball Player)
6F 2-2-2 Jigyohama
Chuo-Ku Fukouka 810, JAPAN

Oh, Sandra (Actor)
c/o Marsha McManus *Principal Entertainment (LA)*
1964 Westwood Blvd Ste 400
Los Angeles, CA 90025-4695, USA

Oh, Soon-Teck (Actor)
5091 N Fresno St Ste 130
Fresno, CA 93710-7617, USA

O?Hagan, Andrew (Editor, Writer)
c/o Staff Member *UNICEF*
Africa House 64-78 Kingsway
London WC2B 6NB, UNITED KINGDOM

O'Hair, Sean (Athlete, Golfer)
c/o Staff Member *Pro Golfers Association (PGA) Tour*
112 Tpc Blvd
Ponte Vedra Beach, FL 32082, USA

O'Halloran, Greg (Athlete, Baseball Player)
1021 Hedge Dr
Mississauga, ON L4Y 1G3, Canada

O'Hanlon, Bill (Writer)
c/o Staff Member *Loretta Barrett Books, Inc.*
220 E 23rd St Fl 11
New York, NY 10010-4693, USA

O'Hanlon, Francis (Athlete, Basketball Player)
27 W Wayne Ave
Easton PA, 18042 USA

O'Hara, Catherine (Actor, Comedian)
c/o Marc Gurvitz *Brillstein Entertainment Partners*
9150 Wilshire Blvd Ste 350
Beverly Hills, CA 90212-3453, USA

O'Hara, David (Actor)
c/o Tammy Rosen *Sanders Armstrong Caserta*
425 N Robertson Blvd
West Hollywood, CA 90048-1735, USA

O'Hara, Jamie
1025 16th Ave S Ste 200
Nashville, TN 37212-2343

O'Hara, Jenny (Actor)
8663 Wonderland Ave
Los Angeles, CA 90046-1452, USA

O'Hara, Kelli (Actor)
c/o Erica Tuchman *One Entertainment (NY)*
12 W 57th St PH 1
New York, NY 10019-3900, USA

O'Hara, Maureen (Actor)
P.O. Box 808
Bantry, Couty Cork, Ireland

O'Hara, Terrence J (Director)
1888 Century Park E Ste 1800
Los Angeles, CA 90067-1722, USA

O'Hare, Denis (Actor)
c/o Staff Member *Innovative Artists (LA)*
1505 10th St
Santa Monica, CA 90401-2805, USA

Oher, Michael (Athlete, Football Player)
c/o Jimmy Sexton *SportsTrust Advisors - TN*
1100 Ridgeway Loop Rd Fl 5
Memphis, TN 38120-4053, USA

Ohl, Don (Athlete, Basketball Player)
2 E Lockhaven Ct
Edwardsville, IL 62025-3703, USA

Ohlendorf, Ross (Athlete, Baseball Player)
2300 Barton Creek Blvd Apt 40
Austin, TX 78735-1687, USA

Ohlsson, Garrick (Musician)
8942 Wilshire Blvd # 219
Beverly Hills, CA 90211-1908, USA

Ohlund, Mattias (Athlete, Hockey Player)
800 Griffiths Way
Vancouver, BC V6B 6G1, Canada

Ohman, Jack (Cartoonist, Editor)
1320 SW Broadway
Portland, OR 97201-3411, USA

Ohman, Will (Athlete, Baseball Player)
4346 N Desert Oasis Cir
Mesa, AZ 85207-7246, USA

Ohme, Kevin (Athlete, Baseball Player)
806 Starlifter Ln
Valrico, FL 33594-2978, USA

Ohno, Apolo Anton (Athlete, Olympic Athlete, Speed Skater)
c/o Lee Kernis *Brillstein Entertainment Partners*
9150 Wilshire Blvd Ste 350
Beverly Hills, CA 90212-3453, USA

Ohoven, Ute-Henriette (Misc)
c/o Staff Member *United Nations Educational, Scientific and Cultural Organization (UNESCO)*
7, place de Fontenoy 75352
Paris 07 SP, France

Ohtani, Monshu Roshin (Religious Leader)
Horikawa-Dori Hanayachosagaru
Shimogyoku
Kyoto 600, JAPAN

O'Hurley, John (Actor)
c/o Marv Dauer *Marv Dauer Management*
11661 San Vicente Blvd Ste 104
Los Angeles, CA 90049-5150, USA

Ohyama, Heilchiro (Conductor)
6305 Via Cabrera
La Jolla, CA 92037-5836, USA

Oimeon, Casper (Skier)
540 S Mountain Ave
Ashland, OR 97520-3242, USA

Oistrakh, Igor D (Musician)
Novolesnaya Str 3 Korp 2 #10
Moscow, RUSSIA

Oiter, Bailey (President)
Palikia Pohnepei FM
Kolonia 96941, MICRONESIA

Oja, Kim (Actor)
c/o Staff Member *Gage Group, The (LA)*
14724 Ventura Blvd Ste 505
Sherman Oaks, CA 91403-3505, USA

Ojala, Kirt (Athlete, Baseball Player)
1902 Forest Lake Dr SE
Grand Rapids, MI 49546-8234, USA

Ojczyk, Cindy (Stylist)
2220 Deer Pass Trl
Saint Paul, MN 55110-1049, USA

Ojeda, Augle (Athlete, Baseball Player)
9402 Dorothy Ave
South Gate, CA 90280-5106, USA

Ojeda, Bob (Athlete, Baseball Player)
20 Somerset Dr
Rumson, NJ 07760-1101, USA

Ojeda, Miguel (Baseball Player)
c/o Staff Member *San Diego Padres*
100 Park Blvd
San Diego, CA 92101-7405, USA

Ojukwu, Chukwuerneka O (General, President)
29 Queen's Dr Ikoyi
Lagos State, NIGERIA

Oka, Masi (Actor, Writer)
c/o Ilan Breil *Mosaic Media Group*
9200 W Sunset Blvd Ste 10
Los Angeles, CA 90069-3608, USA

Oka, Takeshi (Misc)
1463 E Park Pl
Chicago, IL 60637-1835, USA

Okabe, Noroki (Architect, Engineer)
1 Banchi Senshu-Kuko Kita Izumisanoshi
Osake 549, JAPAN

Okafor, Emeka (Athlete, Basketball Player)
c/o Jeff Schwartz *Excel Sports Management*
9665 Wilshire Blvd Ste 500
Beverly Hills, CA 90212-2312, USA

Okamoto, Ayako (Golfer)
22627 Ladeene Ave
Torrance, CA 90505-3438, USA

Okamura, Arthur (Artist)
210 Kale Rd
Bolinas, CA 94924, USA

O'Keefe, Jeremiah J Sr (War Hero)
PO Box 430
Ocean Springs, MS 39566-0430, USA

O'Keefe, Jodie Lyn (Actor)
c/o Vincent Cirrincione *Vincent Cirrincione Associates*
1516 N Fairfax Ave
Los Angeles, CA 90046-2608, USA

O'Keefe, Michael (Actor)
c/o Staff Member *Paradigm (LA)*
360 N Crescent Dr
Beverly Hills, CA 90210-4874, USA

O'Keefe, Miles (Actor)
c/o Alexandra Karrys *Divine Management*
117 N Orlando Ave
Los Angeles, CA 90048-3403, USA

O'Keefe, Paul
225 W 83rd St # 9-5
New York, NY 10024-4952

O'Keefe, Richard (Athlete, Basketball Player)
31 Corte Ortega Apt 7
Greenbrae, CA 94904-1992, USA

O'Keefe, Sean (Government Official)
300 E St SW
Washington, DC 20024-3210, USA

O'Keefe, Tommy (Athlete, Basketball Player)
1000 Potomac Ln
Alexandria, VA 22308-2638, USA

Okera (Stylist)
c/o Staff Member *Dossier*
556 S Fair Oaks Ave # 431
Pasadena, CA 91105-2656, USA

Okhotnikoff, Nikolai P (Opera Singer)
Canal Griboedova 109 #13
Saint Petersburg 190068, RUSSIA

Okobi, Chukky (Athlete, Football Player)
5516 Maple Heights Ct
Pittsburgh, PA 15232-2326, USA

Okogie, Anthony Olubunmi Cardinal (Religious Leader)
PO Box 8 19 Catholic Mission St
Lagos, NIGERIA

Okolowicz, Jeff (Musician)
PO Box 12956
Rochester, NY 14612-0956, USA

Okolowicz, Ted (Musician)
PO Box 12956
Rochester, NY 14612-0956, USA

Okonedo, Sophie (Actor)
c/o Pippa Markham *Markham & Froggatt*
4 Windmill St
London W1T 1HZ, UK

Okoniewski, Steve (Athlete, Football Player)
222 S Oakland Ave
Oconto Falls, WI 54154-1617, USA

O'Koren, Mike (Athlete, Basketball Player)
12 Danbury Ct
Township Of Washington,
NJ 07676-4350, USA

Okoye, Amobi (Athlete, Football Player)
2431 Sara Ridge Ln
Katy, TX 77450-5377, USA

Okoye, Christian E (Athlete, Football Player)
10082 Big Pine Dr
Alta Loma, CA 91737-4247, USA

Okrie, Len (Athlete, Baseball Player)
2636 Burke Ln
Fayetteville, NC 28306-2629, USA

Okubo, Susumu (Physicist)
1209 East Ave
Rochester, NY 14607-2336, USA

Okuda, Hiroshi (Business Person)
1 Toyotacho Toyota City
Aichi Prefecture 471, JAPAN

Okumura, Tomohiro (Musician)
2717 Nichols Ln
Davenport, IA 52803-3620, USA

Okun, Daniel A (Engineer)
750 Weaver Dairy Rd
Chapel Hill, NC 27514-1438, USA

O'Lachlan, Alex (Actor)
c/o Staff Member *June Cann Management*
73 Jersey Rd
Woollahra 2025, AUSTRALIA

Olah, George A (Nobel Prize Laureate)
2252 Gloaming Way
Beverly Hills, CA 90210-1717, USA

Olajuwon, Hakeem (Athlete, Basketball Player)
9010 Sandringham Dr
Houston, TX 77024-5823, USA

Olander, Ed (War Hero)
85 N Maple St
Florence, MA 01062-1324, USA

Olander, Jim (Athlete, Baseball Player)
8421 S Triangle R Ranch Pl
Vail, AZ 85641-8719, USA

Olander, Jimmy (Musician)
2908 Poston Ave
Nashville, TN 37203-1312, USA

Olandt, Ken (Actor)
3500 W Olive Ave Ste 1400
Burbank, CA 91505-5512, USA

Olay, Ruth (Musician)
3100 Neilson Way Apt 216
Santa Monica, CA 90405-5329, USA

Olazabel, Jose Maria (Golfer)
Apartado 26
San Sebastian E-20080, SPAIN

Olberding, Mark (Athlete, Basketball Player)
100 N Santa Rosa St Apt 809
San Antonio, TX 78207-3261, USA

Olberman, Bob (Athlete, Football Player)
4486 Dobbs Xing
Marietta, GA 30068-2714, USA

Olbermann, Keith (Sportscaster, Television Host)
c/o Michael Price *Price Management*
Prefers to be contacted by telephone
Los Angeles, CA 90069, USA

Olczyk, Ed (Athlete, Coach, Hockey Player)
66 Mario Lemieux Pl
Pittsburgh, PA 15219-3504, USA

Old, Lloyd J (Biologist)
1345 Avenue of the Americas
New York, NY 10105-0302, USA

Old Crow Medicine Show (Music Group)
c/o Staff Member *Paradigm (Monterey)*
404 W Franklin St
Monterey, CA 93940-2303, USA

Olde, Jeff (Director, Producer)
c/o Staff Member *VH1 Television*
1515 Broadway
New York, NY 10036-8901, USA

Oldenburg, Claes T (Artist)
556 Broome St
New York, NY 10013-1517, USA

Oldenburg, Richard E (Director)
447 E 57th St
New York, NY 10022-3064, USA

Oldendorf, William (Doctor)
Medical Center Neurology Dept
Los Angeles, CA 90024, USA

Older, Charles (Chuck) (War Hero)
930 Thayer Ave
Los Angeles, CA 90024-3314, USA

Olderman, Murray (Writer)
832 Inverness Dr
Rancho Mirage, CA 92270-1451, USA

Oldershaw, Kelsey (Actor)
c/o Darren Goldberg *Global Creative*
1051 Cole Ave # B
Los Angeles, CA 90038-2601, USA

Oldfield, Bruce (Designer, Fashion Designer)
27 Beauchamp Place
London SW3, UNITED KINGDOM(UK)

Oldfield, Mike (Actor, Composer, Director)
c/o Staff Member *Air-Edel (UK)*
18 Rodmarton Street
London W1H 3F, United Kingdom

Oldfield, Sally (Musician)
Willy-Brandt-Str 39
Erftstadt 50374, GERMANY

Oldham, D Ray (Athlete, Football Player)
1096 Harbor Landing Dr
Soddy Daisy, TN 37379-5755, USA

Oldham, John (Athlete, Basketball Player, Coach)
2127 Sycamore Dr
Bowling Green, KY 42104-3868, USA

Oldham, John (Athlete, Baseball Player)
1845 Anne Way
San Jose, CA 95124-6137, USA

Oldham, Tasha (Director)
c/o Jerry Shandrew *Shandrew Public Relations*
1050 S Stanley Ave
Los Angeles, CA 90019-6634, USA

Oldham, Todd (Designer, Fashion Designer)
c/o Staff Member *Creative Artists Agency (CAA-LA)*
2000 Avenue of the Stars Ste 100
Los Angeles, CA 90067-4705, USA

Oldis, Bob (Athlete, Baseball Player)
306 Virginia Dr
Iowa City, IA 52245-1639, USA

Oldman, Gary (Actor, Director, Producer)
c/o Douglas Urbanski *Douglas Management Group*
9713 Little Santa Monica Blvd
Beverly Hills, CA 90210, USA

Olds, Bill (Athlete, Football Player)
7414 Pohick Rd
Lorton, VA 22079-1518, USA

Olds, Gabriel
PO Box 120551
Nashville, TN 37212-0551

Olds, Robin (Athlete, Football Player, War Hero)
P.O. Box 1478
Steamboat Springs, CO 80477, USA

Olds, Sharon (Writer)
58 W 10th St Attn Englishdept
New York, NY 10011-8702, USA

Olds, Walter (Wally) (Athlete, Hockey Player)
37296 Pincherry Rd
Cohasset, MN 55721-2069, USA

O'Leary, Brian T (Astronaut)
1993 S Kihei Rd # 21200
Kihei, HI 96753-7834, USA

Oleary, Dan (Athlete, Football Player)
3088 Joslyn Rd
Cleveland, OH 44111-1555, USA

O'Leary, George (Coach, Football Coach)
Athletic Dept
Orlando, FL 32918, USA

O'Leary, Hazel R (Secretary)
1000 Independence Ave SW
Washington, DC 20585-0001, USA

O'Leary, John (Actor)
14724 Ventura Blvd Ste 505
Sherman Oaks, CA 91403-3505, USA

O'Leary, Marrissa (Actor)
c/o Staff Member *Select Artists Ltd (CA-Valley Office)*
PO Box 4359
Burbank, CA 91503-4359, USA

O'Leary, Matthew (Actor)
c/o Brian Swardstrom *WmE2 (Endeavor-LA)*
9601 Wilshire Blvd Fl 3
Beverly Hills, CA 90210-5219, USA

O'Leary, Michael (Actor)
38 Prospect Ave
Montclair, NJ 07042-1915, USA

O'Leary, Troy (Athlete, Baseball Player)
1060 W Norwood St
Rialto, CA 92377-8220, USA

O'Leary, William (Actor)
c/o Staff Member *Coast to Coast Talent Group*
3350 Barham Blvd
Los Angeles, CA 90068-1404, USA

Oleg, Deripaska (Business Person)
30 Rochdelskaya St
Moscow 123022, Russia

Olejnik, Craig (Actor)
c/o Robert Stein *Robert Stein Management*
PO Box 3797
Beverly Hills, CA 90212-0797, USA

Oleksy, Jozef (Prime Minister)
Ul Wiktorii Wiedenskiej 5 M 4
Warsaw 02-954, POLAND

Olerich, Dave (Athlete, Football Player)
2138 Wellesley St
Palo Alto, CA 94306-1335, USA

Olerud, John (Athlete, Baseball Player)
PO Box 606
Medina, WA 98039-0606, USA

Olesz, Rostislav (Athlete, Hockey Player)
1 Panther Pkwy
Sunrise, FL 33323-5315, USA

Olevsky, Julian (Musician)
68 Blue Hills Rd
Amherst, MA 01002-2220, USA

Oleynick, Frank (Athlete, Basketball Player)
1164 Brooklawn Ave
Bridgeport, CT 06604-1206, USA

Oleynik, Larisa (Actor)
c/o Staff Member *Savage Agency*
6212 Banner Ave
Los Angeles, CA 90038-2802, USA

Oliceira, Ana Cristina (Actor)
c/o Clifford Gilbert-Lurie *Ziffren Brittenham LLP*
1801 Century Park W Fl 7
Los Angeles, CA 90067-6406, USA

Olin, Ken (Actor)
c/o Staff Member *Creative Artists Agency (CAA-LA)*
2000 Avenue of the Stars Ste 100
Los Angeles, CA 90067-4705, USA

Olin, Lena (Actor)
c/o Chris Schmidt *Paradigm (LA)*
360 N Crescent Dr
Beverly Hills, CA 90210-4874, USA

Olin, Lina (Actor)
c/o Staff Member *Industry Entertainment Partners*
955 Carrillo Dr Ste 300
Los Angeles, CA 90048-5400, USA

Olinger, Marilyn (Baseball Player)
6451 Far Hills Ave
Dayton, OH 45459-2725, USA

Olinski, Harry (Athlete, Football Player)
3205 Furman Blvd
Louisville, KY 40220-1949, USA

Oliphant, Patrick B (Cartoonist)
4520 Main St
Kansas City, MO 64111-1876, USA

Oliphant, Randall (Business Person)
200 Bay St
Toronto, ON M5J 2J3, CANADA

Olitski, Jules (Artist)
PO Box 440
Marlboro, VT 05344-0440, USA

Oliu, Ingrid (Actor)
c/o Staff Member *Cunningham Escott Slevin & Doherty (CESD-LA)*
10635 Santa Monica Blvd Ste 130
Los Angeles, CA 90025-8306, USA

Oliva, L Jay (Educator)
President's Office
New York, NY 10012, USA

Oliva, Sergio (Misc)
7383 N Rogers Ave
Chicago, IL 60626-1524, USA

Oliva, Tony (Athlete, Baseball Player)
212 Spring Valley Dr
Minneapolis, MN 55420-5540, USA

Olivares, Ed (Athlete, Baseball Player)
HC 2 Box 12887
San German, PR 683, USA

Olivares, Omar (Athlete, Baseball Player)
PO Box 1328
San German, PR 00683-1328, USA

Olivares, Ruben (Boxer)
PO Box 113
Montebello, CA 90640-0113, USA

Olivas, John D (Astronaut)
595 36th St
Manhattan Beach, CA 90266-3409, USA

Olive, Jason (Actor, Model)
c/o Staff Member *Kazarian Spencer Ruskin & Assoc.*
11969 Ventura Blvd Ste 300
Studio City, CA 91604-2619, USA

Olive, John (Athlete, Basketball Player)
8652 Harjoan Ave
San Diego, CA 92123-3445, USA

Oliveira, Elmar (Musician)
3436 Springhill Rd
Lafayette, CA 94549-2535, USA

Oliveira, Nathan J (Artist)
785 Santa Maria Ave
Palo Alto, CA 94305-8439, USA

Oliveira, Ray (Stylist)
c/o Staff Member *Jump Management Inc*
455 W 23rd St Apt 1D
New York, NY 10011-2156, USA

Oliver, Albert (Al) (Athlete, Baseball Player)
PO Box 1466
Portsmouth, OH 45662-1466, USA

Oliver, Bilal (Musician)
c/o Staff Member *Creative Artists Agency (CAA-LA)*
2000 Avenue of the Stars Ste 100
Los Angeles, CA 90067-4705, USA

Oliver, Bob (Athlete, Baseball Player)
1716 G St
Rio Linda, CA 95673-4534, USA

Oliver, Christian (Actor)
7211 Mulholland Dr
Los Angeles, CA 90068-2031, USA

Oliver, Clancy (Athlete, Football Player)
233 Springview
Irvine, CA 92620-1970, USA

Oliver, Covey T (Attorney, Attorney General, Diplomat, General)
Ingleton-on-Miles RR 1 Box 194
Easton, MD 21601, USA

Oliver, Daniel (Government Official)
214 Massachusetts Ave NE
Washington, DC 20002-4958, USA

Oliver, Darren (Athlete, Baseball Player)
1804 Larkspur Ct
Southlake, TX 76092-3572, USA

Oliver, Dave (Athlete, Baseball Player)
1709 Timberlake Cir
Lodi, CA 95242-4283, USA

Oliver, Dean (Race Car Driver)
21386 Notus Rd
Greenleaf, ID 83626-8940, USA

Oliver, Hubie (Athlete, Football Player)
136 Blake St
Elyria, OH 44035-5422, USA

Oliver, Jamie (Chef, Television Host)
911 3rd Ave
Huntington, WV 25701-1404, USA

Oliver, Joe (Athlete, Baseball Player)
4137 Bounce Dr
Orlando, FL 32812-8147, USA

Oliver, Louis (Athlete, Football Player)
5082 SW 167th Ave
Miramar, FL 33027-4910, USA

Oliver, Mary (Writer)
PO Box 1071
Sweet Briar, VA 24595-1071, USA

Oliver, Murray C (Athlete, Hockey Player)
5505 McGuire Rd
Minneapolis, MN 55439-1342, USA

Oliver, Nate (Athlete, Baseball Player)
4403 Oak Hill Rd
Oakland, CA 94605-4632, USA

Oliver, Pam (Sportscaster)
205 E 67th St
New York, NY 10065-6050, USA

Oliver, Ron (Director, Writer)
c/o Mark Itkin *WmE2 (Endeavor-LA)*
9601 Wilshire Blvd Fl 3
Beverly Hills, CA 90210-5219, USA

Oliver, Winslow (Athlete, Football Player)
2027 Summerall Ct
Richmond, TX 77406-6737, USA

Oliveres, Rubin
PO Box 113
Montebello, CA 90640-0113

Olivia (Musician)
c/o Staff Member *Interscope Records (LA) - Main*
2220 Colorado Ave
Santa Monica, CA 90404-3506, USA

Olivieri, Dawn (Actor)
c/o Joel Stevens *Joel Stevens Entertainment*
5627 Allott Ave
Van Nuys, CA 91401-4502, USA

Olivo, America (Actor)
PO Box 54228
Cincinnati, OH 45254-0228, USA

Olivo, Joey (Boxer)
9628 Poinciana St
Pico Rivera, CA 90660-4242, USA

Olivo, Karen (Actor)
c/o Brian Liebman *Liebman Entertainment*
25 E 21st St PH
New York, NY 10010-6226, USA

Olivo, Miguel (Athlete, Baseball Player)
10004 Plaza De Oro Dr
Oakdale, CA 95361-9235, USA

Olivor, Jane (Music Group, Musician)
32 Saint Edward Rd
Boston, MA 02128-1263, USA

Olkewicz, Neal (Athlete, Football Player)
5706 English Ct
Bethesda, MD 20817-6258, USA

Olkewicz, Walter (Actor)
3500 W Olive Ave Ste 1400
Burbank, CA 91505-5512, USA

Ollie, Kevin (Athlete, Basketball Player)
210 Thompson St
South Glastonbury, CT 06073-2915, USA

Ollom, Jim (Athlete, Baseball Player)
10916 27th Ave SE
Everett, WA 98208-7807, USA

Olman, Monica (Stylist)
6400 NE 4th Ct
Miami, FL 33138-6110, USA

Olmedo, Alex (Tennis Player)
5067 Woodley Ave
Encino, CA 91436-1472, USA

Olmo, Luis (Athlete, Baseball Player)
620 Calle Jose Ramon Figueroa
San Juan, PR 00907-3928, USA

Olmos, Edward James (Actor)
c/o Staff Member *Olmos Productions Inc*
500 S Buena Vista St Old Animation Mail Code Bldg 3A-6 PMB 1803
Burbank, CA 91521, USA

Olmstead, Matt (Producer)
c/o Staff Member *International Creative Management (ICM-LA)*
10250 Constellation Blvd Fl 7
Los Angeles, CA 90067-6207, USA

Olmsted, Al
1008 Pinecone Trl
Florissant, MO 63031-7436, USA

Olmsted, Al (Athlete, Baseball Player)
1008 Pinecone Trl
Florissant, MO 63031-7436, USA

Olney, Claude W (Educator)
PO Box 686
Scottsdale, AZ 85252-0686, USA

O'Loughlin, Alex (Actor, Producer, Writer)
c/o Sarah Caroline Linsten *Linsten Morris Management*
3 Gladstone St Suite 301
Newtown, New South Wales 2042, Australia

O'Loughlin, Gerald
PO Box 340832
Arleta, CA 91334-0832

O'Loughlin, Gerald S (Actor)
23388 Mulholland Dr # 204
Woodland Hills, CA 91364-2733, USA

Olowaonkandi, Michael (Basketball Player)
c/o Staff Member *Los Angeles Clippers*
1111 S Figueroa St
Los Angeles, CA 90015-1300, USA

Olowokandi, Michael (Basketball Player)
Target Center 600 1st Ave N
Minneapolis, MN 55403, USA

Olsavsky, Bill (Athlete, Football Player)
132 Walnut Ave
Saint Clairsville, OH 43950-1702, USA

Olsavsky, Jerry (Athlete, Football Player)
115 Yorkshire Dr
Pittsburgh, PA 15208-2640, USA

Olsen, Andrew (Baseball Player)
451 93rd Ave N
Saint Petersburg, FL 33702-3147, USA

Olsen, Andy (Athlete, Baseball Player)
451 93rd Ave N
Saint Petersburg, FL 33702-3147, USA

Olsen, Ashley (Actor)
c/o Nicole Caruso *Wolf Kasteler Van Iden & Associates (NY)*
584 Broadway Rm 310
New York, NY 10012-5246, USA

Olsen, Bud (Athlete, Basketball Player)
1602 Gardiner Ln Apt 130
Louisville, KY 40205-2761, USA

Olsen, Eric Christian (Actor)
c/o Ellen Meyer *Ellen Meyer Management*
8899 Beverly Blvd Ste 612
West Hollywood, CA 90048-2429, USA

Olsen, Gregory (Astronaut, Business Person)
3490 US Highway 1 Ste 12
Princeton, NJ 08540-5920, USA

Olsen, Kenneth H (Inventor)
111 Powder Mill Rd
Maynard, MA 01754-1482, USA

Olsen, Kevin (Ballerina)
3353 Dales Dr
Norco, CA 92860-2281, USA

Olsen, Kevin (Athlete, Baseball Player)
3353 Dales Dr
Norco, CA 92860-2281, USA

Olsen, Mary-Kate (Actor)
c/o Steven Kavovit *Thruline Entertainment*
9250 Wilshire Blvd Ground Fl
Beverly Hills, CA 90212, USA

Olsen, Olaf (Archaeologist)
Strevelsiovedvej 2 Alro
Oder 8300, DENMARK

Olsen, Paul E (Misc)
Lamont-Doherty Geological Laboratory
New York, NY 10027, USA

Olsen, Phil (Athlete, Football Player)
112 Hitching Post Rd
Bozeman, MT 59715-8027, USA

Olsen, Robert C Jr (Admiral, Educator)
Superintendent's Office US Coast Guard Academy
New London, CT 6320, USA

Olsen, Scott (Athlete, Baseball Player)
2991 NE 185th St Apt 1701
Aventura, FL 33180-2904, USA

Olsen, Stanford (Musician, Opera Singer)
c/o Staff Member *Columbia Artists Mgmt Inc*
1790 Broadway Fl 6
New York, NY 10019-1537, USA

Olshwanger, Ron (Journalist, Photographer)
1447 Meadowside Dr
Saint Louis, MO 63146-4914, USA

Olson, Allen I (Ex-Governor)
1250 23rd St NW Ste 100
Washington, DC 20037-1100, USA

Olson, Benji (Athlete, Football Player)
2211 Old Natchez Trce
Franklin, TN 37069-1904, USA

Olson, Bree (Adult Film Star)
PO Box 10471
Fort Wayne, IN 46852-0471, USA

Olson, Candice (Designer)
2760 Mornington Dr NW
Atlanta, GA 30327-1216, USA

Olson, Greg (Athlete, Baseball Player)
18592 Saint Mellion Pl
Eden Prairie, MN 55347-3487, USA

Olson, Gregg (Athlete, Baseball Player)
1996 Port Nelson Pl
Newport Beach, CA 92660-6618, USA

Olson, Harold (Athlete, Football Player)
1622 Holly Springs Rd NE
Marietta, GA 30062-2829, USA

Olson, James (Actor)
250 W 57th St Ste 803
New York, NY 10107-0800, USA

Olson, Kaitlin (Actor)
c/o Amy Slomovits *Flutie Entertainment (LA)*
9320 Wilshire Blvd Ste 202
Beverly Hills, CA 90212-3217, USA

Olson, Karl (Athlete, Baseball Player)
1417 Pin Oak Dr
Gardnerville, NV 89410-7388, USA

Olson, Mancur (Economist)
4316 Clagett Pine Way
University Park, MD 20782-1141, USA

Olson, Mark (Musician, Songwriter, Writer)
1222 16th Ave S # 300
Nashville, TN 37212-2926, USA

Olson, Mark (Economist, Government Official)
20th St & Constitution Ave
Washington, DC 20551-0001, USA

Olson, Nancy (Actor)
945 N Alpine Dr
Beverly Hills, CA 90210-2946, USA

Olson, Peter (Congressman, Politician)
312 Cannon Hob
Washington, DC 20515-3207, USA

Olson, R Lute (Athlete, Basketball Player, Coach)
5831 E Finisterra
Tucson, AZ 85750-1008, USA

Olson, Richard E (Business Person)
1 Champion Plz
Stamford, CT 06921-0001, USA

Olson, Tim (Athlete, Baseball Player)
601 Moss Cliff Cir
McKinney, TX 75071-7629, USA

Olson, Weldon (Athlete, Hockey Player)
2623 Goldenrod Ln
Findlay, OH 45840-1025, USA

Olssen, Lance (Athlete, Football Player)
5222 E Timberwood Dr
Newburgh, IN 47630-3014, USA

Olsson, Ann (Ann-Margret) (Actor, Dancer, Musician)
c/o Alan Margulies *AM Productions & Management*
8899 Beverly Blvd Ste 713
Los Angeles, CA 90048-2450, USA

Olstead, Renee (Musician)
c/o Beverly Strong *Strong Management*
9350 Wilshire Blvd Ste 224
Beverly Hills, CA 90212-3204, USA

Olszewski, Jan F (Prime Minister)
Biuro Poselskie Al Ujazdowskie 13
Warsaw 00-567, POLAND

Olwine, Ed (Athlete, Baseball Player)
3419 Jacona Pl
The Villages, FL 32162 6681, USA

Olympia (Music Group, Musician)
c/o Staff Member *Equal Vision Records*
PO Box 38202
Albany, NY 12203-8202, USA

Olyphant, Timothy (Actor)
c/o Colton Gramm *Brillstein Entertainment Partners*
9150 Wilshire Blvd Ste 350
Beverly Hills, CA 90212-3453, USA

Omakuchi, Narasimhann (Actor)
24 Vasudevapuram Besant Rd
Chennai, TN 600 005, INDIA

O'Malley, Jim (Athlete, Football Player)
238 S Berryline Cir
Spring, TX 77381-4824, USA

O'Malley, Joe (Athlete, Football Player)
656 Sugar Creek Trl SE
Conyers, GA 30094-3808, USA

O'Malley, Martin (Governor)
100 State Cir
Annapolis, MD 21401-1924, USA

O'Malley, Mike (Actor, Director, Writer)
c/o Peter Principato *Principato/Young Management*
9465 Wilshire Blvd Ste 430
Beverly Hills, CA 90212-2613, USA

O'Malley, Peter (Baseball Player)
326 S Hudson Ave
Los Angeles, CA 90020-4804, USA

O'Malley, Robert E (War Hero)
PO Box 775
Goldthwaite, TX 76844-0775, USA

O'Malley, Sean Patrick (Religious Leader)
2121 Commonwealth Ave
Brighton, MA 02135-3101, USA

O'Malley, Susan (Misc)
MCI Centre 601 F St NW
Washington, DC 20004, USA

O'Malley, Thomas D (Business Person)
1700 E Putnam Ave # 500
Old Greenwich, CT 06870-1366, USA

O'Malley, Tom (Athlete, Baseball Player)
10 Carriage Sq
Montoursville, PA 17754, USA

Oman, Qaboos Bin Said Sultan of
The Palace
Muscat, OMAN

Omar, Chamassi Said (Prime Minister)
BP 421
Moroni, COMOROS

Omar & The Howlers
PO Box 93
Austin, TX 78767-0093

O'Mara, Jason (Actor)
c/o Michael (Mike) Jelline *United Talent Agency (UTA)*
10250 Constellation Blvd Fl 7
Los Angeles, CA 90067-6207, USA

O'Mara, Mark (Coach, Horse Racer)
629 Laurel Cove Ct Apt 205
Orlando, FL 32825-3220, USA

O'Meara, Jo (Actor, Musician)

O'Meara, Mark (Golfer)
2000 Auburn Dr Ste 330
Beachwood, OH 44122-4327

O'Meara, Peter (Actor)
c/o Staff Member *ROAR (LA)*
9701 Wilshire Blvd Fl 8
Beverly Hills, CA 90212-2008, USA

Omidyar, Pierre (Business Person)
2145 Hamilton Ave
San Jose, CA 95125-5905, USA

Ommanney, Catherine (Reality TV Star)
c/o Staff Member *Bravo (NY)*
30 Rockefeller Plz
New York, NY 10112-0015, USA

Onanian, Edward (Religious Leader)
630 2nd Ave
New York, NY 10016-4806, USA

Onarati, Peter (Actor)
252 N Larchmont Blvd
Los Angeles, CA 90004-3753, USA

Onassis, Athina (Heir/Heiress)
88 Av Foch
Paris, FRANCE F-75116

Ondaatje, Michael (Writer)
English Dept 2275 Bayview
Toronto, ON M4N 3M6, CANADA

Ondetti, Miguel A
79 Hemlock Cir
Princeton, NJ 08540-5405, USA

Ondrasik, John (Musician, Songwriter)
c/o Staff Member *Paradigm (NY)*
360 Park Ave S Fl 16
New York, NY 10010-1708, USA

Ondricek, Miroslav (Cinematographer)
Nad Pomnikem 1
Prague 5, Smichow 15200, CZECH REPUBLIC

One EskimO (Music Group, Musician)
c/o Nick Matthews *Coda Music Agency - UK*
229 Shoreditch High St
London E1 6PJ, UK

ONeal, Alexander (Musician)
18-24 John St
Luton LU1 2JE, UNITED KINGDOM

O'Neal, Griffin (Actor)
21368 Pacific Coast Hwy
Malibu, CA 90265-5203, USA

O'Neal, Jamie (Musician, Songwriter, Writer)
19078 Wedgewood Ave
Nashville, TN 37212, USA

O'Neal, Jermaine (Athlete, Basketball Player)
1500 Ocean Dr Apt 1206
Miami Beach, FL 33139-3147, USA

O'Neal, Leslie C (Athlete, Football Player)
5617 Adobe Falls Rd Unit A
San Diego, CA 92120-4654, USA

O'Neal, Randy (Athlete, Baseball Player)
10015 Honey Tree Ct
Orlando, FL 32836-5937, USA

O'Neal, Ryan (Actor)
c/o David Shapira *David Shapira & Associates*
193 N Robertson Blvd
Beverly Hills, CA 90211-2103, USA

O'Neal, Shaquille (Actor, Athlete, Basketball Player)
c/o Perry Rogers *Venture Management*
10100 W Charleston Blvd Ste 110
Las Vegas, NV 89135-5005, USA

O'Neal, Shaunie (Actor, Reality TV Star)
c/o Patti Webster *W&W PR*
476 Union Ave Ste 2
Middlesex, NJ 08846-1968, USA

O'Neal, Steve (Athlete, Football Player)
2914 Coronado Dr
College Station, TX 77845-7716, USA

O'Neal, Tatum (Actor)
c/o Brian Young *Untitled Entertainment (LA)*
350 S Beverly Dr Ste 200
Beverly Hills, CA 90212-4819, USA

O'Neil, Danny (Stylist)
c/o Staff Member *Artist Untied (LA)*
845 S Mansfield Ave Apt 1
Los Angeles, CA 90036-4979, USA

O'Neil, Edward W (Athlete, Football Player)
6691 Aiken Rd
Lockport, NY 14094-9648, USA

O'Neil, John (Athlete, Baseball Player, Coach)
220 Southwestern Dr Apt 131
Lakewood, NY 14750-2142, USA

O'Neil, Lawrence (Director)
8942 Wilshire Blvd # 219
Beverly Hills, CA 90211-1908, USA

O'Neil, Ron
10100 Santa Monica Blvd Ste 2500
Los Angeles, CA 90067-4116

O'Neil, Susie (Athlete, Swimmer)
177 Bridge Rd
Richmond, Vic 3121, Australia

O'Neil, Tricia (Actor)
c/o Staff Member *David Shapira & Associates*
193 N Robertson Blvd
Beverly Hills, CA 90211-2103, USA

O'Neil, Warren (Baseball Player)
258 Terrace Park
Rochester, NY 14619-2443, USA

O'Neill, Brian (Athlete, Hockey Player)
2600-1800 McGill College Ave
Montreal, QC H3A 3J6, Canada

O'Neill, Ed (Actor)
c/o Marc Gurvitz *Brillstein Entertainment Partners*
9150 Wilshire Blvd Ste 350
Beverly Hills, CA 90212-3453, USA

O'Neill, Eugene F (Engineer)
394 Dogford Rd
Etna, NH 03750-4310, USA

O'Neill, Jennifer (Actor, Model)
30 Hillenglade Dr
Nashville, TN 37207-1797, USA

O'Neill, Kevin (Athlete, Football Player)
1363 Masters Dr
Metamora, MI 48455-8701, USA

O'Neill, Michael (Actor)
c/o Staff Member *Mitchell K Stubbs & Assoc (MKS)*
8675 Washington Blvd Ste 203
Culver City, CA 90232-7486, USA

O'Neill, Michael J (Editor)
23 Cayuga Rd
Scarsdale, NY 10583-6941, USA

O'Neill, Paul (Athlete, Baseball Player)
7785 Hartford Hill Ln
Montgomery, OH 45242-4347, USA

O'Neill, Paul H (Secretary)
3 Von Lent Pl
Pittsburgh, PA 15232-1444, USA

O'Neill, Susan (Susie) (Swimmer)
207 Kent St # 1800
Sydney, NSW 2000, AUSTRALIA

O'Neill, Terence P (Terry) (Photographer)
8 Warwick Ave
London W2 1XB, UNITED KINGDOM (UK)

O'Neill of Bengarve, O Sylvia (Misc)
Cambridge CB3 9DF, UNITED KINGDOM (UK)

OneRepublic (Music Group)
c/o Ron Laffitte *Red Light Management (LA)*
8439 W Sunset Blvd Ste 2
Los Angeles, CA 90069-1925, USA

Onesti, Larry (Athlete, Football Player)
5476 E James Rd
Bloomington, IN 47408-9402, USA

Onetto, Victoria (Actor)
c/o Staff Member *Telefe - Argentina*
Pavon 2444 (C1248AAT)
Buenos Aires, ARGENTINA

Onkotz, Dennis H (Athlete, Football Player)
270 Walker Dr
State College, PA 16801-7097, USA

Ono, Yoko (Director, Musician, Producer)
P.O. Box 1009
Reykjavik 121, Iceland

Onodi, Henrietta (Gymnast)
Magyar Toma Szovetseg
Budapest 1143, HUNGARY

O'Nora, Brian (Baseball Player)
4294 Maureen Dr
Youngstown, OH 44511-1014, USA

O'Nora, Brian (Athlete, Baseball Player)
5265 Nashua Dr
Youngstown, OH 44515-5174, USA

Onorati, Peter
c/o Kay Liberman *Liberman/Zerman Management*
252 N Larchmont Blvd Ste 200
Los Angeles, CA 90004-3754, USA

Ontiveros, Lupe (Actor)
c/o Staff Member *Latin Hollywood Films*
2934 1/2 N Beverly Glen Cir # 262
Los Angeles, CA 90077-1724, USA

Ontiveros, Steve (Athlete, Baseball Player)
9970 E Charter Oak Rd
Scottsdale, AZ 85260-5138, USA

Ontkean, Michael (Actor)
PO Box 51
Kilauea, HI 96754-0051, USA

Onufriyenko, Yuri I (Astronaut, Misc)
Moskovskoi Oblasti
Syvisdny Goroduk 141160, RUSSIA

Oorvasi (Actor, Bollywood)
117 Solai Krishnan Street Janaki Nagar
Chennai, TN 600087, INDIA

Oosterhouse, Carter (Television Host)
c/o Robert Flutie *Flutie Entertainment (LA)*
9320 Wilshire Blvd Ste 202
Beverly Hills, CA 90212-3217, USA

Oosterhuis, Peter (Golfer)
2823 Providence Rd Unit 182
Charlotte, NC 28211-2274, USA

Oosterhuls, Peter (Golfer)
PO Box 27440
Scottsdale, AZ 85255-0140, USA

Opalinski-Harrer, Janice (Athlete, Volleyball Player)
3653 Diamond Head Cir
Honolulu, HI 96815-4430, USA

Opasik, Jim (Artist)
1914 Beverly Rd
Baltimore, MD 21228-4227, USA

Operator (Music Group)
c/o Staff Member *Agency Group Ltd, The (LA)*
1880 Century Park E Ste 711
Los Angeles, CA 90067-1618, USA

Opie, John D (Business Person)
3135 Easton Tpke
Fairfield, CT 06828-0002, USA

Opik, Ernst J (Astronomer)
Dept
College Park, MD 20742-0001, USA

Oppel, Richard A (Editor)
529 14th St NW
Washington, DC 20045-1002, USA

Oppenheim, Dennis A (Artist)
54 Franklin St
New York, NY 10013-4009, USA

Oppenheim, Irwin (Physicist)
140 Upland Rd
Cambridge, MA 02140-3623, USA

Oppenheim-Barnes, Saily (Government Official)
Quietways Highlands Painswick
Glos, UNITED KINGDOM (UK)

Oppenheimer, Alan
1207 Beverly Green Dr
Beverly Hills, CA 90212-4105

Oppenheimer, Allan (Actor)
1207 Beverly Green Dr
Beverly Hills, CA 90212-4105, USA

Oppenheimer, Benjamin R (Astronomer)
Astronomy
Pasadena, CA 91125-0001, USA

Oppenheimer, Deborah (Producer)
c/o Staff Member *United Talent Agency (UTA)*
9560 Wilshire Blvd Fl 5
Beverly Hills, CA 90212-2400, USA

Oppewal, Jeannine (Misc)
c/o Barbara Halperin *Gersh (LA)*
9465 Wilshire Blvd Ste 600
Beverly Hills, CA 90212-2612, USA

Opry, Tonya
1525 E Noble Ave # 160
Visalia, CA 93292-3043

Oquendo, Jose (Athlete, Baseball Player)
13219 Selma Rd
De Soto, MO 63020-5242, USA

O'Quinn, John M (Attorney, Attorney General, General)
440 Louisiana St Ste 440
Houston, TX 77002-1643, USA

O'Quinn, Terry (Actor)
1505 10th St
Santa Monica, CA 90401-2805, USA

Oquist, Mike (Athlete, Baseball Player)
1910 Raton Ave
La Junta, CO 81050-3427, USA

Orange, Walter (Clyde) (Music Group, Musician)
1920 Benson Ave
Saint Paul, MN 55116-3214, USA

Orba, Josephine (Stylist)
3223 N Ravenswood Ave # 2N
Chicago, IL 60657-2003, USA

Orbach, Raymond L (Educator)
4004 Petra Path
Austin, TX 78731-1407, USA

Orbelian, Konstantin A (Composer)
Demirchyan Str 27 #12
Yerevan 3750002, ARMENIA

Orbit, William (Musician)
c/o Staff Member *Creative Artists Agency (CAA-LA)*
2000 Avenue of the Stars Ste 100
Los Angeles, CA 90067-4705, USA

Orci, Roberto (Producer)
c/o Risa Gertner *Creative Artists Agency (CAA-LA)*
2000 Avenue of the Stars Ste 100
Los Angeles, CA 90067-4705, USA

Ord, Maren
1187 W 16th Ave
Vancouver V6H 1S8, CANADA

Ord, Robert L (Bob) III (General)
3020 Ribera Rd
Carmel, CA 93923-9724, USA

Ordonez, Magglio (Athlete, Baseball Player)
181 Nurmi Dr
Fort Lauderdale, FL 33301-1404, USA

Ordonez, Rey (Athlete, Baseball Player)
1000 SE 9th Ave
Hialeah, FL 33010-5810, USA

Ordovos, Jose M (Scientist)
Nutrition Research Center
Medford, MA 2155, USA

Orduna, Joe (Athlete, Football Player)
15 Grant
Irvine, CA 92620-3354, USA

Ordway, Frederick I III (Writer)
3423 Lookout Dr SE
Huntsville, AL 35801-1020, USA

O'Ree, William E (Willie) (Athlete, Hockey Player)
7961 Anders Cir
La Mesa, CA 91942-2304, USA

O'Reilly, Bill (Television Host)
c/o Staff Member *Fox News Channel (NY)*
1211 Ave Of The Americas Level C1
New York, NY 10036-8701, USA

O'Reilly, Cyril (Actor)
6500 Wilshire Blvd # 550
Los Angeles, CA 90048-4920, USA

O'Reilly, Sir Anthony J.F. (Business Person)
2 Fitzwilliam Sq
Dublin 2, Ireland

O'Reilly, Terry (Athlete, Coach, Hockey Player)
PO Box 5544
Salisbury, MA 01952-0544, USA

Oremans, Miriam (Tennis Player)
1751 Pinnacle Dr Ste 1500
McLean, VA 22102-3833, USA

Orend, Jack R
1808 N Van Ness Ave
Hollywood, CA 90028-5674, USA

Orendi, Ron
6323 Salem Park Cir
Mechanicsburg, PA 17050-2839

Orenduff, J Michael (Educator)
President's Office
Las Cruces, NM 88003, USA

Orenstein, Andrew (Producer)
c/o Staff Member *United Talent Agency (UTA)*
9560 Wilshire Blvd Fl 5
Beverly Hills, CA 90212-2400, USA

Oreskaband (Music Group)
c/o Staff Member *Paradigm (Monterey)*
404 W Franklin St
Monterey, CA 93940-2303, USA

Oresko, Nicholas (War Hero)
3 Tenakill Park E Apt 111
Cresskill, NJ 07626-2052, USA

Orgad, Ben-Zion (Composer)
14 Bloch St
Tel-Aviv 64161, ISRAEL

Organ, H Bryan (Artist)
Stables Marston Trussel near Market Harborough
Leics LE16 9TX, UNITED KINGDOM (UK)

Orgy (Music Group)
c/o Staff Member *Creative Artists Agency (CAA-LA)*
2000 Avenue of the Stars Ste 100
Los Angeles, CA 90067-4705, USA

Oriard, Michael (Athlete, Football Player)
3010 NW McKinley Dr
Corvallis, OR 97330-1138, USA

Orie, Kevin (Athlete, Baseball Player)
190 Shadow Ridge Dr
Pittsburgh, PA 15238-2132, USA

Origliasso, Jessica (Actor)
c/o Staff Member *The Harbour Agency*
135 Forbes St
Woolloomooloo NSW 2011, Australia

Origliasso, Lisa (Actor)
c/o Staff Member *The Harbour Agency*
135 Forbes St
Woolloomooloo NSW 2011, Australia

O'Riordan, Dolores (Musician)
c/o Danny Goldberg *Gold Village Entertainment*
37 W 17th St Ste 7W
New York, NY 10011-5525, USA

Orland, Frank J (Doctor)
519 Jackson Blvd
Forest Park, IL 60130-1807, USA

Orlandi, Oluchi (Model)
c/o Staff Member *Model Africa*
Paramount Place 105 Main Road
Green Point, Cape Town 8001, South Africa

Orlando, Bo (Athlete, Football Player)
1360 Armstrong Rd
Bethlehem, PA 18017-1002, USA

Orlando, Eric (Stylist)
c/o Staff Member *Stockland Martel*
343 E 18th St
New York, NY 10003-2802, USA

Orlando, Geoarge J (Misc)
219 Paterson Ave
Little Falls, NJ 07424-1657, USA

Orlando, Tony (Musician)
c/o David Brokaw *Brokaw Company, The*
9255 W Sunset Blvd Ste 804
Los Angeles, CA 90069-3305, USA

Orleans, Joan (Musician)
PO Box 2596
New York, NY 10009-8923, USA

Orlenko, Oksana (Actor)
c/o Staff Member *Sharp Entertainment*
1515 Broadway
New York, NY 10036-8901, USA

Orlich, Dan (Athlete, Football Player)
1030 Porter Cir
Reno, NV 89509-2349, USA

Orlov, Masha (Stylist)
c/o Staff Member *Rex Agency, The*
6311 Romaine St
Los Angeles, CA 90038-2617, USA

Orlov, Yuri
Cornell Univ.Newman Lab.
Ithaca, NY 14853-5001

Orman, Suze (Business Person, Correspondent, Writer)
2000 Powell St Ste 1605
Emeryville, CA 94608-1861, USA

Orme, Stanley (Government Official)
8 Northwood Grove Sale
Cheshire M33 3DZ, UNITED KINGDOM (UK)

Ormond, Julia (Actor)
c/o Staff Member *Artists Independent Management (LA)*
825 Nowita Pl
Venice, CA 90291-3836, USA

Ormond, Paul (Business Person)
333 N Summit St
Toledo, OH 43604-1531, USA

Orms, Barry (Athlete, Basketball Player)
3 Loudon Dr Unit 8
Fishkill, NY 12524-1870, USA

Orndorff, Paul (Athlete, Wrestler)
135 Pamela Ct
Fayetteville, GA 30214-4309, USA

Ornish, Dean (Doctor, Writer)
7 Miller Ave
Sausalito, CA 94965-2039, USA

Ornstein, Donald S (Mathematician)
857 Tolman Dr
Stanford, CA 94305-1025, USA

Ornston, David E. (Producer)
5650 Camellia Ave
North Hollywood, CA 91601-1710, USA

Oropesa, Eddie (Athlete, Baseball Player)
15757 SW 102nd St
Miami, FL 33196-5420, USA

Orosz, Tom (Athlete, Football Player)
425 1/2 5th St
Fairport Harbor, OH 44077-5629, USA

O'Rourke, Charles C (Athlete, Football Player)
220 Bedford St Apt 7A
Bridgewater, MA 02324-3123, USA

O'Rourke, Charlie (Athlete, Baseball Player)
15612 N Little Spokane Dr
Spokane, WA 99208-8527, USA

O'Rourke, PJ (Actor)
c/o Missy Malkin *Brillstein Entertainment Partners*
9150 Wilshire Blvd Ste 350
Beverly Hills, CA 90212-3453, USA

O'Rourke, Tom (Actor)
c/o Staff Member *Law & Order: SVU*
100 Universal City Plz Bldg 2252
Universal City, CA 91608-1002, USA

Orpik, Brooks (Athlete, Hockey Player)
110 Cypress St Unit Ph 1
Brookline, MA 2445, USA

Orr, Bobby (Athlete, Hockey Player)
6413 Mullin St
Jupiter, FL 33458-6666, USA

Orr, Christopher (Actor)
c/o Staff Member *3 Arts Entertainment Inc*
9460 Wilshire Blvd Fl 7
Beverly Hills, CA 90212-2713, USA

Orr, David A (Business Person)
Home Farm House Shackleford
Godalming
Surrey GU8 6AH, UNITED KINGDOM (UK)

Orr, James E (Athlete, Football Player)
3104 Glynn Ave
Brunswick, GA 31520, USA

Orr, John (Johnny) (Athlete, Basketball Player, Coach)
5736 Gallery Ct
West Des Moines, IA 50266-6629, USA

Orr, Louis (Athlete, Basketball Player, Coach)
1333 Pine Valley Dr
Bowling Green, OH 43402-5207, USA

Orr, Pete (Athlete, Baseball Player)
400 Rannie Rd
Newmarket, ON L3X 2N3, Canada

Orr, Terrence S (Dancer)
890 Broadway
New York, NY 10003-1211, USA

Orr, Terry (Athlete, Football Player)
2710 Kellogg Ave
Dallas, TX 75216-3250, USA

Orr III, James E (Business Person)
2211 Congress St
Portland, ME 04122-0002, USA

Orr Jr, James E (Jim) (Athlete, Football Player)
3104 Glynn Ave
Brunswick, GA 31520, USA

Orrall, Robert Ellis (Musician)
3 E 54th St # 1400
New York, NY 10022-3108, USA

Orr-Cahall, Christina (Director)
1451 S Olive Ave
West Palm Beach, FL 33401-7162, USA

Orr-Ewing, Hamish (Business Person)
Fox Mill Purton near Swindon
Wilts SN5 9EF, UNITED KINGDOM (UK)

Orrico, Stacie (Musician)
c/o Staff Member *Creative Artists Agency (CAA-LA)*
2000 Avenue of the Stars Ste 100
Los Angeles, CA 90067-4705, USA

Orser, Brian (Figure Skater)
1600 James Naismith Dr
Gloucester, ON L1B 5N4, CANADA

Orser, Leland (Actor)
c/o Kami Putnam-Heist *WmE2 (Endeavor-LA)*
9601 Wilshire Blvd Fl 3
Beverly Hills, CA 90210-5219, USA

Orsin, Raymond (Cartoonist)
1801 Superior Ave E
Cleveland, OH 44114-2107, USA

Orsini, Myrna J (Artist)
4411 N 7th St
Tacoma, WA 98406-3507, USA

Orsino, John (Athlete, Baseball Player)
6141 Terra Mere Cir
Boynton Beach, FL 33437-4920, USA

Orsulak, Joe (Athlete, Baseball Player)
29 Keansburg Rd
Parsippany, NJ 07054-3508, USA

Orta, Jorge (Athlete, Baseball Player)
1201 Heather Hill Cres
Flossmoor, IL 60422-1425, USA

Ortega, Amancio (Business Person)
Industria de Diseno Textil Avenida de la Diputacion
La Coruna, Arteixo 15142, SPAIN

Ortega, Bill (Athlete, Baseball Player)
4635 NW 95th Ave
Doral, FL 33178-2091, USA

Ortega, Gaspar
38 Branhaven Dr
East Haven, CT 06513-2005

Ortega, Jeannie (Musician)
500 S Buena Vista St
Burbank, CA 91521-0001, USA

Ortega, Keith (Athlete, Football Player)
142 Lucille St
Lake Charles, LA 70601-8423, USA

Ortega, Kenny (Actor, Choreographer, Director, Producer)
c/o Andy Patman *Paradigm (LA)*
360 N Crescent Dr
Beverly Hills, CA 90210-4874, USA

Ortega, Manuel (Actor)
c/o Staff Member *Telefe - Argentina*
Pavon 2444 (C1248AAT)
Buenos Aires, ARGENTINA

Ortega, Phil (Athlete, Baseball Player)
3071 Via Real
Carpinteria, CA 93013-3043, USA

Ortega, Ralph (Athlete, Football Player)
10465 SW 124th St
Miami, FL 33176-4721, USA

Ortega Saavedra, Daniel (President)
Managua, NICARAGUA

Ortega y Alamino, Jaime Cardinal (Religious Leader)
Apartado 594 Calle Habana 152
Havana 10100, CUBA

Ortenberg, Arthur (Business Person)
1441 Broadway
New York, NY 10018-1905, USA

Ortenzio, Frank (Athlete, Baseball Player)
2357 Oak St
Jacksonville, FL 32204, USA

Orth, Lea Diane (Stylist)
15 W 96th St Apt 4
New York, NY 10025-6548, USA

Ortiz, Adalberto (Junior) (Athlete, Baseball Player)
296 Strayer St
Johnstown, PA 15906-1733, USA

Ortiz, Alejo (Actor)
c/o Staff Member *Telefe - Argentina*
Pavon 2444 (C1248AAT)
Buenos Aires, ARGENTINA

Ortiz, Ana (Actor)
c/o Gayle Max *Blue Max Management*
1219 Blackthorn Ln
Deerfield, IL 60015-3103, USA

Ortiz, Cristina (Musician)
12 Penzance Place
London W11 4PA, UNITED KINGDOM (UK)

Ortiz, David (Athlete, Baseball Player)
16 Driftwood Ln
Weston, MA 02493-1416, USA

Ortiz, Domingo (Misc)
400 Foundry St
Athens, GA 30601-2623, USA

Ortiz, Javier (Athlete, Baseball Player)
19520 SW 39th Ct
Miramar, FL 33029-2736, USA

Ortiz, Louis (Baseball Player)
39450 Northfork Rd
Nehalem, OR 97131-9670, USA

Ortiz, Luis (Athlete, Baseball Player)
6408 Rogers Dr
North Richland Hills, TX 76182-4807, USA

Ortiz, Manuel
1 Hall of Fame Dr
Canastota, NY 13032-1175

Ortiz, Russ (Athlete, Baseball Player)
4040 E McLellan Rd Unit 13
Mesa, AZ 85205-3105, USA

Ortiz, Shalim (Actor)
c/o Irene Marie *Irene Marie Management Group*
PO Box 398115
Miami Beach, FL 33239-8115, USA

Ortiz, Tito (Athlete, Boxer)
c/o Staff Member *John Lewis Entertainment Group*
3071 S Valley View Blvd
Las Vegas, NV 89102-7889, USA

Ortiz Jr, Frank V (Diplomat)
663 Garcia St
Santa Fe, NM 87505-2857, USA

Ortlieb, Patrick (Skier)
Obertech
Lech 6764, AUSTRIA

Ortmann, Charles (Athlete, Football Player)
4 River Birch Ln
Savannah, GA 31411-2847, USA

Ortmeier, Dan (Athlete, Baseball Player)
2121 Fairmont Dr
Flower Mound, TX 75028-4606, USA

Ortner, Bev (Bowler)
PO Box 436
Odebolt, IA 51458-0436, USA

Ortolani, Riz
Via Aurelia km 23 400
Torrimpietra, ITALY I-00050

Orton, Beth (Musician)
c/o Beth Holden-Garland *Untitled Entertainment (LA)*
350 S Beverly Dr Ste 200
Beverly Hills, CA 90212-4819, USA

Orton, John (Athlete, Baseball Player)
98 Cherry Blossom Ln
Aptos, CA 95003-4907, USA

Orton, Kyle (Football Player)
c/o Staff Member *Chicago Bears*
1000 Football Dr
Lake Forest, IL 60045

Orton, Randy (Athlete, Wrestler)
c/o Kerry Rodgerson *World Wrestling Entertainment (WWE)*
1241 E Main St
Stamford, CT 06902-3520, USA

Oruche, Phina (Actor)
c/o Staff Member *Bauman Redanty & Shaul Agency*
5757 Wilshire Blvd Suite 473
Beverly Hills, CA 90212, USA

Oruviral, Krishna Rao (Actor)
4/1 Vellala Street Kodambakkam
Chennai, TN 600 024, INDIA

Orvella, Chad (Athlete, Baseball Player)
3327 Sahalee Dr W
Sammamish, WA 98074-6301, USA

Orvick, George M (Religious Leader)
6 Browns Ct
Mankato, MN 56001-6121, USA

Orvis, Herb (Athlete, Football Player)
1475 Abbey Ln
Lafayette, OR 97127-9180, USA

Ory, Meghan (Actor)
c/o Staff Member *Pacific Artists Management*
1285 W Broadway Suite 685
Vancouver, BC V6H 3X8, Canada

Osborn, Danny (Athlete, Baseball Player)
7620 Knox Ct
Westminster, CO 80030-4540, USA

Osborn, David V (Dave) (Athlete, Football Player)
18067 Judicial Way S
Lakeville, MN 55044-8895, USA

Osborn, Jim (Athlete, Football Player)
4 Canyon Ct
Algonquin, IL 60102-6306, USA

Osborn, Kassidy (Musician)
1228 Pineview Ln
Nashville, TN 37211-7422, USA

Osborn, Kelsi (Musician)
1228 Pineview Ln
Nashville, TN 37211-7422, USA

Osborn, Kristyn (Musician, Songwriter, Writer)
1228 Pineview Ln
Nashville, TN 37211-7422, USA

Osborn, William A (Financier)
50 S La Salle St
Chicago, IL 60603-1008, USA

Osborne, Barrie M (Director, Producer)
c/o Staff Member *Emerald City Productions*
9777 Wilshire Blvd Ste 550
Beverly Hills, CA 90212-1905, United States

Osborne, Bobo (Athlete, Baseball Player)
3309 Rough Creek Dr
Woodstock, GA 30189-6137, USA

Osborne, Burl (Editor, Publisher)
Editorial Dept Communications Center
Dallas, TX 75265, USA

Osborne, Burl (Religious Leader)
799 Bloomfield Ave
Verona, NJ 07044-1367, USA

Osborne, Donovan (Athlete, Baseball Player)
1651 Brightstone Ct
Reno, NV 89521-4049, USA

Osborne, Jeffrey (Musician, Songwriter, Writer)
2409 21st Ave S Ste 100
Nashville, TN 37212-5317, USA

Osborne, Joan (Musician, Songwriter)
c/o Staff Member *Paradigm (Monterey)*
404 W Franklin St
Monterey, CA 93940-2303, USA

Osborne, Mary Pope (Writer)
1745 Broadway # B1
New York, NY 10019-4368, USA

Osborne, Richard (Athlete, Football Player)
418 Tango Dr
San Antonio, TX 78216-3564, USA

Osborne, Tom (Athlete, Football Coach, Football Player)
5400 Trotter Rd
Lincoln, NE 68516-3419, USA

Osbourne, Jack (Reality TV Star)
c/o Staff Member *Sharon Osbourne Management*
9292 Civic Center Dr
Beverly Hills, CA 90210-3714, USA

Osbourne, Kelly (Musician)
c/o Staff Member *Sharon Osbourne Management*
9292 Civic Center Dr
Beverly Hills, CA 90210-3714, USA

Osbourne, Ozzy (Musician, Songwriter)
5535 Dixon Trail Rd
Hidden Hills, CA 91302-1185, USA

Osbourne, Sharon (Business Person, Reality TV Star)
5535 Dixon Trail Rd
Hidden Hills, CA 91302-1185, USA

Osburn, Pat (Athlete, Baseball Player)
208 64th Street Ct NW
Bradenton, FL 34209-1625, USA

Osby, Greg (Musician)
35 Clark St Apt A5
Brooklyn, NY 11201-2374, USA

O'Scannlain, Diarmuld F (Judge)
555 SW Yamhill St
Portland, OR 97204-1303, USA

Oscar Scheld, Eusebio Cardinal (Religious Leader)
Rua Benjamin Constant # 23/502
Washington, DC 20241-0001, BRAZIL

Oseary, Guy (Business Person, Producer)
c/o Staff Member *Untitled Entertainment (LA)*
350 S Beverly Dr Ste 200
Beverly Hills, CA 90212-4819, USA

Osgood, Charlie (Athlete, Baseball Player)
3 S Meadow Vig Apt 22
Carver, MA 2330, USA

Osgood, Chris (Athlete, Hockey Player)
6382 Pembrook Dr
Westland, MI 48185-7759, USA

O'Shea, Milo (Actor)
40 W 72nd St Apt 17A
New York, NY 10023-4192, USA

O'Shea, Terry (Athlete, Football Player)
506 Amberson Pl
Greensburg, PA 15601-8684, USA

Osher, John (Business Person)
1001 E Indiantown Rd
Jupiter, FL 33477-5110, USA

Osheroff, Douglas D (Nobel Prize Laureate)
75 Ranch Rd
Woodside, CA 94062-4809, USA

Oshima, Nagisa (Director)
2-15-7 Arasaka Minatoku
Tokyo, JAPAN

Oshodin, Willie (Athlete, Football Player)
8134 Murray Hill Dr
Fort Washington, MD 20744-4416, USA

Osiecki, Sandy (Athlete, Football Player)
11 Bryan Cir
Seymour, CT 06483-3676, USA

Osik, Keith (Athlete, Baseball Player)
5 Pal Ct
Shoreham, NY 11786-2352, USA

Osima, Nagisa
4-11-5 Kugenuma-Matsugaoka
Fujisawa-Shi, JAPAN 251

Osinski, Dan (Athlete, Baseball Player)
9723 W Amber Trl
Sun City, AZ 85351-1346, USA

Osis, Deborah (Stylist)
c/o Staff Member *Perrella Management*
330 W 38th St Rm 1407
New York, NY 10018-8435, USA

Oslin, K T (Musician)
704 18th Ave S
Nashville, TN 37203-3215, USA

Osman, Mat (Musician)
98 White Lion St
London N1 9PF, UNITED KINGDOM (UK)

Osman, Osman Ahmed (Engineer)
34 Adly St
Cairo, EGYPT

Osmar, Dean (Misc)
PO Box 32
Clam Gulch, AK 99568-0032, USA

Osment, Emily (Actor)
c/o Kim Jakwerth *Marleah Leslie & Associates PR*
1645 Vine St Apt 712
Los Angeles, CA 90028-8812, USA

Osment, Haley Joel (Actor)
c/o Meredith Fine *Coast to Coast Talent Group*
3350 Barham Blvd
Los Angeles, CA 90068-1404, USA

Osmond, Cliff (Actor, Director)
630 Bienveneda Ave
Pacific Palisades, CA 90272-3337, USA

Osmond, Donny (Actor, Musician, Producer)
c/o Eric Gardner *Panacea Entertainment*
13587 Andalusia Dr
Santa Rosa Valley, CA 93012-9226, USA

Osmond, Ken (Actor)
9863 Wornom Ave
Sunland, CA 91040-1535, USA

Osmond, Marie (Actor, Musician)
c/o Allison Garman *Rogers & Cowan PR (LA)*
Pacific Design Center 8687 Melrose Ave, 7th Floor
West Hollywood, CA 90069, USA

Osmond Boys
PO Box 7122
Branson, MO 65615-7122

Osnes, Larry G (Educator)
President's Office
Saint Paul, MN 55104, USA

Osorio, Jorge Federico (Musician)
165 W 57th St
New York, NY 10019-2201, USA

Osrin, Raymond H (Cartoonist)
1801 Superior Ave E
Cleveland, OH 44114-2107, USA

Oss Jr, Arnold (Athlete, Hockey Player)
8012 Pennsylvania Rd
Bloomington, MN 55438-1135, USA

Ossana, Diana (Producer, Writer)
c/o Adam Shulman *Anonymous Content (AC-LA)*
2049 Century Park E Ste 2550
Los Angeles, CA 90067-3139, USA

Ost, Friedheim (Government Official)
Heiersmauer 59
Paderborn 33098, GERMANY

Ostaseski, Frank (Director)
273 Page St
San Francisco, CA 94102-5616, USA

Osteen, Claude W (Athlete, Baseball Player)
2313 Duncan Perry Rd
Grand Prairie, TX 75050-2039, USA

Osteen, Darrell (Athlete, Baseball Player)
73901 Cezanne Dr
Palm Desert, CA 92211-4512, USA

Osteen, Joel (Religious Leader)
PO Box 4600
Houston, TX 77210-4600, USA

Osteen Jr, H M (Financier)
1 10th St
Augusta, GA 30901-0100, USA

Oster, Bill (Athlete, Baseball Player)
56 Little Neck Rd
Centerport, NY 11721-1617, USA

Osterbrock, Donald E (Astronomer)
120 Woodside Ave
Santa Cruz, CA 95060-3422, USA

Osterhage, Jeff (Actor)
1342 Lupine Hills Dr
Vista, CA 92081-5387, USA

Osterkorn, Wally (Athlete, Basketball Player)
3202 E Medlock Dr
Phoenix, AZ 85018-1427, USA

Osteroth, Alexander
Steinsdorfstr. 20
Munich, GERMANY 80538

Ostertag, Greg (Athlete, Basketball Player)
7401 Cobblestone Ct
McKinney, TX 75070-5073, USA

Ostheim, Michael (Model)
Ebersberger Str 9
Munich 81679, USA

Osting, Jimmy (Athlete, Baseball Player)
927 Lakeside Dr
Taylorsville, KY 40071-9271, USA

Ostman, Arnold (Conductor)
36 Station Road
London SE20 7BQ, UNITED KINGDOM (UK)

Ostos, Javier (Swimmer)
Isabel La Catolica 13 Desp 401-2
Mexico City 1, DF, MEXICO

Ostriker, Jeremiah P (Physicist)
33 Philip Dr
Princeton, NJ 08540-5409, USA

Ostrom, John H (Misc)
52 Hillhouse Rd
Goshen, CT 06756-1001, USA

Ostroski, Gerald (Athlete, Football Player)
6926 E 115th Pl S
Bixby, OK 74008-8248, USA

Ostrosky, Beth (Actor, Model)
c/o Staff Member *Don Buchwald & Associates Inc (NY)*
10 E 44th St Frnt 1
New York, NY 10017-3654

Ostrosky, David (Actor)
c/o Staff Member *Televisa*
Blvd Adolfo Lopez Mateos 232 Colonia San Angel INN
DF CP 01060, MEXICO

Ostrosser, Brian (Athlete, Baseball Player)
27 Chelsea Cres
Stoney Creek, ON L8E 5R7, Canada

Ostrum, Peter (Actor)
RR 1 Box 43
Glenfield, NY 13343, USA

Ostwald, Martin (Educator)
350 5th Ave Ste 4510
New York, NY 10118-4510, USA

O'Sullevan, Peter J (Sportscaster, Writer)
37 Cranmer Court
London SW3 3HW, UNITED KINGDOM (UK)

O'Sullivan, Dan (Athlete, Basketball Player)
33 Crescent Ave
Summit, NJ 07901-1902, USA

O'Sullivan, Gilbert (Musician)
PO Box 651 Park Road
Oxford OX2 9RB, UNITED KINGDOM (UK)

O'Sullivan, Peter (Editor)
4747 Southwest Fwy
Houston, TX 77027-6901, USA

O'Sullivan, Richard (Actor)
5 Anglers Lane Kentish Town
London NW5 3DG, UNITED KINGDOM (UK)

O'Sullivan, Sonia (Athlete, Track Athlete)
201 High St Hampton Hill
Middx TW12 1NL, UNITED KINGDOM (UK)

Osuna, Al (Athlete, Baseball Player)
8256 Via Rosa
Orlando, FL 32836-8789, USA

Osuna, Antonio (Athlete, Baseball Player)
10345 W Olympic Blvd
Los Angeles, CA 90064-2524, USA

Oswald, J Julian R (Admiral)
Victory Bldg HM Naval Base
Portsmouth PO1 3LS, UNITED KINGDOM (UK)

Oswald, Mark (Race Car Driver)
PO Box 99
Pfafftown, NC 27040-0099, USA

Oswald, Mark (Opera Singer)
266 W 37th St # 2000
New York, NY 10018-6609, USA

Oswald, Paul (Athlete, Football Player)
521 Cambridge Ct
Alpharetta, GA 30005-4216, USA

Oswald, Stephen S (Astronaut)
2101 Nasa Pkwy Spc Center
Houston, TX 77058-3607, USA

Oswalt, Patton (Actor)
c/o Dave Rath *Generate Management*
1545 26th St Ste 200
Santa Monica, CA 90404-3554, USA

Oswalt, Roy (Athlete, Baseball Player)
107 Oakmont Rd
Starkville, MS 39759-5512, USA

Oszajca, John (Musician)
2220 Colorado Ave
Santa Monica, CA 90404-3506, USA

Otaka, Tadaaki (Conductor)
31 Sinclair Road
London W14 0NS, UNITED KINGDOM (UK)

Otanez, Willis (Athlete, Baseball Player)
7904 March Brown Ave
Las Vegas, NV 89149-5101, USA

Otellini, Paul (Business Person)
2200 Mission College Blvd
Santa Clara, CA 95054-1537, USA

Oteri, Cheri (Actor, Comedian)
c/o Lori Sale *Paradigm (LA)*
360 N Crescent Dr
Beverly Hills, CA 90210-4874, USA

Otero, Ricky (Athlete, Baseball Player)
126 Calle Sorbona Urb University Gardens
San Juan, PR 927, USA

Othenin-Girard, Dominque (Director)
327 S Church Ln
Los Angeles, CA 90049-3057, USA

Othick, Trent (Producer)
c/o Staff Member *Creative Artists Agency (CAA-LA)*
2000 Avenue of the Stars Ste 100
Los Angeles, CA 90067-4705, USA

Otis, Amos J (Athlete, Baseball Player)
588 Preakness Stakes St
Henderson, NV 89015-6948, USA

Otis, Carre (Actor, Model)
c/o Staff Member *Storm Model Management*
5 Jubilee Pl 1st Floor
London SW3 3TD, UNITED KINGDOM

Otis, Glenn K (General)
3401 RR 9 LAKE SHORE Rd
Peru, NY 12972, USA

Otis, James L (Jim) (Athlete, Football Player)
14795 Greenleaf Valley Dr
Chesterfield, MO 63017-5542, USA

Otis, Johnny (Musician, Songwriter, Writer)
1226 E Altadena Dr
Altadena, CA 91001-2004, USA

Otman, Assed Mohamed (Prime Minister)
Villa Rissani Route Oued Akrach
Souissi, Rabat, MOROCCO

O'Toole, Annette (Actor)
c/o Harriet Sternberg *Harriet Sternberg Management*
4530 Gloria Ave
Encino, CA 91436-2718, USA

O'Toole, Dennis (Denny) (Athlete, Baseball Player)
9105 Royal Oak Ln
Union, KY 41091-8806, USA

O'Toole, Jim (Athlete, Baseball Player)
1010 Lanette Dr
Cincinnati, OH 45230-3616, USA

O'Toole, S Peter (Actor)
c/o Steven Arcieri *Arcieri & Associates Inc*
305 Madison Ave Ste 2315
New York, NY 10165-5015, USA

otowa, Plaxico (Athlete, Football Player)
47 Huntington Ter
Totowa, NJ 07512-2181, USA

Otstott, Charles P (General)
6152 Pohick Station Dr
Fairfax Station, VA 22039-1646, USA

Otsuka, Akinori (Athlete, Baseball Player)
5238 Ocean Breeze Ct
San Diego, CA 92109-1361, USA

Otsuki, Tamayo (Actor)
20318 Hiawatha St
Chatsworth, CA 91311-2553, USA

Ott, Billy (Athlete, Baseball Player)
132 W Nyack Way
West Nyack, NY 10994-2202, USA

Ott, Ed (Athlete, Baseball Player)
1 Hall Dr Attn Coachingstaff
Little Falls, NJ 07424-2160, USA

Ottaviano, Susan (Stylist)
c/o Staff Member *Ennis*
119 Braintree St
Boston, MA 02134-1628, USA

Otten, Jim (Athlete, Baseball Player)
1417 N Forest
Mesa, AZ 85203-3903, USA

Otten, Mac (Athlete, Basketball Player)
1000 Ashwood Pkwy Apt 1238
Atlanta, GA 30338-7514, USA

Otter, C.L. (Butch) (Governor)
PO Box 83720
Boise, ID 83720-0003, USA

Ottey, Merlene
PO Box 120
Indianapolis, IN 46206-0120

Ottey-Page, Merlene (Athlete, Track Athlete)
Po Box 544
Kingston 10, JAMAICA

Otto, August J (Gus) (Athlete, Football Player)
14411 Open Meadow Ct W
Chesterfield, MO 63017-9627, USA

Otto, Bob (Athlete, Football Player)
8705 Leeward Dr
Las Vegas, NV 89117-2283, USA

Otto, Dave (Athlete, Baseball Player)
1383 Shady Ln
Wheaton, IL 60187-3722, USA

Otto, Frei (Architect)
Berghalde 19 7250 Leonberg
Warmbroun 71229, GERMANY

Otto, James (Musician)
c/o Dan Anderson *Red Light Management (Nashville)*
39 Music Sq E
Nashville, TN 37203-4322, USA

Otto, James E (Jim) (Athlete, Football Player)
100 Estates Dr
Auburn, CA 95602, USA

Otto, Joel (Athlete, Hockey Player)
77 Sunset Way SE
Calgary, AB T2X 3C1, Canada

Otto, Kristin (Swimmer)
Postfach 4040
Mainz 55100, GERMANY

Otto, Michael (Business Person)
3500 Lacey Rd
Downers Grove, IL 60515-5422, USA

Otto, Miranda (Actor)
PO Box 1509
Darlinghurst, NSW 1300, AUSTRALIA

Otto, Sylke (Athlete)
An der Schiessstatte 4
Berchtesgaden 83471, GERMANY

Otto Jr, A T (Misc)
1411 Peterson Ave Ste 201
Park Ridge, IL 60068-5076, USA

Otwell, Ralph M (Editor)
34 Knox Cir
Evanston, IL 60201-1912, USA

Ouaido, Nassour Guelengdoussia (Prime Minister)
N'Djamena, CHAD

Oubre, Louis (Athlete, Football Player)
11008 Curran Blvd
New Orleans, LA 70127-1408, USA

Ouchi, William G (Educator)
Graduate Management School
Los Angeles, CA 90024, USA

Oudin, Melanie (Athlete, Tennis Player)
c/o Sam Duvall *Lagardere Unlimited - (D.C.)*
5335 Wisconsin Ave NW Ste 850
Washington, DC 20015-2052, USA

Ouedraogo, Gerard Kango (Prime Minister)
01 BP 347
Ouagadougou, BURKINA FASO

Ouedraogo, Idrissa (Director)
01 BP 2524
Ouagadougou, BURKINA FASO

Ouedraogo, Kdre Desire (Prime Minister)
Parliament Building
Ouagadougou, BURKINA FASO

Ouellet, Joseph G N Cardinal (Religious Leader)
34 Rue De l'eveche East Cp 730
Rimouski, QC G5L 7C7, CANADA

Ouellette, Dawn (Stylist)
336 E 30th St Apt 2A
New York, NY 10016-8330, USA

Ouellette, Phil (Athlete, Baseball Player)
7421 Poppy St
Corona, CA 92881-3739, USA

Our Lady Peace (Music Group)
c/o Eric Lawrence *Coalition Entertainment Management*
10271 Yonge St Suite 302
Richmond Hill, Ontario L4C 3B5, Canada

Oureiro, Natalia (Musician)
c/o Staff Member *BMG*
1540 Broadway
New York, NY 10036-4039, USA

Ourisson, Guy (Misc)
10 Rue Geiler
Strasbourg 67000, FRANCE

Ousland, Borge (Skier)
Axel Huitfeldts V5
Oslo 1170, NORWAY

Outkast (Music Group)
c/o Charles King *WmE2 (Endeavor-LA)*
9601 Wilshire Blvd Fl 3
Beverly Hills, CA 90210-5219, USA

Outland, Felton (War Hero)
1669 US Highway 158 E
Sunbury, NC 27979-9583, USA

Outlar, Jesse (Writer)
1252 Stephens St SW
Lilburn, GA 30047-4354, USA

Outlaw, Charles (Bo) (Athlete, Basketball Player)
14815 River Ml
San Antonio, TX 78216-7817, USA

Outlaw, Travis (Athlete, Basketball Player)
c/o Bill Duffy *BDA Sports Management (BDA-CA)*
700 Ygnacio Valley Rd Ste 330
Walnut Creek, CA 94596-3838, USA

Outman, Tim (Artist)
57101 N Bank Rd
McKenzie Bridge, OR 97413-9629, USA

OV7 (Music Group)
c/o Staff Member *Sony Music Miami*
605 Lincoln Rd Ste 700
Miami Beach, FL 33139-2901, USA

Ovchinikov, Vladmir P (Musician)
13 Cotswold Mews 30 Battersea Square
London SW11 3RA, UNITED KINGDOM (UK)

Ovechkin, Alexander (Athlete, Hockey Player)
601 F St NW
Washington, DC 20004-1605, USA

Overall, Park (Actor)
1374 Ripley Island Rd
Afton, TN 37616-6102, USA

Overath, Wolfgang
Auf dem Hummerich
Siegburg, GERMANY D-53721

Overbay, Lyle (Athlete, Baseball Player)
107 Captain Ln
Centralia, WA 98531-1614, USA

Overbeek, Jan T G (Misc)
Zweerslaan 35
Bilthoven, HN 3723, NETHERLANDS

Overgard, Robert M (Religious Leader)
PO Box 655
Fergus Falls, MN 56538-0655, USA

Overgard, William (Cartoonist)
200 Madison Ave
New York, NY 10016-3903, USA

Overhauser, Albert W (Physicist)
236 Pawnee Dr
West Lafayette, IN 47906-2115, USA

Overhauser, Chad (Athlete, Football Player)
8303 N No Pac Expy Suite 425B
Austin, TX 78759, USA

Overleese, Joanne (Baseball Player)
849 Coach Blvd
La Jolla, CA 92037, USA

Overman, Ion
c/o Staff Member *GVA Talent Agency Inc*
8981 W Sunset Blvd Ste 101
Los Angeles, CA 90069-1850, USA

Overman, Larry E (Misc)
Chemistry Dept
Irvine, CA 92717, USA

Overmyer, Amanda (Musician)

Overmyer, Eric (Writer)
English Dept
New Haven, CT 6520, USA

Overstreet, Chord (Actor)
c/o Mara Santino *Luber Roklin Management*
8530 Wilshire Blvd Ste 550
Beverly Hills, CA 90211-3133, USA

Overstreet, Paul (Musician, Songwriter, Writer)
475 Annex Ave
Nashville, TN 37209-2747, USA

Overstreet, Tommy (Musician, Songwriter, Writer)
PO Box 455
Brentwood, TN 37024-0455, USA

Overstreet, Will (Athlete, Football Player)
106 Avondale St
Jackson, MS 39216, USA

Overton, Kelly (Actor)
c/o Staff Member *Management 360*
9111 Wilshire Blvd
Beverly Hills, CA 90210-5508, USA

Overton, Rick (Actor)
c/o Staff Member *Sutton Barth & Vennari Inc*
145 S Fairfax Ave Ste 310
Los Angeles, CA 90036-2176, USA

Overy, Mike (Athlete, Baseball Player)
3010 N 152nd Ln
Goodyear, AZ 85395-8636, USA

Ovitz, Michael S (Business Person)
1234 Benedict Canyon Dr
Beverly Hills, CA 90210-2728, USA

Ovshinsky, Stanford R (Engineer, Inventor)
2956 Waterview Dr
Rochester Hills, MI 48309-3484, USA

Owchinko, Bob (Athlete, Baseball Player)
14000 N 94th St Unit 1033
Scottsdale, AZ 85260-7776, USA

Owen, Clive (Actor)
c/o Staff Member *42West (NY)*
220 W 42nd St Fl 12
New York, NY 10036-7200, USA

Owen, Dave (Athlete, Baseball Player)
1921 FM 3136
Cleburne, TX 76031-8792, USA

Owen, David A L (Government Official)
78 Narrow St Limehouse
London E14 8BP, UNITED KINGDOM (UK)

Owen, Edwyn (Bob) (Athlete, Hockey Player)
3630 SW Stratford Rd
Topeka, KS 66604-2544, USA

Owen, Glyn (Stylist)
c/o Staff Member *Art Department*
48 Greene St Fl 4
New York, NY 10013-2663, USA

Owen, Henry (Diplomat)
1775 Massachusetts Ave NW
Washington, DC 20036-2103, USA

Owen, Larry (Athlete, Baseball Player)
804 White Pine St
New Carlisle, OH 45344-1125, USA

Owen, Michael (Soccer Player)
c/o Staff Member *Newcastle United FC*
Saint James Park
Newcastle-Tyne NE1 4ST, UNITED KINGDOM (UK)

Owen, Michael (Athlete, Soccer Player)
c/o Dan Levy *Wasserman Media Group*
10960 Wilshire Blvd Fl 22
Los Angeles, CA 90024-3808, USA

Owen, Randy Y (Musician)
PO Box 529
Fort Payne, AL 35968, USA

Owen, Ray D (Biologist)
1583 Rose Villa St
Pasadena, CA 91106-3524, USA

Owen, Spike (Athlete, Baseball Player)
11211 Musket Rim St
Austin, TX 78738-6613, USA

Owen, Tom (Athlete, Football Player)
PO Box 3
Albany, OK 74721-0003, USA

Owens, Al (Baseball Player)
63 Bluff Ave
La Grange, IL 60525-2507, USA

Owens, Billy (Athlete, Basketball Player)
608 Canary Dr
Carlisle, PA 17013-8768, USA

Owens, Brig (Athlete, Football Player)
6902 Lupine Ln
Mc Lean, VA 22101-1578, USA

Owens, Burgess (Athlete, Football Player)
1430 Telegraph Rd
West Chester, PA 19380-1621, USA

Owens, Charles W (Tinker) (Athlete, Football Player)
2547 McGee Dr
Norman, OK 73072-6704, USA

Owens, Chris (Actor)
c/o Jerry Shandrew *Shandrew Public Relations*
1050 S Stanley Ave
Los Angeles, CA 90019-6634, USA

Owens, Cotton (Race Car Driver)
7065 White Ave
Spartanburg, SC 29303-2058, USA

Owens, Craig (Musician)
c/o Staff Member *Equal Vision Records*
PO Box 38202
Albany, NY 12203-8202, USA

Owens, Dan (Athlete, Football Player)
280 Selkirk Ln
Duluth, GA 30097-8043, USA

Owens, Darrick (Athlete, Football Player)
610 Cypress St
Raceland, LA 70394-2817, USA

Owens, Eric (Athlete, Baseball Player)
22431 N 54th St
Phoenix, AZ 85054-7210, USA

Owens, Gary (Entertainer)
17856 Via Vallarta
Encino, CA 91316-4345, USA

Owens, Jackson (Athlete, Baseball Player)
PO Box 6046
Decatur, IL 62524-6046, USA

Owens, James D (Jim) (Athlete, Coach, Football Coach, Football Player)
14321 Evanston Ave N
Seattle, WA 98133-6844, USA

Owens, Jayhawk (Athlete, Baseball Player)
273 Warwick Pl
Castle Pines, CO 80108-8823, USA

Owens, Jim (Athlete, Baseball Player)
1426 Ramada Dr
Houston, TX 77062-5908, USA

Owens, Joe (Athlete, Football Player)
2754 Highway 13 N
Columbia, MS 39429-8634, USA

Owens, Kem (Musician)
c/o Staff Member *The Paradise Group*
PO Box 69451
West Hollywood, CA 90069-0451, USA

Owens, Lorenzo (Musician)
c/o Staff Member *Paradigm (Monterey)*
404 W Franklin St
Monterey, CA 93940-2303, USA

Owens, Luke (Athlete, Football Player)
2970 Richmond Rd
Beachwood, OH 44122-3248, USA

Owens, Mel (Athlete, Football Player)
1230 Market St Apt 504
San Francisco, CA 94102-4801, USA

Owens, Morris (Athlete, Football Player)
4156 W Michigan Ave
Glendale, AZ 85308-1707, USA

Owens, Rawleigh C (R C) (Athlete, Football Player)
626 E Yosemite Ave
Manteca, CA 95336-5835, USA

Owens, Rena (Actor, Model)
526 N Larchmont Blvd # 201
Los Angeles, CA 90004-1300, USA

Owens, Steve (Athlete, Football Player)
4704 Harrogate Dr
Norman, OK 73072-3958, USA

Owens, Terrell (Athlete, Football Player)
c/o Tammy Brook *FYI Public Relations*
174 5th Ave Ste 400
New York, NY 10010-5935, USA

Owens, Terry (Athlete, Football Player)
2524 Poovey Rd SE
Decatur, AL 35603-5624, USA

Owens, William A (Admiral)
510 Lake St S Apt B302
Kirkland, WA 98033-6486, USA

Owensby, Earl
1 Motion Picture Blvd
Shelby, NC 28152-1044

Owings, Micah (Athlete, Baseball Player)
3208 Druid Hills Reserve Dr NE
Atlanta, GA 30329-2042, USA

Owings, Richard (Stylist)
c/o Staff Member *De Facto*
15 W 26th St Fl 5
New York, NY 10010-1028, USA

Ownbey, Rick (Athlete, Baseball Player)
2166 Via Monserate
Fallbrook, CA 92028-9335, USA

Owsley, Douglas (Misc)
& 17th M Sts NW
Washington, DC 20036, USA

Oxenberg, Catherine (Actor)
c/o Staff Member *Agency for the Performing Arts (APA-LA)*
405 S Beverly Dr Ste 500
Beverly Hills, CA 90212-4425, USA

Oyakawa, Yoshinobu (Yoshi) (Swimmer)
4171 Hutchinson Rd
Cincinnati, OH 45248-2219, USA

Oye, Erlend (Musician)
c/o Staff Member *Paradigm (Monterey)*
404 W Franklin St
Monterey, CA 93940-2303, USA

Oz, Amos (Writer)
Ben Gurion University PO Box 653
Beer-Sheva 84195, ISRAEL

Oz, Dr Mehmet (Correspondent, Doctor, Writer)
30 Rockefeller Plz Studio 6A
New York, NY 10112-0015, USA

Oz, Frank R (Director)
c/o David O'Connor *Creative Artists Agency (CAA-LA)*
2000 Avenue of the Stars Ste 100
Los Angeles, CA 90067-4705, USA

Ozaki, Masashi (Golfer)
14230 Lochridge Blvd Ste G
Covington, GA 30014-4953, USA

Ozark, Daniel L (Danny) (Athlete, Baseball Player, Coach)
PO Box 6666
Vero Beach, FL 32961-6666, USA

Ozawa, Ichiro (Government Official)
Daiichi Giia Kaikan Nagatacho
Chiyodaku
Tokyo 100, JAPAN

Ozbek, Rifat (Designer, Fashion Designer)
18 Haunch of Venison Yard
London W1Y 1AF, UNITED KINGDOM (UK)

Ozio, David (Bowler)
5915 Ventura Ln
Beaumont, TX 77706-3418, USA

Ozolinsh, Sandis (Athlete, Hockey Player)
2000 E Gene Autry Way
Anaheim, CA 92806-6143, USA

Ozomatli (Music Group)
c/o Amy Blackman *Tsunami Entertainment*
2525 Hyperion Ave
Los Angeles, CA 90027-3316, USA

Ozsan, Hal (Actor)
c/o Staff Member *Overbrook Entertainment*
450 N Roxbury Dr Fl 4
Beverly Hills, CA 90210-4218, USA

Ozzie, Raymond (Ray) (Designer)
33 Harbor St
Manchester By The Sea, MA 01944-1461, USA

P

P. Bilbray, Brian (Congressman, Politician)
2410 Rayburn Hob
Washington, DC 20515-0504, USA

P. Duffy, Sean (Congressman, Politician)
1208 Longworth Hob
Washington, DC 20515-0604, USA

P. Frelinghuysen, Rodney (Congressman, Politician)
2369 Rayburn Hob
Washington, DC 20515-3225, USA

P. Gibson, Christopher (Chris) (Congressman, Politician)
502 Cannon Hob
Washington, DC 20515-1003, USA

P. McGovern, James (Congressman, Politician)
438 Cannon Hob
Washington, DC 20515-0519, USA

P. McKeon, Howard H (Congressman, Politician)
2184 Rayburn Hob
Washington, DC 20515-2701, USA

P. Moran, James (Congressman, Politician)
2239 Rayburn Hob
Washington, DC 20515-4608, USA

Paabo, Svante (Director)
Deutscher Platz 6
Leipzig 4103, USA

Paavola, Rodney (Athlete, Hockey Player)
General Delivery
Hancock, MI 49930-9999, USA

Pablo Cruise
PO Box 770850
Orlando, FL 32877-0850

Pacar, Johnny (Actor)
c/o Bradley Lefler *Gersh (LA)*
9465 Wilshire Blvd Ste 600
Beverly Hills, CA 90212-2612, USA

Pace, Darrell O (Athlete)
4394 Hamilton Princeton Rd
Hamilton, OH 45011-9753, USA

Pace, Dominic (Actor)
c/o Budd Burton Moss *Burton Moss*
10533 Strathmore Dr
Los Angeles, CA 90024-2540, USA

Pace, Judy (Actor)
4139 S Cloverdale Ave
Los Angeles, CA 90008-1034, USA

Pace, Justin (Actor)
c/o Todd Justice *Marshak/Zachary Company, The*
8840 Wilshire Blvd Fl 1
Beverly Hills, CA 90211-2606, USA

Pace, Lee (Actor)
c/o Peter Kiernan *Management 360*
9111 Wilshire Blvd
Beverly Hills, CA 90210-5508, USA

Pace, Leslie (Stylist)
823 N Marion St
Oak Park, IL 60302-1532, USA

Pace, Orlando (Athlete, Football Player)
355 Galahad Dr
Weldon Spring, MO 63304-5703, USA

Pace, Peter (General)
Vice Chairman Joint Chiefs of Staff
Pentagon
Washington, DC 20318-0001, USA

Pacella, John (Athlete, Baseball Player)
1500 Abbotsford Green Dr
Powell, OH 43065-8938, USA

Pacheco, Abel (President)
Apdo 520-2010
San Jose 1000, COSTA RICA

Pacheco, Ferdie (Sportscaster)
4151 Gate Ln
Miami, FL 33137-3319, USA

Pacheco, Manuel T (Educator)
President S Ofc
Tucson, AZ 85721-0001, USA

Pacillo, Pat (Athlete, Baseball Player)
8 Rocky Glen Way
Lebanon, NJ 08833-4611, USA

Pacino, Al (Actor)
c/o Jeff Berg *International Creative Management (ICM-LA)*
10250 Constellation Blvd Fl 7
Los Angeles, CA 90067-6207, USA

Paciorek, Jim (Athlete, Baseball Player)
9641 E Waters Edge Pl
Tucson, AZ 85749-7901, USA

Paciorek, John (Athlete, Baseball Player)
8400 Huntington Dr
San Gabriel, CA 91775-1154, USA

Paciorek, Tom (Athlete, Baseball Player)
2389 Broad Creek Dr
Stone Mountain, GA 30087-3755, USA

Packard, Kelly (Actor, Model)
c/o Michael Valeo *Valeo Entertainment*
8265 W Sunset Blvd Ste 103
West Hollywood, CA 90046-2433, USA

Packard, Scott (Baseball Player)
135 Eastview Dr
Horseheads, NY 14845-2548, USA

Packard, Scott (Athlete, Baseball Player)
135 Eastview Dr
Horseheads, NY 14845-2548, USA

Packer, A William (Billy) (Sportscaster)
115 Penn Warren Dr # 300-329
Brentwood, TN 37027-5047, USA

Packer, David (Actor)
c/o Staff Member *Creative Artists Agency (CAA-LA)*
2000 Avenue of the Stars Ste 100
Los Angeles, CA 90067-4705, USA

Packer, James (Business Person)
54 Park St
Sydney NSW 2000, AUSTRALIA

Packwocd, Bob (Ex-Senator, Senator)
2201 Wisconsin Ave NW Ste C120
Washington, DC 20007-4114, USA

Pacquiao, Manny (Athlete, Boxer)
1123 Vine St
Los Angeles, CA 90038-1675, USA

Pactwa, Joe (Athlete, Baseball Player)
147 Winning Colors Dr
Wilmer, TX 75172-2307, USA

Pacula, Joanna (Actor)
1465 Lindacrest Dr
Beverly Hills, CA 90210-2519, USA

Padalecki, Jared (Actor)
c/o Dan Spilo *Industry Entertainment Partners*
955 Carrillo Dr Ste 300
Los Angeles, CA 90048-5400, USA

Padalka, Gennadi I (Cosmonaut)
Moskovskoi Oblasti
Syvisdny Goroduk 141160, RUSSIA

Paddio, Gerald (Athlete, Basketball Player)
5112 Morris St
Las Vegas, NV 89122-7063, USA

Paddock, John (Athlete, Coach, Hockey Player)
1315 Penn Ave
Hershey, PA 17033-1844, USA

Padgett, Jason (Actor)
c/o Staff Member *GVA Talent Agency Inc*
8981 W Sunset Blvd Ste 101
Los Angeles, CA 90069-1850, USA

Padilla, Douglas (Doug) (Athlete, Track Athlete)
182 N 555 W
Orem, UT 84057-1937, USA

Padilla, Mikel (Stylist)
c/o Staff Member *Action Agency Stylists*
8424 Santa Monica Blvd
West Hollywood, CA 90069-6233, USA

Padilla, Vicente (Athlete, Baseball Player)
2112 Royal Dominion Ct
Arlington, TX 76006-4836, USA

Padjen, Gary (Athlete, Football Player)
9314 Tower Bridge Rd Apt B
Indianapolis, IN 46240-5434, USA

Padma-Nathan, Harin (Doctor)
1245 16th St Ste 312
Santa Monica, CA 90404-1239, USA

Padmini (Actor, Bollywood)
9 Palot Madhavan Road Mahalingapuram
Chennai, TN 600034, INDIA

Paepke, Dennis (Athlete, Baseball Player)
4560 Trieste Dr
Carlsbad, CA 92010-3741, USA

Paes, Leander (Athlete, Tennis Player)
c/o Staff Member *ATP Tour*
201 Atp Tour Blvd
Ponte Vedra Beach, FL 32082-3211, USA

Paetkau, David (Actor)
c/o Martin Berneman *Precision Entertainment*
6338 Wilshire Blvd
Los Angeles, CA 90048-5002, USA

Paez, Jorge (Maromero) (Boxer)
233 Paulin Ave
Calexico, CA 92231-2615, USA

Paez, Richard A (Judge)
Court Building 125 S Grand Ave
Pasadena, CA 91105, USA

Paffrath, Amy (Actor)
c/o Scott Karp *Crystal Sky Pictures*
10203 Santa Monica Blvd Ste 500
Los Angeles, CA 90067-6416, USA

Paffrath, Bob (Athlete, Football Player)
11235 SW Meadowbrook Dr Apt 1
Portland, OR 97224-3373, USA

Pafko, Andrew (Andy) (Athlete, Baseball Player)
1890 W Glenlord Rd
Stevensville, MI 49127-9560, USA

Pagac, Fred (Athlete, Football Player)
10261 Normandy Crst
Eden Prairie, MN 55347-4849, USA

Pagan, Dave (Athlete, Baseball Player)
504 10th Ave W
Nipawin, SK S0E 1E0, Canada

Pagan, Jose (Athlete, Baseball Player)
425 Maple Ln
Sebring, FL 33876-6318, USA

Pagan, Reo (Baseball Player)
280 Creekview Trl
Fayetteville, GA 30214-7230, USA

Paganelli, Robert P (Diplomat)
331 S Main St
Albion, NY 14411-1602, USA

Page, Alan C (Athlete, Football Player, Judge)
PO Box 581254
Minneapolis, MN 55458-1254, USA

Page, Ashley (Choreographer, Dancer)
Covent Garden Bow St
London WC2E 9DD, UNITED KINGDOM (UK)

Page, Bettle (Model)
PO Box 56176
Chicago, IL 60656-0176, USA

Page, Corey (Actor)
9200 W Sunset Blvd Ste 900
Los Angeles, CA 90069-3604, USA

Page, David (Artist)
3724 Greenmount Ave
Baltimore, MD 21218-1843, USA

Page, David C (Misc)
9 Cambridge Ctr
Cambridge, MA 02142-1401, USA

Page, Ellen (Actor)
c/o Kish Igbal *Gary Goddard Agency*
10 St Mary St Suite 305
Toronto, ON M4Y 1P9, Canada

Page, Erika (Actor)
400 S Beverly Dr Ste 216
Beverly Hills, CA 90212-4404, USA

Page, Genevieve (Actor)
52 Rue de Vaugirard
Paris 75006, FRANCE

Page, Greg (Boxer)
968 Pinehurst Dr
Las Vegas, NV 89109-1569, USA

Page, Harrison (Actor)
1801 Avenue of the Stars Ste 902
Los Angeles, CA 90067-5981, USA

Page, Jimmy (Musician)
c/o Staff Member *International Talent Booking*
1st Floor, Ariel House 74A Charlotte St
London W1T 4QJ, UNITED KINGDOM

Page, Kimberly (Actor)
c/o Staff Member *The Paradise Group*
PO Box 69451
West Hollywood, CA 90069-0451, USA

Page, Larry (Business Person)
1600 Amphitheatre Pkwy
Mountain View, CA 94043-1351, USA

Page, Michael (Misc)
PO Box 229
North Salem, NY 10560-0229, USA

Page, Mike (Athlete, Baseball Player)
599 Briarcliff Dr
Woodruff, SC 29388-2326, USA

Page, Mitchell (Athlete, Baseball Player)
535 Pierce St
Albany, CA 94706-1000, USA

Page, Murriel (Basketball Player)
MCI Center 601 F St NW
Washington, DC 20004, USA

Page, Oscar C (Educator)
President's Office
Sherman, TX 75090, USA

Page, Patti (Actor, Musician)
404 Loma Larga Dr
Solana Beach, CA 92075-1719, USA

Page, Pierre (Athlete, Coach, Hockey Player)
2000 E Gene Autry Way
Anaheim, CA 92806-6143, USA

Page, Robin (Stylist)
c/o Staff Member *Artists by Timothy Priano (CA)*
8447 Wilshire Blvd Ste 301
Beverly Hills, CA 90211-3206, USA

Page, Sam (Actor)
c/o Lena Roklin *Luber Roklin Management*
8530 Wilshire Blvd Ste 550
Beverly Hills, CA 90211-3133, USA

Page, Solomon (Athlete, Football Player)
9302 Vista Cir
Irving, TX 75063-5060, USA

Page, Steven (Musician)
8730 Wilshire Blvd # 304
Beverly Hills, CA 90211-2716, USA

Page, Tim (Journalist)
1150 15th St NW
Washington, DC 20071-0001, USA

Pagel, Karl (Athlete, Baseball Player)
2698 N Ellis St
Chandler, AZ 85224-1777, USA

Pagel, Mike (Athlete, Football Player)
11981 Coopers Run
Strongsville, OH 44149-9260, USA

Paget, Debra (Actor)
411 Kari Ct
Houston, TX 77024-6804, USA

Pagett, Dana (Athlete, Basketball Player)
120 Yale Ln
Seal Beach, CA 90740-2522, USA

Pagett, Nicola (Actor)
22 Victoria Road Mortlake
London SW14, UNITED KINGDOM (UK)

Paggi, Nicole (Actor)
c/o Kenneth (Kenny) Goodman *Schiff Company, The*
8440 Warner Dr Ste B1
Culver City, CA 90232-2461, USA

Paglia, Camile (Writer)
c/o Staff Member *Random House Publicity*
1745 Broadway
New York, NY 10019-4368, USA

Paglia, Camille (Educator, Writer)
320 S Broad St
Philadelphia, PA 19102-4901, USA

Pagliaroni, Jim (Athlete, Baseball Player)
10388 Partridge Rd
Grass Valley, CA 95945-7449, USA

Pagliarulo, Michael T (Mike) (Athlete, Baseball Player)
11 Fieldstone Dr
Winchester, MA 01890-3257, USA

Pagliei, Joe (Athlete, Football Player)
7 Pine Ridge Ct
Sewell, NJ 08080-3648, USA

Pagnozzi, Thomas A (Tom) (Athlete, Baseball Player)
2319 N Heather Cv
Fayetteville, AR 72701-2991, USA

Pagnucco, Chris (Athlete, Football Player)
937 W Belden Ave
Chicago, IL 60614-3239, USA

Pagonis, William G (General)
202 Smalstig Rd
Evans City, PA 16033-3924, USA

Pahang (Misc)
Pekan
Pahang, MALAYSIA

Pahlavi, Ashraf
12 Ave Montaigne
Paris, FRANCE 75016

Pahukoa, Jeff (Athlete, Football Player)
20191 Cape Coral Ln
Huntington Beach, CA 92646-8514, USA

Paich, David (Musician)
34 N Palm St
Ventura, CA 93001-2600, USA

Paige, Betty
PO Box 56176
Chicago, IL 60656-0176

Paige, Colleen (Business Person)
PO Box 2061
Kingston, WA 98346-2061, USA

Paige, Elaine (Actor, Musician)
DeWalden Court 85 New Cavendish St
London W1M 7RA, UNITED KINGDOM (UK)

Paige, Janis (Actor)
1700 Rising Glen Rd
Los Angeles, CA 90069-1230, USA

Paige, Marcia A (Stylist)
26200 Town Center Dr Ste 185
Novi, MI 48375-1240, USA

Paige, Peter (Actor)
c/o Suzanne (Sue) Wohl *TalentWorks (LA)*
3500 W Olive Ave Ste 1400
Burbank, CA 91505-5512, USA

Paige, Rod (Secretary)
400 Maryland Ave SW
Washington, DC 20202-0001, USA

Paige, Tarah (Actor)
c/o Michael Henderson *Heresun Management*
4119 W Burbank Blvd
Burbank, CA 91505-2122, USA

Paik, Kun Woo (Musician)
12 Rosebery Thomton Heath
Surrey CR7 8PT, UNITED KINGDOM (UK)

Pailes, William A (Astronaut)
411 S Cedar Ridge Cir
Robinson, TX 76706-5681, USA

Paine, Chris
c/o Eddie Michaels *Insignia Public Relations*
1507 20th St Ste D
Santa Monica, CA 90404-3474, USA

Paine, Horner (Athlete, Football Player)
1105 W York Ave
Enid, OK 73703-7104, USA

Paine, John (Musician)
300 Vine St Ste 14
Seattle, WA 98121-1465, USA

Paintal (Actor, Bollywood, Comedian)
B 103 Sun Swept Lokhandwala Complex Andheri
Bombay, MS 400 058, INDIA

Painter, John Mark (Musician)
119 Pebble Creek Rd
Franklin, TN 37064-5525, USA

Painter, Lance (Athlete, Baseball Player)
2683 E Pinto Dr
Gilbert, AZ 85296-8934, USA

Paire-Davis, Lavonne (Baseball Player)
15847 Marlin Pl
Van Nuys, CA 91406-5019, USA

Paisley, Brad (Musician)
c/o Bill Simmons *Fitzgerald Hartley Co (Nashville)*
1908 Wedgewood Ave
Nashville, TN 37212-3733, USA

Paisley, Ian R K (Politician)
17 Cyprus Ave
Belfast BT5 5NT, NORTHERN IRELAND

Pak, Charles (Scientist)
Health Sciences Center
Dallas, TX 75235, USA

Pak, Se Ri (Golfer)
8836 Elliotts Ct
Orlando, FL 32836-5027, USA

Pakeledinaz, Martin (Designer)
232 N Canon Dr
Beverly Hills, CA 90210-5302, USA

Paksas, Rolandus (Prime Minister)
Gediminas 53
Vilnius 232026, LITHUANIA

Palacios, Rey (Athlete, Baseball Player)
160 Heberton Ave Apt 4H
Staten Island, NY 10302-1463, USA

Palagyi, Mike (Athlete, Baseball Player)
167 14th St
Conneaut, OH 44030-1805, USA

Palahniuk, Chuck (Writer)
c/o Howard Sanders *United Talent Agency (UTA)*
9560 Wilshire Blvd Fl 5
Beverly Hills, CA 90212-2400, USA

Palance, Holly
2753 Roscomare Rd
Los Angeles, CA 90077-1632

Palast, Greg (Musician)

Palastra Jr, Joseph T (General)
RR 1 Box 267
Myrtle, MO 65778-9726, USA

Palatella, Lou (Athlete, Football Player)
1532 Kennewick Dr
Sunnyvale, CA 94087-4158, USA

Palau, Doug (Producer)
c/o Staff Member *WmE2 (Endeavor-LA)*
9601 Wilshire Blvd Fl 3
Beverly Hills, CA 90210-5219, USA

Palau, Luis (Misc)
1500 NW 167th Pl
Beaverton, OR 97006-7342, USA

Palazzari, Doug (Athlete, Hockey Player)
2250 W Elizabeth St Apt 531
Fort Collins, CO 80521-4278, USA

Palazzi, Lou (Athlete, Football Player)
6400 Windcrest Dr Apt 826
Plano, TX 75024-3059, USA

Palazzi, Togo (Athlete, Basketball Player)
84 Framingham Rd
Southborough, MA 01772-1206, USA

Paldridge, Curt (Athlete, Football Player)
2820 Country Club Ln
Dekalb, IL 60115-4922, USA

Palekar, Amol (Actor, Bollywood, Director)
Chire Bandee 10th N S Road JVPD Scheme
Mumbai, MS 400049, INDIA

Palelei, Lonnie (Athlete, Football Player)
1808 SW Chief Cir
Blue Springs, MO 64015-5420, USA

Palermo, Olivia (Reality TV Star, Stylist)
c/o Brian Young *Untitled Entertainment (LA)*
350 S Beverly Dr Ste 200
Beverly Hills, CA 90212-4819, USA

Palermo, Stephen M (Steve) (Athlete, Baseball Player)
5102 W 143rd Ter
Overland Park, KS 66224-3746, USA

Palermo, Steve (Athlete, Baseball Player)
5102 W 143rd Ter
Overland Park, KS 66224-3746, USA

Palesh, Shirley (Baseball Player)
120 Grand Ave Apt 213
Wausau, WI 54403-7202, USA

Paleta, Ludwika (Actor)
c/o Staff Member *Televisa*
Blvd Adolfo Lopez Mateos 232 Colonia San Angel INN
DF CP 01060, MEXICO

Paley, Albert R (Artist)
25 N Washington St
Rochester, NY 14614-1110, USA

Paley, Grace (Misc)
PO Box 112
Thetford, VT 05074-0112

Palias, Cecile (Actor)
Drury House 34-43 Russell St
London WC2B 5HA, UNITED KINGDOM (UK)

Palicki, Adrianne (Actor)
c/o Michael Sugar *Anonymous Content (AC-LA)*
3531 Hayden Ave
Culver City, CA 90232, USA

Palillo, Ron (Actor)
322 Bowling Grn
New York, NY 10274, USA

Palin, Bristol (Reality TV Star)
711 H St Ste 620
Anchorage, AK 99501-3454, USA

Palin, Michael (Actor, Writer)
34 Tavistock Street
London WC2E 7PB, UK

Palin, Sarah (Ex-Governor, Politician)
1140 W Parks Hwy
Wasilla, AK 99654-6910, USA

Pall, Donn (Athlete, Baseball Player)
155 Wellington Dr
Bloomingdale, IL 60108-3012, USA

Pall, Gloria (Actor, Model)
12814 Victory Blvd
North Hollywood, CA 91606-3013

Pall, Olga (Skier)
Fahrenweg 28
Absam 6060, AUSTRIA

Palladino, Eric (Actor)
2311 Lyric Ave
Los Angeles, CA 90027-4656, USA

Palladino, Erik (Actor)
c/o Andrew Tetenbaum *ATA Management*
12 Desbrosses St
New York, NY 10013-1704, USA

Palladino, Vincent (Misc)
1727 King St
Alexandria, VA 22314-2700, USA

Pallavi (Actor, Bollywood)
14A Directors Colony Kodambakkam
Chennai, TN 600024, INDIA

Palli, Anne-Marie (Golfer)
4510 N Alta Hacienda Dr
Phoenix, AZ 85018-2004, USA

Pallone, Dave (Athlete, Baseball Player)
4420 Dickason Ave Apt 1135
Dallas, TX 75219-6642, USA

Pallone Jr., Frank (Congressman, Politician)
237 Cannon Hob
Washington, DC 20515-0526, USA

Palm, Mike (Athlete, Baseball Player)
21 Riverview Pl
Scituate, MA 02066-1215, USA

Palm, Siegfried
Dombacher Str 41/III/3
Vienna 1170, AUSTRIA

Palmas, Giorgia (Actor, Model)

Palmeiro, Orlando (Athlete, Baseball Player)
11991 SW 103rd Ter
Miami, FL 33186-2654, USA

Palmeiro, Rafael C (Athlete, Baseball Player)
5216 Reims Ct
Colleyville, TX 76034-5574, USA

Palmer, Alisa (Actor)
c/o Staff Member *Catch Up Agentur*
Gorzer Strasse 35a
Munchen 81669, Germany

Palmer, Amanda (Musician)
c/o Staff Member *High Road Touring*
751 Bridgeway Fl 2
Sausalito, CA 94965-2174, USA

Palmer, Arnold (Athlete, Golfer)
9000 Bay Hill Blvd
Orlando, FL 32819-4880, USA

Palmer, Barbara (Stylist)
805 N Sycamore Ave
Los Angeles, CA 90038-3316, USA

Palmer, Betsy (Actor)
PO Box 55
Disney, OK 74340-0055, USA

Palmer, Bud (Athlete, Basketball Player)
1200 S Flagler Dr Apt 303
West Palm Beach, FL 33401-6740, USA

Palmer, C R (Business Person)
2800 Post Oak Blvd
Houston, TX 77056-6100, USA

Palmer, Carl (Musician)
9 Hillgate St
London W8 7SP, UNITED KINGDOM (UK)

Palmer, Carson (Athlete, Football Player)
25052 Adelanto Dr
Laguna Niguel, CA 92677-1839, USA

Palmer, Dave R (Educator, General)
4531 Blue Ridge Dr
Belton, TX 76513-4906, USA

Palmer, David (Athlete, Baseball Player)
61 Sherman Ave
Glens Falls, NY 12801-2708, USA

Palmer, David (Athlete, Football Player)
PO Box 310871
Birmingham, AL 35231-0871, USA

Palmer, Dean (Athlete, Baseball Player)
3907 W Millers Bridge Rd
Tallahassee, FL 32312-1054, USA

Palmer, Derrell (Athlete, Football Player)
900 Jennifer Ct
Cleburne, TX 76033-5931, USA

Palmer, Geoffrey (Actor)
c/o Liz Nelson *Conway van Gelder*
8-12 Broadwick St
London W1F 8HW, UK

Palmer, Geoffrey W R (Prime Minister)
63 Roxburgh St Mount Victoria
Wellington, NEW ZEALAND

Palmer, Gery (Athlete, Football Player)
6411 E Irish Pl
Centennial, CO 80112-2404, USA

Palmer, Gregg
5726 Graves Ave
Encino, CA 91316-1441

Palmer, Jesse (Athlete, Football Player, Reality TV Star)
c/o Staff Member *San Francisco 49ers*
4949 Centennial Blvd
Santa Clara, CA 95054-1254

Palmer, Jim (Baseball Player, Sportscaster)
239 Sanford Ave
Palm Beach, FL 33480-3619, USA

Palmer, Keke (Actor)
c/o Alissa Vradenburg *Untitled Entertainment (LA)*
350 S Beverly Dr Ste 200
Beverly Hills, CA 90212-4819, USA

Palmer, Lowell (Athlete, Baseball Player)
PO Box 5253
El Dorado Hills, CA 95762-0005, USA

Palmer, Matt (Athlete, Baseball Player)
c/o Staff Member *Los Angeles Dodgers (LA Dodgers)*
1000 Elysian Park Ave
Los Angeles, CA 90090-1112, USA

Palmer, Mitch (Athlete, Football Player)
14420 Cypress Pt
Poway, CA 92064-6600, USA

Palmer, Patsy (Actor)
c/o Staff Member *International Artistes*
Holborn Hall - 4th Floor
London WC1V 7BD, UK

Palmer, Peter (Actor)
216 Kingsway Dr
Temple Terrace, FL 33617-4823, USA

Palmer, Ralph (Baseball Player)
PO Box 25065
Lansing, MI 48909-5065, USA

Palmer, Richard H (Athlete, Football Player)
14420 Cypress Pt
Poway, CA 92064-6600, USA

Palmer, Sandra (Athlete, Golfer)
498 Peralta Ave
Long Beach, CA 90803-2218, USA

Palmer, Scott (Athlete, Football Player)
7408 Lady Suzannes Ct
Austin, TX 78729-7793, USA

Palmer, Teresa (Actor)
c/o David Seltzer *Management 360*
9111 Wilshire Blvd
Beverly Hills, CA 90210-5508, USA

Palmer, Vivienne (Stylist)
c/o Staff Member *Celestine - CA*
1666 20th St Ste 200B
Santa Monica, CA 90404-3828, USA

Palmer, Walter (Athlete, Basketball Player)
87 South St
Rockport, MA 01966-1924, USA

Palmieri, Eddie (Musician)
2608 9th St Ste 301
Berkeley, CA 94710-2556, USA

Palmieri, Paul (Religious Leader)
& 6th Lincoln Sts
Monongahela, PA 15063, USA

Palminteri, Chazz (Actor)
375 Greenwich St
New York, NY 10013-2376, USA

Palmisano, Samuel J (Business Person)
1 N Castle Dr
Armonk, NY 10504-1725, USA

Palmquist, Ed (Athlete, Baseball Player)
2475 Southside Rd
Grants Pass, OR 97527-8981, USA

Palms, John M (Educator)
President's Office
Columbia, SC 29208-0001, USA

Palomeque, Lincoln (Actor)
c/o Staff Member *TV Caracol*
Calle 76 #11 - 35 Piso 10AA
Bogota DC 26484, COLOMBIA

Palomino, Carlos (Boxer)
14242 Burbank Blvd # 8
Sherman Oaks, CA 91401-4937, USA

Paltrow, Gwyneth (Actor)
c/o Aleen Keshishian *Brillstein Entertainment Partners*
9150 Wilshire Blvd Ste 350
Beverly Hills, CA 90212-3453, USA

Paltrow, Jake (Director)
c/o John Lesher *WmE2 (Endeavor-LA)*
9601 Wilshire Blvd Fl 3
Beverly Hills, CA 90210-5219, USA

Palumba, Joe (Athlete, Football Player)
927 Old Garth Rd
Charlottesville, VA 22901-1937, USA

Palys, Stan (Athlete, Baseball Player)
448 Center St
Covington Township, PA 18444-7824, USA

Pampanini, Sylvana
Via Flaminia 322
Rome, ITALY I-00196

Pampling, Rod (Golfer)
9 Campbell Ct
Lewisville, TX 75077-8201, USA

Pamuk, Orhan (Nobel Prize Laureate)
c/o Staff Member *Farrar, Straus and Giroux*
18 W 18th St Fl 7
New York, NY 10011-4675, USA

Pan, Hong (Actor)
Tonghui Menwai
Chengdu City, Sichuan Province, CHINA

Panabaker, Danielle (Actor)
c/o Lainie Sorkin Becky *Management 360*
9111 Wilshire Blvd
Beverly Hills, CA 90210-5508, USA

Panabaker, Kay (Actor)
c/o Lena Roklin *Luber Roklin Management*
8530 Wilshire Blvd Ste 550
Beverly Hills, CA 90211-3133, USA

Panafieu, Bernard L A Cardinal (Religious Leader)
14 Place du Colonel-Edon
Marseille Cedex 07 13284, FRANCE

Panagaris, Orianthi (Musician)
c/o Sterling McIlwaine *19 Entertainment - LA*
8560 W Sunset Blvd Ste 9
West Hollywood, CA 90069-2339, USA

Pancake, Sam (Actor)
c/o Joel King *Pakula/King & Associates*
9229 W Sunset Blvd Ste 315
Los Angeles, CA 90069-3403, USA

Panch, Marvin (Race Car Driver)
1648 Taylor Rd Ste 406
Port Orange, FL 32128-6753, USA

Pancholi, Aditya (Actor, Bollywood)
Hattes Bungalow Gandhigram Road Juhu
Mumbai, MS 400049, INDIA

Pancholy, Maulik (Actor)
c/o Staff Member *ROAR (LA)*
9701 Wilshire Blvd Fl 8
Beverly Hills, CA 90212-2008, USA

Panday, Basdeo (Prime Minister)
Eric Williams Plaza
Port of Spain, TRINIDAD & TOBAGO

Pandey, Chunky (Actor, Bollywood)
1 A/B Monisha Apartments St Andrews Road Bandra
Mumbai, MS 400050, INDIA

Pandian (Actor)
18 5/6 Bharatidasan Street Baskar Colony
Chennai, TN 600 093, INDIA

Pandian, Arun (Actor)
2A Bajaj Apartment NANDANAM
Chennai, TN 600 035, INDIA

Pandiani, Karen (Stylist)
c/o Staff Member *Stockland Martel*
343 E 18th St
New York, NY 10003-2802, USA

Panelli, John (Athlete, Football Player)
17549 Kirkshire Ave
Beverly Hills, MI 48025-3265, USA

Panetta, Leon E (Government Official)
15 Panetta Rd
Carmel Valley, CA 93924-9452, USA

Panettiere, Hayden (Actor)
c/o Emily Gerson Saines *Brookside Artists Management (NY)*
250 W 57th St Ste 2303
New York, NY 10107-2399, USA

Pang, May
1619 3rd Ave Apt 9D
New York, NY 10128-3937

Pang, Qing (Figure Skater)
c/o Staff Member *Champions on Ice*
3500 W 80th St Ste 200
Minneapolis, MN 55431-1090, USA

Panhofer, Walter (Musician)
Erdbergstr 35/9
Vienna 1030, AUSTRIA

Panic, Milan (Business Person, Prime Minister)
1050 Arden Rd
Pasadena, CA 91106-4004, USA

Panic at the Disco (Music Group)
PO Box 1803
Tampa, FL 33601-1803, USA

Panichas, George A (Writer)
PO Box AB
College Park, MD 20741-3025, USA

Panico, Jane (Stylist)
145 E 16th St
New York, NY 10003-3405, USA

Panish, Morton B (Misc)
52 Baldwin Rd
Freeport, ME 04032-6485, USA

Pankey, Irv (Athlete, Football Player)
348 Walker St
Aberdeen, MD 21001-3543, USA

Pankin, Stuart (Actor)
1288 Bienevenda Ave
Pacific Palisades, CA 90272, USA

Pankovits, Jim (Athlete, Baseball Player)
6014 Catalina Dr Unit 115
N Myrtle Bch, SC 29582-8388, USA

Pankow, James (Musician)
3826 Bowsprit Cir
Westlake Village, CA 91361-3814, USA

Pankow, John (Actor)
232 N Canon Dr
Beverly Hills, CA 90210-5302, USA

Panni, Marcello (Composer)
3 Piazza Borghese
Rome 186, ITALY

Panofsky, Wolfgang K H (Physicist)
25671 Chapin Rd
Los Altos Hills, CA 94022-3413, USA

Panos, Joe (Athlete, Football Player)
31010 Chequamegon Dr
Hartland, WI 53029-8560, USA

Panov, Valery M (Ballerina)
119 W 57th St # 903
New York, NY 10019-2303, USA

Panozzo, Chuck (Musician)
c/o Sterling Bacon *TBA Artist Management (Atlanta)*
1111 Alderman Dr Ste 285
Alpharetta, GA 30005-5433, USA

Pantaleo, Nancy (Stylist)
c/o Staff Member *Directions USA*
3717 W Market St Ste C
Greensboro, NC 27403-1155, USA

Panther, Jim (Athlete, Baseball Player)
7936 Tiger Palm Way
Fort Myers, FL 33966-6447, USA

Pantoja, Arnie (Actor)
c/o Julie Balfour *AKA Talent Agency*
6310 San Vicente Blvd Ste 200
Los Angeles, CA 90048-5488, USA

Pantoliano, Joe (Joey Pants) (Actor)
c/o Staff Member *WmE2 (Endeavor-LA)*
9601 Wilshire Blvd Fl 3
Beverly Hills, CA 90210-5219, USA

Pantotiano, Joe (Actor)
600 Willow Ave Apt 3
Hoboken, NJ 07030-6919, USA

Panza dl Blumo, Giuseppe (Misc)
PO Box 3183
Lugano 6901, SWITZERLAND

Paola (Royalty)
Rue de Brederode
Brussels 1000, BELGIUM

Paolini, Christopher (Writer)
c/o Staff Member *Random House*
1540 Broadway
New York, NY 10036-4039, USA

Paolo, Connor (Actor)
c/o Ellen Gilbert *Abrams Artists Agency (LA)*
9200 W Sunset Blvd PH 11
Los Angeles, CA 90069-3601, USA

Paolozzi, Eduardo L (President)
107 Dovehouse
London SW3 6JZ, UNITED KINGDOM (UK)

Papa, Greg (Athlete, Baseball Player)
11 San Andreas Dr
Danville, CA 94506-2035, USA

Papa, John (Athlete, Baseball Player)
275 Mary Ave
Stratford, CT 06614-5329, USA

Papa, Tom (Comedian)
c/o Staff Member *WmE2 (WMA-LA)*
1 William Morris Pl
Beverly Hills, CA 90212-4261, USA

Papa Doo Run Run
PO Box 255
Cupertino, CA 95015-0255

Papa Roach (Music Group)
c/o Staff Member *10th Street Entertainment (NY)*
38 W 21st St Rm 300
New York, NY 10010-6979, USA

Papach, George (Athlete, Football Player)
5454 Hohman Ave
Hammond, IN 46320-1931, USA

Papadopoulos, Tassos (President)
5 Ioannis Ceridos St
Nicosia, CYPRUS

Papajohn, Michael (Actor)
c/o Monique Moss *Moss Public Relations*
8060 Melrose Ave Fl 4
Los Angeles, CA 90046-7038, USA

Papale, Vince (Athlete, Football Player)
2219 S 15th St
Philadelphia, PA 19145-3920, USA

Papamichael, Phedon M (Cinematographer)
1505 10th St
Santa Monica, CA 90401-2805, USA

Papapetrou, Peter (Stylist)
c/o Staff Member *Judy Inc*
1 Yorkville Ave
Toronto ON M4W 1L1, Canada

Papas, Irene (Actor)
38 Xenokratous St
Athens 106 76, GREECE

Papathanassiou, Aspassia (Actor)
38 Xenokratous St
Athens 106 76, GREECE

Papazian, Marty (Actor)
c/o Lin Bickelmann *Encore Artists Management*
3815 W Olive Ave Ste 101
Burbank, CA 91505-4674, USA

Pape, Ken (Athlete, Baseball Player)
2127 Green Creek St
San Antonio, TX 78232-3913, USA

Papelbon, Jonathan (Athlete, Baseball Player)
284 Cornerstone Dr
Brandon, MS 39042-2747, USA

Papert, Seymour (Mathematician)
20 Ames St
Cambridge, MA 02142-1308, USA

Papi, Stan (Athlete, Baseball Player)
1111 W Sierra Madre Ave
Fresno, CA 93705-0433, USA

Papit, Johnny (Athlete, Football Player)
PO Box 8
Brownsburg, VA 24415-0008, USA

Papoose (Musician)
c/o Staff Member *Violator Management*
36 W 25th St Fl 11
New York, NY 10010-2752, USA

Pappalardo, Salvatore Cardinal (Religious Leader)
Via Matteo Bonello 2
Palermo 90134, ITALY

Pappano, Antonio
Covent Garden Bow St
London WC2E 9DD, UNITED KINGDOM (UK)

Pappas, Brenden (Athlete, Golfer)
5320 Fort Buckner Dr
McKinney, TX 75070-7044, USA

Pappas, Deane (Golfer)
2930 S College Dr
Fayetteville, AR 72701-9136, USA

Pappas, Erik (Athlete, Baseball Player)
10248 S Seeley Ave
Chicago, IL 60643, USA

Pappas, George (Bowler)
21108 Blakely Shores Dr
Cornelius, NC 28031-6606, USA

Pappas, Milt (Athlete, Baseball Player)
319 Aspen Dr
Beecher, IL 60401-5140, USA

Pappas, Stephen (Stylist)
c/o Staff Member *Celestine - CA*
1666 20th St Ste 200B
Santa Monica, CA 90404-3828, USA

Pappenheimer, John R (Physicist)
66 Sherman St Apt 113
Cambridge, MA 02140-3528, USA

Pappin, James J (Jim) (Athlete, Hockey Player)
44827 Oro Grande Cir
Indian Wells, CA 92210-7412, USA

Paquette, Craig (Athlete, Baseball Player)
16615 S 27th Ave
Phoenix, AZ 85045-2202, USA

Paquette, Julie (Stylist)
c/o Staff Member *Team*
423 W Broadway Ste 406
Boston, MA 02127-2265, USA

Paquin, Anna (Actor)
c/o JoAnne Colonna *Brillstein Entertainment Partners*
9150 Wilshire Blvd Ste 350
Beverly Hills, CA 90212-3453, USA

Paquin, Kit (Actor)
c/o Staff Member *Trilogy Talent*
13425 Ventura Blvd Fl 2
Sherman Oaks, CA 91423-3974, USA

Paradis, Vanessa (Actor, Model, Musician)
c/o Hank Sacks *Partisan Arts*
1505 Bridgeway Ste 205
Sausalito, CA 94965-1968, USA

Paradise, Bob (Athlete, Hockey Player)
1303 Beechwood Pl
Saint Paul, MN 55116-2202, USA

Parado, Alejandra (Actor)
c/o Gabriel Blanco *Gabriel Blanco Iglesias (Mexico)*
Rio Balsas 35-32 Colonia Cuauhtemoc
DF 6500, Mexico

Parahia, Murray (Musician)
420 W 45th St
New York, NY 10036-3501, USA

Paramore (Music Group, Musician)
c/o Randy Dease *Fly South Music Group*
189 S Orange Ave Ste 1100
Orlando, FL 32801-3256, USA

Paraseghian, Ara
51767 Oakbrook Ct
Granger, IN 46530-8731

Parazaider, Walter (Musician)
8900 Wilshire Blvd Ste 300
Beverly Hills, CA 90211-1959, USA

Parazynski, Scott E (Astronaut)
2015 Wroxton Rd
Houston, TX 77005-1654, USA

Parcells, Duane C (Bill) (Athlete, Coach, Football Coach, Football Player)
2 Campion Ln
Saratoga Springs, NY 12866-8796, USA

Pardee, Arthur B (Misc)
15 Buzzards Bay Ave
Woods Hole, MA 02543-1105, USA

Pardee, John P (Jack) (Athlete, Coach, Football Coach, Football Player)
PO Box 272
Gause, TX 77857-0272, USA

Pardes, Herbert (Misc)
15 Claremont Ave # 93
New York, NY 10027-6809, USA

Pardo, Al (Athlete, Baseball Player)
908 Hillary Cir
Lutz, FL 33548-5052, USA

Pardo, Don (Correspondent)
30 Rockefeller Plz
New York, NY 10112-0015, USA

Pardo, Jimmy (Comedian)
c/o Staff Member *OmniPop Talent Group*
10700 Ventura Blvd Fl 2
Studio City, CA 91604-3561, USA

Pardue, Kip (Actor)
c/o Jason Newman *Untitled Entertainment (LA)*
350 S Beverly Dr Ste 200
Beverly Hills, CA 90212-4819, USA

Pardue, Wendye (Stylist)
10A Clara Dr
Norwalk, CT 06851-3203, USA

Pare, Jessica (Actor)
c/o Nick Frenkel *3 Arts Entertainment Inc*
9460 Wilshire Blvd Fl 7
Beverly Hills, CA 90212-2713, USA

Pare, Michael (Actor)
c/o Staff Member *David Shapira & Associates*
193 N Robertson Blvd
Beverly Hills, CA 90211-2103, USA

Paredes, Marisa (Actor)
Gran Via 63 #3 Izda
Madrid 28013, SPAIN

Parekh, Asha (Actor, Bollywood)
Azad Road Juhu
Mumbai, MS 400049, INDIA

Parekh, Kal (Actor)
c/o Jenn Lederer *AFST Management*
350 W 43rd St Apt 32G
New York, NY 10036-6476, USA

Parent, Gail
2001 Mandeville Canyon Rd
Los Angeles, CA 90049-2226

Parent, Mark (Athlete, Baseball Player)
8829 Midview Dr
Palo Cedro, CA 96073-8635, USA

Parent, Monique (Actor, Model)
PO Box 3458
Ventura, CA 93006-3458, USA

Paret, Peter (Historian, Writer)
Historical Studies School
Princeton, NJ 8540, USA

Paretsky, Sara N (Writer)
1504 E 53rd St # 302
Chicago, IL 60615-4503, USA

Parfit, Derek A (Misc)
Philosophy Dept
Oxford OX1 4AL, UNITED KINGDOM (UK)

Parham, Gus (Athlete, Football Player)
4294 El Camino Real
Los Altos, CA 94022-1048, USA

Parilla, Lana (Actor)
c/o Staff Member *Windfall*
3000 W Alameda Ave
Burbank, CA 91523-0001, USA

Parillaud, Anne (Actor)
c/o Elisabeth Tanner *ArtMedia*
20 avenue Rapp
Paris 75008, France

Parilli, Vito (Babe) (Athlete, Coach, Football Coach, Football Player)
8060 E Girard Ave Apt 218
Denver, CO 80231-4414, USA

Paris, Bubba (Athlete, Football Player)
4096 Beacon Pl
Discovery Bay, CA 94505-1125, USA

Paris, Kelly (Athlete, Baseball Player)
1515 Redwood Cir
Thousand Oaks, CA 91360-6336, USA

Paris, Mica (Musician)
1800 Argyle Ave # 408
Los Angeles, CA 90028-5253, USA

Paris, Twila (Musician, Songwriter, Writer)
PO Box 150867
Nashville, TN 37215-0867, USA

Parise, Louis (Misc)
1125 15th St NW
Washington, DC 20005-2721, USA

Parise, Robert L (Basketball Player)
1307 Windsor Dr
Framingham, MA 01701-5005, USA

Parise, Ronald A (Astronaut)
15419 Good Hope Rd
Silver Spring, MD 20905-4129, USA

Parise, Vanessa (Actor)
c/o Lara Rosenstock *Lara Rosenstock Management*
8371 Blackburn Ave Apt 1
Los Angeles, CA 90048-4245, USA

Parise, Zach (Athlete, Hockey Player)
c/o Wade Arnott *Newport Sports Management*
201 City Centre Dr Suite 400
Mississauga, ON L58 2T4, Canada

Parish, Robert (Athlete, Basketball Player)
1307 Windsor Dr
Framingham, MA 01701-5005, USA

Parisi, Siobhan
c/o Staff Member *Carry Company, The*
3875 Wilshire Blvd Ste 402
Los Angeles, CA 90010-3209, USA

Parisot, Dean (Director)
c/o Staff Member *3 Arts Entertainment Inc*
9460 Wilshire Blvd Fl 7
Beverly Hills, CA 90212-2713, USA

Parisse, Annie (Actor)
c/o Kami Putnam-Heist *WmE2 (Endeavor-LA)*
9601 Wilshire Blvd Fl 3
Beverly Hills, CA 90210-5219, USA

Parizeau, Jacques (Politician)
88 Grand Alle Est
Quebec, PQ G1A 1A2, CANADA

Park, Alyssa (Musician)
165 W 57th St
New York, NY 10019-2201, USA

Park, Chan Ho (Athlete, Baseball Player)
c/o Team Member *New York Yankees*
Yankee Stadium 161st St & River Ave
Bronx, NY 10451, USA

Park, Charles R (Physicist)
305 Wheatfield Cir Apt 134
Brentwood, TN 37027-4475, USA

Park, D Bradford (Brad) (Athlete, Coach, Hockey Player)
100 Legends Way Attn Alumniassociation
Boston, MA 02114-1300, USA

Park, Ernie (Athlete, Football Player)
3160 Private Road 1101
Clyde, TX 79510-4905, USA

Park, Grace (Actor)
c/o Tyman Stewart *Characters Talent Agency, The (Vancouver)*
1505 W 2nd Ave #200
Vancouver, BC V6H 3Y4, Canada

Park, Joon (Actor)
c/o Susan Yoo *Susan Yoo*
Prefers to be contacted via telephone
Los Angeles, CA, USA

Park, Linda (Actor)
c/o Ro Diamond *SDB Partners Inc*
1801 Avenue of the Stars Ste 902
Los Angeles, CA 90067-5981, USA

Park, Linkin (Music Group)
c/o Michael Arfin *Artist Group International (NY)*
150 E 58th St Fl 19
New York, NY 10155-1900, USA

Park, Merle F (Ballerina)
144 Talgarth Road
London W14 9DE, UNITED KINGDOM (UK)

Park, Nicholas W (Nick) (Animator, Director)
Gas Ferry Road
Bristol B51 6UN, UNITED KINGDOM (UK)

Park, Patrick (Musician)
c/o Staff Member *Red Light Management (LA)*
8439 W Sunset Blvd Ste 2
Los Angeles, CA 90069-1925, USA

Park, Ray (Actor)
c/o Dino May *Dino May Management*
6362 Hollywood Blvd
Los Angeles, CA 90028-6323, USA

Park, Reg
Box 1002-Morningside 2057 Sandton
Gauteng, SOUTH AFRICA

Park, Steve (Race Car Driver)
1675 Coddle Creek Hwy
Mooresville, NC 28115-8245, USA

Parke, Evan Dexter (Actor)
c/o Staff Member *McCabe Group, The*
3211 Cahuenga Blvd W Ste 104
Los Angeles, CA 90068-1372, USA

Parkening, Christopher (Musician)
420 W 45th St
New York, NY 10036-3501, USA

Parker, Ace (Athlete, Baseball Player)
210 Snead Fairway
Portsmouth, VA 23701-1641, USA

Parker, Ace (Athlete, Football Player)
210 Snead Fairway
Portsmouth, VA 23701-1641, USA

Parker, Alan W (Director)
c/o Staff Member *Independent Talent Group (ITG-UK)*
Oxford House 76 Oxford St
London W1D 1BS, UK

Parker, Andrea (Actor)
c/o Dan Baron *Agency for the Performing Arts (APA-LA)*
405 S Beverly Dr Ste 500
Beverly Hills, CA 90212-4425, USA

Parker, Angie (Stylist)
c/o Staff Member *Mercury Artists*
8460 Higuera St Fl 2
Culver City, CA 90232-2520, USA

Parker, Anthony (Basketball Player)
Waterhouse Center 8701 Maitland Summit Blvd
Orlando, FL 32810, USA

Parker, Anthony (Athlete, Football Player)
1054 E Geneva Dr
Tempe, AZ 85282-3805, USA

Parker, Artimus (Athlete, Football Player)
4231 47th St
Sacramento, CA 95820-4034, USA

Parker, Bob (Skier)
408 Camino Don Miguel
Santa Fe, NM 87505-5948, USA

Parker, Brant J (Cartoonist)
613 Florence Ave
Waynesboro, VA 22980-6030, USA

Parker, Bruce C (Biologist)
841 Hutcheson Dr
Blacksburg, VA 24060-3211, USA

Parker, Caryl Mack (Musician)
PO Box 120053
Nashville, TN 37212-0053, USA

Parker, Chris (Actor)
Clarendon Road Borehamwood
Herts WD6 1JF, UK

Parker, Christian (Athlete, Baseball Player)
10101 Mesa Arriba Ave NE
Albuquerque, NM 87111-4962, USA

Parker, Christopher (Actor)
13 Radnor Walk
London SW3 4BP, UNITED KINGDOM (UK)

Parker, Clay (Athlete, Baseball Player)
6614 Brickston St
Hixson, TN 37343-2593, USA

Parker, Corey (Actor)
429 Santa Monica Blvd # 520
Santa Monica, CA 90401-3401, USA

Parker, Craig (Actor)
c/o Joe Smith *International Creative Management (ICM-LA)*
10250 Constellation Blvd Fl 7
Los Angeles, CA 90067-6207, USA

Parker, Dave (Athlete, Baseball Player)
7131 Reading Rd
Cincinnati, OH 45237-3806, USA

Parker, Denise (Athlete)
4801 Wallace Ln
Salt Lake City, UT 84117, USA

Parker, Eleanor (Actor)
2195 S La Paz Way
Palm Springs, CA 92264-9529, USA

Parker, Eugene N (Physicist)
1323 Evergreen Rd
Homewood, IL 60430-3410, USA

Parker, Franklin (Writer)
Education & Psychology Dept
Cullowhee, NC 28723, USA

Parker, George M (Misc)
1440 S Byme Rd
Toledo, OH 43614, USA

Parker, Georgie (Actor)
c/o Staff Member *Mark Morrissey and Associates*
16 Princess Ave Rosebery
Sydney NSW 2018, Australia

Parker, Harry (Athlete, Baseball Player)
7305 Dress Blue Cir
Mechanicsville, VA 23116-6569, USA

Parker, Jack D (Jackie) (Athlete, Football Player)
10623 65 Ave NW
Edmonton, AB T6H 1V5, Canada

Parker, James T (Jim) (Athlete, Football Player)
1902 Cedar Circle Dr
Catonsville, MD 21228-3741, USA

Parker, Jameson (Actor)
1604 N Vista St
Los Angeles, CA 90046-2818, USA

Parker, Lani Malone (Stylist)
c/o Staff Member *Celestine - CA*
1666 20th St Ste 200B
Santa Monica, CA 90404-3828, USA

Parker, Lara (Actor)
PO Box 1254
Topanga, CA 90290-1254, USA

Parker, Larry (Athlete, Football Player)
15903 San Marco Pl
Bakersfield, CA 93314-6650, USA

Parker, Lu
12222 Vance Jackson Rd Apt 734
San Antonio, TX 78230-5941

Parker, Maceo (Musician)
109 W Newark Ave
Wildwood, NJ 08260-1038

Parker, Mary-Louise (Actor)
c/o Jillian Fowkes *ID Public Relations (ID-LA)*
7080 Hollywood Blvd Fl 8
Los Angeles, CA 90028-6906, USA

Parker, Molly (Actor)
c/o Staff Member *Dontanville/Frattaroli (D/F)*
270 Lafayette St Ste 402
New York, NY 10012-3327, USA

Parker, Nate (Actor)
c/o Samantha Hill *WKT Public Relations (WKT-LA)*
9350 Wilshire Blvd Ste 450
Beverly Hills, CA 90212-3230, USA

Parker, Nathanial
10100 Santa Monica Blvd Ste 2500
Los Angeles, CA 90067-4116

Parker, Nathaniel (Actor)
Julian House 4 Windmill St
London W1P 1HF, UNITED KINGDOM (UK)

Parker, Nicole (Actor)
c/o Mark Rousso *New Wave Entertainment (LA)*
2660 W Olive Ave
Burbank, CA 91505-4525, USA

Parker, Nicole Ari (Actor)
c/o Maani Golesorkhi *Bluestone Entertainment*
5639 Vista Del Monte Ave
Van Nuys, CA 91411-3356, USA

Parker, Noelle
9300 Wilshire Blvd Ste 555
Beverly Hills, CA 90212-3211

Parker, Oliver
76 Oxford St
London, ENGLAND W1N 0AX

Parker, Olivia (Photographer)
38 Newbury St # 400
Boston, MA 02116-3210, USA

Parker, Orlando (Athlete, Football Player)
4402 Chatham Pl
Montgomery, AL 36108-4902, USA

Parker, Paula Jai (Actor)
c/o Leonard Torgan *Collective*
8383 Wilshire Blvd Ste 1050
Beverly Hills, CA 90211-2415, USA

Parker, Ray Jr (Musician)
8901 Melrose Ave # 200
West Hollywood, CA 90069-5605, USA

Parker, Rick (Athlete, Baseball Player)
2641 NE 74th St
Gladstone, MO 64119-5349, USA

Parker, Riddick (Athlete, Football Player)
11226 NE 68th St Apt 212-B
Kirkland, WA 98033-7181, USA

Parker, Robert A R (Astronaut)
4800 Oak Grove Dr
Pasadena, CA 91109-8001, USA

Parker, Sarah Jessica (Actor, Producer)
c/o Ina Treciokas *Slate Public Relations*
9000 W Sunset Blvd Ste 915
West Hollywood, CA 90069-5809, USA

Parker, Scott (Motorcycle Race, Motorcycle Racer)
6096 Grand Blanc Rd
Swartz Creek, MI 48473-9441, USA

Parker, T Jefferson (Writer)
c/o Staff Member *Trident Media Group LLC*
41 Madison Ave Fl 36
New York, NY 10010-2257, USA

Parker, Tony (Athlete, Basketball Player)
c/o Leon Rose *CAA - NJ*
308 Harper Dr Ste 210
Moorestown, NJ 08057-3245, USA

Parker, Trey (Animator, Writer)
c/o Gabrielle (Gaby) Morgerman *WmE2 (Endeavor-LA)*
9601 Wilshire Blvd Fl 3
Beverly Hills, CA 90210-5219, USA

Parker, Vaughn (Athlete, Football Player)
2500 6th Ave Unit 107
San Diego, CA 92103-6629, USA

Parker, Wes (Athlete, Baseball Player)
1000 Elysian Park Ave Attn Communityrelations
Los Angeles, CA 90090-1112, USA

Parker, Willie (Athlete, Football Player)
9327 Kai Dr
Beach City, TX 77523-2333, USA

Parker-Bowles, Camilla (Royalty)
Stable Yard Gate
London SW1, UNITED KINGDOM (UK)

Parkhill, Barry (Athlete, Basketball Player)
3429 Cesford Grange
Keswick, VA 22947-9127, USA

Parkhurst, Heather
8383 Wilshire Blvd # 954
Beverly Hills, CA 90211-2425

Parkhurst, Heather Elizabeth (Actor)
8491 W Sunset Blvd # 440
West Hollywood, CA 90069-1911, USA

Parkins, Barbara
6399 Wilshire Blvd Ste 414
Los Angeles, CA 90048-5716

Parkinson, Bradford W (Business Person)
2780 Valley Cir
Meadow Vista, CA 95722, USA

Parkinson, Katherine (Actor)
c/o Sarah McCormick *Curtis Brown Group*
Haymarket House 28 - 29 Haymarket
London SW1Y 4SP, UNITED KINGDOM

Parkinson, Michael
Drury House 34/43 Russell St
London WC2B 5HA, UNITED KINGDOM

Parkinson, Roger P (Publisher)
425 Portland Ave
Minneapolis, MN 55488-1511, USA

Parks, Cherokee (Athlete, Basketball Player)
5331 Kadena Garden Ct
North Las Vegas, NV 89031-6605, USA

Parks, Chris (Athlete, Wrestler)
c/o Staff Member *TNA Wrestling*
209 10th Ave S Ste 302
Nashville, TN 37203-0730, USA

Parks, Dallas (Athlete, Baseball Player)
3353 Pittman Grove Church Rd
Raeford, NC 28376-6012, USA

Parks, David W (Dave) (Athlete, Football Player)
12113 Palisades Pkwy
Austin, TX 78732-1244, USA

Parks, Derek (Athlete, Baseball Player)
7828 Day Creek Blvd Apt 1214
Rancho Cucamonga, CA 91739-8580, USA

Parks, Maxie (Athlete, Track Athlete)
4545 E Norwich Ave
Fresno, CA 93726-2726, USA

Parks, Michael (Actor)
11684 Ventura Blvd # 476
Studio City, CA 91604-2699, USA

Parks, Michael (Editor)
202 W 1st St
Los Angeles, CA 90012-4105, USA

Parks, Phaedra (Reality TV Star)
c/o Staff Member *Bravo (NY)*
30 Rockefeller Plz
New York, NY 10112-0015, USA

Parks, Suzan-Lori (Actor, Writer)
c/o Staff Member *Creative Artists Agency (CAA-LA)*
2000 Avenue of the Stars Ste 100
Los Angeles, CA 90067-4705, USA

Parks, Van Dyke (Composer)
2141 Layton St
Pasadena, CA 91104-1805, USA

Parks-Young, Barbara (Baseball Player)
5078 Edinboro Ln
Wilmington, NC 28409-8518, USA

Parlavecchio, Chet (Athlete, Football Player)
178 Brooklake Rd
Florham Park, NJ 07932-2707, USA

Parlen, Megan (Actor)
c/o Staff Member *Cunningham Escott Slevin & Doherty (CESD-LA)*
10635 Santa Monica Blvd Ste 130
Los Angeles, CA 90025-8306, USA

Parlow, Sarah (Stylist)
c/o Staff Member *Mark Edward Inc*
325 W 8th St # 1011
New York, NY 10018, USA

Parmalee, Bernie (Athlete, Football Player)
9208 158th St
Overland Park, KS 66221-7589, USA

Parmenter, Charles S (Misc)
Chemistry Dept
Bloomington, IN 47405, USA

Parmer, Jim (Athlete, Football Player)
2311 S County Road 1120
Midland, TX 79706-4942, USA

Parmet, Philip (Cinematographer)
1080 S Hayworth Ave
Los Angeles, CA 90035-2602, USA

Parnell, Chris (Actor)
c/o Jimmy Miller *Mosaic Media Group*
9200 W Sunset Blvd Ste 10
Los Angeles, CA 90069-3608, USA

Parnell, Lee Roy (Musician)
PO Box 23451
Nashville, TN 37202-3451, USA

Parnell, LeRoy
PO Box 23451
Nashville, TN 37202-3451

Parnell, Mel (Athlete, Baseball Player)
700 Turquoise St
New Orleans, LA 70124-3541, USA

Parnell, Peter (Writer)
c/o Staff Member *United Talent Agency (UTA)*
9560 Wilshire Blvd Fl 5
Beverly Hills, CA 90212-2400, USA

Parnell, Sean (Governor)
PO Box 110001
Juneau, AK 99811-0001, USA

Parnevik, Jesper (Golfer)
17553 SE Conch Bar Ave
Jupiter, FL 33469-1709, USA

Parodi, Starr (Musician)
c/o Staff Member *Evolution Music Partners*
1680 Vine St Ste 500
Hollywood, CA 90028-8800, USA

Paronto, Chad (Athlete, Baseball Player)
617 Benedict Rd
Pittsfield, MA 01201-2899, USA

Parque, Jim (Athlete, Baseball Player)
4109 Crystal Ridge Dr SE
Puyallup, WA 98372-5214, USA

Parr, Carolyn Miller (Judge)
400 2nd St NW
Washington, DC 20217-0001, USA

Parr, Jerry S
4529 38th St NW
Washington, DC 20016-1827, USA

Parr, Ralph S (War Hero)
14831 Heather Valley Way
Houston, TX 77062-2337, USA

Parr, Robert G (Misc)
701 Kenmore Rd
Chapel Hill, NC 27514-2019, USA

Parr, Todd (Writer)
c/o Staff Member *Suppertime Entertainment*
21300 Oxnard St Ste 100
Woodland Hills, CA 91367-5059, USA

Parra, Derek (Speed Skater)
PO Box 450639
Westlake, OH 44145-0611, USA

Parra, Manny (Athlete, Baseball Player)
c/o Joe Urbon *Creative Artists Agency (CAA-NY)*
162 5th Ave Fl 6
New York, NY 10010-6047, USA

Parrella, John (Athlete, Football Player)
8161 Regency Dr
Pleasanton, CA 94588-3136, USA

Parrett, Jeff (Athlete, Baseball Player)
722 Seattle Dr
Lexington, KY 40503-2127, USA

Parrett, William (Business Person)
433 Country Club Rd W
New Canaan, CT 06840-3604, USA

Parrilla, Lana (Actor)
c/o Pamela Kohl *3 Arts Entertainment Inc*
9460 Wilshire Blvd Fl 7
Beverly Hills, CA 90212-2713, USA

Parriott, James (Director)
c/o Jamie Mandelbaum *Jackoway Tyerman Wertheimer Austen Mandelbaum Morris & Klein*
1925 Century Park E Fl 22
Los Angeles, CA 90067-2701, USA

Parris, Fred (Musician)
PO Box 12
Far Hills, NJ 07931-0012, USA

Parris, Gary (Athlete, Football Player)
5170 9th St
Vero Beach, FL 32966-2841, USA

Parris, Steve (Athlete, Baseball Player)
22942 Judith Dr
Plainfield, IL 60586-9653, USA

Parrish, Bernard J (Bernie) (Athlete, Football Player)
140A Toms Creek Rd
Eastanollee, GA 30538, USA

Parrish, Hunter (Actor)
c/o Lainie Sorkin Becky *Management 360*
9111 Wilshire Blvd
Beverly Hills, CA 90210-5508, USA

Parrish, John (Athlete, Baseball Player)
325 Charles Rd
Lancaster, PA 17603-6833, USA

Parrish, Lance M (Athlete, Baseball Player)
1101 Chateau Ln
Nashville, TN 37215-4505, USA

Parrish, Larry A (Athlete, Baseball Player, Coach)
234 Green Haven Ln W
Dundee, FL 33838-4112, USA

Parrish, Lemar (Athlete, Football Player)
52 Brittany Way
Palmetto, GA 30268-8575, USA

Parros, Peter (Actor)
PO Box 3055
West Orange, NJ 07052-0655, USA

Parrot, Andrew
10 Fiske Pl Ste 530
Mount Vernon, NY 10550-3211, USA

Parrott, Ian
Abermad nr. Aberystwyth
Dyfed Wales, ENGLAND SY 23 4RS

Parrott, Mike (Athlete, Baseball Player)
PO Box 1264
Lyons, CO 80540-1264, USA

Parry, Craig (Golfer)
5139 Latrobe Dr
Windermere, FL 34786-8916, USA

Parry, Edward (Athlete, Basketball Player)
6152 Benoit Rd
Clay, MI 48001-3302, USA

Parry, Ken (Actor)
c/o Linda Kremer *Billy Marsh Drama Ltd*
20 Garrick St
London WC2E 9BT, UK

Parry, Robert T (Financier)
720 S Colorado Blvd Ste 290A
Denver, CO 80246-1929, USA

Parry, Vikci (Stylist)
c/o Staff Member *Elite Model Management/Atlanta*
1708 Peachtree St NW Ste 210
Atlanta, GA 30309-2416, USA

Parseghian, Ara (Coach, Football Coach, Sportscaster)
51767 Oakbridge Ct
Granger, IN 46539, USA

Parseghian, Gregory (Business Person)
8200 Jones Branch Dr
McLean, VA 22102-3107, USA

Parshall, George W (Misc)
2401 Pennsylvania Ave Apt 714
Wilmington, DE 19806-1410, USA

Parsia, Fati (Stylist)
c/o Staff Member *Rex Agency, The*
6311 Romaine St
Los Angeles, CA 90038-2617, USA

Parsky, Gerald L (Attorney, Attorney General, General)
1800 Century Park E
Los Angeles, CA 90067-1501, USA

Parsons, Alan (Musician)
c/o Staff Member *Agency Group Ltd, The (NY)*
142 W 57th St Fl 6
New York, NY 10019-3300, USA

Parsons, Benny (Race Car Driver)
1691 Old Harmony Dr NW
Concord, NC 28027-8031, USA

Parsons, Bill (Athlete, Baseball Player)
322 Karen Ave Unit 3901
Las Vegas, NV 89109-0453, USA

Parsons, Bob (Athlete, Football Player)
1098 Stanton Rd
Lake Zurich, IL 60047-1746, USA

Parsons, Casey (Athlete, Baseball Player)
17214 E Galactica Ct
Greenacres, WA 99016-7766, USA

Parsons, David (Choreographer)
476 Broadway
New York, NY 10013-2621, USA

Parsons, Estelle (Actor)
924 W End Ave Apt T5
New York, NY 10025-3543, USA

Parsons, Jim (Actor)
c/o Marsha McManus *Principal Entertainment (LA)*
1964 Westwood Blvd Ste 400
Los Angeles, CA 90025-4695, USA

Parsons, John T (Inventor)
1456 Brigadoon Ct
Traverse City, MI 49686-5921, USA

Parsons, Karyn (Actor)
c/o Matthew Lesher *Insight*
1134 S Cloverdale Ave
Los Angeles, CA 90019-6737, USA

Parsons, Nathan (Actor)
c/o Melissa Hirschenson *Innovative Artists (LA)*
1505 10th St
Santa Monica, CA 90401-2805, USA

Parsons, Nicholas (Actor)
174/178 N Gower St
London NW1 2NB, UNITED KINGDOM (UK)

Parsons, Phil (Athlete, Race Car Driver)
18801 Coveside Ln
Cornelius, NC 28031-5250, USA

Parsons, Robert (Bob)
14455 N Hayden Rd Ste 219
Scottsdale, AZ 85260-6993, USA

Parsons, Tom (Athlete, Baseball Player)
7106 Lorraine Ave NW
North Canton, OH 44720-8832, USA

Parsons-Zipay, Suzanne (Baseball Player)
2310 Englewood Rd
Englewood, FL 34223-6333, USA

Part, Arvo (Composer)
Warwick House 9 Warrick St
London W1R 5RA, UNITED KINGDOM (UK)

Partee, Barbara H (Educator)
50 Hobart Ln
Amherst, MA 01002-1321, USA

Partee, Dennis (Athlete, Football Player)
604 E Rusk St
Marshall, TX 75670-3472, USA

Parten, Ty (Athlete, Football Player)
2926 W Eastman Dr
Anthem, AZ 85086-1501, USA

Partlow, Hope (Musician)
c/o Staff Member *Virgin Records (NY)*
150 5th Ave Fl 7
New York, NY 10011-4372, USA

Parton, Dolly (Actor, Musician, Songwriter)
2700 Dollywood Parks Blvd
Pigeon Forge, TN 37863-4102, USA

Parton, Stella (Musician)
PO Box 120871
Nashville, TN 37212-0871, USA

Partridge, Derek
96 Broadway Bexley Heath
Kent, ENGLAND DA6 7DE

Partridge, John A (Architect)
20 Old Pye St Westminster
London SW1, UNITED KINGDOM (UK)

Partridge, Rick (Athlete, Football Player)
707 Reeder Rd
Paramus, NJ 07652-3721, USA

Parvanov, Georgi (President)
2 Dondukov Blvd
Sofia 1123, BULGARIA

Pasanella, Giovanni (Architect)
330 W 42nd St
New York, NY 10036-6902, USA

Pasanella, Marco (Designer)
45 W 18th St
New York, NY 10011-4609, USA

Pasarell, Charles (Tennis Player)
78200 Miles Ave
Indian Wells, CA 92210-6803, USA

Pascal, Adam (Actor)
c/o Staff Member *Paradigm (LA)*
360 N Crescent Dr
Beverly Hills, CA 90210-4874, USA

Pascal, Francoise
89 Riverview Gdns
London, ENGLAND SW12 9RA

Pascal, Olivia
Merzstr. 14
Munich, GERMANY D-81679

Paschal, Doug (Athlete, Football Player)
4600 Coburn Ct
Charlotte, NC 28277-2553, USA

Paschall, Bill (Athlete, Baseball Player)
7926 Windspray Dr
Summerfield, NC 27358-9715, USA

Paschall, Jim (Race Car Driver)
RR 2 Box 450
Denton, NC 27239, USA

Paschke, Melanie (Athlete, Track Athlete)
Asseweg 2
Braunschweig 38124, GERMANY

Pasco, Richard (Actor)
125 Gloucester Road
London SW7 4TE, UNITED KINGDOM (UK)

Pascoal, Hermeto (Musician)
RVN Vitor Guisard 209
Rio de Janerio 21832, BRAZIL

Pascrell Jr., Bill (Congressman, Politician)
2370 Rayburn Hob
Washington, DC 20515-0906, USA

Pascual, Camilo (Athlete, Baseball Player)
4625 SW 82nd Pl
Miami, FL 33155-5453, USA

Pascual, Carlos (Athlete, Baseball Player)
2540 SW 92nd Ct
Miami, FL 33165-8139, USA

Pascual, Luis (Director)
1 Place Paul Claudel
Paris 75006, FRANCE

Pascual, Mercedes (Biologist)
Ecology & Biology Dept
Ann Arbor, MI 48109, USA

Pascucci, Val (Athlete, Baseball Player)
11163 James Pl
Cerritos, CA 90703-6450, USA

Pasdar, Adrian (Actor)
c/o Leigh Brillstein *International Creative Management (ICM-LA)*
10250 Constellation Blvd Fl 7
Los Angeles, CA 90067-6207, USA

Pashnick, Larry (Athlete, Baseball Player)
506 Highland St
Wyandotte, MI 48192-2433, USA

Pasian, Karina (Musician)
c/o Staff Member *Island Def Jam Music Group*
825 8th Ave Fl 28
New York, NY 10019-7416

Pasik, Mario (Actor)
c/o Staff Member *Telefe - Argentina*
Pavon 2444 (C1248AAT)
Buenos Aires, ARGENTINA

Pasillas, Jose (Musician)
c/o Staff Member *ArtistDirect*
9046 Lindblade St
Culver City, CA 90232-2513, USA

Paskai, Laszio Cardinal (Religious Leader)
Uri Utca 62
Budapest 1014, HUNGARY

Paskvan, George (Athlete, Football Player)
1955 Betty Jane Ct
Saint Paul, MN 55109-4105, USA

Pasley, Kevin (Athlete, Baseball Player)
2701 Lancaster Dr
Sun City Center, FL 33573-6517, USA

Pasmore, E J Victor (Artist)
Dar Gamri
Gudja, MALTA

Pasqua, Dan (Athlete, Baseball Player)
10423 Capistrano Ln
Orland Park, IL 60467-8244, USA

Pasquale, Steven (Actor)
c/o Staff Member *Overbrook Entertainment*
450 N Roxbury Dr Fl 4
Beverly Hills, CA 90210-4218, USA

Pasqualini, Tony (Actor)
c/o Sandra Joseph *SLJ Management*
833 N Edinburgh Ave Ph 11
Los Angeles, CA 90046-6999, USA

Pasqualoni, Paul (Coach, Football Coach)
Athletic
Syracuse, NY 13244-0001, USA

Pasquesi, Anthony (Athlete, Football Player)
463 N Clubview Ct
Addison, IL 60101-2998, USA

Pasquin, John R (Actor, Director, Filmmaker, Producer)
801 Tarcuto Way
Los Angeles, CA 90077-3216, USA

Pass, Patrick (Athlete, Football Player)
4 Spruce Pond Rd
Franklin, MA 02038-2500, USA

Passaglia, Martin (Athlete, Basketball Player)
7377 Capay Ave
Orland, CA 95963-9687, USA

Passarelli, Pasquale (Wrestler)
Ander Froschlache 23
Munster 4400, GERMANY

Passer, Ivan (Director)
8281 Melrose Ave Ste 300
Los Angeles, CA 90046-6891, USA

Passions, The
141 Dunbar Ave
Fords, NJ 08863-1551

Passman, Elizabeth (Stylist)
927 Noyes St
Evanston, IL 60201-6206, USA

Passmore, John A (Misc)
6 Jansz Cres
Manuka, ACT 2603, AUSTRALIA

Passos, Rosa (Musician)
c/o Staff Member *Concord Music Group, Inc*
900 N Rohlwing Rd
Itasca, IL 60143-1161, USA

Paster, Jessica (Stylist)
c/o Staff Member *Magnet (LA)*
6363 Wilshire Blvd Ste 650
Los Angeles, CA 90048-5725, USA

Pasternak, Michael (Actor)
c/o Craig Wyckoff *Epstein-Wyckoff-Corsa-Ross & Associates (LA)*
11350 Ventura Blvd Ste 100
Studio City, CA 91604-3140, USA

Pasternak, Reagan (Actor)
c/o Staff Member *Noble Caplan Abrams*
1260 Yonge St 2nd Floor
Toronto ON M4T 1W6, Canada

Pastor, Ed (Congressman, Politician)
2465 Rayburn Hob
Washington, DC 20515-0304, USA

Pastore, Frank (Athlete, Baseball Player)
1542 Francis Way
Upland, CA 91786-2353, USA

Pastore, Vincent (Actor)
40 Fordham St
Bronx, NY 10464-1405, USA

Pastorini, Darite A (Dan) Jr (Athlete, Football Player)
2703 Stuart Mnr
Houston, TX 77082-3097, USA

Pastornicky, Cliff (Athlete, Baseball Player)
4815 50th Ave W
Bradenton, FL 34210-4907, USA

Pastrana, Arango Andres (President)
Plaza de Bolivar Carrera 8A
Bogota, DE, COLUMBIA

Pastrana, Travis (Athlete)
c/o Staff Member *Familie, The*
1545 Faraday Ave
Carlsbad, CA 92008-7449, USA

Pataki, Governor George E (Ex-Governor, Politician)
30 Rockefeller Plz
New York, NY 10112-0015, USA

Pataky, Elsa (Actor)
3221 Hutchison Ave Ste H
Los Angeles, CA 90034-3298, USA

Patane, Giuseppe
Holbeinstr 6
Munich 81679, GERMANY

Pataric, Sebastian (Stylist)
c/o Staff Member *Zenobia Agency Inc*
PO Box 909
Groveland, CA 95321-0909, USA

Patat, Frederic (Misc)
2 Bis Blvd Tonnelle
Tours Cedex 37032, FRANCE

Pate, Bob (Athlete, Baseball Player)
16834 Superior St
Northridge, CA 91343-1736, USA

Pate, Cynthia (Beauty Pageant Winner)
7907 Stafford Trl
Savage, MN 55378-4308, USA

Pate, Jerry (Golfer)
5 Hyde Park Rd
Pensacola, FL 32503-5830, USA

Pate, Rupert (Athlete, Football Player)
428 Shadowbrook Dr
Burlington, NC 27215-4775, USA

Pate, Steve (Golfer)
1034 Brookview Ave
Westlake Village, CA 91361-1623, USA

Patek, Freddie (Athlete, Baseball Player)
5408 NE Wedgewood Ln
Lees Summit, MO 64064-1220, USA

Patekar, Nana (Actor, Bollywood)
304 Sheetal Apna Ghar Society Samarth Nagar Andheri
Mumbai, MS 400053, INDIA

Patel, Anuradha (Actor, Bollywood)
1001D Abhishek Aptartments Juhu Versova Road Andheri
Mumbai, MS 400058, INDIA

Patel, C Kumar N (Inventor)
1171 Roberto Ln
Los Angeles, CA 90077-2302, USA

Patel, Dev (Actor)
c/o Sarah Spear *Curtis Brown Ltd*
Hay Market House 28-29 Hay Market
London SW1Y 4SP, UK

Patera, Dennis (Athlete, Football Player)
61535 S Highway 97 Apt 9512
Bend, OR 97702-2154, USA

Patera, George (Athlete, Football Player)
7305 172nd St SW
Edmonds, WA 98026-5121, USA

Patera, John A (Jack) (Athlete, Coach, Football Coach, Football Player)
82 Osprey Dr
Cle Elum, WA 98922, USA

Patera, Ken (Athlete)
6932 Stratford Rd
Saint Paul, MN 55125, USA

Patera, Pavel (Athlete, Hockey Player)
175 Kellogg Blvd W
Saint Paul, MN 55102-1206, USA

Paterno, Joseph V (Joe) (Athlete, Coach, Football Coach, Football Player)
830 McKee St
State College, PA 16803-3632, USA

Paterra, Greg (Athlete, Football Player)
305 Douglas Ave
Elizabeth, PA 15037-1724, USA

Paterra, Herb (Athlete, Football Player)
3696 Woodmonte Dr
Rochester, MI 48306-4799, USA

Paterson, Bill (Actor)
15 Kensington High St
London W8 5NP, UNITED KINGDOM (UK)

Pathon, Jerome (Athlete, Football Player)
4827 Eagles Watch Ln
Indianapolis, IN 46254-9531, USA

Patillo, Maria
6300 Wilshire Blvd # 2110
Los Angeles, CA 90048-5204

Patinkin, Mandy (Actor, Musician)
c/o Iris Grossman *International Creative Management (ICM-LA)*
10250 Constellation Blvd Fl 7
Los Angeles, CA 90067-6207, USA

Patitz, Tatjana (Model)
c/o Gordon Rael *JV Entertainment*
27346 English Oak Ct
Canyon Country, CA 91387-6869, USA

Patkau, John (Architect)
560 Beaty St # L110
Vancouver, BC V6B 2L3, CANADA

Paton, Nikki (Stylist)
c/o Staff Member *Independent NY*
15 E 30th St Apt 401
New York, NY 10016-7031, USA

Patrese, Ricardo (Race Car Driver)
Via Umberto 1
Padova 35100, ITALY

Patriarco, Earie (Opera Singer)
40 W 57th St
New York, NY 10019-4001, USA

Patric, Jason (Actor, Producer)
c/o Jason Weinberg *Untitled Entertainment (LA)*
350 S Beverly Dr Ste 200
Beverly Hills, CA 90212-4819, USA

Patrick, Bronswell (Athlete, Baseball Player)
3202 Morton Ln
Greenville, NC 27834-4930, USA

Patrick, Craig (Athlete, Coach, Hockey Player)
66 Mario Lemieux Pl
Pittsburgh, PA 15219-3504, USA

Patrick, Danica (Race Car Driver)
PO Box 155
Roscoe, IL 61073-0155, USA

Patrick, Deval (Governor)
State House, Office of the Governor
Room 280
Boston, MA 2133, USA

Patrick, Frank (Athlete, Football Player)
5689 SW 98th St
Denton, NE 68339-3346, USA

Patrick, Marcus (Actor)
c/o Staff Member *Gar Lester Agency*
4130 Cahuenga Blvd Ste 108
Toluca Lake, CA 91602-2848, USA

Patrick, Mary Anthony
56 Copsterhill Rd.Oldham
Manchester, ENGLAND

Patrick, Nicholas J M (Astronaut)
10811 Oak Creek St
Houston, TX 77024-3016, USA

Patrick, Pat (Misc)
8431 Green Town Rd # 400
Indianapolis, IN 46234, USA

Patrick, Richard (Musician)
c/o Jamie Talbot *Sanctuary Artist Management*
8750 Wilshire Blvd Ste 200
Beverly Hills, CA 90211-2707, USA

Patrick, Robert (Actor, Producer)
c/o Susan Patricola *Patricola Lust PR*
9171 Wilshire Blvd Ste 390
Beverly Hills, CA 90210-5515, USA

Patrick, Ruth (Educator)
& 19th Pkwy
Philadelphia, PA 19103, USA

Patrick, Tera (Adult Film Star)
c/o Jeff Bowler *Insomnia Media Group*
100 Universal City Plaza Drive The Rock Hudson Bldg Suite G
Universal CIty, CA 91608, USA

Patrick, Thomas M (Business Person)
130 E Randolph St
Chicago, IL 60601-6207, USA

Patrick, Tom
Heimeranstr. 51
Munich, GERMANY D-80339

Patrick, Wayne (Athlete, Football Player)
329 Peppertree Dr
Amherst, NY 14228-2955, USA

Patridge, Audrina (Actor, Reality TV Star)
c/o David (Dave) Fleming *Mosaic Media Group*
9200 W Sunset Blvd Ste 10
Los Angeles, CA 90069-3608, USA

Patrone, Shana
209 10th Ave S Ste 229
Nashville, TN 37203-0721

Patten, Joel (Athlete, Football Player)
13415 Marble Rock Dr
Chantilly, VA 20151-2482, USA

Patten of Barnes, Christopher F (Government Official)
The House Of Lords
London SW1A OPW, UK

Patterson, Bob (Athlete, Baseball Player)
1093 7th Street Blvd SE
Hickory, NC 28602-4342, USA

Patterson, Carly (Gymnast)
1937 W Parker Rd
Plano, TX 75023-7503, USA

Patterson, Colin (Athlete, Hockey Player)
128-2100 13th St S
Cranbrook, BC V1C 7J5, Canada

Patterson, Corey (Athlete, Baseball Player)
1115 Gordon Combs Rd NW
Marietta, GA 30064-1225, USA

Patterson, Danny (Athlete, Baseball Player)
13944 E Yucca St
Scottsdale, AZ 85259-4638, USA

Patterson, Daryl (Athlete, Baseball Player)
20145 Tollhouse Rd
Clovis, CA 93619-9760, USA

Patterson, Dave (Athlete, Baseball Player)
8425 Evanston Ave
Raytown, MO 64138-3346, USA

Patterson, Don (Athlete, Football Player)
1558 Halisport Lake Dr NW
Kennesaw, GA 30152-4072, USA

Patterson, Elvis V (Athlete, Football Player)
3939 Alberta St
Houston, TX 77021-4009, USA

Patterson, Francine G (Penny) (Misc)
PO Box 620-640
Woodside, CA 94062, USA

Patterson, Gary (Cartoonist)
25208 Malibu Rd
Malibu, CA 90265-4635, USA

Patterson, Gil (Athlete, Baseball Player)
3910 Little Egret Ct
Lutz, FL 33558-2711, USA

Patterson, James (Business Person, Writer)
466 Lexington Ave
New York, NY 10017-3140, USA

Patterson, Jarrod (Athlete, Baseball Player)
405 6th St N
Clanton, AL 35045-2823, USA

Patterson, Jeff (Athlete, Baseball Player)
27825 Tamara Dr
Yorba Linda, CA 92887-5843, USA

Patterson, John (Athlete, Baseball Player)
2659 E Jade Pl
Chandler, AZ 85286-2697, USA

Patterson, John (Athlete, Baseball Player)
2709 Country Club Dr
Orange, TX 77630-2142, USA

Patterson, John M (Ex-Governor)
P.O. Box 30155
Montgomery, AL 36103, USA

Patterson, Katerine (Writer)
70 Wildersburg Cmn
Barre, VT 05641-9761, USA

Patterson, Ken (Athlete, Baseball Player)
1202 Maverick Trl
Mc Gregor, TX 76657-4078, USA

Patterson, Lorna (Actor)
23852 Pacific Coast Hwy # 355
Malibu, CA 90265-4876, USA

Patterson, Marne (Actor)
c/o Matthew Lesher *Insight*
1134 S Cloverdale Ave
Los Angeles, CA 90019-6737, USA

Patterson, Marnette (Actor)
c/o Matthew Lesher *Insight*
1134 S Cloverdale Ave
Los Angeles, CA 90019-6737, USA

Patterson, Melody (Actor)
141 Sunny Ln
Branson West, MO 65737-9606, USA

Patterson, Michael (Financier)
270 Park Ave
New York, NY 10017-2014, USA

Patterson, Mike (Athlete, Baseball Player)
19306 Chamblee Ave
Cerritos, CA 90703-6751, USA

Patterson, Neva
2498 Mandeville Canyon Rd
Los Angeles, CA 90049-1236

Patterson, Percival J (Prime Minister)
1 Devon Road PO Box 272
Kingston 6, JAMAICA

Patterson, Reggie (Athlete, Baseball Player)
PO Box 55511
Birmingham, AL 35255-5511, USA

Patterson, Richard North (Writer)
PO Box 183
West Tisbury, MA 02575-0183, USA

Patterson, Robert M (War Hero)
907 Ironwood Dr
Henderson, KY 42420-4866, USA

Patterson, Ross (Actor)
c/o Gina Hoffman *Baker Winokur Ryder Public Relations (BWR-LA)*
9100 Wilshire Blvd Ste 500 PMB WEST
Beverly Hills, CA 90212-3426, USA

Patterson, Scott (Actor)
c/o Laina Cohn *Laina Cohn Management*
15066 Sutton St
Sherman Oaks, CA 91403-4020, USA

Patterson, Shawn (Athlete, Football Player)
15711 E Avenida Del Ville Ct
Chandler, AZ 85249, USA

Patterson, Suzanne (Stylist)
13226 Grand Junction Dr
Fairfax, VA 22033-1328, USA

Patterson, Willie (Baseball Player)
409 Tuscaloosa Ave SW Apt 7
Birmingham, AL 35211-1457, USA

Patterson, Worthy (Athlete, Basketball Player)
2091 Kerwood Ave
Los Angeles, CA 90025-6006, USA

Pattillo, Linda (Correspondent)
820 1st St NE
Washington, DC 20002-4243, USA

Pattin, Marty (Athlete, Baseball Player)
3401 Sweetgrass Ct
Lawrence, KS 66049-4245, USA

Pattinson, Robert (Actor)
c/o Nick Frenkel *3 Arts Entertainment Inc*
9460 Wilshire Blvd Fl 7
Beverly Hills, CA 90212-2713, USA

Pattison, Mark (Athlete, Football Player)
415 14th St
Santa Monica, CA 90402-2131, USA

Patton, Donovan (Actor)
c/o Staff Member *Glasser/Black Management*
283 Cedarhurst Ave
Cedarhurst, NY 11516-1671, USA

Patton, Gene (Athlete, Baseball Player)
910 Kingsway Dr
Coatesville, PA 19320-2166, USA

Patton, Jerry (Athlete, Football Player)
219 N 12th St
Saginaw, MI 48601-1718, USA

Patton, Marvcus (Athlete, Football Player)
12994 Wyckland Dr
Clifton, VA 20124-2053, USA

Patton, Mel
2312 Via Del Aquacate
Fallbrook, CA 92028-9697

Patton, Melvin (Mel) (Athlete, Track Athlete)
2312 Via Del Aquacate
Fallbrook, CA 92028-9697, USA

Patton, Paula (Actor, Director)
c/o Melissa Stone *42West (LA)*
11400 W Olympic Blvd Ste 1100
Los Angeles, CA 90064-1579, USA

Patton, Tom (Athlete, Baseball Player)
577 Daisy Dr
New Holland, PA 17557-8708, USA

Patton, Troy (Athlete, Baseball Player)
c/o Staff Member *Baltimore Orioles*
333 W Camden St
Baltimore, MD 21201-2496, USA

Patton, Will (Actor)
c/o Kate Edwards *Grand View Management*
578 Washington Blvd # 688
Marina Del Rey, CA 90292-5442, USA

Patty, Edward
14 Ave De Jurigoz
Lausanne, SWITZERLAND 1006

Patty, J Edward (Budge) (Tennis Player)
La Mame 14 Ave de Jurigoz
Lausanne 1006, SWITZERLAND

Patty, Sandi
c/o Staff Member *Richard De La Font Agency*
3808 W South Park Blvd
Broken Arrow, OK 74011-1261, USA

Patty, Sandi (Music Group, Musician)
PO Box 6
Pendleton, IN 46064-0006, USA

Patu, Saul (Athlete, Football Player)
6001 S Hazel St
Seattle, WA 98178-2450, USA

Patulski, Walter G (Walt) (Athlete, Football Player)
420 Kimber Rd
Syracuse, NY 13224-1836, USA

Patz, Arnall (Doctor)
600 N Wolfe
Baltimore, MD 21287-0005, USA

Patzaichin, Ivan (Athlete)
SC Sportiv Unirea Tricolor Soseaua Stefan Cel Mare 9
Bucharest, ROMANIA

Patzak, PeterJosef
Schottlgasse 23
Klosterneuburg, AUSTRIA A-3400

Patzakis, Michele (Opera Singer)
Plandengasse 7
Vienna 1010, AUSTRIA

Pauk, Gyorgy (Musician)
27 Armitage Road
London NW11, UNITED KINGDOM (UK)

Paukner, Catherine (Stylist)
349 Silver Hill Rd
Easton, CT 06612-1134, USA

Paul, Aaron (Actor)
c/o Loch Powell *Leverage Management*
3030 Pennsylvania Ave
Santa Monica, CA 90404-4112, USA

Paul, Adrian (Actor, Director, Producer)
c/o David (Dave) Fleming *Mosaic Media Group*
9200 W Sunset Blvd Ste 10
Los Angeles, CA 90069-3608, USA

Paul, Alan (Music Group, Musician)
1801 Century Park W
Los Angeles, CA 90067-6409, USA

Paul, Alexandra (Actor)
c/o Chuck Binder *Binder & Associates*
1465 Lindacrest Dr
Beverly Hills, CA 90210-2519, USA

Paul, Billy (Musician)
8215 Winthrop St
Philadelphia, PA 19136-1914, USA

Paul, Chris (Athlete, Basketball Player)
c/o Chris Chambers *The Chamber Group*
416 W 13th St Ste 105
New York, NY 10014-1179, USA

Paul, Christi (Correspondent)
1050 Techwood Dr NW
Atlanta, GA 30318-5604, USA

Paul, Don (Athlete, Football Player)
20100 Delita Dr
Woodland Hills, CA 91364-3519, USA

Paul, Don Michael (Actor, Director)

Paul, Emily (Actor)
c/o Simon Millar *Rumble Media*
1620 Broadway Ste C
Santa Monica, CA 90404-2777, USA

Paul, Henry (Music Group, Musician)
1607 17th Ave S
Nashville, TN 37212-2812, USA

Paul, Jarrad (Actor)
c/o JC Spink *Benderspink*
5870 W Jefferson Blvd Ste E
Los Angeles, CA 90016-3159, USA

Paul, John Michael (Actor)

Paul, Josh (Athlete, Baseball Player)
28751 Windover St
Zephyrhills, FL 33545-4378, USA

Paul, Markus (Athlete, Football Player)
PO Box 423041
Kissimmee, FL 34742-3041, USA

Paul, Mike (Athlete, Baseball Player)
5121 N Circulo Sobrio
Tucson, AZ 85718-6037, USA

Paul, Oakenfold (Musician)
PO Box 19788
London SW15 2FT, UNITED KINGDOM (UK)

Paul, Robert (Figure Skater)
10675 Rochester Ave
Los Angeles, CA 90024-5009, USA

Paul, Ron (Congressman, Politician)
122 W Way St Ste 301
Lake Jackson, TX 77566-5245, USA

Paul, Vinnie (Musician)
361 W Broadway # 200
New York, NY 10013-2209, USA

Paul, Whitney (Athlete, Football Player)
6802 Thornwild Rd
Missouri City, TX 77489-2649, USA

Paul, Wolfgang (Soccer Player)
Postfach 1324
Olsberg-Bigge 59939, GERMANY

Paul & Paula
7251 Lowell Dr # 200
Overland Park, KS 66204-1840

Paula, Alejandro F (Jandi) (Prime Minister)
Fort Amsterdam 17
Willemstad, NETHERLANDS ANTILLES

Paulauskas, Arturas (President)
Gediminas 53
Vilnius 232026, LITHUANIA

Pauley, Jane (Correspondent)
c/o Wayne Kabak *WSK Management, LLC*
888 7th Ave Ste 503
New York, NY 10106-0501, USA

Paulino, Ronny (Athlete, Baseball Player)
129 Cardinal Cir
Pittsburgh, PA 15237-1067, USA

Paulk, Charlie (Athlete, Basketball Player)
3336 Emmons Dr
Memphis, TN 38128-5308, USA

Paulk, Jeff (Athlete, Football Player)
7751 S Bonarden Ln
Tempe, AZ 85284-1569, USA

Paulo (DJ)
c/o Staff Member *Diva Central Inc*
7510 W Sunset Blvd Ste 1445
Los Angeles, CA 90046-3408, USA

Pauls, Raymond (Composer, Music Group, Musician)
Veidenbaum Str 41/43 #26
Riga 226001, LATVIA

Paulsen, Erik (Congressman, Politician)
127 Cannon Hob
Washington, DC 20515-0904, USA

Paulsen, Robert (Rob) (Artist, Voice Over Artist)
c/o Staff Member *Sutton Barth & Vennari Inc*
145 S Fairfax Ave Ste 310
Los Angeles, CA 90036-2176, USA

Paulson, Carl (Golfer)
8211 Tibet Butler Dr
Windermere, FL 34786-5614, USA

Paulson, Dainard (Athlete, Football Player)
2904 Main St
Union Gap, WA 98903-1756, USA

Paulson, Dennis (Golfer)
1872 Shadetree Dr
San Marcos, CA 92078-0902, USA

Paulson, Richard L (Business Person)
601 W Riverside Ave
Spokane, WA 99201-0638, USA

Paulson, Sarah (Actor)
c/o Judy Hofflund *Hofflund/Polone*
9465 Wilshire Blvd Ste 420
Beverly Hills, CA 90212-2603, USA

Paultz, Billy (Athlete, Basketball Player)
1941 Waters Edge Ln
Seabrook, TX 77586-2599, USA

Paulusma, Polly (Musician)
c/o Staff Member *Paradigm (Monterey)*
404 W Franklin St
Monterey, CA 93940-2303, USA

Paup, Bryce E (Athlete, Football Player)
4300 Oak Ridge Cir
De Pere, WI 54115-8327, USA

Pausini, Laura (Musician)
c/o Staff Member *Creative Artists Agency (CAA-LA)*
2000 Avenue of the Stars Ste 100
Los Angeles, CA 90067-4705, USA

Pavan, Marisa (Actor)
4 Allee des Brouillards
Paris 75018, FRANCE

Pavano, Carl (Athlete, Baseball Player)
300 E 55th St Apt 23C
New York, NY 10022-4390, USA

Pavelich, Mark (Athlete, Hockey Player, Olympic Athlete)
19 E Norwood Shrs
Lutsen, MN 55612, USA

Pavelka, Jake (Reality TV Star)
c/o Janice Lee *MLC PR*
7080 Hollywood Blvd Ste 903
Los Angeles, CA 90028-6936, USA

Paven, Corey
2515 McKinney Ave Ste 930 PMB 10
Dallas, TX 75201-1921

Paver, Michelle (Writer)
186 Bickenhall Mansions
London W1U 6BX, UNITED KINGDOM

Pavia, Ria
3500 W Olive Ave Ste 1400
Burbank, CA 91505-5512

Pavin, Corey (Golfer)
4332 Gilbert Ave
Dallas, TX 75219-2908, USA

Pavlas, David (Dave) (Athlete, Baseball Player)
PO Box 1224
Shiner, TX 77984-1224, USA

Pavletic, Viaiko (President)
Pantovcak 241
Zagreb 10000, CROATIA

Pavletich, Don (Athlete, Baseball Player)
13645 Adelaide Ln
Brookfield, WI 53005-4965, USA

Pavlik, Kelly (Boxer)
3908 Howard Hughes Pkwy # 580
Las Vegas, NV 89109, USA

Pavlik, Roger (Athlete, Baseball Player)
622 Beaver Bend Rd
Houston, TX 77037-2004, USA

Pavlovic, Aleksandar (Basketball Player)
Delta Center 301 W South Temple
Salt Lake City, UT 84101, USA

Pavlow, Muriel
2 Conduit St
London, ENGLAND W1R 9TG

Pawelczyk, James A (Jim) (Astronaut)
2101 Nasa Pkwy Spc Center
Houston, TX 77058-3607, USA

Pawloski, Stan (Athlete, Baseball Player)
413 Maryjoe Way
Warrington, PA 18976-1695, USA

Pawlowski, John (Athlete, Baseball Player)
257 Mill Branch Way
North Augusta, SC 29860-8622, USA

Paxman, Jeremy
56 Wood Ln
London, ENGLAND W12 7RJ

Paxon, L William (Bill) (Misc)
1333 New Hampshire Ave NW
Washington, DC 20036-1511, USA

Paxson, Jim (Athlete, Basketball Player)
3225 Southdale Dr Apt 1
Dayton, OH 45409-1130, USA

Paxson, John (Athlete, Basketball Player, Misc)
125 Boardman Ct
Lake Bluff, IL 60044-2454, USA

Paxson, Melanie (Actor)
c/o Staff Member *Brady Brannon & Rich*
5670 Wilshire Blvd Ste 820
Los Angeles, CA 90036-5613, USA

Paxton, Bill (Actor)
c/o Jillian Fowkes *ID Public Relations (ID-LA)*
7080 Hollywood Blvd Fl 8
Los Angeles, CA 90028-6906, USA

Paxton, John (Editor)
175 5th Ave
New York, NY 10010-7703, USA

Paxton, Mike (Athlete, Baseball Player)
1145 S Indian Wells Dr
Collierville, TN 38017-3667, USA

Paxton, Sara (Actor)
c/o TJ Stein *Stein Entertainment Group*
1351 N Crescent Heights Blvd Apt 312
West Hollywood, CA 90046-4549, USA

Paxton, Tom (Music Group, Musician, Songwriter, Writer)
733 N Main St
Ann Arbor, MI 48104-1030, USA

Payak Jr, John (Athlete, Basketball Player)
3550 Hill River Dr
Toledo, OH 43615-1189, USA

Payette, Julie (Astronaut)
Rockliffe Base
Ottawa, ON K1A 1A1, CANADA

Paymer, David (Actor)
327 19th St
Santa Monica, CA 90402-2409, USA

Payne, Alexander (Actor, Director, Producer)
c/o Craig Gering *Creative Artists Agency (CAA-LA)*
2000 Avenue of the Stars Ste 100
Los Angeles, CA 90067-4705, USA

Payne, Allen (Actor)
c/o Tom Harrison *Diverse Talent Group*
9911 W Pico Blvd Ste 340W
Los Angeles, CA 90035-2712, USA

Payne, Anthony E (Composer)
2 Wilton Square
London N1 3DL, UNITED KINGDOM (UK)

Payne, Barbara (Baseball Player)
15897 W Desert Meadow Dr
Surprise, AZ 85374-5636, USA

Payne, Bruce (Actor)
c/o Gordon Gilbertson *Gilbertson Management*
1334 3rd Street Promenade Ste 201
Santa Monica, CA 90401-1320, USA

Payne, David N (Engineer)
Highfield
Southampton SO17 1BJ, UNITED KINGDOM (UK)

Payne, Dougie (Musician)
21 Heathmans Road
London SW6 4TJ, UNITED KINGDOM (UK)

Payne, Freda (Music Group, Musician)
c/o Staff Member *Diva Central Inc*
7510 W Sunset Blvd Ste 1445
Los Angeles, CA 90046-3408, USA

Payne, Harry C (Educator)
President's Office
Williamstown, MA 1267, USA

Payne, Henry (Cartoonist, Editor)
615 W Lafayette Blvd
Detroit, MI 48226-3124, USA

Payne, Julie (Actor)
c/o Staff Member *Pakula/King & Associates*
9229 W Sunset Blvd Ste 315
Los Angeles, CA 90069-3403, USA

Payne, Keith (War Hero)
2 Saint Bee's Ave
Bucasia, QLD 4740, AUSTRALIA

Payne, Ken (Athlete, Football Player)
307 W 108th Pl
Chicago, IL 60628-3344, USA

Payne, Kenny (Athlete, Basketball Player)
655 Goodpasture Island Rd Apt 199
Eugene, OR 97401-1534, USA

Payne, Kherington (Actor)
c/o Staff Member *Luber Roklin Management*
8530 Wilshire Blvd Ste 550
Beverly Hills, CA 90211-3133, USA

Payne, Ladell (Educator)
President's Office
Ashland, VA 23005, USA

Payne, Rod (Athlete, Football Player)
9622 Stonemasters Dr
Loveland, OH 45140-6209, USA

Payne, Roger S (Biologist, Misc)
191 Western Rd
Lincoln, MA 1773, USA

Payne, Scherrie-
433 N Camden Dr Ste 400
Beverly Hills, CA 90210-4408

Payne, Seth (Athlete, Football Player)
5004 Chestnut St
Bellaire, TX 77401-3412, USA

Payne, Tom (Actor)
c/o Beth Holden-Garland *Untitled Entertainment (LA)*
350 S Beverly Dr Ste 200
Beverly Hills, CA 90212-4819, USA

Payne, Waylon (Actor, Musician)
c/o Ben Feigin *Anonymous Content (AC-LA)*
3531 Hayden Ave
Culver City, CA 90232, USA

Paynter, Kristen (Stylist)
c/o Staff Member *Montana Artists Agency*
9150 Wilshire Blvd Ste 100
Beverly Hills, CA 90212-3459, USA

Pays, Amanda (Actor)
c/o Staff Member *Personal Management Company*
425 N Robertson Blvd
West Hollywood, CA 90048-1735, USA

Payton, Benjamin F (Educator)
President's Office
Tuskegee, AL 36088, USA

Payton, Christian (Actor)
c/o Staff Member *WmE2 (WMA-LA)*
1 William Morris Pl
Beverly Hills, CA 90212-4261, USA

Payton, Eddie (Athlete, Football Player)
2656 Hemingway Cir
Jackson, MS 39209-7026, USA

Payton, Gary (Athlete, Basketball Player)
1114 Post Ave
Seattle, WA 98101-2915, USA

Payton, Gary E (Astronaut)
2367 Diamond Creek Dr
Colorado Springs, CO 80921-2916, USA

Payton, James (Actor)
c/o Staff Member *Debbie Edler Management Ltd.*
Little Friars Cottage Lombard St
Eynsham, Oxon OX29 4HT, UK

Payton, Jay (Athlete, Baseball Player)
3000 Cone Manor Ln
Raleigh, NC 27613-6604, USA

payton, khary (Actor)
c/o Theodore B Gekis *Gekis Management*
4217 Verdugo View Dr
Los Angeles, CA 90065-4317, USA

Payton, Melvin (Athlete, Basketball Player)
17310 River Ave
Noblesville, IN 46062-8526, USA

Payton, Nicholas (Musician)
116 Village Blvd Ste 200
Princeton, NJ 08540-5700, USA

Payton, Sean (Football Player)
1 Cowboys Pkwy
Irving, TX 75063-4924, USA

Pazienda, Vinnie
64 Waterman Ave
Cranston, RI 02910-4522

Pazienza, Vinny (Boxer)
c/o Darren Prince *Prince Marketing Group*
18 Carillon Cir
Livingston, NJ 07039-2600, USA

Pazik, Mike (Athlete, Baseball Player)
8413 Comanche Ct
Bethesda, MD 20817-4533, USA

PC Quest
PO Box 720423
Norman, OK 73070-4310

Peace, Larry (Athlete, Football Player)
5278 S Hardwood Ter
Lecanto, FL 34461-9253, USA

Peace, Terry (Actor)
PO Box 74
Allison Park, PA 15101-0074, USA

Peace, Warren (Baseball Player)
27921 NC Highway 903
Robersonville, NC 27871-8904, USA

Peacock, Andrew S (Government Official)
30 Monomeath Ave
Canterbury, VIC 3126, AUSTRALIA

Peacocke, Arthur R (Misc)
St Mark's Rectory 11 Summer
Augusta, ME 4330, USA

Peake, Don (Musician)
c/o Mike Rosen *Working Artists Agency*
13525 Ventura Blvd
Sherman Oaks, CA 91423-3801

Peake, James B (General)
5109 Leesburg Pike
Falls Church, VA 22041-3215, USA

Peaker, E J (Actor)
4935 Densmore Ave
Encino, CA 91436-1537, USA

Peaks, Clarence (Football Player)
2500 Knights Rd Apt 3-2
Bensalem, PA 19020-3413, USA

Peaks, Pandora (Adult Film Star)
6011 Winterpointe Ln Apt 201
Raleigh, NC 27606-2278, USA

Pear, Dave (Athlete, Football Player)
3126 199th Ave SE
Sammamish, WA 98075-9652, USA

Pearce, Guy (Actor)
c/o Ann Churchill-Brown *Shanahan Management*
Level 3 Berman House
Surry Hills 2010, AUSTRALIA

Pearce, Jacqueline (Actor)
6 Langley St #41
London WC2H 9JA, UNITED KINGDOM (UK)

Pearce, Josh (Athlete, Baseball Player)
2607 Draper Rd
Yakima, WA 98903-9216, USA

Pearce, Richard I (Director)
240 Bentley Cir
Los Angeles, CA 90049-2414, USA

Pearcy, James W (Athlete, Football Player)
PO Box 609
Cobbs Creek, VA 23035-0609, USA

Pearl, Barry (Actor)
c/o Staff Member *Coolwaters Productions*
10061 Riverside Dr # 531
Toluca Lake, CA 91602-2560, USA

Pearl Jam (Music Group)
c/o Kelly Curtis *Curtis Management*
1900 S Corgiat Dr
Seattle, WA 98108-2817, USA

Pearlman, Rhea (Actor)
c/o Stan Rosenfield *Stan Rosenfield & Associates*
2029 Century Park E Ste 1190
Los Angeles, CA 90067-2931, USA

Pearlstein, Philip (Artist)
361 W 36th St
New York, NY 10018-6408, USA

Pearlstine, Norman (Writer)
c/o Lynn Nesbit *Janklow & Nesbit Associates*
445 Park Ave Fl 13
New York, NY 10022-8628, USA

Pears, David F (Misc)
7 Sandford Road Littlemore
Oxford OX4 4PU, UNITED KINGDOM (UK)

Pearson, Albie (Athlete, Baseball Player)
55473 Oakhill
La Quinta, CA 92253-4730, USA

Pearson, Barry (Athlete, Football Player)
85 Westledge Rd
West Simsbury, CT 06092-2327, USA

Pearson, Corey (Actor)
c/o Colton Gramm *Brillstein Entertainment Partners*
9150 Wilshire Blvd Ste 350
Beverly Hills, CA 90212-3453, USA

Pearson, David
PO Box 161599
Boiling Springs, SC 29316-0027

Pearson, Drew (Athlete, Football Player)
3721 Mount Vernon Way
Plano, TX 75025-3729, USA

Pearson, Durk
PO Box 1067
Hollywood, FL 33022

Pearson, Jason (Athlete, Baseball Player)
2373 Sunset Dr
Freeport, IL 61032-8348, USA

Pearson, Jayice (Athlete, Football Player)
721 SW Winterhill Ln
Lees Summit, MO 64081-2676, USA

Pearson, Larry (Race Car Driver)
12015 Lazy Willow Ln
Charlotte, NC 28273-6720, USA

Pearson, Lindell (Athlete, Football Player)
5512 NW 114th St
Oklahoma City, OK 73162-3745, USA

Pearson, Malina (Stylist)
c/o Staff Member *Faucher Artists*
636 Broadway Rm 1218
New York, NY 10012-2624, USA

Pearson, Preston (Athlete, Football Player)
9104 Moss Farm Ln
Dallas, TX 75243-7429, USA

Pearson, Rob (Athlete, Hockey Player)
467 Meadow St
Oshawa, ON L1L 1B9, Canada

Pearson, Terry (Athlete, Baseball Player)
3010 Wisteria Ln
Northport, AL 35473-8165, USA

Pearson-Tesseine, Dolly (Baseball Player)
1510A Canterbury Trl
Mount Pleasant, MI 48858-4002, USA

Peart, Neil (Musician)
c/o Staff Member *SRO Management*
189 Carlton St
Toronto, ON M5A 2K7, Canada

Pease, Patsy (Actor)
5416 Fair Ave Apt 6413
N Hollywood, CA 91601-2786

Peasgood, Julie (Actor)
c/o Staff Member *NCI Management Ltd*
51 Queen Ann Street Floor 2
London W1G 9HS, UNITED KINGDOM (UK)

Peatros, Maurice (Baseball Player)
8633 Copper Mine Ave
Las Vegas, NV 89129-7630, USA

Peavy, Jake (Athlete, Baseball Player)
c/o Staff Member *Chicago White Sox*
U.S. Cellular Field 333 Wes 35th St
Chicago, IL 60616, USA

Peay, Francis (Athlete, Football Player)
PO Box 53877
Indianapolis, IN 46253-0877, USA

Peck, Austin (Actor)
13576 Cheltenham Dr
Sherman Oaks, CA 91423-4818, USA

Peck, Ethan (Actor)
c/o Stephanie Ritz *WmE2 (Endeavor-LA)*
9601 Wilshire Blvd Fl 3
Beverly Hills, CA 90210-5219, USA

Peck, J Eddie (Actor)
c/o Kim Dorr *Defining Artists Agency*
10 Universal City Plz Ste 2000
Universal City, CA 91608-1074, USA

Peck, Josh (Actor)
c/o Sam Maydew *Collective*
8383 Wilshire Blvd Ste 1050
Beverly Hills, CA 90211-2415, USA

Peck, Richard (Writer)
c/o Staff Member *Scholastic Entertainment*
557 Broadway
New York, NY 10012-3962, USA

Peck, Tom (Race Car Driver)
417 E North St
Mc Connellsburg, PA 17233-1141, USA

Pecota, Bill (Athlete, Baseball Player)
332 NE Warrington Ct
Lees Summit, MO 64064-1605, USA

Pedersen, Tilly Scott (Actor)
c/o George Englund *George Englund Jr Management*
11661 San Vicente Blvd Ste 609
Los Angeles, CA 90049-5114, USA

Pederson, Stu (Athlete, Baseball Player)
747 Bermuda Dr
San Mateo, CA 94403-1401, USA

Pedre, Jorge (Athlete, Baseball Player)
7894 Bellflower Dr
Buena Park, CA 90620, USA

Pedrigue, Al (Athlete, Baseball Player)
10382 E Oakbrook St
Tucson, AZ 85747-5967, USA

Pedrique, Al (Athlete, Baseball Player, Coach)
10382 E Oakbrook St
Tucson, AZ 85747-5967, USA

Pedroia, Dustin (Athlete, Baseball Player)
c/o Seth Levinson *A.C.E.S*
188 Montague St Fl 6
Brooklyn, NY 11201-3609, USA

Peëa, Elizabeth (Actor, Director)
c/o Staff Member *Rugolo Entertainment*
195 S Beverly Dr Ste 400
Beverly Hills, CA 90212-3044, USA

Peebles, Danny (Athlete, Football Player)
12205 Fieldmist Dr
Raleigh, NC 27614-7539, USA

Peek, Richard (Athlete, Basketball Player)
15631 State Highway 31 W
Tyler, TX 75709-3335, USA

Peeler, Anthony (Athlete, Basketball Player)
4502 E 48th St
Kansas City, MO 64130-2231, USA

Peeples, George (Athlete, Basketball Player)
1032 Loma Lisa Ln
Arcadia, CA 91006-2218, USA

Peeples, Nathaniel (Baseball Player)
536 Lipford St
Memphis, TN 38112-2934, USA

Peeples, Nia (Actor)
c/o Staff Member *Stone Manners Salners Agency (LA)*
9911 W Pico Blvd Ste 1400
Los Angeles, CA 90035-2715, USA

Peet, Amanda (Actor)
c/o Eric Kranzler *Management 360*
9111 Wilshire Blvd
Beverly Hills, CA 90210-5508, USA

Peet, Lizzie (Actor)
4623 Ambrose Ave Apt 1
Los Angeles, CA 90027-1935, USA

Peete, Calvin (Golfer)
128 Garden Gate Dr
Ponte Vedra Beach, FL 32082-3668, USA

Peete, Rodney (Athlete, Football Player, Television Host)
c/o Dolores Robinson *Dolores Robinson Entertainment*
9250 Wilshire Blvd Ste 220
Beverly Hills, CA 90212-3344, USA

Peets, Brian (Athlete, Football Player)
5361 Auburn Blvd
Sacramento, CA 95841-2805, USA

Pegg, Simon (Actor)
c/o Dawn Sedgwick *Dawn Sedgwick Management*
3 Goodwins Ct Covent Garden
London WC2N 4LL, United Kingdom

Pegler, Luke (Actor)
c/o Will Ward *ROAR (LA)*
9701 Wilshire Blvd Fl 8
Beverly Hills, CA 90212-2008, USA

Pegram, Erric (Athlete, Football Player)
5913 Sterling Trl
McKinney, TX 75071-8028, USA

Peguero, Julio (Athlete, Baseball Player)
1500 State Road 1
Socorro, NM 87801-5093, USA

Pegues, Steve (Athlete, Baseball Player)
362 Presidents Dr
Pontotoc, MS 38863-2322, USA

Peguese, Willis (Athlete, Football Player)
7977 W 12th Ave
Hialeah, FL 33014-3534, USA

Pei, I M (Architect)
88 Pine St
New York, NY 10005-1801, USA

Peirce, Kimberly (Director, Producer, Writer)
c/o Staff Member *Creative Artists Agency (CAA-LA)*
2000 Avenue of the Stars Ste 100
Los Angeles, CA 90067-4705, USA

Peirse, Sarah (Actor)
c/o Dallas Smith *United Agents*
12-26 Lexington St
London W1F OLE, UK

Peizerat, Gwendal (Figure Skater)
c/o Staff Member *Champions on Ice*
3500 W 80th St Ste 200
Minneapolis, MN 55431-1090, USA

Pelaez, Alex (Athlete, Baseball Player)
1501 Oleander Ave
Chula Vista, CA 91911-5623, USA

Peldon, Ashley (Actor)
c/o Pamela Wagner *Metropolitan (MTA)*
4526 Wilshire Blvd
Los Angeles, CA 90010-3801, USA

Peldon, Courtney (Actor)
c/o Steve Rodriguez *McGowan Management*
8733 W Sunset Blvd Ste 103
West Hollywood, CA 90069-2241, USA

Pele (Athlete, Soccer Player)
Rua Riachuelo 121-3 Andar-Fones 34-1633/35
Santos SP, Brazil

Pelfrey, Raymond (Athlete, Football Player)
1301 Summit St
Portsmouth, OH 45662-3719, USA

Peli, Oren (Director)
c/o Staff Member *Creative Artists Agency (CAA-LA)*
2000 Avenue of the Stars Ste 100
Los Angeles, CA 90067-4705, USA

Pelikan, Lisa (Actor)
c/o Peter Giagni *Premier Talent Group*
4370 Tujunga Ave Ste 110
Studio City, CA 91604-2753, USA

Pell, Claybourne (Ex-Senator, Senator)
45 Ledge Rd
Newport, RI 02840-4257, USA

Pellegrini, Margaret (Actor)
5018 N 61st Ave
Glendale, AZ 85301-7310, USA

Pellegrini, Robert
1731 Route 9 Unit 97
Ocean View, NJ 08230-1388

Pellegrino, Mark (Actor)
c/o Mary Ellen Mulcahy *Framework Entertainment (LA)*
9057 Nemo St Ste C
West Hollywood, CA 90069-5511, USA

Pelletier, Bronson (Actor)
c/o Staff Member *Carrier Talent Management*
#705-1080 Howe St.
Vancouver BC V6Z 2T1, CANADA

Pelletier, Lysa (Stylist)
c/o Staff Member *Team*
423 W Broadway Ste 406
Boston, MA 02127-2265, USA

Pelley, Scott (Correspondent)
c/o Staff Member *ABC News*
77 W 66th St Fl 3
New York, NY 10023-6201, USA

Pellington, Mark (Director, Producer)
c/o Staff Member *3 Arts Entertainment Inc*
9460 Wilshire Blvd Fl 7
Beverly Hills, CA 90212-2713, USA

Pellow, Kit (Athlete, Baseball Player)
2965 Long Bend Rd
Galena, MO 65656-4865, USA

Pellow, Marti (Musician)
c/o Staff Member *Solo Agency Ltd (UK)*
55 Fulham High St 2nd Floor
London SW6 3JJ, United Kingdom

Pelluer, Steve (Athlete, Football Player)
2632 W Lake Sammamish Pkwy NE
Redmond, WA 98052-5915, USA

Peloffy, Andre (Athlete, Hockey Player)
PO Box 2382
Morehead City, NC 28557-2382, USA

Pelphrey, Tom (Actor)
c/o Cyrena Esposito *Cyrena Esposito Management*
437 W 48th St Apt D
New York, NY 10036-1285, USA

Peltier, Dan (Athlete, Baseball Player)
239 Lapp Rd
Clifton Park, NY 12065-6012, USA

Peltier, Leonard (Writer)
c/o Staff Member *St Martins Press*
175 5th Ave
New York, NY 10010-7703, USA

Peltz, Nicola (Actor)
c/o Cynthia Pett-Dante *Brillstein Entertainment Partners*
9150 Wilshire Blvd Ste 350
Beverly Hills, CA 90212-3453, USA

Peluce, Meeno (Actor)
2445 Metzler Dr
Los Angeles, CA 90031-2830, USA

Pelzer, Dave
PO Box 1846
Rancho Mirage, CA 92270-1081

Pember, Dave (Athlete, Baseball Player)
8823 Shoreham Blvd
Knoxville, TN 37922-1457, USA

Pemberton, Brock (Athlete, Baseball Player)
5763 S 80th East Ave
Tulsa, OK 74145-8611, USA

Pemberton, Rudy (Athlete, Baseball Player)
PO Box 602
Imperial, PA 15126-0602, USA

Pempengco, Charice (Musician)
c/o Liz Rosenberg *Warner Bros Records (NY)*
75 Rockefeller Plz
New York, NY 10019-6908, USA

Pena, Alejandro (Athlete, Baseball Player)
12635 Etris Rd
Roswell, GA 30075-1039, USA

Pena, Brayan (Athlete, Baseball Player)
14217 SW 102nd St
Miami, FL 33186-6970, USA

Pena, Carlos (Athlete, Baseball Player)
8157 Via Bella Notte
Orlando, FL 32836-7705, USA

Pena, Carlos (Musician)
c/o Glenn Hughes III *Gem Entertainment Group*
10701 Wilshire Blvd Apt 1202
Los Angeles, CA 90024-4437, USA

Pena, Federico Secy
3517 Sterling Ave
Alexandria, VA 22304-1834, USA

Pena, Geronimo (Athlete, Baseball Player)
1384 Franklin St
Clearwater, FL 33756-6029, USA

Pena, Hipolito (Athlete, Baseball Player)
11412 Park Blvd
Seminole, FL 33772-4620, USA

Pena, Jim (Athlete, Baseball Player)
3228 E Silverwood Dr
Phoenix, AZ 85048-7257, USA

Pena, Jose
A. Flores #1116 NTE C Jiquilpan
Los Mochia Sinoloa, MEXICO

Pena, Juan (Athlete, Baseball Player)
4940 NW 179th St
Miami Gardens, FL 33055-3244, USA

Pena, Michael (Actor)
c/o Eric Kranzler *Management 360*
9111 Wilshire Blvd
Beverly Hills, CA 90210-5508, USA

Pena, Orlando (Athlete, Baseball Player)
1750 W 46th St Apt 416
Hialeah, FL 33012-2849, USA

Pena, Ramiro (Athlete, Baseball Player)
c/o Team Member *New York Yankees*
Yankee Stadium 161st St & River Ave
Bronx, NY 10451, USA

Pena, Robert (Athlete, Football Player)
77 John Parker Rd
East Falmouth, MA 02536-5116, USA

Pena, Tony (Athlete, Baseball Player, Coach)
161st Street And River Avenue Attn Coaching Staff
Bronx, NY 10451, USA

Pena, Wily Mo (Athlete, Baseball Player)
27520 Breakers Dr
Wesley Chapel, FL 33544-6667, USA

Penaranda, Jairo (Athlete, Football Player)
2023 Lloyd Ctr
Portland, OR 97232-1314, USA

Pence, Hunter (Athlete, Baseball Player)
25344 FM 2100 Rd
Huffman, TX 77336-4102, USA

Penchion, Bob (Athlete, Football Player)
315 County Road 266
Town Creek, AL 35672-3939, USA

Pender, Jerry Lee (Athlete, Basketball Player)
382 Chrystal Way
Rocky Mount, NC 27801-9323, USA

Pender, Mel
4910 Karl's Gate Dr
Marietta, GA 30062

Pendleton, Austin
155 E 76th St
New York, NY 10021-2810

Pendleton, Terry (Athlete, Baseball Player)
2998 Grey Moss Pass
Duluth, GA 30097, USA

Penfold, James (Model)
c/o Staff Member *DNA Model Management*
555 W 25th St Fl 6
New York, NY 10001-5542, USA

Penghlis, Thaao (Actor)
c/o Christopher Barrett *Metropolitan (MTA)*
4526 Wilshire Blvd
Los Angeles, CA 90010-3801, USA

Pengilly, Kirk (Musician)
94-98 Chalmers Street,
Surry Hills, NSW 2010, Australia

Penguins, The
24210 E East Fork Rd Spc 9
Azusa, CA 91702-6249

Penhaligon, Susan
109 Jermyn St
London, ENGLAND SW1

Penhall, Bruce (Race Car Driver)
PO Box 5625
Norco, CA 92860-8021, USA

Peniche, Arturo (Actor)
c/o Staff Member *Televisa*
Blvd Adolfo Lopez Mateos 232 Colonia
San Angel INN
DF CP 01060, MEXICO

Peniche, Kari Ann (Actor)
c/o Ted Maier *Maier Management*
11870 Santa Monica Blvd Ste 106
Los Angeles, CA 90025-5276, USA

Penick, Trevor (Musician)
7380 W Sand Lake Rd # 350
Orlando, FL 32819-5248, USA

Penikett, Tahmoh (Actor)
c/o Robert Stein *Robert Stein Management*
PO Box 3797
Beverly Hills, CA 90212-0797, USA

Peniston, Ce Ce
250 W 57th St # 821
New York, NY 10107-0001

Peniston, CeCe (Musician)
c/o Staff Member *Diva Central Inc*
7510 W Sunset Blvd Ste 1445
Los Angeles, CA 90046-3408, USA

Penky, Joseph F (Engineer)
Chemical Engineering Dept
West Lafayette, IN 47907, USA

Penn, Chris (Athlete, Football Player)
PO Box 123
S Coffeyville, OK 74072-0123, USA

Penn, Hayden (Athlete, Baseball Player)
9150 Canyon Park Ter
Santee, CA 92071-4733, USA

Penn, Jesse (Athlete, Football Player)
8420 Wildcreek Dr
Plano, TX 75025-4150, USA

Penn, Kal (Actor, Producer)
c/o Dan Spilo *Industry Entertainment Partners*
955 Carrillo Dr Ste 300
Los Angeles, CA 90048-5400, USA

Penn, Michael (Musician)
c/o Staff Member *Kraft-Engel Management*
15233 Ventura Blvd Ste 200
Sherman Oaks, CA 91403-2244, USA

Penn, Sean (Actor, Director)
c/o Mara Buxbaum *ID PR (LA)*
7060 Hollywood Blvd Fl 8
Los Angeles, CA 90028-6014, USA

Penn, Shannon (Athlete, Baseball Player)
1535 Blair Ave Apt 1
Cincinnati, OH 45207-1424, USA

Penn & Teller (Comedian, Magician)
4132 S Rainbow Blvd # 377
Las Vegas, NV 89103-3106, USA

Pennacchio, Len A (Misc)
Human Genome Center
Stanford, CA 94305, USA

Pennebaker, Ed (Artist)
428 County Road 9351
Green Forest, AR 72638-9764, USA

Pennell, Larry
15516 W Sunset Blvd Apt 101
Pacific Palisades, CA 90272-3542

Penner, Jonathan (Actor)
c/o Staff Member *Modus Entertainment*
8569 Holloway Dr Apt 1
West Hollywood, CA 90069-6918, USA

Penner, Stanford S (Engineer)
5912 Avenida Chamnez
La Jolla, CA 92037-7402, USA

Penniman, Michael (Mika) (Musician)
c/o Jbeau Lewis *Creative Artists Agency (CAA-LA)*
2000 Avenue of the Stars Ste 100
Los Angeles, CA 90067-4705, USA

Penniman, Micheal (Mika) (Musician)
c/o Jbeau Lewis *Creative Artists Agency (CAA-LA)*
2000 Avenue of the Stars Ste 100
Los Angeles, CA 90067-4705, USA

Pennington, Ann
701 N Oakhurst Dr
Beverly Hills, CA 90210-3532

Pennington, Art (Baseball Player)
922 5th St SE Apt E5
Cedar Rapids, IA 52401-2440, USA

Pennington, Brad (Athlete, Baseball Player)
7220 E State Road 160
Salem, IN 47167-7856, USA

Pennington, Chad (Athlete, Football Player)
c/o Team Member *New York Jets*
5150 Palm Valley Rd Ste 210
Ponte Vedra Beach, FL 32082-4631, USA

Pennington, Janice (Actor, Model)
PO Box 11402
Beverly Hills, CA 90213-4402, USA

Pennington, Julia
PO Box 5617
Beverly Hills, CA 90209-5617

Pennington, Michael (Actor)
Langham House 302/8 Regent St
London W1R 5AL, UNITED KINGDOM (UK)

Pennington, T Durwood (Athlete, Football Player)
480 Peninsula Rd
Gainesville, GA 30506-1705, USA

Pennington, Ty (Actor)
2554 Lincoln Blvd # 660
Venice, CA 90291-5082, USA

Pennison, Jay (Athlete, Football Player)
3007 W Autumn Run Cir
Sugar Land, TX 77479-2624, USA

Pennock, Chris (Actor)
25150 1/2 Malibu Rd
Malibu, CA 90265-4639, USA

Pennock of Norton, Raymond (Business Person)
23 Great Winchester St
London EC2P 2AX, UNITED KINGDOM (UK)

Penny, Brad (Athlete, Baseball Player)
25071 Abercrombie Ln
Calabasas, CA 91302-2360, USA

Penny, Joe (Actor)
c/o Staff Member *Geddes Agency, The*
8430 Santa Monica Blvd Ste 200
Los Angeles, CA 90069-4253, USA

Penny, Roger P (Business Person)
1170 8th Ave
Bethlehem, PA 18018-2255, USA

Penny, Sudney (Actor)
9100 Wilshire Blvd Ste 600
Beverly Hills, CA 90212-3494, USA

Penny, Sydney (Actor)
c/o Bob McGowan *McGowan Management*
8733 W Sunset Blvd Ste 103
West Hollywood, CA 90069-2241, USA

Pennyfeather, Will (Athlete, Baseball Player)
333 Rector St Apt 6D
Perth Amboy, NJ 08861-4277, USA

Penny's
3220 Altura Ave Apt 106
La Crescenta, CA 91214-3304

Pennywell, Carlos (Athlete, Football Player)
3729 Clover Dr
Arcadia, LA 71001-3628, USA

Pennywell, Robert (Athlete, Football Player)
8546 Leake Ave Apt A
Baton Rouge, LA 70810-6954, USA

Penot, Jacques
9 Rue De L'Isly
Paris, FRANCE F-75008

Penrose, Craig R (Athlete, Football Player)
1609 Camino Way
Woodland, CA 95695-5517, USA

Penske, Roger S (Race Car Driver)
200 Penske Way
Mooresville, NC 28115-8022, USA

Pentecost, Del (Actor)
c/o Staff Member *Paradigm (LA)*
360 N Crescent Dr
Beverly Hills, CA 90210-4874, USA

Penthouse Pets
277 Park Ave
New York, NY 10172-0003

Pentland, Alex P (Scientist)
Media Laboratory
Cambridge, MA 2139, USA

Pentz, Gene (Athlete, Baseball Player)
207 Rainbow Dr
Johnstown, PA 15904-2253, USA

Penzias, Arno A (Nobel Prize Laureate)
600 Mountain Ave
New Providence, NJ 07974-2008, USA

People, Village (Music Group, Musician)
c/o Staff Member *WmE2 (WMA-LA)*
1 William Morris Pl
Beverly Hills, CA 90212-4261, USA

Peoples, John (Physicist)
PO Box 500
Batavia, IL 60510-5011, USA

Peoples, Woodrow (Woody) (Athlete, Football Player)
1810 Eufaula Ave
Birmingham, AL 35208-1312, USA

Pepin, Jacques (Chef)
214 Durham Rd
Madison, CT 06443-2451, USA

Pepitone, Joseph A (Joe) (Athlete, Baseball Player)
27 Roosevelt Blvd
Massapequa, NY 11758-6841, USA

Peplinski, Jim (Athlete, Hockey Player)
212 Meridian Rd NE
Calgary, AB T2A 2N6, Canada

Peplowski, Mike (Athlete, Basketball Player)
4110 Harris Rd
Williamston, MI 48895-9204, USA

Peppas, June (Athlete, Baseball Player)
1700 NE Indian River Dr Apt 302
Jensen Beach, FL 34957-5860, USA

Pepper, Barry (Actor)
c/o Nancy Mccarty Iannios *Nancy Iannois Public Relations*
PO Box 430
Signal Mountain, TN 37377-0430, USA

Pepper, Cynthia (Actor)
219 Friendly Ct
Henderson, NV 89052-5660

Pepper, Don (Athlete, Baseball Player)
8145 Reynoldswood Dr
Reynoldsburg, OH 43068-9328, USA

Pepper, Dottie (Golfer)
PO Box 623
Saratoga Springs, NY 12866-0623

Pepper, Dottle (Golfer)
108 Micco Cir
Jupiter, FL 33458-7730, USA

Pepper, Gene (Athlete, Football Player)
105 Park Ridge Dr
O Fallon, MO 63366-1087, USA

Pepper, Laurin (Athlete, Baseball Player)
8932 Davis St
Ocean Springs, MS 39564-3633, USA

Peppers, Julius (Athlete, Football Player)
173 Rehoboth Ln
Mooresville, NC 28117-6711, USA

Peppler, Mary Jo (Athlete, Volleyball Player)
2390 Boswell Rd Ste 400
Chula Vista, CA 91914-3541, USA

Perabo, Piper (Actor)
c/o Tina Thor *TMT Entertainment Group*
648 Broadway Ste 1002
New York, NY 10012-2348, USA

Perak, Sultan of (King)
Istana Bukit Serene
Kula Lumpur, MALAYSIA

Perakis, Nicos
Isabellastr. 19
Munich, GERMANY D-80798

Peralta, Jhonny (Athlete, Baseball Player)
27940 Berringer Run
Westlake, OH 44145-3063, USA

Peralta, Ricardo (Astronaut)
Ciudad Universitaria
Mexico City, DF 4510, MEXICO

Peranoski, Ron (Baseball Player)
4800 Highway A1a Apt 307
Vero Beach, FL 32963-1230, USA

Perayra, Marianela (Television Host)
c/o Michael (Mike) Esterman
Esterman.Com, LLC
Prefers to be contacted via email
MD, USA

Peraza, Alejandro (Stylist)
c/o Staff Member *Mercury Artists*
8460 Higuera St Fl 2
Culver City, CA 90232-2520, USA

Percival, Lance (Actor)
Westbury-on-Trim
Bristol BS9 3DU, UNITED KINGDOM (UK)

Percival, Mac (Athlete, Football Player)
6710 Flowermound Dr
Sugar Land, TX 77479-6000, USA

Percival, Troy E (Athlete, Baseball Player)
2127 Century Ave
Riverside, CA 92506-4653, USA

Perconte, Jack (Athlete, Baseball Player)
6197 Hinterlong Ct
Lisle, IL 60532-2818, USA

Perdue, Bev (Governor)
20301 Mail Service Ctr Ofc of
Raleigh, NC 27699-0300, USA

Perdue, Will (Athlete, Basketball Player)
6310 Innisbrook Dr
Prospect, KY 40059-9223, USA

Perec, Marie-Jose (Athlete, Track Athlete)
10 Rue du Fg Poissonniere
Paris 75480, FRANCE

Peregrym, Missy (Actor)
c/o Jai Khanna *Brillstein Entertainment Partners*
9150 Wilshire Blvd Ste 350
Beverly Hills, CA 90212-3453, USA

Pereira, Aristides M (President)
PO Box 172
Praia, CAPE VERDE

Perek, Lubos (Astronomer)
Budecska 6
Prague 2, CZECH REPUBLIC

Perelman, Ronald O (Business Person)
35 E 62nd St
New York, NY 10065-8014, USA

Perelman, Vadim (Director)
c/o Simon Millar *Rumble Media*
1620 Broadway Ste C
Santa Monica, CA 90404-2777, USA

Perenyi, Miklos (Musician)
Erdoalja Utca 1/B
Budapest 1037, HUNGARY

Peres, Shimon (Nobel Prize Laureate)
Aenot Law House 8 Shaul Hamelech Blvd
Tel Aviv 64733, ISRAEL

Peretokin, Mark (Dancer)
Teatralnaya Pl 1
Moscow 103009, RUSSIA

Perez, Armando (Pitbull) Christian (Musician)
c/o Drew Elliot *Media Artists Group (NY)*
140 E 46th St PH C
New York, NY 10017-2633, USA

Perez, Atanasio (Athlete, Baseball Player)
1717 N Bayshore Dr
Miami, FL 33132-1180, USA

Perez, Chris (Musician)
301 Arizona Ave Ste 200
Santa Monica, CA 90401-1364, USA

Perez, Danny (Athlete, Baseball Player)
10511 Cuesta Brava Ln
El Paso, TX 79935-2210, USA

Perez, Dick (Artist)
PO Box 503
Wayne, PA 19087-0503, USA

Perez, Eddie (Athlete, Baseball Player)
615 Rose Creek Cir
Duluth, GA 30097-7895, USA

Perez, Eduardo (Athlete, Baseball Player)
113 Calle Las Flores
San Juan, PR 00911-2298, USA

Perez, George (Athlete, Baseball Player)
711 S Old Stage Rd
Cave Junction, OR 97523-9362, USA

Perez, Hugo (Soccer Player)
22018 Newbridge Dr
Lake Forest, CA 92630-6511, USA

Perez, Luiz (Louie) (Musician)
3575 Cahuenga Blvd W Ste 450
Los Angeles, CA 90068-1364, USA

Perez, Manny (Actor, Producer, Writer)
c/o Scott Zimmerman *Evolution Entertainment (LA)*
901 N Highland Ave
Los Angeles, CA 90038-2412, USA

Perez, Marty (Athlete, Baseball Player)
30 Willowick Dr
Lithonia, GA 30038-1722, USA

Perez, Melido (Athlete, Baseball Player)
Nigua KM 21 1/2
Santa Domingo, Dominican Republic

Perez, Mike (Athlete, Baseball Player)
800 Kylewood Pl
Ballwin, MO 63021-4796, USA

Perez, Odalis A (Baseball Player)
1000 Elysian Park Ave
Los Angeles, CA 90090-1112, USA

Perez, Oliver (Baseball Player)
c/o Scott Boras *Boras Corporation*
18 Corporate Plaza Dr
Newport Beach, CA 92660-7901, USA

Perez, Pascual (Athlete, Baseball Player)
Salvador Cucurulo #105
Santiago, Dominican Republic

Perez, Rosie (Actor, Producer)
c/o Jodi Gottlieb *ID PR (LA)*
7060 Hollywood Blvd Fl 8
Los Angeles, CA 90028-6014, USA

Perez, Scott (Cartoonist)
1700 Broadway
New York, NY 10019-5905, USA

Perez, Timothy Paul (Actor)
9229 W Sunset Blvd Ste 311
Los Angeles, CA 90069-3403, USA

Perez, Tony (Athlete, Baseball Player, Coach)
1717 N Bayshore Dr Apt A-2735
Miami, FL 33132-1180, USA

Perez, Vincent (Actor)
c/o Staff Member *ArtMedia*
20 avenue Rapp
Paris 75008, France

Perez de Cuellar, Javier (General, Secretary)
Avenida A Miro Quesada
Lima 1071, PERU

Perez de Tagle, Anna Maria (Actor)
c/o Beverly Strong *Strong Management*
3532 Hayden Ave
Culver City, CA 90232-2413, USA

Perez de Tagle, Anna Marie (Actor)
c/o Beverly Strong *Strong Management*
3532 Hayden Ave
Culver City, CA 90232-2413, USA

Perez Esquivel, Adolfo (Nobel Prize Laureate)
Piedras 730
Buenos Aires 1070, ARGENTINA

Perez Fernandez, Pedro (Government Official)
Ferraz 68 y 70
Madrid 28008, SPAIN

Perez Limon, Iyari (Actor)
c/o Mitchell Stubbs *Mitchell K Stubbs & Assoc (MKS)*
8675 Washington Blvd Ste 203
Culver City, CA 90232-7486, USA

Perez-Brown, Maria (Producer)
c/o Staff Member *WmE2 (WMA-LA)*
1 William Morris Pl
Beverly Hills, CA 90212-4261, USA

Perezchica, Tony (Athlete, Baseball Player)
79220 Victoria Dr
La Quinta, CA 92253-4274, USA

Pergine, John (Athlete, Football Player)
5 Jody Dr
Plymouth Meeting, PA 19462-2625, USA

Perick, Christof (Conductor)
130 W 57th St Apt 8G
New York, NY 10019-3311, USA

Perishers, The (Music Group)
c/o Staff Member *Paradigm (Monterey)*
404 W Franklin St
Monterey, CA 93940-2303, USA

Perisho, Matt (Athlete, Baseball Player)
1462 W Cardinal Way
Chandler, AZ 85286-4379, USA

Periyar, Dasan (Actor)
30 Muthaiappa Street Shenoy Nagar
Chennai, TN 600 030, INDIA

Perkins, Broderick (Athlete, Baseball Player)
5367 San Vicente Blvd Apt 237
Los Angeles, CA 90019-2751, USA

Perkins, Bruce (Athlete, Football Player)
19014 E Ryan Rd
Queen Creek, AZ 85142-6877, USA

Perkins, Cecil (Athlete, Baseball Player)
711 Cushwa Rd
Martinsburg, WV 25403-1228, USA

Perkins, Dan (Athlete, Baseball Player)
1509 Kenan St NW
Wilson, NC 27893-2252, USA

Perkins, David D (Biologist)
367 S Baywood Ave
San Jose, CA 95128-5123, USA

Perkins, Donald A (Athlete, Football Player)
808 Vassar Dr NE
Albuquerque, NM 87106-2726, USA

Perkins, Edward J (Diplomat)
2201 C St NW
Washington, DC 20520-0099, USA

Perkins, Elivs (Musician)
c/o Staff Member *Paradigm (Monterey)*
404 W Franklin St
Monterey, CA 93940-2303, USA

Perkins, Elizabeth (Actor)
c/o Leslie Siebert *Gersh (LA)*
9465 Wilshire Blvd Ste 600
Beverly Hills, CA 90212-2612, USA

Perkins, Emily (Actor)
c/o Tyman Stewart *Characters Talent Agency, The (Vancouver)*
8 Elm St 2nd Floor
Toronto, ON M5G 1G7, Canada

Perkins, John (Writer)
c/o Paul Fedorko *Trident Media Group LLC*
41 Madison Ave Fl 36
New York, NY 10010-2257, USA

Perkins, John M (Activist)
1655 Saint Charles St
Jackson, MS 39209-5404, USA

Perkins, Johnny (Athlete, Football Player)
5320 Fairway Cir
Granbury, TX 76049-5184, USA

Perkins, Kathleen Rose (Actor)
c/o Devon Jackson *Trademark Talent*
4758 Allott Ave
Sherman Oaks, CA 91423-2403, USA

Perkins, Kendrick (Basketball Player)
151 Merrimac St # 1
Boston, MA 02114-4714, USA

Perkins, Lucian (Journalist)
3103 17th St NW
Washington, DC 20010-2701, USA

Perkins, Millie (Actor)
2511 Canyon Dr
Los Angeles, CA 90068-2415, USA

Perkins, Oz
7720 W Sunset Blvd
Los Angeles, CA 90046-3962

Perkins, Sam (Athlete, Basketball Player)
14901 Bellbrook Dr
Dallas, TX 75254-7673, USA

Perkins, Tex (Musician)
70 Universal City Plz
Universal City, CA 91608-1011, USA

Perkins, W Ray (Athlete, Coach, Football Coach, Football Player)
57 Honors Ln
Hattiesburg, MS 39402-7100, USA

Perkins, Warren (Athlete, Basketball Player)
717 Fairfield Ave
Gretna, LA 70056-7625, USA

Perkoff, Gerald T (Doctor)
1300 Torrey Pines Dr
Columbia, MO 65203-4826, USA

Perkowski, Harry (Athlete, Baseball Player)
211 McGinnis St
Beckley, WV 25801-5725, USA

Perks, Craig (Golfer)
321 Thibodeaux Dr
Lafayette, LA 70503-4444, USA

Perl, Frank J (Cinematographer)
5020 Biloxi Ave
North Hollywood, CA 91601-4140, USA

Perl, Martin L (Nobel Prize Laureate)
3737 El Centro St
Palo Alto, CA 94306-2642, USA

Perle, George (Composer)
Music Dept
Flushing, NY 11367, USA

Perles, George (Athlete, Football Coach, Football Player)
6153 W Longview Dr
East Lansing, MI 48823-9739, USA

Perley, James (Misc)
1012 14th St NW
Washington, DC 20005-3406, USA

Perlich, Max (Actor)
c/o Staff Member *Metropolitan (MTA)*
4526 Wilshire Blvd
Los Angeles, CA 90010-3801, USA

Perlick-Keating, Edythe (Baseball Player)
3051 S Palm Aire Dr Bldg 34
Pompano Beach, FL 33069-4277, USA

Perlman, Itzhak (Conductor, Musician)
c/o Wray Armstrong *IMG Artists Worldwide (UK)*
The Light Box 111 Power Road
London W4 5PY, United Kingdom

Perlman, Jon (Athlete, Baseball Player)
3225 Bryn Mawr Dr
Dallas, TX 75225-7646, USA

Perlman, Lawrence (Business Person)
3311 E Old Shakopee Rd
Minneapolis, MN 55425-1361, USA

Perlman, Phil
439 S Catalina Ave Apt 102
Pasadena, CA 91106-3343

Perlman, Rhea (Actor, Producer)
c/o Staff Member *Christopher Wright Management*
3207 Winnie Dr
Los Angeles, CA 90068-1439, USA

Perlman, Ron (Actor)
c/o Erik Kritzer *Kritzer Levine Wilkins Entertainment*
11872 La Grange Ave Fl 1
Los Angeles, CA 90025-5283, USA

Perlmutter, Ed (Congressman, Politician)
1221 Longworth Hob
Washington, DC 20515-0517, USA

Perlozzo, Sam (Athlete, Baseball Player, Coach)
18101 Emerald Bay St
Tampa, FL 33647-3316, USA

Perls, Tom (Misc)
2 Harrington Ln
Weston, MA 02493-1355, USA

Perme, Len (Athlete, Baseball Player)
3350 D St
Hayward, CA 94541-4590, USA

Pernandez, Mervyn (Athlete, Football Player)
1546 Morning Star Dr
Morgan Hill, CA 95037-9033, USA

Perner, Wolfgang (Athlete)
Schildlehen 29
ramsau-D 8972, AUSTRIA

Pernice Jr, Tom (Golfer)
c/o Staff Member *Pro Golfers Association (PGA) Tour*
112 Tpc Blvd
Ponte Vedra Beach, FL 32082, USA

Pero, Perry R (Financier)
50 S La Salle St
Chicago, IL 60603-1008, USA

Peron, Isabelita Martinez de (President)
Moreto 3 Los Jeronimos
Madrid 28014, SPAIN

Perot, Pete (Athlete, Football Player)
2401 Hillside Rd
Ruston, LA 71270-2093, USA

Perot, Ross H (Business Person)
c/o Staff Member *Perot Group*
2300 W Plano Pkwy
Plano, TX 75075-8427, USA

Perot Jr, Henry Ross (Business Person)
c/o Staff Member *Perot Group*
2300 W Plano Pkwy
Plano, TX 75075-8427, USA

Perranoski, Ron
4800 Highway A1a Apt 307
Vero Beach, FL 32963-1230

Perranoski, Ronald P (Ron) (Athlete, Baseball Player)
4800 Highway A1a Apt 307
Vero Beach, FL 32963-1230, USA

Perreau, Gigi (Actor)
5841 Cantaloupe Ave
Van Nuys, CA 91401-4311, USA

Perreault, Gilbert (Gil) (Athlete, Hockey Player)
4 Rue De La Serenite
Victoriaville, QC G6P 6S2, CANADA

Perreault, Pete (Athlete, Football Player)
7540 Sunshine Skyway Ln S
Saint Petersburg, FL 33711-5115, USA

Perret, Christine (Stylist)
c/o Staff Member *O'Gorman/Schramm Represents, Inc*
642 Washington St Apt 1A
New York, NY 10014-6327, USA

Perretta, Ralph (Athlete, Football Player)
1305 Calle Scott
Encinitas, CA 92024-5532, USA

Perrette, Pauley (Actor)
c/o Steven Jang *SDB Partners Inc*
1801 Avenue of the Stars Ste 902
Los Angeles, CA 90067-5981, USA

Perrier, Mireille (Actor)
36 Rue de Ponthieu
Paris 75008, FRANCE

Perriman, Brett (Athlete, Football Player)
PO Box 83337
Conyers, GA 30013-8019, USA

Perrin, Benny (Athlete, Football Player)
2509 Burningtree Dr SE
Decatur, AL 35603-5138, USA

Perrin, Lonnie (Athlete, Football Player)
7809 Green St
Clinton, MD 20735-1973, USA

Perrin, Philippe (Astronaut)
11923 Mighty Redwood Dr
Houston, TX 77059-5542, USA

Perrine, Valerie (Actor)
c/o Staff Member *Bensky Entertainment*
15030 Ventura Blvd Ste 343
Sherman Oaks, CA 91403-5470, USA

Perrineau Jr, Harold (Harry) (Actor, Producer)
c/o Stacy Abrams *Abrams Entertainment*
5225 Wilshire Blvd # Suite 515 PMB 515
Los Angeles, CA 90036, USA

Perron, Jean (Coach)
5 Thomas Mellon Cir
San Francisco, CA 94134-2501, USA

Perroni, Maite (Actor)
c/o Staff Member *Televisa S.A. de C.V.*
Av. Vasco de Quirroga 2000
DF 01210, Mexico

Perrotta, Tom (Writer)
175 5th Ave
New York, NY 10010-7703, USA

Perry, Anne (Writer)
Turn Vawr Seafield Postmahomack
Rosshire IV20 1RE, SCOTLAND

Perry, Barbara
6926 La Presa Dr
Los Angeles, CA 90068-3103

Perry, Barry W (Business Person)
101 Wood Ave S
Iselin, NJ 08830-2703, USA

Perry, Bob (Athlete, Baseball Player)
445 Fox Chase Vig
New Bern, NC 28562, USA

Perry, Chan (Athlete, Baseball Player)
788 NE County Road 353
Mayo, FL 32066-5450, USA

Perry, Charles O (Artist)
20 Shorehaven Rd
Norwalk, CT 06855-2807, USA

Perry, Chris (Athlete, Golfer)
170 Valley Run Dr
Powell, OH 43065-9454, USA

Perry, Chris (Athlete, Football Player)
c/o Eugene Parker *Maximum Sports Management*
6435 W Jefferson Blvd # 197
Fort Wayne, IN 46804-6203, USA

Perry, Darren (Athlete, Football Player)
6451 Pinehurst Ln
Mason, OH 45040-2051, USA

Perry, Ed (Athlete, Football Player)
1583 SW 161st Ave
Pembroke Pines, FL 33027-5140, USA

Perry, Elliott (Athlete, Basketball Player)
3230 Scheibler Rd
Memphis, TN 38128-4817, USA

Perry, Felton (Actor)
PO Box 931359
Los Angeles, CA 90093-1359, USA

Perry, Gaylord J (Athlete, Baseball Player)
PO Box 489
Spruce Pine, NC 28777-0489, USA

Perry, Gerald (Athlete, Football Player)
2940 Dell Dr
Columbia, SC 29209-4906, USA

Perry, Gerald (Athlete, Baseball Player)
1348 Waterford Green Close
Marietta, GA 30068-2919, USA

Perry, Gerald E (Athlete, Football Player)
336 5th St
Manhattan Beach, CA 90266-5712, USA

Perry, Herbert (Herb) (Athlete, Baseball Player)
978 N Fletcher Ave
Mayo, FL 32066-4506, USA

Perry, Ira (Stylist)
c/o Staff Member *Axis Models & Talent*
PO Box 367
Ringwood, NJ 07456-0367, USA

Perry, James E (Jim) (Athlete, Baseball Player)
155 Porters Gin
New London, NC 28127, USA

Perry, Jeff (Actor)
2029 Century Park E Ste 1060
Los Angeles, CA 90067-2919, USA

Perry, Joe (Musician, Songwriter)
c/o Staff Member *Paradigm (Monterey)*
404 W Franklin St
Monterey, CA 93940-2303, USA

Perry, John Bennett (Actor)
606 N Larchmont Blvd Ste 309
Los Angeles, CA 90004-1309, USA

Perry, John R (Misc)
Language & Information Study Center
Stanford, CA 94305, USA

Perry, Katy (Musician)
c/o Bradford Cobb *Direct Management Group*
947 N La Cienega Blvd Ste G
Los Angeles, CA 90069-4700, USA

Perry, Kenny (Golfer)
418 Quail Ridge Rd
Franklin, KY 42134-9650, USA

Perry, Leon (Athlete, Football Player)
RR 1 Box 195A
Gloster, MS 39638, USA

Perry, Linda (Musician, Producer)
9615 Brighton Way Ste 300
Beverly Hills, CA 90210-5118, USa

Perry, Luke (Actor)
c/o Steve Himber *Steve Himber Entertainment*
211 S Beverly Dr Apt S
Beverly Hills, CA 90212-3807, USA

Perry, Matthew (Actor)
c/o Lisa Kasteler *WKT Public Relations (WKT-LA)*
9350 Wilshire Blvd Ste 450
Beverly Hills, CA 90212-3230, USA

Perry, Michael Dean (Athlete, Football Player)
PO Box 221771
Charlotte, NC 28222-1771, USA

Perry, Nickolas (Director, Editor, Writer)
c/o Staff Member *WmE2 (WMA-LA)*
1 William Morris Pl
Beverly Hills, CA 90212-4261, USA

Perry, Pat (Athlete, Baseball Player)
1115 W Franklin St
Taylorville, IL 62568-2037, USA

Perry, Rachel (Actor)
c/o Staff Member *Envision Management*
8840 Wilshire Blvd Fl 3
Beverly Hills, CA 90211-2606, USA

Perry, Rick (Governor, Politician)
PO Box 12428
Austin, TX 78711-2428, USA

Perry, Robert P (Biologist)
1808 Bustleton Pike
Churchville, PA 18966-4608, USA

Perry, Rod (Athlete, Football Player)
PO Box 532551
Indianapolis, IN 46253-2551, USA

Perry, Ruth (Prime Minister)
Capitol Hill
Monrovia, LIBERIA

Perry, Scott (Athlete, Football Player)
3708 S Dolphin St
San Pedro, CA 90731-6020, USA

Perry, Steve (Director, Producer)
c/o Staff Member *DH1 Studios*
8730 W Sunset Blvd Fl 6
West Hollywood, CA 90069-2210, USA

Perry, Todd (Athlete, Football Player)
13805 Brittle Rd
Alpharetta, GA 30004-3577, USA

Perry, Tyler (Actor, Director, Producer, Writer)
c/o Keleigh Thomas *Sunshine, Sachs & Associates - LA*
8409 Santa Monica Blvd
West Hollywood, CA 90069-4209, USA

Perry, Vernon (Athlete, Football Player)
PO Box 842201
Houston, TX 77284-2201, USA

Perry, William (Refrigerator) (Athlete, Football Player)
349 Kershaw St NE
Aiken, SC 29801-4432, USA

Perry, Wilmont (Athlete, Football Player)
1757 W River Rd
Franklinton, NC 27525-8293, USA

Perry, Yvonne (Actor)
524 W 57th St
New York, NY 10019-2930, USA

Perryman, Jill
4 Hillside Cres
Gooseberry Hill, AUSTRALIA 6076 W Aus

Perryman, Jim (Athlete, Football Player)
2345 Southwood Dr
Pittsburgh, PA 15241-3344, USA

Perryman, Robert (Athlete, Football Player)
PO Box 8543
Haverhill, MA 01835-0985, USA

Perschy, Maria
Maxingstr. 30
Vienna, AUSTRIA 1130

Persoff, Nahemiah (Actor)
5670 Moonstone Beach Dr
Cambria, CA 93428-2210, USA

Persoff, Nehemiah (Actor)
5670 Moonstone Beach Dr
Cambria, CA 93428-2210, USA

Person, Chuck (Athlete, Basketball Player)
2022 Ruhland Ave
Redondo Beach, CA 90278-2325, USA

Person, Robert (Athlete, Baseball Player)
25 Bellerive Acres
Saint Louis, MO 63121-4328, USA

Person, Wesley (Athlete, Basketball Player)
PO Box 481
Brantley, AL 36009-0481, USA

Persons, Peter (Golfer)
1153 Saint Andrews Dr
Macon, GA 31210-4760, USA

Persson, Goeran (Prime Minister)
Rosenbad 4
Stockholm 103 33, SWEDEN

Persson, Nina (Musician)
Gotabergs Gatan 2
Gothenburg 400 14, SWEDEN

Persson, Stefan (Business Person)
Sverigekontoret
Stockholm SE-106 38, SWEDEN

Persuaders, The
225 W 57th St Ste 500
New York, NY 10019-2136

Pertucceli, Valeria (Actor)
c/o Staff Member *Telefe - Argentina*
Pavon 2444 (C1248AAT)
Buenos Aires, ARGENTINA

Pertwee, Bill
25 Whitehall
London, ENGLAND SW1A 2BS

Peruzovic, Josip (Actor, Wrestler)
c/o Nick Cordasco *Prince Marketing Group*
18 Carillon Cir
Livingston, NJ 07039-2600, USA

Pervical, Troy (Baseball Player)
2127 Century Ave
Riverside, CA 92506-4653, USA

Perzanowski, Stan (Athlete, Baseball Player)
10908 Wheat Rd
New Park, PA 17352-9563, USA

Perzigian, Jerry (Producer, Writer)
c/o Joseph Cohen *Creative Artists Agency (CAA-LA)*
2000 Avenue of the Stars Ste 100
Los Angeles, CA 90067-4705, USA

Pescatelli, Tammy (Actor)
c/o Douglas Edley *Gersh (LA)*
9465 Wilshire Blvd Ste 600
Beverly Hills, CA 90212-2612, USA

Pesce, P J (Director, Writer)
c/o Jordan Bayer *Original Artists (LA)*
9465 Wilshire Blvd Ste 870
Beverly Hills, CA 90212-2610, USA

Pesch, Doro & Warlock
Box 8721
Dusseldorf 1, GERMANY D-(W) 4000

Pesci, Joe (Actor)
c/o Jay Julien *Jay Julien Management*
Prefers to be contacted via telephone
New York, NY 10036, USA

Pescow, Donna (Actor)
8267 Paseo Canyon Dr
Malibu, CA 90265, USA

Pesek, Libor (Conductor)
Media House 3 Burlington Lane
London W4 2TH, UNITED KINGDOM (UK)

Pesi, Gino Anthony (Actor)
c/o Loch Powell *Leverage Management*
3030 Pennsylvania Ave
Santa Monica, CA 90404-4112, USA

Pesky, Johnny (Athlete, Baseball Player, Coach)
25 Parsons Dr
Swampscott, MA 01907-2929, USA

Pesonen, Richard (Athlete, Football Player)
765 Pine Hills Pl
The Villages, FL 32162-1617, USA

Pestana, Simon (Actor)
c/o Staff Member *Telefe - Argentina*
Pavon 2444 (C1248AAT)
Buenos Aires, ARGENTINA

Pestka, Sidney (Misc)
675 Hoes Ln W
Piscataway, NJ 08854-8021, USA

Pet Shop Boys (Music Group)
c/o Staff Member *Creative Artists Agency (CAA-LA)*
2000 Avenue of the Stars Ste 100
Los Angeles, CA 90067-4705, USA

Petagine, Roberto (Athlete, Baseball Player)
1098 Hunting Lodge Dr
Miami Springs, FL 33166-5754, USA

Petcka, Joe (Actor)
c/o Marta Michaud *Cinematic Management*
249 1/2 E 13th St
New York, NY 10003-5602, USA

Peter, Valentine J (Educator, Religious Leader)
Boys Town, NE 68010, USA

Peter II, Edward C (General)
4 Herons Nest
Savannah, GA 31410-3332, USA

Peter Paul & Mary (Music Group, Musician)
121 Mount Hermon Way
Ocean Grove, NJ 07756-1443

Peterdi, Gabor (Artist)
108 Highland Ave
Norwalk, CT 06853-1315, USA

Peterek, Jeff (Athlete, Baseball Player)
8073 Elm Valley Rd
Three Oaks, MI 49128-9552, USA

Peterman, Donald W (Cinematographer)
232 N Canon Dr
Beverly Hills, CA 90210-5302, USA

Peterman, Melissa (Actor, Producer)
c/o Staff Member *Agency for the Performing Arts (APA-LA)*
405 S Beverly Dr Ste 500
Beverly Hills, CA 90212-4425, USA

Peters, Andy (Television Host)
c/o Staff Member *BBC Artist Mail*
PO Box 1116
Belfast BT2 7AJ, United Kingdom

Peters, Anthony L (Tony) (Athlete, Football Player)
2402 Boston St
Muskogee, OK 74401-5233, USA

Peters, Barbara (Director)
1118 Magnolia Blvd
North Hollywood, CA 91601, USA

Peters, Bernadette (Actor, Musician)
c/o Jeff Hunter *WmE2 (WMA-NY)*
1325 Avenue of the Americas
New York, NY 10019-6026, USA

Peters, Bob (Coach)
Athletic Dept
Bernidji, MN 56601, USA

Peters, Caleigh (Musician)
c/o Siri Garber *Platform Public Relations*
2666 N Beachwood Dr
Los Angeles, CA 90068-2308, USA

Peters, Charlie (Writer)
c/o Todd Feldman *Creative Artists Agency (CAA-LA)*
2000 Avenue of the Stars Ste 100
Los Angeles, CA 90067-4705, USA

Peters, Chris (Athlete, Baseball Player)
6091 Irishtown Rd
Bethel Park, PA 15102-2343, USA

Peters, Clarke (Actor)
c/o Staff Member *Writers and Artists Group Intl (NY)*
360 Park Ave # 16
New York, NY 10022-5909, USA

Peters, Dan (Musician)
7 Trinity Row
Florence, MA 01062-1931, USA

Peters, Emmitt (Dog Sled Racer)
General Delivery
Ruby, AK 99768-9999, USA

Peters, Even (Actor)
c/o Megan Silverman *WmE2 (Endeavor-LA)*
9601 Wilshire Blvd Fl 3
Beverly Hills, CA 90210-5219, USA

Peters, Gary C (Athlete, Baseball Player)
7121 N Serenoa Dr
Sarasota, FL 34241-9271, USA

Peters, Gordon
20 Elm Tree Ave.
Ester Surrey, ENGLAND

Peters, Gretchen (Musician, Songwriter, Writer)
PO Box 331242
Nashville, TN 37203-7512, USA

Peters, Jason (Athlete, Football Player)
11611 Secretariat Dr
Walton, NE 68461-9804, USA

Peters, Kate (Stylist)
2121 E 7th Pl Apt 201
Los Angeles, CA 90021-1769, USA

Peters, Maria Liberia (Prime Minister)
Fort Amsterdam
Willemstad, NETHERLANDS ANTILLES

Peters, Marjorie (Baseball Player)
4081 S 122nd St
Greenfield, WI 53228-1823, USA

Peters, Mary (Athlete, Track Athlete)
Willowtree Cottage River Road
Dunmurray, Belfast, NORTHERN IRLAND

Peters, Mike (Cartoonist)
PO Box 957
Bradenton, FL 34206-0957, USA

Peters, Ray (Athlete, Baseball Player)
106 Cifuentes Way
Hot Springs Village, AR 71909-7421, USA

Peters, Rick (Actor)
c/o Patricia (Patty) Woo *Patty Woo Management*
8906 W Olympic Blvd
Beverly Hills, CA 90211-3550, USA

Peters, Rick (Ricky) (Athlete, Baseball Player)
43977 W Juniper Ave
Maricopa, AZ 85138-4072, USA

Peters, Roberta (Actor, Opera Singer)
19356 Cedar Glen Dr
Boca Raton, FL 33434-5129, USA

Peters, Russell (Actor)
c/o Paul Canterna *Seven Summits Pictures & Management*
8906 W Olympic Blvd Ground Floor
Beverly Hills, CA 90211, USA

Peters, Steve (Athlete, Baseball Player)
1524 SW 123rd St
Oklahoma City, OK 73170-4935, USA

Peters, Timothy (Race Car Driver)
PO Box 1708
Mount Juliet, TN 37121-1708, USA

Peters, Tom (Business Person)
555 Hamilton Ave
Palo Alto, CA 94301-2015, USA

Peters, Volney (Athlete, Football Player)
325 Lancaster Rd
Walnut Creek, CA 94595-1760, USA

Petersdorf, Robert G (Physicist)
8001 Sand Point Way NE Unit C71
Seattle, WA 98115-6382, USA

Petersen, Byron (Scientist)
Medical Center
Pittsburgh, PA 15260, USA

Petersen, Chris (Athlete, Baseball Player)
242 Timberland Ave
Longwood, FL 32750-6159, USA

Petersen, Jan (Government Official)
Postboks 8114 Dep
Oslo 32, NORWAY

Petersen, Kurt (Athlete, Football Player)
5520 Linmore Ln
Plano, TX 75093-7619, USA

Petersen, Loy (Athlete, Basketball Player)
475 NE Meadowlark Ln
Madras, OR 97741-9063, USA

Petersen, Melvin (Athlete, Basketball Player)
1412 Princeton Ct Apt C
Wheaton, IL 60189-7535, USA

Petersen, Niels Helveg (Government Official)
Drosselvej 72
Frederiksberg 2000, DENMARK

Petersen, Pat
1634 Veteran Ave
Los Angeles, CA 90024-5517

Petersen, Paul (Actor, Musician)
14530 S Denker Ave
Gardena, CA 90247-2323, USA

Petersen, Robert E (Publisher)
6420 Wilshire Blvd # 100
Los Angeles, CA 90048-5502, USA

Petersen, Stewart
PO Box 64
Cokeville, WY 83114-0064

Petersen, Ted (Athlete, Football Player)
323 Ridge Point Cir Apt 32A
Bridgeville, PA 15017-1566, USA

Petersen, William L (Actor, Producer)
c/o Staff Member *High Horse Films*
25135 Anza Dr Stage 5
Santa Clarita, CA 91355-3416, USA

Petersen, Wolfgang (Director)
c/o Staff Member *Radiant Productions*
914 Montana Ave Fl 2
Santa Monica, CA 90403-1505, USA

Petersmark, Brett (Athlete, Football Player)
2082 Pennsbury Ln
Hanover Park, IL 60133-6715, USA

Peterson, Adam (Athlete, Baseball Player)
6401 NE 144th St
Vancouver, WA 98686-2016, USA

Peterson, Adam (Athlete, Baseball Player)
4359 N Rushwood Ct
Wichita, KS 67226-1487, USA

Peterson, Adrian (Athlete, Football Player)
1087 Mount Vernon Dr
Grayslake, IL 60030-2647, USA

Peterson, Anthony (Boxer)
c/o Staff Member *Top Rank Inc.*
3908 Howard Hughes Pkwy # 580
Las Vegas, NV 89109, USA

Peterson, Anthony (Athlete, Football Player)
1974 Montrose Dr
Atlanta, GA 30344-3003, USA

Peterson, Buzz (Coach)
Athletic
Knoxville, TN 37996-0001, USA

Peterson, Cal (Athlete, Football Player)
22646 Ingomar St
Canoga Park, CA 91304-4622, USA

Peterson, David C (Journalist)
4805 Pinehurst Ct
Pleasant Hill, IA 50327-0959, USA

Peterson, Debbi (Musician)
1341 W Fullerton Ave # 180
Chicago, IL 60614-2362, USA

Peterson, Donald H
427 Pebblebrook Dr
El Lago, TX 77586-6012, USA

Peterson, Donald R (Astronaut)
427 Pebblebrook Dr
El Lago, TX 77586-6012, USA

Peterson, Elly (Activist)
1515 M St NW
Washington, DC 20005, USA

Peterson, Forrest J (Misc)
17 Collins Meadow Dr
Georgetown, SC 29440, USA

Peterson, Fred I (Fritz) (Athlete, Baseball Player)
PO Box 137
East Dubuque, IL 61025-0137, USA

Peterson, Harding (Hardy) (Athlete, Baseball Player)
2822 Sherbrooke Ln Apt C
Palm Harbor, FL 34684-2545, USA

Peterson, Jessie Lee (Radio Personality, Television Host)
PO Box 35090
Los Angeles, CA 90035-0090, USA

Peterson, John (Wrestler)
457 19th Ave
Comstock, WI 54826-9746, USA

Peterson, Kyle (Athlete, Baseball Player)
13253 Hamilton St
Omaha, NE 68154-5293, USA

Peterson, Lars (Doctor)
Surgery Dept
Goteborg 413 45, SWEDEN

Peterson, Maggie
3310 W Warm Springs Rd
Las Vegas, NV 89118-5229

Peterson, Michael (Musician)
1103 17th Ave S
Nashville, TN 37212-2203, USA

Peterson, Michael (Athlete, Football Player)
PO Box 904
Alachua, FL 32616-0904, USA

Peterson, Morris (Basketball Player)
Air Canada Center 40 Bay St
Toronto, ON M5J 2N8, CANADA

Peterson, Patrick (Football Player)
c/o Patrick William Lawlor *Galaxy Sports*
811 E Hillsboro Blvd
Deerfield Beach, FL 33441-3521, USA

Peterson, Paul E (Scientist)
5 Midland Rd
Wellesley, MA 02482-6927, USA

Peterson, Peter G (Business Person, Financier, Secretary)
345 Park Ave
New York, NY 10154-0004, USA

Peterson, Seth (Actor)
3424 Blair Dr
Los Angeles, CA 90068-1412, USA

Peterson, Steven (Architect)
131 E 66th St
New York, NY 10065-6129, USA

Peterson, Todd (Athlete, Football Player)
3249 Chatham Rd NW
Atlanta, GA 30305-1101, USA

Peterson, Vicki (Musician)
1341 W Fullerton Ave # 180
Chicago, IL 60614-2362, USA

Peterson, Walter R (Ex-Governor)
Dunlap Center 25 Concord Rd
Durham, NH 03824-3545, USA

Peterson, William L (Actor)
c/o Kelly Bush *ID PR (LA)*
7060 Hollywood Blvd Fl 8
Los Angeles, CA 90028-6014, USA

Peterson, William W (Athlete, Football Player)
13536 Mijo Ln
Lakeside, CA 92040-4824, USA

Peterson-Fox, Betty Jean (Baseball Player)
PO Box 280
Wyanet, IL 61379-0280, USA

Peterson-Parker, Katie (Golfer)
527 Henkel Cir
Winter Park, FL 32789-5127, USA

Petherbridge, Edward (Actor)
13 Shorts Gardens
London WC2H 9AT, UNITED KINGDOM (UK)

Petievich, Gerald (Producer, Writer)
c/o Brian Lipson *WmE2 (Endeavor-LA)*
9601 Wilshire Blvd Fl 3
Beverly Hills, CA 90210-5219, USA

Petit, Philippe (Misc)
1047 Amsterdam Ave
New York, NY 10025-1747, USA

Petit, Roland (Dancer)
20 Blvd Gabes
Marseilles 13008, FRANCE

Petitbon, John (Athlete, Football Player)
3804 N Labarre Rd
Metairie, LA 70002-1817, USA

Petitbon, Richie (Athlete, Football Coach, Football Player)
9628 Percussion Way
Vienna, VA 22182-3334, USA

Petitgout, Luke (Athlete, Football Player)
267 Prospect St
Ridgewood, NJ 07450-5121, USA

Petke, Mike (Soccer Player)
14120 Newbrook Dr
Chantilly, VA 20151-2273, USA

Petkovic, Andrea (Athlete, Tennis Player)
c/o Staff Member *Women's Tennis Association (WTA (US))*
1 Progress Plz Ste 1500
St Petersburg, FL 33701-4335, USA

Petkovsek, Mark (Athlete, Baseball Player)
5575 Duff St
Beaumont, TX 77706-6307, USA

Peto, Richard (Misc)
Harkness Building
Oxford, ON OX2 6HE, UNITED KINGDOM (UK)

Petra, Yvon (Tennis Player)
Residence du Prieure
Saint Germain en Laye 78100, FRANCE

Petralli, Geno (Athlete, Baseball Player)
119 Laser Ln
Weatherford, TX 76087-4006, USA

Petras, Ernestine (Baseball Player)
5 Greenwood Ave
Haskell, NJ 07420-1417, USA

Petrassi, Gottfredovia
Ferdinando di Savola 3
Rome, ITALY 196

Petrenko, Victor (Figure Skater)
c/o Staff Member *Champions on Ice*
3500 W 80th St Ste 200
Minneapolis, MN 55431-1090, USA

Petrenko, Viktor (Figure Skater)
PO Box 577
Simsbury, CT 06070-0577, USA

Petrey, Dan
1808 Cartlen Dr
Placentia, CA 92870-2734

Petri, Michala (Musician)
Nordskraenten 3
Kokkedal 2980, DENMARK

Petri, Nina (Actor)
Agnesstr 47
Munich 80798, GERMANY

Petrich, Bob (Athlete, Football Player)
1391 Silverberry Ct
El Cajon, CA 92019-2835, USA

Petrick, Ben (Athlete, Baseball Player)
1553 NE Jackson School Rd
Hillsboro, OR 97124-2425, USA

Petrie, Donald (Director)
c/o Alan Gasmer *Alan Gasmer Management Company*
10877 Wilshire Blvd Ste 603
Los Angeles, CA 90024-4348, USA

Petrie, Geoff (Athlete, Basketball Player)
PO Box 272
Clarksburg, CA 95612-0272, USA

Petrocelli, Americo P (Rico) (Athlete, Baseball Player)
37 Green Heron Ln
Nashua, NH 03062-2239, USA

Petrocelli, Daniel (Attorney, Attorney General, General)
11377 W Olympic Blvd
Los Angeles, CA 90064-1625, USA

Petrone, Rocco A (Engineer)
1329 Granvia Altamira
Palos Verdes Estates, CA 90274-2005, USA

Petrone, Shana (Musician)
3310 W End Ave Ste 500
Nashville, TN 37203-1087, USA

Petroni, Michael (Director)
9560 Wilshire Blvd Ste 500
Beverly Hills, CA 90212-2401, USA

Petronio, Stephen (Choreographer, Dancer)
95 Saint Marks Pl
New York, NY 10009-5110, USA

Petroske, John (Athlete, Hockey Player)
PO Box 366
Side Lake, MN 55781-0366, USA

Petrov, Andrei P (Composer)
Petrovskaya Str 42 #75
Saint Petersburg 197046, RUSSIA

Petrov, Nikolai A (Musician)
Kutuzovsky Prosp 26 #23
Moscow 121165, RUSSIA

Petrovic, Tim (Golfer)
11602 Turtle Ln
Austin, TX 78726-1825, USA

Petrovich, George (Athlete, Football Player)
3300 Joyce Dr
Fort Worth, TX 76116-6424, USA

Petrovics, Emil (Composer)
Attila Utca 29
Budapest 1013, HUNDARY

Petrovsky, Daniel J (General)
Commanding General UN Command Korea
APO, AE 96343, USA

Petrucci, John (Musician)
c/o Staff Member *Agency Group Ltd, The (LA)*
1880 Century Park E Ste 711
Los Angeles, CA 90067-1618, USA

Petry, Dan (Athlete, Baseball Player)
30715 Mystic Forest Dr
Farmington Hills, MI 48331-1106, USA

Petsko, Gregory A (Misc)
8 Jason Rd
Belmont, MA 02478-3129, USA

Pett, Joel (Cartoonist)
1010 New Circle Rd NW
Lexington, KY 40511, USA

Pettee, Roger (Athlete, Football Player)
210 S Obrien St
Tampa, FL 33609-3526, USA

Pettengill, Gordon H (Physicist)
Space Research Ctr
Cambridge, MA 2139, USA

Petter, Noel (Stylist)
1716 Hillside Dr
Glendale, CA 91208-2559, USA

Petterson, Donald K (Diplomat)
American Embassy Khartoum #63900
APO, AE 9829, USA

Pettersson, Carl (Athlete, Golfer)
2208 Oak Lawn Way
Wake Forest, NC 27587-4700, USA

Pettibon, Raymond (Artist)
920 Colorado Ave
Santa Monica, CA 90401-2717, USA

Pettibon, Richard A (Richie) (Athlete, Football Player)
9628 Percussion Way
Vienna, VA 22182-3334, USA

Pettibone, Jay (Athlete, Baseball Player)
5112 Via Marcos
Yorba Linda, CA 92887-2530, USA

Petties, Neal (Athlete, Football Player)
767 Jewell Dr
San Diego, CA 92113-2731, USA

Pettiet, Christopher
9255 W Sunset Blvd Ste 620
Los Angeles, CA 90069-3303

Pettiford, Valarie
c/o Jeff Morrone *Jeff Morrone Entertainment*
9350 Wilshire Blvd Ste 224
Beverly Hills, CA 90212-3204, USA

Pettigrew, Antonio (Athlete, Track Athlete)
Athletic Dept
Raleigh, NC 27610, USA

Pettigrew, Gary (Athlete, Football Player)
2707 E 27th Ave # 2B
Spokane, WA 99223-4912, USA

Pettigrew, L Eudora (Educator)
President's Office
Old Westbury, NY 11568, USA

Pettijohn, Francis J (Misc)
11630 Glen Arm Rd # V51
Glen Arm, MD 21057-9403, USA

Pettinato, Rachelle (Actor)
c/o Staff Member *Select Artists Ltd (CA-Westside Office)*
1138 12th St Apt 1
Santa Monica, CA 90403-5459, USA

Pettini, Joe (Athlete, Baseball Player)
112 Logan Ct
Bethany, WV 26032-2016, USA

Pettis, Gary (Athlete, Baseball Player)
3129 Crestline Ct
Antioch, CA 94531-6640, USA

Pettis, Madison (Actor)
c/o Alissa Vradenburg *Untitled Entertainment (LA)*
350 S Beverly Dr Ste 200
Beverly Hills, CA 90212-4819, USA

Pettis, Madsion (Actor)
c/o Alissa Vradenburg *Untitled Entertainment (LA)*
350 S Beverly Dr Ste 200
Beverly Hills, CA 90212-4819, USA

Pettit, Bob (Athlete, Basketball Player)
7 Garden Ln
New Orleans, LA 70124-1024, USA

Pettit, Donald R (Astronaut)
2014 Country Ridge Dr
Houston, TX 77062-3636, USA

Pettit, Paul (Athlete, Baseball Player)
928 Sarazen St
Hemet, CA 92543, USA

Pettit Jr, Robert L (Bob) (Basketball Player)
7 Garden Ln
New Orleans, LA 70124-1024, USA

Pettitte, Andy (Athlete, Baseball Player)
c/o Team Member *New York Yankees*
Yankee Stadium 161st St & River Ave
Bronx, NY 10451, USA

Petty, Kyle (Race Car Driver)
135 Longfield Dr
Mooresville, NC 28115-7342, USA

Petty, Lori (Actor)
c/o Mark J. Holder *Zero Gravity Management*
11578 Canton Dr
Studio City, CA 91604-4160, USA

Petty, Richard L (Race Car Driver)
311 Branson Mill Rd
Randleman, NC 27317-8008, USA

Petty, Tom (Musician, Songwriter)
c/o Staff Member *Warner Bros Records (LA)*
PO Box 6868
Burbank, CA 91510-6868, USA

Pettyfer, Alex (Actor)
c/o Simon Halls *Slate Public Relations*
9000 W Sunset Blvd Ste 915
West Hollywood, CA 90069-5809, USA

Pettyjohn, Adam (Athlete, Baseball Player)
717 Westwood Dr
Exeter, CA 93221-1438, USA

Petzy, Paul Angelo (Stylist)
c/o Staff Member *Ennis*
119 Braintree St
Boston, MA 02134-1628, USA

Pevec, Katja (Actor)
c/o Anne Woodward *ROAR (LA)*
9701 Wilshire Blvd Fl 8
Beverly Hills, CA 90212-2008, USA

Pevey, Marty (Athlete, Baseball Player)
158 Nightwind Trce
Acworth, GA 30101-5981, USA

Peviani, Bob (Athlete, Football Player)
25262 Northrup Dr
Laguna Hills, CA 92653-5223, USA

Peyroux, Madeline (Musician, Songwriter, Writer)
PO Box 158 Station E
Toronto, ON M6H 4E2, CANADA

Peyton, Brad (Director)
c/o Staff Member *WmE2 (Endeavor-LA)*
9601 Wilshire Blvd Fl 3
Beverly Hills, CA 90210-5219, USA

Peyton of Yeovil, John W W (Government Official)
Old Malt House Hinton Saint George
Somerset TA17 8SE, UNITED KINGDOM (UK)

Pezzano, Chuck (Writer)
27 Mountainside Ter
Clifton, NJ 07013-1107, USA

Pfaff, Judy (Artist)
175 E 79th St Apt 2B
New York, NY 10075-0565, USA

Pfann, George R (Athlete, Coach, Football Coach, Football Player)
120 Warwick Pl
Ithaca, NY 14850-1731, USA

Pfeiffer, Dedee (Actor, Model)
c/o David Rose *Innovative Artists (LA)*
1505 10th St
Santa Monica, CA 90401-2805, USA

Pfeiffer, Doug (Editor)
PO Box 1806
Big Bear Lake, CA 92315-1806, USA

Pfeiffer, Michelle (Actor)
c/o Jessica Kolstad *WKT Public Relations (WKT-LA)*
9350 Wilshire Blvd Ste 450
Beverly Hills, CA 90212-3230, USA

Pfeiffer, Norman (Architect)
811 W 7th St
Los Angeles, CA 90017-3408, USA

Pfeil, Bobby (Athlete, Baseball Player)
2358 Pheasant Run Cir
Stockton, CA 95207-5210, USA

Pfeil, Mark (Golfer)
2565 Chelsea Rd
Palos Verdes Estates, CA 90274-4309, USA

Pfister, Dan (Athlete, Baseball Player)
322 Nevada St
Hollywood, FL 33019-3532, USA

Pflug, Jo Ann (Actor)
PO Box 3292
Jupiter, FL 33469-1004, USA

Pfund, Lee (Athlete, Baseball Player)
130 Windsor Park Dr Apt C214
Carol Stream, IL 60188-1998, USA

Pfund, Randy (Athlete, Basketball Player, Coach)
100 S Pointe Dr Apt 1206
Miami Beach, FL 33139-7381, USA

Phair, Liz (Actor, Musician, Songwriter)
c/o Jason Weinberg *Untitled Entertainment (LA)*
350 S Beverly Dr Ste 200
Beverly Hills, CA 90212-4819, USA

Pham, Tuan (Cosmonaut)
4C-1000-Soc Son
Hanoi, VIETNAM

Pham Dinh Tung, Paul J Cardinal (Religious Leader)
Toa Tong Giam Muc Pho Nha Chung
Hanoi 40, VIETNAM

Pham Minh Man, Jean-Baptiste Cardinal (Religious Leader)
180 Nguyen Dink Chieu
Thanh-Pho Ho Chi Minh, VIETNAM

Phan, Dat (Actor, Comedian)
c/o Gayle Divine *Divine Management*
3822 Latrobe St
Los Angeles, CA 90031-1446

Phan, Van Khai (Prime Minister)
Hoang Hoa Thum St
Hanoi, VIETNAM

Phantog (Mountaineer)
Jiagnsu, CHINA

Phegley, Roger (Athlete, Basketball Player)
43 Timberlane Dr
Morton, IL 61550-1146, USA

Pheil, Anna (Actor)
c/o Scott Zimmerman *Evolution Entertainment (LA)*
901 N Highland Ave
Los Angeles, CA 90038-2412, USA

Phelan, Jack (Athlete, Basketball Player)
6404 21st Ave W Apt H502
Bradenton, FL 34209-7878, USA

Phelan, Jim (Athlete, Basketball Player, Coach)
16579 Old Emmitsburg Rd
Emmitsburg, MD 21727-8927, USA

Phelps, Brian
1265 Coldwater Canyon Dr
Beverly Hills, CA 90210-2419

Phelps, Doug (Musician)
212 3rd Ave N Ste 301
Nashville, TN 37201-1632, USA

Phelps, Edmund S (Economist)
45 E 89th St
New York, NY 10128-1251, USA

Phelps, James (Actor)
PO Box 9765 Coldfield
Sutton B75 5XB, UNITED KINGDOM (UK)

Phelps, Jaycie (Gymnast)
3635 Woodridge Blvd
Fairfield, OH 45014-8521, USA

Phelps, Josh (Athlete, Baseball Player)
1503 Regal Mist Loop
Trinity, FL 34655-4974, USA

Phelps, Kelly Joe (Musician)
733 N Main St # 35
Ann Arbor, MI 48104-1030, USA

Phelps, Ken (Athlete, Baseball Player)
6030 E Foothill Dr N
Paradise Valley, AZ 85253-3070, USA

Phelps, Michael (Athlete, Olympic Athlete, Swimmer)
c/o Staff Member *North Baltimore Aquatic Club*
PO Box 20801
Baltimore, MD 21209-0801, USA

Phelps, Oliver (Actor)
c/o Staff Member *JOP Project*
PO Box 9765
Sutton Coldfield B75 5XB, United Kingdom

Phelps, Richard (Athlete)
c/o Staff Member *ESPN (Main)*
ESPN Plaza 935 Middle St
Bristol, CT 06010-1001, USA

Phelps, Richard F (Digger) (Coach)
Sports Dept ESPN Plaza 935 Middle St
Bristol, CT 6010, USA

Phelps, Tommy (Athlete, Baseball Player)
4418 Pawnee Path
Valrico, FL 33594-5529, USA

Phelps, Travis (Athlete, Baseball Player)
PO Box 336
Wheaton, MO 64874-0336, USA

Phelps Jr, Ashton (Publisher)
3800 Howard Ave
New Orleans, LA 70125-1429, USA

Phenix, Perry Lee (Athlete, Football Player)
4849 Frankford Rd Apt 715
Dallas, TX 75287-5309, USA

Phifer, Mekhi (Actor)
c/o Emily Gerson Saines *Brookside Artists Management (NY)*
250 W 57th St Ste 2303
New York, NY 10107-2399, USA

Phifer, Roman Z (Athlete, Football Player)
PO Box 83215
Los Angeles, CA 90083-0215, USA

Philaret, Patriarch (Religious Leader)
10 Osvobozdeniya St
Minsk 22004, BELARUS

Philbin, Gerry (Athlete, Football Player)
9976 Marsala Way
Delray Beach, FL 33446-9727, USA

Philbin, Joy
101 W 67th St Apt 51A
New York, NY 10023-5953

Philbin, Regis (Television Host)
7 Lincoln Sq Fl 5
New York, NY 10023-7219, USA

Philbrick, Denise (Golfer)
5364 Carnegie Loop
Livermore, CA 94550-7136, USA

Philcox, Todd (Athlete, Football Player)
1201 1st St N Apt 703
Jacksonville Beach, FL 32250-8205, USA

Philip (Prince)
London SW1A 1AA, UNITED KINGDOM (UK)

Philip, HRH Prince
Buckingham Palace
London, ENGLAND SW1

Philip, Primate (Religious Leader)
358 Mountain Rd
Englewood, NJ 07631-3727, USA

Philipp, Stephanie (Model)
Icking-Isartal 82057, GERMANY

Philippoussis, Mark (Tennis Player)
1751 Pinnacle Dr Ste 1500
McLean, VA 22102-3833, USA

Philipps, Elizabeth (Busy) (Actor)
c/o Steven Levy *Framework Entertainment (LA)*
9057 Nemo St Ste C
West Hollywood, CA 90069-5511, USA

Philips, Chuck (Journalist)
202 W 1st St
Los Angeles, CA 90012-4105, USA

Philips, Emo (Actor)
c/o Staff Member *OmniPop Talent Group*
10700 Ventura Blvd Fl 2
Studio City, CA 91604-3561, USA

Philips, Gina (Actor)
c/o Erik Kritzer *Kritzer Levine Wilkins Entertainment*
11872 La Grange Ave Fl 1
Los Angeles, CA 90025-5283, USA

Philips, Jeanne (Writer)

Philley, Dave (Athlete, Baseball Player)
1336 E Polk St
Paris, TX 75460-7460, USA

Phillippe, Ryan (Actor)
c/o David Schiff *Schiff Company, The*
8440 Warner Dr Ste B1
Culver City, CA 90232-2461, USA

Phillips, Andy (Athlete, Baseball Player)
420 River Ranch Rd
Gallion, AL 36742-4629, USA

Phillips, Anthony (Musician, Songwriter, Writer)
55 Fulham High St
London SW6 3JJ, UNITED KINGDOM (UK)

Phillips, Bijou (Actor, Model, Musician)
c/o Jennifer Merlino *Untitled Entertainment (LA)*
350 S Beverly Dr Ste 200
Beverly Hills, CA 90212-4819, USA

Phillips, Bill (Writer)
10100 Santa Monica Blvd Ste 1300
Los Angeles, CA 90067-4114, USA

Phillips, Bobbie (Actor)
3001 Heavenly Ridge St
Thousand Oaks, CA 91362-1178, USA

Phillips, Brandon (Athlete, Baseball Player)
586 Rowland Rd
Stone Mountain, GA 30083-4573, USA

Phillips, Bum (Athlete, Football Coach, Football Player)
2981 S Riverdale Ln
Goliad, TX 77963-3723, USA

Phillips, Caryl (Writer)
English Dept
Amherst, MA 1002, USA

Phillips, Chynna (Actor, Musician)
1007 Montana Ave # 230
Santa Monica, CA 90403-1603, USA

Phillips, Davey (Baseball Player)
12 Upper Whitmoor Dr
Weldon Spring, MO 63304-0541, USA

Phillips, Davey (Athlete, Baseball Player)
12 Upper Whitmoor Dr
Weldon Spring, MO 63304-0541, USA

Phillips, Ed (Eddie) (Athlete, Baseball Player)
2022 Tracy Dr Apt 4
Bloomington, IL 61704-7358, USA

Phillips, Eddie (Athlete, Baseball Player)
1323 S Oak Run Pl
Springfield, MO 65809-2024, USA

Phillips, Eddie Lee (Athlete, Basketball Player)
800 McCary St SW
Birmingham, AL 35211-2944, USA

Phillips, Emo (Comedian)
63 William St # 300
East Sydney, NSW 1022, AUSTRALIA

Phillips, Ethan (Actor)
4212 W McFarlane Ave
Burbank, CA 91505-4018, USA

Phillips, Gary (Athlete, Basketball Player)
729 Country Club Dr
Kerrville, TX 78028-2781, USA

Phillips, Gene (Athlete, Basketball Player)
4630 Eldon Run
San Antonio, TX 78247-5520, USA

Phillips, Gersha (Designer)
c/o Staff Member *Paradigm (LA)*
360 N Crescent Dr
Beverly Hills, CA 90210-4874, USA

Phillips, Glasgow (Director)
c/o Brett Hansen *United Talent Agency (UTA)*
9560 Wilshire Blvd Fl 5
Beverly Hills, CA 90212-2400, USA

Phillips, Grant Lee (Musician)
c/o Staff Member *Paradigm (Monterey)*
404 W Franklin St
Monterey, CA 93940-2303, USA

Phillips, Harvey (Misc)
4769 S Harrell Rd
Bloomington, IN 47401-9028, USA

Phillips, Howard (Misc)
47 West St
Boston, MA 02111-1219, USA

Phillips, J R (Athlete, Baseball Player)
12010 N Rio Vista Dr
Sun City, AZ 85351-3663, USA

Phillips, Jack (Athlete, Baseball Player)
721 May Rd
Potsdam, NY 13676-3244, USA

Phillips, James (Red) (Athlete, Football Player)
1948 Wicker Point Rd
Alexander City, AL 35010-6504, USA

Phillips, Jason (Athlete, Football Player)
3001 N Boulevard
Richmond, VA 23230-4331, USA

Phillips, Jason (Athlete, Baseball Player)
7111 Defranzo Loop
Fort George G Meade, MD 20755-4053, USA

Phillips, Jason (Athlete, Baseball Player)
1777 Tara Way
San Marcos, CA 92078-1081, USA

Phillips, Jeffrey
8436 W 3rd St Ste 740
Los Angeles, CA 90048-4130

Phillips, Jess (Athlete, Football Player)
2820 San Antonio St
Beaumont, TX 77701-8036, USA

Phillips, Jim (Athlete, Football Player)
67 Lakeview Dr Unit 10D
Alexander City, AL 35010-6292, USA

Phillips, Joe (Athlete, Football Player)
425 Barker Ave
Oregon City, OR 97045-3449, USA

Phillips, John (Coach)
Athletic Dept
Tulsa, OK 74104, USA

Phillips, John L (Astronaut)
4422 Cedar Ridge Trl
Houston, TX 77059-3116, USA

Phillips, Joseph C
8730 W Sunset Blvd Ste 480
Los Angeles, CA 90069-2277, USA

Phillips, Julianne (Actor)
27727 Pacific Coast Hwy
Malibu, CA 90265-4344, USA

Phillips, Kevin (Actor)
c/o Todd Eisner *Agency for the Performing Arts (APA-LA)*
405 S Beverly Dr Ste 500
Beverly Hills, CA 90212-4425, USA

Phillips, Kim (Stylist)
c/o Staff Member *Elite Model Management/Atlanta*
1708 Peachtree St NW Ste 210
Atlanta, GA 30309-2416, USA

Phillips, Kirk (Athlete, Football Player)
2103 E Alma Ave
Sherman, TX 75090-4008, USA

Phillips, Lawrence (Athlete, Football Player)
9527 Langdon Ave
North Hills, CA 91343-2102, USA

Phillips, Leslie (Actor)
47 Brewer St
London W1R 3FD, UNITED KINGDOM (UK)

Phillips, Lou Diamond (Actor)
c/o JB Roberts *Thruline Entertainment*
9250 Wilshire Blvd Ground Fl
Beverly Hills, CA 90212, USA

Phillips, Loyd (Athlete, Football Player)
General Delivery
Springdale, AR 72764-9999, USA

Phillips, Mackenzie (Actor)
c/o Geneva Bray *GVA Talent Agency Inc*
8981 W Sunset Blvd Ste 101
Los Angeles, CA 90069-1850, USA

Phillips, Mel (Athlete, Football Player)
6368 Milk Wagon Ln
Miami Lakes, FL 33014-6083, USA

Phillips, Michelie (Actor, Musician)
c/o Marc Chancer *Origin Talent Agency*
4705 Laurel Canyon Blvd Ste 306
Studio City, CA 91607-5940, USA

Phillips, Michelle (Actor)
c/o Merritt Blake *The Blake Agency*
23441 Malibu Colony Rd
Malibu, CA 90265-4640, USA

Phillips, Mike (Athlete, Baseball Player)
3322 Ridgefield St
Irving, TX 75062-4157, USA

Phillips, Norma (Activist)
PO Box 819100
Dallas, TX 75381-9100, USA

Phillips, Owen M (Engineer)
462 Quail Ct
Chestertown, MD 21620-1241, USA

Phillips, Paul (Athlete, Baseball Player)
507 N Mine Ave
Demopolis, AL 36732, USA

Phillips, Peter C B (Economist)
PO Box 208281
New Haven, CT 06520-8281, USA

Phillips, Phil (Musician, Songwriter, Writer)
PO Box 105
Jennings, LA 70546-0105, USA

Phillips, Princess Zara (Royalty)
Gatcombe Park Minchinhampton
Stroud GL6 9AT, United Kingdom

Phillips, Richard (Captain)
211 River Rd
Underhill, VT 05489-9417, USA

Phillips, Ricky (Musician)
c/o Sterling Bacon *TBA Artist Management (Atlanta)*
1111 Alderman Dr Ste 285
Alpharetta, GA 30005-5433, USA

Phillips, Sam (Musician, Songwriter, Writer)
12424 Wilshire Blvd Ste 1000
Los Angeles, CA 90025-1071, USA

Phillips, Scott (Musician)
1776 Broadway Ste 430
New York, NY 10019-2002, USA

Phillips, Sean
153 Petherton Rd Highbury
London, ENGLAND N5 2RS

Phillips, Shaun (Athlete, Football Player)
c/o Staff Member *EAG Sports Management*
12910 Agustin Pl
Playa Vista, CA 90094-2301, USA

Phillips, Sian (Actor)
8 Alexa Court 78 Lexham Gdns
London, ENGLAND W8 6JL, UNITED KINGDOM (UK)

Phillips, Stone (Correspondent)
c/o Staff Member *Dateline NBC*
30 Rockefeller Plz Fl 270E
New York, NY 10112-0299, USA

Phillips, Susan M (Financier, Government Official)
20th St & Constitution NW
Washington, DC 20551-0001, USA

Phillips, Tari (Basketball Player)
Madison Square Garden 2 Penn Plaza
New York, NY 10121, USA

Phillips, Taylor (Athlete, Baseball Player)
594 Mein Mitchell Rd
Hiram, GA 30141-5810, USA

Phillips, Teresa (Basketball Player, Coach)
Athletic Dept
Nashville, TN 37209, USA

Phillips, Todd (Actor, Director, Producer, Writer)
c/o Todd Feldman *Creative Artists Agency (CAA-LA)*
2000 Avenue of the Stars Ste 100
Los Angeles, CA 90067-4705, USA

Phillips, Tony (Athlete, Baseball Player)
13341 E Cochise Rd
Scottsdale, AZ 85259-5442, USA

Phillips, Wade (Athlete, Coach, Football Coach, Football Player)
6115 Norway Rd
Dallas, TX 75230-4058, USA

Phillips, Warren H (Publisher)
PO Box 1798
Bridgehampton, NY 11932-1798, USA

Phillips, William D (Nobel Prize Laureate)
13409 Chestnut Oak Dr
Gaithersburg, MD 20878-3541, USA

Phillips, Craig, and Dean (Musician)
c/o Staff Member *INO Records*
210 Jamestown Park Ste 100
Brentwood, TN 37027-7570, USA

Phillips Jr, J Dixon (Judge)
100 Europa Dr
Chapel Hill, NC 27517-2357, USA

Phillips-Bannister, Kristie (Gymnast)
2809 Amity Hill Rd
Statesville, NC 28677-9744, USA

Phillopusis, Mark (Tennis Player)
c/o Staff Member *Octagon (VA)*
1751 Pinnacle Dr Ste 1500
McLean, VA 22102-3833, USA

Philyaw, Charles (Athlete, Football Player)
3929 Eileen Ln
Shreveport, LA 71109-1921, USA

Philyaw, Dino (Athlete, Football Player)
3164 Arrowhead St
Eugene, OR 97404-3858, USA

Phipps, Martin (Composer)
c/o Darrell Alexander *Cool Music Ltd*
1A Fishers Ln Chiswick
London W4 1RX, England

Phipps, Michael E (Mike) (Athlete, Football Player)
2748 NE 25th St
Lighthouse Point, FL 33064-8308, USA

Phipps, Sam
2346 Walgrove Ave
Los Angeles, CA 90066-3504

Phish (Music Group)
c/o Patrick Jordan *Red Light Management (NY)*
44 Wall St Fl 22
New York, NY 10005-2401, USA

Phoebus, Thomas H (Tom) (Athlete, Baseball Player)
2822 SW Lakemont Pl
Palm City, FL 34990-6094, USA

Phoenix, Beth (Wrestler)
c/o Kerry Rodgerson *World Wrestling Entertainment (WWE)*
1241 E Main St
Stamford, CT 06902-3520, USA

Phoenix, Joaquin (Actor)
c/o Jenni Weinman *Patricola Lust PR*
9171 Wilshire Blvd Ste 390
Beverly Hills, CA 90210-5515, USA

Phoenix, Rain (Actor)
c/o Josh Taylor *Val's Artist Management*
3 Greatmeadow Rd
Locust Valley, NY 11560-1005, USA

Phoenix, Steve (Athlete, Baseball Player)
11212 Horizon Hills Dr
El Cajon, CA 92020-8231, USA

Phoenix, Summer (Actor)
c/o Nick Frenkel *3 Arts Entertainment Inc*
9460 Wilshire Blvd Fl 7
Beverly Hills, CA 90212-2713, USA

Pianalto, Sandra (Financier)
1455 E 6th St
Cleveland, OH 44114-2517, USA

Piano, Renzo (Architect, Nobel Prize Laureate)
Via Rubens 29
Genoa 16158, ITALY

Piatkowski, Eric (Athlete, Basketball Player)
2125 S 189th Cir
Omaha, NE 68130-2834, USA

Piatkowski, Walt (Athlete, Basketball Player)
5263 Autumn Pl
Rapid City, SD 57702-8335, USA

Piatt, Adam (Athlete, Baseball Player)
1808 SE 37th Ter
Cape Coral, FL 33904-5036, USA

Piatt, Doug (Athlete, Baseball Player)
29 L St
Beaver, PA 15009-1520, USA

Piazza, Michale J (Mike) (Athlete, Baseball Player)
1000 S Pointe Dr Apt 3101
Miami Beach, FL 33139-7363, USA

Piazza, Vincent (Actor)
c/o Rhonda Price *Gersh (NY)*
41 Madison Ave
New York, NY 10010-2202, USA

Picard, Alexandre (Athlete, Hockey Player)
200 W Nationwide Blvd
Columbus, OH 43215-2563, USA

Picard, Robert
31831 Grand River Ave Unit 55
Farmington, MI 48336-4147

Picardo, Robert (Actor, Writer)
c/o Peter Young *Sovereign Talent Group*
8421 Wilshire Blvd Ste 200
Beverly Hills, CA 90211-3204, USA

Picasso, Paloma (Actor, Designer)
41 Rue Martre
Clichy 92117, France

Picatto, Alexandra (Actor)
c/o Kari Estrin *Paradigm (LA)*
360 N Crescent Dr
Beverly Hills, CA 90210-4874, USA

Piccard, Bertrand (Misc)
Rue de Lausanne 42
Geneva 1201, SWITZERLAND

Piccard, Jacques E J (Scientist)
Place d'Armes
Cully 1096, SWITZERLAND

Picciolo, Rob (Athlete, Baseball Player)
11773 Invierno Dr
San Diego, CA 92124-2814, USA

Picco, Giandomenico
1 United Nations Plz
New York, NY 10017-3515

Piccoli, Camille (Actor)
36 Rue de Ponthieu
Paris 75008, FRANCE

Piccoli, Michel (Actor)
11 Rue des Lions Saint Paul
Paris 75004, FRANCE

Piccolo, Bill (Athlete, Football Player)
2626 E Aurora Rd Apt 101
Twinsburg, OH 44087-2172, USA

Piccone, Lou (Athlete, Football Player)
325 N Forest Rd
Buffalo, NY 14221-5055, USA

Piccone, Robin (Designer, Fashion Designer)
1424 Washington Blvd
Venice, CA 90291, USA

Piccuito, Paul E (Stylist)
16 Olmstead Pl
Norwalk, CT 06855-1318, USA

Picerni, Paul (Actor)
PO Box 88
Llano, CA 93544-0088, USA

Pichardo, Hipolito (Athlete, Baseball Player)
21218 Saint Andrews Blvd Apt 305
Boca Raton, FL 33433-2435, USA

Piche, Ron (Athlete, Baseball Player)
128-100 Rue De Gaspe
Verdun, QC H3E 1E5, Canada

Pichler, Joseph A (Business Person)
1014 Vine St
Cincinnati, OH 45202-1141, USA

Pichlikova, Lenka (Actor)
101 Knickerbocker Ave
Stamford, CT 06907-2520, USA

Pick, Amelie (Actor)
20 Ave Rapp
Paris 75007, FRANCE

Pickard, Nancy (Writer)
7258 Mastin St
Shawnee, KS 66203-4606, USA

Pickel, William (Bill) (Athlete, Football Player)
9 Autumn Ridge Rd
South Salem, NY 10590-1103, USA

Pickens, Bruce (Athlete, Football Player)
2811 Wickeford Mill Dr
Buford, GA 30519-7611, USA

Pickens, Carl M (Athlete, Football Player)
623 Terrace Ave
Murphy, NC 28906, USA

Pickens, Jo Ann (Opera Singer)
56 Lawrie Park Gardens
London SE26 6XJ, UNITED KINGDOM (UK)

Pickens, Robert (Athlete, Football Player)
6701 S Crandon Ave Apt 21B
Chicago, IL 60649-1274, USA

Pickens Jr, James (Actor)
c/o Staff Member *Grey's Anatomy*
500 S Buena Vista St
Burbank, CA 91521-0001, USA

Pickens Jr, T Boone
1 Woodstone St
Amarillo, TX 79106-4151, USA

Pickens Jr., T. Boone (Business Person)
PO Box 12123
Dallas, TX 75225-0123, USA

Pickering, Byron (Artist)
6919 NE Highland Dr
Lincoln City, OR 97367, USA

Pickering, Calvin (Baseball Player)
201 Tanglewood Pl Apt 305
Tampa, FL 33617, USA

Pickering, Donald
Back Court Manor House
Eastleach Glos, ENGLAND

Pickering, Jeff (Cartoonist)
c/o Staff Member *King Features Syndication*
300 W 57th St Fl 15
New York, NY 10019-5238, USA

Pickering, Thomas R (Business Person, Diplomat)
2318 Kimbro St
Alexandria, VA 22307-1822, USA

Pickett, Cindy (Actor)
c/o Andrew Howard *Incognito Management*
9440 Santa Monica Blvd Ste 302
Beverly Hills, CA 90210-4614, USA

Pickett, Jay
24801 Eilat St
Woodland Hills, CA 91367-1036

Pickett, Rex
c/o Daniel A (Dan) Strone *Trident Media Group LLC*
41 Madison Ave Fl 36
New York, NY 10010-2257, USA

Pickett, Ricky (Athlete, Baseball Player)
1017 Wood Ridge Dr
Azle, TX 76020-3759, USA

Pickett, Ryan (Athlete, Football Player)
901 N Broadway
Saint Louis, MO 63101-2800, USA

Pickford, Kevin (Athlete, Baseball Player)
6006 N Harcourt Dr
Coeur D Alene, ID 83815-8473, USA

Pickford, Mary Foundation
9171 Wilshire Blvd # 512
Beverly Hills, CA 90210-5530

Pickitt, John L (General)
38 Sunrise Point Rd
Lake Wylie, SC 29710-9230, USA

Pickler, John M (General)
Director Army Staff Hqusa Pentagon
Washington, DC 20310-0001, USA

Pickler, Kellie (Musician, Reality TV Star)
c/o Staff Member *Fitzgerald Hartley Co (Nashville)*
1908 Wedgewood Ave
Nashville, TN 37212-3733, USA

Pickles, Christina (Actor)
137 S Westgate Ave
Los Angeles, CA 90049-4222, USA

Pickles, Vivian
91 Regent St
London, ENGLAND W1R 8RU

Pickren, Bradley (Actor)
c/o Philip Marcus *Clear Talent Group (LA)*
10950 Ventura Blvd
Studio City, CA 91604-3340, USA

Pickren, Spencer (Actor)
c/o Philip Marcus *Clear Talent Group (LA)*
10950 Ventura Blvd
Studio City, CA 91604-3340, USA

Pickup, Ronald
54 Crouch Hall Rd
London, ENGLAND N8 8HG

Pickus, Karen (Stylist)
175 W 76th St
New York, NY 10023-8302, USA

Pico, Jeff (Athlete, Baseball Player)
3291 Grape Way
Chico, CA 95973-9622, USA

Picone, Mario (Athlete, Baseball Player)
8876 Bay 16th St
Brooklyn, NY 11214-5902, USA

Picoult, Jodi (Writer)
38 Goodfellow Rd
Hanover, NH 03755-4800, USA

Pictor, Bruce (Musician)
1924 Spring St
Paso Robles, CA 93446-1620, USA

Pidgeon, Rebecca (Actor)
46 Albermarle St
London W1X 4PP, UNITED KINGDOM (UK)

Piech, Ferdinand (Business Person)
Braunschweiger Str 63
Schwulper 38179, GERMANY

Pied Pipers, The
25 Cobble Creek Dr Rd # Box 1 PMB 91
Tannersville, PA 18372

Piedmont, Matt (Director, Producer, Writer)
c/o Simon Millar *Rumble Media*
1620 Broadway Ste C
Santa Monica, CA 90404-2777, USA

Piedra, Jorge (Athlete, Baseball Player)
5608 Fairfax Dr
Frisco, TX 75034-5927, USA

Piekarski, Julie (Actor)
#301-100 Donwood Drive
Winnipeg, MB R2G 0W1, CANADA

Pienaar, Jacobus F (Misc)
PO Box 99
Newlands, 7725, SOUTH AFRICA

Piene, Otto (Artist)
383 Old Ayer Rd
Groton, MA 01450-1823, USA

Pierce, Adrienne (Musician)
c/o Staff Member *Paradigm (Monterey)*
404 W Franklin St
Monterey, CA 93940-2303, USA

Pierce, Chester M (Psychic)
17 Prince St
Jamaica Plain, MA 02130-2725, USA

Pierce, David Hyde (Actor)
c/o Cara Tripicchio *WKT Public Relations (WKT-LA)*
9350 Wilshire Blvd Ste 450
Beverly Hills, CA 90212-3230, USA

Pierce, Ed (Athlete, Baseball Player)
702 E Laurel Ave
Glendora, CA 91741-2851, USA

Pierce, Jack (Athlete, Baseball Player)
1002 Cortez St
Laredo, TX 78040-6237, USA

Pierce, Jeff (Athlete, Baseball Player)
1046 Lantern Ln
Circle Pines, MN 55014-1335, USA

Pierce, Jeffrey (Actor)
c/o Gary Pearl *Pearl Pictures & Management*
10956 Weyburn Ave Ste 200
Los Angeles, CA 90024-2835, USA

Pierce, Jill (Actor)
15941 Harlem Ave # 319
Tinley Park, IL 60477-1609, USA

Pierce, John (Musician)
c/o Staff Member *Paradigm (Monterey)*
404 W Franklin St
Monterey, CA 93940-2303, USA

Pierce, Jonathan (Musician)
330 Franklin Rd # 135-8
Brentwood, TN 37027-3280, USA

Pierce, Lincoln (Cartoonist)
200 Madison Ave
New York, NY 10016-3903, USA

Pierce, Paul (Athlete, Basketball Player)
79 Winter St
Lincoln, MA 01773-3502, USA

Pierce, Stack (Actor)
11288 Ventura Blvd # 620
Studio City, CA 91604-3187, USA

Pierce, Tamora (Writer)
612 Westcott St
Syracuse, NY 13210-2536, USA

Pierce, Tony (Athlete, Baseball Player)
6119 Brittany Ct
Columbus, GA 31909-4247, USA

Pierce, W William (Billy) (Athlete, Baseball Player)
1321 Baileys Crossing Dr
Lemont, IL 60439-8540, USA

Pierce, Wendell (Actor)
c/o Staff Member *Paradigm (LA)*
360 N Crescent Dr
Beverly Hills, CA 90210-4874, USA

Pierce The Veil (Music Group, Musician)
c/o Staff Member *Equal Vision Records*
PO Box 38202
Albany, NY 12203-8202, USA

Pierce-Roberts, Tony (Cinematographer)
1 Princes Garden
London W5 1SD, UNITED KINGDOM (UK)

Pierces, The (Music Group)
c/o Staff Member *Paradigm (Monterey)*
404 W Franklin St
Monterey, CA 93940-2303, USA

Piercy, Marge (Writer)
PO Box 1473
Wellfleet, MA 02667-1473, USA

Pieri, Damon (Athlete, Football Player)
1120 W Tuckey Ln
Phoenix, AZ 85013-1049, USA

Pierpoint, Eric (Actor)
2199 Topanga Skyline Dr
Topanga, CA 90290-4050, USA

Pierpoint, Robert (Correspondent)
2020 M St NW
Washington, DC 20036-3304, USA

Pierre, Andrew J (Scientist)
1779 Massachusetts Ave NW
Washington, DC 20036-2109, USA

Pierre, Juan (Athlete, Baseball Player)
6148 NW 65th Ter
Parkland, FL 33067-1553, USA

Pierre of Normandy, Abbe (Activist, Religious Leader)
La Halte d'Emmaus
Esteville 76690, FRANCE

Piers, Julie (Golfer)
5019 SW Hammock Creek Dr
Palm City, FL 34990-7909, USA

Piersall, James A (Jimmy) (Athlete, Baseball Player)
1105 Oakview Dr
Wheaton, IL 60187-3026, USA

Piersoll, Chris (Athlete, Baseball Player)
4275 Kingston Ct
Sarasota, FL 34238-2627, USA

Pierson, Frank R (Director, Writer)
c/o Staff Member *Academy of Motion Pictures Arts & Sciences*
8949 Wilshire Blvd
Beverly Hills, CA 90211-1972, USA

Pierson, Geoff (Actor)
165 W 46th St
New York, NY 10036-2501, USA

Pierson, Kate (Musician)
947 N La Cienega Blvd # 2
Los Angeles, CA 90069-4782, USA

Pierson, Marcus (Artist)
7216 Washington St NE Ste A
Albuquerque, NM 87109-4514, USA

Pierson, Pete (Athlete, Football Player)
17646 Jamestown Way Apt D
Lutz, FL 33558-7777, USA

Pierzynski, Anthony J (AJ) (Athlete, Baseball Player)
2139 N Clifton Ave
Chicago, IL 60614-4115, USA

Pieterse, Sasha (Actor)
c/o Ryan Martin *Agency for the Performing Arts (APA-LA)*
405 S Beverly Dr Ste 500
Beverly Hills, CA 90212-4425, USA

Pietkiewicz, Stan (Athlete, Basketball Player)
2213 Venetian Way
Winter Park, FL 32789-1215, USA

Pietrangeli, Nicola (Tennis Player)
Via Eustachio Manfredi
Rome 15, ITALY

Pietrangelo, Frank (Athlete, Hockey Player)
11 Buttonwood Ln
Avon, CT 6001, USA

Pietrus, Mickael (Basketball Player)
1001 Broadway
Oakland, CA 94607-4019, USA

Pietruski Jr, John M (Business Person)
27 E Corsica Ct
Farmingdale, NJ 07727-4312, USA

Pietrzak, Jim (Athlete, Football Player)
9800 4th St N Ste 400
Saint Petersburg, FL 33702-2464, USA

Pietrzykowski, Zbigniew (Boxer)
Ul Gomicza 5
Bielsko-Blata 43-409, POLAND

Pietsch, Barbara (Stylist)
126 Powell Ln
Upper Darby, PA 19082-3310, USA

Pietz, Amy (Actor)
c/o Scott Howard *Howard Entertainment*
10850 Wilshire Blvd Ste 1260
Los Angeles, CA 90024-4337, USA

Pifferini, Bob Sr (Athlete, Football Player)
4160 Jade St Spc 65
Capitola, CA 95010-3922, USA

Pigford, Eva (Model, Reality TV Star)
c/o Joseph Babineaux *Perspective Public Relations*
9107 Wilshire Blvd Ste 450
Beverly Hills, CA 90210-5535, USA

Piggott, Lester K (Jockey)
Beech Tree House Tostock Bury Saint Edmonds
Suffolk 1P20 9NY, UNITED KINGDOM (UK)

Pignatano, Joe (Athlete, Baseball Player)
150 78th St
Brooklyn, NY 11209-2914, USA

Pignatiellp, Carmen (Athlete, Baseball Player)
4087 Milford Ln
Aurora, IL 60504-2059, USA

Pigott, Mark C (Business Person)
777 106th Ave NE
Bellevue, WA 98004-5027, USA

Pigott, Sebastian (Actor)
c/o Andrew Edwards *Wishlab*
2438 Canyon Oak Dr
Los Angeles, CA 90068-2428, USA

Pigott-Smith, Tim (Actor)
34-43 Russell St
London WC2B 5HA, UNITED KINGDOM (UK)

Pihos, Peter L (Pete) (Athlete, Football Player)
USA

Pikaizen, Viktor A (Musician)
Chekhova Str 31/22 #37
Moscow, RUSSIA

Pike, Deborah (Stylist)
176 Scottswood Rd
Riverside, IL 60546-2268, USA

Pike, Gary (Musician)
10031 Benares Pl
Sun Valley, CA 91352-4207, USA

Pike, Jim (Musician)
9255 W Sunset Blvd Ste 407
Los Angeles, CA 90069-3302, USA

Pike, Rosamund (Actor)
c/o Dallas Smith *United Agents*
12-26 Lexington St
London W1F OLE, UK

Pike, Rosamund (Actor)
c/o Shelley Browning *Magnolia Entertainment (LA)*
9595 Wilshire Blvd Ste 601
Beverly Hills, CA 90212-2506, USA

Pikser, Jeremy (Actor)
c/o Margaret Riley *Brillstein Entertainment Partners*
1041 N Formosa Ave
West Hollywood, CA 90046-6703

Pilarcik, Al (Athlete, Baseball Player)
8790 Parrish Ave
Schererville, IN 46375-2435, USA

Pilarczyk, Daniel E (Religious Leader)
100 E 8th St
Cincinnati, OH 45202-2129, USA

Pileggi, Mitch (Actor)
c/o Joel King *Pakula/King & Associates*
9229 W Sunset Blvd Ste 315
Los Angeles, CA 90069-3403, USA

Pilic, Nicki (Tennis Player)
Otto-Fleck-Schneise 8
Frankfurt/Maim 60528, GERMANY

Piligian, Craig (Producer)
c/o Staff Member *WmE2 (WMA-LA)*
1 William Morris Pl
Beverly Hills, CA 90212-4261, USA

Pilkey, Dav (Writer)
555 Broadway
New York, NY 10012-3919, USA

Pilkey, Dave (Writer)
7406 Summer Trail Dr
Sugar Land, TX 77479-6232, USA

Pilkis, Simon J (Physicist)
Health Sciences Ctr
Stony Brook, NY 11794-0001, USA

Pill, Alison (Actor)
c/o Joanna (Joanie) Burstein *Burstein Company, The*
15304 W Sunset Blvd Ste 208
Pacific Palisades, CA 90272-3656, USA

Pilla, Anthony M (Religious Leader)
3211 4th St NE
Washington, DC 20017-1104, USA

Pillath, Roger (Athlete, Football Player)
N3623 Lepinsky Rd
Peshtigo, WI 54157-9403, USA

Piller, Zach (Athlete, Football Player)
3907 Dunleer Ct
Tallahassee, FL 32309-2630, USA

Pillers, Lawrence (Athlete, Football Player)
4305 Hanging Moss Rd
Jackson, MS 39206-4719, USA

Pillette, Duane (Athlete, Baseball Player)
2925 Carradale Dr
Roseville, CA 95661-4048, USA

Pilliod Jr, Charles J (Business Person, Diplomat)
494 Saint Andrews Dr
Akron, OH 44303-1226, USA

Pillow, Ray (Musician)
2802 Columbine Pl
Nashville, TN 37204-3104, USA

Pillsbury, Edmund P (Director)
3601 Potomac Ave
Fort Worth, TX 76107-1722, USA

Pilotdrift (Music Group)
c/o Staff Member *Paradigm (Monterey)*
404 W Franklin St
Monterey, CA 93940-2303, USA

Pilote, Pierre P (Hockey Player)
25 Mary Jane
Elmwood, ON L0L 2PO, CANADA

Pilska, Paul (Opera Singer)
352 7th Ave
New York, NY 10001-5012, USA

Pimenta, Simon Ignatius Cardinal (Religious Leader)
21 Nathalal Parekh Marg
Mumbai, MS 400 039, INDIA

Pimental, Nancy (Actor, Writer)
c/o Staff Member *WmE2 (Endeavor-LA)*
9601 Wilshire Blvd Fl 3
Beverly Hills, CA 90210-5219, USA

Pinal, Silvia
Av. de las Fuentas 629 Pedregal de San Angel
Mexico DF, MEXICO

Pincay, Laffit
PO Box 250
Lexington, KY 40588-0250

Pinchak, Jimmy (Jax) (Actor)
c/o Staff Member *Agency for the Performing Arts (APA-LA)*
405 S Beverly Dr Ste 500
Beverly Hills, CA 90212-4425, USA

Pinchot, Bronson (Actor)
10061 Riverside Dr
Toluca Lake, CA 91602-2560, USA

Pinckney, Ed (Athlete, Basketball Player)
3350 SW 27th Ave Apt 1004
Miami, FL 33133-5326, USA

Pinckney, Sandra (Chef, Television Host)
c/o Staff Member *Food Network, The*
75 9th Ave
New York, NY 10011-7006, USA

Pinder, Cyril (Athlete, Football Player)
7137 S Luella Ave
Chicago, IL 60649-2511, USA

Pinder, Gary (Athlete, Hockey Player)
320 39 Ave SW
Calgary, AB T2S 0W7, Canada

Pinder, Michael (Mike) (Misc)
53-55 High St Cobham
Surrey KT11 3DP, UNITED KINGDOM (UK)

Pine, Chris (Actor)
c/o John Carrabino *John Carrabino Management*
5900 Wilshire Blvd Ste 406
Los Angeles, CA 90036-5015, USA

Pine, Courtney (Musician)
100 Park St Apt 4
Montclair, NJ 07042-2996, USA

Pine, Phillip (Actor)
3972 Acapulco Ave
Las Vegas, NV 89121-6104, USA

Pine, Robert (Actor)
4212 Ben Ave
Studio City, CA 91604-2021, USA

Pineau-Valencienne, Didler (Business Person)
64/70 J Baptiste Clement
Boulogne-Billancourt 92646, FRANCE

Pineda, Salvador (Actor)
c/o Staff Member *TV Azteca*
Periferico Sur 4121 Colonia Fuentes del Pedregal
DF CP 14141, Mexico

Pinero, Joel (Athlete, Baseball Player)
9406 Lake Washington Blvd NE
Bellevue, WA 98004-5409, USA

Pines, Alexander (Misc)
Chemistry Dept Hildebrand Hall
Berkeley, CA 94720-0001, USA

Pinette, John
c/o Staff Member *International Creative Management (ICM-LA)*
10250 Constellation Blvd Fl 7
Los Angeles, CA 90067-6207, USA

Ping Lu, Kun (Misc)
3300 Brookline Ave
Boston, MA 2215, USA

Pingel, John S (Athlete, Football Player)
80 Celestial Way Apt 203
Juno Beach, FL 33408-2314, USA

Pinger, Mark (Swimmer)
5201 Orduna Dr Apt 6
Coral Gables, FL 33146-2655, USA

Pingree, Chellie (Congressman, Politician)
1318 Longworth Hob
Washington, DC 20515-4332, USA

Piniella, Louis V (Lou) (Athlete, Baseball Player, Coach)
705 Berrocales De Avila
Tampa, FL 33613-1099, USA

Pink (Musician)
c/o Roger Davies *RD Worldwide Management*
59 John St Woollahra
Sydney, New South Wales 2025, Australia

Pink, Steve
c/o Gabrielle (Gaby) Morgerman *WmE2 (Endeavor-LA)*
9601 Wilshire Blvd Fl 3
Beverly Hills, CA 90210-5219, USA

Pink Floyd (Music Group, Musician)
370 City Rd. Islington
London EC1V 2QA, UK

Pinkel, Donald P (Misc)
275 Marlene Dr
San Luis Obispo, CA 93405-1023, USA

Pinkel, Gary (Coach, Football Coach)
Athletic Dept
Columbia, MO 64211, USA

Pinker, Steven (Scientist, Writer)
33 Kirkland St William James Hall 970
Cambridge, MA 02138-2044, USA

Pinkett, Allen (Athlete, Football Player)
2026 Tuam St
Houston, TX 77004-1349, USA

Pinkett Smith, Jada (Actor, Producer, Writer)
c/o Miguel Melendez *Overbrook Entertainment*
450 N Roxbury Dr Fl 4
Beverly Hills, CA 90210-4218, USA

Pinkham Jr, Daniel R (Composer)
150 Chilton St
Cambridge, MA 02138-1227, USA

Pinkins, Tonya (Actor)
1505 10th St
Santa Monica, CA 90401-2805, USA

Pinkston, Rob (Actor)
c/o Staff Member *Mark Robert Management*
2208 Patricia Ave
Los Angeles, CA 90064-2318, USA

Pinkston, Ryan (Actor)
c/o Staff Member *Morra Brezner Steinberg & Tenenbaum (MBST) Entertainment*
345 N Maple Dr Ste 200
Beverly Hills, CA 90210-5174, USA

Pinkston, Todd (Athlete, Football Player)
1 Novacare Way
Philadelphia, PA 19145-5900, USA

Pinmonkey (Music Group)
c/o Staff Member *WmE2 (WMA-TN)*
1600 Division St Ste 300
Nashville, TN 37203-2755, USA

Pinner, Artose (Athlete, Football Player)
102 Big Blue Ct
Hopkinsville, KY 42240-2600, USA

Pinney, Ray (Athlete, Football Player)
6529B NE Windermere Rd
Seattle, WA 98105-2057, USA

Pinnock, Trevor (Conductor, Musician)
35 Gloucester Crescent
London NW1 7DL, UNITED KINGDOM (UK)

Pino, Danny (Actor)
c/o Geordie Frey *GEF Entertainment*
122 N Clark Dr Apt 401
West Hollywood, CA 90048-6315, USA

Pinone, John (Athlete, Basketball Player)
108 Riverview Rd
Glastonbury, CT 06033-3140, USA

Pinos, Carmen (Architect)
Av Diagonal 490 #3/2
Barcelona 8006, SPAIN

Pinsent, Gordon (Actor)
c/o Steve Lovett *Lovett Management*
1327 Brinkley Ave
Los Angeles, CA 90049-3619, USA

Pinsky, Drew (Doctor, Reality TV Star, Television Host)
c/o Valerie Allen *Valerie Allen PR*
2452 Chelsea Pl
Santa Monica, CA 90404-2037, USA

Pinsky, Robert N (Writer)
236 Bay State Rd
Boston, MA 02215-1403, USA

Pinson, Julie (Actor)
13576 Cheltenham Dr
Sherman Oaks, CA 91423-4818, USA

Pinson, Vada
710 31st St
Oakland, CA 94609-2925

Pintauro, Danny (Actor)
c/o Arnold M Preston *Preston Entertainment Inc*
8033 W Sunset Blvd # 7250
Los Angeles, CA 90046-2401

Pintilie, Lucian (Director)
44 Mihail Kogalniceanu Blvd
Bucharest, ROMANIA

Pinto, Freida (Actor)
c/o Staff Member *Performers Management*
258 E 3rd St #B
Vancouver BC V7W 1E7, CANADA

Pintscher, Matthias (Composer)
4 Addison Bridge Place
London W14 8XP, UNITED KINGDOM (UK)

Piotrowski, Tom (Athlete, Basketball Player)
80 Clarks Landing Rd
Port Republic, NJ 08241-9741, USA

Piovanelli, Silvano Cardinal (Religious Leader)
Piazzi S Glovanni 3
Florence 50129, ITALY

Piper, Billie (Actor)
c/o Staff Member *MF Management Limited*
Drury House 34-43 Russell St
London WC2B 5HA, UK

Piper, Jacki (Actor)
17 Westfields Ave Barnes
London SW13 0AT, UNITED KINGDOM (UK)

Piper, Rowdy Roddy (Actor, Athlete, Wrestler)
13110 SW Whitmore Rd
Hillsboro, OR 97123-9073, USA

Pipes, Leah (Actor)
c/o Jason Newman *Untitled Entertainment (LA)*
350 S Beverly Dr Ste 200
Beverly Hills, CA 90212-4819, USA

Pipes, R Byron (Educator)
PO Box 1147
Hudson, OH 44236-6347, USA

Pipettes, The (Music Group)
c/o Staff Member *Paradigm (Monterey)*
404 W Franklin St
Monterey, CA 93940-2303, USA

Pippen, Scottie (Athlete, Basketball Player)
c/o Staff Member *Chicago Bulls*
1901 W Madison St
Chicago, IL 60612-2459, USA

Pippig, Uta (Athlete, Track Athlete)
4279 Niblick Dr
Longmont, CO 80503-8326, USA

Piquet, Nelson (Race Car Driver)
SEN/CDPM Rua da Gasolina #01
Brasilia, DF 7007-400, BRAZIL

Pirae, Marcus Jean (Actor)
c/o Tom Parziali *Visionary Entertainment*
1558 N Stanley Ave
Los Angeles, CA 90046-2711, USA

Piraro, Dan (Cartoonist)
200 Madison Ave
New York, NY 10016-3903, USA

Pirates of the Mississippi
PO Box 17087
Nashville, TN 37217-0087

Pirelli, Leopoldo (Business Person)
Via Gaetano Negri 10
Milan 20123, ITALY

Pires, Alexandre (Musician)
c/o Staff Member *BMG*
1540 Broadway
New York, NY 10036-4039, USA

Pires, Mary Joao (Musician)
165 W 57th St
New York, NY 10019-2201, USA

Pires, Pedro V R (General, Prime Minister)
CP 22 Praia
Santiago, CAPE VERDE

Pires de Miranda, Pedro (Government Official)
Avenida da India 10
Lisbon 1300, PORTUGAL

Pirkl, Greg (Athlete, Baseball Player)
6822 Emerald Bay Ln
Indianapolis, IN 46237-5063, USA

Pirner, Dave (Musician, Songwriter, Writer)
509 Hartnell St
Monterey, CA 93940-2825, USA

Piro, Stephanie (Cartoonist)
PO Box 605
Hampton, NH 03843-0605, USA

Pirok, Pauline (Baseball Player)
13636 86th Ave
Orland Park, IL 60462-1612, USA

Pirri, Jim
9300 Wilshire Blvd Ste 555
Beverly Hills, CA 90212-3211

Pirtle, Gerry (Athlete, Baseball Player)
30306 E 59th St S
Broken Arrow, OK 74014-8434, USA

Pirus, Alex (Athlete, Hockey Player)
15W222 Concord St
Elmhurst, IL 60126-5326, USA

Pisarcik, Joe (Athlete, Football Player)
27 Compass Cir
Mount Laurel, NJ 08054-6106, USA

Pisarkiewicz, Steve (Athlete, Football Player)
1601 Johns Lake Rd Apt 1121
Clermont, FL 34711-6666, USA

Pischetsrider, Bernd (Business Person)
Petuelring 130
Munich 80788, GERMANY

Pisciotta, Marc (Athlete, Baseball Player)
867 Village Greene NW
Marietta, GA 30064-4749, USA

Piscopo, Joe (Actor, Comedian)

Piskula, Grace (Baseball Player)
415 Cherry Hill Dr
Mount Pleasant, WI 53406-3523, USA

Pister, Karl S (Educator)
Chancellor's Office
Santa Cruz, CA 95064, USA

Pistone, Tom (Athlete, Race Car Driver)
12536 Caldwell Rd
Charlotte, NC 28213-3808, USA

Pitchford, Dean
1701 Queens Ct
Los Angeles, CA 90069-1431

Pitcock, Joan (Golfer)
341 E Lester Ave
Fresno, CA 93720-1615, USA

Pithart, Petr (Government Official)
Vakdstejnske Nam 4
Prague 118 11, CZECH REPUBLIC

Pitillo, Maria (Actor)
c/o Jonathan Howard *Innovative Artists (LA)*
1505 10th St
Santa Monica, CA 90401-2805, USA

Pitino, Rick (Athlete, Basketball Player, Coach)
214 Mockingbird Gardens Dr
Louisville, KY 40207-5711, USA

Pitko, Alex (Athlete, Baseball Player)
655 S 79th Way
Mesa, AZ 85208-6320, USA

Pitlock, Skip (Athlete, Baseball Player)
215 Prospect St
Seguin, TX 78155-6018, USA

Pitman, Jennifer S (Race Car Driver)
Weathercock House Upper Lamboum
Hungerford
Berks RG17 8QT, UNITED KINGDOM (UK)

Pitoc, J P
1836 Courtney Ter
Los Angeles, CA 90046-2106, USA

Pitoc, John Paul (Actor)
c/o Amy Slomovits *Flutie Entertainment (LA)*
9320 Wilshire Blvd Ste 202
Beverly Hills, CA 90212-3217, USA

Pitou Zimmerman, Penny (Skier)
560 Sanborn Rd
Sanbornton, NH 03269-2401, USA

Pitt, Brad (Actor)
c/o Cynthia Pett-Dante *Brillstein Entertainment Partners*
9150 Wilshire Blvd Ste 350
Beverly Hills, CA 90212-3453, USA

Pitt, Eugene (Musician)
PO Box 12
Far Hills, NJ 07931-0012, USA

Pitt, Michael (Actor)
c/o Jason Weinberg *Untitled Entertainment (LA)*
350 S Beverly Dr Ste 200
Beverly Hills, CA 90212-4819, USA

Pitt, William
9 Rue Jean Mermoz
Paris, FRANCE F-75008

Pittaro, Chris (Athlete, Baseball Player)
42 Pintinalli Dr
Trenton, NJ 08619-1558, USA

Pittenger, Mark F (Scientist)
2001 Aliceanna St
Baltimore, MD 21231-3043, USA

Pittman, Charles (Athlete, Basketball Player)
16286 N 29th Dr
Phoenix, AZ 85053-3004, USA

Pittman, Danny (Football Player)
University of Wyoming Attn: Alumni Association
Laramie, WY 82071, USA

Pittman, Joe (Athlete, Baseball Player)
809 McKinnon Dr
Columbus, GA 31907-6508, USA

Pittman, R F (Publisher)
202 S Parker St
Tampa, FL 33606-2308, USA

Pittman, Richard A (War Hero)
5380 Dehesa Rd
El Cajon, CA 92019-1807, USA

Pittman Jr, James A (Misc)
5 Ridge Dr
Mountain Brk, AL 35213-3631, USA

Pitts, Chester (Athlete, Football Player)
c/o Staff Member *EAG Sports Management*
12910 Agustin Pl
Playa Vista, CA 90094-2301, USA

Pitts, Frank (Athlete, Football Player)
8249 S Laredo Ave
Baton Rouge, LA 70811-4055, USA

Pitts, Gaylen (Athlete, Baseball Player)
214 Rocky Bluff Ln
Mountain Home, AR 72653-7186, USA

Pitts, Greg
c/o Amy Slomovits *Flutie Entertainment (LA)*
9320 Wilshire Blvd Ste 202
Beverly Hills, CA 90212-3217, USA

Pitts, Hugh (Athlete, Football Player)
3612 Short St
Greenville, TX 75401-3900, USA

Pitts, Jacob (Actor)
c/o Robert Stein *Robert Stein Management*
PO Box 3797
Beverly Hills, CA 90212-0797, USA

Pitts, John (Athlete, Football Player)
4899 W Tyson St
Chandler, AZ 85226-2909, USA

Pitts, Robert (R C) (Athlete, Basketball Player)
12655 E Millburn Ave
Baton Rouge, LA 70815-6827, USA

Pitts, Ron (Sportscaster)
205 E 67th St
New York, NY 10065-6050, USA

Pitts, Ron (Athlete, Football Player)
3811 Davids Rd
Agoura Hills, CA 91301-3643, USA

Pitts, Tyrone S (Religious Leader)
601 50th St NE
Washington, DC 20019-5450, USA

Pittsley, Jim (Athlete, Baseball Player)
5 Old Woods Rd
Du Bois, PA 15801-8711, USA

Pivec, Dave (Athlete, Football Player)
1288 Fenwick Garth
Arnold, MD 21012-2107, USA

Piven, Jeremy (Actor)
c/o Jon Rubinstein *Authentic Talent and Literary Management*
45 Main St Ste 1004
Brooklyn, NY 11201-8200, USA

Pivonka, Michal (Athlete, Hockey Player)
8312 Grand Estuary Trl Unit 102
Bradenton, FL 34212-4264, USA

Piza, Arthur Luiz de (Artist)
16 Rue Dauphine
Paris 75006, FRANCE

Pizarro, Artur (Musician)
c/o Staff Member *Musicians Corporate Management*
PO Box 825
Highland, NY 12528-0825, USA

Pizarro, Juan (Athlete, Baseball Player)
2262 Ave Borinquen
San Juan, PR 00915-4421, USA

Piziou, Peter
16 Belsize Park
London, ENGLAND NW3 4ES

Pizzarelli, John (Musician)
c/o Staff Member *Challenge Records International*
Noorderweg 68
Hilversum 1221 AB, The Netherlands

Pizzo, Angelo (Director, Producer, Writer)
c/o David Greenblatt *Key Creatives*
1800 N Highland Ave Fl 5
Los Angeles, CA 90028-4523, USA

PJ & Duncan
PO Box 122Ashford
Kent, ENGLAND TN27 9BZ

Pjetray, Brittany (Beauty Pageant Winner)
641 Hollylake Rd
Aiken, SC 29803, USA

Place, Mary Kay (Actor)
c/o Staff Member *Gersh (LA)*
9465 Wilshire Blvd Ste 600
Beverly Hills, CA 90212-2612, USA

Placebo (Music Group)
4 South Street Epsom
Surrey KT18 7PF, UNITED KINGDOM

Plachta, Leonard E (Educator)
President S Ofc
Mount Pleasant, MI 48859-0001, USA

Placido, Michele
. 5200 via San Cornelia
Formello-RM, ITALY 60

Pladson, Gordon (Gordie) (Athlete, Baseball Player)
19087 87A Ave
Surrey, BC V4N 3G5, Canada

Plager, Robert B (Bob) (Athlete, Coach, Hockey Player)
362 Branchport Dr
Chesterfield, MO 63017-2902, USA

Plager, S Jay (Judge)
7171 Madison Pl NW
Washington, DC 20439-0001, USA

Plain White T's (Music Group)
c/o Sharrin Summers *Hollywood Records*
500 S Buena Vista St
Burbank, CA 91521-0002, USA

Plainic, Zoran (Basketball Player)
390 Murray Hill Pkwy
East Rutherford, NJ 07073-2109, USA

Plakson, Suzie (Actor)
302 N La Brea Ave # 363
Los Angeles, CA 90036-2518, USA

Plan B (Music Group)
c/o Staff Member *Paradigm (Monterey)*
404 W Franklin St
Monterey, CA 93940-2303, USA

Plana, Tony (Actor)
c/o Todd Eisner *Agency for the Performing Arts (APA-LA)*
405 S Beverly Dr Ste 500
Beverly Hills, CA 90212-4425, USA

Planchon, Roger (Director, Writer)
8 Pl Lazare Goujon
Villeurbanne 69627, FRANCE

Planinc, Milka (Prime Minister)
Bul Lenjina 2
Novi Belgrad 11075, SERBIA-MONTENEGRO

Plank, Doug (Athlete, Football Player)
12622 E Paradise Dr
Scottsdale, AZ 85259-3455, USA

Plank, Ed (Eddie) (Athlete, Baseball Player)
1353 Leawood Rd
Englewood, FL 34223-1714, USA

Plank, Raymond (Business Person)
2000 Post Oak Blvd
Houston, TX 77056-4499, USA

Plano, Richard J (Physicist)
10 Longwood Dr Unit 533
Westwood, MA 02090-1183, USA

Plant, Robert (Musician, Songwriter)
c/o Rod MacSween *International Talent Booking*
1st Floor, Ariel House 74A Charlotte St
London W1T 4QJ, UNITED KINGDOM

Plante, Bruce (Cartoonist)
100 E 11th St Ste 400
Chattanooga, TN 37402-4214, USA

Plante, William M (Correspondent)
2020 M St NW
Washington, DC 20036-3304, USA

Plantenberg, Erik (Athlete, Baseball Player)
1846 Creekside Dr NE
Owatonna, MN 55060-3973, USA

Plantier, Phil (Athlete, Baseball Player)
16001 Martincoit Rd
Poway, CA 92064-2115, USA

Plantu (Cartoonist)
Editorial Dept 21 Bis Rue Claude Bernard
Paris 75005, FRANCE

Planutis, Jerry (Athlete, Football Player)
3776 Stadium Dr
Bridgman, MI 49106-9789, USA

Plaskett, Thomas G (Business Person)
5215 N O Connor Blvd Ste 1070
Irving, TX 75039-3738, USA

Plater-Zyberk, Elizabeth M (Architect)
1023 SW 25th Ave
Miami, FL 33135-4824, USA

Platini, Michel
90 Av Des Champs-Elysees
Paris, FRANCE F-75008

Platinli, Michel (Soccer Player)
17-21 Ave Gen Mangin
Paris Cedex 75024, FRANCE

Platinum Blonde
Box 1223 Sta. F
Toronto, CANADA Ont.M4Y 2T

Platon, Nicolas (Archaeologist)
Leof Alexandras 126
Athens 11471, GREECE

Platov, Yevgeni (Dancer)
300 Alumni Rd
Newington, CT 06111-1868, USA

Platt, David (Soccer Player)
52 Victoria Street
McMahons Point NSW 2060, AUSTRALIA

Platt, Howard (Actor)
9200 W Sunset Blvd Ste 1130
Los Angeles, CA 90069-3606, USA

Platt, Kenneth A (Doctor)
11435 Quivas Way
Westminster, CO 80234-2620, USA

Platt, Lewis E (Lew) (Business Person)
3000 Hanover St
Palo Alto, CA 94304-1112, USA

Platt, Nicholas (Diplomat)
131 E 69th St
New York, NY 10021-5158, USA

Platt, Oliver (Actor, Producer)
c/o Tamar Salup *I/D PR (NY)*
150 W 30th St Fl 19
New York, NY 10001-4003, USA

Platters
2756 N Green Valley Pkwy # 449
Henderson, NV 89014-2120

Platts, Todd (Congressman, Politician)
2455 Rayburn Hob
Washington, DC 20515-2401, USA

Plavinsky, Dmitri P (Artist)
Arbat Str 51 Kotp 2 #97
Moscow 121002, RUSSIA

Playboy Playmates
2112 Broadway
Santa Monica, CA 90404-2912

Player, Gary J (Athlete, Golfer)
2000 Pga Blvd Ste 4450
North Palm Beach, FL 33408-2747, USA

Player, Scott (Athlete, Football Player)
1583 W Saltsage Dr
Phoenix, AZ 85045-1712, USA

Pleasant, Anthony (Athlete, Football Player)
17249 Connor Quay Ct
Cornelius, NC 28031-6503, USA

Pleasant, Reggie (Athlete, Football Player)
8270 Milford Plantation Rd
Pinewood, SC 29125-9249, USA

Pleau, Lawrence W (Larry) (Athlete, Coach, Hockey Player)
12 Atlantic Ave
Seabrook, NH 03874-4803, USA

Pleis, Bill (Athlete, Baseball Player)
16744 4th Ave NE
Bradenton, FL 34212-5510, USA

Plemons, Jesse (Actor)
c/o Staff Member *Simmons & Scott Entertainment*
7942 Mulholland Dr
Los Angeles, CA 90046-1225, USA

Plenty, Patty
1350 E Flamingo Rd # 150
Las Vegas, NV 89119-5263

Plesac, Dan (Athlete, Baseball Player)
245 White Thorne Ln
Valparaiso, IN 46383-9785, USA

Pleshette, John (Actor)
2643 Creston Dr
Los Angeles, CA 90068-2207, USA

Pless, Rance (Athlete, Baseball Player)
5528 Asheville Hwy
Greeneville, TN 37743-2287, USA

Pletcher, Eidon (Cartoonist)
210 Canberra Ct
Slidell, LA 70458-1520, USA

Pletnev, Mikhail V (Musician)
Starpkonyushenny Per 33 #16
Moscow, RUSSIA

Plews, Herb (Athlete, Baseball Player)
350 Ponca Pl
Boulder, CO 80303-3828, USA

Plimpton, Calvin H (Doctor)
450 Clarkson Ave
Brooklyn, NY 11203-2012, USA

Plimpton, Martha (Actor)
c/o Jill Littman *Impression Entertainment*
9229 W Sunset Blvd Ste 700
West Hollywood, CA 90069-3407, USA

Plisetskaya, Maiya M (Ballerina)
Tverskaya 25/9 #31
Moscow 103050, RUSSIA

Plodinec, Tim (Athlete, Baseball Player)
23251 Gilmore St
West Hills, CA 91307-3427, USA

Ploeger, Kurt (Athlete, Football Player)
304 2nd Ave SW
Pipestone, MN 56164-1508, USA

Plotkin, Stanley A (Musician)
3940 Delancey St
Philadelphia, PA 19104-4107, USA

Plott, Charles R (Economist)
881 El Campo Dr
Pasadena, CA 91107-5565, USA

Plough, Thomas (Educator)
President's Office
Fargo, ND 58105, USA

Plowden, David (Photographer, Writer)
609 Cherry St
Winnetka, IL 60093-2614, USA

Plowright, Joan A (Actor)
Malthouse Horsham Road Ashurst Steying
West Sussex BN44 3AR, UNITED KINGDOM (UK)

Plowright, Joan A (Opera Singer)
83 Saint Mark's Ave Salisbury
Wilts SP1 3DW, UNITED KINGDOM (UK)

Pluhar, Erika
Huschkagasse 5
Vienna, AUSTRIA A-1190

Plum, Milton R (Milt) (Athlete, Football Player)
1104 Oakside Ct
Raleigh, NC 27609-3596, USA

Plum, Ted (Athlete, Football Player)
17 Laurel Hill Dr
Cherry Hill, NJ 08003-2658, USA

Plumb, Eve (Actor)
c/o Mark Measures *Abrams Artists Agency (LA)*
9200 W Sunset Blvd PH 11
Los Angeles, CA 90069-3601, USA

Plumer, Patricia (PattiSue) (Athlete, Track Athlete)
4341 Starlight Dr
Indianapolis, IN 46239-1473, USA

Plummer, Amanda (Actor)
c/o Perry Zimel *Oscars Abrams Zimel & Associates, Inc. (OAZ)*
438 Queen St E
Toronto ON M5A 1T4, CANADA

Plummer, Bill (Athlete, Baseball Player, Coach)
2171 Sageway Dr
Redding, CA 96003-9384, USA

Plummer, Christopher (Actor, Musician)
49 Wampum Hill Rd Ste 480
Weston, CT 06883-1228, USA

Plummer, Gary (Athlete, Football Player)
10374 Rue Chamberry
San Diego, CA 92131-2212, USA

Plummer, Gary (Athlete, Basketball Player)
2119 Arthur Ave
Belmont, CA 94002-1660, USA

Plummer, Glenn (Actor)
c/o Brian Wilkins *Kritzer Levine Wilkins Entertainment*
11872 La Grange Ave Fl 1
Los Angeles, CA 90025-5283, USA

Plummer, Scotty
909 Parkview Ave
Lodi, CA 95242-2347

Plummer, Stephen B (General)
Deputy To Assistant Secretary Hqusaf Pentagon
Washington, DC 20330-0001, USA

Plunk, Eric (Athlete, Baseball Player)
9500 Pats Point Dr
Corona, CA 92883-5068, USA

Plunkett, Jim
51 Kilroy Way
Atherton, CA 94027-5405, USA

Plunkett, Maryann
10 E 44th St
New York, NY 10017-3601

Plunkett, Warren (Athlete, Football Player)
309 21st St SW
Austin, MN 55912-1566, USA

Plus One (Music Group)
c/o Teresa Davis *Paradigm (Nashville)*
124 12th Ave S Ste 410
Nashville, TN 37203-3170, USA

Plushenko, Evgeni (Figure Skater)
c/o Staff Member *Champions on Ice*
3500 W 80th St Ste 200
Minneapolis, MN 55431-1090, USA

Ply, Bobby (Athlete, Football Player)
8616 Ash Ave
Raytown, MO 64138-3431, USA

Plympton, Jeff (Athlete, Baseball Player)
8 Robin St
Plainville, MA 02762-1522, USA

Plyushch, Ivan S (Misc)
Verkhovna Rada M Hrushevskoho 5
Kiev 252019, UKRAINE

PM Dawn (Music Group)
857 Atlantic Ave Apt 5
Brooklyn, NY 11238-2797, USA

Pochman, Owen (Athlete, Football Player)
7405 91st Ave SE
Mercer Island, WA 98040-5805, USA

Pocklington, Peter H (Misc)
11230 110th St
Edmonton, AB T5G 3H7, CANADA

Pocoroba, Biff (Athlete, Baseball Player)
3445 Broxton Mill Way
Snellville, GA 30039-4441, USA

POD (Music Group)
c/o Staff Member *Paradigm (Monterey)*
404 W Franklin St
Monterey, CA 93940-2303, USA

Podell, Eyal (Actor)
c/o Samantha Crisp *Kohner Agency, The*
9300 Wilshire Blvd Ste 555
Beverly Hills, CA 90212-3211, USA

Podesta, John (Government Official)
1600 Pennsylvania Ave NW
Washington, DC 20500-0005, USA

Podesta, Rosanna
Via Bartolomeo Ammannati 8
Rome, ITALY I-00197

Podesta, Rossana (Actor)
Via Bartolomeo Ammanatti 8
Rome 187, ITALY

Podeswa, Jeremy (Director, Writer)
c/o Jennifer Levine *Untitled Entertainment (LA)*
350 S Beverly Dr Ste 200
Beverly Hills, CA 90212-4819, USA

Podewell, Cathy (Actor)
17328 S Crest Dr
Los Angeles, CA 90035, USA

Podkopayeva, Lilia
Rue des Oeuches 10
Moutier, SWITZERLAND CP 350 374

Podolak, Edward J (Ed) (Athlete, Football Player)
PO Box 2000
Basalt, CO 81621-2000, USA

Podoley, Jim (Athlete, Football Player)
2706 Gingerview Ln
Annapolis, MD 21401-7290, USA

Podolski, Lukas (Soccer Player)
Heinz-Nixdorf-Straüe 33
Münchengladbach 41179, GERMANY

Podres, Johnny (Athlete, Baseball Player)
1 Colonial Ct
Queensbury, NY 12804-1912, USA

Podsednik, Scott (Athlete, Baseball Player)
c/o Staff Member *Chicago White Sox*
U.S. Cellular Field 333 Wes 35th St
Chicago, IL 60616, USA

Poe, Gregory (Designer, Fashion Designer)
1950 S Santa Fe Ave
Los Angeles, CA 90021-2928, USA

Poe, Johnnie (Athlete, Football Player)
924 Donald F McHenry Pl
East Saint Louis, IL 62201-1046, USA

Poe, Richard
10 Prospect Park SW Apt 17
Brooklyn, NY 11215-5937

Poe, Ted (Congressman, Politician)
320 Cannon Hob
Washington, DC 20515-0603, USA

Poehler, Amy (Actor, Comedian)
c/o David (Dave) Becky *3 Arts Entertainment Inc*
9460 Wilshire Blvd Fl 7
Beverly Hills, CA 90212-2713, USA

Poepping, Mike (Athlete, Baseball Player)
13791 250th Ave
Pierz, MN 56364-2531, USA

Poesy, Clemence (Actor)
c/o Hylda Queally *Creative Artists Agency (CAA-LA)*
2000 Avenue of the Stars Ste 100
Los Angeles, CA 90067-4705, USA

Poff, John (Athlete, Baseball Player)
2786 Mishler Rd
Mio, MI 48647-9505, USA

Pogorelich, Ivo (Musician)
67 Teignmouth Road
London NW2 4EA, UNITED KINGDOM (UK)

Pogrebin, Letty Cottin (Activist, Editor, Writer)
33 W 67th St
New York, NY 10023-6224, USA

Pogue, David (Correspondent)
c/o Staff Member *CNBC*
900 Sylvan Ave
Englewood Cliffs, NJ 07632-3312, USA

Pogue, Donald W (Judge)
1 Federal Plz
New York, NY 10278-0001, USA

Pogue, William R (Astronaut)
15 Wesley Dr
Bella Vista, AR 72715-8461, USA

Pohl, Dan (Golfer)
903 E Bellows St
Mount Pleasant, MI 48858-3903, USA

Pohl, Don (Golfer)
903 E Bellows St
Mount Pleasant, MI 48858-3903, USA

Pohl, Frederick
855 S Harvard Dr
Palatine, IL 60067-7026

Pohlad, Carl (Baseball Player, Business Person)
c/o Staff Member *Minnesota Twins*
Metrodome 34 Kirby Punkett Place
Minneapolis, MN 55412, USA

Pohn, Carol (Stylist)
2259 N Wayne Ave
Chicago, IL 60614-3122, USA

Poimboeuf, Lance (Athlete, Football Player)
309 Fairfield Dr
Thibodaux, LA 70301-3721, USA

Poindexter, Alan G (Astronaut)
20229 Biddle Rd
Monterey, CA 93940-7458, USA

Poindexter, Anthony (Athlete, Football Player)
RR 3 Box 128
Forest, VA 24551, USA

Poindexter, Buster (Musician)
c/o Nina Nisenholtz *N2N Entertainment*
1230 Montana Ave Ste 203
Santa Monica, CA 90403-5987, USA

Poindexter, Christian H (Business Person)
39 W Lexington St
Baltimore, MD 21201-3910, USA

Poindexter, John M (Admiral, Government Official)
10 Barrington Fare
Rockville, MD 20850-3001, USA

Point of Grace (Music Group)
5250 Virginia Way Ste 110
Brentwood, TN 37027-7575, USA

Pointer, Aaron (Baseball Player)
4902 N Scenic View Ln
Tacoma, WA 98407-1365, USA

Pointer, Aaron (Athlete, Baseball Player)
4902 N Scenic View Ln
Tacoma, WA 98407-1365, USA

Pointer, Anita (Musician)
12060 Crest Ct
Beverly Hills, CA 90210-1348, USA

Pointer, Bonnie (Musician)
508 Honey Lake Ct
Danville, CA 94506-1237, USA

Pointer, Noel (Musician)
1650 Broadway Ste 508
New York, NY 10019-6833, USA

Pointer, Priscilla (Actor)
c/o Staff Member *WmE2 (WMA-LA)*
1 William Morris Pl
Beverly Hills, CA 90212-4261, USA

Pointer, Priscilla (Musician)
213 16th St
Santa Monica, CA 90402-2215, USA

Poirier, Anne
32 Rue Lenine
Ivry, FRANCE F-94200

Poirier, Mark (Writer)
c/o Rowena Arguelles *Creative Artists Agency (CAA-LA)*
2000 Avenue of the Stars Ste 100
Los Angeles, CA 90067-4705, USA

Poirier, Patrick
32 Rue Lenine
Ivry, FRANCE F-94200

Poitier, Sidney (Actor)
c/o Staff Member *Verdon-Cedric Productions*
PO Box 2639
Beverly Hills, CA 90213-2639

Polaha, Kristoffer (Actor)
c/o Paul Rosicker *Gersh (LA)*
9465 Wilshire Blvd Ste 600
Beverly Hills, CA 90212-2612, USA

Polamalu, Troy (Athlete, Football Player)
3400 S Water St
Pittsburgh, PA 15203-2349, USA

Polanco, Placido (Athlete, Baseball Player)
8950 SW 63rd Ct
Miami, FL 33156-1830, USA

Polanski, Roman (Director)
c/o Jeff Berg *International Creative Management (ICM-LA)*
10250 Constellation Blvd Fl 7
Los Angeles, CA 90067-6207, USA

Polansky, Abraham
135 S McCarty Dr PH 4
Beverly Hills, CA 90212-2257

Polansky, Mark (Astronaut)
2010 Hillside Oak Ln
Houston, TX 77062-3642, USA

Polanyi, John C (Nobel Prize Laureate)
142 Collier St
Toronto, ON M4W 1M3, CANADA

Polchinski, Joseph G (Physicist)
Physics Institute
Santa Barbara, CA 93106-0001, USA

Polcovich, Kevin (Athlete, Baseball Player)
3 Beardsley St
Auburn, NY 13021-2809, USA

Pole, Dick (Athlete, Baseball Player)
21012 Whitlock Dr
Dearborn Heights, MI 48127-2648, USA

Poledouris, Basil (Composer)
15233 Ventura Blvd Ste 200
Sherman Oaks, CA 91403-2244, USA

Polee, Dwayne (Athlete, Basketball Player)
1169 E 60th St
Los Angeles, CA 90001-1117, USA

Poleshchuk, Alexander F (Cosmonaut)
Syvisdny Goroduk 141160, RUSSIA

Poletiek, Noah (Actor)
c/o Staff Member *Protege Entertainment*
710 E Angeleno Ave
Burbank, CA 91501-2213, USA

Poletto, Severino Cardinal (Religious Leader)
Via Arcivescovado 12
Torino 10121, ITALY

Polgar, Laszlo (Opera Singer)
Abel Jeno Utca 12
Budapest 1113, HUNGARY

Polic, Henry II (Actor)
145 S Fairfax Ave Ste 310
Los Angeles, CA 90036-2176, USA

Police, The (Music Group)
194 Kensington Park Rd
London, ENGLAND W11 2ES, UNITED KINGDOM

Polish, Mark (Actor, Producer, Writer)
c/o Sean Elliott *WmE2 (Endeavor-LA)*
9601 Wilshire Blvd Fl 3
Beverly Hills, CA 90210-5219, USA

Polish, Michael (Director)
9701 Wilshire Blvd Ste 1000
Beverly Hills, CA 90212-2010, USA

Polishchuk, Oleksiy (Figure Skater)
c/o Staff Member *Champions on Ice*
3500 W 80th St Ste 200
Minneapolis, MN 55431-1090, USA

Politis, Irene (Stylist)
201 E 21st St Apt 4C
New York, NY 10010-6405, USA

Polito, Jon (Actor)
c/o Mary Ellen Mulcahy *Framework Entertainment (LA)*
9057 Nemo St Ste C
West Hollywood, CA 90069-5511, USA

Politte, Cliff (Athlete, Baseball Player)
6306 Sprig Oak Ct Apt C
Saint Louis, MO 63128-4336, USA

Politz, Henry A (Judge)
500 Fannin St
Shreveport, LA 71101-3023, USA

Politzer, Hugh David (Nobel Prize Laureate)
1200 E California Blvd
Pasadena, CA 91125-0001, USA

Polizzi, Nicole (Snooki) (Reality TV Star)
c/o Stacey Wechsler *Hired Gun Publicity*
250 W 19th St Apt 15F
New York, NY 10011-4049, USA

Polk, Steven R (General)
Vice Commander Pacific Air Forces
Hickam Air Force Base, HI 96853, USA

Polke, Sigmar (Artist)
4 E 77th St # 200
New York, NY 10075-1727, USA

Polkinghome, John C (Physicist)
Cambridge University
Cambridge CB3 9ET, UNITED KINGDOM (UK)

Poll, Martin H (Producer)
8961 W Sunset Blvd # E
Los Angeles, CA 90069-1807, USA

Polla, Dennis L (Engineer)
Electrical Engineering Dept
Minneapolis, MN 55455, USA

Pollack, Andrea (Swimmer)
Postfach 420140
Kassel 34070, GERMANY

Pollack, Daniel (Musician)
Music Dept
Los Angeles, CA 90089-0001, USA

Pollack, Frank (Athlete, Football Player)
4027 Austin Meadow Dr
Sugar Land, TX 77479-3036, USA

Pollack, Jim (Actor)
1418 N Highland Ave # 102
Los Angeles, CA 90028-7611, USA

Pollack, Joseph (Misc)
1017 12th St NW
Washington, DC 20005-4054, USA

Pollack, Kevin (Actor)
c/o Annett Wolf *WKT Public Relations (WKT-LA)*
9350 Wilshire Blvd Ste 450
Beverly Hills, CA 90212-3230, USA

Pollack, Sam (Misc)
6811 Monkland Ave
Montreal, QC H4B 1J2, CANADA

Pollak, Kevin (Actor, Comedian)
1360 N Crescent Heights Blvd
West Hollywood, CA 90046-4553, USA

Pollan, Tracy (Actor)
c/o Bob Gersh *Gersh (LA)*
9465 Wilshire Blvd Ste 600
Beverly Hills, CA 90212-2612, USA

Pollard, Bob (Athlete, Football Player)
8987 Washington Blvd
Beaumont, TX 77707-2814, USA

Pollard, Frank (Athlete, Football Player)
1526 N 12th St
Waco, TX 76707-2320, USA

Pollard, Marcus (Athlete, Football Player)
2991 Cameo Dr
Carmel, IN 46032-9313, USA

Pollard, Michael J (Actor)
520 S Burnside Ave Apt 12A
Los Angeles, CA 90036-3956, USA

Pollard, Scot (Athlete, Basketball Player)
10389 Windemere
Carmel, IN 46032-8594, USA

Pollard, Sue (Su) (Actor)
c/o Staff Member *Noel Gay Artists*
19 Denmark St
London WC2H 8NA, United Kingdom

Pollard, Tiffany (New York) (Actor, Reality TV Star)
c/o Chuck Binder *Binder & Associates*
1465 Lindacrest Dr
Beverly Hills, CA 90210-2519, USA

Polle, David R (Misc)
501 Broadway
Nashville, TN 37203-3980, USA

Polle, Norman R (Bud) (Athlete, Coach, Hockey Player)
1509-2004 Fullerton Ave
North Vancouver, BC V7P 3G8, Canada

Pollen, Arabella R H (Designer, Fashion Designer)
Canham Mews #8 Canham Road
London W3 7SR, UNITED KINGDOM (UK)

Polley, Dale (Ballerina)
107 Redding Rd
Georgetown, KY 40324-1078, USA

Polley, Dale (Athlete, Baseball Player)
107 Redding Rd
Georgetown, KY 40324-1078, USA

Polley, Eugene J (Inventor)
60 Nicoll Ave Apt 251
Glen Ellyn, IL 60137-8211, USA

Polley, Sarah (Actor, Director, Writer)
c/o Frank Frattaroli *Dontanville/Frattaroli (D/F)*
270 Lafayette St Ste 402
New York, NY 10012-3327, USA

Pollin, Abe (Baseball Player)
Capital Centre 1 Truman Dr
Landover, MD 20785, USA

Pollini, Maurizio (Musician)
Via Manzoni 31
Milan 20120, ITALY

Pollitt-Deschaine, Alice (Baseball Player)
9140 Silver Strand Rd
Levering, MI 49755-9103, USA

Pollock, Alex J (Business Person)
111 E Wacker Dr
Chicago, IL 60601-3757, USA

Pollock, Michael P (Admiral)
Ivy House Churchstoke Montgomery
Powys SY15 6DU, WALES

Polo, Ana Maria (Actor)
c/o Staff Member *Telemundo*
2470 W 8th Ave
Hialeah, FL 33010-2000, USA

Polo, Teri (Actor)
c/o Bob McGowan *McGowan Management*
8733 W Sunset Blvd Ste 103
West Hollywood, CA 90069-2241, USA

Polo, Terri (Actor)
c/o Staff Member *United Talent Agency (UTA)*
9560 Wilshire Blvd Fl 5
Beverly Hills, CA 90212-2400, USA

Polofsky, Gordon (Athlete, Football Player)
8815 Gatwick Dr
Concord, TN 37922-6098, USA

Polone, Gavin (Producer)
c/o Staff Member *WmE2 (Endeavor-LA)*
9601 Wilshire Blvd Fl 3
Beverly Hills, CA 90210-5219, USA

Poloni, John (Athlete, Baseball Player)
1714 Polo Club Dr
Tarpon Springs, FL 34689-8013, USA

Poloujadoff, Michel E (Engineer)
8 Rue Roches
Buthiers 77760, FRANCE

Polowski, Larry (Athlete, Football Player)
365 E Brookhollow Dr
Boise, ID 83706-6730, USA

Polozkova, Lidia P (Speed Skater)
Solianka Str 14/2
Moscow 109240, RUSSIA

Polshak, James Stewart (Architect)
320 W 134th St # 800
New York, NY 10030, USA

Polson, John (Actor)
c/o Robyn Gardiner *RGM Artist Group*
64-76 Kippax St Level 2, Suite 202 & 206
Surry Hills, NSW 2010, Australia

Polson, Ralph (Athlete, Basketball Player)
3846 S Eagle Ln
Spokane Valley, WA 99206-6351, USA

Polyakov, Valeri V (Cosmonaut)
Choroshevskoye Chaussee 76A
Moscow 123007, RUSSIA

Polynice, Olden (Athlete, Basketball Player)
PO Box 220339
Newhall, CA 91322-0339, USA

Polyphonic Spree, The (Music Group)
c/o Staff Member *Paradigm (Monterey)*
404 W Franklin St
Monterey, CA 93940-2303, USA

Pomers, Scarlett
c/o Rhonda Boudreaux *Rhonda Boudreaux Publicity*
Prefers to be contacted via telephone
Oakland, CA 900, USA

Pommier, Jean-Bernard (Musician)
2 Chemin des Cotes de Montmoiret
Lausanne 1012, SWITZERLAND

Pomodora, Arnaldo (Artist)
Via Vigevano 5
Milan 20144, ITALY

Pompedda, Mario Francesco Cardinal (Religious Leader)
Palazzo della Cancelleria Plazza della Cancelleria 1
Rome 186, ITALY

Pompeo, Ellen (Actor)
c/o Judy Hofflund *Hofflund/Polone*
9465 Wilshire Blvd Ste 420
Beverly Hills, CA 90212-2603, USA

Pompeo, Mike (Congressman, Politician)
107 Cannon Hob
Washington, DC 20515-0902, USA

Ponazecki, Joe (Actor)
10 E 44th St
New York, NY 10017-3601, USA

Ponce, Carlos (Musician)
c/o Staff Member *WmE2 (WMA-LA)*
1 William Morris Pl
Beverly Hills, CA 90212-4261, USA

Ponce, Carlos (Athlete, Baseball Player)
590 Kingsbury Ct
Wellington, FL 33414-3919, USA

Ponce, Enrile Juan (Government Official)
2305 Morado St Dasmarinas Village
Makati
Metro Manila, PHILLIPPINES

Ponce, LuAnne (Actor)
3500 W Olive Ave Ste 1400
Burbank, CA 91505-5512, USA

Ponce, Walter (Musician)
165 W 57th St
New York, NY 10019-2201, USA

Poncino, Larry (Baseball Player)
2954 N Calle Ladera
Tucson, AZ 85715-3202, USA

Poncino, Larry (Athlete, Baseball Player)
2954 N Calle Ladera
Tucson, AZ 85715-3202, USA

Pond, Lennie (Race Car Driver)
4301 Caronado Dr
Chester, VA 23831-4502, USA

Pond, Matt (Musician)
c/o Staff Member *Paradigm (Monterey)*
404 W Franklin St
Monterey, CA 93940-2303, USA

Ponder, Christian (Football Player)
c/o Pat Dye Jr *SportsTrust Advisors - GA*
3340 Peachtree Rd NE Fl 16
Atlanta, GA 30326-1000, USA

Ponder, Dave (Athlete, Football Player)
1818 Sandalwood Ln
Grapevine, TX 76051-7344, USA

Pondexter, Cliff (Athlete, Basketball Player)
1135 W Stuart Ave
Fresno, CA 93711-2040, USA

Pons, B Stanley (Misc)
Chemistry Dept Eyring Building
Salt Lake City, UT 84112, USA

Pons, Juan (Opera Singer)
119 W 57th St Ste 1505
New York, NY 10019-2403, USA

Ponson, Sidney (Athlete, Baseball Player)
443 Hendricks Isle Slip 2
Ft Lauderdale, FL 33301-5740, USA

Pontes, Marcos (Astronaut)
16807 Soaring Forest Dr
Houston, TX 77059-4002, USA

Ponti, Cario (Producer)
Palazzo Colonna 1 Piazza d'Ara Coell 1
Rome, ITALY

Ponti, Michael (Musician)
Heubergstr 32
Eschenlohe 83565, GERMANY

Pontius, Chris (Actor, Writer)
c/o Beth Holden-Garland *Untitled Entertainment (LA)*
350 S Beverly Dr Ste 200
Beverly Hills, CA 90212-4819, USA

Pontois, Noella-Chantal (Ballerina)
25 Rue de Maubeuge
Paris 75009, FRANCE

Ponty, Jean-Luc (Composer, Musician)
c/o Staff Member *Paradigm (NY)*
360 Park Ave S Fl 16
New York, NY 10010-1708, USA

Pony, Trick (Music Group)
c/o Staff Member *Creative Artists Agency (CAA-TN)*
3310 W End Ave Fl 5
Nashville, TN 37203-1028, USA

Ponzini, Anthony (Actor)
3500 W Olive Ave Ste 1400
Burbank, CA 91505-5512, USA

Ponzo, Rosemary (Stylist)
181 7th Ave Apt 3B
New York, NY 10011-1855, USA

Pooja, Bhatt (Actor, Bollywood)
601 Kyle More Apartments Behind Mehboob Studios Bandra W
Mumbai, MS 400050, INDIA

Pook, Chris (Race Car Driver)
5350 Lakeview Parkway South Dr
Indianapolis, IN 46268-5129, USA

Pool, David (Athlete, Football Player)
460 Vista Glen Dr
Cincinnati, OH 45246-2366, USA

Pool, John L (Doctor)
1011 Charles St Apt C
Fredericksburg, VA 22401-3852, USA

Poole, Bob (Athlete, Football Player)
7802 Shadyvilla Ln
Houston, TX 77055, USA

Poole, Brian (Musician)
67 Tower Drive Neath Hill
Milton Keynes MK14 6JX, UNITED KINGDOM (UK)

Poole, David J (Artist)
Trinity Flint Bam Weston Lane
Petersfield Hants GU32 3NN, UNITED KINGDOM (UK)

Poole, G Barney (Athlete, Football Player)
213 E Railroad Ave
Gloster, MS 39638, USA

Poole, George B (Athlete, Football Player)
PO Box 278
Gloster, MS 39638-0278, USA

Poole, Jim (Athlete, Baseball Player)
605 Falls Lake Dr
Alpharetta, GA 30022-8059, USA

Poole, Keith (Athlete, Football Player)
4100 S Arizona Ave Ste 4
Chandler, AZ 85248-3988, USA

Poole, Larry (Athlete, Football Player)
15803 Sea Oats Pl
Tampa, FL 33624-1629, USA

Poole, Nathan (Athlete, Football Player)
8686 Longwood St
San Diego, CA 92126-3654, USA

Poole, Oliver (Athlete, Football Player)
PO Box 184
Gloster, MS 39638-0184, USA

Poole, Tyrone (Athlete, Football Player)
3415 Rivers Call Blvd
Atlanta, GA 30339-5662, USA

Poole, William (Government Official)
137 Frontenac Frst
Saint Louis, MO 63131-3220, USA

Pooley, Don (Athlete, Golfer)
5251 N Camino Sumo
Tucson, AZ 85718-6047, USA

Poons, Larry (Artist)
PO Box 115
Islamorada, FL 33036-0115, USA

Poornam, Viswanatha (Actor)
7 Lodi Khan Street T Nagar
Chennai, TN 600 017, INDIA

Poots, Imogen (Actor)
c/o Ted Schachter *Schachter Entertainment*
1157 S Beverly Dr Fl 2
Los Angeles, CA 90035-1119, USA

Pop, Iggy (Actor, Composer, Musician, Songwriter)
c/o Marsha Vlasic *International Creative Management (ICM-LA)*
10250 Constellation Blvd Fl 7
Los Angeles, CA 90067-6207, USA

Popcorn, Faith (Writer)
1 Dag Hammarskjold Plaza 885 Second Ave Fl 16
New York, NY 10017, USA

Pope, Bucky (Athlete, Football Player)
7 Bunker Hill Dr
Washington Crossing, PA 18977-1415, USA

Pope, Carly (Actor, Producer)
c/o Ben Levine *Kritzer Levine Wilkins Entertainment*
11872 La Grange Ave Fl 1
Los Angeles, CA 90025-5283, USA

Pope, Eddie (Soccer Player)
1 Harmon Plz # 300
Secaucus, NJ 07094-2803, USA

Pope, Edwin (Writer)
1 Herald Plz
Miami, FL 33132-1609, USA

Pope, Everett P (War Hero)
40 Patriots Point Rd
Mt Pleasant, SC 29464-4377, USA

Pope, Marguez P (Athlete, Football Player)
PO Box 470487
San Francisco, CA 94147-0487, USA

Pope, Marquez (Athlete, Football Player)
110 Avila St
San Francisco, CA 94123-2010, USA

Pope, Monsanto (Athlete, Football Player)
312 13th St NW Apt 10
Charlottesville, VA 22903-2754, USA

Pope, Odeon (Musician)
122 E 57th St # 300
New York, NY 10022-2623, USA

Pope, Rosie (Reality TV Star)
18 E 41st St Rm 1702
New York, NY 10017-6231, USA

Pope, Willie (Baseball Player)
7616 Bennett St
Pittsburgh, PA 15208-1602, USA

Popiel, Poul P (Athlete, Hockey Player)
2501 Peppermill Ridge Dr
Chesterfield, MO 63005-6707, USA

Popoff, A Jay (Musician)
1223 Wilshire Blvd # 804
Santa Monica, CA 90403-5400, USA

Popoff, Frank P (Business Person)
2030 Dow Ctr
Midland, MI 48674-0001, USA

Popov, Aleksandr (Swimmer)
Sports House Maitland Road #7
Hackett 2602, AUSTRALIA

Popov, Leonid I (Cosmonaut)
Syvisdny Goroduk 141160, RUSSIA

Popovac, Gwynn (Artist)
17270 Robin Rdg
Sonora, CA 95370-8108, USA

Popovich, Gregg (Athlete, Basketball Player, Coach)
41 Vineyard Dr
San Antonio, TX 78257-1236, USA

Popovich, Milt (Athlete, Football Player)
1355 Dewey Blvd
Butte, MT 59701-3415, USA

Popovich, Paul (Athlete, Baseball Player)
2604 Woodlawn Rd
Northbrook, IL 60062-5951, USA

Popowich, Paul (Actor)
c/o Mark Schumacher *Schumacher Management*
1122 San Vicente Blvd
Santa Monica, CA 90402-2008, USA

Popp, Nathaniel (Religious Leader)
PO Box 309
Grass Lake, MI 49240-0309, USA

Poppe, Nils
Fredriksdale Theaterin Domsten
Helsingborg, SWEDEN 25590

Popper, John (Musician)
c/o Staff Member *ArtistDirect*
9046 Lindblade St
Culver City, CA 90232-2513, USA

Popplewell, Anna (Actor)
c/o Staff Member *Sasha Leslie Management*
34 Pember Rd
London NW10 5LS, UNITED KINGDOM

Popson, Dave (Athlete, Basketball Player)
82 Fall St
Ashley, PA 18706-2709, USA

Poquette, Ben (Athlete, Basketball Player)
17917 N Shore Estates Rd
Spring Lake, MI 49456-9114, USA

Poquette, Tom (Athlete, Baseball Player)
3411 Ridgeway Dr
Eau Claire, WI 54701-8142, USA

Porcaro, Jeff
5247 Twin Oaks Rd
Hidden Hills, CA 91302-2417

Porcaro, Steve (Composer)
13596 Contour Dr
Sherman Oaks, CA 91423-4702, USA

Porcaro, Steve (Musician)
34 N Palm St
Ventura, CA 93001-2600, USA

Porch, Colleen (Actor)
c/o Vincent Cirrincione *Vincent Cirrincione Associates*
1516 N Fairfax Ave
Los Angeles, CA 90046-2608, USA

Porcher, Robert (Football Player)
c/o Staff Member *Detroit Lions*
222 Republic Dr
Allen Park, MI 48101-3650, USA

Porfilio, John C (Judge)
1919 Stout St
Denver, CO 80294, USA

Porizkova, Paulina (Actor, Model)
c/o Heather Reynolds *One Entertainment (NY)*
12 W 57th St PH 1
New York, NY 10019-3900, USA

Pork Tornado (Music Group)
c/o Staff Member *Paradigm (Monterey)*
404 W Franklin St
Monterey, CA 93940-2303, USA

Porras, German (Director)
c/o Staff Member *Gabriel Blanco Iglesias (Colombia)*
Dg 127A #20-36 Conjunto Plenitud, Apto 132
Bogota, Colombia

Porretta, Matthew (Actor)
10 Southwick Mews
London W2, UNITED KINGDOM (UK)

Port, Chris (Athlete, Football Player)
452 Walnut St
New Orleans, LA 70118-4932, USA

Port, Whitney (Reality TV Star)
c/o Nicole Perez *PMK/BNC Public Relations (PMK-LA)*
Pacific Design Center 8687 Melrose Ave, 7th Floor
West Hollywood, CA 90069, USA

Portale, Carl (Publisher)
1633 Broadway
New York, NY 10019-6708, USA

Porteous, Peter
Glencot Parkside Cheam
Surrey, ENGLAND SM3 8BS

Porter, Adina (Actor)
c/o Heidi Ifft *Bamboo Management*
17 Buccaneer St
Marina Del Rey, CA 90292-5103, USA

Porter, Andrew (Athlete, Baseball Player)
2502 W 117th St
Hawthorne, CA 90250-1999, USA

Porter, Billy (Musician)
c/o Staff Member *Gersh (LA)*
9465 Wilshire Blvd Ste 600
Beverly Hills, CA 90212-2612, USA

Porter, Bob (Athlete, Baseball Player)
771 Pueblo Ave
Napa, CA 94558-3546, USA

Porter, Chuck (Athlete, Baseball Player)
9321 Snyder Ln
Perry Hall, MD 21128-9414, USA

Porter, Colin (Athlete, Baseball Player)
1612 E Buck Hollow Ct
Tucson, AZ 85737-6011, USA

Porter, Dan (Athlete, Baseball Player)
40275 Colony Dr
Murrieta, CA 92562-5514, USA

Porter, Daryl (Athlete, Football Player)
9053 W Sunrise Blvd
Plantation, FL 33322-5218, USA

Porter, David H (Educator)
President's Office
Saratoga Springs, NY 12866, USA

Porter, Gail (Actor)
18 Broad Wick St 2nd Fl
London W1F 8HS, UNITED KINGDOM

Porter, Gary (Misc)
c/o Staff Member *Feld Entertainment, Inc.*
8607 Westwood Center Dr Ste 500
Vienna, VA 22182-7501, USA

Porter, Jack (Athlete, Football Player)
1027 County Road 1530
Rush Springs, OK 73082-2416, USA

Porter, Jay (Athlete, Baseball Player)
9677 Heather Cir W
Palm Beach Gardens, FL 33410-5467, USA

Porter, Jean (Actor)
200 Glenwood Cir Apt 717
Monterey, CA 93940-6750, USA

Porter, Jody (Musician)
6404 Wilshire Blvd Ste 505
Los Angeles, CA 90048-5507, USA

Porter, Joey (Athlete, Football Player)
c/o Staff Member *Pittsburgh Steelers*
3400 S Water St
Pittsburgh, PA 15203-2358, USA

Porter, Kalan (Musician, Reality TV Star)
c/o Joanne Setterington *BMG Canada Inc*
190 Liberty St #100
Toronto, ON M6K3L5, CANADA

Porter, Lee (Athlete, Golfer)
1604 Birch Ln
Greensboro, NC 27408-6500, USA

Porter, Marina Oswald
1850 Wfm Rd 550
Rockwall, TX 75087

Porter, Marquis (Bo) (Athlete, Baseball Player)
1226 N Teal Estates Cir
Fresno, TX 77545-9676, USA

Porter, Rick
943 Hartzell St
Pacific Palisades, CA 90272-3819

Porter, Ricky (Athlete, Football Player)
5800 Airline Dr
Metairie, LA 70003-3876, USA

Porter, Rufus (Athlete, Football Player)
2255 Eldridge Pkwy OFC
Houston, TX 77077-1694, USA

Porter, Scott (Actor)
c/o Staff Member *Brillstein Entertainment Partners*
9150 Wilshire Blvd Ste 350
Beverly Hills, CA 90212-3453, USA

Porter, Terry (Basketball Player, Coach)
Bradley Center 1001 N 4th St
Milwaukee, WI 53203, USA

Porter, Tracy (Athlete, Football Player)
c/o Roosevelt Barnes *Maximum Sports Management*
6435 W Jefferson Blvd # 197
Fort Wayne, IN 46804-6203, USA

Porterfield, Ellary Hume (Actor)
c/o Marv Dauer *Marv Dauer Management*
11661 San Vicente Blvd Ste 104
Los Angeles, CA 90049-5150, USA

Porterfield, Garry (Athlete, Football Player)
7621 S Harvard Pl
Tulsa, OK 74136-8000, USA

Porter-King, Mary Bea (Golfer)
6412 Kalama Rd
Kapaa, HI 96746-8633, USA

Portes, Richard D (Economist)
90-98 Goswell Road
London EC1V 7RR, UNITED KINGDOM (UK)

Portilla, Jose (Athlete, Football Player)
8831 E Quill St
Mesa, AZ 85207-9706, USA

Portillo, Alfonso (President)
Palacio Nacional
Guatemala City, GUATEMALA

Portis, Charles (Writer)
7417 Kingwood Rd
Little Rock, AR 72207-1734, USA

Portis, Clinton (Athlete, Football Player)
3510 NE 156th Ave
Gainesville, FL 32609-8895, USA

Portisch, Lajos (Misc)
Nephadsereg Utca 10
Budapest 1055, HUNGARY

Portishead (Music Group)
c/o Staff Member *High Road Touring*
751 Bridgeway Fl 2
Sausalito, CA 94965-2174, USA

Portland, Rene (Coach)
Greenberg Complex
University Park, PA 16802, USA

Portman, Natalie (Actor)
c/o Aleen Keshishian *Brillstein Entertainment Partners*
9150 Wilshire Blvd Ste 350
Beverly Hills, CA 90212-3453, USA

Portman, Rachel (Composer)
29/33 Berners St
London W1P 4AA, UNITED KINGDOM (UK)

Portman, Robert (Athlete, Basketball Player)
1412 Winter Sweet Pl
Hillsborough, NC 27278-7382, USA

Porto, James (Photographer)
601 W 26th St Rm 1321
New York, NY 10001-1134, USA

Portugal, Mark (Athlete, Baseball Player)
65 Serpentine Rd
Warren, RI 2885, USA

Portugal. The Man (Music Group, Musician)
c/o Matt Hickey *High Road Touring*
751 Bridgeway Fl 2
Sausalito, CA 94965-2174, USA

Portwich, Ramona (Athlete)
KC Limmer Stockhardweg 3
Hanover 30453, GERMANY

Poryes, Michael (Producer, Writer)
c/o Debbee Klein *Paradigm (LA)*
360 N Crescent Dr
Beverly Hills, CA 90210-4874, USA

Porzio, Mike (Athlete, Baseball Player)
PO Box 2242
Westport, CT 06880-0242, USA

Posada, Jorge (Athlete, Baseball Player)
9335 Balada St
Coral Gables, FL 33156-2333, USA

Posada, Leo (Athlete, Baseball Player)
8200 Grand Canal Dr
Miami, FL 33144-3538, USA

Poschl, Hanno
Singerstr. 13/15
Vienna, AUSTRIA 1010

Pose, Scott (Athlete, Baseball Player)
1216 Kintail Dr
Raleigh, NC 27613-8121, USA

Posehn, Brian (Comedian)
c/o Dave Rath *Generate Management*
1545 26th St Ste 200
Santa Monica, CA 90404-3554, USA

Posen, Zac (Designer)
c/o Susan Posen 115 Spring St
New York, NY 10012, USA

Poses, Frederic M (Business Person)
PO Box 4000
Morristown, NJ 07962-4000, USA

Posey, Bill (Congressman, Politician)
120 Cannon Hob
Washington, DC 20515-2106, USA

Posey, Parker (Actor)
c/o Frank Frattaroli *Dontanville/Frattaroli (D/F)*
270 Lafayette St Ste 402
New York, NY 10012-3327, USA

Posey, Tyler Garcia (Actor)
c/o Sarah Shyn *3 Arts Entertainment Inc*
9460 Wilshire Blvd Fl 7
Beverly Hills, CA 90212-2713, USA

Posner, Mike (Musician)
c/o Jamie Abzug *Sony/RCA Records*
550 Madison Ave Fl 6
New York, NY 10022-3211, USA

Posner, Richard A (Judge)
219 S Dearborn St
Chicago, IL 60604-1702, USA

Posner, Vladimir
1125 16th St NW
Washington, DC 20036-4801

Posokhin, Mikhail M (Architect)
Mosproyekt-2 2 Brestskaya Str 5
Moscow 123056, RUSSIA

Post, Avery D (Religious Leader)
80 Lyme Rd Apt 246
Hanover, NH 03755-1246, USA

Post, Markie (Actor)
c/o Staff Member *Insight*
1134 S Cloverdale Ave
Los Angeles, CA 90019-6737, USA

Post, Mike (Composer)
1007 W Olive Ave
Burbank, CA 91506-2211, USA

Post, Richard (Athlete, Football Player)
1812 Rickey Canyon Rd
Rice, WA 99167-9754, USA

Post, Sandra (Golfer)
100 International Golf Dr
Daytona Beach, FL 32124-1082, USA

Post, Ted (Director)
11030 Santa Monica Blvd
Los Angeles, CA 90025-7530, USA

Post, William (Business Person)
PO Box 52132
Phoenix, AZ 85072-2132, USA

Post III, Glen F (Business Person)
100 Century Park Dr
Monroe, LA 71203, USA

Postaer, Staffan (Writer)
c/o David Krintzman *Morris, Yorn, Barnes, Levine, Krintzman, Rubenstein and Kohner*
2000 Ave Of The Stars 3rd Tower Floor NORTH
Los Angeles, CA 90067, USA

Postell, Lavor (Athlete, Basketball Player)
2008 Murray Hill Ln
Albany, GA 31707-3268, USA

Postema, Pam (Baseball Player)
171 Garver Rd
Mansfield, OH 44903-9056, USA

Poster, Steve (Cinematographer)
PO Box 1156
Studio City, CA 91614-0156, USA

Postlewait, Kathy (Golfer)
111 Saint Johns Landing Dr
Winter Springs, FL 32708-6501, USA

Postman, Marc (Astronomer)
3303 Lightfoot Dr
Pikesville, MD 21208-4417, USA

Postrel, Virginia (Writer)
c/o Staff Member *Simon & Schuster*
1230 Avenue of the Americas Fl CONC1
New York, NY 10020-1586, USA

Pote, Lou (Athlete, Baseball Player)
10601 Orchard Ln
Chicago Ridge, IL 60415-1864, USA

Poteat, Hank (Athlete, Football Player)
19 Welsford Way
Mount Holly, NJ 08060-6728, USA

Potente, Franka (Actor)
c/o Ashley Franklin *Thruline Entertainment*
8383 Wilshire Blvd Ste 1050
Beverly Hills, CA 90211-2415, USA

Pothan, Pratap (Actor)
8-C Peninsula Apartments Tailers Road Kilpauk
Chennai, TN 600 010, INDIA

Poti, Tom (Athlete, Hockey Player)
103 Alvarado Ave
Worcester, MA 01604-1151, USA

Potrykus, Ingo (Scientist)
Plant Sci Dept
Zurich 8093, SWITZERLAND

Potter, Carol
c/o Staff Member *Pakula/King & Associates*
9229 W Sunset Blvd Ste 315
Los Angeles, CA 90069-3403, USA

Potter, Chris (Actor, Director)
c/o Gayle Abrams *Oscars Abrams Zimel & Associates, Inc. (OAZ)*
438 Queen St E
Toronto ON M5A 1T4, CANADA

Potter, Chris (Musician)
c/o Louise Holland *Vision Arts Management*
16 Clint Finger Rd
Saugerties, NY 12477-4360, USA

Potter, Cindy
1189 Ragley Hall Rd NE
Atlanta, GA 30319

Potter, Cynthia (Cindy) (Sportscaster, Swimmer)
1188 Ragley Hall Rd NE
Atlanta, GA 30319-2512, USA

Potter, Dan M (Religious Leader)
21 Forest Dr
Albany, NY 12205-2521, USA

Potter, Huntington (Scientist)
25 Shattuck St
Boston, MA 02115-6027, USA

Potter, John (Government Official)
475 Lenfant Plz SW
Washington, DC 20260-0001, USA

Potter, Mike (Stylist)
c/o Staff Member *Independent NY*
15 E 30th St Apt 401
New York, NY 10016-7031, USA

Potter, Mike (Athlete, Baseball Player)
21582 Archer Cir
Huntington Beach, CA 92646-8017, USA

Potter, Monica (Actor)
c/o Christian Donatelli *Schiff Company, The*
8440 Warner Dr Ste B1
Culver City, CA 90232-2461, USA

Potter, Nelson (Business Person)
3125 Myers St
Riverside, CA 92503-5527, USA

Potter, Philip A (Religious Leader)
3A York Castle Ave
Kingston 6, JAMAICA

Potter, Scott (Athlete, Baseball Player)
1637 Cordova Ave
Daytona Beach, FL 32117-1708, USA

Potter, Steve (Athlete, Football Player)
750 SE 7th Ave
Pompano Beach, FL 33060-9502, USA

Pottinger, Stanley (Writer)
c/o Staff Member *St Martins Press*
175 5th Ave
New York, NY 10010-7703, USA

Pottruck, David S (Financier)
101 Montgomery St
San Francisco, CA 94104-4151, USA

Potts, Annie (Actor, Producer)
16 S Oakland Ave
Pasadena, CA 91101-2043, USA

Potts, Cliff (Actor)
PO Box 131
Topanga, CA 90290-0131, USA

Potts, Erwin (Business Person)
2100
Sacramento, CA 95816, USA

Potts, MC
818 18th Ave S
Nashville, TN 37203-6663

Potts, Mike (Athlete, Baseball Player)
1140 Shonele Ln
Stem, NC 27581-9585, USA

Potts, Roosevelt (Athlete, Football Player)
113 Mounger Rd
Rayville, LA 71269-7407, USA

Potts, Sarah-Jane (Actor)
c/o Staff Member *Anonymous Content (AC-LA)*
3531 Hayden Ave
Culver City, CA 90232, USA

Potts, Tony (Television Host)
c/o Access Hollywood *KNBC (LA)*
3000 W Alameda Ave
Burbank, CA 91523-0002, USA

Potvin, Denis (Athlete, Hockey Player)
6820 NW 101st Ter
Parkland, FL 33076-2921, USA

Potvin, Felix (Athlete, Hockey Player)
1 Fleet St
Boston, MA 02136-2015, USA

Potvin, Jean R (Athlete, Hockey Player)
24 Longwood Dr
Huntington Station, NY 11746-4716, USA

Pough, Ernest (Athlete, Football Player)
2141 Buckman St
Jacksonville, FL 32206-4124, USA

Pouke (Stylist)
Prefers to be contacted via telephone or email
San Francisco, CA, USA

Poul, Alan (Producer)
c/o Andrew Cannava *United Talent Agency (UTA)*
9560 Wilshire Blvd Fl 5
Beverly Hills, CA 90212-2400, USA

Poulin, Dave (Athlete, Coach, Hockey Player)
16771 Orchard Ridge Ct
Granger, IN 46530-5916, USA

Poullain, Frankie (Musician)
c/o Sue Whitehouse *Whitehouse Management*
PO Box 43829
London NW6 3PJ, UNITED KINGDOM

Poulsen, Ken (Athlete, Baseball Player)
PO Box 1699
Oakhurst, CA 93644-1699, USA

Poulson, Josh (Actor)
c/o Staff Member *WmE2 (Endeavor-LA)*
9601 Wilshire Blvd Fl 3
Beverly Hills, CA 90210-5219, USA

Poulter, Ian (Athlete, Golfer)
9791 Covent Garden Dr
Orlando, FL 32827-7066, USA

Pouncey, Mike (Football Player)
c/o Joel Segal *Lagardere Unlimited - NY*
845 United Nations Plz
New York, NY 10017-3540, USA

Pound, Richard W D (Misc)
87 Arlington Ave
Westmount, QC H3Y 2W5, CANADA

Pound, Robert V (Physicist)
87 Pinehurst Rd
Belmont, MA 02478-1502, USA

Pound, The Dog
8942 Wilshire Blvd
Beverly Hills, CA 90211-1908

Pounder, CCH (Actor)
c/o Richard Hoffman *Warren Cowan & Associates PR*
8899 Beverly Blvd Ste 918
Los Angeles, CA 90048-2427, USA

Poundstone, Paula (Actor, Comedian)
c/o William (Bill) Sobel *Edelstein Laird & Sobel*
9255 W Sunset Blvd Ste 800
Los Angeles, CA 90069-3320

Poupard, Paul Cardinal (Religious Leader)
120, VATICAN CITY

Pousette, Lena (Actor)
8040 Ventura Canyon Ave
Panorama City, CA 91402-6313, USA

Poussaint, Alvin F (Educator)
295 Longwood Ave
Boston, MA 02115-5716, USA

Povich, Maury (Talk Show Host)
307 Atlantic St
Stamford, CT 06901-3506, USA

Powe, Karl (Athlete, Football Player)
PO Box 160961
Mobile, AL 36616-1961, USA

Powell, A J Philip (Architect)
16 Little Boltons
London SW10, UNITED KINGDOM (UK)

Powell, Alonzo (Athlete, Baseball Player)
220 N Patterson Blvd
Dayton, OH 45402-1279, USA

Powell, Andre (Athlete, Football Player)
N50W16962 Maple Crest Ln
Menomonee Falls, WI 53051-6689, USA

Powell, Art (Athlete, Football Player)
25221 Via Lido
Laguna Niguel, CA 92677-7307, USA

Powell, Arthur (Art) (Athlete, Football Player)
25221 Via Lido
Laguna Niguel, CA 92677-7307, USA

Powell, Brittany
145 S Fairfax Ave Ste 310
Los Angeles, CA 90036-2176

Powell, Brittney (Actor, Model)
c/o Mike Eisenstadt *Amsel, Eisenstadt & Frazier Talent Agency (AEF)*
5055 Wilshire Blvd Ste 860
Los Angeles, CA 90036-6108, USA

Powell, Cecil (Nobel Prize Laureate, Physicist)
220 Villa Verde Dr SE
Rio Rancho, NM 87124-1341, USA

Powell, Charley (Athlete, Football Player)
4119 Aralia Rd
Altadena, CA 91001-3701, USA

Powell, Cincy (Athlete, Basketball Player)
2541 Brookside Dr
Irving, TX 75063-3173, USA

Powell, Clifton (Actor)
c/o Christopher Black *Opus Entertainment*
5225 Wilshire Blvd Ste 905
Los Angeles, CA 90036-4353, USA

Powell, Colin L (General)
1317 Ballantrae Farm Dr
McLean, VA 22101-3028, USA

Powell, Dante (Athlete, Baseball Player)
6235 Riviera Cir
Long Beach, CA 90815-4756, USA

Powell, Dennis (Athlete, Baseball Player)
1743 Eastgate Ave
Upland, CA 91784-9211, USA

Powell, Dick (Athlete, Baseball Player)
2864 Hunt Valley Dr
Glenwood, MD 21738-9639, USA

Powell, Drew (Actor)
c/o Billy Miller *Billy Miller Management*
8322 Ridpath Dr
Los Angeles, CA 90046-7710, USA

Powell, Hosken (Athlete, Baseball Player)
1289 Tamara Dr
Pensacola, FL 32504-6642, USA

Powell, James R (Inventor)
25 Health Sciences Dr
Stony Brook, NY 11790-3350, USA

Powell, Jay (Athlete, Baseball Player)
155 Butler Dr
Ridgeland, MS 39157-9779, USA

Powell, Jeremy (Athlete, Baseball Player)
3022 W Summit Walk Ct
Anthem, AZ 85086-1012, USA

Powell, Jesse (Musician)
c/o Staff Member *Pyramid Entertainment Group*
377 Rector Pl Apt 21A
New York, NY 10280-1439, USA

Powell, Jesse (Athlete, Football Player)
3507 77th Dr
Lubbock, TX 79423-1213, USA

Powell, John (Composer)
15233 Ventura Blvd Ste 200
Sherman Oaks, CA 91403-2244, USA

Powell, John G (Athlete, Track Athlete)
10445 Mary Ave
Cupertino, CA 95014-1348, USA

Powell, John W (Boog) (Athlete, Baseball Player)
333 W Camden St
Baltimore, MD 21201-2496, USA

Powell, Leroy (Athlete, Baseball Player)
PO Box 4036
Muscle Shoals, AL 35662-4036, USA

Powell, Marvin (Athlete, Football Player)
5441 8th Ave
Los Angeles, CA 90043-2517, USA

Powell, Michael K (Government Official)
1919 M St NW
Washington, DC 20036-3521, USA

Powell, Michael (Mike) (Athlete, Track Athlete)
PO Box 8000-354
Alta Loma, CA 91701, USA

Powell, Mike
1751 Pinnacle Dr Ste 1500
McLean, VA 22102-3833

Powell, Monroe (Musician)
880 E Sahara Ave # 101
Las Vegas, NV 89104-3002, USA

Powell, Nicole (Basketball Player)
100 Hive Dr
Charlotte, NC 28217-4524, USA

Powell, Paul (Athlete, Baseball Player)
5254 E Enrose St
Mesa, AZ 85205-5484, USA

Powell, Randolph
2644 Highland Ave
Santa Monica, CA 90405-4402

Powell, Robert (Actor)
10 Pond Place
London W12 7RJ, UNITED KINGDOM (UK)

Powell, Ross (Athlete, Baseball Player)
605 Bristlewood Dr
McKinney, TX 75070-8361, USA

Powell, Sandy (Designer)
2-4 Noel St
London W1V 3RB, UNITED KINGDOM (UK)

Powell, Susan (Actor)
6333 Bryn Mawr Dr
Los Angeles, CA 90068-2808, USA

Powell, William (Baseball Player)
869 7th St W
Birmingham, AL 35204-3542, USA

Powell III, Earl A (Rusty) (Misc)
Constitution Ave & 4th St NW
Washington, DC 20565, USA

Powell Jr, D Duane (Cartoonist)
215 S McDowell St
Raleigh, NC 27601-1331, USA

Power, Cat (Actor, Composer, Musician)

Power, Dave (Actor)
c/o Steven Siebert *Lighthouse Entertainment*
9220 W Sunset Blvd Ste 200
West Hollywood, CA 90069-3501, USA

Power, J D (Dave) (Business Person)
2625 Townsgate Rd
Westlake Village, CA 91361-5751, USA

Power, Romina(Brindise)
I-72020 Cellino
San Marco, ITALY

Power, Ted (Athlete, Baseball Player)
544 Sutton Pl
Longboat Key, FL 34228-2301, USA

Power, Udana
1962 N Beachwood Dr Apt 202
Los Angeles, CA 90068-4073

Powers, Alexandra (Actor)
9560 Wilshire Blvd Ste 500
Beverly Hills, CA 90212-2401, USA

Powers, Clyde (Athlete, Football Player)
6020 NW Williams Ave
Lawton, OK 73505-1317, USA

Powers, James B (Religious Leader)
4605 N State Line Ave
Texarkana, TX 75503-2916, USA

Powers, Jeff (Athlete)
2124 Main St Ste 210
Huntington Beach, CA 92648-7450, USA

Powers, Ross (Skier)
PO Box 186
Londonderry, VT 05148-0186, USA

Powers, Stefanie (Actor)
c/o Alexandra McLean *McLean-Williams Management*
Gainsborough House 81 Oxford St
London W1D 2EU, UK

Powers, Stephanie (Actor)
c/o Staff Member *McLean-Williams Management*
Gainsborough House 81 Oxford St
London W1D 2EU, UK

Powers, Warren (Athlete, Football Player)
3909 Lausanne Rd
Randallstown, MD 21133-4511, USA

Powers, Warren A (Athlete, Football Player)
14742 Thornbird Manor Pkwy
Chesterfield, MO 63017-2497, USA

Powlus, Ron (Athlete, Football Player)
1012 Ruthann Dr
Berwick, PA 18603-2426, USA

Powter, Daniel (Musician)
c/o Staff Member *Paradigm (Monterey)*
404 W Franklin St
Monterey, CA 93940-2303, USA

Poynter, Dougie (Musician)
c/o Staff Member *Universal Music Group (UMG - LA)*
2220 Colorado Ave
Santa Monica, CA 90404-3506, USA

Poza, Jorge (Actor)
c/o Staff Member *Televisa*
Blvd Adolfo Lopez Mateos 232 Colonia San Angel INN
DF CP 01060, MEXICO

Pozderac, Phil (Athlete, Football Player)
2193 Carmel Dr
Carrollton, TX 75006-2814, USA

Pozdnykova, Tatyana (Athlete, Track Athlete)
4151 NW 43rd St
Gainesville, FL 32606-4582, USA

Pozsgay, Imre (Government Official)
Kossuth Lajos Ter 1
Budapest 1055, HUNGARY

Prabhu (Actor)
16 Chevaliea Sivaji Ganesan Salai T Nagar
Chennai, TN 600 017, INDIA

Prada, Aura Helena (Actor)
c/o Gabriel Blanco *Gabriel Blanco Iglesias (Mexico)*
Rio Balsas 35-32 Colonia Cuauhtemoc
DF 6500, Mexico

Prada, Miuccia (Designer, Fashion Designer)
Via Andrea Maffei 2
Milan 20154, ITALY

Prado, Edgar (Jockey)
c/o Staff Member *HarperCollins Publishers*
10 E 53rd St C/O Author Mail Floor 7
New York, NY 10022, USA

Praed, Michael
11500 W Olympic Blvd Ste 510
Los Angeles, CA 90064-1527

Prager, Dennis (Radio Personality)
18455 Burbank Blvd Ste 407
Tarzana, CA 91356-6651, USA

Prall, Willie (Athlete, Baseball Player)
3 Pheasant Run
Kinnelon, NJ 07405-3022, USA

Pran (Actor, Bollywood)
25 Union Park Khar
Bombay, MS 400 052, INDIA

Prance, Ghilean T (Misc)
Richmond
Surrey TW9 3AE, UNITED KINGDOM (UK)

Prange, Laurie
1519 Sargent Pl
Los Angeles, CA 90026

Prangley, Chris
c/o Jeff Morrone *Jeff Morrone Entertainment*
9350 Wilshire Blvd Ste 224
Beverly Hills, CA 90212-3204, USA

Pras (Musician)
83 Riverside Dr
New York, NY 10024-5713, USA

Prasanna (Actor)
C4 Cauvery Apartments 14 Brindavanam Street
Chennai, TN 600 004, INDIA

Prashanth (Actor)
No 40 North Usman Road Thiagaraja Nagar
Chennai, TN 600 017, INDIA

Pratchett, Terry (Writer)
P.O. Box 6 Gerrards Cross
Bucks SL9 8XA, UNITED KINGDOM (UK)

Prather, Joan (Actor)
31647 Sea Level Dr
Malibu, CA 90265-2633, USA

Pratiwi, Sudarmono (Astronaut)
Jalan Pegangsaan Timur
Jakarta 16, INDONESIA

Pratt, Andy (Athlete, Baseball Player)
1244 Gardenia Ln
Prescott, AZ 86305-6749, USA

Pratt, Awadagin (Musician)
3436 Springhill Rd
Lafayette, CA 94549-2535, USA

Pratt, Chris (Actor)
c/o Jimmy Miller *Mosaic Media Group*
9200 W Sunset Blvd Ste 10
Los Angeles, CA 90069-3608, USA

Pratt, Deborah (Actor, Producer, Writer)
c/o Staff Member *Hirsch Wallerstein Hayum Matlof & Fishman*
10100 Santa Monica Blvd Fl 23
Los Angeles, CA 90067-4003, USA

Pratt, Heidi Montag (Musician, Reality TV Star)
c/o Spencer Pratt *Innovator Management*
8899 Beverly Blvd Ste 622
Los Angeles, CA 90048-2428, USA

Pratt, Judson
8745 Oak Park Ave
Northridge, CA 91325-3211

Pratt, Keri Lynn (Actor)
c/o Steve Caserta *Sanders Armstrong Caserta*
2120 Colorado Ave Ste 120
Santa Monica, CA 90404-3561, USA

Pratt, Kyla (Actor)
c/o Judy Landis *Landis-Simon Productions Talent Management*
2410 Oakshore Dr
Westlake Village, CA 91361-3416, USA

Pratt, Kyle (Actor)
c/o Staff Member *Acme Talent & Literary (LA)*
1400 Atlantic Ave Ste 274
Long Beach, CA 90813-2013, USA

Pratt, Mary (Baseball Player)
1428 Quincy Shore Dr
Quincy, MA 02169-2333, USA

Pratt, Michael (Athlete, Basketball Player)
14603 Landon Ct
Louisville, KY 40245-4190, USA

Pratt, Robert (Athlete, Football Player)
320 Greenway Ln
Richmond, VA 23226-1632, USA

Pratt, Roger (Cinematographer)
10 Nightingale Lane Hornsey
London N8 7QU, UNITED KINGDOM (UK)

Pratt, Spencer (Reality TV Star)
c/o Adam Gelvan *WmE2 (Endeavor-LA)*
9601 Wilshire Blvd Fl 3
Beverly Hills, CA 90210-5219, USA

Pratt, Stephanie (Reality TV Star)
c/o Elizabeth Much *Much and House Public Relations*
8075 W 3rd St Ste 500
Los Angeles, CA 90048-4325, USA

Pratt, Susan C (Actor)
7 Old Pound Rd
Pound Ridge, NY 10576-1737, USA

Pratt, Todd (Athlete, Baseball Player)
5950 Dorset Bridge Rd
Douglasville, GA 30135-6014, USA

Pratt, Vicky
1930 Yonge Street Toronto # 1155
CANADA, CA Ont. M4A 1

Pratt, Victoria (Actor)
c/o Gordon Gilbertson *Gilbertson Management*
1334 3rd Street Promenade Ste 201
Santa Monica, CA 90401-1320, USA

Prchlik, John (Athlete, Football Player)
128 Brokenwood Ln
Crossville, TN 38558-7713, USA

Preas, George (Athlete, Football Player)
2220 Carolina Ave SW Apt 302
Roanoke, VA 24014-1798, USA

Preate Jr, Ernest D (Attorney, Attorney General, General, Government Official)
4th & Walnut
Harrisburg, PA 17120, USA

Prebola, Gene (Athlete, Football Player)
24 Hayward Rd
Sparta, NJ 07871-3119, USA

Precourt, Charles J (Astronaut)
1960 Shoshone Dr
Ogden, UT 84403-4655, USA

Predock, Antoine (Architect)
300 12th St
Northwest Albuquerque, NM 87102, USA

Preece, Steve (Athlete, Football Player)
2723 NW Monte Vista Ter
Portland, OR 97210-3338, USA

Preer Jr, John R (Biologist)
1414 E Maxwell Ln
Bloomington, IN 47401-5143, USA

Pregenzer, John (Athlete, Baseball Player)
6314 104th St E
Puyallup, WA 98373-4127, USA

Pregerson, Harry (Judge)
21800 Oxnard St
Woodland Hills, CA 91367-3633, USA

Pregulman, Merv (Athlete, Football Player)
4 Cherokee Blvd Apt 517
Chattanooga, TN 37405-4904, USA

Prejean, Carrie (Beauty Pageant Winner)
PO Box 691700
Los Angeles, CA 90069-9700, USA

Prejean, Patrick
B5 135 Poissonniere
Paris, FRANCE F-75002

Preki (Soccer Player)
2 Arrowhead Dr
Kansas City, MO 64129-1650, USA

Premice, Josephine
755 W End Ave
New York, NY 10025-6238

Premji, Ajij (Business Person)
Doddakannelli Sarjapur Rd
Bangalore 560 035, India

Prendergast, John (Writer)
c/o Joe Veltre *Gersh (NY)*
41 Madison Ave
New York, NY 10010-2202, USA

Prentice, Dean S (Athlete, Hockey Player)
13-220 Salisbury Ave
Cambridge, ON N1S 1K5, Canada

Prentiss, Lee
122 Middlesex St
London, ENGLAND El 7HY

Prentiss, Paula (Actor, Comedian)
719 Foothill Rd
Beverly Hills, CA 90210-3437, USA

Prepon, Laura (Actor)
c/o Paul M. Brown *New Wave Entertainment (LA)*
2660 W Olive Ave
Burbank, CA 91505-4525, USA

Presar, Barbara (Stylist)
622 E 20th St Apt 7D
New York, NY 10009-1414, USA

Prescott, John L (Government Official)
365 Saltshouse Road Sutton-on-Hull
North Humderside, UNITED KINGDOM (UK)

Prescott, Jon (Actor)
c/o Miles Levy *James/Levy/Jacobson Management Inc*
3500 W Olive Ave Ste 1470
Burbank, CA 91505-5514, USA

Presko, Joe (Athlete, Baseball Player)
1612 NE 77th Ter
Kansas City, MO 64118-1939, USA

Presle, Micheline (Actor)
6 Rue Antoine Dubois
Paris 75006, FRANCE

Presley, Brian (Actor)
c/o Nikki Joel *International Creative Management (ICM-LA)*
10250 Constellation Blvd Fl 7
Los Angeles, CA 90067-6207, USA

Presley, Jim (Athlete, Baseball Player)
2449 Bonanza Dr
Cantonment, FL 32533-7402, USA

Presley, Lisa-Marie (Musician)
c/o Stephen (Scooter) Weintraub *W Management*
75 E 4th St Frnt 1
New York, NY 10003-0831, USA

Presley, Priscilla (Actor, Producer, Writer)
c/o Susan Haber *Haber Entertainment*
434 S Canon Dr Apt 204
Beverly Hills, CA 90212-4501, USA

Presley, Reg (Musician)
PO Box 4 Dartmouth
Devon TQ6 0YD, UNITED KINGDOM (UK)

Presley, Richard (Musician)
c/o Staff Member *WmE2 (WMA-LA)*
1 William Morris Pl
Beverly Hills, CA 90212-4261, USA

Press, Bill (Correspondent)
1050 Techwood Dr NW
Atlanta, GA 30318-5604, USA

Press, Frank (Physicist)
2500 Virginia Ave NW # 616
Washington, DC 20037-1900, USA

Pressel, Morgan (Golfer)
9266 Legare St
Boca Raton, FL 33434-5905, USA

Pressey, Paul (Athlete, Basketball Player, Coach)
782 Haddonstone Cir
Lake Mary, FL 32746-5603, USA

Pressler, H Paul (Attorney, Attorney General, General, Judge)
3711 San Felipe St Unit 9J
Houston, TX 77027-4048, USA

Pressler, Larry L (Senator)
2812 Davis Ave
Alexandria, VA 22302-2507, USA

Pressler, Menahem M J (Musician)
115 College St
Burlington, VT 05401-8424, USA

Pressley, Dominic (Athlete, Basketball Player)
1406 Whooping Ct
Upper Marlboro, MD 20774-7086, USA

Pressley, Harold (Athlete, Basketball Player)
6470 Matheny Way
Citrus Heights, CA 95621-4839, USA

Pressley, Paul (Athlete, Basketball Player)
600 County Road 4694
Timpson, TX 75975, USA

Pressley, Robert (Race Car Driver)
6 Forestdale Dr
Asheville, NC 28803-1811, USA

Pressly, Jaime (Actor, Model)
c/o Lena Roklin *Luber Roklin Management*
8530 Wilshire Blvd Ste 550
Beverly Hills, CA 90211-3133, USA

Pressman, Edward R (Producer)
130 El Camino Dr
Beverly Hills, CA 90212-2700, USA

Pressman, Lawrence (Actor)
15033 Encanto Dr
Sherman Oaks, CA 91403-4409, USA

Pressman, Michael (Actor, Director, Producer)
c/o Judy Hofflund *Hofflund/Polone*
9465 Wilshire Blvd Ste 420
Beverly Hills, CA 90212-2603, USA

Pressman, Sally (Actor)
c/o Staff Member *Abrams Artists Agency (LA)*
9200 W Sunset Blvd PH 11
Los Angeles, CA 90069-3601, USA

Presswood, Henry (Baseball Player)
1445 W 71st Pl
Chicago, IL 60636-3961, USA

Presta, Peter (DJ)
c/o Len Evans *Project Publicity*
312 W 53rd St Ste 202
New York, NY 10019-5743, USA

Prestel, Jim (Athlete, Football Player)
6150 N Hurricane Ct
Parker, CO 80134-5704, USA

Preston, Carrie (Actor)
c/o Steve Caserta *Sanders Armstrong Caserta*
2120 Colorado Ave Ste 120
Santa Monica, CA 90404-3561, USA

Preston, Cynthia (Actor)
c/o Charles Silver *Silver Massetti & Szatmary (SMS) Talent Inc*
8730 W Sunset Blvd Ste 440
Los Angeles, CA 90069-2277, USA

Preston, Duncan
46 Hilltop House Hornsey Ln
London, ENGLAND N6 5NW

Preston, J A (Actor)
10100 Santa Monica Blvd Ste 2500
Los Angeles, CA 90067-4116, USA

Preston, Johhny
PO Box 1875
Gretna, LA 70054-1875

Preston, Kelly (Actor)
c/o Michelle Pesce *WKT Public Relations (WKT-LA)*
9350 Wilshire Blvd Ste 450
Beverly Hills, CA 90212-3230, USA

Preston, Ray (Athlete, Football Player)
304 Great Lakes Cir W Apt D
Avon, IN 46123-3792, USA

Preston, Simon J (Musician)
Little Hardwick Langton Green Tunbridge Wells
Kent TN3 OEY, UNITED KINGDOM (UK)

Preston-Campbell, Brian (Stylist)
214 N Henry St # 2
Brooklyn, NY 11222-3608, USA

Prestridge, Luke (Athlete, Football Player)
17802 Island Spring Ln
Tomball, TX 77377-8155, USA

Pretre, Georges (Conductor)
Chateau de Vaudricourt A Naves
Par Casters 81100, FRANCE

Pretti, Kim Healy (Stylist)
c/o Celebrity Stylist *Zenobia Agency Inc*
PO Box 909
Groveland, CA 95321-0909, USA

Pretty Ricky (Music Group)
c/o Staff Member *Atlantic Records (NY)*
1290 Avenue of the Americas Fl CONC4
New York, NY 10104-0184

Prettyman, Tristan (Musician)
c/o Staff Member *Paradigm (Monterey)*
404 W Franklin St
Monterey, CA 93940-2303, USA

Preus, David W (Religious Leader)
2481 Como Ave
Saint Paul, MN 55108-1445, USA

Previn, Dory (Musician, Songwriter, Writer)
2533 Zorada Dr
Los Angeles, CA 90046-1747, USA

previs, Steve (Athlete, Basketball Player)
3106 Dennison Rd
Bethel Park, PA 15102-1208, USA

Previte, Richard (Business Person)
PO Box 3453
Sunnyvale, CA 94088-3453, USA

Prevost, Josette (Actor)
6767 Forest Lawn Dr Ste 101
Los Angeles, CA 90068-1050, USA

Prew, William A (Business Person, Swimmer)
30600 Telegraph Rd Ste 3110
Bingham Farms, MI 48025-4589, USA

Pribilinec, Jozef (Athlete, Track Athlete)
Moyzesova 75
Lutila 966 22, SLOVAKIA

Price, AJ (Athlete, Basketball Player)
c/o Jeff Schwartz *Excel Sports Management*
9665 Wilshire Blvd Ste 500
Beverly Hills, CA 90212-2312, USA

Price, Alan (Musician, Songwriter, Writer)
PO Box 770850
Orlando, FL 32877-0850, USA

Price, Antony (Designer, Fashion Designer)
468 Kings Road
London SW1, UNITED KINGDOM (UK)

Price, Brent (Athlete, Basketball Player)
1111 W Wynona Ave
Enid, OK 73703-6909, USA

Price, Charles W (Athlete, Football Player)
3712 43rd St
Lubbock, TX 79413-3036, USA

Price, Elex (Athlete, Football Player)
2833 Newport St
Jackson, MS 39213-5335, USA

Price, Ferne (Baseball Player)
720 E Mary Ln
Terre Haute, IN 47802-4617, USA

Price, Frank (Misc)
2425 Olympic Blvd
Santa Monica, CA 90404-4030, USA

Price, Frederick K C (Religious Leader)
7901 S Vermont Ave
Los Angeles, CA 90044-3531, USA

Price, George C (Prime Minister)
Belmopan, BELIZE

Price, Hillary (Cartoonist)
221 Pine St # 4G3
Florence, MA 01062-1267, USA

Price, James G (Doctor)
12205 Mohawk Rd
Leawood, KS 66209-2137, USA

Price, Jim (Athlete, Baseball Player)
57152 Willow Way
Washington, MI 48094-4205, USA

Price, Joe (Athlete, Baseball Player)
1874 Arabian Ct
Hebron, KY 41048-8436, USA

Price, Katie (Jordan) (Actor, Model)
P.O. Box 5036 Argus House, Crowhurst Road
Brighton, East Sussex BN1 8AR, UK

Price, Kelly (Musician)
18653 Ventura Blvd # 340
Tarzana, CA 91356-4103, USA

Price, Larry C (Journalist)
930 S Garfield St
Denver, CO 80209-5006, USA

Price, Lindsay (Actor)
c/o Leslie Sloane *Baker Winokur Ryder Public Relations BWR (BWR-NY)*
292 Madison Ave Fl 12
New York, NY 10017-6415, USA

Price, Lloyd (Musician, Songwriter, Writer)
95 Horseshoe Hill Rd
Pound Ridge, NY 10576-1636, USA

Price, Lonny (Actor)
c/o Joy Gorman *Anonymous Content (AC-LA)*
3531 Hayden Ave
Culver City, CA 90232, USA

Price, M V Leontyne (Opera Singer)
9 Vandam St
New York, NY 10013-1215, USA

Price, Marc (Actor)
8444 Magnolia Dr
Los Angeles, CA 90046-1932, USA

Price, Margaret B (Opera Singer)
Sankt Eriksgatan 100
Stockholm 113 31, SWEDEN

Price, Marvin (Baseball Player)
12136 S Princeton Ave
Chicago, IL 60628-6516, USA

Price, Megyn (Actor)
c/o Leslie Allan-Rice *Leslie Allan-Rice Management*
7524 Mulholland Dr
Los Angeles, CA 90046-1239, USA

Price, Mike (Coach, Football Coach)
Athletic
El Paso, TX 79968-0001, USA

Price, MIke (Athlete, Basketball Player)
4415 Thornleigh Dr
Indianapolis, IN 46226-2165, USA

Price, Mitchell (Athlete, Football Player)
3935 Thousand Oaks Dr Apt 1506
San Antonio, TX 78217-1877, USA

Price, Molly (Actor)
c/o Stephen Hirsch *Gersh (NY)*
41 Madison Ave
New York, NY 10010-2202, USA

Price, Nick (Golfer)
900 S US Highway # Ste 1 PMB 5
Jupiter, FL 33477, USA

Price, Noel (Athlete, Hockey Player)
21 Windeyer Cres
Kanata, ON K2K 2P6, Canada

Price, Paul B (Physicist)
1056 Overlook Rd
Berkeley, CA 94708-1712, USA

Price, Peerless (Athlete, Football Player)
5658 Legends Club Cir
Braselton, GA 30517-6029, USA

Price, Phoebe (Actor)
c/o Staff Member *Bernstein Entertainment*
3869 Tilden Ave Apt 15
Culver City, CA 90232-3965, USA

Price, Randy (Stylist)
c/o Staff Member *Independent Artists*
448 E Riverdale Ave
Orange, CA 92865-1302, USA

Price, Ray (Musician)
c/o Staff Member *Texas Sounds Entertainment*
633 Davis Rd
League City, TX 77573-2847, USA

Price, Reynolds (Writer)
PO Box 99014
Durham, NC 27708-9014, USA

Price, S H (Publisher)
251 W 57th St
New York, NY 10019-1802, USA

Price, Steven (Stylist)
c/o Staff Member *Koko Represents*
166 Geary St Ste 1007
San Francisco, CA 94108-5623, USA

Price, Terry (Athlete, Football Player)
59 Fieldstone Dr
South Glastonbury, CT 06073-3717, USA

Price, Tom (Congressman, Politician)
403 Cannon Hob
Washington, DC 20515-1807, USA

Price, Vanessa (Stylist)
c/o Staff Member *Rex Agency, The*
6311 Romaine St
Los Angeles, CA 90038-2617, USA

Price, W Mark (Basketball Player)
Athletic
Atlanta, GA 30332-0001, USA

Price, Willard D
PO Box 2783
Laguna Hills, CA 92654-2783, USA

Price II, Charles H (Business Person, Diplomat)
1 W Armour Blvd Ste 300
Kansas City, MO 64111-2087, USA

Price-Bunch, Ashil (Golfer)
1629 Country Club Dr
Morristown, TN 37814-3316, USA

Prichard, Peter S (Editor)
1000 Wilson Blvd
Arlington, VA 22209-2230, USA

Priddy, Bob (Athlete, Basketball Player)
PO Box 3169
Boys Ranch, TX 79010-3169, USA

Priddy, Bob (Athlete, Baseball Player)
136 Shingiss St Apt 214
Mc Kees Rocks, PA 15136-5500, USA

Priddy, Nancy (Actor)
11223 Sunshine Ter
Studio City, CA 91604-3123, USA

Pride, Charley (Baseball Player)
3198 Royal Ln Ste 204
Dallas, TX 75229-6921, USA

Pride, Charlie (Musician)
PO Box 670507
Dallas, TX 75367-0507, USA

Pride, Curtis (Athlete, Baseball Player)
1288 Lake Breeze Dr
Wellington, FL 33414-7953, USA

Pride, Dicky (Golfer)
PO Box 844
Windermere, FL 34786-0844, USA

Pride, Lynn (Basketball Player)
Target Center 600 1st Ave N
Minneapolis, MN 55403, USA

Pride, Mack (Baseball Player)
3305 Pierce St
Wheat Ridge, CO 80033-6333, USA

Pridemore, Tom (Athlete, Football Player)
3935 Poplar Springs Rd
Gainesville, GA 30507-8618, USA

Pridy, Todd (Athlete, Baseball Player)
3430 Scenic Dr
Napa, CA 94558-4239, USA

Priesand, Sally J (Religious Leader)
32 Fernwood Dr
Asbury Park, NJ 07712-8713, USA

Priest, Eddie (Athlete, Baseball Player)
445 Ballard Rd
Altoona, AL 35952-6227, USA

Priest, Judas (Music Group, Musician)
c/o Troy Blakely *Agency for the Performing Arts (APA-LA)*
405 S Beverly Dr Ste 500
Beverly Hills, CA 90212-4425, USA

Priest, Maxi (Musician)
150 5th Ave
New York, NY 10011-4311, USA

Priest, Steve (Musician)
296 Nether St Finchley
London N3 1RJ, UNITED KINGDOM (UK)

Priestley, Jason (Actor)
c/o Annett Wolf *WKT Public Relations (WKT-LA)*
9350 Wilshire Blvd Ste 450
Beverly Hills, CA 90212-3230, USA

Priestley, Jr, Thomas (Director, Photographer)
c/o Jay Gilbert *Broder Webb Chervin Silbermann Agency, The (BWCS)*
10250 Constellation Blvd
Los Angeles, CA 90067-6200, USA

Prieto, Ariel (Athlete, Baseball Player)
15325 SW 53rd St
Miami, FL 33185-4265, USA

Prieto, Chris (Athlete, Baseball Player)
3450 Fisher Pl
Carmel, CA 93923-9020, USA

Prieto, Rodrigo (Cinematographer)
PO Box 3338
Beverly Hills, CA 90212-0338, USA

Primack, Joel R (Astronomer)
Astronomy Dept
Santa Cruz, CA 95064, USA

Primatesta, Raul Francisco Cardinal (Religious Leader)
Arzobispado Ave H Irigoyen 98
Cordoba 5000, ARGENTINA

Primeau, Keith (Athlete, Hockey Player)
2 Danforth Dr
Voorhees, NJ 08043-3947, USA

Primeaux, Brian (Stylist)
32 Thompson St Apt 6
New York, NY 10013-1634, USA

Primrose, Neil (Musician)
21 Heathmans Road
London SW6 4TJ, UNITED KINGDOM (UK)

Primus, Barry
2735 Creston Dr
Los Angeles, CA 90068-2209

Prince, Angel (Dancer)
PO Box 1991
Honokaa, HI 96727-1832, USA

Prince, Charles (Chuck) (Financier)
399 Park Ave
New York, NY 10022-4614, USA

Prince, Clayton
3500 W Olive Ave Ste 1400
Burbank, CA 91505-5512

Prince, Don (Athlete, Baseball Player)
11143 James B White Hwy S
Whiteville, NC 28472-6419, USA

Prince, Faith (Actor, Musician)
1505 10th St
Santa Monica, CA 90401-2805, USA

Prince, Harold S (Hal) (Director, Producer)
10 Rockefeller Plz Ste 1104
New York, NY 10020-1903, USA

Prince, Jonathan
1801 San Ysidro Dr
Beverly Hills, CA 90210-1518

Prince, Karim
3313 1/2 Barham Blvd
Los Angeles, CA 90068-1450

Prince, Larry L (Business Person)
2999 Circle 75 Pkwy SE
Atlanta, GA 30339-3050, USA

Prince, Tayshaun (Athlete, Basketball Player)
5550 Leeds Ct
Oakland Township, MI 48306-4911, USA

Prince, Tom (Athlete, Baseball Player)
6816 10th Ave NW
Bradenton, FL 34209-1209, USA

Prince Harry (Prince)
Highgrove House
Gloucestershire, UNITED KINGDOM

Prince Jr, Gregory S (Educator)
President's Office
Amherst, MA 1002, USA

Prince-Bythewood, Gina (Director, Producer, Writer)
c/o Ava DuVernay *The DuVernay Agency*
Prefers to be contact via telephone or email
Los Angeles, CA 90069, USA

Princess Ann Claire (Actor, Musician, Royalty)
c/o Staff Member *Love Is In The Heir*
E! Entertainment Television 5750 Wilshire Blvd
Los Angeles, CA 90036, USA

Princess Beatrice (Royalty)
Buckingham Palace
London SW1A 1AA, United Kingdom

Princess Eugenie (Royalty)
Buckingham Palace
London SW1A 1AA, United Kingdom

Principal, Victoria (Actor, Business Person, Producer)
c/o Staff Member *Victoria Principal Productions*
23852 Pacific Coast Hwy
Malibu, CA 90265-4876, USA

Principe, Dom (Athlete, Football Player)
300 N Highway A1A Apt E303
Jupiter, FL 33477-4542, USA

Principi, Anthony (Secretary)
810 Vermont Ave NW
Washington, DC 20420-0001, USA

Prine, Andrew (Actor)
3364 Longridge Ave
Sherman Oaks, CA 91423, USA

Prine, John (Musician, Songwriter, Writer)
33 Music Sq W Ste 102B
Nashville, TN 37203-6607, USA

Pringle, Joan (Actor)
3500 W Olive Ave Ste 1400
Burbank, CA 91505-5512, USA

Pringley, Mike (Athlete, Football Player)
709 Gilchrist Ave
Linden, NJ 07036-1210, USA

Prinosil, David (Athlete)
Am Schanzl 3
Amberg 92224, GERMANY

Prinz, Bret (Athlete, Baseball Player)
15471 N 88th Ave
Peoria, AZ 85382-3789, USA

Prinze Jr, Freddie (Actor)
c/o Aleen Keshishian *Brillstein Entertainment Partners*
9150 Wilshire Blvd Ste 350
Beverly Hills, CA 90212-3453, USA

Prinzi, Frank (Cinematographer)
571 W 113th St # 24
New York, NY 10025, USA

Prioleau, Pierson (Athlete, Football Player)
2221 Santee River Rd
Alvin, SC 29479-3844, USA

Prior, Anthony (Athlete, Football Player)
3529 Holding St
Riverside, CA 92501-2235, USA

Prior, Maddy (Musician)
PO Box 651 Park Road
Oxford OX2 9RB, UNITED KINGDOM (UK)

Prior, Mark (Athlete, Baseball Player)
3256 Casa Bonita Dr
Bonita, CA 91902-1721, USA

Prior of Brampton, James M L (Government Official)
36 Morpeth Mansions
London SW1, UNITED KINGDOM (UK)

Priory, Richard B (Business Person)
526 S Church St
Charlotte, NC 28202-1802, USA

Pritchard, Barry (Musician)
PO Box 770850
Orlando, FL 32877-0850, USA

Pritchard, Buddy (Athlete, Baseball Player)
507 E Sunny Hills Rd
Fullerton, CA 92835-1357, USA

Pritchard, David E (Physicist)
Physics Dept
Cambridge, MA 2139, USA

Pritchard, Michael (Athlete, Football Player)
23400 E Roxbury Dr Unit 303
Aurora, CO 80016-1397, USA

Pritchard, Ron (Athlete, Football Player)
495 E Coconino Dr
Chandler, AZ 85249-5302, USA

Pritchett, Chris (Athlete, Baseball Player)
959 Fir Tree Pl
Carlsbad, CA 92011-3926, USA

Pritchett, James (Actor)
53 W 74th St
New York, NY 10023-2484, USA

Pritchett, Kelvin (Athlete, Football Player)
4765 Guilford Forest Dr SW
Atlanta, GA 30331-7395, USA

Pritchett, Matt (Cartoonist)
181 Marsh Wall
London E14 9SR, UNITED KINGDOM (UK)

Pritchett, Sir Victor
12 Regent's Park Ter
London, ENGLAND NW1

Pritchett, Stanley (Athlete, Football Player)
523 Monteagle Trce
Stone Mountain, GA 30087-4937, USA

Pritchett, Wes (Athlete, Football Player)
2599 Winnies Way
Johns Island, SC 29455-8037, USA

Pritha, Saratha (Actor, Bollywood)
2 1st Main Road Shenoy Nagar W
Chennai, TN 600030, INDIA

Prithiveeraj (Bablu) (Actor)
146 Anna Nagar W
Chennai, TN 600 040, INDIA

Pritikin, Greg (Director)
c/o Staff Member *Anonymous Content (AC-LA)*
3531 Hayden Ave
Culver City, CA 90232, USA

Pritkin, Roland I (Doctor)
4128 Grove Ave
Stickney, IL 60402-4435, USA

Pritko, Steve (Athlete, Football Player)
328 Chanticlair Dr
Apex, NC 27502-9623, USA

Pritzker, Robert A (Business Person)
1150 17th St NW
Washington, DC 20036-4603, USA

Prix, Wolf (Architect)
3526 Beethoven St
Los Angeles, CA 90066-3039, USA

Probst, Jeff (Game Show Host, Reality TV Star, Television Host)
c/o Sean Perry *WmE2 (Endeavor-LA)*
9601 Wilshire Blvd Fl 3
Beverly Hills, CA 90210-5219, USA

Prochazka, Martin (Athlete, Hockey Player)
40 Bay St
Toronto, ON M5J 2K2, Canada

Prochnow, Jurgen (Actor)
c/o Staff Member *International Creative Management (ICM-LA)*
10250 Constellation Blvd Fl 7
Los Angeles, CA 90067-6207, USA

Prock, Markus (Athlete)
6142 Mieders
AUSTRIA

Proclaimers, The (Music Group)
c/o Staff Member *A.S.S. Concerts & Promotion GMBH*
Rahlstedter Str. 92 A
Hamburg 22149, Germany

Procol Harum
195 Sandycombe Rd
Kew, ENGLAND TW9 2EW

Procter, Emily (Actor)
c/o Brad Slater *WmE2 (Endeavor-LA)*
9601 Wilshire Blvd Fl 3
Beverly Hills, CA 90210-5219, USA

Proctor, Charles N (Skier)
100 Lockewood Ln Apt 238
Scotts Valley, CA 95066-3959, USA

Proctor, David (Baseball Player)
5517 SW 23rd St
Topeka, KS 66614-1727, USA

Proctor, Dewey (Athlete, Football Player)
6004 Robert Ruark Dr SE
Southport, NC 28461-2644, USA

Proctor, James (Jim) (Athlete, Baseball Player)
2 Westmoreland Pl
Saint Louis, MO 63108-1228, USA

Proctor, Scott (Athlete, Baseball Player)
428 NE Bayberry Ln
Jensen Beach, FL 34957-4612, USA

Prodi, Romano (Prime Minister)
200 Rue de la Loi
Brussels, BELGIUM

Prodigy (Music Group)
c/o Staff Member *Maverick Recording Co (LA)*
3300 Warner Blvd
Burbank, CA 91505-4632, USA

Proehl, Ricky (Athlete, Football Player)
3504 Bromley Wood Ln
Greensboro, NC 27410-2181, USA

Professor, Griff (Actor, Musician)
c/o Staff Member *WmE2 (WMA-LA)*
1 William Morris Pl
Beverly Hills, CA 90212-4261, USA

Profit, Gene (Athlete, Football Player)
6116 Nightshade Ct
Rockville, MD 20852-3409, USA

Project 86 (Music Group)
c/o Staff Member *Paradigm (Monterey)*
404 W Franklin St
Monterey, CA 93940-2303, USA

Prokhorov, Mikhail (Business Person)
PO Box 55
Morrisonville, NY 12962-0055, Russia

Prokop, Matt (Actor)
c/o Margot Menzel *Evolution Entertainment (LA)*
9111 Wilshire Blvd
Beverly Hills, CA 90210-5508, USA

Prokopec, Luke (Athlete, Baseball Player)
178 18th St
Renmark, SA 5341, Australia

Proly, Mike (Athlete, Baseball Player)
112 Country Mist Dr
Greer, SC 29651-1919, USA

Promisel-Ryan, Shelley (Stylist)
230 Sunridge St
Playa Del Rey, CA 90293-7750, USA

Pronger, Chris (Athlete, Hockey Player)
345 S Hinchman Ave
Haddonfield, NJ 08033-3716, USA

Pronites, Diane (Stylist)
1767 N 1220 East Rd
Gilman, IL 60938-6106, USA

Pronovost, Jean (Athlete, Hockey Player)
1100 De La Gauchetiere St W Unit 2657
Montreal, QC H3B 2S2, Canada

Pronovost, R Marcel (Athlete, Hockey Player)
4620 Dali Ct
Windsor, ON N9G 2MB, Canada

Proops, Greg (Actor)
c/o Lee Kernis *Brillstein Entertainment Partners*
9150 Wilshire Blvd Ste 350
Beverly Hills, CA 90212-3453, USA

Prophet, Billy (Musician)
PO Box 12
Far Hills, NJ 07931-0012, USA

Prophet, Elizabeth Clare (Religious Leader)
Box A
Livingston, MT 59047, USA

Prophet, Ronnie
1227 Saxon Dr
Nashville, TN 37215-4426

Propp, Brian (Athlete, Hockey Player)
2320 Riverton Rd
Cinnaminson, NJ 08077-3719, USA

Props, Rene (Actor)
9200 W Sunset Blvd Ste 900
Los Angeles, CA 90069-3604, USA

Prospal, Vaclav (Athlete, Hockey Player)
2000 E Gene Autry Way
Anaheim, CA 92806-6143, USA

Prospal, Vactav (Athlete, Hockey Player)
401 Channelside Dr
Tampa, FL 33602-5400, USA

Prosper, Sandra (Actor)
c/o Staff Member *Mitchell K Stubbs & Assoc (MKS)*
8675 Washington Blvd Ste 203
Culver City, CA 90232-7486, USA

Prosser, C Ladd (Misc)
101 W Windsor Rd # 2106
Urbana, IL 61802-6663, USA

Prosser, James (Musician)
209 10th Ave South Cummins Sta # 347
Nashville, TN 37203, USA

Prosser, Robert (Religious Leader)
1978 Union Ave
Memphis, TN 38104-4134, USA

Prost, Alain M P (Race Car Driver)
7 Ave Eugene Freyssinet
Guyancourt 78286, FRANCE

Prost, Sharon (Judge)
717 Madison Pl NW
Washington, DC 20439-0001, USA

Protopopov, Oleg (Figure Skater)
Chalet Hubel
Grindelwald 3818, SWITZERLAND

Proulx, Brooklynn (Actor)
c/o Christopher Rockwell *Global Creative*
1051 Cole Ave # B
Los Angeles, CA 90038-2601, USA

Proulx, E Annie (Writer)
c/o Staff Member *The Sayle Literary Agency*
1 Petersfield
Cambridge CB1 1BB, UK

Prout, Bob (Athlete, Football Player)
23102 N Shepard Rd
Chillicothe, IL 61523-9035, USA

Prout, Brian (Musician)
2908 Poston Ave
Nashville, TN 37203-1312, USA

Proval, David (Actor)
c/o Andrew Howard *Incognito Management*
9440 Santa Monica Blvd Ste 302
Beverly Hills, CA 90210-4614, USA

Provence, Andrew (Athlete, Football Player)
224 Providence Rd
Fayetteville, GA 30215-2844, USA

Provenza, Paul (Actor)
c/o Peter Golden *Golden Entertainment West*
10921 Wilshire Blvd
Los Angeles, CA 90024-3906, United States

Provenzano, Chris (Director, Writer)
c/o David Ginsberg *Insight*
1134 S Cloverdale Ave
Los Angeles, CA 90019-6737, USA

Provost, Jon
627 Montclair Dr
Santa Rosa, CA 95409-2833

Prowse, David (Actor)
c/o Nick Cordasco *Prince Marketing Group*
18 Carillon Cir
Livingston, NJ 07039-2600, USA

Proyas, Alex (Director)
8942 Wilshire Blvd # 219
Beverly Hills, CA 90211-1908, USA

Prudden, Bonnie (Misc)
4330 E Havasu Rd
Tucson, AZ 85718-2518, USA

Prudhomme, Don (Race Car Driver)
1232 Distribution Way
Vista, CA 92081-8816, USA

Prudhomme, Paul (Chef)
40 Allen St
Brockport, NY 14420-2228, USA

Pruett, Harold
8904 Wonderland Ave
Los Angeles, CA 90046-1854

Pruett, Jeanne (Musician, Songwriter, Writer)
2802 Columbine Pl
Nashville, TN 37204-3104, USA

Pruett, Scott (Athlete, Race Car Driver)
9743 W Bray Creek St
Star, ID 83669-5815, USA

Pruitt, Gregory D (Greg) (Athlete, Football Player)
13851 Larchmere Blvd
Cleveland, OH 44120-1349, USA

Pruitt, James (Athlete, Football Player)
PO Box 244483
Boynton Beach, FL 33424-4483, USA

Pruitt, Jason (Baseball Player)
320 Clark Dr Apt 101
Summerfield, NC 27358, USA

Pruitt, Jordan (Musician)
c/o Thor Bradwell *WmE2 (Endeavor-LA)*
9601 Wilshire Blvd Fl 3
Beverly Hills, CA 90210-5219, USA

Pruitt, Ron (Athlete, Baseball Player)
3632 Turnberry Dr
Medina, OH 44256-6827, USA

Pruitt, Toni (Stylist)
c/o Staff Member *Celestine - CA*
1666 20th St Ste 200B
Santa Monica, CA 90404-3828, USA

Pruitt Jr, Basil A (Doctor)
Fort Sam Houston, TX 78234, USA

Prunariu, Dumitru D (Cosmonaut)
Str Sf Spiridon 12 #4
Bucharest 70231, ROMANIA

Prunskiene, Kazimiera (Politician)
Vilnius St 45-13
Vilnius 2001, LITHUANIA

Prusiner, Stanley B (Nobel Prize Laureate)
Biochemistry
San Francisco, CA 94143-0001, USA

Pryce, Jonathan (Actor, Musician)
46 Albermarle St
London, ENGLAND W1X 4PP, UK

Pryce, Travor (Athlete, Football Player)
13655 Broncos Pkwy
Englewood, CO 80112-4150, USA

Pryor, David H (Ex-Governor, Ex-Senator, Senator)
1405 N Pierce St Ste 212
Little Rock, AR 72207-5357, USA

Pryor, Greg (Athlete, Baseball Player)
9726 W 115th Ter
Overland Park, KS 66210-2927, USA

Pryor, Hubert (Editor, Publisher)
3560 S Ocean Blvd Apt 607
Palm Beach, FL 33480-5773, USA

Pryor, Kelli (Writer)
c/o Andrea Simon *Andrea Simon Entertainment*
4230 Woodman Ave
Sherman Oaks, CA 91423-4334, USA

Pryor, Nicholas (Actor)
1801 Avenue of the Stars Ste 902
Los Angeles, CA 90067-5981, USA

Pryor, Peter P (Editor)
5700 Wilshire Blvd Ste 120
Los Angeles, CA 90036-3644, USA

Pryor, Rain (Actor, Producer)
2809 Saint Paul St # 2
Baltimore, MD 21218-4312, USA

Przybilla, Joel (Athlete, Basketball Player)
104 Oakview Cir
Monticello, MN 55362-8973, USA

Psaltis, Jim (Athlete, Football Player)
23115 Samuel St Apt 23
Torrance, CA 90505-3850, USA

Psycho, Les (Musician)
c/o Staff Member *Agency Group Ltd, The (NY)*
142 W 57th St Fl 6
New York, NY 10019-3300, USA

Ptacek, Bob (Athlete, Football Player)
648 Deptford Ave
Dayton, OH 45429-5941, USA

Ptacek, Louis (Misc)
Howard Hughes Institute
Salt Lake City, UT 84112, USA

Ptak, Frank (Business Person)
3600 W Lake Ave
Glenview, IL 60026-1215, USA

Ptashne, Mark S (Misc)
Biochemistry Dept
Cambridge, MA 2138, USA

Public Enemy (Music Group, Musician)
c/o Walter F. Leaphart Jr *Creamworks*
8391 Beverly Blvd Ste 352
Los Angeles, CA 90048-2633, USA

Pucci, Ben (Athlete, Football Player)
8502 Timber West St
San Antonio, TX 78250-4209, USA

Pucci, Bert (Publisher)
1888 Century Park E
Los Angeles, CA 90067-1702, USA

Puck, Wolfgang (Chef)
100 N Crescent Dr Ste 100
Beverly Hills, CA 90210-5447, USA

Puckett, Gary (Musician, Songwriter, Writer)
10710 Seminole Blvd Ste 3
Largo, FL 33778-3316, USA

Puemer, John P (Publisher)
435 N Michigan Ave
Chicago, IL 60611-4066, USA

Puenzo, Luis A (Director)
Lima 319
Buenos Aires 1073, ARGENTINA

Puerner, John P (Publisher)
202 W 1st St
Los Angeles, CA 90012-4105, USA

Puett, Tommy (Actor)
16621 Cerulean Ct
Chino Hills, CA 91709-4690, USA

Puetz, Garry (Athlete, Football Player)
1779 Robinson Rd
Dahlonega, GA 30533-6119, USA

Puffer, Brandon (Athlete, Baseball Player)
1546 Haynie Bnd
Round Rock, TX 78665-1216, USA

Pugacheva, Alia B (Musician)
Bersenevskaya Nab 20/2
Moscow 109072, RUSSIA

Pugh, Larry (Football Player)
RR 4
New Castle, PA 16101, USA

Pugh, Lewis Gordon (Sportscaster)
c/o Staff Member *WmE2 (WMA-LA)*
1 William Morris Pl
Beverly Hills, CA 90212-4261, USA

Pugh, Tim (Athlete, Baseball Player)
7906 N 125th East Cir
Owasso, OK 74055-3539, USA

Pugh, Willard E. (Actor)
c/o Shirley Wilson *Shirley Wilson Agency*
5410 Wilshire Blvd #806 Los Angeles
CA 90036, USA

Pugh Jr, Jethro (Athlete, Football Player)
329 E Colorado Blvd Apt 505
Dallas, TX 75203-1257, USA

Pugliese, Charles (Producer)
c/o Staff Member *Killer Films (US)*
526 W 26th St Rm 715
New York, NY 10001-5524, USA

Pugsley, Don (Actor)
c/o Hazel Shallon *Shallon Star Management*
14320 Ventura Blvd # 624
Sherman Oaks, CA 91423-2717, USA

Puhl, Terry (Athlete, Baseball Player)
918 Gondola St
Sugar Land, TX 77478-3414, USA

Puig, Rich (Athlete, Baseball Player)
2809 Albion Ave
Orlando, FL 32833-4330, USA

Pujats, Janis Cardinal (Religious Leader)
Maza Pils lela 2/A
Riga 1050, LATVIA

Pujol, Laetitia (Ballerina)
Place de l'Opera
Paris 75009, FRANCE

Pujol I Soley, Jordi (Politician)
Placa Sant Jaume S/N
Barcelona 2, SPAIN

Pujols, Albert (Athlete, Baseball Player)
102 Grand Meridien Frst
Chesterfield, MO 63005-4980, USA

Pujols, Luis B (Athlete, Baseball Player, Coach)
3867 Jonathans Way
Boynton Beach, FL 33436-8524, USA

Pulcini, Robert (Director)
c/o Staff Member *Creative Artists Agency (CAA-LA)*
2000 Avenue of the Stars Ste 100
Los Angeles, CA 90067-4705, USA

Puleo, Charlie (Athlete, Baseball Player)
3203 Miser Station Rd
Louisville, TN 37777-3611, USA

Pulford, Robert J (Bob) (Athlete, Hockey Player)
78 Coventry Rd
Northfield, IL 60093-3117, USA

Pulido, Carlos (Athlete, Baseball Player)
PO Box 25323
Miami, FL 33102-5323, USA

Puljic, Vinko Cardinal (Religious Leader)
Nadbiskupski Ordinarijat Kaptol 7
Sarajevo 71000, BOSNIA HERZEGOVINA

Pullard, Anthony (Athlete, Basketball Player)
3518 Monroe St
Lake Charles, LA 70607-3204, USA

Pullen, Melanie Clark (Actor)
c/o Staff Member *Julian Belfrage & Associates*
46 Albemarle St
London W1X 4PP, UK

Pulli, Frank (Baseball Player)
1981 Downing Pl
Palm Harbor, FL 34683-5727, USA

Pulliam, Harvey (Athlete, Baseball Player)
2009 Mount Hamilton Dr
Antioch, CA 94531-8331, USA

Pulliam, Keshia Knight (Actor)
PO Box 866
Teaneck, NJ 07666-0866, USA

Pullman, Bill (Actor, Director)
c/o Staff Member *One Talent Management*
9220 W Sunset Blvd Ste 306
Los Angeles, CA 90069-3503, USA

Pullman, Philip (Writer)
24 Templar Road
Oxford OX2 8LT, UNITED KINGDOM (UK)

Pulman, Bill (Actor, Director, Producer)
c/o Graciella Sanchez *One Talent Management*
9220 W Sunset Blvd Ste 306
Los Angeles, CA 90069-3503, USA

Pulp (Music Group)
c/o Staff Member *Paradigm (Monterey)*
404 W Franklin St
Monterey, CA 93940-2303, USA

Pulsipher, Bill (Athlete, Baseball Player)
1986 SW Certosa Rd
Port Saint Lucie, FL 34953-1393, USA

Pulver, Liselotte (Actor)
Villa Bip Kanton Vaudois
Perroy 1166, SWITZERLAND

Pumpkins, Penelope (Adult Film Star)
1247 14th St # 104
Santa Monica, CA 90404, USA

Punch, Lucy (Actor)
c/o Christian Donatelli *Schiff Company, The*
8440 Warner Dr Ste B1
Culver City, CA 90232-2461, USA

Punk, Daft (Composer, Writer)
c/o Staff Member *Primary Talent International (UK)*
The Primary Building 10-11 Jockeys Fields
London WC1R 4BN, UK

Punsley, Bernard (Actor)
1415 Granvia Altemeia
Palos Verdes Estates, CA 90274, USA

Punto, Nick (Athlete, Baseball Player)
19550 N Grayhawk Dr Unit 1122
Scottsdale, AZ 85255-3986, USA

Puppa, Daren (Athlete, Hockey Player)
4526 Cheval Blvd
Lutz, FL 33558-5331, USA

Puppies, The
15476 NW 77th Ct # 286
Miami Lakes, FL 33016-5823

Pupunu, Alfred (Athlete, Football Player)
415 Conestoga Dr
Moscow, ID 83843-5028, USA

Purcell, Dominic (Actor)
c/o Beth Holden-Garland *Untitled Entertainment (LA)*
350 S Beverly Dr Ste 200
Beverly Hills, CA 90212-4819, USA

Purcell, Herman (Baseball Player)
1031 Cass Ave SE
Grand Rapids, MI 49507-1119, USA

Purcell, James N (Government Official)
6 Chateau-Banquet
Geneva 1202, SWITZERLAND

Purcell, Lee (Actor)
11101 Provence Ln
Tujunga, CA 91042-1263, USA

Purcell, Patrick B (Publisher)
300 Harrison Ave
Boston, MA 02118-2237, USA

Purcell, Philip J (Financier)
1585 Broadway
New York, NY 10036-8200, USA

Purcell, Sarah (Actor)
6525 Esplanade
Playa Del Rey, CA 90293-7521, USA

Purcell, William (Physicist)
Astrophysics
Evanston, IL 60208-0001, USA

Purdee, Nathan (Actor)
56 E 66th St
New York, NY 10065-6538, USA

Purdin, John (Athlete, Baseball Player)
4942 Southgate Pkwy
Myrtle Beach, SC 29579-4147, USA

Purdom, Edmund (Actor)
Via Isonzo 42/C
Rome 198, ITALY

Purdy, Alfred (Writer)
PO Box 219
Madeira Park, BC V0N 2H0, CANADA

Purdy, Ted (Athlete, Golfer)
5600 N 4th St
Phoenix, AZ 85012-1305, USA

Pure Reason Revolution (Music Group)
c/o Staff Member *Paradigm (Monterey)*
404 W Franklin St
Monterey, CA 93940-2303, USA

Purefoy, James (Actor)
c/o JoAnne Colonna *Brillstein Entertainment Partners*
9150 Wilshire Blvd Ste 350
Beverly Hills, CA 90212-3453, USA

Puri, Om (Actor)
703 Trishul II Seven Bangalows Versova Andheri
Bombay, MS 400 061, INDIA

Purim, Flora (Musician)
PO Box 29242
Oakland, CA 94604-9242, USA

Purkey, Bob (Athlete, Baseball Player)
5559 Steeplechase Ct
Bethel Park, PA 15102-4501, USA

Purl, Linda (Actor)
13775A Mono Way # 220
Sonora, CA 95370-8813, USA

Purnell, Ella (Actor)
c/o Oriana Elia *MF Management Limited*
Drury House 34-43 Russell St
London WC2B 5HA, UK

Purnell, Frank (Athlete, Football Player)
PO Box 1387
Seaside, CA 93955-1387, USA

Purpura, Dominick P (Scientist)
1300 Morris Park Ave
Bronx, NY 10461-1900, USA

Purtzer, Tom (Golfer)
9828 E Desert Cove Ave
Scottsdale, AZ 85260-6220, USA

Purves, William (Financier)
87 Chester Square
London SW1W 9HT, UNITED KINGDOM (UK)

Purvis, Jeff (Race Car Driver)
4106 Roberta Rd
Concord, NC 28027, USA

Purvis, Jeff (Race Car Driver)
900 Providence Blvd
Clarksville, TN 37042-4477

Puryear, Martin (Artist)
700 New Hampshire Ave NW # 917
Washington, DC 20037-2407, USA

Pushelberg, Glenn (Designer)
55 Booth Ave
Toronto, ON M4M 2M3, CANADA

Puskaric, Joseph (Athlete, Baseball Player)
201 West Dr N Apt 63
Marshall, MI 49068-1486, USA

Puskarioc, Joseph (Baseball Player)
429 35th St
McKeesport, PA 15132-7226, USA

Pussycat Dolls (Music Group)
c/o Staff Member *WmE2 (WMA-LA)*
1 William Morris Pl
Beverly Hills, CA 90212-4261, USA

Putch, John (Actor)
3972 Sunswept Dr
Studio City, CA 91604-2330, USA

Putilin, Nikolai G (Opera Singer)
Teatralnaya Square 1
Saint Petersburg 190000, RUSSIA

Putin, Vladimir (Politician)
Office of the Prime Minister Krelim
Moscow 103073, Russia

Putin, Vladimir V (President)
Kremlin Staraya Pl 4
Moscow 103132, RUSSIA

Putman, Earl (Athlete, Football Player)
PO Box 18091
Munds Park, AZ 86017-8091, USA

Putman, Ed (Athlete, Baseball Player)
PO Box 3366
Mesquite, NV 89024-3366, USA

Putman, Pat (Baseball Player)
2311 Carrell Rd
Fort Myers, FL 33901-8012, USA

Putnam, David (Actor, Producer)
c/o Staff Member *Enigma Productions*
429 Santa Monica Blvd Ste 700
Santa Monica, CA 90401-3435, USA

Putnam, Duane (Athlete, Football Player)
1545 Magnolia Ave
Ontario, CA 91762-5335, USA

Putnam, Hilary W (Misc)
31 Cleveland St
Arlington, MA 02474-6915, USA

Putnam, Pat (Athlete, Baseball Player)
4040 Staley Rd
Fort Myers, FL 33905-6410, USA

Putti, Frank (Athlete, Baseball Player)
1981 Downing Pl
Palm Harbor, FL 34683-5727, USA

Puttnam, David T (Producer)
29A Tufton St
London SW1P 3QL, UNITED KINGDOM (UK)

Putz, J J (Athlete, Baseball Player)
8375 W La Caille
Peoria, AZ 85383-1305, USA

Putzier, Jeb (Athlete, Football Player)
2641 W 131st Ter
Leawood, KS 66209-1923, USA

Puyana, Rafael (Musician)
88 Rue de Grenelle
Paris 75007, FRANCE

Pyavko, Vladislav I (Opera Singer)
Bryusov Per 2/14 #27
Moscow 103009, RUSSIA

Pyburn, Jack (Athlete, Football Player)
1197 Peachtree St NE Ste 533A
Atlanta, GA 30361-3508, USA

Pyburn, Jim (Athlete, Baseball Player)
259 Longview Dr
Jasper, AL 35504-3715, USA

Pye, Eddie (Athlete, Baseball Player)
307 Polk St
Columbia, TN 38401-4453, USA

Pye, William B (Artist)
43 Hambalt Road Clapham
London SW4 9EQ, UNITED KINGDOM (UK)

Pyeatt, John (Johnny) (Athlete, Football Player)
18374 E Via De Palmas
Queen Creek, AZ 85242, USA

Pyecha, John (Athlete, Baseball Player)
107 Nottingham Dr
Chapel Hill, NC 27517-6569, USA

Pyfrom, Shawn (Actor)
c/o Eric Podwall *Podwall Entertainment*
710 N Orlando Ave Apt 203
Los Angeles, CA 90069-5549, USA

Pygram, Wayne (Actor)
c/o Bob Knotek *McCann - Knotek Associates*
8539 W Sunset Blvd Ste 4-136
Los Angeles, CA 90069-2334, USA

Pyle, Andy (Musician)
29 Ruston Mews
London W11 1RB, UNITED KINGDOM (UK)

Pyle, Michael J (Mike) (Athlete, Football Player)
2436 Saranac Ct
Glenview, IL 60026-1042, USA

Pyle, Missi (Actor)
c/o Mel McKeon *McKeon-Myones Management*
3500 W Olive Ave Ste 770
Burbank, CA 91505-5527, USA

Pyle, Missy (Actor)
10100 Santa Monica Blvd Ste 2500
Los Angeles, CA 90067-4116, USA

Pyle, Palmer (Athlete, Football Player)
2487 Potter Rd E
Traverse City, MI 49696-8572, USA

Pym of Sandy, Francis L (Government Official)
Everton Park Sandy
Beds SG19 2DE, UNITED KINGDOM (UK)

Pyne, George F (Athlete, Football Player)
123 Congress St
Milford, MA 01757-2006, USA

Pyne, Natasha (Actor)
Primrose Hill Studios Fitzroy Road
London NW1 8TR, UNITED KINGDOM (UK)

Pyne, Stephen J (Historian, Writer)
History
Tempe, AZ 85287-0001, USA

Pyott, David E I (Business Person)
2525 Dupont Dr
Irvine, CA 92612-1531, USA

Pyper-Ferguson, John (Actor)
c/o Adena Chawke *Greenlight Management and Production*
13848 Valleyheart Dr
Sherman Oaks, CA 91423-2930, USA

Python, Monty
34 Thistlewaite Rd
London, ENGLAND E5 0QQ

Pyznarski, Tim (Athlete, Baseball Player)
10716 Austin Ave
Chicago Ridge, IL 60415-2224, USA

Q

Q, Maggie (Actor)
c/o Andrew Ooi *Echelon Talent Management*
3674 Oxford St
Vancouver BC V5K 1P3, Canada

Qabas ibn Sa'id al Sa'id (King)
PO Box 252
Muscat, OMAN

Qaiyum, Gregory (GQ) (Actor)
c/o Sandra Joseph *SLJ Management*
833 N Edinburgh Ave Ph 11
Los Angeles, CA 90046-6999, USA

Qarase, Laisenia (Prime Minister)
6 Berkeley Crescent Suva
VITI LEVU, FIJI

Qasimi, Sheikh Saqr bin Muhammad al (President)
Ras Al Khaimah
UNITED ARAB EMIRATES

Qasimi, Sheikh Sultan bin Muhammad al (President)
Sharjah, UNITED ARAB EMIRATES

Qi, Shu (Actor)
c/o Steve Chasman *Ace Media*
9200 W Sunset Blvd Ste 10
Los Angeles, CA 90069-3608, USA

Qin, Shaobo (Actor)
c/o Don Hughes *IAI Presentations*
PO Box 4
Pismo Beach, CA 93448-0004, USA

Q-Tip (Actor, Producer)
c/o Staff Member *Violator Management*
36 W 25th St Fl 11
New York, NY 10010-2752, USA

Quackenbush, Bill
54 Danielle Ct
Lawrenceville, NJ 08648-1452

Quade, John (Actor)
12429 Laurel Terrace Dr
Studio City, CA 91604-2402, USA

Quaerna, Jerry (Athlete, Football Player)
1211 Pheasant Ct
Lake Geneva, WI 53147-1077, USA

Quaid, Dennis (Actor)
c/o Cara Tripicchio *WKT Public Relations (WKT-LA)*
9350 Wilshire Blvd Ste 450
Beverly Hills, CA 90212-3230, USA

Quaid, Randy (Actor)
PO Box 17372
Beverly Hills, CA 90209-3372, USA

Quaintance, Rachel (Comedian)
c/o Staff Member *OmniPop Talent Group*
10700 Ventura Blvd Fl 2
Studio City, CA 91604-3561, USA

Qualife, Pete (Musician)
29 Ruston Mews
London W11 1RB, UNITED KINGDOM (UK)

Qualls, Chad (Athlete, Baseball Player)
1868 260th St
Lomita, CA 90717-3305, USA

Qualls, DJ (Actor)
c/o Staff Member *Principato/Young Management*
9465 Wilshire Blvd Ste 430
Beverly Hills, CA 90212-2613, USA

Qualls, Jim (Athlete, Baseball Player)
410 N County Road 950
Sutter, IL 62373-5021, USA

Qualters, Tom (Athlete, Baseball Player)
236 Lake Rd
Somerset, PA 15501-1644, USA

Quan, Samantha (Actor)
c/o Vincent Cirrincione *Vincent Cirrincione Associates*
1516 N Fairfax Ave
Los Angeles, CA 90046-2608, USA

Quandt, Richard E (Economist)
162 Springdale Rd
Princeton, NJ 08540-4948, USA

Quann, Megan (Swimmer)
8421 Woodland Ave E
Puyallup, WA 98371-6557, USA

Quanstrom, Nissa (Stylist)
c/o Staff Member *Artist Untied (LA)*
845 S Mansfield Ave Apt 1
Los Angeles, CA 90036-4979, USA

Quant, Mary (Designer, Fashion Designer)
3 Ives St
London SW3 2NE, UNITED KINGDOM (UK)

Quantrill, Paul (Athlete, Baseball Player)
334 E Lake Rd
Palm Harbor, FL 34685-2427, USA

Quarashi (Musician)
c/o Staff Member *Creative Artists Agency (CAA-LA)*
2000 Avenue of the Stars Ste 100
Los Angeles, CA 90067-4705, USA

Quaresma, Rhonda Lee (Misc)
PO Box 22033
Kingston, ON K7M 8S5, CANADA

Quarles, Shelton (Athlete, Football Player)
17019 Candeleda De Avila
Tampa, FL 33613-5213, USA

Quarrie, Donald (Don) (Athlete, Track Athlete)
PO Box 272
Kingston 5, JAMAICA

Quarshie, Hugh (Actor)
PO Box 20092
London NW2 6FJ, UNITED KINGDOM (UK)

Quarterflash
5410 SW MacAdam Ave Ste 280
Portland, OR 97239-3825

Quastel, J Hirsch (Biologist, Scientist)
4585 Langara Ave
Vancouver, BC V6R 1C9, CANADA

Quasthoff, Thomas (Musician)
3436 Springhill Rd
Lafayette, CA 94549-2535, USA

Quate, Calvin F (Engineer)
340 Princeton Rd
Menlo Park, CA 94025-5220, USA

Quatro, Suzi (Musician, Songwriter, Writer)
4 Pasteur Courtyard Whittle Road Corby Norths, FL NN17 5DX, UNITED KINGDOM (UK)

Quayle, Anna (Actor)
47 Courtfield Rd
London, ENGLAND SW7 4DB, UNITED KINGDOM (UK)

Quayle, Benjamin (Congressman, Politician)
1419 Longworth Hob
Washington, DC 20515-2008, USA

Quayle, Dan (Politician)
7001 N Scottsdale Rd
Scottsdale, AZ 85253-3658, USA

Quayle, Jenny (Actor)
c/o Staff Member *Michelle Braidman Assoc*
Lower John St Fl 3 #10/11
London W1F 9EB, UNITED KINGDOM (UK)

Qubein, Nido (Business Person)
806 Westchester Dr
High Point, NC 27262-7347, USA

Quddus (Television Host)
c/o Michael (Mike) Esterman *Esterman.Com, LLC*
Prefers to be contacted via email
MD, USA

Queen (Music Group, Musician)
16-A High Street Barnes
London SW13 9LW, UK

Queen, Ida (Musician)
16045 36th Ave NE
Lake Forest Park, WA 98155-6623, USA

Queen, Jeff (Athlete, Football Player)
General Delivery
Oceanside, CA 92054-9999, USA

Queen, Konga (Actor, Wrestler)
PO Box 5050
Carson, CA 90749-5050, USA

Queen, Mel (Athlete, Baseball Player, Coach)
345 Cerrito Pl
Morro Bay, CA 93442-2708, USA

Queen Elizabeth II (Royalty)
London SW1A 1AA, UNITED KINGDOM (UK)

Queen Rania (Royalty)
Amman, JORDAN

Queens of the Stone Age (Music Group)
c/o Staff Member *Creative Artists Agency (CAA-LA)*
2000 Avenue of the Stars Ste 100
Los Angeles, CA 90067-4705, USA

Queensryche (Music Group)
c/o Staff Member *Monterey International (Chicago)*
200 W Superior St Ste 202
Chicago, IL 60654-6422, USA

Queffelec, Anne (Musician)
15 Ave Corneille
Maisons-Laffittle 78600, FRANCE

Queler, Eve (Conductor)
239 W 72nd St Apt 2R
New York, NY 10023-2734, USA

Quellmatz, Udo (Athlete)
Friedhofstr 10
Omgolstandt 85049, GERMANY

Queloz, Didier (Astronomer)
Geneva Observatory
Geneva, SWITZERLAND

Quenneville, Joel (Athlete, Coach, Hockey Player)
835 S Park Ave
Hinsdale, IL 60521-4569, USA

Quenzrd, Nathalie (Actor)
36 Rue de Ponthieu
Paris 75008, FRANCE

Query, Jeff (Athlete, Football Player)
93 Woodlily Pl
Spring, TX 77382-1254, USA

Quester, Hugues (Actor)
36 Rue de Ponthieu
Paris 75008, FRANCE

Questlove (Musician)
6255 W Sunset Blvd
Los Angeles, CA 90028-7403, USA

Questrom, Allen I (Business Person)
6501 Legacy Dr
Plano, TX 75024-3612, USA

Quezada, Milly (Musician)
c/o Staff Member *Sony Music Miami*
605 Lincoln Rd Ste 700
Miami Beach, FL 33139-2901, USA

Quezada Toruno, Rodolfo Cardinal (Religious Leader)
7A Avenida 6-21 Zona 1
Guatemala City 1001, GUATEMALA

Quick, Clarence E (Musician, Songwriter, Writer)
376 Quincy St
Brooklyn, NY 11216-1502, USA

Quick, Diana (Actor)
39 Seymour Walk
London SW10, UNITED KINGDOM (UK)

Quick, James E (Jim) (Actor)
PO Box 12760
Scottsdale, AZ 85267-2760, USA

Quick, Jim (Athlete, Baseball Player)
PO Box 1127
Camino, CA 95709-1127, USA

Quick, Jonathan (Athlete, Hockey Player)
c/o Staff Member *Los Angeles Kings*
1111 S Figueroa St Ste 3100
Los Angeles, CA 90015-1333, USA

Quick, Michael A (Mike) (Athlete, Football Player)
13 Slab Branch Ct
Marlton, NJ 08053-5407, USA

Quick, Rebecca (Talk Show Host)
900 Sylvan Ave
Englewood Cliffs, NJ 07632-3312, USA

Quick, Richard (Coach, Swimmer)
Athletic Dept
Stanford, CA 94305, USA

Quicksilver (Music Group)
c/o Staff Member *Paradigm (Monterey)*
404 W Franklin St
Monterey, CA 93940-2303, USA

Quie, Albert H (Al) (Ex-Governor)
4209 Christy Ln
Minnetonka, MN 55345-3001, USA

Quiet Riot
2002 Hogback Rd Ste 20
Ann Arbor, MI 48105-9736

Quigley, Austin E (Educator)
President's Office
New York, NY 10027, USA

Quigley, Dana (Golfer)
90 Wheeler St
Rehoboth, MA 02769-1110, USA

Quigley, Joan (Psychic)
1055 California St # 14
San Francisco, CA 94108-2203

Quigley, Linnea (Actor)
2608 N Ocean Blvd Ste 1 # 126
Pompano Beach, FL 33062-2955, USA

Quigley, Mike (Congressman, Politician)
3742 W Irving Park Rd
Chicago, IL 60618-3116, USA

Quigley, Philip J (Phil) (Business Person)
130 Keamy St
San Francisco, CA 94108, USA

Quik, D J (Musician)
8942 Wilshire Blvd # 219
Beverly Hills, CA 90211-1908, USA

Quilici, Frank (Athlete, Baseball Player, Coach)
3413 E 126th St
Burnsville, MN 55337-3440, USA

Quill, Leonard W (Financier)
Rodney Square N 1100 N Market St
Wilmington, DE 19801, USA

Quill, Timothy E (Activist)
Medical & Dentistry School
Rochester, NY 14642, USA

Quillan, Frederick (Fred) (Athlete, Football Player)
2924 Bailey Ln
Eugene, OR 97401-6926, USA

Quinaz, Victor (Director)
c/o Chad Hamilton *Anonymous Content (AC-LA)*
3531 Hayden Ave
Culver City, CA 90232, USA

Quinlan, Kathleen (Actor)
PO Box 6728
Malibu, CA 90264-6728, USA

Quinlan, Maeve (Actor)
c/o Staff Member *Main Title Entertainment*
2225 Wilshire Blvd Suite 500
Los Angeles, CA 90036, USA

Quinlan, Maive
1123 N Flores St
West Hollywood, CA 90069-2967

Quinlan, Robb (Athlete, Baseball Player)
1125 Sterling Cir N
Saint Paul, MN 55119-7183, USA

Quinlan, Sally (Golfer)
1419 Laguna St Apt 79
Santa Barbara, CA 93101-1241, USA

Quinlan, Tom (Athlete, Baseball Player)
1061 Sterling St S
Saint Paul, MN 55119-5972, USA

Quinlan, William D (Bill) (Athlete, Football Player)
393 Mount Vernon St
Lawrence, MA 01843-3103, USA

Quinn, Aidan (Actor)
c/o Peg Donegan *Framework Entertainment (LA)*
9057 Nemo St Ste C
West Hollywood, CA 90069-5511, USA

Quinn, Aileen (Actor)
c/o Corey Smith *Gemini Entertainment*
PO Box 1772
New York, NY 10101-1772, USA

Quinn, Brady (Athlete, Football Player)
c/o Team Member *Cleveland Browns*
76 Lou Groza Blvd
Berea, OH 44017-1269

Quinn, Brandon (Actor)
c/o Ben Feigin *Anonymous Content (AC-LA)*
3531 Hayden Ave
Culver City, CA 90232, USA

Quinn, Brian (Coach, Soccer Player)
3550 Stevens Creek Blvd Ste 200
San Jose, CA 95117-1031, USA

Quinn, Carmel (Musician)
230 W Summit Ave # 1
Haddonfield, NJ 08033-3703, USA

Quinn, Colin (Actor, Comedian)
c/o Staff Member *Agency for the Performing Arts (APA-LA)*
405 S Beverly Dr Ste 500
Beverly Hills, CA 90212-4425, USA

Quinn, Colleen (Actor)
5750 Wilshire Blvd # 473
Los Angeles, CA 90036-3697, USA

Quinn, Danny (Actor)
c/o Michael Greenwald *Don Buchwald & Associates Inc (LA)*
6500 Wilshire Blvd Ste 2200
Los Angeles, CA 90048-4942, USA

Quinn, David W (Business Person)
2728 N Harwood St
Dallas, TX 75201-1516, USA

Quinn, DeClan (Cinematographer)
22 Cherry Ave
Cornwall On Hudson, NY 12520-1506, USA

Quinn, Ed (Actor)
c/o Staff Member *Burstein Company, The*
15304 W Sunset Blvd Ste 208
Pacific Palisades, CA 90272-3656, USA

Quinn, Freddy
Am Pfeilshof 35
Hamburg, GERMANY D-22393

Quinn, Glenn (Actor)
2120 Colorado Ave Ste 120
Santa Monica, CA 90404-3561, USA

Quinn, J B Patrick (Pat) (Athlete, Coach, Hockey Player)
40 Bay St
Toronto, ON M5J 2K2, Canada

Quinn, Jane Bryant (Journalist)
251 W 57th St
New York, NY 10019-1802, USA

Quinn, Jim (Misc)
675 S Sierra Ave Unit 32
Solana Beach, CA 92075-3232, USA

Quinn, John A (Engineer)
275 E Wynnewood Rd
Merion Station, PA 19066-1627, USA

Quinn, John C (Editor)
365 S Atlantic Ave
Cocoa Beach, FL 32931-2719, USA

Quinn, Mark (Athlete, Baseball Player)
1941 Terrebonne Ave
San Dimas, CA 91773-1334, USA

Quinn, Martha (Actor, Model)
11684 Ventura Blvd # 453
Studio City, CA 91604-2699, USA

Quinn, Mike (Athlete, Football Player)
10703 Del Monte Dr
Houston, TX 77042-2326, USA

Quinn, Molly C (Actor)
c/o Ellen Meyer *Ellen Meyer Management*
8899 Beverly Blvd Ste 612
West Hollywood, CA 90048-2429, USA

Quinn, Pat (Governor)
Of the Governor 207 State House Ofc
Springfield, IL 62706-0001, USA

Quinn, Patricia (Actor)
11 Garrick Street
London WC2E 9AR, United Kingdom

Quinn, Robert (Football Player)
c/o Carl Carey *Champion Pro Consulting Group*
3547 Ruth St
Houston, TX 77004-5515, USA

Quinn, Sally (Journalist)
3014 N St NW
Washington, DC 20007-3404, USA

Quinn, Stephen (Athlete, Football Player)
RR 1 Box 163
Mount Sterling, IL 62353-9765, USA

Quinnett, Brian (Athlete, Basketball Player)
862 Indian Hills Dr
Moscow, ID 83843-9373, USA

Quinones, John (Correspondent)
c/o Staff Member *ABC News*
77 W 66th St Fl 3
New York, NY 10023-6201, USA

Quinones, Luis (Athlete, Baseball Player)
5821 Calle San Bruno
Ponce, PR 00730-4443, USA

Quinones, Rey (Athlete, Baseball Player)
216 Calle Ronda
San Juan, PR 00926-2351, USA

Quintal, Stephane (Athlete, Hockey Player)
1356A La Fontaine
Montreal, QC H2L 1T5, Canada

Quintana, Chela (Golfer)
100 International Golf Dr
Daytona Beach, FL 32124-1082, USA

Quintanilla, Omar (Athlete, Baseball Player)
12457 Paseo De Arco Ct
El Paso, TX 79928-5669, USA

Quinto, Zachary (Actor)
c/o Jason Weinberg *Untitled Entertainment (LA)*
350 S Beverly Dr Ste 200
Beverly Hills, CA 90212-4819, USA

Quirico, Rafael (Athlete, Baseball Player)
4422 W Rogers Ave
Tampa, FL 33611-5630, USA

Quiring, Frederic (Actor)
36 Rue de Ponthieu
Paris 75008, FRANCE

Quirk, Art (Athlete, Baseball Player)
2 Ensign Ln
Stonington, CT 06378-2944, USA

Quirk, James P (Jamie) (Athlete, Baseball Player)
310 W 123rd Ter
Kansas City, MO 64145-1186, USA

Quirk, Michael J (War Hero)
1700 Kit Ln
Navarre, FL 32566, USA

Quiroga, Elena (Writer)
Diagonal 580
Barcelona 8021, SPAIN

Quiroga, Jorge (Tuto) (President)
Palacio de Gobierno Plaza Murllia
La Paz, BOLIVIA

Quist, Janet (Model)
13446 Poway Rd # 239
Poway, CA 92064-4714, USA

Quitones, John (Correspondent)
77 W 66th St
New York, NY 10023-6201, USA

Quivar, Florence (Opera Singer)
165 W 57th St
New York, NY 10019-2201, USA

Quivers, Robin (Actor, Entertainer, Radio Personality, Talk Show Host)
c/o Staff Member *Don Buchwald & Associates Inc (LA)*
6500 Wilshire Blvd Ste 2200
Los Angeles, CA 90048-4942, USA

Qulgley, Brett (Golfer)
127 Sandpiper Cir
Jupiter, FL 33477-8434, USA

Qulgley, Dana (Golfer)
2670 Tecumseh Dr
West Palm Beach, FL 33409-7421, USA

Quon, Di (Actor)
c/o Loch Powell *Leverage Management*
3030 Pennsylvania Ave
Santa Monica, CA 90404-4112, USA

Quon, Erin (Stylist)
544 Central Ave
San Francisco, CA 94117-1313, USA

Qureia, Ahmed (Prime Minister)
Gara City Gaza Strip
Palestine, ISRAEL

R

R. Carter, John (Congressman, Politician)
409 Cannon Hob
Washington, DC 20515-0911, USA

R. Conseco, Francisco (Congressman, Politician)
1339 Longworth Hob
Washington, DC 20515-1202, USA

R E M (Music Group)
170 College Ave
Athens, GA 30601-2805, US

R. Keating, William (Congressman, Politician)
315 Cannon Hob
Washington, DC 20515-0101, USA

R. Labrador, Raul (Congressman, Politician)
1523 Longworth Hob
Washington, DC 20515-4003, USA

R. Langevin, James (Congressman, Politician)
109 Cannon Hob
Washington, DC 20515-3902, USA

R M A, Bharathimohan (Actor)
3 1/8 Madley Lind Street T Nagar
Chennai, TN 600 017, INDIA

R Pandiarajan (Actor)
18 Sivasailam Street T Nagar
Chennai, TN 600 017, INDIA

R Partheepan (Actor)
Veerappa Nagar
Chennai, TN 600 093, INDIA

R. Pierluisi, Pedro (Congressman, Politician)
1213 Longworth Hob
Washington, DC 20515-1313, USA

R. Pitts, Joseph (Congressman, Politician)
420 Carmon Hob
Washington, DC 20515-0001, USA

Raab, Chris (Actor)
c/o Staff Member *Haber Entertainment*
434 S Canon Dr Apt 204
Beverly Hills, CA 90212-4501, USA

Raab, Marc (Athlete, Football Player)
8500 Sea Pines Pl
McKinney, TX 75070-8412, USA

Raabe, Brian (Athlete, Baseball Player)
38760 Kost Trl
North Branch, MN 55056-6722, USA

Raabe, Max (Opera Singer)
Thuyring 63
Berlin 12101, GERMANY

Raakhee (Actor, Bollywood)
Muktangan Sarojini Naidu Road
Santacruz
Bombay, MS 400 054, INDIA

Raaurn, Gustav (Skier)
PO Box 700
Mercer Island, WA 98040-0700, USA

Raba, Robert (Athlete, Football Player)
16066 Acre St
North Hills, CA 91343-4822, USA

Rabb, John (Johnny) (Athlete, Baseball Player)
1942 W Manchester Ave
Los Angeles, CA 90047-2923, USA

Rabe, Charlie (Athlete, Baseball Player)
6059 E Sierra Blanca St
Mesa, AZ 85215-7753, USA

Rabe, Lily (Actor)
c/o Peg Donegan *Framework Entertainment (LA)*
9057 Nemo St Ste C
West Hollywood, CA 90069-5511, USA

Rabe, Pamela (Actor)
PO Box 1509
Darlinghurst, NSW 1300, AUSTRALIA

Rabelo, Mike (Athlete, Baseball Player)
5813 N 17th St
Tampa, FL 33610-4308, USA

Rabensteiner, Robert (Stylist)
c/o Staff Member *Michele Filomeno New York LLC*
515 Greenwich St Ste 503
New York, NY 10013-1097, USA

Rabin, Trevor (Composer)
15233 Ventura Blvd Ste 200
Sherman Oaks, CA 91403-2244, USA

Rabinovitch, Benton S (Misc)
12530 42nd Ave NE
Seattle, WA 98125-4621, USA

Rabinowitz, Dorothy (Journalist)
200 Liberty St
New York, NY 10281-1003, USA

Rabinowitz, Harry (Composer, Conductor)
11 Mead Road Cranleigh
Surrey GU6 7BG, UNITED KINGDOM (UK)

Rabinowitz, Jesse C (Misc)
Dept
Berkeley, CA 94720-0001, USA

Rabkin, Mitchell T (Doctor)
330 Brookline Ave
Boston, MA 02215-5400, USA

Raburn, Ryan (Athlete, Baseball Player)
6612 Ike Smith Rd
Plant City, FL 33565-3038, USA

Raby, Stuart (Physicist)
Physics Dept
Columbus, OH 43210, USA

Racan, Ivica (Prime Minister)
Jordanovac 71
Zagreb 41000, CROATIA

Racette, Patricia (Opera Singer)
165 W 57th St
New York, NY 10019-2201, USA

Rachal, Latorio (Athlete, Football Player)
3266 Golden Ave
Long Beach, CA 90806-1208, USA

Rachin, Julian (Musician)
165 W 57th St
New York, NY 10019-2201, USA

Rachins, Alan (Actor)
c/o Mark Teitelbaum *Teitelbaum Artists Group*
8840 Wilshire Blvd Fl 3
Beverly Hills, CA 90211-2606, USA

Racicot, Jody (Actor)
c/o Jamie Levitt *Lauren Levitt & Associates Inc*
1525 W 8th St 3rd Fl
Vancouver V6J 1T5, British Columbia

Racicot, Marc F (Ex-Governor)
28013 Swan Cove Dr
Bigfork, MT 59911-7846, USA

Rackers, Neil (Athlete, Football Player)
945 Shady Path Ct
Saint Peters, MO 63376-3898, USA

Rackley, Derek (Athlete, Football Player)
2770 Shumard Oak Dr
Braselton, GA 30517-6024, USA

Rackley, Luther (Athlete, Basketball Player)
36 W 128th St Apt 2
New York, NY 10027-3100, USA

Rackley, Marv (Athlete, Baseball Player)
512 S Bibb St
Westminster, SC 29693-2134, USA

Raczka, Mike (Athlete, Baseball Player)
72 Foley Dr
Southington, CT 06489-4400, USA

Radachowsky, George (Athlete, Football Player)
87 Merrimac St
Danbury, CT 06810-6463, USA

Radcliffe, Daniel (Actor)
c/o Scott Boute *Scott Boute Publicity*
529 W 42nd St Apt 5A
New York, NY 10036-6228, USA

Raddatz, Carl
Stalluponer Allee 54
Berlin, GERMANY 14055

Rade, John (Athlete, Football Player)
611 Deertrail Dr
Hailey, ID 83333-8731, USA

Rademacher, Bill (Athlete, Football Player)
PO Box 11
Haslett, MI 48840-0011, USA

Rademacher, Ingo (Actor)
1801 Avenue of the Stars Ste 902
Los Angeles, CA 90067-5981, USA

Rademacher, Pete
5585 River Styx Rd
Medina, OH 44256-8786

Rademacher, T Peter (Pete) (Boxer)
5585 River Styx Rd
Medina, OH 44256-8786, USA

Rader, Dave (Athlete, Baseball Player)
2345 Summit Dr
Escondido, CA 92025-7513, USA

Rader, Douglas L (Doug) (Athlete, Baseball Player, Coach)
PO Box 2768
Stuart, FL 34995-2768, USA

Rader, Randall R (Judge)
717 Madison Pl NW
Washington, DC 20439-0001, USA

Rader, Stanley
360 Waverly Dr
Pasadena, CA 91105-1820

Radford, Mark (Athlete, Basketball Player)
5160 NE Wistaria Dr
Portland, OR 97213-2557, USA

Radford, Michael (Director)
38 Rickering Mews
London W2 5AD, UNITED KINGDOM (UK)

Radford, Wayne (Athlete, Basketball Player)
4660 Running Brook Ter
Greenwood, IN 46143-9254, USA

Radha Ravi (Actor)
23 Poes Road Teynampet
Chennai, TN 600 018, INDIA

Radhika (Actor, Bollywood)
3 Paul Appasamy Street Abhirampuram
Chennai, TN 600018, INDIA

Radigan, Terry (Musician, Songwriter)
209 10th Ave S Ste 322
Nashville, TN 37203-0744, USA

Radin, Joshua
c/o Debbie Wilson *Wilspro Management*
P.O. Box 9
Point Pleasant, NY 10001, USA

Radinsky, Scott (Athlete, Baseball Player)
2974 Santiago St
Westlake Village, CA 91362-3737, USA

Radiohead (Music Group)
c/o Staff Member *XL Recordings*
1 Codrington Mews
London W11 2EH, UNITED KINGDOM

Radisic, Zivko (President)
Marsala Titz 7
Sarajevo 71000, BOSNIA & HERZEGOVINA

Radke, Brad W (Athlete, Baseball Player)
125 18th St
Belleair Beach, FL 33786-3313, USA

Radko, Christopher (Artist)
PO Box 536
Elmsford, NY 10523-0536, USA

Radloff, Wayne (Athlete, Football Player)
2108 Chambwood Dr
Charlotte, NC 28205-3618, USA

Radlosky, Robert (Rob) (Athlete, Baseball Player)
1219 W Broward St
Lantana, FL 33462-3013, USA

Radmanovich, Ryan (Athlete, Baseball Player)
25 Ware Ave
West Hartford, CT 06119-1532, USA

Radner, Roy (Economist)
30711 Overlook Run
Buena Vista, CO 81211-9836, USA

Radnor, Josh (Actor)
c/o Rhonda Price *Gersh (NY)*
41 Madison Ave
New York, NY 10010-2202, USA

Radojevic, Danilo (Dancer)
890 Broadway
New York, NY 10003-1211, USA

Radosevich, George (Athlete, Football Player)
414 Shaffer Ave
Elizabeth, PA 15037-1840, USA

Radovich, Frank (Athlete, Basketball Player)
121 Lakewood Dr
Statesboro, GA 30458-9041, USA

Radtke, Sheilah (Stylist)
c/o Staff Member *Page.214*
3303 Lee Pkwy Ste 205
Dallas, TX 75219-5145, USA

Raduege Jr, Harry D (General)
Director Defense Information Systems Agency
Arlington, VA 22204, USA

Radwanski, George (Editor)
Editorial Dept 1 Yonge St
Toronto, ON M5E 1E6, CANADA

Rady, Michael (Actor)
c/o Kasra Ajir *Station3*
1051 Cole Ave
Los Angeles, CA 90038-2601, USA

Radziwill, Lee (Misc)
c/o Staff Member *Assouline Publishing, Inc.*
601 W 26th St Fl 18
New York, NY 10001-1101, USA

Rae, Cassidy (Actor)
c/o Ro Diamond 1801 Avenue of the Stars #902
Los Angeles, CA 90067, USA

Rae, Charlotte (Actor)
10790 Wilshire Blvd Apt 903
Los Angeles, CA 90024-4478, USA

Rae, Fiona (Artist)
Burlington House Piccadilly
London W1J 0BD, UK

Rae, Mike (Athlete, Football Player)
18541 Auburn Ave
Santa Ana, CA 92705-2704, USA

Rae, Patricia (Actor)

Rae, Robert K (Bob) (Politician)
250 Yonge St
Toronto, ON M5B 2M6, CANADA

Rae Westley, Jennifer (Actor)
c/o Staff Member *da Vinci Talent*
919 Marie Anne Est
Montreal QC H2J 2B2, CANADA

Raekwon (Musician)
c/o Drew Elliot *Media Artists Group (NY)*
140 E 46th St PH C
New York, NY 10017-2633, USA

Raether, Hal (Athlete, Baseball Player)
6105 Lincoln Dr Apt 133
Minneapolis, MN 55436-1619, USA

Rafalski, Brian (Athlete, Hockey Player)
Continental Arena 50 RR 120 N
East Rutherford, NJ 7073, USA

Rafelson, Bob (Director)
1022 Palm Ave # 3
New Haven, VT 5472, USA

Raffarin, Jean-Pierre (Prime Minister)
15 Rue De Vaugirard Cedex 06
Paris F-75291, FRANCE

Rafferty, Thomas M (Tom) (Athlete, Football Player)
1526 Mount Gilead Rd
Keller, TX 76262-7358, USA

Raffo, Al (Athlete, Baseball Player)
330 Pleasant View Cir
Jasper, TN 37347-7242, USA

Rafikov, Mars Z (Cosmonaut)
Ul M Gorkova 59 KV 44
Almaty 480 002, KAZAKHSTAN

Rafko, Kaye Lani Rae
4932 Frary Ln
Monroe, MI 48161-9708

Rafsanjani, Hashemi (Ex-President, President)
Ali Shariati Ave
Tehran, IRAN

Rafsanjani, Hojatoleslam H (President)
Majilis
Teheran, IRAN

Rafshoon, Gerald
3028 Q St NW
Washington, DC 20007-3080

Rafter, Patrick (Tennis Player)
PO Box 1235
North Sydney, NSW 2059, AUSTRALIA

Raftery, Erin (Actor)
c/o Rachel Rothman *Rothman / Patino / Andres Entertainment*
4370 Tujunga Ave Ste 120
Studio City, CA 91604-2763, USA

Raftery, S Frank (Misc)
1750 New York Ave NW
Washington, DC 20006-5305, USA

Ragan, Dave (Athlete, Golfer)
PO Box 1131
Harrisburg, NC 28075-1131, USA

Ragan, David (Race Car Driver)
c/o Staff Member *National Association of Stock Car Racing (NASCAR)*
1801 W Speedway Blvd
Daytona Beach, FL 32114-1215, USA

Ragavendar (Actor)
2-C Palace View Apartments 788
Santhome High Rd
Chennai, TN 600 028, INDIA

Rage Against The Machine (Music Group, Musician)
c/o Staff Member *Columbia Records UK*
Bedford House 69-79 Fulham High St
London SW6 3JW, United Kingdom

Raggi, Florencia (Actor)
c/o Staff Member *Telefe - Argentina*
Pavon 2444 (C1248AAT)
Buenos Aires, ARGENTINA

Raggio, Brady (Athlete, Baseball Player)
10653 Rue D Azur
Reno, NV 89511-4308, USA

Raggio, Lisa
9300 Wilshire Blvd Ste 410
Beverly Hills, CA 90212-3228

Raghavan, V S (Actor)
6 School View Road Mandavelli
Chennai, TN 600 028, INDIA

Raghavi (Actor, Bollywood)
18 Crescent Park Road T Nagar
Chennai, TN 600017, INDIA

Raghuvaran (Actor)
D-1 Ist Floor Anandsree Apartments 32
Hindi Prachar Saba Street
Chennai, TN 600 017, INDIA

Ragin, Derek Lee (Opera Singer)
111 W 57th St
New York, NY 10019-2211, USA

Ragin, John S (Actor)
5706 Briarcliff Rd
Los Angeles, CA 90068, USA

Ragland, Tom (Athlete, Baseball Player)
20201 Greenlawn St
Detroit, MI 48221-1187, USA

Raglin, Floyd (Athlete, Football Player)
2701 Alister Ave
Tustin, CA 92782-0934, USA

Ragnone, Teresa (Stylist)
5679 SE International Way
Portland, OR 97222-4608, USA

Rago, Pablo (Actor)
c/o Staff Member *Telefe - Argentina*
Pavon 2444 (C1248AAT)
Buenos Aires, ARGENTINA

Ragogna, Mike (Musician, Producer)
204 E Madison Ave
Fairfield, IA 52556-3641, USA

Ragsdale, William (Actor)
1505 10th St
Santa Monica, CA 90401-2805, USA

Ragunas, Vincent (Athlete, Football Player)
4201 W Grace St
Richmond, VA 23230-3803, USA

Rahal, Bashar (Actor)
c/o Victor (Viktor) Kruglov *Victor Kruglov Talent Management*
7461 Beverly Blvd Ste 403
Los Angeles, CA 90036-2774, USA

Rahal, Bobby
1903 N Howe St
Chicago, IL 60614-5127

Rahal, Robert W (Bobby) (Race Car Driver)
4601 Lyman Dr
Hilliard, OH 43026-1249, USA

Rahel (Stylist)
c/o Staff Member *L'Agence*
5901 Peachtree Dunwoody Rd NE Ste C60
Atlanta, GA 30328-7155, USA

Rahlves, Daron (Skier)
PO Box 333
Truckee, CA 96160-0333, USA

Rahm, Kevin (Actor)
9460 Wilshire Blvd Ste 700
Beverly Hills, CA 90212-2713, USA

Rahman, A.R. (Bollywood, Composer)
c/o Sam Schwartz *Gorfaine/Schwartz Agency Inc*
4111 W Alameda Ave Ste 509
Burbank, CA 91505-4171, USA

Rahman, Hamida Betty (Stylist)
2329 NE Clackamas St
Portland, OR 97232-1637, USA

Rahman Khan, Ataur (Prime Minister)
500 A Dhanmondi R/A Road 7
Dhaka, BANGLADESH

Rahul, Roy (Actor, Bollywood)
502 Gildar Villa 17 Master Vinayak X Road Bandra
Mumbai, MS 400050, INDIA

Rahzel (Musician)
c/o Staff Member *Agency Group Ltd, The (NY)*
142 W 57th St Fl 6
New York, NY 10019-3300, USA

Rai, Aishwarya (Actor, Bollywood, Dancer)
402 Ramalaxmi Nowas 16th Road Khar W
Mumbai, MS 400054, India

Rai, Rajeev (Bollywood, Director, Filmmaker, Producer)
22 Sonmarg Nepean Sea Rd
Bombay, MS 400 006, INDIA

Rai, Rajiv (Bollywood, Director, Producer)
B-11 Commerce Center Tardeo
Mumbai, MS 400034, INDIA

Raible, Steve (Athlete, Football Player)
18 W Raye St
Seattle, WA 98119-2362, USA

Raich, Eric (Athlete, Baseball Player)
3963 Edward Dr
Brunswick, OH 44212-1509, USA

Raichle, Marcus E (Doctor)
Medical School Neurology Dept
Saint Louis, MO 63130, USA

Raider-Wexler, Victor (Actor)
c/o Lorraine Berglund *Lorraine Berglund Management*
11537 Hesby St
North Hollywood, CA 91601-3618, USA

Raiken, Sherwin (Athlete, Basketball Player)
2400 McClellan Ave Apt 120B
Pennsauken, NJ 08109-4629, USA

Raikkonen, Kimi (Race Car Driver)
c/o Staff Member *Formula Management Ltd*
PO Box 222 Borehamwood
Herts WD6 3FJ, United Kingdom

Railsback, Steve (Actor)
11684 Ventura Blvd # 581
Studio City, CA 91604-2699, USA

Raimi, Sam (Writer)
c/o Richard Lovett *Creative Artists Agency (CAA-LA)*
2000 Avenue of the Stars Ste 100
Los Angeles, CA 90067-4705, USA

Raimi, Ted (Director, Producer)

Raimond, Jean-Bernard (Government Official)
Servier SA 22 Rue Garnier
Neuilly-sur-Seine 92200, FRANCE

Raimondi, Ben (Athlete, Football Player)
5 Grandview Dr
Holmdel, NJ 07733-2007, USA

Raimondi, Ruggero (Opera Singer)
140 Bis Rue Lecourbe
Paris 75015, USA

Rain, Misty
PO Box 67
Lakewood, CA 90714-0067

Rain, Steve (Athlete, Baseball Player)
20320 E Crestline Dr
Walnut, CA 91789-4605, USA

Raine, Craig A (Writer)
English Dept
Oxford OX1 3BN, UNITED KINGDOM (UK)

Raine, Gillian
13 Billing Rd
London, ENGLAND SW10

Rainer, Luise (Actor)
54 Eaton Square
London SW1, UNITED KINGDOM (UK)

Rainer, Wali (Athlete, Football Player)
4715 Monaco Dr
Sandston, VA 23150-3205, USA

Raines, Cristina
6399 Wilshire Blvd Ste 414
Los Angeles, CA 90048-5716

Raines, Franklin D (Financier, Government Official)
3900 Wisconsin Ave NW
Washington, DC 20016-2806, USA

Raines, Mike (Athlete, Football Player)
5238 Summit Lake Dr
Jacksonville, FL 32258-3325, USA

Raines, Timothy (Tim) (Athlete, Baseball Player)
1242 Saint Albans Loop
Lake Mary, FL 32746-1978, USA

Rainey, Chuck (Athlete, Baseball Player)
6484 Del Cerro Blvd
San Diego, CA 92120-4804, USA

Rainey, Matt (Journalist)
1 Star Ledger Plz
Newark, NJ 07102-1200, USA

Rains, Dan (Athlete, Football Player)
2509 Wigwam Rd
Aliquippa, PA 15001-4340, USA

Rains, Luce (Actor, Producer)
c/o Andrew Stawiarski *ADS Management*
269 S Beverly Dr # 441
Beverly Hills, CA 90212-3851, USA

Rainwater, G L (Business Person)
1901 Chouteau Ave
Saint Louis, MO 63103-3003, USA

Rainwater, Gregg (Actor)
PO Box 291836
Los Angeles, CA 90029-8836, USA

Rainwater, Keech (Musician)
1222 16th Ave S Ste 23
Nashville, TN 37212-2926, USA

Rainwater, Marvin (Musician)
36968 295th St
Aitkin, MN 56431-4374, USA

Raisa, Francia (Actor)
c/o Faras Rabadi *Emerald Talent Group*
10 Universal City Plz Fl 20
Universal City, CA 91608-1074, USA

Raitt, Bonnie L (Musician, Songwriter, Writer)
c/o Staff Member *Paradigm (Monterey)*
404 W Franklin St
Monterey, CA 93940-2303, USA

Raj, Prakash (Actor)
183 Bharathidasan Street Baskar Colony Virugambakka
Chennai, TN 600 092, INDIA

Raja (Actor)
6 Ranjith Road Kotturpuram
Chennai, TN 600 085, INDIA

Rajasulochana (Actor, Bollywood)
70 N G Chetty Road T Nagar
Chennai, TN 600017, INDIA

Rajat, Kapoor (Actor, Bollywood)
Unit No 140 Andheri Indl Est Off Veera Desai Road Andheri (W)
Mumbai, MS 400053, INDIA

Rajeev (Actor)
12/V Ambedkar Street Gandhi Nagar Saligramam
Chennai, TN 600 093, INDIA

Rajeevi (Actor, Bollywood)
32 Raman Street T Nagar
Chennai, TN 600017, INDIA

Rajendran, S S (Actor)
3/3 Eldams Rd
Chennai, TN 600 018, INDIA

Rajesh (Actor)
7 Kannappa Salai Ashok Nagar
Chennai, TN 600 083, INDIA

Rajinikanth (Actor)
18 Raghava Veera Ave Poes Gdn
Chennai, TN 600 086, INDIA

Rajkiran (Actor, Bollywood)
14 5/5 N Boag Road T Nagar
Chennai, TN 600017, INDIA

Rajkumar, Puru (Actor, Bollywood)
57 Worli Sea Face Worli
Mumbai, MS 400018, INDIA

Rajna, Thomas (Composer, Musician)
10 Wyndover Road Claremont
Cape 7700, SOUTH AFRICA

Rajnikant (Actor, Bollywood)
18 Ragava Veera Avenue Poes Gdn
Madras, TN 600 086, INDIA

Rajsich, Dave (Athlete, Baseball Player)
1605 N Main St
Flagstaff, AZ 86004-4917, USA

Rajsich, Gary (Athlete, Baseball Player)
6510 Charleston Dr
Colleyville, TX 76034-5670, USA

Rajskub, Mary Lynn (Actor, Writer)
c/o Christie Smith *Mosaic Media Group*
9200 W Sunset Blvd Ste 10
Los Angeles, CA 90069-3608, USA

Rajtar, John (Stylist)
5032 17th Ave S
Minneapolis, MN 55417-1212, USA

Rakers, Aaron (Athlete, Baseball Player)
553 W 3rd St
Trenton, IL 62293-1013, USA

Rakers, Jason (Athlete, Baseball Player)
547 Hickory Hollow Dr
Canfield, OH 44406-1052, USA

Rakestraw, Larry (Athlete, Football Player)
2462 Welford Ct
Suwanee, GA 30024-3130, USA

Rakhmonov, Emomali (President)
Supreme Soviet
Dushanbe, TAJIKISTAN

Raki, Laya (Actor)
8040 Ventura Canyon Ave
Panorama City, CA 91402-6313, USA

Rakim (Musician)
156 W 56th St # 400
New York, NY 10019-3800, USA

Rakoczy, Gregg (Athlete, Football Player)
8709 Hidden Green Ln
Tampa, FL 33647-2271, USA

Rakotomavo, Pascal (Prime Minister)
Mahazoarivo
Antananarivo, MADAGASCAR

Rakowski, Mieczyslaw F (Prime Minister)
Ul Poznanska 3
Warsaw 00-680, POLAND

Rales, Steven M (Business Person, Producer)
c/o Staff Member *Indian Paintbrush*
1660 Euclid St
Santa Monica, CA 90404-3724, USA

Rall, J Edward (Doctor)
9901 Longs Mill Rd
Rocky Ridge, MD 21778-8817, USA

Rall, Roberta (Stylist)
38 France St
Norwalk, CT 06851-3820, USA

Rall, Ted (Cartoonist)
901 Mission St
San Francisco, CA 94103-2905, USA

Rall, Tommy (Actor)
6442 Coldwater Canyon Ave Ste 206
North Hollywood, CA 91606-1174, USA

Ralph, Christopher (Actor)
c/o Rich Kaplan *Noble Caplan Abrams*
1260 Yonge St 2nd Floor
Toronto ON M4T 1W6, Canada

Ralston, Bob
17027 Tennyson Pl
Granada Hills, CA 91344-1225

Ralston, Dennis (Tennis Player)
2005 San Vincente Dr
Concord, CA 94519-1018, USA

Ralston, John R (Athlete, Coach, Football Coach, Football Player)
8245 Claret Ct
San Jose, CA 95135-1415, USA

Ralston, Steve (Soccer Player)
CMGI Field 1 Patriot Place
Foxboro, MA 2035, USA

Ram, C Venkata (Doctor)
5323 Harry Hines Blvd
Dallas, TX 75390-7201, USA

Rama IX (King)
Bangakok, THAILAND

Rama Rau, Santha (Writer)
496 Leedsville Rd
Amenia, NY 12501-5820, USA

Ramage, Rob (Athlete, Hockey Player)
16127 Wilson Manor Dr
Chesterfield, MO 63005-4583, USA

Ramahata, Victor (Prime Minister)
PO Box 6004
Antanarivo 101, MADAGASCAR

Ramamurthy, Sendhil (Actor)
c/o Mary Erickson *Levine Okwu Erickson Management*
6363 Wilshire Blvd Ste 300
Los Angeles, CA 90048-5729, USA

Raman, Priya (Actor, Bollywood)
Plot No 69 Part II VGP Sea View Palavakkam
Chennai, TN 600041, INDIA

Raman, Ragha (Actor, Bollywood)
Flat 202 II Floor 167 Eldams Road Teynampet
Chennai, TN 600018, INDIA

Ramani, Karthik (Engineer)
3421 Crawford St
West Lafayette, IN 47906-1196, USA

Ramaphosa, M Cyril (Government Official)
PO Box 782922
Sandton 2416, SOUTH AFRICA

Ramarajan (Actor)
1 Ramakrishna Street T Nagar
Chennai, TN 600 017, INDIA

Ramasami, V. K. (Actor, Bollywood)
26 Tilak Street T Nagar
Chennai, TN 600017, INDIA

Ramazzotti, Eros (Musician)
Via Vittoria Colonna
Milan, ITALY I-20149

Ramba (Actor, Bollywood)
184 Bharathidasan Salai Baskaran Colony Saligramam
Chennai, TN 600092, INDIA

Ramba (Actor)
4 4/1 Navaneethammal Street Saligramam
Chennai, TN 600 093, INDIA

Rambahadur, Limbu (War Hero)
Box 420 Bandar Seri Begawan
Negara Brunei Darussalam, BRUNEI

Rambert, Charles J J (Architect)
179 Rue de Courcelles
Paris 75017, FRANCE

Rambin, Leven (Actor)
c/o Rhonda Price *Gersh (NY)*
41 Madison Ave
New York, NY 10010-2202, USA

Rambis, Kurt (Athlete, Basketball Player, Coach)
20 Chatham
Manhattan Beach, CA 90266-7225, USA

Rambo, David L (Religious Leader)
PO Box 35000
Colorado Springs, CO 80935-3500, USA

Rambo, John (Athlete, Track Athlete)
1847 Myrtle Ave
Long Beach, CA 90806-5613, USA

Rambola, Tony (Musician)
c/o Staff Member *WmE2 (WMA-LA)*
1 William Morris Pl
Beverly Hills, CA 90212-4261, USA

Ramey, Louis (Actor, Comedian)
10839 Union Tpke
Forest Hills, NY 11375-6823, USA

Ramey, Samuel E (Opera Singer)
320 Central Park W
New York, NY 10025-7659, USA

Ramgoolam, Navinchandra (Prime Minister)
85 Sir Seewilsagur Ramgoolam St
Port Louis, MAURITIUS

Ramgoolam, Seewosagur (Prime Minister)
85 Desforges St
Port Louis, MAURITIUS

Ramini, TJ (Actor)
c/o Joel King *Pakula/King & Associates*
9229 W Sunset Blvd Ste 315
Los Angeles, CA 90069-3403, USA

Ramirez, Alex (Athlete, Baseball Player)
PO Box 880
Winter Haven, FL 33882-0880, USA

Ramirez, Allan (Athlete, Baseball Player)
8 Line Drive Rd
Victoria, TX 77905-5414, USA

Ramirez, Aramis (Athlete, Baseball Player)
1440 N Lake Shore Dr Apt 10EG
Chicago, IL 60610-1626, USA

Ramirez, Carolina (Actor)
c/o Gabriel Blanco *Gabriel Blanco Iglesias (Mexico)*
Rio Balsas 35-32 Colonia Cuauhtemoc
DF 6500, Mexico

Ramirez, Cierra (Actor)
c/o Thomas Richards *Corsa Agency, The*
11704 Wilshire Blvd Ste 204
Los Angeles, CA 90025-1510, USA

Ramirez, Dania (Actor, Producer)
c/o Jeff Morrone *Jeff Morrone Entertainment*
9350 Wilshire Blvd Ste 224
Beverly Hills, CA 90212-3204, USA

Ramirez, Edgar (Actor)
c/o Leslie Sloane *Baker Winokur Ryder Public Relations BWR (BWR-NY)*
292 Madison Ave Fl 12
New York, NY 10017-6415, USA

Ramirez, Efren (Actor)
c/o Staff Member *James/Levy/Jacobson Management Inc*
3500 W Olive Ave Ste 1470
Burbank, CA 91505-5514, USA

Ramirez, Erasmo (Athlete, Baseball Player)
3605 S Parton St
Santa Ana, CA 92707-4824, USA

Ramirez, Hanley (Athlete, Baseball Player)
3868 Falcon Ridge Cir
Weston, FL 33331-5015, USA

Ramirez, Horacio (Athlete, Baseball Player)
6424 Queens Court Trce
Mableton, GA 30126-7227, USA

Ramirez, Manny (Athlete, Baseball Player)
13737 NW 18th Ct
Pembroke Pines, FL 33028-2602, USA

Ramirez, Mario (Athlete, Baseball Player)
HC 3 Box 14107
Yauco, PR 698, USA

Ramirez, Michael P (Mike) (Cartoonist)
202 W 1st St
Los Angeles, CA 90012-4105, USA

Ramirez, Milt (Athlete, Baseball Player)
7 Calle Tulio Larrinaga
Mayaguez, PR 00682-2447, USA

Ramirez, Pedro J (Editor)
Calle Pradillo 42
Madrid 28002, SPAIN

Ramirez, Raul (Tennis Player)
Avenida Ruiz 65 Sur Ensenada
Baja California, MEXICO

Ramirez, RaulAvenida Ruiz
65 Sur Ensenada
Baja, California MEXICO

Ramirez, Sara (Actor)
c/o Staff Member *Mitchell K Stubbs & Assoc (MKS)*
8675 Washington Blvd Ste 203
Culver City, CA 90232-7486, USA

Ramirez, Twiggy (Musician)
c/o Staff Member *Mitch Schneider Organization, The*
14724 Ventura Blvd Ste 410
Sherman Oaks, CA 91403-3537, USA

Ramirez Vazquez, Pedro (Architect)
Ave de la Fuentes 170
Mexico City, DF 1900, MEXICO

Ramis, Harold (Actor, Director)
160 Euclid Ave
Glencoe, IL 60022-2107, USA

Ramm, Haley (Actor)
c/o Wendi Niad *Niad Management*
15030 Ventura Blvd Bldg 19STE PMB 860
Sherman Oaks, CA 91403-5470, USA

Rammstein (Music Group, Musician)
c/o Staff Member *Pilgrim Management*
Postfach 540 101
Berlin 10042, Germany

Ramo, Simon (Business Person)
9200 W Sunset Blvd # 401
W Hollywood, CA 90069-3502, USA

Ramon, Haim (Government Official)
Jerusalem 91010, ISRAEL

Ramone, Phil (Musician)
c/o Staff Member *Gorfaine/Schwartz Agency Inc*
4111 W Alameda Ave Ste 509
Burbank, CA 91505-4171, USA

Ramones, The (Music Group)
c/o Gary Kurfirst *Kurfirst/Blackwell Management*
601 W 26th St Fl 11
New York, NY 10001-1101

Ramos, Bobby (Athlete, Baseball Player)
15109 SW 62nd St
Miami, FL 33193-2735, USA

Ramos, Constance (Connie) (Actor, Reality TV Star)
c/o Staff Member *Extreme Makeover: Home Edition*
Endemol Entertainment USA 9225 Sunset Blvd #1100
Los Angeles, CA 90069, USA

Ramos, Diego (Actor)
c/o Gabriel Blanco *Gabriel Blanco Iglesias (Mexico)*
Rio Balsas 35-32 Colonia Cuauhtemoc
DF 6500, Mexico

Ramos, Domingo (Athlete, Baseball Player)
Carr Duarte KM 8 1/2 Licey Al Medio
Santiago, Dominican Republic

Ramos, Fidel (President)
Malacanang Palace
Manila, PHILIPPINES

Ramos, John (Athlete, Baseball Player)
4214 W Leona St
Tampa, FL 33629-7714, USA

Ramos, Jorge (Actor)
c/o Staff Member *Univision*
605 3rd Ave Fl 12
New York, NY 10158-0034, USA

Ramos, Ken (Athlete, Baseball Player)
2107 Settlers Dr
Pueblo, CO 81008-1888, USA

Ramos, Mario (Athlete, Baseball Player)
20228 Mustang Island Cir
Pflugerville, TX 78660-7720, USA

Ramos, Mel (Artist)
5941 Ocean View Dr
Oakland, CA 94618-1842, USA

Ramos, Monica (Musician)
PO Box 535
Taby 183 25, SWEDEN

Ramos, Nathalia (Actor)
c/o Loch Powell *Leverage Management*
3030 Pennsylvania Ave
Santa Monica, CA 90404-4112, USA

Ramos, Pedro (Athlete, Baseball Player)
6637 W 22nd Ln
Hialeah, FL 33016-3916, USA

Ramos, Sarah (Actor)
c/o Staff Member *Abrams Artists Agency (LA)*
9200 W Sunset Blvd PH 11
Los Angeles, CA 90069-3601, USA

Ramos, Tab (Athlete, Soccer Player)
17 Blair Rd
Aberdeen, NJ 07747-1242, USA

Ramos-Horta, Jose (Nobel Prize Laureate)
Rua Sao Lazoro 16 #1
Lisbon 1150, PORTUGAL

Rampling, Charlotte (Actor)
c/o Elisabeth Tanner *ArtMedia*
20 avenue Rapp
Paris 75008, France

Ramsay, Anne
c/o Todd Eisner *Agency for the Performing Arts (APA-LA)*
405 S Beverly Dr Ste 500
Beverly Hills, CA 90212-4425, USA

Ramsay, Bruce
9150 Wilshire Blvd Ste 350
Beverly Hills, CA 90212-3453

Ramsay, Craig (Athlete, Coach, Hockey Player)
9701 NW 58th Ct
Parkland, FL 33076-1829, USA

Ramsay, Gordon (Chef)
1 Catherine Place
London sw1c6dx

Ramsay, John T (Jack) (Athlete, Basketball Player, Coach)
11118 Gulf Shore Dr Apt 904
Naples, FL 34108-1731, USA

Ramsay, Keshu (Director, Filmmaker, Producer)
Maharaja Surajmal 'C' New Versova Link Road Andheri
Bombay, MS 400 058, INDIA

Ramsay, Laymon (Baseball Player)
2417 Princeton Ave SW
Birmingham, AL 35211-3144, USA

Ramsay, Lynne (Cinematographer, Director, Writer)
c/o Jon Rubinstein *Authentic Talent and Literary Management*
45 Main St Ste 1004
Brooklyn, NY 11201-8200, USA

Ramsay, Robert (Athlete, Baseball Player)
264 NW Clay Ct
Pullman, WA 99163-3679, USA

Ramsay, Tana (Chef, Writer)
c/o Staff Member *HarperCollins Publishers*
10 E 53rd St C/O Author Mail Floor 7
New York, NY 10022, USA

Ramsay, Wayne (Athlete, Hockey Player)
Oak River, MB R0K 1T0, Canada

Ramsbottom, Nancy (Golfer)
2216 Parkers Hill Dr
Maidens, VA 23102-2243, USA

Ramsey, Bill (Athlete, Baseball Player)
6301 Village Grove Dr
Memphis, TN 38115-8119, USA

Ramsey, Boniface (Writer)
c/o Staff Member *New City Press*
202 Comforter Blvd
Hyde Park, NY 12538-2977, USA

Ramsey, Cal (Athlete, Basketball Player)
181 Mercer St Ofc
New York, NY 10012-1501, USA

Ramsey, Chuck (Athlete, Football Player)
17519 Martel Rd
Lenoir City, TN 37772-4235, USA

Ramsey, David (Actor)
c/o Staff Member *Agency for the Performing Arts (APA-LA)*
405 S Beverly Dr Ste 500
Beverly Hills, CA 90212-4425, USA

Ramsey, Derrick (Athlete, Football Player)
7805 Arbor Grove Dr Apt 212
Hanover, MD 21076-1903, USA

Ramsey, Fernando (Athlete, Baseball Player)
2501 Sandy Trl
Keller, TX 76248-8490, USA

Ramsey, Garrard S (Buster) (Athlete, Football Player)
613 Georgia Ave
Signal Mountain, TN 37377, USA

Ramsey, Gerrard (Athlete, Football Player)
4102 US Highway 411 S
Maryville, TN 37801-9148, USA

Ramsey, John (Misc)
PO Box 243
Cheboygan, MI 49721-0243, USA

Ramsey, Knox (Athlete, Football Player)
1380 Huntington Trails Pkwy
Westminster, CO 80023-8451, USA

Ramsey, Laura (Actor)
c/o Michael Katcher *Creative Artists Agency (CAA-LA)*
2000 Avenue of the Stars Ste 100
Los Angeles, CA 90067-4705, USA

Ramsey, Logan
12923 Killion St
Sherman Oaks, CA 91401-5421

Ramsey, Marion (Actor)
c/o Aine Leicht *Horror & Hilarity*
Prefers to be contacted via telephone
Los Angeles, CA 90067, USA

Ramsey, Mary (Musician)
9200 W Sunset Blvd Ste 900
Los Angeles, CA 90069-3604, USA

Ramsey, Michael (Mike) (Athlete, Hockey Player)
445 W 79th St
Chanhassen, MN 55317-4505, USA

Ramsey, Mike (Athlete, Baseball Player)
PO Box 262
Harlem, GA 30814-0262, USA

Ramsey, Mike (Athlete, Baseball Player)
11564 92nd Way
Largo, FL 33773-4606, USA

Ramsey, Nate (Athlete, Football Player)
1938 Cambridge St
Philadelphia, PA 19130-1508, USA

Ramsey, Ray (Athlete, Basketball Player)
1721 N Albany St
Springfield, IL 62702-3122, USA

Ramsey, Rick (Stylist)
c/o Staff Member *Ken Barboza Associates*
115 W 30th St Rm 203
New York, NY 10001-4088, USA

Ramsey, Tom (Athlete, Football Player)
4999 Beauchamp Ct
San Diego, CA 92130-2742, USA

Ramsey, Wes (Actor)
c/o Robert Attermann *Abrams Artists Agency (LA)*
9200 W Sunset Blvd PH 11
Los Angeles, CA 90069-3601, USA

Ramsey, William E (Admiral)
825 Bayshore Dr
Pensacola, FL 32507-3497, USA

Ramsey Jr, Frank V (Athlete, Basketball Player, Coach)
150 Givens St
Madisonville, KY 42431-1619, USA

Ramsey Jr, Norman F (Nobel Prize Laureate)
24 Monmouth Ct
Brookline, MA 02446-5634, USA

Ramson, Eason (Athlete, Football Player)
1000 Claudia Ct Apt 39
Antioch, CA 94509-3440, USA

Ran, Shulamit (Composer)
5845 S Ellis Ave
Chicago, IL 60637-1476, USA

Rana, Ashutosh (Actor, Bollywood)
23 Bharat Petroleum Colony Aziz Baug Chembur
Mumbai, MS 400074, INDIA

Rancic, Bill (Reality TV Star)
c/o Marki Costello *Creative Management Entertainment Group (CMEG)*
2050 S Bundy Dr Ste 280
Los Angeles, CA 90025-6128, USA

Rancic, Giuliana (Reality TV Star, Television Host)
c/o Pamela Kohl *3 Arts Entertainment Inc*
9460 Wilshire Blvd Fl 7
Beverly Hills, CA 90212-2713, USA

Rancid (Music Group, Musician)
c/o Staff Member *Leave Home Booking*
1400 Foothill Dr Ste 34
Salt Lake City, UT 84108-2392, USA

Rand, Marvin (Photographer)
4344 Glencoe Ave Unit 5
Marina Del Rey, CA 90292-6410, USA

Rand, Reese Mary (Athlete, Track Athlete)
6650 Los Gatos Rd
Atascadero, CA 93422-3608, USA

Rand, Robert W (Educator)
Neurosciences Institute
Los Angeles, CA 90017, USA

Randa, Joe (Athlete, Baseball Player)
6436 Ensley Ln
Mission Hills, KS 66208-1932, USA

Randall, Alice (Writer)
c/o Staff Member *Houghton Mifflin Company (Trade Division)*
222 Berkeley St Adult Editorial Floor 8
Boston, MA 02116-3764, USA

Randall, Bob (Athlete, Baseball Player)
2105 Hillview Dr
Manhattan, KS 66502-1942, USA

Randall, Carolyn D (Judge)
515 Rusk St
Houston, TX 77002-2600, USA

Randall, Claire (Religious Leader)
10015 W Royal Oak Rd Apt 1214
Sun City, AZ 85351-3164, USA

Randall, Frankie (Boxer)
355 Fish Hatchery Rd # 02
Morristown, TN 37813, USA

Randall, James (Sap) (Athlete, Baseball Player)
158 Heather Ln
Ruston, LA 71270 1165, USA

Randall, Jon (Musician)
4405 Belmont Park Ter
Nashville, TN 37215-3609, USA

Randall, Josh (Actor)
8730 W Sunset Blvd Ste 490
Los Angeles, CA 90069-2248, USA

Randall, Mark (Athlete, Basketball Player)
9851 Jefferson Pkwy Apt F3
Englewood, CO 80112-5973, USA

Randall, Rebel (Actor)
PO Box 1405
Riverside, CA 92502-1405, USA

Randall, Scott (Athlete, Baseball Player)
467 Reed Ct
Goleta, CA 93117-2906, USA

Randall, Theresa (Stylist)
c/o Staff Member *The Docherty Agency - OH*
2044 Euclid Ave
Cleveland, OH 44115-2282, USA

Randall, Tom (Athlete, Football Player)
2521 Park Vista Cir
Ames, IA 50014-4568, USA

Randall Johnson, Nicole (Actor)
c/o Paul M. Brown *New Wave Entertainment (LA)*
2660 W Olive Ave
Burbank, CA 91505-4525, USA

Randazzo, Barbara (Stylist)
PO Box 2725
Montauk, NY 11954-0300, USA

Randazzo, Mike (Actor, Talk Show Host)
c/o Mike Randazzo 3469 West Stones Crossing Road
Greenwood, IN 46143-8564, USA

Randazzo, Tony (Athlete, Baseball Player)
2462 Los Alamos Ct
Las Cruces, NM 88011-1657, USA

Randi, James (Misc)
2941 Fairview Park Dr Ste 105
Falls Church, VA 22042-4526, USA

Randie, John (Athlete, Football Player)
PO Box 489
Harrisonburg, VA 22803-0489, USA

Randle, Betsy
9300 Wilshire Blvd Ste 555
Beverly Hills, CA 90212-3211

Randle, Ervin (Athlete, Football Player)
900 Spring Creek Dr
Grapevine, TX 76051-8269, USA

Randle, John (Football Player)
c/o Staff Member *Seattle Seahawks*
12 Seahawks Way
Renton, WA 98056-1572, USA

Randle, Lenny (Athlete, Baseball Player)
39461 Cozumel Ct
Murrieta, CA 92563-2552, USA

Randle, Lynda (Musician)
5565 NW Barry Road PO Box 236
Kansas City, MO 64154, USA

Randle, Tate (Athlete, Football Player)
11116 Sea Hero Ln
Austin, TX 78748-2918, USA

Randle, Theresa (Actor)
c/o Jason Priluck *Agency Group Ltd, The (LA)*
1880 Century Park E Ste 711
Los Angeles, CA 90067-1618, USA

Randle, Ulmo (Sonny) (Athlete, Football Player)
8 Niblick Ln
Verona, VA 24482-2635, USA

Randolph, A Raymond (Judge)
333 Constitution Ave NW
Washington, DC 20001-2802, USA

Randolph, Alvin (Athlete, Football Player)
319 Roble Ave
Redwood City, CA 94061-3732, USA

Randolph, Carl (Musician)
200 W 57th St Ste 308
New York, NY 10019-3211, USA

Randolph, Jackson H (Business Person)
139 E 4th St
Cincinnati, OH 45202-4003, USA

Randolph, Joyce
295 Central Park W Apt 18A
New York, NY 10024-3024

Randolph, Judson G (Doctor)
111 Michigan Ave NW
Washington, DC 20010-2916, USA

Randolph, Robert (Musician)
c/o Coran Capshaw *Red Light Management (VA)*
PO Box 1467
Charlottesville, VA 22902-1467, USA

Randolph, Sam (Golfer)
1305 Briar Ridge Dr
Keller, TX 76248-8376, USA

Randolph, Stephen (Athlete, Baseball Player)
3706 Apache Forest Dr
Austin, TX 78739-4418, USA

Randolph, Willie L (Athlete, Baseball Player, Coach)
715 Jenny Trl
Franklin Lakes, NJ 07417-2907, USA

Randolph, Zach (Athlete, Basketball Player)
c/o Raymond Brothers *International Athlete Management, Inc*
433 N Camden Dr Ste 600
Beverly Hills, CA 90210-4416, USA

Randrup, Michael (Misc)
10 Fairlawn Road Lythamst Annes
Lancashire FY8 5PT, UNITED KINGDOM (UK)

Rands, Bernard (Composer)
Music Dept
Cambridge, MA 2138, USA

Randy Rogers Band (Music Group, Musician)
c/o Joey Lee *WmE2 (WMA-TN)*
1600 Division St Ste 300
Nashville, TN 37203-2755, USA

Ranew, Merritt (Athlete, Baseball Player)
7611 S Duval Island Dr
Floral City, FL 34436-2905, USA

Ranford, William (Bill) (Athlete, Hockey Player)
633 Poirier St
Coquitlam, BC V3J 6B1, Canada

Ranganathan, Suman (Actor, Bollywood)
Gilder Building Turner Road Bandra
Mumbai, MS 400050, INDIA

Rangel, Charles B (Politician)
74 W 132nd St
New York, NY 10037-3313

Ranger, Doug (Songwriter, Writer)
1921 Broadway
Nashville, TN 37203-2719, USA

Rani (Actor, Bollywood)
Anubhav Apts Arunachalam Road
Chennai, TN 600083, INDIA

Ranis, Gustav (Economist)
7 Mulberry Rd
Woodbridge, CT 06525-1716, USA

Ranjani (Actor, Bollywood)
78/A Moubrews Road Alwarpet
Chennai, TN 600018, INDIA

Ranjeet (Actor, Bollywood)
14 Silver Beach A B Nair Road Juhu
Bombay, MS 400 049, INDIA

Ranki, Dezso (Musician)
OrdogoromLejto 11/B
Budapest 1112, HUNGARY

Rankin, Chris (Actor)
c/o Staff Member *Ken McReddie Ltd*
11 Connaught Pl
London W2 2ET, UNITED KINGDOM

Rankin, Ian (Writer)
c/o Staff Member *St Martins Press*
175 5th Ave
New York, NY 10010-7703, USA

Rankin, Judy (Golfer)
2715 Racquet Club Dr
Midland, TX 79705-7432, USA

Rankin, Kenny (Musician, Songwriter)
c/o Staff Member *Variety Artists International Inc*
793 Higuera St Ste 6
Sn Luis Obisp, CA 93401-0500, USA

Rankin, Rose (Stylist)
107 Routt St
San Antonio, TX 78209-4661, USA

Rankin Jr, Alfred M (Business Person)
5875 Landerbrook Dr
Mayfield Heights, OH 44124-6511, USA

Rankine, Terry (Architect)
1050 Massachusetts Ave
Cambridge, MA 02138-5359, USA

Ranks, Shabba (Musician)
c/o Clifton Dillon *Shang Artist Management*
222 NE 27th St
Miami, FL 33137-4522, USA

Ranney, Helen M (Doctor)
99 Mt Holly Rd
Katonah, NY 10536-3537, USA

Ransdell, Gary (Educator)
President's Office
Bowling Green, KY 42101, USA

Ransey, Kelvin (Athlete, Basketball Player)
3195 Monterey Dr
Tupelo, MS 38801-6817, USA

Ransom, Cody (Athlete, Baseball Player)
12217 E Bluebird Pl
Chandler, AZ 85286-1913, USA

Ransom, Derrick (Athlete, Football Player)
6521 Sparrowood Ct
Indianapolis, IN 46236-8122, USA

Ransom, Jeff (Athlete, Baseball Player)
2131 Curtis St
Berkeley, CA 94702-1815, USA

Ransome, Prunella
59 Frith St
London, ENGLAND W1

Ransone, James (Actor)
c/o Kimberlin Dalehite *Magnolia Entertainment (LA)*
9595 Wilshire Blvd Ste 601
Beverly Hills, CA 90212-2506, USA

Rao, Ashok (Actor)
28 17th Cross Malleswaram
Bangalore, KA, INDIA

Rao, C N Ramchandra (Misc)
JNC President's House Indian Science Institute
Bangalore, KA 560012, INDIA

Rao, Calyampudi R (Mathematician)
29 Old Orchard St
Buffalo, NY 14221-2105, USA

Rao, T Rama (Actor, Bollywood, Director, Filmmaker, Producer)
No 14 1st Balaji Street Balaji Avenue T Nagar
Madras, TN 600 017, INDIA

Raoul, Dale (Actor)
c/o Staff Member *JC Robbins Management*
113 S Kilkea Dr
Los Angeles, CA 90048-3525, USA

Rapace, Noomi (Actor)
c/o Jenny Planthaber *Agentfirman Planthaber/Kilden*
Drottninggatan 55
Stockholm 11121, SWEDEN

Rapada, Clay (Athlete, Baseball Player)
37224 Summerglen Ave
Murrieta, CA 92563-5070, USA

Rapaport, Michael (Actor)
c/o Suzan Bymel *Management 360*
9111 Wilshire Blvd
Beverly Hills, CA 90210-5508, USA

Raper, Kenneth B (Misc)
602 N Segoe Rd
Madison, WI 53705-3138, USA

Raphael (Actor)
16125 NE 18th Ave
North Miami Beach, FL 33162-4749, USA

Raphael, Fredric M (Writer)
Largadeile Saint Lauraent la Vallee
Belves 24170, FRANCE

Raphael, June Diane (Actor, Writer)
c/o Jon Rubinstein *Authentic Talent and Literary Management*
45 Main St Ste 1004
Brooklyn, NY 11201-8200, USA

Raphael, Sally Jessy (Entertainer)

Raposo, Greg (Musician)
PO Box 434
Glen Head, NY 11545-0434

Rapp, Anthony (Actor)
c/o Elise Konialian *Untitled Entertainment (NY)*
322 8th Ave Ste 601
New York, NY 10001-6715, USA

Rapp, Pat (Athlete, Baseball Player)
2554 Pete Seay Rd
Sulphur, LA 70663-9377, USA

Rapp, Vern (Athlete, Baseball Player, Coach)
1559 Redwing Ln
Broomfield, CO 80020-0614, USA

Rappa, Tamara (Stylist)
c/o Staff Member *Exclusive Artists Mgmt*
7700 W Sunset Blvd Ste 205
Los Angeles, CA 90046-3913, USA

Rappaport, Sheeri (Actor)
c/o Paul Greenstone *Paul Greenstone Entertainment*
3008 Sorrelwood Dr
San Ramon, CA 94582-5008, USA

Rappeneau, Jean-Paul (Director)
24 Rue Henri Barbusse
Paris 75005, FRANCE

Rapping 4-Tay (Musician)
1800 Argyle Ave # 408
Los Angeles, CA 90028-5253, USA

Rappuoli, Rino (Scientist)
Via Fiorentina 1
Siena 53100, ITALY

Rapuano, Ed (Baseball Player)
10815 Japonica Ct
Boca Raton, FL 33498-4839, USA

Rapuano, Ed (Athlete, Baseball Player)
10815 Japonica Ct
Boca Raton, FL 33498-4839, USA

Rare, Vanessa (Actor)
c/o Staff Member *Auckland Actors*
PO Box 56460 Dominion Road
Auckland, NEW ZEALAND

Rarick, Cindy (Golfer)
PO Box 30001
Tucson, AZ 85751-0001, USA

Rasa Don (Musician)
1325 Avenue of the Americas
New York, NY 10019-6026, USA

Rasby, Walter (Athlete, Football Player)
6413 Brookbury Ct
Charlotte, NC 28226-6131, USA

Rascal, Dizzee (Musician)
c/o Peter Elliot *Primary Talent International (UK)*
The Primary Building 10-11 Jockeys Fields
London WC1R 4BN, UK

Rascal Flatts (Music Group)
c/o Clarence Spalding *Spalding Entertainment*
1025 16th A S Suite 393
Nashville, TN 37212, USA

Rasche, David (Actor)
c/o Brian Liebman *Liebman Entertainment*
25 E 21st St PH
New York, NY 10010-6226, USA

Raschke, Kaylynn (Stylist)
PO Box 392
New York, NY 10108-0392, USA

Rascoe, Robert (Bobby) (Athlete, Basketball Player)
523 Sumpter Ave
Bowling Green, KY 42101-3750, USA

Rascon, Alfred V (War Hero)
10397 Derby Dr
Laurel, MD 20723-5743, USA

Rash, Jim
c/o Jeff Morrone *Jeff Morrone Entertainment*
9350 Wilshire Blvd Ste 224
Beverly Hills, CA 90212-3204, USA

Rash, Steve (Director)
c/o Staff Member *Gersh (LA)*
9465 Wilshire Blvd Ste 600
Beverly Hills, CA 90212-2612, USA

Rashad, Ahmad (Athlete, Football Player)
13220 Verdun Dr
Palm Beach Gardens, FL 33410-1472, USA

Rashad, Phylicia (Actor)
c/o Johnnie Planco *Parseghian Planco LLC*
322 8th Ave Ste 601
New York, NY 10001-6715, USA

Rasheeda (Musician)
c/o Staff Member *International Creative Management (ICM-LA)*
10250 Constellation Blvd Fl 7
Los Angeles, CA 90067-6207, USA

Rashid, Karim (Designer)
357 W 17th St
New York, NY 10011-5060, USA

Rashnikov, Viktor (Business Person)
92 Kirov St
Magnitogorsk, Chelyabinsk
region 455002, Russia

Rasi (Actor, Bollywood)
28B Main Road Zakkaria Colony
Saligramam
Chennai, TN 600094, INDIA

Raskin, Alex (Journalist)
202 W 1st St
Los Angeles, CA 90012-4105, USA

Rasley, Rocky (Athlete, Football Player)
1918 S Mills Ave Apt 4
Lodi, CA 95242-4475, USA

Rasmussen, Anders Fogh (Prime Minister)
prins Jorgens Gard 11
Copenhagen K 2000, DENMARK

Rasmussen, Blair (Athlete, Basketball Player)
3258 74th Ave SE
Mercer Island, WA 98040-3419, USA

Rasmussen, Dennis (Athlete, Baseball Player)
PO Box 547341
Orlando, FL 32854-7341, USA

Rasmussen, Eris (Athlete, Baseball Player)
237 SW 45th St
Cape Coral, FL 33914-5907, USA

Rasmussen, Poul Nyrup (Prime Minister)
Aliegade 6A
Frederiksberg 2000, DENMARK

Rasmussen, Randy (Athlete, Football Player)
3990 114th Ln NW
Coon Rapids, MN 55433-2506, USA

Rasmussen, Randy (Athlete, Football Player)
81 Grumman Hill Rd
Wilton, CT 06897-4508, USA

Rasmussen, Wayne (Athlete, Football Player)
9000 E Maple St
Brandon, SD 57005-1026, USA

Rasner, Darrell (Athlete, Baseball Player)
10712 Misty Meadows Dr
Reno, NV 89521-8234, USA

Raspberry, William J (Journalist)
1150 15th St NW
Washington, DC 20071-0001, USA

Rassas, Nick (Athlete, Football Player)
PO Box 227
Moose, WY 83012-0227, USA

Rasuk, Victor (Actor)
c/o Katherine Atkinson *Washington Square Arts (LA)*
1041 N Formosa Ave Lot Bldg
West Hollywood, CA 90046-6703, USA

Ratchford, Jeremy (Actor)
10100 Santa Monica Blvd Ste 2500
Los Angeles, CA 90067-4116, USA

Ratcliffe, John A (Astronomer)
193 Huntingdon Road
Cambridge CB3 0DL, UNITED KINGDOM (UK)

Ratelle, J G Y Jean (Athlete, Hockey Player)
100 Legends Way Attn Alumniassociation
Boston, MA 02114-1300, USA

Rath, Fred (Athlete, Baseball Player)
7308 Pelican Island Dr
Tampa, FL 33634-7470, USA

Rath, Gary (Athlete, Baseball Player)
15433 Meadow Brook Ct
Gulfport, MS 39503-9465, USA

Rath, Meaghan (Actor)
2101 St Laurent Blvd
Montreal, QC H2X 2T5, CANADA

Rathbone, Jackson (Actor)
c/o Pat Cutler *Cutler Management*
165 Little Park Ln
Los Angeles, CA 90049-4023, USA

Rather, Bo (Athlete, Football Player)
7728 La Jessica Cir
Kalamazoo, MI 49009-7542, USA

Rather, Dan (Correspondent, Television Host)
130 W 42nd St Ste 850
New York, NY 10036-7804, USA

Rathke, Henrich K M H (Religious Leader)
Schleifmuhlenweg 11
Schwering 19061, GERMANY

Rathman, Tom (Athlete, Football Player)
222 Republic Dr
Allen Park, MI 48101-3650, USA

Rathmann, George B (Business Person)
22021 20th Ave SE
Bothell, WA 98021-4406, USA

Rathmann, Jim (Race Car Driver)
14 Marina Isles Blvd # 14G
Indian Harbour Beach, FL 32937-5372, USA

Rathnam, Mani (Bollywood, Director)
3 First Cross Road Venus Colony
Alwarpet, Madras 600018, INDIA

Ratigan, Brian (Athlete, Football Player)
51702 Ashton Ct
Granger, IN 46530-8747, USA

Ratkovicz, George (Athlete, Basketball Player)
1112 Ohstrom Park
Webster, NY 14580-9185, USA

Ratkowski, Ray (Athlete, Football Player)
PO Box 2736
Hyannis, MA 02601-7736, USA

Ratleff, Ed (Athlete, Basketball Player)
4202 Paseo De Oro
Cypress, CA 90630-3420, USA

Ratliff, Don (Athlete, Football Player)
9048 Bay Hill Blvd
Orlando, FL 32819-4880, USA

Ratliff, Gene (Athlete, Baseball Player)
315 Southern Walk Cir
Gray, GA 31032-4528, USA

Ratliff, Jon (Athlete, Baseball Player)
289 Boughton Hill Rd
Honeoye Falls, NY 14472-9706, USA

Ratliff, Theo (Basketball Player)
Rose Garden 1 Center Court St
Portland, OR 97227, USA

Ratliffe, Paul (Athlete, Baseball Player)
78 Campton Pl
Laguna Niguel, CA 92677-4734, USA

Ratner, Brett (Director)
c/o Richard Lovett *Creative Artists Agency (CAA-LA)*
2000 Avenue of the Stars Ste 100
Los Angeles, CA 90067-4705, USA

Ratner, Ellen (Actor, Radio Personality)
c/o Judy Orbach *Judy O Productions*
6136 Glen Holly St
Hollywood, CA 90068-2338, USA

Ratner, Mark A (Misc)
615 Greenleaf Ave
Glencoe, IL 60022-1745, USA

Ratnoff, Oscar D (Doctor)
1801 Chestnut Hills Dr
Cleveland, OH 44106-4626, USA

Rato, Rodrigo (Government Official)
700 19th St NW
Washington, DC 20431-0001, USA

Ratser, Dmitri (Musician)
1401 NE 9th St Apt 38
Fort Lauderdale, FL 33304-4412, USA

Ratsiraka, Didier (Admiral, President)
Iavoloha
Antananarivo, MADAGASCAR

Ratt (Music Group)
11684 Ventura Blvd # 675
Studio City, CA 91604-2699, USA

Ratterman, George (Athlete, Football Player)
4751 E Costilla Ave Apt 115
Centennial, CO 80122-2393, USA

Rattner, Steven (Business Person)
998 5th Ave
New York, NY 10028-0102, USA

Ratushinskaya, Irina B (Writer)
Kuzakova Str 18
Moscow 107005, RUSSIA

Ratzenberger, John (Actor)
9255 W Sunset Blvd Ste 1010
Los Angeles, CA 90069-3307, USA

Ratzer, Steve (Athlete, Baseball Player)
5746 Deer Flag Dr
Lakeland, FL 33811-2001, USA

Ratzinger, Joseph A Cardinal (Religious Leader)
Palazzo del S Uffizio II
Rome 193, ITALY

Rau, Doug (Athlete, Baseball Player)
1615 Treasure Oaks Dr
Katy, TX 77450-5088, USA

Rauch, Bob (Athlete, Baseball Player)
3409 Head River Rd
Virginia Beach, VA 23457-1159, USA

Rauch, Jon (Athlete, Baseball Player)
14081 N Old Forest Trl
Oro Valley, AZ 85755-5789, USa

Rauch, Siegfried (Actor)
c/o Gabriele Frederking *Alexander Agency*
Lamontstrasse 9
Munich D-81679, GERMANY

Raudman, Bob (Athlete, Baseball Player)
440 N 300 W
Tetonia, ID 83452, USA

Rauner-Harrington, Helen (Baseball Player)
2027 Kentucky Ave
Fort Wayne, IN 46805-4442, USA

Raup, David M (Musician)
423 Johnson Dr
Washington Island, WI 54246-9169, USA

Rauschenberg, Robert (Artist)
381 Lafayette St
New York, NY 10003-7022, USA

Rautins, Andy (Athlete, Basketball Player)
c/o Bill Duffy *BDA Sports Management (BDA-CA)*
700 Ygnacio Valley Rd Ste 330
Walnut Creek, CA 94596-3838, USA

Rautins, Leo (Athlete, Basketball Player)
202 Litchfield Dr
Syracuse, NY 13224-2023, USA

Rautio, Nina (Opera Singer)
119 W 57th St Ste 1505
New York, NY 10019-2403, USA

Rautzhan, Lance (Athlete, Baseball Player)
2472 Covington Dr
Myrtle Beach, SC 29579-3123, USA

Raval, Manish (Composer, Musician)
c/o Staff Member *Aperture Music*
PO Box 90010
Pasadena, CA 91109-5010, USA

Ravalec, Blanche (Actor)
6 Square Villaret de Joyeuse
Paris 75017, FRANCE

Ravali (Actor, Bollywood)
159 Thirupathi Nagar Valasaravakkam
Chennai, TN 600087, INDIA

Ravalomanana, Marc (President)
Iavoloha
Antananarivo, MADAGASCAR

Raveena, Tondon (Actor, Bollywood)
Nippon Society Juhu Church
Mumbai, MS 400049, INDIA

Raven, Eddy (Musician, Songwriter, Writer)
PO Box 2476
Hendersonville, TN 37077-2476, USA

Raven, Marion (Musician)
c/o Staff Member *10th Street Entertainment (LA)*
700 N San Vicente Blvd Ste G410
West Hollywood, CA 90069-5060, USA

Raven, Peter H (Misc)
PO Box 299
Saint Louis, MO 63166-0299, USA

Ravensberg, Robert (Athlete, Football Player)
636 Sherwood Dr
Saint Louis, MO 63119-3754, USA

Raver, Kim (Actor)
c/o David (Dave) Fleming *Mosaic Media Group*
9200 W Sunset Blvd Ste 10
Los Angeles, CA 90069-3608, USA

Raver, Lorna

Ravitch, Diane S (Historian)
Press Building Washington Place
New York, NY 10003, USA

Ravony, Francisque (Prime Minister)
Antananarivo, MADAGASCAR

Ravotti, Eric (Athlete, Football Player)
573 Macleod Dr
Gibsonia, PA 15044-8962, USA

Rawail, Rahul (Bollywood, Director, Filmmaker, Producer)
B103 Kailash Juhu Church Road Juhu
Bombay, MS 400 049, INDIA

Rawal, Paresh (Actor, Bollywood, Comedian)
11 Sea Breeze Apartments 12th Road Jvpd Scheme
Bombay, MS 400 049, INDIA

Rawat, Navi (Actor)
c/o Jai Khanna *Brillstein Entertainment Partners*
9150 Wilshire Blvd Ste 350
Beverly Hills, CA 90212-3453, USA

Rawis, Betsy (Golfer)
501 Country Club Dr
Wilmington, DE 19803-2430, USA

Rawley, Shane (Athlete, Baseball Player)
4587 Cherrybark Ct
Sarasota, FL 34241-9213, USA

Rawlings, Adrian (Actor)
91 Regent St
London W1R 7TB, ENGLAND

Rawlings, Pat (Artist)
2200 Space Park Dr Ste 200
Houston, TX 77058-3678, USA

Rawlins, V Lane (Educator)
President S Ofc
Pullman, WA 99164-0001, USA

Rawlinson, Chris (Athlete, Olympic Athlete)
Longford Park Stadium Ryebank Road
Chorlton Cum Hardy, Manchester M21 9TA, UNITED KINGDOM

Rawlinson of Ewell, Peter A G (Government Official)
Wardour Castle Tisbury
Wilts SP3 6RH, UNITED KINGDOM (UK)

Rawls, Betsy (Athlete, Golfer)
101 Lynthwaite Farm Ln
Wilmington, DE 19803-1535, USA

Rawls, Elizabeth E (Betsy) (Golfer)
101 Lynthwaite Farm Ln
Wilmington, DE 19803-1535, USA

Rawls, Sam (Cartoonist)
c/o Staff Member *King Features Syndication*
300 W 57th St Fl 15
New York, NY 10019-5238, USA

Ray, Amy (Musician, Songwriter)
c/o Staff Member *High Road Touring*
751 Bridgeway Fl 2
Sausalito, CA 94965-2174, USA

Ray, Anthony L (Sir Mix-A-Lot) (Musician)
c/o Staff Member *Richard Walters Entertainment, Inc*
PO Box 2789
Toluca Lake, CA 91610-0789, USA

Ray, Chris (Athlete, Baseball Player)
15311 Winding Creek Dr
Tampa, FL 33613-1217, USA

Ray, Darrol (Athlete, Football Player)
13000 Doriath Way
Oklahoma City, OK 73170-2108, USA

Ray, David (Athlete, Football Player)
6962 Bridgewater Dr
Huntington Beach, CA 92647-4023, USA

Ray, Ear (Athlete, Basketball Player)
446 N Lowell St
Casper, WY 82601-2147, USA

Ray, Eddie (Athlete, Football Player)
5319 Avondale Dr
Sugar Land, TX 77479-3814, USA

Ray, Edward J (Educator)
President's Office
Corvallis, OR 97331, USA

Ray, Frankie (Actor)

Ray, Fred Olen (Director)
PO Box 3563
Van Nuys, CA 91407-3563, USA

Ray, James Arthur (Business Person)
PO Box 691689
West Hollywood, CA 90069-9689, USA

Ray, Jimmy (Musician)
35-37 Parkgate Road
London SW11 4NP, UNITED KINGDOM (UK)

Ray, John (Athlete, Football Player)
10 Ranger Ln
Charleston, WV 25309, USA

Ray, Johnny (Athlete, Baseball Player)
20618 Laverton Dr
Katy, TX 77450-1914, USA

Ray, Ken (Athlete, Baseball Player)
6072 Grand Loop Rd
Sugar Hill, GA 30518-8180, USA

Ray, Larry (Athlete, Baseball Player)
2639 E Oakmont Dr
Plainfield, IN 46168, USA

Ray, Lisa (Actor)
c/o Dannielle Thomas *Untitled Entertainment (LA)*
350 S Beverly Dr Ste 200
Beverly Hills, CA 90212-4819, USA

Ray, Marguerite (Actor)
1329 N Vista St Apt 106
Los Angeles, CA 90046-4833, USA

Ray, Rachael (Chef, Talk Show Host)
132 E 43rd St
New York, NY 10017-4019, USA

Ray, Robert D (Ex-Governor)
114 SW 51st St
Des Moines, IA 50312-2142, USA

Ray, Ronald E (War Hero)
2670 Saint Andrews Blvd
Tarpon Springs, FL 34688-6339, USA

Ray, Sugar
c/o Staff Member *Pinnacle Entertainment*
30 Glenn St
White Plains, NY 10603-3254, USA

Ray, Terry (Athlete, Football Player)
42559 Angel Wing Way
Ashburn, VA 20148-5635, USA

Ray, Vanessa (Actor)
c/o Randi Goldstein *Gersh (NY)*
41 Madison Ave
New York, NY 10010-2202, USA

Ray Newman, Jaime (Actor)
c/o Joanna (Joanie) Burstein *Burstein Company, The*
15304 W Sunset Blvd Ste 208
Pacific Palisades, CA 90272-3656, USA

Raybon, Marty (Musician)
15 Music Sq W
Nashville, TN 37203-6200, USA

Raycroft, Andrew (Hockey Player)
c/o Staff Member *Toronto Maple Leafs*
Air Canada Centre 400-40 Bay St
Toronto, ON M5J 2X2, Canada

rayder, franki (Model)
via Zenale, 9
Milano 20123, Italy

Raydon, Curt (Athlete, Baseball Player)
PO Box 124
Jasper, TX 75951-0002, USA

Raye, Collin (Musician)
c/o Dave Fowler *Nashville Artist Management*
Prefers to be contacted via telephone
Nashville, TN, USA

Raye, Lisa (Actor)
c/o Susan Haber *Haber Entertainment*
434 S Canon Dr Apt 204
Beverly Hills, CA 90212-4501, USA

Rayford, Floyd (Athlete, Baseball Player)
11701 Pointe Cir
Fort Myers, FL 33908-2161, USA

Rayhal, Bobby
934A Crescent Blvd
Glenellyn, IL 60137

Rayl, James (Jim) (Athlete, Basketball Player)
201 W Boulevard
Kokomo, IN 46902-2154, USA

Raymer, Cory (Athlete, Football Player)
46629 Hampshire Station Dr
Sterling, VA 20165-7395, USA

Raymo, Maureen (Misc)
Geology Dept
Boston, MA 2215, USA

Raymond, Claude (Athlete, Baseball Player)
3 Rue De La Citiere
Saint-Jean-Sur-Richelieu, QC J2W 1B8, Canada

Raymond, Corey (Athlete, Football Player)
106 Carter St
New Iberia, LA 70560-6214, USA

Raymond, Gary (Actor)
c/o Staff Member *Scott Marshall Partners Ltd*
15 Little Portland St 2nd Floor
London W1W 8BW, UK

Raymond, Guy (Actor)
550 Erskine Dr
Pacific Palisades, CA 90272-4247, USA

Raymond, Jeff
8687 Melrose Ave
West Hollywood, CA 90069-5701, USA

Raymond, Kenneth N (Misc)
Chemistry
Berkeley, CA 94720-0001, USA

Raymond, Lee R (Business Person)
5959 Las Colinas Blvd
Irving, TX 75039-4202, USA

Raymond, Lisa (Tennis Player)
1751 Pinnacle Dr Ste 1500
McLean, VA 22102-3833, USA

Raymond, Paula (Actor)
PO Box 86
Beverly Hills, CA 90213-0086, USA

Raymond, Usher (Actor, Musician)
c/o David Wirtschafter *WmE2 (Endeavor-LA)*
9601 Wilshire Blvd Fl 3
Beverly Hills, CA 90210-5219, USA

Raymonde, Tania (Actor)
c/o Katie Rhodes *Untitled Entertainment (LA)*
350 S Beverly Dr Ste 200
Beverly Hills, CA 90212-4819, USA

Rayner, Chuck
116-5710 201st St
Langley, CANADA BC V3A 8A6

Raynis, Richard (Producer)
c/o Staff Member *Creative Artists Agency (CAA-LA)*
2000 Avenue of the Stars Ste 100
Los Angeles, CA 90067-4705, USA

Raynor, Bruce (Politician)
275 7th Ave
New York, NY 10001-6708, USA

Raynr, David (Actor, Director, Producer)
c/o Simon Millar *Rumble Media*
1620 Broadway Ste C
Santa Monica, CA 90404-2777, USA

Raz, Kavi (Actor)
c/o Staff Member *Almond Talent Agency*
8217 Beverly Blvd Ste 8
Los Angeles, CA 90048-4534, USA

Raz B (Actor, Musician)
c/o Michael (Mike) Esterman
Esterman.Com, LLC
Prefers to be contacted via email
MD, USA

Raza, S Atiq (Business Person)
1 Amd Pl
Sunnyvale, CA 94085-3905, USA

Razafindratandra, Armand Gaetan Cardinal (Religious Leader)
Archeveche Andohalo
Antananarivo 101, MADAGASCAR

Razanamasy, Guy (Prime Minister)
Mahazoarivo
Antananarivo, MADAGASCAR

Razborov, A A (Mathematician)
Mathematics Dept
Princeton, NJ 8540, USA

Raziano, Barry (Athlete, Baseball Player)
1315 4th St
Kenner, LA 70062-7311, USA

Razorlight (Music Group)
364-366 Kensington High St
London W14 8NS, UNITED KINGDOM

Re, Glovanni Battsti Cardinal (Religious Leader)
Palazzo delle Congregazioni Piazza Pio XII #10
Rome 193, ITALY

Rea, Connie (Athlete, Basketball Player)
13 Marina Dr
Winter Haven, FL 33881-9710, USA

Rea, Stephen (Actor, Writer)
c/o Sue Leibman *Barking Dog Entertainment*
9 Desbrosses St Fl 2
New York, NY 10013-1701, USA

Read, Amy (Golfer)
7622 Fall Creek Bnd
Humble, TX 77396-3460, USA

Read, James (Actor)
c/o Staff Member *Pakula/King & Associates*
9229 W Sunset Blvd Ste 315
Los Angeles, CA 90069-3403, USA

Read, Nicolas (Actor)
c/o Carlo Capomazza *Capocom Entertainment*
8970 Norma Pl
Los Angeles, CA 90069-4819, USA

Read, Richard (Journalist)
1320 SW Broadway
Portland, OR 97201-3411, USA

Read, Sister Joel (Educator)
President's Office PO Box 343922
Milwaukee, WI 53234, USA

Readdy, William F (Bill) (Astronaut)
2101 Nasa Pkwy Spc Center
Houston, TX 77058-3607, USA

Reading, John (Musician)
14321 Draft Horse Ln
Wellington, FL 33414-1020, USA

Read-Martin, Dolly
30765 Pacific Coast Hwy # 103
Malibu, CA 90265-3646

Ready, Randy (Athlete, Baseball Player)
4410 Enfield Dr
Dallas, TX 75220-6406, USA

Reagan, Bernice Johnson (Musician)
History Dept
Washington, DC 20016, USA

Reagan, Michael
P.O. Box 6061-405
Sherman Oaks, CA 91412, USA

Reagan, Nancy D (Actor, First Lady)
10880 Wilshire Blvd Ste 870
Los Angeles, CA 90024-4109, USA

Reagan Jr, Ron (Television Host)
c/o Staff Member *MSNBC (NJ)*
NBC/One Microsoft Corporation 1 MSNC Plaza
Secaucus, NJ 7094, USA

Reagor, Montae (Athlete, Football Player)
1511 Drexel Dr
Waxahachie, TX 75165-4409, USA

Real, Roxanne (Musician)
1650 Broadway Ste 508
New York, NY 10019-6833, USA

Real, Terrence (Writer)
754 Massachusetts Ave
Arlington, MA 02476-4712, USA

Reality, Maxim (Musician)
Jenkins Lane Great Hallinsbury
Essex CM22 7QL, UNITED KINGDOM (UK)

Ream, Charles (Athlete, Football Player)
1412 Snowmass Rd
Columbus, OH 43235-2130, USA

Reames, Britt (Athlete, Baseball Player)
806 Dalton Rd
Seneca, SC 29678-3722, USA

Reamon, Tommy (Athlete, Football Player)
709 Galahad Dr
Newport News, VA 23608-1807, USA

Reams, Leroy (Athlete, Baseball Player)
6140 E 17th St
Oakland, CA 94621-4108, USA

Reardon, Jeff (Athlete, Baseball Player)
5 Marlwood Ln
Palm Beach Gardens, FL 33418-6805, USA

Reardon, John (Actor)
c/o Courtney Kivowitz *Schiff Company, The*
8440 Warner Dr Ste B1
Culver City, CA 90232-2461, USA

Reardon, Kerry (Stylist)
580 Broadway Rm 500
New York, NY 10012-5229, USA

Reaser, Elizabeth (Actor)
c/o Perri Kipperman *Kipperman Management*
243 W 72nd St Apt 2
New York, NY 10023-2704, USA

Reason, Rex (Actor)
20105 Rhapsody Rd
Walnut, CA 91789-3533, USA

Reason, Rhodes (Actor)
1339 Trofeo Cir
Palm Springs, CA 92262-5369, USA

Reasons, Gary P (Athlete, Football Player)
805 Glendevon Dr
McKinney, TX 75071-6543, USA

Reaux, Angelina (Opera Singer)
119 W 57th St Ste 1505
New York, NY 10019-2403, USA

Reaves, Ken (Athlete, Football Player)
413 Oakside Dr SW
Atlanta, GA 30331-3724, USA

Reaves, Shawn (Actor)
c/o Claudia Black *Glasser/Black Management*
283 Cedarhurst Ave
Cedarhurst, NY 11516-1671, USA

Reaves, Stephanie (Race Car Driver)
PO Box 55
Bar Mills, ME 04004-0055, USA

Reaves, T Johnson (John) (Athlete, Coach, Football Coach, Football Player)
5716 Bayshore Blvd
Tampa, FL 33611-4726, USA

Reavis, Dave (Athlete, Football Player)
5495 S Newport Cir
Greenwood Village, CO 80111-1601, USA

Rebagliati, Ross
1 Erieview Plz # 1300
Cleveland, OH 44114-1738

Rebardo, Joe (Musician)
8215 Winthrop St
Philadelphia, PA 19136-1914, USA

Rebekah (Musician)
27A Floral St #300
London WC2E 9DQ, UNITED KINGDOM (UK)

Rebel Emergency (Music Group)
c/o Staff Member *Paradigm (Monterey)*
404 W Franklin St
Monterey, CA 93940-2303, USA

Rebennack Jr., Malcolm (Dr. John) (Musician)
c/o Staff Member *Impact Artists Group LLC*
42 Hamilton Ter
New York, NY 10031-6403, USA

Reberger, Frank (Athlete, Baseball Player)
439 Sunset View Ln
Hope, ID 83836-9845, USA

Rebhorn, James (Actor)
145 W 45th St # 1204
New York, NY 10036-4008, USA

Reboulet, Jeff (Athlete, Baseball Player)
7003 Rosecliff Pl
Dayton, OH 45459-1386, USA

Rebowe, Rusty (Athlete, Football Player)
656 Pine St
Norco, LA 70079-2136, USA

Recasner, Eldridge (Athlete, Basketball Player)
6159 164th Ave SE
Bellevue, WA 98006-5613, USA

Recher, Dave (Athlete, Football Player)
970 E Devon Dr
Gilbert, AZ 85296-3620, USA

Rechichar, Albert (Bert) (Athlete, Football Player)
141 W McClain Rd
Belle Vernon, PA 15012-3507, USA

Rechin, Bill (Cartoonist)
235 E 45th St
New York, NY 10017-3305, USA

Rechter, Yacov (Architect)
150 Arlozorov St
Tel Aviv 62098, ISRAEL

Reckell, Peter (Actor)
c/o Staff Member *Rebel Entertainment Partners*
5700 Wilshire Blvd Ste 456
Los Angeles, CA 90036-3648, USA

Reckless Kelly (Music Group)
c/o Staff Member *Paradigm (Monterey)*
404 W Franklin St
Monterey, CA 93940-2303, USA

Records, Max (Actor)
c/o Ara Keshishian *Creative Artists Agency (CAA-LA)*
2000 Avenue of the Stars Ste 100
Los Angeles, CA 90067-4705, USA

Rector, Jeff (Actor)
10153 1/2 Riverside Dr
Toluca Lake, CA 91602-2561, USA

Rector, Milton G (Misc)
288 Monroe Ave
River Edge, NJ 07661-1316, USA

Red Alert, Kool DJ (Musician)
c/o Staff Member *Violator Management*
36 W 25th St Fl 11
New York, NY 10010-2752, USA

Red Hot Chili Peppers (Music Group)
c/o Cliff Burnstein *Q Prime Inc*
729 7th Ave Ste 1600
New York, NY 10019-6880, USA

Redbone, Leon (Musician)
2169 Aquetong Rd
New Hope, PA 18938-1148, USA

Redd, Glen (Athlete, Football Player)
4526 W 1500 N
Ogden, UT 84404-9097, USA

Redd, Michael (Basketball Player)
Bradley Center 1001 N 4th St
Milwaukee, WI 53203, USA

Redden, Barry (Athlete, Football Player)
22503 Diamond Shore Ct
Katy, TX 77450-8053, USA

Reddicliffe, Steven (Editor)
100 Matsonford Rd
Radnor, PA 19087-4559, USA

Redding, Juli
PO Box 1806
Beverly Hills, CA 90213-1806

Redding, Tim (Athlete, Baseball Player)
1801 E Palm Valley Blvd
Round Rock, TX 78664-9469, USA

Reddout, Frank (Athlete, Basketball Player)
379 Niblick Cir
Winter Haven, FL 33881-9572, USA

Reddy, D Raj (Scientist)
Carnegie-Mellon University
Pittsburgh, PA 15213, USA

Reddy, Helen (Musician)
c/o Staff Member *T-Best Talent Agency*
508 Honey Lake Ct
Danville, CA 94506-1237, USA

Redfern, Pete (Athlete, Baseball Player)
12516 Haddon Ave
Sylmar, CA 91342-3636, USA

Redfield, James (Actor, Producer, Writer)
1125 Stoney Ridge Rd
Charlottesville, VA 22902-8719, USA

Redfield, Joe (Athlete, Baseball Player)
307 Glenview Cir
Woodway, TX 76712-3141, USA

Redford, Blair (Actor)
c/o Matt Fletcher *Greene & Associates*
1901 Avenue Of The Stars Ste 130
Los Angeles, CA 90067-6030, USA

Redford, Jamie (Producer)
c/o Jim Ehrich *Rothman Brecher Agency*
9250 Wilshire Blvd Ste 400
Beverly Hills, CA 90212-3397

Redford, Paul (Producer, Writer)
c/o Cori Wellins *WmE2 (Endeavor-LA)*
9601 Wilshire Blvd Fl 3
Beverly Hills, CA 90210-5219, USA

Redford, Robert (Actor, Director)
3101 E Idas Rd
Provo, UT 84604, USA

Redgrave, Corin (Actor)
Primrose Hill Studios Fitzroy Road
London NW1 8TR, UNITED KINGDOM (UK)

Redgrave, Jemma (Actor)
18-21 Jermyn St
London SW1Y 6NB, UNITED KINGDOM (UK)

Redgrave, Vanessa (Actor)
c/o Nicole Caruso *Wolf Kasteler Van Iden & Associates (NY)*
584 Broadway Rm 310
New York, NY 10012-5246, USA

Red-Horse, Valerie (Actor, Director, Producer, Writer)
6028 Calvin Ave
Tarzana, CA 91356-1115, USA

Redick, JJ (Athlete, Basketball Player)
315 E New England Ave Unit 13
Winter Park, FL 32789-4477, USA

Reding, Juli (Actor)
PO Box 1806
Beverly Hills, CA 90213-1806, USA

Redman, Amanda (Actor)
c/o Staff Member *Lip Service Casting Ltd*
60-66 Wardour St
London W1F 0TA, UK

Redman, Dewey (Composer, Musician)
300 Mercer St Apt 3J
New York, NY 10003-6732, USA

Redman, Joshua (Composer, Musician)
323 Broadway
Cambridge, MA 02139-1801, USA

Redman, Joyce (Actor)
34-43 Russell St
London WC2B 5HA, UNITED KINGDOM (UK)

Redman, Magdalen (Baseball Player)
N7780 Vicksburg Way Apt D
Oconomowoc, WI 53066-2016, USA

Redman, Mark (Athlete, Baseball Player)
6818 E 109th St
Tulsa, OK 74133-7153, USA

Redman, Michele (Golfer)
3410 Queensland Ln N
Minneapolis, MN 55447-1153, USA

Redman, Prentice (Athlete, Baseball Player)
106 Jason Dr
Forney, TX 75126-4786, USA

Redman, Susle (Golfer)
137 SW Sarasota Ave
Port Saint Lucle, FL 34952, USA

Redman, Tike (Athlete, Baseball Player)
13838 Bear Creek Rd
Duncanville, AL 35456-2520, USA

Redmann, Teal (Actor)
c/o Amy Abell *Innovative Artists (LA)*
1505 10th St
Santa Monica, CA 90401-2805, USA

Redmayne, Eddie (Actor)
c/o Gene Parseghian *Parseghian Planco LLC*
322 8th Ave Ste 601
New York, NY 10001-6715, USA

Redmon, Glenn (Athlete, Baseball Player)
PO Box 2171
Riverview, FL 33568-2171, USA

Redmond, Marge (Actor)
9200 W Sunset Blvd Ste 1125
Los Angeles, CA 90069-3610, USA

Redmond, Markus (Actor)
c/o Staff Member *Gersh (LA)*
9465 Wilshire Blvd Ste 600
Beverly Hills, CA 90212-2612, USA

Redmond, Marlon (Athlete, Basketball Player)
441 Oak St
San Francisco, CA 94102-5609, USA

Redmond, Michael E (Mickey) (Athlete, Hockey Player)
30699 Harlincin Ct
Franklin, MI 48025-1521, USA

Redmond, Mike (Athlete, Baseball Player)
7321 SW 16th St
Plantation, FL 33317-4963, USA

Redmond, Rudy (Athlete, Football Player)
17091 Melrose St
Southfield, MI 48075-4260, USA

Redmond, Wayne (Athlete, Baseball Player)
18061 Sussex St
Detroit, MI 48235-2835, USA

Rednikova, Yekaterina (Actor)
c/o Larry Hummel 358 North Gardner St
Los Angeles, CA 90036, USA

Redpath, Jean (Musician)
Sunny Knowe Promenade
Leven, Fife, SCOTLAND

Redstone, Summer M (Business Person)
1515 Broadway
New York, NY 10036-8901, USA

Redstone, Sumner (Business Person)
c/o Staff Member *Viacom Entertainment Group*
5555 Melrose Ave
Los Angeles, CA 90038-3989

Redus, Gary (Athlete, Baseball Player)
2202 Mallard Ln SE
Decatur, AL 35601-6759, USA

Redwine, Jarvis J (Athlete, Football Player)
2707 W 79th St
Inglewood, CA 90305-1033, USA

Redwine, Tim
3518 Cahuenga Blvd W # 200
Los Angeles, CA 90068-1304

Reece, Beasley (Athlete, Football Player, Sportscaster)
17 Stirling Way
Lumberton, NJ 08048-5207, USA

Reece, Bob (Athlete, Baseball Player)
3106 Castlewood Cir
Pollock Pines, CA 95726-9522, USA

Reece, Carmen (Musician)
c/o Mark Feist *Real MF Ltd*
22425 Ventura Blvd # 179
Woodland Hills, CA 91364-1524, USA

Reece, Carole (Stylist)
c/o Staff Member *Talent Plus*
1222 Lucas Ave Ste 300
Saint Louis, MO 63103-1937, USA

Reece, Daniel (Danny) (Athlete, Football Player)
5519 S Corning Ave
Los Angeles, CA 90056-1302, USA

Reece, Gabrielle (Gabby) (Athlete, Model, Volleyball Player)
c/o Lisa Shotland *Creative Artists Agency (CAA-LA)*
2000 Avenue of the Stars Ste 100
Los Angeles, CA 90067-4705, USA

Reece, John (Athlete, Football Player)
5927 Cape Hatteras Dr
Houston, TX 77041-5911, USA

Reece, Thomas L (Business Person)
280 Park Ave
New York, NY 10017-1216, USA

Reed, Alvin (Athlete, Football Player)
3910 Abbeywood Dr
Pearland, TX 77584-4943, USA

Reed, Alyson (Actor)
c/o Christopher Black *Opus Entertainment*
5225 Wilshire Blvd Ste 905
Los Angeles, CA 90036-4353, USA

Reed, Andre D (Athlete, Football Player)
16 Gypsy Ln
East Aurora, NY 14052-2108, USA

Reed, Ben
c/o Staff Member *AKA Talent Agency*
6310 San Vicente Blvd Ste 200
Los Angeles, CA 90048-5488, USA

Reed, Bob (Athlete, Baseball Player)
42519 Lake Hospitality Ln
Altoona, FL 32702-9584, USA

Reed, Bruce (Writer)
c/o Staff Member *Public Affairs Books*
1094 Flex Dr
Jackson, TN 38301-5070, USA

Reed, Chad (Motorcycle Racer)
c/o Staff Member *Rockstar Makita Suzuki Factory Racing*
PO Box 27740
Las Vegas, NV 89126-7740, USA

Reed, Crystal (Actor)
c/o Staff Member *Main Title Entertainment*
2225 Wilshire Blvd Suite 500
Los Angeles, CA 90036, USA

Reed, Darren (Athlete, Baseball Player)
8101 Santa Ana Rd
Ventura, CA 93001-9723, USA

Reed, Diana (Beauty Pageant Winner)
PO Box 25
Bettendorf, IA 52722-0001, USA

Reed, Dizzy (Musician)
c/o Joel Miller *Albion Entertainment*
24331 Hatteras St
Woodland Hills, CA 91367, USA

Reed, Ed (Athlete, Football Player)
1 Winning Dr
Owings Mills, MD 21117-4776, USA

Reed, Eddie (Baseball Player)
708 8th Ave S
Great Falls, MT 59405-2052, USA

Reed, Eric (Musician)
300 Mercer St Apt 3J
New York, NY 10003-6732, USA

Reed, Herb (Musician)
990 Massachusetts Ave
Arlington, MA 02476-4532, USA

Reed, Hub (Athlete, Basketball Player)
46601 Garretts Lake Rd
Shawnee, OK 74804-9494, USA

Reed, Jack (Athlete, Baseball Player)
PO Box 728
Tougaloo, MS 39174-0728, USA

Reed, Jeff (Athlete, Baseball Player)
259 Sunrise Dr
Elizabethton, TN 37643-6459, USA

Reed, Jeremy (Athlete, Baseball Player)
977 Hormel Ave
La Verne, CA 91750-3240, USA

Reed, Jerry (Athlete, Baseball Player)
13964 106th Ave
Largo, FL 33774-4543, USA

Reed, Jody (Athlete, Baseball Player)
17299 Solie Rd
Odessa, FL 33556-1943, USA

Reed, Joe (Athlete, Football Player)
106 Whitechapel Ct
Cedar Park, TX 78613-3219, USA

Reed, John H (Ex-Governor)
410 O St SW
Washington, DC 20024-2239, USA

Reed, John S (Financier)
399 Park Ave
New York, NY 10022-4614, USA

Reed, Johnny (Musician)
7251 Lowell Dr # 200
Overland Park, KS 66204-1840, USA

Reed, Keith (Athlete, Baseball Player)
513A S Main St
Rolesville, NC 27571-9666, USA

Reed, Kira
PO Box 251255
Los Angeles, CA 90025-9755

Reed, Lou (Actor, Composer, Musician, Songwriter)
c/o Tom Sarig *Esther Creative Group*
27 W 24th St Ste 404
New York, NY 10010-3289, USA

Reed, Margaret
524 W 57th St # 5330
New York, NY 10019-2930

Reed, Mark A (Doctor)
Electrical Engineering Dept PO Box 2157
New Haven, CT 6520, USA

Reed, Nikki (Actor, Producer, Writer)
c/o Amy Zvi *Thruline Entertainment*
9250 Wilshire Blvd Ground Fl
Beverly Hills, CA 90212, USA

Reed, Oscar (Athlete, Football Player)
700 Elizabeth Ln
Minneapolis, MN 55411-3340, USA

Reed, Pamela (Actor)
1505 10th St
Santa Monica, CA 90401-2805, USA

Reed, Peyton (Actor, Director, Producer)
c/o Staff Member *Moxie Pictures*
5890 W Jefferson Blvd Ste A
Los Angeles, CA 90016-3161, USA

Reed, Rex (Critic)
1 W 72nd St Apt 86
New York, NY 10023-3425, USA

Reed, Richard A (Rick) (Baseball Player)
86 Private Dr 8323
Proctorville, OH 45669-7914, USA

Reed, Richard J (Misc)
Atmospheric Sciences
Seattle, WA 98195-0001, USA

Reed, Rick (Athlete, Baseball Player)
9604 County Road 107 Unit 7
Proctorville, OH 45669-8023, ISA

Reed, Rick (Athlete, Baseball Player)
4938 Crestone Way
Rochester, MI 48306-1682, USA

Reed, Robert (Athlete, Football Player)
21 Wells St
Saratoga Springs, NY 12866-1218, USA

Reed, Ronald L (Ron) (Athlete, Baseball Player, Basketball Player)
2613 Cliffview Dr SW
Lilburn, GA 30047-4794, USA

Reed, Royce (Actor)
c/o Dominic Friesen *Bridge and Tunnel Communications*
9157 W Sunset Blvd
West Hollywood, CA 90069-3127, USA

Reed, Shanna (Actor)
1327 Brinkley Ave
Los Angeles, CA 90049-3619, USA

Reed, Steve (Athlete, Baseball Player)
5335 Pine Ridge Rd
Golden, CO 80403-8030, USA

Reed, Thomas C (Government Official)
PO Box 2240
Healdsburg, CA 95448-2240, USA

Reed, Tony (Athlete, Football Player)
4551 W 107th St Attn Applebee's Human Resources Dept
Overland Park, KS 66207, USA

Reed, Walter
3400 Paul Sweet Rd Unit B209
Santa Cruz, CA 95065-1552

Reed, Willis (Jake) (Athlete, Football Player)
PO Box 1848
Frisco, TX 75034-0031, USA

Reed Jr, Alan
3455 Laurelvale Dr
Studio City, CA 91604-4135, USA

Reed Jr, Willis (Athlete, Basketball Player, Coach)
1250 Poydras St Attn Vp
New Orleans, LA 70113-1804, USA

Reeds, Mark (Athlete, Hockey Player)
7823 Cardinal Ridge Ct
Saint Louis, MO 63119-5014, USA

Reedus, Norman (Actor, Model)
c/o Staff Member *ROAR (LA)*
9701 Wilshire Blvd Fl 8
Beverly Hills, CA 90212-2008, USA

Reel & Reel
Box 480 High Wycombe
Bucks., ENGLAND PH12 4LH

Reep, Jon (Actor, Comedian)
c/o Kara Welker *Generate Management*
1545 26th St Ste 200
Santa Monica, CA 90404-3554, USA

Rees, Andrew (Opera Singer)
4 Addison Bridge Place
London W14 8XP, UNITED KINGDOM (UK)

Rees, Angharad (Actor)
21 Golden Square
London W1R 3PA, UNITED KINGDOM (UK)

Rees, Dai (Designer, Fashion Designer)
c/o Staff Member *Dai Rees*
6 Blackstock Mews Blackstock Road
London, England N42BT, United Kingdom

Rees, Eberhard (Physicist)
69 Revere Way
Huntsville, AL 35801-2847, USA

Rees, Jed (Actor)
c/o Staff Member *Elizabeth Hodgson Management Group*
1688 Cypress St Suite 405
Vancouver, BC V6J 5J1, Canada

Rees, John (Musician)
PO Box 124
Round Corner, NSW 2158, USA

Rees, Martin J (Astronomer)
Astronomy Institute
Cambridge CB2 1ST, UNITED KINGDOM (UK)

Rees, Mina (Mathematician)
301 E 66th St
New York, NY 10065-6205, USA

Rees, Norma S (Educator)
President's Office
Hayward, CA 94542, USA

Rees, Roger (Actor)
1505 10th St
Santa Monica, CA 90401-2805, USA

Rees Jr, Clifford H (Ted) (General)
1620 Mayflower Ct Apt B414
Winter Park, FL 32792-2571, USA

Reese, Brian Adrian (Cassidy) (Musician)
c/o Greg Cohen *Amalgam Management*
3564 Piedmont Rd NE Apt 306
Atlanta, GA 30305-1597, USA

Reese, Calvin (Pokey) (Athlete, Baseball Player)
12416 Sylvan Oak Way
Charlotte, NC 28273-4728, USA

Reese, Della (Actor, Musician)
1910 Bel Air Rd
Los Angeles, CA 90077-2727, USA

Reese, Eddie (Coach, Swimmer)
Athletic Dept
Austin, TX 78712, USA

Reese, Guy (Athlete, Football Player)
2409 Cardinal Way
McKinney, TX 75070-5966, USA

Reese, Izell (Athlete, Football Player)
10270 Willeo Creek Trce
Roswell, GA 30075-3269, USA

Reese, Kevin (Athlete, Baseball Player)
1221 Willow St
San Diego, CA 92106-2538, USA

Reese, Rich (Athlete, Baseball Player)
PO Box 2339
Carefree, AZ 85377-2339, USA

Reese, Steve (Athlete, Football Player)
1146 Parkwood Trce
Stone Mountain, GA 30083-2485, USA

Reeser, Autumn (Actor)
c/o Staff Member *Kritzer Levine Wilkins Entertainment*
11872 La Grange Ave Fl 1
Los Angeles, CA 90025-5283, USA

Rees-Jones, Trevor
Oswestry
Shropshire, ENGLAND

Rees-Mogg of Hinton Bleweet, William (Publisher)
3 Smith Square
London SW1, UNITED KINGDOM (UK)

Reeves, Bryant (Athlete, Basketball Player)
116458 S 4710 Rd
Muldrow, OK 74948-6882, USA

Reeves, Dan (Athlete, Football Player)
785 W Conway Dr NW
Atlanta, GA 30327-3633, USA

Reeves, Diane
PO Box 66
Englishtown, NJ 07726-0066

Reeves, Dianne (Musician)
PO Box 66
Englishtown, NJ 07726-0066, USA

Reeves, Julie
PO Box 300
Russell, KY 41169-0300

Reeves, Keanu (Actor)
c/o Erwin Stoff *3 Arts Entertainment Inc*
9460 Wilshire Blvd Fl 7
Beverly Hills, CA 90212-2713, USA

Reeves, Khalid (Athlete, Basketball Player)
11519 140th St
Jamaica, NY 11436-1018, USA

Reeves, Martha (Musician)
14608 Annapolis Dr
Sterling Hts, MI 48313-3616, USA

Reeves, Melissa
6520 Platt Ave # 634
West Hills, CA 91307-3218

Reeves, Perrey (Actor)
c/o Sarah Lum *Leverage Management*
3030 Pennsylvania Ave
Santa Monica, CA 90404-4112, USA

Reeves, Richard (Misc)
4520 Main St
Kansas City, MO 64111-1876, USA

Reeves, Rodrick (Stylist)
c/o Staff Member *Ford Models (Chicago)*
311 W Superior St
Chicago, IL 60654-3548, USA

Reeves, Ronna
5114 Albert Dr
Brentwood, TN 37027-6810

Reeves, Sarah Gore (Stylist)
c/o Staff Member *Art House Management*
1548 16th St
Santa Monica, CA 90404-3309, USA

Reeves, Saskia (Actor)
Julian House 4 Windmill St
London W1P 1HF, UNITED KINGDOM (UK)

Reeves, Scott (Actor)
6520 Platt Ave # 634
West Hills, CA 91307-3218, USA

Reeves, Walter (Athlete, Football Player)
PO Box 16171
Fort Worth, TX 76162-0171, USA

Refaeli, Bar (Actor, Model)
c/o Scott Lipps *One Model Management*
42 Bond St Apt 2
New York, NY 10012-2428, USA

Regaibuto, Joe (Actor)
724 24th St
Santa Monica, CA 90402-3138, USA

Regalado, Rudy (Athlete, Baseball Player)
PO Box 475
Borrego Springs, CA 92004-0475, USA

Regalbuto, Joe
724 24th St
Santa Monica, CA 90402-3138

Regan, Brian (Actor, Comedian)
c/o Staff Member *WmE2 (Endeavor-LA)*
9601 Wilshire Blvd Fl 3
Beverly Hills, CA 90210-5219, USA

Regan, Bridget (Actor)
c/o Staff Member *TMT Entertainment Group*
648 Broadway Ste 1002
New York, NY 10012-2348, USA

Regan, Chris (Writer)
c/o Staff Member *Gersh (LA)*
9465 Wilshire Blvd Ste 600
Beverly Hills, CA 90212-2612, USA

Regan, Donald T
240 McLaws Cir Ste 142
Williamsburg, VA 23185-6429, USA

Regan, Gerald A (Government Official)
PO Box 828 Station B
Ottawa, ON K1P 5P9, CANADA

Regan, Judith (Talk Show Host, Writer)
c/o Staff Member *Regan Media*
10100 Santa Monica Blvd Fl 10
Los Angeles, CA 90067-4003, USA

Regan, Laura (Actor)
c/o Staff Member *TMT Entertainment Group*
648 Broadway Ste 1002
New York, NY 10012-2348, USA

Regan, Philip R (Phil) (Athlete, Baseball Player, Coach)
1249 Coopers Pass SW
Byron Center, MI 49315-6927, USA

Regas, Karen (Stylist)
3573 Linden Ln
Coconut Grove, FL 33133-5614, USA

Regazzoni, Clay (Race Car Driver)
Via Monzoni 13
Lugano 6900, SWITZERLAND

Regehr, Duncan (Actor)
2501 Main St
Santa Monica, CA 90405, USA

Regen, Elizabeth (Actor)
c/o Mark Measures *Abrams Artists Agency (LA)*
9200 W Sunset Blvd PH 11
Los Angeles, CA 90069-3601, USA

Reger, John (Athlete, Football Player)
14028 Capitol Dr
Tampa, FL 33613-2110, USA

Reger, Nate (Writer)
c/o Staff Member *International Creative Management (ICM-LA)*
10250 Constellation Blvd Fl 7
Los Angeles, CA 90067-6207, USA

Reggiani, Serge (Actor, Musician)
4 Ave Hoche
Paris 75008, FRANCE

Reggio, Godfrey (Director)
PO Box 2404
Santa Fe, NM 87504-2404, USA

Reghanti, Noel (Stylist)
c/o Staff Member *Artist Untied (LA)*
845 S Mansfield Ave Apt 1
Los Angeles, CA 90036-4979, USA

Regilio, Nick (Athlete, Baseball Player)
6505 Raham Ct
Port Orange, FL 32128-6069, USA

Regina, Paul
2911 Canna St
Thousand Oaks, CA 91360-1418

Regine (Business Person)
502 Park Ave
New York, NY 10022-1108, USA

Regis, John (Athlete, Track Athlete)
67 Fairby Road
London SE12, UNITED KINGDOM (UK)

Regner, Tom (Athlete, Football Player)
2231 Big Trail Cir
Reno, NV 89521-8957, USA

Regnier, Charles (Actor, Director)
Neherstr 7
Munich 81675, GERMANY

Rehberg, Scott (Athlete, Football Player)
1120 Kittiwake Dr
Venice, FL 34285-6614, USA

Rehder, Tom (Athlete, Football Player)
181 Rim Rock Rd
Nipomo, CA 93444, USA

Rehm, Diane (Radio Personality)
c/o Staff Member *National Public Radio (NPR)*
635 Massachusetts Ave NW Ste 1
Washington, DC 20001-3753, USA

Rehm, Fred (Athlete, Basketball Player)
19340A Stonehedge Dr
Brookfield, WI 53045-3665, USA

Rehm, Jack D (Publisher)
19 Neponset Ave # 9A
Old Saybrook, CT 06475-3107, USA

Rehm Jr, Daniel R (War Hero)
1043 Del Norte St
Houston, TX 77018-1422, USA

Rehn, Trista (Reality TV Star)
42 Meadow Dr
Vail, CO 81657, USA

Rehr, Frank (Cartoonist)
200 Madison Ave
New York, NY 10016-3903, USA

Rehrer-Carteaux, Rita (Baseball Player)
3210 Kenwood Ave
Fort Wayne, IN 46805-2932, USA

Reich, Charles A (Educator, Lawyer)
225 Park Ave S
New York, NY 10003-1604, USA

Reich, Doris (Stylist)
882 Carroll St
Brooklyn, NY 11215-1702, USA

Reich, Frank M (Athlete, Football Player)
12551 Glendurgan Dr
Carmel, IN 46032-8314, USA

Reich, Herm (Athlete, Baseball Player)
PO Box 1249
Bonsall, CA 92003-1249, USA

Reich, Jason (Writer)
c/o Staff Member *Kaplan Stahler Agency*
8383 Wilshire Blvd Ste 923
Beverly Hills, CA 90211-2443, USA

Reich, John (Director)
724 Bohemia Pkwy
Sayville, NY 11782-3300, USA

Reich, Robert B (Secretary)
1230 Bonita Ave
Berkeley, CA 94709-1923, USA

Reich, Steve M (Composer)
75 Rockefeller Plz
New York, NY 10019-6908, USA

Reichard, Daniel
c/o Jeff Morrone *Jeff Morrone Entertainment*
9350 Wilshire Blvd Ste 224
Beverly Hills, CA 90212-3204, USA

Reichardt, Bill (Athlete, Football Player)
2935 Sioux Ct
Des Moines, IA 50321-1427, USA

Reichardt, Rick (Athlete, Baseball Player)
2605 NW 90th Ter
Gainesville, FL 32606-6742, USA

Reichel, Robert (Athlete, Hockey Player)
40 Bay St
Toronto, ON M5J 2K2, Canada

Reichenbach, Mike (Athlete, Football Player)
2230 Cloverly Cir
Jamison, PA 18929-1555, USA

Reichert, Dan (Athlete, Baseball Player)
445 Cornell Dr
Turlock, CA 95382-0502, USA

Reichert, Jack F (Business Person)
580 Douglas Dr
Lake Forest, IL 60045-3342, USA

Reichert, Tanja (Actor)
1404-510 W Hastings St
Vancouver, BC V6B 1L8, CANADA

Reichl, Ruth M (Editor)
4 Times Sq
New York, NY 10036-6515, USA

Reichman, Fred (Artist)
1235 Stanyan St
San Francisco, CA 94117-3816, USA

Reichow, Garet N (Athlete, Football Player)
PO Box 822
Tesuque, NM 87574-0822, USA

Reid, Andy (Coach, Football Coach)
1 Novacare Way
Philadelphia, PA 19145-5900, USA

Reid, Antonio (L.A.) (Producer)
c/o Staff Member *Hitco Music Publishing*
500 Bishop St NW Ste A4
Atlanta, GA 30318-4380, USA

Reid, Christopher (Actor)
c/o Rod Baron *Baron Entertainment*
13848 Ventura Blvd Ste A
Sherman Oaks, CA 91423-3654

Reid, Daphne (Actor)
c/o Kevin Suber *Suber Group, The*
PO Box 90062
Los Angeles, CA 90009-0062, USA

Reid, Don S (Musician, Songwriter, Writer)
8747 Highway 304
Hernando, MS 38632-8445, USA

Reid, Dorice (Baseball Player)
1165 Via Santa Paulo
Vista, CA 92081-6332, USA

Reid, Elliott
11201 Ventura Blvd
Studio City, CA 91604-3136, USA

Reid, Harold W (Musician, Songwriter, Writer)
8747 Highway 304
Hernando, MS 38632-8445, USA

Reid, J R (Athlete, Basketball Player)
121 Cemetary St
Chester, SC 29706-1620, USA

Reid, Jesse (Athlete, Baseball Player)
2641 Carey Station Rd
Greensboro, GA 30642-2625, USA

Reid, Joe (Athlete, Football Player)
651 Shady Hollow St
Houston, TX 77056-1635, USA

Reid, Michael B (Mike) (Athlete, Composer, Football Player)
825 Overton Ln
Nashville, TN 37220-1515, USA

Reid, Mike (Golfer)
1220 Chadwick Dr
Westminster, MD 21158-6124, USA

Reid, Mike (Athlete, Football Player)
PO Box 362
Pacolet, SC 29372-0362, USA

Reid, Norman R (Misc)
50 Brabourne Rise Park Langley
Beckenham
Kent, UNITED KINGDOM (UK)

Reid, Odgen R (Diplomat, Journalist)
Ophir Hill
Purchase, NY 10577, USA

Reid, Ogden
Ophir Hill
Purchase, NY 10577

Reid, Scott (Athlete, Baseball Player)
10827 S 26th Ave
Phoenix, AZ 85041-9630, USA

Reid, Stephen E (Steve) (Athlete, Doctor, Football Player)
1784 Locust St
Des Plaines, IL 60018-2234, USA

Reid, Tara (Actor)
c/o Darris Hatch *Daris Hatch Management*
10027 Rossbury Pl
Los Angeles, CA 90064-4825, USA

Reid, Terry (Musician)
PO Box 343
Burbank, CA 91503-0343, USA

Reid, Tim (Actor, Director)
c/o Sandra Joseph *SLJ Management*
833 N Edinburgh Ave Ph 11
Los Angeles, CA 90046-6999, USA

Reid, William J (Athlete, Football Player)
315 Ramona St
Palo Alto, CA 94301-1440, USA

Reifsnyder, Robert H (Bob) (Athlete, Football Player)
4 Helm Ct
Berlin, MD 21811-1836, USA

Reightler Jr, Kenneth S (Astronaut)
1602 Honeysuckle Ridge Ct
Annapolis, MD 21401-6425, USA

Reihner, George (Athlete, Football Player)
1010 Electric St
Scranton, PA 18509-1951, USA

Reil, Shannen
PO Box 661
West Van Lear, KY 41268-0661, USA

Reilly, Gabrielle (Model)
PO Box 3145
Shawnee, KS 66203-0145, USA

Reilly, Jennifer
345 N Maple Dr Ste 397
Beverly Hills, CA 90210-5179

Reilly, John (Actor)
c/o Peter Young *Sovereign Talent Group*
8421 Wilshire Blvd Ste 200
Beverly Hills, CA 90211-3204, USA

Reilly, John C (Actor)
c/o Peg Donegan *Framework Entertainment (LA)*
9057 Nemo St Ste C
West Hollywood, CA 90069-5511, USA

Reilly, Kevin (Athlete, Football Player)
1141 Webster Dr
Wilmington, DE 19803-3459, USA

Reilly, Mike (Athlete, Football Player)
708 Loretto Ct
Dubuque, IA 52003-7813, USA

Reilly, Mike (Athlete, Baseball Player)
131 Smithfield Rd
Battle Creek, MI 49015-3545, USA

Reilly, Rick (Writer)
891 14th St Unit 2601
Denver, CO 80202-3272, USA

Reilly, William K (Government Official)
International Studies Institute
Stanford, CA 94305, USA

Reilly II, James F (Astronaut)
15903 Lake Lodge Dr
Houston, TX 77062-4745, USA

Reimer, Dennis J (Denny) (General)
PO Box 889
Oklahoma City, OK 73101-0889, us3

Reimer, Kevin (Athlete, Baseball Player)
PO Box 1111
Arlington, TX 76004-1111, USA

Reimer, Roland (Religious Leader)
8000 W 21st St N
Wichita, KS 67205-1744, USA

Reimers, Bruce (Athlete, Football Player)
2206 W River Dr
Humboldt, IA 50548-2638, USA

Reina (Musician)
c/o Staff Member *Diva Central Inc*
7510 W Sunset Blvd Ste 1445
Los Angeles, CA 90046-3408, USA

Reincke, Heinz
Hof 38
Mondsee, AUSTRIA A-5310

Reineck, Thomas (Athlete)
Graf-Bernadotte-Str 4
Essen 45133, GERMANY

Reiner, Carl (Actor, Director)
c/o Staff Member *Clear Productions*
9171 Wilshire Blvd Ste 350
Beverly Hills, CA 90210-5523, USA

Reiner, ex-DA Ira
1290 Sunset Plaza Dr
Los Angeles, CA 90069-1245

Reiner, John (Cartoonist)
750 3rd Ave
New York, NY 10017-2703, USA

Reiner, Rob (Actor, Director)
c/o Rand Holston *Creative Artists Agency (CAA-LA)*
2000 Avenue of the Stars Ste 100
Los Angeles, CA 90067-4705, USA

Reinfeldt, Mike (Athlete, Football Player)
1204 Waterstone Blvd
Franklin, TN 37069-7208, USA

Reinhard, Bill (Athlete, Football Player)
43683 Old Troon Ct
Indio, CA 92201-8910, USA

Reinhard, Robert R (Bob) (Athlete, Football Player)
37230 Soap Creek Rd
Corvallis, OR 97330-9376, USA

Reinhardt, Doug (Athlete, Baseball Player, Reality TV Star)
c/o Liza Anderson *Anderson Group Public Relations*
8060 Melrose Ave Fl 4
Los Angeles, CA 90046-7038, USA

Reinhardt, John E (Diplomat)
3154 Gracefield Rd Apt 417
Silver Spring, MD 20904-0808, USA

Reinhardt, Stephen R (Judge)
312 N Spring St
Los Angeles, CA 90012-4701, USA

Reinhart, Haley (Musician, Reality TV Star)
216 N Brand Blvd
Glendale, CA 91203-2610, USA

Reinharz, Jehuda (Educator)
President's Office
Waltham, MA 2254, USA

Reinhold, Judge (Actor, Director)
c/o Tiffany Kuzon *Evolution Entertainment (LA)*
901 N Highland Ave
Los Angeles, CA 90038-2412, USA

Reininger, Travis (Athlete, Baseball Player)
3470 Hottman St
Brighton, CO 80601-3424, USA

Reinking, Ann (Actor, Dancer, Director)
40 W 57th St # 1800
New York, NY 10019-4001, USA

Reinsdorf, Jerry (Baseball Player)
40 E Elm St
Chicago, IL 60611-1016, USA

Reis, Tommy (Athlete, Baseball Player)
15456 SW 15th Terrace Rd
Ocala, FL 34473-8862, USA

Reiser, Jerry (Architect)
28 S Washington Ave
Dobbs Ferry, NY 10522-1807, USA

Reiser, Paul (Actor, Producer)
c/o Peter Safran *The Safran Company*
8748 Holloway Dr
West Hollywood, CA 90069-2327, USA

Reiser, Rock
9014 Melrose Ave
West Hollywood, CA 90069-5610

Reisman, Garrett E (Astronaut)
1715 Hedgecroft Dr
Seabrook, TX 77586, USA

Reiss, Howard (Misc)
16656 Oldham St
Encino, CA 91436-3706, USA

Reisz, Michael (Actor)
c/o Staff Member *WmE2 (WMA-LA)*
1 William Morris Pl
Beverly Hills, CA 90212-4261, USA

Reiter, Mario (Skier)
Hauselweg 5
Rankweil 6830, AUSTRIA

Reiter, Thomas (Astronaut)
Linder Hohe Box 906096
Cologne 51127, GERMANY

Reith, Brian (Athlete, Baseball Player)
9706 54th Ct E
Parrish, FL 34219-4440, USA

Reitherman, Bruce (Cinematographer, Producer, Writer)
c/o Staff Member *Pandion Enterprises, Inc.*
2287 Whitney Ave
Summerland, CA 93067, USA

Reitman, Ivan (Director, Producer)
900 Cold Springs Rd
Montecito, CA 93108-1009, USA

Reitman, Jason (Director)
c/o Staff Member *WmE2 (Endeavor-LA)*
9601 Wilshire Blvd Fl 3
Beverly Hills, CA 90210-5219, USA

Reitman, Joe (Actor)
c/o Suzanne (Sue) Wohl *TalentWorks (LA)*
3500 W Olive Ave Ste 1400
Burbank, CA 91505-5512, USA

Reitsma, Chris (Athlete, Baseball Player)
6050 Jim Davis Rd
Parrish, FL 34219-9363, USA

Reitz, Bruce (Doctor)
600 N Wolfe St
Baltimore, MD 21287-0005, USA

Reitz, Ken (Athlete, Baseball Player)
1704 Carbine Ln
Saint Charles, MO 63303-1104, USA

ReK (Artist)
PO Box 1484
Southampton, PA 18966-0832, USA

Rekar, Bryan (Athlete, Baseball Player)
4326 Waterville Ave
Wesley Chapel, FL 33543-7037, USA

Reklow, Jesse (Cartoonist)
2415 College Ave Apt 20
Berkeley, CA 94704-2458, USA

Relaford, Desmond (Athlete, Baseball Player)
12483 Highview Dr
Jacksonville, FL 32225-5725, USA

Relch, Steve (Baseball Player)
28 Scofield Hill Rd
Washington Depot, CT 06794-1012, USA

Reld, Andy (Athlete, Football Coach, Football Player)
1215 Page Ter
Villanova, PA 19085-2132, USA

Relient K (Music Group, Musician)
c/o Kevin Spellman *Vector Management (LA)*
1100 Glendon Ave Ste 2000
Los Angeles, CA 90024-3524, USA

Reliford, Charlie (Baseball Player)
1509 Cypress St
Ashland, KY 41101-3624, USA

Reliford, Charlie (Athlete, Baseball Player)
1509 Cypress St
Ashland, KY 41101-3624, USA

Rellford, Richard (Athlete, Basketball Player)
28 Balfour Rd W
Palm Beach Gardens, FL 33418-7090, USA

Relman, Arnold S (Doctor, Editor)
860 Winter St # 2
Waltham, MA 02451-1449, USA

Remar, James (Actor)
409 N Camden Dr Ste 202
Beverly Hills, CA 90210-4423, USA

Rembert, Johnny (Athlete, Football Player)
1415 Indian Woods Dr
Neptune Beach, FL 32266-3149, USA

Remedios, Alberto T (Opera Singer)
21 Lanhill Road
London W9 2BS, UNITED KINGDOM (UK)

Remek, Vladimir (Cosmonaut)
Veletrzni 17
Prague 7 17000, CZECH REPUBLIC

Remigino, Lindy (Athlete, Track Athlete)
22 Paris Ln
Newington, CT 06111-1628, USA

Remington, Deborah W (Artist)
309 W Broadway
New York, NY 10013-5325, USA

Remini, Leah (Actor)
PO Box 15669
North Hollywood, CA 91615-5669, USA

Remlinger, Mike (Athlete, Baseball Player)
6667 N Mummy Mountain Rd
Paradise Valley, AZ 85253-3380, USA

Remmerswaal, Win (Athlete, Baseball Player)
Doktor Van Praag St 16
Wassenaar, Holland

Remmert, Dennis (Athlete, Football Player)
3933 Briarwood Dr
Cedar Falls, IA 50613-7508, USA

Remnick, David (Writer)
c/o Robert (Bob) Bookman *Creative Artists Agency (CAA-LA)*
2000 Avenue of the Stars Ste 100
Los Angeles, CA 90067-4705, USA

Remnick, David J (Editor, Writer)
257 W 86th St # 11A
New York, NY 10024-3105, USA

Remo, Ken
121 S Orange Dr
Los Angeles, CA 90036-3012

Rempt, Rodney (Admiral, Educator)
Superintendent US Naval Academy
Annapolis, MD 21402, USA

Remy, Gerald P (Jerry) (Athlete, Baseball Player)
33 Viles St
Weston, MA 02493-1743, USA

Renard, Mercedes (Actor)
c/o Evan Hainey *Untitled Entertainment (LA)*
350 S Beverly Dr Ste 200
Beverly Hills, CA 90212-4819, USA

Renaud, Line (Musician)
5 Rue du Bois-de-Boulogne
Paris 75116, FRANCE

Renault, Dennis (Cartoonist)
Editorial Dept 21st & Q Sts
Sacramento, CA 95852, USA

Renbourn, John (Musician)
1671 Appian Way
Santa Monica, CA 90401-3258, USA

Rencher, Terrence (Athlete, Basketball Player)
2001 S MO Pac Expy Apt 924
Austin, TX 78746-7579, USA

Rendall, Mark (Actor)
c/o Staff Member *Artist Management Inc*
464 King St E
Toronto ON M5A 1L7, CANADA

Rendell, Majorie O (Judge)
601 Market St
Philadelphia, PA 19106-1737, USA

Rendell, Ruth
Nusstead's Polstead Suffolk
Colchester, ENGLAND CO6 5DN

Rendell of Barbergh, Ruth B (Writer)
Nussteads Polstead Suffolk
Colchester CO6 5DN, UNITED KINGDOM (UK)

Rene, France-Albert (President)
State House Victoria
Mahe, SEYCHELLES

Reneau, Daniel D (Educator)
President S Ofc
Ruston, LA 71272-0001, USA

Renfrew of Kaimsthorn, Andrew C (Archaeologist)
Downing St
Cambridge CB2 3ER, UNITED KINGDOM (UK)

Renfro, Leonard (Athlete, Football Player)
12190 Bannock St Apt C
Denver, CO 80234-2125, USA

Renfro, Mike (Athlete, Football Player)
PO Box 93073
Southlake, TX 76092-1073, USA

Renfroe, Jay (Producer)
c/o Staff Member *Renegade 83 Entertainment*
5700 Wilshire Blvd Fl 6
Los Angeles, CA 90036-3659, USA

Renfroe, Laddie (Athlete, Baseball Player)
236 Hickory Ln
Batesville, MS 38606-9339, USA

Rengel, Mike (Athlete, Football Player)
1782 Montane Dr E
Golden, CO 80401, USA

Renger, Annemarie (Government Official)
Bundestag Platz der Republik 1
Berlin 11011, GERMANY

Renick, Rick (Athlete, Baseball Player)
7320 Hawkins Rd
Sarasota, FL 34241-9375, USA

Renier, Jeremie (Actor)
20 Ave Rapp
Paris 75007, FRANCE

Renis, Tony (Musician)
501 Deep Valley Dr Fl 1
Rolling Hills Estates, CA 90274-7605, USA

Renk, Silke (Athlete, Track Athlete)
Erhard-Hubner-Str 13
Halle/S 6132, GERMANY

Renko, Steven (Steve) (Athlete, Baseball Player)
15812 W 136th St
Olathe, KS 66062-5310, USA

Renn, Crystal (Model)
c/o Staff Member *Ford Models (NY)*
238 E 4th St
New York, NY 10009-7425

Renna, Bill (Athlete, Baseball Player)
1476 Lesher Ct
San Jose, CA 95125-3936, USA

Renna, Eugene A (Business Person)
3225 Gallows Rd
Fairfax, VA 22037-0001, USA

Renna, Patrick (Actor)
c/o Staff Member *Talent Company, The*
135 E Olive Ave # 4227
Burbank, CA 91502-1820, USA

Renne, Paul (Misc)
2445 Ridge Rd
Berkeley, CA 94709, USA

Rennebohm, J Fred (Religious Leader)
PO Box 1620
Oak Creek, MI 53154, USA

Rennebohm, J Fred (Misc)
Holbeinstr 58
Berlin 12203, GERMANY

Renner, Jeremy (Actor)
c/o Beth Holden-Garland *Untitled Entertainment (LA)*
350 S Beverly Dr Ste 200
Beverly Hills, CA 90212-4819, USA

Rennert, Dutch (Baseball Player)
Walkers Glen 2560 46th Rd
Vero Beach, FL 32966-2053, USA

Rennert, Dutch (Athlete, Baseball Player)
2560 46th Rd
Vero Beach, FL 32966-2053, USA

Rennert, Gunther (Director, Opera Singer)
Holbeinstr 58
Berlin 12203, GERMANY

Renney, Tom (Coach)
Madison Square Garden 2 Penn Plaza
New York, NY 10121, USA

Renni, Gino (Actor)
c/o Staff Member *Telefe - Argentina*
Pavon 2444 (C1248AAT)
Buenos Aires, ARGENTINA

Reno, Jack
PO Box 1001
Florence, KY 41022-1001

Reno, Janet (Attorney, Attorney General, General)
11200 N Kendall Dr
Miami, FL 33176-1108, USA

Reno, Jean (Actor)
c/o Amy Guenther *Gateway Management Company Inc*
860 Via De La Paz Ste F10
Pacific Palisades, CA 90272-3631, USA

Reno, William H (General)
2706 S Ives St
Arlington, VA 22202-2372, USA

Renoth, Heldi (Skier)
Lercheckerweg 23
Berchtesgaden 83471, GERMANY

Rensberger, Robert (Athlete, Basketball Player)
818 Green Pine Ct
Mishawaka, IN 46545-2888, USA

Renteria, Edgar (Athlete, Baseball Player)
PO Box 260898
Pembroke Pines, FL 33026-7898, USA

Renteria, Rich (Athlete, Baseball Player)
930 Pacific Hills Pt Apt B103
Colorado Springs, CO 80906-8407, USA

Renteria, Rick (Athlete, Baseball Player)
43310 Calle Nacido
Temecula, CA 92592-3068, USA

Rentie, Caesar (Athlete, Football Player)
2243 Elderoaks Ln
Dallas, TX 75232-3310, USA

Rentmeester, Co (Photographer)
PO Box 1562
Westhampton Beach, NY 11978-7562, USA

Renton of Mount Harry, R Timothy (Government Official)
Westminster
London SW1A 0PW, UNITED KINGDOM (UK)

Rentzel, Lance (Athlete, Football Player)
12104 Monument Dr Apt 354
Fairfax, VA 22033-4053, USA

Rentzepis, Peter M (Misc)
Chemistry Dept
Irvine, CA 92717, USA

Renucci, Robin
64 Rue Condorcet
Paris, FRANCE 75009

Renvall, Johan (Dancer)
890 Broadway
New York, NY 10003-1211, USA

Renyi, Thomas A (Financier)
1 Wall St
New York, NY 10005-2500, USA

Repeta, Nina (Actor)
14724 Ventura Blvd Ste 505
Van Nuys, CA 91403-3505, USA

Repin, Vadim V (Musician)
Eckholdtweg 2A
Lubeck 23566, GERMANY

Replogle, Andy (Athlete, Baseball Player)
8047 Hidden Hills Dr
Spring Hill, FL 34606-7263, USA

Repoz, Roger (Athlete, Baseball Player)
930 Whitewater Dr
Fullerton, CA 92833-2194, USA

Rerych, Stephen (Steve) (Swimmer)
445 Baltimore Ave
Ashville, NC 28801, USA

Resch, Alexander (Athlete)
An der Schiessstatte 4
Berchtesgaden 83471, GERMANY

Rescher, Nicholas (Misc)
1033 Milton St
Pittsburgh, PA 15218-1228, USA

Resnais, Alain (Director)
70 Rue des Plantes
Paris 75014, FRANCE

Resnik, Regina (Opera Singer)
1430 Broadway
New York, NY 10018-3308, USA

Resop, Chris (Athlete, Baseball Player)
10028 Heather Ln Apt 1102
Naples, FL 34119-9021, USA

Ressler, Glenn E (Athlete, Football Player)
1524 Woodcreek Dr
Mechanicsburg, PA 17055-6766, USA

Ressler, Robert
PO Box 187
Spotsylvania, VA 22553-0187

Restani, Jane A (Judge)
1 Federal Plz
New York, NY 10278-0001, USA

Restani, Kevin (Athlete, Basketball Player)
230 Hawthorne Ave
Larkspur, CA 94939-1308, USA

Restic, Joe (Athlete, Football Player)
18 Penny Ln
Milford, MA 01757-1516, USA

Restless Heart (Music Group)
c/o Staff Member *Agency for the Performing Arts (APA-Nashville)*
3017 Poston Ave
Nashville, TN 37203-1313

Restovich, Michael (Athlete, Baseball Player)
710 11th St SW
Rochester, MN 55902-6339, USA

Reswick, James B (Engineer)
1834 Calf Mountain Rd
Crozet, VA 22932, USA

Retherford, Dave (Athlete, Football Player)
2609 W Watrous Ave
Tampa, FL 33629-5346, USA

Retore, Guy (Director)
Theatre de l'Est Parislen 159 Ave Gambetta
Paris 75020, FRANCE

Rettenmund, Merv (Athlete, Baseball Player)
655 India St Unit 123
San Diego, CA 92101-6738, USA

Retton, Mary Lou (Athlete, Gymnast)
203 Fairmeadow Cir
Houston, PA 15342-1069, USA

Rettondini, Francesca (Actor)
c/o Staff Member *C.D.A. Studio Di Nardo*
Via Cavour
Rome 184, Italy

Retzer, Ken (Athlete, Baseball Player)
95A Abel Ct
Granite City, IL 62040-6700, USA

Retzer, Otto W (Director)
Justinus-Kerner-Str 10
Munich 80686, GERMANY

Retzlaff, Palmer (Pete) (Athlete, Football Player)
669 New Rd
Gilbertsville, PA 19525-9613, USA

Reuben, Gloria (Actor)
c/o Staff Member *Untitled Entertainment (LA)*
350 S Beverly Dr Ste 200
Beverly Hills, CA 90212-4819, USA

Reubens, Paul (Actor, Comedian)
PO Box 29373
Los Angeles, CA 90029-0373, USA

Reukauf, Timothy (Stylist)
c/o Staff Member *Marek & Associates Inc*
508 W 26th St Rm 12C
New York, NY 10001-5541, USA

Reuschel, Paul (Athlete, Baseball Player)
1143 Stacy Ln
Macomb, IL 61455-2646, USA

Reuschel, Ricky E (Rick) (Athlete, Baseball Player)
PO Box 143
Renfrew, PA 16053-0143, USA

Reuss, Jerry (Athlete, Baseball Player, Sportscaster)
1000 Elysian Park Ave Attn Broadcast
Los Angeles, CA 90090-1112, USA

Reusser, Ken L (War Hero)
17345 SW Reusser Ct
Aloha, OR 97007-8772, USA

Reutemann, Carlos
San Martin 3233
Santa Fe, ARGENTINA

Reuten, Thekla (Actor)
c/o Paula Rosenberg *ICA Talent*
818 12th St Apt 9
Santa Monica, CA 90403-1727, USA

Reuter, Edzard (Business Person)
Postfach 800230
Stuttgart 70546, GERMANY

Reutershan, Randy (Athlete, Football Player)
4 Indian Field Ct
Mahwah, NJ 07430-2243, USA

Reutersward, Carl Fredrik (Artist)
6 Rue Montilieu
Bussigny/Lausanne 1030, SWITZERLAND

Revathi (Actor, Bollywood)
7 1st Crescent Road Gandhinagar Adyar
Chennai, TN 600020, INDIA

Reveiz, Fuad (Athlete, Football Player)
2160 Lakeside Centre Way Ste 250
Knoxville, TN 37922-0201, USA

Revell, Graeme (Composer)
PO Box 567
Crow's Nest, NSW 2065, AUSTRALIA

Revenig, Todd (Athlete, Baseball Player)
2412 E Prescott Pl
Chandler, AZ 85249-2946, USA

Revere, Paul (Musician)
108 E Matilija St
Ojai, CA 93023-2639, USA

Reverho, Christine (Actor)
20 Ave Rapp
Paris 75007, FRANCE

Revering, Dave (Athlete, Baseball Player)
1063 Crows Wing Way
Ivins, UT 84738-6364, USA

Revill, Clive (Actor)
15029 Encanto Dr
Sherman Oaks, CA 91403-4409, USA

Revolution Mother (Music Group, Musician)
c/o Staff Member *Velvet Hammer*
9014 Melrose Ave
West Hollywood, CA 90069-5610, USA

Revs, The (Music Group)
c/o Staff Member *Paradigm (Monterey)*
404 W Franklin St
Monterey, CA 93940-2303, USA

Rex (Musician)
361 W Broadway # 200
New York, NY 10013-2209, USA

Rex, Simon (Sebastian) (Actor, Television Host)
c/o Katie Mason *Luber Roklin Management*
8530 Wilshire Blvd Ste 550
Beverly Hills, CA 90211-3133, USA

Rey, Paola (Actor)
c/o Gabriel Blanco *Gabriel Blanco Iglesias (Mexico)*
Rio Balsas 35-32 Colonia Cuauhtemoc
DF 6500, Mexico

Rey, Reynaldo (Actor, Comedian, Writer)
433 N Camden Dr Ste 400
Beverly Hills, CA 90210-4408, USA

Reyes, Anthony (Athlete, Baseball Player)
8929 Watson Ave
Whittier, CA 90605-2035, USA

Reyes, Carlos (Athlete, Baseball Player)
7205 N Cortez Ave
Tampa, FL 33614-2638, USA

Reyes, Judy (Actor)
c/o Leonard Torgan *Collective*
8383 Wilshire Blvd Ste 1050
Beverly Hills, CA 90211-2415, USA

Reyes, Lalo (Actor)
c/o Paul Uvanitte *ProActive Management Group (PMG)*
10944 Bluffside Dr Apt 213
Studio City, CA 91604-3362, USA

Reyes, Sandra (Actor)
c/o Staff Member *TV Caracol*
Calle 76 #11 - 35 Piso 10AA
Bogota DC 26484, COLOMBIA

Reyes, Senen (Sen Dog) (Actor, Composer, Musician)
c/o Randy Cabrera *Brass Artists & Associates*
9025 Wilshire Blvd Ste 400
Beverly Hills, CA 90211-1828, USA

Reyes Jr, Ernie
12561 Willard St
N Hollywood, CA 91605-1244, USA

Reymundo, Alex (Comedian)
c/o Alex D'Andrea *Edmonds Management*
1635 N Cahuenga Blvd Fl 5
Los Angeles, CA 90028-6201, USA

Reynold, Catherine B (Business Person)
PO Box 11346
McLean, VA 22102-9346, USA

Reynolds, Alastair (Writer)
34-43 Russell St
London WC2B 5HA, UNITED KINGDOM (UK)

Reynolds, Albert (Prime Minister)
Mount Carmel House Dublin Road
Longford, IRELAND

Reynolds, Anna (Opera Singer)
Peesten 9
Kasendorf 95359, GERMANY

Reynolds, Archie (Athlete, Baseball Player)
1828 Pinecrest Dr
Tyler, TX 75701-5006, USA

Reynolds, Bob (Athlete, Baseball Player)
952 SW Campus Dr Apt 26D3
Federal Way, WA 98023-5026, USA

Reynolds, Burt (Actor, Director)
c/o Erik Kritzer *Kritzer Levine Wilkins Entertainment*
11872 La Grange Ave Fl 1
Los Angeles, CA 90025-5283, USA

Reynolds, Craig (Athlete, Baseball Player)
4210 Hidden Links Ct
Kingwood, TX 77339-5308, USA

Reynolds, David S (Historian, Writer)
16 Linden Ln
Old Westbury, NY 11568-1610, USA

Reynolds, Debbie (Actor, Musician)
1700 Coldwater Canyon Dr
Beverly Hills, CA 90210-2407, USA

Reynolds, Don (Athlete, Baseball Player)
6035 NE 35th Pl
Portland, OR 97211-7358, USA

Reynolds, Ed (Athlete, Football Player)
2387 Country Side Dr
Fleming Isle, FL 32003-4907, USA

Reynolds, Gene (Actor, Producer)
2034 Castilian Dr
Los Angeles, CA 90068-2609, USA

Reynolds, Glenn F (Inventor)
242 Edgewood Ave
Westfield, NJ 07090-3918, USA

Reynolds, Harold (Athlete, Baseball Player)
2890 NW Angelica Dr
Corvallis, OR 97330-3619, USA

Reynolds, Harry (Butch) (Athlete, Track Athlete)
1025 Thomas Jefferson St NW # 450
Washington, DC 20007-5201, USA

Reynolds, J Guy (Admiral)
1605 Fox Hunt Ct
Alexandria, VA 22307, USA

Reynolds, Jack (Athlete, Football Player)
11480 SW 102nd St
Miami, FL 33176-2588, USA

Reynolds, Jamai (Athlete, Football Player)
PO Box 10628
Green Bay, WI 54307-0628, USA

Reynolds, Jamal (Athlete, Football Player)
76 Lou Groza Blvd
Berea, OH 44017-1238, USA

Reynolds, James (Actor)
1925 Hanscom Dr
South Pasadena, CA 91030-4009, USA

Reynolds, James (Baseball Player)
708 Highpoint Dr
Rocky Hill, CT 06067-1088, USA

Reynolds, Jerry O (Coach)
1 Sports Pkwy
Sacramento, CA 95834-2300, USA

Reynolds, Jim (Athlete, Football Player)
2200 Elkoa's St
Selma, AL 36701, USA

Reynolds, Jim (Athlete, Baseball Player)
708 Highpoint Dr
Rocky Hill, CT 06067-1088, USA

Reynolds, John R (Educator, Physicist)
Physics
Berkeley, CA 94720-0001, USA

Reynolds, Ken (Athlete, Baseball Player)
182 Greenwood St
Marlborough, MA 01752-3307, USA

Reynolds, Kevin (Director, Writer)
c/o Mike Simpson *WmE2 (Endeavor-LA)*
9601 Wilshire Blvd Fl 3
Beverly Hills, CA 90210-5219, USA

Reynolds, Patti
PO Box 530
Fontana, WI 53125-0530

Reynolds, R Shane (Athlete, Baseball Player)
2205 Warwick Way Ste 200
Marriottsville, MD 21104-1632, USA

Reynolds, Rachel (Actor, Model)
c/o Staff Member *Price Is Right, The*
2700 Colorado Ave Fl 4
Santa Monica, CA 90404-3553, USA

Reynolds, Randolph N (Business Person)
PO Box 27003
Richmond, VA 23261-7003, USA

Reynolds, Richard V (General)
Commander Aeronautical Systems
Wright-Patterson Air Force Base, OH 45433, USA

Reynolds, Ricky (Athlete, Football Player)
18032 Java Isle Dr
Tampa, FL 33647-2708, USA

Reynolds, Robert (Musician)
1620 16th Ave S
Nashville, TN 37212-2908, USA

Reynolds, Roxy (Actor)
c/o Staff Member *Sosincere Entertainment*
2054 Nostrand Ave Apt 4F
Brooklyn, NY 11210-2526, USA

Reynolds, Ryan (Actor)
c/o Meredith O'Sullivan *42West (LA)*
11400 W Olympic Blvd Ste 1100
Los Angeles, CA 90064-1579, USA

Reynolds, Sheldon (Musician)
137 N Wetherly Dr Apt 403
Los Angeles, CA 90048-2866, USA

Reynolds, Tom (Athlete, Baseball Player)
640 Jinks Crossing Rd
Bainbridge, GA 39819-1334, USA

Reynolds Booth, Nancy (Skier)
3197 Padaro Ln
Carpinteria, CA 93013-1115, USA

Reynolds Jr, Thomas A (Lawyer)
1 First National Plaza 45 West Wacker Dr
Chicago, IL 60601, USA

Reynoso, Armando (Athlete, Baseball Player)
PO Box 442
Scottsdale, AZ 85252-0442, USA

Reza, Yasmina (Actor, Writer)
14 Rue des Sablons
Paris 75116, FRANCE

Reznor, Trent (Musician)
c/o Marc Geiger *WmE2 (Endeavor-LA)*
9601 Wilshire Blvd Fl 3
Beverly Hills, CA 90210-5219, USA

Rhames, Ving (Actor)
c/o Steven Muller *Innovative Artists (LA)*
1505 10th St
Santa Monica, CA 90401-2805, USA

Rhea, Caroline (Actor, Comedian)
c/o Jonathan Howard *Innovative Artists (LA)*
1505 10th St
Santa Monica, CA 90401-2805, USA

Rhea, Floyd (Athlete, Football Player)
12 Rivo Alto Canal
Long Beach, CA 90803-4036, USA

Rheams, Leonta (Athlete, Football Player)
1712 W Jackson St
Tyler, TX 75701-1209, USA

Rheaume, Manon (Athlete, Hockey Player)
Athletic Dept
Duluth, MN 55812, USA

Rheinecker, John (Athlete, Baseball Player)
7152 State Route 156
Waterloo, IL 62298-2522, USA

Rhett, Alicia (Actor)
PO Box 700
Charleston, SC 29402-0700, USA

Rhett, Errict (Athlete, Football Player)
6 NW 108th Ter
Plantation, FL 33324-1560, USA

Rhimes, Shonda (Actor, Producer, Writer)
4151 Prospect Ave Los Feliz Tower Fl 4
Los Angeles, CA 90027, USA

Rhind-Tutt, Julian (Actor)
c/o Staff Member *The Rights House (UK)*
Drury House 34-43 Russell St
London WC2B 5HA, UK

Rhine Sr, Kendall (Athlete, Basketball Player)
6240 State Route 127 N
Alto Pass, IL 62905-3230, USA

Rhinehart, Coby (Athlete, Football Player)
8209 Meadow Rd Apt 1140
Dallas, TX 75231-3644, USA

Rhines, Peter B (Oceanographer)
5753 61st Ave NE
Seattle, WA 98105-2037, USA

Rhoades, Kerry (Football Player)
c/o Team Member *New York Jets*
5150 Palm Valley Rd Ste 210
Ponte Vedra Beach, FL 32082-4631, USA

Rhoades, Lisa (Stylist)
c/o Staff Member *Perrella Management*
330 W 38th St Rm 1407
New York, NY 10018-8435, USA

Rhoads, George (Artist)
1478 Mecklenburg Rd
Ithaca, NY 14850-9301, USA

Rhoads, James B (Misc)
1300 Fox Run Trl
Platte City, MO 64079-7640, USA

Rhoda, Hilary (Model)
c/o Staff Member *IMG*
304 Park Ave S Fl 12
New York, NY 10010-4314, USA

Rhoden, Richard A (Rick) (Athlete, Baseball Player)
1253 Killarney Dr
Ormond Beach, FL 32174-2828, USA

Rhodes, Arthur (Athlete, Baseball Player)
14114 Phoenix Rd
Phoenix, MD 21131-1020, USA

Rhodes, Cynthia (Actor, Dancer)
15260 Ventura Blvd Ste 2100
Sherman Oaks, CA 91403-5360, USA

Rhodes, Donnelly (Actor)
3500 W Olive Ave Ste 1400
Burbank, CA 91505-5512, USA

Rhodes, Eugene (Athlete, Basketball Player)
132 N Peterson Ave Apt 7
Louisville, KY 40206-2340, USA

Rhodes, Frank H T (Educator)
Geology Dept Snee Hall
Ithaca, NY 14853, USA

Rhodes, Harry (Athlete, Baseball Player)
7207 S Evans Ave
Chicago, IL 60619-1224, USA

Rhodes, Jan (Stylist)
106 Dolores St
San Francisco, CA 94103-2210, USA

Rhodes, Karl (Athlete, Baseball Player)
3622 Ridgeview Dr
Missouri City, TX 77459-4047, USA

Rhodes, Lou (Musician)
c/o Staff Member *Paradigm (Monterey)*
404 W Franklin St
Monterey, CA 93940-2303, USA

Rhodes, Mark (Musician)
c/o Staff Member *QVoice*
193-197 High Holborn 4th Floor, Holborn Hall
London WC1V 7BD, UNITED KINGDOM (UK)

Rhodes, Nick (Musician)
93A Westbourne Park Villas
London W2 5ED, UNITED KINGDOM (UK)

Rhodes, Philip (Musician)
2100 W End Ave Ste 1000
Nashville, TN 37203-5240, USA

Rhodes, Ray (Athlete, Coach, Football Coach, Football Player)
25812 NE 4th Pl
Sammamish, WA 98074-3419, USA

Rhodes, Richard L (Writer)
445 Park Ave # 1300
New York, NY 10022-2606, USA

Rhodes, Rodrick (Athlete, Basketball Player)
PO Box 17704
Sugar Land, TX 77496-7704, USA

Rhodes, Tom (Actor, Comedian, Writer)
c/o Staff Member *WmE2 (WMA-LA)*
1 William Morris Pl
Beverly Hills, CA 90212-4261, USA

Rhodes, Zandra (Designer, Fashion Designer)
79-85 Bermondsey St
London SE1 3XF, UNITED KINGDOM (UK)

Rhomberg, Kevin (Athlete, Baseball Player)
9692 Executive Ct
Mentor, OH 44060-8721, USA

Rhome, Gerald B (Jerry) (Athlete, Coach, Football Coach, Football Player)
3883 Morning Meadow Ln
Buford, GA 30519-4383, USA

Rhone, Earriest C (Ernie) (Athlete, Football Player)
3603 Potomac Ave
Texarkana, TX 75503-3519, USA

Rhone, Sylvia (Business Person)
75 Rockefeller Plz Fl 15
New York, NY 10019-6908

Rhude, Kellan (Actor)
c/o Staff Member *Diverse Talent Group*
9911 W Pico Blvd Ste 340W
Los Angeles, CA 90035-2712, USA

Rhyan, Dick (Golfer)
111 Camp Dr
Georgetown, TX 78633-4874, USA

Rhymer, Don (Writer)
c/o David Kramer *United Talent Agency (UTA)*
9560 Wilshire Blvd Fl 5
Beverly Hills, CA 90212-2400, USA

Rhymes, Busta (Musician)
c/o Staff Member *Violator Management*
36 W 25th St Fl 11
New York, NY 10010-2752, USA

Rhymes, Buster (Athlete, Football Player)
17120 NW 37th Ave
Carol City, FL 33056-4112, USA

Rhys, Matthew (Actor)
c/o Suzan Bymel *Management 360*
9111 Wilshire Blvd
Beverly Hills, CA 90210-5508, USA

Rhys, Paul (Actor)
232 N Canon Dr
Beverly Hills, CA 90210-5302, USA

Rhys, Phillip (Actor)
c/o Joe Vance *Domain Talent*
9229 W Sunset Blvd Ste 710
Los Angeles, CA 90069-3407, USA

Rhys-Davies, John (Actor)
2901 S Robertson Ave
Tyler, TX 75701-6943, USA

Rhys-Jones, HRH Sophie (Duchess of Wessex)
Bagshot Park
Surrey, ENGLAND GUI9 5PN

Rhys-Meyers, Jonathan (Actor)
c/o Meredith O'Sullivan *42West (LA)*
11400 W Olympic Blvd Ste 1100
Los Angeles, CA 90064-1579, USA

Rhythm Syndicate
6255 W Sunset Blvd Ste 2100
Los Angeles, CA 90028-7422

Ri Jong Ok (President, Vice President)
Pyongyang, NORTH KOREA

Ribant, Dennis (Athlete, Baseball Player)
46 Sidra Cv
Newport Coast, CA 92657-2115, USA

Ribas Reig, Oscar (Government Official)
Andorra la Vella, ANDORRA

Ribbs, Willy T (Race Car Driver)
2343 Ribbs Ln
San Jose, CA 95116-2147, USA

Ribeau, Sidney A (Educator)
President S Ofc
Bowling Green, OH 43403-0001, USA

Ribeiro, Alfonso (Actor)
c/o Konrad Leh *Creative Talent Group*
1900 Avenue of the Stars Ste 2475
Los Angeles, CA 90067-4512, USA

Ribeiro, Ignacio (Designer, Fashion Designer)
48 S Molton St
London W1X 1HE, UNITED KINGDOM (UK)

Ribisi, Giovanni (Actor)
c/o Eric Kranzler *Management 360*
9111 Wilshire Blvd
Beverly Hills, CA 90210-5508, USA

Ribisi, Marissa (Actor)
4121 Wilshire Blvd Apt 415
Los Angeles, CA 90010-3525, USA

Ribot, Mark (Composer, Musician)
c/o Staff Member *Concerted Efforts*
PO Box 440326
Somerville, MA 02144-0004, USA

Ricard, Alan (Athlete, Football Player)
4711 Winterset Way Apt 7
Owings Mills, MD 21117-4746, USA

Ricardo, Benny (Athlete, Football Player)
3012 Harding Way
Costa Mesa, CA 92626-2846, USA

Ricardo Y Alberto (Music Group)
c/o Staff Member *Sony Music Miami*
605 Lincoln Rd Ste 700
Miami Beach, FL 33139-2901, USA

Ricca, Jim (Athlete, Football Player)
55 Whittingham Cir
Sterling, VA 20165-6236, USA

Riccelli, Frank (Athlete, Baseball Player)
PO Box 2102
Syracuse, NY 13220-2102, USA

Ricci, Christina (Actor)
c/o David Seltzer *Management 360*
9111 Wilshire Blvd
Beverly Hills, CA 90210-5508, USA

Ricci, Chuck (Athlete, Baseball Player)
110 Moonlight Dr
Greencastle, PA 17225-1059, USA

Ricci, Ruggiero (Musician)
2930 E Delhi Rd
Ann Arbor, MI 48103-9007, USA

Ricciarelli, Katia (Opera Singer)
2 Magellana Via
Washington, DC 20097-0001, ITALY

Rice, Alex (Actor)
c/o Staff Member *Artist Representation Company, The*
1147 S Big Island Rd RR 1
Demorestville ON K0K 1W0, CANADA

Rice, Andy (Athlete, Football Player)
801 N Main St
Hallettsville, TX 77964-2321, USA

Rice, Anne (Writer)
9 Monte Carlo Dr
Kenner, LA 70065-2028, USA

Rice, Bobby G
505 Canton Pass
Madison, TN 37115-5449, USA

Rice, Buddy (Race Car Driver)
4601 Lyman Dr
Hilliard, OH 43026-1249, USA

Rice, Christopher (Writer)
9 Monte Carlo Dr
Kenner, LA 70065-2028, USA

Rice, Condoleezza (Government Official)
Freeman Spogli Institute For International Studies 616 Serra St C100
Stanford, CA 94305-6010, USA

Rice, Damien (Musician)
c/o Staff Member *Paradigm (Monterey)*
404 W Franklin St
Monterey, CA 93940-2303, USA

Rice, Elizabeth (Actor)
c/o Steven Warren *Hansen, Jacobson, Teller, Hoberman, Newman, Warren & Richman*
450 N Roxbury Dr Fl 8
Beverly Hills, CA 90210-4222, USA

Rice, Gene D (Religious Leader)
PO Box 2430
Cleveland, TN 37320-2430, USA

Rice, Gigi (Actor)
14951 Alva Dr
Pacific Palisades, CA 90272-4402, USA

Rice, Glen
9492 Doral Blvd
Miami, FL 33178

Rice, Glenn (Athlete, Basketball Player)
13621 Deering Bay Dr Apt 304
Coral Gables, FL 33158-2845, USA

Rice, James E (Jim) (Athlete, Baseball Player)
35 Bobby Jones Dr
Andover, MA 01810-2880, USA

Rice, James R (Geophysicist, Physicist)
Applied Science Division
Cambridge, MA 2138, USA

Rice, Jerry (Athlete, Football Player)
c/o Jim Steiner *CAA - St. Louis*
222 S Central Ave Ste 1008
Saint Louis, MO 63105-3509, USA

Rice, John (Baseball Player)
2666 E 73rd St Apt 12W
Chicago, IL 60649-2732, USA

Rice, John (Athlete, Baseball Player)
2666 E 73rd St Apt 12W
Chicago, IL 60649-2732, USA

Rice, Ken (Athlete, Football Player)
10619 Big Canoe
Big Canoe, GA 30143-5130, USA

Rice, Norman B (Politician)
600 4th Ave
Seattle, WA 98104-1850, USA

Rice, Pat (Athlete, Baseball Player)
4090 Zurich Dr
Colorado Springs, CO 80920-7521, USA

Rice, Regina (Actor, Producer)
c/o Staff Member *Temptation Management*
1010 S Robertson Blvd Ste 2
Los Angeles, CA 90035-1527, USA

Rice, Ron (Athlete, Football Player)
22880 Twyckingham Way
Southfield, MI 48034-6260, USA

Rice, Simeon (Athlete, Football Player)
1360 E 9th St
Cleveland, OH 44114-1737, USA

Rice, Stuart A (Misc)
5517 S Kimbark Ave
Chicago, IL 60637-1618, USA

Rice, Thomas M (Physicist)
ETH-Hoggerberg
Zurich, 8093, SWITZERLAND

Rice, Timothy M B (Tim) (Musician)
Chiltens France-Hill Dr Camberley
Surrey GU153-30A, UNITED KINGDOM (UK)

Rice-Hughes, Donna
PO Box 888
Fairfax, VA 22038-0888

Rich, Adam (Actor)
4814 Lemona Ave
Sherman Oaks, CA 91403-2010, USA

Rich, Adrienne (Writer)
English Dept
Stanford, CA 94305, USA

Rich, Alexander (Misc)
2 Walnut Ave
Cambridge, MA 02140-2707, USA

Rich, Allan (Actor)
225 E 57th St
New York, NY 10022-2822, USA

Rich, Christopher (Actor)
11500 W Olympic Blvd Ste 510
Los Angeles, CA 90064-1527, USA

Rich, Claude
18 Chemin De La Butte
Orgeval, FRANCE F-78630

Rich, Clayton (Doctor)
Health Services Ctr
Oklahoma City, OK 73190-0001, USA

Rich, Denise (Musician)
785 5th Ave
New York, NY 10022-1608

Rich, Elaine
500 S Sepulveda Blvd
Los Angeles, CA 90049-3540

Rich, John (Musician)
c/o Dale Morris *Morris Management Group, Inc*
818 19th Ave S
Nashville, TN 37203-3202, USA

Rich, Katie
10100 Santa Monica Blvd # 2490
Los Angeles, CA 90067

Rich, Lee (Business Person)
75 Rockefeller Plz
New York, NY 10019-6907, USA

Rich, Matty
9560 Wilshire Blvd Ste 500
Beverly Hills, CA 90212-2401

Rich, Mike (Writer)

Rich, Richie (Fashion Designer)
575 Broadway Fl 2
New York, NY 10012-3230, USA

Rich, Tony (Musician)
220 E 23rd St Ste 303
New York, NY 10010-4676, USA

Richard, Chris (Athlete, Baseball Player)
11389 Ironwood Rd
San Diego, CA 92131-1916, USA

Richard, Cliff (Musician)
Portsmouth Road Box 46C Esher
Surrey KT10 9AA, UK

Richard, Deb (Golfer)
125 Hidden Cove Ln
Ponte Vedra Beach, FL 32082-2154, USA

Richard, Henri (Athlete, Hockey Player)
905-4300 Place De Cageux
Ile Paton Laval, QC H7W 4Z3, Canada

Richard, Ivor S (Government Official)
11 South Square Gray's Inn
London WC1R 5EU, UNITED KINGDOM (UK)

Richard, James Rodney (J R) (Athlete, Baseball Player)
5615 Chimney Rock Rd Apt 338
Houston, TX 77081-1957, USA

Richard, Lee (Athlete, Baseball Player)
1621 14th St
Port Arthur, TX 77640-4482, USA

Richard, Pierre
6 Rue De Vieux-Moulin
Droue-sur-Drouette, FRANCE 28230

Richard, Ruth (Baseball Player)
880 Allentown Rd
Sellersville, PA 18960-1000, USA

Richard III, Oliver G (Business Person)
200 Civic Center Dr
Columbus, OH 43215-4138, USA

Richards, Ariana (Actor)
6500 Wilshire Blvd # 3300
Los Angeles, CA 90048-4920, USA

Richards, Bob (Doctor)
1616 Estates Dr
Waco, TX 76712-2208, USA

Richards, Bobby (Athlete, Football Player)
2881 Fairplay Rd
Rutledge, GA 30663-2000, USA

Richards, Brad (Athlete, Hockey Player)
101 Warren St Apt 3150
New York, NY 10007-1375, USA

Richards, Curvin (Athlete, Football Player)
11000 Gatesden Dr Apt 1311
Tomball, TX 77377-8706, USA

Richards, Dakota Blue (Actor)
c/o Sue Latimer *Artists Rights Group (ARG)*
4 Great Portland St
London W1W 8PA, UNITED KINGDOM (UK)

Richards, David R (Athlete, Football Player)
4209 San Carlos St
Dallas, TX 75205-2049, USA

Richards, DeLeon (Actor)
c/o Staff Member *Britto Agency PR*
234 W 56th St PH
New York, NY 10019-4302, USA

Richards, Denise (Actor)
c/o Ame Van Iden *PMK/BNC Public Relations (PMK-LA)*
8687 Melrose Ave Ste 8
West Hollywood, CA 90069-5746, USA

Richards, Duane (Athlete, Baseball Player)
PO Box 54
Palestine, OH 45352-0054, USA

Richards, Emelie
PO Box 7052
Arlington, VA 22207-0052

Richards, Evan
1800 Avenue of the Stars Ste 400
Los Angeles, CA 90067-4206

Richards, Fred (Athlete, Baseball Player)
1760 Dodge Dr NW
Warren, OH 44485-1823, USA

Richards, Frederic M (Misc)
69 Andrews Rd
Guilford, CT 06437-3715, USA

Richards, Gene (Athlete, Baseball Player)
1193 Spring Sage St
Henderson, NV 89011-0884, USA

Richards, Golden (Athlete, Football Player)
7274 Winesap Ct
Salt Lake City, UT 84121-4439, USA

Richards, Howard (Athlete, Football Player)
PSC 98 Box 30
APO, AE 9830, USA

Richards, I Vivian A (Viv) (Cricketer)
PO Box 616
Saint John's, ANTIGUA & BARBUDA

Richards, J August (Actor)
PO Box 99
China Spring, TX 76633-0099, USA

Richards, J R (Musician)
1325 Avenue of the Americas
New York, NY 10019-6026, USA

Richards, James B (Athlete, Football Player)
733 Vanderbilt Ave
Virginia Beach, VA 23451-3632, USA

Richards, Jasmine (Actor)
c/o Staff Member *Noble Caplan Abrams*
1260 Yonge St 2nd Floor
Toronto, ON M4T 1W6, Canada

Richards, Keith (Musician)
c/o Kenneth Kleinberg *Kleinberg Lopez Lange Brisbin and Cuddy*
2049 Century Park E Ste 3180
Los Angeles, CA 90067-3205, USA

Richards, Kim (Actor)
10326 Orton Ave
Los Angeles, CA 90064-2556, USA

Richards, Kyle (Actor, Reality TV Star)
c/o Bette Smith *Bette Smith Management*
499 N Canon Dr
Beverly Hills, CA 90210-4887, USA

Richards, Lou
2467 Brighton Dr # 2-B
Valencia, CA 91355

Richards, Mark (Misc)
755 Hunter St
Newcastle, NSW 2302, AUSTRALIA

Richards, Michael (Actor, Comedian)
c/o Staff Member *Untitled Entertainment (NY)*
322 8th Ave Ste 601
New York, NY 10001-6715, USA

Richards, Paul G (Misc)
Palisades, NY 10964, USA

Richards, Paul W (Astronaut)
2101 Nasa Pkwy Spc Center
Houston, TX 77058-3607, USA

Richards, Perry (Athlete, Football Player)
30079 Saint Martins St # 311
Livonia, MI 48152-1938, USA

Richards, Renee (Tennis Player)
1604 Union St
San Francisco, CA 94123-4507, USA

Richards, Rex E (Misc)
13 Woodstock Close
Oxford OX2 8DB, UNITED KINGDOM (UK)

Richards, Richard N (Astronaut)
2101 Nasa Pkwy Spc Center
Houston, TX 77058-3607, USA

Richards, Robert E (Bob) (Athlete, Track Athlete)
1616 Estates Dr
Waco, TX 76712-2208, USA

Richards, Rosemary Elam (Stylist)
60 Ross Ave Apt 1
San Anselmo, CA 94960-2832, USA

Richards, Rusty (Athlete, Baseball Player)
PO Box 7966
Horseshoe Bay, TX 78657-7966, USA

Richards, Sanya (Athlete, Olympic Athlete)
c/o Staff Member *Octagon*
2 Union St Ste 300
Portland, ME 04101-4295, USA

Richards, Stephanie (Actor)
733 Seward St PH
Los Angeles, CA 90038-3503, USA

Richards, Viv (Cricketer)
c/o Staff Member *West Indies Cricket Club*
PO Box 616
St John's, ANTIGUA

Richards, Warren J
9075 S 700 E Apt 109
Sandy, UT 84070-2445, USA

Richardson, Al (Athlete, Football Player)
3003 Mary Ashley Ct SE
Conyers, GA 30013-6419, USA

Richardson, Andrew (Stylist)
c/o Staff Member *Streeters*
560 Broadway Rm 203
New York, NY 10012-3945, 212-219-9566

Richardson, Ashley (Model)
c/o Staff Member *Ford Models (NY)*
238 E 4th St
New York, NY 10009-7425

Richardson, Bucky (Athlete, Football Player)
1025 Dulles Ave Apt 1313
Stafford, TX 77477-5747, USA

Richardson, Cameron (Actor)
c/o Staff Member *United Talent Agency (UTA)*
9560 Wilshire Blvd Fl 5
Beverly Hills, CA 90212-2400, USA

Richardson, Cheryl (Actor)
749 Fair Oaks Dr
Alamo, CA 94507-1457, USA

Richardson, Cliff (Athlete, Basketball Player)
6236 Radiance Blvd E # 2
Fife, WA 98424-3868, USA

Richardson, Damien (Athlete, Football Player)
1300 E Cromwell Ave
Fresno, CA 93720-2628, USA

Richardson, Dan (Musician)
c/o Staff Member *Agency Group Ltd, The (NY)*
142 W 57th St Fl 6
New York, NY 10019-3300, USA

Richardson, Donna (Misc)
500 Kirts Blvd
Troy, MI 48084-4134, USA

Richardson, Earl (Educator)
President's Office
Baltimore, MD 21239, USA

Richardson, Eliot
1100 Crest Ln
McLean, VA 22101-1815

Richardson, Eric (Athlete, Football Player)
509 Ely Blvd S
Petaluma, CA 94954-3813, USA

Richardson, Gloster (Athlete, Football Player)
9143 S Euclid Ave
Chicago, IL 60617-3749, USA

Richardson, Gordie (Athlete, Baseball Player)
23 Saint Paul Church Rd
Colquitt, GA 39837-6829, USA

Richardson, Gordon W H (Financier)
25 Cabot Square Canary Wharf
London E14 4QA, UNITED KINGDOM (UK)

Richardson, Grady (Athlete, Football Player)
5804 La Jolla Way
Cypress, CA 90630-3210, USA

Richardson, Greg (Boxer)
382 Camden Ave
Youngstown, OH 44505-4845, USA

Richardson, Hamilton (Tennis Player)
870 United Nations Plz
New York, NY 10017-1807, USA

Richardson, Huey (Athlete, Football Player)
1288 Skyhaven Rd SE
Atlanta, GA 30316-2606, USA

Richardson, Jack (Artist)
12171 Sunset Ave
Grass Valley, CA 95945-8512, USA

Richardson, Jake (Actor)
c/o Meredith Fine *Coast to Coast Talent Group*
3350 Barham Blvd
Los Angeles, CA 90068-1404, USA

Richardson, Jason (Athlete, Basketball Player)
c/o Dan Fegan *Lagardere Unlimited - (LA)*
10866 Wilshire Blvd
Los Angeles, CA 90024-4300, USA

Richardson, Jay (Athlete, Football Player)
c/o Eugene Parker *Maximum Sports Management*
6435 W Jefferson Blvd # 197
Fort Wayne, IN 46804-6203, USA

Richardson, Jeff (Athlete, Baseball Player)
47 Kuester Lk
Grand Island, NE 68801-8609, USA

Richardson, Jeffrey (Jeff) (Athlete, Baseball Player)
11779 W Fordson Dr
Marana, AZ 85653-7722, USA

Richardson, Jerry (Athlete, Football Player)
3200 Fleetwood Dr Apt 14
Amarillo, TX 79109-3218, USA

Richardson, Joely (Actor)
c/o Charles Finch *Finch & Partners*
Top Floor 29-37 Heddon St
London W1B 4BR, UNITED KINGDOM

Richardson, John (Athlete, Football Player)
3053 Eagles Claw Ave
Thousand Oaks, CA 91362-1771, USA

Richardson, John T (Educator)
2233 N Kenmore Ave
Chicago, IL 60614-3547, USA

Richardson, Kevin Michael (Actor)
c/o David Ginsberg *Insight*
1134 S Cloverdale Ave
Los Angeles, CA 90019-6737, USA

Richardson, Kristin (Actor)
c/o Brady McKay *Flutie Entertainment (LA)*
9320 Wilshire Blvd Ste 202
Beverly Hills, CA 90212-3217, USA

Richardson, LaTanya (Actor, Producer)
c/o Staff Member *Paradigm (LA)*
360 N Crescent Dr
Beverly Hills, CA 90210-4874, USA

Richardson, Linda (Opera Singer)
4 Addison Bridge Place
London W14 8XP, UNITED KINGDOM (UK)

Richardson, Michael Ray (Athlete, Basketball Player)
121 N Elk Ct
Aurora, CO 80018-1599, USA

Richardson, Midge T (Editor)
850 3rd Ave
New York, NY 10022-6222, USA

Richardson, Mike (Producer)
c/o Staff Member *Dark Horse Entertainment*
1438 N Gower St Box Bldg 23 PMB 200
Hollywood, CA 90028, USA

Richardson, Mike (Athlete, Football Player)
1619 W Caldwell St
Compton, CA 90220-4333, USA

Richardson, Mike W (Athlete, Football Player)
7310 Covewood Dr
Garland, TX 75044-2624, USA

Richardson, Miranda (Actor)
7 Saint George's Square
London SW1V 2HX, UNITED KINGDOM (UK)

Richardson, Nolan (Coach)
4057 N Hughmount Rd
Fayetteville, AR 72704-6516, USA

Richardson, Patricia (Actor)
c/o Jonathan Howard *Innovative Artists (LA)*
1505 10th St
Santa Monica, CA 90401-2805, USA

Richardson, Quentin (Basketball Player)
Staples Center 1111 S Figueroa St
Los Angeles, CA 90015, USA

Richardson, Robert (Cinematographer)
c/o Spyros Skouras *The Skouras Agency*
1149 3rd St Ste 300
Santa Monica, CA 90403-7201, USA

Richardson, Robert (Race Car Driver)
PO Box 523
McKinney, TX 75070-8139, USA

Richardson, Robert C (Nobel Prize Laureate)
4 Hunter Ln
Ithaca, NY 14850-9662, USA

Richardson, Robert C (Bobby) (Athlete, Baseball Player)
47 Adams Ave
Sumter, SC 29150-4037, USA

Richardson, Sam (Artist)
4121 Sequoyah Rd
Oakland, CA 94605-4539, USA

Richardson, W Franklyn (Religious Leader)
52 S 6th Ave
Mount Vernon, NY 10550-3005, USA

Richardson, Willam C (Educator)
1 Michigan Ave E
Battle Creek, MI 49017-4005, USA

Richardson, Willie (Athlete, Football Player)
5928 Waverly Dr
Jackson, MS 39206-2503, USA

Richardson of Lee, John S (Doctor)
Windcutter Lee
North Devon EX34 8LW, UNITED KINGDOM (UK)

Richardson-Whitfield, Salli (Actor)
c/o Craig Dorfman *Frontline Management*
5670 Wilshire Blvd Ste 1370
Los Angeles, CA 90036-5679, USA

Richardt, Mike (Athlete, Baseball Player)
5286 W Richert Ave
Fresno, CA 93722-9152, USA

Richer, Stephane (Athlete, Hockey Player)
Continental Arena 50 RR 120 N
East Rutherford, NJ 7073, USA

Richert, Nate (Actor)
c/o Iris Burton *Iris Burton Agency*
10100 Santa Monica Blvd Ste 1300
Los Angeles, CA 90067-4114, USA

Richert, Pete (Athlete, Baseball Player)
80 La Cerra Dr
Rancho Mirage, CA 92270-3811, USA

Richeson, Ray (Athlete, Football Player)
1348 Willoughby Rd
Vestavia, AL 35216-2906, USA

Richey, Cliff (Tennis Player)
2936 Cumberland Dr
San Angelo, TX 76904-6163, USA

Richey, Jennifer (Actor)
c/o Staff Member *Cunningham Escott Slevin & Doherty (CESD-LA)*
10635 Santa Monica Blvd Ste 130
Los Angeles, CA 90025-8306, USA

Richey, Nancy (Tennis Player)
2936 Cumberland Dr
San Angelo, TX 76904-6163, USA

Richey, Wade (Athlete, Football Player)
720 Patin Rd
Carencro, LA 70520-5206, USA

Richie, Lionel (Musician, Songwriter)
2850 Ocean Park Blvd Ste 300
Santa Monica, CA 90405-6216, USA

Richie, Michele (Stylist)
2521 Lincoln Ave
Miami, FL 33133-3822, USA

Richie, Nicole (Heir/Heiress, Reality TV Star)
c/o Michael Baum *Impression Entertainment*
9229 W Sunset Blvd Ste 700
West Hollywood, CA 90069-3407, USA

Richie, Rob (Athlete, Baseball Player)
1835 Meadowvale Way
Sparks, NV 89431-2949, USA

Richie, Shane (Actor)
c/o Phil Dale *Qdos Entertainment*
8 King St Covent Garden
London WC2 8HN, UNITED KINGDOM

Riching, Julian (Actor)
c/o Staff Member *Gary Goddard Agency*
10 St Mary St Suite 305
Toronto, ON M4Y 1P9, Canada

Richman, Caryn (Actor)
1805 Via Arriba
Palos Verdes Estates, CA 90274-1236, USA

Richman, Jonathan (Actor, Musician)
751 Bridgeway # 300
Sausalito, CA 94965-2102, USA

Richman, Peter Mark (Actor)
5114 Del Moreno Dr
Woodland Hills, CA 91364-2426, USA

Richmond, Branscombe (Actor)
PO Box 881095
Pukalani, HI 96788-1095, USA

Richmond, Mitch (Athlete, Basketball Player)
25374 Prado De La Felicidad
Calabasas, CA 91302-3649, USA

Richmond, Tequan (Actor)
c/o Temple Poteat *AMP Live Entertainment*
3727 W Magnolia Blvd # 446
Burbank, CA 91505-2818, USA

Richt, Mark (Coach, Football Coach)
PO Box 1472
Athens, GA 30603-1472, USA

Richter, Al (Athlete, Baseball Player)
3810 Atlantic Ave Apt 703
Virginia Beach, VA 23451-2736, USA

Richter, Andy (Actor, Comedian)
c/o Tim Sarkes *Brillstein Entertainment Partners*
9150 Wilshire Blvd Ste 350
Beverly Hills, CA 90212-3453, USA

Richter, Burton (Nobel Prize Laureate)
Linear Accelerator Center PO Box 4349
Stanford, CA 94309, USA

Richter, Frank (Athlete, Football Player)
711 N Slappey Blvd
Albany, GA 31701-1452, USA

Richter, Gerhard (Artist)
Bismarckstr 50
Cologne 50672, GERMANY

Richter, Hans
In der Wasserschopp 43
Heppenheim, GERMANY D-64646

Richter, James A (Jim) (Athlete, Football Player)
8620 Bournemouth Dr
Raleigh, NC 27615-2008, USA

Richter, Jason James (Actor)
9560 Wilshire Blvd Ste 500
Beverly Hills, CA 90212-2401, USA

Richter, John (Athlete, Basketball Player)
2740 Narcissa Rd
Plymouth Meeting, PA 19462-1107, USA

Richter, Leslie A (Les) (Athlete, Football Player)
PO Box 20499
Riverside, CA 92516-0499, USA

Richter, Michael T (Mike) (Athlete, Hockey Player)
2016 Hilltop Rd
Flourtown, PA 19031-1615, USA

Richter, Pat V (Athlete, Football Executive, Football Player)
833 Kings Way
Madison, WI 53704-6046, USA

Richwine, Maria (Actor)
8075 W 3rd St # 303
Los Angeles, CA 90048-4318, USA

Rickards, Ashley (Actor)
c/o Ben Levine *Kritzer Levine Wilkins Entertainment*
11872 La Grange Ave Fl 1
Los Angeles, CA 90025-5283, USA

Ricker, Robert S (Religious Leader)
2002 S Arlington Heights Rd
Arlington Heights, IL 60005-4102, USA

Ricketts, Dave (Athlete, Baseball Player)
12860 Polo Parc Dr
Saint Louis, MO 63146-1504, USA

Ricketts, Jeff (Actor)

Ricketts, Tom (Athlete, Football Player)
720 Warrendale Bayne Rd
Wexford, PA 15090-7492, USA

Rickles, Don (Actor, Comedian)
10249 Century Woods Dr
Los Angeles, CA 90067-6312, USA

Rickman, Alan (Actor, Producer)
c/o Judy Hofflund *Hofflund/Polone*
9465 Wilshire Blvd Ste 420
Beverly Hills, CA 90212-2603, USA

Ricks, Mikhael (Athlete, Football Player)
PO Box 41
Anahuac, TX 77514-0041, USA

Rico, Alfredo (Fred) (Athlete, Baseball Player)
7720 Ensign Ave
Sun Valley, CA 91352-4451, USA

Ricoeur, Paul (Misc)
18 Rue Henri Marrou
Chatenay Malabry 92290, FRANCE

Rida, Flo (Musician)
c/o Nick Carcaterra *Susan Blond Inc (NY)*
50 W 57th St Fl 14
New York, NY 10019-3914, USA

Ridder, P Anthony (Business Person, Publisher)
50 W San Fernando St
San Jose, CA 95113-2429, USA

Riddick, Frank A Jr (Physicist)
150 Broadway St Apt 709
New Orleans, LA 70118-7603, USA

Riddick, Steven (Steve) (Athlete, Track Athlete)
7601 Crittenden St Apt F2
Philadelphia, PA 19118-3225, USA

Riddiford, Lynn M (Biologist)
40733 Manor House Rd
Leesburg, VA 20175-6517, USA

Riddleberger, Denny (Athlete, Baseball Player)
3846 Riverside Dr
Columbus, OH 43220-4560, USA

Riddles, Libby (Dog Sled Racer)
PO Box 15253
Fritz Creek, AK 99603-6253, USA

Riddoch, Greg (Athlete, Baseball Player, Coach)
703 Windflower Dr
Longmont, CO 80504-2770, USA

Ride, Sally K (Astronaut)
PO Box 221
La Jolla, CA 92038-0221, USA

Rider, Amy (Actor)
c/o Amy Slomovits *Flutie Entertainment (LA)*
9320 Wilshire Blvd Ste 202
Beverly Hills, CA 90212-3217, USA

Rider, Isiah (J R) (Athlete, Basketball Player)
P.O. Box 121R
Montchanin, DE 19710, USA

Riders In The Sky
38 Music Sq E Ste 300
Nashville, TN 37203-4304

Riders of the Purple Sage
PO Box 1987
Studio City, CA 91614-0987

Ridge, Houston (Athlete, Football Player)
7027 Benson Ave
San Diego, CA 92114-5908, USA

Ridgeley, Andrew (Musician)
8800 W Sunset Blvd # 401
Los Angeles, CA 90069-2105, USA

Ridgeway, Angle (Golfer)
c/o Staff Member *Pro Golfers Association (PGA) Tour*
112 Tpc Blvd
Ponte Vedra Beach, FL 32082, USA

Ridgeway, Frank (Cartoonist)
c/o Staff Member *King Features Syndication*
300 W 57th St Fl 15
New York, NY 10019-5238, USA

Ridgle, Elston (Athlete, Football Player)
5317 Wilkinson Ave
Studio City, CA 91607-2412, USA

Ridgley, Bob (Actor)
4605 Lankershim Blvd Ste 305
North Hollywood, CA 91602-1875, USA

Ridgway, Brunilde S (Archaeologist)
Archaeology Dept
Bryn Mawr, PA 19010, USA

Ridings, Tag (Athlete, Golfer)
2040 Bantry Dr
Keller, TX 76262-9001, USA

Ridker, Paul (Doctor)
75 Francis St
Boston, MA 02115-6110, USA

Ridlehuber, Preston (Athlete, Football Player)
720 Serramonte Dr
Marietta, GA 30068-4674, USA

Ridley, John (Director, Producer, Writer)
c/o Nancy Josephson *WmE2 (Endeavor-LA)*
9601 Wilshire Blvd Fl 3
Beverly Hills, CA 90210-5219, USA

Ridlon, James A (Athlete, Football Player)
8006 E Lake Rd
Cazenovia, NY 13035, USA

Ridnour, Luke (Basketball Player)
351 Elliott Ave W Ste 500
Seattle, WA 98119-4153, USA

Ridzik, Steve (Athlete, Baseball Player)
7008 11th Ave W
Bradenton, FL 34209-4066, USA

Riedel, Lars (Athlete, Track Athlete)
Reichenhainer Str 154
Chemnitz 9125, GERMANY

Riedlbauch, Vaclav (Composer)
Revolucni 6
Prague 1 110 00, CZECH REPUBLIC

Riedling, John (Athlete, Baseball Player)
2118 Homestead Ln
Franklin, TN 37064-1177, USA

Riegel, Eden (Actor, Musician)
c/o Leigh Brillstein *International Creative Management (ICM-LA)*
10250 Constellation Blvd Fl 7
Los Angeles, CA 90067-6207, USA

Rieger, Max (Skier)
Innsbrucker Str 12
Mittenwald 82481, GERMANY

Riegert, Peter (Actor)
c/o John S Kelly *Bresler Kelly & Associates*
11500 W Olympic Blvd Ste 510
Los Angeles, CA 90064-1527, USA

Riegger, John (Golfer)
768 Tossa De Mar Ave
Henderson, NV 89002-6536, USA

Riegle, Gene (Coach, Horse Racer)
818 Chestnut Cir
Greenville, OH 45331-1075, USA

Riegle Jr, Donald W (Business Person, Ex-Senator, Senator)
700 12th St NW Ste 800
Washington, DC 20005-3949, USA

Riehle, Richard (Actor)
9200 W Sunset Blvd Ste 1125
Los Angeles, CA 90069-3610, USA

Rieker, Rich (Athlete, Baseball Player)
1223 Grey Fox Run
Weldon Spring, MO 63304-0307, USA

Rieker, Richard (Baseball Player)
5337 Foxshire Ct
Orlando, FL 32819-3824, USA

Rienstra, John (Athlete, Football Player)
5056 Briscoglen Dr
Colorado Springs, CO 80906-8612, USA

Riepe, James S (Business Person)
100 E Pratt St
Baltimore, MD 21202-1009, USA

Ries, Christopher D (Artist)
Keelersburg Road
Tunkhannock, PA 18657, USA

Riesenberg, Doug (Athlete, Football Player)
25068 Starr Creek Rd
Corvallis, OR 97333-9576, USA

Riesgo, Nikco (Athlete, Baseball Player)
29625 Bermuda Ln
Southfield, MI 48076-1663, USA

Riesgraf, Beth (Actor)
c/o Matthew Lesher *Insight*
1134 S Cloverdale Ave
Los Angeles, CA 90019-6737, USA

Riess, Adam (Astronomer, Physicist)
3700 San Martin Dr
Baltimore, MD 21218-2410, USA

Riessen, Marty (Tennis Player)
PO Box 5444
Santa Barbara, CA 93150-5444, USA

Ries-Zillmer, Ruth (Baseball Player)
133 Adeline St
Walworth, WI 53184-9522, USA

Rieu, Andre (Musician)
Mozartlaan 25
Hilversum, CM 1217, NETHERLANDS

Rieves, Charles (Athlete, Football Player)
3107 Long Bay Ct
Houston, TX 77059-3720, USA

Rife, Rikki
520 Washington Blvd # 924
Marina del Rey, CA 90292-5442

Riff
PO Box 7257
Paterson, NJ 07509-7257

Rifkin, Adam (Actor, Director, Writer)
c/o Simon Millar *Rumble Media*
1620 Broadway Ste C
Santa Monica, CA 90404-2777, USA

Rifkin, Jeremy (Activist, Writer)
1660 L St NW Ste 216
Washington, DC 20036-5642, USA

Rifkin, Ron (Actor, Musician)
c/o Marcia Hurwitz *Innovative Artists (LA)*
1505 10th St
Santa Monica, CA 90401-2805, USA

Rifkind, Joshua (Conductor, Musician)
100 Montgomery St
Cambridge, MA 02140-1725, USA

Rigali, Justin F Cardinal (Religious Leader)
222 N 17th St
Philadelphia, PA 19103-1202, USA

Rigby, Amy (Musician, Songwriter, Writer)
1229 17th Ave S
Nashville, TN 37212-2801, USA

Rigby, Brad (Athlete, Baseball Player)
1317 Ballentyne Pl
Apopka, FL 32703-6870, USA

Rigby, Jean P (Opera Singer)
31 Sinclair Road
London W14 0NS, UNITED KINGDOM (UK)

Rigby, Paul (Cartoonist)
119 Monterey Pointe Dr
West Palm Beach, FL 33418-5811, USA

Rigby, Randall Jr (General)
Deputy CG US Army Training/Doctrine Command
Fort Monroe, VA 23651, USA

Rigdon, Paul (Athlete, Baseball Player)
9231 Coxwell Ct
Jacksonville, FL 32221-1378, USA

Rigg, Diana (Actor)
Oaklands Park Chichester
West Sussex PO19 6AP, UK

Rigg, Rebecca (Actor)
110 Queen St
Woollahra, NSW 2025, AUSTRALIA

Riggan, Jerrod (Athlete, Baseball Player)
PO Box 1019
Brewster, WA 98812-1019, USA

Riggio, Leonard (Business Person)
122 5th Ave
New York, NY 10011-5605, USA

Riggle, Bob (Athlete, Football Player)
55 Waynesburg Rd
Washington, PA 15301-3224, USA

Riggleman, James D (Jim) (Athlete, Baseball Player, Coach)
14950 Gulf Blvd Apt 1003
Madeira Beach, FL 33708-2047, USA

Riggs, Adam (Athlete, Baseball Player)
26 Pebble Hollow Ct
Spring, TX 77381-4803, USA

Riggs, Chandler (Actor)
c/o Joanna (Joanie) Burstein *Burstein Company, The*
15304 W Sunset Blvd Ste 208
Pacific Palisades, CA 90272-3656, USA

Riggs, Gerald (Athlete, Football Player)
2574 Bright Ct
Decatur, GA 30034-2245, USA

Riggs, Lorrin A (Misc)
80 Lyme Rd Apt 104
Hanover, NH 03755-1229, USA

Riggs, Thron (Athlete, Football Player)
2645 E Southern Ave Apt A496
Tempe, AZ 85282-7791, USA

Righetti, Amanda (Actor, Producer)
c/o David (Dave) Fleming *Mosaic Media Group*
9200 W Sunset Blvd Ste 10
Los Angeles, CA 90069-3608, USA

Righetti, David A (Dave) (Athlete, Baseball Player)
552 Magdalena Ave
Los Altos Hills, CA 94024-5233, USA

Right Said Fred
PO Box 891135
Edam, NETHERLANDS ZJ

Righteous Bros (Music Group)
c/o Staff Member *WmE2 (WMA-LA)*
1 William Morris Pl
Beverly Hills, CA 90212-4261, USA

Rightnowar, Ron (Athlete, Baseball Player)
8926 Stonybrook Blvd
Sylvania, OH 43560-8906, USA

Rights, Graham H (Religious Leader)
459 S Church St
Winston Salem, NC 27101-5314, USA

Rigsbee, Shani (Actor, Bollywood)
c/o Staff Member *Cherokee Productions*
8491 W Sunset Blvd # 277
Los Angeles, CA 90069-1911, USA

Rigsby, Donald (Musician)
31959 Amberlea Rd
Dade City, FL 33523-6289, USA

Rihanna (Musician)
c/o Staff Member *Roc Nation*
1411 Broadway Fl 38
New York, NY 10018-3409, USA

Rijker, Lucia (Actor)
c/o Harlan Werner *Sports Placement Service*
330 W 11th St Apt 105
Los Angeles, CA 90015-2230, USA

Rijo, Jose (Athlete, Baseball Player)
2127 Brickell Ave Apt 2101
Miami, FL 33129-2146, USA

Rikaart, Greg (Actor)
c/o Kyle Fritz *Kyle Fritz Management*
6325 Heather Dr
Los Angeles, CA 90068-1633, USA

Riker, Albert J (Misc)
2760 E 8th St
Tucson, AZ 85716-4712, USA

Riker, Robin (Actor)
c/o Staff Member *Don Buchwald & Associates Inc (LA)*
6500 Wilshire Blvd Ste 2200
Los Angeles, CA 90048-4942, USA

Riker, Tom (Athlete, Basketball Player)
600 Fines Creek Rd
Clyde, NC 28721-9183, USA

Riklis, Meshulam (Business Person)
2901 Las Vegas Blvd S
Las Vegas, NV 89109-1933, USA

Riles, Ernest (Athlete, Baseball Player)
221 Asante Dr
Ellenwood, GA 30294-3187, USA

Riley, Amber (Actor)
c/o Nicki Fioravante *PMK/BNC - LA*
8687 Melrose Ave Ste 8
West Hollywood, CA 90069-5746, USA

Riley, Bill (Athlete, Hockey Player)
286 Buckingham Ave
Riverview, NB E1B 2P2, Canada

Riley, Boots (Musician)
c/o Danny Goldberg *Gold Village Entertainment*
37 W 17th St Ste 7W
New York, NY 10011-5525, USA

Riley, Bridget L (Artist)
31A Bruton Place
London W1X 7A8, UNITED KINGDOM (UK)

Riley, Chris (Golfer)
2289 Surrey Meadows Ave
Henderson, NV 89052-2335, USA

Riley, Eric (Athlete, Basketball Player)
6601 Sands Point Dr Apt 4
Houston, TX 77074-3731, USA

Riley, Forbes (Actor)
c/o Staff Member *Cohen Entertainment*
964 Hancock Ave Apt 305
West Hollywood, CA 90069-4091, USA

Riley, George (Athlete, Baseball Player)
451 Basket Rd
Oley, PA 19547-9245, USA

Riley, Gerald (Jerry) (Dog Sled Racer)
General Delivery
Nenana, AK 99760-9999, USA

Riley, H John Jr (Business Person)
600 Travis St
Houston, TX 77002-3009, USA

Riley, Jack (Actor)
c/o Staff Member *House of Representatives, The*
1434 6th St Ste 1
Santa Monica, CA 90401-2527, USA

Riley, James (Athlete, Football Player)
2201 Cardinal Dr
Edmond, OK 73013-7635, USA

Riley, James C (General)
Commanding General V Corps
APO, AE 9079, USA

Riley, Jeannie C (Musician)
417 Donelson Pike
Nashville, TN 37214-3556, USA

Riley, John P (Jack) (Athlete, Coach, Hockey Player)
PO Box 1302
Marstons Mills, MA 02648-5302, USA

Riley, Ken (Athlete, Football Player)
1865 E Gibbons St
Bartow, FL 33830-6712, USA

Riley, Kim Manske (Stylist)
3802 Ridge Manor Ct # CR
Kingwood, TX 77345-1216, USA

Riley, Lee (Athlete, Football Player)
1511 Yarbro Ln
Paducah, KY 42003-0281, USA

Riley, Madison (Actor)
c/o Mona Loring *MLC PR*
7080 Hollywood Blvd Ste 903
Los Angeles, CA 90028-6936, USA

Riley, Matt (Athlete, Baseball Player)
6 Kirra Ct
Aliso Viejo, CA 92656-4276, USA

Riley, Michael
9200 W Sunset Blvd Ste 900
Los Angeles, CA 90069-3604

Riley, Mike (Coach, Football Coach)
Athletic Dept
Corvallis, OR 97331, USA

Riley, Patrick J (Pat) (Athlete, Basketball Player, Coach)
800 S Pointe Dr # B
Miami Beach, FL 33139-7163, USA

Riley, Raven (Actor)
Prefers to be contacted via email
Phoenix, AZ 85066, USA

Riley, Richard D (Misc)
16 Boathouse Rd
Laconia, NH 03246-1949, USA

Riley, Ruth (Athlete)
3777 Lapeer Rd
Auburn Hills, MI 48326-1733

Riley, Sam (Actor)
c/o Angharad Wood *Tavistock Wood Management*
32 Tavistock St
London WC2B 5HA, UK

Riley, Steve (Athlete, Football Player)
7 Via Cancion
San Clemente, CA 92673-6907, USA

Riley, Talulah (Actor)
c/o Laura Symons *Premier PR (UK)*
91 Berwick St
London W1F 0NE, UK

Riley, Teddy (Musician, Songwriter)
70 Universal City Plz
Universal City, CA 91608-1011, USA

Riley, Terry M (Composer, Musician)
13699 Moonshine Rd
Camptonville, CA 95922-9713, USA

Riley, Victor (Athlete, Football Player)
1430 Bavand Cir Apt 107
Rock Hill, SC 29732-7521, USA

Riley, William Jay (Judge)
PO Box 307
Omaha, NE 68101-0307, USA

Rilling, Helmuth
Johann-Sebastian-Bach-Platz
Stuttgart 70178, GERMANY

Rimando, Nick (Soccer Player)
2400 E Capitol St NE
Washington, DC 20003-1734, USA

Rimer, Jeff (Sportscaster)
9916 Morris Dr
Dublin, OH 43017-8859, USA

Rimes, LeAnn (Musician)
c/o Terry Elam *Fitzgerald Hartley Co (Nashville)*
1908 Wedgewood Ave
Nashville, TN 37212-3733, USA

Rimington, Dave (Athlete, Football Player)
125 W 110th St Apt 5A
New York, NY 10026-4274, USA

Rimington, Stella (Government Official)
PO Box 1604
London SW1P 1XB, UNITED KINGDOM (UK)

Rimmel, James E (Religious Leader)
26049 5 Mile Rd
Detroit, MI 48239-3235, USA

Rinaldi, Kathy (Tennis Player)
1025 Thomas Jefferson St NW # 450
Washington, DC 20007-5201, USA

Rinaldi, Rich (Athlete, Basketball Player)
1117 Perry Ln
Collegeville, PA 19426-1067, USA

Rinaldo, Benjamin (Skier)
2680 Buena Park Dr
North Hollywood, CA 91604, USA

Rincon, Andy (Athlete, Baseball Player)
5425 Los Toros Ave
Pico Rivera, CA 90660-3038, USA

Rincon, Ricardo (Baseball Player)
c/o Staff Member *Oakland Athletics*
7000 Coliseum Way Ste 3
Oakland, CA 94621-1992, USA

Rinearson, Peter M (Journalist)
1120 John St
Seattle, WA 98109-5321, USA

Rineer, Jeff (Athlete, Baseball Player)
325 W Charlotte St
Millersville, PA 17551-9515, USA

Rinehart, Kenneth (Misc)
Chemistry Dept
Urbana, IL 61801, USA

Rines, Robert H (Inventor)
17 Ripley Rd
Belmont, MA 02478-1246, USA

RIng, Royce (Athlete, Baseball Player)
4849 Williamsburg Ln Unit 267
La Mesa, CA 91942-7657, USA

Ringadoo, Veerasamy (President)
Corner of Farquhar & Sir Celicourt Antelme Sts
Quatre-Bornes, MAURITIUS

Ringer, Jenifer (Ballerina)
c/o Staff Member *New York City Ballet*
20 Lincoln Center Plz
New York, NY 10023-6913, USA

Ringer, Robert J (Motivational Speaker, Writer)
c/o Staff Member *The Harry Walker Agency*
355 Lexington Ave Fl 21
New York, NY 10017-6603, USA

Ringwald, Molly (Actor)
c/o Greg Clark *Untitled Entertainment (LA)*
350 S Beverly Dr Ste 200
Beverly Hills, CA 90212-4819, USA

Rini, Mary (Baseball Player)
37592 Charter Oaks Blvd
Clinton Township, MI 48036-2422, USA

Rinker, Larry (Golfer)
1615 Woodland Ave
Winter Park, FL 32789-2774, USA

Rinna, Lisa (Actor)
c/o Steven Grossman *Collective*
8383 Wilshire Blvd Ste 1050
Beverly Hills, CA 90211-2415, USA

Rinser, Luise
via di Marino 49
Rocca di Papa, ITALY I-00040

Rintoul, David
91 Regent St
London, ENGLAND W1R 7TB

Rintoul, Steve (Golfer)
17506 Osprey Manor Way
Lithia, FL 33547-5044, USA

Rintzler, Marius A (Opera Singer)
Friedingstr 18
Dusseldorf 40625, GERMANY

Riordan, Marjorie
1833 Pelham Ave
Los Angeles, CA 90025-4713

Riordan, Mike (Athlete, Basketball Player)
10 N Cherry Grove Ave
Annapolis, MD 21401-3332, USA

Riordan, Richard J (Politician)
355 S Grand Ave Ste 4400
Los Angeles, CA 90071-3106, USA

Rios, Alberto (Writer)
English
Tempe, AZ 85287-0001, USA

Rios, Alexis (Baseball Player)
252 Derby Ave
West Haven, CT 6516, USA

Rios, Armando (Athlete, Baseball Player)
790 Ridenhour Cir
Orlando, FL 32809-7158, USA

Rios, Brandon (Boxer)
c/o Staff Member *Top Rank Inc.*
3908 Howard Hughes Pkwy # 580
Las Vegas, NV 89109, USA

Rios, Danny (Athlete, Baseball Player)
2523 W 9th Ln
Hialeah, FL 33010-1225, USA

Rios, Emily (Actor)
c/o Staff Member *Kass & Stokes Management*
9229 W Sunset Blvd Ste 504
Los Angeles, CA 90069-3405, USA

Rios, Marcelo (Tennis Player)
Via Augusta 200 #400
Barcelona 8021, SPAIN

Rios, Osvaldo (Actor)
c/o Staff Member *TV Caracol*
Calle 76 #11 - 35 Piso 10AA
Bogota DC 26484, COLOMBIA

Riotta, Vincent (Actor)
c/o Staff Member *Scott Marshall Partners Ltd*
15 Little Portland St 2nd Floor
London W1W 8BW, UK

Ripa, Kelly (Actor)
7 Lincoln Sq Fl 5
New York, NY 10023-7219, USA

Ripert, Eric (Chef)
787 7th Ave
New York, NY 10019-6018, USA

Ripken, Billy (Athlete, Baseball Player)
900 Mount Soma Ct
Fallston, MD 21047-1935, USA

Ripken Jr, Cal (Athlete, Baseball Player)
1427 Clarkview Rd Ste 100
Baltimore, MD 21209-0030, USA

Ripley, Alice (Actor, Musician)
c/o Staff Member *Douglas Gorman Rothacker & Wilhelm Inc*
1501 Broadway Ste 703
New York, NY 10036-5501, USA

Ripley, Allen (Athlete, Baseball Player)
50 Dunham St
Attleboro, MA 02703-3052, USA

Rippelmeyer, Ray (Athlete, Baseball Player)
104 Eagle Ct
Waterloo, IL 62298-3158, USA

Rippey, Rodney Allan (Actor)
3941 Veselich Ave # 4-251
Los Angeles, CA 90039-1461, USA

Rippey, Rodney Allen
3939 Veselich Ave # 351
Los Angeles, CA 90039-1460

Ripple, Kenneth F (Judge)
204 S Main St
South Bend, IN 46601-2126, USA

Rippley, Steve (Baseball Player)
3900 Galt Ocean Dr Apt 1406
Fort Lauderdale, FL 33308-6606, USA

Rippley, Steve (Athlete, Baseball Player)
3900 Galt Ocean Dr Apt 1406
Fort Lauderdale, FL 33308-6606, USA

Ris, Hans (Biologist)
2116 Madison St
Madison, WI 53711-2132, USA

Riseborough, Andrea (Actor)
c/o Ciara Parkes *Public Eye Communications*
535 Kings Rd Suite 313 Plaza
London SW10 0SZ, United Kingdom

Risebrough, Doug (Athlete, Coach, Hockey Player)
5809 Schaefer Rd
Edina, MN 55436-1115, USA

Risen, Arnold (Arnie) (Athlete, Basketball Player)
3217 Bremerton Rd
Cleveland, OH 44124-5346, USA

Risher, Alan (Athlete, Football Player)
59350 Stonewall Dr
Plaquemine, LA 70764-7422, USA

Risien, Cody L (Athlete, Football Player)
12060 Lake Ave Apt 401
Lakewood, OH 44107-1865, USA

Risinger, Earlene (Baseball Player)
334 Aurora St SE
Grand Rapids, MI 49507-3124, USA

Risk, Thomas N (Financier)
10 Belford Place
Edinburgh EH4 3DH, SCOTLAND

Riske, Alison (Athlete, Tennis Player)
c/o Staff Member *Women's Tennis Association (WTA (US))*
1 Progress Plz Ste 1500
St Petersburg, FL 33701-4335, USA

Riske, David (Athlete, Baseball Player)
2771 Culloden Ave
Henderson, NV 89044-0233, USA

Risley, Bill (Athlete, Baseball Player)
1160 Prim Rose Cir
Greenwood, AR 72936-3066, USA

Risney, Jodee (Stylist)
3234 Maplethorpe Ln
Soquel, CA 95073-2917, USA

Rispoli, Michael (Actor)
c/o Staff Member *Gersh (LA)*
9465 Wilshire Blvd Ste 600
Beverly Hills, CA 90212-2612, USA

Rissmiller, Ray (Athlete, Football Player)
114 Iken Cir
Goose Creek, SC 29445-7148, USA

Rist, Robbie
PO Box 867
Woodland Hills, CA 91365-0867

Ristorucci, Lisa (Actor)
400 S Beverly Dr Ste 216
Beverly Hills, CA 90212-4404, USA

Ritcher, James A (Jim) (Athlete, Football Player)
8620 Boumemouth Dr
Raleigh, NC 27615, USA

Ritchie, Daniel L (Educator, Television Host)
Chancellor S Ofc
Denver, CO 80208-0001, USA

Ritchie, Guy (Director, Producer, Writer)
c/o Cindy Guagenti *Baker Winokur Ryder Public Relations (BWR-LA)*
9100 Wilshire Blvd Ste 500 PMB WEST
Beverly Hills, CA 90212-3426, USA

Ritchie, Ian (Architect)
110 Three Colt St
London E14 8A2, UNITED KINGDOM (UK)

Ritchie, Jay (Athlete, Baseball Player)
8275 Highway 52
Rockwell, NC 28138-8545, USA

Ritchie, Jill (Actor)
c/o Staff Member *Rugolo Entertainment*
195 S Beverly Dr Ste 400
Beverly Hills, CA 90212-3044, USA

Ritchie, Jim (Artist)
19 E 82nd St
New York, NY 10028-0302, USA

Ritchie, John H (Architect)
Mount Heswall
Wirrai L60 4RD, UNITED KINGDOM (UK)

Ritchie, Jon (Football Player)
c/o Staff Member *Philadelphia Eagles*
1 Novacare Way
Philadelphia, PA 19145-5996

Ritchie, Todd (Athlete, Baseball Player)
114 Hulan Dr
Kerens, TX 75144-6046, USA

Ritchie, Wally (Athlete, Baseball Player)
417 Robert Cir
Santa Clara, UT 84765-5617, USA

Ritchie Family, The
4100 W Flagler St # B-2
Coral Gables, FL 33134-1612

Ritchson, Alan (Actor)
c/o Gayle Divine *Divine Management*
3822 Latrobe St
Los Angeles, CA 90031-1446

Ritenour, Lee (Composer, Musician)
11808 Dorothy St Apt 108
Los Angeles, CA 90049-5469, USA

Ritger, Dick (Bowler)
804 Valley View Dr
River Falls, WI 54022-2724, USA

Rittenhouse, Lenore (Golfer)
295 Bellhaven Dr
Whispering Pines, NC 28327-7133, USA

Ritter, C Dowd (Financier)
1900 5th Ave N
Birmingham, AL 35203-2610, USA

Ritter, Huntley (Actor, Producer)
c/o Sheila Wenzel *Innovative Artists (LA)*
1505 10th St
Santa Monica, CA 90401-2805, USA

Ritter, Jason (Actor)
c/o Joanna (Joanie) Burstein *Burstein Company, The*
15304 W Sunset Blvd Ste 208
Pacific Palisades, CA 90272-3656, USA

Ritter, Krysten (Actor)
c/o Nancy Sanders *Sanders Armstrong Caserta*
2120 Colorado Ave Ste 120
Santa Monica, CA 90404-3561, USA

Ritter, Lawrence (Baseball Player)
424 W End Ave Apt 6D
New York, NY 10024-5777, USA

Ritter, Reggie (Athlete, Baseball Player)
1564 Estep Rd
Donaldson, AR 71941-8987, USA

Ritts, Jim (Golfer, Television Host)
100 International Golf Dr
Daytona Beach, FL 32124-1082, USA

Rittwage, Jim (Athlete, Baseball Player)
23931 Columbus Rd
Bedford, OH 44146-2969, USA

Ritz, David
c/o Daniel A (Dan) Strone *Trident Media Group LLC*
41 Madison Ave Fl 36
New York, NY 10010-2257, USA

Ritz, Kevin (Athlete, Baseball Player)
836 N 6th St
Cambridge, OH 43725-1400, USA

Ritzenhaler, Henry Leon
PO Box 305
Dermott, AR 71638-0305

Ritzman, Alice (Golfer)
614 S Foys Lake Dr
Kalispell, MT 59901-7440, USA

Riutta, Ernest R (Admiral)
US Coast Guard Pacific Coast Guard Island
Alameda, CA 94501, USA

Riva, Diana Maria (Actor)
c/o Amy Guenther *Gateway Management Company Inc*
860 Via De La Paz Ste F10
Pacific Palisades, CA 90272-3631, USA

Riva, Emmanuelle
37 Rue De La Harpe
Paris, FRANCE F-75005

Rivaldo (Soccer Player)
3 Turati Via
Washington, DC 20221-0001, ITALY

Rivas, Daniel Louis (Actor)
c/o Paul Santana *Agency for the Performing Arts (APA-LA)*
405 S Beverly Dr Ste 500
Beverly Hills, CA 90212-4425, USA

Rivas, Gonzalo (Actor)
c/o Staff Member *Televisa*
Blvd Adolfo Lopez Mateos 232 Colonia San Angel INN
DF CP 01060, MEXICO

Rivas Monta??o, Hanna (Actor)
c/o Staff Member *Televisa*
Blvd Adolfo Lopez Mateos 232 Colonia San Angel INN
DF CP 01060, MEXICO

Rivera, Ana Liz (Actor)
c/o Staff Member *Televisa*
Blvd Adolfo Lopez Mateos 232 Colonia San Angel INN
DF CP 01060, MEXICO

Rivera, Angelica (Actor)
c/o Staff Member *Televisa*
Blvd Adolfo Lopez Mateos 232 Colonia San Angel INN
DF CP 01060, MEXICO

Rivera, Chita (Actor, Dancer, Musician)
c/o Staff Member *WmE2 (WMA-LA)*
1 William Morris Pl
Beverly Hills, CA 90212-4261, USA

Rivera, Geraldo (Journalist, Television Host)
c/o Jim Griffin *Paradigm (NY)*
360 Park Ave S Fl 16
New York, NY 10010-1708, USA

Rivera, Jerry (Musician)
c/o Staff Member *BMG*
1540 Broadway
New York, NY 10036-4039, USA

Rivera, Jim (Athlete, Baseball Player)
2311 Abbey Dr Apt 7
Fort Wayne, IN 46835-3150, USA

Rivera, Jose (Producer, Writer)
c/o Rick Berg *Code Entertainment*
9229 W Sunset Blvd Ste 615
Los Angeles, CA 90069-3419, USA

Rivera, Juan (Athlete, Baseball Player)
c/o Staff Member *Los Angeles Dodgers (LA Dodgers)*
1000 Elysian Park Ave
Los Angeles, CA 90090-1112, USA

Rivera, Luis (Athlete, Baseball Player)
16 Calle Lazaro Ramos
Cidra, PR 00739-3424, USA

Rivera, Lupillo (Music Group)
c/o Staff Member *Sony Music Miami*
605 Lincoln Rd Ste 700
Miami Beach, FL 33139-2901, USA

Rivera, Mariano (Athlete, Baseball Player)
147 Anderson Hill Rd
Purchase, NY 10577-2007, USA

Rivera, Maxwell (Musician)
c/o Staff Member *Shore Fire Media*
32 Court St Fl 16
Brooklyn, NY 11201-4441, USA

Rivera, Naya (Actor)
c/o Sharyn Berg *Sharyn Talent Management*
PO Box 18033
Encino, CA 91416-8033, USA

Rivera, Ron (Athlete, Football Player)
9212 Heydon Hall Cir
Charlotte, NC 28210-6063, USA

Rivera Carrera, Norberto Cardinal (Religious Leader)
Aptdo Postal 24-4-33
Mexico City, DF 6700, MEXICO

Rivero, Jorge (Actor)
733 Seward St PH
Los Angeles, CA 90038-3503, USA

Rivers, David (Athlete, Basketball Player)
10509 Greensprings Dr
Tampa, FL 33626-1724, USA

Rivers, Glenn (Doc) (Athlete, Basketball Player, Coach)
5 Isle of Sicily
Winter Park, FL 32789-1505, USA

Rivers, Jamie (Athlete, Football Player)
4006 Lindell Blvd
Saint Louis, MO 63108-3202, USA

Rivers, Joan (Comedian, Producer)
PO Box 1150
New York, NY 10150-1150, USA

Rivers, Johnny (Musician, Songwriter, Writer)
3141 Coldwater Canyon Ln
Beverly Hills, CA 90210-1250, USA

Rivers, Marcellus (Athlete, Football Player)
12003 Eden Ln
Frisco, TX 75033-1146, USA

Rivers, Melissa (Talk Show Host)
c/o Steven Jensen *The Independent Group*
6363 Wilshire Blvd Ste 115
Los Angeles, CA 90048-5734, USA

Rivers, Mickey (Athlete, Baseball Player)
350 NW 48th St
Miami, FL 33127-2459, USA

Rivers, Philip (Athlete, Football Player)
4020 Murphy Canyon Rd
San Diego, CA 92123-4407, USA

Rivers, Reggie (Athlete, Football Player)
5003 E Weaver Pl
Centennial, CO 80121-3520, USA

Riverside, Vincent
c/o Melanie Sharp *Sharp Talent*
117 N Orlando Ave
Los Angeles, CA 90048-3403, USA

Rives, Don (Athlete, Football Player)
PO Box 553
Wheeler, TX 79096-0553, USA

Rivest, Ronald (Scientist)
Cambridge, MA 2139, USA

Rivette, Jacques (Director)
20 Blvd de la Bastille
Paris 75012, FRANCE

Riviere, Marie (Actor, Director)
c/o Staff Member *Dominique Sarais Agence Artistique*
37 rue du Port a l'Anglais
Alfortville 94140, France

Rivlin, Alice M (Government Official)
2842 Chesterfield Pl NW
Washington, DC 20008-1015, USA

Rizzo, Jack (Athlete, Football Player)
1105 Forest Trails Dr
Castle Pines, CO 80108-8280, USA

Rizzo, Jerry (Athlete, Basketball Player)
1751 E Reno Ave Unit 104
Las Vegas, NV 89119-2183, USA

Rizzo, Joe (Athlete, Football Player)
6131 Dorsett Pl
Wilmington, NC 28403-0128, USA

Rizzo, John R (Athlete, Football Player)
1105 Forest Trails Dr
Castle Pines, CO 80108-8280, USA

Rizzo, Patti (Golfer)
2455 Provence Cir
Weston, FL 33327-1303, USA

Rizzo, Rizzo (DJ)
c/o Len Evans *Project Publicity*
312 W 53rd St Ste 202
New York, NY 10019-5743, USA

Rizzo, Todd (Athlete, Baseball Player)
7 Williamsburg Ct
Sewell, NJ 08080-3230, USA

Rizzo-Depardon, Patti (Golfer)
1008 SE 5th Ct
Ft Lauderdale, FL 33301-3004, USA

Rizzotti, Jennifer (Basketball Player, Coach)
Athletic Dept
West Hartford, CT 6117, USA

Roa, Joe (Athlete, Baseball Player)
677 E Brickley Ave
Hazel Park, MI 48030-1270, USA

Roa Bastos, Augusto (Writer)
Berutti 2828 Martinez
Buenos Aires, ARGENTINA

Roach, Jason (Athlete, Baseball Player)
12295 SE Birkdale Run
Jupiter, FL 33469-1746, USA

Roach, Jay (Director, Producer, Writer)
c/o Staff Member *Everyman Pictures*
3000 Olympic Blvd Ste 1500
Santa Monica, CA 90404-5073, USA

Roach, John (Athlete, Football Player)
4101 San Carlos St
Dallas, TX 75205-2047, USA

Roach, Mel (Athlete, Baseball Player)
4131 Southaven Rd
Richmond, VA 23235-1026, USA

Roache, Linus (Actor)
c/o Staff Member *WmE2 (Endeavor-LA)*
9601 Wilshire Blvd Fl 3
Beverly Hills, CA 90210-5219, USA

Roaches, Carl (Athlete, Football Player)
1314 Twining Oaks Ln
Missouri City, TX 77489-2110, USA

Roaf, William L (Willie) (Athlete, Football Player)
1900 E 38th Ave
Pine Bluff, AR 71601-7280, USA

Roan, Michael (Athlete, Football Player)
11275 Green Valley Rd
Sebastopol, CA 95472-9771, USA

Roan, Oscar (Athlete, Football Player)
9 Pringle Ln
Rockwall, TX 75087-8004, USA

Roark, Terry P (Educator)
1752 Edward Dr
Laramie, WY 82072-2331, USA

Roarke, Mike (Athlete, Baseball Player)
940 Quaker Ln Apt 2302
East Greenwich, RI 02818-5085, USA

Roath, Stephen D (Business Person)
141 N Civic Dr
Walnut Creek, CA 94596-3815, USA

Robach, Amy (Correspondent)
c/o Staff Member *MSNBC (NJ)*
NBC/One Microsoft Corporation 1 MSNC Plaza
Secaucus, NJ 7094, USA

Robards, Jake (Actor)
c/o Staff Member *Don Buchwald & Associates Inc (NY)*
10 E 44th St Frnt 1
New York, NY 10017-3654

Robards, Sam (Actor)
1180 S Beverly Dr Ste 601
Los Angeles, CA 90035-1158, USA

Robb, Annasophia (Actor)
c/o Alissa Vradenburg *Untitled Entertainment (LA)*
350 S Beverly Dr Ste 200
Beverly Hills, CA 90212-4819, USA

Robb, David (Actor)
c/o Staff Member *Emptage Hallett*
14 Rathbone Pl
London W1T 1HT, UNITED KINGDOM (UK)

Robb, Doug (Musician)
c/o Staff Member *Island Def Jam Records*
2220 Colorado Ave
Santa Monica, CA 90404-3506, USA

Robb, Lynda Bird Johnson (Misc)
612 Chain Bridge Rd
McLean, VA 22101-1810, USA

Robb, Walter L (Business Person, Inventor)
1358 Ruffner Rd
Niskayuna, NY 12309-2500, USA

Robbers on High Street (Music Group)
c/o Staff Member *Paradigm (Monterey)*
404 W Franklin St
Monterey, CA 93940-2303, USA

Robbie, Margot (Actor)
c/o Chris Huvane *Management 360*
9111 Wilshire Blvd
Beverly Hills, CA 90210-5508, USA

Robbie, Seymour
9980 Liebe Dr
Beverly Hills, CA 90210-1037

Robbie, Timothy J (Tim) (Football Executive)
7500 SW 30th St
Davie, FL 33314-1020, USA

Robbins, Amy (Actor)
c/o Staff Member *Artists Rights Group (ARG)*
4 Great Portland St
London W1W 8PA, UNITED KINGDOM (UK)

Robbins, Anthony (Tony) (Motivational Speaker, Writer)
9888 Carroll Centre Rd Ste 100
San Diego, CA 92126-4581, USA

Robbins, Austin (Athlete, Football Player)
4627 Hilltop Ter SE
Washington, DC 20019-7837, USA

Robbins, Barret (Athlete, Football Player)
25773 Perlman Pl Unit B
Stevenson Ranch, CA 91381-2365, USA

Robbins, Brian (Director)
c/o Staff Member *Tollin/Robbins Management*
4130 Cahuenga Blvd Ste 305
Toluca Lake, CA 91602-2847, USA

Robbins, Bruce (Athlete, Baseball Player)
13023 E 239th St
Noblesville, IN 46060-6988, USA

Robbins, Deanna (Actor)
630 N Keystone St
Burbank, CA 91506-1922, USA

Robbins, Doug (Baseball Player)
915 NW A St
Richmond, IN 47374-4059, USA

Robbins, Jake (Athlete, Baseball Player)
14208 Castle Abbey Ln
Charlotte, NC 28277-1612, USA

Robbins, Jane (Actor)
44 Perry Road
London W3 7NA, UNITED KINGDOM (UK)

Robbins, Kelly (Golfer)
1025 Lincoln Dr
Weidman, MI 48893-9365, USA

Robbins, Lizz (Model)
c/o Michael (Mike) Esterman
Esterman.Com, LLC
Prefers to be contacted via email
MD, USA

Robbins, Mary
PO Box 641032
Miami, FL 33164-1032

Robbins, Randy (Athlete, Football Player)
1131 E Valle Vista Dr
Nogales, AZ 85621-1229, USA

Robbins, Red (Athlete, Basketball Player)
308 Brockenbraugh Ct
Metairie, LA 70005-3322, USA

Robbins, Tim (Actor, Director)
c/o Jen Turner *Wolf Kasteler Van Iden & Associates (NY)*
584 Broadway Rm 310
New York, NY 10012-5246, USA

Robbins, Tom (Writer)
PO Box 338
La Conner, WA 98257-0338, USA

Robbins, Tootie (Athlete, Football Player)
3600 W Ray Rd Apt 1031
Chandler, AZ 85226-7705, USA

Robby Krieger Band (Music Group)
c/o Sammy Boyd *dv8 Entertainment & Productions*
208 Main St Ste 202
Asbury Park, NJ 07712-7033, USA

Robelot, Jane (Correspondent)
51 W 52nd St
New York, NY 10019-6119, USA

Robens of Woldingham, Alfred (Educator, Government Official)
2 Laleham Abbey
Staines, Middx TW18 1SZ, UNITED KINGDOM (UK)

Roberge, Bert (Athlete, Baseball Player)
267 Sunderland Dr
Auburn, ME 04210-9232, USA

Roberson, Antoinette (Musician)
c/o Staff Member *Diva Central Inc*
7510 W Sunset Blvd Ste 1445
Los Angeles, CA 90046-3408, USA

Roberson, Irvin (Bo) (Athlete, Football Player, Track Athlete)
820 N Raymond Ave Apt 47
Pasadena, CA 91103-3151, USA

Roberson, James (Athlete, Football Player)
417 Labarre Ct
Saint Johns, FL 32259-4024, USA

Roberson, James W (Cinematographer)
PO Box 121013
Big Bear Lake, CA 92315-8948, USA

Roberson, Kevin (Athlete, Baseball Player)
1565 E North Port Rd
Decatur, IL 62526-2823, USA

Roberson, Rick (Athlete, Basketball Player)
635 W West Ave
Fullerton, CA 92832-2120, USA

Roberson, Sid (Athlete, Baseball Player)
132 Tulip Tree Ct
Jupiter, FL 33458-7179, USA

Robert, Jacques F (Attorney, Attorney General, General)
14 Villa Saint-Georges
Antony 92160, FRANCE

Robert, Rene (Athlete, Hockey Player)
4020 Rue Savard
Troie Rivieres, QC G8Y 4B8, Canada

Roberts, Alfredo (Athlete, Football Player)
4616 W Beach Park Dr
Tampa, FL 33609-3705, USA

Roberts, Bernard (Musician)
Uwchlaw'r Coed Llanbedr
Gwynedd LL45 2NA, WALES

Roberts, Bert C Jr (Business Person)
500 Clinton Center Dr
Clinton, MS 39056-5678, USA

Roberts, Beverly
16430 Bake Pkwy
Irvine, CA 92618-4665

Roberts, Beverly (Actor)
16430 Bake Pkwy
Irvine, CA 92618-4665, USA

Roberts, Bill (Athlete, Football Player)
5901 Amy Dr
Minneapolis, MN 55436-1933, USA

Roberts, Brad (Musician)
1505 W 2nd Ave # 200
Vancouver, BC V6H 3Y4, CANADA

Roberts, Bret (Actor)
c/o Scott Karp *Crystal Sky Pictures*
10203 Santa Monica Blvd Ste 500
Los Angeles, CA 90067-6416, USA

Roberts, Brian (Athlete, Baseball Player)
3434 Rugby Rd
Durham, NC 27707-5449, USA

Roberts, Brian L (Business Person)
1500 Market St Fl 33E
Philadelphia, PA 19102-2131, USA

Roberts, Bruce (Musician, Songwriter, Writer)
c/o Staff Member *Gorfaine/Schwartz Agency Inc*
4111 W Alameda Ave Ste 509
Burbank, CA 91505-4171, USA

Roberts, Cecil (Misc)
8315 Lee Hwy # 500
Fairfax, VA 22031-2215, USA

Roberts, Corrine (Cokie) (Correspondent)
5315 Bradley Blvd
Bethesda, MD 20814-1244, USA

Roberts, Dale (Athlete, Baseball Player)
8 McDowell Rd
Nicholasville, KY 40356-9323, USA

Roberts, Danny (Reality TV Star)
c/o Staff Member *Heffner Management*
80 Vine St Apt 203
Seattle, WA 98121-1369, USA

Roberts, Dave (Athlete, Baseball Player)
10002 Windover Dr
Fort Ashby, WV 26719-9211, USA

Roberts, Dave (Athlete, Baseball Player)
9705 Sam Bass Trl
Keller, TX 76244-6092, USA

Roberts, Dave (Athlete, Baseball Player)
6937 Laurel Valley Dr
Fort Worth, TX 76132-4461, USA

Roberts, Dave (Athlete, Baseball Player)
1208 Crestview Dr
Cardiff By The Sea, CA 92007-1400, USA

Roberts, David (Dave) (Athlete, Track Athlete)
14310 SW 73rd Ave
Archer, FL 32618-2914, USA

Roberts, Dee (Artist)
2012 N 19th St
Boise, ID 83702-0821, USA

Roberts, Doris (Actor)
6225 Quebec Dr
Los Angeles, CA 90068-2219, USA

Roberts, Emma (Actor)
c/o David Sweeney *Sweeney Management*
8755 Lookout Mountain Ave
Los Angeles, CA 90046-1861, USA

Roberts, Eric (Actor)
c/o Mark Teitelbaum *Teitelbaum Artists Group*
8840 Wilshire Blvd Fl 3
Beverly Hills, CA 90211-2606, USA

Roberts, Fred (Athlete, Basketball Player)
463 Knight Cir
Alpine, UT 84004-1259, USA

Roberts, Gary (Athlete, Hockey Player)
PO Box 848 Station Main
Uxbridge, PM L9P 1N2, Canada

Roberts, Gene (Athlete, Football Player)
10803 E 49 Hwy
Independence, MO 64055, USA

Roberts, Gordon R (War Hero)
445 Ward Koebel Rd
Oregonia, OH 45054-9468, USA

Roberts, Grant (Athlete, Baseball Player)
1299 Vista Captain Dr
El Cajon, CA 92020, USA

Roberts, Gregory David (Writer)
c/o Staff Member *United Talent Agency (UTA)*
9560 Wilshire Blvd Fl 5
Beverly Hills, CA 90212-2400, USA

Roberts, H Edward (Ed) (Designer)
408 Peacock St
Cochran, GA 31014, USA

Roberts, J D (Athlete, Football Coach, Football Player)
6708 Trevi Ct
Oklahoma City, OK 73116-2604, USA

Roberts, Jake (Actor, Writer)
Box 3859
Stamford, CT 6905

Roberts, James A (Jim) (Athlete, Coach, Hockey Player)
137 Ridgecrest Dr
Chesterfield, MO 63017-2653, USA

Roberts, Joe (Athlete)
4100 Redwood Rd Ste 10
Oakland, CA 94619-2363, USA

Roberts, John (Director)
c/o Staff Member *Independent Talent Group (ITG-UK)*
Oxford House 76 Oxford St
London W1D 1BS, UK

Roberts, John (Judge)
1st St NE
Washington, DC 20543-0001, USA

Roberts, John D (Misc)
Chemistry
Pasadena, CA 91125-0001, USA

Roberts, John D (J D) (Athlete, Coach, Football Player)
6708 Trevi Ct
Oklahoma City, OK 73116-2604, USA

Roberts, Julia (Actor)
c/o Marcy Engleman *Engelman & Company*
156 5th Ave Ste 711
New York, NY 10010-7779, USA

Roberts, Julie (Musician)
c/o Staff Member *Creative Artists Agency (CAA-LA)*
2000 Avenue of the Stars Ste 100
Los Angeles, CA 90067-4705, USA

Roberts, Kenny (Motorcycle Race, Motorcycle Racer)
419 Medina Rd
Medina, OH 44256-9619, USA

Roberts, Lawrence G (Scientist)
170 Baytech Dr
San Jose, CA 95134-2302, USA

Roberts, Leon (Athlete, Baseball Player)
4711 Chapel Springs Ct
Arlington, TX 76017-1204, USA

Roberts, Leon (Bip) (Athlete, Baseball Player)
3569 Rosincress Dr
San Ramon, CA 94582-5078, USA

Roberts, Leonard (Business Person)
300 Trinity Campus Cir
Fort Worth, TX 76102-1964, USA

Roberts, Leonard (Actor)
c/o Lena Roklin *Luber Roklin Management*
8530 Wilshire Blvd Ste 550
Beverly Hills, CA 90211-3133, USA

Roberts, Leonard (Athlete, Baseball Player)
1027 Waterford Dr
Dallas, TX 75218-2845, USA

Roberts, Loren (Athlete, Golfer)
8429 Orchard Hill Dr
Germantown, TN 38138-6297, USA

Roberts, Louie
2401 12th Ave S
Nashville, TN 37204-2415

Roberts, Lynn
42 Vespers Way
Okatie, SC 29909-6216, USA

Roberts, M Brigitte (Writer)
29 Fernshaw Road
London SW10 0TG, UNITED KINGDOM (UK)

Roberts, Marcus (Musician)
165 W 57th St
New York, NY 10019-2201, USA

Roberts, Marvin (Athlete, Basketball Player)
1 Gilbert Trl NE
Atlanta, GA 30308-2331, USA

Roberts, Michael D (Actor)
c/o Staff Member *Talent Company, The*
135 E Olive Ave # 4227
Burbank, CA 91502-1820, USA

Roberts, Nora (Writer)
19239 Burnside Bridge Rd
Keedysville, MD 21756-1603, USA

Roberts, Paul H (Mathematician)
PO Box 951567
Los Angeles, CA 90095-1567, USA

Roberts, R Michael (Scientist)
2213 Hominy Branch Ct
Columbia, MO 65201-6113, USA

Roberts, Rachel (Actor, Model)
c/o Staff Member *Models 1*
12 Macklin St Covent Gardens
London WC2B 5SZ, UK

Roberts, Ralph J (Business Person)
1500 Market St
Philadelphia, PA 19102-2109, USA

Roberts, Randy (Actor)
c/o Mary Dangerfield 239 NW 13th Ave Ste 215
Portland, OR 97209, USA

Roberts, Randy (Actor)
Attn: Renee Amaireh 14220 Winterset Dr
Greenwell Springs, LA 70739, USA

Roberts, Richard J (Nobel Prize Laureate)
32 Tozer Rd
Beverly, MA 01915-5510, USA

Roberts, Rick
9150 Wilshire Blvd Ste 350
Beverly Hills, CA 90212-3453

Roberts, Robin (Sportscaster, Television Host)
c/o Staff Member *Good Morning America (NY)*
147 Columbus Ave Fl 6
New York, NY 10023-6503, USA

Roberts, Robin (Athlete, Baseball Player)
504 Terrace Hill Dr
Temple Terrace, FL 33617-3850, USA

Roberts, Shawn (Actor)
c/o Staff Member *Christopher Wright Management*
3207 Winnie Dr
Los Angeles, CA 90068-1439, USA

Roberts, Stanley (Athlete, Basketball Player)
1192 Congaree Rd
Hopkins, SC 29061-9704, USA

Roberts, Steven
5315 Bradley Blvd
Bethesda, MD 20814-1244

Roberts, Tanya (Actor)
c/o Jay Schwartz *Jay D Schwartz & Associates*
3151 Cahuenga Blvd W Ste 220
Los Angeles, CA 90068-1749, USA

Roberts, Tim (Athlete, Football Player)
7248 New Dale Rd
Rex, GA 30273-2186, USA

Roberts, Tony (Actor)
970 Park Ave # 8N
New York, NY 10028-0324, USA

Roberts, Trish (Athlete, Basketball Player)
218 Carver Dr
Monroe, GA 30655-1814, USA

Roberts, Vicki (Actor)
c/o Arthur Andelson *Kismet Talent Agency*
3435 Ocean Park Blvd Ste 107
Santa Monica, CA 90405-3320, USA

Roberts, Walter (Athlete, Football Player)
268 Kenbrook Cir
San Jose, CA 95111-3262, USA

Roberts, Willa (Stylist)
319 Stratford Rd
Brooklyn, NY 11218-4315, USA

Roberts, William H (Athlete, Football Player)
18520 NW 67th Ave Apt 141
Hialeah, FL 33015-3302, USA

Roberts, Willie (Athlete, Baseball Player)
11476 Emuness Rd
Jacksonville, FL 32218, USA

Roberts, Xavier (Business Person, Designer)
PO Box 1438
Cleveland, GA 30528-0027, USA

Robertson, Alvin C (Athlete, Basketball Player)
2919 Biering Peak
San Antonio, TX 78247-3550, USA

Robertson, Andre (Athlete, Baseball Player)
2229 Cross Ln
Orange, TX 77630-2561, USA

Robertson, Belinda (Designer, Fashion Designer)
22 Palmerston Place
Edinburgh EH12 5AL, SCOTLAND

Robertson, Bob (Athlete, Football Player)
411 Belle Monti Ct
Aptos, CA 95003-5208, USA

Robertson, Bob (Athlete, Baseball Player)
10015 Shinnamon Dr SW
Cumberland, MD 21502-6149, USA

Robertson, Brittany (Britt) (Actor)
c/o Francis Okwu *Levine Okwu Erickson Management*
6363 Wilshire Blvd Ste 300
Los Angeles, CA 90048-5729, USA

Robertson, Dale (Actor)
PO Box 850707
Yukon, OK 73085-0707, USA

Robertson, Daryl (Athlete, Baseball Player)
52 Princeton Dr
Midvale, UT 84047-7514, USA

Robertson, David (Athlete, Baseball Player)
c/o Team Member *New York Yankees*
Yankee Stadium 161st St & River Ave
Bronx, NY 10451, USA

Robertson, Davis (Dancer)
70 E Lake St Ste 1300
Chicago, IL 60601-7458, USA

Robertson, DeWayne (Athlete, Football Player)
1000 Fulton Ave
Hempstead, NY 11550-1030, USA

Robertson, Don (Athlete, Baseball Player)
5715 W Monte Vista Rd
Phoenix, AZ 85035-3626, USA

Robertson, Gordon (Religious Leader, Television Host)
c/o 700 Club *Christian Broadcasting Network (CBN)*
977 Centerville Tpke
Virginia Beach, VA 23463-1001, USA

Robertson, Isiah (Athlete, Football Player)
PO Box 1405
Mabank, TX 75147-1405, USA

Robertson, Jenny (Actor)
9255 W Sunset Blvd Ste 1010
Los Angeles, CA 90069-3307, USA

Robertson, Jeriome (Athlete, Baseball Player)
105 Boone Ct
Hallsville, MO 65255-9353, USA

Robertson, Jim (Athlete, Baseball Player)
2515 109th Ave SE
Bellevue, WA 98004-7331, USA

Robertson, Kathleen (Actor)
c/o Staff Member *Jeff Morrone Entertainment*
9350 Wilshire Blvd Ste 224
Beverly Hills, CA 90212-3204, USA

Robertson, Kimmy (Actor)
8383 Wilshire Blvd Ste 850
Beverly Hills, CA 90211-2443, USA

Robertson, Leslie E (Engineer)
211 E 46th St
New York, NY 10017-2935, USA

Robertson, Lisa
1365 Enterprise Dr
West Chester, PA 19380-5959

Robertson, Marcus A (Athlete, Football Player)
3218 Cypress Point Dr
Missouri City, TX 77459-3634, USA

Robertson, Mike (Athlete, Baseball Player)
2626 E Viking Rd
Las Vegas, NV 89121-4114, USA

Robertson, Nate (Athlete, Baseball Player)
621 W Ness St
Valley Center, KS 67147-4922, USA

Robertson, Oscar P (Athlete, Basketball Player)
621 Tusculum Ave
Cincinnati, OH 45226-1771, USA

Robertson, Pat (Religious Leader, Television Host)
c/o 700 Club *Christian Broadcasting Network (CBN)*
977 Centerville Tpke
Virginia Beach, VA 23463-1001, USA

Robertson, RIch (Athlete, Baseball Player)
32202 Sandwedge Dr
Waller, TX 77484-9017, USA

Robertson, Rich (Athlete, Baseball Player)
1201 Crescent Ter
Sunnyvale, CA 94087-2855, USA

Robertson, Robble (Musician, Songwriter, Writer)
323 14th St
Santa Monica, CA 90402-2113, USA

Robertson, Scotty (Athlete, Basketball Player, Coach)
420 Forest Cir
Ruston, LA 71270-2643, USA

Robes, Ernest C (Bill) (Skier)
3 Mile Rd
Etna, NH 3750, USA

Robey, Rick (Athlete, Basketball Player)
15129 Chestnut Ridge Cir
Louisville, KY 40245-5291, USA

Robidoux, Billy Joe (Athlete, Baseball Player)
2 King George Dr
Ware, MA 01082-9799, USA

Robie, Carl (Swimmer)
2525 Sunnybrook Dr
Sarasota, FL 34239-4729, USA

Robinowitz, Joseph R (Editor, Publisher)
100 Matsonford Rd
Radnor, PA 19087-4559, USA

Robins, Lee N (Scientist)
Medical School Psychiatry Dept
Saint Louis, MO 63110, USA

Robins, Oliver (Actor, Director)
c/o Dawn Goodson *Genius Talent Management*
342 1/2 N Genesee Ave
Los Angeles, CA 90036-2261, USA

Robinson, Alexia
3500 W Olive Ave Ste 920
Burbank, CA 91505-5514

Robinson, Alicia (Stylist)
c/o Staff Member *Ford Models (Chicago)*
311 W Superior St
Chicago, IL 60654-3548, USA

Robinson, Andrea (Actor)
c/o Alan Saffron *Saffron Management*
9171 Wilshire Blvd Ste 441
Beverly Hills, CA 90210-5516, USA

Robinson, Andrew (Actor)
2671 Byron Pl
Los Angeles, CA 90046-1021, USA

Robinson, Ann (Actor)
1357 Elysian Park Dr
Los Angeles, CA 90026-3407, USA

Robinson, Anne (Actor, Entertainer)
19 Victoria Grove
London W8 5RW, UNITED KINGDOM (UK)

Robinson, Arthur H (Misc)
7707 N Brookline Dr Apt 302
Madison, WI 53719-3526, USA

Robinson, Bo (Athlete, Football Player)
PO Box 2323
Coppell, TX 75019-8323, USA

Robinson, Brooks (Athlete, Baseball Player)
PO Box 1168
Baltimore, MD 21203-1168, USA

Robinson, Bruce (Athlete, Baseball Player)
1310 Dellcrest Ln
La Jolla, CA 92037-5207, USA

Robinson, Bruce (Director)
c/o Rand Holston *Creative Artists Agency (CAA-LA)*
2000 Avenue of the Stars Ste 100
Los Angeles, CA 90067-4705, USA

Robinson, Bumper (Actor)
c/o David Altman *Altman Greenfield & Selvaggi*
200 Park Ave S Fl 8
New York, NY 10003-1526, United States

Robinson, Cary (Stylist)
c/o Staff Member *Karlee Artist Management*
2658 Griffith Park Blvd # 171
Los Angeles, CA 90039-2520, USA

Robinson, Charles
10000 Santa Monica Blvd # 305
Los Angeles, CA 90067

Robinson, Charles Knox
10637 Burbank Blvd
North Hollywood, CA 91601-2512

Robinson, Chip (Race Car Driver)
3034 Lake Forest Dr
Augusta, GA 30909-3081, USA

Robinson, Chris (Musician)

Robinson, Chris (Director)
c/o Peter Safran *The Safran Company*
8748 Holloway Dr
West Hollywood, CA 90069-2327, USA

Robinson, Christina (Actor)
c/o Bill Perlman *New Talent Management*
PO Box 2939
Beverly Hills, CA 90213-2939, USA

Robinson, Clarence (Arnie) (Athlete, Track Athlete)
2904 Ocean View Blvd
San Diego, CA 92113-1336, USA

Robinson, Cliff (Athlete, Basketball Player)
98 S Bardsbrook Cir
Spring, TX 77382-2858, USA

Robinson, Clifford (Athlete, Basketball Player)
702 Sandia Pl
Franklin Lakes, NJ 07417-2120, USA

Robinson, Craig (Actor)
c/o Mark Schulman *3 Arts Entertainment Inc*
9460 Wilshire Blvd Fl 7
Beverly Hills, CA 90212-2713, USA

Robinson, Daniel (Baseball Player)
10889 Dauphine St
Shreveport, LA 71106-8524, USA

Robinson, Dave (Athlete, Baseball Player)
6140 Camino Del Rincon
San Diego, CA 92120-3112, USA

Robinson, David M (Athlete, Basketball Player)
24165 Ih-I O W
San Antonio, TX 78257, USA

Robinson, Dawn (Actor, Musician)
c/o Jonathan Clardy *CN Publicity*
9107 Wilshire Blvd Ste 450
Beverly Hills, CA 90210-5535, USA

Robinson, Dewey (Athlete, Baseball Player)
1388 Cottonwood Trl
Sarasota, FL 34232-3437, USA

Robinson, Don (Athlete, Baseball Player)
1215 86th Ct NW
Bradenton, FL 34209-9307, USA

Robinson, Dwight P (Financier)
451 7th St SW
Washington, DC 20410-0001, USA

Robinson, Earl (Athlete, Baseball Player)
6895 Oakwood Dr
Oakland, CA 94611-1116, USA

Robinson, Eddie (Athlete, Baseball Player)
6104 Cholla Dr
Fort Worth, TX 76112-1105, USA

Robinson, Elizabeth
12706 E Pacific Cir # 202
Aurora, CO 80014

Robinson, Emily (Musician)
c/o Staff Member *Creative Artists Agency (CAA-LA)*
2000 Avenue of the Stars Ste 100
Los Angeles, CA 90067-4705, USA

Robinson, Emily Erwin (Athlete, Football Player)
4400 Falcon Pkwy
Flowery Branch, GA 30542-3176, USA

Robinson, Fatima
8306 Wilshire Blvd PMB 833
Beverly Hills, CA 90211-2382, USA

Robinson, Floyd (Athlete, Baseball Player)
PO Box 152419
San Diego, CA 92195-2419, USA

Robinson, Flynn (Athlete, Basketball Player)
11875 Manor Dr Apt 1
Hawthorne, CA 90250-2950, USA

Robinson, Frank (Athlete, Football Player)
15401 E Wyoming Dr Unit C
Aurora, CO 80017-4727, USA

Robinson, Frank (Athlete, Baseball Player, Coach)
15557 Aqua Verde Dr
Los Angeles, CA 90077-1503, USA

Robinson, Gerald (Athlete, Football Player)
4708 Scarborough Pl
Stone Mountain, GA 30087-4104, USA

Robinson, Glenn (Basketball Player, Coach)
Athletic Dept
Lancaster, PA 17604, USA

Robinson, Humberto (Athlete, Baseball Player)

Robinson, Jackie (Athlete, Basketball Player)
130 W Harcourt St
Long Beach, CA 90805-2124, USA

Robinson, Jacob (Baseball Player)
1300 Giddings Ave SE
Grand Rapids, MI 49506-3216, USA

Robinson, James (Baseball Player)
65 W 96th St Apt 22G
New York, NY 10025-6533, USA

Robinson, Janice (Musician)
c/o Staff Member *Diva Central Inc*
7510 W Sunset Blvd Ste 1445
Los Angeles, CA 90046-3408, USA

Robinson, Jay (Actor)
13757 Milbank St
Sherman Oaks, CA 91423-2966, USA

Robinson, Jeff (Athlete, Baseball Player)
27 Weber Ln
Trabuco Canyon, CA 92679-5235, USA

Robinson, Jeff (Athlete, Baseball Player)
5317 W 158th Pl
Overland Park, KS 66224-3616, USA

Robinson, Jerry (Athlete, Football Player)
1408 Fairoaks Ct
Merced, CA 95340-2341, USA

Robinson, John A (Athlete, Coach, Football Coach, Football Player)
1513 Village View Rd
Encinitas, CA 92024-5605, USA

Robinson, Johnny N (Athlete, Football Player)
3209 S Grand St
Monroe, LA 71202-5225, USA

Robinson, Julie Anne (Director)
c/o Leslie Maskin *United Talent Agency (UTA)*
9560 Wilshire Blvd Fl 5
Beverly Hills, CA 90212-2400, USA

Robinson, Keith (Actor)
c/o Staff Member *Stone Manners Salners Agency (LA)*
9911 W Pico Blvd Ste 1400
Los Angeles, CA 90035-2715, USA

Robinson, Keith (Musician)
c/o Staff Member *Paradigm (NY)*
360 Park Ave S Fl 16
New York, NY 10010-1708, USA

Robinson, Kenneth (Government Official)
12 Grove Terrace
London NW5, UNITED KINGDOM (UK)

Robinson, Kerry (Athlete, Baseball Player)
133 Vlasis Dr
Ballwin, MO 63011-3055, USA

Robinson, Koren (Athlete, Football Player)
12 Henry Ave
Belmont, NC 28012-3930, USA

Robinson, Larry (Athlete, Coach, Hockey Player)
10709 Winding Stream Way
Bradenton, FL 34212-5255, USA

Robinson, Laura (Actor)
8285 W Sunset Blvd Ste 1
West Hollywood, CA 90046-2420, USA

Robinson, Leon (Leon) (Actor, Producer)
c/o Leo Bozzuto *HYPHENATE*
9701 Wilshire Blvd Fl 10
Beverly Hills, CA 90212-2010, USA

Robinson, Madeleine
63 Av De Chillon
Territet-Veytaux, SWITZERLAN D1820

Robinson, Marcus (Athlete, Football Player)
PO Box 1924
Fort Valley, GA 31030-1924, USA

Robinson, Mark (Athlete, Football Player)
303 Pennsylvania Ave
Palm Harbor, FL 34683-5222, USA

Robinson, Mary (Ex-President)
Aras an Uachtarain Phoenix Park
Dublin 8, IRELAND

Robinson, Matt (Athlete, Football Player)
12374 Mandarin Rd
Jacksonville, FL 32223-1892, USA

Robinson, Nichole (Actor)
c/o Tiffany Kuzon *Evolution Entertainment (LA)*
901 N Highland Ave
Los Angeles, CA 90038-2412, USA

Robinson, Oliver (Athlete, Basketball Player)
9640 Eastpointe Cir
Birmingham, AL 35217-5202, USA

Robinson, Patrick (Designer, Fashion Designer)
1 Harrison St
San Francisco, CA 94105-1683, USA

Robinson, Patrick (Athlete, Football Player)
3875 N Advantage Way Dr Apt 104
Memphis, TN 38128-7239, USA

Robinson, Paul (Athlete, Football Player)
1303 W 26th St
Safford, AZ 85546-3721, USA

Robinson, Rachel
75 Varick St Frnt 2
New York, NY 10013-1947

Robinson, Rafael (Athlete, Football Player)
6203 Wynbrook Dr
Randolph, NJ 07869-1287, USA

Robinson, Randall
1744 R St NW
Washington, DC 20009-2410

Robinson, Rich (Musician)
c/o Staff Member *Paradigm (Monterey)*
404 W Franklin St
Monterey, CA 93940-2303, USA

Robinson, Richard D (Dave) (Athlete, Football Player)
406 S Rose Blvd
Akron, OH 44320-1308, USA

Robinson, Robinson (Director)
c/o Peter Safran *The Safran Company*
8748 Holloway Dr
West Hollywood, CA 90069-2327, USA

Robinson, Ron (Athlete, Baseball Player)
3128 E Race Ave
Visalia, CA 93292-6858, USA

Robinson, Ronnie (Athlete, Basketball Player)
4169 S Germantown Rd
Memphis, TN 38125-2624, USA

Robinson, Roxanne (Stylist)
c/o Staff Member *Jed Root Inc*
61-A Walker St
New York, NY 10013, USA

Robinson, Rumeal (Basketball Player)
2 Championship Dr
Auburn Hills, MI 48326-1753, USA

Robinson, Sam (Athlete, Basketball Player)
130 W Harcourt St
Long Beach, CA 90805-2124, USA

Robinson, Sammy (Baseball Player)
503 Umatilla St SE
Grand Rapids, MI 49507-1218, USA

Robinson, Sandra Dee (Actor)
c/o Vincent Cirrincione *Vincent Cirrincione Associates*
1516 N Fairfax Ave
Los Angeles, CA 90046-2608, USA

Robinson, Shaun (Correspondent)
c/o Susan Haber *Haber Entertainment*
434 S Canon Dr Apt 204
Beverly Hills, CA 90212-4501, USA

Robinson, Shawna (Race Car Driver)
PO Box 1858
New Smyrna Beach, FL 32170-1858, USA

Robinson, Shelton (Athlete, Football Player)
18725 20th Dr SE
Bothell, WA 98012-8721, USA

Robinson, Stacy (Athlete, Football Player)
2409 Starcrest Dr
Silver Spring, MD 20904-5459, USA

Robinson, Stephen K (Astronaut)
2405 Airline Dr
Friendswood, TX 77546-5509, USA

Robinson, T Wayne
PO Box 249
Mc Connellsburg, PA 17233-0249, USA

Robinson, Ted (Sportscaster)
c/o Lou Oppenheim *Headline Media Management*
888 7th Ave Ste 503
New York, NY 10106-0501, USA

Robinson, Tony (Actor, Producer, Writer)
c/o Staff Member *Jeremy Hicks Associates*
114-115 Tottenham Court Rd
London W1T 5AH, UK

Robinson, Tony (Athlete, Football Player)
728 Efferson St
Tallahassee, FL 32303-5321, USA

Robinson, V Gene (Religious Leader)
21 Centre St
Concord, NH 03301-6301, USA

Robinson, Wendy Raquel (Actor)
c/o Patricia (Patty) Woo *Patty Woo Management*
8906 W Olympic Blvd
Beverly Hills, CA 90211-3550, USA

Robinson, Wilbert (Athlete, Basketball Player)
2124 Bedell Rd
Grand Island, NY 14072-1652, USA

Robinson, William (Smokey) (Musician, Producer, Songwriter, Writer)
385 S Lemon Ave Ste E181
Walnut, CA 91789-2727, USA

Robinson, Zuleikha (Actor)
c/o Dan Spilo *Industry Entertainment Partners*
955 Carrillo Dr Ste 300
Los Angeles, CA 90048-5400, USA

Robinson of Woolwich, John (Religious Leader)
Cambridge CB2 1TQ, UNITED KINGDOM (UK)

Robinson-Peete, Holly (Actor)
9250 Wilshire Blvd Ste LL15
Beverly Hills, CA 90212-3342, USA

Robisch, Dave (Athlete, Basketball Player)
1401 Guemes Ct
Springfield, IL 62702-6400, USA

Robiskie, Terry (Athlete, Football Player)
333 Las Olas Way Apt 910
Ft Lauderdale, FL 33301-4300, USA

Robison, Bruce (Musician, Songwriter, Writer)
1016 16th Ave S Apt 101
Nashville, TN 37212-2315, USA

Robison, Charlie (Musician, Songwriter)
c/o Staff Member *Paradigm (Monterey)*
404 W Franklin St
Monterey, CA 93940-2303, USA

Robison, Paula (Musician)
18 Allison Ave
Staten Island, NY 10306-2806, USA

Robison, Tommy (Athlete, Football Player)
711 Biscayne Dr
Mansfield, TX 76063-3236, USA

Robitaille, Luc (Athlete, Hockey Player)
13801 Ventura Blvd
Sherman Oaks, CA 91423-3603, USA

Robl, Harold (Athlete, Football Player)
W1089 County Road C
Gleason, WI 54435-9472, USA

Robles, Jorge (Actor)
c/o Staff Member *Televisa*
Blvd Adolfo Lopez Mateos 232 Colonia San Angel INN
DF CP 01060, MEXICO

Robles, Marisa (Musician)
38 Luttrll Ave
London SW15 6PE, UNITED KINGDOM (UK)

Robles, Mike (Producer)
8942 Wilshire Blvd
Beverly Hills, CA 90211-1908

Roboz, Zsuzsi (Artist)
6 Bryanston Court George St
London W1H 7HA, UNITED KINGDOM (UK)

Robson, Bryan (Soccer Player)
Riverside Stadium Midds
Cleveland TS3 6RS, UNITED KINGDOM (UK)

Robson, TOm (Athlete, Baseball Player)
7331 W Morrow Dr
Glendale, AZ 85308-5848, USA

Robson, Wade (Choreographer)
c/o Andrew Jacobs *McDonald/Selznick Assoc (MSA)*
1611A N El Centro Ave
Hollywood, CA 90028, USA

Robuchon, Joel (Chef)
67 Blvd du Gen M Valin
Paris 75015, FRANCE

Robuck, Nicolas (Nic) (Actor)
c/o Margot Menzel *Evolution Entertainment (LA)*
901 N Highland Ave
Los Angeles, CA 90038-2412, USA

Robustelli, Andrew R (Andy) (Athlete, Football Player)
30 Spring St
Stamford, CT 06901-1701, USA

Robyn (Musician)
73C Saint Charles Square
London W10 6EJ, UNITED KINGDOM (UK)

Rocard, Michel L L (Prime Minister)
Hotel de Ville 63 Rue M Berteaux
Conflans-Sainte-Honorine 78700, FRANCE

Rocca, Constantino (Golfer)
5719 Lake Lindero Dr
Agoura Hills, CA 91301-1444, USA

Rocca, Costentino (Golfer)
5719 Lake Lindero Dr
Agoura Hills, CA 91301-1444, USA

Rocca, Mo (Correspondent)
c/o Don Epstein *Greater Talent Network Inc*
437 5th Ave Fl 7
New York, NY 10016-2205, USA

Rocca, Peter (Swimmer)
534 Hazel Ave
San Bruno, CA 94066-4228, USA

Rocco, Alex (Actor)
c/o Staff Member *Bresler Kelly & Associates*
11500 W Olympic Blvd Ste 510
Los Angeles, CA 90064-1527, USA

Rocco, Rinaldo (Actor)
Via Giuseppe Pisanelli
Rome 196, ITALY

Rocha, Coco (Musician)
c/o Christina Neuman *Full Picture (NY)*
915 Broadway Fl 20
New York, NY 10010-7131, USA

Rocha, Enrique (Actor)
c/o Staff Member *Televisa*
Blvd Adolfo Lopez Mateos 232 Colonia San Angel INN
DF CP 01060, MEXICO

Rocha, Ephraim (Red) (Athlete, Basketball Player, Coach)
815 N 9th St
Philomath, OR 97370-9724, USA

Rocha, Kali (Actor)
c/o Katie Rhodes *Untitled Entertainment (LA)*
350 S Beverly Dr Ste 200
Beverly Hills, CA 90212-4819, USA

Rochberg, George (Composer)
3500 W Chester Pike # CH118
Newtown Square, PA 19073-4101, USA

Roche, Alden (Athlete, Football Player)
1082 Farragut St
New Orleans, LA 70114-2810, USA

Roche, Anthony D (Tony) (Tennis Player)
5 Kapiti St
Saint Ives, NSW 2075, AUSTRALIA

Roche, Brian (Athlete, Football Player)
1358 Oak Tree Cir
Chino Hills, CA 91709-2231, USA

Roche, E Kevin (Architect)
20 Davis St
Hamden, CT 06517-3501, USA

Roche, George A (Financier)
100 E Pratt St
Baltimore, MD 21202-1009, USA

Roche, James G (Secretary)
Secretary S Ofc Pentagon
Washington, DC 20310-0001, USA

Roche, John (Athlete, Basketball Player)
191 Clayton Ln Unit 303
Denver, CO 80206-5679, USA

Rochefort, Jean (Actor)
Le Chene Rogneaux
Grosvre 78125, FRANCE

Rochefort, Normand (Athlete, Hockey Player)
7704 Camminare Dr
Sarasota, FL 34238-4777, USA

Rochester, Paul (Athlete, Football Player)
218 Evans Dr
Jacksonville, FL 32250-2631, USA

Rochford, Mike (Athlete, Baseball Player)
926 N O St
Lake Worth, FL 33460-2746, USA

Rochon, Debbie (Actor)
PO Box 1299
New York, NY 10009-8958

Rochon, Lela (Actor)
232 N Canon Dr
Beverly Hills, CA 90210-5302, USA

Rock (Actor, Wrestler)
1241 E Main St
Stamford, CT 06902-3520, USA

Rock, Angela (Athlete, Volleyball Player)
1210 Cheadle Hall
Santa Barbara, CA 93106-1004, USA

Rock, Chris (Actor, Comedian, Director, Producer)
c/o Leslie Sloane *Baker Winokur Ryder Public Relations BWR (BWR-NY)*
292 Madison Ave Fl 12
New York, NY 10017-6415, USA

Rock, Tony (Comedian)
c/o Staff Member *New Wave Entertainment (LA)*
2660 W Olive Ave
Burbank, CA 91505-4525, USA

Rock, Walt (Athlete, Football Player)
1030 Highams Ct
Woodbridge, VA 22191-1445, USA

Rock City (Music Group, Musician)
c/o Noel Palm *Venture IAB*
3211 Cahuenga Blvd W Ste 104
Los Angeles, CA 90068-1372, USA

Rockburne, Dorothea G (Artist)
140 Grand St
New York, NY 10013-3104, USA

Rockefeller, David (Financier)
146 E 65th St & Lexington Ave
New York, NY 10021, USA

Rockefeller, Laurance S (Misc)
30 Rockefeller Plz # 5600
New York, NY 10112-0015, USA

Rockefeller, Sharon Percy
1940 Shepherd St NW
Washington, DC 20011

Rockenbach, Lyle (Athlete, Football Player)
25 State Road 13 Apt E9-E11
Jacksonville, FL 32259-2842, USA

Rocker, David (Athlete, Football Player)
3833 Seton Hall Dr
Decatur, GA 30034-5540, USA

Rocker, John (Athlete, Baseball Player)
1223 Manor Oaks Ct
Atlanta, GA 30338-2756, USA

Rockett, Pat (Athlete, Baseball Player)
17107 Eagle Hollow Dr
San Antonio, TX 78248-1553, USA

Rockett, Rikki (Musician)
c/o Staff Member *HK Management (LA)*
10866 Wilshire Blvd Ste 200
Los Angeles, CA 90024-4350, USA

Rockford, Jim (Athlete, Football Player)
1829 Camden St
Springfield, IL 62702-3201, USA

Rockwell, Martha (Coach, Skier)
PO Box 9
Hanover, NH 03755-0009, USA

Rockwell, Nancy (Athlete, Baseball Player)
54658 County Road 101
Elkhart, IN 46514-8967, USA

Rockwell, Robert
18428 Coastline Dr
Malibu, CA 90265-5707

Rockwell, Sam (Actor)
c/o Liz Mahoney *ID Public Relations (ID-LA)*
7080 Hollywood Blvd Fl 8
Los Angeles, CA 90028-6906, USA

Rockwood, Marcia (Editor)
PO Box 100
Pleasantville, NY 10570-0100, USA

Rodan, Jay (Actor)
c/o Staff Member *WmE2 (WMA-LA)*
1 William Morris Pl
Beverly Hills, CA 90212-4261, USA

Rodas, Rich (Athlete, Baseball Player)
6877 Bergano Pl
Rancho Cucamonga, CA 91701-8606, USA

Roday, James (Actor, Writer)
c/o Larry Taube *Principal Entertainment (LA)*
1964 Westwood Blvd Ste 400
Los Angeles, CA 90025-4695, USA

Rodd, Marcia (Actor)
11738 Moorpark St Apt C
Studio City, CA 91604-2116, USA

Roddam, Franc (Director)
52/53 Poland Place
London W1F 7LX, UNITED KINGDOM (UK)

Roddick, Andy (Athlete, Tennis Player)
c/o Ken Meyerson *Lagardere Unlimited - Miami*
235 Park Ave S Fl 6
New York, NY 10003-1405, USA

Rodenhauser, Mark (Athlete, Football Player)
1451 Charlotte Hwy
York, SC 29745-8947, USA

Roder, Mirro (Athlete, Football Player)
181 Herrick Rd
Riverside, IL 60546-2045, USA

Roderick, Brande (Actor, Model)
c/o Shannon Barr *Shannon Barr Public Relations*
3313 N Sepulveda Blvd
Manhattan Beach, CA 90266-3626, USA

Rodgers, Aaron (Athlete, Football Player)
c/o David Dunn *Athletes First, LLC*
3300 Irvine Ave Ste 300
Newport Beach, CA 92660-3108, USA

Rodgers, Anton
The White House Lower Basildon
Berkshire, ENGLAND

Rodgers, Del (Athlete, Football Player)
3112 Yosemite Park Way
Elk Grove, CA 95758-4687, USA

Rodgers, Derrick (Athlete, Football Player)
5550 SW 192nd Ter
Southwest Ranches, FL 33332-3333, USA

Rodgers, Jimmie (Musician)
42230 Sandy Bay Rd
Bermuda Dunes, CA 92203-1394, USA

Rodgers, Jimmy (Athlete, Basketball Player, Coach)
4995 Marsh Turtle Trl Unit 101
Estero, FL 33928-3943, USA

Rodgers, Johnny (Athlete, Football Player)
2011 Wirt St
Omaha, NE 68110-2051, USA

Rodgers, Michael (Actor)
c/o Adam Levine *Levine Okwu Erickson Management*
9601 Wilshire Blvd Fl 3
Beverly Hills, CA 90210-5219, USA

Rodgers, Paul (Musician)
19D Pinhold Road
London SW16 5GD, United Kingdom

Rodgers, Phil (Golfer)
4067 N Shore Dr
Akron, OH 44333-8305, USA

Rodgers, Robert (Buck) (Athlete, Baseball Player, Coach)
5181 W Knoll Dr
Yorba Linda, CA 92886-4338, USA

Rodgers-Cromartie, Dominique (Athlete, Football Player)
c/o Eugene Parker *Maximum Sports Management*
6435 W Jefferson Blvd # 197
Fort Wayne, IN 46804-6203, USA

Rodin, Judith S (Educator)
35 Hillhouse Ave
New Haven, CT 06511-8948, USA

Rodina, Irina (Athlete)
13243 Fiji Way # 7
Marina Del Rey, CA 90292-7079, USA

Rodman, Dennis (Athlete, Basketball Player)
4910 Campus Dr
Newport Beach, CA 92660-2119, USA

Rodrigue, George (Artist)
PO Box 51227
Lafayette, LA 70505-1227, USA

Rodrigues, Blenvenido (Baseball Player)
PO Box 42
Santa Isabel, PR 00757-0042, USA

Rodrigues, Darryl (Stylist)
c/o Staff Member *Jed Root Inc*
61-A Walker St
New York, NY 10013, USA

Rodriguez, Adam (Actor)
c/o Abe Hoch *A Management Company*
9107 Wilshire Blvd Ste 650
Beverly Hills, CA 90210-5544, USA

Rodriguez, Alex (Athlete, Baseball Player)
PO Box 190749
Dallas, TX 75219-0749, USA

Rodriguez, Anthony (Golfer)
13602 Summer Glen Dr
San Antonio, TX 78247-3510, USA

Rodriguez, Carlos (Athlete, Baseball Player)
10139 Snyder Church Rd NW
Baltimore, OH 43105-9475, USA

Rodriguez, Eduardo (President)
Palacio de Gobierno Plaza Murilla
La Paz, BOLIVIA

Rodriguez, Edwin (Athlete, Baseball Player)
7901 30th Ave N
Saint Petersburg, FL 33710-1151, USA

Rodriguez, Francisco (Athlete, Baseball Player)
c/o Staff Member *New York Mets*
Roosevelt Ave Shea Stadium 123-01
Flushing, NY 11368-9993, USA

Rodriguez, Freddy (Actor)
c/o Staff Member *Kass & Stokes Management*
9229 W Sunset Blvd Ste 504
Los Angeles, CA 90069-3405, USA

Rodriguez, Freddy (Actor)
c/o Robbie Kass *Kass & Stokes Management*
9229 W Sunset Blvd Ste 504
Los Angeles, CA 90069-3405, USA

Rodriguez, Genesis (Actor)
c/o Staff Member *Select Artists Ltd (CA-Valley Office)*
PO Box 4359
Burbank, CA 91503-4359, USA

Rodriguez, Geoffrey (Stylist)
c/o Staff Member *Mercury Artists*
8460 Higuera St Fl 2
Culver City, CA 90232-2520, USA

Rodriguez, Hector (Baseball Player)
Taxistas Reg 92 Zona 6 Lote 75 Num Cancun
Quintana Roo, MEXICO

Rodriguez, Henry (Athlete, Baseball Player)
295 Wadsworth Ave Apt 3F
New York, NY 10040-4416, USA

Rodriguez, Ivan (Pudge) (Athlete, Baseball Player)
c/o Scott Boras *Boras Corporation*
18 Corporate Plaza Dr
Newport Beach, CA 92660-7901, USA

Rodriguez, Jai (Actor, Television Host)
c/o Michael Einfeld *Michael Einfeld Management*
10630 Moorpark St Unit 101
Toluca Lake, CA 91602-2797, USA

Rodriguez, Javier (Actor)
c/o Staff Member *Select Artists Ltd (CA-Valley Office)*
PO Box 4359
Burbank, CA 91503-4359, USA

Rodriguez, Jesse (Stylist)
c/o Staff Member *Arlene Wilson Management*
807 N Jefferson St # 200
Milwaukee, WI 53202-8150, USA

Rodriguez, Johnny
PO Box 23162
Nashville, TN 37202-3162

Rodriguez, Jose Luis (El Puma) (Musician)
c/o Staff Member *BMG*
1540 Broadway
New York, NY 10036-4039, USA

Rodriguez, Juan (Chi Chi) (Athlete)
3916 Clock Pointe Trl Ste 101
Stow, OH 44224-2932

Rodriguez, Maggie (Anchor)
c/o Staff Member *CBS News Productions*
524 W 57th St Fl 8
New York, NY 10019-2930, USA

Rodriguez, Michelle (Actor)
c/o Jason Weinberg *Untitled Entertainment (LA)*
350 S Beverly Dr Ste 200
Beverly Hills, CA 90212-4819, USA

Rodriguez, Paul (Actor)
c/o Staff Member *International Creative Management (ICM-LA)*
10250 Constellation Blvd Fl 7
Los Angeles, CA 90067-6207, USA

Rodriguez, Raini (Actor)
c/o Traci Harper *Harper PR*
3940 Laurel Canyon Blvd Ste 1010
Studio City, CA 91604-3709, USA

Rodriguez, Ramon (Actor)
c/o Allan Grifka *Alchemy Entertainment*
7024 Melrose Ave Ste 420
Los Angeles, CA 90038-3394, USA

Rodriguez, Rich (Athlete, Baseball Player)
94 Via Katrina
Newbury Park, CA 91320-7019, USA

Rodriguez, Rick (Athlete, Baseball Player)
106 Oneill Ct
Folsom, CA 95630-2379, USA

Rodriguez, Rico (Actor)
c/o Traci Harper *Harper PR*
3940 Laurel Canyon Blvd Ste 1010
Studio City, CA 91604-3709, USA

Rodriguez, Robert (Director, Producer)
c/o Robert Newman *WmE2 (Endeavor-LA)*
9601 Wilshire Blvd Fl 3
Beverly Hills, CA 90210-5219, USA

Rodriguez, Steve (Athlete, Baseball Player)
10430 Orchard View Ln
Riverside, CA 92503-6602, USA

Rodriguez, Vic (Athlete, Baseball Player)
631 SE 9th Pl
Cape Coral, FL 33990-2950, USA

Rodriquez, La Mala (Musician)
c/o Staff Member *Zona Bruta Discos S.L.*
C Clemente Fernandez 56 Local Izda
Madrid 28011, Spain

Roe, Bill (Athlete, Football Player)
9931 E Ohio Ave
Denver, CO 80247-1958, USA

Roe, Elwin (Preacher) (Athlete, Baseball Player)
204 Wildwood Ter
West Plains, MO 65775-2548, USA

Roe, Preacher (Baseball Player)
204 Wildwood Ter
West Plains, MO 65775-2548, USA

Roe, Rocky (Athlete, Baseball Player)
2033 Stefano Ct
Mount Dora, FL 32757-6511, USA

Roe, Tommy
PO Box 26037
Minneapolis, MN 55426-0037

Roebuck, Daniel (Actor)
c/o Leslie Allan-Rice *Leslie Allan-Rice Management*
7524 Mulholland Dr
Los Angeles, CA 90046-1239, USA

Roebuck, Ed (Athlete, Baseball Player)
3434 Warwood Rd
Lakewood, CA 90712-3751, USA

Roedel, Herb (Athlete, Football Player)
4810 201st St
Flushing, NY 11364-1012, USA

Roeg, Nicolas
14 Courtnell St
London, ENGLAND W2 5BX

Roemer, Sarah (Actor, Model)
c/o Staff Member *Luber Roklin Management*
8530 Wilshire Blvd Ste 550
Beverly Hills, CA 90211-3133, USA

Roenick, Jeremy (Hockey Player)
c/o Staff Member *Los Angeles Kings*
1111 S Figueroa St Ste 3100
Los Angeles, CA 90015-1333, USA

Roenicke, Gary (Athlete, Baseball Player)
11023 Rough and Ready Rd
Rough And Ready, CA 95975-9750, USA

Roenicke, Ron (Athlete, Baseball Player)
787 Avenida Salvador
San Clemente, CA 92672-2369, USA

Roeper, Lindsey
4321 W Flamingo Rd
Las Vegas, NV 89103-3903, USA

Roerig, Zach (Actor)
c/o Loch Powell *Leverage Management*
3030 Pennsylvania Ave
Santa Monica, CA 90404-4112, USA

Roesler, Mike (Athlete, Baseball Player)
12033 Fallen Leaf Ct
Fort Wayne, IN 46845-8992, USA

Roethlisberger, Ben (Athlete, Football Player)
c/o Ryan Tollner *REP 1 Sports Group*
2 Corporate Park Ste 106
Irvine, CA 92606-5103, USA

Roffe-Barker, Melanie (Director)
c/o Staff Member *Don Capo Entertainment*
Ste 5 South Bank Terrace Surbiton
Surrey KT6 6DG, UNITED KINGDOM (UK)

Roffe-Barker, Nigel (Director, Producer, Writer)
c/o Staff Member *Don Capo Entertainment*
Ste 5 South Bank Terrace Surbiton
Surrey KT6 6DG, UNITED KINGDOM (UK)

Rogan, Joe (Comedian)
c/o Ivo Fischer *WmE2 (Endeavor-LA)*
9601 Wilshire Blvd Fl 3
Beverly Hills, CA 90210-5219, USA

Rogas, Dan (Athlete, Football Player)
2352 Evalon St
Beaumont, TX 77702-1310, USA

Rogen, Seth (Actor)
c/o Marsha McManus *Principal Entertainment (LA)*
1964 Westwood Blvd Ste 400
Los Angeles, CA 90025-4695, USA

Roger, John (Religious Leader)
2101 Wilshire Blvd
Santa Monica, CA 90403-5744, USA

Rogers, Amerie M M (Musician)
c/o Richard Murphy *International Creative Management (ICM-NY)*
40 W 57th St
New York, NY 10019-4001, USA

Rogers, Bill (Golfer)
12 Halifax Ct
San Antonio, TX 78209-1864, USA

Rogers, Chad (Business Person, Reality TV Star)
250 N Canon Dr
Beverly Hills, CA 90210-5322, USA

Rogers, Dennis (Athlete)
c/o Staff Member *Big Machine Media*
110 E 37th St Fl 4
New York, NY 10016-3029, USA

Rogers, Gene (Misc)
P.O. Box 3537
McAlester, OK 74502-3637, USA

Rogers, George (Athlete, Football Player)
1007 Lofty Pine Dr
Columbia, SC 29212-2037, USA

Rogers, Greg (Writer)
614 Big Hill Cir
McAlester, OK 74501-2591, USA

Rogers, Jane
1485 S Beverly Dr Apt 8
Los Angeles, CA 90035-3021

Rogers, Jimmy (Athlete, Baseball Player)
7235 S Janet St Trlr 10
Oklahoma City, OK 73150-7426, USA

Rogers, Joy
4141 W Kling St Apt 3
Burbank, CA 91505-3309

Rogers, Kenny (Athlete, Baseball Player)
1730 Ottinger Rd
Roanoke, TX 76262, USA

Rogers, Kenny (Musician)
c/o Debbie Cross *Kenny Rogers Inc*
533 Williamsport Dr
Smyrna, TN 37167-6357

Rogers, Kevin (Athlete, Baseball Player)
604 Douglas Ave
Cleveland, MS 38732-2026, USA

Rogers, Lamarr (Baseball Player)
1240 Spring Green Ln
Burnsville, MN 55306-6413, USA

Rogers, Melody
2051 Nichols Canyon Rd
Los Angeles, CA 90046-1727

Rogers, Mimi (Actor)
c/o Staff Member *Millbrook Farm Productions*
11693 San Vicente Blvd # 241
Los Angeles, CA 90049-5105, USA

Rogers, Paul (Actor)
9 Hillside Gdns
London, ENGLAND N6 5SU, United Kingdom

Rogers, Reg (Actor)
c/o Staff Member *Brookside Artists Management (NY)*
250 W 57th St Ste 2303
New York, NY 10107-2399, USA

Rogers, Shorty
PO Box 1711
Bellingham, WA 98227-1711

Rogers, Stephen D (Steve) (Baseball Player)
3746 S Madison Ave
Tulsa, OK 74105-3016, USA

Rogers, Steve (Athlete, Baseball Player)
10112 Taylor Ct
Princeton Junction, NJ 08550-5319, USA

Rogers, Suzanne (Actor)
11266 Canton Dr
Studio City, CA 91604-4154, USA

Rogers, Tracy (Athlete, Football Player)
1011 Tam O Shanter Dr
Bakersfield, CA 93309-2451, USA

Rogers, Wayne (Actor)
11828 La Grange Ave
Los Angeles, CA 90025-5212, USA

Roges, Al (Athlete, Basketball Player)
6217 Scenic Ave
Los Angeles, CA 90068-2914, USA

Rogge, Jacques (Misc)
Chateau de Vidy
Lausanne 1007, SWITZERLAND

Roggeman, Tom (Athlete, Football Player)
51267 Pembridge Ct
Granger, IN 46530-8306, USA

Roggenburk, Garry (Athlete, Baseball Player)
33550 Streamview Dr
Avon, OH 44011-2597, USA

Roggin, Fred
3000 W Alameda Ave
Burbank, CA 91523-0001

Rogiani, Elisabetta (Stylist)
7466 Beverly Blvd
Los Angeles, CA 90036-2760, USA

Rogin, Gilbert L (Editor)
6 Roosevelt Rd
Westport, CT 06880-6840, USA

Rogodzinski, Mike (Athlete, Baseball Player)
1 Emlyn Ct
Clementon, NJ 08021-4871, USA

Rogoff, Ilan (Musician)
Apdo 1098
Palma de Mallorca 7080, SPAIN

Rogow, Stan (Producer)
c/o Staff Member *International Creative Management (ICM-LA)*
10250 Constellation Blvd Fl 7
Los Angeles, CA 90067-6207, USA

Rogue Wave (Music Group)
c/o Staff Member *Paradigm (Monterey)*
404 W Franklin St
Monterey, CA 93940-2303, USA

Rohan, Margo (Stylist)
c/o Staff Member *Halley Resources*
37 W 20th St Ste 603
New York, NY 10011-3718, USA

Rohatgi, Payal (Actor, Bollywood)
c/o Bunty Bahl *Carving Dreams Entertainment*
304-305, Oberoi Chambers II B Wing, Off New Link Road, Andheri West
Mumbai 400053, INDIA

Rohde, Bruce (Business Person)
1 Conagra Dr
Omaha, NE 68102-5003, USA

Rohde, Dave (Athlete, Baseball Player)
1707 Port Barmouth Pl
Newport Beach, CA 92660-5314, USA

Rohde, Kristen (Actor)
c/o Staff Member *Gersh (LA)*
9465 Wilshire Blvd Ste 600
Beverly Hills, CA 90212-2612, USA

Rohde, Len (Athlete, Football Player)
100 W El Camino Real Ste 76
Mountain View, CA 94040-2679, USA

Rohini (Actor, Bollywood)
D-1 Ist Floor Anandsree Apartments 32 Hindi Prachara Saba Street
Chennai, TN 600017, INDIA

Rohlander, Uta (Athlete, Track Athlete)
Liebigstr 9
Leuna 6237, GERMANY

Rohloff, Kenneth (Athlete, Basketball Player)
206 Cedar Ln
Atlantic Beach, NC 28512-5747, USA

Rohm, Elisabeth (Actor)
c/o Katie Mason *Luber Roklin Management*
8530 Wilshire Blvd Ste 550
Beverly Hills, CA 90211-3133, USA

Rohn, Dan (Athlete, Baseball Player)
2406 Arthur Ct
Traverse City, MI 49685-7411, USA

Rohner, Clayton (Actor)
8571 Holloway Dr Apt 2
W Hollywood, CA 90069-6916

Rohner, Georges (Artist)
3 Rue des Saints Peres
Paris 75006, FRANCE

Rohr, Bill (Billy) (Athlete, Baseball Player)
69265 McCallum Way
Cathedral City, CA 92234-2990, USA

Rohr, James E (Financier)
1 Pnc Plaza 249 5th Ave
Pittsburgh, PA 15222, USA

Rohr, Les (Athlete, Baseball Player)
1508 Wicks Ln
Billings, MT 59105-4412, USA

Rohrer, Heinrich (Nobel Prize Laureate)
Saumerstr 4
Ruschilkon 8803, SWITZERLAND

Rohrer, Jeff (Athlete, Football Player)
3201 Executive Cir
Dallas, TX 75234-3764, USA

Rohrmeier, Dan (Athlete, Baseball Player)
1029 Edgetree Ln
Cincinnati, OH 45238-4318, USA

Roig, Tony (Athlete, Baseball Player)
24125 E Lakeridge Dr
Liberty Lake, WA 99019-9612, USA

Roitman, Esther (Stylist)
c/o Staff Member *Walter Schupfer Management Corp*
413 W 14th St Ste 3
New York, NY 10014-1097, USA

Roiz, Sasha (Actor)
c/o Pearl Hanan *Pearl Hanan Management*
7775 W Sunset Blvd Ste 118
Los Angeles, CA 90046-3911, USA

Roizman, Bernard (Biologist)
5555 S Everett Ave
Chicago, IL 60637-5013, USA

Roizman, Owen (Cinematographer)
17533 Magnolia Blvd
Encino, CA 91316, USA

Roja (Actor, Bollywood)
8 Saravana Mudali Street T Nagar
Chennai, TN 600017, INDIA

Roja (Actor)
12 43rd Street 6th Avenue Ashok Nagar
Chennai, TN 600 083, INDIA

Rojas, Goffrey (Prince Royal) (Musician)
c/o Michael Vega *WmE2 (WMA-Miami)*
119 Washington Ave Ste 400
Miami, FL 33139-7202, USA

Rojas, Mel (Athlete, Baseball Player)
15645 Collins Ave Apt 802
North Miami Beach, FL 33160-4790, USA

Rojas, Nydia (Musician)
9171 Wilshire Blvd Ste 426
Beverly Hills, CA 90210-5516, USA

Rojas, Octavio R (Cookie) (Athlete, Baseball Player, Coach)
19195 Mystic Pointe Dr Apt 3002
Aventura, FL 33180-4502, USA

Rojcewicz, Susan (Sue) (Basketball Player)
48 Elena Cir
San Rafael, CA 94903-3342, USA

Rojo, Ana Patricia (Actor)
c/o Staff Member *Televisa*
Blvd Adolfo Lopez Mateos 232 Colonia San Angel INN
DF CP 01060, MEXICO

Rojo, Gustavo (Actor)
c/o Staff Member *Televisa*
Blvd Adolfo Lopez Mateos 232 Colonia San Angel INN
DF CP 01060, MEXICO

Roker, Al (Correspondent, Television Host)
c/o Staff Member *Today Show, The*
30 Rockefeller Plz
New York, NY 10112-0015, USA

Rokk, Marika
Mozartstr. 15
Baden, AUSTRIA A-2500

Rokke, Ervin J (General)
810 Dolan Dr
Monument, CO 80132-2219, USA

Roland, Ed (Musician, Songwriter, Writer)
11845 W Olympic Blvd Ste 1125
Los Angeles, CA 90064-5096, USA

Roland, Jim (Athlete, Baseball Player)
1802 Arbor Way Dr
Shelby, NC 28150-6166, USA

Roland, Joan (Stylist)
370 E 76th St Apt A201
New York, NY 10021-2548, USA

Roland, Johnny E (Athlete, Coach, Football Player)
8701 S Hardy Dr
Tempe, AZ 85284-2800, USA

Rolandi, Gianna (Opera Singer)
165 W 57th St
New York, NY 10019-2201, USA

Rolen, Scott B (Athlete, Baseball Player)
11711 N Pennsylvania St Ste 250
Carmel, IN 46032-4560, USA

Roles-Williams, Barbara (Figure Skater)
3790 Leisure Ln
Las Vegas, NV 89103-2323, USA

Rolfe, Dale
365 Hughson St
Gravenhurst, CANADA ON P1P 1G8

Rolfe, Johnson Anthony (Opera Singer)
40 W 57th St
New York, NY 10019-4001, USA

Rolison, Nathan (Nate) (Athlete, Baseball Player)
89 Bridgefield Ct
Hattiesburg, MS 39402-8689, USA

Rolle, Butch (Athlete, Football Player)
17822 NW 15th St
Pembroke Pines, FL 33029-3134, USA

Rolle, Dave (Athlete, Football Player)
1107 Woodmount Ct
Denton, TX 76209-1424, USA

Roller, Becky (Stylist)
801 S Chester Ave
Park Ridge, IL 60068-4614, USA

Roller, David E (Athlete, Football Player)
1110 Anthony Ct
Suwanee, GA 30024-5431, USA

Rollin, Betty (Correspondent, Writer)
67 Park Ave
New York, NY 10016-2557, USA

Rolling Stones (Music Group, Musician)
c/o Fran Curtis *Rogers & Cowan PR (LA)*
Pacific Design Center 8687 Melrose Ave, 7th Floor
West Hollywood, CA 90069, USA

Rollins, Ed
c/o Staff Member *WmE2 (WMA-LA)*
1 William Morris Pl
Beverly Hills, CA 90212-4261, USA

Rollins, Henry (Musician, Songwriter)
c/o Tiffany Kuzon *Evolution Entertainment (LA)*
901 N Highland Ave
Los Angeles, CA 90038-2412, USA

Rollins, James (Jimmy) (Athlete, Baseball Player)
1137 Rosewood Way
Alameda, CA 94501-5635, USA

Rollins, John (Golfer)
8703 Playground Ct
North Chesterfield, VA 23237-2378, USA

Rollins, Kenneth (Kenny) (Athlete, Basketball Player)
1497 N County Road 175 W
Greencastle, IN 46135-9238, USA

Rollins, Phil (Athlete, Basketball Player)
221 Norbourne Blvd
Louisville, KY 40207-3922, USA

Rollins, Rich (Athlete, Baseball Player)
4146 Evergreen Ln
Richfield, OH 44286-9592, USA

Rollins, Rose (Actor)
c/o David Sweeney *Sweeney Management*
8755 Lookout Mountain Ave
Los Angeles, CA 90046-1861, USA

Rollins, Theodore W (Sonny) (Composer, Musician)
RR 9G
Germantown, NY 12526, USA

Rollins, Wayne (Tree) (Athlete, Basketball Player, Coach)
PO Box 681971
Orlando, FL 32868-1971, USA

Rolls, Damian (Athlete, Baseball Player)
11112 Shadybrook Dr
Tampa, FL 33625-5708, USA

Roloff, Matt
23985 NW Grossen Dr
Hillsboro, OR 97124-8149

Roloson, Dwayne (Athlete, Hockey Player)
175 Kellogg Blvd W
Saint Paul, MN 55102-1206, USA

Rolston, Holmes III (Misc)
Philosophy
Fort Collins, CO 80523-0001, USA

Rolston, Matthew (Photographer)
3630 Eastham Dr
Culver City, CA 90232-2411, USA

Roman, Bill (Athlete, Baseball Player)
1720 Yale Ct
Lake Forest, IL 60045-5117, USA

Roman, Dan (Baseball Player)
10313 Arran Ct
Huntersville, NC 28078-7021, USA

Roman, John (Athlete, Football Player)
13 Mendham Rd
Bernardsville, NJ 7924, USA

Roman, Joseph (Misc)
556 E Town St
Columbus, OH 43215-4802, USA

Roman, Kevin (Stylist)
c/o Staff Member *Ford Models (Chicago)*
311 W Superior St
Chicago, IL 60654-3548, USA

Roman, Lauren
170 Flanders Drakestown Rd
Flanders, NJ 07836-4014

Roman, Petre (Prime Minister)
Str Gogol 2 Sector 1
Bucharest, ROMANIA

Roman, Phil
10635 Riverside Dr
Toluca Lake, CA 91602-2341

Roman, Ric
2967 E 3rd St
Los Angeles, CA 90033-4108

Roman Holiday
Box 475
London, ENGLAND

Romanek, Mark (Director)
c/o Staff Member *Creative Artists Agency (CAA-LA)*
2000 Avenue of the Stars Ste 100
Los Angeles, CA 90067-4705, USA

Romanenko, Roman Y (Cosmonaut)
Moskovskoi Oblasti
Syvisdny Goroduk 141160, RUSSIA

Romanenko, Yuri V (Cosmonaut)
Moskovskoi Oblasti
Syvisdny Goroduk 141160, RUSSIA

Romanick, Ron (Athlete, Baseball Player)
15709 E Cervantes Ct
Fountain Hills, AZ 85268-1820, USA

Romaniszyn, Jim (Athlete, Football Player)
1786 Arash Cir
Port Orange, FL 32128-7301, USA

Romano, Christy Carlson (Actor)
c/o Staff Member *Global Artists Agency*
6253 Hollywood Blvd Apt 508
Los Angeles, CA 90028-8251, USA

Romano, Jason (Athlete, Baseball Player)
1411 Willow Oak Cir
Bradenton, FL 34209-7822, USA

Romano, John (Misc)
212 Valley Rd
Merion Station, PA 19066-1543, USA

Romano, Johnny (Athlete, Baseball Player)
160 W Pago Pago Dr
Naples, FL 34113-8616, USA

Romano, Larry (Actor)
3500 W Olive Ave Ste 1400
Burbank, CA 91505-5512, USA

Romano, Mike (Athlete, Baseball Player)
1202 N Lee Rd
Covington, LA 70433-1738, USA

Romano, Pete (Cinematographer)
5335 McConnell Ave
Los Angeles, CA 90066-7025, USA

Romano, Ray (Actor, Comedian, Producer, Writer)
c/o Rory Rosegarten *Conversation Company*
1044 Northern Blvd Ste 304
Roslyn, NY 11576-1589, USA

Romano, Roberta (Attorney, Educator)
127 Wall St
New Haven, CT 06511-8918, USA

Romano, Tom (Athlete, Baseball Player)
1266 Penora St
Depew, NY 14043-4512, USA

Romano, Umberto (Artist)
162 E 83rd St
New York, NY 10028-1901, USA

Romanos, John J (Jack) Jr (Publisher)
1230 Avenue of the Americas
New York, NY 10020-1513, USA

Romanov, Pyotr V (Government Official)
Bolshoy Komsomlsky Per 8/7
Moscow 10100, RUSSIA

Romanov, Stephanie (Actor)
c/o Staff Member *Diverse Talent Group*
9911 W Pico Blvd Ste 340W
Los Angeles, CA 90035-2712, USA

Romanowski, Bill (Athlete, Football Player)
3706 Mt Diablo Blvd Ste 200
Lafayette, CA 94549-3638, USA

Romansky, Monroe J (Doctor)
5600 Wisconsin Ave
Chevy Chase, MD 20815-4405, USA

Romantics, The
1924 Spring St
Paso Robles, CA 93446-1620

Romanus, Richard (Actor)
8899 Beverly Blvd # 716
Los Angeles, CA 90048-2412, USA

Romanus, Robert (Actor)
c/o Melanie Sharp *Sharp Talent*
117 N Orlando Ave
Los Angeles, CA 90048-3403, USA

Romar, Lorenzo (Athlete, Basketball Player)
4408 164th Ln SE
Issaquah, WA 98027-9046, USA

Romario (Soccer Player)
Rua Alvaro Chaves 41
Rio de Janiero 22231-200, BRAZIL

Romashin, Anatoliy V (Actor)
#60
Moscow 103101, RUSSIA

Romatowski, Jenny (Baseball Player)
3116 Highlands Blvd
Palm Harbor, FL 34684-2700, USA

Romby, Bob (Baseball Player)
38 Holman Mill Rd
Cumberland, VA 23040-2804, USA

Rome, Jim (Actor)
c/o Jeffrey Jacobs *Creative Artists Agency (CAA-LA)*
2000 Avenue of the Stars Ste 100
Los Angeles, CA 90067-4705, USA

Rome, Stan (Athlete, Football Player)
4489 Green Island Rd
Valdosta, GA 31602-0870, USA

Romelfanger, Charles (Misc)
4106 34th Ave
Moline, IL 61265-5501, USA

Romer, Roy R (Ex-Governor)
1150 17th St NW Ste 875
Washington, DC 20036-4630, USA

Romer, Suzanne F C (Prime Minister)
Willemstad, Curacao, NETHERLANDS ANTILLES

Romero, Celino (Musician)
165 W 57th St
New York, NY 10019-2201, USA

Romero, Danny Jr (Boxer)
800 Salida Sandia SW
Albuquerque, NM 87105-7607, USA

Romero, Ed (Athlete, Baseball Player)
1380 Wood Row Way
Wellington, FL 33414-9082, USA

Romero, George
c/o Staff Member *Gersh (LA)*
9465 Wilshire Blvd Ste 600
Beverly Hills, CA 90212-2612, USA

Romero, Gus (Stylist)
c/o Celebrity Stylist *Oliver Piro Inc*
725 Riverside Dr Apt 3A
New York, NY 10031-2460, USA

Romero, Mandy (Athlete, Baseball Player)
19280 SW 216th St
Miami, FL 33170-1214, USA

Romero, Ned (Actor)
19438 Lassen St
Northridge, CA 91324-1121, USA

Romero, Patricia (Stylist)
c/o Staff Member *Perrella Management*
330 W 38th St Rm 1407
New York, NY 10018-8435, USA

Romero, Richard (Actor)
c/o Staff Member *Select Artists Ltd (CA-Valley Office)*
PO Box 4359
Burbank, CA 91503-4359, USA

Romijn, Rebecca (Actor, Model)
c/o Molly Madden *3 Arts Entertainment Inc*
9460 Wilshire Blvd Fl 7
Beverly Hills, CA 90212-2713, USA

Romine, Alton (Athlete, Football Player)
286 Highway 79
Phil Campbell, AL 35581-6314, USA

Romine, Kevin (Athlete, Baseball Player)
8750 Rogue River Ave
Fountain Valley, CA 92708-5517, USA

Rominger, Kent V (Astronaut)
2714 Bridgeport Ave
Salt Lake City, UT 84121-5603, USA

Romita Sr., John (Artist, Cartoonist)
11301 W Olympic Blvd # 587
Los Angeles, CA 90064-1653, USA

Rommel, Ex-Mayor Manfred
Eduard-Steinle-Str 60
Stuttgart, GERMANY D-70619

Rommelaere-Manning, Martha (Baseball Player)
503-3252 Glasgow Ave
Victoria, BC V8X 1M2, CANADA

Romney, Mitt (Business Person, Ex-Governor, Politician)
PO Box 79226
Waverley, MA 02479-0226, USA

Romo, Daniela (Actor)
c/o Staff Member *Televisa*
Blvd Adolfo Lopez Mateos 232 Colonia San Angel INN
DF CP 01060, MEXICO

Romo, Tony (Athlete, Football Player)
c/o Tom Condon *CAA - St. Louis*
222 S Central Ave Ste 1008
Saint Louis, MO 63105-3509, USA

Romonosky, John (Athlete, Baseball Player)
5090 Bixby Rd
Groveport, OH 43125-9564, USA

Rompre, Robert (Athlete, Hockey Player)
105 Cherokee Rd
Beaver Dam, WI 53916-1035, USA

Ron, Moo-hyun (President)
Chong Wa Dae 1 Sejong-no
Seoul, SOUTH KOREA

Ronaldo, Cristiano (Athlete, Soccer Player)
c/o Jorge Mendes *Gestifute (Porto)*
Praceta Do Bom Sucesso 61 Salas 706/7/8
Porto 4150-146, Portugal

Ronan, Marc (Athlete, Baseball Player)
104 Evonshire Dr
Arkadelphia, AR 71923-5449, USA

Ronan, Saoirse (Actor)
c/o Staff Member *Creative Artists Agency (CAA-LA)*
2000 Avenue of the Stars Ste 100
Los Angeles, CA 90067-4705, USA

Ronan, William J (Engineer)
525 S Flagler Dr
West Palm Beach, FL 33401-5922, USA

Rondo, Rajon (Athlete, Basketball Player)
c/o Bill Duffy *BDA Sports Management (BDA-CA)*
700 Ygnacio Valley Rd Ste 330
Walnut Creek, CA 94596-3838, USA

Rondon, Gilberto (Gil) (Athlete, Baseball Player)
6131 Celtic
San Antonio, TX 78240-5703, USA

Ronettes, The
855 E Twain Ave # 123411
Las Vegas, NV 89169-0819

Roney, Matt (Athlete, Baseball Player)
1809 Nighthawk Ct
Edmond, OK 73034-6110, USA

Roney, Paul H (Judge)
100 1st Ave S
Saint Petersburg, FL 33701, USA

Ronney, Paul D (Astronaut)
613 Ranchito Rd
Monrovia, CA 91016-3733, USA

Ronning, Cliff (Athlete, Hockey Player)
316 Newton Dr RR 3
Penticton, BC V2A 8Z5, Canada

Ronningen, Jon (Wrestler)
Mellomasveien 132
Trollasen 1414, NORWAY

Rono, Peter (Athlete, Track Athlete)
Athletic Dept
Emmitsburg, MD 21727, USA

Ronson, Len
2006 SW Eastwood Ave
Gresham, OR 97080-5751

Ronson, Mark (Musician)
c/o Staff Member *Red Ink (Germany)*
Schlegelstr. 26b
Berlin 10115, Germany

Ronson, Samantha (DJ, Musician)
c/o Michael Schweiger *CEG Talent*
251 W 39th St Fl 7
New York, NY 10018-3171, USA

Ronstadt, Linda (Musician)
c/o Sheldon (Shelly) Schultz *Trident Media Group LLC*
41 Madison Ave Fl 36
New York, NY 10010-2257, USA

Roocroft, Amanda (Opera Singer)
26 Wadham Road
London SW15 2LR, UNITED KINGDOM (UK)

Roof, Gene (Athlete, Baseball Player)
175 Spring Valley Dr
Paducah, KY 42003-8894, USA

Roof, Michael (Actor)
c/o Staff Member *3 Arts Entertainment Inc*
9460 Wilshire Blvd Fl 7
Beverly Hills, CA 90212-2713, USA

Roof, Phil (Athlete, Baseball Player)
1301 Pillar Chase
Paducah, KY 42001-6137, USA

Rook, Jerry (Athlete, Basketball Player)
Route 9 Box 124L
Jonesboro, AR 72404, USA

Rook, Susan (Correspondent)
1050 Techwood Dr NW
Atlanta, GA 30318-5604, USA

Rooker, Jim (Athlete, Baseball Player)
1684 Citation Dr
South Park, PA 15129-8831, USA

Rooker, Michael (Actor)
275 S Beverly Dr Ste 215
Beverly Hills, CA 90212-5002, USA

Roomes, Rolando (Athlete, Baseball Player)
11520 E Pratt Ave
Mesa, AZ 85212-1949, USA

Roomful of Blues (Music Group, Musician)
c/o Staff Member *Concerted Efforts*
PO Box 440326
Somerville, MA 02144-0004, USA

Rooney, Daniel M (Football Executive)
940 N Lincoln Ave
Pittsburgh, PA 15233-1814, USA

Rooney, Jim (Soccer Player)
CMGI Field 1 Patriot Place
Foxboro, MA 2035, USA

Rooney, Joe Don (Musician)
1228 Pineview Ln
Nashville, TN 37211-7422, USA

Rooney, Kevin (Actor)
c/o Staff Member *Emptage Hallett*
14 Rathbone Pl
London W1T 1HT, UNITED KINGDOM (UK)

Rooney, Mickey (Actor, Director, Writer)
c/o Robert Malcolm *Artists Group, The (NY)*
1650 Broadway Ste 711
New York, NY 10019-6833, USA

Rooney, Pat (Athlete, Baseball Player)
400 Skokie Blvd Ste 280
Northbrook, IL 60062-7939, USA

Rooney, Patrick W (Business Person)
Lima & Western Aves
Findlay, OH 45840, USA

Rooney, Wayne (Soccer Player)
c/o Staff Member *Ian Monk Associates*
2 Station Rd Gerrards Cross
Buckinghamshire SL9 8EL, UK

Roop, Richard (Business Person)
743 Goldhills Pl S # 239
Woodland Park, CO 80863-1101, USA

Roopenian, Mark (Athlete, Football Player)
358 Charles River Rd
Watertown, MA 02472-2737, USA

Rooper, Jemima (Actor)
c/o Staff Member *Conway van Gelder*
8-12 Broadwick St
London W1F 8HW, UK

Roos, Don (Actor, Producer)
c/o Steve Rabineau *United Talent Agency (UTA)*
9560 Wilshire Blvd Fl 5
Beverly Hills, CA 90212-2400, USA

Rooster (Music Group)
c/o Staff Member *BMG*
1540 Broadway
New York, NY 10036-4039, USA

Rooster, The Red
PO Box 3859
Stamford, CT 6905

Root, Bonnie (Actor)
c/o Tracy Steinsapir *Main Title Entertainment*
2225 Wilshire Blvd Suite 500
Los Angeles, CA 90036, USA

Root, Jim (Athlete, Football Player)
1540 Linkside Dr
Orange Park, FL 32003-7767, USA

Root, Stephen (Steven) (Actor)
c/o Jai Khanna *Brillstein Entertainment Partners*
9150 Wilshire Blvd Ste 350
Beverly Hills, CA 90212-3453, USA

Roots, Melvin H (Misc)
1125 17th St NW
Washington, DC 20036-4709, USA

Roots, The (Music Group)
c/o Cara Lewis *WmE2 (WMA-NY)*
1325 Avenue of the Americas
New York, NY 10019-6026, USA

Roper, Dee Dee (Spinderella) (Musician)
1650 Broadway # 1130
New York, NY 10019-6833, USA

Roper, John (Athlete, Baseball Player)
519 John Roper Ave
Raeford, NC 28376-2211, USA

Roper, John (Athlete, Football Player)
4213 Alice St
Houston, TX 77021-4903, USA

Rorem, Ned (Composer, Writer)
PO Box 764
Nantucket, MA 02554-0764, USA

Rorty, Richard M (Misc)
402 Peacock Dr
Charlottesville, VA 22903-9725, USA

Rosa, John (Educator, General)
President's Office
Charleston, SC 6520, USA

Rosa, Robi Draco (Composer, Musician, Producer)
10866 Wilshire Blvd # 10000
Los Angeles, CA 90024-4300, USA

Rosa, Rosa
6640 W Sunset Blvd # 110
Los Angeles, CA 90028-7104

Rosado, Eduardo (Opera Singer)
Calle 3 Ave Cupules 112A Col G Giberes
Menda, Yucatan 97070, MEXICO

Rosales, Jenny (Athlete, Golfer)
265 S Vine St
Anaheim, CA 92805-4128, USA

Rosamund, John
4 Dean's Yard
London, ENGLAND SW1P

Rosand, David (Historian)
560 Riverside Dr
New York, NY 10027-3202, USA

Rosario, Jimmy (Athlete, Baseball Player)
PO Box 9020739
San Juan, PR 00902-0739, USA

Rosario, Mel (Athlete, Baseball Player)
205 Round Tree Ct
Egg Harbor Township, NJ 08234-7910, USA

Rosario, Santiago (Baseball Player)
HC 1 Box 7982
Guayanilla, PR 00656-9801, USA

Rosas, Cesar (Musician, Songwriter, Writer)
200 W Superior St Ste 202
Chicago, IL 60654-3554, USA

Rosato, Cristina (Actor)
c/o Sandy Martinez *Martinez Creative Management*
7012 St Laurent Blvd Suite 200
Montreal, QC H2S 3E2, Canada

Rosato, Genesia (Ballerina)
Covent Garden Bow St
London WC2E 9DD, UNITED KINGDOM (UK)

Rosato, Tony (Actor, Writer)
c/o Staff Member *Don Capo Entertainment*
Ste 5 South Bank Terrace Surbiton
Surrey KT6 6DG, UNITED KINGDOM (UK)

Rosberg, Keke (Race Car Driver)
7 Rue Gabian
Monte Carlo 9800, MONACO

Rosburg, Bob (Golfer)
2902 Dublin Dr
Austin, TX 78745-3474, USA

Roschkov, Victor (Cartoonist, Editor)
Editorial Dept 1 Yonge St
Toronto, ON M5E 1E5, CANADA

Rose, Adam (Actor)
c/o Steven Siebert *Lighthouse Entertainment*
9220 W Sunset Blvd Ste 200
West Hollywood, CA 90069-3501, USA

Rose, Anika Noni (Actor)
c/o David Williams *David Williams Management*
9614 W Olympic Blvd Apt F
Beverly Hills, CA 90212-3761, USA

Rose, Axl (Musician, Songwriter, Writer)
5055 Latigo Canyon Rd
Malibu, CA 90265-2812, USA

Rose, Barry (Athlete, Football Player)
1761 W White Ash Dr
Balsam Lake, WI 54810-2416, USA

Rose, Bernard (Director, Producer, Writer)
c/o Jenne Casarotto *Casarotto Ramsay & Associates Ltd (UK)*
Waverley House 7-12 Noel St
London W1F 8GQ, UK

Rose, Bobby (Athlete, Baseball Player)
2713 Highview Dr
Bullhead City, AZ 86429-5928, USA

Rose, Brian (Athlete, Baseball Player)
5 Ashland St
South Dartmouth, MA 02748-3211, USA

Rose, Carol (Attorney, Educator)
127 Wall St
New Haven, CT 06511-8918, USA

Rose, Charles (Charlie) (Television Host)
2100 Crystal Dr
Arlington, VA 22202-3784, USA

Rose, Chris (Television Host)
c/o Staff Member *Best Damned Sports Show Period, The*
10201 W Pico Blvd
Los Angeles, CA 90064-2606, USA

Rose, Clarence (Golfer)
106 Harding Pl
Goldsboro, NC 27534-9100, USA

Rose, Cristine (Actor)
c/o Staff Member *Silver Massetti & Szatmary (SMS) Talent Inc*
8730 W Sunset Blvd Ste 440
Los Angeles, CA 90069-2277, USA

Rose, Derrick (Athlete, Basketball Player)
c/o BJ Armstrong *Wasserman Media Group*
10960 Wilshire Blvd Fl 22
Los Angeles, CA 90024-3808, USA

Rose, Don (Athlete, Baseball Player)
16254 Palomino Mesa Way
San Diego, CA 92127-4445, USA

Rose, Donovan (Athlete, Football Player)
103 Lenox Ct
Yorktown, VA 23693-5501, USA

Rose, Emily (Actor)
c/o Connie Tavel *Forward Entertainment*
9255 W Sunset Blvd Ste 805
Los Angeles, CA 90069-3305, USA

Rose, George (Athlete, Football Player)
712 Indian Mound Rd
Brunswick, GA 31525-2124, USA

Rose, H Michael (General)
Wellington Barracks
London SW1E 6HQ, UNITED KINGDOM (UK)

Rose, Irwin A. (Nobel Prize Laureate)
1 Health Sciences Rd # 252
Irvine, CA 92697-0001, USA

Rose, Jalen (Athlete, Basketball Player)
6689 Orchard Lake Rd
West Bloomfield, MI 48322-3404, USA

Rose, Jamie (Actor)
c/o Staff Member *Marshak/Zachary Company, The*
8840 Wilshire Blvd Fl 1
Beverly Hills, CA 90211-2606, USA

Rose, Jessica (Actor)
c/o Brad Marks *BM Management*
Prefers to be contacted via phone
Los Angeles, CA 90069, USA

Rose, Joe (Athlete, Football Player)
3293 SW 138th Way
Davie, FL 33330-4664, USA

Rose, John (Cartoonist)
95 Laurel St
Harrisonburg, VA 22801-2732, USA

Rose, Justin (Golfer)
c/o Staff Member *Pro Golfers Assoc of America (PGA)*
112 Tpc Blvd
Ponte Vedra Beach, FL 32082, USA

Rose, Katy (Musician)
c/o Staff Member *Paradigm (Monterey)*
404 W Franklin St
Monterey, CA 93940-2303, USA

Rose, Ken (Athlete, Football Player)
1736 Bronzewood Ct
Thousand Oaks, CA 91320-4546, USA

Rose, Lee (Director, Producer)
c/o Staff Member *Broder Webb Chervin Silbermann Agency, The (BWCS)*
10250 Constellation Blvd
Los Angeles, CA 90067-6200, USA

Rose, Malik (Athlete, Basketball Player)
PO Box 493
Glen Mills, PA 19342-0493, USA

Rose, Marie (Actor)
6916 Chisholm Ave
Van Nuys, CA 91406-5111, USA

Rose, Matthew (Business Person)
2650 Lou Menk Dr
Fort Worth, TX 76131-2830, USA

Rose, Monica (Stylist)
c/o Staff Member *Rex Agency, The*
6311 Romaine St
Los Angeles, CA 90038-2617, USA

Rose, Murray (Swimmer)
77 Berry Level 3
North Sydney, NSW 2060, AUSTRALIA

Rose, Pete (Athlete, Baseball Player, Coach)
13348 Chandler Blvd
Sherman Oaks, CA 91401-5323, USA

Rose, Peter H (Business Person)
2 Centennial Dr
Peabody, MA 01960-7911, USA

Rose, Richard (Scientist)
Bennochy 1 E Abercromby St
Helensburgh, Dunbartonshire G84 7SP, SCOTLAND

Rose, Shayna (Actor)
C/O Bill Kravitz 1424 N Kings Rd
Los Angeles, CA 90069, USA

Rose, Sherrie (Actor, Model)
1758 Laurel Canyon Blvd
Los Angeles, CA 90046-2134, USA

Rose Jr, Pete (Athlete, Baseball Player)
3921 Legendary Ridge Ln
Cleves, OH 45002-2395, USA

Roseau, Maurice E D (Engineer)
144 Bis Ave du General Leclerc
Sceaux 92330, FRANCE

Rosecrans, James (Athlete, Football Player)
210 Houston Ave
Syracuse, NY 13224-1754, USA

Rosegarten, Rory (Producer)
c/o Staff Member *WmE2 (WMA-LA)*
1 William Morris Pl
Beverly Hills, CA 90212-4261, USA

Rosell, Janet (Stylist)
c/o Staff Member *Clutts Agency, The*
1400 Turtle Creek Blvd # 171
Dallas, TX 75207-3337, USA

Roselle, David P (Educator)
14 Laurel Ridge Ln
Wilmington, DE 19807-1322, USA

Roselli, Bob (Athlete, Baseball Player)
100 Clydesdale Way
Roseville, CA 95678-6032, USA

Roselli, Jimmy
64 Division Ave
Levittown, NY 11756-2999

Rosellini, Albert D (Ex-Governor)
5936 6th Ave S
Seattle, WA 98108-3302, USA

Rosello, Dave (Athlete, Baseball Player)
HC 1 Box 8125
Hormigueros, PR 660, USA

Rosema, Roger (Athlete, Football Player)
3300 S Creek Dr SE Apt 204
Grand Rapids, MI 49512-8385, USA

Roseman, Saul (Scientist)
3020 Essex Rd
Cleveland Heights, OH 44118-3536, USA

Rosemont, Romy (Actor)
c/o Staff Member *Don Buchwald & Associates Inc (LA)*
6500 Wilshire Blvd Ste 2200
Los Angeles, CA 90048-4942, USA

Rosen, Albert (Al) (Conductor)
2101 California St Apt 2
San Francisco, CA 94115-2801, USA

Rosen, Albert L (Al) (Athlete, Baseball Player)
15 Mayfair Dr
Rancho Mirage, CA 92270-2586, USA

Rosen, Beatrice (Actor)
c/o Staff Member *Inspire Entertainment*
315 7th Ave Apt 17E
New York, NY 10001-6011, USA

Rosen, Charles W (Musician)
101 W 78th St
New York, NY 10024-6717, USA

Rosen, Harold A (Engineer, Inventor)
8226 Whittier Blvd
Pico Rivera, CA 90660-2522, USA

Rosen, Jeneffer Jones (Stylist)
255 Shrader St Apt 8
San Francisco, CA 94117-1875, USA

Rosen, Milton W (Engineer, Physicist)
5610 Alta Vista Rd
Bethesda, MD 20817-3512, USA

Rosen, Nathaniel (Musician)
282 Cabrini Blvd Apt 4J
New York, NY 10040-3679, USA

Rosen, Sam (Actor)
c/o Staff Member *Brookside Artists Management (NY)*
250 W 57th St Ste 2303
New York, NY 10107-2399, USA

Rosenbaum, Edward E (Physicist)
333 NW 23rd Ave
Portland, OR 97210-3403, USA

Rosenbaum, Michael (Actor)
c/o Jason Newman *Untitled Entertainment (LA)*
350 S Beverly Dr Ste 200
Beverly Hills, CA 90212-4819, USA

Rosenberg, Alan
PO Box 5617
Beverly Hills, CA 90209-5617

Rosenberg, Alyse (Producer)
c/o Staff Member *The Alpern Group*
15645 Royal Oak Rd
Encino, CA 91436-3905, USA

Rosenberg, Craig (Director, Writer)
c/o Staff Member *Firm, The*
2049 Century Park E Ste 2550
Los Angeles, CA 90067-3139, USA

Rosenberg, Gabrielle (Stylist)
17 Downing St
New York, NY 10014-4750, USA

Rosenberg, Howard (Misc)
5859 Larboard Ln
Agoura Hills, CA 91301-1422, USA

Rosenberg, Joel C (Writer)
C/O Beverly Rykerd PO Box 88180
Colorado Springs, CO 80908, USA

Rosenberg, Michael (Producer)
c/o Staff Member *Imagine Films Entertainment*
1925 Century Park E Ste 800
Los Angeles, CA 90067-2749, USA

Rosenberg, Pierre M (Director)
34-36 Quai du Louvre
Paris 75068, FRANCE

Rosenberg, Scott (Writer)
c/o David O'Connor *Creative Artists Agency (CAA-LA)*
2000 Avenue of the Stars Ste 100
Los Angeles, CA 90067-4705, USA

Rosenberg, Sena (Stylist)
c/o Staff Member *Fifty8 Artists*
58 W Huron St
Chicago, IL 60654-3806, USA

Rosenberg, Steve (Athlete, Baseball Player)
2430 NE 35th St
Lighthouse Point, FL 33064-8155, USA

Rosenberg, Steven A (Doctor)
10104 Iron Gate Rd
Potomac, MD 20854-4728, USA

Rosenberg, Stuart (Director)
1984 Coldwater Canyon Dr
Beverly Hills, CA 90210-1731, USA

Rosenberg, Tina (Writer)
World Policy Institute
New York, NY 10011, USA

Rosenblath, Marshall N (Physicist)
2311 Via Siena
La Jolla, CA 92037-3933, USA

Rosenblatt, Dana (Boxer)
30 Cleveland Rd
Chestnut Hill, MA 02467-1417, USA

Rosenbluth, Leonard (Lennie) (Athlete, Basketball Player)
123 Priestly Creek Dr
Chapel Hill, NC 27514-5432, USA

Rosenbohm, Jim (Baseball Player)
9513 Bedford Ave
Omaha, NE 68134-4607, USA

Rosenburg, Saul A (Doctor)
Oncology Division
Stanford, CA 94305, USA

Rosendahl, Heidemarie (Heide) (Athlete, Track Athlete)
Burscheider Str 426
Leverkusen 51381, GERMANY

Rosenfeld, Arnold S (Editor)
PO Box 105720
Atlanta, GA 30348-5720, USA

Rosenfeld, Isadore (Physicist)
1271 Avenue of the Americas
New York, NY 10020-1300, USA

Rosenfels, Sage (Athlete, Football Player)
1459 White Hawk Ranch Dr
Boulder, CO 80303-1674, USA

Rosenfelt, David (Writer)
c/o Staff Member *St Martins Press*
175 5th Ave
New York, NY 10010-7703, USA

Rosenfield, John Max (Educator)
1573 Cambridge St Apt 711
Cambridge, MA 02138-4381, USA

Rosengarten, David (Writer)
PO Box 20459
New York, NY 10025-1520, USA

Rosenman, Howard (Producer)
c/o Staff Member *Marshak/Zachary Company, The*
8840 Wilshire Blvd Fl 1
Beverly Hills, CA 90211-2606, USA

Rosenmeyer, Grant (Actor)
c/o Staff Member *DreamWorks SKG*
1000 Flower St
Glendale, CA 91201-3007, USA

Rosenn, Max (Judge)
S Main St US Courthouse 197
Wilkes Barre, PA 18701-1686, USA

Rosenquist, James A (Artist)
PO Box 4
Aripeka, FL 34679-0004, USA

Rosenstein, Hank (Athlete, Basketball Player)
3040 Hythe C
Boca Raton, FL 33434-4608, USA

Rosenstein, Samuel M (Judge)
2200 S Ocean Ln
Fort Lauderdale, FL 33316-3836, USA

Rosenthal, Albert J (Attorney, Attorney General, Educator, General)
15 Oak Way
Scarsdale, NY 10583-1415, USA

Rosenthal, Amy Krouse (Writer)
1745 Broadway
New York, NY 10019-4368, USA

Rosenthal, David S (Director, Writer)
1801 Century Park E Ste 2160
Los Angeles, CA 90067-2343

Rosenthal, Dick (Athlete, Basketball Player)
33108 Lake Forest Ct
Niles, MI 49120-7794, USA

Rosenthal, Howard L (Scientist)
Politics
Princeton, NJ 08544-0001, USA

Rosenthal, Jane (Producer)
c/o Staff Member *Tribeca Productions*
375 Greenwich St Fl 7
New York, NY 10013-2379, USA

Rosenthal, Mark D (Writer)
c/o Tom Strickler *WmE2 (Endeavor-LA)*
9601 Wilshire Blvd Fl 3
Beverly Hills, CA 90210-5219, USA

Rosenthal, Mike (Athlete, Football Player)
6112 Every Sail Path
Clarksville, MD 21029-2904, USA

Rosenthal, Philip (Producer)
c/o Adam Berkowitz *Creative Artists Agency (CAA-LA)*
2000 Avenue of the Stars Ste 100
Los Angeles, CA 90067-4705, USA

Rosenthal, Richard L (Rick) (Director, Producer)
c/o Staff Member *Whitewater Films*
11264 La Grange Ave
Los Angeles, CA 90025-5514, USA

Rosenthal, Robert J (Editor)
400 N Broad St
Philadelphia, PA 19130-4015, USA

Rosenthal, Sean (Athlete, Volleyball Player)
715 S Circle Dr
Colorado Springs, CO 80910-2324, USA

Rosenthal, Tony (Artist)
173 E 73rd St
New York, NY 10021-3510, USA

Rosenthal, Wayne (Athlete, Baseball Player)
10224 Allamanda Blvd
Palm Beach Gardens, FL 33410-5206, USA

Rosenzweig, Barney (Producer)
2311 Fisher Island Dr
Miami Beach, FL 33109-0086, USA

Rosenzweig, Mark R (Misc)
Psychology Dept Tolman Hall
Berkeley, CA 94720-0001, USA

Rosenzweig, Robert M (Educator)
1462 Dana Ave
Palo Alto, CA 94301-3115, USA

Roses, Allen D (Doctor)
Medical Center Bryan Research Center
Durham, NC 27706, USA

Rosewall, Ken (Tennis Player)
111 Pentacost Ave
Sydney, NSW 2074, AUSTRALIA

Rosewoman, Michele (Musician)
223 1/2 E 48th St
New York, NY 10017, USA

Roshan, Hrithik (Actor, Bollywood)
c/o Jai Khanna *Brillstein Entertainment Partners*
9150 Wilshire Blvd Ste 350
Beverly Hills, CA 90212-3453, USA

Roshan, Rakesh (Actor, Bollywood, Director, Producer)
c/o Asal Masomi *Asal Masomi Public Relations*
6320 Canoga Ave Ste 1513
Woodland Hills, CA 91367-2526, USA

Rosi, Francesco
Via Gregoriana 36
Rome, ITALY 1-00187

Rosin, Walter L (Religious Leader)
1333 S Kirkwood Rd
Saint Louis, MO 63122-7226, USA

Rosinski, Edward J (Inventor)
1308 Kellogg Ave
Utica, NY 13502-3740, USA

Roskill of Newtown, Eustace W (Judge)
New Court Temple
London EC4, UNITED KINGDOM (UK)

Roskos, John (Athlete, Baseball Player)
PO Box 45514
Rio Rancho, NM 87174-5514, USA

Rosman, Mackenzie (Actor)
c/o Kanica Suy *Sweeney Management*
8755 Lookout Mountain Ave
Los Angeles, CA 90046-1861, USA

Rosner, Robert (Astronomer)
4950 S Greenwood Ave
Chicago, IL 60615-2816, USA

Rosnes, Renee (Musician)
PO Box 961
Burlington, MA 01803-5961, USA

Ross, Al (Cartoonist)
2185 Bolton St
Bronx, NY 10462-1367, USA

Ross, Anne (Stylist)
4640 Vantage Ave
Valley Village, CA 91607-3814, USA

Ross, Ben (Director)
9560 Wilshire Blvd Ste 500
Beverly Hills, CA 90212-2401, USA

Ross, Betsy (Sportscaster)
Sports Dept ESPN Plaza 935 Middle St
Bristol, CT 6010, USA

Ross, Bob (Athlete, Baseball Player)
862 Bergamo Ave
San Jacinto, CA 92583-2967, USA

Ross, Brian (Correspondent)
c/o Staff Member *ABC News*
77 W 66th St Fl 3
New York, NY 10023-6201, USA

Ross, Charlotte (Actor)
c/o Paul Santana *Agency for the Performing Arts (APA-LA)*
405 S Beverly Dr Ste 500
Beverly Hills, CA 90212-4425, USA

Ross, Chelcie (Actor)
c/o Staff Member *Geddes Agency, The*
8430 Santa Monica Blvd Ste 200
Los Angeles, CA 90069-4253, USA

Ross, Cody (Athlete, Baseball Player)
21469 N 83rd St
Scottsdale, AZ 85255-6473, USA

Ross, Daniel R (Dan) (Athlete, Football Player)
10 Manasquan Cir
Londonderry, NH 03053-2636, USA

Ross, Dave (Athlete, Baseball Player)
2768 Millstone Plantation Rd
Tallahassee, FL 32312-3880, USA

Ross, David A (Director)
945 Madison Ave
New York, NY 10021-2764, USA

Ross, Diana (Actor, Musician)
c/o Whitney Tancred *Sunshine, Sachs & Associates - LA*
8409 Santa Monica Blvd
West Hollywood, CA 90069-4209, USA

Ross, Don (Athlete)
PO Box 981
Venice, CA 90294-0981, USA

Ross, Donald R (Judge)
PO Box 307
Omaha, NE 68101-0307, USA

Ross, Douglas T (Scientist)
2 Highwood Dr Ste 200
Tewksbury, MA 01876-1100, USA

Ross, Emma (Stylist)
c/o Staff Member *Michele Karpe*
4328 Ben Ave
Studio City, CA 91604-1703, USA

Ross, Evan (Actor)
c/o Adam Griffin *Kritzer Levine Wilkins Entertainment*
11872 La Grange Ave Fl 1
Los Angeles, CA 90025-5283, USA

Ross, Fairbanks Anne (Swimmer)
10 Grandview Ave
Troy, NY 12180-2113, USA

Ross, Gary (Director, Producer, Writer)
c/o Staff Member *Larger Than Life Productions*
100 Universal City Plz Bldg 5138
Universal City, CA 91608-1002

Ross, Gary (Athlete, Baseball Player)
1729 Cuadro Vis
San Marcos, CA 92078-2102, USA

Ross, George (Business Person, Reality TV Star)
c/o Staff Member *The Apprentice*
725 5th Ave
New York, NY 10022-2519, USA

Ross, Heather (Musician)
6736 Breezy Palm Dr
Riverview, FL 33578-8802, USA

Ross, Ian M (Engineer)
5 Blackpoint Road Horsehoe
Rumson, NJ 7760, USA

Ross, Jeffrey (Actor, Comedian)
c/o Amy Zvi *Thruline Entertainment*
9250 Wilshire Blvd Ground Fl
Beverly Hills, CA 90212, USA

Ross, Jerry L (Astronaut)
2101 Nasa Pkwy Spc Center
Houston, TX 77058-3607, USA

Ross, Jim (Athlete, Wrestler)
605 Shadow View Ct
Norman, OK 73072-4827, USA

Ross, Jimmy D (General)
265 Minorca Beach Way Apt 856
New Smyrna Beach, FL 32169-6058, USA

Ross, John (Misc)
620 Sand Hill Rd Apt 405E
Palo Alto, CA 94304-2078, USA

Ross, Jonathan (Actor)
c/o Staff Member *Off The Kerb Productions*
Hammer House, 3rd Fl 113-117 Wardour St
London W1F 0UN, UK

Ross, Jonathon (Actor, Producer, Writer)
19 Bird St
Lichfield, Staffordshire WS13 6PW, UNITED KINGDOM

Ross, Karie (Sportscaster)
Sports Dept ESPN Plaza 935 Middle St
Bristol, CT 6010, USA

Ross, Katharine
33050 Pacific Coast Hwy
Malibu, CA 90265-2300

Ross, Katherine (Actor)
33050 Pacific Coast Hwy
Malibu, CA 90265-2300, USA

Ross, Kevin (Athlete, Football Player)
146 High St
Woodbury, NJ 08096-2304, USA

Ross, Louis (Athlete, Football Player)
4283 Booker St
Orlando, FL 32811-4662, USA

Ross, Marion (Actor)
4230 Natoma Ave
Woodland Hills, CA 91364-5623, USA

Ross, Mark (Athlete, Baseball Player)
1747 N Wild Hyacinth Dr
Tucson, AZ 85715-5912, USA

Ross, Rick (Musician)
c/o Staff Member *Island Def Jam Music Group*
825 8th Ave Fl 28
New York, NY 10019-7416

Ross, Robert J (Bobby) (Coach, Football Coach)
Athletic Dept
West Point, NY 10996, USA

Ross, Ryan (Actor)
c/o Staff Member *Vincent Cirrincione Associates*
1516 N Fairfax Ave
Los Angeles, CA 90046-2608, USA

Ross, Scott (Athlete, Football Player)
303 Lake View Dr Unit D
Montgomery, TX 77356-5782, USA

Ross, Stan
1410 N Gardner St
Los Angeles, CA 90046-4142

Ross, Tracee Ellis (Actor)
c/o Janean Glover *Screen Partners*
9663 Santa Monica Blvd # 639
Beverly Hills, CA 90210-4303, USA

Ross, Willie (Athlete, Football Player)
1100 S Hamilton Ave
Chicago, IL 60612-4207, USA

Ross, Yolanda (Actor)
c/o Brian Liebman *Liebman Entertainment*
25 E 21st St PH
New York, NY 10010-6226, USA

Rossdale, Gavin (Actor, Musician)
c/o Cynthia Pett-Dante *Brillstein Entertainment Partners*
9150 Wilshire Blvd Ste 350
Beverly Hills, CA 90212-3453, USA

Rosselli, Jimmy
344 Paterson Plank Rd
Jersey City, NJ 07307-1051

Rosselli, Joe (Athlete, Baseball Player)
6231 Le Sage Ave
Woodland Hills, CA 91367-1327, USA

Rossellini, Isabella (Actor)
c/o Cindy Schultzel-Ambers *Art/Work Entertainment*
5900 Wilshire Blvd Ste 2150
Los Angeles, CA 90036-5021, USA

Rossen, Carol
1119 23rd St Unit 8
Santa Monica, CA 90403-5732

Rosser, Ronald (War Hero)
36 James St
Roseville, OH 43777-1228, USA

Rossi, Alice (Scientist)
2131 Century Park Ln Apt 309
Los Angeles, CA 90067-3315, USA

Rossi, Gretchen (Reality TV Star)
c/o Marki Costello *Creative Management Entertainment Group (CMEG)*
2050 S Bundy Dr Ste 280
Los Angeles, CA 90025-6128, USA

Rossi, Luigi Francis (Shorty) (Actor)
12405 Venice Blvd Ste 7
Los Angeles, CA 90066-3803, USA

Rossi, Tony (Ray) (Actor)
c/o Kristene Wallis *Wallis Agency*
210 N Pass Ave Ste 205
Burbank, CA 91505-3936, USA

Rossi, Valentino (Motorcycle Racer)
Koolhovenlaan 101
1119 NC 1119 NC, The Netherlands

Rossio, Terry (Writer)
c/o Brian Siberell *Creative Artists Agency (CAA-LA)*
2000 Avenue of the Stars Ste 100
Los Angeles, CA 90067-4705, USA

Rossovich, Rick
PO Box 5617
Beverly Hills, CA 90209-5617

Rossovich, Tim (Athlete, Football Player)
19811 Wildwood West Dr
Penn Valley, CA 95946-9547, USA

Rossum, Allen (Athlete, Football Player)
2520 Johnson Dr
Mesquite, TX 75181-4619, USA

Rossum, Emmy (Actor, Musician)
c/o Christian Donatelli *Schiff Company, The*
8440 Warner Dr Ste B1
Culver City, CA 90232-2461, USA

Rossy, Rico (Athlete, Baseball Player)
A7 Calle Atenas
Bayamon, PR 00959-4928, USA

Rostenkowski, Dan (Politician)
1372 W Evergreen Ave
Chicago, IL 60642-2363

Rostosky, Pete (Athlete, Football Player)
637 F McMurray Rd
Canonsburg, PA 15317-3430, USA

Rostow, Walt
1 Wildwind Pt
Austin, TX 78746-2434

Rotblatt, Marv (Athlete, Baseball Player)
584 N East River Rd
Des Plaines, IL 60016-1228, USA

Rote, Kyle
24700 Deepwater Point Dr Unit 14
Saint Michaels, MD 21663-2327

Rote, Tobin
7590 Lighthouse Rd
Port Hope, MI 48468-9760

Rote Jr, Kyle
6075 Poplar Ave # 920
Memphis, TN 38119-4740, USA

Rotem, Jonathan (J.R.) (Producer)
c/o Zach Katz *Beluga Heights Management*
10323 Santa Monica Blvd Ste 111
Los Angeles, CA 90025-5056, USA

Roth, Andrea (Actor)
c/o Staff Member *Levine Okwu Erickson Management*
6363 Wilshire Blvd Ste 300
Los Angeles, CA 90048-5729, USA

Roth, David Lee (Musician)
c/o Garry Buck *Monterey International*
PO Box 297
Carmel By The Sea, CA 93921-0297, USA

Roth, Doug (Athlete, Basketball Player)
9975 Spillway Cir Apt 201
Cordova, TN 38016-7152, USA

Roth, Eli (Producer, Writer)
c/o Simon Halls *Slate Public Relations*
9000 W Sunset Blvd Ste 915
West Hollywood, CA 90069-5809, USA

Roth, Ellaine (Baseball Player)
872 Goguac St W
Springfield, MI 49015-1737, USA

Roth, Eric (Writer)
c/o Staff Member *Creative Artists Agency (CAA-LA)*
2000 Avenue of the Stars Ste 100
Los Angeles, CA 90067-4705, USA

Roth, Matt
PO Box 5617
Beverly Hills, CA 90209-5617

Roth, Philip (Writer)
c/o Andrew Wylie *The Andrew Wylie Agency*
250 W 57th St Ste 2114
New York, NY 10107-2114, USA

Roth, Rachel (Actor)
c/o Justine Hunt *Hines and Hunt Entertainment*
1213 W Magnolia Blvd
Burbank, CA 91506-1829, USA

Roth, Tim (Actor)
c/o Pippa Markham *Markham & Froggatt*
4 Windmill St
London W1T 1HZ, UK

Rothemund, Marc (Director)
c/o Daniel J Talbot *International Creative Management (ICM-LA)*
10250 Constellation Blvd Fl 7
Los Angeles, CA 90067-6207, USA

Rothenberg, Irv (Athlete, Basketball Player)
6600 Capistrano Beach Trl
Delray Beach, FL 33446-5664, USA

Rothenberger, Anneliese (Opera Singer)
Quellenhof
Salenstein, TG 8268, SWITZERLAND

Rothery, Teryl (Actor)
c/o Staff Member *Twenty First Century Artists*
501 - 825 Granville St
Vancouver BC V6Z 1K9, CANADA

Rothman, John
9229 W Sunset Blvd Ste 710
Los Angeles, CA 90069-3407

Rothman, Les (Athlete, Basketball Player)
11854 Fountainside Cir
Boynton Beach, FL 33437, USA

Rothrock, Cynthia
20670 Callon Dr
Topanga, CA 90290-3712

Rothschild, Larry (Athlete, Baseball Player, Coach)
4508 W Culbreath Ave
Tampa, FL 33609-4206, USA

Rothstein, Ron (Athlete, Basketball Player, Coach)
60 Edgewater Dr Apt 4E
Coral Gables, FL 33133-6971, USA

Rottino, Vinny (Athlete, Baseball Player)
4939 Crystal Spg
Racine, WI 53406-1526, USA

Rottner, Mickey (Athlete, Basketball Player)
5757 N Sheridan Rd Apt 8B
Chicago, IL 60660-8704, USA

Rotunno, Giuseppe
Via Crescenzio 58
Rome, ITALY 193

Rouen, Tom (Athlete, Football Player)
19947 N 84th St
Scottsdale, AZ 85255, USA

Rouillard, Richard
11750 W Sunset Blvd Apt 117
Los Angeles, CA 90049-2904

Roumel, Katie (Producer)
c/o Staff Member *Killer Films (US)*
526 W 26th St Rm 715
New York, NY 10001-5524, USA

Roundfield, Dan (Athlete, Basketball Player)
340 Spring Lake Ter
Roswell, GA 30076-3234, USA

Rounds, Lil (Musician)

Roundtree, Raleigh (Athlete, Football Player)
2001 Roosevelt Dr
Augusta, GA 30904-5021, USA

Roundtree, Richard (Actor)
7120 Hayvenhurst Ave Ste 409
Van Nuys, CA 91406-3813, USA

Rounsaville, Gene (Athlete, Baseball Player)
3331 Mountaire Dr
Antioch, CA 94509-5661, USA

Rountree, Mary (Athlete, Baseball Player)
8204 NW 80th St
Tamarac, FL 33321-1627, USA

Rourke, Jim (Athlete, Football Player)
466 Plymouth St
Abington, MA 02351-1842, USA

Rourke, Mickey (Actor)
1203 Washington Ave
Miami Beach, FL 33139-4613, USA

Rouse, Curtis (Athlete, Football Player)
301 Hampshire Ct
Clarksville, TN 37043-4661, USA

Rouse, Irving (Misc)
509 Rockavon Rd
Narberth, PA 19072-2318, USA

Rouse, Jeff
302 Gerber Dr
Fredericksburg, VA 22408-2920

Rouse, Jeffrey (Jeff) (Swimmer)
302 Gerber Dr
Fredericksburg, VA 22408-2920, USA

Rouse, Mitch (Actor)
c/o David (Dave) Becky *3 Arts Entertainment Inc*
9460 Wilshire Blvd Fl 7
Beverly Hills, CA 90212-2713, USA

Roush, Jack (Misc)
122 Knob Hill Rd
Mooresville, NC 28117-6847, USA

Rouson, Lee (Athlete, Football Player)
20 Main St
Flanders, NJ 07836-9112, USA

Roussel, Tom (Athlete, Football Player)
13 Heron Ln
Mandeville, LA 70471-6739, USA

Roussell, Thierry
Villa Crystal
St. Moritz, SWITZERLAND CH-7500

Rousselot, Philippe (Cinematographer)
232 N Canon Dr
Beverly Hills, CA 90210-5302, USA

Rousset, Christophe (Musician)
1926 Broadway
New York, NY 10023-6915, USA

Roustabouts, The
PO Box 25371
Charlotte, NC 28229-5371

Routh, Brandon (Actor)
c/o Stewart Strunk *Main Title Entertainment*
2225 Wilshire Blvd Suite 500
Los Angeles, CA 90036, USA

Routledge, Alison (Actor)
Langham House 302/8 Regent St
London W1R 5AL, UNITED KINGDOM (UK)

Routledge, Patricia (Actor)
6 King George Gardens Chichester
W Sussex PO19 6LB, UK

Roux, Albert H (Chef)
43 Upper Brook St
London W1Y 1PF, UNITED KINGDOM (UK)

Roux, Gifford (Athlete, Basketball Player)
69 Linden Ln
Medora, IL 62063-2135, USA

Roux, Jean-Louis (Actor, Director)
4145 Blueridge Cres # 2
Montreal, QC H3H 1S7, CANADA

Roux, Michel A (Chef)
43 Upper Brook St
London W1K 7QR, UK

Rove, Karl (Government Official)
1333 New Hampshire Ave NW Ste 600
Washington, DC 20036-1532, USA

Rovick, Sheriff John
3531 Clifton Pl
Glendale, CA 91208-1350

Rowan, Carl T
3116 Fessenden St NW
Washington, DC 20008-2029, USA

Rowan, Kelly (Actor, Producer)
c/o Brit Reece *PMK/BNC Public Relations (PMK-LA)*
8687 Melrose Ave Ste 8
West Hollywood, CA 90069-5746, USA

Rowand, Aaron (Athlete, Baseball Player)
34 Meadowhawk Ln
Las Vegas, NV 89135-5201, USA

Rowden, William H (Admiral)
1306 Dehlgren Avenue Washington Navy Yard SE
Washington, DC 20374-5055, USA

Rowdon, Wade (Athlete, Baseball Player)
230 Crooked Tree Trl
Deland, FL 32724-3426, USA

Rowe, Alan
8 Sherwood Close
London, ENGLAND SW13

Rowe, Bob (Athlete, Football Player)
1754 Highview Circle Ct
Ballwin, MO 63021-7806, USA

Rowe, Brad (Actor, Producer, Writer)
1327 Brinkley Ave
Los Angeles, CA 90049-3619, USA

Rowe, Dave (Athlete, Football Player)
372 Broken Arrow Trl
Boone, NC 28607-6535, USA

Rowe, John W (Business Person)
10 S Dearborn St
Chicago, IL 60603-2300, USA

Rowe, John W (Business Person)
151 Farmington Ave
Hartford, CT 06156-0001, USA

Rowe, Ken (Athlete, Baseball Player)
347 Princeton Dr
Dallas, GA 30157-0853, USA

Rowe, Maggie (Comedian)
c/o Staff Member *International Creative Management (ICM-LA)*
10250 Constellation Blvd Fl 7
Los Angeles, CA 90067-6207, USA

Rowe, Mike (Television Host)
4730 Woodman Ave Ste 300
Sherman Oaks, CA 91423-2400, USA

Rowe, Misty (Actor)
2193 River Rd
Egg Harbor City, NJ 08215-4745, USA

Rowe, Nicolas
52 Shaftesbury Ave
London, ENGLAND WlV 7DE

Rowe, Patrick (Athlete, Football Player)
6259 Alderley St
San Diego, CA 92114-6715, USA

Rowe, Ray (Athlete, Football Player)
11443 Westonhill Dr
San Diego, CA 92126-1450, USA

Rowe, Red
79 Margarita Ave
Camarillo, CA 93012-8113

Rowe, Sandra M (Editor)
1320 SW Broadway
Portland, OR 97201-3411, USA

Rowe-Jackson, Debbie
435 N Roxbury Dr
Beverly Hills, CA 90210-5008

Rowell, Victoria (Actor)
c/o Tracy Christian *Don Buchwald & Associates Inc (LA)*
6500 Wilshire Blvd Ste 2200
Los Angeles, CA 90048-4942, USA

Rowland, Betty (Dancer)
125 N Barrington Ave Apt 103
Los Angeles, CA 90049-2949, USA

Rowland, Brad (Athlete, Football Player)
552 Rosebud Dr N
Lombard, IL 60148-6166, USA

Rowland, Dave
PO Box 121089
Nashville, TN 37212-1089

Rowland, Derrick (Athlete, Basketball Player)
3 Island View Rd
Cohoes, NY 12047-4929, USA

Rowland, F Sherwood (Nobel Prize Laureate)
4807 Dorchester Rd
Corona Del Mar, CA 92625-2718, USA

Rowland, J David (Business Person)
41 Lothbury
London EC2P 2BP, UNITED KINGDOM (UK)

Rowland, James A (General)
17 Pindari Ave
Mosman, NSW 2088, AUSTRALIA

Rowland, John W (Misc)
5025 Wisconsin Ave NW
Washington, DC 20016-4113, USA

Rowland, Justin (Athlete, Football Player)
1919 NW Loop 410 Ste 200
San Antonio, TX 78213-2325, USA

Rowland, Kelly (Musician)
c/o Mark Schulman *3 Arts Entertainment Inc*
9460 Wilshire Blvd Fl 7
Beverly Hills, CA 90212-2713, USA

Rowland, Landon H (Business Person)
PO Box 219335
Kansas City, MO 64121-9335, USA

Rowland, Mike (Athlete, Baseball Player)
12104 E Mescal St
Scottsdale, AZ 85259-4230, USA

Rowland, Rich (Athlete, Baseball Player)
91 Clark Ave
Cloverdale, CA 95425-3918, USA

Rowland, Rodney (Actor, Model)
11350 Ventura Blvd Ste 206
Studio City, CA 91604-3140, USA

Rowland, Troy (Producer)
c/o Susan Curtis *Curtis Talent Management*
9607 Arby Dr
Beverly Hills, CA 90210-1202, USA

Rowlands, Gena (Actor)
c/o Lou Pitt *Pitt Group, The*
9465 Wilshire Blvd Ste 420
Beverly Hills, CA 90212-2603, USA

Rowlands, Patsy
265 Liverpool Rd
London, ENGLAND N1 1LX

Rowlands, Sherry
5055 Seminary Rd
Alexandria, VA 22311-2033

Rowley, Cynthia (Designer, Fashion Designer)
c/o Staff Member *IMG*
304 Park Ave S Fl 12
New York, NY 10010-4314, USA

Rowley, Denise (Stylist)
PO Box 146
White Sulphur Springs, NY 12787-0146, USA

Rowley, Elwood R (Athlete, Football Player)
13605 Uhl Hwy SE
Cumberland, MD 21502-8433, USA

Rowley, Janet D (Physicist)
5310 S University Ave
Chicago, IL 60615-5106, USA

Rowling, JK (Joanne Kathleen) (Writer)
c/o Staff Member *Christopher Little Literary Agency*
10 Eel Brook Studios
London SW6 4PS, UNITED KINGDOM

Rowlinson, John S (Misc)
12 Pullens Field
Headington OX3 0BU, UNITED KINGDOM (UK)

Rowny, Edward L (General)
6200 Oregon Ave NW Apt 345
Washington, DC 20015-1542, USA

Rowse, Darren (Internet Star)
PO BOX 1295
North Fitzroy, Victoria 3068, AUSTRALIA

Rowser, John (Athlete, Football Player)
17564 Alta Vista Dr
Southfield, MI 48075-1936, USA

Roxborough, Charlene (Stylist)
c/o Staff Member *Mercury Artists*
8460 Higuera St Fl 2
Culver City, CA 90232-2520, USA

Roxburgh, Richard (Actor, Music Group)
c/o Eric Kranzler *Management 360*
9111 Wilshire Blvd
Beverly Hills, CA 90210-5508, USA

Roxette (Music Group)
c/o Staff Member *D&D Management*
Drottning Gatan 55
Stockholm 11121, Sweden

Roxton, Steve
6 Thornton Rd Leytonstone
London, ENGLAND E11

Roy (Misc)
1639 Valley Dr
Las Vegas, NV 89108-2002, USA

Roy, Aruna (Activist)
81 Sahayoga apartments Mayur Vihar - I
Delhi 110 091, India

Roy, Arundhati (Writer)
c/o Kimberly Witherspoon *Inkwell Management*
521 5th Ave
New York, NY 10175-0003, USA

Roy, Brandon (Athlete, Basketball Player)
c/o Arn Tellem *Wasserman Media Group*
10960 Wilshire Blvd Fl 22
Los Angeles, CA 90024-3808, USA

Roy, Deep (Actor)
c/o Victor (Viktor) Kruglov *Victor Kruglov Talent Management*
7461 Beverly Blvd Ste 403
Los Angeles, CA 90036-2774, USA

Roy, Drew (Actor)
c/o Matt Luber *Luber Roklin Management*
8530 Wilshire Blvd Ste 550
Beverly Hills, CA 90211-3133, USA

Roy, James D (Financier)
601 Grant St
Pittsburgh, PA 15219-4405, USA

Roy, Jean-Pierre (Athlete, Baseball Player)
407 Rue Des Harfangs
Saint-Nicolas, QC G7A 3H4, Canada

Roy, John (Actor, Comedian)
c/o Gabrielle Krengel *Domain Talent*
9229 W Sunset Blvd Ste 710
Los Angeles, CA 90069-3407, USA

Roy, Norm (Athlete, Baseball Player)
2 Autumn Leaf Dr Apt 15
Nashua, NH 03060-5510, USA

Roy, Patricia (Baseball Player)
I H S A A 201 E Amkey Way
Carmel, IN 46032-5170, USA

Roy, Patrick (Athlete, Hockey Player)
Colisee Pepsi 250 Boulevard Wilfred-Hamel
Quebec G1L 5A7, Canada

Roy, Reena (Actor, Bollywood)
Pam Villa D'Monte Park Road Bandra
Bombay, MS 400 050, INDIA

Royal, Billy Joe (Musician, Songwriter, Writer)
900 Abner Jones Rd
Havelock, NC 28532-8879, USA

Royal, Darrell K (Athlete, Coach, Football Coach, Football Player)
PO Box 1744
Castle Rock, CO 80104-6244, USA

Royale, Maureen (Stylist)
c/o Staff Member *Marilyn's Inc*
601 Norwalk St
Greensboro, NC 27407-1409, USA

Royals, Mark (Athlete, Football Player)
4035 Courtside Way
Tampa, FL 33618-2748, USA

Royals, Reggie (Athlete, Basketball Player)
121 Maultsby Dr
Whiteville, NC 28472-3149, USA

Royce, Kenneth
3 Abbott's Close Andover
Hants., ENGLAND SP11 7NP

Royce, Mike (Comedian)
c/o Staff Member *United Talent Agency (UTA)*
9560 Wilshire Blvd Fl 5
Beverly Hills, CA 90212-2400, USA

Roye, Orpheus (Athlete, Football Player)
12955 NW 18th Mnr
Pembroke Pines, FL 33028-2522, USA

Royer, Stan (Athlete, Baseball Player)
9301 Christopher Lake Dr
Columbia, IL 62236-3458, USA

Roylance, Juanita (Baseball Player)
PO Box 282
Lorida, FL 33857-0282, USA

Roylance, Pamela
221 S Gale Dr Unit 403
Beverly Hills, CA 90211-5409

Royo, Sanchez Aristides (President)
PO Box 1824
Panama City 1, PANAMA

Royster, Jeron K (Jerry) (Athlete, Baseball Player, Coach)
8717 Classic Dr
Memphis, TN 38125-8826, USA

Royster, Mazio (Athlete, Football Player)
15251 Jeraldo Dr
Victorville, CA 92394-2098, USA

Royster, Willie (Athlete, Baseball Player)
229 55th St NE
Washington, DC 20019-6737, USA

Royston, Ed (Athlete, Football Player)
13 Ford Ct
Bergenfield, NJ 07621-2409, USA

Rozalla (Musician)
c/o Staff Member *Diva Central Inc*
7510 W Sunset Blvd Ste 1445
Los Angeles, CA 90046-3408, USA

Rozanov, Evgeny G (Architect)
Bolshara Dmitrovka 24
Moscow 103284, RUSSIA

Rozelle, Pete (Athlete, Football Player)
23800 Valley Oak Ct
Newhall, CA 91321-3746, USA

Rozema, Dave (Athlete, Baseball Player)
1560 N Renaud Rd
Grosse Pointe Woods, MI 48236-1763, USA

Rozhdestvensky, Gennady N
4 Oak Hill Way
London NW3, UNITED KINGDOM (UK)

Rozhdestvensky, Valery I (Cosmonaut)
Moskovskoi Oblasti
Syvisdny Goroduk 141160, RUSSIA

Rozier, Clifford (Athlete, Basketball Player)
PO Box 1194
Palmetto, FL 34220-1194, USA

Rozier, Mike (Athlete, Football Player)
PO Box 880120
Lincoln, NE 68588-0120, USA

Roznovsky, Vic (Athlete, Baseball Player)
266 W Bluff Ave
Fresno, CA 93711-6930, USA

Rozon, Tim (Actor)
c/o Pearl Hanan *Pearl Hanan Management*
7775 W Sunset Blvd Ste 118
Los Angeles, CA 90046-3911, USA

Rozumek, Dave (Athlete, Football Player)
18 Old Rockingham Rd
Salem, NH 03079-2111, USA

Rozzell, Aubrey (Athlete, Football Player)
PO Box 844
Quitman, MS 39355-0844, USA

Ruah, Daniela (Actor)
c/o Rhonda Price *Gersh (NY)*
41 Madison Ave
New York, NY 10010-2202, USA

Rubalcaba, Gonzalo (Musician)
5930 NW 201st St
Hialeah, FL 33015-4886, USA

Rubbia, Carlo (Nobel Prize Laureate)
Particle Physics Laboratory
Geneva 23 1211, SWITZERLAND

Rubel, Fran (Director, Producer)
c/o Staff Member *Kuzui Enterprises*
8225 Santa Monica Blvd
West Hollywood, CA 90046-5912, USA

Ruben, Joseph P (Joe) (Director)
250 W 57th St # 1905
New York, NY 10107-0001, USA

Rubens, Larry (Athlete, Football Player)
12213 Ansley Ct
Knoxville, TN 37934-1525, USA

Rubenstein, Ann (Correspondent)
30 Rockefeller Plz
New York, NY 10112-0015, USA

Rubenstein, David (Business Person)
1001 Pennsylvania Ave NW
Washington, DC 20004-2502, USA

Rubenstein, Edward (Physicist)
Surgery Dept
Stanford, CA 94305, USA

Ruberto, Sonny (Athlete, Baseball Player)
207 Ambridge Ct Apt 204
Chesterfield, MO 63017-9506, USA

Rubiano, Saenz Pedro Cardinal (Religious Leader)
Arzubispado Carrera 7A N 10-20
Santafe de Bogota, DC 1, COLOMBIA

Rubick, Rob (Athlete, Football Player)
1571 Stonewood Dr
Lapeer, MI 48446-4200, USA

Rubik, Erno (Inventor)
Varosmajor Utca 74
Budapest 1122, HUNGARY

Rubin, Amy (Actor)
PO Box 64249
Los Angeles, CA 90064-0249, USA

Rubin, Benjamin A (Inventor)
1329 173rd St
Hazel Crest, IL 60429-1921, USA

Rubin, Chanda
708 S Saint Antoine St
Lafayette, LA 70501-5740

Rubin, Chandra (Tennis Player)
708 S Saint Antoine St
Lafayette, LA 70501-5740, USA

Rubin, Ellis (Lawyer)
4141 NE 2nd Ave Ste 203A
Miami, FL 33137-3539, USA

Rubin, Gloria (Actor)
c/o Leigh Brillstein *International Creative Management (ICM-LA)*
10250 Constellation Blvd Fl 7
Los Angeles, CA 90067-6207, USA

Rubin, Harry (Biologist)
Molecular Biology
Berkeley, CA 94720-0001, USA

Rubin, Leigh (Cartoonist)
5777 W Century Blvd Ste 700
Los Angeles, CA 90045-5652, USA

Rubin, Louis D Jr (Writer)
702 Gimghoul Rd
Chapel Hill, NC 27514-3811, USA

Rubin, Rick (Musician, Producer)
c/o Staff Member *American Recordings*
3300 Warner Blvd
Burbank, CA 91505-4632, USA

Rubin, Robert (Misc)
32 Fruit St
Boston, MA 02114-2620, USA

Rubin, Robert E (Financier, Secretary)
399 Park Ave
New York, NY 10022-4614, USA

Rubin, Theodore I (Misc)
219 E 62nd St
New York, NY 10065-7685, USA

Rubin, Vanessa (Musician)
300 Mercer St Apt 3J
New York, NY 10003-6732, USA

Rubin, Vera C (Astronomer)
5241 Broad Branch Rd NW
Washington, DC 20015-1305, USA

Rubin, William (Misc)
11 W 53rd St
New York, NY 10019-5401, USA

Rubinek, Saul (Actor)
232 N Canon Dr
Beverly Hills, CA 90210-5302, USA

Rubinfeld, Daniel (Attorney, Educator)
Law School Boalt Hall
Berkeley, CA 94720-0001, USA

Rubini, Cesare (Athlete, Basketball Player, Coach)
Voa A Banfi 8
Milan, Italy

Rubino, Frank A (Lawyer)
6698 SW 92nd St
Miami, FL 33156-1838, USA

Rubinoff, Ira (Biologist)
Unit 0848
APO, AA 34002, USA

Rubinoff, Marla (Actor)
c/o Staff Member *John Glenn Harding Management*
7004 Oakwood Ave
Los Angeles, CA 90036-2660, USA

Rubinstein, John (Actor)
4417 Leydon Ave
Woodland Hills, CA 91364-4847, USA

Rubinstein, Zeida (Actor)
1800 Avenue of the Stars Ste 400
Los Angeles, CA 90067-4206, USA

Rubin-Vega, Daphne (Actor)
c/o Jeremy Katz *Katz Company, The*
1674 Broadway Fl 7
New York, NY 10019-5838, USA

Rubio, Marco (Senator)
B40A Dirksen Senate Office Bldg
Washington, DC 20510-0001, USA

Rubio, Maria
2238BLVD Adolfo Lopez Mateo 5
Placopac San Angel
Mexico DF, MEXICO 1040

Rubio, Paulina (Musician)
c/o Rick Canny *Sanctuary Artist Management*
8750 Wilshire Blvd Ste 200
Beverly Hills, CA 90211-2707, USA

Rubke, Karl (Athlete, Football Player)
1650 Barnes Mill Rd Apt 1425
Marietta, GA 30062-7568, USA

Ruby & The Romantics
1650 Broadway Ste 508
New York, NY 10019-6833

Rucci, Todd (Athlete, Football Player)
5 Southview Ln
Lititz, PA 17543-8205, USA

Ruccolo, Richard (Actor)
301 W 53rd St Apt 4K
New York, NY 10019-5768, USA

Ruch, Charles (Educator)
President S Ofc
Boise, ID 83725-0001, USA

Rucinsky, Martin (Athlete, Hockey Player)
800 Griffiths Way
Vancouver, BC V6B 6G1, Canada

Ruck, Alan (Actor)
c/o Lisa Lieberman *Innovative Artists (NY)*
235 Park Ave S Fl 7
New York, NY 10003-1404, USA

Rucka, Leo (Athlete, Football Player)
814 Crosby Dayton Rd
Crosby, TX 77532-5803, USA

Ruckelshaus, William D (Business Person, Government Official)
PO Box 76
Medina, WA 98039-0076, USA

Ruckenstein, Eli (Engineer)
755 Renaissance Dr Apt 203
Buffalo, NY 14221-8046, USA

Rucker, Anja (Athlete, Track Athlete)
Wollnitzer Str 42
Jena 7749, GERMANY

Rucker, Darius (Musician)
c/o Scott McGhee *McGhee Entertainment*
8730 W Sunset Blvd Ste 175
Los Angeles, CA 90069-2246, USA

Rucker, Dave (Athlete, Baseball Player)
18602 Piper Pl
Yorba Linda, CA 92886-2559, USA

Rucker, Michael (Athlete, Football Player)
5971 Rolling Ridge Dr
Kannapolis, NC 28081-6705, USA

Rucker, Reggie (Athlete, Football Player)
4517 Saint Germain Blvd
Cleveland, OH 44128-6205, USA

Rucker, Reginald J (Reggie) (Athlete, Football Player)
3128 Richmond Rd
Beachwood, OH 44122-3249, USA

Rudbottom, Roy R Jr (Diplomat)
7831 Park Ln Apt 213A
Dallas, TX 75225-2045, USA

Rudd, Delaney (Athlete, Basketball Player)
422 Chesham Dr
Kernersville, NC 27284-7017, USA

Rudd, Dwayne (Athlete, Football Player)
PO Box 273309
Boca Raton, FL 33427-3309, USA

Rudd, John (Athlete, Basketball Player)
4440 Sweet Bay Dr
Lake Charles, LA 70611-3240, USA

Rudd, Kevin (Prime Minister)
Parliament House
Canberra ACT 2600, AUSTRALIA

Rudd, Paul (Actor)
c/o Aleen Keshishian *Brillstein Entertainment Partners*
9150 Wilshire Blvd Ste 350
Beverly Hills, CA 90212-3453, USA

Rudd, Ricky (Race Car Driver)
124 Summerville Dr
Mooresville, NC 28115-7864, USA

Rudd, Xavier (Musician)
c/o Staff Member *Paradigm (Monterey)*
404 W Franklin St
Monterey, CA 93940-2303, USA

Ruddle, Francis H (Biologist)
Biology Dept
New Heaven, CT 6511, USA

Ruddock, Donovan (Razor) (Boxer)
7379 NW 34th St
Lauderhill, FL 33319-4962, USA

Ruddy, Al
1601 Clear View Dr
Beverly Hills, CA 90210-2010

Ruddy, Tim (Athlete, Football Player)
3885 Vale View Ln
Mead, CO 80542-4500, USA

Rude, Jim (Stylist)
935 Alpine Dr
Janesville, WI 53546-1751, USA

Rudel, Julius
101 Central Park W # 11A
New York, NY 10023-4250, USA

Rudenstine, Neil L (Educator)
41 Armour Rd
Princeton, NJ 08540-3003, USA

Ruder, David S (Educator, Government Official)
1 Prudential Plaza 130 East Randolph Dr
Chicago, IL 60601, USA

Rudi, Joseph O (Joe) (Athlete, Baseball Player)
17667 Deer Park Loop
Baker City, OR 97814-8425, USA

Rudie, Evelyn (Actor)
7514 Hollywood Blvd
Los Angeles, CA 90046-2814, USA

Rudin, Scott (Filmmaker, Producer)
120 W 45th St
New York, NY 10036-4041, USA

Rudis-Bestudik, Mary (Baseball Player)
4333 Deeboyar Ave
Lakewood, CA 90712-3703, USA

Rudnay, Jack (Athlete, Football Player)
7219 Whipperwill Rd
Versailles, MO 65084-4033, USA

Rudner, Rita (Actor, Comedian)
c/o Staff Member *International Creative Management (ICM-LA)*
10250 Constellation Blvd Fl 7
Los Angeles, CA 90067-6207, USA

Rudnick, Paul (Writer)
c/o Robert (Bob) Bookman *Creative Artists Agency (CAA-LA)*
2000 Avenue of the Stars Ste 100
Los Angeles, CA 90067-4705, USA

Rudnick, Tim (Athlete, Football Player)
7311 N Octavia Ave
Chicago, IL 60631-4348, USA

Rudolph, Alan
15760 Ventura Blvd Fl 16
Encino, CA 91436-3027

Rudolph, Alan S (Director)
8942 Wilshire Blvd # 219
Beverly Hills, CA 90211-1908, USA

Rudolph, Ben (Athlete, Football Player)
561 E General Gorgas Dr
Mobile, AL 36617-3036, USA

Rudolph, Coleman (Athlete, Football Player)
342 Carmichael Cir
Canton, GA 30115-6862, USA

Rudolph, Council (Athlete, Football Player)
8310 Lago Vista Dr
Tampa, FL 33614-2769, USA

Rudolph, Frederick (Historian)
234 Ide Rd
Williamstown, MA 01267-2800, USA

Rudolph, Ken (Athlete, Baseball Player)
1317 W Sands Ct
Gilbert, AZ 85233-6637, USA

Rudolph, Larry (Producer)
c/o Staff Member *ReignDeer Entertainment*
100 Glendon Ave Suite 1100
Los Angeles, CA 90024, USA

Rudolph, Maya (Actor)
c/o David (Dave) Becky *3 Arts Entertainment Inc*
9460 Wilshire Blvd Fl 7
Beverly Hills, CA 90212-2713, USA

Rudometkin, John (Athlete, Basketball Player)
6181 Wise Rd
Newcastle, CA 95658-9231, USA

Rudzinski, Paul (Athlete, Football Player)
3216 Delahaut St
Green Bay, WI 54301-1551, USA

Rudzinski, Witold (Composer)
Ul Narbutta 50 m 6
Warsaw 02-541, POLAND

Rue, Sara (Actor)
c/o Alan David *Alan David Management*
8840 Wilshire Blvd Ste 200
Beverly Hills, CA 90211-2606, USA

Ruebel, Matt (Athlete, Baseball Player)
7509 W Augusta Blvd
Yorktown, IN 47396-9354, USA

Ruegamer, Grey (Athlete, Football Player)
PO Box 70155
Las Vegas, NV 89170-0155, USA

Ruehe, Volker (Government Official)
Hardthoehe
Honn 53125, GERMANY

Ruehl, Mercedes (Actor)
c/o Jonathan Howard *Innovative Artists (LA)*
1505 10th St
Santa Monica, CA 90401-2805, USA

Ruelas, Gabriel (Gabe) (Athlete, Boxer)
1119 S Hudson Ave
Los Angeles, CA 90019-1807, USA

Ruell, Aaron (Actor, Director, Writer)
c/o Staff Member *Brillstein Entertainment Partners*
9150 Wilshire Blvd Ste 350
Beverly Hills, CA 90212-3453, USA

Ruelle, David P (Mathematician)
1 Ave Charles-Cormar
Bures-sur-Yvette 91440, FRANCE

Rueter, Kirk (Athlete, Baseball Player)
46 Pheasant Ridge Ct
Nashville, IL 62263-5845, USA

Ruether, Mike (Athlete, Football Player)
23014 Gardner Dr
Alpharetta, GA 30009-2179, USA

Ruether, Rosemary R (Misc)
530 Mayflower Rd
Claremont, CA 91711-4237, USA

Ruettgers, Ken (Athlete, Football Player)
16897 Golden Stone Dr
Sisters, OR 97759-9696, USA

Ruettgers, Michael C (Business Person)
35 Parkway Dr
Hopkinton, MA 1748, USA

Rufer, Rudy (Athlete, Baseball Player)
250 N Village Ave Apt B16
Rockville Centre, NY 11570-2324, USA

Ruff, Howard J (Economist, Writer)
PO Box 441
Orem, UT 84059-0441, USA

Ruff, Lindy (Athlete, Coach, Hockey Player)
5006 Winding Ln
Clarence, NY 14031-1500, USA

Ruffalo, Mark (Actor)
c/o Jessica Kolstad *WKT Public Relations (WKT-LA)*
9350 Wilshire Blvd Ste 450
Beverly Hills, CA 90212-3230, USA

Ruffcorn, Scott (Athlete, Baseball Player)
2137 Barton Hills Dr
Austin, TX 78704-4659, USA

Ruffin, Bruce (Athlete, Baseball Player)
3410 Pawnee Pass S
Austin, TX 78738-1709, USA

Ruffin, Jimmy
102 Ryders Ln
East Brunswick, NJ 08816-1328

Ruffin, Johnny (Athlete, Baseball Player)
4229 Trumpworth Ct
Valrico, FL 33596-8494, USA

Ruffini, Attilio (Government Official)
Camera dei Deputati Via della Missione 10
Rome 187, ITALY

Ruffner, Paul (Athlete, Basketball Player)
3352 N 100 E Apt 210
Provo, UT 84604-6661, USA

Ruffo, Victoria (Actor)
c/o Staff Member *Televisa*
Blvd Adolfo Lopez Mateos 232 Colonia San Angel INN
DF CP 01060, MEXICO

Rufus
7250 Beverly Blvd Ste 200
Los Angeles, CA 90036-2560

Ruge, John A (Cartoonist)
240 Bronxville Rd Apt B4
Bronxville, NY 10708-2800, USA

Ruggiano, Justin (Athlete, Baseball Player)
8711 Tallwood Dr
Austin, TX 78759-7529, USA

Ruggiero, Adamo (Actor)
c/o Shari Quallenberg *AMI Artist Management*
464 King St E
Toronto, ON M5A 1L7, Canada

Ruggiero, John (Stylist)
c/o Staff Member *Mercury Artists*
8460 Higuera St Fl 2
Culver City, CA 90232-2520, USA

Rugolo, Pete
4520 Natick Ave Unit 103
Sherman Oaks, CA 91403-2707

Ruhman, Chris (Athlete, Football Player)
13206 Vinery Ct
Cypress, TX 77429-5195, USA

Ruivivar, Anthony Michael (Actor)
c/o Nick Collins *Gersh (LA)*
9465 Wilshire Blvd Ste 600
Beverly Hills, CA 90212-2612, USA

Ruiz, Chico (Athlete, Baseball Player)
267 Calle Tapia
San Juan, PR 00912-4201, USA

Ruiz, John (Boxer)
PO Box 2581
Taunton, MA 02780-0980, USA

Ruiz, Jose Carlos (Actor)
c/o Staff Member *Televisa*
Blvd Adolfo Lopez Mateos 232 Colonia San Angel INN
DF CP 01060, MEXICO

Ruiz, Rodrigo (Actor)
c/o Staff Member *Televisa*
Blvd Adolfo Lopez Mateos 232 Colonia San Angel INN
DF CP 01060, MEXICO

Rukavina, Terry (Baseball Player)
6676 Washington Cir
Franklin, OH 45005-5521, USA

Ruklick, Joe (Athlete, Basketball Player)
1300 Central St Apt 302
Evanston, IL 60201-1678, USA

Ruland, Jeff (Athlete, Basketball Player)
38 Glen Lake Dr
Medford, NJ 08055-3104, USA

Rule, Bob (Athlete, Basketball Player)
4303 Kansas Ave
Riverside, CA 92507-5153, USA

Rule, Gordon (Athlete, Football Player)
716 Manchester Rd
Neenah, WI 54956-4910, USA

Rulin, Olesya (Actor)
c/o Jonathan Baruch *Rain Management Group (RMG)*
1631 21st St
Santa Monica, CA 90404-3914, USA

Rulli, Sebastian (Actor)
c/o Gabriel Blanco *Gabriel Blanco Iglesias (Mexico)*
Rio Balsas 35-32 Colonia Cuauhtemoc
DF 6500, Mexico

Rullo, Jerry (Athlete, Basketball Player)
300 Brookline Blvd
Havertown, PA 19083-3923, USA

Rumer (Music Group, Musician)
c/o Christian Bernhardt *Agency Group Ltd, The (LA)*
1880 Century Park E Ste 810
Los Angeles, CA 90067-1627, USA

Rummells, Dave (Golfer)
1820 Harbor Blvd
Kissimmee, FL 34744-6623, USA

Rumsey, Janet (Athlete, Baseball Player)
7830 W County Road 80 N
Greensburg, IN 47240-7910, USA

Rumsfeld, Donald (Business Person)
1718 M St NW # 366
Washington, DC 20036-4504, USA

Runager, Max (Athlete, Football Player)
PO Box 37971
Rock Hill, SC 29732-0534, USA

Rundgren, Todd (Musician)
c/o Staff Member *Agency Group Ltd, The (NY)*
142 W 57th St Fl 6
New York, NY 10019-3300, USA

Runga, Bic (Musician)
c/o Staff Member *Paradigm (Monterey)*
404 W Franklin St
Monterey, CA 93940-2303, USA

Runge, Brian (Athlete, Baseball Player)
8225 E County Dr
El Cajon, CA 92021-8826, USA

Runge, Paul (Athlete, Baseball Player)
1719 W Community Dr
Jupiter, FL 33458-8218, USA

Runge, Paul (Athlete, Baseball Player)
8225 E County Dr
El Cajon, CA 92021-8826, USA

Runnells, Tom (Athlete, Baseball Player, Coach)
6045 Settlers Ridge Cir
Sylvania, OH 43560-9474, USA

Runnels, Terri (Model, Wrestler)
11520 NW 8th Ln
Gainesville, FL 32606-0408, USA

Runnels, Tom (Athlete, Football Player)
6111 Laredo Ct
Granbury, TX 76049-5220, USA

RunningWolf, Myrton (Actor)
c/o Tracey Mapes *Imperium 7 Talent Agency*
5455 Wilshire Blvd Ste 1706
Los Angeles, CA 90036-4217, USA

Runrig (Music Group)
c/o Staff Member *Sony Music Entertainment Germany*
Neumarkter Str. 28
Muenchen 81673, Germany

Runyan, Jon (Athlete, Football Player)
262 Mount Laurel Rd
Mount Laurel, NJ 8054, USA

Runyan, Marla (Athlete, Track Athlete)
5135 Center Way
Eugene, OR 97405-4673, USA

Runyan, Sean (Athlete, Baseball Player)
1958 Bermuda Pointe Dr
Haines City, FL 33844-2413, USA

Runyon, Jennifer (Actor)
5922 SW Amberwood Ave
Corvallis, OR 97333-2702, USA

Rupe, Josh (Athlete, Baseball Player)
1114 Dane St
Chesapeake, VA 23323-4813, USA

Rupe, Ryan (Athlete, Baseball Player)
2 Windflower Pl
Spring, TX 77381-6274, USA

Rupp, Debra Jo (Actor)
c/o Staff Member *Christopher Wright Management*
3207 Winnie Dr
Los Angeles, CA 90068-1439, USA

Ruprecht, Tom (Writer)
c/o Staff Member *3 Arts Entertainment Inc*
9460 Wilshire Blvd Fl 7
Beverly Hills, CA 90212-2713, USA

Rusch, Glendon (Athlete, Baseball Player)
6428 Chaffee St
Tujunga, CA 91042-2811, USA

Rusedski, Greg (Tennis Player)
PO Box 57
Caernarfon LL55 4WL, UNITED KINGDOM

Rush (Music Group)
c/o Staff Member *Artist Group International (NY)*
150 E 58th St Fl 19
New York, NY 10155-1900, USA

Rush, Barbara (Actor)
1709 Tropical Ave
Beverly Hills, CA 90210, USA

Rush, Bob (Athlete, Baseball Player)
444 S Higley Rd Apt 116
Mesa, AZ 85206-2195, USA

Rush, Deborah (Actor)
c/o Rhonda Price *Gersh (NY)*
41 Madison Ave
New York, NY 10010-2202, USA

Rush, Geoffrey (Actor)
c/o Stan Rosenfield *Stan Rosenfield & Associates*
2029 Century Park E Ste 1190
Los Angeles, CA 90067-2931, USA

Rush, Ian (Athlete, Football Player)
McDonald's Restaurants Ltd: 11 - 59 High Rd, East Finchley
London N2 8AW, UK

Rush, Jennifer (Musician)
c/o Staff Member *Armin Rahn Agency and Management*
Dreimuehlenstr. 7
Muenchen 80469, Germany

Rush, Jerry (Athlete, Football Player)
17536 Oak Dr
Detroit, MI 48221-2747, USA

Rush, Kareem (Athlete, Basketball Player)
2220 Gates Ave
Redondo Beach, CA 90278-2026, USA

Rush, Mathew (Adult Film Star)
c/o Staff Member *Diva Central Inc*
7510 W Sunset Blvd Ste 1445
Los Angeles, CA 90046-3408, USA

Rush, Matthew (Actor, Adult Film Star)
c/o Staff Member *Diva Central Inc*
7510 W Sunset Blvd Ste 1445
Los Angeles, CA 90046-3408, USA

Rush, Merrilee (Musician)
27 L Ambiance Ct
Bardonia, NY 10954-1421, USA

Rush, Robert J (Athlete, Football Player)
8201 Scruggs Dr
Germantown, TN 38138-6119, USA

Rush, Rudy (Comedian)
c/o Staff Member *International Creative Management (ICM-LA)*
10250 Constellation Blvd Fl 7
Los Angeles, CA 90067-6207, USA

Rush, Sarah (Actor)
c/o Staff Member *Acme Talent & Literary (LA)*
1400 Atlantic Ave Ste 274
Long Beach, CA 90813-2013, USA

Rush, Tom (Musician)
PO Box 1570
Wilson, WY 83014-1570, USA

Rushdie, A Salman (Writer)
42 Knightsbridge
London SW1S 7JR, UNITED KINGDOM (UK)

Rushen, Patrice
c/o Staff Member *Soundtrack Music Assoc*
1460 4th St Ste 308
Santa Monica, CA 90401-3483, USA

Rushford, Jim (Athlete, Baseball Player)
11069 Caminito Alegra
San Diego, CA 92131-3504, USA

Rushing, Marion (Athlete, Football Player)
358 Bathon Dr
Pinckneyville, IL 62274-3335, USA

Ruskin, Scott (Athlete, Baseball Player)
27982 Red Pine Ct
Valencia, CA 91354-1888, USA

Rusler, Robert
c/o Staff Member *Ellis Talent Group*
4705 Laurel Canyon Blvd Ste 300
Valley Village, CA 91607-5901, USA

Russ, Steve (Athlete, Football Player)
PO Box 817
Buffalo, NY 14224-0817, USA

Russ, Tim (Actor, Director)
7336 Santa Monica Blvd # 711
West Hollywood, CA 90046-6616, USA

Russell, Andy (Athlete, Football Player)
625 Liberty Ave Ste 3100
Pittsburgh, PA 15222-3115, USA

Russell, Betsy (Actor)
c/o Mark Burg *Evolution Entertainment (LA)*
901 N Highland Ave
Los Angeles, CA 90038-2412, USA

Russell, Bill (Athlete, Basketball Player)
9415 SE 52nd St
Mercer Island, WA 98040-4723, USA

Russell, Bill (Athlete, Baseball Player, Coach)
27982 Red Pine Ct
Valencia, CA 91354-1888, USA

Russell, Bing
229 E Gainsborough Rd
Thousand Oaks, CA 91360-5331

Russell, Brenda (Actor, Musician)
c/o Seth Keller *SKM Artist Management*
PO Box 25906
Los Angeles, CA 90025-0906, USA

Russell, Brian (Football Player)
c/o Team Member *Cleveland Browns*
76 Lou Groza Blvd
Berea, OH 44017-1269

Russell, Campy (Athlete, Basketball Player)
66 Earlmoor Blvd
Pontiac, MI 48341-2816, USA

Russell, Cazzie (Athlete, Basketball Player)
PO Box 3146
Savannah, GA 31402-3146, USA

Russell, Chuck (Director)
c/o Robert Stein *Paradigm (LA)*
360 N Crescent Dr
Beverly Hills, CA 90210-4874, USA

Russell, Dana (Stylist)
c/o Staff Member *Ford Models (Chicago)*
311 W Superior St
Chicago, IL 60654-3548, USA

Russell, David O (Actor, Director, Producer, Writer)
c/o John Lesher *WmE2 (Endeavor-LA)*
9601 Wilshire Blvd Fl 3
Beverly Hills, CA 90210-5219, USA

Russell, Jack (Athlete, Football Player)
PO Box 16505
Fort Worth, TX 76162-0505, USA

Russell, Jeff (Athlete, Baseball Player)
2325 Oak Knoll Dr
Colleyville, TX 76034-4478, USA

Russell, John (Athlete, Baseball Player, Coach)
25643 N 71st Dr
Peoria, AZ 85383-7173, USA

Russell, Johnny
PO Box 37
Hendersonville, TN 37077-0037

Russell, Ken (Director)
c/o Staff Member *Independent Talent Group (ITG-UK)*
Oxford House 76 Oxford St
London W1D 1BS, UK

Russell, Ken (Football Player)
c/o Staff Member *Detroit Lions*
222 Republic Dr
Allen Park, MI 48101-3650, USA

Russell, Keri (Actor)
c/o Joanna (Joanie) Burstein *Burstein Company, The*
15304 W Sunset Blvd Ste 208
Pacific Palisades, CA 90272-3656, USA

Russell, Kimberly
11617 Laurelwood Dr
Studio City, CA 91604-3818

Russell, Kurt (Actor, Producer, Writer)
c/o Michael Cooper *Creative Artists Agency (CAA-LA)*
2000 Avenue of the Stars Ste 100
Los Angeles, CA 90067-4705, USA

Russell, Leon (Musician)
104 W 5th St Ste B
Columbia, TN 38401-3245, USA

Russell, Leonard (Athlete, Football Player)
497 Saint Louis Ave Apt 102
Long Beach, CA 90814-3363, USA

Russell, Lynne (Anchor, Designer)
Lynne Russell Unlimited Inc 880 Marietta Hwy #630-273
Roswell, GA 30075

Russell, Mark
3201 33rd Pl NW
Washington, DC 20008-3304

Russell, Rubin (Athlete, Basketball Player)
P.O. Bix 542742
Grand Prairie, TX 75054, USA

Russell, T E
8271 Melrose Ave Ste 110
Los Angeles, CA 90046-6800, USA

Russell, Theresa (Actor)
c/o Scott Zimmerman *Evolution Entertainment (LA)*
901 N Highland Ave
Los Angeles, CA 90038-2412, USA

Russell, Twan (Athlete, Football Player)
11201 NW 8th St
Plantation, FL 33325-1508, USA

Russell, Victoria (Actor)
c/o Staff Member *Wizzo and Company*
47 Beak St
London W1F 9SE, UK

Russell, William (Actor)
Primrose Hill Studios Fitzroy Road
London NW1 8TR, UNITED KINGDOM (UK)

Russert, Luke (Correspondent)
c/o Staff Member *NBC Nightly News*
30 Rockefeller Plz Fl 270E
New York, NY 10112-0299, USA

Russhon, Chris (Stylist)
1531 E Stephens Dr
Tempe, AZ 85283-4826, USA

Russi, Bernhard
6490 Andermatt
, SWITZERLAND

Russo, Deanna (Actor)
c/o Staff Member *Paradigm (LA)*
360 N Crescent Dr
Beverly Hills, CA 90210-4874, USA

Russo, Gia (Stylist)
c/o Staff Member *Celestine - CA*
1666 20th St Ste 200B
Santa Monica, CA 90404-3828, USA

Russo, James (Actor)
c/o Staff Member *United Talent Agency (UTA)*
9560 Wilshire Blvd Fl 5
Beverly Hills, CA 90212-2400, USA

Russo, Joe (Director, Producer, Writer)
c/o Staff Member *United Talent Agency (UTA)*
9560 Wilshire Blvd Fl 5
Beverly Hills, CA 90212-2400, USA

Russo, John
218 Euclid Ave
Glassport, PA 15045-1331

Russo, Patricia (Business Person)
600 Mountain Ave
New Providence, NJ 07974-2008, USA

Russo, Rene (Actor, Model)
c/o John Crosby *Crosby/Spilo Management*
1310 N Spaulding Ave
Los Angeles, CA 90046-4010, USA

Rust, Rod (Athlete, Football Coach, Football Player)
1 W 13th St
Ocean City, NJ 08226-2945, USA

Rusteck, Dick (Athlete, Baseball Player)
6302 N 87th St
Scottsdale, AZ 85250-5712, USA

Rutan, Elbert L (Burt) (Designer)
6383 E Dewey Cir
Coeur D Alene, ID 83814-7918, USA

Rutan, Richard G (Dick) (Designer)
2833 Delmar Ave
Mojave, CA 93501-1113, USA

Rutgens, Joe (Athlete, Football Player)
227 W Devlin St
Spring Valley, IL 61362-1923, USA

Ruth, Lauren (Cartoonist)
PO Box 200206
New Haven, CT 06520-0206, USA

Ruth, Mike (Athlete, Football Player)
17 Rock Ridge Rd
Atkinson, NH 03811-5117, USA

Rutherford, Ann (Actor)
826 Greenway Dr
Beverly Hills, CA 90210-3006, USA

Rutherford, John S (Johnny) III (Race Car Driver)
4819 Black Oak Ln
River Oaks, TX 76114, USA

Rutherford, Johnny (Race Car Driver)
4919 Black Oak Ln
River Oaks, TX 76114-2933

Rutherford, Johnny (Athlete, Baseball Player)
765 Briar Hill Ln
Bloomfield Hills, MI 48304-1443, USA

Rutherford, Kelly (Actor)
c/o Katie Mason *Luber Roklin Management*
8530 Wilshire Blvd Ste 550
Beverly Hills, CA 90211-3133, USA

Rutherford, Mike (Musician)
55 Fulham High St
London SW6 3JJ, UNITED KINGDOM (UK)

Rutherfurd, Emily (Actor)
c/o Chris Schmidt *Paradigm (LA)*
360 N Crescent Dr
Beverly Hills, CA 90210-4874, USA

Ruthven, Dick (Athlete, Baseball Player)
13480 Providence Lake Dr
Alpharetta, GA 30004-7510, USA

Rutigliano, Sam (Athlete, Coach, Football Coach, Football Player)
9671 Metcalf Rd
Willoughby, OH 44094-9744, USA

Rutkowski, Ed (Athlete, Football Player)
47 Brenton Ln
Hamburg, NY 14075-4327, USA

Rutland, Reggie (Athlete, Football Player)
4265 Jailette Rd
Atlanta, GA 30349-1881, USA

Rutledge, Jeffrey R (Jeff) (Athlete, Coach, Football Coach, Football Player)
6102 W Gary Dr
Chandler, AZ 85226-1193, USA

Rutledge, Johnny (Athlete, Football Player)
948 SW Avenue J
Belle Glade, FL 33430-4232, USA

Rutschman, Adolph (Ad) (Coach, Football Coach)
2142 NW Pinehurst Dr
McMinnville, OR 97128-2426, USA

Ruttan, Susan (Actor)
c/o Christopher Black *Opus Entertainment*
5225 Wilshire Blvd Ste 905
Los Angeles, CA 90036-4353, USA

Rutter, John M (Composer)
Old Lacey's Saint John's Church
Duxford, Cambridge, UNITED KINGDOM (UK)

Ruttgers, Jurgen (Government Official)
Heinemannstr 2
Bonn 53175, GERMANY

Rutting, Barbara
Sommerholz 30
Neumarkt, AUSTRIA 5202

Ruttman, Joe
3 Knob Hill Rd
Mooresville, NC 28115

Ruud, Birger (Skier)
Munstersvei 20
Kongsberg 3600, NORWAY

Ruud, Sigmund (Skier)
Kirkeveien 57
Oslo 3, NORWAY

Ruud, Tom (Athlete, Football Player)
1821 S 33rd St
Lincoln, NE 68506-1905, USA

Ruuska, Percy Sylvia (Swimmer)
4216 College View Way
Carmichael, CA 95608, USA

Ruusuvuori, Aarno E (Architect)
Annankalu 15 B 10
Helsinki 12 120, UNITED KINGDOM (UK)

Ruutel, Arnold (President)
Koidula Str 3-5
Tallinn 10, ESTONIA

Ruwe, Robert P (Judge)
400 2nd St NW
Washington, DC 20217-0001, USA

Ruzek, Roger (Athlete, Football Player)
921 Warwick St
Bedford, TX 76022-7856, USA

Ruzicka, Vladimir (Athlete, Hockey Player)
17 Highland Ct
Needham, MA 02492-3149, USA

Ryal, Mark (Athlete, Baseball Player)
204 E University Dr
Auburn, AL 36832-6703, USA

Ryan, Amy (Actor)
c/o Jennifer Wiley *Framework Entertainment (NY)*
129 W 27th St Fl 12
New York, NY 10001-6206, USA

Ryan, Arthur F (Business Person)
Prudential Plaza 751 Broad St
Newark, NJ 7102, USA

Ryan, B J (Athlete, Baseball Player)
4014 Wisteria Ln
Benton, LA 71006-9368, USA

Ryan, Blanchard (Actor)
c/o Staff Member *Jeff Morrone Entertainment*
9350 Wilshire Blvd Ste 224
Beverly Hills, CA 90212-3204, USA

Ryan, Bobby (Athlete, Hockey Player)
c/o Donald Meehan *Newport Sports Management*
201 City Centre Dr Suite 400
Mississauga, ON L58 2T4, Canada

Ryan, Buddy (Athlete, Football Coach, Football Player)
819 Abingdon Ln
Shelbyville, KY 40065-6310, USA

Ryan, Dave (Musician)
c/o Staff Member *Agency Group Ltd, The (NY)*
142 W 57th St Fl 6
New York, NY 10019-3300, USA

Ryan, Debbie (Actor)
c/o Staff Member *Kritzer Levine Wilkins Entertainment*
11872 La Grange Ave Fl 1
Los Angeles, CA 90025-5283, USA

Ryan, Debble (Comedian)
Athletic Dept PO Box 3785
Charlottesville, VA 22903, USA

Ryan, Debby (Actor)
c/o Jennifer Patredis *Cunningham Escott Slevin & Doherty (CESD-LA)*
10635 Santa Monica Blvd Ste 130
Los Angeles, CA 90025-8306, USA

Ryan, Fran
4204 W Woodland Ave
Burbank, CA 91505-3758

Ryan, Frank (Athlete, Football Player)
PO Box 185
Grafton, VT 05146-0185, USA

Ryan, Jay (Athlete, Baseball Player)
1232 Rocky River Rd W
Charlotte, NC 28213-5034, USA

Ryan, Jeri (Actor)
c/o David Lust *Patricola Lust PR*
9171 Wilshire Blvd Ste 390
Beverly Hills, CA 90210-5515, USA

Ryan, Ken (Athlete, Football Player)
45 Tanager Rd
Seekonk, MA 02771-2707, USA

Ryan, Ken (Athlete, Baseball Player)
45 Tanager Rd
Seekonk, MA 02771-2707, USA

Ryan, Lee (Actor)
c/o Jack Gilardi *International Creative Management (ICM-LA)*
10250 Constellation Blvd Fl 7
Los Angeles, CA 90067-6207, USA

Ryan, Lisa Dean (Actor)
c/o Staff Member *Pakula/King & Associates*
9229 W Sunset Blvd Ste 315
Los Angeles, CA 90069-3403, USA

Ryan, Marisa (Actor)
c/o Bob McGowan *McGowan Management*
8733 W Sunset Blvd Ste 103
West Hollywood, CA 90069-2241, USA

Ryan, Mark (Actor)
c/o Staff Member *Starfish PR*
PO Box 7000-54
Redondo Beach, CA 90277, USA

Ryan, Max (Actor)
c/o Erik Kritzer *Kritzer Levine Wilkins Entertainment*
11872 La Grange Ave Fl 1
Los Angeles, CA 90025-5283, USA

Ryan, Meg (Actor)
c/o Stephen Huvane *Slate Public Relations*
9000 W Sunset Blvd Ste 915
West Hollywood, CA 90069-5809, USA

Ryan, Michael (Athlete, Baseball Player)
521 Water St
Indiana, PA 15701-1927, USA

Ryan, Michelle (Actor)
c/o Philip Grenz *WmE2 (Endeavor-LA)*
9601 Wilshire Blvd Fl 3
Beverly Hills, CA 90210-5219, USA

Ryan, Mike (Athlete, Baseball Player)
592 Stoneham Rd
Wolfeboro, NH 03894-4711, USA

Ryan, Mitchell (Actor)
30355 Mulholland Hwy
Cornell, CA 91301-3117, USA

Ryan, Nolan (Athlete, Baseball Player)
237 Escalera Pkwy
Georgetown, TX 78628-7157, USA

Ryan, Norbert R Jr (Admiral)
2 Navy St
Washington, DC 20370-0002, USA

Ryan, Pat (Athlete, Football Player)
6930 Old Kent Dr
Knoxville, TN 37919-7472, USA

Ryan, Patrick G (Business Person)
200 E Randolf St
Chicago, IL 60601, USA

Ryan, Rex (Athlete, Football Coach)
c/o David Dunn *Athletes First, LLC*
3300 Irvine Ave Ste 300
Newport Beach, CA 92660-3108, USA

Ryan, Rob (Athlete, Baseball Player)
914 E Golden Ct
Spokane, WA 99208-7570, USA

Ryan, Roz (Actor)
c/o Staff Member *Gage Group, The (LA)*
14724 Ventura Blvd Ste 505
Sherman Oaks, CA 91403-3505, USA

Ryan, Ryan (Actor)
c/o Staff Member *Warner Bros Television Production*
4000 Warner Blvd
Burbank, CA 91522-0002

Ryan, Sharon (Stylist)
c/o Staff Member *Halley Resources*
37 W 20th St Ste 603
New York, NY 10011-3718, USA

Ryan, Shawn (Producer)
c/o Staff Member *International Creative Management (ICM-LA)*
10250 Constellation Blvd Fl 7
Los Angeles, CA 90067-6207, USA

Ryan, Thomas M (Business Person)
1 Cvs Dr
Woonsocket, RI 02895-6146, USA

Ryan, Tim E (Athlete, Football Player)
1159 Calle Ventura
San Jose, CA 95120-5503, USA

Ryan, Timothy T (Tim) (Athlete, Football Player)
4901 Sugar Creek Dr
Evansville, IN 47715-7744, USA

Ryan, Tom K (Cartoonist)
235 E 45th St
New York, NY 10017-3305, USA

Ryans, Larry (Athlete, Football Player)
110 Brookfield Dr
Greenwood, SC 29646-8501, USA

Ryazanov, Eldar A (Director)
Bolshoi Tishinski Per 12 #70
Moscow 123557, RUSSIA

Rybak, Alexander (Musician)
c/o Staff Member *Lionheart International AB*
P.O. Box 11108 Nytorgsgatan 40 A
Stockholm SE-10061, Sweden

Rybkin, Ivan (Government Official)
4 Staraya Poischad
Moscow 103073, RUSSIA

Rybska, Agnieszka (Music Group, Musician)
130 W 57th St Apt 9D
New York, NY 10019-3311, USA

Rychlec, Tom (Athlete, Football Player)
71 Round Hill Rd
Southington, CT 06489-3645, USA

Ryckman, Billy (Athlete, Football Player)
513 Doucet Rd
Lafayette, LA 70503-3557, USA

Rycroft, Melissa (Actor)
c/o Susan Madore *Guttman Associates*
118 S Beverly Dr Ste 201
Beverly Hills, CA 90212-3016, USA

Ryczek, Dan (Athlete, Football Player)
3714 Monitor Pl
Olney, MD 20832-2248, USA

Ryczek, Paul (Athlete, Football Player)
9335 Scott Rd
Roswell, GA 30076-3416, USA

Rydal, Emma (Actor)
c/o Lucy Brazier *The Rights House (UK)*
Drury House 34-43 Russell St
London WC2B 5HA, UK

Rydalch, Ron (Athlete, Football Player)
500 E Durfee St
Grantsville, UT 84029-9514, USA

Rydell, Bobby (Actor, Music Group, Musician)
917 Bryn Mawr Ave
Penn Valley, PA 19072-1524, USA

Rydell, Christopher (Actor)
911 N Sweetzer Ave Apt C
Los Angeles, CA 90069-4368, USA

Rydell, Mark (Director)
3110 Main St Ste 220
Santa Monica, CA 90405-5353, USA

Ryder, JoJo (Actor, Producer, Writer)
c/o Staff Member *Untouchable J Productions*
9300 Civic Center Dr # 202
Beverly Hills, CA 90210-3604, USA

Ryder, Lisa (Actor)
c/o Deb Dillistone *Lucas Talent Inc*
100 W. Pender St Sun Tower, 7th Floor
Vancouver, BC V6B 1R8, Canada

Ryder, Michael (Athlete, Hockey Player)
c/o Staff Member *Boston Bruins*
TD Banknorth Garden 100 Legends Way, Suite 250
Boston, MA 2114, USA

Ryder, Mitch (Music Group, Musician)
6400 Pleasant Park Dr
Chanhassen, MN 55317-8804, USA

Ryder, Nick (Athlete, Football Player)
14 Ridgeway
Goshen, NY 10924-1408, USA

Ryder, Thomas O (Publisher)
PO Box 100
Pleasantville, NY 10570-0100, USA

Ryder, Winona (Actor)
c/o Mara Buxbaum *ID PR (LA)*
7060 Hollywood Blvd Fl 8
Los Angeles, CA 90028-6014, USA

Ryders, Ruff (Music Group)
c/o Staff Member *Universal Attractions*
135 W 26th St Fl 12
New York, NY 10001-6872, USA

Rydze, Richard (Misc)
125 7th St
Pittsburgh, PA 15222-3410, USA

Ryerson, Ann
935 Gayley Ave
Los Angeles, CA 90024-2805

Ryerson, Gary (Athlete, Baseball Player)
1059 Terrace Crst
El Cajon, CA 92019-3129, USA

Ryff, Frankie
2055 McGraw Ave
Bronx, NY 10462-8014

Rykiel, Sonia F (Designer, Fashion Designer)
175 Blvd Saint Germain
Paris 75006, FRANCE

Ryknow (Musician)
c/o Staff Member *Agency Group Ltd, The (NY)*
142 W 57th St Fl 6
New York, NY 10019-3300, USA

Rylan, Marcy (Actor)
c/o Marnie Sparer *Innovative Artists (LA)*
1505 10th St
Santa Monica, CA 90401-2805, USA

Rylance, Mark (Actor, Director)
Southwark
London SE1, UNITED KINGDOM (UK)

Ryman, Robert T (Artist)
17 W 16th St
New York, NY 10011-6301, USA

Rymer, Charlie (Golfer)
6026 Crystal View Dr
Orlando, FL 32819-4208, USA

Rymer, Pamela Ann (Judge)
125 S Grand Ave
Pasadena, CA 91105-1643, USA

Rynkiewicz, Mariusz (Artist, Misc)
12401 Alexander Rd
Everett, WA 98204-4715, USA

Rypdal, Terje (Musician)
Utragata 16
Voss 5700, NORWAY

Rysanek, Leony
Altenbeuren, GERMANY D-88682

Ryumin, Valery V (Astronaut, Misc)
Moskovskoi Oblasti
Syvsdny Goroduk 141160, RUSSIA

Ryun, James R (Jim) (Athlete, Track Athlete)
PO Box 826
Topeka, KS 66601-0826, USA

Ryzhkov, Nikolai I (Misc)
Okhotny Ryad 1
Moscow 103009, RUSSIA

RZA (Artist, Musician)
c/o Sophia Chang *Beehive Management*
598 Broadway Apt 10C
New York, NY 10012-3362, USA

Rzeznik, Johnny (Musician)
c/o Staff Member *WmE2 (WMA-LA)*
1 William Morris Pl
Beverly Hills, CA 90212-4261, USA

S

S, Kimberley
c/o Staff Member *Diva Central Inc*
7510 W Sunset Blvd Ste 1445
Los Angeles, CA 90046-3408, USA

S, Kimberly (DJ)
c/o Len Evans *Project Publicity*
312 W 53rd St Ste 202
New York, NY 10019-5743, USA

S Club 7 (Music Group)
c/o Staff Member *Creative Artists Agency (CAA-LA)*
2000 Avenue of the Stars Ste 100
Los Angeles, CA 90067-4705, USA

S. Critz, Mark (Congressman, Politician)
1022 Longworth Hob
Washington, DC 20515-4902, USA

S Jayaram (Actor)
7-MAJESTIC Terrace 48 Arcot Road
Saligramam
Chennai, TN 600 098, INDIA

S. Miller, Candice (Congressman, Politician)
1034 Longworth Hob
Washington, DC 20515-0510, USA

S. Murphy, Christopher (Congressman, Politician)
412 Cannon Hob
Washington, DC 20515-2509, USA

Saad, Mindy (Stylist)
c/o Staff Member *Art House Management*
1548 16th St
Santa Monica, CA 90404-3309, USA

Saadiq, Raphael (Musician)
c/o Eva Arthur *Universal Attractions*
135 W 26th St Fl 12
New York, NY 10001-6872, USA

Saakashvili, Mikhail (President)
Rustaveli Prosp 29
Tbilsi 380008, GEORGIA

Saalfeld, Kelly (Athlete, Football Player)
761 N 153rd Ave
Omaha, NE 68154-1807, USA

Saar, Bettye (Artist)
8074 Willow Glen Rd
Los Angeles, CA 90046-1617, USA

Saari, Roy A (Swimmer)
PO Box 7086
Mammoth Lakes, CA 93546-7086, USA

Saarloos, Kirk (Athlete, Baseball Player)
8608 E Sunnywalk Ln
Anaheim, CA 92808-1689, USA

Saatchi, Charles (Business Person)
36 Golden Square
London W1R 4EE, UNITED KINGDOM (UK)

Saatchi, Maurice (Business Person)
36 Golden Square
London W1R 4EE, UNITED KINGDOM (UK)

Sabah (Stylist)
6267 Bay Club Dr Apt 3
Fort Lauderdale, FL 33308-1502, USA

Sabah, Sheikh Saad al-Abdullah al-Salem (Prime Minister, Prince)
PO Box 4 Safat
Kuwait City 13001, KUWAIT

Saban, Haim (Producer)
c/o Staff Member *Saban Entertainment*
10100 Santa Monica Blvd Fl 26
Los Angeles, CA 90067-4003, USA

Saban, Nick (Athlete, Football Coach, Football Player)
1549 Sharlo Ave
Baton Rouge, LA 70820-4553, USA

Sabara, Daryl (Actor)
9701 Wilshire Blvd Ste 1000
Beverly Hills, CA 90212-2010, USA

Sabathia, CC (Athlete, Baseball Player)
c/o Scott Parker *Legacy Sports Group*
500 Newport Center Dr Ste 800
Newport Beach, CA 92660-7008, USA

Sabatini, Gabriela (Tennis Player)
c/o Staff Member *Women's Tennis Association (WTA (UK))*
Palliser House Palliser Rd
London W149EB, UK

Sabatino, Joe (Actor)
c/o Melanie Sharp *Sharp Talent*
117 N Orlando Ave
Los Angeles, CA 90048-3403, USA

Sabatino, Michael (Actor)
13538 Valleyheart Dr N
Sherman Oaks, CA 91423-3124, USA

Sabato, Ernesto (Writer)
Severino Langeri 3135
Santos Lugares, ARGENTINA

Sabato Jr, Antonio (Actor, Model)
c/o Tracy Steinsapir *Main Title Entertainment*
2225 Wilshire Blvd Suite 500
Los Angeles, CA 90036, USA

Sabb, Dwayne (Athlete, Football Player)
26 Marie Rd
Fords, NJ 08863-1306, USA

Sabbah, Michel (Religious Leader)
PO Box 14152
Jerusalem, ISRAEL

Sabbatini, Rory (Athlete, Golfer)
9472 Sagrada Park
Fort Worth, TX 76126-1915, USA

Sabel, Erik (Athlete, Baseball Player)
4609 Haven Ct
West Lafayette, IN 47906-5600, USA

Sabella, Ernie (Actor, Artist, Voice Over Artist)
c/o Staff Member *Gage Group, The (LA)*
14724 Ventura Blvd Ste 505
Sherman Oaks, CA 91403-3505, USA

Sabelle (Music Group, Musician, Songwriter, Writer)
241 W 36th St Apt 2R
New York, NY 10018-7541, USA

Saberhagen, Bret W (Athlete, Baseball Player)
22817 Ventura Blvd Ste 474
Woodland Hills, CA 91364-1202, USA

Sabihy, Kyle (Actor)
c/o Dino May *Dino May Management*
6362 Hollywood Blvd
Los Angeles, CA 90028-6323, USA

Sabiston Jr, David C (Doctor)
26 Speyside Cir
Pittsboro, NC 27312-8638, USA

Sabo, Christopher A (Chris) (Athlete, Baseball Player)
7455 Stonemeadow Ln
Montgomery, OH 45242-6305, USA

Sabo-Dusanko, Julie (Baseball Player)
7702 E Doubletree Ranch Rd Ste 150
Scottsdale, AZ 85258-2130, USA

Sabuda, Robert (Writer)
350 Broadway Rm 1204
New York, NY 10013-3964, USA

Saca, Elias Antonio (President)
Barrosan Jacinto
San Salvador, El SALVADOR

Sacchi, Robert
203 N Gramercy Pl
Los Angeles, CA 90004-4021

Sacco, Joe (Artist)
c/o Staff Member *Fantagraphics Books*
7563 Lake City Way NE
Seattle, WA 98115-4218, USA

Sacco, Michael (Misc)
5201 Auth Way
Suitland, MD 20746-4211, USA

Saccone, Viviana (Actor)
c/o Staff Member *Telefe - Argentina*
Pavon 2444 (C1248AAT)
Buenos Aires, ARGENTINA

Sachdev, Asha (Actor, Bollywood)
18B Sunset Heights 59 Pali Hill Bandra
Mumbai, MS 40050, INDIA

Sachenbacher, Evi (Skier)
Rthausplatz 1
Reit im Winkl 83242, GERMANY

Sachin (Actor, Bollywood, Director, Filmmaker)
B609 Pearl Apartments 33 Swami Samarth Nagar Cross Road No 3 Andheri
Bombay, MS 400 058, INDIA

Sachs, Andrew (Actor)
2 Henrietta St
London WC2E 8PS, UNITED KINGDOM (UK)

Sachs, Gloria (Designer, Fashion Designer)
117 E 57th St
New York, NY 10022-2002, USA

Sachs, Gunter
101 E 63rd St
New York, NY 10065-7302

Sachs, Jeffrey D (Economist)
535 W 116th St Low Library MC4335
New York, NY 10027-7041, USA

Sachs, Richard (Doctor)
6 Saint Ronan Ter
New Haven, CT 06511-2315, USA

Sachs, William (Director)
3739 Montuso Pl
Encino, CA 91436-4001, USA

Sachu (Actor, Bollywood)
78 Sairam Colony Alwarpet
Chennai, TN 600018, INDIA

Sack, Kevin (Journalist)
202 W 1st St
Los Angeles, CA 90012-4105, USA

Sack, Steve (Cartoonist)
425 Portland Ave
Minneapolis, MN 55488-1511, USA

Sackheim, Daniel (Director, Editor, Producer)
c/o Chris Simonian *Creative Artists Agency (CAA-LA)*
2000 Avenue of the Stars Ste 100
Los Angeles, CA 90067-4705, USA

Sackhoff, Katee (Actor)
c/o Leland LaBarre *Bleu, An Entertainment Company*
5225 Wilshire Blvd Ste 336
Los Angeles, CA 90036-4380, USA

Sackinsky, Brian (Athlete, Baseball Player)
8 Valley Forge Dr
Shrewsbury, MA 01545-1553, USA

Sacks, Greg (Race Car Driver)
6092 Sabal Creek Blvd
Port Orange, FL 32128-7131, USA

Sacks, Jonathan H (Religious Leader)
735 High Road
London N12 0US, UNITED KINGDOM (UK)

Sacks, Oliver W (Doctor, Writer)
2 Horatio St Apt 3G
New York, NY 10014-1638, USA

Sacramone, Alicia (Athlete, Gymnast, Olympic Athlete)
c/o Staff Member *USA Gymnastics*
Pan American Plz #300 201 S Capitol Ave
Indianapolis, IN 46225, USA

Sadanah, Kamal (Actor, Bollywood)
Jal Kamal Plot 202 23rd Road Bandra
Mumbai, MS 400050, INDIA

Sadat, Jehan El- (Activist)
Int L Development Ctr
College Park, MD 20742-0001, USA

Sadat, Madame Jehan
2310 Decatur Pl NW
Washington, DC 20008-4010

Sadecki, Raymond M (Ray) (Athlete, Baseball Player)
4237 E Clovis Ave
Mesa, AZ 85206-1945, USA

Sadek, Mike (Athlete, Baseball Player)
6741 Quartz Mine Rd
Mountain Ranch, CA 95246-9748, USA

Sadik, Nafis (Government Official)
220 E 42nd St
New York, NY 10017-5806, USA

Sadler, Carl (Athlete, Baseball Player)
204 S Hendry Ave
Perry, FL 32347-3417, USA

Sadler, Donnie (Athlete, Baseball Player)
802 Sadler Rd
Valley Mills, TX 76689-4499, USA

Sadler, Elliott (Race Car Driver)
PO Box 32
Emporia, VA 23847-0032, USA

Sadler, Ray (Athlete, Baseball Player)
4423 Lake Shore Villa Dr
Waco, TX 76710-1448, USA

Sadler, William (Actor)
c/o James Suskin *James Suskin Management*
2 Charlton St Apt 5K
New York, NY 10014-4970, USA

Sadoski, Thomas (Actor)
c/o Howard Axel *TMT Entertainment Group*
648 Broadway Ste 1002
New York, NY 10012-2348, USA

Sadoulet, Bernard (Astronomer)
2824 Forest Ave
Berkeley, CA 94705-1309, USA

Sadowski, Bob (Athlete, Baseball Player)
26 Barrington Ct
Sharpsburg, GA 30277-1849, USA

Sadowski, Bob (Athlete, Baseball Player)
1465 Creekside Dr
High Ridge, MO 63049-1314, USA

Sadowski, Jim (Athlete, Baseball Player)
696 Sloop Rd
Pittsburgh, PA 15237-4164, USA

Sadowski, Jonathan (Actor)
c/o Susan Yoo *Susan Yoo*
Prefers to be contacted via telephone
Los Angeles, CA, USA

Saenz, Chris (Athlete, Baseball Player)
7919 N Rondure Loop
Tucson, AZ 85743-7413, USA

Safdie, Moshe (Architect)
100 Rev Nazareno Properzi Way
Somerville, MA 02143-3740, USA

Safer, Morley (Correspondent)
c/o 60 Minutes *CBS News Productions*
524 W 57th St Fl 8
New York, NY 10019-2930, USA

Saferight, Harry (Baseball Player)
2321 Wadebridge Rd
Midlothian, VA 23113-3839, USA

Saffell, Tom (Athlete, Baseball Player)
1503 Clower Creek Dr Apt HA262
Sarasota, FL 34231-1911, USA

Saffiotti, Umberto (Doctor)
5114 Wissioming Rd
Bethesda, MD 20816-2259, USA

Safin, Marat (Tennis Player)
Schirmitzer Weg
Weiden 92637, GERMANY

Safina, Alessandro (Opera Singer)
2220 Colorado Ave
Santa Monica, CA 90404-3506, USA

Safina, Carl (Biologist)
100 W Main St
East Islip, NY 11730-2300, USA

Safina, Dinara (Athlete, Tennis Player)
c/o Staff Member *Women's Tennis Association (WTA (US))*
1 Progress Plz Ste 1500
St Petersburg, FL 33701-4335, USA

Safka, Melanie (Musician)
53 Baymont St
Clearwater, FL 33767-1705, USA

Safran Foer, Jonathan (Writer)
c/o Geoffrey Sanford *Rabineau Wachter & Sanford Literary*
1107 1/2 Glendon Ave
Los Angeles, CA 90024-3501, USA

Safuto, Dominick (Randy) (Music Group, Musician)
PO Box 656507
Fresh Meadows, NY 11365-6507, USA

Safuto, Frank (Music Group, Musician)
PO Box 656507
Fresh Meadows, NY 11365-6507, USA

Sagal, Jean (Actor)
400 S Beverly Dr Ste 216
Beverly Hills, CA 90212-4404, USA

Sagal, Katey (Actor)
c/o Staff Member *B and B Management*
1041 N Formosa Ave Formosa Bldg Rm 194
W Hollywood, CA 90046, USA

Sagal, Liz (Actor)
c/o Staff Member *Gersh (LA)*
9465 Wilshire Blvd Ste 600
Beverly Hills, CA 90212-2612, USA

Sagan, Carl (Astronomer, Writer)
7165 W Sunset Blvd
Los Angeles, CA 90046-4417, USA

Sagansky, Jeff
145 Ocean Avenue Ext
Santa Monica, CA 90402-1211

Sagapolutele, Pio (Athlete, Football Player)
PO Box 110
Bellevue, ID 83313-0110, USA

Sagar, Ramanand (Actor, Director, Filmmaker, Producer)
Natraj Studios 194 M V Road Andheri (E)
Bombay, MS 400 069, INDIA

Sagdeev, Roald Z (Physicist)
Profsoyuznaya 84/32
Moscow B485 11780, RUSSIA

Sage, William (Actor)
232 N Canon Dr
Beverly Hills, CA 90210-5302, USA

Sagebrecht, Marianne (Actor)
Kaulbachstr 61 Ruckgeb
Munich 80539, GERMANY

Sagely, Floyd (Athlete, Football Player)
181 Wildflower Pl E
Edwards, CO 81632, USA

Sagemiller, Melissa (Actor)
c/o Leslie Siebert *Gersh (LA)*
9465 Wilshire Blvd Ste 600
Beverly Hills, CA 90212-2612, USA

Sager, A J (Athlete, Baseball Player)
235 4th St
Kirkersville, OH 43033, USA

Sager, Carole Bayer (Music Group, Musician, Songwriter, Writer)
10761 Bellagio Rd
Los Angeles, CA 90077-3731, USA

Sagers, Rand (Stylist)
c/o Celebrity Stylist *Oliver Piro Inc*
725 Riverside Dr Apt 3A
New York, NY 10031-2460, USA

Saget, Bob (Actor)
c/o Daniel (Danny) Sussman *Brillstein Entertainment Partners*
9150 Wilshire Blvd Ste 350
Beverly Hills, CA 90212-3453, USA

Saglio, Laura (Actor)
36 Rue de Ponthieu
Paris 75008, FRANCE

Sagmoen, Marc (Athlete, Baseball Player)
19715 1st Pl SW
Normandy Park, WA 98166-4007, USA

Sagnier, Ludivine (Actor)
c/o Jon Rubinstein *Authentic Talent and Literary Management*
45 Main St Ste 1004
Brooklyn, NY 11201-8200, USA

Sagona, Katie (Actor)
300 Park Ave S # 200
New York, NY 10010-5313, USA

Sahagun, Elena (Actor)
1180 S Beverly Dr Ste 301
Los Angeles, CA 90035-1154, USA

Sahara Hotnights (Music Group)
c/o Staff Member *Paradigm (Monterey)*
404 W Franklin St
Monterey, CA 93940-2303, USA

Sahgal, Ajay (Actor, Producer, Writer)
c/o Nicole Clemens *International Creative Management (ICM-LA)*
10250 Constellation Blvd Fl 7
Los Angeles, CA 90067-6207, USA

Sahgal, Nayantara (Writer)
181B Rajpur Rd
Dehra Dun, Uttar Pradesh 248009, INDIA

Sahi, Deepa (Actor, Bollywood)
466 Laxmi Bhuvan Sardar Patel Rd
Mumbai, MS 400004, INDIA

Sahl, Mort (Actor, Comedian)
1441 3rd Ave Apt 12C
New York, NY 10028-1976, USA

Sahm, Hans-Werner (Artist)
Zur Wasserburg 7 Bidingen
Schwab, GERMANY

Saidock, Tom (Athlete, Football Player)
20316 Old Colony Rd
Dearborn Heights, MI 48127-2758, USA

Sailer, Anton (Toni) (Skier)
Kitzbuhl 6370, AUSTRIA

Sailer, Toni
Gundhabing 19
Kitzbuhel, AUSTRIA A-6370

Sailors, Kenny (Ken) (Athlete, Basketball Player)
5710 Howe Ln
Laramie, WY 82070-8935, USA

Saimes, George (Athlete, Football Executive, Football Player)
2307 Beechmoor Dr NW
North Canton, OH 44720-5814, USA

Sain, Johnny
707 Avenue Latour
Oak Brook, IL 60523-1085

Saindon, Pat (Athlete, Football Player)
105 King Arthur Pl
Alabaster, AL 35007 9111, USA

Sainsbury of Preston Candover, John D (Business Person)
Stamford House Stamford St
London SE1 9LL, UNITED KINGDOM (UK)

Sainsbury of Turville, David J (Business Person)
4 Charterhouse Mews Charterhouse Square
London EC1M 6BB, UNITED KINGDOM (UK)

Saint, Crosbie E (General)
1116 N Pitt St
Alexandria, VA 22314-1455, USA

Saint, Eva Marie (Actor)
c/o Joel Dean *TalentWorks (LA)*
3500 W Olive Ave Ste 1400
Burbank, CA 91505-5512, USA

Saint, Silva (Adult Film Star)
c/o Staff Member *Atlas Multimedia Inc*
9005 Eton Ave Ste C
Canoga Park, CA 91304-6533, USA

Saint, Sylvia
26500 Agoura Rd # 389
Calabasas, CA 91302-1952

Saint James, Sara
289 S Robertson Blvd # 259
Beverly Hills, CA 90211-2834

Saint James, Susan (Actor)

Sainte-Marie, Buffy (Music Group, Musician, Songwriter, Writer)
1191 Kuhio Hwy
Kapaa, HI 96746, USA

Sainz, Salvador (Actor, Director)
Ave Prat de la Riba 43
Reus (Tarragona) 43201, SPAIN

Saipe, Mike (Athlete, Baseball Player)
4191 Combe Way
San Diego, CA 92122-2511, USA

Sajak, Pat (Game Show Host)
c/o Staff Member *PAT Productions*
10202 W Washington Blvd Robert Young Bldg Suite 2000
Culver City, CA 90232, USA

Sajawal, Aziz (Actor, Bollywood, Director, Filmmaker)
S303 Sameer Society JP Road Seven Bungalows Andheri
Mumbai, MS 400058, INDIA

Sajko, Kristina (Model)
6 W 14th St # 300
New York, NY 10011-7505, USA

Sakamoto, Ryoichi (Composer)
165 W 57th St
New York, NY 10019-2201, USA

Sakamoto, Soichi (Coach, Swimmer)
768 McCully St
Honolulu, HI 96826-5908, USA

Sakamura, Ken (Inventor)
Information Science Dept
Tokyo, JAPAN

Sakata, Lenn (Athlete, Baseball Player)
PO Box 21727
San Jose, CA 95151-1727, USA

Sakata, Theresa Kemper (Stylist)
12515 Portada Pl
San Diego, CA 92130-2208, USA

Sakato, George T (War Hero)
6369 Katherine Way
Denver, CO 80221, USA

Sakharov, Alik (Cinematographer)
6050 Kennedy Blvd E Apt 4D
West New York, NJ 07093-3932, USA

Sakmann, Bert (Nobel Prize Laureate)
Jehnstr 39
Heidelberg 69120, GERMANY

Saks, Gene (Actor, Director)
40 W 57th St # 1800
New York, NY 10019-4001, USA

Sakshaug, Eugene C (Engineer)
18 Grove Ave
Pittsfield, MA 01201-1080, USA

Sala, Edoardo (Actor)
Via Giuseppe Pisanelli
Rome 196, ITALY

Sala, Oskar
Leistikowstr. 5
Berlin, GERMANY 14050

Sala, Richard (Cartoonist)
3131 College Ave
Berkeley, CA 94705-2740, USA

Salaam, Abdul (Athlete, Football Player)
11153 Embassy Dr
Cincinnati, OH 45240-3005, USA

Salaam, Ephraim (Athlete, Football Player)
c/o Staff Member *EAG Sports Management*
12910 Agustin Pl
Playa Vista, CA 90094-2301, USA

Salaam, Rashaan (Athlete, Football Player)
8132 Brookhaven Rd
San Diego, CA 92114-7404, USA

Salac, Joe
2205 Avenue Colisee Quebec
PQ, CANADA GIL 4W7

Salad Hassan, Abdikassim (President)
People's Palace
Mogadishu, SOMALIA

Salahi, Michaele (Reality TV Star)
c/o Staff Member *Bravo (NY)*
30 Rockefeller Plz
New York, NY 10112-0015, USA

Salamanca & Garcia (Writer)
c/o Gabriel Blanco *Gabriel Blanco Iglesias (Mexico)*
Rio Balsas 35-32 Colonia Cuauhtemoc
DF 6500, Mexico

Salanda, Zoe (Actor)
c/o Andrea Pett-Joseph *Brillstein Entertainment Partners*
9150 Wilshire Blvd Ste 350
Beverly Hills, CA 90212-3453, USA

Salans, Lester B (Doctor)
RR 10
Hanover, NJ 7936, USA

Salas, Mark (Athlete, Baseball Player)
1302 6th St SE
Ruskin, FL 33570-5308, USA

Salata, Paul (Athlete, Football Player)
3723 Birch St Ste 11
Newport Beach, CA 92660-2614, USA

Salazar, Alberto (Athlete, Track Athlete)
1 Erieview Plaza 1360 East 9th St # 1300
Cleveland, OH 44114, USA

Salazar, Arion (Musician)
5715 Claremont Ave # C
Oakland, CA 94618-1279, USA

Salazar, Eliseo (Race Car Driver)
19480 Stokes Rd
Waller, TX 77484-8785, USA

Salazar, Luis (Athlete, Baseball Player)
20808 Cabrillo Way
Boca Raton, FL 33428-1201, USA

Saldana, Theresa (Actor)
c/o Staff Member *Leavitt Talent Group*
8255 W Sunset Blvd
West Hollywood, CA 90046-2417, USA

Saldana, Zoe (Actor)
c/o Aleen Keshishian *Brillstein Entertainment Partners*
9150 Wilshire Blvd Ste 350
Beverly Hills, CA 90212-3453, USA

Saldanha, Carlos (Animator, Director)
c/o Staff Member *Blue Sky Studios*
44 S Broadway Fl 17
White Plains, NY 10601-4411, USA

Saldarini, Giovanni Cardinal (Religious Leader)
Archdiocese of Turin Via dell'Archivescovado 12
Turin 10121, ITALY

Saldi, Jay (Athlete, Football Player)
303 Donley Ct
Southlake, TX 76092-5940, USA

Sale, Jamie (Dancer)
12116 NW 128th St
Edmonton, AB T5L 1C3, CANADA

Saleaumua, Dan (Athlete, Football Player)
8234 Marshall Dr
Overland Park, KS 66214-1537, USA

Saleen, Steve
76 Fairbanks
Irvine, CA 92618-1602, USA

Saleh, Ali Abdullah (General, President)
Zubairy St
Sana'a, YEMEN ARAB REPUBLIC

Salem, Dahlia (Actor)
c/o Robert (Rob) Gomez *Precision Entertainment*
6338 Wilshire Blvd
Los Angeles, CA 90048-5002, USA

Salem, Harvey (Athlete, Football Player)
25 Menlo Pl
Berkeley, CA 94707-1532, USA

Salem, Marc (Actor, Comedian)

Salemi, Sam (Athlete, Football Player)
2971 Delaware Ave
Kenmore, NY 14217-2353, USA

Salenger, Meredith (Actor)
c/o Scott Zimmerman *Evolution Entertainment (LA)*
901 N Highland Ave
Los Angeles, CA 90038-2412, USA

Salerno-Sonnenberg, Nadja (Musician)
165 W 57th St
New York, NY 10019-2201, USA

Sales, Eugenio de Araujo Cardinal (Religious Leader)
Palacio Sao Joaquim Rua Gloria 446
Washington, DC 20241-0001, BRAZIL

Sales, Nykesha (Basketball Player)
Mohegan Sun Arena
Uncasville, CT 6382, USA

Salgado, Michael (Musician)
c/o Staff Member *Sony Music Miami*
605 Lincoln Rd Ste 700
Miami Beach, FL 33139-2901, USA

Salgado, Sabastiano R (Photographer)
Fazenda Bulcao
Minas Gerais, BRAZIL

Saliba, Metropolitan Primate Philip (Religious Leader)
358 Mountain Rd
Englewood, NJ 07631-3727, USA

Saliers, Emily (Musician, Songwriter, Writer)
315 W Ponce De Leon Ave # 755
Decatur, GA 30030-2400, USA

Salim, Salim Ahmed (Prime Minister)
PO Box 3243
Addis Ababa, ETHIOPIA

Salinas, Carmen (Actor)
c/o Staff Member *Televisa*
Blvd Adolfo Lopez Mateos 232 Colonia San Angel INN
DF CP 01060, MEXICO

Salinas, Dixie Carter (Producer)
209 10th Ave S Ste 302
Nashville, TN 37203-0730, USA

Salinas, Jorge (Actor)
c/o Staff Member *Televisa*
Blvd Adolfo Lopez Mateos 232 Colonia San Angel INN
DF CP 01060, MEXICO

Salinas, Maria Elena (Actor)
c/o Staff Member *Univision*
605 3rd Ave Fl 12
New York, NY 10158-0034, USA

Salinas, Nora (Actor)
c/o Staff Member *Televisa*
Blvd Adolfo Lopez Mateos 232 Colonia San Angel INN
DF CP 01060, MEXICO

Salinger, Amy (Stylist)
c/o Staff Member *Arlene Wilson Management*
807 N Jefferson St # 200
Milwaukee, WI 53202-8150, USA

Salinger, Diane (Actor)
c/o Robert Depp *Beverly Hecht Agency*
3500 W Olive Ave Ste 1180
Burbank, CA 91505-4651, USA

Salinger, Emmanuel (Actor)
36 Rue de Ponthieu
Paris 75008, FRANCE

Salinger, Matt (Actor)
11500 W Olympic Blvd Ste 510
Los Angeles, CA 90064-1527, USA

Salisbury, Benjamin (Actor)
c/o Staff Member *ICA Talent*
818 12th St Apt 9
Santa Monica, CA 90403-1727, USA

Salisbury, Sean (Athlete, Football Player)
5823 Brushy Creek Trl
Dallas, TX 75252-2341, USA

Salkeld, Roger (Athlete, Baseball Player)
27824 Ridgegrove Dr
Santa Clarita, CA 91350-1747, USA

Salkind, Ilya (Producer)
Iverheath Iver
Bucks SL0 0NH, UNITED KINGDOM (UK)

Salle, David (Artist)
980 Madison Ave PH
New York, NY 10075-1848, USA

Salles, Walter (Director, Producer)
c/o Staff Member *WmE2 (Endeavor-LA)*
9601 Wilshire Blvd Fl 3
Beverly Hills, CA 90210-5219, USA

Salley, John (Athlete, Basketball Player, Television Host)
2533 N Beachwood Dr
Los Angeles, CA 90068-2342

Sallinen, Aulis H (Composer)
Runneberginkatu 37A
Helsinki 10 100, FINLAND

Salling, Mark (Actor)
c/o Jason Solomon *Full Circle Management*
4932 Lankershim Blvd Ste 202
North Hollywood, CA 91601-4452, USA

Sallis, Peter (Actor)
13 Shorts Gardens
London WC2H 9AT, UNITED KINGDOM (UK)

Sally, Jerome (Athlete, Football Player)
4107 Roxbury Ct
Columbia, MO 65203-6832, USA

Salminen, Matti (Opera Singer)
535 El Camino Del Mar
San Francisco, CA 94121-1041, USA

Salming, Borje (Athlete, Hockey Player)
Box 45438
Stockholm 104 31, Sweden

Salmon, Brad (Athlete, Baseball Player)
11102 Herschel Loop
Daphne, AL 36526-6648, USA

Salmon, Colin (Actor)
Julian House 4 Windmill St
London W1P 1HF, UNITED KINGDOM (UK)

Salmon, Tim (Athlete, Baseball Player)
6061 E Sunnyside Dr
Scottsdale, AZ 85254-4977, USA

Salmons, John (Basketball Player)
1st Union Center 3601 South Broad St
Philadelphia, PA 19148, USA

Salo, Mika (Race Car Driver)
Leafield Whitney
Oxon OX8 5PF, UNITED KINGDOM (UK)

Salomon, Mikael (Cinematographer)
PO Box 2230
Los Angeles, CA 90078-2230, USA

Salomon, Sandy (Actor)
36 Rue de Ponthieu
Paris 75008, FRANCE

Salonen, Brian (Athlete, Football Player)
2801 S Russell St Ste 33
Missoula, MT 59801-7914, USA

Salonen, Esa-Pekka (Composer)
Music Center 135 N Grand Ave
Los Angeles, CA 90012, USA

Salonga, Lea (Actor, Musician)
c/o Staff Member *Agency Group Ltd, The (UK)*
361-373 City Rd
London EC1V 1PQ, UK

Salopek, Paul (Journalist)
435 N Michigan Ave
Chicago, IL 60611-4066, USA

Salpeter, Edwin E (Physicist)
116 Westbourne Ln
Ithaca, NY 14850-2414, USA

Salt, Jennifer (Actor)
3742 Sheridge Dr
Sherman Oaks, CA 91403-5005, USA

Saltalamacchia, Jarrod (Athlete, Baseball Player)
12475 58th Pl N
West Palm Beach, FL 33411-8539, USA

Salter, Bryant (Athlete, Football Player)
16810 SW 88th Ct
Palmetto Bay, FL 33157-4537, USA

Salter, Hans
3658 Woodhill Canyon Rd
Studio City, CA 91604-3658

Saltpeter, Edwin E (Misc)
Physical Sciences Dept
Ithaca, NJ 14853, USA

Saltykov, Aleksey A (Director)
Per 4A #104
Moscow 119285, RUSSIA

Saltykov, Boris G (Economist, Government Official)
Bryusov Per 11
Moscow 103009, RUSSIA

Salva, Victor (Director)
c/o Staff Member *Gersh (LA)*
9465 Wilshire Blvd Ste 600
Beverly Hills, CA 90212-2612, USA

Salvador, Henri
6 Place Vendome
Paris, FRANCE 75001

Salvadori, Al (Athlete, Basketball Player)
787 Lindsay Rd
Carnegie, PA 15106-3845, USA

Salvail, Eve (DJ)
c/o Len Evans *Project Publicity*
312 W 53rd St Ste 202
New York, NY 10019-5743, USA

Salvatore, Adamo (Musician)
Avenue Louise 522
Bruxelles 1050, BELGIUM

Salvatore, Robert Anthony (R.A.) (Writer)
c/o Staff Member *Random House*
1540 Broadway
New York, NY 10036-4039, USA

Salvay, Bennett (Composer, Musician)
c/o Staff Member *Gorfaine/Schwartz Agency Inc*
4111 W Alameda Ave Ste 509
Burbank, CA 91505-4171, USA

Salvino, Carmen (Bowler)
65 Stevens Dr
Schaumburg, IL 60173-2176, USA

Sam the Sham (Musician)
6123 Old Brunswick Rd
Arlington, TN 38002-5928, USA

Samaras, Lucas (Artist, Photographer)
32 E 57th St
New York, NY 10022-2513, USA

Samberg, Andy (Actor)
c/o Staff Member *Mosaic Media Group*
9200 W Sunset Blvd Ste 10
Los Angeles, CA 90069-3608, USA

Sambito, Joe (Athlete, Baseball Player)
23 Modesto
Irvine, CA 92602-0929, USA

Sambora, Richie (Music Group, Musician, Songwriter)
c/o Chris Goodman *Outside Organisation, The*
Butler House 177-178 Tottenham Court Rd
London W1T 7NY, UNITED KINGDOM (UK)

Samcoff, Ed (Athlete, Baseball Player)
8153 Maderia Port Ln
Fair Oaks, CA 95628-2833, USA

Samford, Ron (Athlete, Baseball Player)
2144 Kessler Ct
Dallas, TX 75208-2948, USA

Samios, Nicholas P (Misc, Physicist)
Directors's Office 2 Center St
Upton, NY 11973, USA

Samis, Phil
1509 Rue Sherbrooke O
Montreal, CANADA QC H3G 1M1

Sammartino, Bruno (Wrestler)
413 Goldsmith Rd
Pittsburgh, PA 15237-3723, USA

Sammie (Actor)
c/o Staff Member *Green Light Talent Agency*
PO Box 3172
Beverly Hills, CA 90212-0172, USA

Sammons, Clint (Athlete, Baseball Player)
5014 Oak Leaf Ter
Stone Mountain, GA 30087-3281, USA

Samms, Emma (Actor)
2934 1/2 N Beverly Glen Cir # 417
Los Angeles, CA 90077-1724, USA

Sammy, Sugar (Actor)
c/o Jodi Lieberman *Parallel Entertainment*
9420 Wilshire Blvd Ste 250
Beverly Hills, CA 90212-3151, USA

Samoilova, Tatiana Y (Actor)
Spiridonyevsky Per 8/11
Moscow 103104, RUSSIA

Samotsvetov, Anatoly (Athlete, Hockey Player)
501 Broadway
Nashville, TN 37203-3980, USA

Sampaio, Jorge (President)
Palacio de Belem
Lisbon 1300, PORTUGAL

Sampen, Bill (Athlete, Baseball Player)
11 Carnaby Ct
Brownsburg, IN 46112-8834, USA

Sample, Billy (Athlete, Baseball Player)
10 Pascack Rd
Township Of Washington, NJ 07676-5116, USA

Sample, Joe (Musician)
1255 5th Ave Apt 7J
New York, NY 10029-3848, USA

Sample, Steven B (Educator)
President's Office
Los Angeles, CA 90089-0001, USA

Samples, Keith (Director, Producer, Writer)
c/o Rob Kenneally *Creative Artists Agency (CAA-LA)*
2000 Avenue of the Stars Ste 100
Los Angeles, CA 90067-4705, USA

Sampleton, Lawrence (Athlete, Football Player)
2900 Bunny Run
Austin, TX 78746-1702, USA

Sampras, Pete (Tennis Player)
1360 E 9th St Ste 100
Cleveland, OH 44114-1730

Sampson, Benj (Athlete, Baseball Player)
8312 Flat Rock Ct
North Richland Hills, TX 76182-8471, USA

Sampson, Greg (Athlete, Football Player)
3286 Highland Dr
Carlsbad, CA 92008-1918, USA

Sampson, Kelvin (Basketball Player, Coach)
Lloyd Noble Complex
Norman, OK 73019-0001, USA

Sampson, Linda (Stylist)
827 Ursulines Ave
New Orleans, LA 70116-2421, USA

Sampson, Ralph L Jr (Athlete, Basketball Player, Coach)
530 Myrtle St
Harrisonburg, VA 22802-4725, USA

Sampson, Robert (Actor)
4605 Lankershim Blvd Ste 305
North Hollywood, CA 91602-1875, USA

Sams, Dean (Musician)
c/o Staff Member *Borman Entertainment (TN)*
4322 Harding Pike Ste 429
Nashville, TN 37205-2661, USA

Sams, Doris (Baseball Player)
2405 Alberta Dr
Knoxville, TN 37920-4701, USA

Sams, Jeffrey D (Actor)
c/o Toni Benson *Third Hill Entertainment*
195 S Beverly Dr Ste 400
Beverly Hills, CA 90212-3044, USA

Sams, Judy (Golfer)
2603 Wells Ave
Sarasota, FL 34232-3954, USA

Sams, Russell (Actor)
c/o Jon Simmons *Simmons & Scott Entertainment*
7942 Mulholland Dr
Los Angeles, CA 90046-1225, USA

Samson, Savanna (Adult Film Star)
118 Fullerton St # 149
New York, NY 10038, USA

Samuel, Amado (Athlete, Baseball Player)
1931 Yale Dr
Louisville, KY 40205-2038, USA

Samuel, Juan (Athlete, Baseball Player)
1622 E Preston St
Baltimore, MD 21213-3026, USA

Samuel, Xavier (Actor)
c/o David Seltzer *Management 360*
9111 Wilshire Blvd
Beverly Hills, CA 90210-5508, USA

Samuels, Chris (Athlete, Football Player)
8415 Fredericksburg Rd Apt 906
San Antonio, TX 78229-3352, USA

Samuels, Dale (Athlete, Football Player)
7617 Highway X
Three Lakes, WI 54562-9224, USA

Samuels, Jack (Athlete, Baseball Player)
840 Vista Cir
Brea, CA 92821-2317, USA

Samuels, Roger (Athlete, Baseball Player)
4865 Tampico Way
San Jose, CA 95118-2348, USA

Samuels, Ron
PO Box 1690
Rancho Mirage, CA 92270-1058

Samuels, Skyler (Actor)
c/o Paul Nelson *Mosaic Media Group*
9200 W Sunset Blvd Ste 10
Los Angeles, CA 90069-3608, USA

Samuels, Stephanie (Stylist)
1636 W Montrose Ave
Chicago, IL 60613-1214, USA

Samuelson, Pamela (Attorney, Attorney General, General)
Center for Law Technology
Berkeley, CA 94720-0001, USA

Samuelson, Paul A (Nobel Prize Laureate)
94 Somerset St
Belmont, MA 02478-2010, USA

Samuelsson, Bengt I (Nobel Prize Laureate)
Chemistry Dept
Stockholm 171 77, SWEDEN

Samuelsson, Kjell (Athlete, Hockey Player)
5 Simsbury Dr
Voorhees, NJ 08043-3948, USA

Samuelsson, Marcus (Chef)
c/o Staff Member *Discovery Channel*
1 Discovery Pl
Silver Spring, MD 20910-3354, USA

Samuelsson, Ulf (Athlete, Hockey Player)
37 W Hills Dr
Avon, CT 6001, USA

San Basilio, Paloma (Music Group)
c/o Staff Member *Sony Music Miami*
605 Lincoln Rd Ste 700
Miami Beach, FL 33139-2901, USA

Sanabria, Marilyn (Actor)
c/o Laura Walsh *Central Artists*
3310 W Burbank Blvd # A
Burbank, CA 91505-2230, USA

Sanada, Hiroyuki (Actor)
c/o William Choi *Management 360*
9111 Wilshire Blvd
Beverly Hills, CA 90210-5508, USA

Sanborn, David (Musician)
c/o Staff Member *International Creative Management (ICM-LA)*
10250 Constellation Blvd Fl 7
Los Angeles, CA 90067-6207, USA

Sanches, Brian (Athlete, Baseball Player)
903 N 31st St
Nederland, TX 77627-6706, USA

Sanches, Stacy (Model)
c/o Staff Member *Playboy Productions*
2706 Media Center Dr
Los Angeles, CA 90065-1733, USA

Sanchez, Alex (Athlete, Baseball Player)
1400 Mellissa Cir
Antioch, CA 94509-6301, USA

Sanchez, Duaner (Athlete, Baseball Player)
56748 Eastvue Dr
Osceola, IN 46561-9468, USA

Sanchez, Eduardo (Director)
c/o Staff Member *Elements Entertainment*
312 W 5th St Apt 815
Los Angeles, CA 90013-1750, USA

Sanchez, Emilio (Tennis Player)
Sabiono de Avena 28
Barcelona 46, SPAIN

Sanchez, Emma (Stylist)
c/o Staff Member *Marek & Associates Inc*
508 W 26th St Rm 12C
New York, NY 10001-5541, USA

Sanchez, Evet (Stylist)
c/o Staff Member *Fred Segal Beauty*
PO Box 5304
Beverly Hills, CA 90209-5304, USA

Sanchez, Freddy (Athlete, Baseball Player)
227 W Swan Dr
Chandler, AZ 85286-7770, USA

Sanchez, Israel (Athlete, Baseball Player)
5444 N Spaulding Ave
Chicago, IL 60625-4608, USA

Sanchez, Jose T Cardinal (Religious Leader)
Via Rusticucci 13
Rome 193, ITALY

Sanchez, Juan (Pepe) (Basketball Player)
c/o Staff Member *Detroit Pistons*
2 Championship Dr
Auburn Hills, MI 48326-1753, USA

Sanchez, Kiele (Actor)
c/o Dan Spilo *Industry Entertainment Partners*
955 Carrillo Dr Ste 300
Los Angeles, CA 90048-5400, USA

Sanchez, Lupe (Athlete, Football Player)
28870 Road 68
Visalia, CA 93277-9470, USA

Sanchez, Marco (Actor)
c/o Steve Himber *Steve Himber Entertainment*
211 S Beverly Dr Apt S
Beverly Hills, CA 90212-3807, USA

Sanchez, Mark (Athlete, Football Player)
c/o David Dunn *Athletes First, LLC*
3300 Irvine Ave Ste 300
Newport Beach, CA 92660-3108, USA

Sanchez, Monika (Actor)
c/o Gabriel Blanco *Gabriel Blanco Iglesias (Mexico)*
Rio Balsas 35-32 Colonia Cuauhtemoc
DF 6500, Mexico

Sanchez, Pepe (Director)
c/o Staff Member *Gabriel Blanco Iglesias (Colombia)*
Dg 127A #20-36 Conjunto Plenitud, Apto 132
Bogota, Colombia

Sanchez, Raul (Athlete, Baseball Player)
15790 Kingsmoor Way
Hialeah, FL 33014-6574, USA

Sanchez, Rey (Athlete, Baseball Player)
788 Calle Pampero
San Juan, PR 00924-1772, USA

Sanchez, Rick (Correspondent, Journalist)
c/o Staff Member *CNN (Atlanta)*
1 Cnn Ctr NW
Atlanta, GA 30303-2762, USA

Sanchez, Roselyn (Actor)
c/o Lena Roklin *Luber Roklin Management*
8530 Wilshire Blvd Ste 550
Beverly Hills, CA 90211-3133, USA

Sanchez Azuara, Rocio (Actor)
c/o Staff Member *TV Azteca*
Periferico Sur 4121 Colonia Fuentes del Pedregal
DF CP 14141, Mexico

Sanchez Gijon, Aitana (Actor)
Gran Via 63 #3 Izda
Madrid 28013, SPAIN

Sanchez-Vicario, Arantxa (Tennis Player)
Sabino de Arana 28 #6-1A
Barcelona 8028, SPAIN

Sanctus Real (Music Group, Musician)
c/o Dan Spencer *Flat-Out Management*
1800 Blair Blvd
Nashville, TN 37212-5004, USA

Sand, Paul (Actor)
10100 Santa Monica Blvd Ste 2500
Los Angeles, CA 90067-4116, USA

Sand, Shauna
c/o Staff Member *Acme Talent & Literary (LA)*
1400 Atlantic Ave Ste 274
Long Beach, CA 90813-2013, USA

Sand, Todd (Figure Skater)
2973 Harbor Blvd # 468
Costa Mesa, CA 92626-3912, USA

Sanda, Dominique
201 Rue Du Faubourg St Honore
Paris, FRANCE F-75008

Sandage, Allan R (Astronomer)
813 Santa Barbara St
Pasadena, CA 91101-1232, USA

Sandberg, Jared (Athlete, Baseball Player)
4275 NE 125th St
Seattle, WA 98125-4635, USA

Sandberg, Ryne (Athlete, Baseball Player)
26 Biltmore Est
Phoenix, AZ 85016-2823, USA

Sandeno, Kaitlin (Athlete, Swimmer)
c/o Staff Member *Premier Management Group (PMG Sports)*
115 Crescent Commons Dr Ste 250
Cary, NC 27518-8134, USA

Sander, Casey
c/o Jeffrey Leavitt *Leavitt Talent Group*
8255 W Sunset Blvd
West Hollywood, CA 90046-2417, USA

Sander, Ian (Producer)
c/o Staff Member *WmE2 (WMA-LA)*
1 William Morris Pl
Beverly Hills, CA 90212-4261, USA

Sander, Jil (Designer, Fashion Designer)
Osterfeldstr 32-34
Hamburg 22529, GERMANY

Sander, Mark (Athlete, Football Player)
4930 NW 83rd Ave
Lauderhill, FL 33351-5553, USA

Sanderling, Kurt (Conductor)
Am Iderfenngraben 47
Berlin 13156, GERMANY

Sanderman, Bill (Athlete, Football Player)
PO Box 203
Homewood, CA 96141-0203, USA

Sanders, Barry (Athlete, Football Player)
2121 George Halas Dr NW
Canton, OH 44708-2630, USA

Sanders, Beverly (Actor)
12218 Morrison St
Valley Village, CA 91607-3627, USA

Sanders, Bill (Cartoonist)
PO Box 661
Milwaukee, WI 53201-0661, USA

Sanders, Bobby (Baseball Player)
24799 Lake Shore Blvd Apt 712
Euclid, OH 44123-4246, USA

Sanders, Charles A (Charlie) (Athlete, Coach, Football Coach, Football Player)
3418 Palm Aire Ct
Rochester Hills, MI 48309-1040, USA

Sanders, Chris (Director)
c/o Rob Carlson *WmE2 (Endeavor-LA)*
9601 Wilshire Blvd Fl 3
Beverly Hills, CA 90210-5219, USA

Sanders, Christoph (Actor)
c/o Beverly Strong *Strong Management*
3532 Hayden Ave
Culver City, CA 90232-2413, USA

Sanders, Daryl (Athlete, Football Player)
9220 Shawnee Trl
Powell, OH 43065-5012, USA

Sanders, David (Athlete, Baseball Player)
10411 S Ellen St
Mulvane, KS 67110-9374, USA

Sanders, Deion (Athlete, Baseball Player, Football Player)
406 Dartmoor Dr
Celina, TX 75009-4589, USA

Sanders, Doug (Golfer)
1311 Nantucket Dr
Houston, TX 77057-1907, USA

Sanders, Eric D (Athlete, Football Player)
9325 Tailey Cir
Duluth, GA 30097-2451, USA

Sanders, Frank (Athlete, Hockey Player)
670 Lake View Dr
Saint Paul, MN 55129-9228, USA

Sanders, Frank (Athlete, Football Player)
12310 Silver Cup Ct
Reisterstown, MD 21136-6481, USA

Sanders, James (Baseball Player)
1001 43rd Place Ensley
Birmingham, AL 35208-1402, USA

Sanders, Jay O (Actor)
165 W 46th St Ste 409
New York, NY 10036-2522, USA

Sanders, Jeff (Athlete, Basketball Player)
PO Box 374
South Holland, IL 60473-0374, USA

Sanders, John (Athlete, Baseball Player)
3004 Cheshire Ct
Woodstock, GA 30189-6690, USA

Sanders, John M (Athlete, Football Player)
520 Old Whitfield Rd
Pearl, MS 39208-5512, USA

Sanders, Jonathan (Jon) (Yachtsman)
28 Portland St
Redlands, WA 6009, AUSTRALIA

Sanders, Ken (Athlete, Baseball Player)
12141 Parkview Ln
Hales Corners, WI 53130-2341, USA

Sanders, Mariene (Correspondent)
356 W 58th St
New York, NY 10019-1804, USA

Sanders, Marlene
175 Riverside Dr
New York, NY 10024-1616

Sanders, Orban (Athlete, Football Player)
3520 NW Ferris Ave
Lawton, OK 73505-6104, USA

Sanders, Pharoah (Musician)
300 Mercer St Apt 3J
New York, NY 10003-6732, USA

Sanders, Reggie
1764 Williamsburg Cir
Florence, SC 29506-6914

Sanders, Reggie (Athlete, Baseball Player)
122 Vista Del Mar Ln Unit 102
Myrtle Beach, SC 29572-8148, USA

Sanders, Robert J (Athlete, Football Player)
412 Homestead Ave
Metairie, LA 70005-3208, USA

Sanders, Rupert (Director)
c/o Guymon Casady *Management 360*
9111 Wilshire Blvd
Beverly Hills, CA 90210-5508, USA

Sanders, Scott G (Athlete, Baseball Player)
315 Belmont Dr
Thibodaux, LA 70301-2908, USA

Sanders, Summer (Athlete, Swimmer)
731 Martingale Ln
Park City, UT 84098-7559, USA

Sanders, Thomas (Athlete, Football Player)
72 S Fiore Pkwy
Vernon Hills, IL 60061-3269, USA

Sanders, Thomas (Satch) (Basketball Player, Misc)
114 Fenway
Boston, MA 02115-3715, USA

Sanders, W J (Jerry) III (Business Person)
PO Box 3453
Sunnyvale, CA 94088-3453, USA

Sanderson, Cael (Wrestler)
1380 Valley Hills Blvd
Heber City, UT 84032-1111, USA

Sanderson, Derek M (Athlete, Hockey Player)
267 Manning St
Needham, MA 02492-3507, USA

Sanderson, Geoff (Athlete, Hockey Player)
1988 Berkshire Rd
Upper Arlington, OH 43221-3746, USA

Sanderson, Nikki (Actor)
c/o Coronation Sreet Granada Studios, Quay St
Manchester M60 9EA, UNITED KINGDOM

Sanderson, Peter (Artist)
1105 Shell Gate Pl
Alameda, CA 94501-5949, USA

Sanderson, Reggie (Athlete, Football Player)
160 Mara Ave
Ventura, CA 93004-1513, USA

Sanderson, Scott (Athlete, Baseball Player)
945 Newcastle Dr
Lake Forest, IL 60045-4928, USA

Sanderson, Theresa (Tessa) (Athlete, Track Athlete)
Atles Center Oxgate Lane
London NW2 7HU, UNITED KINGDOM (UK)

Sanderson, William (Actor)
c/o Lori DeWaal *Lori DeWaal & Associates PR*
7080 Hollywood Blvd Ste 515
Los Angeles, CA 90028-6932, USA

Sandeson, William S (Cartoonist, Editor)
2230 Muskoday Pass
Fort Wayne, IN 46809-1428, USA

Sandiford, L Erskine (Prime Minister)
Hillvista Porters
Saint James, BARBADOS

Sandig, Curtis (Athlete, Football Player)
2742 Pebble Breeze
San Antonio, TX 78232-4116, USA

Sandin, Bill (Inventor)
Electronic Visualization Lab
Chicago, IL 60607, USA

Sandit, Tom (Athlete)
540 S Ashland Ave
La Grange, IL 60525-2811

Sandler, Adam (Actor, Comedian)
c/o Sandy Wernick *Brillstein Entertainment Partners*
9150 Wilshire Blvd Ste 350
Beverly Hills, CA 90212-3453, USA

Sandler, Herbert M (Financier)
1901 Harrison St
Oakland, CA 94612-3574, USA

Sandler, Marion O (Financier)
1901 Harrison St
Oakland, CA 94612-3574, USA

Sandlock, Mike (Athlete, Baseball Player)
81 Bible St
Cos Cob, CT 06807-2109, USA

Sandlund, Debra (Actor)
1505 10th St
Santa Monica, CA 90401-2805, USA

Sandman, Cindy (Stylist)
c/o Staff Member *Barbara Laurie Photographers*
152 Madison Ave Rm 1803
New York, NY 10016-5424, USA

Sandoval, Arturo (Musician)
PO Box 143936
Coral Gables, FL 33114-3936, USA

Sandoval, Brian (Governor)
101 N Carson St
Carson City, NV 89701-3713, USA

Sandoval, Hope (Music Group, Musician)
66 Golbarne Road
London W10 5PS, UNITED KINGDOM (UK)

Sandoval, Miguel (Actor)
10100 Santa Monica Blvd Ste 2500
Los Angeles, CA 90067-4116, USA

Sandoval, Sonny (Musician)
75 Rockefeller Plz
New York, NY 10019-6908, USA

Sandoval Iniguez, Juan Cardinal (Religious Leader)
Morelos 244
San Pedro Tlaquepaque 45500, MEXICO

Sandow, Nick (Actor)
c/o Tina Thor *TMT Entertainment Group*
648 Broadway Ste 1002
New York, NY 10012-2348, USA

Sandre, Didier (Actor)
201 Faubourg Saint Honore
Paris 75008, FRANCE

Sandrelli, Stefania (Actor)
Viale Parioli 41
Rome 197, ITALY

Sandrich, Jay (Director)
c/o Staff Member *Creative Artists Agency (CAA-LA)*
2000 Avenue of the Stars Ste 100
Los Angeles, CA 90067-4705, USA

Sands, Charlie (Athlete, Baseball Player)
4740 Stratford Ct Apt 1603
Naples, FL 34105-6689, USA

Sands, Julian (Actor)
1287 Ozeta Ter
Los Angeles, CA 90069-1835, USA

Sands, Tommy (Actor, Musician)
916 19th Ave S
Nashville, TN 37212-2108, USA

Sands-Ferguson, Sarah Jane (Baseball Player)
338 Rohrsburg Rd
Orangeville, PA 17859-9108, USA

Sandstrom, Sven (Financier)
4300 Wilson Blvd Fl 11
Arlington, VA 22203-4167, USA

Sandstrom, Tomas (Athlete, Hockey Player)
156 Iron Run Rd
Bethel Park, PA 15102-1081, USA

Sandt, Tommy (Athlete, Baseball Player)
3723 Eleanor Ct
Lake Oswego, OR 97035-4455, USA

Sandusky, Alexander B (Alex) (Athlete, Football Player)
22 Floral Ave
Key West, FL 33040-6243, USA

Sandusky, Mike (Athlete, Football Player)
2786 Amberwood Ct
Naples, FL 34120-7520, USA

Sandvoss, Steve (Actor)
c/o Joan Hyler *Hyler Management*
20 Ocean Park Blvd Unit 25
Santa Monica, CA 90405-3590, USA

Sandy, Baby (Sandra Magee)
6846 Haywood St
Tujunga, CA 91042-2850

Sandy, Gary (Actor)
PO Box 818
Cynthiana, KY 41031-0818, USA

Sandy B (Musician)
2922 Atlantic Ave Ste 200
Atlantic City, NJ 08401-6337, USA

Sandy Jr, Alomar (Baseball Player)
4635 Prestwick Xing
Westlake, OH 44145-5073, USA

Sanford, Chance (Athlete, Baseball Player)
15028 Bardwell Ln
Frisco, TX 75035-0412, USA

Sanford, Ed (Athlete, Hockey Player)
18 Clearwater Rd
Winchester, MA 01890-4011

Sanford, Fred (Athlete, Baseball Player)
1046 W 600 N
Salt Lake City, UT 84116-2637, USA

Sanford, Jack
2300 Presidential Way
West Palm Beach, FL 33401-1510

Sanford, Jennifer S (Misc)
1725 Atlantic Ave
Sullivans Island, SC 29482-9794, USA

Sanford, Leo (Athlete, Football Player)
3044 Gorton Rd
Shreveport, LA 71119-3606, USA

Sanford, Lucius M (Athlete, Football Player)
8745 Carriage Hills Dr
Columbia, MD 21046, USA

Sanford, Meredith (Athlete)
2800 Highway 389
Starkville, MS 39759-8379

Sanford, Mo (Athlete, Baseball Player)
2800 Highway 389
Starkville, MS 39759-8379, USA

Sanford, Richard M (Rick) (Athlete, Football Player)
110 Oak Park Dr Ste B
Irmo, SC 29063-6110, USA

Sanford, Ron (Athlete, Basketball Player)
3129 Santana Ln
Plano, TX 75023-3630, USA

Sangalo, Ivete (Musician)
via Bonafous, 6
Torino 10123, Italy

Sangare, Oumou (Actor, Composer, Musician)
c/o Staff Member *Concerted Efforts*
PO Box 440326
Somerville, MA 02144-0004, USA

Sangavi (Actor, Bollywood)
20 4th Street Dr Subraya Nagar
Kodambakkam
Chennai, TN 600024, INDIA

Sangeetha (Actor, Bollywood)
26A Brindavan Apartments Karumari
Amman Koil Street Vadapalani
Chennai, TN 600026, INDIA

Sanger, David J (Musician)
Embleton Near Cockermouth
Cumbria CA13 9YA, UNITED KINGDOM (UK)

Sanger, Frederick (Nobel Prize Laureate)
Far Leys Fen Lane Swaffham Bulbeck
Cambridge CB5 0NJ, UNITED KINGDOM (UK)

Sanger, Stephan W (Business Person)
PO Box 1113
Minneapolis, MN 55440-1113, USA

SanGiacomo, Laura (Actor)
c/o Staff Member *Rugolo Entertainment*
195 S Beverly Dr Ste 400
Beverly Hills, CA 90212-3044, USA

Sangster, Thomas (Actor)
c/o Duncan Millership *Management 360*
9111 Wilshire Blvd
Beverly Hills, CA 90210-5508, USA

Sangueli, Andrei (Prime Minister)
Prosp 105
Kishineau 277073, MOLDOVA

Sanguillen, Manny (Athlete, Baseball Player)
2838 SW 4th St
Boynton Beach, FL 33435-7902, USA

Sanguinetti Cairolo, Julio Maria (President)
Andres Martinez Trueba 1271
Montevideo, URUGUAY

Sanha, Malam Bacai (President)
Bissau, GUINEA-BISSAU

SanJuan, Olga (Actor)
12100 W Sunset Blvd # 2
Los Angeles, CA 90049-4143, USA

Sanjukta, Singh (Actor, Bollywood)
4th Apts Breach Candy Floor MONA
Mumbai, MS 400036, INDIA

Sano, Roya A (Religious Leader)
PO Box 320
Nashville, TN 37202-0320, USA

Sanobar, Kabir (Actor, Bollywood)
402 Karan Road Versova Andheri W
Building YARI
Mumbai, MS 400061, INDIA

Sansom, Bruce (Ballerina)
c/o Staff Member *Royal Ballet*
Covent Garden Bow St
London WC2E 9DD, UK

Sansom, Chip (Cartoonist)
204 Long Beach Rd
Centerville, MA 02632-3534, USA

Sant, Alfred (Prime Minister)
Mills End Road
Hannum, MALTA

Santa Rosa, Gilberto (Musician)
c/o Staff Member *Richard De La Font Agency*
3808 W South Park Blvd
Broken Arrow, OK 74011-1261, USA

Santamaria, Eduardo (Actor)
c/o Gabriel Blanco *Gabriel Blanco Iglesias (Mexico)*
Rio Balsas 35-32 Colonia Cuauhtemoc
DF 6500, Mexico

Santana, Ava (Actor)
c/o Claudia Speicher *New Orleans Talent Agency*
1347 Magazine St
New Orleans, LA 70130-4240, USA

Santana, Carlos (Musician, Songwriter)
PO Box 10348
San Rafael, CA 94912-0348, USA

Santana, Johan (Athlete, Baseball Player)
5150 Lincoln Dr
Minneapolis, MN 55436-1010, USA

Santana, Juelz (Musician)
c/o Staff Member *Island Def Jam Music Group*
825 8th Ave Fl 28
New York, NY 10019-7416

Santana, Manuel (Tennis Player)
194 Bellevue Ave
Newport, RI 02840-3515, USA

Santana, Maria (Stylist)
c/o Staff Member *Ray Brown Represents*
601 W 26th St Rm 1310
New York, NY 10001-1129, USA

Santana, Rafael (Athlete, Baseball Player)
3220 SE 1st Ave
Cape Coral, FL 33904-4103, USA

Santangelo, F P (Athlete, Baseball Player)
3602 Rocky Ridge Way
El Dorado Hills, CA 95762-4432, USA

Santaolalla, Gustavo (Musician)
c/o Robert Messinger *First Artists Management*
4764 Park Granada Ste 210
Calabasas, CA 91302-3333, USA

Santer, Jacques (Misc)
69 Rue J P Huberty
1742, LUXEMBOURG

Santiago (Stylist)
339 W 48th St
New York, NY 10036-1309, USA

Santiago, Benito R (Athlete, Baseball Player)
PO Box 5759
Lighthouse Point, FL 33074-5759, USA

Santiago, Carlos (Baseball Player)
7 Calle Archilla Cabrera
Mayaguez, PR 00680-3302, USA

Santiago, Daniel (Basketball Player)
c/o Staff Member *Phoenix Suns*
201 E Jefferson St
Phoenix, AZ 85004-2412, USA

Santiago, Danny (Stylist)
c/o Staff Member *Blink Management*
421 Washington Ave Ste 202
Miami Beach, FL 33139-6612, USA

Santiago, Eddie (Musician)
c/o Staff Member *Sony Music Miami*
605 Lincoln Rd Ste 700
Miami Beach, FL 33139-2901, USA

Santiago, Jose (Athlete, Baseball Player)
Z12 Calle Yagrumo
Carolina, PR 00983-3422, USA

Santiago, Ray (Actor)
c/o Scott Zimmerman *Evolution Entertainment (LA)*
901 N Highland Ave
Los Angeles, CA 90038-2412, USA

Santiago, Rodiney (Model, Reality TV Star)
c/o Staff Member *Mega Models (Miami)*
420 Lincoln Rd Ste 408
Miami, FL 33139-3015, USA

Santiago, Tessie (Actor)
c/o Craig Shapiro *International Creative Management (ICM-LA)*
10250 Constellation Blvd Fl 7
Los Angeles, CA 90067-6207, USA

Santiago, Victor (Nore) (Musician)
c/o Staff Member *Violator Management*
36 W 25th St Fl 11
New York, NY 10010-2752, USA

Santiago-Hudson, Ruben (Actor)
c/o Vincent Cirrincione *Vincent Cirrincione Associates*
1516 N Fairfax Ave
Los Angeles, CA 90046-2608, USA

Santini, Geo (Director)
c/o Kieran Maguire *The Arlook Group*
205 S Beverly Dr Ste 209
Beverly Hills, CA 90212-3899, USA

Santo, Ronald (Ron) (Athlete, Baseball Player)
1721 Meadow Ln
Bannockburn, IL 60015-1844, USA

Santo & Johnny
217 Edgewood Ave
Clearwater, FL 33755-5702

Santo Domingo, Rafael (Athlete, Baseball Player)
PO Box 21
Orocovis, PR 00720-0021, USA

Santorelli, Frank (Actor)
c/o Mitch Smelkinson *Stone, Meyer, Genow, Smelkinson and Binder*
9665 Wilshire Blvd Ste 500
Beverly Hills, CA 90212-2312, USA

Santorini, AL (Athlete, Baseball Player)
9 Daniele Dr
Ocean, NJ 07712-7910, USA

Santorini, Paul E (Engineer, Physicist)
PO Box 49
Athens, GREECE

Santoro, Nicoletta (Stylist)
c/o Staff Member *Art + Commerce*
531 W 25th St # 4
New York, NY 10001-5593, USA

Santoro, Rodrigo (Actor)
c/o Aleen Keshishian *Brillstein Entertainment Partners*
9150 Wilshire Blvd Ste 350
Beverly Hills, CA 90212-3453, USA

Santorum, Rick (Ex-Senator, Politician)
c/o Staff Member *Ambassador Speakers Bureau*
PO Box 50358
Nashville, TN 37205-0358, USA

Santos, Al (Actor)
c/o Staff Member *Don Buchwald & Associates Inc (LA)*
6500 Wilshire Blvd Ste 2200
Los Angeles, CA 90048-4942, USA

Santos, Bruno (Model)
c/o Staff Member *WHY NOT Model Agency*
via Zenale 9
Milano 20123, ITALY

Santos, Carlos (Comedian)
c/o Staff Member *WmE2 (WMA-LA)*
1 William Morris Pl
Beverly Hills, CA 90212-4261, USA

Santos, Joe (Actor)
c/o Mike Eistenstadt *Amsel, Eisenstadt & Frazier Talent Agency (AEF)*
5055 Wilshire Blvd Ste 860
Los Angeles, CA 90036-6108, USA

Santos, Rey-Phillip (Actor)
c/o Staff Member *Dramatic Artists Agency*
103 W Alameda Ave Ste 139
Burbank, CA 91502-2253, USA

Santos de Oliveira, Alessandra (Basketball Player)
MCI Center 601 F St NW
Washington, DC 20004, USA

Santovenia, Nelson (Athlete, Baseball Player)
14642 SW 141st Ct
Miami, FL 33186-7260, USA

Sanz, Alejandro (Musician, Songwriter, Writer)
c/o Staff Member *WmE2 (WMA-Miami)*
119 Washington Ave Ste 400
Miami, FL 33139-7202, USA

Sanz, Horatio (Actor)
c/o David (Dave) Becky *3 Arts Entertainment Inc*
9460 Wilshire Blvd Fl 7
Beverly Hills, CA 90212-2713, USA

Saper, Clifford (Doctor)
330 Brookline Ave
Boston, MA 02215-5400, USA

Saperstein, David (Director, Producer, Writer)
c/o Staff Member *Fran Saperstein Organization*
Marina del Rey, CA 90292, USA

Sapienza, Al
10474 Santa Monica Blvd Ste 380
Los Angeles, CA 90025-6943

Sapienza, Americo (Athlete, Football Player)
6 Forenza Rd
Peabody, MA 01960-3732, USA

Saplenza, Al (Actor)
PO Box 691240
West Hollywood, CA 90069-9240, USA

Sapolu, Jesse (Athlete, Football Player)
1123 Buckingham Dr Apt B
Costa Mesa, CA 92626-2185, USA

Saporta, Gabe (Musician)
c/o Staff Member *Fueled By Ramen*
PO Box 1803
Tampa, FL 33601-1803, USA

Sapp, Bob (Actor)
c/o Blake Bandy *Kritzer Levine Wilkins Entertainment*
11872 La Grange Ave Fl 1
Los Angeles, CA 90025-5283, USA

Sapp, Carolyn
1840 41st Ave # 102-227
Capitola, CA 95010-2513

Sapp, Theron (Athlete, Football Player)
892 N Belair Rd
Evans, GA 30809-4222, USA

Sapp, Warren (Athlete, Football Player)
c/o Drew Rosenhaus *Rosenhaus Sports Representation*
6400 Allison Rd
Miami Beach, FL 33141-4540, USA

Sappleton, Wayne (Athlete, Basketball Player)
8040 N Nob Hill Rd Apt 205
Tamarac, FL 33321-7410, USA

Sara, Mia (Actor)
2311 Alto Oak Dr
Los Angeles, CA 90068-2509, USA

Saracco, Joe (Stylist)
4642 E 26th St
Tucson, AZ 85711-5725, USA

Sarachan, Dave (Coach, Soccer Player)
980 N Michigan Ave Ste 1998
Chicago, IL 60611-7504, USA

Sarafian, Richard C (Actor, Director, Writer)
c/o Staff Member *Leavitt Talent Group*
8255 W Sunset Blvd
West Hollywood, CA 90046-2417, USA

Sarah, Duchess of York
Birch Hall
Windlesham Surrey, ENGLAND GU2O 6BN

Sarahyba, Daniella (Model)
c/o Staff Member *IMG Models (NY)*
304 Park Ave S # PH
New York, NY 10010, USA

Saraiva Martins, Jose Cardinal (Religious Leader)
Via Pancrazio Pfeiffer 10
Rome 193, ITALY

Saralegui, Cristina (Correspondent)
c/o Staff Member *Creative Artists Agency (CAA-LA)*
2000 Avenue of the Stars Ste 100
Los Angeles, CA 90067-4705, USA

Sarandon, Chris (Actor)
c/o Miles Levy *James/Levy/Jacobson Management Inc*
3500 W Olive Ave Ste 1470
Burbank, CA 91505-5514, USA

Sarandon, Susan (Actor, Producer)
c/o Meredith Wechter *International Creative Management (ICM-LA)*
10250 Constellation Blvd Fl 7
Los Angeles, CA 90067-6207, USA

Saranya (Actor, Bollywood)
17A Rajaram Directors Colony
Kodambakkam
Chennai, TN 600024, INDIA

Saraste, Jukka-Pekka
4 Addison Bridge Place
London W14 8XP, UNITED KINGDOM (UK)

Sarazen-Smith, Dorothy (Baseball Player)
4774 Eagle Crest Dr
Madison, WI 53704-6426, USA

Sarbanes, Paul (Senator)
320 Suffolk Rd
Baltimore, MD 21218-2521, USA

Sarcev, Ursula
PO Box 25738
Los Angeles, CA 90025-0738

Sardinha, Bronson (Athlete, Baseball Player)
7153 Trysail Cir
Tampa, FL 33607-5844, USA

Sardinha, Dane (Athlete, Baseball Player)
156 Kuulei Rd
Kailua, HI 96734-2718, USA

Sare, Chris
21100 Erwin St
Woodland Hills, CA 91367-3712

Sarfatl, Alain (Architect)
28 Rue Barbet du Jouy
Paris 75007, FRANCE

Sargent, Ben (Cartoonist, Editor)
166 E Riverside Dr
Austin, TX 78704, USA

Sargent, Joseph (Director, Producer)
27432 Latigo Bay View Dr
Malibu, CA 90265-2865, USA

Sargent, Nikki (Stylist)
c/o Staff Member *Celestine - CA*
1666 20th St Ste 200B
Santa Monica, CA 90404-3828, USA

Sargent, Ronald L (Business Person)
PO Box 9265
Framingham, MA 01701-9265, USA

Sargent, Wallace (Astronomer)
400 S Berkeley Ave
Pasadena, CA 91107-5062, USA

Sargeson, Alan M (Misc)
Chemistry Dept
Canberra, ACT 200, AUSTRALIA

Sari, Gabriela (Actor)
c/o Staff Member *Telefe - Argentina*
Pavon 2444 (C1248AAT)
Buenos Aires, ARGENTINA

Sarif, Shamim (Actor, Director, Writer)
77 Cheyne Court
London SW3 5TT, United Kingdom

Saritha (Actor, Bollywood)
Karthik Apartments III Floor, No.46,
Vijayaraghava Road T. Nagar
Chennai, TN 600017, INDIA

Sarkisian, Alex (Athlete, Football Player)
1604 E 142nd St
East Chicago, IN 46312-3008, USA

Sarkozy, Nicolas (President)
55 Rue La Boetie
Paris 75384, FRANCE

Sarna, Craig (Athlete, Hockey Player)
1375 Brown Rd S
Wayzata, MN 55391-9316, USA

Sarne, Tanya (Designer, Fashion Designer)
Ghost Chapel 263 Kensal Road
London W10 5DB, UNITED KINGDOM (UK)

Sarner, Craig (Athlete, Hockey Player)
1375 Brown Rd S
Wayzata, MN 55391-9316, USA

Sarni, Vincent A (Baseball Player, Misc)
PNC Park 115 Federal St
Pittsburgh, PA 15212, USA

Sarnoff, Liz (Actor)
c/o Staff Member *Creative Artists Agency (CAA-LA)*
2000 Avenue of the Stars Ste 100
Los Angeles, CA 90067-4705, USA

Sarnoff, William (Publisher)
1325 Avenue of the Americas
New York, NY 10019-6026, USA

Sarojadevi (Actor, Bollywood)
351 4th Main Road Sadasivanagar
Bangalore, KA 560080, INDIA

Sarosi, Imre (Coach, Swimmer)
1033 Bp Harrer Dal Utca 4
HUNGARY

Sarra, Joe (Stylist)
c/o Staff Member *Elite Model Management/Atlanta*
1708 Peachtree St NW Ste 210
Atlanta, GA 30309-2416, USA

Sarratt, Charles (Athlete, Football Player)
5812 Oak Tree Rd
Edmond, OK 73025-2620, USA

Sarsgaard, Peter (Actor)
c/o Jon Rubinstein *Authentic Talent and Literary Management*
45 Main St Ste 1004
Brooklyn, NY 11201-8200, USA

Sartain, Gailard (Actor)
c/o Michael Livingston *Leavitt Talent Group*
8255 W Sunset Blvd
West Hollywood, CA 90046-2417, USA

Sartzetakis, Christos (President)
7 Vas Georgiou B Odos Zalokosta 10
Athens, GREECE

Sarver, Michael (Musician)

Sarzo, Rudy
1155 N La Cienega Blvd Apt 506
Los Angeles, CA 90069-2437

Sasaki, Kazuhiro (Baseball Player)
PO Box 4100
Seattle, WA 98194-0100, USA

Sasaki, Norio (Coach)
3-10-15 Hongo Bunkyo-ku
Tokyo 113-0033, Japan

Sasdy, Peter (Director)
21 Matham Rd E Molesey
Surrey KT8 0SX, ENGLAND

Sasikala (Actor, Bollywood)
D-10 Parsan Apartments 204 T.T.K. Road
Alwarpet
Chennai, TN 600018, INDIA

Sassano, C E (Business Person)
1 Bausch and Lomb Pl
Rochester, NY 14604-2701, USA

Sassard, Jacqueline
54 Av Montaigne
Paris, FRANCE F-75008

Sasselov, Dimitar (Astronomer)
60 Garden St
Cambridge, MA 02138-1516, USA

Sasser, Clarence E (War Hero)
13414 FM 521 Rd
Rosharon, TX 77583-6608, USA

Sasser, Jason (Athlete, Basketball Player)
4211 Tiffany Trl
Grand Prairie, TX 75052-2823, USA

Sasser, Mackey (Athlete, Baseball Player)
19 Harrington Ln
Dothan, AL 36305-9732, USA

Sasser, Rob (Athlete, Baseball Player)
1004 Delta River Way
Knightdale, NC 27545-7326, USA

Sasso, Will (Actor, Comedian)
c/o Staff Member *Lord Mucker Entertainment*
839 E Orange Grove Ave
Burbank, CA 91501-1404, USA

Sasson, Debra (Opera Singer)
Erlenhaupstr 10
Bensheim 64625, GERMANY

Sassoon, David (Designer, Fashion Designer)
18 Culford Gardens
London SW3 2ST, UNITED KINGDOM (UK)

Sassoon, Vidal (Stylist)
15000 Mulholland Dr
Los Angeles, CA 90077-1617, USA

Sassoon Adams, Beverly (Model)
848 Oso Ave
Canoga Park, CA 91306, USA

Sassou-Nguesso, Denis (President)
Brazzaville, CONGO REPUBLIC

Sastre, Ines (Actor)
c/o Brad Schenck *Paradigm (LA)*
360 N Crescent Dr
Beverly Hills, CA 90210-4874, USA

Satanowski, Robert (Conductor)
Ul Madalinskiego 50/52 m 1
Warsaw 02-581, POLAND

Satcher, David (Misc)
2400 Sand Hill Rd
Menlo Park, CA 94025-6941, USA

Satcher, Leslie (Music Group, Musician, Songwriter, Writer)
3300 Warner Blvd
Burbank, CA 91505-4632, USA

Satchwell, Brooke (Actor)
2 Marston Lane Portsmouth
Hampshire, England PO3 5TW

Sather, Glen C (Athlete, Coach, Hockey Player)
505 Buffalo St
Banff, AB T0L 0C0, Canada

Sathiyaraj (Actor)
13-A Pirakathambal St
Chennai, TN 600 034, INDIA

Sato, Kazuo (Economist)
300 E 71st St Apt 15H
New York, NY 10021-5245, USA

Satra, Sonia (Actor)
1505 10th St
Santa Monica, CA 90401-2805, USA

Satre, Philip G (Business Person)
1023 Cherry Rd
Memphis, TN 38117-5423, USA

Satriani, Joe (Musician)
c/o Staff Member *Solo Agency Ltd (UK)*
55 Fulham High St 2nd Floor
London SW6 3JJ, United Kingdom

Satriano, Tom (Athlete, Baseball Player)
5320 Otis Ave
Tarzana, CA 91356-4214, USA

Satterfield, Paul (Actor)
PO Box 6945
Beverly Hills, CA 90212-6945, USA

Satterwhite, Howard (Athlete, Football Player)
3418 Action Ln
San Antonio, TX 78210-3402, USA

Satturno, William (Archaeologist)
Archaelogy Dept
Durham, NH 3824, USA

Saturday, Jeff (Athlete, Football Player)
2437 Londonberry Blvd
Carmel, IN 46032-8219, USA

Saubert, Jean M (Skier)
PO Box 836
Bigfork, MT 59911-0836, USA

Saucier, Frank (Athlete, Baseball Player)
1615 S Bryan St Apt 9
Amarillo, TX 79102-2326, USA

Saucier, Kevin (Athlete, Baseball Player)
2316 Silversides Loop
Pensacola, FL 32526-1509, USA

Saud, Prince Sultan Bin Abdulaziz al (Government Official)
PO Box 26731 Airport Road
Riyadh 11165, SAUDI ARABIA

Saudek, Jan (Photographer)
Blodkova 6
Prague 3 130 00, CZECH REPUBLIC

Sauderbeck, Scott (Athlete, Baseball Player)
3919 Riverview Blvd
Bradenton, FL 34209-2000, USA

Sauer, Craig (Athlete, Football Player)
6926 Pagenkopf Rd
Maple Plain, MN 55359-8725, USA

Sauer, George H Jr (Athlete, Football Player)
1297 Amberlea Dr E
Columbus, OH 43230-6856, USA

Sauer, Louis (Architect)
3472 Marlowe St
Montreal, QC H4A 2L7, CANADA

Sauer, Richard J (Educator)
7100 Connecticut Ave
Bethesda, MD 20815-4934, USA

Sauerlander, Willibald P W (Historian)
Meiserstr 10
Munich 80333, GERMANY

Sauers, Gene (Golfer)
9 Judsons Ct
Savannah, GA 31410-1060, USA

Saul, April (Journalist)
400 N Broad St
Philadelphia, PA 19130-4015, USA

Saul, Bill (Athlete, Football Player)
8300 Harford Rd
Parkville, MD 21234-5711, USA

Saul, John
229 E 79th St
New York, NY 10075-0866

Saul, John (Writer)
368 N La Cienega Blvd
Los Angeles, CA 90048-1949, USA

Saul, John W III (Writer)
9100 Wilshire Blvd Ste 100W
Beverly Hills, CA 90212-3435, USA

Saul, Ralph S (Business Person)
1400 Waverly Rd Apt V57
Gladwyne, PA 19035-1200, USA

Saul, Stephanie (Journalist)
235 Pinelawn Rd
Melville, NY 11747-4226, USA

Sauli, Daniel (Actor)
c/o James Suskin *James Suskin Management*
2 Charlton St Apt 5K
New York, NY 10014-4970, USA

Sauls, Don (Religious Leader)
PO Box 1568
Dunn, NC 28335-1568, USA

Saulters, Glynn (Athlete, Basketball Player)
240 Country Ln
Quitman, LA 71268-1226, USA

Saum, Sherri (Actor)
c/o Christian Donatelli *Schiff Company, The*
8440 Warner Dr Ste B1
Culver City, CA 90232-2461, USA

Saunders, Dennis (Athlete, Baseball Player)
2854 Rosewood St
Trenton, MI 48183-3602, USA

Saunders, Doug
43 Saint Kitts
Dana Point, CA 92629-4130

Saunders, Doug (Athlete, Baseball Player)
10580 Parkington Ln Unit A
Highlands Ranch, CO 80126-6748, USA

Saunders, George (Writer)
1745 Broadway # B1
New York, NY 10019-4368, USA

Saunders, George L Jr (Attorney, Attorney General, General)
179 E Lake Shore Dr
Chicago, IL 60611-1340, USA

Saunders, Jennifer (Actor)
c/o Maureen Vincent *United Agents*
12-26 Lexington St
London W1F OLE, UK

Saunders, John (Sportscaster)
Sports Dept ESPN Plaza 935 Middle St
Bristol, CT 6010, USA

Saunders, John (Cartoonist)
c/o Staff Member *King Features Syndication*
300 W 57th St Fl 15
New York, NY 10019-5238, USA

Saunders, John R (Race Car Driver)
PO Box 500F
Watkins Glen, NY 14891, USA

Saunders, Lori (Actor)
99 La Vuelta Rd
Santa Barbara, CA 93108-2621, USA

Saunders, Rachel (Beauty Pageant Winner)
203 Bocage Dr
Dothan, AL 36303-2944, USA

Saunders, Tony (Athlete, Baseball Player)
PO Box 126
Hanover, MD 21076-0126, USA

Saunders, Townsend (Wrestler)
733 Chantilly Dr
Sierra Vista, AZ 85635-4733, USA

Saura, Carlos (Director)
Calle Arturo Soria 52 #Edif 2 1-5A
Madrid 28027, SPAIN

Sauve, Marie-Amelie (Stylist)
c/o Staff Member *Management + Artists + Organization*
330 W 38th St Ste 1401
New York, NY 10018-8438, USA

Sauve, Robert (Bob) (Athlete, Hockey Player)
803-3080 Boul Le Carrefour
Laval, QC H7T 2R5, Canada

Sauveur, Rich (Athlete, Baseball Player)
3312 47th Ave E
Bradenton, FL 34203-3947, USA

Sauvion, Mariann (Stylist)
309 E 108th St Apt 2H
New York, NY 10029-4208, USA

Savage, Adam (Television Host)
9701 Wilshire Blvd Ste 800
Beverly Hills, CA 90212-2033, USA

Savage, Andrea (Actor, Producer, Writer)
c/o Julie Darmody *Mosaic Media Group*
9200 W Sunset Blvd Ste 10
Los Angeles, CA 90069-3608, USA

Savage, Ann (Actor)
1541 N Hayworth Ave Apt 203
Los Angeles, CA 90046-3333, USA

Savage, Ben (Actor)
c/o Staff Member *Abrams Artists Agency (LA)*
9200 W Sunset Blvd PH 11
Los Angeles, CA 90069-3601, USA

Savage, Bob (Athlete, Baseball Player)
95 Raycrest Dr
Randolph, NH 03593-5213, USA

Savage, Brian (Athlete, Hockey Player)
8030 E Whistling Wind Way
Scottsdale, AZ 85255-6480, USA

Savage, Chad (Adult Film Star)
c/o Staff Member *Diva Central Inc*
7510 W Sunset Blvd Ste 1445
Los Angeles, CA 90046-3408, USA

Savage, Chantay (Music Group, Musician)
250 W 57th St
New York, NY 10107-0001, USA

Savage, Don (Athlete, Basketball Player)
53 Park Edge # 1E
Berkeley Heights, NJ 07922-1281, USA

Savage, Fred (Actor)
c/o Andy Elkin *Creative Artists Agency (CAA-LA)*
2000 Avenue of the Stars Ste 100
Los Angeles, CA 90067-4705, USA

Savage, Herschel (Adult Film Star)
c/o Staff Member *Vivid Entertainment*
3599 Cahuenga Blvd W # 400
Los Angeles, CA 90068-1397, USA

Savage, Jack (Athlete, Baseball Player)
9920 White Blossom Blvd
Louisville, KY 40241-4163, USA

Savage, John (Actor)
5584 Bonneville Rd
Hidden Hills, CA 91302-1201, USA

Savage, Michael (Radio Personality)
110 Pacific Ave # 135
San Francisco, CA 94111-1962, USA

Savage, Rick (Musician)
c/o Rod MacSween *International Talent Booking*
1st Floor, Ariel House 74A Charlotte St
London W1T 4QJ, UNITED KINGDOM

Savage, Stephanie (Producer, Writer)
c/o Staff Member *Wonderland Sound and Vision*
8739 W Sunset Blvd
W Hollywood, CA 90069-2205, USA

Savage, Ted (Athlete, Baseball Player)
1510 Mallard Landing Ct
Chesterfield, MO 63017-5588, USA

Savage, Tracie
6212 Banner Ave
Los Angeles, CA 90038-2802

Saval, Dany
131 Rue De L'Universite
Paris, FRANCE 75007

Savant, Doug (Actor)
c/o Kay Liberman *Liberman/Zerman Management*
252 N Larchmont Blvd Ste 200
Los Angeles, CA 90004-3754, USA

Savard, Denis (Athlete, Hockey Player)
United Center 1901 W Madison St
Chicago, IL 60612, USA

Savard, Marc (Hockey Player)
c/o Staff Member *Boston Bruins*
TD Banknorth Garden 100 Legends Way, Suite 250
Boston, MA 2114, USA

Savard, Serge A (Athlete, Hockey Player)
1790 Ch Du Golf RR 1
Saint Bruno, QC J3V 4P6, Canada

Savary, Jerome (Director)
1 Place du Trocadero
Paris 75116, FRANCE

Savchenko, Arkadly M (Opera Singer)
Minsk 220002, BELARUS

Save Ferris (Music Group)
c/o Staff Member *Epic Records Group*
550 Madison Ave Fl 6
New York, NY 10022-3211, USA

Saveleva, Lyudmila M (Actor)
Tverskaya Str 19 #76
Moscow 103050, RUSSIA

Saverine, Bob (Athlete, Baseball Player)
228 Slice Dr
Stamford, CT 06907-1137, USA

Saverson, Henry (Baseball Player)
1726 Benjamin Ave NE
Grand Rapids, MI 49505-5434, USA

Saves the Day (Music Group)
c/o Jeff Hanson *Jeff Hanson Management & Promotions*
2813 S Hiawassee Rd Ste 307
Orlando, FL 32835-6690, USA

Savident, John (Actor)
c/o Staff Member *Coronation Street*
Granada Television Quay Street
Manchester M60 9EA, UNITED KINGDOM (UK)

Savidge, Jennifer (Actor)
c/o Staff Member *TalentWorks (LA)*
3500 W Olive Ave Ste 1400
Burbank, CA 91505-5512, USA

Savile, David
28 Colomb St
London, ENGLAND SW10 9EW

Saville, Curtis (Misc)
RFD Box 44
West Charleston, VT 5872, USA

Saville, Fleur (Actor)
c/o Staff Member *Auckland Actors*
PO Box 56460 Dominion Road
Auckland, NEW ZEALAND

Saville, Kathleen (Misc)
RFD Box 44
West Charleston, VT 5872, USA

Saving Jane
9423 Old Forest Ln
Loveland, OH 45140-1065, USA

Savini, Tom
311 Taylor St
Pittsburgh, PA 15224-1862

Savinykh, Viktor P (Misc)
Gorochovskii 4
Moscow 103064, RUSSIA

Savitskaya, Svetalana Y (Misc)
Khovanskaya Str 3
Moscow 129515, RUSSIA

Savitsky, George M (Athlete, Football Player)
350 E Seabright Rd
Ocean City, NJ 08226-4505, USA

Savitt, Dick
19 E 80th St
New York, NY 10075-0117

Savitt, Richard (Dick) (Tennis Player)
19 E 80th St
New York, NY 10075-0117, USA

Savoretti, Jack (Musician)
c/o Michael Moses *Baker Winokur Ryder Public Relations (BWR-LA)*
9100 Wilshire Blvd Ste 500 PMB WEST
Beverly Hills, CA 90212-3426, USA

Savoy, Gene
PO Box 3279
Reno, NV 89505-3279

Savoy, Guy (Chef)
101 Blvd Pereire
Paris 75017, FRANCE

Savransky, Moe (Athlete, Baseball Player)
128 Dorset D
Boca Raton, FL 33434-3076, USA

Savre, Danielle (Actor)
c/o Adam Griffin *Kritzer Levine Wilkins Entertainment*
11872 La Grange Ave Fl 1
Los Angeles, CA 90025-5283, USA

Savvina, Iya S (Actor)
Grunzinskaya St 12 #43
Moscow 123242, RUSSIA

Saw, Maung (General, Prime Minister)
Yangon, MYANMAR

Sawa, Devon (Actor)
c/o Brian Wilkins *Kritzer Levine Wilkins Entertainment*
11872 La Grange Ave Fl 1
Los Angeles, CA 90025-5283, USA

Sawalha, Julia (Actor)
Drury House 34-43 Russell St
London WC2B 5HA, UNITED KINGDOM (UK)

Sawalha, Nadia (Talk Show Host)
Broadcasting House Portland Place
London, UK W1A 1AA

Sawallisch, Wolfgang (Conductor, Musician)
Hinterm Bichi 2
Grassau 83224, GERMANY

Sawyer, Alan (Athlete, Basketball Player)
117 San Juan Dr
Sequim, WA 98382-9326, USA

Sawyer, Amos (President)
Executive Mansion PO Box 9001
Monrovia, LIBERIA

Sawyer, Charles H (Misc)
466 Tuallitan Rd
Los Angeles, CA 90049-1941, USA

Sawyer, Daine (Correspondent)
147 Columbus Ave # 300
New York, NY 10023-6503, USA

Sawyer, Diane (Television Host)
77 W 66th St
New York, NY 10023-6201, USA

Sawyer, Elton (Race Car Driver)
185 McKenzie Rd
Mooresville, NC 28115-7976, USA

Sawyer, Forrest (Correspondent)
30 Rockefeller Plz
New York, NY 10112-0015, USA

Sawyer, James L (Misc)
11 Peabody Sq
Peabody, MA 01960-5600, USA

Sawyer, John (Athlete, Football Player)
23637 Sunnyside Ln
Zachary, LA 70791-6118, USA

Sawyer, Ken (Athlete, Football Player)
667 Violet Ave Lot 36
Hyde Park, NY 12538-1951, USA

Sawyer, Mary Jane (Stylist)
c/o Staff Member *Ennis*
119 Braintree St
Boston, MA 02134-1628, USA

Sawyer, Paul (Race Car Driver)
PO Box 9257
Richmond, VA 23227-0257, USA

Sawyer, Rick (Athlete, Baseball Player)
1201 Calle Extrano
Bakersfield, CA 93309-7116, USA

Sawyer, Robert E (Religious Leader)
459 S Church St
Winston Salem, NC 27101-5314, USA

Sawyer, Talance (Athlete, Football Player)
6150 Brookhaven Dr
Bastrop, LA 71220-1878, USA

Sawyer Brown (Music Group)
c/o Staff Member *Paradigm (Nashville)*
124 12th Ave S Ste 410
Nashville, TN 37203-3170, USA

Sax, Dave (Athlete, Baseball Player)
3352 Eaton Dr
Roseville, CA 95661-7907, USA

Sax, Stephen L (Steve) (Athlete, Baseball Player)
201 Wesley Ct
Roseville, CA 95661-7913, USA

Sax, Steve
201 Wesley Ct
Roseville, CA 95661-7913

Saxbe, William H (Attorney, Attorney General, General, Senator)
4600 N Ocean Blvd Ste 200
Boynton Beach, FL 33435-7365, USA

Saxe, Adrian (Artist)
4835 N Figueroa St
Los Angeles, CA 90042-4408, USA

Saxon, David S (Physicist)
1008 Hilts Ave
Los Angeles, CA 90024-3215, USA

Saxon, Edward (Producer)
c/o Staff Member *Creative Artists Agency (CAA-LA)*
2000 Avenue of the Stars Ste 100
Los Angeles, CA 90067-4705, USA

Saxon, James E (Athlete, Football Player)
RR 3 Box 34X
Beaufort, SC 29906, USA

Saxon, James E (Jimmy) (Athlete, Football Player)
1 Mulberry Ln
West Lake Hills, TX 78746-4321, USA

Saxon, John (Actor)
2432 Banyan Dr
Los Angeles, CA 90049-1240, USA

Saxon, Mike (Athlete, Football Player)
660 W Peninsula Dr
Coppell, TX 75019-6801, USA

Saxton, Brian (Athlete, Football Player)
3604 Tudor Dr
Pompton Plains, NJ 07444-1141, USA

Saxton, Jimmy (Athlete, Football Player)
1 Mulberry Ln
West Lake Hills, TX 78746-4321, USA

Saxton, Johnny (Boxer)
1710 4th Ave N
Lake Worth, FL 33460-2874, USA

Saxton, Shirley Childress (Music Group, Musician)
PO Box 600099
Newtonville, MA 02460-0001, USA

Say, Peggy
438 Lake Shore Dr
Cadiz, KY 42211

Sayed, Mostafa Amr El (Misc)
579 Westover Dr NW
Atlanta, GA 30305-3537, USA

Sayer, Leo (Music Group, Musician, Songwriter, Writer)
Business Center Lower Road
London SE16 2XB, UNITED KINGDOM (UK)

Sayers, E Roger (Educator)
President S Ofc
Tuscaloosa, AL 35487-0001, USA

Sayers, Gale (Athlete, Football Player)
852 Coving Dr
Lawrence, KS 66049-7846, USA

Saykally, Richard J (Misc)
Chemistry Dept Latimer Hall
Berkeley, CA 94720-0001, USA

Sayles, John (Director)
210 13th St
Hoboken, NJ 07030-4435, USA

Sayre, Anne
1268 E 14th St
Brooklyn, NY 11230-5241

Sazio, Ralph (Athlete, Football Player)
4005 Gulf Shore Blvd N Apt 1107
Naples, FL 34103-2674, USA

Sbarge, Raphael (Actor)
c/o Tracy Steinsapir *Main Title Entertainment*
2225 Wilshire Blvd Suite 500
Los Angeles, CA 90036, USA

Sbranti, Ron (Athlete, Football Player)
2925 Roosevelt Ln
Antioch, CA 94509-5040, USA

Scaasi, Arnold (Designer, Fashion Designer)
16 E 52nd St
New York, NY 10022-5306, USA

Scacchi, Greta (Actor)
c/o Susan Smith *Susan Smith Company, The*
1344 N Wetherly Dr
Los Angeles, CA 90069-1817, USA

Scaduto, Al (Cartoonist)
571 Swanson Cres
Milford, CT 06461-2735, USA

Scadyac, Tom (Director)
c/o Staff Member *Creative Artists Agency (CAA-LA)*
2000 Avenue of the Stars Ste 100
Los Angeles, CA 90067-4705, USA

Scafa, Bob (Baseball Player)
2090 Milton Ave
Park Ridge, IL 60068-2320, USA

Scaggs, Boz (Musician)
9460 Wilshire Blvd Ste 310
Beverly Hills, CA 90212-2710

Scaggs, William R (Boz) (Music Group, Musician, Songwriter, Writer)
c/o Staff Member *HK Management (LA)*
10866 Wilshire Blvd Ste 200
Los Angeles, CA 90024-4350, USA

Scagliotti-Smith, Allison (Actor)
c/o Staff Member *Osbrink Talent Agency*
4343 Lankershim Blvd Ste 100
West Toluca Lake, CA 91602-2705, USA

Scales, Charlie (Athlete, Football Player)
4035 Vistaview St
West Mifflin, PA 15122-2134, USA

Scales, Dwight (Athlete, Football Player)
6112 Roosevelt Cir NW
Huntsville, AL 35810-1634, USA

Scales, Greg (Athlete, Football Player)
4118 Carnation Dr
Winston Salem, NC 27105-3219, USA

Scales, Hurles (Athlete, Football Player)
600 N Adams St
Amarillo, TX 79107-5068, USA

Scales, Prunella (Actor)
18-21 Jermyn St
London SW1Y 6NB, UNITED KINGDOM (UK)

Scalia, Jack (Actor)
c/o Alan Ellsweig *Shadow Entertainment*
10 Universal City Plz Fl 20
Universal City, CA 91608-1074, USA

Scalia, Justice Antonin (Judge)
1 1st St NE
Washington, DC 20543-0001, USA

Scalia, Pietro (Actor, Director, Editor, Producer)
c/o Spyros Skouras *The Skouras Agency*
1149 3rd St Ste 300
Santa Monica, CA 90403-7201, USA

Scalians, Bret (Musician)
3005 Brodhead Read # 170
Bethlehem, PA 18020, USA

Scalzitti, Will (Baseball Player)
19321 SW 61st St
Ft Lauderdale, FL 33332-3354, USA

Scalzo, Tony (Musician)
c/o Staff Member *Russell Carter Artist Management*
567 Ralph McGill Blvd NE
Atlanta, GA 30312-1110, USA

Scaminace, Joseph M (Business Person)
101 W Prospect Ave
Cleveland, OH 44115-1093, USA

Scancarelli, Jim (Cartoonist)
PO Box 1892
Santa Rosa, CA 95402-1892, USA

Scandiuzzi, Roberto (Opera Singer)
Maximilianstr 22
Munich 80539, GERMANY

Scanga, Italo (Artist)
7127 Olivetas Ave
La Jolla, CA 92037-5332, USA

Scanlan, Bob (Athlete, Baseball Player)
19546 Dorado Dr
Trabuco Canyon, CA 92679-1612, USA

Scanlan, Hugh P S (Misc)
23 Seven Stones Dr Broadstairs
Kent, UNITED KINGDOM (UK)

Scanlon, Pat (Athlete, Baseball Player)
7400 Portland Ave
Minneapolis, MN 55423-4343, USA

Scarbath, John C (Jack) (Athlete, Football Player)
736 Calvert Rd
Rising Sun, MD 21911-2332, USA

Scarber, Sam (Athlete, Football Player)
12209 Crewe St
North Hollywood, CA 91605-5609, USA

Scarbery, Randy (Athlete, Baseball Player)
5010 E Lewis Ave
Fresno, CA 93727-2418, USA

Scarborough, Joe (Senator, Television Host)
c/o Staff Member *ABC Television Network (NY)*
147 Columbus Ave
New York, NY 10023-5999, USA

Scarborough, Jon (Television Host)
c/o Staff Member *MSNBC (NJ)*
NBC/One Microsoft Corporation 1 MSNC Plaza
Secaucus, NJ 7094, USA

Scarbrough, W Carl (Misc)
1910 Air Lane Dr
Nashville, TN 37210-3810, USA

Scarce, Mac (Athlete, Baseball Player)
1010 Richmond Glen Cir
Alpharetta, GA 30004-8216, USA

Scardelletti, Robert A (Misc)
3 Research Pl
Rockville, MD 20850-3279, USA

Scardino, Albert J (Journalist)
19 Empire House Thurloe Place
London SW7 2RU, UNITED KINGDOM (UK)

Scarf, Herbert E (Economist)
88 Blake Rd
Hamden, CT 06517-3402, USA

Scarf, Maggie (Writer)
c/o Camille McDuffie *Goldberg McDuffie Communications*
250 Park Ave Fl 7
New York, NY 10177-0799, USA

Scarface (Musician)
c/o Staff Member *American Talent Agency*
248 W 35th St Rm 501
New York, NY 10001-2505, USA

Scarfe, Gerald A (Cartoonist)
10 Cheyne Walk
London SW3, UNITED KINGDOM (UK)

Scarfe, Jonathan
4739 Lankershim Blvd
North Hollywood, CA 91602-1803

Scargill, Arthur (Misc)
2 Huddersfield Road
Barnsley, UNITED KINGDOM (UK)

Scarpati, Joseph H (Athlete, Football Player)
32 Lexington Cir
Marlton, NJ 08053-3860, USA

Scarpelli, Glenn
3480 Barham Blvd Apt 320
Los Angeles, CA 90068-1469

Scarpitto, Bob (Athlete, Football Player)
117 White Oaks Ln
Carmel Valley, CA 93924-9650, USA

Scarry, Mike (Athlete, Football Player)
7430 Lake Breeze Dr Apt 104
Fort Myers, FL 33907-8058, USA

Scarsone, Steve (Athlete, Baseball Player)
3935 E Rough Rdr Rd Unit 1158
Phoenix, AZ 85050-7356, USA

Scarwid, Diana (Actor)
PO Box 3614
Savannah, GA 31414-3614, USA

Scates, Al (Coach, Volleyball Player)
Athletic Dept - Volleyball J.D. Morgan Center, P.O. Box 24044
Los Angeles, CA 90024, USA

Scattini, Monica (Actor)
Via Giuseppe Pisanelli
Rome 196, ITALY

Scelba-Shorte, Mercedes (Reality TV Star)
c/o Staff Member *Ty Ty Baby Productions*
8346 W 3rd St # 650
Los Angeles, CA 90048-4311, USA

Schaaf-Behle, Petra
Am Rodeland 22
Willingen, GERMANY D-34508

Schaal, Paul (Athlete, Baseball Player)
681962 Puu Nui St
Waikoloa, HI 96738-5238, USA

Schaal, Richard (Actor)
612 Gulf Blvd # 9
Indian Rocks Beach, FL 33785-2950, USA

Schaal, Wendy (Actor)
14724 Ventura Blvd Ste 505
Sherman Oaks, CA 91403-3505, USA

Schaap, Dick
77 W 66th St
New York, NY 10023-6201

Schabarum, Pete (Athlete, Football Player)
46170 E Eldorado Dr
Indian Wells, CA 92210-8633, USA

Schacher, Mel (Musician)
PO Box 770850
Orlando, FL 32877-0850, USA

Schachman, Howard K (Biologist)
Molecular Biology
Berkeley, CA 94720-0001, USA

Schachnow, Eddie (Stylist)
c/o Staff Member *Celestine - CA*
1666 20th St Ste 200B
Santa Monica, CA 90404-3828, USA

Schacht, Henry B (Business Person)
600 Mountain Ave
New Providence, NJ 07974-2008, USA

Schachter, Blanche (Baseball Player)
163 W 18th St Apt 3A
New York, NY 10011-4144, USA

Schachter, Steven (Director, Writer)
c/o Staff Member *Ken Gross Management*
12135 Stanwood Dr
Los Angeles, CA 90066-1052, USA

Schachter Sisters
182-06 Midland Park Blvd
Jamaica Estates, NY 11432

Schacker, Hal (Athlete, Baseball Player)
4609 N Matanzas Ave
Tampa, FL 33614-6652, USA

Schade, Frank (Athlete, Basketball Player)
826 Nicolet Ave
Oshkosh, WI 54901, USA

Schade, Molly (Actor)
c/o Aron Giannini *Collective*
8383 Wilshire Blvd Ste 1050
Beverly Hills, CA 90211-2415, USA

Schadler, Jay (Correspondent)
c/o Staff Member *Primetime*
147 Columbus Ave
New York, NY 10023-6503, USA

Schadt, James P (Publisher)
Readers Digest Rd
Pleasantville, NY 10570-7001, USA

Schaech, Johnathon (Actor, Producer, Writer)
c/o Eli Selden *Anonymous Content (AC-LA)*
3531 Hayden Ave
Culver City, CA 90232, USA

Schaefer, Bob (Athlete, Baseball Player, Coach)
9070 Old Hickory Cir
Fort Myers, FL 33912-6844, USA

Schaefer, Don (Athlete, Football Player)
286 Birch Pkwy
Wyckoff, NJ 07481-2831, USA

Schaefer, Ernst J (Scientist)
Nutrition Research Center
Medford, MA 2155, USA

Schaefer, George A Jr (Financier)
38 Fountain Square Plz
Cincinnati, OH 45202-3102, USA

Schaefer, Henry F III (Misc)
Computational Quantum Chemistry Ctr
Athens, GA 30602-0001, USA

Schaefer, Jeff (Athlete, Baseball Player)
2110 Woodbend Trl
Fort Mill, SC 29708-8343, USA

Schaefer, Roberto (Cinematographer)
1505 10th St
Santa Monica, CA 90401-2805, USA

Schaefer, Yvonne Maria (Actor, Producer)
343 E 76th St
New York, NY 10021-2404, USA

Schaeffer, Danny (Athlete, Baseball Player)
3400 E Palm Valley Blvd Attn Coachingstaff
Round Rock, TX 78665-3906, USA

Schaeffer, Eric (Actor, Director)
c/o Norman Aladjem *Paradigm (LA)*
360 N Crescent Dr
Beverly Hills, CA 90210-4874, USA

Schaeffer, George
1040 Woodland Dr
Beverly Hills, CA 90210-2936

Schaeffer, Harry (Athlete, Baseball Player)
5000 Mcintyre Cir
Austin, TX 78734-1818, USA

Schaeffer, Leonard (Business Person)
1 Wellpoint Way
Westlake Village, CA 91362-3893, USA

Schaeffer, Mark (Athlete, Baseball Player)
18261 Parthenia St
Northridge, CA 91325-3303, USA

Schaefzel, John R (Writer)
2 Bay Tree Ln
Bethesda, MD 20816-1046, USA

Schaffel, Lewis (Basketball Player, Misc)
601 Biscayne Blvd
Miami, FL 33132-1801, USA

Schaffer, Akiva (Director, Editor, Writer)
c/o Staff Member *Mosaic Media Group*
9200 W Sunset Blvd Ste 10
Los Angeles, CA 90069-3608, USA

Schaffer, Eric (Music Group, Musician)
Washington, DC 20011, USA

Schaffer, Jimmie (Athlete, Baseball Player)
655 Birch Ter
Coopersburg, PA 18036-2407, USA

Schaffermoth, Joe (Athlete, Baseball Player)
20 Marion Ave
Berkeley Heights, NJ 07922-1260, USA

Schafrath, Dick (Athlete, Football Player)
704 Ashland Rd
Mansfield, OH 44905-2536, USA

Schaive, Johnny (Athlete, Baseball Player)
8000 Wilson Ter
Springfield, IL 62712-8952, USA

Schalder, Ben (Athlete, Basketball Player)
808 Bauer Dr
San Carlos, CA 94070-3614, USA

Schall, Alvin A (Judge)
717 Madison Pl NW
Washington, DC 20439-0001, USA

Schall, Benny (Athlete, Basketball Player)
4305 Robinhood Ln
Toledo, OH 43623-2537, USA

Schall, Gene (Athlete, Baseball Player)
1582 Bromley Dr
Harleysville, PA 19438-3056, USA

Schaller, George B (Biologist)
90 Sentry Hill Rd
Roxbury, CT 06783 1306, USA

Schaller, Willie (Soccer Player)
3283 S Indiana St
Lakewood, CO 80228-5499, USA

Schallert, William (Actor)
14920 Ramos Pl
Pacific Palisades, CA 90272-4460, USA

Schallock, Art (Athlete, Baseball Player)
749 Crocus Dr
Sonoma, CA 95476-8325, USA

Schally, Andrew V (Nobel Prize Laureate)
3801 Collins Ave
Miami Beach, FL 33140-3705, USA

Schama, Simon M (Historian, Writer)
Adolphus Hall
Cambridge, MA 2138, USA

Schamehorn, Kevin (Athlete, Hockey Player)
5536 Stoney Brook Rd
Kalamazoo, MI 49009-7703

Schanberg, Sydney H (Journalist)
PO Box 236
Rifton, NY 12471-0236, USA

Schank, Roger C (Doctor, Scientist)
Learning Sciences Institute
Evanston, IL 60201, USA

Schankweiler, Scott (Athlete, Football Player)
11 Bartley Ct
Nottingham, MD 21236-2428, USA

Schanz, Heidi (Actor)
232 N Canon Dr
Beverly Hills, CA 90210-5302, USA

Schapker, Alison (Producer, Writer)
c/o Ilan Breil *Mosaic Media Group*
9200 W Sunset Blvd Ste 10
Los Angeles, CA 90069-3608, USA

Schapp, Dick (Sportscaster)
Sports Dept ESPN Plaza 935 Middle St
Bristol, CT 6010, USA

Schar, Dwight (Business Person)
7601 Lewinsville Rd Ste 300
McLean, VA 22102-2835, USA

Scharansky, Natan (Activist, Scientist)
30 Rehov Agron
Jerusalem 91002, ISRAEL

Scharar, Erich (Athlete)
Grutstrasse 63
Herrliberg 8074, SWITZERLAND

Scharping, Rudolf (Government Official)
Wilhelmstr 5
Lahnstein 56112, GERMANY

Schattinger, Jeff (Athlete, Baseball Player)
PO Box 134
Lake Arrowhead, CA 92352-0134, USA

Schatz, Albert (Biologist)
Research/Endowment Foundation
New Brunswick, NJ 8903, USA

Schatz, Gottfried (Biologist, Misc)
Klingelbergstr 70
Basle 4056, SWITZERLAND

Schatz, Howard (Photographer)
435 W Broadway Fl 2
New York, NY 10012-5902, USA

Schatzberg, Jerry N (Director)
c/o Staff Member *International Creative Management (ICM-LA)*
10250 Constellation Blvd Fl 7
Los Angeles, CA 90067-6207, USA

Schatzeder, Dan (Athlete, Baseball Player)
186 River Mist Dr
Oswego, IL 60543-8358, USA

Schatzman, Evry (Physicist)
11 Rue de l'Eglise Domplerre
Maignelay-Montigny 60420, FRANCE

Schaudt, Martin (Athlete, Horse Racer)
Gerhardstr 10/2
Albstadt 72461, GERMANY

Schaufuss, Peter (Ballerina, Director)
18 Sundial Ave
London SE25 4BX, UNITED KINGDOM (UK)

Schaum, Greg (Athlete, Football Player)
4303 Piney Park Rd
Perry Hall, MD 21128-9524, USA

Schauman, Wilhelm (Athlete, Golfer)
c/o Jim Lehrman *SFX Golf*
36855 W Main St Ste 200
Purcellville, VA 20132-3561, USA

Schaus, Fred (Athlete, Basketball Player)
2024 Georgian Ln
Morgantown, WV 26508-4514, USA

Schayes, Adolph (Dolph) (Athlete, Basketball Player)
PO Box 156
Syracuse, NY 13214-0156, USA

Schayes, Danny (Athlete, Basketball Player)
7035 E Berneil Dr
Paradise Valley, AZ 85253-1944, USA

Scheck, Barry (Attorney, Attorney General, Educator, General)
55 5th Ave
New York, NY 10003-4301, USA

Scheckter, Jody D (Race Car Driver)
39 Ave Princess Grace
Monte Carlo, MONACO

Schecter, Wendy (Stylist)
20 W 27th St Apt 2
New York, NY 10001-6917, USA

Schectman, Ossie (Athlete, Basketball Player)
1332 High Point Pl N Apt A
Delray Beach, FL 33445-1529, USA

Schedeen, Anne (Actor)
c/o Tom Markley *Metropolitan Talent Group*
4526 Wilshire Blvd Fl 3
Los Angeles, CA 90010-3801, USA

Scheer-Demme, Amanda (Business Person, Producer)
c/o Staff Member *Thrive Music*
1024 N Orange Dr
Los Angeles, CA 90038-2336, USA

Scheetz, Larry (Athlete, Football Player)
3175 Grape Bay
Doylestown, PA 18902-1708, USA

Scheffer, Aaron (Athlete, Baseball Player)
1351 Sharon St
Westland, MI 48186-5044, USA

Scheffer, Victor B (Biologist)
14806 SE 54th St
Bellevue, WA 98006-3522, USA

Scheffler, Israel (Misc)
Larsen Hall
Cambridge, MA 2138, USA

Scheffler, Tony (Football Player)
c/o Staff Member *Denver Broncos*
13655 Broncos Pkwy
Englewood, CO 80112-4151, USA

Schefft, Jen (Reality TV Star)
3650 N Magnolia Ave
Chicago, IL 60613-3821, USA

Scheib, Carl (Athlete, Baseball Player)
2922 Old Ranch Rd
San Antonio, TX 78217-5858, USA

Scheibel, Arnold B (Doctor)
16231 Morrison St
Encino, CA 91436-1331, USA

Scheid, Rich (Athlete, Baseball Player)
1 Hancock Ct
East Windsor, NJ 08520-2722, USA

Scheimer, Lou (Producer)
18918 La Montana Pl
Tarzana, CA 91356-4819, USA

Schein, Philip S (Doctor)
6212 Robinwood Rd
Bethesda, MD 20817-6115, USA

Scheinblum, Richie (Athlete, Baseball Player)
1308 Woodstock Dr
Palm Harbor, FL 34684-2246, USA

Schekman, Randy W (Scientist)
4000 Jones Bridge Rd
Chevy Chase, MD 20815-6720, USA

Schell, Catherine (Actor)
Postfach 800504
Cologne 51005, GERMANY

Schell, Jonathan (Journalist)
235 Pinelawn Rd
Melville, NY 11747-4226, USA

Schell, Jozef S (Biologist, Scientist)
11 Pl Marcelin-Berthelot
Paris Cedex 05 75231, FRANCE

Schell, Maximilian (Actor)
16501 Ventura Blvd Ste 304
Encino, CA 91436-2067, USA

Schell, Maximillian (Actor, Director, Writer)
c/o Staff Member *The Blake Agency*
23441 Malibu Colony Rd
Malibu, CA 90265-4640, USA

Schell, Ronnie
4741 Laurel Canyon Blvd Ste 101
Valley Village, CA 91607-5905, USA

Schellenbach, Kate (Musician)
2 Penn Plz # 2600
New York, NY 10121-0101, USA

Schellenberg, August (Actor)
3500 W Olive Ave Ste 1400
Burbank, CA 91505-5512, USA

Schellhase, Dave (Athlete, Basketball Player)
PO Box 48482
Tampa, FL 33646-0121, USA

Schelling, Gunther F K (Engineer)
Rechbauerstr 12
Graz 8010, AUSTRIA

Schelling, Thomas C (Economist)
Economics
College Park, MD 20742-0001, USA

Schellman, John A (Misc)
65 W 30th Ave # 508
Eugene, OR 97405-3373, USA

Schelmerding, Kirk (Race Car Driver)
PO Box 1189
Welcome, NC 27374-1189, USA

Schemansky, Norbert (Misc)
24826 New York St
Dearborn, MI 48124-4485, USA

Schembechler, Bo
13684 Random Ridge Vw
Colorado Springs, CO 80921-7209

Schembechler, Glenn E (Bo) Jr (Athlete, Coach, Football Player)
13684 Random Ridge Vw
Colorado Springs, CO 80921-7209, USA

Schemling, Bill
PO Box 11308
Portland, OR 97211-0308

Schenert, Turk (Athlete, Football Player)
239 Willow Ave
Pompton Lakes, NJ 07442-2443, USA

Schenk, Franziska (Speed Skater)
Mensinger Str 68
Munich 80992, GERMANY

Schenkenberg, Markus (Actor, Model)
c/o Maury DiMauro *Innovative Artists (LA)*
235 Park Ave S Fl 10
New York, NY 10003-1404, USA

Schenker, Nathan (Athlete, Football Player)
5 Conover Xing
Fairport, NY 14450-8979, USA

Schenkkan, Robert F (Writer)
1501 Broadway Ste 701
New York, NY 10036-5505, USA

Schenkman, Eric (Musician)
84 Riverside Dr
New York, NY 10024-5723, USA

Schepisi, Fred (Director)
c/o Staff Member *WmE2 (WMA-LA)*
1 William Morris Pl
Beverly Hills, CA 90212-4261, USA

Schepisl, Frederic A (Director)
159 Eastern Rd
South Melbourne, VIC 3205, AUSTRALIA

Scherbarth, Bob (Athlete, Baseball Player)
PO Box 2337
Eagle River, WI 54521-2337, USA

Scherbo, Vitali (Gymnast)
8308 Aqua Spray Ave
Las Vegas, NV 89128-7432, USA

Scherbo, Vitaly
8308 Aqua Spray Ave
Las Vegas, NV 89128-7432

Scherega, Harold A (Misc)
223 Savage Farm Dr
Ithaca, NY 14850-6501, USA

Scherer, Bernard (Athlete, Football Player)
PO Box 5201
Carmel By The Sea, CA 93921-5201, USA

Scherfig, Lone (Director)
c/o Jodi Shields *Casarotto Ramsay & Associates Ltd (UK)*
Waverley House 7-12 Noel St
London W1F 8GQ, UK

Scherman, Fred (Athlete, Baseball Player)
7454 S Tipp Cowlesville Rd
Tipp City, OH 45371-8351, USA

Scherrer, Bill (Athlete, Baseball Player)
4155 E Rockledge Rd
Phoenix, AZ 85044-6770, USA

Scherrer, Jean-Louis (Designer, Fashion Designer)
51 Ave du Montaigne
Paris 75008, FRANCE

Scherza, Chuck (Athlete, Hockey Player)
51 Manistee St
Pawtucket, RI 02861-4011

Scherzinger, Nicole (Actor, Musician)
c/o Brit Reece *PMK/BNC Public Relations (PMK-LA)*
8687 Melrose Ave Ste 8
West Hollywood, CA 90069-5746, USA

Scheuer, Paul J (Misc)
3271 Melemele Pl
Honolulu, HI 96822-1431, USA

Scheuring, Paul (Director)
c/o Adam Berkowitz *Creative Artists Agency (CAA-LA)*
2000 Avenue of the Stars Ste 100
Los Angeles, CA 90067-4705, USA

Scheve, Carin (Stylist)
c/o Staff Member *ESP (London)*
63 Charlotte St. 1st Floor
London W11 4PG, UK

Schevill, James (Writer)
1309 Oxford St
Berkeley, CA 94709-1424, USA

Schiavo, Mary (Activist, Government Official)
Public Policy Dept
Columbus, OH 43210, USA

Schickel, Richard (Critic, Writer)
9051 Dicks St
Los Angeles, CA 90069-4808, USA

Schickele, Peter (Comedian, Composer)
40 W 57th St # 1800
New York, NY 10019-4001, USA

Schiebold, Hans (Artist)
13705 SW 118th Ct
Tigard, OR 97223-2857, USA

Schieffer, Bob (Correspondent, Television Host)
CBS 2020 Main St NW
Washington, DC 20036-3304, USA

Schierholtz, Nate (Athlete, Baseball Player)
7500 E Deer Valley Rd Unit 118
Scottsdale, AZ 85255-4867, USA

Schiff, Andras (Musician)
711 W End Ave Apt 5KN
New York, NY 10025-0100, USA

Schiff, Heinrich (Musician)
Monckegergallee 41
Hannover 30453, GERMANY

Schiff, John J Jr (Financier)
6200 S Gilmore Rd
Fairfield, OH 45014-5141, USA

Schiff, Mark (Actor, Comedian)
1025 N Kings Rd Apt 113
Los Angeles, CA 90069-6007, USA

Schiff, Richard (Actor, Director)
c/o Michael Garnett *Leverage Management*
3030 Pennsylvania Ave
Santa Monica, CA 90404-4112, USA

Schiff, Robin (Writer)
c/o Staff Member *Broder Webb Chervin Silbermann Agency, The (BWCS)*
10250 Constellation Blvd
Los Angeles, CA 90067-6200, USA

Schiffer, Claudia (Model)
c/o Duncan Heath *Independent Talent Group (ITG-UK)*
Oxford House 76 Oxford St
London W1D 1BS, UK

Schiffer, Eric (Writer)
6965 El Camino Real Ste 105 PMB 517
Carlsbad, CA 92009-4101

Schiffer, Menahem M (Mathematician)
6404 Ruffin Rd
Chevy Chase, MD 20815-5323, USA

Schiffer, Michael (Actor)
c/o David Greenblatt *Key Creatives*
1800 N Highland Ave Fl 5
Los Angeles, CA 90028-4523, USA

Schiffner, Travis (Actor)
c/o Staff Member *Bohemia Group*
1680 Vine St Ste 216
Los Angeles, CA 90028-8829, USA

Schifrin, Lalo (Composer)
710 N Hillcrest Rd
Beverly Hills, CA 90210-3517, USA

Schiller, Harvey W (Misc)
1050 Techwood Dr NW
Atlanta, GA 30318-5604, USA

Schiller, Lawrence J (Director, Writer)
10 W End Ave Apt 30B
New York, NY 10023-7939, USA

Schilling, Chuck (Athlete, Baseball Player)
907 Caroline Ct
New Bern, NC 28560-1804, USA

Schilling, Curtis (Curt) M (Athlete, Baseball Player)
7 Woodridge Rd
Medfield, MA 02052-2526, USA

Schilling, Peter
Geiselgasteigstr. 76
Munich, GERMANY 81545

Schilling, William
626 N Valley St
Burbank, CA 91505-3147

Schimberg, Henry R (Business Person)
2500 Windy Ridge Pkwy SE
Atlanta, GA 30339-5677, USA

Schimberni, Mario (Business Person)
Via IV Novembre
Rome 187, ITALY

Schimmel, Paul R (Biologist, Misc)
10550 N Torrey Pines Rd
La Jolla, CA 92037-1000, USA

Schindelholz, Lorenz (Athlete)
Hardstr 184
Herbetswil 4715, SWITZERLAND

Schindler, Steve (Athlete, Football Player)
6109 Willow Springs Dr
Morrison, CO 80465-2133, USA

Schinkel, Kenneth (Ken) (Athlete, Hockey Player)
19927 Beaulieu Ct
Fort Myers, FL 33908-4832, USA

Schino, Dominic (Producer)
c/o Staff Member *Magic Touch Records*
12-15 36th Ave # 4-E
Long Island City, NY 11106, USA

Schipper, Ron (Coach, Football Coach)
1088 Fountain View Cir Unit 1
Holland, MI 49423-5620, USA

Schiraldi, Calvin (Athlete, Baseball Player)
9108 Tweed Berwick Dr
Austin, TX 78750-3554, USA

Schirinowskij, Wladmir
Sokolnitscheskij wal 38-114
Moscow, RUSSIA 107113

Schirmacher, Carolyn (Stylist)
3307 SW Dosch Rd
Portland, OR 97239-1423, USA

Schirripa, Steve (Actor)
c/o Brad Stokes *Kass & Stokes Management*
9229 W Sunset Blvd Ste 504
Los Angeles, CA 90069-3405, USA

Schisgal, Murray J (Writer)
40 W 57th St # 1800
New York, NY 10019-4001, USA

Schissler, Les (Bowler)
3060 E Bridge St Lot 20
Brighton, CO 80601-2718, USA

Schlafly, Phyllis (Activist)
68 Fairmont Ave
Alton, IL 62002, USA

Schlag, Edward W (Misc)
Osterwaldstr 91
Munich 80805, GERMANY

Schlamme, Thomas (Actor)
c/o Rosalie Swedlin *Anonymous Content (AC-LA)*
3531 Hayden Ave
Culver City, CA 90232, USA

Schlatmann, Gert Jan
Oostzeedijk Gen 39a
Rotterdam, HOLLAND NL 3062 WK

Schlatter, Charlie (Actor)
638 Lindero Canyon Rd # 322
Oak Park, CA 91377-5457, USA

Schlatter, George
400 Robert Ln
Beverly Hills, CA 90210-2632

Schleech, Russ (Misc)
21634 Paseo Maravia
Mission Viejo, CA 92692-4963, USA

Schlegel, Hans W (Astronaut)
DLR Astronaulenburo Linder Hohe
Postfach 906058
Cologne 51140, GERMANY

Schlegel, John P (Educator)
President's Office
San Francisco, CA 94117, USA

Schleich, Vic (Athlete, Football Player)
121 W Keller St
Lock Haven, PA 17745-3920, USA

Schleinzer, Markus (Director)
c/o Doug MacLaren *International Creative Management (ICM-LA)*
10250 Constellation Blvd Fl 7
Los Angeles, CA 90067-6207, USA

Schleinzer, Markus (Director)

Schlereth, Mark (Athlete, Football Player)
c/o Lou Oppenheim *Headline Media Management*
888 7th Ave Ste 503
New York, NY 10106-0501, USA

Schlesinger, Adam (Music Group, Musician, Songwriter, Writer)
6404 Wilshire Blvd Ste 505
Los Angeles, CA 90048-5507, USA

Schlesinger, Cory (Athlete, Football Player)
36 Bradford Ct
Dearborn, MI 48126-4169, USA

Schlesinger, Iliza (Comedian)
c/o Staff Member *Gersh (LA)*
9465 Wilshire Blvd Ste 600
Beverly Hills, CA 90212-2612, USA

Schlesinger, James R (Secretary)
1800 K St NW Ste 400
Washington, DC 20006-2230, USA

Schlesinger, Rudy (Athlete, Baseball Player)
5708 Abelia Ct
Cincinnati, OH 45213-2434, USA

Schlessinger, Laura (Radio Personality, Writer)
PO Box 8120
Van Nuys, CA 91409-8120, USA

Schleyer, Paul Von R (Misc)
Henkestr 41
Erlangen 91469, GERMANY

Schlichtmann, Jan (Attorney, Attorney General, General)
359 Hale St
Beverly, MA 01915-2029, USA

Schlondorff, Volker (Director)
Postfach 900361
Potsdam 14439, GERMANY

Schloredt, Robert S (Bob) (Athlete, Football Player)
1827 N 167th St
Shoreline, WA 98133-5505, USA

Schlossberg, Edwin (Writer)
Columbia Point
New York, NY 2125

Schlossberg, Katie (Actor)
6300 Wilshire Blvd Ste 2100
Los Angeles, CA 90048-5282, USA

Schlossberg, Katle (Actor)
5670 Wilshire Blvd Ste 820
Los Angeles, CA 90036-5613, USA

Schlosser, Eric (Writer)
c/o Staff Member *Houghton Mifflin*
215 Park Ave S Fl 12
New York, NY 10003-1621, USA

Schlueter, Dale (Athlete, Basketball Player)
15555 SW Harcourt Ter
Portland, OR 97224-5234, USA

Schlueter, Jay (Athlete, Baseball Player)
5232 E Shaw Butte Dr
Scottsdale, AZ 85254-4745, USA

Schluter, Poul H (Prime Minister)
Frederiksberg Allee 66
Frederiksberg C 1820, DENMARK

Schmack, Brian (Athlete, Baseball Player)
504 E Wye Mesa
Brookings, SD 57006-4534, USA

Schmautz, Bobby
15544 SE Webster Rd
Portland, OR 97267

Schmelz, Al (Athlete, Baseball Player)
7406 E Camino Rayo De Luz
Scottsdale, AZ 85266-4295, USA

Schmid, Dave
17173 Rayen St
Northridge, CA 91325-2908

Schmid, Kyle (Actor)
c/o Norbert Abrams *Noble Caplan Abrams*
1260 Yonge St 2nd Floor
Toronto ON M4T 1W6, Canada

Schmid, Rudi (Misc)
211 Woodland Rd
Kentfield, CA 94904-2631, USA

Schmid, Sigi (Coach, Soccer Player)
1010 Rose Bowl Dr
Pasadena, CA 91103, USA

Schmidgall, Jennifer (Athlete, Hockey Player)
3640 Wooddale Ave S Unit 103
Minneapolis, MN 55416-5157, USA

Schmidly, David J (Educator)
President's Office
Lubbock, TX 79409, USA

Schmidt, Andreas (Opera Singer)
Fossredder 51
Hamburg 22359, GERMANY

Schmidt, Benno C Jr (Educator)
375 Park Ave
New York, NY 10152-0002, USA

Schmidt, Bob (Athlete, Football Player)
10005 Sky View Way Apt 2106
Fort Myers, FL 33913-6606, USA

Schmidt, Bob (Athlete, Baseball Player)
9 Hardwood Dr
Saint Charles, MO 63303-5942, USA

Schmidt, Curt (Athlete, Baseball Player)
4025 Chara Ln
Billings, MT 59105-5659, USA

Schmidt, Dave (Athlete, Baseball Player)
7172 N Serenoa Dr
Sarasota, FL 34241-9270, USA

Schmidt, Dave (Athlete, Baseball Player)
26636 Portales Ln
Mission Viejo, CA 92691-5122, USA

Schmidt, Eric E (Business Person, Engineer)
c/o Staff Member *Google Inc*
1600 Amphitheatre Pkwy
Mountain View, CA 94043-1351, USA

Schmidt, Freddy (Athlete, Baseball Player)
128 Constitution Ave
Wind Gap, PA 18091-1119, USA

Schmidt, Hank (Athlete, Football Player)
4641 Mission Bell Ln
La Mesa, CA 91941-5450, USA

Schmidt, Harald (Athlete, Track Athlete)
Schulstr 11
Hasselroth 63594, GERMANY

Schmidt, Helmut (Misc)
Neuberger Weg 80
Hamburg 22419, GERMANY

Schmidt, Jason D (Athlete, Baseball Player)
3134 Porter St
Enumclaw, WA 98022-3336, USA

Schmidt, Jeff (Athlete, Baseball Player)
1028 Seminole Hwy
Madison, WI 53711-3021, USA

Schmidt, John (Athlete, Football Player)
2 Mayflower Rd
Glen Head, NY 11545-3120, USA

Schmidt, Joseph P (Joe) (Athlete, Football Coach, Football Player)
226 Norcliff Dr
Bloomfield Hills, MI 48302-1556, USA

Schmidt, Kathryn (Kate) (Athlete, Track Athlete)
1008 Dexter St
Los Angeles, CA 90042-2248, USA

Schmidt, Kendall (Musician)
c/o David Eisenberg *Protege Entertainment*
710 E Angeleno Ave
Burbank, CA 91501-2213, USA

Schmidt, Kenneth (Actor)
c/o Staff Member *Coast to Coast Talent Group*
3350 Barham Blvd
Los Angeles, CA 90068-1404, USA

Schmidt, Kevin (Actor)
c/o David Eisenberg *Protege Entertainment*
710 E Angeleno Ave
Burbank, CA 91501-2213, USA

Schmidt, Maarten (Astronomer)
Astronomy
Pasadena, CA 91125-0001, USA

Schmidt, Mike (Athlete, Baseball Player)
c/o Staff Member *National Baseball Hall of Fame*
PO Box 590
Cooperstown, NY 13326-0590, USA

Schmidt, Milt (Athlete, Hockey Player)
10 Longwood Dr Unit 376
Westwood, MA 02090-1144

Schmidt, Milton C (Milt) (Athlete, Hockey Player)
10 Longwood Dr Unit 376
Westwood, MA 02090-1144, USA

Schmidt, Ole (Composer, Conductor)
Puggaardsgade 17
Copenhagen 1573, DENMARK

Schmidt, Richard (Doctor)
3400 Spruce St
Philadelphia, PA 19104-4208, USA

Schmidt, Roy (Athlete, Football Player)
1844 Highpoint Rd
Snellville, GA 30078-2802, USA

Schmidt, Stephanie (Stylist)
2901 4th St Apt 318
Santa Monica, CA 90405-5514, USA

Schmidt, Steve (Race Car Driver)
6732 Creekridge Trl
Indianapolis, IN 46256-2183, USA

Schmidt, Terry (Athlete, Football Player)
10910 Double Island Rd
Green Mountain, NC 28740-6029, USA

Schmidt, William (Bill) (Athlete, Track Athlete)
1809 Devonwood Ct
Knoxville, TN 37922-6233, USA

Schmidt, Wolfgang (Opera Singer)
Plankengasse 7
Vienna 1010, AUSTRIA

Schmidt, Wolfgang (Athlete, Track Athlete)
Birkheckenstr 116B
Stuttgart 70599, GERMANY

Schmidtmer, Christiane (Actor, Model)
Postfach 120617
Heidelberg 69067, GERMANY

Schmidt-Nielsen, Knut (Doctor)
Zoology Dept
Durham, NC 27706, USA

Schmidtt, Harrison (Ex-Senator, Senator)
PO Box 90730
Albuquerque, NM 87199-0730, USA

Schmidt-Weitzman, Violet (Baseball Player)
225 S Mill St
Mishawaka, IN 46544-2002, USA

Schmiege, Marilyn (Opera Singer)
Maximilianstr 22
Munich 80539, GERMANY

Schmiegel, Klaus K (Inventor)
4507 Staughton Dr
Indianapolis, IN 46226-3127, USA

Schmiesing, Joe (Athlete, Football Player)
19460 County 2
Sauk Centre, MN 56378-4624, USA

Schmit, Timothy B (Musician)
1325 Avenue of the Americas
New York, NY 10019-6026, USA

Schmitt, Harrison H (Jack) (Astronaut, Ex-Senator)
PO Box 90730
Albuquerque, NM 87199-0730, USA

Schmitt, John (Athlete, Football Player)
2 Mayflower Rd
Glen Head, NY 11545-3120, USA

Schmitt, Martin (Skier)
Muhleschweg 4
VA-Tannehim 78052, GERMANY

Schmitz, John A (Johnny) (Athlete, Baseball Player)
3305 Timberline Dr
Wausau, WI 54401-3766, USA

Schmock, Jonathan (Actor)
c/o Judy Orbach *Judy O Productions*
6136 Glen Holly St
Hollywood, CA 90068-2338, USA

Schmoeller, David (Director)
3910 Woodhill Ave
Las Vegas, NV 89121-6245, USA

Schmoll, Steve (Athlete, Baseball Player)
4758 Chastain Dr
Melbourne, FL 32940-1274, USA

Schnabel, Julian (Artist, Director)
c/o Bart Walker *Cinetic Management*
555 W 25th St Fl 4
New York, NY 10001-5542, USA

Schnabel, Marco (Director)
c/o Staff Member *3 Arts Entertainment Inc*
9460 Wilshire Blvd Fl 7
Beverly Hills, CA 90212-2713, USA

Schnackenberg, Roy L (Artist)
1919 N Orchard St
Chicago, IL 60614-5159, USA

Schnarch, David (Writer)
c/o Staff Member *HarperCollins Publishers*
10 E 53rd St C/O Author Mail Floor 7
New York, NY 10022, USA

Schnarre, Monika (Actor, Model)
137 N Larchmont Blvd # 259
Los Angeles, CA 90004-3704, USA

Schnebli, Dolf (Architect)
Sudstr 45
Zurich 8008, SWITZERLAND

Schneck, Dave (Athlete, Baseball Player)
3891 Lehigh Dr
Northampton, PA 18067-9771, USA

Schneck, Mike (Athlete, Football Player)
110 Three Degree Rd
Allison Park, PA 15101, USA

Schneider, Andrew (Journalist)
c/o Richard Weitz *WmE2 (Endeavor-LA)*
9601 Wilshire Blvd Fl 3
Beverly Hills, CA 90210-5219, USA

Schneider, Bernd (Race Car Driver)
Daimlerstr 1
Affalterbach 71563, GERMANY

Schneider, Bob (Musician)
c/o Paul Nugent *Rainmaker Artists*
10925 Estate Ln Ste 124
Dallas, TX 75238-5168, USA

Schneider, Brian (Athlete, Baseball Player)
203 Eagleton Lake Blvd
Palm Beach Gardens, FL 33418-8061, USA

Schneider, Dan (Producer, Writer)
c/o Staff Member *WmE2 (Endeavor-LA)*
9601 Wilshire Blvd Fl 3
Beverly Hills, CA 90210-5219, USA

Schneider, Dan (Athlete, Baseball Player)
PO Box 2421
Tubac, AZ 85646-2421, USA

Schneider, Fred (Musician, Songwriter)
c/o Staff Member *Direct Management Group*
947 N La Cienega Blvd Ste G
Los Angeles, CA 90069-4700, USA

Schneider, Helen (Musician)
c/o Staff Member *UD Promotion*
Uwe Darkow Hauptstr. 64-66
Essen-Kettwig 45219, Germany

Schneider, Helge (Actor)
Schloßstr. 33
Mülheim/Ruhr D-45468, Germany

Schneider, Howie (Cartoonist)
200 Madison Ave
New York, NY 10016-3903, USA

Schneider, Jeff (Athlete, Baseball Player)
268 Pin Oak Dr
Geneseo, IL 61254-1944, USA

Schneider, John (Actor, Musician)
c/o Steven Jensen *Independent Group, The*
6363 Wilshire Blvd Ste 115
Los Angeles, CA 90048-5734, USA

Schneider, Mathieu (Athlete, Hockey Player)
122 Cross St Apt C303
Westerly, RI 02891-2477, USA

Schneider, Paul (Actor)
c/o Jillian Fowkes *ID Public Relations (ID-LA)*
7080 Hollywood Blvd Fl 8
Los Angeles, CA 90028-6906, USA

Schneider, Rob (Actor, Comedian, Producer, Writer)
650 Cape Breton Dr
Pacifica, CA 94044-3811, USA

Schneider, Vreni (Skier)
Dorf
Elm 8767, SWITZERLAND

Schneider, William (Buzz) (Athlete, Hockey Player)
5656 Turtle Lake Rd
Shoreview, MN 55126-4769, USA

Schneider, William G (Misc)
65 Whitemart Dr # 2
Ottawa, ON K1L 8J9, CANADA

Schneiderman, David A (Editor, Publisher)
President's Office 36 Cooper Square
New York, NY 10003, USA

Schneiderman, Leon (Musician)
PO Box 540115
Waltham, MA 02454-0115, USA

Schnelker, Bob (Coach)
85 Silver Oaks Cir Apt 6102
Naples, FL 34119-4665, USA

Schnelldorfer, Manfred (Figure Skater)
Seydlitzstr 55
Munich 80993, GERMANY

Schnellenberger, Howard (Athlete, Coach, Football Coach, Football Player)
5109 N Ocean Blvd Apt G
Ocean Ridge, FL 33435-7066, USA

Schnetzer, Ben (Actor)
c/o Rhonda Price *Gersh (NY)*
41 Madison Ave
New York, NY 10010-2202, USA

Schnetzer, Stephen (Actor)
c/o Matthew Sullivan *Sullivan Talent Group*
305 W 105th St Apt 3B
New York, NY 10025-9116, USA

Schnitker, Mike (Athlete, Football Player)
PO Box 968
Conifer, CO 80433-0968, USA

Schnittker, Richard (Dick) (Athlete, Basketball Player)
203 E Las Granadas
Green Valley, AZ 85614-2233, USA

Schobel, Frank (Actor, Musician)
Wielandstrasse 6
Berlin D-12623, Germany

Schochet, Bob (Cartoonist)
6 Sunset Rd
Highland Mills, NY 10930, USA

Schock, Gina (Musician)
PO Box 720160
San Francisco, CA 94172-0160, USA

Schock, Ron (Athlete, Hockey Player)
1360 Whalen Rd
Penfield, NY 14526-1918, USA

Schockemohle, Alwin (Horse Racer)
Munsterlandstr 51
Muhlen 49439, GERMANY

Schoelen, Jill (Actor)
3500 W Olive Ave Ste 1400
Burbank, CA 91505-5512, USA

Schoellkopf, Carolyn Hunt
100 Crescent Ct Ste 1700
Dallas, TX 75201-6917

Schoen, Gerry (Athlete, Baseball Player)
219 Highway Dr
New Orleans, LA 70121-3429, USA

Schoen, Max H (Doctor)
123 Wellfleet Cir
Folsom, CA 95630-6541, USA

Schoen, Tom (Athlete, Football Player)
437 W Belmont Ave Apt 13
Chicago, IL 60657-4756, USA

Schoenbaechler, Andreas (Skier)
Muhlrustistr 2
Affoltern a A 8910, SWITZERLAND

Schoenberg, Marv (Stylist)
878 W End Ave Apt 10A
New York, NY 10025-4956, USA

Schoenborn, Christoph Cardinal (Religious Leader)
Wollzeile 2
Vienna 1010, AUSTRIA

Schoendienst, Red (Athlete, Baseball Player, Coach)
1105 Jo Carr Dr
Chesterfield, MO 63017-8401, USA

Schoene, Russ (Athlete, Basketball Player)
1136 205th Ave NE
Sammamish, WA 98074-6654, USA

Schoeneweis, Scott (Athlete, Baseball Player)
1204 Suncast Ln Ste 2
El Dorado Hills, CA 95762-9665, USA

Schoenfeld, Jim (Athlete, Coach, Hockey Player)
11745 E Cortez Dr
Scottsdale, AZ 85259-2605, USA

Schoenfield, Al (Athlete, Swimmer)
75 Santa Rosa St
San Luis Obispo, CA 93405-1819, USA

Schoenfield, Dana (Swimmer)
7734 E Lakeview Trl
Orange, CA 92869-2446, USA

Schoenke, Raymond F (Athlete, Football Player)
21151 Woodfield Rd
Gaithersburg, MD 20882-4847, USA

Schoffer, Nicolas (Artist)
Villa Des Arts 15 Rue Hegesippe-Moreau
Paris 75018, FRANCE

Schofield, Annabel (Actor)
345 N Maple Dr # 302
Beverly Hills, CA 90210-3869, USA

Schofield, Dick (Athlete, Baseball Player)
17148 Windsor Crest Blvd
Glencoe, MO 63038-1392, USA

Schofield, Dick (Athlete, Baseball Player)
139 Circle Dr
Springfield, IL 62703-4862, USA

Schofield, Dwight (Athlete, Hockey Player)
5900 N Illinois St
Fairview Heights, IL 62208-2700

Schofield, John (Actor, Producer)
c/o Pete Franciosa *United Talent Agency (UTA)*
9560 Wilshire Blvd Fl 5
Beverly Hills, CA 90212-2400, USA

Schofield, Phillip
56 Wood Ln
London, ENGLAND W12 7RJ

Scholder, Fritz (Artist)
118 Cattletrack Rd
Scottsdale, AZ 85251, USA

Scholes, Clarke (Swimmer)
20671 Wedgewood Dr
Grosse Pointe Woods, MI 48236-1560, USA

Scholes, Myron S (Nobel Prize Laureate)
Graduate Business School
Stanford, CA 94305, USA

Schollander, Don
3576 Lakeview Blvd
Lake Oswego, OR 97035-5544

Schollander, Donald A (Don) (Swimmer)
3576 Lakeview Blvd
Lake Oswego, OR 97035-5544, USA

Scholten, Jim (Music Group, Musician)
5200 Old Harding Rd
Franklin, TN 37064-9406, USA

Scholtz, Bob (Athlete, Football Player)
6721 S 71st East Ave
Tulsa, OK 74133-1818, USA

Scholtz, Bruce (Athlete, Football Player)
6607 Cypress Pt N
Austin, TX 78746-7104, USA

Scholz, Rupert (Government Official)
Postfach 1328
Bonn 1 5300, GERMANY

Scholz, Tom (Musician)
c/o Gail Parenteau *Parenteau Guidance*
132 E 35th St # 3J
New York, NY 10016-3892, USA

Schomberg, A Thomas (Artist)
4923 Snowberry Ln
Evergreen, CO 80439-5622, USA

Schon, Jan Hendrik (Inventor)
600 Mountain Ave
New Providence, NJ 07974-2008, USA

Schon, Kyra (Actor)
930 N Sheridan Ave
Pittsburgh, PA 15206-2261, USA

Schon, Neal (Musician)
c/o Staff Member *WmE2 (WMA-LA)*
1 William Morris Pl
Beverly Hills, CA 90212-4261, USA

Schon, Neil (Musician)
c/o Staff Member *WmE2 (WMA-LA)*
1 William Morris Pl
Beverly Hills, CA 90212-4261, USA

Schone, Lydia
2020 Broadway
Santa Monica, CA 90404-2910

Schonhuber, Franz (Correspondent)
Fraunhoferstr 23
Munich 80469, GERMANY

Schoofs, Mark (Journalist)
32 Cooper Sq
New York, NY 10003-7117, USA

Schooler, Mike (Athlete, Baseball Player)
519 N Buttonwood St
Anaheim, CA 92805-2226, USA

Schoolnik, Gary (Biologist)
Medical School Microbiology Dept
Stanford, CA 94305, USA

Schools, Dave (Musician)
400 Foundry St
Athens, GA 30601-2623, USA

Schoomaker, Peter J (Pete) (General)
Chief of Staff Hqusa Pentagon
Washington, DC 20310-0001, USA

Schoon, Milton (Athlete, Basketball Player)
1218 Blaine Ave
Janesville, WI 53545-1834, USA

Schoonmaker, Jerry (Athlete, Baseball Player)
8343 Schreiber Dr
Munster, IN 46321-1829, USA

Schopf, J William (Biologist)
Study of Evolution Center
Los Angeles, CA 90024, USA

Schorer, Jane (Journalist)
PO Box 957
Des Moines, IA 50306-0957, USA

Schorr, Bill (Cartoonist)
200 Madison Ave
New York, NY 10016-3903, USA

Schott, Stephen (Baseball Player)
12330 Hilltop Dr
Los Altos Hills, CA 94024-5218, USA

Schotte, Jan P Cardinal (Religious Leader)
Sinodo Dei Vescovi
120, VATICAN CITY

Schottenheimer, Marty (Athlete, Football Coach, Football Player)
8204 Prestwick Dr
La Jolla, CA 92037-2046, USA

Schou, Mogens (Doctor)
Institute of Psychiatry
Aarhus, DENMARK

Schourek, Pete (Athlete, Baseball Player)
14917 Cub Run Park Dr
Centreville, VA 20120-1234, USA

Schowalter, Edward R Jr (War Hero)
913 Bibb Ave # 312
Auburn, AL 36830-2715, USA

Schrader, Ken (Race Car Driver)
4403 Stough Rd SW
Concord, NC 28027-8964, USA

Schrader, Maria (Actor)
c/o Davien Littlefield *Davien Littlefield Management*
33 W 67th St PH
New York, NY 10023-6224, USA

Schrader, Paul (Actor, Director, Writer)
c/o Johnnie Planco *Parseghian Planco LLC*
322 8th Ave Ste 601
New York, NY 10001-6715, USA

Schram, Bitty (Actor)
c/o Robert Marsala *Global Creative*
1051 Cole Ave # B
Los Angeles, CA 90038-2601, USA

Schram, Jessy (Actor)
c/o Brian Wilkins *Kritzer Levine Wilkins Entertainment*
11872 La Grange Ave Fl 1
Los Angeles, CA 90025-5283, USA

Schramka, Paul (Athlete, Baseball Player)
W180N9923 Riversbend Cir W
Germantown, WI 53022-4656, USA

Schramm, David (Actor)
3521 Berry Dr
Studio City, CA 91604-3882, USA

Schranz, Karl (Skier)
Hotel Garni
Saint Anton 6580, AUSTRIA

Schreder, Sabina (Stylist)
c/o Staff Member *Walter Schupfer Management Corp*
413 W 14th St Ste 3
New York, NY 10014-1097, USA

Schreiber, Adam (Athlete, Football Player)
2520 River Summit Dr
Duluth, GA 30097-2255, USA

Schreiber, Avery
6399 Wilshire Blvd Ste 414
Los Angeles, CA 90048-5716

Schreiber, Larry (Athlete, Football Player)
388 Albion Ave
Woodside, CA 94062-3603, USA

Schreiber, Liev (Actor)
c/o Ina Treciokas *Slate Public Relations*
9000 W Sunset Blvd Ste 915
West Hollywood, CA 90069-5809, USA

Schreiber, Martin J (Ex-Governor)
2700 S Shore Dr Unit B
Milwaukee, WI 53207-2366, USA

Schreiber, Ted (Athlete, Baseball Player)
116 Nantucket Is
Centerville, GA 31028-8547, USA

Schreler, Peter (Conductor, Opera Singer)
Calberlastr 13
Dresdon 1326, GERMANY

Schremmer, Patty (Golfer)
5547 Avenida Del Mare
Sarasota, FL 34242-1914, USA

Schremp, Bob (Athlete, Football Player)
PO Box 584
Bellflower, CA 90707-0584, USA

Schrempf, Detlef (Athlete, Basketball Player)
9735 NE 1st St
Bellevue, WA 98004-5413, USA

Schrempp, Jurgen E (Business Person)
Plieningerstra
Stuttgart 70546, GERMANY

Schrenk, Steve (Athlete, Baseball Player)
2547 Oakboro Ln
Charlotte, NC 28214-6900, USA

Schreyer, Cindy (Golfer)
18 Cottage Dr
Newnan, GA 30265-5513, USA

Schreyer, Edward R (Ex-Governor)
3069 Henderson Hwy
Winnipeg, MB R2E 0H9, Canada

Schrieber, Paul (Athlete, Baseball Player)
9715 E Gary Rd
Scottsdale, AZ 85260-6225, USA

Schrieffer, John R (Nobel Prize Laureate)
1800 E Paul Dirac Dr
Tallahassee, FL 32310-3706, USA

Schrier, Eric W (Editor)
PO Box 100
Pleasantville, NY 10570-0100, USA

Schriesheim, Alan (Misc)
1440 N Lake Shore Dr Apt 31AC
Chicago, IL 60610-5927, USA

Schrimshaw, Nevin S (Doctor)
Sandwich Notch Farm
Thompton, NH 3223, USA

Schriner, David
3216 Upland Pl. NW Calgary
Alb., CANADA

Schrock, Richard R (Nobel Prize Laureate)
77 Massachusetts Ave Dept of
Cambridge, MA 02139-4301, USA

Schroder, Bob (Athlete, Baseball Player)
2810 Jefferson Dr
Hattiesburg, MS 39402-2047, USA

Schroder, Ernst A (Actor)
Podere Montalto Castellina In Chianti
Siena 53011, ITALY

Schroder, Gerhard
Bundeskanzleramt
Berlin, GERMANY 11012

Schroder, Jochen
Postfach 10 23 46
Bochum, GERMANY D-44723

Schroder, Rick(y) (Actor)
c/o Rebecca (Becca) Kovacik *Hofflund/Polone*
9465 Wilshire Blvd Ste 420
Beverly Hills, CA 90212-2603, USA

Schrody, Eric (Everlast) (Actor, Composer, Musician)
c/o Jeff Rabhan *Three Ring Projects*
111 Westwood Pl Ste 101
Brentwood, TN 37027-5057, USA

Schroeder, Barbet (Director, Producer)
8033 W Sunset Blvd # 51
West Hollywood, CA 90046-2401, USA

Schroeder, Bill (Athlete, Baseball Player)
S75W17724 Harbor Cir
Muskego, WI 53150-9182, USA

Schroeder, Carly (Actor)
c/o Beverly Strong *Strong Management*
9350 Wilshire Blvd Ste 224
Beverly Hills, CA 90212-3204, USA

Schroeder, Gene (Athlete, Football Player)
918 Aaron Ct
Crown Point, IN 46307-7593, USA

Schroeder, Gerhard (Misc)
Willy-Brandt-Str 1
Berlin 10557, GERMANY

Schroeder, Jay (Athlete, Football Player)
730 E Grinnell Dr
Burbank, CA 91501-1720, USA

Schroeder, Jim (Bowler)
3 Greenhaven Ter
Tonawanda, NY 14150-5503, USA

Schroeder, John (Athlete, Golfer)
PO Box 2768
Del Mar, CA 92014-5768, USA

Schroeder, John H (Educator)
Chancellor's Office
Milwaukee, WI 53211, USA

Schroeder, Kenneth L (Business Person)
160 Rio Robles
San Jose, CA 95134-1813, USA

Schroeder, Lisa Golden (Stylist)
39 Apple Orchard Rd
Saint Paul, MN 55110-1234, USA

Schroeder, Manfred R (Physicist)
Rieswartenweg 8
Gottingen 37073, GERMANY

Schroeder, Mary M (Judge)
230 N 1st Ave
Phoenix, AZ 85003-1723, USA

Schroeder, Patricia S (Misc)
c/o Staff Member *21st Century Speakers*
1352 Lake Rd
Gouldsboro, PA 18424, USA

Schroeder, Paul W (Writer)
810 S Wright St
Urbana, IL 61801-3644, USA

Schroeder, Steven A (Doctor, Misc)
10 Paseo Mirasol
Bel Tiburon, CA 94920-2021, USA

Schroeder, Terry (Athlete, Coach)
4901 Lewis Rd
Agoura Hills, CA 91301-2453, USA

Schroedter, Katherine (Stylist)
88 W Schiller St Apt 204
Chicago, IL 60610-2026, USA

Schroll, William (Athlete, Football Player)
2361 McClendon Rd
Magnolia, MS 39652-9419, USA

Schrom, Kenneth M (Ken) (Athlete, Baseball Player)
1002 Black Diamond Ct
Portland, TX 78374-4162, USA

Schroy, Ken (Athlete, Football Player)
79 Russell Rd
Garden City, NY 11530-1933, USA

Schruefer, John J (Doctor)
Ob-Gyn Dept
Washington, DC 20007, USA

Schu, Rick (Athlete, Baseball Player)
2013 Driftwood Cir
El Dorado Hills, CA 95762-3744, USA

Schuba, Beatrice (Trixi) (Figure Skater)
Giorgengasse 2/1/8
Vienna 1190, AUSTRIA

Schubb, Mark
9744 Wilshire Blvd Ste 308
Beverly Hills, CA 90212-1813

Schubert, Eric (Athlete, Football Player)
722 Homestead Ave
Maybrook, NY 12543-1308, USA

Schubert, Mark (Coach, Swimmer)
PO Box 479
Surfside, CA 90743-0479, USA

Schubert, Richard F (Misc)
6615 Madison McLean Dr
McLean, VA 22101-2902, USA

Schubert, Steve (Athlete, Football Player)
7 Douglas Dr
Candia, NH 03034-2304, USA

Schuck, Anett (Athlete)
Defoestry 6A
Leipzig 4159, GERMANY

Schuck, John (Actor)
1501 Broadway Ste 703
New York, NY 10036-5501, USA

Schueler, Jon R (Artist)
40 W 22nd St
New York, NY 10010-5806, USA

Schueler, ROn (Athlete, Baseball Player)
3108 E San Juan Ave
Phoenix, AZ 85016-3725, USA

Schuenke, Donald J (Business Person)
8200 Dixie Rd
Brampton, ON L6T 5P6, CANADA

Schuerholz, John (Baseball Player)
1025 Royal Dr
Canonsburg, PA 15317-5004, USA

Schuessel, Wolfgang (Misc)
Ballhausplatz 2
Vienna 1014, AUSTRIA

Schuessler, Jack (Business Person)
4288 W Dublin Granville Rd
Dublin, OH 43017-1442, USA

Schuh, Harry F (Athlete, Football Player)
2309 Massey Rd
Memphis, TN 38119-6516, USA

Schuh, Jeff (Athlete, Football Player)
5550 Vagabond Ln N
Minneapolis, MN 55446-1323, USA

Schuhmacher, John (Athlete, Football Player)
6000 Reims Rd Apt 3006
Houston, TX 77036-3053, USA

Schul, Robert (Bob) (Athlete, Track Athlete)
320 Wisteria Dr
Dayton, OH 45419-3553, USA

Schuler, Bill (Athlete, Football Player)
201 Cahaba Park Cir Ste 400
Birmingham, AL 35242-8130, USA

Schuler, Carolyn (Swimmer)
26552 Via Del Sol
Mission Viejo, CA 92691-6125, USA

Schuler, Dave (Athlete, Baseball Player)
17210 Chatham St
Lewes, DE 19958-7229, USA

Schulhofer, Scotty (Misc)
PO Box 1581
Waynesville, NC 28786-1581, USA

Schull, Rebecca (Actor)
8383 Wilshire Blvd # 550
Beverly Hills, CA 90211-2425, USA

Schuller, Grete (Artist)
8 Barstow Rd Apt 7G
Great Neck, NY 11021-3547, USA

Schuller, Gunther (Composer, Conductor)
167 Dudley Rd
Newton Center, MA 02459-2830, USA

Schuller, Robert (Religious Leader)
12141 Lewis St
Garden Grove, CA 92840-4627, USA

Schullstrom, Erik (Athlete, Baseball Player)
1425 Court St
Alameda, CA 94501-3145, USA

Schulman, Ariel (Director)
c/o Rowena Arguelles *Creative Artists Agency (CAA-LA)*
2000 Avenue of the Stars Ste 100
Los Angeles, CA 90067-4705, USA

Schult, Art (Athlete, Baseball Player)
9225 SW 90th St
Ocala, FL 34481-8485, USA

Schult, Jurgen (Athlete, Track Athlete)
Drosselweg 6
Leuna 19069, GERMANY

Schulte, Greg (Baseball Player)
20723 N 56th Ave
Glendale, AZ 85308-6276, USA

Schulte, Richard (Athlete, Football Player)
1216 N Kenneth Pl
Chandler, AZ 85226-7210, USA

Schulters, Lance (Athlete, Football Player)
594 Grant Ave
Roselle, NJ 07203-2911, USA

Schultz, Axel (Boxer)
Kloetzrstr 15
Riesa 1587, GERMANY

Schultz, Barney (Athlete, Baseball Player)
400 Fern Brook Ln # 218
Mount Laurel, NJ 08054-9542, USA

Schultz, Bill (Athlete, Football Player)
10302 Lakeland Dr
Fishers, IN 46037-9323, USA

Schultz, Buddy (Athlete, Baseball Player)
5629 E Thunderbird Rd
Scottsdale, AZ 85254-3741, USA

Schultz, Dave (Athlete, Hockey Player)
505 Alpine Ct
Mays Landing, NJ 08330-2213, USA

Schultz, Dave (Race Car Driver)
2365 Lazy River Ln
Fort Myers, FL 33905-2242, USA

Schultz, Dean (Financier)
1079 Hutchinson Rd
Walnut Creek, CA 94598-4543, USA

Schultz, Dwight (Actor)
3172 Dona Susana Dr
Studio City, CA 91604-4356, USA

Schultz, Ed (Radio Personality)
417 38th St S Ste F
Fargo, ND 58103-6508, USA

Schultz, Frederick H (Government Official)
118 W Adams St Fl 6
Jacksonville, FL 32202-3815, USA

Schultz, Howard (Business Person)
2401 Utah Ave S
Seattle, WA 98134-1436, USA

Schultz, Howard H (Howie) (Athlete, Baseball Player, Basketball Player)
1333 McKusick Road Ln N
Stillwater, MN 55082-4163, USA

Schultz, John (Athlete, Football Player)
503 Skyline Dr
Vestal, NY 13850-5321, USA

Schultz, John (Director)
c/o Staff Member *Creative Artists Agency (CAA-LA)*
2000 Avenue of the Stars Ste 100
Los Angeles, CA 90067-4705, USA

Schultz, Kirki (Stylist)
2517 W 52nd St
Minneapolis, MN 55410-2229, USA

Schultz, Kurt (Athlete, Football Player)
5075 Rockledge Dr
Clarence, NY 14031-2426, USA

Schultz, Michael A (Director)
PO Box 1940
Santa Monica, CA 90406-1940, USA

Schultz, Mitch (Stylist)
c/o Staff Member *Ford Models (Chicago)*
311 W Superior St
Chicago, IL 60654-3548, USA

Schultz, Peter C (Inventor)
3473 Satellite Blvd Ste 300
Duluth, GA 30096-4658, USA

Schultz, Peter G (Misc)
10550 N Torrey Pines Rd
La Jolla, CA 92037-1000, USA

Schultz, Richard D (Misc)
1 Olympic Plz
Colorado Springs, CO 80909-5780, USA

Schultze, Charles L (Government Official)
1775 Massachusetts Ave NW
Washington, DC 20036-2103, USA

Schulz, Axel
Zehmeplatz 10
Frankfurt/Oder, GERMANY D-15230

Schulz, Jeff (Athlete, Baseball Player)
1167 S Stockwell Rd
Evansville, IN 47714-0749, USA

Schulz, Jody (Athlete, Football Player)
222 Schulz Ln
Chester, MD 21619-2658, USA

Schulz, Kurt (Athlete, Football Player)
5075 Rockledge Dr
Clarence, NY 14031-2426, USA

Schulz, William (Editor)
PO Box 100
Pleasantville, NY 10570-0100, USA

Schulze, Don (Athlete, Baseball Player)
1851 N Brinton Ave
Dixon, IL 61021-8262, USA

Schulze, Matt (Actor)
c/o David Gardner *Principato/Young Management*
9465 Wilshire Blvd Ste 430
Beverly Hills, CA 90212-2613, USA

Schulze, Paul (Actor)
c/o Staff Member *Kyle Fritz Management*
6325 Heather Dr
Los Angeles, CA 90068-1633, USA

Schulze, Richard M (Business Person)
7601 Penn Ave S
Minneapolis, MN 55423-3645, USA

Schumacher, Gregg (Athlete, Football Player)
104 Surfview Dr Apt 2108
Palm Coast, FL 32137-2348, USA

Schumacher, Joel (Director)
11766 Wilshire Blvd Ste 1610
Los Angeles, CA 90025-6565, USA

Schumacher, Kelly (Basketball Player)
125 S Pennsylvania St
Indianapolis, IN 46204-3610, USA

Schumacher, Kurt (Athlete, Football Player)
673 Northfield Ln
Harleysville, PA 19438-1698, USA

Schumacher, Michael (Race Car Driver)
Brackley
Northants NN13 7BD, UK

Schumacher, Ralf (Race Car Driver)
Trankestr 11
Stuttgart 70597, GERMANY

Schumaker, Jared (Skip) (Athlete, Baseball Player)
6672 Abrego Rd
Goleta, CA 93117-7507, USA

Schuman, Allan L (Business Person)
Ecolab Center 370 Wabasha St N
Saint Paul, MN 55102, USA

Schuman, Melissa (Actor)
c/o Staff Member *Kazarian Spencer Ruskin & Assoc.*
11969 Ventura Blvd Ste 300
Studio City, CA 91604-2619, USA

Schuman, Tom (Musician)
PO Box 435
Highland Mills, NY 10930-0435, USA

Schumann, Jochen (Yachtsman)
Birkenstr 88
Penzberg 48336, GERMANY

Schumann, Ralf (Misc)
Steomach 22
Stockheim 97640, GERMANY

Schur, Michael (Writer)
c/o Staff Member *3 Arts Entertainment Inc*
9460 Wilshire Blvd Fl 7
Beverly Hills, CA 90212-2713, USA

Schurig, Roger (Athlete, Basketball Player)
1031 Brookside
Greensboro, GA 30642-6814, USA

Schurmann, Petra (Swimmer)
Max-Emanuel-Str 7
Starnberg 82319, GERMANY

Schurr, Harry W (War Hero)
1178 Davis Dr
Fairborn, OH 45324-5614, USA

Schurr, Wayne (Athlete, Baseball Player)
10030 W 500 S
Hudson, IN 46747-9705, USA

Schussler Florenza, Elisabeth (Writer)
Theology Dept
Notre Dame, IN 46556, USA

Schuster, Rudolf (President)
Nam Slobody 1
Bratislava 91370, SLOVAKIA

Schute, Anja
Parkstr. 37
Erfstadt, GERMANY D-50374

Schutz, Carl (Athlete, Baseball Player)
PO Box 162
French Settlement, LA 70733-0162, USA

Schutz, Klaus (Government Official)
9 Konstanzerstr
Berlin 10707, GERMANY

Schutz, Stephen (Artist)
PO Box 4549
Boulder, CO 80306-4549, USA

Schutz, Susan Polis (Writer)
PO Box 4549
Boulder, CO 80306-4549, USA

Schuur, Diane (Music Group, Musician)
33042 Ocean Rdg
Dana Point, CA 92629-1078, USA

Schwab, Charles (Business Person, Financier)
211 Main St
San Francisco, CA 94105-1905, USA

Schwab, John J (Doctor)
21 Bradley Rd Apt 117
Woodbridge, CT 06525-2255, USA

Schwabe, Mike (Athlete, Baseball Player)
13341 Presidio Pl
Tustin, CA 92782-8608, USA

Schwall, Don (Athlete, Baseball Player)
2000 Lake Marshall Dr
Gibsonia, PA 15044-7425, USA

Schwantz, Jim (Athlete, Football Player)
1047 W Chatham Dr
Palatine, IL 60067-5817, USA

Schwarthoff, Florian (Athlete, Track Athlete)
Fischweiher 51
Heppenheim 64646, GERMANY

Schwartz, Debbie (Stylist)
c/o Staff Member *Axis Models & Talent*
PO Box 367
Ringwood, NJ 07456-0367, USA

Schwartz, Don (Athlete, Football Player)
19410 NE Redmond Rd
Redmond, WA 98053, USA

Schwartz, Jacob T (Scientist)
Courant Math Sciences Institute
New York, NY 10012, USA

Schwartz, Josh (Producer, Writer)
c/o Mikkel Bondesen *Fuse Entertainment*
1041 N Formosa Ave Formosa Bldg 197
W Hollywood, CA 10046, USA

Schwartz, Lloyd (Journalist)
27 Pennsylvania Ave
Somerville, MA 02145-2217, USA

Schwartz, Maxime (Misc)
25-28 Rue du Docteur-Roux
Paris Cedex 15 75724, FRANCE

Schwartz, Melvin (Nobel Prize Laureate)
PO Box 5068
Ketchum, ID 83340-5068, USA

Schwartz, Neil
3044 Pearl Harbor Dr
Las Vegas, NV 89117-0925, USA

Schwartz, Neil J (Actor)
3044 Pearl Harbor Dr
Las Vegas, NV 89117-0925, USA

Schwartz, Norton A (General)
Commander 11th Air Force
Elmendorf Air Force Base, AK 99506, USA

Schwartz, Randy (Athlete, Baseball Player)
757 El Rancho Dr
El Cajon, CA 92019-1141, USA

Schwartz, Stephen L (Composer, Music Group, Musician, Songwriter, Writer)
545 8th Ave # 14
New York, NY 10018-4307, USA

Schwartz, Thomas A (General)
Commander United Nations Command/US Forces Korea
APO, AP 96205, USA

Schwartzman, Jason (Actor)
c/o Matthew (Matt) Labov *Forefront Media*
5700 Wilshire Blvd Ste 550
Los Angeles, CA 90036-3790, USA

Schwartzman, Robert (Actor)
c/o Joanne Wiles *International Creative Management (ICM-LA)*
10250 Constellation Blvd Fl 7
Los Angeles, CA 90067-6207, USA

Schwarz, Gerard R (Conductor)
1395 Lexington Ave
New York, NY 10128-1612, USA

Schwarz, Hanna (Opera Singer)
Maximilianstr 22
Munich 80539, GERMANY

Schwarz, Jeff (Athlete, Baseball Player)
912 Club Dr
Palm Beach Gardens, FL 33418-7065, USA

Schwarz, John H (Physicist)
Physics
Pasadena, CA 91125-0001, USA

Schwarzbein, Diana (Doctor, Writer)
3201 SW 15th St
Deerfield Beach, FL 33442-8157, USA

Schwarzenegger, Arnold (Actor, Director, Ex-Governor, Producer)
c/o Bryan Lourd *Creative Artists Agency (CAA-LA)*
2000 Avenue of the Stars Ste 100
Los Angeles, CA 90067-4705, USA

Schwarzkopf, H Norman (General)
c/o Author Mail *Bantam-Dell Publishing (NY)*
1745 Broadway
New York, NY 10019-4368, USA

Schwarzman, Stephen (Steve) (Business Person)
345 Park Ave
New York, NY 10154-0004, USA

Schwarzman, Steve (Business Person)
345 Park Ave
New York, NY 10154-0004, USA

Schwarz-Shilling, Christian (Government Official)
Heinrich-von-Stephanstr 1
Bonn 53175, GERMANY

Schwebel, Stephen M (Judge)
PO Box 356
Woodstock, VT 05091-0356, USA

Schweder, John (Athlete, Football Player)
525 Barclay Dr
Bethlehem, PA 18017-3858, USA

Schwedes, Gerhard (Athlete, Football Player)
PO Box 570
Clayton, NY 13624-0570, USA

Schwedes, Scott (Athlete, Football Player)
6871 Claret Cir
Fayetteville, NY 13066-1048, USA

Schweickart, Russell (Rusty) (Astronaut)
1150 Gemini St
Houston, TX 77058-2708, USA

Schweig, Eric (Actor)
PO Box 5163
Vancouver, BC V7B 1M4, CANADA

Schweiger, Til (Actor, Director, Producer)
Saarbrueckerstrasse 36
Berlin 10405, Germany

Schweiker, Richard S (Secretary)
8890 Windy Ridge Way
McLean, VA 22102-1558, USA

Schweikert, J E (Religious Leader)
4200 N Kedvale Ave
Chicago, IL 60641-2215, USA

Schweinsteiger, Bastian (Soccer Player)
Attention Bastian Schweinsteiger Säbener Strasse 51
Munich 81547, GERMANY

Schweitz, John (Athlete, Basketball Player)
813 Smith Dr
Florence, SC 29501-5979, USA

Schweitzer, Brian (Governor)
PO Box 200801
Helena, MT 59620-0801, USA

Schwertsik, Kurt (Composer)
Dorotheerhgasse 10
Vienna 1011, AUSTRIA

Schwery, Henry Cardinal (Religious Leader)
CP 2068
Sion 2 1950, SWITZERLAND

Schwimmer, David (Actor)
c/o Eric Kranzler *Management 360*
9111 Wilshire Blvd
Beverly Hills, CA 90210-5508, USA

Schwimmer, Lacey-Mae (Actor)
c/o Ben Russo *EMC / Bowery*
8155 Santa Monica Blvd Ste 200
West Hollywood, CA 90046-4986, USA

Schwinden, Ted (Ex-Governor)
18811 N 19th Ave Apt 3022
Phoenix, AZ 85027-5283, USA

Schwitters, Roy F (Physicist)
1718 Cromwell Hl
Austin, TX 78703-3307, USA

Schygulla, Hanna (Actor)
Leopoldstr 19
Munich 80802, GERMANY

Schypinski, Jerry (Athlete, Baseball Player)
28014 Shadowood Ln
Harrison Township, MI 48045-2246, USA

Scialfa, Patty (Music Group, Musician)
c/o Staff Member *Sony Music International*
550 Madison Ave Fl 6
New York, NY 10022-3211, USA

Sciarra, John M (Athlete, Football Player)
4420 Woodleigh Ln
Flintridge, CA 91011-3541, USA

Sciascia, Leonardo
Viale Scaduto 10/B
Palermo, ITALY 1-90144

Scifres, Steve (Athlete, Football Player)
2026 Northglen Dr
Colorado Springs, CO 80909-1629, USA

Sciole, Jennifer (Actor, Producer)
c/o Steve Honig *Honig Company, The*
3500 W Olive Ave Ste 300
Burbank, CA 91505-4647, USA

Scioli, Brad (Football Player)
5433 Bay Harbor Dr
Indianapolis, IN 46254-4510, USA

Sciorra, Annabella (Actor)
c/o Staff Member *Dontanville/Frattaroli (D/F)*
270 Lafayette St Ste 402
New York, NY 10012-3327, USA

Scioscia, Michael L (Mike) (Athlete, Baseball Player, Coach)
1915 Falling Star Ave
Westlake Village, CA 91362-5284, USA

Scirica, Anthony J (Judge)
601 Market St
Philadelphia, PA 19106-1737, USA

Scissor Sisters (Music Group)
c/o Darin Harmon *3D Management*
1901 Main St Fl 3
Santa Monica, CA 90405-1075, USA

Sciutto, Nellie (Actor)
c/o Ted Schachter *Schachter Entertainment*
1157 S Beverly Dr Fl 2
Los Angeles, CA 90035-1119, USA

Scodelario, Kaya (Actor)
c/o Kate Staddon *Curtis Brown Group*
Haymarket House 28 - 29 Haymarket
London SW1Y 4SP, UNITED KINGDOM

Scofield, Dean
12304 Santa Monica Blvd Ste 104
Los Angeles, CA 90025-2586

Scofield, Dino (Actor)
3330 Barham Blvd Ste 103
Los Angeles, CA 90068-1476, USA

Scofield, John (Musician)
173 Brighton Ave
Boston, MA 02134-2003, USA

Scofield, Paul (Actor)
Gables Balcombe
Sussex RH17 6ND, UNITED KINGDOM (UK)

Scofield, Richard M (Dick) (General)
3251 Country Club Pkwy
Castle Rock, CO 80108-9078, USA

Scoggins, Eric (Athlete, Football Player)
3513 W 78th St
Inglewood, CA 90305-1205, USA

Scoggins, Matt (Swimmer)
4900 Calhoun Canyon Loop
Austin, TX 78735-6417, USA

Scoggins, Tracy (Actor)
c/o Staff Member *Bette Smith Management*
499 N Canon Dr
Beverly Hills, CA 90210-4887, USA

Scola, Angelo Cardinal (Religious Leader)
S Marco 320/A
Venezia 30124, ITALY

Scola, Ettore (Director)
Via Bertoloni 1/E
Rome 197, ITALY

Scolari, Luiz Felipe (Football Coach)
3 Beruniy St Shaykhontohur District
Tashkent, Uzbekistan

Scolari, Peter (Actor)
c/o Staff Member *Peter Strain & Associates Inc (LA)*
5455 Wilshire Blvd Ste 1812
Los Angeles, CA 90036-4268, USA

Scollay, Gabrielle (Actor)
c/o Fleur Griffin *Mark Morrissey and Associates*
16 Princess Ave Rosebery
Sydney NSW 2018, Australia

Scolnick, Edward M (Doctor, Scientist)
1201 Magnolia Dr
Wayland, MA 01778-2848, USA

Scolnik, Glenn (Athlete, Football Player)
301 Willowgate Dr
Indianapolis, IN 46260-1476, USA

Sconiers, Daryl (Athlete, Baseball Player)
15985 Hibiscus St
Fontana, CA 92335-4460, USA

Scooters, The
15190 Encanto Dr
Sherman Oaks, CA 91403-4410

Scorpions (Music Group)
Musikproduktions- Und Verlags GmbH
Bohlenweg 8
Langenhagen 30835, Germany

Scorsese, Martin (Director)
c/o Rick Yorn *Yorn Management Group*
2000 Avenue Of The Stars 3rd Tower Floor NORTH
Los Angeles, CA 90067, USA

Scorsese, Nicolette (Actor)
c/o Gregory (Greg) Mayo *Orange Grove Group, The*
12178 Ventura Blvd Ste 205
Studio City, CA 91604-2540, USA

Scorupco, Izabella (Actor, Model, Music Group, Musician)
c/o Anne Woodward *ROAR (LA)*
9701 Wilshire Blvd Fl 8
Beverly Hills, CA 90212-2008, USA

Scott, Adam (Golfer)
c/o Staff Member *Pro Golfers Assoc of America (PGA)*
112 Tpc Blvd
Ponte Vedra Beach, FL 32082, USA

Scott, Adam (Actor)
c/o Danielle Thomas *Untitled Entertainment (LA)*
350 S Beverly Dr Ste 200
Beverly Hills, CA 90212-4819, USA

Scott, Alvin (Athlete, Basketball Player)
5786 W Townley Ave
Glendale, AZ 85302-4612, USA

Scott, Andy (Musician)
296 Nether St Finchley
London N3 1RJ, UNITED KINGDOM (UK)

Scott, Arthur (Athlete, Football Player)
634 U St
King Of Prussia, PA 19406-2702, USA

Scott, Ashley (Actor)
c/o Mary Putnam Greene *MPG Management*
9150 Wilshire Blvd Ste 350
Beverly Hills, CA 90212-3453, USA

Scott, Bo (Athlete, Football Player)
1301 Fountain Ln Apt 1
Columbus, OH 43213, USA

Scott, Bobby (Athlete, Football Player)
801 McKinley Pointe Ln
Knoxville, TN 37934-1568, USA

Scott, Byron (Athlete, Basketball Player, Coach)
668 Euclid Ave Unit 527
Cleveland, OH 44114-3014, USA

Scott, Camilla
23773 Via Canon Unit 201
Newhall, CA 91321-4632

Scott, Campbell (Actor)
c/o Clifford Stevens *Paradigm (NY)*
360 Park Ave S Fl 16
New York, NY 10010-1708, USA

Scott, Carlos (Athlete, Football Player)
RR 1 Box 346
Hempstead, TX 77445, USA

Scott, Chad (Athlete, Football Player)
18526 Reliant Dr
Gaithersburg, MD 20879-5421, USA

Scott, Charles (Charlie) (Athlete, Basketball Player)
300 Chastain Manor Dr
Norcross, GA 30071-2186, USA

Scott, Chuck (Athlete, Football Player)
875 Landover Xing
Suwanee, GA 30024-3045, USA

Scott, Clarence (Athlete, Football Player)
3-17-6 NishiAzabu Regency Apt 202
Minato-ku, Tokyo, Japan

Scott, Clarence (Athlete, Football Player)
216 Sisson Ave NE
Atlanta, GA 30317-1422, USA

Scott, Clyde L (Smackover) (Athlete, Football Player, Track Athlete)
12840 Rivercrest Dr
Little Rock, AR 72212-1446, USA

Scott, Coltin
195 S Beverly Dr Ste 400
Beverly Hills, CA 90212-3044

Scott, Dale (Baseball Player)
1283 SW Cardinell Dr
Portland, OR 97201-3114, USA

Scott, Dale (Athlete, Baseball Player)
1283 SW Cardinell Dr
Portland, OR 97201-3114, USA

Scott, Darnay (Athlete, Football Player)
18551 Patton St
Detroit, MI 48219-5202, USA

Scott, Darryl (Athlete, Baseball Player)
8093 E Theresa Dr
Scottsdale, AZ 85255-5421, USA

Scott, Dave (Athlete, Football Player)
3151 Robindale Rd
Decatur, GA 30034-4962, USA

Scott, David
1300 Manhattan Ave Apt B
Manhattan Beach, CA 90266-4776

Scott, David R (Astronaut)
VC Johnson 30 Hackamore Lane #1
Bell Canyon, CA 91307, USA

Scott, Dennis (Athlete, Basketball Player)
9832 Laurel Valley Dr
Windermere, FL 34786-8911, USA

Scott, Dick (Athlete, Baseball Player)
750 E Pinetree Blvd Lot 6
Thomasville, GA 31792-6803, USA

Scott, Dick (Athlete, Baseball Player)
7399 E Cortez Rd
Scottsdale, AZ 85260-5432, USA

Scott, Donnie (Athlete, Baseball Player)
6042 114th Ter N
Pinellas Park, FL 33782-2018, USA

Scott, Donovan (Actor)
6300 Wilshire Blvd Ste 2100
Los Angeles, CA 90048-5282, USA

Scott, Dougray (Actor)
c/o Staff Member *Dontanville/Frattaroli (D/F)*
270 Lafayette St Ste 402
New York, NY 10012-3327, USA

Scott, Edward (Baseball Player)
720 Kasserine Pass
Mobile, AL 36609-6430, USA

Scott, Eric
11934 River Grove Ct
Moorpark, CA 93021-3105

Scott, Freddie (Musician)
1650 Broadway Ste 508
New York, NY 10019-6833, USA

Scott, Freddie L (Athlete, Football Player)
PO Box 197
Coahoma, MS 38617-0197, USA

Scott, Gary (Athlete, Baseball Player)
25 W Elm St Apt 47
Greenwich, CT 06830-2802, USA

Scott, Gavin (Writer)
c/o Jordan Bayer *Original Artists (LA)*
9465 Wilshire Blvd Ste 870
Beverly Hills, CA 90212-2610, USA

Scott, Geoffrey
1126 N Hollywood Way # 203-A
Burbank, CA 91505-2527

Scott, George (Athlete, Baseball Player)
1316 Goodrich St
Greenville, MS 38701-6130, USA

Scott, Gloria Dean Randle (Educator)
President's Office
Greensboro, NC 27401, USA

Scott, H Lee Jr (Business Person)
702 SW 8th St
Bentonville, AR 72712-6209, USA

Scott, Herbert (Athlete, Football Player)
605 Rawhide Ct
Plano, TX 75023-4753, USA

Scott, Jack (Music Group, Musician, Songwriter, Writer)
34039 Coachwood Dr
Sterling Heights, MI 48312-5617, USA

Scott, Jacob E (Jake) Jr (Athlete, Football Player)
PO Box 857
Hanalei, HI 96714-0857, USA

Scott, James (Athlete, Football Player)
10127 Chisholm Trl
Dallas, TX 75243-2511, USA

Scott, James (Actor)
c/o Sandra Siegal *Siegal Company, The*
9025 Wilshire Blvd Ste 400
Beverly Hills, CA 90211-1828, USA

Scott, Jason-Shane (Actor)
c/o Paulo Andres *Link Talent Group*
4741 Laurel Canyon Blvd Ste 106
Valley Village, CA 91607-5907, USA

Scott, Jerry (Cartoonist)
5777 W Century Blvd Ste 700
Los Angeles, CA 90045-5652, USA

Scott, Jill (Actor, Musician)
c/o Shawn Gee *Watch Your Back Management*
417 N 8th St Ste 503
Philadelphia, PA 19123-3920, USA

Scott, Jimmy (Music Group, Musician)
175 Prospect St Apt 20D
East Orange, NJ 07017-2631, ITALY

Scott, John (Athlete, Football Player)
1583 N Ellen Ave
Decatur, IL 62526-3718, USA

Scott, John (Composer, Musician)
c/o Otto Vavrin II *SMC Artists*
4400 Coldwater Canyon Ave Ste 127
Studio City, CA 91604-5038, USA

Scott, John (Athlete, Baseball Player)
917 S Pearl Ave
Compton, CA 90221-4320, USA

Scott, Josey (Music Group, Musician)
Plaza 535 Kings Road
London SW10 0S, UNITED KINGDOM (UK)

Scott, Judson
10000 Santa Monica Blvd # 305
Los Angeles, CA 90067

Scott, Kathryn Leigh (Actor)
3236 Bennett Dr
Los Angeles, CA 90068-1702, USA

Scott, Kevin B (Athlete, Football Player)
2335 Cascade St
Milpitas, CA 95035-7807, USA

Scott, Klea (Actor)
c/o Staff Member *Epstein-Wyckoff-Corsa-Ross & Associates (LA)*
11350 Ventura Blvd Ste 100
Studio City, CA 91604-3140, USA

Scott, Lary R (Business Person)
PO Box 1000
Cherryville, NC 28021-1000, USA

Scott, Lew (Athlete, Football Player)
4 Osprey Ct
Streamwood, IL 60107-2813, USA

Scott, Lindsay (Athlete, Football Player)
214 N Troup St
Valdosta, GA 31601-5738, USA

Scott, Lizabeth (Actor)
8277 Hollywood Blvd
Los Angeles, CA 90069-1611, USA

Scott, Lorna (Actor)
c/o Staff Member *Kjar and Associates*
10153 1/2 Riverside Dr
Toluca Lake, CA 91602-2561, USA

Scott, Luke (Athlete, Baseball Player)
PO Box 39
De Leon Springs, FL 32130-0039, USA

Scott, L'Wren (Fashion Designer, Stylist)
58/63 Tuxedo Ter
Hollywood, CA 90068, USA

Scott, Melody Thomas (Actor)
12068 Crest Ct
Beverly Hills, CA 90210-1354, USA

Scott, Michael W (Mike) (Athlete, Baseball Player)
28355 Chat Dr
Laguna Niguel, CA 92677-1384, USA

Scott, Mickey (Athlete, Baseball Player)
1134 Vestal Ave
Binghamton, NY 13903-1528, USA

Scott, Patricia (Baseball Player)
320 Edwards Ave
Walton, KY 41094-1096, USA

Scott, Paul (Writer)
33 Drumsheugh Gardens
Edinburgh, SCOTLAND

Scott, Pippa (Actor)
10850 Wilshire Blvd # 250
Los Angeles, CA 90024-4305, USA

Scott, Randy (Athlete, Football Player)
1440 Woodland Lake Dr
Snellville, GA 30078-2097, USA

Scott, Ray (Basketball Player, Coach)
33200 Schoolcraft Rd
Livonia, MI 48150-1643, USA

Scott, Richard U (Dick) (Athlete, Football Player)
3369 Upland Ct
Adamstown, MD 21710-9665, USA

Scott, Rick (Governor)
400 S Monroe St
Tallahassee, FL 32399-6536, USA

Scott, Ridley (Director)
c/o Simon Halls *Slate Public Relations*
9000 W Sunset Blvd Ste 915
West Hollywood, CA 90069-5809, USA

Scott, Robert (Baseball Player)
236 W Grand St
Elizabeth, NJ 07202-1284, USA

Scott, Robert L Jr (War Hero, Writer)
PO Box 2469
Warner Robins, GA 31099-2469, USA

Scott, Rodney (Athlete, Baseball Player)
4206 Priscilla Ave
Indianapolis, IN 46226-3334, USA

Scott, Sean (Athlete, Football Player)
3217 Boise St
Berkeley, CA 94702-2607, USA

Scott, Seann William (Actor, Producer)
c/o Christina Papadopoulos *Baker Winokur Ryder Public Relations BWR (BWR-NY)*
292 Madison Ave Fl 12
New York, NY 10017-6415, USA

Scott, Shelby (Misc)
260 Madison Ave
New York, NY 10016-2401, USA

Scott, Stephanie (Stylist)
1208 S Genesee Ave
Los Angeles, CA 90019-2406, USA

Scott, Stephen (Musician)
35 Clark St Apt A5
Brooklyn, NY 11201-2374, USA

Scott, Steven M (Steve) (Athlete, Track Athlete)
4106 La Portalada Dr
Carlsbad, CA 92010-2805, USA

Scott, Stuart
c/o Staff Member *ESPN (Main)*
ESPN Plaza 935 Middle St
Bristol, CT 06010-1001, USA

Scott, Thomas C (Tom) (Athlete, Football Player)
3259 Kirkwood Ct
Keswick, VA 22947, USA

Scott, Tim (Athlete, Baseball Player)
956 W Julia Way
Hanford, CA 93230-8552, USA

Scott, Todd (Athlete, Football Player)
5605 Avenue P
Galveston, TX 77551-5028, USA

Scott, Tom (Musician)
8901 Melrose Ave # 200
West Hollywood, CA 90069-5605, USA

Scott, Tom (Athlete, Football Player)
1012 Peed Dr Apt 8
Greenville, NC 27834-7063, USA

Scott, Tom (Athlete, Football Player)
3359 Kirkwood Ct
Keswick, VA 22947-9138, USA

Scott, Tom Everett (Actor)
c/o John Carrabino *John Carrabino Management*
5900 Wilshire Blvd Ste 406
Los Angeles, CA 90036-5015, USA

Scott, Tony (Director)
c/o Simon Halls *Slate Public Relations*
9000 W Sunset Blvd Ste 915
West Hollywood, CA 90069-5809, USA

Scott, Tony (Athlete, Baseball Player)
120 Seay St
Spartanburg, SC 29306-5342, USA

Scott, W Richard (Misc)
940 Lathrop Pl
Stanford, CA 94305-1060, USA

Scott, Walter (Athlete, Football Player)
1991 Edgefield Rd
Trenton, SC 29847-2435, USA

Scott, Willard (Television Host)
c/o Staff Member *NBC Universal (NY)*
30 Rockefeller Plz Fl 270E
New York, NY 10112-0299, USA

Scott, Willard W Jr (Educator, General)
9115 McNair Dr
Alexandria, VA 22309-3315, USA

Scott, William Lee
c/o Dan Spilo *Industry Entertainment Partners*
955 Carrillo Dr Ste 300
Los Angeles, CA 90048-5400, USA

Scott, Willie (Athlete, Football Player)
1123 Long St
Newberry, SC 29108-4231, USA

Scott, Winston E (Astronaut)
PO Box 1192
Cape Canaveral, FL 32920-1192, USA

Scott Brown, Denise (Architect)
4236 Main St
Philadelphia, PA 19127-1603, USA

Scott Kay, Dominic (Actor)
c/o Rich Hueners *Paradigm (LA)*
360 N Crescent Dr
Beverly Hills, CA 90210-4874, USA

Scott Thomas, Kristin (Actor)
c/o Mara Buxbaum *ID PR (LA)*
7060 Hollywood Blvd Fl 8
Los Angeles, CA 90028-6014, USA

Scott-Brown, Denise (Architect)
Main St Venturi Scott Brown Assoc 423
Philadelphia, PA 19127-2128, USA

Scotti, Benjamin (Athlete, Football Player)
5556 Mallard Trce
Frisco, TX 75034-5045, USA

Scotti, Nick (Actor, Musician)
c/o Elise Konialian *Untitled Entertainment (NY)*
322 8th Ave Ste 601
New York, NY 10001-6715, USA

Scotto, Renata (Opera Singer)
c/o Staff Member *Opera Et Concert*
37, rue de la Chaussée d'Antin
Paris F-75009, France

Scotto, Rosanna (Correspondent)
205 E 67th St
New York, NY 10065-6050, USA

Scottoline, Lisa (Writer)
10 E 53rd St
New York, NY 10022-5244, USA

Scotty K (DJ)
c/o Staff Member *Diva Central Inc*
7510 W Sunset Blvd Ste 1445
Los Angeles, CA 90046-3408, USA

Scouler, Angela (Actor)
60 Old Brompton Road
London SW7 3LQ, UNITED KINGDOM (UK)

Scovell, Nell (Producer)
c/o Staff Member *WmE2 (WMA-LA)*
1 William Morris Pl
Beverly Hills, CA 90212-4261, USA

Scowcroft, Brent (General, Government Official)
350 Park Ave # 2600
New York, NY 10022-6022, USA

Scrafford, Kirk (Athlete, Football Player)
19400 US Highway 93 N
Florence, MT 59833-5914, USA

Scranton, Jim (Athlete, Baseball Player)
27519 Hammack Ave
Perris, CA 92570-7071, USA

Scranton, Nancy (Golfer)
1816 Forest Glen Way
Saint Augustine, FL 32092-1003, USA

Scranton, William W (Ex-Governor)
888 17th St NW Ste 306
Washington, DC 20006-3307, USA

Scratch (Artist, Musician)
1325 Avenue of the Americas
New York, NY 10019-6026, USA

Scream3 (Music Group)
c/o Staff Member *Wind-up Records*
72 Madison Ave Fl 8
New York, NY 10016-8731, USA

Scribner, Bucky (Athlete, Football Player)
1123 Pine St
Santa Monica, CA 90405-3925, USA

Scribner, Rick (Race Car Driver)
8904 Amerigo Ave
Orangevale, CA 95662-4612, USA

Scrimm, Angus (Actor)
PO Box 5193
North Hollywood, CA 91616-5193, USA

Scrimshaw, Nevin S (Doctor)
PO Box 330
Campton, NH 03223-0330, USA

Scripps, Charles E (Publisher)
10 Grandin Ln
Cincinnati, OH 45208-3304, USA

Scrivener, Chuck (Athlete, Baseball Player)
1766 Hazel St
Birmingham, MI 48009-6892, USA

Scroggins, Tracy (Athlete, Football Player)
6001 N Ocean Dr Apt 757
Hollywood, FL 33019-4617, USA

Scruggs, Earl (Musician, Songwriter, Writer)
774 Elysian Rd
Nashville, TN 37204, USA

Scruggs, Eugene (Baseball Player)
618 Dawson Ter NW
Huntsville, AL 35811-1782, USA

Scruggs, Randy (Musician)
c/o Staff Member *Creative Artists Agency (CAA-TN)*
3310 W End Ave Fl 5
Nashville, TN 37203-1028, USA

Scruggs, Tony (Athlete, Baseball Player)
11621 Braddock Dr Apt 17
Culver City, CA 90230-5175, USA

Scudamore, Peter (Jockey)
Mucky Cottage Grangehill Naunton Cheltenham
Glos GL54 3AY, UNITED KINGDOM (UK)

Scudder, Scott (Athlete, Baseball Player)
943 Farm Road 1499
Paris, TX 75460-0602, USA

Scudero, Joe (Athlete, Football Player)
2534 N Railroad Way
Hernando, FL 34442-2988, USA

Scully, John (Athlete, Football Player)
3500 Bankview Dr
Joliet, IL 60431-4804, USA

Scully, Sean P (Artist)
1 Bruton Place
London W1X 7AB, UNITED KINGDOM (UK)

Scully, Vin (Sportscaster)
c/o Staff Member *Los Angeles Dodgers (LA Dodgers)*
1000 Elysian Park Ave
Los Angeles, CA 90090-1112, USA

Scully-Power, Paul D (Astronaut)
Box 2005
Canberra, ACT 2600, AUSTRALIA

Sculthorpe, Peter J (Composer)
91 Holdsworth St
Woollahra, NSW 2025, AUSTRALIA

Scurti, John (Actor)
c/o Jennifer Konawal *Gersh (NY)*
41 Madison Ave
New York, NY 10010-2202, USA

Scutaro, Marco (Athlete, Baseball Player)
19877 E Country Club Dr Apt 3503
Miami, FL 33180-4812, USA

Scutt, Der (Architect)
44 W 28th St
New York, NY 10001-4212, USA

Sczurek, Stan (Athlete, Football Player)
689 Beaver Ridge Trl
Broadview Heights, OH 44147-1972, USA

Sea, Daniela (Actor)
c/o Hannah Roth *Don Buchwald & Associates Inc (LA)*
6500 Wilshire Blvd Ste 2200
Los Angeles, CA 90048-4942, USA

Seabol, Scott (Athlete, Baseball Player)
427 Cedar Dr
Elizabeth, PA 15037-2167, USA

Seabra, Verissimo Correia (General, President)
Bissau, GUINEA-BISSAU

Seabron, Malcolm (Athlete, Football Player)
10418 Cliffwood Dr
Houston, TX 77035-3702, USA

Seacrest, Ryan (Producer, Radio Personality, Television Host)
c/o Melissa Stone *42West (LA)*
11400 W Olympic Blvd Ste 1100
Los Angeles, CA 90064-1579, USA

Seaforth Hayes, Susan (Actor)
11333 Moorpark St # 368
Studio City, CA 91602-2618, USA

Seaga, Edward P G (Prime Minister)
24-26 Grenada Crescent New Kingston
Kingston 5, JAMAICA

Seagal, Steven (Actor)
c/o Michelle Bega *Rogers & Cowan PR (LA)*
Pacific Design Center 8687 Melrose Ave, 7th Floor
West Hollywood, CA 90069, USA

Seagrave, Jocelyn (Actor)
c/o Gregg Steiner *Perspective Film*
15030 Ventura Blvd
Sherman Oaks, CA 91403-5470, USA

Seagraves, Ralph (Race Car Driver)
RR 10 Box 413
Winston Salem, NC 27127, USA

Seagren, Bob
One Hoosier Dome
Indianapolis, IN 46225-1023

Seagren, Robert L (Bob) (Athlete, Track Athlete)
21902 Velicata St
Woodland Hills, CA 91364-3114, USA

Seagrove, Jenny (Actor)
Langham House 302/8 Regent St
London W1R 5AL, UNITED KINGDOM (UK)

Seal (Musician)
c/o Mitch Rose *Creative Artists Agency (CAA-LA)*
2000 Avenue of the Stars Ste 100
Los Angeles, CA 90067-4705, USA

Seal, Paul (Athlete, Football Player)
21599 Hidden Rivers Dr N
Southfield, MI 48075-6110, USA

Seale, John C (Cinematographer)
1801 Century Park E
Los Angeles, CA 90067-2302, USA

Seale, Johnnie (Athlete, Baseball Player)
1941 County Road 207
Durango, CO 81301-7700, USA

Seale, Sam (Athlete, Football Player)
1818 Da Gama Ct
Escondido, CA 92026-1729, USA

Sealey, Tom (Athlete, Basketball Player)
316 Fountain Ave
Brooklyn, NY 11208-4302, USA

Seals, Brady
2100 W End Ave Ste 1000
Nashville, TN 37203-5240

Seals, Bruce (Athlete, Basketball Player)
115 Prospect St
Ashland, MA 01721-2249, USA

Seals, George (Athlete, Football Player)
1101 1st St Unit 204
Coronado, CA 92118-1496, USA

Seals, Ray (Athlete, Football Player)
664 NW Shaw Gln
Lake City, FL 32055-0408, USA

Seals & Croft (Music Group)
c/o Staff Member *4STAR Entertainment LLC*
1675 York Ave Apt 32C
New York, NY 10128-6905, USA

Seaman, Christopher (Conductor)
25 Westfield Dr
Glasgow G52 2SG, SCOTLAND

Seaman, David (Soccer Player)
Avenell Road Highbury
London N5 1BU, UNITED KINGDOM (UK)

Seaman, Kim (Athlete, Baseball Player)
4900 Main St
Moss Point, MS 39563-2735, USA

Sean, Jay (Musician)
c/o Ness *Media Artists Group (LA)*
8255 W Sunset Blvd
West Hollywood, CA 90046-2417, USA

Seanez, Rudy (Athlete, Baseball Player)
1422 McCabe Cove Rd
El Centro, CA 92243-9741, USA

Searage, Ray (Athlete, Baseball Player)
9737 Pine Lake Trl
Saint Petersburg, FL 33708-3571, USA

Searchers, The
2514 Build America Dr
Hampton, VA 23666-3223

Searcy, Leon (Athlete, Football Player)
3841 Biggin Church Rd W
Jacksonville, FL 32224-7985, USA

Searcy, Nick (Actor)
c/o Joseph (Joe) Rice *Abrams Artists Agency (LA)*
9200 W Sunset Blvd PH 11
Los Angeles, CA 90069-3601, USA

Searcy, Steve (Athlete, Baseball Player)
5112 Gouffon Rd
Knoxville, TN 37918-9319, USA

Searfoss, Richard A (Astronaut)
24480 Silver Creek Way
Tehachapi, CA 93561-8399, USA

Searle, Jackie
7214 Chestwood Dr
Tujunga, CA 91042

Searle, John R (Misc)
109 Yosemite Rd
Berkeley, CA 94707, USA

Searle, Ronald (Animator, Cartoonist)
PO Box 1062
Bayonne, NJ 07002-1062, USA

Searles, Kyle (Actor)
c/o Loch Powell *Leverage Management*
3030 Pennsylvania Ave
Santa Monica, CA 90404-4112, USA

Sears, Ken (Athlete, Basketball Player)
40 Cutter Dr
Watsonville, CA 95076-2229, USA

Sears, Paul B (Misc)
17 Las Milpas
Taos, NM 87571, USA

Sears, Todd (Athlete, Baseball Player)
513 NW Chapel Dr
Ankeny, IA 50023-1420, USA

Sears, Victor W (Vic) (Athlete, Football Player)
151 Old Forest Cir
Winchester, VA 22602-6627, USA

Sears, Dr, William
34761 Doheny Pl
Capistrano Beach, CA 92624-1713

Sease, Marvin
PO Box 9287
Jackson, MS 39286-9287, USA

Seaver, Tom (Athlete, Baseball Player)
1761 Diamond Mountain Rd
Calistoga, CA 94515-9672, USA

Seaward, Tracey (Producer)
c/o Staff Member *International Creative Management (ICM-LA)*
10250 Constellation Blvd Fl 7
Los Angeles, CA 90067-6207, USA

Seaward, Tracy (Producer)
c/o Staff Member *Independent Talent Group (ITG-UK)*
Oxford House 76 Oxford St
London W1D 1BS, UK

Seay, Bobby (Athlete, Baseball Player)
1591 Oak Cir N
Sarasota, FL 34232-3478, USA

Seay, Laura (Actor)
c/o Susan Smith *Susan Smith Company, The*
1344 N Wetherly Dr
Los Angeles, CA 90069-1817, USA

Seay, Mark (Athlete, Football Player)
2866 Muscupiabe Dr
San Bernardino, CA 92405-3060, USA

Seay, Virgil (Athlete, Football Player)
5611 Fort Corloran Dr
Burke, VA 22015-2112, USA

Sebaldt, Maria
Geranienstr. 3
Grunwald, GERMANY D-82031

Sebastian (Stylist)
c/o Staff Member *Ford Models (Chicago)*
311 W Superior St
Chicago, IL 60654-3548, USA

Sebastian, Cuthbert (General, Government Official, Governor)
6 Canyon St
Basseterre, Saint Kitts & Nevis

Sebastian, John (Musician)
PO Box 770850
Orlando, FL 32877-0850, USA

Sebastiani, Sergio Cardinal (Religious Leader)
Palazzo delle Congregazioni Lardo del Colonnato 3
Rome 193, ITALY

Sebbah, Kate (Stylist)
c/o Staff Member *Streeters*
560 Broadway Rm 203
New York, NY 10012-3945, 212-219-9566

Sebek, Nick (Athlete, Football Player)
3233 Rachelle Dr
North Tonawanda, NY 14120-1459, USA

Sebert, Kesha (Ke$ha) (Musician)
c/o Nicki Loranger *Vector Management (LA)*
1100 Glendon Ave Ste 2000
Los Angeles, CA 90024-3524, USA

Sebesky, Don (Musician)
c/o Staff Member *Bennett Morgan & Associates*
1022 Route 376 Ste 3
Wappingers Falls, NY 12590-6372, USA

Sebestyen, Marta (Music Group, Musician)
Nonnengasse 15
Fulda 36037, GERMANY

Sebold, Alice (Writer)
c/o Staff Member *Steven Barclay Agency*
12 Western Ave
Petaluma, CA 94952-2907, USA

Sebra, Bob (Athlete, Baseball Player)
20 Misners Trl
Ormond Beach, FL 32174-8531, USA

Secada, Jon (Musician)
c/o Susan Haber *Haber Entertainment*
434 S Canon Dr Apt 204
Beverly Hills, CA 90212-4501, USA

Seck, Idrissa (Prime Minister)
Ave Leopold Sedar Senghor
Dakar, SENEGAL

Secor, Kyle (Actor)
9150 Wilshire Blvd Ste 350
Beverly Hills, CA 90212-3453, USA

Secord, Al (Athlete, Hockey Player)
950 Ginger Ct
Southlake, TX 76092-6063

Secord, John (Music Group, Musician)
PO Box 1013
Putnam, TX 76469-1013, USA

Secord, Richard V (General)
1719 W 2800 S
Ogden, UT 84401-3263, USA

Secrest, Charles (Baseball Player)
215 Orchard Grove Ave
Lewistown, PA 17044-7509, USA

Secret GardenContinental AS, Marcus
Thranesgate 2b
Oslo, NORWAY 473

Secrets, No (Music Group)
PO Box 5247
Bellingham, WA 98227-5247, USA

Secrist, Don (Athlete, Baseball Player)
1003 Davis Creek Ln
Du Quoin, IL 62832-3738, USA

Secules, Scott (Athlete, Football Player)
6907 Helsem Way
Dallas, TX 75230-1920, USA

Secunda, Andrew (Writer)
c/o Staff Member *United Talent Agency (UTA)*
9560 Wilshire Blvd Fl 5
Beverly Hills, CA 90212-2400, USA

Seda, Jon (Actor)
c/o Staff Member *Anthem Entertainment*
9595 Wilshire Blvd Ste 900
Beverly Hills, CA 90212-2509, USA

Sedaka, Neil (Musician)
201 E 66th St Apt 3N
New York, NY 10065-6454, USA

Sedaris, Amy (Actor)
c/o Sarah Fargo *Paradigm (NY)*
360 Park Ave S Fl 16
New York, NY 10010-1708, USA

Sedaris, David (Comedian, Writer)
c/o Staff Member *Little, Brown & Co.*
466 Lexington Ave Lbby 15
New York, NY 10017-3165, USA

Seddon, M Rhea
1709 Shagbark Trl
Murfreesboro, TN 37130-1136, USA

Seddon, Margaret Rhea (Astronaut)
1709 Shagbark Trl
Murfreesboro, TN 37130-1136, USA

Sedelmaier, J Josef (Joe) (Animator, Director)
858 W Armitage Ave # 267
Chicago, IL 60614-4370, USA

Sedgman, Frank (Tennis Player)
28 Bolton Ave
Hampton, VIC 3188, AUSTRALIA

Sedgwick, Kyra (Actor)
c/o Jill Littman *Impression Entertainment*
9229 W Sunset Blvd Ste 700
West Hollywood, CA 90069-3407, USA

Sedgworth, Bill
1811 Volusia Ave
Daytona Beach, FL 32015

Sedlacek, Shawn (Athlete, Baseball Player)
590 Penn Ave NW
Cedar Rapids, IA 52405-1631, USA

Sedlbauer, Ron (Athlete, Hockey Player)
3021 Woodland Park Dr
Burlington, Ontario L7N 1K8, Canada

Sedney, Jules (Prime Minister)
Maystreet 24
Paramaribo, SARINAME

Sedoris, Chris (Athlete, Football Player)
7500 Turner Ridge Rd
Crestwood, KY 40014-8951, USA

Seduction (Music Group)
c/o Staff Member *Diva Central Inc*
7510 W Sunset Blvd Ste 1445
Los Angeles, CA 90046-3408, USA

Sedykh, Yuri G (Athlete, Track Athlete)
Luzhnetskaya Nab 8
Moscow, RUSSIA

See, Carolyn (Writer)
930 3rd St Apt 203
Santa Monica, CA 90403-2561, USA

See, Larry (Athlete, Baseball Player)
1913 W Remington Dr
Chandler, AZ 85286-6231, USA

See, Marshall (Athlete, Basketball Player)
1138 S Canal Cir
Camp Verde, AZ 86322-7014, USA

Seear, Beatrice N S (Government Official)
189B Kennington Road
London SE11 6ST, UNITED KINGDOM (UK)

Seegal, Denise (Business Person)
1441 Broadway
New York, NY 10018-1905, USA

Seeger, Michael
PO Box 1592
Lexington, VA 24450-1592

Seeger, Mike (Composer, Musician)
c/o Staff Member *Forklore Productions*
PO Box 7003
Santa Monica, CA 90406-7003, USA

Seeger, Pete (Musician, Songwriter)
PO Box 431
Beacon, NY 12508-0431, USA

Seehorn, Rhea (Actor)
c/o Randi Ross *Epstein-Wyckoff-Corsa-Ross & Associates (LA)*
11350 Ventura Blvd Ste 100
Studio City, CA 91604-3140, USA

Seelbach, Chris (Athlete, Baseball Player)
302 Fort Howell Dr
Hilton Head Island, SC 29926-2764, USA

Seelbach, Chuck (Athlete, Baseball Player)
13800 Fairhill Rd Apt 501
Cleveland, OH 44120-5510, USA

Seelenfreund, Alan (Business Person)
1 Post St
San Francisco, CA 94104-5201, USA

Seeler, Uwe (Soccer Player)
125 Rothenbaumchaussee
Ashburn, VA 20149-0001, GERMANY

Seeley, Andrew (Actor, Musician)
c/o Ellen Drantch-Billet *EDB Management*
11657 La Grange Ave
Los Angeles, CA 90025-5331, USA

Seeling, Angelle (Motorcycle Race, Motorcycle Racer)
PO Box 1240
Americus, GA 31709, USA

Seely, Jeannie (Music Group, Musician, Songwriter, Writer)
c/o Staff Member *Tessier-Marsh Talent*
505 Canton Pass
Madison, TN 37115-5449, USA

Seelye, Talcott W (Diplomat)
4952 Sentinel Dr Apt 206
Bethesda, MD 20816-3558, USA

Seema (Actor, Bollywood)
25 Madhavan Nair Road Mahalingapuram
Chennai, TN 600034, INDIA

Seether (Music Group)
c/o Staff Member *Wind-up Records*
72 Madison Ave Fl 8
New York, NY 10016-8731, USA

Sefcik, Kevin (Athlete, Baseball Player)
16921 Steeplechase Pkwy
Orland Park, IL 60467-8769, USA

Seffrin, John R (Misc)
1599 Clifton Rd NE
Atlanta, GA 30322-4250, USA

Sega, Ronald M (Astronaut, Engineer)
711A Massey Ln
Alexandria, VA 22314-1268, USA

Segal, Fred (Designer, Fashion Designer)
8100 Melrose Ave
Los Angeles, CA 90046-7012, USA

Segal, George (Actor)
c/o Abe Hoch *A Management Company*
9107 Wilshire Blvd Ste 650
Beverly Hills, CA 90210-5544, USA

Segal, Jason (Actor)
c/o Staff Member *United Talent Agency (UTA)*
9560 Wilshire Blvd Fl 5
Beverly Hills, CA 90212-2400, USA

Segal, Jonathan
PO Box 3059
Tel Aviv, ISRAEL 61030

Segal, Michael
27 Cyprus Ave Finchley
London, ENGLAND N3 1SS

Segal, Peter (Director, Producer, Writer)
c/o Adam Kanter *Creative Artists Agency (CAA-LA)*
2000 Avenue of the Stars Ste 100
Los Angeles, CA 90067-4705, USA

Segal, Uri
28 Sheffield Terrace
London W8 7NA, UNITED KINGDOM (UK)

Segall, Pamela (Actor)
c/o Staff Member *Meghan Schumacher Management*
13351D Riverside Dr # 387
Sherman Oaks, CA 91423-2508, USA

Seganti, Paolo (Actor)
Drury House 34-43 Russell St
London W8 7NA, UNITED KINGDOM (UK)

Ségara, Hélène (Musician)
c/o Staff Member *BG Productions*
10, rue Damré
Paris 75918, France

Segel, Jason (Actor, Producer)
c/o Stacy Abrams *Abrams Entertainment*
5225 Wilshire Blvd # Suite 515 PMB 515
Los Angeles, CA 90036, USA

Segelke, Herman (Athlete, Baseball Player)
PO Box 2513
Antioch, CA 94531-2513, USA

Seger, Bob (Musician, Songwriter)
c/o Staff Member *Creative Artists Agency (CAA-LA)*
2000 Avenue of the Stars Ste 100
Los Angeles, CA 90067-4705, USA

Seger, Shea (Music Group, Musician)
Plaza 535 Kings Road
London SW10 0S, UNITED KINGDOM (UK)

Segerstam, Leif S (Composer)
59 Lansdowne Place
Hove BN3 1FL, UNITED KINGDOM (UK)

Segrist, Kal (Athlete, Baseball Player)
3813 55th St
Lubbock, TX 79413-4619, USA

Segui, David V (Athlete, Baseball Player)
2740 N 131st St
Kansas City, KS 66109-3365, USA

Segui, Diego P (Athlete, Baseball Player)
13421 Leavenworth Rd
Kansas City, KS 66109-3351, USA

Segura, Francisco (Pancho) (Tennis Player)
7690 Camino Real
Carlsbad, CA 92009, USA

Segura, Pancho
. La Costa Hotel
Costa Del Mar Rd, Carlsbad 92009

Seguso, Robert (Tennis Player)
1025 Thomas Jefferson St NW # 450
Washington, DC 20007-5201, USA

Sehorn, Jason (Athlete, Football Player)
3460 Marjorie Way
Sacramento, CA 95820-1952, USA

Seibel, Phil (Athlete, Baseball Player)
351 Woodland Dr
Driftwood, TX 78619-4212, USA

Seibert, Kurt (Athlete, Baseball Player)
95 Amberwood Cir
Irmo, SC 29063-7942, USA

Seibou, Ali (General, President)
National Orientation Higher Council
Niamey, NIGER

Seidel, Frederick (Writer)
c/o Staff Member *Farrar, Straus and Giroux*
18 W 18th St Fl 7
New York, NY 10011-4675, USA

Seidel, Kelly
8441 Balboa Blvd Apt 36
Northridge, CA 91325-4096

Seidel, Martie (Music Group, Musician)
9465 Wilshire Blvd
Beverly Hills, CA 90212-2612, USA

Seidelman, Susan (Director)
225 W 34th St Ste 1012
New York, NY 10122-1012, USA

Seidenberg, Ivan G (Business Person)
1095 Avenue of the Americas
New York, NY 10036-6797, USA

Seidler, David (Writer)
c/o Jeff Aghassi *Jeff Aghassi Management*
2810 S Bedford St
Los Angeles, CA 90034-2523, USA

Seidman, L William (Business Person, Government Official)
1025 Connecticut Ave NW Ste 800
Washington, DC 20036-5419, USA

Seifert, George G (Athlete, Coach, Football Coach, Football Player, Sportscaster)
1276 Estate Dr
Los Altos, CA 94024-6100, USA

Seifert, Mike (Athlete, Football Player)
1605 E Bristlecone Dr
Hartland, WI 53029-8655, USA

Seifert, Mike (Athlete, Football Player)
N5610 Lac Verde Cir
Green Lake, WI 54941-9702, USA

Seigenthaler, John L (Television Host)
c/o Staff Member *MSNBC (NJ)*
NBC/One Microsoft Corporation 1 MSNC Plaza
Secaucus, NJ 7094, USA

Seigner, Emmanuelle (Actor)
20 Ave Rapp
Paris 75007, FRANCE

Seigner, Mathilde (Actor)
20 Ave Rapp
Paris 75007, FRANCE

Seignoret, Clarence H A (President)
24 Cork St
Roseau, DOMINICA

Seiheimer, Rick (Athlete, Baseball Player)
401 Hickory Hollow Ln
Brenham, TX 77833-9240, USA

Seikaly, Rony (Athlete, Basketball Player)
400 Alton Rd Apt 3201
Miami Beach, FL 33139-6756, USA

Seilacher, Adolf (Geophysicist, Physicist)
Geology/Geophysics Laboratory
New Haven, CT 6520, USA

Seinfeld, Jerry (Actor, Comedian)
c/o George Shapiro *Shapiro/West & Associates*
141 El Camino Dr Ste 205
Beverly Hills, CA 90212-2786, USA

Seinfeld, Jessica (Chef)
2971 Bellmore Ave
Bellmore, NY 11710-4313, USA

Seinfeld, John H (Engineer)
363 Patrician Way
Pasadena, CA 91105-1027, USA

Seiple, Larry (Athlete, Football Player)
1361 W Golfview Dr
Pembroke Pines, FL 33026-3112, USA

Seitz, Frederick (Educator, Politician)
1230 York Ave
New York, NY 10065-6307, USA

Seitz, Raymond G H (Diplomat)
1 Broadgate
London EC2M 7HA, UNITED KINGDOM (UK)

Seitzer, Kevin (Athlete, Baseball Player)
13705 Holmes Rd
Kansas City, MO 64145-1591, USA

Seiwald, Robert J (Inventor)
59 Burnside Ave
San Francisco, CA 94131-2904, USA

Seixas, E Victor (Vic) Jr (Tennis Player)
8 Harbor Point Dr Apt 207
Mill Valley, CA 94941-3241, USA

Seixas, Vic
8 Harbor Point Dr Apt 207
Mill Valley, CA 94941-3241

Seizinger, Katja (Skier)
Rudolf-Epp-Str 48
Eberbach 69412, GERMANY

Seka
1122 White Rock Dr
Dixon, IL 61021-9049

Sela, Michael (Doctor, Misc)
Immunology Dept
Rehovot 76100, ISRAEL

Selanne, Teemu (Athlete, Hockey Player)
31731 Madre Selva Ln
Trabuco Canyon, CA 92679-3613, USA

Selby, Bill (Athlete, Baseball Player)
228 Eunice Bonner Rd
Waynesboro, MS 39367-9474, USA

Selby, David (Actor)
8942 Wilshire Blvd # 219
Beverly Hills, CA 90211-1908, USA

Selby, Philip (Composer)
Via 1 Maggio 93 Rignano Flaminio
Rome 68, ITALY

Seldes, Marian (Actor)
c/o Clifford Stevens *Paradigm (NY)*
360 Park Ave S Fl 16
New York, NY 10010-1708, USA

Seldin, Donald W (Doctor)
5323 Harry Hines Blvd
Dallas, TX 75390-7201, USA

Sele, Aaron H (Athlete, Baseball Player)
4 Oak Tree Dr
Newport Beach, CA 92660-4290, USA

Seles, Monica (Athlete, Tennis Player)
2895 Dick Wilson Dr
Sarasota, FL 34240-8729, USA

Seley, Jason (Artist)
Art Dept
Ithaca, NY 14853, USA

Self, Bill (Athlete, Basketball Player, Coach)
1651 Naismith Dr
Lawrence, KS 66045-4069, USA

Self, Clarence (Athlete, Football Player)
43W689 Willow Creek Ct
Elburn, IL 60119-9152, USA

Self, Todd (Athlete, Baseball Player)
10238 Cardiff Dr
Keithville, LA 71047-8980, USA

Selfridge, Andy (Athlete, Football Player)
3400 Dunscroft Ct
Keswick, VA 22947-9141, USA

Selig, Bud (Baseball Player, Misc)
1480 E Standish Pl
Bayside, WI 53217-1958, USA

Seliger, Mark (Photographer)
3 Center Plz
Boston, MA 02108-2003, USA

Seligman, Martin E P (Doctor)
Psychology Dept
Philadelphia, PA 19104, USA

Selig-Prieb, Wendy (Baseball Player)
6620 N Lake Dr
Milwaukee, WI 53217-4245, USA

Selkirk, George N (Government Official)
Rose Lawn Coppice Wimborne
Dorset, UNITED KINGDOM (UK)

Selkoe, Dennis J (Doctor)
221 Longwood Ave
Boston, MA 02115-5804, USA

Selldorf, Annabelle (Architect)
62 White St
New York, NY 10013-3593, USA

Selleca, Connie (Actor)
c/o Chuck Binder *Binder & Associates*
1465 Lindacrest Dr
Beverly Hills, CA 90210-2519, USA

Selleck, Tom (Actor, Producer, Writer)
c/o Bettye McCartt *Agency for Artists*
165 N Arnaz Dr
Beverly Hills, CA 90211-2114, USA

Seller, Peg (Coach, Swimmer)
72 Monkswood Cres
Newmarket, ON L3Y 2K1, CANADA

Sellers, Brad (Athlete, Basketball Player)
682 Arbor Way
Aurora, OH 44202-9113, USA

Sellers, Franklin (Religious Leader)
2001 Frederick Rd
Baltimore, MD 21228-5511, USA

Sellers, Goldie (Athlete, Football Player)
13425 Braun Rd
Golden, CO 80401-1646, USA

Sellers, Jeff (Athlete, Baseball Player)
833 S 224th Ln
Buckeye, AZ 85326-5593, USA

Sellers, Larry (Actor)
c/o Vaughn Hart *Vaughn Hart & Associates*
12304 Santa Monica Blvd Ste 111
Los Angeles, CA 90025-2586, USA

Sellers, Michael (Actor, Producer, Writer)
c/o Staff Member *Quantum Entertainment*
209 E Alameda Ave Ste 203
Burbank, CA 91502-2674, USA

Sellers, Piers J (Astronaut)
16011 Craighurst Dr
Houston, TX 77059-6424, USA

Sellers, Robert (Writer)
c/o Staff Member *Pollinger Limited*
9 Staple Inn Holborn
London WC1V 7QH, UK

Sellers, Ron F (Athlete, Football Player)
129 Via Palacio
Palm Beach Gardens, FL 33418-6212, USA

Sellers, Victoria
1927 Vista Del Mar St
Hollywood, CA 90068-4004

Sellick, Phyllis (Musician)
Beverly House 29A Ranelagh Ave
Barnes SW13 0BN, UNITED KINGDOM (UK)

Sells, Dave (Athlete, Baseball Player)
700 Blue Ridge Ln
Vacaville, CA 95688-2023, USA

Selmon, Dewey W (Athlete, Football Player)
2725 S Berry Rd
Norman, OK 73072-6908, USA

Selmon, Lee Roy (Athlete, Football Player)
15350 Amberly Dr Unit 624
Tampa, FL 33647-1608, USA

Selmon, Lucious (Athlete, Coach, Football Player)
1 Alltel Stadium Pl
Jacksonville, FL 32202-1917, USA

Selten, Reinhard (Nobel Prize Laureate)
Hardtweg 23
Konigswinter 53639, GERMANY

Seltz, Rolland (Basketball Player)
3328 Oswego Heights Rd
Shoreview, MN 55126, USA

Seltzer, David (Director, Producer, Writer)
c/o Dan Aloni *Creative Artists Agency (CAA-LA)*
2000 Avenue of the Stars Ste 100
Los Angeles, CA 90067-4705, USA

Selverstone, Katy (Actor)
c/o Jason Priluck *Agency Group Ltd, The (LA)*
1880 Century Park E Ste 711
Los Angeles, CA 90067-1618, USA

Selvy, Franklin D (Frank) (Athlete, Basketball Player)
18 Oglethorpe Ln
Hilton Head Island, SC 29926-4704, USA

Selwyn, Zach (Actor)
c/o Kenneth (Kenny) Goodman *Schiff Company, The*
8440 Warner Dr Ste B1
Culver City, CA 90232-2461, USA

Selya, Bruce M (Judge)
US Courthouse
Providence, RI 2903, USA

Selzer, Richard (Doctor, Writer)
6 Saint Ronan Ter
New Haven, CT 06511-2315, USA

Selznick, Albie
2800 Neilson Way
Santa Monica, CA 90405-4025

Semak, Michael W (Photographer)
1796 Spruce Hill Rd
Pickering, ON L1V 1S4, CANADA

Sembello, Michael (Musician, Songwriter)
105 Shad Row Ste B
Piermont, NY 10968-3001, USA

Sember, Mike (Athlete, Baseball Player)
285 S Country Club Blvd
Boca Raton, FL 33487-2326, USA

Sembier, Melvin F (Diplomat)
5858 Central Ave
Saint Petersburg, FL 33707-1708, USA

Semel, David (Director)
c/o Staff Member *3 Arts Entertainment Inc*
9460 Wilshire Blvd Fl 7
Beverly Hills, CA 90212-2713, USA

Semel, Terry (Business Person)
701 First Ave
Sunnyvale, CA 94089-1019, USA

Semenova, Juliana (Basketball Player)
Zalalela 4-35
Riga 1010, LATVIA

Semenyaka, Lyudmila (Ballerina)
Teatralnaya Pl 1
Moscow 103009, RUSSIA

Seminara, Frank (Athlete, Baseball Player)
8029 Harbor View Ter
Brooklyn, NY 11209-2822, USA

Semiz, Teata (Bowler)
3131 Kennedy Blvd
North Bergen, NJ 07047-2379, USA

Semizorova, Nina L (Ballerina)
2 Zhukovskaya St #8
Moscow, RUSSIA

Semjonova, Uljana (Athlete, Basketball Player)
Zalaiela 4-35
Riga 1010, Latvia

Semkow, Jerzy G
Ul Dynasy 6 m 1
Warsaw 00-354, POLAND

Semler, Dean (Cinematographer, Director)
4260 Arcola Ave
Toluca Lake, CA 91602-2902, USA

Semmelrogge, Martin
Terhallestr. 11
Munich, GERMANY D-81545

Sempe, Jean-Jacques (Cartoonist)
9 Rue du Cherche-Midi
Paris 75006, FRANCE

Semproch, Ray (Athlete, Baseball Player)
4220 Buechner Ave
Cleveland, OH 44109-5035, USA

Semyonov, Vladilen G (Ballerina)
15/17-504 Roubinshteina St
Saint Petersburg 191002, RUSSIA

Sen, Amartya K (Nobel Prize Laureate)
Economics Dept
Cambridge CB2 1TP, UNITED KINGDOM (UK)

Sen, Moon Moon (Actor)
Ruia Park Flat No 62 'B' Juhu
Bombay, MS 400 049, INDIA

Sen, Mrinal (Director)
4E Motilal Nehru Road
Culcutta 700029, INDIA

Sen, Riya (Actor, Bollywood)
62-B Ruia Park Juhu
Mumbai, MS 400049, INDIA

Sen, Sushmita (Actor, Bollywood)
Beach Queen Yari Road Versova Andheri W Floor 6
Mumbai, MS 400061, INDIA

Sena, Dominic (Director)
c/o Robert Newman *WmE2 (Endeavor-LA)*
9601 Wilshire Blvd Fl 3
Beverly Hills, CA 90210-5219, USA

Sena, Suzanne
6310 San Vicente Blvd Ste 200
Los Angeles, CA 90048-5488

Sendak, Maurice B (Writer)
200 Chestnut Hill Rd
Ridgefield, CT 06877-1200, USA

Sendel, Lorri (Stylist)
c/o Staff Member *AFG Management*
62 Chelsea Piers Ste 203
New York, NY 10011-1015, USA

Sendel, Peter (Athlete)
9 Zallaer St
Olympia, WA 98599-0001, GERMANY

Sendel, Sergio (Actor)
c/o Staff Member *Televisa*
Blvd Adolfo Lopez Mateos 232 Colonia San Angel INN
DF CP 01060, MEXICO

Senderens, Alain (Chef)
9 Place de la Madeleine
Paris 75008, FRANCE

Sendlein, Robin (Athlete, Football Player)
14737 E Mark Ln
Scottsdale, AZ 85262-7814, USA

Senff, Dina (Nida) (Swimmer)
Praam 122
Amstelveen 1186 TL, NETERLANDS

Senior, Peter (Golfer)
c/o Staff Member *Pro Golfers Association (PGA) Tour*
112 Tpc Blvd
Ponte Vedra Beach, FL 32082, USA

Senn, Adam (Model)
c/o Staff Member *NEXT*
188 rue de Rivoli
Paris 75001, FRANCE

Sennewald, Robert W (General)
212 Wolfe St
Alexandria, VA 22314-3858, USA

Senser, Joe (Athlete, Football Player)
4217 W 80th St
Bloomington, MN 55437, USA

Sensibaugh, Mike (Athlete, Football Player)
18414 Woodlands Terrace Dr
Glencoe, MO 63038-1829, USA

Sentelle, David B (Judge)
333 Constitution Ave NW
Washington, DC 20001-2804, USA

Senter, Marc (Actor)
c/o Jennifer Shoucair *S/W Pr Shop*
142 S Crescent Dr
Beverly Hills, CA 90212-3102, USA

Seoane, Manny (Athlete, Baseball Player)
8912 Southbay Dr
Tampa, FL 33615-2770, USA

Seow, Yit Kin (Musician)
8 North Terrace
London SW3 2BA, UNITED KINGDOM (UK)

Sepe, Crescenzio Cardinal (Religious Leader)
Piazza della Citta Leonina 9
Rome 193, ITALY

Seper, Zeynep (Beauty Pageant Winner)
Rue de Dilbeeck 200
Brussels B-1082, BELGIUM

Septimus, Jake (Producer)
c/o Staff Member *Creative Artists Agency (CAA-LA)*
2000 Avenue of the Stars Ste 100
Los Angeles, CA 90067-4705, USA

Sepulveda, Charlie (Musician)
568 Broadway # 608
New York, NY 10012-3225, USA

Sequeira, Luis (Biologist, Scientist)
10 Appomattox Ct
Madison, WI 53705-4202, USA

Serafini, Dan (Athlete, Baseball Player)
430 Alamosa Dr
Sparks, NV 89441-8583, USA

Serafini, Tito A (Biologist)
Neurobiology
San Francisco, CA 94143-0001, USA

Serafinowitz, Peter (Actor, Producer, Writer)
c/o Peter Principato *Principato/Young Management*
9465 Wilshire Blvd Ste 430
Beverly Hills, CA 90212-2613, USA

Serano, Greg (Actor)
c/o Erik Kritzer *Kritzer Levine Wilkins Entertainment*
11872 La Grange Ave Fl 1
Los Angeles, CA 90025-5283, USA

Seraphin, Oliver (Prime Minister)
44 Green's Lane
Goodwill, DOMINICA

Serbedzija, Rade (Actor)
Drury House 34-43 Russell St
London WC2B 5HA, UNITED KINGDOM (UK)

Serebrier, Jose (Composer)
20 Queensgate Gardens
London SW7 5LZ, UNITED KINGDOM (UK)

Serebrov, Alexander A (Misc)
Moskovskoi Oblasti
Syvisdny Goroduk 141160, RUSSIA

Serembus, John (Misc)
25 N 4th St
Philadelphia, PA 19106-2105, USA

Serendipity Singers, The (Music Group)
349 S Main St
Wauconda, IL 60084-1966

Sereno, Paul (Scientist)
Paleontology Dept
Chicago, IL 60537, USA

Seresin, Michael (Cinematographer)
59 North Wharf Road
London W2 1LA, UNITED KINGDOM (UK)

Sereys, Jacques
84 Bd Malesherbes
Paris, FRANCE F-75008

Sergei, Ivan (Actor)
c/o Joanna (Joanie) Burstein *Burstein Company, The*
15304 W Sunset Blvd Ste 208
Pacific Palisades, CA 90272-3656, USA

Serig, Jennifer (Designer, Fashion Designer)
c/o Staff Member *Perception Public Relations LLC*
3940 Laurel Canyon Blvd Ste 169
Studio City, CA 91604-3709, USA

Seriki, Hakeem (Chamillionaire) (Musician)
c/o Sara Ramaker *Paradigm (LA)*
360 N Crescent Dr
Beverly Hills, CA 90210-4874, USA

Serious, Yahoo (Actor)
12/33 E Crescent St
McMahons Point, NSW 2060, AUSTRALIA

Serkin, Peter A (Musician)
150 W 85th St
New York, NY 10024-4402, USA

Serkis, Andy (Actor)
c/o Staff Member *Gersh (LA)*
9465 Wilshire Blvd Ste 600
Beverly Hills, CA 90212-2612, USA

Serlemitsos, Peter J (Astronomer)
Space Flight Center
Greenbelt, MD 20771-0001, USA

Sermon, Eric (Musician)
1800 Argyle Ave # 408
Los Angeles, CA 90028-5253, USA

Serna, Assumpta (Actor)
8306 Wilshire Blvd # 438
Beverly Hills, CA 90211-2382, USA

Serna, Diego (Soccer Player)
1010 Rose Bowl Dr
Pasadena, CA 91103, USA

Serna, Paul (Athlete, Baseball Player)
32421 Outrigger Way
Laguna Niguel, CA 92677-4219, USA

Serna, Pepe (Actor)
127 Ruby Ave
Newport Beach, CA 92662-1125, USA

Serota, Nicholas A (Director)
Millbank
London SW1P 4RG, UNITED KINGDOM (UK)

Serpa, Joseph (Stylist)
c/o Staff Member *Ennis*
119 Braintree St
Boston, MA 02134-1628, USA

Serra, Eduardo (Cinematographer)
c/o Staff Member *United Talent Agency (UTA)*
9560 Wilshire Blvd Fl 5
Beverly Hills, CA 90212-2400, USA

Serra, Pablo (Writer)
c/o Gabriel Blanco *Gabriel Blanco Iglesias (Mexico)*
Rio Balsas 35-32 Colonia Cuauhtemoc
DF 6500, Mexico

Serra, Richard (Artist)
173 Duane St
New York, NY 10013-3334, USA

Serrano, Efrain (Tito El Bambino) (Musician)
c/o Staff Member *EMI Music Publishing (Latin America)*
404 Washington Ave Ste 700
Miami Beach, FL 33139-6615, USA

Serrano, Jimmy (Athlete, Baseball Player)
2943 E Erika Ct
Grand Junction, CO 81504-6963, USA

Serrano, Juan (Musician)
1450 Southgate Ave Apt 206
Daly City, CA 94015-4021, USA

Serrano, Nestor (Actor)
c/o Danielle Galiana-Allman *InnerAct Entertainment*
141 S Barrington Ave Ste E
Los Angeles, CA 90049-3314, USA

Serratos, Christian (Actor)
c/o Katie Rhodes *Untitled Entertainment (LA)*
350 S Beverly Dr Ste 200
Beverly Hills, CA 90212-4819, USA

Serrauot, Michel
201 Rue Du Faubourg-St -Honore
Paris, FRANCE F-75008

Serre, Jean-Pierre (Mathematician)
6 Ave de Montespan
Paris 75116, FRANCE

Serreau, Coline (Director)
20 Ave Rapp
Paris 75007, FRANCE

Serrin, James B (Mathematician)
4422 Dupont Ave S
Minneapolis, MN 55419-4739, USA

Serum, Gary (Athlete, Baseball Player)
10525 Hidden Oaks Ln N
Champlin, MN 55316-3045, USA

Servais, Scott (Athlete, Baseball Player)
4409 Triple Eagle Trl
Larkspur, CO 80118-5744, USA

Servan-Schreiber, Jean-Claude (Journalist)
147 Bis Rue d'Alesia
Paris 75014, FRANCE

Server, Josh (Actor)
c/o Mike Eistenstadt *Amsel, Eisenstadt & Frazier Talent Agency (AEF)*
5055 Wilshire Blvd Ste 860
Los Angeles, CA 90036-6108, USA

Service, Scott (Athlete, Baseball Player)
9920 Prechtel Rd
Cincinnati, OH 45252-2122, USA

Sesame Street
1 Lincoln Plz
New York, NY 10023-7129

Sessions, John
4 Windmill St
London, ENGLAND W1P 1HF

Sessions, William S (Judge)
112 E Pecan St Ste 2900
San Antonio, TX 78205-1549, USA

Sessler, Gerhard M (Inventor)
Fichtenstra 30B
Darmstadt 64285, GERMANY

Setari, Robert (Actor)
c/o Patty Stevens *Vessel Entertainment*
10989 Bluffside Dr Apt 3210
Studio City, CA 91604-4407

Seter, Mordecai (Composer)
1 Kamy St Ramat Aviv
Tel-Aviv, ISRAEL

Seth, Joshua (Actor)
c/o Staff Member *Sutton Barth & Vennari Inc*
145 S Fairfax Ave Ste 310
Los Angeles, CA 90036-2176, USA

Seth, Oliver (Judge)
PO Box 1
Santa Fe, NM 87504-0001, USA

Seth, Vikram (Writer)
Orion House 5 Upper St
London WC2H 9EA, UNITED KINGDOM (UK)

Sethi, Parmeet (Actor, Bollywood)
702/B-1 Sundervan Off Lokhandwala Road Andheri W
Mumbai, MS 400053, INDIA

Sethna, Homi N (Engineer)
Old Yacht Club Chatrapati Shivaji Maharaj
Bombay 400 038, INDIA

Setlow, Richard B (Biologist)
4 Beachland Ave
East Quogue, NY 11942-4941, USA

Settle, John (Athlete, Football Player)
505 E 6th St Unit 1603
Charlotte, NC 28202-3148, USA

Settle, Matthew (Actor)
c/o Jeb Brandon *Kritzer Levine Wilkins Entertainment*
11872 La Grange Ave Fl 1
Los Angeles, CA 90025-5283, USA

Settles, Sandra (Stylist)
423 27th St
San Francisco, CA 94131-1916, USA

Settles, Tawambi (Athlete, Football Player)
4204 Rogers Rd
Chattanooga, TN 37411-3244, USA

Setzer, Brian (Music Group, Musician)
c/o Staff Member *WmE2 (WMA-LA)*
1 William Morris Pl
Beverly Hills, CA 90212-4261, USA

Setziol, LeRoy I (Roy) (Artist)
30450 SW Moriah Ln
Sheridan, OR 97378-9745, USA

Seubert, Rich (Athlete, Football Player)
D1891 County Road C
Stratford, WI 54484-9330, USA

Seurer, Frank (Athlete, Football Player)
16168 S Brookfield St
Olathe, KS 66062-3927, USA

Sevastyanov, Vitayi I (Misc)
Moskovskoi Oblasti
Syvisdny Goroduk 141160, RUSSIA

Sevcik, John (Athlete, Baseball Player)
10107 Shinnecock Hills Dr
Austin, TX 78747-1318, USA

Sevendust (Music Group)
c/o Staff Member *TVT Records*
23 E 4th St Fl 3
New York, NY 10003-7023, USA

Severance, Joan (Actor)
c/o Steven Jensen *Independent Group, The*
6363 Wilshire Blvd Ste 115
Los Angeles, CA 90048-5734, USA

Severeid, Suzanne (Actor, Model)
PO Box 4171
Malibu, CA 90264-4171, USA

Severin, G Timothy (Tim) (Misc)
Inchy Bridge Timoleague
County Cork, IRELAND

Severino, John C (Misc)
401 S Prairie Ave
Inglewood, CA 90301-5001, USA

Severinsen, Al (Athlete, Baseball Player)
133 Warren Ave
Mystic, CT 06355-2136, USA

Severinsen, Carl H (Doc) (Musician)
11812 San Vicente Blvd Ste 200
Los Angeles, CA 90049-6622, USA

Severson, Jeff (Athlete, Football Player)
20625 Sierra Elena
Murrieta, CA 92562-8817, USA

Severson, Rich (Athlete, Baseball Player)
781 Spring Flowers Trl
Brandon, FL 33511-5993, USA

Sevier, Corey (Actor)
c/o Sheila Wenzel *Innovative Artists (LA)*
1505 10th St
Santa Monica, CA 90401-2805, USA

Sevigny, Chloe (Actor)
c/o Daniel (Danny) Sussman *Brillstein Entertainment Partners*
9150 Wilshire Blvd Ste 350
Beverly Hills, CA 90212-3453, USA

Sevilla, Carmen
Plaza de Pablo Ruiz Picasso s/n Torre Picasso Planto 36
Madrid, SPAIN 2800

Sevsec, Pedro (Actor)
c/o Staff Member *Telemundo*
2470 W 8th Ave
Hialeah, FL 33010-2000, USA

Sevy, Jeff (Athlete, Football Player)
5890 Arcadia Ave
Loomis, CA 95650-8734, USA

Seward, George C (Attorney, Attorney General, General)
1 Battery Park Plz
New York, NY 10004-1405, USA

Sewell, George (Actor)
68 Old Brompton Road
London SW7 3LQ, UNITED KINGDOM (UK)

Sewell, Harley (Athlete, Football Player)
1405 Lyra Ln
Arlington, TX 76013-8311, USA

Sewell, Rufus (Actor)
c/o Gene Parseghian *Parseghian Planco LLC*
322 8th Ave Ste 601
New York, NY 10001-6715, USA

Sewell, Steve (Athlete, Football Player)
15918 E Crestridge Pl
Centennial, CO 80015-4219, USA

Seweryn, Andrzej (Actor)
Place Colette
Paris 75001, FRANCE

Sex Pistols
c/o Mitch Schneider *Mitch Schneider Organization, The*
14724 Ventura Blvd Ste 410
Sherman Oaks, CA 91403-3537, USA

Sexauer, Elmer (Athlete, Baseball Player)
3605 Vanneman Ct SE
Atlanta, GA 30339-5731, USA

Sexsmith, Ron (Musician)
c/o Staff Member *Paradigm (Monterey)*
404 W Franklin St
Monterey, CA 93940-2303, USA

Sexson, Richie (Athlete, Baseball Player)
6539 170th Pl SE
Bellevue, WA 98006-6012, USA

Sexto, Camilo (Musician)
c/o Staff Member *BMG*
1540 Broadway
New York, NY 10036-4039, USA

Sexton, Brent (Actor)
c/o Staff Member *Greene & Associates*
1901 Avenue Of The Stars Ste 130
Los Angeles, CA 90067-6030, USA

Sexton, Charlie (Musician)
310 Water St # 201
Vancouver, BC V6B 1B6, CANADA

Sexton, Chris (Athlete, Baseball Player)
7030 Baytowne Dr
Cincinnati, OH 45247-5097, USA

Sexton, Jimmy (Athlete, Baseball Player)
2680 Baxter Rd
Wilmer, AL 36587-8225, USA

Sexton III, Brendan (Actor)
c/o Staff Member *Gersh (LA)*
9465 Wilshire Blvd Ste 600
Beverly Hills, CA 90212-2612, USA

Seydoux, Geraldine (Biologist)
Molecular Biology Dept
Baltimore, MD 21218, USA

Seydoux, Lea (Actor)
c/o Dallas Smith *United Agents*
12-26 Lexington St
London W1F OLE, UK

Seyferth, Dietmar (Misc)
Chemistry Dept
Cambridge, MA 2139, USA

Seyfried, Amanda (Actor)
c/o Evelyn Karamanos *WKT Public Relations (WKT-LA)*
9350 Wilshire Blvd Ste 450
Beverly Hills, CA 90212-3230, USA

Seyfried, Gordon (Athlete, Baseball Player)
56428 Lowe Ave
Yucca Valley, CA 92284-1740, USA

Seyler, Athene (Actor)
Coach House 26 Upper Mall Hammersmith
London W8, UNITED KINGDOM (UK)

Seymour, Cara (Actor)
c/o Vanessa Pereira *Artists Independent Management (LA)*
825 Nowita Pl
Venice, CA 90291-3836, USA

Seymour, Caroline (Actor)
17 Westfields Ave
London SW13 0AT, UNITED KINGDOM (UK)

Seymour, Carolyn (Actor)
8899 Beverly Blvd # 716
Los Angeles, CA 90048-2412, USA

Seymour, Jane (Actor, Producer)
c/o Susan Madore *Guttman Associates*
118 S Beverly Dr Ste 201
Beverly Hills, CA 90212-3016, USA

Seymour, John (Senator)
77655 Iroquois Dr
Indian Wells, CA 92210-6130, USA

Seymour, Lynn (Ballerina)
16 Balderton St
London W1Y 1TF, UNITED KINGDOM (UK)

Seymour, Paul (Athlete, Football Player)
4188 Shoals Dr
Okemos, MI 48864-3431, USA

Seymour, Paul C (Athlete, Football Player)
4188 Shoals Dr
Okemos, MI 48864-3431, USA

Seymour, Richard (Athlete, Football Player)
c/o Eugene Parker *Maximum Sports Management*
6435 W Jefferson Blvd # 197
Fort Wayne, IN 46804-6203, USA

Seymour, Stephanie (Model)
c/o Peg Donegan *Framework Entertainment (LA)*
9057 Nemo St Ste C
West Hollywood, CA 90069-5511, USA

Seymour, Stephanie K (Judge)
333 W 4th St
Tulsa, OK 74103-3839, USA

Seymour, Terri (Actor)
c/o Ivo Fischer *WmE2 (Endeavor-LA)*
9601 Wilshire Blvd Fl 3
Beverly Hills, CA 90210-5219, USA

Seynhaeve, Ingrid
111 E 22nd St Rm 200
New York, NY 10010-5414

Sezer, Ahmet Necdet (President)
Cumhurbaskanlgl Kosku Cankaya
Ankara, TURKEY

Sfar, Rachid (Prime Minister)
278 Ave de Tervuren
Brussels 1150, BELGIUM

Sfeir, Nasrallah Pierre Cardinal (Religious Leader)
Patriarcat Maronite
Bkerke, LEBANON

Sgouros, Dimitris (Musician)
Tompazi 28 Str
Piraeus 18537, GREECE

Shaback, Nick (Athlete, Basketball Player)
3019 49th St Apt 2N
Astoria, NY 11103-1315, USA

Shabala, Adam (Athlete, Baseball Player)
6 M St
Streator, IL 61364-2613, USA

Shack, Edward S P (Eddie) (Athlete, Hockey Player)
508 Fairlawn Ave
North York, ON M5M 1V2, Canada

Shack, William A (Misc)
4131 Rhoda Ave
Oakland, CA 94602-3442, USA

Shackelford, Don (Athlete, Football Player)
P.O. Box 1468
Lansdale, PA 19446, USA

Shackelford, Ted (Actor)
12305 Valleyheart Dr
Studio City, CA 91604-1643, USA

Shackleford, Brian (Athlete, Baseball Player)
2812 N Birch St
McAlester, OK 74501-2412, USA

Shackleford, Charles (Athlete, Basketball Player)
711 Haskett Ct
Kinston, NC 28501-8826, USA

Shackleford, Ray (Athlete, Basketball Player)
15458 Borges Dr
Moorpark, CA 93021-3228, USA

Shackouls, Bobby S (Business Person)
5051 Westheimer Rd
Houston, TX 77056-5622, USA

Shadic-Campbell, Lillian (Baseball Player)
61 Bloody Hill Rd
Craryville, NY 12521-5101, USA

Shadow (DJ)
690 5th St # 208
San Francisco, CA 94107-1517, USA

Shadyac, Tom (Director)
c/o Dan Aloni *Creative Artists Agency (CAA-LA)*
2000 Avenue of the Stars Ste 100
Los Angeles, CA 90067-4705, USA

Shafer, Martin (Business Person)
c/o Staff Member *Castle Rock Entertainment*
335 N Maple Dr Ste 175
Beverly Hills, CA 90210-3867, USA

Shafer, Matthew (Uncle Kracker) (Music Group, Musician)
c/o Jeff Kwatinetz *Prospect Park*
2049 Century Park E Ste 2550
Century City, CA 90067-3139, USA

Shafer, R Donald (Religious Leader)
PO Box 290
Grantham, PA 17027-0290, USA

Shaffer, Akiva (Director, Writer)
c/o Staff Member *Mosaic Media Group*
9200 W Sunset Blvd Ste 10
Los Angeles, CA 90069-3608, USA

Shaffer, Atticus (Actor)
c/o Linda Defilippo *D.C. Talent Management*
Prefers to be contacted via email or telephone
Los Angeles, CA 90069, USA

Shaffer, David H (Publisher)
175 5th Ave
New York, NY 10010-7703, USA

Shaffer, Lee (Athlete, Basketball Player)
3822 Nottaway Rd
Durham, NC 27707-5421, USA

Shaffer, Paul (Musician)
13587 Andalusia Dr
Santa Rosa Valley, CA 93012-9226, USA

Shaffer, Peter (Writer)
200 W 57th St Ste 503
New York, NY 10019-3211, USA

Shafsky, Janet (Stylist)
3920 Omalley Rd
Anchorage, AK 99507-4268, USA

Shagari, Alhaji Shehu Usman Aliu (President)
22 Shehu Crescent PO Box 162 Adarawa
Sokoto State, NIGERIA

Shaggy (Radio Personality)
c/o Staff Member *WPKX*
1331 Main St Ste 4
Springfield, MA 01103-1621, USA

Shah, Idries (Writer)
26/28 Bedford Row
London WC1R 4HL, UNITED KINGDOM (UK)

Shah, Kiran (Actor)
c/o Michael Henderson *Heresun Management*
4119 W Burbank Blvd
Burbank, CA 91505-2122, USA

Shah, Satish (Actor, Bollywood, Comedian)
30A Anand Nagar Forjeet St
Bombay, MS 400 036, INDIA

Shahan, Gil (Musician)
40 W 57th St
New York, NY 10019-4001, USA

Shahi, Sarah (Actor)
c/o Laura Myones *McKeon-Myones Management*
3500 W Olive Ave Ste 770
Burbank, CA 91505-5527, USA

Shahidi, Yara (Actor)
c/o Laura Ackerman *Much and House Public Relations*
8075 W 3rd St Ste 500
Los Angeles, CA 90048-4325, USA

Shaiman, Marc (Composer)
8476 Brier Dr
West Hollywood, CA 90046-1908, USA

Shakar, Martin (Actor)
118 E 37th St
New York, NY 10016-3025, USA

Shake, Christi (Model)
2518 Lodge Forest Dr
Baltimore, MD 21219-1911, USA

Shakespeare, Frank J Jr (Diplomat, Television Host)
303 Coast Blvd
La Jolla, CA 92037-4630, USA

Shakira (Musician)
c/o Ceci Kurzman *Nexus Management Group*
43 Clarkson St Ground Floor
New York, NY 10014, USA

Shakur, Kula
39A Gramercy Park N Apt 1C
New York, NY 10010-6312

Shakurov, Sergei K (Actor)
Bibliotechnava Str 27 #94
Moscow 109544, RUSSIA

Shalala, Donna (Secretary)
President's Office
Coral Gables, FL 33124, USA

Shalamar
707 18th Ave S
Nashville, TN 37203-3214

Shales, Thomas W (Journalist)
1150 15th St NW
Washington, DC 20071-0001, USA

Shales, Tom
1650 Kirby Rd
McLean, VA 22101-3209

Shalets, Victoria (Actor)
c/o Angharad Wood *Tavistock Wood Management*
32 Tavistock St
London WC2B 5HA, UK

Shalhoub, Tony (Actor)
c/o Mary Goldberg *Mary Goldberg Management*
4158 Grand Ave
Ojai, CA 93023-9382, USA

Shal-Houd, Tony
9560 Wilshire Blvd # 516
Beverly Hills, CA 90212-2427

Shalikashvili, John M (Shali) (General)
55 Chapman Loop
Steilacoom, WA 98388-1731, USA

Shalim (Musician)
c/o Staff Member *Sony Music Miami*
605 Lincoln Rd Ste 700
Miami Beach, FL 33139-2901, USA

Shalit, Gene (Critic)
30 Rockefeller Plz
New York, NY 10112-0015, USA

Shallow, Parvati (Reality TV Star)
c/o Ken Jacobson *Ken Jacobson Management*
Preferred to be contacted by phone
Los Angeles, CA 91367, USA

Shamir, Yitzhak (Prime Minister)
Beit Amot Mishpat 8 Shaul Hamelech Blvd
Tel Aviv 64733, ISRAEL

Shamrock, Ken (Actor, Athlete, Wrestler)
c/o Staff Member *UFC*
PO Box 26959
Las Vegas, NV 89126-0959, USA

Shamsky, Art (Athlete, Baseball Player)
PO Box 1400
New York, NY 10163-1400, USA

Shan Kuo-Hsi, Paul Cardinal (Religious Leader)
125 Szu-Wie 3rd Road
Kaohsiung 80203, TAIWAN

Shanahan, Brendan (Athlete, Hockey Player)
823 Park Ave
New York, NY 10021-2849, USA

Shanahan, Greg (Athlete, Baseball Player)
PO Box 6428
Eureka, CA 95502-6428, USA

Shanahan, Mike (Athlete, Coach, Football Coach, Football Player)
20 Cherry Hills Farm Dr
Englewood, CO 80113-7165, USA

Shand, Remy (Music Group, Musician, Songwriter, Writer)
2550 Victoria Park
Toronto, ON M2J 4A2, CANADA

Shandling, Garry (Actor, Comedian)
c/o Ariel (Ari) Emanuel *WmE2 (Endeavor-LA)*
9601 Wilshire Blvd Fl 3
Beverly Hills, CA 90210-5219, USA

Shandrowsky, Alex (Misc)
444 N Capitol St NW
Washington, DC 20001-1512, USA

Shane, Bob (Music Group, Musician)
9410 S 46th St
Phoenix, AZ 85044-7512, USA

Shangri-La's, The
27 L Ambiance Ct
Bardonia, NY 10954-1421

Shanice (Musician)
1800 Argyle Ave # 408
Los Angeles, CA 90028-5253, USA

Shank, Harvey (Athlete, Baseball Player)
201 E Jefferson St
Phoenix, AZ 85004-2412, USA

Shank, Roger C (Scientist)
Learning Sciences Institute
Evanston, IL 60201, USA

Shankar, Anoushka (Musician)
c/o Staff Member *International Creative Management (ICM-LA)*
10250 Constellation Blvd Fl 7
Los Angeles, CA 90067-6207, USA

Shankar, Naren (Producer)
c/o Staff Member *CSI*
7800 Beverly Blvd
Los Angeles, CA 90036-2112, USA

Shankar, Ravi (Composer, Musician)
17 Warden Ct Gowalia Tank Rd
Bombay 36, INDIA

Shanker, Ravi (Composer, Musician)
17 Warden Court Gowalia Tank Road
Bonbay 36, INDIA

Shankley, Amelia
2-4 Noel St
London, ENGLAND W1V 3RB

Shankman, Adam (Choreographer, Director)
c/o BeBe Lerner *ID Public Relations (ID-LA)*
7080 Hollywood Blvd Fl 8
Los Angeles, CA 90028-6906, USA

Shanks, Michael (Actor, Director, Writer)
c/o Jay Schwartz *Jay D Schwartz & Associates*
3151 Cahuenga Blvd W Ste 220
Los Angeles, CA 90068-1749, USA

Shanley, Jim (Athlete, Football Player)
4 Brookside Dr Apt D
Walla Walla, WA 99362, USA

Shanley, John Patrick (Director, Writer)
c/o Staff Member *Creative Artists Agency (CAA-LA)*
2000 Avenue of the Stars Ste 100
Los Angeles, CA 90067-4705, USA

Shannon (Music Group, Musician)
226 5th Ave
New York, NY 10001-7706, USA

Shannon (Musician)
c/o Staff Member *Diva Central Inc*
7510 W Sunset Blvd Ste 1445
Los Angeles, CA 90046-3408, USA

Shannon, Carver (Athlete, Football Player)
6005 S La Cienega Blvd
Los Angeles, CA 90056-1523, USA

Shannon, Howard (Athlete, Basketball Player)
4009 Valdez Ct
Plano, TX 75074-7944, USA

Shannon, Mem (Musician, Songwriter)
1048 Hesper Ave
Metairie, LA 70005-1552, USA

Shannon, Michael (Actor)
c/o Bryna Rifkin *ID PR (LA)*
7060 Hollywood Blvd Fl 8
Los Angeles, CA 90028-6014, USA

Shannon, Michael E (Business Person)
Ecolab Center 370 Wabasha St N
Saint Paul, MN 55102, USA

Shannon, Mike (Athlete, Baseball Player)
620 Market St
Saint Louis, MO 63101-1827, USA

Shannon, Molly (Actor, Comedian)
c/o Steven Levy *Framework Entertainment (LA)*
9057 Nemo St Ste C
West Hollywood, CA 90069-5511, USA

Shannon, Polly (Actor)
c/o Richard Caplan *Noble Caplan Abrams*
1260 Yonge St 2nd Floor
Toronto, ON M4T 1W6, Canada

Shannon, Randy (Athlete, Football Player)
7420 SW 107th Ave Apt 7-207
Miami, FL 33173-2970, USA

Shannon, Vicellous (Actor)
c/o Tony Chargin *Ovation Management*
12028 National Blvd
Los Angeles, CA 90064-3542, USA

Shantz, Robert C (Bobby) (Athlete, Baseball Player)
152 E Mount Pleasant Ave
Ambler, PA 19002-4209, USA

Shanze, Michael
Fichtenweg 8
Feldafing, GERMANY D-82340

Shapar, Howard K (Government Official)
PO Box 30242
Bethesda, MD 20824-0242, USA

Shaparo, Cara (Stylist)
c/o Staff Member *Artists by Timothy Priano (CA)*
8447 Wilshire Blvd Ste 301
Beverly Hills, CA 90211-3206, USA

Shapiro, Ascher H (Engineer)
111 Perkins St
Jamaica Plain, MA 02130-4313, USA

Shapiro, Dani (Writer)
1745 Broadway # B1
New York, NY 10019-4368, USA

Shapiro, Debbie (Actor)
9200 W Sunset Blvd Ste 900
Los Angeles, CA 90069-3604, USA

Shapiro, Harold T (Educator)
10 Campbelton Cir
Princeton, NJ 08540-3010, USA

Shapiro, Irwin I (Physicist)
17 Lantern Ln
Lexington, MA 02421-6029, USA

Shapiro, James (Doctor)
114th St & 89th Ave
Edmonton T6G 2M7, CANADA

Shapiro, Jim (Actor)
Legislative Office Building Room 4028
Hartford, CT 06106 -159, USA

Shapiro, Joel E (Artist)
32 E 57th St
New York, NY 10022-2513, USA

Shapiro, Kevin (Stylist)
c/o Staff Member *Montana Artists Agency*
9150 Wilshire Blvd Ste 100
Beverly Hills, CA 90212-3459, USA

Shapiro, Lorraine (Stylist)
7416 Waring Ave
Los Angeles, CA 90046-7521, USA

Shapiro, Mary L (Government Official)
450 5th St NW
Washington, DC 20001-2739, USA

Shapiro, Maurice M (Physicist)
5225 Pooks Hill Rd Apt 1122S
Bethesda, MD 20814-6721, USA

Shapiro, Mel (Writer)
Theater Film/TV Dept
Los Angeles, CA 90024, USA

Shapiro, Neal (Horse Racer)
296 Sharon Rd
Trenton, NJ 08691-2313, USA

Shapiro, Richard & Esther
617 N Alta Dr
Beverly Hills, CA 90210-3503

Shapiro, Robert (Lawyer)
10250 Constellation Blvd Fl 19
Los Angeles, CA 90067-6219, USA

Shapley, Lloyd S (Economist, Mathematician)
Economics Dept
Los Angeles, CA 90024, USA

Sharapova, Maria (Athlete, Tennis Player)
c/o Max Eisenbud *IMG (Cleveland)*
1360 E 9th St Ste 100
Cleveland, OH 44114-1730, USA

Share, Charlie (Chuck) (Athlete, Basketball Player)
12922 Twin Meadows Ct
Saint Louis, MO 63146-1803, USA

Sharif, Omar (Actor)
BP 41 Bougival
Yvelines 78380, FRANCE

Sharipov, Sallzhan S (Cosmonaut)
Moskovskoi Oblasti
Syvisdny Goroduk 141160, RUSSIA

Sharkey, Ed (Athlete, Football Player)
3615 Russell Rd
Centralia, WA 98531-1666, USA

Sharma, Barbara (Actor)
PO Box 29125
Los Angeles, CA 90029-0125, USA

Sharma, Chris (Athlete)
c/o Staff Member *Sanuk Climbing Team*
64 Fairbanks
Irvine, CA 92618-1602, USA

Sharma, Kawal (Actor, Bollywood)
A 502 Janak Deep Seven Bangalows
Versova Andheri
Bombay, MS 400 049, INDIA

Sharma, Rakesh (Cosmonaut)
Bangalore, KA 560037, INDIA

Sharma, Robin (Motivational Speaker, Writer)
1 W Pearce St Suite 505
Richmond Hill, ON L4B 3K3, Canada

Sharman, Bill (Athlete, Basketball Player)
138 Paseo De Gracia
Redondo Beach, CA 90277-5803, USA

Sharman, Helen (Cosmonaut)
12 Stratton Court Adelade Road Surbiton
Surrey, UNITED KINGDOM (UK)

Sharman, Jim (Director)
49 Daringhurst St
Kings Cross, NSW 2100, AUSTRALIA

Sharmila (Actor, Bollywood)
5 Narsimhan 1st Crossstreet B Reddy Road T Nagar N
Chennai, TN 600017, INDIA

Sharmili (Actor, Bollywood)
5/A Karnan Street Svt Maligai Rangarajapuram
Chennai, TN 600024, INDIA

Sharockman, Ed (Athlete, Football Player)
8955 Thomas Ln
Woodbury, MN 55125-7603, USA

Sharon, Dick (Athlete, Baseball Player)
1143 N 31st St
Billings, MT 59101-0132, USA

Sharp, Bill (Athlete, Baseball Player)
2244 Thornwood Ave
Wilmette, IL 60091-1454, USA

Sharp, Dee Dee (Musician)
8432 NW 31st Ct
Plantation, FL 33322, USA

Sharp, Don
80 Castelnau
London, ENGLAND SW13 9EX

Sharp, Kevin (Musician)
1415 River Landing Way
Woodstock, GA 30188-5345, USA

Sharp, Lesley
76 Oxford St
London, ENGLAND WIN OAX

Sharp, Leslie (Actor)
8942 Wilshire Blvd # 219
Beverly Hills, CA 90211-1908, USA

Sharp, Linda K (Coach)
American West Arena 201 E Jefferson St
Phoenix, AZ 85004, USA

Sharp, Marsha (Coach)
Athletic Dept
Lubbock, TX 79409, USA

Sharp, Mitchell W (Government Official)
33 Monkland Ave
Ottawa, ON K1S 1Y8, CANADA

Sharp, Phillip A (Nobel Prize Laureate)
36 Fairmont Ave
Newton, MA 02458-2506, USA

Sharp, Preston (Actor, Reality TV Star)
c/o Staff Member *Extreme Makeover: Home Edition*
Endemol Entertainment USA 9225 Sunset Blvd #1100
Los Angeles, CA 90069, USA

Sharp, Richard L (Business Person)
9950 Mayland Dr
Richmond, VA 23233-1463, USA

Sharpe, Rochelle P (Journalist)
94 Dudley St # 2
Brookline, MA 02445-5937, USA

Sharpe, Shannon (Athlete, Football Player)
867 Carlton Rdg NE
Atlanta, GA 30342-4346, USA

Sharpe, Sterling (Athlete, Football Player)
81 Running Fox Rd
Columbia, SC 29223-3052, USA

Sharpe, Thomas R (Tom) (Writer)
38 Tunwells Lane Great Shelford
Cambridge CB2 5LJ, UNITED KINGDOM (UK)

Sharpe, William F (Nobel Prize Laureate)
PO Box 610
Los Altos, CA 94023-0610, USA

Sharpe Jr, Luis E (Athlete, Football Player)
13418 S 38th Pl
Phoenix, AZ 85044-8202, USA

Sharper, Darren (Athlete, Football Player)
11613 Heverley Ct
Glen Allen, VA 23059-4829, USA

Sharper, Jamie (Athlete, Football Player)
11613 Heverley Ct
Glen Allen, VA 23059-4829, USA

Sharpless, K Barry (Nobel Prize Laureate)
10650 N Torrey Pines Rd
La Jolla, CA 92037-1001, USA

Sharpton, Al (Activist, Religious Leader)
106 W 145th St
New York, NY 10039-4138, USA

Sharqi, Sheikh Hamad bin Muhammad al (President)
Emiri Court PO Box 1
Fujairah, UNITED ARAB EMIRATES

Sharvani, Isha (Actor, Bollywood)
c/o Bunty Bahl *Carving Dreams Entertainment*
304-305, Oberoi Chambers II B Wing, Off New Link Road, Andheri West
Mumbai 400053, INDIA

Shasky, John (Athlete, Basketball Player)
1755 S Benson Rd
Frankfort, KY 40601-7649, USA

Shatalov, Vladimir A (Cosmonaut)
Moskovskoi Oblasti
Syvisdny Goroduk 141160, RUSSIA

Shatkin, Aaron J (Biologist)
679 Hoes Ln W
Piscataway, NJ 08854-8021, USA

Shatner, Melanie (Actor)
8285 W Sunset Blvd Ste 1
West Hollywood, CA 90046-2420, USA

Shatner, William (Actor)
c/o Larry Thompson *Larry A Thompson Organization*
9663 Santa Monica Blvd Ste 801
Beverly Hills, CA 90210-4303, USA

Shatraw, David
c/o Staff Member *Stone Manners Salners Agency (LA)*
9911 W Pico Blvd Ste 1400
Los Angeles, CA 90035-2715, USA

Shattuck, Kim (Musician)
40 W 57th St # 1800
New York, NY 10019-4001, USA

Shattuck, Molly (Reality TV Star)
c/o Staff Member *Fox Broadasting Company*
PO Box 900
Beverly Hills, CA 90213-0900

Shattuck, Shari (Actor, Writer)
4142 Big Tujunga Canyon Rd
Tujunga, CA 91042-1010

Shaud, Grant (Actor)
8738 Appian Way
Los Angeles, CA 90046-7733, USA

Shaud, John A (General)
1745 Jefferson Davis Hwy Ste 202
Arlington, VA 22202-3423, USA

Shaughnessy, Charles (Actor)
c/o Staff Member *Marshak/Zachary Company, The*
8840 Wilshire Blvd Fl 1
Beverly Hills, CA 90211-2606, USA

Shave, Jon (Athlete, Baseball Player)
1801 Park Way Dr
Fernandina Beach, FL 32034-2417, USA

Shavelson, Mel
11947 Sunshine Ter
North Hollywood, CA 91604-3708

Shaver, Billy Joe (Musician, Songwriter, Writer)
435 N Martel Ave
Los Angeles, CA 90036-2513, USA

Shaver, Helen (Actor)
1505 10th St
Santa Monica, CA 90401-2805, USA

Shaver, Jeff (Athlete, Baseball Player)
9651 E Clinton St
Scottsdale, AZ 85260-6209, USA

Shavers, Ernie (Boxer)
30 Doreen Ave Moretown Wirral
Merseyside CH46 6DN, UNITED KINGDOM (UK)

Shavick, James (Actor, Director, Producer, Writer)

Shaw, Bernard (Correspondent)
7526 Heatherton Ln
Potomac, MD 20854-3222, USA

Shaw, Bryant (Athlete, Football Player)
7900 Churchill Way Apt 1301
Dallas, TX 75251-2010, USA

Shaw, Carolyn Hagner (Publisher)
2620 P St NW
Washington, DC 20007-3062, USA

Shaw, Dennis (Athlete, Football Player)
14844 Priscilla St
San Diego, CA 92129-1525, USA

Shaw, Don (Athlete, Baseball Player)
857 Waterford Villas Dr
Lake Saint Louis, MO 63367-2574, USA

Shaw, Fiona (Actor)
76 Oxford St
London W1N 0AX, UNITED KINGDOM (UK)

Shaw, Jeffrey L (Jeff) (Athlete, Baseball Player)
1215 Storybrook Dr
Washington Court House, OH 43160-2608, USA

Shaw, John H (Geophysicist, Physicist)
Geophysics Dept
Cambridge, MA 2138, USA

Shaw, Kenneth A (Educator)
Presidential S Ofc
Syracuse, NY 13244-0001, USA

Shaw, Lindsey (Actor)
c/o Pat Cutler *Cutler Management*
165 Little Park Ln
Los Angeles, CA 90049-4023, USA

Shaw, Mariena (Musician)
2608 9th St
Berkeley, CA 94710-2550, USA

Shaw, Martin (Actor)
36 - 40 Glasshouse St
London W1B 5DL, UNITED KINGDOM (UK)

Shaw, Pete (Athlete, Football Player)
25052 Pappas Rd
Ramona, CA 92065-4920, USA

Shaw, Robert (Athlete, Football Player)
4013 Centenary Ave
Dallas, TX 75225-5430, USA

Shaw, Robert (Athlete, Football Player)
487 Old Coach Rd Apt D
Westerville, OH 43081-1392, USA

Shaw, Robert J (Bob) (Athlete, Baseball Player)
10 Ocean Dr
Jupiter, FL 33469-3512, USA

Shaw, Run Run (Producer)
Shaw House Lot 220 Clear Water Bar Road
Kowloon, Hong Kong, CHINA

Shaw, Scott (Journalist)
20771 Lake Rd
Cleveland, OH 44116-1335, USA

Shaw, Sedrick (Athlete, Football Player)
1007 Waller St
Austin, TX 78702-2632, USA

Shaw, Stan (Actor)
1505 10th St
Santa Monica, CA 90401-2805, USA

Shaw, Tim
5315 River Ave
Newport Beach, CA 92663-2208

Shaw, Timothy A (Tim) (Swimmer)
5315 River Ave
Newport Beach, CA 92663-2208, USA

Shaw, Tommy (Musician, Songwriter, Writer)
c/o Sterling Bacon *TBA Artist Management (Atlanta)*
1111 Alderman Dr Ste 285
Alpharetta, GA 30005-5433, USA

Shaw, Victoria (Musician, Songwriter, Writer)
PO Box 58175
Nashville, TN 37205-8175, USA

Shaw, Vinessa (Actor)
955 Carrillo Dr Ste 300
Los Angeles, CA 90048-5400, USA

Shaw, William L (Billy) (Athlete, Football Player)
3427 Old Rothell Rd
Toccoa, GA 30577-9436, USA

Shaw Jr, Brewster H (Astronaut)
3519 Rice Blvd
Houston, TX 77005-2937, USA

Shawkat, Alia (Actor, Producer)
c/o Michelle Theodat *Kipperman Management*
243 W 72nd St Apt 2
New York, NY 10023-2704, USA

Shawn, Wallace (Actor, Writer)
c/o Christopher Black *Opus Entertainment*
5225 Wilshire Blvd Ste 905
Los Angeles, CA 90036-4353, USA

Shawyer, David
16 Rylett Rd
London, ENGLAND W12

Shay, Jerry (Athlete, Football Player)
81 E Shasta St
Chula Vista, CA 91910-6127, USA

Shaye, Lin (Actor)
9300 Wilshire Blvd Ste 555
Beverly Hills, CA 90212-3211, USA

Shaye, Skyler (Actor)
c/o Dorothy Koster *Crystal Sky/Artists Only Management*
10203 Santa Monica Blvd Fl 5
Los Angeles, CA 90067-6405, USA

Shchedrin, Rodion K (Composer)
Tverskaya St #31
Moscow 103050, RUSSIA

Shea, Charity (Actor)
c/o Scott Karp *Crystal Sky Pictures*
10203 Santa Monica Blvd Ste 500
Los Angeles, CA 90067-6416, USA

Shea, Dan (Actor)
c/o Staff Member *Talent Plus*
1222 Lucas Ave Ste 300
Saint Louis, MO 63103-1937, USA

Shea, Eric (Actor)
27710 Jubilee Run Rd
Pearblossom, CA 93553-3439, USA

Shea, George Beverly
1300 Harmon Pl
Minneapolis, MN 55403-1925

Shea, Jere (Actor)
8730 W Sunset Blvd Ste 440
Los Angeles, CA 90069-2277, USA

Shea, John (Actor)
40 Carl Hall Rd
Toronto, ON M3K 2B8, CANADA

Shea, Joseph F (Scientist)
15 Dogwood Rd
Weston, MA 02493-2403, USA

Shea, Judith (Artist)
10 Newbury St
Boston, MA 02116-3204, USA

Shea, Katt (Actor)
8942 Wilshire Blvd # 219
Beverly Hills, CA 90211-1908, USA

Shea, Pat (Athlete, Football Player)
1175 Evergreen Dr
Encinitas, CA 92024-3918, USA

Shea, Robert M (General)
2 Navy St
Washington, DC 20380-1775, USA

Shea, Steve (Athlete, Baseball Player)
1 Shepherds Ln
North Hampton, NH 03862-2133, USA

Shea, Terry (Coach, Football Coach)
Athletic
San Jose, CA 95192-0001, USA

Sheaffer, Danny (Athlete, Baseball Player)
165 Savannah Ln
Mount Airy, NC 27030-8688, USA

Shealy, Ryan (Athlete, Baseball Player)
2168 NE 63rd Ct
Fort Lauderdale, FL 33308-1335, USA

Shear, Jules (Actor, Musician, Songwriter, Writer)
c/o Staff Member *Concerted Efforts*
PO Box 440326
Somerville, MA 02144-0004, USA

Shear, Rhonda (Actor, Comedian, Model)
2550 Greenvalley Rd
Los Angeles, CA 90046-1438, USA

Sheard, Kiera Kiki (Musician)
c/o Staff Member *EMI Gospel*
PO Box 5085
Brentwood, TN 37024-5085, USA

Shearer, Al (Actor, Reality TV Star)
c/o Staff Member *Dolores Robinson Entertainment*
9250 Wilshire Blvd Ste 220
Beverly Hills, CA 90212-3344, USA

Shearer, Alan (Soccer Player)
Saint James Park
Newcastle-Tyne NE1 4ST, UNITED KINGDOM (UK)

Shearer, Bob (Golfer)
281 Clarence St Floor 2
Sydney, NSW 2000, AUSTRALIA

Shearer, Harry (Actor, Comedian)
c/o Melanie Greene *Affirmative Entertainment*
425 N Robertson Blvd
West Hollywood, CA 90048-1735, USA

Shearer, Peter M (Geophysicist, Physicist)
Geophysics
La Jolla, CA 92093-0001, USA

Shearer, S Bradford (Brad) (Athlete, Football Player)
1909B Lakeshore Dr Apt B
Austin, TX 78746-2904, USA

Shearin, Joe (Athlete, Football Player)
3533 Stanford Ave
Dallas, TX 75225-7402, USA

Shearmur, Edward (Ed) (Composer, Musician)
c/o Staff Member *Gorfaine/Schwartz Agency Inc*
4111 W Alameda Ave Ste 509
Burbank, CA 91505-4171, USA

Shearn, Tom (Athlete, Baseball Player)
1254 Spring Brook Ct
Westerville, OH 43081-3785, USA

Shears, Jake (Musician)
c/o Staff Member *Paradigm (NY)*
360 Park Ave S Fl 16
New York, NY 10010-1708, USA

Shearsmith, Reece (Actor)
c/o Lorraine Hamilton *Hamilton Hodell Ltd*
66-68 Margaret St Fl 5
London W1W 8SR, UK

Sheckler, Ryan (Actor, Skateboarder)
c/o Nick Styne *Creative Artists Agency (CAA-LA)*
2000 Avenue of the Stars Ste 100
Los Angeles, CA 90067-4705, USA

Shedd, Kenny (Athlete, Football Player)
1928 Tioga Pass Way
Antioch, CA 94531-9054, USA

Sheedy, Ally (Actor)
c/o Bill Veloric *Innovative Artists (NY)*
235 Park Ave S Fl 7
New York, NY 10003-1404, USA

Sheehan, Doug (Actor)
1505 10th St
Santa Monica, CA 90401-2805, USA

Sheehan, Jeremiah J (Business Person)
PO Box 27003
Richmond, VA 23261-7003, USA

Sheehan, Neil (Journalist)
4505 Klingle St NW
Washington, DC 20016-3580, USA

Sheehan, Patrick (Golfer)
2913 Ashton Ter
Oviedo, FL 32765-7949, USA

Sheehan, Patty (Golfer)
c/o Staff Member *Ladies Pro Golf Association (LPGA)*
100 International Golf Dr
Daytona Beach, FL 32124-1092, USA

Sheehan, Susan (Writer)
4505 Klingle St NW
Washington, DC 20016-3580, USA

Sheehy, Timothy (Tim) (Athlete, Hockey Player)
4 Boswell Ln
Southborough, MA 01772-1763, USA

Sheelor, Willie (Baseball Player)
152 Beaumont Ave
Kannapolis, NC 28083-6501, USA

Sheen, Charles (Actor)
4814 Lemara Ave
Sherman Oaks, CA 91403, USA

Sheen, Charlie (Actor)
c/o Mark Burg *Evolution Entertainment (LA)*
901 N Highland Ave
Los Angeles, CA 90038-2412, USA

Sheen, Martin (Actor)
c/o Steve Rohr *Lexicon Public Relations*
1901 Avenue of the Stars Fl 2
Los Angeles, CA 90067-6001, USA

Sheen, Michael (Actor, Producer)
c/o Tammy Rosen *Sanders Armstrong Caserta*
425 N Robertson Blvd
West Hollywood, CA 90048-1735, USA

Sheen, Ramon
6916 Dume Dr
Malibu, CA 90265-4227

Sheer, Ireen
Yachthof B-22
Waldeck, GERMANY D-34513

Sheerer, Gary (Athlete)
1557 Country Club Dr
Los Altos Hills, CA 94024-5908, USA

Sheets, Andy (Athlete, Baseball Player)
104 Villaggio Dr
Lafayette, LA 70508-6795, USA

Sheets, Ben (Athlete, Baseball Player)
730 N Plankinton Ave Unit 8B
Milwaukee, WI 53203-2406, USA

Sheets, Larry (Athlete, Baseball Player)
1411 Chippendale Rd
Lutherville Timonium, MD 21093-1608, USA

Sheffer, Craig (Actor)
5699 Kanan Rd # 275
Agoura, CA 91301-3358, USA

Sheffield, Fred (Athlete, Basketball Player)
11664 McDougall
Tustin, CA 92782-3345, USA

Sheffield, Gary A (Athlete, Baseball Player)
6731 30th St S
Saint Petersburg, FL 33712-5566, USA

Sheffield, John M (Johnny) (Actor)
834 1st Ave
Chula Vista, CA 91911-1451, USA

Sheffield, Johnny
834 1st Ave
Chula Vista, CA 91911-1451

Sheffield, Lois (Baseball Player)
227 Jones St
Wellington, OH 44090-1062, USA

Sheffield, Tony (Baseball Player)
PO Box 164
Tullahoma, TN 37388-0164, USA

Sheffield, William J (Bill) (Ex-Governor)
P.O. Box 911476
Anchorage, AK 99509, USA

Shefft, Jen (Reality TV Star)
c/o Michael (Mike) Esterman
Esterman.Com, LLC
Prefers to be contacted via email
MD, USA

Shehee, Rashaan (Athlete, Football Player)
6120 Bay Club Ct
Bakersfield, CA 93312-6212, USA

Sheibler, Jim
PO Box 60
Venice, CA 90294-0060

Sheik, Duncan (Musician, Songwriter, Writer)
75 Rockefeller Plz
New York, NY 10019-6908, USA

Sheikh, Farooque (Actor, Bollywood)
Rafi Mansion 28th Road Bandra
Mumbai, MS 400050, INDIA

Sheila E (Musician)
1005 N Alfred St Apt 2
West Hollywood, CA 90069-4757, USA

Sheindlin, Judge Judy (Judge, Television Host)
c/o Jane Dystel *Dystel & Goderich Literary Management*
1 Union Sq W Ste 904
New York, NY 10003-3313, USA

Sheiner, David S (Actor)
1827 Veteran Ave Apt 19
Los Angeles, CA 90025-4567, USA

Sheinfeld, David (Composer)
112 Ash Way
San Rafael, CA 94903-2902, USA

Shelby, Carol (Race Car Driver)
19020 Anelo Ave
Gardena, CA 90248-4520

Shelby, Carroll (Race Car Driver)
19020 Anelo Ave
Gardena, CA 90248-4520, USA

Shelby, John (Athlete, Baseball Player)
2232 Broadhead Pl
Lexington, KY 40515-1147, USA

Shelby, Mark (Composer, Musician)
11761 E Speedway Blvd
Tucson, AZ 85748-2017, USA

Sheldon, Bob (Athlete, Baseball Player)
3013 River Lakes Dr
Whitefish, MT 59937-7801, USA

Sheldon, Jack (Musician)
7095 Hollywood Blvd Ste 617
Los Angeles, CA 90028-8912, USA

Sheldon, Rollie (Athlete, Baseball Player)
614 NE Coronado Ave
Lees Summit, MO 64063-2522, USA

Sheldon, Scott (Athlete, Baseball Player)
306 Robin Hill Dr
Altamonte Springs, FL 32701-7824, USA

Shell, Arthur (Art) (Athlete, Coach, Football Coach, Football Player)
469 Creekside Dr
Monroe, GA 30655-7713, USA

Shell, Donnie (Athlete, Football Player)
2945 Shandon Rd
Rock Hill, SC 29730-9521, USA

Shell, Todd (Athlete, Football Player)
4222 E McLellan Cir Unit 15
Mesa, AZ 85205-3119, USA

Shellen, Stephen (Actor)
3655 St Laurent # 205
Montreal, Quebec HX 2V5, Canada

Shellenbeck, Jim (Athlete, Baseball Player)
10627 Dreamy Ln
Parker, AZ 85344-7576, USA

Shelley, Barbara (Actor)
91 Regent St
London W1R 7TB, UNITED KINGDOM (UK)

Shelley, Carole (Actor)
c/o Steve Stone *Cornerstone Talent Agency*
37 W 20th St
New York, NY 10011-3706, USA

Shelley, Howard G (Conductor, Musician)
38 Cholmeley Park
London N6 5ER, UNITED KINGDOM (UK)

Shelley, Rachel (Actor)
c/o Kesha Williams *Affirmative Entertainment*
425 N Robertson Blvd
West Hollywood, CA 90048-1735, USA

Shelly, Randy (Actor)
c/o Ellen Gilbert *Abrams Artists Agency (LA)*
9200 W Sunset Blvd PH 11
Los Angeles, CA 90069-3601, USA

Shelton, Abigail (Actor)
8831 Sunset Blvd # 402
Los Angeles, CA 90069, USA

Shelton, Angela V (Comedian)
c/o Staff Member *Gekis Management*
4217 Verdugo View Dr
Los Angeles, CA 90065-4317, USA

Shelton, Ben (Athlete, Baseball Player)
4925 S Forrestville Ave Apt 2N
Chicago, IL 60615-2470, USA

Shelton, Blake (Musician)
PO Box 1511
Ada, OK 74821-1511, USA

Shelton, Chris (Athlete, Baseball Player)
6382 Shady Grove Cir
Salt Lake City, UT 84121-6508, USA

Shelton, Craig (Athlete, Basketball Player)
8618 Leslie Ave
Glenarden, MD 20706-1528, USA

Shelton, Deborah (Actor)
c/o Marc Bass *Beacon Talent Agency*
170 Apple Ridge Rd
Woodcliff Lake, NJ 07677-8149, USA

Shelton, L J (Athlete, Football Player)
6034 W Trovita Pl
Chandler, AZ 85226-1271, USA

Shelton, Lonnie (Athlete, Basketball Player)
1201 40th St Apt 74
Bakersfield, CA 93301-1171, USA

Shelton, Marley (Actor)
c/o Jason Weinberg *Untitled Entertainment (LA)*
350 S Beverly Dr Ste 200
Beverly Hills, CA 90212-4819, USA

Shelton, Peter (Architect)
56 W 22nd St Fl 12
New York, NY 10010-7279, USA

Shelton, Richard (Athlete, Football Player)
6367 Raw Hyde Trl N
Jacksonville, FL 32210-3821, USA

Shelton, Ricky Van (Musician, Songwriter)
PO Box 111
Woodlawn, VA 24381-0111, USA

Shelton, Ronald W (Director)
c/o Staff Member *WmE2 (WMA-LA)*
1 William Morris Pl
Beverly Hills, CA 90212-4261, USA

Shelton, Samantha (Actor)
c/o Staff Member *Innovative Artists (LA)*
1505 10th St
Santa Monica, CA 90401-2805, USA

Shelton, William E (Educator)
Eastern Michigan University President's Office
Ypsilanti, MI 48197, USA

Shemin, Robert (Business Person, Writer)
c/o PREIG 7965 S 700 E
Sandy, UT 84070, USA

Shen, Parry (Actor)
c/o Staff Member *Lichtman/Salners Company*
12216 Moorpark St
Studio City, CA 91604-5228, USA

Shenandoah (Music Group)
PO Box 680956
Franklin, TN 37068-0956, USA

Shenandoh, Joanne (Musician, Songwriter, Writer)
PO Box 450
Oneida, NY 13421-0450, USA

Shenkman, Ben (Actor)
2 Charlton St Apt 5K
New York, NY 10014-4970, USA

Shepard, Bert (Athlete, Baseball Player)
1116 S Richmond Ave
Tulsa, OK 74112-5212, USA

Shepard, Dax (Actor, Reality TV Star, Writer)
c/o Staff Member *Baker Winokur Ryder Public Relations (BWR-LA)*
9100 Wilshire Blvd Ste 500 PMB WEST
Beverly Hills, CA 90212-3426, USA

Shepard, Devon (Producer, Writer)
c/o Staff Member *Agency for the Performing Arts (APA-LA)*
405 S Beverly Dr Ste 500
Beverly Hills, CA 90212-4425, USA

Shepard, Jean (Musician)
5811 Still Hollow Rd
Nashville, TN 37215-4819, USA

Shepard, Judy (Activist)
301 Thelma Dr # 512
Casper, WY 82609-2325, USA

Shepard, Kenny Wayne (Musician)
c/o Staff Member *Richard De La Font Agency*
3808 W South Park Blvd
Broken Arrow, OK 74011-1261, USA

Shepard, Kiki (Actor)
c/o Staff Member *Cunningham Escott Slevin & Doherty (CESD-LA)*
10635 Santa Monica Blvd Ste 130
Los Angeles, CA 90025-8306, USA

Shepard, Larry (Athlete, Baseball Player, Coach)
8516 Westgate St
Lenexa, KS 66215-2860, USA

Shepard, Roger N (Psychic)
5775 Montclair Ave
Marysville, CA 95901-6820, USA

Shepard, Samuel (Sam) (Actor, Writer)
c/o Staff Member *Eighth Square Entertainment*
606 N Larchmont Blvd Ste 307
Los Angeles, CA 90004-1309, USA

Shepard, Vonda (Actor, Musician, Songwriter, Writer)
c/o Staff Member *Marleah Leslie & Associates PR*
1645 Vine St Apt 712
Los Angeles, CA 90028-8812, USA

Sheperd, Ben (Musician)
6523 California Ave SW # 348
Seattle, WA 98136-1833, USA

Sheperd, Elizabeth (Actor)
2-4 Noel St
London W1V 3RB, UNITED KINGDOM (UK)

Sheperd, Morgan (Race Car Driver)
57 Rhody Creek Loop
Stuart, VA 24171-3011, USA

Shephard, Gillian P (Government Official)
Westminster
London SW1A 0AA, UNITED KINGDOM (UK)

Shepherd, Chris (Director, Writer)
c/o Staff Member *Slinky Pictures*
Old Truman Brewery 91 Brick Ln
London E16 QN, UNITED KINGDOM (UK)

Shepherd, Cybill (Actor)
c/o Judy Hofflund *Hofflund/Polone*
9465 Wilshire Blvd Ste 420
Beverly Hills, CA 90212-2603, USA

Shepherd, Gannon (Athlete, Football Player)
5818 Alvaton Ct
Norcross, GA 30092-3901, USA

Shepherd, Keith (Athlete, Baseball Player)
860 Alber St
Wabash, IN 46992-1635, USA

Shepherd, Ron (Athlete, Baseball Player)
5821 FM 349
Kilgore, TX 75662-6905, USA

Shepherd, Sherri (Actor, Comedian, Talk Show Host)
c/o Elizabeth Morris *Rogers & Cowan PR (LA)*
Pacific Design Center 8687 Melrose Ave, 7th Floor
West Hollywood, CA 90069, USA

Shepherd, Sherrie (Cartoonist)
200 Madison Ave
New York, NY 10016-3903, USA

Shepherd, William M (Astronaut)
18623 Prince William Ln
Houston, TX 77058-4224, USA

Shepis, Tiffany (Actor)
c/o Michael J Roberts *D-Mentd Entertainment*
Prefers to be contact via email or telephone
Wilmington, NC, USA

Sheppard, Delia (Actor, Model)
4795 S Sandhill Rd Ste 9
Las Vegas, NV 89121-6029, USA

Sheppard, Jonathan (Misc)
287 Lamborntown Rd
West Grove, PA 19390-9237, USA

Sheppard, Julian (Comedian)
c/o Staff Member *Gersh (LA)*
9465 Wilshire Blvd Ste 600
Beverly Hills, CA 90212-2612, USA

Sheppard, Mike (Coach, Football Coach)
Athletic
Albuquerque, NM 87131-0001, USA

Sheppard, William Morgan (Actor)
c/o Bri Franchot *Franchot Management*
PO Box 48890A
Los Angeles, CA 90048-0971, USA

Sheps, Cecil G (Biologist)
388 Carolina Meadows Villa
Chapel Hill, NC 27517-7522, USA

Sher, Antony (Actor)
18-21 Jermyn St
London SW1Y 6NB, UNITED KINGDOM (UK)

Sher, Eden (Actor)
c/o Adam Griffin *Kritzer Levine Wilkins Entertainment*
11872 La Grange Ave Fl 1
Los Angeles, CA 90025-5283, USA

Shera, Mark (Actor)
PO Box 15717
Beverly Hills, CA 90209-1717, USA

Sherba, John (Musician)
1235 9th Ave
San Francisco, CA 94122-2306, USA

Sherbedgia, Rade (Actor)
1505 10th St
Santa Monica, CA 90401-2805, USA

Sherer, Dave (Athlete, Football Player)
4212 Colgate Ave
Dallas, TX 75225-6603, USA

Sherffius, John (Cartoonist)
900 N Tucker Blvd
Saint Louis, MO 63101-1069, USA

Sheridan, Bonnie
18011 Martha St
Encino, CA 91316-1052

Sheridan, Bonnie Bramlett (Actor, Musician)
18011 Martha St
Encino, CA 91316-1052, USA

Sheridan, Dave C (Actor, Writer)
c/o Kara Welker *Generate Management*
1545 26th St Ste 200
Santa Monica, CA 90404-3554, USA

Sheridan, Dinah (Actor)
76 Oxford St
London W1N 0AX, UNITED KINGDOM (UK)

Sheridan, Jamey (Actor)
c/o Scott Schachter *International Creative Management (ICM-LA)*
10250 Constellation Blvd Fl 7
Los Angeles, CA 90067-6207, USA

Sheridan, Jim (Actor, Director, Producer, Writer)
21 Mespil Rd.
Dublin 4, Ireland

Sheridan, Lisa (Actor)
c/o Joanna (Joanie) Burstein *Burstein Company, The*
15304 W Sunset Blvd Ste 208
Pacific Palisades, CA 90272-3656, USA

Sheridan, Liz (Actor)
11333 Moorpark St # 427
West Toluca Lake, CA 91602-2618

Sheridan, Neill (Athlete, Baseball Player)
150 Chaucer Ct
Pleasant Hill, CA 94523-4104, USA

Sheridan, Nicole (Adult Film Star)
c/o Staff Member *Atlas Multimedia Inc*
9005 Eton Ave Ste C
Canoga Park, CA 91304-6533, USA

Sheridan, Nicollette (Actor)
c/o Nicole Perna *Baker Winokur Ryder Public Relations (BWR-LA)*
9100 Wilshire Blvd Ste 500 PMB WEST
Beverly Hills, CA 90212-3426, USA

Sheridan, Pat (Athlete, Baseball Player)
31654 Taft St
Wayne, MI 48184-2234, USA

Sheridan, Rondell (Actor)
1025 N Kings Rd Apt 113
Los Angeles, CA 90069-6007, USA

Sheridan, Tony (Musician)
PO Box 1031
Montrose, CA 91021-1031, USA

Sheriff, Haja (Actor)
2 0/1 Desikar St
Chennai, TN 600 026, INDIA

Sherk, Jerry M (Athlete, Football Player)
1819 Bel Air Ter
Encinitas, CA 92024-5502, USA

Sherk, Kathy (Golfer)
1333 Dorval Dr
Oakville, ON L6M 4G2, CANADA

Sherlock, Nancy J (Astronaut)
2101 Nasa Pkwy Spc Center
Houston, TX 77058-3607, USA

Sherlock-Currie, Nancy
2101 Nasa Pkwy
Houston, TX 77058-3607, USA

Sherman, Allie (Athlete, Football Coach, Football Player)
136 E 55th St Apt 12H
New York, NY 10022-4523, USA

Sherman, Bobby (Actor, Musician)
1870 Sunset Plaza Dr
Los Angeles, CA 90069-1314, USA

Sherman, Cindy (Photographer)
519 W 24th St
New York, NY 10011-1104, USA

Sherman, Darrell (Athlete, Baseball Player)
20695 Azalea Terrace Rd
Riverside, CA 92508-3505, USA

Sherman, Edgar A (Coach, Football Coach)
681 Nancy Ln
Newark, OH 43055-4333, USA

Sherman, Heath (Athlete, Football Player)
2785 County Road 247
Wharton, TX 77488-5554, USA

Sherman, Mike (Athlete, Coach, Football Coach, Football Player)
3337 Arapaho Ridge Dr
College Station, TX 77845-4540, USA

Sherman, Richard M (Composer, Musician)
1875 Century Park E Ste 1120
Los Angeles, CA 90067-2529, USA

Sherman, Rod (Football Player)
PO Box 4551
Incline Village, NV 89450-4551, USA

Sherman, Saul (Athlete, Football Player)
1313 N Wood St # 2
Chicago, IL 60622-3204, USA

Sherman-Palladino, Amy (Director, Producer, Writer)
c/o Staff Member *Creative Artists Agency (CAA-LA)*
2000 Avenue of the Stars Ste 100
Los Angeles, CA 90067-4705, USA

Shernoff, William M (Attorney, Attorney General, General)
600 S Indian Hill Blvd
Claremont, CA 91711-5444, USA

Sherod, Edmund (Athlete, Basketball Player)
519 Montvale Ave
Richmond, VA 23222-3020, USA

Sherrard, Michael W (Mike) (Athlete, Football Player)
5661 Colodny Dr
Agoura Hills, CA 91301-2217, USA

Sherrill, Dennis (Athlete, Baseball Player)
1691 Tolley Ter SE
Palm Bay, FL 32909-8831, USA

Sherrill, George (Athlete, Baseball Player)
2092 Lee Pl
Memphis, TN 38104-2804, USA

Sherrill, Jackie W (Coach, Football Coach)
Athletic Dept
Mississippi State, MS 39762, USA

Sherrill, Tim (Athlete, Baseball Player)
PO Box 812
Harrison, AR 72602-0812, USA

Sherrin, Edward G (Ned) (Director)
4 Cornwall Mansions Ashburnham Road
London SW10 0PE, UNITED KINGDOM (UK)

Sherrington, Georgina (Actor)
c/o Staff Member *JGM*
15 Lexham Mews
London W8 6JW, UNITED KINGDOM (UK)

Sherrod, Derek (Football Player)
c/o Adisa P. Bakari *Dow Lohnes PLLC*
1200 New Hampshire Ave NW Ste 800
Washington, DC 20036-6800, USA

Sherry, Norm (Athlete, Baseball Player, Coach)
4383 Nobel Dr Unit 89
San Diego, CA 92122-1575, USA

Sherry, Paul H (Religious Leader)
700 Prospect Ave E
Cleveland, OH 44115-1110, USA

Sherwin, Tim (Athlete, Football Player)
6 Mill Rd
Latham, NY 12110-1184, USA

Sherwood, Brad (Actor, Producer)
c/o Erik Kritzer *Kritzer Levine Wilkins Entertainment*
11872 La Grange Ave Fl 1
Los Angeles, CA 90025-5283, USA

Sheshadri, Meenakshi (Actor, Bollywood)
601 Sheshadri Moonbeam Union Park Khar W
Mumbai, MS 400052, INDIA

Shesol, Jeff (Cartoonist)
5777 W Century Blvd Ste 700
Los Angeles, CA 90045-5652, USA

Shestakova, Tatyana B (Actor)
Rubinstein St 18
Saint Petersburgh, RUSSIA

Shetty, Reshma (Actor)
c/o Smith (Stevie) Stephanie *Station3*
1051 Cole Ave
Los Angeles, CA 90038-2601, USA

Shetty, Shilpa (Actor, Bollywood)
12 Dev Darshan 262 St Anthony Road Chembur
Mumbai, MS 400071, INDIA

Shetty, Sunil (Actor, Bollywood)
18/B Prithvi Apartments Altamont Rd
Mumbai, MS 400026, INDIA

Shevchenko, Arkady N (Politician)
201 E 50th St
New York, NY 10022-7703

Shi, David E (Educator)
President S Ofc
Greenville, SC 29613-0001, USA

Shicoff, Neil (Opera Singer)
Maximilianstr 22
Munich 80539, GERMANY

Shields, Ben (Actor)
1749 N Serrano Ave Apt 213
Los Angeles, CA 90027-3416, USA

Shields, Beth K (Stylist)
3001 Carob St
Newport Beach, CA 92660-3216, USA

Shields, Billy (Athlete, Football Player)
12701 Treeridge Ter
Poway, CA 92064-6426, USA

Shields, Brooke (Actor, Model)
9200 W Sunset Blvd Ste 600
Los Angeles, CA 90069-3196, USA

Shields, Perry (Judge)
400 2nd St NW
Washington, DC 20217-0001, USA

Shields, Robert (Misc)
PO Box 3161
Cottonwood, AZ 86326-2592, USA

Shields, Samona (Samantha Strong) (Adult Film Star)
3324 Castle Heights Ave
Los Angeles, CA 90034-2729, USA

Shields, Scott (Athlete, Football Player)
3317 Kennelworth Ln
Bonita, CA 91902-1507, USA

Shields, Steve (Athlete, Baseball Player)
4969 Leonard Dr
Gadsden, AL 35903-4638, USA

Shields, Tommy (Athlete, Baseball Player)
518 N Elm St
Lititz, PA 17543-1312, USA

Shields, Tyler (Cinematographer)
c/o Eric Podwall *Podwall Entertainment*
710 N Orlando Ave Apt 203
Los Angeles, CA 90069-5549, USA

Shields, Will H (Athlete, Football Player)
13125 W 127th Pl
Overland Park, KS 66213-3846, USA

Shiell, Jason (Athlete, Baseball Player)
301 Sting Ray Ct
Guyton, GA 31312-6592, USA

Shiely, John S (Business Person)
PO Box 702
Milwaukee, WI 53201-0702, USA

Shifflett, Garland (Athlete, Baseball Player)
1095 Cody St
Lakewood, CO 80215-4818, USA

Shifflett, Steve (Athlete, Baseball Player)
24004 E 172nd St
Pleasant Hill, MO 64080-7582, USA

Shifty, Shellshock (Musician)
729 7th Ave Ste 1600
New York, NY 10019-6880, USA

Shigeta, James (Actor)
10635 Santa Monica Blvd Ste 130
Los Angeles, CA 90025-8306, USA

Shih, Wen Yann (Actor)
c/o Vincent Cirrincione *Vincent Cirrincione Associates*
1516 N Fairfax Ave
Los Angeles, CA 90046-2608, USA

Shikler, Aaron (Artist)
44 W 77th St
New York, NY 10024-5150, USA

Shiley, Newhouse Jean (Athlete, Track Athlete)
1100 Sunnybrae Ave
Chatsworth, CA 91311, USA

Shilling, Curt (Baseball Player)
c/o Staff Member *Boston Red Sox*
4 Yawkey Way
Boston, MA 02215-3496, USA

Shilton, Justin (Actor)
c/o Staff Member *Magnolia Entertainment (LA)*
9595 Wilshire Blvd Ste 601
Beverly Hills, CA 90212-2506, USA

Shilton, Peter (Soccer Player)
Hubbards Cottage Bentley Lane
Maxstoke near Coleshill B46 2QR, UNITED KINGDOM (UK)

Shima, Masatoshi (Engineer)
260 Tsurumaki Omika Haramachishi
Fukushima 975-0049, JAPAN

Shimada, Yoko
7245 Hillside Ave Apt 415
Los Angeles, CA 90046-2342

Shimell, William (Opera Singer)
3 Burlington Lane Chiswick
London W4 2TH, UNITED KINGDOM (UK)

Shimerman, Armin (Actor)
1505 10th St
Santa Monica, CA 90401-2805, USA

Shimkis, Joanna
9255 Doheny Rd
Los Angeles, CA 90069-3200

Shimkus, Joanna (Actor)
c/o Staff Member *Creative Artists Agency (CAA-LA)*
2000 Avenue of the Stars Ste 100
Los Angeles, CA 90067-4705, USA

Shimmerman, Armin (Actor)
c/o Staff Member *Innovative Artists (LA)*
1505 10th St
Santa Monica, CA 90401-2805, USA

Shimono, Sab (Actor)
12711 Ventura Blvd Ste 440
Studio City, CA 91604-2456, USA

Shin, Yong Moon (Biologist)
Sillimdong Gwanakgu
Seoul 151-742, SOUTH KOREA

Shinall, Zak (Athlete, Baseball Player)
16605 Sell Cir
Huntington Beach, CA 92649-3299, USA

Shindle, Kate
2 Convention Blvd Ste 1000
Atlantic City, NJ 08401-4137

Shinefield, Henry R (Misc)
2240 Hyde St # 2
San Francisco, CA 94109-1509, USA

Shiner, Dick (Athlete, Football Player)
6683 Terrace Way
Harrisburg, PA 17111-7057, USA

Shines, Anthony (Razor) (Athlete, Baseball Player)
11508 Herb Cv
Austin, TX 78750-3671, USA

Shinko (Stylist)
c/o Staff Member *Rex Agency, The*
6311 Romaine St
Los Angeles, CA 90038-2617, USA

Shinn, Christopher (Comedian)
c/o Staff Member *Gersh (LA)*
9465 Wilshire Blvd Ste 600
Beverly Hills, CA 90212-2612, USA

Shinn, George (Business Person)
210 Park Ave Ste 1850
Oklahoma City, OK 73102-5636, USA

Shinners, John (Athlete, Football Player)
N120W1495 Freistadt Road
Germantown, WI 53022, USA

Shinoda, Mike (Musician)
9560 Wilshire Blvd # 400
Beverly Hills, CA 90212-2427, USA

Shiny Toy Guns (Music Group)
c/o Staff Member *Paradigm (Monterey)*
404 W Franklin St
Monterey, CA 93940-2303, USA

Shipanoff, Dave (Athlete, Baseball Player)
3 Salina Dr
St Albert, AB T8N 0L1, Canada

Shipkey, Jerry (Athlete, Football Player)
PO Box 31259
Laughlin, NV 89028-1259, USA

Shipler, David K (Journalist)
4005 Thornapple St
Bethesda, MD 20815-5037, USA

Shipley, Craig (Athlete, Baseball Player)
4 Yawkey Way Attn V
Boston, MA 02215-3409, USA

Shipley, Joe (Athlete, Baseball Player)
23 Park Dr
Saint Charles, MO 63303-3607, USA

Shipley, Walter V (Financier)
270 Park Ave
New York, NY 10017-2014, USA

Shipman, Clarie (Correspondent)
77 W 66th St
New York, NY 10023-6201, USA

Shipman, Kim (Golfer)
239 Texas Dr
Hideaway, TX 75771-5030, USA

Shipp, E R (Misc)
220 E 42nd St
New York, NY 10017-5806, USA

Shipp, Jackie (Athlete, Football Player)
3117 Trails Ct
Norman, OK 73072-7459, USA

Shipp, Jerry (Athlete, Basketball Player)
PO Box 370
Kingston, OK 73439-0370, USA

Shipp, John Wesley (Actor)
c/o Janette Anderson *Janette Anderson Entertainment*
9682 Via Torino
Burbank, CA 91504-1410, USA

Shipp, William (Athlete, Football Player)
3920 Camellia Dr
Mobile, AL 36693-2814, USA

Shirakawa, Hideki (Nobel Prize Laureate)
Chemistry Dept Sakura-Mura
Ibaraki 305, JAPAN

Shirayanagi, Peter Seiichi Cardinal (Religious Leader)
3-16-15 Sekiguchi Bunkyoku
Tokyo 112, JAPAN

Shire, David L (Composer)
19 Ludlow Ln
Palisades, NY 10964-1606, USA

Shire, Talia (Actor, Director)
10730 Bellagio Rd
Los Angeles, CA 90077-3730, USA

Shirelles, The
PO Box 100
Clifton, NJ 07015-0100

Shirk, Gary (Athlete, Football Player)
5419 Silchester Ln
Charlotte, NC 28215-5307, USA

Shirley, Al (Baseball Player)
PO Box 1235
Chesapeake, VA 23327-1235, USA

Shirley, Bart (Athlete, Baseball Player)
6538 Orangetip Dr
Corpus Christi, TX 78414-6088, USA

Shirley, Bob (Athlete, Baseball Player)
761 W 13th St
Tulsa, OK 74127-9162, USA

Shirley, Caroline (Stylist)
c/o Staff Member *Ennis*
119 Braintree St
Boston, MA 02134-1628, USA

Shirley, George I (Opera Singer)
Music School
Ann Arbor, MI 48109, USA

Shirley, J Dallas (Referee)
5324 Pommel Dr
Mount Airy, MD 21771-8124, USA

Shirley, Steve (Athlete, Baseball Player)
9200 James Pl NE
Albuquerque, NM 87111-3323, USA

Shirley-Quirk, John S (Opera Singer)
511 N Chapel Gate Ln
Baltimore, MD 21229-2403, USA

Shirodkar, Shilpa (Actor, Bollywood)
Venkatesh Vihar 4th Floor 7th Road Khar
Mumbai, MS 400050, INDIA

Shiver, Sanders (Athlete, Football Player)
9217 Christo Ct
Owings Mills, MD 21117-3596, USA

Shivers, Roy (Athlete, Football Player)
2067 Hidden Hollow Ln
Henderson, NV 89012-3203, USA

Shivpuri, Himani (Actor)
16A/24 Pgm Colony Poonam Nagar
Mahakali Caves Road Andheri E
Bombay, MS 400 093, INDIA

Shivpuri, Ritu (Actor, Bollywood)
12 Poonam 29/30 Pali Hill Union Bank Khar
Bombay, MS 400 052, INDIA

Shlaudeman, Harry W (Diplomat)
7006 Pebble Beach Way
San Luis Obispo, CA 93401-8916, USA

Shlomi, Vince (Offer) (Director)
1680 Michigan Ave Ste 700
Miami Beach, FL 33139-2551, USA

Shlyapina, Galina A (Ballerina)
Teatralnaya Pl 1
Moscow 103009, RUSSIA

Shnayerson, Robert B (Editor)
118 Riverside Dr
New York, NY 10024-3708, USA

Shoals, Roger (Athlete, Football Player)
365 Righters Mill Rd
Gladwyne, PA 19035-1542, USA

Shobana (Actor, Bollywood)
7 7/5 Gulmohar Avenue Velachery High Rd
Chennai, TN 600032, INDIA

Shobana, Maganadhi (Actor, Bollywood)
A P 198 16th Street 2nd Sector
Chennai, TN 600078, INDIA

Shobert, Bubba (Race Car Driver)
8905 153rd St
Wolfforth, TX 79382-4305, USA

Shocked, Michelle (Musician)
28 Union St
Whitefield, NH 03598-3503, USA

Shockey, Jeremy (Athlete, Football Player)
c/o Traci Harper *Harper PR*
3940 Laurel Canyon Blvd Ste 1010
Studio City, CA 91604-3709, USA

Shockley, Costen (Athlete, Baseball Player)
403 Wilson St
Georgetown, DE 19947-2340, USA

Shockley, Jeremy (Football Player)
Giants Stadium
East Rutherford, NJ 7073, USA

Shockley, William (Actor)
6345 Balboa Blvd Ste 375
Encino, CA 91316-5238, USA

Shoecraft, John A (Misc)
7430 E Stetson Dr
Scottsdale, AZ 85251-3566, USA

Shoeffling, Michael
PO Box 2563
Canyon Country, CA 91386-2563

Shoemaker, Bill
250 W Main St # 1820
Lexington, KY 40507-1714

Shoemaker, Carolyn S (Astronomer)
1400 W Mars Hill Rd
Flagstaff, AZ 86001-4470, USA

Shoemaker, Craig (Actor)
c/o Staff Member *Osbrink Talent Agency*
4343 Lankershim Blvd Ste 100
West Toluca Lake, CA 91602-2705, USA

Shoemaker, Robert M (General)
PO Box 768
Belton, TX 76513-0768, USA

Shoemaker, Sydney S (Misc)
104 Northway Rd
Ithaca, NY 14850-2241, USA

Shoemate, C Richard (Business Person)
International Plaza 700 Sylvan Ave
Englewood Cliffs, NJ 7632, USA

Shofner, Delbert M (Del) (Athlete, Football Player)
1665 Del Mar Ave
San Marino, CA 91108-2621, USA

Shofner, James (Jim) (Athlete, Football Coach, Football Player)
9620 Champions Dr
Granbury, TX 76049-4447, USA

Shoji, Dave (Coach)
Athletic Dept
Hilo, HI 96720, USA

Shonekan, Ernest A O (President)
12 Alexander Ave Ikoyi
Lagos, NIGERIA

Shonin, Georgi S (Cosmonaut, General)
Moskovskoi Oblasti
Syvisdny Goroduk 141160, RUSSIA

Shoop, Ron
PO Box 92
Rural Valley, PA 16249-0092

Shopay, Tom (Athlete, Baseball Player)
10145 NW 19th St
Doral, FL 33172-2529, USA

Shope, Allan (Architect)
18 W Putnam Ave
Greenwich, CT 06830-5341, USA

Shoppach, Kelly (Athlete, Baseball Player)
6117 Forest River Dr
Fort Worth, TX 76112-1066, USA

Shor, Anya (Stylist)
c/o Staff Member *Judy Inc*
1 Yorkville Ave
Toronto ON M4W 1L1, Canada

Shore, David (Producer, Writer)
c/o Lawrence Shuman *Shuman Company*
3815 Hughes Ave Fl 4
Culver City, CA 90232-2715, USA

Shore, Howard (Actor, Composer, Musician)
c/o Staff Member *Columbia Artists Mgmt Inc*
1790 Broadway Fl 6
New York, NY 10019-1537, USA

Shore, Pauly (Actor, Comedian)
c/o Staff Member *Landing Patch Productions*
8491 W Sunset Blvd # 700
West Hollywood, CA 90069-1911, USA

Shore, Roberta
PO Box 71639
Salt Lake City, UT 84171-0639

Shores, Del (Writer)
13636 Ventura Blvd # 218
Sherman Oaks, CA 91423-3700, USA

Shorr, Lonnie
707 18th Ave S
Nashville, TN 37203-3214

Short, Bill (Athlete, Baseball Player)
2975 57th St
Sarasota, FL 34243-2434, USA

Short, Brandon (Athlete, Football Player)
1717 Sumac St
McKeesport, PA 15132-5470, USA

Short, Columbus (Actor)
c/o Colton Gramm *Brillstein Entertainment Partners*
9150 Wilshire Blvd Ste 350
Beverly Hills, CA 90212-3453, USA

Short, Eugene (Athlete, Basketball Player)
8111 Fondren Lake Dr
Houston, TX 77071-3610, USA

Short, Martin (Actor, Comedian, Musician)
c/o Stacy Mark *WmE2 (Endeavor-LA)*
9601 Wilshire Blvd Fl 3
Beverly Hills, CA 90210-5219, USA

Short, Nigel (Misc)
Peterborough Court Marsh Wall
London E14, UNITED KINGDOM (UK)

Short, Purvis (Athlete, Basketball Player)
8111 Fondren Lake Dr
Houston, TX 77071-3610, USA

Short, Rick (Athlete, Baseball Player)
3021 Forsythe Ct
Peoria, IL 61614-1119, USA

Short, Thomas C (Misc)
1515 Broadway
New York, NY 10036-8901, USA

Shorter, Frank (Athlete, Track Athlete)
558 Utica Ct
Boulder, CO 80304-0773, USA

Shorter, Wayne (Composer, Musician)
278 S Main St # 400
Gloucester, MA 1930, USA

Shorthill, Richard W (Engineer)
Mechanical Engineering Dept
Salt Lake City, UT 84112, USA

Shortridge, Steve (Actor)
1707 Clear View Dr
Beverly Hills, CA 90210-2012, USA

Shorts, Peter (Athlete, Football Player)
810 S Cedar Point Dr
Anaheim, CA 92808-1680, USA

Shostakovich, Maxim D (Musician)
PO Box 105
Jordanville, NY 13361-0105, USA

Shou, Robin (Actor)
10100 Santa Monica Blvd Ste 2500
Los Angeles, CA 90067-4116, USA

Shoults, Paul (Athlete, Football Player)
530 Tanglewood Ln Apt 204
Mishawaka, IN 46545-2654, USA

Shouse, Brian (Athlete, Baseball Player)
3121 W Summerbend Ct
Peoria, IL 61615-8879, USA

Shouse, Dexter (Athlete, Basketball Player)
4523 E Rhonda Dr
Phoenix, AZ 85018-7223, USA

Shout Out Louds (Music Group)
c/o Staff Member *Paradigm (Monterey)*
404 W Franklin St
Monterey, CA 93940-2303, USA

Show, Frida (Actor)
c/o Kim Matuka *Online Talent Group*
Prefers to be contacted via email or telephone
Los Angeles, CA 90069, USA

Show, Grant (Actor)
c/o Heather Reynolds *One Entertainment (NY)*
12 W 57th St PH 1
New York, NY 10019-3900, USA

Showalter III, William N (Buck) (Athlete, Baseball Player, Coach)
9736 Hathaway St
Dallas, TX 75220-2114, USA

Shower, Kathy (Actor, Model)
Provenca 23 1-1
Barcelona, SPAIN

Shraner, Kim (Actor)
c/o Robyn Friedman *Artist Management Inc*
464 King St E
Toronto ON M5A 1L7, CANADA

Shreve, Anita (Writer)

Shreve, Susan R (Writer)
3506 35th St NW
Washington, DC 20016-3114, USA

Shribman, David M (Journalist)
1130 Connecticut Ave NW
Washington, DC 20036-3901, USA

Shrider, Richard (Athlete, Basketball Player)
6666 Morning Sun Rd
Oxford, OH 45056-8843, USA

Shrimpton, Jean (Actor, Model)
Abbey Hotel Penzance
Cornwall, UNITED KINGDOM (UK)

Shriner, Kin (Actor)
6500 Wilshire Blvd Ste 2200
Los Angeles, CA 90048-4942, USA

Shriner, Wil (Entertainer)
5313 Quakertown Ave
Woodland Hills, CA 91364-3542, USA

Shriver, Anthony
100 SE 2nd St # 1990
Miami, FL 33131-2100

Shriver, Bobby
501 Colorado Ave Ste 200
Santa Monica, CA 90401-2426

Shriver, Duward F (Scientist)
1100 Colfax St
Evanston, IL 60201-2611, USA

Shriver, Loren J (Astronaut)
108 Charleston St
Friendswood, TX 77546-4928, USA

Shriver, Maria (Correspondent, Television Host)
3110 Main St Ste 300
Santa Monica, CA 90405-5354, USA

Shriver, Mark Kennedy
10015 Carter Rd
Bethesda, MD 20817

Shriver, Pam
c/o Jill Smoller *WmE2 (Endeavor-LA)*
9601 Wilshire Blvd Fl 3
Beverly Hills, CA 90210-5219, USA

Shriver, R
1325 G St NW
Washington, DC 20005-3104, USA

Shroff, Jackie (Actor, Bollywood)
1302 Le Pepeyon Mount Mary Road Bandra
Mumbai, MS 400050, INDIA

Shrontz, Frank A (Business Person)
2949 81st Pl SE # P
Mercer Island, WA 98040-3059, USA

Shroud, Johnathan (Writer)
17 Alwyne Villas
London N1 2HG, UNITED KINGDOM

Shrowder, Lisa (Race Car Driver)
1650 E Golf Rd
Schaumburg, IL 60196-0001, USA

Shroyer, Sonny (Actor)
12725 Ventura Blvd Ste F
Studio City, CA 91604-2437, USA

Shtalenkov, Mikhail (Athlete, Hockey Player)
501 Broadway
Nashville, TN 37203-3980, USA

Shtokolov, Boris T (Opera Singer)
Teatralnaya Pl 1
Saint Petersburg, RUSSIA

Shuart, James M (Educator)
President's Office
Hempstead, NY 11550, USA

Shuba, George (Athlete, Baseball Player)
3421 Bentwillow Ln
Youngstown, OH 44511-2502, USA

Shubin, Neil H (Biologist)
Biology Dept
Cambridge, MA 2138, USA

Shue, Andrew (Actor)
c/o Jimmy Darmody *Creative Artists Agency (CAA-LA)*
2000 Avenue of the Stars Ste 100
Los Angeles, CA 90067-4705, USA

Shue, Elisabeth (Actor)
c/o David Seltzer *Management 360*
9111 Wilshire Blvd
Beverly Hills, CA 90210-5508, USA

Shue, Gene (Athlete, Basketball Player, Coach)
4338 Redwood Ave Unit 303
Marina Del Rey, CA 90292-7648, USA

Shuey, Paul (Athlete, Baseball Player)
5252 Mill Dam Rd
Wake Forest, NC 27587-6386, USA

Shugart, Alan F (Inventor)
920 Disc Dr
Scotts Valley, CA 95066-4544, USA

Shugart, Clyde (Athlete, Football Player)
1628 Champagne Ave
Gulf Breeze, FL 32563-9036, USA

Shugarts, Bret (Athlete, Football Player)
3724 Knob Hill Farm Rd
Evans, GA 30809-6697, USA

Shuken, Ettie Benjamin (Stylist)
c/o Staff Member *Judy Inc*
1 Yorkville Ave
Toronto ON M4W 1L1, Canada

Shukovsky, Joel (Writer)
4024 Radford Ave
Studio City, CA 91604-2101, USA

Shula, David D (Dave) (Athlete, Coach, Football Coach, Football Player)
10805 Indian Trl
Cooper City, FL 33328-5509, USA

Shula, Donald F (Don) (Athlete, Coach, Football Coach, Football Player)
16 Indian Creek Island Rd
Indian Creek Village, FL 33154-2904, USA

Shula, Mike (Athlete, Coach, Football Coach, Football Player)
19140 Peninsula Club Dr
Cornelius, NC 28031-5122, USA

Shuler, Heath (Athlete, Football Player)
900 Johnnie Dodds Blvd Ste 103
Mount Pleasant, SC 29464-6177, USA

Shuler, Mickey C (Athlete, Football Player)
332 Belle Vista Dr
Marysville, PA 17053-9640, USA

Shuler Jr, Ellie G (Buck) (General)
32 Willow Way W
Alexander City, AL 35010, USA

Shulgin, Alexander (Scientist)
1483 Shulgin Rd
Lafayette, CA 94549-2226, USA

Shulman, Lawrence E (Scientist)
3726 Tudor Arms Ave
Baltimore, MD 21211-2245, USA

Shulman, Robert G (Biologist)
333 Cedar St
New Haven, CT 06510-3206, USA

Shulock, John (Baseball Player)
4180 5th St SW
Vero Beach, FL 32968-3909, USA

Shulock, John (Athlete, Baseball Player)
4180 5th St SW
Vero Beach, FL 32968-3909, USA

Shultz, George P (Politician, Secretary)
Stanford University
Stanford, CA 94305, USA

Shum Jr., Harry (Actor)
c/o Marissa Upchurch *Triniti Management*
12400 Ventura Blvd # 668
Studio City, CA 91604-2406, USA

Shumaker, Anthony (Athlete, Baseball Player)
2213 Jefferson St
Paducah, KY 42001-3108, USA

Shumaker, John W (Educator)
Presidents Ofc
Louisville, KY 40292-0001, USA

Shuman-Juransinski, Amy (Baseball Player)
424 Douglass St
Wyomissing, PA 19610-2906, USA

Shumate, John (Athlete, Basketball Player, Coach)
16406 S 12th Pl
Phoenix, AZ 85048-4045, USA

Shumate, Rachel (Actor)
c/o Sean Fay *Kritzer Levine Wilkins Entertainment*
11872 La Grange Ave Fl 1
Los Angeles, CA 90025-5283, USA

Shumlin, Peter (Governor, Politician)
109 State St Ofc Bldg
Montpelier, VT 05609-0002, USA

Shumpert, Terry (Athlete, Baseball Player)
8432 Fairview Ct
Lone Tree, CO 80124-3181, USA

Shut Up Stella (Music Group)
c/o Staff Member *Paradigm (Monterey)*
404 W Franklin St
Monterey, CA 93940-2303, USA

Shutt, Steve (Athlete, Coach, Hockey Player)
65 Villiers
Toronto, ON M5A 3S1, Canada

Shuttleworth, Mark (Astronaut)
PO Box 1159
Durbanville 7551, SOUTH AFRICA

Shuttz, George P
776 Dolores St
Stanford, CA 94305-8428, USA

Shy, Don (Athlete, Football Player)
1645 Avenida Oceano
Oceanside, CA 92056-6948, USA

Shy, Les (Athlete, Football Player)
512 N McClurg Ct Apt 3611
Chicago, IL 60611-4122, USA

Shyamalan, M Night (Director, Producer, Writer)
c/o Staff Member *Night Chronicles*
c/o Media Rights Capital 1800 Century Park East
Los Angles, CA 90067, USA

Shydner, Ritch (Comedian)
c/o Staff Member *Agency for the Performing Arts (APA-LA)*
405 S Beverly Dr Ste 500
Beverly Hills, CA 90212-4425, USA

Shyer, Charles R (Director, Writer)
227 N Glenroy Ave
Los Angeles, CA 90049-2417, USA

Shys, The (Music Group)
c/o Staff Member *Paradigm (Monterey)*
404 W Franklin St
Monterey, CA 93940-2303, USA

Sia, Beau (Actor)
c/o Staff Member *Creative Artists Agency (CAA-LA)*
2000 Avenue of the Stars Ste 100
Los Angeles, CA 90067-4705, USA

Siana (Model)
2113 Cocoa Cir
Virginia Beach, VA 23454-2213

Siani, Michael J (Mike) (Athlete, Football Player)
9768 Leyland Dr Unit 11
Myrtle Beach, SC 29572-5553, USA

Sias, John B (Publisher)
901 Mission St
San Francisco, CA 94103-2905, USA

Sibbett, Jane (Actor)
c/o John Carrabino *John Carrabino Management*
5900 Wilshire Blvd Ste 406
Los Angeles, CA 90036-5015, USA

Sibert, Sam (Athlete, Basketball Player)
4615 Enchanted Bay Blvd
Arlington, TX 76016-5331, USA

Sibley, Antoinette (Ballerina)
36 Battersea Square
London SW11 3LT, UNITED KINGDOM (UK)

Sibley, David (Actor)
c/o Staff Member *Select Artists Ltd (CA-Westside Office)*
1138 12th St Apt 1
Santa Monica, CA 90403-5459, USA

Sibley, Marilyn (Stylist)
c/o Staff Member *Clutts Agency, The*
1400 Turtle Creek Blvd # 171
Dallas, TX 75207-3337, USA

Sibley, Mark (Athlete, Basketball Player)
334 E McKenna Ct
Elmhurst, IL 60126-5361, USA

Sicard, Pedro (Actor)
c/o Gabriel Blanco *Gabriel Blanco Iglesias (Mexico)*
Rio Balsas 35-32 Colonia Cuauhtemoc
DF 6500, Mexico

Sichting, Jerry (Basketball Player)
3190 N Country Club Rd
Martinsville, IN 46151-7929, USA

Siddall, Joe (Athlete, Baseball Player)
2785 Sierra Dr
Windsor, ON N9E 2Y9, Canada

Siddig, Alexander (Actor)
c/o Pippa Markham *Markham & Froggatt*
4 Windmill St
London W1T 1HZ, UK

Siddiqui, Aamera (Actor)
c/o Staff Member *NUTS*
820 Lilac Dr N Ste 101
Golden Valley, MN 55422-4614, USA

Siddiqui, Farouge (Director, Filmmaker)
16/24 Old Collector Compound Malvani Colony Gate No 5 Malad
Bombay, MS 400 095, INDIA

Siddons, Ann Rivers (Writer)
60 Church St
Charleston, SC 29401-2558

Siddons, Anne R (Writer)
767 Vermont Rd
Atlanta, GA 30319, USA

Sidenbladh, Goran (Architect)
Narvagen 23
Stockholm 114 60, SWEDEN

Sider, Harvey R (Religious Leader)
PO Box 290
Grantham, PA 17027-0290, USA

Sidewalk Prophets (Music Group, Musician)
c/o Scott Bickell *Brickhouse Entertainment*
106 Mission Ct Ste 1202
Franklin, TN 37067-6484, USA

Sidgmore, John (Business Person)
500 Clinton Center Dr
Clinton, MS 39056-5678, USA

Sidibe, Gabourey (Gabby) (Actor)
c/o Jill Kaplan *Principal Entertainment (NY)*
130 W 42nd St Ste 614
New York, NY 10036-7804, USA

Sidime, Lamine (Prime Minister)
Conakry, GUINEA

Sidlin, Murry (Conductor)
Music School
Washington, DC 20064-0001, USA

Sidney, Dainon (Athlete, Football Player)
605 Lakemeade Pt
Old Hickory, TN 37138-2588, USA

Sidor, Susan (Stylist)
361 E 50th St
New York, NY 10022-7954, USA

Sidransky, David (Doctor, Scientist)
1200 Moursand Ave
Houston, TX 77030, USA

Siebel, Jennifer (Actor, Producer)
San Francisco, CA, USA

Sieber, Christopher (Actor)
c/o Richard Fisher *Abrams Artists Agency (NY)*
275 7th Ave Fl 26
New York, NY 10001-6708, USA

Siebern, Norm (Athlete, Baseball Player)
4181 5th Ave NW
Naples, FL 34119-1505, USA

Siebert, Paul (Athlete, Baseball Player)
1711 Acker St
Orlando, FL 32837-6588, USA

Siebert, Sonny
2583 Brush Creek Rd
Saint Louis, MO 63129-5601

Siebert, Wilfred C (Sonny) (Athlete, Baseball Player)
2555 Brush Creek Rd
Saint Louis, MO 63129-5601, USA

Siebler, Dwight (Athlete, Baseball Player)
11565 S 204th St
Gretna, NE 68028-7974, USA

Siega, Marcos (Director)
c/o Staff Member *WmE2 (Endeavor-LA)*
9601 Wilshire Blvd Fl 3
Beverly Hills, CA 90210-5219, USA

Siegal, Bernard (Writer)
61 0X Bow Ln
Woodbridge, CT 06525-1525

Siegal, Jay (Music Group, Musician)
141 Dunbar Ave
Fords, NJ 08863-1551, USA

Siegal, John (Football Player)
Harvey's Bt
Harveys Lake, PA 18618, USA

Siegbahn, Kai M B (Nobel Prize Laureate)
Physics Institute Box 530
Uppasala 75 121, SWEDEN

Siegel, Barry (Journalist)
202 W 1st St
Los Angeles, CA 90012-4105, USA

Siegel, Bernie (Doctor, Writer)
61 Ox Bow Ln
Woodbridge, CT 06525-1525, USA

Siegel, Eric (Actor)
c/o Mickey Berman *United Talent Agency (UTA)*
10250 Constellation Blvd Fl 7
Los Angeles, CA 90067-6207, USA

Siegel, Herbert J (Business Person)
767 5th Ave
New York, NY 10153-0023, USA

Siegel, Ira T (Publisher)
16589 Senterra Dr
Delray Beach, FL 33484-6986, USA

Siegel, Jake (Actor)
c/o Staff Member *JC Robbins Management*
113 S Kilkea Dr
Los Angeles, CA 90048-3525, USA

Siegel, Janis (Musician)
40 W 57th St # 1800
New York, NY 10019-4001, USA

Siegel, L Pendleton (Business Person)
601 W Riverside Ave
Spokane, WA 99201-0638, USA

Siegel, Norman (Attorney)
260 Madison Ave
New York, NY 10016-2401, USA

Siegel, Robert C (Correspondent)
c/o Gregory McKnight *Creative Artists Agency (CAA-LA)*
2000 Avenue of the Stars Ste 100
Los Angeles, CA 90067-4705, USA

Siegert, Wayne (Athlete, Football Player)
401 E 4th St
Pana, IL 62557-1655, USA

Siegfried, Larry (Athlete, Basketball Player)
4178 Covert Rd
Perrysville, OH 44864-9320, USA

Siegfried And (&) Roy (Magician)
3400 Las Vegas Blvd S
Las Vegas, NV 89109-8923, USA

Siekevitz, Philip (Biologist)
290 W End Ave
New York, NY 10023-8106, USA

Siemaszko, Casey (Actor)
232 N Canon Dr
Beverly Hills, CA 90210-5302, USA

Siemaszko, Nina (Actor)
c/o David Rose *Innovative Artists (LA)*
1505 10th St
Santa Monica, CA 90401-2805, USA

Sieminski, Chuck (Athlete, Football Player)
5000 Village Way Apt 406
Marcus Hook, PA 19061-6857, USA

Siemon, Jeffrey G (Jeff) (Athlete, Football Player)
5401 Londonderry Rd
Edina, MN 55436-1026, USA

Sienkiewicz, Troy (Athlete, Football Player)
186 Darcy Ave
Goose Creek, SC 29445-6664, USA

Siepi, Cesare (Opera Singer)
12095 Brookfield Club Dr
Roswell, GA 30075-1261, USA

Sierchio, Tom (Actor, Writer)
c/o Alan Gasmer *Alan Gasmer Management Company*
10877 Wilshire Blvd Ste 603
Los Angeles, CA 90024-4348, USA

Siering, Lauri (Swimmer)
3829 Rotterdam Ave
Modesto, CA 95356-0739, USA

Sierra, Jessica (Musician)
PO Box 447
Herndon, VA 20172-0447, USA

Sierra, Pedro (Baseball Player)
11013 Horde St
Silver Spring, MD 20902-3617, USA

Sierra, Ruben A (Athlete, Baseball Player)
12355 SW 51st St
Miami, FL 33175-5506, USA

Sierra, Rubin
1 Res Jard Selles Apt 2501
Rio Piedras, PR 00924-2964

Siers, Kevin (Cartoonist, Editor)
600 S Tryon St
Charlotte, NC 28202-1842, USA

Sievers, Eric (Athlete, Football Player)
11550 Great Falls Way
Great Falls, VA 22066-1148, USA

Sievers, Roy E (Athlete, Baseball Player)
11505 Bellefontaine Rd
Saint Louis, MO 63138-1706, USA

Sieverts, Thomas C W (Architect)
Buschstr 20
Bonn 53113, GERMANY

Siff, Maggie (Actor)
c/o James Suskin *James Suskin Management*
2 Charlton St Apt 5K
New York, NY 10014-4970, USA

Sifford, Charlie (Golfer)
14220 Lynderwood Ct
Charlotte, NC 28273-3428, USA

Sific, Mokdad (Prime Minister)
Government Palais Al-Moradia
Algiers, ALGERIA

Sigel, Beanie (Musician)
8942 Wilshire Blvd # 219
Beverly Hills, CA 90211-1908, USA

Sigel, Jay (Golfer)
1284 Farm Rd
Berwyn, PA 19312-2000, USA

Sigel, Tom (Cinematographer)
8942 Wilshire Blvd # 219
Beverly Hills, CA 90211-1908, USA

Sigholtz, Bob
5425 Shirley Ave
Tarzana, CA 91356-2910

Sigler, Jamie-Lynn (Actor)
c/o Glenn Gulino *G2 Entertainment LLC*
1 Columbus Pl Apt S25E
New York, NY 10019-8208, USA

Sigman, Stan (Business Person)
5565 Glenridge Connector NE
Atlanta, GA 30342-4756, USA

Signaigo, Joe (Athlete, Football Player)
1687 Bryn Mawr Cir
Germantown, TN 38138-2618, USA

Sigur Ros (Music Group)
c/o Staff Member *Paradigm (Monterey)*
404 W Franklin St
Monterey, CA 93940-2303, USA

Sigurdson, Sig (Athlete, Football Player)
2233 NW 59th St Apt 103
Seattle, WA 98107-3155, USA

Sigwart, Ulrich (Doctor)
Centre Hospitalier Universitaire Vaudois
Lausanne, SWITZERLAND

Siilasvuo, Ensio (General)
Castrenikatu 6A17
Helsinki 53 530, FINLAND

Sikahema, Vai (Athlete, Football Player)
28 Abington Rd
Mount Laurel, NJ 08054-4720, USA

Sikes, Alfred C (Government Official)
10331 Todds Corner Rd
Easton, MD 21601-5405, USA

Sikes, Cynthia (Actor)
250 Delfern Dr
Los Angeles, CA 90077-3543, USA

Sikharulidze, Anton (Figure Skater)
111 Midtown Bridge Approac
Hackensack, NJ 07601-7505, USA

Sikich, Mike P (Athlete, Football Player)
702 Tudor Dr
Janesville, WI 53546-2001, USA

Sikking, James B (Actor)
258 S Carmelina Ave
Los Angeles, CA 90049-3957, USA

Sikma, Jack (Athlete, Basketball Player)
9125 NE 21st Pl
Clyde Hill, WA 98004-2437, USA

Sikora, Joe (Actor)
c/o Myrna Jacoby *MJ Management*
130 W 57th St Apt 11A
New York, NY 10019-3311, USA

Sikorski, Brian (Athlete, Baseball Player)
17930 Wexford St
Roseville, MI 48066-4630, USA

Silas, James (Athlete, Basketball Player)
6800 Thistle Hill Way
Austin, TX 78754-5800, USA

Silas, Paul (Athlete, Basketball Player, Coach)
2463 Peninsula Shores Ct
Denver, NC 28037-7655, USA

Silatolu, Ratu Timoci (Prime Minister)
6 Berkeley Crescent Suva
Viti Levu, FIJI

Silber, John R (Educator)
132 Carlton St
Brookline, MA 02446-4009, USA

Silberling, Bradley (Brad) (Director, Producer)
c/o Staff Member *Reveal Entertainment*
310 N Stanley Ave
Los Angeles, CA 90036-2304, USA

Silberman, Laurence H (Diplomat, Judge)
& 3rd Constitution NW
Washington, DC 20001, USA

Silbermann, Jake (Actor)
c/o Robyn Ziegler *Robyn Ziegler Management*
143 W 29th St Ste 1103
New York, NY 10001-5134, USA

Silberstein, Diane Wichard (Publisher)
Publisher's Office 4 Times Square
New York, NY 10036, USA

Silbey, Robert J (Misc)
Chemistry Dept
Cambridge, MA 2139, USA

Sileo, Dan (Athlete, Football Player)
5000 Culbreath Key Way Apt 1317
Tampa, FL 33611-3054, USA

Silia, Felix (Actor)
8927 Snowden Ave
Arleta, CA 91331-6115, USA

Silja, Anja (Opera Singer)
111 W 57th St
New York, NY 10019-2211, USA

Silk (Artist, Musician)
c/o Staff Member *Faa*
250 W 57th St
New York, NY 10107-0001, USA

Silk, David (Dave) (Athlete, Hockey Player)
265 Franklin St
Boston, MA 02110-3113, USA

Silla, Felix
8927 Snowden Ave
Arleta, CA 91331-6115

Sillas, Karen (Actor)
PO Box 725
Wading River, NY 11792-0725, USA

Siller, Eugenio (Actor)
c/o Tom Harrison *Diverse Talent Group*
9911 W Pico Blvd Ste 340W
Los Angeles, CA 90035-2712, USA

Sillinger, Mike (Athlete, Hockey Player)
7476 E Buteo Dr
Scottsdale, AZ 85255-4628, USA

Sills, Douglas (Actor, Musician)
3500 W Olive Ave Ste 1400
Burbank, CA 91505-5512, USA

Sills, Stephen (Architect, Designer)
30 E 67th St
New York, NY 10065-6155, USA

Silva, Adele (Actor, Model)
c/o Staff Member *McLean-Williams Management*
Gainsborough House 81 Oxford St
London W1D 2EU, UK

Silva, Anderson (Athlete, Wrestler)
c/o Ed Soares *Black House*
Av. Alfredo Balthazar Da Silveira 520
Recreio
Rio De Janeiro 22790071, Brazil

Silva, Daniel (Writer)
3512 Winfield Ln NW
Washington, DC 20007-2344

Silva, Gilberto (Football Player)
Arsenal Stadium Highbury
London N5 1BU, ENGLAND

Silva, Henry (Actor)
8747 Clifton Way Apt 305
Beverly Hills, CA 90211-2125, USA

Silva, Jackie (Athlete, Volleyball Player)
Prefers to be contacted via email or telephone

Silva, Jason (Television Host)
c/o Rob Levy *Untitled Entertainment (LA)*
350 S Beverly Dr Ste 200
Beverly Hills, CA 90212-4819, USA

Silva, Jose (Stylist)
c/o Staff Member *Directions USA*
3717 W Market St Ste C
Greensboro, NC 27403-1155, USA

Silva, Jose (Athlete, Baseball Player)
401 Pappan Dr
Imperial, PA 15126-1192, USA

Silva, Tom (Entertainer)
PO Box 2284
South Burlington, VT 05407-2284, USA

Silva, Zack (Actor)
c/o Michael Dean Valeo 8265 Sunset Blvd Ste 103
Los Angeles, CA 90046, USA

Silver, Beverly (Stylist)
4 E 36th St Apt 5R
New York, NY 10016-3304, USA

Silver, Edward J (Religious Leader)
5118 Clarendon Rd
Brooklyn, NY 11203-5329, USA

Silver, Harvey (Actor)
c/o Staff Member *Anonymous Content (AC-LA)*
3531 Hayden Ave
Culver City, CA 90232, USA

Silver, Horace (Composer, Musician)
35 Clark St Apt A5
Brooklyn, NY 11201-2374, USA

Silver, Jeffrey (Producer)
c/o Staff Member *Outlaw Productions*
9350 Civic Center Dr Ste 100
Beverly Hills, CA 90210-3629, USA

Silver, Joan Macklin (Director)
510 Park Ave Apt 9B
New York, NY 10022-6640, USA

Silver, Joel (Producer)
c/o Staff Member *Silver Pictures*
4000 Warner Blvd Bldg 90
Burbank, CA 91522-0001

Silver, Michael B
9229 W Sunset Blvd Ste 315
Los Angeles, CA 90069-3403, USA

Silver, Pamela (Stylist)
c/o Staff Member *Lachapelle Representation Ltd*
420 E 54th St Apt 14F
New York, NY 10022-5151, USA

Silver, Robert S (Engineer)
Oakbank Breadalbane St
Tobermory, Isle of Mull, SCOTLAND

Silvera, Charlie (Athlete, Baseball Player)
1240 Manzanita Dr
Millbrae, CA 94030-2934, USA

Silverberg, Robert (Writer)
175 5th Ave
New York, NY 10010-7703, USA

Silverbush, Lori (Actor)
c/o Brantley Brown *Schachter Entertainment*
1157 S Beverly Dr Fl 2
Los Angeles, CA 90035-1119, USA

Silverchair
Box 15
Merewether, AUSTRALIA NSW 2291

Silverio, Luis (Athlete, Baseball Player)
3130 NW 89th Ter
Kansas City, MO 64154-1835, USA

Silverman, Al (Publisher)
411 E 53rd St # 16H
New York, NY 10022-5106, USA

Silverman, Barry G (Judge)
230 N 1st St
Phoenix, AZ 85004-2217, USA

Silverman, Benjamin (Producer)
c/o Staff Member *NBC Universal (LA)*
100 Universal City Plz
Universal City, CA 91608-1002, USA

Silverman, Fred
1642 Mandeville Canyon Rd
Los Angeles, CA 90049-2524

Silverman, Henry R (Business Person)
9 W 57th St
New York, NY 10019-2701, USA

Silverman, Jonathan (Actor)
c/o Beth Holden-Garland *Untitled Entertainment (LA)*
350 S Beverly Dr Ste 200
Beverly Hills, CA 90212-4819, USA

Silverman, Sarah (Actor, Comedian)
c/o Amy Zvi *Thruline Entertainment*
9250 Wilshire Blvd Ground Fl
Beverly Hills, CA 90212, USA

Silvers, Robert (Artist)
115 W 18th St
New York, NY 10011-4113, USA

Silverstein, Elliott (Director)
232 N Canon Dr
Beverly Hills, CA 90210-5302, USA

Silverstein, Joseph H (Conductor, Musician)
123 W South Temple
Salt Lake City, UT 84101-1403, USA

Silverstone, Alicia (Actor)
c/o Jason Weinberg *Untitled Entertainment (LA)*
350 S Beverly Dr Ste 200
Beverly Hills, CA 90212-4819, USA

Silverstone, Ben (Actor)
c/o Staff Member *London Management*
2-4 Noel St
London W1V 3RB, UNITED KINGDOM (UK)

Silversun Pickups (Music Group, Musician)
c/o Cliff Burnstein *Q Prime Inc*
729 7th Ave Ste 1600
New York, NY 10019-6880, USA

Silvestre, Armando
Cerro Macultepec 273Col. Campestre Churubusco
Mexico DF, MEXICO

Silvestri, Alan A (Composer, Musician)
c/o Staff Member *Gorfaine/Schwartz Agency Inc*
4111 W Alameda Ave Ste 509
Burbank, CA 91505-4171, USA

Silvestri, Carl (Athlete, Football Player)
980 Cape Marco Dr Unit 1403
Marco Island, FL 34145-6342, USA

Silvestri, Dave (Athlete, Baseball Player)
15511 Country Mill Ct
Chesterfield, MO 63017-5148, USA

Silvestrini, Achille Cardinal (Religious Leader)
Via Conciliazione 34
Rome 193, ITALY

Silvia (Royalty)
Kungliga Slottet Stottsbacken
Stockholm 111 30, SWEDEN

Silvstedt, Victoria (Actor, Model)
c/o Liza Anderson *Anderson Group Public Relations*
8060 Melrose Ave Fl 4
Los Angeles, CA 90046-7038, USA

Sim, Gerald (Actor)
7 Great Russell St
London W1D 1BS, UNITED KINGDOM (UK)

Sim, Sheila
Old Friars Richmond Greene
Surrey, ENGLAND

Simanek, Robert E (War Hero)
25194 Westmoreland Dr
Farmington Hills, MI 48336-1270, USA

Simas, Bill (Athlete, Baseball Player)
1890 E Warwick Ave
Fresno, CA 93720-5633, USA

Simcoe, Anthony (Actor)
c/o Pauline Lee *International Casting Service & Associates*
2/218 Crown St (via Kings Lane)
Darlinghurst NSW 2010, Australia

Sime, David W (Dave) (Athlete, Doctor, Track Athlete)
240 Harbor Dr
Key Biscayne, FL 33149-1218, USA

Simeon II (King, Prime Minister)
1 Dondukov Blvd
Sofia 1000, BULGARIA

Simeoni, Sara (Athlete, Track Athlete)
Via Castello Rivoli Veronese
Verona 37010, ITALY

Simhan, Meera (Actor)
C/O Heidi L Ifft 17 Buccaneer St
Marina Del Rey, CA 90292, USA

Simic, Charles (Writer)
PO Box 192
Strafford, NH 03884-0192, USA

Simien, Tracy (Athlete, Football Player)
3219 Sumac Dr
Pearland, TX 77584-8069, USA

Simien, Wayne (Basketball Player)
c/o Staff Member *Miami Heat*
1 SE 3rd Ave Ste 2300
Miami, FL 33131-1716, USA

Simitis, Costas (Prime Minister)
35 Akadanuas St
Athens 106 72, GREECE

Simkin, Margery (Misc)
606 N Larchmont Blvd # 4B
Los Angeles, CA 90004-1321, USA

Simkus, Arnold (Athlete, Football Player)
4248 Chicago Rd
Warren, MI 48092-1471, USA

Simmel, Johannes Mario
Bohlgutsch 3
Zug, SWITZERLAND CH-6300

Simmes, Misty Blue (Wrestler)
106 Maple St
Hudson Falls, NY 12839-2129, USA

Simmonds, Kennedy A (Prime Minister)
PO Box 167 Earle Mome Development
Basseterre, SAINT KITTS & NEVIS

Simmonds, Sara (Actor)
c/o Steven Jensen *Independent Group, The*
6363 Wilshire Blvd Ste 115
Los Angeles, CA 90048-5734, USA

Simmons, Arthur (Baseball Player)
27 158th Pl Apt 2W
Calumet City, IL 60409-4945, USA

Simmons, Bob (Athlete, Football Player)
16040 Chalfont Cir
Dallas, TX 75248-3544, USA

Simmons, Bobby Ray (B.o.B.) (Musician)
c/o Staff Member *Atlantic Records (NY)*
1290 Avenue of the Americas Fl CONC4
New York, NY 10104-0184

Simmons, Brian (Athlete, Football Player)
9240 Liberty Hill Ct
Cincinnati, OH 45242-4663, USA

Simmons, Brian (Athlete, Baseball Player)
226 Village Dr
Canonsburg, PA 15317-2367, USA

Simmons, Chelan (Actor)
c/o Staff Member *Pacific Artists Management*
1285 W Broadway Suite 685
Vancouver, BC V6H 3X8, Canada

Simmons, Curtis T (Curt) (Athlete, Baseball Player)
200 Park Rd
Ambler, PA 19002-1121, USA

Simmons, Dan (Writer)
c/o Michael Prevett *The Gotham Group Inc*
9255 W Sunset Blvd Ste 515
Los Angeles, CA 90069-3308, USA

Simmons, Dick
3215 E Silvercliff Cir
Prescott, AZ 86303-5708

Simmons, Earl (DMX) (Actor, Musician)
c/o Charles King *WmE2 (Endeavor-LA)*
9601 Wilshire Blvd Fl 3
Beverly Hills, CA 90210-5219, USA

Simmons, Earl (DMX) (Actor, Musician)
c/o Ray Copeland *Bar Entertainment Management*
1501 Broadway Ste 1914
New York, NY 10036-5600, USA

Simmons, Ed (Athlete, Football Player)
PO Box 6632
Kennewick, WA 99336-0639, USA

Simmons, Gene (Business Person, Musician, Reality TV Star)
PO Box 16075
Beverly Hills, CA 90209-2075, USA

Simmons, Grant (Athlete, Basketball Player)
7274 E Costilla Pl
Centennial, CO 80112-1111, USA

Simmons, Harold (Business Person)
6000 Harry Hines Blvd # NB2.300
Dallas, TX 75235-5303, USA

Simmons, Henry (Actor)
c/o Jason Shapiro *United Talent Agency (UTA)*
9560 Wilshire Blvd Fl 5
Beverly Hills, CA 90212-2400, USA

Simmons, Hubert (Baseball Player)
3247 Sonia Trl
Ellicott City, MD 21043-3273, USA

Simmons, Jaason (Actor)
1330 4th St
Santa Monica, CA 90401-1302, USA

Simmons, Jason (Athlete, Football Player)
1225 Resaca Pl
Pittsburgh, PA 15212-4518, USA

Simmons, Jerry (Athlete, Football Player)
2233 S King Dr
Chicago, IL 60616-1415, USA

Simmons, JK (Actor)
c/o Stephen Hirsh *Gersh (NY)*
41 Madison Ave
New York, NY 10010-2202, USA

Simmons, John E (Athlete, Baseball Player, Basketball Player)
9 Lee Dr
Farmingdale, NY 11735-5407, USA

Simmons, Johnny (Actor)
c/o Mimi DiTrani *Schiff Company, The*
8440 Warner Dr Ste B1
Culver City, CA 90232-2461, USA

Simmons, Joseph (Rev Run) (Actor, Producer)
512 Seventh Ave Floor 43
New York, New York 10018, USA

Simmons, Kimora Lee (Designer, Fashion Designer)
c/o Staff Member *Phat Fashions LLC*
512 Seventh Ave
New York, NY 10018, USA

Simmons, Lionel J (Athlete, Basketball Player)
108 Wellesley Ct
Mount Laurel, NJ 08054-5133, USA

Simmons, Richard (Actor, Fitness Expert, Producer)
c/o Rick Hersh *Celebrity Consultants LLC*
3340 Ocean Park Blvd Ste 1030
Santa Monica, CA 90405-3259, USA

Simmons, Richard D (Publisher)
181 Avenue Charles De Gaulie
Riverside, CA 92521-0001, FRANCE

Simmons, Richard P (Business Person)
1000 6 Ppg Pl
Pittsburgh, PA 15222, USA

Simmons, Russell (Producer)
c/o Steve Smooke *Creative Artists Agency (CAA-LA)*
2000 Avenue of the Stars Ste 100
Los Angeles, CA 90067-4705, USA

Simmons, Ruth (Educator)
President S Ofc
Providence, RI 02912-0001, USA

Simmons, Shadia (Actor)
265 GA Highway 30 W
Americus, GA 31719-8502, USA

Simmons, Stacey (Athlete, Football Player)
1780 Harbor Dr
Clearwater, FL 33755-1828, USA

Simmons, Tabitha (Stylist)
c/o Staff Member *Streeters*
560 Broadway Rm 203
New York, NY 10012-3945, 212-219-9566

Simmons, Ted L (Athlete, Baseball Player)
PO Box 26
Chesterfield, MO 63006-0026, USA

Simmons, Todd (Baseball Player)
39778 Pinedale Way
Murrieta, CA 92562-6719, USA

Simmons, Tony (Athlete, Football Player)
366 Grand Ave Apt 319
Oakland, CA 94610-4840, USA

Simmons, Vanessa (Model)
c/o Staff Member *Ford Models (LA)*
9200 W Sunset Blvd Ste 805
West Hollywood, CA 90069-3603, USA

Simmons, Victor (Athlete, Football Player)
5475 W Hirsch St
Chicago, IL 60651-1301, USA

Simms, Chris (Football Player)
c/o Team Member *Tampa Bay Buccaneers*
1 Bucaneer Pl
Tampa, FL 33607, USA

Simms, Joan (Actor)
Southbank House Black Prince Road
London SE1 7SJ, UNITED KINGDOM (UK)

Simms, Julie (Stylist)
1800 S Hobart Blvd
Los Angeles, CA 90006-5237, USA

Simms, Larry (Actor)
1043 Keeho Marina
Honolulu, HI 96819, USA

Simms, Mike (Athlete, Baseball Player)
PO Box 96011
Southlake, TX 76092-0111, USA

Simms, Molly (Actor)
c/o Alissa Vradenburg *Untitled Entertainment (LA)*
350 S Beverly Dr Ste 200
Beverly Hills, CA 90212-4819, USA

Simms, Philip (Phil) (Athlete, Football Player, Sportscaster)
930 Old Mill Rd
Franklin Lakes, NJ 07417-1906, USA

Simms, Primate George Otto (Religious Leader)
62 Cypress Grove Road
Dublin 6, IRELAND

Simollardes, Drew (Musician)
200 W 57th St Ste 308
New York, NY 10019-3211, USA

Simon, Bob (Correspondent)
c/o 60 Minutes *CBS News Productions*
524 W 57th St Fl 8
New York, NY 10019-2930, USA

Simon, Carly (Composer, Musician)
c/o Staff Member *American Entertainment Productions, Inc.*
6120 W Tropicana Ave Ste A16BOX PMB 403
Las Vegas, NV 89103-4489, USA

Simon, Corey (Athlete, Football Player)
6089 Leigh Read Rd
Tallahassee, FL 32309-8929, USA

Simon, Daniella (Designer)
1192 Elinor Rd
Hewlett, NY 11557-2524, USA

Simon, David (Actor, Producer, Writer)
c/o Staff Member *Creative Artists Agency (CAA-LA)*
2000 Avenue of the Stars Ste 100
Los Angeles, CA 90067-4705, USA

Simon, Dick (Race Car Driver)
701 S Girls School Rd
Indianapolis, IN 46231-3132, USA

Simon, George W (Astronaut)
PO Box 62
Sunspot, NM 88349-0062, USA

Simon, James (Athlete, Football Player)
8501 SW 103rd Ave
Gainesville, FL 32608-7206, USA

Simon, Josette (Actor)
18-21 Jermyn St
London SW1Y 6NB, UNITED KINGDOM (UK)

Simon, Neil (Writer)
c/o Staff Member *WmE2 (WMA-LA)*
1 William Morris Pl
Beverly Hills, CA 90212-4261, USA

Simon, Paul (Musician, Songwriter)

Simon, Roger M (Writer)
1627 K St NW
Washington, DC 20006-1704, USA

Simon, Salem (Athlete, Football Player)
2245 Sheridan Rd
Evanston, IL 60201-2918, USA

Simon, Sam
c/o Gary Cosay *United Talent Agency (UTA)*
9560 Wilshire Blvd Fl 5
Beverly Hills, CA 90212-2400, USA

Simon, Scott (Correspondent)
30 Rockefeller Plz
New York, NY 10112-0015, USA

Simon, White (Stylist)
c/o Staff Member *Rex Agency, The*
6311 Romaine St
Los Angeles, CA 90038-2617, USA

Simone, Albert J (Educator)
President's Office
Rochester, NY 14623, USA

Simoneau, Mark (Athlete, Football Player)
17 Waterview Dr
Sicklerville, NJ 08081-1683, USA

Simoneau, Yves (Director, Producer, Writer)
c/o Adam Levine *Levine Okwu Erickson Management*
9601 Wilshire Blvd Fl 3
Beverly Hills, CA 90210-5219, USA

Simonini, Edward (Ed) (Athlete, Football Player)
3825 E 66th St
Tulsa, OK 74136-2820, USA

Simonis, Adrianus J Cardinal (Religious Leader)
Aartbisdom BP 14019 Maliebaan
Utrecht, SB 3508, NETHERLANDS

Simonon, Paul (Musician)
268 Camden Rd
London NW1, UNITED KINGDOM

Simonov, Yuriy I (Conductor)
Gertsema St 13
Moscow, RUSSIA

Simons, Doug (Athlete, Baseball Player)
1988 Mount Olive Rd
Lookout Mountain, GA 30750-4746, USA

Simons, Elwyn L (Misc)
Primate Center 3705 Erwin Road
Durham, NC 27705, USA

Simons, James (Producer)
c/o Staff Member *Paradigm (LA)*
360 N Crescent Dr
Beverly Hills, CA 90210-4874, USA

Simons, Lawrence B (Government Official)
1001 Pennsylvania Ave NW
Washington, DC 20004-2502, USA

Simonsen, Renee (Actor, Model)
c/o Staff Member *Ford Models (NY)*
238 E 4th St
New York, NY 10009-7425

Simonsen, Rob (Composer, Musician)
c/o Neil Kohan *Greenspan Artist Management*
8760 W Sunset Blvd
West Hollywood, CA 90069-2206, USA

Simonson, Dave (Athlete, Football Player)
408 1st St SW
Austin, MN 55912-3254, USA

Simontacchi, Jason (Athlete, Baseball Player)
6924 Birdie Ln
Saint Louis, MO 63129-5408, USA

Simpkins, Dickey (Athlete, Basketball Player)
150 Toulon Dr
Buffalo Grove, IL 60089-7736, USA

Simple Kid (Music Group)
c/o Staff Member *Paradigm (Monterey)*
404 W Franklin St
Monterey, CA 93940-2303, USA

Simple Plan (Music Group)
c/o Staff Member *Creative Artists Agency (CAA-LA)*
2000 Avenue of the Stars Ste 100
Los Angeles, CA 90067-4705, USA

Simpson, Alan (Educator)
Little Compton, RI 2837, USA

Simpson, Alan K (Senator)
1201 Sunshine Ave PO Box 270
Cody, WY 82414, USA

Simpson, Arnelle
11661 San Vicente Blvd # 632
Los Angeles, CA 90049-5103

Simpson, Bill (Athlete, Football Player)
5732 Huntley Ave
Garden Grove, CA 92845-2040, USA

Simpson, Carl (Athlete, Football Player)
12106 Parkview Ln
Alpharetta, GA 30005-5418, USA

Simpson, Carole (Correspondent)
77 W 66th St
New York, NY 10023-6201, USA

Simpson, Charles R (Judge)
400 2nd St NW
Washington, DC 20217-0001, USA

Simpson, Cody (Musician)
c/o Todd Jacobs *WmE2 (Endeavor-LA)*
9601 Wilshire Blvd Fl 3
Beverly Hills, CA 90210-5219, USA

Simpson, Dick (Athlete, Baseball Player)
PO Box 3593
Culver City, CA 90231-3593, USA

Simpson, Duke (Athlete, Baseball Player)
78369 Kistler Way
Palm Desert, CA 92211-2727, USA

Simpson, Geoffrey (Cinematographer)
PO Box 3194
Bellevue Hills, NSW 2023, AUSTRALIA

Simpson, Herbert (Baseball Player)
1462 Farragut St
New Orleans, LA 70114-2818, USA

Simpson, Jason
11661 San Vicente Blvd # 632
Los Angeles, CA 90049-5103

Simpson, Jessica (Musician)
c/o Joe Simpson *JT Entertainment*
1453 3rd Street Promenade Ste 320
Santa Monica, CA 90401-3442, USA

Simpson, Jimmi (Actor)
c/o Staff Member *ROAR (LA)*
9701 Wilshire Blvd Fl 8
Beverly Hills, CA 90212-2008, USA

Simpson, Joanne G (Scientist)
Earth Sciences Ctr Mail Code 912
Greenbelt, MD 20771-0001, USA

Simpson, Joe (Producer)
c/o Staff Member *JT Entertainment*
1453 3rd Street Promenade Ste 320
Santa Monica, CA 90401-3442, USA

Simpson, Joe (Athlete, Baseball Player)
4681 Jefferson Township Ln
Marietta, GA 30066-1737, USA

Simpson, Juliene Brazinski (Athlete, Basketball Player)
PO Box 1267
Stroudsburg, PA 18360-4267, USA

Simpson, Keith (Athlete, Football Player)
20710 Castle Bend Dr
Katy, TX 77450-4911, USA

Simpson, Louis A M (Writer)
7 Stony Rd
Stony Brook, NY 11790-1525, USA

Simpson, Orenthal James (OJ) (Actor, Athlete, Football Player, Sportscaster)
9450 SW 112th St
Miami, FL 33176-3619, USA

Simpson, Ralph (Athlete, Basketball Player)
7578 S Duquesne Way
Aurora, CO 80016-1317, USA

Simpson, Scott (Athlete, Golfer)
8515 Falmouth Ave Apt 224
Playa Del Rey, CA 90293-8714, USA

Simpson, Stern Carol (Misc)
1012 14th St NW
Washington, DC 20005-3406, USA

Simpson, Suzi (Actor, Model)
24338 El Toro Rd # E315
Laguna Woods, CA 92637-2776, USA

Simpson, Terry (Coach)
2000 E Gene Autry Way
Anaheim, CA 92806-6143, USA

Simpson, Wayne K (Athlete, Baseball Player)
330 E Collamer Dr
Carson, CA 90746-1139, USA

Simpson, William (Writer)
c/o Staff Member *HarperCollins Publishers*
10 E 53rd St C/O Author Mail Floor 7
New York, NY 10022, USA

Simpson Sr, John F (Race Car Driver)
Mount Morris Star Route
Waynesburg, PA 15370, USA

Simpson-Wentz, Ashlee (Actor, Musician)
c/o Joe Simpson *JT Entertainment*
1453 3rd Street Promenade Ste 320
Santa Monica, CA 90401-3442, USA

Simpy Red (Music Group)
c/o Staff Member *Lee & Thompson*
15 St Christopher's Pl
London W1M 5HE, UNITED KINGDOM (UK)

Simran (Actor)
C/o Hotel Residency Thyagaraya Nagar
Chennai, TN 600 017, INDIA

Sims, Barry (Athlete, Football Player)
369 Golden Grass Dr
Alamo, CA 94507-2788, USA

Sims, Billy R (Athlete, Football Player)
PO Box 3147
Coppell, TX 75019-9147, USA

Sims, Darryl (Athlete, Football Player)
PO Box 379
Mc Farland, WI 53558-0379, USA

Sims, Duane (Duke) (Athlete, Baseball Player)
10509 Shoalhaven Dr
Las Vegas, NV 89134-7425, USA

Sims, Greg (Athlete, Baseball Player)
6700 Rancho Pico Way
Sacramento, CA 95828-1325, USA

Sims, Joan
17 Esmond Ct Thackery St
London, ENGLAND WE 5HB

Sims, Keith (Athlete, Football Player)
2920 Luckie Rd
Weston, FL 33331-3005, USA

Sims, Ken (Athlete, Football Player)
4898 Converse Ave
East Saint Louis, IL 62207-2533, USA

Sims, Kenneth W (Athlete, Football Player)
PO Box 236
Kosse, TX 76653-0236, USA

Sims, Molly (Actor)
c/o Alissa Vradenburg *Untitled Entertainment (LA)*
350 S Beverly Dr Ste 200
Beverly Hills, CA 90212-4819, USA

Sims, Robert (Athlete, Basketball Player)
915 Highland Ave Apt 3
Duarte, CA 91010-1935, USA

Sin, Jaime L Cardinal (Religious Leader)
121 Arzobispo St Entramuros PO Box 132
Manila 10099, PHILIPPINES

Sinatra, Nancy (Actor, Musician)
c/o Thomas De Lorenzo *SmartPR*
8033 W Sunset Blvd Ste 1033
Los Angeles, CA 90046-2401, USA

Sinatra, Ray
1234 8th Pl
Las Vegas, NV 89104-1555

Sinatra Jr, Frank (Musician)
c/o Seth Shomes *Day After Day Productions*
436 1st St Ste 102
Solvang, CA 93463-3710, USA

Sinatro, Matt (Athlete, Baseball Player)
2619 239th Ave SE
Sammamish, WA 98075-9442, USA

Sinbad (Actor, Comedian)
c/o Linda Jones *The Mass Appeal*
3940 Laurel Canyon Blvd Unit 447
Studio City, CA 91604-3709, USA

Sinceno, Kaseem (Athlete, Football Player)
168B Bradford Ct
Mount Laurel, NJ 08054-3705, USA

Sinceros
25 Buliver St Shephard's Bush
London, ENGLAND W12 8AR

Sinclair, Cameron (Architect, Business Person)
848 Folsom St Ste 201
San Francisco, CA 94107-1173, USA

Sinclair, Clive M (Inventor)
7 York Central 70 York Way
London N1 9AG, UNITED KINGDOM (UK)

Sinclair, Harry (Director, Writer)
c/o Ken Kamins *International Creative Management (ICM-LA)*
10250 Constellation Blvd Fl 7
Los Angeles, CA 90067-6207, USA

Sinclair, Joshua (Actor, Director, Producer, Writer)
c/o Staff Member *Sun Gateway Entertainment*
Taubenheimstr 30
70372, GERMANY

Sinclair, Michael (Athlete, Football Player)
1914 Pannell St
Houston, TX 77020-2339, USA

Sindelar, Jerry
213 Prospect Hill Rd
Horseheads, NY 14845

Sindelar, Joan (Baseball Player)
504 W Sunland Ave
Phoenix, AZ 85041-4822, USA

Sindelar, Joey (Golfer)
18 Prospect Rdg
Horseheads, NY 14845-7988, USA

Sinden, Donald A (Actor)
Rats Castle Isle of Oxney
Kent TN30 7HX, UNITED KINGDOM (UK)

Sinden, Harry (Athlete, Hockey Player)
9 Olde Village Dr
Winchester, MA 01890-2213, USA

Sinegal, James (Business Person)
999 Lake Dr
Issaquah, WA 98027-8990, USA

Sinfelt, John H (Misc)
Clinton Township RR 22E
Annadale, NJ 8801, USA

Sing, Daniel (Actor)
c/o Kathryn Rawlings *Kathryn Rawlings Actors Agency*
4/28 Williamson Ave. Grey Lynn
Auckland, New Zealand

Singer, Bryan (Director)
c/o Staff Member *Bad Hat Harry Productions*
4000 Warner Blvd Bldg 81 PMB 200
Burbank, CA 91522, USA

Singer, Isadore M (Mathematician)
Mathematics Dept
Cambridge, MA 2139, USA

Singer, Lori (Actor)
1465 Lindacrest Dr
Beverly Hills, CA 90210-2519, USA

Singer, Marc (Actor)
11218 Canton Dr
Studio City, CA 91604-4154, USA

Singer, Maxine F (Educator)
5410 39th St NW
Washington, DC 20015-2902, USA

Singer, Peter A D (Misc)
Human Values Ctr
Princeton, NJ 08544-0001, USA

Singer, Ramona (Designer, Reality TV Star)
c/o Staff Member *Bravo (NY)*
30 Rockefeller Plz
New York, NY 10112-0015, USA

Singer, S Fred (Physicist)
4084 University Dr Ste 101
Fairfax, VA 22030-6803, USA

Singer, William R (Bill) (Athlete, Baseball Player)
1119 Mallard Marsh Dr
Osprey, FL 34229-6810, USA

Singh, Amrita (Actor, Bollywood)
Bungalow 5 Lokhandwala Complex
Andheri Link Road
Mumbai, MS 400058, INDIA

Singh, Archana Puran (Actor, Bollywood)
G426 Anjali Apartments Seven Bungalows Anheri
Mumbai, MS 400061, INDIA

Singh, Bipin (Choreographer, Dancer)
15A Bipin Pal Rd
Kolkata, WB 700026, INDIA

Singh, Chandrachur (Actor, Bollywood)
6th Park Off Lokhandwala Complex
Versova Floor OAKLAND
Mumbai, MS 400049, INDIA

Singh, Dara (Actor, Bollywood)
Dara Villa Mamta Apartments Ground Floor A. B. Nair Road Juhu
Mumbai, MS 400049, INDIA

Singh, Manmohan (Prime Minister)
South Block Safdarjung Road
New Delhi, Delhi 110011, INDIA

Singh, Sukhmander (Engineer)
Civil Engineering
Santa Clara, CA 95053-0001, USA

Singh, Tjinder (Musician)
7 Trinity Row
Florence, MA 01062-1931, USA

Singh, Vijay (Golfer)
1275 Ponte Vedra Blvd
Ponte Vedra Beach, FL 32082-4402, USA

Singh, Vishwanath Pratap (Prime Minister)
1 Teen Murti Marg
New Delhi, ND 110001, INDIA

Singletary, Daryl
1000 18th Ave S
Nashville, TN 37212-2105

Singletary, Michael (Mike) (Athlete, Football Player)
18411 Nicklaus Way
Eden Prairie, MN 55347-3441, USA

Singletary, Tony (Director)
c/o Staff Member *Agency for the Performing Arts (APA-LA)*
405 S Beverly Dr Ste 500
Beverly Hills, CA 90212-4425, USA

Singleton, Chris (Athlete, Football Player)
42599 W Sunland Dr
Maricopa, AZ 85138-1632, USA

Singleton, Chris (Athlete, Baseball Player)
2038 Town Manor Ct
Dacula, GA 30019-3247, USA

Singleton, Doris
344 Dalehurst Ave
Los Angeles, CA 90024-2512

Singleton, Duane (Athlete, Baseball Player)
191 MacDonough St
Brooklyn, NY 11216-2507, USA

Singleton, Isaac (Actor)
c/o Jason Mellerstig *Artist International Management (LA)*
9595 Wilshire Blvd Fl 9
Beverly Hills, CA 90212-2512, USA

Singleton, John D (Director, Producer, Writer)
c/o Staff Member *Creative Artists Agency (CAA-LA)*
2000 Avenue of the Stars Ste 100
Los Angeles, CA 90067-4705, USA

Singleton, Kenneth W (Kenny) (Athlete, Baseball Player)
10 Sparks Farm Rd
Sparks Glencoe, MD 21152-9300, USA

Singleton, Margie (Musician)
PO Box 567
Hendersonville, TN 37077-0567, USA

Sinha, Mala (Actor)
8 Turner Road Bandra
Bombay, MS 400 050, INDIA

Sinha, Shatrughan (Actor, Bollywood, Politician)
104 Green Star Apts Rizvi Complex
Sherly Rajan Road Bandra
Bombay, MS 400 050, INDIA

Sinise, Gary (Actor)
c/o Marc Gurvitz *Brillstein Entertainment Partners*
9150 Wilshire Blvd Ste 350
Beverly Hills, CA 90212-3453, USA

Sinn, Pearl (Golfer)
132 21st Pl
Manhattan Beach, CA 90266-4402, USA

Sinner, George A (Ex-Governor)
101 3rd St N
Moorhead, MN 56560-1952, USA

Sinnott, John (Athlete, Football Player)
9 Primrose Ln
North Providence, RI 02904-3840, USA

Sinton, Nell (Artist)
484 Lake Park Ave # 189
Oakland, CA 94610-2730, USA

Sinyavskaya, Tamara I (Opera Singer)
Plankengasse 7
Vienna 1010, AUSTRIA

Siouxsie & The Banshees
1325 Avenue of the Americas
New York, NY 10019-6026

Siouzsie, Sioux (Musician)
Plaza 535 Kings Road
London SW10 0S, UNITED KINGDOM (UK)

Sipchen, Bob (Journalist)
202 W 1st St
Los Angeles, CA 90012-4105, USA

Sipe, Brian W (Athlete, Football Player)
17 E H St
Encinitas, CA 92024-3616, USA

Siphandon, Khamtay (General, President)
Vientiane, LAOS

Sipin, John (Athlete, Baseball Player)
451 Ponza Ln
Soquel, CA 95073, USA

Sipinen, Arto K (Architect)
Arkkitehtitoimistro Arto Sipinen Ky
Ahertajantie 3
Espoo 2100, FINLAND

Sipos, Shaun (Actor)
c/o Sheila Wenzel *Innovative Artists (LA)*
1505 10th St
Santa Monica, CA 90401-2805, USA

Sippy, G P (Actor)
3/G Naaz Rd Building LAMINGTON
Bombay, MS 400 004, INDIA

Sippy, Raj (Bollywood, Director, Filmmaker, Producer)
101 Jal Tarang Kishore Kumar Ganguly Marg Juhu Tara Rd
Bombay, MS 400 049, INDIA

Sippy, Ramesh (Bollywood, Director, Filmmaker, Producer)
379 Sathe House 14th Road Khar
Bombay, MS 400 052, INDIA

Sippy Cups, The (Music Group)
c/o Staff Member *Paradigm (Monterey)*
404 W Franklin St
Monterey, CA 93940-2303, USA

Sir Douglas Quintet
59 Parsons St
Newtonville, MA 2160

Sir Mix-a-lot (Musician)
c/o Eva Arthur *Universal Attractions*
135 W 26th St Fl 12
New York, NY 10001-6872, USA

Siragusa, Tony (Athlete, Football Player)
349 Ashwood Ave
Kenilworth, NJ 07033-2056, USA

Siren, Heikki (Architect)
Tiirasaarentie 35
Heisinki 200, FINLAND

Siren, Katri A H (Architect)
Tiirasaarentie 35
Heisinki 200, FINLAND

Sirgo, Otto (Actor)
c/o Staff Member *Televisa*
Blvd Adolfo Lopez Mateos 232 Colonia San Angel INN
DF CP 01060, MEXICO

Sirhan, Sirhan
#B21014Corcoran State Prison Box 8800
Corcoran, CA 93212

Siri Singh Sahib (Religious Leader)
PO Box 351149
Los Angeles, CA 90035-9549, USA

Siriano, Christian (Designer, Reality TV Star)
c/o Bianca Bianconi *SLATE Public Relations - NY*
307 7th Ave Rm 2401
New York, NY 10001-6019, USA

Sirico, Tony (Actor)
c/o Bob McGowan *McGowan Management*
8733 W Sunset Blvd Ste 103
West Hollywood, CA 90069-2241, USA

Sirikit (Royalty)
Bangkok, THAILAND

Sirmon, Peter (Athlete, Football Player)
5255 McGavock Rd
Brentwood, TN 37027-5197, USA

Sirotka, Mike (Athlete, Baseball Player)
20704 N 90th Pl Unit 1005
Scottsdale, AZ 85255-9135, USA

Sirtis, Marina (Actor)
c/o Alan Saffron *Saffron Management*
9171 Wilshire Blvd Ste 441
Beverly Hills, CA 90210-5516, USA

Sisco, Andrew (Athlete, Baseball Player)
25324 176th Ave SE
Covington, WA 98042-6709, USA

Sisco, Joseph J (Engineer, Government Official)
2702 Parkview Dr
Riva, MD 21140-1017, USA

Sisco, Steve (Athlete, Baseball Player)
630 San Doval Pl
Thousand Oaks, CA 91360-1314, USA

Sisemore, Jerald G (Jerry) (Athlete, Football Player)
17301 Whippoorwill Trl
Lago Vista, TX 78645-9734, USA

Sisk, Bradford (Producer)
c/o Staff Member *Bankable Productions*
226 W 26th St Fl 4
New York, NY 10001-6700, USA

Sisk, Doug (Athlete, Baseball Player)
3610 42nd Ave NE
Tacoma, WA 98422-2480, USA

Sisk, John (Athlete, Football Player)
7814 W Wisconsin Ave
Wauwatosa, WI 53213-3420, USA

Sisk, Tommie (Athlete, Baseball Player)
164 E 4635 N
Provo, UT 84604-5447, USA

Sislen, Myrna (Musician)
1007 Lakewater Dr
Henrico, VA 23229-6011, USA

Sisler, Dave (Athlete, Baseball Player)
11 Hacienda Dr
Saint Louis, MO 63124-1754, USA

Sisqo (Musician)
c/o Jason Priluck *Agency Group Ltd, The (LA)*
1880 Century Park E Ste 711
Los Angeles, CA 90067-1618, USA

Sissel (Musician)
Skuteviksboder 11
Bergen 5035, NORWAY

Sissel, George A (Business Person)
10 Longs Peak Dr
Broomfield, CO 80021-2510, USA

Sissi (Actor)
c/o Staff Member *Univision*
605 3rd Ave Fl 12
New York, NY 10158-0034, USA

Sisson, Scott (Athlete, Football Player)
902 Ravenwood Way
Canton, GA 30115-6421, USA

Sissons, Kimber (Actor)
412 Amaz Dr # 204
Los Angeles, CA 90048, USA

Sister, Max (Designer, Fashion Designer)
Kathmandu, NEPAL

Sister Hazel (Music Group)
c/o Staff Member *Sixthman*
83 Walton St NW
Atlanta, GA 30303-2179, USA

Sister Sledge (Music Group)
c/o Staff Member *Tony Denton Promotions Limited (UK)*
P.O. Box 2839
London W1K 5LE, United Kingdom

Sisters of Mercy
28 Kensington Church St
London, ENGLAND W8 4EP

Sisto, Jeremy (Actor)
c/o Christina Papadopoulos *Baker Winokur Ryder Public Relations BWR (BWR-NY)*
292 Madison Ave Fl 12
New York, NY 10017-6415, USA

Sistrunk, Manny (Athlete, Football Player)
3856 Williams Rd
Montgomery, AL 36110-7660, USA

Sistrunk, Otis (Athlete, Football Player)
PO Box 372
Dupont, WA 98327-0372, USA

Sites, Brian (Actor)
c/o Staff Member *Innovative Artists (LA)*
1505 10th St
Santa Monica, CA 90401-2805, USA

Sites, James W (Producer)
700 N Pennsylvania St
Indianapolis, IN 46204-1129, USA

Sithara (Actor, Bollywood)
556 I Floor Block 2nd Cross R T Nagar 2ND
Bangalore, KA 560032, INDIA

Sitkovetsky, Dmitry (Musician)
165 W 57th St
New York, NY 10019-2201, USA

Sitter, Charles R (Business Person)
5959 Las Colinas Blvd
Irving, TX 75039-4202, USA

Sittler, Darrell (Athlete, Hockey Player)
84 Buttonwood Ct
East Amherst, NY 14051-1644, USA

Sittler, Walter (Actor)
Seinstr 54
Munich 81667, GERMANY

Sitton, Charles (Athlete, Basketball Player)
3035 SW Homesteader Rd
West Linn, OR 97068-9612, USA

Sivad, Darryl (Actor)
c/o Staff Member *Leavitt Talent Group*
8255 W Sunset Blvd
West Hollywood, CA 90046-2417, USA

Sivam, Peeli (Actor)
43 Parthasarathy Pettai II St
Chennai, TN 600 086, INDIA

Sivan, Santosh (Cinematographer, Director, Writer)
c/o Staff Member *Paradigm (LA)*
360 N Crescent Dr
Beverly Hills, CA 90210-4874, USA

Sivaranjani (Ooha) (Actor, Bollywood)
7 Vivekananda Nagar Nesapakkam
Chennai, TN 600092, INDIA

Siwy, Jim (Athlete, Baseball Player)
6919 April Wind Ave
Las Vegas, NV 89131-0119, USA

Six Shooter
PO Box 53
Portland, TN 37148-0053

Sixthman (Music Group, Musician)
1040 Boulevard SE # J
Atlanta, GA 30312-3858, USA

Sixx
9255 W Sunset Blvd Ste 200
Los Angeles, CA 90069-3308

Sixx, Nikki (Musician)
2532 White Rd
Irvine, CA 92614-6236, USA

Siza, Alvaro (Architect)
Architecture School
Oporto, PORTUGAL

Sizemore, Grady (Athlete, Baseball Player)
23518 N 78th St
Scottsdale, AZ 85255-3416, USA

Sizemore, Matt (Adult Film Star)
c/o Staff Member *Diva Central Inc*
7510 W Sunset Blvd Ste 1445
Los Angeles, CA 90046-3408, USA

Sizemore, Ted (Athlete, Baseball Player)
14030 Conway Rd
Chesterfield, MO 63017-3402, USA

Sizemore, Tom (Actor)
c/o Staff Member *Evolution Entertainment (LA)*
901 N Highland Ave
Los Angeles, CA 90038-2412, USA

Sizemore, Tom (Educator)
Essential Schools Coalition
Providence, RI 02912-0001, USA

Sizova, Alla I (Ballerina)
4301 Harewood Rd NE
Washington, DC 20017-1514, USA

Sjoberg, Patrik (Athlete, Track Athlete)
Hokegatan 17
Goteberg 416 66, SWEDEN

Skaggs, Dave (Athlete, Baseball Player)
11131 Arlington Ave
Riverside, CA 92505-2148, USA

Skaggs, Jim (Athlete, Football Player)
421 Falcon Ridge Rd
Ellensburg, WA 98926-5037, USA

Skaggs, Ricky (Actor, Musician)
c/o Bobby Cudd *Paradigm (Nashville)*
124 12th Ave S Ste 410
Nashville, TN 37203-3170, USA

Skah, Khalid (Athlete, Track Athlete)
Boite Postale 2577
Fez, MOROCCO

Skala, Brian T (Actor)
c/o Staff Member *Osbrink Talent Agency*
4343 Lankershim Blvd Ste 100
West Toluca Lake, CA 91602-2705, USA

Skalski, Joe (Athlete, Baseball Player)
630 114th St
Whiting, IN 46394-1006, USA

Skarsgard, Alexander (Actor)
c/o Larry Taube *Principal Entertainment (LA)*
1964 Westwood Blvd Ste 400
Los Angeles, CA 90025-4695, USA

Skarsgard, J Stellan (Actor)
Hogersgatan 40
Stockholm 118 26, SWEDEN

Skarsgard, Stellan
Hogbergsgatan 40 II
Stockholm, SWEDEN S-118 26

Skarsten, Rachel (Actor)
c/o Steve Lovett *Lovett Management*
1327 Brinkley Ave
Los Angeles, CA 90049-3619, USA

Skaugstad, Daryle (Athlete, Football Player)
17216 NE 195th St
Woodinville, WA 98072, USA

Skaugstad, Dave (Athlete, Baseball Player)
16222 Monterey Ln Spc 274
Huntington Beach, CA 92649-2248, USA

Skayskal, Wayne
PO Box 191
Tampa, FL 33601-0191

Skeels, Mark (Baseball Player)
1835 Hilton Head Rd
El Cajon, CA 92019-4472, USA

Skeen, Archie (Baseball Player)
2685 N 4275 W
Ogden, UT 84404-9074, USA

Skeet, DJ Skeet (DJ)
c/o Ron Laffitte *Red Light Management (LA)*
8439 W Sunset Blvd Ste 2
Los Angeles, CA 90069-1925, USA

Skeeters, The (Music Group)
c/o Staff Member *Paradigm (Monterey)*
404 W Franklin St
Monterey, CA 93940-2303, USA

Skeggs, Leonard T Jr (Misc)
10212 Blair Ln
Kirtland, OH 44094-9514, USA

Skeie, Andris (Prime Minister)
Brivibus Bulv 36
Riga, PDP 226170, LATVIA

Skelton, Byron G (Judge)
717 Madison Ave NW
Washington, DC 20439-0001, USA

Skelton, Mike (Writer)
c/o Jon Huddle *United Talent Agency (UTA)*
9560 Wilshire Blvd Fl 5
Beverly Hills, CA 90212-2400, USA

Skerritt, Tom (Actor)
c/o Amy Weiss *Brillstein Entertainment Partners*
9150 Wilshire Blvd Ste 350
Beverly Hills, CA 90212-3453, USA

Skibbie, Lawrence F (General)
2309 S Queen St
Arlington, VA 22202-1550, USA

Skibinski, Joe (Athlete, Football Player)
1912 Pine St
Peru, IL 61354-1828, USA

Skibniewska, Halina (Architect)
Wydzlat Architektury Politechniki Ul Koszykowa 55
Warsaw 00-659, POLAND

Skid Row (Music Group)
720 E Palisade Ave
Englewood Cliffs, NJ 07632-3053, USA

Skidmore, Roe (Athlete, Baseball Player)
964 E Marlin Dr
Decatur, IL 62521-5549, USA

Skiles, Scott (Athlete, Basketball Player)
2350 Woodpath Ln
Highland Park, IL 60035-2046, USA

Skillets (Music Group, Musician)
c/o Staff Member *Q Management Group*
PO Box 273
Franklin, TN 37065-0273, USA

Skilling, Hugh H (Engineer)
11720 E Shore Dr
Whitmore Lake, MI 48189-9104, USA

Skinner, Al (Athlete, Basketball Player)
145 Great Plain Ave
Wellesley, MA 02482-7211, USA

Skinner, Frank (Actor, Comedian)
P.O. Box 168
London, England W10 6WH, UK

Skinner, Jane (Anchor)
c/o Staff Member *Fox News Channel (NY)*
1211 Ave Of The Americas Level C1
New York, NY 10036-8701, USA

Skinner, Jimmy (Athlete, Coach, Hockey Player)
2860 Askin Ave
Windsor, ON N9E 3H9, Canada

Skinner, Joel P (Athlete, Baseball Player, Coach)
275 Pamilla Cir
Avon Lake, OH 44012-1973, USA

Skinner, Jonty (Coach, Swimmer)
Athletic
Tuscaloosa, AL 35487-0001, USA

Skinner, Mike (Race Car Driver)
201 Cessna Blvd Ste 4
Port Orange, FL 32128-6856, USA

Skinner, Robert R (Bob) (Athlete, Baseball Player, Coach)
1576 Diamond St
San Diego, CA 92109-3050, USA

Skinner, Samuel K (Business Person, Secretary)
PO Box 767
Chicago, IL 60690-0767, USA

Skinner, Sonny (Golfer)
114 Northlake Dr
Sylvester, GA 31791-3909, USA

Skinner, Val (Golfer)
44 Bridge Ave
Bay Head, NJ 08742-4747, USA

Skinny Puppy (Music Group, Musician)
c/o Jeremy Holgersen *Agency Group Ltd, The (NY)*
142 W 57th St Fl 6
New York, NY 10019-3300, USA

Skizas, Lou (Athlete, Baseball Player)
2101 W White St Apt 118
Champaign, IL 61821-7203, USA

Skjelbreid, Ann-Elen (Athlete)
5640 Eikelandsosen
NORWAY

Skladany, Thomas E (Tom) (Athlete, Football Player)
6666 Highland Lakes Pl
Westerville, OH 43082-8703, USA

Sklvorecky, Josef (Writer)
English Dept
Toronto, ON M5S 1A5, CANADA

Skoczen, Stan (Athlete, Football Player)
6368 Brecksville Rd
Seven Hills, OH 44131-3405, USA

Skok, Craig (Athlete, Baseball Player)
981 Slash Pine Way
Lawrenceville, GA 30043-3465, USA

Skol, Michael (Diplomat)
PO Box 596
Dennis, MA 02638-0596, USA

Skolimowski, Jerzy (Director)
Ul Mazowiecka 6/8
Warsaw 00-048, POLAND

Skoll, Jeff (Business Person, Producer)
335 N Maple Dr Ste 245
Beverly Hills, CA 90210-5175, USA

Skolnick, Mark H (Scientist)
N Medical Dr
Salt Lake City, UT 84132-0100, USA

Skoog, Meyer (Whitey) (Athlete, Basketball Player, Coach)
1545 Aspen Dr
Saint Peter, MN 56082-1586, USA

Skopil Jr, Otto R (Judge)
555 SW Yamhill St
Portland, OR 97204-1303, USA

Skorich, Nick (Athlete, Football Coach, Football Player)
9 Briarwood Ct
Columbus, NJ 08022-1102, USA

Skoronski, Bob (Athlete, Football Player)
3907 Signature Dr
Middleton, WI 53562-2388, USA

Skorupan, John P (Athlete, Football Player)
142 Crossing Ridge Trl
Cranberry Township, PA 16066-6512, USA

Skotheim, Robert A (Misc)
2120 Place Rd
Port Angeles, WA 98363-9664, USA

Skou, Jens C (Nobel Prize Laureate)
Rislundvej 9
Risskov 8240, DENMARK

Skouras, Thanos (Economist)
8 Chlois St
Athens 145 62, GREECE

Skovhus, Bo (Opera Singer)
Granitweg 2
Zurich 8006, SWITZERLAND

Skowron, Bill (Athlete, Baseball Player)
1118 Beach Comber Dr
Schaumburg, IL 60193-3832, USA

Skowron, Moose (Baseball Player)
1118 Beach Comber Dr
Schaumburg, IL 60193-3832

Skrebneski, Victor (Photographer)
1350 N La Salle Dr
Chicago, IL 60610-1911, USA

Skrepcinski, Denice (Stylist)
5 Spring Ct
Edgewood, NM 87015-9419, USA

Skrepenak, Greg (Athlete, Football Player)
400 Middle Rd
Nanticoke, PA 18634-3821, USA

Skribble (DJ)
c/o Len Evans *Project Publicity*
312 W 53rd St Ste 202
New York, NY 10019-5743, USA

Skrien, Dave (Athlete, Football Player)
445 Enchanted Dr
Mound, MN 55364, USA

Skrmetta, Matt (Athlete, Baseball Player)
827 Poinsetta Dr
Indian Harbour Beach, FL 32937-3548, USA

Skrovan, Steve (Comedian)
c/o Staff Member *WmE2 (WMA-LA)*
1 William Morris Pl
Beverly Hills, CA 90212-4261, USA

Skrowaczewski, Stanislaw (Composer)
1111 Nicollet Mail
Minneapolis, MN 55403, USA

Skrypnk, Metropolitan Mstyslav S (Religious Leader)
PO Box 445
South Bound Brook, NJ 08880-0445, USA

Skube, Bob (Athlete, Baseball Player)
7135 W Foothill Dr
Glendale, AZ 85310-5817, USA

Skvorecky, Josef V (Writer)
487 Sackville St
Montreal, ON M4X 1T6, CANADA

Sky, Jennifer (Actor)
12533 Woodgreen St
Los Angeles, CA 90066-2723, USA

Sky, Nina (Music Group, Musician)
c/o Tammy Brook *FYI Public Relations*
174 5th Ave Ste 400
New York, NY 10010-5935, USA

Sky Eats Airplane (Music Group, Musician)
c/o Brigitte Wright *Brigitte Wright Management*
1674 Broadway Fl 3
New York, NY 10019-5861, USA

Skye, Azura (Actor)
c/o Brian Wilkins *Kritzer Levine Wilkins Entertainment*
11872 La Grange Ave Fl 1
Los Angeles, CA 90025-5283, USA

Skye, Britney (Adult Film Star)
9155-9161 Derring Ave
Chatsworth, CA 91304, USA

Skye, Ione (Actor)
c/o Mike Packenham *Concrete Entertainment*
468 N Camden Dr # 200
Beverly Hills, CA 90210-4507, USA

Skyrms, Brian (Misc)
Philosophy Dept
Irvine, CA 92717, USA

Slaby, Lou (Athlete, Football Player)
6 Elder Pl
Denville, NJ 07834-9312, USA

Slack, Reggie (Athlete, Football Player)
5973 Queen St
Milton, FL 32570-3574, USA

Slade, Bernard N (Writer)
345 N Saltair Ave
Los Angeles, CA 90049-2914, USA

Slade, Chris (Musician)
11 Leominster Road Morden
Surrey SA4 6HN, UNITED KINGDOM (UK)

Slade, Chris (Athlete, Football Player)
4163 Onslow Pl SE
Smyrna, GA 30080-6341, USA

Slade, Jeff (Athlete, Basketball Player)
5354 Farmington Rd
Toledo, OH 43623-2636, USA

Slade, Mark (Actor)
38 Joppa Rd
Worcester, MA 01602-2230, USA

Slade, Roy (Artist)
PO Box 801
Bloomfield Hills, MI 48303-0801, USA

Slagle, James R
13630 Barryknoll Ln
Houston, TX 77079-5928, USA

Slagle, Roger (Athlete, Baseball Player)
158 Brooksboro Ter
Nashville, TN 37217-3372, USA

Slaney, Mary Decker (Athlete, Track Athlete)
87141 Kellmore St
Eugene, OR 97402-9128, USA

Slash (Musician)
PO Box 57593
Sherman Oaks, CA 91413-2593, USA

Slaten, Doug (Athlete, Baseball Player)
233 Rennie Ave
Venice, CA 90291-2645, USA

Slater, Bob (Baseball Player)
4322 Avenida Rio Del Oro
Yorba Linda, CA 92886-3011, USA

Slater, Christian (Actor)
c/o Jason Newman *Untitled Entertainment (LA)*
350 S Beverly Dr Ste 200
Beverly Hills, CA 90212-4819, USA

Slater, Helen (Actor)
c/o Lisa DiSante-Frank *DiSante Frank & Company*
10061 Riverside Dr # 377
Toluca Lake, CA 91602-2560, USA

Slater, Jackie (Athlete, Football Player)
PO Box 6411
Orange, CA 92863-6411, USA

Slater, Jock C K (John) (Admiral)
Victory Bldg HM Naval Base
Portsmouth PO1 3LS, UNITED KINGDOM (UK)

Slater, Kelly (Actor, Athlete)
31652 2nd Ave
Laguna Beach, CA 92651-8244, USA

Slater, Mark (Athlete, Football Player)
10545 Rome Ave
Young America, MN 55397-9468, USA

Slater, Ryan
3500 W Olive Ave Ste 1400
Burbank, CA 91505-5512

Slater, Suzanne
10000 Riverside Dr Ste 10
Toluca Lake, CA 91602-2537

Slatkin, Leonard E (Conductor, Musician)
c/o Staff Member *Askonas Holt Ltd*
Lincoln House 300 High Holborn
London WC1V 7JH, UK

Slaton, Jim (Athlete, Baseball Player)
4082 N Arbor Ln
Buckeye, AZ 85396-3603, USA

Slaton, Mike (Athlete, Football Player)
7691 Park Village Rd
San Diego, CA 92129-4514, USA

Slaton, Tony (Athlete, Football Player)
122 E Childs Ave
Merced, CA 95341-6346, USA

Slattery, John M (Actor)
c/o Chris Kanarick *ID Public Relations (ID-NY)*
7060 Hollywood Blvd # 8
Los Angeles, CA 90028-6014, USA

Slattvik, Simon (Athlete)
Bankgata 22
Lillehammer 2600, NORWAY

Slaught, Don (Athlete, Baseball Player)
27 Middleridge Ln S
Rolling Hills, CA 90274-4055, USA

Slaughter (Music Group)
c/o Staff Member *Artist Representation & Management*
1257 Arcade St
Saint Paul, MN 55106-2022

Slaughter, Frank (Doctor)
Box 14 Ortega Station
Jacksonville, FL 32210, USA

Slaughter, J Mack (Actor)
c/o Jeff Golenberg *Collective*
8383 Wilshire Blvd Ste 1050
Beverly Hills, CA 90211-2415, USA

Slaughter, John B (Educator)
President's Office
Los Angeles, CA 90041, USA

Slaughter, Mickey (Athlete, Football Player)
1402 Mesa Ave
Ruston, LA 71270-2032, USA

Slaughter, Stering (Athlete, Baseball Player)
742 E Avenida Sierra Madre
Gilbert, AZ 85296-1108, USA

Slaughter, Webster (Athlete, Football Player)
3706 Rory Ct
Missouri City, TX 77459-6662, USA

Slavin, Randall (Actor)
3500 W Olive Ave Ste 1400
Burbank, CA 91505-5512, USA

Slavitt, David R (Writer)
35 West St Apt 5
Cambridge, MA 02139-1723, USA

Slay, Brandon (Wrestler)
6155 Lehman Dr
Colorado Springs, CO 80918-3456, USA

Slayback, Bill (Athlete, Baseball Player)
25710 Armstrong Cir Unit E
Stevenson Ranch, CA 91381-2336, USA

Slayton, Bobby (Comedian)
c/o Sherry Marsh *Marsh Entertainment*
12444 Ventura Blvd Ste 203
Studio City, CA 91604-2409, USA

Sleater, Lou (Athlete, Baseball Player)
12 Bandon Ct Unit 102
Lutherville Timonium, MD 21093-7504, USA

Sledd, William L (Internet Star)
PO Box 3714
Paducah, KY 42002-3714, USA

Sledge, Kathy (Musician)
c/o Staff Member *Webster & Associates PR*
3573 Couchville Pike
Hermitage, TN 37076-4012, USA

Sledge, Leroy (Athlete, Football Player)
6036 Golden Gate Cir
Dallas, TX 75241-5258, USA

Sledge, Percy (Musician)
9430 Palmetto Ln
Shreveport, LA 71118-4012, USA

Sledge, Termel (Athlete, Baseball Player)
30041 Medford Pl
Castaic, CA 91384-4565, USA

Sleep, Wayne (Actor, Choreographer, Dancer)
22 Queensberry Mews West
London SW7 2DY, UNITED KINGDOM (UK)

Sleepy Jackson, The (Music Group)
c/o Staff Member *Paradigm (Monterey)*
404 W Franklin St
Monterey, CA 93940-2303, USA

Slegr, Jiri (Athlete, Hockey Player)
800 Griffiths Way
Vancouver, BC V6B 6G1, Canada

Slegr, Jirl (Athlete, Hockey Player)
1 Fleet St
Boston, MA 02136-2015, USA

Slezak, Erika (Actor)
40 W 57th St # 1800
New York, NY 10019-4001, USA

Slice, Kimbo (Athlete, Wrestler)
c/o Staff Member *UFC*
PO Box 26959
Las Vegas, NV 89126-0959, USA

Slichter, Charles P (Physicist)
61 Chestnut Ct
Champaign, IL 61822-7121, USA

Slichter, Jacob (Musician)
509 Hartnell St
Monterey, CA 93940-2825, USA

Slick, Grace (Musician, Songwriter, Writer)
c/o Staff Member *Warner Books (Author Mail)*
237 Park Ave
New York, NY 10017-3140, USA

Slick, Rick (Musician)
250 W 57th St
New York, NY 10107-0001, USA

Sliger, Bernard F (Educator)
3496 Lakeshore Dr
Tallahassee, FL 32312-1485, USA

Slightly Stoopid (Music Group)
c/o Staff Member *Paradigm (Monterey)*
404 W Franklin St
Monterey, CA 93940-2303, USA

Slim Helu, Carlos (Business Person)
Lago Alberto 366
Mexico DF 11320, Mexico

Slipknot (Musician)
c/o Staff Member *Agency Group Ltd, The (NY)*
142 W 57th St Fl 6
New York, NY 10019-3300, USA

Sliwiak, Dina (Stylist)
c/o Staff Member *Montana Artists Agency*
9150 Wilshire Blvd Ste 100
Beverly Hills, CA 90212-3459, USA

Sliwinska, Edyta (Dancer, Reality TV Star)
c/o Bob Knotek *McCann - Knotek Associates*
8539 W Sunset Blvd Ste 4-136
Los Angeles, CA 90069-2334, USA

Sloan (Music Group)
c/o Staff Member *Paradigm (Monterey)*
404 W Franklin St
Monterey, CA 93940-2303, USA

Sloan, Amy (Actor)
c/o Marion Campbell *TalentWorks (LA)*
3500 W Olive Ave Ste 1400
Burbank, CA 91505-5512, USA

Sloan, David (Athlete, Football Player)
2711 Nottingham St
Houston, TX 77005-2421, USA

Sloan, Ed (Musician)
216 Lincoln St
West Columbia, SC 29170-1812, USA

Sloan, Gerald E (Jerry) (Basketball Player, Coach)
300 S Washington St
Mc Leansboro, IL 62859-1141, USA

Sloan, Holly Goldberg (Director)
1015 Gayley Ave # 300
Los Angeles, CA 90024-3413, USA

Sloan, Jerry (Athlete, Basketball Player)
5583 W 13680 S
Herriman, UT 84096-1713, USA

Sloan, Michael (Actor, Producer)
c/o Mickey Freiberg *Acme Talent & Literary (LA)*
1400 Atlantic Ave Ste 274
Long Beach, CA 90813-2013, USA

Sloan, P F (Musician, Songwriter, Writer)
PO Box 164
Cedarhurst, NY 11516-0164, USA

Sloan, Stephen C (Steve) (Coach, Football Coach, Football Player)
Athletic
Orlando, FL 32816-0001, USA

Sloan Jr, Robert B (Educator)
Bayor University President's Office
Waco, TX 76798, USA

Sloane, Carol (Musician)
705 Centre St # 300
Boston, MA 02130-2598, USA

Sloane, Hilary (Stylist)
1616 Fremont Ave
South Pasadena, CA 91030-4407, USA

Sloane, Lindsay (Actor)
c/o Ron West *Thruline Entertainment*
9250 Wilshire Blvd Ground Fl
Beverly Hills, CA 90212, USA

Sloat, Micah (Actor)
c/o Alex Cole *Elevate Entertainment*
2029 Century Park E Ste 300
Los Angeles, CA 90067-2904, USA

Sloatman, Lala
11917 Vose St
North Hollywood, CA 91605-5750

Slobodyanik, Alexander (Musician)
165 W 57th St
New York, NY 10019-2201, USA

Slocombe, Douglas (Cinematographer)
2-4 Noel St
London W1V 3RB, UNITED KINGDOM (UK)

Slocum, Heath (Golfer)
5640 Keystone Rd
Pensacola, FL 32504-8416, USA

Slocum, Ron (Athlete, Baseball Player)
29646 Pebble Beach Dr
Sun City, CA 92586-5129, USA

Slocumb, Heathcliff (Heath) (Athlete, Baseball Player)
1045 Arthur St
Uniondale, NY 11553-3103, USA

Slon, Steve (Editor)
601 E St NW
Washington, DC 20049-0001, USA

Slonimsky, Sergey M (Composer)
9 Kanal Griboedova #97
Saint Petersburg, RUSSIA

Slosburg, Phil (Athlete, Football Player)
201 Glen Ln
Elkins Park, PA 19027-1761, USA

Slotnick, Joey (Actor)
232 N Canon Dr
Beverly Hills, CA 90210-5302, USA

Slotnick, Mortimer H (Artist)
43 Amherst Dr
New Rochelle, NY 10804-1814, USA

Slotnick, R Nathan (Doctor)
825 Fairfax Ave
Norfolk, VA 23507-1914, USA

Slovan, Eric (Comedian)
c/o Staff Member *WmE2 (WMA-LA)*
1 William Morris Pl
Beverly Hills, CA 90212-4261, USA

Slover, Karl (Actor)
504 Firetower Rd
Dublin, GA 31021-2642, USA

Slovin, Eric (Writer)
c/o Staff Member *Principato/Young Management*
9465 Wilshire Blvd Ste 430
Beverly Hills, CA 90212-2613, USA

Sloviter, Dolores K (Judge)
601 Market St
Philadelphia, PA 19106-1737, USA

Slowes, Charles (Baseball Player, Sportscaster)
3936 Mimosa Pl
Palm Harbor, FL 34685-3674, USA

Sloyan, James (Actor)
920 Kagawa St
Pacific Palisades, CA 90272-3833, USA

Sluby, Tom (Athlete, Basketball Player)
39 Poplar St
Ramsey, NJ 07446-1535, USA

Sluman, Jeff (Golfer)
808 McKinley Ln
Hinsdale, IL 60521-4831, USA

Slusarski, Joe (Athlete, Baseball Player)
11 Rodelle Woods Dr
Weldon Spring, MO 63304-7875, USA

Slutskaya, Irina (Figure Skater)
c/o Staff Member *Champions on Ice*
3500 W 80th St Ste 200
Minneapolis, MN 55431-1090, USA

Slutsky, Lorie A (Misc)
2 Park Ave
New York, NY 10016-5675, USA

Sly, Darryl (Athlete, Hockey Player)
Highway 26
Collingwood, ON L9Y 1W6, Canada

Slyman, Darin (Stylist)
c/o Staff Member *Talent Plus*
1222 Lucas Ave Ste 300
Saint Louis, MO 63103-1937, USA

Smagala, Stan (Athlete, Football Player)
13155 Meadow Hill Ln
Lemont, IL 60439-6743, USA

Smagorinsky, Joseph (Misc)
72 Gabriel Ct
Hillsborough, NJ 08844-1450, USA

Smajstria, Craig (Athlete, Baseball Player)
4606 Honey Creek Ct
Pearland, TX 77584-1285, USA

Smale, Stephen (Mathematician)
68 Highgate Rd
Kensington, CA 94707, USA

Small, Aaron (Athlete, Baseball Player)
775 Loudon Rd
Loudon, TN 37774-6705, USA

Small, Hank (Athlete, Baseball Player)
4715 Millbrook Dr NW
Atlanta, GA 30327-3548, USA

Small, Jim (Athlete, Baseball Player)
7960 Island Ct
Stanwood, MI 49346-8920, USA

Small, Lawrence W (Financier)
1000 Jefferson Dr SW
Washington, DC 20560-0008, USA

Small, Mark (Athlete, Baseball Player)
10605 229th Pl SW
Edmonds, WA 98020-6151, USA

Small, Mary
165 W 66th St
New York, NY 10023-6508

Small, Marya (Actor)
843 N Sycamore Ave
Los Angeles, CA 90038-3316, USA

Small, Torrance (Athlete, Football Player)
66 Chateau Mouton Dr
Kenner, LA 70065-1903, USA

Small, William N (Admiral)
1605 Bluecher Ct
Virginia Beach, VA 23454-2501, USA

Smalley, Roy Jr (Athlete, Baseball Player)
6319 Timber Trl
Minneapolis, MN 55439-1049, USA

Smalley Sr, Roy (Athlete, Baseball Player)
922 N Kenneth Dr
Green Valley, AZ 85614-5225, USA

Smallwood, Dwana (Dancer)
211 W 61st St # 300
New York, NY 10023-7832, USA

Smallwood, Richard (Music Group, Musician)
1035 Bates Ct
Hendersonville, TN 37075-8864, USA

Smart, Amy (Actor)
c/o Jennifer Merlino *Untitled Entertainment (LA)*
350 S Beverly Dr Ste 200
Beverly Hills, CA 90212-4819, USA

Smart, J D (Athlete, Baseball Player)
1325 Lost Creek Blvd
Austin, TX 78746-6331, USA

Smart, Jean (Actor)
c/o Jennifer Levine *Untitled Entertainment (LA)*
350 S Beverly Dr Ste 200
Beverly Hills, CA 90212-4819, USA

Smart, Keith (Athlete, Basketball Player, Coach)
5306 Asterwood Dr
Dublin, CA 94568-7718, USA

Smart, Pamela
#93G0356 Bedford Hills Corr. Fac.
Bedford Hills, NY 10507-2496

Smash Mouth (Music Group, Musician)
c/o Staff Member *Creative Artists Agency (CAA-LA)*
2000 Avenue of the Stars Ste 100
Los Angeles, CA 90067-4705, USA

Smashing Pumpkins (Music Group)
c/o Staff Member *Creative Artists Agency (CAA-LA)*
2000 Avenue of the Stars Ste 100
Los Angeles, CA 90067-4705, USA

Smeal, Eleanor C (Activist)
900 N Stafford St Apt 1217
Arlington, VA 22203-1845, USA

Smeaton, Bruce
585 Nepean Hwy Carrum
Victoria, AUSTRALIA 3197

Smedley, Geoffrey (Artist)
RR 3 Gambier Island
Gibsons, BC V0N 1V0, CANADA

Smedvig, Rolf (Musician)
165 W 57th St
New York, NY 10019-2201, USA

Smeenge, Joel (Athlete, Football Player)
9148 Sugarland Dr
Jacksonville, FL 32256-9611, USA

Smehlik, Richard (Athlete, Hockey Player)
8824 Hearthstone Dr
East Amherst, NY 14051-2354, USA

Smerek, Don (Athlete, Football Player)
1298 Valhalla Dr
Denver, NC 28037-5503, USA

Smerlas, Fred (Athlete, Football Player)
11 Saddle Ridge Rd
Sudbury, MA 01776-2770, USA

Smid, Ladislav (Athlete, Hockey Player)
2000 E Gene Autry Way
Anaheim, CA 92806-6143, USA

Smigel, Irwin (Doctor)
635 Madison Ave
New York, NY 10022-1009, USA

Smigel, Robert (Actor, Writer)
c/o Staff Member *Creative Artists Agency (CAA-LA)*
2000 Avenue of the Stars Ste 100
Los Angeles, CA 90067-4705, USA

Smigelsky, Dave (Athlete, Football Player)
4332 Nesting Pl
Oakwood, GA 30566-3247, USA

Smiley, Don (Baseball Player, President)
10539 NW 10th St
Plantation, FL 33322-6546, USA

Smiley, Jane (Writer)
c/o Lynn Pleshette *Lynn Pleshette Literary Agency*
2700 N Beachwood Dr
Los Angeles, CA 90068-1922, USA

Smiley, John (Athlete, Baseball Player)
208 W 3rd Ave
Trappe, PA 19426-2212, USA

Smiley, Rickey (Comedian)
c/o Kevin Wasson *Breakwind Entertainment*
PO Box 59784
Birmingham, AL 35259-9784, USA

Smiley, Tavis (Radio Personality, Television Host)
4401 Sunset Blvd
Los Angeles, CA 90027, USA

Smiley, Tommie B (Athlete, Football Player)
5340 Timberline Ln
Beaumont, TX 77706-7343, USA

Smirnoff, Karina (Dancer)
c/o Staff Member *Continuum Entertainment*
Prefers to be contact via telephone or email
Los Angeles, CA 90069, USA

Smirnoff, Yakov (Actor, Comedian)
c/o Staff Member *Richard De La Font Agency*
3808 W South Park Blvd
Broken Arrow, OK 74011-1261, USA

Smirnov, Nikolai I (Admiral)
4 Staraya Pl
Moscow 103073, RUSSIA

Smith, Aaron (Athlete, Football Player)
711 Copper Creek Ln
Wexford, PA 15090-6822, USA

Smith, Adrian (Musician)
1976 E High St Ste 101
Pottstown, PA 19464-3277, USA

Smith, Adrian (Athlete, Basketball Player)
2829 Saddleback Dr
Cincinnati, OH 45244-3914, USA

Smith, Akili (Athlete, Football Player)
7771 Gribble St
San Diego, CA 92114-6018, USA

Smith, Al (Athlete, Football Player)
15 Pembroke St
Sugar Land, TX 77479-2929, USA

Smith, Al (Athlete, Basketball Player)
308 S Sterling Ave
Peoria, IL 61604-6063, USA

Smith, Al (Athlete, Baseball Player)
1101 Ogilvie St
Bossier City, LA 71111-4639, USA

Smith, Aldon (Football Player)
c/o Tom Condon *CAA - St. Louis*
222 S Central Ave Ste 1008
Saint Louis, MO 63105-3509, USA

Smith, Alexander J C (Financier)
1166 Avenue of the Americas
New York, NY 10036-2708, USA

Smith, Alexis (Artist)
215 Windward Ave
Venice, CA 90291-3764, USA

Smith, Alice (Musician)
c/o Staff Member *Paradigm (Monterey)*
404 W Franklin St
Monterey, CA 93940-2303, USA

Smith, Allen D (Athlete, Football Player)
1220 Walker Dr Apt A
Decatur, GA 30030-5709, USA

Smith, Allison (Actor)
1505 10th St
Santa Monica, CA 90401-2805, USA

Smith, Amber (Actor, Model)
c/o Jerry Shandrew *Shandrew Public Relations*
1050 S Stanley Ave
Los Angeles, CA 90019-6634, USA

Smith, Amy J (Stylist)
611 Main St # A
Sausalito, CA 94965-2318, USA

Smith, Ann (Athlete, Tennis Player)
3737 Cole Ave Apt 110
Dallas, TX 75204-1594, USA

Smith, Anna Deavere (Actor, Producer, Writer)
c/o Johnnie Planco *Parseghian Planco LLC*
322 8th Ave Ste 601
New York, NY 10001-6715, USA

Smith, Anthony (Athlete, Football Player)
PO Box 573
Fontana, CA 92334-0573, USA

Smith, Anthony W (Educator)
PO Box 573
Fontana, CA 92334-0573, USA

Smith, Antowain (Athlete, Football Player)
2121 Hepburn St Apt 917
Houston, TX 77054-3221, USA

Smith, April (Writer)
427 7th St
Santa Monica, CA 90402-1907, USA

Smith, Art (Chef)
c/o Staff Member *Premier Management Group (PMG Sports)*
115 Crescent Commons Dr Ste 250
Cary, NC 27518-8134, USA

Smith, Arthur (Producer)
9911 W Pico Blvd Ste 250
Los Angeles, CA 90035-2737, USA

Smith, Arthur K Jr (Educator)
45 Wexford Club Dr
Hilton Head Island, SC 29928-3356, USA

Smith, Artie (Athlete, Football Player)
3809 W 68th St
Stillwater, OK 74074-2428, USA

Smith, Barbara (Business Person)
1120 Avenue of the Americas Fl 4
New York, NY 10036-6700, USA

Smith, Barry (Athlete, Football Player)
4048 Corkwood Ct
Palm Harbor, FL 34684-3608, USA

Smith, Barty (Athlete, Football Player)
2290 Dabney Rd
Richmond, VA 23230-3344, USA

Smith, Beau (Cartoonist)
PO Box 706
Ceredo, WV 25507-0706, USA

Smith, Ben (Athlete, Coach, Hockey Player)
20 Leonard St Unit 3
Gloucester, MA 01930-1364, USA

Smith, Ben (Cartoonist)
c/o Staff Member *King Features Syndication*
300 W 57th St Fl 15
New York, NY 10019-5238, USA

Smith, Ben (Athlete, Football Player)
1127 Riverbend Club Dr SE
Atlanta, GA 30339-2817, USA

Smith, Bennett W (Religious Leader)
601 50th St NE
Washington, DC 20019-5450, USA

Smith, Bernie (Athlete, Baseball Player)
PO Box 513
Lutcher, LA 70071-0513, USA

Smith, Bill (Athlete, Football Player)
153 Wa Grubb Rd
Lexington, NC 27295-6649, USA

Smith, Billy (Athlete, Hockey Player)
8356 Quail Meadow Way
West Palm Beach, FL 33412-1505, USA

Smith, Billy (Athlete, Baseball Player)
333 Rolling Hills Dr
Conroe, TX 77304-1280, USA

Smith, Billy (Athlete, Baseball Player)
5328 E Lancaster Ave
Fort Worth, TX 76112-6360, USA

Smith, Billy Ray Jr (Athlete, Football Player)
6160 Cornerstone Ct E Ste 100
San Diego, CA 92121-3724, USA

Smith, Bob (Golfer)
PO Box 6511
Ventura, CA 93006-6511, USA

Smith, Bob (Athlete, Baseball Player)
221 Hackberry Ln
Aiken, SC 29803-2733, USA

Smith, Bobby (Athlete, Hockey Player)
10800 E Cactus Rd Unit 46
Scottsdale, AZ 85259-2505, USA

Smith, Bobby (Athlete, Baseball Player)
2822 60th Ave
Oakland, CA 94605-1502, USA

Smith, Bobby Gene (Athlete, Baseball Player)
1267 Tucker Rd Unit 15
Hood River, OR 97031-8601, USA

Smith, Brad (Musician)
9229 W Sunset Blvd Ste 607
Los Angeles, CA 90069-3406, USA

Smith, Brent (Athlete, Football Player)
258 Ridgewood Dr
Pontotoc, MS 38863-3532, USA

Smith, Brian (Athlete, Baseball Player)
203 Bo Howard Rd
Toney, AL 35773-9235, USA

Smith, Brick (Athlete, Baseball Player)
4743 Amity Pl
Charlotte, NC 28212-5305, USA

Smith, Brooke (Actor)
c/o Sue Leibman *Barking Dog Entertainment*
9 Desbrosses St Fl 2
New York, NY 10013-1701, USA

Smith, Bruce (Athlete, Football Player)
111 S Saint Joseph St
South Bend, IN 46601-1901, USA

Smith, Bruce W (Director)
c/o Staff Member *Jambalaya Studio*
111 N Maryland Ave # 300
Glendale, CA 91206-4238, USA

Smith, Bryn (Athlete, Baseball Player)
1239 Highway 1
Santa Maria, CA 93455-5909, USA

Smith, Calvin (Athlete, Track Athlete)
16703 Sheffield Park Dr
Lutz, FL 33549-6833, USA

Smith, Carl (Musician)
2510 Franklin Pike
Nashville, TN 37204-2714, USA

Smith, Carl R (General)
2345 S Queen St
Arlington, VA 22202-1550, USA

Smith, Carolyn Renee
PO Box 813
North Hollywood, CA 91603-0813

Smith, Chad (Musician)
c/o Peter Mensch *Q Prime South*
729 7th Ave Fl 16
New York, NY 10019-6831, USA

Smith, Charles (Athlete, Basketball Player)
PO Box 433
Cedar Grove, NJ 07009-0433, USA

Smith, Charles Martin (Actor, Director)
c/o David Saunders *Agency for the Performing Arts (APA-LA)*
405 S Beverly Dr Ste 500
Beverly Hills, CA 90212-4425, USA

Smith, Charlie E (Athlete, Football Player)
1906 Crescent Dr
Monroe, LA 71202-3024, USA

Smith, Charlie H (Athlete, Football Player)
14074 Skyline Blvd
Oakland, CA 94619-3622, USA

Smith, Chelsi
335 E San Augustine St
Deer Park, TX 77536-4175

Smith, Chris (Athlete, Baseball Player)
4206 Dawn Ln
Oceanside, CA 92056-4716, USA

Smith, Chris (Golfer)
208 S Bellerive Dr
Peru, IN 46970-8060, USA

Smith, Chris M (Athlete, Football Player)
1424 Martway Cir Apt A
Olathe, KS 66061-5820, USA

Smith, Chuck (Athlete, Baseball Player)
10271 SW 9th Ln
Pembroke Pines, FL 33025-3584, USA

Smith, Chuck (Athlete, Football Player)
848 Big Horn Holw
Suwanee, GA 30024-1766, USA

Smith, Clifford (Method Man) (Musician, Television Host)
c/o Shauna Garr *Smart Girl Productions*
8335 W Sunset Blvd Ste 222
Los Angeles, CA 90069-1534, USA

Smith, Clinton J (Clint) (Athlete, Hockey Player)
501-1919 Bellview Ave
West Vancouver, BC V7V 1B7, Canada

Smith, Connie (Music Group, Musician)
1204B Cedar Ln
Nashville, TN 37212-5910, USA

Smith, Cotter (Actor)
15332 Antioch St # 800
Pacific Palisades, CA 90272-3628, USA

Smith, D Brooks (Judge)
319 Washington St
Johnstown, PA 15901-1624, USA

Smith, Dan (Athlete, Baseball Player)
5205 Balmoral Ln
Flower Mound, TX 75028-1669, USA

Smith, Dan (Athlete, Baseball Player)
4411 Adonis Dr
Salt Lake City, UT 84124-3901, USA

Smith, Daniel E. (Actor)
c/o James Kellem *JKA Talent*
12725 Ventura Blvd Ste H
Studio City, CA 91604-2437, USA

Smith, Danny (Actor)
c/o Lisa Harrison *WmE2 (Endeavor-LA)*
9601 Wilshire Blvd Fl 3
Beverly Hills, CA 90210-5219, USA

Smith, Dante (Mos Def) (Actor, Musician)
c/o Linda Carbone *Covers Media*
138 W 25th St Fl 9
New York, NY 10001-7405, USA

Smith, Darden (Music Group, Musician, Songwriter, Writer)
30 W 21st St # 700
New York, NY 10010-6905, USA

Smith, Darrin (Athlete, Football Player)
7395 NW 19th Ct
Hollywood, FL 33024-1015, USA

Smith, Daryl (Athlete, Baseball Player)
3 Sunny Mills Ct
Randallstown, MD 21133-4449, USA

Smith, Daryl (Athlete, Football Player)
1636 Norton Hill Dr
Jacksonville, FL 32225-4937, USA

Smith, Daryle (Athlete, Football Player)
6275 Country Club Dr
Huntington, WV 25705-2009, USA

Smith, Dave (Athlete, Baseball Player)
16330 Jersey Dr
Jersey Village, TX 77040-2020, USA

Smith, Dave (Athlete, Football Player)
11828 W Maui Ln
El Mirage, AZ 85335-6945, USA

Smith, Dave (Athlete, Football Player)
650 S 13th St Apt 123-20
Indiana, PA 15701-3566, USA

Smith, Dave (Athlete, Baseball Player)
3925 San Gregorio Way
San Diego, CA 92130-2263, USA

Smith, Dean E (Athlete, Basketball Player, Coach)
105 Fox Run
Chapel Hill, NC 27516-0608, USA

Smith, Delia (Actor, Chef, Writer)
PO Box 1124
Knaphill GU21 9AA, United Kingdom

Smith, Dennis (Athlete, Football Player)
2450 Achilles Dr
Los Angeles, CA 90046-1626, USA

Smith, Derek (Athlete, Hockey Player)
201 Bramblewood Ln
East Amherst, NY 14051-2228, USA

Smith, Derek (Athlete, Football Player)
4949 Centennial Blvd
Santa Clara, CA 95054-1229, USA

Smith, Dick (Business Person)
10 Cassola Pl
Penrith 2750, Australia

Smith, Dick (Athlete, Coach, Swimmer)
PO Box 1831
Dewey, AZ 86327-1831, USA

Smith, Dick (Athlete, Baseball Player)
1926 Norwood Ln
State College, PA 16803-1326, USA

Smith, Dick (Athlete, Baseball Player)
2615 Gates Rd
Lincolnton, NC 28092-7968, USA

Smith, Dick (Athlete, Baseball Player)
6850 Downing Rd Spc 35
Central Point, OR 97502-3418, USA

Smith, Donald L (Athlete, Football Player)
3338 Pineview Dr
Holiday, FL 34691-9732, USA

Smith, Doug (Athlete, Basketball Player)
21930 Winchester St
Southfield, MI 48076-4892, USA

Smith, Doug (Coach, Football Coach, Football Player)
Heritage Hall
Los Angeles, CA 90089-0001, USA

Smith, Doug (Athlete, Football Player)
25661 Pacific Crest Dr
Mission Viejo, CA 92692-5040, USA

Smith, Douglas (Doug) (Actor)
c/o Beverly Strong *Strong Management*
3532 Hayden Ave
Culver City, CA 90232-2413, USA

Smith, Dr. Robin (Writer)
PO Box 4061
Philadelphia, PA 19118-8061, USA

Smith, Dwight (Athlete, Baseball Player)
PO Box 98
Varnville, SC 29944-0098, USA

Smith, Earl (Athlete, Baseball Player)
2764 N Leonard Ave
Fresno, CA 93737-9720, USA

Smith, Ed (Athlete, Football Player)
429 Inland Cir
Azle, TX 76020-4908, USA

Smith, Elliot (Athlete, Football Player)
1343 Cadillac Dr
Jackson, MS 39213-4811, USA

Smith, Elmore (Athlete, Basketball Player)
PO Box 241475
Cleveland, OH 44124-8475, USA

Smith, Emil L (Biologist, Physicist)
Medical School
Los Angeles, CA 90024, USA

Smith, Emmitt (Athlete, Football Player)
15001 Winnwood Rd
Dallas, TX 75254-7629, USA

Smith, Eugene (Baseball Player)
8337 Flora Ave
Saint Louis, MO 63114-6203, USA

Smith, F Dean (Athlete, Track Athlete)
PO Box 71
Breckenridge, TX 76424-0071, USA

Smith, Floyd (Athlete, Hockey Player)
138 Stonehenge Dr
Orchard Park, NY 14127-2845, USA

Smith, Forry
3500 W Olive Ave Ste 1400
Burbank, CA 91505-5512

Smith, Frankie (Athlete, Football Player)
620 N Grayson St
Groesbeck, TX 76642-1157, USA

Smith, Frederick W (Business Person)
942 S Shady Grove Rd
Memphis, TN 38120-4117, USA

Smith, G E
24 Thorndike St
Cambridge, MA 02141-1882, USA

Smith, G Elaine (Religious Leader)
PO Box 851
Valley Forge, PA 19482-0851, USA

Smith, Garfield (Athlete, Basketball Player)
2006 Idylwild Ct
Richmond, KY 40475-3606, USA

Smith, Gary (Athlete, Hockey Player)
Villa Cortina 4451 Albert St #102
Burnaby, BC V5C 2G4, Canada

Smith, George (Cartoonist)
4520 Main St
Kansas City, MO 64111-1876, USA

Smith, George E. (Nobel Prize Laureate)
600 Mountain Ave
New Providence, NJ 07974-2008, USA

Smith, Gerald (Misc)
133 1st St NE
Saint Petersburg, FL 33701-3307, USA

Smith, Gerald C (Government Official)
2425 Tracy Pl NW
Washington, DC 20008-1628, USA

Smith, Greg (Athlete, Baseball Player)
27435 Hanes Rd E
Davenport, WA 99122-9443, USA

Smith, Greg (Athlete, Basketball Player)
9930 SW Lumbee Ln
Tualatin, OR 97062-7355, USA

Smith, Gregory (Actor, Producer)
c/o JJ Harris *One Talent Management*
9220 W Sunset Blvd Ste 306
Los Angeles, CA 90069-3503, USA

Smith, Gregory White (Writer)
129 1st Ave SW
Aiken, SC 29801-4862, USA

Smith, Hal (Athlete, Baseball Player)
9514 Londonderry Ct
Fort Smith, AR 72908-9520, USA

Smith, Hal (Athlete, Baseball Player)
637 Houston St
Columbus, TX 78934-2618, USA

Smith, Hal (Athlete, Football Player)
PO Box 570517
Tarzana, CA 91357-0517, USA

Smith, Hamilton O (Nobel Prize Laureate)
13607 Hanover Pike
Reisterstown, MD 21136-4520, USA

Smith, Harry (Correspondent)
c/o Staff Member *Early Show, The (NY)*
524 W 57th St
New York, NY 10019-2924, USA

Smith, Harry (Bowler)
580 E Cuyahoga Falls Ave
Akron, OH 44310-1540, USA

Smith, Harry E (Black Jack) (Athlete, Coach, Football Coach, Football Player)
805 Leawood Ter
Columbia, MO 65203-2729, USA

Smith, Hedrick L (Journalist)
4204 Rosemary St
Chevy Chase, MD 20815-5218, USA

Smith, Helen (Baseball Player)
2104 Turtle Run Dr Apt 6
Richmond, VA 23233-3673, USA

Smith, Hillary B
8730 W Sunset Blvd Ste 480
Los Angeles, CA 90069-2277, USA

Smith, Hunter (Athlete, Football Player)
9601 E 300 S
Zionsville, IN 46077-8825, USA

Smith, Ivor (Architect)
Station Officer's House Prawle Pointe Kingsbridge
Devon TQ7 2BX, UNITED KINGDOM (UK)

Smith, J D (Athlete, Football Player)
1615 County Road 204
Richland Springs, TX 76871, USA

Smith, J D Jr (Athlete, Football Player)
3332 Florida St
Oakland, CA 94602-3808, USA

Smith, J Robert (Athlete, Football Player)
6102 Timberlake Ct
Flower Mound, TX 75022-5627, USA

Smith, J T (Athlete, Football Player)
10110 Planters Row Dr
Frisco, TX 75033-0255, USA

Smith, Jack (Athlete, Baseball Player)
250 Doubles Dr
Covington, GA 30016-1736, USA

Smith, Jackie L (Athlete, Football Player)
1566 Walpole Dr
Chesterfield, MO 63017-4615, USA

Smith, Jaclyn (Actor)
10398 W Sunset Blvd
Los Angeles, CA 90077-3613, USA

Smith, Jacob (Actor)
c/o Elaine Lively *Elaine Entertainment*
Prefers to be contacted via telephone
Northridge, CA 91324, USA

Smith, Jaden (Actor)
c/o Miguel Melendez *Overbrook Entertainment*
450 N Roxbury Dr Fl 4
Beverly Hills, CA 90210-4218, USA

Smith, James (Bonecrusher) (Boxer)
355 Keith Hills Rd
Lillington, NC 27546, USA

Smith, Jamie Renee (Actor)
c/o Pam Grimes *Hervey/Grimes Talent Agency*
10561 Missouri Ave Apt 2
Los Angeles, CA 90025-5940, USA

Smith, Jason (Athlete, Baseball Player)
6350 Golden Acres Dr
Cottondale, AL 35453-3917, USA

Smith, Jean (Baseball Player)
5400 5 Mile Creek Rd
Harbor Springs, MI 49740-9783, USA

Smith, Jean Kennedy (Misc)
2700 F St NW
Washington, DC 20566-0001, USA

Smith, Jennifer M (Prime Minister)
Cabinet Building 105 Front St
Hamilton, HM 12, BERMUDA

Smith, Jermaine (Athlete, Football Player)
1345 12th St
Augusta, GA 30901-3260, USA

Smith, Jerry (Judge)
515 Rusk St
Houston, TX 77002-2600, USA

Smith, Jerry (Athlete, Football Coach, Football Player)
7227 Sugar Maple Dr
Irving, TX 75063-5519, USA

Smith, Jim (Athlete, Baseball Player)
1730 S Arroyo Ln
Gilbert, AZ 85295-4815, USA

Smith, Jim (Athlete, Football Player)
8600 Doral Ct W
Flower Mound, TX 75022-6480, USA

Smith, Jim Field (Actor, Director)
c/o Trevor Engelson *Underground Management*
447 S Highland Ave
Los Angeles, CA 90036-3530, USA

Smith, Jim Ray (Athlete, Football Player)
7049 Cliffbrook Dr
Dallas, TX 75254-7909, USA

Smith, Jimmy Lee (Athlete, Football Player)
105 Long Leaf Pl
Madison, MS 39110-6956, USA

Smith, Joe (Basketball Player)
7639 Leafwood Dr
Norfolk, VA 23518-4536, USA

Smith, John (Actor)
c/o Alan Ellsweig *Shadow Entertainment*
10 Universal City Plz Fl 20
Universal City, CA 91608-1074, USA

Smith, John L (Coach, Football Coach)
Daugherty Field House
East Lansing, MI 48824, USA

Smith, John M (Athlete, Football Player)
184 Centre St
Dover, MA 02030-2413, USA

Smith, John W (Wrestler)
5315 S Sangre Rd
Stillwater, OK 74074-2071, USA

Smith, Josh (Misc)
240 S 33rd St
Philadelphia, PA 19104-6316, USA

Smith, Justin (Athlete, Football Player)
5045 Rollman Estates Dr
Cincinnati, OH 45236-1455, USA

Smith, Karin
2300 Palisades Ave
Los Osos, CA 93402-3910

Smith, Kathy (Misc)
PO Box 491433
Los Angeles, CA 90049-9433, USA

Smith, Katie (Athlete, Basketball Player)
2494 Farleigh Rd
Columbus, OH 43221-2618, USA

Smith, Kayla (Stylist)
663 W 2575 N
Clearfield, UT 84015-9744, USA

Smith, Keith (Athlete, Baseball Player)
5823 13th St E
Bradenton, FL 34203-6819, USA

Smith, Keith (Athlete, Baseball Player)
15711 Ada St
Canyon Country, CA 91387-1891, USA

Smith, Kellita (Actor)
c/o Lynn Jeter *Lynn Jeter & Associates*
3699 Wilshire Blvd Ste 850
Los Angeles, CA 90010-2737, USA

Smith, Ken (Architect)
80 Warren St Apt 28
New York, NY 10007 1029, USA

Smith, Ken (Athlete, Baseball Player)
100 Lansdowne Blvd
Youngstown, OH 44506-1137, USA

Smith, Kenneth L (Athlete, Baseball Player, Football Player)
3802 Athens Dr
Pasadena, TX 77505-3349, USA

Smith, Kenny (Sportscaster)
c/o Staff Member *Octagon Home Office*
1751 Pinnacle Dr Fl 15
McLean, VA 22102-3833, USA

Smith, Kerr (Actor, Director)
c/o Steven Kavovit *Thruline Entertainment*
9250 Wilshire Blvd Ground Fl
Beverly Hills, CA 90212, USA

Smith, Kevin (Actor, Director, Producer, Writer)
c/o Tony Angellotti *Angellotti Company*
12423 Ventura Ct
Studio City, CA 91604-2417, USA

Smith, Kevin (Athlete, Football Player)
7001 Parkwood Blvd Apt 3204
Plano, TX 75024-7176, USA

Smith, Kim (Actor)
c/o Staff Member *Clipse Management*
279 W Main St
Dallas, TX 75034, USA

Smith, Kurtwood (Actor)
c/o Kelly Garner *Pop Art Management*
PO Box 55363
Sherman Oaks, CA 91413-0363, USA

Smith, Labradford (Athlete, Basketball Player)
410 Thompson Dr
Bay City, TX 77414-7910, USA

Smith, Lance (Athlete, Football Player)
PO Box 948
Kannapolis, NC 28082-0948, USA

Smith, Larry (Athlete, Basketball Player)
1767 Lakeside Dr
Vicksburg, MS 39180-9369, USA

Smith, Larry (Athlete, Football Player)
3601 Bayshore Blvd
Tampa, FL 33629-8942, USA

Smith, Lauren Lee (Actor)
c/o Eric Black *Anonymous Content (AC-LA)*
3531 Hayden Ave
Culver City, CA 90232, USA

Smith, Laury (Stylist)
c/o Staff Member *Mercury Artists*
8460 Higuera St Fl 2
Culver City, CA 90232-2520, USA

Smith, Laverne (Athlete, Football Player)
2122 N Homestead St
Wichita, KS 67208-1872, USA

Smith, Lawrence Leighton
611 W Main St
Louisville, KY 40202-2963, USA

Smith, Lee (Athlete, Baseball Player)
PO Box 399
Castor, LA 71016-0399, USA

Smith, Lee A (Baseball Player)
2124 Highway 507
Castor, LA 71016-4069, USA

Smith, Leonard P (Athlete, Football Player)
PO Box 82718
Baton Rouge, LA 70884-2718, USA

Smith, Lewis
8271 Melrose Ave Ste 110
Los Angeles, CA 90046-6800

Smith, Lois (Actor)
c/o Steve Stone *Cornerstone Talent Agency*
37 W 20th St
New York, NY 10011-3706, USA

Smith, Lonnie (Athlete, Baseball Player)
145 Wesley Forest Dr
Fayetteville, GA 30214-1094, USA

Smith, Loren A (Judge)
717 Madison Pl NW
Washington, DC 20439-0001, USA

Smith, Lovie (Athlete, Coach, Football Coach, Football Player)
1000 Football Dr
Lake Forest, IL 60045, USA

Smith, M Elizabeth (Liz) (Writer)
160 E 38th St
New York, NY 10016-2651, USA

Smith, Madeline (Actor)
Sunbury Island Sunbury on Thames
Middx, UNITED KINGDOM (UK)

Smith, Maggie (Actor)
c/o Toni Howard *International Creative Management (ICM-LA)*
10250 Constellation Blvd Fl 7
Los Angeles, CA 90067-6207, USA

Smith, Margaret (Producer, Writer)
c/o Gail Stocker *Gail Stocker Presents*
1025 N Kings Rd Apt 113
Los Angeles, CA 90069-6007, USA

Smith, Margo (Musician, Songwriter, Writer)
PO Box 3367
Brentwood, TN 37024-3367, USA

Smith, Marilynn (Golfer)
3784 N 162nd Ln
Goodyear, AZ 85395-8017, USA

Smith, Mark (Athlete, Baseball Player)
907 Forest Green Rd
Reedville, VA 22539-3577, USA

Smith, Mark (Athlete, Baseball Player)
1312 Elmhurst Ln
Flower Mound, TX 75028-3847, USA

Smith, Marquis (Athlete, Football Player)
843 51st St
San Diego, CA 92114-1002, USA

Smith, Martha (Actor, Model)
9690 Heather Rd
Beverly Hills, CA 90210-1757, USA

Smith, Marvel (Athlete, Football Player)
30 Waterfront Dr
Pittsburgh, PA 15222-4748, USA

Smith, Marvin (Smitty) (Musician)
300 Mercer St Apt 3J
New York, NY 10003-6732, USA

Smith, Matt (Actor)
c/o Michael Duff *Troika*
74 Clerkenwell Rd 3rd Floor
London EC1M 5QA, United Kingdom

Smith, Melanie (Actor)
1505 10th St
Santa Monica, CA 90401-2805, USA

Smith, Michael (Athlete, Basketball Player)
PO Box 91912
Washington, DC 20090-1912, USA

Smith, Michael Bailey (Actor)
c/o Alexandra Karrys *Divine Management*
117 N Orlando Ave
Los Angeles, CA 90048-3403, USA

Smith, Michael W (Musician, Songwriter, Writer)
c/o Staff Member *Creative Artists Agency (CAA-TN)*
3310 W End Ave Fl 5
Nashville, TN 37203-1028, USA

Smith, Mike (Cartoonist)
Editorial Dept 2275 Corporate Circle Dr
Henderson, NV 89074, USA

Smith, Mike (Misc)
310 Townsend St
San Francisco, CA 94107-1653, USA

Smith, Mike (Athlete, Baseball Player)
3226 Livingston Rd
Jackson, MS 39213-6106, USA

Smith, Mike (Athlete, Baseball Player)
2717 Seville Blvd Apt 8306
Clearwater, FL 33764-1169, USA

Smith, Mike (Athlete, Baseball Player)
7605 Antique Oak St
Live Oak, TX 78233-3102, USA

Smith, Mike (Athlete, Football Player)
619 Feamster Dr
Houston, TX 77022-2505, USA

Smith, Mindy (Musician, Songwriter, Writer)
2700 Pennsylvania Ave
Santa Monica, CA 90404-4066, USA

Smith, Moishe (Artist)
Dept
Logan, UT 84322-0001, USA

Smith, Monika (Actor)
c/o David Gardner *Principato/Young Management*
9465 Wilshire Blvd Ste 430
Beverly Hills, CA 90212-2613, USA

Smith, Myron (Athlete, Football Player)
6604 Sandgate Dr
Arlington, TX 76002-5549, USA

Smith, Nate (Athlete, Baseball Player)
6365 Tahoe Dr
Atlanta, GA 30349-4052, USA

Smith, Neil (Athlete, Football Player)
9423 Nall Ave
Overland Park, KS 66207-2529, USA

Smith, Nicholas (Actor)
10/11 Lower John St
London, ENGLAND W1R 3PE, UNITED KINGDOM (UK)

Smith, Noland (Athlete, Football Player)
4338 Watkins Dr
Jackson, MS 39206-4450, USA

Smith, O C
1650 Broadway Ste 508
New York, NY 10019-6833, USA

Smith, O Guinn (Athlete, Track Athlete)
1 Hawthorne Pl Apt 3P
Boston, MA 02114-2333, USA

Smith, Orin R (Business Person)
101 Wood Ave S
Iselin, NJ 08830-2703, USA

Smith, Orlando (Tubby) (Coach)
Athletic
Lexington, KY 40536-0001, USA

Smith, Osborne E (Ozzie) (Athlete, Baseball Player)
201 Kendall Bluff Ct
Chesterfield, MO 63017-2158, USA

Smith, Otis (Athlete, Basketball Player)
607 Applewood Ave
Altamonte Springs, FL 32714-7301, USA

Smith, Patti (Musician, Songwriter)
2-12 Pentonville Rd Fl 5
Sausalito, London N1 9PL, UNITED KINGDOM

Smith, Paul (Athlete, Baseball Player)
711 Trevino Ln
Conroe, TX 77302-3835, USA

Smith, Paul B (Designer, Fashion Designer)
41/44 Floral St Covent Garden
London WC2E 9DG, UNITED KINGDOM (UK)

Smith, Pete (Athlete, Baseball Player)
10030 Halstead Dr
Suwanee, GA 30024-5397, USA

Smith, Pete (Athlete, Baseball Player)
3512 Dixon Ln
The Villages, FL 32162-7150, USA

Smith, Putter
318 Fairview Ave
South Pasadena, CA 91030-1715

Smith, Quincy (Baseball Player)
715 S 14th St
Terre Haute, IN 47807-4920, USA

Smith, Quinn (Actor)
1738 Whitley Ave
Hollywood, CA 90028-4809

Smith, R Jackson (Swimmer)
122 Palmers Hill Rd Unit 3101
Stamford, CT 06902-2147, USA

Smith, Rachel (Beauty Pageant Winner)

Smith, Ralph (Athlete, Football Player)
PO Box 1406
McComb, MS 39649-1406, USA

Smith, Ralph (Cartoonist)
c/o Staff Member *King Features Syndication*
300 W 57th St Fl 15
New York, NY 10019-5238, USA

Smith, Randy (Athlete, Basketball Player)
2694 Villa Cortona Way
San Jose, CA 95125-6250, USA

Smith, Ray (Athlete, Baseball Player)
17183 Poblado Ct
San Diego, CA 92127-1431, USA

Smith, Ray E (Religious Leader)
2020 Bell Ave
Des Moines, IA 50315-1031, USA

Smith, Raymond W (Business Person, Financier)
1251 Avenue of the Americas
New York, NY 10020-1104, USA

Smith, Reggie (Athlete, Basketball Player)
6975 Claywood Way
San Jose, CA 95120-2241, USA

Smith, Rex (Actor)
16986 Encino Hills Dr
Encino, CA 91436-4008, USA

Smith, Richard A (Publisher)
275 Washington St
Newton, MA 02458-1611, USA

Smith, Richard M (Editor)
251 W 57th St
New York, NY 10019-1802, USA

Smith, Rico (Athlete, Football Player)
8976 Foothill Blvd Unit B7-389
Rancho Cucamonga, CA 91730-3400, USA

Smith, Riley (Actor)
c/o Mark Armstrong *Sanders Armstrong Caserta*
2120 Colorado Ave Ste 120
Santa Monica, CA 90404-3561, USA

Smith, Robert (Musician)
c/o Staff Member *Geffen Records*
9126 Sunset Blvd
West Hollywood, CA 90069, USA

Smith, Robert B (Athlete, Football Player)
1012 S Royal St
Bogalusa, LA 70427-5457, USA

Smith, Robert C (Editor)
100 Matsonford Rd
Radnor, PA 19087-4559, USA

Smith, Robert C (Bob) (Senator)
9012 Rocky Lake Ct
Sarasota, FL 34238-4008, USA

Smith, Robert Gray (Graysmith) (Cartoonist)
901 Mission St
San Francisco, CA 94103-2905, USA

Smith, Robert L (Athlete, Football Player)
426 Cape Lookout Dr
Corpus Christi, TX 78412-2636, USA

Smith, Robert S (Athlete, Football Player)
5668 Harrison Ave
Maple Heights, OH 44137-3331, USA

Smith, Robyn (Jockey)
1155 San Ysidro Dr
Beverly Hills, CA 90210-2102, USA

Smith, Rod (Athlete, Football Player)
821 W 4th St
Charlotte, NC 28202-1103, USA

Smith, Roger (Actor)
2707 Benedict Canyon Dr
Beverly Hills, CA 90210-1024, USA

Smith, Roger Guenveur (Actor, Writer)
2018 Vine St
Los Angeles, CA 90068-3915, USA

Smith, Rolland (Correspondent)
524 W 57th St
New York, NY 10019-2930, USA

Smith, Ron (Athlete, Football Player)
266 York St
Trussville, AL 35173-3224, USA

Smith, Ron (Athlete, Football Player)
1804 Park Ave
Richmond, VA 23220-2821, USA

Smith, Ronnie Ray (Athlete, Track Athlete)
752 W Athens Blvd
Los Angeles, CA 90044-3921, USA

Smith, Roy (Athlete, Baseball Player)
908 Woodbridge Ct
Safety Harbor, FL 34695-2951, USA

Smith, Roy (Athlete, Baseball Player)
472 Gramatan Ave Apt G2
Mount Vernon, NY 10552-2940, USA

Smith, Royce (Athlete, Football Player)
404 S College St
Claxton, GA 30417-1820, USA

Smith, Russell (Musician)
PO Box 965
Antioch, TN 37011-0965, USA

Smith, Sam (Athlete, Basketball Player)
246 Calvary Colony Rd
Memphis, TN 38127-3100, USA

Smith, Shawnee (Actor)
c/o Brian Wilkins *Kritzer Levine Wilkins Entertainment*
11872 La Grange Ave Fl 1
Los Angeles, CA 90025-5283, USA

Smith, Shelley (Actor)
4184 Colfax Ave
Studio City, CA 91604-2165, USA

Smith, Sherman (Athlete, Football Player)
41165 Black Branch Pkwy
Leesburg, VA 20175-4807, USA

Smith, Shevin (Athlete, Football Player)
PO Box 14331
Saint Petersburg, FL 33733-4331, USA

Smith, Sid (Athlete, Football Player)
1939 Melody Ln
Richmond, TX 77406-2411, USA

Smith, Sinjin (Athlete, Volleyball Player)
PO Box 1714
Pacific Palisades, CA 90272-1714, USA

Smith, Sonny (Baseball Player)
3549 N College Ave
Indianapolis, IN 46205-3733, USA

Smith, Stan
194 Bellevue Ave
Newport, RI 02840-3515

Smith, Stanley R (Stan) (Tennis Player)
1101 Woodrow Wilson Blvd # 1800
Arlington, VA 22209, USA

Smith, Stephen A (Correspondent, Radio Personality)
c/o Staff Member *WmE2 (WMA-LA)*
1 William Morris Pl
Beverly Hills, CA 90212-4261, USA

Smith, Steve (Producer)
c/o Staff Member *Hall Webber*
1200 Bay St Suite 400
Toronto, ON M5R 2A5, Canada

Smith, Steve (Athlete, Football Player)
1104 Lake Shore Dr N
Barrington, IL 60010-3427, USA

Smith, Steve (Athlete, Hockey Player)
117 W 4th St
Hinsdale, IL 60521-4023, USA

Smith, Steve A (Athlete, Football Player)
2717 Millwood Dr
Richardson, TX 75082-3832, USA

Smith, Steven (Misc)
1630 Duke St
Alexandria, VA 22314-3467, USA

Smith, Steven D (Steve) (Basketball Player)
c/o Staff Member *Charlotte Bobcats*
333 E Trade St Ste A
Charlotte, NC 28202-2332, USA

Smith, Steven L (Astronaut)
15728 Lake Lodge Dr
Houston, TX 77062, USA

Smith, Susan
2809 Airport Rd
Greenwood, SC 29649-9212

Smith, Taran (Actor)
12665 Kling St
North Hollywood, CA 91604-1143, USA

Smith, Tasha (Actor)
c/o Staff Member *Luber Roklin Management*
8530 Wilshire Blvd Ste 550
Beverly Hills, CA 90211-3133, USA

Smith, Thomas (Athlete, Football Player)
RR 1 Box 198
Gates, NC 27937, USA

Smith, Tommie (Athlete, Football Player, Track Athlete)
1800 Lilburn Stone Mountain Rd
Stone Mountain, GA 30087-1720, USA

Smith, Tommy (Athlete, Baseball Player)
1299 E Cannon Ave
Albemarle, NC 28001-4360, USA

Smith, Tony (Athlete, Football Player)
10400 Katelyn Dr
Charlotte, NC 28269-1463, USA

Smith, Tony (Athlete, Basketball Player)
2645 N 40th St
Milwaukee, WI 53210-2505, USA

Smith, Travian (Athlete, Football Player)
13941 County Road 2167D
Tatum, TX 75691-3214, USA

Smith, Travis (Athlete, Baseball Player)
1865 Cherry St
Clarkston, WA 99403-8717, USA

Smith, Troy (Football Player)
c/o Staff Member *Baltimore Ravens*
1 Winning Dr
Owings Mills, MD 21117-4776, USA

Smith, Tyron (Football Player)
c/o Joe Panos *Lock Metz Milanovic LLC*
6900 E Camelback Rd Ste 600
Scottsdale, AZ 85251-8044, USA

Smith, Vernice (Athlete, Football Player)
4347 Arajo Ct
Belle Isle, FL 32812-2854, USA

Smith, Vernon L (Nobel Prize Laureate)
1305 E Everett Pl
Orange, CA 92867-7007, USA

Smith, Vince (Musician)
439 Wiley Ave
Franklin, PA 16323-2834, USA

Smith, W Lawrence (Athlete, Football Player)
3601 Bayshore Blvd
Tampa, FL 33629-8942, USA

Smith, Wallace B (Religious Leader)
PO Box 1059
Independence, MO 64051-0559, USA

Smith, Walter (Designer, Engineer)
1 Microsoft Way
Redmond, WA 98052-8300, USA

Smith, Walter H F (Oceanographer)
Commerce
Washington, DC 20230-0001, USA

Smith, Wayne (Athlete, Football Player)
7730 S Bishop St
Chicago, IL 60620-4127, USA

Smith, Wilbur (Writer)
3 Bryanston Place #3
London W1H 7FN, UNITED KINGDOM (UK)

Smith, Will (Actor, Musician, Producer)
c/o James Lassiter *Overbook Entertainment*
450 N Roxbury Dr Fl 4
Beverly Hills, CA 90210-4218, USA

Smith, William (Actor)
3202 Anacapa St
Santa Barbara, CA 93105, USA

Smith, William (Stylist)
80 Cranberry St # 12-K
Brooklyn, NY 11201-1726, USA

Smith, William A. (Athlete, Basketball Player)
4379 Tami Ln
Central Point, OR 97502-1040, USA

Smith, William D (Admiral)
7025 Fairway Oaks
Fayetteville, PA 17222-9416, USA

Smith, William Jay (Writer)
62 LUTHER SHAW ROAD RR 1 Box 151
Cummington, MA 1026, USA

Smith, William Y (General)
6541 Brooks Pl
Falls Church, VA 22044-1106, USA

Smith, Willie (Football Player)
Ravens Stadium 11001 Russell St
Baltimore, MD 21230, USA

Smith, Willie (Athlete, Baseball Player)
1330 E 68th St
Savannah, GA 31404-5718, USA

Smith, Willow (Actor)
c/o Miguel Melendez *Overbrook Entertainment*
450 N Roxbury Dr Fl 4
Beverly Hills, CA 90210-4218, USA

Smith, Yeardley (Actor)
c/o Meredith O'Sullivan *42West (LA)*
11400 W Olympic Blvd Ste 1100
Los Angeles, CA 90064-1579, USA

Smith, Zadie (Writer)
1745 Broadway # B1
New York, NY 10019-4368, USA

Smith, Zane (Athlete, Baseball Player)
420 Windship Pl NW
Atlanta, GA 30327-4967, USA

Smith Court, Margaret (Tennis Player)
21 Lewanna Way City Bch
Perth, WA 6010, AUSTRALIA

Smith III, Earl (J.R.) (Athlete, Basketball Player)
c/o Shawn Zanotti *Exact Publicity Sports PR & Marketing*
1 S Dearborn St Ste 2100
Chicago, IL 60603-2307, USA

Smith Jr, John F (Jack) (Business Person)
100 Renaissance Ctr
Detroit, MI 48243-1114, USA

Smith Jr, Lonnie Liston (Musician)
1995 Broadway # 501
New York, NY 10023-5882, USA

Smith Jr, William R (Lawyer)
PO Box 3239
Tampa, FL 33601-3239, USA

Smith Osborne, Madolyn (Actor)
9560 Wilshire Blvd Ste 500
Beverly Hills, CA 90212-2401, USA

Smithberg, Roger (Athlete, Baseball Player)
988 Glenmore Ln
Elgin, IL 60124-2303, USA

Smitherman, Stephen (Athlete, Baseball Player)
HC 74 Box 240-10
Hartshorne, OK 74547, USA

Smithers, Jan (Actor)
c/o Staff Member *Innovative Artists (LA)*
1505 10th St
Santa Monica, CA 90401-2805, USA

Smithers, William (Actor)
2202 Anacapa St
Santa Barbara, CA 93105-3506, USA

Smithies, Oliver (Misc)
318 Umstead Dr
Chapel Hill, NC 27516, USA

Smith-McCulloch, Colleen (Baseball Player)
3-7168 Ash Cres
Vancouver, BC V6P 3K7, CANADA

Smith-McPhee, Sianoa (Actor)
c/o Kenneth (Kenny) Goodman *Schiff Company, The*
8440 Warner Dr Ste B1
Culver City, CA 90232-2461, USA

Smithson, Carly (Musician)

Smithson, Mike (Athlete, Baseball Player)
2540 Swan Creek Rd
Centerville, TN 37033-4374, USA

Smithson, Ryan (Writer)
c/o Staff Member *HarperCollins Publishers*
10 E 53rd St C/O Author Mail Floor 7
New York, NY 10022, USA

Smit-McPhee, Kodi (Actor)
c/o Kenneth (Kenny) Goodman *Schiff Company, The*
8440 Warner Dr Ste B1
Culver City, CA 90232-2461, USA

Smitrovich, Bill (Actor)
c/o Steven Siebert *Lighthouse Entertainment*
9220 W Sunset Blvd Ste 200
West Hollywood, CA 90069-3501, USA

Smits, Jimmy (Actor)
c/o Daniel (Danny) Sussman *Brillstein Entertainment Partners*
9150 Wilshire Blvd Ste 350
Beverly Hills, CA 90212-3453, USA

Smits, Rik (Athlete, Basketball Player)
8346 E 550 S
Zionsville, IN 46077-8610, USA

Smogolski, Henry R (Financier)
2300 N Western Ave
Chicago, IL 60647-3179, USA

Smolan, Rick (Artist, Photographer)
225 Varick St Fl 9
New York, NY 10014-4381, USA

Smoler, Carol (Stylist)
1825 N Sedgwick St
Chicago, IL 60614-5305, USA

Smolinski, Mark (Athlete, Football Player)
3300 Country Club Rd
Petoskey, MI 49770-8211, USA

Smolka, James W (Misc)
PO Box 2123
Lancaster, CA 93539-2123, USA

Smollett, Jurnee (Actor)
c/o Jon Leshay *Storefront Entertainment*
647 N Martel Ave Ste 102
Los Angeles, CA 90036-1930, USA

Smoltz, John A (Athlete, Baseball Player)
700 Foxhollow Run
Alpharetta, GA 30004-0962, USA

Smoot, Fred (Football Player)
c/o Staff Member *Washington Redskins*
1600 Fedex Way
Landover, MD 20785-4534, USA

Smoot III, George F. (Nobel Prize Laureate, Physicist)
Lbl Bldg # 50/5005
Berkeley, CA 94720-0001, USA

Smoove, J.B. (Actor, Writer)
c/o Staff Member *Rain Management Group (RMG)*
1631 21st St
Santa Monica, CA 90404-3914, USA

Smothers, Dick (Actor, Comedian)
c/o Staff Member *WmE2 (WMA-LA)*
1 William Morris Pl
Beverly Hills, CA 90212-4261, USA

Smothers, Tom (Actor, Comedian)
6442 Coldwater Canyon Ave Ste 107B
North Hollywood, CA 91606-1137, USA

Smothers Brothers, The (Comedian)
c/o Staff Member *WmE2 (WMA-LA)*
1 William Morris Pl
Beverly Hills, CA 90212-4261, USA

Smuin, Michael (Ballerina, Choreographer)
1314 34th Ave
San Francisco, CA 94122-1309, USA

Smulders, Cobie (Actor)
c/o Staff Member *ROAR (LA)*
9701 Wilshire Blvd Fl 8
Beverly Hills, CA 90212-2008, USA

Smurfit, Victoria (Actor)
c/o Richard (Rich) Cook *Lisa Richards Agency*
108 Upper Leeson St
Dublin 4, Ireland

Smyl, Stan (Athlete, Hockey Player)
202-130 W 5th St
North Vancouver, BC V7M 1J8, Canada

Smyres, Clancy (Athlete, Baseball Player)
38864 Edgemont Dr
Palmdale, CA 93551-4069, USA

Smyth, Charles P (Misc)
245 Prospect Ave
Princeton, NJ 08540-5303, USA

Smyth, Craig H (Historian)
PO Box 39
Cresskill, NJ 07626-0039, USA

Smyth, Joe (Music Group, Musician)
5200 Old Harding Rd
Franklin, TN 37064-9406, USA

Smyth, Patty (Musician)
23712 Malibu Colony Rd
Malibu, CA 90265-6629, USA

Smyth, Randy (Yachtsman)
17136 Bluewater Ln
Huntington Beach, CA 92649-2934, USA

Smyth, Ryan (Athlete, Hockey Player)
601-201 City Centre Dr
Mississauga, ON L5B 2T4, Canada

Smyth, Steve (Athlete, Baseball Player)
44005 Northgate Ave
Temecula, CA 92592-3000, YSA

Smythe, Marcus (Actor)
c/o Bob Waters *Bob Waters Agency*
9301 Wilshire Blvd Ste 300
Beverly Hills, CA 90210-6119, USA

Snare, Ryan (Athlete, Baseball Player)
2671 Derby Walk NE
Atlanta, GA 30319-3657, USA

Snarr, Trevor (Actor)
c/o Elizabeth Knight *KnightStar Multimedia*
PO Box 893
Lehi, UT 84043-0893, USA

Snead, Esix (Athlete, Baseball Player)
1332 42nd St
Orlando, FL 32839-1276, USA

Snead, Jesse Caryle (J C) (Golfer)
PO Box 782170
Wichita, KS 67278-2170, USA

Snead, Norman B (Norm) (Athlete, Football Player)
508 Veranda Way Apt C204
Naples, FL 34104-6049, USA

Snead, W T Sr (Religious Leader)
1404 Firestone Blvd
Los Angeles, CA 90001-3827, USA

Sneaker Pimps (Music Group)
c/o Staff Member *Paradigm (Monterey)*
404 W Franklin St
Monterey, CA 93940-2303, USA

Snedden, Stephen (Actor)
c/o Don Carroll *Don Carroll Management*
14211 Hatteras St
Sherman Oaks, CA 91401-4207, USA

Sneddon, Bob (Athlete, Football Player)
9564 Brentford Dr
Highlands Ranch, CO 80130-3782, USA

Snedeker, Brandt (Golfer)
4307 Glen Eden Dr
Nashville, TN 37205-3432, USA

Sneed, Ed (Golfer)
4155 Nottinghill Gate Rd
Columbus, OH 43220-3942, USA

Sneed, Floyd (Musician)
5171 Caliente St Unit 134
Las Vegas, NV 89119-2198, USA

Sneed, Joseph T (Judge)
Court Building 95 7th St
San Francisco, CA 94103, USA

Snelder, Richard L (Diplomat)
211 Central Park W
New York, NY 10024-6020, USA

Snell, Esmond E (Misc)
819 Tempted Ways Dr
Longmont, CO 80504-8467, USA

Snell, Ian (Athlete, Baseball Player)
90 Beechwood Ave
Dover, DE 19901-5236, USA

Snell, Matthews (Matt) (Athlete, Football Player)
175 Clendenny Ave
Jersey City, NJ 07304-1201, USA

Snell, Nate (Athlete, Baseball Player)
7299 Old State Rd
Holly Hill, SC 29059-8514, USA

Snell, Peter (Athlete, Track Athlete)
6452 Dunstan Ln
Dallas, TX 75214-2239, USA

Snell, Ray (Athlete, Football Player)
1411 W Linebaugh Ave
Tampa, FL 33612-7641, USA

Sneva, Tom (Race Car Driver)
3301 E Valley Vista Ln
Paradise Valley, AZ 85253-3739, USA

Sniadecki, Jim (Athlete, Football Player)
3267 Congressional Cir
Fairfield, CA 94534-7869, USA

Snicket, Lemony (Writer)
10 E 53rd St
New York, NY 10022-5244, USA

Snider, Dee (Musician)
9511 Weldon Cir Apt 316
Fort Lauderdale, FL 33321-0922, USA

Snider, Edward M (Ed) (Athlete, Hockey Player)
PO Box 25088
Philadelphia, PA 19147-0288, USA

Snider, Mike
PO Box 140710
Nashville, TN 37214-0710

Snider, R Michael (Scientist)
Eastern Point Rd
Groton, CT 06340-5196, USA

Snider, Todd (Music Group, Musician, Songwriter, Writer)
33 Music Sq W Ste 102B
Nashville, TN 37203-6607, USA

Snider, Van (Athlete, Baseball Player)
1615 Windsor Dr
Cleveland, OH 44124-3616, USA

Snidow, Ron (Football Player)
18742 Via San Marco
Irvine, CA 92603-3436, USA

Snipes, Wesley (Actor)
c/o David Schiff *Schiff Company, The*
8440 Warner Dr Ste B1
Culver City, CA 90232-2461, USA

Snipscheer, Fred (Athlete, Hockey Player)
13404 Macaw Pl
Carmel, IN 46033-8964, USA

Snitzier, Larry (Musician)
5 Loblolly Ct
Pinehurst, NC 28374-9349, USA

Snodgrass, William D (Writer)
3061 Hughes Rd
Erieville, NY 13061-4128, USA

Snook, Frank (Athlete, Baseball Player)
2580 Elysium Ave
Eugene, OR 97401-7441, USA

Snopek, Chris (Athlete, Baseball Player)
103 Bradford Dr
Cynrhiana, KY 41031, USA

Snow (Artist, Musician, Songwriter, Writer)
2076 Sherobee Rd # 510
Mississauga, ON L5A 4C4, CANADA

Snow, Brittany (Actor)
c/o Marcel Pariseau *True Public Relations*
6725 W Sunset Blvd Ste 470
Los Angeles, CA 90028-7180, USA

Snow, DeShawn (Reality TV Star)
c/o Richard Heard *DeShawn Snow Enterprises, L.L.C.*
5665 Atlanta Hwy Ste 103-370
Alpharetta, GA 30004-3959, USA

Snow, Eric (Athlete, Basketball Player)
5665 Atlanta Hwy Ste 103
Alpharetta, GA 30004-3932, USA

Snow, J T (Athlete, Baseball Player)
15 Bridle Ct
Hillsborough, CA 94010-7451, USA

Snow, John W (Secretary)
1500 Pennsylvania Ave NW
Washington, DC 20220-0001, USA

Snow, Justin (Athlete, Football Player)
1826 Milford St
Carmel, IN 46032-7207, USA

Snow, Kate (Television Host)
c/o Staff Member *Good Morning America (NY)*
147 Columbus Ave Fl 6
New York, NY 10023-6503, USA

Snow, Mark (Composer, Musician)
c/o Staff Member *Robert Urband & Associates*
8981 W Sunset Blvd Ste 311
W Hollywood, CA 90069-1881, USA

Snow, Percy L (Football Player)
2010 48th St NE
Canton, OH 44705-3082, USA

Snow, Richard F (Editor)
60 5th Ave
New York, NY 10011-8868, USA

Snow Patrol (Music Group)
c/o Staff Member *Paradigm (Monterey)*
404 W Franklin St
Monterey, CA 93940-2303, USA

Snowden, Alison (Director, Writer)
c/o Melissa Myers *WmE2 (Endeavor-LA)*
9601 Wilshire Blvd Fl 3
Beverly Hills, CA 90210-5219, USA

Snowden, Earl of (A C R Armstrong-Jones) (Photographer)
22 Launceston Place
London W8 5RL, UNITED KINGDOM (UK)

Snowden, Lisa (Model)
c/o Marki Costello *Creative Management Entertainment Group (CMEG)*
2050 S Bundy Dr Ste 280
Los Angeles, CA 90025-6128, USA

Snowdon, Lisa (Actor)
c/o Marki Costello *Creative Management Entertainment Group (CMEG)*
2050 S Bundy Dr Ste 280
Los Angeles, CA 90025-6128, USA

Snowdon, Lord
22 Lauceston Pl
London, ENGLAND W1

Snuggerud, Dave (Athlete, Hockey Player)
4529 Saddlewood Dr
Minnetonka, MN 55345-2656, USA

Snuka, Jimmy (Superfly) (Actor, Wrestler)
647 Pacific Ave
Atco, NJ 08004-2117

Snyder, Allan W (Scientist)
Optical Science Center
Canberra, ACT 2601, AUSTRALIA

Snyder, Ben (Comedian)
c/o Staff Member *Gersh (LA)*
9465 Wilshire Blvd Ste 600
Beverly Hills, CA 90212-2612, USA

Snyder, Bill (Coach, Football Coach)
Athletic Dept
Manhattan, KS 66506, USA

Snyder, Brian (Athlete, Baseball Player)
14834 Wood Home Rd
Centreville, VA 20120-1546, USA

Snyder, Cory (Athlete, Baseball Player)
468 N Loafer Dr
Payson, UT 84651-4535, USA

Snyder, Daniel (Football Executive)
c/o Staff Member *Washington Redskins*
1600 Fedex Way
Landover, MD 20785-4534, USA

Snyder, Dick (Athlete, Basketball Player)
4621 E Mockingbird Ln
Paradise Valley, AZ 85253-2420, USA

Snyder, Earl (Athlete, Baseball Player)
58 Diamond Ave
Plainville, CT 06062-2904, USA

Snyder, Evan (Doctor)
25 Shattuck St
Boston, MA 02115-6027, USA

Snyder, Fonda (Actor)
c/o Staff Member *WmE2 (WMA-LA)*
1 William Morris Pl
Beverly Hills, CA 90212-4261, USA

Snyder, Gary S (Writer)
18442 MacNab Cypress Rd
Nevada City, CA 95959-8504, USA

Snyder, James (Actor)
c/o Brad Schenck *Paradigm (LA)*
360 N Crescent Dr
Beverly Hills, CA 90210-4874, USA

Snyder, Jerry (Athlete, Baseball Player)
2553 Wild Oak Forest Ln
Seabrook, TX 77586-2632, USA

Snyder, Jim (Athlete, Baseball Player)
7516 Dunbridge Dr
Odessa, FL 33556-2270, USA

Snyder, Jim (Athlete, Baseball Player, Coach)
7516 Dunbridge Dr
Odessa, FL 33556-2270, USA

Snyder, Joan (Artist)
21 E 70th St
New York, NY 10021-4982, USA

Snyder, John (Athlete, Baseball Player)
17729 W Port Royale Ln
Surprise, AZ 85388-7593, USA

Snyder, Joshua (Actor)
c/o Staff Member *Main Title Entertainment*
2225 Wilshire Blvd Suite 500
Los Angeles, CA 90036, USA

Snyder, Kyle (Athlete, Baseball Player)
1869 Upper Cove Ter
Sarasota, FL 34231-5437, USA

Snyder, Liza (Actor)
c/o Susan Smith *Susan Smith Company, The*
1344 N Wetherly Dr
Los Angeles, CA 90069-1817, USA

Snyder, Loren (Athlete, Football Player)
7727 Via Cortona
San Diego, CA 92127-3824, USA

Snyder, Rick (Governor)
PO Box 30013
Lansing, MI 48909-7513, USA

Snyder, Russ (Athlete, Baseball Player)
PO Box 264
Nelson, NE 68961-0264, USA

Snyder, Solomon H (Doctor)
3801 Canterbury Rd Unit 1001
Baltimore, MD 21218-2379, USA

Snyder, Suzanne (Actor)
1875 Century Park E Ste 2250
Los Angeles, CA 90067-2563, USA

Snyder, Todd (Football Player)
850 S Valley Ln
Palatine, IL 60067-7185, USA

Snyder, William (Journalist)
508 Young St
Dallas, TX 75202-4808, USA

Snyder, William D (Journalist, Photographer)
Communivations Center Editorial Dept
Dallas, TX 75265, USA

Snyder, Zack (Director, Writer)
c/o Todd Feldman *Creative Artists Agency (CAA-LA)*
2000 Avenue of the Stars Ste 100
Los Angeles, CA 90067-4705, USA

Snyderman, Nancy (Doctor, Entertainer)
1220 L St NW Ste 850
Washington, DC 20005-4095, USA

So, Linda (Model)
6130 W Tropicana Ave # 280
Las Vegas, NV 89103-4604

So Solid Crew (Music Group)
c/o Staff Member *Mission Control Artists Agency*
Unit 3 City Business Centre St Olav's Court, Lower Road
London SE16 2XB, UNITED KINGDOM (UK)

Soares, Mario A N L (President)
Rue Dr Joao Soares #2-3
Lisbon 1600, PORTUGAL

Sobel, Barry
9000 W Sunset Blvd Ste 1200
Los Angeles, CA 90069-5812

Sobers, Garfield S (Gary) (Cricketer)
9 Appleblossom Petit Valley
Diego Martin, TRINIDAD

Sobers, Rickey (Athlete, Basketball Player)
6530 Annie Oakley Dr Apt 1414
Henderson, NV 89014-2171, USA

Sobieski, Leelee (Actor)
c/o Shelley Browning *Magnolia Entertainment (LA)*
9595 Wilshire Blvd Ste 601
Beverly Hills, CA 90212-2506, USA

Sobkowiak, Scott (Athlete, Baseball Player)
1732 Borman Pl
Downers Grove, IL 60516-3743, USA

Soble, Ron (Actor)
4637 Willowcrest Ave
North Hollywood, CA 91602-1464, USA

Sobule, Jill (Musician, Songwriter, Writer)
c/o Jonny (Jon) Podell *Podell Talent Agency LLC*
22 W 21st St Fl 9
New York, NY 10010-7095, USA

Socha, Lauren (Actor)
c/o Nicola Van Gelder *Conway van Gelder*
8-12 Broadwick St
London W1F 8HW, UK

Socha, Michael (Actor)
c/o Saskia Mulder *Ken McReddie Ltd*
11 Connaught Pl
London W2 2ET, UNITED KINGDOM

Sochor, James (Jim) (Coach, Football Coach)
1018 Kent Dr
Davis, CA 95616-0933, USA

Social Distortion (Music Group, Musician)
c/o Jim Guerinot *Rebel Waltz Inc*
31652 2nd Ave
Laguna Beach, CA 92651-8244, USA

Society, Honor (Music Group, Musician)
c/o Staff Member *Walt Disney Music*
500 S Buena Vista St Animation 2E16
Burbank, CA 91521-0007

Socolofsky, Shelley (Artist)
3285 Sumac Dr S
Salem, OR 97302-4080, USA

Sodano, Angelo Cardinal (Religious Leader)
Palazzo Apostolico
120, VATICAN CITY

Soderbaum, Kristina
St.-Jakobs-platz 10 D-
Munich, GERMANY 80331

Soderberg, E Loren (Photographer)
PO Box 313
Sausalito, CA 94966-0313, USA

Soderbergh, Steven (Director, Producer)
c/o Michael Sugar *Anonymous Content (AC-LA)*
3531 Hayden Ave
Culver City, CA 90232, USA

Soderholm, Eric (Athlete, Baseball Player)
10S360 Hampshire Ln
Willowbrook, IL 60527, USA

Soderstrom, Elisabeth (Opera Singer)
19 Hersbyvagen
Lidingo 181 42, SWEDEN

Soderstrom, Elizabeth
19 Jersbyvagen
Lidingo, SWEDEN 181-42

Soderstrom, Steve (Athlete, Baseball Player)
301 N Faith Home Rd
Turlock, CA 95380-9458, USA

Sodowsky, Client (Athlete, Baseball Player)
2801 Tropicana Ave
Norman, OK 73071-1711, USA

Sofaer, Abraham D (Lawyer)
120 Bryant St
Palo Alto, CA 94301, USA

Sofer, Rena (Actor)
c/o Nancy Iannios *Nancy Iannios PR*
PO Box 430
Signal Mountain, TN 37377-0430, USA

Soff, Ray (Athlete, Baseball Player)
146 Drew Ave
Deerfield, MI 49238-9787, USA

Soffer, Jesse Lee (Actor)
c/o Marnie Sparer *Innovative Artists (LA)*
1505 10th St
Santa Monica, CA 90401-2805, USA

Sofie von Otter, Anne (Musician)
c/o Staff Member *International Creative Management (ICM-LA)*
10250 Constellation Blvd Fl 7
Los Angeles, CA 90067-6207, USA

Sofield, Rick (Athlete, Baseball Player)
1 University Blvd
Okatie, SC 29909-6085, USA

Softley, Iain (Director)
32A Camaby St
London, W1V 1PA UNITED KIN

Sohmer, Steve
2625 Larmar Rd
Los Angeles, CA 90068-2631

Sohn Kee-Chung (Athlete, Track Athlete)
International PO Box 1106
Seoul, SOUTH KOREA

Sojo, Luis (Athlete, Baseball Player)
17647 SW 20th St
Miramar, FL 33029-5238, USA

Soklosky, Bing (Cinematographer)
4654 Cartwright Ave
Toluca Lake, CA 91602-1451, USA

Sokol, Marilyn (Actor)
24 W 40th St # 1700
New York, NY 10018-3904, USA

Sokoloff, Louis (Misc)
9000 Rockville Pike
Bethesda, MD 20892-0001, USA

Sokoloff, Marla (Actor)
9100 Wilshire Blvd Ste 100W
Beverly Hills, CA 90212-3435, USA

Sokolosky, John (Football Player)
13240 Leech Dr
Sterling Heights, MI 48312-3253, USA

Sokolov, Grigory L (Musician)
1926 Broadway
New York, NY 10023-6915, USA

Sokolove, James G (Lawyer)
1 Boston Pl
Boston, MA 02108-4400, USA

Sokomanu, A George (President)
Mele Village PO Box 1319
Port Villa, VANUATU

Sokurov, Alexander N (Director)
Smolenskaya Nab 4 #222
Saint Petersburg 199048, RUSSIA

Solana Madariaga, Javier (Government Official)
Rue de la Loi
Brussels 1048, BELGIUM

Solano, Jose (Actor)
c/o Staff Member *Stephany Hurkos Management*
11935 Kling St
Valley Village, CA 91607-4072, USA

Solars, Stephen
241 Dover St
Brooklyn, NY 11235-3721

Solberg, Magnar (Athlete)
Stabellvn 60
Trondheim 7000, NORWAY

Solder, Nate (Football Player)
c/o David Dunn *Athletes First, LLC*
3300 Irvine Ave Ste 300
Newport Beach, CA 92660-3108, USA

Soleil, Stella (Music Group, Musician)
350 W End Ave Apt 1A
New York, NY 10024-6818, USA

Soleri, Paolo (Architect)
6433 Doubletree Rd
Scottsdale, AZ 85253, USA

Soles, Pamela Jayne (PJ) (Actor)
c/o Bill Philputt *Re-Evolution*
Prefers to be contacted via telephone
Los Angeles Area, CA 90069, USA

Solh, Rashid (Prime Minister)
Place de l'Etoile
Beirut, LABANON

Solich, Frank (Coach, Football Coach)
Athletic Dept
Lincoln, NE 68588, USA

Solis, Christina
9300 Wilshire Blvd Ste 555
Beverly Hills, CA 90212-3211

Sollscher, Goran (Musician)
Plankengasse 7
Vienna 1010, AUSTRIA

Soloman, Anthony M (Financier)
46 Convent Ct
San Rafael, CA 94901-1334, USA

Soloman, Freddie (Football Player)
803 Turtle River Ct
Plant City, FL 33567-2474, USA

Solomon, Ariel (Football Player)
5045 51st St
Boulder, CO 80301-4309, USA

Solomon, Arthur K (Physicist)
27 Craigie St
Cambridge, MA 02138-3457, USA

Solomon, Bruce
3518 Cahuenga Blvd W # 316
Los Angeles, CA 90068-1304

Solomon, David H (Scientist)
3640 Dragonfly Dr Apt 202
Thousand Oaks, CA 91360-8445, USA

Solomon, Ed (Writer)
c/o Todd Feldman *Creative Artists Agency (CAA-LA)*
2000 Avenue of the Stars Ste 100
Los Angeles, CA 90067-4705, USA

Solomon, Edward I (Misc)
Chemistry Dept
Stanford, CA 94305, USA

Solomon, Freddie (Athlete, Football Player)
803 Turtle River Ct
Plant City, FL 33567-2474, USA

Solomon, Harold (Tennis Player)
1 Erieview Plaza 1360 East 9th St # 1300
Cleveland, OH 44114, USA

Solomon, Jesse (Football Player)
401 SW Bunker St
Madison, FL 32340-1902, USA

Solomon, Richard H (Diplomat, Scientist)
1200 17th St NW Ste 200
Washington, DC 20036-3011, USA

Solomon, Sophie (Musician)
c/o Staff Member *Paradigm (Monterey)*
404 W Franklin St
Monterey, CA 93940-2303, USA

Solomon, Susan (Misc)
325 Broadway St
Boulder, CO 80305-3337, USA

Solomon, Yonty (Musician)
56 Canonbury Park N
London N1 2JT, UNITED KINGDOM (UK)

Solondz, Todd (Director, Writer)
955 Carrillo Dr Ste 300
Los Angeles, CA 90048-5400, USA

Solovey, Sam (Actor)
c/o Staff Member *Ruth Webb Enterprises*
10580 Des Moines Ave
Northridge, CA 91326-2926, USA

Soloviyev, Vladimir A (Cosmonaut)
Khovanskaya Ui D 3 Kv 28
Moscow 129515, RUSSIA

Solovyev, Anatoli Y (Cosmonaut)
Moskovskoi Oblasti
Syvisdny Goroduk 141160, RUSSIA

Solovyev, Sergei A (Director, Writer)
Akademika Pilyugina Str 8 Korp 1 #330
Moscow 11393, RUSSIA

Solow, Robert M (Nobel Prize Laureate)
1010 Waltham St Apt 328
Lexington, MA 02421-8057, USA

Soloway, Jill (Producer)
c/o Staff Member *International Creative Management (ICM-LA)*
10250 Constellation Blvd Fl 7
Los Angeles, CA 90067-6207, USA

Solt, Ron (Football Player)
1200 Thornhurst Rd
Bear Creek Township, PA 18702-8212, USA

Soltan, Jerzy (Architect)
148 Boylston St
Watertown, MA 02472-1907, USA

Soltau, Gordie (Football Player)
620 Sand Hill Rd Apt 105E
Palo Alto, CA 94304-2605, USA

Soltau, Gordon (Gordy) (Football Player)
620 Sand Hill Rd Apt 105E
Palo Alto, CA 94304-2605, USA

Soltau, Gordy
1111 Hamilton Ave
Palo Alto, CA 94301-2217

Soluna (Music Group)
c/o Staff Member *Creative Artists Agency (CAA-LA)*
2000 Avenue of the Stars Ste 100
Los Angeles, CA 90067-4705, USA

Solvay, Jacques (Business Person)
Rue de Prince Albert 33
Brussels 1050, BELGIUM

Solymosi, Zoltan (Dancer)
Covent GArden Bow St
London WC2E 9DD, UNITED KINGDOM (UK)

Solyom, Janos P (Musician)
Norr Malarstrand 54 VII
Stockholm 11220, SWEDEN

Solzhenitsyn, Ignat (Musician)
165 W 57th St
New York, NY 10019-2201, USA

Somare, Michael T (Prime Minister)
Karan Murik Lakes
East Sepik, PAPUA NEW GUINEA

Sombrotto, Vincent R (Misc)
100 Indiana Ave NW
Washington, DC 20001-2143, USA

Somerhalder, Ian (Actor)
c/o Alissa Vradenburg *Untitled Entertainment (LA)*
350 S Beverly Dr Ste 200
Beverly Hills, CA 90212-4819, USA

Somers, Gwen (Actor, Model)
1927 Vista Del Mar St
Los Angeles, CA 90068-4004, USA

Somers, Suzanne (Actor)
23677 Calabasas Rd # 663
Calabasas, CA 91302-1502, USA

Somerset, Willie (Athlete, Basketball Player)
6441 Oak View Dr
Harrisburg, PA 17112-1889, USA

Somerville, Bonnie (Actor)
c/o Staff Member *McKeon-Myones Management*
3500 W Olive Ave Ste 770
Burbank, CA 91505-5527, USA

Something Corporate (Music Group)
c/o Staff Member *Agency for the Performing Arts (APA-LA)*
405 S Beverly Dr Ste 500
Beverly Hills, CA 90212-4425, USA

Sommaruga, Cornelio (Misc)
19 Ave de la Paix
Genoa 1202, SWITZERLAND

Sommer, Elke (Actor)
Atzelaberger Str 46
Marloffstein D-91080, GERMANY

Sommer, Rich (Actor)
c/o Staff Member *Davis Spylios Management*
244 W 54th St Ste 707
New York, NY 10019-5515

Sommerfeld, Kent (Sportscaster)
13935 W Maria Dr
New Berlin, WI 53151-6891, USA

Sommers, Gordon L (Religious Leader)
1021 Center St
Bethlehem, PA 18018-2838, USA

Sommers, Joanie (Musician)
900 SE 3rd Ave Ste 201
Fort Lauderdale, FL 33316-1118, USA

Sommers, Stephen (Director, Producer, Writer)
c/o Stuart Rosenthal *Bloom Hergott Diemer Rosenthal Laviolette & Feldman*
150 S Rodeo Dr Fl 3
Beverly Hills, CA 90212-2410, USA

Sommore (Comedian)
c/o Staff Member *International Creative Management (ICM-LA)*
10250 Constellation Blvd Fl 7
Los Angeles, CA 90067-6207, USA

Somogyi, Jennie R (Ballerina)
c/o Staff Member *New York City Ballet*
20 Lincoln Center Plz
New York, NY 10023-6913, USA

Somogyi, Jozsef (Artist)
Marton Utca 3/5
Budapest 1038, HUNGARY

Somorjai, Gabor A (Misc)
665 San Luis Rd
Berkeley, CA 94707-1725, USA

Sondeckis, Saulls (Conductor)
Ciurlionio 28
Vilnius, LITHUANIA

Sondheim, Stephen (Composer, Musician)
265 Wollaton Vale
Wollaton, Nottingham NG8 2PX, UNITED KINGDOM (UK)

Sondrini, Joe (Athlete, Baseball Player)
9523 Laguna Ave NW
Concord, NC 28027-3553, USA

Song, Brenda (Actor)
c/o Richard Konigsberg *RKM*
400 N Mansfield Ave
Los Angeles, CA 90036-2622, USA

Song, Xiaodong (Misc)
Lamont-Doherty Earth Observatory
New York, NY 10027, USA

Songaila, Antoinette (Astronomer)
Astronomy Dept
Honolulu, HI 96822, USA

Songz, Trey (Musician)
c/o Dana Sims *International Creative Management (ICM-LA)*
10250 Constellation Blvd Fl 7
Los Angeles, CA 90067-6207, USA

Soni, Rebecca (Athlete, Swimmer)
c/o Staff Member *USA Swimming Association*
1 Olympic Plz
Colorado Springs, CO 80909-5780, USA

Sonja (Royalty)
Det Kongelige Slott Drammensveien 1
Oslo 10, NORWAY

Sonnanstine, Andy (Athlete, Baseball Player)
1848 Sailfish Rd S
Saint Petersburg, FL 33707-3832, USA

Sonnenfeld, Barry (Director)
c/o Richard Lovett *Creative Artists Agency (CAA-LA)*
2000 Avenue of the Stars Ste 100
Los Angeles, CA 90067-4705, USA

Sonnenschein, Hugo F (Educator)
President's Office
Chicago, IL 60637, USA

Sonnenschein, Klaus
Breisgauer Str. 15a
Berlin, GERMANY D-14129

Sonnier, Jo-El (Musician)
2409 21st Ave S Ste 100
Nashville, TN 37212-5317, USA

Sons of the Desert (Music Group)
c/o Staff Member *WmE2 (WMA-TN)*
1600 Division St Ste 300
Nashville, TN 37203-2755, USA

Sons of the Pioneers
117 Berms Cir # 45
Branson, MO 65616-4051

Sonsini, Larry W (Lawyer)
650 Page Mill Rd
Palo Alto, CA 94304-1001, USA

Sood, Veena (Actor, Producer)
c/o Robyn Friedman *Artist Management Inc*
464 King St E
Toronto ON M5A 1L7, CANADA

Soomekh, Bahar (Actor)
c/o Paul Kohner *Kohner Agency, The*
9300 Wilshire Blvd Ste 555
Beverly Hills, CA 90212-3211, USA

Sophia (Royalty)
Madrid 28071, SPAIN

Sopko, Michael D (Business Person)
145 King St W
Toronto, ON M5H 4B7, CANADA

Sopkovic, Kay (Athlete, Baseball Player)
6540 W Butler Dr Unit 62
Glendale, AZ 85302-4313, USA

Sorbo, Kevin (Actor)
c/o Matt Luber *Luber Roklin Management*
8530 Wilshire Blvd Ste 550
Beverly Hills, CA 90211-3133, USA

Sorel, Edward (Artist)
156 Franklin St
New York, NY 10013-2908, USA

Sorel, Jean (Actor)
36 Rue de Ponthieu
Paris 75008, FRANCE

Sorel, Louise (Actor)
20 E 74th St # 3F
New York, NY 10021-2654, USA

Sorel, Ted (Actor)
c/o Staff Member *Kerin-Goldberg Associates*
155 E 55th St Ste 5D
New York, NY 10022-4038, USA

Sorensen, Jacki F (Misc)
129 1/2 N Woodland Blvd Ste 5
Deland, FL 32720-4269, USA

Sorensen, Lary (Athlete, Baseball Player)
42515 Northville Place Dr Apt 406
Northville, MI 48167-3186, USA

Sorensen, Nick (Football Player)
305 Grandview Dr
Blacksburg, VA 24060-6222, USA

Sorenson, Heidi (Actor, Model)
13775A Mono Way # 220
Sonora, CA 95370-8813, USA

Sorenson, Theodore
1285 Avenue of the Americas
New York, NY 10019-6028

Sorenson, Zach (Athlete, Baseball Player)
1322 S 2670 E
Saint George, UT 84790-6197, USA

Sorenstam, Annika (Golfer)
c/o Staff Member *IMG (Cleveland)*
1360 E 9th St Ste 100
Cleveland, OH 44114-1730, USA

Sorenstam, Charlotta (Golfer)
1411 W Whitman Ct
Anthem, AZ 85086-3927, USA

Sorey, Revie (Football Player)
485 Saint Moritz Dr
Glen Ellyn, IL 60137-4320, USA

Sorgers, Jana (Athlete)
An Der Pirschheide
Potsdam 14471, GERMANY

Sorgi, Jim (Athlete, Football Player)
72 Hollaway Blvd
Brownsburg, IN 46112-8355, USA

Soriano, Alfonso G (Baseball Player)
1000 Ballpark Way
Arlington, TX 76011-5168, USA

Soriano, Edward (General)
Vice Commander I Corps/Fort Lewis
Fort Lewis, WA 98433, USA

Soriano, Rafael (Athlete, Baseball Player)
6820 81st Dr NE
Marysville, WA 98270-6598, USA

Sorkin, Aaron (Producer, Writer)
c/o Rick Rosen *WmE2 (Endeavor-LA)*
9601 Wilshire Blvd Fl 3
Beverly Hills, CA 90210-5219, USA

Sorkin, Andrew Ross (Correspondent)
c/o Staff Member *The New York Times Company*
229 W 43rd St
New York, NY 10036-3913, USA

Sorkin, Arleen (Actor)
623 S Beverly Glen Blvd
Los Angeles, CA 90024-2531, USA

Sorlie, Donald M (Misc)
14612 44th Avenue Ct NW
Gig Harbor, WA 98332-9048, USA

Sorokin, Peter P (Physicist)
5 Ashwood Rd
South Salem, NY 10590-1601, USA

Soros, George (Business Person, Financier)
888 7th Ave # 3300
New York, NY 10106-0001, USA

Soroya, Princess
Ave. Montaigne
Paris, FRANCE 75008

Sorrell, Bill (Athlete, Baseball Player)
12255 Ranch House Rd
San Diego, CA 92128-1229, USA

Sorrentino, Mike (The Situation) (Reality TV Star)
4400 US Highway 9 Ste 1000
Freehold, NJ 07728-1383, USA

Sorrento, Paul (Athlete, Baseball Player)
5918 Mont Blanc Pl NW
Issaquah, WA 98027-7859, USA

Sorrento, Paul A (Baseball Player)
5918 Mont Blanc Pl NW
Issaquah, WA 98027-7859, USA

Sorsa, T Kalevi (Prime Minister)
Hakaniemenranta 16D
Helsinki 530, FINLAND

Sorte, Maria (Actor)
c/o Staff Member *Televisa*
Blvd Adolfo Lopez Mateos 232 Colonia
San Angel INN
DF CP 01060, MEXICO

Sortun, Henrik (Athlete, Football Player)
6708 16th Ave NW
Seattle, WA 98117-5513, USA

Sorum, Matt (Musician)
c/o Todd Cameron *Abrams Artists Agency (LA)*
806 N Crescent Heights Blvd
Los Angeles, CA 90046-6902, USA

Sorvino, Mira (Actor)
c/o Jason Weinberg *Untitled Entertainment (LA)*
350 S Beverly Dr Ste 200
Beverly Hills, CA 90212-4819, USA

Sorvino, Paul (Actor)
c/o Steven Muller *Innovative Artists (LA)*
1505 10th St
Santa Monica, CA 90401-2805, USA

Sosa, Elias (Athlete, Baseball Player)
3126 Summerfield Ridge Ln
Matthews, NC 28105-8509, USA

Sosa, Samuel (Sammy) (Athlete, Baseball Player)
1060 W Addison St Attn
Alumniassociation
Chicago, IL 60613-4566, USA

Sossaman, Shannyn (Actor)
c/o Matt Eskander *Paradigm (LA)*
360 N Crescent Dr
Beverly Hills, CA 90210-4874, USA

Sossamon, Lou (Athlete, Football Player)
6308 Exum Dr
West Columbia, SC 29169-7184, USA

Soter, Paul (Comedian)
c/o Staff Member *United Talent Agency (UTA)*
9560 Wilshire Blvd Fl 5
Beverly Hills, CA 90212-2400, USA

Sotin, Hans (Opera Singer)
Schulheide 10
Bendestorf 21227, GERMANY

Sotirhos, Michael A (Diplomat)
A Leoforos Vassilissis Sofias 91
Athens 106 60, GREECE

Sotkilava, Zurab L (Opera Singer)
Teatralnaya Pi 1
Moscow 103009, RUSSIA

Soto, Gabriel (Actor)
c/o Staff Member *Televisa*
Blvd Adolfo Lopez Mateos 232 Colonia
San Angel INN
DF CP 01060, MEXICO

Soto, Geovany (Athlete, Baseball Player)
6319 Perch Creek Dr
Houston, TX 77049-3447, USA

Soto, Mario M (Athlete, Baseball Player)
6319 Perch Creek Dr
Houston, TX 77049-3447, USA

Soto, Talisa (Actor)
c/o Peg Donegan *Framework Entertainment (LA)*
9057 Nemo St Ste C
West Hollywood, CA 90069-5511, USA

Sotomayor, Antonio (Artist)
3 Leroy Pl
San Francisco, CA 94109-4224, USA

Sotomayor, Nancy (Stylist)
1 Penn Plz Frnt 9
New York, NY 10119-0204, USA

Sotomayor Sanabria, Javier (Athlete, Track Athlete)
1 Erieview Plaza 1360 East 9th St # 1300
Cleveland, OH 44114, USA

Sottsass Jr, Ettore (Designer)
Via Manzoni 14
Milan 20121, ITALY

Souch, Carolyn (Stylist)
c/o Staff Member *Judy Inc*
1 Yorkville Ave
Toronto ON M4W 1L1, Canada

Souders, Cecil (Football Player)
1803 Channingway Ct E
Reynoldsburg, OH 43068, USA

Soul, David (Actor, Musician)
1505 10th St
Santa Monica, CA 90401-2805, USA

Soul Asylum (Music Group, Musician)
955 Carrillo Dr Ste 300
Los Angeles, CA 90048-5400, USA

Soul II Soul (Music Group)
c/o Staff Member *Profile Artists Agency*
Unit 10, J Block Tower Bridge Business Complex, 110 Clements Road
London SE16 4DG, United Kingdom

Soulages, Pierre (Artist)
18 Rue des Trois-Portes
Paris 75005, FRANCE

SoulDecision (Music Group)
c/o Staff Member *Bruce Allen Talent*
425 Carrall St Suite 500
Vancouver, BC V6B 6E3, Canada

Sound Tribe Sector 9 (Music Group)
c/o Staff Member *Paradigm (Monterey)*
404 W Franklin St
Monterey, CA 93940-2303, USA

Sousa, Mauricio de (Cartoonist)
Rua do Curtume 745
Sao Paulo SP, BRAZIL

Soutar, Dave (Bowler)
6910 Chickasaw Falls Ave
Bradenton, FL 34203, USA

Soutar, Judy (Bowler)
3914 102nd Pl N
Clearwater, FL 33762-5404, USA

Soutendijk, Renee (Actor)
PO Box 69826
West Hollywood, CA 90069-0826, USA

Souter, David H (Judge)
1 1st St NE
Washington, DC 20543-0001, USA

South, Joe (Musician, Songwriter, Writer)
3051 Claremont Rd NE
Atlanta, GA 30329, USA

South, Mike
PO Box 1288
Tucker, GA 30085-1288

Southcott, Susan (Stylist)
12313 Culver Dr
Culver City, CA 90230-5920, USA

Souther, J D (Musician, Songwriter, Writer)
8263 Hollywood Blvd
Los Angeles, CA 90069-1611, USA

Southern, Silas (Eddie) (Athlete, Track Athlete)
2006 Custer Pkwy
Richardson, TX 75080-3403, USA

Southern Belles
11150 W Olympic Blvd Ste 1100
Los Angeles, CA 90064-1845

Southworth, Bill (Athlete, Baseball Player)
320 Dobbin Rd
Saint Louis, MO 63119-4515, USA

Southworth, Carrie (Actor)
c/o Van Johnson *Van Johnson Company*
350 S Beverly Dr Ste 200
Beverly Hills, CA 90212-4819, USA

Souza, Mark (Athlete, Baseball Player)
10001 Woodcreek Oaks Blvd Unit 817
Roseville, CA 95747-5105, USA

Sova, Peter M (Cinematographer)
1492 Roses Brook Rd
South Kortright, NY 13842-2514, USA

Sovereign, Lady (Musician)
c/o Staff Member *Paradigm (Monterey)*
404 W Franklin St
Monterey, CA 93940-2303, USA

Sovern, Michael I (Educator)
435 W 116th St
New York, NY 10027-7237, USA

Sovey, William P (Business Person)
20 E Milwaukee St Ste 212
Janesville, WI 53545-3061, USA

Sovran, Gino (Athlete, Basketball Player)
2669 Cheswick Dr
Troy, MI 48084-1069, USA

Soward, R J (Football Player)
7660 Chipwood Ln
Jacksonville, FL 32256-2338, USA

Sowell, Arnold (Arnie) (Athlete, Track Athlete)
1647 Waterstone Ln # 1
Charlotte, NC 28262-3176, USA

Sowell, Thomas (Economist)
Hoover Institution
Stanford, CA 94305, USA

Sowells, Rich (Football Player)
6711 McCullum Rd
Missouri City, TX 77489-3430, USA

Sowers, Barbara (Baseball Player)
5601 Duncan Rd Lot 199
Punta Gorda, FL 33982-4762, USA

Soyer, David (Musician)
PO Box 307
Brattleboro, VT 05302-0307, USA

Soyinka, Wole (Nobel Prize Laureate)
Creative Writing Dept
Las Vegas, NV 89154, USA

Soyster, Harry E (General)
5403 Heatherford Ct
Fairfax, VA 22030-7273, USA

Spaak, Catherine
Viale Parioli 59
Rome, ITALY 197

Spacek, Jaroslav (Athlete, Hockey Player)
200 W Nationwide Blvd
Columbus, OH 43215-2563, USA

Spacek, Sissy (Actor)
PO Box 22
Cobham, VA 22947-0022, USA

Spacey, Kevin (Actor, Producer)
c/o Joanne Horowitz *Joanne Horowitz Management*
9350 Wilshire Blvd Ste 224
Beverly Hills, CA 90212-3204, USA

Spaddky, Boris V (Misc)
Skatertny Pereulok 4
Moscow, RUSSIA

Spade, David (Actor, Comedian)
c/o Marc Gurvitz *Brillstein Entertainment Partners*
9150 Wilshire Blvd Ste 350
Beverly Hills, CA 90212-3453, USA

Spade, Kate (Designer, Fashion Designer)
48 W 25th St Fl 4
New York, NY 10010-2786, USA

Spader, James (Actor)
254 S Windsor Blvd
Los Angeles, CA 90004-3820, USA

Spafford, Eugene (Educator)
Education Research Center
West Lafayette, IN 47907, USA

Spagnardi, Darren (Athlete, Baseball Player)
2364 W Center Street Ext
Lexington, NC 27295-5943, USA

Spagnola, John S (Football Player)
414 Hillbrook Rd
Bryn Mawr, PA 19010-3634, USA

Spahn, Ryan (Actor)
c/o Ann Kelly *Ann Kelly Management*
245 W 51st St Apt 411
New York, NY 10019-6281, USA

Spahr, Charles E (Business Person)
800 Beach Rd
Vero Beach, FL 32963-3392, USA

Spain, Douglas (Actor)
1505 10th St
Santa Monica, CA 90401-2805, USA

Spain, Gary (Stylist)
c/o Staff Member *Clutts Agency, The*
1400 Turtle Creek Blvd # 171
Dallas, TX 75207-3337, USA

Spalding, Esperanza (Musician)
c/o Daniel Florestano *Montuno Productions*
C/ Rosselló 248, 5º - 2
Barcelona 8008, Spain

Spalding, Leslie (Athlete, Golfer)
1055 O Malley Dr
Billings, MT 59102-2524, USA

Spali, Timothy (Actor)
Julian House 4 Windmill St
London W1P 1HF, UNITED KINGDOM (UK)

Spall, Timothy (Actor)
c/o Laura Berwick *Hofflund/Polone*
9465 Wilshire Blvd Ste 420
Beverly Hills, CA 90212-2603, USA

Spanarkel, Jim (Athlete, Basketball Player)
436 Edgewood Pl
Rutherford, NJ 07070-2662, USA

Spanger, Amy (Actor)
c/o Maureen Taran *New Wave Entertainment (LA)*
2660 W Olive Ave
Burbank, CA 91505-4525, USA

Spangler, Al (Athlete, Baseball Player)
27202 Afton Way
Huffman, TX 77336-3601, USA

Spani, Gary (Football Player)
3920 NE Sequoia St
Lees Summit, MO 64064-1574, USA

Spanic, Gabriela (Actor)
c/o Staff Member *Televisa*
Blvd Adolfo Lopez Mateos 232 Colonia San Angel INN
DF CP 01060, MEXICO

Spanjers, Martin (Actor)
c/o Sommer Smith *Innovative Artists (LA)*
1505 10th St
Santa Monica, CA 90401-2805, USA

Spano, Joe (Actor)
10315 Woodley Ave Ste 110
Granada Hills, CA 91344-6900, USA

Spano, Nick (Actor)
c/o Justin Evans *The Independent Group*
6363 Wilshire Blvd Ste 115
Los Angeles, CA 90048-5734, USA

Spano, Robert (Musician)
c/o Staff Member *International Creative Management (ICM-LA)*
10250 Constellation Blvd Fl 7
Los Angeles, CA 90067-6207, USA

Spano, Vincent (Actor)
c/o Jo Kincaid *Gilbertson Management*
1334 3rd Street Promenade Ste 201
Santa Monica, CA 90401-1320, USA

Spanoulis, Vassilis (Athlete, Basketball Player)
c/o Jeff Schwartz *Excel Sports Management*
9665 Wilshire Blvd Ste 500
Beverly Hills, CA 90212-2312, USA

Spanswick, Bill (Athlete, Baseball Player)
71 Judith St
Springfield, MA 01118-1042, USA

Sparks
106 N Buffalo St Ste 200
Warsaw, IN 46580-2755

Sparks, Dana (Actor)
5670 Wilshire Blvd Ste 820
Los Angeles, CA 90036-5613, USA

Sparks, Daniel (Athlete, Basketball Player)
2396 N Bruceville Rd
Vincennes, IN 47591-9698, USA

Sparks, Hal (Actor, Comedian, Musician, Producer)
c/o Alison Leslie *Marleah Leslie & Associates PR*
1645 Vine St Apt 712
Los Angeles, CA 90028-8812, USA

Sparks, Hayley
5757 Wilshire Blvd # 512
Los Angeles, CA 90036-5810

Sparks, Jeff (Athlete, Baseball Player)
714 W 42nd St
Houston, TX 77018-4429, USA

Sparks, Jordin (Musician)
c/o Brian Manning *Creative Artists Agency (CAA-LA)*
2000 Avenue of the Stars Ste 100
Los Angeles, CA 90067-4705, USA

Sparks, Kylie (Actor)
c/o Myrna Lieberman *Myrna Lieberman Management*
3001 Hollyridge Dr
Hollywood, CA 90068-1951, USA

Sparks, Mike (Referee)
c/o Staff Member *World Wrestling Entertainment (WWE)*
1241 E Main St
Stamford, CT 06902-3520, USA

Sparks, Nicholas (Writer)
c/o Staff Member *United Talent Agency (UTA)*
9560 Wilshire Blvd Fl 5
Beverly Hills, CA 90212-2400, USA

Sparks, Phillippi (Football Player)
3315 W Walter Way
Phoenix, AZ 85027-1084, USA

Sparks, Stephanie (Golfer)
48 Redwood Ln
Wheeling, WV 26003-4854, USA

Sparks, Steve (Athlete, Baseball Player)
4019 Colony Oaks Dr
Sugar Land, TX 77479-2420, USA

Sparks, Steve (Athlete, Baseball Player)
23378 Wilson Dr
Loxley, AL 36551-8559, USA

Sparlis, Alexander (Al) (Football Player)
HC 4 Box 243
Porterville, CA 93257-9706, USA

Sparrow, Guy (Athlete, Basketball Player)
210 Hortense Dr
Kirkland, IL 60146-9751, USA

Sparrow, Rory (Athlete, Basketball Player)
111 Valley Rd
Montclair, NJ 07042-2322, USA

Sparv, Camilla (Actor)
957 Cole Ave
Los Angeles, CA 90038-2610, USA

Sparxxx, Bubba (Musician)
c/o Staff Member *Paradigm (Monterey)*
404 W Franklin St
Monterey, CA 93940-2303, USA

Spassky, Boris
Skatertny Pereulok 5
Moscow, CA RUSSIA

Speake, Bob (Athlete, Baseball Player)
4742 SW Urish Rd
Topeka, KS 66610-9758, USA

Speakman, Jeff (Actor)
11141 Woodview Dr
Rch Cucamonga, CA 91730-6728, USA

Speakman-Pitt, William (War Hero)
Old Admiralty Building
London SW1A 2BL, UNITED KINGDOM (UK)

Speaks, Ruben L (Religious Leader)
PO Box 32843
Charlotte, NC 28232-2843, USA

Spear, Kristin (Stylist)
c/o Staff Member *Zenobia Agency Inc*
PO Box 909
Groveland, CA 95321-0909, USA

Spear, Laurinda H (Architect)
550 Brickell Ave # 200
Miami, FL 33131, USA

Spearman, Alvin (Athlete, Baseball Player)
635 E 49th St Apt 3
Chicago, IL 60615-1556, USA

Spearritt, Hannah (Actor, Musician)
c/o Jeb Brandon *Kritzer Levine Wilkins Entertainment*
11872 La Grange Ave Fl 1
Los Angeles, CA 90025-5283, USA

Spears, Aries (Actor)
c/o Leigh Brillstein *International Creative Management (ICM-LA)*
10250 Constellation Blvd Fl 7
Los Angeles, CA 90067-6207, USA

Spears, Billie Jo (Musician)
PO Box 23470
Nashville, TN 37202-3470, USA

Spears, Britney (Actor, Musician, Producer)
23505 Prado De Los Suena
Calabasas, CA 91302-3648, USA

Spears, Eddie (Actor)
c/o Jennie Saks *NASS Talent Management*
5865 Trail Creek Rd
Bozeman, MT 59715-8044, USA

Spears, Ernest (Athlete, Football Player)
33 Hudson St Apt 1706
Jersey City, NJ 07302-6583, USA

Spears, Jamie Lynn (Actor)
c/o Nick Styne *Creative Artists Agency (CAA-LA)*
2000 Avenue of the Stars Ste 100
Los Angeles, CA 90067-4705, USA

Spears, Lynne (Educator, Writer)
c/o Staff Member *Thomas Nelson Inc*
PO Box 141000
Nashville, TN 37214-1000, USA

Spears, Marcus (Athlete, Football Player)
18634 Cypress Lake Village Dr
Cypress, TX 77429-5556, USA

Spears, Peter (Actor)
c/o Jaclyn Travers *Creative Artists Agency (CAA-LA)*
2000 Avenue of the Stars Ste 100
Los Angeles, CA 90067-4705, USA

Spears, Randy (Adult Film Star)
c/o Staff Member *Wicked Pictures*
9040 Eton Ave
Canoga Park, CA 91304-1616, USA

Spears, William D (Football Player)
63 Waterbridge Pl
Ponte Vedra Beach, FL 32082-2323, USA

Speck, Cliff (Athlete, Baseball Player)
823 S Nueva Vista Dr
Palm Springs, CA 92264-3425, USA

Specter, Arlen (Senator)
310 Spruce St
Scranton, PA 18503-1413, USA

Specter, Rachel (Actor)
c/o Adam Griffin *Kritzer Levine Wilkins Entertainment*
11872 La Grange Ave Fl 1
Los Angeles, CA 90025-5283, USA

Spector, Phil (Business Person, Songwriter, Writer)
686 S Arroyo Pkwy # 175
Pasadena, CA 91105-3233, USA

Spector, Ronnie (Musician)
8490 W Sunset Blvd # 403
West Hollywood, CA 90069-1912, USA

Speech (Artist, Musician)
1325 Avenue of the Americas
New York, NY 10019-6026, USA

Speed, Horace (Athlete, Baseball Player)
6821 State Boulevard Ext
Meridian, MS 39305-8420, USA

Speed, Lake (Race Car Driver)
4027 Old Salisbury Rd
Kannapolis, NC 28083, USA

Speed, Lizz (Producer)
c/o Staff Member *Jackoway Tyerman Wertheimer Austen Mandelbaum Morris & Klein*
1925 Century Park E Fl 22
Los Angeles, CA 90067-2701, USA

Speedman, Scott (Actor)
c/o Frank Frattaroli *Dontanville/Frattaroli (D/F)*
270 Lafayette St Ste 402
New York, NY 10012-3327, USA

Speedwagon, REO (Music Group, Musician)
c/o Keith Naisbitt *Agency Group Ltd, The (LA)*
1880 Century Park E Ste 711
Los Angeles, CA 90067-1618, USA

Speer, Del (Football Player)
17620 NW 40th Ave
Miami Gardens, FL 33055-3864, USA

Speer, Hugo (Actor)
c/o Fiona McLoughlin *Independent Talent Group (ITG-UK)*
Oxford House 76 Oxford St
London W1D 1BS, UK

Speers, Ted (Athlete, Hockey Player)
61515 Brookway Dr
South Lyon, MI 48178-7056, USA

Spehr, Tim (Athlete, Baseball Player)
8524 Briargrove Dr
Woodway, TX 76712-2305, USA

Speier, Chris (Athlete, Baseball Player)
3102 N Manor Dr W
Phoenix, AZ 85014-5525, USA

Speier, Justin (Athlete, Baseball Player)
9405 S 51st St
Phoenix, AZ 85044-5686, USA

Speight, Derrick (Producer)
c/o Staff Member *Screen Door Entertainment*
5709 Fairview Pl
Agoura Hills, CA 91301-2229, USA

Speight, Lester (Rasta) (Actor)
c/o Staff Member *WmE2 (Endeavor-LA)*
9601 Wilshire Blvd Fl 3
Beverly Hills, CA 90210-5219, USA

Speigner, Levale (Athlete, Baseball Player)
1041 Bond St
Thomasville, GA 31757-0221, USA

Speir, Chris
6114 E Montecito Ave
Scottsdale, AZ 85251-1936

Speiser, Jerry (Musician)
PO Box 124
Round Corner, NSW, AUSTRALIA

Spektor, Regina (Actor, Musician)
c/o Ron Shapiro *Ron Shapiro Management & Consulting*
135 W 26th St Ste 4A
New York, NY 10001-6809, USA

Spelke, Elizabeth S (Doctor)
Psychology Dept
Cambridge, MA 2138, USA

Spelling, Candy (Actor)
c/o Kevin Sasaki *Kevin Sasaki Public Relations & Media Counsel*
8491 W Sunset Blvd Ste 224
Los Angeles, CA 90069-1911, USA

Spelling, Randy (Actor)
c/o Staff Member *Innovative Artists (LA)*
1505 10th St
Santa Monica, CA 90401-2805, USA

Spelling, Tori (Actor)
c/o Meghan Prophet *PMK/BNC Public Relations (PMK-LA)*
8687 Melrose Ave Ste 8
West Hollywood, CA 90069-5746, USA

Spellman, Alonzo R (Football Player)
1300 Marigold Way
Pflugerville, TX 78660-4137, USA

Spellman, John D (Ex-Governor)
Columbia Center 701 5th Ave.
Seattle, WA 98104, USA

Spelvin, Georgina
3121 Ledgewood Dr
Hollywood, CA 90068-1913

Spence, A Michael (Nobel Prize Laureate)
768 Mayfield Ave
Stanford, CA 94305-1044, USA

Spence, Blake (Athlete, Football Player)
3655 W Tropicana Ave
Las Vegas, NV 89103-5638, USA

Spence, Bob (Athlete, Baseball Player)
3081 Bonita Woods Dr
Bonita, CA 91902-2020, USA

Spence, Bruce (Actor)
c/o Imogen Johnson *Johnson and Laird Management*
P.O. Box 78340
Grey Lynn Auckland 1245, New Zealand

Spence, Dave (Misc)
RR 2 Box 71C
Englishtown, NJ 7726, USA

Spence, Gerry (Lawyer)
15 S Jackson St
Jackson, WY 83001, USA

Spence, Jonathan D (Historian, Writer)
691 Forest Rd
West Haven, CT 06516-7932, USA

Spence, Sebastian (Actor)
1005 Cambie St
Vancouver, BC V6B 5L7, CANADA

Spence, Stan (Athlete, Baseball Player)
3100 NE 188th St
Ridgefield, WA 98642-9515, USA

Spencer, Abigail (Actor)
c/o Jon Rubinstein *Authentic Talent and Literary Management*
45 Main St Ste 1004
Brooklyn, NY 11201-8200, USA

Spencer, Andre (Athlete, Basketball Player)
1315 W Gage Ave
Los Angeles, CA 90044-2733, USA

Spencer, Anthony (Athlete, Football Player)
c/o Eugene Parker *Maximum Sports Management*
6435 W Jefferson Blvd # 197
Fort Wayne, IN 46804-6203, USA

Spencer, Bud (Actor)
Via Archmede 24
Rome 187, ITALY

Spencer, Chaske (Actor)
c/o Staff Member *Josselyne Herman & Associates*
345 E 56th St Apt 3B
New York, NY 10022-3745, USA

Spencer, Chris (Actor)
c/o Julia Buchwald *Don Buchwald & Associates Inc (LA)*
6500 Wilshire Blvd Ste 2200
Los Angeles, CA 90048-4942, USA

Spencer, Danielle (Actor)
c/o Martin Bedford *Bedford & Pearce Management Martin Bedford*
2/263-269 Alfred St N
North Sydney NSW 2060, Australia

Spencer, Darryl (Athlete, Football Player)
166 Lura Ln
Merritt Island, FL 32953-4746, USA

Spencer, Daryl (Athlete, Baseball Player)
2740 S Larkin Dr
Wichita, KS 67216-1258, USA

Spencer, Earl Charles (Government Official)
Althorp
Northampton NN7 4HQ, UNITED KINGDOM (UK)

Spencer, Elizabeth (Writer)
402 Longleaf Dr
Chapel Hill, NC 27517-3042, USA

Spencer, Elmore (Athlete, Basketball Player)
2770 Foxlair Trl
Atlanta, GA 30349-4436, USA

Spencer, Felton (Athlete, Basketball Player)
4102 Nicholas Roy Ct
Prospect, KY 40059-8209, USA

Spencer, Frank Cole (Doctor, Educator)
560 1st Ave
New York, NY 10016-6402, USA

Spencer, George (Athlete, Baseball Player)
8160 Hickory Ave
Galena, OH 43021-8508, USA

Spencer, J Robert (Actor)
c/o Nyle Brenner *Brenner Management*
9171 Wilshire Blvd Ste 441
Beverly Hills, CA 90210-5516, USA

Spencer, Jesse (Actor)
c/o Jason Weinberg *Untitled Entertainment (LA)*
350 S Beverly Dr Ste 200
Beverly Hills, CA 90212-4819, USA

Spencer, Jimmy (Football Player)
5331 Talavero Pl
Parker, CO 80134-2799, USA

Spencer, John (Athlete, Misc)
17 Knowles St Radcliffe
Lancs M26 0DN, UNITED KINGDOM (UK)

Spencer, Lara (Television Host)
c/o Jonathan Rosen *WmE2 (WMA-NY)*
1325 Avenue of the Americas
New York, NY 10019-6026, USA

Spencer, Marc (Radio Personality)
c/o Staff Member *WPKX*
1331 Main St Ste 4
Springfield, MA 01103-1621, USA

Spencer, Maurice (Football Player)
61 W 62nd St
New York, NY 10023-7015, USA

Spencer, Melvin J (Attorney, Attorney General, General, Religious Leader)
5910 N Shawnee Ave
Oklahoma City, OK 73112-1627, USA

Spencer, Octavia (Actor)
c/o Melissa Kates *Viewpoint Inc*
8820 Wilshire Blvd Ste 220
Beverly Hills, CA 90211-2622, USA

Spencer, Roderick
602 Bay St
Santa Monica, CA 90405-1215

Spencer, Sean (Athlete, Baseball Player)
3584 E Calistoga Ct
Port Orchard, WA 98366-4084, USA

Spencer, Shane (Athlete, Baseball Player)
2858 Manzanita View Rd
Alpine, CA 91901-3988, USA

Spencer, Susan (Correspondent)
2020 M St NW
Washington, DC 20036-3304, USA

Spencer, Timothy (Tim) (Football Player)
1435 Sherborne Ln
Powell, OH 43065-7604, USA

Spencer, Tom (Athlete, Baseball Player)
2021 E Conner Stra
Tucson, AZ 85719-3206, USA

Spencer, Tracie (Musician)
6340 Breckenridge Run
Rex, GA 30273-1841, USA

Spencer, Willie (Football Player)
1109 Johnson St SE
Massillon, OH 44646-8266, USA

Spencer-Churchill, Victor
6 Cumberland Geo St
London, ENGLAND W1

Spencer-Devlin, Muffin (Golfer)
1278 Glenneyre St Apt 155
Laguna Beach, CA 92651-3103, USA

Spender, Percy C (Judge)
Headingley House 11 Wellington St
Woolhara
Sydney, NSW 2025, AUSTRAILIA

Spenn, Fred (Athlete, Baseball Player)
105 Heather Ln
Parrish, FL 34219-8912, USA

Sperber Carter, Paula (Bowler)
10331 SW 102nd Ave
Miami, FL 33176-3507, USA

Spergel, David (Misc)
Astrophysicist
Princeton, NJ 08544-0001, USA

Sperling, Gene (Government Official, Politician)
1600 Pennsylvania Ave NW
Washington, DC 20506, USA

Spero, Nancy
530 Laguardia Pl
New York, NY 10012-1427, USA

Sperring, Rob (Athlete, Baseball Player)
13302 Chriswood Dr
Cypress, TX 77429-2066, USA

Speth, George (Football Player)
10705 Footprint Ln
Port Richey, FL 34668-2713, USA

Spevack, Jason (Actor)
c/o Dana Wdrick Fletcher *Coast to Coast Talent Group*
3350 Barham Blvd
Los Angeles, CA 90068-1404, USA

Speyrer, Cotton (Football Player)
PO Box 13537
Austin, TX 78711-3537, USA

Spheeris, Penelope (Director)
PO Box 1128
Studio City, CA 91614-0128, USA

Spice 1 (Artist, Musician)
18653 Ventura Blvd # 340
Tarzana, CA 91356-4103, USA

Spice Girls (Music Group)
35 Parkgate Road Ransome Dock # 32
London, ENGLAND SW11 4NP

Spicer, Bob (Athlete, Baseball Player)
423 McPhee Dr
Fayetteville, NC 28305-5129, USA

Spicer III, William E (Physicist)
620 Sand Hill Rd Apt 305E
Palo Alto, CA 94304-2610, USA

SPider Loc (Musician)
c/o Staff Member *Interscope Records (NY)*
1755 Broadway
New York, NY 10019-3743, USA

Spidia, Vladimir (Prime Minister)
Hradecek
Prague 1 119 08, CZECH REPUBLIC

Spidlik, Tomas Cardinal (Religious Leader)
Borgo S Spirito 4 CP 6139
Rome-Prati 195, ITALY

Spiegel, Henry W (Economist)
6848 Nashville Rd
Lanham Seabrook, MD 20706-3742, USA

Spiegelman, Art (Writer)
c/o Staff Member *Steven Barclay Agency*
12 Western Ave
Petaluma, CA 94952-2907, USA

Spieier, Patrick (Baseball Player)
6635 S 108th Ave
Omaha, NE 68137-4733, USA

Spielberg, David (Actor)
10537 Cushdon Ave
Los Angeles, CA 90064-3315, USA

Spielberg, Steven (Director, Producer)
c/o Richard Lovett *Creative Artists Agency (CAA-LA)*
2000 Avenue of the Stars Ste 100
Los Angeles, CA 90067-4705, USA

Spieler, Patrick (Athlete, Baseball Player)
12818 Chandler St
Omaha, NE 68138-6018, USA

Spielman, C Christopher (Chris) (Football Player, Sportscaster)
2094 Edgemont Rd
Columbus, OH 43212-1970, USA

Spier, Peter E (Artist)
PO Box 566
Shoreham, NY 11786-0566, USA

Spier, Wolfgang
Kaiserdamm 98
Berlin, GERMANY 14057

Spiers, Bill (Athlete, Baseball Player)
9233 Old State Rd
Cameron, SC 29030-8129, USA

Spiers, Judi
1-3 Charlotte St
London, ENGLAND W1P 1HD

Spiers, Ronald I (Diplomat)
1176 Middletown Rd
South Londonderry, VT 05155-9143, USA

Spies, Joshua (Artist)
PO Box 90
Watertown, SD 57201-0090, USA

Spiezio, Ed (Athlete, Baseball Player)
2550 Gore Rd
Morris, IL 60450-8686, USA

Spiezio, Scott (Athlete, Baseball Player)
2550 Gore Rd
Morris, IL 60450-8686, USA

Spikes, Cameron (Football Player)
3001 Fraternity Row # 132
College Station, TX 77845-6504, USA

Spikes, Charlie (Athlete, Baseball Player)
531 N Border Dr
Bogalusa, LA 70427-3307, USA

Spikes, Jack E (Football Player)
9537 Highland View Dr
Dallas, TX 75238-1025, USA

Spikes, Takeo (Athlete, Football Player)
5005 Heatherwood Ct
Roswell, GA 30075-2285, USA

Spilborghs, Ryan (Athlete, Baseball Player)
2220 Elise Way
Santa Barbara, CA 93109-1814, USA

Spilde, Jenna (Model, Reality TV Star)
c/o Staff Member *The Sports Illustrated Fresh Faces Competition*
3000 W Alameda Ave # 5366
Burbank, CA 91523-0001, USA

Spilker, Angela
425 N Oakhurst Dr
Beverly Hills, CA 90210-3982

Spiller, Michael A (Cinematographer)
2418 Roscomare Rd
Los Angeles, CA 90077, USA

Spillner, Dan (Athlete, Baseball Player)
18505 SE Newport Way Unit C113
Issaquah, WA 98027-9032, USA

Spilman, Harry (Athlete, Baseball Player)
4423 Saint Phillips Rd S
Mount Vernon, IN 47620-9629, USA

Spin Doctors, The (Music Group)
c/o Staff Member *Paradigm (Monterey)*
404 W Franklin St
Monterey, CA 93940-2303, USA

Spindt, Capp (Inventor)
333 Ravenswood Ave
Menlo Park, CA 94025-3453, USA

Spinella, Stephen (Actor)
c/o Staff Member *Innovative Artists (LA)*
1505 10th St
Santa Monica, CA 90401-2805, USA

Spiner, Brent (Actor)
c/o Rebecca (Becca) Kovacik *Hofflund/Polone*
9465 Wilshire Blvd Ste 420
Beverly Hills, CA 90212-2603, USA

Spinetta, Jean-Cyril (Business Person)
Group Air France 45 Rue de Paris
Roissy CDG Cedex 95747, FRANCE

Spinetti, Victor (Actor)
15 Devonshire Place Brighton
Sussex, UNITED KINGDOM (UK)

Spinks, Michael (Boxer)
250 W 57th St Ste 311
New York, NY 10107-0303, USA

Spinks, Scipio (Athlete, Baseball Player)
11422 Rock Bridge Ln
Sugar Land, TX 77498-0923, USA

Spinners, The
65 W 55th St Apt 6C
New York, NY 10019-4917

Spinney, Caroll (Actor)
940 Brickyard Rd
Woodstock, CT 06281-1302, USA

Spinotti, Dante (Cinematographer)
PO Box 1156
Studio City, CA 91614-0156, USA

Spires, Greg (Football Player)
175 Centre St # 520
Quincy, MA 02169-8600, USA

Spiro, Jordana (Actor)
c/o Larry Taube *Principal Entertainment (LA)*
1964 Westwood Blvd Ste 400
Los Angeles, CA 90025-4695, USA

Spiro, Lev L (Director)
c/o Staff Member *WmE2 (Endeavor-LA)*
9601 Wilshire Blvd Fl 3
Beverly Hills, CA 90210-5219, USA

Spirtas, Kevin (Actor)
c/o Robert Baird *Baird Artists Management*
P.O. Box 5016 Station A
Toronto, ON M5W 1N4, Canada

Spittka, Marko (Athlete)
Zielona-Gora-Str 9
Frankfurt/Ober 15230, GERMANY

Spitz, Mark A (Athlete, Swimmer)
c/o Staff Member *Premier Management Group (PMG Sports)*
115 Crescent Commons Dr Ste 250
Cary, NC 27518-8134, USA

Spitzer, Eliot (Ex-Governor, Talk Show Host)
985 5th Ave
New York, NY 10075-0142, USA

Spitzer, Robert (Doctor, Psychic)
Psychiatry School
New York, NY 10027, USA

Spivakov, Vladmir T (Musician)
Vspolny Per 17 #14
Moscow, RUSSIA

Spivey, Junior (Athlete, Baseball Player)
4140 S Ambrosia Dr
Chandler, AZ 85248-4804, USA

Spivey, Sebron (Football Player)
435 Capitol View Dr
Columbus, OH 43203-1037, USA

Splatt, Rachel (Race Car Driver)
12631 N Tatum Blvd
Phoenix, AZ 85032-7710, USA

Split Ends
136 New Kings Rd
London, ENGLAND SW6

Splittorff Jr, Paul W (Athlete, Baseball Player)
4204 SW Hickory Ln
Blue Springs, MO 64015-4517, USA

Spoelstra, Art (Athlete, Basketball Player)
1606 N Meadow Rd
Evansville, IN 47715-2002, USA

Spohr, Arnold T (Director)
380 Graham Ave
Winnipeg, MB R3C 4K2, CANADA

Spoiler, The
3615 W Waters Ave # 110
Tampa, FL 33614-2783

Spoljario, Paul (Baseball Player)
13261 N 73rd Ave
Peoria, AZ 85381-6054, USA

Sponenburgh, Mark (Artist)
5562 NW Pacific Coast Hwy
Seal Rock, OR 97376-9619, USA

Spong, Annie (Stylist)
c/o Staff Member *Cloutier Agency*
2632 La Cienega Ave
Los Angeles, CA 90034-2641, USA

Spong, John S (Religious Leader)
24 Puddingstone Rd
Morris Plains, NJ 07950-1114, USA

Spooner, John (Financier, Writer)
222 Berkeley St # 700
Boston, MA 02116-3748, USA

Spooneybarger, Tim (Athlete, Baseball Player)
7815 Eight Mile Creek Rd
Pensacola, FL 32526-8783, USA

Spoonhour, Charles (Charlie) (Coach)
Athletic Dept
Las Vegas, NV 89154, USA

Spork, Shirley (Golfer)
PO Box 637
Palm Desert, CA 92261-0637, USA

Sporkin, Stanley (Government Official, Judge)
Courthouse 3rd & Constitution NW
Washington, DC 20001, USA

Sporleder, Gregory (Actor)
c/o Julia Buchwald *Don Buchwald & Associates Inc (LA)*
6500 Wilshire Blvd Ste 2200
Los Angeles, CA 90048-4942, USA

Sposa, Mike (Golfer)
40 Tahoe Ln
Dillard, GA 30537-2618, USA

Spottiswoode, Roger (Director)
c/o Staff Member *International Creative Management (ICM-LA)*
10250 Constellation Blvd Fl 7
Los Angeles, CA 90067-6207, USA

Spottsville, Ray (Baseball Player)
PO Box 591
Colfax, LA 71417-0591, USA

Spound, Michael (Actor)
3500 W Olive Ave Ste 1470
Burbank, CA 91505-5514, USA

Spradlin, Danny (Football Player)
1011 Laurie St
Maryville, TN 37803-6731, USA

Spradlin, G D (Actor)
PO Box 1294
San Luis Obispo, CA 93406-1294, USA

Spradlin, Jerry (Athlete, Baseball Player)
2824 E Diana Ave
Anaheim, CA 92806-4412, USA

Spradling, Charlie (Actor)
c/o Staff Member *Don Buchwald & Associates Inc (NY)*
10 E 44th St Frnt 1
New York, NY 10017-3654

Spragan, Donnie (Football Player)
312 Riviera Dr
Union City, CA 94587-3722, USA

Sprague, Ed (Athlete, Baseball Player)
4677 Pine Valley Cir
Stockton, CA 95219-1881, USA

Sprague, Ed (Athlete, Baseball Player)
19015 N Davis Rd
Lodi, CA 95242-9203, USA

Spratlan, Lewis (Composer)
Music Dept
Amherst, MA 1002, USA

Sprayberry, James M (War Hero)
426 Holiday Dr
Titus, AL 36080-2520, USA

Spreitler, Taylor (Actor)
c/o Cameron Curtis *Curtis Talent Management*
9607 Arby Dr
Beverly Hills, CA 90210-1202, USA

Sprewell, Latrell (Athlete, Basketball Player)
850 W Dean Rd
Milwaukee, WI 53217-2527, USA

Spriggs, George (Athlete, Baseball Player)
77A W Bay Front Rd
Lothian, MD 20711-9711, USA

Spriggs, Larry (Athlete, Basketball Player)
23900 Cancuna Ct
Huson, MT 59846-9756, USA

Spring, Jack (Athlete, Baseball Player)
PO Box 118
Colbert, WA 99005-0118, USA

Spring, Sherwood C (Astronaut)
2116 McDonough Ln
San Diego, CA 92106-6087, USA

Springer, Dennis (Athlete, Baseball Player)
1060 W Windsor Ct
Hanford, CA 93230-6572, USA

Springer, Jerry (Talk Show Host)
The Rich Forum Theater, Stamford Center For The Perf Arts 61 Atlantic St
Stamford, CT 6901, USA

Springer, Michael (Golfer)
1482 E Forest Oaks Dr
Fresno, CA 93730-3443, USA

Springer, Mike (Golfer)
1482 E Forest Oaks Dr
Fresno, CA 93730-3443, USA

Springer, Robert C (Astronaut)
202 Village Cir
Sheffield, AL 35660-5632, USA

Springer, Russ (Athlete, Baseball Player)
PO Box 185
Pollock, LA 71467-0185, USA

Springer, Steve (Athlete, Baseball Player)
6962 Carla Cir
Huntington Beach, CA 92647-4315, USA

Springfield, Marty (Athlete, Baseball Player)
5164 Flicker Field Cir
Sarasota, FL 34231-3242, USA

Springfield, Rick (Actor, Musician)
c/o Staff Member *Doyle-Kos Entertainment*
1 Penn Plz Ste 2107
New York, NY 10119-2107, USA

Springgs, Marcus (Football Player)
830 Regal St
Houston, TX 77034-1231, USA

Springs, Alice (Photographer)
7 Ave Saint-Ramon #T1008
Monte Carlo, MONACO

Springs, Kirk (Football Player)
4925 Paddock Rd
Cincinnati, OH 45237-5548, USA

Springs, Ron (Football Player)
128 Ron Springs Dr
Williamsburg, VA 23185-6014, USA

Springs, Shawn (Football Player)
21300 Redskin Park Dr
Ashburn, VA 20147-6100, USA

Springstead, Marty (Baseball Player)
5164 Flicker Field Cir
Sarasota, FL 34231-3242, USA

Springsteen, Bruce (Musician, Songwriter)
c/o Jon Landau *Jon Landau Management*
80 Mason St
Greenwich, CT 06830-5515, USA

Springsteen, Pamela (Actor, Photographer)
c/o Caryn Weiss *Weiss Artists*
6311 Romaine St # 7234
Los Angeles, CA 90038-2617, USA

Sprinkel, Beryl W (Government Official)
16625 Waters Edge Ct # 101
Fort Myers, FL 33908-4304, USA

Sprinkel, Patrick (Stylist)
c/o Staff Member *Zenobia Agency Inc*
PO Box 909
Groveland, CA 95321-0909, USA

Sprinkle, Edward A (Ed) (Football Player)
3 Saint Moritz Dr
Palos Park, IL 60464-3057, USA

Sprotte, Jimmy (Football Player)
2163 E Palmcroft Dr
Tempe, AZ 85282-3062, USA

Sprouse, Cole (Actor)
c/o Megan Moss Pachon *ID Public Relations (ID-LA)*
7080 Hollywood Blvd Fl 8
Los Angeles, CA 90028-6906, USA

Sprouse, Dylan (Actor)
c/o Megan Moss Pachon *ID Public Relations (ID-LA)*
7080 Hollywood Blvd Fl 8
Los Angeles, CA 90028-6906, USA

Sprouse, James M (Judge)
PO Box 401
Lewisburg, WV 24901-0401, USA

Sprout, Bob (Athlete, Baseball Player)
32515 Quiet Harbor Ave Apt 101
Leesburg, FL 34788-7695, USA

Sprowl, Bobby (Athlete, Baseball Player)
4711 Leeward Ave
Northport, AL 35473-1934, USA

Spruce, Andy (Athlete, Hockey Player)
12 Rathgar St
London, ON N5Z 1Y4, Canada

Spruill, Jim (Football Player)
710 9th St
Levelland, TX 79336-4534, USA

Spurgeon, Jay (Athlete, Baseball Player)
212 Hartsdale Rd
Rochester, NY 14622-2007, USA

Spurling, Chris (Athlete, Baseball Player)
6031 Bowen Daniel Dr Unit 101
Tampa, FL 33616-1375, USA

Spurlock, Morgan (Actor)
c/o Richard Arlook *The Arlook Group*
205 S Beverly Dr Ste 209
Beverly Hills, CA 90212-3899, USA

Spurrier, Paul
Beccles Rd. 47
Lowestoft/Norfolk, ENGLAND

Spurrier, Stephen O (Steve) (Athlete, Coach, Football Coach, Football Player)
126 Beaver Ridge Dr
Elgin, SC 29045-8210, USA

Spurrior, Stephen O (Steve) (Coach, Football Player)
17050 Silver Charm Pl
Leesburg, VA 20176-7152, USA

Spuzich, Sandra (Golfer)
100 International Golf Dr
Daytona Beach, FL 32124-1082, USA

Spyro Gyro
200 W Superior St Ste 202
Chicago, IL 60654-3554, USA

Squierek, Jack (Football Player)
4051 Vezber Dr
Seven Hills, OH 44131-6233, USA

Squirek, Jack (Football Player)
4051 Vezber Dr
Seven Hills, OH 44131-6233, USA

Squires, Mike (Athlete, Baseball Player)
9548 Autumnwood Cir
Kalamazoo, MI 49009-9385, USA

Squirrel Nut Zippers
2756 N Green Valley Pkwy # 449
Henderson, NV 89014-2120

Squyres, Steven W (Scientist)
Planetary Science Dept
Ithaca, NY 14853, USA

SR-71 (Music Group)
c/o Staff Member *Jeff Hanson Management & Promotions*
2813 S Hiawassee Rd Ste 307
Orlando, FL 32835-6690, USA

Sranowski, Wally
Mill Rd.
Toronto, CANADA Ont M9C 1Y

Srb, Adrian M (Misc)
411 Cayuga Heights Rd
Ithaca, NY 14850-1401, USA

Sri Chinmoy (Religious Leader)
85-45 Sri Chinmoy St
Jamaica, NY 11432, USA

Sridevi (Actor, Bollywood)
Green Acres 7 Bungalows Lokhandwala Complex Andheri(W)
Mumbai, 400058 MS, INDIA

Sridevi (Actor, Bollywood)
1 Bishop Wallers Avenue C I T Colony S
Chennai, TN 600004, INDIA

Sripriya (Actor, Bollywood)
10 Muthu Pandian Avenue Santhome
Chennai, TN 600004, INDIA

Srividhya (Actor, Bollywood)
22 N Street Sriram Nagar
Chennai, TN 600018, INDIA

St, Clair Carl
1231 E Dyer Rd
Santa Ana, CA 92705-5606, USA

St. Clair, Jessica (Actor)
c/o Christie Smith *Mosaic Media Group*
9200 W Sunset Blvd Ste 10
Los Angeles, CA 90069-3608, USA

St Clair, Mike (Football Player)
1606 Birchwood Ave
Cincinnati, OH 45224-2002, USA

St Clair, Robert B (Bob) (Athlete, Football Player)
3312 Parker Hill Rd
Saratoga, CA 95070, USA

St Claire, Randy (Athlete, Baseball Player)
7117 State Route 8
Brant Lake, NY 12815-2234, USA

St Florian, Friedrich G (Architect)
Architecture Dept
Providence, RI 2903, USA

St George, William R (Admiral)
862 San Antonio Pl
San Diego, CA 92106-3057, USA

St James, James (Jimmy) (Actor, Radio Personality)
7510 W Sunset Blvd # 333
West Hollywood, CA 90046-3408, USA

St. James, Rebecca (Musician)
c/o Staff Member *Smallbone Management*
PO Box 1524
Franklin, TN 37065-1524, USA

St Jean, Garry (Basketball Player, Coach)
1001 Broadway
Oakland, CA 94607-4019, USA

St Jean, Len (Football Player)
32 Ledgebrook Ave
Stoughton, MA 02072-1054, USA

St John, Andrew (Actor)
c/o Loch Powell *Leverage Management*
3030 Pennsylvania Ave
Santa Monica, CA 90404-4112, USA

St John, Gina (Actor, Television Host)
10657 Riverside Dr
Toluca Lake, CA 91602-2341, USA

St John, Jill (Actor)
c/o Staff Member *Borinstein Oreck Bogart Agency*
8271 Melrose Ave Ste 110
Los Angeles, CA 90046-6800, USA

St John, Kristoff (Actor)
c/o Steve Rohr *Lexicon Public Relations*
1901 Avenue of the Stars Fl 2
Los Angeles, CA 90067-6001, USA

St John, Lara (Musician)
165 W 57th St
New York, NY 10019-2201, USA

St John, Mia (Boxer)
c/o Staff Member *Amsel, Eisenstadt & Frazier Talent Agency (AEF)*
5055 Wilshire Blvd Ste 860
Los Angeles, CA 90036-6108, USA

St John of Fawsley, Norman A F
(Government Official)
Old Rectory Preston Capes Daventry
Northants NN11 6TE, UNITED KINGDOM (UK)

St Louis, Martin (Athlete, Hockey Player)
401 Channelside Dr
Tampa, FL 33602-5400, USA

St Patrick, Mathew (Actor)
c/o Todd Eisner *Agency for the Performing Arts (APA-LA)*
405 S Beverly Dr Ste 500
Beverly Hills, CA 90212-4425, USA

St Patrick, Matthew (Actor)
c/o Staff Member *Untitled Entertainment (LA)*
350 S Beverly Dr Ste 200
Beverly Hills, CA 90212-4819, USA

St. Pierre, Georges (Athlete)
c/o Staff Member *CAA Sports (LA)*
2000 Avenue of the Stars
Los Angeles, CA 90067-4700, USA

Staab, Rebecca (Actor)
6500 Wilshire Blvd Ste 2200
Los Angeles, CA 90048-4942, USA

Staats, Dewayne (Baseball Player, Sportscaster)
1170 Gulf Blvd Apt 1601
Clearwater Beach, FL 33767-2785, USA

Staats, Elmer B (Government Official)
712 Jackson Pl NW
Washington, DC 20006-4901, USA

Stabile, Nick
c/o Staff Member *Diverse Talent Group*
9911 W Pico Blvd Ste 340W
Los Angeles, CA 90035-2712, USA

Stablein, George (Athlete, Baseball Player)
2903 Penman
Tustin, CA 92782-3314, USA

Stabler, Ken
260 N Joachim St
Mobile, AL 36603-6472

Stabler, Ken M (Kenny) (Football Player)
260 N Joachim St
Mobile, AL 36603-6472, USA

Stables, Kelly (Actor)
c/o Kurt Patino *Rothman / Patino / Andres Entertainment*
4370 Tujunga Ave Ste 120
Studio City, CA 91604-2763, USA

Stacco, Ed (Football Player)
1909 Hudson Ct
Oldsmar, FL 34677-2505, USA

Stacey, Caitlin (Actor)
21 Esmond Rd
London W4 1JG, UNITED KINGDOM

Stacey, Siran (Football Player)
PO Box 131
Hartford, AL 36344-0131, USA

Stacey Q (Actor, Music Group, Musician)
641 S Palm St Ste D
La Habra, CA 90631-5758, USA

Stack, Brian (Writer)
c/o Staff Member *3 Arts Entertainment Inc*
9460 Wilshire Blvd Fl 7
Beverly Hills, CA 90212-2713, USA

Stack, Timothy
10635 Santa Monica Blvd Ste 130
Los Angeles, CA 90025-8306

Stackhouse, Charles (Football Player)
240 Shady Grove St
Marion, AR 72364-9412, USA

Stackhouse, Jerry (Athlete, Basketball Player)
19 Abbey Woods Ln
Dallas, TX 75248-7900, USA

Stackpole, H C (Hank) (General)
2058 Maluhia Rd
Honolulu, HI 96815-1949, USA

Stacom, Kevin (Athlete, Basketball Player)
14 Florida Ave
Jamestown, RI 02835-1548, USA

Stacy, Billy (Football Player)
400 Colonial Cir
Starkville, MS 39759-4214, USA

Stacy, Hollis (Golfer)
9400 W 10th Ave
Lakewood, CO 80215-4700, USA

Stacy, James (Actor)
478 Severn Ave
Tampa, FL 33606-3842, USA

Stadlen, Lewis J. (Actor)
c/o Staff Member *Access Talent Voice Overs*
171 Madison Ave Ste 900
New York, NY 10016-5110

Stadler, Craig (Golfer)
113 Elk Xing
Evergreen, CO 80439-4114, USA

Stadler, Sergei V (Musician)
Kaiserstr 43
Munich 80801, GERMANY

Stadtman, Earl R (Misc)
16907 Redland Rd
Derwood, MD 20855-1954, USA

Stadtman, Thressa C (Misc)
16907 Redland Rd
Derwood, MD 20855-1954, USA

Staehle, Marv (Athlete, Baseball Player)
19421 Cromwell Ct Apt 208
Fort Myers, FL 33912-0386, USA

Staff, Kathy
17 Maple Mews
London, ENGLAND NW6

Staffieri, Joe (Football Player)
6825 Polo Fields Pkwy
Cumming, GA 30040-5731, USA

Stafford, Harrison (Football Player)
RR 1 Box 216
Edna, TX 77957-9801, USA

Stafford, James Francis Cardinal
(Religious Leader)
Piazza S Calisto 16
Rome 153, ITALY

Stafford, Jerry (Baseball Player)
2316 Catalina Cir Apt 276
Oceanside, CA 92056-5395, USA

Stafford, Jim (Music Group, Musician, Songwriter, Writer)
PO Box 6366
Branson, MO 65615-6366, USA

Stafford, Jimmy (Musician)
80 Mason St
Greenwich, CT 06830-5515, USA

Stafford, John R (Business Person)
11 Arden Ln
Essex Fells, NJ 07021-1204, USA

Stafford, Matthew (Athlete, Football Player)
c/o Tom Condon *CAA - St. Louis*
222 S Central Ave Ste 1008
Saint Louis, MO 63105-3509, USA

Stafford, Michelle (Actor)
c/o Marlan Willardson *MWPR*
10153 Riverside Dr # 157
Toluca Lake, CA 91602-2562, USA

Stafford, Nancy (Actor)
PO Box 11807
Marina Del Rey, CA 90295-2807, USA

Stafford, Thomas
1006 Cameron St
Alexandria, VA 22314-2427

Stafford, Thomas P (Astronaut, General)
PO Box 604
Glenn Dale, MD 20769-0604, USA

Stageman-Roberts, Donna (Baseball Player)
1831 Jerome Pl
Helena, MT 59601-4735, USA

Staggers, Jon (Football Player)
3835 Oakes Dr
Hayward, CA 94542-1720, USA

Staggs, Jeff (Football Player)
4641 Jeri Way
El Cajon, CA 92020-8329, USA

Staggs, Steve (Athlete, Baseball Player)
4001 Bentbrook Pl
Norman, OK 73072-4020, USA

Stagliano, John
14141 Covello St
Van Nuys, CA 91405-1489

Stagus, Gus (Coach, Swimmer)
Athletic Dept
Ann Arbor, MI 48104, USA

Stahl, Jerry (Actor, Writer)
c/o Staff Member *United Talent Agency (UTA)*
9560 Wilshire Blvd Fl 5
Beverly Hills, CA 90212-2400, USA

Stahl, Larry (Athlete, Baseball Player)
1506 E Main St # A
Belleville, IL 62221-5436, USA

Stahl, Lesley (Correspondent)
c/o Staff Member *WmE2 (WMA-LA)*
1 William Morris Pl
Beverly Hills, CA 90212-4261, USA

Stahl, Leslie (Actor)
c/o Staff Member *WmE2 (WMA-LA)*
1 William Morris Pl
Beverly Hills, CA 90212-4261, USA

Stahl, Lisa (Actor)
6500 Wilshire Blvd Ste 2200
Los Angeles, CA 90048-4942, USA

Stahl, Nick (Actor)
c/o Sean Fay *Kritzer Levine Wilkins Entertainment*
11872 La Grange Ave Fl 1
Los Angeles, CA 90025-5283, USA

Stahl, Norman H (Judge)
McCormack Federal Building
Boston, MA 2109, USA

Stahler, Jeff (Cartoonist, Editor)
125 E Court St
Cincinnati, OH 45202-1212, USA

Stahley, Adele (Baseball Player)
3700 SE Jennings Rd Apt 214W
Port St Lucie, FL 34952-7701, USA

Stahoviak, Scott (Athlete, Baseball Player)
507 Balmoral Ct
Grayslake, IL 60030-9303, USA

Stai, Brendon (Football Player)
1431 Teal Trce
Pittsburgh, PA 15237-3848, USA

Staiger, Roy (Athlete, Baseball Player)
1233 Tyler Dr
Lebanon, MO 65536-4121, USA

Staind (Music Group)
c/o Staff Member *Mitch Schneider Organization, The*
14724 Ventura Blvd Ste 410
Sherman Oaks, CA 91403-3537, USA

Stairs, Matt (Athlete, Baseball Player)
76 Skyline Rd
Bangor, ME 4401, USA

Staite, Jewel (Actor)
c/o Nils Larsen *Elements Entertainment*
312 W 5th St Apt 815
Los Angeles, CA 90013-1750, USA

Stajola, Enzo
Piazza Augusto Albini 5
Rome, ITALY I-00154

Stalcup, Jerry (Football Player)
1023 Westchester Dr
Rockford, IL 61107-3442, USA

Staley, Bill (Football Player)
9210 Todd Rd
Potter Valley, CA 95469-9727, USA

Staley, Dawn (Athlete, Basketball Player)
1224 Glenwood Rd
Columbia, SC 29204-3351, USA

Staley, Dawn M (Basketball Player, Coach)
1228 Callowhill St # 603
Philadelphia, PA 19123, USA

Staley, Gerry (Athlete, Baseball Player)
2517 NE 100th St
Vancouver, WA 98686-5744, USA

Staley, Jerry (Athlete)
2517 NE 100th St
Vancouver, WA 98686-5744

Staley, Joan (Actor)
24516 Windsor Dr Unit B
Valencia, CA 91355-4430, USA

Staley, Lex (Radio Personality)
c/o Staff Member *The Lex & Terry Morning Radio Network*
11700 Central Pkwy
Jacksonville, FL 32224-2600, USA

Staley, Matthew R (Actor, Musician)
PO Box 590
New York, NY 10108-0590, USA

Staley, Walter (Athlete, Hockey Player)
214 Teal Lake Rd
Mexico, MO 65265-3705, USA

Stallard, Tracy (Athlete, Baseball Player)
PO Box 905
Wise, VA 24293-0905, USA

Staller, Ilona 'Cicciolina' (Adult Film Star, Politician)
Via Cassia 1818
Rome I-00123, ITALY

Stallings, Gene (Athlete, Football Coach, Football Player)
6508 County Road 43200
Powderly, TX 75473-5320, USA

Stallings, Larry (Football Player)
207 S Mason Rd
Saint Louis, MO 63141-8026, USA

Stallone, Frank (Actor, Musician)
c/o Staff Member *Noris Media Management*
Postfach 2117
Fürth 90711, Germany

Stallone, Jackie (Actor)
PO Box 491550
Los Angeles, CA 90049-9550, USA

Stallone, Sylvester (Actor, Director, Producer)
c/o Michelle Bega *Rogers & Cowan PR (LA)*
Pacific Design Center 8687 Melrose Ave, 7th Floor
West Hollywood, CA 90069, USA

Stalls, David (Football Player)
2100 Stout St
Denver, CO 80205-2827, USA

Stallworth, Bud (Athlete, Basketball Player)
14 Westwood Rd
Lawrence, KS 66044-4560, USA

Stallworth, Dave (Athlete, Basketball Player)
4400 N Rushwood St
Wichita, KS 67226-1475, USA

Stallworth, Donte (Athlete, Football Player)
6 Arvis Ct
Sacramento, CA 95835-1643, USA

Stallworth, Johnny L (John) (Athlete, Football Player)
302 Osman Dr
Madison, AL 35756-3499, USA

Stallworth, Ron (Football Player)
1834 Parkview Dr S
Montgomery, AL 36117-7701, USA

Stalmaster, Lynn
12400 Wilshire Blvd Ste 920
Los Angeles, CA 90025-1040

Stam, Jessica (Model)
c/o Staff Member *IMG*
304 Park Ave S Fl 12
New York, NY 10010-4314, USA

Stam, Katie (Beauty Pageant Winner)
222 New Rd Ste 700
Linwood, NJ 08221-1286, USA

Stamatopoulos, Dino (Writer)
c/o Greg Cavic *Creative Artists Agency (CAA-LA)*
2000 Avenue of the Stars Ste 100
Los Angeles, CA 90067-4705, USA

Stamberg, Josh (Actor)
c/o James Suskin *James Suskin Management*
2 Charlton St Apt 5K
New York, NY 10014-4970, USA

Stamler, Jonathan (Misc)
Medical Center Hematology Dept
Durham, NC 27708-0001, USA

Stamm, Michael (Mike) (Athlete, Swimmer)
3929 Everett Ave
Oakland, CA 94602-1763, USA

Stamos, John (Actor, Musician)
c/o Daniel (Danny) Sussman *Brillstein Entertainment Partners*
9150 Wilshire Blvd Ste 350
Beverly Hills, CA 90212-3453, USA

Stamos, Theodoros (Artist)
37 W 83rd St
New York, NY 10024-5201, USA

Stamp, Terence (Actor)
c/o Beth Holden-Garland *Untitled Entertainment (LA)*
350 S Beverly Dr Ste 200
Beverly Hills, CA 90212-4819, USA

Stamps, Sylvester (Football Player)
1831 Eisenhower Dr
Vicksburg, MS 39180-3757, USA

Stams, Frank (Football Player)
2870 Marcia Blvd
Cuyahoga Falls, OH 44223-1146, USA

Stan, Jason (Musician)
Level 6/3 Bowen Crs
Victoria, Melbourne 3000, AUSTRALIA

Stan, Sebastian (Actor)
c/o Emily Gerson Saines *Brookside Artists Management (NY)*
250 W 57th St Ste 2303
New York, NY 10107-2399, USA

Stanat, Dug (Artist)
46828 Bradley St
Fremont, CA 94539-7104, USA

Stanback, Haskel (Football Player)
1530 Kingston Dr
Kannapolis, NC 28083-9280, USA

Standal, Barb (Stylist)
4115 Juneau Ln N
Plymouth, MN 55446-2723, USA

Standhardt, Kenneth (Artist)
620 Elwood Dr
Eugene, OR 97401-6012, USA

Standing, John (Actor)
76 Oxford St
London W1N 0AX, UNITED KINGDOM (UK)

Standly, Mike (Golfer)
2306 Columbia Cir
League City, TX 77573-7622, USA

Standridge, Jason (Athlete, Baseball Player)
6228 Cardinal Dr
Pinson, AL 35126-3492, USA

Stanek, Al (Athlete, Baseball Player)
96 Allyn St
Holyoke, MA 01040-2549, USA

Stanfel, Richard (Dick) (Coach, Football Player)
1104 Juniper Pkwy
Libertyville, IL 60048-3543, USA

Stanfield, Kevin (Athlete, Baseball Player)
7565 Newcomb St
San Bernardino, CA 92410-4333, USA

Stanfill, Dennis
908 Oak Grove Ave
San Marino, CA 91108-1022

Stanfill, William T (Bill) (Athlete, Football Player)
3117 Wisteria Ct
Albany, GA 31721-2988, USA

Stanford, Aaron (Actor)
c/o Lainie Sorkin Becky *Management 360*
9111 Wilshire Blvd
Beverly Hills, CA 90210-5508, USA

Stanford, Angela (Golfer)
525 Buckstone Dr
Saginaw, TX 76179-1245, USA

Stanford, Jason (Athlete, Baseball Player)
4505 W Mesquital Del Oro
Tucson, AZ 85742-9704, USA

Stang, Peter J (Misc)
Chemistry Dept
Salt Lake City, UT 84112, USA

Stangassinger, Thomas (Skier)
Hofgasse 19
Durenberg-Hallein 5422, AUSTRIA

Stange, Lee (Athlete, Baseball Player)
436 Dolphin St
Melbourne Beach, FL 32951-2916, USA

Stange, Maya (Actor)
c/o Lindy King *United Agents*
12-26 Lexington St
London W1F OLE, UK

Stangel, Eric (Producer, Writer)
c/o Staff Member *3 Arts Entertainment Inc*
9460 Wilshire Blvd Fl 7
Beverly Hills, CA 90212-2713, USA

Stangel, Justin (Producer, Writer)
c/o Staff Member *3 Arts Entertainment Inc*
9460 Wilshire Blvd Fl 7
Beverly Hills, CA 90212-2713, USA

Stanger, Patti (Business Person, Reality TV Star)
c/o Lance Klein *WmE2 (Endeavor-LA)*
9601 Wilshire Blvd Fl 3
Beverly Hills, CA 90210-5219, USA

Stanhouse, Don (Athlete, Baseball Player)
4 Creekmere Dr
Roanoke, TX 76262-9755, USA

Stanicek, Pete (Athlete, Baseball Player)
525 Wilson St
Downers Grove, IL 60515-3845, USA

Stanicek, Steve (Athlete, Baseball Player)
16354 Lanfear Dr
Lockport, IL 60441-4747, USA

Stanifer, Rob (Athlete, Baseball Player)
13547 Las Palmas Dr
Largo, FL 33774-4632, USA

Stanis, Bernadette (Actor)
c/o Vanessa Morman 11152 Westheimer Rd #299
Houston, TX 77042, USA

Stanka, Joe (Athlete, Baseball Player)
32718 Weymouth Ct
Fulshear, TX 77441-4164, USA

Stankalla, Stefan (Skier)
Furstenstr 14
Gramisch-Partenkirchen 82467, GERMANY

Stankavage, Scott (Football Player)
3843 Somerset Dr
Durham, NC 27707-5016, USA

Stankiewicz, Andy (Athlete, Baseball Player)
9729 Wren Bluff Dr
San Diego, CA 92127-3462, USA

Stankovic, Borislav (Boris) (Athlete, Basketball Player, Misc)
P.O. Box 7005
Munich D-81479, Germany

Stankowski, Paul (Athlete, Golfer)
4713 Rangewood Dr
Flower Mound, TX 75028-1695, USA

Stanlch, George (Athlete, Basketball Player, Track Athlete)
15816 Marigold Ave
Gardena, CA 90249-4837, USA

Stanler, John W (Misc)
440 Strand
London SC2R 0QS, UNITED KINGDOM (UK)

Stanley, Allan H (Athlete, Hockey Player)
RR 3
Fennelon Falls, ON K0M 1N0, Canada

Stanley, Bob (Athlete, Baseball Player)
30 Tansy Ave
Stratham, NH 03885-2288, USA

Stanley, Chad (Athlete, Football Player)
21451 Merlot Ln
Tyler, TX 75703-9202, USA

Stanley, Frank (Cinematographer)
PO Box 2230
Los Angeles, CA 90078-2230, USA

Stanley, Fred (Athlete, Baseball Player)
2109 Winthrop Hill Rd
Argyle, TX 76226-2103, USA

Stanley, Israel (Football Player)
3850 S Miner St
Milwaukee, WI 53221-1250, USA

Stanley, James (Producer)
c/o Staff Member *United Talent Agency (UTA)*
9560 Wilshire Blvd Fl 5
Beverly Hills, CA 90212-2400, USA

Stanley, Marianne Crawford (Coach)
Madison Square Garden 2 Penn Plaza
New York, NY 10121, USA

Stanley, Marlanne Crawford (Basketball Player, Coach)
MCI Center 601 F St NW
Washington, DC 20004, USA

Stanley, Mike (Athlete, Baseball Player)
1108 NE 10th Ave
Fort Lauderdale, FL 33304-2115, USA

Stanley, Mitchell J (Mickey) (Athlete, Baseball Player)
6370 Cunningham Lake Rd
Brighton, MI 48116-5222, USA

Stanley, Paul (Musician)
8730 W Sunset Blvd # 195
Los Angeles, CA 90069-2210, USA

Stanley, Ralph (Music Group, Musician)
2607 Westwood Dr
Nashville, TN 37204-2709, USA

Stanley, Steven M (Misc)
4308 Folly Quarter Rd
Ellicott City, MD 21042-1424, USA

Stanley, Walter (Athlete, Football Player)
23977 E Alamo Pl
Aurora, CO 80016-4247, USA

Stansbury, Terrace (Athlete, Basketball Player)
901 N Franklin St # 2
Wilmington, DE 19806-4529, USA

Stansfield, Claire
9300 Wilshire Blvd Ste 555
Beverly Hills, CA 90212-3211

Stansfield, Lisa (Music Group, Musician, Songwriter, Writer)
PO Box 59 Ashwell
Herts SG7 5NG, UNITED KINGDOM (UK)

Stansfield Smith, Colin (Architect)
Three Ministers House 76 High St
Winchester
Hants SO23 8UL, UNITED KINGDOM (UK)

Stansky, Peter D L (Historian)
375 Pinehill Rd
Hillsborough, CA 94010-6612, USA

Stantis, Scott (Cartoonist, Editor)
2200 4th Ave N
Birmingham, AL 35203-3802, USA

Stanton, Andrew (Animator, Director, Writer)
1200 Park Ave
Emeryville, CA 94608-3677, USA

Stanton, Frank N (Misc)
25 W 52nd St
New York, NY 10019-6104, USA

Stanton, Harry Dean (Actor)
14527 Mulholland Dr
Los Angeles, CA 90077-1713, USA

Stanton, Jeff (Race Car Driver)
1137 Athens Rd
Sherwood, MI 49089-9721, USA

Stanton, Mike (Athlete, Baseball Player)
3801 E Van Buren St
Phoenix, AZ 85008, USA

Stanton, Molly (Actor)
c/o Rick Kurtzman *Creative Artists Agency (CAA-LA)*
2000 Avenue of the Stars Ste 100
Los Angeles, CA 90067-4705, USA

Stanton, Paul (Athlete, Hockey Player)
2150 Sheepshead Dr
Naples, FL 34102-1506, USA

Stanton, Phil (Entertainer)
3900 Las Vegas Blvd S
Las Vegas, NV 89119-1004, USA

Stapf, David (Business Person)
c/o Staff Member *CBS Paramount Network Television*
4024 Radford Ave
Studio City, CA 91604-2190, USA

Stapinski, Helene (Writer)
175 5th Ave
New York, NY 10010-7703, USA

Staple Singers, The
PO Box 170429
San Francisco, CA 94117-0429

Staples, Mavis (Music Group, Musician)
PO Box 498360
Chicago, IL 60649-8360, USA

Stapleton, Dave (Athlete, Baseball Player)
51 N Bayview St
Fairhope, AL 36532-2537, USA

Stapleton, Dave (Athlete, Baseball Player)
418 S Galaxy Dr
Chandler, AZ 85226-4644

Stapleton, Jacinta (Actor)
c/o Stacey Testro *Stacey Testro International*
8265 W Sunset Blvd Ste 102
West Hollywood, CA 90046-2433, USA

Stapleton, Jean (Actor)
155 W 68th St Apt 29C
New York, NY 10023-5835, USA

Stapleton, Kevin (Actor)
232 N Canon Dr
Beverly Hills, CA 90210-5302, USA

Stapleton, Oliver (Cinematographer)
1640 5th St Ste 205
Santa Monica, CA 90401-3325, USA

Stapleton, Parish (Stylist)
c/o Staff Member *Independent Artists*
448 E Riverdale Ave
Orange, CA 92865-1302, USA

Stapleton, Walter K (Judge)
844 N King St
Wilmington, DE 19801-3519, USA

Stapp, Scott (Musician)
c/o Staff Member *Wind-up Records*
72 Madison Ave Fl 8
New York, NY 10016-8731, USA

Star, Darren (Doctor, Producer, Writer)
c/o Tracey Jacobs *United Talent Agency (UTA)*
9560 Wilshire Blvd Fl 5
Beverly Hills, CA 90212-2400, USA

Star, Marilyn (Adult Film Star)
1521 Alton Rd # 369
Miami Beach, FL 33139-3301, USA

Star, Ryan (Musician)
c/o Michael (Mike) Esterman
Esterman.Com, LLC
Prefers to be contacted via email
MD, USA

Star Sailor (Musician)
c/o Staff Member *Solo Agency Ltd (UK)*
55 Fulham High St 2nd Floor
London SW6 3JJ, United Kingdom

Starbird, Kate (Basketball Player)
125 S Pennsylvania St
Indianapolis, IN 46204-3610, USA

Starbuck, Jo Jo (Figure Skater)
33 Pomeroy Rd
Madison, NJ 07940-2638, USA

Starch, Ken (Football Player)
603 E Hillcrest Dr
Verona, WI 53593-1517, USA

Starck, Philippe (Architect, Designer)
3 Rue Faisans
Shiltigheim 67300, FRANCE

Starfield, Barbara H (Doctor)
624 N Broadway
Baltimore, MD 21205-1900, USA

Stargell, Tony (Athlete, Football Player)
131 Jenny Rd
Grantville, GA 30220-2134, USA

Stark, Chad (Football Player)
300 Broadway N Apt 401
Fargo, ND 58102-4726, USA

Stark, Collin (Actor)
c/o Peter Himberger *Impact Artists Group LLC*
42 Hamilton Ter
New York, NY 10031-6403, USA

Stark, Dennis (Athlete, Baseball Player)
213 N Elm St
Edgerton, OH 43517-9672, USA

Stark, Don (Actor)
c/o Tom Harrison *Diverse Talent Group*
9911 W Pico Blvd Ste 340W
Los Angeles, CA 90035-2712, USA

Stark, Freya M (Writer)
Via Canova Asolo
Treviso, ITALY

Stark, Graham (Actor)
76 Oxford St
London W1N 0AX, UNITED KINGDOM (UK)

Stark, Koo (Actor)
52 Shaftesbury Ave
London W1V 7DE, UNITED KINGDOM (UK)

Stark, Matt (Athlete, Baseball Player)
721 Shirehampton Dr
Las Vegas, NV 89178-1233, USA

Stark, Melissa (Correspondent, Sportscaster)
30 Rockefeller Plz
New York, NY 10112-0015, USA

Stark, Nathan J (Lawyer)
4000 Cathedral Ave NW # 132
Washington, DC 20016-5249, USA

Stark, Rohn T (Football Player)
PO Box 10067
Lahaina, HI 96761-0067, USA

Starke, Anthony (Actor)
c/o Staff Member *Paradigm (LA)*
360 N Crescent Dr
Beverly Hills, CA 90210-4874, USA

Starker, James
1241 S Winfield Rd
Bloomington, IN 47401-6147

Starker, Janos (Musician)
1241 S Winfield Rd
Bloomington, IN 47401-6147, USA

Starkey, Jason (Athlete, Football Player)
1525 Washington Ave # 1
Huntington, WV 25704-1520, USA

Starks, Duane (Football Player)
811 NW 199th St
Miami, FL 33169-2847, USA

Starks, John (Athlete, Basketball Player)
PO Box 8146
Stamford, CT 06905-8146, USA

Starks, Max (Athlete, Football Player)
c/o Eugene Parker *Maximum Sports Management*
6435 W Jefferson Blvd # 197
Fort Wayne, IN 46804-6203, USA

Starkweather, Gary K (Engineer)
10274 Parkwood Dr Apt 7
Cupertino, CA 95014-1441, USA

Starling, Carol (Stylist)
759 Belmont Ave Apt 3
Charlottesville, VA 22902-5756, USA

Starling, James D (General)
3581 Joshua Rd
Shingle Springs, CA 95682-9478, USA

Starn, Douglas (Photographer)
163 Mercer St # 1
New York, NY 10012-3203, USA

Starn, Mike (Photographer)
163 Mercer St # 1
New York, NY 10012-3203, USA

Starner, Shelby (Music Group, Musician)
30 Hillcrest Ave
Morristown, NJ 07960-5090, USA

Starnes, John G (Football Player)
8826 Shade Tree
San Antonio, TX 78254-6821, USA

Staroba, Paul (Football Player)
9235 McWain Rd
Grand Blanc, MI 48439-8006, USA

Starr, Albert (Doctor)
5050 SW Patton Rd
Portland, OR 97221-2263, USA

Starr, Bart (Athlete, Football Coach, Football Player)
2647 Rocky Ridge Ln
Birmingham, AL 35216-4809, USA

Starr, Beau (Actor)
c/o Geneva Bray *GVA Talent Agency Inc*
8981 W Sunset Blvd Ste 101
Los Angeles, CA 90069-1850, USA

Starr, Brenda K (Music Group, Musician)
141 Dunbar Ave
Fords, NJ 08863-1551, USA

Starr, Chauncey (Engineer)
12375 Melody Ln
Los Altos Hills, CA 94022-3238, USA

Starr, Dick (Athlete, Baseball Player)
613 N Crescent Dr
Kittanning, PA 16201-2214, USA

Starr, Fredro (Actor, Artist, Musician)
c/o Keith Brown *KBiz Entertainment*
22425 Ventura Blvd # 106
Woodland Hills, CA 91364-1524, USA

Starr, Garrison (Musician)
c/o Staff Member *MCT Management*
520 8th Ave Rm 2205
New York, NY 10018-4160, USA

Starr, Kay (Music Group, Musician)
708 Palisades Dr
Pacific Palisades, CA 90272-2800, USA

Starr, Keith (Athlete, Basketball Player)
1583 Graystone Canyon Ave
Las Vegas, NV 89183-6309, USA

Starr, Kenneth (Government Official, Judge)
24255 Pacific Coast Hwy
Malibu, CA 90263-0001, USA

Starr, Leonard (Cartoonist)
435 N Michigan Ave Ste 1500
Chicago, IL 60611-4012, USA

Starr, Martin (Actor)
c/o Ben Feigin *Anonymous Content (AC-LA)*
3531 Hayden Ave
Culver City, CA 90232, USA

Starr, Paul E (Misc)
Green Hall
Princeton, NJ 08544-1020, USA

Starr, Randy (Music Group, Musician, Songwriter, Writer)
230 Park Ave
New York, NY 10169-0005, USA

Starr, Ringo (Actor, Musician)
90 Jermyn St 1st Floor
London UK, SW1Y 6JD

Starr, Steve (Journalist, Photographer)
Colorado Springs, CO 80903, USA

Starrette, Herm (Athlete, Baseball Player)
103 Howard Pond Loop
Statesville, NC 28625-2280, USA

Starring, Stephen (Football Player)
6120 W Tropicana Ave Ste A PMB 16
Las Vegas, NV 89103-4489, USA

Starsailor (Music Group)
c/o Staff Member *Paradigm (Monterey)*
404 W Franklin St
Monterey, CA 93940-2303, USA

Starship
9850 Sandalfoot Blvd # 458
Boca Raton, FL 33428-6645

Starting Line (Music Group)
c/o Staff Member *Virgin Records (NY)*
150 5th Ave Fl 7
New York, NY 10011-4372, USA

Starzewski, Tomasz (Designer, Fashion Designer)
15-17 Pont St
London SW1X 9EH, UNITED KINGDOM (UK)

Starzl, Thomas E (Doctor)
Medical School Surgery
Pittsburgh, PA 15261-0001, USA

Stasey, Caitlin (Actor)
c/o Shelley Browning *Magnolia Entertainment (LA)*
9595 Wilshire Blvd Ste 601
Beverly Hills, CA 90212-2506, USA

Stashwick, Todd (Actor)
c/o Staff Member *Meghan Schumacher Management*
13351D Riverside Dr # 387
Sherman Oaks, CA 91423-2508, USA

Stastny, Anton (Athlete, Hockey Player)
Montoileu 11
Bussigney-Lausanne 1030, Switzerland

Stastny, Peter (Athlete, Hockey Player)
465 S Mason Rd
Saint Louis, MO 63141-8519, USA

Stata, Raymond S (Business Person)
1 Technology Way
Norwood, MA 02062-2634, USA

Statham, Jason (Actor)
c/o Steve Chasman *Ace Media*
9200 W Sunset Blvd Ste 10
Los Angeles, CA 90069-3608, USA

Static, Wayne (Musician)
9100 Wilshire Blvd Ste 400W
Beverly Hills, CA 90212-3464, USA

Statler Brothers (Music Group)
PO Box 2703
Staunton, VA 24402-2703, USA

Staton, Aaron (Actor)
c/o Carol Goll *International Creative Management (ICM-LA)*
10250 Constellation Blvd Fl 7
Los Angeles, CA 90067-6207, USA

Staton, Candi (Music Group, Musician)
1201 N St NW # A5
Washington, DC 20005-5115, USA

Staton, Dave (Athlete, Baseball Player)
2175 Arnold Dr
Rocklin, CA 95765-5901, USA

Staton, Joe (Athlete, Baseball Player)
2929 76th Ave SE Apt 201
Mercer Island, WA 98040-2715, USA

Staton, Leroy (Athlete, Baseball Player)
1751 N Norwood Ln
Florence, SC 29506-6901, USA

Staton, Mike (Athlete, Baseball Player)
19602 Indigo Lake Dr
Magnolia, TX 77355-3158, USA

Status Quo (Music Group, Musician)
c/o Simon Porter *Duroc Media Ltd.*
Riverside House 10-12 Victoria Road
Uxbridge, Middlesex UB8 2TW, UK

Statuto, Art (Football Player)
3701 Poplar Ct
Carrollton, TX 75007-1927, USA

Staub, Chelsea (Actor)
c/o Margot Menzel *Evolution Entertainment (LA)*
9111 Wilshire Blvd
Beverly Hills, CA 90210-5508, USA

Staub, Daniel J (Rusty) (Athlete, Baseball Player)
9 Broadcast Plz
Secaucus, NJ 07094-2913, USA

Staub, Danielle (Reality TV Star)
c/o Jeffre Phillips *Ja-Tail Enterprises*
8306 Wilshire Blvd Ste 528
Beverly Hills, CA 90211-2382, USA

Staubach, Roger T (Athlete, Football Player)
5242 Ravine Dr
Dallas, TX 75220-2260, USA

Staubach, Scott (Football Player)
6701 Miwok Ct
Bakersfield, CA 93309-3436, USA

Stauber, Liz (Actor)
c/o Sally Ware *Gersh (NY)*
41 Madison Ave
New York, NY 10010-2202, USA

Stauffer, Tim (Athlete, Baseball Player)
1464 Summit Ave
Cardiff By The Sea, CA 92007-2432, USA

Stauffer, William A (Bill) (Athlete, Basketball Player)
13808 Sheridan Ave
Urbandale, IA 50323-2188, USA

Staunton, Imelda (Actor)
Drury House 34-43 Russell St
London WC2B 5HA, UNITED KINGDOM (UK)

Staurovsky, Jason (Football Player)
4822 E 87th Pl
Tulsa, OK 74137-2825, USA

Stause, Chrishell (Actor)
c/o Staff Member *Rooster Films*
5225 Wilshire Blvd Ste 701
Los Angeles, CA 90036-4351, USA

Stautberg, Gerald (Athlete, Football Player)
3200 Park Rd
Monkton, MD 21111, USA

Staveley, William D M (Admiral)
40 Eastbourne Terrace
London W2 3QR, UNITED KINGDOM (UK)

Stavropoulos, William S (Business Person)
2030 Dow Ctr
Midland, MI 48674-0001, USA

Stayskal, Wayne (Cartoonist, Editor)
200 S Parker St
Tampa, FL 33606-2308, USA

Staysniak, Joseph A (Joe) (Football Player)
4094 Forest Dr
Brownsburg, IN 46112-8672, USA

Stead, Eugene A Jr (Doctor)
3017 Daventry Ln
Raleigh, NC 27613-6506, USA

Steadman, Alison (Actor)
Drury House 34-43 Russell St
London WC2B 5HA, UNITED KINGDOM (UK)

Steadman, J Richard (Doctor)
181 W Meadow Dr Ste 400
Vail, CO 81657-5058, USA

Steadman, Mark (Writer)
450 Pin-Du-Lac Dr
Central, SC 29630, USA

Steadman, Ralph I (Cartoonist)
Old Loose Court Loose Valley Maidstone
Kent ME15 9SE, UNITED KINGDOM (UK)

Steadman, Robert L (Cinematographer)
15925 Temecula St
Pacific Palisades, CA 90272-4239, USA

Stearns, Cheryl (Misc)
613 Saddlebred Ln
Raeford, NC 28376-5535, USA

Stearns, Jeff
9200 W Sunset Blvd Ste 1130
Los Angeles, CA 90069-3606

Stearns, John (Athlete, Baseball Player)
1155 W Mound St
Columbus, OH 43223-2211, USA

Stecher, Renate Meissner- (Athlete, Track Athlete)
Haydnstr 11 #526/38
Jena 7749, GERMANY

Stecher, Theodore P (Astronomer)
Space Flight Center
Greenbelt, MD 20771-0001, USA

Steckel, Les (Athlete, Football Coach, Football Player)
195 Blew Ct
E Brunswick, NJ 08816-1834, USA

Steckler, Ray Dennis (Director)
2375 E Tropicana Ave
Las Vegas, NV 89119-6564, USA

Steck-Weiss, Elma (Baseball Player)
7555 W Kimberly Way
Glendale, AZ 85308-5954, USA

Steding, Katy (Athlete, Basketball Player)
21625 SW 100th Dr
Tualatin, OR 97062-8581, USA

Steeb, Carl-Uwe
18 Chemin Des Jardillets
Hauterive, SWITZERLAND CH-2068

Steed, Joel (Football Player)
2639 Holly St
Denver, CO 80207-3229, USA

Steege, Deb (Stylist)
c/o Staff Member *Help Me Rhonda*
541 10th St NW # 294
Atlanta, GA 30318-5713, USA

Steel, Amy (Actor)
1505 10th St
Santa Monica, CA 90401-2805, USA

Steel, David M S (Government Official)
Aikwood Tower Ettrick Bridge
Selkirkshire, SCOTLAND

Steel, John (Musician)
PO Box 770850
Orlando, FL 32877-0850, USA

Steel Magnolia (Music Group, Musician)
c/o Staff Member *Big Machine Records*
1219 16th Ave S
Nashville, TN 37212-2901, USA

Steele, Allan (Actor)
c/o Staff Member *Baumgarten Management*
406 Wilshire Blvd
Santa Monica, CA 90401-1410, USA

Steele, Barbara (Actor)
2460 Benedict Canyon Dr
Beverly Hills, CA 90210-1433, USA

Steele, Billy (DJ)
c/o Len Evans *Project Publicity*
312 W 53rd St Ste 202
New York, NY 10019-5743, USA

Steele, Brian (Actor)
c/o Joan Vento-Hall *Law Offices of Joan Vento-Hall, The*
10250 Constellation Blvd Fl 19
Los Angeles, CA 90067-6219, USA

Steele, Cassie (Actor)
c/o Staff Member *Noble Caplan Abrams*
1260 Yonge St 2nd Floor
Toronto ON M4T 1W6, Canada

Steele, Danielle (Writer)
c/o Staff Member *Doubleday/ RandomHouse*
1745 Broadway
New York, NY 10019-4368, USA

Steele, Ernie (Athlete, Football Player)
4407 244th St SE
Woodinville, WA 98072-8623, USA

Steele, Glen (Football Player)
303 E 5th St
Ligonier, IN 46767-2205, USA

Steele, Joyce (Athlete, Baseball Player)
627 Sr 4010
Mehoopany, PA 18629-8841, USA

Steele, Larry (Athlete, Basketball Player)
27448 NW Saint Helens Rd Slip 470
Scappoose, OR 97056-3233, USA

Steele, Michael (Musician)
1341 W Fullerton Ave # 180
Chicago, IL 60614-2362, USA

Steele, Michael (Politician)
310 1st St SE
Washington, DC 20003-1885, USA

Steele, Nick (Stylist)
c/o Celebrity Stylist *Oliver Piro Inc*
725 Riverside Dr Apt 3A
New York, NY 10031-2460, USA

Steele, Richard (Boxer, Referee)
2438 Antler Point Dr
Henderson, NV 89074-6269, USA

Steele, Robert (Football Player)
PO Box 681478
Marietta, GA 30068-0025, USA

Steele, Shelby (Writer)
English
San Jose, CA 95192-0001, USA

Steele, Tommy (Actor, Musician)
Media House 3 Burlington Lane
London W4 2TH, UNITED KINGDOM (UK)

Steele, William M (Mike) (General)
Commanding General Combined Arms Center
Fort Leavenworth, KS 66207, USA

Steele-Perkins, Christopher H (Photographer)
5 Saint John's Buildings Canterbury St
London SW9 7QB, UNITED KINGDOM (UK)

Steels, Jim (Athlete, Baseball Player)
1654 Via Rico
Santa Maria, CA 93454-2609, USA

Steely Dan (Music Group)
c/o Barry Dickins *International Talent Booking*
1st Floor, Ariel House 74A Charlotte St
London W1T 4QJ, UNITED KINGDOM

Steen, Jessica (Actor)
1505 10th St
Santa Monica, CA 90401-2805, USA

Steenburgen, Mary (Actor)
c/o Eric Kranzler *Management 360*
9111 Wilshire Blvd
Beverly Hills, CA 90210-5508, USA

Steenstra, Ken (Athlete, Baseball Player)
1228 Pheasant Ct
Liberty, MO 64068-8464, USA

Steeples, Eddie (Actor)
c/o Staff Member *LRB Publicity*
2206 Rockefeller Ln Unit 1
Redondo Beach, CA 90278-3723, USA

Steere, Richard (Football Player)
1810 Fox Bridge Ct
Fallbrook, CA 92028-8745, USA

Steers, Burr (Director)
c/o Shawn Simon *Anonymous Content (AC-LA)*
3531 Hayden Ave
Culver City, CA 90232, USA

Steevens, Morrie (Athlete, Baseball Player)
14465 Cadillac Dr
San Antonio, TX 78248-1001, USA

Stefan, Greg (Athlete, Hockey Player)
37648 Baywood Dr Unit 33
Farmington Hills, MI 48335-3604, USA

Stefani, Gwen (Fashion Designer, Musician, Songwriter)
c/o Jim Guerinot *Rebel Waltz Inc*
31652 2nd Ave
Laguna Beach, CA 92651-8244, USA

Stefanich, Jim (Athlete, Bowler)
1444 Coral Bell Dr
Joliet, IL 60435-3979, USA

Stefanson, Leslie (Actor)
c/o Andy Cohen *Gersh (LA)*
10250 Constellation Blvd Fl 7
Los Angeles, CA 90067-6207, USA

Stefanyshyn-Piper, Heidemarie M (Astronaut)
6875 Rolling Creek Way
Alexandria, VA 22315-6122, USA

Stefero, John (Athlete, Baseball Player)
6239 Chestnut Oak Ln
Linthicum Heights, MD 21090-2148, USA

Steffen, Dave (Baseball Player)
30531 Maple View Ln
Flat Rock, MI 48134-2744, USA

Steffen, Jim (Football Player)
1440 Westway
Arnold, MD 21012-2428, USA

Steffes, Kent (Athlete, Volleyball Player)
14675 Titus St
Panorama City, CA 91402-4922, USA

Steffy, Joseph B (Joe) Jr (Football Player)
25 Water Way
Newburgh, NY 12550-1989, USA

Stefy (Music Group)
72 Madison Ave Fl 8
New York, NY 10016-8731, USA

Stegall, Keith (Musician)
c/o Staff Member *Sony Music Nashville*
8 Music Sq W
Nashville, TN 37203-3204, USA

Stegent, Larry (Football Player)
1177 West Loop S # 525
Houston, TX 77027-9006, USA

Steger, Joseph A (Educator)
President S Ofc
Cincinnati, OH 45221-0001, USA

Steger, Michael (Actor)
c/o Staff Member *Marianne Daniels & Associates*
8491 W Sunset Blvd # 416
Los Angeles, CA 90069-1911, USA

Steger, Will (Misc)
990 3rd St E
Saint Paul, MN 55106-5243, USA

Stegman, Dave (Athlete, Baseball Player)
3234 Simmons Dr
Grove City, OH 43123-1835, USA

Stegman, Millie (Actor)
c/o Staff Member *Telefe - Argentina*
Pavon 2444 (C1248AAT)
Buenos Aires, ARGENTINA

Stehlin, Savannah (Actor)
c/o Sharon Lane *Lane Management Group*
13017 Woodbridge St
Studio City, CA 91604-1431, USA

Steiger, Ueli (Cinematographer)
2222 Kenilworth Ave
Los Angeles, CA 90039-3010, USA

Stein, Ben (Actor, Comedian, Producer, Writer)
8787 Shoreham Dr Apt 810
West Hollywood, CA 90069-2230, USA

Stein, Bill (Athlete, Baseball Player)
7816 Rogue River Trl
Fort Worth, TX 76137-4329, USA

Stein, Blake (Athlete, Baseball Player)
115 Bonne Vie Dr
Brandon, MS 39047-8789, USA

Stein, Bob (Basketball Player, Misc)
Target Center 600 1st Ave N
Minneapolis, MN 55403, USA

Stein, Carolyn (Stylist)
1901 S Oak Haven Cir
Miami, FL 33179-2834, USA

Stein, Chris (Musician)
32 Court St Ste 1600
Brooklyn, NY 11201-4441, USA

Stein, Ed (Cartoonist, Editor)
Editorial Dept 400 W Colfax Ave
Denver, CO 80204, USA

Stein, Elias M (Mathematician)
132 Dodds Ln
Princeton, NJ 08540-4106, USA

Stein, Garth (Writer)
c/o Staff Member *HarperCollins Publishers*
10 E 53rd St C/O Author Mail Floor 7
New York, NY 10022, USA

Stein, Gilbert (Gil) (Athlete, Hockey Player)
650 5th Ave Apt 3300
New York, NY 10019-6108, USA

Stein, James (Business Person)
3353 Michelson Dr
Irvine, CA 92612-7622, USA

Stein, Joseph (Writer)
1130 Park Ave
New York, NY 10128-1255, USA

Stein, Mark (Music Group, Musician)
280 Riverside Dr Apt 12L
New York, NY 10025-9032, USA

Stein, Pamela Jean
2112 Broadway
Santa Monica, CA 90404-2912

Stein, Randy (Athlete, Baseball Player)
8627 Mandarin Ave
Rancho Cucamonga, CA 91701-2626, USA

Stein, Robert (Editor)
375 Lexington Ave
New York, NY 10017-5514, USA

Steinbach, Alice (Journalist)
501 N Calvert St
Baltimore, MD 21278-1000, USA

Steinbach, Terry (Athlete, Baseball Player)
PO Box 181
Hamel, MN 55340-0181, USA

Steinberg, Leigh (Attorney, Attorney General, General)
1280 Bison Ave
Newport Beach, CA 92660-4258, USA

Steinberg, Paul (Cartoonist)
4 Times Sq
New York, NY 10036-6515, USA

Steinberg, Ruth (Stylist)
PO Box 5242
Santa Monica, CA 90409-5242, USA

Steinberg, Saul P (Business Person)
5 Hanover Sq # 1700
New York, NY 10004-2614, USA

Steinberg, Tristam (Stylist)
c/o Staff Member *Koko Represents*
166 Geary St Ste 1007
San Francisco, CA 94108-5623, USA

Steinberger, Jack (Nobel Prize Laureate)
25 Chemin des Merles 1213 Onex
Geneva, SWITZERLAND

Steindler, Mary-Helen (Stylist)
2725 N Hermitage Ave
Chicago, IL 60614-4804, USA

Steindorff, Scott (Producer, Writer)
c/o Staff Member *Stone Village Entertainment*
1036 Carol Dr
West Hollywood, CA 90069-3108, USA

Steinem, Gloria (Journalist, Writer)
118 E 73rd St
New York, NY 10021-4238, USA

Steiner, Andre (Athlete)
Bismarckstr 4
Berlin 14109, GERMANY

Steiner, George (Writer)
32 Barrow Road
Cambridge, UNITED KINGDOM (UK)

Steiner, Mel (Baseball Player)
27217 White Alder Ct
Murrieta, CA 92562-4592, USA

Steiner, Paul (Cartoonist)
3600 New York Ave NE
Washington, DC 20002-1947, USA

Steiner, Peter (Cartoonist)
4 Times Sq
New York, NY 10036-6515, USA

Steiner, Rebel (Athlete, Football Player)
112 Aaronvale Cir
Birmingham, AL 35242-7353, USA

Steiner, Reed (Producer)
c/o Staff Member *WmE2 (WMA-LA)*
1 William Morris Pl
Beverly Hills, CA 90212-4261, USA

Steines, Mark (Television Host)
c/o Staff Member *Entertainment Tonight (ET)*
4024 Radford Ave
Studio City, CA 91604-2101, USA

Steinfeld, Hailee (Actor)
c/o David Eisenberg *Protege Entertainment*
710 E Angeleno Ave
Burbank, CA 91501-2213, USA

Steinfeld, Jake (Actor, Athlete, Wrestler)
622 Toyopa Dr
Pacific Palisades, CA 90272-4471

Steinfield, Jake (Actor, Misc, Wrestler)
622 Toyopa Dr
Pacific Palisades, CA 90272-4471, USA

Steinfort, Fred (Athlete, Football Player)
PO Box 24981
Denver, CO 80224-0981, USA

Steinhardt, Arnold (Musician)
266 W 37th St # 2000
New York, NY 10018-6609, USA

Steinhardt, Gillian (Stylist)
c/o Staff Member *Judy Inc*
1 Yorkville Ave
Toronto ON M4W 1L1, Canada

Steinhardt, Paul J (Physicist)
1000 Cedar Grove Rd
Wynnewood, PA 19096-2006, USA

Steinhardt, Richard (Biologist)
Biology
Berkeley, CA 94720-0001, USA

Steinhauer, Sherri (Golfer)
5010 Hammersley Rd
Madison, WI 53711-2616, USA

Steinkraus, William (Bill) (Horse Racer)
PO Box 3038
Darien, CT 06820-8038, USA

Steinkuhler, Dean E (Football Player)
1135 Oak St
Syracuse, NE 68446-9483, USA

Steinman, Jim (Songwriter, Writer)
83 Riverside Dr
New York, NY 10024-5713, USA

Steinmetz, Richard (Actor)
c/o Staff Member *Personal Management Company*
425 N Robertson Blvd
West Hollywood, CA 90048-1735, USA

Steinsaltz, Adin (Religious Leader)
PO Box 1458
Jerusalem, ISRAEL

Steinseifer Bates, Carrie (Swimmer)
9309 Benzon Dr
Pleasanton, CA 94588-4767, USA

Steirer, Ricky (Athlete, Baseball Player)
1015 Haverhill Rd
Baltimore, MD 21229-5115, USA

Steitz, Joan A (Misc)
45 Prospect Hill Rd
Branford, CT 06405-5711, USA

Stela, Annie (Musician)
c/o Staff Member *Paradigm (Monterey)*
404 W Franklin St
Monterey, CA 93940-2303, USA

Stella, Frank P (Artist, Misc)
17 Jones St
New York, NY 10014-4131, USA

Stella, Martina (Actor)
c/o Daniela di Santo *Moviement*
Via P Cavallini 24
Rome 193, ITALY

Stelle, Kellogg S (Physicist)
Prince Consort Road
London SW7 2BZ, UNITED KINGDOM (UK)

Stelmaszek, Rick (Athlete, Baseball Player)
2734 E 97th St
Chicago, IL 60617-4928

Stember, Jeff (Athlete, Baseball Player)
9517 E Altadena Ave
Scottsdale, AZ 85260-5865, USA

Stemie, Steve (Athlete, Baseball Player)
4011 Weatherby Way
New Albany, IN 47150-9676, USA

Stempel, Robert C (Business Person)
1647 W Maple Rd
Troy, MI 48084, USA

Stempniak, Lee (Athlete, Hockey Player)
4469 Clinton St
Buffalo, NY 14224-1700, USA

Stemrick, Greg (Football Player)
1012 Matthews Dr
Cincinnati, OH 45215-1804, USA

Stenberg, Brigitta
11484th St # 116
Santa Monica, CA 90403

Stenger, Brian (Football Player)
7921 Kellogg Creek Dr
Mentor, OH 44060-7111, USA

Stenhouse, Dave (Athlete, Baseball Player)
20 Hayward St
Cranston, RI 02910-2701, USA

Stenhouse, Mike (Athlete, Baseball Player)
70 Woodbury Rd
Cranston, RI 02905-3317, USA

Stenko, Paul (Football Player)
149 Tunxis Ave
Bloomfield, CT 06002-2038, USA

Stenmark, Ingemar (Skier)
Residence l'Annonciade 17 Av de l'Anncenciade
Monte Carlo 98000, MONACO

Stennett, Rennie (Athlete, Baseball Player)
6519 Boticelli Dr
Lake Worth, FL 33467-7037, USA

Stensrud, Mike (Football Player)
304 S Winnebago St
Lake Mills, IA 50450-1637, USA

Stenstrom, Steve (Athlete, Football Player)
70 Valley Ct
Atherton, CA 94027-6472, USA

Stepanova, Maria (Basketball Player)
American West Arena 201 E Jefferson St
Phoenix, AZ 85004, USA

Stepashin, Sergei V (General, Prime Minister)
Government of Russia Kasnopresneskaya Embankment 2
Moscow 103274, RUSSIA

Stephanie (Royalty)
Maison Clos St Martin
Saint Remy de Provence, FRANCE

Stephanopolous, Constantine (Costis) (President)
7 Vas Georgiou B Odos Zalokosta 10
Athens, GREECE

Stephanopoulos, George R (Journalist, Television Host)
c/o Staff Member *ABC News*
77 W 66th St Fl 3
New York, NY 10023-6201, USA

Stephen, Buzz (Athlete, Baseball Player)
15512 Sycamore St
Porterville, CA 93257-2594, USA

Stephens, Darryl (Actor)
c/o Staff Member *Noah's Arc*
75 Charles Rowen House Merlin Street
London WC1X OEJ, UNITED KINGDOM

Stephens, Everette (Athlete, Basketball Player)
1347 Adams Ave
Saint Charles, IL 60174-3307, USA

Stephens, Gene (Athlete, Baseball Player)
602 Erin Ave
Monroe, LA 71201-4710, USA

Stephens, Hal (Football Player)
221 W Virginia St
Rocky Mount, NC 27804-4940, USA

Stephens, Jack (Athlete, Basketball Player)
40 Woodscape Ct
Pekin, IL 61554-5301, USA

Stephens, Jamain (Athlete, Football Player)
105 W 6th St
Tabor City, NC 28463-1633, USA

Stephens, James
8271 Melrose Ave Ste 110
Los Angeles, CA 90046-6800

Stephens, Janaya (Actor)
c/o Penny Noble *Noble Caplan Abrams*
1260 Yonge St 2nd Floor
Toronto ON M4T 1W6, Canada

Stephens, John (Athlete, Football Player)
P.O. Box 496
Shreveport, LA 71107-7407, USA

Stephens, John (Athlete, Baseball Player)
1325 Oak Point Ct
Venice, FL 34292-1635, USA

Stephens, Laraine
10800 Chalon Rd
Los Angeles, CA 90077-3220

Stephens, Ray (Athlete, Baseball Player)
1065 Council Rd NE
Charleston, TN 37310-6232, USA

Stephens, Robert (Business Person)
691 S Milpitas Blvd
Milpitas, CA 95035-5476, USA

Stephens, Santo (Football Player)
2720 Benson Dr
Marietta, GA 30062-4901, USA

Stephens, Scott (Football Player)
4132 Palm Tree Ct
La Mesa, CA 91941-7238, USA

Stephens, Toby (Actor)
c/o Simon Halls *Slate Public Relations*
9000 W Sunset Blvd Ste 915
West Hollywood, CA 90069-5809, USA

Stephens, Tom (Football Player)
69 Orchard Rd
Swampscott, MA 01907-2349, USA

Stephenson, Bob (Athlete, Baseball Player)
1518 Brookhaven Blvd
Norman, OK 73072-3206, USA

Stephenson, Debra
2 Henrietta St
London, ENGLAND WC2E 8PS

Stephenson, Dwight E (Football Player)
4785 Tree Fern Dr
Delray Beach, FL 33445-7025, USA

Stephenson, Earl (Athlete, Baseball Player)
4043 Zacks Mill Rd
Angier, NC 27501-7185, USA

Stephenson, Garrett (Athlete, Baseball Player)
3075 W Balata Ct
Meridian, ID 83646-5180, USA

Stephenson, Gordon (Architect)
55/14 Albert St
Claremont, WA 6010, AUSTRALIA

Stephenson, Jerry (Athlete, Baseball Player)
1425 Marelen Dr
Fullerton, CA 92835-3709, USA

Stephenson, John (Actor, Voice Over Artist)
c/o Staff Member *International Creative Management (ICM-LA)*
10250 Constellation Blvd Fl 7
Los Angeles, CA 90067-6207, USA

Stephenson, John (Athlete, Baseball Player)
7 Mauroner Dr
Hammond, LA 70401-1728, USA

Stephenson, Kay (Athlete, Football Player)
310 Plantation Hill Rd
Gulf Breeze, FL 32561-4818, USA

Stephenson, Pamela (Actor)
2 Triq Il-Barriera
Balzen BZN 06, Malta

Stephenson, Phil (Athlete, Baseball Player)
1307 Hancock St
Dodge City, KS 67801-3451, USA

Stepp, Craig
6310 San Vicente Blvd Ste 520
Los Angeles, CA 90048-5421

Steppe, Brook (Athlete, Basketball Player)
3486 Clare Cottage Trce SW
Marietta, GA 30008-6075, USA

Steppenwolf (John Kay)
108 E Matilija St
Ojai, CA 93023-2639

Steptoe, Jack (Football Player)
77777 Country Club Dr Apt 109
Palm Desert, CA 92211-0460, USA

Steranko, Jim (Cartoonist)
PO Box 974
Reading, PA 19603-0974, USA

Sterban, Richard (Musician)
88 New Shackle Island Rd
Hendersonville, TN 37075-2393, USA

Stereo Fuse (Music Group)
c/o Staff Member *Wind-up Records*
72 Madison Ave Fl 8
New York, NY 10016-8731, USA

Stereo MC's (Music Group)
c/o Staff Member *Paradigm (Monterey)*
404 W Franklin St
Monterey, CA 93940-2303, USA

Stereophonics (Music Group)
c/o Staff Member *Nettwerk Management (Canada)*
1850 W Second Ave
Vancouver BC V6J 4R3, CANADA

Sterger, Jenn (Model, Television Host)
PO Box 2642
Lutz, FL 33548-2642, USA

Sterkel, Jill (Swimmer)
3025 S Snoddy Rd
Bloomington, IN 47401-9671, USA

Sterling, Annette (Music Group, Musician)
332 Southdown Rd
Lloyd Harbor, NY 11743-1053, USA

Sterling, Ashleigh (Actor)
10 Silkleaf
Irvine, CA 92614-5404, USA

Sterling, Mindy (Actor)
7307 Melrose Ave
Los Angeles, CA 90046-7512, USA

Sterling, Nici (Adult Film Star)
c/o Staff Member *Atlas Multimedia Inc*
9005 Eton Ave Ste C
Canoga Park, CA 91304-6533, USA

Sterling, Rachel (Actor)
c/o Leland LaBarre *Bleu, An Entertainment Company*
5225 Wilshire Blvd Ste 336
Los Angeles, CA 90036-4380, USA

Sterling, Randy (Athlete, Baseball Player)
2516 Linda Ave
Key West, FL 33040-5114, USA

Sterling, Tisha (Actor)
PO Box 788
Ketchum, ID 83340-0788, USA

Stern, Andrew L (Misc)
1313 L St NW
Washington, DC 20005-4110, USA

Stern, Bert (Photographer)
330 E 39th St
New York, NY 10016-2187, USA

Stern, Daniel (Actor)
PO Box 6788
Malibu, CA 90264-6788, USA

Stern, David J (Basketball Player, Misc)
122 E 55th St
New York, NY 10022-4535, USA

Stern, Dawn (Actor)
c/o Holly Shelton *Precision Entertainment*
6338 Wilshire Blvd
Los Angeles, CA 90048-5002, USA

Stern, Ellen (Stylist)
6231 SW 116th Pl
Miami, FL 33173-4792, USA

Stern, Fritz R (Historian)
15 Claremont Ave
New York, NY 10027-6809, USA

Stern, Gardner (Producer, Writer)
c/o Rick Rosen *WmE2 (Endeavor-LA)*
9601 Wilshire Blvd Fl 3
Beverly Hills, CA 90210-5219, USA

Stern, Gary H (Financier, Government Official)
PO Box 291
Minneapolis, MN 55480-0291, USA

Stern, Howard (Radio Personality, Talk Show Host)
1221 Avenue of the Americas
New York, NY 10020-1001, USA

Stern, Howard K (Attorney, Reality TV Star)
c/o Staff Member *E! Entertainment Television (LA)*
5750 Wilshire Blvd
Los Angeles, CA 90036-3697, USA

Stern, Joseph (Actor, Producer)
c/o Chris Simonian *Creative Artists Agency (CAA-LA)*
2000 Avenue of the Stars Ste 100
Los Angeles, CA 90067-4705, USA

Stern, Michael (Mike) (Musician)
163 3rd Ave # 206
New York, NY 10003-2523, USA

Stern, Richard G (Writer)
English Dept
Chicago, IL 60637, USA

Stern, Robert A M (Architect)
460 W 34th St
New York, NY 10001-2320, USA

Stern, Shoshannah (Actor)
c/o David Ginsberg *Insight*
1134 S Cloverdale Ave
Los Angeles, CA 90019-6737, USA

Sternberg, Thomas (Business Person)
PO Box 9265
Framingham, MA 01701-9265, USA

Sternecky, Neal (Cartoonist)
52 Bluebird Ln
Naperville, IL 60565-1347, USA

Sternhagen, Frances (Actor)
152 Sutton Manor Rd
New Rochelle, NY 10801-5756, USA

Sternin, Joshua (Actor)
c/o Staff Member *International Creative Management (ICM-LA)*
10250 Constellation Blvd Fl 7
Los Angeles, CA 90067-6207, USA

Sternoff, Miriam (Stylist)
c/o Celebrity Stylist *Oliver Piro Inc*
725 Riverside Dr Apt 3A
New York, NY 10031-2460, USA

Sterrett, Samuel B (Judge)
400 2nd St NW
Washington, DC 20217-0001, USA

Sterzinsky, Georg Maximilian Cardinal (Religious Leader)
Wundstr 48/50
Berlin 14057, GERMANY

Stetson, Mark (Designer, Special Effects Designer)
c/o Staff Member *International Creative Management (ICM-LA)*
10250 Constellation Blvd Fl 7
Los Angeles, CA 90067-6207, USA

Stetter, Karl (Biologist)
Universitatsstr 31
Regensburg 93053, GERMANY

Stetter, Mitch (Athlete, Baseball Player)
3120 N Marigold Dr
Phoenix, AZ 85018-6741, USA

Steuert-Armstrong, Beverly (Baseball Player)
211 Cathi Ln
Kernersville, NC 27284-9363, USA

Steussie, Todd E (Athlete, Football Player)
34535 Emigrant Trl
Shingletown, CA 96088-9342, USA

Steve Miller Band (Music Group)
c/o Staff Member *Paradigm (Nashville)*
124 12th Ave S Ste 410
Nashville, TN 37203-3170, USA

Stevens, Amber (Actor)
c/o Robert Enriquez *Red Baron Management*
1600 Rosecrans Ave PMB 4
Manhattan Beach, CA 90266-3708, USA

Stevens, Andrew (Actor)
9300 Wilshire Blvd Ste 410
Beverly Hills, CA 90212-3228, USA

Stevens, April (Music Group, Musician)
19530 Superior St
Northridge, CA 91324-1648, USA

Stevens, Bob (Producer)
c/o Staff Member *United Talent Agency (UTA)*
9560 Wilshire Blvd Fl 5
Beverly Hills, CA 90212-2400, USA

Stevens, Brinke (Actor, Athlete)
PO Box 7112
Van Nuys, CA 91409-7112, USA

Stevens, Cat
Steinhauser Str. 3
Munich, GERMANY 81677

Stevens, Cat (Yusef Islam) (Music Group, Musician, Songwriter, Writer)
Ariola Steinhauser Str 3
Munich 81667, USA

Stevens, Chuck (Photographer)
PO Box 422782
San Francisco, CA 94142-2782, USA

Stevens, Chuck (Athlete, Baseball Player)
12591 George Reyburn Rd
Garden Grove, CA 92845-2404, USA

Stevens, Connie (Actor, Music Group, Musician)
243 Delfern Dr
Los Angeles, CA 90077-3544, USA

Stevens, Courtenay J (Actor)
943 Queen St E2nd Fl
Toronto, ON M4M 1J6, CANADA

Stevens, Dave (Athlete, Baseball Player)
2630 Candlewood Way
La Habra, CA 90631-6203, USA

Stevens, Dodie (Musician)
c/o Jim Wagner *American Management*
19948 Mayall St
Chatsworth, CA 91311-3522, USA

Stevens, Earl (E-40) (Musician)
c/o Staff Member *Warner Bros Records (LA)*
PO Box 6868
Burbank, CA 91510-6868, USA

Stevens, Ed (Athlete, Baseball Player)
805 S Holland St
Bellville, TX 77418-2513, USA

Stevens, Eileen (Activist)
126 Marion St
Sayville, NY 11782-1806, USA

Stevens, Fisher (Actor)
329 N Orange Grove Ave
Los Angeles, CA 90036-2135, USA

Stevens, George Jr (Producer)
John F Kennedy Ctr
Washington, DC 20566-0001, USA

Stevens, Howard (Football Player)
834 Saint Catherines Dr
Wake Forest, NC 27587-6639, USA

Stevens, Jeremy (Actor, Producer, Writer)
c/o Staff Member *WmE2 (WMA-LA)*
1 William Morris Pl
Beverly Hills, CA 90212-4261, USA

Stevens, Jerramy (Athlete, Football Player)
10047 Main St Apt 515
Bellevue, WA 98004-5319, USA

Stevens, John Paul (Judge)
1 1st St NE
Washington, DC 20543-0001, USA

Stevens, Katie (Musician)
c/o Simon Fuller *XIX Entertainment*
33/32 Ransomes Dock 35-37 Parkgate Rd
London SW11 4NP, UK

Stevens, Kenneth N (Engineer)
15298 SE Oregon Trail Dr
Clackamas, OR 97015-5421, USA

Stevens, Kevin M (Athlete, Hockey Player)
37 Hawkins Pl
Duxbury, MA 02332-4537, USA

Stevens, Laraine
10800 Chalon Rd
Los Angeles, CA 90077-3220

Stevens, Lee (Athlete, Baseball Player)
9157 Buck Hill Dr
Highlands Ranch, CO 80126-5042, USA

Stevens, Mick
PO Box 344
West Tisbury, MA 02575-0344

Stevens, R C (Athlete, Baseball Player)
1405 Mound St
Davenport, IA 52803-3333, USA

Stevens, Rachel (Actor, Musician)
c/o Kat Gosling *Finch & Partners*
Top Floor 29-37 Heddon St
London W1B 4BR, UNITED KINGDOM

Stevens, Ray (Musician, Songwriter, Writer)
1707 Grand Ave
Nashville, TN 37212-2205, USA

Stevens, Richard (Football Player)
4100 Cimmaron Trl
Granbury, TX 76049-5252, USA

Stevens, Rise (Opera Singer)
930 5th Ave
New York, NY 10021-2651, USA

Stevens, Robert B (Educator)
Leconfield House Curzon St
London W1Y 8AS, UNITED KINGDOM (UK)

Stevens, Robert J (Business Person)
6801 Rockledge Dr
Bethesda, MD 20817-1803, USA

Stevens, Rogers (Musician)
9229 W Sunset Blvd Ste 607
Los Angeles, CA 90069-3406, USA

Stevens, Ronnie (Actor)
125 Gloucester Road
London SW7 4IE, UNITED KINGDOM (UK)

Stevens, Scott (Athlete, Hockey Player)
280 Spook Hollow Rd
Far Hills, NJ 07931-2707, USA

Stevens, Shadoe (Radio Personality)
2934 N Beverly Glen Cir # 399
Los Angeles, CA 90077-1724, USA

Stevens, Shakin' (Music Group, Musician)
c/o Ed Stringfellow *Agency Group Ltd, The (UK)*
361-373 City Rd
London EC1V 1PQ, UK

Stevens, Stella (Actor, Model)
c/o Maria Calabrese *MC Squared Entertainment*
17545 Weddington St
Encino, CA 91316-2566, USA

Stevens, Steve (Musician)
c/o Staff Member *J H Cohn LLP*
720 E Palisade Ave
Englewood Cliffs, NJ 07632-3053, USA

Stevens, Steven (Actor)
3518 Cahuenga Blvd W
Los Angeles, CA 90068-1304, USA

Stevens, Sufjan (Musician)
c/o Ali Hedrick *Billions Corporation, The*
3522 W Armitage Ave
Chicago, IL 60647-3603, USA

Stevens, Tony (Musician)
PO Box 770850
Orlando, FL 32877-0850, USA

Stevens, Warren (Actor)
14155 Magnolia Blvd Apt 27
Sherman Oaks, CA 91423-1143, USA

Stevens, William S (Football Player)
PO Box 221320
El Paso, TX 79913-4320, USA

Stevenson, Cynthia (Actor)
c/o Elizabeth Much *Much and House Public Relations*
8075 W 3rd St Ste 500
Los Angeles, CA 90048-4325, USA

Stevenson, DeShawn (Basketball Player)
Delta Center 301 W South Temple
Salt Lake City, UT 84101, USA

Stevenson, James (Actor)
c/o Melissa Prophet *Melissa Prophet Management*
Prefers to be contacted by telephone
CA, USA

Stevenson, Juliet (Actor)
68 Pall Mall
London SW1Y 5ES, UNITED KINGDOM (UK)

Stevenson, Parker (Actor)
c/o Laina Cohn *Laina Cohn Management*
15066 Sutton St
Sherman Oaks, CA 91403-4020, USA

Stevenson, Ray (Actor)
c/o Liz Nelson *Conway van Gelder*
8-12 Broadwick St
London W1F 8HW, UK

Stevenson, Rosemary (Baseball Player)
19123 120th Ave
Nunica, MI 49448-9460, USA

Stevenson, Teofilo
Hotel Havana Libre
Havana, CUBA

Stevenson Lorenzo, Teofilo (Boxer)
Hotel Havana Libre
Havana, CUBA

Stever, H Guyford (Educator, Engineer)
59 Randolph Hill Rd
Randolph, NH 03593-5138, USA

Steverson, Todd (Athlete, Baseball Player)
109 W Glenhaven Dr
Phoenix, AZ 85045-0717, USA

Steward, Emanuel (Boxer, Misc)
19244 Bretton Dr
Detroit, MI 48223-1364, USA

Steward, Robert L
2864 S Circle Dr Ste 800
Colorado Springs, CO 80906-4163, USA

Stewart, Al (Music Group, Musician, Songwriter, Writer)
14011 Ventura Blvd Ste 405
Sherman Oaks, CA 91423-5230, USA

Stewart, Alana (Actor)
c/o Arnold Robinson *Rogers & Cowan PR (LA)*
Pacific Design Center 8687 Melrose Ave, 7th Floor
West Hollywood, CA 90069, USA

Stewart, Alec (Cricketer)
Kennington Oval
London SE11 5SS, UNITED KINGDOM (UK)

Stewart, Alexandra
37 Ave De La Dame Blanche
Fontenay-Bois, FRANCE 94120

Stewart, Amy (Actor)
c/o Lisa DiSante-Frank *DiSante Frank & Company*
10061 Riverside Dr # 377
Toluca Lake, CA 91602-2560, USA

Stewart, Andy (Athlete, Baseball Player)
641 Geddes St
Wilmington, DE 19805-3718, USA

Stewart, Bill (Musician)
6920 W Sunset Blvd
Los Angeles, CA 90028-7010, USA

Stewart, Bill (Athlete, Baseball Player)
44842 Aspen Ridge Dr
Northville, MI 48168-4435, USA

Stewart, Boo Boo (Actor)
c/o Staff Member *Osbrink Talent Agency*
4343 Lankershim Blvd Ste 100
West Toluca Lake, CA 91602-2705, USA

Stewart, Catherine Mary (Actor)
350 Dupont St
Toronto, ON M5R 1Z9, Canada

Stewart, Curtis (Football Player)
873 April Ct
Montgomery, AL 36105-2430, USA

Stewart, Danica (Actor)
c/o Terrance Hines *Hines and Hunt Entertainment*
1213 W Magnolia Blvd
Burbank, CA 91506-1829, USA

Stewart, Dave (Athlete, Baseball Player)
17762 Vineyard Ln
Poway, CA 92064-1061, USA

Stewart, David A (Dave) (Composer, Musician)
c/o Allison Elbl *ID PR (LA)*
7060 Hollywood Blvd Fl 8
Los Angeles, CA 90028-6014, USA

Stewart, David K (Dave) (Baseball Player)
17762 Vineyard Ln
Poway, CA 92064-1061, USA

Stewart, Elizabeth (Stylist)
c/o Staff Member *Cloutier Agency*
2632 La Cienega Ave
Los Angeles, CA 90034-2641, USA

Stewart, Freddie
4862 Excelente Dr
Woodland Hills, CA 91364-4011

Stewart, French (Actor)
c/o J.C. (JC) Robbins *JC Robbins Management*
113 S Kilkea Dr
Los Angeles, CA 90048-3525, USA

Stewart, Ian (Government Official)
Westminster
London SW1A 0AA, UNITED KINGDOM (UK)

Stewart, James B (Journalist)
200 Liberty St
New York, NY 10281-1003, USA

Stewart, James C (War Hero)
8793 Grape Wagon Cir
San Jose, CA 95135-2161, USA

Stewart, Jermaine (Music Group, Musician)
1800 Argyle Ave # 408
Los Angeles, CA 90028-5253, USA

Stewart, Jimmy (Athlete, Football Player)
3609 Tartan Dr
Metairie, LA 70003-1637, USA

Stewart, Jimmy (Athlete, Baseball Player)
15644 Eastbourn Dr
Odessa, FL 33556-2850, USA

Stewart, John Y (Jackie) (Race Car Driver)
Silverstone Cicuit
Northamptonshire NN12 8TN, UNITED KINGDOM (UK)

Stewart, Jon (Actor, Comedian, Television Host)
604 W 52nd St
New York, NY 10019-5013, USA

Stewart, Josh (Actor)
c/o Lena Roklin *Luber Roklin Management*
8530 Wilshire Blvd Ste 550
Beverly Hills, CA 90211-3133, USA

Stewart, Josh (Athlete, Baseball Player)
182 Stewart Ln
Ledbetter, KY 42058-9549, USA

Stewart, Kimberly (Actor, Model)
c/o Kenya Knight *Nous Model Management*
117 N Robertson Blvd
Los Angeles, CA 90048-3101, USA

Stewart, Kordell (Athlete, Football Player)
5950 Sherry Ln Ste 700
Dallas, TX 75225-6562, USA

Stewart, Kristen (Actor)
c/o Ruth Bernstein *Viewpoint Inc*
8820 Wilshire Blvd Ste 220
Beverly Hills, CA 90211-2622, USA

Stewart, Lisa (Musician)
1344 Lexington Ave
New York, NY 10128-1507, USA

Stewart, Lisa (Actor, Producer)
c/o Staff Member *Vinyl Films*
5555 Melrose Ave
Los Angeles, CA 90038-3989, USA

Stewart, Martha (Business Person, Talk Show Host)
601 W 26th St Fl 9
New York, NY 10001-1101, USA

Stewart, Mary (Writer)
House of Letterawe Lock Awe
Argyll PA33 1AH, SCOTLAND

Stewart, Maxine (Actor)
180 Comanche
Topanga, CA 90290-4426, USA

Stewart, Melvin Jr (Swimmer)
c/o Scott Karp *Crystal Sky Pictures*
10203 Santa Monica Blvd Ste 500
Los Angeles, CA 90067-6416, USA

Stewart, Michael (Football Player)
717 Palo Verde St
Bakersfield, CA 93309-1863, USA

Stewart, Natalie (Musician, Songwriter, Writer)
9268 W 3rd St
Beverly Hills, CA 90210-3713, USA

Stewart, Norman (Athlete, Basketball Player)
5550 Highway 63 Athletic S Dept
Columbia, MO 65201, USA

Stewart, Norman W (Stylist)
c/o Staff Member *Zenobia Agency Inc*
PO Box 909
Groveland, CA 95321-0909, USA

Stewart, Patrick (Actor, Director, Producer)
c/o Staff Member *ID Public Relations (ID-LA)*
7080 Hollywood Blvd Fl 8
Los Angeles, CA 90028-6906, USA

Stewart, Paul Anthony (Actor)
c/o Paul Reisman *Abrams Artists Agency (NY)*
275 7th Ave Fl 26
New York, NY 10001-6708, USA

Stewart, Peggy (Actor)
PO Box 2468
N Hollywood, CA 91602-1878, USA

Stewart, Potter (Judge)
100 E 5th St
Cincinnati, OH 45202-3905, USA

Stewart, Ray (Golfer)
2777 Dehavilland Pl
Abbotsford, BC V2T 5E2, CANADA

Stewart, Robert L (Astronaut, General)
815 Sun Valley Dr
Woodland Park, CO 80863-7729, USA

Stewart, Rod (Actor, Musician)
1435 S Ocean Blvd
Palm Beach, FL 33480-5005, USA

Stewart, Ronald G (Ron) (Athlete, Hockey Player)
4010 N 11th St Apt 3
Phoenix, AZ 85014-4835, USA

Stewart, Ryan (Football Player)
2715 Owens Ave SW
Marietta, GA 30064-4253, USA

Stewart, Sammy (Athlete, Baseball Player)
Craggy Correctional Center P.O. Box 399 #0390745
Asheville, NC 28814, USA

Stewart, Scott (Actor)
c/o Jeff Okin *Anonymous Content (AC-LA)*
3531 Hayden Ave
Culver City, CA 90232, USA

Stewart, Scott (Athlete, Baseball Player)
5243 Hickory Knoll Ln
Mount Holly, NC 28120-9344, USA

Stewart, Shannon (Athlete, Baseball Player)
14348 SW 156th Ave
Miami, FL 33196-6072, USA

Stewart, Shannon H (Athlete, Baseball Player)
14348 SW 156th Ave
Miami, FL 33196-6072, USA

Stewart, Steve (Football Player)
1161 Jeans Ln
Amery, WI 54001-5109, USA

Stewart, Thomas J Jr (Opera Singer)
165 W 57th St
New York, NY 10019-2201, USA

Stewart, Tonea (Actor)
Theater Arts Dept
Montgomery, AL 36101, USA

Stewart, Tony (Race Car Driver)
5644 W 74th St
Indianapolis, IN 46278-1752, USA

Stewart, Tyler (Musician)
8730 Wilshire Blvd # 304
Beverly Hills, CA 90211-2716, USA

Stewart, Will Foster (Actor)
8730 Santa Monica Blvd # 1
Los Angeles, CA 90069-4547, USA

Stewart-Hardway, Donna (Actor)
PO Box 777
Pinch, WV 25156-0777, USA

Steyn, Mark (Writer)
PO Box 30
Woodsville, NH 03785-0030, USA

Stezer, Philip (Musician)
3 Burlington Lane Chiswick
London W4 2TH, UNITED KINGDOM (UK)

Stich, Michael (Tennis Player)
Ernst-Barlach-Str 44
Elmshom 25336, GERMANY

Sticht, J Paul (Business Person)
11732 Lake House Ct
North Palm Beach, FL 33408-3320, USA

Stickel, Fred A (Publisher)
1320 SW Broadway
Portland, OR 97201-3411, USA

Stickler, Alfons M Cardinal (Religious Leader)
Piazza del S Uffizio 11
Rome 193, ITALY

Stickles, Montford (Monty) (Football Player)
1363 3rd Ave
San Francisco, CA 94122-2718, USA

Stickles, Ted (Swimmer)
1142 Sharynwood Dr
Baton Rouge, LA 70808-6069, USA

Stidham, Howard (Athlete, Football Player)
438 John Mark Ct
Manchester, TN 37355-8491, USA

Stidham, Phil (Athlete, Baseball Player)
5025 Malabar Blvd
Melbourne Beach, FL 32951-3268, USA

Stieb, David (Dave) A (Athlete, Baseball Player)
10860 Shay Ln
Reno, NV 89511-9505, USA

Stieber, Tamar (Journalist)
7777 Jefferson St NE
Albuquerque, NM 87109-4343, USA

Stief, Dave (Football Player)
PO Box 343
Corbett, OR 97019-0343, USA

Stiefel, Ethan (Ballerina)
890 Broadway
New York, NY 10003-1211, USA

Stiegler, Josef (Pepi) (Skier)
PO Box 290
Teton Village, WY 83025-0290, USA

Stienke, Jim (Football Player)
4707 Interlachen Ln
Austin, TX 78747-1457, USA

Stiers, David Ogden (Actor)
c/o Staff Member *Mitchell K Stubbs & Assoc (MKS)*
8675 Washington Blvd Ste 203
Culver City, CA 90232-7486, USA

Stieve, Terry (Athlete, Football Player)
1407 Vail Pl
Saint Louis, MO 63104-2570, USA

Stigers, Curtis (Actor, Musician)
32 Court St Fl 16
Brooklyn, NY 11201-4441, USA

Stiglitz, Joseph E (Nobel Prize Laureate)
International Affairs Building
New York, NY 10027, USA

Stigman, Dick (Athlete, Baseball Player)
12914 5th Ave S
Burnsville, MN 55337-3504, USA

Stigwood, Robert
122 E 42nd St
New York, NY 10168-0002

Stigwood, Robert C (Producer)
Whippingham East Cowes
Isle of Wight PO32 6LB, UNITED KINGDOM (UK)

Stiles, Darron (Athlete, Golfer)
130 Wild Turkey Run
Pinehurst, NC 28374-9658, USA

Stiles, Jackie (Basketball Player)
115 E Hamilton St
Claflin, KS 67525-5200, USA

Stiles, Julia (Actor)
c/o Jason Weinberg *Untitled Entertainment (LA)*
350 S Beverly Dr Ste 200
Beverly Hills, CA 90212-4819, USA

Stiles, Ryan (Actor, Comedian)
c/o Kay Liberman *Liberman/Zerman Management*
252 N Larchmont Blvd Ste 200
Los Angeles, CA 90004-3754, USA

Stilgoe, Richard (Songwriter, Writer)
24 Denmark St
London WC2H 8NJ, UNITED KINGDOM (UK)

Still, Arthur B (Art) (Athlete, Football Player)
9813 Betsy Ross Ct
Liberty, MO 64068-8418, USA

Still, Bryan (Football Player)
3812 Brennen Robert Pl
Glen Allen, VA 23060-2505, USA

Still, Ken (Golfer)
1210 Princeton St
Fircrest, WA 98466-6035, USA

Still, Ray (Conductor, Musician)
41 W McKinsey Rd # 206
Severna Park, MD 21146-4546, USA

Still, Susan L (Astronaut)
2101 Nasa Pkwy Spc Center
Houston, TX 77058-3607, USA

Still, William C Jr (Misc)
Chemistry Dept
New York, NY 10027, USA

Stiller, Ben (Actor, Comedian, Director)
c/o Kelly Bush *ID PR (LA)*
7060 Hollywood Blvd Fl 8
Los Angeles, CA 90028-6014, USA

Stiller, Jerry (Actor, Comedian)
c/o Pearl Wexler *Kohner Agency, The*
9300 Wilshire Blvd Ste 555
Beverly Hills, CA 90212-3211, USA

Stiller, Stephen (Music Group, Musician)
17525 Ventura Blvd Ste 210
Encino, CA 91316-5111, USA

Stillman, Denise (Stylist)
PO Box 7692
Laguna Niguel, CA 92607-7692, USA

Stillman, Royle (Athlete, Baseball Player)
580 Jb Ct
Glenwood Springs, CO 81601-8733, USA

Stillman, Whit (Director)
8942 Wilshire Blvd # 219
Beverly Hills, CA 90211-1908, USA

Stills, Chris (Musician)
9229 W Sunset Blvd Ste 900
Los Angeles, CA 90069-3410, USA

Stills, Ken (Football Player)
647 Michael St
Oceanside, CA 92057-3505, USA

Stills, Stephen (Musician)
c/o Marsha Vlasic *International Creative Management (ICM-LA)*
10250 Constellation Blvd Fl 7
Los Angeles, CA 90067-6207, USA

Stills, The (Music Group)
c/o Staff Member *Paradigm (Monterey)*
404 W Franklin St
Monterey, CA 93940-2303, USA

Stillwagon, Jim R (Football Player)
3999 Parkway Ln
Hilliard, OH 43026-1252, USA

Stillwell, Kurt (Athlete, Baseball Player)
1105 Lassen View Dr
Westwood, CA 96137-9537, USA

Stillwell, Richard D (Opera Singer)
1969 Rockingham St
McLean, VA 22101-4923, USA

Stillwell, Roger (Football Player)
25 Woodland Ct
Novato, CA 94947-7504, USA

Stillwell, Ron (Athlete, Baseball Player)
1105 Lassen View Dr
Westwood, CA 96137-9537, USA

Stilson, Jeff (Producer)
c/o Staff Member *Creative Artists Agency (CAA-LA)*
2000 Avenue of the Stars Ste 100
Los Angeles, CA 90067-4705, USA

Stilwell, Victoria (Television Host)
c/o Cristina Dennstedt *Sarah Hall Productions Inc*
670 Broadway Rm 504
New York, NY 10012-2318, USA

Stinchcomb, Matt (Athlete, Football Player)
312 Bradford Way
Peachtree City, GA 30269-2311, USA

Stincic, Thomas (Football Player)
2121 E Oasis St
Mesa, AZ 85213-9743, USA

Stine, Richard (Cartoonist, Editor)
PO Box 348
Hansville, WA 98340-0348, USA

Stine, Robert L (R L) (Writer)
555 Broadway
New York, NY 10012-3919, USA

Stine, Robert (RL) (Writer)
225 W 71st St
New York, NY 10023-3726, USA

Sting (Actor, Musician, Producer)
c/o Kathy Schenker *KSM Inc.*
1776 Broadway Ste 1000
New York, NY 10019-2012, USA

Sting, Charlotte (Athlete, Basketball Player)
333 E Trade St
Charlotte, NC 28202-2331, USA

Stingley, Darryl (Football Player)
400 E Randolph St # K125
Chicago, IL 60601-7329, USA

Stinnett, Kelly (Athlete, Baseball Player)
3950 E McLellan Rd Unit 6
Mesa, AZ 85205-3820, USA

Stinson, Bob (Athlete, Baseball Player)
1309 Bando Ln
The Villages, FL 32162-0115, USA

Stipe, Michael (Musician)
1016 Palm Ave
West Hollywood, CA 90069-4059, USA

Stiritz, William P (Business Person)
Checkerboard Sq
Saint Louis, MO 63164-0001, USA

Stirling, Rachel (Actor)
c/o Staff Member *Management Inc*
2032 Pinehurst Rd
Los Angeles, CA 90068-3732

Stirling, Steve (Athlete, Coach, Hockey Player)
11 Hempstead Tpke
Uniondate, NY 11553, USA

Stirvins, Alex (Athlete, Basketball Player)
11330 N Sundown Dr
Scottsdale, AZ 85260-5538, USA

Stitch, Stephen P (Misc)
Philosophy Dept
New Brunswick, NJ 8901, USA

Stith, Bryant (Athlete, Basketball Player)
20697 Governor Harrison Pkwy
Freeman, VA 23856-2451, USA

Stith, Samuel (Athlete, Basketball Player)
36 Madison St NE
Washington, DC 20011-2352, USA

Stith, Thomas (Athlete, Basketball Player)
105 Overlook Dr
Farmingville, NY 11738-3107, USA

Stits, Bill (Football Player)
1177 Eolus Ave
Encinitas, CA 92024-1727, USA

Stobart, John (Artist)
61 3/4 Bat Club Dr
Fort Lauderdale, FL 33308, USA

Stobbs, Chuck (Athlete, Baseball Player)
1731 Riviera Cir
Sarasota, FL 34232-3509, USA

Stock, Barbara (Actor)
22532 Margarita Dr
Woodland Hills, CA 91364-4030, USA

Stock, Mark (Football Player)
9344 Crest Hill Rd
Marshall, VA 20115-3017, USA

Stock, Wes (Athlete, Baseball Player)
PO Box 1309
Allyn, WA 98524-1309, USA

Stockdale, Charlotte (Stylist)
c/o Staff Member *Camilla Lowther Managment (CLM Represents)*
30-32 Ericsson Pl
New York, NY 10013, USA

Stockdale, Gretchen
520 Washington Blvd # 248
Marina del Rey, CA 90292

Stockdale, James
Hoover Inst
Stanford, CA 94305-6010, USA

Stockemer, Ralph (Athlete, Football Player)
4001 Madison Cir
Plano, TX 75023-5910, USA

Stocker, Kevin (Athlete, Baseball Player)
1204 N Murray Ln
Liberty Lake, WA 99019-7555, USA

Stocker-Bottazzi, Jeanette (Baseball Player)
1440 W Walnut St Apt 811
Allentown, PA 18102-4444, USA

Stockhausen, Karl-Heinz
Stockhausen-Verlag
Kuerten, GERMANY D-51515

Stockhausen, Karlheinz (Composer)
Stockhausen-Vertag
Kurten 51515, GERMANY

Stockman, David A (Financier, Government Official)
345 Park Ave
New York, NY 10154-0004, USA

Stockman, Shawn (Music Group, Musician)
c/o Steve C Smith *Creative Talent Management Group (CTMG)*
433 N Camden Dr Ste 600
Beverly Hills, CA 90210-4416, USA

Stockmayer, Walter H (Doctor, Misc)
Willey Hill
Norwich, VT 5055, USA

Stockton, Dave K (Golfer)
30378 Copper Hill Ct
Redlands, CA 92373-7373, USA

Stockton, David (Golfer)
30378 Copper Hill Ct
Redlands, CA 92373-7373, USA

Stockton, David Jr (Golfer)
10 Carrera Pl
Rancho Mirage, CA 92270-3227, USA

Stockton, Dick (Sportscaster)
2519 NW 59th St
Boca Raton, FL 33496-2224, USA

Stockton, John H (Athlete, Basketball Player)
800 N Hamilton St
Spokane, WA 99202-2047, USA

Stockton, Richard L (Dick) (Tennis Player)
715 Stadium Dr
San Antonio, TX 78212-7201, USA

Stockwell, Dean (Actor)
95723 Highway 99 W
Junction City, OR 97448-9395, USA

Stockwell, Jeff (Writer)
c/o Staff Member *United Talent Agency (UTA)*
9560 Wilshire Blvd Fl 5
Beverly Hills, CA 90212-2400, USA

Stockwell, John (Actor)
9560 Wilshire Blvd Ste 500
Beverly Hills, CA 90212-2401, USA

Stoddard, Bob (Athlete, Baseball Player)
15760 Sunnyside Ave
Morgan Hill, CA 95037-5331, USA

Stoddard, Brandon
241 N Glenroy Ave
Los Angeles, CA 90049

Stoddard, Tim (Athlete, Baseball Player)
4545 Gettysburg Dr
Rolling Meadows, IL 60008-1105, USA

Stofa, John (Football Player)
7344 Jefferson Meadows Dr
Blacklick, OH 43004-9813, USA

Stofer, Ken (Football Player)
25742 Candlewick Ct
Westlake, OH 44145-1476, USA

Stoicheff, Boris P (Physicist)
66 Collier St # 6B
Toronto, ON M4W 1L9, CANADA

Stoilov, Nickolai (Actor)
c/o Monique Moss *Warren Cowan & Associates PR*
8899 Beverly Blvd Ste 918
Los Angeles, CA 90048-2427, USA

Stoitchkov, Hristo (Soccer Player)
14120 Newbrook Dr
Chantilly, VA 20151-2273, USA

Stojko, Elvis (Figure Skater)
2 Saint Clair Ave E
Toronto, ON M4T 2T, CANADA

Stokes, Chris (Business Person, Director, Musician)
c/o Staff Member *Tobin & Associates PR*
4929 Wilshire Blvd Ste 245
Los Angeles, CA 90010-3859, USA

Stokes, Fred (Football Player)
4673 Anson Ln
Orlando, FL 32814-6074, USA

Stokes, Greg (Athlete, Basketball Player)
2505 Plymouth St
Marion, IA 52302-5609, USA

Stokes, Jesse (Football Player)
5810 Cayuga Dr
San Antonio, TX 78228-4325, USA

Stokes, Sims (Football Player)
1011 Wind Ridge Cir
Duncanville, TX 75137-3741, USA

Stokes of Leyland, Donald G (Business Person)
2 Branksome Cliff Westminster Road
Poole
Dorset BH13 6JW, UNITED KINGDOM (UK)

Stokkan, Bill (Race Car Driver)
5350 Lakeview Parkway South Dr
Indianapolis, IN 46268-5129, USA

Stokley, Brandon (Athlete, Football Player)
12479 Autumn Gate Way
Carmel, IN 46033-8284, USA

Stoklos, Randy (Athlete, Volleyball Player)
PO Box 1714
Pacific Palisades, CA 90272-1714, USA

Stole, Mink (Actor)
635 Colorado Ave Apt 3B
Baltimore, MD 21210-2135, USA

Stolhandske, Tom (Football Player)
518 Mirepoix
San Antonio, TX 78232-1950, USA

Stolhanske, Erik (Comedian)
c/o Staff Member *United Talent Agency (UTA)*
9560 Wilshire Blvd Fl 5
Beverly Hills, CA 90212-2400, USA

Stolle, Frederick S (Tennis Player)
19735 Turnberry Way
Miami, FL 33180-2797, USA

Stoller, Mike (Composer)
9000 W Sunset Blvd
West Hollywood, CA 90069-5801, USA

Stoller, Nicholas (Director)

Stollery, David (Actor)
3203 Bern Ct
Laguna Beach, CA 92651-2007, USA

Stolley, Paul D (Doctor)
10205 Wincopin Cir Apt 312
Columbia, MD 21044-3435, USA

Stolley, Richard B (Editor)
Time-Life Building Rockefeller Center
New York, NY 10020, USA

Stolojan, Theodor (Prime Minister)
1818 H St NW
Washington, DC 20433-0001, USA

Stolper, Pinchas (Religious Leader)
11 Broadway
New York, NY 10004-1301, USA

Stoltenberg, Bryan (Football Player)
3207 W Farmington Ln
Sugar Land, TX 77479-1883, USA

Stoltz, Eric (Actor, Director, Producer)
c/o Helen Sugland *Landmark Artists*
4116 W Magnolia Blvd Ste 101
Burbank, CA 91505-2700, USA

Stolze, Lena (Actor)
Neuroeder Str 1C
Planegg 82152, GERMANY

Stomare, Peter
1129 N Poinsettia Pl
West Hollywood, CA 90046-5715

Stone, Albert L (Race Car Driver)
700 Central Ave PO Box 8427
Louisville, KY 40208, USA

Stone, Andrew L (Director)
2132 Century Park Ln Apt 212
Los Angeles, CA 90067-3320, USA

Stone, Angie (Musician)
c/o Reina King *Paradigm (LA)*
360 N Crescent Dr
Beverly Hills, CA 90210-4874, USA

Stone, Benjamin (Actor)
c/o Mara Santino *Luber Roklin Management*
8530 Wilshire Blvd Ste 550
Beverly Hills, CA 90211-3133, USA

Stone, Curtis (Chef, Television Host)
c/o Todd Jacobs *WmE2 (Endeavor-LA)*
9601 Wilshire Blvd Fl 3
Beverly Hills, CA 90210-5219, USA

Stone, Dean (Athlete, Baseball Player)
213 13th St
Silvis, IL 61282-1267, USA

Stone, Debbie (Stylist)
c/o Staff Member *Independent NY*
15 E 30th St Apt 401
New York, NY 10016-7031, USA

Stone, Dee Wallace (Actor)
c/o Laura Pallas *Pallas Management*
5301 Bellaire Ave
Valley Village, CA 91607-2329, US

Stone, Doug (Musician)
PO Box 943
Springfield, TN 37172-0943

Stone, Eddie (Adult Film Star)
c/o Staff Member *Diva Central Inc*
7510 W Sunset Blvd Ste 1445
Los Angeles, CA 90046-3408, USA

Stone, Edward C Jr (Physicist)
4800 Oak Grove Dr # 180-904
Pasadena, CA 91109-8001, USA

Stone, Emma (Actor)
c/o Doug Wald *Anonymous Content (AC-LA)*
545 Veteran Ave
Los Angeles, CA 90024-1915, USA

Stone, Gene (Athlete, Baseball Player)
6897 Highway 262 SE
Othello, WA 99344-9761, USA

Stone, George H (Athlete, Baseball Player)
1304 Fairfield Dr
Ruston, LA 71270-3540, USA

Stone, Jack (Religious Leader)
6401 Paseo Blvd
Kansas City, MO 64131-1213, USA

Stone, Jack (Football Player)
16125 Crestridge Ave
Sonora, CA 95370-8542, USA

Stone, James L (War Hero)
3102 Avon Dr
Arlington, TX 76015-2001, USA

Stone, Jeff (Athlete, Baseball Player)
RR 2 Box 392
Portageville, MO 63873, USA

Stone, Jennifer (Actor)
c/o Laura Ackerman *Much and House Public Relations*
8075 W 3rd St Ste 500
Los Angeles, CA 90048-4325, USA

Stone, Joss (Musician, Songwriter)
c/o Patrick Confrey *Sunshine, Sachs & Associates*
149 5th Ave Fl 7
New York, NY 10010-6824, USA

Stone, Ken (Football Player)
16 W Riverside Dr
Jupiter, FL 33469-2960, USA

Stone, Lara (Model)
c/o Staff Member *IMG (NY)*
432 W 45th St Fl 5
New York, NY 10036-3503, USA

Stone, Leonard (Actor)
6404 Wilshire Blvd Ste 950
Los Angeles, CA 90048-5529, USA

Stone, Matt (Animator, Writer)
c/o Mike Simpson *WmE2 (Endeavor-LA)*
9601 Wilshire Blvd Fl 3
Beverly Hills, CA 90210-5219, USA

Stone, Michael (Athlete, Football Player)
c/o Eugene Parker *Maximum Sports Management*
6435 W Jefferson Blvd # 197
Fort Wayne, IN 46804-6203, USA

Stone, Nikki (Skier)
PO Box 680-332
Park City, UT 84068, USA

Stone, Oliver (Actor, Director, Producer, Writer)
c/o Bryan Lourd *Creative Artists Agency (CAA-LA)*
2000 Avenue of the Stars Ste 100
Los Angeles, CA 90067-4705, USA

Stone, Ricky (Athlete, Baseball Player)
6494 Lakeview Ct
Hamilton, OH 45011-8139, USA

Stone, Rob
8033 W Sunset Blvd # 450
Los Angeles, CA 90046-2401

Stone, Robert A (Writer)
121 W 27th St Ste 704
New York, NY 10001-6262, USA

Stone, Robert B. (Writer)
Sand Not. 24, North Building Former-Estate Guadalupe
Chimalistac, Mexico

Stone, Roger D (Politician)
34 W 88th St
New York, NY 10024-2558, USA

Stone, Ron (Athlete, Baseball Player)
11720 NW Lovejoy St
Portland, OR 97229-5028, USA

Stone, Sammy
PO Box 2825
Port Arthur, TX 77643-2825

Stone, Sharon (Actor)
c/o Chuck Binder *Binder & Associates*
1465 Lindacrest Dr
Beverly Hills, CA 90210-2519, USA

Stone, Steven M (Steve) (Athlete, Baseball Player, Sportscaster)
9261 N 128th Way
Scottsdale, AZ 85259-6233, USA

Stone, William J (Football Player)
618 Woodland Knolls Rd
Germantown Hills, IL 61548-9429, USA

Stone Foxes, The (Music Group, Musician)
c/o Rob Weldon *Wingman Music*
Prefers to be contacted by email or telephone
CA, USA

Stone III, Charles (Actor, Director, Writer)
c/o Barbara Dreyfus *United Talent Agency (UTA)*
9560 Wilshire Blvd Fl 5
Beverly Hills, CA 90212-2400, USA

Stone Sour (Music Group)
c/o Cory Brennan *Sanctuary Artist Management (NY)*
75 9th Ave
New York, NY 10011-7006, USA

Stone Temple Pilots (Music Group)
c/o Rod MacSween *International Talent Booking*
1st Floor, Ariel House 74A Charlotte St
London W1T 4QJ, UNITED KINGDOM

Stonebreaker, Mike (Football Player)
3300 Delaware Ave Apt A
Kenner, LA 70065-3689, USA

Stonecipher, David A (Financier)
100 N Greene St
Greensboro, NC 27401-2547, USA

Stonecipher, Harry C (Business Person)
PO Box 3707
Seattle, WA 98124-2207, USA

Stoneman, Bill (Athlete, Baseball Player)
2519 N San Miguel Dr
Orange, CA 92867-8604, USA

Stoner, Alyson (Musician)
c/o Cindy Osbrink *Osbrink Talent Agency*
4343 Lankershim Blvd Ste 100
West Toluca Lake, CA 91602-2705, USA

Stoner, Sherri (Actor, Producer, Writer)
c/o Tom Strickler *WmE2 (Endeavor-LA)*
9601 Wilshire Blvd Fl 3
Beverly Hills, CA 90210-5219, USA

Stone-Richards, Lucille (Baseball Player)
65 Anchor Ct
Marco Island, FL 34145-4703, USA

Stones
4790 Irvine Blvd Ste 105
Irvine, CA 92620-1998

Stones, Dwight E (Athlete, Track Athlete)
4790 Irvine Blvd Ste 105
Irvine, CA 92620-1998, USA

Stonesifer, Don (Football Player)
557 McHenry Rd Apt 218
Wheeling, IL 60090-9207, USA

Stonesipher, Don (Football Player)
557 McHenry Rd Apt 218
Wheeling, IL 60090-9207, USA

Stonestreet, Eric (Actor)
c/o Suzanne (Sue) Wohl *TalentWorks (LA)*
3500 W Olive Ave Ste 1400
Burbank, CA 91505-5512, USA

Stookey, Paul (Music Group, Musician, Songwriter, Writer)
RR 175
South Blue Hill Falls, ME 4615, USA

Stoops, Bob (Coach, Football Coach)
Athletic Dept 108 Brooks St
Norman, OK 73069, USA

Stoops, Jim (Athlete, Baseball Player)
205 Foster Dr
Oswego, IL 60543-4053, USA

Stoops, Mike (Coach, Football Coach)
Athletes
Tempe, AZ 85287-0001, USA

Stopanovich, Steve (Athlete, Basketball Player)
14 Ridgecreek
Saint Louis, MO 63141-8042, USA

Stopel, Terry (Football Player)
804 Saddlebrook Dr S
Bedford, TX 76021-5360, USA

Stoppard, Tom S (Writer)
Drury House 34-43 Russell St
London WC2B 5HA, UNITED KINGDOM (UK)

Storaro, Vittorio (Cinematographer)
Via Divino Amore 2
Frattocchie Merino 40, ITALY

Storch, Larry (Actor)
330 W End Ave # 17F
New York, NY 10023-8171, USA

Storch, Scott (Producer)
c/o Tracy Christian *Don Buchwald & Associates Inc (LA)*
6500 Wilshire Blvd Ste 2200
Los Angeles, CA 90048-4942, USA

Storer, Chris (Stylist)
c/o Staff Member *Judy Inc*
1 Yorkville Ave
Toronto ON M4W 1L1, Canada

Storey, David M (Writer)
2 Lyndhurst Gardens
London NW3, UNITED KINGDOM (UK)

Storey, June
338 Morgan Pl
Vista, CA 92083-8018

Storey, Lisa (Stylist)
c/o Staff Member *Independent NY*
15 E 30th St Apt 401
New York, NY 10016-7031, USA

Storey, Meredith (Stylist)
c/o Staff Member *Clutts Agency, The*
1400 Turtle Creek Blvd # 171
Dallas, TX 75207-3337, USA

Stori, Moneca (Actor)
c/o Elena Kirschner *Lucas Talent Inc*
100 W. Pender St Sun Tower, 7th Floor
Vancouver, BC V6B 1R8, Canada

Stork, Gilbert (Misc)
188 Chestnut St
Englewood Cliffs, NJ 07632-1908, USA

Stork, Jeff (Athlete, Coach, Volleyball Player)
18111 Nordhoff St
Northridge, CA 91330-0001, USA

Storke, Adam (Actor)
c/o Marc Epstein *Marc Epstein Entertainment*
108 Breeze Ave
Venice, CA 90291-3360, USA

Storm, Avery (Musician)
c/o Staff Member *Derrty Entertainment*
9648 Olive Blvd # 230
Saint Louis, MO 63132-3002, USA

Storm, Crystal
2139 N University Dr # 297
Coral Springs, FL 33071-6134

Storm, Hannah (Correspondent, Sportscaster)
c/o Staff Member *ESPN (Main)*
ESPN Plaza 935 Middle St
Bristol, CT 06010-1001, USA

Storm, Jim
13576 Cheltenham Dr
Sherman Oaks, CA 91423-4818

Storm, Lauren (Actor)
c/o Staff Member *Aquarius Public Relations*
5320 Sylmar Ave
Sherman Oaks, CA 91401-5612, USA

Storm, Tempest (Dancer)
3905 Cambridge St Unit 3
Las Vegas, NV 89119-7402, USA

Stormare, Peter (Actor)
c/o Jeff Golenberg *Collective*
8383 Wilshire Blvd Ste 1050
Beverly Hills, CA 90211-2415, USA

Stormer, Horst L (Nobel Prize Laureate)
20 E 9th St # 14P
New York, NY 10003-5944, USA

Storms, Kirsten (Actor)
c/o Nils Larsen *Elements Entertainment*
312 W 5th St Apt 815
Los Angeles, CA 90013-1750, USA

Storraro, Vittorio (Cinematographer)
c/o Paul Hook *International Creative Management (ICM-LA)*
10250 Constellation Blvd Fl 7
Los Angeles, CA 90067-6207, USA

Story, Tim (Director)
c/o Staff Member *WmE2 (WMA-LA)*
1 William Morris Pl
Beverly Hills, CA 90212-4261, USA

Story, Winston (Actor)
c/o Brian McCabe *Venture IAB*
8285 W Sunset Blvd Ste 1
West Hollywood, CA 90046-2420, USA

Storz, Erik (Football Player)
114 Andrea Dr
Rockaway, NJ 07866-3702, USA

Stossel, John (Correspondent, Television Host)
c/o Staff Member *NS Bienstock Inc*
250 W 57th St Ste 333
New York, NY 10107-0302, USA

Stott, Kathryn L (Musician)
Mire House West Martor near Skipton
Yorks BD23 3UQ, UNITED KINGDOM (UK)

Stott, Nicole P (Astronaut)
2101 Nasa Pkwy Spc Center
Houston, TX 77058-3607, USA

Stottlemyre, Melvin L (Mel) (Athlete, Baseball Player)
26004 SE 27th St
Sammamish, WA 98075-9140, USA

Stottlemyre, Todd (Athlete, Baseball Player)
6918 E Bronco Dr
Paradise Valley, AZ 85253-3123, USA

Stottlemyre Jr, Mel (Athlete, Baseball Player)
3314 Meadowlark Dr
Lewiston, ID 83501-8609, USA

Stotts, Terry (Coach)
1001 Broadway
Oakland, CA 94607-4019, USA

Stoudamire, Damon (Athlete, Basketball Player)
c/o Lon Rosen *Lagardere Unlimited - (D.C.)*
5335 Wisconsin Ave NW Ste 850
Washington, DC 20015-2052, USA

Stoudemire, Amare (Athlete, Basketball Player)
c/o Happy Walters *Immortal Sports*
12200 W Olympic Blvd Ste 400
Los Angeles, CA 90064-1047, USA

Stouder, Sharon M (Swimmer)
144 Loucks Ave
Los Altos, CA 94022-1045, USA

Stoudt, Bud (Bowler)
431 Lehman St
Lebanon, PA 17046-3639, USA

Stoudt, Cliff (Football Player)
326 Doe Run Cir
Henderson, NV 89012-2701, USA

Stouffer, Kelly (Football Player)
HC 81 Box 55
Rushville, NE 69360-9729, USA

Stovall, Da Rond (Athlete, Baseball Player)
1107 Goelz Dr
East Saint Louis, IL 62203-1917, USA

Stovall, Jerry L (Football Player)
7948 Wrenwood Blvd Apt C
Baton Rouge, LA 70809-1787, USA

Stove, Betty (Tennis Player)
1025 Thomas Jefferson St NW # 450
Washington, DC 20007-5201, USA

Stover, George (Actor)
PO Box 10005
Baltimore, MD 21285-0005, USA

Stover, Irwin Russ Juno (Athlete, Swimmer)
512 Lanai Cir
Union City, CA 94587-4113, USA

Stover, Jeff (Athlete, Football Player)
260 Cohasset Rd Ste 190
Chico, CA 95926-2282, USA

Stover, Matt (Football Player)
10024 Rustleleaf Dr
Dallas, TX 75238-2143, USA

Stover, Stewart (Football Player)
9334 La Highway 82
Abbeville, LA 70510-2356, USA

Stowe, David H Jr (Business Person)
John Deere Road
Moline, IL 61265, USA

Stowe, Hal (Athlete, Baseball Player)
1361 Union New Hope Rd
Gastonia, NC 28056-8574, USA

Stowe, Madeleine (Actor)
c/o Cynthia Pett-Dante *Brillstein Entertainment Partners*
9150 Wilshire Blvd Ste 350
Beverly Hills, CA 90212-3453, USA

Stowe, Medeleine (Actor)
9560 Wilshire Blvd Ste 500
Beverly Hills, CA 90212-2401, USA

Stowe, Otto (Football Player)
546 Mills Way
Goleta, CA 93117-4021, USA

Stowers, Chris (Athlete, Baseball Player)
3773 Wakefield Hall Sq SE
Smyrna, GA 30080-4917, USA

Stowers, Tommie (Football Player)
2435 NW Valley View Dr
Lees Summit, MO 64081-1977, USA

Stoyanov, Krasimir M (Misc)
Moskovskoi Oblasti
Syvisdny Goroduk 141160, RUSSIA

Stoyanovich, Peter (Pete) (Athlete, Football Player)
18185 Parkshore Dr
Northville, MI 48168-8591, USA

Stracey, John (Boxer)
Van Laeken 4 Norsey Road Billericay
Essex CM11 2AD, UNITED KINGDOM (UK)

Strachan, Mike (Football Player)
PO Box 642007
Kenner, LA 70064-2007, USA

Strachan, Rod (Swimmer)
11632 Ranch Hl
Santa Ana, CA 92705-3130, USA

Strachan, Steve (Football Player)
46 Crimson Rd
Billerica, MA 01821-5420, USA

Straczynski, J Michael (Actor)
c/o Chris Harbert *Creative Artists Agency (CAA-LA)*
2000 Avenue of the Stars Ste 100
Los Angeles, CA 90067-4705, USA

Strader, Cam (Athlete, Race Car Driver)
10974 Heritage Green Dr
Cornelius, NC 28031-7407, USA

Stradford, Troy (Athlete, Football Player)
6600 N Andrews Ave Ste 160
Fort Lauderdale, FL 33309-2188, USA

Stradlin, Izzy (Musician)
301 Arizona Ave Ste 200
Santa Monica, CA 90401-1364, USA

Stradling, Harry A Jr (Cinematographer)
1518 E Valley Rd
Santa Barbara, CA 93108-2103, USA

Strahan, Michael A (Athlete, Football Player)
2018 Cias Trail Ln
Spring, TX 77386-1832, USA

Strahler, Mike (Athlete, Baseball Player)
8 Canyon Draw
Alamogordo, NM 88310-3613, USA

Strahovski, Yvonne (Actor)
c/o Laura Myones *McKeon-Myones Management*
3500 W Olive Ave Ste 770
Burbank, CA 91505-5527, USA

Straight, Bering (Music Group)
c/o Staff Member *Creative Artists Agency (CAA-TN)*
3310 W End Ave Fl 5
Nashville, TN 37203-1028, USA

Strain, Joe (Athlete, Baseball Player)
8668 E Otero Cir
Centennial, CO 80112-3351, USA

Strain, Julie (Actor, Model)
8491 W Sunset Blvd Ste 1850
West Hollywood, CA 90069-1911, USA

Strain, Sammy (Music Group, Musician)
1995 Broadway # 501
New York, NY 10023-5882, USA

Strait, Donald (War Hero)
6 Burning Tree Pl
Jackson Springs, NC 27281-9756, USA

Strait, George (Musician)
c/o Staff Member *Erv Woolsey Agency, The*
1000 18th Ave S
Nashville, TN 37212-2184, USA

Strait, Steven (Actor)
c/o Chris Andrews *Creative Artists Agency (CAA-LA)*
2000 Avenue of the Stars Ste 100
Los Angeles, CA 90067-4705, USA

Straka, Martin (Athlete, Hockey Player)
66 Mario Lemieux Pl
Pittsburgh, PA 15219-3504, USA

Straker, Lee (Athlete, Baseball Player)
1 Citizens Bank Way Attn Venezulanbaseballacademy
Philadelphia, PA 19148-5205, USA

Strampe, Bob (Bowler)
5875 W Michigan Ave
Saginaw, MI 48638-5989, USA

Strampe, Bob (Athlete, Baseball Player)
19210 W Lance Hill Rd
Cheney, WA 99004-7907, USA

Stranahan, Frank (Golfer)
8400 Heritage Club Dr
West Palm Bch, FL 33412-1571, USA

Strand, Robin (Actor)
4118 Elmer Ave
North Hollywood, CA 91602-3312, USA

Strane, John (War Hero)
18230 Mirasol Dr
San Diego, CA 92128-1226, USA

Strang, Deborah (Actor)
8285 W Sunset Blvd Ste 1
West Hollywood, CA 90046-2420, USA

Strang, William G (Mathematician)
7 Southgate Rd
Wellesley, MA 02482-6606, USA

Strange, Doug (Athlete, Baseball Player)
435 Heights Dr
Gibsonia, PA 15044-6032, USA

Strange, Pat (Athlete, Baseball Player)
156 Mill St
Springfield, MA 01108-1022, USA

Strange, Sarah (Actor)
c/o Ryan Martin *Agency for the Performing Arts (APA-LA)*
405 S Beverly Dr Ste 500
Beverly Hills, CA 90212-4425, USA

Strange Boys, The (Music Group)
c/o Staff Member *Paradigm (Monterey)*
404 W Franklin St
Monterey, CA 93940-2303, USA

Strange-Hansen, Martin (Actor)
c/o Staff Member *Gersh (LA)*
9465 Wilshire Blvd Ste 600
Beverly Hills, CA 90212-2612, USA

Stransky, Bob (Football Player)
5970 W Colgate Pl
Denver, CO 80227-3814, USA

Strasser, Teresa (Comedian, Television Host)
c/o Staff Member *OmniPop Talent Group*
10700 Ventura Blvd Fl 2
Studio City, CA 91604-3561, USA

Strassman, Marcia (Actor)
c/o Staff Member *Bette Smith Management*
499 N Canon Dr
Beverly Hills, CA 90210-4887, USA

Stratas, Teresa (Opera Singer)
481 8th Ave # 340
New York, NY 10001-1809, USA

Strathairn, David (Actor)
c/o Madeline Ryan 461 South Ogden Dr
Los Angeles, CA 90036, USA

Stratham, Jason (Actor)
8942 Wilshire Blvd # 219
Beverly Hills, CA 90211-1908, USA

Strathiam, David (Actor)
9560 Wilshire Blvd Ste 500
Beverly Hills, CA 90212-2401, USA

Stratton, Dan
65 Broadway Ste 504
New York, NY 10006-2541, USA

Stratton, Frederick P Jr (Business Person)
PO Box 702
Milwaukee, WI 53201-0702, USA

Stratton, Mike (Football Player)
2611 Shore Line Rd
Knoxville, TN 37932-1724, USA

Stratus, Trish (Wrestler)
5468 Dundas St W # 579
Toronto, ON M9B 6E3, CANADA

Straub, Peter
53 W 85th St
New York, NY 10024-4132

Straub, Peter F (Writer)
53 W 85th St
New York, NY 10024-4132, USA

Straus, Robert (Scientist)
656 Raintree Rd
Lexington, KY 40502-2874, USA

Strauss, Neil (Writer)
8491 W Sunset Blvd # 348
West Hollywood, CA 90069-1911, USA

Strauss, Peter (Actor)
335 N Maple Dr Ste 351
Beverly Hills, CA 90210-5174, USA

Strauss, Robert S (Diplomat, Politician)
1700 Pacific Ave Ste 4100
Dallas, TX 75201-4624, USA

Strauss-Schulson, Todd (Director)
c/o Christie Smith *Mosaic Media Group*
9200 W Sunset Blvd Ste 10
Los Angeles, CA 90069-3608, USA

Straw, John W (Jack) (Government Official)
Westminster
London SW1A 0AA, UNITED KINGDOM (UK)

Straw, Syd (Musician)
c/o Staff Member *Agency Group Ltd, The (NY)*
142 W 57th St Fl 6
New York, NY 10019-3300, USA

Strawberry, Darryl E (Athlete, Baseball Player)
4215 235th St
Douglaston, NY 11363-1526, USA

Strawberry Blondes
Box 33 Pontypool
Gwent, ENGLAND NP4 6YU

Strawder, Joe (Athlete, Basketball Player)
3037 SW Taylors Ferry Rd
Portland, OR 97219-5552, USA

Stray Cats (Music Group, Musician)
c/o Dave Kaplan *Dave Kaplan Management*
1126 S Coast Hwy Suite 101
Encinitas, CA 92024, USA

Strayhorn, Les (Football Player)
109 Sir Richard Ln
Chapel Hill, NC 27517-5531, USA

Streater, Sonja (Stylist)
c/o Staff Member *Celestine - CA*
1666 20th St Ste 200B
Santa Monica, CA 90404-3828, USA

Streep, Meryl (Actor)
c/o Michelle Benson *42West (NY)*
220 W 42nd St Fl 12
New York, NY 10036-7200, USA

Street, Huston (Athlete, Baseball Player)
107 Wood Trl
West Lake Hills, TX 78746-5241, USA

Street, John (Politician)
23 N Juniper St
Philadelphia, PA 19107, USA

Street, Picabo (Skier)
PO Box 321
Hailey, ID 83333-0321, USA

Street, Rebecca (Actor)
255 Cabrini Blvd
New York, NY 10040-3612, USA

Streeter, George (Athlete, Football Player)
35 Brentwood Pl
Fort Thomas, KY 41075-2446, USA

Streetman, Ben G (Engineer)
3915 Glengarry Dr
Austin, TX 78731-3835, USA

Streiber, Whitley (Writer)
c/o Paul Canterna *Seven Summits Pictures & Management*
8906 W Olympic Blvd Ground Floor
Beverly Hills, CA 90211, USA

Streisand, Barbra (Actor, Director, Musician, Producer)
c/o Martin Erlichman *Martin Erlichman Associates*
5670 Wilshire Blvd Ste 2400
Los Angeles, CA 90036-5626

Streit, Clarence K (Journalist)
2853 Ontario Rd NW
Washington, DC 20009-2224, USA

Streitwieser Jr, Andrew (Misc)
Chemistry
Berkeley, CA 94720-0001, USA

Strekalov, Gennadi M (Cosmonaut)
36 Mira Prospekt
Moscow 129090, RUSSIA

Strenger, Rich (Football Player)
1064 Arbroak Way
Lake Orion, MI 48362-2500, USA

Streuli, Wait (Athlete, Baseball Player)
1107 Westminster Dr
Greensboro, NC 27410-4545, USA

Stribling, Bill (Football Player)
PO Box 820046
Vicksburg, MS 39182-0046, USA

Stricker, Bill (Athlete, Basketball Player)
2930 Driftwood Pl Apt 70
Stockton, CA 95219-8027, USA

Stricker, Steve (Athlete, Golfer)
5804 N Sherman Ave
Madison, WI 53704-2147, USA

Strickland, Donald (Athlete, Football Player)
1110 Gilman Ave
San Francisco, CA 94124-3623, USA

Strickland, Gail (Actor)
14732 Oracle Pl
Pacific Palisades, CA 90272-2642, USA

Strickland, George (Athlete, Baseball Player, Coach)
6328 Constance St
New Orleans, LA 70118-5813, USA

Strickland, Jim (Athlete, Baseball Player)
2139 Equestrian Rd
Paso Robles, CA 93446-4149, USA

Strickland, KaDee (Actor)
c/o Jason Trawick *WmE2 (Endeavor-LA)*
9601 Wilshire Blvd Fl 3
Beverly Hills, CA 90210-5219, USA

Strickland, Rod (Athlete, Basketball Player)
3120 Hemingway Ln
Lexington, KY 40513-1858, USA

Strickland, Scott (Athlete, Baseball Player)
415 Enchanted River Dr
Spring, TX 77388-5981, USA

Strieber, Whitley (Writer)
c/o Staff Member *Gersh (LA)*
9465 Wilshire Blvd Ste 600
Beverly Hills, CA 90212-2612, USA

Striker, Jake (Athlete, Baseball Player)
1963 SE Gregory Dr
Dallas, OR 97338-2746, USA

Strincevich, Nick (Athlete, Baseball Player)
1308 Camelot Mnr
Portage, IN 46368-5318, USA

Stringer, C Vivian (Coach)
Athletic Dept
New Brunswick, NJ 8903, USA

Stringer, Howard (Business Person)
Sony Drive
Park Ridge, NJ 7656, USA

Stringer, Lou (Athlete, Baseball Player)
23442 El Toro Rd Bldg 2
Lake Forest, CA 92630-6992, USA

Stringer, Rob (Business Person)
c/o Staff Member *Epic Records Group*
550 Madison Ave Fl 6
New York, NY 10022-3211, USA

Stringert, Hal (Football Player)
1711 Dole St Apt 603
Honolulu, HI 96822-4946, USA

Stringfield, Sherry (Actor)
c/o Leanne Coronel *Coronel Group*
1100 Glendon Ave Fl 17
Los Angeles, CA 90024-3588, USA

Stritch, Elaine (Actor, Musician)
c/o Staff Member *International Creative Management (ICM-LA)*
10250 Constellation Blvd Fl 7
Los Angeles, CA 90067-6207, USA

Strittmatter, Mark (Athlete, Baseball Player)
6533 Dutch Creek St
Highlands Ranch, CO 80130-3859, USA

Strobel, Eric (Athlete, Hockey Player)
6617 129th St W
Apple Valley, MN 55124-7967, USA

Stroble, Bobby (Golfer)
526 W 2nd Ave
Albany, GA 31701-2205, USA

Strock, Donald J (Don) (Coach, Football Coach, Football Player)
1512 Passion Vine Cir
Weston, FL 33326-3656, USA

Strohmayer, John (Athlete, Baseball Player)
1825 Crosby Ln
Redding, CA 96003-7754, USA

Strohmayer, Tod (Astronomer)
Nasa/Gsfc
Greenbelt, MD 20771-0001, USA

Strolz, Hubert (Skier)
6767 Warth 19
AUSTRIA

Strom, Brent (Athlete, Baseball Player)
2202 N Catalina Vista Loop
Tucson, AZ 85749-7908, USA

Strom, Brock T (Football Player)
4301 W 110th St
Leawood, KS 66211-1424, USA

Strom, Karin (Stylist)
150 Polkville Rd
Columbia, NJ 07832-2419, USA

Strom, Rick (Football Player)
8905 Moor Park Run
Duluth, GA 30097-6622, USA

Stroma, Freddie (Actor)
c/o Danny Mancini *Affirmative Entertainment*
425 N Robertson Blvd
West Hollywood, CA 90048-1735, USA

Stroman, Susan (Director)
c/o Leslee Dart *42West (NY)*
220 W 42nd St Fl 12
New York, NY 10036-7200, USA

Stromberg, Mike (Football Player)
PO Box 1510
Shelter Island, NY 11964-1510, USA

Strominger, Jack L (Misc)
44 Binney St
Boston, MA 02115-6013, USA

Stronach, Belinda (Business Person)
600 Wilshire Dr
Troy, MI 48084-1625, USA

Strong, Brenda (Actor)
c/o Kay Liberman *Liberman/Zerman Management*
252 N Larchmont Blvd Ste 200
Los Angeles, CA 90004-3754, USA

Strong, Danny (Actor, Producer, Writer)
c/o Staff Member *The Gotham Group Inc*
9255 W Sunset Blvd Ste 515
Los Angeles, CA 90069-3308, USA

Strong, Derek (Athlete, Basketball Player)
5434 Hillcrest Dr
Los Angeles, CA 90043-2323, USA

Strong, Jeremy (Actor)
c/o Meredith Wechter *International Creative Management (ICM-LA)*
10250 Constellation Blvd Fl 7
Los Angeles, CA 90067-6207, USA

Strong, Jim (Football Player)
9303 Oxted Ln
Spring, TX 77379-6621, USA

Strong, Joe (Athlete, Baseball Player)
1340 Corcoran Ave
Vallejo, CA 94589-1878, USA

Strong, Johnny (Actor)
c/o Beverly Strong *Strong Management*
9350 Wilshire Blvd Ste 224
Beverly Hills, CA 90212-3204, USA

Strong, Mack (Football Player)
c/o Staff Member *Maxx Sports & Entertainment*
546 5th Ave Fl 6
New York, NY 10036-5000, USA

Strong, Mark (Actor)
c/o Pippa Markham *Markham & Froggatt*
4 Windmill St
London W1T 1HZ, UK

Strong, Maurice F (Government Official)
255 Consummers Rd # 401
Toronto, ON M2J 5B6, CANADA

Strong, Rider (Actor)
c/o Ellen Meyer *Ellen Meyer Management*
8899 Beverly Blvd Ste 612
West Hollywood, CA 90048-2429, USA

Strong, Tara (Actor)
c/o Jeff Danis *Danis, Panaro, Nist (DPN)*
9201 W Olympic Blvd
Beverly Hills, CA 90212-4605, USA

Strongin-Weiss, Randy (Stylist)
10 Bittersweet Ct
Centerport, NY 11721-1703, USA

Stroock, Daniel W (Mathematician)
55 Frost St
Cambridge, MA 02140-2247, USA

Strossen, Nadine (Lawyer)
57 Worth St
New York, NY 10013-2926, USA

Stroud, Carlos (Misc)
Physics Dept 1230 York Ave
Cambridge, MA 2138, USA

Stroud, Don (Actor)
500 Lunalilo Home Rd Apt 16A
Honolulu, HI 96825-1718, USA

Stroud, Ed (Athlete, Baseball Player)
1696 Oak St SW
Warren, OH 44485-3568, USA

Stroud, Les (Cinematographer, Director, Writer)
c/o Staff Member *Les Stroud Productions Inc.*
1235 Deerhurst Dr
Huntsville, Ontario P1H 2E8, Canada

Stroud, Morris (Athlete, Football Player)
11214 College Ave
Kansas City, MO 64137-2221, USA

Stroughter, Steve (Athlete, Baseball Player)
247 E Ashland Ave
Visalia, CA 93277-6702, USA

Stroup, Jessica (Actor)
c/o Erica Tarin *ID Public Relations (ID-LA)*
7080 Hollywood Blvd Fl 8
Los Angeles, CA 90028-6906, USA

Stroup Jr, Theodore G (Ted) (General)
2085 Hopewood Dr
Falls Church, VA 22043-1820, USA

Strouse, Charles (Composer)
171 W 57th St
New York, NY 10019-2203, USA

Strube, Juergen F (Business Person)
Carl-Bosch Str 38
Ludwigshafen 67063, GERMANY

Struber, Larry (Producer)
c/o Staff Member *WmE2 (WMA-LA)*
1 William Morris Pl
Beverly Hills, CA 90212-4261, USA

Struchkova, Raisa S (Ballerina)
Tverskaya 22B
Moscow 103050, RUSSIA

Strudwick, Suzanne (Golfer)
5500 Crestwood Dr
Knoxville, TN 37914-5108, USA

Struever, Stuart M (Misc)
200 Sheridan Rd
Evanston, IL 60208-0001, USA

Strug, Kerri (Athlete, Gymnast)
1099 1st St
Coronado, CA 92118-1357, USA

Strugnell, John (Misc)
45 Francis Ave
Cambridge, MA 02138-2115, USA

Strus, Lusia (Actor)
c/o Staff Member *Steve Himber Entertainment*
211 S Beverly Dr Apt S
Beverly Hills, CA 90212-3807, USA

Struthers, Sally (Actor)
c/o Vincent Cirrincione *Vincent Cirrincione Associates*
1516 N Fairfax Ave
Los Angeles, CA 90046-2608, USA

Struycken, Carel (Actor)
PO Box 1365
Avalon, CA 90704-1365, USA

Stryker, Bradley (Actor)
c/o Staff Member *House of Representatives, The*
1434 6th St Ste 1
Santa Monica, CA 90401-2527, USA

Strykert, Ron (Musician)
PO Box 124
Round Corner, NSW 2158, AUSTRALIA

Strzelczyk, Justin (Athlete, Football Player)
420 Fort Duquesne Blvd
Pittsburgh, PA 15222-1435, USA

Stuart, Barbara (Actor)
6332 Farmdale Ave
North Hollywood, CA 91606-3605, USA

Stuart, Eric (Actor, Musician)
330 Carroll St
Brooklyn, NY 11231-5008, USA

Stuart, Jason (Actor, Comedian)
c/o Bonny Dore *Bonny Dore Management*
8530 Wilshire Blvd Ste 400
Beverly Hills, CA 90211-3131

Stuart, Katie (Actor)
c/o Russ Mortensen *Pacific Artists Management*
1285 W Broadway Suite 685
Vancouver, BC V6H 3X8, Canada

Stuart, Katie (Actor)
c/o Blaine Greenberg *Speak Softly Legal Management*
13540 Ventura Blvd
Sherman Oaks, CA 91423-3826, USA

Stuart, Lyle (Publisher)
1530 Palisade Ave Apt 6L
Fort Lee, NJ 07024-5402, USA

Stuart, Marty (Musician, Songwriter)
c/o Staff Member *Paradigm (Monterey)*
404 W Franklin St
Monterey, CA 93940-2303, USA

Stuart, Maxine (Actor)
1801 Avenue of the Stars Ste 902
Los Angeles, CA 90067-5981, USA

Stuart, Roy (Athlete, Football Player)
6800 S Granite Ave Apt 339
Tulsa, OK 74136-7043, USA

Stubbins Jr, Hugh Asher (Architect)
6110 N Ocean Blvd
Boynton Beach, FL 33435-5204, USA

Stubblefield, Dana W (Athlete, Football Player)
5226 Pisa Ct
San Jose, CA 95138-2122, USA

Stubblefield, Marga (Golfer)
PO Box 140
Kailua, HI 96734-0140, USA

Stubblefield, Mickey (Baseball Player)
4870 Seldon Way SE
Smyrna, GA 30080-9266, USA

Stubbs, Franklin (Athlete, Baseball Player)
PO Box 325
Goshen, KY 40026-0325, USA

Stubbs, Imogen M (Actor)
76 Oxford St
London W1N 0AX, UNITED KINGDOM (UK)

Stubing, Larry (Moose) (Athlete, Baseball Player, Coach)
10821 Laconia Dr
Villa Park, CA 92861-6408, USA

Stuck, Hans-Joachim (Race Car Driver)
Harmstatt 3
Ellmau/Tirol 6352, AUSTRIA

Stuckey, Henry (Athlete, Football Player)
3615 Winchester Ave
Atlantic City, NJ 08401-3544, USA

Stuckey, James (Jim) (Football Player)
2044 Egret Ln
Charleston, SC 29414-5302, USA

Stuckey, Joe (Stylist)
c/o Staff Member *L'Agence*
5901 Peachtree Dunwoody Rd NE Ste C60
Atlanta, GA 30328-7155, USA

Stuckey, Rodney (Athlete, Basketball Player)
c/o Steve Banks *Banks Sports Ventures*
1126 17th Ave
Seattle, WA 98122-4645, USA

Studaway, Mark (Football Player)
4524 Saint Honore Dr
Memphis, TN 38116-2012, USA

Studdard, Ruben (Musician)
c/o Cara Lewis *WmE2 (WMA-NY)*
1325 Avenue of the Americas
New York, NY 10019-6026, USA

Studdard, Vern (Football Player)
11449 Tara Blvd
Lovejoy, GA 30250, USA

Studer, Cheryl (Opera Singer)
165 W 57th St
New York, NY 10019-2201, USA

Studi, Wes (Actor)
c/o Nevin Dolcefino *Innovative Artists (LA)*
1505 10th St
Santa Monica, CA 90401-2805, USA

Studnicki-Caden, Mary Lou (Baseball Player)
29 Mazarron Dr
Hot Springs Village, AR 71909-5827, USA

Studstill, Patrick L (Pat) (Football Player)
2235 Linda Flora Dr
Los Angeles, CA 90077-1410, USA

Studt, Amy (Musician)

Studwell, Scott (Football Player)
10415 Brown Farm Cir
Eden Prairie, MN 55347-4926, USA

Stuffel, Paul (Athlete, Baseball Player)
25501 Trost Blvd
Bonita Springs, FL 34135-6422, USA

Stuhlbarg, Michael (Actor)
c/o Lisa Loosemore *Viking Entertainment*
445 W 23rd St Ste 1A
New York, NY 10011-1445, USA

Stuhr, Jerzy (Actor, Director)
Ul SW Gertrudy 5
Cracow 31-107, POLAND

Stuhr-Thompson, Beverly (Baseball Player)
6379 N Muscatel Ave
San Gabriel, CA 91775-1843, USA

Stukes, Charles (Football Player)
2040 Bishop St
Petersburg, VA 23805-2220, USA

Stull, Everett (Athlete, Baseball Player)
1667 Fieldgreen Overlook
Stone Mountain, GA 30088-3112, USA

Stults, Geoff (Actor)
c/o Ashley Franklin *Thruline Entertainment*
8383 Wilshire Blvd Ste 1050
Beverly Hills, CA 90211-2415, USA

Stults, George (Actor)
c/o Staff Member *Bleu, An Entertainment Company*
5225 Wilshire Blvd Ste 336
Los Angeles, CA 90036-4380, USA

Stump, David (Cinematographer)
394 E Glaucus St
Encinitas, CA 92024-1734, USA

Stump, Gene (Athlete, Basketball Player)
542 S Hampton Ave
Orlando, FL 32803-6514, USA

Stump, Jim (Athlete, Baseball Player)
7432 Creekside Dr
Lansing, MI 48917-9693, USA

Stump, Patrick (Musician)
c/o Staff Member *Fueled By Ramen*
PO Box 1803
Tampa, FL 33601-1803, USA

Stumpf, Kenneth E (War Hero)
16528 State Highway 131
Tomah, WI 54660-6803, USA

Stumpf, Paul K (Misc)
1515 Shasta Dr Apt 2219
Davis, CA 95616-6683, USA

Stumps, Kathy (Actor)
c/o Staff Member *Gersh (LA)*
9465 Wilshire Blvd Ste 600
Beverly Hills, CA 90212-2612, USA

Stuper, John (Athlete, Baseball Player)
38 Lake St
Hamden, CT 06517-2315, USA

Stura, Paul (Stylist)
c/o Staff Member *Katy Barker Agency Inc*
6606 10th Ave Apt 3R
Brooklyn, NY 11219-5804, USA

Sturckow, Frederick W (Rick) (Astronaut)
RR 2 Box 14
Dickinson, TX 77539, USA

Sturdivant, John N (Misc)
80 F St NW
Washington, DC 20001-1528, USA

Sturgeon, Bob
3903 Lewis Ave
Long Beach, CA 90807-3617

Sturgess, Jim (Actor)
c/o Jodi Gottlieb *ID PR (LA)*
7060 Hollywood Blvd Fl 8
Los Angeles, CA 90028-6014, USA

Sturgess, Shannon (Actor)
1223 Wilshire Blvd # 577
Santa Monica, CA 90403-5400, USA

Sturm, Jerry (Football Player)
3 Niblick Ln
Littleton, CO 80123-6621, USA

Sturm, John F (Misc)
1921 Gallows Rd # 4
Vienna, VA 22182-3900, USA

Sturm, Marco (Athlete, Hockey Player)
11611 W Lanktree Gulch Rd
Star, ID 83669-5175, USA

Sturm, Yfke (Model)
c/o Staff Member *Storm Model Management*
5 Jubilee Pl 1st Floor
London SW3 3TD, UNITED KINGDOM

Sturman, Eugene (Artist)
1108 W Washington Blvd
Venice, CA 90291, USA

Sturr, Jimmy (Musician)
PO Box 1
Florida, NY 10921-0001, USA

Sturridge, Charles (Director)
Drury House 34-43 Russell St
London WC2B 5HA, UNITED KINGDOM (UK)

Sturridge, Tom (Actor)
c/o Sarah Spear *Curtis Brown Ltd*
Hay Market House 28-29 Hay Market
London SW1Y 4SP, UK

Sturt, Fred (Football Player)
120 N Berkey Southern Rd
Swanton, OH 43558-8907, USA

Sturtevant, Julian M (Misc)
14025 3rd Ave NW
Seattle, WA 98177-3923, USA

Sturtze, Tanyon (Athlete, Baseball Player)
501 Knights Run Ave Apt 2316
Tampa, FL 33602-5948, USA

Sturza, Ion (Prime Minister)
Piaca Maril Atuner Nacional
Chishinev 277033, MOLDOVA

Stutter, Jason (Director, Producer, Writer)
c/o Simon Millar *Rumble Media*
1620 Broadway Ste C
Santa Monica, CA 90404-2777, USA

Stuttering John (Radio Personality)
c/o Staff Member *Howard Stern Show*
1221 Avenue of the Americas
New York, NY 10020-1001, USA

Stutzmann, Nathalie (Opera Singer)
119 W 57th St Ste 1505
New York, NY 10019-2403, USA

Styler, Kara
PO Box 8002
Honolulu, HI 96830-0002

Styler, Trudie (Actor, Director, Producer)
c/o Staff Member *Xingu Films*
12 Cleveland Row St James
London SW1A 1DH, UNITED KINGDOM (UK)

Styles, Stephanie (Stylist)
622 Washington St Apt 2A
New York, NY 10014-3342, USA

Stynes, Chris (Athlete, Baseball Player)
1980 NE 7th St Ste 106
Deerfield Beach, FL 33441-3778, USA

Styx (Music Group, Musician)
c/o Keith Naisbitt *Agency Group Ltd, The (LA)*
1880 Century Park E Ste 711
Los Angeles, CA 90067-1618, USA

Suarez, Carlos (Actor)
c/o Staff Member *Televisa*
Blvd Adolfo Lopez Mateos 232 Colonia San Angel INN
DF CP 01060, MEXICO

Suarez, Ken (Athlete, Baseball Player)
6000 Forest Ln
Fort Worth, TX 76112-1060, USA

Suarez Gomez, Hector (Actor)
c/o Gabriel Blanco *Gabriel Blanco Iglesias (Mexico)*
Rio Balsas 35-32 Colonia Cuauhtemoc
DF 6500, Mexico

Suarez Gonzalez, Adolfo (Prime Minister)
Sagasta 33
Madrid 4, SPAIN

Suarez Rivera, Adolfo A Cardinal (Religious Leader)
Apartado Postal 7 Loma Larga 2429 Sierra Madre
Monterrey 64000, MEXICO

Suau, Anthony (Journalist)
PO Box 1709
Denver, CO 80201-1709, USA

Suazo, Chloe (Actor)
c/o Cindy Osbrink *Osbrink Talent Agency*
4343 Lankershim Blvd Ste 100
West Toluca Lake, CA 91602-2705, USA

Subhash, B (Actor, Bollywood)
1 Coelho House Juhu Tara Road Juhu
Mumbai, MS 400049, INDIA

Sublime (Music Group, Musician)
c/o Jon Phillips *Silverback Professional Artist Management*
1013 N Orange Dr
Los Angeles, CA 90038-2317, USA

Subotnick, Morton L (Composer)
25 Minetta Ln Apt 4B
New York, NY 10012-1253, USA

Subways, The (Music Group)
c/o Staff Member *Paradigm (Monterey)*
404 W Franklin St
Monterey, CA 93940-2303, USA

Such, Alec John (Musician)
248 W 17th St Apt 501
New York, NY 10011-5330, USA

Such, Dick (Athlete, Baseball Player)
7614 Divot Dr
Sanford, NC 27332-8804, USA

Sucherman, Todd (Musician)
c/o Sterling Bacon *TBA Artist Management (Atlanta)*
1111 Alderman Dr Ste 285
Alpharetta, GA 30005-5433, USA

Suchet, David (Actor, Producer)
c/o Sarah Jackson *Seven Summits Pictures & Management*
8906 W Olympic Blvd Ground Floor
Beverly Hills, CA 90211, USA

Suchocka, Hanna (Prime Minister)
Urzad Rady Ministrow Al Ujazdowskie 1/3
Warsaw 00-567, POLAND

Suci, Robert (Football Player)
2341 Morton Ave
Flint, MI 48507-4445, USA

Sudakis, Bill
16641 Algonquin St
Huntington Beach, CA 92649-3270

Sudakis, Bill (Athlete, Baseball Player)
81150 Avenida Graneros
Indio, CA 92203-7894, USA

Sudan, Madhu (Scientist)
81 Benton Rd
Somerville, MA 02143-1104, USA

Sudduth, Jill (Athlete, Swimmer)
9917 Calabasas Ave
Las Vegas, NV 89117-7513, USA

Sudduth, Skipp (Actor)
c/o Heather Reynolds *One Entertainment (NY)*
12 W 57th St PH 1
New York, NY 10019-3900, USA

Sudeikis, Jason (Actor, Comedian)
c/o Geoff Cheddy *Brillstein Entertainment Partners*
9150 Wilshire Blvd Ste 350
Beverly Hills, CA 90212-3453, USA

Sudersham, Ennackel (Physicist)
Physics Dept
Austin, TX 78713, USA

Sudharmono (General, Government Official)
Senopati St 44B
Jakarta Selatan, INDONESIA

Sudol, Alison (Actor, Musician)
c/o Julie Colbert *WmE2 (Endeavor-LA)*
9601 Wilshire Blvd Fl 3
Beverly Hills, CA 90210-5219, USA

Suede
PO Box 3431
London, ENGLAND N1 7LW

Sues, Alan (Actor)
9014 Dorrington Ave
West Hollywood, CA 90048-1713, USA

Suess, Hans E (Misc)
Chemistry
La Jolla, CA 92093-0001, USA

Suganya (Actor, Bollywood)
4/5 Oorur Alcot 5thavenue Besant Nagar
Chennai, TN 600090, INDIA

Sugar, Alan (Business Person, Reality TV Star)
Brentwood House 169 Kings Rd
Brentwood, Essex CM14 4EF, UK

Sugar, Bert Randolph (Writer)
6 Southview Rd
Chappaqua, NY 10514-1708, USA

Sugar, Leo T (Football Player)
7161 Golden Eagle Ct Apt 1012
Fort Myers, FL 33912-1708, USA

Sugarcult (Actor)
545 N Rossmore Ave Apt 3
Los Angeles, CA 90004-2440

Sugarland (Music Group)
c/o Staff Member *Gail Gellman Management*
23852 Pacific Coast Hwy
Malibu, CA 90265-4876, USA

Sugarman, Burt (Producer)
9440 Santa Monica Blvd Ste 407
Beverly Hills, CA 90210-4607, USA

Sugarman, Joseph (Joe) (Business Person, Writer)
3350 Palm Center Dr
Las Vegas, NV 89103-5668, USA

Sugarman, Josh (Activist)
1650 Harvard St NW
Washington, DC 20009-3706, USA

Sugg, Diana K (Journalist)
501 N Calvert St
Baltimore, MD 21278-1000, USA

Suggs, M Louise (Golfer)
424 Royal Crescent Ct
Saint Augustine, FL 32092-2786, USA

Suggs, Shafer (Athlete, Football Player)
12849 Barrow Ln
Plainfield, IL 60585-4214, USA

Suggs, Terrell (Athlete, Football Player)
Ravens Stadium 11001 Russell St
Baltimore, MD 21230, USA

Suggs, Walt (Football Player)
11105 Bradyville Pike
Readyville, TN 37149-4513, USA

Suh, Ndamukong (Athlete, Football Player)
c/o Roosevelt Barnes *Maximum Sports Management*
6435 W Jefferson Blvd # 197
Fort Wayne, IN 46804-6203, USA

Suharto, Mohamed (General, President)
8 Jalan Cendana
Jakarta, INDONESIA

Suhey, Matthew J (Matt) (Football Player)
550 Carriage Way
Deerfield, IL 60015-4535, USA

Suhl, Harry (Physicist)
9500 Gilman Dr
La Jolla, CA 92093-5003, USA

Suhonen, Alpo (Coach)
United Center 1901 W Madison St
Chicago, IL 60612, USA

Suhor, Yvonne (Actor)
233 Park Ave S # 1000
New York, NY 10003-1606, USA

Suhrheinrich, Richard F (Judge)
4725 Jadestone Dr
Williamston, MI 48895-9319, USA

Suhrstedt, Timothy (Cinematographer)
232 N Canon Dr
Beverly Hills, CA 90210-5302, USA

Suitner, Otmar
Platanestr 13
Berlin-Niederschonhausen 13156, GERMANY

Suits, Julia (Cartoonist)
5777 W Century Blvd Ste 700
Los Angeles, CA 90045-5652, USA

Suk, Josef (Musician)
Karlovo Namesti 5
Prague 2 12000, CZECH REPUBLIC

Sukla, Ed (Athlete, Baseball Player)
16 Perch
Irvine, CA 92604-3688, USA

Sukova, Helena (Tennis Player)
1 Ave Grande Bretagne
Monte Carlo, MONACO

Sukowa, Barbara (Actor)
20 Ave Rapp
Paris 75007, FRANCE

Sukselainen, Vieno J (Prime Minister)
Palvattarenpolku 2
Tapiola 2100, FINALND

Sulaiman, Jose (Misc)
Genova 33 Colonia Juarez
Cuahtetemoc 660, MEXICO

Sularz, Guy (Athlete, Baseball Player)
10818 N 83rd St
Scottsdale, AZ 85260-6550, USa

Suleman, Nadya (Octumom) (Reality TV Star)
2149 Marblecrest Dr
Hacienda Heights, CA 91745-5736, USA

Suleymanoglu, Naim (Wrestler)
Sisli Buyukdere Cad 18 Tankaya
Istanbul, TURKEY

Sulin, Suzanne (Stylist)
c/o Staff Member *Ford Models (Chicago)*
311 W Superior St
Chicago, IL 60654-3548, USA

Suliotis, Elena (Opera Singer)
Villa il Poderino Via Incontri
Florence 38, ITALY

Sulkin, Gregg (Actor)
c/o Danielle Allman-Del *D2 Management*
141 S Barrington Ave
Los Angeles, CA 90049-3368, USA

Sullivan, Charlotte (Actor)
c/o Evan Hainey *Untitled Entertainment (LA)*
350 S Beverly Dr Ste 200
Beverly Hills, CA 90212-4819, USA

Sullivan, Chip (Golfer)
49 Homestead Cir
Troutville, VA 24175-6995, USA

Sullivan, CHris (Football Player)
64 Wagon Wheel Rd
North Attleboro, MA 02760-3576, USA

Sullivan, Dan (Football Player)
25 Algonquin Ave
Andover, MA 01810-5527, USA

Sullivan, Daniel (Producer, Writer)
c/o Alan Wertheimer *Jackoway Tyerman Wertheimer Austen Mandelbaum Morris & Klein*
1925 Century Park E Fl 22
Los Angeles, CA 90067-2701, USA

Sullivan, Dennis P (Mathematician)
33 W 42nd St Dept 308
New York, NY 10036-8005, USA

Sullivan, Erik Per (Actor)
c/o Suzanne Smith *Suzanne Smith Management*
451 Greenwich St Rm 500
New York, NY 10013-1757, USA

Sullivan, Frank (Athlete)
PO Box 1873
Lihue, HI 96766-5873

Sullivan, Franklin L (Frank) (Athlete, Baseball Player)
PO Box 1873
Lihue, HI 96766-5873, USA

Sullivan, George (Football Player)
41 Howard St
Norwood, MA 02062-2323, USA

Sullivan, Greg (Musician)
200 W 57th St Ste 308
New York, NY 10019-3211, USA

Sullivan, Jazmine (Musician)
c/o Staff Member *WmE2 (WMA-NY)*
1325 Avenue of the Americas
New York, NY 10019-6026, USA

Sullivan, John (Athlete, Baseball Player)
24 Highland Ave
Dansville, NY 14437-1648, USA

Sullivan, Julie (Stylist)
c/o Staff Member *Artist Agency, THE (NY)*
230 W 55th St Apt 29D
New York, NY 10019-5206

Sullivan, Kathleen (Correspondent)
1025 N Kings Rd Apt 202
West Hollywood, CA 90069-6008, USA

Sullivan, Kathryn D (Astronaut)
795 Old Oak Trce
Columbus, OH 43235-1761, USA

Sullivan, Kevin (Journalist)
1150 15th St NW
Washington, DC 20071-0001, USA

Sullivan, Kevin Rodney (Actor, Director, Producer, Writer)
c/o Arnold Robinson *Rogers & Cowan PR (LA)*
Pacific Design Center 8687 Melrose Ave, 7th Floor
West Hollywood, CA 90069, USA

Sullivan, Louis W (Secretary)
720 Westview Dr SW
Atlanta, GA 30310-1458, USA

Sullivan, Marc (Athlete, Baseball Player)
2038 W First St Ste 100
Fort Myers, FL 33901-3109, USA

Sullivan, Michael J (Mike) (Ex-Governor)
123 W 1st St Ste 200
Casper, WY 82601-2480, USA

Sullivan, Mike (Athlete, Coach, Hockey Player)
256 Washington St
Duxbury, MA 02332-4548, USA

Sullivan, Mike (Athlete, Football Player)
76 Lou Groza Blvd Attn Coachingstaff
Berea, OH 44017-1238, USA

Sullivan, Nicole (Actor)
c/o Jonathan Howard *Innovative Artists (LA)*
1505 10th St
Santa Monica, CA 90401-2805, USA

Sullivan, Pattrick J (Pat) (Coach, Football Coach, Football Player)
1717 Indian Creek Dr
Vestavia, AL 35243-1745, USA

Sullivan, Phil (Football Player)
4113 Rollingwood Ct
Jacksonville, FL 32257-7665, USA

Sullivan, Russ (Athlete, Baseball Player)
1701 Hill N Dale St
Fredericksburg, VA 22405-2735, USA

Sullivan, Scott (Athlete, Baseball Player)
1649 Mayfair Ct
Auburn, AL 36830-2128, USA

Sullivan, Susan (Actor)
c/o Staff Member *Paradigm (LA)*
360 N Crescent Dr
Beverly Hills, CA 90210-4874, USA

Sullivan, Tim (Director)
9200 W Sunset Blvd Ste 900
Los Angeles, CA 90069-3604, USA

Sullivan, Timothy J (Educator)
President's Office
Williamsburg, VA 23187, USA

Sullivan, Tom (Actor, Writer)
c/o Chris Ridenhour *Evolution Entertainment (LA)*
901 N Highland Ave
Los Angeles, CA 90038-2412, USA

Sullivan, William J (Educator)
President's Office
Seattle, WA 98122, USA

Sullivan Jr, Brendan V (Lawyer)
725 12th St NW
Washington, DC 20005-3901, USA

Sullivan Jr, Brendon V
725 12th St NW
Washington, DC 20005-3901, USA

Sulston, John E (Nobel Prize Laureate)
39 Mingle Lane Stapleford
Cambridge CB2 5BG, UNITED KINGDOM (UK)

Sultan, Altoon (Artist)
PO Box 2
Groton, VT 05046-0002, USA

Sultan, Donald K (Artist)
19 E 70th St
New York, NY 10021-4982, USA

Sultan of Brunei
Bandar Seri
Begawan, BRUNEI

Sultan Salman, Abdulaziz Al-Saud (Astronaut)
PO Box 18368
Riyadh 11415, SAUDI ARABIA

Sultanov, Alexel (Musician)
165 W 57th St
New York, NY 10019-2201, USA

Sultonov, Outkir T (Prime Minister)
Mustarilik 5
Tashkent 70008, UZBEKISTAN

Sum 41 (Music Group)
c/o Ron Laffitte *Red Light Management (LA)*
8439 W Sunset Blvd Ste 2
Los Angeles, CA 90069-1925, USA

Suman, Shekhar (Actor, Bollywood, Comedian, Talk Show Host)
1 Krishna Apartments 168 Sher-E-Punjab Colony Mahakali Caves Road Andheri E
Bombay, MS 400 093, INDIA

Sumaye, Frederick T (Prime Minister)
PO Box 980
Dodoma, TANZANIA

Sumerfelt, Josh
6550 Yucca St Apt 310
Los Angeles, CA 90028-4226

Sumika, Aya (Actor)
c/o Jill Littman *Impression Entertainment*
9229 W Sunset Blvd Ste 700
West Hollywood, CA 90069-3407, USA

Sumino, Naoko (Astronaut)
Tsukuba Space Center 2-1-1 Sengen Tukubashi
Ibaraka 305, JAPAN

Suminski, Dave (Football Player)
221 11th Ave E
Ashland, WI 54806-2022, USA

Summer, Cree (Actor)
509 Hartnell St
Monterey, CA 93940-2825, USA

Summer, Donna (Musician)
458 N Oakhurst Dr Apt 102
Beverly Hills, CA 90210-5701, USA

Summerall, Pat (Football Player)
710 S White Chapel Blvd
Southlake, TX 76092-7319, USA

Summer-Francks, Cree
PO Box 5617
Beverly Hills, CA 90209-5617

Summerhays, Bob (Athlete, Football Player)
12345 SE 91st Ave
Summerfield, FL 34491-8251, USA

Summerhays, Boyd (Athlete, Golfer)
9269 E Desert Vw
Scottsdale, AZ 85255-6218, USA

Summerleigh, George A (Pat) (Football Player)
710 S White Chapel Blvd
Southlake, TX 76092-7319, USA

Summers, Andy (Musician)
21A Noel St
London W1V 3PD, UNITED KINGDOM (UK)

Summers, Carol (Artist)
2817 Smith Grade
Santa Cruz, CA 95060-9764, USA

Summers, Champ (Athlete, Baseball Player)
13708 SW 111th Ave
Dunnellon, FL 34432-8797, USA

Summers, Dana (Cartoonist)
633 N Orange Ave
Orlando, FL 32801-1300, USA

Summers, Henry (Stylist)
69 Edgewood Ave
Clifton, NJ 07012-1839, USA

Summers, Isabel (Stylist)
300 Mercer St Apt 9H
New York, NY 10003-6734, USA

Summers, Jerry (Musician)
2011 Ferry Ave Apt U19
Camden, NJ 08104-1900, USA

Summers, Lawrence H (Larry) (Educator, Secretary)
President's Office
Cambridge, MA 2138, USA

Summers, Marc (Actor, Chef, Director, Producer, Television Host)
c/o Staff Member *Marc Summers Productions*
23705 Vanowen St Ste 105
Canoga Park, CA 91307-3030, USA

Summers, Tara (Actor)
c/o Lena Roklin *Luber Roklin Management*
8530 Wilshire Blvd Ste 550
Beverly Hills, CA 90211-3133, USA

Summers, Wilbur (Football Player)
PO Box 72734
Louisville, KY 40272-0734, USA

Summers, Yale (Actor)
c/o Staff Member *Screen Actors Guild (SAG-LA)*
5757 Wilshire Blvd
Los Angeles, CA 90036-5810, USA

Summitt, Pat Head (Athlete, Basketball Player, Coach)
3720 River Trace Ln
Knoxville, TN 37920-7118, USA

Sumner, Peter (Actor)
15/71 Avenue Road
Mosman 2088, AUSTRALIA

Sumner, Walt (Football Player)
PO Box 112
Ocilla, GA 31774-0112, USA

Sumpter, Jeremy (Actor)
c/o Mark Robert *Mark Robert Management*
2208 Patricia Ave
Los Angeles, CA 90064-2318, USA

Sumpter, Tony (Football Player)
702 S Gray St
Stillwater, OK 74074-4331, USA

Sun Dao Lin (Actor, Director)
595 Tsao Hsi North Road
Shanghai 200030, CHINA

Sundance, Robert (Activist)
225 W 8th St
Los Angeles, CA 90014-3209, USA

Sunday, Gabriel (Actor)
c/o Judy Savage *Savage Agency*
6212 Banner Ave
Los Angeles, CA 90038-2802, USA

Sundberg, Jim (Athlete, Baseball Player)
2308 Newforest Ct
Arlington, TX 76017-2638, USA

Sunde, Milt (Football Player)
6008 W 104th St
Bloomington, MN 55438-1826, USA

Sunderland, Zac (Athlete)
1710 N Moorpark Rd # 212
Thousand Oaks, CA 91360-5133, USA

Sundhage, Pia (Coach)
Women's National Team 1801 S. Prairie Ave.
Chicago, IL 60616, USA

Sundin, Gordie (Athlete, Baseball Player)
15600 Old 41 N
Naples, FL 34110-8420, USA

Sundvold, Jon (Athlete, Basketball Player)
2700 Westbrook Way
Columbia, MO 65203-5221, USA

Sung, Elizabeth (Actor)
9229 W Sunset Blvd Ste 320
Los Angeles, CA 90069-3403, USA

Sunjata, Daniel (Actor)
c/o Meg Mortimer *Principal Entertainment (NY)*
130 W 42nd St Ste 614
New York, NY 10036-7804, USA

Sunshine Underground, The (Music Group)
c/o Staff Member *Paradigm (Monterey)*
404 W Franklin St
Monterey, CA 93940-2303, USA

Sununu, John H (Ex-Governor)
49 Linden Rd
Hampton Falls, NH 03844-2035, USA

Superdrag (Music Group)
c/o Staff Member *Paradigm (Monterey)*
404 W Franklin St
Monterey, CA 93940-2303, USA

Supergrass (Music Group)
c/o Staff Member *Paradigm (Monterey)*
404 W Franklin St
Monterey, CA 93940-2303, USA

Supernaw, Kywin (Football Player)
1123 Clairborne Ct
Indianapolis, IN 46280-1100, USA

Supertramp
16530 Ventura Blvd Ste 201
Encino, CA 91436-4586

Suplee, Ethan (Actor)
6500 Wilshire Blvd Ste 2200
Los Angeles, CA 90048-4942, USA

Suppan, Jeff (Athlete, Baseball Player)
25315 Prado De La Felicidad
Calabasas, CA 91302-3651, USA

Suppes, Patrick (Psychic)
678 Mirada Ave
Stanford, CA 94305-8475, USA

Supremes, The (Music Group)
PO Box 1821
Ojai, CA 93024-1821

Suquia Goicoechea, Angel Cardinal (Religious Leader)
El Cardenal Arxobispo San Justo 2
Madrid 28074, SPAIN

Sura, Bob (Basketball Player)
190 Marietta St NW
Atlanta, GA 30303-2762, USA

Sure, Al B (Musician)
c/o Staff Member *International Creative Management (ICM-LA)*
10250 Constellation Blvd Fl 7
Los Angeles, CA 90067-6207, USA

Surhoff, Rick (Athlete, Baseball Player)
1839 White Oak Dr
Reading, PA 19608-9468, USA

Surhoff, William J (BJ) (Athlete, Baseball Player)
2205 Pine Hill Farms Ln
Cockeysville, MD 21030-1023, USA

Surin, Bruny (Athlete, Track Athlete)
PO Box 2 Succ Saint Michel
Montreal, QC H2A 3L8, CANADA

Surkowski-Delmonico, Lee (Baseball Player)
10 Via Las Colinas Apt 1
Rancho Mirage, CA 92270-6015, USA

Surkowski-Deyotte, Anne (Baseball Player)
632 Southwind Dr
Kelowna, BC V1W 3G1, CANADA

Surman, Jamie (Stylist)
c/o Staff Member *Jed Root Inc*
61-A Walker St
New York, NY 10013, USA

Surratt, Al (Baseball Player)
3448 E 54th St
Kansas City, MO 64130-4027, USA

Sursok, Tammin (Actor)
c/o David Gardner *Principato/Young Management*
9465 Wilshire Blvd Ste 430
Beverly Hills, CA 90212-2613, USA

Surtain, Patrick (Athlete, Football Player)
2704 Boot Ln
Weston, FL 33331-3004, USA

Surtees, Bruce (Cinematographer)
36 Linda Vista Pl
Monterey, CA 93940-4345, USA

Surtees, John (Race Car Driver)
Fircroft Way Edenbridge
Kent TN8 6EJ, UNITED KINGDOM (UK)

Survivor
PO Box 1821
Ojai, CA 93024-1821

Susa, Conrad (Composer)
433 Eureka St
San Francisco, CA 94114-2714, USA

Susana, Marta (Actor)
c/o Staff Member *Univision*
605 3rd Ave Fl 12
New York, NY 10158-0034, USA

Susanka, Sarah (Architect, Writer)
c/o Suzanne Fedoruk *Fedoruk & Associates*
P.O. Box 43298
Minneapolis, MN 55423, USA

Susce, George (Athlete, Baseball Player)
2852 Velma St
Matlacha, FL 33993-9747, USA

Suschitzky, J Peter (Cinematographer)
13 priory Road
London NW6 4NN, UNITED KINGDOM (UK)

Suschitzky, Wolfgang (Cinematographer)
Douglas House 6 Maida Ave #11
London W2 1TG, UNITED KINGDOM (UK)

Susclick, Kenneth S (Misc)
Chemistry Dept
Champaign, IL 61820, USA

Susco, Stephen (Producer, Writer)
c/o Chris Ridenhour *Evolution Entertainment (LA)*
901 N Highland Ave
Los Angeles, CA 90038-2412, USA

Susi, Carol Ann (Actor)
846 N Sweetzer Ave
Los Angeles, CA 90069-5942, USA

Susman, Todd (Actor)
9229 W Sunset Blvd Ste 315
Los Angeles, CA 90069-3403, USA

Sussin, Christen (Actor)
c/o Elizabeth Much *Much and House Public Relations*
8075 W 3rd St Ste 500
Los Angeles, CA 90048-4325, USA

Sussman, Adam (Writer)
c/o Staff Member *McKuin Frankel Whitehead*
141 El Camino Dr Ste 100
Beverly Hills, CA 90212-2717, USA

Sussman, Kevin (Actor)
c/o Jill McGrath *Abrams Artists Agency (NY)*
275 7th Ave Fl 26
New York, NY 10001-6708, USA

Sussman, Susan
927 Noyes St
Evanston, IL 60201-6206

Sutcliffe, David (Actor)
c/o Robert Stein *Robert Stein Management*
PO Box 3797
Beverly Hills, CA 90212-0797, USA

Sutcliffe, Richard L (Rick) (Athlete, Baseball Player)
616 NE Seabrook Ct
Lees Summit, MO 64064-1261, USA

Suter, Bob (Athlete, Hockey Player)
2961 Waubesa Ave
Madison, WI 53711-5964, USA

Suter, Gary (Athlete, Hockey Player)
2128 County Road D
Lac Du Flambu, WI 54538-9726, USA

Sutera, Paul
11365 Ventura Blvd Ste 100
Studio City, CA 91604-3148

Sutherland, Bill (Actor)
c/o Staff Member *Select Artists Ltd (CA-Westside Office)*
1138 12th St Apt 1
Santa Monica, CA 90403-5459, USA

Sutherland, Darrell (Athlete, Baseball Player)
1011 NW Jeffrey Pl
Beaverton, OR 97006-6335, USA

Sutherland, David (Golfer)
5431 Tree Side Dr
Carmichael, CA 95608-5958, USA

Sutherland, Donald (Actor, Musician, Producer, Writer)
c/o Allen Eichhorn *PMK/BNC Public Relations (PMK-NY)*
622 3rd Ave Fl 8
New York, NY 10017-6707, USA

Sutherland, Doug (Football Player)
511 Kenilworth Ave
Duluth, MN 55803-2113, USA

Sutherland, Gary (Athlete, Baseball Player)
338 Oakcliff Rd
Monrovia, CA 91016-1823, USA

Sutherland, Kevin (Golfer)
1230 Carter Rd
Sacramento, CA 95864-5328, USA

Sutherland, Kiefer (Actor, Director, Producer)
c/o Suzan Bymel *Management 360*
9111 Wilshire Blvd
Beverly Hills, CA 90210-5508, USA

Sutherland, Kristine (Actor)
c/o Staff Member *Silver Massetti & Szatmary (SMS) Talent Inc*
8730 W Sunset Blvd Ste 440
Los Angeles, CA 90069-2277, USA

Sutherland, Leo (Athlete, Baseball Player)
12082 Nieta Dr
Garden Grove, CA 92840-3524, USA

Sutherland, Peter D (Government Official)
68 Eglinton Road
Dublin 4, IRELAND

Sutherland, Shirley (Athlete, Baseball Player)
9613 Ritter Dr
Machesney Park, IL 61115-1759, USA

Sutherland, Thomas
229 Columbine Ct
Fort Collins, CO 80521-1715

Sutko, Glenn (Athlete, Baseball Player)
1715 Holcomb Lake Rd
Marietta, GA 30062-2093, USA

Sutkus, Mary (Stylist)
720 Limedale Ln
Florissant, MO 63031, USA

Sutor, George (Athlete, Basketball Player)
29840 State Highway 27
Holcombe, WI 54745-8798, USA

Sutorius, James
14014 Milbank St Unit 1
Sherman Oaks, CA 91423-2983

Sutter, Brent (Athlete, Hockey Player)
2551 Thaddeus Cir Apt S
Glen Ellyn, IL 60137, USA

Sutter, Brian (Athlete, Coach, Hockey Player)
1901 W Madison St
Chicago, IL 60612-2459, USA

Sutter, Bruce (Athlete, Baseball Player)
59 Waterside Dr SE
Cartersville, GA 30121-6615, USA

Sutter, Darryl (Athlete, Coach, Hockey Player)
P.O. Box 1540 Station M
Calgary, AB T2P 3B9, Canada

Sutter, Duane (Athlete, Hockey Player)
3703 High Pine Dr
Coral Springs, FL 33065-6014, USA

Sutter, Eddie (Football Player)
5104 N Bevalon Pl
Peoria, IL 61614-4606, USA

Sutter, Rich (Athlete, Hockey Player)
PO Box 1832
Whitefish, MT 59937-1832, USA

Sutter, Ryan (Football Player)
9543 Cedarhurst Ln Unit C
Highlands Ranch, CO 80129-2565, USA

Sutter, Trista (Reality TV Star)
42 W Meadow Dr
Vail, CO 81657-5705, USA

Sutterluty, Elizabeth (Actor)
36 Rue de Ponthieu
Paris 75008, FRANCE

Suttle, Dane (Athlete, Basketball Player)
138 W 69th St
Los Angeles, CA 90003-1824, USA

Sutton, Don (Athlete, Baseball Player)
611 Riverlawn Ct
Atlanta, GA 30339-2993, USA

Sutton, Greg (Athlete, Basketball Player)
PO Box 1801
Edmond, OK 73083-1801, USA

Sutton, Hal (Golfer)
40 Duck Haven Pt
Bossier City, LA 71111-8173, USA

Sutton, Joe (Football Player)
508 44th Ave E Lot K48
Bradenton, FL 34203-7526, USA

Sutton, John (Athlete, Baseball Player)
536 Blueberry Blvd
Dallas, TX 75217-4201, USA

Sutton, Larry (Athlete, Baseball Player)
14209 Woodward St
Overland Park, KS 66223-2561, USA

Sutton, Michael (Actor)
8840 Wilshire Blvd # 200
Beverly Hills, CA 90211-2606, USA

Sutton, Percy E (Politician)
10 W 135th St
New York, NY 10037-2602, USA

Sutton, Randi (Stylist)
7 Victoria Falls Dr
Rancho Mirage, CA 92270-1615, USA

Sutton, Ricky (Football Player)
1112 To Lani Farm Rd
Stone Mountain, GA 30083-5364, USA

Suu Kyi, Aung San (Nobel Prize Laureate)
54 University Ave
Yangon 11181, Myanmar

Suvadova, Silvia (Actor)
c/o Michael Henderson *Heresun Management*
4119 W Burbank Blvd
Burbank, CA 91505-2122, USA

Suvalatsumi (Actor)
58 2nd Street Venkatesh Nagar
Virugambakkam
Chennai, TN 600 092, INDIA

Suvaluxmi (Actor, Bollywood)
Matri Aasis 22/1/1/1 Monohar Pukur Road
PO Rash Behari Avenue
Kolkata, WB 700029, INDIA

Suvari, Mena (Actor)
c/o Jason Barrett *Alchemy Entertainment*
7024 Melrose Ave Ste 420
Los Angeles, CA 90038-3394, USA

Suwa, Gen (Misc)
Human Evolutionary Science Lab
Berkeley, CA 94720-0001, USA

Suwyn, Mark A (Business Person)
111 SW 5th Ave
Portland, OR 97204-3604, USA

Suzman, Janet (Actor)
11 Keats Grove Hampstead
London NW3, UNITED KINGDOM (UK)

Suzor, Mark (Athlete, Hockey Player)
1639 Hillcrest Dr
Sheridan, WY 82801-3242, USA

Suzuki, David (Correspondent, Scientist, Writer)
2211 W 4th Ave Suite 219
Vancouver, BC V6K 4S2, CANADA

Suzuki, Ichiro (Athlete, Baseball Player)
17186 SE 58th St
Bellevue, WA 98006-6609, USA

Suzuki, Pat
343 E 30th St
New York, NY 10016-6417

Suzuki, Robert (Educator)
President's Office
Bakersfield, CA 93311, USA

Suzy (Writer)
18 E 68th St # 1B
New York, NY 10065-5807, USA

Svankmajer, Jan (Director)
Ceminska 5
Prague 1 118 00, CZECH REPUBLIC

Svare, Harland (Athlete, Coach, Football Coach, Football Player)
629 Pine St Unit 105
Steamboat Springs, CO 80487-5115, USA

Svenden, Birgitta (Musician)
Sankt Eriksgatan 100
Stockholm 113 31, SWEDEN

Svendsen, George (Football Player)
163 Wayzata Blvd W Apt 315
Wayzata, MN 55391-1566, USA

Svendsen, Louise A (Misc)
16 Park Ave
New York, NY 10016-4329, USA

Sveningsson, Magnus (Musician)
Gotabergs Gatan 2
Gothenburg 400 14, SWEDEN

Svenson, Bo (Actor)
247 S Beverly Dr # 102
Beverly Hills, CA 90212-3830, USA

Svensson, Peter (Musician, Songwriter, Writer)
Gotabergs Gatan 2
Gothenburg 400 14, SWEDEN

Sverak, Jan (Director)
PO Box 33
Prague 515 155 00, CZECH REPUBLIC

Sveum, Dale (Athlete, Baseball Player)
13483 E Estrella Ave
Scottsdale, AZ 85259-5417, USA

Svihus, Bob (Football Player)
23000 Guidotti Dr
Salinas, CA 93908-1022, USA

Svoboda, Petr (Athlete, Hockey Player)
1119 S Jefferson St
Allentown, PA 18103-3026, USA

Swaby, Don (Actor)
c/o Staff Member *Stone Manners Salners Agency (LA)*
9911 W Pico Blvd Ste 1400
Los Angeles, CA 90035-2715, USA

Swados, Elizabeth A (Composer, Writer)
360 Central Park W Apt 16G
New York, NY 10025-6588, USA

Swagerty, Jane (Swimmer)
9128 N 70th St
Paradise Valley, AZ 85253-1960, USA

Swagerty, Keith (Athlete, Basketball Player)
22232 17th Ave SE Ste 205
Bothell, WA 98021-7411, USA

Swaggart, Jimmy L (Misc)
PO Box 262550
Baton Rouge, LA 70826-2550, USA

Swaggert, Jimmy
8912 World Ministry Ave
Baton Rouge, LA 70810

Swaggerty, Bill (Athlete, Baseball Player)
116 S Forney Ave
Hanover, PA 17331-3711, USA

Swail, Julie (Athlete, Coach)
Athletic
Irvine, CA 92697-0001, USA

Swaim, Caskey
1605 N Cahuenga Blvd # 202
Los Angeles, CA 90028-6201

Swain, Bennie (Athlete, Basketball Player)
3819 Florinda St
Houston, TX 77021-2550, USA

Swain, Brennan (Athlete)
c/o Jerry Shandrew *Shandrew Public Relations*
1050 S Stanley Ave
Los Angeles, CA 90019-6634, USA

Swain, Chelse (Actor)
c/o Staff Member *Identity Talent Agency (ID)*
9107 Wilshire Blvd Ste 500
Beverly Hills, CA 90210-5526, USA

Swain, Dominique (Actor)
c/o Michael Garnett *Leverage Management*
3030 Pennsylvania Ave
Santa Monica, CA 90404-4112, USA

Swain, John (Football Player)
409 E 135th St
Burnsville, MN 55337-4019, USA

Swaminathan, Monkombu S (Scientist)
3 Cross St Taramani
Chennai, TN 600113, INDIA

Swan, Billy (Musician, Songwriter, Writer)
202 Fulham Road Chelsea
London SW10 9PJ, UNITED KINGDOM (UK)

Swan, Craig (Athlete, Baseball Player)
296 Sound Beach Ave
Old Greenwich, CT 06870-1626, USA

Swan, John W D (President)
26 Victoria St
Hamilton HM12, BERMUDA

Swan, Michael (Actor)
13576 Cheltenham Dr
Sherman Oaks, CA 91423-4818, USA

Swan, Richard G (Mathematician)
700 Melrose Ave Apt M3
Winter Park, FL 32789-5610, USA

Swan, Serinda (Actor)
c/o Alex Cole *Elevate Entertainment*
10100 Santa Monica Blvd Ste 300
Los Angeles, CA 90067-4107, USA

Swanagon, Mary Lou (Baseball Player)
2193 E Amarillo Way
Palm Springs, CA 92264-8637, USA

Swanepoel, Candice (Model)
c/o Staff Member *MC2 Israel*
26 Hayarkon St 2nd Floor
Tel Aviv 68011, Israel

Swank, Hilary (Actor)
c/o Kim Hodgert *Creative Artists Agency (CAA-LA)*
2000 Avenue of the Stars Ste 100
Los Angeles, CA 90067-4705, USA

Swanke, Karl (Football Player)
4 Butternut Ct
Essex Junction, VT 05452-3959, USA

Swann, Lynn C (Athlete, Football Player, Sportscaster)
506 Hegner Way # 2
Sewickley, PA 15143-1552, USA

Swann, Pedro (Athlete, Baseball Player)
9 Westbury Dr
New Castle, DE 19720-8812, USA

Swanson, August G (Physicist)
3146 Portage Bay Pl E Apt H
Seattle, WA 98102-3847, USA

Swanson, Jackie (Actor)
15155 Albright St
Pacific Palisades, CA 90272-2511, USA

Swanson, Judith (Actor)
40 E 9th St
New York, NY 10003-6421, USA

Swanson, Kristy (Actor, Model)
c/o Leo Bozzuto *HYPHENATE*
9701 Wilshire Blvd Fl 10
Beverly Hills, CA 90212-2010, USA

Swanson, Red (Athlete, Baseball Player)
1139 Chippenham Dr
Baton Rouge, LA 70808-5694, USA

Swanson, Stan (Athlete, Baseball Player)
1705 E Whaley St
Longview, TX 75601-6833, USA

Swanson, Steven R (Astronomer)
16403 Bougainvilla Ln
Friendswood, TX 77546-3105, USA

Sward, Melinda (Actor)
c/o Sheila Wenzel *Innovative Artists (LA)*
1505 10th St
Santa Monica, CA 90401-2805, USA

Swardson, Nick (Actor, Musician)
c/o Tim Sarkes *Brillstein Entertainment Partners*
9150 Wilshire Blvd Ste 350
Beverly Hills, CA 90212-3453, USA

Swarn, George (Football Player)
442 Daisy St
Mansfield, OH 44903-1305, USA

Swaroop, Shikha (Actor, Bollywood)
13/14 Atmanand Saraswat Colony
Santacruz
Mumbai, MS 400054, INDIA

Swartwoudt, Gregg (Football Player)
202 Anderson Rd
Esko, MN 55733-9413, USA

Swartz, Jacob T (Scientist)
251 Mercer St
New York, NY 10012-1110, USA

Swartzbaugh, Dave (Athlete, Baseball Player)
113 Orchard St
Middletown, OH 45044-4920, USA

Swatek, Barret (Actor)
c/o Tammy Rosen *Sanders Armstrong Caserta*
425 N Robertson Blvd
West Hollywood, CA 90048-1735, USA

Swathi (Actor, Bollywood)
Flat No 4-42 47th Street 9thAvenue
Ashok Nagar
Chennai, TN 600083, INDIA

Swatland, Richard (Football Player)
178 Club Rd
Stamford, CT 06905-2120, USA

Sway (Television Host)
c/o Staff Member *Music Television (MTV) Networks (NY)*
1515 Broadway
New York, NY 10036-8901, USA

Swayne, Harry (Football Player)
2702 Baublitz Rd
Reisterstown, MD 21136-5504, USA

Swayze, Don
247 S Beverly Dr # 102
Beverly Hills, CA 90212-3830

Swe, U Ba (Prime Minister)
84 Innes Road
Yangon, MYANMAR

Swearingen, John E Jr (Business Person)
1420 N Lake Shore Dr
Chicago, IL 60610-6657, USA

Sweat, Keith (Musician, Songwriter)
c/o Michael Irving *Emancipated Talent*
215 Clinton St
Brooklyn, NY 11201, USA

Swedberg, Heidi (Actor)
c/o Staff Member *Marathon Entertainment*
8060 Melrose Ave Ste 400
Los Angeles, CA 90046-7038

Swedlin, Rosalie (Producer)
c/o Staff Member *Jackoway Tyerman Wertheimer Austen Mandelbaum Morris & Klein*
1925 Century Park E Fl 22
Los Angeles, CA 90067-2701, USA

Sweeney, Alison (Actor)
c/o Elissa Leeds-Fickman *Reel Talent Management*
PO Box 491035
Los Angeles, CA 90049-9035, USA

Sweeney, Brian (Athlete, Baseball Player)
199 Morsemere Ave
Yonkers, NY 10703-2007, USA

Sweeney, Calvin (Athlete, Football Player)
4120 Olympiad Dr
Los Angeles, CA 90043-1632, USA

Sweeney, D B (Actor)
c/o Staff Member *Lighthouse Entertainment*
9220 W Sunset Blvd Ste 200
West Hollywood, CA 90069-3501, USA

Sweeney, James (Jim) (Coach, Football Coach)
119 Justabout Rd
Venetia, PA 15367-1230, USA

Sweeney, John J (Politician)
1750 New York Ave NW
Washington, DC 20006-5305, USA

Sweeney, Julia (Actor, Comedian)
c/o Staff Member *WmE2 (Endeavor-LA)*
9601 Wilshire Blvd Fl 3
Beverly Hills, CA 90210-5219, USA

Sweeney, Kevin (Athlete, Football Player)
12401 N Via Tuscania Ave
Clovis, CA 93619-8382, USA

Sweeney, Mark (Athlete, Baseball Player)
1821 Horseman Ln
Rcho Santa Fe, CA 92091-4605, USA

Sweeney, Michael J (Mike) (Athlete, Baseball Player)
PO Box 1193
Rancho Santa Fe, CA 92067-1193, USA

Sweeney, Pepper
1930 Century Park W # 403
Los Angeles, CA 90067-6802

Sweeney, Sunny (Musician)
c/o Staff Member *WmE2 (WMA-TN)*
1600 Division St Ste 300
Nashville, TN 37203-2755, USA

Sweeney, Terry (Actor, Comedian, Writer)
c/o Staff Member *Creative Artists Agency (CAA-LA)*
2000 Avenue of the Stars Ste 100
Los Angeles, CA 90067-4705, USA

Sweeney, Walter F (Walt) (Athlete, Football Player)
6048 Gullstrand St
San Diego, CA 92122-3822, USA

Sweet, Joe (Athlete, Football Player)
1503 NE 89th Ct
Vancouver, WA 98664-6413, USA

Sweet, Matthew (Musician, Songwriter, Writer)
315 W Ponce De Leon Ave Ste 755
Decatur, GA 30030-2497, USA

Sweet, Rachel (Producer)
c/o Staff Member *WmE2 (Endeavor-LA)*
9601 Wilshire Blvd Fl 3
Beverly Hills, CA 90210-5219, USA

Sweet, Rick (Athlete, Baseball Player)
1503 NE 89th Ct
Vancouver, WA 98664-6413, USA

Sweet, Sharon (Opera Singer)
165 W 57th St
New York, NY 10019-2201, USA

Sweet, Shay (Adult Film Star)
c/o Staff Member *Atlas Multimedia Inc*
9005 Eton Ave Ste C
Canoga Park, CA 91304-6533, USA

Sweeten, Madylin (Actor)
c/o Dino May *Dino May Management*
6362 Hollywood Blvd
Los Angeles, CA 90028-6323, USA

Sweethearts of the Rodeo
5101 Overton Rd
Nashville, TN 37220-1920

Sweetin, Jodie (Actor)
c/o Staff Member *Savage Agency*
6212 Banner Ave
Los Angeles, CA 90038-2802, USA

Sweetlin, Jodie
6212 Banner Ave
Los Angeles, CA 90038-2802

Sweetman, Julie (Stylist)
c/o Staff Member *Artist Agency, THE (NY)*
230 W 55th St Apt 29D
New York, NY 10019-5206

Sweetney, Mike (Basketball Player)
Madison Square Garden 2 Penn Plaza
New York, NY 10121, USA

Swensen, Joseph A (Composer, Conductor)
4 Addison Bridge Place
London W14 8XP, UNITED KINGDOM (UK)

Swenson, August
1702 Azores Dr
Pflurgerville, TX 78880

Swenson, Eliza (Actor, Musician)
5118 Vineland Ave # 102
North Hollywood, CA 91601-3814, USA

Swenson, Inga (Actor, Musician)
3351 Halderman St
Los Angeles, CA 90066-1719, USA

Swenson, Rick (Dog Sled Racer)
PO Box 16205
Two Rivers, AK 99716-0205, USA

Swenson, Robert C (Bob) (Athlete, Football Player)
910 Cypress Ln
Louisville, CO 80027-9428, USA

Swenson, Ruth Ann (Opera Singer)
165 W 57th St
New York, NY 10019-2201, USA

Swensson, Earl S (Architect)
2100 W End Ave Ste 1200
Nashville, TN 37203-5239, USA

Swerling Jr, Jo
25745 Vista Verde Dr
Calabasas, CA 91302-2165, USA

Swiatek, Kazimierz Cardinal (Religious Leader)
Pl Swobody 9
Minsk 220030, BELARUS

Swick, Mike (Athlete)
c/o Staff Member *Zinkin Entertainment & Sports Management*
5 E River Park Pl W Ste 203
Fresno, CA 93720-1557, USA

Swiczinsky, Helmut (Architect)
16/11A Seilerstatte
Pueblo, CO 81010-0001, AUSTRIA

Swider, Larry (Athlete, Football Player)
1903 W 93rd Ave
Crown Point, IN 46307-1809, USA

Swienton, Gregory T (Business Person)
3600 NW 82nd Ave
Doral, FL 33166-6623, USA

Swift, Clive (Actor)
8 Silver Place
London W1R 3LJ, UNITED KINGDOM (UK)

Swift, Doug (Athlete, Football Player)
265 S 25th St
Philadelphia, PA 19103-5551, USA

Swift, Graham C (Writer)
20 John St
London WC1N 2DR, UNITED KINGDOM (UK)

Swift, Harley (Athlete, Basketball Player)
357 Cliffside Dr
Kingsport, TN 37660-7103, USA

Swift, Hewson H (Biologist)
Cell Biology Dept
Chicago, IL 60637, USA

Swift, Stephanie (Adult Film Star)
PO Box 9864
Canoga Park, CA 91309-0864, USA

Swift, Stephen J (Judge)
400 2nd St NW
Washington, DC 20217-0001, USA

Swift, Stromile (Athlete, Basketball Player)
1111 Lincoln Rd Fl 4
Miami Beach, FL 33139-2439, USA

Swift, Taylor (Musician)
c/o Robert Allen *13 Management*
170 E Main St Ste D
Hendersonville, TN 37075-3952, USA

Swift, William C (Bill) (Athlete, Baseball Player)
5880 E Sapphire Ln
Paradise Valley, AZ 85253-2200, USA

Swilley, Dennis (Athlete, Football Player)
1020 Gruene River Dr
New Braunfels, TX 78132-3298, USA

Swindell, F Gregory (Greg) (Athlete, Baseball Player)
2706 Rivercrest Dr
Austin, TX 78746-1722, USA

Swindells, William Jr (Business Person)
1300 SW 5th Ave
Portland, OR 97201-5667, USA

Swindle, Orson
500 University Ave Apt 309
Honolulu, HI 96826-4903

Swindoll, Luci (Writer)
PO Box 141000
Nashville, TN 37214-1000, USA

Swinford, Wayne (Athlete, Football Player)
100 Beacham Dr
Athens, GA 30606-4004, USA

Swing Out Sister
132 Liverpool Rd Islington
London, ENGLAND N1 1LA

Swingfly
c/o Staff Member *United Stage Artist*
Box 11029
Stockholm S-10061, Sweden

Swingle, Paul (Athlete, Baseball Player)
6844 S Whetstone Pl
Chandler, AZ 85249-9149, USA

Swingley, Doug (Dog Sled Racer)
General Delivery
Lincoln, MT 59639-9999, USA

Swink, James E (Jim) (Athlete, Football Player)
723 Euclid Ave
Rusk, TX 75785-1919, USA

Swinny, Wayne (Musician)
535 Kings Road
London SW10 0S, UNITED KINGDOM (UK)

Swinson, Aaron (Athlete, Basketball Player)
1004 Longley Cv
Heathrow, FL 32746-1921, USA

Swinton, Tilda (Actor)
c/o Christian Hodell *Hamilton Hodell Ltd*
66-68 Margaret St Fl 5
London W1W 8SR, UK

Swisher, Carl C (Misc)
1288 9th St
Berkeley, CA 94710-1501, USA

Swisher, Nick (Athlete, Baseball Player)
c/o Team Member *New York Yankees*
Yankee Stadium 161st St & River Ave
Bronx, NY 10451, USA

Swisher, Steve (Athlete, Baseball Player)
432 60th St
Vienna, WV 26105-8091, USA

Swisten, Amanda (Actor)
c/o Staff Member *WNWN Media*
348 Hauser Blvd # PH414
Los Angeles, CA 90036-3276, USA

Swistowicz, Mike (Athlete, Football Player)
2519 S Drake Ave
Chicago, IL 60623-3919, USA

Swit, Loretta (Actor)
23852 Pacific Coast Hwy
Malibu, CA 90265-4876, USA

Switchfoot (Music Group)
c/o Staff Member *Red Light Management (LA)*
8439 W Sunset Blvd Ste 2
Los Angeles, CA 90069-1925, USA

Switzer, Barry (Basketball Player)
PO Box 43021
Lubbock, TX 79409-3021, USA

Switzer, Barry (Athlete, Coach, Football Coach, Football Player)
700 W Timberdell Rd
Norman, OK 73072-6323, USA

Switzer, Jon (Athlete, Baseball Player)
3915 Oakmont Blvd
Austin, TX 78731-6048, USA

Switzer, Veryl (Athlete, Football Player)
1412 Wreath Ave
Manhattan, KS 66503-2402, USA

Swoboda, Ron (Athlete, Baseball Player)
315 Alonzo St
New Orleans, LA 70115-2119, USA

Swope, Tracy Brooks
8730 W Sunset Blvd Ste 480
Los Angeles, CA 90069-2277

Sword, Sam (Athlete, Football Player)
2781 San Leandro Blvd
San Leandro, CA 94578-2583, USA

SWV
6464 W Sunset Blvd Ste 610
Hollywood, CA 90028-7527

Swygert, H Patrick (Educator)
President S Ofc
Washington, DC 20059-0001, USA

Syal, Meera (Actor)
c/o Dallas Smith *United Agents*
12-26 Lexington St
London W1F OLE, UK

Syberberg, Hans-Jurgen (Director)
Genter Str 15A
Munich 80805, GERMANY

Sybil (Musician)
Business Center Lower Road
London SE16 2XB, UNITED KINGDOM (UK)

Sydney, Harry (Athlete, Football Player)
1558 Cardinal Ln
Green Bay, WI 54313-7117, USA

Sykes, Bob (Athlete, Baseball Player)
1451 County Road 900 E
Carmi, IL 62821-4924, USA

Sykes, Eric (Actor)
9 Orme Court
London W2 4RL, UNITED KINGDOM (UK)

Sykes, Eugene (Gene) (Athlete, Football Player)
8155 Jefferson Hwy Apt 903
Baton Rouge, LA 70809-1616, USA

Sykes, Lynn R (Geophysicist, Physicist)
RR 1 Box 248 100 Washington Spring Road
Palisades, NY 10964, USA

Sykes, Melanie (Actor)
c/o Staff Member *Money Management*
22 Noel Street
London W1f 8GS, United Kingdom

Sykes, Peter (Director)
76 Oxford St
London W1N 0AX, UNITED KINGDOM (UK)

Sykes, Phil (Athlete, Hockey Player)
2312 Hill Ln
Redondo Beach, CA 90278-5218, USA

Sykes, Wanda (Actor, Comedian)
c/o Danica Smith *PMK/BNC Public Relations (PMK-LA)*
8687 Melrose Ave Ste 8
West Hollywood, CA 90069-5746, USA

Sykora, Petr (Athlete, Hockey Player)
2548 Appletree Dr
Pittsburgh, PA 15241-2587, USA

Sylbert, Anthea (Designer)
13949 Ventura Blvd # 309
Sherman Oaks, CA 91423-3584, USA

Sylver, Marshall (Misc)
1027 S Rainbow Blvd Ste 281
Las Vegas, NV 89145-6232, USA

Sylvester, George H (General)
4571 Conicville Rd
Mount Jackson, VA 22842-2713, USA

Sylvester, Harold (Actor)
8942 Wilshire Blvd # 219
Beverly Hills, CA 90211-1908, USA

Sylvester, Michael (Opera Singer)
165 W 57th St
New York, NY 10019-2201, USA

Sylvester, Steven P (Athlete, Football Player)
10425 Londonderry Ct
Cincinnati, OH 45242-5029, USA

Sylvia (Musician)
PO Box 120426
Nashville, TN 37212-0426, USA

Symmonds, Nick (Athlete, Olympic Athlete, Track Athlete)
c/o Staff Member *Total Sports Management*
507 Laurel Ave
Johnson City, TN 37604-6643, USA

Symms, Steven D (Senator)
43527 Butler Pl
Leesburg, VA 20176-7428, USA

Symone, Raven (Actor)
c/o Todd Diener *Collective*
8383 Wilshire Blvd Ste 1050
Beverly Hills, CA 90211-2415, USA

Symonette, Josh (Athlete, Football Player)
4923 Forrest Run
Lithonia, GA 30038-2794, USA

Syms, Sylvia (Actor)
47 West Square
London SE11 4SP, UNITED KINGDOM (UK)

Synkowski, Judy (Stylist)
305 E 76th St Apt 2D
New York, NY 10021-2428, USA

Sypek, Ryan (Actor)
c/o Leonard Torgan *Collective*
8383 Wilshire Blvd Ste 1050
Beverly Hills, CA 90211-2415, USA

Syreeta
6255 W Sunset Blvd Ste 1800
Los Angeles, CA 90028-7419

Syron, Richard F (Financier, Government Official)
500 Kendall St
Cambridge, MA 02142-1108, USA

System of a Down (Music Group)
c/o David Benveniste *Velvet Hammer*
9014 Melrose Ave
West Hollywood, CA 90069-5610, USA

Sytsma, John F (Politician)
1370 Ontario St
Cleveland, OH 44113-1701, USA

Szabo, Istvan (Director)
Rona Utca 174
Budapest 1149, HUNGARY

Szajda, Pawel (Actor)
c/o Staff Member *Stone Manners Salners Agency (LA)*
9911 W Pico Blvd Ste 1400
Los Angeles, CA 90035-2715, USA

Szarabajka, Keith (Actor)
c/o Staff Member *Bauman Redanty & Shaul Agency*
5757 Wilshire Blvd Suite 473
Beverly Hills, CA 90212, USA

Szasz, Thomas S (Doctor)
4739 Limberlost Ln
Manlius, NY 13104-1405, USA

Szczerbiak, Walt (Wally) (Athlete, Basketball Player)
20 Peabody Rd
Cold Spring Harbor, NY 11724-1709, USA

Szekely, Eva (Swimmer)
Szepvolgyi Utca 4/B
Budapest 1025, HUNGARY

Szekessy, Karen (Photographer)
Haynstr 2
Hamburg 20249, GERMANY

Szep, Paul M (Cartoonist, Editor)
7 Stetson St
Brookline, MA 02446-7106, USA

Szewczenki, Tanya (Figure Skater)
Niederbeerbacher Str 10
Muhital 64367, GERMANY

Szigmond, Vilmos (Cinematographer)
PO Box 2230
Los Angeles, CA 90078-2230, USA

Szmanda, Eric (Actor)
c/o Michael Gruber *After Dark Management Group*
Prefers to be contacted via telephone
Los Angeles, CA 90069, USA

Szohr, Jessica (Actor)
c/o Lena Roklin *Luber Roklin Management*
8530 Wilshire Blvd Ste 550
Beverly Hills, CA 90211-3133, USA

Szoka, Edmund C Cardinal (Religious Leader)
Vatican City 120, VATICAN CITY

Szostak, Jack W. (Nobel Prize Laureate)
Simches Research Ctr CPZN# 7320 185 Cambridge St
Boston, MA 2114, USA

Szotkiewicz, Ken (Athlete, Baseball Player)
849 Dusky Sap Ct
Griffin, GA 30223-5994, USA

Szott, David (Athlete, Football Player)
11 Manor Dr
Morristown, NJ 07960-2600, USA

Szukala, Stan (Athlete, Basketball Player)
2510 N Mozart St
Chicago, IL 60647-2616, USA

Szuminski, Jason (Athlete, Baseball Player)
680 Serra St Apt W402
Stanford, CA 94305-7327, USA

Szymanski, Jim (Athlete, Football Player)
541 Riverwalk Dr
Mason, MI 48854-9361, USA

Szymanski, Richard (Dick) (Athlete, Football Player)
5270 Forest Edge Ct
Sanford, FL 32771-7160, USA

Szymborska, Wislawa (Nobel Prize Laureate)
Stowarzyszenie Pissarzy Polskich Ul Kanonicza 7
Cracow 31-002, POLAND

T

T Hooft, Gerardus (Nobel Prize Laureate)
Leuvenlaan 4 Postbus 80.195
Utrecht 3508, NETHERLANDS

T. King, Peter (Congressman, Politician)
339 Cannon Hob
Washington, DC 20515-3003, USA

T. McCaul, Michael (Congressman, Politician)
131 Cannon Hob
Washington, DC 20515-2501, USA

T Pain (Musician)
c/o Staff Member *Jive Records*
550 Madison Ave Fl 6
New York, NY 10022-3211, USA

T Rajendar (Actor)
33 Hindi Prachar Sabha Road T Nagar
Chennai, TN 600 017, INDIA

Tabachnik, Michel (Composer, Conductor)
59 Lansdowne Place
Hove BN3 1FL, UNITED KINGDOM (UK)

Tabackin, Lewis B (Lew) (Musician)
38 W 94th St
New York, NY 10025-7123, USA

Tabai, Ieremia T (President)
Ratu Su Kuna Rd GPO Box 856
Suva, FIJI

Tabak, Zan (Athlete, Basketball Player)
230 W Superior St Ste 510
Chicago, IL 60654-3584, USA

Tabaka, Jeff (Athlete, Baseball Player)
1481 Norview Dr
Clinton, OH 44216-8804, USA

Tabakov, Oleg P (Actor, Director)
#3
Moscow 103062, RUSSIA

Tabaksblat, Morris (Business Person)
Weena 455
Rotterdam, DK 3000, NETHERLANDS

Tabassum (Actor, Bollywood, Talk Show Host, Television Host)
11A Pooja Apartments Master Vinayak Road Bandra
Bombay, MS 400 050, INDIA

Tabb, Jerry (Athlete, Baseball Player)
7819 Gable Bridge Ln
Richmond, TX 77407-5586, USA

Taber, Catherine (Actor)
c/o Staff Member *Charles Riley*
7122 Beverly Blvd Ste F
Los Angeles, CA 90036-2572, USA

Tabitha, Masentle (Royalty)
PO Box 524
Maseru, LESOTHO

Tabler, Pat (Athlete, Baseball Player, Sportscaster)
1 Blue Jays Way Suite Attn Broadcast Dept 3200
Toronto, ON M5V 1J1, Canada

Tabois, Sean (Stylist)
c/o Staff Member *Stockland Martel*
343 E 18th St
New York, NY 10003-2802, USA

Tabone, Anton (President)
33 Carmel St
Slierna, MALTA

Tabor, David (Physicist)
8 Rutherford Road
Cambridge CB2 2HH, UNITED KINGDOM (UK)

Tabor, Greg (Athlete, Baseball Player)
29317 Whalebone Way
Hayward, CA 94544-6427, USA

Tabor, Herbert (Scientist)
8 Center Dr
Bethesda, MD 20892-0001, USA

Tabor, Paul (Athlete, Football Player)
3308 Riverwalk Dr
Norman, OK 73072-4852, USA

Tabor, Phil (Athlete, Football Player)
806 Wood N Creek Rd
Ardmore, OK 73401-2940, USA

Tabori, Kristoffer (Actor)
235 Regent St
London W1R 8AX, USA

Tabori, Laszlo (Athlete, Track Athlete)
2221 W Olive Ave
Burbank, CA 91506-2659, USA

Tabu (Actor, Bollywood)
Anukool 2nd Floor 7 Bungalows Versova Andheri (W)
Mumbai, MS 400058, INDIA

Taccone, Jorma (Writer)
c/o Julie Darmody *Mosaic Media Group*
9200 W Sunset Blvd Ste 10
Los Angeles, CA 90069-3608, USA

Tacha, Deanell R (Judge)
4830 Bob Billings Pkwy
Lawrence, KS 66049-4091, USA

Tackett, Jeffrey (Jeff) (Athlete, Baseball Player)
1574 Frazier St
Camarillo, CA 93012-4431, USA

Taco (Musician)
8124 W 3rd St Ste 204
Los Angeles, CA 90048-4341, USA

Tada, Joni Eareckson (Writer)
PO Box 3333
Agoura Hills, CA 91376-3333, USA

Taddei, Giuseppe (Opera Singer)
Lincoln Center Plaza
New York, NY 10023, USA

Tadic, Boris (President)
Nemanjina 11
Belgrade 11000, SERBIA

Taeger, Ralph
5619 Mother Lode Dr
Placerville, CA 95667-8232

Taff, Russ
PO Box 570815
Tarzana, CA 91357-0815

Taffoni, Joe (Athlete, Football Player)
605 Golf Links Ct
Chapin, SC 29036-7108, USA

Tafoya, Michele (Sportscaster)
c/o Staff Member *ESPN (Main)*
ESPN Plaza 935 Middle St
Bristol, CT 06010-1001, USA

Tafoya, Michele (Sportscaster)
51 W 52nd St
New York, NY 10019-6119, USA

Taft, Robert
2933 Lower Bellbrook Rd
Spring Valley, OH 45370-8761

Taft, William H IV (Government Official)
1001 Pennsylvania Ave NW
Washington, DC 20004-2502, USA

Tagawa, Cary-Hiroyuki (Actor)
c/o Joseph (Joe) Rice *Abrams Artists Agency (LA)*
9200 W Sunset Blvd PH 11
Los Angeles, CA 90069-3601, USA

Tagge, Jerry (Athlete, Football Player)
15033 Patterson Cir
Omaha, NE 68137-5127, USA

Taghmaoui, Said (Actor)
c/o Leonard Torgan *Collective*
8383 Wilshire Blvd Ste 1050
Beverly Hills, CA 90211-2415, USA

Tagliabue, Paul (Football Executive)
280 Park Ave Fl 12W
New York, NY 10017-1298

Tagliabue, Paul J (Football Executive)
280 Park Ave Fl 12W
New York, NY 10017-1298, USA

Taglianetti, Peter (Athlete, Hockey Player)
67 Bayhill Dr
Bridgeville, PA 15017-1088, USA

Taguchi, So (Athlete, Baseball Player)
320 N Bemiston Ave
Saint Louis, MO 63105-3830, USA

Tahil, Dalip (Actor, Bollywood)
19 Deepali St Cyril Road Bandra
Mumbai, MS 400050, INDIA

Tahir, Faran (Actor)

Tai, Kobe (Adult Film Star)
c/o Staff Member *Atlas Multimedia Inc*
9005 Eton Ave Ste C
Canoga Park, CA 91304-6533, USA

Taichman, Tamara (Stylist)
c/o Staff Member *Marek & Associates Inc*
508 W 26th St Rm 12C
New York, NY 10001-5541, USA

Taillibert, Roger R (Architect)
163 Rue de la Ponpe
Paris 75116, FRANCE

Tait, John (Athlete, Football Player)
3004 S Market St Apt 1010
Gilbert, AZ 85295-1351, USA

Tait, John E (Business Person)
Independence Sq
Philadelphia, PA 19172-0001, USA

Tait, Tristan (Actor)
10100 Santa Monica Blvd Ste 2500
Los Angeles, CA 90067-4116, USA

Taittinger, Jean (Business Person)
58 Blvd Gouvion Saint-Cyr
Paris 75017, FRANCE

Tak, Saawan Kumar (Bollywood, Director, Filmmaker, Producer)
A/11 Dakshina Park 10th Road Juhu
Bombay, MS 400 049, INDIA

Taka, Miiko
14560 Round Valley Dr
Sherman Oaks, CA 91403-4631

Takac, Robby (Musician)
c/o Staff Member *Atlas/Third Rail Entertainment*
9200 W Sunset Blvd Ste 10
Los Angeles, CA 90069-3608, USA

Takacs, Tibor (Director)
IP 104 Richview Ave
Toronto, ON M5P 3E9, CANADA

Takacs-Nagy, Gabor (Musician)
Case Postale 196
Collonge-Bellerive 1245, SWITZERLAND

Takahashi, Joseph S (Scientist)
2153 N Campus Dr
Evanston, IL 60208-0877, USA

Takahashi, Michiaki (Scientist)
Microbe Diseases Research Institute
Osaka, JAPAN

Takamatsu, Shin (Architect)
195 Jobodaiincho Takeda
Kyoto, JAPAN

Take 6 (Music Group, Musician)
c/o Staff Member *Agency for the Performing Arts (APA-LA)*
405 S Beverly Dr Ste 500
Beverly Hills, CA 90212-4425, USA

Take That
69-79 Fulham High St
London, ENGLAND SW6 3JW

Takei, George (Actor)
c/o Michael Greenwald *Don Buchwald & Associates Inc (LA)*
6500 Wilshire Blvd Ste 2200
Los Angeles, CA 90048-4942, USA

Takenouchi, Naoko (Artist)
PO Box 58922
Renton, WA 98058-1922, USA

Takezawa, Kyoko (Musician)
40 W 57th St
New York, NY 10019-4001, USA

Takle, Darien (Actor)
c/o Staff Member *Robert Bruce Agency*
218 Richmond Rd Grey Lynn
Auckland 2, New Zealand

Tal, Alona (Actor)
c/o Laura Myones *McKeon-Myones Management*
3500 W Olive Ave Ste 770
Burbank, CA 91505-5527, USA

Talalay, Paul (Scientist)
5512 Boxhill Ln
Baltimore, MD 21210-2039, USA

Talalay, Rachel (Director)
1047 Grant St
Santa Monica, CA 90405-1411, USA

Talamini, Robert (Athlete, Football Player)
1312 Calle Lajas
Las Cruces, NM 88007-8809, USA

Talancon, Ana Claudia (Actor)
c/o Carlos Carreras *Paradigm (LA)*
360 N Crescent Dr
Beverly Hills, CA 90210-4874, USA

Talavera, Tracee (Gymnast)
1487 Marion Ave
Tallahassee, FL 32303-5828, USA

Talbert, Billy (Athlete)
194 Bellevue Ave
Newport, RI 02840-3515, USA

Talbert, Diron (Athlete, Football Player)
PO Box 388
Rosenberg, TX 77471-0388, USA

Talbert, Don (Athlete, Football Player)
PO Box 261
Richmond, TX 77406-0007, USA

Talbot, Bob (Athlete, Baseball Player)
608 W Kaweah Ave
Visalia, CA 93277-2510, USA

Talbot, Dale (Baseball Player)
608 W Kaweah Ave
Visalia, CA 93277-2510, USA

Talbot, Diron V (Athlete, Football Player)
3803 B F Terry Blvd
Rosenberg, TX 77471-5657, USA

Talbot, Don (Coach, Swimmer)
333 River Road Vanier
Ottawa, ON K1L 8B9, CANADA

Talbot, Fred (Athlete, Baseball Player)
7701 Lunceford Ln
Falls Church, VA 22043-1207, USA

Talbot, Joby (Composer, Musician)
c/o Catherine Manners *Manners McDade Artist Management*
46 Copperfield St
London SE1 0DY, UK

Talbot, Nita (Actor)
3420 Merrimac Rd
Los Angeles, CA 90049-1034, USA

Talbot, Susan (Actor)
6300 Wilshire Blvd Ste 1470
Los Angeles, CA 90048-5200, USA

Talbott, Gloria (Actor)
2066 Montecito Dr
Glendale, CA 91208-1824, USA

Talbott, John H (Doctor)
177 Ocean Lane Dr
Key Biscayne, FL 33149-1426, USA

Talbott, John R (Writer)
c/o Staff Member *St Martins Press*
175 5th Ave
New York, NY 10010-7703, USA

Talbott, Michael (Actor)
2011 Euclid Ave
Waverly, IA 50677-9700, USA

Talbott, Strobe (Journalist)
2201 C St NW
Washington, DC 20520-0099, USA

Talese, Gay (Writer)
154 E Atlantic Blvd
Ocean City, NJ 08226-4511, USA

Taliaferro, George (Athlete, Football Player)
2708 S Olcott Blvd
Bloomington, IN 47401-4417, USA

Taliaferro, Mike (Athlete, Football Player)
7332 Oakbluff Dr
Dallas, TX 75254-2739, USA

Talla (DJ)
c/o Staff Member *Diva Central Inc*
7510 W Sunset Blvd Ste 1445
Los Angeles, CA 90046-3408, USA

Tallchief, Maria (Dancer)
48 Prospect Ave
Highland Park, IL 60035-3329, USA

Tallet, Brian (Athlete, Baseball Player)
3167 McClendon Ct
Baton Rouge, LA 70810 8376, USA

Talley, Darryl V (Athlete, Football Player)
1620 George Jenkins Blvd
Lakeland, FL 33815-3700, USA

Talley, Gary (Musician)
PO Box 8770
Endwell, NY 13762-8770, USA

Talley, Joel E (War Hero)
20 Lakeshore Dr
Shalimar, FL 32579-2210, USA

Talley, Stan (Athlete, Football Player)
24241 Porto Cristo
Dana Point, CA 92629-4511, USA

Tallman, Patricia (Actor)
1801 E Tropicana Ave Ste 9
Las Vegas, NV 89119-6559, USA

Tallman, Richard C (Judge)
5th Ave US Courthouse 1010
Seattle, WA 98104-3191, USA

Talor, Vanessa
11271 Ventura Blvd # 396
Studio City, CA 91604-3136

Talsania, Tiku (Actor, Bollywood)
22-A Shruti Yashudham Enclave Filmcity Rd Goregaon E
Mumbai, MS 400053, INDIA

Talton, Tim (Athlete, Baseball Player)
130 Hardy Talton Rd NW
Pikeville, NC 27863-8601, USA

Tam, Amy (Stylist)
c/o Staff Member *L'Agence*
5901 Peachtree Dunwoody Rd NE Ste C60
Atlanta, GA 30328-7155, USA

Tam, Jeffrey (Jeff) (Athlete, Baseball Player)
5255 Pina Vista Dr
Melbourne, FL 32934-7897, USA

Tamahori, Lee W (Director)
8942 Wilshire Blvd # 219
Beverly Hills, CA 90211-1908, USA

Tamargo, John (Athlete, Baseball Player)
19018 Fern Meadow Loop
Lutz, FL 33558-4000, USA

Tamaro, Janet (Journalist)
c/o Rob Kenneally *Creative Artists Agency (CAA-LA)*
2000 Avenue of the Stars Ste 100
Los Angeles, CA 90067-4705, USA

Tamayo, Mendez Amaldo (Cosmonaut)
Calle 16 #504 C/5A y 7MA
Miramar, Ciudad Havana 11300, CUBA

Tambellini, Roger (Athlete, Golfer)
32531 N Scottsdale Rd Ste 105
Scottsdale, AZ 85266-1519, USA

Tamberino, Paul (Referee)
349 Homeland Southway
Baltimore, MD 21212-4153, USA

Tambiah, Stanley J (Misc)
Anthropology Dept
Cambridge, MA 2138, USA

Tamblyn, Amber (Actor)
c/o Joan Hyler *Hyler Management*
20 Ocean Park Blvd Unit 25
Santa Monica, CA 90405-3590, USA

Tamblyn, Russ (Actor, Dancer)
2310 6th St Apt 2
Santa Monica, CA 90405-2443, USA

Tambone, Jeanne D (Stylist)
9 Lauri Ln
Middlesex, NJ 08846-1408, USA

Tambor, Jeffrey (Actor)
c/o Leslie Siebert *Gersh (LA)*
9465 Wilshire Blvd Ste 600
Beverly Hills, CA 90212-2612, USA

Tambor, Jeffrey (Actor)
9150 Wilshire Blvd Ste 350
Beverly Hills, CA 90212-3453, USA

Tamburello, Ben (Athlete, Football Player)
4385 Milner Rd W
Birmingham, AL 35242-7355, USA

Tamke, George W (Business Person)
PO Box 4100
Saint Louis, MO 63136-8506, USA

Tamm, Peter (Publisher)
Elbchaussee 277
Hamburg 22605, GERMANY

Tamm, Ralph (Athlete, Football Player)
2670 Atlantic Ave
Bensalem, PA 19020-3507, USA

Tan, Amy (Writer)
c/o Staff Member *Steven Barclay Agency*
12 Western Ave
Petaluma, CA 94952-2907, USA

Tan, Dun (Composer)
Arts School Dodge Hall
New York, NY 10027, USA

Tan, Elaine (Actor)
19 Denmark Street
London WC2H 8NA, UNITED KINGDOM (UK)

Tan, Melvyn (Musician)
4 Winsley St #305
London W1N 7AR, UNITED KINGDOM (UK)

Tan, Phillip (Actor)
c/o Michael Henderson *Heresun Management*
4119 W Burbank Blvd
Burbank, CA 91505-2122, USA

Tanaev, Nikoly (Prime Minister)
Ul Perromayskaya 57
Bishkek, KYRGYZSTAN

Tanaka, Koichi (Nobel Prize Laureate)
1 Nishinokyo-Kuwabaracho Nakagoku
Kyoto 604-8511, JAPAN

Tanaka, Machiko (Stylist)
2378 Silver Ridge Ave
Los Angeles, CA 90039-3646, USA

Tanaka, Shoji (Physicist)
1-10-13 Shinonome Kotoku
Tokyo 135, JAPAN

Tanana, Frank D (Athlete, Baseball Player)
28492 S Harwich Dr
Farmington Hills, MI 48334-4281, USA

Tancredo, Tom (Politician)
15342 W Iliff Dr
Lakewood, CO 80228-6443, USA

Tandon, Raveena (Actor, Bollywood)
Tandon House Nippon Society Juhu Church
Mumbai, MS 400049, INDIA

Tandon, Ravi (Bollywood, Director, Filmmaker, Producer)
B/58 Ravi Kiran New Linking Road
Bombay, MS 400 058, INDIA

Tanford, Charles (Doctor)
Tarlswood Back Lane
Easingwold, York YO6 3BG, UNITED KINGDOM (UK)

Tang, David (Designer)
Guangdong Investment Tower 23rd Floor
148 Connaught Road Central
Central Hong Kong, HONG KONG

Tangerine Dream
PO Box 29242
Oakland, CA 94604-9242

Tani, Daniel M (Astronaut)
14827 Sparkling Bay Ln
Houston, TX 77062-2325, USA

Taniguchi, Tadatsugu (Biologist)
Molecular & Cellular Biology Dept
Osaka, JAPAN

Tanka, Aiko (Model)
PO Box 1025
Beverly Hills, CA 90213-1025, USA

Tankersley, Dennis (Athlete, Baseball Player)
1032 Pearview Dr
Saint Peters, MO 63376-2269, USA

Tankersley, Taylor (Athlete, Baseball Player)
853 Chartier Ct
Asheboro, NC 27205-0545, USA

Tankian, Serj (Musician)
c/o David Holmes *3D Management*
1901 Main St Fl 3
Santa Monica, CA 90405-1075, USA

Tanksley, Steven D (Scientist)
Plant Genetics Dept Emerson Hall
Ithaca, NY 14853, USA

Tannen, Steve (Athlete, Football Player)
735 N Niagara St
Burbank, CA 91505-3006, USA

Tannenwald, Theodore Jr (Judge)
400 2nd St NW
Washington, DC 20217-0001, USA

Tanner, Alain (Director)
Chemin Point-du-Jour 12
Geneva 1202, SWITZERLAND

Tanner, Barron (Athlete, Football Player)
7556 W Oregon Ave
Glendale, AZ 85303-5685, USA

Tanner, Bruce (Athlete, Baseball Player)
324 Hearthstone Dr
New Castle, PA 16105-1374, USA

Tanner, Charles W (Chuck) (Athlete, Baseball Player, Coach)
327 Brownhome Rd
New Castle, PA 16101-9533, USA

Tanner, Hamp (Athlete, Football Player)
5960 Cherokee Trce
Cumming, GA 30041-5478, USA

Tanner, John (Athlete, Football Player)
235 Ash Dr
Merritt Island, FL 32953-4361, USA

Tanner, Joseph R (Astronaut)
PO Box 17546
Boulder, CO 80308-0546, USA

Tannous, Afif I (Government Official)
6912 Oak Ct
Annandale, VA 22003-5929, USA

Tanuja (Actor, Bollywood)
14 Usha Kiran 15 M L Dhahanukar Marg
Mumbai, MS 400026, INDIA

Tanumafili, Malietoa II (President)
Valima, Apia, SAMOA

Tanzi, Vito (Economist)
5912 Walhonding Rd
Bethesda, MD 20816-2354, USA

Tapani, Kevin (Athlete, Baseball Player)
781 Ferndale Rd N
Wayzata, MN 55391-1010, USA

Tape, Gerald F (Physicist)
90 Camino Espejo
Santa Fe, NM 87507-7603, USA

Tapert, Robert (Director, Producer, Writer)
c/o Staff Member *Renaissance Pictures / Ghost House Pictures*
315 S Beverly Dr Ste 216
Beverly Hills, CA 90212-4310, USA

Tapes N Tapes (Music Group)
c/o Staff Member *Paradigm (Monterey)*
404 W Franklin St
Monterey, CA 93940-2303, USA

Tapia, Johnny (Athlete, Boxer)
1800 Fran Rd Se
Rio Rancho, NM 87124-2741, USA

Tapia, Roberto (Musician)
c/o Staff Member *Universal Music Group (UMG - LA)*
2220 Colorado Ave
Santa Monica, CA 90404-3506, USA

Tappan V, Alfredo (Director)
c/o Gabriel Blanco *Gabriel Blanco Iglesias (Mexico)*
Rio Balsas 35-32 Colonia Cuauhtemoc
DF 6500, Mexico

Tappe, Ted (Athlete, Baseball Player)
1415 Koetters Ln
Quincy, IL 62305-1149, USA

Tapping, Amanda (Actor)
c/o Staff Member *Stargate SG-1*
10250 Constellation Blvd
Los Angeles, CA 90067-6200, USA

Tapply, William G. (Writer)
c/o Staff Member *St Martins Press*
175 5th Ave
New York, NY 10010-7703, USA

Tapscott, Mark
5663 Ruthwood Dr
Calabasas, CA 91302-1053

Tarand, Andres (Prime Minister)
Riigikogu Lossi Plats 1A
New York, NY 10130-0001, ESTONIA

Tarantina, Brian (Actor)
c/o Staff Member *Cunningham Escott Slevin & Doherty (CESD-LA)*
10635 Santa Monica Blvd Ste 130
Los Angeles, CA 90025-8306, USA

Tarantino, Quentin (Actor, Director, Producer, Writer)
c/o Paula Woods *Paula Woods Consultants*
Prefers to be contacted via email
Los Angeles, CA 90069, USA

Taranu, Cornel (Composer, Conductor)
Str Nicolae Iorga
Ckuj-Napoca 3400, ROMANIA

Tarasco, Tony (Athlete, Baseball Player)
3528 Maplewood Ave
Los Angeles, CA 90066-3020, USA

Tarasova, Tatiana (Coach, Figure Skater)
300 Alumni Rd
Newington, CT 06111-1868, USA

Tarasovic, George (Athlete, Football Player)
1503 Michael Dr
Pittsburgh, PA 15227-3958, USA

Tarbuck, Jimmy (Comedian)
c/o Staff Member *International Artistes*
Holborn Hall - 4th Floor
London WC1V 7BD, UK

Tardiff, Marc (Athlete, Hockey Player)
6070 Boul Du Jardin
Charlesbourg, PQ G1G 3Z8, Canada

Tardits, Richard (Athlete, Football Player)
3590 Round Bottom Rd
Cincinnati, OH 45244-3026, USA

Tarjan, Robert E (Mathematician)
4 Constitution Hl E
Princeton, NJ 08540-6740, USA

Tarkan (Musician)
c/o Staff Member *Mydonose Productions*
No 22 K 14 Park Plaza Eski Buyukdere Cad
Maslak, Istanbul, Turkey

Tarkanian, Jerry (Athlete, Basketball Player, Coach)
4767 Ocean Blvd Unit 1005
San Diego, CA 92109-8903, USA

Tarkenton, Francis A (Fran) (Athlete, Business Person, Football Player)
3340 Peachtree Rd NE Ste 2570
Atlanta, GA 30326-1088, USA

Tarle, Jim (Athlete, Football Player)
2125 Willesdon Dr E
Jacksonville, FL 32246-0549, USA

Tarmichael, Stephen (Stylist)
PO Box 1121
Palm Springs, CA 92263-1121, USA

Tarpey, Erin
77 W 66th St
New York, NY 10023-6201

Tarpley, Ron (Athlete, Basketball Player)
819 Foxridge Dr
Arlington, TX 76017-6451, USA

Tarr, Curtis W (Business Person, Government Official)
5445 Corporate Dr Ste 200
Troy, MI 48098-2683, USA

Tarr Jr, Robert J (Publisher)
58 River Marsh Ln
Johns Island, SC 29455-5202, USA

Tarrant, Chris (Game Show Host)
c/o Staff Member *Who Wants to Be a Millionaire*
30 W 67th St
New York, NY 10023-0038

Tarrant, Jim (Athlete, Football Player)
5509 Heath Row Dr
Birmingham, AL 35242-3142, USA

Tarses, Matt (Producer)
c/o Staff Member *WmE2 (Endeavor-LA)*
9601 Wilshire Blvd Fl 3
Beverly Hills, CA 90210-5219, USA

Tart, Levern (Athlete, Basketball Player)
735 W Maplewood Ave
Fullerton, CA 92832-2623, USA

Tartabull, Danilio (Dan) (Athlete, Baseball Player)
8200 Redlands St Apt 112
Playa Del Rey, CA 90293-6101, USA

Tartabull, Jose (Athlete, Baseball Player)
6605 Winfield Blvd Apt 32
Margate, FL 33063-7133, USA

Tartaglia, John (Actor, Producer, Writer)
1681 Broadway
New York, NY 10019-5827, USA

Tartakovsky, Genndy (Director, Producer, Writer)
c/o Staff Member *WmE2 (WMA-LA)*
1 William Morris Pl
Beverly Hills, CA 90212-4261, USA

Tarter, Jill (Astronomer, Physicist)
2035 Mountain Vw
Mountain View, CA 94043, USA

Tarver, John (Athlete, Football Player)
12056 SE Mount Scott Blvd
Happy Valley, OR 97086-6939, USA

Tarver, Laschelle (Athlete, Baseball Player)
4410 N Emerson Ave
Fresno, CA 93705-1203, USA

Tarzier, Carol (Artist)
1217 32nd St
Oakland, CA 94608-4201, USA

Tasby, Willie (Athlete, Baseball Player)
1210 E Renfro St
Plant City, FL 33563-5850, USA

Taschner, Jack (Athlete, Baseball Player)
2170 Hidden Creek Rd
Neenah, WI 54956-8916, USA

Taseff, Carl (Athlete, Football Player)
2548 Bay Pointe Dr
Weston, FL 33327-1421, USA

Tashima, A Wallace (Judge)
125 S Grand Ave
Pasadena, CA 91105-1643, USA

Tasker, Steven J (Steve) (Athlete, Football Player, Sportscaster)
16 Gypsy Ln
East Aurora, NY 14052-2108, USA

Tata, Joe E (Actor)
c/o Jeffrey Leavitt *Leavitt Talent Group*
8255 W Sunset Blvd
West Hollywood, CA 90046-2417, USA

Tata, Ratan (Business Person)
Bombay House 24 Homi Mody St
Mumbai 400 001, India

Tata, Terry (Athlete, Baseball Player)
23 Stonegate Cir
Cheshire, CT 06410-3461, USA

Tatar, Jerome F (Business Person)
Courthouse Plaza N
Dayton, OH 45463, USA

Tatarek, Bob (Athlete, Football Player)
5829 Southhall Rd
Birmingham, AL 35213-1017, USA

Tataurangi, Phil (Golfer)
PO Box 15325
Irvine, CA 92623-5325, USA

Tate, Albert Jr (Judge)
600 Camp St
New Orleans, LA 70130-3425, USA

Tate, Bruce (Musician)
24210 E East Fork Rd Spc 9
Azusa, CA 91702-6249, USA

Tate, Catherine (Actor, Writer)
c/o Doctor Who
Cardiff CF5 2YQ, United Kingdom

Tate, David (Athlete, Football Player)
3481 S Blackhawk Way
Aurora, CO 80014-3984, USA

Tate, Frank (Boxer)
12731 Water Oak Dr
Missouri City, TX 77489-3903, USA

Tate, James V (Writer)
PO Box 9668
North Amherst, MA 01059-9668, USA

Tate, Jeffrey P
2 Coningsby Road
London W5 4HR, UNITED KINGDOM (UK)

Tate, Kevin
6834 Hollywood Blvd # 303
Hollywood, CA 90028-6116

Tate, Lahmard (Actor)
c/o Rob D'Avola *Rob DAvola & Associates*
9107 Wilshire Blvd Ste 450
Beverly Hills, CA 90210-5535, USA

Tate, Larena
4116 W Magnolia Blvd Ste 101
Burbank, CA 91505-2700

Tate, Larenz (Actor)
c/o Thea Ellis *Fifteen Minutes (LA)*
8436 W 3rd St Ste 650
Los Angeles, CA 90048-4131, USA

Tate, Lee (Athlete, Baseball Player)
6905 Pratt St
Omaha, NE 68104-2528, USA

Tate, Randy (Politician)
100 Center Vl
Virginia Beach, VA 23463-0001, USA

Tate, Randy (Athlete, Baseball Player)
106 King St
Muscle Shoals, AL 35661-3698, USA

Tate, Stu (Athlete, Baseball Player)
1436 Nocoseka Trl Apt N1
Anniston, AL 36207-6739, USA

Tatel, David S (Judge)
333 Constitution Ave NW
Washington, DC 20001-2804, USA

Tatiana (Model)
c/o Staff Member *Ford Models (NY)*
238 E 4th St
New York, NY 10009-7425

Tatlitug, Kivanc (Actor)
c/o Gaye Sokmen *Gaye Sökmen Talent Agency*
Karanfil Caddesi Yolal Sokak Ic Levent No:3
Istanbul 34330, Turkey

Tatrai, Vilmos (Musician)
R Wallenberg Utca 4
Budapest XIII 1136, HUNGARY

TATU (Music Group)
c/o Robert Hayes *Sound Management*
1525 S Winchester Blvd
San Jose, CA 95128-4335, USA

Tatum, Bradford
1505 10th St
Santa Monica, CA 90401-2805

Tatum, Channing (Actor)
c/o William Choi *Management 360*
9111 Wilshire Blvd
Beverly Hills, CA 90210-5508, USA

Tatum, Earl (Athlete, Basketball Player)
2300 W Skyline Rd
Milwaukee, WI 53209-2176, USA

Tatum, Jim (Athlete, Baseball Player)
7433 Indian Wells Cv
Lone Tree, CO 80124-4207, USA

Tatum, John D (Jack) (Athlete, Football Player)
10620 Mark St
Oakland, CA 94605-5340, USA

Tatum, Ken (Athlete, Baseball Player)
19 Oakdale Dr
Montevallo, AL 35115-5435, USA

Tatum, Kinnon (Athlete, Football Player)
4109 Knollwood Dr
Fayetteville, NC 28304-5208, USA

Taube, Sven-Bertil
113CHEYNE Walk
London, ENGLAND SWl0 OES

Taubensee, Ed (Athlete, Baseball Player)
2234 Fountain Key Cir
Windermere, FL 34786-5804, USA

Taubman, A Alfred (Business Person)
200 E Long Lake Rd
Bloomfield Hills, MI 48304-2360, USA

Taupin, Bernie (Musician, Songwriter, Writer)
2905 Roundup Rd
Santa Ynez, CA 93460-9558, USA

Tauran, Jean-Louis Cardinal (Religious Leader)
Palazzo Apostolico
Vatican City 120, VATICAN CITY

Taurasi, Diana (Basketball Player)
c/o Staff Member *Phoenix Mercury*
201 E Jefferson St
Phoenix, AZ 85004-2412, USA

Taurel, Sidney (Business Person)
Lilly Corporate Ctr
Indianapolis, IN 46285-0001, USA

Tausch, Terry (Athlete, Football Player)
2804 Ryder Ct
Plano, TX 75093-3426, USA

Tauscher, Hansjorg (Skier)
Schwand 7
Oberstdorf 87561, GERMANY

Tauscher, Mark (Athlete, Football Player)
2245 Red Tail Gin
De Pere, WI 54115, USA

Taussig, Don (Athlete, Baseball Player)
1111 Ocean Dunes Cir
Jupiter, FL 33477-9128, USA

Tautalatasi, Junior (Athlete, Football Player)
1032 Eagle Ave Apt A
Alameda, CA 94501-1111, USA

Tautolo, Terry (Athlete, Football Player)
5713 E Huntdale St
Long Beach, CA 90808-2717, USA

Tautou, Audrey (Actor)
c/o Claire Blondel *ArtMedia*
20 avenue Rapp
Paris 75008, France

Tauziat, Nathalie (Tennis Player)
1 Ave Gordon Bennett
Paris 75016, FRANCE

Tavard, Georges H (Misc)
330 Market St
Brighton, MA 02135-2131, USA

Tavare, Jay (Actor)
c/o Paul Greenstone *Paul Greenstone Entertainment*
3008 Sorrelwood Dr
San Ramon, CA 94582-5008, USA

Tavares, Alex (Athlete, Baseball Player)
Calle 7B #18
Reparto Perello Santiago, Dominican Republic

Tavares, John (Athlete, Hockey Player)
c/o Pat Brisson *Creative Artists Agency (CAA-LA)*
2000 Avenue of the Stars Ste 100
Los Angeles, CA 90067-4705, USA

Tavarez, Christopher (Actor, Football Player)
c/o Staff Member *Ella Bee*
Prefers to be contacted by telephone or email
Atlanta, GA, USA

Tavarez, Julian (Athlete, Baseball Player)
1108 Fireside Trl
Broadview Heights, OH 44147-3625, USA

Tavener, John H (Athlete, Football Player)
241 N Oregon St
Johnstown, OH 43031-1024, USA

Tavener, John K (Composer)
8-9 Firth St
London W1V 5TZ, UNITED KINGDOM (UK)

Taverner, Sonia (Ballerina)
PO Box 129
Stony Plain, AB, CANADA

Tavernier, Bertrand R M (Director)
7-9 Rue Arthur Groussler
Paris 75010, FRANCE

Taviani, Paolo (Director)
Via Tuscolana 1055
Rome 173, ITALY

Taviani, Vittorio (Director)
Via Tuscolana 1055
Rome 173, ITALY

Taxier, Arthur (Actor)
9229 W Sunset Blvd Ste 315
Los Angeles, CA 90069-3403, USA

Taya, Maawiya Ould Sid'Ahmed (President)
Boite Postale 184
Nouakchott, MAURITANIA

Taylor, Aaron (Athlete, Baseball Player)
4518 GA Highway 23 S
Millen, GA 30442-5437, USA

Taylor, Alphonso (Athlete, Football Player)
254 W Trenton Ave Apt 314B
Morrisville, PA 19067-2077, USA

Taylor, Altie (Athlete, Football Player)
5349 Whitehaven Way
Antelope, CA 95843-5992, USA

Taylor, Andy (Musician)
93A Westbourne Park Villas
London W2 5ED, UNITED KINGDOM (UK)

Taylor, Anthony (Athlete, Basketball Player)
5300 Parkview Dr Apt 1093
Lake Oswego, OR 97035-8728, USA

Taylor, Arthur R (Business Person, Educator)
President's Office
Allentown, PA 18104, USA

Taylor, Ben (Football Player)

Taylor, Benedict
4 Great Queen St
London, ENGLAND WC28 5DG

Taylor, Bill (Athlete, Baseball Player)
PO Box 146
Acton, CA 93510-0146, USA

Taylor, Billy (Athlete, Baseball Player)
201 Washington Pl
Thomasville, GA 31792-4785, USA

Taylor, Billy (Athlete, Football Player)
3 Greenwich Dr Apt 86
Jersey City, NJ 07305-1158, USA

Taylor, Bob (Athlete, Baseball Player)
27 Sunnybrook Rd
Springfield, MA 01119-2209, USA

Taylor, Brian (Athlete, Basketball Player)
3622 Green Vista Dr
Encino, CA 91436-4038, USA

Taylor, Brien (Baseball Player)
147 Brien Taylor Ln
Beaufort, NC 28516-6664, USA

Taylor, Bruce (Athlete, Baseball Player)
8 Highland Park Rd
Rutland, MA 01543-1742, USA

Taylor, Bruce L. (Athlete, Football Player)
10324 Pontofino Cir
Trinity, FL 34655-7056, USA

Taylor, Buck (Actor)
1305 Clyde Dr
Marrero, LA 70072-3609, USA

Taylor, Carl (Athlete, Baseball Player)
2356 Riviera Dr
Sarasota, FL 34232-3522, USA

Taylor, Carl E (Physicist)
10625 Hickory Crest Ln
Columbia, MD 21044-4558, USA

Taylor, Cecil P (Composer, Musician)
300 Mercer St Apt 3J
New York, NY 10003-6732, USA

Taylor, Chad (Musician)
1790 Broadway # 131
New York, NY 10019-1412, USA

Taylor, Charles R (Charley) (Athlete, Football Executive, Football Player)
12023 Canter Ln
Reston, VA 20191-2129, USA

Taylor, Christian (Actor)
c/o Staff Member *KST Productions*
5543 Edmondson Pike # 1
Nashville, TN 37211-5808, USA

Taylor, Christine (Actor)
c/o Kimberlin Dalehite *Magnolia Entertainment (LA)*
9595 Wilshire Blvd Ste 601
Beverly Hills, CA 90212-2506, USA

Taylor, Christy (Actor)
10990 Massachusetts Ave Apt 3
Los Angeles, CA 90024-5530, USA

Taylor, Chuck (Athlete, Baseball Player)
1535 Georgetown Ln
Murfreesboro, TN 37129-1783, USA

Taylor, Cindy (Actor)
c/o Allee Newhoff *Elite Model Management*
119 Washington Ave Ste 501
Miami Beach, FL 33139-7228, USA

Taylor, Clarice (Actor)
380 Elkwood Ter
Englewood, NJ 07631-1935, USA

Taylor, Cordell (Athlete, Football Player)
1825 Chasewood Park Dr
Marietta, GA 30066-4298, USA

Taylor, Corey (Musician)
c/o Staff Member *Agency Group Ltd, The (LA)*
1880 Century Park E Ste 711
Los Angeles, CA 90067-1618, USA

Taylor, Dana (Actor)
100 S Sunrise Way # 468
Palm Springs, CA 92262-6779, USA

Taylor, Dave (Athlete, Hockey Player)
18920 Pasadero Dr
Tarzana, CA 91356-5122, USA

Taylor, David (Athlete, Football Player)
304 Paddington Rd
Baltimore, MD 21212-3812, USA

Taylor, David (Writer)
c/o Author Mail *Bantam-Dell Publishing (NY)*
1745 Broadway
New York, NY 10019-4368, USA

Taylor, Delores (Actor)
PO Box 840
Moorpark, CA 93020-0840, USA

Taylor, Dorn (Athlete, Baseball Player)
405 Avenue D
Horsham, PA 19044-2020, USA

Taylor, Dwight (Athlete, Baseball Player)
5163 Queen Mary Ln
Jackson, MS 39209-3141, USA

Taylor, Ed (Athlete, Football Player)
2901 Clarke Rd
Memphis, TN 38115-2402, USA

Taylor, Eric (Artist)
13 Tredgold Ave Branhope near Leeds
West Yorkshire LS16 9BS, UNITED KINGDOM (UK)

Taylor, Eunice (Baseball Player)
955 Carroll Ln
Mount Dora, FL 32757-3726, USA

Taylor, Femi (Actor)
23 Noel St
London W1V 3RD, UNITED KINGDOM (UK)

Taylor, Fred (Athlete, Football Player)
16925 Berkshire Ct
Southwest Ranches, FL 33331-1357, USA

Taylor, Gary (Athlete, Baseball Player)
995 Beaumont Rd
Highland, MI 48356-3202, USA

Taylor, Gilbert (Cinematographer)
11 Croft Gerrards Cross
Bucks SL9 9E, UNITED KINGDOM (UK)

Taylor, Glen (Basketball Player)
Target Center 600 1st Ave N
Minneapolis, MN 55403, USA

Taylor, Harry (Athlete, Baseball Player)
2125 Cooks Ln
Fort Worth, TX 76120-5301, USA

Taylor, Henry S (Writer)
1120 Aqua Vista Dr NW
Gig Harbor, WA 98335-1536, USA

Taylor, Holland (Actor)
c/o Bob Gersh *Gersh (LA)*
9465 Wilshire Blvd Ste 600
Beverly Hills, CA 90212-2612, USA

Taylor, Hosea (Athlete, Football Player)
208 Bobby St
Longview, TX 75602-3804, USA

Taylor, J Herbert (Biologist)
110 Wood Rd Apt H210
Los Gatos, CA 95030-6734, USA

Taylor, J T (Musician)
250 W 57th St
New York, NY 10107-0001, USA

Taylor, Jack (Business Person)
600 Corporate Park Dr
Saint Louis, MO 63105-4204, USA

Taylor, Jackie Lynn (Actor)
PO Box 3182
Citrus Heights, CA 95611-3182, USA

Taylor, James (Musician, Songwriter)
c/o Rob Light *Creative Artists Agency (CAA-LA)*
2000 Avenue of the Stars Ste 100
Los Angeles, CA 90067-4705, USA

Taylor, James A (War Hero)
PO Box 284
Trinity Center, CA 96091-0284, USA

Taylor, James Arnold (Actor, Voice Over Artist)
c/o Pat Brady *Cunningham Escott Slevin & Doherty (CESD-LA)*
10635 Santa Monica Blvd Ste 130
Los Angeles, CA 90025-8306, USA

Taylor, James C (Jim) (Athlete, Football Player)
7840 Walden Rd
Baton Rouge, LA 70808-5939, USA

Taylor, Jason (Rugby Player)
PO BOX 2666
North Parramatta, NSW 1750, AUSTRALIA

Taylor, Jason (Athlete, Football Player)
2980 Paddock Rd
Weston, FL 33331-3604, USA

Taylor, Jay (Business Person)
1600-1055 Dunsmuir St
Vancouver, BC V7X 1P1, CANADA

Taylor, Jennifer Bini (Actor)
c/o Brad Warshaw *Brad Warshaw*
PO Box 931332
Los Angeles, CA 90093-1332, USA

Taylor, Jim (Writer)
c/o Staff Member *WmE2 (WMA-LA)*
1 William Morris Pl
Beverly Hills, CA 90212-4261, USA

Taylor, John (Athlete, Football Player)
PO Box 326
Fresno, CA 93708-0326, USA

Taylor, Jonathan (Producer)
c/o Staff Member *United Talent Agency (UTA)*
9560 Wilshire Blvd Fl 5
Beverly Hills, CA 90212-2400, USA

Taylor, Joseph H Jr (Nobel Prize Laureate)
272 Hartley Ave
Princeton, NJ 08540-5656, USA

Taylor, Josh (Actor)
4151 Vanalden Ave
Tarzana, CA 91356-5527, USA

Taylor, Judson H (Educator)
President's Office
Cortland, NY 13045, USA

Taylor, Karen (Comedian)
c/o Staff Member *Avalon Management*
4A Exmoor St
London W10 6BD, UK

Taylor, Kerry (Athlete, Baseball Player)
647 Keene Cir
Dandridge, TN 37725-6191, USA

Taylor, Kim (Musician)
c/o Staff Member *Paradigm (Monterey)*
404 W Franklin St
Monterey, CA 93940-2303, USA

Taylor, Kitrick L (Athlete, Football Player)
18215 Foothill Blvd Apt 94
Fontana, CA 92335-8512, USA

Taylor, Lance J (Economist)
PO Box 378
Washington, ME 04574-0378, USA

Taylor, Lauriston S (Physicist)
10450 Lottsford Rd # 1-5
Bowie, MD 20721-2734, USA

Taylor, Lawrence (Athlete, Football Player)
2850 Lost Lakes Way
Powder Springs, GA 30127-6017, USA

Taylor, Lee (Stylist)
c/o Staff Member *Directions USA*
3717 W Market St Ste C
Greensboro, NC 27403-1155, USA

Taylor, Lili (Actor)
c/o Staff Member *Dontanville/Frattaroli (D/F)*
270 Lafayette St Ste 402
New York, NY 10012-3327, USA

Taylor, Lionel (Athlete, Coach, Football Coach, Football Player)
201 Pinnacle Dr SE Apt 3614
Rio Rancho, NM 87124-0458, USA

Taylor, Livingston (Musician)
1906 Chet Atkins Pl Apt 502
Nashville, TN 37212-2122, USA

Taylor, Marianne (Actor)
5118 Vineland Ave # 102
North Hollywood, CA 91601-3814, USA

Taylor, Mark (Athlete, Hockey Player)
10388 Nordel Crt
North Delya, BC V4G 1J7, Canada

Taylor, Mark L (Actor)
7919 Norton Ave
West Hollywood, CA 90046-5204, USA

Taylor, Maurice (Basketball Player)
Toyota Center 2 E Greenway Plaza
Houston, TX 77046, USA

Taylor, Meshach (Actor)
c/o Staff Member *Gilbertson Management*
1334 3rd Street Promenade Ste 201
Santa Monica, CA 90401-1320, USA

Taylor, Michael (Athlete, Football Player)
5014 Crane St
Detroit, MI 48213-2917, USA

Taylor, Mick (Musician)
60 Madison Ave Ste 1026
New York, NY 10010-1666, USA

Taylor, Mike (Athlete, Football Player)
19632 Quiet Bay Ln
Huntington Beach, CA 92648-2614, USA

Taylor, Natascha (Actor)
c/o Staff Member *International Creative Management (ICM-LA)*
10250 Constellation Blvd Fl 7
Los Angeles, CA 90067-6207, USA

Taylor, Niki (Actor, Model)
c/o Lou Taylor *Tri Star Sports & Entertainment Group*
215 Ward Cir Ste 200
Brentwood, TN 37027-2306, USA

Taylor, Noah (Actor)
110 Quenn St
Woolahra, NSW 2025, AUSTRALIA

Taylor, Ollie (Athlete, Basketball Player)
6405 Hillock Ln
Pearland, TX 77584-9293, USA

Taylor, Otis (Athlete, Football Player)
6608 Woodson Rd
Raytown, MO 64133-5400, USA

Taylor, Paul B (Choreographer, Dancer)
551 Grand St Lbby A
New York, NY 10002-4282, USA

Taylor, Penny (Basketball Player)
1 Center Ct
Cleveland, OH 44115-4001, USA

Taylor, Phil (Football Player)
c/o Peter Schaffer *All Pro Sports and Entertainment*
36 Steele St Ste 100
Denver, CO 80206-5709, USA

Taylor, Priscilla (Actor, Model)
c/o Staff Member *Crystal Sky Pictures*
10203 Santa Monica Blvd Ste 500
Los Angeles, CA 90067-6416, USA

Taylor, Rachael (Actor)
c/o Annett Wolf *WKT Public Relations (WKT-LA)*
9350 Wilshire Blvd Ste 450
Beverly Hills, CA 90212-3230, USA

Taylor, Reggie (Athlete, Baseball Player)
6257 Vinings Vintage Dr
Mableton, GA 30126-7203, USA

Taylor, Regina (Actor)
8048 Dusenberg Ct
Sacramento, CA 95828-5834, USA

Taylor, Renee (Actor)
606 N Larchmont Blvd Ste 309
Los Angeles, CA 90004-1309, USA

Taylor, Richard E (Nobel Prize Laureate)
757 Mayfield Ave
Stanford, CA 94305-1043, USA

Taylor, Rip (Actor, Comedian)
1133 N Clark St
Los Angeles, CA 90069-2073, USA

Taylor, Robert (Hawk) (Athlete, Baseball Player)
136 Skyway Dr
Murray, KY 42071-5401, USA

Taylor, Rod (Actor)
2375 Bowmont Dr
Beverly Hills, CA 90210-1808, USA

Taylor, Roger (Musician)
c/o Staff Member *DD Productions*
93A Westbourne Park Villas
London W2 5ED, UNITED KINGDOM (UK)

Taylor, Roger (Tennis Player)
39 Newstead Way
Wimbledon SW19, UNITED KINGDOM (UK)

Taylor, Ron (Athlete, Baseball Player)
19 Alvin Ave
Toronto, ON M4T 2A7, Canada

Taylor, Ron (Athlete, Basketball Player)
1813 Barry Ave
Los Angeles, CA 90025-5306, USA

Taylor, Roosevelt (Athlete, Football Player)
7331 Ebbtide Dr
New Orleans, LA 70126-2057, USA

Taylor, Sam (Sammy) (Athlete, Baseball Player)
PO Box 152
Woodruff, SC 29388-0152, USA

Taylor, Sandra (Actor, Model)
c/o Craig Wyckoff *Epstein-Wyckoff-Corsa-Ross & Associates (LA)*
11350 Ventura Blvd Ste 100
Studio City, CA 91604-3140, USA

Taylor, Scott (Athlete, Baseball Player)
925 Indian Bridge Ln
Defiance, OH 43512-1944, USA

Taylor, Stephen Monroe (Actor)
c/o Staff Member *Main Title Entertainment*
2225 Wilshire Blvd Suite 500
Los Angeles, CA 90036, USA

Taylor, Susan (Editor)
135 W 50th St Fl 4
New York, NY 10020-1201, USA

Taylor, Tamara (Actor)
c/o Ira Liss *Manifest Talent Group*
5225 Wilshire Blvd Ste 524
Los Angeles, CA 90036-4349, USA

Taylor, Terry (Athlete, Baseball Player)
743 W Walnut Ave
Crestview, FL 32536-3919, USA

Taylor, Tommy (Baseball Player)
524 Whitehall St
Jackson, TN 38301-5535, USA

Taylor, Tony (Athlete, Baseball Player)
8415 NW 165th Ter
Hialeah, FL 33016-6137, USA

Taylor, Tracy (Stylist)
c/o Staff Member *Kramer + Kramer*
156 5th Ave Ste 415
New York, NY 10010-7774, USA

Taylor, Vaughn (Golfer)
2536 Queens Ct
Grovetown, GA 30813-4520, USA

Taylor, Wade (Athlete, Baseball Player)
6 Sleepy Hollow Cv
Longwood, FL 32750-3845, USA

Taylor, William O (Publisher)
135 William T Morrissey Blvd
Dorchester, MA 02125-3310, USA

Taylor, Wilson H (Business Person)
1 Place Liberty 1650 Market St
Philadelphia, PA 19192-0001, USA

Taylor Jr, William (Billy) (Composer, Musician)
555 Kappock St
Bronx, NY 10463-6420, USA

Taylor-Compton, Scout (Actor)
c/o Nicki Fioravante *PMK/BNC - LA*
8687 Melrose Ave Ste 8
West Hollywood, CA 90069-5746, USA

Taylor-Cotter, Eliza (Actor)
c/o Staff Member *Nickelodeon UK*
PO Box 6425
LONDON W1A 6UR, UNITED KINGDOM

Taylor-Grauman, Joan
9920 Robin Dr
Los Angeles, CA 90069

Taylor-Lukin, Norna (Baseball Player)
7934 W Maple Grove Rd
Andrews, IN 46702-9518, USA

Taylor-Taylor, Courtney (Musician)
PO Box 5908
Portland, OR 97228-5908, USA

Taylor-Young, Leigh (Actor)
11300 W Olympic Blvd Ste 610
Los Angeles, CA 90064-1643, USA

Taymor, Julie (Director, Producer, Writer)
c/o Bart Walker *Cinetic Management*
555 W 25th St Fl 4
New York, NY 10001-5542, USA

Tchaikovsky, Aleksandr V (Composer, Musician)
Leningradsky Prosp 14 #4
Moscow 125040, RUSSIA

Tcherkassky, Marianna (Ballerina)
890 Broadway
New York, NY 10003-1211, USA

Te Kanawa, Kiri (Opera Singer)
Postfach 4113
Lucerne 6002, SWITZERLAND

Tea Leaf Green (Music Group)
c/o Staff Member *Paradigm (Monterey)*
404 W Franklin St
Monterey, CA 93940-2303, USA

Teaff, Grant (Coach, Football Coach)
8265 Forest Ridge Dr
Waco, TX 76712-2405, USA

Teagle, Terry (Athlete, Basketball Player)
2111 Heatherwood Dr
Missouri City, TX 77489-3277, USA

Teague, George (Athlete, Football Player)
6561 Meadow Lark Dr
Montgomery, AL 36116-4227, USA

Teague, Lewis
2190 N Beverly Glen Blvd
Los Angeles, CA 90077-2404

Teague, Marshall (Actor)
c/o Richard Lewis *Geddes Agency, The*
8430 Santa Monica Blvd Ste 200
Los Angeles, CA 90069-4253, USA

Teahen, Mark (Athlete, Baseball Player)
4950 Central St Apt 305
Kansas City, MO 64112-2524, USA

Teal, Jim F (Athlete, Football Player)
38444 Kingsway Ct
Farmington Hills, MI 48331-1651, USA

Teal, Jimmy D (Athlete, Football Player)
2636 Spring Branch Rd
Mesquite, TX 75181-2668, USA

Teal, Willie (Athlete, Football Player)
1322 Westchester Dr
Baton Rouge, LA 70810-5234, USA

Teannaki, Teatao (President)
PO Box 68 Bairiki
Tarawa Atoll, KIRBATI

Tear, Robert (Opera Singer)
11 Ravenscourt Court
London W6, UNITED KINGDOM (UK)

Tearry, Larry (Athlete, Football Player)
1334 Kienast Dr
Fayetteville, NC 28314-5422, USA

Tears For Fears (Music Group)
c/o Staff Member *Creative Artists Agency (CAA-LA)*
2000 Avenue of the Stars Ste 100
Los Angeles, CA 90067-4705, USA

Teasley, Nikki (Basketball Player)
Staples Center 1111 S Figueroa St
Los Angeles, CA 90015, USA

Teasley, Ron (Baseball Player)
19317 Coyle St
Detroit, MI 48235-2039, USA

Tebbit of Chingford, Norman B (Government Official)
Westminsiter
London SW1A 0PW, UNITED KINGDOM (UK)

Tebbutt, Arthur R (Mathematician)
1511 Pelican Point Dr
Sarasota, FL 34231-1711, USA

Tebow, Tim (Athlete, Football Player)
c/o Jimmy Sexton *SportsTrust Advisors - TN*
1100 Ridgeway Loop Rd Fl 5
Memphis, TN 38120-4053, USA

Techine, Andre J F (Director)
20 Ave Rapp
Paris 75007, FRANCE

Tedeschi, Susan (Musician)
761 Washington Ave N
Minneapolis, MN 55401-1101, USA

Tedford, Travis (Actor)
c/o Staff Member *Acme Talent & Literary (LA)*
1400 Atlantic Ave Ste 274
Long Beach, CA 90813-2013, USA

Teed, Dick (Athlete, Baseball Player)
45 Taylor St
Windsor, CT 06095-2437, USA

Teegarden, Aimee (Actor)
c/o Tara Friedlander *ID PR (LA)*
7060 Hollywood Blvd Fl 8
Los Angeles, CA 90028-6014, USA

Teerlinck, John (Athlete, Football Player)
9713 Bay Hill Dr
Lone Tree, CO 80124-3182, USA

Teeter, Mike (Athlete, Football Player)
4393 E Mount Garfield Rd
Fruitport, MI 49415-9782, USA

Teeuws, Len (Athlete, Football Player)
1314 Selkirk Ln
Indianapolis, IN 46260-1230, USA

Teevens, Buddy (Coach, Football Coach)
Athletic Dept
Stanford, CA 94395, USA

Tefkin, Blair (Actor)
8022 Sunset Blvd # 4049
Los Angeles, CA 90046, USA

Tegan and Sara (Music Group)
c/o Staff Member *Paquin Entertainment Agency*
468 Stradbrook Ave
Winnipeg, Manitoba R3L 0J9, Canada

Tegart Dalton, Judy (Tennis Player)
72 Grange Rd
Toorak, VIC 3412, AUSTRALIA

Teich, Kim (Stylist)
c/o Staff Member *Team*
423 W Broadway Ste 406
Boston, MA 02127-2265, USA

Teich, Malvin C (Engineer)
Electrical/Computer Engineering Dept
Boston, MA 2215, USA

Teichner, Helmut (Skier)
4250 N Marine Dr Apt 2101
Chicago, IL 60613-1733, USA

Teillet-Schick, Yolande (Baseball Player)
1016 Chevrier Blvd Ft Garry
Winnipeg, MB R3T 1X9, CANADA

Teitel, Robert (Producer)
c/o Staff Member *Creative Artists Agency (CAA-LA)*
2000 Avenue of the Stars Ste 100
Los Angeles, CA 90067-4705, USA

Teitelbaum, Philip (Doctor)
Psychology
Gainesville, FL 32611-0001, USA

Teitell, Conrad L (Lawyer)
16 Marlow Ct
Riverside, CT 06878-2614, USA

Teitler, William (Producer)
c/o Staff Member *International Creative Management (ICM-LA)*
10250 Constellation Blvd Fl 7
Los Angeles, CA 90067-6207, USA

Teixeira, Mark (Athlete, Baseball Player)
c/o Scott Boras *Boras Corporation*
18 Corporate Plaza Dr
Newport Beach, CA 92660-7901, USA

Tejada, Miguel O M (Athlete, Baseball Player)
10 E Lee St Apt 2505
Baltimore, MD 21202-6025, USA

Tejera, Michael (Athlete, Baseball Player)
14271 SW 18th St
Miami, FL 33175-7062, USA

Tekulve, Kenton C (Kent) (Athlete, Baseball Player)
PO Box 4480
Hidden Valley, PA 15502-4480, USA

Telemaco, Amaury (Athlete, Baseball Player)
830 S Webster Ave
Scranton, PA 18505-4384, USA

Telfer, Paul (Actor)
c/o Michael Greenwald *Don Buchwald & Associates Inc (LA)*
6500 Wilshire Blvd Ste 2200
Los Angeles, CA 90048-4942, USA

Telford, Anthony (Athlete, Baseball Player)
9109 Cypress Keep Ln
Odessa, FL 33556-3150, USA

Telford, Jennifer (Stylist)
c/o Staff Member *Zenobia Agency Inc*
PO Box 909
Groveland, CA 95321-0909, USA

Telgdi, Valentine L (Physicist)
Eidgenossosche Technische Hochschule
Houggerberg
Zurich, SWITZERLAND

Telgheder, David (Athlete, Baseball Player)
50 Orchard Crest Dr
Westtown, NY 10998-3425, USA

Tellem, Nancy (Business Person)
c/o Staff Member *CBS Paramount International Television*
7800 Beverly Blvd
Los Angeles, CA 90036-2112, USA

Teller (Actor, Comedian, Magician)
4132 S Rainbow Blvd
Las Vegas, NV 89103-3106, USA

Teller, Edward (Doctor)
PO Box 808
Livermore, CA 94551-0808, USA

Telles, Rick (Director, Producer)
c/o Josh Levenbrown *Agency for the Performing Arts (APA-LA)*
405 S Beverly Dr Ste 500
Beverly Hills, CA 90212-4425, USA

Tellez, Steve (Actor)
c/o Staff Member *Innovative Artists (LA)*
1505 10th St
Santa Monica, CA 90401-2805, USA

Tellman, Tom (Athlete, Baseball Player)
1021 Yankee Bush Rd
Warren, PA 16365-8536, USA

Telnaes, Ann (Cartoonist)
435 N Michigan Ave Ste 1500
Chicago, IL 60611-4012, USA

Teltscher, Eliot (Coach, Tennis Player)
Athletic Dept
Malibu, CA 90265, USA

Teltschik, John (Athlete, Football Player)
9624 Nathan Way
Plano, TX 75025-5896, USA

Telushkin, Rabbi Joseph (Writer)
2316 Delaware Ave # Ste 266 PMB 4-B
Buffalo, NY 14216-2687, USA

Temchen, Sybil (Actor)
c/o Staff Member *Untitled Entertainment (LA)*
350 S Beverly Dr Ste 200
Beverly Hills, CA 90212-4819, USA

Temesvari, Andrea (Tennis Player)
1101 Woodrow Wilson Blvd # 1800
Arlington, VA 22209, USA

Temirkanov, Yuri K
Mikhailovskaya 2
Saint Petersburg, RUSSIA

Temko, Allan B (Journalist)
Editorial Dept 901 Mission
San Francisco, CA 94103, USA

Temp, Jim (Athlete, Football Player)
311 Roselawn Blvd
Green Bay, WI 54301-1305, USA

Temple, Collins (Athlete, Basketball Player)
2614 Dalrymple Dr
Baton Rouge, LA 70808-2038, USA

Temple, Josh (Television Host)
c/o Steven Neibert *Imperium 7 Talent Agency*
5455 Wilshire Blvd Ste 1706
Los Angeles, CA 90036-4217, USA

Temple, Juno (Actor)
c/o Jessica Kolstad *WKT Public Relations (WKT-LA)*
9350 Wilshire Blvd Ste 450
Beverly Hills, CA 90212-3230, USA

Temple, Lew (Actor)
c/o Peter Young *Sovereign Talent Group*
8421 Wilshire Blvd Ste 200
Beverly Hills, CA 90211-3204, USA

Temple Black, Shirley (Actor, Musician)
400 S Hope St
Los Angeles, CA 90071-2801, USA

Templeman of White Lackington, Sydney W (Judge)
Manor Heath Know Hill Woking
Surrey GU22 7HL, UNITED KINGDOM (UK)

Templeton, Ben (Cartoonist)
435 N Michigan Ave Ste 1500
Chicago, IL 60611-4012, USA

Templeton, Garry L (Athlete, Baseball Player)
13552 Del Poniente Rd
Poway, CA 92064-2230, USA

Templeton, John M (Financier)
Box N7776
Nassau, BAHAMAS

Temptations, The (Music Group)
c/o Mark Cheatham *International Creative Management (ICM-LA)*
10250 Constellation Blvd Fl 7
Los Angeles, CA 90067-6207, USA

Ten Napel, Garth (Athlete, Football Player)
PO Box 26
Carmen, ID 83462-0026, USA

Tena, Natalia (Actor)
c/o Sarah Spear *Curtis Brown Ltd*
Hay Market House 28-29 Hay Market
London SW1Y 4SP, UK

Tenace, F Gene (Athlete, Baseball Player, Coach)
2650 Cliff Hawk Ct
Redmond, OR 97756-7301, USA

Tendulkar, Priya (Actor, Bollywood)
1 Anookul Apartments Harminder Singh Marg Seven Bangalows Versova Andheri
Bombay, MS 400 061, INDIA

Tengbom, Anders (Architect)
Kornhaminstorg 6
Stockholm 11127, SWEDEN

Teng-Hui, Lee (President)
Chaehshou Hall Chung King South Rd.
Taipei 10728, TAIWAN

Tennant, Andy (Actor, Director, Writer)
c/o Eddie Michaels *Insignia Public Relations*
1507 20th St Ste D
Santa Monica, CA 90404-3474, USA

Tennant, David (Actor)
c/o Staff Member *Novello Theatre (formerly The Strand)*
Hamlet Aldwych
London WC2, United Kingdom

Tennant, Stella (Model)
Archer House 43 King St
London WC2E 8RJ, UNITED KINGDOM (UK)

Tennant, Veronica (Ballerina)
157 King St E
Toronto, ON M5C 1G9, CANADA

Tennant, Victoria (Actor)
PO Box 929
Beverly Hills, CA 90213-0929, USA

Tenney, Jon (Actor)
c/o Brian Wilkins *Kritzer Levine Wilkins Entertainment*
11872 La Grange Ave Fl 1
Los Angeles, CA 90025-5283, USA

Tennille, Toni (Actor, Musician)
c/o Staff Member *Chaplin Entertainment*
1650 Broadway Ste 303
New York, NY 10019-6970, USA

Tennison, Chalee (Musician)
1204 17th Ave S
Nashville, TN 37212-2802, USA

Tennon, Julius (Actor)
c/o Jim Kelly *Charles Talent Agency*
11950 Ventura Blvd Ste 3
Studio City, CA 91604-2635, USA

Tenorio, Pedro P (Ex-Governor)
P.O. Box 567
Saipan, MP 96950, USA

Tensi, Steve (Athlete, Football Player)
300 Flannery Fork Rd
Blowing Rock, NC 28605-9333, USA

Tenth Avenue North (Musician)
c/o Staff Member *Reunion Records*
741 Cool Springs Blvd
Franklin, TN 37067-2697, USA

Tenuta, Judy (Actor, Comedian)
c/o Monique Moss *Moss Public Relations*
8060 Melrose Ave Fl 4
Los Angeles, CA 90046-7038, USA

Tepedino, Frank (Athlete, Baseball Player)
2 Pear Ct
Saint James, NY 11780-2143, USA

Tepper, Lou (Coach, Football Coach)
Assembly Hall
Champaign, IL 61820, USA

Tepsic, Joe (Athlete, Baseball Player)
2470 Bald Eagle Pike
Tyrone, PA 16686-7720, USA

Tequila (Nguyen), Tila (Model, Reality TV Star)
1603 Cloverfield # 420
Santa Monica, CA 90404, USA

Ter Horst, Jerald F (Government Official, Journalist)
21 N Oak Forest Dr
Asheville, NC 28803-3333, USA

Teran, Arlet (Actor)
c/o Gabriel Blanco *Gabriel Blanco Iglesias (Mexico)*
Rio Balsas 35-32 Colonia Cuauhtemoc
DF 6500, Mexico

Teraoka, Masami (Artist)
41-048 Kaulu St
Waimanalo, HI 96795-1612, USA

TerBlanche, Esta (Actor)
c/o Chris Schmidt *Paradigm (LA)*
360 N Crescent Dr
Beverly Hills, CA 90210-4874, USA

Terekhova, Margarita B (Actor)
Bolshaya Gruzinskaya Str 57 #92
Moscow 123056, RUSSIA

Terentyeva, Nina N (Opera Singer)
Teatralnaya Pl 1
Moscow 103009, RUSSIA

Tereschenko, Sergei A (Prime Minister)
Dom Pravieelstra
Alma-Ata 148008, KAZAKHSTAN

Tereshinski, Joe (Athlete, Football Player)
6508 Millwood Rd
Bethesda, MD 20817-6056, USA

Tereshkova, Valentina V (Cosmonaut)
Vozdvizhenka Str 14-18
Moscow 103885, RUSSIA

Tergesen, Lee (Actor)
232 N Canon Dr
Beverly Hills, CA 90210-5302, USA

Terlecki, Bob (Athlete, Baseball Player)
113 Shady Brook Dr
Langhorne, PA 19047-8028, USA

Terlecky, Greg (Athlete, Baseball Player)
2130 Camino Laurel
San Clemente, CA 92673-5650, USA

Terlep, George (Athlete, Football Player)
4524 Golf Club Ln
Brooksville, FL 34609-0303, USA

Terlesky, John (Actor)
14229 Dickens St Apt 5
Sherman Oaks, CA 91423-4107, USA

Termeer, Henricus A (Business Person)
1 Kendall Sq
Cambridge, MA 02139-1562, USA

Terminator X (Musician)
c/o Staff Member *WmE2 (WMA-LA)*
1 William Morris Pl
Beverly Hills, CA 90212-4261, USA

Termo, Leonard (Actor)
1041 N Formosa Ave # 200
West Hollywood, CA 90046-6703, USA

Ter-Petrosyan, Levon A (President)
Marshal Baghramjan Prospect # 19
Memphis, TN 37501-0001, ARMENIA

Terpko, Jeff (Athlete, Baseball Player)
3546 Riverside Dr
Sayre, PA 18840-7864, USA

Terra, Scott (Actor)
c/o Mike Cutler *DMG*
9713 Little Santa Monica Blvd
Beverly Hills, CA 90210, USA

Terrani, Lucia Valenti
Via Venti Settembre 72
Padova, ITALY I-35122

Terranova, Joe (Musician)
PO Box 279
Williamstown, NJ 08094-0279, USA

Terranova, Phil (Boxer)
30 Bogardus Pl
New York, NY 10040-2320, USA

Terrasson, Jacky (Musician)
300 Mercer St Apt 3J
New York, NY 10003-6732, USA

Terrazas Sandoval, Julio Cardinal (Religious Leader)
Arzobispado Casilla 25 Calle Ingavi 49
Santa Cruz, BOLIVIA

Terrell, David (Athlete, Football Player)
43628 Cather Ct
Ashburn, VA 20147-4789, USA

Terrell, Ernie
11136 S Parnell Ave
Chicago, IL 60628-4012

Terrell, Ira (Athlete, Basketball Player)
1327 Fernwood Ave
Dallas, TX 75216-1265, USA

Terrell, Jerry (Athlete, Baseball Player)
1301 NE Sunny Creek Ln
Blue Springs, MO 64014-2041, USA

Terrell, Pat (Athlete, Football Player)
40 Hidden Lake Dr
Burr Ridge, IL 60527-8371, USA

Terrell, Walt (Athlete, Baseball Player)
1304 Oxley Ct
Union, KY 41091-7145, USA

Terreri, Chris (Athlete, Hockey Player)
170 Dezenzo Ln
West Orange, NJ 07052-4125, USA

Terrero, Jessy (Director, Producer)
c/o Charles King *WmE2 (Endeavor-LA)*
9601 Wilshire Blvd Fl 3
Beverly Hills, CA 90210-5219, USA

Terrile, Richard (Astronomer)
2121 E Woodlyn Rd
Pasadena, CA 91104-3334, USA

Terrio, Deney (Dancer, Entertainer)
PO Box 12
Far Hills, NJ 07931-0012, USA

Terris, Malcolm
14 England's Ln
London, ENGLAND NW3

Terry, Clark (Musician)
4720 S Beech St
Pine Bluff, AR 71603-7327, USA

Terry, Claude (Athlete, Basketball Player)
14815 E Sandstone Ct
Fountain Hills, AZ 85268-6335, USA

Terry, Hilda (Cartoonist)
8 Henderson Pl
New York, NY 10028-7557, USA

Terry, Jason (Basketball Player)
190 Marietta St NW
Atlanta, GA 30303-2762, USA

Terry, John (Soccer Player)
25 Soho Square
London W1D 4FA, UNITED KINGDOM

Terry, John (Actor)
c/o Darren Goldberg *Global Creative*
1051 Cole Ave # B
Los Angeles, CA 90038-2601, USA

Terry, John Q (Architect)
Old Exchange Dedham Colchester
Essex CO7 6HA, UNITED KINGDOM (UK)

Terry, Megan D (Writer)
2309 Hanscom Blvd
Omaha, NE 68105-3143, USA

Terry, Nat (Athlete, Football Player)
3003 W Palmetto St
Tampa, FL 33607-2936, USA

Terry, Nigel (Actor)
c/o Staff Member *BBC Artist Mail*
PO Box 1116
Belfast BT2 7AJ, United Kingdom

Terry, Ralph W (Athlete, Baseball Player)
801 Park St
Larned, KS 67550-2632, USA

Terry, Randall A (Activist)
PO Box 360221
Melbourne, FL 32936-0221, USA

Terry, Richard E (Business Person)
130 E Randolph St
Chicago, IL 60601-6207, USA

Terry, Rick (Athlete, Football Player)
109 Highgate Ln
Lexington, NC 27292-5372, USA

Terry, Ruth (Actor, Musician)
622 Hospitality Dr
Rancho Mirage, CA 92270-1312, USA

Terry, Scott (Athlete, Baseball Player)
4943 Montford Dr
Saint Louis, MO 63128-3134, USA

Terry, Tony (Musician)
1800 Argyle Ave # 408
Los Angeles, CA 90028-5253, USA

Terwilliger, Wayne (Athlete, Baseball Player)
1909 Clear Creek Dr
Weatherford, TX 76087-3802, USA

Terzian, Jacques (Artist)
PO Box 883753
San Francisco, CA 94188-3753, USA

Terzieff, Laurent D A (Actor, Director)
8 Rue du Dragon
Paris 75006, FRANCE

Tesh, John (Composer, Entertainer, Musician)
PO Box 6010
Sherman Oaks, CA 91413-6010, USA

Teske, Rachel (Golfer)
c/o Staff Member *Pro Golfers Association (PGA) Tour*
112 Tpc Blvd
Ponte Vedra Beach, FL 32082, USA

Tesori, Kathleen (Fitness Expert, Model)
2075 N Main St Apt D106
Layton, UT 84041-4987, USA

Tess, John (Business Person)
123 NW 2nd Ave Ste 200
Portland, OR 97209-3927

Tessler-Lavigne, Marc (Doctor)
361 Ridgeway Rd
Woodside, CA 94062-2343, USA

Tessmer, Jay (Athlete, Baseball Player)
5312 NW Akbar Ct
Port Saint Lucie, FL 34986-3562, USA

Testa, M David (Financier)
100 E Pratt St
Baltimore, MD 21202-1009, USA

Testa, Nick (Athlete, Baseball Player)
537 Riverdale Ave
Yonkers, NY 10705-5501, USA

Testaverde, Vincent F (Vinny) (Athlete, Football Player)
17122 Gunn Hwy
Odessa, FL 33556-1909, USA

Tester, Hans
6310 San Vicente Blvd Ste 401
Los Angeles, CA 90048-5427

Testerman, Don (Athlete, Football Player)
1055 Hacktown Rd
Keswick, VA 22947-2621, USA

Testi, Fabio
Via Francesco Siacci 38
Rome, ITALY I-00197

Testl, Fabio (Actor)
Via Siacci 38
Rome 197, ITALY

Teteak, Deral (Athlete, Football Player)
8067 Palomino Dr
Naples, FL 34113-2684, USA

Tetley, Glen (Choreographer, Director)
15 W 9th St
New York, NY 10011-8918, USA

Tetrault, Roger E (Business Person)
1450 Poydras St
New Orleans, LA 70112-1227, USA

Tetro-Atkinson, Barbara (Baseball Player)
2824 Forest Ln
Waukegan, IL 60087-2835, USA

Tettamanzi, Dlonigi Cardinal (Religious Leader)
Plazza Matteotti 4
Genoa 16123, ITALY

Tettleton, Mickey (Athlete, Baseball Player)
346 W Franklin Rd
Norman, OK 73069-8105, USA

Tetzlaff, Christian (Musician)
120 W 58th St # 80
New York, NY 10019-2141, USA

Teufel, Tim (Athlete, Baseball Player)
PO Box 3517
Jupiter, FL 33469-1009, USA

Teut, Nate (Athlete, Baseball Player)
2010 Sugar Creek Dr
Waukee, IA 50263-8093, USA

Teutul Sr, Paul (Reality TV Star, Television Host)
c/o Staff Member *WmE2 (Endeavor-LA)*
9601 Wilshire Blvd Fl 3
Beverly Hills, CA 90210-5219, USA

Tewell, Doug (Athlete, Golfer)
15216 Fairview Farm Rd
Edmond, OK 73013-1327, USA

Tewes, Lauren (Actor)
c/o Staff Member *The Actor's Group Talent and Literary Agency*
3400 Beacon Ave S
Seattle, WA 98144-6702, USA

Tewkesbury, Joan F (Director, Writer)
c/o Staff Member *Creative Artists Agency (CAA-LA)*
2000 Avenue of the Stars Ste 100
Los Angeles, CA 90067-4705, USA

Tewksbury, Bob (Athlete, Baseball Player)
63 Ridge Rd
Concord, NH 03301-3034, USA

Tewksbury, Mark
2380 Pierre Depuy Ave
Montreal, CANADA PQ H3C 3R4

Tews, Andreas (Boxer)
Hamburger Allee 1
Schwerin 19063, GERMANY

Texada, Tia (Actor)
c/o Staff Member *Rogers & Cowan PR (LA)*
Pacific Design Center 8687 Melrose Ave, 7th Floor
West Hollywood, CA 90069, USA

Tezak-Papesh, Virginia (Baseball Player)
1400 Clement St
Joliet, IL 60435-4209, USA

Thabu (Actor, Bollywood)
Ankul II Floor 7 Bungalows Andheri West
Mumbai, MS 400054, INDIA

Thacker, Brian M (War Hero)
11413 Monterrey Dr
Wheaton, MD 20902-2657, USA

Thacker, Tom (Athlete, Basketball Player)
3655 Dogwood Ln
Cincinnati, OH 45213-2601, USA

Thackery, Jimmy (Musician)
743 Center Blvd
Fairfax, CA 94930-1764, USA

Thaddeus, Patrick (Physicist)
58 Garfield St
Cambridge, MA 02138-1802, USA

Thagard, Norman E (Astronaut, Physicist)
502 N Ride
Tallahassee, FL 32303-5127, USA

Thain, John (Financier)
11 Wall St
New York, NY 10005-1905, USA

Thaksin, Shinawatra (Prime Minister)
Govt House Luke Road
Bangkok 10300/2, THAILAND

Thal, Eric (Actor)
c/o Phillip Carlson *Carlson Menashe Agency*
149 5th Ave Ste 1204
New York, NY 10010-6801

Thalheimer, Mona (Stylist)
630 Washington Ave
Santa Monica, CA 90403-3906, USA

Thalia (Actor, Musician)
c/o Staff Member *WmE2 (WMA-LA)*
1 William Morris Pl
Beverly Hills, CA 90212-4261, USA

Thames, Marcus (Athlete, Baseball Player)
101 Mount Moriah Cir
Louisville, MS 39339-2825, USA

Than, Shwe (General, Prime Minister)
Theinbyu Road Botahtaung
Yangon, MYANMAR

Thani, Sheikh Abdul Aziz Ibn Khalifa al (Prime Minister)
Dohar, QATAR

Thani, Sheikh Hamad bin Khalifa al (Royalty)
PO Box 923
Dohar, QATAR

Thapa, Surya Bahadur (Prime Minister)
Tangal
Kathmandu, NEPAL

Tharp, Twyla (Choreographer, Dancer)
336 Central Park W Apt 17B
New York, NY 10025-7127, USA

Tharpe, Larry (Athlete, Football Player)
3665 Greenbriar Rd E
Macon, GA 31204-4228, USA

Thatcher, Joe (Athlete, Baseball Player)
310 Ruddell Dr
Kokomo, IN 46901-4249, USA

Thatcher, Roland (Golfer)
18 Flowertuft Ct
Spring, TX 77380-1529, USA

Thatcher of Lincolnshire, Margaret H (Prime Minister)
11 Dutwich Gate Dulwich
London SE12, UNITED KINGDOM (UK)

Thaxter, Phyllis (Actor)
90 Wisteria Dr
Longwood, FL 32779-4935

Thaxton, Galand (Athlete, Football Player)
1424 Thaxton Ct Apt C
Laramie, WY 82072-1976, USA

Thaxton, James (Athlete, Football Player)
4319 Deergrove Rd
Memphis, TN 38141-7021, USA

Thayer, Bill (Misc)
PO Box 233
Snohomish, WA 98291-0233, USA

Thayer, Brynn (Actor)
c/o Steven Neibert *Imperium 7 Talent Agency*
5455 Wilshire Blvd Ste 1706
Los Angeles, CA 90036-4217, USA

Thayer, Greg (Athlete, Baseball Player)
1000 3rd St N
Sauk Rapids, MN 56379-2417, USA

Thayer, Helen (Skier)
PO Box 233
Snohomish, WA 98291-0233, USA

Thayer, Maria (Actor)
c/o Barry McPherson *Agency for the Performing Arts (APA-LA)*
405 S Beverly Dr Ste 500
Beverly Hills, CA 90212-4425, USA

Thayer, Tom (Athlete, Football Player)
330 W Diversey Pkwy Apt 2303
Chicago, IL 60657-6204, USA

Thayer, W Paul (Business Person, Government Official)
10200 Hollow Way Rd
Dallas, TX 75229-6635, USA

The Academy Is (Music Group)
c/o Bob McLynn *Crush Management*
60-62 E 11th St Floor 7
New York, NY 10003, USA

The Band Perry (Music Group, Musician)
c/o Rob Beckham *WmE2 (WMA-TN)*
1600 Division St Ste 300
Nashville, TN 37203-2755, USA

The Bronx (Music Group)
c/o Jonathan Daniel *Crush Management*
60-62 E 11th St Floor 7
New York, NY 10003, USA

The Color Fred (Music Group, Musician)
c/o Matt Galle *Paradigm (NY)*
360 Park Ave S Fl 16
New York, NY 10010-1708, USA

The Darkness (Music Group)
c/o Sue Whitehouse *Whitehouse Management*
PO Box 43829
London NW6 3PJ, UNITED KINGDOM

The Dear & Departed (Music Group, Musician)
c/o Stephen Looker *Knives Out Management*
PO Box 480519
Los Angeles, CA 90048-1519, USA

The Decemberists (Music Group)
c/o Ron Laffitte *Red Light Management (LA)*
8439 W Sunset Blvd Ste 2
Los Angeles, CA 90069-1925, USA

The Expendables (Music Group, Musician)
c/o Jon Phillips *Silverback Professional Artist Management*
1013 N Orange Dr
Los Angeles, CA 90038-2317, USA

The Fabulous Thunderbirds (Music Group)
c/o Patrick McAuliff *Monterey International (Chicago)*
200 W Superior St Ste 202
Chicago, IL 60654-6422, USA

The Fall of Troy (Music Group)
c/o David Benveniste *Velvet Hammer*
9014 Melrose Ave
West Hollywood, CA 90069-5610, USA

The Fray (Music Group)
c/o Joseph Carozza *Epic Records Group*
550 Madison Ave Fl 6
New York, NY 10022-3211, USA

The Game (Musician)
c/o Staff Member *Interscope Records (LA) - Main*
2220 Colorado Ave
Santa Monica, CA 90404-3506, USA

The Godfathers (Music Group, Musician)
c/o Matt Suhar *Tantrum Management*
3341 W Berteau Ave
Chicago, IL 60618-2305, USA

The Good The Bad & The Queen (Music Group)
c/o Staff Member *Paradigm (Monterey)*
404 W Franklin St
Monterey, CA 93940-2303, USA

The Great Khali (Writer)
c/o Kerry Rodgerson *World Wrestling Entertainment (WWE)*
1241 E Main St
Stamford, CT 06902-3520, USA

The Imponderables (Music Group, Musician)
c/o Monique Moss *Moss Public Relations*
8060 Melrose Ave Fl 4
Los Angeles, CA 90046-7038, USA

The Insult Comic Dog, Triumph (Actor, Comedian)
c/o Staff Member *Creative Artists Agency (CAA-LA)*
2000 Avenue of the Stars Ste 100
Los Angeles, CA 90067-4705, USA

The Jets (Music Group)
c/o Staff Member *Lustig Talent Enterprises Inc*
PO Box 770850
Orlando, FL 32877-0850, USA

The Jonas Brothers (Music Group)
c/o Staff Member *Hollywood Records*
500 S Buena Vista St
Burbank, CA 91521-0002, USA

The Killers (Music Group)
c/o Staff Member *Island Records*
825 8th Ave Rm C2
New York, NY 10019-7472, USA

The Lonely Island (Music Group)
c/o Staff Member *Silva Artist Management (SAM)*
722 Seward St
Los Angeles, CA 90038-3504, USA

The Maine (Music Group)
13772 Goldenwest St # 545
Westminster, CA 92683-3123, USA

The Moody Blues (Music Group, Musician)
c/o Ivy Stewart *Threshold Recording Co. Ltd.*
53 High St
Cobham KT11 3DP, UK

The National (Music Group)
c/o Dawn Berger *Post Hoc Management*
320 7th Ave # 145
Brooklyn, NY 11215-4194, USA

The Neptunes (Musician, Producer)
c/o Staff Member *Star Trak Entertainment*
1755 Broadway Frnt 3
New York, NY 10019-3743, USA

The Offspring (Music Group, Musician)
c/o Jim Guerinot *Rebel Waltz Inc*
31652 2nd Ave
Laguna Beach, CA 92651-8244, USA

The Pointer Sisters (Music Group, Musician)
c/o Konrad Leh *Creative Talent Group*
1900 Avenue of the Stars Ste 2475
Los Angeles, CA 90067-4512, USA

The Pretenders (Music Group)
c/o Staff Member *WmE2 (WMA-LA)*
1 William Morris Pl
Beverly Hills, CA 90212-4261, USA

The Prize Fighter Inferno (Music Group, Musician)
c/o Blaze James *Black Sheep Fellowship*
3134 Glenmanor Pl
Los Angeles, CA 90039-1713, USA

The Rasmus (Music Group)
c/o Staff Member *Playground Music Scandinavia*
Box 3171
Malm s-200 22, SWEDEN

The Rockers
PO Box 3859
Stamford, CT 6905

The Saturdays (Music Group, Musician)
c/o Staff Member *Maximum Artist Management*
20 Bedford St, 4th Floor Covent Garden
London WC2E 9HQ, UK

The Saw Doctors (Music Group)
3 St Mary's Terrace
Galway, IRELAND

The Script (Music Group, Musician)
c/o Cindi Berger *PMK/BNC Public Relations (PMK-NY)*
622 3rd Ave Fl 8
New York, NY 10017-6707, USA

The Snake The Cross The Crown (Music Group, Musician)
c/o Staff Member *Equal Vision Records*
PO Box 38202
Albany, NY 12203-8202, USA

The The (Music Group)
c/o Staff Member *Paradigm (Monterey)*
404 W Franklin St
Monterey, CA 93940-2303, USA

The Vaccines (Music Group, Musician)
c/o Staff Member *Paradigm (NY)*
360 Park Ave S Fl 16
New York, NY 10010-1708, USA

The Veronicas (Music Group, Musician)
c/o Staff Member *Wilhelmina Dan Agency*
1503 Union Ave Ste 211
Memphis, TN 38104-3739, USA

The Wiggles (Music Group, Musician)
P.O. Box 7873
Baulkham Hills, BC NSW 2153, Australia

The Yellowjackets (Music Group)
9715 Belmar Ave
Northridge, CA 91324-1606, USA

Theberge, James D (Diplomat)
4462 Cathedral Ave NW
Washington, DC 20016, USA

Thedford, Marcello (Actor)
c/o J.C. (JC) Robbins *JC Robbins Management*
113 S Kilkea Dr
Los Angeles, CA 90048-3525, USA

Theile, David (Swimmer)
84 Woodville St Hendea
Brisbane, QLD 4011, AUSTRALIA

Theis, Dave (Athlete, Baseball Player)
7250 Lewis Ridge Pkwy Apt 206
Minneapolis, MN 55439-1938, USA

Theismann, Joseph R (Joe) (Athlete, Football Player, Sportscaster)
PO Box 186
Leesburg, VA 20178-0186, USA

Theiss, Duane (Athlete, Baseball Player)
66 Juniper Ave
Westerville, OH 43081-1700, USA

Thelan, Jodi
8428 Melrose Pl Ste C
Los Angeles, CA 90069-5300

Themmen, Paris (Actor)
2109 S Wilbur Ave
Walla Walla, WA 99362-9048, USA

Theo Paphitis, Theo Paphitis (Business Person)
Ryman House , Savoy Rd Crewe
Cheshire CW1 6NA, UK

Theobald, Ron (Athlete, Baseball Player)
319 Jacaranda Pl
Fullerton, CA 92832-1434, USA

Theodorakis, Mikis (Composer)
Epifanous 1 Akropolis
Athens, GREECE

Theodore, Donna
10000 Santa Monica Blvd # 305
Los Angeles, CA 90067

Theodore, George (Athlete, Baseball Player)
1388 Princeton Ave
Salt Lake City, UT 84105-1921, USA

Theodore, Jose (Athlete, Hockey Player)
1260 De La Gauchetiere W
Montreal, QC H3B 5EB, Canada

Theodorescu, Monica (Athlete)
Gestit Lindenhof
Sassenberg 48336, GERMANY

Theodorou, Susie (Stylist)
c/o Staff Member *Jean Conlon*
461 Broome St
New York, NY 10013-2653, USA

Theodosakis, Jason (Doctor, Writer)
175 5th Ave
New York, NY 10010-7703, USA

Theodosius, Primate Metropolitian (Religious Leader)
PO Box 675 RR 25A
Syosset, NY 11791, USA

Theofiledes, Harry (Athlete, Football Player)
17806 Carrollwood Dr
Dallas, TX 75252-6357, USA

Therefore I Am (Music Group, Musician)
c/o Cody DeLong *Kenmore Agency, The*
59 Park St Ste 2
Beverly, MA 01915-4255, USA

Theriot, Ryan (Athlete, Baseball Player)
17502 Karen Dr
Prairieville, LA 70769-4660, USA

Theron, Charlize (Actor, Model)
c/o JJ Harris *One Talent Management*
9220 W Sunset Blvd Ste 306
Los Angeles, CA 90069-3503, USA

Theroux, Justin (Actor)
c/o Nick Frenkel *3 Arts Entertainment Inc*
9460 Wilshire Blvd Fl 7
Beverly Hills, CA 90212-2713, USA

Theroux, Louis (Television Host)
c/o Staff Member *BBC Artist Mail*
PO Box 1116
Belfast BT2 7AJ, United Kingdom

Theroux, Paul E (Writer)
35 Elsynge Road
London SW18 2NR, UNITED KINGDOM (UK)

Therrien, Gaston (Athlete, Hockey Player)
RDS 1775 Rene-Levesque Blvd E Bureau 300
Montreal, QC H2K 4P6, Canada

Theuriau, Melissa (Television Host)
4 Sente Des Robertines
Chanteloup-les-Vignes 78570, FRANCE

Theus, Reggie (Athlete, Basketball Player)
4259 Enoro Dr
Los Angeles, CA 90008-4802, USA

Thewlis, David (Actor)
c/o Steve Dontanville *Dontanville/ Frattaroli (D/F)*
8609 Washington Blvd # 8607
Culver City, CA 90232-7441, USA

Thiandoum, Hyacinthe Cardinal (Religious Leader)
Archeveche Ave Jean XXIII
Dakar 1908, SENEGAL

Thibaud, Todd (Musician)
c/o Staff Member *Paradigm (Monterey)*
404 W Franklin St
Monterey, CA 93940-2303, USA

Thibaudet, Jean-Yves (Musician)
3601 Griffith Park Blvd
Los Angeles, CA 90027-1406, USA

Thibault, Charles (Doctor)
4 Place Jussieu
Paris 75005, FRANCE

Thibaut, Jim (Athlete, Football Player)
PO Box 251
Kenner, LA 70063-0251, USA

Thibeaux, Peter (Athlete, Basketball Player)
2036 Paradise Dr Apt 2
Belvedere Tiburon, CA 94920-1985, USA

Thibert, Jim (Athlete, Football Player)
1365 County Road L
Swanton, OH 43558-9791, USA

Thibiant, Aida (Designer, Fashion Designer)
449 N Canon Dr
Beverly Hills, CA 90210-4819, USA

Thibodeaux, Keith (Actor)
5372 Jamaica Dr
Jackson, MS 39211-4057, USA

Thicke, Alan (Actor)
7110 Gobernador Canyon Rd
Carpinteria, CA 93013-3127, USA

Thicke, Robin (Musician)
c/o Miguel Melendez *Overbrook Entertainment*
450 N Roxbury Dr Fl 4
Beverly Hills, CA 90210-4218, USA

Thieben, Bill (Athlete, Basketball Player)
225 Jayne Ave
Patchogue, NY 11772-2628, USA

Thiedemann, Fritz (Misc)
Ostreherweg 28
Heide 25746, GERMANY

Thiel, Bert (Athlete, Baseball Player)
W11077 County Road D
Marion, WI 54950-9068, USA

Thiele, Gerhard P J (Astronaut)
Linder Hohe
Cologne 51147, GERMANY

Thielemann, Ray C (R C) (Athlete, Football Player)
210 Rose Meadow Ln
Alpharetta, GA 30005-8339, USA

Thielemans, Jean B (Toots) (Musician)
2575 Palisade Ave Apt 11H
Bronx, NY 10463-6149, USA

Thielen, Gunter (Business Person)
Carl-Bertelsmann-Str 270
Guetersloh 33311, GERMANY

Thiemann, Charles Lee (Financier)
PO Box 598
Cincinnati, OH 45201-0598, USA

Thieme, Paul (Misc)
Wilhelmstr 7
Tubingen 72074, GERMANY

Thier, Samuel O (Educator, Physicist)
99-20 Florence St Apt 4B
Chestnut Hill, MA 02467-1929, USA

Thieriot, Max (Actor)
c/o Ruth Bernstein *Viewpoint Inc*
8820 Wilshire Blvd Ste 220
Beverly Hills, CA 90211-2622, USA

Thierry, John F (Athlete, Football Player)
1431 Federal Rd
Opelousas, LA 70570-1172, USA

Thies, Jake (Athlete, Baseball Player)
4 Cornflower Ct
Florissant, MO 63033-6530, USA

Thiessen, Tiffani (Actor)
c/o Jai Khanna *Brillstein Entertainment Partners*
9150 Wilshire Blvd Ste 350
Beverly Hills, CA 90212-3453, USA

Thievery Corporation (Music Group, Musician)
c/o Sandee Fenton *Fresh and Clean Media*
12701 Venice Blvd
Los Angeles, CA 90066-3705, USA

Thigpen, Bobby (Athlete, Baseball Player)
1857 Brightwaters Blvd NE
Saint Petersburg, FL 33704-3005, USA

Thigpen, Curtis (Athlete, Baseball Player)
10637 Greenbrier Cir
Forney, TX 75126-6640, USA

Thile, Chris (Actor, Musician)
c/o Staff Member *IMG Artists Worldwide (NY)*
825 7th Ave
New York, NY 10019-6014, USA

Thimmesch, Nicholas (Journalist)
6301 Broad Branch Rd
Chevy Chase, MD 20815-3343, USA

Thinnes, Roy (Actor)
c/o Staff Member *Phoenix Artists*
321 W 44th St Ste 401
New York, NY 10036-5470, USA

Third Day (Music Group)
c/o Staff Member *Red Light Management (LA)*
8439 W Sunset Blvd Ste 2
Los Angeles, CA 90069-1925, USA

Third Eye Blind (Music Group)
c/o Carla Parisi *Kid Logic*
156 Liberty St Apt 12
Little Ferry, NJ 07643-1768, USA

Third World (Music Group)
PO Box 5231
Hollywood, FL 33083-5231, USA

Thirlby, Olivia (Actor)
c/o William Choi *Management 360*
9111 Wilshire Blvd
Beverly Hills, CA 90210-5508, USA

Thirsk, Robert B (Astronaut)
6767 Route De Aeroport
Saint-Hubert, QC J3Y 8Y9, CANADA

This Time Next Year (Music Group, Musician)
c/o Staff Member *Equal Vision Records*
PO Box 38202
Albany, NY 12203-8202, USA

Thobe, J J (Athlete, Baseball Player)
902 Grovemont St
Santa Ana, CA 92706-2046, USA

Thode, Henry G (Scientist)
Nuclear Research Dept
Hamilton, ON L8S 4M1, CANADA

Thoenen, Dick (Athlete, Baseball Player)
862 Smith St
Harrisburg, OR 97446-9505, USA

Thom, Sandi (Musician)
c/o Staff Member *Paradigm (Monterey)*
404 W Franklin St
Monterey, CA 93940-2303, USA

Thoma, Dieter (Skier)
Am Rossleberg 35
Hinterzarten 79856, GERMANY

Thoma, Georg (Skier)
Bisten 6
Hinterzarten 79856, GERMANY

Thomalla, Georg (Actor)
Hans Nefer
Bad Gastein 5640, AUSTRIA

Thomas, Aaron (Athlete, Football Player)
2906 NW Golf Course Dr S
Bend, OR 97701-5504, USA

Thomas, Adalius (Athlete, Football Player)
1 Willow Bend Dr
Hattiesburg, MS 39402-8552, USA

Thomas, Alex (Actor)
c/o Staff Member *Identity Talent Agency (ID)*
9107 Wilshire Blvd Ste 500
Beverly Hills, CA 90210-5526, USA

Thomas, Andrew S W (Andy) (Astronaut)
2101 Nasa Pkwy Spc Center
Houston, TX 77058-3607, USA

Thomas, Aurelius (Athlete, Football Player)
PO Box 91157
Columbus, OH 43209-7157, USA

Thomas, B J (Musician, Songwriter, Writer)
1324 Crownhill Dr
Arlington, TX 76012, USA

Thomas, Barbara S (Government Official)
1 Virginia St
London E1 9XY, UNITED KINGDOM (UK)

Thomas, Ben (Athlete, Football Player)
2155 Herndon St
Auburn, AL 36830-6603, USA

Thomas, Betty (Actor, Director, Producer)
c/o Bryan Lourd *Creative Artists Agency (CAA-LA)*
2000 Avenue of the Stars Ste 100
Los Angeles, CA 90067-4705, USA

Thomas, Billy M (General)
626 Sweetbrush
San Antonio, TX 78258-4119, USA

Thomas, BJ (Musician)
c/o Staff Member *Gloria Thomas Inc*
1424 Crownhill Dr
Arlington, TX 76012-2816, USA

Thomas, Blair (Athlete, Football Player)
401 Gulph Ridge Dr
King Of Prussia, PA 19406-3213, USA

Thomas, Broderick (Athlete, Football Player)
12004 Opal Creek Dr
Pearland, TX 77584-1647, USA

Thomas, Bruce (Actor)
c/o Jerry Shandrew *Shandrew Public Relations*
1050 S Stanley Ave
Los Angeles, CA 90019-6634, USA

Thomas, Calvin (Athlete, Football Player)
908 Manchester Ave
Westchester, IL 60154-2719, USA

Thomas, Carl (Musician)
c/o Staff Member *Red Entertainment Agency*
16 Penn Plz Ste 824
New York, NY 10001-1809, USA

Thomas, Carl (Athlete, Baseball Player)
7910 E Camelback Rd Unit 202
Scottsdale, AZ 85251-8609, USA

Thomas, Carotine Bedell (Physicist)
2401 Calvert St NW Apt 504
Washington, DC 20008-2669, USA

Thomas, Charles (Athlete, Baseball Player)
137 Black Oak Dr
Asheville, NC 28804-1835, USA

Thomas, Chris (Musician)
1995 Broadway # 501
New York, NY 10023-5882, USA

Thomas, Chuck (Athlete, Football Player)
2201 Purple Majesty Ct
Las Vegas, NV 89117-2747, USA

Thomas, Clendon (Athlete, Football Player)
7508 Rumsey Rd
Oklahoma City, OK 73132-5335, USA

Thomas, Craig (Actor)
Quay Street
Manchester M60 9EA, UK

Thomas, Damien
31 Kensington Church St
London, ENGLAND W8 4LL

Thomas, Dave (Comedian)
c/o David Boxerbaum *Agency for the Performing Arts (APA-LA)*
405 S Beverly Dr Ste 500
Beverly Hills, CA 90212-4425, USA

Thomas, Dave G (Athlete, Football Player)
2127 Brickell Ave Apt 3404
Miami, FL 33129-2105, USA

Thomas, David (Athlete, Football Player)
c/o Staff Member *New England Patriots*
Gillette Stadium One Patriots Pl
Foxboro, MA 02035-1388, USA

Thomas, David (Business Person)
Metro Center 1 Station Pl
Stanford, CT 6902, USA

Thomas, David (Musician)
74 Hyde Vale Greenwich
London SE10 8HP, UNITED KINGDOM (UK)

Thomas, Debra J (Deb) (Figure Skater)
202 S Michigan St Ste 810
South Bend, IN 46601-2012, USA

Thomas, Dennis (DT) (Musician)
c/o Staff Member *Pyramid Entertainment Group*
377 Rector Pl Apt 21A
New York, NY 10280-1439, USA

Thomas, Derrel (Athlete, Baseball Player)
112 Juniperhill Ln
Riverside, CA 92506-6217, USA

Thomas, Dominic R (Religious Leader)
& 6th Lincoln Sts
Monongahela, PA 15063, USA

Thomas, Donald A (Astronaut)
1029 Hart Rd
Towson, MD 21286-1630, USA

Thomas, Donald Michael (D M) (Writer)
Coach House Rashleigh Vale Tregolls Rd
Truro, Cornwall TR1 1TJ, UNITED KINGDOM (UK)

Thomas, Doug (Athlete, Football Player)
11220 NE 53rd St
Kirkland, WA 98033-7505, USA

Thomas, Duane (Athlete, Football Player)
PO Box 862
Del Mar, CA 92014-0862, USA

Thomas, E Donnall (Nobel Prize Laureate)
PO Box 19024
Seattle, WA 98109-1024, USA

Thomas, Earl (Athlete, Football Player)
1000 Farrah Ln Apt 825
Stafford, TX 77477-6046, USA

Thomas, Earlie (Athlete, Football Player)
PO Box 1445
Laporte, CO 80535-1445, USA

Thomas, Eddie Kaye (Actor)
c/o Greg Clark *Untitled Entertainment (LA)*
350 S Beverly Dr Ste 200
Beverly Hills, CA 90212-4819, USA

Thomas, Elizabeth Marshall (Writer)
80 E Mountain Rd
Peterborough, NH 03458-2318, USA

Thomas, Emmitt (Athlete, Football Player)
4603 NE Dick Howser Cir
Lees Summit, MO 64064-1678, USA

Thomas, Ernest (Actor)
3350 Barham Blvd
Los Angeles, CA 90068-1404, USA

Thomas, Etan (Basketball Player)
c/o Staff Member *Washington Wizards*
601 F St NW
Washington, DC 20004-1605, USA

Thomas, Evan (Writer)
c/o Staff Member *Public Affairs Books*
1094 Flex Dr
Jackson, TN 38301-5070, USA

Thomas, Frank E (Athlete, Baseball Player)
1540 Villa Rica Dr
Henderson, NV 89052-4050, USA

Thomas, Frank J (Athlete, Baseball Player)
118 Doray Dr
Pittsburgh, PA 15237-3681, USA

Thomas, Fred (Government Official, Lawyer)
300 Indiana Ave NW
Washington, DC 20001-2108, USA

Thomas, Gareth (Actor)
c/o Staff Member *Julian Belfrage & Associates*
46 Albemarle St
London W1X 4PP, UK

Thomas, Gareth (Engineer)
Materials Science
Berkeley, CA 94720-0001, USA

Thomas, Gorman (Athlete, Baseball Player)
W331S5179 Hood Pkwy
North Prairie, WI 53153-9719, USA

Thomas, Heather (Actor)
c/o Larry Kennar *Code Entertainment*
9229 W Sunset Blvd Ste 615
Los Angeles, CA 90069-3419, USA

Thomas, Heidi (Actor)

Thomas, Helen A (Journalist)
2501 Calvert St NW
Washington, DC 20008-2611, USA

Thomas, Henry (Actor)
c/o Colton Gramm *Brillstein Entertainment Partners*
9150 Wilshire Blvd Ste 350
Beverly Hills, CA 90212-3453, USA

Thomas, Henry L Jr (Athlete, Football Player)
16811 Southern Oaks Dr
Houston, TX 77068-1509, USA

Thomas, Henry W (Writer)
3214 Warder St NW
Washington, DC 20010-2521, USA

Thomas, Hollis (Athlete, Football Player)
920 Yeadon Ave
Lansdowne, PA 19050-3713, USA

Thomas, Irma (Musician)
c/o Staff Member *Concerted Efforts*
PO Box 440326
Somerville, MA 02144-0004, USA

Thomas, Irving (Athlete, Basketball Player)
5117 Lakosee Ct
Orlando, FL 32818-8330, USA

Thomas, Isaac (Athlete, Football Player)
510 Grady Ln
Cedar Hill, TX 75104-4212, USA

Thomas, J T (Athlete, Football Player)
408 Arden Dr
Monroeville, PA 15146-4855, USA

Thomas, Jack Ward (Biologist, Government Official)
Biology
Missoula, MT 59812-0001, USA

Thomas, Jake (Actor)
c/o Connie Tavel *Forward Entertainment*
9255 W Sunset Blvd Ste 805
Los Angeles, CA 90069-3305, USA

Thomas, Jay (Actor)
c/o Christine Holder *Zero Gravity Management (II)*
5225 Wilshire Blvd Ste 600
Los Angeles, CA 90036-4351, USA

Thomas, Jean (Artist)
1427 Summit Rd
Berkeley, CA 94708-2214, USA

Thomas, Jeremy (Filmmaker, Producer)
8-12 Broadwick St
London W1V 1FH, UNITED KINGDOM (UK)

Thomas, Jesse (Athlete, Football Player)
4955 Woodward Gdns
Columbia, MD 21044-1525, USA

Thomas, Joe L (Musician)
c/o Staff Member *Kedar Entertainment*
365 Bridge St Apt 20C
Brooklyn, NY 11201-3821, USA

Thomas, Joey (Athlete, Football Player)
c/o Eugene Parker *Maximum Sports Management*
6435 W Jefferson Blvd # 197
Fort Wayne, IN 46804-6203, USA

Thomas, John (Basketball Player)
Air Canada Center 40 Bay St
Toronto, ON M5J 2N8, CANADA

Thomas, John (Bud) (Athlete, Baseball Player)
2475 Woodland Dr
Sedalia, MO 65301-8915, USA

Thomas, John C (Athlete, Track Athlete)
51 Mulberry St
Brockton, MA 02302-2327, USA

Thomas, John M (Scientist)
21 Albemarle St
London W1X 4BS, UNITED KINGDOM (UK)

Thomas, Johnny (Athlete, Football Player)
1818 Darby Ln
Fresno, TX 77545-9233, USA

Thomas, Jonathan Taylor (Actor)
c/o Abby Bluestone *Innovative Artists (LA)*
1505 10th St
Santa Monica, CA 90401-2805, USA

Thomas, Justice Clarence (Judge)
1 1st St NE
Washington, DC 20543-0001, USA

Thomas, Khleo (Actor)
c/o Staff Member *Beverly Hecht Agency*
3500 W Olive Ave Ste 1180
Burbank, CA 91505-4651, USA

Thomas, Kleo (Musician)

Thomas, Kurt (Athlete, Basketball Player)
1826 Brook Terrace Trl
Dallas, TX 75232-3708, USA

Thomas, Lamar (Athlete, Football Player)
10524 NW 13th Ln
Gainesville, FL 32606-8091, USA

Thomas, Larry (Athlete, Baseball Player)
3825 Graham Ln
Eight Mile, AL 36613-2306, USA

Thomas, Larry (Actor)
c/o Dora Whitaker *Whitaker Agency, The*
4924 Vineland Ave
N Hollywood, CA 91601-3847, USA

Thomas, LaToya (Basketball Player)
1 at and T Center Pkwy
San Antonio, TX 78219-3604, USA

Thomas, Lavale (Athlete, Football Player)
712 Bradford Creek Trl # M
Duluth, GA 30096-1402, USA

Thomas, Lee (Athlete, Baseball Player)
14260 Manderleigh Woods Dr
Chesterfield, MO 63017-8051, USA

Thomas, Mark A (Athlete, Football Player)
556 Hillsboro St
Monticello, GA 31064-1046, USA

Thomas, Marlo (Actor)
c/o Johnnie Planco *Parseghian Planco LLC*
322 8th Ave Ste 601
New York, NY 10001-6715, USA

Thomas, Mary (Musician)
PO Box 371371
Las Vegas, NV 89137-1371, USA

Thomas, Mava Lee (Baseball Player)
PO Box 830242
Ocala, FL 34483-0242, USA

Thomas, Merilisa (Stylist)
84912 Sunset Blvd # 262
Los Angeles, CA 90069, USA

Thomas, Michael Tilson (Conductor, Musician)
Davies Symphony Hall
San Francisco, CA 94102, USA

Thomas, Michelle Rene (Actor)
9200 W Sunset Blvd Ste 900
Los Angeles, CA 90069-3604

Thomas, Mike (Athlete, Baseball Player)
1572 County Road 766
Jonesboro, AR 72401-8296, USA

Thomas, Mike (Athlete, Football Player)
PO Box 446
Missouri City, TX 77459-0446, USA

Thomas, Norris (Athlete, Football Player)
4510 Chippewa Ave
Pascagoula, MS 39581-2501, USA

Thomas, Pamela (Business Person)
c/o Staff Member *CNBC*
900 Sylvan Ave
Englewood Cliffs, NJ 07632-3312, USA

Thomas, Pat (Athlete, Football Player)
612 Middle Cove Dr
Plano, TX 75023-4802, USA

Thomas, Philip Michael (Actor)
PO Box 23714
Brooklyn, NY 11202-3714, USA

Thomas, Ralph (Athlete, Football Player)
3270 Alum Creek Ct
Reno, NV 89509-7117, USA

Thomas, Randy (Athlete, Football Player)
2254 Nelms Dr SW
Atlanta, GA 30315-6404, USA

Thomas, Ray (Nobel Prize Laureate)
1222 16th Ave S # 300
Nashville, TN 37212-2926, USA

Thomas, Reginald
18 Belgrave Mews W
London, ENGLAND SW1X 8HT

Thomas, Richard (Actor)
c/o Emily Gerson Saines *Brookside Artists Management (NY)*
250 W 57th St Ste 2303
New York, NY 10107-2399, USA

Thomas, Ricky (Athlete, Football Player)
4621 Melbourne Rd
Indianapolis, IN 46228-2773, USA

Thomas, Rob (Musician, Songwriter)
c/o Michael Lippman *Lippman Entertainment*
23586 Calabasas Rd Ste 208
Calabasas, CA 91302-1361, USA

Thomas, Rob (Director, Producer, Writer)
c/o Ari Greenburg *WmE2 (Endeavor-LA)*
9601 Wilshire Blvd Fl 3
Beverly Hills, CA 90210-5219, USA

Thomas, Robb (Athlete, Football Player)
179 NW Outlook Vista Dr
Bend, OR 97701-5472, USA

Thomas, Robert D (Publisher)
223 Mariomi Rd
New Canaan, CT 06840-3315, USA

Thomas, Robert L (Athlete, Football Player)
2810 W Slauson Ave Apt 5
Los Angeles, CA 90043-2583, USA

Thomas, Robert R (Athlete, Football Player)
259 Linden St
Glen Ellyn, IL 60137-4009, USA

Thomas, Robin (Actor)
c/o Staff Member *Marshak/Zachary Company, The*
8840 Wilshire Blvd Fl 1
Beverly Hills, CA 90211-2606, USA

Thomas, Ross (Actor)
c/o Bryan Bukowski *Simmons & Scott Entertainment*
7942 Mulholland Dr
Los Angeles, CA 90046-1225, USA

Thomas, Roy (Athlete, Baseball Player)
6881 SW 167th Pl
Beaverton, OR 97007-6312, USA

Thomas, Rozonda (Chili) (Musician)
c/o Staff Member *WmE2 (WMA-LA)*
1 William Morris Pl
Beverly Hills, CA 90212-4261, USA

Thomas, Sean Patrick (Actor)
c/o Karen Samfilippo *Image Management PR*
1810 14th St Ste 205
Santa Monica, CA 90404-4662, USA

Thomas, Serena Scott (Actor)
8730 W Sunset Blvd Ste 440
Los Angeles, CA 90069 2277, USA

Thomas, Skip (Athlete, Football Player)
3021 N 63rd St
Kansas City, KS 66104-1935, USA

Thomas, Speedy (Athlete, Football Player)
7534 Weyburn St
Houston, TX 77028-2418, USA

Thomas, Stan (Athlete, Baseball Player)
10827 159th Ct NE
Redmond, WA 98052-2691, USA

Thomas, Steve (Athlete, Hockey Player)
289 Bering Ave
Toronto, ON M8Z 3A5, Canada

Thomas, Steve (Entertainer)
PO Box 2284
South Burlington, VT 05407-2284, USA

Thomas, Taylor Lea (Designer, Entertainer)
c/o Staff Member *Elite Soiree*
1221 Brickell Ave Ste 800
Miami, FL 33131-3231, USA

Thomas, Ted (Business Person)
234 Willard St
Cocoa, FL 32922-7984, USA

Thomas, Thurman L (Athlete, Football Player)
240 Pound Rd
Elma, NY 14059-9681, USA

Thomas, Tony (Actor, Producer)
11901 Santa Monica Blvd Ste 596
West Los Angeles, CA 90025-5188, USA

Thomas, Tra (Athlete, Football Player)
1 Novacare Way
Philadelphia, PA 19145-5900, USA

Thomas, Valmy (Athlete, Baseball Player)
PO Box 811
Christiansted, VI 00821-0811, USA

Thomas, Wayne (Athlete, Hockey Player)
200 Hudson Rd E
Cleveland, OH 44115, USA

Thomas, William H Jr (Athlete, Football Player)
2401 Echo Dr
Amarillo, TX 79107-6405, USA

Thomas, William J (Athlete, Football Player)
16 Russell St
Waltham, MA 02453-8505, USA

Thomas, Zach (Athlete, Football Player)
1051 NW 122nd Ave
Plantation, FL 33323-2529, USA

Thomas III, Isiah L (Athlete, Basketball Player)
400 Renaissance Ctr Ste 300
Detroit, MI 48243-1502, USA

Thomas Jr, James (Athlete, Basketball Player)
4499 Willow Hill Rd
Portal, GA 30450-5344, USA

Thomas of Swynnerton, Hugh S (Historian)
Well House
Sudbourne, Suffolk, UNITED KINGDOM (UK)

Thomaselli, Rich (Athlete, Football Player)
96A Seneca St
Weirton, WV 26062-2627, USA

Thomason, Bob (Athlete, Football Player)
2645 Bucknell Ave
Charlotte, NC 28207-2649, USA

Thomason, CJ (Actor)
c/o Staff Member *Robert Stein Management*
PO Box 3797
Beverly Hills, CA 90212-0797, USA

Thomason, Erskine (Athlete, Baseball Player)
932 Dial Pl
Laurens, SC 29360-8850, USA

Thomason, Harry (Producer)
c/o Staff Member *Mozark Productions*
4024 Radford Ave Bldg 5 PMB 104
Studio City, CA 91604, USA

Thomason, Harry Z (Producer)
10732 Riverside Dr
North Hollywood, CA 91602-2313, USA

Thomason, Marsha (Actor)
c/o Kesha Williams *Affirmative Entertainment*
425 N Robertson Blvd
West Hollywood, CA 90048-1735, USA

Thomassin, Florence (Actor)
20 Ave Rapp
Paris 75007, FRANCE

Thomasson, Gary (Athlete, Baseball Player)
8300 N 53rd St
Paradise Valley, AZ 85253-2512, USA

Thome, James H (Jim) (Athlete, Baseball Player)
125 E 8th St
Hinsdale, IL 60521-4520, USA

Thomerson, Tim (Actor)
2635 28th St Apt 14
Santa Monica, CA 90405-2960, USA

Thomlinson, John (Baseball Player)
2351 Beach Way SW
Atlanta, GA 30310-1005, USA

Thomopoulos, Anthony (Business Person)
5357 Long Shadow Ct
Westlake Village, CA 91362-5223, USA

Thomopoulos, Tony
1280 Stone Canyon Rd
Los Angeles, CA 90077-2920

Thompson, Ahmir-Khalib (Musician)
c/o Sara Ramaker *Paradigm (LA)*
360 N Crescent Dr
Beverly Hills, CA 90210-4874, USA

Thompson, Andrea (Actor)
8306 Wilshire Blvd # 56
Beverly Hills, CA 90211-2382, USA

Thompson, Andy (Athlete, Baseball Player)
4801 Culbreath Isles Way
Tampa, FL 33629-4846, USA

Thompson, Anthony (Coach, Football Coach, Football Player)
Athletic Dept
Bloomington, IN 47405, USA

Thompson, Arland (Athlete, Football Player)
6692 S Routt St
Littleton, CO 80127-4962, USA

Thompson, Aundra (Athlete, Football Player)
12060 Galva Dr
Dallas, TX 75243-3702, USA

Thompson, Barbara (Baseball Player)
1721 Edgebrook Dr
Rockford, IL 61107-1320, USA

Thompson, Bennie (Athlete, Football Player)
11001 Russell St
Baltimore, MD 21230, USA

Thompson, Billy (Athlete, Basketball Player)
54 Pinecrest St
Lake Placid, FL 33852-8118, USA

Thompson, Bobby (Athlete, Baseball Player)
7006 Hunters Glen Dr
Charlotte, NC 28214-2271, USA

Thompson, Bobby (Athlete, Football Player)
23600 Lahser Rd
Southfield, MI 48033-3202, USA

Thompson, Brian
1010 Olive Ln
La Canada, CA 91011-2367

Thompson, Brooks (Athlete, Basketball Player)
29222 Oakview Rdg
Boerne, TX 78015-4457, USA

Thompson, Caroline W (Director, Producer, Writer)
c/o Brian Sher *Category 5 Entertainment*
10250 Constellation Blvd Fl 7
Los Angeles, CA 90067-6207, USA

Thompson, Christopher (Astronomer)
Astrophysics
Chapel Hill, NC 27599-0001, USA

Thompson, Clifford (Athlete, Coach, Hockey Player)
3 Summit Dr Apt 16
Reading, MA 01867-4025, USA

Thompson, Cornelius (Athlete, Basketball Player)
207 Lamentation Dr
Berlin, CT 06037-3727, USA

Thompson, Craig (Athlete, Football Player)
913 C St
Hartsville, SC 29550-3166, USA

Thompson, Daley (Athlete)
1 Church Row Wandsworth Pln
London, ENGLAND SW18 1ES

Thompson, Darrell (Athlete, Football Player)
4220 Oakview Ln N
Plymouth, MN 55442-2773, USA

Thompson, David O (Athlete, Basketball Player)

Thompson, David R (Judge)
940 Front St
San Diego, CA 92101-8971, USA

Thompson, David W (Scientist)
21839 Atlantic Blvd
Sterling, VA 20166-6850, USA

Thompson, Derek (Athlete, Baseball Player)
3212 Pine Shadow Dr
Land O Lakes, FL 34639-4516, USA

Thompson, Donnell (Athlete, Football Player)
1302 Village Crossing Dr
Chapel Hill, NC 27517-7572, USA

Thompson, Edward K (Editor)
PO Box 350
Mahopac, NY 10541-0350, USA

Thompson, Edward T (Editor)
11 Cotswold Dr
North Salem, NY 10560-2708, USA

Thompson, Emma (Actor)
c/o Catherine Olim *PMK/BNC Public Relations (PMK-LA)*
8687 Melrose Ave Ste 8
West Hollywood, CA 90069-5746, USA

Thompson, Ernest
Rt. #1 Box 3248
Ashland, NH 3217

Thompson, F M (Daley) (Athlete, Track Athlete)
1 Wadsworth Plain
London SW18 1EH, UNITED KINGDOM (UK)

Thompson, Fred Dalton (Actor, Ex-Senator, Politician)
PO Box 143
Hermitage, TN 37076-0143, USA

Thompson, G Kennedy (Financier)
1 First Union Ctr
Charlotte, NC 28288-0001, USA

Thompson, G Ralph (Religious Leader)
12501 Old Columbia Pike
Silver Spring, MD 20904-6601, USA

Thompson, Gary (Basketball Player)
2531 Park Vista Cir
Ames, IA 50014-4568, USA

Thompson, Gary Scott (Producer, Writer)
c/o Rob Carlson *WmE2 (Endeavor-LA)*
1 William Morris Pl
Beverly Hills, CA 90212-4261, USA

Thompson, Gina (Musician)
1800 Argyle Ave # 408
Los Angeles, CA 90028-5253, USA

Thompson, Hank (Musician, Songwriter, Writer)
2000 Vista Rd
Keller, TX 76262-8803, USA

Thompson, Hilarie
13202 Weddington St
Sherman Oaks, CA 91401-6034

Thompson, Hugh L (Educator)
President's Office
Topeka, KS 66621, USA

Thompson, Ian
44 Perryn Rd
London, ENGLAND W3 7NA

Thompson, J Lee
9595 Lime Orchard Rd
Beverly Hills, CA 90210-1315, USA

Thompson, Jack (Actor)
110 Queen St
Woollahra, NSW 2025, AUSTRALIA

Thompson, Jack (Athlete, Football Player)
643 NW 85th St
Seattle, WA 98117-3144, USA

Thompson, Jack E (Business Person)
650 California St
San Francisco, CA 94108-2702, USA

Thompson, James B Jr (Misc)
1010 Waltham St # F1
Lexington, MA 02421-8044, USA

Thompson, James R (Jim) Jr (Ex-Governor)
35 W Wacker Dr
Chicago, IL 60601-1723, USA

Thompson, James R Jr (Misc)
5046 Somerby Dr SE
Huntsville, AL 35802-1267, USA

Thompson, Jason (Athlete, Baseball Player)
10359 Trillium Dr
Las Vegas, NV 89135-4055, USA

Thompson, Jason (Actor)
c/o Ryan Daly *Zero Gravity Management*
11578 Canton Dr
Studio City, CA 91604-4160, USA

Thompson, Jason D (Athlete, Baseball Player)
4056 Summerfield Dr
Troy, MI 48085-7033, USA

Thompson, Jennifer (Jenny) (Swimmer)
1 Olympic Plz
Colorado Springs, CO 80909-5780, USA

Thompson, Jenny
1 Olympic Plz
Colorado Springs, CO 80909-5780

Thompson, Jill (Cartoonist)
1700 Broadway
New York, NY 10019-5905, USA

Thompson, John G (Mathematician)
Mathematics
Gainesville, FL 32611-0001, USA

Thompson, Junior (Athlete, Baseball Player)
8325 E Hazelwood St
Scottsdale, AZ 85251-1751, USA

Thompson, Justin (Athlete, Baseball Player)
37111 Edgewater Dr
Pinehurst, TX 77362-1936, USA

Thompson, Kenan (Actor)
c/o Michael Goldman *Michael Goldman Management*
7471 Melrose Ave Ste 11
Los Angeles, CA 90046-7551, USA

Thompson, Kenneth L (Scientist)
600 Mountain Ave
New Providence, NJ 07974-2008, USA

Thompson, Kevin (Athlete, Basketball Player)
204 Asbury Dr
Kernersville, NC 27284-2195, USA

Thompson, Lasalle (Athlete, Basketball Player)
399 Du Bois Ave
Sacramento, CA 95838-2546, USA

Thompson, Laura Ann (Stylist)
c/o Staff Member *Zenobia Agency Inc*
PO Box 909
Groveland, CA 95321-0909, USA

Thompson, Lea (Actor)
c/o Lisa Lieberman *Innovative Artists (NY)*
235 Park Ave S Fl 7
New York, NY 10003-1404, USA

Thompson, Leonard (Golfer)
9010 Marsh View Ct
Ponte Vedra Beach, FL 32082-1928, USA

Thompson, Leonard (Athlete, Football Player)
5534 W Glenrosa Ave
Phoenix, AZ 85031-2220, USA

Thompson, Leroy (Athlete, Football Player)
5005 Princess Ann Ct
Knoxville, TN 37918-9274, USA

Thompson, Linda (Actor)
25254 Eldorado Meadow Rd
Hidden Hills, CA 91302-1242, USA

Thompson, Linda (Musician)
751 Bridgeway # 300
Sausalito, CA 94965-2102, USA

Thompson, Lonnie (Scientist)
Geology Dept
Columbus, OH 43210, USA

Thompson, Mark (Athlete, Baseball Player)
2600 Chandler Dr Apt 1311
Bowling Green, KY 42104-6235, USA

Thompson, Martel (Stylist)
c/o Staff Member *Montana Artists Agency*
9150 Wilshire Blvd Ste 100
Beverly Hills, CA 90212-3459, USA

Thompson, Marty (Athlete, Football Player)
1290 Lone Star Ct
Calimesa, CA 92320-1501, USA

Thompson, Mike (Cartoonist, Editor)
600 W Fort St
Detroit, MI 48226-3138, USA

Thompson, Mike (Athlete, Baseball Player)
7565 Turner Dr
Denver, CO 80221-3432, USA

Thompson, Milt (Athlete, Baseball Player)
PO Box 663
Williamstown, NJ 08094-0663, USA

Thompson, Morgan
c/o Jeff Morrone *Jeff Morrone Entertainment*
9350 Wilshire Blvd Ste 224
Beverly Hills, CA 90212-3204, USA

Thompson, Mychal (Athlete, Basketball Player)
11 Paverstone Ln
Ladera Ranch, CA 92694-0454, USA

Thompson, Norm (Athlete, Football Player)
PO Box 4552
Hayward, CA 94540-4552, USA

Thompson, Obadele (Athlete, Track Athlete)
PO Box 46
Bridgetown, BARBADOS

Thompson, Paul (Athlete, Basketball Player)
3422 N 40th St
Milwaukee, WI 53216-3637, USA

Thompson, Paul H (Educator)
President S Ofc
Ogden, UT 84408-0001, USA

Thompson, Ray (Athlete, Football Player)
1501 N Johnson St Apt A208
New Orleans, LA 70116, USA

Thompson, Raynoch (Athlete, Football Player)
1739 2nd St
New Orleans, LA 70113-1657, USA

Thompson, Reyna (Athlete, Football Player)
1502 NW 183rd Ter
Pembroke Pines, FL 33029-3095, USA

Thompson, Rich (Athlete, Baseball Player)
7 Chambers Ct
Huntington Station, NY 11746-2620, USA

Thompson, Rich (Athlete, Baseball Player)
47 Murray St
Binghamton, NY 13905-4522, USA

Thompson, Richard (Musician, Songwriter, Writer)
100 Park St Apt 4
Montclair, NJ 07042-2996, USA

Thompson, Richard K (Religious Leader)
PO Box 32843
Charlotte, NC 28232-2843, USA

Thompson, Ricky (Athlete, Football Player)
1277 Brazos Bluff Dr
China Spring, TX 76633-2865, USA

Thompson, Robert (Athlete, Football Player)
910 SW 15th St
Deerfield Beach, FL 33441-6222, USA

Thompson, Robert G K (General)
Pitcott House Winsford Minehead
Somerset, UNITED KINGDOM (UK)

Thompson, Robert L (Athlete, Football Player)
16924 White Pine Way
Canyon Country, CA 91387-3992, USA

Thompson, Robert R (Robby) (Athlete, Baseball Player)
4438 Gun Club Rd
West Palm Beach, FL 33406-2961, USA

Thompson, Ryan (Athlete, Baseball Player)
2153 Fullerton Dr
Indianapolis, IN 46214-2130, USA

Thompson, Sarah (Actor)
c/o Gerry Harrington *Brillstein Entertainment Partners*
9150 Wilshire Blvd Ste 350
Beverly Hills, CA 90212-3453, USA

Thompson, Scot (Athlete, Baseball Player)
6142 Penn Dr
Butler, PA 16002-0406, USA

Thompson, Scott (Carrot Top) (Actor, Comedian)
c/o Steve Levine *International Creative Management (ICM-LA)*
10250 Constellation Blvd Fl 7
Los Angeles, CA 90067-6207, USA

Thompson, Scottie (Actor)
c/o Mary Putnam Greene *MPG Management*
1136 Roxbury Dr
Los Angeles, CA 90035-1066, USA

Thompson, Shawn
5319 Biloxi Ave
North Hollywood, CA 91601-3514

Thompson, Sophie (Actor)
13 Shorts Gardens
London WC2H 9AT, UNITED KINGDOM (UK)

Thompson, Starley L (Scientist)
PO Box 3000
Boulder, CO 80307-3000, USA

Thompson, Steve M (Athlete, Football Player)
11115 Vernon Rd
Lake Stevens, WA 98258-8541, USA

Thompson, Sue (Musician)
3907 W Alameda Ave Ste 200
Burbank, CA 91505-4359, USA

Thompson, Susanna
PO Box 15717
Beverly Hills, CA 90209-1717

Thompson, Tara (Actor)
c/o Staff Member *Innovative Artists (LA)*
1505 10th St
Santa Monica, CA 90401-2805, USA

Thompson, Ted (Athlete, Football Player)
PO Box 10628
Green Bay, WI 54307-0628, USA

Thompson, Tessa (Actor)
c/o Eric Black *Anonymous Content (AC-LA)*
3531 Hayden Ave
Culver City, CA 90232, USA

Thompson, Tim (Athlete, Baseball Player)
536 Summit Dr
Lewistown, PA 17044-1252, USA

Thompson, Tommy (Athlete, Football Player)
PO Box 687
Calico Rock, AR 72519-0687, USA

Thompson, Tommy (Politician)
1313 Manassas Trl
Madison, WI 53718-8243, USA

Thompson, Tommy G (Secretary)
200 Independence SW
Washington, DC 20201-0004, USA

Thompson, Weegie (Athlete, Football Player)
14501 Felbridge Way
Midlothian, VA 23113-6721, USA

Thompson, Wilbur (Moose) (Athlete, Track Athlete)
1111 Stevely Ave
Long Beach, CA 90815-4946, USA

Thompson, William A (Athlete, Football Player)
120 S Fraser Cir
Aurora, CO 80012-1556, USA

Thompson, William P (Religious Leader)
475 Riverside Dr
New York, NY 10115-0002, USA

Thompson Square (Music Group, Musician)
c/o Staff Member *WmE2 (WMA-TN)*
1600 Division St Ste 300
Nashville, TN 37203-2755, USA

Thompson Twins
9 Eccleston St
London, ENGLAND SW1W 9LX

Thompson-Griffin, Viola (Baseball Player)
200 Edgewood Dr
Belton, SC 29627-1615, USA

Thoms, Art (Athlete, Football Player)
90 Goodfellow Dr
Moraga, CA 94556-1584, USA

Thoms, Tracie (Actor)
c/o Ted Schachter *Schachter Entertainment*
1157 S Beverly Dr Fl 2
Los Angeles, CA 90035-1119, USA

Thomsen, Cecilie (Actor)
c/o Staff Member *Special Artists Agency*
9465 Wilshire Blvd Ste 820
Beverly Hills, CA 90212-2607, USA

Thomsen, Mary Sue (Stylist)
8 Oak Pl
Belvedere, CA 94920-2411, USA

Thomsen, Ulrich (Actor)
10100 Santa Monica Blvd Ste 2500
Los Angeles, CA 90067-4116, USA

Thomson, Anna (Actor)
1505 10th St
Santa Monica, CA 90401-2805, USA

Thomson, Brian E (Designer)
5 Little Dowling St
Paddington, NSW 2021, AUSTRALIA

Thomson, Cyndi (Musician)
9100 Wilshire Blvd Ste 100W
Beverly Hills, CA 90212-3435, USA

Thomson, David (Business Person)
Metro Center 1 Station Place
Stamford, CT 6902, USA

Thomson, Dorrie
3349 Cahuenga Blvd W Ste 2
Los Angeles, CA 90068-1379

Thomson, Gordon (Actor)
3914 Fredonia Dr
Los Angeles, CA 90068-1214, USA

Thomson, H C (Hank) (Misc)
PO Box 38
Mullett Lake, MI 49761-0038, USA

Thomson, James A (Biologist)
Medical School Biology Dept
Madison, WI 53706, USA

Thomson, John (Athlete, Baseball Player)
1414 E Kent Dr
Sulphur, LA 70663-5017, USA

Thomson, June (Correspondent)
3000 W Alameda Ave
Burbank, CA 91523-0001, USA

Thomson, Peter (Golfer)
44 Mathoura St
Toorak, VIC 3142, AUSTRALIA

Thomson, Robert B (Bobby) (Athlete, Baseball Player)
13 Saltwind Cir
Savannah, GA 31411-3067, USA

Thomson, Scott (DJ)
c/o Staff Member *Sharp Talent*
117 N Orlando Ave
Los Angeles, CA 90048-3403, USA

Thon, Dickie (Athlete, Baseball Player)
C17 Calle Lirio Del Mar
Dorado, PR 00646-2126, USA

Thon, Olaf (Activist)
Postfach 200861
Gelsenkirchen 45843, GERMANY

Thone, Charles (Ex-Governor)
301 S 13th St Ste 400
Lincoln, NE 68508-2532, USA

Thoni, Gustav (Coach, Skier)
39026 Prato Allo
Stelvio-Prao, BZ, ITALY

Thor, Brad (Writer)
c/o Staff Member *Sanford J Greenburger Associates Inc*
55 5th Ave
New York, NY 10003-4301, USA

Thora (Actor)
10635 Santa Monica Blvd Ste 130
Los Angeles, CA 90025-8306, USA

Thorell, Clarke (Actor)
5757 Wilshire Blvd Ste 473
Los Angeles, CA 90036-3632

Thoren, Skip (Athlete, Basketball Player)
330 Buckland Trce
Louisville, KY 40245-4272, USA

Thorin, Christopher (Musician)
9229 W Sunset Blvd Ste 607
Los Angeles, CA 90069-3406, USA

Thormodsgard, Paul (Athlete, Baseball Player)
7752 E Rose Ln
Scottsdale, AZ 85250-4724, USA

Thorn, Gaston (Prime Minister)
1 Rue de la Forge
Luxembourg, LUXEMBOURG

Thorn, Paul (Musician)
c/o Staff Member *Paradigm (Monterey)*
404 W Franklin St
Monterey, CA 93940-2303, USA

Thorn, Rod (Athlete, Basketball Player)
20 Loewen Ct
Rye, NY 10580-2823, USA

Thorn, Tracey (Musician)
Acklam Worshops 10 Acklam Road
London W10 5QZ, UNITED KINGDOM (UK)

Thornbladh, Robert (Athlete, Football Player)
PO Box 1391
Ann Arbor, MI 48106-1391, USA

Thornburgh, Richard (Dick) (Ex-Governor)
1601 K St NW
Washington, DC 20006-1682, USA

Thornburgh, Richard L (Dick) (Ex-Governor)
1601 K St NW
Washington, DC 20006-1682, USA

Thorne, Bella (Actor)
c/o Adam Griffin *Kritzer Levine Wilkins Entertainment*
11872 La Grange Ave Fl 1
Los Angeles, CA 90025-5283, USA

Thorne, Callie (Actor)
c/o Lindsay Porter *Gersh (NY)*
41 Madison Ave
New York, NY 10010-2202, USA

Thorne, Dyanne (Actor)
8721 W Sunset Blvd Ste 101
Los Angeles, CA 90069-2271, USA

Thorne, Frank (Cartoonist)
1967 Grenville Rd
Scotch Plains, NJ 07076-2907, USA

Thorne, Gary (Correspondent)
77 W 66th St
New York, NY 10023-6201, USA

Thorne, Kip S (Physicist)
Physics
Pasadena, CA 91125-0001, USA

Thorne, Remy (Actor)
c/o Adam Griffin *Kritzer Levine Wilkins Entertainment*
11872 La Grange Ave Fl 1
Los Angeles, CA 90025-5283, USA

Thornell, Jack R (Journalist, Photographer)
6815 Madewood Dr
Metairie, LA 70003-4529, USA

Thorne-Smith, Courtney (Actor, Model)
c/o Staff Member *IMPR*
1810 14th St Ste 205
Santa Monica, CA 90404-4662, USA

Thornhill, Arthur H Jr (Publisher)
50 S School St
Portsmouth, NH 03801-5258, USA

Thornhill, Josh (Athlete, Football Player)
1580 Haddon Hall Dr
Holt, MI 48842-8688, USA

Thornhill, Leeroy (Dancer)
Jenkins Lane
Great Hallinsburry, Essex CM22 9QL, UNITED KINGDOM (UK)

Thornhill, Lisa (Actor)
208-11 Anin St Bedford Nova
Scotia B4A 4E3, CANADA

Thornton, Andre (Athlete, Baseball Player)
PO Box 395
Chagrin Falls, OH 44022-0395, USA

Thornton, Bill (Athlete, Football Player)
2709 Poppy Way
Columbia, MO 65202-1264, USA

Thornton, Billy Bob (Actor, Director)
c/o Geyer Kosinski *Media Talent Group*
9200 W Sunset Blvd Ste 550
Los Angeles, CA 90069-3611, USA

Thornton, Bob (Athlete, Basketball Player)
27865 Espinoza
Mission Viejo, CA 92692-2151, USA

Thornton, Bruce (Athlete, Football Player)
3117 Hazlewood Ct
Bedford, TX 76021-2953, USA

Thornton, Frank (Actor)
586A King Road
London SW6 2DX, UNITED KINGDOM (UK)

Thornton, George (Athlete, Football Player)
2830 Marti Ln
Montgomery, AL 36116-3139, USA

Thornton, James (Athlete, Football Player)
1010 Fuller Rd
Gurnee, IL 60031-1834, USA

Thornton, Joe (Athlete, Hockey Player)
c/o Staff Member *San Jose Sharks*
525 W Santa Clara St
San Jose, CA 95113-1500, USA

Thornton, John (Athlete, Football Player)
6192 Otoole Ln
Mount Morris, MI 48458-2628, USA

Thornton, John (Athlete, Football Player)
7340 Indian Hill Rd
Cincinnati, OH 45243-4022, USA

Thornton, Kalen (Athlete, Football Player)
c/o Eugene Parker *Maximum Sports Management*
6435 W Jefferson Blvd # 197
Fort Wayne, IN 46804-6203, USA

Thornton, Kathryn C (Astronaut)
100 Bedford Pl
Charlottesville, VA 22903-4622, USA

Thornton, Lou (Athlete, Baseball Player)
725 Henderson Rd
Hope Hull, AL 36043-4429, USA

Thornton, Matt (Athlete, Baseball Player)
21208 N 82nd Ln
Peoria, AZ 85382-3480, USA

Thornton, Melody (Musician)
c/o Page Jeter *Entertainment Fusion Group*
8899 Beverly Blvd Ste 412
West Hollywood, CA 90048-2431, USA

Thornton, Michael (War Hero)
16856 Falcon Sound Dr
Montgomery, TX 77356-8386, USA

Thornton, Otis (Athlete, Baseball Player)
4312 Avenue L
Birmingham, AL 35208-1812, USA

Thornton, Shawn (Athlete)
12 Sackville St Unit 2
Charlestown, MA 02129-1923, USA

Thornton, Sidney (Athlete, Football Player)
748 Royal St
Natchitoches, LA 71457-5741, USA

Thornton, Sigrid (Actor)
147 King St
Sydney, NSW 2000, AUSTRALIA

Thornton, Tiffany (Actor)
c/o Eileen Stringer *Howard Entertainment*
10850 Wilshire Blvd Ste 1260
Los Angeles, CA 90024-4337, USA

Thornton, William E (Astronaut)
7640 Pimlico Ln
Boerne, TX 78015-4820, USA

Thornton, Zach (Soccer Player)
980 N Michigan Ave Ste 1998
Chicago, IL 60611-7504, USA

Thorogood, George (Musician)
PO Box 807
Lewisburg, WV 24901-0807, USA

Thorp, Amanda (Actor)

Thorpe, Alexis (Actor)
c/o Marv Dauer *Marv Dauer Management*
11661 San Vicente Blvd Ste 104
Los Angeles, CA 90049-5150, USA

Thorpe, Ian (Swimmer)
PO Box 427
Milsons Point, NSW 2061, AUSTRALIA

Thorpe, James (Director)
20 Loeffler Rd Apt T320
Bloomfield, CT 06002-2277, USA

Thorpe, Jeremy J (Government Official)
2 Orme Square Bayswater
London W2, UNITED KINGDOM (UK)

Thorpe, Jim (Golfer)
1612 Kersley Cir
Lake Mary, FL 32746-1923, USA

Thorpe, Otis H (Athlete, Basketball Player)
PO Box 400
Canfield, OH 44406-0400, USA

Thorsell, William (Editor)
444 Front St W
Toronto, ON M5V 2S9, CANADA

Thorsness, Leo K (War Hero)
239 Watterson Way
Madison, AL 35756-6426, USA

Thorson, Celeste (Producer, Writer)
c/o Alex Fox *Cunningham Escott Slevin & Doherty (CESD-LA)*
10635 Santa Monica Blvd Ste 130
Los Angeles, CA 90025-8306, USA

Thorson, Linda (Actor)
8730 W Sunset Blvd Ste 440
Los Angeles, CA 90069-2277, USA

Those, Tom (Athlete, Baseball Player)
740 E Mingus Ave Apt 1012
Cottonwood, AZ 86326-3780, USA

Thousand Foot Krutch (Music Group)
PO Box 12698
Seattle, WA 98111-4698, USA

Thout, Pierre
22897 Thornbury Dr
Hollywood, MD 20636-4228

Thranhardt, Carlo
Brauweilerstr. 14
Koln, GERMANY D-50859

Thrash, James (Athlete, Football Player)
16005 Hampton Rd
Hamilton, VA 20158-3311, USA

Threadgill, Henry L (Composer, Musician)
300 Mercer St Apt 3J
New York, NY 10003-6732, USA

Threats, Jabbar (Athlete, Football Player)
2015 Miracle Mile
Springfield, OH 45503-2836, USA

Threatt, Sedale (Athlete, Basketball Player)
8400 E Dixileta Dr Unit 191
Scottsdale, AZ 85266-2270, USA

Three 6 Mafia (Music Group, Musician)
c/o Jennifer Wilson *Entertainment Fusion Group*
8899 Beverly Blvd Ste 412
West Hollywood, CA 90048-2431, USA

Three Degrees
19 The Willows Maidenhead Rd.
Windsor Berkshire, ENGLAND

Three Dog Night

Threets, Erick (Athlete, Baseball Player)
2080 Vintage Ln
Livermore, CA 94550-8202, USA

Threlfall, David (Actor)
c/o Staff Member *James Sharkey Assoc*
15 Golden Sq Fl 3
London W1R 3PA, UNITED KINGDOM (UK)

Threlkeld, Richard D (Correspondent)
51 W 52nd St
New York, NY 10019-6119, USA

Threshie, R David Jr (Publisher)
625 N Grand Ave
Santa Ana, CA 92701-4347, USA

Thrice (Music Group)
c/o Staff Member *Nick Ben-Meir CPA*
652 N Doheny Dr
West Hollywood, CA 90069-5526, USA

Thrift, Cliff (Athlete, Football Player)
705 Trisha Ln
Norman, OK 73072-3718, USA

Throne, Malachi (Actor)
11805 Mayfield Ave Apt 306
Los Angeles, CA 90049-5748, USA

Throop, George (Athlete, Baseball Player)
239 Windwood Ln
Sierra Madre, CA 91024-2677, USA

Thrower, Jim (Athlete, Football Player)
17421 Pontchartrain Blvd
Detroit, MI 48203-1720, USA

Throwing Muses (Composer, Musician)
c/o Staff Member *Concerted Efforts*
PO Box 440326
Somerville, MA 02144-0004, USA

Thumann, Chad (Writer)
c/o Josh Kesselman *Jericho Entertainment*
2121 Avenue of the Stars Ste 2900
Los Angeles, CA 90067-5057

Thunman, Nils R (Admiral)
1516 S Willemore Ave
Springfield, IL 62704-3374, USA

Thuot, Pierre
21700 Atlantic Blvd
Dulles, VA 20166-6860

Thuot, Pierre J (Astronaut)
22897 Thornbury Dr
Hollywood, MD 20636-4228, USA

Thurlow, Steve (Athlete, Football Player)
198 Shore Rd
Old Greenwich, CT 06870-2421, USA

Thurm, Maren (Actor)
Ordensmeisterstr 15-16
Berlin 12099, GERMANY

Thurman, Corey (Athlete, Baseball Player)
713 S Duke St
York, PA 17401-3113, USA

Thurman, Dennis L (Athlete, Football Player)
1 Jets Dr
Florham Park, NJ 07932-1215, USA

Thurman, Gary (Athlete, Baseball Player)
225 W 32nd St
Indianapolis, IN 46208-4603, USA

Thurman, Mike (Athlete, Baseball Player)
1360 7th St
West Linn, OR 97068-4718, USA

Thurman, Uma (Actor, Producer)
c/o Jason Weinberg *Untitled Entertainment (LA)*
350 S Beverly Dr Ste 200
Beverly Hills, CA 90212-4819, USA

Thurman, William E (General)
10 Firestone Dr
Pinehurst, NC 28374-7091, USA

Thurmond, Mark (Athlete, Baseball Player)
1614 Kings Castle Dr
Katy, TX 77450-4300, USA

Thurmond, Nate (Athlete, Basketball Player)
1665 Folsom St
San Francisco, CA 94103-3722, USA

Thurow, Lester C (Economist)
Economics Dept
Cambridge, MA 2139, USA

Thursday (Music Group)
c/o Staff Member *Island Records*
825 8th Ave Rm C2
New York, NY 10019-7472, USA

Thurston, Frederick C (Fuzzy) (Athlete, Football Player)
E1462 Grandview Rd
Waupaca, WI 54981-9136, USA

Thurston, Joe (Athlete, Baseball Player)
2219 Fairfield Ave
Fairfield, CA 94533-2017, USA

Thyssen, Greta (Actor)
444 E 82nd St
New York, NY 10028-5903, USA

T.I. (Musician)
c/o Staff Member *Grand Hustle*
541 10th St NW PMB 161
Atlanta, GA 30318-5713, USA

Tian, Jiyun (Government Official)
State Council
Beijing, CHINA

Tiant, Luis (Athlete, Baseball Player)
24 Southwood Dr
Southborough, MA 01772-1976, USA

Tibbets, Paul W
5574 Knollwood Dr
Columbus, OH 43232-1543, USA

Tibbets, Paul W Jr (War Hero)
5574 Knollwood Dr
Columbus, OH 43232-1543, USA

Tibbs, Jay (Athlete, Baseball Player)
905 Smith Rd
Oneonta, AL 35121-7181, USA

Tice, George A (Photographer)
581 Kings Hwy E
Atlantic Highlands, NJ 07716-2326, USA

Tice, John (Athlete, Football Player)
26 Winhaven Ct
Highland Falls, NY 10928-1640, USA

Tice, Michael P (Mike) (Athlete, Football Coach, Football Player)
1213 Ashbury Ln
Libertyville, IL 60048-2976, USA

Tichmarsh, Alan (Actor, Writer)
c/o Staff Member *Arlington Enterprises Ltd*
1-3 Charlotte St
London W1P 1HD, UNITED KINGDOM (UK)

Tichnor, Alan (Religious Leader)
155 5th Ave
New York, NY 10010-6802, USA

Tickner, Charles (Charlie) (Figure Skater)
5410 Sunset Dr
Littleton, CO 80123-1422, USA

Ticotin, Rachel (Actor)
c/o Staff Member *Stone Manners Salners Agency (LA)*
9911 W Pico Blvd Ste 1400
Los Angeles, CA 90035-2715, USA

Tiddy, Kim (Actor)
1 Deer Park Rd Merton
London SW19 9TL, ENGLAND

Tidrow, Dick (Athlete, Baseball Player)
324 NE Warrington Ct
Lees Summit, MO 64064-1605, USA

Tidwell, Moody R III (Judge)
717 Madison Pl NW
Washington, DC 20439-0001, USA

Tidwell, Travis (Athlete, Football Player)
3300 Caseys Xing
Birmingham, AL 35215-1072, USA

Tiefenbach, Dov (Actor)
c/o Staff Member *Bauman Redanty & Shaul Agency*
5757 Wilshire Blvd Suite 473
Beverly Hills, CA 90212, USA

Tiefenthaler, Verfe (Athlete, Baseball Player)
1852 Quint Ave
Carroll, IA 51401-3567, USA

Tiegs, Cheryl (Model, Television Host)
9663 Santa Monica Blvd # 339
Beverly Hills, CA 90210-4303, USA

Tieman, Dan (Athlete, Basketball Player)
8 Janet Dr
Taylor Mill, KY 41015-1731, USA

Tiemann, Norbert T (Ex-Governor)
7511 Pebblestone Dr
Dallas, TX 75230-4454, USA

Tiernan, Andrew (Actor)
c/o Paula Rosenberg *ICA Talent*
818 12th St Apt 9
Santa Monica, CA 90403-1727, USA

Tierney, Maura (Actor)
c/o Christina Papadopoulos *Baker Winokur Ryder Public Relations BWR (BWR-NY)*
292 Madison Ave Fl 12
New York, NY 10017-6415, USA

Tiffany (Musician)
c/o Charlie Davis *Paradise Artists*
PO Box 1821
Ojai, CA 93024-1821, USA

Tiffee, Terry (Athlete, Baseball Player)
2620 Calico Creek Dr
North Little Rock, AR 72116-7638, USA

Tiffin, Pamela (Actor)
15 W 67th St
New York, NY 10023-6226, USA

Tiger, Lionel (Scientist)
248 W 23rd St # 400
New York, NY 10011-2304, USA

Tigerman, Stanley (Architect)
444 N Wells St
Chicago, IL 60654-4501, USA

Tighe, Kevin (Actor)
c/o Joanna (Joanie) Burstein *Burstein Company, The*
15304 W Sunset Blvd Ste 208
Pacific Palisades, CA 90272-3656, USA

Tikkanen, Esa (Athlete, Hockey Player)
Curtiusstr 2
Essen 45144, Germany

Tilberg, Tasha (Model)
c/o Staff Member *Next (LA)*
8447 Wilshire Blvd Ste 301
Beverly Hills, CA 90211-3206, USA

Tilford, Terrell (Actor)
c/o Staff Member *Silver Massetti & Szatmary (SMS) Talent Inc*
8730 W Sunset Blvd Ste 440
Los Angeles, CA 90069-2277, USA

Tilghman, Shirley M C (Biologist, Educator)
President S Ofc
Princeton, NJ 08544-0001, USA

Tilker, Ewald (Athlete)
2767 40th Ave
San Francisco, CA 94116-2707, USA

Till, Lucas (Actor)
c/o Ellen Meyer *Ellen Meyer Management*
8899 Beverly Blvd Ste 612
West Hollywood, CA 90048-2429, USA

Tilleman, Mike (Athlete, Football Player)
180 County Road 800 NW
Havre, MT 59501, USA

Tiller, Joe (Coach, Football Coach)
Athletic Dept
W Lafayette, IN 47907, USA

Tiller, Nadja (Actor)
Via Tamporiva 26
Castagnola 6976, SWITZERLAND

Tilley, Patrick L (Pat) (Athlete, Coach, Football Coach, Football Player)
PO Box 4523
Shreveport, LA 71134-0523, USA

Tillis, Mel (Musician, Songwriter, Writer)
PO Box 305
Silver Springs, FL 34489-0305, USA

Tillis, Pam (Musician, Songwriter, Writer)
1908 Wedgewood Ave
Nashville, TN 37212-3733, USA

Tillison, Ed (Athlete, Football Player)
38504 James Crosby Rd
Pearl River, LA 70452-3431, USA

Tillman, Andre (Athlete, Football Player)
PO Box 743204
Dallas, TX 75374-3204, USA

Tillman, Lewis (Athlete, Football Player)
PO Box 166
Madison, MS 39130-0166, USA

Tillman, Robert L (Business Person)
1605 Curtis Bridge Rd
Wilkesboro, NC 28697-2231, USA

Tillman, Rusty (Athlete, Baseball Player)
8711 Newton Rd Apt 61
Jacksonville, FL 32216-4661, USA

Tillman Jr, George (Director, Producer, Writer)
10201 W Pico Blvd Bldg 52RM PMB 123
Los Angeles, CA 90064-2606, USA

Tillotson, Johnny (Musician)
19948 Mayall St
Chatsworth, CA 91311-3522, USA

Tillotson, Thad (Athlete, Baseball Player)
PO Box 1942
Winton, CA 95388-1942, USA

Tilly, Jennifer (Actor)
c/o Brad Marks *BM Management*
Prefers to be contacted via phone
Los Angeles, CA 90069, USA

Tilly, Meg (Actor)
c/o Staff Member *IFA Talent Agency*
8730 W Sunset Blvd Ste 490
Los Angeles, CA 90069-2248, USA

Tilson, Joseph (Joe) (Artist)
2 Brook Street Mansions 41 Davies St
London W1Y 1FJ, UNITED KINGDOM (UK)

Tilton, Charlene (Actor)
c/o Staff Member *Bohemia Group*
1680 Vine St Ste 216
Los Angeles, CA 90028-8829, USA

Tilton, Charline (Actor)
c/o Staff Member *Bohemia Group*
1680 Vine St Ste 216
Los Angeles, CA 90028-8829, USA

Tilton, Glenn F (Business Person)
1200 E Algonquin Rd
Arlington Heights, IL 60005-4712, USA

Tilton, Robert (Misc)
PO Box 819000
Dallas, TX 75381, USA

Timbaland (Musician)
c/o David Zedeck *Creative Artists Agency (CAA-NY)*
162 5th Ave Fl 6
New York, NY 10010-6047, USA

Timberlake, Gary (Athlete, Baseball Player)
14016 Waters Edge Dr
Louisville, KY 40245-5250, USA

Timberlake, George (Athlete, Football Player)
13880 Canoe Brook Dr Apt 4D
Seal Beach, CA 90740-3856, USA

Timberlake, Justin (Actor, Musician, Producer)
c/o Rick Yorn *Yorn Management Group*
2000 Avenue Of The Stars 3rd Tower Floor NORTH
Los Angeles, CA 90067, USA

Timberlake, Robert W (Bob) (Athlete, Football Player)
2219 E Jarvis St
Milwaukee, WI 53211-2149, USA

Timchal, Cindy (Coach)
Athletic
College Park, MD 20742-0001, USA

Times, Ken (Athlete, Football Player)
2603 S Sanford Ave
Sanford, FL 32773-5298, USA

Timken, William R Jr (Business Person)
1835 Dueber Ave SW
Canton, OH 44706-2728, USA

Timlin, Mike (Athlete, Baseball Player)
355 High Ridge Way
Castle Pines, CO 80108-3422, USA

Timm, Bruce (Animator)
c/o Staff Member *Peter Strain & Associates Inc (LA)*
5455 Wilshire Blvd Ste 1812
Los Angeles, CA 90036-4268, USA

Timme, Robert (Architect)
2370 Rice Blvd Ste 112
Houston, TX 77005-2644, USA

Timmerman, Adam (Athlete, Football Player)
6209 Mid Rivers Mall Dr
Saint Peters, MO 63304-1102, USA

Timmermann, Tom (Athlete, Baseball Player)
197 Coyote Ct
Pinckney, MI 48169-8022, USA

Timmermann, Ulf (Athlete, Track Athlete)
Conrad Blenkle Str 34
Berlin 1055, GERMANY

Timmins, Call (Actor)
1800 Avenue of the Stars Ste 400
Los Angeles, CA 90067-4206, USA

Timmons, Harold
PO Box 140571
Nashville, TN 37214-0571

Timmons, Jeff (Musician)
83 Riverside Dr
New York, NY 10024-5713, USA

Timmons, Margo (Musician)
1505 W 2nd Ave # 200
Vancouver, BC V6H 3Y4, CANADA

Timmons, Michael (Musician, Songwriter, Writer)
1505 W 2nd Ave # 200
Vancouver, BC V6H 3Y4, CANADA

Timmons, Ozzie (Athlete, Baseball Player)
4901 S 83rd St
Tampa, FL 33619-7101, USA

Timmons, Peter (Musician)
1505 W 2nd Ave # 200
Vancouver, BC V6H 3Y4, CANADA

Timmons, Tim (Baseball Player)
PO Box 574
New Albany, OH 43054-0574, USA

Timmons, Tim (Athlete, Baseball Player)
PO Box 574
New Albany, OH 43054-0574, USA

Timofeev, Valeri (Artist)
464 Blue Mountain Lk
East Stroudsburg, PA 18301-8654, USA

Timofeyeva, Nina V (Ballerina)
Teatralnaya Pl 1
Moscow 103009, RUSSIA

Timpson, Michael D (Athlete, Football Player)
3020 Crested Cir
Orlando, FL 32837-6956, USA

Tin Tin, Rin
PO Box 27
Crockett, TX 75835-0027

Tina, Fasano-Cucci (Stylist)
3286 Polo Pl
Bronx, NY 10465-1310, USA

Tindermans, Leo (Prime Minister)
Jan Verbertiel 24
Edegem 2520, BELGIUM

Tindle, David (Astronaut)
20 Cork St
London W1, UNITED KINGDOM (UK)

Ting, Samuel C C (Nobel Prize Laureate)
2 Eliot Pl
Jamaica Plain, MA 02130-4021, USA

Ting, Walasse (Artist)
100 W 25th St
New York, NY 10001, USA

Ting Tings, The (Music Group)

Tingelhoff, Mick (Athlete, Football Player)
20517 Kalmeadow Ct
Lakeville, MN 55044-6705, USA

Tinglehoff, H Michael (Mick) (Athlete, Football Player)
19288 Judicial Rd
Prior Lake, MN 55372, USA

Tingley, Leeann (Beauty Pageant Winner)
PO Box 3509
Cranston, RI 02910-0509, USA

Tingley, Ron (Athlete, Baseball Player)
349 Omni Dr
Sparks, NV 89441-7295, USA

Tinker, Grant (Business Person)
541 Perugia Way
Los Angeles, CA 90077-3708, USA

Tinkham, Michael (Physicist)
6126 SE Grant St
Portland, OR 97215-4055, USA

Tinoco, Joe
118 N Keeler St
Olathe, KS 66061-3716

Tinsley, Bruce (Cartoonist, Editor)
c/o Staff Member *King Features Syndication*
300 W 57th St Fl 15
New York, NY 10019-5238, USA

Tinsley, Buddy (Athlete, Football Player)
10-6645 Roblin Blvd
Winnipeg, MB R3R 3S4, Canada

Tinsley, George (Athlete, Basketball Player)
PO Box 1442
Auburndale, FL 33823-1442, USA

Tinsley, Jackson B (Jack) (Editor)
400 W 7th St
Fort Worth, TX 76102-4701, USA

Tinsley, Jamaal (Basketball Player)
125 S Pennsylvania St
Indianapolis, IN 46204-3610, USA

Tinsley, Lee (Athlete, Baseball Player)
237 Tenor St
Shelbyville, KY 40065-9255, USA

Tinsley, Scott (Athlete, Football Player)
26852 Sommerset Ln
Lake Forest, CA 92630-5800, USA

Tint, Francine (Stylist)
1 University Pl PH 22B
New York, NY 10003-4516, USA

Tippet, Andre B (Athlete, Football Player)
17 Knob Hill St
Sharon, MA 02067-3119, USA

Tippett, Dave (Athlete, Coach, Hockey Player)
116 Great Brook Rd
Groton, CT 06340-7701, USA

Tippett, Sir Michael
48 Great Marborough St
London, ENGLAND W1V 2BN

Tippin, Aaron (Musician, Songwriter)
PO Box 41689
Nashville, TN 37204-1689, USA

Tippins, Ken (Athlete, Football Player)
RR 2 Box 173
Adel, GA 31620, USA

Tipton, Daniel (Religious Leader)
PO Box 30
Circleville, OH 43113-0030, USA

Tipton, Dave L (Athlete, Football Player)
915 Bonneville Way
Sunnyvale, CA 94087-3038, USA

Tiriac, Ion (Coach, Tennis Player)
Blvd. D'Italie 44
Monte Carlo, MONACO

Tirico, Mike (Sportscaster)
77 W 66th St
New York, NY 10023-6201, USA

Tirimo, Martino (Musician)
1 Romeyn Road
London SW16 2NU, UNITED KINGDOM (UK)

Tirole, Jean M (Economist)
Toulouse, FRANCE

Tisch, James S (Business Person)
667 Madison Ave
New York, NY 10065-8029, USA

Tisch, Preston R (Business Person, Government Official)
667 Madison Ave
New York, NY 10065-8029, USA

Tisch, Steve (Writer)
1162 Tower Rd
Beverly Hills, CA 90210-2131, USA

Tischiski, Tom (Athlete, Baseball Player)
9905 N Donnelly Ave
Kansas City, MO 64157-7861, USA

Tisdale, Ashley (Actor)
c/o Bill Perlman *New Talent Management*
PO Box 2939
Beverly Hills, CA 90213-2939, USA

Tisdale, Jennifer (Actor)
c/o Bill Perlman *New Talent Management*
PO Box 2939
Beverly Hills, CA 90213-2939, USA

Tishby, Noa (Actor)
c/o Bob McGowan *McGowan Management*
8733 W Sunset Blvd Ste 103
West Hollywood, CA 90069-2241, USA

Tishchenko, Boris I (Composer)
79 Rimsky-Korsakoff Ave #10
Saint Petersburg 190121, RUSSIA

Tisser, Orna (Stylist)
c/o Staff Member *Celestine - CA*
1666 20th St Ste 200B
Santa Monica, CA 90404-3828, USA

Titanic Historical Society
PO Box 51053
Indian Orchard, MA 01151-5053

Titchenal, Bob (Athlete, Football Player)
1401 Fountaingrove Pkwy Unit 200
Santa Rosa, CA 95403-5762, USA

Titchmarsh, Alan (Talk Show Host)
New Mills Slad Rd
Stroud, Gloucestershire Engl GL5 1RN, UNITED KINGDOM (UK)

Titensor, Glen (Athlete, Football Player)
729 Montrose Ct
Flower Mound, TX 75022-8000, USA

Tito, Dennis (Astronaut)
1800 Alta Mura Rd
Pacific Palisades, CA 90272-2700, USA

Tito, Teburoro (President)
Tarawa, KIRIBATI

Titone, Jackie (Actor)
c/o Staff Member *WmE2 (Endeavor-LA)*
9601 Wilshire Blvd Fl 3
Beverly Hills, CA 90210-5219, USA

Titov, German (Athlete, Hockey Player)
2000 E Gene Autry Way
Anaheim, CA 92806-6143, USA

Titov, Vladimir
3 Hovanskaya Str 8
Moscow, RUSSIA 129515

Titov, Vladimir G (Cosmonaut)
Moskovskoi Oblasti
Syvisdny Goroduk 141160, RUSSIA

Titov, Yuri E (Gymnast)
Kolokolnikov Per 6 #19
Moscow 103045, RUSSUA

Tits, Jacques L (Mathematician)
12 Rue du Moulin des Pres
Paris 75013, FRANCE

Tittle, Y A (Athlete, Football Player)
PO Box 1960
San Jose, CA 95109-1960, USA

Tittle, Yelberton A (Y A) (Athlete, Football Player)
2500 E Camino Real
Palo Alto, CA 94306, USA

Titus, Christopher (Writer)
c/o Max Burgos *Collective*
8383 Wilshire Blvd Ste 1050
Beverly Hills, CA 90211-2415, USA

Titus-Carmel, Gerard (Artist)
La Grand Maison
Oulchy Le Chateau 2210, FRANCE

Tixby, Dexter (Musician)
24210 E East Fork Rd Spc 9
Azusa, CA 91702-6249, USA

Tizard, Catherine A (Ex-Governor)
12A Wallace St
Herne Bay, Auckland 1, New Zealand

Tiziani, Mario (Athlete, Golfer)
c/o Jim Lehrman *SFX Golf*
36855 W Main St Ste 200
Purcellville, VA 20132-3561, USA

Tizon, Albert (Journalist)
1120 John St
Seattle, WA 98109-5321, USA

Tizzio, Thomas R Sr (Business Person)
70 Pine St
New York, NY 10270-0001, USA

Tjeknavorian, Loris-Zare (Composer, Conductor)
Mashtotsi Prospekt 46
Yerevan, ARMENIA

Tjoflat, Gerald B (Judge)
311 W Monroe St
Jacksonville, FL 32202-4242, USA

Tkachuk, Keith (Athlete, Hockey Player)
11243 Hunters Pond Rd
Creve Coeur, MO 63141-7672, USA

Tkaczuk, Ivan (Religious Leader)
3 Davenport Ave Apt 2A
New Rochelle, NY 10805-3438, USA

Tkaczuk, Walter R (Walt) (Athlete, Hockey Player)
RR 3
Saint Mary's, ON N0M 2G0, Canada

TLC (Music Group)
c/o Staff Member *Creative Artists Agency (CAA-LA)*
2000 Avenue of the Stars Ste 100
Los Angeles, CA 90067-4705, USA

TNA Wrestling (Wrestler)
c/o Staff Member *Paradigm (Monterey)*
404 W Franklin St
Monterey, CA 93940-2303, USA

To, Tony (Director, Producer)
3000 Olympic Blvd Ste 2405
Santa Monica, CA 90404-5073, USA

Toale, Will (Actor)
c/o Jennifer Wiley *Framework Entertainment (NY)*
129 W 27th St Fl 12
New York, NY 10001-6206, USA

Toback, James (Director)
8942 Wilshire Blvd # 219
Beverly Hills, CA 90211-1908, USA

Tobeck, Robbie (Athlete, Football Player)
2018 Newport Way NW
Issaquah, WA 98027-5392, USA

Tober, Ronnie (Business Person)
Tober Jochems VOF Stadskade 258
Apeldoorn 7311 XV, NETHERLANDS

Tobey, James (Actor)
10100 Santa Monica Blvd Ste 2500
Los Angeles, CA 90067-4116, USA

Tobian, GAry M (Misc)
9171 Belted Kingfisher Rd
Blaine, WA 98230-5701, USA

Tobias, Andrew (Business Person, Writer)
787 NE 71st St
Miami, FL 33138-5717, USA

Tobias, Oliver (Actor)
2D Wimpole St
London W1G 0EB, UNITED KINGDOM (UK)

Tobias, Phillip V (Scientist)
7 York Road
Johannesburg 2193, SOUTH AFRICA

Tobias, Randall L (Business Person)
Lilly Corporate Ctr
Indianapolis, IN 46285-0001, USA

Tobias, Robert M (Misc)
901 E St NW
Washington, DC 20004-2013, USA

Tobias, Stephen C (Business Person)
3 Commercial Pl
Norfolk, VA 23510-2108, USA

Tobik, Dave (Athlete, Baseball Player)
848 Chancellor Heights Dr
Ballwin, MO 63011-3580, USA

Tobin, Don (Cartoonist)
12312 Ranchwood Rd
Santa Ana, CA 92705-3349, USA

Tobin, Vince (Athlete, Coach, Football Coach, Football Player)
15997 W Monterey Way
Goodyear, AZ 85395-8054, USA

Tobolowsky, Stephen (Actor, Director, Writer)
c/o Steven Levy *Framework Entertainment (LA)*
9057 Nemo St Ste C
West Hollywood, CA 90069-5511, USA

Toburen, Nelson (Athlete, Football Player)
1007 Village Dr
Pittsburg, KS 66762-3552, USA

Tobymac (Musician)
c/o Staff Member *True Artist Management*
227 3rd Ave N
Franklin, TN 37064-2504, USa

Toca, Jorge (Athlete, Baseball Player)
7940 NW 167th Ter
Hialeah, FL 33016-3424, USA

Tocchet, Rick (Athlete, Hockey Player)
933 Osage Rd
Pittsburgh, PA 15243-1011, USA

Toczyska, Stefania (Opera Singer)
165 W 57th St
New York, NY 10019-2201, USA

Todd, Anne E (Actor)
2419 Oregon St
Berkeley, CA 94705-1113, USA

Todd, Hallie (Actor)
550 Erskine Dr
Pacific Palisades, CA 90272-4247, USA

Todd, Jackson (Athlete, Baseball Player)
8958 E 76th St
Tulsa, OK 74133-4406, USA

Todd, James R (Jim) (Athlete, Baseball Player)
21639 Hill Gail Way
Parker, CO 80138-7249, USA

Todd, Jeanine (Stylist)
360 W 22nd St
New York, NY 10011-2600, USA

Todd, Josh (Musician)
9100 Wilshire Blvd Ste 100W
Beverly Hills, CA 90212-3435, USA

Todd, Kate (Actor)
c/o Robert Lanni *Coalition Entertainment Management*
10271 Yonge St Suite 302
Richmond Hill, Ontario L4C 3B5, Canada

Todd, Kendra (Business Person, Reality TV Star)
423 W 55th St Fl 2
New York, NY 10019-4460, USA

Todd, Mark (Horse Racer)
PO Box 507
Cambridge, NEW ZEALAND

Todd, Rachel (Actor)
6310 San Vicente Blvd Ste 520
Los Angeles, CA 90048-5421, USA

Todd, Richard (Football Player)
PO Box 471
Sheffield, AL 35660-0471, USA

Todd, Tony (Actor)
c/o Jeff Goldberg *Jeff Goldberg Management*
817 Monte Leon Dr
Beverly Hills, CA 90210-2629, USA

Todd, Trisha (Actor)
c/o Staff Member *Henry Downey Talent Management*
4045 Vineland Ave PH 538
Studio City, CA 91604-4481, USA

Todd, Virgil H (Religious Leader)
168 E Parkway S
Memphis, TN 38104-4340, USA

Todorov, Stanko (Prime Minister)
Narodno Sobranie
Sofia, BULGARIA

Todorovsky, Piotr Y (Director)
Vernadskogo Prospect 70A #23
Moscow 117454, RUSSIA

Toennies, Jan Peter (Physicist)
Ewaldstr 7
Gottingen 37075, GERMANY

Toerzs, Gregor (Actor)
c/o Beate Wolgast *Die Agenten*
Auguststraße 34
Berlin 10119, Germany

Toews, Jeffrey M (Jeff) (Athlete, Football Player)
11924 Silver Oak Dr
Davie, FL 33330-1911, USA

Toews, Jonathan (Athlete, Hockey Player)
c/o Pat Brisson *Creative Artists Agency (CAA-LA)*
2000 Avenue of the Stars Ste 100
Los Angeles, CA 90067-4705, USA

Toews, Loren (Athlete, Football Player)
165 Hawthorne Ave
Los Altos, CA 94022-3704, USA

Tofani, Loretta A (Journalist)
400 N Broad St
Philadelphia, PA 19130-4015, USA

Tofflemire, Joe (Athlete, Football Player)
2482 196th Ave SE
Sammamish, WA 98075-7448, USA

Toffler, Alvin (Writer)
1745 Broadway # B1
New York, NY 10019-4368, USA

Toffoli, Brian (Stylist)
c/o Staff Member *Cloutier Agency*
2632 La Cienega Ave
Los Angeles, CA 90034-2641, USA

Toft, Rod (Bowler)
11350 12th St N
Lake Elmo, MN 55042-8621, USA

Tognini, Michel (Cosmonaut)
5413 Newcastle St
Bellaire, TX 77401-2713, USA

Tognoni, Gina (Actor)
c/o Marnie Sparer *Innovative Artists (LA)*
1505 10th St
Santa Monica, CA 90401-2805, USA

Togo, Jonathan (Actor)
c/o Cynthia Shelton-Droke *Sweet Mud Group*
648 Broadway # 1002
New York, NY 10012-2348, USA

Togunde, Victor (Actor)
c/o Staff Member *GVA Talent Agency Inc*
8981 W Sunset Blvd Ste 101
Los Angeles, CA 90069-1850, USA

Tointon, Kara (Actor)
c/o Staff Member *RKM Communications*
4 New Burlington St 5th Floor
London W1S 2JG, UK

Tokarev, Valeri I (Cosmonaut)
Moskovskoi Oblasti
Syvisdny Goroduk 141160, RUSSIA

Tokes, Laszlo (Politician, Religious Leader)
Calvin Str 1
Oradea 3700, ROMANIA

Tokio Hotel (Music Group, Musician)
c/o Staff Member *Universal Music Deutschland*
Stralauer Allee 1
Berlin 10245, Germany

Tokody, Ilona (Opera Singer)
Andrassy Utca 22
Budapest 1062, HUNGARY

Tolan, Peter (Actor, Director, Producer, Writer)

Tolan, Robert (Bobby) (Athlete, Baseball Player)
804 Woodstock St
Bellaire, TX 77401-4716, USA

Tolar, Kevin (Athlete, Baseball Player)
6412 Lake Joanna Cir
Panama City, FL 32404-3401, USA

Tolbert, Berlinda (Actor)
c/o Staff Member *Pallas Management*
5301 Bellaire Ave
Valley Village, CA 91607-2329, US

Tolbert, Jim (Athlete, Football Player)
2435 Corinna Ct
San Diego, CA 92105-5303, USA

Tolbert, Ray (Athlete, Basketball Player)
2205 Crestwood Dr
Anderson, IN 46016-2751, USA

Tolbert, Tom (Athlete, Basketball Player)
368 Creedon Cir
Alameda, CA 94502-7793, USA

Tolbert, Tony L (Athlete, Football Player)
475 S White Chapel Blvd
Southlake, TX 76092-7314, USA

Toldeo, Esteban (Golfer)
135 Spring Vly
Irvine, CA 92602-0919, USA

Toledo, Alejandro (President)
Plaza de Armas S/N
Lima 1, PERU

Tolentino, Jose (Athlete, Baseball Player)
26711 Caceres Cir
Mission Viejo, CA 92691-5503, USA

Toler, Ken (Athlete, Football Player)
4560 Eastwood Rd
Jackson, MS 39211-6115, USA

Toles, Alvin (Athlete, Football Player)
106 Todd Creek Pl
Forsyth, GA 31029, USA

Toles, Thomas G (Tom) (Cartoonist, Editor)
4625 46th St NW
Washington, DC 20016-4477, USA

Tolins, Jonathan (Writer)
c/o Cori Wellins *WmE2 (Endeavor-LA)*
9601 Wilshire Blvd Fl 3
Beverly Hills, CA 90210-5219, USA

Toliver, Freddie (Athlete, Baseball Player)
674 Medical Center Dr
San Bernardino, CA 92411-2520, USA

Tolkan, James (Actor)
10100 Santa Monica Blvd Ste 2500
Los Angeles, CA 90067-4116, USA

Tollberg, Brian (Athlete, Baseball Player)
2104 39th St W
Bradenton, FL 34205-1334, USA

Tolle, Eckhart (Writer)
P.O. Box 93661 Nelson Park RPO
Vancouver, BC V6E 4L7, CANADA

Tollerod, Siri (Model)
c/o Staff Member *Modelwerk Modelagentur GmbH*
Rothenbaum Chaussee 1
Hamburg 20148, Germany

Tolles, Tommy (Golfer)
c/o Staff Member *Pro Golfers Association (PGA) Tour*
112 Tpc Blvd
Ponte Vedra Beach, FL 32082, USA

Tolleson, Wayne (Athlete, Baseball Player)
313 Mossycup Oak Ct
Spartanburg, SC 29306-6627, USA

Tollin, Michael (Director, Producer, Writer)
c/o Staff Member *Tollin/Robbins Management*
4130 Cahuenga Blvd Ste 305
Toluca Lake, CA 91602-2847, USA

Tolliver, Billy Joe (Athlete, Football Player)
9837 Neesonwood Dr
Shreveport, LA 71106-7738, USA

Tolman, Tim (Athlete, Baseball Player)
11425 N Ingot Loop
Tucson, AZ 85737-9450, USA

Tolsky, Susan (Actor)
10815 Acama St
North Hollywood, CA 91602-3204, USA

Tolson, Billy
2710 N Stemmons Fwy Ste 700
Dallas, TX 75207-2208

Tolson, Byron (Athlete, Basketball Player)
4012 N Orchard St
Tacoma, WA 98407-4215, USA

Tom, Braatz (Athlete, Football Player)
3131 NE 55th Ct
Fort Lauderdale, FL 33308-3428, USA

Tom, David
3033 Vista Crest Dr
Los Angeles, CA 90068-1824

Tom, Heather (Actor)
c/o Staff Member *Michael Einfeld Management*
10630 Moorpark St Unit 101
Toluca Lake, CA 91602-2797, USA

Tom, Kiana (Actor, Fitness Expert)
555 N El Camino Real Ste A401
San Clemente, CA 92672-6740, USA

Tom, Lauren (Actor)
c/o Kelly Garner *Pop Art Management*
PO Box 55363
Sherman Oaks, CA 91413-0363, USA

Tom, Mel (Athlete, Football Player)
1118 Via Grande Apt 255
Cathedral City, CA 92234-4300, USA

Tom, Nicholle (Actor)
c/o Michael Einfeld *Michael Einfeld Management*
10630 Moorpark St Unit 101
Toluca Lake, CA 91602-2797, USA

Tom, Nicolle
3033 Vista Crest Dr
Los Angeles, CA 90068-1824

Tom Scholz (Music Group, Musician)
c/o Gail Parenteau *Parenteau Guidance*
132 E 35th St # 3J
New York, NY 10016-3892, USA

Toma, David
PO Box 854
Clark, NJ 07066-0854

Tomaini, Amadeo (Athlete, Football Player)
3750 Oakhill Dr
Titusville, FL 32780-3521, USA

Tomanek, Dick (Athlete, Baseball Player)
165 Duff Dr
Avon Lake, OH 44012-1234, USA

Tomanovich, Dara
8016 Willow Glen Rd
Los Angeles, CA 90046-1617

Tomas, Hildi Santo (Actor, Television Host)
741 Parkside Trl NW
Marietta, GA 30064-4714, USA

Tomasetti, Louis (Athlete, Football Player)
100 Powell St
Old Forge, PA 18518-1728, USA

Tomasic, Andrew J (Andy) (Athlete, Baseball Player, Football Player)
3 Tonto Ct
Albrightsville, PA 18210-3510, USA

Tomasik, Kathleen (Director)
c/o David Krintzman *Morris, Yorn, Barnes, Levine, Krintzman, Rubenstein and Kohner*
2000 Ave Of The Stars 3rd Tower Floor NORTH
Los Angeles, CA 90067, USA

Tomasina Keough, Jeana (Reality TV Star)
c/o Patrick Hughes *Hughes Capital Entertainment*
22817 Ventura Blvd # 471
Woodland Hills, CA 91364-1202, USA

Tomasson, Helgi (Ballerina, Director)
455 Franklin St
San Francisco, CA 94102-4438, USA

Tomba, Alberto (Skier)
Castel dei Britti
Bologna 40100, ITALY

Tomberlin, Andy (Athlete, Baseball Player)
7411 Crooked Creek Church Rd
Monroe, NC 28110-8283, USA

Tomberlin, Pat (Athlete, Football Player)
891 Arthur Moore Dr
Green Cove Springs, FL 32043-9510, USA

Tomblin, Earl Ray (Governor)
State Capitol Bldg
Charleston, WV 25305, USA

Tombs, Tina (Golfer)
5919 N 45th St
Phoenix, AZ 85018-1230, USA

Tomczak, Michael J (Mike) (Athlete, Football Player)
400 Broad St Ste 106
Sewickley, PA 15143-1500, USA

Tomei, Concetta (Actor)
765 Linda Flora Dr
Los Angeles, CA 90049-1626, USA

Tomei, Marisa (Actor)
c/o Jason Weinberg *Untitled Entertainment (LA)*
350 S Beverly Dr Ste 200
Beverly Hills, CA 90212-4819, USA

Tomel, Marisa (Actor)
9460 Wilshire Blvd Ste 700
Beverly Hills, CA 90212-2713, USA

Tomey, Dick (Coach, Football Coach)
4949 Centennial Blvd
Santa Clara, CA 95054-1229, USA

Tomfohrde, Heinn F (Business Person)
1361 Alps Rd
Wayne, NJ 07470-3700, USA

Tomich, Jared (Athlete, Football Player)
2222 Red River Dr
Schererville, IN 46375-4492, USA

Tomita, Stan (Photographer)
2439 Saint Louis Dr
Honolulu, HI 96816-2030, USA

Tomita, Tamlyn (Actor)
c/o Nancy Moon-Broadstreet *Geddes Agency, The*
8430 Santa Monica Blvd Ste 200
Los Angeles, CA 90069-4253, USA

Tomjanovich, Rudolph (Rudy) (Athlete, Basketball Player, Coach)
19 West Ln
Houston, TX 77019-1007, USA

Tomko, Brett (Athlete, Baseball Player)
14008 Lake Poway Rd
Poway, CA 92064-1421, USA

Tomko, Jozef Cardinal (Religious Leader)
Via Urbano VIII-16
Rome 165, ITALY

Tomlin, Chris (Musician)
c/o Shelley Giglio *Six Steps Records*
PO Box 5
Roswell, GA 30077-0005, USA

Tomlin, Dave (Athlete, Baseball Player)
2020 Clayton Pike
Manchester, OH 45144-9429, USA

Tomlin, Lily (Actor, Comedian)
c/o Scott Henderson *WmE2 (Endeavor-LA)*
9601 Wilshire Blvd Fl 3
Beverly Hills, CA 90210-5219, USA

Tomlin, Mike (Athlete, Football Coach, Football Player)
1224 Shady Ave
Pittsburgh, PA 15232-2812, USA

Tomlin, Randy (Athlete, Baseball Player)
153 Ridgeview Ln
Madison Heights, VA 24572-6037, USA

Tomlinson, Charles (Writer)
English Dept
Bristol BS8 1TH, UNITED KINGDOM (UK)

Tomlinson, John (Opera Singer)
13 Ardilaun Road Highbury
London N5 2QR, UNITED KINGDOM (UK)

Tomlinson, LaDainian (Football Player)
c/o Tom Condon *Creative Artists Agency (CAA-LA)*
2000 Avenue of the Stars Ste 100
Los Angeles, CA 90067-4705, USA

Tomlinson, Mel A (Ballerina)
790 Riverside Dr Apt 6B
New York, NY 10032-7445, USA

Tommy Tutone (Music Group, Musician)
c/o Jake Hooker *Hook Entertainment*
26033 Mulholland Hwy
Woodland Hls, CA 91302-1946, USA

Tomowa-Sintow, Anna (Opera Singer)
165 W 57th St
New York, NY 10019-2201, USA

Tompkins, Allie (Baseball Player)
931 1/2 Clarissa St
Pittsburgh, PA 15219-5770, USA

Tompkins, Angel (Actor)
11935 Kling St Apt 10
Valley Village, CA 91607-5406, USA

Tompkins, Dariene (Actor)
15413 Hall Rd # 230
Macomb, MI 48044-3840, USA

Tompkins, Ron (Athlete, Baseball Player)
25072 Leucadia St Unit G
Laguna Niguel, CA 92677-7598, USA

Tompkins, Susie (Designer, Fashion Designer)
2500 Steiner St PH
San Francisco, CA 94115-1100, USA

Toms, David (Golfer)
6606 Gilbert Dr
Shreveport, LA 71106-2300, USA

Toms, Tommy (Athlete, Baseball Player)
126 Leadbetter Rd
Wayne, ME 04284-3144, USA

Tomsco, George (Musician)
1224 Cottonwood St
Raton, NM 87740-3513, USA

Tomsic, Dubravka (Musician)
1926 Broadway
New York, NY 10023-6915, USA

Tomsic, Ronald (Ron) (Athlete, Basketball Player)
22 Twilight Blf
Newport Coast, CA 92657-2126, USA

Tone Loc (Musician)
c/o Bobby Bessone *Entertainment Artists*
PO Box 120824
Nashville, TN 37212-0824, USA

Toneff, Robert (Bob) (Athlete, Football Player)
18 Dutch Valley Ln
San Anselmo, CA 94960-1016, USA

Tonegawa, Susumu (Nobel Prize Laureate)
Biology Dept
Cambridge, MA 2139, USA

Toner, Mike (Journalist)
72 Marietta St NW
Atlanta, GA 30303-2804, USA

Toner Jr, Ed (Athlete, Football Player)
12 Preston Ct
Swampscott, MA 01907-1650, USA

Toner Sr, Ed (Athlete, Football Player)
225 Ocean St
Lynn, MA 01902-3269, USA

Toney, Andrew (Athlete, Basketball Player)
1613 14th Ave N
Birmingham, AL 35204-2726, USA

Toney, James
6305 Wellesley Dr
West Bloomfield, MI 48322-2407

Toney, Sedric (Athlete, Basketball Player)
3831 Sweetwater Dr
Brecksville, OH 44141-4102, USA

Tong, Jian (Figure Skater)
c/o Staff Member *Champions on Ice*
3500 W 80th St Ste 200
Minneapolis, MN 55431-1090, USA

Tong, Pete (DJ, Musician)
c/o Joel Zimmerman *WmE2 (WMA-NY)*
1325 Avenue of the Americas
New York, NY 10019-6026, USA

Tong, Stanley (Director)
c/o Ramses Ishak *United Talent Agency (UTA)*
9560 Wilshire Blvd Fl 5
Beverly Hills, CA 90212-2400, USA

Tongue, Marco (Athlete, Football Player)
8051 Winding Wood Rd
Glen Burnie, MD 21061-5020, USA

Tonic (Music Group)
652 N Doheny Dr
Los Angeles, CA 90069-5526

Tonini, Ersilio Cardinal (Religious Leader)
Ravenna 48100, ITALY

Tonioli, Bruno (Actor)
c/o Duncan Heath *Independent Talent Group (ITG-UK)*
Oxford House 76 Oxford St
London W1D 1BS, UK

Tonis, Mike (Athlete, Baseball Player)
9231 Bella Vista Pl
Elk Grove, CA 95624-2152, USA

Tonkovich, Andy (Athlete, Basketball Player)
2400 Forest Dr Apt 210
Inverness, FL 34453-3705, USA

Tonnema, Pat (Stylist)
2455 1/2 Cheremoya Ave
Los Angeles, CA 90068-3069, USA

Tony! Toni! Tone!
1995 Broadway # 501
New York, NY 10023-5882

Too, Slim (Musician)
1921 Broadway
Nashville, TN 37203-2719, USA

Too Short (Musician)
c/o Staff Member *American Talent Agency*
248 W 35th St Rm 501
New York, NY 10001-2505, USA

Tooker, George (Artist)
PO Box 385
Hartland, VT 05048-0385, USA

Tool (Music Group)
2311 W Empire Ave
Burbank, CA 91504-3318, USA

Toole, Tara (Stylist)
c/o Staff Member *Crews*
828 Clemont Dr NE
Atlanta, GA 30306-3694, USA

Toolson, Andy (Athlete, Basketball Player)
722 Ranch Cir
Alpine, UT 84004-1971, USA

Toomay, John (Athlete, Basketball Player)
4020 Edgehill Rd
Fort Worth, TX 76116-7325, USA

Toomay, Pat (Athlete, Football Player)
221 Tornasol Ln NE
Albuquerque, NM 87113-1214, USA

Toomer, Amani (Athlete, Football Player)
25 Regency Pl
Weehawken, NJ 07086-6600, USA

Toomey, Toomey (Cartoonist, Writer)
4520 Main St
Kansas City, MO 64111-1876, USA

Toomey, William A (Bill) (Athlete, Track Athlete)
4360 Park Terrace Dr Ste 160
Westlake Village, CA 91361-4452, USA

Toomin Straus, Amy (Writer)
c/o Staff Member *United Talent Agency (UTA)*
9560 Wilshire Blvd Fl 5
Beverly Hills, CA 90212-2400, USA

Toon, Al (Athlete, Football Player)
3113 Kirkwall St
Fitchburg, WI 53711-7215, USA

Tootoosis, Gordon (Actor)
c/o Staff Member *Artist Representation Company, The*
1147 S Big Island Rd RR 1
Demorestville ON K0K 1W0, CANADA

Toots & The Maytals (Music Group)
c/o Staff Member *WmE2 (WMA-NY)*
1325 Avenue of the Americas
New York, NY 10019-6026, USA

Toploader (Music Group)
c/o Staff Member *Helter Skelter (UK)*
535 Kings Rd The Plaza
London SW10 0SZ, UNITED KINGDOM (UK)

Topol, Chaim (Actor)
22 Vale Court Maidville
London W9 1RT, UNITED KINGDOM (UK)

Topor, Ted (Athlete, Football Player)
2840 Condit St
Highland, IN 46322-1605, USA

Topp, Robert (Athlete, Football Player)
10351 Douglas Ave
Plainwell, MI 49080-9664, USA

Topper, John (Musician)
509 Hartnell St
Monterey, CA 93940-2825, USA

Toppin, Rupe (Athlete, Baseball Player)
PO Box 25724
Miami, FL 33102-5724, USA

Topping, Seymour (Editor)
5 Heathcote Rd
Scarsdale, NY 10583-4413, USA

Toppo, Telesphore P Cardinal (Religious Leader)
PO Box 5 Purulia Road
Ranchi, Jharkhand 834001, INDIA

Toradze, Alexander (Musician)
165 W 57th St
New York, NY 10019-2201, USA

Torborg, Jeffrey A (Jeff) (Athlete, Baseball Player, Coach)
47 Railroad Ave
Manahawkin, NJ 08050-3932, USA

Torcato, Tony (Athlete, Baseball Player)
798 SE Miller Ave
Dallas, OR 97338-2637, USA

Torczon, Laverne J (Athlete, Football Player)
6472 Country Club Dr
Columbus, NE 68601-8338, USA

Torgensen, Paul E (Educator)
President S Ofc
Blacksburg, VA 24061-0001, USA

Torgeson, Lavern (Athlete, Football Player)
17672 Gainsford Ln
Huntington Beach, CA 92649-4723, USA

Tork, Peter (Musician)
524 Anselmo Ave # 102
San Anselmo, CA 94960, USA

Torkelson, Eric (Athlete, Football Player)
1196 Pleasant Valley Dr
Oneida, WI 54155-8634, USA

Torkildsen, Justin
7800 Beverly Blvd # 3371
Los Angeles, CA 90036-2112

Torme, Daisy (Actor)
c/o Steven Neibert *Imperium 7 Talent Agency*
5455 Wilshire Blvd Ste 1706
Los Angeles, CA 90036-4217, USA

Torme, Steve March (Actor, Musician)
c/o Mark Lourie *Skyline Music*
28 Union St
Whitefield, NH 03598-3503, USA

Tormohlen, Gene (Athlete, Basketball Player)
2248 Walker Dr
Lawrenceville, GA 30043-2472, USA

Torn, Rip (Actor)
c/o Alan Somers *Pure Arts Entertainment*
1925 Century Park E Ste 2320
Los Angeles, CA 90067-2724, USA

Tornatore, Giuseppe (Director)
c/o Staff Member *Marco Patrizi*
Viale Giuseppe Mazzini, 11
Roma 195, Italy

Torp, Niels A (Architect)
PO Box 5387
Oslo 304, NORWAY

Torrance, Sam (Golfer)
The Glassmill Battersea Bridge Rd
London SW11 3BZ, UNITED KINGDOM (UK)

Torrance, Thomas F (Educator, Religious Leader)
37 Braid Farm Road
Edinburgh EH10 6LE, SCOTLAND

Torre, Frank (Athlete, Baseball Player)
13901 Palm Grove Pl
West Palm Beach, FL 33418-6977, USA

Torre, Joe (Athlete, Baseball Player, Coach)
245 Park Ave
New York, NY 10167-0002, USA

Torre, Jose Maria (Actor)
c/o Staff Member *Televisa*
Blvd Adolfo Lopez Mateos 232 Colonia San Angel INN
DF CP 01060, MEXICO

Torrence, Gwendolyn (Gwen) (Athlete, Track Athlete)
1750 14th St
Boulder, CO 80302-6332, USA

Torrens, David (Actor)
c/o Gabriel Blanco *Gabriel Blanco Iglesias (Mexico)*
Rio Balsas 35-32 Colonia Cuauhtemoc
DF 6500, Mexico

Torres, Dara (Athlete, Model, Swimmer)
c/o Staff Member *Premier Management Group (PMG Sports)*
115 Crescent Commons Dr Ste 250
Cary, NC 27518-8134, USA

Torres, Diego (Actor)
c/o Jon Simmons *Simmons & Scott Entertainment*
7942 Mulholland Dr
Los Angeles, CA 90046-1225, USA

Torres, Felix (Athlete, Baseball Player)
HC 1 Box 6424
Santa Isabel, PR 00757-9777, USA

Torres, Gina (Actor)
c/o Christopher Barrett *Metropolitan (MTA)*
4526 Wilshire Blvd
Los Angeles, CA 90010-3801, USA

Torres, Harold (Musician)
141 Dunbar Ave
Fords, NJ 08863-1551, USA

Torres, Hector (Athlete, Baseball Player)
2386 Sumatran Way Apt 64
Clearwater, FL 33763-1815, USA

Torres, Jacques (Chef, Television Host)
c/o Staff Member *Food Network, The*
75 9th Ave
New York, NY 10011-7006, USA

Torres, Jose (Boxer)
2 Chelsea Ridge Dr
Wappingers Fl, NY 12590-5625, USA

Torres, Liz (Actor, Musician)
1680 Vine St Ste 617
Hollywood, CA 90028-8833, USA

Torres, Oscar (Athlete, Basketball Player)
c/o Michael Esola *WmE2 (Endeavor-LA)*
9601 Wilshire Blvd Fl 3
Beverly Hills, CA 90210-5219, USA

Torres, Raffi (Athlete, Hockey Player)
11230 110th St
Edmonton, AB T5G 3H7, Canada

Torres, Rusty (Athlete, Baseball Player)
250 N Cedar St
Massapequa, NY 11758-2822, USA

Torres, Salomon (Athlete, Baseball Player)
101 Crimson Dr
Pittsburgh, PA 15237-1069, USA

Torres, Tia Maria (Reality TV Star)
PO Box 1544
Canyon Country, CA 91386-1544, USA

Torres, Tico (Musician)
248 W 17th St Apt 501
New York, NY 10011-5330, USA

Torres, Tommy (Musician)
c/o Staff Member *Sony Music Miami*
605 Lincoln Rd Ste 700
Miami Beach, FL 33139-2901, USA

Torretta, Gino L (Athlete, Football Player)
3000 Groves Edge Ln
Waxhaw, NC 28173-8291, USA

Torrey, Bill (Misc)
2740 Clubhouse Pointe
West Palm Beach, FL 33409-2018, USA

Torrey, Rich (Cartoonist)
c/o Staff Member *King Features Syndication*
300 W 57th St Fl 15
New York, NY 10019-5238, USA

Torrez, Mike (Athlete, Baseball Player)
1015 Frances Ct
Naperville, IL 60563-3370, USA

Torriero, Talan (Actor)
c/o Scott Karp *Crystal Sky Pictures*
10203 Santa Monica Blvd Ste 500
Los Angeles, CA 90067-6416, USA

Torrijos, Martin (President)
Valija 50
Panama City 1, PANAMA

Torrini, Emiliana (Musician)
c/o Staff Member *Paradigm (Monterey)*
404 W Franklin St
Monterey, CA 93940-2303, USA

Torrissen, Birger (Skier)
PO Box 216
Lakeville, CT 06039-0216, USA

Torruella, Juan R (Judge)
150 Ave Carlos Chardon Ste 119
San Juan, PR 00918-1706, USA

Torry, Guy (Actor, Comedian)
c/o Janean Glover *Screen Partners*
9663 Santa Monica Blvd # 639
Beverly Hills, CA 90210-4303, USA

Torry, Joe (Comedian)
c/o Staff Member *WmE2 (WMA-LA)*
1 William Morris Pl
Beverly Hills, CA 90212-4261, USA

Torteller, Yan Pascal (Musician)
Building Gaceau 11 Ave Delcasse
Paris 75635, FRANCE

Torti, Robert (Actor)
5722 Ranchito Ave
Van Nuys, CA 91401-4343, USA

Tortorella, John (Coach)
2801 Northwood Hills Dr
Valrico, FL 33594, USA

Tortorella, Nico (Actor)
c/o Brian Wilkins *Kritzer Levine Wilkins Entertainment*
11872 La Grange Ave Fl 1
Los Angeles, CA 90025-5283, USA

Tortorici, Nick (Stylist)
c/o Staff Member *Solo Artists*
2148 Federal Ave
Los Angeles, CA 90025-5327, USA

Torv, Anna
c/o Christine Tripicchio *WKT Public Relations (WKT-LA)*
9350 Wilshire Blvd Ste 450
Beverly Hills, CA 90212-3230, USA

Torvaids, Linus (Designer)
3990 Freedom Cir
Santa Clara, CA 95054-1204, USA

Torvalds, Linus (Designer, Engineer)
12725 SW Millikan Way
Beaverton, OR 97005-1678, USA

Torve, Kelvin (Athlete, Baseball Player)
18701 Hammock Ln
Davidson, NC 28036-8836, USA

Torvill, Jayne (Dancer)
PO Box 32
Heathfield, East Sussex TN21 0BW, UNITED KINGDOM (UK)

Tosca, Carlos (Athlete, Baseball Player, Coach)
PO Box 3623
Brandon, FL 33509-3623, USA

Toscano, Harry (Golfer)
231 Rose Hill Dr
New Castle, PA 16105-9107, USA

Tosh, Daniel (Comedian)
c/o Staff Member *Mosaic Media Group*
9200 W Sunset Blvd Ste 10
Los Angeles, CA 90069-3608, USA

Tosheff, Bill (Athlete, Basketball Player)
13101 Hartfield Ave
San Diego, CA 92130-1511, USA

Toski, Bob (Golfer)
20914 Hamaca Ct
Boca Raton, FL 33433-2716, USA

Tostenson, Laura (Stylist)
c/o Staff Member *Page.214*
3303 Lee Pkwy Ste 205
Dallas, TX 75219-5145, USA

Totenberg, Nina (Correspondent)
News Dept 615 Main Ave NW
Washington, DC 20024, USA

Toth, Nick (Athlete, Football Player)
1 Diaz Ave
San Francisco, CA 94132-2434, USA

Toth, Tom (Athlete, Football Player)
13723 Lindsay Dr
Orland Park, IL 60462-7011, USA

Toth, Zollie (Athlete, Football Player)
1612 Hideaway Ct
Baton Rouge, LA 70806-7674, USA

Totmianina, Tatyana (Figure Skater)
c/o Staff Member *Champions on Ice*
3500 W 80th St Ste 200
Minneapolis, MN 55431-1090, USA

Totten, Robert (Director)
PO Box 7180
Big Bear Lake, CA 92315-7180, USA

Totter, Audrey (Actor)
23388 Mulholland Dr
Woodland Hills, CA 91364-2733, USA

Totushek, John B (Admiral)
Naval Reserve Force Hqusn Pentagon
Washington, DC 20350-0001, USA

Toulouse, Gerard (Physicist)
24 Rue Lhomond
Paris 75231, FRANCE

Tountas, Pete (Bowler)
10100 N Calle Del Camero
Tucson, AZ 85737, USA

Touraine, Jean-Louis (Biologist)
Place d'Arsonval
Lyons Cedex 03 69437, FRANCE

Toure, Younoussi (Prime Minister)
01 BP 543
Quagadougou 01, Burkina Faso, MALI

Tournier, Michel (Writer)
Le Presbytree Choisel
Chevreuse 78460, FRANCE

Toussaint, Allen (Composer, Musician)
272 Abalon Ct
New Orleans, LA 70114-1374, USA

Toussaint, Beth (Actor)
c/o Staff Member *Don Buchwald & Associates Inc (LA)*
6500 Wilshire Blvd Ste 2200
Los Angeles, CA 90048-4942, USA

Toussaint, Lorraine (Actor)
c/o Jonathan Howard *Innovative Artists (LA)*
1505 10th St
Santa Monica, CA 90401-2805, USA

Tovar, Lupita
1527 N Tigertail Rd
Los Angeles, CA 90049-1430

Tovar, Steven E (Steve) (Athlete, Football Player)
1026 Brower Rd
Lima, OH 45801-2316, USA

Tovoli, Luciano (Cinematographer)
9560 Wilshire Blvd Ste 500
Beverly Hills, CA 90212-2401, USA

Towe, Monte (Athlete, Basketball Player, Coach)
2125 Gold Valley Dr
Murfreesboro, TN 37130-8423, USA

Tower, Joan P (Composer)
Music Dept
Annandale-on-Hudson, NY 12504, USA

Tower, Keith (Athlete, Basketball Player)
12530 Aldershot Ln
Windermere, FL 34786-6610, USA

Tower of Power (Music Group, Musician)
c/o Staff Member *CT Creative Talent GmbH*
Koepenicker Strasse 48/49
New York, NY 10179-0001, GERMANY

Towers, Constance (Actor)
c/o Staff Member *Stone Manners Salners Agency (LA)*
9911 W Pico Blvd Ste 1400
Los Angeles, CA 90035-2715, USA

Towers, Josh (Athlete, Baseball Player)
1033 Crescent Falls St
Henderson, NV 89011-2506, USA

Towery, Blackie (Athlete, Basketball Player)
314 W Carlisle St
Marion, KY 42064-1506, USA

Towle, Stephen R (Steve) (Athlete, Football Player)
609 NE Lake Pointe Dr
Lees Summit, MO 64064-1193, USA

Towles, J R (Athlete, Baseball Player)
19210 J R Towles Dr
Crosby, TX 77532-7562, USA

Towles, Tom (Actor)
c/o Craig Dorfman *Frontline Management*
5670 Wilshire Blvd Ste 1370
Los Angeles, CA 90036-5679, USA

Towne, Katharine (Actor)
9560 Wilshire Blvd Ste 500
Beverly Hills, CA 90212-2401, USA

Towne, Robert (Director, Writer)
1417 San Remo Dr
Pacific Palisades, CA 90272, USA

Towner, Ralph N (Musician)
173 Brighton Ave
Boston, MA 02134-2003, USA

Townes, Charles H (Nobel Prize Laureate)
1850 Alice St Apt 713
Oakland, CA 94612-4114, USA

Townes, Linton (Athlete, Basketball Player)
PO Box 254
Luray, VA 22835-0254, USA

Townes, Willie (Athlete, Football Player)
5714 Logancraft Dr
Dallas, TX 75227-2847, USA

Towns, Bobby (Athlete, Football Player)
1351 Jennings Mill Rd Unit A
Bogart, GA 30622-2537, USA

Towns, Morris (Athlete, Football Player)
7102 Rustling Oaks Dr
Richmond, TX 77469-7338, USA

Townsell, Jo Jo (Athlete, Football Player)
1857 Borda Way
Gardnerville, NV 89410-6679, USA

Townsend, Andre (Athlete, Football Player)
6206 Providence Club Dr
Mableton, GA 30126-3697, USA

Townsend, Colleen (Actor)
645 E Champlain Dr Apt 150
Fresno, CA 93730-1295, USA

Townsend, John W Jr (Scientist)
6532 79th St
Cabin John, MD 20818-1201, USA

Townsend, Raymond (Athlete, Basketball Player)
5160 Cribari Knls
San Jose, CA 95135-1327, USA

Townsend, Robert (Actor, Director, Producer, Writer)
c/o Jeff Witjas *Agency for the Performing Arts (APA-LA)*
405 S Beverly Dr Ste 500
Beverly Hills, CA 90212-4425, USA

Townsend, Roscoe (Religious Leader)
2018 W Maple St
Wichita, KS 67213-3314, USA

Townsend, Stuart (Actor)
c/o Vanessa Pereira *Artists Independent Management (LA)*
825 Nowita Pl
Venice, CA 90291-3836, USA

Townsend, Tammy (Actor)
c/o Marni Goldman *Abrams Artists Agency (LA)*
9200 W Sunset Blvd PH 11
Los Angeles, CA 90069-3601, USA

Townsend, Wade (Athlete, Baseball Player)
PO Box 2744
Columbus, GA 31902-2744, USA

Townshend, Peter D B (Musician, Songwriter, Writer)
4 Friars Ln
Richmond, Surrey TW9 1NL, UK

Toya (Musician)

Toye, Wendy (Ballerina, Choreographer)
2-4 Noel St
London W1V 3RB, UNITED KINGDOM (UK)

Toyoda, Shoichiro (Business Person)
1-9-4 Ohtemachi Chuyodaku
Tokyo 100, JAPAN

Tozzi, Giorgio (Opera Singer)
Via Berchet 2
Milan 20100, ITALY

Tozzi, Tahyna (Actor)
c/o Elise Konialian *Untitled Entertainment (NY)*
322 8th Ave Ste 601
New York, NY 10001-6715, USA

Tozzi, Umberto
Heussweg 25
Hamburg, GERMANY D-20255

T-Pain (Musician)
c/o Michael Moses *Baker Winokur Ryder Public Relations (BWR-LA)*
9100 Wilshire Blvd Ste 500 PMB WEST
Beverly Hills, CA 90212-3426, USA

Traa (Musician)
75 Rockefeller Plz
New York, NY 10019-6908, USA

Traber, Billy (Athlete, Baseball Player)
836 Lomita St
El Segundo, CA 90245-2541, USA

Traber, Jim (Athlete, Baseball Player)
1917 Rosebrook
Norman, OK 73072-3104, USA

Trabert, M Anthony (Tony) (Tennis Player)
115 Knotty Pine Trl
Ponte Vedra Beach, FL 32082-3024, USA

Trabert, Tony
115 Knotty Pine Trl
Ponte Vedra, FL 32082-3024

Tracewski, Dick (Athlete, Baseball Player, Coach)
5 Flora Dr
Peckville, PA 18452-1004, USA

Trachsel, Stephen P (Steve) (Athlete, Baseball Player)
18750 Heritage Dr
Poway, CA 92064-6643, USA

Trachta, Jeff (Actor)
590 S Indian Trl
Palm Springs, CA 92264-7623, USA

Trachte, Don (Cartoonist)
c/o Staff Member *King Features Syndication*
300 W 57th St Fl 15
New York, NY 10019-5238, USA

Trachtenberg, Lyle
18619 Collins St Apt F7
Tarzana, CA 91356-2169

Trachtenberg, Michelle (Actor)
c/o Peg Donegan *Framework Entertainment (LA)*
9057 Nemo St Ste C
West Hollywood, CA 90069-5511, USA

Trachtenberg, Stephen J (Educator)
President S Ofc
Washington, DC 20052-0001, USA

Track, Emma (Stylist)
c/o Staff Member *Smashbox Beauty*
8549 Higuera St Bldg B
Culver City, CA 90232-2521, USA

Tracy, Andy (Athlete, Baseball Player)
138 S Monroe St
Blissfield, MI 49228-1263, USA

Tracy, Brian (Business Person, Writer)
462 Stevens Ave Ste 202
Solana Beach, CA 92075-2065, USA

Tracy, Chad (Athlete, Baseball Player)
9422 Sir Huon Ln
Waxhaw, NC 28173-0112, USA

Tracy, James E (Jim) (Athlete, Baseball Player, Coach)
7112 Woodhall Ct
Presto, PA 15142-1511, USA

Tracy, Jeanie (Musician)
c/o Staff Member *Diva Central Inc*
7510 W Sunset Blvd Ste 1445
Los Angeles, CA 90046-3408, USA

Tracy, Keegan Connor (Actor)
c/o Deb Dillistone *Lucas Talent Inc*
100 W. Pender St Sun Tower, 7th Floor
Vancouver, BC V6B 1R8, Canada

Tracy, Michael C (Dancer, Director)
PO Box 388
Washington Depot, CT 06794-0388, USA

Tracy, Paul (Race Car Driver)
PO Box 956
Reading, PA 19603-0956, USA

Trafficant, James (Politician)
125 Market St
Youngstown, OH 44503-1780

Trafton, Stephanie Brown (Athlete, Track Athlete)
c/o Staff Member *USA Track & Field*
132 E Washington St Ste 800
Indianapolis, IN 46204-3674, USA

Trager, Milton (Doctor)
3800 Park East Dr Ste 100
Beachwood, OH 44122-4322, USA

Trager, William (Biologist)
1230 York Ave
New York, NY 10065-6307, USA

Traill, Phil (Director)
c/o Rosalie Swedlin *Anonymous Content (AC-LA)*
3531 Hayden Ave
Culver City, CA 90232, USA

Train (Music Group)
c/o Jonathan Daniel *Crush Management*
60-62 E 11th St Floor 7
New York, NY 10003, USA

Train, Harry D II (Admiral)
401 College Pl Apt 10
Norfolk, VA 23510-1130, USA

Train, Russell E (Government Official)
1250 24th St NW
Washington, DC 20037-1124, USA

Trainor, Bernard E (General)
46874 Grissom St
Sterling, VA 20165-3574, USA

Trainor, Jerry (Actor)
c/o Staff Member *Burstein Company, The*
15304 W Sunset Blvd Ste 208
Pacific Palisades, CA 90272-3656, USA

Trainor, Mary Ellen (Actor)
c/o Staff Member *Creative Artists Agency (CAA-LA)*
2000 Avenue of the Stars Ste 100
Los Angeles, CA 90067-4705, USA

Trammell, Alan (Athlete, Baseball Player, Coach)
1060 W Addison St Attn Coachingstaff
Chicago, IL 60613-4566, USA

Trammell, Sam (Actor)
c/o Gene Parseghian *Parseghian Planco LLC*
322 8th Ave Ste 601
New York, NY 10001-6715, USA

Trammell, Terry (Doctor)
1801 Senate Blvd # 200
Indianapolis, IN 46202-1228, USA

Trammell, Thomas (Bubba) (Athlete, Baseball Player)
614 Saxony Blvd
Saint Petersburg, FL 33716-1284, USA

Tramps, The
102 Ryders Ln
East Brunswick, NJ 08816-1328

Tran, Duc Luong (President)
Hoang Hoa Tham St
St Hanoi, VIETNAM

Tran, Huy K (Stylist)
c/o Staff Member *Artist Untied (LA)*
845 S Mansfield Ave Apt 1
Los Angeles, CA 90036-4979, USA

Tranelli, Deborah (Actor, Musician)
c/o Staff Member *Image Entertainment*
20525 Nordhoff St Ste 200
Chatsworth, CA 91311-6104, USA

Trang, Thuy
12651 Olaf Pl
Granada Hills, CA 91344-1052

Trani, Eugene P (Educator)
President's Office
Richmond, VA 23284, USA

Traore, Rokia (Actor, Composer)
c/o Staff Member *Concerted Efforts*
PO Box 440326
Somerville, MA 02144-0004, USA

Trapani, Gina (Internet Star)

Trapilo, Steve (Athlete, Football Player)
879 Main St
Norwell, MA 02061-2317, USA

Trapp, John (Athlete, Basketball Player)
12237 Concho Ct
Lusby, MD 20657-4819, USA

Trask, Emma (Stylist)
c/o Staff Member *Mercury Artists*
8460 Higuera St Fl 2
Culver City, CA 90232-2520, USA

Trask, Stephen (Composer)
c/o Brice Gaeta *Broder Webb Chervin Silbermann Agency, The (BWCS)*
10250 Constellation Blvd
Los Angeles, CA 90067-6200, USA

Trask, Thomas E (Religious Leader)
1445 N Boonville Ave
Springfield, MO 65802-1894, USA

Traub, Charles (Photographer)
39 E 10th St
New York, NY 10003-6154, USA

Traue, Antje (Actor)
c/o Staff Member *Anthem Entertainment*
9595 Wilshire Blvd Ste 900
Beverly Hills, CA 90212-2509, USA

Trauth, AJ (Actor)
c/o Felicia Sager *Sager Management*
260 S Beverly Dr # 205
Beverly Hills, CA 90212-3805, USA

Trautmann, Richard (Athlete)
Horemansstr 29
Munich 80636, GERMANY

Trautwein, John (Athlete, Baseball Player)
882 Beach Rd
Sanibel, FL 33957-6907, USA

Trautwig, Al (Sportscaster)
77 W 66th St
New York, NY 10023-6201, USA

Travanti, Daniel J (Actor)
10866 Wilshire Blvd Fl 10
Los Angeles, CA 90024-4350, USA

Travers, Bill (Athlete, Baseball Player)
10 Shoreline Dr
Foxboro, MA 02035-1115, USA

Travers, Pat (Musician)
1257 Arcade St
Saint Paul, MN 55106-2022, USA

Travis (Music Group)
c/o Staff Member *MCT Management*
520 8th Ave Rm 2205
New York, NY 10018-4160, USA

Travis, Kylie (Actor, Model)
1196 Summit Dr
Beverly Hills, CA 90210-2248, USA

Travis, Mack (Athlete, Football Player)
605 Holland Ave
Las Vegas, NV 89106-2651, USA

Travis, Nancy (Actor, Producer)
c/o David Lust *Patricola Lust PR*
9171 Wilshire Blvd Ste 390
Beverly Hills, CA 90210-5515, USA

Travis, Randy (Musician, Songwriter)
PO Box 121712
Nashville, TN 37212-1712, USA

Travis, Stacey (Actor)
c/o Brian Alexander *Essential Talent Management*
6399 Wilshire Blvd Ste 401
Los Angeles, CA 90048-5716, USA

Traviss, Adrienne (Stylist)
c/o Staff Member *Judy Inc*
1 Yorkville Ave
Toronto ON M4W 1L1, Canada

Travis-Visich, Gene (Baseball Player)
777 Wearimus Rd
Westwood, NJ 7675, USA

Travolta, Ellen (Actor)
6470 E Sunnyside Rd
Coeur D Alene, ID 83814-9503, USA

Travolta, Joey (Actor)
c/o Staff Member *Stephany Hurkos Management*
11935 Kling St
Valley Village, CA 91607-4072, USA

Travolta, John (Actor)
1401 NE 77th St
Ocala, FL 34479-1347, USA

Traya, Misti (Actor)
c/o Darren Goldberg *Global Creative*
1051 Cole Ave # B
Los Angeles, CA 90038-2601, USA

Trayham, Jerry (Athlete, Football Player)
6606 S Tomaker Ln
Spokane, WA 99223-6202, USA

Traylor, B Keith (Athlete, Football Player)
1000 Football Dr
Lake Forest, IL 60045, USA

Traylor, Keith (Athlete, Football Player)
11043 S 4317
Chouteau, OK 74337-6063, USA

Traylor, Robert (Basketball Player)
1501 Girod St
New Orleans, LA 70113-3124, USA

Traylor, Susan (Actor)
1741 Ivar Ave
Los Angeles, CA 90028-5105, USA

Traynham, Wade (Athlete, Football Player)
PO Box 176
Wake, VA 23176-0176, USA

Traynor, Jay (Musician)
17 Pauline Ct
Rensselaer, NY 12144-9780, USA

Traynowicz, Mark (Athlete, Football Player)
1668 Sioux St
Lincoln, NE 68502-4737, USA

Treach (Musician)
8942 Wilshire Blvd # 219
Beverly Hills, CA 90211-1908, USA

Treacy, Philip (Designer, Fashion Designer)
69 Elizabeth St
London SW1W 9PJ, UNITED KINGDOM (UK)

Treadaway, John (Athlete, Football Player)
3140 N 83rd Ave
Phoenix, AZ 85033-4724, USA

Treadway, Edward A (Politician)
5565 Sterrett Pl
Columbia, MD 21044-2665, USA

Treadway, James C Jr (Government Official)
Croton Lake Road RR 4
Mount Kisco, NY 10549, USA

Treadway, Jeff (Athlete, Baseball Player)
8812 Estes Rd
Macon, GA 31220-5649, USA

Treadway, Kenneth (Misc)
Adams Building
Bartlesville, OK 74003, USA

Treadway, Nick (Athlete, Baseball Player)
50 Treasure Island Dr
Troy, MO 63379-2337, USA

Treadway, Ty (Actor)
c/o Frank Gonzales *The Agency (CA)*
3711 Ocean Front Walk # 1
Marina Del Rey, CA 90292-5705, USA

Treadwell, David (Athlete, Football Player)
5445 Dtc Pkey Suite 800
Greenwood Village, CO 80111, USA

Treanor, Matt (Athlete, Baseball Player)
460 NW 115th Way
Coral Springs, FL 33071-4121, USA

Trebek, Alex (Game Show Host)
c/o Steven Arcieri *Arcieri & Associates Inc*
305 Madison Ave Ste 2315
New York, NY 10165-5015, USA

Trebelhorn, Thomas L (Tom) (Athlete, Baseball Player, Coach)
7333 W Camden St
Baltimore, MD 21201-2435, USA

Trebunskaya, Anna (Dancer, Reality TV Star)
c/o Staff Member *American Broadcasting Company (ABC LA)*
500 S Buena Vista St
Burbank, CA 91521-0001, USA

Tree, Michael (Musician)
45 E 89th St
New York, NY 10128-1251, USA

Trefilov, Andrei
PO Box 1540 Station M
Calgary, AB T2P 3B9, CANADA

Trejo, Danny (Actor)
c/o Gloria Hinojosa *Amsel, Eisenstadt & Frazier Talent Agency (AEF)*
5055 Wilshire Blvd Ste 860
Los Angeles, CA 90036-6108, USA

Trejos, Fernandez Jose J (President)
Apartado 10 096
San Jose 1000, COSTA RICA

Trelford, Donald G (Editor)
15 Fowler Road
London N1 2EA, UNITED KINGDOM (UK)

Tremblay, Mario (Athlete, Coach, Hockey Player)
714 Mistassini
Lachenaie, QC J6W 5H2, Canada

Tremblay, Michel (Writer)
294 Carre Saint Louis # 5E
Montreal, QC H2X 1A4, CANADA

Trembley, Dave (Athlete, Baseball Player, Coach)
333 W Camden St Attn Managers
Baltimore, MD 21201-2496, USA

Tremel, Bill (Athlete, Baseball Player)
315 E 23rd Ave
Altoona, PA 16601-4002, USA

Tremie, Chris (Athlete, Baseball Player)
484 Marion Ln
New Waverly, TX 77358-4504, USA

Tremko, Anne
10100 Santa Monica Blvd Ste 2500
Los Angeles, CA 90067-4116

Tremlett, David R (Artist)
Broadlawns Chipperfield Road
Bovingdon, Herts, UNITED KINGDOM (UK)

Tremont, Ray C (Religious Leader)
3939 N Causeway Blvd Ste 400
Metairie, LA 70002-1777, USA

Trendy, Bobby (Designer)
c/o Darryl Marshak *Marshak/Zachary Company, The*
8840 Wilshire Blvd Fl 1
Beverly Hills, CA 90211-2606, USA

Trenhaile, John
4 Wailands Crescent Lewes
E. Sussex, ENGLAND BNT 2QT

Treniers, The
520 N Camden Dr
Beverly Hills, CA 90210-3202

Trent, Buck (Musician)
118 Hampshire Dr
Branson, MO 65616-3765, USA

Trent, Gary (Athlete, Basketball Player)
1150 Northwood Cir
New Albany, OH 43054-9056, USA

Trenyce (Reality TV Star)
c/o Staff Member *Diva Central Inc*
7510 W Sunset Blvd Ste 1445
Los Angeles, CA 90046-3408, USA

Treschev, Sergei Y (Cosmonaut)
Moskovskoi Oblasti
Syvisdny Goroduk 141160, RUSSIA

Trese, Adam (Actor)
c/o Staff Member *Robert Stein Management*
PO Box 3797
Beverly Hills, CA 90212-0797, USA

Tresh, Tom (Athlete, Baseball Player)
1751 Waxwing Cir
Venice, FL 34293-1461, USA

Tressel, Jim (Coach, Football Coach)
Athletic Dept
Columbus, OH 43210, USA

Trestman, Marc (Football Player)
PO Box 888
Phoenix, AZ 85001-0888, USA

Tresvant, John (Athlete, Basketball Player)
14814 61st Dr SE
Snohomish, WA 98296-4221, USA

Tretlak, Vladislav (Athlete, Coach, Hockey Player)
94 Festival Dr
Toronto, ON M2R 3V1, Canada

Tretyak, Ivan (General)
34 Manerezhnaya M Thoreza
Moscow, RUSSIA

Treu, Adam (Athlete, Football Player)
3176 NW Shevlin Meadows Dr
Bend, OR 97701-1476, USA

Trevanian (Writer)
375 Hudson St
New York, NY 10014-3658, USA

Trever, John (Cartoonist, Editor)
Editorial Dept 717 Silver Ave SW
Albuquerque, NM 87102, USA

Treves, Frederick
5 St Catherine's Mews Milner St
London, ENGLAND SW3 2PX

Trevi, Gloria (Musician)
Avenida Parque 67 Napoles
Mexico City, DF 3810, MEXICO

Trevino, Alex (Athlete, Baseball Player)
PO Box 288
Houston, TX 77001-0288, USA

Trevino, Lee B (Golfer)
1901 W 47th Pl Ste 200
Westwood, KS 66205-1834, USA

Trevino, Michael (Actor)
c/o Lena Roklin *Luber Roklin Management*
8530 Wilshire Blvd Ste 550
Beverly Hills, CA 90211-3133, USA

Trevino, Rick (Musician)
2100 W End Ave Ste 1000
Nashville, TN 37203-5240, USA

Trevor, William (Writer)
Drury House 34-43 Russell St
London WC2B 5HA, UNITED KINGDOM (UK)

Triandos, C Gus (Athlete, Baseball Player)
PO Box 5642
San Jose, CA 95150-5642, USA

Trias, Jasmine (Musician)

Tribbett, Tye (Musician)
c/o Staff Member *Sony Music International*
550 Madison Ave Fl 6
New York, NY 10022-3211, USA

Tribe, Laurence H (Attorney, Attorney General, Educator, General)
Law School Griswold Hall
Cambridge, MA 2138, USA

Trible, Paul S Jr (Educator, Senator)
50 University Pl
Newport News, VA 23606-2949, USA

Trichter, Judd
10264 Rochester Ave
Los Angeles, CA 90024-5331

Trick, Cheap (Music Group, Musician)
c/o Dave Frey *Red Light Management (VA)*
PO Box 1467
Charlottesville, VA 22902-1467, USA

Trickey, Paula
PO Box 261098
Encino, CA 91426-1098

Trickle, Dick (Race Car Driver)
PO Box 645
Skyland, NC 28776-0645, USA

Trickle, Dick (Race Car Driver)
5011 Old Midlothian Tpke
Richmond, VA 23224-1119, USA

Trickside (Music Group)
c/o Staff Member *Wind-up Records*
72 Madison Ave Fl 8
New York, NY 10016-8731, USA

Triffle, Carol (Director)
17 SE 8th Ave
Portland, OR 97214-1239, USA

Trigg, Alex (Baseball Player)
900 Turner Ln
Shreveport, LA 71106-4528, USA

Trigger, Sarah (Actor)
10100 Santa Monica Blvd Ste 2500
Los Angeles, CA 90067-4116, USA

Triggs, Trini
3178 Allen Marthaville Rd
Robeline, LA 71469-4528

Trillin, Calvin M (Writer)
4 Times Sq
New York, NY 10036-6515, USA

Trillo, Manny (Athlete, Baseball Player)
7309 W Coyle Ave
Chicago, IL 60631-1110, USA

Trimble, David (Nobel Prize Laureate)
2 Queen St Lurgen
County Arnagh BT66 8BQ, NORTHERN IRELAND

Trimble, Joe (Athlete, Baseball Player)
14 Fair Oaks Dr
Lincoln, RI 02865-4520, USA

Trimble, Solomon (Actor)
c/o Kaili Canfield *Arthouse Talent and Literary*
107 SE Washington St Ste 156
Portland, OR 97214-2105, USA

Trimble, Vance H (Editor)
25 Oakhurst St
Wewoka, OK 74884-3714, USA

Trimble, Vivian (Musician)
2 Penn Plz # 2600
New York, NY 10121-0101, USA

Trina (Musician)
c/o Staff Member *Pyramid Entertainment Group*
377 Rector Pl Apt 21A
New York, NY 10280-1439, USA

Trineer, Connor (Actor)
c/o Gregg A Klein *Abrams Artists Agency (LA)*
9200 W Sunset Blvd PH 11
Los Angeles, CA 90069-3601, USA

Trinh, Eugene (Astronaut)
300 E St SW
Washington, DC 20546-0002, USA

Trinidad, Felix (Tito) (Boxer)
RR 6 Box 11479
Rio Piedras, PR 926, USA

Trinkaus, Erik (Biologist)
Paleontology Dept
Saint Louis, MO 63130, USA

Trinneer, Connor (Actor)
c/o Staff Member *Abrams Artists Agency (LA)*
9200 W Sunset Blvd PH 11
Los Angeles, CA 90069-3601, USA

Trintignant, Jean-Louis (Actor)
20 Ave Rapp
Paris 75007, FRANCE

Triola, Michelle
23215 Mariposa De Oro St
Malibu, CA 90265-4909

Triplet, Kirk (Golfer)
4527 N 61st Pl
Scottsdale, AZ 85251-1945, USA

Triplett, Kirk (Golfer)
4527 N 61st Pl
Scottsdale, AZ 85251-1945, USA

Triplett, Wally (Athlete, Football Player)
4250 Fullerton St
Detroit, MI 48238-3235, USA

Tripp, Linda
27285 Boyce Mill Rd
Greensboro, MD 21639-1332

Tripp, Valerie (Writer)
PO Box 620991
Middleton, WI 53562-0991, USA

Trippi, Charles L (Charlie) (Athlete, Football Player)
125 Riverhill Ct
Athens, GA 30606-4034, USA

Tripplehorn, Jeanne (Actor)
c/o Cynthia Pett-Dante *Brillstein Entertainment Partners*
9150 Wilshire Blvd Ste 350
Beverly Hills, CA 90212-3453, USA

Tripplett, Larry (Athlete, Football Player)
5324 Overdale Dr
Los Angeles, CA 90043-2023, USA

Triptow, Dick (Athlete, Basketball Player)
325 Birkdale Rd
Lake Bluff, IL 60044-2334, USA

Tripucka, Kelly (Athlete, Basketball Player)
14 Devon Rd
Boonton, NJ 07005-9305, USA

Tritt, Travis (Actor, Musician)
c/o Duke Cooper *Quantum Management*
5340 Forest Acres Dr
Nashville, TN 37220-2123, USA

Trivanovich, Cristina (Stylist)
c/o Staff Member *Creative Talent Columbus*
5864 Nike Dr
Hilliard, OH 43026-8756, USA

Trivium (Music Group)
c/o Staff Member *Roadrunner Records Inc*
902 Broadway Fl 8
New York, NY 10010-6037, USA

Trixter
210 Westfield Ave
Clark, NJ 07066-1539

Trlicek, Rick (Athlete, Baseball Player)
PO Box 1109
La Grange, TX 78945-1109, USA

Troche, Rose (Actor, Director, Producer, Writer)
c/o Staff Member *Gersh (NY)*
41 Madison Ave
New York, NY 10010-2202, USA

Troedson, Rich (Athlete, Baseball Player)
899 Bowen Ave
San Jose, CA 95123-5303, USA

Troger, Christian-Alexander (Swimmer)
Josefstr 26
Deisenhofen 82941, GERMANY

Troisgros, Pierre E R (Business Person)
Roanne 42300, FRANCE

Troitskaya, Natalia L (Opera Singer)
Klostergasse 37
Vienna 1170, AUSTRIA

Troliope, Joanna (Writer)
Drury House 34-43 Russell St
London WC2B 5HA, UNITED KINGDOM (UK)

Trombley, Mike (Athlete, Baseball Player)
2 Hilltop Park
Wilbraham, MA 01095-1753, USA

Trondheim, Lewis (Artist)
c/o Staff Member *Fantagraphics Books*
7563 Lake City Way NE
Seattle, WA 98115-4218, USA

Trone, Roland (Don) (Musician)
27 L Ambiance Ct
Bardonia, NY 10954-1421, USA

Tronnier, Ellen (Baseball Player)
PO Box 255
Palmyra, WI 53156-0255, USA

Trosch, Gene (Athlete, Football Player)
6393 Oak Tree Dr
Mc Calla, AL 35111-3926, USA

Trosky Jr, Hal (Athlete, Baseball Player)
1414 Curtis Bridge Rd NE
Swisher, IA 52338-9588, USA

Trosper, Jennifer Harris (Scientist)
4800 Oak Grove Dr
Pasadena, CA 91109-8001, USA

Trost, Barry M (Scientist)
24510 Amigos Ct
Los Altos Hills, CA 94024-4773, USA

Trost, Carlisle A H (Admiral)
11 Compromise St
Annapolis, MD 21401-1806, USA

Trott, Stephen S (Judge)
550 W Fort St
Boise, ID 83724-0201, USA

Trottier, Bryan
3868 Forest Dr
Doylestown, PA 18902-8100

Trottier, Bryan J (Athlete, Coach, Hockey Player)
356 Birdsong Way
Doylestown, PA 18901-4885, USA

Trouble, Valli (Musician)
729 7th Ave Ste 1600
New York, NY 10019-6880, USA

Troup, Bill (Athlete, Football Player)
4 Quail Wood Ct
Parkton, MD 21120-9444, USA

Troup, Tom
8829 Ashcroft Ave
West Hollywood, CA 90048-2401

Troupe, Tom (Actor)
8829 Ashcroft Ave
West Hollywood, CA 90048-2401, USA

Trousdale, Chris (Actor, Musician)
c/o Staff Member *Adonis Productions*
175 Skillman St
Brooklyn, NY 11205-3901, USA

Trout, David (Athlete, Football Player)
408 Paddock Ct
Sewell, NJ 08080-2509, USA

Trout, Steve (Athlete, Baseball Player)
PO Box 1155
Tinley Park, IL 60477-7955, USA

Troutt, William E (Educator)
President's Office
Nashville, TN 37212, USA

Trova, Ernest T (Artist)
7706 Arthur Ave
Saint Louis, MO 63117-1519, USA

Trowbridge, Alexander B Jr (Secretary)
1823 23rd St NW
Washington, DC 20008-4030, USA

Trower, Robin (Musician)
4600 Franklin Ave
Los Angeles, CA 90027-4202, USA

Troxel, Gary
11471 Earle Dr
Mount Vernon, WA 98273-7261, USA

Troyat, Henri (Writer)
23 Quai de Conti
Paris 75006, FRANCE

Troyer, Verne (Actor)
c/o Elaina Bertnolli *Fonolli Management*
11218 Osborne St
Lake View Ter, CA 91342-6604, USA

Truax, Billy (Athlete, Football Player)
735 Ruth Ave
Gulfport, MS 39501-1056, USA

Truax, Dalton (Athlete, Football Player)
77 Chateau Magdelaine Dr
Kenner, LA 70065-2026, USA

Truby, Chris (Athlete, Baseball Player)
12244 Silverado Dr
Fishers, IN 46037-8328, USA

Trucco, Michael (Actor)
3500 W Olive Ave Ste 770
Burbank, CA 91505-5527, USA

Trucks, Virgil O (Fire) (Athlete, Baseball Player)
1016 Waterford Trl
Calera, AL 35040-7613, USA

Trudeau, Garry (Cartoonist)
459 Columbus Ave # 200
New York, NY 10024-5129, USA

Trudeau, Jack F (Athlete, Football Player)
9150 Timberwolf Ln
Zionsville, IN 46077-8320, USA

Trudeau, Paul (Stylist)
c/o Staff Member *Team*
423 W Broadway Ste 406
Boston, MA 02127-2265, USA

TRUE, Rachel (Actor)
c/o Lorrie Bartlett *International Creative Management (ICM-LA)*
10250 Constellation Blvd Fl 7
Los Angeles, CA 90067-6207, USA

True Vibe (Music Group)
c/o Staff Member *Creative Artists Agency (CAA-LA)*
2000 Avenue of the Stars Ste 100
Los Angeles, CA 90067-4705, USA

Trueco, Michael (Actor)
c/o Staff Member *Raw Talent Management*
545 Veteran Ave
Los Angeles, CA 90024-1915, USA

Truesdale, Yanic (Actor)
c/o Danielle Allman-Del *D2 Management*
141 S Barrington Ave
Los Angeles, CA 90049-3368, USA

Trufant, Marcus (Athlete, Football Player)
11220 NE 53rd St
Kirkland, WA 98033-7505, USA

Truhitte, Dan
4630 Sapp Rd
Concord, NC 28025-1567

Truitt, Anne D (Artist)
29 Boutonville Rd
South Salem, NY 10590-1517, USA

Truitt, Ansley (Athlete, Basketball Player)
18680 Lurin Ave
Riverside, CA 92508-8006, USA

Truitt, Olanda (Athlete, Football Player)
1901 16th Way N
Bessemer, AL 35020-3930, USA

Trujillo, Chadwick (Astronomer)
Astronomy
Pasadena, CA 91125-0001, USA

Trujillo, J J (Athlete, Baseball Player)
1329 York Ave
Corpus Christi, TX 78415-4337, USA

Trujillo, Mike (Athlete, Baseball Player)
16373 6475 Rd
Montrose, CO 81403-8578, USA

Trujillo, Solomon D (Business Person)
1801 California St
Denver, CO 80202-2658, USA

Trull, Don (Athlete, Football Player)
16435 Elmwood Point Ln
Sugar Land, TX 77498-7134, USA

Truly, Richard N (Admiral, Astronaut)
2340 Juniper Ct
Golden, CO 80401-8087, USA

Truman, Dan (Musician)
2908 Poston Ave
Nashville, TN 37203-1312, USA

Truman, James (Editor)
4 Times Sq
New York, NY 10036-6515, USA

Trumbo, Karen (Actor)
c/o Staff Member *Creative Artists Management (OR)*
909 SW Saint Clair Ave
Portland, OR 97205-1300, USA

Trumka, Richard L (Politician)
1750 New York Ave NW
Washington, DC 20006-5305, USA

Trump, Blaine
166 Avenue of the Americas
New York, NY 10013-1207, USA

Trump, Donald (Business Person, Reality TV Star)
c/o Staff Member *Trump Organization*
725 5th Ave Bsmt
New York, NY 10022-2516, USA

Trump, Ivana (Business Person, Model)
PO Box 8104
West Palm Beach, FL 33407-0104, USA

Trump, Ivanka (Business Person, Heir/Heiress)
725 5th Ave
New York, NY 10022-2519, USA

Trump, Melania (Model)
c/o Marc Beckman *Designers Management Agency*
446 Broadway Fl 4
New York, NY 10013-2546, USA

Trumpy, Robert T (Bob) Jr (Athlete, Football Player, Sportscaster)
75 Oak St
Cincinnati, OH 45246-4437, USA

Trundy, Natalie (Actor)
2109 S Wilbur Ave
Walla Walla, WA 99362-9048, USA

Truran, James W Jr (Physicist)
210 Wysteria Dr
Olympia Fields, IL 60461-1202, USA

Truscott, Lucian K IV (Writer)
1350 Avenue of the Americas
New York, NY 10019-4702, USA

Truth, Hurts (Actor, Songwriter, Writer)
2220 Colorado Ave
Santa Monica, CA 90404-3506, USA

Truvillion, Eric (Athlete, Football Player)
10436 Saint Tropez Pl
Tampa, FL 33615-4213, USA

Truvillion, Tobias (Actor)
c/o Kim Matuka *Online Talent Group*
Prefers to be contacted via email or telephone
Los Angeles, CA 90069, USA

Tryba, Ted (Athlete, Golfer)
6321 Cheryl St
Orlando, FL 32819-7511, USA

Tryon, Ty (Golfer)
8713 the Esplanade Apt 1
Orlando, FL 32836-8784, USA

Tsai, Cheryl (Actor)
c/o Jason Solomon *Full Circle Management*
4932 Lankershim Blvd Ste 202
North Hollywood, CA 91601-4452, USA

Tsai, Sue (Stylist)
c/o Staff Member *Exclusive Artists Mgmt*
7700 W Sunset Blvd Ste 205
Los Angeles, CA 90046-3913, USA

Tsakalidis, Iakovos (Jake) (Basketball Player)
175 Toyota Plz Ste 150
Memphis, TN 38103-6601, USA

Tsamis, George (Athlete, Baseball Player)
12 Sweetbriar Ct
Colchester, CT 06415-1887, USA

Tsang, Bion (Musician)
165 W 57th St
New York, NY 10019-2201, USA

Tsantiris, Len (Football Player)
Athletic Dept
Storrs Mansfield, CT, USA

Tsao, I Fu (Engineer)
Chemical Engineering Dept
Ann Arbor, MI 48109, USA

Tschechowa, Vera (Actor)
c/o Ute Nicolai *Agentur Ute Nicolai*
Gosslerstrasse 2
Berlin 12161, Germany

Tschida, Tim (Baseball Player)
274 15 1/2 Ave
Turtle Lake, WI 54889-8825, USA

Tschida, Tim (Athlete, Baseball Player)
274 15 1/2 Ave
Turtle Lake, WI 54889-8825, USA

Tschogl, John (Athlete, Basketball Player)
295 Shirley St
Chula Vista, CA 91910-1101, USA

Tschumi, Bernard (Architect)
7 Rue Pecquay
Paris 75004, FRANCE

Tsibliyev, Vasili V (Cosmonaut)
Moskovskoi Oblasti
Syvisdny Goroduk 141160, RUSSIA

Tsioropoulos, Lou (Athlete, Basketball Player)
2404 Chattesworth Ct
Louisville, KY 40242-2852, USA

Tsitouris, John (Athlete, Baseball Player)
5207 Austin Rd
Monroe, NC 28112-7948, USA

Tskitishvili, Nikoloz (Basketball Player)
Pepsi Center 1000 Chopper Circle
Denver, CO 80204, USA

Tsoucalas, Nicholas (Judge)
1 Federal Plz
New York, NY 10278-0001, USA

Tsu, Irene (Actor)
c/o Richard A. Castleberry *Castleberry Talent*
636 Acanto St Apt 205
Los Angeles, CA 90049-2128, USA

Tsui, Daniel C (Nobel Prize Laureate)
53 College Rd W
Princeton, NJ 08540-5049, USA

Tsui, Lap-Chee (Biologist)
555 University Ave
Toronto, ON M5G 1X8, CANADA

Tsukasa, Helene (Stylist)
2100 Federal Ave
Los Angeles, CA 90025-5327, USA

Tu, Francesca (Actor)
c/o Staff Member *Agentur Jovanovic*
Theresienstrasse 124
Munchen 80333, Germany

Tuanku, Salehuddin Abdul Aziz Shah (King, Royalty)
Istana Bukit Serene
Kuala Lumpur 50502, MALAYSIA

Tuaolo, Esera (Athlete, Football Player)
6520 Promontory Dr
Eden Prairie, MN 55346-1915, USA

Tubbs, Billy (Coach)
Athletic Dept
Beaumont, TX 77710, USA

Tubbs, Gerald J (Jerry) (Athlete, Football Player)
3813 Centenary Ave
Dallas, TX 75225-5226, USA

Tubbs, Greg (Athlete, Baseball Player)
833 Clay Ave
Cookeville, TN 38501-2261, USA

Tubbs, Winfred (Athlete, Football Player)
RR 1 Box 800
Oakwood, TX 75855, USA

Tubert, Marcelo (Actor)
c/o Staff Member *Richard Schwartz Management*
2934 1/2 N Beverly Glen Cir # 107
Los Angeles, CA 90077-1724, USA

Tuberville, Tommy (Coach, Football Coach)
Athletic
Auburn University, AL 36849-0001, USA

Tubiola, Nicole (Actor)
c/o Charlton Blackburne *A Management Company*
9107 Wilshire Blvd Ste 650
Beverly Hills, CA 90210-5544, USA

Tucci, Michael (Actor)
1425 Irving Ave
Glendale, CA 91201-1274, USA

Tucci, Roberto Cardinal (Religious Leader)
Palazzo Pio Piazza Pia 3
Rome 193, ITALY

Tucci, Stanley (Actor, Director)
c/o Jennifer Plante *SLATE Public Relations - NY*
307 7th Ave Rm 2401
New York, NY 10001-6019, USA

Tuchman, Maurice (Misc)
150 E 57th St PH PMB 1A
New York, NY 10022-2700, USA

Tuck, Hillary (Actor)
c/o Justin Evans *The Independent Group*
6363 Wilshire Blvd Ste 115
Los Angeles, CA 90048-5734, USA

Tuck, Jessica (Actor)
448 W 44th St
New York, NY 10036-5205, USA

Tucker, Barbara (Musician)
c/o Staff Member *Diva Central Inc*
7510 W Sunset Blvd Ste 1445
Los Angeles, CA 90046-3408, USA

Tucker, Bill (Boxer)
26126 Meadowcrest Blvd
Huntington Woods, MI 48070-1534, USA

Tucker, Chris (Actor, Comedian)
c/o Tracy Krammer *Toltec Artists*
7674 Woodrow Wilson Dr
Los Angeles, CA 90046-1252, USA

Tucker, Corin (Musician)
7 Trinity Row
Florence, MA 01062-1931, USA

Tucker, Eddie (Athlete, Baseball Player)
2216 Red Maple Ln
Dawsonville, GA 30534-8032, USA

Tucker, Elizabeth (Baseball Player)
4037 N Fremont Ave
Tucson, AZ 85719-1065, USA

Tucker, Jason (Athlete, Football Player)
620 Remington Park
Robinson, TX 76706-7255, USA

Tucker, Jonathan (Actor)
8265 W Sunset Blvd Ste 201
Los Angeles, CA 90046-2470, USA

Tucker, Marshall Band (Music Group)
c/o Ron Rainey *Ron Rainey Management Inc.*
315 S Beverly Dr Ste 300
Beverly Hills, CA 90212-4309, USa

Tucker, Michael (Actor, Producer)
PO Box 843
Santa Ynez, CA 93460-0843, USA

Tucker, Michael (Athlete, Baseball Player)
407 Maple Ave N
Lehigh Acres, FL 33972-4001, USA

Tucker, Rex (Athlete, Football Player)
2300 Culpeper Dr
Midland, TX 79705-6314, USA

Tucker, Robert L (Bob) Jr (Athlete, Football Player)
8 Hunter Rd
Hazleton, PA 18201-6817, USA

Tucker, Robin (Stylist)
9120 Beverlywood St
Los Angeles, CA 90034-1912, USA

Tucker, Ryan (Athlete, Football Player)
c/o Team Member *Cleveland Browns*
76 Lou Groza Blvd
Berea, OH 44017-1269

Tucker, T J (Athlete, Baseball Player)
6616 Ridge Top Dr
New Port Richey, FL 34655-5614, USA

Tucker, Tanya (Musician)
c/o Frank Wing *Agency for the Performing Arts (APA-Nashville)*
3017 Poston Ave
Nashville, TN 37203-1313

Tucker, Tony (Boxer)
1619 E 7th Ave
Tampa, FL 33605-3705, USA

Tucker, Travis (Athlete, Football Player)
1568 Lee Terrace Dr
Wickliffe, OH 44092-1604, USA

Tucker, Trent (Athlete, Basketball Player)
433 River St
Minneapolis, MN 55401-2515, USA

Tucker, Wendell (Athlete, Football Player)
2042 E 171st Pl
South Holland, IL 60473-3718, USA

Tucker, William E (Educator)
Chancellor S Ofc
Fort Worth, TX 76129-0001, USA

Tucker, Y Arnold (Athlete, Football Player)
P.O. Box 514
Hilbert, WI 54129, USA

Tuckwell, Barry E
13140 Fountain Head Rd
Hagerstown, MD 21742-2839, USA

Tudor, John T (Athlete, Baseball Player)
5 Nathan Ln
Middleton, MA 01949-1531, USA

Tudyk, Alan (Actor)
c/o Nick Collins *Gersh (LA)*
9465 Wilshire Blvd Ste 600
Beverly Hills, CA 90212-2612, USA

Tueting, Sarah (Athlete, Hockey Player)
488 Ash St
Winnetka, IL 60093-2604, USA

Tufts, Bob (Athlete, Baseball Player)
6738 108th St Apt A27
Forest Hills, NY 11375-2358, USA

Tuggle, Anthony (Athlete, Football Player)
12345 Plymouth Dr
Baton Rouge, LA 70807-1961, USA

Tuggle, Jessie (Athlete, Football Player)
540 Avala Ct
Alpharetta, GA 30022-5576, USA

Tuiasosopo, Marques (Athlete, Football Player)
5569 Gold Creek Dr
Castro Valley, CA 94552-5442, USA

Tuiasosopo, Peter Navy (Actor)
c/o Harold Gray *Shirley Wilson Agency*
5410 Wilshire Blvd #806 Los Angeles CA 90036, USA

Tuibahadur, Pun (War Hero)
Old Admiralty Building
London SW1A 2BL, UNITED KINGDOM (UK)

Tuilaepa, Sailele Maljelegaio (Prime Minister)
PO Box 193
Apia, SAMOA

Tuinei, Tom (Athlete, Football Player)
714 Kihapai Pl Apt B2
Kailua, HI 96734-2677, USA

Tuininga, Heidi (Stylist)
c/o Staff Member *Zenobia Agency Inc*
PO Box 909
Groveland, CA 95321-0909, USA

Tuipala, Joe (Athlete, Football Player)
43845 Thornberry Sq Unit 103
Leesburg, VA 20176-3403, USA

Tull, Thomas (Producer)
4000 Warner Blvd Bldg 76
Burbank, CA 91522-0001, ISA

Tullis, Willie (Athlete, Football Player)
10018 Knoboak Dr Apt 4
Houston, TX 77080-6445, USA

Tully, Darrow (Publisher)
9862 Bridgeton Dr
Tampa, FL 33626-1802, USA

Tully, Susan (Actor, Director)
c/o Bryn Newton *Saraband Associates*
265 Liverpool Rd
London N1 1LX, UNITED KINGDOM (UK)

Tulowitzki, Troy (Athlete, Baseball Player)
2986 Taper Ave
Santa Clara, CA 95051-2343, USA

Tulving, Endel (Misc)
45 Baby Point Cres
York, ON M6S 2B7, CANADA

Tumi, Christian W Cardinal (Religious Leader)
Archveche BP 179
Douala, CAMEROON

Tumulty, Tom (Athlete, Football Player)
167 Woodside Ln
Verona, PA 15147-3425, USA

Tune, Thomas J (Tommy) (Actor, Dancer)
222 Park Ave S Apt 12C
New York, NY 10003-1508, USA

Tung, Chee-Hwa (Misc)
3 Garden Road
Hong Kong, CHINA

Tunie, Tamara (Actor)
c/o Jean-Pierre (JP) Henraux *Shelter Entertainment*
9454 Wilshire Blvd Ste 715
Beverly Hills, CA 90212-2925, USA

Tunnell, Denise (Stylist)
c/o Staff Member *Help Me Rhonda*
541 10th St NW # 294
Atlanta, GA 30318-5713, USA

Tunnell, Janice (Stylist)
c/o Staff Member *Help Me Rhonda*
541 10th St NW # 294
Atlanta, GA 30318-5713, USA

Tunnell, Lee (Athlete, Baseball Player)
6000 Kingsbridge Dr
Oklahoma City, OK 73162-3208, USA

Tunney, John V (Senator)
304 Chautauqua Blvd
Pacific Palisades, CA 90272-4405, USA

Tunney, Robin (Actor)
c/o Joan Hyler *Hyler Management*
20 Ocean Park Blvd Unit 25
Santa Monica, CA 90405-3590, USA

Tupa, Thomas J (Tom) (Athlete, Football Player)
5921 Fawn Ln
Brecksville, OH 44141-2849, USA

Tupouto'a (Prince)
PO Box 6
Nuku'alofa, TONGA

Tupper, James (Actor)
c/o Jason Weinberg *Untitled Entertainment (LA)*
350 S Beverly Dr Ste 200
Beverly Hills, CA 90212-4819, USA

Tupper, Jeff (Athlete, Football Player)
3263 W 164th Ter
Stilwell, KS 66085-8822, USA

Turang, Brian (Athlete, Baseball Player)
3014 McNab Ave
Long Beach, CA 90808-4002, USA

Turco, Marty (Athlete, Hockey Player)
841 Shorewood Dr
Coppell, TX 75019-5665, USA

Turco, Paige (Actor)
c/o Rhonda Price *Gersh (NY)*
41 Madison Ave
New York, NY 10010-2202, USA

Turco, Richard P (Scientist)
4340 Admiralty Way
Marina del Rey, CA 90292, USA

Turcotte, Donald L (Don) (Geophysicist, Physicist)
27104 Middle Golf Dr
El Macero, CA 95618-1054, USA

Turcotte, Jean-Claude Cardinal (Religious Leader)
1071 Rue De La Cathedrale
Montreal, QC H2B 2V4, CANADA

Turcotte, Ron (Jockey)
82 Seattle Slew Dr
Howell, NJ 07731-3106, USA

Tureaud, Lawrence (Mr T) (Actor)
c/o Barry M. Greenberg *Celebrity Connection*
812 N Highland Ave
Los Angeles, CA 90038-3417, USA

Turgeon, Pierre (Athlete, Hockey Player)
1075 E Oxford Ln
Englewood, CO 80113-4822, USA

Turiaf, Ronny (Athlete, Basketball Player)
c/o Mark Bartelstein *Priority Sports & Entertainment - Chicago*
312 N La Salle # 650
Chicago, IL 60610, USA

Turin Brakes (Music Group)
c/o Staff Member *Paradigm (Monterey)*
404 W Franklin St
Monterey, CA 93940-2303, USA

Turk, Brian (Actor)
c/o Staff Member *House of Representatives, The*
1434 6th St Ste 1
Santa Monica, CA 90401-2527, USA

Turk, Godwin (Athlete, Football Player)
1303 Magnolia Cir
Orange, TX 77632-8996, USA

Turk, Stephen (Cartoonist)
927 Westbourne Dr
Los Angeles, CA 90069-4113, USA

Turkel, Ann (Actor)
c/o Mark Baintree *Brian Baintree Agency*
4 W 58th St
New York, NY 10019-2515, USA

Turkoglu, Hidayet (Hedo) (Athlete, Basketball Player)
100 S Eola Dr Unit 1603
Orlando, FL 32801-6601, USA

Turkson, Peter K A Cardinal (Religious Leader)
PO Box 112
Cape Coast, GHANA

Turley, Bob (Athlete, Baseball Player)
3327 Duluth Highway 120 Ste 101
Duluth, GA 30096-3334, USA

Turley, Kyle (Football Player)
c/o Staff Member *Saint Louis Rams*
1 Rams Way
Earth City, MO 63045-1525, USA

Turley, Robert L (Bob) (Athlete, Baseball Player)
3327 Duluth Highway 120 Ste 101
Duluth, GA 30096-3334, USA

Turlington, Christy (Model)
c/o Lisa Jacobson *United Talent Agency (UTA)*
9560 Wilshire Blvd Fl 5
Beverly Hills, CA 90212-2400, USA

Turman, Glynn (Actor, Director, Musician)
c/o Staff Member *Elkins Management*
8306 Wilshire Blvd # 438
Beverly Hills, CA 90211-2382, USA

Turnage, Mark-Anthony (Composer)
Great Marlborough St
London W1V 2BN, UNITED KINGDOM (UK)

Turnbow, Derrick (Athlete, Baseball Player)
2224 Brienz Valley Dr
Franklin, TN 37064-1401, USA

Turnbow, Scot (Baseball Player)
404 Newbary Ct
Franklin, TN 37069-1848, USA

Turnbull, Alistair (Stylist)
c/o Staff Member *Pat Bates & Associates*
300 W 12th St
New York, NY 10014-1939, USA

Turnbull, David (Physicist)
29 Concord Ave Apt 715
Cambridge, MA 02138-2330, USA

Turnbull, Wendy (Tennis Player)
822 Boylston St Ste 203
Chestnut Hill, MA 02467-2504, USA

Turnbull, William (Artist)
11 Cork St
London W1, UNITED KINGDOM (UK)

Turner, Aiden (Actor)
c/o Marnie Sparer *Innovative Artists (LA)*
1505 10th St
Santa Monica, CA 90401-2805, USA

Turner, Bake (Athlete, Football Player)
PO Box 277
Alpine, TX 79831-0277, USA

Turner, Bree (Actor)
c/o Jai Khanna *Brillstein Entertainment Partners*
9150 Wilshire Blvd Ste 350
Beverly Hills, CA 90212-3453, USA

Turner, Cathy (Speed Skater)
251 East Ave
Hilton, NY 14468-1333, USA

Turner, Cecil (Athlete, Football Player)
2717 Dog Leg Trl
McKinney, TX 75069-8043, USA

Turner, Chris (Athlete, Baseball Player)
28553 N Quarry Dr
Elberta, AL 36530-5792, USA

Turner, Debbye (Doctor)
PO Box 12450
Saint Louis, MO 63132-0150, USA

Turner, Edwin L (Physicist)
Astro Physical Science
Princeton, NJ 08544-0001, USA

Turner, Elston (Athlete, Basketball Player)
23 Commanders Cv
Missouri City, TX 77459-6517, USA

Turner, Floyd (Athlete, Football Player)
9626 Garden Row Dr
Sugar Land, TX 77498-1033, USA

Turner, Fred L (Business Person)
McDonald's Plaza 1 Kroc Dr
Oak Brook, IL 60523, USA

Turner, Gideon (Actor)
c/o Staff Member *Ken McReddie Ltd*
11 Connaught Pl
London W2 2ET, UNITED KINGDOM

Turner, Glenn (Business Person)
PO Box 952608
Lake Mary, FL 32795-2608, USA

Turner, Grant
PO Box 414
Brentwood, TN 37024-0414

Turner, Guinevere (Actor)
41 Madison Ave # 3300
New York, NY 10010-2202, USA

Turner, Hamp (Athlete, Football Player)
430172 Milledge Ter
Athens, GA 30605, USA

Turner, Herschel (Athlete, Football Player)
16622 Equestrian Ln
Chesterfield, MO 63005-4880, USA

Turner, Hersh (Athlete, Basketball Player)
1706 Lamberton Creek Ct NE
Grand Rapids, MI 49505-7702, USA

Turner, Jackie Lee (Athlete, Basketball Player)
2402 H St
Bedford, IN 47421-5122, USA

Turner, James A (Jim) (Athlete, Football Player)
14155 W 59th Pl
Arvada, CO 80004-3724, USA

Turner, James Jr (Business Person)
3190 Fairview Park Dr
Falls Church, VA 22042-4530, USA

Turner, James T (Judge)
717 Madison Pl NW
Washington, DC 20439-0001, USA

Turner, Janine (Actor, Model)
c/o Tiffany Smith *Binder & Associates*
1465 Lindacrest Dr
Beverly Hills, CA 90210-2519, USA

Turner, Jerry (Athlete, Baseball Player)
1935 18th St Apt B
Santa Monica, CA 90404-4732, USA

Turner, Jesse
1502 N 5th St
Boise, ID 83702-3703

Turner, Jim (Actor)
c/o Margrit Polak *Margrit Polak Management*
1954 Hillhurst Ave Ste 405
Los Angeles, CA 90027-2722, USA

Turner, John (Athlete, Football Player)
3217 Cedar Ave S
Minneapolis, MN 55407-3802, USA

Turner, John N (Prime Minister)
27 Dunice Rd
Toronto, ON M4V 2W4, CANADA

Turner, Josh (Musician)
c/o Michael (Mike) Esterman
Esterman.Com, LLC
Prefers to be contacted via email
MD, USA

Turner, Karri (Actor)
1875 Century Park E Ste 2250
Los Angeles, CA 90067-2563, USA

Turner, Kathleen (Actor)
c/o Alan Nierob *Rogers & Cowan PR (LA)*
Pacific Design Center 8687 Melrose Ave, 7th Floor
West Hollywood, CA 90069, USA

Turner, Keena (Athlete, Coach, Football Coach, Football Player)
8200 W Erb Way
Tracy, CA 95304-8896, USA

Turner, Ken (Athlete, Baseball Player)
PO Box 252
San Marcos, CA 92079-0252, USA

Turner, Kevin (Athlete, Football Player)
215 Liberty Lake Dr
Vestavia, AL 35242-7567, USA

Turner, Kriss (Producer)
c/o Staff Member *WmE2 (WMA-LA)*
1 William Morris Pl
Beverly Hills, CA 90212-4261, USA

Turner, Kristin (Stylist)
c/o Staff Member *Perrella Management*
330 W 38th St Rm 1407
New York, NY 10018-8435, USA

Turner, Kristopher (Actor)
c/o Shelley Browning *Magnolia Entertainment (LA)*
9595 Wilshire Blvd Ste 601
Beverly Hills, CA 90212-2506, USA

Turner, Lane (Musician)
c/o Staff Member *Paradigm (Monterey)*
404 W Franklin St
Monterey, CA 93940-2303, USA

Turner, Lowri (Actor)
c/o Staff Member *Noel Gay Artists*
19 Denmark St
London WC2H 8NA, United Kingdom

Turner, Marcus (Athlete, Football Player)
5032 Meadow Wood Ave
Lakewood, CA 90712-2855, USA

Turner, Matt (Athlete, Baseball Player)
829 Della Dr
Lexington, KY 40504-2319, USA

Turner, Maurice (Athlete, Football Player)
3558 Tiffany Ln
Shoreview, MN 55126-3072, USA

Turner, Michael (Football Player)
c/o Staff Member *Atlanta Falcons*
4400 Falcon Pkwy
Flowery Branch, GA 30542-3176, USA

Turner, Morrie (Cartoonist)
127 Touchstone Pl
West Sacramento, CA 95691-4612, USA

Turner, Norv (Athlete, Coach, Football Coach, Football Player)
PO Box 400
Del Mar, CA 92014-0400, USA

Turner, Odessa (Athlete, Football Player)
1416 Perry Ave
Bastrop, LA 71220-4213, USA

Turner, Richard (Athlete, Football Player)
408 Piney Oak Dr
Norman, OK 73072-4603, USA

Turner, Ryan (Baseball Player)
1221 Shafter St
San Mateo, CA 94402-2901, USA

Turner, Shane (Athlete, Baseball Player)
3032 Van Reed Rd
Reading, PA 19608-1037, USA

Turner, Shelly N (Stylist)
232 President St Apt 3L
Brooklyn, NY 11231-4325, USA

Turner, Sherri (Athlete, Golfer)
5 Alpine St
Carbondale, CO 81623-9090, USA

Turner, Stacie (Business Person, Reality TV Star)
c/o Staff Member *Bravo (NY)*
30 Rockefeller Plz
New York, NY 10112-0015, USA

Turner, Stansfield
600 New Hampshire Ave NW # 800
Washington, DC 20037-2403, USA

Turner, Ted (Business Person, Producer)
133 Luckie St NW Fl 2
Atlanta, GA 30303-2038, USA

Turner, Thomas (Baseball Player)
4817 Delhi Arnheim Rd
Georgetown, OH 45121-8229, USA

Turner, Tina (Musician)
c/o Steven Manzano *RDWM America*
1158 26th St Ste 564
Santa Monica, CA 90403-4698, USA

Turner, Tyrin (Actor)
c/o David Saunders *Agency for the Performing Arts (APA-LA)*
405 S Beverly Dr Ste 500
Beverly Hills, CA 90212-4425, USA

Turner, Vernon (Athlete, Football Player)
86 Crosshill St
Staten Island, NY 10301-3308, USA

Turner, William (Athlete, Basketball Player)
3271 Wisteria Tree St
Las Vegas, NV 89135-1787, USA

Turnesa, Jim (Golfer)
24 Poplar St
Elmsford, NY 10523-3726, USA

Turnesa, Mike (Golfer)
c/o Staff Member *Pro Golfers Association (PGA) Tour*
112 Tpc Blvd
Ponte Vedra Beach, FL 32082, USA

Turnesa, Willie (Golfer)
41 Sheraton Dr
Poughkeepsie, NY 12601-5629, USA

Turney, Maura
PO Box 5617
Beverly Hills, CA 90209-5617

Turow, Scott (Writer)
c/o Robert (Bob) Bookman *Creative Artists Agency (CAA-LA)*
2000 Avenue of the Stars Ste 100
Los Angeles, CA 90067-4705, USA

Turpin, Mel (Athlete, Basketball Player)
1004 Spring Run Rd
Lexington, KY 40514-1027, USA

Turpin, Miles (Athlete, Football Player)
471 Lexington Cir
Oceanside, CA 92057-7355, USA

Turteltaub, Jon (Director)
500 S Buena Vista St Animation Building Ste 1B
Burbank, CA 91521, USA

Turtles, The
PO Box 1821
Ojai, CA 93024-1821

Turturro, Aida (Actor)
c/o Peg Donegan *Framework Entertainment (LA)*
9057 Nemo St Ste C
West Hollywood, CA 90069-5511, USA

Turturro, John (Actor)
c/o Bart Walker *Cinetic Management*
555 W 25th St Fl 4
New York, NY 10001-5542, USA

Turturro, Nicholas (Actor)
c/o Staff Member *Agency for the Performing Arts (APA-LA)*
405 S Beverly Dr Ste 500
Beverly Hills, CA 90212-4425, USA

Turturro, Nick (Actor)
c/o Adam Griffin *Kritzer Levine Wilkins Entertainment*
11872 La Grange Ave Fl 1
Los Angeles, CA 90025-5283, USA

Tush, Bill
1 City Cnn Ctr Box 105366
Atlanta, GA 30348-5366

Tushingham, Rita
4 Kingly St
London, ENGLAND W1R 5LF

Tuso, Gena (Stylist)
c/o Celebrity Stylist *Cloutier Agency*
2632 La Cienega Ave
Los Angeles, CA 90034-2641, USA

Tuten, Rick (Athlete, Football Player)
1146 SE 15th St
Ocala, FL 34471-4514, USA

Tutera, David (Reality TV Star)
c/o Eda Kalkay *EKPR*
470 Fashion Ave Fl 11
New York, NY 10018-7195, USA

Tutin, Dame Dorothy
13 St Martin's Rd
London, ENGLAND SW9 0SP

Tutson, Tom (Athlete, Football Player)
6655 Poplar Grove Way
Stone Mountain, GA 30087-4791, USA

Tuttle, Matthew Chal (Stylist)
281 Whetstone Creek Rd
Stoneville, NC 27048-7678, USA

Tuttle, Perry (Athlete, Football Player)
14224 King Eider Dr
Charlotte, NC 28273-6714, USA

Tutu, Desmond (Religious Leader)
PO Box 1092
Milnerton, Cape Town 7435, SOUTH AFRICA

Twain, Shania (Actor, Musician)
c/o Peter Mensch *Q Prime South*
729 7th Ave Fl 16
New York, NY 10019-6831, USA

Twardzik, Dave (Athlete, Basketball Player)
1670 Balmy Beach Dr
Apopka, FL 32703-7853, USA

Tway, Bob (Golfer)
6300 Oak Heritage Trl
Edmond, OK 73025-2766, USA

Tweed, Shannon (Actor, Model, Reality TV Star)
c/o Danielle Allman-Del *D2 Management*
141 S Barrington Ave
Los Angeles, CA 90049-3368, USA

Tweeden, Leeann (Actor, Model, Sportscaster)
c/o Jon Orlando *WNWN Media*
348 Hauser Blvd # PH414
Los Angeles, CA 90036-3276, USA

Tweet, Rodney (Athlete, Football Player)
2096 Placita De Vida
Santa Fe, NM 87505-5489, USA

Twiggs, Greg (Golfer)
c/o Staff Member *Pro Golfers Association (PGA) Tour*
112 Tpc Blvd
Ponte Vedra Beach, FL 32082, USA

Twilight Singers (Music Group)
c/o Staff Member *Paradigm (Monterey)*
404 W Franklin St
Monterey, CA 93940-2303, USA

Twilley, Howard J Jr (Athlete, Football Player)
7040 Hill Forest Dr
Dallas, TX 75230-2347, USA

Twilly, Dwight
PO Box 1821
Ojai, CA 93024-1821

Twista (Actor, Musician)
c/o Staff Member *Violator Management*
36 W 25th St Fl 11
New York, NY 10010-2752, USA

Twitchell, Wayne (Athlete, Baseball Player)
5719 SW Brugger St
Portland, OR 97219-4905, USA

Twitty, Howard (Golfer)
8007 E Mercer Ln
Scottsdale, AZ 85260-6563, USA

Twitty, Jeff (Athlete, Baseball Player)
812 Willow Cove Rd
Chapin, SC 29036-8733, USA

Twohy, David (Actor)
c/o John Burnham *International Creative Management (ICM-LA)*
10250 Constellation Blvd Fl 7
Los Angeles, CA 90067-6207, USA

Twohy, Mike (Cartoonist)
605 Beloit Ave
Kensington, CA 94708-1117, USA

Twohy, Robert (Cartoonist)
4 Times Sq
New York, NY 10036-6515, USA

Twyford, Dwan (Business Person)
15 Gramercy Park S Fl 3
New York, NY 10003-1793, USA

Twyman, John K (Jack) (Athlete, Basketball Player, Business Person)
8955 Indian Ridge Ln
Cincinnati, OH 45243-3740, USA

Tydings, Joseph D (Senator)
2705 Pocock Rd
Monkton, MD 21111-2311, USA

Tyers, Kathy (Writer)
204 Park Ave
Madison, NJ 07940-1128, USA

Tykwer, Tom (Actor, Composer, Director, Producer, Writer)
Kurfürstenstrasse 57
Berlin 10785, Germany

Tyler, Aisha (Actor, Comedian)
c/o Jordan Tilzer *ROAR (LA)*
9701 Wilshire Blvd Fl 8
Beverly Hills, CA 90212-2008, USA

Tyler, Anne (Writer)
c/o Staff Member *Random House Publicity*
1745 Broadway
New York, NY 10019-4368, USA

Tyler, Bonnie (Musician, Songwriter, Writer)
c/o Joe Smith *International Creative Management (ICM-LA)*
10250 Constellation Blvd Fl 7
Los Angeles, CA 90067-6207, USA

Tyler, Cory
9955 Balboa Blvd
Northridge, CA 91325-1610

Tyler, Harold R Jr (Attorney, Attorney General, General)
30 Rockefeller Plz
New York, NY 10112-0015, USA

Tyler, James Michael (Actor)
c/o Craig Mobbs *AKA Talent Agency*
6310 San Vicente Blvd Ste 200
Los Angeles, CA 90048-5488, USA

Tyler, Jess (Radio Personality)
c/o Staff Member *WPKX*
1331 Main St Ste 4
Springfield, MA 01103-1621, USA

Tyler, Karmyn (Actor, Musician)
c/o Staff Member *BMI (LA)*
8730 W Sunset Blvd Fl 3
Los Angeles, CA 90069-2210

Tyler, Liv (Actor)
c/o Jason Weinberg *Untitled Entertainment (LA)*
350 S Beverly Dr Ste 200
Beverly Hills, CA 90212-4819, USA

Tyler, Maurice (Athlete, Football Player)
7066 Whitfield Dr
Riverdale, GA 30296-2161, USA

Tyler, Mia (Actor)
c/o Staff Member *Core/Lapides Lear Entertainment*
14724 Ventura Blvd PH
Sherman Oaks, CA 91403-3513, USA

Tyler, Nikki
4F S Main St PMB 307
West Bridgewater, MA 02379-1766

Tyler, Richard (Designer, Fashion Designer)
c/o Staff Member *Richard Tyler*
525 Mission St
S Pasadena, CA 91030-3035, USA

Tyler, Robert (Actor)
1505 10th St
Santa Monica, CA 90401-2805, USA

Tyler, Steven (Musician, Songwriter)
c/o Irving Azoff *Azoff Music Management/ Front Line*
1100 Glendon Ave
Los Angeles, CA 90024-3503, USA

Tyler, Terry (Athlete, Basketball Player)
6500 Tauton Rd NW
Albuquerque, NM 87120-2061, USA

Tyler, Wendell A (Athlete, Football Player)
4083 W Avenue L Apt 294
Quartz Hill, CA 93536-4202, USA

Tyler, Willie
1650 Broadway # 705
New York, NY 10019-6833

Tylo, Hunter (Actor)
11684 Ventura Blvd # 910
Studio City, CA 91604-2699

Tylo, Michael (Actor)
11684 Ventura Blvd # 910
Studio City, CA 91604-2699, USA

Tylo, Noa (DJ)
c/o Len Evans *Project Publicity*
312 W 53rd St Ste 202
New York, NY 10019-5743, USA

Tylski, Richard (Athlete, Football Player)
5456 Tierra Verde Ln
Jacksonville, FL 32258-2281, USA

Tynan, Ronan (Musician)
c/o Lynnette Crouse *CMI Entertainment*
925 E 9th St
Port Angeles, WA 98362-8012, USA

Tyne, George
1449 Benedict Canyon Dr
Beverly Hills, CA 90210-2021

Tyner, Charles (Actor)
6442 Coldwater Canyon Ave Ste 206
Valley Glen, CA 91606-1174, USA

Tyner, Jason (Athlete, Baseball Player)
5535 Sul Ross Ln
Beaumont, TX 77706-3435, USA

Tyner, Tray (Athlete, Golfer)
208 Plantation Path
Boerne, TX 78006-3879, USA

Type O Negative (Music Group)
c/o Staff Member *Helter Skelter (UK)*
535 Kings Rd The Plaza
London SW10 0SZ, UNITED KINGDOM (UK)

Tyree, David (Athlete, Football Player)
15 Fox Hill Dr
Wayne, NJ 07470-2539, USA

Tyree, Jim (Athlete, Football Player)
PO Box 701295
Tulsa, OK 74170-1295, USA

Tyrell, Steve (Musician)
c/o Staff Member *WmE2 (WMA-LA)*
1 William Morris Pl
Beverly Hills, CA 90212-4261, USA

Tyrell, Susan
1489 Scott Ave
Los Angeles, CA 90026-2671

Tyrone, Jim (Athlete, Baseball Player)
1115 Park Vista Dr Apt 703
Arlington, TX 76012-2349, USA

Tyrone, Wayne (Athlete, Baseball Player)
505 Tish Cir Apt 404
Arlington, TX 76006-3549, USA

Tyrrell, Genevieve (Stylist)
c/o Staff Member *Montana Artists Agency*
9150 Wilshire Blvd Ste 100
Beverly Hills, CA 90212-3459, USA

Tyrrell, Susan (Actor)
c/o Staff Member *Don Buchwald & Associates Inc (LA)*
6500 Wilshire Blvd Ste 2200
Los Angeles, CA 90048-4942, USA

Tyrrell, Tim (Athlete, Football Player)
17 Fallstone Dr
Streamwood, IL 60107-1071, USA

Tysoe, Ronald W (Business Person)
151 W 34th St
New York, NY 10001-2101, USA

Tyson, Cathy (Actor)
34-43 Russell St
London WC2B 5HA, UNITED KINGDOM (UK)

Tyson, Cicely (Actor)
c/o Staff Member *WmE2 (WMA-LA)*
1 William Morris Pl
Beverly Hills, CA 90212-4261, USA

Tyson, Dick (Athlete, Football Player)
PO Box 4307
Kansas City, KS 66104-0307, USA

Tyson, Ian (Musician)
60 McGill St
Toronto, ON M5B 1H2, CANADA

Tyson, Mike (Athlete, Baseball Player)
479 Thunderhead Canyon Dr
Ballwin, MO 63011-1736, USA

Tyson, Mike (Athlete, Boxer)
c/o Harlan Werner *Sports Placement Service*
330 W 11th St Apt 105
Los Angeles, CA 90015-2230, USA

Tyson, Neil de Grasse (Physicist)
W 81st St & Central Park
New York, NY 10024, USA

Tyson, Richard (Actor)
c/o Staff Member *Cunningham Escott Slevin & Doherty (CESD-LA)*
10635 Santa Monica Blvd Ste 130
Los Angeles, CA 90025-8306, USA

Tyurin, Mikhail (Cosmonaut)
Moskovskoi Oblasti
Syvisdny Goroduk 141160, RUSSIA

Tyus, Wyomia (Athlete, Track Athlete)
1102 Keniston Ave
Los Angeles, CA 90019-1709, USA

Tzadua, Paulos Cardinal (Religious Leader)
PO Box 2141
Addis Abeba, ETHIOPIA

U

U2 (Musician)
c/o Keryn Kalpan *Principle Management*
250 W 57th St Ste 2120
New York, NY 10107-0001, USA

UB 40
Kensal House 553-579 Harrow Rd.
London, ENGLAND W10 4RH

UB40 (Music Group)
c/o Staff Member *International Talent Booking (ITB - UK)*
27A Floral St Fl 3 Covent Garden
London WC2E 9, UNITED KINGDOM

Ubach, Alanna (Actor)
c/o Staff Member *Margrit Polak Management*
1954 Hillhurst Ave Ste 405
Los Angeles, CA 90027-2722, USA

Uberroth, Peter (Baseball Player)
184 Emerald Bay
Laguna Beach, CA 92651-1209, USA

Ubriaco, Gene (Coach)
2301 Ravine Way
Glenview, IL 60025-7627, USA

Uchida, Irene A (Scientist)
20 N Shore Blvd W
Burlington, ON L7T 1A1, CANADA

Uchida, Mitsuko (Musician)
1133 Broadway Ste 1025
New York, NY 10010-7985, USA

Udenio, Fabiana (Actor)
8730 W Sunset Blvd Ste 220W
Los Angeles, CA 90069-2275, USA

Uderzo, Albert
26 Av Victor Hugo
Paris, FRANCE F-75116

Udhas, Pankaj (Musician)
20-A, Vijay Chambers Opp Dreamlead Cinema, Tribhuvan Rd
Mumbai 400 004, India

Udvari, Frank (Referee)
2-379 Gage Ave
Kitchener, ON N2M 5E1, CANADA

Udy, Helene (Actor)
10877 Wilshire Blvd # 15
Los Angeles, CA 90024-4341, USA

Ueberroth, John A (Business Person)
311 S Wacker Dr Ste 1900
Chicago, IL 60606-6676, USA

Ueberroth, Peter
184 Emerald Bay
Laguna Beach, CA 92651-1209

Ueberroth, Peter V (Misc)
755 Crossover Ln
Memphis, TN 38117-4906, USA

Uecker, Bob (Athlete, Baseball Player)
c/o Deborah Miller *Deborah Miller & Company Management*
9454 Wilshire Blvd Ste 715
Beverly Hills, CA 90212-2925, USA

Uecker, Gunther (Artist)
Dusseldorfer Str 29A
Dusseldorf 40545, GERMANY

Uecker, Keith (Athlete, Football Player)
1230 Sunset View Dr
Akron, OH 44313-7839, USA

Uehara, Koji (Athlete)
c/o Staff Member *SFX Sports Management*
5335 Wisconsin Ave NW Ste 850
Washington, DC 20015-2052, USA

Uelses, John (Athlete, Track Athlete)
30660 Rolling Hills Dr
Valley Center, CA 92082-3351, USA

Uelsmann, Jerry N (Photographer)
5701 SW 17th Dr
Gainesville, FL 32608-5365, USA

Ueltschi, Albert L (Business Person)
Marine Air Terminal LaGuardia Airport
Flushing, NY 11371, USA

Ufland, Len (Actor, Director)
4400 Hillcrest Dr Apt 901
Hollywood, FL 33021-7979, USA

UFO
10 Sutherland
London, ENGLAND W9 24Q

Uggams, Leslie (Actor, Musician)
72 N Village Ave
Rockville Centre, NY 11570-4600, USA

Uggla, Dan (Athlete, Baseball Player)
1400 Jewell Dr
Columbia, TN 38401-5211, USA

Ughi, Uto (Musician)
Cannareggio 4990/E
Venice 30121, ITALY

U-God (Artist)
250 W 57th St
New York, NY 10107-0001, USA

Ugueto, Luis (Athlete, Baseball Player)
6009 188th Ln NE Apt 201
Redmond, WA 98052-6735, USA

Uh Huh Her (Music Group)
c/o Staff Member *Paradigm (Monterey)*
404 W Franklin St
Monterey, CA 93940-2303, USA

Uhl, George (Biologist)
Medical Center Genetics Dept
Baltimore, MD 21218, USA

Uhl, Petr (Activist)
Anglicka 8
Prague 2 120 00, CZECH REPUBLIC

Uhlenbeck, Karen K (Mathematician)
Mathematics Dept
Austin, TX 78712, USA

Uhlenhake, Jeffrey (Athlete, Football Player)
635 Marburn Dr
Columbus, OH 43214-3417, USA

Uhlig, Anneliese
1519 Escalona Dr
Santa Cruz, CA 95060-3311

Uhry, Alfred F (Writer)
226 W 47th St Ste 900
New York, NY 10036-1413, USA

Ujdur, Jerry (Athlete, Baseball Player)
112 Riveness Rd
Duluth, MN 55811-2873, USA

Ukropina, James R (Attorney, Attorney General, Business Person, General)
400 S Hope St
Los Angeles, CA 90071-2801, USA

Ulene, Art (Doctor)
6511 Moore Dr
Los Angeles, CA 90048-5325, USA

Ulevich, Neal (Journalist, Photographer)
2841 Perry St
Iowa City, IA 52245, USA

Ulinski, Ed (Athlete, Football Player)
2860 Lander Rd
Cleveland, OH 44124-4820, USA

Ulion, Gretchen (Athlete, Hockey Player)
22181 Toro Hills Dr
Salinas, CA 93908-1132, USA

Ullger, Scott (Athlete, Baseball Player)
400 Spring St Apt 441
Saint Paul, MN 55102-4454, USA

Ulliel, Gaspard (Actor)
c/o Brinda Bhatt *Innovative Artists (LA)*
9560 Wilshire Blvd Fl 5
Beverly Hills, CA 90212-2401, USA

Ullman, Norman V A (Norm) (Athlete, Hockey Player)
819-25 Austin Dr
Unionville, ON L3R 8H4, Canada

Ullman, Ricky (Actor)
c/o Terry Saperstein *Nani/Saperstein Management*
481 8th Ave # 1575
New York, NY 10001-1809, USA

Ullman, Tracey (Actor, Comedian)
c/o Brian Swardstrom *WmE2 (Endeavor-LA)*
9601 Wilshire Blvd Fl 3
Beverly Hills, CA 90210-5219, USA

Ullmann, Liv J (Actor)
Hafrsfjordgata 7
Oslo N-0273, Norway

Ulloa, Christina (Actor)
c/o Michael Greenwald *Don Buchwald & Associates Inc (LA)*
6500 Wilshire Blvd Ste 2200
Los Angeles, CA 90048-4942, USA

Ullsten, Ola (Prime Minister)
PO Box 6508
Stockholm 11383, SWEDEN

Ulmar, Bin Hassan (Musician)
1775 Broadway Ste 433
New York, NY 10019-1903, USA

Ulmer, Arthur (Athlete, Football Player)
1133 Lloyd Dr
Forest Park, GA 30297-1516, USA

Ulmer, Kristen (Athlete)
3734 Thousand Oaks Cir
Salt Lake City, UT 84124-3905, USA

Ulrich, Chuck (Athlete, Football Player)
4921 Bluffton Pkwy Apt 838
Bluffton, SC 29910-4669, USA

Ulrich, Henry (Admiral)
Commander Naval Striking Force Central Europe & 6th Fleet
FPO, AE 9609, USA

Ulrich, Kim Johnston (Actor)
1801 Avenue of the Stars Ste 902
Los Angeles, CA 90067-5981, USA

Ulrich, Lars (Musician)
729 7th Ave Ste 1600
New York, NY 10019-6880, USA

Ulrich, Laurel T (Historian)
History Dept
Durham, NH 3824, USA

Ulrich, Robert (Business Person)
1000 Nicollet Mall
Minneapolis, MN 55403-2542

Ulrich, Robert J (Business Person)
1000 Nicollet Mall
Minneapolis, MN 55403-2542, USA

Ulrich, Skeet (Actor)
c/o Andrea Pett-Joseph *Brillstein Entertainment Partners*
9150 Wilshire Blvd Ste 350
Beverly Hills, CA 90212-3453, USA

Ulrich, Thomas (Boxer)
Brunsbutteler Damm 29
Berlin 13581, GERMANY

Ultra, Nate (Musician)
451 Washington Ave Apt 5A
Brooklyn, NY 11238-1838, USA

Ulufa'alu, Bartholomew (Prime Minister)
Legakiki Ridge Honiara
Guadacanal, SOLOMON ISLANDS

Ulusu, Bulent (Admiral, Prime Minister)
Ciftehavuzlar Yesilbahar 50K 8/27
Kadikoy/Istanbul, TURKEY

Ulvaeus, Bjorn (Composer, Musician)
Sodra Brobanken 41A Skeppsholmen
Stockholm 11149, SWEDEN

Ulvang, Vegard (Skier)
Fiellveien 53
Kirkenes 9900, NORWAY

Ulyanov, Mikhail A (Actor, Director)
26 Arbat
Moscow 121002, RUSSIA

Umana, Christina (Actor)
c/o Staff Member *TV Caracol*
Calle 76 #11 - 35 Piso 10AA
Bogota DC 26484, COLOMBIA

Umbach, Arnie (Athlete, Baseball Player)
760 Moores Mill Rd
Auburn, AL 36830-6032, USA

Umbarger, Jim (Athlete, Baseball Player)
3082 Maritime Forest Dr
Johns Island, SC 29455, USA

Umberger, Andy (Actor)
c/o Claire Miller *Bauman Redanty & Shaul Agency*
5757 Wilshire Blvd Suite 473
Beverly Hills, CA 90212, USA

Umbers, Mark (Actor)
c/o Nick Frenkel *3 Arts Entertainment Inc*
9460 Wilshire Blvd Fl 7
Beverly Hills, CA 90212-2713, USA

Umermoto, Nanako (Architect)
118 E 59th St
New York, NY 10022-1310, USA

Umphlett, Tommy (Athlete, Baseball Player)
104 Berkley Rd
Ahoskie, NC 27910-9575, USA

Umphrey's McGee (Music Group)
c/o Staff Member *Paradigm (Monterey)*
404 W Franklin St
Monterey, CA 93940-2303, USA

Umrao, Singh (War Hero)
Old Admiralty Building
London SW1A 2BL, UNITED KINGDOM (UK)

Umrigar, Jeannine (Stylist)
c/o Staff Member *Stockland Martel*
343 E 18th St
New York, NY 10003-2802, USA

Unanue, Emil R (Misc)
Medical School Pathology Dept
Saint Louis, MO 63110, USA

Underhill, Barbara (Figure Skater)
c/o Staff Member *Guelph Storm Hockey Club*
55 Wyndham St N
Guelph, ON N1H 7T8, Canada

Underwood, Blair (Actor)
c/o Ron West *Thruline Entertainment*
9250 Wilshire Blvd Ground Fl
Beverly Hills, CA 90212, USA

Underwood, Carrie (Musician)
c/o Ann Edulblute *19 Entertainment - LA*
33/32 Ransomes Dock 35-37 Parkgate Rd
London SW11 4NP, UK

Underwood, Jacob (Musician)
7380 W Sand Lake Rd # 350
Orlando, FL 32819-5248, USA

Underwood, Jay (Actor)
6100 Wilshire Blvd Ste 1170
Los Angeles, CA 90048-5116, USA

Underwood, Matthew (Actor)
c/o Glenn Hughes III *Gem Entertainment Group*
10701 Wilshire Blvd Apt 1202
Los Angeles, CA 90024-4437, USA

Underwood, Olen (Athlete, Football Player)
302 N Main St
Conroe, TX 77301-2810, USA

Underwood, Pat (Athlete, Baseball Player)
708 Riverview Dr
Kokomo, IN 46901-7024, USA

Underwood, Ron (Director)
9560 Wilshire Blvd Ste 500
Beverly Hills, CA 90212-2401, USA

Underwood, Sarah Jean (Actor)
c/o Matt Cohen *IAG Entertainment & Sports*
5189 Argonne Ct
San Diego, CA 92117-1054, USA

Underwood, Scott (Musician)
80 Mason St
Greenwich, CT 06830-5515, USA

Underwood, Tom (Athlete, Baseball Player)
13595 83rd Ln N
West Palm Beach, FL 33412-2331, USA

Ungaro, Emanuel M (Designer, Fashion Designer)
2 Ave du Montaigne
Paris 75008, FRANCE

Ungaro, Susan Kelliher (Editor)
375 Lexington Ave
New York, NY 10017-5514, USA

Unger, Brian
5750 Wilshire Blvd
Los Angeles, CA 90036-3697

Unger, Brian (Television Host)
c/o Staff Member *Extra (LA)*
1840 Victory Blvd
Glendale, CA 91201-2558, USA

Unger, Deborah Kara (Actor)
c/o Sarah Jackson *Seven Summits Pictures & Management*
8906 W Olympic Blvd Ground Floor
Beverly Hills, CA 90211, USA

Unger, Garry D (Athlete, Hockey Player)
5315 E 93rd St
Tulsa, OK 74137-4415, USA

Unger, Jim (Cartoonist)
4520 Main St
Kansas City, MO 64111-1876, USA

Unger, Leonard (Diplomat)
31 Amherst Rd
Belmont, MA 02478-2102, USA

Ungers, Oswald M (Architect)
Belvederestr 60
Cologne 50933, GERMANY

Union, Gabrielle (Actor)
c/o Jeff Morrone *Jeff Morrone Entertainment*
9350 Wilshire Blvd Ste 224
Beverly Hills, CA 90212-3204, USA

Union, Sarah (Actor)
c/o Jason Barrett *Alchemy Entertainment*
7024 Melrose Ave Ste 420
Los Angeles, CA 90038-3394, USA

Unkefer, Ronald A (Business Person)
1600 Harbor Bay Pkwy
Alameda, CA 94502-3085, USA

Uno, Osamu (Business Person)
1-46 Showacho Hamadera Sakai
Osaka 592, JAPAN

Unroe, Tim (Athlete, Baseball Player)
2719 S Joplin
Mesa, AZ 85209-2508, USA

Unruh, James A (Business Person)
5426 E Morrison Ln
Paradise Valley, AZ 85253-3017, USA

Unseld, Westley S (Wes) (Athlete, Basketball Player, Coach)
2210 Cedar Circle Dr
Catonsville, MD 21228, USA

Unser, Alfred (Al) Jr (Race Car Driver)
PO Box 56696
Albuquerque, NM 87187-6696, USA

Unser, Del (Athlete, Baseball Player)
33516 N 79th Way
Scottsdale, AZ 85266-4244, USA

Unser, Robert W (Bobby) (Race Car Driver)
7700 Central Ave SW
Albuquerque, NM 87121-2113, USA

Unser Sr, Alfred (Al) (Race Car Driver)
7625 Central Ave NW
Albuquerque, NM 87121-2115, USA

Unutoa, Morris (Athlete, Football Player)
821B Country Club Pkwy
Mount Laurel, NJ 08054-2714, USA

Upatnieks, Juris (Engineer)
2662 Valley Dr
Ann Arbor, MI 48103-2748, USA

Upbin, Lori (Stylist)
37 Greenacres Ave
Scarsdale, NY 10583-1413, USA

Upchurch, Rickie (Rick) (Athlete, Football Player)
463 Hagens Aly
Mesquite, NV 89027-5815, USA

Upham, Dr Steadman (Educator)
President's Office
Tulsa, OK 74104, USA

Upham, John (Athlete, Baseball Player)
1502 Pierre Ave
Windsor, ON N8X 4P5, Canada

Upham, Misty (Actor)
c/o Molly Conners *Rogues Gallery*
20 Clinton St Apt C7
New York, NY 10002-1755, USA

Uphoff-Becker, Nicole (Horse Racer)
Freiherr-von-Lanen-Str 15
Warendorf 48231, GERMANY

Upshaw, Marv (Athlete, Football Player)
3851 Madrone Ave
Oakland, CA 94619-2731, USA

Upshaw, Regan (Athlete, Football Player)
21300 Redskin Park Dr
Ashburn, VA 20147-6100, USA

Upshaw, Willie (Athlete, Baseball Player)
193 Osborne Ln
Southport, CT 06890-1192, USA

Upton, Arthur C (Physicist)
250 E Alameda St Apt 636
Santa Fe, NM 87501-6205, USA

Upton, Fred (Congressman, Politician)
157 S Kalamazoo Mall Ste 180
Kalamazoo, MI 49007-4827, USA

Upton, Melvin (B J) (Athlete, Baseball Player)
637 Riviera Dr
Tampa, FL 33606-3809, USA

Upton, Tom (Athlete, Baseball Player)
4753 Canehill Ave
Lakewood, CA 90713-2411, USA

Urb, Johann (Actor)
c/o Lena Roklin *Luber Roklin Management*
8530 Wilshire Blvd Ste 550
Beverly Hills, CA 90211-3133, USA

Urban, Karl (Actor)
c/o Jennifer Rawlings *WmE2 (Endeavor-LA)*
9601 Wilshire Blvd Fl 3
Beverly Hills, CA 90210-5219, USA

Urban, Keith (Musician)
c/o Gary Borman *Moir / Borman Entertainment*
1250 6th St Ste 401
Santa Monica, CA 90401-1638, USA

Urban, Thomas N (Business Person)
Capital Square 400 Locust St
Des Moines, IA 50309, USA

Urban, Tim (Musician)
c/o Simon Fuller *XIX Entertainment*
33/32 Ransomes Dock 35-37 Parkgate Rd
London SW11 4NP, UK

Urbanchek, Jon (Coach)
Athletic Dept
Ann Arbor, MI 48109, USA

Urbanek, Karel (President)
Kvetna 54
Brno, CZECHOSLOVAKIA

Urbani, Tom (Athlete, Baseball Player)
578 Country Oaks
Greenville, TX 75401-1074, USA

Urbano, Mike (Musician)
c/o Staff Member *Creative Artists Agency (CAA-LA)*
2000 Avenue of the Stars Ste 100
Los Angeles, CA 90067-4705, USA

Urbanova, Eva (Opera Singer)
Narodni Divadlo
Prague 1, CZECH REPUBLIC

Urbanski, Douglas (Actor, Producer, Writer)
9713 Little Santa Monica Blvd Suite 218
Beverly Hills, CA 90210, USA

Urbina, Ugueth U (Athlete, Baseball Player)
Venezuela

Urch, Scott (Athlete, Football Player)
645 Foxboro Dr
Avon, IN 46123-7185, USA

Ure, Midge (Musician)
#8 Glenthome 115A Glenhome Hammersm
London W6 0LJ, UNITED KINGDOM (UK)

Uremovich, Emil P (Athlete, Football Player)
2935 S County Road 210
Knox, IN 46534-7968, USA

Urenda, Herman (Athlete, Football Player)
4105 Mountcastle Way
San Jose, CA 95136-1755, USA

Uresti, Omar (Golfer)
2503 Pebble Beach Dr
Austin, TX 78747-1618, USA

Urguhart, Lawrence M (Business Person)
Business Park Theale
Reading RG7 4SA, UNITED KINGDOM (UK)

Uribe, Diane (Actor)
23874 Via Jacara
Valencia, CA 91355-2520, USA

Urich, Justin (Actor)
5670 Wilshire Blvd Ste 820
Los Angeles, CA 90036-5613, USA

Urie, Brendon (Musician)
c/o Staff Member *Fueled By Ramen*
PO Box 1803
Tampa, FL 33601-1803, USA

Urie, Michael (Actor)
c/o Sarah Jackson *Seven Summits Pictures & Management*
8906 W Olympic Blvd Ground Floor
Beverly Hills, CA 90211, USA

Urkal, Oklay (Boxer)
Bautzener Str 4
Berlin 10829, GERMANY

Urlacher, Brian (Football Player)
c/o Staff Member *Chicago Bears*
1000 Football Dr
Lake Forest, IL 60045

Urmanov, Aleksei (Figure Skater)
Luzhnetskaya Nab 8
Moscow 119871, RUSSIA

Urmanov, Alexei
Luzhnetskaya nab. 8
Moscow, RUSSIA 119871

Urmson, Claire (Model)
c/o Staff Member *Ford Models (NY)*
238 E 4th St
New York, NY 10009-7425

Urquhart, Brian E (Diplomat)
Howard Farms Jerusalem Road
Tyringham, MA 1264, USA

Urrea, John (Athlete, Baseball Player)
9312 Palm St Apt 201
Bellflower, CA 90706-6263, USA

Urseth, Bonnie (Actor)
c/o Staff Member *Gage Group, The (LA)*
14724 Ventura Blvd Ste 505
Sherman Oaks, CA 91403-3505, USA

Urshan, Nathaniel A (Religious Leader)
8855 Dunn Rd
Hazelwood, MO 63042-2212, USA

Ursi, Corrado Cardinal (Religious Leader)
Via Capodimonte 13
Naples 80136, ITALY

Usachyov, Yuri V (Cosmonaut)
Moskovskoi Oblasti
Syvisdny Goroduk 141160, RUSSIA

Usaher (Actor, Artist)
3996 Pleasantville Rd # 104A
Dovaville, GA 30340, USA

Used, The (Music Group)
c/o Staff Member *Freeze Artist Management*
27783 Hidden Trail Rd
Laguna Hills, CA 92653-7821

Usery, William J Jr (Secretary)
1101 S Arlington Ridge Rd
Arlington, VA 22202-1951, USA

Usher, Bob (Athlete, Baseball Player)
1022 N 5th St
San Jose, CA 95112-4413, USA

Usher, Paul (Actor)
c/o Staff Member *Qdos Entertainment*
8 King St Covent Garden
London WC2 8HN, UNITED KINGDOM

Usher, Thomas J (Business Person)
600 Grant St
Pittsburgh, PA 15219-2702, USA

Ushkowitz, Jenna (Actor)
c/o Jill Fritzo *PMK/BNC Public Relations (PMK-NY)*
622 3rd Ave Fl 8
New York, NY 10017-6707, USA

Uslan, Michael (Producer, Writer)
333 Crestmont Rd
Cedar Grove, NJ 07009-1907, USA

Usova, Maya (Figure Skater)
300 Alumni Rd
Newington, CT 06111-1868, USA

Ustvolskaya, Galina I (Composer)
Prospect Gagarina 27 #72
Saint Petersburg 196135, RUSSIA

Ut, Nick (Photographer)
221 S Figueroa St Ste 300
Los Angeles, CA 90012-2552, USA

Utay, William (Actor)
c/o Staff Member *Days of Our Lives*
3000 W Alameda Ave
Burbank, CA 91523-0001, USA

Uteem, Cassam (President)
Le Redult
Port Louis, MAURITIUS

Utley, Adrian (Musician)
Saga Centre 326 Kensal Road
London W10 5BZ, UNITED KINGDOM (UK)

Utley, Chase (Athlete, Baseball Player)
620 Avery Pl
Long Beach, CA 90807-3102, USA

Utley, Garrick (Correspondent)
News Dept 8 Carburton St
London W1P 7DT, UNITED KINGDOM (UK)

Utley, Mike (Athlete, Football Player)
PO Box 349
Orondo, WA 98843-0349, USA

Utley, Stan (Golfer)
20701 N Scottsdale Rd # 107-619
Scottsdale, AZ 85255-6413, USA

Utt, Ben (Athlete, Football Player)
143 Blackland Rd NW
Atlanta, GA 30342-4419, USA

Utzon, Jorn (Architect)
Hellebaek 3150, DENMARK

Uyeda, Seiya (Geophysicist, Physicist)
2-39-6 Daizawa Setagayaku
Tokyo 113, JAPAN

Uzawa, Hirofumi (Economist)
Higashi 1-3-6 Hoya
Tokyo, JAPAN

V

V, Michael (Stylist)
c/o Staff Member *Koko Represents*
166 Geary St Ste 1007
San Francisco, CA 94108-5623, USA

V Gopalakrishnan (Actor)
11D4 Habibullah Road T Nagar
Chennai, TN 600 017, INDIA

V. Gutterrez, Luis (Congressman, Politician)
2266 Rayburn Hob
Washington, DC 20515-0308, USA

V. Johnson, Timothy (Congressman, Politician)
1207 Longworth Hob
Washington, DC 20515-4201, USA

V M T Chaarllee (Actor)
Plot No 11 Kamarajar Nagar II Street
Sathya Gardens Saligramam
Chennai, TN 600 093, INDIA

Vaamonde, Lisa (Stylist)
c/o Staff Member *Team*
423 W Broadway Ste 406
Boston, MA 02127-2265, USA

Vaca, Joselito (Soccer Player)
14800 Quorum Dr Ste 300
Dallas, TX 75254-1442, USA

Vacano, Jost (Cinematographer)
Leoprechtingstr 18
Munich 81739, GERMANY

Vacanti, Charles A (Doctor)
Anesthesiology Dept
Worcester, MA 2139, USA

Vacariou, Nicolae (Prime Minister)
Piata Revolutiei
Bucharest 71243, ROMANIA

Vacariu, Alina (Model)
c/o Staff Member *Elite Model Management - Los Angeles*
345 N Maple Dr Ste 176
Beverly Hills, CA 90210-5193, USA

Vaccaro, Brenda (Actor)
c/o Stephen (Steve) LaManna *Innovative Artists (LA)*
1505 10th St
Santa Monica, CA 90401-2805, USA

Vacendak, Steve (Athlete, Basketball Player)
608 Gaston St Ste 100
Raleigh, NC 27603-1258, USA

Vachon, Christine (Producer)
c/o Staff Member *Killer Films (US)*
63 Flushing Ave Unit 341
Brooklyn, NY 11205-1084, USA

Vachon, Louis-Albert Cardinal (Religious Leader)
1 Rue Des Remparts
Quebec, QC G1R 5LY, CANADA

Vachon, Paul (Wrestler)
RR 4
Mansonville, QC J0E 1X0, CANADA

Vachon, Rogatien R (Rogie) (Athlete, Coach, Hockey Player)
2228 Glyndon Ave
Venice, CA 90291-4043, USA

Vactor, Ted (Athlete, Football Player)
11504 Channing Dr
Wheaton, MD 20902-2908, USA

Vadivukkarasi (Actor, Bollywood)
49/1A Sadulla St
Chennai, TN 600017, INDIA

Vadsaria, Dilshad (Actor)
c/o Staff Member *Kass & Stokes Management*
9229 W Sunset Blvd Ste 504
Los Angeles, CA 90069-3405, USA

Vaduva, Leontina (Opera Singer)
Glaburgstr 95
Frankfurt 60318, GERMANY

Vaea of Houma, Baron (Prime Minister)
Nuku'alofa, TONGA

Vagelos, P Roy (Biologist, Business Person)
1 Crossroads Dr # 500
Bedminster, NJ 07921-2688, USA

Vaglica, James (Actor)
c/o Lisa Lobel *Boston Casting Inc*
129 Braintree St Ste 107
Boston, MA 02134-1613, USA

Vago, Constantin (Misc)
Place Eugene Bataillon
Montpellier 34095, FRANCE

Vahi, Tiit (Prime Minister)
Kuhlbarsi 1
Tallinn 104, ESTONIA

Vai, Steve (Musician)
c/o Ruta Seopetys *Sepetys Entertainment Group*
5543 Edmondson Pike Ste 8A
Nashville, TN 37211-5808, USA

Vaidisova, Nicole (Tennis Player)
c/o Staff Member *IMG (Cleveland)*
1360 E 9th St Ste 100
Cleveland, OH 44114-1730, USA

Vaidyanathan, Aparna (Actor, Bollywood)
520 19th Cross 14th Main Benasankari 2nd Stage
Bangalore, KA 560070, INDIA

Vail, Justina (Actor)
651 N Kilkea Dr
Los Angeles, CA 90048-2213, USA

Vail, Mike (Athlete, Baseball Player)
2348 Aztec Ruin Way
Henderson, NV 89044-4496, USA

Vail, Thomas (Editor)
1801 Superior Ave E
Cleveland, OH 44114-2107, USA

Vaishnavi (Actor, Bollywood)
2 Sambandam Street G North Chetty Rd
Chennai, TN 600017, INDIA

Vajiralongkorn (Prince)
Chirtalad a Villa
Bangkok, THAILAND

Vajna, Andrew (Andy) (Filmmaker, Producer)
c/o Staff Member *C-2 Pictures*
2308 Broadway
Santa Monica, CA 90404-2916, USA

Vajpayee, Atal Bihari (Prime Minister)
6 Raisina Rd
New Delhi, Delhi 110011, INDIA

Valabik, Boris (Athlete, Hockey Player)
13 S Avenue SE
Atlanta, GA 30315, USA

Valance, Holly (Musician)
c/o Andrew Edwards *Wishlab*
2438 Canyon Oak Dr
Los Angeles, CA 90068-2428, USA

Valandrey, Charlotte (Actor)
c/o Staff Member *ArtMedia*
20 avenue Rapp
Paris 75008, France

Valar, Paul (Skier)
34 Hubertus Ring
Franconia, NH 03580-5114, USA

Valastro, Buddy (Chef)
95 Washington St
Hoboken, NJ 07030-4533, USA

Valderrama, Carlos (Soccer Player)
555 17th St Ste 3350
Denver, CO 80202-3909, USA

Valderrama, Wilmer (Actor)
c/o Glenn Rigberg *HYPHENATE*
9701 Wilshire Blvd Fl 10
Beverly Hills, CA 90212-2010, USA

Valdes, Jesus (Chucho) (Musician)
278 Main St
Gloucester, MA 01930-6022, USA

Valdes, Mark (Athlete, Baseball Player)
7519 Paula Dr
Tampa, FL 33615-4113, USA

Valdes, Maximiano (Conductor)
3436 Springhill Rd
Lafayette, CA 94549-2535, USA

Valdes, Roy (Athlete, Baseball Player)
8725 SW 83rd St
Miami, FL 33173-4135, USA

Valdespino, Sandy (Athlete, Baseball Player)
3937 Lilac Haze St
Las Vegas, NV 89147-6841, USA

Valdes-Rodriguez, Alisa (Writer)
c/o Staff Member *Greater Talent Network Inc*
437 5th Ave Fl 7
New York, NY 10016-2205, USA

Valdez, Ismael (Athlete, Baseball Player)
4001 26th St
Vero Beach, FL 32960-1930, USA

Valdez, Luis (Writer)
705 4th St
San Juan Bautista, CA 95045, USA

Valdivielso, Jose (Athlete, Baseball Player)
14 Rita Dr
Mount Sinai, NY 11766-2215, USA

Vale, Angelica (Actor)
c/o Staff Member *Televisa*
Blvd Adolfo Lopez Mateos 232 Colonia San Angel INN
DF CP 01060, MEXICO

Vale, Jerry (Musician)
40960 Glenmore Dr
Palm Desert, CA 92260-1665, USA

Vale, Tina (Musician)
9268 W 3rd St
Beverly Hills, CA 90210-3713, USA

Vale, Virginia
4039 Edenhurst Ave
Los Angeles, CA 90039-1469

Valek, Vladimir (Conductor)
Na Vapennem 6
Prague 4 140 00, CZECH REPUBLIC

Valen, Nancy (Actor)
c/o Michael Livingston *Leavitt Talent Group*
8255 W Sunset Blvd
West Hollywood, CA 90046-2417, USA

Valensi, Nick (Musician)
c/o Staff Member *MVO Ltd*
307 7th Ave Rm 807
New York, NY 10001-6066, USA

Valent, Eric (Athlete, Baseball Player)
107 Lengle Ave
Wernersville, PA 19565-1331, USA

Valente, Catarina (Musician)
Villa Corallo Via Ai Ronci
Danbury, CT 06816-0001, SWITZERLAND

Valente, Caterina (Musician)
Casella Postale 91 6976 Castagnola
SWITZERLAND

Valenti, Carl M (Publisher)
200 Liberty St
New York, NY 10281-1003, USA

Valentin, Barbara (Actor)
Hans-Sachs-Str 22
Munich 80469, GERMANY

Valentin, Dave (Musician)
103 Westwood Dr
Miami Springs, FL 33166, USA

Valentin, John (Athlete, Baseball Player)
37 Golden Ln
Hazlet, NJ 07730-2538, USA

Valentin, Jose (Athlete, Baseball Player)
PO Box 50746
Phoenix, AZ 85076-0746, USA

Valentine, Bill (Baseball Player)
15 Blue Ridge Cir
Little Rock, AR 72207-1901, USA

Valentine, Bill (Athlete, Baseball Player)
15 Blue Ridge Cir
Little Rock, AR 72207-1901, USA

Valentine, Brooke (Musician)
c/o Staff Member *Virgin Records (NY)*
150 5th Ave Fl 7
New York, NY 10011-4372, USA

Valentine, Chris (Athlete, Hockey Player)
1565 Maple Grove Rd
Kanata, ON K2V 1A3, Canada

Valentine, Dan (Business Person)
1551 McCarthy Blvd
Milpitas, CA 95035-7437, USA

Valentine, Darnell (Athlete, Basketball Player)
7546 SW Ashford St
Portland, OR 97224-7143, USA

Valentine, Donald T (Business Person)
495 E Java Dr
Sunnyvale, CA 94089-1125, USA

Valentine, Ellis (Athlete, Baseball Player)
2708 Bridgemarker Dr
Grand Prairie, TX 75054-7262, USA

Valentine, Fred (Athlete, Baseball Player)
4838 Blagden Ave NW
Washington, DC 20011-3716, USA

Valentine, Gary (Actor, Comedian)
c/o Staff Member *Anonymous Content (AC-LA)*
3531 Hayden Ave
Culver City, CA 90232, USA

Valentine, James (Musician)
c/o Staff Member *Creative Artists Agency (CAA-LA)*
2000 Avenue of the Stars Ste 100
Los Angeles, CA 90067-4705, USA

Valentine, James W (Biologist)
1351 Glendale Ave
Berkeley, CA 94708-2025, USA

Valentine, Joe (Athlete, Baseball Player)
4168 Chiffon Ln
North Port, FL 34287-3236, USA

Valentine, Karen (Actor)
PO Box 1410
Washington Depot, CT 06793-0410, USA

Valentine, Kym (Actor)
P O Box 463
Elwood, Victoria 3184, AUSTRALIA

Valentine, Raymond C (Misc)
Plant Growth Laboratory
Davis, CA 95616, USA

Valentine, Robert J (Bobby) (Athlete, Baseball Player, Coach)
71 Wynnewood Ln
Stamford, CT 06903-1931, USA

Valentine, Scott (Actor)
17465 Flanders St
Granada Hills, CA 91344-2211, USA

Valentine, Stacy (Adult Film Star)
200 W Houston St
New York, NY 10014-4828, USA

Valentine, Steve (Actor)
c/o Nicholas Bogner *Affirmative Entertainment*
425 N Robertson Blvd
West Hollywood, CA 90048-1735, USA

Valentine, Victoria
PO Box 12324
La Crescenta, CA 91224-5324

Valentine, William N (Doctor)
2128 Quail Point Cir
Medford, OR 97504-4523, USA

Valentine, Zack (Athlete, Football Player)
162 Harvest Rd
Swedesboro, NJ 08085-1427, USA

Valentinetti, Vito (Athlete, Baseball Player)
271 Summit Ave
Mount Vernon, NY 10552-3309, USA

Valentino, Bobby (Musician)
c/o Staff Member *Island Def Jam Music Group*
825 8th Ave Fl 28
New York, NY 10019-7416

Valentino, Kristen (Stylist)
c/o Staff Member *Crews*
828 Clemont Dr NE
Atlanta, GA 30306-3694, USA

Valenzuela, Fernando (Athlete, Baseball Player)
2123 N Beachwood Dr
Los Angeles, CA 90068-3403, USA

Valeriani, Richard G (Correspondent)
23 Island View Dr
Sherman, CT 06784-2036, USA

Valetta, Amber (Model)
c/o Dan Spilo *Industry Entertainment Partners*
955 Carrillo Dr Ste 300
Los Angeles, CA 90048-5400, USA

Valiant, Leslie G (Scientist)
50 Tyler Rd
Belmont, MA 02478-2023, USA

Valiee, Bert L (Doctor)
300 Boyksti St # 712
Boston, MA 2116, USA

Valle, Aurora (Actor)
c/o Staff Member *TV Azteca*
Periferico Sur 4121 Colonia Fuentes del Pedregal
DF CP 14141, Mexico

Valle, Dave (Athlete, Baseball Player)
2260 95th Ave NE
Clyde Hill, WA 98004-2516, USA

Valle, Hector (Athlete, Baseball Player)
P.O. Box 5909 College Sta
Mayaguez, PR 681, USA

Vallely, James (Jim) (Writer)
c/o Staff Member *Creative Artists Agency (CAA-LA)*
2000 Avenue of the Stars Ste 100
Los Angeles, CA 90067-4705, USA

Vallely, John (Athlete, Basketball Player)
2042 Commodore Rd
Newport Beach, CA 92660-4306, USA

Valletta, Amber (Actor, Model)
c/o Lee Daniels *Lee Daniels Entertainment*
315 W 36th St Rm 1002
New York, NY 10018-6526, USA

Valley, Mark (Actor)
c/o Christine Tripicchio *WKT Public Relations (WKT-LA)*
9350 Wilshire Blvd Ste 450
Beverly Hills, CA 90212-3230, USA

Vallez, Emilio (Football Player)
General Delivery
Polvadera, NM 87828-9999, USA

Valli, Frankie (Musician)
c/o Staff Member *Motown Records (LA)*
6255 W Sunset Blvd Fl 18
Los Angeles, CA 90028-7419, USA

Vallien, Bertil (Artist)
Roleks Vall 93 Visby
621, SWEDEN

Vallina, Dea (Stylist)
14521 Crossway Ct
Chesterfield, MO 63017-8017, USA

Vallone, Raf
Viale R. Bacone 14
Rome, ITALY

Valo, Ville (Musician)
P.O. Box 194
Helsinki FIN-00121, Finland

Valot, Daniel L (Business Person)
900 19th St
Denver, CO 80202, USA

Valtman, Edmund S (Cartoonist, Editor)
9 Rundelane
Bloomfield, CT 06002-1522, USA

Valverde, Jose (Athlete, Baseball Player)
773 W Raven Dr
Chandler, AZ 85286-4484, USA

Valverde, Rawley
15207 Magnolia Blvd Unit 106
Sherman Oaks, CA 91403-1105

Van, Allen (Athlete, Hockey Player)
4890 Ashley Ln Apt 206
Inver Grove Heights, MN 55077-1234, USA

Van, Joey
48607 Presidential Dr # 2
Macomb, MI 48044-1985

Van Allsburg, Chris (Writer)
c/o Houghton Mifflin Children's Books
222 Berkeley St 8th Fl
Boston, MA 2116, USA

Van Ark, Joan (Actor)
c/o Konrad Leh *Creative Talent Group*
1900 Avenue of the Stars Ste 2475
Los Angeles, CA 90067-4512, USA

Van Benschoten, John (Athlete, Baseball Player)
5918 Milburne Dr
Milford, OH 45150-4101, USA

Van Brabant, Ozzie (Athlete, Baseball Player)
5389 William Dr
Lexington, MI 48450-8864, USA

Van Breda Kolff, Jan (Athlete, Basketball Player)
1102 French Town Ln
Franklin, TN 37067-4666, USA

Van Buren, Ebert (Athlete, Football Player)
2100 Highway 165 S
Monroe, LA 71202-8219, USA

Van Buren, Jermaine (Athlete, Baseball Player)
557 Acree Ln
Columbus, OH 43228-8907, USA

Van Buren, Steve (Athlete, Football Player)
2121 George Halas Dr NW
Canton, OH 44708-2630, USA

Van Burkleo, Ty (Athlete, Baseball Player)
19681 Rabon Valley Rd
Grass Valley, CA 95949-8166, USA

Van Cuyk, Johnny (Athlete, Baseball Player)
2096 11th Ave SE Apt A
Rochester, MN 55904-2943, USA

Van Dam, Rob (Actor)
c/o Staff Member *Coast to Coast Talent Group*
3350 Barham Blvd
Los Angeles, CA 90068-1404, USA

Van Damme, Jean-Claude (Actor)
4502 Wood St
Erie, PA 16509-1639, USA

Van Der Beek, James (Actor)
c/o Daniel (Danny) Sussman *Brillstein Entertainment Partners*
9150 Wilshire Blvd Ste 350
Beverly Hills, CA 90212-3453, USA

Van Der Meer, Johnny
4005 W Leona St
Tampa, FL 33629-8506

Van Der Perren, Kevin (Figure Skater)
Dr W Drees laan 35
Goes 4463 XE, NETHERLANDS

Van der Pol, Anneliese (Actor, Musician)
c/o Victoria Morris *Kazarian Spencer Ruskin & Assoc.*
11969 Ventura Blvd Ste 300
Studio City, CA 91604-2619, USA

Van Derbur-Alter, Marilyn
1401 17th St Ste 600
Denver, CO 80202-1485

Van Devere, Trish (Actor)
7036 Grasswood Ave
Malibu, CA 90265-4247, USA

Van Dien, Casper (Actor)
c/o Barry McPherson *Agency for the Performing Arts (APA-LA)*
405 S Beverly Dr Ste 500
Beverly Hills, CA 90212-4425, USA

Van Doren, Mamie (Actor)
3419 Via Lido # 184
Newport Beach, CA 92663-3908, USA

Van Dusen, Fred (Athlete, Baseball Player)
331 Gillette Dr
Franklin, TN 37069-4195, USA

Van Dusen, Granville
10974 Alta View Dr
Studio City, CA 91604-3903

Van Dyk, Paul (DJ, Musician)
c/o Joel Zimmerman *WmE2 (WMA-NY)*
1325 Avenue of the Americas
New York, NY 10019-6026, USA

Van Dyke, Barry (Actor)
27800 Blythedale Rd
Agoura, CA 91301-1824, USA

Van Dyke, Bruce (Athlete, Football Player)
143 Lakeview Dr
Mc Murray, PA 15317-2747, USA

Van Dyke, Dick (Actor)
23215 Mariposa De Oro St
Malibu, CA 90265-4909, USA

Van Dyke, Jerry
c/o Staff Member *J Cast Productions*
2550 Greenvalley Rd
Los Angeles, CA 90046-1438

Van Dyke, Leroy
29000 Highway V
Smithton, MO 65350-3629

Van Eeghen, Mark (Athlete, Football Player)
2207 Station Cir
Dedham, MA 02026-4588, USA

Van Egmond, Tim (Athlete, Baseball Player)
8839 Callaway Rd
Gay, GA 30218-1817, USA

Van Eman, Charles
12304 Santa Monica Blvd Ste 104
Los Angeles, CA 90025-2586

Van Every, Hal (Athlete, Football Player)
2700 W 54th St
Minneapolis, MN 55410-2510, USA

Van Exel, Nick (Athlete, Basketball Player)
3102 Noble Lakes Ln
Houston, TX 77082-6809, USA

Van Galder, Tim (Athlete, Football Player)
11851 Charlemagne Dr
Maryland Heights, MO 63043-1505, USA

Van Gorder, Dave (Athlete, Baseball Player)
212 Black Eagle Ave
Henderson, NV 89002-9234, USA

Van Gorkum, Harry (Actor)
2490 Cheremoya Ave
Los Angeles, CA 90068-3070, USA

Van Gundy, Jeff (Sportscaster)
c/o Staff Member *WmE2 (WMA-LA)*
1 William Morris Pl
Beverly Hills, CA 90212-4261, USA

Van Halen (Music Group)
c/o Jonny (Jon) Podell *Podell Talent Agency LLC*
22 W 21st St Fl 9
New York, NY 10010-7095, USA

Van Halen, Alex (Musician)
c/o Irving Azoff *Azoff Music Management/ Front Line*
1100 Glendon Ave
Los Angeles, CA 90024-3503, USA

Van Halen, Eddie (Musician)
c/o Irving Azoff *Azoff Music Management/ Front Line*
1100 Glendon Ave
Los Angeles, CA 90024-3503, USA

Van Hekken, Andy (Athlete, Baseball Player)
4742 64th St
Holland, MI 49423-8980, USA

Van Heusen, Billy (Athlete, Football Player)
835 Hudson St
Denver, CO 80220-4436, USA

Van Hollen, Chris (Congressman, Politician)
51 Monroe St Ste 507
Rockville, MD 20850-2406, USA

Van Holt, Brian (Actor)
c/o Brad Schenck *Paradigm (LA)*
360 N Crescent Dr
Beverly Hills, CA 90210-4874, USA

Van Horn, Doug (Athlete, Football Player)
149 Feronia Way
Rutherford, NJ 07070-2437, USA

Van Horn, Kelly (Producer, Writer)
c/o Staff Member *Mirisch Agency*
8840 Wilshire Blvd Ste 100
Beverly Hills, CA 90211-2606, USA

Van Horn, Patrick
9200 W Sunset Blvd Ste 1130
Los Angeles, CA 90069-3606

Van Horne, Keith (Football Player)
c/o Staff Member *Dallas Mavericks*
2500 Victory Ave
Dallas, TX 75219-7601, USA

Van Houten, Leslie
#W13378 Bed #1B314U CA Inst. for Women16756 Chino Corona
Frontera, CA 91720

Van Impe, Ed (Athlete, Hockey Player)
3601 S Broad St Ste 2
Philadelphia, PA 19148-5250, USA

van Johnson, Rodney (Actor)
c/o Staff Member *Passions*
4024 Radford Ave
Studio City, CA 91604-2101, USA

Van Kemp, Merete
10000 Santa Monica Blvd # 305
Los Angeles, CA 90067

Van Kempen, Simon (Reality TV Star)
c/o Staff Member *Bravo (NY)*
30 Rockefeller Plz
New York, NY 10112-0015, USA

Van Keulen, Isabelle (Musician)
c/o Staff Member *Columbia Artists Mgmt Inc*
1790 Broadway Fl 6
New York, NY 10019-1537, USA

Van Landingham, William (Athlete, Baseball Player)
3023 Old Hillsboro Rd
Franklin, TN 37064-9544, USA

van Nistelrooy, Ruud (Soccer Player)
c/o Staff Member *Manchester United PLC*
Sir Matt Busby Way Old Trafford
Manchester M160RA, UNITED KINGDOM

Van Note, Jeff (Athlete, Football Player)
345 Hollyberry Dr
Roswell, GA 30076-1215, USA

Van Noy, Jay (Athlete, Baseball Player)
1092 N 1700 E
Logan, UT 84341-3024, USA

Van Patten, Dick (Actor)
c/o Daniel Bernstein *Bernstein Entertainment*
3869 Tilden Ave Apt 15
Culver City, CA 90232-3965, USA

Van Patten, James
14411 Riverside Dr Apt 15
Sherman Oaks, CA 91423-1739

Van Patten, Joyce
c/o Staff Member *Silver Massetti & Szatmary (SMS) Talent Inc*
8730 W Sunset Blvd Ste 440
Los Angeles, CA 90069-2277, USA

Van Patten, Nels
14411 Riverside Dr Apt 18
Sherman Oaks, CA 91423-1740

Van Patten, Tim (Actor, Director, Writer)
c/o Jeffrey Jacobs *Creative Artists Agency (CAA-LA)*
2000 Avenue of the Stars Ste 100
Los Angeles, CA 90067-4705, USA

Van Patten, Timothy
13920 Magnolia Blvd
Sherman Oaks, CA 91423-1230

Van Patten, Vincent
13926 Magnolia Blvd
Sherman Oaks, CA 91423-1230

Van Peebles, Mario (Actor, Director, Producer)
c/o Vincent Cirrincione *Vincent Cirrincione Associates*
1516 N Fairfax Ave
Los Angeles, CA 90046-2608, USA

Van Pelt, Alex (Athlete, Football Player)
6621 Stonington Dr N
Tampa, FL 33647-1177, USA

Van Pelt, Bo (Athlete, Golfer)
c/o Jim Lehrman *SFX Golf*
36855 W Main St Ste 200
Purcellville, VA 20132-3561, USA

Van Pier, Andre
PO Box 555
New York, NY 10156-0555, USA

Van Poppel, Todd (Athlete, Baseball Player)
340 Springfield Bnd
Argyle, TX 76226-6848, USA

Van Praagh, James (Actor, Producer, Writer)
PO Box 60517
Pasadena, CA 91116-6517, USA

Van Raaphorst, Dick (Athlete, Football Player)
720 Devon Ct
San Diego, CA 92109-8005, USA

Van Ryn, Ben (Athlete, Baseball Player)
PO Box 672572
Chugiak, AK 99567-2572, USA

Van Sant, Doug G (Director)
c/o Gabrielle (Gaby) Morgerman *WmE2 (Endeavor-LA)*
9601 Wilshire Blvd Fl 3
Beverly Hills, CA 90210-5219, USA

Van Sant, Gus (Actor, Director, Producer, Writer)
c/o Gabrielle (Gaby) Morgerman *WmE2 (Endeavor-LA)*
9601 Wilshire Blvd Fl 3
Beverly Hills, CA 90210-5219, USA

Van Sant-Machado, Helene (Baseball Player)
8172 Walnut Villa Way
Fair Oaks, CA 95628-2775, USA

Van Slyke, Andy (Athlete, Baseball Player)
710 S Price Rd
Saint Louis, MO 63124-1867, USA

Van Susteren, Greta (Television Host)
c/o Staff Member *Fox News Channel (NY)*
1211 Ave Of The Americas Level C1
New York, NY 10036-8701, USA

Van Valkenberg, Pete (Athlete, Football Player)
3072 Ninebark Cir
Saint George, UT 84790-8226, USA

Van Valkenburgh, Deborah
2025 Stanley Hills Dr
Los Angeles, CA 90046-7752

Van Varenberg, Kristopher (Actor)
c/o Jack Gilardi *International Creative Management (ICM-LA)*
10250 Constellation Blvd Fl 7
Los Angeles, CA 90067-6207, USA

Van Vleet, Michael (Baseball Player)
118 Dreamfield Dr
Battle Creek, MI 49014-7846, USA

Van Vleet, Michael (Athlete, Baseball Player)
8462 Grapevine Cir
Mattawan, MI 49071-8433, USA

Van Vooren, Monique
165 E 66th St
New York, NY 10065-6132

Van Wageningen, Yorick (Actor)
c/o Staff Member *Nine Yards Entertainment*
8530 Wilshire Blvd Ste 550
Beverly Hills, CA 90211-3133, USA

Van Wagner, James (Athlete, Football Player)
5246 N Royal Dr
Traverse City, MI 49684-6984, USA

Van Winkle, Travis (Actor)
c/o Scott Fish *Vital Management Group (VMG)*
5225 Wilshire Blvd Ste 303
Los Angeles, CA 90036-4347, USA

Van Wormer, Steve (Actor)
c/o Staff Member *Innovative Artists (LA)*
1505 10th St
Santa Monica, CA 90401-2805, USA

Van Zandt, Caitlin (Actor)
40 E 9th St Apt 11J
New York, NY 10003-6426, USA

Van Zandt, Steven (Actor)
c/o Staff Member *Renegade Nation Holdings*
434 Sixth Ave Suite 6R
New York, NY 10011, USA

Van Zant, Donnie (Musician)
c/o Staff Member *Vector Management*
PO Box 120479
Nashville, TN 37212-0479, USA

Van Zee, Margie (Stylist)
17207 E Rand Dr
Fountain Hills, AZ 85268-5033, USA

Van Zeeland, Kathy (Designer)
1359 Broadway Fl 21
New York, NY 10018-7824, USA

VanAllen, James A (Physicist)
PO Box 1460
Iowa City, IA 52244-1460, USA

VanAllen, Richard (Opera Singer)
18 Octavia St
London SW11 3DN, UNITED KINGDOM (UK)

VanAlmsick, Franziska (Franzi) (Swimmer)
Bizetstr 1
Berlin 13088, GERMANY

VanAmerongen, Jerry (Cartoonist)
10926 Owensmouth Ave
Chatsworth, CA 91311-1342, USA

VanArsdale, Dick (Athlete, Basketball Player)
5816 N Dragoon Ln
Paradise Valley, AZ 85253-5210, USA

VanArsdale, Tom (Athlete, Basketball Player)
7510 N Eucalyptus Dr
Paradise Valley, AZ 85253-3319, USA

Vanasse, Karine (Actor)
c/o Lainie Sorkin Becky *Management 360*
9111 Wilshire Blvd
Beverly Hills, CA 90210-5508, USA

VanAuken, John A (Misc)
PO Box 1538
Sydney, NS B1P 6R7, CANADA

VanBasten, Marco (Soccer Player)
Via Turati 3
Milan 20121, ITALY

VanBerg, John C (Jack) (Coach)
420 Fair Hill Dr # 1
Elkton, MD 21921-2573, USA

Vanbiesbrouck, John (Athlete, Hockey Player)
PO Box 1514
Sault Sainte Marie, MI 49783-7514, USA

VanCamp, Emily (Actor)
c/o Marc Hamou *Thruline Entertainment*
9250 Wilshire Blvd Ground Fl
Beverly Hills, CA 90212, USA

Vance, Cory (Athlete, Baseball Player)
1321 Surrey Rd
Vandalia, OH 45377-1646, USA

Vance, Courtney B (Actor, Producer)
c/o Steven Siebert *Lighthouse Entertainment*
9220 W Sunset Blvd Ste 200
West Hollywood, CA 90069-3501, USA

Vance, Cyrus
425 Lexington Ave
New York, NY 10017-3903

Vance, Eric (Athlete, Football Player)
17613 Archland Pass Rd
Lutz, FL 33558-8034, USA

Vance, Gene (Athlete, Basketball Player)
6 Carriage Way
Champaign, IL 61821-5119, USA

Vance, Judy (Stylist)
720 S Stone Ave
La Grange, IL 60525-2724, USA

Vance, Kenny (Musician)
PO Box 116
Fort Tilden, NY 11695-0116, USA

Vance, Robert S (Judge)
1800 5th Ave N
Birmingham, AL 35203-2111, USA

Vance, Sandy (Athlete, Baseball Player)
5863 Chelton Dr
Oakland, CA 94611-2423, USA

VanCitters, Robert L (Psychic)
Medical School Physiology Dept
Seattle, WA 98815, USA

VanClief, D G (Race Car Driver)
PO Box 8
Esmont, VA 22937-0008, USA

VanCulin, Samuel (Religious Leader)
43 Trinity Square
London EC3N 4DJ, UNITED KINGDOM (UK)

VanDam, Jose (Opera Singer)
Rutistr 52
Zurich, Gockhausen 8044, SWITZERLAND

VanDantzig, Rudi (Choreographer)
Emma-Straat 27
Amsterdam, NETHERLANDS

Vande Berg, Ed (Athlete, Baseball Player)
4903 S Meadows Pl
Chandler, AZ 85248-5460, USA

Vandeman, George
1600 Waverly Rd
San Marino, CA 91108-2038

Vanden Bosch, Kyle (Athlete, Football Player)
2331 E Cedar Pl
Chandler, AZ 85249-4101, USA

VandenBerg, Lodewijk (Astronaut)
7887 Bryan Dairy Rd Ste 100
Largo, FL 33777-1452, USA

VandenBergh, M A (Business Person)
30 Van Bylandtlaan
Hague, HR 2596, NETHERLANDS

VanDenHoogenband, Pieter (Athlete, Swimmer)
PO Box 302
Amhem, AH 6800, NETHERLANDS

Vander, Jagt Guy (Misc)
1050 Connecticut Ave NW
Washington, DC 20036-5303, USA

Vander, Musetta (Actor)
c/o Jeff Goldberg *Jeff Goldberg Management*
817 Monte Leon Dr
Beverly Hills, CA 90210-2629, USA

Vander Wal, John (Athlete, Baseball Player)
5142 Abbeydale Dr SE
Grand Rapids, MI 49546-7565, USA

Vanderbeek, Matt (Athlete, Football Player)
4 Monstad St
Aliso Viejo, CA 92656-6246, USA

Vanderberg Shaw, Helen (Coach)
301 14th St NW
Calgary, AB T2N 2A1, CANADA

Vanderbilt, Gloria (Writer)
c/o Staff Member *HarperCollins Publishers*
10 E 53rd St C/O Author Mail Floor 7
New York, NY 10022, USA

Vanderbundt, Skip (Athlete, Football Player)
4225 Los Coches Way
Sacramento, CA 95864-5241, USA

Vanderhoef, Larry N (Educator)
President's Office
Davis, CA 95616, USA

Vanderkelen, Ron (Athlete, Football Player)
5300 Vernon Ave S Apt 102
Edina, MN 55436-2328, USA

Vanderlip-Ozburn, Dolly (Baseball Player)
N2844 Smith Valley Rd # RR2
La Crosse, WI 54601-2935, USA

Vanderloo, Mark (Model)
300 Park Ave S # 200
New York, NY 10010-5313, USA

VanDerMeer, Simon (Nobel Prize Laureate)
4 Chemin Des Corbillettes
Saconnex, GD 1218, SWITZERLAND

Vandermeersch, Bernard (Misc)
Anthropology Dept
Bordeaux, FRANCE

Vanderpump, Lisa (Business Person, Reality TV Star)
c/o Bette Smith *Bette Smith Management*
499 N Canon Dr
Beverly Hills, CA 90210-4887, USA

Vandersea, Phil (Athlete, Football Player)
34 Hunting Ave
Shrewsbury, MA 01545-3177, USA

Vanderveen, Loet (Artist)
Lime Creek 5
Big Sur, CA 93920, USA

VanDerveer, Tara (Athlete, Basketball Player, Coach)
1036 Cascade Dr
Menlo Park, CA 94025-6629, USA

Vandervoort, Laura (Actor)
c/o Staff Member *Levine Okwu Erickson Management*
6363 Wilshire Blvd Ste 300
Los Angeles, CA 90048-5729, USA

VandeSande, Theo A (Cinematographer)
2337 High Oak Dr
Los Angeles, CA 90068-2515, USA

Vandeweghe, Coco (Athlete, Tennis Player)
c/o Staff Member *Women's Tennis Association (WTA (UK))*
Palliser House Palliser Rd
London W149EB, UK

Vandeweghe, Ernie (Athlete, Basketball Player)
18025 Green Meadow Dr
Encino, CA 91316-4424, USA

Vandeweghe, Kiki (Athlete, Basketball Player)
c/o Staff Member *Denver Nuggets*
1000 Chopper Cir
Denver, CO 80204-5805, USA

VandeWetering, John E (Educator)
2500 East Ave Apt 4X
Rochester, NY 14610-3170, USA

Vandis, Titos
1930 Century Park W # 303
Los Angeles, CA 90067-6802

VanDusen, Granville (Actor)
10974 Alta View Dr
Studio City, CA 91604-3903, USA

VanDyke, Philip (Actor)
1464 Madera Rd # 108N
Simi Valley, CA 93065-3077, USA

Vaneck, Pierre (Actor)
c/o Staff Member *Cineart*
36 Rue de Ponthieu
Paris F-75008, France

Vangelis (Musician)
c/o Staff Member *Robert Urband & Associates*
8981 W Sunset Blvd Ste 311
W Hollywood, CA 90069-1881, USA

VanGundy, Stan (Coach)
c/o Team Member *Orlando Magic*
8701 Maitland Summit Blvd
Orlando, FL 32810-5915, USA

VanHorn, Buddy (Director)
4409 Ponca Ave
Toluca Lake, CA 91602-2513, USA

Vanilla Fudge
141 Dunbar Ave
Fords, NJ 08863-1551

Vann, Marc (Actor)
c/o Staff Member *McCabe Group, The*
3211 Cahuenga Blvd W Ste 104
Los Angeles, CA 90068-1372, USA

Vannelli, Gino
28205 Agoura Rd
Agoura Hills, CA 91301-2482

Vanner, Sue
26 Wellesley Rd Cheswick
London, ENGLAND W4 4BN

Vanous, Lucky (Actor, Model)
28345 La Calenta Msn
Vlejo, CA 92692, USA

Vanover, Larry (Baseball Player)
801 Glenn Ct
Owensboro, KY 42303-0520, USA

Vanover, Larry (Athlete, Baseball Player)
3037 Sterling Ct
Owensboro, KY 42303-6393, USA

Vanover, Tamarick (Athlete, Football Player)
703 NW Wilson St
Lake City, FL 32055-1863, USA

Vanoy, Vern (Athlete, Football Player)
3710 E 51st St Apt 409
Kansas City, MO 64130-3061, USA

VanSanten, Shantel (Actor)
c/o Loch Powell *Leverage Management*
3030 Pennsylvania Ave
Santa Monica, CA 90404-4112, USA

Vansina, Jan M J (Historian)
2810 Ridge Rd
Madison, WI 53705-5224, USA

Vanska, Osmo
1111 Nicollet Ave
Minneapolis, MN 55403-2406, USA

VanValkenburgh, Deborah (Actor)
PO Box 1515
Studio City, CA 91614-0515, USA

Vanvieren, Pete (Baseball Player, Sportscaster)
12260 Magnolia Cir
Alpharetta, GA 30005-7234, USA

Vanzant, Iyanla (Reality TV Star, Writer)
c/o Jerome Martin *Jerome Martin Management*
Prefers to be contacted via telephone
Los Angeles, CA 90024, USA

Vapors, The
44 Valmoral Dr. Woking
Surrey, ENGLAND

Varada, Vaclav (Athlete, Hockey Player)
9042 Stonebriar Dr
Clarence Center, NY 14032, USA

Varda, Agnes (Director)
86 Rue Daguerre
Paris 75014, FRANCE

Vardalos, Nia (Actor)
c/o Peter Safran *The Safran Company*
8748 Holloway Dr
West Hollywood, CA 90069-2327, USA

Vardell, Tommy (Athlete, Football Player)
2424 E Ruby Hill Dr
Pleasanton, CA 94566-5100, USA

Varela, Leonor (Actor)
c/o Adam Griffin *Kritzer Levine Wilkins Entertainment*
11872 La Grange Ave Fl 1
Los Angeles, CA 90025-5283, USA

Varga, Imre (Artist)
Bartha Utca 1
Budapest XII, HUNGARY

Vargas, Elizabeth (Television Host)
c/o Staff Member *ABC News*
77 W 66th St Fl 3
New York, NY 10023-6201, USA

Vargas, Jacob (Actor)
c/o Matt Luber *Luber Roklin Management*
8530 Wilshire Blvd Ste 550
Beverly Hills, CA 90211-3133, USA

Vargas, Jason (Athlete, Baseball Player)
14775 Keota Ln
Apple Valley, CA 92307-5137, USA

Vargas, Jay R (War Hero)
12466 Thombrush Ct
San Diego, CA 92131, USA

Vargas, Ramon (Opera Singer)
165 W 57th St
New York, NY 10019-2201, USA

Vargas, Roberto (Baseball Player)
Urb Runoz Rivera 24 Calle Brizaida
Guaynabo, PR 00969-3529, USA

Vargas, Valentina (Actor)
5 Rue Norvins
Paris 75018, FRANCE

Vargo, Ed (Athlete, Baseball Player)
101 Freedom Rd
Butler, PA 16001-1304, USA

Vargo, Larry (Athlete, Football Player)
23337 S Colonial Ct
Saint Clair Shores, MI 48080-2605, USA

Vargo, Tim (Business Person)
123 S Front St
Memphis, TN 38103-3607, USA

Varian, Hal R (Economist)
576 Del Amigo Rd
Danville, CA 94526-3215, USA

Varitek, Jason (Athlete, Baseball Player)
c/o Scott Boras *Boras Corporation*
18 Corporate Plaza Dr
Newport Beach, CA 92660-7901, USA

Varma, Indira (Actor)
c/o Tammy Rosen *Sanders Armstrong Caserta*
425 N Robertson Blvd
West Hollywood, CA 90048-1735, USA

Varmus, Harold E (Nobel Prize Laureate)
1275 York Ave
New York, NY 10065-6007, USA

Varnado, Victor (Actor, Comedian)
1600 Broadway # 410
New York, NY 10019-7413, USA

Varney, Pete (Athlete, Baseball Player)
14 Juniper Ridge Rd
Acton, MA 01720-2213, USA

Varo, Marton (Artist)
PO Box 5807
Carmel, CA 93921-5807, USA

Varoni, Miguel (Actor)
c/o Oswaldo Pisfil *NCM Productions*
10770 NW 66th St Apt 512
Doral, FL 33178-3781, USA

Varrela, Leonor (Actor)
c/o Mimi DiTrani *Schiff Company, The*
8440 Warner Dr Ste B1
Culver City, CA 90232-2461, USA

Varrichione, Frank
55 Dinsmore Ave Apt 103
Framingham, MA 01702-6054

Varrichone, Frank (Athlete, Football Player)
RR 72 Box 319
Alton, NJ 3809, USA

Varshavsky, Alexander (Biologist)
Cell Biology
Pasadena, CA 91125-0001, USA

Varsho, Gary (Athlete, Baseball Player, Coach)
11921 Starr Rd
Chili, WI 54420-9502, USA

Vartan, Michael (Actor)
c/o Stephen Hanks *Stephen Hanks Management*
252 N Larchmont Blvd Ste 200
Los Angeles, CA 90004-3754, USA

Vartan, Sylvie (Musician)
706 N Beverly Dr
Beverly Hills, CA 90210-3322, USA

Varty, Keith (Designer, Fashion Designer)
Bosco di San Francesco #6
Sirolo, ITALY

Varvatos, John (Designer, Fashion Designer)
315 Bowery
New York, NY 10003-7151, USA

Vasarely, Victor
83 Rue Aux Religues
Annet-sur-Marne, FRANCE F-77410

Vasary, Tamas (Musician)
9 Village Road
London N3, UNITED KINGDOM (UK)

Vasicek, Victor (Athlete, Football Player)
1502 Douglas Ave
Midland, TX 79701-4056, USA

Vasilak, Peg (Stylist)
5544 N Glenwood Ave
Chicago, IL 60640-1235, USA

Vasile, Radu (Prime Minister)
Piata Vicotriel 1
Bucharest 71201, ROMANIA

Vasilyev, Vladimir V (Ballerina, Dancer)
Teatralnaya Pl 1
Moscow 103009, RUSSIA

Vasquez, Juan F (Judge)
400 2nd St NW
Washington, DC 20217-0001, USA

Vasquez, Junior (DJ, Musician)
647 9th Ave Apt 3
New York, NY 10036-3661, USA

Vasquez, LaLa (Television Host)
c/o Deborah Williams *Deborah Williams Management*
28 W 96th St Apt 5
New York, NY 10025-6596, USA

Vasquez, Rana Mario (Publisher)
Guillermo Prieto 7
Mexico City, DF, MEXICO

Vasquez, Randy
10600 Holman Ave Apt 1
Los Angeles, CA 90024-5931

Vass, Irene (Stylist)
270 Park Ave S Apt 8D
New York, NY 10010-6105, USA

Vass, Zita (Actor)
c/o Kim Matuka *Online Talent Group*
Prefers to be contacted via email or telephone
Los Angeles, CA 90069, USA

Vasser, Jimmy (Race Car Driver)
2398 Broadway St
San Francisco, CA 94115-1234, USA

Vassey, Liz (Actor)
c/o Nevin Dolcefino *Innovative Artists (LA)*
1505 10th St
Santa Monica, CA 90401-2805, USA

Vassilieva, Sofia (Actor)
c/o Jason Trawick *WmE2 (Endeavor-LA)*
9601 Wilshire Blvd Fl 3
Beverly Hills, CA 90210-5219, USA

Vassillou, George V (President)
PO Box 874 21 Academiou Ave
Aglandjia, Nicosia, CYPRUS

Vasu, P (Actor, Bollywood)
25 D Tilak Street T Nagar
Chennai, TN 600017, INDIA

Vaswani, Vivek (Actor, Bollywood)
141 142 Dalamal Park Cuffe Parade
Bombay, MS 400 005, INDIA

Vasys, Arunas (Athlete, Football Player)
2525 Hanford Ln
Aurora, IL 60502-6971, USA

Vasyuchenko, Yuri (Ballerina, Dancer)
Teatralnaya Pl 1
Moscow 103009, RUSSIA

Vasyutin, Vladimir V (Cricketer)
Moskovskoi Oblasti
Syvisdny Goroduk 141160, RUSSIA

Vataha, Randy (Athlete, Football Player)
36 Longmeadow Rd
Lincoln, MA 01773-4810, USA

Vatcher, Jim (Athlete, Baseball Player)
16039 Northfield St
Pacific Palisades, CA 90272-4261, USA

Vatterott, Charles (Athlete, Football Player)
662 W Forest Dr
Houston, TX 77079-6916, USA

Vaughan, Charlie (Athlete, Baseball Player)
5717 Brazilwood Ct
Harlingen, TX 78552-2027, USA

Vaughan, Denis E (Musician)
c/o Staff Member *Schofer/Gold Agency*
51 Riverside Dr
New York, NY 10024, USA

Vaughan, Greg (Actor)
c/o Alex Cole *Elevate Entertainment*
10100 Santa Monica Blvd Ste 300
Los Angeles, CA 90067-4107, USA

Vaughan, Jimmie (Musician)
c/o Staff Member *Monterey International (Chicago)*
200 W Superior St Ste 202
Chicago, IL 60654-6422, USA

Vaughan, Martha (Biologist)
11608 W Hill Dr
Rockville, MD 20852-3751, USA

Vaughan, Peter (Actor)
76 Oxford St
London W1N 0AX, UNITED KINGDOM (UK)

Vaughan, Porter (Athlete, Baseball Player)
2931 Polo Pkwy
Midlothian, VA 23113-1453, USA

Vaughan, Stoll (Musician)
c/o Staff Member *Paradigm (Monterey)*
404 W Franklin St
Monterey, CA 93940-2303, USA

Vaughn, Bruce (Golfer)
5615 N Monroe St
Hutchinson, KS 67502-3251, USA

Vaughn, Charles (Athlete, Basketball Player)
PO Box 95
Cairo, IL 62914-0095, USA

Vaughn, Countess (Actor)
c/o Staff Member *Amsel, Eisenstadt & Frazier Talent Agency (AEF)*
5055 Wilshire Blvd Ste 860
Los Angeles, CA 90036-6108, USA

Vaughn, Damian (Athlete, Football Player)
423 Danvers Ct
Orrville, OH 44667-9579, USA

Vaughn, David (Basketball Player)
390 Murray Hill Pkwy
East Rutherford, NJ 07073-2109, USA

Vaughn, Dewayne (Athlete, Baseball Player)
5501 NW 37th St
Warr Acres, OK 73122-2210, USA

Vaughn, Gregory L (Greg) (Athlete, Baseball Player)
10830 Sheldon Woods Way
Elk Grove, CA 95624-9630, USA

Vaughn, Jacque (Basketball Player)
190 Marietta St NW
Atlanta, GA 30303-2762, USA

Vaughn, Jimmie (Musician)
PO Box 29480
Austin, TX 78755-6480, USA

Vaughn, John H (Johnny) (Athlete, Coach, Football Player)
Highway 6 W
Oxford, MS 38655, USA

Vaughn, Jonathan S (Jon) (Athlete, Football Player)
224 N US Highway 67
Florissant, MO 63031-5904, USA

Vaughn, Kip (Baseball Player)
1820 Wildbrook Ct Apt C
Concord, CA 94521-1464, USA

Vaughn, Linda (Race Car Driver)
PO Box 352
Newville, PA 17241-0352, USA

Vaughn, Matthew (Actor)
c/o Cynthia Pett-Dante *Brillstein Entertainment Partners*
9150 Wilshire Blvd Ste 350
Beverly Hills, CA 90212-3453, USA

Vaughn, Maurice S (Mo) (Athlete, Baseball Player)
28 Ave at Port Imperial Apt 340
West New York, NJ 07093-8387, USA

Vaughn, Ned (Actor)
3500 W Olive Ave Ste 920
Burbank, CA 91505-5514, USA

Vaughn, Robert (Actor)
PO Box 2071
Los Angeles, CA 90051-0071, USA

Vaughn, Terri J (Actor)
c/o Sandra Siegal *Siegal Company, The*
9025 Wilshire Blvd Ste 400
Beverly Hills, CA 90211-1828, USA

Vaughn, Thomas R (Athlete, Football Player)
860 E Linda Ln
Gilbert, AZ 85234-5969, USA

Vaughn, Vince (Actor)
c/o Alan Nierob *Rogers & Cowan PR (LA)*
Pacific Design Center 8687 Melrose Ave, 7th Floor
West Hollywood, CA 90069, USA

Vaught, Loy (Athlete, Basketball Player)
1289 Perkins Ave NE
Grand Rapids, MI 49505-5625, USA

Vaugier, Emmanuelle (Actor)
c/o David (Dave) Fleming *Mosaic Media Group*
9200 W Sunset Blvd Ste 10
Los Angeles, CA 90069-3608, USA

Vavra, Otakar (Director, Writer)
Smetanova Nabrezo 2
Prague 1 11000, CZECH REPUBLIC

Vayda, Brandon Michael (Actor)
c/o Omar Mayet *Gel Entertainment*
9255 W Sunset Blvd Ste 803
Los Angeles, CA 90069-3305, USA

Vaynerchuk, Gary (Business Person, Writer)
c/o Staff Member *Vaynermedia*
586 Morris Ave
Springfield, NJ 07081-1017, USA

Vaziri, Khosrow (Wrestler)
c/o Nick Cordasco *Prince Marketing Group*
18 Carillon Cir
Livingston, NJ 07039-2600, USA

Vazquez, Armondo (Baseball Player)
160 W 85th St Apt 1K
New York, NY 10024-4410, USA

Vazquez, Javier (Athlete, Baseball Player)
1441 S Prairie Ave
Chicago, IL 60605-2886, USA

Vazquez, LaLa (Actor)
c/o Shannon Barr *Shannon Barr Public Relations*
3313 N Sepulveda Blvd
Manhattan Beach, CA 90266-3626, USA

Vazquez, Yul (Actor)
c/o Sarah Fargo *Paradigm (NY)*
360 N Crescent Dr
Beverly Hills, CA 90210-4874, USA

Veal, Coot (Athlete, Baseball Player)
238 Stonegables Dr
Gray, GA 31032-5526, USA

Veale, Robert A (Bob) (Athlete, Baseball Player)
2833 Bush Blvd
Birmingham, AL 35208-2227, USA

Veals, Elton (Athlete, Football Player)
2981 Joyce Dr
Baton Rouge, LA 70814-2568, USA

Veasey, Josephine (Opera Singer)
5 Meadow Biew Whitechurch
Hunts RG28 7BL, UNITED KINGDOM (UK)

Vecchione, Mike (Scientist)
14th & Constitution
Washington, DC 20230, USA

Vecsei, Eva H (Architect)
1425 Rue Du Ft
Montreal, QC H3H 2C2, CANADA

Vedder, Eddie (Musician)
c/o Kelly Curtis *Curtis Management*
1900 S Corgiat Dr
Seattle, WA 98108-2817, USA

Vee, Bobby (Musician, Songwriter, Writer)
St Ives Eden Road
Gordon, Berwickshire TD3 6JT, Scotland

Veerapha, P S (Actor, Bollywood)
Porur
Chennai, TN 600116, INDIA

Vega, Alexa (Actor, Musician)
1801 Avenue of the Stars Ste 902
Los Angeles, CA 90067-5981, USA

Vega, Antonio (Stylist)
c/o Staff Member *Zenobia Agency Inc*
PO Box 909
Groveland, CA 95321-0909, USA

Vega, Paz (Actor)
c/o Scott Henderson *WmE2 (Endeavor-LA)*
9601 Wilshire Blvd Fl 3
Beverly Hills, CA 90210-5219, USA

Vega, Suzanne (Musician)
c/o Staff Member *WmE2 (WMA-NY)*
1325 Avenue of the Americas
New York, NY 10019-6026, USA

Vega 4 (Music Group)
c/o Staff Member *Paradigm (Monterey)*
404 W Franklin St
Monterey, CA 93940-2303, USA

Vegas, Dirty (Music Group)
c/o Staff Member *Creative Artists Agency (CAA-LA)*
2000 Avenue of the Stars Ste 100
Los Angeles, CA 90067-4705, USA

Veigel, Al (Athlete, Baseball Player)
1907 Dover Ave
Dover, OH 44622-2426, USA

Veil, Simone (Government Official)
11 Place Vauban
Paris 75007, FRANCE

Veils, The (Music Group)
c/o Staff Member *Paradigm (Monterey)*
404 W Franklin St
Monterey, CA 93940-2303, USA

Veingrad, Alan (Athlete, Football Player)
614 SE 26th Ave
Fort Lauderdale, FL 33301-2708, USA

Vejar, Chico (Boxer)
56 Glenbrook Rd # 3214
Stamford, CT 6902, USA

Vejtasa, Stanley W (Swede) (War Hero)
1649 Summit Ln
Escondido, CA 92025-7535, USA

Vel Johnson, Reginald (Actor)
1501 Broadway Ste 703
New York, NY 10036-5501

Velaquez, Nydia M. (Congressman, Politician)
266 Broadway Ste 201
Brooklyn, NY 11211-6306, USA

Velarde, Randy (Athlete, Baseball Player)
4902 Thames Ct
Midland, TX 79705-1796, USA

Velasquez, Cain (Athlete)
c/o Bob Cook *Zinkin Entertainment & Sports Management*
5 E River Park Pl W Ste 203
Fresno, CA 93720-1557, USA

Velasquez, Guillermo (Athlete, Baseball Player)
13842 Clear Trail Ln
Houston, TX 77034-2158, USA

Velasquez, Jaci (Musician)
PO Box 158659
Nashville, TN 37215-8659, USA

Velasquez, Jorge
770 Allerton Ave
Bronx, NY 10467-8879

Velasquez, Jorge L Jr (Jockey)
770 Allerton Ave
Bronx, NY 10467-8879, USA

Velasquez, Patricia (Actor, Model)
c/o Ivan De Paz *DePaz Management*
2011 N Vermont Ave
Los Angeles, CA 90027-1931, USA

Velazquez, Freddie (Athlete, Baseball Player)
Jose Amado Soler No. 70
Santo Domingo, Dominican Republic

Velazquez, Nadine (Actor, Model)
c/o Courtney Kivowitz *Schiff Company, The*
8440 Warner Dr Ste B1
Culver City, CA 90232-2461, USA

Velez, Eddie (Actor)
c/o Staff Member *Stone Manners Salners Agency (LA)*
9911 W Pico Blvd Ste 1400
Los Angeles, CA 90035-2715, USA

Velez, Gloria (Model)
c/o Michael (Mike) Esterman
Esterman.Com, LLC
Prefers to be contacted via email
MD, USA

Velez, Lauren (Actor)
c/o Staff Member *Gersh (LA)*
9465 Wilshire Blvd Ste 600
Beverly Hills, CA 90212-2612, USA

Velez, Lisa Lisa (Musician)
c/o Staff Member *WmE2 (WMA-LA)*
1 William Morris Pl
Beverly Hills, CA 90212-4261, USA

Velez, Mia (Stylist)
c/o Staff Member *Blink Management*
421 Washington Ave Ste 202
Miami Beach, FL 33139-6612, USA

Velez, Otto (Baseball Player)
33 Villas De Cambalache
Rio Grande, PR 966, USA

Velez-Mitchell, Jane (Actor, Correspondent)
c/o Staff Member *NS Bienstock Inc*
250 W 57th St Ste 333
New York, NY 10107-0302, USA

Velga, Carlos A Wahnon de C (Prime Minister)
Varzea CP 16
Praia, Santiago, CAPE VERDE

Velikhov, Yevgeni P (Physicist)
Kurchatovskiy Institute Kurchatova Pl 1
Moscow 12182, RUSSIA

Veljohnson, Reginald (Actor)
9637 Allenwood Dr
Los Angeles, CA 90046, USA

Vella, John (Athlete, Football Player)
1890 Saint George Rd
Danville, CA 94526-6253, USA

Veloso, Caetano (Musician, Songwriter, Writer)
Rua Marquis Sao Vincente
Rio de Janiero, BRAZIL

Veltman, Martinus J G (Nobel Prize Laureate)
Sachubertiaan 15
Bilthoven 3723, NETHERLANDS

Velvet, Jimmy
PO Box 808
Lititz, PA 17543-0538

Velvet Revolver (Music Group)
c/o Staff Member *RCA Records (LA)*
8750 Wilshire Blvd Fl 2
Beverly Hills, CA 90211-2715, USA

Vemtrone, Raymond (Athlete, Hockey Player)
c/o Staff Member *Boston Bruins*
TD Banknorth Garden 100 Legends Way, Suite 250
Boston, MA 2114, USA

Venable, Mac (Athlete, Baseball Player)
107 Clark St
San Rafael, CA 94901-3604, USA

Venable, Max (Athlete, Baseball Player, Coach)
PO Box 535
Lake Elsinore, CA 92531-0535, USA

Venables, Terry F (Coach, Football Coach)
213 Putney Bridge Road
London SW15 2NY, UNITED KINGDOM (UK)

Venafro, Mike (Athlete, Baseball Player)
15271 McGregor Blvd Ste 16
Fort Myers, FL 33908-1900, USA

Venditti, Antonello
Via Zara 12
Rome, ITALY

Venet, Bernar (Artist)
533 Canal St
New York, NY 10013-1328, USA

Veneziale, Mike (Baseball Player)
110 Cloverdale Ln
Williamstown, NJ 08094-2341, USA

Vengerov, Maxim (Musician)
6 Henrietta St
London WC2E 8LA, UNITED KINGDOM (UK)

Venitucci, Michele (Actor)
Vla Giuseppe Pisanelli
Rome 196, ITALY

Venkataraman, Prof. G. (Physicist)
Ex Vice Chancellor Sri Sathya Sai Institute of Higher Learning
Prashantinilayam, Anantapur Dist.
A.P. 515 134, India

Venniraadai, Murthy (Actor, Bollywood)
44 4th Main Road Kottur Gdn
Chennai, TN 600085, INDIA

Venora, Diane (Actor)
1505 10th St
Santa Monica, CA 90401-2805, USA

Ventimiglia, John (Actor)
c/o Stacy Abrams *Abrams Entertainment*
5225 Wilshire Blvd # Suite 515 PMB 515
Los Angeles, CA 90036, USA

Ventimiglia, John
9150 Wilshire Blvd Ste 350
Beverly Hills, CA 90212-3453

Ventimiglia, Milo (Actor)
c/o Jason Heyman *Creative Artists Agency (CAA-LA)*
2000 Avenue of the Stars Ste 100
Los Angeles, CA 90067-4705, USA

Ventimilia, Jeffrey (Actor)
c/o Staff Member *International Creative Management (ICM-LA)*
10250 Constellation Blvd Fl 7
Los Angeles, CA 90067-6207, USA

Vento, Mike (Athlete, Baseball Player)
7142 Kendall Heath Way
Land O Lakes, FL 34637-7554, USA

Ventresca, Vincent (Actor)
9057 Nemo St # C
West Hollywood, CA 90069-5511, USA

Ventrone, Raymond (Athlete, Football Player)
c/o Staff Member *New England Patriots*
Gillette Stadium One Patriots Pl
Foxboro, MA 02035-1388, USA

Ventura, Cassandra (Cassie) (Musician)
c/o Tommy Mottola *Mottola Company, The*
745 5th Ave # 800
New York, NY 10151-0099, USA

Ventura, Jesse (Politician, Talk Show Host)
c/o Barry Bloom *Braverman/Bloom Company*
14320 Ventura Blvd Ste 632
Sherman Oaks, CA 91423-2717, USA

Ventura, Robin (Athlete, Baseball Player)
1088 Newsom Springs Rd
Arroyo Grande, CA 93420-3618, USA

Ventura, Robin M (Baseball Player)
106 Dingletown Rd
Greenwich, CT 06830-3540, USA

Ventura-Manina, Virginia (Baseball Player)
PO Box 2306
Garfield, NJ 07026-4306, USA

Ventures, The (Music Group)
11761 E Speedway Blvd
Tucson, AZ 85748-2017, USA

Venturi, Ken (Golfer)
161 Waterford Cir
Rancho Mirage, CA 92270-3100, USA

Venturi, Rick (Athlete, Football Coach, Football Player)
1935 Sumter Ridge Ct
Chesterfield, MO 63017-8733, USA

Venus Hum (Music Group)
c/o Staff Member *Paradigm (Monterey)*
404 W Franklin St
Monterey, CA 93940-2303, USA

Ver Ploeg, Marcia (Stylist)
c/o Staff Member *VP Communications*
22 Gladbrook Rd
Pittsford, NY 14534-3546, USA

Vera, Audry (Actor)
c/o Staff Member *Televisa*
Blvd Adolfo Lopez Mateos 232 Colonia San Angel INN
DF CP 01060, MEXICO

Veras, Quilvio (Athlete, Baseball Player)
4244 Vineyard Cir
Weston, FL 33332-2153, USA

Verba, Ross (Athlete, Football Player)
222 Republic Dr
Allen Park, MI 48101-3650, USA

Verbanic, Joe (Athlete, Baseball Player)
85462 Lorane Hwy
Eugene, OR 97405-9409, USA

Verbeek, Lotte (Actor)
c/o Lindsay Galin *Lantern PR*
Prefers to be contacted via telephone and email
New York, NY, USA

Verbinski, Gore (Director, Producer)
c/o Dave Morrison *Anonymous Content (AC-LA)*
3531 Hayden Ave
Culver City, CA 90232, USA

Verble, Gene (Athlete, Baseball Player)
633 Camrose Cir NE
Concord, NC 28025-3280, USA

Verboom, Hanna (Actor)
c/o Greg Siegel *WmE2 (Endeavor-LA)*
9601 Wilshire Blvd Fl 3
Beverly Hills, CA 90210-5219, USA

Verchota, Phil (Athlete, Hockey Player, Olympic Athlete)
PO Box 1181
Bemidji, MN 56619-1181, USA

Verdi, Frank (Athlete, Baseball Player)
10961 Peppertree Ln
Port Richey, FL 34668-2420, USA

Verdi, Robert (Stylist, Television Host)
c/o Jeff Googel *WmE2 (WMA-NY)*
1325 Avenue of the Americas
New York, NY 10019-6026, USA

Verdin, Clarence (Athlete, Football Player)
6221 Eastover Dr
New Orleans, LA 70128-3619, USA

Verdugo, Elena
PO Box 2048
Chula Vista, CA 91912-2048

Vereen, Ben (Actor, Dancer, Musician)
729 7th Ave
New York, NY 10019-6831, USA

Vereen, Carl (Athlete, Football Player)
300 River Glen Dr
Roswell, GA 30075-4873, USA

Veres, Dave (Athlete, Baseball Player)
871 Diamond Ridge Cir
Castle Rock, CO 80108-7812, USA

Veres, Randy (Athlete, Baseball Player)
9213 W Frank Ave
Peoria, AZ 85382-5364, USA

Vergara, Sofia (Actor, Musician)
c/o Evan Hainey *Untitled Entertainment (LA)*
350 S Beverly Dr Ste 200
Beverly Hills, CA 90212-4819, USA

Verhoeven, John (Athlete, Baseball Player)
20805 Paseo De La Rambla
Yorba Linda, CA 92887-2429, USA

Verhoeven, Lis
Merzstrasse 14
Munich, GERMANY D-81679

Verhoeven, Paul (Director, Writer)
c/o Staff Member *Marion Rosenberg Office, The*
PO Box 69826
Los Angeles, CA 90069-0826, USA

Verhoeven, Peter (Athlete, Basketball Player)
12722 Fargo Ave
Hanford, CA 93230-9645, USA

Verica, Tom (Actor)
c/o Laura Fogelman *Independent Artists Agency*
9601 Wilshire Blvd Ste 750
Beverly Hills, CA 90210-5228, USA

Veris, Garin (Athlete, Football Player)
2 Christine Dr
Atkinson, NH 03811-2303, USA

Verlander, Justin (Athlete, Baseball Player)
744 Grasslands Village Cir
Lakeland, FL 33803-5480, USA

Verma, Deven (Actor, Bollywood)
7B Todiwala Rd
Pune, MS 400041, INDIA

Vermeil, Dick (Athlete, Coach, Football Coach, Football Player)
775 Fairview Rd
Coatesville, PA 19320-4453, USA

Vermilyea, Jamie (Athlete, Baseball Player)
7051 E Calle Arandas
Tucson, AZ 85750-2563, USA

Vernon, Conrad (Actor)
c/o Ilan Breil *Mosaic Media Group*
9200 W Sunset Blvd Ste 10
Los Angeles, CA 90069-3608, USA

Vernon, Kate (Actor)
c/o Staff Member *Shelter Entertainment*
9454 Wilshire Blvd Ste 715
Beverly Hills, CA 90212-2925, USA

Vernon Jr, Gary Wayne (Gary Levox) (Musician)
c/o Staff Member *Lyric Street Records*
500 S Buena Vista St
Burbank, CA 91521-0001, USA

Veroni, Craig (Actor)
c/o Staff Member *Muse Artists Management*
401-207 W Hastings St
Vancouver, BC V6B 1H7, Canada

Verplank, Scott (Athlete, Golfer)
1850 W Waterloo Rd
Edmond, OK 73025-1801, USA

Verraros, Jim (Musician)
c/o Jeff Ballard *Jeff Ballard PR*
4814 Lemona Ave
Sherman Oaks, CA 91403-2010, USA

Verreos, Nick (Fashion Designer)
3579 Tacoma Ave
Los Angeles, CA 90065-1725, USA

Versace, Donatella (Designer, Fashion Designer)
Via Manzoni 38
Milan 20121, ITALY

Verser, David (Athlete, Football Player)
21 Bellemonte Ave
Lakeside Park, KY 41017-3111, USA

Versini, Marie
23 res. Elysses 78170 La Celle-St Cloud, FRANCE

Vertical Horizon (Music Group)
c/o Staff Member *Paradigm (Monterey)*
404 W Franklin St
Monterey, CA 93940-2303, USA

Veruca Salt (Music Group)
PO Box 291105
Los Angeles, CA 90029-9105, USA

Verve Pipe, The (Music Group)
c/o Staff Member *Paradigm (Monterey)*
404 W Franklin St
Monterey, CA 93940-2303, USA

Verve, The (Music Group)
c/o Staff Member *Paradigm (Monterey)*
404 W Franklin St
Monterey, CA 93940-2303, USA

Verveen, Arie (Actor)
c/o Scott Karp *Crystal Sky Pictures*
10203 Santa Monica Blvd Ste 500
Los Angeles, CA 90067-6416, USA

Verwey, Bob (Golfer)
1360 E 9th St Ste 100
Cleveland, OH 44114-1730, USA

Veryzer, Tom (Athlete, Baseball Player)
41 Union Ave
Islip, NY 11751-3919, USA

Verzi, Linda (Stylist)
2913 Payton Rd NE
Atlanta, GA 30345-2639, USA

Vessey, Tricia (Actor)
c/o Staff Member *Brillstein Entertainment Partners*
9150 Wilshire Blvd Ste 350
Beverly Hills, CA 90212-3453, USA

Vest, R Lamar (Religious Leader)
PO Box 2430
Cleveland, TN 37320-2430, USA

Vetri, Victoria (Actor)
610 N Van Ness Ave
Los Angeles, CA 90004-1536, USA

Vetrov, Aleksandr (Ballerina, Dancer)
Teatralnaya Pl 1
Moscow 103009, RUSSIA

Vetter, Jack (Athlete, Football Player)
1021 Cedars Dr # 215
McPherson, KS 67460-2735, USA

Vettori, Ernst (Skier)
Fohrenweg 1
Absam, Eichat 6060, AUSTRIA

Vettrus, Richard J (Religious Leader)
12229 W 80th Ave
Arvada, CO 80005-3351, USA

Vey, Michelle (Stylist)
c/o Staff Member *Arlene Wilson Management*
807 N Jefferson St # 200
Milwaukee, WI 53202-8150, USA

Vez, El
3322 Hamilton Way
Los Angeles, CA 90026-2112

Viaene, David (Athlete, Football Player)
W9859 School Rd
Hortonville, WI 54944-9630, USA

Vian, Sissy (Stylist)
c/o Staff Member *Michele Filomeno New York LLC*
515 Greenwich St Ste 503
New York, NY 10013-1097, USA

Viardo, Vladimir V (Musician)
457 Piermont Rd
Cresskill, NJ 07626-1524, USA

Vichitra (Actor, Bollywood)
821 Jeevanandam Salai
Chennai, TN 600078, INDIA

Vicius, Nicole (Actor)
c/o Mimi DiTrani *Schiff Company, The*
8440 Warner Dr Ste B1
Culver City, CA 90232-2461, USA

Vick, Michael (Athlete, Football Player)
c/o Rick French *French/West/Vaughan*
185 Madison Ave Rm 401
New York, NY 10016-0032, USA

Vick, Roger (Athlete, Football Player)
12919 Windfern Rd Apt 1902
Houston, TX 77064-3068, USA

Vickaryous, Scott (Actor)
c/o Staff Member *Artists Only Management*
10203 Santa Monica Blvd
Los Angeles, CA 90067-6405, USA

Vickers, Brian (Race Car Driver)
136 Knob Hill Rd
Mooresville, NC 28117-6847, USA

Vickers, Jonathan S (Jon) (Opera Singer)
Collingtree 18 Riddlells Bay Road
Warwick WK 04, BERMUDA

Vickers, Kipp (Athlete, Football Player)
PO Box 78365
Indianapolis, IN 46278-0365, USA

Vickers, Steve (Athlete, Hockey Player)
209 Washington Ave
Batavia, NY 14020-2211, USA

Victor, James
1944 Whitley Ave Apt 306
Los Angeles, CA 90068-4100

Victoria (Royalty)
Kung Slottet Stottsbacken
Stockholm 11130, SWEDEN

Victorin (Ursache), Archbishop (Religious Leader)
19959 Riopelle St
Detroit, MI 48203-1249, USA

Victorino, Shane (Athlete, Baseball Player)
498 S Alu Rd
Wailuku, HI 96793-1508, USA

Vida Blue (Music Group)
c/o Staff Member *Paradigm (Monterey)*
404 W Franklin St
Monterey, CA 93940-2303, USA

Vidal, Christina (Actor)
c/o Bob McGowan *McGowan Management*
8733 W Sunset Blvd Ste 103
West Hollywood, CA 90069-2241, USA

Vidal, Deborah (Golfer)
2033 Paramount Dr
Los Angeles, CA 90068-3120, USA

Vidal, Gore (Writer)
c/o Robert (Bob) Bookman *Creative Artists Agency (CAA-LA)*
2000 Avenue of the Stars Ste 100
Los Angeles, CA 90067-4705, USA

Vidal, Jean-Pierre (Skier)
50 Rue de Marquisats BP 51
Annecy Cedex 74011, FRANCE

Vidal, Lisa (Actor)
c/o Bob McGowan *McGowan Management*
8733 W Sunset Blvd Ste 103
West Hollywood, CA 90069-2241, USA

Vidal, Raquel (Stylist)
c/o Staff Member *Anyway Productions*
870 Avenue of the Americas
New York, NY 10001-4111, USA

Vidal, Ricardo J Cardinal (Religious Leader)
PO Box 52
Ansonia, CT 06401-0052, PHILIPINES

Vidal, Rodrigo (Actor)
c/o Staff Member *Televisa*
Blvd Adolfo Lopez Mateos 232 Colonia
San Angel INN
DF CP 01060, MEXICO

Vidali, Lynn (Swimmer)
14750 Mosegard Ln
Morgan Hill, CA 95037-9604, USA

Vider, Ricky (Stylist)
c/o Staff Member *Walter Schupfer Management Corp*
413 W 14th St Ste 3
New York, NY 10014-1097, USA

Vidmar, Peter (Gymnast)
18 Downfield Way
Trabuco Canyon, CA 92679-5004, USA

Vidro, Jose A C (Athlete, Baseball Player)
159 Wentworth Ave
Brockton, MA 02301-6357, USA

Vie, Richard C (Business Person)
PO Box 191
Lake Forest, IL 60045-0191, USA

Viehboeck, Franz (Cosmonaut)
Brunnerbergstr 3021
Perchtoldsdorf 2380, AUSTRIA

Vieillard, Roger (Artist)
7 Rue de l'Estrapade
Paris 75005, FRANCE

Vieira, Meredith (Game Show Host, Television Host)
c/o Staff Member *Today Show, The*
30 Rockefeller Plz
New York, NY 10112-0015, USA

Vieira, Patrick (Soccer Player)
Corso Galileo Ferraris 32
Turin 10128, ITALY

Vieluf, Vince (Actor)
c/o Tammy Rosen *Sanders Armstrong Caserta*
425 N Robertson Blvd
West Hollywood, CA 90048-1735, USA

Vien, Dominique (Stylist)
c/o Staff Member *Judy Inc*
1 Yorkville Ave
Toronto ON M4W 1L1, Canada

Viener, John (Actor)
c/o Kevin Crotty *International Creative Management (ICM-LA)*
10250 Constellation Blvd Fl 7
Los Angeles, CA 90067-6207, USA

Viera, Joey
4253 Navajo Ave
Toluca Lake, CA 91602-2913

Viereck, Peter (Writer)
1346 Murrell Ave
Columbus, OH 43212-3558, USA

Viertel, Peter Wyhergut
7250 Klosters
Grisons, SWITZERLAND

Vieth, Michelle (Actor)
c/o Staff Member *Televisa*
Blvd Adolfo Lopez Mateos 232 Colonia
San Angel INN
DF CP 01060, MEXICO

View, The (Music Group)
c/o Staff Member *Paradigm (Monterey)*
404 W Franklin St
Monterey, CA 93940-2303, USA

Vieyra, Veronica (Actor)
c/o Staff Member *Telefe - Argentina*
Pavon 2444 (C1248AAT)
Buenos Aires, ARGENTINA

Vig, Butch (Musician)
c/o Staff Member *Borman Entertainment (TN)*
4322 Harding Pike Ste 429
Nashville, TN 37205-2661, USA

Vigman, Gillian (Actor)
c/o Jeanne Newman *Hansen, Jacobson, Teller, Hoberman, Newman, Warren & Richman*
450 N Roxbury Dr Fl 8
Beverly Hills, CA 90210-4222, USA

Vigneault, Alain (Athlete, Coach, Hockey Player)
1401 Clark Ave
Saint Louis, MO 63103-2700, USA

Vigneron, Thierry (Athlete, Track Athlete)
5675 N Blackstock Rd
Spartanburg, SC 29303-6329, USA

Vignesh (Actor, Bollywood)
AP 210 9th Street 2nd Sector
Chennai, TN 600078, INDIA

Vigoda, Abe (Actor)
c/o Staff Member *Cunningham Escott Slevin & Doherty (CESD-LA)*
10635 Santa Monica Blvd Ste 130
Los Angeles, CA 90025-8306, USA

Vigorito, Tommy (Athlete, Football Player)
184 Smith Lake Rd
Roscoe, NY 12776-5902, USA

Viguerie, Richard
7777 Leesburg Pike
Falls Church, VA 22043-2411

Vijay, S A (Actor, Bollywood)
64 Kaveri Street Saligramam
Chennai, TN 600093, INDIA

Vijaya K R (Actor, Bollywood)
9 Raman St
Chennai, TN 600018, INDIA

Vijayakanth (Actor, Bollywood)
54 Kannambal Street Kannapiran Colony
Saligramam
Chennai, TN 600093, INDIA

Vijayakumar, Manjula (Actor, Bollywood)
236 & 237 8th Street Asthalakshmi Nagar
Chennai, TN 600116, INDIA

Vila, Bob (Actor, Producer, Television Host)
162 5th Ave Attn Agnieszka
New York, NY 10010-5902, USA

Vilanch, Bruce (Comedian, Writer)
c/o Joan Hyler *Hyler Management*
20 Ocean Park Blvd Unit 25
Santa Monica, CA 90405-3590, USA

Vilanich, Bruce (Comedian)
c/o Staff Member *WmE2 (WMA-LA)*
1 William Morris Pl
Beverly Hills, CA 90212-4261, USA

Vilar, Tracy (Actor)
c/o Doug Wald *Anonymous Content (AC-LA)*
545 Veteran Ave
Los Angeles, CA 90024-1915, USA

Vilas, Guillermo
86 av. Foch F-75116
Paris, FRANCE

Vilasuso, Jordi (Actor)
c/o Jeb Brandon *Kritzer Levine Wilkins Entertainment*
11872 La Grange Ave Fl 1
Los Angeles, CA 90025-5283, USA

Vilasuso, Jordie (Actor)
c/o Staff Member *Innovative Artists (LA)*
1505 10th St
Santa Monica, CA 90401-2805, USA

Vilella, Edward
905 Lincoln Blvd
Miami, FL 33139

Viljoen, Marais (President)
PO Box 5555
Pretoria 1, SOUTH AFRICA

Villacis, Eduardo (Athlete, Baseball Player, Coach)
PO Box 1293
Casper, WY 82602-1293, USA

Villacorta (Stylist)
c/o Staff Member *Action Agency Stylists*
8424 Santa Monica Blvd
West Hollywood, CA 90069-6233, USA

Villa-Cryan, Marge (Athlete, Baseball Player)
16305 Summershade Dr
La Mirada, CA 90638-2742, USA

Villafuerte, Brandon (Athlete, Baseball Player)
PO Box 188
North Bridgton, ME 04057-0188, USA

Villalon, Jade Valerie (Musician)
c/o Staff Member *Universal Records*
825 8th Ave Fl C2B
New York, NY 10019-7472, USA

Villano, Mike (Baseball Player)
PO Box 36
Macomb, IL 61455-0036, USA

Villanueva, Carlos (Athlete)
c/o Staff Member *SFX Sports Management*
5335 Wisconsin Ave NW Ste 850
Washington, DC 20015-2052, USA

Villanueva, Charlie (Athlete, Basketball Player)
c/o Jeff Schwartz *Excel Sports Management*
9665 Wilshire Blvd Ste 500
Beverly Hills, CA 90212-2312, USA

Villanueva, Danny (Athlete, Football Player)
PO Box 258
Somis, CA 93066-0258, USA

Villapiano, Phillip J (Phil) (Athlete, Football Player)
21 Riverside Dr
Rumson, NJ 07760-1026, USA

Villaraigosa, Antonio (Politician)
200 N Spring St Ste 303
Los Angeles, CA 90012-3239, USA

Villari, Guy (Musician)
293 Airport Rd
Liberty, NY 12754-2613, USA

Villarrial, Chris (Athlete, Football Player)
254 Hidden Meadow Ln
Ebensburg, PA 15931-7511, USA

Villarroel, Vernoica (Opera Singer)
165 W 57th St
New York, NY 10019-2201, USA

Villegas, Camilo (Athlete, Golfer)
c/o Staff Member *IMG Miami*
Miami, FL, USA

Villella, Edward J (Ballerina, Choreographer)
2200 Liberty Ave
Miami Beach, FL 33139-1641, USA

Villeneuve, Jacques (Race Car Driver)
PO Box 5014 Brackley
Northants NN13 7YY, UNITED KINGDOM (UK)

Villiers, Christopher (Actor)
c/o Staff Member *Katie Threlfall Associates*
2A Gladstone Rd
London SW19 1QT, UNITED KINGDOM (UK)

Villiers, James (Actor)
76 Oxford St
London W1N 0AX, UNITED KINGDOM (UK)

Villone, Ron (Athlete, Baseball Player)
3 Schindler Ct
Upper Saddle River, NJ 07458-2363, USA

Viloria, Brian (Boxer)

Viltz, Theo (Athlete, Football Player)
2729 E De Soto St
Long Beach, CA 90814-2337, USA

Vimond, Paul M (Architect)
91 Ave Niel
Paris 75017, USA

Vina, Fernando (Athlete, Baseball Player)
9464 Clementine Way
Elk Grove, CA 95758-3910, USA

Vinatieri, Adam (Athlete, Football Player)
12850 Horseferry Rd
Carmel, IN 46032-7266, USA

Vince, Pruitt Taylor (Actor)
c/o Joanna (Joanie) Burstein *Burstein Company, The*
15304 W Sunset Blvd Ste 208
Pacific Palisades, CA 90272-3656, USA

Vince, Taylor (Misc)
20160 NW 9th Dr
Pembroke Pines, FL 33029-3422, USA

Vincent, Brooke (Actor)
c/o Staff Member *Laine Management*
Laine House 131 victoria road
Salford M6 8LF, UNITED KINGDOM

Vincent, Cerina (Actor)
c/o Adam Seid *Bohemia Group*
1680 Vine St Ste 216
Los Angeles, CA 90028-8829, USA

Vincent, Christian (Actor)
c/o Staff Member *Noah's Arc*
75 Charles Rowen House Merlin Street
London WC1X OEJ, UNITED KINGDOM

Vincent, Fay (Athlete, Baseball Player)
290 Harbor Dr
Stamford, CT 06902-8700, USA

Vincent, Jan-Michael (Actor, Producer)
c/o Staff Member *Genesis Creations*
Contact through website
unknown, CA 0, USA

Vincent, Jay (Athlete, Basketball Player)
PO Box 27459
Lansing, MI 48909-0459, USA

Vincent, June
1541 Via Entrada Del Lago
Lake San Marcos, CA 92069

Vincent, Marjorie
1325 Boardwalk
Atlantic City, NJ 08401-7240

Vincent, Rhonda (Musician)
c/o Scott Clayton *Creative Artists Agency (CAA-TN)*
3310 W End Ave Fl 5
Nashville, TN 37203-1028, USA

Vincent, Richard F (Misc)
Westminster
London SW1A 0PW, UNITED KINGDOM (UK)

Vincent, Rick (Musician, Songwriter, Writer)
1028 18th Ave S # B
Nashville, TN 37212-2105, USA

Vincent, Sam (Athlete, Basketball Player)
PO Box 27459
Lansing, MI 48909-0459, USA

Vincent, Troy (Athlete, Football Player)
18900 Longhouse Pl
Leesburg, VA 20176-6464, USA

Vincent, Virginia (Actor)
1001 Hammond St
Los Angeles, CA 90069-3829, USA

Vincz, Melanie (Actor)
2212 Earle Ct
Redondo Beach, CA 90278-5003, USA

Vineetha (Actor, Bollywood)
Flat No 3B Chandrika Apartments 5 & 6
Ashok Avenue Directors Colony
Kodambakkam
Chennai, TN 600024, INDIA

Vinegrad, Kat (Stylist)
c/o Staff Member *Smashbox Beauty*
8549 Higuera St Bldg B
Culver City, CA 90232-2521, USA

Vines, C Jerry (Religious Leader)
124 W Ashley St
Jacksonville, FL 32202-3104, USA

Vines, Ellsworth
4680 Irvine Blvd # 203
Irvine, CA 92620

Vines, The (Music Group)
c/o Rick Roskin *Creative Artists Agency (CAA-LA)*
2000 Avenue of the Stars Ste 100
Los Angeles, CA 90067-4705, USA

Vineyard, Dave (Athlete, Baseball Player)
1850 Tariff Rd
Left Hand, WV 25251-9542, USA

Vinge, Vernor (Writer)
175 5th Ave
New York, NY 10010-7703, USA

Vining, David (Doctor, Scientist)
2210 Bellefontaine St Unit D
Houston, TX 77030-3281, USA

Vining, Ken (Athlete, Baseball Player)
517 Mount Elon Church Rd
Hopkins, SC 29061-8666, USA

Vinith, R (Actor, Bollywood)
Flat G 1 68 Halls Road Kilpauk
Chennai, TN 600010, INDIA

Vinnie (Artist, Music Group)
8942 Wilshire Blvd # 219
Beverly Hills, CA 90211-1908, USA

Vinogradov, Oleg M (Ballerina)
Teatralnaya Square 1
Saint Petersburg 190000, RUSSIA

Vinoly, Rafael (Architect)
1016 5th Ave
New York, NY 10028-0132, USA

Vinothini (Actor, Bollywood)
3 Alagar Perumal Koil St
Chennai, TN 600026, INDIA

Vinson, Charlie (Athlete, Baseball Player)
3821 Walters Ln
District Heights, MD 20747-3943, USA

Vinson, Fernandus (Athlete, Football Player)
6572 Glenwood Ave Apt 221
Raleigh, NC 27612-7156, USA

Vinson, Fred (Athlete, Football Player)
11220 NE 53rd St
Kirkland, WA 98033-7505, USA

Vinson, Fred (Athlete, Basketball Player)
925 1/2 E Fairview Blvd
Inglewood, CA 90302-1426, USA

Vinson, James S (Educator)
President S Ofc
Evansville, IN 47722-0001, USA

Vint, Jesse
10637 Burbank Blvd
North Hollywood, CA 91601-2512

Vint, Jesse Lee III (Actor)
13563 1/2 Ventura Blvd # 200
Sherman Oaks, CA 91423, USA

Vinton, Bobby (Musician)
c/o Staff Member *MPI Talent Agency*
1801 Avenue of the Stars Ste 1420
Los Angeles, CA 90067-5899, USA

Vinton, Will (Animator, Director, Producer)
c/o Rob Kenneally *Creative Artists Agency (CAA-LA)*
2000 Avenue of the Stars Ste 100
Los Angeles, CA 90067-4705, USA

Viola, Bill (Artist)
282 Granada Ave
Long Beach, CA 90803-5520, USA

Viola, Frank
844 Sweetwater Island Cir
Longwood, FL 32779-2345

Viola, Frank J Jr (Athlete, Baseball Player)
9868 Kilgore Rd
Orlando, FL 32836-5708, USA

Viola, Lisa (Dancer)
552 Broadway
New York, NY 10012-3922, USA

Violent Femmes (Music Group)
15030 Ventura Blvd # 710
Sherman Oaks, CA 91403-5470, USA

Violette, Chris (Actor)
c/o Staff Member *Power Rangers SPD*
500 S Buena Vista St
Burbank, CA 91521-0001, USA

Virata, Cesar E (Prime Minister)
63 E Maya Dr
Quezon City, PHILIPPINES

Virden, Claude (Athlete, Basketball Player)
337 Fernwood Dr
Akron, OH 44320-2317, USA

Virdon, William C (Bill) (Athlete, Baseball Player, Coach)
1311 E River Rd
Springfield, MO 65804-7901, USA

Viren, Lasse (Athlete, Track Athlete)
Suomen Urhellulirto Ry Box 25202
Helsinki 25 250, FINLAND

Virgil Jr, Ozzie (Athlete, Baseball Player)
5444 W Creedance Blvd
Glendale, AZ 85310-3724, USA

Virgil Sr, Ozzie (Athlete, Baseball Player)
CAlle Frank Felix Miranda #1 ENS, Naco
Attn: Special Catching Instructor
Santa Domingo, Dominican Republic

Virgins, The (Music Group)
c/o Staff Member *Paradigm (Monterey)*
404 W Franklin St
Monterey, CA 93940-2303, USA

Virts, Terry W Jr (Astronaut)
1904 Edgewater Dr
Friendswood, TX 77546-7845, USA

Virtue, Doreen (Writer)
PO Box 5100
Carlsbad, CA 92018-5100

Virtue, Frank (Musician)
8309 Rising Sun Ave
Philadelphia, PA 19111, USA

Virtue, Thomas (Tom) (Actor)
c/o Staff Member *Gage Group, The (LA)*
14724 Ventura Blvd Ste 505
Sherman Oaks, CA 91403-3505, USA

Virzaladze, Elizo K (Music Group, Musician)
Bolshaya Nikitskaya Str 13
Moscow, RUSSIA

Vis, Anthony (Religious Leader)
475 Riverside Dr
New York, NY 10115-0002, USA

Viscardi, Johnston Catherine (Publisher)
200 Madison Ave
New York, NY 10016-3903, USA

Visclosky, Pete (Congressman, Politician)
7895 Broadway Ste A
Merrillville, IN 46410-5529, USA

Visconti, Tony (Musician, Producer)
c/o Joe D'Ambrosio *Joe D'Ambrosio Management Inc*
1311 Mamaroneck Ave Ste 220
White Plains, NY 10605-5222, USA

Visculo, Sal
6491 Ivarene Ave
Los Angeles, CA 90068-2823

Viscuso, Sal (Actor)
6491 Ivarene Ave
Los Angeles, CA 90068-2823, USA

Vise, David A (Journalist)
1150 15th St NW
Washington, DC 20071-0001, USA

Vishnevskaya, Galina P (Opera Singer)
Gazetny Per 13 #79
Moscow 103009, RUSSIA

Vishnyova, Diana V (Ballerina)
Teatralnaya Square 1
Saint Petersburg 190000, RUSSIA

Visitor, Nana (Actor)
c/o Joanne Halpern *Halpern Management*
PO Box 5042
Santa Monica, CA 90409-5042, USA

Visnic, Larry (Athlete, Football Player)
846 Master Dr
Galloway, OH 43119-8238, USA

Visnjic, Goran (Actor)
c/o Elyse Scherz *WmE2 (Endeavor-LA)*
9601 Wilshire Blvd Fl 3
Beverly Hills, CA 90210-5219, USA

Viso, Michel (Misc)
7 Domaine Chateau-Gaillard
Maison-d' Alfort 94700, FRANCE

Visscher, Maurice B (Doctor)
120 Melbourne Ave SE
Minneapolis, MN 55414-3516, USA

Visser, Lesley (Sportscaster)
c/o Staff Member *CBS Television*
51 W 52nd St
New York, NY 10019-6119, USA

Visu (Actor, Bollywood)
11 Agastheya Nagar Kilpaul Gdn
Chennai, TN 600012, INDIA

Vitale, Dick (Athlete, Basketball Player, Coach, Sportscaster)
7810 Mathern Ct
Lakewood Ranch, FL 34202-2592, USA

Vitale, Joe (Business Person, Writer)
121 Canyon Gap Rd
Wimberley, TX 78676-6314, USA

Vitale, Tony (Actor, Director, Writer)
c/o Staff Member *Hansen, Jacobson, Teller, Hoberman, Newman, Warren & Richman*
450 N Roxbury Dr Fl 8
Beverly Hills, CA 90210-4222, USA

Vitamin-C (Actor, Musician)
c/o Carter Cohn *International Creative Management (ICM-LA)*
10250 Constellation Blvd Fl 7
Los Angeles, CA 90067-6207, USA

Viterbi, Andrew J (Engineer, Scientist)
5775 Morehouse Dr
San Diego, CA 92121-1714, USA

Vitez, Michael (Journalist)
400 N Broad St
Philadelphia, PA 19130-4015, USA

Vithayathil, Varkey Cardinal (Religious Leader)
Syro-Malabar Archiepiscopal Curia
Bharath Matha College
Kerala, INDIA

Vitiello, Joe (Athlete, Baseball Player)
13615 Old El Camino Real
San Diego, CA 92130-3088, USA

Vitiello, Sandro (Athlete, Football Player)
9 Dwight Cir
Commack, NY 11725-3313, USA

Vitko, Joe (Athlete, Baseball Player)
1853 Frankstown Rd Apt 1
Johnstown, PA 15902-4504, USA

Vitolo, Dennis (Race Car Driver)
2130 Intracoastal Dr
Fort Lauderdale, FL 33305-3638, USA

Vitousek, Peter M (Misc)
Biological Science Dept
Stanford, CT 94305, USA

Vitti, Monica (Actor)
Via F Siacci 38
Rome 197, ITALY

Vittori, Roberto (Astronaut)
Linder Hole Box 906096
Cologne 51127, GERMANY

Vitukhnovskaya, Alina A (Writer)
Leningradskoye Shosse 80 #89
Moscow 125565, RUSSIA

Vivas, Juan Carlos (Actor)
c/o Gabriel Blanco *Gabriel Blanco Iglesias (Mexico)*
Rio Balsas 35-32 Colonia Cuauhtemoc
DF 6500, Mexico

Vivek (Actor, Bollywood)
9 Subhiksha Apts 5 Tank Street U I Colony
Chennai, TN 600024, INDIA

Viviano, Joseph P (Business Person)
100 Crystal A Dr
Hershey, PA 17033-9524, USA

Vizcaino, Jose (Athlete, Baseball Player)
5976 Germaine Ln
La Jolla, CA 92037-7430, USA

Vizquel, Omar E (Athlete, Baseball Player)
26630 SE Issaquah Fall City Rd
Issaquah, WA 98029-9183, USA

Vlacil, Frantisek (Director)
Cinska 5
Prague 6 160 00, CZECH REPUBLIC

Vladeck, Judith P (Attorney, Attorney General, General)
1501 Broadway
New York, NY 10036-5601, USA

Vladimir, Potanin (Business Person, Politician)
40 Bolshaya Yakimanka St
Moscow 119049, Russia

Vlady, Marina (Actor)
10 Ave de Marivaux
Mission Lafitte 78800, FRANCE

Vlardo, Vladimir V (Musician)
457 Piermont Rd
Cresskill, NJ 07626-1524, USA

Vlasic, Mark (Athlete, Football Player)
12809 Catalina St
Leawood, KS 66209-3327, USA

Vlassic, Robert
716 Ocean Dr
Juno Beach, FL 33408-1911

Vlk, Miloslav Cardinal (Religious Leader)
Arcibiskupstvi Hradcanske Nam 16/56
Prague 1 119 02, CZECH REPUBLIC

Vo Nguyen Giap (General)
Dang Cong San Vietnam 1C Blvd Hoang Van Thu
Hanoi, VIETNAM

Voce, Gary (Athlete, Basketball Player)
25912 147th Ave
Rosedale, NY 11422-3321, USA

Vodianova, Natalia (Model)
c/o Staff Member *DNA Model Management*
555 W 25th St Fl 6
New York, NY 10001-5542, USA

Voevodsky, Vladimir (Mathematician)
22 Earle Ln
Princeton, NJ 08540-4925, USA

Vogel, Bob (Athlete, Football Player)
2065 N Galena Rd
Sunbury, OH 43074-9588, USA

Vogel, Dariene (Actor)
8730 W Sunset Blvd Ste 220W
Los Angeles, CA 90069-2275, USA

Vogel, Darlene (Actor)
c/o Staff Member *The Paradise Group*
PO Box 69451
West Hollywood, CA 90069-0451, USA

Vogel, Hans-Jochen (Government Official)
Stresemanstr 6
Bonn-Bad Godesberg 53123, GERMANY

Vogel, Mark (Composer)
c/o Staff Member *Gorfaine/Schwartz Agency Inc*
4111 W Alameda Ave Ste 509
Burbank, CA 91505-4171, USA

Vogel, Mike (Actor)
c/o Geordie Frey *GEF Entertainment*
122 N Clark Dr Apt 401
West Hollywood, CA 90048-6315, USA

Vogel, Mitch (Actor)
3335 Honeysuckle Ave
Palmdale, CA 93550-1305, USA

Vogelsong, Ryan (Athlete, Baseball Player)
637 W Jardin Dr
Casa Grande, AZ 85122-5117, USA

Vogelstein, Bert (Doctor, Scientist)
Medical School Oncology Center
Baltimore, MD 21218, USA

Vogler, Karl Michael
Auweg 8
Seehausen, GERMANY D-82418

Vogler, Tim (Athlete, Football Player)
6710 Woodland Dr
Hamburg, NY 14075-6521, USA

Vogt, Lars (Musician)
c/o Staff Member *International Creative Management (ICM-NY)*
40 W 57th St
New York, NY 10019-4001, USA

Vogt, Paul (Actor)
c/o Judy Coppage *Coppage Company, The*
5411 Camellia Ave
North Hollywood, CA 91601-2615, USA

Vogt, Peter K (Misc, Scientist)
2011 Zonal Ave
Los Angeles, CA 90089-0110, USA

Vogt, Rochus E (Astronomer, Physicist)
Bridge Laboratory
Pasadena, CA 91125-0001, USA

Vogts, Hans-Hubert (Berti) (Soccer Player)
Mozartweg 2
Korschenbroich 41352, GERMANY

Voight, Jon (Actor, Producer, Writer)
c/o Dorothy Koster *Crystal Sky/Artists Only Management*
10203 Santa Monica Blvd Fl 5
Los Angeles, CA 90067-6405, USA

Voight, Karen (Fitness Expert)
827 Chautauqua Blvd
Pacific Palisades, CA 90272-3802, USA

Voight, Stu (Athlete, Football Player)
8832 Hunters Way
Apple Valley, MN 55124-9478, USA

Voigt, Jack (Athlete, Baseball Player)
1759 Bayshore Rd
Nokomis, FL 34275-1413, USA

Voinovich, George V (Ex-Governor, Senator)
524 Hart Senate Ofc Building
Washington, DC 20510-0001, USA

Voisard, Mark (Baseball Player)
222 Meadowlane Dr
Sidney, OH 45365-7000, USA

Volberding, Paul (Scientist)
995 Potrero Ave
San Francisco, CA 94110-2859, USA

Volcker, Paul (Government Official)
151 E 79th St
New York, NY 10075-0417, USA

Voldstad, John (Actor)
24812 Van Owen St
West Hills, CA 91300, USA

Volibracht, Michaele (Artist, Designer, Fashion Designer)
Safety Harbor, FL 34695, USA

Volk, Igor P (Misc)
Moskovskoi Oblasti
Syvisdny Goroduk 141160, RUSSIA

Volk, Patricia (Writer)
133 E 35th St
New York, NY 10016-3886, USA

Volk, Phil (Musician)
108 E Matilija St
Ojai, CA 93023-2639, USA

Volk, Richard R (Rick) (Athlete, Football Player)
15860 Irish Ave
Monkton, MD 21111-2120, USA

Volker, Sandra (Swimmer)
Mensingen Str 68
Munich 80992, GERMANY

Volkert, Stephan (Athlete)
Semmelweisstr 42
Cologne 51061, GERMANY

Volkov, Aleksandr A (Misc)
Moskovskoi Oblasti
Syvisdny Goroduk 141160, RUSSIA

Volkov, Alexander (Athlete, Basketball Player)
1413 Waterford Green Dr
Marietta, GA 30068-2910, USA

Voll, Rich (Actor)

Vollebak, Knut (Government Official)
2720 34th St NW
Washington, DC 20008-2705, USA

Vollenweider, Andreas (Musician)
Sempacher Str 16
Zurich 8032, SWITZERLAND

Volodos, Arcadl (Musician)
165 W 57th St
New York, NY 10019-2201, USA

Voloshin, Valeri (Cosmonaut)
Moskovskoi Oblasti
Syvisdny Goroduk 141160, RUSSIA

Volstad, John (Actor)
c/o Brandon Pender *Ithaca Entertainment Media Group*
PO Box 1880
Studio City, CA 91614-0880, USA

Voltaggio, Vic (Baseball Player)
1049 Florian Way
Spring Hill, FL 34609-9021, USA

VOltaggio, Vic (Athlete, Baseball Player)
1049 Florian Way
Spring Hill, FL 34609-9021, USA

Voltz, Jeanne (Stylist)
305 W 98th St
New York, NY 10025-5500, USA

Volynov, Boris V (Misc)
Moskovskoi Oblasti
Syvisdny Goroduk 141160, RUSSIA

Volz, Wilbur (Athlete, Football Player)
35 Seminary Hl Apt C-31
West Lebanon, NH 03784-1728, USA

Volz, Wolfgang (Actor)
Konstanzer Strasse 8
Berlin D-10707, Germany

Von Bargen, Daniel (Actor)
c/o Mitchell Stubbs *Mitchell K Stubbs & Assoc (MKS)*
8675 Washington Blvd Ste 203
Culver City, CA 90232-7486, USA

Von Daniken, Eric (Writer)
Chalet Aelpli
Portsmouth, NH 03803-0001, Switzerland

von Detten, Erik (Actor)
c/o Elissa Leeds-Fickman *Reel Talent Management*
PO Box 491035
Los Angeles, CA 90049-9035, USA

von Dohlen, Lenny (Actor)
c/o Martin Gage *Gage Group, The (LA)*
14724 Ventura Blvd Ste 505
Sherman Oaks, CA 91403-3505, USA

Von Drachenberg, Katherine (Artist, Reality TV Star)
1259 N La Brea Ave
West Hollywood, CA 90038-1023, USA

Von Erich, Jaret (Actor, Musician)
c/o Linda Kordek *Agency Group Ltd, The (LA)*
1880 Century Park E Ste 711
Los Angeles, CA 90067-1618, USA

Von Frankenstein, Clement (Actor)
c/o Staff Member *Matt Sherman Management*
9107 Wilshire Blvd Ste 225
Beverly Hills, CA 90210-5546, USA

Von Furstenberg, Betsy (Actor)
230 Central Park W
New York, NY 10024-6029, USA

Von Furstenberg, Diane (Fashion Designer)
440 W 14th St
New York, NY 10014-1004, USA

Von Hoff, Bruce (Athlete, Baseball Player)
423 S Riverhills Dr
Temple Terrace, FL 33617-7861, USA

Von Hohenzollern, Maja Synke (Prince, Princess)
11605 W Pico Blvd # 200
Los Angeles, CA 90064-2908, USA

von Kusserow, Ingeborg
16-D Avercorn Pl
London, ENGLAND NW8

Von Nieda, Whitey (Athlete, Basketball Player)
1105 James Buchanan Dr
Elizabethtown, PA 17022-3169, USA

Von Ohlen, Dave (Athlete, Baseball Player)
653 Windmill Ave
West Babylon, NY 11704-4403, USA

Von Oy, Jenna (Actor)
19 Saddle Ridge Rd
Newtown, CT 06470-2417, USA

von Pfetten, Stefanie (Actor)
c/o Marina D'Amico *Precision Entertainment*
6338 Wilshire Blvd
Los Angeles, CA 90048-5002, USA

Von Schamann, Uwe (Athlete, Football Player)
PO Box 5562
Norman, OK 73070-5562, USA

Von Scherler Mayer, Daisy (Director)
c/o Keith Addis *Industry Entertainment Partners*
955 Carrillo Dr Ste 300
Los Angeles, CA 90048-5400, USA

Von Stade, Frederica (Opera Singer)
333 Kennedy St
Oakland, CA 94606-5319, USA

Von Sydow, Max (Actor)
c/o Staff Member *United Talent Agency (UTA)*
9560 Wilshire Blvd Fl 5
Beverly Hills, CA 90212-2400, USA

Von Teese, Dita (Dancer, Model)
PO Box 1760
Eagle, ID 83616-9106, USA

von Trier, Lars (Director, Writer)
c/o Staff Member *Jeff Morrone Entertainment*
9350 Wilshire Blvd Ste 224
Beverly Hills, CA 90212-3204, USA

von Weizsacker, Carl
Alpenstr. 15
Socking, GERMANY D-82319

von Weizsacker, Richard (Ex-President, President)
Meisenstr 6
Berlin D-14195, GERMANY

von Wietersheim, Sharon
Leopoldstr. 19
Munich, GERMANY D-80802

VonBulow, Vicco (Loriot) (Actor)
Hohenweg 19
Munsing-Ammerland 82451, GERMANY

Vonderau, Kathryn (Athlete, Baseball Player)
7224 Hawthorn Ave NE
Albuquerque, NM 87113-2084, USA

VonDohnanyi, Christoph (Conductor)
Severance Hall
Cleveland, OH 44106, USA

VonErich, Waldo (Wrestler)
9-145 Columbia W
Waterloo, ON N2L 3L2, CANADA

VonEschenbach, Andrew (Doctor)
9000 Rockville Pike
Bethesda, MD 20892-0001, USA

VonFurstenberg, Betsy (Actor)
230 Central Park W
New York, NY 10024-6029, USA

VonFurstenberg, Egon (Designer, Fashion Designer)
50 E 72nd St
New York, NY 10021-4246, USA

VonGarnier, Katja (Director, Writer)
c/o John Campisi *Creative Artists Agency (CAA-LA)*
2000 Avenue of the Stars Ste 100
Los Angeles, CA 90067-4705, USA

Vongerichten, Jean-Geoges (Chef)
19 Greene St
New York, NY 10013-2535, USA

VonGerkan, Meinhard (Architect)
Elbchaussee 139
Hamburg 22763, GERMANY

VonGrunigen, Michael (Skier)
Chalet Sunneblick
Schonried 3778, SWITZERLAND

VonHabsburg-Lothringem, Otto (Government Official)
Hindenburgstrasse 15
Poecking D-82343, USA

VonHippel, Peter H (Misc)
1900 Crest Dr
Eugene, OR 97405-1753, USA

VonKlitzing, Klaus (Nobel Prize Laureate)
Heisenbergstr 1
Stuttgart 70569, GERMANY

VonMehren, Arthur T (Attorney, Attorney General, Educator, General)
68 Sparks St
Cambridge, MA 02138-2238, USA

VonMehren, Arthur T (Attorney, Attorney General, General)
925 Park Ave
New York, NY 10028-0210, USA

Vonn, Lindsey (Athlete, Skier)
c/o Staff Member *US Ski And Snowboard Association*
Box 199
Park City, UT 84060, USA

Vonnegut Jr, Kurt (Writer)
140 Watts St
New York, NY 10013-1738, USA

Vonoelhoffen, Kimo (Athlete, Football Player)
1503 Scarlet Oak Dr
Wexford, PA 15090-6931, USA

Vonohlen, Dave (Baseball Player)
74 Elizabeth St
Floral Park, NY 11001-2129, USA

Vonoimoana, Eric
715 S Circle Dr
Colorado Springs, CO 80910-2324

VonOtter, Anne Sofie (Opera Singer)
40 W 57th St
New York, NY 10019-4001, USA

VonOy, Jenna (Actor)
19 Saddle Ridge Rd
Newtown, CT 06470-2417, USA

VonPierer, Heinrich (Business Person)
Wittelsbacherplatz 2
Munich 80333, GERMANY

VonQuast, Veronika (Actor)
Leopoldstr 19
Munich 80802, GERMANY

VonRunkle, Theodora (Designer, Fashion Designer)
8805 Lookout Mountain Ave
Los Angeles, CA 90046-1819, USA

VonSaltza Olmstead, S Christine (Chris) (Swimmer)
7060 Fairway Pl
Carmel, CA 93923-9586, USA

Vonsonn, Andrew (Athlete, Football Player)
PO Box 791538
Paia, HI 96779-1538, USA

VonStrateen, Frans (Artist)
Samuel Muller Plein 17C
Rotterdam 3023, DENMARK

VonWeizsacker, Carl Friedrich (Misc)
Aplenstr 15
Socking 82319, GERMANY

VonWeizsacker, Richard (President)
Meisenstr 6
Berlin 14195, GERMANY

Voog, Ana (Music Group, Musician, Songwriter, Writer)
1755 Broadway
New York, NY 10019-3743, USA

Voorhees, John J (Doctor)
3965 Waldenwood Dr
Ann Arbor, MI 48105-3008, USA

Voorhies, Lark (Actor)
10635 Santa Monica Blvd Ste 130
Los Angeles, CA 90025-8306, USA

Vorgan, Gigi (Actor)
3637 Stone Cyn
Sherman Oaks, CA 91403, USA

Vorhies, Lark (Actor)
c/o Geoff Cheddy *Brillstein Entertainment Partners*
9150 Wilshire Blvd Ste 350
Beverly Hills, CA 90212-3453, USA

Voris, Roy M (Butch) (Misc)
14563 Fruitvale Ave
Saratoga, CA 95070-6152, USA

Voronin, Vladimir (President)
23 Nicolae Iorge Str
Chishinev 277033, MOLDOVA

Voronina, Irina (Model)
7119 W Sunset Blvd # 293
Los Angeles, CA 90046-4411, USA

Vos, Rich (Actor, Comedian)
c/o Jason Steinberg *Steinberg Talent Management Group*
1560 Broadway # 405
New York, NY 10036-1537, US

Vosberg, Ed (Athlete, Baseball Player)
7839 E Marquise Dr
Tucson, AZ 85715-3774, USA

Vosloo, Arnold (Actor)
c/o James (Jim) Gosnell *Agency for the Performing Arts (APA-LA)*
405 S Beverly Dr Ste 500
Beverly Hills, CA 90212-4425, USA

Voss, Bill (Athlete, Baseball Player)
10625 E Oak Creek Trl
Cornville, AZ 86325-5824, USA

Voss, Brian (Bowler)
340 Banyon Brook Pt
Roswell, GA 30076-3672, USA

Voss, James S (Astronaut)
4207 Indian Sunrise Ct
Houston, TX 77059-5533, USA

Voss, Janice E (Astronaut)
1807 Plumbwood Way
Houston, TX 77058-2251, USA

Voss, Lloyd (Athlete, Football Player)
1127 Greentree Rd
Pittsburgh, PA 15220-3130, USA

Votaw, Ty (Golfer)
100 International Golf Dr
Daytona Beach, FL 32124-1082, USA

Voth, Julia (Actor)
c/o Alex Fox *Cunningham Escott Slevin & Doherty (CESD-LA)*
10635 Santa Monica Blvd Ste 130
Los Angeles, CA 90025-8306, USA

Votto, Joey (Athlete, Baseball Player)
c/o Staff Member *Cincinnati Reds*
Great American Ball Park 100 Main St
Cincinnati, OH 45202-4109, USA

Vouyer, Vince (Adult Film Star)
9020 Eton Ave Ste G
Canoga Park, CA 91304-6514, USA

Vowell, Sarah (Actor, Writer)
c/o Staff Member *Steven Barclay Agency*
12 Western Ave
Petaluma, CA 94952-2907, USA

Voyce, Inez (Baseball Player)
2107 Ashland Ave
Santa Monica, CA 90405-6025, USA

Voyles, Brad (Athlete, Baseball Player)
314 East Ave
Casco, WI 54205-9679, USA

Voytek, Edward (Athlete, Football Player)
2111 NW 13th St
Blue Springs, MO 64015-7734, USA

Voznesensky, Andrei A (Writer)
Kotelnicheskaya Nab 1/15 Bl W #62
Moscow 109240, RUSSIA

Vraa, Sanna (Actor, Model)
9300 Wilshire Blvd Ste 410
Beverly Hills, CA 90212-3228, USA

Vrabel, Mike (Athlete, Football Player)
777 W Orange Rd
Delaware, OH 43015-9365, USA

Vrabel, Mike (Athlete, Football Player)
74 Concerto Ct
North Easton, MA 02356-2762, USA

Vraciu, Alexander (Alex) (War Hero)
309 Merrilee Pl
Danville, CA 94526-4315, USA

Vranes, Danny (Athlete, Basketball Player)
3540 Bengal Blvd
Salt Lake City, UT 84121-5902, USA

Vranes, Slavko (Basketball Player)
c/o Staff Member *Portland Trail Blazers*
1 N Center Court St Ste 200
Portland, OR 97227-2103, USA

Vranitzky, Franz
Ballhausplatz 2
Vienna, AUSTRIA 1015

Vuarnet, Jean (Skier)
Chalet Squaw Peak
Auoriaz 74110, FRANCE

Vucinich, Milt (Athlete, Football Player)
23 Belford Way
San Mateo, CA 94402-1205, USA

Vuckovich, Peter D (Pete) (Athlete, Baseball Player)
86 Leonard St
Johnstown, PA 15902-1234, USA

Vujtek, Vladimir (Athlete, Hockey Player)
66 Mario Lemieux Pl
Pittsburgh, PA 15219-3504, USA

Vukovich, George (Athlete, Baseball Player)
305 W Calle Gota
Sahuarita, AZ 85629-7845, USA

Vulkovich, Frances (Baseball Player)
2172 Smithdale Rd
West Newton, PA 15089-9603, USA

Vullo, Jennifer (Stylist)
c/o Staff Member *Crews*
828 Clemont Dr NE
Atlanta, GA 30306-3694, USA

Vuono, Carl E (General)
5796 Westchester St
Alexandria, VA 22310-1146, USA

Vyent, Louise (Model)
379 W Broadway # 502
New York, NY 10012-5121, USA

W

W, Kristine (Musician)
c/o Staff Member *Diva Central Inc*
7510 W Sunset Blvd Ste 1445
Los Angeles, CA 90046-3408, USA

W. Boustany Jr., Charles (Congressman, Politician)
1431 Longworth Hob
Washington, DC 20515-4802, USA

W. Dent, Charles (Congressman, Politician)
1009 Longworth Hob
Washington, DC 20515-3511, USA

W. Meeks, Gregory (Congressman, Politician)
2234 Rayburn Hob
Washington, DC 20515-2202, USA

W. Olver, John (Congressman, Politician)
1111 Longworth Hob
Washington, DC 20515-3229, USA

Waadataar, Paar (Musician)
11 Elvaston Place #300
London SW 7 5QC, UNITED KINGDOM (UK)

Waalkes, Otto
Papenhuder Str. 61
Hamburg, GERMANY D-22087

Wach, Caitlin (Actor)
c/o David Brownstein *Art Work Entertainment*
5900 Wilshire Blvd Ste 2150
Los Angeles, CA 90036-5021, USA

Wachowski, Andy (Director, Producer, Writer)
c/o Lawrence Mattis *Circle of Confusion LLC (NY)*
10723 71st Rd # 300
Forest Hills, NY 11375-4707, USA

Wachowski, Larry (Director, Producer, Writer)
c/o Lawrence Mattis *Circle of Confusion LLC (NY)*
10723 71st Rd # 300
Forest Hills, NY 11375-4707, USA

Wachs, Caitlin (Actor)
c/o Shelley Browning *Magnolia Entertainment (LA)*
9595 Wilshire Blvd Ste 601
Beverly Hills, CA 90212-2506, USA

Wachtel, Christine (Athlete, Track Athlete)
Rostock
Mecklenburg-Vorpommoem, GERMANY

Wachter, Anita (Skier)
Gantschierstr 579
Schruns 6780, AUSTRIA

Wacksman, Sara (Stylist)
c/o Staff Member *Apostrophe (NY)*
527 W 29th St
New York, NY 10001-1342, USA

Waddell, Charles (Athlete, Football Player)
3600 Bon Rea Dr
Charlotte, NC 28226-3146, USA

Waddell, Ernest (Actor)
c/o Bob McGowan *McGowan Management*
8733 W Sunset Blvd Ste 103
West Hollywood, CA 90069-2241, USA

Waddell, John Henry (Artist)
Star Route 2273 Oak Creek Village Road
Cornville, AZ 86325, USA

Waddell, Justine (Actor)
8942 Wilshire Blvd # 219
Beverly Hills, CA 90211-1908, USA

Waddell, Tom (Athlete, Baseball Player)
10171 E Achi St
Tucson, AZ 85748-1803, USA

Waddell-Wyatt, Helen (Baseball Player)
7714 Deerfield Rd
Loves Park, IL 61111-3218, USA

Waddington, Steven (Actor)
Adam House 14 New Burlington Street
London W1S 3BQ, UNITED KINGDOM (UK)

Waddle, Tom (Athlete, Football Player)
184 W Onwentsia Rd
Lake Forest, IL 60045-2840, USA

Waddy, Billy (Athlete, Football Player)
2838 Highway 88
Minneapolis, MN 55418-3243, USA

Wade, Abdoulaye (President)
Ave Roume
Dakar BPI 168, SENEGAL

Wade, Adam (Musician)
118 E 25th St # 600
New York, NY 10010-2915, USA

Wade, Charlie (Athlete, Football Player)
3109 E Raines Rd
Memphis, TN 38118-6756, USA

Wade, Cory (Athlete, Baseball Player)
c/o Staff Member *Los Angeles Dodgers (LA Dodgers)*
1000 Elysian Park Ave
Los Angeles, CA 90090-1112, USA

Wade, Dwayne (Athlete, Basketball Player)
c/o Henry Thomas *CAA Sports (LA)*
2000 Avenue of the Stars
Los Angeles, CA 90067-4700, USA

Wade, Dwyane (Athlete, Basketball Player)
c/o Leon Rose *CAA - NJ*
308 Harper Dr Ste 210
Moorestown, NJ 08057-3245, USA

Wade, Ed (Actor)
436 SW 50th Ave
Pratt, KS 67124-7731, USA

Wade, Edgar L (Religious Leader)
4466 Elvis Presley Blvd Ste 222
Memphis, TN 38116-7100, USA

Wade, Gale (Athlete, Baseball Player)
10240 NC 226 S
Nebo, NC 28761-5810, USA

Wade, Jason (Musician)
9268 W 3rd St
Beverly Hills, CA 90210-3713, USA

Wade, Kevin (Writer)
c/o David Lonner *Oasis Media Group*
8730 W Sunset Blvd Ste 700
Los Angeles, CA 90069-2249, USA

Wade, Mark (Athlete, Basketball Player)
405 S Centre St Apt 37
San Pedro, CA 90731-2732, USA

Wade, Russell
47287 W Eldorado Dr
Indian Wells, CA 92210-8654

Wade, Terrell (Athlete, Baseball Player)
6380 Dinkins Mill Rd
Rembert, SC 29128-9789, USA

Wade, Todd (Athlete, Football Player)
217 Hendricks Isle Apt 302
Fort Lauderdale, FL 33301-5753, USA

Wade, Tom (Athlete, Football Player)
3309 Oak Knoll Dr
Tyler, TX 75707-1619, USA

Wade, Virginia (Tennis Player)
Sharstead Court Sittingbourne
Kent, UNITED KINGDOM (UK)

Wade, William J (Bill) Jr (Athlete, Football Player)
7740 Buffalo Rd
Nashville, TN 37221-5501, USA

Wadhams, Wayne (Musician)
73 Hemenway St
Boston, MA 02115-2941, USA

Wadhawan, Avinash (Actor, Bollywood)
305 Skyway Shastri Nagar Off J P Road Andheri
Mumbai, MS 400058, INDIA

Wadkins, Bobby (Golfer)
204 Kinloch Rd
Manakin Sabot, VA 23103-2911, USA

Wadkins, Lanny (Golfer)
6002 Kettering Ct
Dallas, TX 75248-2137, USA

Wadsworth, Andre (Athlete, Football Player)
14003 N 99th Way
Scottsdale, AZ 85260-8851, USA

Wadsworth, Charles W (Musician)
PO Box 157
Charleston, SC 29402-0157, USA

Wadsworth, Fred (Golfer)
823 Byron Rd
Columbia, SC 29209-2303, USA

Waechter, Doug (Athlete, Baseball Player)
4590 13th Way NE
Saint Petersburg, FL 33703-5324, USA

Waelsch, Salome G (Doctor, Scientist)
90 Morningside Dr
New York, NY 10027-7124, USA

Wages, Harmon (Athlete, Football Player)
1846 Margaret St Apt 3C
Jacksonville, FL 32204-4423, USA

Wages, Robert E (Misc)
PO Box 2812
Denver, CO 80201-2812, USA

Wages, William (Cinematographer)
1505 10th St
Santa Monica, CA 90401-2805, USA

Waggoner, Bashie (Stylist)
6333 Monterey Rd
Los Angeles, CA 90042-4332, USA

Waggoner, Lyle (Actor)
1124 Oak Mirage Pl
Westlake Village, CA 91362-5622, USA

Waggoner, Paul E (Misc)
314 Vineyard Point Rd
Guilford, CT 06437-3255, USA

Wagner, Amanda
2627 S Cherry St Apt 234
Tomball, TX 77375-6848

Wagner, Bret (Baseball Player)
489 Ridge Rd
Lewisberry, PA 17339-9308, USA

Wagner, Bruce (Writer)
9560 Wilshire Blvd Ste 500
Beverly Hills, CA 90212-2401, USA

Wagner, Bryan (Athlete, Football Player)
6020 Arlyne Ln
Medina, OH 44256-6852, USA

Wagner, Chuck (Actor, Musician)
1200 Maldonado Dr
Pensacola Beach, FL 32561-2244, USA

Wagner, Dajuan (Basketball Player)
1 Center Ct
Cleveland, OH 44115-4001, USA

Wagner, Fred (Cartoonist)
c/o Staff Member *King Features Syndication*
300 W 57th St Fl 15
New York, NY 10019-5238, USA

Wagner, Gary (Athlete, Baseball Player)
1707 Northbrook Ct
Seymour, IN 47274-4801, USA

Wagner, Harold A (Business Person)
7201 Hamilton Blvd
Allentown, PA 18195-9642, USA

Wagner, Jack (Actor, Musician)
314 Waverly Place Ct
Chesterfield, MO 63017-7819, USA

Wagner, Jane
PO Box 27700
Los Angeles, CA 90027-0700

Wagner, Jill (Actor)
c/o Jeff Golenberg *Collective*
8383 Wilshire Blvd Ste 1050
Beverly Hills, CA 90211-2415, USA

Wagner, John (Cartoonist)
101 McDonald Dr
Lawrence, KS 66044-1056, USA

Wagner, Katey (Actor)
1500 Old Oak Rd
Los Angeles, CA 90049-2504, USA

Wagner, Katie (Actor, Television Host)
c/o Staff Member *TV Guide Channel*
7140 S Lewis Ave
Tulsa, OK 74136-5437, USA

Wagner, Lindsay (Actor)
PO Box 57593
Sherman Oaks, CA 91413-2593, USA

Wagner, Lou (Actor)
21224 Celtic St
Chatsworth, CA 91311-1468, USA

Wagner, Louis C Jr (General)
6336 Manchester Way
Alexandria, VA 22304-3534, USA

Wagner, Lowell (Athlete, Football Player)
3013 254th Ave SE
Sammamish, WA 98075-9435, USA

Wagner, Maggie (Actor)
11935 Kling St Apt 10
Valley Village, CA 91607-5406, USA

Wagner, Mark (Athlete, Baseball Player)
1038 Willow Arms Dr
Ashtabula, OH 44004-7810, USA

Wagner, Matt (Cartoonist)
1700 Broadway
New York, NY 10019-5905, USA

Wagner, Matt (Athlete, Baseball Player)
1112 Lilac Ln
Cedar Falls, IA 50613-5342, USA

Wagner, Melinda (Composer)
588 N Gulph Rd
King Of Prussia, PA 19406-2831, USA

Wagner, Michael R (Mike) (Athlete, Football Player)
203 E Cherry Dr
Mars, PA 16046, USA

Wagner, Mike (Athlete, Football Player)
2607 Lakeview Way
Plant City, FL 33566-6774, USA

Wagner, Natasha Gregson (Actor)
c/o Amy Guenther *Gateway Management Company Inc*
860 Via De La Paz Ste F10
Pacific Palisades, CA 90272-3631, USA

Wagner, Paul (Athlete, Baseball Player)
N1960 State Road 67
Neosho, WI 53059-9723, USA

Wagner, Paula (Producer)
3000 Olympic Blvd Bldg 1 PMB 2515
Santa Monica, CA 90404, USA

Wagner, Philip M (Writer)
32 Montgomery St
Boston, MA 02116-6111, USA

Wagner, Phillip (Athlete, Basketball Player)
328 Glenloch Ln
Stockbridge, GA 30281-5920, USA

Wagner, Robert (Actor)
c/o Chuck Binder *Binder & Associates*
1465 Lindacrest Dr
Beverly Hills, CA 90210-2519, USA

Wagner, Robin S A (Designer)
890 Broadway
New York, NY 10003-1211, USA

Wagner, Roy H (Actor, Director)
c/o Lisa Helsing Lenhoff *Lenhoff & Lenhoff*
830 Palm Ave
West Hollywood, CA 90069-4009

Wagner, Ryan (Athlete, Baseball Player)
50 County Road 311
Yoakum, TX 77995, USA

Wagner, William E (Billy) (Athlete, Baseball Player)
5066 Jones Mill Rd
Crozet, VA 22932-2610, USA

Wagner, Wolfgang M M (Director, Opera Singer)
Postfach 100262
Bayreuth 95402, GERMANY

Wagoner, Dan (Choreographer, Dancer)
17 Duke's Road
London WC1H 9AB, UNITED KINGDOM (UK)

Wagoner, Dan (Athlete, Football Player)
PO Box 476
Lyman, SC 29365-0476, USA

Wagoner, David R (Writer)
5416 154th Pl SW
Edmonds, WA 98026-4348, USA

Wagoner, G Richard (Business Person)
100 Renaissance Ctr
Detroit, MI 48243-1114, USA

Wagoner, Harold E (Architect)
331 Lindsey Dr
Berwyn, PA 19312-1822, USA

Wahl, Deborah (Stylist)
4010 Band Shell Ct
Chesapeake Beach, MD 20732-3164, USA

Wahl, Ken (Actor)
c/o Susan Balistocky *Law Offices of Sysan Balistocky*
1901 Avenue of the Stars Ste 1900
Los Angeles, CA 90067-6020, USA

Wahlberg, Donnie (Actor, Musician)
c/o Jonathan Baruch *Rain Management Group (RMG)*
1631 21st St
Santa Monica, CA 90404-3914, USA

Wahlberg, Mark (Actor, Model, Musician)
c/o Stephen (Steve) Levinson *Leverage Management*
3030 Pennsylvania Ave
Santa Monica, CA 90404-4112, USA

Wahle, Mike (Athlete, Football Player)
914 Laurie Dr
Madison, WI 53711-2417, USA

Wahler, Jason (Reality TV Star)
c/o Staff Member *MTV Networks (LA)*
2600 Colorado Ave
Santa Monica, CA 90404-3519

Wahlgren, Olof G C (Editor)
Nicoloviusgatan 5B
Malmo 217 57, SWEDEN

Wahlquist, Heather (Actor)
c/o Troy Begnaud *Evolution Entertainment (LA)*
901 N Highland Ave
Los Angeles, CA 90038-2412, USA

Wahlstrom, Becky (Actor)
c/o Rob D'Avola *Rob DAvola & Associates*
9107 Wilshire Blvd Ste 450
Beverly Hills, CA 90210-5535, USA

Wahlstrom, Jarl H (Religious Leader)
Borgstrominkuja 1A10
Helsinki 84 840, FINLAND

Waigel, Theodor (Government Official)
Oberrohr
Ursberg 86513, GERMANY

Waihee, John D III (Ex-Governor)
333 Queen St Ste 608
Honolulu, HI 96813-4716, USA

Wain, Bea (Musician)
9955 Durant Dr Unit 305
Beverly Hills, CA 90212-1601, USA

Wainhouse, Dave (Athlete, Baseball Player)
6101 85th Pl SE
Mercer Island, WA 98040-4916, USA

Wainscott, Loyd (Athlete, Football Player)
401 Tarpey Rd
Texas City, TX 77591-3159, USA

Wainwright, Adam (Athlete, Baseball Player)
401 Pebble Trce
Saint Simons Island, GA 31522-3744, USA

Wainwright, James (Actor)
937 N Sinova
Mesa, AZ 85205-5438, USA

Wainwright, Loudon (Actor)
c/o Harriet Sternberg *Harriet Sternberg Management*
4530 Gloria Ave
Encino, CA 91436-2718, USA

Wainwright, Loudon III (Musician, Songwriter, Writer)
521 SW Halpatiokee St
Stuart, FL 34994-2815, USA

Wainwright, Rufus (Musician)
c/o Staff Member *MCT Management*
520 8th Ave Rm 2205
New York, NY 10018-4160, USA

Wainwright, Rupert (Director)
c/o Staff Member *United Talent Agency (UTA)*
9560 Wilshire Blvd Fl 5
Beverly Hills, CA 90212-2400, USA

Waite, John (Musician, Songwriter, Writer)
506 Walt Whitman Rd
Melville, NY 11747-2109, USA

Waite, Liam
c/o Staff Member *Gersh (LA)*
9465 Wilshire Blvd Ste 600
Beverly Hills, CA 90212-2612, USA

Waite, Ralph (Actor)
c/o Staff Member *Marshak/Zachary Company, The*
8840 Wilshire Blvd Fl 1
Beverly Hills, CA 90211-2606, USA

Waite, Terence H (Terry) (Religious Leader)
Wheelrights Green Harvest Bury Saint Demunds
Suffolk IP29 4DH, UNITED KINGDOM (UK)

Waite, Terry
The Green Harvest Bury St. Edmunds
Suffolk, ENGLAND 1P29 4DH

Waiters, Granville (Athlete, Basketball Player)
3740 Moor Ridge Ln
Canal Winchester, OH 43110-8082, USA

Waiters, Van (Athlete, Football Player)
6021 NW 201st Ln
Hialeah, FL 33015-4865, USA

Waitley, Denis (Business Person)
PO Box 197
Rancho Santa Fe, CA 92067-0197, USA

Waitley, Denis (Writer)
PO Box 197
Rancho Santa Fe, CA 92067-0197, USA

Waits, Rick (Athlete, Baseball Player)
PO Box 1001
Patagonia, AZ 85624-1001, USA

Waits, Tom (Music Group, Musician, Songwriter, Writer)
c/o Adam Isaacs *WmE2 (Endeavor-LA)*
9601 Wilshire Blvd Fl 3
Beverly Hills, CA 90210-5219, USA

Waitt, Theodore W (Ted) (Business Person)
7565 Irvine Center Dr
Irvine, CA 92618-2930, USA

Waitz, Grete (Athlete, Track Athlete)
Birgitte Hammers Vei 15G
Oslo 1169, NORWAY

Waitz, Richard H (Cinematographer)
405 Zenith Ave
Lafayette, CO 80026-3104, USA

Wajda, Andrezei
u1 Jezefa Hauke Boska 14
Warsaw, POLAND 01-540

Wajda, Andrzej (Director)
Ul Konopnickiej 26
Cracow 30-302, POLAND

Wakamatsu, Don (Athlete, Baseball Player)
8740 Ramblewood Ct
Keller, TX 76248-0361, USA

Wakasugi, Hiroshi
Monckebergallee 41
Hanover 30453, GERMANY

Wakata, Koichi (Astronaut)
2101 Nasa Pkwy Spc Center
Houston, TX 77058-3607, USA

Wakefield, Abbey-May (Actor)
c/o Simon Millar *Rumble Media*
1620 Broadway Ste C
Santa Monica, CA 90404-2777, USA

Wakefield, Andre (Athlete, Basketball Player)
320 Wisconsin Ave Apt 519
Oak Park, IL 60302-3459, USA

Wakefield, Bill (Athlete, Baseball Player)
1 Baypoint Village Dr
San Rafael, CA 94901-8409, USA

Wakefield, Cameron (Actor)
c/o Simon Millar *Rumble Media*
1620 Broadway Ste C
Santa Monica, CA 90404-2777, USA

Wakefield, Rhys (Actor)
c/o Darren Statt *Creative Artists Agency (CAA-LA)*
2000 Avenue of the Stars Ste 100
Los Angeles, CA 90067-4705, USA

Wakefield, Tim (Athlete, Baseball Player)
241 Lansing Island Dr
Indian Harbour Beach, FL 32937-5102, USA

Wakeham of Maldon, John (Government Official)
Westminster
London SW1A 0PW, UNITED KINGDOM (UK)

Wakeland, Chris (Athlete, Baseball Player)
60997 Luttrell Ln
Saint Helens, OR 97051-9126, USA

Wakeley, Amanda (Designer, Fashion Designer)
79-91 New Kings Road
London SW6 4SQ, UNITED KINGDOM (UK)

Wakeman, Frederic E Jr (Historian)
702 Gonzalez Dr
San Francisco, CA 94132-2234, USA

Wakeman, Rick (Musician, Songwriter, Writer)
Bajonor House 2 Bridge St Peel
Isle of Man, UNITED KINGDOM (UK)

Waknin, Deborah (Stylist)
c/o Staff Member *Smashbox Beauty*
8549 Higuera St Bldg B
Culver City, CA 90232-2521, USA

Wako, Gabriel Zubeir Cardinal (Religious Leader)
PO Box 49
Khartoum, SUDAN

Wakoski, Diane (Writer)
607 Division St
East Lansing, MI 48823-3428, USA

Walbeck, Matt (Athlete, Baseball Player)
8216 Olive Ave
Fair Oaks, CA 95628-7623, USA

Walberg, Mark L. (Actor, Television Host)
c/o Staff Member *WmE2 (Endeavor-LA)*
9601 Wilshire Blvd Fl 3
Beverly Hills, CA 90210-5219, USA

Walcott, Derek (Nobel Prize Laureate)
c/o Staff Member *Farrar, Straus and Giroux*
18 W 18th St Fl 7
New York, NY 10011-4675, USA

Walcott, Gregory (Actor)
22246 Saticoy St
Canoga Park, CA 91303-1043, USA

Walcott, Jennifer (Model)
4400 N Scottsdale Rd Ste 9
Scottsdale, AZ 85251-3331, USA

Walcutt, John (Actor)
c/o Staff Member *MC Talent Management*
4821 Lankershim Blvd # F329
N Hollywood, CA 91601-4538, USA

Walczak, Mark (Athlete, Football Player)
PO Box 372
Scottsdale, AZ 85252-0372, USA

Wald, Charles F (General)
Deputy Cofs for Air Space Operations
Hqusaf Pentaton
Washington, DC 20330-0001, USA

Wald, Jeff (Producer)
c/o Jeff Wald *Jeff Wald Entertainment*
3000 Olympic Blvd Bldg 2 PMB 1400
Santa Monica, CA 90404-5073, USA

Wald, Patricia M (Judge)
& 3rd Constitution NW
Washington, DC 20001, USA

Waldegrave, William (Government Official)
66 Palace Gardens Terrace
London W8 4RR, UNITED KINGDOM (UK)

Waldemore, Stan (Athlete, Football Player)
PO Box 611
New Vernon, NJ 07976-0611, USA

Walden, Robert (Actor)
c/o Staff Member *Bret Adams Agency*
448 W 44th St
New York, NY 10036-5220, USA

Walden, Robert E (Bobby) (Athlete, Football Player)
1403 Douglas Dr
Bainbridge, GA 39819-5176, USA

Walden, Ronnie (Athlete, Baseball Player)
1007 Autumn Way
Blanchard, OK 73010-8961, USA

Walder, Katie
c/o Jeff Morrone *Jeff Morrone Entertainment*
9350 Wilshire Blvd Ste 224
Beverly Hills, CA 90212-3204, USA

Waldheim, Kurt (President)
1 Lobkowitz Platz
Vienna 1010, AUSTRIA

Waldhorn, Gary (Actor)
2-4 Noel St
London W1V 3RB, UNITED KINGDOM (UK)

Waldie, Marc (Athlete, Volleyball Player)
3545 Camino Del Rio S Ste C
San Diego, CA 92108-4025, USA

Waldner, Jan-Ove (Athlete, Tennis Player)
Skiulstagatan 1O
Eskilstuna 632 29, SWEDEN

Waldo, Janet
15735 Royal Oak Rd
Encino, CA 91316

Waldorf, Duffy (Golfer)
17100 Halsted St
Northridge, CA 91325-1960, USA

Waldorf, Julie (Stylist)
c/o Staff Member *Fred Segal Beauty*
PO Box 5304
Beverly Hills, CA 90209-5304, USA

Waldron, Jeremy J (Educator)
1061 Keith Ave
Berkeley, CA 94708-1604, USA

Wales, Ross (Swimmer)
2730 Walsh Rd
Cincinnati, OH 45208-3425, USA

Walesa, Lech (Nobel Prize Laureate, President)
Ul Polanki 54
Gdansk-Oliwa 80-308, POLAND

Walewander, Jim (Athlete, Baseball Player)
6149 Loch Raven Dr
Mc Lean, VA 22101-3131, USA

Walger, Sonya (Actor)
c/o Jon Rubinstein *Authentic Talent and Literary Management*
45 Main St Ste 1004
Brooklyn, NY 11201-8200, USA

Walheim, Rex J (Astronaut)
142 Hidden Lake Dr
League City, TX 77573-6976, USA

Walia, Sonu (Actor, Bollywood)
20 The Anchorage Juhu-Versova Link Road Andheri W
Bombay, MS 400 058, INDIA

Walik, Billy (Athlete, Football Player)
PO Box 10712
Bainbridge Island, WA 98110-0712, USA

Walk, Bob (Athlete, Baseball Player)
2494 Shadowbrook Dr
Wexford, PA 15090-7982, USA

Walk, Neal (Athlete, Basketball Player)
6030 N 11th Ave
Phoenix, AZ 85013-1415, USA

Walkabouts, The
PO Box 360524
Berlin, GERMANY 10975

Walken, Christopher (Actor)
c/o Mara Buxbaum *ID PR (LA)*
7060 Hollywood Blvd Fl 8
Los Angeles, CA 90028-6014, USA

Walker, Adam (Athlete, Football Player)
923 Bucknell Ave
Johnstown, PA 15905-2215, USA

Walker, Alan (Misc)
Medical School Cell Biology/Anatomy Dept
Baltimore, MD 21205, USA

Walker, Alice M (Activist, Producer, Writer)
670 San Luis Rd
Berkeley, CA 94707-1744, USA

Walker, Ally (Actor)
c/o Katie Mason *Luber Roklin Management*
8530 Wilshire Blvd Ste 550
Beverly Hills, CA 90211-3133, USA

Walker, Anetia
19551 Turtle Ridge Ln
Northridge, CA 91326-3808

Walker, Ann (Actor)
c/o Pam Ellis *Ellis Talent Group*
4705 Laurel Canyon Blvd Ste 300
Valley Village, CA 91607-5901, USA

Walker, Antoine (Athlete, Basketball Player)
3950 Wood Ave
Miami, FL 33133-6429, USA

Walker, Arnetia (Actor)
19551 Turtle Ridge Ln
Northridge, CA 91326-3808, USA

Walker, B J (Financier)
1 First Union Ctr
Charlotte, NC 28288-0001, USA

Walker, Bree
3347 Tareco Dr
Los Angeles, CA 90068-1527

Walker, Brian (Cartoonist)
c/o Staff Member *King Features Syndication*
300 W 57th St Fl 15
New York, NY 10019-5238, USA

Walker, Bruce (Athlete, Football Player)
279 Eastlawn St
Detroit, MI 48215-3072, USA

Walker, Butch (Musician)
c/o Jonathan Daniel *Crush Management*
60-62 E 11th St Floor 7
New York, NY 10003, USA

Walker, Caroline (Actor)
c/o Staff Member *Badgley-Connor-King*
9229 W Sunset Blvd Ste 311
Los Angeles, CA 90069-3403, USA

Walker, Catherine (Designer, Fashion Designer)
65 Sydney St Chelsea
London SW3 6PX, UNITED KINGDOM (UK)

Walker, Charles D (Astronaut)
1200 Wilson Blvd # MCRS00
Arlington, VA 22209-2300, USA

Walker, Charls E (Economist)
19207 Racine Ct
Montgomery Village, MD 20886-3900, USA

Walker, Chet (Athlete, Basketball Player)
PO Box 9451
Marina Del Rey, CA 90295-1851, USA

Walker, Chico (Athlete, Baseball Player)
450 W Huron St
Chicago, IL 60654-3495, USA

Walker, Chris (Actor)
121 Gloucester Place
London W1H 3PJ, UNITED KINGDOM (UK)

Walker, Chuck (Athlete, Football Player)
1613 Tradd Ct
Chesterfield, MO 63017-5627, USA

Walker, Clay (Musician)
c/o Liza Prijate *Susan Blond Inc (NY)*
50 W 57th St Fl 14
New York, NY 10019-3914, USA

Walker, Cleo (Athlete, Football Player)
512 Tecumseh Dr
Shepherdsville, KY 40165-7060, USA

Walker, Colleen (Golfer)
3612 Sugar Loaf Ln
Valrico, FL 33596-6062, USA

Walker, Darnell (Athlete, Football Player)
715 N Terrace Blvd
Muskogee, OK 74401-3717, USA

Walker, Darrell (Athlete, Basketball Player, Coach)
16122 Patriot Dr
Little Rock, AR 72212-2669, USA

Walker, David (Government Official)
441 G St NW
Washington, DC 20548-0001, USA

Walker, Denard (Athlete, Football Player)
17214 Lechlade Ln
Dallas, TX 75252-4208, USA

Walker, Derek (Architect)
2 General Sage Dr
Santa Fe, NM 87505-6333, USA

Walker, Derrick (Race Car Driver)
147 Midland Rd Royston Bamsley
S York S71 4B1, UNITED KINGDOM (UK)

Walker, Dreama (Actor)
c/o Randi Goldstein *Gersh (NY)*
41 Madison Ave
New York, NY 10010-2202, USA

Walker, Duane (Athlete, Baseball Player)
2509 Georgia Ave
Deer Park, TX 77536-4732, USA

Walker, Dwight (Athlete, Football Player)
3112 Phoenix St Apt B
Kenner, LA 70065-5115, USA

Walker, Eamonn (Actor)
c/o Scott Schachter *International Creative Management (ICM-LA)*
10250 Constellation Blvd Fl 7
Los Angeles, CA 90067-6207, USA

Walker, Fiona (Writer)
c/o Susan Fletcher *Hodder & Stoughton Limited*
338 Euston Rd
London NW1 3BH, UK

Walker, George T Jr (Composer)
323 Grove St
Montclair, NJ 07042-4223, USA

Walker, Glen (Athlete, Football Player)
5592 Nelson St
Cypress, CA 90630-3147, USA

Walker, Greg (Cartoonist)
c/o Staff Member *King Features Syndication*
300 W 57th St Fl 15
New York, NY 10019-5238, USA

Walker, Greg (Athlete, Baseball Player)
530 N Lake Shore Dr Apt 1009
Chicago, IL 60611-7426, USA

Walker, Harry
2120 Montevallo Rd
Leeds, AL 35094-3738

Walker, Herschel (Athlete, Football Player)
2210 King Fisher Dr
Westlake, TX 76262-4815, USA

Walker, Hezekiah (Musician)
c/o Staff Member *The Alliance Agency*
1035 Bates Ct
Hendersonville, TN 37075-8864, USA

Walker, Hugh (Baseball Player)
24 Georgeann Dr
Jacksonville, AR 72076-5352, USA

Walker, Jackie (Athlete, Football Player)
13014 N Dale Mabry Hwy # 120
Tampa, FL 33618-2808, USA

Walker, James E (Educator)
President S Ofc
Murfreesboro, TN 37132-0001, USA

Walker, James L (Jimmy) (Misc)
1100 Circle 75 Pkwy SE
Atlanta, GA 30339-3064, USA

Walker, Jamie (Athlete, Baseball Player)
11450 W 187th St
Spring Hill, KS 66083-7593, USA

Walker, Jason (Musician)
c/o Len Evans *Project Publicity*
312 W 53rd St Ste 202
New York, NY 10019-5743, USA

Walker, Javon (Athlete, Football Player)
7375 Talon Trl
Parker, CO 80138-7956, USA

Walker, Jeff (Athlete, Football Player)
3712 Ringgold Rd Apt 204
Chattanooga, TN 37412-1638, USA

Walker, Jerry (Athlete, Baseball Player)
2015 Collins Blvd
Ada, OK 74820-7015, USA

Walker, Jerry Jeff (Musician, Songwriter)
PO Box 39
Austin, TX 78767-0039, USA

Walker, Jimmie (J J) (Actor, Comedian)
c/o Wes Stevens *Vox*
6420 Wilshire Blvd Ste 1080
Los Angeles, CA 90048-5539, USA

Walker, Joe Louis (Musician)
714 Brookside Ln
Sierra Madre, CA 91024-1426, USA

Walker, John (Athlete, Track Athlete)
Jeffs Road
RD Papatoetoe, NEW ZEALAND

Walker, John E (Nobel Prize Laureate)
Hills Road
Cambridge CB2 2QH, UNITED KINGDOM (UK)

Walker, Johnny (Baseball Player)
718 Franklin St SE
Grand Rapids, MI 49507-1307, USA

Walker, Junior
141 Dunbar Ave
Fords, NJ 08863-1551

Walker, Kenny (Athlete, Basketball Player)
2252 Terrace Woods Park
Lexington, KY 40513-1611, USA

Walker, Kenyatta (Athlete, Football Player)
14813 Tudor Chase Dr
Tampa, FL 33626-3353, USA

Walker, Kevin (Athlete, Baseball Player)
3701 Riviera Dr Apt 8
San Diego, CA 92109-6600, USA

Walker, Larry (Athlete, Baseball Player)
1667 Flagler Pkwy
West Palm Beach, FL 33411-1874, USA

Walker, Leroy T (Coach, Educator)
PO Box 110105
Durham, NC 27709-5105, USA

Walker, Luke (Athlete, Baseball Player)
316 Loma Linda St
Wake Village, TX 75501-8638, USA

Walker, Malcolm (Athlete, Football Player)
7140 Winterwood Ln
Dallas, TX 75248-5246, USA

Walker, Marquis (Athlete, Football Player)
17576 Cherrylawn St
Detroit, MI 48221-2508, USA

Walker, Mickey (Athlete, Football Player)
22828 S Maple Point Rd
Pickford, MI 49774-9145, USA

Walker, Mike (Athlete, Baseball Player)
23195 Tankersley Rd
Brooksville, FL 34601-4818, USA

Walker, Mike (Athlete, Baseball Player)
24616 Marks Rd
Splendora, TX 77372-3407, USA

Walker, Mort (Cartoonist)
61 Studio Rd
Stamford, CT 06903-4724, USA

Walker, Nicholas
1900 Avenue of the Stars Ste 1640
Los Angeles, CA 90067-4407

Walker, Paul (Actor)
c/o Matt Luber *Luber Roklin Management*
8530 Wilshire Blvd Ste 550
Beverly Hills, CA 90211-3133, USA

Walker, Paul L (Religious Leader)
PO Box 2430
Cleveland, TN 37320-2430, USA

Walker, Pete (Athlete, Baseball Player)
2 White Oak Ln
Quaker Hill, CT 06375-1045, USA

Walker, Peter (Director)
23 Bentick St
London W1, UNITED KINGDOM (UK)

Walker, Phillip (Athlete, Basketball Player)
720 E Phil Ellena St
Philadelphia, PA 19119-1531, USA

Walker, Polly (Actor)
c/o Jon Rubinstein *Authentic Talent and Literary Management*
45 Main St Ste 1004
Brooklyn, NY 11201-8200, USA

Walker, Rick (Athlete, Football Player)
906 Winstead St
Great Falls, VA 22066-2546, USA

Walker, Robert M (Physicist)
1 Brookings Dr # CB1105
Saint Louis, MO 63130-4862, USA

Walker, Roger N (Architect)
8 Brougham St Mount Victoria
Wellington, NEW ZEALAND

Walker, Ronald C (Publisher)
900 Jefferson Dr SW
Washington, DC 20560-0004, USA

Walker, Sammy (Athlete, Football Player)
1031 Kings Row
Mc Kinney, TX 75069-6207, USA

Walker, Sandra (Opera Singer)
165 W 57th St
New York, NY 10019-2201, USA

Walker, Sarah E B (Opera Singer)
152 Inchmery Road
London SE6 1DF, UNITED KINGDOM (UK)

Walker, Scott (Governor, Politician)
PO Box 7863
Madison, WI 53707-7863, USA

Walker, Scott (Director)
c/o Michael Esola *WmE2 (Endeavor-LA)*
9601 Wilshire Blvd Fl 3
Beverly Hills, CA 90210-5219, USA

Walker, Todd (Athlete, Baseball Player)
212 Madonna Dr
Benton, LA 71006-4217, USA

Walker, Tom (Athlete, Baseball Player)
817 Whippoorwill Hill Rd
Gibsonia, PA 15044-8985, USA

Walker, Tony (Athlete, Baseball Player)
2030 Goldenrod Ln
San Ramon, CA 94582-5543, USA

Walker, Tyler (Athlete, Baseball Player)
400 Sansome St
San Francisco, CA 94111-3353, USA

Walker, Val Joe (Athlete, Football Player)
3857 S Versailles Ave
Dallas, TX 75209-5927, USA

Walker, Wally (Athlete, Basketball Player)
154 Lombard St Apt 58
San Francisco, CA 94111-1125, USA

Walker, Wayne (Athlete, Football Player)
2033 S White Pine Ln
Boise, ID 83706-4048, USA

Walker, Wesley D (Athlete, Football Player)
PO Box 20438
Huntington Station, NY 11746-0857, USA

Walker, William D (Business Person)
26600 Sourtwest Pkwy
Wilsonville, OR 97070, USA

Walker Jr, Robert (Actor)
23410 Civic Center Way Ste C1
Malibu, CA 90265-5925, USA

Walker of Worchester, Peter E (Government Official)
Abbots Morton Manor Grooms Hill
Abbots Morton
Worc WR7 4LT, UNITED KINGDOM (UK)

Wall, Brian A (Artist)
306 Lombard St
San Francisco, CA 94133-2415, USA

Wall, Carolyn (Publisher)
251 W 57th St
New York, NY 10019-1802, USA

Wall, David (Ballerina)
Covent Garden Bow St
London WC2E 9DD, UNITED KINGDOM (UK)

Wall, Donne (Athlete, Baseball Player)
116 River Breeze Way
Saint Louis, MO 63129-4855, USA

Wall, Frederick T (Athlete, Football Player)
2044 Kerwood Ave
Los Angeles, CA 90025-6007, USA

Wall, John (Athlete, Basketball Player)
c/o Dan Fegan *Lagardere Unlimited - (LA)*
10866 Wilshire Blvd
Los Angeles, CA 90024-4300, USA

Wall, John F (General)
507 Hanover St
Fredericksburg, VA 22401-5711, USA

Wall, Lindsay (Hockey Player)
Athletic Dept
Minneapolis, MN 55455, USA

Wall, Paul (Musician)
c/o Drew Elliot *Media Artists Group (NY)*
140 E 46th St PH C
New York, NY 10017-2633, USA

Wall, Shana (Actor)
c/o Elizabeth Much *Much and House Public Relations*
8075 W 3rd St Ste 500
Los Angeles, CA 90048-4325, USA

Wall, Stan (Athlete, Baseball Player)
9907 E 80th St
Raytown, MO 64138-1929, USA

Wallace, Aaron (Athlete, Football Player)
9327 Edinburgh Ln
Frisco, TX 75035-3119, USA

Wallace, Anthony F C (Misc)
Anthropology Dept
Philadelphia, PA 19014, USA

Wallace, Aria (Actor)
c/o DebraLynn Findon *Discover Inc Management*
11425 Moorpark St
Studio City, CA 91602-2009, USA

Wallace, B J (Baseball Player)
12775 River Creek Dr
Fairhope, AL 36532-6501, USA

Wallace, B Steven (Steve) (Athlete, Football Player)
305 Heards Ferry Rd NW
Atlanta, GA 30328-4716, USA

Wallace, Ben (Basketball Player)
c/o Staff Member *Chicago Bulls*
1901 W Madison St
Chicago, IL 60612-2459, USA

Wallace, Bob (Athlete, Football Player)
44111 N 43rd Dr
New River, AZ 85087-5956, USA

Wallace, Bruce (Doctor, Scientist)
940 McBryde Ln
Blacksburg, VA 24060-3221, USA

Wallace, Carol (Editor)
Editorial Dept Time-Life Building
New York, NY 10020, USA

Wallace, Cathy (Stylist)
PO Box 140725
Irving, TX 75014-0725, USA

Wallace, Chris (Correspondent)
c/o Staff Member *ABC News*
77 W 66th St Fl 3
New York, NY 10023-6201, USA

Wallace, Christopher (Chris) (Correspondent)
205 E 67th St
New York, NY 10065-6050, USA

Wallace, Clifford J (Judge)
940 Front St
San Diego, CA 92101-8971, USA

Wallace, Cooper (Athlete, Football Player)
c/o Chad Speck *Allegiant Athletic Agency*
35 Market Sq Ste 201
Knoxville, TN 37902-1420, USA

Wallace, Craig K (Doctor)
9000 Rockville Pike
Bethesda, MD 20892-0001, USA

Wallace, Dave (Athlete, Baseball Player)
82 Whipple Brook Rd
Wrentham, MA 02093-2512, USA

Wallace, Derek (Athlete, Baseball Player)
4250 SE Boxleaf Pl
Stuart, FL 34997-2253, USA

Wallace, Don (Actor)
c/o Staff Member *Silver Massetti & Szatmary (SMS) Talent Inc*
8730 W Sunset Blvd Ste 440
Los Angeles, CA 90069-2277, USA

Wallace, Don (Athlete, Baseball Player)
23 Kris Ln
Manitou Springs, CO 80829-2709, USA

Wallace, George (Musician)
c/o Staff Member *Paradigm (Monterey)*
404 W Franklin St
Monterey, CA 93940-2303, USA

Wallace, Gerald (Athlete, Basketball Player)
8381 Providence Rd
Charlotte, NC 28277-9753, USA

Wallace, Jane (Entertainer)
4303 W Verdugo Ave
Burbank, CA 91505-3358, USA

Wallace, Jeff (Athlete, Baseball Player)
2904 Federal Ave
Alliance, OH 44601-4550, USA

Wallace, Jennifer (Stylist)
c/o Staff Member *Fred Segal Beauty*
PO Box 5304
Beverly Hills, CA 90209-5304, USA

Wallace, Julie T (Actor)
9 Newburgh St
London W1V 1LH, UNITED KINGDOM (UK)

Wallace, Kenny (Race Car Driver)
8929 Harris Rd
Concord, NC 28027, USA

Wallace, Laurie
PO Box 3023
Guttenberg, NJ 07093-6023

Wallace, Marcia (Actor)
c/o Sandie Schnarr *Sandie Schnarr Talent Agency*
5670 Wilshire Blvd Ste 1930
Los Angeles, CA 90036-5603, USa

Wallace, Mike (Correspondent)

Wallace, Mike (Athlete, Baseball Player)
12483 Elk Run Rd
Midland, VA 22728-2316, USA

Wallace, Randall (Actor, Director, Producer, Writer)
c/o Staff Member *Wheelhouse, The*
142 S Woodburn Dr
Los Angeles, CA 90049-3041

Wallace, Rasheed (Athlete, Basketball Player)
1979 Arthurs Way
Rochester Hills, MI 48306-3363, USA

Wallace, Ray (Athlete, Football Player)
2480 Port Kembla Dr
Mount Juliet, TN 37122-7512, USA

Wallace, Rheagan (Actor)
c/o Linda McAlister *Linda McAlister Talent*
100 Oak Ln
Waxahachie, TX 75167-8412, USA

Wallace, Rodney (Athlete, Football Player)
20566 E Maplewood Pl
Centennial, CO 80016-1264, USA

Wallace, Roger (Athlete, Football Player)
408 N Oakland St
Urbana, OH 43078-1521, USA

Wallace, Rusty (Athlete, Race Car Driver)
149 Knob Hill Rd
Mooresville, NC 28117-6847, USA

Wallace, Steve (Race Car Driver)
c/o Staff Member *Rusty Wallace Racing, LLC*
149 Knob Hill Rd
Mooresville, NC 28117-6847, USA

Wallace, Tommy Lee (Director)
1505 10th St
Santa Monica, CA 90401-2805, USA

Wallace, Will (Actor)
c/o Andrew Stawiarski *ADS Management*
269 S Beverly Dr # 441
Beverly Hills, CA 90212-3851, USA

Wallace, William (General)
Commanding General V Corps
APO, AE 9079, USA

Wallach, Eli (Actor)
90 Riverside Dr
New York, NY 10024-5306, USA

Wallach, Evan J (Judge)
1 Federal Plz
New York, NY 10278-0001, USA

Wallach, Tim (Athlete, Baseball Player)
21750 Deveron Cv
Yorba Linda, CA 92887-2662, USA

Wallack, Anna (Stylist)
c/o Staff Member *Team*
423 W Broadway Ste 406
Boston, MA 02127-2265, USA

Wallechinsky, David (Writer)
c/o Staff Member *HarperCollins Publishers*
10 E 53rd St C/O Author Mail Floor 7
New York, NY 10022, USA

Wallenberg, Raoul Committee
823 United Nations Plz Fl 8
New York, NY 10017-3543

Wallendas, The Great
138 Frog Hollow Rd
Churchville, PA 18966-1031

Waller, Dwight (Athlete, Basketball Player)
1038 S Brookside Dr
Gallatin, TN 37066-5612, USA

Waller, Jamie (Athlete, Basketball Player)
904 Owens Ave
South Boston, VA 24592-3728, USA

Waller, Jo (Stylist)
18 E 18th St Apt 5E
New York, NY 10003-1933, USA

Waller, Michael (Editor)
285 Broad St
Hartford, CT 06115-3785, USA

Waller, Peter
7 Passage St Owley
Cornwall, ENGLAND PL23 IDE

Waller, Robert James (Writer)
708 3rd Ave Rm 2300
New York, NY 10017-4211, USA

Waller, Ron (Athlete, Football Player)
900 Concord Rd
Seaford, DE 19973, USA

Waller, Ty (Athlete, Baseball Player)
16963 Silver Crest Dr
San Diego, CA 92127-2816, USA

Waller, William L (Ex-Governor)
220 S President St
Jackson, MS 39201-4307, USA

Wallerstein, Ralph G (Misc)
3447 Clay St
San Francisco, CA 94118-2008, USA

Wallflowers, The (Music Group)
c/o Rick Roskin *Creative Artists Agency (CAA-LA)*
2000 Avenue of the Stars Ste 100
Los Angeles, CA 90067-4705, USA

Walliams, David (Actor, Producer, Writer)
c/o Kevin McLaughlin *Baker Winokur Ryder Public Relations (BWR-LA)*
9100 Wilshire Blvd Ste 500 PMB WEST
Beverly Hills, CA 90212-3426, USA

Walling, Camryn (Actor)
c/o Staff Member *Abrams Artists Agency (LA)*
9200 W Sunset Blvd PH 11
Los Angeles, CA 90069-3601, USA

Walling, Cheves T (Misc)
318 Rivermead Rd
Peterborough, NH 03458-1762, USA

Walling, Denny (Athlete, Baseball Player)
PO Box 1312
Waynesboro, VA 22980-0902, USA

Wallis, Annabelle (Actor)
c/o Cynthia Campos-Greenberg *Anthem Entertainment*
9595 Wilshire Blvd Ste 900
Beverly Hills, CA 90212-2509, USA

Wallis, Joe (Athlete, Baseball Player)
PO Box 659
Chesterfield, MO 63006-0659, USA

Wallis, Shani (Actor)
PO Box 3604
Dana Point, CA 92629-8604, USA

Walliser, Maria (Skier)
Selfwingert
Malans 7208, SWITZERLAND

Wallop, Malcolm (Senator)
58 Canyon Ranch Rd
Big Horn, WY 82833, USA

Walls, Denise (Nee-C) (Musician, Songwriter, Writer)
2113 South Ave
Youngstown, OH 44502-2255, USA

Walls, Everson C (Athlete, Football Player)
4812 Portrait Ln
Plano, TX 75024-3803, USA

Walls, Herkie (Athlete, Football Player)
1002 Cherrywood Dr
Garland, TX 75040-7437, USA

Walls, Jeannette (Writer)
c/o Staff Member *Keppler Associates*
4350 Fairfax Dr Ste 700
Arlington, VA 22203-1620, USA

Walls, Lenny (Athlete, Football Player)
2800 Bush St
San Francisco, CA 94115-2905, USA

Walls, Wesley (Athlete, Football Player)
8711 Lake Challis Ln
Charlotte, NC 28226-2666, USA

Walmsley, Jon (Actor)
217 Grand Ave Apt 5
Long Beach, CA 90803-6135, USA

Walpot, Heike (Astronaut)
Abt Raumflugbetrieb
Cologne 51170, GERMANY

Walrond, Les (Athlete, Baseball Player)
113 Autumn Oaks Ct
Brentwood, TN 37027-8818, USA

Walser, Don (Musician, Songwriter, Writer)
6618 Wolfcreek Pass
Austin, TX 78749-1744, USA

Walser, Martin
Zum Hecht 36
Uberlingen, GERMANY D-88662

Walsh, Addie (Writer)
c/o Staff Member *WmE2 (WMA-LA)*
1 William Morris Pl
Beverly Hills, CA 90212-4261, USA

Walsh, Amanda (Actor)
c/o Laina Cohn *Laina Cohn Management*
15066 Sutton St
Sherman Oaks, CA 91403-4020, USA

Walsh, Arthur
12360 Riverside Dr
Valley Village, CA 91607-3644

Walsh, Bradley (Actor)
c/o Debi Allen *Debi Allen Associates*
22 Torrington Pl
London WC1E 7HP, UK

Walsh, Catherine (Stylist)
3800 Overdale Dr
Columbus, OH 43220-4749, USA

Walsh, Chris (Athlete, Football Player)
1850 Bryant St
Palo Alto, CA 94301-3709, USA

Walsh, Dave (Athlete, Baseball Player)
500 Concord Ln
Edmond, OK 73003-6127, USA

Walsh, David M (Cinematographer)
15436 Valley Vista Blvd
Sherman Oaks, CA 91403-3812, USA

Walsh, Diana Chapman (Educator)
President's Office
Wellesley, MA 2181, USA

Walsh, Don (Athlete, Swimmer)
14758 Sitkum Ln
Myrtle Point, OR 97458-9692, USA

Walsh, Donnie (Basketball Player, Coach)
125 S Pennsylvania St
Indianapolis, IN 46204-3610, USA

Walsh, Dylan (Actor)
c/o Bob McGowan *McGowan Management*
8733 W Sunset Blvd Ste 103
West Hollywood, CA 90069-2241, USA

Walsh, Frances (Fran) (Producer, Writer)
c/o Staff Member *WingNut Films*
PO Box 15-208 Miramar
Wellington 6003, NEW ZEALAND

Walsh, Gwynyth (Actor)
c/o Staff Member *Characters Talent Agency, The (Vancouver)*
1505 W 2nd Ave #200
Vancouver, BC V6H 3Y4, Canada

Walsh, Joe (Musician, Songwriter)
400 Porter St
Easton, PA 18042-1726, USA

Walsh, John (Television Host)
c/o Sean Perry *WmE2 (Endeavor-LA)*
9601 Wilshire Blvd Fl 3
Beverly Hills, CA 90210-5219, USA

Walsh, Kate (Actor)
c/o Justin Grey Stone *Untitled Entertainment (LA)*
350 S Beverly Dr Ste 200
Beverly Hills, CA 90212-4819, USA

Walsh, Kerri (Athlete, Volleyball Player)
PO Box 33053
Los Gatos, CA 95031-3053, USA

Walsh, Kimberley (Actor, Musician)
c/o Staff Member *Artists Rights Group (ARG)*
4 Great Portland St
London W1W 8PA, UNITED KINGDOM (UK)

Walsh, Lawrence E (Attorney, Attorney General, General, Government Official)
1902 Bedford Dr
Nichols Hills, OK 73116-5306, USA

Walsh, M Emmet (Actor)
4173 Motor Ave
Culver City, CA 90232-3414, USA

Walsh, M. Emmett (Actor)
c/o Sandra Joseph *SLJ Management*
833 N Edinburgh Ave Ph 11
Los Angeles, CA 90046-6999, USA

Walsh, Maiara (Actor)
c/o Staff Member *Mattie Management*
2216 Alcyona Dr
Los Angeles, CA 90068-2805, USA

Walsh, Martin (Misc)
910 16th St NW
Washington, DC 20006-2903, USA

Walsh, Matt (Comedian)
c/o Staff Member *United Talent Agency (UTA)*
9560 Wilshire Blvd Fl 5
Beverly Hills, CA 90212-2400, USA

Walsh, Patrick C (Doctor)
Brady Urological Institute
Baltimore, MD 21205, USA

Walsh, Peter (Designer)
15030 Ventura Blvd # 19-881
Sherman Oaks, CA 91403-5470, USA

Walsh, Sheila (Musician, Writer)
PO Box 150783
Nashville, TN 37215-0783, USA

Walsh, Shelia (Musician, Writer)
PO Box 1516
Celina, TX 75009-1516, USA

Walsh, Stephen J (Steve) (Athlete, Football Player)
8801 Wellington View Dr
West Palm Beach, FL 33411-5311, USA

Walsh, Steve
Box 6 Wickford
Essex, ENGLAND SS12 9D0

Walsh, Sydney (Actor)
1505 10th St
Santa Monica, CA 90401-2805, USA

Walsh, Tom (Artist)
PO Box 133
Philomath, OR 97370-0133, USA

Walsh, Ward (Athlete, Football Player)
1658 W Carson St Ste C
Torrance, CA 90501-2897, USA

Walshe, Tommy (Actor, Television Host)
c/o Staff Member *Arlington Enterprises Ltd*
1-3 Charlotte St
London W1P 1HD, UNITED KINGDOM (UK)

Walske, Steven (Business Person)
140 Kendrick St
Needham Heights, MA 02494-2739, USA

Walsman, Leanna (Actor)
c/o Chris Andrews *Creative Artists Agency (CAA-LA)*
2000 Avenue of the Stars Ste 100
Los Angeles, CA 90067-4705, USA

Walte, Grant (Golfer)
9380 S Magnolia Ave
Ocala, FL 34476-7535, USA

Walter, Gene (Athlete, Baseball Player)
1901 Fairway Dr
La Grange, KY 40031-9697, USA

Walter, Harriet (Actor)
c/o Jeremy Conway *Conway van Gelder*
8-12 Broadwick St
London W1F 8HW, UK

Walter, Jessica (Actor)
c/o Sandra Chang *Industry Entertainment Partners*
955 Carrillo Dr Ste 300
Los Angeles, CA 90048-5400, USA

Walter, Joe (Athlete, Football Player)
4136 Binley Dr
Richardson, TX 75082-3723, USA

Walter, Lisa Ann (Actor)
c/o Mel McKeon *McKeon-Myones Management*
3500 W Olive Ave Ste 770
Burbank, CA 91505-5527, USA

Walter, Michael (Athlete, Football Player)
6900 SW Knollwood St
Tualatin, OR 97062-7717, USA

Walter, Mike (Athlete, Football Player)
6900 SW Knollwood St
Tualatin, OR 97062-7717, USA

Walter, Paul H L (Misc)
95 Skidaway Island Park Rd Apt 121
Savannah, GA 31411-1112, USA

Walter, Robert D (Business Person)
7000 Cardinal Pl
Dublin, OH 43017-1091, USA

Walter, Tracey (Actor)
257 N Rexford Dr
Beverly Hills, CA 90210-4907, USA

Walter, Ulrich (Astronaut)
Schonaicherstr 220
Boblingen 71032, GERMANY

Walters, Barbara (Journalist, Talk Show Host)
c/o Cindi Berger *PMK/BNC Public Relations (PMK-NY)*
622 3rd Ave Fl 8
New York, NY 10017-6707, USA

Walters, Charles (Director)
23922 De Ville Way Apt A
Malibu, CA 90265-4844, USA

Walters, Charlie (Athlete, Baseball Player)
1717 Sutton Ln
Saint Paul, MN 55118-3717, USA

Walters, Dan (Athlete, Baseball Player)

Walters, Donna (Stylist)
6611 W 62nd St
Mission, KS 66202-3208, USA

Walters, Harry N (Government Official)
125 Thomas Dl
Williamsburg, VA 23185-6576, USA

Walters, Hugh
15 Christchurch Ave
London, ENGLAND NW6 7QP

Walters, Jamie (Actor, Musician)
4702 Ethel Ave
Sherman Oaks, CA 91423-3315, USA

Walters, Julie (Actor)
c/o Tom Burke *International Creative Management (ICM-LA)*
10250 Constellation Blvd Fl 7
Los Angeles, CA 90067-6207, USA

Walters, Ken (Athlete, Baseball Player)
3175 Edgewood Ln
Newcastle, CA 95658-9315, USA

Walters, Lisa (Athlete, Golfer)
211 S Westland Ave Unit 2
Tampa, FL 33606-1721, USA

Walters, Melora (Actor)
c/o Staff Member *Platform Public Relations*
2666 N Beachwood Dr
Los Angeles, CA 90068-2308, USA

Walters, Michael (Stylist)
10 Circle Way
Mill Valley, CA 94941-3420, USA

Walters, Mike (Athlete, Baseball Player)
79070 Desert Stream Dr
La Quinta, CA 92253-4295, USA

Walters, Peter I (Business Person)
22 Hill St
London W1X 7FU, UNITED KINGDOM (UK)

Walters, Rex (Athlete, Basketball Player)
21602 W 99th St
Lenexa, KS 66220-2678, USA

Walters, Roger T (Architect)
46 Princess Road
London NW1 8JL, UNITED KINGDOM (UK)

Walters, Stan (Athlete, Football Player)
10 Lcklingham Wood
Sewell, NJ 8080, USA

Walters, Susan (Actor)
c/o Gabrielle Krengel *Domain Talent*
9229 W Sunset Blvd Ste 710
Los Angeles, CA 90069-3407, USA

Walters, Tom (Athlete, Football Player)
8 Heritage Ln
Magnolia, TX 77354-1337, USA

Walters, Tome H Jr (General)
Defense Security Cooperation Agency
1111 Davis Highway
Arlington, VA 22202, USA

Walterschield, Len (Athlete, Football Player)
2312 I Rd
Grand Junction, CO 81505-9646, USA

Walther, Herbert (Physicist)
Egenhoferstr 7A
Munich 81243, GERMANY

Walther, Paul (Athlete, Basketball Player)
6555 Riverside Dr NW
Atlanta, GA 30328-2705, USA

Walton, Alice (Business Person)
702 SW 8th St
Bentonville, AR 72716-6209, USA

Walton, Anna (Actor)
c/o Rupert Fowler *ID Public Relations*
Pall Mall Deposit 124-128 Barlby Rd Unit 27A
London W10 6BL, UK

Walton, Anthony J (Tony) (Designer)
40 W 57th St # 1800
New York, NY 10019-4001, USA

Walton, Bennie (Baseball Player)
188 S Palm Villas Way
Palm Springs, FL 33461-1084, USA

Walton, Bruce (Athlete, Baseball Player)
10704 Sunset Canyon Dr
Bakersfield, CA 93311-2746, USA

Walton, Cedar A Jr (Musician)
35 Clark St Apt A5
Brooklyn, NY 11201-2374, USA

Walton, Christy (Business Person)
702 SW 8th St
Bentonville, AR 72716-6209, USA

Walton, Danny (Athlete, Baseball Player)
PO Box 296
Huntsville, UT 84317-0296, USA

Walton, David (Actor)
c/o Eric Black *Anonymous Content (AC-LA)*
3531 Hayden Ave
Culver City, CA 90232, USA

Walton, Jerome (Athlete, Baseball Player)
8015 Clearview Cir
Riverdale, GA 30296-3389, USA

Walton, Jess (Actor)
c/o Staff Member *Stone Manners Salners Agency (LA)*
9911 W Pico Blvd Ste 1400
Los Angeles, CA 90035-2715, USA

Walton, Jim (Business Person)
PO Box 2030
Bentonville, AR 72712-2030, USA

Walton, John (Athlete, Football Player)
401 New York Ave
Elizabeth City, NC 27909-5939, USA

Walton, Joseph (Joe) (Athlete, Coach, Football Coach, Football Player)
8 Windycrest Dr
Beaver Falls, PA 15010-3041, USA

Walton, Lawrence (Athlete, Football Player)
PO Box 32204
Phoenix, AZ 85064-2204, USA

Walton, Luke (Athlete, Basketball Player)
1613 Gates Ave
Manhattan Beach, CA 90266-7028, USA

Walton, Reggie (Athlete, Baseball Player)
1142 S Curson Ave
Los Angeles, CA 90019-6611, USA

Walton, Robin (Golfer)
604 Rittenhouse Ct
Winston Salem, NC 27104-5103, USA

Walton, S Robson (Rob) (Business Person)
702 SW 8th St
Bentonville, AR 72716-6209, USA

Walton, Whip (Athlete, Football Player)
748 E Solana Cir
Solana Beach, CA 92075-2356, USA

Walton, William T (Bill) III (Athlete, Basketball Player, Sportscaster)
1010 Myrtle Way
San Diego, CA 92103-5123, USA

Waltrip, Darrell L (Race Car Driver)
PO Box 381
Harrisburg, NC 28075-0381, USA

Waltrip, Michael (Race Car Driver)
20310 Chartwell Center Dr
Cornelius, NC 28031-5253, USA

Waltrip, Robert L (Business Person)
1929 Allen Pkwy
Houston, TX 77019-2506, USA

Waltz, Christoph (Actor)
c/o Craig Bankey *WKT Public Relations (WKT-LA)*
9350 Wilshire Blvd Ste 450
Beverly Hills, CA 90212-3230, USA

Waltz, Lisa (Actor)
c/o Donald Spradlin *Essential Talent Management*
6399 Wilshire Blvd Ste 401
Los Angeles, CA 90048-5716, USA

Walulik-Kiely, Helen (Baseball Player)
493 W Hill Rd
Glen Gardner, NJ 08826-3341, USA

Walz, Carl E (Astronaut)
129 Lake Point Dr
League City, TX 77573-6973, USA

Walz, Zach (Athlete, Football Player)
6270 E Wilshire Dr
Scottsdale, AZ 85257-1114, USA

Wamala, Emmanuel Cardinal (Religious Leader)
PO Box 14125 Mengo
Kampala, UGANDA

Wambach, Abby (Soccer Player)
1600 Parkwood Cir SE Ste 600
Atlanta, GA 30339-2147, USA

Wambaugh, Joseph (Writer)
3520 Kellogg Way
San Diego, CA 92106-3346, USA

Wambold, Richard L (Business Person)
1900 W Field Ct
Lake Forest, IL 60045-4828, USA

Wan, James (Director)
c/o Stacey Testro *Stacey Testro International*
8265 W Sunset Blvd Ste 102
West Hollywood, CA 90046-2433, USA

Wan, Li (Government Official)
People's Congress Tian An Men Square
Beijing, CHINA

Wanamaker, Zoe (Actor)
18-21 Jermyn St
London SW1Y 6NB, UNITED KINGDOM (UK)

Wang, Alexander (Fashion Designer)
386 Broadway Fl 3
New York, NY 10013-6021, USA

Wang, Garrett (Actor)
501 E Del Mar Blvd Apt 310
Pasadena, CA 91101-3613, USA

Wang, Hannah
c/o Staff Member *Nickelodeon UK*
PO Box 6425
LONDON W1A 6UR, UNITED KINGDOM

Wang, Henry Y (Engineer)
Chemical Engineering Dept
Ann Arbor, MI 48109, USA

Wang, Jida (Artist)
7612 35th Ave Apt 3E
Jackson Heights, NY 11372-4612, USA

Wang, Junxia (Athlete, Track Athlete)
9 Tlyuguan Road Chongwen District
Beijing 10061, CHINA

Wang, Taylor G (Astronaut, Physicist)
1224 Amo Dr
Sierra Madre, CA 91024, USA

Wang, Tian-Ren (Artist)
Longshoucun Xi'am
Shaanxi 710016, CHINA

Wang, Vera (Designer, Fashion Designer)
225 W 39th St # 1000
New York, NY 10018-3103, USA

Wang, Wayne (Director)
1888 Century Park E Ste 1888
Los Angeles, CA 90067-1722, USA

Wang, Zhen-Yi (Doctor, Scientist)
Rul Jin Road 11
Shanghai 200025, CHINA

Wang Zhl Zhi (Basketball Player)
601 Biscayne Blvd
Miami, FL 33132-1801, USA

Wangchuck, Dasho Jigme Khesar Namgyal (Prince)
Tashichhodzong
Thimpu, BHUTAN

Wangchuck, Jigme Singye (King)
Tashichhodzong
Thimpu, BHUTAN

Wanner, H Eric (Misc)
112 E 64th St
New York, NY 10065-7307, USA

Wannsdedt, David R (Dave) (Coach, Football Coach)
12600 N Stonebrook Cir
Davie, FL 33330-1288, USA

Wannstedt, David R (Dave) (Athlete, Coach, Football Coach, Football Player)
3011 Cloverbank Rd Unit 26
Hamburg, NY 14075-3459, USA

Wansel, Dexter (Musician)
PO Box 27641
Philadelphia, PA 19118-0641, USA

Wanzer, Robert F (Bobby) (Athlete, Basketball Player)
28 Greenwood Park
Pittsford, NY 14534-2965, USA

Waples, Keith (Horse Racer)
PO Box 632
Durham, ON N0G 1R0, CANADA

Wapner, Joseph (Joe) (Actor, Judge)
2388 Century Hl
Los Angeles, CA 90067-3514, USA

Wapnick, Steve (Athlete, Baseball Player)
5934 Woodcliffe Dr
Windsor, CO 80550-8025, USA

War
250 W 57th St # 407
New York, NY 10107-0001

Warbeck, Stephen (Composer)
c/o Staff Member *Soundtrack Music Assoc*
1460 4th St Ste 308
Santa Monica, CA 90401-3483, USA

Warburton, Patrick (Actor)
c/o Dolores Robinson *Dolores Robinson Entertainment*
9250 Wilshire Blvd Ste 220
Beverly Hills, CA 90212-3344, USA

Ward, Anita (Musician)
c/o Staff Member *Diva Central Inc*
7510 W Sunset Blvd Ste 1445
Los Angeles, CA 90046-3408, USA

Ward, Bert (Actor)
c/o Wes Stevens *Vox*
6420 Wilshire Blvd Ste 1080
Los Angeles, CA 90048-5539, USA

Ward, Bryan (Athlete, Baseball Player)
140 Bannock Ct
East Dundee, IL 60118-1626, USA

Ward, Charlie (Athlete, Basketball Player, Football Player)
3717 Drake St
Houston, TX 77005-1117, USA

Ward, Chris (Athlete, Baseball Player)
12858 Williams Ranch Rd
Moorpark, CA 93021-2109, USA

Ward, Chris (Athlete, Football Player)
325 Manning Ct
Atlanta, GA 30349-8785, USA

Ward, Christopher L (Chris) (Athlete, Football Player)
PO Box 1365
Inglewood, CA 90308-1365, USA

Ward, Colby (Athlete, Baseball Player)
1508 Hobble Creek Dr
Springville, UT 84663-2890, USA

Ward, Colin (Athlete, Baseball Player)
PO Box 21413
Mesa, AZ 85277-1413, USA

Ward, Dale (Musician)
PO Box 23066
London W11 3FR, UNITED KINGDOM (UK)

Ward, Daryle (Athlete, Baseball Player)
18073 Granite Ave
Riverside, CA 92508-9777, USA

Ward, David (Opera Singer)
1 Kennedy Crescent
Lake Wanaka, NEW ZEALAND

Ward, Dedric (Athlete, Football Player)
3435 N 45th St
Phoenix, AZ 85018-6028, USA

Ward, Fred (Actor)
c/o Ben Levine *Kritzer Levine Wilkins Entertainment*
11872 La Grange Ave Fl 1
Los Angeles, CA 90025-5283, USA

Ward, Gary (Athlete, Baseball Player)
18073 Granite Ave
Riverside, CA 92508-9777, USA

Ward, Gemma (Actor, Model)
c/o Staff Member *Caliber Media Company*
9229 W Sunset Blvd Ste 705
West Hollywood, CA 90069-3407, USA

Ward, Hines (Athlete, Football Player)
6215 Riverside Dr NW
Sandy Springs, GA 30328-3623, USA

Ward, Jay (Athlete, Baseball Player)
432 Hickory Tree Hollow Rd
Sevierville, TN 37876-9506, USA

Ward, John (Athlete, Football Player)
9501 Silver Lake Dr
Oklahoma City, OK 73162-7547, USA

Ward, John F (Business Person)
755 Lee St
Alexander City, AL 35010-2638, USA

Ward, John Milton (Educator)
20 Follen St
Cambridge, MA 02138-3503, USA

Ward, Jon P (Business Person)
77 W Wacker Dr
Chicago, IL 60601-1604, USA

Ward, Jonathan (Actor)
Po Box 56460 Dominion Road
Auckland 1030, NEW ZELAND

Ward, Kevin (Athlete, Baseball Player)
160 F Ave
Coronado, CA 92118-1212, USA

Ward, Lala (Actor)
2-4 Noel St
London W1V 3RB, UNITED KINGDOM (UK)

Ward, Maggie Hill (Stylist)
24317 Glyndon Ave
Venice, CA 90291, USA

Ward, Mary (Actor)
643 Saint Kilda Rd
Melbourne, VIC 3004, AUSTRALIA

Ward, Mary B (Actor)
1505 10th St
Santa Monica, CA 90401-2805, USA

Ward, Megan (Actor)
PO Box 481219
Los Angeles, CA 90036, USA

Ward, Michael P (Doctor, Mountaineer)
Bow St
London E3 3NT, UNITED KINGDOM (UK)

Ward, Micky (Athlete, Boxer)
c/o Nick Cordasco *Prince Marketing Group*
18 Carillon Cir
Livingston, NJ 07039-2600, USA

Ward, Pete (Athlete, Baseball Player)
575 G Ave
Lake Oswego, OR 97034-2272, USA

Ward, Preston (Athlete, Baseball Player)
4371 De Silva Pl
Las Vegas, NV 89121-5347, USA

Ward, R Duane (Athlete, Baseball Player)
PO Box 312
Durango, CO 81302-0312, USA

Ward, Rachel (Actor)
c/o Kate Richter *HLA Management*
PO Box 1536
Strawberry Hills 2012, AUSTRALIA

Ward, Robert (Composer, Musician)
2701 Pickett Rd Apt 4022
Durham, NC 27705-5652, USA

Ward, Robert R (Bob) (Athlete, Football Player)
PO Box 535
Riva, MD 21140-0535, USA

Ward, Ronald L (Ron) (Athlete, Hockey Player)
3178 W 140th St
Cleveland, OH 44111-1442, USA

Ward, Sela (Actor)
c/o David Seltzer *Management 360*
9111 Wilshire Blvd
Beverly Hills, CA 90210-5508, USA

Ward, Simon (Actor)
13 Radner Walk
London SW3 4BP, UNITED KINGDOM (UK)

Ward, Sterling (Religious Leader)
524 College Ave
Ashland, OH 44805-3703, USA

Ward, Susan (Actor)
c/o Staff Member *Agency Group Ltd, The (LA)*
1880 Century Park E Ste 711
Los Angeles, CA 90067-1618, USA

Ward, Turner M (Athlete, Baseball Player)
232 Autumn Dr
Saraland, AL 36571-2619, USA

Ward, Vincent (Director)
PO Box 423 Kings Cross
Sydney, NSW 2011, AUSTRALIA

Ward, Wendy (Golfer)
12850 Sassin Station Rd N
Edwall, WA 99008-9564, USA

Ward, Zach (Actor)
1875 Century Park E Ste 2250
Los Angeles, CA 90067-2563, USA

Warden, John (Attorney, Attorney General, General)
125 Broad St
New York, NY 10004-2400, USA

Warden, Jon (Athlete, Baseball Player)
9573 Loveland Madeira Rd
Loveland, OH 45140-8947, USA

Wardlaw, Kim McLane (Judge)
125 S Grand Ave
Pasadena, CA 91105-1643, USA

Wardle, Curt (Athlete, Baseball Player)
13900 Pheasant Knoll Ln
Moreno Valley, CA 92553-5330, USA

Ware, Andre (Athlete, Football Player)
3910 Wood Park
Sugar Land, TX 77479-2838, USA

Ware, Chris (Artist)
c/o Staff Member *Fantagraphics Books*
7563 Lake City Way NE
Seattle, WA 98115-4218, USA

Ware, Clyde (Director, Producer, Writer)
1765 N Sycamore Ave Apt 218
Los Angeles, CA 90028-3912, USA

Ware, DeMarcus (Athlete, Football Player)
c/o Bill Johnson *ProFiles Sports Inc*
3340 Peachtree Rd NE Fl 16
Atlanta, GA 30326-1000, USA

Ware, Derek (Athlete, Football Player)
4318 E South Fork Dr
Phoenix, AZ 85044-3738, USA

Ware, Jeff (Athlete, Baseball Player)
2560 Mulberry Loop
Virginia Beach, VA 23456-7818, USA

Warfield, Eric (Athlete, Football Player)
718 Meadows Rd
Texarkana, AR 71854-8341, USA

Warfield, Paul D (Athlete, Football Player)
16 Normandy Way
Rancho Mirage, CA 92270-1635, USA

Wargo, Tom (Athlete, Golfer)
2801 Putter Dr
Centralia, IL 62801-6183, USA

Warhols, James (Writer)
PO Box 748
Rhinebeck, NY 12572-0748, USA

Warhop, George (Athlete, Football Coach, Football Player)
4100 Symphony Ln
Cleveland, OH 44124-5691, USA

Wariner, Steve (Musician, Songwriter, Writer)
PO Box 1647
Franklin, TN 37065-1647, USA

Waring, Amanda
8 Chester Close Queens Ride
Barnes, ENGLAND

Waring, Richard
1 Chester Close Queens Ride
London, ENGLAND SW13 OJE

Waring, Todd (Actor)
1180 S Beverly Dr Ste 301
Los Angeles, CA 90035-1154, USA

Wark, Robert R (Misc)
1151 Oxford Rd
San Marino, CA 91108-1218, USA

Warlick, Ernie (Athlete, Football Player)
121 Presidents Walk
Buffalo, NY 14221-2447, USA

Warlock, Billy (Actor)
c/o Staff Member *Peter Strain & Associates Inc (LA)*
5455 Wilshire Blvd Ste 1812
Los Angeles, CA 90036-4268, USA

Warmenhoven, Daniel (Business Person)
495 E Java Dr
Sunnyvale, CA 94089-1125, USA

Warmerdam, Cornelius
3976 N 1st St
Fresno, CA 93726-4304

Warne, Jim (Athlete, Football Player)
5850 Hardy Ave Apt 112
San Diego, CA 92115, USA

Warnecke, John Carl (Architect)
190 Cortsen Rd
Pleasant Hill, CA 94523-3114, USA

Warnecke, Mark (Swimmer)
Am Schichtmeister 100
Witten 58453, GERMANY

Warner, Amelia (Actor)
c/o Jon Rubinstein *Authentic Talent and Literary Management*
45 Main St Ste 1004
Brooklyn, NY 11201-8200, USA

Warner, Charley (Athlete, Football Player)
1890 Rena St
Beaumont, TX 77705-4729, USA

Warner, Chris (Cartoonist)
10956 SE Main St
Portland, OR 97222-7644, USA

Warner, Cornell (Athlete, Basketball Player)
2479 Glen Meadow Ln
Escondido, CA 92027-2810, USA

Warner, Curt (Athlete, Football Player)
PO Box 4357
Troy, MI 48099-4357, USA

Warner, Dan (Actor)
c/o Staff Member *Players Talent Agency*
7700 W Sunset Blvd # 1
Los Angeles, CA 90046-3913, USA

Warner, David (Actor)
46 Albermarle St
London W1X 4PP, UNITED KINGDOM (UK)

Warner, Douglas A III (Financier)
270 Park Ave
New York, NY 10017-2014, USA

Warner, Jack (Athlete, Baseball Player)
5938 W Calle Lejos
Glendale, AZ 85310-3505, USA

Warner, Jackie (Athlete, Baseball Player)
19136 US Highway 18
Apple Valley, CA 92307-2507, USA

Warner, Jackie (Fitness Expert, Reality TV Star)
8500 Wilshire Blvd
Beverly Hills, CA 90211-3109, USA

Warner, Jane
166 Ditching Rd
Brighton, CA BN1 6JA EN

Warner, John (Senator)
PO Box 1320
Middleburg, VA 20118-1320, USA

Warner, Julie (Actor, Director, Producer)
c/o Nevin Dolcefino *Innovative Artists (LA)*
1505 10th St
Santa Monica, CA 90401-2805, USA

Warner, Kirk (Athlete, Football Player)
110 S 5th St
Cochran, GA 31014-6632, USA

Warner, Kurt (Athlete, Football Player)
10105 E Via Linda Ste 103
Scottsdale, AZ 85258-5346, USA

Warner, Malcolm Jamal (Actor)
c/o Adam Griffin *Kritzer Levine Wilkins Entertainment*
11872 La Grange Ave Fl 1
Los Angeles, CA 90025-5283, USA

Warner, Margaret (Correspondent)
2700 S Quincy St
Arlington, VA 22206-2242, USA

Warner, T C (Actor)
1801 Avenue of the Stars Ste 902
Los Angeles, CA 90067-5981, USA

Warner, Todd (Artist)
8799 Boyne City Rd
Charlevoix, MI 49720-9102, USA

Warner, Tom (Producer)
4024 Radford Ave Bldg 3
Studio City, CA 91604-2101, USA

Warner, Ty (Designer)
PO Box 5377
Oak Brook, IL 60522-5377, USA

Warner, William W (Writer)
2243 47th St NW
Washington, DC 20007-1034, USA

Warnes, Jennifer (Musician, Songwriter, Writer)
12746 Kling St
Studio City, CA 91604-1125, USA

Warnke, Paul
5037 Garfield St NW
Washington, DC 20016-3465

Warnock, John (Business Person)
345 Park Ave
San Jose, CA 95110-2704, USA

Warren, Chris (Athlete, Football Player)
13707 Black Spruce Way
Chantilly, VA 20151-2346, USA

Warren, Cicero (Baseball Player)
3820 Saratoga Dr
Raleigh, NC 27604-3445, USA

Warren, Diane (Musician, Songwriter)
6363 W Sunset Blvd # 810
Los Angeles, CA 90028-7317, USA

Warren, Don (Athlete, Football Player)
6001 Union Mill Rd Attn Athletic
Clifton, VA 20124-1128, USA

Warren, Estalia (Actor, Model)
200 Park Ave # 800
New York, NY 10166-0005, USA

Warren, Estella (Actor, Model)
c/o Stephanie Simon *Untitled Entertainment (LA)*
350 S Beverly Dr Ste 200
Beverly Hills, CA 90212-4819, USA

Warren, Fran (Musician)
173 Cobble Creek Dr
Tannersville, PA 18372-7849, USA

Warren, Frank (Internet Star)
13345 Copper Ridge Rd
Germantown, MD 20874-3454, USA

Warren, Frederick M (Architect)
65 Cambridge Terrace
Christchurch 1, NEW ZEALAND

Warren, Gerard (Football Player)
c/o Staff Member *Denver Broncos*
13655 Broncos Pkwy
Englewood, CO 80112-4151, USA

Warren, Gloria (Actor, Musician)
16872 Bosque Dr
Encino, CA 91436-3531, USA

Warren, Jennifer (Actor)
1675 Old Oak Rd
Los Angeles, CA 90049-2505, USA

Warren, Jim (Athlete, Football Player)
2200 Riverfront Dr Apt 3113
Little Rock, AR 72202-2242, USA

Warren, John Robin (Nobel Prize Laureate)
GPO Box X2213
Perth 6001, Western Australia

Warren, Karle (Actor)
c/o Justine Hunt *Hines and Hunt Entertainment*
1213 W Magnolia Blvd
Burbank, CA 91506-1829, USA

Warren, Kenneth S (Doctor, Scientist)
350 Community Dr
Manhasset, NY 11030-3816, USA

Warren, Kiersten (Actor)
c/o Staff Member *Mitchell K Stubbs & Assoc (MKS)*
8675 Washington Blvd Ste 203
Culver City, CA 90232-7486, USA

Warren, L D (Cartoonist, Editor)
1815 William Howard Taft Rd Apt 203
Cincinnati, OH 45206-1842, USA

Warren, Lesley Ann (Actor)
c/o Staff Member *Untitled Entertainment (LA)*
350 S Beverly Dr Ste 200
Beverly Hills, CA 90212-4819, USA

Warren, Martina (Adult Film Star)
8675 Washington Blvd Ste 203
Culver City, CA 90232-7486, USA

Warren, Michael
11500 W Olympic Blvd Ste 510
Los Angeles, CA 90064-1527

Warren, Michael (Mike) (Actor, Basketball Player)
21216 Escondido St
Woodland Hills, CA 91364-5905, USA

Warren, Mike (Athlete, Baseball Player)
12281 Diane St
Garden Grove, CA 92840-3224, USA

Warren, Neil Clark
c/o Eharmony.com P.O. Box 60157
Pasadena, CA 91116, USA

Warren, Rick (Religious Leader, Writer)
1 Saddleback Pkwy
Lake Forest, CA 92630-8700, USA

Warren, Robert (Athlete, Basketball Player)
989 Hardin Wadesboro Rd
Hardin, KY 42048, USA

Warren, Ron (Baseball Player)
4025 Paddock Rd Apt 401
Cincinnati, OH 45229-1635, USA

Warren, Rosanna (Writer)
11 Robinwood Ave
Needham, MA 02492-2112, USA

Warren, Sahron (Actor)
c/o Kathryn Boole *Studio Talent Group*
1328 12th St
Santa Monica, CA 90401-2051, United states

Warren, Thomas L (Misc)
11100 Wildlife Center Dr
Reston, VA 20190-5361, USA

Warren, Tom (Athlete)
2393 La Marque St
San Diego, CA 92109-2342, USA

Warren, Ty (Athlete, Football Player)
c/o Staff Member *New England Patriots*
Gillette Stadium One Patriots Pl
Foxboro, MA 02035-1388, USA

Warren Brothers
PO Box 120479
Nashville, TN 37212-0479, USA

Warren Brothers, The (Music Group)
c/o Staff Member *Creative Artists Agency (CAA-TN)*
3310 W End Ave Fl 5
Nashville, TN 37203-1028, USA

Warren G (Artist, Music Group, Musician)
1800 Argyle Ave # 408
Los Angeles, CA 90028-5253, USA

Warren Jr, Christopher C (Chris) (Athlete, Football Player)
1020 W Casino Rd
Everett, WA 98204-7900, USA

Warren-Green, Christopher (Conductor, Musician)
165 W 57th St
New York, NY 10019-2201, USA

Warrenskjold, Dorothy
165 W 57th St
New York, NY 10019-2201

Warrick, Peter (Athlete, Football Player)
4305 17th St E
Ellenton, FL 34222-2688, USA

Warsi, Arshad (Actor, Bollywood)
Kohinoor Apartments 503 Yari Road
Versova Andheri
Mumbai, MS 400061, INDIA

Warthen, Dan (Athlete, Baseball Player)
3933 SW Wapato Ave
Portland, OR 97239-1412, USA

Warwick, Carl (Athlete, Baseball Player)
14102 Bonney Brier Dr
Houston, TX 77069-1324, USA

Warwick, Dionne (Musician)
c/o Kevin Sasaki *Kevin Sasaki Public Relations & Media Counsel*
8491 W Sunset Blvd Ste 224
Los Angeles, CA 90069-1911, USA

Warwick, Lonnie (Athlete, Football Player)
828 Main St
Mount Hope, WV 25880-1321, USA

Warzeka, Ron (Athlete, Football Player)
9390 W Ustick Rd Unit 32
Boise, ID 83704-5501, USA

Was, Don (Composer, Musician)
10984 Bellagio Rd
Los Angeles, CA 90077, USA

Wasdin, John (Athlete, Baseball Player)
6331 Crawfordville Rd
Tallahassee, FL 32305-9158, USA

Wash, Martha (Musician)
c/o Staff Member *Diva Central Inc*
7510 W Sunset Blvd Ste 1445
Los Angeles, CA 90046-3408, USA

Washburn, Abigail (Musician)
c/o Staff Member *Paradigm (Monterey)*
404 W Franklin St
Monterey, CA 93940-2303, USA

Washburn, Barbara (Misc)
1010 Waltham St Apt D327
Lexington, MA 02421-8044, USA

Washburn, Beverly (Actor)
2561 Olivia Heights Ave
Henderson, NV 89052-7130, USA

Washburn, Greg (Athlete, Baseball Player)
1685 E Stellon St
Diamond, IL 60416-6028, USA

Washburn, Jarrod M (Athlete, Baseball Player)
10003 Olinger Rd
Webster, WI 54893-7435, USA

Washburn, Ray C (Athlete, Baseball Player)
1103 N 49th St
Seattle, WA 98103-6630, USA

Washburn Jr, H Bradford (Misc)
1010 Waltham St Apt D237
Lexington, MA 02421-8044, USA

Washetz, Joel A (Stylist)
1435 12th St
Key West, FL 33040-4062, USA

Washington, Algernod Lanier (Plies) (Musician)
c/o Cara Donatto *Atlantic Records (LA)*
3400 W Olive Ave Fl 2
Burbank, CA 91505-5538, USA

Washington, Alonzo (Cartoonist)
PO Box 171046
Kansas City, KS 66117-0046, USA

Washington, Baby (Musician)
1650 Broadway Ste 508
New York, NY 10019-6833, USA

Washington, Chris (Athlete, Football Player)
PO Box 17823
San Diego, CA 92177-7823, USA

Washington, Claudell (Athlete, Baseball Player)
4081 Clayton Rd Apt 227
Concord, CA 94521-2615, USA

Washington, Denzel (Actor)
c/o Alan Nierob *Rogers & Cowan PR (LA)*
Pacific Design Center 8687 Melrose Ave, 7th Floor
West Hollywood, CA 90069, USA

Washington, Dewayne (Athlete, Football Player)
6205 Rocky Creek Way
Wake Forest, NC 27587-6267, USA

Washington, Dwayne (Pearl) (Basketball Player)
206 Grenadier Dr # 206C
Liverpool, NY 13090-2744, USA

Washington, Eugene (Gene) (Athlete, Football Player)
2725 Jewel Ln N
Plymouth, MN 55447-1737, USA

Washington, Gene A (Athlete, Football Player)
10521 Bellagio Rd
Los Angeles, CA 90077-3820, USA

Washington, Hayma (Producer)
c/o Lindsay Williams *The Gotham Group Inc*
9255 W Sunset Blvd Ste 515
Los Angeles, CA 90069-3308, USA

Washington, Herb (Athlete, Baseball Player)
640 Saddlebrook Dr
Youngstown, OH 44512-4781, USA

Washington, Isaiah (Actor)
c/o Adel Nur *Three Tier Entertainment*
645 W 9th St Apt 406
Los Angeles, CA 90015-1648, USA

Washington, Jascha (Actor)
c/o Staff Member *House of Representatives, The*
1434 6th St Ste 1
Santa Monica, CA 90401-2527, USA

Washington, Jim (Athlete, Basketball Player)
1108 Cardinal Way SW
Atlanta, GA 30311-2417, USA

Washington, Joe (Athlete, Football Player)
434 E 42nd Pl
Chicago, IL 60653-2916, USA

Washington, Joe (Athlete, Football Player)
4 Treadwell Ct
Lutherville Timonium, MD 21093-3716, USA

Washington, Joe D (Athlete, Football Player)
2350 W Joppa Rd
Lutherville, MD 21093-4616, USA

Washington, Keith (Athlete, Football Player)
548 Parkview Dr
Grand Prairie, TX 75052-3168, USA

Washington, Kelley (Athlete, Football Player)
c/o Chad Speck *Allegiant Athletic Agency*
35 Market Sq Ste 201
Knoxville, TN 37902-1420, USA

Washington, Kermit (Athlete, Basketball Player)
7208 NE Hazel Dell Ave
Vancouver, WA 98665-8341, USA

Washington, Kerry (Actor)
c/o Kathy Atkinson *Washington Square Arts (LA)*
1041 N Formosa Ave Lot Bldg
West Hollywood, CA 90046-6703, USA

Washington, Larue (Athlete, Baseball Player)
6323 Reseda Blvd Unit 16
Tarzana, CA 91335-6981, USA

Washington, Lionel (Athlete, Football Player)
5 Gleneagles Dr
La Place, LA 70068-1612, USA

Washington, MaliVai (Tennis Player)
5 S Roscoe Blvd
Ponte Vedra Beach, FL 32082-3813, USA

Washington, Mickey (Athlete, Football Player)
9420 Riggs St
Beaumont, TX 77707-1164, USA

Washington, Mike L (Athlete, Football Player)
3235 Hernon Rd
Montgomery, AL 36106, USA

Washington, Richard (Athlete, Basketball Player)
4606 SE Logus Rd
Portland, OR 97222-5150, USA

Washington, Ron (Athlete, Baseball Player, Coach)
2406 Copper Ridge Rd
Arlington, TX 76006-2726, USA

Washington, Ronnie (Athlete, Football Player)
2204 Burg Jones Ln
Monroe, LA 71202-4411, USA

Washington, Russ (Athlete, Football Player)
9060 Gramercy Dr
San Diego, CA 92123-2395, USA

Washington, Sam (Athlete, Football Player)
7111 Cumberland Pl
Tampa, FL 33617-8423, USA

Washington, Ted (Athlete, Football Player)
PO Box 434
Waxhaw, NC 28173-1047, USA

Washington, Theodore (Ted) (Athlete, Football Player)
3522 E 26th Ave
Tampa, FL 33605-1602, USA

Washington, U L (Athlete, Baseball Player)
PO Box 164
Stringtown, OK 74569-0164, USA

Washington, Vic (Athlete, Football Player)
1851 E Morten Ave Apt 152
Phoenix, AZ 85020-4696, USA

Washington, Wilson (Athlete, Basketball Player)
2625 Mapleton Ave
Norfolk, VA 23504-3717, USA

Wasikowska, Mia (Actor)
c/o Christine Tripicchio *WKT Public Relations (WKT-LA)*
9350 Wilshire Blvd Ste 450
Beverly Hills, CA 90212-3230, USA

Wasilewski, Paul Thomas (Paul Wesley) (Actor)
c/o Susan Calogerakis *Thruline Entertainment*
9250 Wilshire Blvd Ground Fl
Beverly Hills, CA 90212, USA

Wasim, Akram (Cricketer)
Old Trafford
Manchester M16 0PX, UNITED KINGDOM (UK)

Wasinger, Mark (Athlete, Baseball Player)
303 S Seneca St
Wichita, KS 67213-5539, USA

Waskiewicz, Jim (Athlete, Football Player)
4360 Nelson Dr
Broomfield, CO 80023-9598, USA

Waskow, Thomas C (General)
Unit 5068
Apo, AP 96328-5068, USA

Waslewski, Gary (Athlete, Baseball Player)
106 McKenzie Dr
Southington, CT 06489-4149, USA

Wasmeier, Markus (Skier)
Breitensteinstr 14B
Schliersee-Neuhaus 83727, GERMANY

Wass, Ted (Actor)

Wasserburg, Gerald J (Geophysicist, Physicist, Scientist)
PO Box 2959
Florence, OR 97439-0167, USA

Wasserman, Allan (Actor)
c/o Judy Orbach *Judy O Productions*
6136 Glen Holly St
Hollywood, CA 90068-2338, USA

Wasserman, Dale (Writer)
Casa Blanca Estates #37
Paradise Valley, AZ 95253, USA

Wasserman, Dan (Cartoonist, Editor)
135 William T Morrissey Blvd
Dorchester, MA 02125-3310, USA

Wasserman, Kevin (Noodles) (Musician)
c/o Staff Member *Sugaroo! LLC*
3650 Helms Ave
Culver City, CA 90232-2417, USA

Wasserman, Lew
722 N Rexford Dr
Beverly Hills, CA 90210-3314

Wasserman, Lisa (Stylist)
1420 W Oceanfront Apt 2
Newport Beach, CA 92661-1000, USA

Wasserman, Rob (Musician)
PO Box 245
Sausalito, CA 94966-0245, USA

Wasserman, Robert H (Doctor)
Veterinary Medicine College
Ithaca, NY 14853, USA

Wasserstein, Bruce (Business Person)
30 Rockefeller Plz
New York, NY 10112-0015, USA

Wasserstein, Wendy (Writer)
c/o Robert (Bob) Bookman *Creative Artists Agency (CAA-LA)*
2000 Avenue of the Stars Ste 100
Los Angeles, CA 90067-4705, USA

Wasson, Erin (Model)
304 Park Ave S # 1200
New York, NY 10010-4301, USA

Waszgis, B J (Athlete, Baseball Player)
2708 Dover Ln
Albany, GA 31721-1583, USA

Watanabe, Gedde
325 Cherry Dr
Pasadena, CA 91105-2150

Watanabe, Ken (Actor)
c/o Will Ward *ROAR (LA)*
9701 Wilshire Blvd Fl 8
Beverly Hills, CA 90212-2008, USA

Watanabe, Milio (Scientist)
Computer Labs 5-33-1 Shiba
Tokyo, JAPAN

Watanabe, Sadao (Musician)
278 S Main St # 400
Gloucester, MA 1930, USA

Waterboys
3 Monmouth Rd
London, ENGLAND W2

Waterbury, Steve (Athlete, Baseball Player)
710 N Garfield St
Marion, IL 62959-3429, USA

Waterhouse, Matthew (Actor)
1 Kingsway House Albion Rd
London N16 0TA, UNITED KINGDOM (UK)

Waterman, Denis
Pinewood Studios Iverheath
Iver SL0 0NH, UNITED KINGDOM (UK)

Waterman, Felicity (Actor)
PO Box 234
Elk, CA 95432-0234, USA

Waterman, Michael (Mathematician)
Mathematics Dept
Los Angeles, CA 90089-0001, USA

Waters, Alice (Chef)
1517 Shattuck Ave
Berkeley, CA 94709-1516, USA

Waters, Andre (Athlete, Football Player)
7715 Carriage Pointe Dr
Gibsonton, FL 33534-3004, USA

Waters, Brian (Athlete, Football Player)
7209 W 144th Pl
Overland Park, KS 66223-2284, USA

Waters, Charles T (Charlie) (Athlete, Coach, Football Coach, Football Player)
9305 Moss Trl
Dallas, TX 75231-1409, USA

Waters, Crystal (Musician)
270 Lafayette St # 602
New York, NY 10012-3311, USA

Waters, Derek (Actor)
c/o Naomi Odenkirk *Odenkirk Provissiero Entertainment*
650 N Bronson Ave Bldg B145
Los Angeles, CA 90004-1404, USA

Waters, Frank (Muddy) (Coach, Football Coach)
4850 Gratiot Rd No 2D
Saginaw, MI 48638-6202, USA

Waters, John (Director)
c/o Steven Trachtenbroit *Big Hassle*
44 Wall St Ste 2201
New York, NY 10005-2427, USA

Waters, John B (Government Official)
405 Burridge Waters Edge
Sevierville, TN 37862, USA

Waters, Lou (Correspondent)
1050 Techwood Dr NW
Atlanta, GA 30318-5604, USA

Waters, Mark (Director)
c/o Robert (Bob) Bookman *Creative Artists Agency (CAA-LA)*
2000 Avenue of the Stars Ste 100
Los Angeles, CA 90067-4705, USA

Waters, Richard (Publisher)
13919 Woods Run Ct
Centreville, VA 20121-3078, USA

Waters, Roger (Musician)
106 Gifford St
London N1 0DF, UK

Waterston, James (Actor)
c/o Beth Colt *Gateway Management Company Inc*
860 Via De La Paz Ste F10
Pacific Palisades, CA 90272-3631, USA

Waterston, Katherine (Actor)
c/o Allison Band *Gersh (LA)*
9465 Wilshire Blvd Ste 600
Beverly Hills, CA 90212-2612, USA

Waterston, Robert (Biologist)
Biology Dept
Saint Louis, MO 63130, USA

Waterston, Sam (Actor)
c/o Keith Addis *Industry Entertainment Partners*
955 Carrillo Dr Ste 300
Los Angeles, CA 90048-5400, USA

Wathan, Dusty (Athlete, Baseball Player)
1132 Turnbridge Rd
Charlotte, NC 28226-5862, USA

Wathan, John D (Athlete, Baseball Player, Coach)
1354 NE Todd George Rd
Lees Summit, MO 64086-5337, USA

Watkins, Bob (Athlete, Baseball Player)
4417 W 58th Pl
Los Angeles, CA 90043-3409, USA

Watkins, Bobby (Athlete, Football Player)
1112 Devonshire Dr
Desoto, TX 75115-3756, USA

Watkins, Carlene (Actor)
104 Fremont Pl
Los Angeles, CA 90005-3867, USA

Watkins, Danny (Football Player)
c/o Joe Panos *Lock Metz Milanovic LLC*
6900 E Camelback Rd Ste 600
Scottsdale, AZ 85251-8044, USA

Watkins, Dave (Athlete, Baseball Player)
506 Ridgewood Rd
Louisville, KY 40207-1325, USA

Watkins, Dean A (Business Person, Inventor)
401 River Oaks Pkwy
San Jose, CA 95134-1916, USA

Watkins, James D (Admiral, Secretary)
411 Prince St
Alexandria, VA 22314-3113, USA

Watkins, Lloyd I (Economist)
PO Box 111
Bloomington, IL 61702-0111, USA

Watkins, Marilyn
217 N San Marino Ave
San Gabriel, CA 91775-2909

Watkins, Michaela (Actor, Comedian)
c/o Amy Slomovits *Flutie Entertainment (LA)*
9320 Wilshire Blvd Ste 202
Beverly Hills, CA 90212-3217, USA

Watkins, Michelle (Actor)
6404 Wilshire Blvd Ste 950
Los Angeles, CA 90048-5529, USA

Watkins, Pat (Athlete, Baseball Player)
1205 Fowler Dr
Garner, NC 27529-4420, USA

Watkins, Rhonda (Stylist)
4007 Huntingdon Dr
Minnetonka, MN 55305-5116, USA

Watkins, Robert A (Athlete, Football Player)
6 White Alder Way
South Dartmouth, MA 02748-1429, USA

Watkins, Scott (Athlete, Baseball Player)
14660 W 18th St S
Sand Springs, OK 74063-4405, USA

Watkins, Steve (Athlete, Baseball Player)
3408 Evanston Ave
Lubbock, TX 79407-4039, USA

Watkins, Tasker (Judge, War Hero)
5 Pump Court Middle Temple
London EC4, UNITED KINGDOM (UK)

Watkins, Tionne (T-Boz) (Artist, Musician)
c/o Jack Iannaci *Brass Artists & Associates*
9025 Wilshire Blvd Ste 400
Beverly Hills, CA 90211-1828, USA

Watkins, Tom (Athlete, Football Player)
5008 Bartley Way
Mc Leansville, NC 27301-9293, USA

Watkins, Tuc (Actor)
c/o Brad Warshaw *Brad Warshaw*
PO Box 931332
Los Angeles, CA 90093-1332, USA

Watkins, William D (Business Person)
920 Disc Dr
Scotts Valley, CA 95066-4544, USA

Watkinson of Working, Harold A (Government Official)
Tyma House Bosham near Chichester
Sussex, UNITED KINGDOM (UK)

Watley, Jody (Musician)
9100 Wilshire Blvd Ste 600
Beverly Hills, CA 90212-3494, USA

Watling, Deborah
183 Trevelyan Rd
London, ENGLAND SW17 9LW

Watling, Leonor (Actor)
c/o Staff Member *WmE2 (Endeavor-LA)*
9601 Wilshire Blvd Fl 3
Beverly Hills, CA 90210-5219, USA

Watlington, Neal (Athlete, Baseball Player)
PO Box 418
Yanceyville, NC 27379-0418, USA

Watney, Nick (Athlete, Golfer)
c/o Staff Member *Gaylord Sports Management*
13845 N Northsight Blvd Ste 200
Scottsdale, AZ 85260-3609, USA

Watros, Cynthia (Actor)
c/o Marsha McManus *Principal Entertainment (LA)*
1964 Westwood Blvd Ste 400
Los Angeles, CA 90025-4695, USA

Watrous, Cynthia (Actor)
c/o Staff Member *Innovative Artists (LA)*
1505 10th St
Santa Monica, CA 90401-2805, USA

Watson, A J (Engineer, Race Car Driver)
5420 Crawfordsville Rd
Indianapolis, IN 46224-5407, USA

Watson, Albert M (Photographer)
44 Laight St Apt 1A
New York, NY 10013-2148, USA

Watson, Alberta (Actor)
c/o Staff Member *Cathy Atkinson*
2629 Main St PMB 129
Santa Monica, CA 90405-4001, USA

Watson, Alexander F (Diplomat)
4245 Fairfax Dr Ste 100
Arlington, VA 22203-1637, USA

Watson, Allen (Athlete, Baseball Player)
6144 65th St
Middle Village, NY 11379-1027, USA

Watson, Angela (Actor)
c/o Tom Chasin *Chasin Agency, The*
8899 Beverly Blvd Ste 714
Los Angeles, CA 90048-2449, USA

Watson, Barry (Actor)
c/o Ruth Bernstein *Viewpoint Inc*
8820 Wilshire Blvd Ste 220
Beverly Hills, CA 90211-2622, USA

Watson, Benjamin (Athlete, Football Player)
c/o Staff Member *New England Patriots*
Gillette Stadium One Patriots Pl
Foxboro, MA 02035-1388, USA

Watson, Bob (Athlete, Baseball Player)
9319 Montridge Dr
Houston, TX 77080-5429, USA

Watson, Cecil J (Doctor)
2727 Chicago Ave
Minneapolis, MN 55407-3707, USA

Watson, Dale (Musician)
602 Wayside Dr
Wimberley, TX 78676-5151, USA

Watson, Denis (Athlete, Golfer)
14209 Evans Rd
Pacific Palisades, CA 90272, USA

Watson, Doc (Musician)
5479 Larryon Dr
Woodland Hills, CA 91367, USA

Watson, Elizabeth M (Judge)
Chief's Office 1200 Travis St
Houston, TX 77002, USA

Watson, Emily (Actor)
c/o George Freeman *WmE2 (Endeavor-LA)*
9601 Wilshire Blvd Fl 3
Beverly Hills, CA 90210-5219, USA

Watson, Emma (Actor)
c/o Staff Member *Storm Model Management*
5 Jubilee Pl 1st Floor
London SW3 3TD, UNITED KINGDOM

Watson, Gene (Musician)
909 Meadowlark Ln
Goodlettsville, TN 37072-2309, USA

Watson, James D (Nobel Prize Laureate)
PO Box 100
Cold Spring Harbor, NY 11724-0100, USA

Watson, Jamie (Athlete, Basketball Player)
PO Box 761
Elm City, NC 27822-0761, USA

Watson, Joe (Athlete, Football Player)
112 Baldwin Rd
Hillsborough, NC 27278-7389, USA

Watson, Kenneth M (Oceanographer, Physicist)
8515 Costa Verde Blvd Unit 2008
San Diego, CA 92122-1150, USA

Watson, Mark (Athlete, Baseball Player)
555 Spender Trce
Atlanta, GA 30350-5017, USA

Watson, Martha (Athlete, Track Athlete)
5509 Royal Vista Ln
Las Vegas, NV 89149-6644, USA

Watson, Max P Jr (Business Person)
2101 Citywest Blvd
Houston, TX 77042-2829, USA

Watson, Mills (Actor)
2824 Dell Ave
Venice, CA 90291-4547, USA

Watson, Pamela (Stylist)
c/o Staff Member *The Montgomery Group*
210 W 29th St Fl 6
New York, NY 10001-5205, USA

Watson, Paul (Journalist, Photographer)
Editorial Dept 1 Yonge St
Toronto, ON M5E 1E6, CANADA

Watson, Paul (Misc)
PO Box 2616
Friday Harbor, WA 98250-2616, USA

Watson, Polly Jo (Misc)
Anthropology Dept
Saint Louis, MO 63130, USA

Watson, Robert (Athlete, Basketball Player)
1625 Sherwood Dr
Owensboro, KY 42301-3578, USA

Watson, Robert A (Religious Leader)
615 Slaters Ln
Alexandria, VA 22314-1112, USA

Watson, Robert M (Bobby) Jr (Musician)
11 Ridge Rd
Chappaqua, NY 10514-2508, USA

Watson, Russell (Musician)
Box 806
Manchester M60 2XS, UNITED KINGDOM (UK)

Watson, Sheri (Stylist)
4440 Ambrose Ave Apt 110
Los Angeles, CA 90027-2148, USA

Watson, Sid (Athlete, Football Player)
3150 Binnacle Dr Apt 212
Naples, FL 34103-2712, USA

Watson, Stephen E (Business Person)
1000 Nicollet Mall
Minneapolis, MN 55403-2542, USA

Watson, Stephen R (Athlete, Football Player)
4675 S Vine Way
Englewood, CO 80113-6044, USA

Watson, Thomas S (Tom) (Athlete, Golfer)
16104 Riggs Rd
Stilwell, KS 66085-9256, USA

Watson, Tim (Athlete, Football Player)
113 Crestwood Dr RR 13
Fort Valley, GA 31030, USA

Watson, Wayne (Musician)
300 10th Ave S
Nashville, TN 37203-4125, USA

Watson Jr, Jack H (Government Official)
1900 K St NW
Washington, DC 20006-1110, USA

Watson Richardson, Lillian (Pockey) (Swimmer)
4960 Maunalani Cir
Honolulu, HI 96816-4016, USA

Watson-Johnson, Vernee (Actor)
14724 Ventura Blvd Ste 505
Sherman Oaks, CA 91403-3505, USA

Watt, Ben (Musician, Songwriter, Writer)
Acklam Workshops 10 Acklam Road
London W10 5QZ, UNITED KINGDOM (UK)

Watt, Eddie (Athlete, Baseball Player)
940 Locust St
North Bend, NE 68649-4543, USA

Watt, James G (Designer, Secretary)
PO Box 3705
Jackson Hole, WY 83001-3705, USA

Watt, J.J. (Football Player)
c/o Tom Condon *CAA - St. Louis*
222 S Central Ave Ste 1008
Saint Louis, MO 63105-3509, USA

Watt, Mike (Musician)
c/o Staff Member *Agency Group Ltd, The (NY)*
142 W 57th St Fl 6
New York, NY 10019-3300, USA

Watt, Tom (Athlete, Coach, Hockey Player)
P.O. Box 1540 Station M
Calgary, AB T2P 3B9, Canada

Wattelet, Frank (Athlete, Football Player)
4 Deer Run Dr
Joplin, MO 64804-5832, USA

Wattenberg, Ben J (Television Host)
4455 Connecticut Ave NW Ste C100
Washington, DC 20008-2372, USA

Watters, Bill (Correspondent)
c/o Staff Member *Landmark Sport Group*
1 City Centre Dr Suite 605
Mississauga, Ontario L5B 1M2, Canada

Watters, Richard J (Rickie) (Athlete, Football Player)
11100 NE 8th St Ste 600
Bellevue, WA 98004-4402, USA

Watters, Ricky (Athlete, Football Player)
6107 Springford Dr Apt S3
Harrisburg, PA 17111-4941, USA

Watters, Tim (Athlete, Hockey Player)
804 Oak Grove Pkwy
Houghton, MI 49931-2707, USA

Watterson, John B (Brett) (Astronaut)
2508 Via Anacapa
Palos Verdes Estates, CA 90274-4333, USA

Wattleton, A Faye (Entertainer)
250 W 57th St
New York, NY 10107-0001, USA

Watts, Andre (Musician)
205 W 57th St
New York, NY 10019-2105, USA

Watts, Brian (Athlete, Golfer)
2309 Arbor Trl
Colleyville, TX 76034-5034, USA

Watts, Charles R (Charlie) (Musician)
Halsdon Farm Dolton Winkleigh
Devon EX19 8RF, UK

Watts, D Henry (Business Person)
3 Commercial Pl
Norfolk, VA 23510-2108, USA

Watts, Ernest J (Ernie) (Musician)
4031 Panama Ct
Piedmont, CA 94611-4930, USA

Watts, Ernie (Designer, Director)
40 W 57th St # 1800
New York, NY 10019-4001, USA

Watts, Helen J (Opera Singer)
Rock House Wallis Ambleston Haverford-West
Dyfed SA62 5RA, WALES

Watts, JC (Correspondent, Politician)
600 13th St NW Ste 790
Washington, DC 20005-3021, USA

Watts, Kristi (Religious Leader, Television Host)
c/o 700 Club *Christian Broadcasting Network (CBN)*
977 Centerville Tpke
Virginia Beach, VA 23463-1001, USA

Watts, Naomi (Actor)
c/o Jason Weinberg *Untitled Entertainment (LA)*
350 S Beverly Dr Ste 200
Beverly Hills, CA 90212-4819, USA

Watts, Quincy (Athlete, Track Athlete)
PO Box 67581
Los Angeles, CA 90067-0581, USA

Watts, Robert (Athlete, Football Player)
99 Villa Dr
San Pablo, CA 94806-3736, USA

Watts, Ronald (Athlete, Basketball Player)
11800 Sunset Hills Rd Apt 908
Reston, VA 20190-4787, USA

Watts III, Claudius E (Educator, General)
President S Ofc
Charleston, SC 29409-0001, USA

Waugh, Jim (Athlete, Baseball Player)
501 Bourland Rd Apt 3106
Keller, TX 76248-3578, USA

Waugh, John S (Misc)
Chemistry Dept
Cambridge, MA 2139, USA

Waugh, Stephen (Steve) (Cricketer)
1751 Pinnacle Dr Ste 1500
McLean, VA 22102-3833, USA

Wawryshyn-Moroz, Evelyn (Baseball Player)
139 Royal Ave
Winnipeg, MB R2V 1H5, CANADA

Wax, Ruby (Actor, Comedian)
c/o Nicola Richardson *QVoice*
193-197 High Holborn 4th Floor, Holborn Hall
London WC1V 7BD, UNITED KINGDOM (UK)

Waxenberg, Alan M (Publisher)
959 8th Ave
New York, NY 10019-3737, USA

Waxman, Henry (Politician)
6913 Ayr Ln
Bethesda, MD 20817-4901

Waxman, Keoni (Director, Writer)
c/o Jeff Okin *Anonymous Content (AC-LA)*
3531 Hayden Ave
Culver City, CA 90232, USA

Wayans, Damien Dante (Actor, Director, Producer)
c/o Kim Dixon *Dominion3*
1420 Camden Ave Apt 5
Los Angeles, CA 90025-3449, USA

Wayans, Damon (Actor)
c/o Kim Dixon *Dominion3*
1420 Camden Ave Apt 5
Los Angeles, CA 90025-3449, USA

Wayans, Keenen Ivory (Actor, Director, Producer)
c/o Lisa Suzanne Blum *Modus Entertainment*
8569 Holloway Dr Apt 1
West Hollywood, CA 90069-6918, USA

Wayans, Kim (Actor)
c/o Staff Member *Wayans Brothers Entertainment*
8730 W Sunset Blvd Ste 290
W Hollywood, CA 90069-2247, USA

Wayans, Marlon (Actor, Comedian)
c/o Lisa Suzanne Blum *Modus Entertainment*
8569 Holloway Dr Apt 1
West Hollywood, CA 90069-6918, USA

Wayans, Shawn (Actor)
c/o Staff Member *Wayans Brothers Entertainment*
8730 W Sunset Blvd Ste 290
W Hollywood, CA 90069-2247, USA

Wayans Jr, Damon (Actor)
c/o Cecy Galvan *Bleu Entertainment*
10750 Palms Blvd Apt 108
Los Angeles, CA 90034-5570, USA

Wayda, Stephen (Photographer)
680 N Lake Shore Dr
Chicago, IL 60611-4546, USA

Wayne, Fredd
117 Strand St
Santa Monica, CA 90405-2293

Wayne, Gary (Athlete, Baseball Player)
5762 W Asbury Pl
Lakewood, CO 80227-2550, USA

Wayne, Jeff (Composer)
Lyndhurst Green St Shenley
Hertfordshire WD7 9BD, UK

Wayne, Jimmy (Musician)
1219 16th Ave S
Nashville, TN 37212-2901, USA

Wayne, John (Bowler)
5018 S Barley Ct
Gilbert, AZ 85298-8633, USA

Wayne, June (Artist)
1108 Tamarind Ave
Los Angeles, CA 90038-1906, USA

Wayne, Justin (Athlete, Baseball Player)
302 Muirfield Ct
Jupiter, FL 33458-8060, USA

Wayne, Nathaniel (Athlete, Football Player)
2878 Grey Moss Pass
Duluth, GA 30097-5226, USA

Wayne, Patrick (Actor)
10502 Whipple St
Toluca Lake, CA 91602-2838, USA

Wayne, Reggie (Athlete, Football Player)
7001 W 56th St
Indianapolis, IN 46254-9725, USA

Wayt, Russell (Athlete, Football Player)
PO Box 9
White Oak, TX 75693-0009, USA

Wazed, Sheik Hasina (Prime Minister)
Gono Bhaban Sher-e-Banglanagar
Dakar, BANGLADESH

Wazniak, Steve (Business Person, Inventor)
16400 Blackberry Hill Rd
Los Gatos, CA 95030-7513, USA

We Came As Romans (Music Group, Musician)
c/o Matthew Stewart *Outerloop Management*
2200 Clarendon Blvd Ste 1400
Arlington, VA 22201-3331, USA

We The Kings (Musician)
c/o Staff Member *Ozone Entertainment*
60-62 E 11th St Floor 7
New York, NY 10003, USA

Weah, George (Soccer Player)
3 Turati Via
Washington, DC 20221-0001, ITALY

Wearstler, Kelly (Writer)
c/o Staff Member *HarperCollins Publishers*
10 E 53rd St C/O Author Mail Floor 7
New York, NY 10022, USA

Weatherill, B Bruce (Government Official)
Emmets House Ide Hill
Kent TN14 6BA, UNITED KINGDOM (UK)

Weatherly, Gerald (Athlete, Football Player)
506 1/2 E Clayton St
Cuero, TX 77954-2820, USA

Weatherly, Jim (Athlete, Football Player)
23679 Calabasas Rd Apt 558
Calabasas, CA 91302-1502, USA

Weatherly, Michael (Actor)
c/o Jai Khanna *Brillstein Entertainment Partners*
9150 Wilshire Blvd Ste 350
Beverly Hills, CA 90212-3453, USA

Weatherly, Shwan (Actor, Beauty Pageant Winner)
135 N Westgate Ave
Los Angeles, CA 90049-2916, USA

Weathers, Carl (Actor)
c/o Mark Measures *Abrams Artists Agency (LA)*
9200 W Sunset Blvd PH 11
Los Angeles, CA 90069-3601, USA

Weathers, Carl (Athlete, Football Player)
2228 Walnut Ave
Venice, CA 90291-4035, USA

Weathers, Dave (Athlete, Baseball Player)
979 Lexington Hwy
Loretto, TN 38469-2732, USA

Weatherspoon, Cephus (Athlete, Football Player)
321 E Fir St
Brea, CA 92821-6538, USA

Weatherspoon, Clarence (Athlete, Basketball Player)
PO Box 117
Crawford, MS 39743-0117, USA

Weatherspoon, Nick (Athlete, Basketball Player)
2413 Midway Ave NE
Canton, OH 44705-3457, USA

Weatherspoon, Teresa G (Basketball Player)
Staples Center 1111 S Figueroa St
Los Angeles, CA 90015, USA

Weatherwax, Bob
1768 Rocking Horse Dr
Simi Valley, CA 93065-5909

Weatherwax, Jim (Athlete, Football Player)
2725 Abarr Dr
Loveland, CO 80538-3159, USA

Weaver, Dewitt (Athlete, Golfer)
5640 Golf Club Dr
Braselton, GA 30517-2426, USA

Weaver, Earl (Athlete, Baseball Player, Coach)
501 Cypress Pointe Dr W
Pembroke Pines, FL 33027-1356, USA

Weaver, Eric (Athlete, Baseball Player)
2641 Weaver Rd
Illiopolis, IL 62539-3640, USA

Weaver, Floyd (Athlete, Baseball Player)
93 County Road 35930
Powderly, TX 75473-3307, USA

Weaver, Fritz (Actor)
161 W 75th St
New York, NY 10023-1801, USA

Weaver, Gary (Athlete, Football Player)
3496 Arden Rd
Hayward, CA 94545-3906, USA

Weaver, Herman (Athlete, Football Player)
8105 Hamilton Mill Dr
Chattanooga, TN 37421-2766, USA

Weaver, Jacki (Actor)
c/o Alex Cole *Elevate Entertainment*
10100 Santa Monica Blvd Ste 300
Los Angeles, CA 90067-4107, USA

Weaver, Jason (Actor)
c/o Lisa Chance *Kyle Avery Public Relations*
1107 Fair Oaks Ave # 321
S Pasadena, CA 91030-3311, USA

Weaver, Jed (Athlete, Football Player)
696 E 16th Aly
Eugene, OR 97401-4480, USA

Weaver, Jeff (Athlete, Baseball Player)
2246 Birchglen St Unit 125
Simi Valley, CA 93063-6508, USA

Weaver, Jered (Athlete, Baseball Player)
c/o Staff Member *Los Angeles Dodgers (LA Dodgers)*
1000 Elysian Park Ave
Los Angeles, CA 90090-1112, USA

Weaver, Jim (Athlete, Baseball Player)
6916 8th Ave W
Bradenton, FL 34209-3416, USA

Weaver, Jim (Athlete, Baseball Player)
626 Prince George Dr
Lancaster, PA 17601-8802, USA

Weaver, John (Athlete, Football Player)
520 E Ward St
Versailles, OH 45380-1436, USA

Weaver, Michael (Actor)
c/o Siri Garber *Platform Public Relations*
2666 N Beachwood Dr
Los Angeles, CA 90068-2308, USA

Weaver, Reg (Misc)
1201 16th St NW
Washington, DC 20036-3201, USA

Weaver, Roger (Athlete, Baseball Player)
65 Moyer St
Canajoharie, NY 13317-1430, USA

Weaver, Rufus (Inventor)
77 Adelaide St
New London, CT 06320-6522, USA

Weaver, Sigourney (Actor)
c/o Michelle Benson *42West (NY)*
220 W 42nd St Fl 12
New York, NY 10036-7200, USA

Weaver, Warren E (Misc)
7607 Horsepen Rd
Richmond, VA 23229, USA

Weaver, Wayne (Football Executive)
1 Alltel Stadium Pl
Jacksonville, FL 32202-1917, USA

Weaving, Hugo (Actor)
c/o Ann Churchill-Brown *Shanahan Management*
Level 3 Berman House
Surry Hills 2010, AUSTRALIA

Weaving, Ryan (Stylist)
c/o Staff Member *Judy Inc*
1 Yorkville Ave
Toronto ON M4W 1L1, Canada

Webb, Brandon (Athlete, Baseball Player)
8814 E Ann Way
Scottsdale, AZ 85260-5010, USA

Webb, Charley (Actor)
c/o Staff Member *Emmerdale Yorkshire Television*
Yorkshire Television Centre Leeds
West Yorkshire LS3 1JS, UK

Webb, Chloe (Actor)
PO Box 2824
Venice, CA 90294-2824, USA

Webb, Christiaan (Musician, Songwriter, Writer)
109B Regents Park Road
London NW1 8UR, UNITED KINGDOM (UK)

Webb, Hank (Athlete, Baseball Player)
4527 Lake Valencia Blvd W
Palm Harbor, FL 34684-3920, USA

Webb, James R (Jimmy) (Athlete, Football Player)
1319 S Prairie Flower Rd
Turlock, CA 95380-9367, USA

Webb, Jeff (Athlete, Basketball Player)
8011 FM 621
Martindale, TX 78655-2521, USA

Webb, Justin (Musician, Songwriter, Writer)
109B Regents Park Road
London NW1 8UR, UNITED KINGDOM (UK)

Webb, Karrie (Athlete, Golfer)
725 Presidential Dr
Boynton Beach, FL 33435-2431, USA

Webb, Lee (Religious Leader, Television Host)
c/o 700 Club *Christian Broadcasting Network (CBN)*
977 Centerville Tpke
Virginia Beach, VA 23463-1001, USA

Webb, Lucy (Actor, Comedian)
1360 N Crescent Heights Blvd # 38
West Hollywood, CA 90046-4553, USA

Webb, Marc (Director)
c/o Michael Sugar *Anonymous Content (AC-LA)*
3531 Hayden Ave
Culver City, CA 90232, USA

Webb, Richmond J (Athlete, Football Player)
4120 Humphrey Dr
Dallas, TX 75216-4908, USA

Webb, Russell (Athlete)
611 Knob Hill Ave
Redondo Beach, CA 90277-4255, USA

Webb, Sonny (Baseball Player)
3194 Jordan Rd
Pleasant Plain, OH 45162-9238, USA

Webb, Spud (Athlete, Basketball Player)
1453 Mosslake Dr
Desoto, TX 75115-7709, USA

Webb, Tamilee (Athlete)
7031 Calle Portone
Rancho Santa Fe, CA 92091-0262, USA

Webb, Veronica (Actor, Model)
c/o Rae Ruff *Don Buchwald & Associates Inc (NY)*
10 E 44th St Frnt 1
New York, NY 10017-3654

Webb, Wayne (Bowler)
4413 McGuire St
North Las Vegas, NV 89081-2709, USA

Webb, Wellington E (Misc)
1437 Bannock St
Denver, CO 80202-5337, USA

Webb, William H (Business Person)
120 Park Ave
New York, NY 10017-5577, USA

Webber, Chris (Athlete, Basketball Player)
c/o Leon Rose *CAA - NJ*
308 Harper Dr Ste 210
Moorestown, NJ 08057-3245, USA

Webber, Julian Lloyd (Musician)
165 W 57th St
New York, NY 10019-2201, USA

Webber, Lord Andrew Lloyd (Composer, Musician, Producer)
c/o Staff Member *The Really Useful Group*
22 Tower St
London WC2H 9NS, UK

Webber, Mark (Actor)
c/o Abby Bluestone *Innovative Artists (LA)*
1505 10th St
Santa Monica, CA 90401-2805, USA

Webber, Tristan (Designer, Fashion Designer)
74 Gloucester Place
London W1H 3HN, UNITED KINGDOM (UK)

Weber, Amy (Actor)
c/o Staff Member *Select Artists Ltd (CA-Westside Office)*
1138 12th St Apt 1
Santa Monica, CA 90403-5459, USA

Weber, Arnold R (Educator)
Chancellor S Ofc
Evanston, IL 60208-0001, USA

Weber, Ben (Actor)
c/o Amy Guenther *Gateway Management Company Inc*
860 Via De La Paz Ste F10
Pacific Palisades, CA 90272-3631, USA

Weber, Ben (Athlete, Baseball Player)
5550 Baird St
Groves, TX 77619-3231, USA

Weber, Bruce (Coach)
Athletic Dept Assembly Hall
Champaign, IL 61820, USA

Weber, Bruce (Photographer)
526 W 26th St Rm 10A
New York, NY 10001-5541, USA

Weber, Charlie (Actor)
c/o Liza Anderson *Anderson Group Public Relations*
8060 Melrose Ave Fl 4
Los Angeles, CA 90046-7038, USA

Weber, Chuck (Athlete, Football Player)
12740 Cobblestone Creek Rd
Poway, CA 92064-5348, USA

Weber, Eberhard (Composer, Musician)
173 Brighton Ave
Boston, MA 02134-2003, USA

Weber, Eugen J (Historian)
11579 W Sunset Blvd
Los Angeles, CA 90049-2048, USA

Weber, George B (Misc)
Chemin Moise-Duboule 19
Geneva 1209, SWITZERLAND

Weber, Jack (Actor)
232 N Canon Dr
Beverly Hills, CA 90210-5302, USA

Weber, Jake (Actor)
c/o Staff Member *Gersh (LA)*
9465 Wilshire Blvd Ste 600
Beverly Hills, CA 90212-2612, USA

Weber, Leyna Juliet
c/o Staff Member *Atlas Talent Agency Inc*
36 W 44th St
New York, NY 10036-8102, USA

Weber, Mary E (Astronaut)
14 Hawkview St
Portola Valley, CA 94028-8037, USA

Weber, Neil (Athlete, Baseball Player)
1 Morning Vw
Irvine, CA 92603-3716, USA

Weber, Peter D (Pete) (Bowler)
10500 Saint Xavier Ln
Saint Ann, MO 63074-2607, USA

Weber, Robert M (Bob) (Cartoonist)
4 Times Sq
New York, NY 10036-6515, USA

Weber, Stephen L (Educator)
President's Office
Oswego, NY 13126, USA

Weber, Steven (Actor)
c/o Daniel (Danny) Sussman *Brillstein Entertainment Partners*
9150 Wilshire Blvd Ste 350
Beverly Hills, CA 90212-3453, USA

Weber, Vin (Misc)
1776 I St NW
Washington, DC 20006-3700, USA

Weber Jr, Bob (Cartoonist)
c/o Staff Member *King Features Syndication*
300 W 57th St Fl 15
New York, NY 10019-5238, USA

Webre, Septime (Choreographer)
3515 Wisconsin Ave NW
Washington, DC 20016-3010, USA

Webster, Alexander (Alex) (Athlete, Coach, Football Coach, Football Player)
8461 SE Palm Hammock Ln
Hobe Sound, FL 33455-8227, USA

Webster, Corey (Athlete, Football Player)
c/o Jimmy Sexton *SportsTrust Advisors - TN*
1100 Ridgeway Loop Rd Fl 5
Memphis, TN 38120-4053, USA

Webster, Cornell (Athlete, Football Player)
4575 Palm Ave Apt H
Riverside, CA 92501-3966, USA

Webster, George D (Athlete, Football Player)
6215 E Lake Dr
Haslett, MI 48840-8990, USA

Webster, Jason (Athlete, Football Player)
c/o Staff Member *New England Patriots*
Gillette Stadium One Patriots Pl
Foxboro, MA 02035-1388, USA

Webster, Jeff (Athlete, Basketball Player)
10405 SE 15th St
Oklahoma City, OK 73130-5714, USA

Webster, Larry (Athlete, Football Player)
12 Oakridge Ct
Elkton, MD 21921-3928, USA

Webster, Lenny (Athlete, Baseball Player)
6211 Bridgeport Dr
Charlotte, NC 28215-2319, USA

Webster, Marvin (Athlete, Basketball Player)
PO Box 237
Virginia Beach, VA 23458-0237, USA

Webster, Mitch (Athlete, Baseball Player)
5260 Timber Creek Rd
Great Bend, KS 67530-6633, USA

Webster, R Howard (Baseball Player, Publisher)
444 Front St W
Toronto, ON M5V 2S9, CANADA

Webster, Ray (Athlete, Baseball Player)
311 5th St
Marysville, CA 95901-5714, USA

Webster, Robert D (Bob) (Athlete, Swimmer)
269 Hacienda Carmel
Carmel, CA 93923-7947, USA

Webster, Tom (Athlete, Coach, Hockey Player)
1750 Longfellow Dr
Canton, MI 48187-2995, USA

Webster, Victor (Actor)
c/o Courtney Kivowitz *Schiff Company, The*
8440 Warner Dr Ste B1
Culver City, CA 90232-2461, USA

Webster, William H (Government Official)
4777 Dexter St NW
Washington, DC 20007-1060, USA

Wechsler, Nick (Actor)
c/o Benjamin Tappan *Tappan Entertainment*
8324 Fountain Ave Apt C
Los Angeles, CA 90069-2916, USA

Wecht, Cyril H
5420 Darlington Rd
Pittsburgh, PA 15217-1506, USA

Weck, Peter
Bambauer Keplerstr. 2
Munich, GERMANY D-81679

Wecker, Andreas (Gymnast)
Am Dorfplatz 1
Klein-Ziethen 16766, GERMANY

Weddington, Mike (Athlete, Football Player)
237 Sycamore Grove St
Simi Valley, TX 93605-7342, USA

Weddington, Sarah R (Attorney, Attorney General, General)
709 W 14th St
Austin, TX 78701-1707, USA

Weddle-Hines, Mary (Baseball Player)
329 Park Hills Rd
Corbin, KY 40701-2583, USA

Wedeen, Kelsey (Actor)
c/o Staff Member *Select Artists Ltd (CA-Westside Office)*
1138 12th St Apt 1
Santa Monica, CA 90403-5459, USA

Wedel, Dieter (Director)
Hamburg 22045, GERMANY

Weder, Gustav (Athlete)
Haltenstr 2
Stachen/TG, SWITZERLAND

Wedge, Chris (Actor, Director, Writer)
c/o Staff Member *Blue Sky Studios*
44 S Broadway Fl 17
White Plains, NY 10601-4411, USA

Wedge, Eric M (Athlete, Baseball Player, Coach)
31422 Saint Andrews
Westlake, OH 44145-5054, USA

Wedgeworth, Ann (Actor)
70 Riverside Dr
New York, NY 10024-5714, USA

Wedman, Scott (Athlete, Basketball Player)
7912 NW Scenic Dr
Kansas City, MO 64152-1645, USA

Weed, Kent (Director, Producer, Writer)
c/o Staff Member *Arthur Smith & Co*
1811 Centinela Ave
Santa Monica, CA 90404-4203, USA

Weed, Maurice James (Composer, Musician)
308 Overlook Rd # 55
Asheville, NC 28803-3319, USA

Weege, Reinhold (Producer)
2035 Via Don Benito
La Jolla, CA 92037-6427, USA

Weekend Players (Music Group)
c/o Staff Member *Paradigm (Monterey)*
404 W Franklin St
Monterey, CA 93940-2303, USA

Weekley, Thomas (Boo) (Athlete, Golfer)
2555 New York St
Jay, FL 32565-2956, USA

Weeks, Claire
11048 Chimineas Ave
Northridge, CA 91326-2820

Weeks, John D (Misc)
15301 Watergate Rd
Silver Spring, MD 20905-5779, USA

Weeks, John R (Architect)
39 Jackson's Lane Highgate
London N6 5SR, UNITED KINGDOM (UK)

Weeks, Michelle
c/o Staff Member *Diva Central Inc*
7510 W Sunset Blvd Ste 1445
Los Angeles, CA 90046-3408, USA

Weeks, Rickie (Athlete, Baseball Player)
550 Birch Ct
Altamonte Springs, FL 32714-1364, USA

Weeks, Rollo (Actor)
270 Lafayette St Ste 402
New York, NY 10012-3327, 212-343-3216

Weeks, Rosey (Baseball Player)
1290 Menna St
Jacksonville, FL 32205-8330, USA

Ween (Music Group, Musician)
ATTN: Mickey Melchiondo P.O. Box 324
New Hope, PA 18938, USA

Weezer (Music Group)
c/o Don Muller *WmE2 (Endeavor-LA)*
1 William Morris Pl
Beverly Hills, CA 90212-4261, USA

Wefald, Jon (Educator)
President's Office
Manhattan, KS 66506, USA

Wegener, Mike (Athlete, Baseball Player)
1507 Bennett Rd
Madison, OH 44057-1415, USA

Weger, Mike (Athlete, Football Player)
825 Markwood Dr
Oxford, MI 48370-2929, USA

Wegman, Bill (Athlete, Baseball Player)
20521 Heather Ct
Lawrenceburg, IN 47025-9396, USA

Wegman, Marie (Baseball Player)
4158 Westwood Northern Blvd
Cincinnati, OH 45211-2444, USA

Wegman, William G (Artist, Photographer)
239 W 18th St
New York, NY 10011-4502, USA

Wegner, Hans J (Designer)
Tinglevej 17
Gentoftte 2820, DENMARK

Wegner, Mark (Baseball Player)
3215 Stevenson St
Plant City, FL 33566-9517, USA

Wegner, Mark (Athlete, Baseball Player)
2607 Lakeview Way
Plant City, FL 33566-6774, USA

Wehba, Ray (Athlete, Football Player)
10312 Sunrise Blvd
Oklahoma City, OK 73120-2329, USA

Wehling, Ulrich (Athlete)
Hubertusstr 1
Munich 81477, GERMANY

Wehner, John (Athlete, Baseball Player)
105 Averys Way
Cranberry Twp, PA 16066-3303, USA

Wehr, Dick (Athlete, Basketball Player)
4425 Thomas Dr Unit 813A
Panama City, FL 32408-8320, USA

Wehrli, Roger R (Athlete, Football Player)
204 Fox Haven Ct
O Fallon, MO 63368-6596, USA

Wehrmeister, Dave (Athlete, Baseball Player)
4216 Dubhe Ct
Concord, CA 94521-1820, USA

Wei, Dan-Wen (Musician)
165 W 57th St
New York, NY 10019-2201, USA

Wei, James (Engineer)
571 Lake Dr
Princeton, NJ 08540-5632, USA

Weibel, Robert (Doctor)
Med School Pediatrics Dept
Philadelphia, PA 19104, USA

Weibring, D A (Athlete, Golfer)
5865 Versailles Ave
Frisco, TX 75034-5957, USA

Weich, Gillian (Musician)
1017 16th Ave S
Nashville, TN 37212-2324, USA

Weicker, Lowell P Jr (Ex-Governor, Ex-Senator)
1730 M St NW Ste 900
Washington, DC 20036-4547, USA

Weida, Johnny (Educator, General)
Superintendent US Air Force Academy
Colorado Springs, CO 80840, USA

Weide, Bob (Director)
4804 Laurel Canyon Blvd PMB 502
North Hollywood, CA 91607-3717, USA

Weide, Robert B (Director, Producer)
c/o Jonathan Brandstein *Morra Brezner Steinberg & Tenenbaum (MBST) Entertainment*
345 N Maple Dr Ste 200
Beverly Hills, CA 90210-5174, USA

Weidemann, Jakob (Artist)
Ringsveen
Lillehammer 2600, NORWAY

Weidenbaum, Murray L (Economist, Government Official)
6231 Rosebury Ave
Saint Louis, MO 63105-3243, USA

Weidenfeld of Chelsea, Arthur G (Publisher)
9 Chelsea Embankment
London SW3 4LE, UNITED KINGDOM (UK)

Weider, Joe (Publisher)
21100 Erwin St
Woodland Hills, CA 91367-3712, USA

Weidinger, Christine (Opera Singer)
801 W 181st St Apt 20
New York, NY 10033-4518, USA

Weidlinger, Paul (Engineer)
375 Hudson St
New York, NY 10014-3658, USA

Weidner, Bert (Athlete, Football Player)
517 NW 106th Ave
Plantation, FL 33324-1629, USA

Weidner, Brant (Athlete, Basketball Player)
1111 Colfax St
Evanston, IL 60201-2610, USA

Weigel, Teri (Adult Film Star)
4924 Balboa Blvd
Castaic, CA 91310, USA

Weigert, Robin (Actor)
c/o Staff Member *Frontline Management*
5670 Wilshire Blvd Ste 1370
Los Angeles, CA 90036-5679, USA

Weight, Doug (Athlete, Hockey Player)
1401 Clark Ave
Saint Louis, MO 63103-2700, USA

Weihenmayer, Erik (Mountaineer)
682 Partridge Cir
Golden, CO 80403-1548, USA

Weikel, M Keith (Business Person)
333 N Summit St
Toledo, OH 43604-1531, USA

Weikl, Bernd (Opera Singer)
Sankt Eriksgatan 100
Stockholm 113 31, SWEDEN

Weil, Andrew (Doctor, Writer)
c/o Richard S. Pine *Inkwell Management*
521 5th Ave
New York, NY 10175-0003, USA

Weil, Bruno (Composer, Conductor)
130 W 57th St Apt 8G
New York, NY 10019-3311, USA

Weil, Cynthia (Musician, Songwriter)
c/o Staff Member *Gorfaine/Schwartz Agency Inc*
4111 W Alameda Ave Ste 509
Burbank, CA 91505-4171, USA

Weil, Frank A (Misc)
900 Jefferson Dr SW
Washington, DC 20560-0004, USA

Weil, Liza (Actor)
c/o Kim Hodgert *Creative Artists Agency (CAA-LA)*
2000 Avenue of the Stars Ste 100
Los Angeles, CA 90067-4705, USA

Weiland, Scott (Musician, Songwriter)
c/o Andrea Pett-Joseph *Brillstein Entertainment Partners*
9150 Wilshire Blvd Ste 350
Beverly Hills, CA 90212-3453, USA

Weill, Claudia B (Director)
2800 Seattle Dr
Los Angeles, CA 90046-1209, USA

Weill, David (Dave) (Athlete, Track Athlete)
120 Mountain Spring Ave
San Francisco, CA 94114-2120, USA

Weill, Sanford I (Sandy) (Business Person)
399 Park Ave
New York, NY 10022-4614, USA

Weinbach, Arthur F (Business Person)
1 Adp Blvd
Roseland, NJ 07068-1728, USA

Weinbach, Lawrence A (Business Person)
Unisys Way
Blue Bell, PA 19424-0001, USA

Weinberg, Mike (Actor)
c/o Elissa Leeds-Fickman *Reel Talent Management*
PO Box 491035
Los Angeles, CA 90049-9035, USA

Weinberg, Rebecca (Stylist)
c/o Staff Member *Judy Casey Inc*
114 E 13th St
New York, NY 10003-5329, USA

Weinberg, Robert A (Doctor, Scientist)
9 Cambridge Ctr
Cambridge, MA 02142-1401, USA

Weinberg, Steven (Nobel Prize Laureate)
Physics Dept 2613 Wichita St
Austin, TX 78712, USA

Weinberger, Caspar (Publisher, Secretary)
2001 K St NW
Washington, DC 20006-1037, USA

Weinbrecht, Donna (Skier)
West Milford, NJ 7480, USA

Weiner, Art E (Athlete, Football Player)
404 Kimberly Dr
Greensboro, NC 27408-5020, USA

Weiner, Eric (Producer, Writer)
c/o Staff Member *International Creative Management (ICM-LA)*
10250 Constellation Blvd Fl 7
Los Angeles, CA 90067-6207, USA

Weiner, Gerry (Government Official)
40 Fredmir St
Dollard-des-Ormeaux, PQ H9A 2R3, CANADA

Weiner, Matthew (Producer)
c/o Ted Miller *Creative Artists Agency (CAA-LA)*
2000 Avenue of the Stars Ste 100
Los Angeles, CA 90067-4705, USA

Weiner, Timothy E (Tim) (Journalist)
1627 I St NW
Washington, DC 20006-4007, USA

Weiner-Davis, Michele (Writer)
c/o Staff Member *21st Century Speakers*
1352 Lake Rd
Gouldsboro, PA 18424, USA

Weingarten, David M (Architect)
330 2nd St
Oakland, CA 94607-4149, USA

Weingarten, Reid (Attorney, Attorney General, General)
4603 Harrison St
Chevy Chase, MD 20815-3721, USA

Weinke, Chris (Athlete, Football Player)
5718 Providence Country Club Dr
Charlotte, NC 28277-2621, USA

Weinman, Roz (Producer)
c/o Staff Member *Wolf Films Inc (LA)*
100 Universal City Plz Bldg 2252
Universal City, CA 91608-1002, USA

Weinstein, Bob (Business Person, Producer)
c/o Staff Member *Weinstein Company, The*
345 Hudson St Rm 1301
New York, NY 10014-7118, USA

Weinstein, Diane Gilbert (Judge)
717 Madison Pl NW
Washington, DC 20439-0001, USA

Weinstein, Eric
c/o Staff Member *Home Box Office (HBO-LA)*
2500 Broadway Ste 400
Santa Monica, CA 90404-3176, USA

Weinstein, Harvey (Actor, Business Person, Director, Producer)
c/o Staff Member *Weinstein Company, The*
345 Hudson St Rm 1301
New York, NY 10014-7118, USA

Weinstein, Jack B (Judge)
US Courthouse 225 Cadman Plaze E
Brooklyn, NY 11201, USA

Weinstein, Sidney T (General)
11936 Holly Branch Ct
Great Falls, VA 22066-1216, USA

Weintraub, Carl
10390 Santa Monica Blvd Ste 300
Los Angeles, CA 90025-5091

Weintraub, Jerry (Producer)
27740 Pacific Coast Hwy
Malibu, CA 90265-4341, USA

Weir, Arabella (Actor)
c/o Staff Member *Lip Service Casting Ltd*
60-66 Wardour St
London W1F 0TA, UK

Weir, Bill (Correspondent)
c/o Staff Member *Good Morning America (NY)*
147 Columbus Ave Fl 6
New York, NY 10023-6503, USA

Weir, Bob (Musician)
PO Box 1073
San Rafael, CA 94915-1073, USA

Weir, Gillian C (Musician)
78 Robin Way Tilehurst
Berks RG3 5SW, UNITED KINGDOM (UK)

Weir, Johnny (Athlete, Figure Skater)
c/o Tara Modlin *Fireworks Sorts Marketing*
475 Park Ave S Fl 6
New York, NY 10016-6901, USA

Weir, Judith (Composer)
8/9 Frith St
London W1V 5TZ, UNITED KINGDOM (UK)

Weir, Mike (Athlete, Golfer)
2960 Oberland Rd
Sandy, UT 84092-7128, USA

Weir, Peter (Director)
PO Box 29
Palm Beach, NSW 2108, AUSTRALIA

Weir, Stephanie (Actor)
c/o Dan Baron *Agency for the Performing Arts (APA-LA)*
405 S Beverly Dr Ste 500
Beverly Hills, CA 90212-4425, USA

Weirs, Peter (Director)
c/o Staff Member *Anonymous Content (AC-LA)*
3531 Hayden Ave
Culver City, CA 90232, USA

Weis, Al (Athlete, Baseball Player)
902 S Poplar Ave
Elmhurst, IL 60126-4547, USA

Weis, Charlie (Athlete, Coach, Football Coach, Football Player)
50905 Fox Trl Rail # T-5
Granger, IN 46530, USA

Weis, Heidelinde
Schleissheimer Str. 207
Munich, GERMANY D-80809

Weis, Joseph F Jr (Judge)
Grant St US Courthouse 700
Pittsburgh, PA 15219-2459, USA

Weis, Lianne (Stylist)
c/o Staff Member *Sally Bjornsen Represents*
2008 3rd Ave N
Seattle, WA 98109-2510, USA

Weisacosky, Ed (Athlete, Football Player)
14112 Lawrence 1137
Mount Vernon, MO 65712-8454, USA

Weisberg, Ruth (Artist)
11452 W Washington Blvd
Los Angeles, CA 90066-6013, USA

Weisberg, Tim (Musician)
c/o Staff Member *Pyramid Entertainment Group*
377 Rector Pl Apt 21A
New York, NY 10280-1439, USA

Weisburg, Alyssa (Producer)
c/o Staff Member *Casting Society of America*
606 N Larchmont Blvd Ste 4B
Los Angeles, CA 90004-1309, USA

Weiser-Most, Franz (Conductor)
4 Addison Bridge Place
London W14 8XP, UNITED KINGDOM (UK)

Weishoff, Paula (Athlete, Coach, Volleyball Player)
Athletic Dept Galen Center, 3400 S Figueroa St
Los Angeles, CA 90089-0001, USA

Weishuhn, Clayton (Athlete, Football Player)
4521 Kropala Rd
San Angelo, TX 76905-7412, USA

Weiskopf, Tom (Athlete, Golfer)
7580 E Gray Rd Ste 204
Scottsdale, AZ 85260-3408, USA

Weiskrantz, Lawrence (Doctor)
Experimental Psychology Dept
Oxford OX1 3UD, UNITED KINGDOM (UK)

Weisman, Annie (Comedian)
c/o Staff Member *Gersh (LA)*
9465 Wilshire Blvd Ste 600
Beverly Hills, CA 90212-2612, USA

Weisman, Kevin (Actor)
c/o Holly Lebed *Holly Lebed Personal Management*
10535 Wilshire Blvd Apt 808
Los Angeles, CA 90024-4556, USA

Weisman, Sam (Actor, Director)
9560 Wilshire Blvd Ste 500
Beverly Hills, CA 90212-2401, USA

Weisner, Maurice F (Admiral)
3000 Steeplechase
Alpharetta, GA 30004-1443, USA

Weiss, Brian L (Writer)
c/o Staff Member *WmE2 (WMA-LA)*
1 William Morris Pl
Beverly Hills, CA 90212-4261, USA

Weiss, Frank (Athlete, Football Player)
729 Fairfax Dr
Salinas, CA 93901-1250, USA

Weiss, Gary (Athlete, Baseball Player)
1700 Weiss Ln
Brenham, TX 77833-7063, USA

Weiss, Glenn (Director)
c/o Staff Member *WmE2 (WMA-LA)*
1 William Morris Pl
Beverly Hills, CA 90212-4261, USA

Weiss, Heinz
Rosskopfstr. 10
Grunwald, GERMANY D-82031

Weiss, Janet (Musician)
7 Trinity Row
Florence, MA 01062-1931, USA

Weiss, Julie (Designer)
8942 Wilshire Blvd # 219
Beverly Hills, CA 90211-1908, USA

Weiss, Karen (Athlete, Golfer)
13575 40th St S
Afton, MN 55001-9638, USA

Weiss, Kirsten Kjaer (Stylist)
c/o Staff Member *Independent NY*
15 E 30th St Apt 401
New York, NY 10016-7031, USA

Weiss, Margaret (Writer)
PO Box 707
Renton, WA 98057-0707, USA

Weiss, Melvyn I (Attorney, Attorney General, General)
1 Pennsylvania Plz
New York, NY 10119, USA

Weiss, Michael (Figure Skater)
PO Box 12311
Burke, VA 22009-2311, USA

Weiss, Michael T (Actor, Director)
c/o Robert Stein *Robert Stein Management*
PO Box 3797
Beverly Hills, CA 90212-0797, USA

Weiss, Morry (Business Person)
1 American Rd
Cleveland, OH 44144-2301, USA

Weiss, Robert W (Bob) (Athlete, Basketball Player, Coach)
3309 E St Andrews Way
Seattle, WA 98112-3749, USA

Weiss, Roberta (Actor)
3500 W Olive Ave Ste 300
Burbank, CA 91505-4647, USA

Weiss, Shaun
c/o Jeff Morrone *Jeff Morrone Entertainment*
9350 Wilshire Blvd Ste 224
Beverly Hills, CA 90212-3204, USA

Weiss, Walter W (Walt) (Athlete, Baseball Player)
1275 Castle Pointe Dr
Castle Rock, CO 80104-3258, USA

Weissenberg, Alexis (Musician)
59 E 54th St Rm 83
New York, NY 10022-9206, USA

Weissenhofer, Ron (Athlete, Football Player)
16156 Seneca Lake Cir
Crest Hill, IL 60403-1500, USA

Weisser, Morgan (Actor)
c/o Jeri Scott *Jeri Scott Management*
291 S La Cienega Blvd Ste 104
Beverly Hills, CA 90211-3308, USA

Weissflog, Jens (Skier)
Markt 2
Kurort Oberweisenthal 9484, GERMANY

Weissman, Irving L (Biologist, Doctor)
Pathology Dept Beckman Center
Stanford, CA 94305, USA

Weissman, Robert (Business Person)
1499 Post Rd
Fairfield, CT 06824-5940, USA

Weissman, Steven (Artist)
c/o Staff Member *Fantagraphics Books*
7563 Lake City Way NE
Seattle, WA 98115-4218, USA

Weisz, Martin (Director)
c/o Doreen Wilcox Little *Anonymous Content (AC-LA)*
3531 Hayden Ave
Culver City, CA 90232, USA

Weisz, Paul B (Engineer, Physicist)
Bio-Engineering Dept
Philadelphia, PA 19104, USA

Weisz, Rachel (Actor)
c/o Stacy O'Neil *Brillstein Entertainment Partners*
9150 Wilshire Blvd Ste 350
Beverly Hills, CA 90212-3453, USA

Weithaas, Antje (Musician)
12 Penzance Place
London W11 4PA, UNITED KINGDOM (UK)

Weitz, Bruce (Actor)
18826 Erwin St
Tarzana, CA 91335-6827, USA

Weitz, Chris (Actor, Director, Writer)
c/o David Lubliner *WmE2 (WMA-LA)*
1 William Morris Pl
Beverly Hills, CA 90212-4261, USA

Weitz, Paul (Director, Writer)
1424 2nd St Fl 3
Santa Monica, CA 90401-2379, USA

Weitz, Paul J (Astronaut)
3086 N Tam Oshanter Dr
Flagstaff, AZ 86004-7405, USA

Weitzman, Howard (Attorney, Attorney General, General)
1999 Ave of Stars Ste 1400
Los Angeles, CA 90067-6047, USA

Weitzman, Rick (Athlete, Basketball Player)
76 Birch St
Peabody, MA 01960-2059, USA

Weixler, Jess (Actor)
c/o Rhonda Price *Gersh (NY)*
41 Madison Ave
New York, NY 10010-2202, USA

Wejbe, Jolean (Actor)
c/o Bob McGowan *McGowan Management*
8733 W Sunset Blvd Ste 103
West Hollywood, CA 90069-2241, USA

Wek, Alek (Model)
c/o Staff Member *IMG*
304 Park Ave S Fl 12
New York, NY 10010-4314, USA

Welbourn, John (Athlete, Football Player)
3301 Palos Verdes Dr N
Palos Verdes Estates, CA 90274-1030, USA

Welbring, D A (Golfer)
c/o Staff Member *Pro Golfers Association (PGA) Tour*
112 Tpc Blvd
Ponte Vedra Beach, FL 32082, USA

Welch, Brian (Head) (Musician)
4025 E Chandler Blvd Ste 70-B3
Phoenix, AZ 85048-8829, USA

Welch, Claxton (Athlete, Football Player)
9721 SE Ankeny St
Portland, OR 97216-2311, USA

Welch, Gillian (Musician)
c/o Peter Mensch *Q Prime South*
729 7th Ave Fl 16
New York, NY 10019-6831, USA

Welch, Herb (Athlete, Football Player)
999 La Senda
Santa Barbara, CA 93105-4512, USA

Welch, Jack (Business Person)
c/o Staff Member *21st Century Speakers*
1352 Lake Rd
Gouldsboro, PA 18424, USA

Welch, Jack (Astronomer)
Electrical Engineering
Berkeley, CA 94720-0001, USA

Welch, Justin (Musician)
Ransomes Dock 35037 Parkgate Road
London SW11 4NP, UNITED KINGDOM (UK)

Welch, Lenny (Musician)
141 Dunbar Ave
Fords, NJ 08863-1551, USA

Welch, Michael (Actor)
c/o Susan Curtis *Curtis Talent Management*
9607 Arby Dr
Beverly Hills, CA 90210-1202, USA

Welch, Mike (Athlete, Baseball Player)
3 Inca Dr
Nashua, NH 03063-3544, USA

Welch, Milt (Athlete, Baseball Player)
818 Jannette Ct
Springfield, OR 97477-3694, USA

Welch, Raquel (Actor)
c/o Julie Nathanson *Rogers & Cowan PR (LA)*
Pacific Design Center 8687 Melrose Ave, 7th Floor
West Hollywood, CA 90069, USA

Welch, Robert L (Bob) (Athlete, Baseball Player)
11055 E Gold Dust Ave
Scottsdale, AZ 85259-4801, USA

Welch, Tahnee (Actor, Model)
PO Box 823
Beverly Hills, CA 90213-0823, USA

Welch Jr, John F (Business Person)
3135 Easton Tpke
Fairfield, CT 06828-0002, USA

Welchel, Don (Athlete, Baseball Player)
21518 Patton Ave
Lago Vista, TX 78645-6770, USA

Weld, Susan (Tuesday) (Actor)
c/o Alexa Pagonas *Michael Black Management*
9701 Wilshire Blvd Fl 10
Beverly Hills, CA 90212-2010, USA

Weld, William F (Ex-Governor)
120 Zaccheus Mead Ln
Greenwich, CT 06831-3751, USA

Weldon, Ann (Actor)
c/o Staff Member *Sutton Barth & Vennari Inc*
145 S Fairfax Ave Ste 310
Los Angeles, CA 90036-2176, USA

Weldon, Fay (Writer)
National House 62/66 Wardour
London W1V 3HP, UNITED KINGDOM (UK)

Weldon, Joan (Actor)
67 E 78th St
New York, NY 10075-0273, USA

Weldon, W Casey (Athlete, Football Player)
380 Castleton Cir
Tallahassee, FL 32312-1404, USA

Welk, Lawrence (All Stars)
901 Winding River Rd
Vero Beach, FL 32963-2548

Welke, Tim (Baseball Player)
7790 Doubletree Ct
Kalamazoo, MI 49009-9771, USA

Welke, William (Bill) (Athlete, Baseball Player)
54 Country Hls
Marshall, MI 49068-9674, USA

Welker, Frank (Actor)
c/o Staff Member *Cunningham Escott Slevin & Doherty (CESD-LA)*
10635 Santa Monica Blvd Ste 130
Los Angeles, CA 90025-8306, USA

Welker, Wes (Athlete, Football Player)
c/o Staff Member *New England Patriots*
Gillette Stadium One Patriots Pl
Foxboro, MA 02035-1388, USA

Welland, Colin (Actor, Writer)
68 Old Brompton Road
London SW7 3LQ, UNITED KINGDOM (UK)

Wellborn, Joe (Athlete, Football Player)
803 Paulus St
Schulenburg, TX 78956-1424, USA

Wellemeyer, Todd (Athlete, Baseball Player)
8402 Westover Dr
Prospect, KY 40059-9497, USA

Weller, Freddie (Musician, Songwriter, Writer)
PO Box 428
Portland, TN 37148-0428, USA

Weller, Paul (Musician)
c/o Staff Member *Variety Artists International Inc*
793 Higuera St Ste 6
Sn Luis Obisp, CA 93401-0500, USA

Weller, Peter (Actor)
c/o Bill Treusch *Bill Treusch Management*
853 7th Ave Apt 9A
New York, NY 10019-5222, USA

Weller, Rene (Boxer)
Hirsauerstrasse 50
Pforzheim D-75180, Germany

Weller, Robb (Television Host)
4249 Beck Ave
Studio City, CA 91604-2913

Weller, Watter (Musician)
Doblinger Hauptstr 40
Vienna 1190, AUSTRIA

Wellford, Harry W (Judge)
167 N Main St
Memphis, TN 38103-1814, USA

Welling, Tom (Actor, Director)
c/o Simon Halls *Slate Public Relations*
9000 W Sunset Blvd Ste 915
West Hollywood, CA 90069-5809, USA

Wellington, Harry H (Educator)
57 Worth St
New York, NY 10013-2926, USA

Welliver, Titus (Actor)
c/o Chris Schmidt *Paradigm (LA)*
360 N Crescent Dr
Beverly Hills, CA 90210-4874, USA

Wellman, Brad (Athlete, Baseball Player)
733 Graham Ct
Danville, CA 94526-4326, USA

Wellman, Gary (Athlete, Football Player)
1638 Wellington Pl
Westlake Village, CA 91361-1535, USA

Wellman Jr, William (Actor)
15935 Meadowcrest Rd
Sherman Oaks, CA 91403-4715, USA

Wells, Annie (Journalist, Photographer)
427 Mendocino Ave
Santa Rosa, CA 95401-6313, USA

Wells, Audrey (Director, Writer)
c/o David Lonner *Oasis Media Group*
8730 W Sunset Blvd Ste 700
Los Angeles, CA 90069-2249, USA

Wells, Bob (Athlete, Baseball Player)
154 Wilcox Rd
Cowiche, WA 98923-9775, USA

Wells, Carole (Actor)
c/o Staff Member *Burton Moss*
10533 Strathmore Dr
Los Angeles, CA 90024-2540, USA

Wells, Charles (Baseball Player)
1035 Beaver Creek Dr
Duncanville, TX 75137-3731, USA

Wells, Claudia (Actor)
c/o Staff Member *Privilege Talent Agency*
PO Box 260860
Encino, CA 91426-0860, USA

Wells, Cory (Musician)
PO Box 96597
Las Vegas, NV 89193-6597, USA

Wells, Dan (Actor)
c/o Jon Simmons *Simmons & Scott Entertainment*
7942 Mulholland Dr
Los Angeles, CA 90046-1225, USA

Wells, David (Dave) (Athlete, Baseball Player)
6170 Via Posada Del Norte
Rancho Santa Fe, CA 92067, USA

Wells, Dawn (Actor)
c/o Wes Stevens *Vox*
6420 Wilshire Blvd Ste 1080
Los Angeles, CA 90048-5539, USA

Wells, Dean (Athlete, Football Player)
1146 Copperfield Dr
Georgetown, IN 47122-9082, USA

Wells, Gawen D (Bonzi) (Basketball Player)
c/o Staff Member *Sacramento Kings*
1 Sports Pkwy
Sacramento, CA 95834-2301

Wells, Greg (Athlete, Baseball Player)
1 Sterling Ct
Cartersville, GA 30120-6469, USA

Wells, Harold (Athlete, Football Player)
2315 New Bern Ave
Raleigh, NC 27610-2434, USA

Wells, Jane (Correspondent)
c/o Staff Member *CNBC*
900 Sylvan Ave
Englewood Cliffs, NJ 07632-3312, USA

Wells, Joel (Athlete, Football Player)
11 Flicker Pt
Greenville, SC 29609-6646, USA

Wells, John (Producer)
c/o Staff Member *John Wells Productions*
4000 Warner Blvd Bldg 1
Burbank, CA 91522-0001

Wells, Kip (Athlete, Baseball Player)
3063 Tam O Shanter Ln
Missouri City, TX 77459-3114, USA

Wells, Kitty (Musician)
240 E Old Hickory Blvd
Madison, TN 37115-3935, USA

Wells, LLewellyn (Producer)
c/o Wayne Fitterman *United Talent Agency (UTA)*
9560 Wilshire Blvd Fl 5
Beverly Hills, CA 90212-2400, USA

Wells, Mark (Athlete, Hockey Player)
2341 Union Rd Apt 132
West Seneca, NY 14224-1469, USA

Wells, Norman (Athlete, Football Player)
600 Lakes Edge Dr
Oxford, MI 48371-5229, USA

Wells, Patricia (Journalist)
10 E 53rd St
New York, NY 10022-5244, USA

Wells, Terry (Athlete, Football Player)
25036 Polktown Rd
Lucedale, MS 39452, USA

Wells, Terry (Athlete, Baseball Player)
110 Seymour Creek Dr
Cary, NC 27519-5870, USA

Wells, Thelma (Writer)
1934 Lanark Ave
Dallas, TX 75203-4523, USA

Wells, Thomas B (Judge)
400 2nd St NW
Washington, DC 20217-0001, USA

Wells, Vernon (Athlete, Baseball Player)
2251 King Fisher Dr
Westlake, TX 76262-4816, USA

Wells, Warren (Athlete, Football Player)
1399 Pipkin St
Beaumont, TX 77705-2056, USA

Wells-Hawkes, Sharlene (Beauty Pageant Winner)
77 W Lund Ln
Centerville, UT 84014-2710, USA

Welp, Christian (Athlete, Basketball Player)
10235 Central Valley Rd NW
Poulsbo, WA 98370-8195, USA

Welser-Most, Franz (Conductor)
Euclid Ave Severance Hall 11001
Cleveland, OH 44106-4791, USA

Welsh, Chris (Athlete, Baseball Player)
12640 Huey Ln
Walton, KY 41094-9511, USA

Welsh, Irvine (Writer)
c/o Laura Hassan *Random House Group Limited*
The Book Service Limited 20 Vauxhall Bridge Road
London SW1V 2SA, United Kingdom

Welsh, Moray M (Musician)
28 Somerfield Ave Queens Park
London NW6 6JY, UNITED KINGDOM (UK)

Welsh, Stephanie (Journalist, Photographer)
PO Box 277
Wayne, ME 04284-0277, USA

Welsom, Eleen (Journalist)
7777 Jefferson St NE
Albuquerque, NM 87109-4343, USA

Welteroth, Dick (Athlete, Baseball Player)
122 Eldred St
Williamsport, PA 17701-3434, USA

Welti, Lisa (Actor)
c/o Staff Member *Select Artists Ltd (CA-Westside Office)*
1138 12th St Apt 1
Santa Monica, CA 90403-5459, USA

Welty, John D (Educator)
4411 N Van Ness Blvd
Fresno, CA 93704-3725, USA

Wen, Jinbao (Prime Minister)
Zhonganahai
Beijing, CHINA

Wendell, Krissy (Hockey Player)
Athletic Dept
Minneapolis, MN 55455, USA

Wendell, Martin (Athlete, Football Player)
405 W Olive Ave
Prospect Heights, IL 60070-1430, USA

Wendell, Ryan (Athlete, Football Player)
c/o Staff Member *New England Patriots*
Gillette Stadium One Patriots Pl
Foxboro, MA 02035-1388, USA

Wendell, Turk (Athlete, Baseball Player)
227 Hidden Valley Ln
Castle Rock, CO 80108-3487, USA

Wendelstedt, Hunter (Athlete, Baseball Player)
101 Hawthorne Hollow Dr
Madisonville, LA 70447-9340, USA

Wendelstedt Jr, Harry H (Baseball Player, Referee)
3044 SW 98th Way
Gainesville, FL 32608-8682, USA

Wenden, Michael (Swimmer)
Thrower Dr
Palm Beach Queens, AUSTRALIA

Wenders, Wim (Director)
Clausewitzstra 4
Berlin 10629, GERMANY

Wendkos, Gina (Writer)
c/o Staff Member *Industry Entertainment Partners*
955 Carrillo Dr Ste 300
Los Angeles, CA 90048-5400, USA

Wendryhoski, Joe (Athlete, Football Player)
312 Williams Blvd
Kenner, LA 70062-7630, USA

Wendt, George (Actor)
3856 Vantage Ave
Studio City, CA 91604-3636, USA

Wenge, Ralph (Correspondent)
1050 Techwood Dr NW
Atlanta, GA 30318-5604, USA

Wenger, Arsene (Coach)
Highbury House 75 Drayton Park
London N5 1BU, UNITED KINGDOM

Wengert, Don (Athlete, Baseball Player)
13100 Cedarwood Ave
Clive, IA 50325-8568, USA

Wenglikowski, Alan (Athlete, Football Player)
422 Lake Ave
Franklin, OH 45005-3521, USA

Wengren, Mike (Musician)
c/o Staff Member *Mitch Schneider Organization, The*
14724 Ventura Blvd Ste 410
Sherman Oaks, CA 91403-3537, USA

Wenham, David (Actor, Producer)
c/o Julie Curran *Shanahan Management*
Level 3, Berman House 91 Campbell St
Surry Hills NSW 2010, Australia

Wenner, Jann S (Publisher)
1290 Avenue of the Americas
New York, NY 10104-0101, USA

Wennington, Bill (Athlete, Basketball Player)
1085 Oak Grove Ln
Lake Forest, IL 60045-1629, USA

Wenstrom, Matt (Athlete, Basketball Player)
15714 Blanco Trails Ln
Cypress, TX 77429-4618, USA

Went, Joseph J (General)
9204 Kristin Ln
Fairfax, VA 22032-1809, USA

Wente, Jean R (Business Person)
PO Box 422940
San Francisco, CA 94142-2940, USA

Wentworth, Alexandra (Ali) (Actor, Comedian)
c/o Rhonda Price *Gersh (NY)*
41 Madison Ave
New York, NY 10010-2202, USA

Wentz, Pete (Musician)
c/o Nick Styne *Creative Artists Agency (CAA-LA)*
2000 Avenue of the Stars Ste 100
Los Angeles, CA 90067-4705, USA

Wenz, Fred (Athlete, Baseball Player)
1 Circle Dr
Branchburg, NJ 08876-3905, USA

Wenzel, Andreas (Skier)
Oberhul 151
Liechtenstein-Gamprin, LIECHENSTEIN

Wenzel, Hanni Weirather- (Skier)
Fanalwegle 4
Schaan 9494, LIECHENSTEIN

Wenzel, Ralph M (Athlete, Football Player)
2432 Pebble Beach Dr
League City, TX 77573-6417, USA

Wenzel, Ralph R (Athlete, Football Player)
921 Creek Dr
Annapolis, MD 21403-2309, USA

Wenzell, Marge (Baseball Player)
78287 Brookhaven Ln
Palm Desert, CA 92211-2735, USA

Wepner, Chuck (Boxer)
153 Avenue E
Bayonne, NJ 07002-4434, USA

Wepper, Fritz (Actor)
c/o Staff Member *NDF*
Joseph-Dollinger-Bogen 26
München 80807, Germany

Werbach, Adam (Misc)
85 2nd St Ste 200
San Francisco, CA 94105-3456, USA

Werber, William M (Bill) (Athlete, Baseball Player)
5800 Old Providence Rd
Charlotte, NC 28226-6872, USA

Werbowy, Daria (Model)
c/o Staff Member *IMG*
304 Park Ave S Fl 12
New York, NY 10010-4314, USA

Werdann, Robert (Athlete, Basketball Player)
4739 40th St Apt 5F
Sunnyside, NY 11104-4035, USA

Werhas, Johnny (Athlete, Baseball Player)
23705 Via Del Rio
Yorba Linda, CA 92887-2717, USA

Werkheiser, Devon (Actor)
c/o Cameron Curtis *Curtis Talent Management*
9607 Arby Dr
Beverly Hills, CA 90210-1202, USA

Werle, Bill (Athlete, Baseball Player)

Werley, George (Athlete, Baseball Player)
1374 Clarkston Clayton Cir
Ellisville, MO 63011, USA

Werner, Anna (Correspondent)
1945 Allen Pkwy
Houston, TX 77019-2506, USA

Werner, Clyde (Athlete, Football Player)
3009 Islandview Ct
Gig Harbor, WA 98335-1258, USA

Werner, Don (Athlete, Baseball Player)
2204 Briarwood Blvd
Arlington, TX 76013-3316, USA

Werner, Marianne (Athlete, Track Athlete)
Gauseland 2A
Dortmund 44227, GERMANY

Werner, Michael (Misc)
21 E 67th St
New York, NY 10065-5817, USA

Werner, Roger L Jr (Television Host)
10000 Santa Monica Blvd
Los Angeles, CA 90067, USA

Werner, Tom (Producer)
c/o Staff Member *Carsey-Werner-Mandabach*
16027 Ventura Blvd Ste 600
Encino, CA 91436-2798, USA

Wersching, Annie (Actor)
c/o Tara Friedlander *ID PR (LA)*
7060 Hollywood Blvd Fl 8
Los Angeles, CA 90028-6014, USA

Wersching, Raimund (Ray) (Athlete, Football Player)
18 Buttercup Ln
San Carlos, CA 94070-1528, USA

Wert, Don (Athlete, Baseball Player)
341 Smithville Rd
New Providence, PA 17560-9729, USA

Werth, Dennis (Athlete, Baseball Player)
2505 Tartan Way
Springfield, IL 62711-6755, USA

Werth, Isabell (Horse Racer)
Winterswicker Feld 4
Rheinberg 47495, USA

Werth, Jayson (Athlete, Baseball Player)
PO Box 13457
Springfield, IL 62791-3457, USA

Wertheim, Jorge (Misc)
Director's Office UN Plaza
New York, NY 10017, USA

Wertheimer, Fredric M (Misc)
3502 Macomb St NW
Washington, DC 20016-3162, USA

Wertheimer, Linda (Correspondent)
2025 M St NW
Washington, DC 20036-3399, USA

Werthein, Julio
c/o Staff Member *United Nations Educational, Scientific and Cultural Organization (UNESCO)*
7, place de Fontenoy 75352
Paris 07 SP, France

Wertimer, Ned (Actor)
4727 Wilshire Blvd Ste 333
Los Angeles, CA 90010-3874, USA

Wertis, Ray (Athlete, Basketball Player)
7840 NW 3rd St # 103
Pembroke Pines, FL 33024-1265, USA

Wertmuller, Lina (Director)
Piazza Clotilde
Rome 196, ITALY

Wertz, Bill (Athlete, Baseball Player)
26514 Mingo Dr
Perrysburg, OH 43551-5437, USA

Wescott, Scott (Athlete, Snowboarder)
c/o Ben Morrill *Octagon*
2 Union St Ste 300
Portland, ME 04101-4295, USA

Wesker, Arnold (Writer)
37 Ashley Road
London N19 3AG, UNITED KINGDOM (UK)

Wesley, Dante (Athlete, Football Player)
104 Fawn Cv
White Hall, AR 71602-4774, USA

Wesley, David (Athlete, Basketball Player)
16440 Marvin Rd
Charlotte, NC 28277-1950, USA

Wesley, James (Musician)
c/o Staff Member *Broken Bow Records*
209 10th Ave South Cummins Sta Suite 230
Nashville, TN 37203, USA

Wesley, Norman (Business Person)
300 Tower Pkwy
Lincolnshire, IL 60069-3640, USA

Wesley, Paul (Actor)
c/o Susan Calogerakis *Thruline Entertainment*
9250 Wilshire Blvd Ground Fl
Beverly Hills, CA 90212, USA

Wesley, Rutina (Actor)
c/o Holly Shakoor *42West (LA)*
11400 W Olympic Blvd Ste 1100
Los Angeles, CA 90064-1579, USA

Wesley, Walt (Athlete, Basketball Player)
6417 Scott Ln
Fort Myers, FL 33966-4713, USA

WesleySmith, Michael (Actor)
c/o Staff Member *Sharon Power Management*
Pope Street
Camborne, Wellington, New Zealand

Wessinger, Jim (Athlete, Baseball Player)
4275 Altair Crse
Liverpool, NY 13090-2230, USA

Wessling, John (Actor, Comedian)
c/o Nick Nuciforo *Creative Artists Agency (CAA-LA)*
2000 Avenue of the Stars Ste 100
Los Angeles, CA 90067-4705, USA

Wesson, Barry (Athlete, Baseball Player)
36 Shore Dr NE
Brookhaven, MS 39601-8756, USA

West, Adam (Actor)
c/o Tom Chasin *Chasin Agency, The*
8899 Beverly Blvd Ste 714
Los Angeles, CA 90048-2449, USA

West, Adam (Actor)
c/o Wes Stevens *Vox*
6420 Wilshire Blvd Ste 1080
Los Angeles, CA 90048-5539, USA

West, Billy (Artist, Voice Over Artist)
c/o Jeff Danis *Danis, Panaro, Nist (DPN)*
9201 W Olympic Blvd
Beverly Hills, CA 90212-4605, USA

West, Bob (Athlete, Football Player)
3915 Boston Ave
San Diego, CA 92113-3318, USA

West, Chandra
c/o Staff Member *Industry Entertainment Partners*
955 Carrillo Dr Ste 300
Los Angeles, CA 90048-5400, USA

West, Cornel (Activist)
Afro American Studies Dept
Cambridge, MA 2138, USA

West, David (Basketball Player)
1501 Girod St
New Orleans, LA 70113-3124, USA

West, David (Athlete, Baseball Player)
1242 SW Seahawk Way
Palm City, FL 34990-4246, USA

West, Delonte (Athlete, Basketball Player)
c/o Aaron Goodwin *Goodwin Sports Management*
Prefers to be contacted via email or telephone
Seattle, WA, USA

West, Dominic (Actor, Director)
c/o Angharad Wood *Tavistock Wood Management*
32 Tavistock St
London WC2B 5HA, UK

West, Doug (Athlete, Basketball Player)
1131 Meridian Dr
Presto, PA 15142-1031, USA

West, Ed (Athlete, Football Player)
1930 Ma Lee Dr
Moody, AL 35004-2813, USA

West, Ernest E (War Hero)
912 Adams Ave
Wurtland, KY 41144-1504, USA

West, Jake (Misc)
1750 New York Ave NW
Washington, DC 20006-5305, USA

West, James E (Inventor)
724 Berkeley Ave
Plainfield, NJ 07062-2010, USA

West, Jeff (Athlete, Football Player)
12376 Adair Creek Way NE
Redmond, WA 98053-5686, USA

West, Jerry (Athlete, Basketball Player)
1210 Moraga Dr
Los Angeles, CA 90049-1646, USA

West, Joe (Athlete, Baseball Player)
4904 N Travelers Palm Ln
Tamarac, FL 33319-3161, USA

West, Joel (Model)
1325 Avenue of the Americas
New York, NY 10019-6026, USA

West, John B (Scientist)
9626 Black Gold Rd
La Jolla, CA 92037-1110, USA

West, Jon Fredric (Opera Singer)
Maximillianstr 22
Munich 80539, GERMANY

West, Kanye (Actor, Musician, Producer)
c/o Michael Green *Collective*
8383 Wilshire Blvd Ste 1050
Beverly Hills, CA 90211-2415, USA

West, Leslie (Musician)
318 Wynn Ln
Port Jefferson, NY 11777-1670, USA

West, Lizzie (Musician)
3300 Warner Blvd
Burbank, CA 91505-4632, USA

West, Lori (Golfer)
2110 Augusta Dr SE
Marietta, GA 30067-8215, USA

West, Lyle (Athlete, Football Player)
719 1st St SE
Moultrie, GA 31768-5509, USA

West, Mark (Athlete, Basketball Player)
1659 E Sharon Dr
Phoenix, AZ 85022-5035, USA

West, Matthew (Musician)
c/o Mandy Parsons *Savvy Media Solutions*
133 Holiday Ct
Franklin, TN 37067-1384, USA

West, Nathan (Actor)
c/o Jason Egenberg *United Talent Agency (UTA)*
9560 Wilshire Blvd Fl 5
Beverly Hills, CA 90212-2400, USA

West, Paula (Musician)
PO Box 2142
San Francisco, CA 94126-2142, USA

West, Peter
4708 Largo Way
Las Vegas, NV 89121-2836

West, Price (Baseball Player)
3540 Mill Point Dr SE
Grand Rapids, MI 49512-9337, USA

West, Red (Actor)
6676 Memphis-Arlington
Bartlett, TN 38135

West, Richard L (War Hero)
6341 Crosswoods Dr
Falls Church, VA 22044-1209, USA

West, Roland (Athlete, Basketball Player)
7464 Shaker Run Ln
West Chester, OH 45069-6301, USA

West, Ronnie (Athlete, Football Player)
PO Box 110
Pineview, GA 31071-0110, USA

West, Sam
34-43 Russell
London, ENGLAND WC2B 5HA

West, Samuel (Actor)
Drury House 34-43 Russell St
London WC2B 5HA, UNITED KINGDOM (UK)

West, Shane (Actor)
c/o Matt Luber *Luber Roklin Management*
8530 Wilshire Blvd Ste 550
Beverly Hills, CA 90211-3133, USA

West, Simon (Director)
c/o Staff Member *Simon West Productions*
5555 Melrose Ave Dressing Room Building 109
Los Angeles, CA 90038, USA

West, Stan (Athlete, Football Player)
2455 Manchester Dr Unit 3
Oklahoma City, OK 73120-3771, USA

West, Timothy L (Actor)
2D Wimpote St
London W1G 0EB, UNITED KINGDOM (UK)

West, Troy (Athlete, Football Player)
725 N Greenberry Ave
West Covina, CA 91790-1331, USA

West, Willie (Athlete, Football Player)
PO Box 50430
Eugene, OR 97405-0980, USA

West Jr, Togo D (Secretary)
922 N Cameron Ave
Winston Salem, NC 27101-3316, USA

Westbrook, Bryant (Athlete, Football Player)
28017 N 17th Dr
Phoenix, AZ 85085-5350, USA

Westbrook, Dexter (Athlete, Basketball Player)
200 E Church Ln Apt 405
Philadelphia, PA 19144-2245, USa

Westbrook, Jake (Athlete, Baseball Player)
3136 Booger Hill Rd
Danielsville, GA 30633-6017, USA

Westbrook, Marie (Actor)

Westbrook, Michael (Athlete, Football Player)
1585 Oregon Trl
Elk Grove Village, IL 60007-2853, USA

Westbrooks, Greg (Athlete, Football Player)
3832 10th Avenue Pl
Moline, IL 61265-2429, USA

Westcott, Seth (Athlete, Snowboarder)
c/o Staff Member *US Ski And Snowboard Association*
Box 199
Park City, UT 84060, USA

Westenhoefer, Suzanne (Actor, Comedian)
100 S 4th St
Los Angeles, California 90046

Westenra, Hayley (Actor)
c/o Staff Member *Decca Music Group Limited*
347-353 Chiswick High Rd
London W4 4HS, UNITED KINGDOM

Wester, Travis (Actor)
c/o Abby Bluestone *Innovative Artists (LA)*
1505 10th St
Santa Monica, CA 90401-2805, USA

Westerberg, Paul (Musician, Songwriter)
c/o Staff Member *WmE2 (WMA-LA)*
1 William Morris Pl
Beverly Hills, CA 90212-4261, USA

Westerfield, Putney (Publisher)
10 Greenview Ln
Hillsborough, CA 94010-6424, USA

Westerman-Austin, Helen (Baseball Player)
1837 Stonehenge Rd
Springfield, IL 62702-3244, USA

Western, Johnny (Musician)
19 E 16th Ave
Hutchinson, KS 67501-5533, USA

Western Underground (Music Group)
c/o Staff Member *Paradigm (Monterey)*
404 W Franklin St
Monterey, CA 93940-2303, USA

Westfall, Ed
PO Box 39
Locust Valley, NY 11560-0039

Westfall, V Edward (Ed) (Athlete, Hockey Player)
699 Hillside Ave
New Hyde Park, NY 11040-2512, USA

Westfeldt, Jennifer (Actor)
c/o Courtney Kivowitz *Schiff Company, The*
8440 Warner Dr Ste B1
Culver City, CA 90232-2461, USA

Westhead, Barb (Golfer)
9820 E Thompson Peak Pkwy Unit 707
Scottsdale, AZ 85255-6656, USA

Westhead, Paul (Athlete, Basketball Player, Coach)
2217 Via Alamitos
Palos Verdes Estates, CA 90274-1652, USA

Westheimer, Doctor Ruth (Doctor)
c/o Staff Member *Cunningham Escott Slevin & Doherty (CESD-LA)*
10635 Santa Monica Blvd Ste 130
Los Angeles, CA 90025-8306, USA

Westheimer, Gerald (Doctor, Misc)
582 Santa Barbara Rd
Berkeley, CA 94707-1746, USA

Westlake, Wally (Athlete, Baseball Player)
3800 61st St
Sacramento, CA 95820-2421, USA

Westlife (Music Group, Musician)
c/o Staff Member *Solo Agency Ltd (UK)*
55 Fulham High St 2nd Floor
London SW6 3JJ, United Kingdom

Westling, Jon (Educator)
285 Goddard Ave
Brookline, MA 02445-7411, USA

Westling, Wayde (Stylist)
c/o Staff Member *Celestine - CA*
1666 20th St Ste 200B
Santa Monica, CA 90404-3828, USA

Westmore, McKenzie (Actor)
3904 Laurel Canyon Blvd # 766
Studio City, CA 91604, USA

Westmoreland, Dick (Athlete, Football Player)
5601 Sea Reef Pl
San Diego, CA 92154, USA

Westmoreland, James (Actor)
8019 1/2 Norton Ave
West Hollywood, CA 90046-5002, USA

Weston, Celia (Actor)
c/o Staff Member *Innovative Artists (LA)*
1505 10th St
Santa Monica, CA 90401-2805, USA

Weston, David
123-A Grosvenor Rd
London, ENGLAND SW1

Weston, J Fred (Educator)
3484 Hardin Way
Soquel, CA 95073-2745, USA

Weston, Jeff (Athlete, Football Player)
7235 Alakoko St
Honolulu, HI 96825-2712, USA

Weston, Kim (Musician)
5434 W Sample Rd PMB 533
Margate, FL 33073-3453, USA

Weston, Mickey (Athlete, Baseball Player)
2702 Eisenhower Ave
Valparaiso, IN 46383-3273, USA

Weston, P John (Government Official)
13 Denbigh Gardens Richmond
Surrey TW10 6EN, UNITED KINGDOM (UK)

Weston, Randolph (Randy) (Musician)
PO Box 749
Maplewood, NJ 07040-0749, USA

Weston, Wesley (Lil' Flip) (Musician)
c/o Staff Member *Sony Music Entertainment*
555 Madison Ave
New York, NY 10022-3301, USA

Westphal, Paul D (Athlete, Basketball Player, Coach)
1424 Granvia Altamira
Palos Verdes Estates, CA 90274-2131, USA

Westwick, Ed (Actor)
c/o Melanie Greene *Affirmative Entertainment*
425 N Robertson Blvd
West Hollywood, CA 90048-1735, USA

Westwood, Lee (Athlete, Golfer)
c/o Andrew ""Chubby"" Chandler *International Sports Management Ltd (ISM UK)*
Cherry Tree Farm Cherry Tree Lane
Rostherne, Cheshire WA14 3RZ, UNITED KINGDOM

Westwood, Vivienne (Designer, Fashion Designer)
9-15 Elcho St
London SW11 4AU, UNITED KINGDOM (UK)

Wetherbee, James D (Astronaut)
3818 Trailstone Ln
Katy, TX 77494-2472, USA

Wetherby, Jeff (Athlete, Baseball Player)
28410 Great Bend Pl
Wesley Chapel, FL 33543-5726, USA

Wetherell, T R (Educator)
Athletic
Tallahassee, FL 32306-0001, USA

Wetherill, George W (Geophysicist, Physicist)
Terrestrial Magnetism Dept
Washington, DC 20015, USA

Wethington, Charles T Jr (Educator)
2926 Four Pines Dr
Lexington, KY 40502-2969, USA

Wetnight, Ryan S (Athlete, Football Player)
3156 Griffon Ct
Simi Valley, CA 93065-0500, USA

Wetoska, Robert (Athlete, Football Player)
1295 Forest Glen Dr S
Winnetka, IL 60093-1427, USA

Wetteland, John (Athlete, Baseball Player)
1229 Kentucky Derby Dr
Argyle, TX 76226-7005, USA

Wetter, Friedrich Cardinal (Religious Leader)
Kardinal-Faulhaber-Str 7
Munich 80333, GERMANY

Wetterich, Brett (Athlete, Golfer)
149 Morning Dew Cir
Jupiter, FL 33458-5278, USA

Wettig, Patricia (Actor)
c/o Lori Jonas *Jonas Public Relations*
240 26th St Ste 3
Santa Monica, CA 90402-2542, USA

Wetton, John (Musician)
133 W 25th St # 500
New York, NY 10001-7206, USA

Wetzel, Gary G (War Hero)
PO Box 84
Oak Creek, WI 53154-0084, USA

Wetzel, John (Athlete, Basketball Player, Coach)
13011 N Sunrise Canyon Ln
Marana, AZ 85658-4035, USA

Wetzel, Robert L (General)
1425 Dartmouth Rd
Columbus, GA 31904-1902, USA

Wetzel, Rosemarie
111 E 22nd St Rm 200
New York, NY 10010-5414

Wever, Stefan (Athlete, Baseball Player)
7 Corte Los Sombras
Greenbrae, CA 94904-1149, USA

Wexler, Anne (Government Official)
1317 F St NW Ste 600
Washington, DC 20004-1105, USA

Wexler, Haskell (Cinematographer)
1247 Lincoln Blvd # 585
Santa Monica, CA 90401-1700, USA

Wexner, Leslie H (Business Person)
PO Box 16000
Columbus, OH 43216-6000, USA

Weyand, Frederick C (General)
PO Box 3708
Honolulu, HI 96811-3708, USA

Weyerhaeuser, George (Business Person)
33663 32nd Ave S
Federal Ave, WA 98023, USA

Whalen, Dorothy (Baseball Player)
8315 125th St
Kew Gardens, NY 11415-2705, USA

Whalen, Jim (Athlete, Football Player)
9 Wauketa Rd
Gloucester, MA 01930-1423, USA

Whalen, Laurence J (Judge)
400 2nd St NW
Washington, DC 20217-0001, USA

Whalen, Lindsay (Basketball Player)
Mohegan Sun Arena
Uncasville, CT 6382, USA

Whaley, Frank (Actor)
c/o Staff Member *Shelter Entertainment*
9454 Wilshire Blvd Ste 715
Beverly Hills, CA 90212-2925, USA

Whaley, Joanne (Actor)
c/o Staff Member *Creative Artists Agency (CAA-LA)*
2000 Avenue of the Stars Ste 100
Los Angeles, CA 90067-4705, USA

Whalin, Justin
3604 Holboro Dr
Los Angeles, CA 90027-1432

Whalley, Joanne (Actor)
1435 Lindacrest Dr
Beverly Hills, CA 90210-2519, USA

Whalum, Kirk (Musician)
PO Box 231
Canoga Park, CA 91305-0231, USA

Wham, Tom (Athlete, Football Player)
415 John St
Greer, SC 29651-1412, USA

Whang, Suzanne (Actor)
c/o Staff Member *Kragen & Company*
14039 Aubrey Rd
Beverly Hills, CA 90210-1062, USA

Whannell, Leigh (Actor, Writer)
c/o Stacey Testro *Stacey Testro International*
8265 W Sunset Blvd Ste 102
West Hollywood, CA 90046-2433, USA

Wharton, Bernard (Architect)
18 W Putnam Ave
Greenwich, CT 06830-5341, USA

Wharton, Hogan (Athlete, Football Player)
5736 W Airport Blvd
Houston, TX 77035-4314, USA

Whatley, Ennis (Athlete, Basketball Player)
42 Brinkwood Rd
Brookeville, MD 20833-2303, USA

Wheat, Lee (Athlete, Baseball Player)
4010 Galt Ocean Dr Apt 1406
Fort Lauderdale, FL 33308-6519, USA

Wheatley, E H (Publisher)
2250 Granville St
Vancouver, BC V6H 3G2, CANADA

Wheatley, Terrence (Athlete, Football Player)
c/o Staff Member *New England Patriots*
Gillette Stadium One Patriots Pl
Foxboro, MA 02035-1388, USA

Wheatley, Tyrone (Athlete, Football Player)
3090 Andora Dr
Ypsilanti, MI 48198-9649, USA

Wheaton, David (Tennis Player)
20045 Cottagewood Ave
Excelsior, MN 55331-9239, USA

Wheaton, Kenny (Athlete, Football Player)
6427 S 21st Pl
Phoenix, AZ 85042-4652, USA

Wheaton, Wil (Actor)
2603 Sea Pine Ln
La Crescenta, CA 91214-1443, USA

Wheaton, Will (Actor)
c/o Tom Harrison *Diverse Talent Group*
9911 W Pico Blvd Ste 340W
Los Angeles, CA 90035-2712, USA

Wheatus (Music Group)
c/o Robert Hollingsworth *So Called Management*
1055 Homer St #1006
Vancouver, BC V6B 1G3, CANADA

Whedon, Joss (Director, Producer, Writer)
c/o Chris Harbert *Creative Artists Agency (CAA-LA)*
2000 Avenue of the Stars Ste 100
Los Angeles, CA 90067-4705, USA

Wheeler, Blake (Athlete, Hockey Player)
c/o Staff Member *Boston Bruins*
TD Banknorth Garden 100 Legends Way, Suite 250
Boston, MA 2114, USA

Wheeler, Charles F (Cinematographer)
79125 Jack Rabbit Trl
La Quinta, CA 92253-4514, USA

Wheeler, Cheryl (Musician, Songwriter, Writer)
PO Box 1770
Hendersonville, TN 37077-1770, USA

Wheeler, Clinton (Athlete, Basketball Player)
199 Scenic View Ln
Stone Mountain, GA 30087-6222, USA

Wheeler, Daniel (Dan) (Athlete, Baseball Player)
215 Harrison Ave
Belleair Beach, FL 33786-3619, USA

Wheeler, Daniel S (Editor)
700 N Pennsylvania St
Indianapolis, IN 46204-1129, USA

Wheeler, Dwight (Athlete, Football Player)
2124 Blair Blvd
Nashville, TN 37212-4902, USA

Wheeler, Ellen
13576 Cheltenham Dr
Sherman Oaks, CA 91423-4818

Wheeler, H Anthony (Architect)
Hawthornbank House Dean Village
Edinburgh EH4 3BH, SCOTLAND

Wheeler, John (Actor)
8484 Wilshire Blvd Ste 745
Beverly Hills, CA 90211-3235, USA

Wheeler, Joni (Stylist)
2803 Woodlawn Dr
Nashville, TN 37215-1136, USA

Wheeler, Maggie (Actor)
c/o Belle Zwerdling *Progressive Artists Agency*
1041 N Formosa Ave
West Hollywood, CA 90046-6703, USA

Wheeler, Margaret
4950 Cahuenga Blvd
Valley Village, CA 91601-4706

Wheeler, Mark (Athlete, Football Player)
101 Meadowridge Cv
San Marcos, TX 78666-2251, USA

Wheelock, Gary (Athlete, Baseball Player)
3724 N Springfield St
Buckeye, AZ 85396-3537, USA

Whelan, Bill (Composer)
2100 Colorado Ave
Santa Monica, CA 90404-3504, USA

Whelan, Jill (Actor)
c/o Staff Member *Scott Stander & Associates*
4533 Van Nuys Blvd Ste 401
Sherman Oaks, CA 91403-2950, USA

Whelan, Julia (Actor)
c/o Tracy Brennan *Creative Artists Agency (CAA-LA)*
2000 Avenue of the Stars Ste 100
Los Angeles, CA 90067-4705, USA

Whelan, Nicky (Actor)
c/o Justin Grey Stone *Untitled Entertainment (LA)*
350 S Beverly Dr Ste 200
Beverly Hills, CA 90212-4819, USA

Whelan, Wendy (Ballerina)
Lincoln Center Plaza
New York, NY 10023, USA

Whelchel, Lisa (Actor)
5210 Long Prairie Rd Apt 1016
Flower Mound, TX 75028-2277, USA

Wheless, Jamy (Animator)
405 Fair St
Petaluma, CA 94952-2519, USA

Whelpley, John (Actor)
c/o Staff Member *Lenhoff & Lenhoff*
830 Palm Ave
West Hollywood, CA 90069-4009

Whibley, Deryck (Musician)
15445 Varden St
Sherman Oaks, CA 91403-3815, USA

Whicker, Alan D (Correspondent)
Le Gallais Chambers Saint Helier
Jersey, UNITED KINGDOM (UK)

Whigham, Larry (Athlete, Football Player)
6110 Midway Rd
Raymond, MS 39154-8357, USA

Whigham, Shea (Actor)
c/o Larry Taube *Principal Entertainment (LA)*
1964 Westwood Blvd Ste 400
Los Angeles, CA 90025-4695, USA

Whillock, Jack (Athlete, Baseball Player)
2118 River Ridge Rd
Arlington, TX 76017-2758, USA

Whinnery, Barbara (Actor)
3575 Cahuenga Blvd W Ste 500
Los Angeles, CA 90068-1344, USA

Whinnery, John R (Engineer)
576 San Luis Rd
Berkeley, CA 94707-1743, USA

Whirry, Shannon (Actor)
8827 Beverly Blvd
Los Angeles, CA 90048-2405, USA

Whisenant, Matt (Athlete, Baseball Player)
1035 Fairview Dr
La Canada Flintridge, CA 91011-2351, USA

Whisenhunt, Ken (Athlete, Football Player)
6905 E Cheney Dr
Paradise Valley, AZ 85253-3582, USA

Whisenton, Larry (Athlete, Baseball Player)
524 Main St
Canton, MS 39046-3208, USA

Whishaw, Anthony (Artist)
7A Albert Place Victoria Road
London W8 5PD, UNITED KINGDOM (UK)

Whishaw, Ben (Actor)
c/o Clair Dobbs *Public Eye Communications*
535 Kings Rd Suite 313 Plaza
London SW10 0SZ, United Kingdom

Whiskey Myers (Music Group, Musician)
c/o Joey Lee *WmE2 (WMA-TN)*
1600 Division St Ste 300
Nashville, TN 37203-2755, USA

Whisler, J Steven (Business Person)
1 N Central Ave
Phoenix, AZ 85004-4414, USA

Whisman, Greg (Athlete, Golfer)
1908 129th Pl SE
Everett, WA 98208-7121, USA

Whiston, Don (Athlete, Hockey Player)
2 Jeffreys Neck Rd
Ipswich, MA 01938-1328, USA

Whitacre, Edward E Jr (Business Person)
175 E Houston St
San Antonio, TX 78205-2255, USA

Whitaker, Alaina (Musician)
PO Box 703165
Tulsa, OK 74170-3165, USA

Whitaker, Denzel (Actor)
c/o Brad Slater *WmE2 (Endeavor-LA)*
9601 Wilshire Blvd Fl 3
Beverly Hills, CA 90210-5219, USA

Whitaker, Forest (Actor, Director, Producer)
c/o Jennifer Plante *SLATE Public Relations - NY*
307 7th Ave Rm 2401
New York, NY 10001-6019, USA

Whitaker, Johnny
4924 Vineland Ave
No. Hollywood, CA 9160l

Whitaker, Louis R (Lou) Jr (Athlete, Baseball Player)
17 Brownstone Ln
Greensboro, NC 27410-5145, USA

Whitaker, Mark (Editor)
251 W 57th St
New York, NY 10019-1802, USA

Whitaker, Meade (Judge)
400 2nd St NW
Washington, DC 20217-0001, USA

Whitaker, Pernell (Boxer)
3808 Cranberry Ct
Virginia Beach, VA 23456-8109, USA

Whitaker, Roger
1730 Tree Blvd Ste 2
Saint Augustine, FL 32084-4193

Whitaker, Steve (Athlete, Baseball Player)
805 SE 8th St
Fort Lauderdale, FL 33316-1205, USA

Whitaker, William (Athlete, Football Player)
Lake Road 135
Gravois Mills, MO 65037, USA

Whitbank, Ben (Baseball Player)
203 E Apollo Ln
Milton, DE 19968-9781, USA

Whitbread, Fatima (Athlete, Track Athlete)
Elozabeth Road Grays
Essex RM16 6QZ, UNITED KINGDOM (UK)

Whitby, Bill (Athlete, Baseball Player)
13926 Huntersville Concord Rd
Huntersville, NC 28078-6262, USA

Whitcomb, Bob (Race Car Driver)
9201 Garrison Rd
Charlotte, NC 28278, USA

Whitcomb, Edgar D (Ex-Governor)
3905 Highwater Rd
Cannelton, IN 47520-5869, USA

Whitcomb, Ian (Musician, Songwriter, Writer)
PO Box 451
Altadena, CA 91003-0451, USA

Whitcomb, Richard T (Inventor)
119 Tide Mill Ln
Hampton, VA 23666-5204, USA

White, Adrian (Athlete, Football Player)
686 Allen Ln
Orange Park, FL 32073-3986, USA

White, Alan (Musician)
54 Linhope St
London NW1 6HL, UNITED KINGDOM (UK)

White, Albert (Baseball Player)
32 Jessana Hts
Colorado Springs, CO 80906-7902, USA

White, Andre (Athlete, Football Player)
5122 Hunters Luck
Stone Mountain, GA 30088-3123, USA

White, Anna
9950 Durant Dr Unit 402
Beverly Hills, CA 90212-1610

White, Betty (Actor, Comedian)
PO Box 491965
Los Angeles, CA 90049-8965, USA

White, Bob W (Athlete, Football Player)
763D Espada Dr
El Paso, TX 79912-1913, USA

White, Bradley
8730 W Sunset Blvd Ste 480
Los Angeles, CA 90069-2277

White, Brian (Actor)
c/o Staff Member *United Talent Agency (UTA)*
9560 Wilshire Blvd Fl 5
Beverly Hills, CA 90212-2400, USA

White, Brooke (Musician)
c/o Rick Canny *Sanctuary Artist Management*
8750 Wilshire Blvd Ste 200
Beverly Hills, CA 90211-2707, USA

White, Bryan (Musician, Songwriter, Writer)
3415 W End Ave Ste 101G
Nashville, TN 37203-6878, USA

White, Cheryl (Musician)
713 18th Ave S
Nashville, TN 37203-3214, USA

White, Chris (Musician)
PO Box 770850
Orlando, FL 32877-0850, USA

White, Colin (Athlete, Hockey Player)
81 Western Ave
Morristown, NJ 07960-9005, USA

White, Dana (Business Person)
2960 W Sahara Ave Ste 200
Las Vegas, NV 89102-1709, USA

White, Danny (Athlete, Coach, Football Player)
111 S Saint Joseph St
South Bend, IN 46601-1901, USA

White, Derrick (Athlete, Baseball Player)
35 Oak Grove Dr
Novato, CA 94949-7220, USA

White, Devon M (Athlete, Baseball Player)
6440 E Sierra Vista Dr
Paradise Valley, AZ 85253-4351, USA

White, DeVoreaux
4505 Santa Rosalia Dr
Los Angeles, CA 90008-1571

White, Diz (Actor)
203 N Plymouth Blvd
Los Angeles, CA 90004-3833, USA

White, Donna (Athlete, Golfer)
200 Caribe Ct
Greenacres, FL 33413-2150, USA

White, Dwayne (Athlete, Football Player)
1916 Dickinson St
Philadelphia, PA 19146-4662, USA

White, Ed
1225 Grand View Dr
Berkeley, CA 94705-1629

White, Ed (Athlete, Football Player)
PO Box 1437
Julian, CA 92036-1437, USA

White, Edit (Stylist)
2155 W Touhy Ave
Chicago, IL 60645-3505, USA

White, Edmund (Writer)
185 Nassau St Rm 224
Princeton, NJ 08544-2003, USA

White, Edward A (Ed) (Athlete, Football Player)
PO Box 1437
Julian, CA 92036-1437, USA

White, Elder (Athlete, Baseball Player)
919 Colony Ave N
Ahoskie, NC 27910-2107, USA

White, Eric (Athlete, Basketball Player)
1945 Bush St Apt K
San Francisco, CA 94115-3226, USA

White, Eugene (Baseball Player)
4166 Lockhart Dr N
Jacksonville, FL 32209-1928, USA

White, Frank (Athlete, Baseball Player)
412 NE Parks Edge Dr
Lees Summit, MO 64064-1270, USA

White, Gabe (Athlete, Baseball Player)
1571 Lakeview Dr
Sebring, FL 33870-7940, USA

White, Gene C (Athlete, Football Player)
5 Lacosta Ln
Pinehurst, NC 28374-8317, USA

White, Gerald (Athlete, Football Player)
1501 Halo Dr
Troy, MI 48084, USA

White, Gilbert F (Misc)
624 Pearl St Apt 302
Boulder, CO 80302-5072, USA

White, Hubie (Athlete, Basketball Player)
101 E Gowen Ave
Philadelphia, PA 19119-1613, USA

White, Jack (Musician)
c/o Staff Member *WmE2 (WMA-LA)*
1 William Morris Pl
Beverly Hills, CA 90212-4261, USA

White, Jahidi (Athlete, Basketball Player)
c/o Staff Member *Washington Wizards*
601 F St NW
Washington, DC 20004-1605, USA

White, Jaleel (Actor)
c/o Joy Tom *Imperium 7 Talent Agency*
5455 Wilshire Blvd Ste 1706
Los Angeles, CA 90036-4217, USA

White, James
7529 Franklin Ave
Los Angeles, CA 90046-2241

White, James B (Attorney, Attorney General, Educator, General)
1606 Morton Ave
Ann Arbor, MI 48104-4441, USA

White, James C (Athlete, Football Player)
14430 Andrea Way Ln
Houston, TX 77083-7712, USA

White, James (Whirlwind) (Misc)
c/o Staff Member *Peller Artistes Limited*
39 Princes Ave
London N3 2DA, UK

White, Jamie (Radio Personality)
c/o Staff Member *Star 98.7 FM*
3400 W Olive Ave Ste 550
Burbank, CA 91505-5544, USA

White, Jan (Athlete, Football Player)
6507 Burkwood Dr
Clayton, OH 45315-9602, USA

White, Jeris (Athlete, Football Player)
PO Box 3031
Frederick, MD 21705-3031, USA

White, Jerry (Athlete, Baseball Player)
581 Glen Dr
San Leandro, CA 94577-2900, USA

White, Jessica (Model)
c/o Staff Member *IMG*
304 Park Ave S Fl 12
New York, NY 10010-4314, USA

White, Jonah (Business Person)
PO Box 389
Hardin, IL 62047-0389, USA

White, Joseph (Jo Jo) (Basketball Player)
2 Mansfield Rd
Middleton, MA 01949-1515, USA

White, Joy Lynn (Musician)
38 Music Sq E Ste 300
Nashville, TN 37203-4304, USA

White, Judith M (Biologist)
Biology Dept
San Francisco, CA 94117, USA

White, Julie (Actor)
c/o Staff Member *Steve Himber Entertainment*
211 S Beverly Dr Apt S
Beverly Hills, CA 90212-3807, USA

White, Karyn (Musician)
3300 Warner Blvd
Burbank, CA 91505-4632, USA

White, Kate (Editor)
224 W 57th St
New York, NY 10019-3212, USA

White, L Robert (Bob) (Athlete, Football Player)
1044 Grouse Way
Venice, FL 34285-6613, USA

White, Lari (Actor)
c/o Staff Member *WmE2 (WMA-LA)*
1 William Morris Pl
Beverly Hills, CA 90212-4261, USA

White, Larri (Musician, Songwriter, Writer)
1028 18th Ave S # B
Nashville, TN 37212-2105, USA

White, Larry (Athlete, Baseball Player)
19053 N 37th Pl
Phoenix, AZ 85050-2699, USA

White, Lee (Athlete, Football Player)
600 Langtry Dr
Las Vegas, NV 89107-2019, USA

White, Leon (Athlete, Football Player)
11033 Paseo Castanada
La Mesa, CA 91941-7330, USA

White, Lorenzo (Athlete, Football Player)
3450 NW 7th St
Fort Lauderdale, FL 33311-6505, USA

White, Marco P (Chef)
The Restaurant 66 Knightsbridge
London SW1X 7LA, UNITED KINGDOM (UK)

White, Marilyn (Athlete, Track Athlete)
9605 S 6th Ave
Inglewood, CA 90305-3207, USA

White, Mark (Musician)
84 Riverside Dr
New York, NY 10024-5723, USA

White, Marsh (Athlete, Football Player)
7502 Bayhill Dr
Rowlett, TX 75088-5465, USA

White, Martha G (Publisher)
369 York St
London, ON N6A 4G1, CANADA

White, Matt (Athlete, Baseball Player)
1853 Old Route 9
Windsor, MA 01270-9397, USA

White, Meg (Music Group, Musician)
Muenchner Str 45
Unterfoehring 85774, GERMANY

White, Michael Jai (Actor)
c/o Craig Baumgarten *Baumgarten Management*
406 Wilshire Blvd
Santa Monica, CA 90401-1410, USA

White, Michael S (Producer)
48 Dean St
London W1V 5HL, UNITED KINGDOM (UK)

White, Mike (Athlete, Coach, Football Coach, Football Player)
115 Grand Canal
Newport Beach, CA 92662-1329, USA

White, Mike (Athlete, Baseball Player)
26438 S Jardin Dr
Sun Lakes, AZ 85248-7114, USA

White, Mike (Actor)
c/o Staff Member *Black and White Productions*
100 Universal City Plz Bldg 4113
Universal City, CA 91608-1002, USA

White, Miles D (Business Person)
100 Abbott Park Rd
Abbott Park, IL 60064-3502, USA

White, Myron (Athlete, Baseball Player)
3201 S Deegan Dr
Santa Ana, CA 92704-6614, USA

White, Nera D (Athlete, Basketball Player)
Route 3 Box 165
Lafayette, TN 37083, USA

White, Paula (Religious Leader, Television Host, Writer)
PO Box 25151
Tampa, FL 33622-5151, USA

White, Persia (Actor)
c/o Staff Member *Acme Talent & Literary (LA)*
1400 Atlantic Ave Ste 274
Long Beach, CA 90813-2013, USA

White, Peter (Actor)
8730 W Sunset Blvd Ste 440
Los Angeles, CA 90069-2277, USA

White, Randy L (Athlete, Football Player)
9225 Preston Rd
Frisco, TX 75033-3916, USA

White, Raymond P Jr (Doctor)
205 Cedar Meadows Ln
Chapel Hill, NC 27517-7221, USA

White, Reggie (Athlete, Football Player)
17325 Connor Quay Ct
Cornelius, NC 28031-6502, USA

White, Reggie (Athlete, Football Player)
3631 Washington Ave
Baltimore, MD 21244-3776, USA

White, Rex (Race Car Driver)
187 Rivers Rd Lot 222
Fayetteville, GA 30214-3250, USA

White, Ric (Stylist)
c/o Staff Member *Judy Inc*
1 Yorkville Ave
Toronto ON M4W 1L1, Canada

White, Rick (Athlete, Baseball Player)
1527 Oldham Dr
Springfield, OH 45503-7704, USA

White, Robert A (Athlete, Football Player)
11 Jackson St
Jefferson, MA 01522-1429, USA

White, Robert M (General)
PO Box 2488 APO
AE, NY 9063, USA

White, Robert M (Misc)
5610 Wisconsin Ave Apt 1506
Bethesda, MD 20815-4439, USA

White, Robert M II (Journalist)
4871 Glenbrook Rd NW
Washington, DC 20016-3245, USA

White, Rodney (Basketball Player)
Pepsi Center 1000 Chopper Circle
Denver, CO 80204, USA

White, Ron (Actor)
c/o Michael Oscars *Oscars Abrams Zimel & Associates*
438 Queen St. E
Toronto ON M5A 1T4, Canada

White, Ron (Actor, Comedian, Writer)
c/o John MacDonald *MacDonald-Murray Management*
11846 Ventura Blvd Ste 202
Studio City, CA 91604-2620, USA

White, Rondell (Athlete, Baseball Player)
407 Creekside Dr
Gray, GA 31032-6213, USA

White, Rory (Athlete, Basketball Player)
5303 32nd St S
Fargo, ND 58104-6743, USA

White, RoseDenville Hall
62 Ducks Hill Rd Northwood
Middlesex, ENGLAND HA6 2SB

White, Roy (Athlete, Baseball Player)
534 Mill Pond Way
Eatontown, NJ 07724-2477, USA

White, Roy H (Baseball Player)
1001 2nd St
Sacramento, CA 95814-3201, USA

White, Russell (Athlete, Football Player)
17450 Vanowen St Unit 4
Van Nuys, CA 91406-4312, USA

White, Sammy (Athlete, Football Player)
102 Margaret Dr
Monroe, LA 71203-9588, USA

White, Sharon
380 Forest Retreat
Hendersonville, TN 37075

White, Shaun (Athlete, Snowboarder)
c/o Staff Member *US Ski And Snowboard Association*
Box 199
Park City, UT 84060, USA

White, Sheldon (Athlete, Football Player)
PO Box 622
Novi, MI 48376-0622, USA

White, Sherman (Athlete, Football Player)
2710 Summerland Rd
Aromas, CA 95004-9117, USA

White, Shernan E (Sherm) (Athlete, Football Player)
PO Box 1856
Pebble Beach, CA 93953-1856, USA

White, Stan (Athlete, Football Player)
10716 Pot Spring Rd
Cockeysville, MD 21030-3021, USA

White, Stephen (Writer)
375 Hudson St
New York, NY 10014-3658, USA

White, Steve (Athlete, Football Player)
11928 Middlebury Dr
Tampa, FL 33626-2520, USA

White, Steven A (Admiral, Business Person)
4 Mount Royal Ave # 3420
Marlborough, MA 01752-1961, USA

White, Sue (Stylist)
218 Forbes Ave
San Rafael, CA 94901-1745, USA

White, Timothy D (Misc)
Hiuman Evolutionary Studies Lab
Berkeley, CA 94720-0001, USA

White, Tony (Athlete, Basketball Player)
1213 Holston Park Rd
Knoxville, TN 37914-5733, USA

White, Tony L (Business Person)
710 Bridgeport Ave
Shelton, CT 06484-4750, USA

White, Vanna (Entertainer, Model)
c/o Staff Member *PAT Productions*
10202 W Washington Blvd Robert Young Bldg Suite 2000
Culver City, CA 90232, USA

White, Verdine (Musician)
c/o Staff Member *Atlas/Third Rail Entertainment*
9200 W Sunset Blvd Ste 10
Los Angeles, CA 90069-3608, USA

White, Walter (Athlete, Football Player)
504 NW 44th Ter
Kansas City, MO 64116-1580, USA

White, Wilford (Athlete, Football Player)
30A S MacDonald
Mesa, AZ 85210-1322, USA

White, Willard W (Opera Singer)
10 Montague Ave
London SE4 1YP, UNITED KINGDOM (UK)

White, William (Athlete, Football Player)
2323 Woodland Hall Dr
Powell, OH 43065-7141, USA

White, William B (Bill) (Athlete, Baseball Player)

White, Willye B (Athlete, Track Athlete)
5882 S Ensenada St
Aurora, CO 80015-5110, USA

White Jr, Josh (Musician)
23625 Ripple Crk
Novi, MI 48375-3546, USA

White of Rhymney, Eirene L (Government Official)
64 Vandon Court Petty France
London SW1H 9HF, UNITED KINGDOM (UK)

White Stripes, The (Music Group, Musician)
c/o Ian Montone *Monotone Inc.*
820 Seward St
Los Angeles, CA 90038-3602, USA

Whited, Ed (Athlete, Baseball Player)
13201 Ditch Rd
Carmel, IN 46032-9470, USA

Whitefield, A D (Athlete, Football Player)
807 Tangle Way Ct
Cedar Hill, TX 75104-7817, USA

Whitehead, Alfred K (Misc)
1750 New York Ave NW
Washington, DC 20006-5305, USA

Whitehead, Barb (Athlete, Golfer)
9820 E Thompson Peak Pkwy Unit 707
Scottsdale, AZ 85255-6656, USA

Whitehead, Bud (Athlete, Football Player)
5438 N Brooks Ave
Fresno, CA 93711-2913, USA

Whitehead, Cindy (Stylist)
2804 Ingleside Dr
Hermosa Beach, CA 90254-2145, USA

Whitehead, Geoffrey
81 Shaftesbury Ave
London, ENGLAND W1

Whitehead, George W (Mathematician)
299 Cambridge St Unit 424
Winchester, MA 01890-2392, USA

Whitehead, Jerome (Athlete, Basketball Player)
1543 Merritt Dr
El Cajon, CA 92020-7847, USA

Whitehead, John C (Financier, Government Official)
131 Old Chester Rd
Essex Fells, NJ 07021-1625, USA

Whitehead, John C (Scientist)
1775 Massachusetts Ave NW
Washington, DC 20036-2103, USA

Whitehead, Lorne (Inventor)
3015 12th Ave W
Vancouver, BC V6K 2R4, CANADA

Whitehead, Nicholas (Stylist)
c/o Staff Member *Rex Agency, The*
6311 Romaine St
Los Angeles, CA 90038-2617, USA

Whitehead, Paxton (Actor)
c/o Robert Attermann *Abrams Artists Agency (LA)*
9200 W Sunset Blvd PH 11
Los Angeles, CA 90069-3601, USA

Whitehead, Richard F (Admiral)
135 S La Salle St
Chicago, IL 60603-4177, USA

Whitehead, Steven (Stylist)
c/o Staff Member *Artists by Timothy Priano (NY)*
15 Watts St Fl 6
New York, NY 10013-1677, USA

Whitehouse, Len (Athlete, Baseball Player)
300 Shore Rd
Burlington, VT 05408-2632, USA

Whitehurst, C David (Athlete, Football Player)
11010 Linbrook Ln
Duluth, GA 30097-1772, USA

Whitehurst, Wally (Athlete, Baseball Player)
104 Lost Lake Dr
Lafayette, LA 70506-6430, USA

Whitelaw, Billie (Actor)
Rose Cottage Plum St Glensford
Suffolk C010 7PX, UNITED KINGDOM (UK)

Whitemore, Hugh (Writer)
c/o Staff Member *Creative Artists Agency (CAA-LA)*
2000 Avenue of the Stars Ste 100
Los Angeles, CA 90067-4705, USA

Whitemore, Willet F Jr (Doctor, Scientist)
2 Hawthorne Ln
Plandome, NY 11030-1505, USA

Whiten, Mark (Athlete, Baseball Player)
5810 Jefferson Park Dr
Tampa, FL 33625-3313, USA

Whiten, Richard (Actor)
247 S Beverly Dr # 102
Beverly Hills, CA 90212-3830, USA

Whiteread, Rachel (Artist)
22 Dering St
London W1R 9AA, UNITED KINGDOM (UK)

White's
PO Box 2158
Hendersonville, TN 37077-2158

Whitesell, Emily (Producer, Writer)
c/o Staff Member *WmE2 (Endeavor-LA)*
9601 Wilshire Blvd Fl 3
Beverly Hills, CA 90210-5219, USA

Whitesell, Sean (Actor, Producer)
c/o Staff Member *United Talent Agency (UTA)*
9560 Wilshire Blvd Fl 5
Beverly Hills, CA 90212-2400, USA

Whiteside, Eli (Athlete, Baseball Player)
PO Box 467
New Albany, MS 38652-0467, USA

Whiteside, Matt (Athlete, Baseball Player)
255 Palisades Ridge Ct
Eureka, MO 63025-3706, USA

Whiteside, Sean (Athlete, Baseball Player)
3506 N Hills Dr
Haleyville, AL 35565-6746, USA

Whitesides, George M (Misc)
124 Grasmere St
Newton, MA 02458-2235, USA

Whitesnake (Music Group)
c/o Rod MacSween *International Talent Booking*
1st Floor, Ariel House 74A Charlotte St
London W1T 4QJ, UNITED KINGDOM

Whitfield, Annelie (Actor)
c/o Catriona Ribon *The Rights House (UK)*
Drury House 34-43 Russell St
London WC2B 5HA, UK

Whitfield, Dondre T (Actor)
c/o Sheree Cohen *Kohner Agency, The*
9300 Wilshire Blvd Ste 555
Beverly Hills, CA 90212-3211, USA

Whitfield, Fred (Athlete, Baseball Player)
2532 Fairview Rd
Gadsden, AL 35904-3102, USA

Whitfield, Karen (Stylist)
854 Katella St
Laguna Beach, CA 92651-3704, USA

Whitfield, Lynn (Actor)
c/o Staff Member *Innovative Artists (LA)*
1505 10th St
Santa Monica, CA 90401-2805, USA

Whitfield, Mal
1 Hoosier Dome
Indianapolis, IN 46225-1023

Whitfield, Sheree (Designer, Reality TV Star)
c/o Staff Member *Bravo (NY)*
30 Rockefeller Plz
New York, NY 10112-0015, USA

Whitfield, Terry (Athlete, Baseball Player)
849 Clearfield Dr
Millbrae, CA 94030-2148, USA

Whitford, Brad (Musician)
PO Box 38410
Charlotte, NC 28278-1007, USA

Whitford, Bradley (Actor)
c/o Adena Chawke *Greenlight Management and Production*
13848 Valleyheart Dr
Sherman Oaks, CA 91423-2930, USA

Whiting, Leonard
7 Leicester Pl
London, ENGLAND WC2H 7BP

Whiting, Margaret (Musician)
7 Ambrose Ln
Northport, NY 11768-3203, USA

Whitlam, Gough (Prime Minister)
Westfiel Towers 100 William St
Sydney, NSW 2001, AUSTRALIA

Whitley, Curtis (Athlete, Football Player)
1290 Whitley Farm Rd
Smithfield, NC 27577-9463, USA

Whitley, Keith Society
PO Box 222
Sandy Hook, KY 41171-0222

Whitley, Kim E (Actor, Producer)
c/o Judy Apperson *Morra Brezner Steinberg & Tenenbaum (MBST) Entertainment*
345 N Maple Dr Ste 200
Beverly Hills, CA 90210-5174, USA

Whitley, Kym (Actor, Producer)
c/o Adam Williamson *Thruline Entertainment*
9250 Wilshire Blvd Ground Fl
Beverly Hills, CA 90212, USA

Whitlow, Bob (Athlete, Football Player)
315 W Gordon Pike Trl
Bloomington, IN 47403, USA

Whitman, Kari (Actor, Model)
1155 N La Cienega Blvd Apt 104
West Hollywood, CA 90069-2430, USA

Whitman, Kenedy (Stylist)
157 E J St
Benicia, CA 94510-3234, USA

Whitman, Mae (Actor)
c/o Dan Spilo *Industry Entertainment Partners*
955 Carrillo Dr Ste 300
Los Angeles, CA 90048-5400, USA

Whitman, Marina Von Neumann (Economist)
Public Policy School
Ann Arbor, MI 48109, USA

Whitman, Meg (Business Person)
2145 Hamilton Ave
San Jose, CA 95125-5905, USA

Whitman, Slim (Musician)
3830 Old Jennings Rd
Middleburg, FL 32068-3738, USA

Whitman, Stuart (Actor)
749 San Ysidro Rd
Santa Barbara, CA 93108-1328, USA

Whitmer, Dan (Athlete, Baseball Player)
823 Robinhood Ln
Redlands, CA 92373-6665, USA

Whitmire, Steve (Actor)
c/o Staff Member *Jim Henson Company (LA)*
1416 N La Brea Ave
Hollywood, CA 90028-7506

Whitmore, Darrell (Athlete, Baseball Player)
301 E 15th St
Front Royal, VA 22630-4112, USA

Whitmore, Kay (Athlete, Hockey Player)
16 Springwood Rd
Farmington, CT 06032-1105, USA

Whitmyer, Nat (Athlete, Football Player)
5344 Fairview Blvd # 1
Los Angeles, CA 90056-2308, USA

Whitney, Ashley (Swimmer)
124 Hearthstone Manor Cir
Brentwood, TN 37027-4344, USA

Whitney, CeCe (Actor)
16857 San Fernando Mission Blvd Unit 46
Granada Hills, CA 91344-4261, USA

Whitney, David (Baseball Player)
2178 Popps Ferry Rd
Biloxi, MS 39532-4233, USA

Whitney, Jane (Entertainer)
5 Tv Pl
Needham, MA 02494-2302, USA

Whitney, Russ (Business Person, Misc)
1612 Cape Coral Pkwy E
Cape Coral, FL 33904-9618, USA

Whitney-Dearfield, Norma (Baseball Player)
786 Camp Hollow Rd
West Mifflin, PA 15122-3387, USA

Whitney-Lee, Grace (Actor)
PO Box 79
Coarsegold, CA 93614, USA

Whitsett, Vivicca (Actor)
c/o Karin Olsen *Amazon PR*
269 S Beverly Dr # 750
Beverly Hills, CA 90212-3851, USA

Whitson, Ed (Athlete, Baseball Player)
10473 MacKenzie Way
Dublin, OH 43017-8775, USA

Whitson, Peggy A (Astronaut)
306 Lakeview Cir
El Lago, TX 77586-5846, USA

Whitt, Ernie (Athlete, Baseball Player)
37370 Moravian Dr
Clinton Township, MI 48036-3604, USA

Whittaker, James (Jim) (Mountaineer)
2023 E Sims Way # 277
Port Townsend, WA 98368-6905, USA

Whittaker, Roger (Musician, Songwriter, Writer)
426 Marsh Point Cir
Saint Augustine, FL 32080-5863, USA

Whitted, Alvis (Athlete, Football Player)
3 New Bedford Ct
Durham, NC 27704-2240, USA

Whittenton, Jesse (Athlete, Football Player)
PO Box 1626
Santa Teresa, NM 88008-1626, USA

Whittinghill, Dick
11310 Valley Spring Ln
Toluca Lake, CA 91602-2613

Whittington, Art (Athlete, Football Player)
6709 La Tijera Blvd Apt 190
Los Angeles, CA 90045-2017, USA

Whittington, C L (Athlete, Football Player)
3040 Eagles Way Dr Apt 1213
Lafayette, IN 47909-4023, USA

Whittington, Michael S (Athlete, Football Player)
4246 Turtle Mound Rd
Melbourne, FL 32934-8505, USA

Whittle, Ricky (Athlete, Football Player)
514 Tulare St
Fresno, CA 93706-3723, USA

Whitw, Shelbe (Philanthropist)
6 Divinity Ave
Cambridge, MA 02138-2020, USA

Whitwam, David R (Business Person)
2000 N State St RR 63
Benton Harbor, MI 49022, USA

Whitwell, Mike (Athlete, Football Player)
PO Box 6
Cotulla, TX 78014-0006, USA

Whitworth, Johnny
c/o Lena Roklin *Luber Roklin Management*
8530 Wilshire Blvd Ste 550
Beverly Hills, CA 90211-3133, USA

Whitworth, Kathy
5990 Lindenshire Ln Apt 101
Dallas, TX 75230-2726

Whitworth, Kathy (Athlete, Golfer)
1735 Mistletoe Dr
Flower Mound, TX 75022-5316, USA

Wholey, Dennis (Television Host)
1333 H St NW
Washington, DC 20005-4707, USA

Whoppers, Wendy (Actor)
c/o Staff Member *Wow Entertainment Inc*
8362 Pines Blvd # 296
Pembroke Pines, FL 33024-6600, USA

Whyte, Kenneth (Writer)
c/o Staff Member *Counterpoint*
1919 5th St
Berkeley, CA 94710-1916, USA

Whyte, Sandra (Athlete, Hockey Player)
81 Golden Hills Rd
Saugus, MA 01906-4010, USA

WI, Charlie (Athlete, Golfer)
9400 Burnet Ave Unit 109
North Hills, CA 91343-7907, USA

Wiberg, Kenneth B (Misc)
160 Carmalt Rd
Hamden, CT 06517-1904, USA

Wiberg, Pernilla (Skier)
Katterunsvagen 32
Norrkopping 60 210, SWEDEN

Wick, Charles Z (Government Official)
400 C St SW
Washington, DC 20024-2800, USA

Wickander, Kevin (Athlete, Baseball Player)
4319 W Banff Ln
Glendale, AZ 85306-3601, USA

Wicker, Floyd (Athlete, Baseball Player)
1758 W Greensboro Chapel Hill Rd
Snow Camp, NC 27349-9544, USA

Wickersham, Dave (Athlete, Baseball Player)
9118 W 104th Ter
Overland Park, KS 66212-5517, USA

Wickert, Tom (Athlete, Football Player)
3717 Beach Dr SW
Seattle, WA 98116-3060, USA

Wickham, Daniel (Athlete, Baseball Player)
3221 E Mountain Vista Dr
Phoenix, AZ 85048-5802, USA

Wickham, John A Jr (General)
13590 N Fawnbrooke Dr
Tucson, AZ 85737, USA

Wicki-Fink, Agnes (Actor)
Weisgerberstr 2
Munich 80805, GERMANY

Wickman, Robert J (Bob) (Athlete, Baseball Player)
6568 Cheyenne Dr
Abrams, WI 54101-9434, USA

Wicks, Ben (Cartoonist, Editor)
38 Yorkville Ave
Toronto, ON M4W 1L5, CANADA

Wicks, Chuck (Musician)
c/o Staff Member *Webster & Associates PR*
3573 Couchville Pike
Hermitage, TN 37076-4012, USA

Wicks, Sidney (Athlete, Basketball Player)
8650 Cashio St # 5
Los Angeles, CA 90035-3554, USA

Wicks, Sue (Basketball Player)
Madison Square Garden 2 Penn Plaza
New York, NY 10121, USA

Wicoff, Erika (Athlete, Golfer)
7815 Four Leaf Dr
Greenville, IN 47124-9524, USA

Widby, G Ronald (Ron) (Athlete, Basketball Player, Football Player)
542 Mahler Rd
Wichita Falls, TX 76310-0326, USA

Widdoes, Kathleen (Actor)
524 W 57th St
New York, NY 10019-2930, USA

Widdoes, Kathleen (Actor)
24 E 11th St
New York, NY 10003-4402, USA

Widdrington, Peter N T (Business Person)
3221 N Service Rd
Burlington, ON L7R 3Y8, CANADA

Widell, Dave (Athlete, Football Player)
13050 Wexford Hollow Rd N
Jacksonville, FL 32224-9625, USA

Widell, Doug (Athlete, Football Player)
870 21st St
Vero Beach, FL 32960-5314, USA

Wideman, John Edgar (Writer)
Englesh Dept
Amherst, MA 1003, USA

Widener Jr, H Emroy (Judge)
PO Box 1689
Bristol, VA 24203-1689, USA

Widger, Chris (Athlete, Baseball Player)
95 Fort Mott Rd
Pennsville, NJ 08070-2839, USA

Widjaja, David (Stylist)
c/o Staff Member *Frame Representatives*
275 West St
New York, NY 10013, USA

Widman, Herbert (Herb) (Athlete, Swimmer)
844 Monarch Cir
San Jose, CA 95138-1343, USA

Widmer, Corey (Athlete, Football Player)
PO Box 1201
Manhattan, MT 59741-1201, USA

Widom, Benjamin (Misc)
204 the Pkwy
Ithaca, NY 14850-2247, USA

Wie, Michelle (Athlete, Golfer)
17217 Leal Ave
Cerritos, CA 90703-1339, USA

Wieand, Ted (Athlete, Baseball Player)
216 S Walnut St
Slatington, PA 18080-2026, USA

Wiebe, Mark (Athlete, Golfer)
4123 S Elkhart St
Aurora, CO 80014-8100, USA

Wiebe, Susanne (Designer, Fashion Designer)
Amalienstr 39
Munich 80799, GERMANY

Wiedemann, Josef (Architect)
Im Eichgeholz # 11
Colorado Springs, CO 80997-0001, GERMANY

Wiedenbauer, Tom (Athlete, Baseball Player)
1460 Kilrush Dr
Ormond Beach, FL 32174-2882, USA

Wiedlin, Jane (Musician)
c/o Staff Member *WmE2 (WMA-LA)*
1 William Morris Pl
Beverly Hills, CA 90212-4261, USA

Wiedorfer, Paul J (War Hero)
3210 Chesley Ave
Parkville, MD 21234-7816, USA

Wiegart, Zach (Athlete, Football Player)
3747 Saltmeadow Ct S
Jacksonville, FL 32224-9652, USA

Wiegert, Zach (Athlete, Football Player)
919 N 264th St
Waterloo, NE 68069-6207, USA

Wieghaus, Tom (Athlete, Baseball Player)
9724 E 8000N Rd
Grant Park, IL 60940-5364, USA

Wiegmann, Casey (Athlete, Football Player)
30051 N Waukegan Rd
North Chicago, IL 60064, USA

Wiehl, Christopher (Actor)
c/o Staff Member *Gersh (LA)*
9465 Wilshire Blvd Ste 600
Beverly Hills, CA 90212-2612, USA

Wielicki, Krzysztof (Mountaineer)
Ul A Frycza Modrzewskiego 21
Tychy 43-100, POLAND

Wieman, Carl E (Nobel Prize Laureate)
440 Physics Campus Box
Boulder, CO 80309-0001, USA

Wiemer, Jason (Athlete, Hockey Player)
428-5201 Dalhousie Dr NW
Calgary, AB T3A 5Y7, Canada

Wiener, Amy (Stylist)
2026 County Road 1503
Athens, TX 75751-5635, USA

Wiener, Jacques L Jr (Judge)
500 Fannin St
Shreveport, LA 71101-3023, USA

Wier, Murray (Athlete, Basketball Player, Coach)
118 Goodwater St
Georgetown, TX 78633-4505, USA

Wiese, John P (Judge)
717 Madison Pl NW
Washington, DC 20439-0001, USA

Wiesel, Elie (Nobel Prize Laureate, Writer)
745 Commonwealth Ave
Boston, MA 02215-1401, USA

Wiesen, Bernard (Director)
Weisgerberstr 2
Munich 80805, GERMANY

Wiesenhahn, Robert (Athlete, Basketball Player)
3315 Hickorycreek Dr
Cincinnati, OH 45244-2533, USA

Wiesler, Bob (Athlete, Baseball Player)
2325 Indiancup Dr
Florissant, MO 63033-1736, USA

Wiesner, Kenneth (Ken) (Athlete, Track Athlete)
3601 Meta Lake Rd
Eagle River, WI 54521-9119, USA

Wiest, Dianne (Actor)
230 W 79th St
New York, NY 10024-6246, USA

Wiggin, Paul (Athlete, Coach, Football Coach, Football Player)
5013 Ridge Rd
Edina, MN 55436-1013, USA

Wiggins, Audrey (Musician)
2100 W End Ave Ste 1000
Nashville, TN 37203-5240, USA

Wiggins, Candice (Athlete, Basketball Player)
700 Ygnacio Valley Rd Ste 330
Walnut Creek, CA 94596-3838, USA

Wiggins, Jermaine (Athlete, Football Player)
403 Overlook Dr
Beckley, WV 25801-9255, USA

Wiggins, John (Musician)
2100 W End Ave Ste 1000
Nashville, TN 37203-5240, USA

Wiggins, Mitchell (Athlete, Basketball Player)
PO Box 5072
Kinston, NC 28503-5072, USA

Wiggins, Scott (Athlete, Baseball Player)
17 N Crescent Ave
Fort Thomas, KY 41075-2109, USA

Wigginton, Ty (Athlete, Baseball Player)
147 Nantz Woods Ln
Troutman, NC 28166-9572, USA

Wigglesworth, Marian McKean (Skier)
Wilson, WY 83014, USA

Wiggs, Susan (Writer)
PO Box 4469
Rollingbay, WA 98061-0469, USA

Wight, Paul (Big Show) (Athlete, Wrestler)
c/o Staff Member *World Wrestling Entertainment (WWE)*
1241 E Main St
Stamford, CT 06902-3520, USA

Wightman, Arthur S (Mathematician, Physicist)
16 Balsam Ln
Princeton, NJ 08540-5327, USA

Wightman, Donald E (Misc)
815 16th St NW
Washington, DC 20006-4101, USA

Wigiser, Margaret (Baseball Player)
7101 SE Quincy Ter
Hobe Sound, FL 33455-7357, USA

Wigle, Ernest D (Doctor)
101 College St
Toronto, ON M56 1L7, CANADA

Wihtol, Sandy (Athlete, Baseball Player)
1927 Stanley Ave
Santa Clara, CA 95050-5716, USA

Wiig, Kristen (Actor)
c/o Naomi Odenkirk *Odenkirk Provissiero Entertainment*
650 N Bronson Ave Bldg B145
Los Angeles, CA 90004-1404, USA

Wiik, Sven (Skier)
PO Box 774484
Steamboat Springs, CO 80477-4484, USA

Wijdenbosch, Jules A (President)
Onafhankelikheidsplein 1
Paramaribo, SURINAME

Wiklund, Stefan (Stylist)
c/o Staff Member *Halley Resources*
37 W 20th St Ste 603
New York, NY 10011-3718, USA

Wilander, Mats (Tennis Player)
Vickervagen 2
Vaxjo 352 53, SWEDEN

Wilber, Doreen V H (Athlete)
1401 W Lincolnway St
Jefferson, IA 50129-1675, USA

Wilborn, Ted (Athlete, Baseball Player)
6671 Pocket Rd
Sacramento, CA 95831-1904, USA

Wilbraham, John H G (Musician)
9 D Cuthbert St Wells
Somerset BA5 2AW, UNITED KINGDOM (UK)

Wilbur, John (Athlete, Football Player)
PO Box 10002
Honolulu, HI 96816-0002, USA

Wilbur, Richard C (Judge)
400 2nd St NW
Washington, DC 20217-0001, USA

Wilbur, Richard P (Writer)
88 Dodwells Rd
Cummington, MA 01026-9705, USA

Wilbur, Richard S (Doctor)
985 Hawthorne Pl
Lake Forest, IL 60045, USA

Wilburn, J R (Athlete, Football Player)
2211 Chalkwell Dr
Midlothian, VA 23113-3897, USA

Wilburn, Ken (Athlete, Basketball Player)
17 E Meyran Ave
Somers Point, NJ 08244-2720, USA

Wilburn Brothers
PO Box 50
Goodlettsville, TN 37070-0050, USA

Wilby, James (Actor)
52/53 Poland Place
London W1F 7KX, UNITED KINGDOM (UK)

Wilcher, Mary (Actor)
c/o Staff Member *Levine Management*
9028 W Sunset Blvd PH 1
Los Angeles, CA 90069-1830, USA

Wilcox, Chris (Athlete, Basketball Player)
c/o Jeff Schwartz *Excel Sports Management*
9665 Wilshire Blvd Ste 500
Beverly Hills, CA 90212-2312, USA

Wilcox, Christopher (Editor)
Readers Digest Rd
Pleasantville, NY 10570-7001, USA

Wilcox, David (Composer, Music Group, Musician, Songwriter, Writer)
c/o Staff Member *Concerted Efforts*
PO Box 440326
Somerville, MA 02144-0004, USA

Wilcox, Davie (Dave) (Athlete, Football Player)
94471 Willamette Dr
Junction City, OR 97448-9606, USA

Wilcox, John (Athlete, Football Player)
82038 S Fork Walla Walla River Rd
Milton Freewater, OR 97862-7025, USA

Wilcox, Larry (Actor)
10 Appaloosa Ln
Bell Canyon, CA 91307-1002, USA

Wilcox, Lisa (Actor)
6500 Wilshire Blvd # 550
Los Angeles, CA 90048-4920, USA

Wilcox, Milt (Athlete, Baseball Player)
5513 Barrington Ct
Jacksonville, FL 32244-6941, USA

Wilcox, Shannon (Actor)
1753 Centinela Ave Apt A
Santa Monica, CA 90404-4204, USA

Wilcutt, Terence W (Terry) (Astronaut)
1216 Red Wing Dr
Friendswood, TX 77546-5888, USA

Wilczek, Frank (Nobel Prize Laureate)
77 Massachusetts Ave
Cambridge, MA 02139-4301, USA

Wild, Rebecca (Actor, Model)
PO Box 1074
Westerville, OH 43086-7074, USA

Wild Orchid
PO Box 90370
City Of Industry, CA 91715-0370

Wild Orchid (Music Group)
c/o Staff Member *Diva Central Inc*
7510 W Sunset Blvd Ste 1445
Los Angeles, CA 90046-3408, USA

Wilde, Abby
c/o Ileane Rusch *Superior Talent Agency*
2206 N 6th St
Burbank, CA 91504-2437, USA

Wilde, Kim (Musician, Songwriter, Writer)
294-296 Nether St Finchley
Lake Forest N31 RJ, UNITED KINGDOM (UK)

Wilde, Olivia (Actor)
c/o Robbie Kass *Kass & Stokes Management*
9229 W Sunset Blvd Ste 504
Los Angeles, CA 90069-3405, USA

Wilde, Patricia (Artist, Ballerina, Director)
2900 Liberty Ave
Pittsburgh, PA 15201-1511, USA

Wilder, Alan (Musician)
295 Greenwich St # 109
New York, NY 10007-1049, USA

Wilder, Bert (Athlete, Football Player)
501 Willow View Dr
Greensboro, NC 27455-1379, USA

Wilder, Don (Cartoonist)
235 E 45th St
New York, NY 10017-3305, USA

Wilder, Gene (Actor, Director, Writer)
476 Scofieldtown Rd
Stamford, CT 06903-3306, USA

Wilder, James (Actor)
6500 Wilshire Blvd # 550
Los Angeles, CA 90048-4920, USA

Wilder, Sharon (Athlete, Golfer)
72730 Homestead Rd
Palm Desert, CA 92260-6581, USA

Wilder, Yvonne
11836 Hesby St
Valley Village, CA 91607-3218

Wilding, Anna (Actor)
c/o Staff Member *Carpe Diem Films LLC*
9663 Santa Monica Blvd # 557
Beverly Hills, CA 90210-4303, USA

Wildman, George (Cartoonist)
1640 Shepard Ave
Hamden, CT 06518-2036, USA

Wildman, Valerie (Actor)
110 Hurricane St Apt 305
Marina Del Rey, CA 90292-5935, USA

Wildmon, Donald (Activist)
PO Box 1398
Tupelo, MS 38802-1398, USA

Wilds, Tristan (Actor)
c/o Elise Koseff *J Mitchell Management*
70 W 36th St Rm 1006
New York, NY 10018-8015, USA

Wildung, Richard K (Dick) (Athlete, Football Player)
10368 Rich Rd
Bloomington, MN 55437-2505, USA

Wiles, Andrew J (Mathematician)
Mathematics
Princeton, NJ 08544-0001, USA

Wiles, Jason (Actor)
c/o Joanne Wiles *International Creative Management (ICM-LA)*
10250 Constellation Blvd Fl 7
Los Angeles, CA 90067-6207, USA

Wiles, Randy (Athlete, Baseball Player)
3716 Lake Catherine Dr
Harvey, LA 70058-5509, USA

Wiley, Enloe Steve (Baseball Player)
1222 Cedar St
Clarksville, TN 37040-3515, USA

Wiley, Lee (Musician)
7787 Monterey St
Gilroy, CA 95020-5217, USA

Wiley, Marcellus (Athlete, Football Player)
PO Box 83070
Los Angeles, CA 90083-0070, USA

Wiley, Mark (Athlete, Baseball Player)
22273 Vista Lago Dr
Boca Raton, FL 33428-4765, USA

Wiley, Michael (Athlete, Basketball Player)
2461 Elm Ave Apt 2
Long Beach, CA 90806-3142, USA

Wiley, Michael E (Business Person)
333 S Hope St
Los Angeles, CA 90071-1406, USA

Wiley, Morlon (Athlete, Basketball Player)
2521 Fallview Ln
Carrollton, TX 75007-1934, USA

Wiley, William T (Artist)
PO Box 661
Forest Knolls, CA 94933-0661, USA

Wiley-Sears, Janet (Baseball Player)
19629 Gilmer St
South Bend, IN 46614-5605, USA

Wilfong, Rob (Athlete, Baseball Player)
126 Maverick Dr
San Dimas, CA 91773-1127, USA

Wilford, John Noble Jr (Journalist)
232 W 10th St
New York, NY 10014-2976, USA

Wilfork, Vince (Athlete, Football Player)
c/o Staff Member *New England Patriots*
Gillette Stadium One Patriots Pl
Foxboro, MA 02035-1388, USA

Wilheim, Jim (Athlete, Baseball Player)
348 Laurel Way
Mill Valley, CA 94941-4046, USA

Wilhelm, Erik (Athlete, Football Player)
6426 SE Division St
Portland, OR 97206-1276, USA

Wilhelm, John W (Misc)
1219 28th St NW
Washington, DC 20007-3362, USA

Wilhelm, Kati (Athlete)
Bierbachstr 68
Zella-Mehlis 98544, USA

Wilhite, Jonathan (Athlete, Football Player)
c/o Staff Member *New England Patriots*
Gillette Stadium One Patriots Pl
Foxboro, MA 02035-1388, USA

Wilhoite, Kathleen
PO Box 5617
Beverly Hills, CA 90209-5617

Wilk, Brad (Musician)
8935 Lindblade St
Culver City, CA 90232-2438, USA

Wilk, Vic (Athlete, Golfer)
1350 N Town Center Dr Unit 2082
Las Vegas, NV 89144-0587, USA

Wilkening, Laurel L (Educator)
Chancellor's Office
Irvine, CA 92717, USA

Wilkens, Lanny
2660 Peachtree Rd NW Apt 39F
Atlanta, GA 30305-3683

Wilkens Jr, Leonard R (Lenny) (Athlete, Basketball Player, Coach)
3429 Evergreen Point Rd
Medina, WA 98039-1022, USA

Wilkerson, Bob (Bobby) (Athlete, Basketball Player)
PO Box 7453
Upper Marlboro, MD 20792-7453, USA

Wilkerson, Brad (Athlete, Baseball Player)
6076 State Route 144
Owensboro, KY 42303-9571, USA

Wilkerson, Bruce (Athlete, Football Player)
2013 Breakers Pt
Knoxville, TN 37922-5676, USA

Wilkerson, Curtis (Athlete, Baseball Player)
PO Box 182993
Arlington, TX 76096-2993, USA

Wilkerson, Doug (Athlete, Football Player)
PO Box 7090
Rancho Santa Fe, CA 92067-7090, USA

Wilkerson, Muhammad (Football Player)
c/o Chad Wiestling *Integrated Sports Management*
2120 Texas St Apt 2204
Houston, TX 77003-3054, USA

Wilkes, Donna
16228 Maplegrove St
La Puente, CA 91744-1348

Wilkes, Glenn (Basketball Player, Coach)
Athletic Dept Campus Box 8359
DeLand, FL 32720, USA

Wilkes, Jamal (Athlete, Basketball Player)
7846 W 81st St
Playa Del Rey, CA 90293-7911, USA

Wilkes, Jimmy (Baseball Player)
26-C Oakhill Dr
Brantford, ON N3T 1R1, CANADA

Wilkes, Maurice V (Engineer)
24A Trumpington St
Cambridge CB2 1QA, UNITED KINGDOM (UK)

Wilkes, Reggie (Athlete, Football Player)
6912 Wissahickon Ave
Philadelphia, PA 19119-3728, USA

Wilkie, Chris (Musician)
2-12 Petonville Road
London N1 9PL, UNITED KINGDOM (UK)

Wilkie, David (Swimmer)
Oaklands Queens Hill Ascot
Berkshire, UNITED KINGDOM (UK)

Wilkin, Richard E (Religious Leader)
950 N Main St
Findlay, OH 45840-3652, USA

Wilkins, Bobby (Athlete, Baseball Player)
357 Janie Ln
Shreveport, LA 71106-6028, USA

Wilkins, Dean (Athlete, Baseball Player)
10974 Tobago Rd
San Diego, CA 92126-2040, USA

Wilkins, Donna (Athlete, Golfer)
3617 Bancroft Main NW
Kennesaw, GA 30144-6011, USA

Wilkins, Eddie Lee (Athlete, Basketball Player)
3045 Mockingbird Ln
Atlanta, GA 30344-5679, USA

Wilkins, Eric (Athlete, Baseball Player)
1650 W Joshua St
Meridian, ID 83642-6194, USA

Wilkins, J Dominique (Athlete, Basketball Player)
4415 Felix Way SE
Smyrna, GA 30082-4700, USA

Wilkins, Laisha (Actor)
c/o Staff Member *Televisa*
Blvd Adolfo Lopez Mateos 232 Colonia San Angel INN
DF CP 01060, MEXICO

Wilkins, Marc (Athlete, Baseball Player)
1636 State Route 314 N
Mansfield, OH 44903-7405, USA

Wilkins, Mardell (Athlete, Golfer)
26982 Durango Ln
Mission Viejo, CA 92691-4431, USA

Wilkins, Maurice (Mac) (Athlete, Track Athlete)
PO Box 1058
Soquel, CA 95073-1058, USA

Wilkins, Rick (Athlete, Baseball Player)
12766 Longview Dr W
Jacksonville, FL 32223-2620, USA

Wilkins, Roger (Journalist)
207 East Building
Fairfax, VA 22030, USA

Wilkins, William W Jr (Judge)
PO Box 10857
Greenville, SC 29603-0857, USA

Wilkinson, Adrienne (Actor)
9157 W Sunset Blvd Ste 215
West Hollywood, CA 90069-3167, USA

Wilkinson, Amanda (Music Group, Musician)
1908 Wedgewood Ave
Nashville, TN 37212-3733, USA

Wilkinson, Bill (Athlete, Baseball Player)
17320 Lindon Dr
Parker, CO 80134-7536, USA

Wilkinson, Bruce (Writer)
6400 Atlantic Blvd
Norcross, GA 30071-1291, USA

Wilkinson, Dale (Athlete, Basketball Player)
3045 Goldfield Dr
Pocatello, ID 83201-2778, USA

Wilkinson, Dan (Athlete, Football Player)
222 Republic Dr
Allen Park, MI 48101-3650, USA

Wilkinson, Geoffrey (Nobel Prize Laureate)
Chemistry Dept
London SW7 2AY, UNITED KINGDOM (UK)

Wilkinson, J Harvie III (Judge)
255 W Main St
Charlottesville, VA 22902-5058, USA

Wilkinson, Jonathan (Jonny) (Athlete, Soccer Player)
c/o Staff Member *Newcastle Falcons RFC*
Kingston Park Brunton Rd, Kenton Bank Foot
Newcastle NE138AF, UK

Wilkinson, Joseph B Jr (Admiral)
340 Chesapeake Dr
Great Falls, VA 22066-3815, USA

Wilkinson, June (Actor, Model)
4060 E Grenora Way
Long Beach, CA 90815-2613, USA

Wilkinson, Kendra (Model, Reality TV Star)
c/o Liza Anderson *Anderson Group Public Relations*
8060 Melrose Ave Fl 4
Los Angeles, CA 90046-7038, USA

Wilkinson, Laura (Athlete, Swimmer)
201 S Capitol Ave Ste 300
Indianapolis, IN 46225-1058, USA

Wilkinson, Signe (Cartoonist, Editor)
400 N Broad St
Philadelphia, PA 19130-4015, USA

Wilkinson, Steve (Musician)
1908 Wedgewood Ave
Nashville, TN 37212-3733, USA

Wilkinson, Tom (Actor)
37 Berwick St
London W1V 3RF, UNITED KINGDOM (UK)

Wilkinson, Tyler (Musician)
1908 Wedgewood Ave
Nashville, TN 37212-3733, USA

Wilks, Jim (Athlete, Football Player)
4314 Leaflock Ln
Katy, TX 77450-8251, USA

Will, Bob (Athlete, Baseball Player)
1001 Chestnut Mountain Rd
Banner Elk, NC 28604, USA

Will, George (Writer)
9 Grafton St
Chevy Chase, MD 20815-3427, USA

Will to Power (Music Group)
c/o Staff Member *Diva Central Inc*
7510 W Sunset Blvd Ste 1445
Los Angeles, CA 90046-3408, USA

Willard, Fred (Actor, Comedian)
c/o Glenn Schwartz *Glenn Schwartz Company*
4046 Declaration Ave
Calabasas, CA 91302-5741, USA

Willard, Jerry (Athlete, Baseball Player)
1421 Kumquat Pl
Oxnard, CA 93036-6219, USA

Willard, Kenneth H (Ken) (Athlete, Football Player)
3071 Viewpoint Rd
Midlothian, VA 23113, USA

Willcocks, David V (Musician)
13 Grange Road
Cambridge CB3 9AS, UNITED KINGDOM (UK)

Willcox, Toyah (Actor)
c/o Staff Member *Roseman Organisation, The*
51 Queen Anne St
London W1G 9HS, UK

Willebrands, Johannes Cardinal (Religious Leader)
Via dell'Erba I
Rome 120, ITALY

Willem-Alexander (Prince)
Hague, NETHERLANDS

Willerth, Jeffrey
6615 W Tamarack Ave
Sun Valley, CA 91352

Willet, E Crosby (Artist)
10 E Moreland Ave
Philadelphia, PA 19118-3541, USA

Willets, Kathy
3251 Spanish River Dr
Pompano Beach, FL 33062-6809

Willett, Chad
PO Box 5617
Beverly Hills, CA 90209-5617

Willett, Malcolm (Cartoonist)
4520 Main St
Kansas City, MO 64111-1876, USA

Willett, Walter (Doctor, Scientist)
25 Shattuck St
Boston, MA 02115-6027, USA

Willette, Jo Ann
9300 Wilshire Blvd Ste 400
Beverly Hills, CA 90212-3210

Willey, Cary (Athlete, Baseball Player)
PO Box 64
Cherryfield, ME 04622-0064, USA

Willey, Kathleen
2642 New Timber Way
Powhatan, VA 23139-5220

Willey, Norm (Athlete, Football Player)
133 Netherlands Dr
Middletown, DE 19709-9679, USA

Will-Halpin, Maggie (Athlete, Golfer)
12423 Carnoustie Ln
North Chesterfield, VA 23236-4172, USA

Willhite, Gerald (Athlete, Football Player)
10464 Cliff Ct
Rancho Cordova, CA 95670, USA

Willhite, Kevin (Athlete, Football Player)
9784 W Taron Dr
Elk Grove, CA 95757-8193, USA

Willhite, Nick (Athlete, Baseball Player)
792 Meadow Ln
Alpine, UT 84004-1527, USA

Will.I.Am (Musician)
c/o Seth Friedman *DAS Communications*
83 Riverside Dr
New York, NY 10024-5713, USA

William (Prince)
Stable Yard Gate
London SW1, UNITED KINGDOM (UK)

William, David (Actor, Director)
194 Langarth St E
London, ON N6C 1Z5, CANADA

William, Edward (Religious Leader)
5118 Clarendon Rd
Brooklyn, NY 11203-5329, USA

Williams, Adrian (Basketball Player)
American West Arena 201 E Jefferson St
Phoenix, AZ 85004, USA

Williams, Aeneas D (Athlete, Football Player)
PO Box 16291
Saint Louis, MO 63105-0991, USA

Williams, Al (Athlete, Basketball Player)
2809 S 36th St
Fort Smith, AR 72903-4501, USA

Williams, Alfred H (Athlete, Football Player)
7800 E Orchard Rd Ste 400
Greenwood Village, CO 80111-2599, USA

Williams, Alvin (Basketball Player)
Air Canada Center 40 Bay St
Toronto, ON M5J 2N8, CANADA

Williams, Andy (Musician)
c/o Staff Member *WmE2 (WMA-LA)*
1 William Morris Pl
Beverly Hills, CA 90212-4261, USA

Williams, Anson (Actor)
c/o Art Rutter *Shapiro-Lichtman Talent Agency*
1010 Lexington Rd
Beverly Hills, CA 90210-2935, USA

Williams, Anthony A (Politician)
District Building 14th & E Sts NW
Washington, DC 20004, USA

Williams, Ashley (Actor)
c/o Lena Roklin *Luber Roklin Management*
8530 Wilshire Blvd Ste 550
Beverly Hills, CA 90211-3133, USA

Williams, Barbara (Actor)
1505 10th St
Santa Monica, CA 90401-2805, USA

Williams, Barry (Actor, Musician)
c/o Staff Member *Good Guy Entertainment*
3733 Oakfield Dr
Sherman Oaks, CA 91423-4430, USA

Williams, Bernabe (Bernie) (Athlete, Baseball Player)
5 Hallock Pl
Armonk, NY 10504-1131, USA

Williams, Bernard (Athlete, Football Player)
1570 Waverly Ave
Memphis, TN 38106-2424, USA

Williams, Bert (Actor)
8281 Melrose Ave Ste 200
Los Angeles, CA 90046-6890, USA

Williams, Betty (Nobel Prize Laureate)
Orchardville Gardens Finaghy
Belfast 10, NORTHERN IRELAND

Williams, Billy (Cinematographer)
Coah House Hawkshill Place Esher
Surrey KT10 9HY, UNITED KINGDOM (UK)

Williams, Billy (Athlete, Baseball Player)
586 Prince Edward Rd
Glen Ellyn, IL 60137-6711, USA

Williams, Billy (Athlete, Baseball Player)
3227 Randolph Ave
Oakland, CA 94602-1539, USA

Williams, Billy Dee (Actor)
c/o Bradley Kramer *Kramer Management*
5699 Kanan Rd # 275
Agoura Hills, CA 91301-3358, USA

Williams, Bob A (Athlete, Football Player)
602 Stone Bam Rd
Towson, MD 21286, USA

Williams, Branden (Actor)
c/o Staff Member *Edward Horowitz*
16862 Calle De Sarah
Pacific Palisades, CA 90272-1951, USA

Williams, Brian (Correspondent, Television Host)
c/o Staff Member *NBC Nightly News*
30 Rockefeller Plz Fl 270E
New York, NY 10112-0299, USA

Williams, Brian (Athlete, Football Player)
1725 Charleston Ln
Waconia, MN 55387-4539, USA

Williams, Brian (Athlete, Football Player)
5319 Lyoncrest Ct
Dallas, TX 75287-5500, USA

Williams, Brian (Athlete, Baseball Player)
2409 Colt Ln
Crowley, TX 76036-4703, USA

Williams, Bruce (Entertainer)
PO Box 7150
Hudson, FL 34674-7150, USA

Williams, Bryan (Baby) (Musician)
c/o Staff Member *Universal Music Group (UMG - LA)*
2220 Colorado Ave
Santa Monica, CA 90404-3506, USA

Williams, Buck (Athlete, Basketball Player)
9219 Fox Meadow Ln
Potomac, MD 20854-4619, USA

Williams, C K (Writer)
English
Princeton, NJ 08544-0001, USA

Williams, Calvin (Athlete, Football Player)
5032 Yellowwood Ave
Baltimore, MD 21209-4602, USA

Williams, Cara (Actor)
9903 Santa Monica Blvd # 606
Beverly Hills, CA 90212-1671, USA

Williams, Carlton (Athlete, Football Player)
5 Pinegate Ct
Peachtree City, GA 30269-1144, USA

Williams, Carnell (Cadillac) (Football Player)
c/o Jim Steiner *CAA - St. Louis*
222 S Central Ave Ste 1008
Saint Louis, MO 63105-3509, USA

Williams, Charlie (Athlete, Football Player)
3052 England Pkwy
Grand Prairie, TX 75054-6639, USA

Williams, Charlie (Athlete, Basketball Player)
374 S Belvoir Blvd
Cleveland, OH 44121-2349, USA

Williams, Charlie (Athlete, Baseball Player)
44 Frederick Ave
Port Orange, FL 32127-8628, USA

Williams, Chris (Actor)
c/o Carolyn Govers *Artist Management*
1119 Colorado Ave Ste 12
Santa Monica, CA 90401-3009, USA

Williams, Chris (Athlete, Football Player)
2851 E Nunneley Rd
Gilbert, AZ 85296-8887, USA

Williams, Chris A (Athlete, Football Player)
2800 Christopher Blvd
Hamburg, NY 14075-3456, USA

Williams, Christopher (Musician)
c/o Ken Maldonado *Zia Artists*
506 Fort Washington Ave Apt 1H
New York, NY 10033-2081, USA

Williams, Christy (Artist)
2745 NE 89th St
Seattle, WA 98115-3459, USA

Williams, Cindy (Actor)
c/o Staff Member *Bette Smith Management*
499 N Canon Dr
Beverly Hills, CA 90210-4887, USA

Williams, Clarence (Journalist)
202 W 1st St
Los Angeles, CA 90012-4105, USA

Williams, Clarence (Athlete, Football Player)
4724 Vine St
Cincinnati, OH 45217-1254, USA

Williams, Cliff (Musician)
11 Leominster Road Morden
Surrey SA4 6HN, UNITED KINGDOM (UK)

Williams, Clyde (Athlete, Football Player)
9754 Highway 79
Bethany, LA 71007, USA

Williams, Clyde (Baseball Player)
17135 San Juan Dr
Detroit, MI 48221-2622, USA

Williams, Colleen (Correspondent)
3000 W Alameda Ave
Burbank, CA 91523-0001, USA

Williams, Cress (Actor)
c/o Marni Rosenzweig *Abrams Artists Agency (LA)*
9200 W Sunset Blvd PH 11
Los Angeles, CA 90069-3601, USA

Williams, Curtis (Musician)
9966 Majorca Pl
Boca Raton, FL 33434-3714, USA

Williams, Cynda (Actor)
1505 10th St
Santa Monica, CA 90401-2805, USA

Williams, Dafydd R (David) (Astronaut)
2101 Nasa Pkwy Spc Center
Houston, TX 77058-3607, USA

Williams, Dallas (Athlete, Baseball Player)
7638 Allenwood Cir
Indianapolis, IN 46268-4738, USA

Williams, Dana (Musician)
2908 Poston Ave
Nashville, TN 37203-1312, USA

Williams, Dana (Athlete, Baseball Player)
121 Arlene Dr
North Versailles, PA 15137-2432, USA

Williams, Daniel (General)
Botanical Gardens
Saint George's, GRENADA

Williams, Danny (Boxer)
c/o Frank Warren *Sports Network*
Centurion House Bircherley Green
Hertford HERTS SG14 1AP, UNITED KINGDOM

Williams, Darnell (Actor)
6500 Wilshire Blvd # 550
Los Angeles, CA 90048-4920, USA

Williams, Darryl (Athlete, Football Player)
7351 Peppertree Cir S
Davie, FL 33314-6922, USA

Williams, Dave (Athlete, Baseball Player)
157 Carter Ln
Camden, DE 19934-1212, USA

Williams, Davey (Athlete, Baseball Player)
14802 Enterprise Dr Apt 30C
Dallas, TX 75234-3004, USA

Williams, David (Athlete, Football Player)
109 E Oxford St
Valley Stream, NY 11580-4622, USA

Williams, David (Athlete, Football Player)
650 Flying Hawk Trl
Waynesville, NC 28786-6193, USA

Williams, David (Athlete, Football Player)
30826 Tanoa Rd
Evergreen, CO 80439-7963, USA

Williams, David G T (Educator)
Cambridge CB2 3AP, UNITED KINGDOM (UK)

Williams, David W (Athlete, Football Player)
108 E Oxford St
Valley Stream, NY 11580, USA

Williams, Davida (Actor)
c/o Marvet Britto *Britto Agency PR*
234 W 56th St PH
New York, NY 10019-4302, USA

Williams, Delvin (Athlete, Football Player)
173 Sierra Vista Ave Apt 11
Mountain View, CA 94043-4468, USA

Williams, Deniece (Musician)
PO Box 3172
Beverly Hills, CA 90212-0172, USA

Williams, Deron (Athlete, Basketball Player)
c/o Bob McClaren *McClaren Sports*
1401 McKinney St Ste 2222
Houston, TX 77010-4038, USA

Williams, Derwin (Athlete, Football Player)
12014 Windermere Crossing Cir
Winter Garden, FL 34787-5518, USA

Williams, Dick
3680 Madrid St
Las Vegas, NV 89121-3415

Williams, Dick Anthony (Actor)
c/o Staff Member *Abrams Artists Agency (LA)*
9200 W Sunset Blvd PH 11
Los Angeles, CA 90069-3601, USA

Williams, Don (Musician, Songwriter, Writer)
5100 Harris Ave
Kansas City, MO 64133-2331, USA

Williams, Don (Athlete, Basketball Player)
6109 Rosedale Dr
Hyattsville, MD 20782-2296, USA

Williams, Don (Athlete, Baseball Player)
2114 Christiansburg Pike NE
Floyd, VA 24091-2179, USA

Williams, Donald E (Astronaut)
2200 Space Park Dr Ste 200
Houston, TX 77058-3678, USA

Williams, Doug (Comedian)
c/o James Kellem *JKA Talent*
12725 Ventura Blvd Ste H
Studio City, CA 91604-2437, USA

Williams, Douglas L (Doug) (Athlete, Coach, Football Coach, Football Player)
10120 Lemon Rd
Zachary, LA 70791-6407, USA

Williams, Dudley (Dancer)
211 W 61st St # 300
New York, NY 10023-7832, USA

Williams, E Virginia (Choreographer, Director)
19 Clarendon St
Boston, MA 02116-6107, USA

Williams, Earl (Athlete, Baseball Player)
61 Winston Dr
Somerset, NJ 08873-2333, USA

Williams, Easy (Actor)
606 N Larchmont Blvd Ste 309
Los Angeles, CA 90004-1309, USA

Williams, Ed (Athlete, Football Player)
521 Royal Ave
Oklahoma City, OK 73130-2719, USA

Williams, Eddie (Athlete, Baseball Player)
6229 Meadowgrass Ln
Las Vegas, NV 89103-1137, USA

Williams, Edy (Actor, Model)
PO Box 6325
Woodland Hills, CA 91365-6325, USA

Williams, Eli (Baseball Player)
214 Thomas Ct NW
Fort Walton Beach, FL 32548-4139, USA

Williams, Ellery (Athlete, Football Player)
1987 Wimbledon Pl
Los Altos, CA 94024-7062, USA

Williams, Elmo (Director, Producer)
1249 Iris St
Brookings, OR 97415-9643, USA

Williams, Eric (Basketball Player)
c/o Staff Member *Toronto Raptors*
400-40 Bay St
Toronto, Ontario M5J 2X2, Canada

Williams, Eric (Football Player)
c/o Staff Member *Pittsburgh Steelers*
3400 S Water St
Pittsburgh, PA 15203-2358, USA

Williams, Eric (Football Player)
c/o Staff Member *Saint Louis Cardinals (St Louis Cardinals)*
700 Clark St
Saint Louis, MO 63102-1727, USA

Williams, Eric M (Athlete, Football Player)
13330 Noel Rd Apt 825
Dallas, TX 75240-5092, USA

Williams, Erik (Athlete, Football Player)
1 Wortham Ct
Bear, DE 19701-2060, USA

Williams, Ernie (Athlete, Football Player)
45 Oakwood Dr
Chapel Hill, NC 27517-5650, USA

Williams, Erwin (Athlete, Football Player)
33 Manly St
Portsmouth, VA 23702-1019, USA

Williams, Esther (Actor, Swimmer)
9377 Readcrest Dr
Beverly Hills, CA 90210-2532, USA

Williams, Eugene (Baseball Player)
110 Townsend Rd
Oak Ridge, TN 37830-5566, USA

Williams, Frank (Basketball Player)
Madison Square Garden 2 Penn Plaza
New York, NY 10121, USA

Williams, Frank (Baseball Player)
9283 Medallion Way
Sacramento, CA 95826-4643, USA

Williams, Freeman (Athlete, Basketball Player)
450 W 41st Pl
Los Angeles, CA 90037-2119, USA

Williams, Gary (Basketball Player, Coach)
Athletic
College Park, MD 20742-0001, USA

Williams, Gary Anthony (Actor)
c/o Staff Member *Innovative Artists (LA)*
1505 10th St
Santa Monica, CA 90401-2805, USA

Williams, George (Athlete, Baseball Player)
26090 Summerdale Dr
Southfield, MI 48033-2228, USA

Williams, George (Athlete, Baseball Player)
N5250 County Road M
West Salem, WI 54669-9202, USA

Williams, Gerald (Athlete, Football Player)
9613 Callis Ct
Harrisburg, NC 28075-9619, USA

Williams, Gerald (Athlete, Baseball Player)
17011 Candeleda De Avila
Tampa, FL 33613-5213, USA

Williams, Gerri (Stylist)
c/o Staff Member *Marnie Rose Agency*
37 Lower Shad Rd
Pound Ridge, NY 10576-2216, USA

Williams, Gluyas (Cartoonist)
4 Times Sq
New York, NY 10036-6515, USA

Williams, Greg (Actor)
1680 Vine St Ste 604
Los Angeles, CA 90028-8833, USA

Williams, Gregg (Athlete, Coach, Football Coach, Football Player)
325 Dandridge Dr
Franklin, TN 37067-8403, USA

Williams, Gregory Alan (Actor)
c/o Staff Member *Pakula/King & Associates*
9229 W Sunset Blvd Ste 315
Los Angeles, CA 90069-3403, USA

Williams, Gus (Athlete, Basketball Player)
PO Box 262
Mount Vernon, NY 10552-0262, USA

Williams, Hal (Actor)
PO Box 14227
Palm Desert, CA 92255-4227, USA

Williams, Harland (Actor)
c/o Jeff Witjas *Agency for the Performing Arts (APA-LA)*
405 S Beverly Dr Ste 500
Beverly Hills, CA 90212-4425, USA

Williams, Harold M (Misc)
Getty Center 1200 Getty Center Dr
Los Angeles, CA 90049, USA

Williams, Hayley (Musician)
c/o Mark Mercado *Fly South Music Group*
189 S Orange Ave Ste 1100
Orlando, FL 32801-3256, USA

Williams, Herb (Basketball Player)
4500 Bentley Dr
Plano, TX 75093-7149, USA

Williams, Hershel W (War Hero)
3450 Wire Branch Rd
Ona, WV 25545-9513, USA

Williams, Howard E (Howie) (Basketball Player)
1940 Hamilton Ln
Carmel, IN 46032-3521, USA

Williams, Howard L (Howie) (Athlete, Football Player)
4731 Proctor Ave
Oakland, CA 94618-2540, USA

Williams, Hype (Actor, Director, Producer)
c/o Staff Member *Creative Artists Agency (CAA-LA)*
2000 Avenue of the Stars Ste 100
Los Angeles, CA 90067-4705, USA

Williams, Ivy (Writer)
834 N Harper Ave
Los Angeles, CA 90046-6804, USA

Williams, Jaimie (Actor)
1019 Kane Concourse Ste 202
Bay Harbor Islands, FL 33154-2138, USA

Williams, Jamal (Athlete, Football Player)
4020 Murphy Canyon Rd
San Diego, CA 92123-4407, USA

Williams, James A (General)
8928 Maurice Ln
Annandale, VA 22003-3914, USA

Williams, James A (Froggy) (Athlete, Football Player)
296 Sugarberry Cir
Houston, TX 77024-7248, USA

Williams, James D (Admiral)
20 Johnson Ln
Westport Island, ME 04578-3006, USA

Williams, James F (Jimy) (Athlete, Baseball Player, Coach)
1401 Olde Post Rd
Palm Harbor, FL 34683-1470, USA

Williams, James (Fly) (Athlete, Basketball Player)
682 Ralph Ave Apt 2E
Brooklyn, NY 11212-3853, USA

Williams, James O (Athlete, Football Player)
330 S Western Ave
Lake Forest, IL 60045-3245, USA

Williams, Jason (Athlete, Basketball Player)
6103 Louise Cove Dr
Windermere, FL 34786-8939, USA

Williams, Jay (Basketball Player)
United Center 1901 W Madison St
Chicago, IL 60612, USA

Williams, Jay (Athlete, Football Player)
1503 Alydar Ct
Waxhaw, NC 28173-6672, USA

Williams, Jayson (Basketball Player, Sportscaster)
30 Rockefeller Plz
New York, NY 10112-0015, USA

Williams, Jeff (Athlete, Football Player)
9710 15th Ave NW
Seattle, WA 98117-2314, USA

Williams, Jeffrey N (Astronaut)
4918 Cross Creek Ln
League City, TX 77573-6267, USA

Williams, Jerome (Athlete, Basketball Player)
c/o Staff Member *Toronto Raptors*
400-40 Bay St
Toronto, Ontario M5J 2X2, Canada

Williams, Jerrol (Athlete, Football Player)
2562 Mizzoni Cir
Henderson, NV 89052-4926, USA

Williams, Jerry (Athlete, Football Player)
941 W Oden Bay Rd
Sandpoint, ID 83864-8615, USA

Williams, Jesse (Actor)
c/o Staff Member *ROAR (LA)*
9701 Wilshire Blvd Fl 8
Beverly Hills, CA 90212-2008, USA

Williams, Jessica (Musician)
c/o Staff Member *Diva Central Inc*
7510 W Sunset Blvd Ste 1445
Los Angeles, CA 90046-3408, USA

Williams, Jim (Athlete, Baseball Player)
16 Stone Pne
Aliso Viejo, CA 92656-2132, USA

Williams, JoBeth (Actor)
c/o Staff Member *Innovative Artists (LA)*
1505 10th St
Santa Monica, CA 90401-2805, USA

Williams, Jody (Nobel Prize Laureate)
663 Lancaster St
Fredericksburg, VA 22405-2447, USA

Williams, Joel (Athlete, Football Player)
PO Box 311802
Atlanta, GA 31131-1802, USA

Williams, Joel (Athlete, Football Player)
1515 Penn Ave Apt 305
Wilkinsburg, PA 15221-2659, USA

Williams, John (Composer, Musician)
27 Chancery Lane
London WC2A 1PF, UNITED KINGDOM (UK)

Williams, John A (Writer)
693 Forest Ave
Teaneck, NJ 07666-2042, USA

Williams, John C (Athlete)
833 Cordova Ave
Ormond Beach, FL 32174-7639, USA

Williams, John E (Athlete, Football Player)
33211 Blue Fin Dr
Dana Point, CA 92629-1416, USA

Williams, John L (Athlete, Football Player)
1709 Husson Ave
Palatka, FL 32177-5809, USA

Williams, John M (Athlete, Football Player)
2222 Victory Memorial Dr
Minneapolis, MN 55412-1116, USA

Williams, John T (Composer, Conductor, Musician)
c/o Staff Member *Chasen & Company*
8899 Beverly Blvd Ste 405
Los Angeles, CA 90048-2431, USA

Williams, John T (Actor, Composer)
c/o Staff Member *Gorfaine/Schwartz Agency Inc*
4111 W Alameda Ave Ste 509
Burbank, CA 91505-4171, USA

Williams, Joseph R (Publisher)
495 Union Ave
Memphis, TN 38103-3217, USA

Williams, Juan (Correspondent)
c/o 21st Century Speakers Box 1422
Gouldsboro, Pennsylvania 18424, USA

Williams, Justin (Athlete, Hockey Player)
1850 Manhattan Ave
Hermosa Beach, CA 90254-3460, USA

Williams, Kameelah (Musician)
c/o Staff Member *Creative Artists Agency (CAA-LA)*
2000 Avenue of the Stars Ste 100
Los Angeles, CA 90067-4705, USA

Williams, Karen (Comedian)
PO Box 32147
Cleveland, OH 44132-0147, USA

Williams, Karl (Athlete, Football Player)
6502 Falcon St
Rowlett, TX 75089-8260, USA

Williams, Katt (Actor, Comedian)
c/o Staff Member *Collective*
8383 Wilshire Blvd Ste 1050
Beverly Hills, CA 90211-2415, USA

Williams, Keith (Athlete, Baseball Player)
1756 N Avignon Ln
Clovis, CA 93619-3799, USA

Williams, Kelli (Actor, Musician)
c/o John Carrabino *John Carrabino Management*
5900 Wilshire Blvd Ste 406
Los Angeles, CA 90036-5015, USA

Williams, Ken (Athlete, Baseball Player)
6430 E Sierra Vista Dr
Paradise Valley, AZ 85253-4351, USA

Williams, Kevin (Athlete, Football Player)
9520 Viking Dr
Eden Prairie, MN 55344-3825, USA

Williams, Kevin (Athlete, Football Player)
5715 Baltimore Dr Unit 148
La Mesa, CA 91942-4246, USA

Williams, Kevin (Athlete, Football Player)
2201 Wembley Downs Dr
Arlington, TX 76017-4548, USA

Williams, Kevin (Athlete, Basketball Player)
1102 Blake Ave # 2
Brooklyn, NY 11208-3634, USA

Williams, Kiely Alexis (Actor, Director, Musician)
c/o Laurie Pozmantier *WmE2 (Endeavor-LA)*
9601 Wilshire Blvd Fl 3
Beverly Hills, CA 90210-5219, USA

Williams, Kim (Athlete, Golfer)
1116 Tobacco Row Ct
Zebulon, NC 27597-6253, USA

Williams, Kimberly (Actor, Producer)
c/o Michael Nilon *Creative Artists Agency (CAA-LA)*
2000 Avenue of the Stars Ste 100
Los Angeles, CA 90067-4705, USA

Williams, Kimberly Kevon (Actor)
c/o TJ Stein *Stein Entertainment Group*
1351 N Crescent Heights Blvd Apt 312
West Hollywood, CA 90046-4549, USA

Williams, Lauryn (Athlete, Track Athlete)
PO Box 8008
Gray, TN 37615-0008, USA

Williams, Lee E (Athlete, Football Player)
11651 NW 4th St
Plantation, FL 33325-2509, USA

Williams, Lewis T (Scientist)
5323 Harry Hines Blvd
Dallas, TX 75390-7201, USA

Williams, Lorenzo (Athlete, Basketball Player)
2731 Via Capri Unit 924
Clearwater, FL 33764-3993, USA

Williams, Lucinda (Musician, Songwriter)
c/o Staff Member *FCC Management*
209 10th Ave S Ste 322
Nashville, TN 37203-0744

Williams, Lynn R (Misc)
79 Kennedy Rd
Cambridge, MA 02138-3352, USA

Williams, Madieu (Athlete, Football Player)
12750 Gladys Retreat Cir
Bowie, MD 20720-3350, USA

Williams, Maiya (Producer)
c/o Staff Member *Principal Entertainment (LA)*
1964 Westwood Blvd Ste 400
Los Angeles, CA 90025-4695, USA

Williams, Malinda (Actor)
c/o Staff Member *Leverage Management*
3030 Pennsylvania Ave
Santa Monica, CA 90404-4112, USA

Williams, Mark (Bowler)
719 2nd Ave Ste 701
Seattle, WA 98104-1747, USA

Williams, Mark (Athlete, Baseball Player)
1453 Trumansburg Rd
Ithaca, NY 14850-9530, USA

Williams, Mary Alice (Correspondent)
c/o Staff Member *CBS News Productions*
524 W 57th St Fl 8
New York, NY 10019-2930, USA

Williams, Mason (Composer, Musician)
13479 SE Lost Lake Dr
Prineville, OR 97754-8487, USA

Williams, Matt (Writer)
211 E 48th St
New York, NY 10017-1538, USA

Williams, Matt (Athlete, Baseball Player)
205 Tearose Ln
Lake Jackson, TX 77566-6043, USA

Williams, Matt (Athlete, Baseball Player)
4400 N Scottsdale Rd Ste 381
Scottsdale, AZ 85251-3331, USA

Williams, Maurice (Musician)
PO Box 509
Orangeburg, SC 29116-0509, USA

Williams, Maurice J (Misc)
1875 Connecticut Ave NW
Washington, DC 20009-5728, USA

Williams, Maxie (Athlete, Football Player)
624 Squaw Run Rd
Ellwood City, PA 16117-6958, USA

Williams, Merriwether (Producer)
c/o Bruce Gellman *Felker, Toczek, Gellman, Suddleson*
10880 Wilshire Blvd Ste 2070
Los Angeles, CA 90024-4118, USA

Williams, Michael (Athlete, Basketball Player)
1005 Lakeridge Ct
Colleyville, TX 76034-2825, USA

Williams, Michael D (Mike) (Athlete, Baseball Player)
302 Horseshoe Farm Rd
Pembroke, VA 24136-3478, USA

Williams, Michael J (General)
2 Navy St
Washington, DC 20380-1775, USA

Williams, Michael Kenneth (Actor)
c/o Tracy Christian *Don Buchwald & Associates Inc (LA)*
6500 Wilshire Blvd Ste 2200
Los Angeles, CA 90048-4942, USA

Williams, Michael L (Actor)
46 Albermarle St
London W1X 4PP, UNITED KINGDOM (UK)

Williams, Micheal (Basketball Player)
1415 Reynoldston Ln
Dallas, TX 75232-2411, USA

Williams, Michelle (Actor, Director, Producer, Writer)
c/o Frank Frattaroli *Dontanville/Frattaroli (D/F)*
270 Lafayette St Ste 402
New York, NY 10012-3327, USA

Williams, Michelle (Musician)
c/o Matthew Knowles *Music World Entertainment*
1505 Hadley St
Houston, TX 77002-8927, USA

Williams, Mike (Athlete, Football Player)
1 Bills Dr
Orchard Park, NY 14127-2237, USA

Williams, Mike (Athlete, Football Player)
2152 NW 74th Ave
Hollywood, FL 33024-1058, USA

Williams, Mikell (Athlete, Football Player)
222 W Edwards St
Covington, LA 70433-1626, USA

Williams, Mitch (Athlete, Baseball Player)
67 Highbridge Blvd
Medford, NJ 08055-3341, USA

Williams, Montel B (Actor, Producer, Talk Show Host)
c/o Evan Warner *WmE2 (Endeavor-LA)*
9601 Wilshire Blvd Fl 3
Beverly Hills, CA 90210-5219, USA

Williams, Natalie (Basketball Player)
125 S Pennsylvania St
Indianapolis, IN 46204-3610, USA

Williams, Natashia (Actor)
c/o Teresa Valente *Beverly Hecht Agency*
3500 W Olive Ave Ste 1180
Burbank, CA 91505-4651, USA

Williams, Nick (Athlete, Football Player)
21760 Parklane St
Farmington Hills, MI 48335-4221, USA

Williams, O L (Religious Leader)
1101 University St
Kinston, NC 28501, USA

Williams, Oliver (Athlete, Football Player)
11924 Daleside Ave
Hawthorne, CA 90250-1925, USA

Williams, Olivia (Actor)
c/o Risa Shapiro *Schiff Company, The*
8440 Warner Dr Ste B1
Culver City, CA 90232-2461, USA

Williams, Parker (Adult Film Star)
c/o Staff Member *Diva Central Inc*
7510 W Sunset Blvd Ste 1445
Los Angeles, CA 90046-3408, USA

Williams, Pat (Football Player)
c/o Danielle Gibbs 1968 W Adams Blvd Ste 205
Los Angeles, CA 90018, USA

Williams, Patrick (Musician)
3156 Mandeville Canyon Rd
Los Angeles, CA 90049-1014, USA

Williams, Paul (Writer)
c/o Chris Fenton *H2F Entertainment*
644 N Cherokee Ave
Los Angeles, CA 90004-1009, USA

Williams, Perry (Athlete, Football Player)
480 Canyon Oaks Dr Apt A
Oakland, CA 94605-3858, USA

Williams, Perry (Athlete, Football Player)
273 Old Laurinburg Rd
Hamlet, NC 28345-8069, USA

Williams, Pete (Writer)
c/o Chris Fenton *H2F Entertainment*
644 N Cherokee Ave
Los Angeles, CA 90004-1009, USA

Williams, Pharrell (Actor, Composer)
c/o Staff Member *Brillstein Entertainment Partners*
9150 Wilshire Blvd Ste 350
Beverly Hills, CA 90212-3453, USA

Williams, Phillip L (Publisher)
202 W 1st St
Los Angeles, CA 90012-4105, USA

Williams, Prince Charles (Boxer)
3675 Polley Dr
Austintown, OH 44515-3349, USA

Williams, R J
1505 10th St
Santa Monica, CA 90401-2805, USA

Williams, Randy (Athlete, Track Athlete)
5655 N Marty Ave Apt 204
Fresno, CA 93711-1575, USA

Williams, Randy (Athlete, Baseball Player)
11410 Fm 586 S
Brookesmith, TX 76827-4010, USA

Williams, Reggie (Athlete, Baseball Player)
RR 6 Box 68
Laurens, SC 29360, USA

Williams, Reggie (Athlete, Basketball Player)
2016 Callaway St
Temple Hills, MD 20748-4354, USA

Williams, Reggie (Athlete, Baseball Player)
9300 Clearstone Cv
Collierville, TN 38017-9414, USA

Williams, Reginald (Reggie) (Athlete, Football Player)
503 Jennifer Ln
Windermere, FL 34786-8400, USA

Williams, Reuben (Baseball Player)
PO Box 3982
Winter Haven, FL 33885-3982, USA

Williams, Richard H (Dick) (Athlete, Baseball Player, Coach)
PO Box 778327
Henderson, NV 89077-8327, USA

Williams, Rick (Athlete, Baseball Player)
1217 Wessmith Way
Madera, CA 93638-1854, USA

Williams, Ricky (Athlete, Football Player)
c/o Drew Rosenhaus *Rosenhaus Sports Representation*
6400 Allison Rd
Miami Beach, FL 33141-4540, USA

Williams, Robert (Artist)
c/o Staff Member *Fantagraphics Books*
7563 Lake City Way NE
Seattle, WA 98115-4218, USA

Williams, Robert (Baseball Player)
6233 Delancey St
Philadelphia, PA 19143-1019, USA

Williams, Robert A (Athlete, Football Player)
602 Stone Barn Rd
Towson, MD 21286-1418, USA

Williams, Robert C (Athlete, Football Player)
347 Walnut Grove Ln
Coppell, TX 75019-5342, USA

Williams, Robert Cary
c/o Staff Member *Robert Cary Williams*
5 Claremont Villas, Southampton Way
Camberwell
London, England 8E4 96W, United Kingdom

Williams, Robert J (Ben) (Athlete, Football Player)
5961 Huntview Dr
Jackson, MS 39206-2128, USA

Williams, Robert (Robbie) (Musician)
c/o Josie Cliff *IE Music Ltd*
111 Frithville Gardens Shepherds Bush
London W12 7JQ, United Kingdom

Williams, Robin (Actor, Comedian, Voice Over Artist, Writer)
c/o David Steinberg *Morra Brezner Steinberg & Tenenbaum (MBST) Entertainment*
345 N Maple Dr Ste 200
Beverly Hills, CA 90210-5174, USA

Williams, Roderick (Opera Singer)
4 Addison Bridge Place
London W14 8XP, UNITED KINGDOM (UK)

Williams, Rodney (Athlete, Football Player)
44520 15th St E Unit 3
Lancaster, CA 93535-6321, USA

Williams, Roger (Musician)
c/o Staff Member *International Ventures*
25115 Avenue Stanford Ste 102
Valencia, CA 91355-4777, USA

Williams, Roland (Athlete, Football Player)
6209 Mid Rivers Mall Dr
Saint Peters, MO 63304-1102, USA

Williams, Rosel (Baseball Player)
204 Little Mountain Rd
Ninety Six, SC 29666-9253, USA

Williams, Roshumba (Model)
c/o Gail Parenteau *Parenteau Guidance*
132 E 35th St # 3J
New York, NY 10016-3892, USA

Williams, Rowan (Religious Leader)
London SE1 9JU, UNITED KINGDOM (UK)

Williams, Roy (Athlete, Football Player)
1 Cowboys Pkwy
Irving, TX 75063-4924, USA

Williams, Sam (Athlete, Football Player)
28960 Westfield St
Livonia, MI 48150-3137, USA

Williams, Sam (Athlete, Basketball Player)
9751 W Teresa Ln
Milwaukee, WI 53224-4651, USA

Williams, Sam B (Inventor)
2280 E West Maple Rd
Commerce Township, MI 48390-3828, USA

Williams, Samuel (Athlete, Basketball Player)
6116 S Verdun Ave
Los Angeles, CA 90043-3632, USA

Williams, Scott (Basketball Player)
201 E Jefferson St
Phoenix, AZ 85004-2412, USA

Williams, Scott (Athlete, Football Player)
284 Heathrow Dr
Riverdale, GA 30274-2729, USA

Williams, Serena (Athlete, Tennis Player)
6231 Pga Blvd Ste 104 PMB 256
Palm Beach Gardens, FL 33418-4033, USA

Williams, Shad (Athlete, Baseball Player)
4682 E Cornell Ave
Fresno, CA 93703-1607, USA

Williams, Shaun (Athlete, Football Player)
11738 Gruen St
Lake View Terrace, CA 91342-6117, USA

Williams, Sherman (Athlete, Football Player)
119 Patricia Ave
Prichard, AL 36610-2114, USA

Williams, Sidney (Athlete, Football Player)
1044 W 82nd St
Los Angeles, CA 90044-3518, USA

Williams, Simon (Actor)
69A Kings Road
London SW3 4NX, UNITED KINGDOM (UK)

Williams, Stanley W (Stan) (Athlete, Baseball Player)
4702 Hayter Ave
Lakewood, CA 90712-3509, USA

Williams, Stepfret (Athlete, Football Player)
913 S Talton St
Minden, LA 71055-5448, USA

Williams, Stephanie E (Actor)
8730 W Sunset Blvd Ste 440
Los Angeles, CA 90069-2277, USA

Williams, Stephen (Misc)
1017 Foothills Trl
Santa Fe, NM 87505-4537, USA

Williams, Stephen F (Judge)
333 Constitution Ave NW
Washington, DC 20001-2802, USA

Williams, Steven (Actor)
8430 Santa Monica Blvd Ste 200
West Hollywood, CA 90069-4253, USA

Williams, Sunita L (Astronomer)
1522 Festival Dr
Houston, TX 77062-4526, USA

Williams, T Franklin (Doctor)
Director's Office
Rochester, NY 14620, USA

Williams, Tamika (Basketball Player)
Target Center 600 1st Ave N
Minneapolis, MN 55403, USA

Williams, Tank (Athlete, Football Player)
c/o Staff Member *New England Patriots*
Gillette Stadium One Patriots Pl
Foxboro, MA 02035-1388, USA

Williams, Tavares (Monty) (Athlete, Basketball Player)
316 Dorrington Blvd
Metairie, LA 70005-3816, USA

Williams, Terrie (Biologist)
Biology Dept
Santa Cruz, CA 95064, USA

Williams, Terry (Musician)
16 Lambton Place
London W11 2SH, UNITED KINGDOM (UK)

Williams, Terry Tempest
1501 Broadway
New York, NY 10036-5601

Williams, Thomas S Cardinal (Religious Leader)
Viard 21 Eccleston Hill Po Box 198
Wellington 1, NEW ZELAND

Williams, Todd (Athlete, Baseball Player)
16707 Whispering Glen Dr
Lutz, FL 33558-4960, USA

Williams, Todd (Actor)
c/o Steve Caserta *Sanders Armstrong Caserta*
2120 Colorado Ave Ste 120
Santa Monica, CA 90404-3561, USA

Williams, Tonya Lee (Actor)
1180 S Beverly Dr Ste 301
Los Angeles, CA 90035-1154, USA

Williams, Treat (Actor)
c/o Melanie Greene *Affirmative Entertainment*
425 N Robertson Blvd
West Hollywood, CA 90048-1735, USA

Williams, Trent (Athlete, Football Player)
c/o Eugene Parker *Maximum Sports Management*
6435 W Jefferson Blvd # 197
Fort Wayne, IN 46804-6203, USA

Williams, Tyler James (Actor)
c/o Staff Member *Osbrink Talent Agency*
4343 Lankershim Blvd Ste 100
West Toluca Lake, CA 91602-2705, USA

Williams, Tyrone (Athlete, Football Player)
9516 Valley Ranch Pkwy E Apt 1024
Irving, TX 75063-7851, USA

Williams, Ulis (Athlete, Track Athlete)
2511 29th St
Santa Monica, CA 90405-2913, USA

Williams, Van (Actor)
612 Lighthouse Ave # 220
Pacific Grove, CA 93950-2615, USA

Williams, Van (Athlete, Football Player)
1804 Parkwood Ln Apt 26
Johnson City, TN 37604-7784, USA

Williams, Vanessa L (Actor, Musician)
c/o Geordie Frey *GEF Entertainment*
122 N Clark Dr Apt 401
West Hollywood, CA 90048-6315, USA

Williams, Vanessa P (Actor)
c/o Melisa Spamer *Domain Talent*
9229 W Sunset Blvd Ste 710
Los Angeles, CA 90069-3407, USA

Williams, Venus (Athlete, Tennis Player)
c/o Todd Rubenstein *Morris, Yorn, Barnes, Levine, Krintzman, Rubenstein and Kohner*
2000 Ave Of The Stars 3rd Tower Floor NORTH
Los Angeles, CA 90067, USA

Williams, Victor L (Actor, Musician)

Williams, Victoria (Musician, Songwriter, Writer)
PO Box 342
Joshua Tree, CA 92252-0342, USA

Williams, Virginia (Actor)
c/o Lisa Suzanne Blum *Modus Entertainment*
8569 Holloway Dr Apt 1
West Hollywood, CA 90069-6918, USA

Williams, W Clyde (Religious Leader)
4466 E Presley Blvd
Memphis, TN 38116, USA

Williams, Wade (Actor, Director, Producer, Writer)
c/o Stacey Bock-McLaughlin *Principal Entertainment (LA)*
1964 Westwood Blvd Ste 400
Los Angeles, CA 90025-4695, USA

Williams, Wallace (Baseball Player)
213 Yosemite Dr
Pittsburgh, PA 15235-2045, USA

Williams, Walt (Athlete, Basketball Player)
3240 Beaumont St
Temple Hills, MD 20748-4541, USA

Williams, Walt (Athlete, Baseball Player)
2417 Monterey St
Brownwood, TX 76801-7808, USA

Williams, Walter (Musician)
1995 Broadway # 501
New York, NY 10023-5882, USA

Williams, Walter (Baseball Player)
15700 Good Hope Rd
Silver Spring, MD 20905-4034, USA

Williams, Walter E. (Economist, Writer)
333 Enterprise Hall Department Of Economics Msn 3G4
Fairfax, Virginia 22030-4444, USA

Williams, Wendy (Radio Personality, Talk Show Host)
433 W 53rd St
New York, NY 10019-5603, USA

Williams, Wendy Lian (Swimmer)
1025 Thomas Jefferson St NW # 450
Washington, DC 20007-5201, USA

Williams, William (Stylist)
c/o Staff Member *Rex Agency, The*
6311 Romaine St
Los Angeles, CA 90038-2617, USA

Williams, William A (Astronaut)
200 SW 35th St
Corvallis, OR 97333-4902, USA

Williams, Willie (Baseball Player)
2729 20th St
Sarasota, FL 34234-7807, USA

Williams, Willie (Athlete, Football Player)
PO Box 871445
Mesquite, TX 75187-1445, USA

Williams, Willie (Athlete, Football Player)
1402 Forest Edge Ct
Wexford, PA 15090-9598, USA

Williams, Woody (Athlete, Baseball Player)
5110 Newpoint Dr
Fresno, TX 77545-9212, USA

Williams & Ree
PO Box 163
Hendersonville, TN 37077-0163

Williams III, Clarance (Actor)
c/o Staff Member *Abrams Artists Agency (LA)*
9200 W Sunset Blvd PH 11
Los Angeles, CA 90069-3601, USA

Williams III, James (Fly) (Actor)
c/o Margaret Matuka *Schuller Talent Agency*
276 5th Ave Rm 206
New York, NY 10001-4509, USA

Williams III, Shelton Hank (Musician)
c/o Mitch Schneider *Mitch Schneider Organization, The*
14724 Ventura Blvd Ste 410
Sherman Oaks, CA 91403-3537, USA

Williams Jr, Hank (Actor, Musician, Songwriter)
c/o Ken Levitan *Vector Management*
PO Box 120479
Nashville, TN 37212-0479, USA

Williams Jr, Redford B (Misc)
Medical School Box 3708
Durham, NC 27706, USA

Williams Jr, Robin M (Scientist)
414 Oak Ave
Ithaca, NY 14850-4822, USA

Williams Jr, Walter Ray (Bowler)
6503 NW 223rd St
Micanopy, FL 32667-7539, USA

Williams Jr, Warren (Athlete, Football Player)
1935 Pauldo St
Fort Myers, FL 33916-4122, USA

Williams of Crosby, Shirley V T B (Government Official)
Westminster
London SW1A 0PW, UNITED KINGDOM (UK)

Williams of Elvel, Charles C P (Government Official)
48 Thurloe Square
London SW7 2SX, UNITED KINGDOM (UK)

Williamson, Antone (Athlete, Baseball Player)
9419 S Stanley Pl
Tempe, AZ 85284-4109, USA

Williamson, Corliss (Basketball Player)
c/o Staff Member *Sacramento Kings*
1 Sports Pkwy
Sacramento, CA 95834-2301

Williamson, Cris (Musician)
PO Box 30067
Seattle, WA 98113-2067, USA

Williamson, Fred (Actor, Athlete, Football Player)
c/o Stephany Hurkos *Stephany Hurkos Management*
11935 Kling St
Valley Village, CA 91607-4072, USA

Williamson, Jay (Athlete, Golfer)
24 Clermont Ln
Saint Louis, MO 63124-1346, USA

Williamson, Joe (Stylist)
c/o Staff Member *Arends, Frank Inc*
216 W 18th St # 703-B
New York, NY 10011, USA

Williamson, Keith A (Misc)
Fakenham
Norfolk, UNITED KINGDOM (UK)

Williamson, Kerry (Writer)
c/o Staff Member *Gersh (LA)*
9465 Wilshire Blvd Ste 600
Beverly Hills, CA 90212-2612, USA

Williamson, Kevin (Director, Producer, Writer)
c/o Staff Member *Outerbanks Entertainment*
1149 N Gower St # 101
Los Angeles, CA 90038-1801, USA

Williamson, Marianne (Radio Personality, Writer)
PO Box 1269
Monument, CO 80132-1269, USA

Williamson, Mark (Athlete, Baseball Player)
1260 Hidden Mountain Dr
El Cajon, CA 92019-3639, USA

Williamson, Martha (Producer)
c/o Bob Broder *International Creative Management (ICM-LA)*
10250 Constellation Blvd
Los Angeles, CA 90067-6200, USA

Williamson, Michael (Writer)
10400 Hutting Pl
Silver Spring, MD 20902-4952, USA

Williamson, Michael (Journalist)
1150 15th St NW
Washington, DC 20071-0001, USA

Williamson, Mykelti (Actor)
c/o Jim Hess *Hess Entertainment*
360 N Crescent Dr
Beverly Hills, CA 90210-4874, USA

Williamson, Nicol (Actor)
13 Shorts Gardens
London WC2H 9AT, UNITED KINGDOM (UK)

Williamson, Oliver E (Economist)
Economics
Berkeley, CA 94720-0001, USA

Williamson, Richard (Athlete, Football Coach, Football Player)
621 E Mehring Way Apt 14
Cincinnati, OH 45202-3557, USA

Williamson, Scott (Athlete, Baseball Player)
21563 Fox Rd
Guilford, IN 47022-9706, USA

Williamson, Shaun (Actor)
Thornton House Thornton Road
London SW19 4NG, ENGLAND

Williamson Jr, Samuel R (Educator)
President's Office
Sewanee, TN 37375, USA

Williford, Duncan (Athlete, Basketball Player)
3703 Westfield St
High Point, NC 27265-2113, USA

Willig, Matt (Athlete, Football Player)
22652 Erwin St
Woodland Hls, CA 91367-1711, USA

Willingham, Josh (Athlete, Baseball Player)
108 Cascade Dr
Florence, AL 35633-7621, USA

Willingham, Larry (Athlete, Football Player)
983 W Lagoon Ave
Gulf Shores, AL 36542-6301, USA

Willingham, Tyrone (Coach, Football Coach)
Athletic
Seattle, WA 98195-0001, USA

Willis, Bruce (Actor)
c/o Paul Bloch *Rogers & Cowan PR (LA)*
Pacific Design Center 8687 Melrose Ave, 7th Floor
West Hollywood, CA 90069, USA

Willis, Carl (Athlete, Baseball Player)
6811 Lipscomb Dr
Durham, NC 27712-9292, USA

Willis, Connie (Voice Over Artist)
301 E Pine St Ste 175
Orlando, FL 32801-2735, USA

Willis, Dale (Athlete, Baseball Player)
3415 Hayes Bayou Dr
Ruskin, FL 33570-6157, USA

Willis, Dave (Writer)
c/o Staff Member *WmE2 (WMA-LA)*
1 William Morris Pl
Beverly Hills, CA 90212-4261, USA

Willis, Dontrelle (Athlete, Baseball Player)
9820 E Thompson Peak Pkwy Unit 726
Scottsdale, AZ 85255-6657, USA

Willis, Fred (Athlete, Football Player)
31 Blithewood Ave Apt 601
Worcester, MA 01604-3558, USA

Willis, Garrett (Athlete, Golfer)
528 Mountain Pass Ln
Knoxville, TN 37923-5723, USA

Willis, Gordon (Cinematographer)
11849 W Olympic Blvd # 100
Los Angeles, CA 90064-1155, USA

Willis, Jim (Artist)
5323 SW 53rd Ct
Portland, OR 97221-1937, USA

Willis, Jim (Athlete, Baseball Player)
PO Box 35
Boyce, LA 71409-0035, USA

Willis, Katherine (Actor)
c/o Heather Collier *Collier Talent Agency*
2313 Lake Austin Blvd Ste 103
Austin, TX 78703-4545, USA

Willis, Keith (Athlete, Football Player)
116 Coffeeberry Ct
Garner, NC 27529-5934, USA

Willis, Kelly (Musician)
c/o Staff Member *Davis McLarty Agency*
708 S Lamar Blvd Ste D
Austin, TX 78704-1541, USA

Willis, Kevin A (Athlete, Basketball Player)
1481 Jones Rd
Roswell, GA 30075-2723, USA

Willis, Mark (Musician)
c/o Staff Member *WmE2 (WMA-TN)*
1600 Division St Ste 300
Nashville, TN 37203-2755, USA

Willis, Mike (Athlete, Baseball Player)
6234 Taggart St
Houston, TX 77007-2051, USA

Willis, Mitch (Athlete, Football Player)
1398 Fairhaven Dr
Mansfield, TX 76063-3765, USA

Willis, Nadine (Model)
c/o Staff Member *New York Model Management*
596 Broadway # 701
New York, NY 10012-3396, USA

Willis, Patrick (Athlete, Football Player)
c/o Denise White *EAG Sports Management*
12910 Agustin Pl
Playa Vista, CA 90094-2301, USA

Willis, Pete (Musician)
729 7th Ave Ste 1400
New York, NY 10019-6889, USA

Willis, Peter Tom (Athlete, Football Player)
PO Box 237
Morris, AL 35116-0237, USA

Willis, Rumer (Actor)
c/o Michael Kives *Creative Artists Agency (CAA-LA)*
2000 Avenue of the Stars Ste 100
Los Angeles, CA 90067-4705, USA

Willison, Mike (Musician)
2 Penn Plz # 2600
New York, NY 10121-0101, USA

Willman, David (Journalist)
202 W 1st St
Los Angeles, CA 90012-4105, USA

Willmon, Trent (Musician)
c/o Shelia Shipley Biddy 713 18th Ave S
Nashville, TN 37203, USA

Willms, Andre (Athlete)
Rennebogen 94
Magdeburg 39130, GERMANY

Willoch, Kare I (Prime Minister)
Fr Nansens V 17
Lysaker 1324, NORWAY

Willoughby, Bill (Basketball Player)
350 W Englewood Ave
Englewood, NJ 07631-3239, USA

Willoughby, Jim (Athlete, Baseball Player)
PO Box 707
Eufaula, OK 74432-0707, USA

Wills, Elliott (Bump) (Athlete, Baseball Player)
1802 Briar Meadow Dr
Arlington, TX 76014-2510, USA

Wills, Frank (Athlete, Baseball Player)
733 General Pershing St
New Orleans, LA 70115-1448, USA

Wills, Garry (Historian, Writer)
History Dept
Evanston, IL 60201, USA

Wills, Maurice M (Maury) (Athlete, Baseball Player, Coach)
5 Dalton Valley Dr
Saint Peters, MO 63376-7720, USA

Wills, Rick (Musician)
16501 Ventura Blvd Ste 602
Encino, CA 91436-2072, USA

Wills, Ted (Athlete, Baseball Player)
10585 E Duckpoint Way
Clovis, CA 93619-4629, USA

Willson, Don (Athlete, Hockey Player)
1303 Rendezvous Dr
Windsor, ON N8P 1K7, Canada

Willson, John (Business Person)
1600-1055 Dunsmuir St
Vancouver, BC V7X 1P1, CANADA

Willumstad, Robert (Financier)
277 Park Ave Fl 35
New York, NY 10172-2904, USA

Wilmarth, Dick (Misc)
1111 F St
Anchorage, AK 99501-4344, USA

Wilmer, Douglas (Actor)
46 Albermarle St
London W1X 4PP, UNITED KINGDOM (UK)

Wilmer, Harry A (Psychic)
Psychiatric Dept
San Antonio, TX 78284, USA

Wilmes, Gary (Actor)
c/o Ruthanne Secunda *United Talent Agency (UTA)*
9560 Wilshire Blvd Fl 5
Beverly Hills, CA 90212-2400, USA

Wilmet, Paul (Athlete, Baseball Player)
PO Box 330074
Nashville, TN 37203-7500, USA

Wilmore, Barry E (Astronaut)
3002 Bryant Ln
Webster, TX 77598-6011, USA

Wilmsmeyer, Klaus (Athlete, Football Player)
1509 Bellingham Ct
Louisville, KY 40245-4488, USA

Wilmut, Ian (Misc)
Roslin Bio Centre
Midlothian EH25 9PS, SCOTLAND

Wilpon, Fred (Baseball Player)
100 Sheep Ln
Locust Valley, NY 11560-1115, USA

Wilson, A N (Writer)
21 Arlington Road
London NW1 7ER, UNITED KINGDOM (UK)

Wilson, Adrian (Athlete, Football Player)
c/o Eugene Parker *Maximum Sports Management*
6435 W Jefferson Blvd # 197
Fort Wayne, IN 46804-6203, USA

Wilson, Al (Athlete, Football Player)
11561 Warrington Ct
Parker, CO 80138-8735, USA

Wilson, Alexander G (Sandy) (Composer, Writer)
2 Southwell Gardens #4
London SW7 4SB, UNITED KINGDOM (UK)

Wilson, Alexandra (Actor)
c/o Staff Member *GVA Talent Agency Inc*
8981 W Sunset Blvd Ste 101
Los Angeles, CA 90069-1850, USA

Wilson, Allan B (Biologist)
Molecular Biology Dept
Berkeley, CA 94724, USA

Wilson, Ann (Actor, Musician)
c/o Carol Peters *Peters Management Syndicate*
PO Box 1710
Topanga, CA 90290-1710, USA

Wilson, Artie (Athlete, Baseball Player)
2226 NE 10th Ave
Portland, OR 97212-4018, USA

Wilson, Ben (Athlete, Football Player)
7707 Virgil St
Houston, TX 77088-7105, USA

Wilson, Bill (Athlete, Baseball Player)
132 Wickenby Ct
Roseville, CA 95661-4044, USA

Wilson, Billy (Athlete, Football Player)
PO Box 84
Clio, CA 96106-0084, USA

Wilson, Blaine (Athlete, Gymnast)
2660 Carters Corner Rd
Sunbury, OH 43074-8962, USA

Wilson, Blenda J (Educator)
President S Ofc
Northridge, CA 91330-0001, USA

Wilson, Brian (Musician, Songwriter)
c/o Jean Sievers *CO5 Media*
2271 Cheremoya Ave
Los Angeles, CA 90068-3006, USA

Wilson, Brian (Athlete, Basketball Player)
1201 Hummingbird Hill Rd
Chapel Hill, NC 27517-7791, USA

Wilson, Brian Anthony (Actor)
352 7th Ave
New York, NY 10001-5012, USA

Wilson, C A S John (Architect)
27 Horsell Road
London N5 1XL, UNITED KINGDOM (UK)

Wilson, Carnie (Musician)
c/o Terry Anzaldo *Good Guy Entertainment*
3733 Oakfield Dr
Sherman Oaks, CA 91423-4430, USA

Wilson, Casey (Actor)
c/o Staff Member *Odenkirk Provissiero Entertainment*
650 N Bronson Ave Bldg B145
Los Angeles, CA 90004-1404, USA

Wilson, Cassandra (Musician)
4346 Redwood Ave Unit 307
Marina Del Rey, CA 90292-6495, USA

Wilson, Chandra (Actor)
c/o Staff Member *Station3*
1051 Cole Ave
Los Angeles, CA 90038-2601, USA

Wilson, Charles (Athlete, Football Player)
5444 Calder Dr
Tallahassee, FL 32317-1429, USA

Wilson, Charlie (Musician)
c/o Carlos Keyes *Red Entertainment Agency*
16 Penn Plz Ste 824
New York, NY 10001-1809, USA

Wilson, Cherilyn (Actor)
c/o Jon Simmons *Simmons & Scott Entertainment*
7942 Mulholland Dr
Los Angeles, CA 90046-1225, USA

Wilson, Chris (Musician)
c/o Staff Member *Fein Music*
81 Pondfield Rd
Bronxville, NY 10708-3818, USA

Wilson, Cindy (Musician)
947 N La Cienega Blvd # 2
Los Angeles, CA 90069-4782, USA

Wilson, Colin H (Writer)
Tetherdown Trewallock Lane Gorran Haven
Cornwall, UNITED KINGDOM (UK)

Wilson, Craig (Misc)
1423 Lake Blvd
Davis, CA 95616-2620, USA

Wilson, Craig (Athlete, Baseball Player)
8241 Drybank Dr
Huntington Beach, CA 92646-3811, USA

Wilson, Craig (Athlete, Baseball Player)
3427 E Tere St
Phoenix, AZ 85044-3625, USA

Wilson, Dan (Musician, Songwriter, Writer)
509 Hartnell St
Monterey, CA 93940-2825, USA

Wilson, Daniel A (Dan) (Athlete, Baseball Player)
2161 E Interlaken Blvd
Seattle, WA 98112-3432, USA

Wilson, Dave (Athlete, Football Player)
4301 San Rufino Cir
Yorba Linda, CA 92886-2351, USA

Wilson, Dean (Athlete, Golfer)
10914 Iris Canyon Ln
Las Vegas, NV 89135-1719, USA

Wilson, De'Angelo (Actor)
c/o Staff Member *Overbrook Entertainment*
450 N Roxbury Dr Fl 4
Beverly Hills, CA 90210-4218, USA

Wilson, Debra (Actor)
c/o Joan Rosenberg *Joan Rosenberg & Assoc Ltd*
3 Adam St
New York, NY 11001, USA

Wilson, Desi (Athlete, Baseball Player)
8 Janet Ln
Glen Cove, NY 11542-2809, USA

Wilson, Don The Dragon
178 S Victory Blvd Ste 205
Burbank, CA 91502-2881

Wilson, Dorien (Actor)
c/o Susie Tobin *Peter Strain & Associates Inc (LA)*
5455 Wilshire Blvd Ste 1812
Los Angeles, CA 90036-4268, USA

Wilson, Doug (Athlete, Hockey Player)
5620 Country Club Pkwy
San Jose, CA 95138-2220, USA

Wilson, Duane (Athlete, Baseball Player)
3301 W 18th St N
Wichita, KS 67203-1142, USA

Wilson, Earl (Athlete, Football Player)
122 W Reading Ave
Pleasantville, NJ 08232-1317, USA

Wilson, Earle L (Religious Leader)
PO Box 50434
Indianapolis, IN 46250-0434, USA

Wilson, Edward O (Writer)
1010 Waltham St # A208
Lexington, MA 02421-8044, USA

Wilson, Elizabeth (Actor)
c/o Staff Member *Paradigm (NY)*
360 Park Ave S Fl 16
New York, NY 10010-1708, USA

Wilson, Eric C T (War Hero)
Woodside Cottage Stowell Sherbome
Dorset, UNITED KINGDOM (UK)

Wilson, Eugene (Skier)
25775 Ranchview Ln N # 1
Plymouth, MN 55447, USA

Wilson, F Perry (Engineer)
225 N 56th St # 217
Lincoln, NE 68504-3519, USA

Wilson, Frank (Race Car Driver)
PO Box 500
Rockingham, NC 28380, USA

Wilson, Gahan (Cartoonist)
4 Times Sq
New York, NY 10036-6515, USA

Wilson, Gary (Athlete, Baseball Player)
1021 Glendale Dr Spc 9
McKinleyville, CA 95519-9763, USA

Wilson, Gary (Athlete, Baseball Player)
713 Ouachita 64
Camden, AR 71701-9616, USA

Wilson, George (Athlete, Basketball Player)
151 Twin Lakes Dr
Fairfield, OH 45014-5257, USA

Wilson, Georges (Director)
Moulin de Vilgris
Rambouillet 78120, FRANCE

Wilson, Gerald S (Composer, Musician)
4625 Brynhurst Ave
Los Angeles, CA 90043-1205, USA

Wilson, Glenn (Athlete, Baseball Player)
300 Tara Park
Conroe, TX 77302-3756, USA

Wilson, Gretchen (Musician)
c/o Staff Member *WmE2 (WMA-LA)*
1 William Morris Pl
Beverly Hills, CA 90212-4261, USA

Wilson, Harry (Athlete, Football Player)
2600 N Lawrence St Apt 307
Philadelphia, PA 19133-3140, USA

Wilson, Harry C (Religious Leader)
6060 Castleway West Dr
Indianapolis, IN 46250-1930, USA

Wilson, Hugh (Director, Producer, Writer)
c/o Staff Member *International Creative Management (ICM-LA)*
10250 Constellation Blvd Fl 7
Los Angeles, CA 90067-6207, USA

Wilson, J C (Athlete, Football Player)
13410 Buchanan Dr
Fort Washington, MD 20744-2931, USA

Wilson, J C (Athlete, Football Player)
4785 Young Rd
Waldorf, MD 20601-4483, USA

Wilson, J Tylee (Business Person)
PO Box 2057
Ponte Vedra Beach, FL 32004-2057, USA

Wilson, James (Athlete, Football Player)
877 NW Charlie Horse Dr
Lake City, FL 32055-9294, USA

Wilson, James B (Admiral)
321 Crosslands Dr
Kennett Square, PA 19348-2007, USA

Wilson, James M (Misc)
Med Center Genetics Dept
Philadelphia, PA 19104, USA

Wilson, James Q (Educator)
Graduate Management School
Los Angeles, CA 90024, USA

Wilson, Janet (Stylist)
1644 Summit Lake Blvd
Akron, OH 44314-3367, USA

Wilson, Jean D (Doctor)
5323 Harry Hines Blvd
Dallas, TX 75390-7201, USA

Wilson, Jeannie (Actor)
General Delivery
Ketchum, ID 83340-9999, USA

Wilson, Jennifer
1947 Lake Shore Dr
Branson, MO 65616-9476

Wilson, Jerrel (Athlete, Football Player)
13860 W Main St
Larose, LA 70373-3006, USA

Wilson, Jerry (Athlete, Football Player)
2117 Mountain View Dr
Vestavia, AL 35216-2023, USA

Wilson, Jerry (Athlete, Football Player)
4272 Ironwood Ct
Weston, FL 33331-3827, USA

Wilson, Jim (Athlete, Baseball Player)
8112 NW Bacon Rd
Vancouver, WA 98665-6634, USA

Wilson, Jim M (Athlete, Football Player)
2674 Tucson Way
Powder Springs, GA 30127-1562, USA

Wilson, Joe (Athlete, Football Player)
328 Valley View Ln
Chester Springs, PA 19425-9605, USA

Wilson, Julie (Actor, Musician)
415 W 55th St
New York, NY 10019-4435, USA

Wilson, Justin (Musician)
200 W 57th St Ste 308
New York, NY 10019-3211, USA

Wilson, Kenneth G (Nobel Prize Laureate)
174 W 18th Ave
Columbus, OH 43210-1106, USA

Wilson, Kim (Musician)
28205 Agoura Rd
Agoura Hills, CA 91301-2482, USA

Wilson, Kris (Athlete, Baseball Player)
PO Box 15
Chillicothe, MO 64601-0015, USA

Wilson, Kristen (Actor)
c/o Norman Aladjem *Paradigm (LA)*
360 N Crescent Dr
Beverly Hills, CA 90210-4874, USA

Wilson, Lambert (Actor)
c/o Estelle Lasher *Principal Entertainment (LA)*
1964 Westwood Blvd Ste 400
Los Angeles, CA 90025-4695, USA

Wilson, Lawrence F (Larry) (Athlete, Football Player)
11834 N Blackheath Rd
Scottsdale, AZ 85254-4809, USA

Wilson, Luke (Actor)
c/o Mara Buxbaum *ID PR (LA)*
7060 Hollywood Blvd Fl 8
Los Angeles, CA 90028-6014, USA

Wilson, Mara (Actor)
c/o Bonnie Liedtke *Principato/Young Management*
9465 Wilshire Blvd Ste 430
Beverly Hills, CA 90212-2613, USA

Wilson, Marc (Athlete, Football Player)
18020 157th Ave NE
Woodinville, WA 98072-9238, USA

Wilson, Marc D (Athlete, Football Player)
113113 Mount Wallace Ct
Alta Loma, CA 91737, USA

Wilson, Marie
6 Oakdale
Irvine, CA 92604-3221

Wilson, Mark (Athlete, Golfer)
N41W27751 Ishnala Trl
Pewaukee, WI 53072-2140, USA

Wilson, Marty (Musician)
c/o Staff Member *VocalPoint*
25 Denmark St Fl 1
London WC2H 8NJ, UNITED KINGDOM (UK)

Wilson, Melanie (Actor)
9300 Wilshire Blvd Ste 410
Beverly Hills, CA 90212-3228, USA

Wilson, Michael G (Producer)
c/o Staff Member *Danjag*
2400 Colorado Ave Suite 310
Santa Monica, CA 90404, USA

Wilson, Michael H (Government Official)
235 Queen's St
Ottawa, ON K1A OH5, CANADA

Wilson, Michael (Tack) (Athlete, Baseball Player)
768 Forest St Apt 6
Roswell, GA 30075-6527, USA

Wilson, Mike D (Athlete, Football Player)
1967 Litchfield Ave
Dayton, OH 45406-3811, USA

Wilson, Mike R (Athlete, Football Player)
2908 N Poinsettia Ave
Manhattan Beach, CA 90266-2405, USA

Wilson, Mookie (Athlete, Baseball Player)
1111 Heyward Wilson Rd
Eastover, SC 29044-9627, USA

Wilson, Nancy (Actor, Composer, Musician)
c/o Carol Peters *Peters Management Syndicate*
PO Box 1710
Topanga, CA 90290-1710, USA

Wilson, Natalie (Stylist)
8950 W Olympic Blvd Ste 299
Beverly Hills, CA 90211-3565, USA

Wilson, Neal C (Religious Leader)
12501 Old Columbus Pike
Silver Spring, MD 20904, USA

Wilson, Neil (Athlete, Baseball Player)
4300 Highway 412 W
Lexington, TN 38351-5423, USA

Wilson, Nemiah (Athlete, Football Player)
11000 E Idaho Pl
Aurora, CO 80012-4118, USA

Wilson, Nigel (Athlete, Baseball Player)
35 Sabbe Cres
Ajax, ON L1T 4E3, Canada

Wilson, Olin C (Astronomer)
1508 Circa Del Lago Unit B110
San Marcos, CA 92078-7204, USA

Wilson, Othell (Athlete, Basketball Player)
3413 Caledonia Cir
Woodbridge, VA 22192-1069, USA

Wilson, Otis (Athlete, Football Player)
7B W 15th St
Chicago, IL 60605-2723, USA

Wilson, Owen C (Actor)
c/o Ina Treciokas *Slate Public Relations*
9000 W Sunset Blvd Ste 915
West Hollywood, CA 90069-5809, USA

Wilson, Patrick (Actor, Musician)
c/o Jennifer Plante *SLATE Public Relations - NY*
307 7th Ave Rm 2401
New York, NY 10001-6019, USA

Wilson, Patti (Stylist)
c/o Staff Member *Management + Artists + Organization*
330 W 38th St Ste 1401
New York, NY 10018-8438, USA

Wilson, Paul (Athlete, Baseball Player)
949 Lenmore Ct
Orlando, FL 32812-1980, USA

Wilson, Peta (Actor)
c/o Gordon Gilbertson *Gilbertson Management*
1334 3rd Street Promenade Ste 201
Santa Monica, CA 90401-1320, USA

Wilson, Preston (Athlete, Baseball Player)
136 Paloma Dr
Coral Gables, FL 33143-6545, USA

Wilson, Rainn (Actor)
c/o Mark Schulman *3 Arts Entertainment Inc*
9460 Wilshire Blvd Fl 7
Beverly Hills, CA 90212-2713, USA

Wilson, Ralph C Jr (Misc)
1 Bills Dr
Orchard Park, NY 14127-2237, USA

Wilson, Red (Athlete, Baseball Player)
806 Cabot Ln
Madison, WI 53711-2810, USA

Wilson, Reinard (Athlete, Football Player)
2595 NW 49th Ave Apt 108
Lauderdale Lakes, FL 33313-3354, USA

Wilson, Rick (Race Car Driver)
PO Box 304
Mulberry, FL 33860-0304, USA

Wilson, Rick (Athlete, Coach, Hockey Player)
166 E Bethel Rd
Coppell, TX 75019-4085, USA

Wilson, Rick (Athlete, Basketball Player)
535 E Ormsby Ave
Louisville, KY 40203-2620, USA

Wilson, Ricky (Athlete, Basketball Player)
8007 Oat Ridge Ct
Bowie, MD 20715-4620, USA

Wilson, Rita (Actor)
c/o Heidi Schaeffer *PMK/BNC Public Relations (PMK-LA)*
8687 Melrose Ave Ste 8
West Hollywood, CA 90069-5746, USA

Wilson, Robert Charles (Writer)
175 5th Ave
New York, NY 10010-7703, USA

Wilson, Robert E (Bobby) (Athlete, Football Player)
1034 Liberty Park Dr Apt 408R
Austin, TX 78746-6854, USA

Wilson, Robert M (Actor)
131 Varick St Ste 908
New York, NY 10013-1444, USA

Wilson, Robert N (Business Person)
1 Johnson and Johnson Plz
New Brunswick, NJ 08933-0001, USA

Wilson, Robert W (Nobel Prize Laureate)
94 Lucille Ave
Dumont, NJ 07628-2034, USA

Wilson, Robin (Musician)
2100 W End Ave Ste 1000
Nashville, TN 37203-5240, USA

Wilson, Roger (Actor)
c/o Staff Member *Joel Stevens Entertainment*
5627 Allott Ave
Van Nuys, CA 91401-4502, USA

Wilson, Ron (Athlete, Coach, Hockey Player)
525 W Santa Clara St
San Jose, CA 95113-1520, USA

Wilson, Ryan (Actor)
c/o Cindy Osbrink *Osbrink Talent Agency*
4343 Lankershim Blvd Ste 100
West Toluca Lake, CA 91602-2705, USA

Wilson, Samuel W (Educator, General)
President's Office
Hampden-Sydney, VA 23943, USA

Wilson, Scott
PO Box 5617
Beverly Hills, CA 90209-5617

Wilson, Sherlee (Actor)
c/o Staff Member *Cunningham Escott Slevin & Doherty (CESD-LA)*
10635 Santa Monica Blvd Ste 130
Los Angeles, CA 90025-8306, USA

Wilson, Sophie (Stylist)
c/o Staff Member *Directions USA*
3717 W Market St Ste C
Greensboro, NC 27403-1155, USA

Wilson, Stephanie D (Astronaut)
14910 Hollydale Dr
Houston, TX 77062-2907, USA

Wilson, Stephen (Athlete, Basketball Player)
West Jefferson Middle School 9449 Barnes Ave
Conifer, CO 80433, USA

Wilson, Steve (Athlete, Baseball Player)
23-1041 Comox St
Vancouver, BC V6E 1K1, Canada

Wilson, Steve (Athlete, Football Player)
3503 Brymore Ct
Pearland, TX 77584, USA

Wilson, Stuart (Actor)
c/o Staff Member *Curtis Brown Group*
Haymarket House 28 - 29 Haymarket
London SW1Y 4SP, UNITED KINGDOM

Wilson, Thomas L (Athlete, Football Player)
PO Box 9135
Pittsburg, CA 94565-9135, USA

Wilson, Thomas (Tom) F (Actor)
c/o Alex Murray *McDonald-Murray Management*
11846 Ventura Blvd Ste 202
Studio City, CA 91604-2620, USA

Wilson, Tom (Athlete, Baseball Player)
2679 Tanglewood Ct
Lake Havasu City, AZ 86403-3225, USA

Wilson, Torrie (Model, Wrestler)
c/o Staff Member *Good Guy Entertainment*
3733 Oakfield Dr
Sherman Oaks, CA 91423-4430, USA

Wilson, Trevor (Athlete, Baseball Player)
11857 White Ln
Oregon City, OR 97045-5716, USA

Wilson, Trevor (Athlete, Basketball Player)
824 15th St
Hermosa Beach, CA 90254-3202, USA

Wilson, Troy (Athlete, Football Player)
14213 W 138th Pl
Olathe, KS 66062-5877, USA

Wilson, Vance (Athlete, Baseball Player)
6368 Elizabeth Ave
Springdale, AR 72762-4234, USA

Wilson, Wade (Athlete, Football Player)
6126 Mimosa Ln
Dallas, TX 75230-5042, USA

Wilson, Wayne (Athlete, Football Player)
5430 Lynx Ln Apt 152
Columbia, MD 21044-2319, USA

Wilson, William (Athlete, Basketball Player)
130 Belmont St
Englewood, NJ 07631-1502, USA

Wilson, William J (Activist)
Kennedy Government School
Cambridge, MA 2138, USA

Wilson, Willie (Athlete, Baseball Player)
18 Vianney Ave
Scarborough, ON M1L 4V4, Canada

Wilson, Woody (Cartoonist)
c/o Staff Member *King Features Syndication*
300 W 57th St Fl 15
New York, NY 10019-5238, USA

Wilson David, Mackenzie (Director)
Castletown
Isle of Man IM9 1LD, UNITED KINGDOM (UK)

Wilson Jr, George B (Mike) (Athlete, Football Player)
1062 E Lancaster Ave
Bryn Mawr, PA 19010-1500, USA

Wilson Jr, Louis H (General, War Hero)
100 University Park Dr
Birmingham, AL 35209-6766, USA

Wilson of Tillyorn, David C (Government Official)
Westminster
London SW1A 0PW, UNITED KINGDOM (UK)

Wilson Phillips
1290 Avenue of the Americas # 4200
New York, NY 10104-0101

Wilson-Johnson, David R (Opera Singer)
28 Englefield Road
London N1 4ET, UNITED KINGDOM (UK)

Wilson-Sampras, Bridgette (Actor)
c/o Andrea Pett-Joseph *Brillstein Entertainment Partners*
9150 Wilshire Blvd Ste 350
Beverly Hills, CA 90212-3453, USA

Wimmer, Brian (Actor)
c/o Jean-Pierre (JP) Henraux *Shelter Entertainment*
9454 Wilshire Blvd Ste 715
Beverly Hills, CA 90212-2925, USA

Wimmer, Chris (Athlete, Baseball Player, Olympic Athlete)
4027 E Countryside Plz
Wichita, KS 67218-4103, USA

Wimmer, Kurt (Actor, Director, Producer, Writer)
c/o Tom Strickler *WmE2 (Endeavor-LA)*
9601 Wilshire Blvd Fl 3
Beverly Hills, CA 90210-5219, USA

Wimmer, Scott (Race Car Driver)
425 Industrial Dr
Welcome, NC 27374, USA

Winans
1420 Coleman Rd
Franklin, TN 37064-7452

Winans, BeBe (Musician)
c/o Staff Member *Agency for the Performing Arts (APA-LA)*
405 S Beverly Dr Ste 500
Beverly Hills, CA 90212-4425, USA

Winans, CeCe (Musician)
2300 Franklin Rd # 2B
Franklin, TN 37064, USA

Winans, Jeff (Athlete, Football Player)
175 21st Ave SE
Saint Petersburg, FL 33705-2826, USA

Winans, Mario (Musician)
c/o Staff Member *Bad Boy Worldwide Entertainment*
1440 Broadway Fl 16
New York, NY 10018-2320, USA

Winans, Matthew (Matt) (Athlete, Baseball Player)
21 Saint George Pl
Sandy Hook, CT 06482-1089, USA

Winans, Tydus (Athlete, Football Player)
92 W Hall Ave
Clovis, CA 93612, USA

Winans, Vickie (Musician)
c/o Staff Member *Covenant Agency, The*
123 California Ave Apt 116
Santa Monica, CA 90403-3560, USA

Winborne, Jamie (Athlete, Football Player)
195 Roscoe Lee Cir
Wetumpka, AL 36092-3681, USA

Winbush, Angela (Musician, Songwriter, Writer)
370 Harrison Ave
Harrison, NY 10528-2714, USA

Winbush, Camille (Actor)
c/o Staff Member *Innovative Artists (LA)*
1505 10th St
Santa Monica, CA 90401-2805, USA

Winbush, Troy (Actor)
c/o Staff Member *Paradigm (LA)*
360 N Crescent Dr
Beverly Hills, CA 90210-4874, USA

Winceniak, Ed (Athlete, Baseball Player)
10828 S Avenue O
Chicago, IL 60617-6543, USA

Wincer, Simon (Director, Producer)
c/o Adam Kanter *Creative Artists Agency (CAA-LA)*
2000 Avenue of the Stars Ste 100
Los Angeles, CA 90067-4705, USA

Wincer, Simon G (Director)
PO Box 241
Toorak, VIC 3142, AUSTRALIA

Winchester, Jesse (Musician, Songwriter, Writer)
1025 17th Ave S # 200
Nashville, TN 37212-2211, USA

Winchester, Philip (Actor)
c/o Guido Giordano *International Creative Management (ICM-LA)*
10250 Constellation Blvd Fl 7
Los Angeles, CA 90067-6207, USA

Winchester, Scott (Athlete, Baseball Player)
4705 Oakridge Dr
Midland, MI 48640-7409, USA

Wincott, Jeff P (Actor)
606 N Larchmont Blvd
Los Angeles, CA 90004-1321

Winder, Sammy (Athlete, Football Player)
4823 Greens Crossing Rd
Ridgeland, MS 39157-5042, USA

Winders, Rich (Bowler)
720 Augusta St
Racine, WI 53402-4412, USA

Winders, Wim (Director)
9300 Wilshire Blvd Ste 555
Beverly Hills, CA 90212-3211, USA

Windham, Melissa (Stylist)
33752 Norfolk St
Livonia, MI 48152-1227, USA

Windhorn, Gordie (Athlete, Baseball Player)
145 Bent Creek Rd
Danville, VA 24540-5213, USA

Windis, Tony (Athlete, Basketball Player)
404 1st St
Rawlins, WY 82301-5502, USA

Windle, William F (Misc)
229 Cherry St
Granville, OH 43023-1195, USA

Windon, Stephen (Cinematographer)
PO Box 659 Northbridge
Sydney, NSW 2063, AUSTRALIA

Windsor, Barbara (Actor, Comedian)
104 Crouch Hill
London NB 9EA, UNITED KINGDOM (UK)

Windsor, Robert E (Athlete, Football Player)
2625 Legends Way
Ellicott City, MD 21042-2257, USA

Windsor-Smith, Barry (Artist)
c/o Staff Member *Fantagraphics Books*
7563 Lake City Way NE
Seattle, WA 98115-4218, USA

Wine, Bobby (Athlete, Baseball Player, Coach)
2614 Woodland Ave
Norristown, PA 19403-1636, USA

Wine, David M (Religious Leader)
1451 Dundee Ave
Elgin, IL 60120-1674, USA

Wine, Robbie (Athlete, Baseball Player)
240 Bryce Jordan Ctr
University Park, PA 16802-7102, USA

Winegardner, Mark (Writer)
1745 Broadway
New York, NY 10019-4368, USA

Winer, Jason (Director)
c/o Michael Lasker *Mosaic Media Group*
9200 W Sunset Blvd Ste 10
Los Angeles, CA 90069-3608, USA

Winfield, Antoine (Athlete, Football Player)
10451 White Tail Xing
Eden Prairie, MN 55347-5026, USA

Winfield, David (Dave) (Athlete, Baseball Player)
2235 Stratford Cir
Los Angeles, CA 90077-1316, USA

Winfield, Lee (Athlete, Basketball Player)
7638 Forest View Dr
Saint Louis, MO 63121-2418, USA

Winfield, Peter (Actor)
c/o Staff Member *Screen Actors Guild (SAG-LA)*
5757 Wilshire Blvd
Los Angeles, CA 90036-5810, USA

Winfrey, Oprah (Actor, Producer, Talk Show Host)
c/o Staff Member *Harpo Productions*
110 N Carpenter St
Chicago, IL 60607-2146, USA

Winfrey, Travis (Actor)
c/o Peter Kluge *Impact Artist Group LLC (LA)*
244 California St Floor 1
Burbank, CA 91505, USA

Winfrey, W C (Bill) (Misc)
7802 Sierra Trl
Spring Lake, NC 28390, USA

Wingate, David (Athlete, Basketball Player)
11404 Glaetzer Ln
Charlotte, NC 28270-1574, USA

Wingate, Elmer (Athlete, Football Player)
807 Wellington Rd
Baltimore, MD 21212-1931, USA

Wingate, J W (Baseball Player)
3215 Case St
Beaumont, TX 77703-3607, USA

Winger, Debra (Actor)
c/o Tim Curtis *WmE2 (Endeavor-LA)*
9601 Wilshire Blvd Fl 3
Beverly Hills, CA 90210-5219, USA

Winger, Kip (Musician)
2740 W Magnolia Blvd Unit 204
Burbank, CA 91505-3051, USA

Wingfield, Dontonio (Athlete, Basketball Player)
1602 Gadsden Dr
Albany, GA 31701-3566, USA

Wingle, Blake (Athlete, Football Player)
8200 Stockdale Hwy Apt 10
Bakersfield, CA 93311-1091, USA

Wing-Merrill, Toby
PO Box 889
Mathews, VA 23109-0889

Wingo, Harthorne (Athlete, Basketball Player)
862 Macon St Apt 2B
Brooklyn, NY 11233-5405, USA

Wingreen, Jason
4224 Teesdale Ave
Studio City, CA 91604-1544

Wingrove-Earl, Elsie (Baseball Player)
PO Box 61
N Portal, SK S0C 1W0, CANADA

Winiger, Melanie (Actor, Model)
ch Carmenstr 32
Zurich 8032, SWITZERLAND

Winings, Meagan (Beauty Pageant Winner)
PO Box 21
Atkinson, NE 68713-0021, USA

Winkelsas, Joe (Athlete, Baseball Player)
213 Virgil Ave
Buffalo, NY 14216-1836, USA

Winkleman, Sophie (Actor)
c/o Staff Member *Creative Artists Agency (CAA-LA)*
2000 Avenue of the Stars Ste 100
Los Angeles, CA 90067-4705, USA

Winkler, David (Director)
1180 S Beverly Dr Ste 604
Los Angeles, CA 90035-1158, USA

Winkler, Francis M (Athlete, Football Player)
8223 Creekside Cir S
Cordova, TN 38016-5117, USA

Winkler, Gerard (Actor)
Alsertra 26-3A
Vienna 1090, AUSTRIA

Winkler, Hans-Gunter (Misc)
Dr Rau Allee 48
Warendorf 48231, GERMANY

Winkler, Henry (Actor, Producer)
c/o Leigh Brillstein *International Creative Management (ICM-LA)*
10250 Constellation Blvd Fl 7
Los Angeles, CA 90067-6207, USA

Winkler, Irwin (Director, Producer)
211 S Beverly Dr # 220
Beverly Hills, CA 90212-3807, USA

Winkler, Marvin (Athlete, Basketball Player)
PO Box 759
Zapata, TX 78076-0759, USA

Winkles, Bobby B (Athlete, Baseball Player, Coach)
78452 Calle Huerta
La Quinta, CA 92253-2372, USA

Winn, D Randolph (Randy) (Athlete, Baseball Player)
59 Leeds Ct E
Danville, CA 94526-4348, USA

Winn, Jim (Athlete, Baseball Player)
3440 S Delaware Ave Apt 123
Springfield, MO 65804-6447, USA

Winner, Charley (Athlete, Football Coach, Football Player)
14970 Lake Olive Dr
Fort Myers, FL 33919-8336, USA

Winner, Michael R (Director, Producer)
31 Melbury Road
London W14 8AB, UNITED KINGDOM (UK)

Winnick, Katheryn (Actor)
c/o Jason Barrett *Alchemy Entertainment*
7024 Melrose Ave Ste 420
Los Angeles, CA 90038-3394, USA

Winningham, Herm (Athlete, Baseball Player)
1542 Belleville Rd
Orangeburg, SC 29115-3702, USA

Winningham, Mare (Actor)
c/o Margrit Polak *Margrit Polak Management*
1954 Hillhurst Ave Ste 405
Los Angeles, CA 90027-2722, USA

Winograd, Shmuel (Mathematician, Scientist)
235 Glendale Rd
Scarsdale, NY 10583-1533, USA

Winokur, Marissa Jaret (Actor)
c/o Michael Valeo *Valeo Entertainment*
8265 W Sunset Blvd Ste 103
West Hollywood, CA 90046-2433, USA

Winslet, Kate (Actor)
c/o Heidi Slan *42West (LA)*
11400 W Olympic Blvd Ste 1100
Los Angeles, CA 90064-1579, USA

Winslow, Dan (Musician)
3807 114th Ln NE
Minneapolis, MN 55449-7031, USA

Winslow, George (Athlete, Football Player)
14 Daisy Ln
Maple Glen, PA 19002-2326, USA

Winslow, Michael (Actor, Comedian)
c/o Damon Frank *Venture IAB*
3211 Cahuenga Blvd W Ste 104
Los Angeles, CA 90068-1372, USA

Winslow Jr, Kellen (Athlete, Football Player)
c/o Staff Member *EAG Sports Management*
12910 Agustin Pl
Playa Vista, CA 90094-2301, USA

Winsor, Jackie (Artist)
534 W 21st St
New York, NY 10011-2812, USA

Winstead, Mary Elizabeth (Actor)
c/o Jim Toth *Creative Artists Agency (CAA-LA)*
2000 Avenue of the Stars Ste 100
Los Angeles, CA 90067-4705, USA

Winston, Dennis (Athlete, Football Player)
150 Chesterfield Ln Apt 8
Maumee, OH 43537-3881, USA

Winston, George (Composer, Musician)
PO Box 639
Santa Cruz, CA 95061-0639, USA

Winston, Hattie (Actor)
13025 Jarvis Ave
Los Angeles, CA 90061-2247, USA

Winston, Mary Ellen (Stylist)
11 E 68th St
New York, NY 10065-4955, USA

Winston, Patrick H (Engineer, Scientist)
Technology Square
Cambridge, MA 2139, USA

Winston, Roland (Physicist)
3384 Locksley Ct
Merced, CA 95340-0751, USA

Winston, Roy C (Athlete, Football Player)
708 Highway 401
Napoleonville, LA 70390-3205, USA

Winstone, Ray (Actor)
c/o Michael Wiggs *Creative Artists Management (CAM (UK))*
1st Floor 55-59 Shaftesbury Ave
London W1D 6LD, UK

Winter, Alex (Actor)
c/o Chris Ridenhour *Evolution Entertainment (LA)*
901 N Highland Ave
Los Angeles, CA 90038-2412, USA

Winter, Antje (Stylist)
c/o Staff Member *Art Partner*
145 Hudson St Frnt 2
New York, NY 10013-2122, USA

Winter, Blaise (Athlete, Football Player)
W5837 Royaltroon Dr
Menasha, WI 54952-9712, USA

Winter, Edgar
26033 Mulholland Hwy
Calabasas, CA 91302-1946

Winter, Edgar (Musician)
26033 Mulholland Hwy
Calabasas, CA 91302-1946, USA

Winter, Eric (Actor)
c/o Colton Gramm *Brillstein Entertainment Partners*
9150 Wilshire Blvd Ste 350
Beverly Hills, CA 90212-3453, USA

Winter, Fred (Tex) (Coach)
Staples Center 1111 S Figueroa St
Los Angeles, CA 90015, USA

Winter, Harrison L (Judge)
101 W Lombard St
Baltimore, MD 21201-2605, USA

Winter, Johnny (Musician)
35 Hayward Ave
Colchester, CT 06415-1221, USA

Winter, Judy
Merzstr. 14
Munich, GERMANY D-81679

Winter, Olaf (Athlete)
An der Pirschheide 28
Potsdam 14471, GERMANY

Winter, Paul T (Musician)
PO Box 72
Litchfield, CT 06759-0072, USA

Winter, Ralph (Producer)
c/o Staff Member *Ralph Winter Productions*
10201 W Pico Blvd Bldg 6 PMB 101
Los Angeles, CA 90064-2606, USA

Winter, Terence (Producer)
c/o Staff Member *Creative Artists Agency (CAA-LA)*
2000 Avenue of the Stars Ste 100
Los Angeles, CA 90067-4705, USA

Winter, Terrence (Producer, Writer)
c/o Staff Member *Jackoway Tyerman Wertheimer Austen Mandelbaum Morris & Klein*
1925 Century Park E Fl 22
Los Angeles, CA 90067-2701, USA

Winter, William F (Ex-Governor)
190 E Capitol St Ste 800
Jackson, MS 39201-2155, USA

Winter Jr, Ralph K (Judge)
55 Whitney Ave
New Haven, CT 06510-1300, USA

Winterbottom, Michael (Director, Producer, Writer)
c/o Staff Member *Revolution Films*
9A Dallington St
London EC1V 0BQ, UNITED KINGDOM (UK)

Winters, Brian (Athlete, Basketball Player)
6144 S Moline Way
Englewood, CO 80111-5845, USA

Winters, Chris (Actor, Model)
933 Backspin Ct
Newport News, VA 23602-9428, USA

Winters, Dean (Actor)
c/o Bill Butler *Industry Entertainment Partners*
955 Carrillo Dr Ste 300
Los Angeles, CA 90048-5400, USA

Winters, Frank (Football Player)
820 17th St
Union City, NJ 07087-1928, USA

Winters, Jonathan (Actor, Comedian)
c/o Staff Member *Abrams Artists Agency (LA)*
9200 W Sunset Blvd PH 11
Los Angeles, CA 90069-3601, USA

Winters, Matt (Athlete, Baseball Player)
1201 Foxfire Dr
Greensboro, NC 27410-3253, USA

Winters, Mike (Athlete, Baseball Player)
13644 Boquita Dr
Del Mar, CA 92014-3408, USA

Winters, Patricia (Stylist)
2122 Century Park Ln Apt 114
Los Angeles, CA 90067-3317, USA

Winters, Scott William (Actor)
c/o Staff Member *Levine Okwu Erickson Management*
6363 Wilshire Blvd Ste 300
Los Angeles, CA 90048-5729, USA

Winters, Voise (Athlete, Basketball Player)
7305 S Rockwell St
Chicago, IL 60629-2037, USA

Winther, Richard (Athlete, Football Player)
1620 6th Way NW
Center Point, AL 35215-5374, USA

Wintour, Anna (Editor)
350 Madison Ave
New York, NY 10017-3700, USA

Winwood, Steve (Musician)
Tirley
Gloucs GL19 4EU, UNITED KINGDOM (UK)

Winzenried, Jesse D (Financier)
805 15th St NW
Washington, DC 20005-2207, USA

Wire II, William S (Business Person)
706 Overton Park
Nashville, TN 37215-2452, USA

Wirgowski, Dennis (Athlete, Football Player)
1127 Brissette Beach Rd
Kawkawlin, MI 48631-9454, USA

Wirth, Alan (Athlete, Baseball Player)
2858 E Jasmine St
Mesa, AZ 85213-3123, USA

Wirth, Billy (Actor, Director)
c/o Molly Conners *Rogues Gallery*
20 Clinton St Apt C7
New York, NY 10002-1755, USA

Wirth, Timothy E (Senator)
1301 Connecticut Ave NW
Washington, DC 20036-1815, USA

Wirtz, W Willard (Secretary)
1211 Connecticut Ave NW
Washington, DC 20036-2700, USA

Wisdom, Norman (Actor, Comedian)
Ballalaugh Lhen Andreas Ramsey
Isle of Man IM7 3EH, UNITED KINGDOM (UK)

Wisdom, Robert (Actor)
10100 Santa Monica Blvd Fl 25
Los Angeles, CA 90067-4003

Wisdom, Sir Norman
The Lhen
Andreas Ramsay ISLE OF MAN, UK 1M7 3EH

Wise, Dewayne (Athlete, Baseball Player)
709 Old Lexington Hwy
Chapin, SC 29036-7980, USA

Wise, Matt (Athlete, Baseball Player)
11627 E Twilight Ct
Chandler, AZ 85249-4546, USA

Wise, Ray (Actor)
c/o Brady McKay *Flutie Entertainment (LA)*
9320 Wilshire Blvd Ste 202
Beverly Hills, CA 90212-3217, USA

Wise, Richard C (Rick) (Athlete, Baseball Player)
8235 SW 184th Ave
Beaverton, OR 97007-5764, USA

Wise, Roy (Athlete, Baseball Player)
14851 Jeffrey Rd Spc 326
Irvine, CA 92618-8326, USA

Wise, William A (Business Person)
1001 Louisiana St
Houston, TX 77002-5089, USA

Wise, Willie (Athlete, Basketball Player)
21929 95th Pl S
Kent, WA 98031, USA

Wisecarver, Ellsworth (Sonny)
305 Mill Creek Rd
Mentone, CA 92359

Wiseman, Frederick (Producer)
1 Richdale Ave Unit 4
Cambridge, MA 02140-2610, USA

Wiseman, Len (Director, Writer)
c/o Nick Reed *International Creative Management (ICM-LA)*
10250 Constellation Blvd Fl 7
Los Angeles, CA 90067-6207, USA

Wiseman, Mac (Musician)
PO Box 17028
Nashville, TN 37217-0028, USA

Wisener, Gary (Athlete, Football Player)
10 Encantado Way
Hot Springs Village, AR 71909-7405, USA

Wish Bone (Actor, Composer, Musician)
c/o Staff Member *Creative Artists Agency (CAA-LA)*
2000 Avenue of the Stars Ste 100
Los Angeles, CA 90067-4705, USA

Wishart III, Leonard P (General)
19360 Magnolia Grove Sq Unit 315
Leesburg, VA 20176-6896, USA

Wisin and Yandel (Musician)
c/o Staff Member *Universal Music Publishing Group (Latin)*
420 Lincoln Rd Ste 200
Miami Beach, FL 33139-3014, USA

Wiska, Jeffrey R (Athlete, Football Player)
18579 Fox Hollow Ct
Northville, MI 48168-8848, USA

Wismann, Pete (Athlete, Football Player)
7923 Caledonia Dr
San Jose, CA 95135-2112, USA

Wisner, Frank G (Diplomat)
70 Pine St # 1800
New York, NY 10270-0001, USA

Wisniewski, Andreas (Actor)
14724 Ventura Blvd Ste 505
Sherman Oaks, CA 91403-3505, USA

Wisniewski, Leo (Athlete, Football Player)
1900 Village Rd
Pittsburgh, PA 15205-1578, USA

Wisniewski, Stephen A (Steve) (Athlete, Football Player)
36 El Alamo Ct
Danville, CA 94526-1455, USA

Wisoff, Peter J K (Jeff) (Astronaut)
4268 Brindisi Pl
Pleasanton, CA 94566-2238, USA

Wissel, Sharon (Figure Skater)
c/o Staff Member *Bobby Ball Talent Agency*
4116 W Magnolia Blvd Ste 205
Burbank, CA 91505-2700, USA

Wissman, Dave (Athlete, Baseball Player)
PO Box 38
Derby, VT 05829-0038, USA

Wistert, Albert A (Ox) (Athlete, Football Player)
PO Box 141
Merlin, OR 97532-0141, USA

Wistert, Alvin L (Moose) (Athlete, Football Player)
10250 7 Mile Rd
Northville, MI 48167-9107, USA

Wistrom, Grant (Athlete, Football Player)
5769 S Fox Hollow Ave
Springfield, MO 65810-2326, USA

Witasick, Jay (Athlete, Baseball Player)
6514 Ambrosia Dr
San Diego, CA 92124-3162, USA

with Spencer Davis, Strawberry Alarm Clock (Music Group)
c/o Geoffrey Blumenauer *Geoffrey Blumenauer Artists*
PO Box 343
Burbank, CA 91503-0343, USA

Withem, Shannon (Athlete, Baseball Player)
39668 Dorchester Cir
Canton, MI 48188-5016, USA

Witherell, Joann (Stylist)
c/o Staff Member *THW Productions*
1801 N Kingsley Dr Apt 103
Los Angeles, CA 90027-3707, USA

Withers, Bill (Musician, Songwriter, Writer)
PO Box 16698
Beverly Hills, CA 90209-2698, USA

Withers, Googie (Actor)
17 Broad Court
London WC2B 5QN, UNITED KINGDOM (UK)

Withers, Jane (Actor)
13701 Riverside Dr Ste 201
Sherman Oaks, CA 91423-2447, USA

Withers, Pick (Musician)
Damage Mgmt 16 Lambton Place
London W11 2SH, UNITED KINGDOM (UK)

Witherspoon, John (Actor, Comedian)
c/o Matt Schuler *Levity Entertainment Group*
6701 Center Dr W Ste 1111
Los Angeles, CA 90045-1552, USA

Witherspoon, Reese (Actor, Producer)
c/o Evelyn O'Neill *Management 360*
9111 Wilshire Blvd
Beverly Hills, CA 90210-5508, USA

Withrow, Phil (Athlete, Football Player)
730 Oakland Hills Cir Apt 106
Lake Mary, FL 32746-5833, USA

Withrow, Ray (Astronomer, Baseball Player)
3842 Bordeaux Loop S
Owensboro, KY 42303-2550, USA

Witiuk, Doris (Baseball Player)
11821 N Hemlock St
Spokane, WA 99218-2718, USA

Witkin, Isaac (Artist)
Art Dept
Bennington, VT 5201, USA

Witkin, Joel-Peter (Photographer)
1707 Five Points Rd SW
Albuquerque, NM 87105-3017, USA

Witkop, Bernhard (Misc)
3807 Montrose Driveway
Chevy Chase, MD 20815, USA

Witman, Jon (Athlete, Football Player)
568 Woodsview Ln
Hellam, PA 17406-9344, USA

Witmeyer, Ron (Athlete, Baseball Player)
PO Box 763
Rancho Santa Fe, CA 92067-0763, USA

Witt, Alexander (Director)
c/o Ann Murtha *Murtha Agency*
1025 Colorado Ave Ste B
Santa Monica, CA 90401-2847, USA

Witt, Alicia (Actor)
c/o Daniel (Danny) Sussman *Brillstein Entertainment Partners*
9150 Wilshire Blvd Ste 350
Beverly Hills, CA 90212-3453, USA

Witt, Bobby (Athlete, Baseball Player)
4601 Winewood Ct
Colleyville, TX 76034-4887, USA

Witt, George (Athlete, Baseball Player)
2209 Catalina
Laguna Beach, CA 92651-3607, USA

Witt, Katarina (Figure Skater)
c/o Gail Parenteau *Parenteau Guidance*
132 E 35th St # 3J
New York, NY 10016-3892, USA

Witt, Kevin (Athlete, Baseball Player)
6350 Concho Bay Dr
Houston, TX 77041-6171, USA

Witt, Michael A (Mike) (Athlete, Baseball Player)
37 Poppy Hills Rd
Laguna Niguel, CA 92677-1010, USA

Witt, Robert E (Educator)
President S Ofc
Tuscaloosa, AL 35487-0001, USA

Witte, Luke (Athlete, Basketball Player)
3223 Arbor Pointe Dr
Charlotte, NC 28210-7994, USA

Witten, Edward (Physicist)
Einstein Lane
Princeton, NJ 8540, USA

Witten, Jason (Athlete, Football Player)
501 King Ranch Rd
Southlake, TX 76092-2029, USA

Witter, Karen (Actor, Model)
247 S Beverly Dr # 102
Beverly Hills, CA 90212-3830, USA

Wittman, Randy (Athlete, Basketball Player, Coach)
8646 French Curv
Eden Prairie, MN 55347-5359, USA

Wittrock, Finn (Actor)
c/o Jim Weissenbach *Weissenbach Management*
5951 Airdrome St
Los Angeles, CA 90035-4635, USA

Wittum, Tom (Athlete, Football Player)
6704 Johnsburg Rd
Spring Grove, IL 60081-9364, USA

Witucki, Casimir (Athlete, Football Player)
3909 Spring Ter
Temple Hills, MD 20748-3439, USA

Witwer, Sam (Actor)
c/o Gordon Gilbertson *Gilbertson Management*
1334 3rd Street Promenade Ste 201
Santa Monica, CA 90401-1320, USA

Wizbicki, Alex (Athlete, Football Player)
10B Hayes Ct
Superior, WI 54880-2939, USA

Wobst, Frank (Financier)
Huntington Center 41 South High St
Columbus, OH 43287-0001, USA

Wockenfuss, Anett (Model)
Private Bag 38
Darlinghurst NSW 2010, AUSTRALIA

Wockenfuss, John (Athlete, Baseball Player)
26 Wallamsey Ln
Chesapeake City, MD 21915-1821, USA

Wocket-Eckert, Barbel (Athlete)
Im Bangert 61
Lutzelbach 64750, GERMANY

Woerner, Scott (Athlete, Football Player)
11268 Turner Rd
Hampton, GA 30228-1534, USA

Woese, Carl R (Biologist)
806 W Delaware Ave
Urbana, IL 61801-4809, USA

Woessner, Mark M (Business Person, Publisher)
Erich-Kastner-Str 25
Gutersloh 33332, GERMANY

Wofford, Harris L (Senator)
955 26th St NW Apt 501
Washington, DC 20037-2040, USA

Wogan, Gerald N (Misc)
Toxicology Div
Cambridge, MA 2139, USA

Woggon, Bill (Cartoonist)
2724 Cabot Ct
Thousand Oaks, CA 91360-1640, USA

Wohl, Dave (Athlete, Basketball Player, Coach)
297 Concord Ave
Oceanside, NY 11572-5417, USA

Wohlers, Mark E (Athlete, Baseball Player)
135 Old Cedar Ln
Alpharetta, GA 30004-3795, USA

Wohlford, Jim (Athlete, Baseball Player)
3700 W Mineral King Ave
Visalia, CA 93291-5531, USA

Wohlhuter, Richard C (Rick) (Athlete, Track Athlete)
175 Dickinson Dr
Wheaton, IL 60189-7473, USA

Wohlwender-Fricker, Marian (Baseball Player)
15210 Portside Dr Apt 401
Fort Myers, FL 33908-6827, USA

Woit, Dick (Misc)
2700 N Lehmann Ct
Chicago, IL 60614, USA

Woiwode, Larry (Writer)
English Dept
Binghamton, NY 13901, USA

Wojciechowski, John (Athlete, Football Player)
13317 Clyde Rd
Holly, MI 48442-9010, USA

Wojciechowski, Steve (Athlete, Baseball Player)
4646 Thornberry Hill Ct NE
Grand Rapids, MI 49525-9489, USA

Wojcik, John (Athlete, Baseball Player)
8303 Salford Way
Louisville, KY 40222-5529, USA

Wojna, Ed (Athlete, Baseball Player)
53 S Jeffery St
Beverly Hills, FL 34465-3637, USA

Wojtowicz, R P (Misc)
3 Research Pl
Rockville, MD 20850-3279, USA

Wolaner, Robin P (Publisher)
80 Willow Rd
Menlo Park, CA 94025-3661, USA

Wolcott, Bob (Athlete, Baseball Player)
3323 Bryson Way
Medford, OR 97504-5811, USA

Wolf, Brana (Stylist)
c/o Staff Member *Art + Commerce*
531 W 25th St # 4
New York, NY 10001-5593, USA

Wolf, Caryn (Stylist)
8651 N Burke Dr
Tucson, AZ 85742-9033, USA

Wolf, David A (Astronaut)
1714 Neptune Ln
Houston, TX 77062-6108, USA

Wolf, Dick (Producer, Writer)
c/o Staff Member *Wolf Films Inc (LA)*
100 Universal City Plz Bldg 2252
Universal City, CA 91608-1002, USA

Wolf, Jim (Athlete, Baseball Player)
1507 E Glenhaven Dr
Phoenix, AZ 85048-9446, USA

Wolf, Joe (Athlete, Football Player)
2324 Lehigh Pkwy N
Allentown, PA 18103-3748, USA

Wolf, Naomi (Writer)
1745 Broadway # B1
New York, NY 10019-4368, USA

Wolf, Randall C (Randy) (Athlete, Baseball Player)
1431 Wesleys Run
Gladwyne, PA 19035-1049, USA

Wolf, Scott (Actor)
c/o Sam Maydew *Collective*
8383 Wilshire Blvd Ste 1050
Beverly Hills, CA 90211-2415, USA

Wolf, Sigrid (Skier)
Elbigenalp 45 A
6652, AUSTRIA

Wolf, Stephanie (Stylist)
c/o Staff Member *Cloutier Agency*
2632 La Cienega Ave
Los Angeles, CA 90034-2641, USA

Wolf, Wally (Athlete, Baseball Player)
18580 Corte Fresco
Rancho Santa Fe, CA 92091-0227, USA

Wolfe, David (Writer)
C/O Angela Hartman 1259 N. Crescent Hts Blvd. Suite D
West Hollywood, CA 90046, USA

Wolfe, Ed (Athlete, Baseball Player)
5038 Gold River Ct
Riverbank, CA 95367-9447, USA

Wolfe, George C (Director)
425 Lafayette St
New York, NY 10003-7021, USA

Wolfe, Kenneth L (Business Person)
100 Crystal A Dr
Hershey, PA 17033-9524, USA

Wolfe, Larry (Athlete, Baseball Player)
4285 Rimini Way
El Dorado Hills, CA 95762-5466, USA

Wolfe, Michael (Producer)
c/o Rosanna Bilow *CAA Sports (LA)*
2000 Avenue of the Stars
Los Angeles, CA 90067-4700, USA

Wolfe, Ralph S (Biologist)
Microbiology Dept Burnill Hall
Urbana, IL 61801, USA

Wolfe, Sterling (Actor)
2609 W Wyoming Ave Ste A
Burbank, CA 91505-1950, USA

Wolfe, Thad A (General)
4790 Longwood Pt
Colorado Springs, CO 80906-8609, USA

Wolfe, Tom (Composer, Musician)
c/o Staff Member *Aperture Music*
PO Box 90010
Pasadena, CA 91109-5010, USA

Wolfe, Traci (Actor)
c/o Staff Member *Cunningham Escott Slevin & Doherty (CESD-LA)*
10635 Santa Monica Blvd Ste 130
Los Angeles, CA 90025-8306, USA

Wolfe Jr, Thomas K (Tom) (Writer)
21 E 79th St
New York, NY 10075-0125, USA

Wolfenden of Westcott, John F (Educator)
White House Guildford Road Westcott near Dorking
Surrey, UNITED KINGDOM (UK)

Wolfenstein, Lincoln (Physicist)
Physics Dept
Pittsburgh, PA 15213, USA

Wolfermann, Klaus (Athlete, Track Athlete)
Fasenenweg 13A
Herzogenaurach 91074, GERMANY

Wolff, Alex (Musician)
c/o Cindi Berger *PMK/BNC Public Relations (PMK-NY)*
622 3rd Ave Fl 8
New York, NY 10017-6707, USA

Wolff, Christian
Zinnkopfstr. 6
Aschau/Chiemsee, GERMANY D-83229

Wolff, Christoph J (Educator)
182 Washington St
Belmont, MA 02478-3560, USA

Wolff, Hugh (Conductor)
4 Addison Bridge Place
London W14 8XP, UNITED KINGDOM (UK)

Wolff, Jon A (Misc)
3506 Lake Mendota Dr
Madison, WI 53705-1473, USA

Wolff, Jonathan (Composer, Musician)
c/o Steve Winogradsky *Winogradsky Co, The*
12650 Riverside Dr Ste 200
Valley Village, CA 91607-3443, USA

Wolff, Nat (Musician)
c/o Yovia 1909 N 3rd Street
Jacksonville Beach, FL 32250, USA

Wolff, Sanford I (Misc)
8141 Broadway
New York, NY 10023, USA

Wolff, Toblas J A (Writer)
English Dept
Stanford, CA 94305, USA

Wolff, Torben (Biologist)
Hesseltoften
Hellerup 2900, DENMARK

Wolfley, Craig (Athlete, Football Player)
331 Station St
Bridgeville, PA 15017-1844, USA

Wolford, Will (Athlete, Football Player)
205 Waterleaf Way
Louisville, KY 40207-5720, USA

Wolfowitz, Paul D (Financier, Government Official)
1818 H St NW
Washington, DC 20433-0001, USA

Wolfson, Louis E (Business Person)
10205 Collins Ave
Bal Harbour, FL 33154-1403, USA

Wolk, Jimmy (Actor)
c/o Adena Chawke *Greenlight Management and Production*
13848 Valleyheart Dr
Sherman Oaks, CA 91423-2930, USA

Wolken, Jonathan (Artist, Dancer, Director)
PO Box 388
Washington Depot, CT 06794-0388, USA

Woll, Deborah Ann (Actor)
c/o Darryl Marshak *Marshak/Zachary Company, The*
8840 Wilshire Blvd Fl 1
Beverly Hills, CA 90211-2606, USA

Wollman, Harvey L (Ex-Governor)
40004 184th St
Frankfort, SD 57440-7311, USA

Wollman, Roger L (Judge)
400 S Phillips Ave
Sioux Falls, SD 57104-6848, USA

Wolman, Kira (Stylist)
348 N Avenue 59
Los Angeles, CA 90042-3408, USA

Wolman, M Gordon (Geophysicist, Physicist)
2104 W Rogers Ave
Baltimore, MD 21209-4553, USA

Wolov, Julia Lea (Actor, Writer)
c/o Jonathan Brandstein *Morra Brezner Steinberg & Tenenbaum (MBST) Entertainment*
345 N Maple Dr Ste 200
Beverly Hills, CA 90210-5174, USA

Wolpe, Lenny (Actor)
c/o Staff Member *Gage Group, The (LA)*
14724 Ventura Blvd Ste 505
Sherman Oaks, CA 91403-3505, USA

Wolpert, Julian (Geophysicist, Physicist)
322 W 72nd St
New York, NY 10023-2676, USA

Wolski, Bill (Athlete, Football Player)
14435 Freemanville Rd
Alpharetta, GA 30004-3176, USA

Wolski, Dariusz (Director)
4705 Laurel Canyon Blvd Ste 204
Valley Village, CA 91607-3998, USA

Wolszczan, Aleksander (Astronomer)
Astronomy Dept
University Park, PA 16802, USA

Wolter, Sherilyn (Actor)
128 Old Topanga Canyon Rd
Topanga, CA 90290-3807

Wolters, Kara (Basketball Player)
137 Westfield Dr
Holliston, MA 01746-1256, USA

Womack, Bobby (Actor, Musician)
c/o Jeremy Rosen *Selverne & Co.*
3450 Cahuenga Blvd W Apt 906
Los Angeles, CA 90068-1594, USA

Womack, Bruce L (Athlete, Football Player)
2834 Triway Ln
Houston, TX 77043-1809, USA

Womack, Dooley (Athlete, Baseball Player)
209 Weeping Cherry Ln
Columbia, SC 29212-8617, USA

Womack, Floyd (Athlete, Football Player)
c/o Eugene Parker *Maximum Sports Management*
6435 W Jefferson Blvd # 197
Fort Wayne, IN 46804-6203, USA

Womack, James E (Scientist)
2105 Farley
College Station, TX 77845-5601, USA

Womack, Lee Ann (Actor, Musician)
c/o Tiffany Shipp *Sunshine, Sachs & Associates*
149 5th Ave Fl 7
New York, NY 10010-6824, USA

Womack, Tony (Athlete, Baseball Player)
8301 Marcliffe Ct
Waxhaw, NC 28173-5500, USA

Woman, Nancy
PO Box 3601
Torrance, CA 90510-3601

Wombats, The (Music Group)
c/o Staff Member *Paradigm (Monterey)*
404 W Franklin St
Monterey, CA 93940-2303, USA

Womble, Royce (Athlete, Football Player)
6350 Newt Patterson Rd
Mansfield, TX 76063-6157, USA

Wonder, Stevie (Musician, Songwriter)
4616 W Magnolia Blvd
Burbank, CA 91505-2731, USA

Wong, Albert (Engineer)
26796 Vista Ter
Lake Forest, CA 92630-8113, USA

Wong, B D (Actor)
c/o Staff Member *Innovative Artists (LA)*
1505 10th St
Santa Monica, CA 90401-2805, USA

Wong, Kailee (Athlete, Football Player)
5410 Valerie St
Bellaire, TX 77401-4709, USA

Wong, Kim (Stylist)
4499 Via Marisol Apt 206 # A
Los Angeles, CA 90042-5126, USA

Wong, Russell (Actor)
8942 Wilshire Blvd # 219
Beverly Hills, CA 90211-1908, USA

Wong-Staal, Flossie (Biologist)
Molecular Biology
La Jolla, CA 92093-0001, USA

Wonsley, George (Athlete, Football Player)
6418 Amblewood Pl
Jackson, MS 39213-7803, USA

Woo, John (Director, Producer)
c/o Staff Member *Lion Rock Productions*
5100 W Goldleaf Cir Ste 230
Los Angeles, CA 90056-1272

Wood, Brenton (Musician)
PO Box 4127
Inglewood, CA 90309-4127, USA

Wood, C Norman (General)
5440 Mount Corcoran Pl
Burke, VA 22015-2147, USA

Wood, Carolyn (Swimmer)
4380 SW 86th Ave
Portland, OR 97225-2428, USA

Wood, Carri (Athlete, Golfer)
2001 Sabal Ridge Ct Apt H
Palm Beach Gardens, FL 33418-8922, USA

Wood, Charles G (Writer)
2-4 Noel St
London W1V 3RB, UNITED KINGDOM (UK)

Wood, Danny (Musician)
c/o Kristin Foster *PMK/BNC Public Relations (PMK-NY)*
622 3rd Ave Fl 8
New York, NY 10017-6707, USA

Wood, David (Athlete, Basketball Player)
5915 Crescent Moon Ct
Reno, NV 89511-4357, USA

Wood, Dennis (Stylist)
c/o Staff Member *Judy Inc*
1 Yorkville Ave
Toronto ON M4W 1L1, Canada

Wood, Dick (Athlete, Football Player)
41 Audubon Pl
Newnan, GA 30265-2003, USA

Wood, Duane (Athlete, Football Player)
407 W Caddo Ave
Wilburton, OK 74578-3431, USA

Wood, Elijah (Actor)
c/o Annick Muller *ID Public Relations (ID-NY)*
150 W 30th St Fl 19
New York, NY 10001-4003, USA

Wood, Evan Rachel (Actor)
c/o Hylda Queally *Creative Artists Agency (CAA-LA)*
2000 Avenue of the Stars Ste 100
Los Angeles, CA 90067-4705, USA

Wood, Gene
PO Box 805
Culver City, CA 90232-0805

Wood, Glen (Race Car Driver)
57 Rhody Creek Loop
Stuart, VA 24171-3011, USA

Wood, Gordon S (Historian)
77 Keene St
Providence, RI 02906-1507, USA

Wood, Jake (Athlete, Baseball Player)
9129 Daytona Dr
Pensacola, FL 32506-2904, USA

Wood, James (Business Person)
2 Paragon Dr
Montvale, NJ 07645-1718, USA

Wood, James N (Director)
111 S Michigan Ave
Chicago, IL 60603-6110, USA

Wood, Janet (Actor)
4727 Wilshire Blvd Ste 333
Los Angeles, CA 90010-3874, USA

Wood, Jason (Stylist)
c/o Staff Member *Arends, Frank Inc*
216 W 18th St # 703-B
New York, NY 10011, USA

Wood, Jason (Athlete, Baseball Player)
9899 N Cascade Dr
Fresno, CA 93730-0864, USA

Wood, John (Actor)
Stratford-on-Avon
Warwickshire CV37 6BB, UNITED KINGDOM (UK)

Wood, John A (Geophysicist, Physicist)
1716 Cambridge St Apt 16
Cambridge, MA 02138-4343, USA

Wood, Jon (Race Car Driver)
4400 Papa Joe Hendrick Blvd
Charlotte, NC 28262-5703, USA

Wood, Ken (Athlete, Baseball Player)
600 10th Ave S Unit A
North Myrtle Beach, SC 29582-3597, USA

Wood, Kerry (Athlete, Baseball Player)
6 Olive St
Ladera Ranch, CA 92694-0885, USA

Wood, Kimba M (Judge)
40 Foley Sq
New York, NY 10007-1502, USA

Wood, Lana (Actor)
1131 Oriole Cir
Fillmore, CA 93015-1601, USA

Wood, Leon (Athlete, Basketball Player)
4217 Faculty Ave
Long Beach, CA 90808-1601, USA

Wood, Maurice (Doctor)
RR 2 Box 543B
Hot Springs, VA 24445, USA

Wood, Mike (Athlete, Football Player)
630 N Geyer Rd
Saint Louis, MO 63122-2756, USA

Wood, Mike (Athlete, Baseball Player)
1199 Cherlynn Ter
West Palm Beach, FL 33406-5272, USA

Wood, Rachel Hurd (Actor)
c/o Michael Lazo *Untitled Entertainment (LA)*
350 S Beverly Dr Ste 200
Beverly Hills, CA 90212-4819, USA

Wood, Richard (Athlete, Football Player)
5413 Windbrush Dr
Tampa, FL 33625-4051, USA

Wood, Robert (Athlete, Basketball Player)
12930 Echo Dr
Rockton, IL 61072-2816, USA

Wood, Robert E (Publisher)
435 N Michigan Ave # 1609
Chicago, IL 60611-4066, USA

Wood, Robert J (Astronaut)
PO Box 516
Saint Louis, MO 63166-0516, USA

Wood, Ron
Sandy Mount House
County Kildare S., IRELAND

Wood, Ronald (Ron) (Musician)
Butler House 177-178 Tottenham Court Road
London W1T 7NY, United Kingdom

Wood, Sharon (Misc)
PO Box 1482
Canmore, AB T0L 0M0, CANADA

Wood, Sidney B B (Athlete, Tennis Player)
170 Chilean Ave Apt 5C
Palm Beach, FL 33480-6741, USA

Wood, Stuart (Woody) (Musician)
27 Preston Grange Road Preston Pans E Lothlan, SCOTLAND

Wood, Ted (Athlete, Baseball Player)
1810 Beckley Pl NW
Kennesaw, GA 30152-4265, USA

Wood, Thomas (Stylist)
c/o Staff Member *Blink Management*
421 Washington Ave Ste 202
Miami Beach, FL 33139-6612, USA

Wood, Tom
6310 San Vicente Blvd Ste 520
Los Angeles, CA 90048-5421

Wood, Wilbur F (Athlete, Baseball Player)
3 Elmbrook Rd
Bedford, MA 01730-1810, USA

Wood, William V (Athlete, Football Player)
7941 16th St NW
Washington, DC 20012-1230, USA

Wood, William V (Willie) (Athlete, Football Player)
7941 16th St NW
Washington, DC 20012-1230, USA

Wood, Willie (Athlete, Golfer)
6309 Oak Tree Dr
Edmond, OK 73025-2678, USA

Wood Brothers, The (Music Group)
c/o Staff Member *Paradigm (Monterey)*
404 W Franklin St
Monterey, CA 93940-2303, USA

Wood III, William B (Biologist)
Molecular Biology
Boulder, CO 80309-0001, USA

Wood Jr, Harlington (Judge)
600 E Monroe St
Springfield, IL 62701-1626, USA

Woodall, Al (Athlete, Football Player)
131 Field Crest Rd
New Canaan, CT 06840-6331, USA

Woodall, Brad (Athlete, Baseball Player)
3539 John Muir Dr
Middleton, WI 53562-5144, USA

Woodall, Jerry M (Engineer, Inventor)
Microelectronic Materials Ctr 105 Wall
New Haven, CT 6511, USA

Woodard, Alfre (Actor)
c/o Steve Dontanville *Dontanville/ Frattaroli (D/F)*
8609 Washington Blvd # 8607
Culver City, CA 90232-7441, USA

Woodard, Bob (Writer)
2907 Q St NW
Washington, DC 20007-3010, USA

Woodard, Charlayne (Actor, Writer)
c/o Alan Harris *Alan M Harris Management*
3278 Wilshire Blvd Apt 901
Los Angeles, CA 90010-1425, USA

Woodard, Darrell (Athlete, Baseball Player)
1227 E 69th St
Los Angeles, CA 90001-1657, USA

Woodard, Lynette (Athlete, Basketball Player)
4206 Quail Pointe Ter
Lawrence, KS 66047-1902, USA

Woodard, Mike (Athlete, Baseball Player)
PO Box 35
Maywood, IL 60153-0035, USA

Woodard, Ray (Athlete, Football Player)
1917 FM 352
Corrigan, TX 75939-6822, USA

Woodard, Rickey (Musician)
3800 Barham Blvd Ste 409
Los Angeles, CA 90068-1042, USA

Woodard, Steven L (Steve) (Athlete, Baseball Player)
800 Frost Ct SW
Hartselle, AL 35640-2714, USA

Woodbine, Bokeem (Actor)
c/o Johnny Gallo *Artist Representation Group*
9701 Wilshire Blvd Fl 10
Beverly Hills, CA 90212-2010, USA

Woodbridge, Todd (Tennis Player)
PO Box 3297
North Burnley, VIC 3121, AUSTRALIA

Woodburn, Danny (Actor)
c/o Marni Anhalt *Imperium 7 Talent Agency*
5455 Wilshire Blvd Ste 1706
Los Angeles, CA 90036-4217, USA

Woodcock, Leonard
2404 Vinewood Blvd
Ann Arbor, MI 48104-2768

Woodcock, Leonard (Actor)
140 Matthew Dr
Hendersonville, NC 28739-9325, USA

Wooden, Shawn (Athlete, Football Player)
17741 SW 12th St
Pembroke Pines, FL 33029-4811, USA

Woodeshick, Hal (Athlete, Baseball Player)
803 Wycliffe Dr
Houston, TX 77079-3511, USA

Woodeshivk, Tom (Athlete, Football Player)
PO Box 716
Blakeslee, PA 18610-0716, USA

Woodforde, Mark (Athlete, Tennis Player)
c/o Staff Member *Octagon (VA)*
7100 Forest Ave Ste 201
Richmond, VA 23226-3742, USA

Woodhead, Cynthia (Swimmer)
PO Box 1193
Riverside, CA 92502-1193, USA

Wooding, Michelle (Athlete, Golfer)
3825 E Camelback Rd Unit 148
Phoenix, AZ 85018-2645, USA

Woodland, Lauren
c/o Jerry Shandrew *Shandrew Public Relations*
1050 S Stanley Ave
Los Angeles, CA 90019-6634, USA

Woodlawn, Holly
PO Box 27766
Los Angeles, CA 90027-0766

Woodley, Shailene (Actor)
c/o Nils Larsen *Elements Entertainment*
312 W 5th St Apt 815
Los Angeles, CA 90013-1750, USA

Woodlief, Doug (Athlete, Football Player)
7928 Wilkinson Ave
N Hollywood, CA 91605-2209, USA

Woodmansee Jr, John W (General)
23 Cattail Pond Dr
Frisco, TX 75034-8584, USA

Woodring, Jim (Artist)
c/o Staff Member *Fantagraphics Books*
7563 Lake City Way NE
Seattle, WA 98115-4218, USA

Woodring, Wendell P (Misc)
6647 El Colegio Rd
Goleta, CA 93117-4203, USA

Woodruff, Billie (Actor)
c/o Joe Gatta *Gersh (NY)*
41 Madison Ave
New York, NY 10010-2202, USA

Woodruff, Blake (Actor)
c/o Justine Hunt *Hines and Hunt Entertainment*
1213 W Magnolia Blvd
Burbank, CA 91506-1829, USA

Woodruff, Bob (Journalist)
c/o Staff Member *ABC News*
77 W 66th St Fl 3
New York, NY 10023-6201, USA

Woodruff, Dwayne (Athlete, Football Player)
10382 Grubbs Rd
Wexford, PA 15090-9420, USA

Woodruff, Frank
170 N Crescent Dr
Beverly Hills, CA 90210-5423

Woodruff, Judy C (Correspondent, Television Host)
820 1st St NE
Washington, DC 20002-4243, USA

Woods, Al (Athlete, Baseball Player)
2600 San Leandro Blvd Apt 1004
San Leandro, CA 94578-5032, USA

Woods, Aubrey (Actor)
21 Golden Square
London W1R 3PA, UNITED KINGDOM (UK)

Woods, Barbara Alyn (Actor)
2930 Falaise Ave SW # H1
Calgary, AL T3E 7J2, CANADA

Woods, Chris (Athlete, Football Player)
202 Stone Ridge Trl
Irondale, AL 35210-1730, USA

Woods, Christine (Actor)
c/o Elizabeth Morris *Rogers & Cowan PR (LA)*
Pacific Design Center 8687 Melrose Ave, 7th Floor
West Hollywood, CA 90069, USA

Woods, Dan (Actor)
89 Bloor St W Fl 3
Toronto, ON M5S 1M1, CANADA

Woods, Don (Athlete, Football Player)
10415 Johncock Ave SW
Albuquerque, NM 87121-9414, USA

Woods, Elbert (Ickey) (Athlete, Football Player)
505 E Sharon Rd # A
Cincinnati, OH 45246-4726, USA

Woods, Gary (Athlete, Baseball Player)
PO Box 151
Solvang, CA 93464-0151, USA

Woods, George (Athlete, Track Athlete)
7631 Green Hedge Rd
Edwardsville, IL 62025-6135, USA

Woods, James (Actor)
c/o Chris Andrews *Creative Artists Agency (CAA-LA)*
2000 Avenue of the Stars Ste 100
Los Angeles, CA 90067-4705, USA

Woods, James A (Actor)
c/o Justin Evans *The Independent Group*
6363 Wilshire Blvd Ste 115
Los Angeles, CA 90048-5734, USA

Woods, Jerome (Athlete, Football Player)
1 Arrowhead Dr
Kansas City, MO 64129-1651, USA

Woods, Jerry L (Athlete, Football Player)
8976 Stratford Ct
Minneapolis, MN 55443-2976, USA

Woods, Jim (Athlete, Baseball Player)
4509 Gardenia Ave
Keyes, CA 95328-9701, USA

Woods, Michael (Actor)
c/o Staff Member *GVA Talent Agency Inc*
8981 W Sunset Blvd Ste 101
Los Angeles, CA 90069-1850, USA

Woods, Paul (Athlete, Hockey Player)
4276 S Shore St
Waterford, MI 48328-1157, USA

Woods, Philip (Composer, Musician)
PO Box 278
Delaware Water Gap, PA 18327-0278, USA

Woods, Pierre (Athlete, Football Player)
c/o Staff Member *New England Patriots*
Gillette Stadium One Patriots Pl
Foxboro, MA 02035-1388, USA

Woods, Qyntel (Basketball Player)
Rose Garden 1 Center Court St
Portland, OR 97227, USA

Woods, Rick (Athlete, Football Player)
713 Baldwin St
Meadville, PA 16335-1959, USA

Woods, Robert E (Athlete, Football Player)
4922 Devonshire Ave
Memphis, TN 38117-4208, USA

Woods, Robert S (Actor)
PO Box 492
Kinderhook, NY 12106-0492, USA

Woods, Ron (Athlete, Baseball Player)
5209 Desert Star Dr
Las Vegas, NV 89130-0159, USA

Woods, Simon (Actor)
c/o Staff Member *International Creative Management (ICM-LA)*
10250 Constellation Blvd Fl 7
Los Angeles, CA 90067-6207, USA

Woods, Stuart (Writer)
10 E 53rd St
New York, NY 10022-5244, USA

Woods, Tiger (Athlete, Golfer)
1 Tiger Woods Way
Anaheim, CA 92801-5039, USA

Woods, Victoria (Musician)
c/o John Elias *Three Twins Entertainment, Inc*
PO Box 100210
Staten Island, NY 10310-0210, USA

Woodside, DB (Actor)
10100 Santa Monica Blvd Ste 2500
Los Angeles, CA 90067-4116, USA

Woodside, Keith (Football Player)
1903 Laura Anne Dr
Houston, TX 77049-3832, USA

Woodson, Abraham B (Abe) (Football Player)
3680 Waynesvill St
Las Vegas, NV 89122-4111, USA

Woodson, Alli (Musician)
PO Box 371371
Las Vegas, NV 89137-1371, USA

Woodson, Charles (Football Player)
9080 Great Heron Cir
Orlando, FL 32836-5483, USA

Woodson, Darren R (Athlete, Football Player)
2215 Cedar Springs Rd Apt 902
Dallas, TX 75201-1835, USA

Woodson, Dick (Athlete, Baseball Player)
27879 Panorama Hills Dr
Menifee, CA 92584-7401, USA

Woodson, Herbert H (Engineer)
1034 Liberty Park Dr
Austin, TX 78746-6891, USA

Woodson, Kerry (Athlete, Baseball Player)
19392 La Serena Dr
Fort Myers, FL 33967-0525, USA

Woodson, Michael (Mike) (Athlete, Basketball Player)
19918 Parsons Green Ct
Katy, TX 77450-5214, USA

Woodson, Robert L (Activist)
1424 16th St NW
Washington, DC 20036-2211, USA

Woodson, Rod (Athlete, Football Player)
c/o Eugene Parker *Maximum Sports Management*
6435 W Jefferson Blvd # 197
Fort Wayne, IN 46804-6203, USA

Woodson, Sean (Football Player)
753 Glencross Dr
Jackson, MS 39206-2557, USA

Woodson, Tracy (Athlete, Baseball Player)
1559 Byfield Pkwy
Valparaiso, IN 46385-9115, USA

Woodson, Warren V (Coach, Football Coach)
12680 Hillcrest Rd Apt 1106
Dallas, TX 75230-2019, USA

Woodville, Kate (Actor)
20141 S Sweetbriar Rd
West Linn, OR 97068-9337, USA

Woodward, Bob (Writer)
c/o Staff Member *Simon & Schuster*
1230 Avenue of the Americas Fl CONC1
New York, NY 10020-1586, USA

Woodward, Chris (Athlete, Baseball Player)
15049 Howellhurst Dr
Baldwin Park, CA 91706-5625, USA

Woodward, Jim (Athlete, Golfer)
1413 Oak Springs Ln
Edmond, OK 73034-2321, USA

Woodward, Joanne (Actor)
c/o Toni Howard *International Creative Management (ICM-LA)*
10250 Constellation Blvd Fl 7
Los Angeles, CA 90067-6207, USA

Woodward, Kirsten (Designer, Fashion Designer)
26 Portobello Green Arcade
London W10, UNITED KINGDOM (UK)

Woodward, Louise
Elton, ENGLAND

Woodward, Morgan (Actor)
2111 Rockledge Rd
Los Angeles, CA 90068-3135, USA

Woodward, Peter (Actor)
c/o Vincent Cirrincione *Vincent Cirrincione Associates*
1516 N Fairfax Ave
Los Angeles, CA 90046-2608, USA

Woodward, Rob (Athlete, Baseball Player)
58 Eastman Hill Rd
Lebanon, NH 03766-2103, USA

Woodward, Robert D (Bob) (Journalist)
2907 Q St NW
Washington, DC 20007-3010, USA

Woodward, Roger R (Composer, Conductor, Musician)
2/37 Hendy Ave
Coogee, NSW 2034, AUSTRALIA

Woodward, Woody (Athlete, Baseball Player)
10 San Marco Ct
Palm Coast, FL 32137-2104, USA

Woodward III, Neil W (Astronaut)
1935 Edgemont Pl W
Seattle, WA 98199-3914, USA

Woodwell, George M (Scientist)
13 Church St
Woods Hole, MA 02543-1007, USA

Woody, Damien (Football Player)
12170 Ashland Heights Rd
Ashland, VA 23005-7634, USA

Woody, Paul (Misc)
1921 Broadway
Nashville, TN 37203-2719, USA

Woogon, Bill (Cartoonist)
2724 Cabot Ct
Thousand Oaks, CA 91360-1640, USA

Wool, Christopher (Artist)
531 W 24th St
New York, NY 10011-1104, USA

Wooldridge, Dean E (Business Person)
355 S Grand Ave Ste 2600
Los Angeles, CA 90071-1505, USA

Wooldridge, Floyd (Athlete, Baseball Player)
214 Barber St
Greenfield, MO 65661-1110, USA

Woolery, Chuck (Actor, Television Host)
26135 Plymouth Rd
Redford, MI 48239-2173, USA

Woolfolk, Andre (Football Player)
460 Great Circle Rd
Nashville, TN 37228-1404, USA

Woolfolk, Harold (Butch) (Football Player)
4519 Magnolia Ln
Sugar Land, TX 77478-5457, USA

Woolford, Donnell (Athlete, Football Player)
725 Lumber Ln
Charlotte, NC 28214-0043, USA

Woolford, Gary (Athlete, Football Player)
6321 S Four Peaks Pl
Chandler, AZ 85249-3946, USA

Woollard, Bob (Athlete, Basketball Player)
Route 1 Box 456
Hamptonville, NC 27020, USA

Woolley, Catherine (Writer)
PO Box 67
Orleans, MA 02653-0067, USA

Woolley, Jordan (Actor)
c/o Suzanne Bennett-Harrison *Diverse Talent Group*
9911 W Pico Blvd Ste 340W
Los Angeles, CA 90035-2712, USA

Woolley, Kenneth F (Architect)
790 George St Lv 5
Sydney, NSW 2000, AUSTRALIA

Woolley, Sheb
PO Box 2124
Hendersonville, TN 37077-2124

Woolridge, Orlando (Athlete, Basketball Player)
308 Johnson St
Tampa, FL 33646, USA

Woolridge, Susan
4 Windmill St
London, ENGLAND W1P 1HF

Woolsey, Elizabeth D (Skier)
Trail Creek Ranch
Wilson, WY 83014, USA

Woolsey, R James (Lawyer)
1800 Massachusetts Ave NW
Washington, DC 20036-1222, USA

Woolsey, Ralph A (Cinematographer)
23388 Mulholland Dr # 109
Woodland Hills, CA 91364-2733, USA

Woolsey, Roland (Football Player)
24100 N Can Ada Rd
Star, ID 83669-5026, USA

Woolstenhulme, Rick (Musician)
c/o Staff Member *Untitled Entertainment (LA)*
350 S Beverly Dr Ste 200
Beverly Hills, CA 90212-4819, USA

Woomble, Roddy (Musician)
370 City Road
London EC1V 2QA, UNITED KINGDOM (UK)

Woosnam, Ian H (Athlete, Golfer)
1360 E 9th St Ste 100
Cleveland, OH 44114-1730, USA

Woosnam, Phil (Athlete, Misc)
2211 Mainsail Dr
Marietta, GA 30062-1765, USA

Wooten, Jim (Correspondent)
5010 Creston St
Hyattsville, MD 20781-1216, USA

Wooten, John (Athlete, Football Player)
505 Boronia Rd
Arlington, TX 76002-4515, USA

Wooten, Morgan (Coach)
Athletic Dept
Hyattsville, MD 20781, USA

Wooten, Nicholas (Producer)
c/o Staff Member *WmE2 (Endeavor-LA)*
9601 Wilshire Blvd Fl 3
Beverly Hills, CA 90210-5219, USA

Wooten, Ron (Football Player)
2401 Lewis Grove Ln
Raleigh, NC 27608-1380, USA

Wooten, Shawn (Athlete, Baseball Player)
17535 49th Ave N
Minneapolis, MN 55446-1741, USA

Wooten, Victor (Musician)
c/o Danetta Albetta *Monarch Music Inc*
1839 Gerritsen Ave
Brooklyn, NY 11229-2611, USA

Wooton, John (Football Player)
13520 Darley Ave
Cleveland, OH 44110-2122, USA

Wootten, Morgan (Athlete, Basketball Player)
6912 Wells Pkwy
University Park, MD 20782-1051, USA

Wootton, Charles G (Diplomat)
555 Market St
San Francisco, CA 94105-2800, USA

Wopat, Tom (Actor, Musician)
c/o David Brokaw *Brokaw Company, The*
9255 W Sunset Blvd Ste 804
Los Angeles, CA 90069-3305, USA

Word, Barry (Athlete, Football Player)
5746 Janneys Mill Cir
Haymarket, VA 20169-6196, USA

Word, Roscoe (Football Player)
175 Richardson Rd
Ridgeland, MS 39157-9781, USA

Word, Weldon R (Engineer)
633 Private Road 7908
Hawkins, TX 75765, USA

Worden, Alfred M (Astronaut)
PO Box 8065
Vero Beach, FL 32963, USA

Worden, Neil (Football Player)
2 Indian Camp Trl
Portage, IN 46368-1001, USA

Working Title, The (Music Group)
c/o Staff Member *Paradigm (Monterey)*
404 W Franklin St
Monterey, CA 93940-2303, USA

Workman, Hank (Athlete, Baseball Player)
307 19th St
Santa Monica, CA 90402-2409, USA

Workman, Haywoode (Athlete, Basketball Player)
PO Box 47932
Tampa, FL 33646-0117, USA

Workman, Jacque (Stylist)
1753 Pinebrook Ct
Ashland, OH 44805-4804, USA

Workman, Tom (Athlete, Basketball Player)
422 NE Roth St
Portland, OR 97211-1084, USA

Workman, Vincent (Vince) (Athlete, Football Player)
1265 Brookwood Dr
Green Bay, WI 54304-4043, USA

World Party (Music Group)
c/o Staff Member *Paradigm (Monterey)*
404 W Franklin St
Monterey, CA 93940-2303, USA

World Wrestling Entertainment (WWE)
1241 E Main St
Stamford, CT 06902-3520

Worlds Apart
PO Box 21
London, ENGLAND W10 6BR

Worley, Darryl (Musician)
c/o Randy Lovelady *RLM / Mission Management*
1102 17th Ave S Ste 402
Nashville, TN 37212-2208, USA

Worley, Jo Anne (Actor)
c/o Staff Member *Amsel, Eisenstadt & Frazier Talent Agency (AEF)*
5055 Wilshire Blvd Ste 860
Los Angeles, CA 90036-6108, USA

Worley, Tim (Athlete, Football Player)
531 Sydnor Ave
Ridgecrest, CA 93555-3143, USA

Wormald, Kenny (Actor)
c/o Dallas Sonnier *Caliber Media Company*
9229 W Sunset Blvd Ste 705
West Hollywood, CA 90069-3407, USA

Worndl, Frank (Skier)
Burgsiedlung 19C
Sonthofen 87527, GERMANY

Woroniecka, Aleksandra (Stylist)
c/o Staff Member *Management + Artists + Organization*
330 W 38th St Ste 1401
New York, NY 10018-8438, USA

Woronov, Mary (Actor)
4350 1/4 Beverly Blvd
Los Angeles, CA 90004, USA

Worrell, Tim (Athlete, Baseball Player)
4719 W El Cortez Pl
Phoenix, AZ 85083-2206, USA

Worrell, Todd (Athlete, Baseball Player)
810 Simmons Ave
Saint Louis, MO 63122-2754, USA

Worsley, Lorne J (Gump) (Athlete, Hockey Player)
421 Bonaire Ave
Beloeil, QC H3G L1L, Canada

Worth, Jody (Actor, Producer)
c/o Jeffrey Jacobs *Creative Artists Agency (CAA-LA)*
2000 Avenue of the Stars Ste 100
Los Angeles, CA 90067-4705, USA

Wortham, Barron (Athlete, Football Player)
8608 Busch Gardens Dr
Fort Worth, TX 76123-1445, USA

Wortham, Rich (Athlete, Baseball Player)
1708 Mira Vis
Leander, TX 78641-8821, USA

Worthen, John E (Educator)
President S Ofc
Muncie, IN 47306-0001, USA

Worthen, Sam (Athlete, Basketball Player)
PO Box 7267
North Bergen, NJ 07047-0967, USA

Worthington, Al (Athlete, Baseball Player)
12070 Highway 55
Sterrett, AL 35147-9601, USA

Worthington, Cal
3815 Florin Rd
Sacramento, CA 95823-1801

Worthington, Craig (Athlete, Baseball Player)
10019 Mattock Ave
Downey, CA 90240-3528, USA

Worthington, Melvin L (Religious Leader)
PO Box 5002
Antioch, TN 37011-5002, USA

Worthington, Sam (Actor)
c/o Sandra Chang *Industry Entertainment Partners*
955 Carrillo Dr Ste 300
Los Angeles, CA 90048-5400, USA

Worthy, James (Athlete, Basketball Player, Sportscaster)
5750 Corbett St
Los Angeles, CA 90016-4545, USA

Worthy, Rick (Richard) (Actor)
c/o Charles Silver *Silver Massetti & Szatmary (SMS) Talent Inc*
8730 W Sunset Blvd Ste 440
Los Angeles, CA 90069-2277, USA

Wortman, Keith (Football Player)
240 Big Sky Dr
Saint Charles, MO 63304-7170, USA

Wottie, David J (Dave) (Athlete, Track Athlete)
9245 Forest Hill Ln
Germantown, TN 38139-7906, USA

Wottle, Dave
9245 Forest Hill Ln
Germantown, TN 38139-7906

Wotus, Ron (Athlete, Baseball Player)
PO Box 2484
Martinez, CA 94553-7484, USA

Woudenberg, John (Football Player)
3116 S Roosevelt St
Tempe, AZ 85282-2008, USA

Wouk, Herman (Writer)
303 W Crestview Dr
Palm Springs, CA 92264-8920, USA

Wow, Bow (Actor, Musician)
c/o Sal Bonaventura *CEG Talent*
251 W 39th St Fl 7
New York, NY 10018-3171, USA

Woytowicz-Rudnicka, Stefania (Musician)
Al Przyiaciol 2 m
Warsaw 00-565, POLAND

Wozniacki, Caroline (Athlete, Tennis Player)
c/o Staff Member *Women's Tennis Association (WTA (US))*
1 Progress Plz Ste 1500
St Petersburg, FL 33701-4335, USA

Wozniak, Steve (Designer, Inventor)
c/o Staff Member *Beverly Hecht Agency*
3500 W Olive Ave Ste 1180
Burbank, CA 91505-4651, USA

Wragg, John (Artist)
6 Castle Lane Devizes
Wilts, SN10 1HJ, UNITED KINGDOM (UK)

Wrangler, Jack
7 Ambrose Ln
Northport, NY 11768-3203

Wray, Gordon R (Designer, Engineer)
Stonestack Rempstone Loughborough
Leics LE12 6RH, UNITED KINGDOM (UK)

Wregget, Ken (Athlete, Hockey Player)
120 Devon Rd
Bloomfield Hills, MI 48302-1123, USA

Wren, Claire
5757 Wilshire Blvd Ste 473
Los Angeles, CA 90036-3632

Wren, Darryl (Football Player)
1418 Skipjack Dr
Fort Washington, MD 20744-4216, USA

Wrenn, Robert (Bob) (Athlete, Golfer)
8908 Watlington Rd
Henrico, VA 23229-7141, USA

Wressell, Christina (Stylist)
c/o Staff Member *Faucher Artists*
636 Broadway Rm 1218
New York, NY 10012-2624, USA

Wright, Alexander (Athlete, Football Player)
501 S Mississippi St
Amarillo, TX 79106-8735, USA

Wright, Ben (Sportscaster)
51 W 52nd St
New York, NY 10019-6119, USA

Wright, Betty (Musician)
1048 Tattnall St
Macon, GA 31201-1537, USA

Wright, Bonnie (Actor)
c/o Ruth Young *United Agents*
12-26 Lexington St
London W1F OLE, UK

Wright, Bracey (Basketball Player)
c/o Staff Member *Minnesota Timberwolves*
600 1st Ave N
Minneapolis, MN 55403-1400, USA

Wright, Brad (Athlete, Basketball Player)
1050 S Cloverdale Ave
Los Angeles, CA 90019-6732, USA

Wright, Bruce A (General)
Vice Commander Air Combat Command
Langley Air Force Base, VA 23665, USA

Wright, Charles (Football Player)
2698 Wakefield Ln
Westlake, OH 44145-3837, USA

Wright, Chase (Athlete, Baseball Player)
1323 Westridge Ln
Iowa Park, TX 76367-1142, USA

Wright, Chely (Musician)
c/o Staff Member *Russell Carter Artist Management*
567 Ralph McGill Blvd NE
Atlanta, GA 30312-1110, USA

Wright, Clyde (Athlete, Baseball Player)
528 S Jeanine St
Anaheim, CA 92806-4415, USA

Wright, Craig M (Architect)
722 N La Cienega Blvd
West Hollywood, CA 90069-5204, USA

Wright, Dan (Athlete, Baseball Player)
310 Vernon Dr
Batesville, AR 72501-4112, USA

Wright, David (Athlete, Baseball Player)
1105 Hillston Ct
Chesapeake, VA 23322-9534, USA

Wright, Dick (Cartoonist)
34 S 3rd St
Columbus, OH 43215-4201, USA

Wright, Donald C (Don) (Cartoonist)
PO Box 1176
Palm Beach, FL 33480-1176, USA

Wright, Dorell (Athlete, Basketball Player)
158 Twin Peaks Dr
Walnut Creek, CA 94595-1728, USA

Wright, Doug (Writer)
c/o Staff Member *International Creative Management (ICM-NY)*
40 W 57th St
New York, NY 10019-4001, USA

Wright, Elmo (Football Player)
11419 Olympia Dr
Houston, TX 77077-6419, USA

Wright, Eric (Athlete, Football Player)
c/o Tony Fleming *Impact Sports - LA*
11331 Ventura Blvd Ste 1A
Studio City, CA 91604-3147, USA

Wright, Evan (Writer)
c/o Susan Solomon *Principato/Young Management*
9465 Wilshire Blvd Ste 430
Beverly Hills, CA 90212-2613, USA

Wright, Felix (Football Player)
2698 Wakefield Ln
Westlake, OH 44145-3837, USA

Wright, Felix E (Business Person)
1 Leggett Rd
Carthage, MO 64836-9649, USA

Wright, Geoffrey (Actor)
1505 10th St
Santa Monica, CA 90401-2805, USA

Wright, George (Athlete, Baseball Player)
4228 NE 18th St
Oklahoma City, OK 73121-7210, USA

Wright, George (Football Player)
10627 Seaford Dr
Houston, TX 77089-1425, USA

Wright, Gerald (Director)
725 Vineland Pl
Minneapolis, MN 55403-1139, USA

Wright, Heather
1 Sunnyside Wimbledon
London, ENGLAND SW19

Wright, Howard (Athlete, Basketball Player)
3019 Kingswood Way
Louisville, KY 40216-4914, USA

Wright, Hugh (Musician)
2100 W End Ave Ste 1000
Nashville, TN 37203-5240, USA

Wright, Ian (Television Host)
c/o Staff Member *Arena Entertainment Consultants*
Regent's Court 39 Harrogate Rd
Leeds LS7 3PD, UK

Wright, Irving S (Doctor)
25 E End Ave
New York, NY 10028-7052, USA

Wright, J Oliver (Diplomat)
Burstow Hall Hortey
Surrey H6 9SR, USA

Wright, James E (Historian)
7 Quail Dr
Etna, NH 03750-4404, USA

Wright, Jamey (Athlete, Baseball Player)
4325 Fairfax Ave
Dallas, TX 75205-3026, USA

Wright, Jaret (Athlete, Baseball Player)
1423 Santiago Dr
Newport Beach, CA 92660-4947, USA

Wright, Jay (Writer)
Piermont, NH 3779, USA

Wright, Jeff (Football Player)
420 W Bluejay Dr
Chandler, AZ 85286-3907, USA

Wright, Jeff (Athlete, Football Player)
23426 N 21st Pl
Phoenix, AZ 85024-8631, USA

Wright, Jeffrey (Actor)
c/o Jimmy Darmody *Creative Artists Agency (CAA-LA)*
2000 Avenue of the Stars Ste 100
Los Angeles, CA 90067-4705, USA

Wright, Jim (Athlete, Baseball Player)
513 W Wyndermere Ct
Peoria, IL 61614-2919, USA

Wright, Jim (Athlete, Baseball Player)
549 E Randall St
Coopersville, MI 49404-9649, USA

Wright, Joby (Athlete, Basketball Player)
P.O. Box 3434 Athletic Dept
Laramie, WY 82071, USA

Wright, John (Football Player)
1673 County Road 2500 E
Saint Joseph, IL 61873-9704, USA

Wright, Johnny (Producer)
7680 Universal Blvd Ste 500
Orlando, FL 32819-8998, USA

Wright, Judith A (Writer)
17 Devonport St # 1
Lyons, ACT 2060, AUSTRALIA

Wright, Keith (Athlete, Football Player)
1525 Rs County Road 3400
Emory, TX 75440-4095, USA

Wright, Ken (Athlete, Baseball Player)
1651 Ora Dr
Pensacola, FL 32506-8250, USA

Wright, Lawrence A (Judge)
400 2nd St NW
Washington, DC 20217-0001, USA

Wright, Louie (Football Player)
2263 S Quentin Way # 301
Aurora, CO 80014-7316, USA

Wright, Louis B (Historian)
3702 Leland St
Chevy Chase, MD 20815-4904, USA

Wright, Louis D (Football Player)
3140 S Peoria St # K274
Aurora, CO 80014-3178, USA

Wright, Margaret H (Mathematician)
600 Mountain Ave
New Providence, NJ 07974-2008, USA

Wright, Max (Actor)
11500 W Olympic Blvd Ste 510
Los Angeles, CA 90064-1527, USA

Wright, Michael (Actor)
c/o Steven Arcieri *Arcieri & Associates Inc*
305 Madison Ave Ste 2315
New York, NY 10165-5015, USA

Wright, Michael W (Business Person)
11840 Valley View Rd
Eden Prairie, MN 55344-3643, USA

Wright, Michelle (Musician)
205 Powell Pl # 214
Brentwood, TN 37027-7522, USA

Wright, Mickey
2972 SE Treasure Island Rd
Port St Lucie, FL 34952-5773

Wright, Mickey (Athlete, Golfer)
2972 SE Treasure Island Rd
Port Saint Lucie, FL 34952-5773, USA

Wright, Mike (Athlete, Football Player)
c/o Staff Member *New England Patriots*
Gillette Stadium One Patriots Pl
Foxboro, MA 02035-1388, USA

Wright, Nathaniel (Nate) (Football Player)
11247 Zorita Ct
San Diego, CA 92124-2207, USA

Wright, N'Bushe
1505 10th St
Santa Monica, CA 90401-2805

Wright, Pamela (Athlete, Golfer)
11333 N 92nd St Unit 2006
Scottsdale, AZ 85260-6154, USA

Wright, Pat (Musician)
PO Box 371371
Las Vegas, NV 89137-1371, USA

Wright, Peter R (Choreographer, Dancer)
10 Chiswick Wharf
London W4 2SR, UNITED KINGDOM (UK)

Wright, Petra (Actor)
c/o Bob Glennon *One Talent Management*
9220 W Sunset Blvd Ste 306
Los Angeles, CA 90069-3503, USA

Wright, Randy (Football Player)
2890 Commerce Park Dr
Fitchburg, WI 53719-5129, USA

Wright, Raymond R (War Hero)
10 Holt Cir
Fletcher, NC 28732-8427, USA

Wright, Rick (Musician)
370 City Road
London EC1V 2QA, UNITED KINGDOM (UK)

Wright, Ricky (Athlete, Baseball Player)
2502 Clark Ln
Paris, TX 75460-6220, USA

Wright, Robin (Actor, Producer)
c/o Michael Sugar *Anonymous Content (AC-LA)*
3531 Hayden Ave
Culver City, CA 90232, USA

Wright, Ron (Athlete, Baseball Player)
310 S 2100 E
Saint George, UT 84790-1465, USA

Wright, Ronald (Winkie) (Boxer)
c/o James Prince *Prince Boxing Enterprises*
3030 Jensen Dr
Houston, TX 77026-5511, USA

Wright, Roy (Athlete, Baseball Player)
331 Pinehurst Cir
Chickamauga, GA 30707-1459, USA

Wright, Samuel E (Actor)
c/o Marvin Josephson *Marvin A Josephson Management*
225 E 36th St Apt 10R
New York, NY 10016-3615, USA

Wright, Sarah (Actor)
c/o Ellen Meyer *Ellen Meyer Management*
8899 Beverly Blvd Ste 612
West Hollywood, CA 90048-2429, USA

Wright, Sharone (Athlete, Basketball Player)
6080 Lakeview Rd Apt 3504
Warner Robins, GA 31088-9157, USA

Wright, Stephen T (Athlete, Football Player)
14 Conifer Sq
Augusta, GA 30909-4505, USA

Wright, Steve (Athlete, Football Player)
15 Camel Point Dr
Laguna Beach, CA 92651-6988, USA

Wright, Steven (Actor, Comedian)
c/o Tim Sarkes *Brillstein Entertainment Partners*
9150 Wilshire Blvd Ste 350
Beverly Hills, CA 90212-3453, USA

Wright, Tom (Athlete, Baseball Player)
1116 Poplar Springs Church Rd
Shelby, NC 28152-8071, USA

Wright, Tom (Actor)
c/o Steven Siebert *Lighthouse Entertainment*
9220 W Sunset Blvd Ste 200
West Hollywood, CA 90069-3501, USA

Wright, Trevor (Actor)
c/o Tiffany Kuzon *Evolution Entertainment (LA)*
901 N Highland Ave
Los Angeles, CA 90038-2412, USA

Wright, Van Earl (Actor)
c/o Jill Smoller *WmE2 (Endeavor-LA)*
9601 Wilshire Blvd Fl 3
Beverly Hills, CA 90210-5219, USA

Wright, Weldon (Athlete, Football Player)
1700 Holly Spring Ct
Arlington, TX 76018-4925, USA

Wright, Willie (Athlete, Football Player)
13456 Dry Gulch Rd
Paonia, CO 81428-7119, USA

Wright Jr, Charles P (Writer)
940 Locust Ave
Charlottesville, VA 22901-4030, USA

Wright Jr, Cobina (Actor)
1326 Dove Meadow Rd
Solvang, CA 93463-9621, USA

Wright Jr, John M (General)
5195 Cottingham Pl
Alexandria, VA 22304-3556, USA

Wrightman, Tim (Football Player)
3505 S Denison Ave
San Pedro, CA 90731-6803, USA

Wrightson, Bernard (Bernie) (Swimmer)
924 Birch Ave
Escondido, CA 92027-3903, USA

Wrigley, Edward A (Historian)
13 Sedley Taylor Rd
Cambridge CB2 2PW, UNITED KINGDOM (UK)

Wrigley Jr, William (Business Person)
410 N Michigan Ave
Chicago, IL 60611-4213, USA

Wrona, Rick (Athlete, Baseball Player)
2946 E 57th St
Tulsa, OK 74105-7404, USA

Wszola, Jacek (Athlete, Track Athlete)
Ul Chrzanowskiego 7 m 70
Warsaw 04-381, POLAND

Wu, Alice (Writer)
c/o Staff Member *Creative Artists Agency (CAA-LA)*
2000 Avenue of the Stars Ste 100
Los Angeles, CA 90067-4705, USA

Wu, Gordon Y S (Business Person)
Hopewell Center 183 Queen Road East
Hong Kong, CHINA

Wu, Kristy (Actor)
c/o Craig Dorfman *Frontline Management*
5670 Wilshire Blvd Ste 1370
Los Angeles, CA 90036-5679, USA

Wu, Lisa (Reality TV Star)
c/o Staff Member *Bravo (NY)*
30 Rockefeller Plz
New York, NY 10112-0015, USA

Wu, Madame Sylvia
1515 Capri Dr
Pacific Palisades, CA 90272-2709

Wu, Sau Lan (Physicist)
29 Oxford St
Cambridge, MA 02138-2933, USA

Wu, Tai Tsun (Physicist)
29 Oxford St
Cambridge, MA 02138-2933, USA

Wu, Vivian (Actor)
c/o Laura Myones 9100 Wilshire Blvd Ste 350W
Beverly Hills, CA 90212, USA

Wu Yigong (Director)
52 Yong Fu Road
Shanghai, CHINA

Wuertz, Michael (Athlete, Baseball Player)
701 19th St SW
Austin, MN 55912-1548, USA

Wuethrich, Kurt (Nobel Prize Laureate)
ETH Zentrum
Zurich 8092, SWITZERLAND

Wuhl, Robert (Actor)
c/o Jimmy Miller *Mosaic Media Group*
9200 W Sunset Blvd Ste 10
Los Angeles, CA 90069-3608, USA

Wuhrer, Kari (Actor)
PO Box 69188
Los Angeles, CA 90069-0188, USA

Wunderlich, Paul (Artist)
Haynstr 2
Hamburg 20949, GERMANY

Wunsch, Carl I (Oceanographer)
78 Washington Ave
Cambridge, MA 02140-2708, USA

Wunsch, Jerry (Football Player)
2601 Red Maple Rd
Wausau, WI 54401-9151, USA

Wunsch, Kelly (Athlete, Baseball Player)
11613 Hunters Green Trl
Austin, TX 78732-2055, USA

Wuorinen, Charles P (Composer)
870 W End Ave
New York, NY 10025-4918, USA

Wurtzel, Elizabeth (Actor, Writer)
c/o Staff Member *Artist Agency, THE (NY)*
230 W 55th St Apt 29D
New York, NY 10019-5206

Wurz, Alexander (Race Car Driver)
Albert Dr Woking
Surrey GU21 5JY, UNITED KINGDOM (UK)

Wu-Tang
1540 Broadway Ste 3500
New York, NY 10036-4039

Wuycik, Dennis (Athlete, Basketball Player)
31 Rogerson Dr
Chapel Hill, NC 27517-4037, USA

Wyant, Fred (Football Player)
516 Westwood Ave
Morgantown, WV 26505-2125, USA

Wyatt, Alvin (Football Player)
PO Box 244
Daytona Beach, FL 32115-0244, USA

Wyatt, Doug (Athlete, Football Player)
4055 Hogan Dr Apt 301
Tyler, TX 75709-6931, USA

Wyatt, Jennifer (Golfer)
2321 Devine St Ste A
Columbia, SC 29205-2428, USA

Wyatt, Keke (Musician)
145 W 57th St # 1500
New York, NY 10019-2220, USA

Wyatt, Leslie (Educator)
President's Office
State University, AR 72467, USA

Wyatt, Shannon (Actor)
8949 Falling Creek Ct
Annandale, VA 22003-4108, USA

Wyatt, Sharon (Actor)
16830 Ventura Blvd Ste 300
Encino, CA 91436-1715, USA

Wyatt, Summer (Beauty Pageant Winner)
6 Presidio Pl
Charleston, WV 25313-3442, USA

Wyatt Jr, Oscar S (Business Person)
6955 Union Park Ctr Ste 540
Midvale, UT 84047-6520, USA

Wyche, Samuel D (Sam) (Athlete, Coach, Football Coach, Football Player, Sportscaster)
PO Box 1570
Pickens, SC 29671-1570, USA

Wycheck, Frank (Football Player)
4674 Sunrise Ave
Bensalem, PA 19020-1112, USA

Wycinsky, Craig (Football Player)
6890 E Sunrise Dr Ste 120
Tucson, AZ 85750-0739, USA

Wycoff, Brooks (Athlete)
1 Mohegan Sun Blvd
Uncasville, CT 06382-1355

Wyeth, James Browning (Artist)
701 Smiths Bridge Rd
Wilmington, DE 19807-1325, USA

Wyeth, Jamie (Artist)
PO Box 445
Tenants Harbor, ME 04860-0445, USA

Wygal, Terry (Business Person)
3005 Woodland Hills Dr
Kingwood, TX 77339-1403, USA

Wylde, Chris
3313 1/2 Barham Blvd
Los Angeles, CA 90068-1450

Wylde, Zakk (Musician)
c/o Bob Ringe *Survival Management*
30765 Pacific Coast Hwy Ste 325
Malibu, CA 90265-3643, USA

Wylde Bunch, The (Music Group)
c/o Staff Member *Paradigm (Monterey)*
404 W Franklin St
Monterey, CA 93940-2303, USA

Wyle, Noah (Actor, Director, Producer)
c/o Daniel (Danny) Sussman *Brillstein Entertainment Partners*
9150 Wilshire Blvd Ste 350
Beverly Hills, CA 90212-3453, USA

Wylie, Adam
14011 Ventura Blvd Ste 202
Sherman Oaks, CA 91423-3594

Wyludda, Ilke (Athlete, Track Athlete)
Relchengainer Str 154
Chemnitz 9125, GERMANY

Wyman, Bill (Actor, Composer, Musician)
344 Kings Road
London SW3 5UR, United Kingdom

Wyman, David (Football Player)
2114 204th Pl NE
Sammamish, WA 98074-4390, USA

Wyman, Joel (Producer, Writer)
c/o Staff Member *Creative Artists Agency (CAA-LA)*
2000 Avenue of the Stars Ste 100
Los Angeles, CA 90067-4705, USA

Wymore, Patrice (Actor)
Port Antonio
JAMAICA BWI, WEST INDIES

Wynalda, Eric (Soccer Player)
2313 Stormcroft Ct
Westlake Village, CA 91361-2054, USA

Wynant, H M
300 S Raymond Ave Ste 11
Pasadena, CA 91105-2639, USA

Wyn-Davies, Geraint (Actor)
Oscars Abrams Zimel 438 Queen St E
Toronto, ON M5A 1T4, CANADA

Wynder, A J (Athlete, Basketball Player)
1 Cardenti Ct
Newark, DE 19702-6833, USA

Wynegar, Butch (Athlete, Baseball Player)
PO Box 915811
Longwood, FL 32791-5811, USA

Wyner, George (Actor)
3450 Laurie Pl
Studio City, CA 91604-3881, USA

Wyngaarden, James B (Doctor)
2101 Columbus Ave NW
Washington, DC 20418-0001, USA

Wynn, Bob (Athlete, Golfer)
78455 Calle Orense
La Quinta, CA 92253-2370, USA

Wynn, Jimmy (Athlete, Baseball Player)
5507 Sandy Field Ct
Rosharon, TX 77583-2040, USA

Wynn, Renaldo (Football Player)
19805 Rothschild Ct
Ashburn, VA 20147-4124, USA

Wynn, Spergon (Football Player)
614 32nd St
Galveston, TX 77550-1325, USA

Wynn, Stephen A (Business Person)
3800 Howard Hughes Pkwy
Las Vegas, NV 89169-0925, USA

Wynn, Steve (Business Person)
3800 Howard Hughes Pkwy
Las Vegas, NV 89169-0925

Wynn, Tracy Keenan
700 W Third St
Los Angeles, CA 90048

Wynne, Billy (Athlete, Baseball Player)
7722 Greenwich Ct W
Jacksonville, FL 32277-0924, USA

Wynne, Marvell (Athlete, Baseball Player)
39640 Del Val Dr
Murrieta, CA 92562-4038, USA

Wynter, Sarah (Actor)
c/o David (Dave) Fleming *Mosaic Media Group*
9200 W Sunset Blvd Ste 10
Los Angeles, CA 90069-3608, USA

Wyss, Amanda (Actor)
c/o Staff Member *Badgley-Connor-King*
9229 W Sunset Blvd Ste 311
Los Angeles, CA 90069-3403, USA

X

Xiaoshuang, Li
Rue Tiyukuan 9
Beijing, Peoples Republic of China

Xie Bingxin (Writer)
Residential Qtrs
Beijing 100081, CHINA

Xie Jin (Director)
595 Caoxi Beilu
Shanghai, CHINA

Xscape (Musician)
c/o Staff Member *So So Def Recordings Inc*
1350 Spring St NW Ste 750
Atlanta, GA 30309-2870, USA

Xu Bing (Artist)
540 Metropolitan Ave
Brooklyn, NY 11211-3554, USA

Xu Shuyang (Artist)
PO Box 169
Hangzhou, CHINA

Xue Wei (Musician)
134 Sheaveshill Ave
London NW9, UNITED KINGDOM (UK)

Xuereb, Emanuel (Actor)
c/o Staff Member *Pantheon Talent*
1801 Century Park E Ste 1910
Los Angeles, CA 90067-2321, USA

Xuereb, Salvator (Actor)
c/o Martin Berneman *Precision Entertainment*
6338 Wilshire Blvd
Los Angeles, CA 90048-5002, USA

Xzibit (Musician)
c/o John Boyle *Sanctuary Artist Management*
8750 Wilshire Blvd Ste 200
Beverly Hills, CA 90211-2707, USA

Y

Yabians, Frank (Producer)
88 Bull Path
East Hampton, NY 11937-4622, USA

Yablans, Frank
100 Bull Path
East Hampton, NY 11937-4601

Yablokov, Alexey V (Biologist)
Vaviloca Str 26
Moscow 117808, RUSSIA

Yabu, Keiichi (Athlete, Baseball Player)
c/o Team Member *San Francisco Giants*
SBC Park 24 Willie Mays Plaza
San Francisco, CA 94107, USA

Yaeger, Andrea (Tennis Player)
1490 S Ute Ave
Aspen, CO 81611-2814, USA

Yaffe, Martin (Physicist)
Biophysics Dept
Toronto, ON M4W 1J3, CANADA

Yager, Faye (Activist)
902 Curlew Ct NW
Atlanta, GA 30327, USA

Yager, Rick (Cartoonist)
235 E 45th St
New York, NY 10017-3305, USA

Yagher, Jeff
15057 Sherview Pl
Sherman Oaks, CA 91403-5037

Yago, Gideon (Journalist, Television Host)
c/o Staff Member *Music Television (MTV) Networks (NY)*
1515 Broadway
New York, NY 10036-8901, USA

Yaguda, Stan (Musician)
370 Harrison Ave
Harrison, NY 10528-2714, USA

Yagudin, Alexei (Figure Skater)
300 Alumini Rd
Newington, CT 6111, USA

Yahr, Betty (Athlete, Baseball Player)
10360 Timber Ridge Dr
Milan, MI 48160-8929, USA

Yakavonis, Ray (Athlete, Football Player)
8 Strand St
Hanover Township, PA 18706-4011, USA

Yake, Terry (Athlete, Hockey Player)
3 Stratford Park
Bloomfield, CT 06002-2143, USA

Yakovlev, Aleksandr N (Government Official)
Ul Iljinka 8/4
Moscow 103132, RUSSIA

Yale, Brian (Musician)
c/o Staff Member *Creative Artists Agency (CAA-LA)*
2000 Avenue of the Stars Ste 100
Los Angeles, CA 90067-4705, USA

Yallop, Frank (Coach)
3550 Stevens Creek Blvd Ste 200
San Jose, CA 95117-1031, USA

Yalow, Rosalyn S (Nobel Prize Laureate)
3242 Tibbett Ave
Bronx, NY 10463-3801, USA

Yalow, Roslyn
3242 Tibbett Ave
Bronx, NY 10463-3801

Yamagata, Hiro (Artist)
1080 Ave D
Redondo Beach, CA 90277, USA

Yamagata, Rachel (Musician)
c/o Staff Member *Paradigm (Monterey)*
404 W Franklin St
Monterey, CA 93940-2303, USA

Yamaguchi, Kristi (Athlete, Figure Skater)
1203 Preservation Park Way Ste 102
Oakland, CA 94612-1246, USA

Yamaguchi, Roy (Business Person)
Kai Corporate Plaza 6600 Kalaniaole Hwy
Honolulu, HI 96825, USA

Yamame, Marlene Mitsuko (Actor)
10801 National Blvd Ste 101
Los Angeles, CA 90064-4140, USA

Yamamoto, Keith R (Biologist)
332 Douglass St
San Francisco, CA 94114-2452, USA

Yamamoto, Kenichi (Business Person)
4-6-19 Funairi-Minami Minamiku
Hiroshima, JAPAN

Yamamoto, Takuma (Business Person)
1-6-1 Marunouchi Chiyodaku
Tokyo 100, JAPAN

Yamamoto, Yohji (Designer, Fashion Designer)
14-15 Conduit St
London W1R 9TG, UNITED KINGDOM (UK)

Yamanaka, Tsuyoshi (Swimmer)
6-10-33-212 Akasaka Minatoku
Tokyo, JAPAN

Yamani, Sheikh Ahmed Zaki (Government Official)
Chermignon near Crans-Montana
Valais, SWITZERLAND

Yamaoka, Seigen H (Religious Leader)
1710 Octavia St
San Francisco, CA 94109-4341, USA

Yamasaki, Taro M (Journalist)
Time-Life Building
New York, NY 10020, USA

Yamashita, Yasuhiro (Athlete, Coach)
1117 Kitakaname
Hitatsuka Kanagawa 259-1207, JAPAN

Yamin, Elliott (Actor, Musician)
c/o Mark Gorlick *Collective*
8383 Wilshire Blvd Ste 1050
Beverly Hills, CA 90211-2415, USA

Yancey, Emily
247 S Beverly Dr # 102
Beverly Hills, CA 90212-3830

Yanchar, William (Athlete, Football Player)
PO Box 460141
Aurora, CO 80046-0141, USA

Yancy, Emily (Actor)
8285 W Sunset Blvd Ste 1
West Hollywood, CA 90046-2420, USA

Yancy, Hugh (Athlete, Baseball Player)
1708 Marilyn Ave
Bradenton, FL 34207-4633, USA

Yandle, Leigh Ann (Stylist)
c/o Staff Member *The Talent Connection*
338 N Elm St Ste 204
Greensboro, NC 27401-2146, USA

Yanez, Eduardo (Actor)
c/o Thomas Richards *Corsa Agency, The*
11704 Wilshire Blvd Ste 204
Los Angeles, CA 90025-1510, USA

Yang, C K
PO Box 7855-39 Tsoying
Kaoshking, TAIWAN R.O.C., TAIWAN R O C

Yang, Chuan-Kwang (C K) (Athlete, Track Athlete)
PO Box 7855-39 Tsoying
Kaohsking, TAIWAN

Yang, Jeanne (Stylist)
c/o Staff Member *Cloutier Agency*
2632 La Cienega Ave
Los Angeles, CA 90034-2641, USA

Yang, Jerry (Business Person, Engineer)
701 First Ave
Sunnyvale, CA 94089-1019, USA

Yang, Liwei (Misc)
Jiuquan
Gansu Province, CHINA

Yang, Shang-Fa (Misc)
118 Villanova Dr
Davis, CA 95616, USA

Yang, Young A (Athlete, Golfer)
5451 Millenia Lakes Blvd Apt 302
Orlando, FL 32839-6314, USA

Yankee, Daddy (Musician)
c/o Lizzie Grubman *Lizzie Grubman Public Relations*
270 Lafayette St Ste 504
New York, NY 10012-0048, USA

Yankelovich, Daniel (Scientist)
6 E 39th St # 900
New York, NY 10016-0112, USA

Yankovic, Al (Weird Al) (Actor, Comedian, Musician, Songwriter)
8033 W Sunset Blvd # 4018
Los Angeles, CA 90046-2401, USA

Yankovsky, Oleg I (Actor)
Komsomolsky Prospekt 41 #10
Moscow 119270, RUSSIA

Yankowski, George (Athlete, Baseball Player)
12 Potter Pond
Lexington, MA 02421-8243, USA

Yankowski, Ron (Athlete, Football Player)
1318 Saint Paul Rd
Ballwin, MO 63021-8208, USA

Yannas, I V (Engineer, Scientist)
Engineering School
Cambridge, MA 2139, USA

Yanni (Musician, Songwriter, Writer)
100 5th Ave Fl 11
New York, NY 10011-6903, USA

Yanofsky, Charles (Biologist)
725 Mayfield Ave
Stanford, CA 94305-1016, USA

Yao, Andrew (Mathematician)
Mathematics
Princeton, NJ 08544-0001, USA

Yaralian, Zaven (Athlete, Football Player)
7770 S Peoria St
Englewood, CO 80112-4138, USA

Yarber, Eric (Athlete, Football Player)
325 Valley Football Ctr Attn Footballprogram
Corvallis, OR 97331-8544, USA

Yarborough, Glenn
PO Box 158
Malibu, CA 90265-0158

Yarborough, W Caleb (Cale) (Race Car Driver)
2723 W Palmetto St
Florence, SC 29501-5929, USA

Yarborough, William P (General)
16205 Timid Creek Ct
Dumfries, VA 22025-3613, USA

Yarbrough, Cedric (Actor)
c/o Jenni Weinman *Patricola Lust PR*
9171 Wilshire Blvd Ste 390
Beverly Hills, CA 90210-5515, USA

Yarbrough, Curtis (Religious Leader)
100 Stinson Dr
Poplar Bluff, MO 63901-8736, USA

Yarbrough, Glenn (Musician, Songwriter, Writer)
150 Avenida Presidio
San Clemente, CA 92672-3170, USA

Yarbrough, Jim (Athlete, Football Player)
720 N Phelps Ave
Winter Park, FL 32789-2757, USA

Yarbrough, Jim (Athlete, Football Player)
440 Capricorn St
Cedar Hill, TX 75104-8106, USA

Yard, Mollie
1000 16th St. W
Washington, DC

Yardbirds, The
PO Box 1821
Ojai, CA 93024-1821

Yared, Gabriel (Composer)
c/o Staff Member *Evolution Music Partners*
1680 Vine St Ste 500
Hollywood, CA 90028-8800, USA

Yarkin, Cori (Musician)
c/o Allan Greene PO Box 151234
Altamonte Springs, FL 32715-1234, USA

Yarlett, Claire (Actor)
c/o Lorraine Berglund *Lorraine Berglund Management*
11537 Hesby St
North Hollywood, CA 91601-3618, USA

Yarmuth, John A (Congressman, Politician)
600 Dr Martin Luther King Pl Bldg Ste
Louisville, KY 40202-2239, USA

Yarnall, Celeste (Actor)
2899 Agoura Rd # 315
Westlake Vlg, CA 91361-3218, USA

Yarnell, Ed (Athlete, Baseball Player)
9837 Vouvray Dr
Baton Rouge, LA 70817-7646, USA

Yarno, George (Athlete, Football Player)
1081 White Pine Flats Rd
Troy, ID 83871-9674, USA

Yarno, John (Athlete, Football Player)
10535 158th Ave NE
Redmond, WA 98052-2659, USA

Yarritu, David (Stylist)
c/o Staff Member *Pat Bates & Associates*
300 W 12th St
New York, NY 10014-1939, USA

Yarrow, Peter (Musician, Songwriter, Writer)
27 W 67th St # 5E
New York, NY 10023-6258, USA

Yary, A Ronald (Ron) (Athlete, Football Player)
38886 Calle De Companero
Murrieta, CA 92562-8877, USA

Yasbeck, Amy (Actor)
c/o Jonathan Howard *Innovative Artists (LA)*
1505 10th St
Santa Monica, CA 90401-2805, USA

Yashin, Alexei (Athlete, Hockey Player)
10 Hempstead Tpke
Uniondale, NY 11553, USA

Yassky, David (Stylist)
c/o Celebrity Stylist *Oliver Piro Inc*
725 Riverside Dr Apt 3A
New York, NY 10031-2460, USA

Yastrzemski, Carl
255 State St
Boston, MA 02109-2617, USA

Yastrzemski, Carl (Athlete, Baseball Player)
255 State St
Boston, MA 02109-2617, USA

Yasutake, Patti
145 S Fairfax Ave Ste 310
Los Angeles, CA 90036-2176

Yates, Al (Athlete, Baseball Player)
999 Inlet Cir Apt A104
Venice, FL 34285-1036, USA

Yates, Albert C (Educator)
President's Office
Denver, CO 80202, USA

Yates, Bill (Cartoonist)
c/o Staff Member *King Features Syndication*
300 W 57th St Fl 15
New York, NY 10019-5238, USA

Yates, Billy (Athlete, Football Player)
c/o Staff Member *New England Patriots*
Gillette Stadium One Patriots Pl
Foxboro, MA 02035-1388, USA

Yates, Bob (Athlete, Football Player)
391 Bentwood Dr
Spring Branch, TX 78070-6016, USA

Yates, Jim (Race Car Driver)
4740 Eisenhower Ave
Alexandria, VA 22304-4806, USA

Yates, Mary Beth (Stylist)
c/o Staff Member *Therese Ryan Mahar Inc*
167 Lexington Ave # 200
New York, NY 10016-7305, USA

Yates, Ronald W (Ron) (General)
525 Silhouette Way
Monument, CO 80132-8503, USA

Yates, Tyler (Athlete, Baseball Player)
3718 Omao Rd
Koloa, HI 96756-9628, USA

Yates, Wayne (Athlete, Basketball Player)
210 Yates Rd
Robeline, LA 71469, USA

Yates, Yvette (Producer)
c/o Staff Member *Payaso Entertainment*
5555 Melrose Ave Bldg 256 PMB 233
Los Angeles, CA 90038, USA

Yau, Shing-Tung (Mathematician)
1 Oxford St
Cambridge, MA 02138-2901, USA

Yauch, Adam (MCA) (Musician)
511 Canal St # 5E
New York, NY 10013-1301, USA

Yavari, Leila (Actor)
c/o Staff Member *Cunningham Escott Slevin & Doherty (CESD-LA)*
10635 Santa Monica Blvd Ste 130
Los Angeles, CA 90025-8306, USA

Yavneh, Cyrus (Producer)
c/o Staff Member *International Creative Management (ICM-LA)*
10250 Constellation Blvd Fl 7
Los Angeles, CA 90067-6207, USA

Yayo, Tony (Musician)
c/o Staff Member *Interscope Records (NY)*
1755 Broadway
New York, NY 10019-3743, USA

Yazpik, Jose Maria (Actor)
c/o Carlos Carreras *Paradigm (LA)*
360 N Crescent Dr
Beverly Hills, CA 90210-4874, USA

Ybarra y Churruca, Emilio de (Financier)
Plaza de San Nicolas 4
Bilboa 48005, SPAIN

Yeager, Andrea
3137 Devin Dr
Grand Junction, CO 81504-6057

Yeager, Bunny (Model, Photographer)
585 NE 92nd St
Miami Shores, FL 33138-3162, USA

Yeager, Charles E (Chuck) (General)
PO Box 579
Penn Valley, CA 95946-0579, USA

Yeager, Jeana (Misc)
4005 Meadowview Dr
Campbell, TX 75422-1875, USA

Yeager, Stephen W (Steve) (Athlete, Baseball Player)
PO Box 34184
Granada Hills, CA 91394-4184, USA

Yeagley, Jerry (Coach)
1418 S Sare Rd
Bloomington, IN 47401-4431, USA

Yeagley, Susan (Actor)
c/o Devon Jackson *Jackson-Medavoy Entertainment*
10203 Santa Monica Blvd Fl 4
Los Angeles, CA 90067-6439, USA

Yeah Yeah Yeahs (Music Group)
249 Metropolitan Ave
Brooklyn, NY 11211-4009, USA

Yeakel, G Scott (Astronaut)
14224 E Kalil Dr
Scottsdale, AZ 85259-4624, USA

Yearley, Douglas C (Business Person)
1 N Central Ave
Phoenix, AZ 85004-4414, USA

Yearwood, Trisha (Musician)
c/o Ken Levitan *Vector Management*
PO Box 120479
Nashville, TN 37212-0479, USA

Yeates, Jeff (Athlete, Football Player)
3793 Club Dr NE
Atlanta, GA 30319-1107, USA

Yelchin, Anton (Actor)
c/o Cynthia Pett-Dante *Brillstein Entertainment Partners*
9150 Wilshire Blvd Ste 350
Beverly Hills, CA 90212-3453, USA

Yelding, Eric (Athlete, Baseball Player)
PO Box 325
Montrose, AL 36559-0325, USA

Yeley, JJ (Race Car Driver)
PO Box 607
Plainfield, IN 46168-0607, USA

Yeliseyev, Aleksei S (Cosmonaut)
Baumanskaya Ul 5
Moscow 107005, RUSSIA

Yellen, Janet L (Financier, Government Official)
2721 O St NW
Washington, DC 20007-3128, USA

Yellen, Larry (Athlete, Baseball Player)
3886 Toccoa Falls Dr
Duluth, GA 30097-8105, USA

Yellen, Linda B (Director, Producer)
3 Sheridan Sq
New York, NY 10014-6828, USA

Yellowcard (Musician)
1750 Vine St # T-06
Hollywood, CA 90028-5209, USA

Yellowjackets
9220 W Sunset Blvd # 320
Los Angeles, CA 90069-3501

Yelvington, Richard J (Athlete, Football Player)
2105 Barbe St
Lake Charles, LA 70601-9017, USA

Yen, Donnie (Actor)
c/o Andrew Ruf *Paradigm (LA)*
360 N Crescent Dr
Beverly Hills, CA 90210-4874, USA

Yeo, Gwendoline (Actor)
c/o Anne Geddes *Geddes Agency, The*
8430 Santa Monica Blvd Ste 200
Los Angeles, CA 90069-4253, USA

Yeoh, Michelle (Actor)
c/o Lee Stollman *The Gotham Group Inc*
9255 W Sunset Blvd Ste 515
Los Angeles, CA 90069-3308, USA

Yeoman, Owain (Actor)
c/o Tom Drumm *The Safran Company*
8748 Holloway Dr
West Hollywood, CA 90069-2327, USA

Yeoman, William F (Bill) (Athlete, Coach, Football Coach, Football Player)
3030 Country Club Blvd
Sugar Land, TX 77478-3630, USA

Yeosock, John J (General)
223 Newport Dr
Peachtree City, GA 30269-4277, USA

Yepremian, Garabed S (Garo) (Athlete, Football Player)
613 Martin Dr
Avondale, PA 19311-1316, USA

Yerby, Frank
Avenida del America 37
Madrid, SPAIN E-28002

Yerman, Jack (Athlete, Track Athlete)
753 Camellia Dr
Paradise, CA 95969-3817, USA

Yes (Music Group)
c/o Staff Member *10th Street Entertainment (LA)*
700 N San Vicente Blvd Ste G410
West Hollywood, CA 90069-5060, USA

Yeston, Maury (Composer)
Music Dept
New Haven, CT 6520, USA

Yetnikoff, Walter
c/o Daniel A (Dan) Strone *Trident Media Group LLC*
41 Madison Ave Fl 36
New York, NY 10010-2257, USA

Yett, Rich (Athlete, Baseball Player)
5840 E Fairbrook Cir
Mesa, AZ 85205-5559, USA

Yeun, Steven (Actor)
c/o Bruce Economou *Pine River Entertainment*
1200 S Corning St Apt 101
Los Angeles, CA 90035-2465, USA

Yeutter, Clayton K (Secretary)
10955 Martingale Ct
Potomac, MD 20854-1500, USA

Yevtushenko, Yevgeny A (Writer)
Kutuzovski Prospekt 2/1 #101
Moscow 121248, RUSSIA

Yewcic, Thomas (Tom) (Athlete, Baseball Player, Football Player)
15 Danby Rd
Stoneham, MA 02180-3003, USA

Yi, Charlyne (Actor, Producer, Writer)
c/o Christie Smith *Mosaic Media Group*
9200 W Sunset Blvd Ste 10
Los Angeles, CA 90069-3608, USA

Yilmaz, A Mesut (Prime Minister)
Basbakanlik Bakanliklar
Ankara, TURKEY

Yimou, Zhang (Actor, Director, Producer, Writer)
c/o William (Bill) Kong *Edko Films*
1212 Tower 2 Admiralty Centre
Hong Kong, CHINA

Ying Yang Twins (Music Group)
23 E 4th St Fl 3
New York, NY 10003-7023, USA

Yip, David
15 Golden Sq # 315
London, ENGLAND W1R 3AG

Yip, Francoise (Actor)
10 - 206 East 6th Ave
Vancouver, BC V5T 1J8, CANADA

Yip, Vern (Designer)
80 Palisades Rd NE
Atlanta, GA 30309-1545

Ylonen, Juha (Athlete, Hockey Player)
1000 Palladium Dr
Kanata, ON K2V 1A4, Canada

Ylonen, Lauri Johannes (Musician)
c/o Staff Member *Rasmus, The*
Playground Music Scandinavia Box 3171
Malm s-200 22, SWEDEN

Yo Yo Ma (Actor, Musician)
c/o Staff Member *International Creative Management (ICM-LA)*
10250 Constellation Blvd Fl 7
Los Angeles, CA 90067-6207, USA

Yoakam, Dwight (Musician, Songwriter, Writer)
c/o Rick Shipp *WmE2 (WMA-TN)*
1600 Division St Ste 300
Nashville, TN 37203-2755, USA

Yoakum, Dwight (Musician)
1250 6th St Ste 401
Santa Monica, CA 90401-1638

Yoba, Malik (Actor)
c/o Matt Luber *Luber Roklin Management*
8530 Wilshire Blvd Ste 550
Beverly Hills, CA 90211-3133, USA

Yoccoz, Jean-Christophe (Mathematician)
Orsay-Cedex-Bait 91405, FRANCE

Yochim, Len (Athlete, Baseball Player)
316 Nelson Dr
New Orleans, LA 70123-1958, USA

Yock, Robert J (Judge)
717 Madison Pl NW
Washington, DC 20439-0001, USA

Yodoyman, Joseph (Prime Minister)
N'Djamena, CHAD

Yogaraj (Actor, Bollywood)
18 34th Street Ashok Nagar
Chennai, TN 600083, INDIA

Yoh, Ramona (Stylist)
1055 Barrow Ct
Westlake Village, CA 91361-1802, USA

Yohn, John (Athlete, Football Player)
12 Riverview Dr
Middletown, PA 17057-3433, USA

Yoho, Mack (Athlete, Football Player)
2205 Sacramento St Apt 304
San Francisco, CA 94115-2394, USA

Yoken, Mel B (Writer)
261 Carroll St
New Bedford, MA 02740-1412, USA

Yokes, Diane (Stylist)
3721 N 83rd St
Milwaukee, WI 53222-2950, USA

Yonaker, John (Athlete, Football Player)
20450 Lake Shore Blvd
Cleveland, OH 44123-1845, USA

Yonakor, Rich (Athlete, Basketball Player)
38140 Tamarac Blvd Apt 106
Willoughby, OH 44094-3448, USA

Yonder Mountain String Band (Music Group)
c/o Staff Member *Paradigm (Monterey)*
404 W Franklin St
Monterey, CA 93940-2303, USA

Yoo, Aaron (Actor)
c/o Tony Cloer *Blue Ridge Entertainment*
41 Union Sq W Ste 809
New York, NY 10003-3264, USA

Yoo, Paula (Writer)
c/o Nancy Etz *International Creative Management (ICM-LA)*
10250 Constellation Blvd Fl 7
Los Angeles, CA 90067-6207, USA

Yore, Jim (Athlete, Football Player)
1084 Westlake Woods Dr
Springfield, MI 49037-7665, USA

York, Barbara (Stylist)
2314 Sibley St
Alexandria, VA 22311-5744, USA

York, Francine (Actor)
6430 W Sunset Blvd Ste 1205
Los Angeles, CA 90028-8002, USA

York, Glen P (War Hero)
1620 E Driftwood Dr
Tempe, AZ 85283-2168, USA

York, Jim (Athlete, Baseball Player)
31262 Via Del Verde
San Juan Capistrano, CA 92675-6315, USA

York, John J (Actor)
4804 Laurel Canyon Blvd # 212
Valley Village, CA 91607-3717, USA

York, Kathleen (Actor)
11500 W Olympic Blvd Ste 510
Los Angeles, CA 90064-1527, USA

York, Michael (Actor)
c/o Staff Member *Peter Strain & Associates Inc (LA)*
5455 Wilshire Blvd Ste 1812
Los Angeles, CA 90036-4268, USA

York, Michael M (Journalist)
Editorial Dept Main & Midland
Lexington, KY 40507, USA

York, Michael (Mike) (Athlete, Hockey Player)
11230 110th St
Edmonton, AB T5G 3H7, Canada

York, Mike (Athlete, Baseball Player)
8001 S 84th Ct
Justice, IL 60458-1420, USA

York, Morgan (Actor)
c/o Meredith Fine *Coast to Coast Talent Group*
3350 Barham Blvd
Los Angeles, CA 90068-1404, USA

York, Ray (Jockey)
27918 Highway 119
Taft, CA 93268-9612, USA

York, Wndy Jill (Stylist)
47 Barney St
Rumford, RI 02916-1201, USA

Yorke, Thom (Musician)
c/o Staff Member *Creative Artists Agency (CAA-LA)*
2000 Avenue of the Stars Ste 100
Los Angeles, CA 90067-4705, USA

Yorkin, Alan (Bud) (Director, Producer)
250 Delfem Dr
Los Angeles, CA 90077, USA

Yorkin, Bud
250 Delfern Dr
Los Angeles, CA 90077-3543

Yorkin, Peg (Politician)
1600 Wilson Blvd Ste 704
Arlington, VA 22209-2505, USA

Yorn, Peter (Musician, Songwriter, Writer)
c/o Rick Yorn *Yorn Management Group*
2000 Avenue Of The Stars 3rd Tower Floor NORTH
Los Angeles, CA 90067, USA

Yorzyk, William A (Bill) (Swimmer)
162 W Sturbridge Rd # 7
East Brookfield, MA 01515-2017, USA

Yoseliani, Otar D (Director)
Mitskewitch 1 Korp 1 #38
Tbilisi 380060, GEORGIA

Yoshida, Hiroshi (Stylist)
c/o Staff Member *Artist Untied (LA)*
845 S Mansfield Ave Apt 1
Los Angeles, CA 90036-4979, USA

Yost, David (Actor)
8837 Cortina Cir
Roseville, CA 95678-2940, USA

Yost, Dennis
PO Box 8770
Endwell, NY 13762-8770

Yost, Edward F J (Eddie) (Athlete, Baseball Player, Coach)
48 Oakridge Rd
Wellesley Hills, MA 02481-2504, USA

Yost, Ned (Athlete, Baseball Player, Coach)
1 Brewers Way Attn Managers
Milwaukee, WI 53214-3655, USA

Yost, Paul A Jr (Admiral)
200 K St NW
Washington, DC 20001-5500, USA

Yothers, Tina (Actor, Musician)
12368 Apple Dr
Chino, CA 91710-2706, USA

Youel, Jim (Athlete, Football Player)
1102 Avenue F
Fort Madison, IA 52627-2743, USA

Youkhannah, David (Stylist)
c/o Staff Member *Cloutier Agency*
2632 La Cienega Ave
Los Angeles, CA 90034-2641, USA

Youkillis, Kevin (Athlete, Baseball Player)
19475 N Grayhawk Dr Unit 1083
Scottsdale, AZ 85255-7420, USA

Youmans, Floyd (Athlete, Baseball Player)
1915 E Noel St
Tampa, FL 33610-6157, USA

Youmans, Maury (Athlete, Football Player)
300 Beach Dr NE Apt 2104
Saint Petersburg, FL 33701-3461, USA

Young, Ace (Musician)
c/o Staff Member *Marleah Leslie & Associates PR*
1645 Vine St Apt 712
Los Angeles, CA 90028-8812, USA

Young, Aden (Actor)
110 Queen St
Woollahra, NSW 2025, AUSTRALIA

Young, Adrian (Musician)
31652 2nd Ave
Laguna Beach, CA 92651-8244, USA

Young, Al (Athlete, Football Player)
1947 Green Forest Dr
North Augusta, SC 29841-2174, USA

Young, Alan (Actor)
c/o Staff Member *Tisherman Gilbert Motley Drozdoski Talent Agency (TGMD)*
6767 Forest Lawn Dr Ste 101
Los Angeles, CA 90068-1050, USA

Young, Almon (Athlete, Football Player)
PO Box 983
Mc Crory, AR 72101-0983, USA

Young, Andre (Dr Dre) (Actor, Musician)
7251 W Lake Mead Blvd
Las Vegas, NV 89128-8351, USA

Young, Angus (Musician, Songwriter, Writer)
c/o Christopher Dalston *Creative Artists Agency (CAA-LA)*
2000 Avenue of the Stars Ste 100
Los Angeles, CA 90067-4705, USA

Young, Anthony (Athlete, Baseball Player)
13107 Ellesmere Dr
Houston, TX 77015-2111, USA

Young, Anthony (Athlete, Football Player)
914 Colonial Ct
Coatesville, PA 19320-1685, USA

Young, Archie (Baseball Player)
1804 Ethel Ave SW
Birmingham, AL 35211-4914, USA

Young, Barbara
23-B Deodar Rd
London, ENGLAND SWI5- 2NP

Young, Bellamy (Actor)
c/o Katie Rhodes *Untitled Entertainment (LA)*
350 S Beverly Dr Ste 200
Beverly Hills, CA 90212-4819, USA

Young, Bob (Cartoonist)
c/o Staff Member *King Features Syndication*
300 W 57th St Fl 15
New York, NY 10019-5238, USA

Young, Boyd (Misc)
3340 Perimeter Hill Dr
Nashville, TN 37211-4123, USA

Young, Brian (Musician)
6404 Wilshire Blvd Ste 505
Los Angeles, CA 90048-5507, USA

Young, Bryant C (Athlete, Football Player)
8454 NW 64th Ln
Gainesville, FL 32653-2987, USA

Young, Burt (Actor)
11 Pioneer Building Suite 4
Mesquite, NV 98027, USA

Young, Charle E (Athlete, Football Player)
16035 Mink Rd NE
Woodinville, WA 98077-9460, USA

Young, Charles E (Athlete, Football Player)
16035 Mink Rd NE
Woodinville, WA 98077-9460, USA

Young, Charles L (Athlete, Football Player)
2120 Daufuskie Dr
Raleigh, NC 27604-2074, USA

Young, Chris (Athlete, Baseball Player)
c/o Staff Member *Arizona Diamondbacks*
PO Box 2095
Phoenix, AZ 85001-2095, USA

Young, Chris T
5959 Triumph St
Commerce, CA 90040-1609, USA

Young, Christoper (Composer)
15233 Ventura Blvd Ste 200
Sherman Oaks, CA 91403-2244, USA

Young, Colville N (General, Governor)
Belize House
Belnopan, BELIZE

Young, Corey
11553 Sunshine Ter
Studio City, CA 91604-3835

Young, Curt (Athlete, Baseball Player)
10800 E Cactus Rd Unit 2
Scottsdale, AZ 85259-2503, USA

Young, C.W. (Bill) (Congressman, Politician)
9120 113th St
Seminole, FL 33772, USA

Young, Danny (Athlete, Baseball Player)
1841 Lascassas Pike Apt J153
Murfreesboro, TN 37130-0609, USA

Young, Dean (Cartoonist)
c/o Staff Member *King Features Syndication*
300 W 57th St Fl 15
New York, NY 10019-5238, USA

Young, Delmon (Athlete, Baseball Player)
2234 Klamath Dr
Camarillo, CA 93010-2120, USA

Young, Dick (Athlete, Baseball Player)
250 W Broadway Apt 224
Eugene, OR 97401-3022, USA

Young, Dmitri (Athlete, Baseball Player)
525 Bennaville Ave
Birmingham, MI 48009-3663, USA

Young, Don (Athlete, Baseball Player)
22495 N 77th Pl
Scottsdale, AZ 85255-4830, USA

Young, Don (Congressman, Politician)
2111 Rayburn House Ofc Building
Washington, DC 20515-0001, USA

Young, Duane (Athlete, Football Player)
2255 River Run Dr
San Diego, CA 92108-5888, USA

Young, Earl (Athlete, Track Athlete)
4344 Livingston Ave
Dallas, TX 75205-2608, USA

Young, Eric O (Athlete, Baseball Player)
120 Brewster Ave
Piscataway, NJ 08854-2205, USA

Young, Ernie (Athlete, Baseball Player)
8995 E Palm Ridge Dr
Scottsdale, AZ 85260-7533, USA

Young, Frank E (Government Official, Scientist)
5600 Fishers Ln
Rockville, MD 20852-1750, USA

Young, Fred (Musician)
212 3rd Ave N Ste 301
Nashville, TN 37201-1632, USA

Young, Fredd (Athlete, Football Player)
4200 Real Del Sur
Las Cruces, NM 88011-7204, USA

Young, George L (Athlete, Track Athlete)
8926 N Cox Rd
Casa Grande, AZ 85194-7230, USA

Young, Gerald (Athlete, Baseball Player)
10014 Rain Cloud Dr
Houston, TX 77095-2442, USA

Young, Glenn (Athlete, Football Player)
8035 Burchmore Rd
Three Lakes, WI 54562-9264, USA

Young, H Edwin (Religious Leader)
901 Commerce St
Nashville, TN 37203-3620, USA

Young, Howard (Howie) (Athlete, Hockey Player)
5527 N 22nd Dr
Phoenix, AZ 85015-2316, USA

Young, J Warren (Publisher)
1325 W Walnut Hill Ln
Irving, TX 75038-3008, USA

Young, Jacob (Actor)
c/o Alex D'Andrea *Edmonds Management*
1635 N Cahuenga Blvd Fl 5
Los Angeles, CA 90028-6201, USA

Young, Jason (Athlete, Baseball Player)
565 Arastradero Rd Apt 108
Palo Alto, CA 94306-4320, USA

Young, Jesse Colin (Musician, Songwriter, Writer)
PO Box 31
Lancaster, NH 03584-0031, USA

Young, Jewell L (Basketball Player)
4480 Fairways Blvd Building 8 PMB 203
Bradenton, FL 34209, USA

Young, Jim (Coach, Football Coach)
Athletic Dept
West Point, NY 10966, USA

Young, Joe (Athlete, Football Player)
33261 Windtree Ave
Wildomar, CA 92595-8235, USA

Young, John (Athlete, Baseball Player)
124 W 57th St
Los Angeles, CA 90037-4114, USA

Young, John A (Business Person)
122 E 1700 S
Provo, UT 84606-7379, USA

Young, John W (Astronaut)
2101 Nasa Pkwy Spc Center
Houston, TX 77058-3607, USA

Young, John Zachary (Misc)
1 Crossroads Brill
Bucks HP18 9TL, UNITED KINGDOM (UK)

Young, Judith Knight (Actor)
330 W 42nd St # 1800
New York, NY 10036-6902, USA

Young, Kate (Stylist)
c/o Staff Member *Management + Artists + Organization*
330 W 38th St Ste 1401
New York, NY 10018-8438, USA

Young, Kathie (Stylist)
c/o Staff Member *Axis Models & Talent*
PO Box 367
Ringwood, NJ 07456-0367, USA

Young, Kathryn (Athlete, Golfer)
323 Date Ave
Imperial Beach, CA 91932-1915, USA

Young, Kathy (Musician)
1161 NW 76th Ave
Plantation, FL 33322-5120, USA

Young, Keone (Actor)
14724 Ventura Blvd Ste 505
Sherman Oaks, CA 91403-3505, USA

Young, Kevin (Athlete, Track Athlete)
8860 Corbin Ave
Northridge, CA 91324-3309, USA

Young, Kevin (Athlete, Baseball Player)
4793 E Charles Dr
Paradise Valley, AZ 85253-2427, USA

Young, Kip (Athlete, Baseball Player)
2570 US Highway 62
Winchester, OH 45697-9517, USA

Young, Larry (Athlete, Baseball Player)
PO Box 255
Roscoe, IL 61073-0255, USA

Young, Laurence Retman (Astronaut)
217 Thorndike St Apt 108
Cambridge, MA 02141-1504, USA

Young, Lee Thompson (Actor)
c/o Jonathan Baruch *Rain Management Group (RMG)*
1631 21st St
Santa Monica, CA 90404-3914, USA

Young, Lonnie (Athlete, Football Player)
6437 S Cedar St
Lansing, MI 48911-5960, USA

Young, M Adrian (Athlete, Football Player)
10300 4th St Ste 100
Rancho Cucamonga, CA 91730-5808, USA

Young, Martin D (Misc)
1110 Marshall Rd # 2007
Greenwood, SC 29646-4216, USA

Young, Matt (Athlete, Baseball Player)
471 Maylin St
Pasadena, CA 91105-1629, USA

Young, Maurice (Trick Daddy) (Music Group, Musician)
c/o Roy Rosental *Energon Entertainment*
276 5th Ave Rm 704
New York, NY 10001-4527, USA

Young, Melissa (Actor)
9229 W Sunset Blvd Ste 311
Los Angeles, CA 90069-3403, USA

Young, Michael (Athlete, Basketball Player)
6707 Broad Oaks Dr
Richmond, TX 77406-7629, USA

Young, Michael (Athlete, Baseball Player)
3508 Bryn Mawr Dr
Dallas, TX 75225-7438, USA

Young, Mighty Joe (Musician)
3430 Bayberry Dr
Northbrook, IL 60062-2217, USA

Young, Mike (Athlete, Football Player)
844 S El Molino Ave
Pasadena, CA 91106-4412, USA

Young, Mike (Athlete, Baseball Player)
1166 Rockspring Way
Antioch, CA 94531-8308, USA

Young, Mimi (Stylist)
c/o Staff Member *Sarah Laird Inc*
12 Charles Ln
New York, NY 10014-2526, USA

Young, Neil (Musician)
c/o Elliot Roberts *Lookout Management*
1460 4th St
Santa Monica, CA 90401-2329

Young, Nina (Actor)
c/o Staff Member *BBC Television Centre*
Incoming Mail Wood Lane
London W12 7RJ, United Kingdom

Young, Parker (Actor)
c/o David Dean Portelli *Precision Entertainment*
6338 Wilshire Blvd
Los Angeles, CA 90048-5002, USA

Young, Paul (Musician)
PO Box 1463
Culver City, CA 90232-1463, USA

Young, Pete (Athlete, Baseball Player)
PO Box 95
Summit, MS 39666-0095, USA

Young, Peter (Misc)
1902 Coldwater Canyon Dr
Beverly Hills, CA 90210-1731, USA

Young, Ray (Misc)
3360 Barham Blvd
Los Angeles, CA 90068-1473, USA

Young, Raymond
7 Church St
Littlehampton, ENGLAND BN1Y 5EL

Young, Ric (Actor)
c/o Staff Member *Coast to Coast Talent Group*
3350 Barham Blvd
Los Angeles, CA 90068-1404, USA

Young, Richard
1275 Westwood Blvd
Los Angeles, CA 90024-4811

Young, Richard E (Scientist)
4800 Oak Grove Dr
Pasadena, CA 91109-8001, USA

Young, Richard S (Photographer)
110 Highlever Road
London W10 6PL, UNITED KINGDOM (UK)

Young, Richard S (Educator)
137 Saint Croix Ave
Cocoa Beach, FL 32931-3334, USA

Young, Rickey (Athlete, Football Player)
13670 Valley View Rd Apt 116
Eden Prairie, MN 55344-1977, USA

Young, Robert (Athlete, Football Player)
RR 7 Box 306
Carthage, MS 39051, USA

Young, Robert (Bob) (Athlete, Track Athlete)
8705 Fairfield Dr
Bakersfield, CA 93311-1593, USA

Young, Ron Jr (War Hero)
c/o Staff Member *Premiere Speakers Bureau*
109 International Dr Ste 300
Franklin, TN 37067-1764, USA

Young, Roynell (Athlete, Football Player)
11823 Beinhorn Dr
Houston, TX 77065-1607, USA

Young, Sean (Actor)
c/o Staff Member *Diverse Talent Group*
9911 W Pico Blvd Ste 340W
Los Angeles, CA 90035-2712, USA

Young, Shelby (Actor)
c/o Katie Mason *Luber Roklin Management*
8530 Wilshire Blvd Ste 550
Beverly Hills, CA 90211-3133, USA

Young, Steve (Football Player, Sportscaster)
c/o Staff Member *ESPN (Main)*
ESPN Plaza 935 Middle St
Bristol, CT 06010-1001, USA

Young, Steve (Athlete, Football Player)
3780 Edgewood Dr
Provo, UT 84604, USA

Young, Steve (Misc)
1501 Broadway Ste 800
New York, NY 10036-5505, USA

Young, Tim (Athlete, Baseball Player)
20730 SE Sherry Ave
Blountstown, FL 32424-2265, USA

Young, Tom (Coach)
MCI Centre 601 F St NW
Washington, DC 20004, USA

Young, Tracy (DJ)
c/o Len Evans *Project Publicity*
312 W 53rd St Ste 202
New York, NY 10019-5743, USA

Young, Vince (Athlete, Football Player)
12006 Legend Manor Dr
Houston, TX 77082-3092, USA

Young, Vincent (Actor)
c/o Alan Ellsweig *Shadow Entertainment*
10 Universal City Plz Fl 20
Universal City, CA 91608-1074, USA

Young, Walter (Athlete, Baseball Player)
134 Center St
Purvis, MS 39475-4540, USA

Young, Wilbur (Athlete, Football Player)
121 W Bannister Rd
Kansas City, MO 64114-4010, USA

Young, Will (Musician)
c/o Angharad Wood *Tavistock Wood Management*
32 Tavistock St
London WC2B 5HA, UK

Young, William Allen (Actor)
c/o Bruce Tufeld *Tufeld Entertainment Group*
19521 Rosita Stt
Tarzana, CA 91356, USA

Young, Wise (Scientist)
Collaborative Neuroscience Center
New Brunswick, NJ 8901, USA

Young Gunz (Musician)
c/o Staff Member *Roc-A-Fella Records*
825 8th Ave Fl 29
New York, NY 10019-7416, USA

Young Jeezy (Musician)
c/o Tracy Nguyen *IPR + MKTG*
1515 Broadway Fl 40
New York, NY 10036-8901, USA

Young Jr, Walter R (Business Person)
2710 University Dr
Auburn Hills, MI 48326, USA

Young Knives, The (Music Group)
c/o Staff Member *Paradigm (Monterey)*
404 W Franklin St
Monterey, CA 93940-2303, USA

Young MC (Musician)
145 W 57th St # 1500
New York, NY 10019-2220, USA

Young Money (Music Group, Musician)
c/o Staff Member *Motown Records (NY)*
1755 Broadway Fl 7
New York, NY 10019-3743, USA

Youngberg, Renae (Baseball Player)
2001 Gasparilla Rd # 25
Placida, FL 33946-2603, USA

Youngblood, George (Athlete, Football Player)
11811 Edgewood Ln
Garden Grove, CA 92840-1845, USA

Youngblood, H Jackson (Jack) (Athlete, Football Player, Sportscaster)
4377 Steed Ter
Winter Park, FL 32792-7630, USA

Youngblood, Jimmy L (Jim) (Athlete, Football Player)
534 N Manhattan Pl
Los Angeles, CA 90004-2513, USA

Youngblood, Joel (Athlete, Baseball Player)
4446 E Camelback Rd Unit 113
Phoenix, AZ 85018-2837, USA

Youngblood, Rob
1604 N Vista St
Los Angeles, CA 90046-2818

Youngblood, Sydney
Postfach 20 13 43
Hamburg, GERMANY D-29243

Youngen, Lois (Baseball Player)
45 Prall Ln
Eugene, OR 97405-3335, USA

Younger, Ben (Director, Writer)
c/o Joseph Cohen *Creative Artists Agency (CAA-LA)*
2000 Avenue of the Stars Ste 100
Los Angeles, CA 90067-4705, USA

Youngerman, Jack (Artist)
PO Box 508
Bridgehampton, NY 11932-0508, USA

Youngfellow, Barrie (Actor)
c/o Staff Member *Gage Group, The (LA)*
14724 Ventura Blvd Ste 505
Sherman Oaks, CA 91403-3505, USA

Younis, Waqar (Cricketer)
Kennington Oval
London SE11 5SS, UNITED KINGDOM (UK)

Yount, Larry (Athlete, Baseball Player)
5701 E Mockingbird Ln
Paradise Valley, AZ 85253-2221, USA

Yount, Robin (Athlete, Baseball Player)
5040 E Shea Blvd Ste 254
Scottsdale, AZ 85254-4687, USA

Yount, Robin R (Athlete, Baseball Player)
5040 E Shea Blvd Ste 254
Scottsdale, AZ 85254-4687, USA

Youso, Frank (Athlete, Football Player)
PO Box 1046
International Falls, MN 56649-1046, USA

Youssoufi, Abdderrahmane El (Prime Minister)
Rabat, MOROCCO

Yow, Kay (Athlete, Basketball Player)
745 Crabtree Crossing Pkwy
Cary, NC 27513-3479, USA

Yowarsky, Walt (Athlete, Football Player)
395 Dogwood Pl NW
Cleveland, TN 37312-4414, USA

Yo-Yo (Musician)
1325 Avenue of the Americas
New York, NY 10019-6026, USA

Yu, Ronnie (Director, Producer, Writer)
c/o Richard Arlook *The Arlook Group*
205 S Beverly Dr Ste 209
Beverly Hills, CA 90212-3899, USA

Yu Chuan Yong (Architect)
149 Guangming Road
Weihai PR, CHINA

Yuan, Ron (Actor)
c/o Laura Pallas *Pallas Management*
5301 Bellaire Ave
Valley Village, CA 91607-2329, US

Yuan Enfeng (Musician)
Xian, Shaanxi, CHINA

Yuan Zhongyi (Archaeologist, Misc)
Lintong, Xi'an, CHINA

Yuasa, Joji (Composer, Musician)
1517 Shields Ave
Encinitas, CA 92024-2911, USA

Yudof, Mark G (Educator)
President's Office
Minneapolis, MN 55455, USA

Yue Jingyu (Swimmer)
9 Tiyuguan Road
Beijing, CHINA

Yuen, Corey (Actor, Director)
c/o Steve Chasman *Acc Media*
9200 W Sunset Blvd Ste 10
Los Angeles, CA 90069 3608, USA

Yulin, Harris (Actor)
40 W 86th St # 5C
New York, NY 10024-3605, USA

Yun Lee, Will (Actor)
c/o Sam Maydew *Collective*
8383 Wilshire Blvd Ste 1050
Beverly Hills, CA 90211-2415, USA

Yune, Johnny
1921 Scenic Sunrise Dr
Las Vegas, NV 89117-7237

Yune, Rick (Actor)
c/o David Gardner *Principato/Young Management*
9465 Wilshire Blvd Ste 430
Beverly Hills, CA 90212-2613, USA

Yun-Fat, Chow (Actor)
c/o Lee Stollman *The Gotham Group Inc*
9255 W Sunset Blvd Ste 515
Los Angeles, CA 90069-3308, USA

Yunis, Jorge J (Misc)
Jefferson Medical College
Philadelphia, PA 19107, USA

Yunus, Muhammad (Nobel Prize Laureate)
500 W Cummings Park Ste 5200
Woburn, MA 01801-6577, USA

Yurak, Jeff (Athlete, Baseball Player)
PO Box 1931
Sumner, WA 98390-0420, USA

Yurchikhin, Fyodor N (Cosmonaut)
2101 Nasa Pkwy Spc Center
Houston, TX 77058-3607, USA

Yushchenko, Victor (President)
Bankova Str 11
Kiev 1220, UKRAINE

Yushkevich, Dmitri (Athlete, Hockey Player)
878 Ridge View Way
Franklin Lakes, NJ 07417-1524, USA

Yustman, Odette (Actor)
c/o Tiffany Kuzon *Evolution Entertainment (LA)*
901 N Highland Ave
Los Angeles, CA 90038-2412, USA

Yusuke, Yamamoto (Actor)
c/o Staff Member *Ever Green Entertainment*
3-12-7-1009 Kita Aoyama Minato
Tokyo, Japan

Yuvarani (Actor, Bollywood)
Plot No 28 Annamalai Colony
Virugambakkam
Chennai, TN 600092, INDIA

Yvars, Sal (Athlete, Baseball Player)
1 Allen St
Valhalla, NY 10595-1429, USA

Ywecic, Tom (Athlete, Football Player)
15 Danby Rd
Stoneham, MA 02180-3003, USA

Yzaguirre, Raul (Activist)
1111 19th St NW Ste 1000
Washington, DC 20036-3622, USA

Yzerman, Steve (Athlete, Hockey Player)
PO Box 488
Bloomfield Hills, MI 48303-0488, USA

Z

Z, Jenna (Model)
PO Box 39624
N Ridgeville, OH 44039-0624, USA

Z. Bordallo, Madeleine (Congressman, Politician)
2441 Rayburn Hob
Washington, DC 20515-1604, USA

Zaa, Charlie (Musician)
c/o Staff Member *Sony Music Miami*
605 Lincoln Rd Ste 700
Miami Beach, FL 33139-2901, USA

Zabaleta, Nicanor (Musician)
Villa Izar Aldapeta
San Sebasatian 20009, SPAIN

Zabarain, Ines (Actor)
c/o Staff Member *TV Caracol*
Calle 76 #11 - 35 Piso 10AA
Bogota DC 26484, COLOMBIA

Zabel, Mark (Athlete)
Grosse Fischerei 18A
Calbe/Saale 39240, GERMANY

Zabel, Steven G (Steve) (Athlete, Football Player)
6000 Oak Tree Rd
Edmond, OK 73025-2625, USA

Zabiela, James (DJ, Musician)
c/o Joel Zimmerman *WmE2 (WMA-NY)*
1325 Avenue of the Americas
New York, NY 10019-6026, USA

Zaborowski, Robert R J M (Religious Leader)
2803 10th St
Wyandotte, MI 48192-4907, USA

Zabriski, Bruce (Athlete, Golfer)
6228 Winding Lake Dr
Jupiter, FL 33458-3787, USA

Zabriskie, Grace (Actor)
c/o David Rose *Innovative Artists (LA)*
1505 10th St
Santa Monica, CA 90401-2805, USA

Zac Brown Band (Music Group, Musician)
c/o Staff Member *ROAR (LA)*
9701 Wilshire Blvd Fl 8
Beverly Hills, CA 90212-2008, USA

Zachar, Jacob (Actor)
c/o Jamie Freed *Paris Hilton Entertainment*
8383 Wilshire Blvd Ste 1050
Beverly Hills, CA 90211-2415, USA

Zachara, Jan (Boxer)
Sladkovicova 13
Nova Dubnica 1851, CZECH REPUBLIC

Zachary, Ken (Football Player)
General Delivery
Newalla, OK 74857-9999, USA

Zacherle, John (Actor)
125 W 96th St Apt 4B
New York, NY 10025-6423, USA

Zachry, Pat (Athlete, Baseball Player)
7611 Bosque Blvd
Woodway, TX 76712-3766, USA

Zadan, Craig (Producer)
c/o Staff Member *WmE2 (WMA-LA)*
1 William Morris Pl
Beverly Hills, CA 90212-4261, USA

Zadeh, Lofti A (Scientist)
904 Mendocino Ave
Berkeley, CA 94707-1925, USA

Zadel, C William (Business Person)
80 Ashby Rd
Bedford, MA 01730-2200, USA

Zadora, Pia (Actor)
69 Hawk Ridge Dr
Las Vegas, NV 89135-7864, USA

Zaentz, Saul (Producer)
c/o Staff Member *Saul Zaentz Film Center*
2600 Durant Ave
Berkeley, CA 94704-1711, USA

Zaeske, Paul (Athlete, Football Player)
12250 S Kirkwood Rd Apt 1818
Stafford, TX 77477-2129, USA

Zaffaroni, Alejandro C (Misc)
1950 Charleston Rd
Mountain View, CA 94043-1218, USA

Zafferani, Rosa (Misc)
Government Palace
47031, SAN MARINO

Zagaria, Anita (Actor)
Via Giuseppe Pisanelli
Rome 196, ITALY

Zaglmann-Willinger, Cornelia (Director)
Siegfriedstr 9
Munich 80802, GERMANY

Zagorin, Perez (Historian)
3050 Military Rd NW Apt 4002
Washington, DC 20015-1387, USA

Zagurski, Mike (Athlete, Baseball Player)
11 Raven Oak Rd
Kimberling City, MO 65686-9478, USA

Zahn, Geoffrey C (geof) (Athlete, Baseball Player)
6536 Walsh Rd
Dexter, MI 48130-9656, USA

Zahn, Paula (Journalist)
c/o Richard Leibner *NS Bienstock Inc*
250 W 57th St Ste 333
New York, NY 10107-0302, USA

Zahn, Steve (Actor)
c/o Marsha McManus *Principal Entertainment (LA)*
1964 Westwood Blvd Ste 400
Los Angeles, CA 90025-4695, USA

Zahn, Timothy (Writer)
PO Box 1755
Coos Bay, OR 97420-0340, USA

Zahn, Wayne (Bowler)
2143 E Center Ln
Tempe, AZ 85281-7719, USA

Zaklinsky, Konstantin (Dancer)
Teatralnaya Square 1
Saint Petersburg 190000, RUSSIA

Zaks, Jerry (Director)
c/o Susan Weaving *WmE2 (WMA-NY)*
1325 Avenue of the Americas
New York, NY 10019-6026, USA

Zal, Roxana (Actor)
c/o Staff Member *Main Title Entertainment*
2225 Wilshire Blvd Suite 500
Los Angeles, CA 90036, USA

Zalapski, Zarley (Athlete, Hockey Player)
308 Kingsberry Cir
Pittsburgh, PA 15234-1069, USA

Zale, Richard N (Misc)
724 Santa Ynez St
Stanford, CA 94305-8441, USA

Zalejski, Ernie (Athlete, Football Player)
427 S Grant St
South Bend, IN 46619-3533, USA

Zaloom, Paul (Actor, Writer)
c/o Staff Member *Washington Square Arts (LA)*
1041 N Formosa Ave Lot Bldg
West Hollywood, CA 90046-6703, USA

Zalyotin, Sergei V (Cosmonaut)
Moskovskoi Oblasti
Syvisdny Goroduk 141160, RUSSIA

Zamba, Frieda (Misc)
2706 S Central Ave
Flagler Beach, FL 32136-4037, USA

Zambrano, Carlos (Athlete, Baseball Player)
c/o Staff Member *Chicago Cubs Spring Training*
HoHoKam Stadium 1235 N St
Mesa, AZ 85201, USA

Zambri, Chris (Athlete, Golfer)
1329 La Culebra Cit
Camarillo, CA 93012-5551, USA

Zamecnik, Paul (Misc)
101 Chestnut St
Boston, MA 02108-1032, USA

Zamecnik, Paul C (Doctor)
222 Maple Ave
Shrewsbury, MA 01545-2732, USA

Zamka, George D (Astronaut)
1936 Mandy Ln
League City, TX 77573-3991, USA

Zamorska, Basia (Stylist)
c/o Staff Member *Aartist Loft*
580 Broadway Rm 606
New York, NY 10012-3258, USA

Zampini, Carina (Actor)
c/o Staff Member *Telefe - Argentina*
Pavon 2444 (C1248AAT)
Buenos Aires, ARGENTINA

Zamprogna, Dominic (Actor)
c/o Margie Weiner *Margie Weiner Management*
8205 Santa Monica Blvd Ste 1450
West Hollywood, CA 90046-5967, USA

Zander, Carl (Athlete, Football Player)
2536 W Palomino Dr
Chandler, AZ 85224-1639, USA

Zander, Robin (Musician)
509 Hartnell St
Monterey, CA 93940-2825, USA

Zander, Thomas (Wrestler)
Grundfeldstr 23
Aalen 73432, GERMANY

Zanders, Emanuel (Athlete, Football Player)
11015 Goodwood Blvd
Baton Rouge, LA 70815-5222, USA

Zane, Billy (Actor)
c/o Matt Luber *Luber Roklin Management*
8530 Wilshire Blvd Ste 550
Beverly Hills, CA 90211-3133, USA

Zane, Lisa (Actor)
505 N Lake Shore Dr Apt 5407
Chicago, IL 60611-6446, USA

Zanes, Dan (Musician, Songwriter, Writer)
c/o Harriet Sternberg *Harriet Sternberg Management*
4530 Gloria Ave
Encino, CA 91436-2718, USA

Zanetti, Eugenio (Actor, Director)
c/o Frank Wuliger *Gersh (LA)*
9465 Wilshire Blvd Ste 600
Beverly Hills, CA 90212-2612, USA

Zanni, Dom (Athlete, Baseball Player)
7 Sussex Ave
Massapequa, NY 11758-2434, USA

Zano, Nick (Actor)
c/o John Carrabino *John Carrabino Management*
5900 Wilshire Blvd Ste 406
Los Angeles, CA 90036-5015, USA

Zanuck, Lili Fini (Director, Producer)
9465 Wilshire Blvd Ste 308
Beverly Hills, CA 90212-2602, USA

Zanuck, Richard D (Producer)
9465 Wilshire Blvd Ste 308
Beverly Hills, CA 90212-2602, USA

Zanussi, Krzysztof (Director)
Ul Kaniowska 114
Warsaw 01-529, POLAND

Zapalac, Willie (Athlete, Football Player)
1400 Shannon Oaks Trl
Austin, TX 78746-7345, USA

Zapata, Carmen (Actor)
6107 Ethel Ave
Van Nuys, CA 91401-3218, USA

Zapata, Laura (Actor)
c/o Staff Member *Televisa*
Blvd Adolfo Lopez Mateos 232 Colonia San Angel INN
DF CP 01060, MEXICO

Zapatero, José Luis Rodríguez (Government Official, Prime Minister)
Complejo De La Moncloa
Madrid 28071, Spain

Zapp, Jim (Baseball Player)
820 Youngs Ln
Nashville, TN 37207-4828, USA

Zappa, Dweezil (Actor, Musician)
7885 Woodrow Wilson Dr
Los Angeles, CA 90046-1213, USA

Zappa, Moon
PO Box 5265
North Hollywood, CA 91616-5265

Zappa, Moon Unit (Actor, Musician)
10377 Oletha Ln
Los Angeles, CA 90077-2417, USA

Zara, Lucy (Actor, Model)
c/o Staff Member *Don Capo Entertainment*
Ste 5 South Bank Terrace Surbiton
Surrey KT6 6DG, UNITED KINGDOM (UK)

Zarate, Carlos (Boxer)
PO Box 113
Montebello, CA 90640-0113, USA

Zardon, Jose (Athlete, Baseball Player)
7825 SW 18th Ter
Miami, FL 33155-1346, USA

Zarin, Jill (Reality TV Star)
c/o Staff Member *Bravo (NY)*
30 Rockefeller Plz
New York, NY 10112-0015, USA

Zarley, Kermit (Athlete, Golfer)
16600 N Thompson Peak Pkwy Unit 2081
Scottsdale, AZ 85260-2185, USA

Zarnas, August C (Gust) (Athlete, Football Player)
850 Jennings St
Bethlehem, PA 18017-7010, USA

Zaske, Jeff (Athlete, Baseball Player)
2404 185th Pl SE
Bothell, WA 98012-6999, USA

Zatcoff, Barbara (Stylist)
3003 Van Ness St NW
Washington, DC 20008-4701, USA

Zatkoff, Roger (Athlete, Football Player)
882 Hidden Ravines Ct
Birmingham, MI 48009-1681, USA

Zatopkova, Dana (Athlete, Track Athlete)
Nad Kazankov 3
Prague 7 171 00, CZECH REPUBLIC

Zaun, Gregg (Athlete, Baseball Player)
8405 Shady Oaks Dr
North Richland Hills, TX 76182-8451, USA

Zaunbrecher, Godfrey (Athlete, Football Player)
3126 N 205th St
Elkhorn, NE 68022-4708, USA

Zavaleta, Cara (Actor, Model)
PO Box 543
Bowling Green, OH 43402-0543, USA

Zavaras, Clint (Athlete, Baseball Player)
9675 S Thimbleberry Way
Parker, CO 80134-8860, USA

Zaveri, Anjala (Actor, Bollywood)
604 Jupiter Apts Yari Road Andheri W
Mumbai, MS 400058, INDIA

Zaveri, Anjali (Actor, Bollywood)
604 Jupiter Apartments Yari Rd
Andheri, Mumbai 400058, India

Zawadzkas, Gerald (Athlete, Football Player)
2712 Alcazar St NE
Albuquerque, NM 87110-3514, USA

Zayas, David (Actor)
c/o Andrew Tetenbaum *ATA Management*
12 Desbrosses St
New York, NY 10013-1704, USA

Zdeb, Joe (Athlete, Baseball Player)
5717 Greenwood St
Shawnee, KS 66216-4676, USA

Zdrok, Victoria (Adult Film Star)
PO Box 332
Pompton Lakes, NJ 07442-0332, USA

Zea, Natalie (Actor)
c/o Robert Semon *True Management*
8964 W 25th St
Los Angeles, CA 90034-2012, USA

Zeal, Meredith (Actor)
c/o Marv Dauer *Marv Dauer Management*
11661 San Vicente Blvd Ste 104
Los Angeles, CA 90049-5150, USA

Zeamer Jr, Jay (War Hero)
108 Emery Ln
Boothbay Harbor, ME 04538-1966, USA

Zeber, George (Athlete, Baseball Player)
18826 Winnwood Ln
Santa Ana, CA 92705-1233, USA

Zech, Rosel
Agensstr. 47
Munich, GERMANY 80798

Zecher, Rich (Athlete, Football Player)
PO Box 1859
Eureka, MT 59917-1859, USA

Zeckhauser, Richard J (Economist)
138 Irving St
Cambridge, MA 02138-1929, USA

Zedillo Ponce de Leon, Ernesto (Politician, President)
Insurges N 61
Mexico City, DF 6350, MEXICO

Zedlitz, Jean (Athlete, Golfer)
4587 Gatetree Cir
Pleasanton, CA 94566-6031, USA

Zednik, Richard (Athlete, Hockey Player)
4401 N Federal Hwy Ste 201
Boca Raton, FL 33431-5164, USA

Zee, Joe (Stylist)
c/o Staff Member *Jed Root Inc*
61-A Walker St
New York, NY 10013, USA

Zee, Ona (Adult Film Star)
2523A Folsom St
San Francisco, CA 94110-2621, USA

Zegers, Kevin (Actor)
c/o Justin Grey Stone *Untitled Entertainment (LA)*
350 S Beverly Dr Ste 200
Beverly Hills, CA 90212-4819, USA

Zeh, Geoffrey N (Misc)
12050 Woodward Ave
Detroit, MI 48203-3578, USA

Zehetner, Nora (Actor)
c/o Staff Member *Anonymous Content (AC-LA)*
3531 Hayden Ave
Culver City, CA 90232, USA

Zeidel, Larry (Athlete, Hockey Player)
16 W Montgomery Ave Apt 16
Ardmore, PA 19003-1428, USA

Zeidler, Eberard H (Architect)
315 Queen St W
Toronto, ON M5V 2X2, CANADA

Zeier, Eric (Athlete, Football Player)
PO Box 327
Nashville, GA 31639-0327, USA

Zeigler, Alma (Athlete, Baseball Player)
403 Gold St
Auburn, CA 95603-5521, USA

Zeigler, Dusty (Athlete, Football Player)
440 Hodgeville Rd
Guyton, GA 31312-7103, USA

Zeigler, Heidi (Actor)
c/o Staff Member *Mary Grady Agency (MGA)*
4400 Coldwater Canyon Ave Ste 135
Studio City, CA 91604-5038, USA

Zeigler, Larry
10620 Woodchase Cir
Orlando, FL 32836-5885

Zeigler, Marie (Athlete, Baseball Player)
2502 N 22nd Ave
Phoenix, AZ 85009-1926, USA

Zeile, Todd E (Actor, Athlete, Baseball Player, Producer)
2324 Crombie Ct
Thousand Oaks, CA 91361-5322, USA

Zeilic, Mauricio (Actor)
c/o Staff Member *Telemundo*
2470 W 8th Ave
Hialeah, FL 33010-2000, USA

Zeitlin, Zvi (Musician)
204 Warren Ave
Rochester, NY 14618-4316, USA

Zekauskas, Ann (Stylist)
21 W 89th St
New York, NY 10024-2051, USA

Zelepukin, Valeri (Athlete, Hockey Player)
9595 Collins Ave Apt 610
Surfside, FL 33154-2636, USA

Zelezny, Jan (Athlete, Track Athlete)
Rue Armady 683
Boleslav, CZECH REPUBLIC

Zell, Samuel (Business Person)
2 N Riverside Plz
Chicago, IL 60606-2600, USA

Zellars, Ray (Athlete, Football Player)
1327 Island Ave
Pittsburgh, PA 15212-2845, USA

Zeller, Bart (Athlete, Baseball Player)
13885 E Lupine Ave
Scottsdale, AZ 85259-3719, USA

Zeller, David (Athlete, Basketball Player)
2260 Greenlawn Dr
Toledo, OH 43614-5122, USA

Zellner, Peppi (Athlete, Football Player)
31 Dew Pl
Forsyth, GA 31029-3302, USA

Zellweger, Renee (Actor, Musician, Producer)
c/o John Carrabino *John Carrabino Management*
5900 Wilshire Blvd Ste 406
Los Angeles, CA 90036-5015, USA

Zelman, Aaron (Writer)
c/o Staff Member *International Creative Management (ICM-LA)*
10250 Constellation Blvd Fl 7
Los Angeles, CA 90067-6207, USA

Zelmani, Sophie (Musician)
PO Box 11029
Stockholm 100 61, SWEDEN

Zeman, E Robert (Athlete, Football Player)
6333 La Jolla Blvd Unit 268
La Jolla, CA 92037-6619, USA

Zeman, Ed (Athlete, Football Player)
3002 Jeffrey Dr Apt C
Costa Mesa, CA 92626-2929, USA

Zeman, Jacklyn (Actor)
6500 Wilshire Blvd # 550
Los Angeles, CA 90048-4920, USA

Zeman, Milos (Prime Minister)
Nabrezi E Benese 4
Prague 1 118 01, CZECH REPUBLIC

Zeman, Zoe (Adult Film Star)
PO Box 343
Walpole, MA 02081-0343, USA

Zemanova, Veronica (Model)
G Noodtstr 12 SW
Nijmegen 6511, NETHERLANDS

Zembriski, Walter (Athlete, Golfer)
6507 Doubletrace Ln
Orlando, FL 32819-4653, USA

Zemeckis, Robert L (Director, Producer, Writer)
100 Universal City Plz PMB 484
Universal City, CA 91608-1002, USA

Zenawi, Hailu (Prime Minister)
PO Box 1013
Addis Ababa, ETHIOPIA

Zenawi, Meles (President)
PO Box 5707
Addis Ababa, ETHIOPIA

Zendejas, Luis (Athlete, Football Player)
6609 S 47th Pl
Phoenix, AZ 85042-5352, USA

Zender, Hans (Composer)
Am Rosenheck
Bad Soden 65812, GERMANY

Zender, Stuart (Musician)
Chapel 26A Munster St
London SW6 4EN, UNITED KINGDOM (UK)

Zeno, Lance (Athlete, Football Player)
530 Landfair Ave
Los Angeles, CA 90024-2104, USA

Zeno, Tony (Athlete, Basketball Player)
4419 Fulton Ave Apt 30
Sherman Oaks, CA 91423-5116, USA

Zentmyer Jr, George A (Misc)
955 S El Camino Real # 216
San Mateo, CA 94402-2346, USA

Zentner, Sy
4825 Fairfax Ave
Las Vegas, NV 89120-1739

Zepeda, David (Actor)
c/o Raul Xumalin *MAFAE Artist Management*
8491 NW 17th St
Doral, FL 33126-1025, USA

Zephaniah, Benjamin (Actor, Writer)
18 Fountain Street
Ulverston LA12 7EQ, UNITED KINGDOM

Zepp, Bill (Athlete, Baseball Player)
15000 Farmbrook Dr
Plymouth, MI 48170-2748, USA

Zeppelin, Dread (Musician)
6404 Wilshire Blvd Ste 700
Los Angeles, CA 90048-5509

Zeppelin, Led (Music Group, Musician)
c/o Seth Rappaport *Agency Group Ltd, The (NY)*
142 W 57th St Fl 6
New York, NY 10019-3300, USA

Zerbe, Anthony (Actor)
1175 High Rd
Santa Barbara, CA 93108-2430, USA

Zerbe, Chad (Athlete, Baseball Player)
7248 Palomino St
Highland, CA 92346-5032, USA

Zereoue, Amos (Athlete, Football Player)
116 Tanglewood Dr
Wexford, PA 15090-8692, USA

Zerhouni, Elias A (Doctor, Government Official)
9000 Rockville Pike
Bethesda, MD 20892-0001, USA

Zero, Mark (Musician)
PO Box 656507
Fresh Meadows, NY 11365-6507, USA

Zervas, Nicholas T (Doctor)
100 Canton Ave
Milton, MA 02186-3507, USA

Zeta-Jones, Catherine (Actor)
c/o CeCe Yorke *True Public Relations*
6725 W Sunset Blvd Ste 470
Los Angeles, CA 90028-7180, USA

Zetsche, Dieter (Business Person)
Plieningstr
Stuggart 70546, GERMANY

Zettler, Michael E (General)
Deputy Chief of Staff for Logistics Hqusa Pentagon
Washington, DC 20310-0001, USA

Zettler, Rob (Athlete, Hockey Player)
31 Tadcaster Pl
Saulte Sainte Marie, ON P6B 5E3, Canada

Zewail, Ahmed H (Nobel Prize Laureate)
871 Winston Ave
San Marino, CA 91108-1430, USA

Zgonina, Jeff (Athlete, Football Player)
41 Hawthorne Ln
Barrington, IL 60010-5109, USA

Zhamnov, Alexei (Athlete, Hockey Player)
1950 N Orchard St
Chicago, IL 60614-5130, USA

Zhang, Aiping (General, Government Official)
State Council
Beijing, CHINA

Zhang, Xianliang (Writer)
Yinchuan City, CHINA

Zhang, Ziyi (Actor)
c/o Kelly Bush *ID PR (LA)*
7060 Hollywood Blvd Fl 8
Los Angeles, CA 90028-6014, USA

Zhang, Ziyl (Actor)
c/o Ling Lucas *Nine Muses and Apollo Inc*
525 Broadway Rm 201
New York, NY 10012-4482, USA

Zhenan, Bao (Inventor)
600 Mountain Ave
New Providence, NJ 07974-2008, USA

Zheng, Wei (Astronomer)
Astronomy Dept
Baltimore, MD 21218, USA

Zhe-Xi Lo (Misc)
4400 Forbes Ave
Pittsburgh, PA 15213-4007, USA

Zhirinovsky, Vladimir V (Government Official)
1st Basmanny Per 3
Moscow 103045, RUSSIA

Zhislin, Grigory Y (Musician)
25 Whiteball Gardens
London W3 9RD, UNITED KINGDOM (UK)

Zhitnik, Alexel (Athlete, Hockey Player)
1 Seymour St
Buffalo, NY 14210, USA

Zholobov, Vitall M (Cosmonaut)
Ul Yanvarskovo Vostaniya D 12
Klev 252010, UKRAINE

Zhou Long (Composer)
Music Dept
Kansas City, MO 64110, USA

Zhudov, Vyacheslav D (Cosmonaut)
Moskovskoi Oblasti
Syvisdny Goroduk 141160, RUSSIA

Zhumaliyev, Kubanychbek M
Bishkek 7200003, KYRGYZSTAN

Zhvanetsky, Mikhail M (Actor, Writer)
Lesnaya Str 4 #63
Moscow 125047, RUSSIA

Zia, B Khaleda (Prime Minister)
Gono Bhaban Sher-e-Banglanagar
Dakah, BANGLADESH

Ziblijew, Wassili (Cosmonaut)
Moskovskoi Oblasti
Syvisdny Goroduk 141160, RUSSIA

Zicherman, Stu (Director)
c/o Staff Member *WmE2 (WMA-LA)*
1 William Morris Pl
Beverly Hills, CA 90212-4261, USA

Zick, Bob (Athlete, Baseball Player)
12028 S 45th St
Phoenix, AZ 85044-2436, USA

Zidane, Zinedine (Soccer Player)
Olympique Croix De Savoie 74 SASP 56
Av. De Général De Gaulle
Thonon-les-Bains F-74200, France

Zidek, George (Athlete, Basketball Player)
551 Landfair Ave
Los Angeles, CA 90024-2172, USA

Zidlicky, Marek (Athlete, Hockey Player)
2006 Sweetbriar Ave
Nashville, TN 37212-5412, USA

Ziegler, Alicia (Actor)
c/o Peter Himberger *Impact Artists Group LLC*
42 Hamilton Ter
New York, NY 10031-6403, USA

Ziegler, Dolorea (Opera Singer)
2702 Crestworth Ln
Buford, GA 30519-6483, USA

Ziegler, Jack (Cartoonist)
4 Times Sq
New York, NY 10036-6515, USA

Ziegler, Larry (Athlete, Golfer)
10315 Luton Ct
Orlando, FL 32836-3733, USA

Ziegler, Ron
413 N Lee St # 1417-D49
Alexandria, VA 22314-2301

Ziegler, Shui (Stylist)
203 Teets Rd
Rochester, PA 15074-2732, USA

Ziegler Jr, John A (Misc)
38525 Woodward Ave
Bloomfield, MI 48304-5088, USA

Ziem, Steve (Athlete, Baseball Player)
1309 Avalon Ave
Beaumont, CA 92223-1528, USA

Ziemann, Sonia (Actor)
Via del Alp Dorf
Saint Moritz 7500, SWITZERLAND

Ziemann, Sonja
Neherstr. 7
Munich, GERMANY D-81675

Zien, Chip (Actor)
c/o Staff Member *Gersh (LA)*
9465 Wilshire Blvd Ste 600
Beverly Hills, CA 90212-2612, USA

Zien, Sam (Chef, Producer, Television Host, Writer)
c/o Staff Member *Wiley John & Sons Incorporated*
Author's Mail (Publicity) 111 River St
Hoboken, NJ 07030-5774, USA

Ziering, Ian (Actor)
c/o Monica Barkett *Global Artists Agency*
6253 Hollywood Blvd Apt 508
Los Angeles, CA 90028-8251, USA

Ziering, Nikki (Actor)
c/o Jerry Shandrew *Shandrew Public Relations*
1050 S Stanley Ave
Los Angeles, CA 90019-6634, USA

Ziffren, Kenneth (Lawyer)
1801 Century Park W
Los Angeles, CA 90067-6409, USA

Ziglar, Zig (Business Person)
5055 W Park Blvd Ste 700
Plano, TX 75093-2006, USA

Zigler, Edward F (Educator)
Bush Child Development Center
New Haven, CT 6520, USA

Zikarsky, Bengt (Swimmer)
Oberer Bogenweg 1
Wurzburg 97074, GERMANY

Zikarsky, Bjorn (Swimmer)
555 California St Ste 2600
San Francisco, CA 94104-1602, USA

Zikes, Les (Bowler)
424 S Stuart Ln
Palatine, IL 60067-6730, USA

Zilinskas, Annette (Actor, Musician)
c/o Staff Member *Creative Artists Agency (CAA-LA)*
2000 Avenue of the Stars Ste 100
Los Angeles, CA 90067-4705, USA

Zilly, Jack (Athlete, Football Player)
67 Tupelo Trl
Narragansett, RI 02882-2743, USA

Zils, John (Engineer)
N1513 Shore Haven Dr
Fontana, WI 53125-1947, USA

Zim Zum (Musician)
c/o Staff Member *Mitch Schneider Organization, The*
14724 Ventura Blvd Ste 410
Sherman Oaks, CA 91403-3537, USA

Zima, Madeline (Actor)
c/o Steven Levy *Framework Entertainment (LA)*
9057 Nemo St Ste C
West Hollywood, CA 90069-5511, USA

Zima, Yvonne (Actor)
c/o Danny Mancini *Affirmative Entertainment*
425 N Robertson Blvd
West Hollywood, CA 90048-1735, USA

Zimbalist, Stephanie (Actor, Writer)
c/o Staff Member *Gage Group, The (LA)*
14724 Ventura Blvd Ste 505
Sherman Oaks, CA 91403-3505, USA

Zimbalist III, Efrem (Business Person)
Times Mirror Square
Los Angeles, CA 90053, USA

Zimbalist Jr, Efrem (Actor)
1448 Holsted Dr
Solvang, CA 93463-2054, USA

Zimerman, Krystian (Musician)
165 W 57th St
New York, NY 10019-2201, USA

Zimm, Bruno H (Misc)
3762 Dupont St
San Diego, CA 92106-3226, USA

Zimmer, Constance (Actor)
c/o David Sweeney *Sweeney Management*
8755 Lookout Mountain Ave
Los Angeles, CA 90046-1861, USA

Zimmer, Donald W (Don) (Athlete, Baseball Player, Coach)
7069 Key Haven Rd Apt 201
Seminole, FL 33777-3870, USA

Zimmer, Hans (Composer, Musician)
c/o Sam Schwartz *Gorfaine/Schwartz Agency Inc*
4111 W Alameda Ave Ste 509
Burbank, CA 91505-4171, USA

Zimmer, Norma (Actor)
31200 Santiago Rd
Temecula, CA 92592-3110

Zimmerer, Wolfgang (Athlete)
Schwaigangerstr 22
Mumau 82418, GERMANY

Zimmerlink, Geno (Athlete, Football Player)
318 Crestwood Dr
Milltown, NJ 08850-1849, USA

Zimmerman, Adria (Stylist)
2704 Holly Dr
Greensboro, NC 27408-3628, USA

Zimmerman, Don (Athlete, Football Player)
107 Coretta St
Monroe, LA 71202-6901, USA

Zimmerman, Gary W (Athlete, Football Player)
17450 Skyliners Rd
Bend, OR 97701-5203, USA

Zimmerman, H Leroy (Athlete, Football Player)
808 Willis Ace
Madera, CA 93637, USA

Zimmerman, Howard E (Misc)
7813 Westchester Dr
Middleton, WI 53562-3671, USA

Zimmerman, James M (Business Person)
151 W 34th St
New York, NY 10001-2101, USA

Zimmerman, Jeff (Athlete, Baseball Player)
3930 Glade Rd Ste 108
Colleyville, TX 76034-7923, USA

Zimmerman, John T (Scientist)
Medical School Neurology Dept
Denver, CO 80202, USA

Zimmerman, Jordan (Athlete, Baseball Player)
15400 W Alexandria Way
Surprise, AZ 85379-8107, USA

Zimmerman, Kent (Publisher)
1999 Shepard Rd
Saint Paul, MN 55116-3210, USA

Zimmerman, Mary Beth (Athlete, Golfer)
6452 Century Park Pl SE
Mableton, GA 30126-7737, USA

Zimmerman, Matt
562 Eastern Ave Lford
Essex, ENGLAND 1G2 6PH

Zimmerman, Philip (Phil) (Designer)
4677 Old Ironsides Dr
Santa Clara, CA 95054-1809, USA

Zimmerman, Ryan (Athlete, Baseball Player)
c/o Staff Member *Washington Nationals*
1500 S Capitol St SE
Washington, DC 20003-3599, USA

Zimmermann, Egon (Skier)
Am Arlberg 67644, AUSTRIA

Zimmermann, Frank P (Musician)
Concertgebouwplein 15
Amsterdam 1071 LL, NETHERLANDS

Zimmermann, Markus (Athlete)
Waldhauserstr 51-33
Schonau am Konigsee 83471, GERMANY

Zimmermann, Udo (Composer)
Augustusptatz
Leipzig 4109, GERMANY

Zimny, Bob (Athlete, Football Player)
1143 Meridian St
Shelbyville, IN 46176-2536, USA

Zinke, Olaf (Speed Skater)
Johannes Bobrowski Str 22
Berlin 12627, GERMANY

Zinkernagel, Rolf M (Nobel Prize Laureate)
Rebhusstr 47
Zumikon 8126, SWITZERLAND

Zinman, David J (Conductor)
1212 Cathedral St
Baltimore, MD 21201-5556, USA

Zinner, Nick (Musician)
249 Metropolitan Ave
Brooklyn, NY 11211-4009, USA

Zinter, Alan (Athlete, Baseball Player)
3064 E Trigger Way
Gilbert, AZ 85297-6038, USA

Zipfel, Bud (Athlete, Baseball Player)
57 Whiteside Dr
Belleville, IL 62221-2542, USA

Zippel, David (Musician)
15233 Ventura Blvd Ste 200
Sherman Oaks, CA 91403-2244, USA

Zisk, Richard W (Richie) (Athlete, Baseball Player)
4231 NE 26th Ter
Lighthouse Point, FL 33064-8053, USA

Ziskin, Laura
c/o Staff Member *WmE2 (WMA-LA)*
1 William Morris Pl
Beverly Hills, CA 90212-4261, USA

Zito, Barry (Athlete, Baseball Player)
647 Santa Rosita
Solana Beach, CA 92075-1530, USA

Zito, Chuck (Actor, Boxer)
c/o Darren Prince *Prince Marketing Group*
18 Carillon Cir
Livingston, NJ 07039-2600, USA

Ziv, Assaf (Stylist)
c/o Staff Member *Ennis*
119 Braintree St
Boston, MA 02134-1628, USA

Zivkovic, Zoran (Prime Minister)
Nemanjina 11
Belgrade 11000, SERBIA

Ziyi, Zhang (Actor)
c/o Ling Lucas *Nine Muses and Apollo Inc*
525 Broadway Rm 201
New York, NY 10012-4482, USA

Zlatoper, Ronald J (Zap) (Admiral)
1001 Kamokila Blvd
Kapolei, HI 96707-2030, USA

Zlotoff, Lee (Director)
c/o Wendi Niad *Niad Management*
15030 Ventura Blvd Bldg 19STE PMB 860
Sherman Oaks, CA 91403-5470, USA

Zmed, Adrian (Actor)
c/o Staff Member *Tisherman Gilbert Motley Drozdoski Talent Agency (TGMD)*
6767 Forest Lawn Dr Ste 101
Los Angeles, CA 90068-1050, USA

Zmeskal, Kim (Gymnast)
3635 Woodridge Blvd
Fairfield, OH 45014-8521, USA

Zmievskaya Petrenko, Galina (Nina) (Coach)
PO Box 577
Simsbury, CT 06070-0577, USA

Zmuda, Bob (Actor, Comedian)
c/o Monique Moss *Warren Cowan & Associates PR*
8899 Beverly Blvd Ste 918
Los Angeles, CA 90048-2427, USA

Zoccolillo, Pete (Athlete, Baseball Player)
5 Spruce Dr
White Plains, NY 10605-4209, USA

Zoe (Stylist)
c/o Staff Member *Artists by Timothy Priano (CA)*
8447 Wilshire Blvd Ste 301
Beverly Hills, CA 90211-3206, USA

Zoe, Deborah (Actor)
c/o Kim Matuka *Online Talent Group*
Prefers to be contacted via email or telephone
Los Angeles, CA 90069, USA

Zoe, Rachel (Reality TV Star, Stylist)
c/o Staff Member *Todd Shemarya Artists*
2550 Outpost Dr
Los Angeles, CA 90068-2647, USA

ZoeGirl (Music Group)
101 Winners Cir N
Brentwood, TN 37027-5352, USA

Zoeller, Fuzzy (Athlete, Golfer)
418 Deer Run Trce
Floyds Knobs, IN 47119-8505

Zofko, Mickey (Athlete, Football Player)
321 W Fern Ave
Foley, AL 36535-2128, USA

Zohn, Ethan (Motivational Speaker, Reality TV Star)
PO Box 440560
Aurora, CO 80044-0560, USA

Zokol, Richard (Athlete, Golfer)
1663 7th Ave W
Vancouver, BC V6J 1S4, CANADA

Zolak, Scott (Athlete, Football Player)
40 Comstock Dr
Wrentham, MA 02093-1852, USA

Zolciak, Kim (Musician, Reality TV Star)
c/o Staff Member *Bravo (NY)*
30 Rockefeller Plz
New York, NY 10112-0015, USA

Zolotow, Charlotte (Writer)
29 Elm Pl
Hastings On Hudson, NY 10706-1703, USA

Zomalt, Eric (Athlete, Football Player)
25387 Delphinium Ave
Moreno Valley, CA 92553-7153, USA

Zombie, Rob (Musician)
c/o Jeremy Platt *Spectacle Entertainment Group*
2800 Olympic Blvd # 1
Santa Monica, CA 90404-4101, USA

Zombie, Sheri Moon (Actor)
8491 W Sunset Blvd # 215
West Hollywood, CA 90069-1911, USA

Zombo, Rick (Athlete, Hockey Player)
557 Vista Hills Ct
Eureka, MO 63025

Zook, John E (Athlete, Football Player)
4302 N Spyglass Cir
Wichita, KS 67226-3355, USA

Zook, Ron (Coach, Football Coach)
Athletic Dept
Champaign, IL 61820, USA

Zopf, Bill (Athlete, Basketball Player)
103 Oakhaven Dr
Wexford, PA 15090-8531, USA

Zophres, Mary (Designer)
c/o Staff Member *United Talent Agency (UTA)*
9560 Wilshire Blvd Fl 5
Beverly Hills, CA 90212-2400, USA

Zordich, Mike (Athlete, Football Player)
373 S Hazelwood Ave
Youngstown, OH 44509-2228, USA

Zorich, Christopher R (Chris) (Athlete, Football Player)
47 W Polk St Ste 100
Chicago, IL 60605-2085, USA

Zorich, Louis (Actor)
c/o Staff Member *Susan Smith Company, The*
1344 N Wetherly Dr
Los Angeles, CA 90069-1817, USA

Zorn, James A (Jim) (Coach, Football Coach)
c/o Staff Member *Washington Redskins*
1600 Fedex Way
Landover, MD 20785-4534, USA

Zorrilla, Alberto (Swimmer)
580 Park Ave
New York, NY 10065-7313, USA

Zorrilla, China (Actor)
c/o Staff Member *Telefe - Argentina*
Pavon 2444 (C1248AAT)
Buenos Aires, ARGENTINA

Zosky, Eddie (Athlete, Baseball Player)
13453 Raceland Rd
La Mirada, CA 90638-2927, USA

Zsigmond, Vilmos (Cinematographer)
c/o Shari Shankewitz *Innovative Artists (LA)*
1505 10th St
Santa Monica, CA 90401-2805, USA

Zubak, Kresimir (President)
Marsala Titz 7A
Sarajevo 71000, BOSNIA-HERZEGOVINA

Zuber, Jon (Athlete, Baseball Player)
197 Fernwood Dr
Moraga, CA 94556-2315, USA

Zuber, Maria (Geophysicist, Physicist)
Geophysics Dept
Cambridge, MA 2139, USA

Zucco, Victor (Athlete, Football Player)
2276 Wulfert Rd
Sanibel, FL 33957-2209, USA

Zucker, David (Director, Producer)
c/o Staff Member *Zucker/Netter Productions*
1645 Abbot Kinney Blvd Unit 320
Venice, CA 90291-5673, USA

Zucker, Irwin (Business Person)
6464 W Sunset Blvd Ste 755
Hollywood, CA 90028-8001, 323-461-3921

Zucker, Jeff (Business Person)
c/o Staff Member *NBC Universal (LA)*
100 Universal City Plz
Universal City, CA 91608-1002, USA

Zucker, Jerry (Director, Producer)
c/o Staff Member *Zucker Productions*
2401 Mandeville Canyon Rd
Los Angeles, CA 90049-1235

Zuckerberg, Mark (Business Person)
156 University Ave
Palo Alto, CA 94301-1688, USA

Zuckerman, Andrew (Director, Producer)
c/o Jon Rubinstein *Authentic Talent and Literary Management*
45 Main St Ste 1004
Brooklyn, NY 11201-8200, USA

Zuckerman, Josh (Actor)
c/o Anne Woodward *ROAR (LA)*
9701 Wilshire Blvd Fl 8
Beverly Hills, CA 90212-2008, USA

Zuckerman, Mortimer (Publisher)
599 Lexington Ave
New York, NY 10022-6030, USA

Zuckerman, Pinchas (Conductor, Musician)
711 W End Ave Apt 5KN
New York, NY 10025-0100, USA

Zuckoff, Mitchell (Writer)
c/o Richard Abate *3 Arts Entertainment - NY*
49 W 27th St Fl 5
New York, NY 10001-6936, USA

Zugsmith, Albert (Director)
23388 Mulholland Dr
Woodland Hills, CA 91364-2733, USA

Zuiker, Anthony E (Producer)
c/o Margaret Riley *Brillstein Entertainment Partners*
9150 Wilshire Blvd Ste 350
Beverly Hills, CA 90212-3453, USA

Zukav, Gary (Writer)
1230 Avenue of the Americas
New York, NY 10020-1513, USA

Zuker, Danny (Producer, Writer)
c/o Staff Member *Creative Artists Agency (CAA-LA)*
2000 Avenue of the Stars Ste 100
Los Angeles, CA 90067-4705, USA

Zukerman, Eugenia (Musician)
Bedford & H Aves
Brooklyn, NY 11210, USA

Zukerman, Pinchas (Conductor, Musician)
c/o Staff Member *Shirley Kirshbaum & Associates*
711 W End Ave Apt 5KN
New York, NY 10025-0100, USA

Zuleta, Julio (Athlete, Baseball Player)
3553 E Lexington Ct
Gilbert, AZ 85234-4237, USA

Zullo, Alan (Cartoonist)
435 N Michigan Ave Ste 1500
Chicago, IL 60611-4012, USA

Zumaya, Joel (Athlete, Baseball Player)
13722 Milton Dr
Belleville, MI 48111-2353, USA

Zunic, Matthew (Athlete, Basketball Player)
9330 W Fort Island Trl Apt 3
Crystal River, FL 34429-5372, USA

Zuniga, Daphne (Actor)
c/o Jonathan Baruch *Rain Management Group (RMG)*
1631 21st St
Santa Monica, CA 90404-3914, USA

Zuniga, Jose (Actor)
c/o Dan Baron *Agency for the Performing Arts (APA-LA)*
405 S Beverly Dr Ste 500
Beverly Hills, CA 90212-4425, USA

Zuniga, Markos Moulitsas (Writer)
c/o Staff Member *Puffin Publicity, Penguin Books (UK)*
80 Strand
London WC2R 0LR, UK

Zuniga, Miles (Musician)
c/o Staff Member *Russell Carter Artist Management*
567 Ralph McGill Blvd NE
Atlanta, GA 30312-1110, USA

Zupcic, Bob (Athlete, Baseball Player)
5409 Silver Creek Dr
Waxhaw, NC 28173-6761, USA

Zurbriggen, Pirmin (Skier)
3905 Saas-Almagell
SWITZERLAND

Zurer, Ayelet (Actor)
c/o Ilene Feldman *IFA Talent Agency*
8730 W Sunset Blvd Ste 490
Los Angeles, CA 90069-2248, USA

Zurkowski-Holmes, Agnes (Baseball Player)
206-2339 Lorne St
Regina, SK S4P 2N2, CANADA

Zuvella, Paul (Athlete, Baseball Player)
2040 Canyon Crest Ave
San Ramon, CA 94582-4841, USA

Zuverink, George (Athlete, Baseball Player)
1027 E McNair Dr
Tempe, AZ 85283-4733, USA

Zuvic, Daniella Monet (Actor)
c/o Staff Member *Elaine Entertainment*
Prefers to be contacted via telephone
Northridge, CA 91324, USA

Zvereva, Natalya (Tennis Player)
c/o Staff Member *Women's Tennis Association (WTA (US))*
133 1st St NE
St Petersburg, FL 33701-3307, USA

Zwanzig, Robert (Scientist)
8300 Burdette Rd Apt 423
Bethesda, MD 20817-2828, USA

Zwart, Harald (Director)
c/o Nicole Clemens *International Creative Management (ICM-LA)*
10250 Constellation Blvd Fl 7
Los Angeles, CA 90067-6207, USA

Zweibel, Alan (Writer)
c/o Lee Kernis *Brillstein Entertainment Partners*
9150 Wilshire Blvd Ste 350
Beverly Hills, CA 90212-3453, USA

Zweig, George (Physicist)
PO Box 1663
Los Alamos, NM 87544-0600, USA

Zweig, Ivan (Athlete, Baseball Player)
6502 Duffield Dr
Dallas, TX 75248-1314, USA

Zwerling, Darrell (Actor)
c/o Staff Member *CLInc Talent*
843 N Sycamore Ave
Los Angeles, CA 90038-3316, USA

Zwick, Charles J (Financier)
4210 Santa Maria St
Miami, FL 33146-1125, USA

Zwick, Edward M (Actor, Director, Producer, Writer)
c/o Staff Member *Bedford Falls Company, The*
409 Santa Monica Blvd PH
Santa Monica, CA 90401-2232, USA

Zwick, Joel (Director)
c/o Staff Member *Irv Schechter Company*
9460 Wilshire Blvd Ste 300
Beverly Hills, CA 90212-2710, USA

Zwierski, Ilona (Stylist)
838 N Taylor Ave
Oak Park, IL 60302-1456, USA

Zwilich, Ellen Taaffe (Composer)
c/o Staff Member *Music Association of America*
224 King St
Englewood, NJ 07631-3026, USA

Zycinski, Jozef (Religious Leader)
Ul Prumasa St Wyszynskiego 2 Skr Poczt 198
Lublin 20-950, POLAND

Zydeco, Buckwheat (Musician)
c/o Staff Member *Concerted Efforts*
PO Box 440326
Somerville, MA 02144-0004, USA

Zykina, Lyudmila G (Musician)
Kotelnicheskaya Nab Y15 Korp B #64
Moscow, RUSSIA

Zylberstein, Elsa (Actor)
c/o Staff Member *Agence Intertalent*
5 Rue Gay Lusac
Paris 75008, France

Zylis-Gara, Teresa (Opera Singer)
16A Blvd de Belgique
Monaco-Ville, MONACO

Zylka, Chris (Actor)
c/o Jon Simmons *Simmons & Scott Entertainment*
7942 Mulholland Dr
Los Angeles, CA 90046-1225, USA

ZZ Top (Music Group, Musician)
c/o Staff Member *Sanctuary Artist Management (UK)*
Sanctuary House 45-53 Sinclair Road
London W14 0NS, UNITED KINGDOM

CPSIA information can be obtained at www.ICGtesting.com
Printed in the USA
LVOW091442121112

306986LV00004B/1/P